Encyclopedia of Computer Science

FOURTH EDITION

Encyclopedia of Computer Science

FOURTH EDITION

Editors:

Anthony Ralston
Edwin D. Reilly
David Hemmendinger

WILEY

Copyright © 2003 John Wiley & Sons, Ltd,
The Atrium, Southern Gate,
Chichester, West Sussex,
PO19 8SQ, England

Telephone (+44) 1243 779777

Email (for orders and customer service enquiries):
cs-books@wiley.co.uk
Visit our Home Page on www.wileyeurope.com or
www.wiley.com

Originally published by Nature Publishing Group, 2000.
Errors identified in previous printings of this edition have been corrected
in this impression.

Other Wiley Editorial Offices

John Wiley & Sons, Inc., 111 River Street,
Hoboken, NJ 07030, USA

Jossey-Bass, 989 Market Street,
San Francisco, CA 94103-1741, USA

Wiley-VCH Verlag GmbH, Boschstr. 12,
D-69469 Weinheim, Germany

John Wiley & Sons Australia Ltd, 33 Park Road,
Milton, Queensland 4064, Australia

John Wiley & Sons (Asia) Pte Ltd, 2 Clementi Loop #02-01,
Jin Xing Distripark, Singapore 129809

John Wiley & Sons (Canada) Ltd, 22 Worcester Road,
Etobicoke, Ontario, Canada M9W 1L1

Wiley also publishes its books in a variety of electronic formats. Some content
that appears in print may not be available in electronic books.

British Library Cataloguing in Publication Data

A catalogue record for this book is available from the British Library

ISBN 0-470-86412-5

Typeset in $9\frac{1}{2}$/12pt by Aarontype Limited, Bristol.
Printed and bound in Great Britain by Bath Press Ltd, Bath.
This book is printed on acid-free paper responsibly manufactured from
sustainable forestry in which at least two trees are planted for each one used
for paper production.

Contents

Contributors

(Numbers after each name indicate the pages at which contributions by each author begin.)

Mark Halpern, Tandem Computers, Inc. 141, 159, 609, 1043
Sven Hammarling, Numerical Algorithms Group, UK 1850
Richard Hamming 674
Chris Hankin, Imperial College, London 462
Mary Ellen Hanley, Kaludis Consulting Group 26
Blake Hannaford, University of Washington 1748
David R. Hanson, Microsoft Research 1694
Richard J. Hanson, Visual Numerics, Houston 963
Vicky J. Hardman, University College, London 131, 445, 481
Donna Harman, National Institute of Standards and Technology 858
Fred H. Harris, University of Tennessee 879
David L. Hart, San Diego Supercomputer Center 1718
Brian Harvey, University of California at Berkeley 1035
Ulf Hashagen, Heinz Nixdorf Museum Forum 1239
John Hatcliff, Kansas State University 1370
Patrick J. Hayes, University of West Florida 947
David G. Hays 210
Herbert Hellerman 425, 928
David Hemmendinger, Union College 169, 439, 572, 691, 928, 1244, 1324, 1412, 1414, 1441, 1444, 1470, 1475, 1674, 1737, 1865
Gabor T. Herman, University of Pennsylvania 51, 1783
Leonard Herman, Videotopia Advisory Board 1827
Bertram Herzog, University of Michigan 274, 448
Vincent P. Heuring, University of Colorado at Boulder 1144
Francis Heylighen, Free University of Brussels 470
Jessica K. Hodgins, Georgia Institute of Technology 301
Jay P. Hoeflinger, University of Illinois at Urbana-Champaign 1710
Clyde W. Holsapple, University of Kentucky 759
Per A. Holst, Stavenger College, Norway 53
John E. Hopcroft, Cornell University 42
Ellis Horowitz, University of Southern California 45
H. K. Huang, University of California at San Francisco 1118
Richard J. Hughes, Los Alamos National Laboratory 1493
Horst Hünke, Commission of the European Communities, Brussels 1945
Harry D. Huskey, University of California at Santa Cruz—retired 435, 626, 649, 934, 1557, 1725, 1851
Velma R. Huskey 1040
W. John Hutchins, University of East Anglia, UK 1059
Michel Israel, Université d'Evry, France 768
Kenneth E. Iverson, Iverson Software 67
Robert J. K. Jacob, Tufts University 1821
H. V. Jagadish, AT&T Laboratories 516
Charles V. Jones, Ball State University 980, 1373
Phillippe Jorrand, Université de Grenoble, France 1945
Cliff Joslyn, Los Alamos National Laboratory 470
David K. Kahaner, Asian Technology Information Program 1260
Ravi Kalakota, Georgia State University 628
Alain Kaloyeros, State University of NY at Albany 892
Laveen N. Kanal, University of Maryland 1383
Arthur I. Karshmer, New Mexico State University 735
Major Keary, Translation consultant 868
Brian W. Kernighan, AT&T Laboratories 171

Robin H. Kerr 134
Helene G. Kershner, State University of NY at Buffalo 395
Clark Kimberling, University of Evansville, Indiana 1101
David R. Kincaid, University of Texas at Austin 1367
William R. King, Systems and Computer Technology Corporation 26
Peter T. Kirstein, University College, London 131, 445, 481
Philip Klahr, Inference Corporation 684
Graham Knight, University College, London 902
Donald E. Knuth, Stanford University 1153, 1756
Jill C. Knuth, Writer 1153, 1756
Tom Koch, Simon Fraser University, Canada 941
Elliot B. Koffman, Temple University 616
Robert R. Korfhage 36, 154, 1409
Robert Kowalski, Imperial College, London 1017
H. T. Kung, Harvard University 1741
Thomas E. Kurtz, Dartmouth College 131
Andrew Laine, Columbia University 1233
Stephen W. Lam, State University of NY at Buffalo 1326
Rolf Landauer 984
Steven P. Landry, University of Southwestern Louisiana 520
Phil M. Lane, University College, London 481
Charles L. Lawson, NASA JPL (California Institute of Technology) 963
Harold W. Lawson, Lawson Konsult AB, Sweden 1643
Norman Layer, IBM—retired 828
Edward D. Lazowska, University of Washington 1311
Joseph J. Lazzaro, Massachusetts Commission for the Blind 585
Doug Lea, State University of NY at Oswego 595
David B. Leake, Indiana University 196
Burton M. Leavenworth, Drexel University—retired 1244
Olivier Lecarme, Université de Nice, France 1174
J. A. N. Lee, Virginia Polytechnic Institute 250, 750, 751, 835, 1365, 1451, 1475, 1514, 1708
Victor R. Lesser, University of Massachusetts 1194
Nancy Leveson, Massachusetts Institute of Technology 646
Paul Levinson, Fordham University 162
Brian T. Lewis, Sun Microsystems 465
Bernard Levrat, Université de Genève 624
Jochen Liedtke, Universität Karlsruhe, Germany 1311
Anthony Liekens, Universiteit Antwerpen 93
Peter F. Linington, University of Kent, UK 488, 1288
Thomas Little, Boston University 1196
Joyce Currie Little, Towson State University 1400
C. L. Liu, University of Illinois 235
Keith R. London 602
Ralph L. London, University of California at Irvine 1458
Margot Lovejoy, State University of NY at Purchase 320
Henry Lowood, Stanford University 1250
Michael R. Lowry, NASA Ames Laboratory 119
William F. Luebbert 785
Daniel C. Lynch, Interop Company 915
Jack Lynch, Rutgers University 645
John MacKrell, CIMdata, Inc. 274
Silvano Maffeis, SoftWired AG, Switzerland 215
Michael S. Mahoney, Princeton University 1613
Jos Marlowe, Sun Microsystems 595
George Marsaglia, Florida State University 1192, 1499
Joanne Martin, IBM 137

Preface to the Fourth Edition

It is now seven years since the publication of the third edition of this *Encyclopedia*. In the Preface to the third edition it was noted that the pace of change in computing "is still more rapid than in any other scientific or technical discipline," but that it "may not be as breakneck as it once was." The former claim is still correct; the latter, however, probably is not. The advent of the Internet and the rapidly falling prices and increasing capability of personal computers, among other things, made the 1990s a period of very rapid change indeed. Thus seven years is such a long time between editions that this is a very different volume from its predecessors.

How different? The third edition contained 605 articles from 370 contributors (compared with 550 and 301 in the second edition and 470 and 210 in the first edition). This edition has 623 articles from over 450 contributors of which

♦ 103 are new articles
♦ 29 are rewritten articles on subjects covered in the third edition
♦ 132 are third edition articles that have been extensively modified and brought up to date.

Also, this edition has 16 color pages whereas the third edition, the first to have any color at all, had only 12.

As in the previous editions, in addition to articles on the history of computing itself, many articles discuss the history of their subjects. There are five new biographies of major figures in computing, but we have adopted a policy of not adding any new biographies of living people. There are also new articles on the history of ten important programming languages. Almost all articles from the third edition that have been retained have undergone at least minor modification, and many were extensively revised or replaced. In order that the fourth edition be not too much larger than the third, some articles from that edition have been merged into other articles while others have been deleted because their subject matter was deemed both obsolete and not of historical significance.

The seven appendices in the third edition have been retained, and two new ones have been added. One lists all articles in earlier editions that no longer appear, so that readers can find certain topics not covered in this edition. The other lists the presidents of various professional societies; previous editions included them in separate articles. The expanded Appendix IX, the Timeline of Significant Computing Milestones, remains, we hope, both informative and irreverent.

The overall result is a fourth edition in which over 40% of the material was either not contained in the third edition or has been significantly modified. The Classification of Articles in the front of this volume is an important tool for readers looking for subject matter in a specific area. In addition, there are two extensive indexes, a Subject Index and a Name Index. The latter contains the names of all persons mentioned somewhere in the *Encyclopedia* (except for authors of uncited items in bibliographies).

It is intended to make this edition available by subscription on the World Wide Web. And because current technology makes it easy and affordable, we hope to update the Web edition regularly to provide a more up-to-date resource than a printed book can ever be. This updated edition will then be used to publish fifth (and later!) editions. Indeed, before too long—but probably not for the fifth edition—this *Encyclopedia* may become entirely electronic.

Finally, a word about the title. It is the same as that of the first and third editions, whereas the second was called *The Encyclopedia of Computer Science and Engineering*. In the preface to the third edition it was light-heartedly suggested that we would henceforth use "Engineering" in the even numbered editions and omit it from the odd-numbered editions. The engineering aspects of computing, both hardware and software, are fully represented in this edition, but we have chosen to retain the more succinct title of the third edition.

Anthony Ralston   ar9@doc.ic.ac.uk
Edwin D. Reilly   reilly@cs.albany.edu
David Hemmendinger hemmendd@union.edu

January, 2000

NOTE: The editors and publisher welcome comments on how this *Encyclopedia* could be improved in both coverage and style as well as reports on any errors of fact or typographical errors. All correspondence should be sent by email to one of the addresses above or The Development Editor, *Encyclopedia of Computer Science*, John Wiley & Sons Ltd, The Atrium, Southern Gate, Chichester, West Sussex, PO19 8SQ, UK. (Email: encomsci@wiley.co.uk)

Editors' Foreword

The most important purpose of an encyclopedia in a particular discipline is to be a basic reference work for readers who need information on subjects in which they are not expert. The implication of "basic" is that an encyclopedia, while it should attempt to be comprehensive in *breadth* of coverage, cannot be comprehensive in the *depth* with which it treats most topics. An encyclopedia should, however, direct the reader to information at a deeper level, as this one does through bibliographic references and cross-references to other articles. In this edition for the first time many articles also list pertinent Websites (but the reader should be warned: uniform resource locators for Websites are often ephemeral so that the fraction of those in this *Encyclopedia* that are accurate will decline with time).

What constitutes breadth of coverage is always a difficult question, and it is especially so for computer science and computer engineering, relatively new disciplines that have evolved over the past five decades and are still changing rapidly. Their boundaries are not well defined because there is no general agreement, even among computer scientists and engineers as to whether certain areas are or are not part of these disciplines. Thus the choice of specific topics for this *Encyclopedia* has required our judgment of what is basic and important, modulated by the practical problems of finding appropriate authors to write the articles. While there may be disagreement about the inclusion or exclusion of certain topics, we hope and believe that little of major importance has been omitted.

Articles in this *Encyclopedia* normally contain definitions of the article titles (typically early in the article in a sentence or paragraph where the article title is italicized), but even the shortest articles also contain explanatory information to broaden and deepen the reader's understanding. There are numerous historical articles, and long articles contain historical and survey material that integrate the subject matter and put it into perspective. Overall, the *Encyclopedia* is a general reference to computer science and engineering, as well as a broad picture of the discipline, its history, and its direction.

Organization

The organization of this volume is alphabetical by article titles. Special characters collate in accord with their ASCII sequence except that hyphens are treated as spaces. Thus, for example, COMPUTER-AIDED SOFTWARE ENGINEERING comes before COMPUTER ALGEBRA. Titles have been chosen so that the first word is generally the one most likely to be selected by the reader searching for a given topic. In addition, there are cross-reference entries when the reader might have sought more than one word in a title, or when the article could have been given an alternative synonymous title.

There are five additional aids to the reader. The first aid is the Classification of Articles, which follows this Foreword. This classification is intended to guide the reader to clusters of related articles. It may also be useful in helping readers to follow a coherent self-study regime in a particular subfield. The second such aid is the list of cross-references at the beginning of each article, which cite titles of closely related articles, and the third aid is the frequent use of the notations (*q.v.*) and "*See*" in articles to indicate the title of an article related to the point under discussion.

The nine appendices at the back of the book constitute the fourth aid. These are abbreviations and acronyms; notation; journals and magazines relevant to computing; academic departments of computer science and engineering; presidents of computer societies; computer languages; a five-language glossary of important computer terms; articles in prior editions deleted from this one; and an extensive timeline of important milestones in computing.

The fifth aid is the pair of indexes. In a dictionary or glossary, all terms being defined appear as entries, making an index superfluous. But in an encyclopedia only the most important terms are used as article titles or even main cross-references, making an index essential. We have tried to make the General Index comprehensive but to make it easier to use, we have placed most references to people in a separate Name Index that precedes the General Index. The General Index contains all terms that should appear in a *dictionary* of computer science, but also contains entries that would not normally appear in a computer dictionary, such as references to subcategories and important words in general usage. Thus the index will often provide pointers to unfamiliar terms whose exploration the reader might find useful and interesting.

Anthony Ralston

Edwin D. Reilly

David Hemmendinger

Classification of Articles

This classification of articles embodies a taxonomy that should be helpful to the reader in grasping the scope of the material contained in this volume. Articles are classified under nine categories:

1. Hardware
2. Computer Systems
3. Information and Data
4. Software
5. Mathematics of Computing
6. Theory of Computation
7. Methodologies
8. Applications
9. Computing Milieux

Each Encyclopedia article appears at least once in this classification. Some titles appear more than once in order to avoid the clutter of cross-references. Most classification headings are themselves article titles, in which case the title is followed by the page on which it begins. Headings preceded by an asterisk (*), however, are not actual titles but rather were invented to provide coherence to the classification. (Note: Appendix VIII contains a list of all articles in previous editions that are not in this edition.)

1. *HARDWARE

*TYPES OF COMPUTERS

COMPUTER ARCHITECTURE   304

3. *INFORMATION AND DATA

6. *THEORY OF COMPUTATION

7. *METHODOLOGIES

9. *COMPUTING MILIEUX

Trademarked Items Mentioned in ─ Encyclopedia Articles ─

Item	Article	Owner
A+	Personnel in the Computer Field	Computing Technology Industry Association
Access	Personnel in the Computer Field	Microsoft
ACSL	Simulation	MGA Software
Alpha	Intermediate Languages	Digital Equipment Corporation
Amphion	Automatic Programming	NASA
Aptiva	IBM PC	IBM
Axiom	Computer Algebra: Systems	Numerical Algorithms Group
BONeS Designer	Simulation	Alta Group
Buddy List	Online Conversation	AOL
Capability Maturity Model	Software Engineering Institute	Software Engineering Institute
CERT	Software Engineering Institute	Software Engineering Institute
Chem	Computer Science	NASA
COMNET III	Simulation	CACI Products
Corel Amicus Attorney	Legal Applications	Gavel and Gown Software Inc.
CPSim	Simulation	BoyanTech
CPUMark99	Benchmarks	Ziff-Davis, Inc.
CSIM18	Simulation	Mesquite Software
DataGlove	Virtual Reality	VPL Research
DB-2	Computer Science	IBM
dBase	Computer Science	dBASE, Inc.
DECNET	Computer Science	Digital Equipment Corporation
Derive	Computer Algebra: Systems	Soft Warehouse
Eispack	Computer Science	Netlib
Excel	Software History	Microsoft
Extend	Simulation	Imagine That
FLAMES	Simulation	Ternion
GPSS/H	Standards	Wolverine Software
HotDocs	Legal Applications	Capsoft Development
Hypercard	Computer Science	Apple Computer, Inc.
IBM PC	Intermediate Languages	IBM
ICQ	Online Conversation	Mirabalis
Ingres	Computer Science	Computer Associates
Instant Messaging	Online Conversation	AOL
Intel Pentium	Microcomputer Chip	Intel
Intel 48	Microcomputer Chip	Intel
Intermedia	Computer Science	Intermedia Communications
ITEMS	Simulation	CAE Electronics

Item	Article	Owner
Java	Java (and many others)	Sun Microsystems
Jaz	Memory: Auxiliary	Iomega Corporation
JFS Docket Station	Legal Applications	Bowne & Co.
JFS JazzNotes	Legal Applications	Bowne & Co.
JFS Litigator's Notebook	Legal Applications	Bowne & Co.
Lego	LOGO	Lego Company
Linpack	Computer Science	Netlib
listserv	Electronic Mail	L-Soft International
Lotus 1-2-3	Software History	Lotus
Mach	Computer Science	Carnegie Mellon University
Macintosh	Windows Environments (and many others)	Apple Computer, Inc.
MacOS	Computer Science	Apple Computer, Inc.
Macsyma	Computer Algebra: Systems	Macsyma, Inc.
Majordomo	Electronic Mail	Great Circle Associates
Maple	Computer Science *and* Mathematics, Computers In *and* Computer Algebra: Systems	Waterloo Maple, Inc.
Mathematica	Computer Science *and* Mathematics, Computers In	Wolfram Reasearch, Inc.
Metafont	Metafont	Addison-Wesley Publishing Co.
Microsoft Messenger	Online Conversation	Microsoft
Microsoft Word	Text Editing Systems	Microsoft
MODSIM	Simulation	CACI Products
MPIOC	Input–Output Operations	MasPar
MS-DOC	Computer Science	Microsoft
Multi-Edit	Text Editing Systems	American Cybernetics
Multics	Computer Science	Honeywell
MultiGenII	Simulation	Multigen
MuPAD	Computer Algebra: Systems	Sciface Software GmbH
NLS	Computer Science	Stanford Research Institute
NoteCards	Computer Science	Xerox
Omnipage Pro	Optical Character Recognition	Caere Corporation
OS/2	Computer Science	IBM
Personal Software Process	Software Engineering Institute	Software Engineering Institute
PlanWare	Automatic Programming	Invest-Tech, Ltd.
Portége	Portable Computers	Toshiba
Powerbuilder	Personnel in the Computer Field	Sybase, Inc.
Quattro Pro	Software History	Corel Corporation
RealAudio	Bulletin Board	Real Networks, Inc.
RealVideo	Bulletin Board	Real Networks, Inc.
SAS System	Access methods	SAS Institute
SciNapse	Automatic Programming	SciComp, Inc.
Silicon Graphics 320	Workstation	Silicon Graphics Inc.
SIMAN/Cinema	Simulation	Systems Modeling
SIMGRAPHICS	Simulation	CACI Products
SimPack	Simulation	University of Florida
Simscript II.5	Simulation	CACI Products
SLAM II	Simulation	Pritsker Associates
Sparc	Intermediate Languages	Sun Microsystems
SuperCard	Computer Science	Digital Media Group, Ltd.
Sybase	Computer Science	Sybase, Inc.
SYSmark	Benchmarks	BAPCo
System R	Computer Science	IBM
Taylor II	Simulation	F&H Simulations
TEX	TEX	American Mathematical Society
Thinkpad	IBM PC	IBM
Unix	Unix (and many others)	AT&T Bell Laboratories
Virtual Basic	Basic	Microsoft
Virtual Classroom	Computer Conferencing	New Jersey Institute of Technology
Visicalc	Software History	Trellix Corporation
Visual Basic	Personnel in the Computer Field	Microsoft
VMS	Computer Science	Digital Equipment Corporation
VRLink	Simulation	MAK Technologies
Web	Computer Science	NASA
WinBench	Benchmarks	Ziff Davis, Inc.

Item	Article	Owner
Windows	Text Editing System (and many others)	Microsoft
Windows NT	Computer Science	Microsoft
Winstone	Benchmarks	Ziff Davis, Inc.
Workbench	Simulation	SES
Xanadu	Computer Science	NASA
Yahoo! Messenger	Online Conversation	Yahoo!
Zip	Memory: Auxiliary	Iomega Corporation
Zip + 4	Optical Character Recognition	US Postal Service

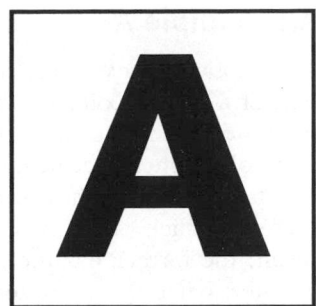

ABSTRACT DATA TYPE

For articles on related subjects *see* CLASS; DATA TYPE;
DATA STRUCTURES; ENCAPSULATION; INFORMATION HIDING;
OBJECT–ORIENTED PROGRAMMING; PROGRAM SPECIFICATION;
SOFTWARE REUSABILITY; and STRUCTURED PROGRAMMING.

The purpose of abstract data types is to allow the modular construction of software systems through the composition of components whose individual behavior is well understood.

An *abstract data type* (ADT) is a programmer-defined data type, comprising a specification and at least one implementation. The specification gives an abstract description of the behavior of instances of the type, independently of any particular implementation. The provider of an abstract type implementation is obliged to ensure that it obeys the specification perfectly. So long as this is the case, users of the type need only understand the specification, rather than the implementation, to know how values of the type will behave.

This approach to software construction has a number of advantages. The specification may be given in a language other than the programming language used to implement it, and in particular an axiomatic specification language such as Z or VDL (*see* VIENNA DEFINITION LANGUAGE) may be used. This allows the user of an abstract data type to gain a very clear understanding of its operational behavior without having to understand the lower-level details of its implementation. Different implementations can be substituted, for example for performance reasons, without affecting the user code. Finally, the user code can be written before any implementation exists, allowing parallel construction in a large system.

The implementation itself consists of a concrete representation, a set of operations that may be performed on that representation, and an interface to those operations. The interface must, of course, correspond to that given as part of the specification. It is a critical requirement for an abstract data type that the interface operations provide the only access by which the concrete representation is manipulated. In this case, whether or not the interface provides a correct implementation of the abstract specification depends only on the coding of the interface operations, independently of any pattern of use.

Some programming languages provide explicit support for abstract data types; some provide implicit support, and some provide no support at all. However, the concept of abstract typing may be usefully thought of as a programming discipline rather than a syntactic construct, and it is possible to program in this discipline in many languages that do not possess explicit syntactic support, as well as in those which do.

Most languages that explicitly support pure models of abstract data types have evolved in the research domain, and include, for example, Alphard, CLU, Euclid, ML (arguably a commercial language), Napier88, and Quest. Commercial languages with at least some support for the key concepts include Ada (*q.v.*), C++ (*q.v.*), Java (*q.v.*), and some dialects of Pascal (*q.v.*).

An Example ADT

As a motivating example, consider an abstract definition of a simple counter, the kind a shepherd might use for counting sheep. We will give one in English for want of a better specification language. The abstract interface consists of the operations "click," "look," and "reset." "Click" and "reset" have no argument or result; the former has the effect of incrementing the counter, while the latter zeros it. "Look" also has no argument, but returns a natural number, representing the current value of the counter.

Notice that the specification is completely independent of the programming language used for coding. However, although the definition might be completely abstract, it is still necessary to find sufficient commonality between the specification and coding languages for the interface operations to be defined in both. In this case we can manage with a programming language that provides procedures and integers; here is an obvious implementation in an imaginary language:

```
let counterRep := 0

procedure click() ; counterRep :=
                            counterRep + 1
procedure reset() ; counterRep := 0
procedure look() -> integer ;
                        return( counterRep )
```

However, this implementation of the abstract description does not make an abstract type, as the operational interface can be compromised by a change to the variable counterRep from another context, without using click or reset. Neither is it completely correct, since we should really note in the specification that it should be used only for flocks up to the maximum integer size! Although this may seem pedantic, such detail is important in the construction of large systems.

First- and Second-Order Information Hiding

There are two ways in which the concrete representation of an abstract data type can be protected from unlawful manipulation: by making it incapable of being denoted in the language, or by giving it a type that precludes illegal operations. Mechanisms in these classes are known respectively as first-order and second-order information hiding. The critical difference is that second-order mechanisms allow instances of the abstract type itself to appear in the operational signature (the specification of the types of the operations in terms of the types of their operands and return values). The use of first-order information hiding is thus restricted to state transformation models, where the abstract instance is hidden behind interface operations that affect and report aspects of its state (*see* PROGRAM-

MING LANGUAGE SEMANTICS). Second-order hiding is more flexible, as it allows abstract values to be passed around along with operations that may be applied to them.

In the example, instances of the counter itself do not appear in the interface, and therefore first-order information hiding may be used. We give the example coded in an imaginary block-structured language with higher-order (first-class) procedures (*see* BLOCK STRUCTURE; and FUNCTIONAL PROGRAMMING). Higher-order procedure types can be used to give the type of the interface ("counter") without relying upon specific abstract type syntax, and block structure can be used to prevent the concrete representation from being accessed other than by the interface procedures. After the initializing block has been executed, the variable counterRep is out of scope with respect to the rest of the program. The implementation of the higher-order procedure mechanism must of course preserve the location for as long as the procedures are accessible.

```
type counter is structure
            ( click, reset : procedure(),
              look         : procedure()
                                -> integer )
let myCounter =
{
  let counterRep := 0
    structure
    (
    click = procedure() ;
            counterRep := counterRep + 1,
    reset = procedure() ;
            counterRep := 0,
    look = procedure() -> integer ;
            return( counterRep )
    )
}
```

This kind of procedural encapsulation follows essentially the same model as that of many object-oriented languages, and differs only by the syntactic mechanism by which the instance variables (corresponding to the concrete representation) are kept inaccessible from other parts of the code. It is reasonable to regard some instances of classes, in some object-oriented languages, as abstract data types. However, other object-oriented languages have models of typing and dynamic method binding (*q.v.*) that make it impossible to define abstract types, as no guarantee can be given that the concrete representation is accessed only by the originally defined interface procedures.

To introduce a second-order example we will model the same kind of counter, but slightly change the abstract definition to model a collection of counters. Each has the same interface operations, modeled now as procedures that operate on counters, and two new interface functions are introduced: one to create a counter, and one to test whether one counter has a greater value than another. Given the identifier `counter` to represent the type of the new counter, the abstract interface is as follows:

```
structure
(
 newCounter  : procedure() -> counter,
 click       : procedure( counter ),
 reset       : procedure( counter ),
 look        : procedure( counter )
                                  -> integer,
 greater     : procedure( counter, counter )
                                  -> boolean
)
```

The procedure `greater` exemplifies one of the major differences in expressive power between the two classes of information hiding, in that second-order hiding allows the neat definition of operators that act over more than a single instance of the type. With first-order information hiding, as in the pure object-oriented paradigm, such operators do not fit neatly and can only be expressed artificially, either asymmetrically or by using the published interface at a different level of abstraction. Second-order hiding, however, allows the definition of arbitrary abstract algebras (mathematical systems of operations on the types).

To provide second-order hiding, a host language must have some mechanism that allows the type of the data to be opaquely abstracted in order to prevent operations other than those in the interface being applied. There are three well-known mechanisms in this category: the abstract type model first used by the language ML, the existential types model proposed by Mitchell and Plotkin, and the class abstraction of many object-oriented programming languages.

ML-Style Information Hiding

ML abstract type syntax allows the association of a new type name with a representation and a set of operators. The signatures of the operators may include the new name, which is interpreted within their bodies as the representation type. After the end of the definition, the names of the operators and the name of the new type are in scope, but its representation may no longer be used.

The following pseudocode captures the essence of the ML mechanism. The counter is represented by an integer location, as before, and this is signified by the first line of the type definition. Within the body of the definition, the type `counter` is interpreted as an integer location. After the end of the definition, however, this use of the type is withdrawn: two values typed as `counter` are known to have the same type, but no other information about the type may be used.

```
abstype counter <=> location( integer ) with
 newCounter = procedure() -> counter
    return( location( 0 ) )
 click       = procedure( x : counter )
    x := at( x ) + 1
 reset       = procedure( x : counter )
    x := 0
 look        = procedure( x : counter )
                                  -> integer
    return( at( x ) )
 greater     = procedure( x,y : counter )
                                  -> boolean
    return( at( x ) > at( y ) )
```

Mitchell and Plotkin's Abstract Packages

Although superbly elegant in its minimal capture of the concept, the very simplicity of the ML model stops it from being ideally suited for large software systems. The name of the abstract type is inherently tied to only a single implementation, making the model inflexible. Furthermore, the type and operator names have global scope, making the composition of independently prepared subsystems problematic due to name clashes. This problem is solved by the model proposed by Mitchell and Plotkin. Here, the type of the abstract package is declared separately from the implementation, with a bound identifier signifying the abstract type:

```
type cPack is AbstractPackage[ counter ]
(
 newCounter : procedure() -> counter,
 click      : procedure( counter ),
 reset      : procedure( counter ),
 look       : procedure( counter )
                                  -> integer,
 greater    : procedure( counter, counter )
                                  -> boolean
)
```

Instances are subsequently created by placing values with known types into an instance of the algebra type. In the following example, the type of the value `repPack` is `cPack`, and the type information denoted by `counter` (an integer location, in this example) may not be subsequently rediscovered. In the example syntax here, the typename `cPack` is overloaded as a constructor function that returns an instance of the `cPack` type.

```
let repPack = cPack()
(
 newCounter = procedure() -> counter
    return( location( 0 ) )
 click       = procedure( x : counter )
    x := at( x ) + 1
 reset       = procedure( x : counter )
    x := 0
 look        = procedure( x : counter )
                                  -> integer
    return( at( x ) )
 greater     = procedure( x,y : counter )
                                  -> boolean
    return( at( x ) > at( y ) )
)
```

This model makes the abstract algebra a structural type, the abstract type name a bound variable of the algebra, and the operators fields of the algebra instance. This approach avoids introducing any significant names with the creation of an instance. Furthermore, it decouples the definition of the algebra signature from the creation of its instances, making it possible for a number of different implementations to coexist. It is essential that a further syntactic mechanism is introduced in order to avoid the mixing of operations between instances. One such mechanism is the open clause, which introduces a new constant binding (myCPack) for the abstract package. Any construct that ensures a constant binding may be used, although the open clause also provides a convenient syntax for introducing an identifier to stand for the abstract type:

```
open repPack as myCPack[ counterType ] in
{
 let newCounter = myCPack.newCounter
 let click = myCPack.click
 let myCounter = newCounter()
                  // value of type counterType

 click( myCounter )
}
```

OBJECT-ORIENTED INFORMATION HIDING

The final well-known mechanism that allows the abstraction required for second-order information hiding is the *class* mechanism of object-oriented languages. Such mechanisms control the scoping of instance variables and methods, and can be used to describe abstract data types. Once again note that the converse is not the case, and many classes described in such languages cannot usefully be regarded as abstract types because they lack the necessary static properties. The following shows the example coded in Java:

```
class Counter
{
 private:
   int counterRep;
 public:
   Counter()    { counterRep = 0 ; }
   void click() { counterRep++ ; }
   void reset() { counterRep = 0 ; }
   int look()   { return counterRep ; }
   static bool greater( Counter x, Counter y )
     { return( x.counterRep > y.counterRep ) ; }
};
```

Object-oriented information hiding is an interesting mix between first- and second-order models. The concept of an object is essentially a first-order model, and is normally used in the state transformation paradigm. However, the scoping rules for method definition can allow the coding of second-order models by giving access to the internal state of more than one object of the same class, as in the above example. This is a com-

mon paradigm in the languages C++ and Java. While neither language provides a perfect degree of safety with respect to the criteria identified earlier, both give a reasonable degree of confidence in the absence of malicious interference.

For code using this class, only the class name Counter and the names of the public interface functions may be accessed. Only the identifier Counter is required to be in global scope and unique within the composition of modules, making less of a problem in system composition than the ML mechanism. The other operator names are effectively labels brought into scope by the dereferencing of an instance of the class or, in the case of static functions, the class itself.

```
class UseCounter
{
 public:
   int useCounter()
   {
    Counter a,b;

    a = new( Counter );
    b = new( Counter );
    a->click();
    return( Counter::greater( a,b ) );
   }
}
```

Also deserving mention in the context of object-oriented programming and abstract data types, is the concept of "componentware" models of programming (*see* COMPONENT SOFTWARE), as typified by CORBA and DCOM. Such models again give practical, if not enforced, guarantees of the externally observable consistent behavior, and the componentware paradigm is arguably that of geographically distributed abstract data types.

Conclusion

To summarize the main concepts presented, it is most helpful to view an abstract data type as a programming discipline that helps with the construction of large software systems by providing components whose behavior may be understood at an abstract level. To achieve this, it must have a precise abstract specification, an interface and implementation that capture the specification, and a sufficient degree of protection from deliberate or accidental misuse.

Bibliography

1981. Liskov, B., Atkinson, R., Bloom, T., Moss, E., Schaffert, J. C., Scheifler, R., and Synder, A. *CLU Reference Manual.* New York: Springer-Verlag.

1990. Milner, R., and Harper, R. *The Definition of Standard ML.* Cambridge, MA: MIT Press.

1994. Schmidt, D. A. *The Structure of Typed Programming Languages.* Cambridge, MA: MIT Press.

1996. Paulson, L. *Standard ML for the Working Programmer*, 2nd Ed. Cambridge: Cambridge University Press.

1997. Meyer, B. *Object-Oriented Software Construction*, 2nd Ed. Upper Saddle River, NJ: Prentice Hall.

1999. Henning, M. and Vinoski, S. *Advanced CORBA Programming with C++*. Reading, MA: Addison-Wesley.

Richard Connor

ACCESS METHODS

For articles on related subjects *see* ACCESS TIME; DATABASE MANAGEMENT SYSTEM; FILE; INFORMATION ACCESS; INPUT–OUTPUT CONTROL SYSTEM; INPUT–OUTPUT OPERATIONS; RECORD; and SEARCHING.

Introduction

An *access method* is a technique for accessing data that has been placed on some kind of mass storage device; magnetic tape at one time, but now most often a hard disk (*q.v.*). While the term *access method* is most properly used to *describe* the method used to retrieve the data, it is also frequently used as a synonym for the program or routine that *implements* the method. All computer manufacturers provide service routines to implement access methods, generally as a component of an operating system (*q.v.*). Instead of *access method*, terms such as data management, file control program, and I/O (input or output) supervisor are sometimes used, depending on the manufacturer. The terminology used in this article is common to several manufacturers, including IBM (*q.v.*), but not all manufacturers support every variant described.

Evolution of Access Methods

In the earliest days of computers, each programmer had to program the flow of data to and from I/O devices, including auxiliary storage units such as disks, drums, and tapes. This required that the programmer be familiar with the characteristics of particular devices and write code for functions such as testing for avail-

able channels (*q.v.*), testing for I/O errors, and programming error recovery. Many of these functions were time dependent. Programming I/O in this manner tended to bind the programs to a particular device. When the storage device changed, program code had to be substantially modified.

Since I/O programming tended to be fairly similar from one program to the next, it was not long before utility service programs (or access methods) were developed. Such programs perform, in a generalized manner, all of the interactions with the storage device. The programmer need merely be concerned with requesting a record and providing a location in storage for it. The division of functions is depicted in Fig. 1. Note the assumption in this figure that the application program can continue processing while data is being transferred, a point to which we return below.

The interface between the application program and the access method tends to be fairly simple and standardized and is generally reducible to a set of parameters. The usual technique is to place the input and output parameters in a table. This table may be called (among other names) the DTF (Define The File), DD (Data Definition), or FCT (File Control Table). The parameters include a pointer (*q.v.*) to an area of storage to and from which the data transfer is to be made (i.e. the record *buffer*—*q.v.*), the size of the record, whether electronic labels are to be written or read at the front of the file, and pointers to special error-handling routines. The application program need only place the necessary data into the table. This is a far easier task than having to write a customized I/O routine. When invoked by the application, the access method uses the contents of the table to perform the task requested. When a new storage device becomes available, only the access method, not the application program's main logic, need be modified. Such device independence, a form of *transparency* (*q.v.*), implies that, to the user of an application, changes in storage devices are invisible, i.e. they need not be concerned with them.

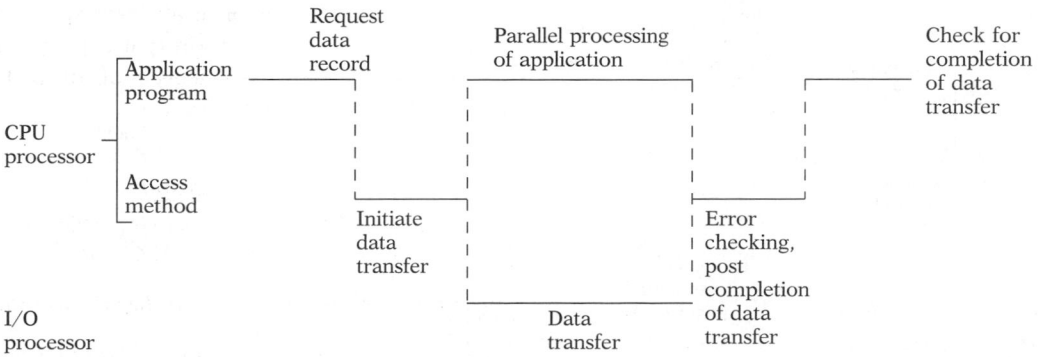

Figure 1. Division of functions.

On early computers without multiprogramming (*q.v.*), it was important that each individually running program use the central processing unit (CPU—*q.v.*) as efficiently as possible. Fig. 1 illustrates an application that continues processing while data transfer takes place. This is achieved by having the access method return control to the application program as soon as it starts the data transfer. When data transfer is complete, the interrupt mechanism gives control to the access method again. The access method performs checking for data transfer errors and, assuming no problem, "posts" or flags the file parameter table that the data transfer is complete. Control is then returned to the application program. The responsibility for insuring that processing of input data does not begin until the data transfer is complete is left to the application program, which must check the parameter table for completion of the data transfer.

Sequential Access Methods

SAM—SEQUENTIAL ACCESS METHOD
The most widely used auxiliary storage device on early computers was magnetic tape. Because records on such a medium must be stored sequentially, they must also be processed sequentially for optimum efficiency. The standard tape access method thus became known as SAM (Sequential Access Method). Using SAM, there was little processing that an application program could do on input while waiting for the next record (although, on output, it could start to generate the next record). A better method was needed to take advantage of the predictability that the next one of the sequentially stored records would be read. Thus a new access method was designed to achieve what the application program generally could not—namely, to overlap processing with data transfer. When reading data, this is achieved by looking ahead and performing the access for the next record while the application program is processing the last (or current) record. This modification of the model of Fig. 1 is illustrated in Fig. 2.

QSAM—QUEUED SEQUENTIAL ACCESS METHOD
As Fig. 2 illustrates, the data transmission proceeds in parallel with the application processing, with a brief time-out at the end of the transmission for the access method to handle the details of error checking. In this case, the access method does not have to post the completion of data transfer to the application, since the application is still working with the last record. Fig. 2 illustrates the normal situation, but clearly there are situations where the application finishes its work before the data transfer is complete. In this case, some waiting is necessary, but nevertheless some overlap of processing and data transfer has been achieved that otherwise would not have been. This access method is known as QSAM (Queued Sequential Access Method) and, to distinguish it from SAM, sequential access was renamed BSAM (Basic Sequential Access Method). QSAM for input was just described, but applies equally well to output. On output, QSAM also assumes responsibility for blocking (packing) records onto a physical storage device (*see* BLOCK AND BLOCKING FACTOR).

Direct Access Methods

BSAM and QSAM were well suited to handling tape files that are inherently sequential. With the advent of direct (random) access storage devices, the need arose to support direct access of a record without passing (and inspecting) all previous records in the file. This need gave rise to two additional access methods.

BDAM—BASIC DIRECT ACCESS METHOD
In the first of these, it is assumed that the application program has the ability to compute the location of the data on the direct access device relative to the beginning of the file and to instruct the access method to retrieve (or replace) the data at that location. This access method is known as DAM (Direct Access Method) or BDAM (Basic Direct Access Method). As with BSAM, the application program is required to check that the input (or output) is complete before

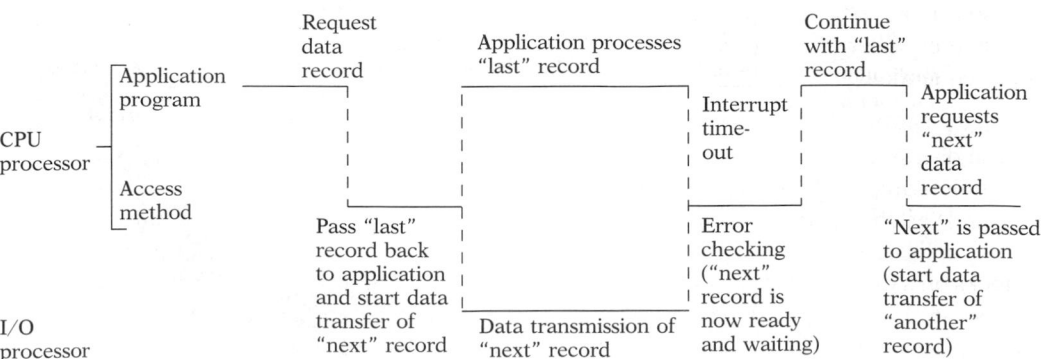

Figure 2. Overlap of processing with data transfer.

using the data. Since the location of the data is computed by the application program, there can be no "lookahead" by the access method itself, but overall computer efficiency can still be maintained if BDAM is used in multiprogramming systems where some application is executing while another is waiting.

ISAM—INDEXED SEQUENTIAL ACCESS METHOD

The second direct access method introduced combined the advantages of sequential and direct access. Known as ISAM (Indexed Sequential Access Method), it combines the two modes of basic and queued access depending on whether the operation requires that the application check for completion (Basic) or permits "lookahead" (Queued). Thus, generically, ISAM, means both BISAM (Basic ISAM) and QISAM (Queued ISAM). ISAM permits the application to process records sequentially, by the key within the record, or directly, by means of maintaining a separate index of keys (or list of pointers) to all records.

With ISAM, record keys become important. Typical examples of record keys are employee names in an alphabetized file or social security numbers in a file ordered numerically. Since BSAM and QSAM always retrieve the next sequential record, a key has no significance in accessing the record. In the case of ISAM, however, the records are not necessarily stored next to each other and a key is essential for locating a particular record. ISAM, in principle, keeps a list of keys and pointers to the appropriate records. In this manner, working from the index list, the records can be presented back to the application program in sequence by key (when all or a significant portion of the file is to be processed) or a unique record can be obtained directly without having to "pass over" any of the records logically preceding it. Since records in a file accessed by ISAM need not be stored in sequential order, the insertion of a new record into a large file is much more efficient than for files accessed by QSAM or BSAM, since a record can be placed anywhere and the index of the key list updated so that it may be found subsequently. Nonetheless, the characteristics of disk storage devices still make data transfer more efficient when the records most likely to be used in a certain order are stored sequentially.

An example of how ISAM uses indexes is shown in Table 1. Since use of a single index sometimes results in a search of a quite long list, it is common to use a hierarchy of indexes, as shown in the table. The table assumes that an employee file with 10,000 records is stored in 100 blocks on a disk, with the first block starting at disk address 46217. Each block would store an average of 100 employee records, but would have the capacity to store more than 100 records so that change

Table 1. A hierarchical block-oriented index.

Index level 1	Index level 2	Block number	Block starting address
	00000–00713	1	46217
	00718–01426	2	46337
	.	.	.
00000–08756			
	07823–08756	10	47395
.			
	41063–42217	41	50362
	.	.	.
41063–52071			
	.	.	.
	49278–50593	49	51612
	50614–52071	50	51738
	.	.	
	.	.	

to, and growth of, the file would be possible before it is reorganized and the indexes updated. Table 1 also assumes that employee numbers are in the range 00000–99999. To retrieve the record for the employee whose number is 49731, the first level index would be searched until, say, the fifth entry (41063–52071) was found; then the second level would be searched, starting at 41063–42217, until the ninth entry (49278–50593) was found; finally, address 51612 (the start of block 49) on the disk would be searched sequentially until the record with key 49731 was found. Note how much more efficient this is than searching the entire file sequentially. Note also how much more efficient a two-level index is than a single index search would be.

VSAM—VIRTUAL STORAGE ACCESS METHOD

The next advance in access methods was the Virtual Storage Access Method (VSAM), introduced in conjunction with IBM's Virtual Storage Operating Systems some time after the concept was used by Burroughs and several other manufacturers. VSAM combines many of the features of ISAM, QSAM, and BDAM into one comprehensive access method. It also incorporates improved techniques for the positioning of records on the disk and for increasing the degree of overlap of computation and I/O processing (buffering). VSAM can operate like ISAM in that records can be accessed by keys, like QSAM in that records can be accessed by the order on the storage device, or like BDAM, where the record is accessed by a "relative" position in the file. However, VSAM operates in only one of these modes for any given file, so if ISAM mode is chosen for a file, it must always be accessed by VSAM in "ISAM mode."

Database Management Systems

A further step in the evolution of data organization is the advent of the concept of the Database Manager, a system software program that manages the data resources for a series of programs. An access method is concerned only with moving data back and forth from main storage to a peripheral storage device. A Database Manager has a wider spectrum of concerns, including maintaining relationships between different sets of data, converting the data format to fit that required by the application programs, and simultaneous use of the same data by different application programs. As organizations move towards a database environment, applications are using Database Managers where they formerly used access methods. Most Database Managers call upon the established access methods to perform input and output. The access methods used are generally based on BDAM or, occasionally, on VSAM.

Teleprocessing

Another aspect of access methods is related to the advent of online processing, in which there is a need for the application program to interact with an online terminal (*see* TELEPROCESSING SYSTEMS). Many of the traditional problems solved by access methods are also apparent here: blocking, buffering, error recovery, communication protocols, etc. But there are differences—there is no storage medium involved and the devices are intended for interacting with people. Communication with such devices is heavily influenced by communications (e.g. phone line) capabilities. Just as device access methods evolved in parallel with operating systems, so telecommunication access methods evolved in parallel with telecommunication monitors. Telecommunication access methods are, however, far less standard than mass storage device access methods.

Storage device access methods evolved to enable the application to process data stored on a variety of devices in several ways in an efficient manner and to isolate the application from the physical characteristics of the device; telecommunication access methods evolved to allow the application to communicate with a variety of terminal devices and in a number of different ways in an efficient manner and to isolate it from the physical characteristics of the device. Thus, terminal access methods have evolved from BTAM (Basic Telecommunications Access Method), whereby a terminal is locked to an application under a specific communications monitor, to VTAM (Virtual Telecommunications Access Method), where a terminal may be connected to any application under a variety of telecommunications monitors.

Bibliography

1977. Hannula, R. *System 360/370 Job Control Language and Access Methods*. Reading, MA: Addison-Wesley.
1986. Lowe, D. *VSAM: Access Method Services and Application Programming*. Fresno, CA: Mike Murach & Associates.
1996. Lowe, D. *Processing VSAM Files with the SAS System*. Cary, NC: SAS Institute Inc.

Fred Braddock

ACCESS TIME

For articles on related subjects *see* CYLINDER; DISKETTE; HARD DISK; and MEMORY: AUXILIARY.

Access time is the elapsed time between the initiation of a request for data and receipt of the first bit or byte of that data.

Direct access devices require varying times to position a read–write head over a particular record. In the case of a moving-head hard disk drive, this involves positioning the *comb* (head assembly, as in Fig. 1) to the designated *cylinder* (*q.v.*), plus rotation of the selected track to the desired record.

For a disk, total access time is the sum of comb-movement (seek) and rotational times to reach a particular record (plus the time to switch from reading or writing one surface to another; however, since this is done at electronic speeds, it contributes almost nothing to the access time). There is a different access time for each record retrieved at random from a disk drive, since it is necessary to move from cylinder C_1 to cylinder C_2 (Fig. 2), and then await rotational positioning of record R.

Consider a 1999 18 GB disk drive (which might have 16,384 cylinders) that rotates at 7,200 rpm, or 8.3 ms/rotation. Typical times for comb-movement are 20 ms maximum, 9 ms average and 2 ms minimum seek

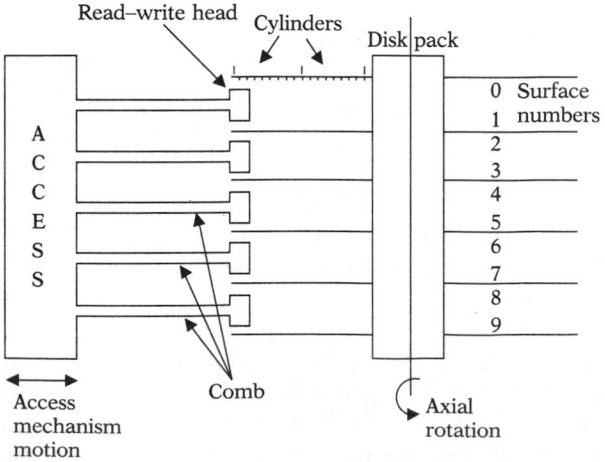

Figure 1. Side view of typical disk drive.

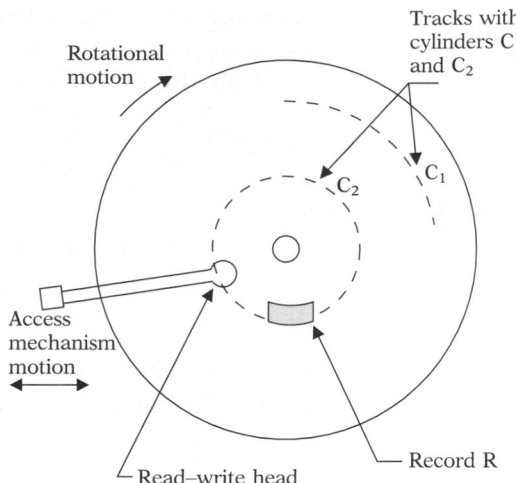

Figure 2. Top view of typical disk drive.

times. Thus the *maximum access time* for this disk is $20 + 8 = 28$ ms, the *average access time* is 13 ms (half a rotation $+ 9$ ms), and the *minimum access time* for data on an adjacent cylinder is 2 ms. The last time is also called the *track-to-track* seek time. Of course, the minimum access time for successive records on a single cylinder approaches 0.

Average access time is an important parameter for analytical planning of a real-time computer application, e.g. an online inquiry system. Minimum access time is more important for sequential usage of disk drives. The dominant component of delay for sequential retrieval of records from a disk drive is the average time for a half rotation (4.17 ms for the drive just described).

During the past 30 years, rotational speeds for hard disk drives have improved modestly; 3,600 rpm was typical, but 7,200, or even 10,800 rpm have become common. During the same period, bit density per track has increased by a factor of 50 to 100, so that average transfer speeds have increased by a factor of 50, taking into account the overhead of transferring data between disk and memory. During this time, average seek times have dropped by a factor of 4 as hydraulic actuators were replaced by "voice coil" actuators for comb-movement. Since seek time depends only on the speed and acceleration of the comb and on the size of the disk, an increase in the number of cylinders due to greater track density does not change the seek time.

For a floppy disk drive, average access time ranges from 12 to 25 ms; the access times for compact disc read-only memories (CD-ROMs) are approximately twice as long as for floppy disks.

For the drums and fixed-head disks that were once used, average access time is a half-revolution and maximum access time is a full revolution, since both have heads that are fixed over the data areas. Average access time for a 3,000 rpm drum is 10 ms.

David N. Freeman

ACCOUNTING SYSTEM, COMPUTER

For articles on related systems *see* BENCHMARKS; DATA SECURITY; OPERATING SYSTEMS; and SOFTWARE MONITOR.

As computer and software systems developed, there arose a need to develop an accounting system for the resources of the system. As with any accounting system, the goal of this capability must be to charge the user for the cost of services rendered in such a fashion that the user is motivated to evaluate the benefits of those services. Furthermore, the resources used by any one user must be limited in order to prevent that user from degrading the total effective services available to others.

Accountability is important both to the computing center staff and to its users. In order to perform their duties as financial planners for the center, the administrators require some form of accounting system. Such a system may be expected to yield statistics on hardware utilization and individual spending. These statistics can then be used to form the basis for monthly and yearly reports.

A completely automated accounting and resource control system does the following:

♦ It provides minute details concerning both hardware and software utilization, along with job statistics on account spending.

♦ It prevents unauthorized users from accessing hardware and software facilities for which they have not received permission.

♦ It prevents users from exceeding their allocated funds or other account limits.

♦ It enforces job limitations on such things as page or line limits, computer time, memory size, and disk file space.

♦ It assists the operating system in providing more effective control of resources such as main memory, auxiliary memory, and peripheral devices.

For each user of a computer system, the accounting system must know (1) who is responsible for the charges, (2) what type of service this user is entitled to (and with what constraints), (3) what resources have been allocated to the user, and (4) what price schedules apply. Further, the pricing structure must allow the user to estimate and predict costs easily, and should require only small amounts of system resources for the accounting.

The introduction of multiuser systems allowed one user to provide services to another. The result is that users are billed by both the computing center (for hardware use, expendable supplies, etc.) and other users (for proprietary software use). Thus, the accounting system must be cognizant of the use of such proprietary software and should, in fact, allow a "higher-order" user to suballocate resources to another user. For instance, it should be possible for one user to develop and maintain a subsystem, fully consistent with the operating and accounting systems, which bills the individual users for actual resources used (both hardware and software).

Another example might be the instructor who allocates fixed amounts of time or money to each student in a course in such a fashion that no student can use more than a fair share. Obviously, the person responsible for the account must be able to reallocate the resources without exceeding the total allotted. In addition, it should be possible to place limits, which may not be uniform, on each student account so that special projects may use extra memory or disk space, special hardware, etc.

Costs of an Automated Accounting System and Charges Levied

The costs of an automated accounting system are a function of the resources used to gather and maintain the accounting information. In order that the overhead of collecting the information not interfere with normal system operation, the charges themselves must reflect the unique characteristics of the system. Typically, charges are based on such things as:

1. CPU time used.
2. Memory residence time (e.g. number of pages referenced).
3. Connect time or port cost.
4. I/O operations performed (e.g. disk reads and writes).
5. Network packets sent and received.
6. Physical I/O units used:
   (a) pages printed;
   (b) file space used; and
   (c) magnetic tapes and disk packs mounted.

Through the use of automated accounting systems both operators and users can try to optimize their interaction with it so as to increase its effective utilization.

Bibliography

1987. Milenkovic, M. *Operating Systems: Concepts and Design.* New York: McGraw-Hill.

Richard H. Eckhouse

ACM

See ASSOCIATION FOR COMPUTING MACHINERY.

ACTIVATION RECORD

For articles on related subjects *see* BLOCK STRUCTURE; CALLING SEQUENCE; and PARAMETER PASSING.

An *activation record* consists of all of the information pushed onto the system stack (*q.v.*) during execution of a procedure call in a high-level block-structured language. The activation record has only transient existence during execution of the called procedure. Typically, the record contains arguments used by the programmer as part of the procedure's *calling sequence*, current contents of important system registers (*q.v.*) pushed by the machine command used to invoke the procedure, and local variables pushed by the procedure itself.

Fig. 1, adapted from Calingaert (1979), shows schematically in part (a) the static structure (nesting of blocks) of a portion of a block-structured program and its corresponding activation record stack. Assume that blocks A, B, C, D, and E are activated in that order and that E is a procedure which calls itself recursively. In addition to key parametric information, the stacked activation records of Fig. 1b must contain *static links* which indicate which procedure encloses (or precedes) a given activation record's procedure, and *dynamic links* which point to the activation record of the procedure which called a given stacked record's procedure. Static links, shown at the right of Fig. 1(b), are needed to allow access to local and nonlocal identifiers. Dynamic links are shown at the left in that same figure. The stacked activation records do not contain executable machine code; single reentrant copies of each procedure are stored elsewhere in memory.

Suppose that, on the Digital Equipment Corporation VAX, a main program calls *proc1*, which then calls *proc2*, which in turn calls *proc3*. Fig. 2 shows how the stack would then appear. Each activation record results from execution of a procedure call, and each called procedure terminates execution by executing a

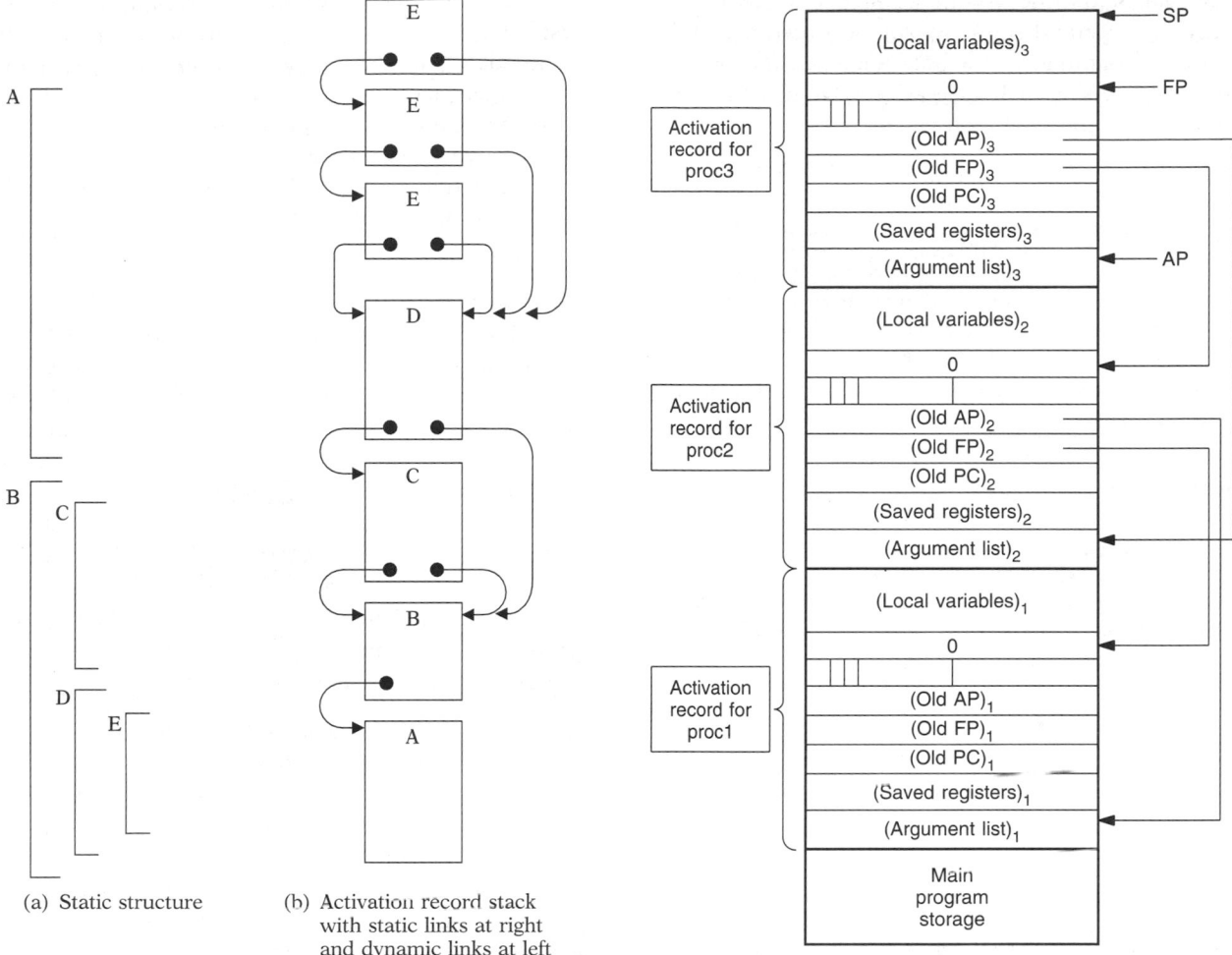

Figure 1. Run-time representation of nested procedures.

Figure 2. VAX activation records on a stack.

return command, which removes the topmost activation record from the stack (by merely resetting the stack pointer, SP in the figure). As first *proc3* and then *proc2* and finally *proc1* finish, their corresponding activation records will be removed from the stack, and thus the stack will return to its status prior to the call of *proc1*. Among the important registers saved by each procedure call are the PC, the program counter, a dynamic link which is needed so that the corresponding *return* can transfer control to exactly the right place in the calling routine. The registers labeled AP and FP, called the Argument Pointer and the Frame Pointer, are static links used by the procedure in order to reference procedure arguments and local variables respectively, and, by following the FP chain of links, nonlocal variables that lie within the scope defined by usual block structure rules.

On some systems, the terms *activation record* and *stack frame* are synonymous, but VAX terminology is that a stack frame consists of just that part of the activation record that is created by the command that invoked the procedure, not those parts consisting of arguments pushed by the calling procedure and local variables pushed by the called procedure. For the topmost activation record, the FP at the top right of the diagram points to the beginning of the stack frame, and the AP directly below it points just beyond the end of the frame, that is, to the argument list which is the last component of the activation record.

In the figure, the second and third nested procedures are called *proc2* and *proc3*, but the essence of the figure would be no different if those procedures happened to be later activations of *proc1* itself. This is equivalent to picturing how the stack would look just after recursive procedure *proc1* has called itself twice (*see* RECURSION). As far as the recursive logic is concerned, additional activation records may be created indefinitely, bounded only by the amount of memory available to enlarge the stack. But lack of such a resource is exactly what usually causes a runaway recursive procedure to abort. A properly written recursive routine will contain terminal conditions and an inductive step that relates to those conditions in such a way that the stack will accumulate activation records only until a terminal condition is reached, and then recede to its original status as each successive stage feeds information back to the stage that called it.

Bibliography

1979. Calingaert, P. *Assemblers, Compilers, and Program Translation.* Potomac, MD: Computer Science Press.
1991. Federighi, F. D., and Reilly, E. D. *VAX Assembly Language Programming.* New York: Macmillan.
1996. Sethi, R. *Programming Languages: Concepts and Structures,* 2nd Ed. Reading, MA: Addison-Wesley.

Edwin D. Reilly

ADA

For articles on related subjects *see* ABSTRACT DATA TYPE; CONCURRENT PROGRAMMING; EMBEDDED SYSTEM; INFORMATION HIDING; OBJECT-ORIENTED PROGRAMMING; PACKAGE; PROGRAMMING LANGUAGES; REAL-TIME SYSTEMS; and STRUCTURED PROGRAMMING.

HISTORY

Ada was initiated for a utopian purpose, to supersede the hundreds of languages then in use in the US Department of Defense (DoD) for critical systems. It was the outcome of an engineering project initiated and technically managed at the Office of the Director of Defense Research and Engineering.

Software cost and reliability was a major DoD problem, but the question was what could be done. More specifically, what could be done at DoD? The proliferation of programming languages made it effectively impossible to organize any reduction of costs, with each of the armed services developing unique languages, computer architectures (*q.v.*), and hardware. A common language for use throughout the DoD would be a first step toward building an engineering discipline for software.

The logic of the initiative was: the use of a high-level language reduces programming costs, increases the readability of programs and the ease of their modification, and facilitates maintenance, thus addressing the DoD concern of life-cycle costs.

A new high-level language (HLL) was needed to let real-time, parallel, and input–output portions of programs be expressed at that level rather than in assembly language inserts that destroy most of the readability and transportability advantages of using an HLL. The language had to provide error-checking for reliable programs, and to have exacting compilers to ensure safety and reliability in software engineering (*q.v.*) of high-integrity DoD systems.

The target was DoD "software in the very large," not just subsystems of 200,000 lines of code, but the hundreds of millions of lines produced by the DoD. This larger picture drove other requirements, such as machine independence and enforced validation. These could be realized only if the technology was applied over the whole of the DoD, generating economies by sharing compiler/tool/training efforts and component reuse.

The DoD High Order Language Working Group (HOLWG) was chartered in 1975 to formulate the requirements, to evaluate existing languages against those requirements, and to implement the minimal set (perhaps one) of high-level computer programming languages appropriate for DoD embedded computer systems. David Fisher, acting as Secretariat for the HOLWG, assembled, sifted, correlated, and integrated the requirements. He was the technical heart of the project. This was not a research effort. It was to produce a practical language using established techniques for a specific customer base. The HOLWG was a committee of users, not language designers.

An initial requirements document (STRAWMAN), was circulated to the Military Departments, other government agencies, the academic community, and industry, including technical experts outside the USA. Requirements proceeded through further generations with world wide technical input (WOODENMAN, TIN-MAN, IRONMAN) to STEELMAN. The final name, Ada, was chosen to honor Augusta Ada Byron (*see* LOVELACE, COUNTESS OF).

The requirements document provided a design philosophy, indicated general structure, and constrained certain detailed properties of the common language; but did not identify specific language features. One significant point agreed to was that the requirements for all branches of the DoD and their applications were consistent with a single language. Up to this point there had been an argument about "the minimum number of languages."

The next phase of the program was the award of contracts for the design. A driving concern was to insure that the designs were guided by a strong responsible principal investigator; however, picking only one contractor to do the job and trusting to luck would have been imprudent. The procurement was through multiple competitive contracts, with the best products to be selected to continue to full rigorous definition and developmental implementation.

Four contractors were funded to produce competitive prototypes. A first-phase evaluation reduced the designs to two (Cii Honeywell-Bull and Intermetrics) which were continued through a second phase. A number of teams representing various interests, applications, and organizations, analyzed reports from many reviewers. On 2 May 1979, a meeting of the HOLWG, including the representatives of the UK, France, and Germany, unanimously selected the design (code-named "Green") of the international Cii team led by Jean Ichbiah, "the designer of Ada." The cost of the program from the beginning through final language selection and the beginning of the validation effort was $4.1 million.

A language validation capability (the *test-code suite*) and associated facilities were established to assure that compilers using the name "Ada" complied with the language definition. The name Ada was initially protected by a DoD-owned trademark.

All Ada compilers were to be validated. There were to be no subset or superset compilers for Ada. This was readily accepted by the military and the users. However, it was a continuous battle with the implementers, primarily academic. Few of these subset advocates ever intended to go to a complete compiler. Some more serious attempts were made to define a standard subset of the language but failed to produce a proposal since everyone had a different idea of what features to include.

The DoD established an Ada Joint Program Office (JPO), a follow-on to the HOLWG, to continue support of Ada. Through the usual Ada open process, the definition was refined to MIL-STD 1815A, and this was endorsed by ANSI in February 1983, and as ISO Standard 8652 in 1987.

As required by standards processes, an "Ada 9X" project was launched to update Ada, in the tradition of Ada openness and international participation. The project leader at the primary contractor, Intermetrics, was Tucker Taft. The principal thrust was to facilitate object-oriented programming while remaining almost entirely compatible with the existing 1983 Ada. In February 1995, the International Organization for Standardization adopted the revision of Ada as ANSI/ISO/IEC 8652:1995. The American National Standards Institute (ANSI) adopted the new standard, called Ada 95, in April 1995. The original became Ada 83, and "Ada" now generally refers to Ada 95.

The Ada process itself remains significant. The development was extraordinarily open. Not only were thousands kept informed; they had a chance to actively participate—and did. The requirements were extensively circulated externally, certainly far more so than any other language effort has done before or since.

Ada, the project and the language, was driven by the goal of encouraging good software design and programming practice. The modularity provided by packages and the separation of specifications and bodies is exceptionally useful in this regard. Properly managed, it is applicable to all levels of the design process, and provides a foundation for software engineering. Ada facilitates the effective direction of a development effort involving hundreds of people, even in different organizations, and the controlled maintenance and modification of software over many years.

Ada has achieved a high level of acceptance. It is an ANSI and ISO standard in its second generation. It is used by many other large organizations worldwide. The project succeeded in that it is the best language for large critical systems. Most DoD code is in Ada and it has significant non-military applications (commercial aircraft, international air traffic control, railways, commercial satellites). For example, the Boeing 777, Airbus 340, French TGV rail system, Channel Tunnel, and many Global Positioning System projects contain significant quantities of software written in Ada.

Bibliography

1978. *Steelman Requirements Document.* htpp:// wuarchive.wustl.edu/languages/ada/ajpo/docs/ reports/steelman/intro.htm.

1983. *Ada '83 Language Reference Manual.* Washington, DC: Ada Joint Program Office. Also at http:// wuarchive.wustl.edu/languages/ada/ajpo/ standards/83lrm/html/Welcome.html.

1986. Ichbiah, J. D., Barnes, G. P., Firth, R. J., and Woodger, M. *Rationale for the Design of the Ada Programming Language.* Washington, DC: Ada Joint Program Office. Also at http:// wuarchive.wustl.edu/languages/ada/ajpo/ standards/83rat/html/Welcome.html.

1995. Intermetrics, Inc. *Ada 95 Language Reference Manual.* Washington, DC: Ada Joint Program Office. Also at http:// wuarchive.wustl.edu/languages/ada/ajpo/ standards/95lrm/, in several formats.

1995. Intermetrics, Inc. *Ada 95 Rationale.* Washington, DC: Ada Joint Program Office. Also at http://wuarchive.wustl. edu/languages/ada/ajpo/standards/95rat/ RAThtml/rat95-copyright.html.

1996. Whitaker, W. A. "Ada—The Project: The DoD High Order Language Working Group," in *History of Programming Languages—II* (eds. T. J. Bergin, Jr. and R. G. Gibson), Ch. V, 173–232. Reading, MA: Addison-Wesley. A longer version of this article is at http://wuarchive.wustl. edu/languages/ada/ajpo/pol-hist/history/ holwg-93/holwg-93.htm.

William A. Whitaker

THE LANGUAGE

Ada was developed for the purpose of reducing software development and maintenance costs, especially for large, constantly changing programs with long lifetimes. It was originally designed during the period 1975–1980 and standardized in 1983, and was specifically intended to support modern programming techniques such as structured programming, information hiding, abstract data types, and concurrent processing. A recent revision of the language standard, adopted in 1995, strengthened the support for object-oriented programming and for concurrency, and added a program-partitioning scheme for distributed systems (*q.v.*). The Ada language standard is taken seriously by compiler developers and users.

The development of Ada was originally motivated by the needs of military command-and-control applications, particularly for computers "embedded" in weapons, aircraft, or other military equipment (*see* EMBEDDED SYSTEM). Although these applications have some special requirements such as real-time processing, concurrency, and nonstandard I/O, the requirements that emerged were suitable for a general-purpose programming language. The design proceeded in that spirit, and as a result Ada has found wide use in industrial, business, and university facilities as well as in the military. A few of the many nonmilitary projects making heavy use of Ada are the Boeing 777 and other recent commercial aircraft, the air traffic control systems of many countries, the French TGV rail system, the Channel Tunnel, and Switzerland's electronic funds transfer (*q.v.*) system.

This article describes the technical characteristics of the language. Ada users generally refer just to Ada and assume Ada 95 is meant; "83" or "95" is added where an explicit distinction is necessary. Ada compilers are currently available for virtually every hardware architecture, from personal computers (*q.v.*) to supercomputers (*q.v.*). These include Ada Core Technologies' very popular GNU Ada 95 compilation system (GNAT), which is freely available for most platforms, as well as compilers and related tools from several other companies.

Language Characteristics

Given Ada's origins and intended use in critical applications, it is not surprising that Ada's basic model of program development is a "front-loaded" one in which a compiler that was validated—heavily tested for compliance with the standard—follows tightly defined rules for determining the validity of operations on data. This model shifts much of the human effort in program debugging from execution time to compilation time. Once an Ada compiler is satisfied with a program, that program is less likely to produce unexpected run-time behavior than are programs written in less strict languages.

Although the early Ada development was heavily influenced by Pascal (*q.v.*), extensive syntactic changes and semantic extensions make it a very different language. The major additions to the basic Pascal block-structured model include:

◆ Module structures and interface specifications for large-program organizations and separate compilation;

◆ Encapsulation (*q.v.*) facilities and generic definitions to support abstract data types;

◆ Support for concurrent (multithreaded or multitasking) processing; and

◆ Control over low-level implementation issues related to the architecture of target machines.

There are three major abstraction tools in Ada. The *package* (*q.v*) is used for encapsulating a set of related definitions and isolating them from the rest of the program. The *type* (*see* TYPES, THEORY OF) determines the states (values) an object (variable or data structure) may take on and its predefined behaviors (set of valid operations). The *generic* definition allows many similar instances of a definition to be generated from a single template. There is also support for parallel processing (*q.v.*), including concurrently executable code segments called *tasks* and language facilities for synchronization. Support for low-level matters includes control over a type's storage layout and a loophole mechanism that provides access to machine-dependent features.

An Example

To give the flavor of the language, consider this object-oriented program to support a set of instruments in a vehicle dashboard. This example illustrates encapsulated packages, type extension and polymorphism, and generic templates. The example is adapted from Feldman (1998), which was, in turn, expanded from an example in the GNAT demonstration library. Output from running the program is

```
Speed : 45 Miles per Hour
Fuel  : 60 %
Water : (*****************....)
Oil   : (******.............)
```

Fig. 1 shows a *package interface*, which specifies Instrument as a *tagged record*, i.e. a composite data structure (*see* RECORD) that can be extended to add

```
package Instruments is

  type Instrument is abstract tagged record
    Name: String(1 .. 14):=(others = ' ');
  end record;
  procedure Set_Name(I: in out Instrument; S:
          in String);
  procedure Display_Value(I: in Instrument);

end Instruments;
```

Figure 1. Interface for Instruments. "in out" designates a parameter that can be both read and updated; "in" denotes a read-only parameter.

```
with Ada.Text_IO; use Ada.Text_IO;
package body Instruments is

  procedure Set_Name(I: in out Instrument;
           S: in String) is
  begin
    I.Name (1..S'Length) := S;
  end Set_Name;

  procedure Display_Value(I: in Instrument) is
  begin
    New_Line;
    Put(I.Name);
    Put(": ");
  end Display_Value;

end Instruments;
```

Figure 2. Implementation of `Instruments`.

other components, thus producing more specialized types *derived* from it. An `Instrument` has a name (a string initialized to blanks) but no value part, so we mark it `abstract` to prevent declaration of objects of this type. `Instrument` serves as a root of a type hierarchy. It has two *primitive methods*, `Set_Name` and `Display_Value`. These will be called by the methods of other types to be derived from `Instrument`.

Fig. 2 shows the *package implementation*, which Ada calls the *body*. `Set_Name` stores the instrument name in the slice, or substring, of the name field; `Display_Value` uses the standard library package `Ada.Text_IO` to display the instrument name.

```
package Instruments.Basic is

  subtype Speeds is Integer range 0 .. 85; -- mph
  type Speedometer is new Instrument with
      record
    Value: Speeds;
  end record;
  procedure Set_Value(S: in out Speedometer; V:
           in Speeds);
  procedure Display_Value(S: in Speedometer);

  subtype Percent is Integer range 0 .. 100;
  type Gauge is new Instrument with record
    Value: Percent;
  end record;
  procedure Display_Value(G: in Gauge);

  type Graphic_Gauge is new Gauge with record
    Size : Integer:= 20;
    Fill : Character:= '*';
    Empty: Character:= '.';
  end record;
  procedure Display_Value(G: in Graphic_Gauge);

end Instruments.Basic;
```

Figure 3. Deriving `Instrument` types from the abstract `Instrument`.

```
with Instruments.Basic; use Instruments.Basic;
package Instruments.Aux is

  type InstrumentPointer is access all
      Instrument'Class;

  Speed      : aliased Speedometer;
  Fuel       : aliased Gauge;
  Oil, Water : aliased Graphic_Gauge;

  procedure Display (P: InstrumentPointer);

end Instruments.Aux;
```

Figure 4. Some `Instrument` objects.

Fig. 3 shows the interface for a *child package* `Instruments.Basic`, which derives two kinds of definite instruments—`Speedometer` and `Gauge`—from the abstract one, and moreover derives `Graphic_Gauge` from `Gauge`. In each case, the derived type inherits the structure of its parent type, but extends its parent by adding one or more new components. Each kind of instrument has its own `Display_Value`, which overrides the `Display_Value` method of its parent. The package body is omitted; it is analogous to the body of the root package `Instruments`, giving the implementations of all the methods.

Fig. 4 shows another child package, this one declaring some instrument objects, namely `Speed`, `Fuel`, `Oil`, and `Water`. These are *aliased* variables; that is, variables that are intended to be pointed to by pointers (*q.v.*) of the type `InstrumentPointer`. The phrase `access all Instrument'Class` indicates that these pointers can point to stack- or heap-allocated objects of type `Instrument` or of any type derived from `Instrument`. Fig. 5 shows the body of this package. The `Display` method shows dynamic dispatch (polymorphism). `P` points to an object of one of several instrument types; `P.all` dereferences the pointer, and the appropriate `Display_Value` is selected and called at run time.

It is now time to construct a dashboard filled with instruments. To illustrate generic templates, the dashboard is implemented as a heterogeneous linked list (*see* LIST PROCESSING), each of whose nodes contains a pointer to an instrument. Fig. 6 shows the interface to

```
package body Instruments.Aux is
  procedure Display (P: InstrumentPointer) is
  begin
    Display_Value (P.all);    -- dispatches at
                                 run time to
  end Display;                -- the appropriate
                                 Display_Value
end Instruments.Aux;
```

Figure 5. Illustrating dynamic dispatch.

```
with Ada.Finalization;
generic
  type ElementType is private;
  with procedure DisplayElement
                   (Item: in ElementType);
package Lists_Generic is

  type List is private;

  procedure MakeEmpty (L : in out List);
  procedure AddToEnd
    (L: in out List; Element: in ElementType);
  function "="(L1, L2: List) return Boolean;
  procedure Display (L: in List);

private

  type ListNode;
  type ListPtr is access ListNode;
  type ListNode is record
    Element: ElementType;
    Next: ListPtr;
  end record;

  type List is new Ada.Finalization.Controlled
  with record
    Head: ListPtr;
    Tail: ListPtr;
  end record;

  procedure Initialize (L : in out List);
  procedure Finalize (L: in out List);
  procedure Adjust (L : in out List);

end Lists_Generic;
```

Figure 6. Interface of generic linked list package.

a simple generic linked list template package. This package is parameterized by a formal generic type—the type of the element to be stored in the list nodes—and on a formal procedure parameter DisplayElement which will display the contents of one node on the screen. The element parameter is shown as private, which means that any type will match it, including a private type. In Ada, all types, including private ones, have the assignment and equality-test operations predefined. Only limited private types, which have no predefined operations at all, are excluded here.

The type List is declared to be private. This means that it has no predefined operations other than assignment and equality-test, and effectively prohibits client

```
procedure Display(L: in List) is
  Current: ListPtr := L.Head;
begin
  while Current /= Null loop
    DisplayElement(Current.Element);
    Current := Current.Next;
  end loop;
end Display;
```

Figure 7. Traversing and displaying a list.

```
with Lists_Generic;
with Instruments.Aux;
package Dashboards is new Lists_Generic
  (ElementType => Instruments.Aux.
        InstrumentPointer,
   DisplayElement => Instruments.Aux.Display);
```

Figure 8. An instantiation of Lists_Generic.

programs from explicitly referencing its Head and Tail components. Four methods are provided; the most interesting is an overloading of the equality-test operator "=" (*see* OPERATOR OVERLOADING). The implementation of this operator does a "deep" equality test, traversing the two lists and comparing the elements pairwise. The procedure Display in Fig. 7 traverses the list and displays the contents of each node, calling DisplayElement to do so. The only unfamiliar syntax is /=, which means "not equal."

The private section of this interface declares a list node and a pointer to list nodes, and then derives the list type from Ada.Finalization.Controlled. The latter, a standard library package, provides primitive methods Initialize, Finalize, and Adjust. Overriding these, as is done here, implements user-defined garbage collection (*q.v.*). Initialize is called automatically whenever the declaration of a list object is reached; Finalize is called when that declaration goes out of scope, and Adjust is called whenever one list variable is assigned to another (as in L1 := L2).

```
with Instruments.Basic; use Instruments.Ba-
sic;
with Instruments.Aux; use Instruments.Aux;
with Dashboards; use Dashboards;
procedure Show_Dashboard is

  Dashboard : List;

begin

  Set_Name (Speed, "Speed");
  Set_Name (Fuel, "Fuel");
  Set_Name (Water, "Water");
  Set_Name (Oil, "Oil");

  Speed.Value := 45; -- mph
  Fuel.Value := 60; -- %
  Water.Value := 80; -- %
  Oil.Value := 30; -- %

  AddToEnd (Dashboard, Speed'Access);
  AddToEnd (Dashboard, Fuel'Access);
  AddToEnd (Dashboard, Water'Access);
  AddToEnd (Dashboard, Oil'Access);

  Display (Dashboard);

end Show_Dashboard;
```

Figure 9. The main program in the Dashboard example.

Finalize walks the list and gives each node back to the heap (garbage collection); Initialize first finalizes the object; Adjust first finalizes L1, then does a deep copy of L2 to L1. These bodies appear in the package body and are not shown; their code is straightforward.

Fig. 8 shows an *instantiation* of the generic package, to provide for lists of instruments. Finally, Fig. 9 shows a main program that pulls everything together. The instrument names are set, the names and values are set, the instruments are added to the dashboard list, and the result is displayed.

Information Resources

A wealth of Ada 95 information and software is available on the World Wide Web. A useful starting point is the Ada Language Resources site operated by the ACM Special Interest Group on Ada (SIGAda), which contains links to all the other main sites. In paper form, there are at least 16 textbooks on Ada 95, with target audiences ranging from introductory to advanced. These are in addition to the "official" *Ada 95 Reference Manual* (Taft and Duff, 1998) and *Ada 95 Rationale* (Barnes, 1997). These books are all described in an annotated bibliography on the SIGAda Website (http://www.acm.org/sigada/).

Bibliography

1997. Barnes, J. G. P. (ed.) *Ada 95 Rationale.* New York: Springer-Verlag.
1998. Feldman, M. B. "Ada 95 in Context," in *Handbook of Programming Languages*, Vol. 1. London: Macmillan Technical Publishing.
1998. Taft, S. T., and Duff, R. A. *Ada 95 Reference Manual.* New York: Springer-Verlag.
1999. SIGAda. *Ada Languages Resources.* http://www.acm.org/sigada/education/.
1999. Taft, S. T., and Duff, R. A. (eds.) *Ada 95 Reference Manual: Language and Standard Libraries, International Standard ISO/IEC 8652:1995(E).* New York: Springer-Verlag.

Michael Feldman

ADA, AUGUSTA

See LOVELACE, COUNTESS OF.

ADDER

For articles on related subjects *see* ARITHMETIC, COMPUTER; ARITHMETIC-LOGIC UNIT; LOGIC DESIGN; and PIPELINE.

An *adder* is a logic network that forms the sum of two or more numbers represented by digit vectors (strings of digits). The simplest adder is the binary one-position adder, or *full adder* (*see* Fig. 1), in which the ith bits of two summands (X_i, Y_i) and the carry C_i from the (pre-

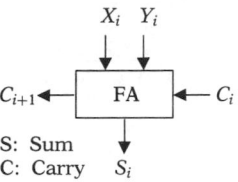

S: Sum
C: Carry

(a) Diagram

X_i	Y_i	C_i	S_i	C_{i+1}
0	0	0	0	0
0	0	1	1	0
0	1	0	1	0
0	1	1	0	1
1	0	0	1	0
1	0	1	0	1
1	1	0	0	1
1	1	1	1	1

(b) Function (truth) table

Figure 1. The binary full adder (FA).

vious) stage ($i - 1$) are added to form the ith sum bit S_i and the carry C_{i+1} to the (next) stage ($i + 1$). A *ripple-carry adder* for two n-bit binary numbers is formed by connecting n full adders in cascade (Fig. 2). The addition time of the ripple-carry adder corresponds to the worst-case delay, which is n times the time required to form the C_{i+1} (carry) output by one full adder, plus the time to form the S_i output, given the C_i input.

Higher speeds of two-operand addition can be attained by the use of *carry-completion sensing, carry-look-ahead, carry-select,* and *conditional-sum* techniques (Koren, 1993). In these techniques, additional logic elements are employed to reduce the carry propagation delay in the adder network.

One-position adders for a higher radix r (for example, 4, 8, 10, or 16) are similar to the full adder of Fig. 1. The digits X_i and Y_i assume values 0 to $r - 1$, and they are represented by two or more binary variables. The values of S_i and C_{i+1} for any radix $r \geq 2$ are determined by the following expressions:

$$C_{i+1} = \begin{cases} 0 & \text{if } X_i + Y_i + C_i \leq r - 1 \\ 1 & \text{if } X_i + Y_i + C_i \geq r \end{cases}$$

for $i = 0, 1, \ldots, n - 1$ with $C_0 = 0$

$$S_i = X_i + Y_i + C_i - r \times C_{i+1}$$

for $i = 0, 1, \ldots, n-1$ with $S_n = C_n$.

The adder speed-up techniques discussed for radix 2 also apply to two-operand addition of higher radix numbers.

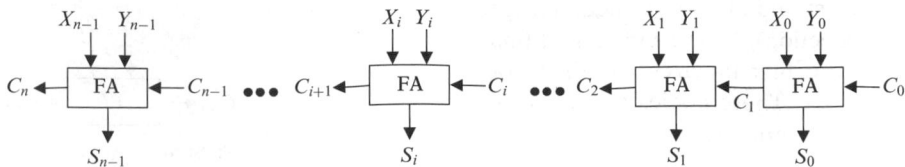

Figure 2. Binary ripple-carry adder.

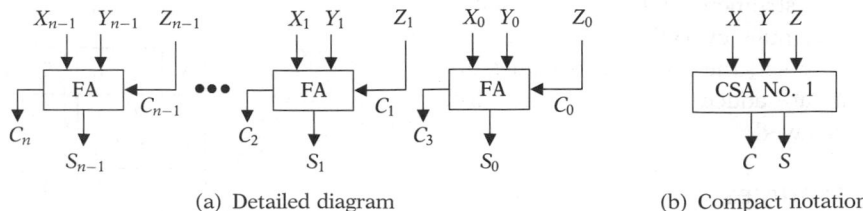

(a) Detailed diagram (b) Compact notation

Figure 3. Three-operand binary carry-save adder.

Fast summation of three or more operands can be accomplished by the use of *carry-save* adders (CSA). A binary three-operand n-bit CSA is shown in Fig. 3. The third n-bit operand Z is entered on the C_i inputs of n binary full adders. The C_{i+1} outputs form a second output result $C = (C_n \ldots C_1)$ and the sum of the three input operands X, Y, Z is represented by two output results, C and $S = (S_{n-1} \ldots S_0)$. The time required to form C and S is equal to the time required by one binary full adder. The final sum, which is the sum of C and S, is then obtained in a two-operand adder, which may employ any of the speed-up techniques discussed above.

The summation of more than three operands uses CSAs in a similar manner to reduce the sum to two results. Fig. 4 illustrates the CSA configuration for nine operands P, Q, T, U, V, W, X, Y, Z. The abbreviated notation

of Fig. 3b is employed. The time required to form the results $C7$ and $S7$ (representing the sum of the nine input operands) is equal to four full-adder operation times, regardless of the length of the operands.

Carry-save adders are frequently employed to implement fast multiplication by means of multiple-operand summation. The technique of *pipelining* may be employed to improve further the effective speed of CSA utilization.

A *signed-digit adder* is a two-operand adder in which numbers are stored in a form such that carry propagation is not needed and the addition time is independent of the length of the operands. The addition of two signed-digit numbers of *any* length requires only the time needed to add two one-digit numbers (Avižienis, 1990).

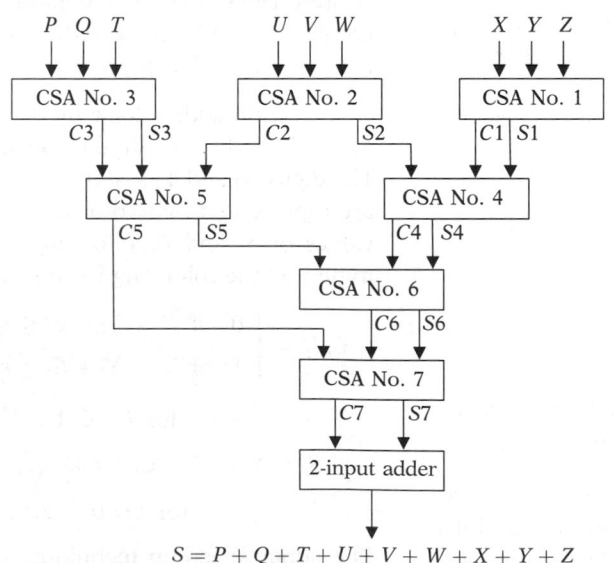

$$S = P + Q + T + U + V + W + X + Y + Z$$

Figure 4. CSA summation of nine operands.

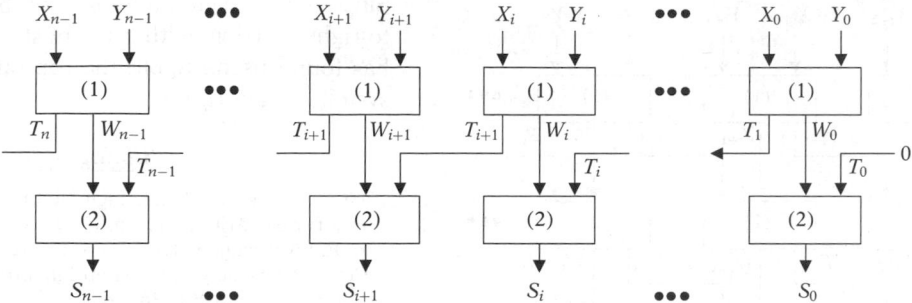

Figure 5. Two-step signed-digit addition for radix $r \geq 3$.

Signed-digit (SD) numbers for radix $r \geq 3$ are digit vectors in which the digits (X_i, Y_i) assume a set of values $\{-a, \ldots, -1, 0, 1, \ldots, a\}$, with $r - 1 \geq a \geq \lfloor r/2 + 1 \rfloor$ and with the place values corresponding to powers of the radix as with conventional radix r numbers. Thus, not only may there be more than one value of a for a given r but, in addition, there may be more than one SD number corresponding to a single radix r number. For example, with $r = 10$ and $a = 6$, the decimal number -2396 may be expressed in SD form as $-2\ -4\ 0\ 4$ or $-3\ 6\ 0\ 4$. However, the conversion algorithm described below assigns a specific SD number to each radix r number.

Thus radix 10 may use the set $\{-a$ to $a\}$ with $a = 6, 7, 8$ or 9 and radix 16 may have $a = 9, 10, 11, 12, 13, 14$ or 15 but radix 4 must have $a = 3$. Radix 2 is a special case with the digit values $\{-1, 0, 1\}$ and is discussed below.

Two-step signed-digit addition for a radix $r \geq 3$ (Fig. 5) is done as follows:

1. Add $X_i + Y_i$ to form the *interim sum* W_i and the *transfer digit* T_{i+1} for all positions $i = 0, 1, \ldots, n - 1$ as follows:

$$T_{i+1} = \begin{cases} 1 & \text{if } X_i + Y_i \geq a \\ 0 & \text{if } -a < (X_i + Y_i) < a \\ -1 & \text{if } X_i + Y_i \leq -a \end{cases}$$

$$W_i = X_i + Y_i - r \times T_{i+1},$$
$$\text{with } -(a - 1) \leq W_i \leq a - 1.$$

2. Form the *sum* digit $S_i = W_i + T_i$, with $-a \leq S_i \leq a$, given $T_0 = 0$ and $S_n = T_n$.

A radix 10 SD addition with $a = 6$ is illustrated below. Note that the bar over a digit value (e.g. $\bar{3}$) designates a *negative* value (-3).

Example 1
Add two SD operands (with $r = 10$, $a = 6$):

	$i =$	4	3	2	1	0
	$X_i =$		$\bar{3}$	6	0	4
	$Y_i =$		$\bar{2}$	6	$\bar{6}$	2
	$X_i + Y_i =$		$\bar{5}$	12	$\bar{6}$	6
(1)	$T_{i+1} =$	0	1	$\bar{1}$	1	
	$W_i =$		$\bar{5}$	2	4	$\bar{4}$
(2)	$T_i =$	0	1	$\bar{1}$	1	$0 \leftarrow T_0$
	$S_i =$	0	$\bar{4}$	1	5	$\bar{4}$

It can be shown that if one of the two operands (X or Y) is in conventional form (digit values 0 to $r - 1$), then the sum digits S_i will still satisfy the constraint $-a \leq S_i \leq a$. Therefore the *conversion* from conventional to SD form is done by adding the conventional form to zero (or to an SD form) in an SD adder. The conversion from SD to conventional form is performed by separating the SD form into two conventional forms: one composed of the positive digits, the other composed of the negative digits, and adding them in a two-operand adder with carry propagation.

Example 2
Convert the conventional $X = -2396$ to SD form with $a = 6$ by adding it to $Y = 0\ 0\ 0\ 0$ in an SD adder.

		$i =$	4	3	2	1	0
(1)		$X_i =$		$\bar{2}$	$\bar{3}$	$\bar{9}$	$\bar{6}$
		$Y_i =$		0	0	0	0
		$X_i + Y_i =$		$\bar{2}$	$\bar{3}$	$\bar{9}$	$\bar{6}$
(2)		$T_{i+1} =$	0	0	$\bar{1}$	$\bar{1}$	
		$W_i =$		$\bar{2}$	$\bar{3}$	1	4
		$T_i =$	0	0	$\bar{1}$	$\bar{1}$	0
		$S_i =$	0	$\bar{2}$	$\bar{4}$	0	4

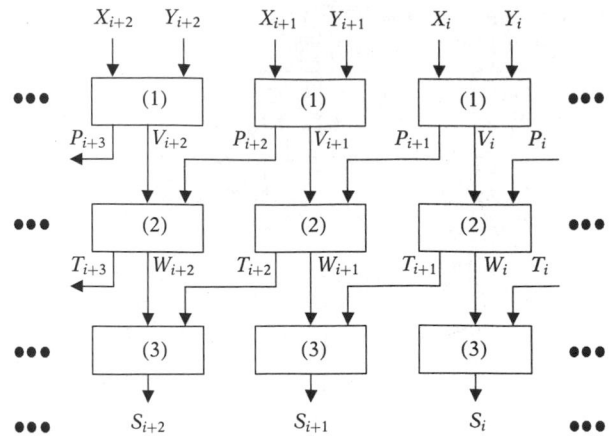

Figure 6. Three-step signed-digit addition for radix $r = 2$.

To perform the *subtraction* $X - Y$, first the signs of all non-zero digits of Y are changed to get $-Y$, and then the SD addition $X + (-Y)$ is carried out.

Three-step signed-digit addition for radix $r = 2$ (Fig. 6) is done as follows:

1. Add $X_i + Y_i$ to form the *pre-interim sum* V_i and the *pre-transfer digit* P_i for all positions $i = 0, 1, \ldots, n - 1$ as follows:

$$
P_{i+1} = \begin{cases} 1 & \text{if } X_i + Y_i \geq 1 \\ 0 & \text{if } X_i + Y_i = 0 \\ -1 & \text{if } X_i + Y_i \leq -1 \end{cases}
$$

$$
V_i = X_i + Y_i - 2P_{i+1}.
$$

2. Add $P_i + V_i$ to form the *interim sum* W_i and the *transfer digit* T_{i+1} for positions $i = 0, 1, \ldots, n$, given $P_0 = 0$ and $V_n = 0$ as follows:

$$
T_{i+1} = \begin{cases} 1 & \text{if } V_i + P_i = 2 \\ 0 & \text{if } -1 \leq V_i + P_i \leq 1 \\ -1 & \text{if } V_i + P_i = -2 \end{cases}
$$

$$
W_i = V_i + P_i - 2T_{i+1}.
$$

3. Form the sum digit $S_i = W_i + T_i$, given $T_0 = 0$ and $S_{n+1} = T_{n+1}$.

The algorithm above is called *two-transfer SD addition* and is applicable to higher radices as well. The time required to add two operands of any length is the time to complete steps 1, 2, and 3 above.

Similar to carry-save adders, pipelining can be used in SD addition to increase the rate at which the sums are generated.

Since signed-digit addition can be carried out left-to-right starting with the most significant digits, it has found useful application in, among other places, systolic arrays (*q.v.*).

Bibliography

1990. Avižienis, A. "Signed-digit Number Representations for Fast Parallel Arithmetic," in *Computer Arithmetic*, Vol. II (ed. E. E. Swartzlander Jr), 54–65. Los Alamitos, CA: IEEE Computer Society Press. (Reprinted from *IRE Trans. El. Comp.*, **EC-10**, 1961, 389–400).
1993. Koren, I. *Computer Arithmetic Algorithms*. Upper Saddle River, NJ: Prentice Hall.

Algirdas Avižienis

ADDRESSING

For articles on related subjects *see* BYTE ORDERING; COMPUTERS, MULTIPLE ADDRESS; GENERAL REGISTER; INDEX REGISTER; INSTRUCTION SET; MACHINE AND ASSEMBLY LANGUAGE PROGRAMMING; POINTER; STORAGE ALLOCATION; and VIRTUAL MEMORY.

BASIC TERMINOLOGY AND HARDWARE CONCEPTS

A typical computer instruction must indicate not only the operation to be performed but also the location of one or more operands (*q.v.*), the location where the result of the computation is to be deposited, and, for certain kinds of instructions, the location where the next instruction is to be found. Normally, all parts of the instruction are either explicitly or implicitly given. We will first consider the hardware techniques by which an *address* (or location) in the computer may be specified. In what follows, we shall consider primarily storage in which each location has associated with it a sequentially assigned numerical address. An alternative method of determining a desired storage location will be considered briefly in the later section "Content-Addressable Storage."

Historically and presently, computer hardware allows addresses to be specified in a variety of ways. The most straightforward approach would be to put the entire address directly into the instruction, representing a specific location of a word or part of a word in storage. Thus, on the IBM 650, an early decimal computer, the two-digit operation code and the two four-digit addresses representing the location of the data and the location of the next instruction, respectively, were represented in the instruction itself. (On modern computers, except for the case of decision-making instructions, the address of the next instruction is always taken implicitly to be the next sequential location after that of the instruction being executed.) The operation code in the 650 (as on some modern computers) implied the location of one of the operands and the location of the result.

Op code	Data address	Next inst. address
2 digit	4 digit	4 digit

For example, the operation code AU (add to upper) implied that the upper half of the accumulator register was one of the operands, along with the explicitly named operand, and the result was to remain in the upper half of the accumulator.

As the amount of storage increases, however, and the number of bits needed to represent an address becomes large relative to the size of the instruction, it is no longer feasible to represent an entire address each time it occurs in an instruction. This is especially true when the address part of an instruction must be able to accommodate the largest possible storage that might be attached to a particular model of computer, even though a particular computer configuration might currently have only a small part of that storage. In such cases, the addresses actually occurring would use only a portion of that part of the instruction allocated for addresses. The remaining portion must always contain zeros, representing a waste of a valuable resource.

Several hardware devices are employed to obtain, from one of a small number of larger registers, most of the information needed to specify an address, with the instruction itself containing only the information needed to complete the address. A number of these methods were employed in the Control Data Corp. (CDC) 160 and 160A computers, early small machines that started out with 4,096 12-bit words of storage. In the CDC 160, which dates back to 1959, six bits were used for the operation code, while the other six bits (with only 64 possible values) were used in the determination of an address. By choosing an appropriate operation code, the address would be interpreted to be in one of

five modes: direct address (d); indirect address (i); relative address forward (f) and backward (b); and no address (n).

The direct addressing mode (d-mode) corresponds to the IBM 650 situation discussed above, in that the address referred to a 12-bit operand in one of the first 64 words of storage.

Relative addressing provided for operand addresses and jump addresses that were near the storage location containing the current instruction. In relative addressing forward (f), the six-bit address portion was added to the current contents of the program counter (PC—q.v.). This register held the full 12-bit address of the current instruction. The new value was then used for obtaining the operand or to jump to one of the 63 addresses forward from the address holding the instruction that was being executed. For relative addressing backward (b), the operand or jump address was obtained by subtracting the six-bit address from the current contents of the PC.

In the no-address mode (n), which is usually now referred to as the *immediate address* mode, the six-bit address part was not treated as an address, but as a constant to be used in the actual computation.

In the CDC 160A, seven banks of 4,096 words each were added to the storage, thus complicating the specification of an address. The modes of addressing already available were retained, but several three-bit registers were added to contain the number of the bank (0–7) in which a designated address would be found, and different operations referred to different bank registers. Additional operations were provided so that the programmer could set the values of these registers as necessary. This later machine also provided for two-word instructions in which the second word might be a 12-bit immediate operand as well.

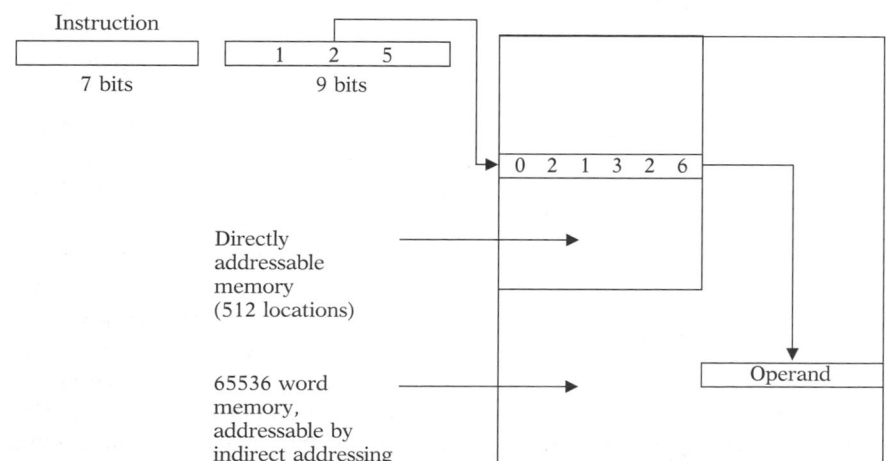

Figure 1. Extension of addressing through indirect addressing.

Indirect Addressing

One way to address a memory larger than the address part of an instruction allows is to have the instruction address point to another address that stores the operand address. This facility, called *indirect addressing* or *deferred addressing*, was available on the CDC 160 and on many subsequent computers up to the advent of reduced instruction set computers (RISC—*q.v.*). Fig. 1 illustrates this situation on a hypothetical 16-bit computer with a 7-bit instruction field and a 9-bit address field that permits the direct addressing of only $512 (= 2^9)$ memory locations. Indirect addressing can be used to address a memory of up to 65,536 words. In the example in Fig. 1, the program has placed the operand address 021326 (where we express addresses in octal for convenience) at a specific address (125) in the first 512 words of memory. If the instruction is, for example, an "add indirect" instruction, the address 125 is interpreted as an indirect address or pointer to the actual operand at location 021326. The address stored at 125 (namely, 021326) becomes the *effective address*.

Some systems allow multilevel indirect addressing. Thus, the number stored at 021326 may have a bit set that indicates that it, itself, is an indirect address that points to another location that contains the operand address. Indirect addressing may be combined in various ways with the use of index registers to produce complex addressing chains.

Index Registers

The concept of an index register, sometimes called a "tally register" or "base register" grew out of the B-line or B-register (named in contrast to the Accumulator, the "A-register"). It was introduced on some of the earliest computers developed in the UK at the University of Manchester (*see* MANCHESTER UNIVERSITY COMPUTERS). This represented a major advance in computer design. Index registers are hardware registers that can be set, incremented, tested, etc., by machine instructions. Each instruction contains an indication as to whether its address is to be added to (or subtracted from) the contents of a designated index register to form the effective address. One of the main purposes, as suggested by the name, was to allow the effective address to be used as an index into a set of contiguous memory locations commonly referred to as an *array*. Without changing the part of the address that was in the instruction itself, one could refer to one after another of the contiguous locations merely by changing the contents of the index register successively. This replaced the more time- and space-consuming sequence of instructions that would normally put an instruction containing an address into an arithmetic register, modify it by ordinary addition, and then store it back to replace its former value. (This modified instruction was then executed, and it would refer to a different storage location.)

The use of index registers eliminated the need for modification of the instruction itself by allowing the index register to be modified by special instructions for that purpose. With the advent of newer systems in which more than one task may be executing the same instructions at the same time, it has become very important that instructions not be modified during execution, since the modification by one task might be inappropriate for another task executing the same set of instructions (*see* REENTRANT PROGRAM).

General Registers

The use of variable-length instructions became widespread in the 1960s and 1970s. The IBM System/360/370/390 (*q.v.*), for example, uses instructions that may take one, two, or three half-words for their representation. In the System/360, 16 *general registers* are provided, each capable of acting as an arithmetic register, a base register for relative addressing, or as an index register. An instruction might refer to only one or two of these registers, in which case only four bits would be needed in the instruction for each one, and it could fit in a half-word (16 bits).

A full-word instruction could accommodate one reference to a general register (4 bits) and a reference to a storage address. The latter could be a combination of a base register (4 bits), an index register designation (4 bits), and a 12-bit displacement, which could be used as a local offset from the contents of the base register. Fig. 2 illustrates the determination of an effective address from a System/360 instruction.

Relocation Registers

Many computers have one or more hardware *relocation registers*, which aid in the implementation and running of multiprogramming (*q.v.*) systems. An example is the CDC Cyber series. A number of different programs may be in the computer memory, each occupying a contiguous area. Thus, program A might occupy the area from 40,000 to 67,777, but this program (as well as all other programs in memory) is written and loaded into memory as if the area it occupies actually has the addresses 0 to 27,777. When program A is given control, the address 40,000 is stored in the hardware relocation register, and this constant is automatically added to all memory reference addresses while program A is running. The program could have been loaded anywhere else in memory, and can be loaded into different areas at different times. It will always produce the correct memory addresses, since all addressing

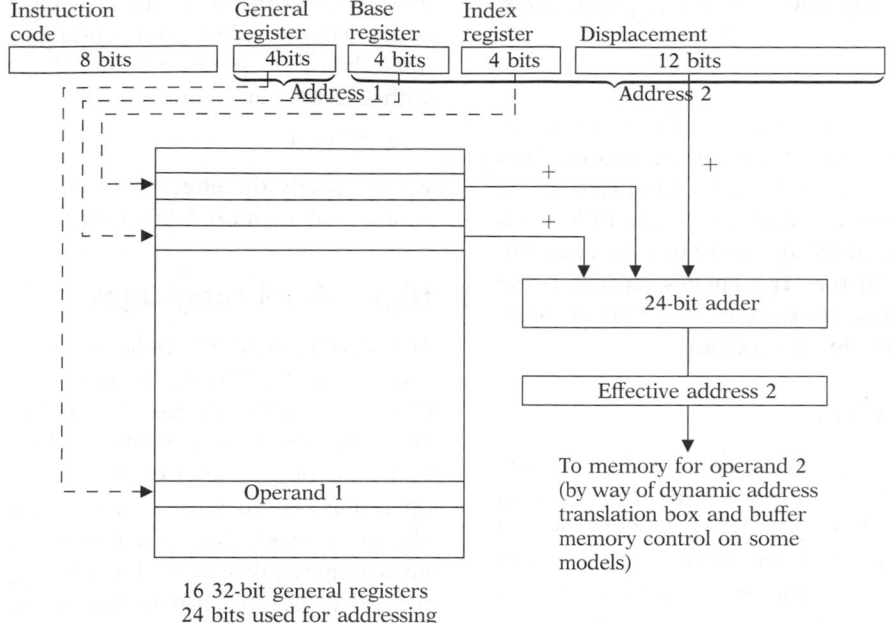

Figure 2. Effective address calculation on the IBM 360.

is automatically made relative to the starting address of the area into which the program has been loaded.

In computers of this type, another hardware register will contain the *field length* or program size. Any attempt to reference beyond the area occupied by the program will be trapped, and an error condition will be signalled.

In a machine with two relocation registers, like the Univac 1100 series, a program may consist of two segments: for example, a program segment and a data segment, which can be placed independently anywhere in memory. The starting addresses of each of the two segments are placed in the two relocation registers, and every effective address has an associated bit that specifies which relocation register is to be added.

A relocation register is quite different in nature from an index register or a register used as a base for relative addressing. The relocation register is a special hardware register whose contents can be accessed and changed only through the use of privileged instructions (*q.v.*) under control of the operating system.

Content-Addressable Storage

Content-addressable or associative memories (*q.v.*) are quite different in concept from the more conventionally addressed memories described above. In a content-addressable memory, the data itself contains a key, usually a specified field. This key is, in effect, the address of the item. The key may be the whole data item itself. The desired data item is located by means of an examination of all relevant keys. This could be done

by software in a computer system with conventional memory addressing, but it would be quite slow.

In an associative or content-addressable memory, comparison circuits are used to provide a hardware-assisted and presumably very fast search through all data items to find the one that matches the key. Small memories of this type have been used to speed up address translation in virtual memory (*q.v.*) systems. Larger systems in which all addressing is associative have been proposed and some experimental models have been built.

The use of content-addressable memory was very expensive in terms of earlier technologies, but has proved practical with modern very large-scale integration (VLSI) technology. There are a number of important application areas in which associative memories can be very useful, such as cache memory (*q.v.*).

Bernard A. Galler and Saul Rosen

SOFTWARE ASPECTS

Corresponding to each hardware addressing mode, there must be one or more techniques by which the programmer specifies addresses in the program.

Absolute Addressing

In the earliest and most elementary programming systems, a programmer would assign instructions and data to locations in memory, and instructions would refer to absolute locations in memory. Thus, using a decimal computer for convenience, a programmer might write

```
267 ADD 3256
```

and, as a result of the eventual loading process, the instruction ADD 3256 would appear in location 267. It was the responsibility of the programmer to make sure that the appropriate data word was in location 3256 at the time the program was to be run. These are absolute addresses in that 267 always represents the same physical location in memory and 3256 similarly represents a specific physical location.

Relative Addressing

Some of the first advances in programming involved permitting the programmer to write programs or parts of programs without having to be aware of the absolute physical locations in which the instructions and data were to be stored. One of the early approaches to this goal was by way of regional or relative programming. The program would be divided into a number of regions, A, B, C, D, etc. Addresses would then be relative to the start of a region. A programmer might write

```
A5 ADD B15
```

to specify that an instruction located in the fifth location in region A is to add (to the accumulator) the data located in the fifteenth location in region B. A translator and loader would eventually take all regional addresses and convert them into absolute addresses.

There are a number of important advantages to this procedure. The programmer does not have to make arbitrary decisions about how large the regions are going to be. Separate sections of the program can be written independently, and unexpected or undesirable interactions can be avoided.

Indirect Addressing

In a computer that allows indirect addressing, the assembly language programmer typically indicates an indirect address by adding a character such as * to the absolute or symbolic address, or by enclosing it in parentheses. Thus,

```
INCR ADD ALPHA*
```

would indicate that the effective address is not ALPHA, but is in the location specified by ALPHA.

Indexing

If an index register is to be used in calculating an effective address, this is normally specified following the instruction address. For example,

```
ADD A,4
```

indicates that the contents of index register 4 is to be added (subtracted on some computers) to A to determine the effective address. Indexing can be combined with indirect addressing so that

```
ADD A*,4
```

would specify the effective address as the sum of the contents of location A and index register 4.

Higher-level Languages

The development of higher-level programming languages has relieved the programmer of the responsibility for many aspects of memory management. However, that responsibility must reside somewhere: either the programmer or the language processor and operating system must take on the responsibility for allocating space for instructions and data and for producing the programs that make appropriate use of the addressing structure of the computer. The software features of addressing discussed in this article are therefore mainly of interest to the assembly language programmer. The programmer who writes in a higher-level language such as C++ (q.v.) or Ada (q.v.) does not have to be aware of the details of memory addressing in the computer on which a program will run, but may be sure that the compiler (q.v.) being used is very much aware of these details, and usually expends a great deal of effort to take advantage of the memory-addressing hardware features provided on the computer.

Saul Rosen, revised by the Editors

VIRTUAL MEMORY

Overlays

Many programs are too long to fit into the space in main memory that can be allocated to them at run time. In a uniprogramming system, this will be true when the amount of space required by the program is greater than the total memory available to problem programs. In a multiprogramming system it may be true because the amount of space that is needed is more than the operating system is willing to allocate to this particular program. In either case, it becomes necessary to break the program up into sections, segments, or overlays so that the entire program need not be in main memory at the same time. The term *folding* has sometimes been used for this process.

In many old systems, the programmer had the responsibility for breaking the program into overlays and for providing the loading instructions that bring necessary overlays into main memory as they are needed. Many software systems provided aids to overlay planning. The user could name the overlays so that all symbolic addresses in an overlay would automatically be tagged with a special identifier that indicated which overlay they belonged to. A loader or linker (*see* LINKERS AND LOADERS) created an object program organized as a set of overlays and a root segment containing information about the overlay structure. The root segment would be loaded into main memory along with the segments needed to get the program started. Any reference to a symbolic address in a segment not in main memory would cause a call on the supervisor to load the required segment, overlaying other segments if necessary.

There were a number of efforts to produce software systems that provided automatic folding of programs. In such systems, a programmer would write a program as if there were enough main memory to contain the whole program, and the software system would organize the program into overlays to fit the actual amount of storage that would be available. Efforts to produce software systems of this type date back to the earliest computers, but none was particularly successful until the advent of so-called *virtual memory* systems that first made their appearance around 1959, became increasingly common in the 1970s, and became ubiquitous in the 1990s.

The Atlas System

The Atlas (*q.v.*) computer was the first virtual memory system. Its designers called it a *single-level storage* system. The idea was that a programmer would program as if all available memory were on a single level and directly addressable, whereas in fact memory was on two levels. In the Atlas, the two levels were magnetic drum and core (*see* MEMORY).

A program for the Atlas could be written as if it were to run in a homogeneous memory consisting of $2^{20} = 1,048,576$ words. Memory was organized into *pages* of $2^9 = 512$ words each. The physical core memory might consist of only 32 or 64 such pages. However, the "address space" (i.e. the addresses that a user could address) consisted of $2^{11} = 2,048$ such pages. Thus, an address in the Atlas consisted of an 11-bit page number and a 9-bit number indicating the location within the page.

A hardware page-address register is associated with each physical page (or *page frame*, as it is sometimes called). A typical running program might consist of 50 pages, of which 20 pages at a particular time would be located in core memory and the other 30 located on the drum.

Each page of the program represents a set of 512 consecutive addresses with the same page number (i.e. the same 11 leftmost bits). The program page number is kept in the page address register of the physical page that is occupied by that program page. Thus, any program (or logical) page may occupy any physical page, and it may occupy different physical pages at different times during the running of the program.

Assume now (see Fig. 3) that the next instruction to be executed refers to an operand whose address (in octal) is 0231443. This is a reference to location 443 in page 231. Note that core memory of the machine contains nowhere near 231 pages, and there are only 50 pages in

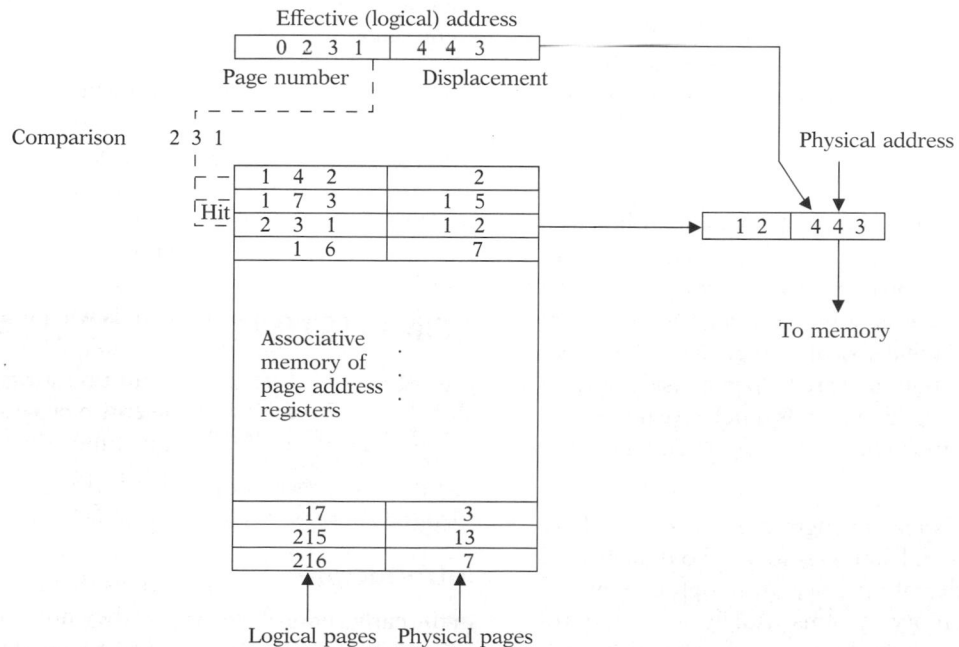

Figure 3. Address translation on the Atlas computer.

the program being executed. The programmer does not have to confine the program to the first 50 pages or to any contiguous block of 50 pages. He or she can use any areas in virtual memory that are convenient. Thus, the programmer does not have to know beforehand how long the code areas and data areas are going to be. The program can be broken up into segments and placed far enough apart in virtual memory so that their memory allocations will not overlap. There is no point at all to scattering a program at random over a large virtual memory; in fact, such programs will usually perform very inefficiently. One wants a very large virtual memory in order to be able to assign areas, whose ultimate sizes are not necessarily known in advance, to program and data modules that do not overlap and that form the structural units of a program. The segmented, two-dimensional virtual memories discussed below were introduced to make this type of modular programming (*q.v.*) more automatic and more convenient.

The page address registers form an associative or content-addressable memory. They are subject to a very rapid hardware scan to determine if one of them is page 231. If it is (say, if page 231 is in physical page 12, as in Fig. 3), then the operand sought is in physical location 12443, and the operand is fetched from that location. If, on the other hand, page 231 of this program is not in core memory, it must be fetched from the drum. An interrupt (*q.v.*) called a *page fault* occurs, and the operating system initiates a transfer of that page from drum into core. Assume that physical page 16 is available. The supervisor will cause program page 231 to be loaded into physical page 16, and will place the number 231 in the corresponding page address register. It then returns control to the program, which tries again to access an operand in virtual location 231443. This time it finds logical page 231 in physical page 16 and translates the address 231443 to 16443.

Segments and Pages

The Atlas system is an example of a one-dimensional or single-segment virtual memory system. The programmer or the language processor must provide symbolic or absolute addresses in the one-dimensional virtual memory. Many of the classical storage allocation problems remain, although they are helped considerably by the fact that the virtual memory is much larger than the actual central memory of the computer on which the program is run.

From the point of view of program organization, there are a number of advantages to a two-dimensional organization of virtual memory. Although two-dimensional virtual memory systems usually are multiprogrammed systems, it is convenient to think of each program in the multiprogrammed environment as if it were running in its own virtual memory. In such a system, a program runs in a large virtual memory consisting of a number of segments. An address then consists of a segment name (or number) and a displacement relative to the beginning of the segment. This is somewhat analogous to the regional organization of programs in earlier computer generations and has some of the same advantages. The programmer or the language processor can assign programs and data to different segments without worrying about the relative position of the segments in the total addressing space. This is especially true if the segments are large enough so that possible segment overflow is not a problem. The segments themselves may be organized into pages.

A *job* (or *process*) is then represented in central memory by a segment table that provides a set of pointers (*q.v.*) to page tables corresponding to the active segments of the process. Each active segment will usually have one or more pages in memory. The actual address space or virtual memory is very large, and in most practical situations it consists mostly of unused space. Of the part of virtual memory that is actually used by a program, only a relatively few pages will be in central memory; the rest will reside on a disk (originally on a drum or disk that was reserved specifically for paging). The segment may serve as a unit of sharing among programs. The same segment (i.e. a pointer to the same page table) may appear in several segment tables that correspond to several jobs that are simultaneously active. The possibility of sharing segments was one of the strong motivations for the development of the segmented virtual memory systems.

A more detailed discussion of contemporary virtual memory systems can be found in the article of that name, and in STORAGE ALLOCATION.

Bibliography

1982. Siewiorek, D. P., Bell, C. G., and Newell, A. *Computer Structures: Principles and Examples*. New York: McGraw-Hill.
1996. Hamacher, C. V., Vranesic, Z. G., and Zaky, S. G. *Computer Organization*, 4th Ed. New York: McGraw-Hill.

Saul Rosen, revised by Edwin D. Reilly

ADMINISTRATIVE APPLICATIONS

For articles on related subjects *see* DATA PROCESSING; ELECTRONIC COMMERCE; ELECTRONIC FUNDS TRANSFER; ELECTRONIC OFFICE; INFORMATION PROCESSING; INFORMATION SYSTEMS; MANAGEMENT INFORMATION SYSTEMS; NETWORKS, COMPUTER; TELEPROCESSING SYSTEMS; TRANSACTION PROCESSING; and Y2K PROBLEM.

Introduction

In the early years of electronic computing, applications were classified simply as either "scientific" or "business." The essence of the distinction was that scientific applications involved substantial arithmetic operations on rather small volumes of data, whereas business applications involved modest arithmetic operations on substantial amounts of data. Internal computer speed (CPU instruction cycle time and memory access time) was the crucial variable in scientific computing applications, while input and output speed and versatility (punched card input–output (I/O), printed output, magnetic tape I/O, disk I/O, etc.) were the crucial variables in business data processing. The two types of applications were called "CPU-intensive" (sometimes "CPU-bound") or "input–output-intensive" ("I/O-bound"). Matrix inversion was "typical" of scientific applications, and insurance company premium transactions processing was "typical" of business applications. With the passage of time and with the pervasive evolution of computer applications, the original two-category distinction no longer sufficed.

First, government transactions processing grew no less rapidly than did business transactions processing, as government agencies, like the US Social Security Administration, established pioneering large-scale government administrative applications that were strikingly similar to business applications. This led to the recognition that the term "administrative" applications was a more descriptive term than "business" applications, since both the private and public sectors "administer," while only the private sector does "business" in the commercial sense of the word.

Second, these simple classifications fell by the wayside with the establishment of other significant varieties of computer applications, such as process control, information retrieval (*q.v.*), voice and message switching, and advanced technical applications such as computer-aided design (*see* COMPUTER-AIDED DESIGN/COMPUTER-AIDED MANUFACTURING) and computer-assisted instruction (CAI).

Today, administrative applications are widely considered to be those that involve the use of computers for processing information in support of the operational, logistical, and functional activities performed by all organizations, and may be classified in a number of different ways. One is by organization type, e.g. banking, insurance, manufacturing, and government (which may be further subdivided into many different categories, such as defense, education, revenue, health services, etc.), among others. Another is by type of function (e.g. accounting, budgeting, payroll, property control, and many others).

This article describes the evolution and growth of administrative applications, the organization of data processing activity, and the increasingly complex administrative processing environment of the late 1990s and into the next millennium.

The Evolution of Administrative and Business Applications

Interestingly, the five evolutionary stages of commercially viable computing systems roughly correspond to each of the last five decades of the twentieth century. While the earliest computers were developed during the Second World War for specific defense applications—some of the first computers were used to calculate artillery firing coordinates—these systems did not become commercially marketable for a number of reasons: they were special-purpose, designed for military applications; they were extremely large, occupying huge warehouses; they consumed enormous amounts of electricity, generated immense amounts of heat, required tons of chilled air, and broke down every few hours. No organization but the government could afford to own and operate one.

The first commercial systems were installed in the 1950s and ran such "business" applications as accounting, billing, payroll, and inventory control. This was a logical first step in the application of computers to solve business-related problems for several reasons:

♦ These activities were well understood and reasonably well documented, which facilitated their computerization.

♦ These applications were well suited to the one-at-a-time sequential processing of data typically performed by the early computers.

♦ In many cases, these applications were already being performed on punched card tabulating equipment, which allowed them to be converted easily to the earliest punched card (*q.v.*) and magnetic tape-based computers.

♦ Computerization of these functions was readily justified by clerical staff reductions and by savings realized through replacement of outmoded and more expensive punched-card equipment.

These early computer systems processed data in batches, that is, they executed one program at a time and handled transactions (say, an accounting entry, such as payment of a bill) one at a time from a predefined sequence of transactions (such as all payments in a batch presorted by account number). They required considerable amounts of manual intervention and the applications they performed were limited in scope. The computers of the 1950s also tended to be physically large, internally slow, and somewhat unreliable in terms of system availability. They used vacuum tubes which limited their price–performance ratio and, thus, both the numbers and kinds of applications that were run on them.

The next major advance in systems came in the early 1960s, with the invention of the transistor and its implementation in the next generation of computers. These systems were smaller, faster, and more reliable. They still ran applications one at a time, but their speed encouraged development of more administrative applications. During the 1960s, virtually all large organizations computerized most of their primary "business" functions.

In the 1970s, the arrival of integrated circuitry (*q.v.*) resulted in fast and reliable computer systems. Advances in operating system technology precipitated the rapid spread of multiuser systems, and data communications systems enabled more and more applications to be accessed from remote locations by employees working at CRT (Cathode Ray Tube—*see* MONITOR, DISPLAY) terminals. The applications began to provide information that resulted in a wide range of benefits, from significantly improved customer service to tighter management control over widely dispersed operations and functions.

In the 1980s, the microcomputer brought low-cost computer power to virtually anyone who wished to use it. Office automation eased the administrative workload in even the smallest offices. User-friendly word processing (*q.v.*), spreadsheets (*q.v.*), databases, and similar applications made it cost-effective to computerize.

In the decade of the 1990s, administrative applications evolved into tools for the strategic use of an organization's information assets to create a competitive advantage for the organization. Advances in electronic technology improved the cost–performance of computer systems; they continued to shrink in size and increase in power. These high-performance systems allowed the integration of graphics, digital audio, and video into previously text-only systems.

Advances in communication technology placed more and more information at the fingertips of the average worker, as systems were tied into local, national, and international networks. The use of the Internet (*q.v.*) and the World Wide Web (WWW—*q.v.*) has become ubiquitous in a few short years.

Commuting costs have increased as telecomputing costs have decreased, so that many employees are now working at home—*telecommuting*—at least part of the time.

The Challenges of the New Millennium

Increasing emphasis is now being placed on a number of critical issues:

◆ The hiring of technically competent staff and their continued technical training. While the power of computing hardware continues to increase, and its relative cost is constantly decreasing, the total unit consumer cost remains relatively constant, primarily because of the increasing cost of skilled technical labor.

◆ Adoption of standards for software, hardware, operating systems, telecommunication systems, and the like; non-standard applications and interfaces have historically ended up costing users millions, if not billions, of dollars to resolve.

◆ Organizations are increasingly recognizing that they can cut maintenance costs, improve response time, and control the cost of additional computing power by moving applications from the mainframe to the desktop.

◆ The security of information, from the point of its creation or gathering through its transmission and storage on permanent or semipermanent media, has become increasingly important, as network access to systems has become pervasive.

◆ With the onset of desktop computing and networks connecting the desktops, the "paperless office" has become not just a possibility, but a reality. "Documents" created on the desktop can be saved in machine-readable form (*q.v.*), transmitted to their intended recipient(s) electronically, pulled up on the screen, and saved or deleted, without ever having been printed by an expensive laser printer, using an expensive toner cartridge, on expensive paper. The potential for savings is driving this new technology. Electronic document archiving and instantaneous retrieval are other important side-benefits of this technology.

The Y2K problem (*q.v.*) alerted managers to the need to examine all software to assure that problems not considered when the software was written do not cause problems later. The importance of these and other issues, and the value of information as an organizational asset will cause many organizations to develop strategic plans for management of their information resources.

Competition for a portion of the high technology market will continue to increase. The Japanese use automated factories to produce one-of-a-kind custom cars built to order, and they plan 10 years into the future. Korea, Singapore and Taiwan are serious competition for Japan. Other countries, including the USA, will have to keep pace, or lose their competitive advantage in world markets.

The Applications Development Environment

Administrative application systems extend over a broadly based clientele, ranging from municipal governments to private corporations to public and state organizations supporting their day-to-day as well as decision-support operations. As the machine- and data center-centralized environments of the 1970s and 1980s evolved into the cooperative and client–server environments of the 1990s, new computer technology increasingly supported the user by fostering information-centered distributed systems (*q.v.*). The applications evolution has followed the expanding hardware capabilities of the computer with its four major physical components: the central processing unit, main storage, auxiliary storage, and input–output devices.

Administrative applications (software) are written by technical staff identified as "programmers," "programmer analysts," and "software engineers," to name a few titles. Even though most software development projects are moving perceptibly closer to the end user, a majority of software projects are still developed in organizational departments known as data centers. These centers may be called data processing offices, management information systems offices, information services, etc., and they are responsible for a number of functions:

◆ Providing good quality service to all customers.

◆ Providing liaison activities to customer offices.

◆ Keeping current with state-of-the-art systems and emerging standards.

◆ Planning, scheduling, and managing resources for operational economy and adequate service levels to customers.

◆ Providing separate development and operating responsibilities to increase auditing controls and to ensure formal procedures for purchasing, developing, and changing administrative software systems.

◆ Providing separate data processing functions and responsibilities so that security systems can be developed to maintain proper controls over the data, particularly for restricting direct control over assets, disbursement of funds, issuance of inventory, etc.

Some specific functional areas generally associated with administrative processing are:

◆ The support of one or more major development areas, for example, bridge construction, aircraft design, software development of new products, or nuclear reactor research.

◆ The support of operational functions, such as airline and hotel reservations, manufacturing control, demand deposit accounting, and electronic funds transfer (*q.v.*).

◆ The support of management systems, like financial management, payroll, personnel, budgeting, cost control, college admission, or student registration.

◆ The provision of a computer utility serving authorized users.

The efficiency impacts of computer software in administrative applications are primarily visible as reductions in transaction processing costs that can reflect reductions in clerical costs, inventory costs, and measures of economy, such as office automation and desktop publishing (*q.v.*). Further effectiveness lies in uses of the growing body of management science, econometrics, and other advanced methodologies of informational analysis. Some administrative analytical applications are valuable at the lowest physical level in organizations, as in the daily scheduling of refinery output with the help of linear programming models.

Traditional Organization of Data Processing Activity

The organization of applications processing activities varies from organization to organization; however, there are a number of required areas of support:

◆ *Systems development.* This activity is usually divided into two parts: systems analysis, and design and applications programming (*q.v.*). The basic organizational unit is project driven, either developing, installing, or modifying systems.

◆ *Operations.* Major divisions within operational functions are production support and hardware/ peripheral operations. All of the planning, scheduling, control, job setup, and logistical work is done in a production organization distinct from the actual "machine room floor." Included in production support is the scheduling and coordination unit. This group monitors production job streams, adjusts problems, and serves as a customer contact point. A second unit, job control, manages individual jobs as they flow through the systems. Controls are established, a job log is maintained, inputs are reviewed and edited, and outputs are reviewed and prepared for customer distribution. Within the computer operations group are all computer console and online peripheral support operators.

◆ *Library and services.* This unit maintains the tape and disk library and provides support services (such as supplies inventory) to the operations group.

◆ *Technical support.* The division of duties within the technical support group will vary within the data processing environment. Typical functions associated here are standards, database administration, user assistance (help desk), desktop support, and training.

◆ *Management.* The director/manager of data processing performs long- and short-range planning, establishes and administers project management systems, monitors resource utilization, maintains financial management systems and is responsible for personnel and budget, and manages hardware and software upgrades/acquisitions. Network communications and contingency planning are frequently a part of this person's management responsibilities.

The Administrative Applications Environment of the Year 2000

"Cooperative processing" and "client–server" environments serve work group domains by using traditional mainframes or, increasingly, powerful network servers, as "warehouses" for data and switching points for communication (*see* DATA WAREHOUSING and FILE SERVER). They also provide security and manage data access and throughput (*q.v.*) for systems of interlocking, distributed, and integrated databases, featuring enhanced system integrity, and a cost-effective array of hardware options, applications software, and data processing personnel.

Since their inception, personal computers have experienced rapidly increasing power (as measured in megahertz), and they have become viable alternatives to centralized mainframe (*q.v.*) hardware for jobs that require robust security, task interleaving with other data processing jobs, and high rates of transaction processing (*q.v.*). Data centers have had to adapt to this new environment by becoming "information utilities," with new organizational structures for properly and successfully supporting distributed processing across microcomputer-based LANs (*see* LOCAL AREA NETWORK), wide area networks, and global Internet structures.

The 24 hours per day, seven days per week applications processing schedule that is standard operating procedure in most large organizations will continue, but in many organizations these will be "lights out" operations, with machines so reliable and operations so automated that they require little or no human intervention, even to the extent of automatically restarting after the infrequent occasions when they fail. This demanding environment includes distributed complexes that are collections of geographically diverse data centers coupled by wideband, wide area communication capabilities. Fail-safe operation and disaster recovery plans are integral components of these operations.

Increasingly, data processing management will seek to improve organizational performance through the formation of partnerships with outside vendors. Termed *outsourcing*, these relationships will decrease the traditional emphasis on operational optimization and increase the emphasis on value creation and management of changing technologies before they are fully or broadly mastered for particular business purposes.

In order to manage and control applications processing, mainframe-based expert systems (*q.v.*) will be widely used. Expert systems may replace the humans who are now required to make the thousands of decisions needed to run data processing complexes on a daily basis. Emphasis on software portability (*q.v.*) and integration of multi-vendor hardware and software systems will become the key to the use of these expert systems. Peripherals, particularly traditional rotating disks and optical discs, will be heavily used, as will image processing (*q.v.*) and microfiche equipment.

Administrative software applications will continue to drive the need for faster processing. Application developers will use new languages and tools that dramatically reduce the time required to develop new applications. Some of these will reside in the fourth generation language (4GL) environment, and some will occur in the computer-aided software engineering (CASE—*q.v.*) environment. Software will be forward and reverse engineered and software design recovery will become common within data centers. Most of these systems will be required to deal with Cobol code, estimated currently at approximately 100 billion lines. Migration to CASE and 4GL will be difficult because of this extensive coding—much of which has no applications documentation and exists only as machine code. The previously mentioned Y2K problem has driven much of the needed software reengineering.

Applications are becoming "net-centric," i.e. developers know that their clients will be geographically dispersed, and will almost certainly access their systems through some type of network connection. Applications will be Web-based, meaning anyone with the proper access authorization may use the application via a single, standard look-and-feel World Wide Web interface.

In the asset management extension of applications functionality, standard software features will also include:

◆ global functionality

◆ support for multiple organizations

- analytical processing
- workflow integration
- Electronic Data Interchange (EDI) standardization
- extensibility allowing integration paths to external and legacy systems
- ties to data warehousing (*q.v.*)
- productivity tools

The trend toward increased computer literacy (*q.v.*) will continue well beyond 2000. A result of this will be that data center professionals will experience changing roles with client offices and will continue to find their expertise being used at higher levels within the organization.

Bibliography

1985. Licker, P. S. *The Art of Managing Software Development People.* New York: John Wiley. (How to manage highly creative and technically oriented staff.)

1987. Vella, C. M., and McGonagle, J. J. Jr. *Competitive Intelligence in the Computer Age.* New York: Quorum Books. (Explores the concept of locating publicly available information and converting it to useful strategic advantage over competitors.)

1990. Penrod, J. I., Dolence, M. G., and Douglas, J. V. *The Chief Information Officer in Higher Education.* Boulder, CO: CAUSE, The Association for the Management of Information Technology in Higher Education. (Description of the role and organizational placement of the CIO.)

1991. Primozic, K., Primozic, E., and Leben, J. *Strategic Choices: Supremacy, Survival, or Sayonara.* New York: McGraw-Hill. (Description of the process of formulating strategic plans for achieving competitive advantage.)

1994. Bogan, C., and English, M. *Benchmarking for Best Practices: Winning Through Innovative Adaptation.* New York: McGraw-Hill. (Discusses designing for implementation success, strategic planning, business process reengineering, change management.)

1997. *CIO Online.* http://www.cio.com. ("The leading resource for those interested in the strategic application of information technology.")

1997. McClure, P. A., Smith, J. W., and Sitko, T. D. *Crisis in Information Technology Support: Has Our Current Model Reached Its Limit?* Boulder, CO: CAUSE Information Resources Library, PUB3016. http://www.educause.edu/ir/ir-library.html. ("...focuses on one of the most serious problems facing our profession today: the difficulty of providing the level and quality of support demanded by our customers.")

1999. Gartner Group. *IT Journal.* http://gartner11.gartnerweb.com/gg/static/itjournal/. A daily update of IT news.

**William R. King and Mary Ellen Hanley
in fond memory of Dr. Aaron Finerman**

AGENT

See MULTI-AGENT SYSTEMS.

AIKEN, HOWARD

For articles on related subjects *see* DIGITAL COMPUTERS, HISTORY OF: EARLY; HOPPER, GRACE MURRAY; MARK I, HARVARD; and WATSON, THOMAS J., SR.

Howard Hathaway Aiken (Fig. 1) was born 8 March 1900, in Hoboken, NJ, and died 14 March 1973, in St Louis, MO. He grew up in Indianapolis, where he attended Arsenal Technical High School while working 12 hours a night at the Indianapolis Light and Heat Company. Upon graduation he went to work for the Madison (Wisconsin) Gas Company, a position that allowed him to go to the University of Wisconsin. He received his B.A. degree in 1923 and was immediately promoted to chief engineer at Madison Gas.

In 1935 he returned to study, first at the University of Chicago and then at Harvard. His doctoral thesis at Harvard, resulting in a Ph.D. in 1939, was on the theory of space charge conduction. The research required laborious calculations of nonlinear differential equations. This experience led him to investigate the possibility of performing these types of calculations with machine assistance. His thoughts on this subject led him in 1937 to circulate a memo entitled, "Proposed Automatic Calculating Machine" (reprinted in *Spectrum*, August 1964, 62–69).

Harvard was not the most likely environment to get support for this type of research. Fortunately, Harvard professors Ted Brown (Business) and Harlow Shapley (Astronomy) were impressed with his work, and both knew of the interest of Thomas Watson Sr. in projects of this nature. With their encouragement, and the knowledge that IBM had the necessary technology, Aiken approached Watson. A contract was signed in 1939 whereby IBM would build the Automatic Sequence

Figure 1. Howard Aiken.

Controlled Calculator (Harvard Mark I). The machine was running in 1944, and Aiken and Grace Hopper described it in a paper in *Electrical Engineering* (Vol. 65, 1946, 384–391, 449–454, 522–528; reprinted in Randell, 1982).

The Mark I was followed by the Mark II (a relay machine built for the US Naval Proving Ground at Dahlgren, VA, and completed in 1946), the Mark III (an electronic machine, also for Dahlgren, completed in 1950), and the Mark IV (an electronic machine built for and delivered to the US Air Force in 1952). With the completion of Mark IV, Aiken got out of the business of building computers.

It is difficult to evaluate precisely the impact of Aiken's series of machines and the Harvard Computation Laboratory, which he founded. Fortunately, the documents are available to anyone interested. One need only look at the log books of the computation lab for this period to see the worldwide range of people who visited the laboratory. Another source of Aiken's work is the many publications in the "Annals of the Harvard Computation Laboratory" series. The Harvard catalog also provides clear evidence of the existence of courses in "computer science" a decade before the emergence of this program at most universities.

In 1947 and again in 1949 Aiken organized symposia on large-scale digital devices at Harvard. Programs from both meetings strongly reflect his hand and his philosophy at that time. Perhaps his most profound impact was in the environment he created at Harvard, which enabled the University to become a vital training ground for many people who became outstanding in the field. A perusal of those who did their doctoral dissertations under his direction is an excellent example of this impact.

Aiken retired from Harvard in 1961 and moved to Fort Lauderdale, FL, where he formed Aiken Industries. He also joined the faculty of the University of Miami as Distinguished Professor of Information Technology. In this latter position, he helped the University develop a computer science program and design a computing center.

His honors include honorary degrees (University of Wisconsin, Wayne State University, and Technische Hochschule, Darmstadt), prizes (Rochlitz Prize, Edison Medal of IEEE, the John Price Award of the Franklin Institute) as well as medals from both the US (Air Force and Navy for distinguished service) and other governments (Sweden, Belgium, France, and Spain).

Howard Aiken felt that he had to be continuously involved in challenging endeavors in order to stay alive both physically and intellectually. His career is a document of that creed. Some of his detractors accused him of living in the past, but nothing could be further from the truth. He was a man of rare vision, whose insights have had a profound effect on the entire computing profession.

Bibliography

1973. Oettinger, A. G. "Howard Aiken," *Comm. of the ACM*, **16**, 298–299.
1982. Randell, B. (ed.). *The Origins of Digital Computers*, 3rd Ed. New York: Springer-Verlag.
1984. Williams, M. R. "Howard Aiken and the Harvard Computation Laboratory," *Annals of the History of Computing*, **6**, *2*, 157–159.
1984. Hurd, C. C. "Aiken Observed," *Annals of the History of Computing* **6**, *2*, 160–162.
1999. Cohen, I. B. *Howard Aiken: Portrait of a Computer Pioneer*. Cambridge, MA: MIT Press.
1999. Cohen, I. B., Campbell, R. V. D., and Welch, G. (eds). *Makin' Numbers: Howard Aiken and the Computer*. Cambridge, MA: MIT Press.

Henry S. Tropp

ALGOL

For articles on related subjects *see* ALGOL 68; BLOCK STRUCTURE; PROCEDURE-ORIENTED LANGUAGES: SURVEY; and PROGRAMMING LANGUAGES.

The driving concern in the development of the programming language Algol was to establish a notation for programs that would be a suitable carrier of algorithms and programs among computers of different types and capabilities.

Algol was the result of a collaboration of American and European committees. When the work was initiated in 1956, the computing scene in Europe was still dominated by one-of-a-kind computers, while in the USA the most commonly used computers were from manufacturers' standard series.

The problems of designing adequate programs were becoming acute everywhere. One approach to overcoming these problems was to replace the cumbersome machine languages by more convenient notations. The selection of such notations was guided by the applications of computers in science and engineering that dominated the early years of their invention, namely, solving the problems of mathematical analysis by techniques developed in numerical analysis (*q.v.*). Numerical techniques build principally on operands of programs that are numerals in floating-point form. Thus programming notations came to be inspired by the algebraic notations that had a long tradition in mathematical analysis. Experiments with using such notations for programs were being made in many places.

Another approach to alleviating the problems of programming was to organize collections of subroutines for common processes, which were parametrized so as to allow them to be included in complete programs. Libraries of subroutines had in fact long been established around computer installations.

The idea of establishing a programming notation that would be equally suitable in programming computers of different makes and types and for exchange of programs was first proposed in Europe in 1955, and became the subject of a working group of GAMM (Gesellschaft für angewandte Mathematik und Mechanik). In 1957 this group joined a similar effort conducted within ACM (*q.v.*). In June 1958 a GAMM-ACM working conference in Zurich worked out a proposal, later known as the Zürich Report or Algol 58, for an algebraic programming language designed for use in programming a variety of computers, as well as for describing algorithms in publications.

The Zürich Report gave rise to intense public discussion. As a result, a 13-person committee met in Paris in January 1960, where a new version of the language, Algol 60, was discussed and agreed upon. Some minor corrections to Algol 60 were published in the *Revised Report on the Algorithmic Language Algol 60* in 1962.

The problems discussed and solved during the development of Algol were those that were imposed by the aim that the resulting notation would be suitable both for wide communication and for programming of many different computers. This implied the requirements that both the meaning of the computational processes described in the notation and the description of the notation itself would be clear and unambiguous, using forms of description that would make computer-independent sense and that would support implementation equivalently across a range of computers of different makes and types.

An induced requirement was that, for reasons of expediency, the computational processes made available to the user of the notation had to allow effective description in brief terms. This requirement led to another, namely that mechanisms made available to the user of the notation had, as far as possible, to be describable in terms of a few rules that were generally valid, without exceptions.

The first proposal for the language, Algol 58, solved many of the problems. It introduced the idea that there would be three *representations* of the language (reference, publication, and hardware), such that the meaning of texts expressed in the language would only be defined in terms of the reference representation, while the typographical forms used in the publication and hardware representations were left to be chosen by users and implementers.

In Algol 58, as in earlier programming languages such as Fortran (*q.v.*), the meaning of each identifier used in a program had to be defined in an explicit or implicit declaration. In Algol 58 each identifier could be declared to denote either an integer or real numeral (intended to be implemented as a floating-point representation), an array of integers or reals having fixed subscript bounds, a label, a switch, a function, or a procedure.

The functions and procedures of Algol 58 were designed to be effective in communicating computational processes in publication. Thus they provided for flexible control through parameters of a variety of types and forms.

The problems raised by Algol 58 and solved in Algol 60 were mostly induced by the incompleteness and ambiguity of Algol 58. However, it was found that the most effective solutions of the problems might be achieved, not by minor corrections of the earlier description, but through radical redesign, aiming at generality and simplicity of both the language mechanisms and of their description.

The major part of the redesign of the language mechanisms related to:

◆ the scope of identifiers: to allow programs to include procedures taken from a library, the language had to provide means for restricting the meaning and use of any identifier to the text of one procedure;

◆ dynamic declarations: while Algol 58 provided only for arrays whose size was fixed with the program, Algol 60 provided for arrays whose size depended on quantities calculated by the program;

◆ the structure of programs: solving the problems of the scope of identifiers and the dynamics of declarations depended on establishing suitable static and dynamic program structures;

◆ the static and dynamic handling of procedure parameters.

The solutions adopted in Algol 60 rested on a static program structure of nested blocks. Each declaration of the meaning of an identifier belonged statically to a block, being valid for any inner nested blocks unless superseded by another declaration of the same identifier within that inner block. The dynamic meaning of a declaration was determined at the moment of entry of program control into the block in which the declaration belonged.

The dynamic meaning of a procedure parameter might be determined by the programmer either at the moment of the procedure call (call by value), or at the moment of reference to the parameter (call by name).

As an incidental consequence of the solutions adopted for the program and procedure structures, Algol 60 provided for recursive activations of procedures.

The description of Algol 60 employed a formal notation of productions, later called Backus–Naur form (BNF—*q.v.*). With this notation, the syntactic descriptions of language constructs were coupled to the descriptions of their dynamic meanings through the use of identical designations.

After 1960, Algol 60 was soon implemented and used for the programming of many computers, particularly in Europe. The language posed some challenges to implementers, particularly in the area of dynamic storage allocation whose solution contributed to the development of implementation techniques for programming languages in general.

Algol 60 became a much-used language for the publication of algorithms. Several journals set up departments for the publication and discussion of such algorithms, and within a few years the number of published Algol algorithms ran into the hundreds.

Given below is a typical Algol program whose purpose is to compute certain simple operations on vectors. Let **x** and **y** be two vectors with n components, given in a sequential input medium that may be accessed by successive calls of a procedure, read, such that the first n and then the elements of first **x** and then **y**, become available as the values of the parameter of the call of read. Then the program determines and prints, successively, (1) the elements of the vector sum **x** + **y**, (2) the elements of the vector difference **x** − **y**, and (3) the elements of the projection P of **y** on **x**, assumed to be nonvanishing: $P = \mathbf{x}(\mathbf{xy})/(\mathbf{xx})$, where (**xy**) denotes the scalar product of **x** and **y** and (**xx**) the scalar product of **x** with itself. The Algol 60 implementations is:

```
begin
  integer n;

  procedure inputvector(vec); array vec;
  comment Reads the next n numerals from the
  input medium and assigns them as the elements
  of the vector vec;
    begin integer k;
        for k := 1 step 1 until n do
            read(vec[k])
    end inputvector;
  procedure outputvector(q, element);
    integer q; real element;
  comment Prints in order the n numbers
  obtained from the expression element when the
  parameter q is given the values 1, 2, ..., n;
    begin
    for q :=1 step 1 until n do print(element)
    end outputvector;
```

```
real procedure scalarproduct(a,b);
  array a, b;
comment Computes the scalar product of the
n-vectors a and b;
  begin integer k; real s;
      s := 0;
      for k := 1 step 1 until n do
          s := s + a[k] × b[k];
      scalarproduct := s
  end scalarproduct;

read(n);
begin array x, y[1:n]; real norm;
    integer i;
inputvector(x);
inputvector(y);
outputvector(i, x[i] + y[i]);
outputvector(i, x[i] - y[i]);
norm :=
    scalarproduct(x, y)/scalarproduct(x, x);
outputvector(i, x[i] × norm);
end
end
```

The influence of Algol 60 on many later programming language developments is visible both in the capabilities of such languages and in the terminology employed in describing them. Several significant later languages, such as Simula (*q.v.*) and Pascal (*q.v.*), extended Algol 60 by providing for further operand types. Algol 68 was a radical redesign aiming at a high degree of formality of description of the language.

Bibliography

1963. Naur, P. (ed.) "Revised Report on the Algorithmic Language ALGOL 60," *Communications of the ACM*, **6**, *1*, 1–17. Reprinted in 1987. *Programming Languages: A Grand Tour* (ed. E. Horowitz), 3rd Ed., 44–60. Rockville, MD: Computer Science Press.

1981. Wexelblat, R. (ed.) *History of Programming Languages.* New York: Academic Press. Contains A. J. Perlis, "The American Side of the Development of ALGOL," 75–91; P. Naur, "The European Side of the Last Phase of the Development of ALGOL 60," 92–139.

Peter Naur

ALGOL 68

For articles on related subjects *see* ALGOL; BLOCK STRUCTURE; EXTENSIBLE LANGUAGE; PROCEDURE-ORIENTED LANGUAGES; and PROGRAMMING LANGUAGES.

Algol 68 was designed by a working group (WG 2.1) of the International Federation for Information Processing (IFIP) in order to provide a general-purpose programming language that would be suitable for communicating algorithms, executing them efficiently on different computers, and teaching computer science. Although Algol 68 was a successor to Algol 60, it was designed as a completely new language. Algol 68 thus differs from Algol 60 in many essential aspects. Algol 68 design reflects the 1968 understanding of a number of fundamental concepts of programming languages and computer science.

Algol 68 has great expressive power and yet a very elegant and interesting basic structure. It features five primitive types of values (called "modes"): `bool` (Boolean), `char` (character), `int` (integer), `real` and `format`; and five rules for constructing new modes from the ones already defined. For example, values of mode `[]real` are one-dimensional arrays or *multiple values* of reals. Values of mode `struct([]char name, bool sex, int age)` are personal records or *structured values* (*see* RECORD). Values of mode `union(real, int)` are either reals or integers, but no value of this mode can be both of mode `real` and `int`. *References* are values that refer (point—*see* POINTER) to other values. For example, values of mode `ref []char` are references to one-dimensional arrays of characters. Values of mode `proc(int, real) bool` are *routines* (i.e. procedures) that take two arguments of respective modes `int` and `real` and return a value of mode `bool`.

Since references and routines are values, they can be manipulated like any other values. In particular, they can be passed as parameters in procedure calls. Because of this, it is possible to achieve the effects of three types of procedure call found in other programming languages: call by value, call by name, and call by reference. For example, values of mode `proc(ref [] char, int)int` are routines with the first formal parameter called by reference.

Different sorts of declarations (*q.v.*) (for example, array declarations and switch declarations) found in other programming languages are captured in the *identity declaration* of Algol 68. This concept is also the basis of the parameter-passing (*q.v.*) mechanism of Algol 68; it allows construction of an infinite number of new modes from the ones already defined and permits declaration of arithmetic and logical operators and their priorities.

The identity declaration and the concept of a reference clarify the distinction between a variable and a constant. An identity declaration in a program defines the value possessed by the declared identifier. This value may be a reference to another value, in which case the identifier is declared as a variable.

An example of an initialized variable declaration (i.e. one that includes assignment) is `real x := 3.1416`. This declaration gives rise to the following scheme: identifier $x \rightarrow$ reference-to-a-real-value $\rightarrow 3.1416$. An example of a declaration that establishes *pi* as a constant 3.1416 is `real pi=3.1416`. This gives rise to the following scheme: identifier $pi=3.1416$.

The effect of a standard assignment statement is achieved by making the reference possessed by an identifier refer to the value specified in the statement. This is not possible if the value possessed by an identifier is not a reference, i.e. if this intermediate link is not present.

This careful distinction permits, in particular, the definition of constant and variable procedures. For example, the declaration `proc f=(real x, real y) real:(x+y)/2-sqrt(x*y)` establishes *f* as a constant, as opposed to `proc f:=(real x, real y) real: (x+y)/2-sqrt(x*y)`, which defines a variable procedure. In the latter case we can, at another point in the program, assign some other value of mode `proc(real,real)real` to *f*. For example, we can write `f := (real x, real y) real: (x+y)/2`.

A number of standard statements are available in Algol 68: assignment, e.g. `x:=(a+b)/2`; repetition, e.g. `for i from 2 to n do f:=f*i`; go to, e.g. `go to loop`; conditional, e.g. `if successful then grade:="a" else grade:="c" fi`, etc. In addition to the conventional serial statement execution, it is possible to specify parallel or *collateral* execution. In the latter case, execution of statements is merged in time in a way to be specified by the implementation. Parallel programming facilities in Algol 68 include elementary means of control or synchronization of collateral execution. These are language-defined values called *semaphores.*

The Algol 60 concept of a *block* appears in a more general form in Algol 68 as a *range*. An example of a range is a sequence of declarations and statements placed between generalized parentheses. Examples of pairs of these parentheses are `begin` and `end`, `if` and `then`, `then` and `else`, and `else` and `fi`. References possessed by the identifiers declared in a range may be local to that range. Since the hardware representation of a reference is a memory location, storage is allocated dynamically to local variables. In addition to these stack-controlled values, Algol 68 also has values whose lifetimes are managed by the *heap*.

Algol 68 was designed at roughly the same time as Pascal (*q.v.*), which was also intended to be a successor to Algol 60. While Pascal was widely accepted and heavily used, Algol 68 was not. Pascal is a much smaller and simpler language than Algol 68. Algol 68 is not only more complex, but the generality that it offers is not always necessary or of the right kind. Even though the orthogonal design adopted in Algol 68 is conceptually correct and attractive, it still leads to complexity both in the language and in its implementation techniques. For example, one implication of orthogonality in Algol 68 is that references are values, too. But having references explicitly in the language has the well-known undesirable consequence of allowing incorrect uses of computer memory addresses (*see* POINTER).

Algol 68 is considerably more difficult to learn than Pascal, partly due to the unusual terminology of Algol 68, which has not been widely accepted. The defining document of Algol 68 is much more elaborate and precise than the Pascal Report, but is also much more difficult to understand than the shorter and less formal Pascal document. This applies, in particular, to the two-level context-sensitive grammar used in the Algol 68 report in comparison to the usual BNF (*q.v.*) syntax used for Pascal.

A decisive factor in the poor acceptance of Algol 68 was that it was much more difficult to implement full Algol 68 than Pascal. Unlike the implementation techniques of Algol 68, well-known, widely used, portable and efficient implementation techniques were developed for Pascal.

In spite of major conceptual advances over Algol 60, both Algol 68 and Pascal lacked some programming abstractions that were only subsequently widely accepted as fundamental for modern programming paradigms. The most important such lack in both languages is the notion of an *abstract data type* (*q.v.*). In fact, a programming language designed around the notion of an abstract data type can accomplish all the generality of Algol 68, and a lot more. At the same time, such a language attains the simplicity that is lacking in Algol 68.

Bibliography

1969. van Wijngaarden, A., Mailloux, B., Peck, J., and Koster, C. "Report on the Algorithmic Language ALGOL 68," *Numerische Mathematik*, **14**, *2*, 79–218.
1971. Branquart, P., Lewi, J., Sintzoff, M., and Wodon, P. L. "The Composition of Semantics in Algol 68," *Comm. of the ACM*, **14**, *11*, 697–708.
1971. Lindsey, C. H., and van der Meulen, S. G. *Informal Introduction to Algol 68*. Amsterdam: North-Holland.
1975. van Wijngaarden, A., Mailloux, B. J., Peck, J. E. L., Koster, C. H. A., Sintzoff, M., Lindsey, C. H., Meertens, L. G. L. T., and Fisher, R. G. "Revised Report on the Algorithmic Language Algol 68," *Acta Informatica*, **5**, *1–3*, 1–236.
1976. Tanenbaum, A. S. "A Tutorial on Algol 68," *Computing Surveys*, **8**, *2*, 155–190.
1978. Tanenbaum, A. S. "A Comparison of Pascal and Algol 68," *Computer Journal*, **21**, *4*, 316–323.

Suad Alagic

ALGORITHM

For articles on related subjects *see* ALGORITHMIC PROBLEM SOLVING; ALGORITHMICS; ALGORITHMS, ANALYSIS OF; ALGORITHMS, DESIGN AND CLASSIFICATION OF; ALGORITHMS, THEORY OF; ERROR ANALYSIS; PROGRAM VERIFICATION; SEARCHING; SORTING; and TURING MACHINE.

In discussing problem solving, we presuppose both a problem and a device to be used in solving the problem. The problem may be mathematical or non-mathematical in nature, simple or complex. The basic requirements for a well-posed problem are that (1) the known information is clearly specified; (2) we can determine when the problem has been solved; and (3) the problem does not change during its attempted solution. The second requirement does not mean that the solution to the problem is known *a priori*, but only that we know when the solution has been attained. For example, in some numerical problems we obtain repeated approximations to the answer, terminating the solution process when two successive approximations are "sufficiently close" together. We can specify in the problem statement the exact meaning of "sufficiently close" without knowing the exact answer. The device to be used for problem solution may be human or machine, or a combination of the two.

Definition

Given both the problem and the device, an *algorithm* is the precise characterization of a method of solving the problem, presented in a notation interpretable by the device. In particular, an algorithm is characterized by these properties:

1. Application of the algorithm to a particular input set or problem description results in a finite sequence of actions.

2. The sequence of actions has a unique initial action.

3. Each action in the sequence has a unique successor.

4. The sequence terminates with either a solution to the problem, or a statement that the problem is unsolvable for that set of data.

We illustrate these concepts with an example: "Find the square root of the real number x." As it is stated, this problem is algorithmically either trivial or unsolvable, owing to the irrationality of most square roots. If we accept $\sqrt{2}$ as the square root of 2, for example, the solution is trivial: the answer is the square root sign ($\sqrt{}$) concatenated with the input. However, if we want a decimal expression, then the square root of 2 can never be calculated exactly. Hence the requirement of a finite number of actions is violated.

A modified statement of the problem is more suited to our purposes. "Find the positive square root of the real number x to four decimal places." This statement has three useful properties:

1. It explicitly names the *positive* square root as the desired one, whereas the earlier statement left that quality ambiguous.

ALGORITHM **37**

2. It eliminates the string $\sqrt{x}$ as a problem solution.

3. By stating "four decimal places" (or any other fixed number of places), it provides a test for termination.

A conceivable but questionable method of solution is:

1. Choose a number y and compute y^2.

2. If $|y^2 - x| < 5 \times 10^{-5}$, the solution is y; if not, return to step (1).

This method fails to be an algorithm, since no procedure is specified for choosing either the initial value y or subsequent values. And, even if there is a solution, there is no guarantee that this method will find it.

Now consider another method:

1. Let $y = 1$.

2. Compute y^2.

3. If $|y^2 - x| < 5 \times 10^{-5}$, the solution is y, HALT; if not, continue with step 4.

4. Replace y by $((x/y) + y)/2$; go to step 2.

This procedure is a special case of a general technique known as the Newton–Raphson method, which has the precise definition of each step required of an algorithm. Moreover, whenever applied to a non-negative real number x, the method will produce the proper solution in a finite number of steps. However, whenever applied to a negative number, the method will endlessly recompute y without recognizing the futility of the task. This is typical of a class of methods called *semi-algorithms*: they will halt in a finite number of steps if the problem posed has a solution, but will not necessarily halt if there is no solution.

To transform this method into an algorithm, two things must be done:

1. Add a step, (0); if $x < 0$, there is no solution; HALT; and

2. Rewrite the given method in a notation suitable for the proposed device. (For English speakers the language as given above is satisfactory; for a computer, a programming language must be used. For example, the following algorithm in pseudocode can easily be converted to any procedure-oriented language (*q.v.*).)

> **Input** x
> **Output** y [An approximation to $\sqrt{x}$]
> **Algorithm** SquareRoot
>   **print** Find the square root of x

>   **if** $x \geq 0$ **then**
> $y \leftarrow 1$
>   **repeat until** $|y^2 - x| < .00005$
> $y \leftarrow ((x/y) + y)/2$
>   **endrepeat**
>   **print** The square root of x is y.
>   **else**
>   **print** There is no real square root for x.
>   **endif**

This algorithm requests input data and then responds with the square root of the input, or a message that there is no real square root. When implemented in most common programming languages with the results to be printed to 5 decimal places, successive runs with the inputs 3, 107, 1, 0, −4, and 3.14159 give the following results:

```
Find the square root of 3
The square root of 3.00000 is 1.73205.
Find the square root of 107
The square root of 107.00000 is 10.34408.
Find the square root of 1
The square root of 1.00000 is 1.00000.
Find the square root of 0
The square root of 0.00000 is 0.00391.
Find the square root of −4
There is no real square root for −4.00000.
Find the square root of 3.14159
The square root of 3.14159 is 1.77245.
```

Note that the result is not correct to 4 decimal places when $x = 0$. Since $(.00391)^2 \approx .00002 < .00005$, $y = .00391$ satisfies the error test. Alas, the problem is that the error test in algorithm SquareRoot only requires that the square of y have four decimal places correct. For very small x this is not sufficient to make y itself have four correct places. Furthermore, when implemented on a real computer with a necessarily finite number of digits in its numbers, programs for algorithm SquareRoot will not even terminate for some very large x. Various techniques may be used to extend the range of values for which correct answers are produced (see below).

Although the algorithm above concerns the solution of a numerical problem, algorithms can be and are applied to a wide variety of nonnumerical problems, for example the algorithms used for searching and sorting.

Significance of Algorithms

While the concept of an algorithm is useful in crystallizing the informal notation of a "method of solution" for a problem, it has a much deeper significance. Whereas it was at one time assumed that any properly stated mathematical problem was solvable, mathematicians in the 1920s began to question this, asking what precisely it meant to say that we could "solve a problem" or "compute a function." Several important areas of mathematics have resulted from attempts to answer these questions, including the theory of Turing machines (*q.v.*) and the theory of algorithms (*see* ALGORITHMS, THEORY OF). All the concepts proposed proved to be equivalent: any problem that is solvable according to one concept is solvable according to all other concepts. Thus, while an algorithm may not be the only way to solve a problem, it appears to be essentially equivalent to any other *formal* method of problem solving.

Quality Judgments on Algorithms

Any computer program is at least a semi-algorithm, and any program that always halts is an algorithm. (Of course, it may not solve the problem for which the programmer intended it.) Given a solvable problem, there are many algorithms (programs) to solve it, not all of equal quality. The primary practical criteria by which the quality of an algorithm is judged are time and memory requirements, accuracy of solution, and generality. To cite an extreme example, since a properly defined game of chess has only a finite number of possible moves, there exists an algorithm to determine the "perfect" chess game. Simply examine all possible move sequences, in some specified order. Unfortunately, the time required to execute any algorithm based on this idea is measured in huge multiples of the age of the universe, even at today's computer speeds. The memory requirements for such an algorithm are similarly overbearing.

On a more practical plane, several numerical methods for solving problems fail to yield satisfactory algorithms because the rate of convergence is so slow that thousands or millions of iterations may be needed to determine the answer. For other numerical methods, rounding or truncation errors may accumulate so rapidly that they destroy the answer (*see* ERROR ANALYSIS).

One characteristic of an algorithm, which is almost always important for numerical algorithms, is its accuracy. For example, the square root algorithm previously presented is not very accurate. Changing the test constant from 0.00005 to 0.00000000005 in the square root program will produce 0.00000381 as the square root of zero at the cost of more iterations through the loop of the algorithm. No additional memory is required, and the additional iterations require only a small fraction of a second. Further improvement may be obtained using double-precision arithmetic (*see* ARITHMETIC, COMPUTER) at a (small) cost of both run time and additional memory space. In each case the basic algorithmic concept is unchanged.

Altering the basic algorithmic concept may provide an improved algorithm to accomplish a given task. For example, three multiplications and two additions are required to evaluate the quadratic expression $ax^2 + bx + c$ in the order $((ax^2) + (bx)) + c$. Changing the evaluation algorithm to $(((ax) + b)x) + c$ eliminates one multiplication, resulting in a more efficient process. This will not only improve the speed of solution of the problem, but will sometimes also improve the accuracy of the result.

The remaining important characteristic of an algorithm is its generality. While there are occasions when an algorithm is needed to solve a single isolated problem, more often algorithms are designed to handle a range of input data. Generality, like accuracy, is often attained at the cost of speed and memory requirements. A general polynomial root finder may be more costly in both time and storage than an algorithm for extracting the roots of a quadratic equation. But the increased generality may justify the cost. This is a pragmatic decision. In another example, an information retrieval (*q.v.*) system based on a free vocabulary is generally more expensive to design and operate than one based on a fixed or coded vocabulary. But the difference in utility may far outweigh the additional cost burden.

Questions of the minimal time and storage requirements posed by a given class of problems, and of the time and storage requirements of any proposed algorithm, have, despite the increasing speed of computers and decreasing cost of storage, become increasingly important as we attempt to solve larger and more complex problems. In recent years, much of the work in algorithm theory has been focused on questions of algorithmic complexity (*see also* COMPUTATIONAL COMPLEXITY).

Bibliography

1983. Aho, A. V., Hopcroft, J. E., and Ullman, J. D. *Data Structures and Algorithms.* Reading, MA: Addison-Wesley.
1987. Korfhage, R. R., and Gibbs, N. E. *Principles of Data Structures and Algorithms with Pascal.* Dubuque, IA: Wm. C. Brown Publishers.
1990. Cormen, T. H., Leiserson, C. E., and Rivest, R. L. *Introduction to Algorithms.* Cambridge, MA: MIT Press.
1992. Sedgewick, R. *Algorithms in C++.* Reading, MA: Addison-Wesley.

Robert R. Korfhage

ALGORITHMIC PROBLEM SOLVING

For articles on related subjects *see* ALGORITHM; ALGORITHMICS; ALGORITHMS, ANALYSIS OF; COMBINATORICS; COMPUTER ALGEBRA; NUMBER THEORETIC CALCULATIONS; and PROBABILISTIC ALGORITHMS.

What is Algorithmic Problem Solving?

Suppose you want to find the solution S to a mathematical problem in some domain. Depending upon the type of operations under consideration that lead to the construction of a solution S, one can distinguish between "pure mathematics" (which uses tools such as infinite union, limits, etc.) and "algorithmic mathematics" (whose tools are substitution, if–then–else, recursion, etc.). Algorithmic mathematics is interested only in those solutions that can be expressed by constructs whose effects can be realized by (idealized) machines. Hence, *the essence of algorithmic problem solving hinges on the algorithmic realization of solutions "relative" to given "black box" (i.e. idealized machine) operations.*

The process by which mathematics, in particular, algorithmic problem solving, is actually carried out is, inevitably, different from this "static" description.

Often, the first insight into a problem is gained by *observation*. Then, based on individual facts—which might be obtained by computer experiments—a *conjecture* is formulated.

The next and crucial step is to transform the conjecture into a *theorem*. This is done by deriving a sequence of steps that shows that the conjectured assertion is true *for all* instances, not only for the particular observed ones. One of the essential features of a "good" theorem is its potential to reduce certain types of problems to other, ideally simpler, problems.

Algorithmic mathematics, in particular, considers those theorems to be "good" from which *algorithms* can be extracted. The extraction of algorithms (formulated in a particular algorithmic language) from theorems may be called *programming*.

Buchberger (1997) (which also discusses various other aspects of "doing mathematics by computer" and which we strongly recommend for further reading) calls the above the steps of the "creativity spiral," emphasizing the fact that after proceeding through such a spiral, one ideally arrives at a "higher level"; i.e. by producing new "good" theorems/algorithms that again can be used to advance the spiral.

In practice, the solution of a problem is achieved by proceeding, iteratively, through several "spirals" or "subspirals." However, in this "dynamic" view, the essence of algorithmic problem solving is that for the crucial, nontrivial steps of *proving*, *algorithms* are used—instead of human insight or ingenuity. A recent algorithmic breakthrough, described in the next section, will serve for illustration.

How to do Combinatorial Sums Using a Computer

Decision procedures, like Risch's *integration* algorithm (used to do analytic integration in computer algebra (*q.v.*) systems), nowadays are routinely used in "subspirals" of the "creativity spiral." Gosper's (1978) algorithm presents a method for indefinite *summation* of *hypergeometric terms* $F(k)$, (i.e. terms for which $F(k+1)/F(k)$ is a rational function of k). However, only recently Zeilberger (1991) showed how Gosper's algorithm can be extended for algorithmic treatment of combinatorial sums such as the binomial theorem, $\sum_k \binom{n}{k} x^k = (1 + x)^n$, or much more complicated, definite summations over *proper hypergeometric terms*. These are terms of the form

$$F(n, k) = P(n, k) \frac{\prod_{i=1}^{I} (a_i n + b_i k + c_i)!}{\prod_{j=1}^{J} (u_j n + v_j k + w_j)!} x^n y^k,$$

in which $P(n, k)$ is a polynomial in n and k, where the quantities c_i, w_j, x, y may depend on parameters (over, say, the complex numbers) and where a_i, b_i, u_j, v_j, I, J are fixed specific integers.

Before Zeilberger's observation, automatic treatment of definite hypergeometric sums had been considered algorithmically infeasible (*see* e.g. Knuth (1968), Exercise 1.2.6.63, p. 73).

As an example, given a sum $\sum_k F(n, k)$ where $F(n, k)$ is as above and which is zero outside the integer interval in k from 0 to n, the key step in Zeilberger's algorithm consists in deriving a recurrence—valid for all nonnegative integers n—of the type

$$\sum_{j=0}^{d} p_j(n) \left(\sum_k F(n+j, k) \right) = 0, \qquad (1)$$

where d is a nonnegative integer and $p_j(n)$ are polynomials in n.

Such sums typically arise in enumeration problems; some of these have a closed form evaluation as a hypergeometric term $S(n)$ (e.g. in the binomial theorem, $F(n, k) = \binom{n}{k} x^k$ and $S(n) = (1 + x)^n$).

Now, having the output recurrence (1) of Zeilberger's algorithm in hand, the proof of the formula

$$\forall n \geq 0: \sum_k F(n, k) = S(n)$$

is equivalent to showing that for all $n \geq 0$, $S(n)$ satisfies the recurrence

$$\sum_{j=0}^{d} p_j(n) S(n+j) = 0 \qquad (2)$$

and to verify that the initial values of $S(n)$ and the sum coincide for n from 0 to $d - 1$.

By definition, $S(n+1)/S(n)$ is a rational function of n; this is also true for

$$S(n+2)/S(n)(=S(n+2)/S(n+1) \times S(n+1)/S(n))$$

up to $S(n+d)/S(n)$. Consequently, after dividing out $S(n)$, the problem of proving (2) for all $n \geq 0$ reduces to the simple verification that the resulting rational function in n is 0.

Another application is *finding* a hypergeometric "closed form" evaluation $S(n)$ of $\sum_k F(n, k)$. For this, one only needs an algorithm for finding hypergeometric solutions $S(n)$ of (2). For further details we refer the reader to the marvelous book by Petkovšek *et al.* (1996).

From the theoretical point of view, these methods can be considered as an algorithmic supplement to classic hypergeometric function machinery (*see*, e.g. Andrews, 1974). However, their impact on algorithmic problem solving is a striking success. For instance, in Nemes *et al.* (1997) it is explained how 27 problems that have appeared in *The American Mathematical Monthly* over the years, can all be solved algorithmically.

In order to give a concrete illustration we take a problem stated in Petkovšek *et al.* (1996): "You've been up all night working on your new theory, you found the answer, and it's in the form of a sum such as

$$S(n) := \sum_{k=0}^{n} (-1)^k \binom{x-k+1}{k} \binom{x-2k}{n-k}.$$

You know that many sums like this one have simple evaluations and you would like to know, quite definitively, if this one does, or does not." If you are using Maple, then get the package EKHAD from the World Wide Website `http://www.cis.upenn.edu/~wilf/AeqB.html`; if you are using Mathematica pick up the program `zb_alg.m` from the site `http://www.risc.uni-linz.ac.at/research/combinat/risc/`. In both cases the programs deliver $S(n+2) - S(n) = 0$ as the recurrence for the sum. Since $S(0) = 1$ and $S(1) = 0$, you have found that $S(n) = 1$ if n is even, and $S(n) = 0$ if n is odd, and you are finished.

Conclusion

Zeilberger's extension of Gosper's algorithm—via its use for proving a result (or finding one)—enables algorithmic problem solving for a huge variety of problems in various contexts. Besides its applicability in "pure mathematics" (enumerative combinatorics, number theory, special functions, etc.) it can also be put into action for problems in computer science (e.g. analysis of algorithms) or physics (e.g. statistical mechanics). But, despite the impressive problem-solving power of methods like Zeilberger's, algorithmic problem solving

is not restricted to the use of such "special provers" (decision procedures).

If one agrees that proving is the essence of (mathematical) problem solving, then there is also the task of building "provers" for much more general domains. Such a list, for instance, would include "A general equational theorem prover," "Theorem provers for the theory of real closed fields" (e.g. Collins' (1975) prover) and "Theorem provers for certain classes of geometrical theorems based on algebraic techniques" (like Gröbner bases (Buchberger, 1985) and characteristic sets).

We conclude with the prospect that a variety of "general purpose" provers and special provers for particular domains will be made available in future computer algebra systems. Of course, many problems still remain to be solved; e.g. the interplay of the special provers. However, there is already an active discussion about various approaches, such as the use of a hierarchy of *functors* (Buchberger, 1996).

Bibliography

1974. Andrews, G. E. "Applications of Basic Hypergeometric Functions," *SIAM Review*, **16**, 441–483.

1975. Collins, G. E. "Quantifier Elimination for Real Closed Fields by Cylindrical Algebraic Decomposition," in *Proc. 2nd GI Conference on Automata Theory and Formal Languages.* Berlin: Springer-Verlag.

1978. Gosper, R. W. Jr. "Decision Procedure for Indefinite Hypergeometric Summation," *Proc. Natl. Acad. Sci. USA*, **75**, 40–42.

1985. Buchberger, B. "Gröbner Bases—An Algorithmic Method in Polynomial Ideal Theory," in *Multidimensional Systems Theory* (ed. N. K. Bose), Chapter 6, 184–232. Dordrecht: Reidel.

1991. Zeilberger, D. "The Method of Creative Telescoping," *J. Symb. Comput.*, **11**, 195–204.

1996. Buchberger, B. "Symbolic Computation: Computer Algebra and Logic," in *Frontiers of Combining Systems* (eds. F. Baader and K. Schulz), 193–220. Dordrecht: Kluwer.

1996. Petkovšek, M., Wilf, H. S., and Zeilberger, D. *A=B.* Natick, MA: Peters.

1997. Buchberger, B. "Mathematica: Doing Mathematics by Computer," in *Advances in the Design of Symbolic Computation Systems.* Texts and Monographs in Symbolic Computation (eds. A. Miola and M. Temperini), 2–20. New York: Springer-Verlag.

1997. Knuth, D. E. *The Art of Computer Programming*, Vol. I, 3rd Ed. Reading, MA: Addison-Wesley.

1997. Nemes, I., Petkovšek, M., Wilf, H. S., and Zeilberger, D. "How To Do MONTHLY Problems With Your Computer," *Amer. Math. Monthly*, **104**, 505–519.

Peter Paule

ALGORITHMICS

For articles on related subjects *see* ALGORITHM; ALGORITHMIC PROBLEM SOLVING; ALGORITHMS, ANALYSIS OF; ALGORITHMS, DESIGN AND CLASSIFICATION OF; ALGORITHMS, THEORY OF; COMPUTATIONAL COMPLEXITY; LOOP INVARIANT; and PROGRAM VERIFICATION.

Algorithmics is the systematic study of algorithms—how to devise them, describe them, validate them, and compare their relative merits. As the study of algorithms, algorithmics might be deemed a synonym for computer science. And, to be sure, "algorithmics" appears in the names of an increasing number of computer science courses, journals, books, research groups, and consulting firms. However, the term is perhaps still used primarily by mathematicians and mathematics educators, for whom it connotes an approach to *mathematics* where the study of the calculations by which answers are obtained is as important as determining that answers exist. This is quite different from the approach to mathematics during most of the twentieth century. At the school level, there was much *doing* of algorithms, but in a rote way. At the university level, the emphasis was on the existence and structure of mathematical objects. But now, with computers, such large and complicated problems are tackled that it is natural to be more systematic about the methodology for computing answers. Thus, algorithmics means not only being explicit about the use of algorithms to do mathematics (for instance, by using *algorithmic language* (i.e. pseudocode) to describe solution methods), but it also means regarding algorithms themselves as worthy objects of mathematical study.

Algorithmics is usually divided into three parts: design, verification, and analysis. Design is the process of creating algorithms and the study of good creation approaches (for instance, reducing to smaller cases and top-down planning). Verification is proving algorithms correct; the primary technique is mathematical induction, often expressed in terms of loop invariants (*q.v.*). Analysis is the determination of the efficiency of an algorithm (how long it takes to run as a function of input size, or how much memory is required) and, when more than one algorithm is known to solve a problem, a comparison of their relative efficiencies (*see* ALGORITHMS, ANALYSIS OF). Better yet, but usually quite difficult, is to determine or at least bound the optimal efficiency for any method that solves the problem at hand. Determining the optimum over all algorithms for a problem is called determining the *computational complexity* (*q.v.*) of the problem.

Here is a simple example. Consider the problem of evaluating a polynomial $p(x) = a_n x^n + \cdots + a_1 x + a_0$. From a classical mathematics standpoint, there isn't any "problem" here; of course the polynomial has a value. But what if n is *very* large and/or we must compute $p(x)$ for many values of x? (These situations can arise in coding theory or in approximating functions with polynomials.) Then it is worthwhile to devise competing evaluation methods and compare them.

For instance, if the standard representation above is evaluated directly, it takes n multiplications to compute $a_n x^n$, $n - 1$ to compute $a_{n-1} x^{n-1}$, etc., for a total of $n(n + 1)/2$ multiplications and n additions. If powers of x are not recomputed, then the number of multiplications is $2n - 1$. This saving can be accomplished by computing $a_n x^n$ first, but saving the intermediate powers x^2, x^3, ... obtained along the way and recalling them when lower-order terms like $a_{n-1} x^{n-1}$ are computed. However, even these memory requirements can be avoided if terms are computed from the low end, as shown in the pseudocode below.

Further savings are obtained if $p(x)$ is rewritten in nested form,

$$p(x) = x(\cdots x(a_n x + a_{n-1}) \cdots) + a_0$$

Then only n multiplications and n additions are needed. This method is perhaps best understood if we write it and the preceding, more standard, approach in algorithmic language.

STANDARD ALGORITHM

$Poly \leftarrow a_0 + a_1 * x$
$Power \leftarrow x$
for $k = 2$ **to** n
$\quad Power \leftarrow Power * x$
$\quad Poly \leftarrow Poly + a_k * Power$
endfor
Output *Poly*

NESTED ALGORITHM

$Poly \leftarrow a_n$
$\quad$**for** $i = 1$ **to** n
$\quad\quad Poly \leftarrow Poly * x + a_{n-i}$
$\quad$**endfor**
Output *Poly*

Perhaps the least evident part of the discussion above is the claim that the nested algorithm is valid. This claim follows from checking that the following is a loop invariant: At the end of the ith pass through the loop, $Poly = \sum_{j=0}^{i} a_{n-j} x^{i-j}$. Upon termination, $i = n$, so it follows from this invariant that $Poly = p(x)$ at the end.

Devising these algorithms, validating them, and analyzing their efficiency illustrate the main parts of algorithmics. In fact, it can be shown that the nested method is an optimal algorithm in a strong sense. (Nested evaluation itself is quite old; Newton used it, though it usually goes under the name Horner's Method. Proofs of its optimality are much more recent.) More to the point here, the idea that evaluating polynomials is indeed a problem gets at the heart of algorithmics. When one looks for algorithmic issues in mathematics, both in elementary and advanced material, many new avenues for exploration are opened.

Bibliography

1977. Engel, A. "Elementarmathematik von algorithmischen Standpunkt," Stuttgart: Ernst Klett Verlag, translated as "Elementary Mathematics from an Algorithmic Standpoint" by F. R. Watson, Staffordshire, UK: KMEP, University of Keele.

1985. Maurer, S. "The Algorithmic Way of Life is Best," *College Math J*, **16** (January), 2–18 (forum piece and reply to responses).

1992. Harel, D. *Algorithmics: The Spirit of Computing*, 2nd Ed. Reading, MA: Addison-Wesley.

1998. Maurer, S. "What are Algorithms? What is an Answer?," in *The Teaching and Learning of Algorithms in School Mathematics* (1998 Yearbook), 21–31. Reston, VA: National Council of Teachers of Mathematics.

ACM *Journal of Experimental Algorithmics*, electronic journal at http://www.jea.acm.org.

Stephen B. Maurer

ALGORITHMS, ANALYSIS OF

For articles on related subjects *see* ALGORITHM; ALGORITHMIC PROBLEM SOLVING; ALGORITHMICS; ALGORITHMS, DESIGN AND CLASSIFICATION OF; ALGORITHMS, THEORY OF; COMBINATORICS; COMPUTATIONAL COMPLEXITY; GRAPH THEORY; NP-COMPLETE PROBLEMS; SEARCHING; and SORTING.

The analysis of algorithms can be partitioned into two areas: algorithm complexity and problem complexity. The former is concerned with consideration of a specific algorithm for a problem and the analysis of its behavior with respect to the amount of memory space, time, or other resource used. The latter is concerned with the class of all algorithms for a particular problem and the determination of its minimum requirements with respect to space and time or other resources. Such analyses are second in importance only to the determination of the correctness of an algorithm. They provide the means to choose algorithms intelligently and improve them.

One might suspect that, as the speed of computers increases, the effects of the efficiency of the algorithms used will decrease. Actually, just the opposite is true. The reason is that the asymptotic behavior of the algorithm becomes more important, as we will now illustrate.

With each problem, we associate an integer that we call the *size* of the problem. For example, the size of a matrix inversion problem is the dimension of the matrix, the size of a graph problem is the number of edges, and so forth. The growth rate of the execution time of the algorithm is determined as a function of the size of the problem. The limiting behavior of the growth rate is called the asymptotic growth rate. For example, the asymptotic behavior of the function $17 + 5n + 2n^2$ is $2n^2$, since, for sufficiently large n, $2n^2$ approximates $17 + 5n + 2n^2$ to arbitrary accuracy. For $n > 100$, the lower-order terms account for less than 3%.

The notation used to describe the asymptotic growth rate (also called asymptotic running time) of an algorithm is given in terms of functions whose domain set is $\mathbb{N}$, the natural numbers. We measure the asymptotic running time by *upper bounds* and *lower bounds*. We denote an *asymptotic upper bound* for a function by O-notation to give an upper bound on the function to within a constant factor. Given a function $g(n)$, $O(g(n))$ is defined as $O(g(n)) = \{f(n)|$ there exist positive constants c, n_0 such that $0 \leq f(n) \leq cg(n)$ for all $n \geq n_0\}$. Intuitively, $f(n)$ is in $O(g(n))$ if the graph of $f(n)$ lies on or below the graph of $cg(n)$ for all values of n greater than n_0. We denote an *asymptotic lower bound* for a function by Ω-notation to give a lower bound on the function to within a constant factor. Given a function $g(n)$, $\Omega(g(n))$ is defined as $\Omega(g(n)) = \{f(n)|$ there exist positive constants c, n_0 such that $0 \leq cg(n) \leq f(n)$ for all $n \geq n_0\}$. Intuitively, $f(n)$ is in $\Omega(g(n))$ if the graph of $f(n)$ lies on or above the graph of $cg(n)$ for all values of n greater than n_0. If a function is both an upper bound and a lower bound, we say the function is an *asymptotically tight bound* and denote it by Θ-notation. Given a function $g(n)$, $\Theta(g(n))$ is defined as $\Theta(g(n)) = \{f(n)|$ there exist positive constants c_1, c_2, n_0 such that $0 \leq c_1g(n) \leq f(n) \leq c_2g(n)$ for all $n \geq n_0\}$. Intuitively, $f(n)$ is in $\Theta(g(n))$ if the graph of $f(n)$ always lies between the graphs of $c_1g(n)$ and $c_2g(n)$ for all values of n greater than n_0.

In performing a hand computation, the size of the problem is usually small, and consequently the asymptotic growth rate is unimportant. On such small problems, most algorithms perform reasonably well. However, on a high-speed computer, the problem size normally encountered is large and the asymptotic growth rate becomes important. Given two algorithms with growth rates $O(n^2)$ and $O(2^n)$ and similar values of c, for problems up to size 6, the difference in execution times is never more than a factor of 2. However, with a computer, a problem of size 100 might be encountered. In this case, the $O(n^2)$ algorithm is easily executed, whereas the $O(2^n)$ algorithm would require centuries to compute. This example illustrates why so much effort is devoted to the analysis of algorithms.

Algorithm Complexity

SPACE AND TIME

Economy of space and time are the most important aspects of algorithm complexity. Since both are limited, it is advisable to determine how much space and time an algorithm requires. An algorithm that requires relatively little memory space for execution may have a greater running time than another algorithm that requires more space, while both algorithms may provide a solution to the same problem. Thus, there is frequently a trade-off between space and time.

As an example of a space–time trade-off, consider an algorithm that requires the storage of an undirected graph. (An undirected graph is a set V of n vertices, $V = (v_1, v_2, \ldots, v_n)$, and a set E of edges, where an edge is an unordered pair of vertices.) The algorithm stores the graph as an $n \times n$ *adjacency matrix* A, where

$$a_{ij} = \begin{cases} 1 & \text{if } (v_i, v_j) \text{ is an edge in } E, \\ 0 & \text{otherwise.} \end{cases}$$

This requires n^2 bits of memory, regardless of the number of edges.

Assume that the algorithm is used only for planar graphs. (A planar graph is an undirected graph that can be drawn on a plane surface so that no edges intersect.) Let G be a planar graph with n vertices. Then G can be represented in the computer by an array of n linked lists (*see* LIST PROCESSING), one for each vertex. The data structure associated with each vertex v_i is a linked list of all vertices adjacent to v_i. Such a graph representation is referred to as an *adjacency list*. Since each edge (v_i, v_j) of G is stored twice (v_j is on the list of vertices adjacent to v_i, and v_i is on the list of vertices adjacent to v_j), the memory required to store the adjacency list representation of G is proportional to the number of edges. For planar graphs it can be shown that the number of edges is bounded by $3n - 6$, where n is the number of vertices. Thus, the memory required is bounded by $C \times n$, where C is a constant, rather than the n^2 that was required for the adjacency matrix representation. If the algorithm is required to determine whether vertex v_i is connected to vertex v_j, then a trade-off between space and time occurs, since only one operation is needed with the connection matrix representation, whereas the list representation requires searching the entire list of vertices adjacent to v_i to see whether v_j is on the list.

FREQUENCY ANALYSIS

A *frequency analysis* of an algorithm reveals the number of times certain parts of the algorithm are executed. Such an analysis indicates which parts of the algorithm consume large quantities of time and hence where efforts should be directed toward improving the algorithm. For example, the following Pascal-like function calculates

$$\sum_{i=0}^{N} a_i x^i$$

```
(1)  function sum (a:array [0..N] of real;
                                x:real): real;
(2)  var
(3)      i,j: integer;
(4)      power_of_x: real;
(5)      term: array [1..N] of real;
(6)    begin
(7)    for i:= 1 to N do begin
(8)        power_of_x := 1.0;              N
(9)        for j := 1 to i do
(10)         power_of_x:=
                  power_of_x*x        N(N+1)/2
(11)         term[i] := a[i]*power_of_x;   N
(12)     end;
(13)     sum:= a[0];                        1
(14)     for i := 1 to N do
(15)         sum := sum+term[i];            N
(16)  end
```

The function is poorly written and just about every statement can be changed to decrease the amount of time required. To the right of each assignment statement is the number of times it is executed. As N increases, the function spends proportionately more and more time executing the statement inside the loop on j than it does for the statements on lines 8, 11, 13, and 15. The asymptotic running time of this function is $O(N^2)$. It is futile to try to improve the function by decreasing the time spent executing the latter statements without first decreasing the time spent executing the innermost statement on line 10. The function can be improved by using Horner's rule for polynomial evaluation. Again, the number of times each assignment statement is executed is given at its right.

```
(1)  function sum (a:array [0..N] of real;
                                x:real): real;
(2)  begin
(3)      sum:= a[N];                        1
(4)      for i:=N-1 downto 0 do
(5)          sum:= sum*x + a[i];            N
(6)  end;
```

Execution Time

To determine the actual execution time of an algorithm in seconds requires a knowledge of the operation times for each instruction of the computer on which the algorithm is to be executed and how the compiler generates code. In order to avoid becoming involved in the specific details of operation of a particular computer, it is customary to find upper and lower bounds c_1 and c_2, such that the execution time of every instruction is between c_1 and c_2. Then the execution time of an algorithm can be estimated from a count of the number of operations that are executed. This frees the analysis of the algorithm from peculiarities of individual computers.

Frequently, the time required by an algorithm is data dependent. In this case, one of two types of analysis is possible. The first is called the *worst case analysis*, in which that set of data of given size requiring the most work is determined and the behavior of the algorithm is analyzed for that specific set of data. The other alternative is to assume a probability distribution for the possible input data and compute the distribution of the execution time as a function of the input distribution. Usually, this computation is so difficult that only the expected or average execution time as a function of size is computed. This is called the *average case analysis*.

Problem Complexity

In problem complexity we are concerned with analyzing a problem rather than an algorithm. The analysis provides us with lower bounds on the amount of time and space required for a solution to the problem, independent of the algorithm used. The lower bounds may be either "worst case" or "average case" bounds. These lower bounds can serve as an indication of how well an algorithm fits the problem and whether it can be improved. For example, such an analysis shows that any algorithm that evaluates an arbitrary n-degree polynomial represented by its coefficients requires at least n multiplications and n additions. Thus, Horner's rule cannot be improved upon.

On the other hand, an analysis of matrix multiplication gives a lower bound of order $\Omega(n^2)$ operations for multiplying two matrices of dimension n. The usual matrix multiplication algorithm has an asymptotic growth rate of $O(n^3)$. Thus there is substantial interest in trying either to find a better lower bound or to improve on the current matrix multiplication algorithms. At the current state of knowledge, the fastest algorithm has an asymptotic growth rate of $O(n^{2.376})$, and thus there is a large gap between the best known lower bound and the performance of the best known algorithm.

In problem analysis, it is often important to consider the frequency of occurrence of a specific operation. The reason is that reducing the number of occurrences of a specific operation can lead to a recursive algorithm with a lower asymptotic growth rate. Consider multiplying two n-digit numbers, where n is a power of 2. The usual algorithm learned in elementary school requires of the order of $O(n^2)$ operations. A recursive method of multiplying two n-digit numbers x and y is to write $x = a10^{n/2} + c$ and $y = b10^{n/2} + d$, where a, b, c, and d are $n/2$-digit numbers. Compute ab, cd, and $ad + bc$. Then

$$xy = ab10^n + (ad + bc)10^{n/2} + cd$$

The problem of computing xy is reduced to the problem of computing ab, cd, and $ad + bc$, which are computed by the three multiplications ab, cd, and

$(a + c)(b + d)$. The formula $ad + bc$ is obtained by $(a + c)(b + d) - ab - cd$. Let $T(n)$ be the time to compute the product of two n-digit numbers. Then $T(n) = 3T(n/2) + kn$, where $3T(n/2)$ is the time to compute the three multiplications, k is a nonnegative constant, and kn is the time to compute the necessary sums. Successively applying the formula above to each product, we obtain

$$T(n) = kn(1 + (3/2) + (3/2)^2 + \cdots + (3/2)^{\log_2 n})$$
$$\simeq 3kn^{\log_2 3} \simeq 3kn^{1.58}$$

The asymptotic growth rate of $O(n^{1.58})$ is better than the $O(n^2)$ of the more elementary method. The important observation is that, in computing ab, cd, and $ad + bc$, the number of multiplications was reduced from four to three at the expense of increasing the number of additions from one to four. The reason for doing this is that the exponent in the asymptotic growth rate is affected by the number of multiplications, whereas the number of additions affects only the constant.

A major difficulty with problem analysis is that it is concerned with the class of all algorithms for a given problem. One can no longer postulate a computer with a given structure and instruction set. Instead, one must envision an abstract computer that is sufficiently general to encompass any physically implementable algorithm. The difficulties involved are of such magnitude that one is forced to obtain bounds for certain limited classes of programs. For example, sorting n integers can be shown to require $n \log n$ operations if restricted to the class of algorithms that sort by binary (two at a time) comparisons. This follows from the simple information-theoretic argument that there are $n!$ possible permutations of n items, and each comparison can at best divide the set of possible permutations by a factor of 2. Since the asymptotic growth rate of $\log(n!)$ is $O(n \log n)$, it takes at least $\Omega(n \log n)$ comparisons to determine the actual permutation uniquely. Of course, if one sorts by some method other than by comparisons (radix sort, for example—*see* SORTING), then the bound is no longer valid.

A typical assumption for a class of programs might be that the computation uses only the arithmetic operations of addition, subtraction, multiplication, and division. Then it is necessary to specify the underlying algebraic structure. For example, the complexity of computing an algebraic expression may depend on whether the underlying structure is the rational, real, or complex number system.

One of the most powerful techniques for establishing results of this nature is due to Winograd, who showed that any algorithm for computing the product of a matrix M and an arbitrary vector $\mathbf{V}$ requires a number of multiplications at least as great as the number of independent columns of M. It immediately follows from this result that Horner's rule evaluates arbitrary n-degree polynomials with the minimum number of multiplications. Let $\mathbf{X} = (x, \ldots, x^{N-1}, x^N)$ and let $\mathbf{A} = (a_1, \ldots, a_{N-1}, a_N)^T$. Then

$$\sum_{i=0}^{N} a_i x^i = a_0 + \sum_{i=1}^{N} a_i x^i = a_0 + \mathbf{XA}$$

$\mathbf{X}$ has N independent columns, which implies that N multiplications are required. The result applies to algorithms that can evaluate any polynomial, given its coefficients. Specific polynomials can often be evaluated with fewer multiplications. Similarly, if the polynomial is specified by parameters other than its coefficients, a saving in the number of multiplications is possible.

The one facet of problem complexity that is most intriguing is the lack of nontrivial lower bounds for various problems. Almost all known lower bounds are either linear in the size of the problem or have been obtained by restricting the classes of algorithms. The notable exceptions are lower bounds obtained by the diagonalization techniques of recursive function theory. One of the major goals of computer scientists working in the analysis of algorithms is to close the gaps in our knowledge of problem complexity.

Bibliography

1974. Aho, A. V., Hopcroft, J. E., and Ullman, J. D. *The Design and Analysis of Computer Algorithms.* Reading, MA: Addison-Wesley.
1976. Wirth, N. *Algorithms + Data Structures = Programs.* Upper Saddle River, NJ: Prentice Hall.
1990. Cormen, T. H., Leiserson, C. E., and Rivest, R. L. *Introduction to Algorithms.* Cambridge, MA: MIT Press.
1997, 1997, 1998. Knuth, D. E. *The Art of Computer Programming,* Vols. 1 (3rd Ed.), 2 (3rd Ed.), 3 (2nd Ed.). Reading, MA: Addison-Wesley.

John E. Hopcroft and Daniela Rus

ALGORITHMS, DESIGN AND CLASSIFICATION OF

For articles on related subjects *see* ALGORITHM; ALGORITHMIC PROBLEM SOLVING; ALGORITHMICS; ALGORITHMS, ANALYSIS OF; ALGORITHMS, THEORY OF; COMBINATORICS; COMPUTATIONAL COMPLEXITY; GRAPH THEORY; SEARCHING; and SORTING.

Introduction

Algorithms are a central field of computer science. A great deal of emphasis has been placed on the analysis of algorithms, determining the time and space required for an algorithm during execution. An equally important topic is the *design and classification of algorithms.*

The design of algorithms attempts to answer the question: "How does one devise an algorithm in the first place?" When faced with a problem for which an algorithm is needed, one might first ask if an algorithm for this problem even exists (*see* ALGORITHMS, THEORY OF and UNDECIDABLE PROBLEMS). Although it is very difficult to determine that *no* algorithm exists for a particular problem, since it is usually the case that at least one does, the challenge is to find it. Once an algorithm is found, one can then analyze its time and space efficiency. But that leads to the question of whether another faster algorithm for this problem exists. So, algorithm design is a subject as important as algorithm analysis.

The study of algorithm design techniques has two important payoffs. First, it leads to an organized way to devise new algorithms. Algorithm design techniques give guidance and direction on how to create a new algorithm. Though there are literally thousands of algorithms, there are very few design techniques. Second, the study of these techniques helps us to categorize or organize the algorithms we know and in that way to understand them better.

The remainder of this article discusses a basic set of design strategies. Each section describes the strategy in general terms and gives one concrete example. It concludes with some well-known algorithms that are specific cases of the design technique.

Divide-and-Conquer

The divide-and-conquer strategy suggests that a problem should be split into subproblems, which are somehow solved, and then the solutions are combined into a solution for the original problem. Usually, the subproblems are solved in the same way—by splitting, solving, and combining—and this can often be done recursively (*see* RECURSION). It is generally advisable to split the problems into roughly equal size subproblems.

An ideal example of divide-and-conquer is *mergesort*, a method for sorting a set. The method proceeds as follows: divide the set into two approximately equal size sets. Then sort each set individually. Next, take the resulting sorted subsets and merge them to produce a single sorted set for the entire data. The algorithm is recursive so that, to sort one-half of the data, that data is again divided into two roughly equal parts, sorted in the same manner, and then merged. A recursive version of this algorithm written in Pascal is shown in Fig. 1.

Procedure `mergesort` is written to sort the consecutive elements in the array x from index `low` to `high`. The procedure is started with `low=1` and `high=n`. If, for some invocation of `mergesort`, `low ≥ high`, the

```
procedure mergesort (var x: afile; low, high:
                              integer)
{the consecutive elements (x[low],..., x[high])
                                    are sorted.}
var mid: integer;
begin
  if low < high then
    begin
      mid := (low + high) div 2;
      mergesort (x,low,mid); {apply algorithm
                                    recursively}
      mergesort (x,mid+1,high); {apply algorithm
                                    recursively}
      merge (x,low,high); {merge the two results}
    end
end; {mergesort}
```

Figure 1. A Pascal version of mergesort.

procedure ends without doing anything. Otherwise, the index of a middle element is computed and assigned to *mid*. This determines two subsets, which are sorted using recursive calls to `mergesort`. We assume that the `merge` procedure is smart enough to merge the two ordered sequences *x[low],...,* *x[mid]* and *x[mid + 1],...,x[high]* into a single ordered sequence stored in *x[low],...,x[high]*.

Additional examples of divide-and-conquer algorithms are quicksort and Strassen's matrix multiplication algorithm (*see* STRUCTURED PROGRAMMING for an implementation of quicksort).

Greedy Method

The greedy method is possibly the simplest of the design techniques. In its most general form, it is applied to an optimization problem. An *optimization problem* has *n* inputs and requires an algorithm that finds a subset of the inputs that satisfy a certain constraint. Any subset that satisfies these constraints is called a *feasible* solution. But in an optimization problem, we need to find not only a feasible solution, but one that either maximizes or minimizes a given objective function. A feasible solution that does this is called an *optimal* solution. Often it is easy to determine feasible solutions, but much harder to determine optimal solutions.

Given a set of *n* inputs and some criteria for determining when a solution is both feasible and optimal, the greedy method suggests an algorithm that works in stages. At each stage, a decision is made regarding whether an input combination is feasible and better or worse than the previous solution. At the end of the final stage, the best solution is obtained. In some cases greedy algorithms will produce the optimal result. In other cases they can be used to derive approximate solutions when the optimal algorithm takes intolerably long.

OPTIMAL GREEDY SOLUTIONS

The greedy strategy leads to a simple sorting algorithm that works this way: look at the remaining elements to be sorted, select the smallest, and place it at the end of the list of already sorted elements. This is called selection sort, and its computing time on *n* elements is $O(n^2)$. Though it is simple to conceive and simple to write, it does not produce a very efficient algorithm (*see* SORTING for a Pascal implementation).

Another problem for which the greedy method produces an optimal solution is the so-called "change-making problem" (for US coins, though not for all possible coin values). This is the problem of making change using the fewest number of coins. For example if the cost of an item is 37 cents, and the customer hands the clerk a one dollar bill, then the clerk might return a 50 cent coin, a 10 cent coin and 3 pennies. These 5 coins are the *minimum* number of coins that could be used to make up the difference between one dollar and 37 cents. The greedy strategy leads us to postulate an algorithm that at each stage returns the largest coin possible without going over the one-dollar limit. A proof that this strategy yields the minimum number of coins is not hard. The computing time of the algorithm is minimal, as each step requires only a few comparisons, and the number of steps is the smallest possible for any equivalent algorithm.

APPROXIMATE GREEDY SOLUTIONS

As an example of how the greedy method can be used to create an approximation algorithm, suppose you have *m* machines, all identical, and you have a set of *n* jobs that need to be carried out on the machines, *n > m*. The times for the *n* jobs vary. You want to schedule the jobs on the machines so as to complete all the jobs in the shortest time possible. For example, suppose you have three machines and seven jobs with times 13, 13, 13, 14, 14, 15, and 15 hours. One sample schedule would be to place job 1 on machine 1, job 2 on machine 2, and job 3 on machine 3. All three machines will be available after 13 hours, so then we can assign job 4 to machine 1, job 5 to machine 2, and job 6 to machine 3. Finally, job 7 is placed on machine 1. The finish time for this schedule, the time the last job finishes, is 42 hours.

A superior assignment is to place jobs 7 and 5 on machine 1, jobs 6 and 4 on machine 2, and jobs 1, 2, and 3 on machine 3. For this assignment of jobs to machines, the finish time is 39 hours.

The best known algorithm that always finds the optimal (shortest time) assignment of jobs to processors for arbitrary *m*, *n*, and job times takes exponential time. For most reasonable size problems, that makes the exact solution infeasible. Therefore, an algorithm that produces a reasonably good approximation quickly is desirable. The greedy method provides such a strategy. It suggests that we consider only one job at a time, assigning it to the next processor that becomes free. We add something a little extra, namely that the jobs should first be placed in decreasing (or non-increasing) order. For our example above, that places job 7 on machine 1, job 6 on machine 2, and job 5 on machine 3 at time zero. In 14 hours we can place job 4 on machine 3, and then job 3 on machine 1 and job 2 on machine 2. Finally, job 1 is placed on machine 1. The total time to process all jobs is 41 hours. Ron Graham has shown that this approximation algorithm, using the greedy heuristic (*q.v.*), will always produce an answer that is within four-thirds of the optimal result. Thus, the greedy method gives an algorithm whose time is the time required to sort n elements and whose answer is thus guaranteed never to get too bad.

Further examples of successful greedy algorithms are optimal storage on tapes, Huffman codes (*see* DATA COMPRESSION), and finding minimal spanning trees or a shortest path on a graph (*see* GRAPH THEORY).

Dynamic Programming

Dynamic programming arises when the only algorithm we can think of is enumerating all possible configurations of the given data and testing each one to see if it is a solution. An essential idea is to keep a table that contains all previously computed configurations and their results. If the total number of configurations is large, the dynamic programming algorithm will require substantial time and space. However, if there are only a small number of distinct configurations, dynamic programming avoids recomputing the solution to these problems over and over.

To determine that there are only a small number of distinct configurations, one needs to detect when the so-called *principle of optimality* holds. This principle asserts that every decision that contributes to the final solution must be optimal with respect to the initial state. When this principle holds, dynamic programming drastically reduces the amount of computation by avoiding the enumeration of some decision sequences that cannot possibly be optimal.

As a simple example, consider computing the nth Fibonacci number, F_n, where $F_n = F_{n-1} + F_{n-2}$, and $F_0 = F_1 = 1$. The first few elements of this famous sequence are 1, 1, 2, 3, 5, 8, 13, 21, 34, ... The obvious recursive algorithm for computing F_n suffers from the fact that many values of F_i are computed over and over again. The total time for this recursive version is exponential. However, if we follow the dynamic programming strategy and create a table that contains all

values of F_i as they are computed, a linear time algorithm results.

Some examples of dynamic programming algorithms are optimal binary search trees, optimal matrix arrangements, and the shortest path problem for all pairs of vertices in a graph.

Basic Traversal and Search

Often, complex objects are stored in a computer using a specific data structure (*q.v.*). The data structure consists of nodes that contain fields. These fields may contain either data or pointers to some other nodes. Thus, a particular instance of some object may include many nodes, all connected in an intricate pattern. Some typical examples of objects would be lists, trees (*q.v.*), binary trees, and graphs.

Often, one wants to devise an algorithm that computes a function of the data object. The traversal-and-search strategy for developing such an algorithm is to move along the data structure from node to node and collect information. After all nodes have been reached, the final answer should be known.

One simple example is the evaluation of an expression (*q.v.*) stored in a tree. For simplicity, we shall consider a binary tree. Fig. 2 shows such a tree, with its contents being the expression shown at the bottom of the figure. Fig. 3 has the definition of a binary tree type and the pseudocode for an algorithm that traverses a binary tree in such a way that all children of a node are examined before the node itself. When `postorder` (*see* TREE) has processed a node's children, it uses the `evalop` procedure to evaluate the operator on its arguments. When a tree leaf contains a variable such as `x`, `postorder` simply stores its value in the leaf with `lookup`.

Some well-known examples of traversal-and-search algorithms are preorder, postorder, and inorder trav-

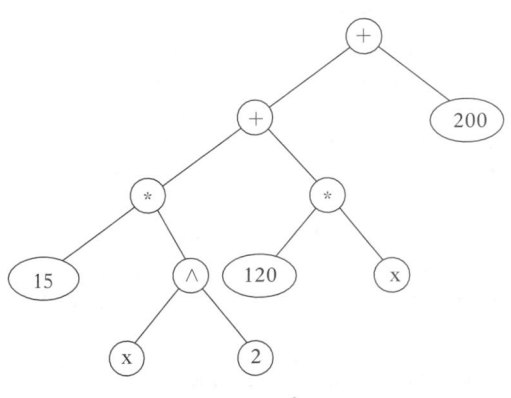

$$15x^2 + 120x + 200$$

Figure 2. A binary tree containing an arithmetic expression.

```
type expressiontree =          [An expression tree is a leaf which
  leaf(integer) or                      holds an integer or
  leaf(variable) or                        a variable or a
  node(expressiontree, operator,    node with an operator and two
    expressiontree)                 expression trees as subtrees]

procedure postorder(expr: expressiontree)   [visit the expression in postorder]
  if leaf(expr) then
    if variable(expr) then           [replace the variable in a
      lookup(expr)                      variable leaf by its value;
    endif                          do nothing for an integer leaf]
  else
    postorder(leftchild(expr))       [evaluate the left argument,
    postorder(rightchild(expr))      evaluate the right argument,
    evalop(expr)                       apply the operator to its
  endif                               evaluated arguments]
endproc
```

Figure 3. An algorithm for postorder traversal of a binary tree.

ersal of binary trees, evaluation of postfix expressions, breadth-first and depth-first traversal of graphs, code optimization, "and/or" graphs of artificial intelligence (*q.v.*), and finding connected and biconnected components of a graph.

Backtracking

Backtracking is an appropriate algorithm design strategy when the desired solution is expressible in the form $(x_1, \ldots, x_n)$, where each of the x_i is chosen from a finite set S_i. Often, the problem calls for finding one vector that maximizes, minimizes or satisfies some criterion function. Sometimes it seeks all such vectors. If the size of S_i is m_i, there are $m = m_1 \times \cdots \times m_n$ n-tuples that are possible candidates. The brute force approach would generate all of these n-tuples and evaluate each one. The idea of backtracking is to build up the vector one component at a time, using modified functions to test whether the vector being formed has any chance of success. Backtracking becomes most efficient when the modified functions are able to eliminate large sets of possible vectors.

A classic combinatorial problem is to place eight queens on an 8×8 chessboard so that no two "attack" that is, so that no two of them are in the same row, column, or diagonal. Assume that the rows and columns of the chessboard, as well as the eight queens, are numbered 1 to 8. We see that each queen will be on a separate row, so we can represent a solution to this problem by a vector, $(x_1, \ldots, x_8)$, where x_i is the column on which queen i is placed. There are $8^8 = 16,777,218$ tuples, so if an algorithm attempts to enumerate all of these and requires 1/10 of a second to generate each one, the algorithm will require over 19 days to get its answer.

The backtracking solution makes use of two important facts that help to prune the number of vectors it must consider. No two x_is can be the same (all queens in different columns). This reduces the number of tuples to $8! = 40,320$. Also no two x_is can be on the same diagonal. The backtracking algorithm will proceed by generating a tuple so that, if $(x_1, \ldots, x_i)$ has already been picked, x_{i+1} is chosen so that $(x_1, \ldots, x_{i+1})$ represents a chessboard configuration in which no two queens are attacking.

Fig. 4 shows a chessboard on which queens have been placed in columns 1 to 5. But with the configuration shown, no queen can be placed in column 6. So we *backtrack* to column 5 and move the queen down column 5 looking for another "safe" square. However, none exists so we backtrack again to column 4 and move the queen in this column down to row 7, which is also safe. Then we try again to put a queen in column 5, etc. Eventually, we find a solution: (1,1), (5,2), (8,3), (6,4), (3,5), (7,6), (2,7), (4,8). This is one

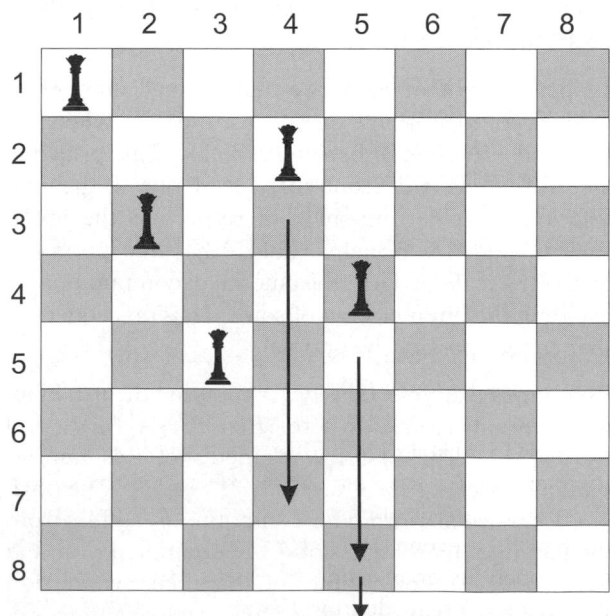

Figure 4. Backtracking in the eight queens problem.

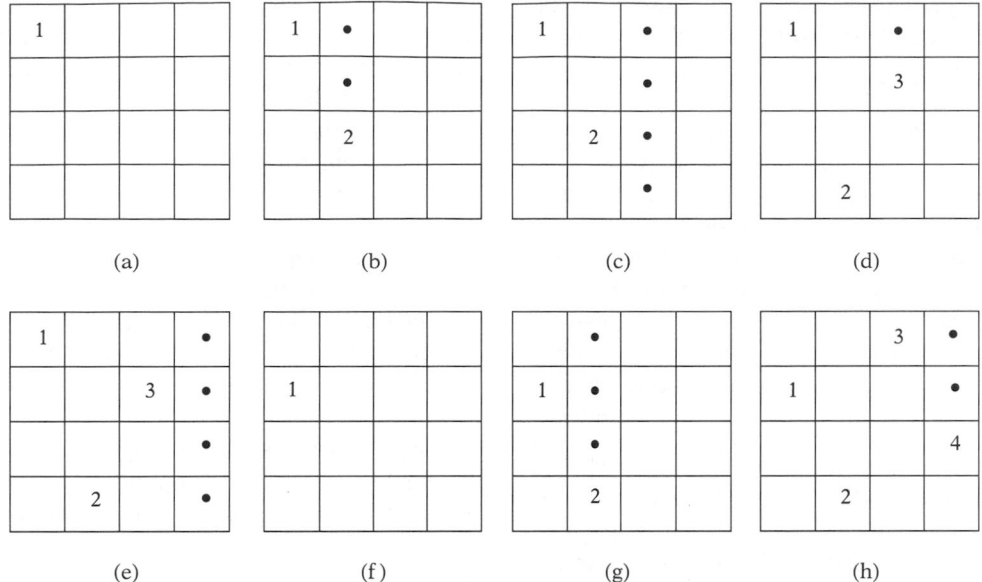

Figure 5. Arriving at one solution for the four queens problem. The dots represent unsuccessful attempts to place a queen. Backtracking occurs after displays (c) and (e).

of 92 solutions, only 12 of which are really distinct (i.e. not related to each other by some type of symmetry). All 92 solutions could be found by continuing as above by backtracking to column 7 after each solution is found. Fig. 5 shows the entire backtracking process when we try to place four queens on a 4×4 board.

Backtracking algorithms have been very successful for games such as checkers and chess. Backtracking is also very valuable for solving various combinatorial optimization problems such as the knapsack and traveling salesman problems (*see* NP-COMPLETE PROBLEMS).

Randomization Algorithms

Another algorithm design strategy is based upon the principles of probability theory. The general idea is to use a random number generator (*q.v.*) (called a *randomizer*) to produce a set of inputs. The inputs are given to an algorithm that tests for the result. Probability theory is used to establish the fact that the algorithm is likely to find the correct result in a short amount of time.

No doubt you have tossed a coin and watched how many times heads or tails appears. For three tosses of a coin there are eight possible outcomes {HHH, HHT, HTH, HTT, THH, THT, TTH, TTT} where H stands for Head and T for Tail. There are 2^8 possible events (i.e. combinations of possible outcomes), e.g. the probability of the event {HHT, HTT, TTT} is $\frac{3}{8}$. In general, the probability of an event is the ratio of the number of possible events divided by the total number of events that could occur, termed the *state space*. If one flips a coin 100 times, then the probability that the first outcome is T is $\frac{1}{2}$. The probability that the second outcome is also T is $\frac{1}{4}$, and the probability of obtaining 100 Ts in a row is $(\frac{1}{2})^{100}$.

Some of the decisions taken within a randomization algorithm are based upon the random values. Since the output of the randomizer will vary from execution to execution, so too can the results of the algorithm. There are two categories of randomized algorithms. *Las Vegas algorithms* always produce the same (correct) output for the same input. The execution time of a Las Vegas algorithm depends upon the output of the randomizer. *Monte Carlo algorithms* are characterized by outputs that might differ from execution to execution despite the same input. For a Monte Carlo algorithm, we require that the probability of an incorrect answer be low. Monte Carlo algorithms generally take the same amount of time to execute, whereas the time for the Las Vegas algorithms can vary widely (*see* MONTE CARLO METHOD).

A SIMPLE EXAMPLE
Consider an array a of n numbers that has $n/2$ distinct elements and $n/2$ copies of another element. Any deterministic algorithm to discover the repeated element will require $(n/2) + 2$ comparisons in the worst case. A Las Vegas algorithm works as follows: two random elements are chosen and compared for equality. One must check that the random array indices are distinct before checking that the array elements are distinct. It is easy to show that the probability that the algorithm terminates in 10 iterations or less is greater than 0.94. The probability that

the algorithm does not terminate in 100 iterations for $n > 20$ is about $(3/4)^{100}$ or approximately 3×10^{-13}, a very small number.

A FAMOUS EXAMPLE

Given an integer n, the problem of deciding whether n is a prime is known as *primality testing* (*see* NUMBER THEORETIC CALCULATIONS). One method is to test all numbers up to the square root of n to see if any one is a factor. This is an exponential time algorithm in the size of the input (which is $\log n$ bits long). It is possible to create a Monte Carlo algorithm for primality testing which is polynomial in running time (proportional to $(\log n)^2$) and has a high probability of being correct.

Randomly choose an $a < n$ and check whether a^{n-1} *is congruent to* 1 (mod n). This is called Fermat's equation. If Fermat's equation is not satisfied, n is composite. If Fermat's equation is satisfied, we try more random as. For each a that Fermat's equation is satisfied, we output "n is prime." How well does this algorithm perform? Sadly, there is a set of numbers, called Carmichael numbers, for which every a that is less than and relatively prime to n will satisfy Fermat's equation. But Miller and Rabin have observed that by confining our attention to nontrivial square roots of n we avoid the problem of Carmichael numbers. Their algorithm will never give an incorrect answer if the input is prime, since Fermat's equation will always be satisfied and no nontrivial square root of 1 modulo n can be found. If n is composite, the algorithm will detect the compositeness of n if either the randomly chosen a leads to the discovery of a nontrivial square root of 1 or it violates Fermat's equation.

In conclusion, randomized algorithms are generally simple and more efficient than the deterministic version. In many cases the probability of producing an incorrect answer is smaller than the probability of the computer's hardware failing. For problems such as primality testing they are ideal.

Other Algorithm Design Techniques

Some other design techniques which we describe only briefly are:

- *Branch-and-bound*: this design strategy is similar to backtracking in that it attempts to find one or more vectors that satisfy some criteria. It differs in the way that elements of a possible solution are generated and explored. Instead of generating a solution vector element by element, all possible candidates for the next entry are produced and stored in a set. Elements in this set are said to be "alive." One is chosen for expansion, and functions are used to prune the set of candidate elements.

To see more concretely the difference between backtracking and branch-and-bound, consider again the four queens problem. The backtracking algorithm assumed that the first queen is placed on location [1,1] of the chessboard. It then computes a single placement for the second queen. In branch-and-bound, all possible queens in column 1, namely those occupying rows 1, 2, 3, and 4, are produced. These are kept in a list and one is removed (say the queen at position [1,1]). Now all possibilities for the second queen are generated, namely the queens in column 2, rows 1, 2, 3, and 4. The queen in column 2, row 1 is considered and rejected according to the "non-attacking" criterion. In branch-and-bound parlance, this is termed the bounding function. Eventually, all solutions will be produced. With effective bounding functions, branch-and-bound can be quite efficient.

- *Transformation of domain*: sometimes it is easier to transform the data for a problem into another domain, solve the problem in the new domain, and then transform the solution back into the original domain.

One example is the way a digital computer does arithmetic. Though it accepts and displays numbers using decimal notation, it translates all numbers into binary notation before doing arithmetic on them. It is easier for a computer to work with binary numbers than with decimal numbers.

Other examples of domain transformation include the Fast Fourier Transform (*q.v.*), the Schwartz–Christoffel transformation of complex variable theory, and algebraic operations such as polynomial arithmetic, greatest common divisor calculations, and factorization.

- *Preconditioning*: if we have an algorithm that we know will be executed many times, sometimes we can improve its speed by precomputing a set of values. As these values are available during execution, the algorithm can work faster.

Suppose we have a binary tree and we are given a pair of nodes, i and j. We want to answer the question: is i an ancestor of j? We could use the algorithm given earlier to traverse the tree and, if j is in a subtree whose root is i, then i must be an ancestor of j. However, the time for this algorithm is linear in the number of nodes in the tree. Though preconditioning gives us the idea that precomputing some values will give us a faster algorithm, the challenge is to determine what precomputed values would be useful. The idea is to first traverse the tree in preorder and then in postorder, assigning consecutive integers to the nodes as one goes. (In preorder, an integer is assigned the first time a node is reached.) Then i is an ancestor of j if and only if the $preorder(i) \leq preorder(j)$ and $postorder(i) \geq postorder(j)$. Therefore, if we are given any i, j pair of nodes, only two comparisons are needed to answer the question of ancestry.

Other examples of successful use of preconditioning are repeated evaluation of a polynomial and searching for a pattern within a string (*see* STRING PROCESSING).

Bibliography

1966. Nemhauser, G. *Introduction to Dynamic Programming.* New York: John Wiley.

1976. Lawler, E. L. *Combinatorial Optimization: Networks and Matroids.* New York: Holt, Reinhart, and Winston.

1978. Sahni, S., and Horowitz, E. "Combinatorial Problems: Reducibility and Approximation," *Operations Research*, **26**, *4*, 718–759.

1984. Bentley, J. "Programming Pearls: Algorithm Design Techniques," *Comm. of the ACM*, **27**, *9*, 865–871.

1988. Brassard, G., and Bratley, P. *Algorithmics: Theory and Practice.* Upper Saddle River, NJ: Prentice Hall.

1989. Manber, U. *Introduction to Algorithms: A Creative Approach.* Reading, MA: Addison-Wesley.

1997. Horowitz, E., Sahni, S., and Rajasekaran, S. *Computer Algorithms/C++.* New York: Computer Science Press, imprint of W. H. Freeman and Co.

Ellis Horowitz

ALGORITHMS, THEORY OF

For articles on related subjects *see* ALGORITHM; ALGORITHMICS; ALGORITHMS, ANALYSIS OF; COMPUTATIONAL COMPLEXITY; FORMAL LANGUAGES; NP-COMPLETE PROBLEMS; TURING MACHINE; and UNDECIDABLE PROBLEMS.

The meaning of the word *algorithm* is somewhat vague. In order to have a *theory of algorithms*, we need a mathematically precise definition of algorithm. Many authors have tried to capture the essence of the intuitive notion of an algorithm. We give four examples.

Hermes (1965). "An algorithm is a general procedure such that for any appropriate question the answer can be obtained by the use of a simple computation according to a specified method ... [A] general procedure [is] a process the execution of which is clearly specified to the smallest details."

Minsky (1967). "... an effective procedure is a set of rules which tells us, from moment to moment, precisely how to behave."

Rogers (1967). "... an algorithm is a clerical (i.e. deterministic, bookkeeping) procedure which can be applied to any of a certain class of symbolic inputs and which will eventually yield, for each such output, a corresponding symbolic *output*."

Hopcroft and Ullman (1979). "A *procedure* is a finite sequence of instructions that can be mechanically carried out, such as a computer program.... A procedure which always terminates is called an *algorithm*."

Note that what Hermes calls a "general procedure" is what Minsky calls an "effective procedure" and what Hopcroft and Ullman call a "procedure." Other terms are also used in the literature, and some authors use the word "algorithm" to denote any procedure whatsoever. In the remainder of this article, the Hopcroft and Ullman terminology will be used.

The notion of a procedure cannot be divorced from the environment in which it operates. What may be a procedure in certain situations may not be considered a procedure in other situations. For example, the instructions of a computer program are not usually understood by most people. Alternatively, the description of a chess game that appears in a newspaper is a perfectly clear algorithm for a chess player who wants to reproduce the game, but it is quite meaningless to people who do not play chess. Thus, when we talk about a procedure as a finite sequence of instructions, we assume that whoever is supposed to carry out those instructions, be it human or machine, understands them in the same way as whoever gave those instructions.

Another sense in which the environment influences the notions of procedure and algorithm is indicated by the following examples. If the instruction requires us to take the integral part of the square root of a number, such an instruction can be carried out if we are dealing with positive integers only, but it cannot always be carried out if we are dealing with both positive and negative integers. Thus the same set of instructions may or may not be a procedure, depending on the subset of integers for which it is intended. Alternatively, we can easily give a procedure that, given an integer x, keeps subtracting 1 until 0 is reached and then stops. Such a procedure will be an algorithm if we intend to use it for positive integers only, but it will not be an algorithm if we also intend to apply it to negative integers.

The recognition of whether or not a sequence of instructions is a procedure or an algorithm is a subjective affair. No precise theory can be built on the vague definitions given above. In trying to build a precise theory, one must examine the situations in which the notion of algorithm is used. In the theory of computation, one is mainly concerned with algorithms that are used either for computing functions or for deciding predicates.

A *function* f with domain D and range R is a definite correspondence by which there is associated with each element x of the domain D (referred to as the "argument") a single element $f(x)$ of the range R (called the "value"). The function f is said to be *computable* (in the intuitive sense) if there exists an algorithm that, for any given x in D, provides us with the value $f(x)$. An example of a computable function is one that associates, with any pair of positive integers, their greatest common divisor. It is computable by the well-known Euclidean algorithm (Knuth, 1997).

A *predicate* P with domain D is a property of the elements of D that each particular element of D either has or does not have. If x in D has the property P, we say that $P(x)$ is true; otherwise, we say that $P(x)$ is false. The predicate P is said to be *decidable* (in the intuitive sense) if there exists an algorithm that, for any given x in D, provides us with a definite answer to the question of whether or not $P(x)$ is true. An example of a decidable predicate over the set of integers greater than 1 is the predicate that determines whether a number is or is not *prime*. An algorithm for implementing this predicate is described by Hopcroft and Ullman (1979).

The computability of functions and the decidability of predicates are very closely related notions because we can associate with each predicate P a function f with range $\{0, 1\}$ such that, for all x in the common domain D of P and f, $f(x) = 0$ if $P(x)$ is true and $f(x) = 1$ if $P(x)$ is false. Clearly, P is decidable if and only if f is computable. For this reason we will hereafter restrict our attention to the computability of functions.

A further restriction customary in the theory of algorithms is to consider only functions whose domains and range are both the set of nonnegative integers. This is reasonable, since, in those situations where the notion of a procedure makes any sense at all, it is usually possible to *represent* elements of the domain and the range by nonnegative integers. For example, if the domain comprises pairs of nonnegative integers, as in the case with an arithmetic function of two arguments, we can represent the pair (a,b) by the number $2^a 3^b$ in an effective one-to-one fashion. If the domain comprises strings of symbols over an alphabet of 15 letters, we can consider the letters to be non-zero hexadecimal digits, and assign that nonnegative integer to a string that is denoted by the string in the hexadecimal notation. The device of representing elements of a set D by nonnegative integers is referred to as *arithmetization* or *Gödel numbering*, after the logician Kurt Gödel, who used it to prove the undecidability of certain predicates about formal logic. From now on we will be exclusively concerned with functions whose domain and range are subsets of the set of nonnegative integers.

In order to show that a certain function is computable, it is sufficient to give an algorithm that computes it. But, without a precise definition of an algorithm, all such demonstrations are open to question. The situation is even more uncertain if we want to show that a given function is uncomputable, i.e. that no algorithm whatsoever computes it. In order to avoid such uncertainty, we need a mathematically precise definition of a computable function. One possible way of making the concept precise is to define an appropriate type of machine, and then define a function to be computable if and only if it can be computed by such a machine. This has indeed been done. The machine usually used for this purpose is the *Turing machine* (*q.v.*). This simple device has a tape and a read–write head, together with a control that may be in one of finitely many states. The tape is used to represent numbers. A function f is called computable if there exists a Turing machine that, given a tape representing an argument x, eventually halts with the tape representing the value $f(x)$. Since a precise definition of a Turing machine can be given, the notion of a computable function has become a precise mathematical notion.

The question arises whether or not it is indeed the case that a function is computable in the intuitive sense if and only if it is computable by a Turing machine. The claim that this is true is usually referred to as *Church's thesis* (sometimes as *Turing's thesis*). Such a claim can never be "proved," since one of the two notions whose equivalence is claimed is mathematically imprecise. However, there are many convincing arguments in support of Church's thesis, and an overwhelming majority of workers in the theory of algorithms accept its validity. One of the strongest arguments in support of Church's thesis is the fact that all of the many diverse attempts at precisely defining the concept of computable function have ended up with defining exactly the same set of functions as can be computed by a Turing machine.

Given a precise definition of a computable function, it is now possible to show for particular functions whether they are or are not computable. We will give two examples (*see also* UNDECIDABLE PROBLEMS).

Example 1

Consider the following problem. Give an algorithm that, for any Turing machine, decides whether or not the machine eventually stops if it is started on an empty tape. This problem is called the "blank-tape halting problem." The required algorithm would be considered a *solution* of the problem. A proof that there is no such algorithm would be said to show the (effective) *unsolvability* of the problem.

The blank-tape halting problem is in fact unsolvable. This is proved by rephrasing it as a problem about the computability of a function, as follows: Turing machines can be Gödel-numbered in an effective manner: i.e. there exists an algorithm that for any Turing machine will give its Gödel number. Furthermore, this can be done in such a way that every nonnegative integer is the Gödel number of some Turing machine. Let f be the function defined as follows.

$$f(n) = \begin{cases} 0 & \text{if } n \text{ is the Gödel number of a Turing} \\ & \text{machine that eventually stops if} \\ & \text{started on the blank tape} \\ 1 & \text{otherwise} \end{cases}$$

It is easy to see that f is computable if and only if the blank-tape halting problem is solvable. The unsolvability of the blank-tape halting problem is proved by showing that the assumption that f is computable leads to a contradiction; for details see Minsky (1967).

Example 2

Our second example indicates that there are unsolvable problems in classical mathematics. The following problem is known as "Hilbert's tenth problem" (after the German mathematician David Hilbert, 1862–1943):

Given a diophantine equation [an equation of the form $E = 0$, where E is a polynomial with integer coefficients; e.g. $xy^2 - 2x^2 + 3 = 0$] with any number of variables, give a procedure with which it is possible to decide after a finite number of operations whether or not the equation has a solution in integers.

This problem was stated by Hilbert in 1900 (long before there was such a thing as a theory of algorithms). In 1970 the Russian mathematician Y. Matiyasevich showed it to be unsolvable.

That there are clearly defined problems, like the two given above, that cannot be solved by any computer-like device is probably the most striking aspect of the theory of algorithms. A whole superstructure has been built on such results, and there are methods to find out not only whether something is uncomputable, but also how badly it is uncomputable (*see* Rogers, 1967).

A typical question that one may ask is the following: Suppose we had a device that, for any given Turing machine, told us whether or not the Turing machine will eventually stop on the blank tape. Can we write an "algorithm" that makes use of this device and solves Hilbert's tenth problem? It has been known for some time that such an "algorithm" exists. In this sense, Hilbert's tenth problem is *reducible* to the blank-tape halting problem. It is the proof that the reverse is also true that gave us the unsolvability of Hilbert's tenth problem. Two problems that are both reducible to the other are said to be *equivalent*. Most of the theory of algorithms has, until recently, concerned itself with questions of the reducibility and equivalence of various unsolvable problems.

In recent years, much of the activity in the theory of algorithms has been concerned with computable functions, decidable predicates, and solvable problems. Questions about the nature of the algorithms, the type of devices that can be used for the computation, and about the difficulty or complexity of the computation have been investigated and are discussed in other articles. A book with a large collection of practical algorithms is Cormen *et al.* (1990).

Bibliography

1965. Hermes, H. *Enumerability, Decidability, Computability*. Berlin: Springer-Verlag.
1967. Minsky, M. *Computation: Finite and Infinite Machines*. Englewood Cliffs, NJ: Prentice Hall.
1967. Rogers, H. *Theory of Recursive Functions and Effective Computability*. New York: McGraw-Hill.
1979. Hopcroft, J. E., and Ullman, J. D. *Introduction to Automata, Languages, and Computation*. Reading, MA: Addison-Wesley.
1990. Cormen, T. H., Leiserson, C. E., and Rivest, R. L. *Introduction to Algorithms*. Cambridge, MA: MIT Press.
1993. Matiyasevich, Yuri V. *Hilbert's Tenth Problem*. Cambridge, MA: MIT Press.
1997. Knuth, D. E. *The Art of Computer Programming: Fundamental Algorithms*, 3rd Ed. Reading, MA: Addison-Wesley.

Gabor T. Herman

ALU

See ARITHMETIC-LOGIC UNIT.

ANALOG COMPUTER

For articles on related subjects *see* ANALOG-TO-DIGITAL AND DIGITAL-TO-ANALOG CONVERTERS; CONTROL APPLICATIONS; DIFFERENTIAL ANALYZER; DIGITAL COMPUTER; NUMERICAL ANALYSIS; and SIMULATION.

Introduction

The word *analog* is derived from the Greek *ana-logon*, meaning "according to a ratio." Simply, it means a similarity in proportional relationships transcending structure or material. For example, the wing of an airplane, a submerged hydrofoil, and a sail filled with wind are different in structure, but analogous in function in the way they transfer physical forces. In an electronic *analog computer* the output voltage of an operational amplifier varies in response to its input signals analogously to how a variable in the physical system being *modeled* responds to its conditions.

Analog studies are generally applied to the study of objects that are difficult or costly to investigate directly. Many analog computations seek to narrow the range of relevant process parameters and coefficients, so that important full scale values and responses can be anticipated with relative certainty. Important observations which are made on the analog representations are subsequently related to and interpreted in the world of "real" variables through a set of appropriate *scale factors*.

The use of analog computation goes back to antiquity. The areas of irregularly shaped tracts of land were "measured" by cutting pieces of paper similar in shape to the land and weighing them, thus obtaining an analogous measure of the total land. A number of physical principles have been used throughout the ages for analog computations, such as marks on a burning candle and the streaming sand in an hourglass to indicate the passage of time. Yesteryear's slide rules were analog computers that juxtaposed sliding scales to add or subtract logarithms.

Cutting and weighing paper pieces and using the slide rule represented, at best, *static analog computing*. Such methods fulfilled the need to carry out simple arithmetic calculations and pin down some important numbers. But they offered little or no help in solving differential equations, the principal means for expressing scientific and technical knowledge. For this, the process of integration was required and is carried out by *dynamic analog computing*.

Early Developments

The emergence of dynamic analog computing may be dated from the invention of the mechanical integrator by Professor James Thomson in 1876 (Fig. 1) and its immediate adaptation to scientific problem-solving by his brother, Sir William Thomson, later Lord Kelvin. The mechanical integrator inspired Lord Kelvin to solve certain differential equations in entirely new ways. Kelvin (1876) wrote:

Every linear differential equation of the second order may, as is known, be reduced to the form

$$\frac{d}{dx}\left(\frac{1}{P}\frac{du}{dx}\right) = u, \qquad (1)$$

where *P* is any given function of *x*.

. . .

So far I had gone and was satisfied, feeling I had done what I wished to do for many years. But then came a

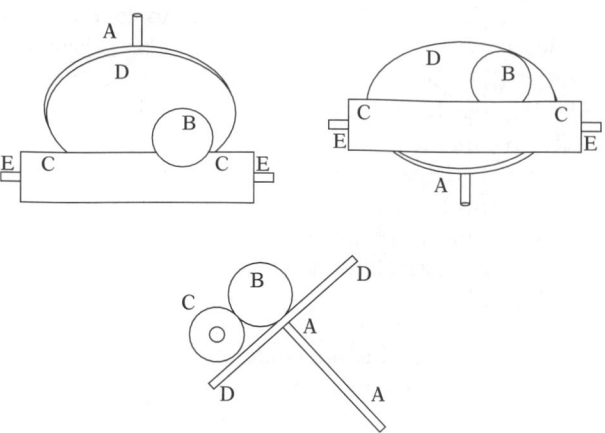

Figure 1. James Thomson's mechanical integrator (reproduced from the article Harmonic Analyzer, in *Proceedings of the Royal Society of London*, Vol. **XXVII**, London 1878, 371–373).

A—Input drive shaft, the turning of which represents the independent variable.
B—Heavy ball transferring by friction the rotation of the disk D to the cylinder C.
C—Receiving cylinder firmly attached to shaft E, the turning of which represents the dependent variable (the integration result).
D—Integrator disk coupled firmly to shaft A.

pleasing surprise. Compel agreement between the function fed into the double [integrator] machine and that given out by it.

. . .

. . . I was led to a conclusion which was quite unexpected; and it seems to me very remarkable that the general differential equation of the second order with variable coefficients may be rigorously, continuously, and in a single process solved by a machine.

Kelvin's setup included two mechanical integrators in series as shown in Fig. 2. Implicit in Kelvin's analysis was the discovery of the *closed-loop principle*, with the output of an integrating device fed back to form its inputs. Thus, to solve the differential equation (1), the value of *u* in Fig. 2 would be *fed back* as the input to the first integrator. This feedback principle is the key to all dynamic analog computing. As another example, consider the general third order linear differential equation

$$y''' + ay'' + by' + cy + d = 0$$

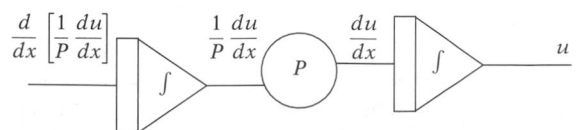

Figure 2. Series integration of a second derivative showing the standard symbols for an integrator and a constant multiplier.

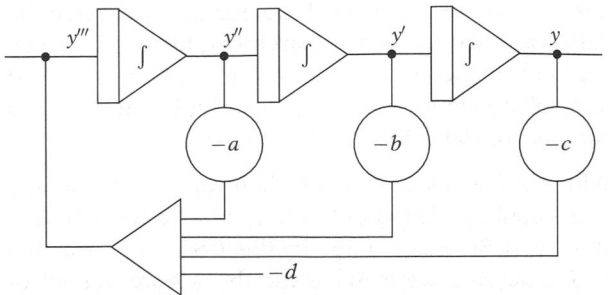

Figure 3. Analog computer setup to solve a third-order linear differential equation. The triangle is the symbol for a summing amplifier whose output is just the sum of its inputs.

which can be reformulated as

$$y''' = -ay'' - by' - cy - d.$$

This simple equation says that the integrand, y''', is made up from a constant term $(-d)$ plus three *negative feedbacks*, $-ay''$, $-by'$, and $-cy$. The variables are all generated by integrations, since integrating y''' yields y''; integrating y'' yields y'; and integrating y' yields y. In other words: a series of three integrations is all that is necessary to achieve what Lord Kelvin

discovered, "that the general differential equation ... may be rigorously, continuously, and in a single process solved by a machine." In this case the circuit for solving the equation is shown in Fig. 3. This circuit disregards initial conditions, that is, the values of the integration constants which are part of all integrations. In practical terms this is achieved by adding constant values, the initial conditions, to the output of each integrator. For example, the output y'' should be added to the initial value of y''.

A very useful aspect of the mechanical integrator was its ability to integrate with respect to a spatial variable: a rotational or linear displacement. This important attribute made the integrator suitable for integration with respect to several independent variables, leading to methods for solving certain types of partial differential equations (*q.v.*).

Lord Kelvin went on to use mechanical integrators in several useful inventions. The new ability to solve differential equations made it practical to build analytical instruments, for example, for harmonic analysis of periodic functions. Within a few years Kelvin had constructed several analyzers and had determined the

H. G. FORD

POWER TRANSMITTING MECHANISM

APPLICATION FILED DEC. 28, 1916, RENEWED JAN. 2. 1919

1,317,916

Patented Oct. 7, 1919.

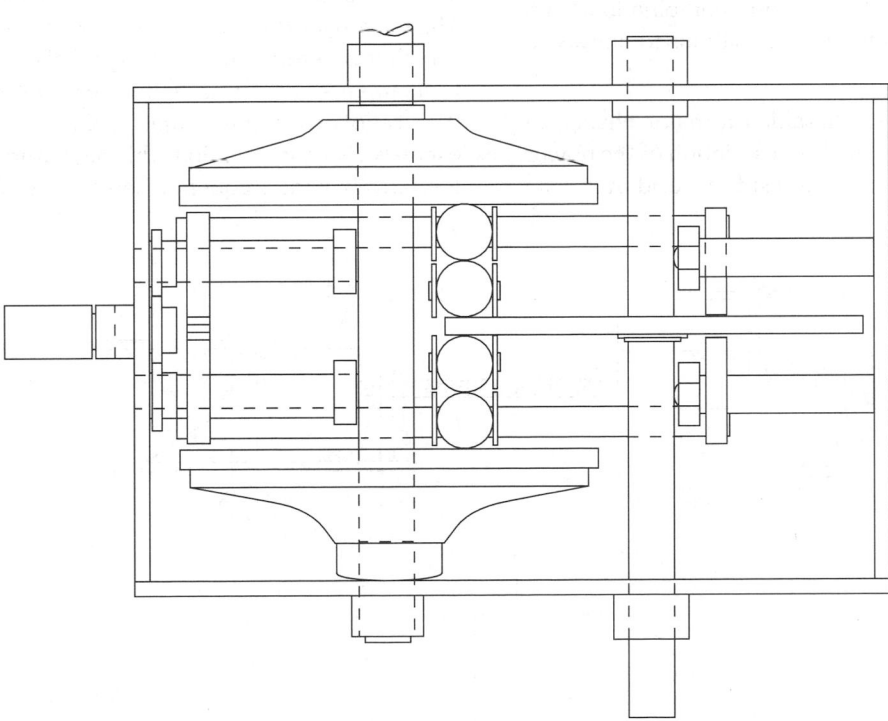

Figure 4. Hannibald C. Ford's patented variable mechanical gear. A form of it was used as the integrator in ballistic gun control systems developed by his firm for the US Navy. A movable twin set of two steel balls conveys rotational motion of the input disks (top and bottom left) to the output disk (middle, right). This gear could transmit a strong force and needed no torque amplifier.

periodicity of naturally occurring phenomena, most notably the tides. This allowed him to construct accurate tide predictors that turned out to be very valuable for ships sailing out of English ports.

Mechanical integration was also the principle of several gun-directing systems used in US Navy ships through the Second World War. The inventor, Hannibald Ford, constructed a complete *mechanical analog computer* in 1918 (*see* Fig. 4). The gun-directing systems were made to order by the Ford Instrument Company in New York City. Ford's integrators were similar in design to those of James Thomson, but they used a double ball which provided a remarkably easy way of producing the integrand and also delivered a high output torque of several horsepower that could drive most gun-directing mechanisms directly.

The next notable mechanical integrator developments occurred around 1930 at the Massachusetts Institute of Technology (MIT), where Vannevar Bush (*q.v.*) used the *Gonnella wheel* (Fig. 5) for mechanical integration: a knife-edged wheel rolling on a disk and radially displaced according to the integrand. As an integrator the Gonnella wheel is accurate, but it requires torque amplification to be useful. At MIT, this was achieved using a design derived from bus servo-steering systems. Bush announced the completion of a purely mechanical equation solver in 1931 that he called a *differential analyzer*. Containing six mechanical integrators, it was capable of integrating with respect to six independent variables and thus could solve any combination from six first-order linear differential equations to one sixth-order equation.

The differential analyzer heralded a major change in scientific investigation. Bush's description of the power of the analyzer stimulated interest the world over. The analyzer promised to revolutionize the way scientific data was analyzed and research conducted. To scientists and engineers it seemed as if almost anyone could now solve equations that previously had been either too complex or too cumbersome to solve.

Within a few years large mechanical differential analyzers could be found in Dublin, Manchester, London, Oslo, and St. Petersburg. In the USA, copies of the MIT analyzers were made for the Moore School of Engineering at the University of Pennsylvania, Philadelphia, and for the Aberdeen Proving Ground near Baltimore, MD.

The Electronic Integrator

In an electronic analog computer differential equations are solved in much the same way as Kelvin first proposed. The key difference is the use of real time as the independent variable, progressing linearly from an initial value to the desired end point. To carry out the required integrations from higher to lower order terms, a series of electronic integrators is used. Each integrator is an adaptation of a high gain operational amplifier in which a capacitor is the only feedback element.

Starting and stopping the integration process requires a simple switching mechanism, connecting the input of the operational amplifier to either the integrand input or to the feedback circuit during *initial condition* (IC) setup. The functional circuit for this is shown in Fig. 6. The term *operational amplifier* refers to an electronic unit that generates an output signal of opposite polarity to its input signal. It has extremely high amplification (the ratio of output-to-input voltage signal typically exceeds 10^8) and it exhibits this high amplification over a relatively wide frequency band, generally from zero

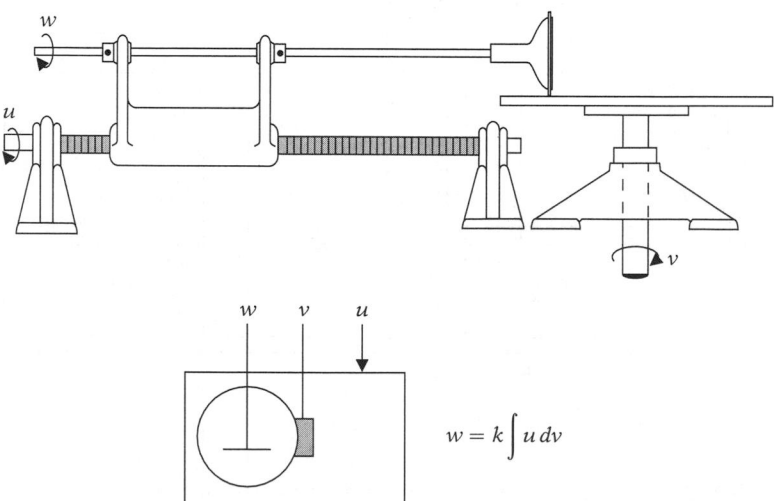

$$w = k \int u \, dv$$

Figure 5. The Gonnella wheel used as integrator. The principle of the integrator: a thin, light wheel rolling by friction on a hard, smooth disk, and its symbolic representation.

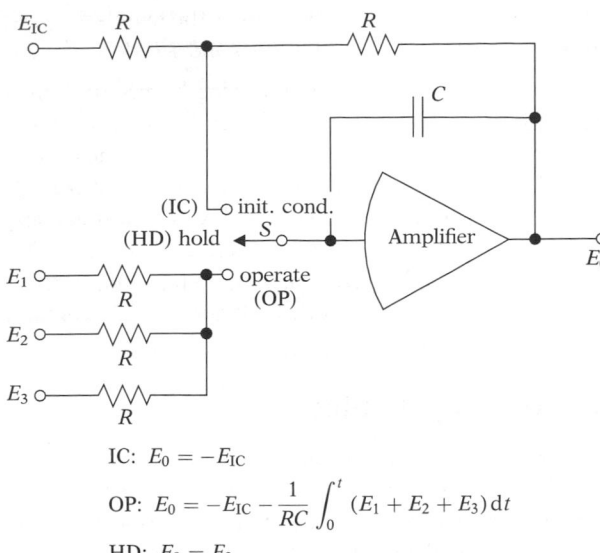

IC: $E_0 = -E_{IC}$

OP: $E_0 = -E_{IC} - \dfrac{1}{RC} \displaystyle\int_0^t (E_1 + E_2 + E_3)\,\mathrm{d}t$

HD: $E_0 = E_0$

Figure 6. The operational amplifier connected as an electronic integrator. When the switch S is in the initial condition (IC) position, the feedback capacitor C is charged to a voltage E_0 equal to the input voltage E_{IC}. This represents tracking or acquiring the initial condition (start value) for the integration. When the switch S is in the hold position (HD), there is no input signal connected to the integrator, and the output voltage remains steady; when the switch S is in the operate position (OP), the feedback capacitor is continuously charged to an output voltage corresponding to the time integral of the sum of the integrand input signals.

(dc) to several megahertz. Reliable computing performance also requires a highly stable circuit design (i.e. the amplifier should exhibit low temperature dependence), and its output stage should deliver a sufficiently large current to "drive" other computational units with a signal-to-noise ratio that typically exceeds 10^5 to 1.

Solving Differential Equations in Real Time

Electronic analog computers solve differential equations in accordance with the feedback principle discussed earlier. The possibility of solving sets of simultaneous differential equations emerged with the availability of many integrators in one computer (*see* Fig. 7). In addition, some large analog computers operated in so-called *real time*, that is, when one second of clock time equals one unit of time of the independent variable.

Solutions carried out in real time lasted minutes or hours, sometimes even days, and rendered output signals that agreed closely with the physical variables they *simulated*. In many cases the analog computers were connected to specific hardware and involved so-called *person-in-the-loop* applications. Several key NASA studies in the early 1960s were of this kind, putting pilots or astronauts into capsules that were "flown" in simulated orbits or under the sea. Such

$$4\frac{d^3x}{dt^3} + 5\frac{d^2x}{dt^2} + 7x\frac{dx}{dt} - 3x + 36 = 0$$

$$-\frac{d^3x}{dt^3} = \frac{5}{4}\frac{d^2x}{dt^2} + \frac{7}{4}x\frac{dx}{dt} - \frac{3}{4}x + 9$$

(a)

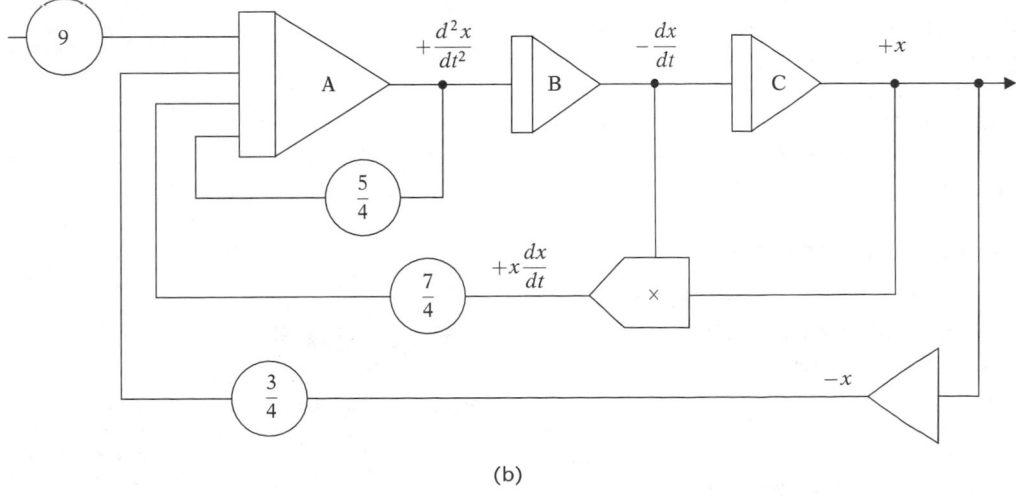

(b)

Figure 7. An analog computer circuit. (a) A third-order nonlinear differential equation in its original form and then in the form suitable for programming. (b) Three integrators (A, B, and C) connected in series to generate the variable x from its first, second and third time derivatives. The first (leftmost) integrator A receives as its input four variables that in sum represent the d^3x/dt^3 term. When integrated, this generates the d^2x/dt^2 term which is the input of integrator B, and so on. Here, as opposed to Figs. 2 and 3, we have used the common convention that integrators, multipliers, and summing amplifiers also invert the sign of the result.

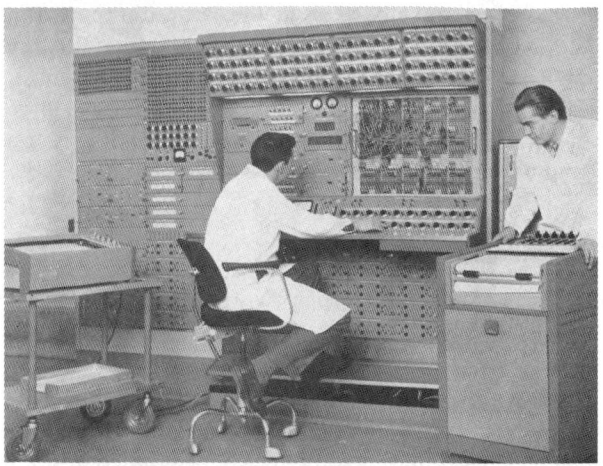

Figure 8. The EAI 231-R electronic analog computer from Electronic Associates. This was one of the first and most important analog computers and provided the capabilities for extensive and complex simulations of process dynamics, spaceflights, airplane stability analysis and medical (drug) evaluations from about 1956 to the late 1960s.

person-in-the-loop simulations were very effective in evaluating engineering solutions where it would be too risky or too costly to experiment directly.

Several specialty firms produced electronic real-time analog computers in the 30 years after the Second World War. Such computers were generally large and assembled to form integrated systems made up of many analog consoles. A large system typically contained dozens of real-time integrators and hundreds of operational amplifiers. Early American producers of large systems were Reeves Electronics of New York, Electronic Associates Inc., of West Long Branch, NJ, Berkley Division of Beckman Instruments, Los Angeles, Applied Dynamics, Inc. of Ann Arbor, MI, among others. Smaller electronic analog computers were made for teaching purposes or more limited engineering simulations. Typical of these were the desktop analog computers made by Donner Associates, Inc. of Los Angeles and Computer Products Corp. of Newton, MA, as well as by Electronics Associates (Fig. 8).

High-Speed Analog Computers

Generally, the smaller the capacitor, the faster the charge rate. Thus, with smaller capacitors, analog computations could proceed faster than real time. So-called *high-speed analog computers* used this principle to generate solutions that were 1000 to 3000 times faster than real time. Such rapid solutions, lasting only fractions of a second, could be repeated many times a second and displayed on an oscilloscope, generating a "steady" picture of the solutions. With standard analog coefficient potentiometers, the user could interact with the high-speed solutions and immediately observe the

effects of parameter changes. This was the basis for so-called *repetitive operation analog computers.*

An early pioneer in individual analog computing units and high-speed integrators for repetitive operations was the Boston firm Geo. A. Philbrick Researches, Inc., later Teledyne Philbrick Inc. Its founder, George A. Philbrick, promoted the use of analog computing using his "black boxes" as flexible and effective engineering analysis tools. In the years from 1946 to 1966, his firm was in the forefront of both high-speed and real-time electronic analog computing.

Iterative Capabilities

In most real-time analog computers the mode control switch S in Fig. 6 was usually one or two simple mechanical relays which needed a few hundred milliseconds to close or open. In the 1960s, when such relays were replaced by high-speed electronic switching circuits, it became possible to control the function of the integrator at much higher speeds, and on an individual basis. Electronic switches were also compatible with electronic logic signals, generated by combining the outputs of *analog signal comparators* with logic devices such as *and-, or-,* and *nor-gates, flip-flops* and *counters* (see LOGIC DESIGN). The advent of logic

Figure 9. The high-speed iterative analog computer from GPS Instrument Company. The microsecond electronic integrator switching controls enabled the user to solve boundary value problems, employ multiple time scales (two or more time dimensions) in solving certain partial differential equations, and in general, through repetitive simulation techniques find embedded optimum solutions. The iterative group was first demonstrated at the Fall Joint Computer Conference in 1961.

control made it possible to program the operations of the integrators according to the progress made in the analog computations, so that analog computations could be controlled in ways similar to branching instructions in digital computer programs.

The first such *iterative electronic analog computer* was unveiled at the Fall Joint Computer Conference, in Washington DC, in December 1961, by GPS Instrument Co. of Newton, MA (Fig. 9). This logic-controlled analog computer enabled the user to apply iterative techniques to the solution of analog problems, with signals (voltages) transferred from one solution or iteration to the next by so-called "track-and-hold" techniques.

Examples of the use of logic control include step-by-step approximation methods, searching for unknown boundary values, solving double or multiple integration problems, and determining complex stochastic (statistical) measures based on thousands of simulations with randomly varying conditions. An example of the latter was the simulation of wind gust effects on a large rocket during its ascent through the lower atmosphere.

Hybrid (Analog and Digital) Computers

During the period from the early 1960s to the early 1970s electronic analog computers were increasingly combined with a digital computer in *hybrid systems*. The idea was to combine the easy programmability of a general purpose digital computer with the ability of a large electronic analog computer to solve substantial, complex problems, notably large sets of nonlinear differential equations, or to simulate challenging spaceflights and "person-in-the-loop" situations in real time.

A number of specialty hybrid systems emerged in the mid- to late 1960s and early 1970s. Many of these were tailor-made for one or just a few very demanding applications. An unusual such system was the Trice digital analog computer developed by the Packard Bell Company and used by NASA for spaceflight simulation. Trice used a pulse frequency modulated signal as the information carrier. The count of pulses received per time unit represented the information conveyed. A high count represented a positive number; a low count was a negative one. Integration consisted simply in counting pulses received during a specific time interval and subtracting the number that corresponded to zero.

The End of an Era

Analog and hybrid computers were generally phased out during the late 1970s. Most users realized they faced the end of an era, brought on by the ever-increas-

ing speed, power, and memory capacity of digital computers. By the late 1970s it was obvious that soon digital solutions would be faster—and considerably more accurate and convenient to use—than even high-speed analog or hybrid computers were. The old axiom that "... when digital computers are programmed to solve equations as fast as analogs, they are less accurate; and when programmed to be as accurate, digital computers are much slower," was no longer true.

The paradigm shift occurred with the advent of digital computer programs and special programming languages. These made it possible to use Kelvin's method of successive integrations on a digital computer. The Continuous System Modeling Program (CSMP) for IBM computers, the SIMSCRIPT language (*see* SIMULATION) and a number of others opened a new era and allowed users to solve sets of differential equations with ease and accuracy.

One advance that made this possible was the development of integration algorithms that delivered accurate numerical solutions. With these methods complex sets of differential equations are now solved as effortlessly and accurately as arithmetic equations so that there is a very limited market for electronic analog computers to solve such problems. Thus, the development has, in a way, come full circle. Lord Kelvin"s "feedback" method of successive numerical integrations, pioneered in 1876, is now in general use on digital computers but with little recognition given to its deep significance.

Bibliography

1876. Thomson, Sir W. "Mechanical Integration of Linear Differential Equation of the Second Order with Variable Coefficients," *Proceedings of the Royal Society of London*, **28**, 269–271.
1962. Holst, P. A. "Iterative Analog Computations," *Annales de l'Association Internationales pour le Calcul Analogique*, **6**, 2, 89–104.
1971. Hausner, A. *Analog and Hybrid Computer Programming*. Upper Saddle River, NJ: Prentice Hall.
1972. Korn, G. A., and Korn, T. M. *Electronic Analog and Hybrid Computers*, 2nd Ed. New York: McGraw-Hill.

Per A. Holst

ANALOG-TO-DIGITAL AND DIGITAL-TO-ANALOG CONVERTERS

For articles on related subjects *see* ANALOG COMPUTER; CODES; COMPUTER CIRCUITRY; CONTROL APPLICATIONS; and DATA COMMUNICATIONS.

Whenever it is necessary to communicate between analog and digital systems, *analog-to-digital* (A-D) and/or *digital-to-analog* (D-A) converters are required. These converters form basic links between the world

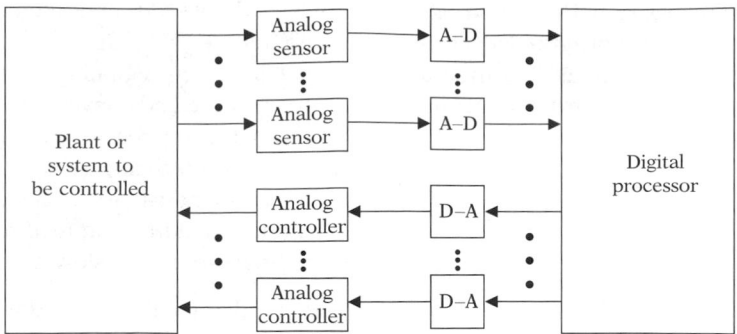

Figure 1. Digital control system.

of "real" phenomena, where the variables are generally continuous analog quantities, and the world of digital information processing (*q.v.*) and data communications, where the variables are discrete quantities.

The number of applications and types of converters available has grown significantly in recent years. This has resulted from increased recognition of the capabilities of digital, as opposed to analog, signal processing and data transmission. The importance of these capabilities is application-dependent; however, in general, the advantages of digital processing and transmission lie in the increased accuracy, noise immunity, processing flexibility, and storage facilities afforded by the digital format. This increasing use of digital processing of analog signals has been aided by the rapid development of sophisticated, yet inexpensive microcomputer systems and by the ability to integrate both analog and digital functions on single VLSI (Very Large-Scale Integration) chips.

Some Applications

A simple classification of application areas where A-D and D-A converters are used is given below.

DIGITAL CONTROL SYSTEMS

Fig. 1 is a block diagram of a digital control system. Variables originate within the plant or system, are sensed by an analog sensor, digitized by an A-D converter, and then transmitted to a digital processor. If the processor merely manipulates and stores this information, the system is a simple data acquisition system. If, on the basis of the input information, control signals determined by the processor are returned to the plant, then a digital control system is present. A variation on this system requiring fewer converters can be designed based on multiplexing (*q.v.*) if the signal frequencies and number of sensors and controllers are not excessive (Fig. 2).

COMMUNICATIONS AND ENTERTAINMENT SYSTEMS

The advantages of digital data transmission have resulted in extensive use of converters as parts of telemetering, voice communications, and entertainment systems. In telemetering systems, analog signals originating in remote locations are first converted into digital signals and then transmitted to the central station. Remote weather and defense-related monitoring systems fall in this category.

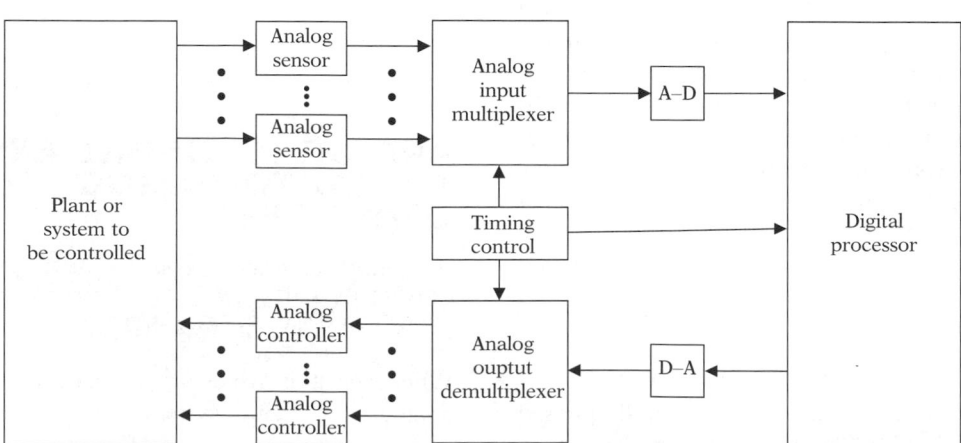

Figure 2. Digital control system with multiplexers.

Voice communications systems are also increasingly oriented toward digital signal processing. In this situation, analog voice signals are digitized with A-D converters and subsequently transmitted over time-shared channels, with many conversations being "simultaneously" carried over the same channel. Such systems can be designed to be flexible and handle both speech and data at the same time, while making nearly optimum use of a system's bandwidth (*q.v.*).

In the entertainment industry, digital recording and playback systems of audio signals are now commonplace. Compact disc (CD) and digital audio tape systems make extensive use of A-D and D-A converters.

TEST, MEASUREMENT, AND MONITORING

Many applications of A-D converters can be found in test and measurement equipment. Digital voltmeters, for example, are now commonplace, and the inclusion of digital readouts alongside analog displays on oscilloscopes has gained widespread acceptance. More complex measurement and monitoring applications, such as online real-time patient monitoring, also have converters as key system elements.

The Basic Relationship

Analog variables such as position, temperature, pressure, and process rate are typically first converted during measurement into analog voltages and cur-

Table 1. Three-bit natural binary code.

Decimal value	Binary value	BIT 1 MSB	BIT 2	BIT 3 LSB
0	0.000	0	0	0
$\frac{1}{8}$	0.001	0	0	1
$\frac{2}{8}$	0.010	0	1	0
$\frac{3}{8}$	0.011	0	1	1
$\frac{4}{8}$	0.100	1	0	0
$\frac{5}{8}$	0.101	1	0	1
$\frac{6}{8}$	0.110	1	1	0
$\frac{7}{8}$	0.111	1	1	1

rents. Conversely, to control the analog variables, analog voltages and currents are usually supplied to the inputs of a controlling transducer. Rather than deal with the basic analog variable (e.g. temperature), it is therefore convenient to deal with the voltages or currents available at the output, or produced for the input, of the transducer. The analog variable considered here is thus a pure voltage or current, and questions concerning transducer operation, signal amplification, and signal conditioning are not discussed.

Digital information is generally represented by the presence or absence of a fixed voltage or current level. Each unit of information ("bit") thus has two states, referred to as the *one* and *zero* states. On a single input line, information can be represented serially by

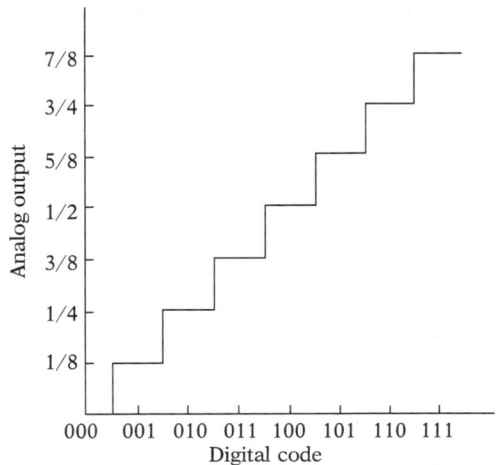

(a) Transfer function of a D–A converter

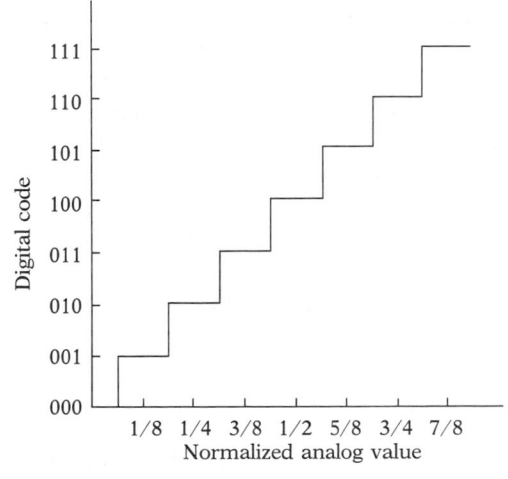

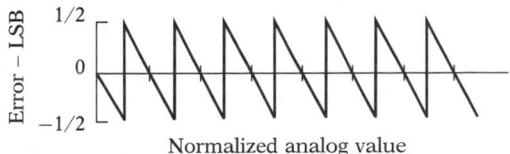

(b) Transfer function of an A–D converter

Figure 3. The basic ideal relationships.

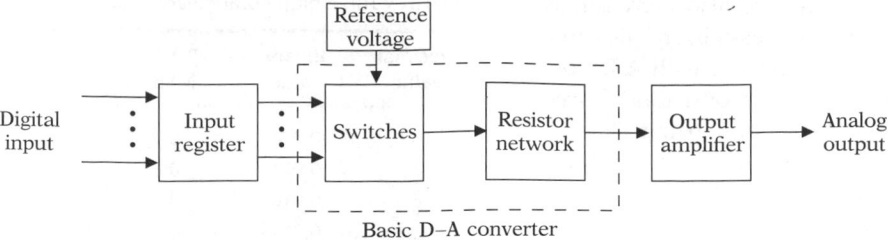

Figure 4. D-A converter and accessories.

periodically changing the voltage level or state of the line. A set of parallel lines or a grouping of serial bits can be used to represent a digital word, where the meaning of this word depends on the number or symbol assigned to each possible combination of bits. This is referred to as the *code*. Different types of codes are used with A-D and D-A converters (e.g. offset binary, ones complement, twos complement). However, for simplicity, this article considers only the *unipolar* or *natural binary* code. Table 1 presents this code for a three-bit word. In general, each word may have n bits, with the bit at left, the most significant bit (MSB), having a weight of 2^{-1}, the bit at right, the least significant bit (LSB), having a weight of 2^{-n}, and the ith bit ($1 \leq i \leq n$) having a weight of 2^{-i}.

The basic conversion relationship for a three-bit binary code is given in Fig. 3a and 3b. Any three-bit digital sequence entering into the D-A converter results in producing one of eight distinct voltage outputs, as seen in Fig. 3a. Similarly, any voltage input into the A-D converter results in producing a distinct three-bit output code. The *ideal resolution* of these converters is equal to the value of the LSB, 2^{-n} for an n-bit converter. Associated with A-D resolution is an inherent quantization error, which reflects an uncertainty in the results of conversion due to quantification of the analog signal. For the system above, transitions occur in the middle of each voltage range, thus minimizing the quantification error to an optimum $\pm 1/2$ LSB. Other errors, such as noise and various nonlinearities, may increase this above $\pm 1/2$ LSB in real systems.

D-A Converters

Fig. 4 shows a block diagram for a D-A converter. The typical D-A converter contains switches and a resistor network. The switches are controlled by the digital input code and establish connections within the network needed to obtain the proper analog voltage.

Fig. 5 shows a simple 3-bit (plus sign) D-A converter. The dashed lines indicate that the switch is controlled by the associated digital bit input. The switches are generally integrated circuits that ideally would have no

resistance when closed and infinite resistance when open. For the 0100-input switch configuration shown, the output voltage V_0 is easily seen to be $V_R/2$. Similarly, the nth bit present can be shown to produce an output voltage increment equal to $2^{-n}V_R$; hence, the resulting output voltage is proportional to the binary input. A sign bit is present that controls a voltage reference switch. Its absence (0) indicates a positive digital input and results in switching in the positive reference voltage $+V_R$. Its presence (1) indicates a negative input, and the negative reference voltage $-V_R$ is applied.

A-D Converters

A simple form of A-D converter is shown in Fig. 6. A conversion begins after the reset signal clears the counter. The counter now receives clock pulses and is incremented with each pulse. The counter output is a digital word representing a voltage level. This word, received by the D-A converter, results in an analog signal, which is compared with the incoming analog signal. When the comparator signal becomes positive, the counter at that point holds the correct digital

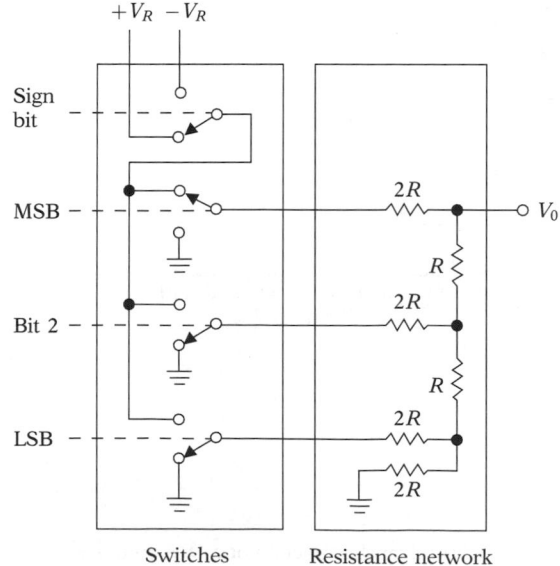

Figure 5. R/2R D-A converter.

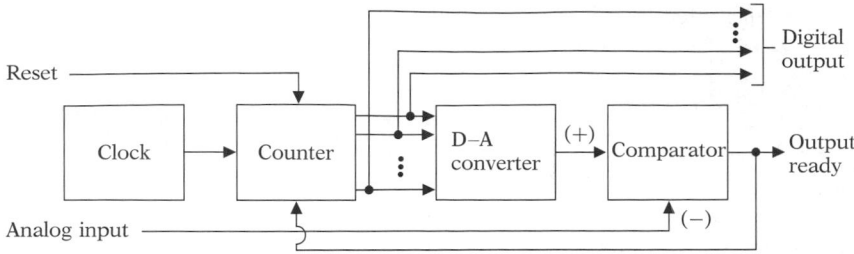

Figure 6. Counter A-D converter.

representation of the analog signal. An "output ready" signal indicates that this has occurred.

The method, though simple, requires a relatively long time for a complete A-D conversion due to the counting process. This time increases by a factor of two for each additional bit and makes the method unsuitable for certain applications. A modification to the above technique, which speeds up the converter, calls for the incrementing counter to be replaced with an "up-down" counter. Here, once a comparison has been made, the counter is designed to increment or decrement on each clock pulse, depending on the output of the comparator. The counter thus follows the analog signal and the full counting process is not necessary on each conversion if large changes in the analog input do not occur.

With the "Successive-Approximation" converter, the counter box is assumed to contain a register and control logic. The converter operates by successively considering each bit position in the register and setting that bit to a one or a zero on the basis of the comparator output. The MSB is first set to a one with all other bit positions set to zero. This word then enters the D-A converter and the D-A output is compared with the analog input. If the result indicates the analog input is larger, then the one in the MSB is kept; otherwise, it is set to zero. The remaining bit positions are considered successively in the same manner and a decision is made on each bit position. After the LSB is considered, the results of conversion are found in the register. Unlike the counting method, the conversion time with this method is constant for every possible analog input, and this approach is often used in high-speed converter design.

A somewhat lower-speed but high-accuracy A-D converter is the "integrating" converter. A "dual slope" version is shown in Fig. 7. The converter operates by first integrating the unknown analog input voltage for a fixed period of time. During this time period, a voltage proportional to the input builds up on the integrating capacitor. After resetting the counter to zero, a fixed reference voltage of opposite polarity is now applied to the integrator and the counter is started. When the null

comparator recognizes that the integrator output has reached zero, the control logic is notified and the counter is stopped. The output count is proportional to the ratio of the input voltage and referenced voltage. Since the reference voltage is known, the count is therefore a binary representation of the analog input. Triple and quad slope architectures that greatly increase the conversion speed at the cost of added complexity are also possible.

A more recent design that has gained widespread acceptance in those applications requiring high dynamic range, accuracy, and superior noise properties (e.g. digital audio) is the Sigma Delta A-D converter (Fig. 8). The high gain negative feedback loop provides for sampling of the analog input at a rate substantially higher than the bandwidth of interest. The loop comparator output is fed into a digital filter that, by weighting successive bits appropriately, creates the desired output (Boser and Wooley, 1988). The design exploits technology developments that permit effective integration of analog and digital functions on the same VLSI chip.

For higher-speed A-D conversion, parallel methods are available. The simplest method uses an analog comparator for each quantization (Fig. 9). Each comparator (C) represents a voltage level, and these levels are coded into the appropriate three-bit codes with an encoding network. Though conversion effectively requires only a single step, the cost increases rapidly with the number of bits n, since the number of comparators needed is $2^n - 1$.

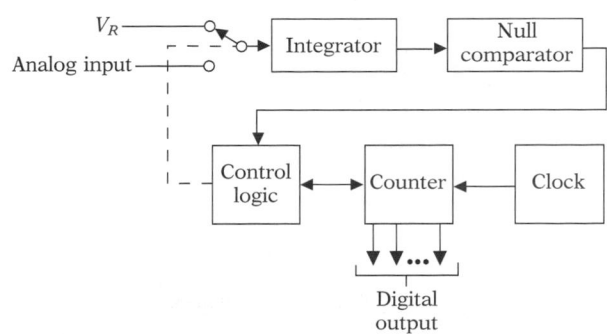

Figure 7. Dual slope integrating A-D converter.

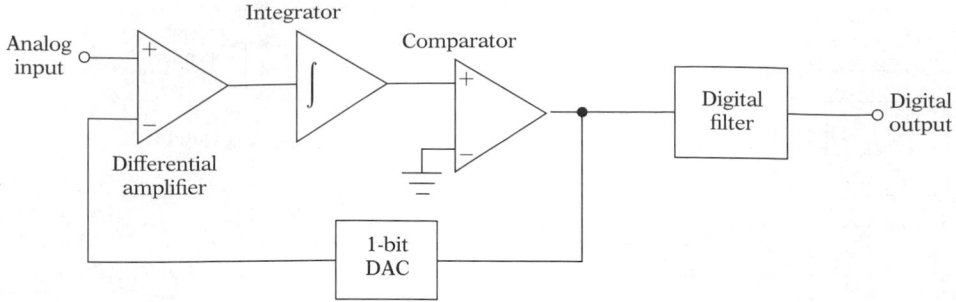

Figure 8. First-order Sigma-Delta A-D converter.

Specification of Converters

A number of measures are normally used in specifying converter accuracy and speed. These measures in part isolate and indicate the various sources of error. With D-A converters, *accuracy* or *absolute accuracy* refers to the deviation of actual analog output from the output predicted by the ideal transfer function. Though this may vary over the range of the unit, specifications are normally given in terms of a single number representing the maximum error over the range. This may be stated as ± a percentage of full scale or ± a fraction of LSB. *Relative* accuracy measures the largest deviation of the analog output from a straight line drawn through the end points of a converter's transfer function.

Several common error types that contribute to a loss of accuracy are illustrated in Fig. 10. Fig. 10a shows *nonlinearity* in the conversion transfer function. The nonlinearity is, however, *monotonic*, since increasing digital values produce increasing analog values.

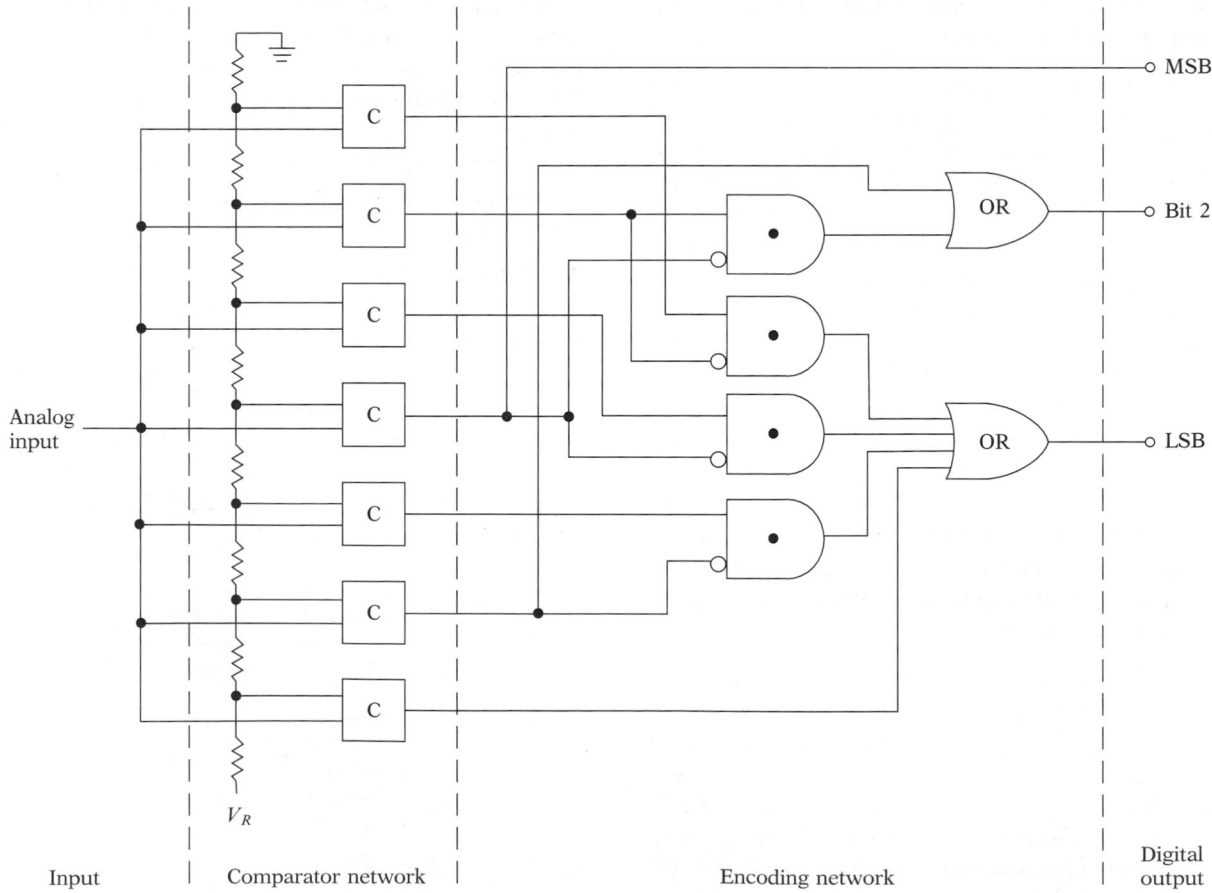

Figure 9. Three-bit parallel A-D converter..

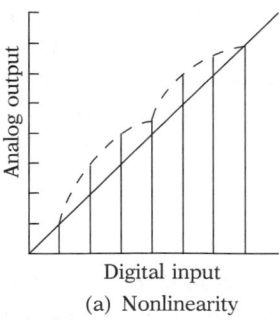
(a) Nonlinearity

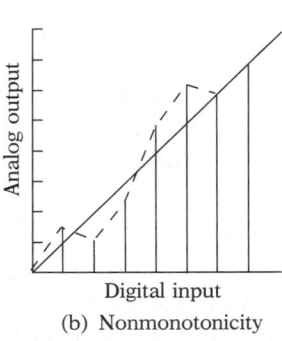
(b) Nonmonotonicity

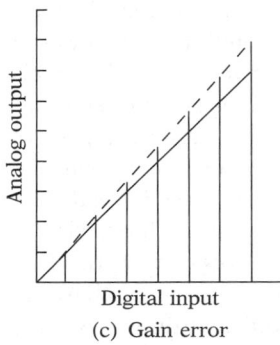
(c) Gain error

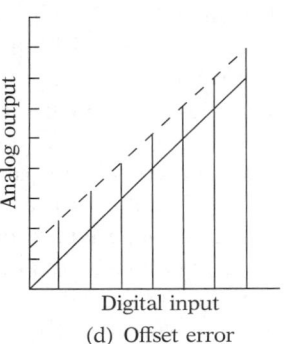
(d) Offset error

Figure 10. D/A errors (Sheingold, 1986).

Fig. 10b shows a *nonmonotonic* nonlinearity. Such a nonlinearity could yield the same analog value for two different digital input codes, a result that might cause oscillations to occur in certain control applications (*q.v.*). Figs. 10c and 10d illustrate *gain* and *offset* errors, which respectively change the slope and zero crossing of the transfer function. The difference between the dotted line in the figures and the solid 45° angle line is the error associated with each digital input code.

Dynamic characteristics of D-A converters are normally specified in terms of a *setting time*. This is the time between arrival of the digital code and settling of the analog output to within certain specified limits of accuracy. The shorter the settling time, the higher the conversion rate. For a high-speed converter, the full scale maximum settling time specification might read 100 μs to settle within $\pm 1/2$ LSB.

For A-D converters, accuracy refers to the deviation of the analog level represented by the digital output from the actual analog input. As with D-A converters, this is normally stated as either a percentage of full scale or a fraction of the LSB. The relative accuracy of an A-D converter measures the largest deviation of the converter's transfer function from a straight line drawn through its endpoints and is also expressed as a percentage of full scale or a fraction of the LSB. Errors here may be divided into two parts. The first, *quantization error*—discussed earlier in this article—results in an inherent error of $\pm 1/2$ LSB, which can be reduced only by increasing the number of bits. All other errors are equipment errors, and error types directly corresponding to those found in D-A converters may be present. Offset, gain (scale factor), and nonlinearity errors have analogous definitions. The error corresponding to nonmonotonic nonlinearity is termed the *differential linearity error* and may result in entire digital outputs being missed.

The dynamic characteristics of A-D converters are normally specified in terms of the total conversion time. This is the time necessary for a complete measurement,

its inverse being the *conversion rate* of the converter. The National Semiconductor ADC0808 high-speed 8-bit A-D converter, for example, has a conversion time of 100 μs and a relative accuracy of $\pm 1/2$ LSB.

Conclusion

A-D and D-A converters are finding increasing use as the scope of digital processing and communications widens. There is every indication that this trend will continue and be augmented by further gains in performance and decreases in converter cost. This will result in large part from the growing use of monolithic and VLSI circuit technologies. A proliferation of new products can be expected with increasing emphasis placed on ease of interfacing these products with microprocessors (*q.v.*) and standard communications systems and buses.

Bibliography

1978. Kurth, C. F. (ed.) Special issue on analog/digital conversion, *IEEE Trans. on Circuits and Systems,* **CAS-25** (July).
1986. Sheingold, D. H. (ed.) *Analog-Digital Conversion Handbook.* Upper Saddle River, NJ: Prentice Hall.
1988. Boser, B. E., and Wooley, B. A. "The Design of Sigma-Delta Modulation Analog-to-Digital Converters," *IEEE Journal of Solid State Circuits,* **23**, 6.
1994. Noeschele, D. F., Jr. *Analog-to-Digital and Digital-to-Analog Conversion Techniques.* New York: John Wiley.
1996. Norsworthy, S. R., Schneier, R., and Temes, G. C. (eds.) *Delta-Sigma Data Converters: Theory, Design, and Simulation.* New York: IEEE Press.

Mark A. Franklin

ANALYSIS OF ALGORITHMS

See ALGORITHMS, ANALYSIS OF.

ANALYTICAL ENGINE

For articles on related subjects *see* BABBAGE, CHARLES; DIFFERENCE ENGINE; and DIGITAL COMPUTERS, HISTORY OF: ORIGINS.

The Analytical Engine, designed by Charles Babbage between 1833 and 1846, anticipated many features of electronic computing devices invented in the 1940s and 1950s. Although mechanical in all its operations, the Analytical Engine could carry out calculations of arbitrary complexity under the control of punched cards. Conditional branching was possible, and Babbage had prepared test programs that included elaborate calculations based on nested loop structures. In a beautiful anticipation of twentieth-century thinking, Babbage showed that, given sufficient time, any finite calculation could be carried out by the Analytical Engine.

Babbage commenced work on the design of the Analytical Engine in 1833 after the collapse of the project to build his Difference Engine (*q.v.*). Babbage had realized that the second difference of the sine function is proportional to the sine itself. If the difference engine could be rearranged so that the tabulated value of the sine could be "fed back" to become the second difference, the sine could be calculated directly without an intermediate polynomial approximation. This image of the engine "eating its own tail" led Babbage to place the number stores of the Difference Engine around a set of central gear wheels that served as a "data bus" to transmit numbers from one store, or "register," to another.

Unfortunately, it requires a multiplication to form the second difference of the sine function. Babbage realized that this multiplication could be implemented as a sequence of shift and addition operations. This would be excessively slow, however, if the addition used the ripple-carry of the Difference Engine. Babbage's *anticipating carry*, a mechanical equivalent of carry-lookahead (*see* ADDER), greatly speeded multiplication. But its complexity led Babbage to separate the Analytical Engine into two distinct parts—the *store*, in which numbers are normally kept, and the *mill*, to which they are brought for calculations.

Division needs little more calculating apparatus than multiplication, but its control is more complex, as division is inherently a trial-and-error process. To control the Analytical Engine, Babbage developed *barrels*, similar in principle to a music box, in which each row of pins puts into gear those parts of the calculating mechanism that must act during one cycle of the drive shaft. Multiplication and division each require many cycles, and the barrels step backwards and forwards from one row of pins to another to control the various stages of each operation. Some pins on the barrel control this movement, which may be conditional upon an intermediate calculational result. In effect, the barrel is a microprogram store, and complex operations are implemented by microprograms represented by rows of pins on the barrel.

Babbage envisioned that the overall calculation performed by the Analytical Engine would be specified by a further barrel that initiated sequences of operations by the barrel just described; that is, a hierarchical organization of control. But in June 1836, Babbage borrowed from the Jacquard pattern-weaving loom the idea of a sequence of punched cards to provide a more flexible alternative to this "user program" barrel.

By late 1837, Babbage had developed all of the essential ideas for a flexible programmed calculating machine. Subsequent work on the Analytical Engine was more technical in nature. Babbage repeatedly re-examined all of the basic elements to see whether they could be simplified or speeded up, conflicting tasks at which he proved remarkably imaginative and productive. Much work was applied to the "architecture" of the Analytical Engine—the functional arrangement of the component mechanisms and the all-important microprograms for multiplication, division, and other operations.

Some of the microprograms are remarkably sophisticated. Signed addition, for example, is "pipelined" so that several additions are in progress simultaneously. Each stage of the pipeline is controlled by its own barrel. These step independently through their own microprograms while cooperating to maximize the flow of operands through the pipeline. It would be an impressive piece of technical design even today.

In contrast, Babbage's user-level programs are a disappointment. Most were prepared in the early years of Babbage's work on the Analytical Engine, and almost all are elementary. They are well described in the notes by Ada Lovelace (*see* LOVELACE, COUNTESS OF), where the idea of nested loops is developed in painful detail. On the strength of these notes, Ada Lovelace has been considered the "world's first programmer," but the accolade is unwarranted. The notes were written at Babbage's direction, as he had earlier directed papers by Lardner and Menabrea, and the example programs were prepared by Babbage, mostly many years before. In later years, Babbage's interest in user-level programs was almost nonexistent. However, his reputation as a "programmer" rests secure in the very sophisticated microprograms of the barrels.

Disenchanted by the attempt to build the Difference Engine, Babbage did not attempt to build the Analytical Engine at this time, but treated the design as merely an intellectual pursuit. In the mid-1850s, however, Babbage returned to the analytical engine and simplified it so that it might be built within his own means. Although this period showed remarkable technological innovation, and a test piece using diecast components was nearing completion at the time of his death in 1871, the brilliance of the earlier years was missing.

Bibliography

1987. Bromley, A. G. "The Evolution of Babbage's Calculating Engines," *Annals of the History of Computing*, **9**, 113–138.

1990. Bromley, A. G. "Difference and Analytical Engines," in *Computing Before Computers*, (ed. W. Aspray). Ames, IA: Iowa State University Press.

1998. Collier, B., MacLachlan, J. H., and Gingerich, O. *Charles Babbage and the Engine of Perfection*. Oxford: Oxford University Press.

Allan G. Bromley

ANIMATION

See COMPUTER ANIMATION.

APL

For an article on a related subject *see* FUNCTIONAL PROGRAMMING.

APL (A Programming Language) was first developed as a notation for teaching in a master's program in *Automatic Data Processing* introduced at Harvard University by Professor Howard Aiken (*q.v.*) in 1955, and was first implemented at IBM in 1965. Its early development, including references to the people involved, is documented in "The Design of APL" (Falkoff and Iverson, 1973) and "The Evolution of APL" (Falkoff and Iverson, 1978).

APL is distinguished by three main properties: (1) the use of functions that apply to arguments of a single type, called *arrays* of various ranks; (2) the use of *operators* (in the sense of Heaviside) that apply to functions to produce related functions (as do adverbs to verbs in natural languages); and (3) the systematic use of *ambivalent* functions, modeled on the use of the minus sign in mathematics for both subtraction ($x - y$) and negation ($-y$) (*see* OPERATOR OVERLOADING). As is characteristic of any functional language, when APL is given an expression that is not being assigned a variable, the value of the expression is printed. Thus:

```
ι6              ⍝ "iota 6" => print the
                ⍝ 1st 6 integers starting at 0
0 1 2 3 4 5

a ← 2 3 5 7     ⍝ a is (assigned) a rank-1
                ⍝ array (vector)

a + a
4 6 10 14

+/a             ⍝ / is an operator; +/ is the
                ⍝ sum-over function

17
a +.× a         ⍝ Outer product operator
 4  6 10 14     ⍝ +.× produces rank-2 (matrix)
 6  9 15 21
10 15 25 35
14 21 35 49
```

```
a * a           ⍝ Example of ambivalence
4 27 3125 823543  ⍝ (* => power for dyadic case)

*a              ⍝ Exponential (* a => exp(a))
7.38906 20.0855   ⍝ for monadic case)
 148.413 1096.63
```

A convenient (but overemphasized) mnemonic characteristic of APL is the use of nonstandard characters (such as ← for *assignment*, × for *times*, ⍝ for *comment*, and Greek letters for certain operators) made possible by use of a special typefont ball on the IBM Selectric typewriter (newly available at the time of the first implementation). The implementation developed into a general-purpose programming language widely available on time-sharing systems within IBM. Dialects of the language (notably APLSV and APL2 developed within IBM) are documented in the 1991 entries in the bibliography. Commercially available dialects were developed in many other companies, beginning in 1969 with *SHARP APL* (I.P. Sharp Associates) and continuing with *APL*PLUS* (Scientific Time Sharing), *Dyalog APL* (Dyadic Systems), and many others. Most comply with (and extend) the ISO standard adopted in 1985. The language J (Iverson, 1991) is a major new implementation that simplifies and extends the original design.

As befits a general-purpose language, and as attested in the proceedings of the almost-yearly international conferences devoted to it since 1969, the uses of APL have been widely varied. Special interest groups have formed in many countries, and APL journals have been established, notably *APL Quote Quad* (Association for Computing Machinery—*q.v.*) and *Vector* (British Computer Society—*q.v.*).

Notable developments since the 1985 adoption of the ISO standard include the following (not common to all dialects):

(a) An *enclose* function that produces a scalar (rank 0) encoding of any array.

(b) Extension of the domain of operators to include user-defined functions (assumed in the original language, but not provided in early implementations).

(c) User-defined operators.

(d) Portability of systems between machines (based on implementation in C).

(e) Portability of APL application programs between systems.

(f) Complex numbers in the domains of all relevant functions.

(g) Implementations under Windows, supporting OLE and other facilities.

(h) Because of the use of operators, APL systems almost qualify as *functional* languages.

The addition of a few facilities make some of the newer APL dialects fully functional languages that support *tacit* definitions, definitions in which no explicit mention is made of the arguments of the function being defined. Some examples from the language J, invented by the author and Roger Hui, follow. J uses the ASCII character set.

`=.`	is used for both assignment and "is defined as"
`NB.`	introduces a comment
`^@`	is the exponential operator
`-:`	takes half of whatever follows
`i.`	is the APL iota function

Thus

```
   i.6
0 1 2 3 4 5

   mean=. +/ % #          NB. Define mean to be sum
                          divided by number of items

   mean 2 3 4 5
3.5

   f=.  ^@-:              NB. Exponential atop
                          half (e to one-half x)

   f 0 1 2 3 4
1 1.64872 2.71828 4.48169 7.38906

   ]c=. f t. i.6          NB. First six Taylor
                          coefficients for e^x/2
1 0.5 0.125 0.02083333 0.002604167
   0.0002604167

   c p. 0 1 2 3 4         NB. Polynomial evaluation
                          using Taylor approximation
1 1.6487 2.71667 4.46172 7.26667
```

Bibliography

1973. Falkoff, A. D., and Iverson, K. E. "The Design of APL," *IBM Journal of Research and Development*, **17**, 4 (July).

1978. Falkoff, A. D., and Iverson, K. E. "The Evolution of APL," *ACM Sigplan Notices*, **13** (August).

1991. Falkoff, A .D., "The IBM Family of APL Systems," *IBM Systems Journal*, **30**, 4.

1991. Brown, J. A., and Crowder, H. P. "APL2: Getting Started," *IBM Systems Journal*, **30**, 4.

1991. Iverson, K E., "A Personal View of APL," *IBM Systems Journal*, **30**, 4.

1999. ACM SIG-APL. http://www.acm.org/sigapl/. Contains many references to the language J.

Kenneth E. Iverson

APPLE COMPUTER, INC.

For articles on related subjects *see* DIGITAL COMPUTERS, HISTORY OF; ENTREPRENEURS; and PERSONAL COMPUTING.

Apple's Beginnings

Twenty years after it was founded, Apple is no longer the major power it once was in personal computing. Apple was the first mainstream vendor of personal computers and is still an important player, setting the pace for ease of use and graphical interfaces, but Apple has become a niche player. The company was born out of the desire of two spirited innovators, Steve Wozniak and Steve Jobs (Fig. 1), who wanted to bring computing power to ordinary people.

With the microprocessor, the semiconductor industry had provided the compact, inexpensive electronic brain needed to build a personal-sized computer. But it was individual computer enthusiasts, not the established mainframe (*q.v.*) and minicomputer (*q.v.*) companies which took the next steps. Fascinated with the computers they designed and programmed by day, many young engineers longed to have their own computers on which to work and play at night. They avidly read the handful of available hobbyist magazines, formed clubs, and swapped ideas.

Stephen G. Wozniak was a regular attendee of the Homebrew Computer Club that began meeting in 1975 in Menlo Park, CA, at the northern edge of what was already called Silicon Valley. Wozniak had become enthralled with computers in high school and had dropped out of the engineering program at the University of California, Berkeley, to work for Hewlett-Packard, a manufacturer of calculators and minicomputers. It was at a Homebrew meeting that Wozniak heard about the first personal computers that were being offered as mail-order kits.

By mid-1976, Wozniak, 26, had written a Basic (*q.v.*) programming language interpreter for a new microprocessor from MOS Technology, the 6502, and designed a computer to run it. Wozniak proudly passed

Figure 1. Apple co-founders Steve Wozniak (left) and Steve Jobs with the original motherboard of the Apple I (courtesy of Apple Computer, Inc.).

out photocopies of his design to Homebrew friends and helped them build their own machines from the plans.

Steven P. Jobs, age 21 in 1976, shared Wozniak's passion for computers. The two had collaborated on several electronics projects, including creating the video game Breakout for Atari, Inc., where Jobs worked. Convinced of the marketability of Wozniak's design, Jobs persuaded his friend to sell the Apple I kits to other hobbyists.

They sold Jobs's Volkswagen van and Wozniak's programmable calculator to raise enough money to get started. Jobs then landed an order for 50 Apple I computers from one of the first computer retail stores in the country, and, on the strength of that order, the two young men secured credit at an electronic parts house. In the garage of Jobs's parents' home in Cupertino, CA, Apple Computer went into business.

"I had wanted a computer my whole life—that was the big thing in my life," Wozniak remembers. "All of a sudden I realized that microprocessors were cheap enough to let me build one myself. Steve [Jobs] went a little further. Steve saw it as a product that you could actually deliver and sell, and someone else could use."

Like all early personal computers, the Apple I was designed for experts who could put it together and write their own programs. But Jobs had a vision for Apple Computer that went far beyond the hobbyist market. He sought advice on realizing his goals from successful industry figures, such as Nolan Bushnell, founder of Atari; Don Valentine, a venture capitalist; Regis McKenna, who owned a rising Silicon Valley advertising and public relations agency; and A. C. "Mike" Markkula, who, at age 33, had retired from a lucrative marketing career at Intel.

Wozniak began designing a second computer that would be technically far superior to the Apple I, incorporating a keyboard, power supply, and the ability to generate color graphics, and to use the Basic programming language. Convinced that this product—the Apple II—would spark demand for personal computers beyond the hobbyist market, Mike Markkula wrote a business plan for the young company and then invested in it. He officially joined Apple when it incorporated in January 1977, and has since served in various executive positions, including president. Apple blossomed during that first year. It introduced the Apple II (Fig. 2) to rave reviews at the first West Coast Computer Faire. Markkula signed up dealers across the country to sell the Apple II. Regis McKenna's agency helped establish an immediate presence for Apple with an eye-catching rainbow logo, ads placed in national consumer publications, and a public relations campaign that leveraged Apple's "American dream" beginnings. An infusion of $3 million in venture capital gave Apple an enormous

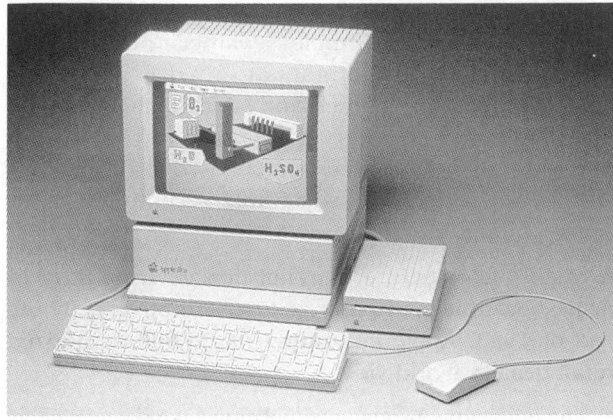

Figure 2. The popular Apple IIGS computer—the last of the Apple II line—which launched Apple computer in 1977 (courtesy of Apple Computer, Inc.).

advantage over many of its struggling competitors. Apple finished its first fiscal year with $774,000 in sales and a $42,000 profit.

An Industry Grows Up

During the next four years, the personal computer industry exploded into the consciousness of everyday lives—in the USA and elsewhere. Large, well-established manufacturers of mainframe computers, office systems, and telecommunications products, such as IBM (*q.v.*), Digital Equipment Corporation (*q.v.*) and AT&T, recognized the opportunity for personal computers and entered the market with zeal. By the end of 1982, more than 100 companies were manufacturing PCs, including Atari, Commodore, Tandy, and a host of start-ups. The boom was kindled by an avalanche of software programs that turned computers into special-purpose tools: for typing and rearranging text, analyzing financial data, sorting and filing information, and thousands of other uses never imagined by the computers' creators.

Apple contributed key products that catalyzed the development of software for the Apple II, including the Disk II floppy disk drive and disk operating system, and several programming languages and aids. As a result, landmark programs, including VisiCalc (*see* SPREADSHEET), Personal Filing System, and other business-oriented applications, were developed first for the Apple II. The benefit of these software packages cannot be underestimated: of the 130,000 Apple II computers sold by September 1980, an estimated 25,000 were purchased specifically for their ability to run VisiCalc.

Apple also secured early dominance in the closely linked education and consumer markets by continually improving its Apple II line with the Apple II Plus in

1979, the Apple IIe in 1983, and the Apple IIc in 1984. Beginning in 1979, Apple awarded hundreds of thousands of dollars in grants to schools and individuals for the development of educational software. The large software library that ensued is a key reason that more than 50% of computers used in US primary and secondary schools were until recently, at least, Apple computers.

A huge infrastructure of retail dealers sprang up to deliver personal computer products to buyers. By the end of 1982, Apple had more than 3,000 authorized retail dealers worldwide.

Even with enormous competition, Apple revenues continued to grow at unprecedented rates, reaching $583.1 million for fiscal 1982, the company's fifth year of operation. The company's initial public stock offering—in December 1980—was one of the largest in Wall Street's history, raising approximately $100 million. In 1983, Apple entered the Fortune 500 and gained additional Wall Street renown by recruiting Pepsi-Cola's president John Sculley as its new chief executive.

However, Apple was not immune to difficulties. Driven by the prospect of IBM and other deep-pocketed firms entering the personal computer industry, Apple raced to produce a third computer designed especially for business users. It began shipping the ill-fated Apple III in late 1980 before the system could be fully tested and without some promised features. The Apple III never recovered from its stumbling start and was eventually discontinued.

IBM's personal computer, introduced in August 1981, stirred up a frenzy in the industry, as software and accessory developers rushed to create products compatible with it. Development for the Apple II and Apple III, though still strong, dwindled by comparison. Awareness of personal computers grew and was symbolized by *Time* magazine's naming the computer as its 1982 "Man of the Year." Scores of companies were vying for market share.

In early 1983, Apple launched its fourth computer, the Lisa. It was a radical change for Apple and the entire personal computer industry, because of its "user-friendly" graphical user interface (GUI), much of it based on technology first created by computer scientists at the Xerox Palo Alto Research Center (PARC) in California. Jobs and others at Apple were convinced that complex and cryptic software was confining the use of personal computers to people who were willing to become experts—just as the earliest microcomputer kits had been useful only to hobbyists. Apple invested $100 million to develop software based on a user-friendly graphical interface so that the Lisa could offer software that was simple and easy to understand.

The news media gave the Lisa a rapturous reception, as did Wall Street. Apple stock, which had traded as low as $10 in 1982, rose to $63 a share. But the Lisa's noisy debut masked grave difficulties. The computer was slow, and users couldn't swap information among programs. There was no network capability. Lisa failed in the marketplace, but it paved the way for the similar but smaller Macintosh. The Macintosh user interface, introduced in January 1984, included icons, windows, pull-down menus, and a mouse (*q.v.*), and set new standards for ease of use. Later, the coupling of the Macintosh and the Apple LaserWriter printer became the catalyst for a new application for personal computers—desktop publishing (*q.v.*).

The year 1985 was an extremely difficult one for Apple. Founder Steve Wozniak resigned from the company that February to start a new video electronics business, feeling that Apple was becoming too corporate. Macintosh and Apple II sales fell dramatically. Apple eliminated 1,200 jobs, sharply cut operating costs, and closed three factories. The company sustained its first quarterly loss.

The biggest blow—especially psychologically—came in September 1985 when the innovative founder Steve Jobs quit Apple, forced out by John Sculley, whom he had hired only two years before. The painful chasm between Jobs and Sculley, once close business partners, demoralized many Apple employees and had many in the industry wondering if the innovative spark that Jobs had ignited would be snuffed out by marketeer Sculley.

However, sales did pick up in 1986 as some businesses bought Macintoshes, spurred by introduction of the faster and more powerful Macintosh Plus (Fig. 3), enhancements to the Apple II, dozens of software and accessory products from Apple and third-party developers, and the new desktop publishing applications.

Meanwhile, claiming innovation at Apple was dead, Jobs launched a rival company, NeXT, Inc., to make high-powered workstations (*q.v.*) for universities and businesses.

From 1987 through 1991, Apple continued to introduce new versions of the Macintosh that made it faster, more powerful, and more able to network with computers based on the MS-DOS operating system. While Apple remained dominant in the education market, by 1991 its share of the business market was just slightly more than 10%, with low-priced clones proving to be extremely tough competition.

After years of pursuing a strategy of high gross margins, Apple realized it would remain a niche player, especially in the business market, unless it lowered its prices and expanded its market share. This decision

Figure 3. The Macintosh Plus—one of the earliest Macintosh computers (courtesy of Apple Computer, Inc.).

required several company reorganizations, and executive management hirings and firings that included the dramatic exit of technology visionary Jean-Louis Gassee, president of Apple Products, who had stepped into the void left by Jobs as the company's technological leader. Gassee quit Apple in March 1990 when he and Sculley failed to agree on product development direction.

In October 1990, Apple instituted an aggressive strategy to gain share in all segments of the market with the introduction of lower-priced Macintosh systems—The Macintosh Classic, the Macintosh LC, and the Macintosh IIsi and lower-priced laser printers. As a result, Apple's market share began to increase despite an overall industry downturn. The downturn, which continued into 1991, and overspending inside Apple led to the company's second massive layoff in a decade when, again, 1,200 people lost their jobs.

In May 1991, Apple began delivery of System 7, a new version of its proprietary operating system intended to make the system even easier to use and more powerful.

The Alliance

In October 1991, Apple Computer reached an agreement that startled and confused both customers and employees, by pairing Apple with its arch rival, IBM. In an alliance called Taligent, the companies planned to create new technologies, especially cross-platform operating systems, that both companies believed crucial to their futures. Both companies invested dollars, staff, and intellectual property in the hope of competing with tough competitors like Microsoft (*q.v.*). But cultural differences and technological difficulties got in the way, and Taligent became an IBM subsidiary in December 1995.

Other parts of the IBM-Apple partnership survived. They agreed to create, with the help of Motorola, Inc., a new family of Reduced Instruction Set Computing (RISC—*q.v.*) microprocessors optimized for personal computers and entry-level workstations. Derived from IBM's single-chip implementation of its POWER RISC architecture, the PowerPC chips are made by Motorola and IBM for both Apple Macintosh and IBM computers and successfully marketed by both. They form the basis for the current Apple product line.

Two years after introducing the "luggable" 15-pound Macintosh Portable, Apple in October 1991 finally caught up with the rest of the portable makers (*see* PORTABLE COMPUTERS) by introducing its PowerBook laptop line. (That has been followed in the late 1990s with Apple's current G3 portable, considered a formidable high-end machine, but Apple now needed a low-end strategy.)

By the end of fiscal 1991, Apple reported net sales of $6.3 billion, a 14% increase over fiscal 1990. Apple started fiscal 1992 (in October 1991) by announcing more CPU products than in any previous year in its history. Apple appeared to have survived the personal computer industry's second major downturn and positioned itself with new products and new alliances to capture higher market share during the personal computer industry's second decade.

In 1992, Apple entered the personal digital assistant (PDA) business with its Newton handheld computer. Based on the ARM RISC chip, the device permitted data entry by handwriting recognition and offered note taking, address book, and calendar functions. Ambitious communications plans and the hopes of a Newton software industry (it used a different operating system than the Macintosh) surrounded its flashy announcement, but the machine's technology was premature and faulty, especially its initial handwriting recognizer. It was lampooned in the popular press and featured in the *Doonesbury* cartoon strip. After a number of attempts to upgrade and rescue the product (and the growth of a sizable base of niche users and applications, particularly in education and mobile markets like real estate, the military, and nursing), the product was discontinued in 1998. This followed the lateral movement of the product into a separate company, Newton, Inc. in 1997.

A child of the Newton was the Apple eMate300, a 1996 attempt to develop a rugged and inexpensive portable for the school market. Cleverly designed and appealing to use, it died with the Newton in 1998. Perhaps the planned low-cost mobile will embody some of its clever design elements.

In June 1993, John Sculley moved up to Chairman. He was succeeded, as Chairman and CEO, by Michael

Spindler. Soon, Sculley would move on, following his vision in other parts of the information industry.

1994 was the year of the PowerPC chip, when Apple brought out its first PowerMacs, based on the IBM RISC chip. Sales were brisk. PowerMac sales buoyed Apple's market share so that, in the third quarter, Apple was reported to be Number One in overall PC sales in the USA, with over 13% market share. It would be the last good news for quite some time.

1995 announcements had an Internet (*q.v.*) focus, including an Apple Internet Server for the World Wide Web (*q.v.*). It was natural that Apple, whose graphic arts customers were building the Web, would notice early and try to play a role. eWorld, a revisiting of Apple's earlier AppleLink online community, went Internet, too. New PowerBooks, PowerMacs, and Newtons were announced, as well as a new version of the Newton operating system. But sales were not holding up and faith in Michael Spindler was running out.

In early 1996, Dr. Gilbert Amelio from National Semiconductor succeeded Spindler as CEO and President of Apple. In this period several very important activities occurred with long-term importance. Apple was the first major vendor to support Linux, both with activities at the Open Software Foundation (OSF—*see* FREEWARE AND SHAREWARE) and also with the announcement of a product that September.

Amelio needed to find a new operating system for Apple and in choosing to acquire NeXT (Steve Jobs's company), he probably caused his own undoing. Not only did he find himself presiding over a debacle with valuable employees fleeing, market share melting, and attempts to integrate the NeXT OS floundering, the beloved and strongly charismatic founder, Jobs, was in position to take his place. In spite of a series of strong strategy statements in early 1997 on the Internet and a new operating system, nothing went right for Amelio and he resigned in July 1997.

This was followed by a restructuring of the company under a new board of directors, including Bill Campbell, now CEO of Intuit (and formerly Vice President of Sales and Marketing at Apple), Larry Ellison (CEO of Oracle and a friend of Jobs), and Jobs himself. OS 8 was shipped and in a show of Apple's enduring strength, 1.2 million copies were purchased in the first two weeks.

In August of 1997, Steve Jobs made a dramatic appearance at MacWorld and announced that he had struck an important alliance with Microsoft. Microsoft would provide a next-generation version of Macintosh Office, allegedly better than that on the Windows platform, and guarantee future versions. It would also make

a $150 million investment in Apple. In turn, Apple would use the Microsoft Internet Explorer browser on the Macintosh and cross-license patents, in part to settle prior litigation. In spite of many groans over deals with "the enemy," it was a brilliant strategy and has served Apple well, getting it both cash and required software, as well as convincing others to write for the platform.

A few months later Jobs agreed to become interim CEO of Apple, a position he held until January 2000 when he agreed to drop the "interim". Apple then acquired Power Computing (an Apple clone manufacturer) for $100 million, bringing to an end the competition of the clones and the hope that Apple might succeed, through licensing, to build a broader market.

In 1998 Apple brought the G3 desktops, servers, and PowerBooks to the market, based on the powerful new PowerPC G3 chip. This provided processor speeds of up to 400 MHz, with a built-in ATI RAGE 128 graphics card. A unique design lets the computer flip open for easy access. All G3s include the IEEE standard FireWire bus for connecting digital cameras and other high-speed devices. This was followed later in the year with the iMac, focused on the consumer market. With its bright color and friendly style, and its emphasis on consumer marketing messages, it reminded the industry of Jobs's earlier triumph with the Macintosh. In early 1999 he announced iMacs in other more brilliant colors as well as the cheery news that more than 800,000 had been sold in only five months. The iBook that followed, a G3-powered notebook computer with a unique clamshell design, is also proving very popular

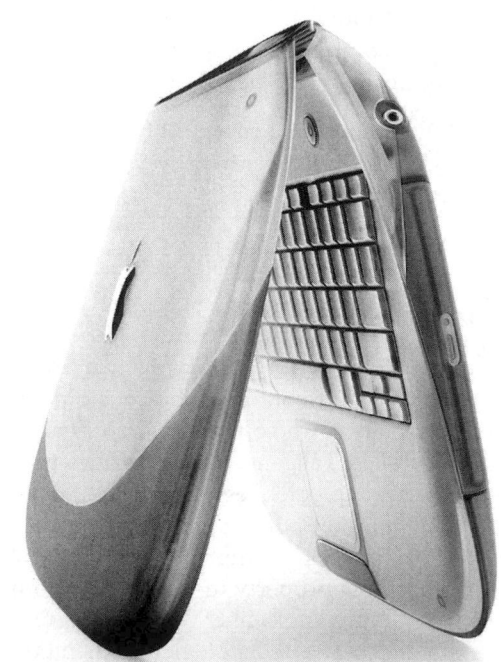

Figure 4. The iBook (courtesy of the Apple Picture Library).

(*see* Fig. 4). The OS X Server (with the long-promised integration of NeXT and Macintosh technologies) was also announced, as well as hints of a low-cost mobile product for the consumer and education markets soon.

Jobs has served Apple well, returning it to profitability and focusing it sharply on markets where loyalty to Apple may ensure its success. This has, however, made Apple more of a niche player, doing best in the graphics and education markets. Apple also continues to be an important consumer market player, but is no longer among the top volume players in the PC market. If Jobs pulls off the feat of making Apple successful in the 21st century, he will earn himself two places in the history books.

Bibliography

1993. Stross, R. E. *Steve Jobs and the Next Big Thing.* New York: Atheneum.
1995. Levy, S. *Insanely Great: The Life and Times of Macintosh, the Computer That Changed Everything.* London: Penguin.
1997. Carlton, J. *Apple: The Inside Story of Intrigue, Egomania and Business Blunders.* New York: HarperBusiness.
1999. Hall, T. "Poor Little Lisa," *Amer. Heritage of Invention and Technology,* **15**, *1* (Summer), 64.
1999. Linzmayer, O. W. *Apple Confidential: The Real Story of Apple Computer, Inc.* San Francisco: No Starch Press.

Mary A. C. Fallon, revised by Amy Wohl

APPLICATIONS PROGRAMMING

For articles on related subjects *see* COMPUTER SOFTWARE; PROGRAMMING LANGUAGES; and SYSTEMS PROGRAMMING.

Applications programs are programs written to solve specific problems, to produce specific reports, or to update specific files. The term is used in contradistinction to *systems programming*, which deals with the development of the software tools that the applications programmer uses. The programming languages that are used most often in applications programming are Fortran, Ada, and C (*q.v.*) for scientific applications and Cobol for data processing applications. Special Report Program Generator (RPG) languages are used on small data processing computers, and languages like Basic, Pascal, and APL were used extensively in early time-sharing systems.

The ultimate aim of all software is to make it possible for the applications programmer to perform well and to write programs that produce results and make effective and efficient use of the computing system. Applications programs make use of subroutine libraries and special packages such as sort–merge systems and data access and database management systems. Most well-designed operating systems provide the applications programmer with special tools for analyzing and debugging programs.

There are very large applications systems such as airline reservations systems and online banking and merchandising systems in which many considerations of systems programming and of applications programming are intermixed. Increasingly, such applications are programmed in an object-oriented language such as C^{++} (*q.v.*) or Java (*q.v.*) .

Saul Rosen

APPLICATIVE PROGRAMMING

See FUNCTIONAL PROGRAMMING.

APPROXIMATION THEORY

For articles on related subjects *see* CHEBYSHEV APPROXIMATION; LEAST-SQUARES APPROXIMATION; NUMERICAL ANALYSIS; and SPLINE.

Approximation theory concerns the following problem: Given a function $f(x)$ defined for x in a prescribed set X, a family of functions G, and a metric $d(f, g)$ (a mathematical prescription for measuring the distance between two functions), determine a function $g(x)$ in G that is "close" to $f(x)$ for x in X. For computer applications, $f(x)$ is typically a continuous function of one real variable, X is a real interval, G is a family of polynomials or of rational functions (ratios of polynomials), or of piecewise polynomials (splines), and the metric is either a least-squares metric

$$d_2(f, g, w) = \int_x [f(x) - g(x)]^2 w(x)\, dx,$$

or the Chebyshev metric

$$d_\infty(f, g, w) = \max_x |[f(x) - g(x)] w(x)|$$

where $w(x)$ is a weight function. For the Chebyshev metric, the weight is usually either $w(x) = 1$ or $w(x) = 1/f(x)$, where $f(x)$ is assumed not to vanish for x in X. This latter weighting is most useful when $f(x)$ varies considerably in magnitude across the interval X. Basic theorems examine the existence, uniqueness, and characterization of $g(x)$, sometimes in very abstract settings. In this article we shall concentrate on polynomials as the most important approximating family, and on the Chebyshev metric, which is more important than the least-squares metric in the generation of approximations to functions to be used on a computer.

Let $f(x)$ be defined and continuous over a finite real interval X. The theoretical justification for using the

Chebyshev metric (with $w(x) = 1$) is the Weierstrass approximation theorem, which asserts the existence of real polynomials that are arbitrarily close to $f(x)$ over the entire interval X. These polynomials are often obtained by appropriately truncating an infinite power series expansion of the function,

$$f(x) = \sum_{k=0}^{\infty} a_k x^k,$$

provided the series converges to $f(x)$ over X, i.e. provided that for any fixed value of x in X and any $\varepsilon > 0$, there is an integer N such that all partial sums

$$s_n(x) = \sum_{k=0}^{n} a_k x^k \qquad n > N$$

differ from $f(x)$ by less than ε. Such expansions are unique whenever they exist.

Some of the more important methods for generating series expansions are based upon the analytic properties of the function. Let $f(x)$ be continuous and have continuous derivatives of all orders at some point x_0 in X. Then the *Taylor series* expansion of $f(x)$ about x_0 is given by

$$f(x) = \sum_{k=0}^{\infty} a_k (x - x_0)^k$$

where

$$a_k = f^{(k)}(x_0)/k! = \frac{1}{k!} \left. \frac{d^k f(x)}{dx^k} \right|_{x=x_0}.$$

Since this expansion is based upon a detailed knowledge of the function at x_0, the Taylor polynomials $g_n(x)$ of degree n, obtained by truncating the series, approximate $f(x)$ well for small $|x - x_0|$, but the error $f(x) - g_n(x)$ typically grows monotonically in magnitude with increasing $|x - x_0|$. Frequently $\max_x |f(x) - g_n(x)|$ occurs at one of the boundaries of X. For example, Fig. 1 shows the error associated with the fourth-degree Taylor polynomial approximation of e^x over $[-1, 1]$, where the Taylor series is

$$e^x = 1 + x + \frac{x^2}{2} + \frac{x^3}{6} + \frac{x^4}{24} + \cdots + \frac{x^n}{n!} + \cdots. \quad (1)$$

If the Taylor series expansion for $f(x)$ exists, then the *Padé table* for $f(x)$ is the array of rational approximations

$$R_{mn}(x) = \frac{p_0 + p_1 x + \cdots + p_m x^m}{1 + q_1 x + \cdots + q_n x^n},$$

characterized by the property that the power series expansion of $R_{mn}(x)$ is identical to the Taylor series expansion through terms in x^{m+n}. The entries $R_{m0}(x)$ are the Taylor polynomials, and the entries $R_{00}(x)$, $R_{01}(x)$, $R_{11}(x), \ldots$ along and just above the main diagonal are the successive convergents of the Stieltjes continued fraction, or *S-fraction*, expansion of $f(x)$:

$$f(x) = \cfrac{a_0}{1 - \cfrac{a_1 x}{1 - a_2 x}}$$

Padé approximants $R_{mn}(x)$ are often better approximations to $f(x)$ than are the Taylor polynomials of degree $m + n$. All elements of the Padé table agree with $f(x)$ exactly at the point of expansion, but $f(x) - R_{mn}(x)$ tends to grow as x moves away from that point. As an example, the Padé approximation $R_{22}(x)$ to e^x can be obtained by solving the linear equations which result from requiring that the difference between the ratio of two quadratic polynomials and the first five terms of the expansion (1) has no numerator terms of degree less than 5. The result is

$$R_{22}(x) = \frac{12 + 6x + x^2}{12 - 6x + x^2}$$

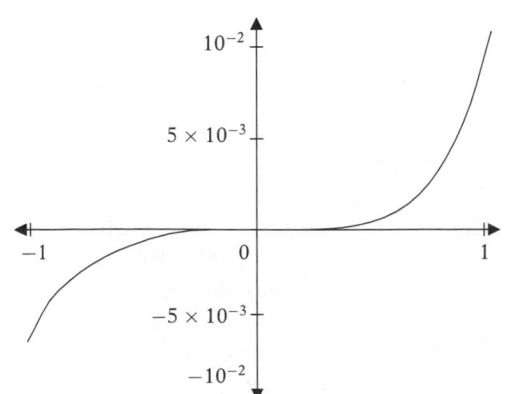

Figure 1. Error $e^x - g_4(x)$ where

$$g_4(x) = 1 + x + \frac{x^2}{2!} + \frac{x^3}{3!} + \frac{x^4}{4!}$$

for approximation over $[-1, 1]$ by fourth-degree Taylor polynomial.

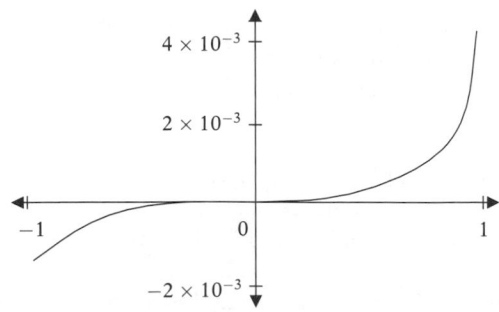

Figure 2. Error $e^x - R_{22}(x)$ for approximation over $[-1, 1]$ by Padé table element.

Fig. 2 shows the error $e^x - R_{22}(x)$ over the interval $[-1, 1]$. Note that the maximum error is less than half of that associated with the fourth-degree Taylor polynomial.

By sacrificing accuracy in the neighborhood of the point of expansion, it is possible to distribute the error over the interval of approximation and to obtain better approximations to $f(x)$ over X in the sense of the Chebyshev metric. The rational Chebyshev, or *minimax*, approximation to $f(x)$ of degree (m, n) is that rational function $R_{mn}^*(x)$, which minimizes $d_\infty(f, R_{mn}, w)$. Basic theorems assert that such an $R_{mn}^*(x)$ exists, is unique, and is characterized by the error $[f(x) - R_{mn}^*(x)]w(x)$ achieving its maximum magnitude with alternating sign a prescribed number of times as x moves across the interval X. The determination of $R_{mn}^*(x)$ is not easy, but the characterization theorem leads to algorithms, such as the Remes algorithm, for computing approximations close to $R_{mn}^*(x)$.

The Chebyshev polynomials are defined as

$$T_n(x) = \cos(n \cos^{-1} x), \qquad -1 \le x \le 1,$$

so that $T_0(x) = 1$ and $T_1(x) = x$. It can be shown that

$$T_{n+1}(x) = 2x T_n(x) - T_{n-1}(x).$$

These polynomials are instrumental in the generation of near-minimax polynomial approximations. If $f(x)$ is continuous and sufficiently smooth, then

$$f(x) = \frac{1}{2} a_0 T_0(x) + \sum_{k=1}^{\infty} a_k T_k(x), \qquad -1 \le x \le 1,$$

where

$$a_k = \frac{2}{\pi} \int_1^1 \frac{f(x) T_k(x)}{(1 - x^2)^{1/2}} \, dx,$$

is the Chebyshev polynomial expansion of $f(x)$. The partial sums of this expansion are the best polynomial approximations to $f(x)$ for the metric $d_2[f, g, 1/(1 - x^2)^{1/2}]$ and are very close to the minimax polynomial approximation to $f(x)$ in most cases. As an example, the coefficients in the Chebyshev series expansion for e^x are $a_k = 2 I_k(1)$, where the I_k are modified Bessel functions. Truncation of this series after five terms leads to the approximation

$$g(x) = 1.000045 + 0.997308x + 0.499197x^2$$
$$+ 0.177347x^3 + 0.043794x^4$$

for the interval $[-1, 1]$. The maximum error associated with this approximation is only about one-twentieth of that associated with the fourth-degree Taylor polynomial (*see* Fig. 3).

Legendre, Jacobi, Hermite, Laguerre, and Gegenbauer polynomials are other important families of polyno-

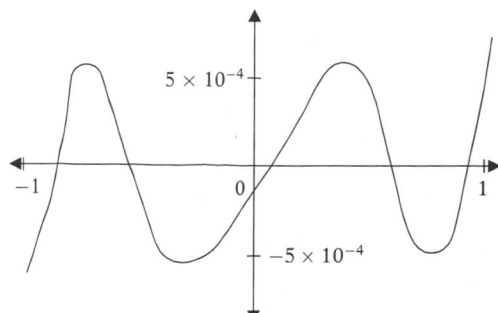

Figure 3. Error $e^x - \sum_{k=0}^{4} a_k T_k(x)$ for approximation over $[-1, 1]$ by truncated Chebyshev series.

mials similarly associated with particular choices of weights and intervals in least-squares approximation. Since power series expansions are unique, the expansion of $f(x)$ in polynomials from any of these families can be formally obtained by replacing each x^k in the power series by its exact representation in polynomials of the family and then collecting terms. This "rearrangement" of the power series may alter the convergence of the series so that the new series may converge for a larger (or smaller) interval than the original series.

Lanczos's telescoping, or *economizing*, process is similar to this rearrangement process. Starting from a truncated power series, such as a Taylor polynomial, over the interval $[-1, 1]$, the degree of the polynomial is lowered by successively replacing the highest-order power of x, x^n, by the polynomial

$$P_{n-1}(x) = x^n - \frac{1}{2^{n-1}} T_n(x),$$

which is the minimax approximation to x^n by a polynomial of degree less than n. Note that $P_{n-1}(x)$ is a polynomial of degree $n - 1$ because the leading coefficient of $T_n(x)$ is 2^{n-1} which follows from the recurrence for the Chebyshev polynomials given earlier. The approximation error introduced at each step tends to distribute the cumulative error over the interval of approximation so that the polynomials in the resulting sequence tend to be better approximations to $f(x)$ than the corresponding truncations of the original power series, but they are not as good as those obtained by truncating the Chebyshev polynomial expansion. For example, the approximation

$$g(x) = 1 + \frac{383}{384} x + \frac{1}{2} x^2 + \frac{17}{96} x^3 + \frac{1}{24} x^4$$

to e^x is obtained by truncating the Taylor series after six terms and replacing x^5 by $P_4(x) = (20x^3 - 5x)/16$. The corresponding maximum error over $[-1, 1]$ is more than four times that of the corresponding truncated Chebyshev series, but only one-fifth that of the fourth-degree Taylor polynomial (*see* Fig. 4).

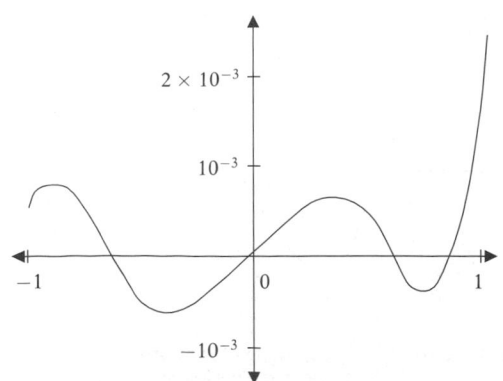

Figure 4. Error $e^x - g(x)$ for approximation over $[-1, 1]$ by fifth-degree Taylor polynomial telescoped to fourth degree.

An extensive theory of approximation exists for functions of a complex variable and for multivariate functions (functions of two or more real variables). The theory relies heavily upon convergent or asymptotic power series and continued fraction expansions. The Taylor series and the Padé table extend to the complex case directly. While the theory of minimax approximation generalizes to these functions, the generalizations are not very useful (e.g. uniqueness is lost in the multivariate case) and reliable algorithms for generating the approximations do not exist. Except for certain elementary functions, direct approximations to complex or multivariate functions are not often used in computer applications although multivariate approximations are used increasingly for studying neural networks (*q.v.*). Instead, indirect evaluation methods based upon recurrence relations, differential equations, etc., are usually used for these kinds of functions.

Bibliography

1967. Meinardus, G. *Approximation of Functions: Theory and Numerical Methods* (translated by L. Schumaker). New York: Springer-Verlag.
1970. Cheney, E. W. *Introduction to Approximation Theory*. New York: McGraw-Hill.
1982. Powell, M. J. D. *Approximation Theory and Methods*. Cambridge: Cambridge University Press.
1990. Mason, J. C., and Cox, M. G. *Algorithms for Approximation 2*. London: Chapman & Hall.

William J. Cody

ARCHITECTURE, COMPUTER

See COMPUTER ARCHITECTURE.

ARGUMENT

For articles on related subjects *see* DATA TYPE; GLOBAL AND LOCAL VARIABLES; MACRO; OPERAND; PARAMETER PASSING; and SUBPROGRAM.

In close analogy to mathematics, where an argument of a function is the value of a variable used to evaluate the function, an *argument* in computing is a value supplied to a procedure, a function, or a macro which is required in order to evaluate the procedure, function, or macro. Another term sometimes used instead of argument is *parameter*.

Two different kinds of argument need to be distinguished: *dummy* or *formal* arguments, and *actual* or *calling* arguments. A dummy argument is an argument used in the definition of a procedure, function, or macro; an actual argument is that which is substituted when the procedure, function, or macro is invoked. For example, Fig. 1 displays a Pascal procedure to compute the solution of a quadratic equation.

$$ax^2 + bx + c = 0$$

The variables a, b, c, mode, x1, and x2 in Fig. 1 are all dummy arguments. If this procedure were to be used to compute the roots of

$$10.7X^2 + (R1 + 6.23)X + S^2 = 0 \tag{1}$$

where $R1$ and S are variables appearing elsewhere in the program, the statement

```
QUAD(y, z, j, 10.7, R1 + 6.23, S * S)
```

might be given. Each argument in this statement is an actual argument, i.e. the argument that will be associated with the dummy argument in the subroutine definition. Thus, when QUAD is executed in response to the call above:

- The values used for a, b, and c will be, respectively, 10.7, R1 + 6.23, and S * S, with the latter two being evaluated using the current calling program values for R1 and S.

- The variable j in the calling program will be set equal to the value of mode in the procedure, where this value indicates whether the quadratic equation has 0 roots, 1 root, two real roots, or two complex roots.

- The main program variables y and z will contain the results of the solution of Eq. (1) after execution of QUAD.

The dummy arguments that are preceded by **var** in Fig. 1, x1 x2 and mode, are *call-by-reference* arguments in that only the storage locations but not the values of the calling arguments are transferred to the procedure. In this way, the values given to x1, x2, and mode in the procedure are returned directly to the calling program. On the other hand, a, b, and c are call-by-value arguments in that their values are

```
procedure QUAD (var x1,x2: real; var mode: integer; a,b,c: real)
    var disc: real;                                        {discriminant}
    begin
    if a = 0 then                                 {Check for leading 0 coefficient}
        if b = 0 then                                        {a = b = 0?}
            mode := 0                                {indicates no root possible}
        else begin
            x1 := -c/b;
            mode := 1                               {indicates a single real root}
        end
    else begin                                     {a ≠ 0 so there are two roots}
        disc := b * b - 4.0 * a * c;
        if disc < 0 then begin                              {complex roots}
            x1 := -b/(2.0 * a);                             {real part: x1}
            x2 := sqrt(-disc)/(2.0 * a);             {imaginary part: x2}
            mode := 2                               {indicates complex roots}
        end
        else begin                                          {real roots}
            if b < 0 then                   {x1 is root of larger magnitude}
                x1 := (-b + sqrt(disc))/(2.0 * a)
            else
                x1 := (-b - sqrt(disc))/(2.0 * a);
            if x1 = 0 then
                x2 := 0
            else
                x2 := c / (x1 * a);
            mode := 3                               {indicates two real roots}
        end
    end
end
```

Figure 1. A quadratic-equation solver. Computation of real roots computes root of larger magnitude (*x*1) first to avoid ever taking difference of two nearly equal quantities.

transmitted to the procedure, since there is no need to send new values of these arguments back to the calling program.

In procedural languages, formal arguments are always required to be identifiers, but, as the example above indicates, actual arguments may be identifiers, numbers, or arithmetic expressions. Most languages allow great generality in the form of the actual arguments, although there may be requirements that the calling arguments have the same *type* as the formal arguments (i.e. a real calling argument if the formal argument denotes a real variable).

Subprogram arguments may also be classified as *input* or *output* arguments, with the former denoting arguments provided to the subprogram and the latter the arguments that convey results back to the main program. In the example given in Fig. 1, a, b, and c are input arguments and mode, x1, and x2 are output arguments. Sometimes an argument may be both an input and output argument; for example, when a procedure to compute the next prime number receives as input the variable P denoting the current prime number and returns the value of the next prime number to P. Sometimes the arguments of a subprogram may be *implicit*; i.e. they are not stated explicitly in the statement heading the subprogram. This happens, for example, when a procedure in a subblock uses variables global to that block.

Calling arguments need not, as above, always be ordered as are the dummy arguments. In languages (like Ada), which allow *keyword* arguments, a procedure like QUAD could be called as

```
QUAD(a=>10.7, b=>R1+6.23, c=>S*S, mode=>j,
    x1=>y, x2=>z).
```

In addition, arguments need not have numeric types like those above. For example, an argument may have type *record* or *set*, or may be a *list* (as in Lisp) or even another procedure. In languages such as ML, Haskell, or Prolog, a formal argument may be a *pattern* that the procedure call compares with the structure of the actual argument, matching corresponding parts of formal and actual arguments.

Anthony Ralston

ARITHMETIC-LOGIC UNIT (ALU)

For articles on related subjects *see* ADDER; ARITHMETIC, COMPUTER; BUS; CENTRAL PROCESSING UNIT; COMPLEMENT; INSTRUCTION SET; NUMBERS AND NUMBER SYSTEMS; OPERAND; REGISTER; and SHIFTING.

The *arithmetic-logic unit* (ALU) is that functional part of the digital computer that carries out arithmetic and logic operations on machine words that represent operands. It is usually a part of the central processing unit (CPU—*q.v.*). In many CPUs, separate units exist for arithmetic operations (the arithmetic unit, AU) and for logic operations (the logic unit, LU).

Many processors contain more than one AU. For example, a separate Index AU is frequently employed to perform addition or subtraction operations on address parts of instructions for the purpose of indexing, boundary tests for memory protection, etc. High-performance processors employ separate AUs for different classes of operands and/or algorithms; for example, the Pentium II contains an integer AU and a floating-point AU.

A complete discussion of an ALU must describe its three fundamental attributes:

1. Operands and results

2. Functional organization

3. Algorithms

Operands and Results

Two kinds of ALU organization can be distinguished with respect to the length of machine words. In machines with *fixed word length*, all words consist of the same number of bits. In machines with *variable word length*, one byte (or sometimes just one bit) is the shortest machine word. Longer machine words consist of some integral number of bytes.

The operands and results of the ALU are machine words of two kinds: *arithmetic words*, which represent numerical values in digital form, and *logic words*, which represent arbitrary sets of digitally encoded symbols.

Arithmetic words consist of digit vectors (strings of digits). Conventional radix r number representations allow r values for one digit: $0, 1, \ldots, r - 1$. Practical design considerations have limited the choice of radices to the values $2, 4, 8, 10,$ and 16. The value of every digit is represented by a set of bits. Radices $2, 4, 8,$ and 16 employ binary numbers having lengths of $1, 2, 3,$ and 4 bits, respectively, to represent the values of one digit (*see* NUMBERS AND NUMBER SYSTEMS). Radix-10 digit values are represented by four bits. Most commonly used is the four-bit BCD (binary-coded decimal) encoding (*see* CODES).

Two methods have been employed to represent negative numbers. In the sign-and-magnitude form, a separate *sign bit* is attached to the string of digits to represent the + and − signs. (Usually, 0 represents the + sign, and 1 represents the − sign.) In the true-and-complement form, the negative value $-x$ is represented as the complement (*q.v.*) with respect to A of the value x; i.e.

$$-x \text{ is represented by } A - x$$

The value of A used in ALUs is either $A = r^{n+1}$ or $A = r^{n+1} - 1$, when x is represented by n digits in the sign-and-magnitude form (*see* COMPLEMENT).

The choice of $A = r^{n+1}$ is called *range* (or *radix*) complement; in binary arithmetic ($r = 2$) it is usually called *twos complement*. It is the prevalent choice in contemporary ALUs. The choice of $A = r^{n+1} - 1$ is called *digit* (or *diminished radix*) complement, usually called *ones complement* for $r = 2$. It has the disadvantages of an "end-around carry" in modulo A addition and two zero representations ($+0$ and -0), and is little used in contemporary ALUs.

The use of complements to represent negative values makes it possible to replace the subtraction algorithm in an ALU by a complementation followed by an addition modulo A; therefore a subtractor is not needed in the ALU.

Other important properties of operands and results are:

1. Location of the radix point: fractions or integers.

2. Use of multiple-precision representations.

3. Use of floating-point forms (*see* ARITHMETIC, COMPUTER).

4. Explicit designation of the number of significant digits (*q.v.*) in a representation.

5. Encoding in error-detecting (or error-correcting) "*An*" or residue codes.

Nonconventional number representations are used in special-purpose processors as a means to increase the speed of arithmetic. They are *residue* number systems (Koren, 1993) and *signed-digit* number systems (Avižienis, 1990) with carry-free addition and subtraction (*see* ADDER).

Logic words that serve as operands represent alphanumeric information and are subject only to logic algorithms that are applied to individual bits of the operands. These algorithms are (1) negation for one operand, and (2) all or some of the 16 two-variable logic operations for corresponding bits of two operands (*see* BOOLEAN ALGEBRA).

Functional Organization of an ALU

An ALU consists of three types of functional parts: storage registers, operations logic, and sequencing logic, as shown in Fig. 1. The inputs and outputs of the ALU are connected to other functional units of the CPU, such as the cache memory and the program execution control unit. At one time a *bus* (*q.v.*) was used as the means of connection, but in microprocessors today the ALU and other CPU elements are all on a single chip.

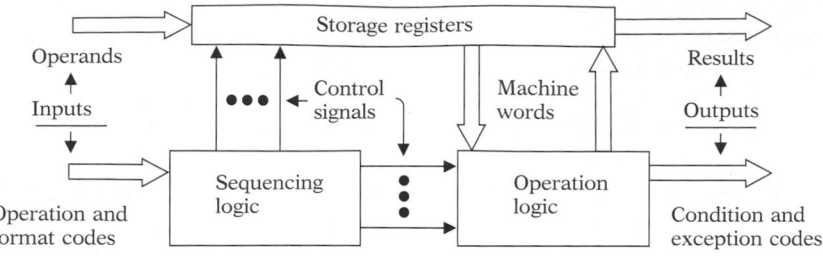

Figure 1. Functions of an ALU.

The input information received by the ALU consists of operands, operation codes, and format codes. The operands are machine words that represent numeric or alphanumeric information. The operation code identifies one operation from the set of available arithmetic and logic operations, and also designates the location (within local storage—q.v.) of the operands and of the results. The designation of operands is omitted in ALUs with limited local storage; for example, an ADD operation code in a single-accumulator ALU always means the addition of the incoming operand to the operand in the accumulator register and storage of the sum in the accumulator. The format code is used when the ALU can operate on more than one type of operand; for example, the ADD operation can be specified for either fixed-point or floating-point operands. Often, the operation code and the format code are represented by a single set of bits.

The output information delivered by the ALU consists of results, *condition codes*, and *exception codes*. The results are machine words generated by the specified operations and stored in the local storage registers. The condition codes are bits or sets of bits that identify specific conditions associated with a result, such as that

the value of the result is positive, negative, zero; that the result consists of all zeros, all ones, etc. The exception codes indicate that the specified operation does not yield a representable result. Examples of exceptions are *overflow*, i.e. the value of the result exceeds the allowed range; attempted division by zero; excessive loss of precision in floating-point operations; and error caused by a logic fault. Exception codes usually set a flag bit in the machine status register.

Internally, the ALU is composed of storage registers, logic circuits that perform arithmetic and logic algorithms, and logic circuits that control the sequence of inter-register transfer operations within the ALU. The diagram of a simple ALU is shown in Fig. 2. The ALU contains four registers: the Operand register, OPR, the double-length Accumulator, ACC, composed of shift registers ACC1 and ACC2, and the multiplier-quotient shift register, MQR. Each register contains one machine word of n bits. In the classic von Neumann IAS (Institute for Advanced Studies) computer, the MQR also served as the ACC2 register.

The transfer of words into the ALU registers and from the registers via the operation circuits back to ALU

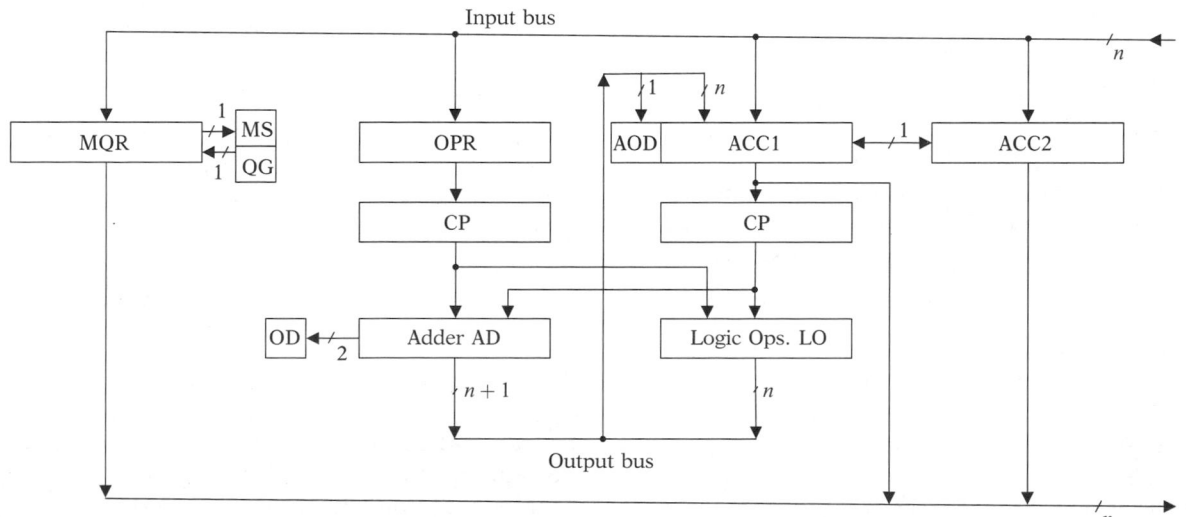

Figure 2. Organization of a fixed-point ALU.

registers or out of the ALU is controlled by the sequencing logic shown in Fig. 1. Each sequence corresponds to one of the algorithms provided within the ALU. The sequencing logic is implemented either in "hard wired" form, using a state machine and decoding circuits, or by means of a microprogrammed control unit (*see* MICROPROGRAMMING). The sequence of control signals is initiated by the receipt of the operation and format codes in the ALU.

ALU Algorithms

The operation circuits consist of the complementers (CP), the adder (AD), and the logic operator circuits (LO). The adder forms the modulo A sum of the *addend* in OPR and the *augend* in ACC1 and returns the sum to ACC1. When the length of the sum exceeds the standard word length, the overflow detection (OD) circuit issues an overflow exception code, and the excess digit of the sum is placed into an overflow digit position (AOD), which is located at the left end of the ACC1. Subtraction is implemented as complementation of the *subtrahend* in OPR, followed by an addition modulo A to the *minuend* in ACC1.

Left-shift and right-shift operations are performed on the words in the shift registers ACC1, ACC2, and MQR. A single-shift operation displaces every digit in the register to the adjacent position on the left or on the right. Shifts are specified either for one ACC register or for both ACC registers simultaneously, with the rightmost position of ACC1 adjoining the leftmost position of ACC2. There are three classes of shift:

1. *Circular shifts (rotations).* The rightmost and the leftmost positions of a register are treated as adjacent during the shift.

2. *Logical shifts.* Digits are discarded from end positions and zeros are inserted; e.g. during a single right shift, the rightmost digit is lost and the leftmost position is filled in with zero.

3. *Arithmetic shifts.* The purpose of an arithmetic shift is to multiply (shift left) or to divide (shift right) the operand by the radix r. For complement forms that represent negative numbers, the leftmost "sign" bit must be treated with special care (*see* SHIFTING).

Multiplication and division are carried out as a sequence of additions or subtractions and arithmetic shifts. The MQR register serves as the multiplier or quotient register for these operations. In *multiplication*, the multiplicand $x = (x_{n-1}, \ldots, x_1, x_0)$ is placed into the OPR register and the multiplier $y = (y_{n-1}, \ldots, y_1, y_0)$ into the MQR register of Fig. 2, while ACC is cleared to zero. The least significant digit y_0 of the multiplier is sensed by the multiplier sensing (MS) circuit, and x is added y_0 times to the contents of ACC. Then ACC1, ACC2, and MQR registers are arithmetically shifted one position to the right, and the next multiplier digit, y_1, is sensed by the MS circuit. After all n digits of y have been sensed, the double-length product xy is located in ACC1 and ACC2 registers. A *roundoff* operation is needed to reduce the product to single-word length. The algorithm for *integers* x, y is described by the arithmetic recurrence relation:

$$p(j+1) = \frac{1}{r} \times [p(j) + (r^n \times x) \times y_j]$$

for $j = 0, 1, \ldots, n-1$; and radix $r \geq 2$, where $p(0) = 0$, $p(j)$ is the jth partial product, and $p(n)$ is the (final) product xy. For *fractions* x, y the term r^n is deleted in the recurrence.

To perform *division*, the *dividend* y is placed into the ACC1. If the dividend is of double length ($2n$ digits), the ACC2 register receives its less significant half. The *divisor* x is placed into the OPR register, and division is carried out as a sequence of trial subtractions (done as complementation of x, followed by addition modulo A) and left arithmetic shifts. Digits of the *quotient* $q = (q_{n-1}, \ldots, q_1, q_0)$ are generated one at a time in the quotient generation (QG) circuit and inserted at the right end of the MQR register after each shift, beginning with the most significant quotient digit, q_{n-1}. After n steps, the quotient q is located in the MQR register and the *remainder* $z(n)$ in the ACC1 register. The algorithm for *integers* x, y is described by the arithmetic recurrence expression:

$$z(j+1) = r \times z(j) - (r^n \times x) \times q_{n-1-j}$$

for $j = 0, 1, \ldots, n-1$; and radix $r = 2$, where $z(0) = y$ is the dividend, x is the divisor, q is the quotient, $z(j)$ is the jth partial remainder, and $z(n)$ is the (final) remainder, which satisfies the condition $0 \leq |z(n)| < |x|$, and sign $z(n) = $ sign $z(0)$. The results q and $z(n)$ satisfy the condition: $y = q \times x + z(n)$.

An initial *overflow test* is made to see if $|z(0)| < x \times r^n$; if it is true, then the quotient q can be represented by n digits; otherwise q will need more than n digits. The quotient digits q_{n-1-j} are chosen so that $z(j+1)$ is as small as possible without changing its sign to differ from the sign of $z(j)$. For fractions x, y the term r^n is deleted in the recurrence and the overflow test.

The logic operator LO circuits perform the specified logic operation on pairs of bits in corresponding positions a_i of ACC1 and x_i of OPR. The bits of the result are returned to ACC1. The usual set of operations includes NOT (one bit: $\bar{a}_i$ or $\bar{x}_i$), AND ($a_i \wedge x_i$), OR ($a_i \vee x_1$), EXCLUSIVE-OR ($a_i \oplus x_i$), EQUIVALENCE

$(a_i \equiv x_i)$, NAND $(\bar{a}_i \vee \bar{x}_i)$, and NOR $(\bar{a}_i \wedge \bar{x}_1)$; sometimes all 16 two-variable logic operations are provided.

An ALU may be bit-serial, byte-serial, or parallel, depending on how many digits are processed simultaneously in the adder (or logic operator) circuits of Fig. 2. In a serial ALU, the adder adds one pair of digits at once; in a byte-serial ALU, it adds a pair of bytes (consisting of two or more digits); in a parallel ALU, it adds two full machine words. Machines with variable word length have byte-serial ALUs, since the words consist of a varying number of bytes. The time required to complete one addition in the adder circuits is a basic time unit of ALU operation.

The speed of execution of the algorithms in a parallel ALU may be increased by the use of various techniques (Koren, 1993). Addition speed is increased by use of *carry-completion sensing, carry-lookahead,* or *conditional-sum adders.* Multiplication is accelerated by multiplier recoding and by the use of multiple-operand carry-save adders (*see* ADDER). Division employs redundant quotient recoding techniques with approximate estimates (Ercegovac and Lang, 1994) or convergence, which uses fast multiplication to generate the quotient (Koren, 1993). The technique of *pipelining* (*q.v.*) has also been employed to increase the effective throughput of an ALU.

The use of more storage registers within the ALU increases the speed of computing by reducing the number of memory accesses. Therefore, 8, 16, or more ALU registers are often used instead of the four registers shown in Fig. 2; each register may perform the function of ACC, OPR, MQR, or index register (*q.v.*) and hence qualify as *general registers* (*q.v.*). In some architectures, several ALU registers may be used to hold a *stack* (*q.v.*) of ALU operands and results.

Bibliography

1990. Avižienis, A. "Signed-digit Number Representations for Fast Parallel Arithmetic," in *Computer Arithmetic*, Vol. II (ed. E. E. Swartzlander Jr), 54–65. Los Alamitos, CA: IEEE Computer Society Press. (Reprinted from *IRE Trans. El. Comp.*, **EC-10** (1961), 389–400.)

1993. Koren, I. *Computer Arithmetic Algorithms.* Upper Saddle River, NJ: Prentice Hall.

1994. Ercegovac, M., and Lang, T. *Division and Square Root.* Boston: Kluwer Academic Publishers.

Algirdas Avižienis

ARITHMETIC, COMPUTER

For articles on related subjects *see* BYTE ORDERING; COMPLEMENT; INTERVAL ARITHMETIC; NUMBERS AND NUMBER SYSTEMS; PRECISION; ROUNDOFF ERROR; SHIFTING; and SIGNIFICANT DIGIT.

The earliest electronic computers were developed in the 1940s to provide arithmetic engines capable of solving a variety of problems, many of them military. Computers, as general symbol manipulators, now solve other intriguing problems, but numerical calculations are still of vital importance in computer applications. How computers store numbers and perform arithmetic and how *computer arithmetic* differs from ordinary hand computation are topics that should be understood by everyone who uses computers.

Computer Storage of Numbers

A memory *cell* is the smallest unit of addressable computer memory. Older word-oriented computers typically used large cell sizes, such as 60 or 64 bits. Newer byte, or character, addressable computers address memory in small units called *bytes.* (In this article, a byte is assumed to be an 8-bit cell. In the hexadecimal number system, a byte is represented as two 4-bit hexadecimal digits, or *hexits.*) In word-oriented computers, a number is stored in one word, while in byte-oriented computers, a number is stored in multiple bytes (2, 4, 8, and 16 bytes have been commonly used). "Single-precision" numbers typically occupy 32 bits of storage (4 bytes) and "double-precision" numbers occupy 64 bits (8 bytes).

A given number may be stored in one of two formats: *fixed-point* or *floating-point.* Fig. 1 illustrates the storage of two numbers, 0.15625 and 57.8125, as fixed-point numbers in a 32-bit format. Throughout this article, numbers in the text will be cited in decimal but their stored representations will be shown in binary. For convenience, only positive numbers will be used in examples. Storage of negative numbers can be either in absolute value and sign form or in complement form (*see* COMPLEMENT).

Two points are worth noting about the numbers in Fig. 1:

1. The left-hand bit (S or bit 0) represents the sign of the number; 0 is used for positive numbers and 1 for negative numbers.

2. The normal binary point (radix point) is assumed to be at the left end of the number, just to the right of the sign bit. The programmer, however, may choose a different or *implicit binary point,* so long as computation is done consistently with respect to the chosen alternative position. A computer calculating with fixed-point numbers assumes that the binary point is always in the same, fixed location— hence the name "fixed-point." In this article and in many computers until recently, this assumption is as shown in Fig. 1, but most computers now

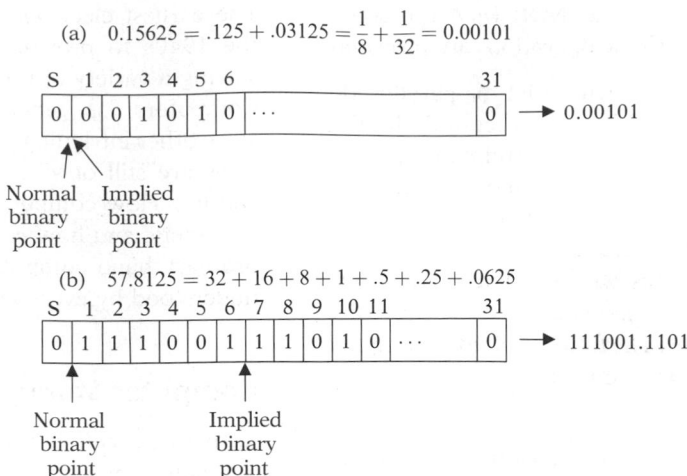

(a) $0.15625 = .125 + .03125 = \frac{1}{8} + \frac{1}{32} = 0.00101$

(b) $57.8125 = 32 + 16 + 8 + 1 + .5 + .25 + .0625$

Figure 1. Fixed-point numbers

assume the binary point to be at the right-hand end of the number. When the latter is done, all bit patterns normally represent whole numbers, or *integers*. Integer arithmetic is discussed later.

Hardware for storing and manipulating numbers in fixed-point form was the only kind available in early computers. The arithmetic of fixed-point numbers created several major problems.

1. How could numbers with magnitudes of 1 or greater be handled? Such numbers can be stored as fixed-point numbers, but when using these numbers in computations, programmers must be careful to keep track of the implicit locations of the radix point.

2. More significant problems occur when two numbers have implicit radix points in different positions. How could these be added? Fig. 1b uses an implied radix point to show how 57.8125 could be stored. As an example of these two problems, consider adding the numbers in Figs 1a and 1b. Before bit-by-bit addition can be done, one of the numbers must be shifted relative to the other.

The term *scaling* is used for the twin activities of shifting the numbers and choosing the location of the implicit binary point. Numbers are usually scaled before they are stored or used in computations. Scaling is difficult and tedious for all but the simplest calculations. Scaling problems led to the introduction of floating-point hardware capabilities, which are now used for virtually all numerical calculations on computers.

Numbers stored in "floating-point" format closely resemble "scientific notation." A number in scientific notation is represented as $f \times R^E$, where f is a fraction

in the range $0 \leq f < 1$, R is the radix (usually 10), and E is the signed integral power (exponent) of the radix. Thus, the number 57.8125 in Fig. 1b would be represented as 0.578125×10^2, where 0.578125 is the fraction, 10 is the radix, and 2 is the exponent. Using floating-point terminology, the fraction 0.578125 is called the *mantissa*. The term *floating-point* is used because the radix point is not fixed, but can move, or "float," depending on the value of the exponent. Floating-point implementations provide solutions to scaling problems and also facilitate computations with a larger range of numbers than can be handled effectively with fixed-point systems.

To store a single-precision floating-point number in a byte-addressable memory, separate portions of the four bytes must be assigned to the sign bit, the exponent, and the fraction. A floating-point format for N bits is labeled (X, Y), where

1. $X + Y + 1 = N$

2. X bits are allocated to the exponent

3. Y bits are allocated to the mantissa.

For any fixed number of bits N, increasing X increases the range of representable numbers but decreases their precision while decreasing X produces a greater precision but smaller numeric range. Fig. 2 displays 32-bit binary floating-point formats for 0.15625 and 57.8125. Fig. 2a shows 0.15625 in (7,24) format, and Fig. 2b shows 57.8125 in (8,23) format.

Thus the floating point numbers are a finite subset of the real numbers which lie between **MINREAL** (the negative number of largest magnitude representable on a particular machine) and **MAXREAL** (the positive number of largest magnitude). The points within those limits are not evenly distributed and, given knowledge

(a) .15625 in (7, 24) Format

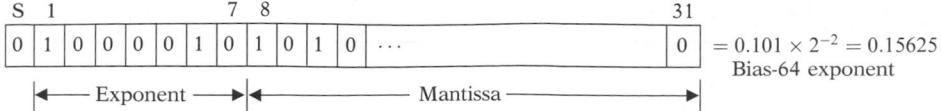

$= 0.101 \times 2^{-2} = 0.15625$
Bias-64 exponent

(b) 57.8125 in (8, 23) Format

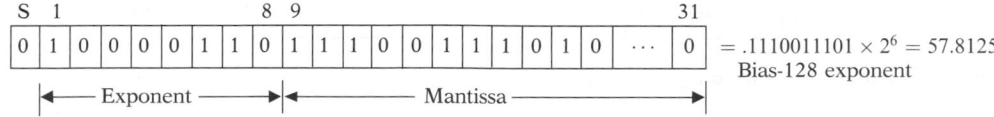

$= .1110011101 \times 2^6 = 57.8125$
Bias-128 exponent

Figure 2. Floating-point numbers.

of any valid point x, it is not trivially easy to compute the next higher valid number. But some C, C++, and Fortran libraries contain a function called `nextafter(x)` that does so.

The following two comments pertain to Fig. 2.

1. As with fixed-point numbers, the binary point of the mantissa is assumed to be in the same place, usually at the left end, but at least one older implementation (Burroughs) positioned the binary point at the right-hand end. The sign bit (S or bit 0) always represents the sign of the mantissa.

2. Special techniques are needed to represent exponents, which may be zero, positive, or negative. One technique is to let bit 1 denote the sign of the exponent, but, more commonly, "biased" exponents are used. The format in Fig. 2a uses "bias-64" to represent any signed exponent -64 to $+63$ by using unsigned numbers 0 to $2^7 - 1 = 127$. Thus 1000000 represents the exponent 0, 1000001 represents 1, 0111111 represents -1, and so forth. Fig. 2b uses "bias-128" and can represent any signed exponent from -128 to $+127$. For floating-point hardware to work correctly, the computer system's arithmetic logic unit (*q.v.*) must be able to interpret the biased exponents correctly. A biased exponent is called a *characteristic*. The advantage of using biased exponents placed to the left of the floating-point word is that a sequence of such numbers can be sorted as if they were integers. (On most computers, integer comparisons are significantly faster than floating-point comparisons.)

Floating-point mantissas are usually stored in a "normalized" form, which requires the most significant digit to be nonzero. Systems using binary formats often "imply" the most significant bit (since it is always 1), but do not store it, while systems using hexadecimal cannot imply a nonzero most significant

hexit, as it could be any of $1, 2, \ldots, F$. The apparent 24-bit precision of the mantissa on the IBM 360 and its successors degenerates to just 21 bits—the equivalent of six decimal digits—whenever a mantissa begins with hexadecimal 1 (binary 0001). In contrast, the apparent 23-bit precision of the mantissas on the DEC VAX actually provides 24-bit precision (about 7 decimal digits) through appendage to the implied 1 bit.

Most computers automatically create normalized numbers as the result of floating-point arithmetic operations and, in so doing, retain the maximum number of significant bits. Some computer systems allow the programmer to choose whether the result should be normalized. Advocates of leaving floating-point results unnormalized claim it gives better accuracy in retained results (see Fig. 10 for an example).

Double-precision floating-point numbers typically are stored in 64-bits; common formats include (7,56), (8,55), and (11,52). "Extended" implementations include 80-bit (15,64) and 128-bit (15,112) formats.

Fixed-Point Arithmetic

Fixed-point arithmetic is done essentially like ordinary binary arithmetic, except for the restriction that negative numbers are generally stored in some complement form. However, some aspects of fixed-point arithmetic need to be considered explicitly. In the following examples, we assume that fixed-point numbers are binary fractions of magnitude less than 1 and that the binary point is at the left.

Fixed-point addition and subtraction are subject to the exceptional condition known as *overflow*. Since not only the two addends but also the result in addition and subtraction must be less than 1 in magnitude, a result greater than 1 will not be correctly handled. To be precise, when adding positive numbers *overflow occurs when bit-1 has a carry-out*, as is shown

Figure 3. Overflow in fixed-point addition.

in Fig. 3. In some computers, this carry-out bit is discarded, while in others it replaces the sign bit, resulting in an artificial negative number. In any case, the result is incorrect, and most computer architectures maintain an overflow bit, which allows a programmer to test for overflow by using a *Branch-On-Overflow* instruction.

Overflow cannot occur in fixed-point multiplication, since the product of two factors less than 1 in magnitude must be less than 1. But multiplying two n-bit numbers produces a $2n$-bit product, which cannot be accommodated in an n-bit register. Normally, the least significant n-bits are placed in a second register. Fig. 4 shows such a multiplication, assuming a word length of 5 bits. Assembly language programmers can retain the bits in the second register, but normally only the rounded results are kept, as shown in Fig. 4.

Fixed-point division can result in overflow if the dividend has magnitude as great or greater than the divisor. A fixed-point divide overflow causes an exceptional condition (different from fixed-point addition overflow) that is usually testable by programmers.

The dividend in fixed-point division is usually double-length (or precision) and occupies two paired registers.

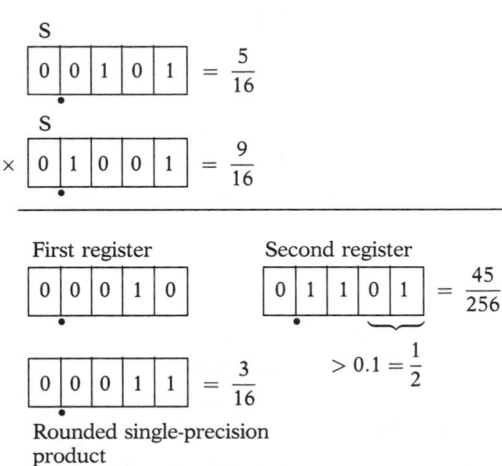

Figure 4. Fixed-point multiplication.

The single-precision quotient is commonly placed in one register and the remainder in another, as illustrated in Fig. 5.

Integer Calculations

In modern computers, fixed-point calculations are performed using integer quantities. The fixed-point

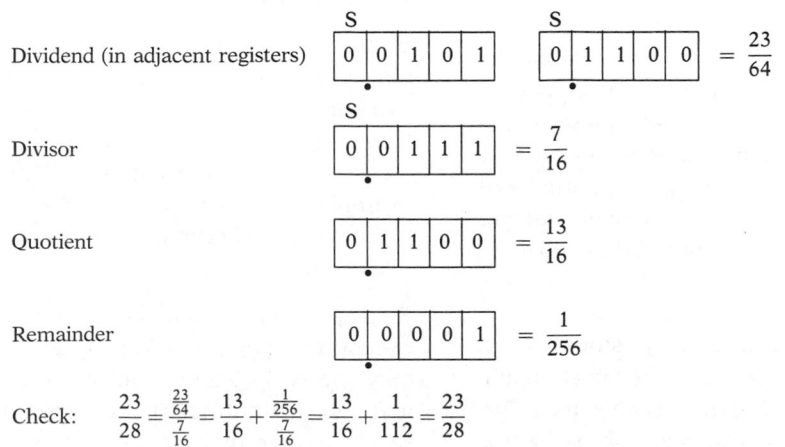

Figure 5. Fixed-point division.

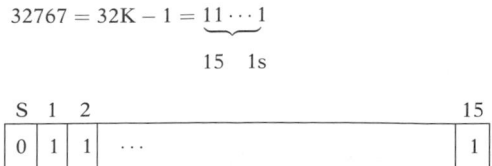

Figure 6. Representation of 32767 in 16-bit integer format.

format used to represent negative integers is usually 2s complement with 1s complement being much less common. Fig. 6 shows the integer representation of 32,767 in a 16-bit format.

Appropriate adjustments must be made to handle the "overflow" problem that occurs when a sum or product is larger than the specified number of bits allowed for integers. Some languages handle overflow by wrapping the overflow around without indicating an error. For example, using 16-bit 2s complement integers, the maximum expressible integer is 32,767, and overflows wrap around the value $2^{16} = 65,536$ (thus $32767 + 2 = -32767$ and $1024 \times 33 = -31744$).

Integer division causes remainders to be dropped. Fig. 7 illustrates what happens in our hypothetical four-bit-plus-sign computer in the evaluation of the Fortran statement K=14/5. Because the remainder is discarded, K evaluates to 2.

Floating-Point Arithmetic

To add or subtract two floating-point numbers, the exponents must be the same. If the rightmost mantissa digit of a floating-point number is 0, shifting the mantissa one digit to the right and increasing the exponent by one produces an equivalent floating-point number. The following algorithm for floating-point addition uses this shifting technique. Suppose A and B are to be added, producing C as a result. Let the exponent and fractional parts be denoted by E_a, E_b, and E_c; and F_a, F_b, and F_c, respectively.

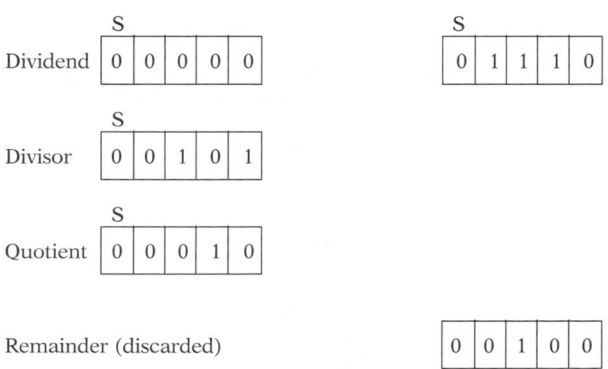

Figure 7. Integer division in Fortran.

Step 1. Set E_c = the larger of E_a and E_b. (Assume in what follows that $E_a \geq E_b$.)

Step 2. Align the exponents. Shift F_b to the right $E_a - E_b$ places (which causes F_a and F_b to have the same exponent, but may cause a loss of precision).

Step 3. Add the mantissas. Set $F_c = F_a + F_b$.

Step 4. Normalize. Shift F_c to make its most significant bit 1, and adjust E_c accordingly.

This four-step algorithm is illustrated in Fig. 8, assuming a hypothetical computer with a binary (5,10) floating-point format using bias-16 exponents.

In proceeding through the four steps, several points are noteworthy:

1. Step 3 of Fig. 8b results in overflow. No error results because the "overflow" bit is always retained and shifted right in Step 4. The calculation in Fig. 8a has no overflow, and normalization is not necessary in Step 4.

2. The computed result is accurate in Fig. 8b, but the computed result in Fig. 8a is 57.9375, while the theoretical result is 57.96875. The error is caused when F_b has to be right-shifted eight places, resulting in a loss of 1 bit of precision.

3. Many computers have instructions that allow programmers to choose unnormalized floating-point operations. Thus, Step 4 in our algorithm can be avoided using unnormalized instructions. Most procedural language processors use normalized instructions; unnormalized instructions are normally available only to assembly language programmers.

4. Floating-point subtraction, or addition of numbers with differing signs, may result in a normalization that requires a left shift of F_c. In some computing systems, the bits shifted right in Step 2 will be retained, and these will now be shifted left to avoid the loss of precision that would be caused if zeros were inserted on the right. Some computers also retain *guard bit(s)* that can be shifted left during normalization.

Overflow can occur in any operation where the magnitude of the result exceeds the floating-point capacity. No matter how many bits are allotted to floating-point operations, examples illustrating overflows can easily be constructed. Fig. 9 shows an example of an addition causing an overflow in our hypothetical (5,10) system. Such an overflow can be handled in three different ways: using the largest possible number, setting an indicator that the programmer can test, or,

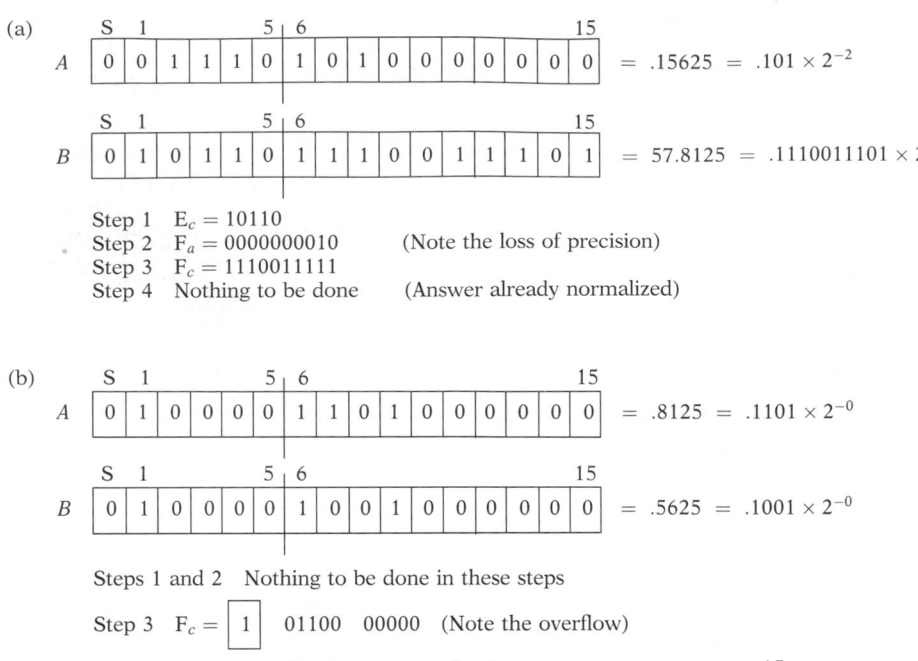

Figure 8. Floating-point addition.

finally, aborting the program with an appropriate error message.

Underflow results from an attempt to produce a non-zero result smaller in magnitude than the smallest possible positive floating-point number. The usual method of handling underflow is to generate a zero result, but sometimes an underflow indicator is also set, which the programmer can test. Fig. 9 shows an example of underflow.

Floating-point multiplication and division techniques do not require exponent alignment. Instead, the appropriate operation is performed on the mantissas, the result rounded, the exponents added (for multiplication) or subtracted (for division), and then the result normalized, if necessary. Examples are shown in Fig. 10.

Floating-Point Standards

Modern computers normally provide some hardware support (either machine instructions or math coprocessors) for floating-point arithmetic. At least 20 different

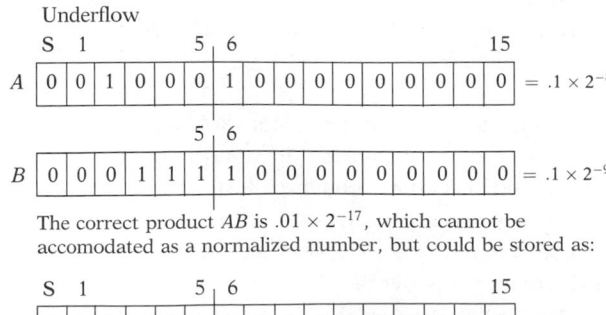

Figure 9. Floating-point overflow and underflow.

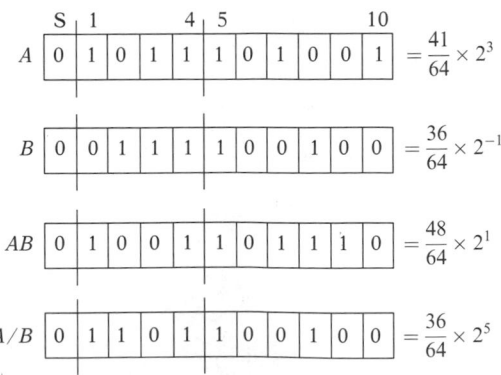

Figure 10. Floating-point multiplication and division.

Table 1. Floating-point formats.

Bits in:	IBM/370		DEC VAX			IEEE	
	S	D	S	D	H	S	D
Total bits	32	64	32	64	64	32	64
Mantissa	6 HX	14 HX	23 B	55 B	52 B	23 B	52 B
Exponent bits	7	7	8	8	11	8	11
Exponent bias	64	64	128	128	128	127	127
Radix	16	16	2	2	2	2	2
Hidden '1'	No	No	Yes	Yes	Yes	Yes	Yes
Maximum	16^{63}	16^{63}	2^{127}	2^{127}	2^{1023}	2^{127}	2^{1023}
number	10^{76}	10^{76}	10^{38}	10^{38}	10^{308}	10^{38}	10^{308}
Minimum	16^{-64}	16^{-64}	2^{-127}	2^{-127}	2^{-1023}	2^{-126}	2^{-1022}
number	10^{-77}	10^{-77}	10^{-38}	10^{-38}	10^{-308}	10^{-38}	10^{-308}
Precision	16^{-6}	16^{-14}	2^{-24}	2^{-56}	2^{-53}	2^{-24}	2^{-53}
	10^{-7}	10^{-17}	10^{-7}	10^{-17}	10^{-16}	10^{-7}	10^{-16}

Notes: S = single-precision, D = double-precision, H = second VAX 64-bit form, HX = hexadecimal digits, B = bits.

floating-point formats have been implemented, and different computer systems may produce slightly different calculated results from identical floating-point inputs.

In 1978, the Institute of Electrical and Electronics Engineers (IEEE) established a committee to develop a floating-point standard. Early work was spearheaded by W. Kahan, J. Coonen, and H. Stone (1979). Draft 8.0 was circulated (Cody, 1981), and the 754 Standard, with only minor changes from Draft 8.0, was published in 1985. The standard describes various conditions, including: Rounding Options, Invalid Operations, Overflow, Division by Zero, Underflow, and Inexact Result. It introduced extremal numbers called Infinities, DeNormal Numbers, and NaNs (not a number); reserved bit patterns for these cases; and discussed how these conditions could be handled effectively.

IBM and Digital Equipment Corporation (DEC) had floating-point hardware implementations before 1980 and thus, to preserve upward compatibility to newer products, did not rush to conform to the IEEE standard. The standard has benefited newer designers, as math coprocessors from Intel, Motorola, Sun, MIPS, and others now conform to the standard. DEC's latest product, the Alpha, is capable of either VAX or IEEE floating-point operations at the discretion of the programmer. The IBM/370, DEC VAX, and (the two shortest) IEEE floating-point formats are given in Table 1.

The IBM, Digital, and IEEE formats include "extended" capabilities of 128, 128, and 80 bits, respectively, but these are not shown or discussed here. Some comments, relating to the "single-precision" formats presented in Fig. 11, are as follows.

1. The IBM format uses 7-bit hexadecimal "bias-64" exponents and 6-hexit (24-bit) mantissas, thus increasing the exponent range over the binary

```
The Fortran Program        The C Program
                           main()
   X = 78931.15            { float x = 78931.15; float inc = 0.01; int i;
   DO 20 I = 1,3             for (1; i<=3; i++)
     X = X + 0.01             { x = x + inc;
     PRINT *,X                  printf("%7.2f \n", x);
20 CONTINUE                   }
   STOP                     return 0;
   END                    }

The results

         IBM 360      VAX/VMX      Intel Pentium PC
         Fortran      Fortran      C
         78931.12     78931.16     78931.16
         78931.12     78931.16     78931.17
         78931.12     78931.17     78931.17
```

Figure 11. Different floating-point results.

formats. Shifting for alignment and normalization occurs 4 bits at a time, which often causes different computed results from those generated using pure binary formats.

2. The VAX and IEEE formats use 8-bit binary biased exponents. Digital uses "bias-128" exponents, while the IEEE specification, in order to reserve both the exponents $0...0$ and $1...1$ for exceptional conditions, uses "bias-127" exponents.

3. The IBM "*true zero*" consists of "a 0 sign, a $0...0$ exponent, and a $0...0$ mantissa" (a whole word of 0s). The *VAX zero* is "a 0 sign, an exponent of $0...0$, and any mantissa." The IEEE bias-127 format represents *zero* as "any sign, an exponent of $0...0$, and a mantissa of $0...0$." The IEEE thus has two zeros, while the VAX has 2^{23} different zeros. Special rules were needed in the latter two cases, because otherwise the implicit 1 bit would imply that "all 0 bits" represents a tiny number but not literally zero.

4. The IEEE defines "denormalized" numbers (*denormals*) as "any sign, an exponent of $0...0$, and a non-zero mantissa"; an "infinity" as "any sign, an exponent of $1...1$, and a mantissa of $0...0$"; and "Not a Number" or "NaN" as "any sign, an exponent of $1...1$, and a nonzero mantissa."

5. The combination of the implied leading digit, the implied binary point, and all the fraction bits is called the "significand." The range of significands, SN, for the three formats is: *IBM*: $1/16 = 0.0625 \leqslant \text{SN} < 1$; *VAX*: $1/2 = 0.5 \leqslant \text{SN} < 1$; and *IEEE*: $1.0 \leqslant \text{SN} < 2$. The latter two bounds reflect a difference in treatment of the implicit 1 bit: in the IEEE format, a mantissa f represents $1.f$, whereas on the VAX, f represents $.1f$—i.e. $1/2(1.f)$. This difference, plus the difference in bias, means that any given VAX floating-point bit pattern would have four times the value if interpreted under IEEE rules (which, of course, it should not be).

Fig. 11 contains a short program that uses the 32-bit, single-precision formats and that illustrates the output differences in computed numbers on different machines.

The problem on all three machines is that the 7-digit number 78931.15 is right on the edge of accurate representation in 32-bit floating-point format. Each decimal digit is equivalent to about 3.3 bits, so a mantissa of at least 23 bits is needed. But the IBM 360 hexadecimal normalization provides, in the worst case, only 21 bits of precision. On that machine, even the initial approximation to 78931.15 fell short by .03; its

next higher floating-point number would be greater than 78931.15. Relative to 78931.12, .01 is essentially zero, so nothing happens when ".01" is added three times. The VAX and the PC (which uses the IEEE standard) do much better because each uses a 24-bit mantissa.

Computer Arithmetic and Real Arithmetic

Four common arithmetic laws that apply to mathematical real numbers a, b, and c are:

1. Closure:

   Addition: $a + b$ is a real number.

   Multiplication: $a \times b$ is a real number.

2. Associative laws:

   Addition: $a + (b + c) = (a + b) + c$.

   Multiplication: $a \times (b \times c) = (a \times b) \times c$.

3. Distributive law:

   $a \times (b + c) = a \times b + a \times c$.

4. Cancellation Property:

   $a + b = a + c$ implies $b = c$.

For real numbers, these laws depend on two facts:

1. There are infinitely many reals.

2. Between any two reals is another real.

But the numbers called "real" by high-level languages provide only an abstraction to mathematical real numbers.

Because of the finiteness of floating-point numbers, the shifting required in additions, and underflow/overflow handling, *none of these laws is valid for all floating-point number combinations*. The failure of these laws for floating-point numbers is sometimes easily overcome, but often computed results differ dramatically from what is expected. A comprehensive treatment of floating-point numbers and their anomalies is found in Sterbenz (1974).

Despite increasing use of the IEEE Standard, finding better implementations of "real number" arithmetic on computers remains an active research area. The 32-bit Symmetric Level Index (SLI) method (Clenshaw *et al.*, 1989) significantly increases both the range and precision of expressible numbers and better handles closure and underflow/overflow problems. But SLI is approximately 10 times slower than floating-point arithmetic and thus has seldom been implemented.

Bibliography

1974. Sterbenz, P. H. *Floating Point Computation.* Upper Saddle River, NJ: Prentice Hall.

1979. Coonen, J., Kahan, W., Palmer, J., Pittman, T., and Stevenson, D. "A Proposed Standard for Floating-point Arithmetic," *ACM SIGNUM Newsletter*, **14**, *35*(October), 4–12.

1981. Cody, W. J. "Analysis of Proposals for the Floating-point Standard," *IEEE Computer*, **14**, *3* (March).

1981. Coonen, J. "Underflow and the Denormalized Numbers," *IEEE Computer*, **14**, *3* (March), 75–87.

1982. Waser, S., and Flynn, M. *Introduction to Arithmetic for Digital Systems Designers.* New York: Holt, Reinhart, and Winston.

1985. *Binary Floating-Point Arithmetic*, IEEE Standard 754, IEEE.

1989. Clenshaw, C., Olver, F., and Turner, P. "Level-index Arithmetic: An Introductory Survey," in *Numerical Analysis and Parallel Processing* (ed. P. Turner), LNM 1397. New York: Springer-Verlag.

1989. Levy, H. M., and Eckhouse, R. H., Jr. *Computer Programming and Architecture, The VAX*, 2nd Ed. Bedford, MA: Digital Press.

1991. Goldberg, D. "What Every Computer Scientist Should Know about Floating-point Arithmetic," *ACM Computing Surveys*, **23**, *1* (March), 5–48.

1991. Swartzlander, E. E., Jr. *Computer Arithmetic*, Vols. I and II. Los Alamitos, CA: IEEE Computer Society Press.

Thomas J. Scott

ART, COMPUTER

See COMPUTER ART.

ARTIFICIAL INTELLIGENCE (AI)

For articles on related subjects *see* ARTIFICIAL LIFE; AUTOMATED PLANNING; COGNITIVE SCIENCE; COMPUTER CHESS; COMPUTER GAMES; COMPUTER MUSIC; COMPUTER VISION; EXPERT SYSTEMS; GENETIC ALGORITHMS; HEURISTIC; KNOWLEDGE REPRESENTATION; MACHINE LEARNING; MACHINE TRANSLATION; MULTI-AGENT SYSTEMS; NATURAL LANGUAGE PROCESSING; NEURAL NETWORKS; NONMONOTONIC LOGIC; PATTERN RECOGNITION; PERCEPTRON; ROBOTICS; SEARCHING; SIMON, HERBERT A.; SPEECH RECOGNITION AND SYNTHESIS; THEOREM PROVING; TURING TEST; and TURING, ALAN M.

Introduction

Artificial Intelligence (AI) is a field of computer science and engineering concerned with the computational understanding of what is commonly called intelligent behavior, and with the creation of artifacts that exhibit such behavior. This definition may be examined more closely by considering the field from three points of view: computational psychology, computational philosophy, and machine intelligence.

COMPUTATIONAL PSYCHOLOGY

The goal of computational psychology is to understand human intelligent behavior by creating computer programs that behave in the same way that people do. For this goal it is important that the algorithm expressed by the program be the same algorithm that people actually use, and that the data structures used by the program be the same data structures used by the human mind. The program should do quickly what people do quickly, should do more slowly what people have difficulty doing, and should even tend to make mistakes where people tend to make mistakes. If the program were put into the same experimental situations that humans are subjected to, the program's results should be within the range of human variability.

COMPUTATIONAL PHILOSOPHY

The goal of computational philosophy is to form a computational understanding of human-level intelligent behavior, without being restricted to the algorithms and data structures that the human mind actually does (or conceivably might) use. By "computational understanding" is meant a model that is expressed as a procedure that is at least implementable (if not actually implemented) on a computer. By "human-level intelligent behavior" is meant behavior that, when engaged in by people, is commonly taken as being part of human intelligent cognitive behavior. It is acceptable, though not required, if the implemented model perform some tasks better than any person would. Bearing in mind Church's Thesis (*see* CHURCH, ALONZO), this goal might be reworded as asking the question, "Is intelligence a computable function?"

In the AI areas of computer vision (*q.v.*) and robotics (*q.v.*), computational philosophy is sometimes replaced by computational natural philosophy (science). For example, some computer vision researchers are interested in the computational optics question of how the information contained in light waves reflected from an object can be used to reconstruct the object. Notice that this is a different question from the computational psychology question of how the human visual system uses light waves falling on the retina to identify objects in the world, or even the computational philosophy question of how any intelligent entity could use light waves falling on a two-dimensional retinal grid to discriminate one three-dimensional object-in-the-world from a set of other possible objects.

MACHINE INTELLIGENCE

The goal of machine intelligence is to push outwards the frontier of what we know how to program on computers, especially in the direction of tasks that, although we don't know how to program them, people can perform. This goal led to one of the oldest definitions of AI: the attempt to program computers to do what, until recently, only people could do. Although this expresses the idea of pushing out the frontier, it is also perpetually self-defeating in that, as soon as a task is conquered, it no longer falls within the domain of AI. Thus, AI is left with only its failures; its successes become other areas of computer science. The most famous example is the area of symbolic calculus (*see* COMPUTER ALGEBRA). When James Slagle wrote the SAINT program, it was the first program that could solve symbolic integration problems at the level of freshman calculus students, and was considered an AI project. Now that there are multiple systems on the market that can do much more than what SAINT did, most people do not consider these to be AI systems. The goal of machine intelligence differs from computational psychology and computational philosophy in being task-oriented rather than oriented toward the understanding of general intelligent behavior. A machine intelligence approach to a task is to use any technique that helps accomplish the task, even if the technique is not used by humans and would probably not be used by generally intelligent entities.

SUBSYMBOLIC AI

Computational psychology, computational philosophy, and machine intelligence are subareas of AI divided by their goals. Cutting across these goals, however, is a recent division of approach into "symbolic" AI and "subsymbolic" AI. The key assumption of symbolic AI is that knowledge is represented by structures of semantically meaningful symbols, each symbol representing some entity, be it abstract or concrete, that the intelligent system or agent is discussing, observing, reasoning about, or operating on. On the contrary, the key assumption of subsymbolic AI is that intelligent behavior can be attained without semantically meaningful symbols. Much of subsymbolic AI is included in the field of *soft computing*:

In contrast to the traditional, hard computing, soft computing is tolerant of imprecision, uncertainty and partial truth. The basic premises of soft computing are:

◆ imprecision and uncertainty are pervasive

◆ precision and certainty carry a cost

The guiding principle of soft computing is:

◆ exploit the tolerance for imprecision, uncertainty and partial truth to achieve tractability, robustness and low solution cost.

Soft computing is not a single methodology; rather, it is a partnership of methodologies. At this juncture, the principal constituents of soft computing (SC) are: fuzzy logic (FL—*q.v.*), neurocomputing (NC) (*see* NEURAL NETWORKS), and genetic algorithms (GA—*q.v.*). The principal contribution of FL is a methodology for approximate reasoning and, in particular, for computing with words; that of NC is curve fitting, learning and system identification; and that of GA is systematized random search and optimization (Zadeh, 1995).

HEURISTIC PROGRAMMING

Another way of distinguishing AI as a field is by noting the AI researcher's interest in *heuristics* (*q.v.*) rather than in *algorithms* (*q.v.*). Here I am taking a wide interpretation of a *heuristic* as any problem-solving procedure that fails to be an algorithm, or that has not been shown to be an algorithm, for any reason. An interesting view of the tasks that AI researchers consider to be their own may be gained by considering those ways in which a procedure may fail to qualify as an algorithm.

By common definition, an algorithm for a general problem P is an unambiguous procedure that, for every particular instance of P, terminates and produces the correct answer. The most common reasons that a heuristic H fails to be an algorithm are that it does not terminate for some instances of P, it has not been proved correct for all instances of P because of some problem with H, or it has not been proved correct for all instances of P because P is not well defined. Common examples of heuristic AI programs that do not terminate for all instances of the problem they have been designed for include searching (*q.v.*) and theorem-proving (*q.v.*) programs. Any search procedure will run forever if given an infinite search space that contains no solution state. Gödel's Incompleteness Theorem states that there are formal theories that contain true but unprovable propositions. In actual practice, AI programs for these problems stop after some prespecified time, space, or work bound has been reached. They can then report only that they were unable to find a solution even though—in any given case—a little more work *might* have produced an answer. An example of an AI heuristic that has not been proved correct is any static evaluation function used in a program for playing computer chess (*q.v.*). The static evaluation function returns an estimate of the value of some state of the board. To be correct, it would return $+\infty$ if the state were a sure win for the side to move, $-\infty$ if it were a sure win for the opponent, and 0 if it were a forced draw. Moreover, for any state it is theoretically possible to find the correct answer algorithmically by doing a full minimax search of the game tree rooted in the state being examined. Such a full search is infeasible for most states, however, because of the size of the game tree. Nonetheless, static evaluation functions are still useful, even without being proved correct.

An example of a heuristic AI program that has not been proved correct because the problem for which it has been designed is not well defined is any natural language understanding program or natural language interface. Since no one has any well-defined criteria for whether a person understands a given language, there cannot be any well-defined criteria for programs either.

Early History

Although the dream of creating intelligent artifacts has existed for many centuries, the field of artificial intelligence is considered to have had its birth at a conference held at Dartmouth College in the summer of 1956. The conference was organized by Marvin Minsky and John McCarthy, and McCarthy coined the name "Artificial Intelligence" for the proposal to obtain funding for the conference. Among the attendees were Herbert Simon (*q.v.*) and Allen Newell, who had already implemented the Logic Theorist program at the Rand Corporation. These four people are considered the fathers of AI. Minsky and McCarthy founded the AI Laboratory at MIT; Simon and Newell founded the AI laboratory at Carnegie Mellon University. McCarthy later moved from MIT to Stanford University, where he founded the AI laboratory there. These three universities, along with Edinburgh University, whose Department of Machine Intelligence was founded by Donald Michie, have remained the premier research universities in the field. The name Artificial Intelligence remained controversial for some years, even among people doing research in the area, but it eventually was accepted.

The first AI text was *Computers and Thought*, edited by Edward Feigenbaum and Julian Feldman, and published by McGraw-Hill in 1963. This is a collection of 21 papers, some of them short versions of Ph.D. dissertations, by early AI researchers. Most of the papers in this collection are still considered classics of AI, but of particular note is a reprint of Alan M. Turing's 1950 paper in which the Turing Test (*q.v.*) was introduced.

Regular AI conferences began in the mid to late 1960s. The Machine Intelligence Workshops series began in 1965 in Edinburgh. A conference at Case Western University in spring, 1968 drew many of the US AI researchers of the time, and the first biennial International Joint Conference on Artificial Intelligence was held in Washington, DC in May, 1969. *Artificial Intelligence*, still the premier journal of AI research, began publication in 1970.

For a more complete history of AI, see McCorduck (1979).

Neighboring Disciplines

Artificial intelligence is generally considered to be a subfield of computer science. There are several disciplines outside computer science, however, that strongly affect AI and that, in turn, AI strongly affects.

Cognitive psychology is the subfield of psychology that uses experimental methods to study human cognitive behavior. The goal of AI called computational psychology earlier is obviously closely related to cognitive psychology, differing mainly in the use of computational models rather than experiments on human subjects. However, most AI researchers pay some attention to the results of cognitive psychology, and cognitive psychologists tend to pay attention to AI as suggesting possible cognitive procedures that they might look for in humans.

Cognitive science (*q.v.*) is an interdisciplinary field that studies human cognitive behavior under the hypothesis that cognition is (or can usefully be modeled as) computation. Although the overlap between AI and cognitive science is large, there are researchers in each field who would not consider themselves to be in the other. AI researchers whose primary goal is what was called machine intelligence earlier in this article generally do not consider themselves to be doing cognitive science, and cognitive science contains not only AI researchers, but also cognitive psychologists, linguists, philosophers, anthropologists, and others, all using the methodologies of their own disciplines on a common problem—that of understanding human cognitive behavior.

Computational linguists use computers, or at least the computational paradigm, to study and process human languages. Like cognitive science, computational linguistics overlaps, but is not coextensive with, AI. It includes those areas of AI called natural language understanding, natural language generation, speech recognition and synthesis (*q.v.*), and machine translation (*q.v.*), but also non-AI areas such as the use of statistical methods to find index keywords useful for retrieving a document.

AI-Complete Tasks

There are many subtopics in the field of AI—subtopics that vary from the consideration of a very particular, technical problem, to broad areas of research. Several of these broad areas can be considered *AI-complete*, in the sense that solving the problem of the area is equivalent to solving the entire AI problem—producing a generally intelligent computer program. Researchers in each of these areas may see themselves as attacking the entire AI problem from a particular direction. The following sections discuss some of the AI-complete areas.

NATURAL LANGUAGE

The AI subarea of natural language is essentially the overlap of AI and computational linguistics (see above). The goal is to form a computational understanding of how people learn and use their native languages, and to produce a computer program that can use a human language at the same level of competence as a native human speaker. Virtually all human knowledge has been (or could be) encoded in human language. Moreover, research in natural language understanding has shown that encyclopedic knowledge is required to understand natural language. Therefore, a complete natural language system will also be a complete intelligent system.

PROBLEM SOLVING AND SEARCH

Problem solving is the area of AI that is concerned with finding or constructing the solution to a problem. That sounds like a very general area, and it is. The distinctive characteristic of the area is probably its approach of seeing tasks as problems to be solved, and of seeing problems as spaces of potential solutions that must be searched to find the true one or the best one. Thus, the AI area of search is very much connected to problem solving. Since any area investigated by AI researchers may be seen as consisting of problems to be solved, all of AI may be seen as involving problem solving and search.

KNOWLEDGE REPRESENTATION AND REASONING

Knowledge representation (*q.v.*) is the area of AI concerned with the formal symbolic languages used to represent the knowledge (data) used by intelligent systems, and the data structures (*q.v.*) used to implement those formal languages. However, one cannot study static representation formalisms and know anything about how useful they are. Instead, one must study how they are helpful for their intended use. In most cases, this use is to use explicitly stored knowledge to produce additional explicit knowledge. This is what reasoning is. Together, knowledge representation and reasoning can be seen to be both necessary and sufficient for producing general intelligence—it is another AI-complete area. Although they are bound up with each other, knowledge representation and reasoning can be teased apart according to whether the particular study is more about the representation language/data structure, or about the active process of drawing conclusions.

LEARNING

Learning is often cited as the critical characteristic of intelligence, and it has always seemed like the easy way to produce intelligent systems: why build an intelligent system when we could just build a learning system and send it to school? Learning includes all styles of learning, from rote learning to the design and analysis of experiments, and all subject areas. If the ultimate learning machine is ever created, it will acquire general intelligence, which is why learning is AI-complete.

VISION

Vision, or image understanding, has to do with interpreting visual images that fall on the human retina or the camera lens (*see* COMPUTER VISION). The actual scene being viewed could be two-dimensional, such as a printed page of text, or three-dimensional, such as the world about us. If we take "interpreting" broadly enough, it is clear that general intelligence may be needed to do the interpretation, and that correct interpretation implies general intelligence, so this is another AI-complete area.

ROBOTICS

Robotics (*q.v.*) is concerned with artifacts that can move about in the actual physical world and/or that can manipulate other objects in the world. Intelligent robots must be able to accommodate to new circumstances, and to do this they need to be able to solve problems and to learn. Thus intelligent robotics is also an AI-complete area.

INTEGRATED SYSTEMS

The most direct work on the problem of generally intelligent systems is to use a robot that has vision and/or other senses, plans and solves problems, and communicates via natural language. Periodically throughout the history of AI, research groups have assembled such integrated robots as tests of the current state of AI.

AUTONOMOUS AGENTS

"Autonomous agents are computer systems that are capable of independent action in dynamic, unpredictable environments" (from the Call for Papers for the Second International Conference on Autonomous Agents). Autonomous agents are like integrated robots, except that they needn't have physical bodies nor need they operate in the real, physical world. Instead, they may be completely software agents, sometimes called "softbots" or just "bots," and may operate in the world of the Internet, crawling around from file to file, collecting information for their human clients. To the extent that a softbot needs to be able to understand the files it comes across, it needs to be able to understand natural language, and to the extent that it needs to solve navigational problems to find the information it was asked for, it may need general-purpose reasoning.

Applications

Throughout the existence of the field, AI research has produced spinoffs into other areas of computer science. Lately, however, programming techniques developed by AI researchers have found application to many programming problems. This has largely come about through the subarea of AI known as expert systems (*q.v.*). Whether or not any particular program should be considered intelligent or an expert according to the common use of those words is largely irrelevant to the workers in and the observers of the expert systems area. From their point of view they have tools and a methodology that are more useful for solving their problems than traditional programming tools and methodologies. From the point of view of AI as a whole, probably the best thing about this development is that after many years of being criticized as following an impossible dream by inappropriate and inadequate means, AI has been recognized by the general public as having applications to everyday problems.

Note: This article is a revised version of Shapiro, S. C. "Artificial Intelligence," in S. C. Shapiro (ed.) (1991) *Encyclopedia of Artificial Intelligence*, 2nd Ed. New York: John Wiley.

Bibliography

1950. Turing, A. M. "Computing Machinery and Intelligence," *Mind*, **59** (October), 433–460.

1956. Newell, A., and Simon, H. A. "The Logic Theory Machine," *IRE Transactions on Information Theory*, **IT-2**, 61–79.

1963. Feigenbaum, E. A., and Feldman, J. (eds.). *Computers and Thought*. New York: McGraw-Hill.

1963. Slagle, J. "A Heuristic Program that Solves Symbolic Integration Problems in Freshman Calculus," *Journal of the Association for Computing Machinery*, **10**, 507–520.

1979. McCorduck, P. *Machines Who Think*. San Francisco: W. H. Freeman.

1981, 1981, 1982. Barr, A., and Feigenbaum, E. A. (eds.) *The Handbook of Artificial Intelligence*, Vols. I, II, III. San Francisco: Morgan Kaufmann.

1989. Barr, A., Cohen, P. R., and Feigenbaum, E. A. (eds.) *The Handbook of Artificial Intelligence*, Vol. IV. Reading, MA: Addison-Wesley.

1990. Kurzweil, R. *The Age of Intelligent Machines*. Cambridge, MA: MIT Press.

1991. Shapiro, S. C. (ed.). *Encyclopedia of Artificial Intelligence*, 2nd Ed. New York: John Wiley.

1995. Zadeh, L. "Foreword for Inaugural Issue," *Intelligent Automation and Soft Computing*, http://internet.roadrunner.com/~js/Autosoft/autosoft-Zadeh_foreword.html.

1995. Russell, S. J., and Norvig, P. *Artificial Intelligence: A Modern Approach*. Upper Saddle River, NJ: Prentice Hall.

1996. Doyle, J., Dean, T., *et al.* "Strategic Directions in Artificial Intelligence," *ACM Computing Surveys*, **28** (December), 653–670.

1997. Waltz, D. L. "Artificial Intelligence: Realizing the Ultimate Promise of Computing," in *Computing Research: A National Investment for Leadership in the 21st Century*, 27–31. Washington, DC: Computing Research Association.

Stuart C. Shapiro

ARTIFICIAL LIFE

For articles on related subjects *see* ARTIFICIAL INTELLIGENCE; BIOCOMPUTING ; CELLULAR AUTOMATA; COMPUTER ANIMATION; COMPUTER ART; COMPUTER GRAPHICS; GENETIC ALGORITHMS; MACHINE LEARNING; NEURAL NETWORKS; and ROBOTICS.

Introduction

As defined by Langton (1992), "*Artificial Life* (AL, or *Alife*) is a new discipline that studies 'natural' life by attempting to recreate biological phenomena, from scratch, within computers and other 'artificial' media. AL complements the traditional analytic approach of traditional biology with a synthetic approach in which, rather than studying biological phenomena by taking apart living organisms to see how they work, one attempts to put together systems that behave like living organisms."

Assembling new chemical compounds not found in nature has been very successful in the scientific research known as *synthetic chemistry*. It has not only contributed enormously to our theoretical understanding of chemical phenomena, but has also allowed us to fabricate new materials and chemicals that are of great practical use in industry and technology.

Artificial Life amounts to the practice of "synthetic biology," which attempts to recreate biological phenomena in alternative media. It is the study of *life-as-it-could-be*, rather than the biological *life-as-we-know-it*. Its goal is not only better theoretical understanding of the phenomena under study, but also practical applications of biological principles in the technology of computer hardware and software, mobile robots (Brooks, 1991), spacecraft, medicine, nanotechnology, industrial fabrication and assembly, and other engineering projects.

AL draws researchers from different disciplines such as computer science, physics, biology, chemistry, economics, and philosophy. It complements traditional biological research by exploring new paths in the quest toward understanding the grand, ancient puzzle called life. The term "artificial" signifies that the systems in question are human made; the basic components might be computer programs or robots. Even mathematics or art can be a suitable medium for artificial life.

The issues raised in AL research pertain to existing biological phenomena as well as to complex systems in general. Thus AL pursues a two-fold goal: (1) an increased understanding of nature and (2) an enhanced insight into artificial models with a view to improving their performance.

The research of John von Neumann (*q.v.*), who posed the question as to whether a machine can reproduce (von Neumann, 1966) is an example of the first goal. More specifically, can an artificial machine create a copy of itself, which in turn could create still more copies, in analogy to nature? Levy (1993) gives a good description of von Neumann's (positive) answer to the question. Von Neumann defined a formal reproductive process that uses assembly instructions in the form of computer code and data interpreted by a robotic device executing a computer program. Other biological phenomena studied are models of the origin of life, evolution, cell construction, animal behavior, and ecology.

An example of the second goal, improving the performance of artificial models such as programming tasks, is software development through evolution (genetic programming), as done by Koza *et al.* (1999). Today, computer programs are written by human programmers. Over the years, there has been a steady rise in software complexity, as computers are given more complicated tasks. Tools used by computer scientists, but which originated in biological systems, are genetic algorithms, neural networks, ant colony behavior, etc.

Evolution

Koza's method, termed *genetic programming*, is based on John Holland's research on genetic algorithms (Holland, 1975). While a programmer develops a single program, attempting to perfect it as much as possible, genetic programming involves a population of programs. Generations of programs are formed by evolution so that in time the population comes to consist of fitter programs (more suitable to solve a given problem), using genetic operators such as mutation, crossover, and selection. The evolution proceeds without human intervention. After the task is set, an initial population is generated at random and evolution continues until a satisfying solution is found (a program that solves the problem posed to the evolutionary programming system).

An evolutionary method, such as evolutionary programming, is advantageous not only in solving difficult problems but also in offering better adaptability. Current computer programs are well known for their brittleness; that is, they are not *robust*. Evolution offers the possibility of adaptation to a dynamic environment; when an unforeseen event occurs, the system could, by analogy with nature, evolve and adapt to the new situation.

Evolution is central to AL research. The major open problem facing biologists is the origin of life: as a necessary precursor to evolution, how did the first self-replicating organisms appear? The underlying conditions necessary for self-reproduction in nature are under intense investigation. The study of artificial life

can contribute to this research by exploring new paths that complement those of biology.

Evolution in nature has received renewed attention over the past two decades. Darwin's fundamental theory of evolution is still sound, but may need expansion. For example, the principle of natural selection is sometimes regarded as sufficient to mold organisms into perfectly adapted creatures. The work of Kauffman (1993) has revealed that other factors can influence evolution besides natural selection. He demonstrated that certain complex systems tend to self-organize; that is, order can arise spontaneously. Self-organization may thus also play a role in evolutionary change.

Another principle of Darwin's theory is that of *gradualism*; small changes accumulate slowly in a species. According to some, paleontological findings discovered over the years have revealed a different picture— long periods of relative stasis, interrupted by short bursts of rapid change. This phenomenon has been named *punctuated equilibria* by biologist Stephen Jay Gould (Gould, 1995). While a full explanation does not yet exist, the phenomenon has been recently observed in a number of AL projects, suggesting that it may be inherent in certain evolutionary systems, biological or not.

Emergence

Along with evolution, a second process is essential in AL systems: *emergence*. By *emergence* is meant that phenomena at a certain level arise from interactions at lower levels. In physical systems, temperature and pressure are examples of emergent phenomena; they occur in large ensembles of molecules due to interactions at the molecular level. An individual molecule possesses neither temperature nor pressure, which are higher-level emergent phenomena.

AL systems consist of large collections of simple, basic units whose interesting properties are those that emerge at higher levels. One example is the work of Craig Reynolds (1987) on flocking behavior. To investigate how flocks of birds fly without apparent coordination of a central guiding mechanism, Reynolds created a virtual bird with basic flight capability, called a *boid*. He populated a computerized world with a collection of boids, flying in accordance with three rules: collision avoidance (avoid collisions with nearby boids), velocity matching (attempt to match velocity with nearby boids) and flock centering (attempt to stay as close as possible to the perceived center of mass of nearby boids). These three rules sufficed for the emergence of flocking behavior even though none of them specifically directs the formation of an orderly flock. The boids fly in a cohesive group and when obstacles

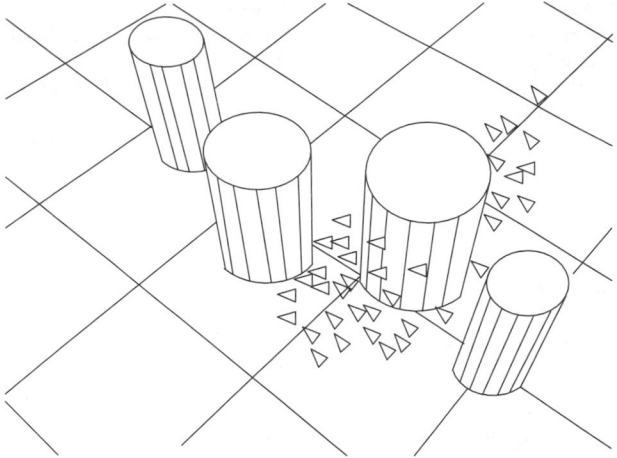

Figure 1. A flock of "boids" separating to avoid obstacles.

appear in their way they spontaneously split up into two subgroups, without any central guidance, rejoining again after clearing the obstruction (*see* Fig. 1). The boids model has been used to produce photorealistic imagery for the feature motion pictures *Batman Returns*, *The Lion King*, and *Cliffhanger*.

Reynolds' model demonstrates the basic architecture of AL systems: a large number of elementary units, relatively simple, interacting with a small number of nearby neighbors, with no central controller. High-level phenomena emerge from these low-level interactions. Although the boids are artificial, the flocking behavior is as real as that observed in nature.

Artificial Intelligence and Artificial Life

The underlying principles of artificial life stand at the core of Rodney Brooks' work. His method for building sophisticated robots demonstrates the AL approach. His robots possess "brains" comprising a hierarchy of layers, each one performing a more complex function than the one beneath. This scheme allows incremental construction of robots by adding to existing layers, thus enabling some form of robotic evolution. Artificial Intelligence (AI) employs a top-down methodology where complex behaviors are identified and an attempt is made to build a system that presents all the details of a behavior (e.g. chess playing—*see* COMPUTER CHESS). Artificial Life operates in a bottom-up manner, starting from simple elemental units, gradually building its way upward through evolution and emergence.

AL and AI also investigate different issues. Whereas AI has traditionally concentrated on complex human functions, AL concentrates on basic natural behaviors, emphasizing survivability in complex environments.

Websites and Recent Projects

The Website `http://www.genarts.com/karl/evolved-virtual-creatures.html` describes Karl Sims' work entitled Evolved Virtual Creatures (Sims, 1994). A population of several hundred creatures is created within a supercomputer (*q.v.*), and each creature is tested for its ability to perform a given task, such as to swim in a simulated water environment. Those that are most successful survive, and their virtual genes containing coded instructions for their growth, are copied, combined, and mutated to make offspring for a new population. As cycles of variation and selection continue, creatures with more and more successful behaviors emerge. The creatures shown in Fig. 2 on Color Page CP-1 result from many independent simulations in which they were selected for their ability to swim, walk, jump, follow a target, and compete for control of a green cube.

The Website `http://www.genarts.com/karl/primordial-dance.html` describes a 1991 project of Karl Sims called Primordial Dance. The pictures of Fig. 3 on Color Page CP-1 are evolved using evolutionary programming. Every pixel is the result of a complex function embedded in artificial "genes." The effects were created using an interactive process of "artificial evolution." The artist and computer collaborate to produce images and movements that neither could easily produce alone. The computer generates and displays a collection of experimental abstract images. The artist chooses the most esthetically interesting images, and these survive and are "bred" to produce a new collection of images. The equations, or artificial genes, of the survivors are copied, mutated, and mated by the computer to generate new offspring pictures. This process of variation and selection is repeated, and with each cycle more complex and interesting results can occur. Finally, movements are created by performing "genetic interpolations" between these evolved images. The figure depicts three interpolations, each applied to a different set of evolved images.

Craig Reynolds' work on the flocking of "boids" is described at `http://www.cs.toronto.edu/~dt/siggraph97-course/cwr87/` and `http://www.red.com/cwr/boids.html`.

Moshe Sipper, whose home page is `http://lslwww.epfl.ch/Staff/MS/MS.html`, has done interesting work on the connections between cellular automata (*q.v.*) and evolutionary biology in general and emergence in particular. His Website describes some of his own work and provides links to other related AL work.

The Santa Fe Institute Website `http://alife.santafe.edu/` contains considerable information on different topics in AL, including references to important papers and conference dates. The comp. ai.alife FAQ Website, written and maintained by the author of this article, is located at `http://alife.nerdhero.org`.

Conclusion

Artificial Life offers opportunities for conducting experiments that are extremely complicated in traditional biology or not feasible at all. AL complements traditional biological research, raising the possibility of joint ventures leading to valuable new scientific discoveries. AL also has the potential to develop new technologies—software evolution, sophisticated robots, ecological monitoring tools, educational systems, and so on. The discipline combines both scientific endeavor and applied research. Although still young, this field has produced exciting results that hold promise for a bright future.

Bibliography

1966. von Neumann, J. in *Theory of Self-Reproducing Automata* (ed. A.W. Burks). Urbana, IL: University of Illinois Press.

1975. Holland, J. H. *Adaptation in Natural and Artificial Systems.* Ann Arbor, MI: University of Michigan Press.

1987. Reynolds, C. W. "Flocks, Herds, and Schools: a Distributed Behavioral," *Computer Graphics*, **21**, *4* (July), 25–34 (ACM SIGGRAPH '87 Conference Proceedings).

1991. Brooks, R. A. "New Approaches to Robotics," *Science*, **253**, *5025* (September), 1227–1232.

1992. Langton, C. G. "Preface," in *Artificial Life II* (eds. C. G. Langton, C. Taylor, J. D. Farmer, and S. Rasmussen). Volume X of SFI Studies in the Sciences of Complexity. Redwood City, CA: Addison-Wesley.

1992. Waldrop, M. M. *Complexity: The Emerging Science at the Edge of Order and Chaos.* New York: Simon & Schuster. Contains an extensive discussion of the philosophy and early AL work of Christopher Langton.

1992. Ray, T. S. "An Approach to the Synthesis of Life," in *Artificial Life II* (eds. C. G. Langton, C. Taylor, J. D. Farmer, and S. Rasmussen). Volume X of SFI Studies in the Sciences of Complexity. Redwood City, CA: Addison-Wesley.

1993. Kauffman, S. A. *The Origins of Order.* New York: Oxford University Press.

1993. Levy, S. *Artificial Life: A Report from the Frontier Where Computers Meet Biology.* New York: Vintage Books.

1994. Sims, K. "Evolving 3D Morphology and Behavior by Competition," in *Artificial Life IV Proceedings* (eds. R. A. Brooks and P. Maes). Cambridge, MA: MIT Press.

1995. Sipper, M. "An Introduction to Artificial Life," in *Explorations in Artificial Life* (special issue of *AI Expert*). San Francisco: Miller Freeman.

1995. Gould, S. J. *The Dinosaur in the Haystack*, 127–136. New York: Harmony Books.

1996. Emmeche, C. *The Garden in the Machine: The Emerging Science of Artificial Life.* Princeton, NJ: Princeton University Press.

1997. Langton, C. (ed.) *Artificial Life: An Overview.* Cambridge, MA: Bradford Books.

1997. Sipper, M. M. *Evolution of Parallel Cellular Machines: The Cellular Programming Approach.* Berlin: Springer-Verlag.

1998. Adami, C. *Introduction to Artificial Life.* New York: Springer-Verlag.

1999. Koza, J. R., Bennett, F. H., Keane, M. A., and Andre, D. *Genetic Programming III: Darwinian Invention and Problem Solving.* San Francisco: Morgan Kaufmann.

1999. Morris, R. *Artificial Worlds: Computers, Complexity, and the Riddle of Life.* New York: Plenum Press.

1999. Terzopoulos, D. "Artificial Life for Computer Graphics," *Comm. of the ACM*, **42**, *8* (August), 33–42.

Anthony Liekens

ASCII

See CHARACTER CODES.

ASSEMBLER

> For articles on related subjects *see* ADDRESSING; CALLING SEQUENCE; COMPILER; CROSS ASSEMBLERS AND COMPILERS; GENERAL REGISTER; INDEX REGISTER; INSTRUCTION SET; LANGUAGE PROCESSORS; LINKERS AND LOADERS; MACHINE AND ASSEMBLY LANGUAGE PROGRAMMING; MACRO; NO-OP; OPERAND; PREPROCESSOR; PROGRAM COUNTER; and REGISTER.

An *assembler* is a program that facilitates the preparation of programs at the machine language level by taking symbolic representations of individual (instruction or data) words and converting them into a form (binary or byte) called *object code* (*see* OBJECT PROGRAM) suitable for input to a linker or loader. It permits the use of mnemonic operation codes, allows symbolic names to be assigned to memory locations, provides facilities for address calculations in terms of such symbolic names, and (usually) enables the user to introduce numerical and character constants in various forms. Assemblers are used for systems programming (*q.v.*) when the need to access all the facilities of the "raw" machine precludes the use of a high-level language. If a micro is too small to support an assembler, a *cross-assembler* is used, an assembler that runs on one (usually larger) machine producing *object code* for another (usually smaller) machine.

Although the term "assembly subroutine" was used as long ago as 1951 for a routine that assembled a master routine and a number of subroutines into a single program (Wilkes, Wheeler, and Gill, 1951), this function is now typically called *linking*. The established connotation of the term "assembler" derives from its function of assembling the internal binary form of the program from symbolic definitions.

History

Although the use of a symbolic representation of machine language programs now seems obviously desirable, this was not always so. Right from the start there was a dichotomy of view between the Cambridge group (EDSAC—*q.v.*), which advocated a measure of symbolic programming, and the Manchester group (MARK I—*see* MANCHESTER UNIVERSITY COMPUTERS), which believed that the programmer should write the program in a form as close as possible to the internal form (Wilkes, 1956).

The EDSAC had a rudimentary assembler called *Initial Orders*, which allowed the user to write machine instructions consisting of a single-letter operation code, a decimal address, and a terminating letter, which caused one of 12 constants preset by the programmer to be added to the address at assembly time. (The Initial Orders were implemented in a form of read-only memory (*q.v.*) consisting of a wired telephone uniselector.)

The first widely used assembler in the sense of this article was SOAP (Symbolic Optimizer and Assembly Program) on the IBM 650 computer in the mid-1950s. However, the symbolic assembly features of SOAP were not its main feature (the 650 was a decimal computer anyway, which removed some of the difficulties of direct machine language coding). The 650 had a magnetic drum memory and an instruction code in which each instruction specified the address of its successor. For maximum efficiency, instructions had to be placed on the drum in positions such that the execution of each instruction overlapped as far as possible the time for the drum to rotate to the next instruction position, thus minimizing the latency waiting for instructions. Such minimum-access coding involved a very difficult optimizing process, and it was this that SOAP achieved.

A significant event in the history of assemblers was the introduction of the Symbolic Assembly Program (SAP) for the IBM 704. The original SAP assembler (UASAP) was written by programmers at United Aircraft Corporation and was distributed by the SHARE organization. SAP set the external form of an assembly language that was to be a model for all its successors and which persists almost unchanged to the present day. On later versions of the 700 series computers, SAP was replaced by FAP (Fortran Assembly Program).

Facilities

A typical machine instruction consists of an operation code, an address, and one or more register fields. The address may refer to a data area or to another instruction (e.g. the destination of a transfer of control). A SAP-like assembler provides a fixed set of mnemonic operation codes and an open-ended set of programmer-defined symbols for use in address parts. Such address symbols may be defined explicitly or implicitly by attaching them as labels to particular instructions or data words. Although a symbol stands for an address,

the assembler cannot convert label symbols directly into addresses, since the address in storage into which a particular instruction will be loaded is not known at assembly time. (It is finally determined only when a number of routines are linked to form a complete program.) The difficulty is resolved by recording as the value of the label symbol the displacement of the instruction in question from the beginning of the code for the subroutine, and marking it in the assembler output as a relative or relocatable value, to be adjusted later by the linker or loader.

Thus, SAP introduced the basic structure of a symbolic instruction as being made up of three fields:

1. *Location* (possibly blank). A symbol placed here takes as its value the address of the memory cell in which the corresponding instruction or data word will be stored: thus it serves as a label by which it can be referenced by other instructions. The assembler has a *location counter* that holds the current address relative to the start of the program.

2. *Operation code*. The symbol here is one of a fixed repertoire of operation-code symbols.

3. *Operand*. This field is usually made up of a number of subfields, reflecting the address/register structure of the computer. The subfields may be simple integer constants or may be expressions made up of symbols (representing addresses), constants, and simple arithmetic operations (usually plus and minus). Alternatively, a literal operand may be supplied: the assembler will store this and substitute the appropriate address in the instruction.

The following fragment of SAP coding illustrates this structure.

```
        TRA     ALPHA
        LOC     16385
ALPHA   CLA     BETA
        STO     DELTA
SYMB    FAD     = 3.14159
        SXO     SYMB-2,4
        STO     SYMB
```

Each instruction in this example is made up of three fields: location (label), operation code, and address. The operation codes are mnemonic: TRA = transfer control, CLA = clear accumulator, FAD = floating add, etc. The address fields show the various possible constructions. In the first line the address is a symbol ALPHA, as yet undefined. (It appears as a label on a later instruction.) In line 2 the address is explicit, and in lines 3 and 4 symbols (presumably defined elsewhere in the program of which this fragment forms a part) are used. Line 5 illustrates the use of a literal operand: the "equals" indicates that the 3.14159 following is the actual value to be loaded by the FAD, not the address of the operand. The next line illustrates a more complex address: it is a two-field form in which the first component is a storage address and the second component identifies an index register (*q.v.*) to be used; in this example the storage address is specified as an expression.

The following excerpt of assembler code for current IBM mainframe computers, whose purpose is to sum 13 numbers, shows how little things have changed.

```
        L     3,=F'0'    CLEAR REGISTER
        L     5,=F'0'    USING LITERAL
        LH    4,=H'14'   LOAD REGISTER
        B     BCNT       ENTER LOOP
BNTER   AH    5,STZ(3)   INDEX STZ BY REG 3
        AH    3,=H'2'    INCREMENT INDEX
BCNT    BCT   4,BNTER    BRANCH ON COUNT
        ST    5,BSUM
STZ     DC    H'15,225,1,52,10,48,76,42,88,
              26,14,4,32'
BSUM    DC    F'0'
```

The three-field format is still used, though the mnemonics have changed. With the exception of the branch (B) order, which has a label as its address, the address field is made up of a register designator and a second field, which in these examples is either a symbolic store address or a literal. (For certain instructions it might be another register designator.)

Literals are introduced by "equals," but now include a type code (F = full word, H = half word). Indexing (modification) is illustrated in the line starting BNTER, and finally there are specifications of a number of constants introduced by the DC (Define Constants) pseudo-operation. The comments on the right are part of the programmer's documentation of the program.

Assembler Directives

Assembler directives serve two purposes. One is to provide information to control the assembly process; the other is to provide a way of defining data words in a program. Assembler directives are often called *pseudo-operations* (a terminology introduced by SAP), since they are commonly designated by special codes in the operation field. A SAP-like pseudo-operation is

symbol BSS *integer constant*

which sets the symbol equal to the location counter, and then advances the location counter by the amount designated by the constant. The effect is thus to reserve a block of memory and label it for future reference. Another typical pseudo-operation is

symbol SET *expression*

which assigns an explicit value to a symbol. Other uses of directives to control the assembly include setting the origin, marking entry points, and defining external symbols.

We have seen an example of a data-generating pseudo-operation in the fragment of IBM S/370 coding given above. Here the pseudo-operation DC (define constants) is followed by a list of constants, each with a type code. A simpler facility provided in some assemblers requires all the constants to be of the same type; e.g. the pseudo-operation DEC introduces a list of decimal constants in the address field.

Listings

Assembler output usually provides a variety of information about the program assembled. Besides details of any obvious errors, such as incorrect syntax or multiple definition of symbols, the following may be provided.

1. Listing of symbolic instructions side by side with generated binary or binary-symbolic code.

2. Table of symbols defined in a routine, with or without their values.

3. Table of symbols used in a routine.

4. Cross-reference table: for each symbol defined, its name, value, and a list of all the instructions that reference it.

The form of the listing is generally controlled by one or more pseudo-operations; for example:

```
LIST FULL
LIST NONE
LIST SYMBOLS
```

The listing corresponding to the program fragment for the IBM S/370 (given in the section "Facilities") is shown in Fig. 1.

Quite different symbolic instructions can nonetheless generate the same sequence of object code bytes. Consider the excerpt from a DEC VAX assembler listing shown in Fig. 2. This listing shows that the assembly language programmer submitted eight different directives and one symbolic instruction to the assembler, yet the assembler generated exactly the same four bytes of object code for each of the nine lines of source code. The sequence of source code instructions has no practical significance other than to demonstrate the single most important concept of stored-program computation: the *context-dependency of stored information*. By this is meant that there is no intrinsic

LOC	OBJECT CODE	ADDR1	ADDR2	ST#	NAME	OP	OPERANDS	
.								
.								
.								
00000C	5830 2030		00038	8		L	3, = F'0'	CLEAR REGISTER
000010	5850 2030		00038	9		L	5, = F'0'	USING LITERAL
000014	4840 2034		0003C	10		LH	4, = H'14'	LOAD REGISTER
000018	47F0 201C		00024	11		B	BCNT	ENTER LOOP
00001C	4A53 2038		0004C	12	BNTER	AH	5,STZ(3)	INDEX STZ BY REG 3
000020	4A30 2036		0003E	13		AH	3, = H'2'	INCREMENT INDEX
000024	4640 2014		0001C	14	BCNT	BCT	4,BNTER	BRANCH ON COUNT
000028	5050 2054		0005C	15		ST	5,BSUM	STORE SUM
				16	*			
000040	000F00E100010034 ⎫			17	STZ	DC	H'15,225,1,52,10,48,76,42,88,26,14,4,32'	
000048	000A0030004C002A ⎪ (Hexadecimal equivalents							
000050	0058001A000E0004 ⎬ of 13 numbers)							
000058	0020 ⎭							
00005A	0000 ← (Filler needed to align next instruction properly)							
00005C	00000000			18	BSUM	DC	F'0'	

Figure 1. Example of listing from System/370 assembler. The LOC column shows the address of each instruction relative to the beginning of the program. The OBJECT CODE columns show the contents of the instruction as they will appear in memory. The ADDR1 (not used in this example) and ADDR2 columns give the effective addresses of the operands. In this example, register 2 holds the constant base-address value 8. The object code for the first instruction has 58, the opcode for L (load), followed by 3 (the destination register). Then comes 0 (no index register), 2 (the base register), 030 (the offset added to the base register to get the effective address). This value, 38, appears in the ADDR2 column. The ST# column is a sequential line number for the programmer's convenience. Note that columns to left of ST# are all given in hexadecimal.

meaning to any arbitrary object-code byte sequence; one must be told how the sequence will be used before it can be ascertained whether the bytes will be executed as an instruction or interpreted as data and, if the latter, the type of data intended.

Macro Assemblers

An important attribute of an assembler is the ability to define and use *macros* (*q.v.*). It often happens that a certain pattern of instructions occurs in several places in a program with only minor variations. This is particularly the case if there is a common operation that requires several machine orders for its execution; for example, the calling sequence for a call of another routine. Thus, to call the SAP routine SUB with parameters A and B, it might be necessary to write

```
LDX 4,*
TFR SUB
NOP A
NOP B
```

The first instruction loads into register 4 the address of itself; i.e. its location in storage. From this the subroutine can compute the return address to resume operation of the main program after the calling sequence. The parameters A and B are assumed to be addresses, and have been placed as the address parts of two no-operation (i.e. null) instructions (*see* NO-OP). Evidently, it would be convenient for the programmer to be able to write

```
CALL SUB,A,B
```

and have the system generate the four-line *calling sequence* given above. The advantages of this approach are threefold. The programmer writes less; the program is more readable; and if at some future stage the calling sequence is changed, a change at one place in the program will insure that all CALLs are changed without the need to alter each one individually.

A macro assembler allows the programmer to define macroinstructions as sequences of ordinary instructions, and provides a means of inserting variable information in the generated sequences.

Macros can be used to generate built-in data sequences, as well as executable instruction sequences.

Successive hex bytes	Address	Line #	Source code
81 72 64 65	10E1	12	.BYTE 101,100,114,129
81 72 64 65	10E5	13	.BYTE 101,100,114,-127
8172 6465	10E9	14	.WORD 25701,33138
8172 6465	10ED	15	.WORD 25701,-32398
81726465	10F1	16	.LONG 2171757669
81726465	10F5	17	.LONG -2123209627
81 72 64 65	10F9	18	.ASCII/edr/<129>
81726465	10FD	19	.FLOAT 4.2336319e+21
81 72 64 65	1101	20	MULD3 (r4),-(r2),(r1)+

Figure 2. Generating object code from assembler instructions.

The following DEC VAX assembler macro generalizes construction of any table whose values can be formed by applying a formula supplied by the user of the macro:

```
.MACRO table n, first, last, fofn
   n = first    ; initialize symbol n
   .repeat last-first+1
               ; argument is repeat count
    .long fofn  ; creates a longword integer
    n=n+1       ; redefine symbol n
   .endr
.ENDM table
```

Arguments *first* and *last* specify the first and last values to be used for whatever actual argument is used in place of *n*, and *fofn* ("*f* of *n*") is a formula that involves *n*. To generate 20 odd numbers, the user could then write

```
odds: table k,0,19,2*k+1
```

Similarly, to generate a *table* of cubes from 5^3 to 15^3 inclusive, the user could write

```
cubes: table j,5,15,j*j*j
```

Such invocations of the macro `table` must, of course, be strategically placed in the source code such that flow-of-control never reaches the labels `odds` or `cubes` (or any place interior to the generated tables).

Conditional Assembly

A feature of many assemblers is the ability to assemble pieces of program selectively. This is particularly useful in package programs that have to provide a large number of options. In its simplest form this facility is provided by a pseudo-instruction that controls the assembly of the immediately following instruction, but usually a more elaborate facility of assembly-time jumps and labels is provided. Typically, assembly-time labels (or sequence symbols) are preceded by a period and appear in the label field. However, they are ignored by the assembler except in the context of pseudo-instructions typically named AGO and AIF. (The mnemonics are derived from "assembler GOTO" and "assembler IF") Let .SS be a sequence symbol; then

```
AGO.SS
```

causes assembly to be continued from the line in which the symbol .SS appears in the label field (usually this must be a forward jump), and

```
AIF(symbol-1 relation symbol-2) .SS
```

causes assembly to be continued from the line labeled .SS if the condition is true; otherwise, assembly continues with the next line of code, as usual.

Conditional assembly is an especially powerful tool when used in conjunction with macro definition. Consider this DEC VAX macro, which places the average of operands *a* and *b* in *result*:

```
.MACRO average a, b, result
   addl a,b,result      ; result <- a+b
   ashl #-1,result,result ; result <- (a+b)/2
.ENDM average
```

The second instruction generated shifts the tentative result right one place (i.e. *sh*ift *l*eft −1 places) as a fast way of dividing by 2. Now, in response to the user who calls the macro via

```
average low, high, mean
```

the macro will be expanded (replaced in-place by) the two instructions

```
addl low, high, mean ; mean <- low+high
ashl #-1, mean, mean ; mean <- (low+high)/2
```

(Amusingly, even the formal arguments used in the comments are replaced by their actual argument counterparts, and the expanded comments happen to be correct!)

But now consider the invocation

```
average R0, R0, ans
```

Macro expansion will still generate two instructions, even though the only one needed would be:

```
movl R0, ans ; ans <- R0
```

(i.e. the average of two identical items is a copy of either). No astute programmer would use the macro in lieu of the move instruction, but a preprocessor (*q.v.*) or a compiler (*q.v.*) might. The solution is to use conditional assembly to generate one instruction whenever the first two operands are *symbolically* identical, and two otherwise:

```
.MACRO average a,b,result
    .if IDENTICAL a,b
        movl a, result
    .if_false
        addl a,b,result
        ashl #-1,result,result
    .endc ; end conditional clause
.ENDM average
```

It must be emphasized that the "condition" tested by conditional assembly must be one testable at assembly time, not execution time. In the earlier invocation

```
average low, high, mean
```

it might happen that the run-time *values* of symbols `low` and `high` are the same, but, since their names were not the same at assembly time, there is no way to avoid generation of the inefficient two-instruction sequence.

The Working of the Assembler

The "classic" assembler takes a routine (or subprogram) and converts it into binary symbolic form for subsequent processing by a linker. The conversion is accomplished in two passes (i.e. the source program is scanned twice). The basic strategy is very simple. The *first pass* through the source program collects all the symbol definitions into a symbol table, and the *second pass* converts the program to binary symbolic form using the definitions collected in the first pass.

During the second pass, the assembler will have to recognize three sorts of quantities: absolute quantities, relocatable quantities, and references to externally defined symbols. In the simplest case, all relocatable quantities are expressed relative to an origin at the beginning of the routine. The assembler therefore has to categorize the symbols as it builds up the symbol table, and then check for illegal combinations in expressions. (For example, it is meaningless to add two relocatable symbols, though their difference may be a respectable absolute quantity.) The exact form of the output from the assembler depends on the linker. Typically, the assembler might produce the following output:

Header	Name of routine.
RLB	Relocatable binary section: consists of binary symbolic code and relocation information.
Definition table	Definitions of global symbols defined in the routine (i.e. symbols that will be referenced in other routines).
Use table	Details of use of global and COMMON symbols in the routine (i.e. symbols used here but defined elsewhere).

The *definition table* carries information about symbols defined in this routine which are to have a global meaning. Since these may be absolute or relative, the table must carry this information as well as the value. In the case of a relative symbol the value is relative to the beginning of the routine.

The *use table* is more complex, since it records all occurrences of global symbols within the routine. Its exact form will depend on the facilities provided by the assembler—in particular, the circumstances in which global symbols can be used.

If multiple location counters are used, an extra block must be output giving the amount of space used by the routine relative to each location counter. Each relocatable item will carry with it an indication of the relevant location counter.

Meta Assemblers

Assemblers for different machines have much in common. They organize symbol tables, evaluate expres-

sions, and generate binary words from a number of symbolic fields. The idea of a meta assembler is to provide a system with these general capabilities, together with a means of describing (in machine-independent form) the assembly rules for a particular machine. The meta assembler accepts this description and then functions apparently as a normal assembler.

The idea of a meta assembler originated with Ferguson (1966) and was used in the Utmost assembler for the Univac III, Sleuth II for the Univac 1107/8, and in Metasymbol for the SDS 900 series. An important feature of these systems is that the syntax of the input to a meta assembler is fixed. The semantics (meaning) of the symbolic information can be defined by the user, but the user cannot change the syntax. Thus, although it is possible in using a meta assembler to write an assembler for most machines, it is not possible to mimic an existing assembler whose syntax will almost certainly be different from that of the meta assembler. (This is one of the many differences between a meta assembler and a *compiler-compiler*: see COMPILER).

The essentially new features of a meta assembler are (1) the provision of assembly-time procedures and functions, and (2) a mechanism whereby the programmer can define binary output formats and cause such binary output to be generated.

Superficially, the input to a meta assembler looks like input to any assembler; each line has three fields—label, operation, and operand. The label is optional: if there is a symbol in this field, it is assigned a value equal to the current location-counter value. The operation may be the name of a built-in system operation, in which case it is no different from a pseudo-operation in a conventional assembler. If the operation is not the name of a built-in operation, it is assumed to be the name of a programmer-defined procedure, which will be obeyed, taking the operand field as an argument. This procedure may have the effect of generating some code, or may just perform housekeeping operations such as entering items in a table. It should be particularly noted that the procedure is obeyed during assembly. It is in many ways comparable to a macro, but instead of textual substitution we obey a piece of program written in *meta*-assembly language. This may itself contain calls to other procedures.

The operand field contains an expression, or group of expressions, made up of symbols and constants. These expressions are evaluated by the system in the same way that a normal assembler evaluates its address field. Unlike a normal assembler, the expressions may contain calls to user-defined functions.

Included in the built-in procedures are GEN and GENB, which output the values of the operand set as a sequence of words or bytes, respectively, and FORM, which allows the user to define a named template for binary output. Thus,

    INSTR FORM 6, 3, 15

defines (for a 24-bit word machine) a template made up of three fields consisting of 6, 3, and 15 bits, and attaches the name INSTR to this template. FORM is a built-in operation. Suppose that subsequent to the definition of INSTR, we write

    INSTR LDA, 7, ALPHA + 1

(Here INSTR is in the operation field, and the operand field is a set of three expressions.) This will cause the three elements of the operand set to be evaluated, truncated, and concatenated to form a 24-bit binary output word. (Note that this technique would allow the operation code of an instruction to be written as an expression!)

The meta assembler does not have any conventional built-in operations for machine instructions. The code emitted for what seems to be an assembly-language instruction is actually determined by a procedure having the name of the desired machine instruction. In this way, and using procedures to produce the required effect for pseudo-instructions, a "conventional" assembler image can be built up.

"High-Level" Assemblers

An assembly language program is necessarily written at a fine level of detail, with each instruction representing a single primitive operation. An unfortunate effect of working at this level of detail is that assembly language programs are rarely as easily understood as programs written in a high-level language can be.

There has been a development in the direction of *high-level* or *Algol-like* assembly languages that attempt to combine fine control over machine registers and storage with a structure that reflects the overall structure of the program; for example, repetition loops, conditional statements, and functions and procedures. The facilities provided in such a language must correspond fairly closely to the actual hardware. The precise facilities provided in a system depend on the particular machine, but typically include the following.

1. Symbolic names (identifiers) with associated types. The types will correspond to the storage units manipulated by the machine instructions; for example, on the Digital Equipment Corporation VAX Series they would include byte, word, and longword.

2. Reserved identifiers for machine registers. A synonym facility may also be provided to associate other names with registers.

3. Block structure, giving scopes to identifiers.

4. Conditional and compound statements.

5. One-dimensional arrays, but not multidimensional arrays (these cannot be accessed by simple indexing on most machines).

6. Procedures and functions (with parameters passed as addresses in general-purpose registers or in a *stack—q.v.*).

7. Simple expressions (but nothing involving temporary storage; all operators are of equal precedence, and evaluation is by a simple left-to-right scan).

8. Provision for including basic assembly language (e.g. for input operations).

The first high-level assembler was the PL/360 system described by Wirth (1968) in a classic paper. As its name implies, it was designed for the IBM System 360 machines. An interesting development in this area is that the only assembler provided by the manufacturers of the GEC 4000 series machines was a high-level assembler called BABBAGE.

Disassemblers

A *disassembler* is a language processor that accepts machine language object code as input and produces assembly language source code as output. Suppose that a valuable object file exists whose corresponding source file has been lost or accidentally destroyed. The object code can be executed indefinitely, but the time will inevitably come when modifications are called for. There are ways to "patch" the object code to add new or modified code, but doing so is very tedious and error prone. What else might be done?

Most real-world processes are inherently irreversible, but a few are not. With the right scanning equipment, printed text can be read and converted back to a text file virtually identical to the one from which it was printed. Might something similar be done with orphaned object code? The answer is yes, but certain concessions must be made. If the original (but lost) source code contained the instruction ADD ACE,KING, which an assembler turned into the hexadecimal sequence A7 3B80 DFF7, then a disassembler that encounters this sequence might output something like ADD P04,S12. The "ADD" can be reconstructed, but the disassembler, having no way of knowing what symbols the original programmer used as operands, must synthesize alternative symbols. In this example, the disassembler being used invents symbols in the order A00, A01, A02, etc., up through Z99, and has reached (at least) S12.

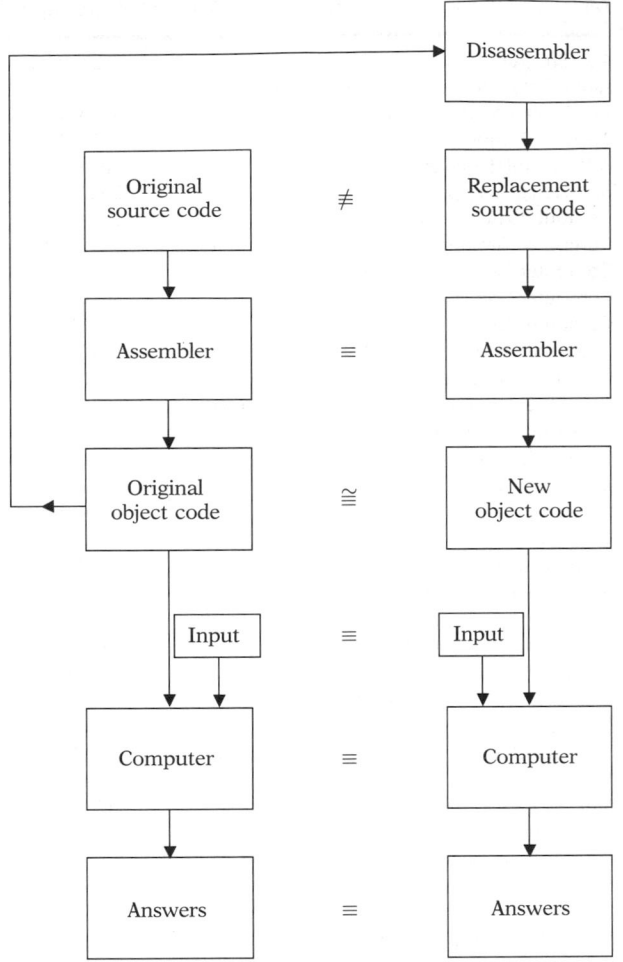

Figure 3. The interrelation of assembly and disassembly. The symbols ≡, ≢, and ≅ are to be read "is identical to," "is not identical to," and "is close to identical to," respectively.

The disassembler must be consistent, of course. If hexadecimal address 3B80 is assigned symbol P04 the first time it is encountered, then it must be replaced with the same symbol every later time it is encountered. Moreover, the disassembler must allocate a particular piece of memory of appropriate size to correspond to symbol P04, a size that is determined from knowledge that the computer's ADD command must be applied to operands of a certain type (such as integers or real numbers).

None of the comments that were embedded in the original source code can be reconstructed, and the synthesized source code will usually be far less readable than the original. What we hope to obtain through disassembly, however, is a new source file that is *logically* equivalent to the original; one that, when assembled and executed, will produce the same answers as the original. When the new source code

does assemble cleanly and function as stated, it then provides a platform for modification and maintenance. The process is shown in Fig. 3.

Bibliography

1956. Wilkes, M. V. *Automatic Digital Computers.* London: Methuen & Co.

1966. Ferguson, D. E. "The Evolution of the Meta-assembly Program," *Comm. of the ACM,* **9**, 190.

1968. Wirth, N. "PL/360, A Programming Language for the 360 Computers," *Journal of the ACM,* **15**, 37.

1978. Barron, D. W. *Assemblers and Loaders,* 3rd Ed. New York: American-Elsevier.

1984. Wilkes, M. V., Wheeler, D. J., and Gill, S. *The Preparation of Programs for an Electronic Digital Computer.* Charles Babbage Institute Reprint Series, 1. Cambridge, MA: MIT Press (originally published by Addison-Wesley, 1951).

1991. Federighi, F. D., and Reilly, E. D. *VAX Assembly Language.* New York: Macmillan.

1994. Abel, P. *IBM PC Assembly Language and Programming,* 3rd Ed. Upper Saddle River, NJ: Prentice Hall.

1994. Clements, A. *68000 Family Assembly Language.* Boston, MA: PWS Publishing Co.

1995. Runnion, W. C. *Structured Programming in Assembly Language for the IBM PC and PS/2.* New York: PWS Publishing Co.

David W. Barron and Edwin D. Reilly

ASSOCIATION FOR COMPUTING MACHINERY (ACM)

For articles on related subjects *see* COMPUTER SOCIETIES; INSTITUTE OF ELECTRICAL AND ELECTRONIC ENGINEERS— COMPUTER SOCIETY; INTERNATIONAL FEDERATION FOR INFORMATION PROCESSING; LITERATURE OF COMPUTING; and TURING AWARD WINNERS.

The *Association for Computing Machinery* (ACM) is an international scientific and educational association of computer professionals which traces its beginnings to the founding of the Eastern Association for Computing Machinery in 1947, followed in 1954 by the incorporation of The Association for Computing Machinery. The word "machinery" in its name has always bothered some ACM leaders, but all attempts at changes to other names, such as *The Association of Computing* or *The Association for Computer Science*, have failed to garner the requisite membership support.

ACM, with a current membership of 80,000, was formed to advance the art, science, engineering, and application of information technology, serving both professional and public interests by fostering the open interchange of information and by promoting the highest professional and ethical standards. To these ends it annually sponsors or co-sponsors over 100 conferences, meetings, workshops, and symposia and engages in an extensive publication program. Its publications include periodicals, books, monographs, tutorials, transactions, and conference proceedings. ACM Press Books, a collaboration with Addison Wesley Longman, publishes about a dozen new titles each year and now has a backlist of several dozen volumes. The leading ACM periodicals are its monthly *Communications of the ACM*, which contains general articles and news about computing as well as some technical articles and which goes to all ACM members; its bi-monthly *Journal*, which is a research journal covering a wide swath of computer science; the quarterly *Computing Surveys*, which provides tutorials on a wide range of computing topics; and the monthly *Computing Reviews* (CR), which for more than 25 years was the only periodical printing critical reviews of the literature of computing. (In 1999 ACM was considering the publication of an online review service, *Online Computing Reviews Service*, which, if it proves viable, may eventually result in the discontinuation of the print publication.) In addition to publishing transactions in 12 different subject areas (Table 1), ACM cooperates with the IEEE Computer Society in the publication of *Transactions on Networking*. The *ACM Guide to Computing Literature* and the ACM Computing Classification System are described in the article LITERATURE OF COMPUTING.

Technical activities are carried out by 36 semi-autonomous Special Interest Groups (SIGs) whose subject areas are shown in Table 2. Depending on their size and strength, the SIGs act like little societies, holding meetings and conferences, and publishing newsletters and conference proceedings. ACM conducts an active awards program honoring technical achievements and service to the profession, society, and ACM itself. Some awards are not limited to ACM members (*see* TURING AWARD WINNERS). It has 125 professional chapters, almost a third outside the USA, and 420 student chapters, including 45 outside the USA, all of which can benefit from the ACM Lectureship Program, which provides speakers on a wide variety of topics.

On 1 January 1999, ACM, as an international organization, became a full member of the International

Table 1. ACM Transactions.

Transactions on Computational Logic
Transactions on Computer–Human Interaction
Transactions on Computer Systems
Transactions on Database Systems
Transactions on Design Automation of Electronic Systems
Transactions on Graphics
Transactions on Information and System Security
Transactions on Information Systems
Transactions on Mathematical Software
Transactions on Modeling and Computer Simulation
IEEE/ACM Transactions on Networking
Transactions on Programming Languages and Systems
Transactions on Software Engineering and Methodology

Table 2. ACM Special Interest Groups (SIGs) and their acronyms.

Ada Programming Language	SIGAda
Algorithms and Computational Theory	SIGACT
APL Programming Language	SIGAPL
Applied Computing	SIGAPP
Artificial Intelligence	SIGART
Biomedical Computing	SIGBIO
Computer Architecture	SIGARCH
Computer Graphics and Interactive Techniques	SIGGRAPH
Computer Personnel Research	SIGCPR
Computer Science Education	SIGCSE
Computer Uses in Education	SIGCUE
Computer–Human Interaction	SIGCHI
Computers and Society	SIGCAS
Computers and the Physically Handicapped	SIGCAPH
Data Communication	SIGCOMM
Design Automation	SIGDA
Electronic Commerce	SIGECOM
Electronic Forum on Sound Technology	SIGSOUND
Groupware	SIGGROUP
Hypertext, Hypermedia and Web	SIGWEB
Information Retrieval	SIGIR
Knowledge Discovery in Data	SIGKDD
Management Information Systems	SIGMIS
Management of Data	SIGMOD
Measurement and Evaluation	SIGMETRICS
Microprogramming	SIGMICRO
Mobility of Systems, Users, Data and Computing	SIGMOBILE
Multimedia	SIGMULTI
Operating Systems	SIGOPS
Programming Languages	SIGPLAN
Security, Audit and Control	SIGSAC
Simulation and Modeling	SIGSIM
Software Engineering	SIGSOFT
Symbolic and Algebraic Manipulation	SIGSAM
Systems Documentation	SIGDOC
University and College Computing Services	SIGUCS

Federation for Information Processing (IFIP—*q.v.*) having previously been one of the two members (with the IEEE-CS) of FOCUS, which until 31 December 1998 represented the USA in IFIP. ACM is also is a constituent society of the Institute for Certification of Computing Professionals (*q.v.*), and is a professional member of the Internet Society (*see* INTERNET). ACM has joint membership arrangements with the IEEE-CS and with 24 computing societies outside the USA. In addition to its headquarters, located in the city of its birth, New York (One Astor Place, 1515 Broadway, New York, NY 10036-5701, acmhelp@acm.org), it has a US Public Policy Office in Washington (666 Pennsylvania Avenue SE, Suite 302B, Washington, DC 20003), and a European Service Centre to provide administrative services to its large non-US membership (108 Cowley Road, Oxford OX4 1JF, UK).

ACM's presidents since its inception are listed in Appendix V.

Eric A. Weiss

ASSOCIATIVE MEMORY

For articles on related subjects *see* ADDRESSING; CACHE MEMORY; MEMORY HIERARCHY; NEURAL NETWORKS; and VIRTUAL MEMORY.

Data in an *associative* or *content-addressable memory* is looked up by properties of its value, rather than by its address as in conventional memory. Such a property might be a pattern of bits at the start of a word or set of words of storage, for example, that serves as an identifying tag. Associative memory is used in multi-level memory systems (*see* MEMORY HIERARCHY), in which a small fast memory such as a cache may hold copies of some blocks of a larger memory for rapid access.

To retrieve a word from associative memory, a search key (or *descriptor*) must be presented that represents particular values of all or some of the bits of the word. This key is compared in parallel with the corresponding lock or tag bits of all stored words, and all words matching this key are signaled to be available. If the key is *loose*, with few attributes, it will access many words. The memory might indicate the number of such words and would in any case normally provide each of these in turn for examination. The order in which they are presented is usually related to their order in physical storage and tells nothing of their value. Once available, each word can be used or, if not wanted, flagged (by a change of a single search bit) so that succeeding words can be retrieved.

Associative search can be fairly complex if the search key has few elements and the association is loose. A limiting case is that in which at most one occurrence of a search key match exists. This occurs in the use of associative stores between levels in a memory hierarchy where the associative store is a scratch pad that may hold a copy of a record in the next higher-level store.

Various attempts have been made to build associative processors in which the main memory is partially or completely associative (Lewin, 1972). In this case each memory word, in addition to match or equality logic on each bit, has other facilities such as "greater than" detection.

Fig. 1 illustrates the logical structure of an associative store, showing the possibility of ("don't care") search inputs whose value results in a positive match independent of the bit stored in the associative memory. Such a store can be implemented using integrated circuitry (*q.v.*), though the additional logic that it requires makes it slower than conventional memory. In addition to the associative search mechanism, the memory is usually equipped with conventional read–write facilities (not shown in Fig. 1).

A flip-flop is shown as the basic storage element and is shaded to indicate its current state. An equivalence circuit (denoted by "=") is used to make the comparison with the search key. The circuit generates a 1 output for a match and 0 for no match. An

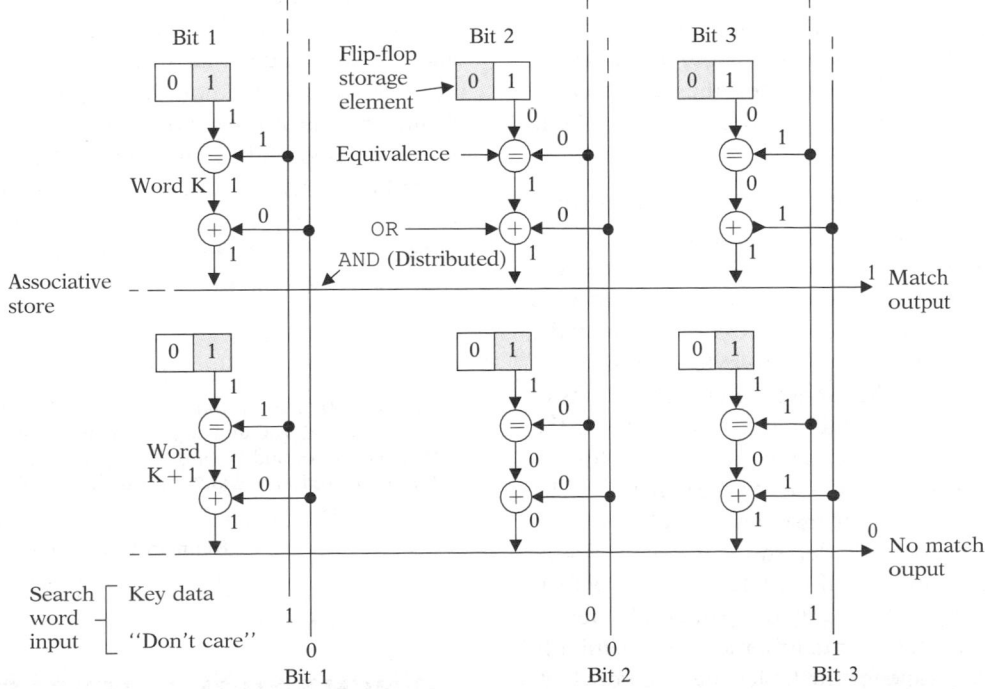

Figure 1. Schematic of an associative store of two words of three bits each being accessed by match on two bits and by "don't care" on one.

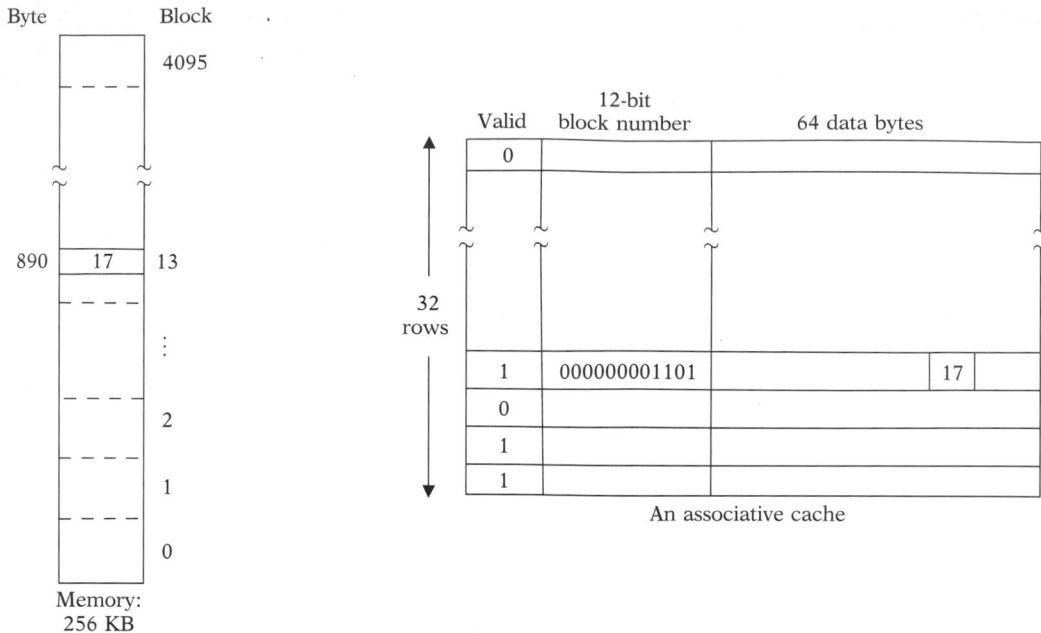

Figure 2. A cache organized as 32 rows, each holding 64 data bytes. The block number (tag) is formed from the high 12 bits of a memory address, and the low 6 bits of the address specify the position of a byte within a cache row. Byte 890 (000000001101 111010 in binary) is in block 13, at position 58 within the cache row, and contains 17. The cache valid bits indicate which rows currently hold data.

additional OR circuit (denoted by "+") per bit allows the use of a "don't care" search condition, producing the logical OR of the match-result and the corresponding don't-care bit. The outputs from the ORs for each bit are combined in an AND, represented by the horizontal lines on the figure. A match output is 1 if and only if the stored data and key data bits match everywhere that "don't care" inputs are zero. Fig. 1 shows a match between a stored value of (1,0,0) and a search key of (1,0,X), where X indicates the "don't care" condition, denoted by the 1-bit in the "don't care" line of bit 3 in the figure.

Associative memory might be used to implement a cache memory as follows. Suppose that a 2 KB cache is organized as 32 rows, each holding 64 bytes, and that the main memory is an (unrealistically small) 256 KB $(= 2^{18}$ bytes), so that a main address is 18 bits wide. If blocks of memory aligned on 64-byte address boundaries are loaded into the cache, then the top 12 bits of an address serve as a tag that marks its presence in the cache (each row of the cache will have 12 bits for the tag plus a "valid data" bit—*see* Fig. 2). If the cache stores these tag bits in an associative memory, then the associative lookup will determine if any particular block is in the cache, and if so, where it is. In effect, the cache can respond directly to the query, "where is the copy of block N?" Virtual memory may similarly use associative storage for the tables that record which portions of the virtual address space are currently held in the main memory.

Associative memory is expensive to implement in integrated circuit technology. Other approaches have recently been studied. A massively parallel processing (*q.v.*) system with small processors and efficient message-broadcast mechanisms can function associatively. If each processor holds a line of text, for example, a broadcast query, "Where does 'associative' appear?," will get affirmative responses from nodes whose text includes that word. Neural networks can model associative memory in a slightly different sense of the term, providing the ability to retrieve information associated with a given input. Such associations might be similarities of meaning in natural language processing (*q.v.*) or pattern similarities in pattern recognition (*q.v.*). *See* Krikelis and Weems (1997) for a survey of these approaches.

Bibliography

1972. Lewin, D. *Theory and Design of Digital Computers,* Chapters 6 and 9. Camden, NJ: Thomas Nelson.
1997. Krikelis, A., and Weems, C. C. (eds.) *Associative Processing and Processors.* Los Alamitos, CA: Computer Society Press.

Kenneth C. Smith and Adel S. Sedra

ASYNCHRONOUS OPERATION

See SYNCHRONOUS/ASYNCHRONOUS OPERATION.

ASYNCHRONOUS TRANSFER MODE (ATM)

For articles on related subjects *see* LOCAL AREA NETWORK; MULTIMEDIA; OPEN SYSTEMS INTERCONNECTION; PACKET SWITCHING; PROTOCOL; and TCP/IP.

ATM is the switching technology that underlies the new (1990s) Broadband Integrated Services Digital Network (B-ISDN). Early in the 21st century, B-ISDN will offer a variety of services including high-speed data transport, local area network (LAN) interconnection, video on demand, interactive television, multimedia email, CD-quality music, videoconferencing and telephony. Also known as *cell relay* (because the basic unit of transmission is called a cell), ATM defines a packet switching protocol which roughly maps on to the physical and datalink layers of the Open Systems Interconnection (OSI) reference model, although some of the functions of the network and transport layers are also included. It is asynchronous in that cells from different sources (applications) share the communication channel on an "as needed" basis, using a scheme known as statistical or asynchronous time division multiplexing (*see* MULTIPLEXING).

The basic features of ATM are:

◆ Fixed-size cells for fast (Gb/sec) switching.

◆ Fiber optic technology, rates of 155–622 Mb/sec.

◆ Constant and variable rate traffic transported.

◆ Connection oriented service with sequenced cell delivery.

◆ Integration with older LANs through LAN emulation and support of IP (Internet Protocol—*see* TCP/IP) over ATM.

Switching

An ATM switch has some number (16–1024) of input and output lines, usually the same number. Cells arrive asynchronously on the input lines, and are switched to the right output lines as they go through the switching fabric (Fig. 1). Switching is synchronous, working in cycles controlled by a master clock. The switching

Table 1.

Field	Bits	Function
GFC	4	Generic Flow Control; at the UNI (User-Network Interface) only; not used at present
VPI	8 (UNI) or 12 (NNI)	Virtual Path Identifier—at the NNI (Network–Network Interface), the 4 bits used for GFC also form part of the VPI
VCI	16	Virtual Channel Identifier
PTI	3	Payload Type; see Table 2
CLP	1	Cell Loss Priority
HEC	8	Header Error Checksum
Data	384	ATM payload, i.e. the data itself

fabric operates at speeds of gigabits per second. Contention for output ports may occur if, in a given cycle, two or more cells arrive wanting the same output port. This may be resolved by queueing or cell discarding. Cell sequence must be preserved within each virtual connection, and cell discard rates should be as low as possible, no more than 1 in 10^{12}.

Cell Format

Each data cell is structured as in Table 1. The VPI and VCI fields identify the end users or applications which own the cell and are also used in routing the cell from source to destination. A fuller discussion appears below.

The CLP bit decides whether a cell may be dropped in the event of network congestion. The HEC allows for single-bit error correction. About 90% of multibit errors will usually be detected.

The PTI field can assume one of eight values, as detailed in Table 2. The cell type bit is used under some circumstances, to distinguish between the first or intermediate cells of a sequence (value 0) and the last (value 1).

Table 2.

PTI	Meaning
000	User data, cell type 0, no congestion
001	User data, cell type 1, no congestion
010	User data, cell type 0, network congestion
011	User data, cell type 1, network congestion
100	Maintenance information between adjacent switches
101	Maintenance information between source and destination switches
110	Resource management, ABR traffic
111	Reserved for future use

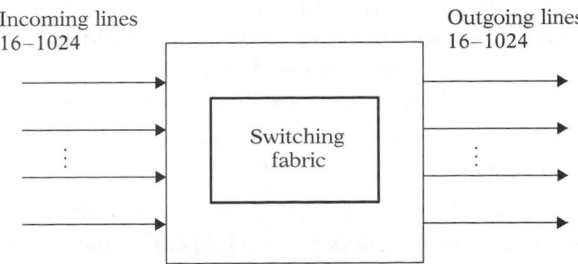

Incoming lines 16–1024 → Switching fabric → Outgoing lines 16–1024

Figure 1. An ATM switch.

After the header come 48 bytes of payload. However, only 44 are usually available to the user as 4 bytes are reserved for system use.

Classes of Service

The different classes of service correspond to the types of traffic that will use the network.

Constant Bit Rate (CBR) is intended for voice-grade Pulse Code Modulation (PCM) and also constant bit rate audio and video streams in real time. Bits are put in at one end and come off the other end. No flow/error control or other processing is done. Quality of Service (QoS) requirements include delay, i.e. mean delay experienced by the cells in going from source to destination and delay variation, i.e. the variance of the distribution of cell delays.

Variable Bit Rate (VBR) is intended for compressed video. This type of traffic has stringent delay and delay variation requirements.

Available Bit Rate (ABR) service is for bursty traffic where the bandwidth (*q.v.*) requirement is known roughly. The network guarantees some bandwidth, but may tell the user to slow down if congestion occurs.

Unspecified Bit Rate (UBR) service makes no promises and gives no congestion notification. If congestion occurs, cells are discarded. Being low priority but cheap, it is attractive for non-urgent applications.

Virtual Channels and Paths

The ATM protocol is connection oriented. Before data exchange can take place, the two parties (user processes or applications) concerned go through a preliminary exchange of messages to "establish a connection." This includes an agreement to participate, negotiation of various operational and quality of service parameters, ensuring the availability of the necessary network resources, and deciding on a path or route through the network. Once this is done, a Virtual Connection (VC) is said to exist between the two processes. It is like a telephone connection, but with an important distinction. The connection is not dedicated, in that the network links on the selected route may be shared by other users and VCs. It is thus termed a logical or *virtual* connection.

VCs may be bundled together for part of the route if they share a common path. These bundles are called virtual paths (VPs) and serve to simplify routing and connection management. Several virtual paths may share the same physical or transmission path (cable). These concepts are illustrated in Fig. 2.

Virtual Connections may be leased on a permanent basis (PVC) or set up as required (Switched Virtual

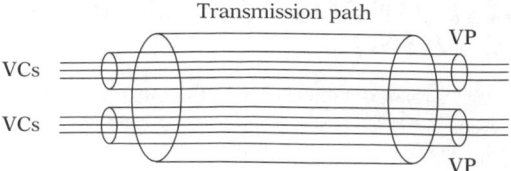

Figure 2. A transmission path showing virtual connections (VC) bundled into virtual paths (VP).

Connection or SVC). An alternative method is to establish (or acquire permanently) a virtual path to the required destination. All VCs within the path can be allocated by the user, without involving the switches.

The setup request contains the destination address. Three forms of ATM address are used. Two are based on the 20 byte hierarchical OSI address. The third uses 15-digit decimal telephone numbers as found on Integrated Services Digital Networks (*see* ISDN).

As the connection setup message goes through the network, the route for the VC is determined. A given VC between a source and a destination will have different VPI/VCIs assigned to it for each hop along the way. Each switch maintains routing table entries for each VC going through it.

When a VC is established, a service contract is negotiated. This includes bandwidth requirements, peak and mean bit rates, service class and compliance requirements. The contract requires the user to restrict the traffic input to the agreed levels, and the carrier to provide the agreed level of service.

Bibliography

1995. Halsall, F. *Data Communications, Computer Networks and OSI*. Reading, MA: Addison-Wesley.
1996. Tanenbaum, A. S. *Computer Networks*, 3rd Ed. Upper Saddle River, NJ: Prentice Hall.
1997. Stallings, W. *Data and Computer Communications*, 5th Ed. Upper Saddle River, NJ: Prentice Hall.

Sati McKenzie

ATANASOFF–BERRY COMPUTER

The Atanasoff–Berry Computer, or ABC, named for its inventor, John V. Atanasoff (*q.v.*), and his graduate assistant, Clifford E. Berry, was the world's first electronic computer. Atanasoff conceived the basic plan of the ABC during the 1937–38 academic year at Iowa State College (now University), where he was a professor of both physics and mathematics.

He spent the next year working out the details of its central computing apparatus: vacuum tube add–subtract mechanisms, rotating drum memory, and vacuum tube regeneration mechanisms to refresh the

Figure 1. The ABC computer.

memory's capacitor elements. He and Berry completed a successful model of that central apparatus by December 1939, and the computer itself by May 1942.

The digital (binary) ABC was designed to solve systems of up to 29 simultaneous linear equations (*see* Fig. 1). Based on an original variant of Gaussian elimination, it used repeated additions and subtractions, sign-sensing, shifting, and automatic sequential controls for the main step of eliminating a designated variable from a pair of equations.

The binary digits of such a pair of equations were represented as high or low charges on capacitors housed in two drums on a common axle. As the drums rotated, their signals were transmitted in parallel to the separate arithmetic unit, where 30 add–subtract mechanisms, together with an associated carry–borrow drum, performed the appropriate additions or subtractions and sent the results back to the memory drum from which a coefficient was being eliminated. Meanwhile, 30 restore-shift mechanisms refreshed the addends or subtrahends and sent those back to the other memory drum, shifting them if necessary for the next rotation.

Computing in the binary system required base conversion in and out. The successive elimination of variables from such long equations also required a great many intermediate binary input–output steps, for which Atanasoff devised an electronically controlled carbon-arc method of punching and reading cards.

In the end, an error of extremely small frequency in this latter system spoiled results for sets of more than five equations, a difficulty Atanasoff and Berry were unable to resolve before they left Iowa for war research positions in 1942. The capacitor memory

and the vacuum tube arithmetic unit worked exactly as intended, however, and established the feasibility of electronic computing, as well as many of its principles, for all time.

The electronic switching principles of the ABC were used throughout the ENIAC (*q.v.*), and its principles of both regenerative storage and logical switching adders were also used in the ensuing EDVAC (*q.v.*). Later computers have used all of these principles, plus those of mechanically rotated memories and capacitor memory elements.

A replica of the ABC was built at Iowa State University and was first demonstrated in October 1997.

Bibliography

1988. Burks, A. R., and Burks, A. W. *The First Electronic Computer: The Atanasoff Story*. Ann Arbor, MI: University of Michigan Press.
1988. Mackintosh, A. R. "Dr. Atanasoff's Computer," *Scientific American*, **259**, 2, 90–96.

Website

1998. Helmer, G. http://www.scl.ameslab.gov/ABC/ABC.html.

Arthur W. Burks and Alice R. Burks

ATANASOFF, JOHN VINCENT

For an article on a related subject *see* ATANASOFF–BERRY COMPUTER.

John V. Atanasoff (Fig. 1) is now widely recognized as the inventor of the world's first electronic computer, the digital Atanasoff–Berry Computer (*q.v.*), or ABC, so named to acknowledge the contribution of his graduate assistant, Clifford E. Berry.

Because the special-purpose ABC led directly to the general-purpose ENIAC (*q.v.*) and on to the EDVAC (*q.v.*) and other first-generation stored-program computers, Atanasoff is also widely recognized as the initiator of the modern computer revolution.

Atanasoff was born in Hamilton, NY, on 4 October 1903 (d. Monrovia, MD, 15 June 1995). He received his B.S. in electrical engineering from Florida State University in 1925, his M.S. in mathematics from Iowa State College (now University) in 1926, and his Ph.D. in experimental physics from the University of Wisconsin in 1930. He taught mathematics and physics at Iowa State until 1942, when he left for war research at the Naval Ordnance Laboratory in Washington, DC.

Atanasoff did not return to teaching, or to computers, when he left government service in 1952, but devoted

Figure 1. John Vincent Atanasoff.

the balance of his career to business enterprises, including the founding of two engineering companies: Ordnance Engineering Corporation and Cybernetics, Inc. Although unsuccessful in patenting the ABC, he obtained over 20 other patents.

Atanasoff's greatest achievement, of course, was his invention of the electronic computer. He conceived its basic plan at Iowa State during the 1937–1938 academic year, worked out critical details the next year, and, with Berry's help, built a working model of the central computing apparatus in late 1939. He and Berry then proceeded with the computer itself, completing construction in the spring of 1942.

Atanasoff designed this computer to solve unprecedentedly large systems of simultaneous linear equations, which he saw as applicable to a wide variety of problems in physics, engineering, and applied mathematics. For this purpose, he devised an original variant of the traditional Gaussian elimination method.

The ABC featured binary arithmetic, rotating drum memories, capacitor memory elements, continuous electronic regeneration of those elements from a separate arithmetic unit, electronic (vacuum tube) switching and logical switching adders, base conversion, punched-card input–output systems, automatic sequential controls, modular units, and parallel operations.

Atanasoff's priority over John W. Mauchly (*q.v.*) and J. Presper Eckert (*q.v.*), whose ENIAC had been unveiled as the first electronic computer in 1946, was not established until 1973, when Federal District Judge Earl R. Larson ruled in the now famous Honeywell vs. Sperry Rand suit. In his unappealed decision, Larson found that "Eckert and Mauchly did not themselves first invent the automatic electronic digital computer, but instead derived that subject matter from one Dr. John Vincent Atanasoff."

Mauchly's contacts with Atanasoff included a five-day visit to Iowa in 1941, during which he was allowed to examine both the machine and a detailed written description of it.

Atanasoff received several awards in the 1940s for his contributions as chief of the Naval Ordnance Laboratory's acoustics division, including the US Navy Distinguished Service Award. In his later years he received many honorary degrees and other citations for his work at Iowa State, culminating in the 1990 National Medal of Technology "for inventing the electronic digital computer."

Bibliography

1988. Burks, A. R., and Burks, A. W. *The First Electronic Computer: The Atanasoff Story.* Ann Arbor, MI: University of Michigan Press.
1988. Mollenhoff, C. R. *Atanasoff: Forgotten Father of the Computer.* Ames, IA: Iowa State University Press.
1988. Mackintosh, A. R. "Dr. Atanasoff's Computer," *Scientific American*, **259**, 2, 90–96.

Arthur W. Burks and Alice R. Burks

ATLAS

For articles on related subject *see* DIGITAL COMPUTERS, HISTORY OF: EARLY; KILBURN, TOM; and MANCHESTER UNIVERSITY COMPUTERS.

The Atlas computer was the third in a series of early computers designed in the UK by a team under Tom Kilburn in the Department of Electrical Engineering, University of Manchester, in association with Ferranti Ltd (later ICT Ltd and then ICL Ltd). Previous systems were the Ferranti Mark I and Ferranti Mark II (Mercury).

Design of Atlas began in 1958, and ultimately three systems, known as Atlas 1, were constructed and installed at the University of Manchester (1962), University of London (1963), and the Atlas Laboratory, Chilton, next to the Atomic Energy Research Establishment at Harwell (1963). [In the late 1950s one response to the increasing expense of scientific equipment at universities was to share centralized facilities. The Atlas computer was set up by the common academic nuclear science establishment, the National Institute for Research in Nuclear Science (NIRNS).] All were operated until the early 1970s, with the Chilton machine being the last to be switched off in March 1973.

In many respects, Atlas led the way in design of an integrated computer system, combining many novel hardware features with an advanced software operating system. Among the new concepts that Atlas successfully introduced were multiprogramming (*q.v.*), one-level store, and paging. It was the first major system designed for multiprogramming and was provided with a composite memory consisting of ferrite cores and magnetic drums linked by program to provide the user with a one-level memory (*see* VIRTUAL MEMORY). This was achieved by a paging system in which page switching was controlled by a simple learning program, or swapping algorithm. There was also a wiremesh/ferrite rod (hairbrush) memory of 8,000 words to hold the supervisor. The standard word length was 48 bits, equivalent to one single-address instruction with two modifiers and allowing for up to 2^{20} addresses. Additionally, 128 index registers (*q.v.*) were provided. Instructions were normally executed at an average rate of 0.5 ms, about a hundred times faster than the Mercury computer.

The magnetic tape system used 1-inch tapes, although standard 0.5-inch tapes could also be used. Magnetic disks were not standard, but were fitted later to the Manchester and Chilton machines. Multiple I/O channels (*q.v.*) provided for both paper-tape and punched-card peripherals as well as line printers.

Other features of the supervisor program, which was produced by a small team under D. J. Howarth (1961), were the facilities for scheduling and streaming of jobs, automatic control of peripherals, detailed job accounting, and a sophisticated level of operator control. It was normal, with some discretion in selecting the job mix, to obtain 60–80% effective use of the CPU.

A modified version of Atlas, known as Atlas 2, was produced with increased core memory and no magnetic drums (thereby dispensing with paging), the prototype being the Titan computer at the University of Cambridge, which was taken out of service at the end of 1973. Two others in this series were installed: one at the Atomic Weapons Research Establishment, Aldermaston, and one at the Computer-Aided Design Centre, Cambridge.

Although technical and economic reasons, partly due to advances in component manufacture, prevented the Atlas computers from achieving commercial success, they represent an important landmark in the development of advanced computer systems.

Bibliography

1961. Howarth, D. J., Payne, R. B., and Sumner, F. H. "The Manchester University Atlas Operating System; Part II, Users' Description," *Computer J.*, **4**, 226–229.

1961. Kilburn, T., Howarth, D. J., Payne, R. B., and Sumner, F. H. "The Manchester University Atlas Operating System; Part I, Internal Organisation," *Computer J.*, **4**, 222–225.

1962. Howarth, D. J., Jones, P. D., and Wyld, M. T. "The Atlas Scheduling System," *Computer J.*, **5**, 238–244.

1962. Kilburn, T., Edwards, B. G., Lanigan, M. J., and Sumner, F. H. "One-level Storage System," *IRE Trans.*, **EC-11**, 2, 223–235.

1984. Hendry, J. "Prolonged Negotiations: The British Fast Computer Project and the Early History of the British Computer Industry," *Business History*, **26**, 280–306.

Richard A. Buckingham

ATM

See ASYNCHRONOUS TRANSFER MODE.

AUTHENTICATION

For articles on related subjects, *see* CRYPTOGRAPHY, COMPUTERS IN; DIGITAL SIGNATURE; PASSWORD; and PRETTY GOOD PRIVACY

The term *authentication* is used to refer to several distinct, though related, processes. The earliest use, as described in Needham and Schroeder's paper (1978), is to arrange that two entities engaged in communication, generically referred to as principals, should each be confident as to the other's identity. A more demanding requirement is for each to be able to convince a referee or arbiter that a certain transaction was performed by the other—generally known as non-repudiation. Finally, document content may need to be authenticated in the sense that its integrity is guaranteed in addition to original authorship. In theory, authentication is quite distinct from the provision of confidentiality, but in practice they often go together.

While some principals are people and could be identified biometrically, that is by physical characteristics, in computing not all are—consider file systems, printers, and so on, which do not have any anatomy. Accordingly authentication is usually on the basis of knowledge of something, or by possession of a token or a by combination of the two, as in the use of passwords, physical keys, or an ATM card with a PIN. There are many different protocols for this type of authentication, but they all depend on a very simple principle: if I receive a message which shows unequivocal knowledge of something that only Joe knows, then it came from Joe. Cryptography enters such protocols basically in order to demonstrate knowledge of Joe's secret, without advertising the secret itself. In detail there are differences. If we are dealing with symmetric cryptography the reasoning is usually "Only Joe and I know X, and I didn't send this message so Joe did," and if we are dealing with asymmetric cryptography it will be "Only Joe knows the X needed to send that which I can unpick with X^{-1}" (the inverse of X).

This principle may be simple, but the detail is not. Authentication protocols are subject to numerous errors of design, and it is quite remarkable how many of them, typically programs of no more than five statements long, are incorrect. It is not unknown for insecurities to be noticed ten years after publication of a protocol. It has been conjectured (Anderson and Needham, 1995) that this is because programmers are not used to designing programs to be robust in the face of deliberately malevolent action in the execution environment. In response to these problems, during the 1990s many tools were developed to check protocol designs for various sorts of insecurity. These range from special-purpose logics (Burrows et al., 1990) to programs that follow all possible execution traces. Meadows (1995) gives a useful survey. Some principles are emerging, notably the need for explicitness in all messages. Thus it is very desirable that a message should include, as an integral part, statements of the source and intended destination, the identity of the protocol being used, and the message number, even if they are "obvious." These matters are discussed further in Abadi and Needham (1996).

Protocols of the sort just discussed and detailed further in the references are directed at causing the parties, usually called A and B, to be satisfied as to the other's identity. They are not necessarily appropriate to convincing a third party of anything—for example for A to convince an arbiter in a dispute that an action really had been undertaken at B's request. This is the second form of authentication. For A and B to share a secret gets us nowhere, because any use B could make of it could also have been made by A. This is where asymmetric cryptography comes seriously into its own, since B can only deny having made use of his private key by saying that it is compromised, casting doubt on all B's other commitments. It is, however, necessary to have some system of trusted infrastructure to satisfy A beyond reasonable doubt that B's alleged public key is real. It is possible to achieve similar effects in a symmetric-key world by using trusted machines with a function reminiscent of a notary, but this is surely an inferior solution. Nonrepudiation is not a completely technical matter; it is basically concerned with the generation of evidence that will be considered by a (human) arbiter.

The third sort of authentication is usually done by computing a "one-way function" of the content, and authenticating it by digital signature. Such one-way functions have to have the property that, given a message and its signed *digest*, as such functions are usually called, it is impracticable to construct a different message with the same digest. Designing digest functions is difficult, and the field is moving very fast. Some of the issues are set out in Schneier (1996), which is also an excellent general reference.

Bibliography

1978. Needham, R. M., and Schroeder, M. D. "Using Encryption for Authentication in Large Networks of Computers," *Comm. of the ACM*, **21**, *12* (December), 993–999.
1990. Burrows, M., Abadi, M., and Needham, R. M. "A Logic of Authentication," *ACM Transactions on Computer Systems*, **8**, *1* (February), 18–36.
1995. Anderson, R. J., and Needham, R. M. "Programming Satan's Computer," in *Computer Science Today* (ed. Jan van Leeuwen), 426–440, LNCS 1000. New York: Springer-Verlag.
1995. Meadows, C. "Formal Verification of Cryptographic Protocols—a Survey," in *Advances in Cryptology—AsiaCrypt 95*, 133–150. New York: Springer-Verlag.
1996. Abadi, M., and Needham, R. M. "Prudent Engineering Practice for Cryptographic Protocols," *IEEE Transactions on Software Engineering*, **22**, *1* (January), 6–15.
1996. Schneier, B. *Applied Cryptography*, 2nd Ed. New York: John Wiley.

Roger M. Needham

AUTOMATA THEORY

For articles on related subjects *see* CELLULAR AUTOMATA; FORMAL LANGUAGES; GRAMMARS; NEURAL NETWORKS; PERCEPTRON; PROBABILISTIC AUTOMATA; QUANTUM COMPUTING; SEQUENTIAL MACHINE; and TURING MACHINE.

Introduction and Definitions

Automata theory is a mathematical discipline concerned with the invention and study of mathematically abstract, idealized machines called *automata*. These automata are usually abstractions of information processing devices, such as computers, rather than of devices that move about, such as robots, mechanical toys, or automobiles.

This article gives a short informal survey of the major classes of automata that automata theorists have seen fit to study, and indicates the primary motivations (from the point of view of computer science) for the study of each of these classes of automata.

For the most part, the automata discussed here process strings of symbols from some finite alphabet of symbols. Let A be any alphabet (finite set of symbols). For example, A might be $\{a, b, c, \ldots, z\}$ or $\{0, 1\}$. We write A^* to mean the set of *all* finite strings of symbols chosen from A. If A is $\{a, b, c, \ldots, z\}$, then A^* contains strings representing English words, such as "cat" and "mouse," along with nonsense strings such as "czzxyh." If A is $\{0, 1\}$, then A^* contains the strings representing the nonnegative integers in binary notation $(0, 1, 10, 11, 100, \ldots)$ and also these same strings but with extra zeros on the left (e.g. 00010).

Automata generally perform one (or both) of two symbol-processing tasks. They compute partial functions from X^* to Y^* for some finite alphabets X and Y, or they *recognize* languages over some alphabet X.

A *partial function* f from X^* to Y^* is a correspondence between some subset D of X^* and the set Y^* that associates with each element of D a unique element in Y^*. D is called the *domain* of f, that is, $D = \{x \in X^* | f(x)$ is defined$\}$. For example, let $X = Y = \{0, 1\}$ and let D be the elements x of X^* such that x begins with 1 or consists of a single 0. If f associates with x the string in Y^* that denotes the binary number representing twice the binary number represented by x, then f is a partial function from X^* to Y^*. If $f(x)$ is not defined, it is *desirable* that automaton α on input x should eventually halt and print some sort of *error message*. However, this is not always possible—there are computable partial functions f all of whose automata fail to halt at all on some input x outside the domain of f.

We say roughly that an automaton α *computes* a partial function f from X^* to Y^* when, if α is given any input x in X^* such that $f(x)$ is defined, α eventually produces an output $y \in Y^*$ such that $f(x) = y$, and otherwise α produces no output.

Automata usually receive their inputs on a linear or one-dimensional tape which they may read one symbol at a time. The manner in which they read symbols on an input tape (left to right, back and forth, with or without changing symbols, etc.) depends on the particular class of automata under consideration. Automata for computing partial functions produce their output on a tape (perhaps the input tape, perhaps a different tape) in a manner also prescribed by the particular class of automata under consideration.

There are also automata whose storage structures more closely resemble *registers* (*q.v.*), such as are found in a typical computer or pocket calculator, than linear tapes.

A *language* over an alphabet X is just a subset of X^*. For example, if $X = \{a, b, c, \ldots, z\}$, then $\{a, aa, aaa, \ldots\}$ and $\{x \in X^* | x$ is a word in the English language$\}$ are both languages over X.

We say that an automaton α *recognizes* a language L over X if, when α reads an input $x \in X^*$ on its input tape in the manner of automata of its type then, if $x \in L$, α eventually performs some particular act of recognition. Examples of such acts of recognition are (1) halting, (2) entering a special internal state called a *final*, or *accepting*, state, or (3) emptying a designated

storage tape, for instance a *pushdown store*. If $x \notin L$, then α, on input x, never performs such an act of recognition. Exactly what constitutes an act of recognition depends on the particular class of automata under consideration.

It is presumably clear why it is of interest to computer scientists to study automata that compute (partial) functions, since computer science is the computation business. Among the interesting questions to ask are whether some function is or is not computable by some representative of a particular class of automata and, if it is computable, how efficiently (with respect to some mathematically precise measure of efficiency) can it be so computed.

We motivate the study of automata that recognize languages by some examples. Let X be the set of allowable symbols for some programming language P. Include in X the necessary punctuation symbols and the blank symbol. Let $L = \{x \in X^* | x$ is a valid program of P$\}$. In the process of compiling from P into some other language, it is useful (among other things) to *recognize* the valid programs of P as being valid. Automata theory gives some insight into the sort of computing ability that may be required to recognize valid programs. For example, *pushdown automata* (to be defined below) are capable of recognizing the valid syntactic classes of all Algol-like languages (*see* ALGOL). Generally, there are many results of the form: the languages recognized by a particular class of automata are exactly those formal languages generated by a particular class of grammars.

Automatic *theorem proving* (*q.v.*), a subarea of artificial intelligence (*q.v.*), is also concerned with language recognition. The language to be recognized is the set of propositions derivable from some set of axioms. Automatic theorem proving has been applied to discover new mathematical theorems, to question-answering systems, and to robotics (*q.v.*)

Types of Automata

Most (but not all) types of automata are special cases of the *Turing machine* (*see* Fig. 1). Turing machines may be operated either to recognize languages or to compute partial functions. Very roughly, a Turing machine is a finite-state deterministic device with read and write heads (which read or write one symbol at a time) attached to one or more tapes. *Finite state* means that the number of distinguishable internal configurations of the device is finite, and *deterministic* means that the next state of the device and its subsequent action (writing or motion) on the tapes is completely determined by its current state and the symbols it is currently reading on its tapes.

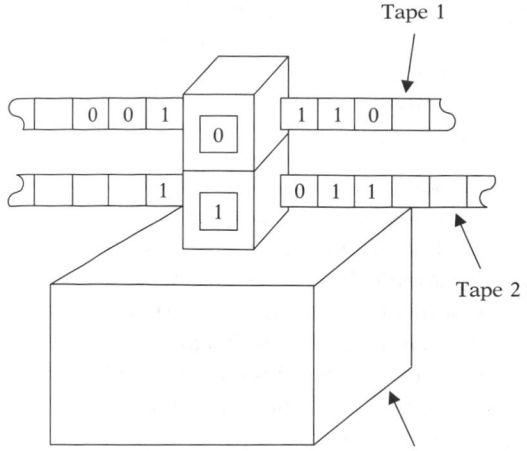

Figure 1. A two-tape Turing machine. Each tape is scanned by a single read–write head. Tape 1 contains the string of nonblank symbols 0010110, with the underlined 0 currently being read. Tape 2 contains 11011, with the underlined 1 being currently read. If the tapes can move in only one direction, the same diagram would depict a two-tape finite automation.

Turing machines were first introduced independently by Turing (*q.v.*) and Post in 1936 to give a precise mathematical definition of *effective procedure* (*see* ALGORITHMS, THEORY OF). There is considerable evidence that the partial functions computed by (languages recognized by) Turing machines are exactly those computed (recognized) by informal effective procedures or algorithms (*q.v.*). Any computation or recognition problem for which there is a known informal algorithm can be handled by a Turing machine. Turing machines with many (in general, *n*-dimensional) tapes and read–write heads can compute and recognize *no more* than can Turing machines with a single one-dimensional tape and single read–write head, although they may compute and recognize more efficiently.

Attempts to define effective procedures in terms of automata that more closely resemble modern electronic stored-program digital computers have led to the *unlimited register machines* of Shepherdson and Sturgis and to the *random access stored-program* machines of Elgot and Robinson. These machines can be shown to compute the same partial functions (recognize the same languages) computed by Turing machines.

Turing machines model the most general sort of computation processes, in part by virtue of their ability to move about freely on their tapes without fear of running out of tape. In general no *a priori* bound can be set on the amount of tape a Turing machine computation will require. Some Turing machine computations may require more tape than is available in the

universe! This partially motivates our consideration of the next class of automata, *finite automata*. We will limit our discussion to finite automata considered as recognizers of languages, and will leave their application as input–output devices to the article SEQUENTIAL MACHINES.

A *finite automaton* is a deterministic finite-state device equipped with a read (only) head attached to a single input tape. A special subset of the finite set of states of a finite automaton is designated as the set of *final*, or *recognition*, states. A finite automaton α processes a string of symbols thus: α begins in a special initial, or start, state and automatically reads the symbols of x (on its tape) from left to right, changing its states in a manner depending only on its previous state and the symbol just read. If, after the last (rightmost) symbol of x is read, α goes into a final state, α recognizes x; otherwise, α does not recognize x. Let $A = \{0, 1\}$. It is possible, for example, to design a finite automaton α such that α recognizes $L = \{x \in A^* \mid x$ ends in two consecutive 1s and does not contain two consecutive 0s$\}$; *see* Fig. 2. On the other hand, it can be shown that *no* finite automaton can recognize $L' = \{x \in A^* \mid x$ consists of a consecutive string of n^2 1s, for some positive integer $n\}$. As might be expected, however, a Turing machine can be designated to recognize L'.

In Fig. 2 the circles represent the different states of α, and the number inside each circle is a name for the state that circle represents. Hence 0 is the start state of α and 4 is its only final state. An arrow (labeled with an alphabet symbol) from one state to another means that if α is in the first state while scanning the alphabet symbol that labels the arrow, then it goes next into the second state. For example, if α is in state 1 scanning a 0, it goes next into state 2; whereas, if it is in state 1

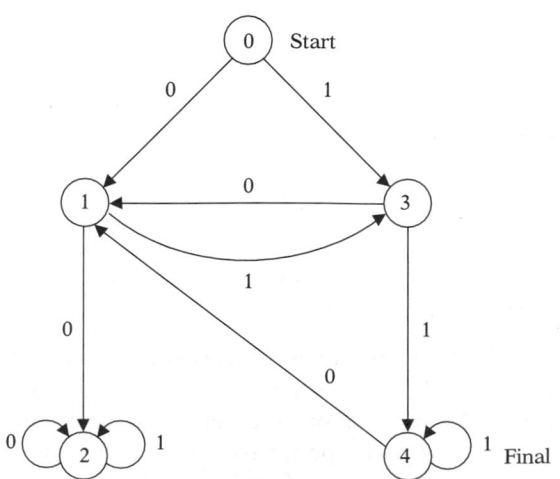

Figure 2. The state diagram of a finite-state automaton for recognizing $\{x \in \{0, 1\}^* \mid x$ ends in two consecutive 1s and does not contain two consecutive 0s$\}$.

scanning a 1, it goes next into state 3. If α is given the input string 010111, beginning in state 0, the successive states into which it is thereafter driven are (in order) 1,3,1,3,4,4. Since 4 is a final state, α (correctly) recognizes the input string 010111. If α is given 10011, beginning in state 0, the successive states into which it is thereafter driven are (in order) 3,1,2,2,2. Since 2 is *not* a final state, α (correctly) fails to recognize 10011.

A *nondeterministic finite automaton* is a device just like a finite automaton except that the next state is not completely determined by the current state and symbol read. Instead, a set of next *possible* states is so determined. A nondeterministic finite automaton α may be thought of as processing a string of symbols x, just like an ordinary finite automaton, except that it has to be run over again several times so that each of the different possible state-change behaviors is eventually realized. One should imagine there being a separate, deterministic control device C which runs α and completely determines α's *actual* state-change behavior each time it is run. There are but finitely many different possible state-change behaviors for α in processing x, and C simply systematically runs α first one way, then another, then another, etc., until all possibilities have been exhausted.

A nondeterministic finite automaton α *recognizes* x if at least one of the possible ways of running α on input x results in getting α into a final state after the last symbol of x has been read (*see* Fig. 3).

In Fig. 3, α_1 is nondeterministic because, for example, from state 0, if it is scanning a it can go into either state 0 or state 1 next. From state 1, if it is scanning b,

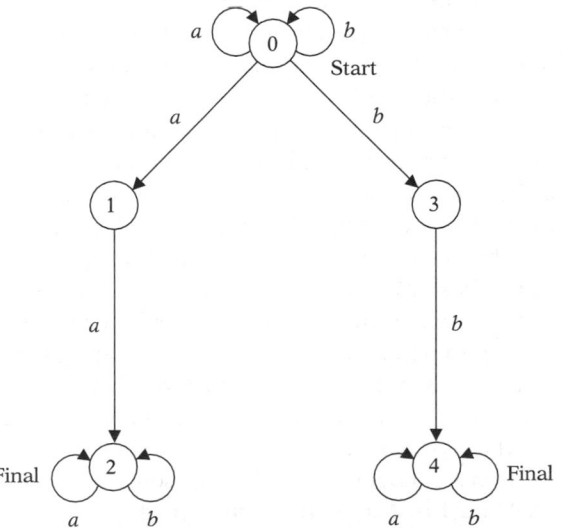

Figure 3. The state diagram of a nondeterministic finite-state automaton α_1 for recognizing $\{x \in \{a, b\}^* \mid x$ contains two consecutive as or two consecutive bs (or both)$\}$.

it *jams*, since the set of next possible states is empty. If α_1 is given the input string *abababba*, beginning in state 0, one possible succession of states is (in order) 0,0,0,0,0,0,0,1. Here, 1 is not one of the final states, so this way of running α_1 does not lead to recognition. Another possible succession of states is (in order) 0,0,0,1, jam. Another is 1, jam. However, 0,0,0,0,0,3, 4,4 is still another possible succession of states. Since 4 is a final state, α_1 (correctly) recognizes *abababba*. It is easy to check that if α_1 is given *babababab*, beginning in state 0, then *none* of the possible ways of running α_1 leads to a final state; hence, α_1 (correctly) does *not* recognize *babababab*.

Interestingly (and perhaps unexpectedly), it can be shown that nondeterministic finite automata recognize exactly the same class of languages as ordinary finite automata. Turing machine recognizers that operate nondeterministically can also be defined, but they, too, cannot recognize more languages than can ordinary Turing machines. For nondeterministic Turing machine recognizers, as well as for some of the other nondeterministic devices to be discussed below, some of the different possible ways to process a given string x may take infinitely many steps. For such devices it is convenient to imagine the separate, deterministic control device C as operating in a parallel mode.

A point of nondeterminism is that it is often conceptually easier to program or design machines that operate nondeterministically. In fact, there are theoretical results to the effect that, for many types of automata, nondeterministic machines are significantly more compact, succinct, or powerful than the corresponding deterministic ones. Furthermore, many practically important recognition tasks can be solved by easy-to-design nondeterministic Turing machines that run in time bounded by a polynomial in the size of their input strings. A famous open question in computer science asks whether these tasks can be done at all in polynomial time by deterministic Turing machines (*see* COMPUTATIONAL COMPLEXITY and NP-COMPLETE PROBLEMS).

In addition to ordinary and nondeterministic automata, a variety of automata called *probabilistic* automata have been studied. A probability of occurrence is assigned to each of the possible next states in a probabilistic automaton. Recently, *quantum Turing machines* have been studied. These theoretically make use of quantum mechanical superposition of states (with error correction) to achieve the effect of parallel processing (with high probability of success). A number of practical problems not known to be solvable in polynomial time deterministically have now been shown so solvable by quantum Turing machines! The exciting possibility is that in the near future it may be possible to construct practical versions of such machines in the real world (*see* QUANTUM COMPUTING).

In 1943, McCulloch and Pitts introduced nets of formalized neurons and showed (in essence) that such neural nets could realize the state-change behavior of any finite automaton. These nets were composed of synchronized elements, each capable of realizing some Boolean function such as *and, or,* or *not*. It has been suggested that von Neumann (*q.v.*) had these networks in mind when he established his logical design (*q.v.*) for digital computers. In 1948, von Neumann added to the computational and logical questions of automata theory by introducing new questions pertaining to construction and self-replication of automata. The iterated arrays of interconnected finite automata which he introduced have also been used to study pattern processing for patterns of symbols, including one-dimensional strings of symbols, among others.

Automata theory, especially finite automata theory, impinges on both mathematical systems theory and modern algebra. In mathematical systems theory, one is interested in the problem of which (if any) input sequences will drive an automaton to some desired internal state. In modern algebra one can study the relations between semigroups and automata. For example, certain decomposition theorems in group theory give information about decomposition of automata into particularly simple component automata.

A *linear-bounded automaton* is a (possibly nondeterministic) one-tape Turing machine whose read–write head is restricted to move only on the section of tape initially containing the input. Special end markers are placed on each side of an input string to prevent the tape head from leaving this restricted section of tape. A form of deterministic linear-bounded automata was first studied by Myhill in an attempt to find models of computation more realistic than the completely general Turing machines, but less restricted than the finite automata. Later it was shown that linear-bounded automata recognize all (and only) the *context-sensitive* languages, an important and natural class of languages which is more restricted than the languages recognizable by Turing machines, but more general than the *context-free* languages. It is an open question whether the linear-bounded automata can recognize more languages than the deterministic linear-bounded automata. Recently, Immerman and Szelepcsényi independently showed that if a language is accepted by some (possibly nondeterministic) linear-bounded automata, then the set of strings (involving the same alphabet) *not* in that language is also accepted by some (different) linear-bounded automata. This answered a long open question.

A *pushdown* automaton is a (possibly nondeterministic) finite automaton with a special sort of auxiliary tape called a *pushdown store*. A pushdown store is a tape quite like the stack (*q.v.*) of plates found on a spring in cafeterias. It is a *last in, first out* store. A special read–write head always scans the top symbol on the pushdown store. The pushdown store is initially loaded with a single special *start* symbol. The top symbol can be replaced by any finite string of symbols (stack of plates), including the empty string of symbols. Replacing the top symbol by the empty string has the effect of completely removing the top symbol and setting the read–write head to scan the next symbol down. The read (only) head on the input tape reads one symbol at a time from left to right, just as in a finite automaton, except that it is allowed (if desired) to stop scanning the input tape momentarily while only the pushdown store is operated.

Pushdown automata recognize a string x by one of two conventions. Either x is recognized by the device as it gets into one of its final states or by the pushdown store as it empties just after the rightmost symbol of x is read. The class of languages recognized by emptying the pushdown store is the same as that recognized by final states. Let $A = \{0, 1\}$. For $x \in A^*$, let x^R be x written backwards. For example, 001110^R is 011100. A string x is a *palindrome* if x and x^R are the same; for instance, 0 and 1001 are palindromes. The language $L = \{x \in A^* | \; x$ is a palindrome$\}$ is recognizable by a suitable nondeterministic pushdown automaton; however, L is *not* recognizable by any finite automaton or even by any deterministic pushdown automaton. A *center-marked palindrome* is a palindrome of odd length with a distinguished symbol for its center symbol. For example, with c as distinguished symbol and the other symbols chosen from $\{0, 1\}$, $001110c011100$ is a center-marked palindrome, but $001110c001110$ and 001110011100 are not. Here, informally, is how to recognize the set of the center-marked palindromes (with c as the distinguished symbol and the other symbols chosen from $\{0, 1\}$) employing a *deterministic* pushdown automaton, where acceptance will be by emptying the stack. Start the machine with a c as the only symbol on its stack and, then, read the input tape. As long as 0s and 1s are seen, put them on the stack (in the order in which they are seen); after, if ever a c is seen, begin to pop items off the stack comparing them with the next symbol on the input tape. If there is a mismatch (either a symbol from the stack does not match the symbol read or the stack runs out of symbols before the tape is finished) or something other than a 0 or a 1 is seen on the input tape, put a c on the stack and stop the machine. If there is no mismatch and the input tape is all read, pop one more symbol off the stack and stop the machine. The machine will halt with an empty stack if and only if the input was a center-marked palindrome (with c as the distinguished symbol and the other symbols chosen from $\{0, 1\}$). Pushdown automata recognize all (and only) the context-free (or equivalently, Algol-like) languages; deterministic pushdown automata are important in compiler design.

Many variations on a slight generalization of pushdown automata have been studied. A *stack automaton* is just like a pushdown automaton except that the read (only) head of the input tape is allowed to move both ways (but not off the section of tape containing the input) and the read–write head on the pushdown store is allowed to scan the entire pushdown list in a *read-only* mode. The class of languages recognized by stack automata is intermediate between context-sensitive and Turing-machine recognizable (*see* CHOMSKY HIERARCHY).

Many other types of automata that have been and could be studied employ some other sort of limited data structure (*q.v.*) for their auxiliary storage or receive inputs in some form other than a string of symbols. For example, *tree* automata process inputs in the form of trees, usually trees associated with parsing expressions in context-free languages.

Automata theory is a growing, open-ended mathematical discipline. It readily admits of extensions of existing concepts and the introduction of totally new ideas. The motivations to make such extensions are esthetic on the one hand, and the need or desire to model some existing or proposed computational phenomenon on the other.

Bibliography

1966. von Neumann, J. *Theory of Self-Reproducing Automata* (edited and completed by A. W. Burks). Urbana, IL: University of Illinois Press.
1967. Minsky, M. *Computation: Finite and Infinite Machines.* Upper Saddle River, NJ: Prentice Hall.
1969. Hopcroft, J. E., and Ullman, J. D. *Formal Languages and Their Relation to Automata.* Reading, MA: Addison-Wesley.
1979. Hopcroft, J. E., and Ullman, J. D. *Introduction to Automata Theory, Languages, and the Theory of Computation.* Reading, MA: Addison-Wesley.
1988. Minsky, M., and Papert, S. *Perceptrons* (expanded edition). Cambridge, MA: MIT Press.
1994. Davis, M., Sigal, R., and Weyuker, E. *Computability, Complexity, and Languages: Fundamentals of Theoretical Computer Science,* 2nd Ed. New York: Academic Press.
1994. Royer, J., and Case, J. *Subrecursive Programming Systems: Complexity and Succinctness.* Boston, MA: Birkhäuser.
1997. Hemaspaandra, L., and Selman, A. (eds.) *Complexity Theory Retrospective II.* Berlin: Springer-Verlag.
1998. Immerman, N. *Descriptive Complexity.* Berlin: Springer-Verlag.
1998. Lewis, H., and Papadimitriou, C. *Elements of the Theory of Computation,* 2nd Ed. Upper Saddle River, NJ: Prentice Hall.

John Case

AUTOMATED PLANNING

For articles on related topics *see* ARTIFICIAL INTELLIGENCE; CASE-BASED REASONING; EXPERT SYSTEMS; LOGIC PROGRAMMING; MACHINE LEARNING; MULTI-AGENT SYSTEMS; and ROBOTICS.

Automated planning is the process of algorithmically creating behavior specifications—or *plans*—for agents, which the agents then follow. By "agent" is meant any kind of entity that behaves, including people, robots, servers on networks, or groups of agents. Because of the variety of agents, and the variety of ways in which behavior might be constrained, there are many different subfields of automated planning.

Taxonomy

One of the simplest and most widely studied kinds of planning is *classical planning*, in which plans are assumed to be sequences of actions that the agent executes one after another; that nothing happens except the actions of the agents; and that the planner has perfect information about the initial world situation and the effects of every action. The goal is to find any sequence of actions, or *tasks*, which, if executed starting in the initial situation, will bring about a situation in which a given *goal predicate* is satisfied. One example is a manufacturing problem in which the initial situation is a set of raw materials, the actions are possible manufacturing steps, and the goal predicate describes the desired product.

An algorithm for classical planning must be supplied with a description of the initial situation and a description of the effects of each action. These are usually expressed in a "STRIPS-style notation," after STRIPS, an early planning algorithm. This notation uses predicate calculus to describe world situations and action effects, although it describes effects in terms of changes to situations, not in strictly logical terms. This notation has the useful property that given a desired effect, it is possible to compute, for every possible action, what precondition must be true before the action in order that the desired effect be true after the action. This computation is called *regressing* the desired effects through the action. For example, rules for robot travel among rooms might include IF inroom(robot, R1) AND connects(door, R1, R2) THEN moveto(robot, R2). If the rule is executed, the situation changes from one in which the robot is in R1 to one in which it is in R2, so that the inroom(robot, R1) predicate would be deleted from the situation description, and inroom(robot, R2) would be added. Such rules might be used if the robot has the task of finding a box and moving it from room to room.

The assumptions of classical planning, and the usual mechanisms for solving it, are rather restrictive, and most real problems are nonclassical. For example, one might want to relax the assumption that the world situation is known after every action and let plans include tests of what is true, followed by *conditional actions* whose execution depends on the results of the tests. Taken to an extreme, plans can be thought of as programs for agents, when planning becomes the problem of automatic programming (*q.v.*) for agents in incompletely specified environments. This is *behavioral planning*.

If the requirement that a single agent be involved is eliminated, then the result is *multi-agent planning*, in which each agent plans, among other things, how to communicate its intentions and requests to other agents. Often it is not enough to find an arbitrary plan, but instead one wants a good or even optimal plan, measured by some objective function. Even very simple planning problems are intractable (NP-hard or worse— *see* COMPUTATIONAL COMPLEXITY), so special cases are of great interest (although they are usually intractable, too). One such case is *scheduling*, in which the input is a set of *tasks* and the desired output is an order in which they are to be executed so as to optimize some objective function. The tasks compete for resources in various ways.

Another important special case is *robot motion planning*, in which situations are specified geometrically, actions are possible joint motions, and the goal predicate is a final position for the robot. This problem can be viewed as a subproblem of *assembly planning*, in which a collection of parts are to be assembled by a robot, using many motion sequences. *Robot navigation planning* is a version of motion planning for mobile robots in which the space moved through is large enough that the details of the robot's shape may be neglected. It focuses on representing, acquiring, and using *maps* to tell the robot which way to move.

Planning algorithms can be classified according to whether they are *offline* or *online*. In offline planning, the planning algorithm is given a problem and solves it without regard to the relation between the time when the resulting plan will be executed and the time when planning is occurring. In online planning, the time spent planning is counted as part of the cost of a plan, so that it can become desirable to stop planning when a "good enough" plan has been found, and further planning might cost more than would be gained. Online planning is inevitable if a plan fails during execution, so that the agent must replan part way through the plan. A planning algorithm is particularly suited for online planning if it has the "anytime" property, i.e. if it finds legal plans quickly, and improves them if given more time.

Planning is a fertile domain for studying *learning* (*see* MACHINE LEARNING), and there has been much research on learning to plan better. One way to do that is to solve a new problem by adapting the solution to a past problem that resembles it; this is called *case-based planning*.

Techniques

For classical planning, the dominant algorithmic framework is *refinement planning*. A refinement planner finds a plan by searching a space of *partial plans*, starting with an empty plan, and adding plan steps until a solution plan is found (if possible). The word "refinement" is used because each partial plan can be taken to stand for a set of possible completions, and planning operations reduce the size of that set by eliminating some of its elements. This framework allows for many variations, especially in the definition of a partial plan. Two basic alternatives are planners that take a partial plan to be a totally ordered (linear) sequence of steps, and those that take a partial plan to be a partially ordered (possibly branching) set of steps. Total-order planners often allow steps to be added only at the end of the sequence; there is no standard term for such an algorithm, but it might be called a *forward-chaining* planner. Partial-order planners allow steps to be added anywhere. There are hybrid systems in which a partial-order planner is used to choose among steps to add to a growing sequence of steps.

The advantage of a forward-chaining planner is that it has a complete model of the world situation at the end of the sequence built so far, which allows detailed computations about what needs to be done next. The advantage of a partial-order planner is that if a goal has two conjuncts whose plans interact only weakly or not at all, then the plans for the two goals can be created separately, without having to commit prematurely to the order in which the two plans will be interleaved. Most researchers feel that this is a decisive advantage, so partial-order planning has become the dominant paradigm for classical planning.

Unfortunately, in spite of their elegance, pure refinement planners require computation time that grows exponentially as problem-size grows, and so cannot solve practical problems of realistic size. For practical purposes, such methods are usually embedded in *hierarchical planners*, in which what is manipulated are sets of "canned" plans from a *plan library*. The library entries are larger than the action definitions in a STRIPS-style notation. They may specify standard sequences of many tasks, each of which has its own set of standard plans. The plan library is created by consultation with experts in the domain the planner operates in (building construction, for instance). The job of the planner is to choose among standard procedures and then put them together into a coherent whole. Good results from such algorithms are reported in the literature, although it is hard to generalize from one domain to another.

Recently there has been interest in *propositional algorithms* for planning, which depart from the refinement framework. These work by instantiating predicate calculus terms for actions in all possible ways, then using fast techniques for *constraint satisfaction* and *graph manipulation* (*see* GRAPH THEORY) to choose action terms that fit into a coherent whole. For small problems, these techniques can work quite rapidly, although work remains to be done on how to avoid instantiating too many terms as the problems get bigger.

There is a huge variety of possible algorithms to solve scheduling problems. Some of them involve refinement-style searches, in which tasks are added to the end of partial schedules, like forward-chaining planners. Others start with an infeasible schedule and postpone various tasks in order to eliminate resource clashes. Others reduce scheduling to an *integer programming* problem (*see* MATHEMATICAL PROGRAMMING). Even in cases where optimality is too costly to achieve, heuristic algorithms can find better schedules than humans could find alone.

Robot motion planning can be thought of as a computational geometry (*q.v.*) problem, in a space with as many dimensions as there are degrees of freedom in the robot that is to execute the plan. There is typically one degree of freedom per joint, so a robot with six joints is operating in a six-dimensional *configuration space*. Part of this space is physically impossible for the robot to occupy; the rest is *free space*. The motion-planning problem is to find a path through free space for a point representing the robot's state. The problem is known to be NP-complete (*q.v.*), measuring problem size as the number of degrees of freedom, so for realistic robots one must use heuristic (*q.v.*) or probabilistic methods. Some of these methods appear to work quite well in practice.

Bibliography

1988. Wilkins, D. *Practical Planning: Extending the Classical AI Planning Paradigm*. San Francisco: Morgan Kaufmann.

1990. Allen, J., Hendler, J., and Tate, A. (eds.) *Readings in Planning*. San Francisco: Morgan Kaufmann.

1991. Latombe, J.-C. *Robot Motion Planning*. Boston: Kluwer Academic.

1994. Zweben, M., and Fox, M. S. *Intelligent Scheduling Systems*. San Francisco: Morgan Kaufmann.

1995. McDermott, D., and Hendler, J., *Artificial Intelligence* **76**, Special Issue on Planning and Scheduling.

Drew McDermott

AUTOMATIC PROGRAMMING

For articles on related subjects *see* COMPUTER-AIDED SOFTWARE ENGINEERING; FORMAL METHODS FOR COMPUTER SYSTEMS; LOGIC PROGRAMMING; LOGICS OF PROGRAMS; NONPROCEDURAL LANGUAGES; PARTIAL EVALUATION; PROBLEM-ORIENTED LANGUAGES; PROGRAM SPECIFICATION; PROGRAM VERIFICATION; PROGRAMMING SUPPORT ENVIRONMENTS; SOFTWARE ENGINEERING; and SOFTWARE REUSABILITY.

The goal of *automatic programming* is to allow human programmers to specify *what* a program should do, and let the programming system generate the code that says *how* to do it.

Early programmers wrote their programs as strings of 0s and 1s. This machine-language programming was far removed from the level at which humans conceive of algorithms for solving problems. The *compiler* (*q.v.*) was one of the first automatic programming tools developed, enabling knowledge to be encoded in languages like Fortran (*q.v.*) in algebraic formulas and high-level control structures (*q.v.*). Indeed, those who used Grace Hopper's (*q.v.*) compilers A-0 and A-2 in the early 1950s were considered to be engaged in "automatic programming," and that view prevailed into the Fortran and Cobol era that began in the late 1950s.

In the 1960s and early 1970s several fields emerged that have contributed to the foundations of automatic programming: compiler theory, programming language semantics, formal methods, and artificial intelligence (*q.v.*). Tools for generating compilers were introduced in the mid-1960s. An example of such a tool is a *parser generator*, which generates a parser for a programming language from a definition of the grammar of the language (*see* GRAMMARS). A standard parser-generator today is *yacc* (yet another compiler-compiler) available with the Unix operating system (*q.v.*).

The goal of programming language semantics is to assign precise mathematical meanings to programs. Anthony Hoare introduced an axiomatic approach to programming language semantics (*q.v.*) using preconditions and post-conditions: a post-condition is a predicate that is true of the state of the machine after a statement is executed *if* the pre-condition is satisfied prior to the execution of the statement (*see* PROGRAM VERIFICATION). The related field of formal methods provides systems of rules for precise reasoning about programs; such a system is called a *calculus*.

Approaches to Automatic Programming

Artificial intelligence had already developed computer systems in the 1950s that reasoned soundly according to a formal calculus, such as Newell and Simon's Logic Theorist (1956). In 1969 Green and Waldinger both used a logical technique called *deductive synthesis* to generate computer programs automatically. Deductive synthesis takes as input a set of axioms that describe programming knowledge, such as a set of axioms in the style of Hoare, and the specification of a desired program. The specification is most often given in the form of a *precondition* on the input variables, and a *postcondition* satisfied by the output variables after the desired program is executed. Deductive synthesis then *proves* that a program satisfying the specification exists by actually generating the program as part of the proof process. As program size grows, however, the time required for deductive synthesis grows exponentially.

Two alternatives to deductive synthesis are the *transformational* and the *expert systems* (*q.v.*) approaches. In the transformational approach, a specification written in the source language is incrementally transformed into a program in the target language through repeated application of a set of transformations. It has the advantage of being common to the different disciplines contributing to automatic programming. In compilers, transformations are used after the initial parsing phase to compute semantic attributes of a source language program, and transformations are also used in the final code generation phase. A transformation can be verified to be correct through proofs based on the programming language semantics of the source and target languages. Artificial intelligence approaches span a wide range of types of transformation from formal transformations rigorously based on programming language semantics to informally defined transformations implemented as small problem-solving expert systems. The transformational approach is still widely used both in practice and in research settings. However, as in deductive synthesis, because the number of distinct transformations that can be applied at each stage is large, then the time it takes to generate programs can grow exponentially with the size of the program. This problem can be avoided by restricting the number of possible transformations applicable at each stage. This restriction limits the range of programs that can be generated, however.

The expert system approach, which dates back to Herbert Simon's 1963 Heuristic Compiler, is to develop programs that reason with the many different kinds of knowledge used by humans in software development. This approach became known as *knowledge-based software engineering* (KBSE).

The US Air Force sponsored a research program called the Knowledge-Based Software Assistant (KBSA—Green *et al.*, 1986) to develop machine assistants for all the major phases of software development, including assistants to help develop requirements, acquire specifications, generate programs, and optimize programs for efficiency, as well as an assistant to help manage the process of software development. This research program ran through the mid-1990s, and resulted in a number of influential research demonstrations.

One outcome of the KBSA program in the 1990s was the development of better ways of organizing knowledge for automated software development. Building on foundational work in algebraic specification languages, researchers have developed a framework for organizing software engineering knowledge through parameterized theories, and mappings between theories. A map between theories is a correspondence between the languages of the source and target theories that preserves semantics; that is, axioms in the source are mapped to theorems in the target. Deductive theorem provers (*see* THEOREM PROVING) can be used to verify that the correspondence preserves semantics. In essence, the parameterized theories provide a flexible module system for reusing knowledge, and the mappings provide a formal foundation for transformations of modules. Deductive synthesis can be applied to modules separately, thereby addressing some of the scaling issues.

Current Practice

James Martin (1982) advocated the use of special-purpose compilers called *application generators*, for both programmers and end-users, as a way to end the backlog of demand for business application programs and to increase software development productivity by orders of magnitude. A decade later, application generators are widespread, each for a narrow range of programs. This narrow focus simplifies what a developer needs to specify in order to generate an application program. Some application generators can be used by people with no training in software engineering, and are found in the database and spreadsheet (*q.v.*) components of so-called "office suites" on personal computers. Examples of application generators include:

◆ Graphical user interface (GUI) generators, which produce the presentation aspect of graphical user interfaces. The layout of the GUI is itself usually developed graphically, through point-and-click actions by the GUI developer.

◆ Database application generators. These enable non-programmers to develop business applications that use a database to record information and perform calculations to generate reports.

◆ Application generator generators. These are tools for generating application generators, and include tools such as parser generators and template-based code *instantiators* that specialize generic programs.

Most application generators in current use have few sophisticated knowledge representation (*q.v.*) structures or automated reasoning capabilities. The most widely used methods come from standard compiler technology: principally parsing followed either by standard code generation or an interpreter connected to a relational database (*q.v.*). When these don't suffice, program transformations are used to provide more sophisticated capabilities.

Current Research

The systems surveyed in this section illustrate various aspects of the state of the art in automatic programming in 1999.

SINAPSE

Sinapse (now *SciNapse*) was designed to generate programs that simulate wave propagation through diverse media. Examples are shock wave propagation through rocks when explosions are set off in exploratory oil drillings to analyze geological structure, and gravitational waves in black holes (Kant, 1993). It is written in Mathematica (*see* COMPUTER ALGEBRA: SYSTEMS).

The input to Sinapse is a model of a problem, expressed in basic physical and mathematical terms. Sinapse may take a typical 50-line input and generate a program of between 200 and 4,000 lines of target-language code. These programs are highly optimized, and can be targeted to different platforms, including parallel computers.

To achieve this level of performance requires encoding substantial amounts of scientific programming knowledge. The knowledge is encoded as a hierarchy of sets of transformations. Given a symbolic model of the physics of an application, Sinapse first applies domain knowledge and algebraic manipulation to derive a mathematical model. It then chooses an algorithm class, which may require human guidance, and generates an algorithm. It applies transformation rules to refine the algorithm structure to yield a generic program description, which is refined with successive choices such as, for example, whether to store or recompute values.

Sinapse is a good example of a high-performance program synthesis system. It is focused on a particular domain, numerical scientific computing, and encodes a substantial amount of knowledge about this domain. It has been applied to several numerical domains, such as programs that apply sophisticated mathematical models to stock option pricing, but the skill and labor required to produce a high-performance program synthesis system has limited the number of such applications.

AMPHION

Amphion uses deductive synthesis and has two advantages over traditional deductive synthesis systems. The first is that instead of generating source code line-by-line, it generates software from components whose behavior is defined through their pre- and post-conditions. For the same amount of automated deduction effort, Amphion can do much more than a line-by-line system. The second advantage is that each instantiation of this framework is focused on a particular application domain, making it possible to give better guidance for rule-selection during deductive synthesis. Both advantages scale up the performance of deductive synthesis to larger problems. Amphion has been used at NASA to generate space observation geometry programs, which are composed from subroutines in NASA's Jet Propulsion Laboratory NAIF (Navigation and Ancillary Information Facility) toolkit.

In later work, Amphion was extended to Meta-Amphion, which generates domain-specific program synthesis systems themselves. Mathematically rich theories can often best be solved through special purpose inference techniques called *decision procedures* rather than through general-purpose theorem provers. Meta-Amphion uses a library of decision procedures as components for assembling a domain-specific program synthesis system. It takes a domain theory as input and generates a hybrid domain-specific program synthesis system in which some mathematical parts in the domain theory are replaced by decision procedures from Meta-Amphion's library. Meta-Amphion can generate computationally efficient synthesis systems, and is able to generate efficient systems for different formulations of the domain theory. This provides some evidence that program synthesis systems based on automated reasoning will one day be as easy to develop as application generators are today.

PLANWARE

This system applies synthesis technology to the routine production of high-performance, specialized planning and scheduling tools. It has been used in military logistics, job shop, and nuclear power maintenance scheduling.

Planware uses parameterized theories that encapsulate generic, reusable concepts. A domain expert who is not trained in program synthesis can nonetheless produce and maintain efficient schedulers. The user specifies task features, resource features, and cost information by choosing from an existing library of theories, or by adding new task and resource definitions. Planware can then either generate the scheduler fully automatically, or allow a more sophisticated user to guide the implementation decisions, which can result in more efficient code.

Planware has several types of knowledge, all encoded through parameterized theories. The first is knowledge of the scheduling domain, including the constraints on use of the different types of resources, such as reusable or sharable resources. Another type of knowledge is *algorithm knowledge*, such as generate-and-test, branch-and-bound, divide-and-conquer, dynamic programming, and hill-climbing (*see* ALGORITHMS, DESIGN AND CLASSIFICATION OF). By codifying them as parameterized theories, algorithms can be automatically derived for a given very-high-level problem specification, given appropriate domain axioms. A third type of knowledge is *implementation knowledge*, which defines how higher-level constructs such as sets can be encoded as more implementation-level constructs such as lists or bit-vectors.

All of these tools use advanced knowledge representation and automated reasoning capabilities. Although research tools today, they represent the degree of programming automation that may become commercially available within a decade.

Bibliography

1956. Newell, A., and Simon, H. A. "The Logic Theory Machine," *IRE Transactions on Information Theory*, **IT-2**, 3 (March), 61–79.

1963. Simon, H. A. "Experiments with a Heuristic Compiler," *Journal of the ACM*, **10**, 493–506.

1982. Martin, J. *Application Development without Programmers*. Upper Saddle River, NJ: Prentice Hall.

1986. Green, C., Luckham, D., Balzer, R., Cheatham, T., and Rich, C. "Report on a Knowledge-based Software Assistant," in *Readings in Artificial Intelligence and Software Engineering* (eds. C. Rich and R. C. Waters). San Francisco: Morgan Kaufmann.

1990. Rich, C., and Waters, R. C. *The Programmer's Apprentice*. Reading, MA: Addison-Wesley.

1991. Lowry, M. R., and McCartney, R. D. (eds.) *Automating Software Design*. Cambridge, MA: MIT Press.

1993. Kant, E. "Synthesis of Mathematical Modeling Software," *IEEE Software*, **10**, 3 (May), 30–41.

1995. Flener, P. *Logic Program Synthesis from Incomplete Information*. Boston: Kluwer Academic Publishers.

1996. Smith, D. R., Parra, E. A., and Westfold, S. J. "Synthesis of Planning and Scheduling Software," in *Advanced Planning Technology* (ed. A. Tate), 226–234. Menlo Park, CA: AAAI Press.

1997. Browne, T., Davila, D., Rugaber, S., and Stirewalt, K. "Using Declarative Descriptions to Model User Interfaces with MASTERMIND," in *Formal Methods in Human Computer Interaction* (eds. F. Paterno and P. Palanque). New York: Springer-Verlag.

1998. Bibel, W., and Schmitt, P. *Automated Deduction. A Basis for Applications*. Boston: Kluwer Academic Press.

Websites

Amphion. `http://ic-www.arc.nasa.gov/ic/projects/amphion/`.

Mastermind. `http://www.cc.gatech.edu/gvu/user_interfaces/Mastermind/`.

Planware. `http://www.kestrel.edu/HTML/projects/arpa-plan2/`.

SciNapse. `http://www.scicomp.com/about/technology.html`.

Michael R. Lowry

AUTOMATION

> For articles on related subjects *see* AUTOMATA THEORY; COMPUTER-AIDED DESIGN/COMPUTER-AIDED MANUFACTURING; COMPUTER-AIDED ENGINEERING; CONTROL APPLICATIONS; ELECTRONIC OFFICE; MANAGEMENT INFORMATION SYSTEMS; ROBOTICS; and TELEROBOTICS.

Automation is the conversion of a work process, a procedure, or equipment to automatic rather than human operation or control. Automation does not simply transfer human functions to machines, but involves a deep reorganization of the work process, during which both the human and the machine functions are redefined. Early automation relied on mechanical and electromechanical control devices; during the last 40 years, however, the computer gradually became the leading vehicle of automation. Modern automation is usually associated with computerization.

This article examines the major phases of historical development and social and economic aspects of industrial automation, focusing on the computerization of production, engineering, and managerial tasks. Other areas of computer-based automation include administrative applications (*q.v.*), communication via electronic mail (*q.v.*), banking applications, medical applications (*q.v.*), and library automation (*see* DIGITAL LIBRARIES).

Phase I: Mechanization and Rationalization of Labor

The mechanization of machine tools for production began during the Industrial Revolution at the end of the 18th century with the introduction of the Watt steam engine, the Jacquard loom, the lathe, and the screw machine. Mechanization replaced human or animal power with machine power; those mechanisms, however, were not automatic but controlled by factory workers. The factory system, with its large-volume, standardized production, and division of labor, replaced the old work organization, where broadly skilled craftsmen and artisans produced small quantities of diverse products. In the late 19th century Frederick W. Taylor rationalized the factory system by introducing the principles of "scientific management." He viewed the body of each worker as a machine whose movements had to be optimized in order to minimize time required to complete each task and thus increase overall productivity. "Scientific management" strictly separated mental work from manual labor:

workers were not to think but to follow detailed instructions prepared for them by managers. The rationalized factory system gave birth to a new managerial class and large clerical bureaucracies. The Taylorist principles served as a basis for Henry Ford's system of mass production. In 1913 the Ford Motor Company introduced a moving assembly line, drastically cutting assembly time. The assembly line imposed a strict order on production by forcing workers to keep pace with the motion of the conveyor belt. Mass production relied on the standardization of components and final products and routinization of manufacturing and assembly jobs. The Ford assembly line became a symbol of efficiency of American manufacturing; for workers and social critics, however, it epitomized the monotony and relentless pressure of mechanized work.

Phase II: Automation of Production

In 1947 the Ford Company brought the term "automation" into wide circulation by establishing the first Automation Department, charged with designing electromechanical, hydraulic, and pneumatic parts-handling, work-feeding, and work-removing mechanisms to connect standalone machines and increase the rate of production. In 1950 Ford put into operation the first "automated" engine plant. Although early automation was "hard," or fixed in the hardware, and did not involve automatic feedback control, this concept provoked great public enthusiasm for "unmanned factories" controlled by "buttons that push themselves," as well as causing growing concern about the prospects of mass unemployment.

To meet US Air Force demands for a high-performance fighter aircraft whose complex structural members could not be manufactured by traditional machining methods, a technology of Numerical Control (NC) of machine tools was developed in the early 1950s. NC laid foundation for programmable, or "soft," automation, in which the sequence of processing operations was not fixed but could be changed for each new product style. Commercial NC machines for batch production appeared in the mid-1950s. Designed to military specifications, early NC equipment proved too complex and therefore unreliable, as well as prohibitively expensive, and was applied mostly in the state-subsidized aircraft industry.

The abstract, formal approach of NC, based on mathematical modeling of the machining process, superseded the record–playback technique of direct machine imitation of workers' actions. While the record–playback approach relied on the skill and discretion of the worker, NC technology allowed engineers and managers to exercise greater control over the production process.

Phase III: Computer-Aided Manufacturing (CAM)

The first industrial applications of digital computers occurred in the electrical power, dairy, chemical, and petroleum refinery industries for automatic process control. In 1959, TRW installed the first digital computer designed specifically for plant process control at Texaco's Port Arthur refinery. Early applications were open-loop control systems: gathering data from measuring devices and sensors throughout the plant, the computers monitored technological processes, performed calculations, and printed out "operator guides"; subsequent adjustments were made by human operators. In the 1960s closed-loop feedback control systems appeared. These computers were connected directly to servo-control valves and made adjustments automatically (*see* CYBERNETICS).

In the late 1960s, with the development of time sharing (*q.v.*) on large mainframe computers (*q.v.*), standalone NC machines were brought under Direct Numerical Control (DNC) of a central computer. DNC systems proved vulnerable to frequent failures due to malfunctioning of the central computer and the interference of factory power cables with the data transmission cables of the DNC system.

With the introduction of microprocessors (*q.v.*) in the 1970s, centralized DNC systems in manufacturing were largely replaced by Computer Numerical Control (CNC) systems with distributed control, in which each NC machine was controlled by its own microcomputer. This blending of information and production technologies produced a new breed of machinist-programmer who could operate CNC equipment by generating and debugging NC programs, thus breaking down the traditional distinction between white-collar and blue-collar jobs.

Robotics combined the techniques of NC and remote control to replace human workers with numerically controlled mechanical manipulators. The first commercial robots appeared in the early 1960s. Robots proved very efficient in performing specialized tasks that demanded high precision or had to be done in hazardous environments. To approach the human level of flexibility, robots were supplied with sophisticated techniques of feedback, vision and tactile sensors, reasoning capabilities, and adaptive control. In the 1980s industrial applications of robots slowed down, as their increasing complexity resulted in growing costs and insufficient reliability.

Hierarchical Numerical Control Systems combined DNC and CNC features: they linked each standalone computer controller to a central computer that maintained a large library of CNC programs and monitored production. This approach aspired to replace the human operator's expertise by engineering knowledge formalized in CNC programs. In such systems, human operators generally no longer programmed CNC equipment on the shop floor, and production was brought under remote supervision of a central management-controlled computer.

Flexible Manufacturing Systems (FMS) combined DNC equipment with machines for automated loading, unloading, and transfer of workpieces. These systems permitted varying process routes and sequences of operations, allowing automatic machining of different products in small batches in the same system. Centralized FMS have often proved too complex, however, and they are increasingly subdivided into smaller flexible manufacturing cells (FMC) that include several CNC machines, robots, and transfer devices controlled by a single computer, the "cell controller."

Phase IV: Automated Engineering

In the 1960s large aerospace manufacturers, such as McDonnell-Douglas and Boeing, developed proprietary computer-aided design (CAD) systems, which provided computer graphics (*q.v.*) tools for drafting, analyzing, and modifying aircraft designs. In 1970 Computer-Vision Corporation introduced the first complete turn-key commercial CAD system for industrial designers, which provided all the necessary hardware and software in one package. In the 1970s, combined CAD/CAM systems emerged which used the parameters of a geometrical model created with the help of CAD to generate programs for CNC machine tools and develop manufacturing plans and schedules. While CAD systems are often packaged and standardized, CAM (Computer-Aided Manufacturing) applications tend to be industry-specific and proprietary. With the introduction of Computer-Aided Engineering (CAE) systems for standard techniques of engineering analysis, the whole range of engineering tasks—from conceptual design to analysis to detailed design to drafting and documentation to manufacturing design—became automated. The distinction between blue-collar and white-collar jobs was further blurred, as engineers, clerks, and managers became integrated in an automated office.

Phase V: Automated Management

Among the earliest applications of information technology was the automation of information-processing tasks. The first stored-program digital computer purchased by a nongovernment customer was UNIVAC (*q.v.*), installed by GE in 1954 to automate basic transaction processing: payroll, inventory control and material scheduling, billing and order service, and general cost accounting. Large clerical bureaucracies, which processed huge amounts of data generated in mass production and mass marketing, became a primary target of automation and job reduction in the 1960s and 1970s. By 1970 the profession of bookkeeper was almost completely eliminated in the USA. In the mid-1960s the first management-information systems (MIS) appeared, providing management with data, models of analysis, and algorithms for decision-making; eventually they became a standard tool for operation control, management control, and strategic planning.

Phase VI: Computer-Integrated Manufacturing (CIM)

In the late 1980s an integration of the automated factory and the electronic office (*q.v.*) began. CIM combines flexible automation (robots, numerically controlled machines, and flexible manufacturing systems), CAD/CAM systems, and management-information systems to build integrated production systems that cover the complete operations of a manufacturing firm, including purchasing, logistics, maintenance, engineering, and business operations. CIM emphasizes horizontal links between different organizational units of a firm and provides the possibility of sharing data and computing resources, making it possible to break the traditional institutional barriers between departments and create flexible functional groups to perform tasks more speedily and efficiently.

Social and Economic Dimensions of Automation

Views of automation range between two extremes—unabashed optimism and utmost pessimism. The optimists believe in a technological utopia, an imagined bright future in which machines will relieve people of all hard work and bring prosperity to humankind. The pessimists view machines as instruments of subjugation and control by a ruling elite, argue that automation leads to the degradation of human beings, and depict the future as a grim technological dystopia. Both sides view automatic technology as an autonomous force determining the direction of human history. Automation itself, however, is a social process shaped by various social and economic forces. This process may take various directions and may have diverse consequences depending on the socioeconomic and organizational choices made during automation.

The Productivity Paradox

While productivity in major industries in the USA rose sharply during production automation in the 1950s and 60s, its growth has slowed significantly since the 1970s, precisely at the time of widespread computerization of the factory and the office. The link between computerization and productivity remains problematic. The advantages most commonly associated with computer-aided manufacturing include increased production rates, better product quality, more efficient use of materials, shorter lead times, reduced work hours, and improved work safety—all factors leading to higher productivity. Among its main disadvantages, analysts usually cite the high cost of designing, building, and maintaining computerized equipment; vulnerability to downtime; relatively low flexibility compared with humans; and worker displacement and emotional stress—all leading to lower productivity. It is particularly difficult to compare directly productivity before and after computerization, since it brings with it not merely technological, but also organizational change which transforms the entire nature of production and brings with it the most benefits and losses.

As manufacturers who introduced computer-aided manufacturing systems affirm, the largest payoff from computerization comes not from speeding up old operations but from making work organization more flexible and efficient. On the other hand, if computers are used to conserve old inefficient organization, computerization can only accelerate negative trends. As John Bessant has remarked, "When you put a computer into a chaotic factory the only thing you get is computerized chaos" (quoted in Ayres, 1991–1992, Vol. 4, p. 94). Most successful manufacturers streamline operations before computerization, following the dictum, "Simplify, then automate!" Efficient computerization takes far more than merely installing a computer: it requires changes in the entire workstyle.

Worker Displacement, Skill, and Working Conditions

A leading concern among workers, labor leaders, and social critics has been the issue of worker displacement—a loss of work, transfer to a different job, or geographic dislocation—due to automation. Such categories as welders, carpenters, insulators, machinists, and clerical staff have been most heavily affected. At the same time, automation creates new highly-skilled jobs in programming, operating, and maintaining computerized production machinery. Workers need extensive retraining programs, however, to prepare for such jobs.

Another risk is the danger of employees losing essential working skills as work becomes increasingly mediated by the computer. With automation, the worker has gone through a series of transformations—from a direct producer of goods and services to the operator of production equipment to the programmer of the computer that operates and controls that equipment. Engineering changed from hands-on tinkering with machinery to the use of standard design and analysis procedures that tell the computer how to design and build a needed part. Management evolved from direct supervision of labor to "management by numbers," based on numerical data reports and pre-programmed computer algorithms for decision-making. When operators must step in and take control in case of an emergency at an automatically controlled nuclear power plant, would they possess the necessary skills if their training and daily experience mainly concerned work with a computerized control system?

Because of the high cost of downtime, efficient maintenance and fast repairs become crucial in automated production, which places a great burden of responsibility and tight time constraints on maintenance and repair crews. Computerized equipment can be used to enhance the flexibility of work organization, leaving one in charge of planning one's work time, but it may also be used to impose a strict and inflexible work regime on factory and office workers by closely monitoring their performance. As a result, automation can make work either easier or more exhausting and stressful, depending on the type of work organization.

Technocentric vs. Human-Centered Approaches

Historically the predominant approach to automation has been technocentric: a goal of automation is to reduce and ultimately entirely eliminate human participation in production and eventually arrive at an unmanned factory. From this standpoint, workers are seen as a source of potential errors, disturbance, and unreliability; on the other hand, automatic machinery is viewed as inherently more precise, reliable, and controllable. The technocentric approach extends the principles of Taylorist work organization to modern information-processing and production systems. It is based on further subdivision of labor, with more complex and intelligent tasks trusted to flexible computer systems and simpler tasks left to low-skilled workers who assume a residual role. Skill gradually passes from people to machines, and control functions are also transferred in the same direction.

The technocentric approach faces a fundamental paradox: it aspires to replace human skill with highly flexible computerized machinery, but this machinery requires even more human skill to operate, maintain, and repair it. Instead of "freeing" production from the "human element," automation only increases the importance of highly qualified, versatile, and motivated workers. Accidents at the nuclear power plants at Three Mile Island and Chernobyl testify that automation does not eliminate the possibility of human error; it only makes this error more costly.

The Taylorist logic of seeking productivity by accelerating the pace of work may not apply in a computerized workplace. With computerization, companies do not simply automate, but "informate" their operations. Computer-based control of production becomes an information-processing task; workers turn into analyzers of information rather than simple machine minders. Improving the quality of this analysis, instead of speeding up workers' movements, becomes a crucial problem of automation.

An alternative approach aspires to change the workforce from being part of the manufacturing problem into part of the solution. Instead of taking skills, responsibility, and control away from the worker and absorbing them into the machine, human-centered CIM systems mobilize the intellectual resources of all employees. Leading Japanese companies, such as Matsushita and Toyota, achieved much greater productivity gains from automation than their American competitors by decentralizing control and reorganizing the factory layout into production islands controlled by semi-autonomous multi-skilled teams responsible for all operations. Reversing the Taylorist trend of subdivision of labor, the human-centered approach integrates functions and skills in flexible teams, where workers can rotate jobs and choose the optimal order and pace of work. Instead of being forced to follow instructions handed to them from above, workers are motivated to play a greater role in decision-making by programming CNC equipment on the shop floor. In the late 1960s and early 1970s only a handful of American companies, such as Procter & Gamble, Cummins Engine, and Gaines Foods, realized that greater productivity did not come automatically with more sophisticated equipment but required profound organizational change. In 1974 Volvo built a highly productive plant at Kalmar, Sweden, which implemented the "sociotechnical systems" approach, elaborated in Britain. Based on group assembly instead of a conventional assembly line, this new design gave workers more initiative, flexibility, and control over product quality. In the 1980s major American manufacturers began experimenting with worker involvement in decision-making, a recent example being GM's Saturn project. The human-centered approach finds a source of productivity in more efficient utilization of human abilities, rather than in the utopian efforts to eliminate people from production.

Bibliography

1967. Bright, J. R. "The Development of Automation," in *Technology in Western Civilization*, Vol. II (eds. M. Kranzberg and C. W. Pursell, Jr.), 635–654. New York: Oxford University Press.

1984. Noble, D. F. *Forces of Production: A Social History of Industrial Automation.* New York: Knopf/Random House.

1988. Zuboff, S. *In the Age of the Smart Machine: The Future of Work and Power.* New York: Basic Books.

1989. Forester, T. (ed.) *Computers in the Human Context: Information Technology, Productivity, and People.* Cambridge, MA: MIT Press.

1992. Ayres, R. U., Haywood, W., and Tchijov, I. (eds.) *Computer Integrated Manufacturing.* 4 Vols. London: Chapman & Hall.

1994. Allen, T. J., and Scott Morton, M. S. (eds.) *Information Technology and the Corporation of the 1990s: Research Studies.* New York: Oxford University Press.

1996. Kling, R. (ed.) *Computerization and Controversy: Value Conflicts and Social Choices*, 2nd Ed. San Diego, CA: Academic Press.

1997. Rochlin, G. I. *Trapped in the Net: The Unanticipated Consequences of Computerization.* Princeton, NJ: Princeton University Press.

Slava Gerovitch

AUXILIARY MEMORY

See MEMORY: AUXILIARY.

B

BABBAGE, CHARLES

For articles on related subjects see ANALYTICAL ENGINE; DIFFERENCE ENGINE; DIGITAL COMPUTERS, HISTORY OF: ORIGINS; and LOVELACE, COUNTESS OF.

Charles Babbage (Fig. 1) was born in London on 26 December 1791. His education was mostly private and he went up to Cambridge University in 1810. Cambridge studies were then strongly oriented toward mathematics. Babbage, however, soon discovered that Newton's ideas still dominated the Cambridge curriculum, whereas he had been exposed to, and was much drawn toward, the type of mathematics then receiving attention in Europe. He preferred to spend time on these studies rather than to undertake the grind that competing for the place of Senior Wrangler would have implied.

Although he did not join the competition, he acquired a high mathematical reputation that increased with the years, so much so that in 1828 he was appointed Lucasian Professor, a position that Newton himself had held many years before. The stipend in Babbage's time was only £80 to £90 per annum. He did not reside in Cambridge nor lecture there, though he performed some of the other duties of the Professorship, such as examining for the Smith's Prize.

In a long life, Babbage turned his attention to many subjects, including mathematics, railroads, lighthouses, cryptography, economics, the ophthalmoscope, politics, and public controversies of various kinds. But the dominating interest of his life was calculating machinery. While still a student he began to work on his *Difference Engine.* This was intended to facilitate the production of mathematical tables, with the emphasis on making them more accurate by reducing the opportunity for human error. The output would be a stereo mold for a printing plate, ready for the printer. Babbage's own attempt at implementing the Difference Engine failed, in spite of financial support from the British government. Another implementation by Georg and Edvard Scheutz, who had read of Babbage's ideas in a magazine, was more successful. Two copies were made and used for a time, but they did not prove to be the panacea that Babbage had predicted, and they soon dropped out of use.

It is his work on the *Analytical Engine* that gives Babbage his real claim to fame. This was to have been an automatically sequenced, general-purpose computer. Here he was profoundly original. He published some of his ideas and others have come down to us in his manuscript notebooks. The real breakthrough came in 1834 and the years immediately following, but Babbage continued to work on the subject for the remainder of his life.

Babbage's thoughts on the Analytical Engine were entirely in mechanical terms, with no suggestion, even in later years, that electricity might be called in aid. The Analytical Engine was to be decimal, although Babbage considered other scales of notation. Numbers were to be stored on wheels, with ten distinguishable positions, and transferred by a system of racks to a central *mill*, or processor, where all arithmetic would be performed. He had in mind storage capacity for a

Figure 1. Charles Babbage (courtesy of the Mary Evans Picture Library).

thousand numbers of 50 decimal digits. He studied exhaustively a wide variety of schemes for performing the four operations of arithmetic, and he invented the idea of *anticipatory carry*, which, in a mechanical computer, is much faster than carrying successively from one stage to another. He also knew about *hoarding carry*, by which a whole series of additions could be performed with one carrying operation at the end.

Punched cards laced together as in a Jacquard loom were to be used both for sequencing the analytical engine and for the input of numbers. For sequencing, Babbage proposed to have two independently stepping card mechanisms, one for operation cards, controlling the mill, and one for variable cards, controlling the store. Thus Babbage had operation codes and he had addresses, but he did not have the concept of instructions in which they were permanently combined. Operation codes and addresses became associated only at run time.

For sequencing within an operation, he proposed to use a system that bears an uncanny resemblance to modern microprogramming (*q.v.*), using rotating drums with projecting studs for the read-only memory (*q.v.*). He well understood the principles of microprogramming, as the large number of *notations* (microprograms) that he left behind make clear. In his published writings there is no hint of the range and originality of his thoughts on this subject.

Nearly all the notations refer to multiplication, division, and other complex operations, to which Babbage gave much thought. By contrast, one must search long before one finds material dealing with smaller operations, conditional jumps in particular. This may be because Babbage saw little difficulty in these operations. But it is also obvious that he attached less importance to the user interface than we do, and had no concept of formalizing it.

Much of what we know about how the Analytical Engine would have appeared to a user derives from an account written in French by L. F. Menebrea of a series of presentations given by Babbage in Turin in 1842 and published in a Geneva journal. This was ably translated into English by Lady Lovelace, the daughter of Lord Byron, who added extensive notes written under Babbage's close supervision. For this Lady Lovelace has left us much in her debt, although there has been a tendency to exaggerate both her mathematical ability and her importance in the Babbage saga. One of the notes contains a sketch of a program—in the absence of a formal instruction set, it could only have been a sketch—for computing Bernoulli numbers. The arithmetic operations are given explicitly, but there are no jump operations, the formation of the main loop being indicated merely by a comment.

Although the locations in the store were numbered, the hardware of the Engine had no knowledge of the ordering that this implies to a user. It was not possible for the programmer to step through the store by incrementing an address or to generate an address for the program to use. This restricted Babbage's ability to design programs with the generality that he would have wished. He was aware that there was a problem, without being able to pinpoint it. If he been inspired to provide a means of modifying addresses, it is likely that he would have recognized it as a major breakthrough. The lack of the capability deprives the Engine of any claim to be described as a stored program computer in the modern sense.

Although he had workmen in his employ until the end of his life, Babbage failed to implement the Analytical Engine. We must conclude, as did some of his contemporaries, that he was temperamentally incapable of carrying a project through. Unfortunately, this time, there were no Scheutzes to take up his ideas. His detailed design studies lay buried in his unpublished notebooks and were forgotten. Of his genius, however, no one who has studied these notebooks will have any doubt.

Babbage went on believing in the Difference Engine until the end of his life, and left behind him drawings of an improved version, Difference Engine No. 2. These were sufficiently detailed to enable the Engine to be built at the Science Museum in London and demonstrated in 1991 at the time of the bicentennial of Babbage's birth.

Babbage died in London on 18 October 1871. His youngest son, Henry, who had spent most of his life in various military and civil appointments in India, did what he could to carry on his father's work, and published a collection of papers relating to it. The eldest son, Herschel, migrated in 1851 to South Australia, where he became a prominent member of the colony.

Bibliography

1864. Babbage, C. *Passages from the Life of a Philosopher.* London, 1864; facsimile edition, London, 1968; reprint (ed. M. Campbell-Kelly) London: Pickering, 1994.

1889. Babbage, H. P. (ed.) *Babbage's Calculating Engines.* London. This book has now been reprinted as vol. 2 of the Babbage Institute reprint series, I. Tomash (ed.), Cambridge, MA: MIT Press, 1984.

1971. Wilkes, M. V. "Babbage as a Computer Pioneer," Report of the Babbage Memorial Meeting, British Computer Society. Reprinted in *Historica Mathematica*, **4**, 415 (1977).

1982. Hyman, A. *Charles Babbage.* Princeton, NJ: Princeton University Press.

1989. Campbell-Kelly, M. (ed.) *The Works of Charles Babbage.* 11 volumes. London: Pickering and Chatto.

1990. Wilkes, M. V. "Herschel, Peacock, Babbage, and the Development of the Cambridge Curriculum," *Notes and Records of the Royal Society*, **44**, 205.

Maurice V. Wilkes

BACKUS–NAUR FORM (BNF)

For articles on related subjects *see* ALGOL; GRAMMARS; METALANGUAGE; PROCEDURE-ORIENTED LANGUAGES: SURVEY; PROGRAMMING LINGUISTICS; SYNTAX, SEMANTICS, AND PRAGMATICS; and VIENNA DEFINITION LANGUAGE.

Backus–Naur Form, named after John W. Backus of the US and Peter Naur of Denmark, and usually written BNF, is the best-known example of a *metalanguage* (q.v.), i.e. one that syntactically describes a programming language. Using BNF it is possible to specify which sequences of symbols constitute a syntactically valid program in a given language. (The question of *semantics*—i.e. what such valid strings of symbols mean—must be specified separately.) A discussion of the basic concepts of BNF follows.

A *metalinguistic variable* (or *metavariable*), also called a *syntactic unit*, is one whose values are strings of symbols chosen from among the symbols permitted in the given language. In BNF, metalinguistic variables are enclosed in brackets, ⟨ ⟩, for clarity and to distinguish them from symbols in the language itself, which are called terminal symbols or just *terminals*. The symbol ::= is used to indicate metalinguistic equivalence; a vertical bar (|) is used to indicate that a choice is to be made among the items so indicated; and concatenation (linking together in a series) is indicated simply by juxtaposing the elements to be concatenated. In the form that this notation was introduced in the *Algol Report*, a *metalinguistic variable* name should

be a word or phrase that describes a language element (e.g. unsigned integer), and that is also used in presenting the semantics of that element. Our examples follow this practice.

For an example, here is how the definition of an Algol (*q.v.*) integer is built up. First, we have a definition of what a digit is, according to the usual meaning:

```
⟨digit⟩ ::= 0 | 1 | 2 | 3 | 4 | 5 | 6 | 7 | 8 | 9
```

Next we have a statement that an unsigned integer consists either of a single digit or an unsigned integer followed by another digit:

```
⟨unsigned integer⟩ ::= ⟨digit⟩
                      | ⟨unsigned integer⟩⟨digit⟩
```

This definition may be applied *recursively* to build up unsigned integers of any length whatever. Since there must be a limit on the number of digits in any actual computer implementation, this would have to be stated separately in conjunction with each particular implementation or, as in some extensions to BNF, by an addition to the definition of *unsigned integer* (e.g. placing [10] above ::= could indicate a limit of 10 digits). Finally, the definition of an integer is completed by noting that it may be preceded by a plus sign, a minus sign, or neither:

```
⟨integer⟩ ::= ⟨unsigned integer⟩
            | + ⟨unsigned integer⟩
            | - ⟨unsigned integer⟩
```

For a second example, suppose that the metalinguistic variables ⟨unsigned number⟩, ⟨variable⟩, ⟨function designator⟩, and ⟨Boolean expression⟩ have all been defined earlier, with their usual meanings, and that the vertical arrow stands for exponentiation. Here, then, is the complete sequence of definitions that culminates with the definition of an Algol ⟨arithmetic expression⟩:

```
⟨adding operator⟩ ::= + | -
⟨multiplying operator⟩ ::= × | / | ÷
⟨primary⟩ ::= ⟨unsigned number⟩
    | ⟨variable⟩
    | ⟨function designator⟩
    | (⟨arithmetic expression⟩)
⟨factor⟩ ::= ⟨primary⟩
    | ⟨factor⟩↑⟨primary⟩
⟨term⟩ ::= ⟨factor⟩
    | ⟨term⟩⟨multiplying operator⟩⟨factor⟩
⟨simple arithmetic expression⟩ ::=
        ⟨term⟩
    | ⟨adding operator⟩⟨term⟩
    | ⟨simple arithmetic expression⟩
        ⟨adding operator⟩⟨term⟩
⟨if clause⟩ ::= if
        ⟨boolean expression⟩ then
⟨arithmetic expression⟩ ::=
        ⟨simple arithmetic expression⟩
    | ⟨if clause⟩
        ⟨simple arithmetic expression⟩
        else ⟨arithmetic expression⟩
```

It is no error that the third definition contains ⟨arithmetic expression⟩, enclosed in parentheses, even though it is ⟨arithmetic expression⟩ that we are trying to define. This is another example of a recursive definition, and simply says in this case that one choice for a ⟨primary⟩ is just any ⟨arithmetic expression⟩ enclosed in parentheses.

The words **if**, **then**, and **else**, since they are not enclosed in metalinguistic brackets, stand for themselves; they are, like the character set, basic elements of the Algol language that are not further defined.

An extended version of BNF (EBNF) is used in the *Pascal User Manual and Report* (Jensen *et al.*, 1985) and in the definition of Modula-2 (Wirth, 1985). An EBNF specification of the syntax of a programming language consists of a collection of rules (*productions*), collectively called a *grammar*, that describe the formation of sentences in the language. Each production consists of a nonterminal symbol and an EBNF expression separated by an equal sign and terminated by a period. The nonterminal symbol is a *meta-identifier* (a syntactic constant denoted by an English word), and the EBNF expression is its definition. An EBNF expression is composed of zero or more terminal symbols, nonterminals, and metasymbols, summarized in Table 1.

The superficial difference between BNF and EBNF is that, in the former, nonterminals need to be delimited (by angle brackets) and terminals are allowed to stand for themselves, whereas in EBNF terminals must be delimited (by quotation marks) and nonterminals are allowed to stand for themselves. The more profound difference is that the bracket and brace notation of EBNF allows a simpler presentation of definitions that must be expressed recursively in BNF. Consider, for example, these contrasting definitions of a Pascal ⟨identifier⟩:

```
BNF: ⟨identifier⟩ ::= ⟨letter⟩
              | ⟨identifier⟩ ⟨letter⟩
              | ⟨identifier⟩ ⟨digit⟩
```

Table 1. Metasymbols in EBNF

Metasymbol	Meaning
=	is defined to be
|	alternatively
.	end of production
[X]	0 or 1 instance of X
{X}	0 or more instances of X
(X|Y)	a grouping: either X or Y
"XYZ"	the terminal symbol XYZ
MetaIdentifier	the nonterminal symbol MetaIdentifier

Meaning: an identifier is either a single letter or else something that is already a valid identifier followed by either a letter or a digit.

```
EBNF:  Identifier = Letter
                   {Letter | Digit}.
```

Meaning: an identifier is a single letter followed by any number of letters or digits, possibly none.

The information conveyed through an EBNF production can be displayed pictorially through the use of *syntax diagrams* (*railroad diagrams*), a technique popularized by the Pascal report of Jensen *et al.* (1985). The syntax diagram for a Pascal identifier is shown in Fig. 1a.

The term "railroad diagram" stems from comparison of the directed line segments to tracks along which a train can proceed on any physically realizable path. Since the train cannot avoid passing through ⟨letter⟩, an identifier consists of at least a single letter. Thereafter, the train may pass straight through to the right, indicating that a single letter is a sufficiently complete definition of an ⟨identifier⟩, or else it may traverse either the top or bottom circuits any number of times in arbitrary order (before finally using the main track to end the definition).

A more complex syntax diagram, one that defines a ⟨signed real⟩ number in Pascal, is shown in Fig. 1b.

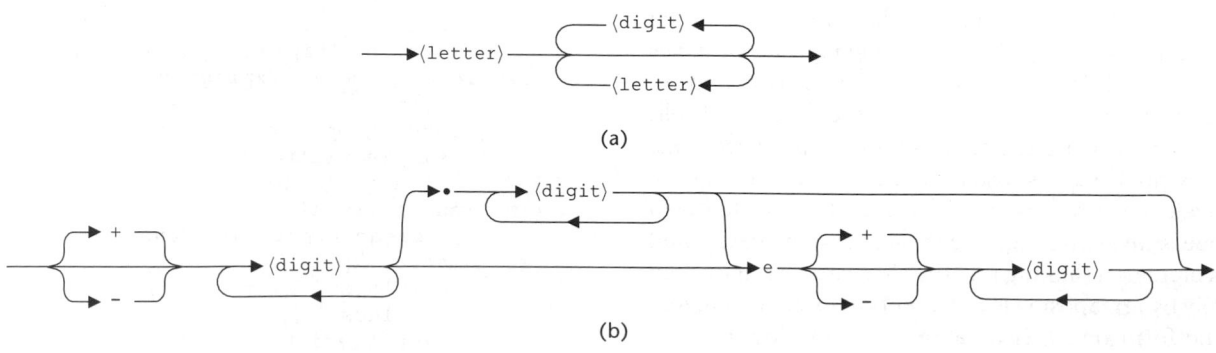

(a)

(b)

Figure 1. (a) ⟨identifier⟩ (b) ⟨signed real⟩.

The diagram can be used to show that such character strings as `5.7`, `-19.0`, `+3.9`, `-7.36e-3`, and `123e4` are valid signed real numbers but that `-7.`, `.2`, and `123.e4` are not.

BNF (or EBNF or syntax diagrams) can be used to describe any context-free language (*see* GRAMMARS), and hence, since most programming languages are context-free, most programming languages. There are competitive notations, however, such as the Vienna Definition Language (*q.v.*), used to describe PL/I, and the notation typically used to describe Cobol, which is closer to EBNF than to BNF.

Bibliography

1985. Jensen, K., Wirth, N., Mickel, A. B., and Miner, J. F. *Pascal User Manual and Report, 3rd Ed.: ISO Pascal Standard.* New York: Springer-Verlag.
1985. Wirth, N. *Programming in Modula-2, Third Corrected Edition.* New York: Springer-Verlag.

Daniel D. McCracken and Edwin D. Reilly

BANDWIDTH

For articles on related subjects *see* COMMUNICATIONS AND COMPUTERS; and DATA COMMUNICATIONS.

The *bandwidth* of an analog communication network is a measure of the range of frequencies it can transmit at or near maximum power levels. As an example, consider a normal telephone system, which still has analog parts in its communication network (line to the customer) normally designed to carry voice traffic in the frequency range 300–3,400 Hz. The equipment in the telephone exchange collects incoming data from the sound spectrum and arranges to attenuate the signals sharply outside that part of the spectrum. Within the preserved range, however, there is still attenuation, since the power of signals passing through the telephone transmission system is reduced. A typical measurement of attenuation on the US telephone network is shown in Fig. 1, which indicates that somewhere below 300 Hz and above 3–4 KHz, the attenuation rises very rapidly. The range of frequencies in which the power level stays at above one-half its peak value (the so-called 3 dB (decibel) points) is the *nominal bandwidth* of the circuit. This is typically 3 KHz in a switched telephone line.

The term *bandwidth* is now also applied—somewhat erroneously—to a digital communication network. In this context the term means the speed at which digital data can be transmitted. Thus, in digital communications, bandwidth has become a synonym for what had been known as the information *transfer rate*. For example, the bandwidth or capacity of an Ethernet network may be 100 (or more) Mb/sec. The digital

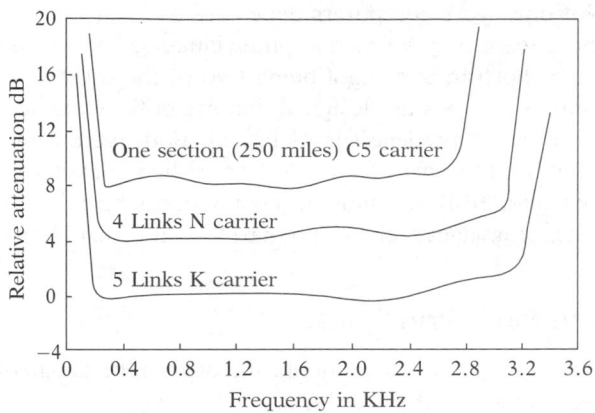

Figure 1. Attenuation for frequency division multiplexing (FDM) systems (reproduced from *Communication-Networks for Computers* by D. W. Davies and D. L. A. Barber, New York: Wiley, 1973, Fig. 2.16).

bandwidth of a channel, or *capacity*, depends directly upon the analog or "electrical" bandwidth of the communication medium and the channel's noise levels. The channel capacity is governed by the Hartley–Shannon law of information theory (*q.v.*).

Bibliography

1999. Bateman, A. *Digital Communications: Design for the Real World.* Reading, MA: Addison-Wesley.

Vicky J. Hardman and Peter T. Kirstein

BAR CODE

See UNIVERSAL PRODUCT CODE.

BASIC

For articles on related subjects, *see* PROGRAMMING LANGUAGES; PROCEDURE-ORIENTED LANGUAGES; STRUCTURED PROGRAMMING; and TIME-SHARING.

The Birth of Basic

Basic (Beginner's All-purpose Symbolic Instruction Code) was invented at Dartmouth College in 1964 to allow all students, especially those with no interest in science, to learn about the computer, i.e. to write simple programs. The students used Basic on a time-sharing system, which allowed them to reach the computer using terminals in their dorms. (The reader should realize that almost all computer work in those days required punched cards to be carried to the computer center. The only terminals were electric typewriters, such as the Teletype, which printed at 10 characters per second. There were no video terminals or personal computers.)

Not only were computers expensive and hard to use, there were only a few computer languages to choose from, Fortran and Algol being two of the most common. Fortran was designed for scientific work and Algol was a predecessor of Pascal. Both were somewhat hard to learn. C and C++ (*q.v.*) had not yet been invented. So Basic came into being partly because the other languages seemed too hard for students to learn.

The Basic Principles

To keep it simple for students and others, the design of Basic followed these criteria:

1. *Free form input and default output*
   Fortran required key-punching numbers on cards in a fixed way, and also required stating how to print the output numbers. Basic allowed numbers to be entered as the user pleased and printed its output to reasonable precision without requiring formatting rules.

2. *English words rather than punctuation*
   Fortran and Algol both used tricky punctuation with semicolons or commas. Basic used English words chosen to suggest what was actually going on. Compare the Fortran loop statement with those of Algol and Basic:

   Fortran:
   ```
           DO 200,I=1,100,3
       200   SUM=SUM+X(I)
   ```

   Algol:
   ```
        for i := 1 step 3 until 100 do
           sum := sum + x(i);
   ```

   Basic:
   ```
      FOR I = 1 TO 100 STEP 3
       LET SUM = SUM + X(I)
      NEXT I
   ```

   Most versions of Basic, though not all, changed all lower-case letters to upper-case.

3. *One line = one statement*
   A statement in a computer language is like a sentence in a written language. Fortran allowed statements longer than could be punched onto one card. Algol allowed short statements to be bunched on the same line. Still other languages used the period to end the statement, as in English. Basic simplified all this: one line equals one statement.

4. *Each statement starts with a keyword*
   In most languages all statements except the assignment statement start with a keyword. But it was felt that students might not understand

   ```
      X = X + 1
   ```

   as an assignment. So LET was picked, to give

   ```
      LET X = X + 1
   ```

5. *Formulas like ordinary algebra*
   Since all college students must have studied high-school algebra, they could type formulas in Basic in the same way. The only differences were that fractions had to be on a single line (using the /) and raising to a power used the ^ —a character on the Teletype—rather than superscripts.

6. *Only one number type*
   Computer experts have always been concerned about how numbers were stored inside the computer: single-precision floating-point, double-precision floating-point, single-precision integer, etc. It is hard to imagine that most non-specialist students and teachers need these distinctions. So Basic decided to shield the users from such technical details and made all its numbers double-precision floating-point.

7. *Line numbers double as GO TO targets*
   Early time-sharing systems used typewriter-like machines called Teletypes; there was nothing like today's word processors. So, to tell Basic how to organize and modify a program, each line had to begin with a line number. Since Basic used GO TO statements to loop back and jump around in the program, the line numbers served also as GO TO targets.

   This is one design feature of the original Basic that quickly disappeared. Word processors now allow writing a program just as you might write a paper, and structured programming (*q.v.*) has taught us how to avoid the use, and therefore the misuse, of GO TO statements.

Features that Never Made the Grade

Several features of the original Basic never made the grade, and are best forgotten. Originally, simple variable names were limited to single letters, or single letters followed by single digits. And confusingly, arrays could be named with the same letter as a simple variable. Multicharacter variable names began to appear in the 1970s. Once there were plenty of variable names possible, there was no need to allow a simple variable and an array to have the same name.

A related feature was that spaces were ignored. For example,

```
   LET X = 3
```

could be written as LETX=3, since the keyword LET was required. Indeed, some early versions actually removed spaces to save valuable memory. Use of spaces became necessary when multicharacter variable names came into being, and besides, programs are much easier for people to read when spaces are judiciously used.

Along Came Personal Computers

In the late 1960s and early 1970s, Basic was the most common language on time-sharing systems. Although there were variations, most were patterned after the original Dartmouth Basic.

Personal computers began their explosive growth in the early 1980s. These machines used TV-like displays for output, and had extremely small memories by today's standards. Because Basic was already the most commonly used language and was still the simplest, it was the language of choice for these new machines. Thus Basic, the most popular language on time-sharing systems, became the most popular language for early personal computers.

Makers of these machines specified additional variations in the Basic interpreters. Two of the most common were graphing commands and number typing. The former was a giant step forward since, to paraphrase, "one graph is worth a thousand numbers." The latter was usually done by adding a character to the end of the variable name. For example, if X were to stand for an integer, a % was added to make it X%. Thus did design criterion 6 disappear. A third addition were the PEEK and POKE instructions, which required the programmer to know details about memory.

Many users objected to typing LET for assignments, so that keyword became optional.

Modern Basic

All modern versions of Basic now are fully structured, that is, you don't have to use GO TO statements. All have sophisticated ways to organize large programs using subroutines and modules. The original Basic included a simple subroutine structure using the GOSUB statement along with line numbers. Parameters (*see* ARGUMENT) were not allowed. Gradually that disappeared in favor of named subroutines with parameters, which allowed the subroutines to be stored separately from the main program.

Modules allow the grouping of several subroutines together with their own private data, thus allowing perhaps the most important ingredient of object-oriented programming (*q.v.*): data abstraction (*see* ABSTRACT DATA TYPE).

Most of the modern features are contained in Standard Basic, a direct descendant of the original Dartmouth Basic. But the most popular version of Basic today is Microsoft's Visual Basic. It differs from Standard Basic in two major ways: it retains the distinction between different types of number (floating-point, integer,

etc.), and it adds data typing and structuring. While such features are desirable (though not necessary) for large applications, they are harder for beginners and students to learn and use.

Of the original design criteria, only 1, 2, and 5 remain in all versions of Basic. Most versions allow some form of line continuation for very long statements, and some versions allow more than one statement on a line. Most versions allow multiple number types, and allow writing programs without using line numbers at all. However, one can still write simple three-line programs and get results quickly. Thus, Basic, on the one hand, is still one of the easiest languages to learn, and, on the other hand, can be used to construct all but the largest applications.

Bibliography

1968. Kemeny, J. G., and Kurtz, T. E. "Dartmouth Time Sharing," *Science*, **162**, 223–238.
1981. Kurtz, T. E. "BASIC," in *History of Programming Languages* (ed. R. L. Wexelblat), 515–549. New York: Academic Press.

Thomas E. Kurtz

BAUD

For an article on a related subject *see* BAUDOT CODE.

The *baud* is a unit of signaling speed and refers to the number of times the state (or condition) of a data communication line changes per second. It is the reciprocal of the length (in seconds) of the shortest element in the signaling code. Historically, it is a contraction of the surname of the Frenchman J. M. E. Baudot, whose five-bit code was adopted by the French telegraph system in 1877. By contrast, a bit is the smallest unit of information in a binary system. The baud rate is therefore equal to the bit rate only if each signal element represents one bit of information.

The relationship between baud and bits per second is illustrated in Fig. 1, where amplitude is used as a coding method. In this particular case, there are four line conditions (amplitudes), one for each of the four combinations of two bits. Each line-change signal element (amplitude) therefore represents two bits of information, and if we have one line-condition change per millisecond the baud rate is 1,000, whereas the bit rate is actually 2,000 bits per second. Similarly, if the signals are coded into eight possible states, one line condition could represent three bits and one baud would then equal three bits per second, etc.

Unfortunately, in much of today's literature, the terms "baud" and "bits per second" are used synonymously. This is correct in cases where pure two-state signaling

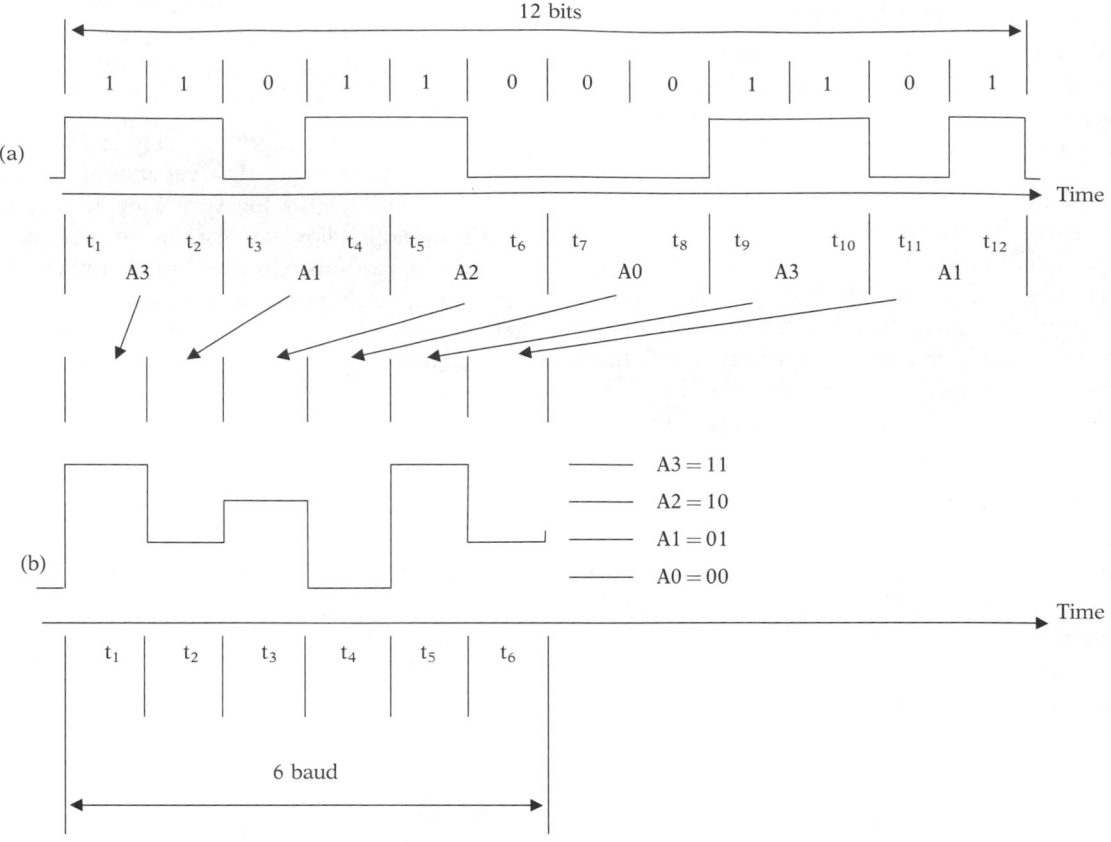

Figure 1. Relationship between baud and bits per second. Each combination of two bits [(a)] is encoded as one of four possible amplitudes [(b)]; hence for this particular case, one baud is equal to two bits per second.

is used, as in Fig. 1a, but is incorrect in general. For this reason, the term "baud" is gradually being replaced by "bits per second," since the latter is independent of the coding method and truly represents the information rate.

John S. Sobolewski

BAUDOT CODE

For articles on related subjects *see* BAUD; CODES; and ERROR CORRECTING AND DETECTING CODE.

The *Baudot code*, also known as the International Telegraph Code No. 1, is named after its inventor, J. M. E. Baudot (1845–1903). It was invented about 1880, and by the mid-twentieth century it had become one of the standards for international telegraph communication.

Baudot is a fixed character-length code in which each character is represented by five binary digits. The five-digit character length allows only 32 $(= 2^5)$ unique combinations, not enough to represent the 26 letters of the alphabet, the 10 digits, and the punctuation characters needed for telegraph messages. This problem is

solved by defining two unique shift-control characters, and interpreting all subsequent characters in terms of the last shift-control character received. The shift-control characters are called "letter shift" and "figure shift." This arrangement is very similar to that of a shift-lock key on a terminal, i.e. once the shift lock has been depressed, all subsequent characters are typed in the same shift.

Using the technique of two unique shift characters, a five-bit code can then represent 62 $(= 2^6 - 2)$ characters. However, in the Baudot code, the total number of characters is less than this because other control characters such as "line feed" and "carriage return" are given representations.

The Baudot code does not have the capability of detecting errors because all combinations of the five bits are valid characters within the code. During transmission, therefore, a character can be transformed into another character by the loss or gain of one or more bits. Particularly harmful is an error in a shift-control character because all characters after the transformed shift-control character up to the next shift-control character would be interpreted in the wrong shift. For example, in the message PAY 810

Table 1. Baudot code characters

Letters	Code	Figures
A	10000	1
B	00110	8
C	10110	9
D	11110	Ø
E	01000	2
F	01110	NA
G	01010	7
H	11010	+
I	01100	NA
J	10010	6
K	10011	(
L	11011	=
M	01011	)
N	01111	NA
O	11100	5
P	11111	%
Q	10111	/
R	00111	–
S	00101	.
T	10101	NA
U	10100	4
V	11101	'
W	01101	?
X	01001	,
Y	00100	3
Z	11001	:
LS	00001	LS
FS	00010	FS
CR	11000	CR
LF	10001	LF
ER	00011	ER
NA	00000	NA

Symbols: LS = Letter Shift, FS = Figure Shift, CR = Carriage Return, LF = Line Feed, ER = Error, NA = Not Assigned, Space = LS or FS.

DOLLARS, if the "figure shift" character between the PAY and the 810 were transformed into, say, a J (i.e. 00010 to 10010), then the message would be received as PAYJBAD DOLLARS (*see* Table 1 for letter-shift and figure-shift equivalents). In order to alleviate this problem, telegraph systems frequently retransmit at the end of the message all figures that occur in the message.

The five-level code most used today is the International Telegraph Code No. 2 (Murray code), invented about 20 years after the Baudot code. In computer manufacturers' literature, there is some confusion concerning the use of the term "baudot code." It is sometimes used to apply to all five-level codes and is frequently applied to International Telegraph Code No. 2.

George D. Detlefsen and Robin H. Kerr

BCD (BINARY-CODED DECIMAL)

See CODES.

BELL LABS RELAY COMPUTERS

For articles on related subjects *see* DIGITAL COMPUTERS, HISTORY OF: EARLY; ENIAC; and STIBITZ, GEORGE.

Between 1939 and 1951, Bell Telephone Laboratories (Bell Labs) built a total of seven digital computing machines of ever-greater sophistication. Each used electromechanical relays and switching equipment for its basic computing elements. The last computers of this series were as functionally powerful as the electronic computers being built elsewhere at that time, but their use of relay switching meant that they would always remain an order of magnitude slower in arithmetic speeds. The inspiration for the initial machines came from George Stibitz, a mathematician at Bell Labs, with the engineering design due at first to Sam Williams and later to E. G. Andrews.

The Model I contained about 400 relays and performed the operations of complex arithmetic on 8-digit decimal numbers. Numbers were internally coded in excess-three binary-coded decimal (Stibitz code). The machine was accessed through a modified teletype terminal (Fig. 1). At Bell Labs, three such terminals allowed multiple (but not simultaneous)

Figure 1 Operator H. L. Marvin seated at one of three consoles for the Bell Labs Complex Number Computer, 1940. (Photo: AT&T Bell Laboratories)

access. That the terminals need not be physically near the processor was dramatically demonstrated at a 1940 meeting of the American Mathematical Society in Hanover, New Hampshire, where a terminal was connected to the computer back at the Labs in New York City. Such remote access to digital equipment would not occur again for ten years.

The Model II, completed in 1943, contained about 440 relays and was optimized for work relating to the development of the M-9 gun director during the Second World War. It used paper tape for input, output, and simple sequences of operations related to interpolation of functions. Its memory capacity was seven decimal numbers of from two to five digits in length.

The Models III and IV were somewhat more powerful, containing about 1,400 relays each and having a memory capacity of ten numbers. They were installed in 1944 at Fort Bliss, Texas, and in 1945 at the Naval Research Laboratory in Washington, DC. Like the Model II, these computers were optimized for fire-control problems, although their programmability meant they could be (and were) reprogrammed to solve many other problems once the war ended.

The Model V was the most ambitious of all the Bell Labs machines, and ranks with the "Giant Brains" of the era, such as the ENIAC or Harvard Mark I (*q.v.*). Two copies were built in 1946–1947, and were installed at the National Advisory Committee for Aeronautics at Langley Field, Virginia, and the Ballistic Research Laboratory at Aberdeen, Maryland. Each machine contained over 9,000 relays, a memory capacity of 30 numbers, and hard-wired floating-point arithmetic unusual for the time.

Decimal numbers were encoded as groups of two and five relays, somewhat like the beads on a Chinese abacus. This *bi-quinary* code allowed for elaborate error checking, which ensured that the machine would stop and alert an operator before ever delivering a wrong answer. Relay computers, unlike their electronic counterparts, had to have error-detecting circuits because a relay can fail intermittently, usually when a piece of dust interferes with a few contact cycles before being dislodged. Such intermittent errors would have been almost impossible to detect without some sort of internal redundancy. By contrast, vacuum tubes failed catastrophically, with a resulting computer failure obvious to its operators.

A Model V could be configured so that several problems could be coded, each on a different paper tape, all of them ready to go. If an error was detected during the run of one problem, the machine would automatically switch over to another tape and begin solving another problem, using different parts of the processor and memory. This early and rudimentary form of *multiprogramming* (*q.v.*) allowed the machine to be run unattended through the night with the assurance that in the morning most, if not all, of the computing work would have been done. That, plus the floating-point arithmetic, helped compensate for the machine's inherently slow speed of about one multiplication per second as compared to the ENIAC's 360 multiplications per second.

The final machine in the series, the Model VI, was built and installed at the Labs for internal use in 1949. It was essentially a simplified version of the Model V, without the multiple independent processors. Apparently it was felt that the complexity of the Model V was not worth it. The Model VI did have an ability to execute short sequences of arithmetic with single commands punched on the tape, a concept new at the time and one rediscovered and named later as "macro" commands. It interpreted these commands through ingenious electromagnetic circuits that, in effect, "microprogrammed" the machine. It is not historically misleading to use that term, since those features were seen and noticed by Maurice Wilkes (*q.v.*), who later developed that concept for stored program electronic computers.

None of the Bell machines used the stored program principle, although the Models V and VI had full conditional branching capabilities. But that made the solving of complex, iterative problems a somewhat baroque exercise involving loops of tape, multiple tape drives, partitioned processors, and other mechanical tricks. Thus, the Model V went about as far as one could with not only relay technology, but also external, paper tape programming.

The Bell Labs computers were powerful, reliable, and balanced machines. They often outperformed their vacuum tube contemporaries in solving problems for which slower speed was not decisive. But once the von Neumann-inspired notions of computer architecture (*q.v.*) became known and accepted, that advantage was lost, as designers elsewhere learned to build electronic computers with none of the architectural drawbacks suffered by machines like the ENIAC. Thus, the Bell Labs machines represent an evolutionary dead end, although their contribution to the mainstream history of digital computing was profound.

Bibliography

1951. Andrews, E. G. "A Review of the Bell Laboratories' Digital Computer Developments," in *Review of Electronic Digital Computers*. Joint AIEE-IRE Computer Conference, 10–12 December, Philadelphia (New York: AIEE, 1952), 101–105.

Paul E. Ceruzzi

BENCHMARKS

For articles on related subjects *see* PARALLEL PROCESSING; and PERFORMANCE MEASUREMENT AND EVALUATION.

INTRODUCTION

The term *benchmark* is drawn from its use in surveying, where it represents a mark on a stationary object whose position and elevation have been measured. The mark, once made, is used subsequently as a reference point in tidal observations and surveys. Analogously, benchmarking of computer systems is intended to measure the performance of new systems relative to a reference point on current systems. In particular, the benchmarks are standardized computer programs for which there is a history of measurement data (typically timings) for executions of the programs with specifically defined input and reproducible output.

Major Benchmark Program Sets

A number of benchmarks have evolved for both scientific and commercial processors. Among the best known for scientific computing are the Livermore Fortran Kernels (McMahon, 1986), the Los Alamos Benchmarks, the NAS Kernels, the Linpack tests (1997), and the Top500 (1996). Recently, due to a growing concern in the supercomputing community that existing benchmarks are too simplistic to represent fully scientific computing, attempts have been made to define new standards. These efforts include the Standard Performance Evaluation Corporation (SPEC), formerly the System Performance Evaluation Cooperative, which is a vendor-sponsored benchmarking project, and the PARKBench (PARallel Kernels and BENCHmarks) collection, which is an academic effort to established a comprehensive set of parallel benchmarks. Each of these collections represents aspects of scientific computation and therefore provides some information about the computational speed of the systems being tested.

The founding members of SPEC were Apollo, Hewlett-Packard, MIPS, and Sun. Joining the consortium later were AT&T, Bull, CDC, Compaq, Data General, DEC, Dupont, Fujitsu, IBM, Intel, Intergraph, Motorola, NCR, Siemens Nixdorf, Silicon Graphics, Solbourne, Stardent, and Unisys. The first set of 10 SPEC benchmarks comprising 150,000 lines of source code was released in October 1989 and was distributed only under a licensing agreement. A performance index called the SPECmark is defined as the geometric mean of the relative performance of the ten separate programs in the SPEC suite. In 1992 SPEC replaced its use of the SPECmark mean by a set of separate benchmarks, including the CPU benchmarks SPECint92 and SPECfp92 (for integer and floating point computations). The current SPEC set of benchmarks includes SPECint95 and SPECfp95 as well as benchmark suites to evaluate the performance of file servers (*q.v.*), WWW (*q.v.*) servers and Java (*q.v.*) Virtual Machine platforms.

The PARKBench committee goals are to establish a comprehensive set of parallel benchmarks that is generally accepted by both users and vendors of parallel systems, provide a focus for parallel benchmark activities and avoid unnecessary duplication of effort and proliferation of benchmarks, to set standards for benchmarking methodology and result-reporting together with a control database/repository for both the benchmarks and the results, and to make the benchmarks and results freely available in the public domain. The initial focus of PARKBench is on the new generation of scalable distributed memory message-passing architectures for which there is a notable lack of existing benchmarks. For this reason the initial benchmark release concentrates on message-passing codes using the widely available MPI and PVM message-passing interfaces for portability.

The first program designed especially for benchmarking was the Whetstone benchmark published in 1976 by H. J. Curnow and B. A. Wichmann of the National Physical Laboratory (NPL) in Great Britain. The benchmark, originally published in Algol 60 but now more often used in its Fortran (*q.v.*) or Pascal (*q.v.*) version, is named for the Whetstone Algol compiler in use at the NPL in the mid-1970s. The Whetstone benchmark gives heavy weight to floating point operations and was of value in testing the effectiveness of various *floating-point coprocessors* that could be optionally added to various microprocessors (*q.v.*). There are now so many different versions of the Whetstone benchmark that comparison of results obtained with one version vs. another is quite difficult.

The Dhrystone benchmark, named in whimsical contradistinction to Whetstone, was published by R. P. Weicker in 1984. Originally written in a Pascal subset of Ada (*q.v.*), the benchmark is now used principally in its C (*q.v.*) version. The Dhrystone benchmark places no emphasis on floating-point operations, but instead contains a mix of statements typical of nonnumeric and systems programming (*q.v.*) environments. Relative to scientific and engineering computations, such programs typically contain fewer loops, simpler computations involving just integer and logical data types, and more conditional statements and procedure calls. Dhrystone is widely distributed via Usenet (*see* INTERNET).

The Top500 looks at the 500 most powerful computer systems installed around the world. This list is updated every six months and provides a look at trends in high-performance computing. The metric used in the evaluation of computer systems is the Linpack benchmark.

One of the most popular benchmarks used on personal computers, though not necessarily a good one, is a Pascal version of the algorithm known as the Sieve of Eratosthenes. It computes all prime numbers up to some limit by eliminating (sieving out) the composite numbers from an original list of all integers less than the limit. The benchmark has been widely used, or perhaps misused, to tout the alleged superiority of one compiler over another with respect to either rate of compilation, speed of execution of object programs, size of object programs, or all three.

In contrast to other benchmarks, which measure the time taken to do a fixed task, the SLALOM benchmark measures the amount of work that can be performed in a fixed time. The rationale is that this will allow comparison over a broader range of machines. The benchmark consists of a radiosity problem (*see* COMPUTER GRAPHICS) together with I/O and matrix setup routines. The problem solved is similar to that of the Linpack benchmark.

The performance of computers, a complicated issue, is a function of many interrelated quantities. These include the application, algorithm, size of the problem, the choices of high-level language and implementation, the level of human effort used to optimize the problem and the compiler's ability to optimize, as well as the operating system, architecture, and hardware characteristics of the system under test. Thus, the results presented for benchmark suites should not be viewed as measures of total system performance, but rather as reference points for further evaluations.

Benchmarks are typically used as one of many data points by algorithm designers seeking the optimal coding style for a given system, by system developers seeking to match machine characteristics to the requirements defined by their target workloads and represented to them through the benchmarks, and by individuals and groups seeking to procure the appropriate computing system for a given installation.

Benchmarking methods (ways to use and abuse benchmarks) are discussed in more detail in Dongarra *et al.* (1987) and in the second part of this article. An overview of common benchmarks is given by Weicker (1990). There have been numerous benchmark programs designed for PCs.

Bibliography

1986. McMahon, F. H. *The Livermore Fortran Kernels: A Computer Test of Numerical Performance Range.* Lawrence Livermore National Laboratory Report UCRL-53745 (October).
1987. Dongarra, J., Martin, J., and Worlton, J. "Evaluating Computers and their Performance: Perspectives, Pitfalls, and Paths," *IEEE Spectrum*, **24** (June).
1990. Weicker, R. P. "An Overview of Common Benchmarks." *IEEE Computer*, **23**, *12* (December), 65–75.
1997. *Performance of Various Computers Using Standard Linear Equations Software in a Fortran Environment.* University of Tennessee, Computer Science Technical Report, CS-89-85, September.
1998. Langer, S. H. "A Comparison of the Floating-point Performance of Current Computers," *Computers in Physics*, *12*, *4* (July/Aug), 338–345.

Website

For an extensive collection of benchmark programs and information on systems from PC to Workstations to Supercomputers, see http://www.netlib.org/benchweb/.

Jack Dongarra and Joanne Martin

RESULTS

Some benchmarking organizations collect results, which they publish in periodic reports or on the World Wide Web. Figs. 1–4 give samples of such reports taken from the Web information of the BAPCo, the SPEC, and the NAS benchmark organizations in May 1999. The intent of these figures is to illustrate the available type of benchmarking information. Additional information would be necessary to interpret the given numbers correctly, for which the reader is referred to the Web pages given in each figure.

In addition there are academic institutions maintaining benchmark result repositories as part of their research efforts. A well-established site is the Performance Database Server at the University of Tennessee (http://performance.netlib.org/performance/html/PDStop.html).

Most of these benchmarks measure the overall speed of computer applications and algorithms. There are a variety of benchmarks that measure the performance of individual system components. For example, one may measure the overall speed of a disk operation, the speed of graphical display functions, the effective bandwidth (*q.v.*) of a network, or the response time of a database query. A large benchmarking organization that deals with the measurement of database transactions is the Transaction Processing Council (TPC—http://www.tpc.org/bench.descrip.html).

With the massive market for PC systems, PC benchmarks have become widely available as well. The term "benchmark" is often loosely used for any tests that can give insight into performance characteristics of an overall system or a component. Many performance metrics in addition to computer speed are of interest. Examples are the performance of graphics systems and the battery life of notebooks. Representative of PC benchmarks are SYSmark, Winstone, WinBench and CPUMark99.

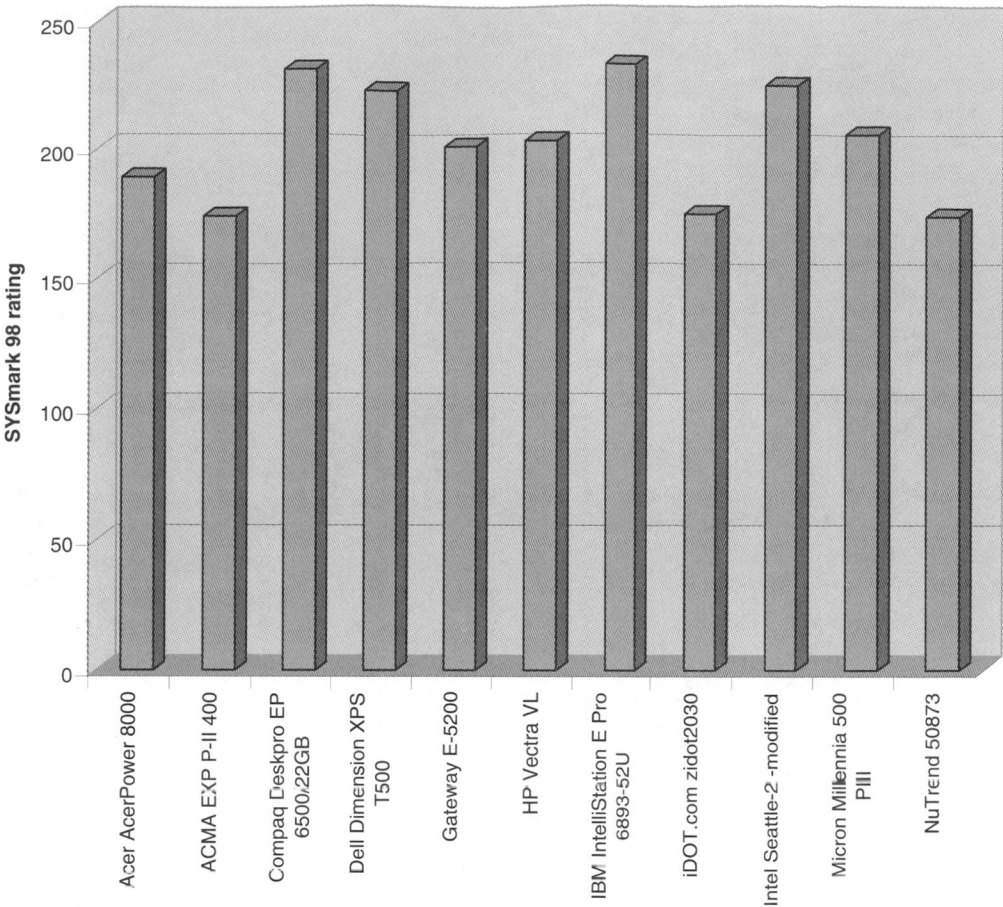

Figure 1. Sample SYSmark benchmark results from `http://www.bapco.com`. The benchmarks represent PC applications ranging from traditional office productivity to Internet content creation and speech recognition.

Many benchmark results with commercial interest are found from sources such as company advertisements and computer-oriented magazines. For example, the PC-oriented benchmarks WinBench and BYTEmark are supported by *PC Magazine* and *BYTE* magazine, respectively.

Issues in Benchmark Use

For the consumer of benchmark results, one of the biggest questions is whether the information is accurate and unbiased. There is an abundance of so-called benchmark publications on the World Wide Web, often accompanied by disclaimers of responsibility for the posted information. Questions to ask when reading benchmark results are: whether or not reported results are approved by a trusted board of experts, whether the benchmarking site has commercial interests, whether the benchmarks are typical of applications that are of interest to the reader, and whether the results have been generated under well-defined benchmark run and reporting rules. Examples of such pitfalls

are to measure kernels instead of full applications, to apply inappropriate program optimizations, to use non-representative input data, to compare with obsolete systems and to use obscure metrics.

To be useful, benchmarks need continuous updating. One reason is that benchmarks have to reflect current applications and current practices in executing these applications on modern computer systems. As computer applications change, so must the benchmarks that serve as reference points for computer performance. Furthermore, the increasing sophistication of computer systems technology requires benchmark updates. For example, for some of the early benchmarks, today's computers would simply recognize the expected outcome and produce an almost instant answer, rather than running the program to obtain a real performance measure.

Another reason for continuous updates of benchmarks is that computer technology tends to "adapt" to benchmarks. Many engineers of computer manufacturers study benchmark suites and tune their hardware and

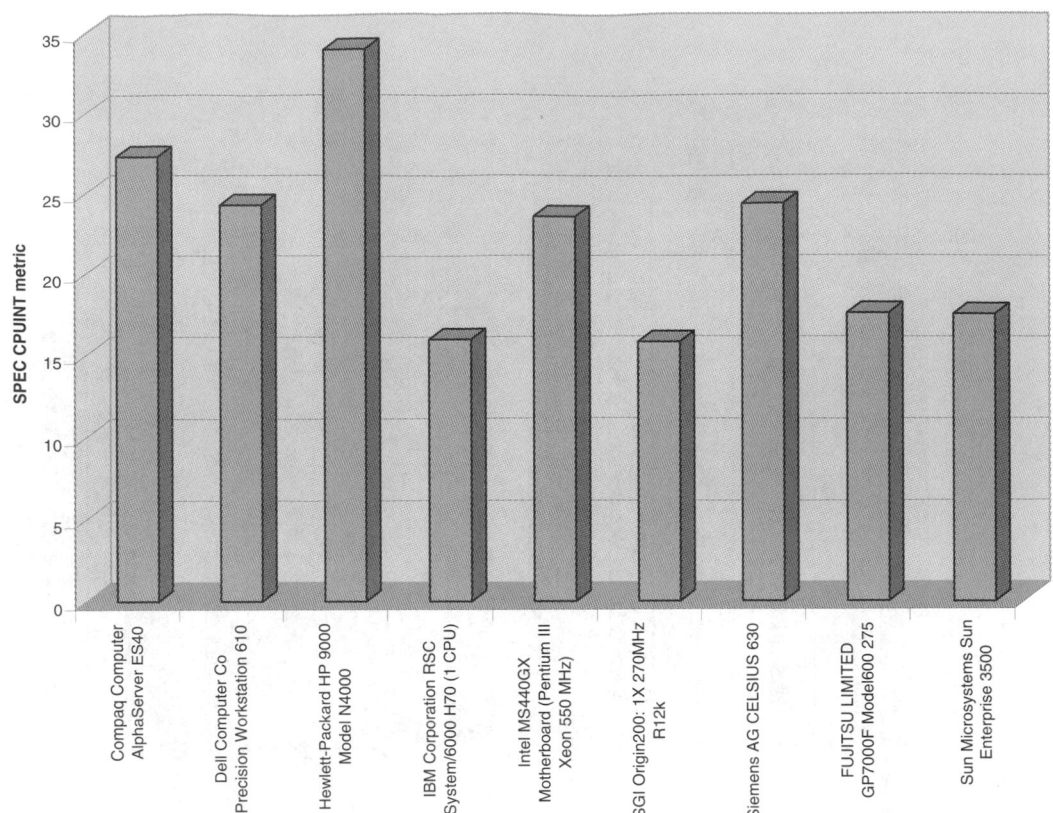

Figure 2. Sample SPEC CINT95 benchmark results from `http://www.spec.org/osg/cpu95`. CINT95 numbers give an indication of the performance of a computer system on programs such as games, program compilers, and image-processing algorithms. The metric indicates the performance of the computer system relative to a Sun SPARCstation 10/40.

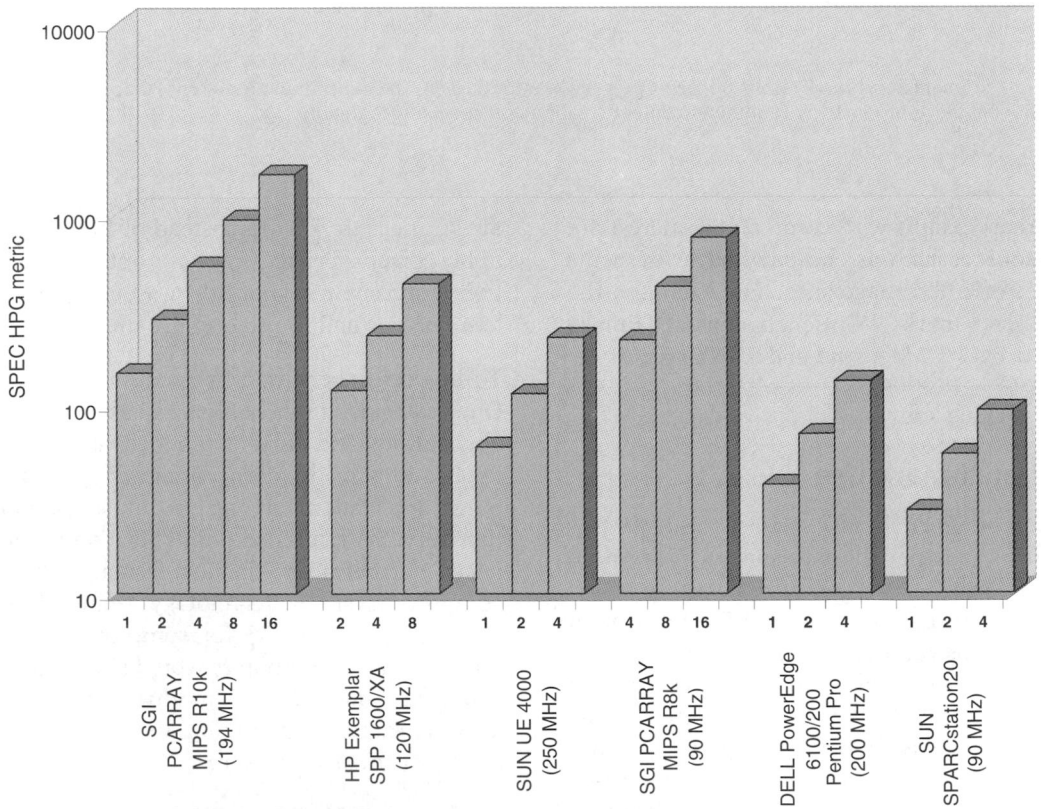

Figure 3. Sample SPEC HPC benchmark results from `http://www.spec.org/hpg/`. HPC numbers give an indication of the performance of a high-performance computer system on scientific and engineering applications. The metric is defined as

$$\frac{86,400 \text{ (seconds in a day)}}{\text{execution time of the benchmark}}.$$

Typically, results are reported for various numbers of processors. Note that the figure uses a logarithmic scale.

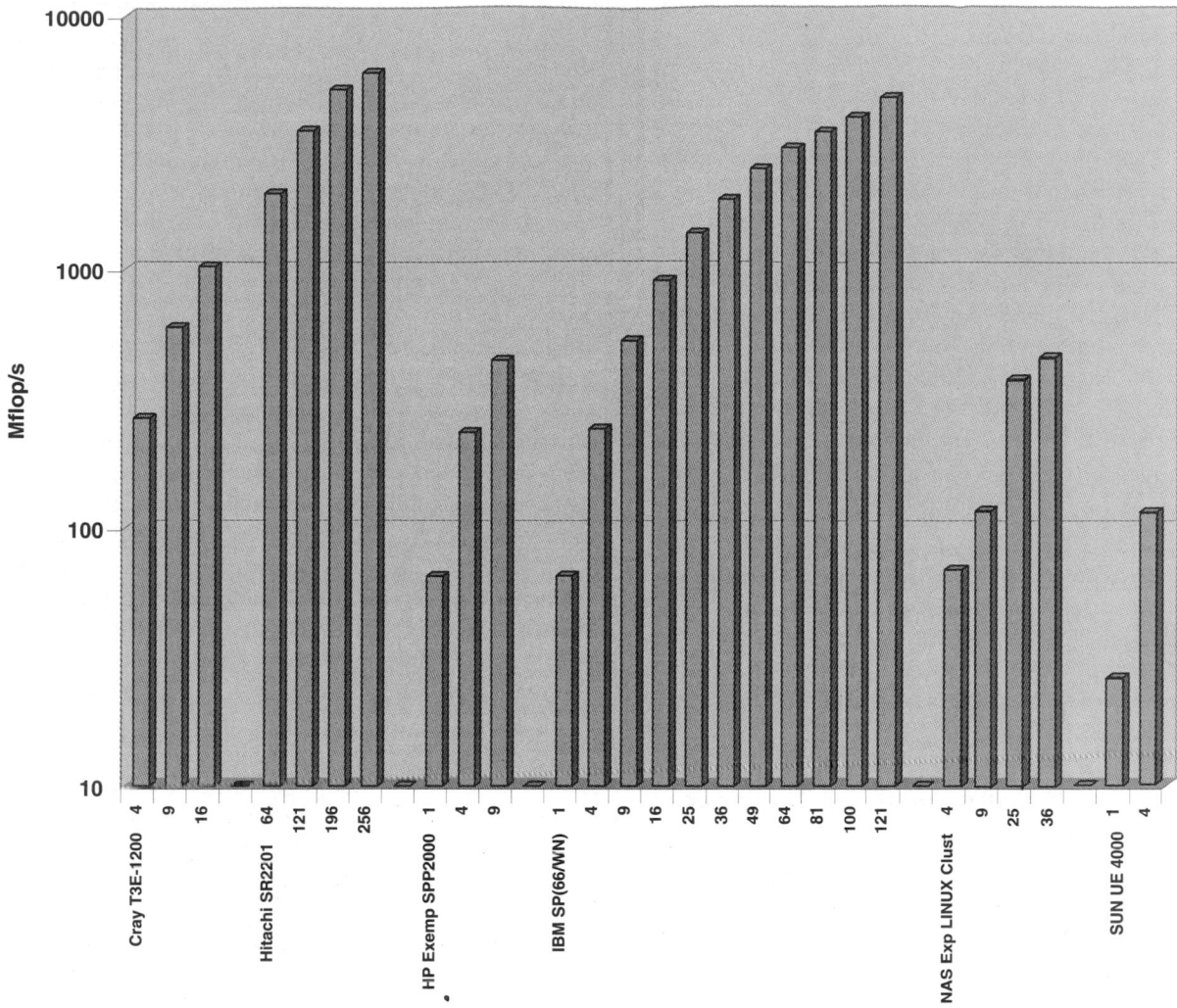

Figure 4. Sample NAS benchmarks results from `http://science.nas.nasa.gov/Software/NPB/`. The benchmarks represent computational fluid dynamics applications used by NASA on high-performance computers. The performance is given as the number of floating-point operations per second (FLOPS), which is one of several metrics given in the NAS reports. Results are reported for various numbers of processors. Note that the figure uses a logarithmic scale.

software systems to produce the best possible performance. Benchmarking efforts have been criticized for this phenomenon. However, one may consider this a natural competitive process and periodic benchmark updates as the appropriate response.

Rudi Eigenmann

BINARY ARITHMETIC

See ARITHMETIC, COMPUTER; COMPLEMENT; and NUMBERS AND NUMBER SYSTEMS.

BINARY-CODED DECIMAL (BCD)

See CODES.

BINARY SEARCH

See SEARCHING.

BINARY TREE

See TREE.

BINDING

For articles on related subjects *see* ASSEMBLER; COMPILER; LANGUAGE PROCESSORS; MACHINE AND ASSEMBLY LANGUAGE PROGRAMMING; and PROGRAMMING LANGUAGES.

Binding means translating an expression in a program into a form immediately interpretable by the machine on which the program is to run; *binding time* is the moment at which this translation is achieved. An expression is c*ompletely* bound, therefore, when translated into an absolute machine representation (*see* "Definition of ML" in MACHINE AND ASSEMBLY LANGUAGE PROGRAMMING) at a fixed location in a storage device. When the context so indicates, however, *binding* can refer to an intermediate point in this process, and *binding time* can mean the point at which the translator has gone as far toward binding the expression as it can. For example, a compiler may intentionally leave the binding of some class of expressions to be completed by a linker (*q.v.*), or even defer binding of some to run time. Similarly, a translator may partly bind a file specification by transforming it into a file descriptor block that needs further interpretation by an input–output (I/O) package or operating system before it can be used for actual I/O procedures.

Some attributes of data objects are bound from the moment the object is defined, even though no specific values may be assigned to them until the language processor has digested the entire source program, or until the object program runs. Many programming languages require that such type attributes as *real*, *integer*, *string*, and so on, be assigned when a variable is introduced, thus enabling the compiler to test statements involving the variable for formal correctness as they are encountered at compile time.

One issue in specifying binding time is efficiency. In general, early binding means more efficient processing of a source program, usually at some cost in flexibility and potentially useful information. The information sacrificed might have supported the use of arrays whose dimensions could vary at run time, or the issuing of more informative error messages, or the ability to compile the same program for various configurations of the target system. The rate at which binding is to take place, therefore, is an important design consideration in virtually all kinds of system software.

Another issue is safety. Early binding generally provides greater safety; if more attributes of a program object are known early, a compiler can better check if it is being used correctly. The programmer can also know these attributes—for example, the size of an array whose bounds are specified early. Conversely, late binding times provide flexibility.

An important form of early binding is also called *lexical* binding (*see* BLOCK STRUCTURE). In most current programming languages, any name used in a subprogram (*q.v.*) definition refers to the most recently declared object with that name, as determined by the nesting of program blocks at that point in the definition. Thus, the textual or lexical context of the subprogram definition determines the attributes of the name. By contrast, *dynamic* binding makes the meaning of a name in a subprogram depend on the context when the subprogram is used, and not when it is defined. Such dynamic binding allows a name like x to refer to a different variable in each call of a subprogram, making it difficult to understand the precise effect of that subprogram. Although some early languages like Lisp (*q.v.*) used dynamic binding, and some scripting languages still do, lexical binding rules are now more common.

As processors have become faster and compilation techniques more sophisticated, efficiency has become a less important issue in deciding upon binding time. A compiler may offer the choice of optimizing a program once it is believed to be correct, or of preserving more of its original form to facilitate debugging (*q.v.*). In many respects, the history of software development is the history of ever-later binding time, with user convenience and program adaptability given progressively greater emphasis, but also with the security of early binding still provided. A language with polymorphic functions (*see* FUNCTIONAL PROGRAMMING) will still check at compile time that the function treats its arguments consistently. Likewise, object-oriented programming (*q.v.*), which makes run-time resolution of attributes and linkages a major feature, preserves static (early) checking of type attributes. (The OOP feature called *inheritance* is, in effect, a systematic approach to distinguishing those attributes of an object that are to be bound at compile time from those to be bound at run time.)

This postponement of binding in the compilation of programs is analogous to the postponement of detailed decisions in the top-down design of programs; in both, the principle is that options should be kept open as long as possible. But in addition to sharing this general principle (one that applies well beyond the designing and compiling of programs, in fact), each of these processes has its own private reason for late binding. In the compiling process, binding involves the loss of information (e.g. the mnemonic name of a program variable) that can be helpful, even essential, in dealing with bugs or other conditions requiring program modification. In the design process, premature binding clutters the designer's vision with unnecessary detail (e.g. the mnemonic name of a program variable), a distraction from the business at hand.

Some translators have attempted to put the issue of binding time, to some degree, in the user's hands. One, at least (Strachey, 1968), has for experimental purposes gone all the way, letting the user specify for each expression the time at which it is to be bound.

Bibliography

1968. Strachey, C. "A General Purpose Macro Generator," *The Computer Journal*, **8**, 225–241.

1996. Pratt, T. W., and Zelkowitz, M. V. *Programming Languages: Design and Implementation*. Upper Saddle River, NJ: Prentice Hall.

Mark Halpern

BIOCOMPUTING

For articles on related subjects *see* COMPUTER GRAPHICS; DATA MINING; GENETIC ALGORITHMS; HOSPITAL INFORMATION SYSTEMS; IMAGE PROCESSING; MEDICAL APPLICATIONS; MEDICAL IMAGING; NEURAL NETWORKS; SCIENTIFIC APPLICATIONS; SCIENTIFIC VISUALIZATION; SIMULATION; TOMOGRAPHY, COMPUTERIZED; and VIRTUAL REALITY.

Modeling Living Systems

Beginning in the late 1800s, mathematicians began to realize that biology and ecology were sources of intriguing mathematical problems. The very complexity that made life difficult for experimental biologists intrigued mathematicians and led to the formation of the field of *mathematical biology*. More recently, as computers became more cost-effective, simulation modeling became more widely used for incorporating the necessary biological complexity into the original, often simplified, mathematical models.

The experimentalists felt that the theoretical analyses were deficient in a variety of areas. The models were too simple to be useful in clinical or practical biological application. They lacked crucial biological and medical realism. Mathematical modelers balked at the demands for increased levels of biological complexity. The addition of the required biological reality often led to significant alterations in the mathematical models, thereby making them intractable to formal mathematical analysis.

With the advent of the new computer technologies, biological and biomedical reality is finally within the grasp of the biomodeler. Mathematical complexity is no longer as serious an issue because computation speeds are now sufficient to enable large modeling computations to be performed. Large memory is now routinely available, and high-speed, efficient, optimized numerical algorithms are constantly being developed.

Visualization

Visualization is a method of presenting computational results. It transforms the symbolic/numeric into the geometric, thereby enabling researchers to observe their simulations and computations. The life sciences are, by their very nature, visual sciences. They are visual in two ways: (1) directly, in that they handle data from images (X-ray, molecular modeling, computational chemistry) and (2) indirectly, in that they handle complex data and transform it to a visual representation (mathematical and computer models, enzymic reaction simulations, physiological process models, image reconstruction, medical diagnostics). In a sense, the computer becomes the laboratory. And, as a consequence, what was once done *in* the tube is now being done *on* the tube.

IMAGING

A natural use of computers for visualization is the handling of patient image data and the construction or reconstruction of medical image data for clinical diagnosis and analysis. Imaging includes three major problem classes: (1) simple rebuilding of two-dimensional image (graphics) data into a useful two-dimensional image on a screen, (2) reconstruction of three-dimensional images from two-dimensional scans, and (3) visualization of an image in a real-time interactive mode. Given a 3D image of the pelvis, for example, can we manipulate it, in real time, for the purposes of clinical examination? As an outgrowth of attempts to address these three areas from the computer science perspective, clinical medicine and diagnosis have become more powerful. Nowhere has this been better demonstrated than in the areas of noninvasive medicine and image reconstruction; CAT, PET, and NMR scanners now inhabit most hospital complexes of any reasonable size. A further extension of this area of investigation may be found in the surgical planning systems at the Mayo Clinic and at the Mallinkrodt Institute (Washington University at St Louis). With these systems, physicians are now able to simulate a surgical procedure before it is performed on the patient, thereby minimizing potential hazard to the patient, and increasing surgical accuracy. In fact, recent virtual reality surgical systems not only allow us to train surgeons and other types of medical practitioner before they operate on a human, but also allow us to perform virtual reality data analysis of complex, multidimensional biomedical datasets, thereby enhancing our ability to extract usable information from those same datasets. Experimental science benefits as well. These same methods, when applied to experimental biology, allow us to begin to understand the biological and physiological functions of various organs and organ systems. For example, brain mapping studies have allowed us to investigate the cognitive function, as well as the physiological behavior, of the brain.

As an outgrowth of such analyses, we find that interesting questions arise in the area of visualization of multiple datasets of different types. For example, how can one effectively visualize the combined CAT,

PET, NMR, and simulation data for a particular patient so that it is possible to visualize the bone, muscle, and metabolic data at the same time?

Computational Genetics and Molecular Biology

Among the numerous interesting and important questions about genetic structure is the issue of the evolution of the structure and complexity of the human genome. The recent advances in molecular biology and gene sequencing have allowed us to obtain massive amounts of complex strings of data which must be searched, correlated, aligned, and analyzed. This sudden surge in molecular information associated with the human genome and other animal genome sequencing projects has two computational foci: (1) a field that is currently and typically referred to as "computational biology" and which is really what we have chosen to think of as "computational molecular biology and genetics" and (2) molecular informatics. These two fields deal with the issues of data analysis and data management problems arising in the experimental domain of gene sequencing and molecular analysis.

As experimental molecular biology sequences more and more of the genes in various species, we have a greater database of information which can be used to study evolutionary biology (*see* Matrix of Biological Knowledge, below). Questions in evolutionary biology involve complex tree searches that are not easily parallelizable. Tree search algorithms, implemented on parallel computers and on networks of smaller workstations (*q.v.*) operating in parallel, can assist scientists in evaluating genetic evolutionary trees and help them to understand the evolution of these genomic structures. In addition, these same algorithms can be used to study the related problem of the origins of the species. Linkage analysis, a complex mathematical analysis involving tree search algorithms, is used to locate and to map gene structures for the purposes of understanding inherited disorders.

At the gene sequencing level, mathematical and computational algorithms are used to align gene sequences, to match gene sequences, to reconstruct gene sequences from sequence fragments, and to construct theoretical three-dimensional structures based upon those sequences. These hypothesized structures are then compared with the experimental data, and binding and transcription predictions can be made and analyzed for new insights into the biological dynamics of the gene. Harris *et al.* (Abbott-Northwestern Hospital) have developed a hypothesis for a simple code for site-specific recognition at the genetic level. Their work, based upon information derived from genetic sequence comparisons, X-ray crystallography data,

and point mutation studies is intensely computer-oriented at a number of levels. Supercomputer (*q.v.*) simulations of the DNA–protein binding predicted by their model have substantiated their predictions.

Computational Chemistry

The field of computational chemistry is readily divided into the following three major topic areas: (1) *biophysical properties*, such as crystallographic reconstruction and molecular visualization, (2) *molecular biochemistry*, which encompasses such areas as structure/function studies, enzyme/substrate studies (reaction studies, pathway analysis), and protein dynamics and their properties, and (3) *Pharmacokinetics/pharmacodynamics*, which encompasses such areas as interactive molecular modeling, drug design and interactions (cancer chemotherapy, orphan drugs), binding studies (binding site properties), structure/function relationships as applied to drug effectiveness, and cell receptor structures. All of these areas involve intensive numeric computation and subsequent real-time graphics for the visualization of the final molecular or chemical structures. The computations are so intensive that there are a number of specialized high-speed superworkstations marketed for real-time rapid visualization of chemical and pharmacological problems. Within the discipline of computational chemistry, the field of neural nets is taking hold. Neural nets (Wilcox at Minnesota Supercomputing Center, Liebman at Amoco Technology Corporation) are being used to learn to identify similar protein structures based upon recognition of pattern representations for the three-dimensional structure of proteins. This work is so intensive, particularly in the early learning stages, that it is performed on a vector supercomputer.

Computational Cell Biology

The dynamics of cell populations is of great interest to both biologists and clinicians. Understanding the cell cycle would contribute to understanding how better to control the development of various forms of cancer, of how to treat AIDS, and of how to address issues of aging. From a therapeutic perspective, a mathematical model or enhanced simulation of cellular processes could be used to test treatment protocols and regimens before they were actually implemented upon the patient. Early work in this area was performed by Morrison, Aroesty, and Lincoln at the Rand Corporation. These investigators developed a sophisticated mathematical model and computer simulation of cancer growth and treatment using ara-c, an extremely toxic chemotherapeutic agent. More recently, mathematical models of cell population growth for the purposes of studying AIDS progression and treatment have been developed and studied by Webb (Vanderbilt University), cancer progression and treatment by Tucker and Zimmerman (M. D. Anderson Cancer Center), aging and its interplay with cancer development and progression by Witten (University of Michigan, Ann Arbor), cell cycle progression by Tyson (Virginia State), and by many others. These mathematical and computer simulation models have attempted to examine cell growth, cell cycle progression, and cell population dynamics from a variety of perspectives.

Computational Physiology

Human physiology attempts to explain the physical and the chemical factors that are responsible for the origin, the development, and the progression of human life. Human beings are complex machines built from equally complex systems (immune system, digestive system, nervous system, etc.). These systems contain multiple parts or organs (each, itself, a complex hierarchy of systems and subsystems). Realistic models of these systems can lead to deeper understanding of the basic biology of these interacting bodily systems. As the models become more sophisticated, they can lead to a deeper understanding of the important synergism between the systems.

REPRODUCTIVE BIOLOGY

The ovaries are the repository of the female reproductive component, the follicles. Of the approximately 500,000 follicles present in the two ovaries at birth, only about 375 of these follicles will eventually develop into ova (eggs). Worldwide, it has been demonstrated that there are increasing levels of infertility in both sexes. This is particularly true in the USA and in Poland. It is not at all clear what is causing such an increase to occur. As a consequence of this fact, it is of no small importance that the dynamics of the reproductive cycle be studied in detail. Such models might give insight into how the environment and other factors might affect the level of infertility displayed in a particular country or population. In addition, such models can be used to study the dynamics of aging in the mammalian reproductive system. Mathematical models of the development of a follicle have been made by a number of groups; Lacker (Courant Institute for Mathematical Sciences), Gosden *et al.* (UK), and Witten (University of Michigan, Ann Arbor). These models represent various levels of complexity in the mathematical modeling process. The basic premise of all of these models is that the follicle undergoes a series of stages or steps in its growth. These stages, and the transitions between them, are modeled by differential equations. This class of compartmental or Markov models can generate extremely large systems of equations. The model system of Witten, for example, involves the solution of anywhere from 50,000 to over 200,000 nonlinear differential equations describing a probability distribution for a given number of follicles, in each stage (compartment) of development. Male reproductive biology can also be addressed. Mathematical models of swimming tails (sperm without heads) have been studied by Fauci (Tulane University). The solution of a swimming object in a viscous fluid is a numerically intensive problem in computational fluid dynamics.

CARDIAC DYNAMICS

The heart and cardiovascular system are central to human life. Arthur Winfree of the University of Arizona is involved in the mathematical modeling and computer simulation of nonlinear waves in excitable media. One particular example of an excitable medium is the heart muscle. Winfree has been studying circulating, vortex-like excitation (re-entrant tachycardia) in the heart as it is related to the onset of fibrillation (when the heart suddenly loses the rhythmic movement that allows it to pump blood). Within the context of his theory and simulations, Winfree has shown that normal healthy heart muscle is an excitable medium. Further, he has shown that two- and three-dimensional vortices arise in excitable media such as heart muscle and that they do so in ways that are predicted by his theory. Other individuals have looked at such problems as modeling the SA node–atrial interactions through single cell and network models, while still others have looked at the problem of modeling and simulating cardiac anatomy for more accurate prediction of cardiac dynamics.

At the University of Calgary, Wayne Giles heads a research team that is investigating the electrical energy of the heart and its effect upon the organ's natural rhythm. He is particularly interested in how such a model could be used to study the interaction of cardiac function and cardiac drugs. Peter Backx and H. terKeurs of the University of Calgary and S. Goldman of the University of Guelph have been studying the property of propagated after-contractions in cardiac preparations. Their mathematical model, involving up to 40,000 coupled ordinary differential equations, is numerically integrated to study the dynamics of calcium-mediated contractile waves in cardiac preparations.

Charles Peskin of the Courant Institute for Mathematical Sciences has been performing two- and three-dimensional modeling of the heart, including valves and ventricles, and is now involved in adding atria and other vessels. This working model beats and moves the blood through the chambers of the heart. The model is a complex one involving a coupled system of equations modeling the wall, the blood, and the valve motion. The purpose of the Peskin research project is to develop a model that will allow for the design of artificial valves and their subsequent testing. In addition, he proposes to study the effect of heart function on the valve design.

Peskin points out that such a model can be used for a number of other investigatory questions. For example, such a model may be used to examine the timing between the atrial and ventricular contraction (a clinically important facet of cardiac function, as sophisticated pacemakers can now separately pace the chambers). Finally, Peskin points out that such a model can be used to study heart disease and its effect on cardiac dynamics. He was able to use his model to show that weakened capillary muscles lead to valve prolapse. Similar work has also been done by Keener and Panfilov, who have looked at the effects of geometry and fiber orientation on propagation and extracellular potentials in the myocardium.

THE NERVOUS SYSTEM

The nervous system (along with the endocrine system) provides the control functions for the human body. The nervous system is responsible for rapid activities of the body, such as muscular contraction, rapidly changing visceral events, and even the rates of secretion of some of the endocrine glands. It is a unique system in that it can control and perform a vast complex of actions. The human brain is estimated to contain approximately 10^{12} neurons. Many of these neurons are connected to 10,000 other neurons. Thus, in many ways, the brain is itself a sophisticated supercomputer.

At the single neuron level, Steve Young and Mark Ellisman of the Laboratory for Neurocytology at UC San Diego are using a supercomputer to reconstruct single neurons. The neurons are frozen, sliced into sections $0.25–5.0 \, \mu m$ thick, and photographed through a high-voltage electron microscope. The computer is then used to reconstruct the slices and to subsequently view them on a graphics workstation (*q.v.*). Ultimately such techniques can be integrated with advanced simulation modeling to allow the scientist to investigate and to simulate tissue activities and structural and functional relationships. As these techniques are refined, one can envision methods for viewing Alzheimer's disease, which plays havoc with the aged in our population, at the single cell level.

T. D. Lagerlund of the Mayo Clinic has been examining the effects of axial diffusion, via mathematical modeling and computer simulation, on oxygen delivery in the peripheral nerves. It is known that victims of diabetes often suffer changes in their system of blood vessels. These changes reduce the supply of oxygen and nutrients to the tissue and subsequently damage the kidneys, retinas, and nerves. The work of Lagerlund has been to examine the mechanism of tissue damage in diabetes and how nutrients reach the cells. His work has been primarily concerned with diffusion of various nutrient and other substances through nerve tissue. A deeper understanding of these mechanisms could well lead to a deeper understanding of, and a subsequent treatment for, a variety of nerve diseases caused by diabetes and other related conditions.

At a higher level of neural organization is the brain itself. Lagerlund, in addition to his kidney work, has developed computer models for modeling various features of the electroencephalogram or EEG as recorded by scalp electrodes. Their model has been an attempt to understand the mechanisms that are responsible for the generation of the rhythmic fluctuations in potential.

COMPUTING THE KIDNEY

The kidneys play a major role in human metabolism through their regulation of bodily fluids. Don Marsh of the University of Southern California School of Medicine is leading a group of investigators in large-scale mathematical modeling and simulation of the kidney. He and his group have looked at two problems: (1) the concentrating mechanism of the inner medulla of the kidney and (2) the oscillation in tubular pressure initiated by the kidney's nonlinear control mechanism. The concentrating mechanism was modeled using a 3D model of the kidney structure. It included longitudinal symmetry, tubules, and blood vessels. The group was able to demonstrate that the longitudinal symmetry played no part in the concentrating mechanism of the kidney. In their study of the oscillation in tubular pressure, Marsh's group is using a sophisticated system of partial differential equation models to describe the physiological control of the kidney tubular pressure. They have been able to show the existence of what appears to be a chaotic attractor in the system and that there is a period-doubling bifurcation in the development of hypertension (*see* FRACTALS and SCIENTIFIC APPLICATIONS). Tewarson and his group at SUNY Stony Brook have been examining the dynamics of parallel processor models for renal concentrating mechanisms in the loop of Henle.

MODELING THE DYNAMICS OF THE BODY

Mathematical and computer models of limb motion are of importance in a number of areas, from robotics (*q.v.*) to biomechanics. Karl Newell of the University of Illinois Urbana-Champaign simulates limb movements using spring–mass models. Such models are currently used as a metaphor for the neuromuscular organization of limb motion. At the cellular level, Cy Frank and Raj Rangayyan of the University of Calgary are examining ligament injuries and methods of treatment. Collagen fibrils, the basic building blocks of normal healthy ligament, are in nearly parallel arrangement when the ligament is healthy. In injured tissue, the arrangement is highly random. These investigators have been able to demonstrate that the randomness of the distribution depends upon the nature of the injury sustained and the stage of healing. As the tissues heal, the collagen fibrils realign in a process called *collagen remodeling*. Using a supercomputer for sophisticated and intense image processing, these investigators are attempting to interpret the realignment stages and to use such knowledge to treat trauma to the limbs more accurately. Other researchers have looked at such problems as modeling cerebral aneurysms, leucocyte deformability, and fracture prediction for various bones in the body.

PATIENT-BASED PHYSIOLOGICAL SIMULATION

Patient-based physiological modeling has come of age. More and more computer systems are being used for taking patient image data and reconstructing it so that a physician can view/review, in 3D, a patient's X-ray, CAT, PET, NMR, or other clinical image data. Computerized surgery systems are currently in place at the Washington University of St Louis Mallinkrodt Institute and at the Mayo Clinic. Facial reconstruction and surgical simulation are now a practiced reality.

Such workstation-based and mainframe-based systems allow one to dream of a new class of ultra-large-scale patient-based physiological simulations that could be performed with a high-performance computing engine. At the VA Medical Center Minneapolis, T. K. Johnson and R. L. Vessella are developing a patient-based simulation of radioactive decay in the organs of the body. Such a problem is computer-intensive in that it requires the mapping of the three-dimensional spatial distribution of radio-labeled compounds. In addition, the difficulty of the problem is enhanced by the fact that the radiation may travel some distance before it interacts with matter, and the irregular shapes of the organs do not lend themselves to simple dose–distance relationships.

Project DaVinci at the University of Illinois is attempting to build a 3D simulation of the human body. Witten (University of Michigan, Ann Arbor) has examined the problem of ultra-large-scale simulation of cellular systems and the interaction between aging cellular systems and cancerous ones. The increased graying of the US population and the increased evidence of age-related cancer indicates that there will be increased costs to be borne by the healthcare system. Understanding of the dynamics of such a complex biological system will allow us to understand better how to treat cancer in an individual of advanced years.

PROJECT HUMAN

Beyond the complexity of such ultra-large-scale simulations and models is the no longer unreasonable goal of an ultra-large-scale simulation of a human being. Such a simulation would rely upon the patient's image data, noninvasive measurements of physiological functions, and assorted clinical tests. One can begin to hypothesize scenarios in which chemotherapy can be simulated, in a given patient, before the therapy is performed. Radical and new drug treatments can be simulated and the results can be examined and evaluated, not based upon an idealized mathematical model, but rather upon an integrated model and patient system. Eventually, one can envision the possibility of actually testing newly designed drugs in computer-based large-scale simulations. While it will be a long time before such a complex simulation and modeling system can be put into place, it is possible to imagine its existence. Project Human is slowly becoming a practical reality.

Computational Population Biology

The study of populations, particularly human populations, is called *demography*. Models, in this area, are generally hyperbolic partial differential equations or their approximations. The canonical system is the McKendrick/Von Foerster system given by

$$\begin{cases} \dfrac{\partial n(t, a)}{\partial t} + \dfrac{\partial n(t, a)}{\partial a} = -\mu(t, a, \dots)n(t, a) \\ n(t, 0) = \displaystyle\int_0^\infty \lambda(t, a, \dots)n(t, a)\,\mathrm{d}a \\ n(0, a) = n_0(a) \end{cases}$$

where $n(t, a)$ is the number (or density) of individuals of age a at time t, $\mu(t, a, \dots)$ is the per capita mortality rate, $\lambda(t, a, \dots)$ is the per capita birth rate, and $n_0(a)$ is the given initial population distribution. Should we choose to discretize a into a discrete age-class structure, we obtain a system of ordinary differential equations which approximates the original partial differential equation system. The study of such models is of great interest for a number of reasons. In particular, given the increasing cost of health care and the associated increase of the aged component of the population, it is of great importance to understand the dynamics of the human population in an effort to hold down the cost of health care. In addition, models of this type arise in the study of toxicological effects of the environment upon a population (ecotoxicology). For example, how does PCB exposure (at the molecular level—computational molecular biology) affect the dynamics of the liver (at the organ level—computational physiology)? And how is this result seen at the population level (the demographic level—computational population biology)?

Mathematical modeling of diseases, particularly of such diseases as AIDS and Lyme disease, requires the use of computational methods. The models are routinely complex, often stochastic in nature, and quite frequently intractable analytically. Models of this class have been studied by Hyman *et al.* at Los Alamos National Laboratories and Levin *et al.* at Cornell University.

Epidemiology and biostatistics study population dynamics and characteristics from a probabilistic perspective. Clinical trials often generate large data sets. Statistical analysis of these data sets is often intense, due to the sample size and the complexity of the interactions. In addition, there are often issues of multicenter trials and the more recent problems arising in metastatistical analysis, the integration of originally disjoint data sets for the purposes of statistical analysis. In general, this class of problem is both computer-dependent and computer-intensive, not only from the point of view of numerical computation, but also from the point of graphic visualization of the resultant computations.

Computational Dentistry

What can be done to visualize the bones and muscles in the torso can also be done to visualize the jaw and the facial muscles. Many dental schools are collaborating with mechanical and biomedical engineers for the purpose of finite element (*q.v.*) modeling of the jaw (e.g. Michael Day at the University of Louisville). The resultant models are then applied to examining the problems of orthodonture and of computer-automated patient-based, dental prosthetics design. Numerous researchers have used high-performance computing methods to study dental implant design.

One of the greatest dental healthcare costs is TMJ (Temporal Mandibular Joint syndrome). ETA Systems, in collaboration with the School of Dentistry at the University of Texas Health Science Center, San Antonio, is developing a neuromuscular joint model in an effort to study TMJ syndrome. The model involves not only the use of sophisticated mathematical equations to describe the dynamics of the bones and muscles of the jaw, but also patient-based data as the input for describing these same structures. Thus, the models will be based upon real patient data rather than hypothesized or idealized dental structures. Such models require the supercomputer to be used not only as a computation engine for model simulation, but also as an image processing system to facilitate the handling of patient-based image data (CAT, NMR, PET, etc.).

Second only to the problem of TMJ syndrome is the problem of periodontal disease. This complex interplay between the bacterial ecology of the patient's mouth and the basic physiology of the patient is not very well understood. Research into the development of an ultra-large-scale simulation of the mouth and its bacterial environment could save millions of dollars in treatments for periodontal disease. The purpose of such a project would be to develop a method for better understanding of how periodontal disease occurs, what factors may influence the progression of the disease, and how it can be better treated.

Agricultural/Veterinary Applications

The same issues that arise in human populations, in such areas as disease spread, environmental impact analysis, and epidemiology, also arise in animal and insect populations. In addition to the obvious areas of investigation, one can investigate, via simulation modeling, such issues as crop yield, milk yield, nutritional demands, and more complex problems such as the interaction between genotype and environment as it relates to dairy herd location. Other investigators have looked at breeding scheme problems in an effort to study the effects of genetic changes and genetic drift, with the goal of maximizing milk yield in a dairy herd or meat yield in a swine population. Finally, other investigators have been examining the question of how competing plants interact in an environment containing limited resources. These models and simulations have been extended to include pest management methods. Similar models exist for fisheries and for forestry management.

The Matrix of Biological Knowledge

Current understanding of biology and biomedicine involves complex relationships rooted in enormous amounts of data—data obtained from numerous experiments and observations and gleaned from diverse disciplines. As a consequence of these harsh realities, few scientists are capable of staying abreast of the ever-increasing knowledge base, let alone searching that database for new or unsuspected biological phenomena. While data mining technologies are being implemented for the vast credit card and marketing databases found in the business world, little effort is being applied to solving the same classes of problem in the scientific world. Data mining is becoming more attractive in the biotechnology arena. It is used as a means to glean new information from databases of sequence and structure information. Yet, hidden within the complete database of published biological experiments—*the matrix of biological knowledge*—lies the potential for developing a new and powerful tool for the investigation of biological principles. Many databases of biological information already exist. Perhaps the best known of these is GenBank, the database of all known gene sequences. This project is, in some sense, an outgrowth of the Human Genome Project, a worldwide effort to sequence the entire human genome. The Human Genome Project requires massive computer support in such areas as numerical computation, searching algorithms, and database design. As these databases increase in size and complexity, it becomes increasingly important that effective and efficient user interfaces be developed. One can envision user interfaces (*q.v.*) incorporating knowledge engineering, advanced graphics and mathematical capabilities, and simulation engines. The future of biocomputing is one of great excitement and great potential.

Bibliography

1987. Witten, M. (ed.) *Advances in Mathematics and Computers in Medicine.* New York: Pergamon Press.

1987. Winfree, A.T. *When Time Breaks Down.* Princeton, NJ: Princeton University Press.

1987. Morowitz, H., and Smith, T. *Report of The Matrix of Biological Knowledge Workshop.* Santa Fe Institute, New Mexico.

1988. Weiss, R. "High-tech Tooth Repair," *Science News*, **134**, 376–379.

1989. Witten, M. (ed.) *Advances in Mathematics and Computers in Medicine 2.* New York: Pergamon Press.

1989. Witten, M. "Modeling the Aging–Cancer Interface: Some Thoughts on a Complex Biological Dynamics," *J. Gerontology*, **44**, *6*, 72–80.

1990. Bell, G. I., and Marr, T. G. (eds.) *Computers and DNA.* Reading, MA: Addison-Wesley.

1995. Hademenos, G. J. "The Physics of Cerebral Aneurysms," *Physics Today*, **48**, *2* (February), 24–30.

1995. Schulze-Kremer, S. *Molecular Bioinformatics.* Berlin: Walter de Gruyter.

1995. Shirley, B. A. *Protein Stability and Folding: Theory and Practice.* Totowa, NJ: Humana Press.

1995. Witten, M. (ed.) *Building a Man in the Machine*, Vols 1–3. Singapore: World Scientific Press.

1997. Panfilov, A. V., and Holden, A. V. (eds.) *Computational Biology of the Heart.* Chichester, UK: John Wiley.

Tarynn M. Witten

BIOS

For articles on related subjects *see* IBM PC; INPUT–OUTPUT CONTROL SYSTEM; KERNEL; and LOGIN FILE.

The *basic input output system* (BIOS) of the disk operating system (DOS) for a typical microcomputer is the portion of the operating system (*q.v.*) that provides an interface between the DOS kernel and the underlying hardware. The *kernel* is the portion of DOS closest to the application software. It is responsible for process control, memory management, file management, and peripheral support. The kernel passes commands from the application software to the BIOS for translation into hardware-specific requests.

The BIOS consists of two parts. The *firmware* (*q.v.*) portion is encoded in PROM chips that cannot be erased by the user. This portion is essentially a table of interrupts (*q.v.*) and some executable code for servicing the interrupt requests. A changeable and extensible portion of the BIOS sits in files, usually hidden, on the boot disk (*see* BOOTSTRAP). On IBM PCs (*q.v.*) and PC-compatibles, these files are named IO.SYS or IBMBIO.COM.

The BIOS is responsible for system checking at startup time. It is also the module that translates commands to specific peripherals and devices into a language that the hardware can handle. The original IBM BIOS for the PC also contained part of the language Basic (*q.v.*), but this is no longer common.

To avoid copyright infringement, manufacturers of IBM-compatible micros emulate the functions of the IBM BIOS without copying the actual code. The relative ease with which this can be done was a major factor in the rise of so many vendors capable of producing low-cost microcomputers that are 100% compatible with the IBM PC. As long as software operates through the BIOS and only through the BIOS, compatibility can be assured.

The BIOS, however, does not support all of the hardware's capabilities. Hardware designers cannot conceive all the uses that software might want to make of new devices. The BIOS is also quite slow at many tasks, especially video graphics. Many software authors choose to bypass the BIOS and program the hardware directly. This leads to increased performance, but there is then a danger that the program will not work on all machines, especially ones whose plug-in boards and other devices are slightly nonstandard.

Devices that were not available when BIOS code was originally burned into PROM can be accommodated by DEVICE commands in CONFIG.SYS files, commands that access the extensible portion of the BIOS that resides on disk (*see* LOGIN FILE).

More recently, BIOS code has been made extensible by the use of *flash memory* chips. These chips are normally divided into blocks. Each block can be erased and programmed independently. Blocks can also be locked to prevent accidental reprogramming. This ability to program the BIOS after it has been installed forestalls the obsolescence of BIOS chips as new hardware features are installed. In this way the BIOS can be updated by modem (*q.v.*) or directly from a diskette (*q.v.*) to bring the code in line with new hardware capabilities.

Modern BIOS chips must be able to perform the basic set of boot instructions; carry out Power On Self Tests (POST); track system date and time; test memory parity; set *wait states* (*q.v.*); set the boot sequence, display type, and keyboard type; set CPU speed; set sign-on password (*q.v.*); provide boot sector virus protection; manage multiple processors and configurations; and even sense and update new *Plug and Play* devices where I/O ports, interrupts, and DIP switch settings no longer need to be set by the user. They are written directly to the BIOS by the Plug and Play system. The latest systems, especially portables, also need to manage battery power effectively to maximize time of use. BIOS chips play a role in managing the power to the various portions of the system using the specifications of the Advanced Power Management (APM) standard.

BIOS chips also assist in *local area network* (*q.v.*) management using the Desktop Management Interface (DMI). System administrators use this interface to gather information about clients and server system hardware, software, and use for individual computers over the network.

As add-on cards have become more sophisticated and been equipped with their own special CPUs, BIOS chips have been installed to track and manage the variety of settings native to these peripheral and control cards. Thus high-performance PCs and workstations no longer use a single BIOS chip; they have as many as they have CPUs.

Stephen J. Rogowski

BIT SLICING

For articles on related subjects *see* ARITHMETIC-LOGIC UNIT (ALU); and INTEGRATED CIRCUITRY.

Bit slicing refers to the technique of constructing an *m*-bit arithmetic-logic unit (ALU) by interconnecting a set of identical *n*-bit ($n \leq m$) LSI chips called *bit slices*. Bit slice chips—typically, one, two, or four bits wide—contain all of the circuits necessary to perform a large number of ALU functions, including arithmetic, logic, register storage, and even I/O, for their segment of a processor word. Then, for example, four four-bit slices may be combined to form the CPU of a 16-bit computer (*see* Fig. 1).

Bit slicing was used before VLSI (Very Large Scale Integration—*see* INTEGRATED CIRCUITRY) became

common in the early 1980s. Its major advantage was to provide a rational basis for packaging very high-speed, high-performance circuits in a reasonable number of IC chips, each with limitations on die area, pin count, and power dissipation. With this approach, high-speed, high-power bipolar circuit technology could be used. For example, the Schottky TTL AMD 2900 series four-bit chip set operates with a 100 ns microcycle, while the ECL M10800 four-bit family performed typical micro-operations in tens of nanoseconds.

The same motives for bit slicing also extend to memory construction. Thus, a semiconductor memory system could be sliced vertically, each *m* bit word being resident in several *n* bit ($n \leq m$) slices.

Bibliography

1999. Tanenbaum, A. S. *Structured Computer Organization,* 4th Ed. Upper Saddle River, NJ: Prentice Hall.

Kenneth C. Smith

BLOCK AND BLOCKING FACTOR

For articles on related subjects *see* FILE; MEMORY: AUXILIARY; OPEN AND CLOSE A FILE; and RECORD.

The term *block* is synonymous with *physical record*: a sequence of words or characters written contiguously by a computer on an external storage medium. Typically, all blocks have the same length and exactly one block is written each time a WRITE command is executed by an I/O channel (or equivalent I/O facility). Analogously, one block is read from an external medium each time that a READ command is executed by the channel.

The idea of a *block* is distinguished from that of a *logical record* as follows: A block is defined by the physical characteristics and constraints of the external storage medium and hence is a hardware design parameter. A logical record is defined by a particular data structure in a processing program; whether all such records have the same length or vary in size is a choice made by the programmer. Logical records (often shortened to "records", although this term is also loosely used for "blocks") are aggregates of data, such as bits, numbers and character strings, which are naturally and conveniently transmitted at one time from the main storage of a computer to an external medium. One type of data aggregate is a *master record*, comprising all attributes associated with a member of some population.

On magnetic tape, blocks are separated by *interblock gaps*, so that large blocks waste the least space on the tape. But the larger the block, the larger the main

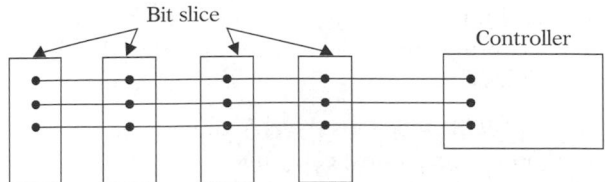

Figure 1. Conceptual view of a (16-bit) ALU consisting of four four-bit slices operated in parallel by a (shared) controller. Only three of the many control lines are shown.

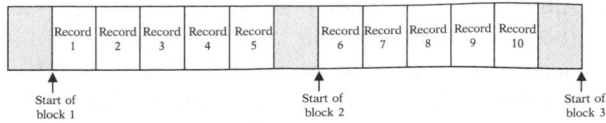

Figure 1. Fixed-length records; blocking factor = 5; all records have the same length; block length = 5 × (record length).

memory buffer needed to accept data read from a block, and the more likely it becomes that the programmer may not be able to fill all of each block with useful data. Unfilled blocks waste tape space and sacrifice processing speed because of the time needed to pass over unused portions of blocks.

To cope with the probably incommensurate sizes of logical and physical records, the programmer must seek to distribute records as efficiently as possible. There are three situations: (a) records have a fixed size smaller than a block, (b) records vary in length but none exceeds the size of a block, and (c) records vary in length but some or all exceed the size of a block.

The first case is shown in Fig. 1. As many records as possible are packed into a block, and the number of records that fit is called the *blocking factor*. The second case is shown in Fig. 2. One or more records are packed into each block, but since the number will vary, one may speak only of an *average* blocking factor. The third case is shown in Fig. 3. Since records

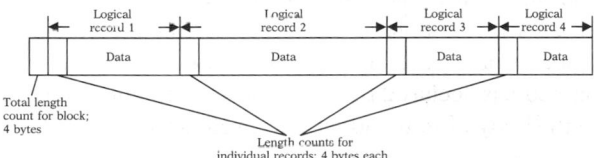

Figure 2. Variable-length records (no logical record larger than one physical block): block length = 4 + [(length of record 1) + 4] + [(length of record 2) + 4] + ···

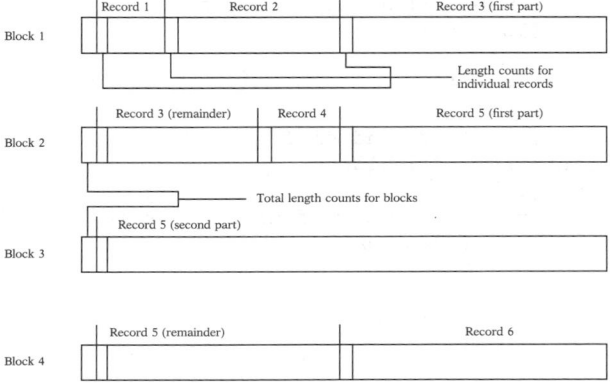

Figure 3. Variable-length records (which may be larger than fixed-length physical blocks).

must often be extended over two or more blocks, the concept of a blocking factor is not applicable and the layout is called *spanned record format*.

David N. Freeman and Edwin D. Reilly

BLOCK STRUCTURE

For articles on related subjects *see* ACTIVATION RECORD; CLASS; CONTROL STRUCTURE; PROCEDURE-ORIENTED LANGUAGES; PROGRAMMING LANGUAGES; and STRUCTURED PROGRAMMING.

Block structure is a programming language concept that allows related declarations and statements to be grouped together. When used judiciously, it can help transform a large, unwieldy program into a disciplined, well-structured, easy-to-understand program.

Because of the important function it performs, block structure (first introduced in Algol 60—*q.v.*) is found in some form in most procedural programming languages developed after Algol 60.

Use of Block Structure in Programming

The block structure mechanism is used to partition a large program into smaller and more manageable *blocks*. Since a block may contain other blocks as components, block structure can be used to decompose a large program into an orderly hierarchy of blocks. This is perhaps the most important use of block structure from the programmer's point of view, since it allows programs to be constructed in a hierarchical fashion which often results in increased program clarity and elegance.

A programming language-specific notation indicates the start and end of a block. Algol 60 and Pascal use the reserved words **begin** and **end**, C uses braces (**{** and **}**).

Block structure is used for two purposes:

1. It allows a sequence of executable statements to be grouped into a single *compound statement*. This allows the compound statement to be used in places where the programming language allows only a single statement (e.g. in any branch of an **if-then-else** statement).

2. It allows the programmer to control where symbols (variables, types, constants, etc.) can be modified and used. Each block introduces a new *scope* (i.e. a domain for the definition of symbols). Symbols declared within a block (i.e. *local* to the block) may be used only within that block (and within any contained block). Thus, variables declared within a

block can have no effect on the program outside of the block. This provides a degree of data security (*q.v.*), since a programmer can use a block to "hide" variables (*information hiding—q.v.*) and thereby make them inaccessible outside of this block.

Conceptually, storage is allocated for variables declared in a block when the block is entered and is deallocated when execution leaves the block. This means that data objects with dynamically determined sizes (e.g. arrays with lower and/or upper bounds that are determined by run-time values) can have a different size each time that the block containing the object is entered during program execution. Most modern compilers will optimize allocation of storage for blocks in a way that is consistent with this concept, but that may economize on the work actually done at each block entry and exit.

The Algol 60 code segment in Fig. 1. illustrates the uses of block structure described above. The first block is used to declare the global variables *sumx*, *sumxx*, *x*, *xxsize*, and *y*. The second block is used to introduce the new variables *p*, *y*, and *xx*. These variables may only be used during execution of the second block. The size of the array *xx* is determined from the value of the global variable *xxsize*. The third block is used to group three assignment statements so that they behave as one statement in the body of the **for** loop.

Scope Rules

A block *body* is a sequence of executable statements and a block is itself an executable statement. Therefore, blocks may be nested to any depth. This has several consequences:

1. Although an identifier may be used only once as the name of an object in a block, the same identifier may be used to name different objects in different blocks. A good programmer will use this facility sparingly (e.g. for utility variables like i, j, k used as counters and loop indices). Widespread reuse of identifiers can make a program difficult to understand.

2. If the same identifier is used to name objects in several nested blocks, the programming language's *scope rule* is used to disambiguate references to the identifier. The *Algol 60 scope rule* (used in most procedural languages) starts at the point where the identifier is used and searches blocks starting with the block containing the use of the identifier and working outward through containing blocks toward the main program block until a declaration of the identifier is found. Note that with this rule the redeclaration of an identifier in an inner block will make the object named by the same identifier in an outer block inaccessible. For example, in Fig. 1, the declaration of an integer variable y in the second block makes the real array y declared in the main program inaccessible in the second block (and in all contained blocks).

Fig. 2 illustrates these points. The identifier b is used to name variables in both the first and fourth blocks. (The outermost, global block has no delimiters in C.) In the second block (body of the function P), the variable x declared in the first block is inaccessible because the identifier x was also used to name a formal parameter of P; the variable c declared in the first block is inaccessible in the body of P because another variable named c is declared there. In the assignment statement in the body of P, the identifier c refers to the variable c

```
begin    comment first block - main program;
    integer sumx, sumxx, xxsize;
    integer array x[1:100];
    real array y[1:50];
    . . .
    begin    comment second block;
        integer p,y;
        integer array xx[1:xxsize];
        sumx := sumxx := 0;
        for p := 1 step 1 until 100 do
            begin    comment third block;
                sumx := sumx + x[p];
                xx[p] := x[p] * x[p];
                sumxx := sumxx + xx[p]
            end;
        . . .
    end
end;
```

Figure 1. An Algol program demonstrating block structure.

```
/* global declarations--first block*/
double c, b, x ;
/* declaration of function P */
int P(double x, float y)
    {/* second block - body of P */
    float c ;
    . . .
    b = x + c ;
    . . .
    }        /* end of P */
main() /* third block */
    {. . .
    if ( c <= x ) /* fourth block */
        {float b ;
        b = c ;
        c = x ;
        x = b ;
        }
    . . .
    }
```

Figure 2. C block structure example.

declared in P, the identifier x refers to a formal parameter of P, and the identifier b refers to the variable b declared in the first block. In the fourth block the variable b declared in the first block is inaccessible because a local variable b has been declared there.

Blocks provide a hierarchical method for controlling access to variables. Other programming language mechanisms, for example modules and classes (*q.v.*), provide more structured access control.

Bibliography

1964. Randell, B. and Russell, L. S. *Algol 60 Implementation*. New York: Academic Press.
1996. Pratt, T. W. and Zelkowitz, M. *The Design and Implementation of Programming Languages*, 3rd Ed. Upper Saddle River, NJ: Prentice Hall.

David B. Wortman

BNF

See BACKUS–NAUR FORM.

BOOLE, GEORGE

For articles on related subjects *see* BOOLEAN ALGEBRA; and LOGIC DESIGN.

George Boole (b. Lincoln, England, 1815; d. Cork, Ireland, 1864), *see* Fig. 1, was one of those rarities in an era of increasing specialization: the self-taught man who followed his own path to the penetration of territory untouched by his contemporaries. Due to the family's sparse financial resources, Boole's formal education was limited to elementary school and a short stint in a commercial school. Beyond this he was almost totally self-educated.

Boole's first scientific publication was an address on Newton to mark the presentation of a bust of Newton to the Mechanics Institution in Lincoln. In 1840 he wrote his first paper for the *Cambridge Mathematical Journal*. In 1849, despite his lack of formal training, he was appointed to a professorship of mathematics in the newly established Queen's College, Cork, Ireland.

During his career he published approximately 50 scientific papers, two textbooks (on differential equations, 1859; and finite differences, 1860), and his two famous volumes on mathematical logic (*see* Bibliography). In 1844, the Royal Society awarded him a medal for his papers on differential operators, and in 1857 it elected him a Fellow. He was married in 1855 to Mary Everest, a niece of Sir George Everest, after whom Mount Everest was named.

Figure 1. George Boole (courtesy of the Mary Evans Picture Library).

Although Boole made significant contributions in a number of areas of mathematics, his immortality stems from his two works that gave decisive impetus to the need to express logical concepts in mathematical form: "The Mathematical Analysis of Logic, Being an Essay Towards a Calculus of Deductive Reasoning" (1847) and "An Investigation of the Laws of Thought, on Which are Founded the Mathematical Theories of Logic and Probability" (1854). Through these works he truly became the founder of modern symbolic logic. He reduced logic to a propositional calculus, now often called *Boolean algebra*, which was extremely simple and based upon classical logic.

Under the influence of his work, a school of symbolic logic evolved that made a determined effort to unify logic and mathematics. As is usual, the impact of this effort was not realized until the latter part of the nineteenth century. Although De Morgan and Jevons expounded on his work during Boole's lifetime, it remained for Frege, Peano, and C. S. Peirce to relight the torch that finally led to the "Principia Mathematica" (1910–1913) of Russell and Whitehead.

Boole's discovery that the symbolism of algebra could be used in logic has had wide impact in the twentieth century. Today, Boolean algebra is important not only in logic, but also in the theory of probability, the theory of lattices, the geometry of sets, and information theory (*q.v.*). It has also led to the design of electronic computers through the interpretation of Boolean combinations of sets as switching circuits (*q.v.*). For example, the logical sum of two sets corresponds to a circuit with two switches in parallel and the logical product corresponds to a pair of switches in series.

Bibliography

1916. MacFarlane, A. *Lectures on Ten British Mathematicians of the Nineteenth Century*, 50–63. New York: John Wiley.

1937. Bell, E. T. *Men of Mathematics*. New York: Simon & Schuster.

1970. Broadbent, T. A. A. "George Boole," in *Dictionary of Scientific Biography* **II**, 293–298. New York: Scribners. (This is an outstanding biography with an excellent bibliography of both primary and secondary sources.)

1982. Smith, G. C. *The Boole–DeMorgan Correspondence*. Oxford: Clarendon Press.

1985. MacHale, D. *George Boole: His Life and Work*. Dublin: Boole Press.

Henry S. Tropp

BOOLEAN ALGEBRA

For articles on related subjects *see* ARITHMETIC, COMPUTER; BOOLE, GEORGE; DISCRETE MATHEMATICS; LOGIC DESIGN; and LOGIC PROGRAMMING.

The concept of a Boolean algebra was first proposed by the English mathematician George Boole in 1847. Since that time, Boole's original conception has been extensively developed and refined by algebraists and logicians. The relationships between Boolean algebra, set algebra, logic, and binary arithmetic have given Boolean algebras a central role in the development of electronic digital computers.

Set Algebras

The most intuitive development of Boolean algebras arises from the concept of a *set algebra*. Let $S = \{a, b, c\}$ and $T = \{a, b, c, d, e\}$ be two sets consisting of three and five elements, respectively. We say that S is a *subset* of T, since every element of S (namely, a, b, and c) belongs to T. Since T has five elements, there are 2^5 subsets of T, for we may choose any individual element to be included or omitted from a subset. Note that these 32 subsets include T itself and the empty set ($\emptyset$), which contains no elements at all. If T contains all elements in the *domain of discourse*, it is called the *universal set*. Given a subset of T, such as S, we may define the *complement* of S with respect to a universal set T to consist of precisely those elements of T that are not included in the given subset. Thus, S as defined above has as its complement (with respect to T) $\bar{S} = \{d, e\}$. The *union* of any two sets consists of those elements that are in one or the other or in both given sets; the *intersection* of two sets consists of those elements that are in both given sets. We use the symbol $\cup$ to denote the union of two sets and $\cap$ to denote the intersection of two sets. For example, if $B = \{b, d, e\}$, then $B \cup S = \{a, b, c, d, e\}$, and $B \cap S = \{b\}$. While other set operations may be defined, the operations of complementation, union and intersection are of primary importance.

Table 1.

Distributivity:	$a(b + c) = ab + ac$ $a + (bc) = (a + b)(a + c)$
Idempotency:	$a + a = a$ $aa = a$
Absorption laws:	$a + ab = a$ $a(a + b) = a$
DeMorgan's laws:	$(a + b)' = a'b'$ $(ab)' = a' + b'$

A *Boolean algebra* is a finite or infinite set of elements together with three operations—negation, addition, and multiplication—that correspond to the set operations of complementation, union, and intersection, respectively. Among the elements of a Boolean algebra are two distinguished elements: 0, corresponding to the empty set; and 1, corresponding to the universal set. For any given element a of a Boolean algebra, there is a unique complement a' with the property that $a + a' = 1$ and $aa' = 0$. (Often a bar, as in $\bar{a}$, is used for complementation, in which case, the second of the preceding formulas would be $a\bar{a} = 0$.) Boolean addition and multiplication are associative and commutative, as are ordinary addition and multiplication, but otherwise have somewhat different properties. The principal properties are given in Table 1, where a, b, and c are any elements of a Boolean algebra.

Since a finite set of n elements has exactly 2^n subsets, and it can be shown that the finite Boolean algebras are precisely the finite set algebras, each finite Boolean algebra consists of exactly 2^n elements for some integer n. For example, the set algebra for the set T defined above corresponds to a Boolean algebra of 32 elements. Tables 2 and 3 define the Boolean operations for Boolean algebras of two and four elements, respectively.

Table 2. Two elements.

$a+b$	0 1
0	0 1
1	1 1

$a \cdot b$	0 1
0	0 0
1	0 1

a	a'
0	1
1	0

Table 3. Four elements.

$a+b$	0 p p' 1
0	0 p p' 1
p	p p 1 1
p'	p' 1 p' 1
1	1 1 1 1

$a \cdot b$	0 p p' 1
0	0 0 0 0
p	0 p 0 p
p'	0 0 p' p'
1	0 p p' 1

a	a'
0	1
p	p'
p'	p
1	0

While it is possible to use a different symbol to denote each element of a Boolean algebra, it is often more useful to represent the 2^n elements of a finite Boolean algebra by binary vectors having n components. With such a representation the operations of the Boolean algebra are accomplished componentwise by considering each component as an independent two-element Boolean algebra. This corresponds to representing subsets of a finite set by binary vectors. For example, since the set T has five elements, we may represent its subsets by five-component binary vectors, each component denoting an element of the set T. A numeral 1 in the ith component of the vector denotes the inclusion of the ith element of that particular subset; a 0 denotes its exclusion. Thus, the subset $S = \{a, b, c\}$ has the binary vector representation $[1,1,1,0,0]$. The set operations become Boolean operations on the components of the vectors. This representation of sets, and the correspondence to Boolean or logical operations, is very useful in database applications. By means of it, sets of document and query characteristics may be easily and rapidly matched.

Propositional Calculus

In database work, and in identifying Boolean algebras as set algebras, we find that various logical connectives, such as "and," "or," and "not" recur frequently. Thus, it is not surprising to find that the two-element Boolean algebra can be identified with elementary logic or propositional calculus. A *proposition* is a statement that can be said to be either true or false. We will denote propositions by letters such as p, q, and r.

The connectives or operators "and" and "or" combine two such propositions into a new one. If we consider two propositions, p and q, each may, independently of the other, assume the value true (T) or false (F). Hence, together, the ordered pair $\langle p, q \rangle$ may assume $2 \times 2 = 4$ combinations of truth values: $\langle T, T \rangle$, $\langle T, F \rangle$, $\langle F, T \rangle$, and $\langle F, F \rangle$. If $\circ$ denotes a binary operator, then $p \circ q$ may be either T or F independently for each of these four T–F combinations. Thus, we can define $2^4 = 16$ distinct binary logical operators, as shown in Table 4. Of the 16 binary logical operators that can be defined, five are commonly used and are more than sufficient to define the remaining operators.

The "negation" or "not" operation, $\neg p$, is defined to form a proposition that is true precisely when the proposition p is false, and false whenever p is true. If we equate the truth values "true" and "false" with the Boolean values 1 and 0, respectively, then we find that negation corresponds to Boolean complementation. That is, $\neg p$ replaces the value "true" with "false," and vice versa, just as p' replaces the value "1" with "0," and vice versa. (In Table 4, column 13 is $\neg p$ and column 11 is $\neg q$.)

The logical "conjunction" or "and," $p \land q$, forms a proposition that is true precisely when both p and q are true, and is false otherwise. This corresponds to the boolean operation of multiplication, with the Boolean expression pq having the value 1 if and only if both p and q have the value 1. (See Table 4, column 8.)

In ordinary usage the word "or" has two distinct meanings, referred to as the "inclusive or" and the "exclusive or." In the inclusive sense, the statement "p or q" is true if p or q or both are true; in the exclusive sense, the same statement is true if either p or q, but not both, is true. The logical "disjunction" or "or," $p \lor q$, is defined to be the inclusive "or." That is, $p \lor q$ is true precisely when at least one of the statements p and q is true. Thus, this operation corresponds to Boolean addition as we have defined it. (*See* Table 4, column 2.)

The "exclusive or," $p \not\equiv q$, is called *inequivalence*, since it defines a proposition that is true precisely when p and q have opposite or inequivalent truth values. This corresponds to any of several more complex Boolean operations such as $pq' + p'q$, and $(p + q)(pq)'$. (*See* Table 4, column 10.)

The remaining conventional logical operator is the *conditional* or *implication*, $p \Rightarrow q$, corresponding to the statement "if p then q." The conditional proposition $p \Rightarrow q$ takes the value "false" if p is true and q is false, and takes the value "true" otherwise. Thus, it corresponds to the boolean operation $p' + q$. Note that if p is false, then $p \Rightarrow q$ is true, regardless of the value of q. This corresponds to the statement that one can prove anything (q, whether true or false) from a false hypothesis (p). (*See* Table 4, column 5.)

While the logical operators that we have defined suffice to define all logical operators, it is only necessary to use two of the above operators, namely negation, and one of the operators conjunction, disjunction, or conditional. However, it is important in computer design that we may define all logical operators in terms of one basic operator, either the "nand" or the "nor" operator. These are the negation of the conjunction and disjunction operators, respectively. That is, the "nand" operator defines a statement, $p \mid q$, which has the value "false" precisely when both p and q are true, and the

Table 4.

p	q	1	2	3	4	5	6	7	8	9	10	11	12	13	14	15	16
T	T	T	T	T	T	T	T	T	T	F	F	F	F	F	F	F	F
T	F	T	T	T	T	F	F	F	F	T	T	T	T	F	F	F	F
F	T	T	T	F	F	T	T	F	F	T	T	F	F	T	T	F	F
F	F	T	F	T	F	T	F	T	F	T	F	T	F	T	F	T	F

Table 5.

$p\ q\ r$	(1) $p\equiv q$	(2) $p\vee\neg r$	(3) $\neg p\vee q$	(4) (2)∧(3)	(5) (4)⇒r	(6) ¬(5)	Expression (1)⇒(6)
T T T	T	T	T	T	T	F	F
T T F	T	T	T	T	F	T	T
T F T	F	T	F	F	T	F	T
T F F	F	T	F	F	T	F	T
F T T	F	F	T	F	T	F	T
F T F	F	T	T	T	F	T	T
F F T	T	F	T	F	T	F	F
F F F	T	T	T	T	F	T	T

value "true" otherwise. The "nor" operator defines a statement, $p\downarrow q$, which has the value "true" precisely when both p and q are false, and the value "false" otherwise. (*See* Table 4, columns 9 and 15.)

Truth Tables

A *truth table* gives the truth values of a logical expression for each combination of the truth values of its variables. Thus, for a logical expression in n variables, the truth table contains 2^n lines, one for each combination of the truth values of its variables. Since the truth value of an expression is determined from the truth values of various subexpressions, the truth table may be given in an extended form, which explicitly lists all subexpressions or a standard form in which the subexpressions are not separately listed. Tables 5 and 6 illustrate these two forms of a truth table for the logical expression

$$(p\equiv q)\Rightarrow\neg(((p\vee\neg r)\wedge(\neg p\vee q))\Rightarrow r).$$

In each of these tables the truth values for the given expression are in the boxed column.

The truth table for an unknown logical function can be used to generate an expression for that function. The expression thus generated is called a *disjunctive normal form* or, in Boolean algebra, a *sum of products form*. The development of this expression is illustrated in Table 7. For each line of the table wherein the unknown function has the value "true," an expression

is formed by taking the conjunction of all variables that are true in that line and the negations of all variables that are false in that line. The expression for the function f is then the disjunction of all expressions formed for the single lines. In Table 7, f is given in this form, and in the corresponding Boolean algebra form, as well as in a shorter form developed by direct inspection of the function values. (Equivalence, $\equiv$, is defined by column 7 of Table 4.)

The development of the disjunctive normal form shows that the logical operators conjunction, disjunction, and negation are sufficient to develop an expression for any logical function. Furthermore, we may use DeMorgan's laws (Table 1) to transform conjunctions to disjunctions, or vice versa. Thus, as we previously asserted, any logical function can be developed from the operators negation and either conjunction or disjunction. Table 8 shows the development of the five common logical operators in terms of these two minimal combinations of operators. In turn, Table 9 shows the development of negation, conjunction, and disjunction in terms of both the "nand" and the "nor" operators, thus indicating that every logical operator can be defined in terms of either one of these latter two operators.

Table 6.

$p\ q\ r$	$(p\equiv q)$	⇒	¬	\(((p∨¬r)∧(¬p∨q))⇒r\)
T T T	T	F	F	T T T T T
T T F	T	T	T	T T T T F
T F T	F	T	F	T F F T T
T F F	F	T	F	T F F T T
F T T	F	T	F	F F T T T
F T F	F	T	T	T T T T F
F F T	T	F	F	F F T T T
F F F	T	T	T	T T T T F

Table 7.

$p\ q\ r$	$f(p,q,r)$	Generated expression
T T T	F	–
T T F	T	$p\wedge q\wedge\neg r$
T F T	T	$p\wedge\neg q\wedge r$
T F F	F	–
F T T	T	$\neg p\wedge q\wedge r$
F T F	F	–
F F T	F	–
F F F	T	$\neg p\wedge\neg q\wedge\neg r$

$$f(p,q,r)=(p\wedge q\wedge\neg r)\vee(p\wedge\neg q\wedge r)$$
$$\vee(\neg p\wedge q\wedge r)(\neg p\wedge\neg q\wedge\neg r)$$
$$f(p,q,r)=pqr'+pq'r+p'qr+p'q'r'$$
$$f(p,q,r)=p\equiv(q\not\equiv r)$$

Table 8.

	$\wedge, \neg$	$\vee, \neg$
$\neg p$	$\neg p$	$\neg p$
$p \wedge q$	$p \wedge q$	$\neg(\neg p \vee \neg q)$
$p \vee q$	$\neg(\neg p \wedge \neg q)$	$p \vee q$
$p \Rightarrow q$	$\neg(p \wedge \neg q)$	$\neg p \vee q$
$p \equiv q$	$\neg(\neg(p \wedge q) \wedge \neg(\neg p \wedge \neg q))$	$\neg(p \vee q) \vee \neg(\neg p \vee \neg q)$

Table 9.

	$\mid$	$\downarrow$
$\neg p$	$p \mid p$	$p \downarrow p$
$p \wedge q$	$(p \mid q) \mid (p \mid q)$	$(p \downarrow p) \downarrow (q \downarrow q)$
$p \vee q$	$(p \mid p) \mid (q \mid q)$	$(p \downarrow q) \downarrow (p \downarrow q)$

Duality

There is a symmetry in the operations of addition and multiplication with a Boolean algebra, which is captured in the Principle of Duality.

> If a given proposition holds in a Boolean algebra, then so does the formula obtained by interchanging addition and multiplication, and the elements 0 and 1 throughout the given formula.

The properties of commutativity and associativity, together with those shown in Table 1, are all examples of the Principle of Duality. The value of this principle lies in the fact that if one formula can be established, the second follows immediately. A separate proof of the second formula is not necessary, although in fact the steps in such a proof would be the duals of the steps in the proof of the first formula. Here are other dual pairs of statements:

$$a + 1 = 1 \qquad a0 = 0$$
$$0' = 1 \qquad 1' = 0$$
$$a + a' = 1 \qquad aa' = 0$$
$$a + (a'b) = a + b \qquad a(a' + b) = ab$$

Computer Arithmetic

The identification of the logical constants T and F with the Boolean constants 1 and 0, respectively, leads to the development of the arithmetic properties of the computer in terms of its logical or Boolean operators. In binary arithmetic, the multiplication of bits is exactly the same as Boolean multiplication: the product of two bits is 1 if and only if both bits are 1. However, the addition of two bits is quite different from Boolean addition. This is apparent, since in Boolean arithmetic $1 + 1 = 1$, while in binary arithmetic $1 + 1 = 10$.

We also observe that in binary arithmetic the sum bit is 1 if and only if one, but not both, summands have the value 1, while the carry bit is 1 if and only if both summands have the value 1. Thus, we can compute the sum bit by using the logical inequivalence (exclusive or) operation, and the carry bit by using the logical conjunction or Boolean multiplication operation. Finally, we observe that, since the negative of an integer may be represented in the computer by a complementary bit pattern (1s complement), arithmetic negation can be accomplished by logical negation, or Boolean complementation, with a slight modification if 2s complement arithmetic is used (*see* COMPLEMENT).

Logical Design

Logical (or logic) design of a computer is the development of computer circuitry to perform the desired functions for a particular machine. It is necessary that the circuitry be accurate and reliable, and desirable that it be relatively simple so that it is inexpensive and easy to maintain. While logical design must include consideration of timing problems and the various electromechanical attachments to the computer, the heart of the problem resides in the development of logical circuitry to perform the desired functions.

Of the various devices designed to systematize study of this logic, the *Venn diagram* and *Karnaugh map* are particularly simple and highly effective for functions of 2, 3, 4, or 5 variables. However, the use of these devices becomes increasingly difficult as the number of variables increases beyond five. The classical Venn diagram consists of a rectangle, representing the universe, containing a circle or other simple closed curve for each variable represented. The interpretation is that within the circle the given variable has the value 1, while outside it has the value 0. These circles are arranged in such a way as to include all possible combinations of 1s and 0s for the variables. The Venn diagram for a three-variable problem is given in Fig. 1, with the various regions labeled in Fig. 1a and certain regions shaded to represent the Boolean function $pq + pr + p'r$ in Fig. 1b. In this form the Venn diagram is relatively ineffective for logical analysis. The varying shapes of the regions cause some difficulty in visualizing possible combinations of these regions, particularly if four or more variables are involved.

The Karnaugh map is a practical modification of the Venn diagram, with each region of the diagram represented by a square within a larger rectangle. The Karnaugh maps for two-, three-, and four-variable problems are given in Fig. 2. The region represented by each square is determined by the product of the letters on the edges of the rectangle. For example, the square marked A in the four-variable rectangle

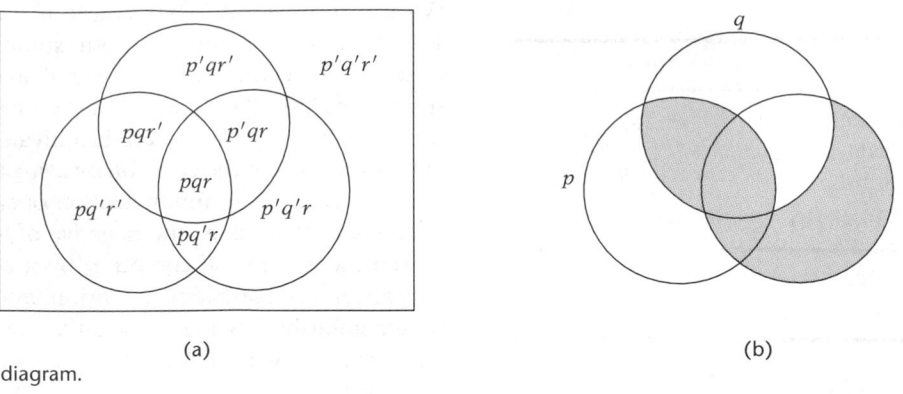

(a)   (b)

Figure 1. Venn diagram.

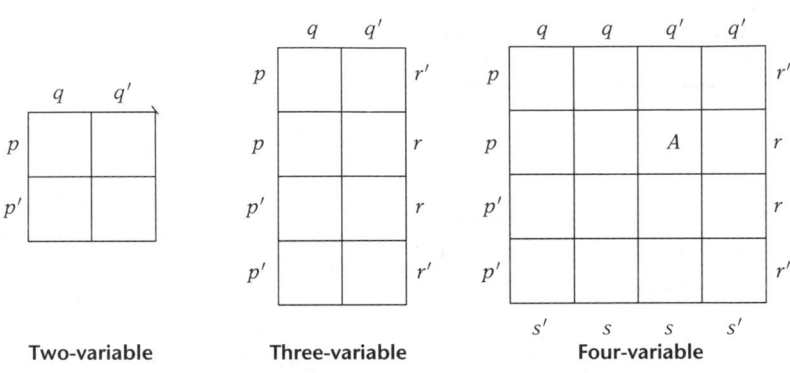

Two-variable   Three-variable   Four-variable

Figure 2. Karnaugh maps.

represents the region $pq'rs$. To represent a Boolean function, say $pq + pr + q'r$, on a Karnaugh map, first expand each term of the function to include all variables present:

$$pq + pr + q'r$$
$$= pq \cdot 1 + p \cdot 1 \cdot r + 1 \cdot q'r$$
$$= pq(r + r') + p(q + q')r + (p + p')q'r$$
$$= pqr + pqr' + pqr + pq'r + pq'r + p'q'r$$
$$= pqr + pqr' + pq'r + p'q'r.$$

Then mark each square corresponding to a term in the expanded expression.

Thus, the Boolean function $pq + pr + q'r$ is represented by the squares marked "1" in Fig. 3, while 0s fill those squares not included in the representation. Note that $pq + q'r$ is also represented by the same four marked squares, and hence is equivalent to the given function. It is also possible to label a square d, denoting "don't care," if the value of that square is irrelevant to the particular function being represented.

Minimization of Boolean Functions

In the interest of economy, it is often desirable to use the simplest possible expression for a Boolean function in the design of computer circuitry. For example, since the expression $pq + pr + q'r$ is equivalent to the

expression $pq + q'r$ in the sense that these expressions have the same value for any argument values, the former expression may be replaced by the latter whenever it occurs in a given circuit design. The determination of the simplest expression equivalent to a given one is known as *minimization*. Minimization is understood to be with respect to a given function form, such as the sum of products form, since a change in permissible operators often lets one find an expression that is simpler yet. Karnaugh maps and a variety of algebraic or geometrical algorithms have been used to accomplish Boolean function minimization.

When computers were constructed from discrete individual logic components, minimization of the number of components or *gates* was a significant task.

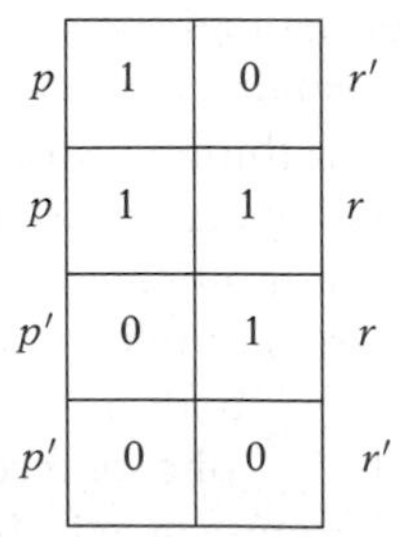

	q	q'	
p	1	0	r'
p	1	1	r
p'	0	1	r
p'	0	0	r'

Figure 3. Karnaugh map for $pq + pr + q'r$.

However, with the development of integrated circuit technology and the shift to Very Large Scale Integration (VLSI), the importance of the individual logic gates in the overall cost of the computer has much diminished. In VLSI technology, each computer chip may contain hundreds or thousands of logic gates. Hence the focus of minimization effort has shifted away from individual gates toward the problem of finding the best combination of logic gates to fit on a chip to perform a given set of functions. That is, the question is not "What is the minimal number of gates to perform this function?" but "What is the minimum number of gates to perform the given set of functions when some may share subsystems of gates?" The concepts of minimization are still relevant, but the designer may be willing to trade a less efficient computation of one function for a more efficient computation of the entire set of functions.

Bibliography

1984. Korfhage, R. R. *Discrete Computational Structures*, 2nd Ed. New York: Academic Press.
1995. Whitesitt, J. E. *Boolean Algebra and Its Applications*. New York: Dover.
1998. Maurer, S. B., and Ralston, A. *Discrete Algorithmic Mathematics* (second corrected edition). Wellesey, MA: A. K. Peters.

Robert R. Korfhage

BOOTSTRAP

For articles on related subjects *see* BIOS; and LOGIN FILE.

To *bootstrap*– more commonly, just *boot*—is to accomplish a task by means of a procedure that gives its user a "free" head start. The term was first used in a computing context to describe the process whereby a loader program, whose job it is to get other pieces of software into a machine, is itself loaded. This task, which at first glance seems to threaten infinite regression, was made possible by a very simple loader wired into the hardware; this was just adequate to load the loader program, which then loaded everything else.

From this beginning, *bootstrapping* has become a generic term for the use of any procedure that requires its user to do only some relatively trivial part of what would seem a major task, with the procedure itself then doing the rest. Such a procedure lets you achieve a result with so much less effort than you would normally expect that it seems unnatural, like lifting oneself by one's own bootstraps.

Bootstrapping is applied equally to software and hardware processes; it is used, for example, to describe the programming of a complete translator for some language L by means of an already-implemented translator for a small subset of L that is adequate—not necessarily good—for writing a translator. Such a subset can be used for the programming of a complete language-L translator, with the resulting translator run through the subset-translator to yield a running translator of the whole language, bootstrapped into existence by means of the already running fragment.

On the hardware side, the term is commonly used now to denote bringing a computer to an operational state—that is, a state in which it accepts user commands—from either an unpowered state, or a powered but unresponsive state. Booting a PC, for example, from an unpowered state—a *cold boot*—is initiated simply by switching the PC on—a one-touch operation that initiates a great deal of hardware testing and loading of software. Booting from a powered state— a *warm boot*—is usually initiated by pressing one or more keys (on a PC, for example, the key combination Ctrl-Alt-Del); it is normally done only to recover from a condition in which user commands are not being responded to. In some extreme conditions—e.g. a "frozen" keyboard—the only recourse the user has is to initiate a cold boot by switching the machine off, then on again.

The boot process, however initiated, then proceeds to load system files, configure the machine according to settings made by the manufacturer and the user, and finally display an interface through which the user can assume control. From the user's standpoint, all these rather complex actions follow from the simple act of switching the machine on, or of pressing a combination of a few keys. At that point, a small program, typically resident in read-only memory (*q.v.*), executes in order to initialize all the services of the much larger operating system (*q.v.*), and it may seem to the user that what has been accomplished is akin to lifting oneself by one's own bootstraps.

Mark Halpern

BRITISH COMPUTER SOCIETY (BCS)

For articles on related subjects *see* ASSOCIATION FOR COMPUTING MACHINERY; COMPUTER SOCIETIES; INSTITUTE OF ELECTRICAL AND ELECTRONIC ENGINEERS—COMPUTER SOCIETY; and INTERNATIONAL FEDERATION FOR INFORMATION PROCESSING.

The *BCS*, formed in 1957, has 35,000 members and is the chartered body in the UK for all information technology professionals. Society membership is limited to those who have satisfactorily passed a two-part examination. A 1984 Royal Charter gives the BCS unique and exclusive responsibilities and authority. It takes responsibilities for education and training, for public awareness, and for standards, quality, and professionalism, and issues and enforces both a code of conduct and a code of practice. It advises Parliament and the government and their agencies as well as the Banking and Building Society Ombudsmen. It examines and pronounces on topical issues concerning computers.

Table 1. BCS specialist groups.

Advanced Programming
British APL
Business Information Systems
CASE (Computer-Aided Systems Engineering)
Client Server
Computer Audit
Computer Conservation Society
Computer Graphics and Displays
Computer Systems Technology
Configuration Management
Cybernetic Machine
Data Management
Developing Countries
Disability Group
Distributed Systems
Document Imaging
Electronic & Multimedia Publishing
Expert Systems
Financial Services
Formal Aspects of Computer Science
Fortran
Healthcare Information
Human Computer Interaction
Independent Computer Contractors
Information Retrieval
Information Security
Information Systems Methodologies
Internet
Law
Manufacturing Automation and Control
Mathematical Programming
Medical London
Medical Northern
Medical Scotland
Methods and Tools
Modular Languages
Natural Language Translation
Networks
Nursing
OOPS
Parallel Processing
Pattern Analysis & Robotics
Payroll
Performance Engineering
Poplog and Pop Languages
Primary Health Care
Project Management
National Quality Specialist Interest Group
RAF
Requirements Systems Engineering
Safety Critical Systems Club
Software Process Improvement Network (SPIN)
Software Protection
Software Reuse
Software Testing

It inspects university and polytechnic courses in computer science and information technology (*q.v.*) and conducts its own examinations. It is the UK member of the International Federation for Information Processing. It organizes an ambitious Professional Development Scheme for young professionals and established practitioners. It is represented on the advisory committees of national examining and educational bodies.

The BCS publishes seven journals. *The Computer Bulletin* is a general interest publication which goes to all members. The others are *The Computer Journal* (which covers computer science broadly), and five more specialized journals: *Software Proceedings, Formal Aspects of Computing, Interacting with Computers, Journal of Digital Information,* and *Distributed System Engineering Journal.* In tandem with its hard copy publications, the BCS increasingly publishes electronically. The Society and its special interest groups publish several series of books and monographs.

The 55 BCS specialist groups (see Table 1) and 41 local branches conduct conferences and meetings both large and small, a dozen or two each month, that insure that the influence of BCS is felt throughout Britain and elsewhere through its overseas sections (in Hong Kong, Malta, Sri Lanka, The Netherlands, and Switzerland) and international conferences.

Its address is 1 Sanford Street, Swindon SN1 1HJ, United Kingdom: bcshq@bcs.org.uk; `http://www.bcs.org.uk`.

The presidents of BCS since its inception are listed in Appendix V.

Eric A. Weiss

BROWSER

See WORLD WIDE WEB.

BUFFER

For articles on related subjects *see* CACHE MEMORY; and INPUT–OUTPUT CONTROL SYSTEM (IOCS).

A *buffer* is an area of storage that temporarily holds data that will be subsequently delivered to a processor or input–output (I/O) peripheral. Buffers exist as an integral part of many peripherals, e.g. bits arriving serially over a telephone line are collected in a buffer before the character is presented from a modem (*q.v.*) to a processor. Similarly, the bits representing a given character remain in a modem buffer while being serialized for transmission. Since the buffer is an integral part of the peripheral, it is usually dedicated to the peripheral and not shared with any other device.

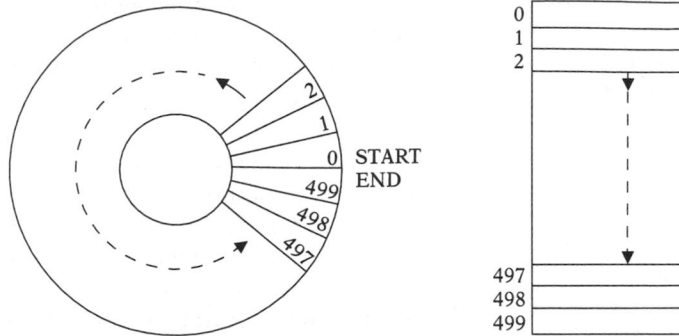

Figure 1. Circular buffer organization shown logically (left) and as it actually appears in memory (right).

A technique called *double buffering* permits one set of data to be used while another is collected. It is used with graphics displays, where one frame buffer holds the current screen image while another acquires the bits that will make up the next image. When it is ready, the buffers are switched, the new screen is displayed, and the process continues. This technique is also used in the standard RS-232 interface between modem and computer, where one buffer holds the current character while the other acquires the bits for the next one.

Buffers are also used in conjunction with a computer's input–output control system (IOCS) to hold the data that is the object of various I/O commands. In this case, the buffer is usually a portion of main storage and is often dynamically allocated and freed by software. In either case, a buffer exists in order to accommodate the different rates at which data is produced or consumed by the processor or peripherals involved.

In a typical situation, a processor will be capable of producing data several orders of magnitude faster than a peripheral (e.g. a printer) can accept it. In order to make most efficient use of the processor, the data will be placed in a buffer and its location made known to the peripheral. The peripheral then proceeds to empty the buffer while the processor is freed for other work.

Various buffering techniques have evolved for use with an IOCS. These techniques can be analyzed according to the policy used for (1) receiving data from the producer and (2) delivering data to the consumer.

When receiving data, two techniques are common: (1) a pool of buffers and (2) circular buffering. With the buffer-pooling technique, a number of buffers are available to the IOCS. Usually, each buffer is large enough to hold the single physical record that is being transferred. When a record is produced, a buffer is taken from the pool and used to hold the data. Data is then consumed on a first in, first out basis (FIFO), and when all data has been transferred, the buffer is returned to the pool.

Circular buffering, in contrast, typically uses a single buffer, usually one that is larger than a single physical record and which is managed as a queue. The basic strategy is to give the appearance that the buffer is organized in a circle, with data "wrapping around" as shown in Fig. 1. This appearance of circular organization is accomplished by using two pointers, IN and OUT, associated with the buffer; the starting and ending addresses of the buffer (START and END) are also known. Initially, START = IN = OUT. Data received from the producer fills the buffer, starting from START and incrementing the pointer IN. The consumer takes data from the buffer, incrementing the pointer OUT (and taking care not to go past IN −1). When the last word of the buffer had been filled (IN = END), then IN is reset to START and subsequent data will wrap around to the start of the buffer.

Similarly, when OUT reaches END, it is reset to START and also wraps around. Clearly, the following restrictions hold:

1. If IN > OUT, then OUT must not become greater than IN −1.

2. If OUT > IN, then IN must not become greater than OUT −1.

If either of these two conditions is violated, then either the consumer is trying to access data that has not been produced, *or* the producer is attempting to overwrite data that has not yet been consumed.

As random access memory (RAM) has become less expensive, designers have increased average buffer size. This usually helps I/O response and throughput (*q.v.*) by exploiting local referencing patterns and achieving a cache effect in the I/O system. Mainframe systems of the 1990s used very large "extended" RAM memories to optimize this effect to the greatest extent possible.

Robert W. Taylor

BUG

For articles on related subjects *see* DEBUGGING; ERRORS; PROGRAM VERIFICATION; and SOFTWARE TESTING.

A *bug* is an error in either the syntax or the logic of a computer program or circuit. Because the story has been retold so often by well-meaning people, many believe that the term originated when a moth was removed ("debugged") from an errant Mark I (*q.v.*) relay circuit in the early 1940s. Though this may very well have happened, the term bug was used in exactly its current context by Thomas Edison in an 1878 letter to Theodore Puskas.

Most syntactical bugs can be detected during the translation from the symbolic languages that programmers use into the (binary) language that is eventually executed. For example, the assignment operator in the Ada (*q.v.*) programming language is `:=`, and if a programmer writes x=x+1 in an assignment statement, the Ada compiler will detect the syntax error and print a diagnostic message, since this operation is illegal.

It is a more serious error if the programmer writes the legal Ada code x:=x-1 when x:=x+1 was intended. This is a bug in program logic, and no compiler will catch it. In the C programming language, which uses == for equality comparison and = for assignment, a statement beginning if (x=1)..., a common slip when (x==1) is intended, is actually a logic error, since (x=1) is a legal expression here. It gives x the value 1 and also returns 1, meaning "true" in C, so the error creates a constantly true value in the if statement, almost certainly not what the programmer intended.

Properly speaking, the elimination of the first type of bug is the process of debugging, whereas the detection and elimination of the second type is the process of software testing. Program bugs can be so extremely subtle that they may resist great efforts to eliminate them. It is commonly accepted that all very large computer programs (such as compilers) have bugs remaining in them. The number of possible paths through a large computer program is enormous, and it is physically impossible to explore all of them. The single path containing a bug may not be followed in actual production runs for a long time (if ever) after the program has been certified as correct by its author or others.

Fred Gruenberger

BULLETIN BOARD

For articles on related subjects *see* DATA COMMUNICATIONS; ELECTRONIC MAIL; GROUPWARE; NETWORKS, COMPUTER; ONLINE CONVERSATION; VIDEOTEX; and WORLD WIDE WEB.

An electronic *bulletin board* is a medium for posting and discussing announcements and messages of interest to a community of online users. Implementation and maintenance of a bulletin board requires three types of equipment: a personal computer or other means of generating text, sounds, and/or graphic material to be posted for viewing and/or hearing; a modem or similar device connected to a phone, cable, or wireless "cell" line, which allows transmission of computer-generated data to and from the bulletin board; and a central computer on which this data can be stored, organized, and made available for transmission to readers. Participants must also have word processing (*q.v.*) and telecommunications software (e.g. a Web browser) for their personal computers.

The first bulletin boards began in the 1960s, with the US Defense Department's ARPA network of interconnected mainframe (*q.v.*) computers. This system required participants to have direct links to a mainframe, usually from a military installation or other official office.

The spread of low-cost personal computers and efficient modems (*q.v.*) in the 1980s engendered the development of numerous bulletin boards or "online systems" that were fully accessible to the public. By the end of the 1990s, more than 100 million people accessed thousands of bulletin boards around the USA and the world at all times of day from their homes and places of business.

Bulletin boards now differ greatly in quality of data available, cost to the user, and services rendered to the user. The most common kinds of bulletin board are found on the Internet and the World Wide Web, and support discussions on a variety of topics, ranging from politics to the latest computer software and hardware (*see* Fig. 1). Some of these bulletin boards specialize in specific areas, such as news, science fiction, computer games, stock quotations, or sports. Friendships, business undertakings, and romantic involvements are some of the many human relationships that regularly develop on bulletin board systems. Although many bulletin boards have facilities for "real-time" communication or "chats" (*see* ONLINE CONVERSATION) most communication takes place through asynchronous exchange of messages. These messages often contain sophisticated images and sound—RealVideo and Real-Audio—but the common denominator of most bulletin board systems is text, usually in a hypertext language (such as HTML—*see* MARKUP LANGUAGES) that allows links to other texts anywhere on the Web.

Bulletin boards are closely related to electronic mail (email) systems, but in the latter, a correspondent typically addresses a message to a particular named recipient or selected group of recipients. The users of a

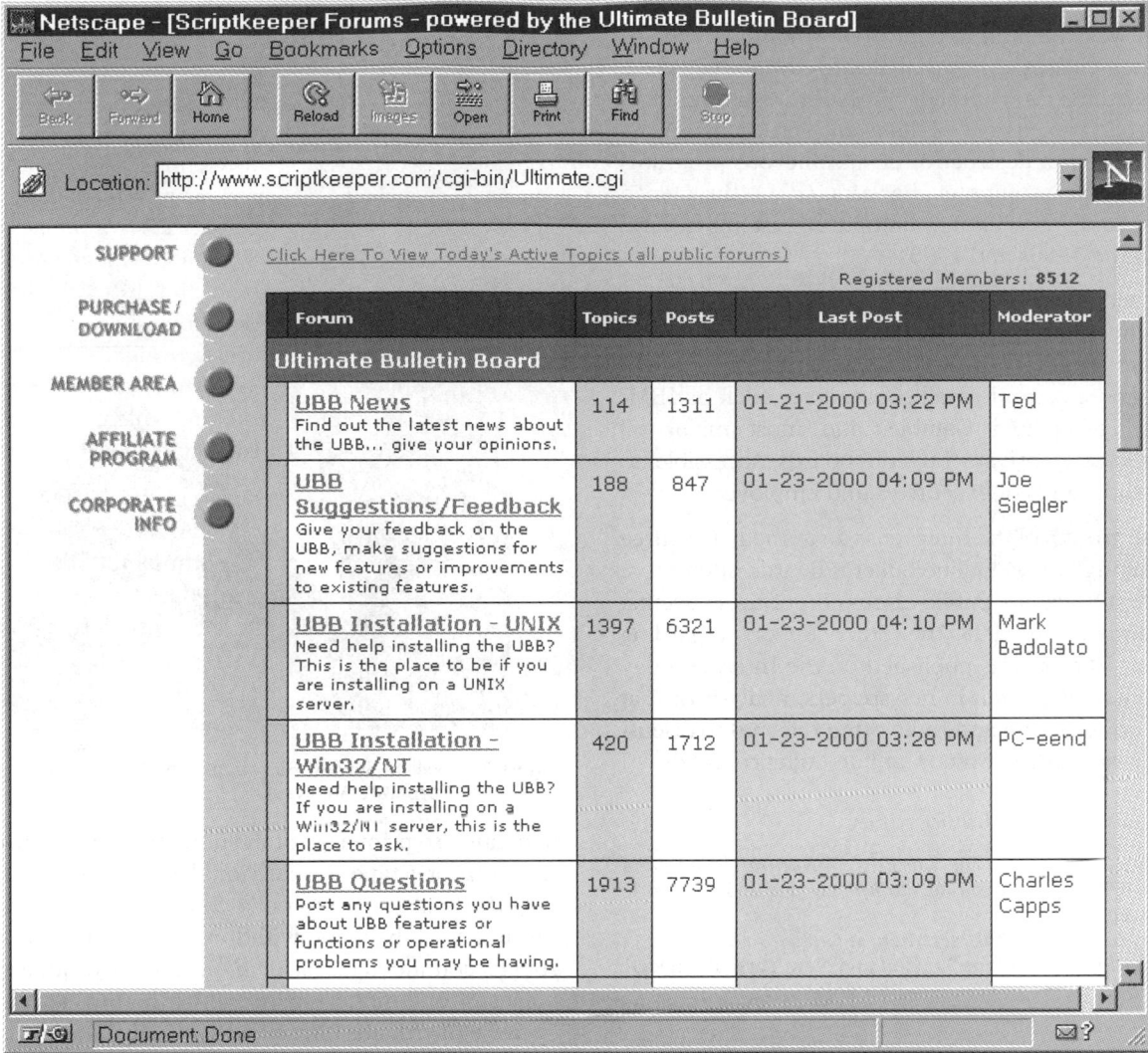

Figure 1. A frame of a commercial bulletin board service (courtesy of Infopop Corporation).

bulletin board service post messages for all users to see, and browse through selected categories of messages posted by others.

Commercial online systems charge their customers monthly rates for unlimited access to their in-depth databases, hundreds of topics for discussion, and the Web at large. In 1999 America Online had nearly 20 million users, and along with its subsidiary, Compu-Serve, offers such services as electronic banking via computer, online encyclopedias, and numerous databases, such as Books-in-Print, medical and legal information, ability to reserve airline flights, and numerous discussions of professional and personal interest. Other well-known US online systems are Prodigy and Genie. Unlike local Web providers that usually serve a city or small limited geographical area, large commercial online systems are accessible via a local phone call from most places in their home country and some parts of the world.

One of the most successful services of bulletin boards is online education. Since 1985, Connected Education has been offering courses for master's level credit granted by major US universities. Students from 45 states in the USA and 20 nations around the world have attended classes entirely via personal computer and modem, without ever leaving their homes or places of business. Courses take place on a special bulletin board called an "electronic campus," where faculty and students enter and read lecture and discussion messages, pursue research, access papers in an online library, and engage in social conversation at times of their own choosing. Such education, like all online services, is especially valuable to people who for reasons of physical disability, geographic isolation, or pressure of business are unable to attend conventional classrooms.

The use of bulletin boards for such serious activities has raised issues of intellectual property and authors' rights not fully addressed by current copyright laws.

The ease and speed of dissemination of electronic text makes it very difficult to control by traditional means. Computer viruses (*q.v.*) that destroy or impair computer systems are another problem resulting from uncontrolled exchange of data and programs. Mass dissemination of destructive or mischievous programs introduced by computer hackers (*q.v.*) threatened national and international computer systems several times in the 1980s and 1990s.

Corporations and business operations, especially those with activities dispersed internationally or around a particular country, make extensive use of bulletin boards and electronic mail. Companies such as IBM, AT&T, Procter and Gamble, and most major oil companies use private bulletin boards accessible to tens of thousands of executives and employees.

With the growth of the Internet as an immediate source of "breaking" news, online bulletin boards often serve as the first place for public discussion of these events. For example, in 1998 the Starr Report regarding President Clinton was published on the Internet a day prior to its publication in newspapers; analysis of that Report on television and radio often referred to discussions already under way on online bulletin boards.

Bibliography

1997/1998. Levinson, P. *The Soft Edge: A Natural History and Future of the Information Revolution.* London and New York: Routledge.
1999. Levinson, P. *Digital McLuhan: A Guide to the Information Millennium.* London and New York: Routledge.

Paul Levinson

BURROUGHS, WILLIAM S.

For an article on a related subject *see* CALCULATING MACHINES.

Williams Seward Burroughs (Fig. 1) was born on 28 January 1855 in Auburn, New York, and died on 5 September 1898 in Citronelle, Alabama. He is immortalized in the name of the Burroughs firm, but, unlike some of the other early manufacturers of mechanical calculators, his firm did not adopt that name until after Burroughs himself had died. It was through his early experience as a junior bank clerk that he developed an appreciation for the types of calculations that were required in a business environment. In 1881 he moved to St Louis and worked in his father's shop, making models for castings, which gave him the background knowledge required for his mechanical inventions.

Inspired by other mechanical calculators, particularly the key-driven comptometers invented by Dorr E. Felt, Burroughs set about inventing one that would not only

Figure 1. William Seward Burroughs (courtesy UNISYS Corporate Archives).

add, but also print a list of the numbers entered and the final total on a tape. An early model, capable of printing only the final total, was not a commercial success, and his financial backers withdrew their support. Burroughs continued on his own, eventually producing 50 copies of one model—all of which had to be recalled because Burroughs himself was the only one who could make them operate in a consistently reliable way.

In 1886 the American Arithmometer Company was formed by Burroughs and three associates. The company manufactured and marketed an improved calculating machine that could list both the individual entries and the totals. The earlier mechanical problems had been overcome by the introduction of a shock absorbing dashpot that cushioned the action of the activating lever on the mechanism. Upon payment of $475.00, the first customers received their machines in December 1892. By 18 January 1908, the firm, by then known as the Burroughs Adding Machine Company, could boast that it had supplied a total of 63,574 machines of 58 different types.

Bibliography

1914. Horsburgh, E. M. *Handbook of the Napier Tercentenary Celebration of Modern Instruments and Methods of Calculation.* Edinburgh: The Royal Society of Edinburgh (reprinted by MIT Press and Tomash Publishers, 1982).
1921. Turck, J. A. V. *Origin of Modern Calculating Machines.* Chicago: The Western Society of Engineers.

Michael R. Williams

BUS

For articles on related subjects *see* CHANNEL; IBM PC; OPEN ARCHITECTURE; PERSONAL COMPUTING; and SYNCHRONOUS/ASYNCHRONOUS OPERATION.

Introduction

A *bus*, sometimes also called a *trunk*, is an electronic highway in a digital computer that provides a communication path for data to flow between the central processing unit (CPU—*q.v.*) and its memory and between and among the CPU and the various peripheral devices connected to the computer. A bus contains one wire for each bit needed to specify the address of a device or location in memory, plus additional wires that distinguish among the various data transfer operations to be performed. A bus can transmit data in either direction between any two components of the computing system. Without a bus, a computer would need separate wires for all possible connections between components—clearly an intolerable situation.

Mainframe and Minicomputer Buses

There are a number of proprietary bus systems used on mainframes (*q.v.*) and minicomputers (*q.v.*). Examples are the Digital Equipment Corporation (*q.v.*) *Unibus* and the Intel *Multibus*. The Unibus, used on the PDP-11 and VAX series computers, has 56 bidirectional lines and a transfer rate of almost 3 MB/sec. Another widely used bus is the General-Purpose Interface Bus (GPIB) defined by the standard ANSI/IEEE 488-1978.

Bus-Tech, Inc. and Harbor Systems Management, Ltd market a bus that provides data movement between S/390 mainframes and large enterprise servers such as IBM RS/6000, HP/UX, Sun Solaris, and Windows NT at transfer rates in excess of 10 MB/sec. The bus provides mainframe-based backup/restore for NT Exchange servers, as well as database agent technology for Oracle, SAP R/3, and SQL-BackTrack servers, which provide support for Informix, Sybase, and SQL-Server.

Polaris Communications markets a Model 6100 PCI Bus/Tag Channel Interface that may be used to attach a PC to an IBM or plug-compatible mainframe channel and is capable of transferring and receiving data at the rate of up to 4.5 MB/sec. The microprocessor and memory on board the Model 6100 provide the processing environment for handling the IBM Bus/Tag channel protocol. The bus is programmable and can emulate any IBM control unit, allowing mainframe applications and utilities to run without modification.

The diversity of buses intrinsic to large computers does not seem to have played a pivotal role in industry competitiveness, but since the very opposite is true for microcomputers, the remainder of this article is devoted to the evolution of the microcomputer bus.

Microcomputer Buses

On a microcomputer, the bus is usually called an *expansion bus* because its design determines the degree to which the minimum configuration of the system can be expanded with regard to memory, processing speed, graphics capability, and peripheral support. The expansion bus is the collection of wires, paths, connectors, and controllers responsible for distributing the data and instructions from the microprocessor to the peripheral expansion cards. *Slots* connected to the bus provide places to plug those cards in, and the bus then provides a mechanism for communicating with them.

When microcomputers were first introduced during the 1970s, there were no standard mechanisms for expanding a computer's capabilities. Every manufacturer had a different scheme, and some manufacturers had not even standardized across different models in a single product line.

S-100 BUS

When Altair introduced its 8080 computer, it came with an expansion bus with a published specification that used common parts and connectors. This *open architecture* soon became a standard. One hundred pins were provided for various signals on what became known as the S-100 bus. This meant that new video cards, more memory, and serial and parallel ports could be added to the computer as needed. They could even be purchased from someone other than Altair. The add-on board business was born, and more than 100 companies manufactured S-100 products. The S-100 bus was even capable of 16-bit addressing, but it had some shortcomings. It was subject to interference and crosstalk between nearby wires, it did not perform reliably with high-frequency signals, and there were ambiguities in the standard that led some manufacturers to define specific pins in multiple ways.

ISA BUS

Just as groups of interested parties were meeting in 1981 to improve the S-100 bus, IBM announced its new personal computer, the IBM PC (*q.v.*). The machine was a success, due in no small part to its open architecture and the flexibility of its expansion bus, whose design details were placed in the public domain. The new IBM bus came to be known as the Industry Standard Architecture (ISA) bus. In some ways it was inferior to the S-100 bus. It used a strictly

8-bit architecture with parity protection and had only 62 pins consisting of 3 grounds, 5 voltage supply lines, 20 address lines, 8 data lines, 10 lines devoted to interrupts, and a variety of special-purpose signal lines. The ISA bus was processor-specific and its edge-triggered interrupts meant that each expansion card could have only one interrupt (q.v.). An entire industry flourished in the shadow of IBM, making products that could be placed in the expansion slots of IBM PCs and a plethora of compatible machines. The ISA bus has survived to this day, but in a radically modified form.

ISA AT Bus

By 1984, microcomputing was a multibillion dollar industry. Users were demanding more power and performance than an 8-bit bus could deliver. IBM announced its Advanced Technology (AT) machine, built around the 16-bit Intel 80286 chip, which could be run as fast as 12 MHz. An additional connector was added next to the 8-bit ISA connector, which allowed additional address and control signals while maintaining downward compatibility with ISA expansion boards. A *wait state* (q.v.) generator was added to allow the microprocessor to keep up with bus components that might be too slow. AT address lines were unlatched, allowing 16-bit cards to determine, as early in the bus cycle as possible, whether signals were intended for them. Information could be transferred at up to 2 MB/sec on this bus, but its rating of 8 MHz ultimately proved to be too slow. Processor speeds for the 80286 began to outrun the bus.

Micro-Channel Architecture (MCA)

At the peak of popularity of the IBM AT-compatible computers, most were not actually made by IBM. A serious erosion of market share as well as a desire to enhance bus performance soon led IBM down a different path. In April 1987, IBM announced a new computer line, the Personal System/2 (PS/2), designed to recapture market share lost to the clone makers. It featured a new expansion bus based on a concept called *Micro-Channel Architecture* (MCA), which IBM intended to license, not give away. The MCA increased data throughput to 20 MB/sec, more than 10 times the speed of the AT ISA bus. The PS/2 was still an *open architecture* (q.v.) machine in some sense, but emulation would no longer be cost-free to the clone makers.

MCA expansion cards were smaller than those used with the ISA bus and were designed to take advantage of assembly advances using surface-mount components. It was a full 32-bit bus. Every fourth pin was a ground, markedly reducing interference and allowing much faster cycle times. Expansion cards could now communicate directly with the Video Graphics Array (VGA) card. They could also now be configured by the microprocessor: no switches specific to the hardware had to be set. Interrupts were level-sensitive and remained active during the entire cycle, making it easier to address multiple cards with the same interrupt.

Most significantly, expansion cards could now have their own processors and memory. No longer was the main processor the sole repository of computing power. Cards could now be more powerful and intelligent, freeing the main CPU for additional tasks. The primary disadvantage of the MCA was that it was not downward compatible with the old ISA cards. The MCA standard never caught on.

Extended Industry Standard Architecture (EISA)

Not surprisingly, clone makers were reluctant to give up their market position and were even more reluctant to pay IBM royalties on every card and machine made. They saw a need to expand the ISA bus, but not at their own expense. A group of computer manufacturers formed the "Gang of Nine": Wyse, AST, Tandy, Compaq, Hewlett-Packard, Zenith, Olivetti, NEC, and Epson. They agreed to develop a joint standard, publish it, and stick to it.

Through use of a clever connector scheme, EISA remained compatible with the old ISA boards. EISA was a 32-bit standard, even faster than the MCA, with a maximum transfer rate of 33 MB/sec. The expansion cards were almost twice as large, allowing for more components. The parts could also be stock; surface-mounted components were not required. The power rating of the EISA boards was 45 W. At +5 V, the MCA card can draw only 1.6 A, while an EISA card can draw 4.5 A. Bus mastering and no-switch configuration were also part of the EISA standard. The EISA bus is synchronous and can perform transfers in long rapid-fire bursts. Only the 80386 and 80486 chips can use EISA. With the Pentium (80586) interrupts are no longer edge-triggered and can be shared.

Nu-Bus

Apple Computer (q.v.) also came to recognize the benefits of an open, published, expandable architecture when it introduced its NU-Bus. Until the introduction of this bus in the late 1980s, the Macintosh had been a closed machine. This was widely cited, along with higher cost, as the reason for Apple's inability to match the market share of IBM compatibles. The 32-bit NU-Bus was introduced with the Mac II. It operates on a 10 MHz synchronous clock, providing access to all main logic board resources through six Euro-DIN connectors. This has led to many enhancements for the Mac that might not otherwise have occurred.

LOCAL BUS ARCHITECTURES

As computers became more powerful, it was clear that a wider bus structure was needed. Two competing architectures evolved—VESA and PCI. The Peripheral Component Interface (PCI) is a 32/64-bit local bus architecture developed by DEC, IBM, Intel, and others that is widely used in Pentium-based PCs. The PCI bus provides a high-bandwidth data channel between the system-board components such as the CPU and devices such as hard disks and video adapters. The VL-Bus or VESA Local Bus architecture was developed by the Video Electronics Standards Association—a consortium of computer manufacturers responsible for the SVGA video standard—and is primarily used in older 80486 PCs. The PCI bus is currently the dominant bus structure. It accommodates a 100 MHz data rate and supports Plug and Play, Hot Plug, Bus Power Management, bus mastering, error detection, and CPU independence. The PCI bus can be designed into portable or desktop machines and is backward compatible with 8 and 16-bit ISA expansion cards.

OTHER BUSES

The Small Computer Systems Interface (SCSI—pronounced "scuzzy") was standardized in 1986, and updated in 1994 to SCSI-2. SCSI is a high-speed interface, originally designed for disk drives and now used for devices such as CD-ROMs and scanners as well. It is the standard disk interface on Apple Macintoshes and on Unix workstations, as well as on Intel PCs that are used as servers. The original SCSI, now SCSI-1, had a clock speed of 5 MHz and a data transfer rate of 5 MB/sec. SCSI-2 now runs at 10 MHz and, with a 16-bit rather than 8-bit datapath, has a transfer rate of 20MB/sec. As of 1999, SCSI-3 standards are being developed.

SCSI devices are connected in a serial *daisy chain* to an SCSI controller, which can manage seven devices. In addition to its high transfer-rate, an SCSI controller can send commands to multiple devices concurrently, so that it can initiate a read on one disk in the chain while doing a write to another.

The buses described so far have been designed for high capacity. For low-speed devices like mice, keyboards, and joysticks, the Universal Serial Bus (USB) is a new PC bus designed to make it easy to attach such devices to a computer. With the USB, devices do not need separate bus interface cards with switches that need to be set correctly. Multiple devices can be attached to an external USB socket or *hub*. The USB has a bandwidth of 1.5 MB/sec, which is shared among all devices connected to it.

Bibliography

1997. Schmidt, F. *The SCSI Bus and IDE Interface: Protocols, Applications and Programming.* Reading, MA: Addison-Wesley.
1997. Anderson, D. *USB System Architecture.* Reading, MA: Addison-Wesley.
1999. Rosch, W. L. *Winn L. Rosch Hardware Bible*, 5th Ed. Indianapolis, IN: Que Publications.

Stephen J. Rogowski

BUSH, VANNEVAR

For an article on a related subject *see* DIFFERENTIAL ANALYZER.

Vannevar Bush (Fig. 1), the son of a clergyman, was born in Massachusetts on 11 March 1890. He attended Tufts University in the years before the First World War and earned both B.S. and M.S. degrees. He then continued on for a doctorate, which was conferred upon him in 1916 simultaneously by both Harvard and MIT. While a graduate student, he worked for General Electric and the US Navy, and taught mathematics at Tufts. In 1919 he joined the teaching staff of MIT, obtaining a full professorship in 1923 and becoming Vice President and Dean of the Engineering School in 1932. He remained with MIT until 1938, when he was elected President of the Carnegie Institution in Washington, a position he held until retiring from active public life in 1955.

During his formative years, Bush showed an interest in mechanical construction, and invented or improved

Figure 1. Vannevar Bush (courtesy of the MIT Museum).

upon several instruments. The most famous of these (invented during his college days) was an automatic surveying machine, resembling a child's scooter, that he constructed from two bicycle wheels with an instrument box mounted between them. It could be pushed over a trail and would automatically create a profile of the terrain over which it had traversed.

His inventive insight was immensely useful to him in later life. Coupled with a zest for hard work, it aided him in the creation of several analog computers (*q.v.*), the most noteworthy of which were his network analyzer and differential analyzer.

Bush's first major calculating machine project resulted from his efforts to solve some very difficult differential equations describing the behavior of a power line network. After several months of effort attempting to find an analytical solution to the equations, he came to the conclusion that it would be more economical to spend his time in the design and construction of special analog machines to solve the problem by simulating the system.

The machines for which he is most famous are his mechanical differential analyzer and the more sophisticated electrical version, known as the second Rockefeller Differential Analyzer, or RDA2. These machines used mechanical integrators to perform the key step in the solution of differential equations, the results being registered as a rotation of an output shaft. The element that then allowed these to be combined into a total solution was a "torque amplifier" which enabled the values to be added and subtracted by feeding them into various gear combinations. The RDA2 replaced these rotating shafts and gears by electrically driven systems, but retained the mechanical analog integrators. Several different examples of the mechanical differential analyzer were constructed just prior to the Second World War, and these became the central instruments in such work as the calculation of ballistic trajectories for artillery firing tables.

Another one of his projects resulted from his realization that it is not sufficient to have some information, you must also be able to access it in a timely way. Together with John H. Howard of MIT, he developed a device known as the Rapid Selector, which was designed to facilitate information retrieval (*q.v.*). A special binary code was created to label specific items of information. This code, when recorded on the edge of a microfilm, could be scanned quickly by photoelectric scanners and the required items retrieved much faster than if one had to read the entire film.

The work with information retrieval technology led Bush to imagine a machine that he called "memex"—essentially an extension of the personal memory and knowledge base of any one individual. It was an attempt to describe a device that would emulate a mind in its associative linking of items of information and their retrieval (*see* HYPERTEXT). Although the memex could never have been constructed during Bush's lifetime, it formed a background to all his thinking and constantly recurred in his thoughts and some of his later publications. Although the memex has been called the first personal workstation (*q.v.*), it is still not available in its full generality.

In terms of computing, Bush is best known for his analog devices, but he had a much more lasting impact in his work behind the scenes. He was the *éminence grise* of American science during and in the decade following the Second World War. In 1940, President Roosevelt appointed him to be chairman of the National Defense Research Committee, a group set up to coordinate and expand military research projects. This position led to his being named first Director of the Office of Scientific Research and Development when it was founded in 1941. In this capacity he was essentially in charge of the entire US scientific research program and could command virtually unlimited budgets and workforce. While not directly involved in computer developments, he started several umbrella projects in which major computational advances were to take place. In 1942 he wrote the report that resulted in the establishment of the Manhattan Project, and it was under his coordination that the development of tactical radar took place.

After the war and up until his death on 28 June 1974, he wrote of his ideas and experiences in a number of books. These were to have a profound effect on the conduct of scientific research and changed the way that basic research was done in America. One of his writings (*Science, the Endless Frontier*, July 1945, Washington, US Govt. Printing Office), a report of his wartime experiences and insights into the organization of research teams, foreshadowed the 1951 establishment of the National Science Foundation. His *Modern Arms and Free Men* (1949, New York: Simon and Schuster), a discussion of how science can play a role in preserving democracy, was one of the key works that resulted in the explosive development of military research that so characterized the cold war era.

Bibliography

1970. Bush, V. *Pieces of the Action*. New York: William Morrow & Co.

1986. Owens, L. "Vannevar Bush and the Differential Analyzer: The Text and Context of an Early Computer," *Technology and Culture*, **27**, *1*, 63–95.

1991. Nyce, J. M. and Kahn, P. *From Memex to Hypertext: Vannevar Bush and the Mind's Machine*. Boston: Academic Press. Includes Bush's essays on hypertext: "As We May Think" and "Memex II".

1994. Burke, C. *Information and Secrecy: Vannevar Bush, Ultra, and the Other Memex.* Metuchen, NJ: Scarecrow Press.
1997. Zachary, G. P. *Endless Frontier: Vannevar Bush, Engineer of the American Century.* New York: The Free Press.

Michael R. Williams

BUSINESS APPLICATIONS

See ADMINISTRATIVE APPLICATIONS; ELECTRONIC COMMERCE; ELECTRONIC FUNDS TRANSFER; and TRANSACTION PROCESSING.

BYTE ORDERING

> For articles on related topics *see* ADDRESSING; COMPATIBILITY; COMPUTER ARCHITECTURE; and NETWORK PROTOCOLS.

In early computers, a *cell*, the smallest addressable unit of main memory, was the same as a *word*, the collection of bits that could be transferred between memory and the CPU in one operation. Typical word sizes varied from 24 bits (CDC 3100) to 64 bits (IBM Stretch—*q.v.*). If a programmer wanted to process less than a full word, he or she would have to fetch the entire word and then use appropriate machine instructions to extract the desired portion.

More recent computers are byte-addressable; that is, a cell is an 8-bit byte, but a word is typically two, four, or eight bytes. Such computers have instructions that fetch an entire word holding an integer value, and others that fetch a byte holding a single character (see CHARACTER CODES).

The computer architects who design such a processor must choose how to store integers. Suppose that a word is 32 bits, a typical storage size for an integer. If the address of a word is 1000, which includes byte addresses 1000–1003, should byte 1000 hold the most-significant bits of the integer (leftmost in the normal way of writing them), or should it hold the least-significant bits (rightmost)? The former choice is called *big-endian* (the address of the integer is the address of the most-significant byte); the latter *little-endian* (the integer address is the address of the least-significant byte). The terms come from Swift's *Gulliver's Travels* (in which opposing camps argue about which end of an

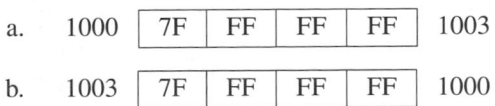

Figure 1. Storage of an integer, 7FFFFFFF, in (a) big-endian and (b) little-endian order, at word-address 1000, consisting of bytes 1000–1003. In both cases, the integer has been written with the most significant byte at the left, but the address at which this is stored depends on the "endianity."

egg to eat first); Cohen (1981) introduced them in the present context. Fig. 1 shows the two ways of storing the hexadecimal value 7FFFFFFF ($2^{31} - 1$).

The two organizations of storage are equally good for computers, and we have big-endian processors (Motorola, Sparc) and little-endian ones (Intel, DEC). A major reason for choosing either format is compatibility with an earlier processor, and some processors can now be set either way by the operating system (MIPS, PowerPC). From the human standpoint, each organization has a virtue. The big-endian representation lets us write the integer in the conventional left-to-right order of digits, with byte-addresses that grow left-to-right as well. However, it is also common to number bits within a byte from 0 on the right to 7 on the left. Hence in the little-endian representation, when an integer is written in the standard way, bit numbering and byte addresses both grow right-to-left.

The existence of these two different schemes creates a problem when data is exchanged between big- and little-endian computers. If an integer is transferred byte-by-byte from a big- to a little-endian machine, the order of the bytes within a word must be reversed between sender and receiver, so that the most significant byte, which is in the lowest address of the sender's word, goes into the highest byte address of the receiver's word. If that reversal is not done, the intended 7FFFFFFF, which is ($2^{31} - 1$), becomes FFFFFF7F, which is −129 in the standard 2s complement representation (*see* COMPLEMENT). However, if a block of bytes holds a string of characters, then no such reordering should occur during the exchange. Any data exchange between computers must therefore take the data types (*q.v.*) into account.

Because this problem commonly arises when computers of different "endianity" are networked, there is now a standard network *byte ordering*. It specifies that the most significant byte of an integer is to be transmitted first (i.e. integers are sent in big-endian order, however they are stored). The software on each side, which is written to take into account the endianity of the computer on which it runs, can then transmit or store the bytes appropriately. As a historical note, the original version of the Unix "talk" program, which let users carry on a written conversation between networked computers, failed to work between Sun (big-endian) and DEC (little-endian) computers because it did not use such a rule.

Bibliography

1981. Cohen, D. "On Holy Wars and a Plea for Peace," *IEEE Computer Magazine,* **14** (October), 48–54.
1999. Tanenbaum, A. S. *Structured Computer Organization,* 4th Ed. Upper Saddle River, NJ: Prentice Hall.

David Hemmendinger and Edwin D. Reilly

C

For articles on related subjects see C++; JAVA; PROCEDURE-ORIENTED LANGUAGES; PROGRAMMING LANGUAGES; STRUCTURED PROGRAMMING; SYSTEMS PROGRAMMING; and UNIX OPERATING SYSTEM.

C is a general-purpose programming language featuring economy of expression, basic control flow and data structure capabilities, and a rich set of operators and data types.

C was originally best known as the primary language of the Unix operating system, but it has become in effect the *lingua franca* of computing: most programmers know C and many large programs are written in C or a descendant like C++ or Java.

C was originally designed and implemented by Dennis Ritchie in 1972–1973 for the DEC PDP-11. C has its roots in BCPL (Richards and Whitbey-Stevens, 1979) in much the same way that, for example, Pascal (*q.v.*) sprang from Algol (*q.v.*). C is the successor to a short-lived BCPL-like language called B that was developed at Bell Labs; thus, the very name "C" derives from BCPL.

C is a traditional procedural language. It is compact, oriented towards system programming, and easily compiled. Its data types and operations map directly into the capabilities of conventional computers, so compilers are small and generated code is efficient. C relies on library routines for input–output and other interactions with an operating system. At the same time, it is sufficiently high level that, with care, large programs can be written and managed, and portability among machines and operating systems can be achieved.

C is not tied to any particular hardware or operating system; C compilers run on virtually all machines. An ANSI/ISO standard for C and its basic libraries was defined in 1988. Accordingly, most C programs can be moved without change to any system that supports C and the standard run-time library. In particular, this has meant that the Unix operating system itself, which is largely written in C, has been ported to a variety of computers with relatively modest effort.

The standard reference on C is Kernighan and Ritchie (1988); detailed information on the history of the language may be found in Ritchie (1995).

Language Components

CONTROL FLOW

Control flow in C is relatively conventional:

```
if (expr) stat1 else stat2
while (expr) stat
for (expr1; expr2; expr3) stat
do stat while (expr)
switch (expr) {
    case const1: stat1
    case const2: stat2
    ...
    default: stat
}
```

In each of these, *expr* is an expression and *stat* is a statement, either simple or a group of statements enclosed in braces. Within a loop, **break** causes an immediate exit and **continue** causes the next iteration to begin; **break** also terminates cases of a **switch** statement. There are also labels and a **goto** though its use is discouraged (*see* STRUCTURED PROGRAMMING).

DATA TYPES

The basic data types (*q.v.*) in C are char (usually an eight-bit byte); int, short, and long; and float and double (floating-point numbers). Integer types come in signed and unsigned variants. An int usually corresponds to the natural word size of the machine (32 or 64 bits) while short is often 16 bits and long the longest possible integer.

In addition, there is a conceptually infinite hierarchy of derived types. If T is a type, then there are pointers (*q.v.*) to objects of type T, arrays of Ts, and structures and unions (records and variant records, in Pascal terminology) that may contain Ts. There are also pointers to functions, and enumeration types (i.e. ones whose discrete members are explicitly listed by the programmer).

C does not have a string data type; strings are represented as arrays of chars, usually with a null byte as terminator, and manipulated by library functions.

Pointer arithmetic is an integral part of C, and the use of pointers to create and access dynamic data structures is one of its most characteristic features. Pointers are more constrained than mere machine addresses, however. Pointers to different types cannot be assigned or combined without explicit coercion (*q.v.*). If *p* is of type pointer to T, and currently points to an element of an array of Ts, then $p + 1$ is a pointer to the next element of the array. That is, arithmetic operations on pointers are scaled by the size of the object to which the pointer points; the programmer is not (and should not be) concerned with the actual size.

OPERATORS AND EXPRESSIONS

In addition to the usual +, –, etc., C has a relatively rich set of operators. Two classes are worth special mention. Any binary operator such as + has a corresponding "assignment operator" (here +=) so that the statement

    v = v + expr;

can be more concisely written

    v += expr;

The unary operators ++ and -- increment or decrement their operand:

    ++v;

is the preferred way to write

    v = v + 1;

An expression (*q.v.*) may be coerced (converted or *cast*) to another type by preceding the expression with a type name, as in

    x = sqrt((double) integer expression);

The coercion in this example converts the *integer expression* into double precision, the type required by the function sqrt. Standard coercions (for example, integer type to floating-point type or vice versa) are performed implicitly, so in this example the cast is unnecessary.

Program Structure

A C program is a set of declarations of variables and functions in one or more source files that may be compiled separately. Function definitions may not be nested, but variables may be declared or redeclared within any block (*see* BLOCK STRUCTURE).

Functions or external variables at the top level are declared either global (i.e. available to all functions) or visible only within the source file where they are declared. Variables internal to a function are either *automatic* (they appear when the function is entered and disappear when it is exited) or *static* (they retain their values from one call of the function to the next). Variables may be initialized at the point of declaration.

All functions may be called recursively. Function arguments are passed by value, but passing a pointer provides call by reference when necessary (*see* PARAMETER PASSING). Function arguments and return values may have any basic type or may be pointers, structures, unions and enumerations. Arrays are passed as a pointer to the first element.

A preprocessor (*q.v.*) provides source file inclusion, conditional compilation, and macro (*q.v.*) processing for symbolic names and short inline functions.

Run-time Environment

C does not provide input–output (I/O) statements as part of the syntax of the language, nor does it support storage management or string manipulation. Similarly, even though C was originally designed for systems programming applications, it provides only single-thread control flow constructs—no multiprogramming (*q.v.*), parallel operations, synchronization, or co-routines (*q.v.*). All of these higher-level facilities must be provided by separate functions. A library that is part of the standard provides a uniform run-time environment for most C programs, so that programs that confine their operating system interactions to the facilities of this library can be moved without change to any system that supports standard C.

An Example

The following program computes and prints the powers of 2 up to 2^{30}.

```
#define LIMIT 30
void main()  /* test power function */
{
    int i;
    long power(int, int);
    for (i = 0; i <= LIMIT; ++i)
        printf("%d %ld\n", i, power(2,i));
}
long power(int x, int n)
            /* raise x to nth power; n >= 0 */
{
    int i;
    long p;
    p = 1;
    for (i = 1; i <= n; ++i)
        p = p * x;
    return p;
}
```

Execution begins at `main`. The standard library function `printf` does formatted output conversion according to the specification in its first argument. Here, `%d` signals an ordinary integer and `%ld` a long integer; `\n` is a newline character.

The function `power` would normally be written more concisely by experienced C programmers:

```
long power(int x, int n)
            /* raise x to nth power; n >= 0 */
{
    long p = 1;
    while (--n >= 0)
            /* decrement n before testing */
        p *= x;
    return p;
}
```

Assessment

C has been remarkably successful in its own right. Its combination of expressiveness, efficiency, and portability have made it probably the most widely used language ever. In addition, it has been the genesis of several other successful languages, most notably its direct descendant C++, which uses C's basic syntax and semantics and adds constructs for classes, inheritance, polymorphism, and the like (*see* OBJECT-ORIENTED PROGRAMMING). C++ is usually object-compatible (linkable) with C so that libraries can be shared, and for many years, the standard C++ implementation (cfront) was a compiler that translated C++ into C, thus reinforcing the half-joking comment that "C is the universal assembly language." Many other languages have also used this path to efficient portable implementations.

Java is a more recent descendant that draws on both C and C++ and lies between them in many respects.

Other languages that have borrowed or adapted C's surface syntax include Awk, Perl and Javascript (*see* SCRIPTING LANGUAGES).

C's success was also due in part to the success of Unix, which made the language available in an attractive form to a wide audience. Of course this was a symbiotic relationship: C's portability contributed greatly to the spread of Unix. C also profited significantly from the development of the personal computer, for which a compact, efficient language was a good match.

C is a small, simple language whose types and operations match those provided by real machines, and learning how to write time- and space-efficient programs is not difficult. At the same time the language is sufficiently abstracted from machine details that program portability can be achieved.

C and its central library support have always remained in touch with a real environment. It was not designed to espouse a particular point of view or programming style, but as a tool to write useful programs, to interact with an operating system, and to build larger tools. C is parsimonious and pragmatic. It covers the essential needs of many programmers, but does not try to supply too much, nor to dictate approach or behavior: although C tries to protect programmers from their errors, the programmer has the final say.

Finally, the C language has remained remarkably stable and unified compared with those of similarly widespread currency, for example Pascal and Fortran, and has remained freer of proprietary extensions than other languages. Although C was not originally designed with portability as a prime goal, it has been used to write programs, even operating systems, on machines ranging from the smallest personal computers to the mightiest supercomputers (*q.v.*).

Ultimately, C has succeeded because it has satisfied a need for a system implementation language sufficiently abstract and fluent to describe algorithms and interactions in a wide variety of environments, yet efficient enough to displace assembly language.

Bibliography

1978. Ritchie, D. M., Johnson, S. C., Lesk, M. E., and Kernighan, B. W. "UNIX Time-sharing System: the C Programming Language," *Bell Sys. Tech. J.*, **57**, *6*, 1991–2019.

1979. Richards, M., and Whitbey-Strevens, C. *BCPL: The Language and its Compiler*. Cambridge: Cambridge University Press.

1988. Kernighan, B. W., and Ritchie, D. M. *The C Programming Language*, 2nd Ed. Upper Saddle River, NJ: Prentice Hall.

1995. Ritchie, D. M. "The Development of the C Language," in *History of Programming Languages II* (ed. T. J. Bergin, and R. G. Gibson), 671–698. Reading, MA: Addison-Wesley.

Brian W. Kernighan and Dennis M. Ritchie

C++

For articles on related subjects *see* ABSTRACT DATA TYPE; C; CLASS; OBJECT-ORIENTED PROGRAMMING; PROGRAMMING LANGUAGES; and PROCEDURE-ORIENTED LANGUAGES: SURVEY.

Chronology

C++ was designed and originally implemented by Bjarne Stroustrup in AT&T Bell Labs' Computer Science Research Center in Murray Hill, New Jersey. The work on what became C++ started in 1979 and led to a first commercial release from AT&T in October 1985. At this point, the language was defined by the first edition of *The C++ Programming Language* (Stroustrup, 1986). The early C++ added better type checking, support for data abstraction, and support for object-oriented programming to the C programming language.

After its initial commercial release in the form of a highly-portable compiler front-end, C++ became widely used and supported by many implementations on all major kinds of computers—including the then newly prominent personal computers (PCs). By 1992, organizations such as Apple (*q.v.*), Borland, DEC (*q.v.*), The Free Software Foundation (*q.v.*), Hewlett-Packard, IBM (*q.v.*), Microsoft (*q.v.*), and Zortech were shipping C++ implementations. During this period, Stroustrup refined C++, based on user feedback, and documented it in *The Annotated C++ Reference Manual* (Ellis and Stroustrup, 1990) and *The C++ Programming Language*, 2nd Ed. (Stroustrup, 1991).

In late 1989, formal standardization of C++ under the auspices of the American National Standards Institute (ANSI) started. In 1991, this effort became international leading to an ISO standard in 1998 (X3 Secretariat, 1998). The C++ language evolved further during standardization and a significant standard library was added. The resulting language, standard library, and the primary programming techniques supported by Standard C++ (also called ANSI C++ and ISO C++) were documented in *The C++ Programming Language*, 3rd Ed. (Stroustrup, 1997).

A detailed history of C++ can be found in Stroustrup (1996) and an extensive discussion of its design in Stroustrup (1994).

The Initial Design of C++

A programming language has two roles:

1. It serves as a medium in which a programmer can express ideas as a means of communication among programmers.

2. It serves as a means of instructing computers to perform specific actions.

The Simula 67 language (*see* SIMULA) with its support for object-oriented programming (then called object-based programming) and object-oriented design was a good match for the first role. The C programming language was a good match for the second role. Thus, C++ was designed to provide Simula's facilities for program organization together with C's efficiency and flexibility for systems programming (*q.v.*).

C++ was designed as a response to specific problems that did not have satisfactory solutions in existing programming languages. In 1979–1980, I was trying to partition an operating system kernel (*q.v.*) to distribute it across several computers connected by a variety of means. No language then combined the ability to do the most demanding systems programming and real-time programming tasks (such as writing device drivers and systems for control of robots) with facilities to express directly the logical structure of large complex systems.

The further evolution of C++ was guided by real problems that my colleagues and I experienced. For many years, new language and library facilities were first tried out in Bell Labs projects and modified through users' feedback before being made more widely available. The aim of C++ was always to produce a good tool for practicing programmers.

The early versions of C++ were called "C with Classes." The name C++, signifying "incremental improvement of C" and "successor to C," came into use in 1984.

Abstraction and Efficiency

Consider designing a simulation of traffic flow through a city to estimate response times for emergency vehicles or commute times. We use concepts such as road, hospital, traffic light, car, motorcycle, and ambulance as we think about our problem. In our program, we want to represent these concepts as directly and as conveniently as possible. A major design aim of C++ was to allow the programmer to specify concepts such as `road`, `hospital`, `traffic_light`, `car`, `motorcycle`, and `ambulance` as user-defined types. Such user-defined types, called *classes*, receive the same degree of support from the language as do built-in types such as integers and characters. Thinking in terms of user-defined types and hiding implementation details within the implementations of these types is commonly called *data abstraction*. Enabling a style of programming based on efficient user-defined data types was a major aim of C++. The benefits are comprehensibility, maintainability and easier debugging.

However, just having classes doesn't raise the level of programming to the level at which we use concepts. For example, we talk of vehicles, rather than always listing the various kinds of vehicles. Thus, C++ had to provide the programmer with the tools to specify relationships among concepts. For example, it is easy to specify that a `motorcycle`, a `car`, and an `ambulance` are `vehicles`, and that an `ambulance` and a `police_car` are `emergency_vehicles`. Representing commonality among concepts in a hierarchical fashion leads to what is referred to as *class hierarchies*. For example:

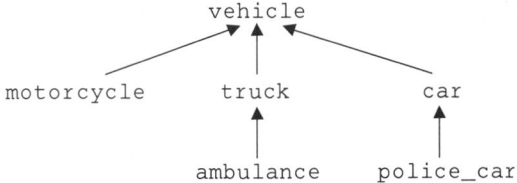

In a program, it is then possible to specify an action such as "the vehicle turns right" without listing the kinds of vehicles that we want to turn; each individual vehicle performs the action appropriate for its type. This style of programming is called *object-oriented programming*, and can be used to design very flexible and extensible systems.

The data abstraction and object-oriented styles of programming are useful not just for traffic simulations. For example, data flows in computer and telephone networks can be handled similarly. The techniques of data abstraction and object-oriented programming are very general and have been successfully applied in C++ to essentially all areas of system design and implementation; for example, scientific computation, commercial data processing systems (Berg, Cline, and Girou, 1995) and telecommunications (Kamath, Smilan, and Smith, 1993).

Class hierarchies provide a way of representing commonality among concepts and their representation as classes in a program. From the earliest days of C with Classes, I was aware of another way of expressing commonality. For example, "vector of integer" and "vector of line segments" are both vectors, but expressing their commonality by deriving two classes from a common base vector would not be a good idea: "being a vector" is not naturally expressed as a set of data and functions that could serve as the common base for two classes `vector<int>` and `vector<line_segment>`. What is needed is a way to parameterize a vector by its element type. The first attempt to achieve this used C-style macros (definitions for the C preprocessor; *see* MACRO), but that resulted in ugly, hard-to-write, and unmaintainable code. From about 1985, work focused on proper language facilities for parameterizing functions and classes with types (*generic*

programming). However, the mechanism supporting this, called a *template*, was not added to C++ until 1989. It took several more years to get the template concept refined enough and well-enough implemented for parameterization by type to serve its proper role in C++ design and programming.

Throughout the development of C++, C compatibility played an important role. C++ shares most of its syntax, its built-in data types, and most forms of statements and expressions with C. The constant aim was to be able to link C and C++ compiled code (*see* LINKERS AND LOADERS) and to allow C code to be compiled by a C++ compiler wherever this would not violate C++'s stronger compile-time type checking. In addition, it was considered crucial that C++ code deliver as good run-time and space efficiency as equivalent C code. Over the years, some of the most contentious issues in the design of C++ related to C compatibility. Some wanted 100% C compatibility (which would seriously compromise C++'s mechanisms for abstraction and type checking) and others wanted to make C++ into a much higher-level language by jettisoning much of its C heritage. The result was that C++ has a very large C subset; well-written C tends to be C++. In particular, every example in the defining textbook for C (Kernighan and Ritchie, 1988) is also a C++ program.

Thus C++ became a language that

♦ is a better C;

♦ supports data abstraction;

♦ supports object-oriented programming;

♦ supports generic programming.

I considered it essential that programmers should not be forced to choose between high-level and efficient code. Thus, all C++ facilities are efficient enough to be useful for the most demanding tasks. The main language support for generic programming, templates with type parameters, is a compile-time mechanism that imposes no run-time overheads, and the primary support for object-oriented programming, a virtual function call, takes only a few percent longer than an ordinary function call.

Evolution and Standardization

During the 1980s use of C++ grew rapidly. By 1991, there were at least 400,000 C++ users worldwide and about a dozen purveyors of C++ implementations. Consequently, formal standardization became necessary. The ANSI and ISO C++ standards committees (founded in 1989 and 1991, respectively), with Dmitry

Lenkov from Hewlett-Packard as chairman, quickly became the focus for discussions of C++, its implementation, and its proper use.

At the start of standardization, the general course for C++ was already set. Consequently, the work focused on technical details and on facilities needed to complete the support for the styles of programming supported by C++. The standard basically confirmed the language as defined by the reference manual in Stroustrup (1991) (including exception handling—q.v., mechanisms and templates) and resulted in a more precise and comprehensive specification. In addition, facilities for run-time identification, a mechanism for namespace control, and about a dozen minor features were added.

At the start of the standards effort, C++ lacked a good standard library. For years, it was uncertain whether the committee could do anything to address this serious issue. The fundamental problem was that they did not know how to design and implement a library that provided sufficiently safe, general, and efficient containers (lists, vectors, maps, etc.). In addition, many organizations already relied on extensive foundation libraries of their own, and none of those was sufficiently better than the rest to please a large majority of the C++ community.

Then, at the invitation of Andrew Koenig, Alex Stepanov from Hewlett-Packard Labs presented a novel framework of containers and algorithms to the committee. This framework called the STL (Standard Template Library), used templates in fairly advanced ways to achieve a hitherto unknown combination of efficiency and generality for type-safe containers and generic algorithms (such as sorting, searching, and traversal) (Stepanov and Lee, 1994; Koenig and Moo, 1997; Stroustrup, 1997). After about a year's study and minor modification, the STL was accepted as a central part of the C++ standard library. The C++ standard library also provides for type-safe extensible input–output, strings of arbitrary character sets, and support for numeric computation (Stroustrup, 1997).

In retrospect, C++ grew within my original view of what it was supposed to become. The evolution of language features and programming techniques critically depended on feedback from its massive use.

Bibliography

1986. Stroustrup, B. *The C++ Programming Language.* Reading, MA: Addison-Wesley.
1988. Kernighan, B., and Ritchie, D. *The C Programming Language*, 2nd Ed. Upper Saddle River, NJ: Prentice Hall.
1990. Ellis, M. A., and Stroustrup, B. *The Annotated C++ Reference Manual.* Reading, MA: Addison-Wesley.
1991. Stroustrup, B. *The C++ Programming Language*, 2nd Ed. Reading, MA: Addison-Wesley.
1993. Kamath, Y. H., Smilan, R. E., and Smith, J. G. "Reaping Benefits with Object-oriented Technology," *AT&T Technical Journal*, **72**, 5 (September/October), 14–24.
1994. Stroustrup, B. *The Design and Evolution of C++.* Reading, MA: Addison-Wesley.
1994. Stepanov, A., and Lee, M. *The Standard Template Library.* HP Labs Technical Report HPL-94-34 (R. 1).
1995. Berg, W., Cline, M., and Girou, M. "Lessons Learned from the OS/400 OO Project," *Comm. of the ACM*, **38**, 10 (October).
1996. Stroustrup, B. "A History of C++: 1979–1991," in *The History of Programming Languages* (eds. T. J. Bergin and R. G. Gibson), 699–754. Reading, MA: Addison-Wesley. Originally published in *Proc. ACM History of Programming Languages Conference (HOPL-2). ACM SIGPLAN Notices*, **28**, 3, March 1993.
1997. Koenig, A., and Moo, B. *Ruminations on C++.* Reading, MA: Addison Wesley Longman.
1997. Stroustrup, B. *The C++ Programming Language*, 3rd Ed. Reading, MA: Addison-Wesley.
1998. X3 Secretariat. *Standard—The C++ Language.* X3J16/98-14882. Washington DC: Information Technology Council (NSITC).

Bjarne Stroustrup

CACHE COHERENCY

For articles on related subjects *see* BUFFER; BUS; CACHE MEMORY; MEMORY: MAIN; and MULTIPROCESSING.

Introduction

The use of caches in a computer system is a cost-effective way of reducing a CPU's average memory latency (access delay) by taking advantage of temporal and spatial locality that frequently exists in software. In order to reduce the latency to a minimum, caches are placed as close as possible to the CPU. On-chip caches have been common in microprocessor design for some time. A typical multiprocessor system arrangement is shown in Fig. 1 (a uniprocessor system would have a single CPU and cache).

Here, each CPU has its own cache and accesses a globally shared main memory through a bus or other type of interconnection. Such an organization allows any piece of shared data to be cached in multiple locations. To illustrate this, let us consider a two-processor system where a shared variable x with an initial value

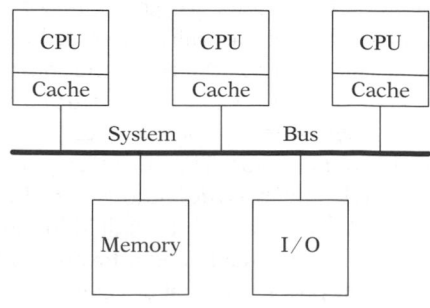

Figure 1.

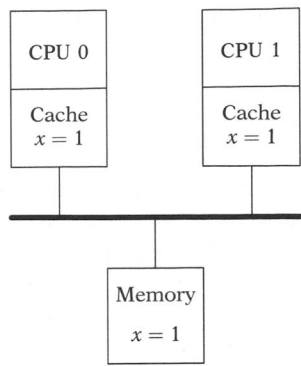

Figure 2.

of 1 is in main memory. If both processors load this variable, they will both be caching the initial value (Fig. 2).

At this point, all caches and main memory present a consistent view of the value of x. If processor 0 now changes the value of x to 2 and write-back caching is used (which does not copy the new value from cache to memory until an entire cache line is replaced), the situation of Fig. 3 results.

The value of x is now inconsistent between the two caches as they have different values for the same shared variable. The value cached by processor 1 is said to be *stale*. Such a situation will usually cause the program to produce incorrect results, so these inconsistencies must be avoided.

When multiple caches maintain the value of a shared location, they are said to be *consistent* or *coherent* if they all reflect the same value of the data. Maintaining *cache coherency* therefore presents a unified view of main memory to all processors in the system. (The terms *cache coherency* and *cache consistency* are synonymous.)

Observe that cache coherency is a problem on uniprocessor systems as well. Inconsistencies can arise if an I/O device updates main memory via direct

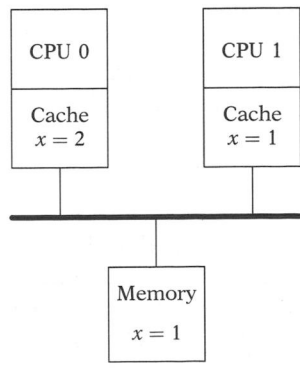

Figure 3.

memory access (DMA—*see* INPUT–OUTPUT OPERATIONS) if the locations being updated are also being cached. Again, this causes the cached data to become stale.

Cache coherency is enforced by the use of a coherency algorithm or protocol (*q.v.*), and may be maintained by either software or hardware techniques.

Cache Coherency Protocols—An Analogy

Let us illustrate the process of maintaining cache coherency by using an analogy. Consider how stock market quotes were communicated to stockbrokers' offices in the days of the ticker tape machine. The stock exchange always maintained the current price of all stocks traded there. It was also typical for each stockbroker office to have a large blackboard where the price of stocks of local interest were listed. This would, of course, be a subset of the stocks traded at the exchange. When a stock price changed, its new price was broadcast to all stockbrokers via the ticker tape machine. A clerk in each broker's office would read the ticker tape and update the office's blackboard for any price changes for the stocks listed there. This way, the blackboard in each office reflected the last known price for the stocks.

To map this analogy to a computer system, the blackboards represent caches and the prices maintained by the stock exchange represent shared data in main memory. The ticker tape represents the memory interconnect and the clerk in each office represents the cache controller. Cache coherency is maintained by broadcasting updates to main memory (i.e. changes in stock prices) to all caches in the system. If the cache was storing the old data, it is updated with the new data, thereby removing any stale data from the cache. These actions represent a cache coherency protocol.

This example is simplified in that the individual brokerage offices do not update the stock prices themselves. All changes are made at the exchange and then the updates are broadcast to the brokerage offices. In a computer system, the CPUs need to update the values in their caches to achieve low latency to memory, so the coherency protocol becomes more complex.

Categories of Protocols

There are many cache coherency protocols, but they can all be divided into two broad categories: *write-invalidate* protocols and *write-update* protocols. The difference between the two categories concerns what actions are taken when shared data is modified: the data in the caches can either be invalidated, so that the next reference the CPU makes to the data causes it to read the new value from main memory, or any cached copies of the data can be updated with the new value. The stockbroker analogy above is an example of a write-update protocol. Because they tend to involve less communication between caches in the system, write-invalidate protocols are the most commonly used. The next two sections illustrate two protocols from this category. Details regarding several write-update protocols can be found in the references cited below.

The Write-Through Invalidate Protocol

One of the simplest cache coherence protocols is the write-through invalidate protocol. As its name implies, write-through caching is used by all caches in the system. This protocol is implemented in hardware using a technique called *snooping* or *bus watching*. This technique, commonly used in bus-based multi-pro-cessor systems to maintain coherence, involves having each cache monitor or snoop the system bus for activity by other caches or for DMA operations. Actions by other caches or I/O devices that affect data stored in the cache can then be detected and appropriate steps are taken to eliminate stale data. The exact steps taken are dictated by the particular protocol being used. The write-through invalidate protocol operates as follows.

When a CPU accesses data that is not present in its cache, it causes a cache miss and it reads the needed value from main memory. Since all caches in the system are using write-through, the data in main memory is always up to date. It is therefore impossible to fetch stale data from main memory on a cache miss. If other CPUs read the same data, they too will read it from main memory and cache a copy of the data. When one CPU writes to shared data in its cache, this action causes any other copies of that data in other caches to become stale. The protocol must therefore eliminate this stale data. Since write-through caching is used, the CPU performing the write immediately sends the data to main memory via the system bus, keeping the value in main memory up to date. The bus operation that updates main memory is then snooped by the other caches in the system. They each check their contents to see whether the same shared data is being cached. If not, then nothing need be done. If it is cached, then the cached copy has been made stale by the CPU that did the write, so the stale copy is invalidated from the cache. The other CPUs must then re-read the updated value of the data from memory when they next access it and coherency is therefore maintained. Since the system bus can only be used by one processor at a time, multiple CPUs writing to the same shared data at the same time will be sequentially ordered, which again ensures coherency. Snooping handles I/O DMA as well. If an I/O device updates main memory, the caches snoop these bus operations as well and invalidate any data made stale by the DMA.

The disadvantage of the write-through invalidate protocol is that it requires a bus operation for each store done by any CPU in the system. This increases the memory latency on stores, wastes bus bandwidth (*q.v.*), and reduces the benefit of using caches. The use of write-back caches is a highly desirable way to solve these problems. However, the protocol described here cannot support write-back caches. The problem is that the protocol causes caches that miss on shared data to read the data from main memory. Write-through caching ensures that the copy in main memory is always up to date. Using write-back caches removes this assurance, which means the copy in main memory may be stale. The simple write-through invalidate protocol is unable to handle stale data in main memory. Because of this, more sophisticated protocols have been developed so that write-back caching may be used while still maintaining coherency.

MESI Protocols

A class of protocols called *MESI protocols* (pronounced as *messy*) have been developed to handle cache coherence for systems using write-back caches. The individual protocols have slight variations between them, but they all use the fundamental concept of *ownership* of a piece of shared data. Since caches organize data into *lines*, the ownership concept usually extends to one line's worth of data, and each cache line's worth of data in main memory may be owned by a different cache at different times. By tracking which cache (if any) owns a particular line of data, the location of the up-to-date copy is always known. Once a cache owns a line, it can update it using write-back without the risk of another CPU accessing the now stale copy of the line in main memory. MESI protocols rely on snooping to avoid stale data.

MESI protocols derive their name from the first letter in each of the states a cache line can have: modified, exclusive, shared, and invalid. The states are recorded as additional flag bits in the cache tags. Write-back caches that lack hardware cache coherency have two state bits: a valid bit and a modified bit. MESI protocols add two additional bits to flag the exclusive and shared states of the line. The protocol then operates as follows.

The *modified* state means that the line is modified in the cache and the copy of the line in main memory is stale. It also implies that this particular cache is the exclusive owner of the line. With MESI protocols, only one cache is allowed to have a modified copy of the data. This cache is the owner of the line. If another

CPU tries to read the same line of data, it is guaranteed to miss in its cache, since another cache currently owns the data. The CPU that missed will try to read the data from main memory. Since all caches are snooping the bus, the cache that owns the line will see the access and intervene. Instead of allowing the stale data to be read from main memory, it will send the modified contents of the line to the cache that's requesting the data. The new cache becomes the owner of the line and the previous owner marks its copy *invalid*.

If a CPU misses in its cache on a load and no other cache contains the line, then it can safely read the line from main memory. The data from main memory is loaded into the cache in the *exclusive* state, since it is the sole cache with a copy. The line stays in the exclusive state as long as the data remains unmodified. If the data is modified by the CPU, the line enters the modified state and behaves as just described.

If a line is in the exclusive state in one cache and another cache tries to read the same line, the cache currently owning the line snoops this action and both caches will now store the line in the *shared* state. The shared state means that multiple caches have a copy of the line, but none has modified it. The line remains in the shared state until one cache attempts to modify the line. When a modification to a shared line occurs, the cache sends a bus transaction which the other caches will snoop. Since a modified line can have only a single owner, the other caches *invalidate* their copies of the line in response to this bus transaction. This allows the line to enter the modified state in the cache in which the update occurred.

Coherency is maintained since MESI protocols allow only a single cache to own a particular line of data in the modified state at one time. Multiple caches may share an unmodified copy of a line, but the sharing ends on the first modification to the line. This allows the write-back caching policy to be used, which reduces bus traffic and can improve overall performance.

Directory-Based Cache Coherency

Snooping the system bus is a convenient way to maintain cache coherency. However, not all systems are bus-based. A single system bus has limited bandwidth which can be saturated if there are too many CPUs or I/O devices connected to it. In short, the bus becomes a bottleneck. To get around the limitations of a single bus, designers have turned to systems that contain either multiple buses or to completely different memory interconnect techniques such as the *crossbar*. The purpose of these designs is to distribute memory traffic across multiple paths such that the aggregate band-width of all the paths together is greater than a single bus could provide. Only a portion of the CPUs and I/O devices in the system are connected to each path so that each path does not become a bottleneck.

A result of these designs is that snooping-based protocols cannot be used since the caches can see only the traffic on the path to memory on which they are connected. Activities on the other paths cannot be snooped, which means some other method of maintaining coherency is needed.

Instead of snooping a shared bus, these systems use a *directory* to maintain coherency. A directory consists of a number of additional bits stored with the data in main memory. These bits are maintained by the hardware and are not visible to the software. In its simplest form, there is one bit in the directory for each CPU in the system. If the bit is set, it means that a CPU may have a copy of that portion of memory in its cache. In essence, the directory is a centralized repository showing which caches have copies of the data. With this information, the standard protocols can be made to operate. For example, if a write-invalidate protocol is used, the directory tells the hardware which CPUs need to be sent invalidations if one CPU modifies a piece of shared data cached in multiple places. Similarly, if a write-update protocol is used, the directory identifies which CPUs the update should be sent to. So the use of a directory eliminates the need to broadcast each invalidate or update throughout the entire system. Such broadcasts are to be avoided since they would waste bandwidth and defeat the purpose of having multiple paths to memory in the system.

Software Coherency, Multi-Level Caches, Split Caches, and Other Topics

Cache coherency raises other issues. For example, coherency can be maintained by either hardware or software or by a combination of both. In modern multiprocessor systems, use of hardware is almost universal since it leads to the best performance. The use of software cache consistency is generally limited to small machines. For instance, many desktop computers using DMA maintain cache coherency by operating system software to save the expense of the hardware that would be needed to snoop DMA operations.

Most computers today employ more than one cache in their memory hierarchy (*q.v.*). A fast primary cache located on the CPU chip itself coupled with a larger external secondary cache is quite common. Having more than one cache, however, creates a coherency problem between the two. In general, this problem is solved by requiring that the primary cache is always a subset of the secondary cache. This way only the secondary cache needs to snoop the bus to maintain proper coherency. Any required updates or invalidates are then relayed to the primary cache.

Finally, some CPUs use separate caches for program instructions and data. This is frequently referred to as a *split cache* and allows greater overall performance since the CPU can be fetching an instruction from the instruction cache while also fetching data from the data cache. However, having separate caches creates the need to maintain consistency between the two. For example, if the operating system were to copy a program from one location to another, it would get copied through the data cache. If write-back caching was used and the operating system now attempted to execute the program, some of the instructions could still be in the data cache, meaning that the instruction cache would not execute the correct instructions unless special actions were taken. Typically, coherency between split caches is left to the operating system.

Bibliography

1993. Tomasevic, M., and Milutinovic, V. *The Cache Coherence Problem in Shared-Memory Multiprocessors: Hardware Solutions.* Los Alamitos, CA: IEEE Computer Society Press.
1994. Schimmel, C. *UNIX Systems for Modern Architectures: Symmetric Multiprocessing and Caching for Kernel Programmers.* Reading, MA: Addison-Wesley.
This book presents a thorough treatment of the architecture and operation of caches and cache coherency on both uniprocessor and multiprocessor systems.

Curt Schimmel

CACHE MEMORY

For articles on related subjects *see* ASSOCIATIVE MEMORY; CACHE COHERENCY; COMPUTER ARCHITECTURE; MEMORY; MEMORY HIERARCHY; and VIRTUAL MEMORY.

Introduction

A *cache memory* is a small, high-speed buffer memory used to hold temporarily those portions of the contents of some larger memory that are (believed to be) currently in use. The most common use of a cache memory is in the CPU of a computer system, where it holds or buffers the contents of main memory. Cache memories can also be used to hold the contents of the disk (a disk cache) or mass storage (e.g. a tape cache). Caching is also used in a wide variety of environments, such as for caching file lookups in a directory system and Web pages on a Web server. In this article, we concentrate on the use of caches in CPUs, but also provide brief discussions of some of the other applications of caching.

A cache memory is normally both significantly faster and significantly smaller than the memory whose contents it caches. Like any component of the memory hierarchy, it is only useful if it can satisfy a large fraction of the references to the larger memory. (For convenience we'll refer to this larger memory as the *main memory*, and the unit using it as the *processor* or *CPU*, but much of our discussion is applicable to a wider class of caches.) In practice, caches are very effective in a wide variety of situations because of the *principle of locality* (*see* WORKING SET), which is an empirical observation that, most of the time, the information in use is either the same information that was recently in use (temporal locality), or is information "nearby" the information recently used (spatial locality). Thus a cache typically operates by retaining copies of blocks of storage, each containing recently used information.

Caches are usually transparent or invisible to the processor. The CPU generates a main memory address when it wishes to read or write data. When a cache is added to this design, it is interposed between the CPU and the main memory. The cache thus receives the main memory address, and determines, through some sort of associative search using the main memory address as the key, whether it already holds the data corresponding to that address. If so, in the case of a read, it replies to the CPU with the data, and the main memory is not referenced. (The case of a write is discussed briefly below.) The only way that the CPU can tell that there is a cache memory is by the timing— the cache is faster. When the data sought is retrieved from the cache, there is a cache *hit*, and a *miss* otherwise.

CPU performance is most often limited by the performance of the cache memory. The mean access time to the cache memory, T, is given by $T = T_h + m \times T_m + E$, where T_h is the time to access the cache when the data is present (time for a hit), m is the probability that the data is not in the cache (the *miss ratio*), T_m is the additional delay for a fetch from main memory after a miss (the *miss delay*), and E accounts for a number of other lesser factors, listed and discussed below. These three factors are the crucial determinants of the cache performance. Since the *hit ratio* (the probability of a hit; i.e. $1 -$ miss ratio) is typically well over 90% in CPU cache memories, the access time, T_h for a hit is critically important. Since the ratio T_m / T_h is typically large (5–100 for current technology), the miss ratio is also critically important. T_m is also very important too, but because it is often difficult to decrease T_m, it is less well studied than the other two parameters.

There are a number of other things which affect access time, but to a lesser extent than the three major factors discussed above. We have grouped the effect of these other things in the parameter E: any extra time for a write to the cache; delays to update memory after data is modified; queueing delays to access main memory due to competing accesses from other processors in a multiprocessor system or due to I/O; and cache cycles taken by consistency (coherency) operations and prefetch operations. These additional factors are briefly discussed later.

The next section first describes a very simple CPU cache, and then describes the operation of a typical CPU memory cache in more detail. The following section discusses each of the major factors in cache design, and the last section considers other kinds of caches.

Cache Operation

A CPU (central processing unit) typically consists of three major components: the *instruction unit*, which fetches and decodes instructions (*see* INSTRUCTION DECODING); the *execution unit*, which executes the instructions (and includes components such as the fixed and floating-point adders and multipliers, and the register file); and the *storage unit*, which contains the cache, the TLB (translation lookaside buffer) and the translator. The operation of the cache is inseparable from the operation of the rest of the storage unit, and we discuss the cache in that context.

Fig. 1 is a diagram showing the CPU and main memory. Fig. 2 presents a very simple design for a CPU cache memory, showing that the cache consists of a number of entries. Each entry consists of an address tag, a valid bit, and a *line* or *block* of data. (The terms "line" and "block" are used interchangeably to refer to the unit of storage in the cache memory.) If the valid bit is set to 1, the data is a copy of the data held in the main memory locations identified by the address tag. If the valid bit is set to 0, then the corresponding data field does not currently hold valid data as a result of changes to the contents of main memory. When the instruction (I) or execution (E) units of the CPU generate a main memory address, that address is presented to the cache, which associatively and simultaneously com-

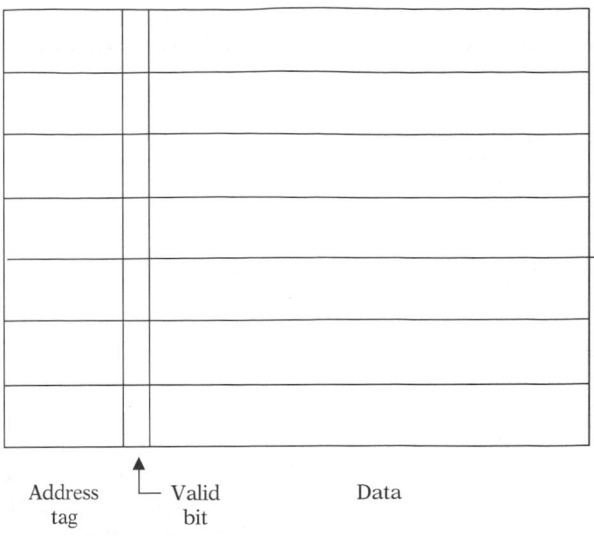

Address   Valid   Data
tag   bit

Figure 2. Elements of a simple cache memory.

pares the address with the address field of each entry for which the valid bit is on. If a match is found (a *hit*), on a read the cache then replies to the I- or E-unit with the requested information. If there is no match, then the cache fetches the line containing the desired information from main memory, extracts the target information and sends it to the I- or E-unit, and also stores the line in a cache entry, replacing the previous contents of that entry. In the case of a write, the data in the cache is updated and, concurrently, the write is also transmitted to main memory, where the main memory copy of the data is updated.

Cache memories are generally more complex than is shown in Fig. 2, for two reasons. Fig. 2 does not reflect the use of virtual memory, and because associative memories are difficult to build and slow, most caches are not fully associative. These two considerations lead to the typical design discussed below and shown in Figs. 4 and 5.

Modern computers all use *virtual memory* by which virtual addresses generated by the instruction and execution units are translated using segment and/or page tables to obtain real main memory addresses. The *translator* is the functional unit that translates virtual to real addresses. The *TLB* (*translation lookaside buffer*) is itself a cache for virtual to real address translations, and is used to improve the performance of the storage unit. (The translation lookaside buffer is also known by other names, including translation buffer (TB), address translation cache (ATC), and directory lookaside table (DLAT).) For the purposes of our discussion, we will assume a 16 KB page, 32-bit virtual and real addresses, a 4-byte word, and a 64-byte line. Fig. 3 shows a virtual address, with fields

CPU

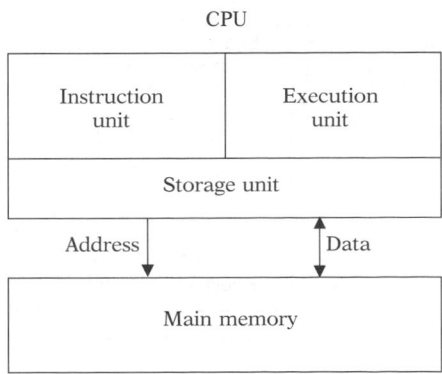

Instruction unit | Execution unit

Storage unit

Address   Data

Main memory

Figure 1. A CPU and main memory.

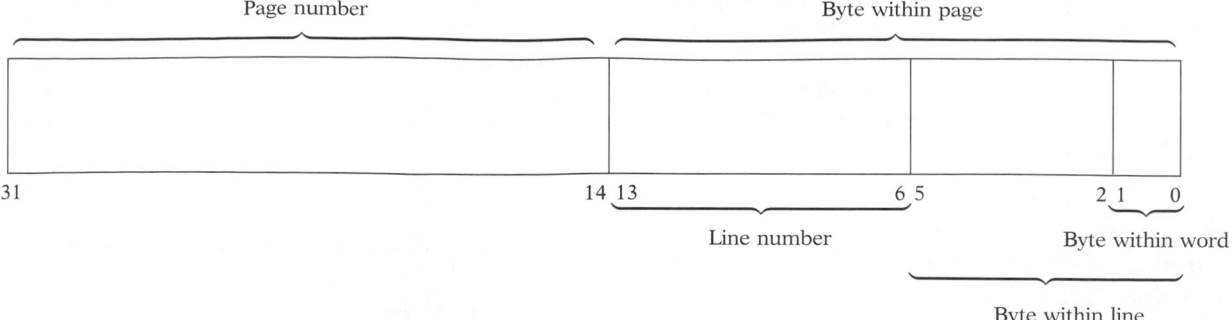

Figure 3. Parts of a virtual address.

and subfields identified. The low-order 14 bits are used to specify the byte within the page, and the upper 18 bits specify the page number, which must be translated to obtain the location of the page frame in main memory. The numbers of bits that would be used for these purposes vary with the page size and virtual address size.

Fig. 4 is a flowchart showing how the cache and storage unit operate, and Fig. 5 shows the major components of the storage unit and the flow of data through them. Fig. 6 shows an entry in the cache and a cache set. In this section, we explain these figures. Note that a variety of designs for a cache are possible; for this initial discussion, we assume a typical design. We also consider only a read from the cache; writes are discussed briefly in the next section.

Both the TLB and cache are shown as organized in a *set associative* manner. In an associative memory, access is on the basis of a key, not on the basis of a storage location; for a CPU cache, the key is the main

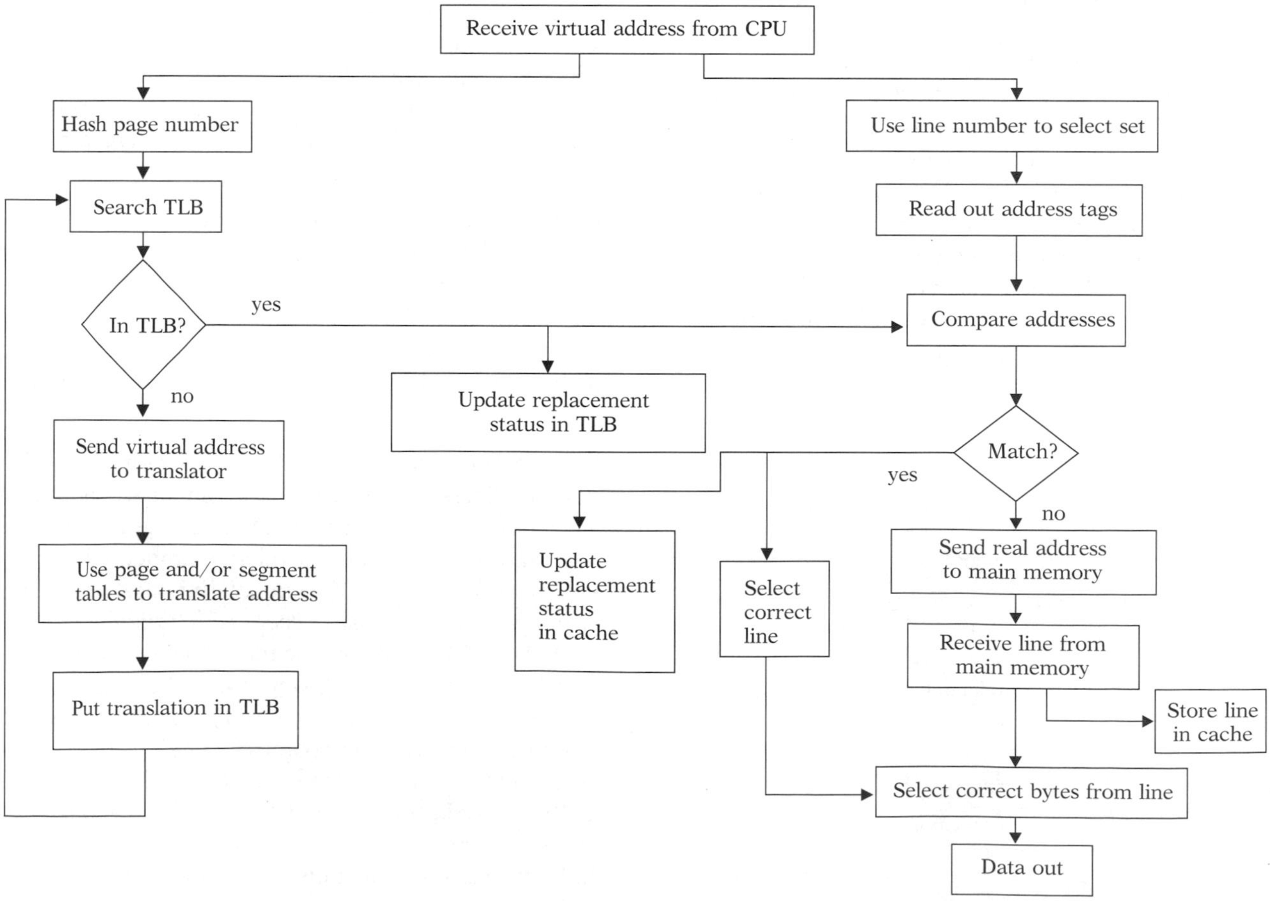

Figure 4. Flowchart of cache operation.

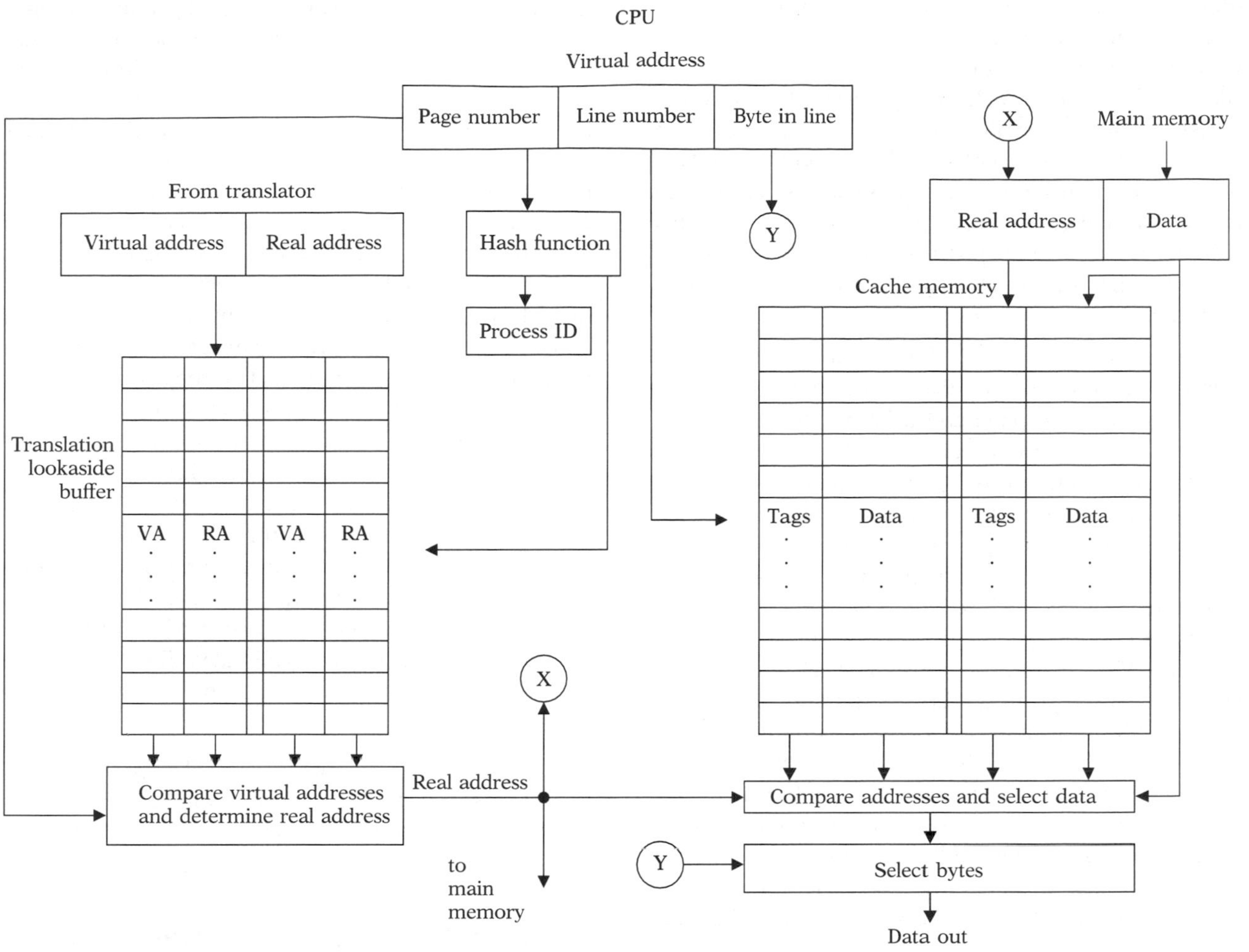

CPU

Virtual address

Page number	Line number	Byte in line

From translator

Virtual address	Real address

Hash function

Process ID

X   Main memory

Real address	Data

Cache memory

Translation lookaside buffer

VA	RA	VA	RA
.	.	.	.
.	.	.	.
.	.	.	.

Tags	Data	Tags	Data
.	.	.	.
.	.	.	.
.	.	.	.

Y

X

Compare virtual addresses and determine real address	Real address

X

Compare addresses and select data

to main memory

Y   Select bytes

Data out

Figure 5. Cache components and information flow through them. The pair of Xs represent a connection, as do the Ys.

memory address (not an address in the cache), and for the TLB, the key is the (virtual) page number. As noted above, large fully associative memories are difficult to build and are usually slow. In a set associative memory, the memory is partitioned into "sets"; the set is determined by some characteristic of the key (e.g. certain bits) and then the elements within the set are searched associatively. Set associative designs typically yield good performance at a reasonable cost.

If each set has one element, the memory is referred to as *direct mapped*. If there is only one set, the memory is referred to as *fully associative*. CPU caches are almost always set associative or direct mapped. TLBs are usually set associative, but are sometimes fully associative.

In Figs. 5 and 6, the cache has *real address tags*. This means that the key to the associative search of the

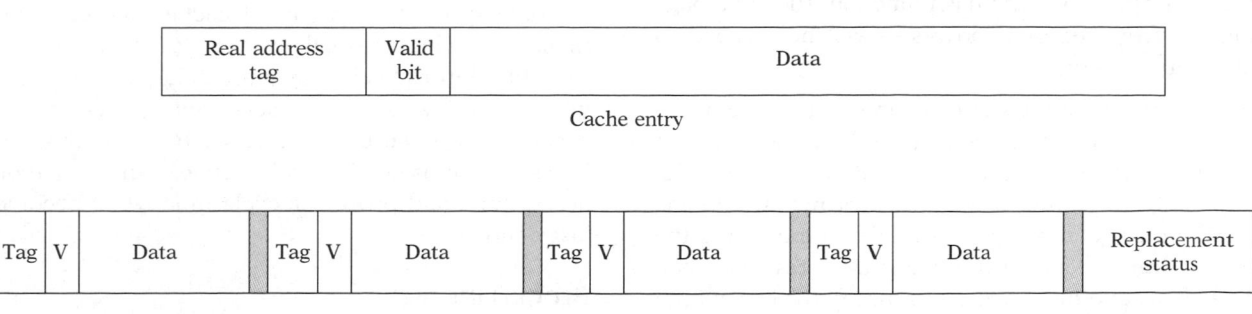

Real address tag	Valid bit	Data

Cache entry

Tag	V	Data		Tag	V	Data		Tag	V	Data		Tag	V	Data		Replacement status

Cache set

Figure 6. A single cache entry and a set of entries.

cache is a real (main memory) address, not the virtual address generated by the CPU. In the most straightforward implementation of a cache system, the virtual address would be translated to a real address by the translator, and the cache would then be accessed based on that real address. Such a design is too slow for two reasons: the translator is very slow, and serializing the translation and cache access is also too slow. For this reason, the translation process is accelerated through the use of the TLB, and the translation is partially overlapped with cache access.

As shown in Figs. 3 and 5, the virtual address may be partitioned into three portions. The high-end 18 bits (assuming a 16 KB page and a 32 bit virtual address) constitute the page number. Typically, the page number is hashed (randomized), as shown in Figs. 4 and 5, often in conjunction with the process ID, and then the low-order bits of that quantity are used to select a set in the TLB. For example, if the TLB had 64 sets, the low-order 6 bits would be used. Each set in the TLB consists of a number of pairs of virtual address–real address ⟨VA, RA⟩ translations. The virtual address field of each entry in a TLB set is read into a comparator, and the page number is compared to each entry of that set. If there is a match, the corresponding real address is output. If there is no match, a no-match signal and the page number are sent to the translator, which uses the segment and page tables of the virtual memory system to perform the translation and load the ⟨VA,RA⟩ pair into the TLB, after which the TLB access is restarted.

The reason for the use of the TLB is that the TLB access takes only a few nanoseconds, whereas the translator requires several hundreds of nanoseconds to do a translation. Most processes have their address spaces start at zero, which means that there is a much higher probability of referencing a page with a low page number than a high one. If access to the TLB were not hashed (randomized), most of the entries would cluster in the lower numbered sets of the TLB, and the TLB would be used very inefficiently. In any multiprogrammed computer system, there is some number that serves as a process identifier (PID). By including the PID in the hash function, the same page number from different processes will be mapped to different TLB entries.

The low 14 bits of the virtual address (in our example) specify the byte within the page and are therefore not translated. Data within the cache is stored in *blocks*; these blocks are often called *lines*. The byte-within-line bits therefore can be split into a line number and the byte within the line. If the line is 64 bytes long, then the low-order 6 bits are used to specify the byte within the line, and the remaining 8 bits specify the byte within the page (*see* Fig. 3).

As Figs. 4 and 5 show, some or all of the line number bits may be used to select the set in the cache. Each cache set consists of a number of ⟨real address, data⟩ pairs, as shown in Fig. 6. If there were 128 sets in the cache, then the low order 7 bits of the line number would be used to select the set. (Each set also has a replacement status field, which is used when one of the elements must be replaced. Each cache (and TLB) entry has a valid bit, which indicates whether the data in that entry is valid.) The address field for each entry in the selected set is read into a comparator, where the real address from the TLB is compared in parallel with the real address tags for that set. If the set size were 4, then four simultaneous comparisons would take place. If there is a match, the corresponding data is read out. If there is no match (a miss), then a signal is sent to the main memory controller, which reads the line from main memory. The cache control logic then loads the entry into the cache, replacing some other existing entry. If the replaced entry has been modified since the time it was fetched from main memory, it must also be copied back to main memory. Finally, the desired word is read from the line, and is sent to the instruction or execution units.

Typically, CPU cache memories will experience 95–99.9% hits and TLBs generally will have 98–99.9% hits, depending on the cache size, line size, and workload.

Cache Optimizations and Parameters

The cache design and operation described above is typical, but it may be varied or optimized in numerous ways. In this section, we provide a brief discussion of the principal issues.

CACHE SIZE AND LOCATION
The larger the cache, the higher the hit ratio, but there are two considerations limiting the size of the cache. First, there may be only a limited amount of chip area when the storage unit is on the same chip as the instruction and execution units. Second, cache speed decreases with greater cache size.

In some systems, a multilevel cache may be implemented, in which a small and very fast cache (e.g. on the CPU chip) is backed by a much larger (and somewhat slower) second level cache. Some Intel Pentium designs (in 1999) use a two-level cache. More than two levels can be used if the ratio between main memory access time and processor cycle time (*q.v.*) becomes large enough.

BLOCK/LINE SIZE
Selecting the block (or line) size is an important optimization factor. The time to fetch a line is usually

of the form $X/A + B$, where X is the line size, B is the latency, and A is the transfer rate. The miss ratio varies with the line size and the cache size. For given values of A, B, and the cache size, an optimal line size may be selected.

FETCH ALGORITHM

Normally, lines are loaded into the cache *on demand*, i.e. when the line is referenced by the CPU. If the line is not present, the CPU waits while the cache fetches it from main memory. As an alternative, the cache can *prefetch* lines by guessing which lines are likely to be needed in the future. Prefetching is seldom worthwhile because it is hard to guess which lines will be needed in advance, the line may not have arrived by the time it is needed, and prefetch operations interfere with normal cache and main memory use.

ORGANIZATION

As explained earlier, caches may be fully associative, set associative, or direct mapped. Fully associative caches are expensive to build and are usually slow. Direct mapped caches are the fastest, but because of the constrained mapping, miss ratios may be high. That is, multiple lines which are concurrently active may map into the same slot in the cache. The best performance is usually obtained from either a set associative or direct mapped design, depending on the cache size, logic speed, main memory and CPU speeds, miss ratio, and other factors.

WRITES AND MAIN MEMORY UPDATE

The discussion above omitted consideration of writes to memory. Writes to memory are normally implemented in one of two ways in a system with a cache. With *write-through*, writes are made simultaneously to the cache and main memory, so that main memory is always up to date. *Write-back buffers* may be provided for buffering pending writes. With *copy-back*, writes are made initially only to the cache, and when the (modified) line is replaced it is copied back to main memory. Copy-back generally provides superior performance, but it is more complex to implement, especially in a multiprocessor system. The main difficulty with write-through is that every write causes a write to main memory, and the data path to main memory (frequently a bus) or main memory bandwidth, can be a bottleneck.

INSTRUCTION AND DATA CACHES

The typical cache described above holds both instructions and data, and is accessed by both the instruction unit and the execution unit. An alternative design is a pair of caches, one for instructions and one for data. This latter design permits higher performance, because instruction and data accesses can take place in parallel, but require that most of the cache control logic be duplicated. In computer systems running old code, instructions and data may be interspersed (as frequently occurs with Fortran) or there may be self-modifying code. In that case, care must be taken to ensure that the instruction cache can detect writes to information it contains, and update or purge its contents accordingly.

MULTICACHE CONSISTENCY (COHERENCY)

In multiprocessor systems, it is common to have several CPUs, each with its own cache, sharing a main memory. In that case, there is the danger that the same data item may be present in more than one cache, and after being modified, may have different values in the different caches. This problem is called the *cache consistency problem* (or the *cache coherency* (q.v.) *problem*). The way this problem is solved in general is that state bits are associated with each line in each cache (or alternately with a central directory which knows which cache has which lines), specifying whether the line is present in more than one cache and whether it has been modified since the time it was read from main memory. Modifications to the state of a line may require communication with other caches or with main memory in order to insure that all copies of the line are consistent.

INPUT–OUTPUT

In all computer systems, there are I/O devices which are continually reading from and writing to main memory. The cache must be implemented in such a way that if the cache holds modified data (i.e. data that is different from that in main memory), a transfer from memory to the I/O device gets the data from the cache. Similarly, a transfer from the I/O device to memory must either update or invalidate the data in the cache if it is present.

VIRTUAL AND REAL ADDRESSING

In most caches, as with our typical cache described above, the address tags in the cache contain real addresses. In a *virtual address cache*, the tags contain virtual addresses. The advantage to a virtual address cache is that access can be faster, since there is no delay for translation. The difficulty is that there may be multiple virtual addresses ("synonyms") that map to the same real address. Unless care is taken, inconsistencies can result from the presence of synonyms in virtual address caches.

REPLACEMENT ALGORITHM

When a line is brought into the cache, it is normally necessary to replace a line that is already there. Usually, some approximation to least-recently-used (LRU) is employed. Note that the replacement must always be of a line in the same set (in a set associative cache) because the mapping is constrained.

TLB Design

The TLB is itself a specialized cache; it caches virtual to real address translations. It can be optimized in terms of its size (number of entries), organization (set associative, fully associative, etc.), replacement algorithm, hash algorithm, and if and how it uses a process identifier. The TLB translates virtual to real addresses, and when the active process changes, the VA → RA mapping changes. To avoid mistranslation after a process switch, either the entries in the TLB must be tagged with a process identifier or the TLB must be purged.

Pipelining, Arbitration

Depending on the timing and design of the CPU, a cache access may take multiple CPU cycles. In that case, it may be useful to pipeline (q.v.) the CPU, so that multiple accesses may be in progress at the same time.

There may also be multiple functional units (e.g. instruction unit, execution unit(s), I/O controller, main memory, cache consistency controller) requesting cache access at the same time. It is necessary to arbitrate among these simultaneous requests so as to produce correct and deadlock-free operation and to maximize performance.

In modern CPUs, several instructions can often be executed at the same time. In that case, the cache must be able to accommodate several accesses at the same time. There are a number of circuit and logic design techniques that may be used to accomplish this.

Implementation Tricks

Many research articles and patents address how to speed up the access time or decrease the miss ratio in a cache memory. Among the more interesting ideas are the victim cache, and the guessing of matches in set-associative caches. The purpose of the "victim cache," when using a direct mapped or set-associative cache, is to keep some of the recently replaced lines in a special buffer (the victim cache), since there is a fairly high probability that they will be referenced again soon. This allows the cache to have a miss ratio close to that of a fully associative cache while still having the faster access time of a direct mapped or set associative cache.

In each set, there is a most recently used (MRU) line, and the probability that a reference to that set is to the MRU line is quite high. Therefore, the cache can guess that the reference is to the MRU line and read it out immediately. If the guess is wrong, an additional delay is incurred while the correct data is forwarded.

Other Types of Cache

Caches can be used in numerous ways in computer systems. A common type of cache is the *disk cache*. The disk cache holds portions of the material on the disk in some sort of faster storage, usually semiconductor storage. The disk cache can be located within the disk enclosure, in which case it is managed by the (single) disk controller in a file server or multidisk controller, or the CPU can do the disk caching itself by using a portion of main memory for that purpose. Disk caches are reasonably effective, with typical read hit ratios in the range of 70–90%. Issues in disk cache design are similar to those for CPU caches; the designer must consider the cache size, the cache location (CPU, server, disk controller), the write policy (write-through, copy-back), replacement algorithm, fetch algorithm, and block size. A particularly important consideration in disk cache design is the problem of reliability in the case of system failure or power loss. In general, an operating system assumes that data written to disk is completely safe and immune to system failure. If data "written" to disk is actually in the disk cache, this assumption is violated, with potentially severe consequences for system integrity. Either write-through or battery backup is typically used for disk caches in systems that are expected to be highly reliable.

Database systems almost always do some amount of caching; typically, they maintain a region in main memory which is used to hold recently referenced blocks of data. This is similar in concept and operation to disk caching.

Caching is used within operating systems to avoid lengthy and redundant computations. For example, the directory structure is used to translate file names to file descriptors, and frequently the same name is translated repeatedly. By caching recently performed translations, use of the directory structure can be avoided.

Caching is used in various ways in accessing the World Wide Web (q.v.). A Web browser caches recently used pages locally at the user's computer. Typically, a Web server will cache recently referenced pages, so that it isn't necessary to retrieve popular pages from disk each time they are referenced. Sometimes, copies of Web pages are cached in various servers scattered around the Web in order to avoid bottlenecks at the location from which they originate.

Note that before the term "cache" became widespread to refer to the types of functions and devices described here, the term "buffer" was often used. A *buffer* (q.v.), of course, is generally any temporary storage device, and the use of that term to refer to what we now call a cache has become uncommon. Conversely, however, the term "cache" is sometimes used to refer to types of buffers that are rather different than the caches described above. Sometimes it may be necessary to determine from the context what sort of cache or buffer is actually referred to.

Conclusions

Memory access time is frequently the critical factor in modern CPU performance and CPU cache memories are the most effective way to improve access time. Cache memories and caching are also useful and are widely used in a variety of other applications. Despite the apparent simplicity of the concept of caching, however, the variety of possible cache designs and the subtlety of some of the issues make cache design a difficult and tricky problem, as may be evident from the number of papers and patents on the topic.

Further Reading

A very good introduction to computer architecture is Hennessy and Patterson (1990); a tutorial discussion of caches and memory hierarchies may be found there. The standard and comprehensive reference for cache memories is Smith (1982), which considers the issues reviewed here (and others) in considerable detail. Smith (1987) looks at the issue of line size, and also provides "design target miss ratios," which are typical miss ratios to be expected from typical workloads. Lilja (1993) provides a thorough survey of the cache consistency issue. Research on cache memories is typically done using *trace-driven simulation*, which is surveyed in Uhlig and Mudge (1997). Peir *et al.* (1999) provide a survey of implementation tricks for CPU cache memories. Smith (1985) considers disk caches.

Bibliography

1982. Smith, A. J. "Cache Memories," *ACM Computing Surveys*, **14**, 3, 473–530.
1985. Smith, A. J. "Disk Cache—Miss Ratio Analysis and Design Considerations," *ACM Transactions on Computer Systems*, **3**, 3, 161–203.
1987. Smith, A. J. "Line (Block) Size Selection in CPU Cache Memories," *IEEE Transactions on Computers*, **C-36**, 9, 1063–1075.
1990. Hennessy, J. L., and Patterson, D. A. *Computer Architecture: A Quantitative Approach*. San Francisco: Morgan-Kaufmann.
1993. Lilja, D. "Cache Coherence in Large-scale Shared Memory Multiprocessors: Issues and Comparisons," *ACM Computing Surveys*, **25**, 3, 303–338.
1997. Uhlig, R. A., and Mudge, T. N. "Trace-driven Memory Simulation: A Survey," *ACM Computing Surveys*, **29**, 2, 128–170.
1999. Peir, J.-K., Hsu, W., and Smith, A. J. "Implementation Issues in Modern Cache Memories," *IEEE Trans. on Computers*, 48, 2, 100–110.

Alan Jay Smith

CAD/CAM

See COMPUTER-AIDED DESIGN/COMPUTER-AIDED MANUFACTURING.

CAI

See COMPUTER-ASSISTED LEARNING AND TEACHING.

CALCULATING MACHINES

For articles on related subjects *see* BURROUGHS, WILLIAM S.; CALCULATORS, ELECTRONIC AND PROGRAMMABLE; LEIBNIZ, GOTTFRIED WILHELM; NAPIER, JOHN; and PASCAL, BLAISE.

The art of mechanical calculation could be said to date back to whenever people first used pebbles or grains of corn to keep track of their belongings. However, the subject is usually thought of as starting when mechanical calculators were invented. A *mechanical calculator* is a device that has three properties: a mechanism that will act as a register to store a number; a mechanism to add a fixed amount to the number stored in that register; and an addition mechanism having the ability to deal automatically with any carry, from one digit to the next, that is generated during the addition process.

The first known device of this kind (Fig. 1a) was produced by the German scholar Wilhelm Schickard (1592–1635) in 1623 as a response to a request for calculating help from the astronomer Johann Kepler. Unfortunately, the machine was destroyed in a fire before Kepler ever saw it, but descriptions and drawings have been found in their correspondence that are sufficiently detailed to enable reconstructions. The upper portion of the machine contains a multiplication table in the form of cylindrical Napier's bones with slides that allow one row at a time to be seen. The lower part contains a very simple register,

Figure 1a. Schickard's calculator.

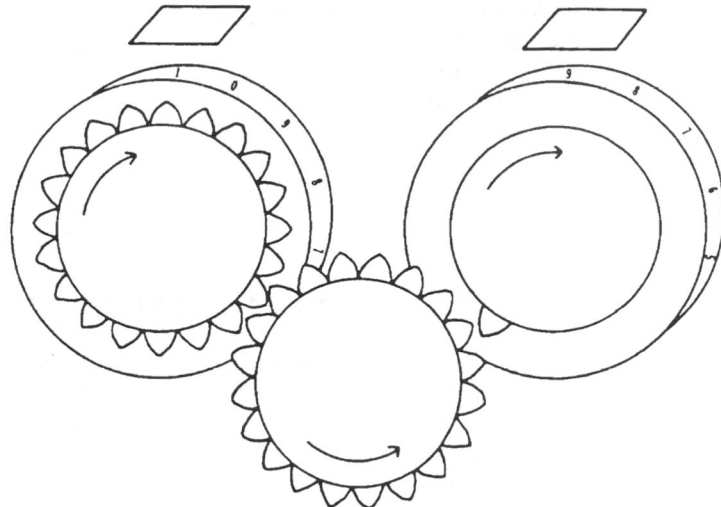

Figure 1b. The Schickard carry mechanism.

much like an automobile odometer, each digit of which contains a single tooth which, when it rotates from 9 to 0, will cause the next wheel on the left to rotate one digit position.

There are two major problems with this "single-tooth" carry mechanism (Fig. 1b). The first is that the addition $99,999 + 1$ will result in a carry being propagated right through the register. This means that considerable force must be used in turning the units digit wheel—enough force to break gears that are not manufactured out of modern high-strength materials. The second problem is more subtle. As can be seen in the diagram, the process of carrying a one to the next digit position is done by the single-tooth gear entering the teeth of the intermediate gear, rotating it 36 degrees (1/10 of a revolution), and exiting from the intermediate gear teeth, all while rotating only 36 degrees itself. This problem led to some very interesting gear designs.

The next major advance in mechanical calculation came 19 years later when Blaise Pascal (*q.v.*), the famous French mathematician and philosopher, invented an adding machine with a gravity-assisted carry mechanism (Fig. 2a). The two difficulties with the single-tooth carry were overcome in Pascaline, as he called his machine, by the simple expedient of having a weight lift up as the digits of the register rotate (Fig. 2b). When a carry was necessary, the weight would fall and "kick" the adjacent digit of the register over one position. By having each digit-carry mechanism driven by gravity, the problem of having to use excess force on the right-hand digit of the register to propagate a carry several digit places was eliminated. The only force needed was to turn the rightmost wheel; the carry weight would drop and that force would turn the wheel next to it, etc. Pascal was then faced with the problem of creating an

"over-rotation preventer" to stop the left digit from rotating too far when a "carry-kick" was given by a digit on the right. Pascal experimented for several years with different versions of his machine, even attempting to interest people in purchasing them for help with their accounting chores. His commercial ventures were unsuccessful, but it did result in about 60 of the machines surviving to modern times.

The story now switches back to Germany and Gottfried Wilhelm Leibniz (*q.v.*). During one of his many trips to France as a diplomat, he saw a copy of the Pascal machine and became intrigued with the concept. When he attempted to add extra gearing on top in order to form a machine with which he could multiply, he discovered that the internal mechanism was not capable of simultaneous action on all digits at once. For the next 20 years he toyed with different ideas, but even after he had envisioned what is today called the *Leibniz stepped-drum principle*, he was unable to construct his machine until he encountered

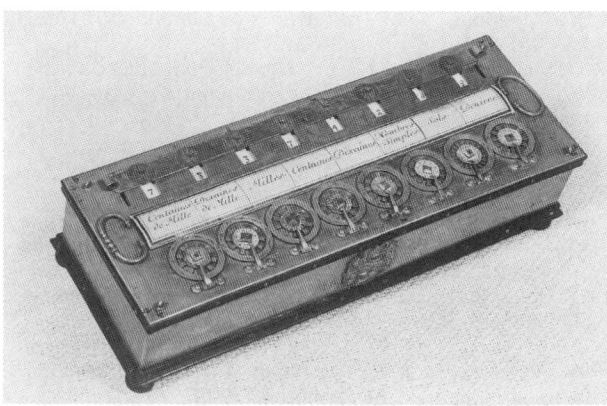

Figure 2a. Pascal's calculating machine (photograph courtesy of IBM Archives).

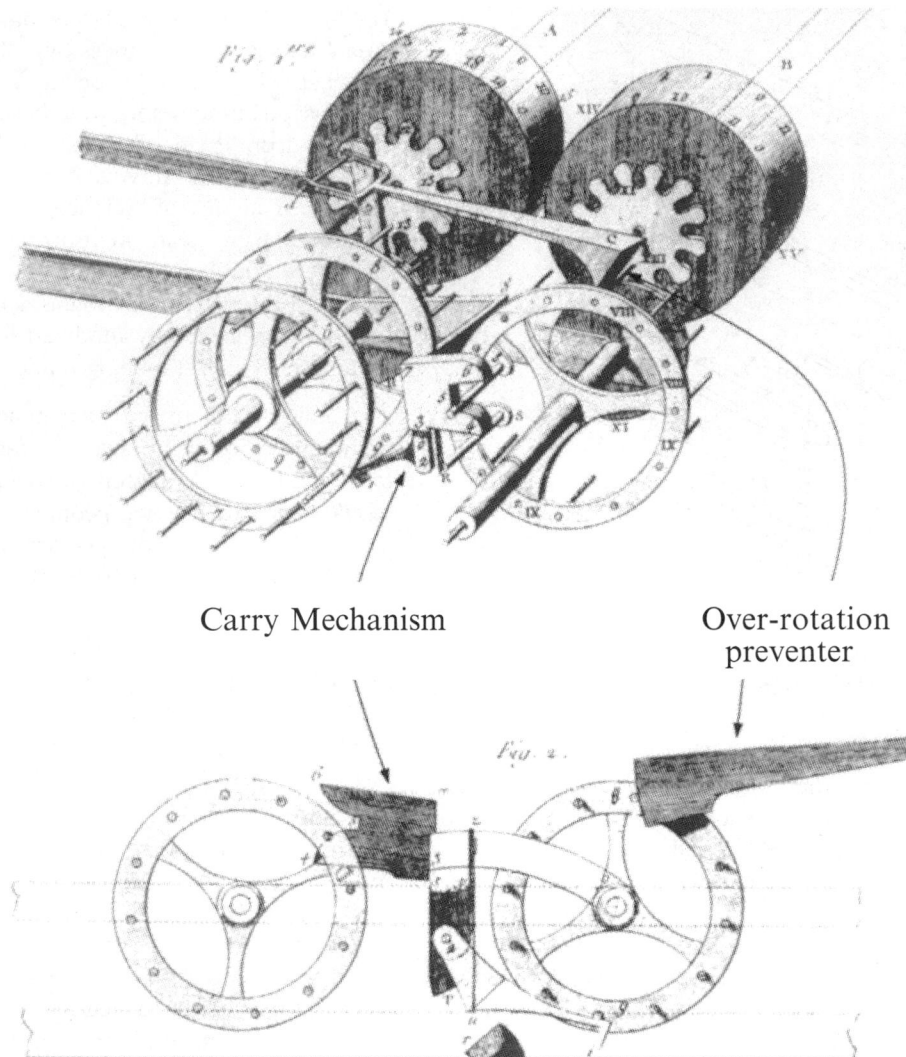

Carry Mechanism   Over-rotation
                              preventer

Figure 2b. Single-tooth carry mechanism.

a French clockmaker named Olivier who had the necessary skills. The Leibniz machine, which was to be the basic pattern for many mechanical calculating machines for the next 300 years, was constructed during the summer of 1674.

Leibniz's inventive genius led him to create a machine in which a number could be set up on an input mechanism and, once set, could be added to the result register by simply turning a crank. Thus, to multiply a number such as 375 by 15, it was only necessary to put 375 on the setup mechanism and turn the crank 15 times. Leibniz saw that the more efficient way would be to have the setup mechanism movable along the gearing that formed the result register—this allowed one to set 375 on the setup, turn the crank five times (adding $375 \times 5 = 1,875$ to the result register), shift the input mechanism one place to the left (effectively making the setup take on the value of 3,750), and then turn the crank once (adding 3,750 to the result register). The movable setup section is clearly visible in the picture of the Leibniz machine (Fig. 3).

The concept of how the machine functioned can be seen by noting the diagram (Fig. 4) showing a single digit of the machine (without any of the mechanical apparatus that controlled the carry operation). The result wheel, shown at the end of the square shaft, showed the current digit being stored. To add a value, say 8, to this wheel, it was necessary to rotate the

Figure 3. The Leibniz calculating machine (photograph courtesy of IBM Archives).

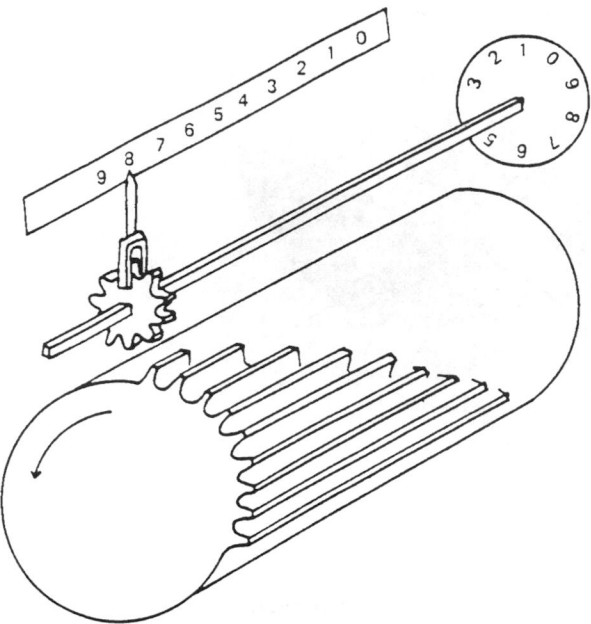

Figure 4. A drawing of Leibniz's stepped-drum mechanism.

square shaft eight positions. That could be accomplished by moving the small gear up or down the square shaft until it was in such a position that, when the large drum was rotated one full revolution, eight of its long teeth would interact with the gear on the square shaft to move the result wheel eight positions around. Once the mechanism had been set up to hold a number (375 being done by having the small gear on the units digit set to the 5 position, the tens gear set to the 7, and the hundreds to the 3), a single turn of the crank would cause all the large stepped-drum gears to rotate through a full revolution and add 375 to the result wheels.

Needless to say, the entire mechanism was more complex than that shown here, the carry mechanism being the most complicated portion. Even then, it sometimes required the operator to stop and help the machine if a carry of more than two decimal places was needed. Nonetheless, this stepped-drum concept was central to most of the attempts at constructing calculating machines for the next 200 years.

Many others made calculating machines of one form or another (some fully functional, others only marginally so), but none was a commercial success. Occasional machines were actually sold by their manufacturers, but they were usually not used for anything except display purposes to show that their owners could afford the latest in scientific toys. The exception to this was the machine made by Charles Xavier Thomas (1785–1870), sometimes known as Thomas de Colmar, a French insurance executive. He was familiar enough with the manufacturing processes available around

1820 to design a workable mechanical calculator and create a successful business by selling them to people who actually wanted to perform computations. The Thomas Arithmometer was based on the Leibniz stepped-drum principle, but had a fully working carry mechanism. It was first demonstrated to the French Academy of Science in 1820, and several thousand were sold in Europe, and occasionally elsewhere, until about 1900. This same technology was used by many other manufacturers and could be found, often in greatly modified form, in mechanical adding machines still being made in the 1970s.

The major problem with any machine based on the Leibniz stepped drum was the fact that it was both large and heavy. A machine with a many-digit capacity would often require two people to move it from place to place. The Leibniz drum essentially provided a gear with a variable number (0–9) of teeth, but at the cost of size and weight. A number of attempts at producing a true variable-toothed gear that would literally change the number of teeth protruding from its surface were unsuccessful until the solution was found, essentially simultaneously, by Willgodt T. Odhner (1845–1905), a Swede working in Russia, and Frank S. Baldwin (1830–1925), an American, in about the year 1874.

As can be seen in the illustration (Fig. 5), the movement of the lever would cause the circular cam to force different numbers of pins through the edge surface of the gear, the pins acting as gear teeth when the whole mechanism was rotated about the central axis. Odhner first produced his "pin wheel" calculator in 1874 at a factory he had set up in St. Petersburg. The concept quickly spread and soon the famous Brunsviga firm was producing them in Germany, the

Figure 5. An illustration of the variable-toothed gear.

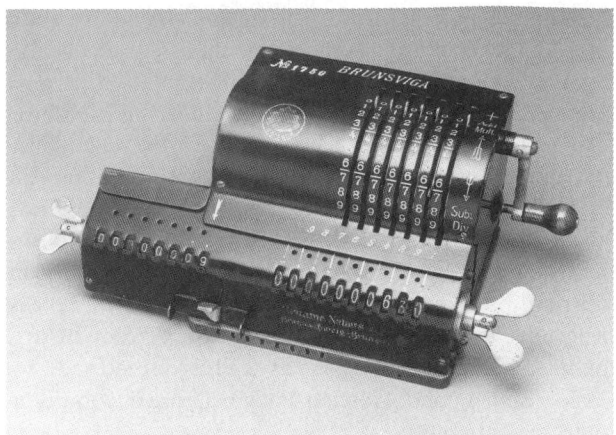

Figure 6. A Brunsviga Calculator (courtesy of Smithsonian Institution).

Baldwin calculators were being made in America, and the original Odhner firm was continuing to produce them in Russia. By 1912 the Brunsviga firm alone had produced over 20,000 machines (Fig. 6) and the total worldwide production was likely many times that number.

The only significant advance on the technology of the variable-toothed gear was the key-driven adding machine. It had long been recognized that the act of moving a setting lever actually contained enough energy to perform the addition if a suitable mechanical mechanism could be invented. Dorr E. Felt (1862–1930), an American, produced the first workable system in 1886, which he named the Comptometer (Fig. 7). By combining the action of entering a number with the action of actually adding it to a mechanical register, the process of performing simple addition was speeded up by several orders of magnitude. This allowed the Comptometer—and similar machines made by Burroughs and others—to become practical tools for the business office.

Figure 7. An early Comptometer (courtesy of Smithsonian Institution).

Figure 8. The Curta (courtesy of Smithsonian Institution).

There were, of course, many improvements to these very basic devices over the years. The addition of a printing mechanism allowed users to keep track of their computations. The replacement of human motive power by electric motors allowed both faster computation and less fatigue for the operator. The improvements in engineering technology shrunk the size and weight of the machines to the point where the Curta calculator (Fig. 8), ironically enough based on the Leibniz stepped drum, could not only be carried in pockets, but was actually used by holding it in one hand. Designed by Curt Herzstark (1902–1988) in 1943 while imprisoned in Buchenwald, over 14,000 Curta calculators were sold from 1948 to 1972. It will undoubtedly remain the smallest mechanical calculator ever built. However the speed, flexibility, and ultralight weight of electronic calculators began to replace the mechanical ones in the modern era. By the early 1970s, even the Curta had ceased production.

In the middle years of the twentieth century, electromechanical desktop calculating machines manufactured by Brunsviga, Facit, Friden, Marchant, and Monroe, among others, were widely used but, with the advent of the handheld electronic calculator, they disappeared.

Bibliography

1914. Horsburgh, E. M. *Handbook of the Napier Tercentenary Celebration on Modern Instruments and Methods of Calculation.* Edinburgh: The Royal Society of Edinburgh (reprinted by MIT Press and Tomash Publishers, 1982).

1921. Turck, J. V. A. *Origin of Modern Calculating Machines.* Chicago: The Western Society of Engineers.

1989. Aspray, W. (ed.) *Computing Before Computers.* Ames, IA: The Iowa State University Press.

Michael R. Williams

CALCULATORS, ELECTRONIC AND PROGRAMMABLE

For articles on related subjects *see* CALCULATING MACHINES; DIGITAL COMPUTERS, HISTORY OF; and PORTABLE COMPUTERS.

It is believed that the first mechanical calculating device was the abacus. There is evidence that the abacus was invented prior to 500 BC. Visitors to the Far East will know that the abacus is still a common form of desk calculator and is used with great dexterity and speed.

Modern calculators are descendants of a digital arithmetic machine devised by Blaise Pascal (*q.v.*) in 1642. In 1671, Gottfried Leibniz (*q.v.*) designed a calculating machine that could add and multiply, with multiplication being performed by repeated addition. During the late 19th century and early 20th century, inventors produced calculators that were progressively smaller and less and less laborious to use.

Prior to the 1950s, desktop calculators were either key driven or used a rotating drum to enter sums punched into a keyboard. Eventually, this drum was spun by an electric motor. The invention of the transistor in 1948 and the integrated circuit in 1964 were the two events that formed the basis for the electronic calculator revolution. Miniature solid state electronics enabled calculators to progress past the basic four arithmetic functions to the point where they are capable of performing almost any function that can be expressed as a programmable sequence or a mathematical formula.

By 1974, calculators using modern electronic technology cost less than $50 and could outperform mechanical calculators that had once sold for up to $1500. Today, some handheld calculators can be purchased for less than $5; and $100 will buy an extremely sophisticated calculator.

Some electronic calculators are intended for desk use, but since 1970 numerous hand models have been available, some as small as a credit card. At the same time, solar or other long-life batteries brought about calculators that can operate for thousands of hours without energy source replacements.

Nearly all calculators have programmed microinstructions; their circuitry can do any of several different things depending on coded commands stored in the system. Some electronic calculators are programmed externally. In this case, a sequence of operations is entered into the calculator, much as occurs during the programming of a computer.

As electronic calculators increase in capabilities, the gap closes between the capabilities of a computer and the capabilities of an electronic calculator. The pro-

grammable calculator was first introduced in 1974 by Hewlett-Packard. Today, calculators such as the Texas Instruments TI-92, shown in Fig. 1, can translate calculus and other types of engineering problems into pictures. Enter an equation and the calculator can draw the result, complete with annotations, on its 5×9 cm liquid crystal display. The calculator has 130K of RAM and can interface with a Windows or Macintosh computer both to save and recall information from the computer as well as to access programs through the Internet. Other Texas Instruments graphing calculators, as well as some made by Casio, Sharp, and Hewlett-Packard, have computer interface capability.

Texas instruments now has *flash technology* (reprogrammable read-only memory—*q.v.*), so their models 83 and 92 calculators can be upgraded. Casio calculators use three colors in their graphing mode and the Sharp EL9600c has some unique teaching features such as Slide Show and EZ modes to facilitate teaching and learning. All three of these companies' advanced calculators are capable of using adapters to collect data such as motion, temperature, and voltage from actual experiments.

Electronic calculators are designed to perform their functions using either algebraic notation or RPN—Reverse Polish Notation (*see* POLISH NOTATION). Algebraic notation permits entry of calculations as normally written (e.g. ②⊞③) with the arithmetic function between the two numbers—infix notation. With RPN, the operator is placed after the two numbers, (②③⊞), and therefore the operator is input *after* both numbers have been entered (postfix notation). The former requires parenthesizing for all but the simplest calculations, whereas RPN allows any sequence of calculations to be entered without parentheses. It is unfamiliar to most people, however, and practice is needed before it can be used easily. Other calculators have been programmed so that the "order of operations" rules are

Figure 1. The TI-92 Plus scientific calculator (courtesy of Texas Instruments).

followed, thereby eliminating much of the need for entering parentheses (*see* OPERATOR PRECEDENCE).

Calculators typically compute nonzero numbers in a range from 10^{-99} to 10^{99} and print from 8 to 12 digits in the display. If the answer is larger than the display, many calculators will automatically express the answer in scientific notation. A typical advanced nonprogrammable electronic calculator would normally include the following scientific functions: x^2, $\sqrt{x}$, $1/x$, y^x, $x\text{--}y$ interchange, normal and inverse trigonometric functions, logarithms to the bases 10 and e, e^x, 10^x, $x!$, and degree to radian conversions. Statistical functions often included are summation, mean, and standard deviation. Other common calculator capabilities are the ability to store a number in memory, to add to memory, to multiply or divide a number saved in memory, and to exchange the display with memory.

Hand-held technology, especially graphing calculators, is becoming a necessity in the high schools and colleges in the USA. Mathematics and science teachers are adapting their curricula to use the calculators. The Scholastic Aptitude Test (SAT) administered by the Educational Testing Service now permits the use of graphing calculators. This test is used by many colleges and universities in the USA as part of their entrance requirements. The New York State Regents Exam in mathematics (Test B), given after three years of high school mathematics, is to require the use of a graphing calculator after June 2001. Texas Instruments, Sharp, and Casio provide extensive support through conferences, workshops, and educational materials to aid teachers. Addison-Wesley and Holt, Reinhart, Winston are two US publishers who are publishing textbooks that integrate the use of the graphing calculator.

Texas Instruments has produced the TI-73 graphing calculator and Casio the fx7400 for middle school mathematics applications. The TI-73 has 25K RAM and graph functions, as well as support for statistical calculations, such as mean, standard deviation, and linear and quadratic regressions, among others. It has list capabilities and is able to graph statistical data in pie chart, histogram, pictorial and line form. It is programmable and is still able to work with fractions and trigonometric functions. These calculators are available for under $80.

Special-purpose calculators have been designed for many professions and hobbies, including finance, statistics, business, mathematics, science, economics, accounting, real estate, sports, and time management. An inexpensive calculator developed by Sharp Electronics, the EL-509RH (Fig. 2), is able to add, subtract, multiply, divide, and reduce fractions along with a multiline playback and the ability to calculate two-variable statistics.

Americans have been purchasing in excess of four million calculators per year for nearly two decades. Texas Instruments, Casio, Sharp, and Hewlett-Packard are the sales leaders.

Jerald L. Mikesell, revised by Charles G. Ames

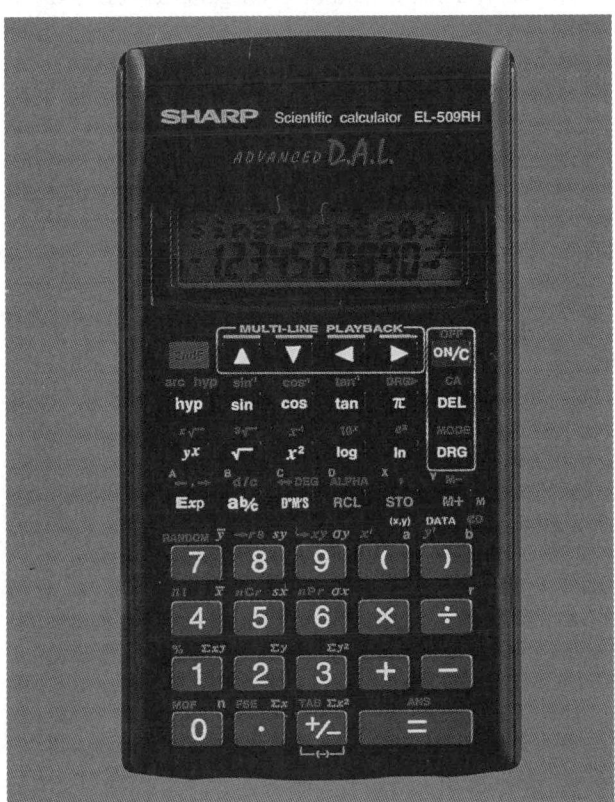

Figure 2. The Sharp EL-509RH calculator (courtesy of Sharp Electronics).

CALLING SEQUENCE

For articles on related subjects *see* ACTIVATION RECORD, PARAMETER PASSING; and SUBPROGRAM.

A *calling sequence* is the precise sequence of one or more commands or statements needed to invoke a subordinate procedure. In a high-level language like Pascal, procedures are called by stating their name, followed by a parenthesized list of the actual parameters that the procedure needs to do its work. An example is

```
search(haystack,150,'needle',locations)
```

which invokes a procedure that searches an array of 150 character strings called *haystack* and places in an array called *locations* the indices (subscripts) of all *haystack* locations that contain *'needle'*.

The single-statement calling sequence just cited is properly formed only if it contains exactly the right number of parameters expected by the called procedure, the parameters are specified in the expected order, and the data type of each parameter (integer, real, string, etc.) is what is expected.

The mechanism used for parameter passing (*q.v.*) may limit the form of the expression used to cite actual parameters. For example, if the second parameter used with procedure `search` is to be an integer passed by value, then the actual parameter used in this position could be an expression such as $n - j + 2$, just as well as a particular number like 150. But if the first and last parameters are passed by reference (VAR parameters in the vocabulary of Pascal), the actual parameters used in those positions must be variable names, as they are in the example given. (When a parameter is passed "by reference," the address where it may be found is transmitted rather than the value stored at that address.)

The term *calling sequence* predates the use of high-level languages. In an assembly language, such as is used with the Digital Equipment Corporation VAX computer, the calling sequence for a machine-language version of `search` would be

```
PUSHAL locations  ;Push the address of
                  ; symbol "locations"
PUSHAL item       ;Push the address of
                  ; the 1st byte of
                  ; string sought
PUSHL #150        ;Push the value 150
PUSHAL haystack   ;Push the address of
                  ; symbol "haystack"
CALLS #4,search   ;Call search with 4
                  ; parameters
```

Note that, with respect to the one-statement Pascal calling sequence, parameters are pushed in right-to-left order so that the first parameter, the address of *haystack*, ends up at the top of the run-time stack. Each push command ends with "L" because, on the VAX, both addresses and the most commonly used form of integer occupy longwords (32 bits). The # symbol is the VAX way of specifying an immediate value. In accord with the assumptions made, only the 150 is passed by value (through use of PUSHL). The addresses of the other three parameters, not their values, are stacked through use of PUSHAL (the "A" indicating "address of") in accord with the procedure's expectation that these parameters are being passed by reference.

The right-to-left order in this example characterizes the VAX Pascal compiler, but a compiler for a different system might use a different order, depending on the architectural details of that system. The order in which procedure parameters are evaluated and placed on the stack or in registers is generally not specified by the language itself.

Edwin D. Reilly

CAPABILITY-BASED ADDRESSING

For articles on related subjects *see* ADDRESSING; COMPUTER ARCHITECTURE; OPERATING SYSTEMS; REGISTER; and VIRTUAL MEMORY.

An operating system must manage access rights, which protect the data of one process from interference by other processes, while also permitting appropriate sharing of data. *Capability-based addressing* achieves this by using protected pointers (*q.v.*), known as *capabilities*, to map from the operand field of an instruction to an operand in memory. A capability contains the *unique identifier* of an object, together with a set of *access rights* that it possesses to that object (Fig. 1). For example, a capability for an array might contain the array's unique identifier, and a single access right allowing the holder of the capability to read (but not write) the array. Or a capability might identify an employee record within a personnel system, and grant the right to inspect the employee's job title, department, and work location, but not the employee's salary.

Capability-based addressing can achieve two major advantages: protection of information, and context independence. Capability systems provide stronger protection than other addressing schemes, because a process can address only objects for which it possesses a capability. Thus it cannot even generate an address for an object it is not allowed to access. Other addressing schemes allow a process to generate an arbitrary address, and then rely on the system to disallow access if the process lacks authority to access the object at that address. Thus failures in capability addressing tend to prevent a process from accessing an object, while failures in other addressing schemes may allow a process to access information illegally.

Capability systems provide context-independent addressing. Because it contains an identifier that is *unique systemwide*, the same capability used by any process will access the same object. This permits processes to share objects just by sharing capabilities for these objects. Contrast this with an "ordinary" (context dependent) virtual memory system where each process has its own virtual address space; address 10000 within one process is the address of a completely different datum than address 10000 within another process. Thus, in a noncapability system, it

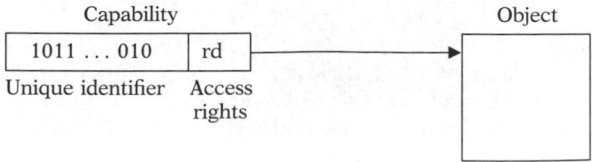

Figure 1. A capability that designates read (rd) access.

is often impossible for a process to share part of its virtual address space with another process, and even when it is possible, it is usually not very flexible (e.g. two processes may be able to share the base of their stacks, or all of their nonstack memory, but they cannot share arbitrary data structures within their address space).

Although capability-based addressing is conceptually very simple, implementing it efficiently is a difficult engineering problem. A process must not be allowed to modify a capability, as this would again permit it to access arbitrary regions of memory. Different systems have used four different means of protecting capabilities:

- Tagging each word of memory with a bit or bits that indicate whether the word contains a capability or an ordinary data item. User processes can read or write ordinary data items, but cannot modify capabilities. (Some systems have used tags for data typing as well, allowing the same machine instruction to operate on several types of data, e.g. integer, floating-point). This is known as *tagged memory* (*see* INSTRUCTION SET).

- Restricting them to special segments, which a process could use for addressing, but in which it could not write. This is known as *partitioned memory* (Fig. 2).

- Restricting them to one end of every segment. For example, the zero offset within a segment might be somewhere in the middle of the segment. Capabilities would be found at negative offsets, while ordinary data would have positive offsets. This approach is sometimes called *fenced segments* (Fig. 3).

- *Encrypting capabilities*, so that any modification by a process would almost surely result in an invalid capability. In this approach, when a capability is created by the kernel (*q.v.*), it is transformed by an algorithm that maps it to a much longer encrypted version.

Protecting capabilities is not the only hurdle in implementing capability addressing. It is also necessary to design an efficient way of mapping from an

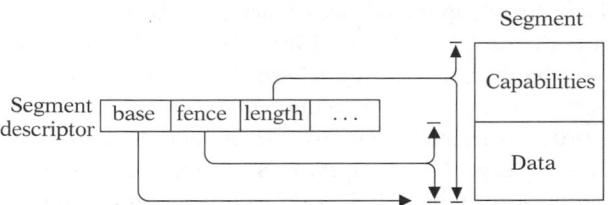

Figure 3. Fenced segment memory.

instruction operand (*q.v.*) to a capability and then to the memory containing the operand. It is usually done like this (Fig. 4):

- An operand in an instruction contains a capability-register number and possibly an offset.

- The processor contains a number of capability registers, each of which holds one capability.

- When a capability register is loaded (from an entry in a *capability list*), the system consults a mapping table, which is similar to a segment table. It looks up the unique identifier in the mapping table, and finds its base address and length. The base and length are loaded into an extension of the capability register.

- Thus, when an instruction refers to a capability register, it finds the address of the object, and can thus complete the reference.

For flexibility of switching from one protection domain to another (e.g. when a system call is performed), a process usually has several capability lists rather than one. Also, if objects are small, the mapping table tends to become large and difficult to manage. However, if these hurdles can be overcome, capabilities can provide very flexible protection. For example, a process could call a library routine, passing it a capability for the object on which it is to operate. The library routine would not have the ability to access anything in the caller's address space but the object passed as a parameter. A system that supports this kind of protection can often provide operating system services *within the user process*, and consequently avoid the need to spawn or activate a separate process to provide the service.

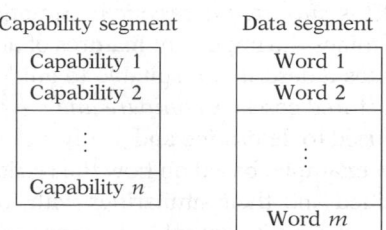

Figure 2. Partitioned memory.

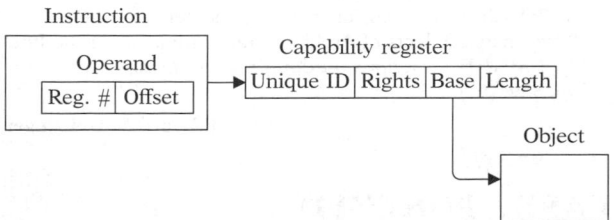

Figure 4. Finding an object that is specified in an instruction.

The term "capability" was coined by Earl Van Horn (Dennis and Van Horn, 1966), but the history goes back further, to the original Rice University computer, designed in 1958. This machine introduced "codewords" to designate regions of main memory accessible to a process. These codewords became "descriptors" in the Burroughs B5000 (1961); capabilities are merely a generalization of this notion. Capabilities were first implemented in the Chicago Magic Number Computer, built at the University of Chicago in the late 1960s. Several research systems followed at universities in the USA and Britain. Notable among these were the CAP project (Wilkes and Needham, 1979) at Cambridge University and the Hydra (Wulf *et al.*, 1981) and STAROS systems at Carnegie Mellon University. The first commercial capability system was the Plessey System 250, which was widely used in telecommunications in the UK in the 1970s. The IBM System 38 (later the AS/400), introduced in 1978, was the first commercial system to employ capabilities in a single large 64-bit virtual address space that was shared by all processes. In the early 1980s, Intel embarked on a very ambitious project to support capabilities and multiprocessing in silicon. The resulting Intel 432 was a very general but very inefficient architecture (Colwell *et al.*, 1988) which sold probably fewer than a hundred units before it was discontinued.

Research activity in capability-based addressing has waned considerably in the past 15 years. Some interest remains from the standpoint of security, and from the standpoint of supporting persistent objects and object-oriented databases. Many of the persistent architectures can be traced back to the MONADS project, which began in 1976 at Monash University in Australia. It is in these two areas—security and persistence—that capabilities have made their greatest contribution.

Bibliography

1966. Dennis, J. B., and Van Horn, E. C. "Programming Semantics for Multiprogrammed Computations," *Comm. of the ACM*, **9**, 3, 143–155.
1979. Wilkes, M. V., and Needham, R. M. *The Cambridge CAP Computer and its Operating System.* New York: North-Holland.
1981. Wulf, W. A., Levin, R., and Harbison, S. P. *HYDRA/C.mmp: An Experimental Computer System.* New York: McGraw-Hill.
1984. Levy, H. M. *Capability-Based Computer Systems.* Bedford, MA: Digital Press.
1988. Colwell, R. P., Gehringer, E. F., and Jensen, E. D. "Performance Effects of Architectural Complexity in the Intel 432," *ACM Transactions on Computer Systems*, **6**, 3, 296–339.

Edward F. Gehringer

CARD, PUNCHED

See PUNCHED CARD; and PUNCHED CARD MACHINERY.

CASE-BASED REASONING

For articles on related subjects *see* ARTIFICIAL INTELLIGENCE; COGNITIVE SCIENCE; EXPERT SYSTEMS; and MACHINE LEARNING.

Case-based reasoning (CBR) is an artificial intelligence paradigm for reasoning and learning. Case-based reasoning solves new problems by retrieving stored records of prior problem-solving episodes (*cases*) and adapting their solutions to fit new circumstances. Each processing episode provides a new case that is stored for future reuse, making learning a natural side-effect of the reasoning process. Case-based reasoning is also studied within cognitive science as a model of human reasoning: studies show that people use recollections of prior problems to guide their reasoning in a wide range of tasks, such as programming, mathematical problem solving, diagnosis, decision making, and design.

One motivation for using case-based reasoning instead of traditional rule-based problem-solving is to increase efficiency by reusing prior reasoning rather than generating solutions from scratch (for example, an architectural design system can save effort by remembering and revising similar previous designs). Other motivations include facilitating reasoning and knowledge acquisition for domains that are imperfectly understood or hard to codify (it is easier to represent information in the form of an ungeneralized case than to distill rules about how each aspect contributes to the whole); the ability to deploy CBR systems with a small set of "seed cases" that are augmented by learning, rather than having to endow the systems with complete sets of rules; the ability to use the pre-existing libraries of cases that are routinely maintained for some tasks; and the ability of CBR systems to explain their conclusions to a user by pointing to real episodes in which similar conclusions applied, rather than relying on generalized rules that the user may not understand or accept.

The CBR process

Case-based reasoning can be used for two purposes, problem-solving and interpretation. Interpretive CBR forms judgments or classifications based on prior cases (e.g. to interpret the law when making legal arguments, or to classify an illness). The first step of interpretive CBR is *situation assessment*. Situation assessment determines the important features of an example and generates a description suitable to guide *retrieval* of relevant stored cases. A *compare and contrast* process is then used to determine and justify a classification for the new example, based on how the retrieved cases were classified and their similarities with, and differences from, the new example. A record of the new reasoning episode, along with any feedback on whether the classification was correct, is saved as a new case for future use. In problem-solving CBR, situation assessment and retrieval of cases from similar problems is followed by *case adaptation* to revise the previous solutions to fit new needs. The resulting solution and feedback on its effectiveness are saved as a new case for future use. Successes are used as the starting point for future reasoning in similar situations; failures are used to warn about potential pitfalls to avoid.

Issues

Major issues in case-based reasoning include knowledge access—memory organization and retrieval—similarity assessment, and case adaptation. A fundamental problem is the *indexing problem* of assuring that stored cases are accessed when appropriate. Because the indices used to organize cases in memory may not correspond to the available features of an input situation, CBR systems often redescribe input cases in order to retrieve relevant cases despite dissimilar appearances. Once cases are retrieved, similarity assessment determines relevant differences to be repaired by case adaptation. Key principles have been established for indexing and retrieval; deepening understanding of case adaptation is a current challenge.

Uses of CBR

Case-based reasoning systems have been developed to perform tasks such as planning, diagnosis, interpretation during legal reasoning, story understanding, creative explanation, and design. They have also been used in combination with traditional expert systems. In combined systems, initial rule-based problem-solving is used to build up a case library, while CBR provides more efficient problem-solving when relevant prior cases are available.

Case-based reasoning is also used in interactive "retrieve and propose" systems that aid human reasoning by maintaining a library of cases and suggesting relevant cases for the human reasoner to consider. Such systems are being applied to support tasks such as software quality control, diagnosis, and design. Compared to traditional information retrieval (*q.v.*) and database systems, case-based systems take a more active role in formulating queries to memory. Unlike database systems, they use flexible retrieval criteria to retrieve the most similar cases even if those cases have conflicts with the query. Retrieve and propose systems are widely used in automated help desks that suggest relevant prior problems and solutions to customer-service personnel and augment their case libraries when novel problems are solved. The accumulated case libraries provide a form of "corporate memory" that enables knowledge sharing.

Educational systems are a growing application area of CBR. In these systems, the cognitive model of CBR provides criteria to help answer design questions such as what makes a good problem to present to students and the range of problems students should solve, while CBR methods are used to organize and retrieve relevant cases (e.g. in the form of video clips of experts' stories) at the right times to support student learning. Riesbeck and Schank (1989) and Schank *et al.* (1994) present detailed studies of a number of seminal case-based reasoning systems. Kolodner's (1993) textbook provides an in-depth examination of principles and methods for CBR. Leake (1996) provides a tutorial introduction to CBR, an overview of new directions, and case studies of important issues and applications.

Bibliography

1989. Riesbeck, C., and Schank, R. C. *Inside Case-Based Reasoning*. Hillsdale, NJ: Lawrence Erlbaum.
1993. Kolodner, J. *Case-Based Reasoning*. San Francisco: Morgan Kaufmann.
1994. Schank, R. C., Riesbeck, C., and Kass, A. (eds.) *Inside Case-Based Explanation*. Hillsdale, NJ: Lawrence Erlbaum.
1996. Leake, D. (ed.) *Case-Based Reasoning: Experiences, Lessons, and Future Directions*. Menlo Park, CA: AAAI Press.

Websites

The American Association for Artificial Intelligence. `http://www.aaai.org/Resources/CB-Reasoning/cbr-resources.html`.
The University of Kaiserlauten, Germany. `http://www.cbr-web.org`.

David B. Leake

CASE

See COMPUTER-ASSISTED SOFTWARE ENGINEERING.

CAT SCAN

See MEDICAL IMAGING; and TOMOGRAPHY, COMPUTERIZED.

CBI

See CHARLES BABBAGE INSTITUTE.

CD-ROM

See OPTICAL STORAGE.

CDC

See CONTROL DATA CORPORATION.

CELLULAR AUTOMATA

For articles on related subjects *see* AUTOMATA THEORY; and PARALLEL PROCESSING.

A *cellular automaton*, or *polyautomaton*, is a theoretical model of a parallel computer, subject to various restrictions to make formal investigation of its computing powers tractable. All versions of the model share these properties: each is an interconnection of identical cells, where a cell is a model of a computer with finite memory—i.e. a finite state machine. Each cell computes an output from inputs it receives from a finite set of cells forming its neighborhood, and possibly from an external source.

All cells compute one output simultaneously and each cell computes an output at each tick of a clock, i.e. after each unit time step. The output of a cell is distributed to its neighborhood and possibly to an external receiver.

A version of the cellular automaton model exists for each set of choices in the following dichotomies: an infinite or a finite number of cells; a uniform interconnection scheme (all cells have neighborhoods of the same shape, e.g. that in Fig. 1) or a nonuniform scheme (Fig. 2); deterministic or non-deterministic cells (a choice of exactly one output value at each unit time step or a set of several values); the absence or presence of an external input (output), and, in the case of an external input (output), connecting it to all cells or to only a subset; Moore-type or Mealy-type cells (unit time or zero time required, respectively, between inputs and the associated output); a static or dynamic interconnection scheme (neighborhood does or does not remain fixed in time). Some of the names associated with one or more of these versions are cellular automaton, cellular space, tessellation automaton, modular array, iterative automaton, intelligent graph, Lindenmayer system, and cellular network.

Historically, the first version of the cellular automaton was the cellular space obtained by selecting the first choice in each dichotomy above, but with no external input or output. It can be visualized in two dimensions as an infinite chessboard, each square representing a cell. It has been used to prove the existence of non-

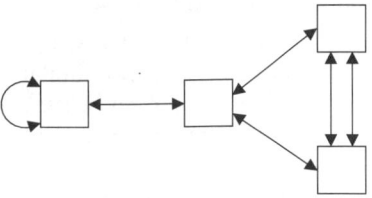

Figure 2. A cellular automaton with nonuniform neighborhood.

trivial self-reproducing machines, is capable of computing any computable function with only three states per cell and the four nearest cells as the neighborhood (Fig. 1), and can exhibit *Garden of Eden configurations*; i.e. patterns of cell states at one time, which can never arise in a given cellular space except at time zero. If an external input is assumed distributed to each cell, then the cellular space becomes what is usually called a *tessellation* space.

The cellular automaton is obtained from the cellular space by admitting only a finite, connected set of cells on the chessboard (Fig. 3). A cell with a neighbor missing has a special boundary signal substituted instead. The cellular automaton is particularly useful as a pattern recognizer, where the pattern comprises the states of the cells at time zero, especially if non-deterministic cells are allowed. A famous problem for the (deterministic) cellular automaton, the Firing Squad problem, calls each cell a soldier with one of them as the general—i.e. all cells but one are "off" initially—and asks if all soldiers can begin firing simultaneously by going into the same state. The Firing Squad theorem, which solves this problem, guarantees a yes.

The Firing Squad theorem remains valid even when a nonuniform interconnection scheme is allowed. Thus, another version of the cellular automaton, the graphical cellular automaton (Fig. 2), requires only that the number of neighbors be fixed, not that they be in any fixed geometric relationship with a cell.

The final type of cellular automaton to be mentioned, the dynamic cellular automaton, or *Lindenmayer system* (or *L-system*), allows a cell to divide into child cells—regardless of the position of that cell in the

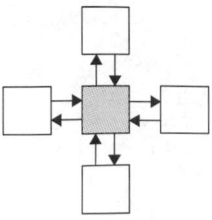

Figure 1. A cell (tinted) and its neighborhood.

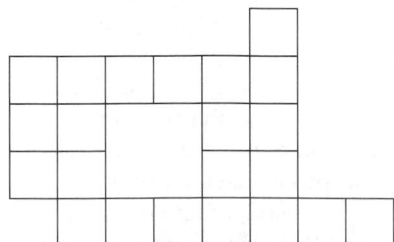

Figure 3. A cellular automaton with uniform neighborhood of Fig. 1 assumed.

initial array of cells—and allows the disappearance, or death, of cells. This version, with its dynamic interconnection scheme, is of interest to theoretical biologists as a model for the growth and development of living things (Prusinkiewicz and Lindenmayer, 1996). During the 1990s there have been numerous papers applying L-systems to the growth of realistic plants and trees (Fig. 4, see Color Page CP-2).

The infinite chessboard cellular automaton model gained much public popularity in the 1970s as the so-called *Game of Life* (Gardner, 1971). A resurgence of interest in the 1980s accompanied application of simple two-state, one-dimensional cellular automata (now often abbreviated CA) to fractals (*q.v.*) and dynamic chaos, rich new subjects that arose during that decade, propelled by inexpensive computer graphics (*q.v.*).

Bibliography

1968. Codd, E. F. *Cellular Automata*, ACM Monograph Series. New York: Academic Press.

1971. Gardner, M. "On Cellular Automata, Self-reproduction, the Garden of Eden, and the Game of Life." Mathematical Games Department, *Scientific American*, **224**, 112–117.

1976. Lindenmayer, A. and Rozenberg, G. (eds.) *Automata, Languages, Development*. Amsterdam: North Holland.

1984. Smith, A. R. "Plants, Fractals, and Formal Languages." *Computer Graphics*, **18**, 1–10.

1986. Wolfram, S. (ed.) *Theory and Applications of Cellular Automata*. Singapore: World Scientific.

1991. Smith, A. R. "Simple Nontrivial Self-reproducing Machines." *Artificial Life II, Santa Fe Institute Studies in the Sciences of Complexity*, vol. X (eds. C. G. Langton, C. Taylor, J. D. Farmer, and S. Rasmussen), Reading, MA: Addison-Wesley.

1996. Prusinkiewicz, P. and Lindenmayer, A. *The Algorithmic Beauty of Plants*, 2nd Ed. New York: Springer-Verlag.

Alvy Ray Smith

CENTRAL PROCESSING UNIT (CPU)

For articles on related subjects *see* ARITHMETIC–LOGIC UNIT; COMPUTER SYSTEM; DIGITAL COMPUTER; INSTRUCTION DECODING; MEMORY: MAIN; and STORED PROGRAM CONCEPT.

A digital computer consists of a selection of units of various types, all interconnected and functioning harmoniously under central control. Most of the units in a system are called "peripheral" devices, or just "peripherals," and serve either as the means of feeding raw data or file data into the system or of receiving results or updated files from the system.

The "central processor," or *central processing unit* (CPU), which the peripherals serve, carries out a variety of essential data manipulation and controlling tasks at the heart of the computer. The principal element of the CPU, the one required to carry out arithmetic and other, mainly logical, operations on data, is usually called the *arithmetic-logic unit* (ALU). It is designed to operate on a pair of numbers and carry out on them the processes of addition, subtraction, multiplication, and division, as well as logical operations on individual bits of numbers. It can compare numbers and determine whether one is the greater or whether they are equal. These operations are carried out at very high speeds; even the slowest computers can do at least several million such operations in a second, and the really fast "number crunchers" handle several billion per second.

The other important element of the CPU is the *control unit* required to supervise the functioning of the machine as a whole, calling into operation the various units as required by the program. It receives the program instructions one by one in sequence, interprets them, and sends appropriate control signals to the various units. It acts in many ways as a very sophisticated telephone switchboard operator, making interconnections among various parts of the system. When the control unit recognizes special signals (e.g. that the result of a subtraction is negative), it can depart from the strict sequence of program instructions and jump to a different part of the program that is designed to deal with those circumstances.

The arithmetic and the control units depend heavily on a third element of a computer, the main storage (memory) unit. The main storage is not part of the CPU *per se*, but together with the CPU it forms what may be called the *processor subsystem*. The arithmetic unit needs numbers on which to operate and needs to store intermediate results until the end of the calculation. The control unit needs program instructions in rapid succession. Both data and instructions are held in memory. The program for a given job is read into memory from an input unit or auxiliary storage device as part of the initiation procedure for the job. Data flows into memory from such devices as keyboards on terminals and magnetic disk units, and is manipulated while in storage to produce results that are output, for example, to a printer.

Memory is also used to store a complex of programs known as the *operating system* (*see* OPERATING SYSTEMS: GENERAL PRINCIPLES); this system is designed to supervise the total operation of the computer in as efficient a manner as possible. These programs function in some ways analogous to "traffic controllers," as they have to monitor the flow of data around the computer, giving some streams right of way over others, opening up clearways for top priority messages, looking out for emergency signals, and generally keeping things flowing smoothly.

The central processing unit thus consists of the control unit and the arithmetic-logic unit. It is aptly named, since it is very much at the center of computer activity, and it completes a massive amount of processing work, both directly to produce the desired results and generally to supervise the efficient operation of the computer system as a whole. With the advent of microprocessors (*see* MICROPROCESSORS AND MICRO-COMPUTERS), entire CPUs are now contained on a single integrated circuit (*see* INTEGRATED CIRCUITRY) chip ("CPU on a chip"). These CPUs are as fast and as powerful as those that required entire cabinets of hardware from decades ago.

Graham J. Morris

CHANNEL

For articles on related subjects *see* ASYNCHRONOUS TRANSFER MODE; BUFFER; BUS; COMMUNICATION CONTROL UNIT; DATA COMMUNICATIONS; INPUT–OUTPUT CONTROL SYSTEM; INPUT–OUTPUT OPERATIONS; INTERRUPT; MEMORY: AUXILIARY; MULTIPLEXING; MULTITASKING; POLLING; PORT, I/O; and SYNCHRONOUS/ASYNCHRONOUS OPERATION.

Introduction

In the design of early computing systems it was usual to provide for only a minimum of input and output devices, such as paper tape (*q.v.*) or card readers and punches, and perhaps a line printer. All these peripherals were essentially slow. In such cases, data could be transferred to and from the peripheral, character by character, and each unit had its special input or output line. Normally, data transferred between an input–output (I/O) device and memory passed through the processor. Later it was found necessary to provide many I/O devices. With the advent of magnetic tape and disk units, which are faster devices with short crisis times (i.e. a need to be serviced very quickly if data was not to be lost), multicharacter block transfers became necessary.

In all cases, however, it was necessary to provide some indication of the status of the I/O device in use, such as "ready" or "busy." If the device called upon was busy, the program had to stop and wait for the unit to become available. The need for block transfers and the avoidance of delays due to unsuitable peripheral conditions led to the use of *buffered* peripherals and the development of continuously operating *channels* communicating directly with memory. Thus, in the sense of this article, a channel is a processor that performs I/O for a mainframe computer. Additionally, the channel provides overlap of I/O processing with logical and arithmetic processing, thereby obtaining high throughput (*q.v.*) by performing different operations in parallel. The channel also provides a standard interface for a range of I/O devices that may be connected to one processor in many combinations.

Autonomous Channel Operation

The eventual availability of buffered peripherals called for the fast transfer of data to and from those peripherals. If these transfers were controlled by the central processing unit (CPU—*q.v.*), much time would be lost since character transfer is slow compared with other CPU operations. Methods of autonomous transfer were needed whereby a whole block of data is transferred rapidly, word by word, to and from the main store, the cycles of the storage time taken for the word transfer being "stolen" from those available to the CPU. This *cycle stealing* (*q.v.*) usually causes only a slight hesitation of the CPU, whose storage cycle time of 10–50 nanoseconds should be compared with that of a high-speed disk drive whose transfer rate is, at best, about 100–200 ns per byte.

To facilitate block transfers directly between the store and the peripheral units, a controller called a *data channel* was introduced. A large mainframe (*q.v.*) has several such channels. A data channel is essentially a small, special-purpose computer. An I/O operation is initiated by the processor that selects a channel and a device to be connected to it. The channel then accesses a unique location in main memory where the processor has stored the address of the first instruction to be issued to the channel. Usually, a list of instructions called a *channel program*, is set up in storage. Each instruction is a particular operation that the channel must execute. The CPU sends to the channel the address of the block of consecutive storage words (or bytes) to be transferred and the number of words to be transferred. If the channel is not already busy and the channel equipment is available and ready to operate, the channel initiates the transfer.

Instructions relating to channel operations commonly consist of two or more parts. The first part will specify and initiate the action of reading or writing, will give the address to which transfer of control will be made in the case of the rejection of the operation, and will contain the address of a *control word*, the second part of the channel instruction. The control word contains the length and initial address of the block to be transferred and is that information that is actually passed to the data channel. It is also possible to allow a sequence of data blocks to be transferred by providing a chain of control words that are sent one after another to the channel.

The control word also provides a *function code* that specifies and provides for certain types of variation of the normal mode of transfer of data, such as skipping, reading, or writing zeros, or terminating data transfer before the specified number of words indicated in the control word is actually transferred. A channel unit may also receive a variety of special orders from the processor, such as channel and equipment selection and channel and equipment status inquiry.

In the case in which there is more than one channel, the channels are connected at the processor end to a scanner circuit called a *director*. The director polls the various data channels in turn and, when data is ready to be transferred, selects an available channel and provides it with an origin (for reading) or destination address (for writing) for the first byte to be transferred. This scanning is done sufficiently rapidly to avoid any crisis. The director has direct access to memory and activates the input to and the output from memory. It scans the channels in a defined order of priority. One director may service as many as 32 channels.

Channel Capacity

The rate at which a channel can transmit data to or from an I/O device, or to or from main storage, is called the *transfer rate* or *channel capacity*. This is usually given in megabytes per second (MB/sec). The channel capacity must, of course, be great enough to service the fastest I/O device connected to it. Channel specifications usually cite figures for data transfer rates under the assumption of ideal conditions. Actual data transmission rates are usually lower. If the channel hardware and the CPU hardware use the same registers (*q.v.*), the channel may have to wait on the CPU for available registers (and vice versa), thus affecting transfer rates in a manner that cannot be determined *a priori*. The maximum rates given for discrete channels may also be degraded by the operation of other channels with which they are *multiplexed* and by relative channel priorities.

Since *multiplexer* or *selector* channels are essentially independent computers controlling I/O, they will, of course, have their transfer rates affected by the way they are programmed. If the data is entered into a contiguous area of storage, the effective data transfer rate will be greater than if it is entered into a noncontiguous set of areas, where all sorts of addresses must be computed and the CPU notified as to which storage area is being affected. This use of noncontiguous memory for a data set is known as *data chaining*. Of course, data chaining creates more conflict with the CPU, slowing either data transmission or processing or both.

Channel Commands

A computer program consists of a set of instructions that are decoded and executed by the CPU. *Channel commands* are instructions that are decoded and executed by the I/O channels. A sequence of commands constitutes a channel program. Commands are stored in the main storage just as though they were instructions. They are fetched from main storage and are common to all I/O devices, but modifier bits are used to specify device-dependent conditions. The modifier bits of the command may also be used to order the I/O device to execute certain functions that are not involved in data transfer, such as tape rewinding or repositioning of a hard disk (*q.v.*) access arm.

During program execution, the CPU will initiate relevant I/O operations. A command will specify a channel, a device, and an operation to be performed, and perhaps a storage area to be used, and perhaps also some memory protection information about the storage area involved. All this information may appear in the command word, or the command may tell the channel in which locations in memory to seek the necessary information. Upon receipt of this information, the multiplexer channel will attempt to select the desired device by sending the device address to all I/O units (including controllers) attached to the channel. A unit that recognizes its address connects itself logically to the channel. Once the connection is made, the channel will send the executable command to the I/O device. The device will respond to the channel, indicating whether it can execute the command and make this information available to the CPU.

An I/O operation involving data transfer to or from a series of noncontiguous memory locations may involve a series of channel commands. Termination of an I/O operation involves channel-end and device-end conditions. These conditions are brought to the attention of the CPU via interrupts or programmed interrogation of the I/O device. The channel-end condition occurs when the data transmission is completed. The channel is considered busy until this condition is accepted by the CPU. The device-end signal is given when the I/O device has terminated execution of the operation. The device remains unavailable until it is cleared by the CPU.

LOCKOUT

The memory of a computer cannot be accessed continuously, only at specific times. The time interval within which memory may be accessed by the processor or an I/O channel is known as a *memory cycle*. Most memory cycle times are measured in nanoseconds (billionths of a second). The CPU is essentially involved in processing data that is in main memory, whereas channels are concerned with the flow of data between I/O devices and main memory. Main memory is a high-speed data store, whereas peripherals are comparatively low-speed data stores. The channels and the CPU are busy moving data into and out of main memory. A conflict arises if they both need access to data at the same time (*see* CONTENTION). Since memory behaves the same way whether the source or destination of the data is an I/O channel or the CPU, some method is needed to resolve the conflict.

Suppose a request for memory access is initiated by a second channel while a memory cycle is being used by the first. Since all requests must eventually be granted, but some more quickly than others, a priority system must be used. It is the comparatively slow I/O devices, rather than the high-speed CPU, that must have their requests answered first. A disk spinning under a read head must give up its data before the next block of data passes that read head; otherwise data will be lost. The moving I/O devices must always have open space to accept more data and cannot be concerned with memory access problems. The CPU, on the other hand, goes from one stable state to another. Once information is in its registers, it can wait. This will slow processing, but will not lose information. Therefore, a priority lock is set whereby the CPU is locked out from access to memory at the instant that the channels need to access memory.

SELECTING A PERIPHERAL

To select a particular peripheral unit, a special function code must be transferred to the channel, indicating the identity of the unit required. This is done by sending a *connect function* to the channel. Usually, a channel unit with a variety of attached equipment is connected in what a communications specialist might call a multi-drop manner; all device controllers are connected by the same communication path to the channel (*see* Fig. 1). Some device controllers may be connected to more than one channel in case the channel initially selected is busy.

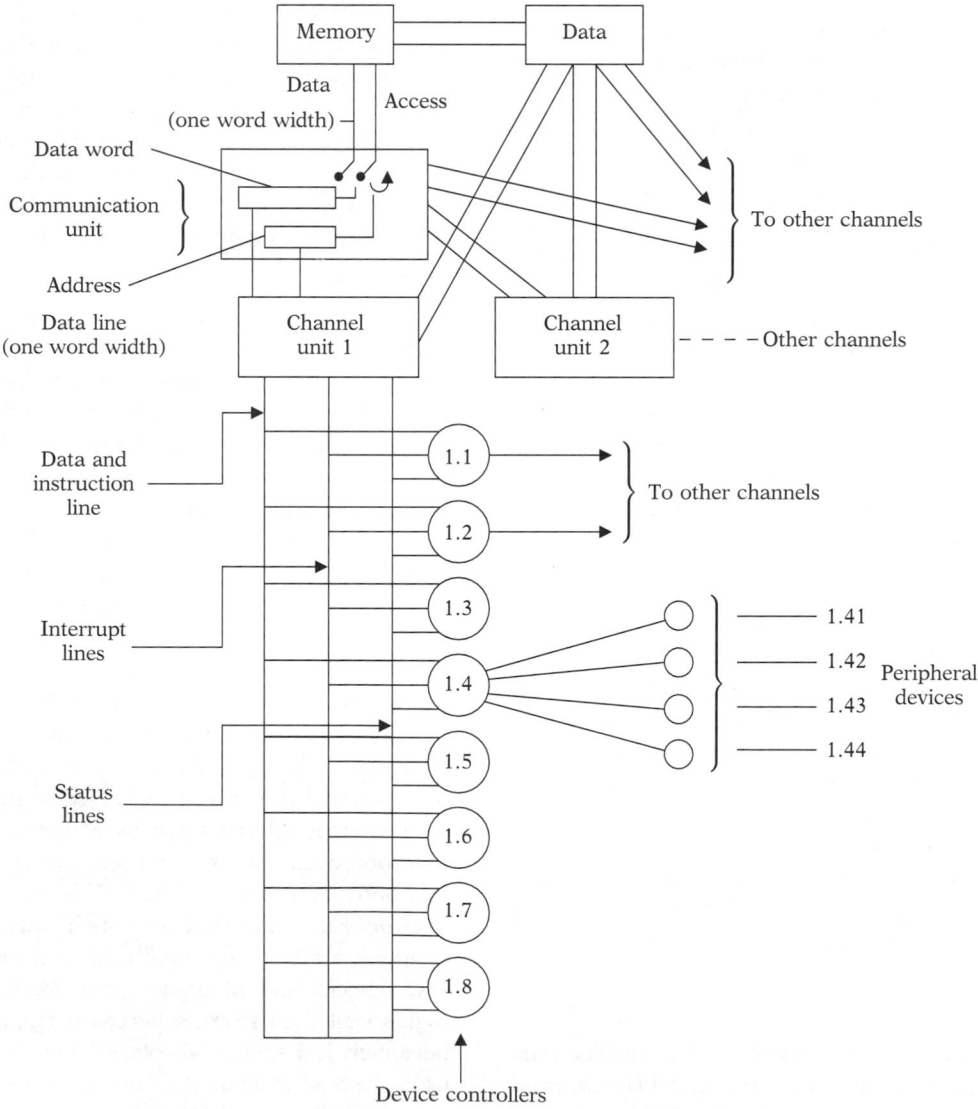

Figure 1. Selector channel organization.

SETTING A PERIPHERAL

A special function code sent to a selected peripheral by its connected channel may specify operating conditions within which the external equipment is to operate or a condition in which an interrupt may occur, such as stopping the channel activity, selecting an interrupt on detection of a parity error, or stopping the operation.

STATUS

A channel must provide a status code to indicate its operating condition. Depending upon the kind of equipment to which the channel is connected, certain bits in the code indicate that a parity error is present, that a read or write is in progress, or that the operation is complete. Other codes in the status instruction cause the current data address and the word count to be sent to the CPU and/or the current control word address to be sent to other CPU registers. Detection of a busy channel or equipment status may be used appropriately to transfer control to a different program until a further interrupt recalls attention to the channel and its user program.

CLEAR CHANNEL

When initiating a program, or starting from a dead-stop condition or a recoverable difficulty, it may be necessary (1) to clear a channel by disconnecting all peripheral devices from the specific channel and preventing any communication until a connect instruction is provided; or (2) to disconnect all units within a compound device (e.g. disks on a multiple disk controller) and to clear the channel control words. The *clear channel* instruction is also needed in case of difficulty with a channel operation and may be initiated by the operator.

INTERRUPTS

Selecting an interrupt condition is performed by a function instruction that can select occurrences of address and data and channel transmission parity errors. Associated with each channel, there is usually a special register in a channel unit that indicates the occurrence of one or more of these conditions. There is usually one bit in the register for each equipment condition. Additional bits are reserved for the use of the channel itself, such as an interrupt from the channel, channel data parity error, or control-word parity errors.

Most systems operate in either *normal* or *privileged* mode. In the latter all interrupts are held inactive when processing an earlier interrupt. The activity state of an interrupt can be set by a special function instruction that sets interrupts active and returns the processor to

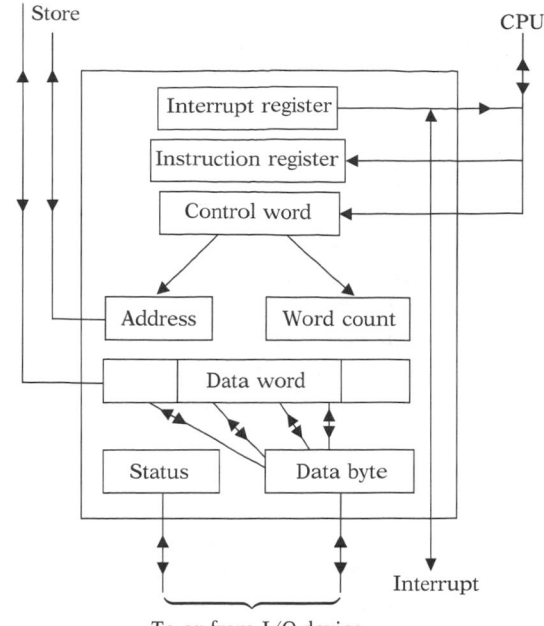

Figure 2. Channel unit.

the unprivileged state. The privileged status is automatically set on the detection of an interrupt when in normal state.

The structure of a channel unit is illustrated in Fig. 2. This shows the channel interrupt register, which indicates the conditions of the interrupt itself; the instruction register of the instruction which is received from the CPU; the control word, which gives the address and the number of words to be transferred; and the data word assembly registers, from which the data is to be sent from storage. In addition to this there is the status register, which is used to indicate the status of the connected unit of the channel.

Selector, Byte-Multiplexer, and Block-Multiplexer Channels

Channels may be classified by the modes of operation they perform. The channel facilities required for an I/O operation is called a *subchannel*. The capability of a channel to perform multiplexing requires more than one subchannel.

SELECTOR CHANNEL

A selector channel has only one subchannel and therefore forces the I/O device to transfer data in *burst mode*. The transmission of data continues uninterrupted until the whole block of data (or series of blocks of data) is transmitted. There can be only one data transfer operating at a time on a selector channel. Devices attached to the channel may be performing operations not requiring communication with the channel while data transfer is occurring in burst mode. When no data is being transferred, the selector channel monitors attached devices for status information.

BYTE-MULTIPLEXER CHANNEL

The byte-multiplexer channel contains numerous subchannels and may operate in burst or in byte-interleave mode. The mode of operation is determined by the device. In burst mode, only one device on the channel may transfer data. In byte-interleave mode, more than one device may operate simultaneously, each using a separate subchannel.

BLOCK-MULTIPLEXER CHANNEL

The block multiplexer channel also has multiple subchannels. It forces I/O devices to transfer data in burst mode, but the burst extends over only one block of data. Multiplexing or interleaving of blocks occurs between channel commands. Multiplexing between blocks may be inhibited by appropriate channel instructions. Byte-multiplexer and block-multiplexer channels can sustain more than one I/O operation per subchannel, provided that the total load on the channel does not exceed its capacity. Each subchannel of a multiplexer channel appears to the program as an independent selector channel. When a multiplexer channel transfers data in burst mode, the subchannel it is using controls the data-transfer facilities of the channel. Other subchannels on the multiplexer channel cannot respond to device requests until the burst is completed.

Conclusion. The term "channel processor" originally denoted a special purpose I/O processor that shared memory with a mainframe CPU. Today, high-performance computers frequently have separate microprocessors to carry out I/O; these serve the same functions as specialized channel processors. One way that such front-end processors are used now is as interfaces between high-bandwidth servers and the World Wide Web, to provide good response time at heavily used sites.

Bibliography

1978. Kuck, D. J. *The Structure of Computers and Communications.* New York: John Wiley.

Trevor Pearcey and Milton Pine

CHARACTER CODES

For articles on related subjects *see* BAUDOT CODE; CODES; ERROR CORRECTING AND DETECTING CODE; PUNCHED CARD; and UNIVERSAL PRODUCT CODE.

Since computers are binary machines, they must represent the characters which humans wish to input into a computer as sequences of ones and zeros. Various schemes have been developed to encode these characters. This article will discuss some of the most important.

BCD

Binary-coded decimal was an early and widely used code for representing single decimal digits in binary form. Table 1 shows the binary equivalent of each decimal digit in BCD. It quickly fell into disuse as computers no longer stored numbers as sequences of decimal digits but rather as the binary equivalents of multi-digit decimal numbers.

EBCDIC

The Extended Binary-Coded Decimal Interchange Code was an 8-bit code developed by IBM for use in its System/360 and later computers. While IBM was dominant in the computer industry, EBCDIC was widely used and important, but as that dominance decreased so did the importance of EBCDIC which has been superseded on all computers, even IBM ones, by ASCII. Table 2 shows the EBCDIC equivalents of letters, numbers, and special characters. The leftmost four bits and their hexadecimal equivalents are shown at the top, while the rightmost four bits and their hexadecimal equivalents are shown at the left.

ASCII

The American Standard Code for Information Interchange is a seven-bit code also known as the USA Standard Code for Information Interchange (USASCII). Table 3 exhibits ASCII; blank cells are reserved for the control character codes that are used in computer communications. The leftmost three bits and their

Table 1. BCD. Each combination is the binary representation of the corresponding digit.

Digit	BCD combination
0	0000
1	0001
2	0010
3	0011
4	0100
5	0101
6	0110
7	0111
8	1000
9	1001

Table 2. EBCDIC codes for letters, numbers and special characters. Codes for which the first hexadecimal digit is less than 4 are used for control characters. Blank spaces are unused. Position 40 (SP) represents the space character. Special character symbols vary a bit among different versions of EBCDIC; those given here are the Cobol (*q.v.*) symbols and may be found at http://www.synkronix.com/programmers_guide/ebcdic.html.

Bit positions 4, 5, 6, 7	Second hexadecimal digit	0100 / 4	0101 / 5	0110 / 6	0111 / 7	1000 / 8	1001 / 9	1010 / A	1011 / B	1100 / C	1101 / D	1110 / E	1111 / F	Bit positions 0, 1, 2, 3 First hexadecimal digit
0000	0	SP	&	−									0	
0001	1			/		a	j			A	J		1	
0010	2					b	k	s		B	K	S	2	
0011	3					c	l	t		C	L	T	3	
0100	4					d	m	u		D	M	U	4	
0101	5					e	n	v		E	N	V	5	
0110	6					f	o	w		F	O	W	6	
0111	7					g	p	x		G	P	X	7	
1000	8					h	q	y		H	Q	Y	8	
1001	9					i	r	z		I	R	Z	9	
1010	A	[	]	|	:									
1011	B	.	$	,	#									
1100	C	<	*	%	@									
1101	D	(	)	−	'									
1110	E	+	;	>	=									
1111	F	!	^	?	"									

Table 3. ASCII codes for letters, numbers, special characters and some control characters. All codes with first digit 0 or 1 are for control characters. The meanings of those shown are: BS—Backspace, HT—Horizontal Tab, LF—Line Feed, VT—Vertical Tab, FF—Form Feed, CR—Carriage Return and DEL (in location 7F)—Delete. Also, SP in location 20 is the space character. For the complete ASCII character set see http://webopedia.internet.com/TERM/A/ASCII.html.

Bit positions 4, 5, 6, 7	Hexadecimal digit	000 / 0	001 / 1	010 / 2	011 / 3	100 / 4	101 / 5	110 / 6	111 / 7	Bit positions 1, 2, 3 Decimal digit
0000	0			SP	0	@	P	`	p	
0001	1			!	1	A	Q	a	q	
0010	2			"	2	B	R	b	r	
0011	3			#	3	C	S	c	s	
0100	4			$	4	D	T	d	t	
0101	5			%	5	E	U	e	u	
0110	6			&	6	F	V	f	v	
0111	7			'	7	G	W	g	w	
1000	8	BS		(	8	H	X	h	x	
1001	9	HT		)	9	I	Y	i	y	
1010	A	LF		*	:	J	Z	j	z	
1011	B	VT		+	;	K	[	k	{	
1100	C	FF		,	<	L	\	l	|	
1101	D	CR		−	=	M	]	m	}	
1110	E			.	>	N	^	n	~	
1111	F			/	?	O	−	o	DEL	

decimal equivalents are shown at the top while the rightmost four bits and their hexadecimal equivalents are shown at the left.

Because 8-bit bytes are common on computers, ASCII is commonly embedded in an 8-bit field in which the high order (leftmost) bit is either used as a parity bit or is set to zero. There are various extensions of ASCII to 8 bits, among which are the IBM extended character set with characters for elementary graphics and the ISO 8859 standard, which includes Latin-1 (the standard ISO 8-bit extension to ASCII (ISO 8859) for Western European alphabets). Since even 8-bit ASCII is capable of encoding only 256 characters, it is unsuitable for the large number of characters and symbols needed in order to store characters from the many languages which do not use the Latin alphabet or which (like French and German) have an effective alphabet of more than 26 characters because of the use of accents, umlauts, etc.

Unicode

Unicode is a 16-bit code and can therefore represent 2^{16} or 65,536 characters. Blocks of codes in Unicode have been assigned to various languages and special character groups (e.g. a block of 94 codes for the Latin alphabet, 104 for Greek (including 14 Coptic characters), 76 for punctuation and 242 for mathematics symbols). Extensions of Unicode to 20 bits enable the representation of 2^{20} or 1,048,576 characters.

The current version 2.1 of Unicode had, as of 4 September 1998, encoded 38,887 characters from the world's alphabets, ideograph sets, and symbol collections. These characters cover the principal written languages of the Americas, Europe, the Middle East, Africa, India, Asia, and the Pacific. Some modern written languages enjoy only partial support or none at all due to a need for further research into the unique coding needs of their scripts. Unicode has been made into a standard (10646) of the International Organization for Standardization.

Unicode makes it much easier for developers to store and process characters for a given language because each Unicode value refers to a unique character. This means that an *E* in English is the same as an *E* in French, because both English and French are both based on the Latin alphabet. This code is not the same as an *E* in Russian, which shares the same glyph—symbol shape—as the Latin *E* but belongs to the Cyrillic script.

An important concept of Unicode is the distinction between *characters* and *glyphs*. A glyph is a visual depiction of a character. A character itself has no inherent image. This distinction is in contrast to the common understanding which equates these two concepts. For example, a *font* is often described as being composed of characters. In contrast, according to the view adopted by Unicode, a font contains glyphs, not "characters." Therefore, a character set should not encode glyphs, since the number of glyphs is much larger than the number of characters which should be encoded.

Table 4. Unicode values for the glyphs in the Armenian language.

	053	054	055	056	057	058
0	▧	Հ 0540	Ր 0550	▧	հ 0570	ռ 0580
1	Ա 0531	Ձ 0541	Ց 0551	ա 0561	ձ 0571	ս 0581
2	Բ 0532	Ղ 0542	Ւ 0552	բ 0562	ղ 0572	վ 0582
3	Գ 0533	Ճ 0543	Փ 0553	գ 0563	ճ 0573	տ 0583
4	Դ 0534	Մ 0544	Ք 0554	դ 0564	մ 0574	ր 0584
5	Ե 0535	Յ 0545	Օ 0555	ե 0565	յ 0575	ց 0585
6	Զ 0536	Ն 0546	Ֆ 0556	զ 0566	ն 0576	ւ 0586
7	Է 0537	Շ 0547	▧	է 0567	շ 0577	փ 0587
8	Ը 0538	Ո 0548	▧	ը 0568	ո 0578	▧
9	Թ 0539	Չ 0549	ʻ 0559	թ 0569	չ 0579	: 0589
A	Ժ 053A	Պ 054A	ʼ 055A	ժ 056A	պ 057A	▧
B	Ի 053B	Ջ 054B	ʹ 055B	ի 056B	ջ 057B	▧
C	Լ 053C	Ռ 054C	ˋ 055C	լ 056C	ռ 057C	▧
D	Խ 053D	Ս 054D	` 055D	խ 056D	ս 057D	▧
E	Ծ 053E	Վ 054E	◠ 055E	ծ 056E	վ 057E	▧
F	Կ 053F	Տ 054F	◡ 055F	կ 056F	տ 057F	▧

Table 4 gives the four hexadecimal digits of the Unicode values for the glyphs generally used for writing the Armenian language.

Unicode is not without its problems, particularly because of the size of files coded using a 16-bit instead of a 7- or 8-bit code. This has so far limited its use and usefulness. In addition, for example, oriental languages are not readily convertible to the Unicode standard. Many language fonts are so unwieldy that a number of partial fonts may be required to convert them into Unicode.

Bibliography

1996. *The Unicode Standard, Version 2.0.* Reading, MA: Addison Wesley Longman. (See also `http://www.unicode.org`)

Stephen J. Rogowski

CHARACTER SET

See CHARACTER CODES.

CHARLES BABBAGE INSTITUTE

For an article on a related subject *see* DIGITAL COMPUTERS, HISTORY OF.

The *Charles Babbage Institute* was the first academic research center devoted to the history of computing, the computer industry, and of computer technology. It houses the most extensive academic archive of the history of computing, and conducts an extensive oral history program to provide further documentation of that history. To encourage younger scholars in the field, the Institute has, since 1978, annually awarded a fellowship to a graduate student in the history of computing or a closely related field.

History

CBI was founded by a group of computer industry executives in 1977 to capture and to record the history of computing. It also won support from the American Federation of Information Processing Societies, and was established at the University of Minnesota, its current home, in 1980. From 1981–1993, Arthur Norberg, the first director of CBI, built up a strong program in computer history that took the world as its arena and the encouragement of scholarship in the history of computing as its mission. Assisted by Associate Directors William Aspray and Judith O'Neill, he launched the oral history program, the archives program, several funded research projects, and a lecture series in the history of computing. Among the fruits of this labor were several hundred oral history transcripts, Aspray's book *John von Neumann and the Origins of Modern Computing,* and Norberg and O'Neill's *Transforming Computer Technology.* In 1994, Norberg was succeeded by Robert W. Seidel as Director of CBI. At that time, CBI began planning for a new home to be erected by the year 2000 at the University of Minnesota, launched new research initiatives in the history of scientific computing, and continued the archives development program. In 1999, Norberg again became CBI Director.

The Charles Babbage Foundation

The Charles Babbage Foundation has endowed the Engineering Research Associates Land-Grant College Chair of the History of Technology, which is held by a member of the faculty of the History of Science and Technology Program at the University of Minnesota, usually the Director of CBI. CBF continues to seek support for CBI from those interested in the history of computing. The chairman of the Foundation in 1999 is James Cortada of IBM Consulting. The Foundation raises funds through the Friends of CBI, whose gifts are tax-deductible and provide funds for the continuation and expansion of the Institute.

Activities

CBI publishes a quarterly Newsletter and maintains a home page on the World Wide Web (`http://www.cbi.umn.edu`) that includes detailed aids for finding material in its own collections. Its archives include manuscripts, computer manuals, trade publications, oral histories, and an extensive photograph collection. Among the many publications of the historical staff are the history of the Defense Advance Research Projects Agency's Information Processing Techniques Office, the biography of John von Neumann (*q.v.*), and the forthcoming history of the early computing industry in Minnesota.

CBI's current research includes a project to write the history of the computer as a scientific instrument and an investigation of the use of computers in nuclear weapons design and development.

Contact information:
Charles Babbage Institute
103 Walter Library
University of Minnesota
117 Pleasant Street
Minneapolis, MN 55455
USA
Phone: 1-612-624-5050

Robert W. Seidel

CHEBYSHEV APPROXIMATION

For articles on related subjects *see* APPROXIMATION THEORY; LEAST-SQUARES APPROXIMATION; and NUMERICAL ANALYSIS.

Many computations on computers require the calculation of values of one or more functions, such as square roots, sines, cosines, logarithms, exponentials, and other elementary functions, or more complicated functions, such as Bessel functions. Since computers can only perform the operations of arithmetic, these functions cannot be evaluated directly, but must be *approximated* by some other functions that can be evaluated arithmetically. For example, you might approximate $\sin x$ by the first few terms of its Maclaurin series:

$$\sin x \approx x - x^3/3! + x^5/5!$$

but this approximation, while very accurate for values of x near 0, has an error which increases rapidly as the magnitude of x increases. In general, we can do much better than approximations like that above. How to do this is the subject of this article.

The general problem we wish to consider here is: given a function $f(x)$ and an interval $[a, b]$ on which we wish to approximate $f(x)$, find an approximation to $f(x)$ on this interval—which can be computed arithmetically—of minimum error. But what do we mean by minimum error? In many problems in mathematics this would mean the minimum least squares (*see* LEAST-SQUARES APPROXIMATION) error over the interval. But in approximating functions for computers we are usually more interested in minimizing the maximum error on the interval, for then the user of the approximation always knows that the worst possible case is as favorable as it can be. Rigorously stated, we wish to find an approximation $R(x)$ which has the property that

$$r = \max_{[a,b]} |f(x) - R(x)|$$

is smaller than for any other approximation. Such a *minimum–maximum error approximation*, or *minimax approximation*, is usually called a *Chebyshev approximation*, after the great Russian mathematician P. L. Chebyshev (1821–1894), whose surname may be transliterated from the Russian in a variety of other ways (e.g. Tchebycheff).

The question remains of what form $R(x)$ should have. If it is to be evaluated arithmetically, the most general function it can be is a *rational function*, i.e. the ratio of two polynomials. For example, the Chebyshev approximation to the exponential function e^x on the interval $[-1, 1]$, which is the ratio of two quadratic polynomials, is given by

$$R(x) = \frac{1.00007255 + 0.50863618x + 0.08582937x^2}{1.0 - 0.49109193x + 0.07770847x^2}$$

for which $r = 0.86899 \times 10^{-4}$. The error, $E(x) = e^x - R(x)$, is shown in Fig. 1. It exhibits the characteristic property of Chebyshev approximations of alternating between its greatest and least values two more times than the sum of the degrees of numerator and denominator of $R(x)$ or, in the example above, $2 + 2 + 2 = 6$ times.

Bibliography

1978. Ralston, A., and Rabinowitz, P. *A First Course in Numerical Analysis*, 2nd Ed. New York: McGraw-Hill.
1990. Rivlin, T. J. *Chebyshev Polynomials: From Approximation Theory to Algebra and Number Theory*. New York: John Wiley.

Anthony Ralston

CHECKPOINT

For articles on related subjects *see* DEBUGGING; and PROGRAMMING SUPPORT ENVIRONMENTS.

A *checkpoint* is a designated place in a program at which normal processing is interrupted specifically to preserve the status information necessary to allow resumption of processing at some arbitrary time in the future.

The primary purpose of a checkpoint is to avoid repeating the execution of a program from its beginning should an error or malfunction occur somewhere in the middle of processing. This is especially important and effective in runs involving several hours of machine time, although such durations are becoming

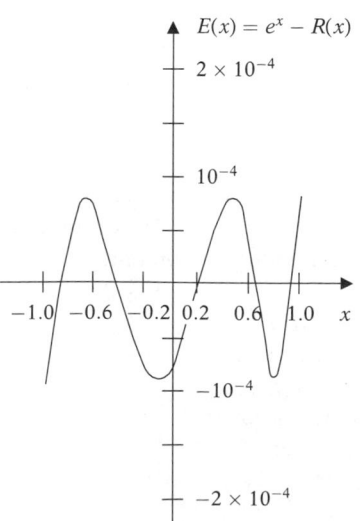

Figure 1. Error in Chebyshev approximation to e^x on $[-1, 1]$ as a ratio of two quadratics.

rare. For such situations it is often appropriate to set up checkpoints at a number of strategic places in the program, either with all checkpoint information being saved, or by using a less conservative system in which the information captured at the most recent checkpoint replaces (overwrites) the previous set. Then, should difficulties arise, it is possible to take corrective action and resume processing from the last checkpoint, rather than starting over. Since the manipulations associated with checkpoint/restart procedures can consume substantial amounts of time and storage, it is possible to have situations in which it is more economical to avoid checkpoints.

A checkpoint capability is implemented by means of a procedure (often termed a *checkpoint routine*) that captures the status of the program at the particular instant when it stopped and copies it onto an auxiliary storage medium. This data includes the contents of the special registers, storage locations associated with the program, and other information relating to the status of input–output devices. Later on, another procedure (a *restart routine*) can reset the system to resume processing by reading in and restoring the checkpoint information.

In a sense, multiprogramming (*q.v.*) operating systems implement an automatic form of checkpoint/restart. Depending on the scheduling algorithm (*q.v.*), a particular process may be interrupted to make its storage (and other resources) available to other processes. The status of the interrupted process is saved so that the process can be continued at a later time.

An automatic facility for checkpoint/restart is also desirable in the context of distributed computing (*see* DISTRIBUTED SYSTEMS). In this setting, a problem is subdivided into pieces that execute on computers that are not under the direct control of the programmer. It may not be possible to determine the fate of any individual piece. Checkpointing serves to record those pieces that have completed. When it appears unlikely that a given piece will complete, it can be interrupted and then restarted.

Seymour V. Pollack and Ron K. Cytron

CHESS, COMPUTER

See COMPUTER CHESS.

CHIEF PROGRAMMER TEAM

For articles on related subjects *see* SOFTWARE ENGINEERING; SOFTWARE PROJECT MANAGEMENT; and STRUCTURED PROGRAMMING.

A *Chief Programmer Team* is a concept coupling a functionally specialized programming organization with the use of software engineering techniques, such as structured programming and top-down development, to produce effective software systems of high quality. The idea originated with Harlan D. Mills, who in 1968 was concerned about the inefficiencies apparent in large-scale software development. He believed that a structured, multi-disciplinary organization using standardized methods and tools could develop systems of higher quality and achieve improved productivity.

A team begins as a nucleus of a *chief programmer*, a *backup programmer*, and a *programming librarian*. The chief programmer is the technical manager of the organization, responsible for all aspects of the design and development of a software system. The backup programmer is the chief's alter ego, serving both as a check and balance and as an insurance policy in case of the illness or departure of the chief. The programming librarian provides clerical support for both programming and documentation activities. (In Mills's original concept, the librarian physically managed all the programming materials of the project—hence the name.) This organizational nucleus begins a project by performing systems analysis, software architecture, and top-level design work, and then develops the code needed to make the framework of the system operational. Specialists (e.g. additional programmers, testers, technical writers) are then added to complete the development, testing, and documentation of the full system. All work is viewed as the shared and public property of the team, rather than as the private property of each participant. *Walkthroughs* (a precursor of inspections) are performed on all elements of design, code, and documentation. The organization was consciously designed to take advantage of the methods of top-down (incremental) development and structured programming, which in 1968 were viewed as radical and untried.

The team idea was first applied on a contract that the IBM Federal Systems Division held with *The New York Times* for development of *The New York Times Information Bank*. The system was designed to be an interactive replacement for the newspaper's internal library, both to be used by staffers and to be marketed to outside users. Use of the team organization and methodology on this contract resulted in delivery in 1971 of a system of over 83,000 source lines. The software had only 21 errors identified during five weeks of acceptance testing and only 25 errors during its first year of use, just one of which resulted in termination of operations. Productivity was 35 lines per person-day over the entire project, and 65 lines per person-day for the software development phase. Although software metrics (*q.v.*) for comparable projects were not generally available at the time, these levels of quality and productivity were viewed as significantly better than those being achieved elsewhere.

The team idea was tried on other projects, both within IBM and by outside organizations. The formal team structure, the roles of the participants, and the degree of discipline expected proved difficult for people to accept; they preferred a less formal structure. Also, while the team was well adapted to small- and medium-sized projects, it proved difficult to scale up to large ones; the chief programmer had difficulty in performing both architectural and management duties. Fred Brooks proposed a slightly enlarged team organization, but still saw difficulty in scaling it up to really large projects. The real value of the early experiments proved to be in demonstrating that structured programming and top-down development, which later became integral components of software engineering (*q.v.*), were in fact practical outside of the academic environment where they originated.

Bibliography

1972. Baker, F. T. "System Quality Through Structured Programming," *AFIPS Proceedings of the 1972 Fall Joint Computer Conference*, **41**, 339–343. Montvale, NJ: AFIPS Press.

1972. Baker, F. T. "Chief Programmer Team Management of Structured Programming," *IBM Systems Journal*, **11**, *1* (January), 56–73.

1995. Brooks, F. P., Jr. *The Mythical Man-Month: Essays on Software Engineering (Anniversary Edition)*, 29–37. Reading, MA: Addison-Wesley.

F. Terry Baker

CHIP

See INTEGRATED CIRCUITRY; MICROCOMPUTER CHIP; and MICROPROCESSORS AND MICROCOMPUTERS.

CHOMSKY HIERARCHY

For articles on related subjects *see* AUTOMATA THEORY; FORMAL LANGUAGES; GRAMMARS; MACHINE TRANSLATION; PROGRAMMING LINGUISTICS; and TURING MACHINE.

For the mathematician, an *alphabet* is a set of symbols and a language is a set, finite or infinite, of strings formed from that alphabet. A *grammar* is a finite system that characterizes a language. Customarily, grammars work by substitution (i.e. by production). Take the alphabet (or, as it is usually called, the *terminal* alphabet) of the language V_T, add a *nonterminal* alphabet V_N, and a special symbol S that belongs to neither V_T nor V_N. A *production* or rule of substitution, R, is an ordered pair of strings, $R = T_1 \rightarrow T_2$. A grammar is a system, $G = \langle V_N, V_T, P, S \rangle$, where P

denotes the set of allowable productions. To use the grammar, start with S and find a rule (i.e. a production) $S \rightarrow T_1$ and substitute T_1 for S. Find another rule $S_1 \rightarrow T_2$, such that S_1 matches part or all of T_1, and substitute T_2 for the matched part of T_1. Continue with any member of P until the result is a string that contains only terminal symbols. This sequential process is called the *derivation* of the string, and the final string belongs to the language. The language consists of exactly the strings that can be so derived.

If, in a grammar, every rule has the form $n \rightarrow nt$, $n \rightarrow t$, or $n \rightarrow \varepsilon$ where n is a non-terminal symbol, t is a terminal symbol, and ε is the empty string, the grammar is *regular* and characterizes a *regular language*.

If every rule has the form $n \rightarrow T$, where T is a string over the combined terminal and nonterminal alphabets, the grammar is *context-free* (the substitution $n \rightarrow T$ can be made wherever n occurs). A context-free grammar generates a context-free language.

If every rule has the form $S'nS'' \rightarrow S'TS''$, where S' and S'' are strings over the combined alphabet of terminal and nonterminal symbols, the grammar is *context-sensitive* (the substitution $n \rightarrow T$ can be made only in the context $S' \ldots S''$). A context-sensitive grammar characterizes a context-sensitive language.

Changing the restrictions on the forms of rules changes the power of the grammar. Without restrictions on the form of rules, a grammar can characterize any *recursively enumerable* set of strings, that is, any language that can be characterized at all (call this class of languages type 0). Not every recursively enumerable set (i.e. type 0 language) is a context-sensitive language, but every context-sensitive language is a recursively enumerable set (call the context-sensitive systems type 1). Again, the context-sensitive systems characterize all context-free languages, but the context-free systems (type 2) cannot characterize some context-sensitive languages. Finally, a regular language can be characterized by a system of any type,

Class of grammar, G_i	Grammatical characterization	Machine characterization
Type 0	Unrestricted (or phrase structure)	Turing machine
Type 1	Context-sensitive	Linear-bounded automaton
Type 2	Context-free	Pushdown automaton
Type 3	Regular (or right linear)	Finite state machine

Figure 1. The Chomsky hierarchy. Each class of grammars in the hierarchy contains all lower levels. Thus $G_3 \subset G_2 \subset G_1 \subset G_0$.

but regular grammars (type 3) cannot characterize all context-free languages. The hierarchy of types 0, 1, 2, 3 is commonly called the *Chomsky hierarchy* (see Fig. 1), named after the linguist Noam Chomsky, who described it in 1956.

To each type of grammar corresponds a kind of machine that *produces* or *accepts* a language of the given type: Turing machines (type 0), linear-bounded automata (type 1), nondeterministic pushdown automata (type 2), and finite-state machines (type 3).

The following example illustrates differences among the four classes of the Chomsky hierarchy. If the terminal alphabet is $\{0,1\}$, then $\{0^n1^m\}$, the set of strings with any number of 0s followed by any number of 1s, is a regular language. The set of strings with any number of 0s followed by the *same* number of 1s, $\{0^n1^n\}$, is context-free but not regular, because an accepting automaton for this language would have to be capable of counting arbitrarily high, which no finite-state machine can do. A pushdown automaton has an unbounded stack (*q.v.*) and can record any count of initial 0s and match that with the count of 1s. However, the language with any number of 0s followed by the same number of 1s and then by the same number of 0s again, $\{0^n1^n0^n\}$, would require two such matching mechanisms, to match the initial and final strings of 0s, and to match those with the number of 1s. That exceeds the power of a pushdown automaton, and this language is context-sensitive.

Strictly type 0 languages arise in the theory of Turing machines and of recursive functions (*see* RECURSION). Every Turing machine with the alphabet $\{0,1\}$ can be encoded in a unique way as a string of 0s and 1s. It is then possible to define a universal Turing machine that, given the encoding of any such Turing machine M joined with an input string I, will accept that concatenated string just in case M would halt on input I. The set of strings accepted by this universal Turing machine is of type 0 but is not context-sensitive.

Bibliography

1956. Chomsky, N. "Three Models for the Description of Language," *IRE Trans. Information Theory*, **IT-2**, 113–124.
1969. Salomaa, A. *Theory of Automata*. Oxford: Pergamon Press.
1997. Sudkamp, T. A. *Languages and Machines*, 2nd Ed. Reading, MA: Addison-Wesley.

David G. Hays

CHURCH, ALONZO

For articles on related subjects *see* ALGORITHMS, THEORY OF; LAMBDA CALCULUS; LOGIC PROGRAMMING; TURING, ALAN M.; and TURING MACHINE.

Alonzo Church was born in Washington, DC, on 14 June 1903, the son of Samuel Robbins Church, Justice of the Municipal Court of the District of Columbia, and Mildred Hannah Church (née Parker). The Church family was of considerable civic and academic distinction; Church's great grandfather, also named Alonzo Church, was a professor of mathematics and later president from 1829 to 1859 of the college in Athens, GA, that became the University of Georgia. Church did his undergraduate work at Princeton University, where his mathematical, logical, and foundational abilities were recognized and nurtured by Oswald Veblen, the brilliant American geometer and postulate theorist who was to become the first professor of the Institute for Advanced Study at Princeton. Church received an A.B. from Princeton in 1924 and was further encouraged by Veblen to stay on for graduate work in mathematics and logic, and in particular to study the foundational research being developed by David Hilbert and his school. Throughout his life, Church warmly acknowledged his friendship and indebtedness to Veblen, whom he referred to as "my sponsor."

In 1927, Church received a Ph.D. for a dissertation directed by Veblen on the effects of modifying the axiom of choice in set theory. This was followed by a two-year National Research Fellowship, the first year of which was spent at Harvard working with Birkhoff and Huntington. In the second year (1928–1929), Church went to Europe. He worked at Göttingen, where he met members of the Hilbert school, including Hilbert himself and Bernays. In Amsterdam, he met Brouwer, the famous intuitionistic mathematician. On his return to the USA in late 1929, he began

Figure 1. Alonzo Church.

teaching as an Assistant Professor of Mathematics at Princeton, a position that Veblen was instrumental in arranging. He continued teaching at Princeton as Professor of Mathematics and Philosophy, a title he received in 1961, until his "retirement" in 1967. In that year he was appointed with the same title at UCLA, where he maintained an active schedule of research, lecturing, and teaching through the spring semester of 1990, when he retired from teaching. He died at Hudson, OH, on 11 August 1995 and was buried in the Princeton Cemetery.

Church received many honors. In 1967, he was elected to the American Academy of Arts and Sciences and to the Académie Internationale de Philosophie des Sciences. In 1967, he received an honorary doctorate from Case Western Reserve University. In 1978, he was elected to the National Academy of Sciences and to the British Academy. In 1980, Princeton University awarded him an honorary doctor of science degree, and in 1990 an international symposium in his honor was held at the State University of New York at Buffalo in conjunction with the conferral of another honorary doctorate.

Church's contributions to logic are extensive, ranging from the practical, the pedagogical, and the philosophical to the scholarly, the historical, and the mathematical. There is no area of modern logic that has not been influenced by his work. His creation of the lambda calculus (q.v.), which makes possible logically precise expression of mathematical propositions, continues to exert a profound influence on logic, mathematics, and computer science. Although originally created for foundational research, lambda calculus has served as a model for functional programming languages, including Lisp (q.v.). He was one of the first logicians, along with Hilbert, Tarski, and Gödel, to grasp and exploit the syntactical, character-manipulating, and computational aspects of logic and postulate theory. He was the first to articulate the widely accepted principle, now known as *Church's Thesis* (and also as the Church–Turing Thesis) that every effectively calculable number-theoretic function is lambda-definable. This principle, which at first was highly controversial, boldly connects syntactical/computational aspects of mathematics to the abstract/numerical: while calculability has to do with string manipulation, lambda definability is abstract and numerical. By the proven equivalence of lambda definability and Turing computability, the Thesis is that effectively calculable number-theoretic functions are exactly the Turing-computable ones (*see* TURING MACHINE). Church's work on the Hilbert decision problem led to the discovery and proof of Church's Theorem—basically, that the set of formulas that do not express tautological propositions cannot be

computer-generated and thus that there is no computational method for deciding whether a given "conclusion" is not logically implied by given "premises." Church's Theorem identifies one outer limit of what is achievable in automated theorem-proving (*q.v.*). It thereby plays a role in modern computer science analogous to the role of the second law of thermodynamics in engineering. Church's lambda calculus and his formalizations of type theory (*q.v.*) jointly and separately continue to influence research by mathematically oriented computer scientists.

Church was also a highly successful teacher; the list of his doctoral students is a virtual *Who's Who* of modern logic and computer science. It includes William Boone, Martin Davis, Stephen Kleene, Hartley Rogers, Barkley Rosser, Dana Scott, Raymond Smullyan, Leon Henkin, Peter Andrews, and Alan Turing.

Throughout his life, Church maintained a deep and abiding interest in the practical aspects of logic. His practical interests in logic included not only applications of logic in computer science, but also institutions that foster the creation and dissemination of logical knowledge. He was an editor of *The Journal of Symbolic Logic* from its inception in 1936 until 1980, when he turned over the world-famous reviews section to a successor.

In the opinion of many logicians, Church's 1956 masterpiece *Introduction to Mathematical Logic* is still unsurpassed for its purpose.

Bibliography

1956. Church, A. *Introduction To Mathematical Logic.* Princeton, NJ: Princeton University Press.
1965. Davis, M. *The Undecidable: Basic Papers on Undecidable Propositions, Unsolvable Problems, and Computable Functions.* Hackett, NY: Raven Press.
1991. Scanlan, M. "Who Were the American Postulate Theorists?" *The Journal of Symbolic Logic*, **56**, 981–1002.
1997. Sieg, W. "Step by Recursive Step: Church's Analysis of Effective Calculability." *The Bulletin of Symbolic Logic*, **3**, 154–180.
1997. Barendregt, H. "The Impact of the Lambda Calculus in Logic and Computer Science," *The Bulletin of Symbolic Logic*, **3**, 181–215.

John Corcoran and Michael Scanlan

CIRCUITRY

See COMPUTER CIRCUITRY; and INTEGRATED CICRUITRY.

CLASS

For articles on related subjects *see* ABSTRACT DATA TYPE; BLOCK STRUCTURE; DATA STRUCTURES; DATA TYPE; and OBJECT-ORIENTED PROGRAMMING.

The concept of *class* was introduced in the programming language Simula 67 as an extension to the block structure and procedure mechanisms of Algol 60 (*q.v.*). As a technique for structuring programs, it is an alternative to the strict nesting of blocks in Algol 60. More recently the class concept has been used in the C++ (*q.v.*) and Java (*q.v.*) programming languages, primarily as a mechanism for building abstract data types (*q.v.*).

Classes in Simula 67

A Simula 67 class declaration resembles a procedure declaration in Algol 60. It was the inspiration for the *abstract data type* mechanism that is an important feature of several modern programming languages. A class may have formal parameters like a procedure. In general, a class declaration includes declarations for variables, functions, and procedures that are local to the class, followed by the body of the class, which is usually a block. An example of class declaration is given in Fig. 1. Unlike an Algol 60 procedure declaration, a class declaration does not by itself cause storage to be allocated or executable code to be compiled. A class declaration is a *template* that can be used to create instances of the class. In Simula 67, these class instances are called *objects*. Simula 67 allows the declaration of variables that are references to objects. The built-in operation **new** is used to create objects (class instances). For example, if z is a variable that is a reference to the class C declared in Fig. 1, then the statement

```
z := new C (100)
```

would create an instance of the class C. The formal parameter n of the class is used to specify the characteristics of the object created from the class (e.g. the upper bound of the array A). In Simula 67, "dot notation" is used to reference variables within objects (e.g. $z.A$ is a reference to the array A in the object z and $z.A[j]$ is a reference to the jth component of A in z).

Note that there may be many objects of a given class, each with its own set of variables in existence at any given time. Thus, the strict Algol 60 nesting of block invocations has been replaced by a more flexible regime. In most implementations of classes the variables declared in a class are treated in much the same way that fields declared in a record (*q.v.*) are treated. Each object has its own copy of the class variables.

The class concept also involves a different rule for the execution of the statements in a class. When an object is created, control is transferred to the executable statements in the body of the class. Three situations are possible:

1. Control passes through the class definition to the end of the block; the object is terminated; execution cannot reenter the object, but its local storage remains allocated. This possibility is usually used to initialize class variables as required.

2. A **detach** statement is executed in the body of the object; in this case, the object becomes an independently executing entity; its lifetime may exceed that of the block in which it was created, allowing objects to be used to create *processes* in a multi-processing system; e.g. an operating system could be structured as a set of cooperating concurrently executing class objects.

3. A **resume** statement is executed in the body of the object. Execution of the body is suspended at the point of the **resume** statement until it is reactivated

```
class C(n);
      integer n;
      begin
           integer array A[1:n];
           integer k;
           procedure clear;
                begin
                     integer i;
                     for i := 1 step 1 until n do
                        A[i] := 0
                end;
           ...
           comment end of declarations;
           comment execution of class object starts here;
           k := 0;
           resume;
           k := k + 1;
           ...
      end;
```

Figure 1. Simula 67 class declaration.

```
C class D(x);
    real x;
    begin
        real y;
        real array B[1:100];
        ...
        comment note the use of variables from C and D;
        y := x + A[k];
        ...
    end;
```

Figure 2. Simula 67 subclass declaration.

by a **resume** statement from outside of the object. For example, if the class C in Fig. 1 is used to create the object named Z, as shown above, then the statement

```
resume (Z)A:
```

would cause execution to continue in the body of the object Z at the statement $k := k + 1$. This allows coroutine (*q.v.*) structures to be built using objects.

Simula 67 Subclasses

The power and flexibility of the class concept is enhanced by the ability to declare subclasses. A subclass is formed by logically concatenating the formal parameters, local variables, procedures, and executable statements of an existing class with those of a class being declared. A subclass is created when the name of a class is used as a prefix to a class declaration. In the example in Fig. 2, the declaration of class D has class C as a prefix. The class D has formal parameters n and x, local variables A, k, y, and B, and a body consisting of the body of C followed by the body of D.

Classes in C++

In the language C++ the class concept occurs in a somewhat different form. In C++, classes are used primarily as a tool for building abstract data types.

```
template <class T, int size>
    class Stack
    {
    public:
            push(T newVal);
            pop(void);
            T top(void);
            int isEmpty(void);
    private:
            T s[size];
            int sp;
    }
...
Stack <int, 1024> intStack;
Stack <float, 512> floatStack;
```

Figure 3. C++ class template example.

A mechanism called *inheritance* allows subclassing as in Simula 67 so that the programmer can control the functionality, from none to all, that the subclass inherits from its base class.

C++ extends the class concept of Simula-67 in several ways:

♦ The designer of a class has explicit control over access to variables declared in the class. Variables can be declared to be accessible (**public**), accessible only to inheriting classes (**protected**) or inaccessible (**private**).

♦ The designer of the class can provide a *constructor* function which can be used to guarantee that variables in a class are properly initialized. The designer can also declare a *destructor* function that is called immediately before the data in a class is to be deallocated in order to perform any finalization that is required.

♦ A **template** mechanism allows classes to have value parameters as in Simula 67 and class (i.e. type) parameters that can be used to determine the types of variables declared in the class.

♦ *Virtual* function declarations allow the designer of a base class to specify an interface that must be provided by inheriting classes. This mechanism helps guarantee a consistent interface across all derived classes of a base class.

Fig. 3 illustrates the use of a template class declaration to create a family of bounded data stacks.

Bibliography

1972. Dahl, O. J., and Hoare, C. A. R. "Hierarchical Program Structures," in *Structured Programming* (eds. O. J. Dahl, E. W. Dijkstra, and C. A. R. Hoare), 175–220. London: Academic Press.

1973. Birtwistle, G. M., Dahl, O. J., Myhrhaug, B., and Nygaard, K. *SIMULA Begin*. Philadelphia: Auerbach.

1990. Ellis, M.A. and Stroustrup, B. *The Annotated C++ Reference Manual*. Reading, MA: Addison-Wesley.

1996. Gosling J., Joy, B., and Steele, G. *The Java Language Specification*. Reading, MA: Addison-Wesley.

David B. Wortman

CLIENT–SERVER COMPUTING

For articles on related subjects *see* DISTRIBUTED SYSTEMS; ELECTRONIC COMMERCE; OPERATING SYSTEMS: CONTEMPORARY ISSUES; and TCP/IP.

Introduction

Client–server computing is a distributed computing model in which *client* applications request services from *server* processes. Clients and servers typically run on different computers interconnected by a computer network. Any use of the Internet (*q.v.*), such as information retrieval (*q.v.*) from the World Wide Web (*q.v.*), is an example of client–server computing. However, the term is generally applied to systems in which an organization runs programs with multiple components distributed among computers in a network. The concept is frequently associated with *enterprise computing*, which makes the computing resources of an organization available to every part of its operation.

A *client* application is a process or program that sends messages to a server via the network. Those messages request the server to perform a specific task, such as looking up a customer record in a database or returning a portion of a file on the server's hard disk. The client manages local resources such as a display, keyboard, local disks, and other peripherals.

The *server* process or program listens for client requests that are transmitted via the network. Servers receive those requests and perform actions such as database queries and reading files. Server processes typically run on powerful PCs, workstations (*q.v.*), or mainframe (*q.v.*) computers.

An example of a client–server system is a banking application that allows a clerk to access account information on a central database server. All access is done via a PC client that provides a graphical user interface (GUI). An account number can be entered into the GUI along with how much money is to be withdrawn or deposited, respectively. The PC client validates the data provided by the clerk, transmits the data to the database server, and displays the results that are returned by the server.

The client–server model is an extension of the *object-based* (or *modular*) programming model, where large pieces of software are structured into smaller components that have well defined interfaces. This decentralized approach helps to make complex programs maintainable and extensible. Components interact by exchanging messages or by *Remote Procedure Calling* (*RPC* — *see* DISTRIBUTED SYSTEMS). The calling component becomes the client and the called component the server.

A client–server environment may use a variety of operating systems and hardware from multiple vendors; standard network protocols like TCP/IP provide compatibility. Vendor independence and freedom of choice are further advantages of the model. Inexpensive PC equipment can be interconnected with mainframe servers, for example.

Client–server systems can be scaled up in size more readily than centralized solutions since server functions can be distributed across more and more server computers as the number of clients increases. Server processes can thus run in parallel, each process serving its own set of clients. However, when there are multiple servers that update information, there must be some coordination mechanism to avoid inconsistencies.

The drawbacks of the client–server model are that security is more difficult to ensure in a distributed environment than it is in a centralized one, that the administration of distributed equipment can be much more expensive than the maintenance of a centralized system, that data distributed across servers needs to be kept consistent, and that the failure of one server can render a large client–server system unavailable. If a server fails, none of its clients can make further progress, unless the system is designed to be fault-tolerant (*see* FAULT-TOLERANT COMPUTING).

The computer network can also become a performance or reliability bottleneck: if the network fails, all servers become unreachable. If one client produces high network traffic then all clients may suffer from long response times.

Design Considerations

An important design consideration for large client–server systems is whether a client talks directly to the server, or whether an *intermediary process* is introduced between the client and the server. The former is a two-tier architecture, the latter is a three-tier architecture.

The *two-tier architecture* is easier to implement and is typically used in small environments (one or two servers with one or two dozens of clients). However, a two-tier architecture is less scalable than a three-tier architecture.

In the *three-tier architecture*, the intermediate process is used for decoupling clients and servers. The intermediary can *cache* frequently used server data to ensure better performance and scalability (*see* CACHE MEMORY). Performance can be further increased by having the intermediate process distribute client requests to several servers so that requests execute in parallel.

The intermediary can also act as a translation service by converting requests and replies from one format to another or as a security service that grants server access only to trusted clients.

Other important design considerations are:

- ◆ **Fat vs. thin client:** A client may implement anything from a simple data entry form to a complex business application. An important design consideration is how to partition application logic into client and server components. This has an impact on the scalability and maintainability of a client–server system. A "thin" client receives information in its final form from the server and does little or no data processing. A "fat" client does more processing, thereby lightening the load on the server.

- ◆ **Stateful vs. stateless:** Another design consideration is whether a server should be stateful or stateless. A *stateless* server retains no information about the data that clients are using. Client requests are fully self-contained and do not depend on the internal state of the server. The advantage of the stateless model is that it is easier to implement and that the failure of a server or client is easier to handle, as no state information about active clients is maintained. However, applications where clients need to acquire and release locks on the records stored at a database server usually require a *stateful* model, because locking information is maintained by the server for each individual client (*see* DATABASE CONCURRENCY CONTROL).

- ◆ **Authentication:** For security purposes servers must also address the problem of authentication (*q.v.*). In a networked environment, an unauthorized client may attempt to access sensitive data stored on a server. Authentication of clients is handled by using cryptographic techniques such as *public key encryption* (*see* CRYPTOGRAPHY, COMPUTERS IN) or special *authentication* (*q.v.*) servers such as in the OSF DCE system described below.

  In public key encryption, the client application "signs" requests with its private cryptographic key (*see* DIGITAL SIGNATURE), and encrypts the data in the request with a secret session key known only to the server and to the client. On receipt of the request, the server validates the signature of the client and decrypts the request only if the client is authorized to access the server.

- ◆ **Fault tolerance:** Applications such as flight-reservation systems and real-time market data feeds must be fault-tolerant. This means that important services remain available in spite of the failure of part of the computer system on which the servers are running (high availability), and that no information

is lost or corrupted when a failure occurs (consistency). For the sake of high availability, critical servers can be replicated, which means they are provided redundantly on multiple computers. If one replica fails then the other replicas still remain accessible by the clients. To ensure consistent modification of database records stored on multiple servers, a transaction processing (TP—*q.v.*) monitor can be installed. TP monitors are intermediate processes that specialize in managing client requests across multiple servers. The TP monitor ensures that such requests happen in an "all-or-nothing" fashion and that all servers involved in such requests are left in a consistent state, in spite of failures.

Distributed Object Computing

Distributed object computing (DOC) is a generalization of the client–server model. Object-oriented modeling and programming are applied to the development of client–server systems. Objects are pieces of software that encapsulate an internal state and make it accessible through a well-defined *interface*. In DOC, the interface consists of object operations and attributes that are remotely accessible. Client applications may connect to a remote instance of the interface with the help of a naming service. Finally, the clients invoke the operations on the remote object. The remote object thus acts as a server.

This use of objects naturally accommodates heterogeneity and autonomy. It supports heterogeneity since requests sent to server objects depend only on their interfaces and not on their internals. It permits autonomy because object implementations can change transparently, provided they maintain their interfaces.

If complex client–server systems are to be assembled out of objects, then objects must be compatible. Client–server objects have to interact with each other even if they are written in different programming languages and run on different hardware and operating system platforms.

Standards are required for objects to interoperate in heterogeneous environments. One of the widely adopted vendor-independent DOC standards is the OMG (Object Management Group) CORBA (Common Object Request Broker Architecture) specification. CORBA consists of the following building blocks:

- ◆ **Interface Definition Language:** Object interfaces are described in a language called IDL (Interface Definition Language). IDL is a purely declarative language resembling C++. It provides the notion of interfaces (similar to classes), of interface inheritance, of operations with input and output arguments, and of data types (*q.v.*) that can be passed along with an operation. IDL serves for declaring remotely accessible server objects in a platform- and programming language-neutral manner, but not for implementing those objects. CORBA objects are implemented in widely used languages such as C++, C, Java, and Smalltalk.

◆ **Object Request Broker:** The purpose of the ORB (Object Request Broker) is to find the server object for a client request, to prepare the object to receive the request, to transmit the request from the client to the server object, and to return output arguments back to the client application. The ORB mainly provides an object-oriented RPC facility.

◆ **Basic Object Adapter:** The BOA (Basic Object Adapter) is the primary interface used by a server object to gain access to ORB functions. The BOA exports operations to create object references, to register and activate server objects, and to authenticate requests. An object reference is a data structure that denotes a server object in a network. A server installs its reference in a *name server* so that a client application can retrieve the reference and invoke the server. The object reference provides the same interface as the server object that it represents. Details of the underlying communication infrastructure are hidden from the client.

◆ **Dynamic Invocation Interface:** The DII (Dynamic Invocation Interface) defines functions for creating request messages and for delivering them to server objects. The DII is a low-level equivalent of the communication stubs (message-passing interfaces) that are generated from an IDL declaration.

◆ **Internet Inter-ORB Protocol:** The Internet Inter-ORB Protocol (IIOP) allows CORBA ORBs from different vendors to interoperate via a TCP/IP connection. IIOP is a simplified RPC protocol used to invoke server objects via the Internet in a portable and efficient manner.

◆ **Interface and Implementation Repository:** The CORBA Interface Repository is a database containing type information (interface names, interface operations, and argument types) for the interfaces available in a CORBA system. This information is used for dynamic invocation via the DII, for revision control, and so forth. The Implementation Repository provides information allowing an ORB to locate and launch server objects.

Client–Server Toolkits

A wide range of software toolkits for building client–server software is available on the market today. Client–server toolkits are also referred to as *middle-* *ware.* CORBA implementations are an example of well-known client–server middleware. Other examples are OSF DCE, DCOM, message-oriented middleware, and transaction processing monitors.

◆ **OSF DCE:** The Open Software Foundation (OSF) Distributed Computing Environment (DCE) is a *de facto* standard for multivendor client–server systems. DCE is a collection of tools and services that help programmers in developing heterogeneous client–server applications. DCE is a large and complex software package; it mainly includes a remote procedure call facility, a naming service, a clock synchronization service, a client–server security infrastructure, and a *threads* package (*see* MULTITASKING).

◆ **DCOM:** Distributed Component Object Model (DCOM) is Microsoft's object protocol that enables *ActiveX* components to communicate with each other across a computer network. An ActiveX component is a remote accessible object that has a well-defined interface and is self-contained. ActiveX components can be embedded into Web documents, so that they download to the client automatically to execute in the client's Web browser (*see* WORLD WIDE WEB). DCOM provides a remote instantiation facility allowing clients to create remote server objects. It also provides a security model to let programmers restrict who may create a server object and who may invoke it. Finally, an Interface Definition Language (IDL) is provided for defining remotely accessible object interfaces and composing remote procedure calls.

◆ **MOM:** Message-Oriented Middleware (MOM) allows the components of a client–server system to interoperate by exchanging general purpose messages. A client application communicates with a server by placing messages into a *message queue.* The client is relieved of the tasks involved in transmitting the messages to the server reliably. After the client has placed a message into a message queue, it continues other work until the MOM informs the client that the server's reply has arrived. This kind of communication is called *asynchronous messaging,* since client and server are decoupled by message queues. MOM functions much like electronic mail, storing and forwarding messages on behalf of client and server applications. Messages may be submitted even when the receiver happens to be temporarily unavailable, and are thus inherently more flexible and fault-tolerant than RPC. Examples of MOM are IBM's MQSeries product and the OMG Event Service. Web *push technologies* such as Marimba's *Castanet* also fall into the category of message-oriented middleware.

◆ **Transaction Processing (TP) Monitors:** Transaction processing (*q.v.*) monitors allow a client application to perform a series of requests on multiple remote servers while preserving consistency among the servers. Such a series of requests is called a *transaction*. The TP monitor ensures that either all requests that are part of a transaction succeed, or that the servers are *rolled back* to the state they had before the unsuccessful transaction was started. A transaction fails when one of the involved computers or applications goes down, or when any of the applications decides to *abort* the transaction. TP monitors are part of client–server products such as Novell's Tuxedo and Transarc's Encina.

A TP monitor can be used within a banking system when funds are withdrawn from an account on one database server and deposited in an account on another database server. The monitor makes sure that the transaction occurs in an "all or nothing" fashion. If any of the servers fails during the transfer then the transaction is rolled back such that both accounts are in the state they were before transaction was started.

Bibliography

1995. Mowbray, T. J., and Zahavi, R. *The Essential CORBA.* New York: John Wiley.
1996. Andrade, J. M. (ed.), Dwyer, T., Felts, S., and Carges, M. *The Tuxedo System: Software for Constructing and Managing Distributed Business Applications.* Reading, MA: Addison-Wesley.
1997. Shan, Y.-P., Earle, R. H., and Lenzi, M. A. *Enterprise Computing With Objects: From Client/Server Environments to the Internet.* Reading, MA: Addison-Wesley.
1998. Orfali, R., and Harkey, D. *Client/Server Programming with Java and CORBA,* 2nd Ed. New York: John Wiley.

Websites

Client–server frequently asked questions URLs: `http://www.abs.net/~lloyd/csfaq.txt`.
OMG CORBA documentation URL: `http://www.omg.org`.
OSF DCE documentation URL: `http://www.rdg.opengroup.org/public/pubs/catalog/dz.htm`.
Microsoft ActiveX and related technology URL: `http://www.microsoft.com/com`.

Silvano Maffeis

CLUSTER COMPUTING

For articles on related subjects *see* CLIENT–SERVER COMPUTING; COOPERATIVE COMPUTING; DATABASE MANAGEMENT SYSTEM; DISTRIBUTED SYSTEMS; MULTIPROCESSING; NETWORKS, COMPUTER; PARALLEL PROCESSING; and SUPERCOMPUTERS.

Introduction

A cluster of computers, or simply a *cluster*, is a collection of computers that are connected together and used as a single computing resource. Clusters have been used from the dawn of electronic computing as a straightforward way to obtain greater capacity and higher reliability than a single computer can provide. Clusters can be an informal, if not anarchic, computer organization. Often they have not been built by computer manufacturers but rather assembled by customers on an *ad hoc* basis to solve a problem at hand.

The first cluster probably appeared in the late 1950s or early 1960s when some company's finance officer, realizing that payroll checks wouldn't get printed if the computer broke down, purchased a spare. Software tools for managing groups of computers and submitting batch jobs to them, such as IBM's Remote Job Entry (RJE) System, became commercially available in the mid-1970s. By the late 1970s, Tandem Computers began selling highly reliable systems that were clusters, with software to make them appear to access a single database system. However, it was not until the early 1980s that DEC (Digital Equipment Corporation—*q.v.*) coined the term *cluster* for a collection of software and hardware that made several VAX minicomputers (*q.v.*) appear to be a single time-sharing (*q.v.*) system called the VAXcluster.

With the appearance of very high performance personal workstations (*q.v.*) in the early 1990s, technical computer users began replacing expensive supercomputers with clusters of those workstations which they assembled themselves. Computer manufacturers responded with prepackaged workstation clusters, which became the standard form of supercomputers by the mid-1990s; a system of this type with special-purpose added hardware achieved the milestone of defeating the reigning human chess champion, Garry Kasparov (*see* COMPUTER CHESS). By 1998, even those systems were being challenged by user-constructed clusters of increasingly powerful personal computers. A very large, highly diffuse and informal cluster—using spare time on approximately 22,000 personal computers owned by volunteers, connected only occasionally though the Internet—succeeded in February 1998 in decoding a "challenge" message encrypted using the Data Encryption Standard system with a 56-bit key (*see* CRYPTOGRAPHY, COMPUTERS IN). The answer was found by simply trying one after another of the 63 quadrillion possible keys; success came after taking only 39 days to examine 85% of the keys. Appropriately, the decoded message read "Many hands make light work."

Individual spectacular feats such as this are not, however, the reason that computer industry analysts estimated that half of all high performance server computer systems would be clusters by the turn of the century. Clusters provide a practical means of increasing performance and providing high system availability. The next sections describe some of the techniques used to achieve these purposes

Performance Scaling

Many hands make light work only if they all work on different parts of the job. If there is a single large problem to solve, such as decoding a message or simulating the airflow over an airplane, techniques must be used that break the problem down into many separate parts that can be worked on separately by the different computers in a cluster. Such techniques are described in PARALLEL PROCESSING: ALGORITHMS, and can lead to the ability to use massive numbers of computers on the same problem, even though the vast majority of clusters have few—two to four—computers; see "Related Concepts" below. Techniques to do this can be complex, but in some cases they are quite straightforward. For example, the decryption problem mentioned above was broken into parts by simply giving to each computer a different set of keys to test.

Most often in so-called "commercial" computing, which is by far the most common use of computers, there isn't one single large problem. Instead, there are naturally many smaller ones, and the aim is to process more of them. For example, a server of World Wide Web pages on the Internet needs to respond to many separate requests. It need not speed up its response to each individual request, but it is useful to be able to handle more of them at a time.

This is very easily done using a cluster, if read-only (unchanging) Web pages are what are being returned to users. For example, one computer in the cluster can be singled out as the "dispatcher." It receives all requests, but does not examine them; instead it quickly forwards them to a collection of "server" computers, uniformly distributing the requests so that each server need handle only a fraction of the total work. The servers perform the actual processing required: they analyze the Uniform Resource Locator (URL) sent by the user, retrieve the information requested, and transmit it back. Each server can have its own copy of all the requestable files, or they can all access yet another separate computer that holds that data, keeping ("caching") their own copies of frequently requested files such as home pages. Adding more servers to the cluster increases the capacity of the system to handle more requests at once, at least until the dispatcher is overloaded; in practice, that has not proven a problem even with hundreds of servers.

Websites providing the ability to purchase merchandise are more complex because they must alter information that all the servers must have access to, for example a table indicating how many items of each kind are in stock (*see* ELECTRONIC COMMERCE). This is usually accomplished by keeping such information in a database, which the servers all access. The database system itself can be designed to operate in parallel across a cluster of computers, and in fact every major database vendor has a version of its product that does this. A cluster-parallel database can be run directly on the servers themselves, or on separate dedicated computers.

High Availability

While important, using clusters for increased performance is actually less common than using them to provide high system availability. Businesses and livelihoods now depend on computers operating around the clock, seven days a week, throughout the year; stores are open 24 hours a day, global businesses span time zones across the globe, the Internet is always open for business—and if your Web server is down, a competitor is just a mouse-click away. Estimates of what computer failures cost vary, but for a large corporation it would not be unusual to find that $10,000 is lost for every hour that an important computer system is not working. In some areas, such as stock exchanges, the amount lost per hour is far higher than that.

Failover is the basic technique used to achieve high availability in clusters: computer failure is detected, and the work it was doing is "failed over" to another in the cluster. To implement failover, monitoring "heartbeat" messages are regularly sent by each computer to one or more others in the cluster, inquiring if they are operational. If a computer does not respond to a heartbeat message, the computer that sent that message cannot immediately assume the other has failed; for example, a network card or cable carrying the heartbeat could have failed. Instead, loss of heartbeat is communicated to the other computers in the cluster, which also monitor each other; if all of them, consolidating their information, reach a consensus that one computer is no longer operational, then the work that was being performed on that computer is failed over to one or more others in the cluster and the system as a whole continues operating, perhaps at lower capacity if a spare system was not part of the configuration.

Failover can be quite complex. If the work being done by the cluster is not homogeneous, as it was in the Web server example above, redistributing the work of the failed computer among the others to achieve the best system throughput (*q.v.*) is often difficult. Furthermore, not every kind of work can necessarily be run on every machine of the cluster; only some computers may have access to the disks holding the required data, for example. Such resource dependencies, coupled with heterogeneous workloads, make the worst case very difficult. Fortunately, many practical situations are homogeneous and simple.

Clusters take time to failover, anywhere from a few seconds to several minutes, and so cannot be used in applications like medical equipment or autopilots where seconds of outage can be disastrous. Instead, special-purpose hardware that is fault-tolerant (*see* FAULT-TOLERANT COMPUTING) is used for those cases. Clusters are, however, usable in many situations; and since they are composed of everyday computers sold in large numbers, they are much less expensive than the alternatives.

In addition, unlike fault-tolerant hardware, clusters can be used to avoid not just failures but planned outages such as taking a computer down to upgrade it. The system operator simply tells the cluster to "act as if" one computer has failed; when the work has been moved off that computer, it can be turned off and upgraded. The ability to avoid both failures and planned outages make clusters the only technique that can be used to make computer systems that never stop working.

Related Concepts

A Network of Workstations (NOW) or Cluster of Workstations (COW) is a type of cluster formed from individuals' workstations (*q.v.*) already present in their offices, connected by the local area network (LAN— *q.v.*) already in place. Unused capacity on those systems, particularly during off-hours, can be effectively used this way. In practice this is useful, but usually needs to be supplemented by a rack full of workstations or servers, placed elsewhere and dedicated solely to cluster computing. This is often enhanced by adding a fast communications network within the rack. The entire collection, including the rack of systems, is then called a NOW or COW.

The term Massively Parallel Processor (MPP) refers to any parallel computer containing a very large number of computing elements, typically 500 or more, and often thousands. As of the late 1990s, the computing elements in most such systems were whole computers, effectively making such systems clusters. (Some were NUMA; see below.) The large number of nodes involved, however, requires special packaging that is more compact than usual; it also usually requires an inter-system communication network that is more compact and with higher bandwidth (*q.v.*) than usual. For example, the ASCI Blue supercomputer, a one-off contract commissioned by the US government as part of the Advanced Scientific Computing Initiative (ASCI) to simulate nuclear processes well enough to

avoid nuclear bomb testing, is indeed a massive cluster. It has 1,464 computers, each with four processors for a total of 5,856 processors, capable of a theoretical maximum performance of 3.88 Teraflops (Trillion Floating-Point Operations per Second)—10,000 times the average desktop PC. Each of the 1,464 computers has a 300 MB/sec communications link to a switch connecting them all (24 times as fast as a 100 Mbit/sec LAN), and many can be active simultaneously (unlike a LAN, typically shared by 10 to 20 workstations). Clearly, "massive" requirements result in MPP designs that are physically as different from most clusters (two to four nodes, on average) as the Sears Tower is from a single family home.

Nonuniform Memory Access (NUMA) systems are sometimes confused with clusters, but are not clusters. NUMA systems connect what seem to be separate computers through their memory subsystems, allowing direct access from any processor to memory anywhere in the complex; the term "nonuniform" is used in the name because it is faster to access nearby memory than remote memory. The processors in clusters, in contrast, have no direct access to nonlocal memory; communication is only by messages. NUMA systems have the advantage of using a single operating system, which makes them easier to administer than a cluster. The direct memory access arguably makes them easier to program in some circumstances. However, they have the disadvantage of not being highly available, since if the single operating system crashes the entire system goes down (it is a single point of failure). The direct memory access also creates hardware-based single points of failure. In addition, it is harder, though not impossible, to scale their size to MPP levels, since the single operating system must be made to work at those levels; clusters' multiple operating systems avoid that issue.

Conclusion

Clusters are a form of distributed or parallel processing that has been used since the dawn of computing, but not always dignified by being a recognized and studied computer system organization. By the mid-1990s, however, they were the dominant form of supercomputing; and by the turn of the century half of all server computers were clusters. This is partly because they provide increased performance, but more importantly because they provide increased system availability, allowing a computer system to keep running despite failures.

Many other parallel and distributed organizations of computers may be invented, but whatever they are, their users will find it valuable to group them into clusters.

Bibliography

1989. Gray, J., and Reuter, A. *Transaction Processing: Concepts and Techniques.* San Francisco: Morgan Kaufmann.

1994. Almasi, G. S., and Gottlieb, A. *Highly Parallel Computing,* 2nd Ed. New York: Benjamin/Cummings.

1998. Hwang, K., and Xu, Z. *Scalable Parallel Computing: Technology, Architecture, Programming.* New York: WCB/McGraw-Hill.

1998. Pfister, G. F. *In Search of Clusters,* 2nd Ed. Upper Saddle River, NJ: Prentice Hall.

Gregory F. Pfister

COBOL

For an article on a related subject *see* PROGRAMMING LANGUAGES.

A Short History of Early Cobol

THE CREATION OF COBOL

This article is a tiny portion of the material in Sammet (1981), which provides full documentation about the creation of Cobol, including lists of participants. That paper was based on the hand notes, correspondence, and official documents created at the time of the work on the initial Cobol, and still in the possession of the author. One persistent myth should be corrected at the beginning; namely that Cobol was created by a single person. As will be shown below, Cobol was created by a committee and nobody can be described or listed as the "developer" or "creator" of Cobol.

THE CREATION OF THE SHORT-RANGE COMMITTEE

On 28–29 May 1959, a meeting was held at the Pentagon. It was chaired by Charles A. Phillips, then Director of the Data Systems Research Staff, Office of the Assistant Secretary of Defense (Comptroller). About 50 people attended the meeting, including representatives of seven government organizations, 11 users and consultants, and 15 representatives of manufacturers. I was present as the senior of two representatives from Sylvania Electric Products. (A complete listing of the attendees at this crucial meeting is in Sammet (1985, p. 240).)

The reason for calling the meeting was to consider the potential need for, or desirability of, a common business language. The DoD was concerned about the inability to run the same business data processing programs on differing computers (e.g. UNIVAC (*q.v.*), IBM 705). BDP programs involved a lot of data and datafiles, but relatively little calculation. The only programming language in significant use was Fortran, and that certainly did not have the necessary capabilities.

At that time, FLOW-MATIC was the only programming language in use for business data processing. It was developed by a group at Remington-Rand UNIVAC under the leadership of Grace Hopper (*q.v.*). A language called AIMACO was also available, but it was essentially a dialect of FLOW-MATIC developed by the Air Force Air Materiel Command under the leadership of Col. Alfred Asch. There was (only) a manual for a new BDP language called COMTRAN (soon renamed Commercial Translator) produced by a group at IBM under the leadership of Robert Bemer; it had not been implemented.

There were several results of the May 1959 meeting, but the four most important were

1. The development of a listing of desired characteristics of a proposed Common Business Language. A crucial item on that list was the use of English language (rather than mathematical symbolism), so that programs could be easily written and read.

2. The creation of three committees with short-, medium- and long-range objectives, and a (self-appointed) Executive Committee to coordinate the efforts of these groups.

3. A mission for the short-range committee (described below).

4. The creation of CODASYL (Committee on Data Systems Languages) and its Executive Committee.

Phillips' report of the meeting stated the Mission of the Short-Range Language Committee as

> "To report by September 1, 1959, the results of its study of the strengths and weaknesses of existing automatic compilers (especially AIMACO, FLOW-MATIC and COMTRAN); and to recommend a short range composite approach (good for at least the next year or two) to a common business language for programming digital computers. . . ."

(The remainder of the mission statement is in Sammet (1985, p. 202).) This wording is ambiguous, and it was certainly not clear that we were directed to create a new language.

THE WORK OF THE SHORT-RANGE COMMITTEE

The Short-Range Committee consisted of representatives from six computer manufacturers (Burroughs, Honeywell, IBM, RCA, Sperry Rand, Sylvania), and three government organizations (Air Force, David Taylor Model Basin, National Bureau of Standards). For a complete listing of all the people who participated in the committee work in 1959, *see* Sammet (1985, p. 214).

I am convinced that had the Short-Range Committee realized at the outset that the language it created (i.e. Cobol) was going to be used for such a long period of time, it would have gone about the task quite differently. Most of us viewed our work as (only) a stopgap measure to prevent a proliferation of new programming languages for business data processing. However, nobody ever produced a replacement language for Cobol.

I have been asked to speculate on how our work might have been done differently if we had known that it would still be widely used several decades later. For one thing, we would have insisted upon having more time. Assuming we were given six months at the beginning (and then assuming we would have asked for more time), we certainly would have included initially some features that were put in later—in particular, the SORT command, and a Report Writer. We might also have found a somewhat better solution to the problem of describing data in a machine-independent way. We would probably also have spent more time discussing some of the trickier aspects, rather than forcing them to a faster vote. However, I think the basic structure of the language would have remained the same, because I believe it was consistent with our basic mission and the state of the art in 1959.

The Short-Range Committee (and its subcommittees) held several meetings, and turned in a preliminary report in September as required, but asked for an extension until December 1959 to complete the work. That preliminary report made it clear that a new language was being developed.

After several more meetings of the committee, it was clear that we were bogged down by the size of the Short-Range committee. In October a six-person subcommittee was appointed to try to produce a set of specifications. The six persons were Gertrude Tierney and William Selden (IBM), Howard Bromberg and Norman Discount (RCA), and Vernon Reeves and Jean Sammet (Sylvania).

This subcommittee—which met for two weeks in November 1959, including several around the clock sessions (literally)—did the bulk of the work in creating the Cobol specifications; the full Short-Range Committee then reviewed and modified their work to produce the final set of specifications. In December 1959, the specifications for Cobol were given to the CODASYL Executive Committee, which accepted the report "for publication and recommended its adoption for usage by the entire data processing community...". Frances (Betty) Holberton (David Taylor Model Basin) then did some editing and the Cobol specifications were officially released as a government report in April 1960.

A listing of all the people who participated in the work of the Short-Range Committee at one time or another is in Sammet (1985, p. 214).

Technical Characteristics of Cobol

Space does not permit any lengthy discussion of the technical aspects of Cobol. The major concepts were:

1. Creation of four divisions in a program: PROCEDURE, DATA, ENVIRONMENT, and IDENTIFICATION. The PROCEDURE Division contained the statements (i.e. commands) and was (meant to be) machine-independent. The DATA Division contained a description of the data to be used, and was moderately machine-independent. The ENVIRONMENT Division was completely machine-dependent and listed the computer, compiler, etc. to be used by the program. The IDENTIFICATION Division just contained information needed to identify the programmer, date, etc.

2. Use of the English language throughout for commands, and data names, including allowance of 30 characters for data names. (This allowed the writing of SOCIAL-SECURITY-NUMBER rather than an abbreviation.)

   Commands were of the form

   ```
   MOVE data-name-1 to data-name-2
   IF data-name-3 IS GREATER THAN
           data-name-4 THEN READ file-name
   ```

3. Data could be organized into files, which contained records (q.v.), then subrecords, and fields within (sub)records; each level could be named and described. One method of describing fields was by using a PICTURE clause indicating the number and type of characters, location of a decimal point (if any) and other characteristics. For example

   ```
   ALPHA PICTURE 9(12)
   ```

   meant that a field named ALPHA had 12 digits. (The number 9 was used to denote a digit.)

   ```
   BETA PICTURE A(2)
   ```

   indicated a two letter field.

   ```
   GAMMA PICTURE $$,$$9.99
   ```

   means that GAMMA is an edited character string. Its value is a series of characters representing a price from $0.00 to $99,999.99.

4. As a by-product, the committee developed a metalanguage (q.v.) which has been widely used (although sometimes with a few modifications) for programming language definitions ever since (see PROGRAMMING LINGUISTICS).

Later Versions and Standardization

As with all other programming languages receiving significant use, Cobol has changed significantly over the years, while still maintaining its basic structure. Even before the Cobol-60 specifications were released, a committee (containing some people from the original Short Range Committee, plus some new individuals and/or organizations) went to work on some improvements, resulting in Cobol-61. This was the first version to be widely implemented. This was followed by Cobol-61 Extended (issued in 1962), and Cobol-65. The first Cobol ANSI standard was issued in 1968, based on Cobol-65; it set the precedent for later standards of not making changes to the specifications but possibly removing some of the features, and/or reorganizing the specifications. Later standards were issued in 1974 and 1985. The latter is being revised, but a new standard is not expected until at least 2000.

Much more information, and many more details, on the creation and evolution of Cobol are in the *Annals* (1985). In particular, the article by Sammet and Garfunkel in that issue summarizes the technical changes made from version to version.

Conclusions

Although Cobol has been scorned by many computer scientists, it has nevertheless lasted for almost 40 years. Many people have claimed it is the most widely used programming language. However, it is impossible to either confirm or reject that hypothesis because of the lack of adequate data.

Bibliography

1981. Sammet, J. E. "The Early History of Cobol," in *History of Programming Languages* (ed. R. L. Wexelblat), Ch. V, 199–276. New York: Academic Press.
1985. Sammet, J. E., and Garfunkel, J. "Summary of Changes in Cobol, 1960–1985," *Annals of the History of Computing,* **7**, *4* (October), 342–347.
1985. *Annals of the History of Computing* (Special Cobol 25th Anniversary Issue), **7**, *4* (October).

Jean E. Sammet

CODES

For articles on related subjects *see* BAUDOT CODE; CHARACTER CODES; ERROR CORRECTING AND DETECTING CODE; and UNIVERSAL PRODUCT CODE.

The term *code* has a particular meaning in cryptography, and is also sometimes used as a synonym for *program* or part of a program. But for the purposes of this article, a *code* is a non-secret mapping between a symbol of an alphabet (e.g. our alphabet of letters) and a number of digits of a number system (e.g. six bits for base 2). To be more precise, the mathematician would say that a code is a pair $(\Sigma; \Pi)$ where Σ is the symbol space (the set of symbols to be coded) and the Π are numeric combinations (the codes). Suppose that S is some symbol in the symbol space Σ and P is one of the permutations of the digits in a numeric counting system Π. We might say "S is mapped into P" or that "S is represented by P," using the symbols:

$$S \rightarrow P \quad \text{or} \quad S \equiv P. \tag{1}$$

Each P in Π is called a *combination*. When P consists of n digits, it can be written as

$$P = P_1 P_2 P_3 \cdots P_n \tag{2}$$

where P_i is any digit of the counting system with radix r, i.e.

$$P_i = 0, 1, 2, \ldots, \text{ or } r - 1. \tag{3}$$

To make this more concrete, let us examine the case where the symbol space Σ_A consists of letters of the alphabet. Let each combination P consist of two decimal digits; thus, $r = 10$ and $n = 2$. A very simple code might assign numbers consecutively to the letters so that we would have

$$A \equiv 01, \ B \equiv 02, \ C \equiv 03, \ldots, Z \equiv 26. \tag{4}$$

It is convenient here to introduce the notation $|s|$ for the number of elements in a set, i.e. its *cardinality*. For our example

$$|\Sigma_A| = 26 \quad \text{and} \quad |\Pi| = 100. \tag{5}$$

Since there are many more elements in Π than there are symbols in the symbol space, many numeric combinations are unassigned. These are sometimes called *forbidden combinations*.

Need

Data is an abstraction of information in the real world. People keep this information in the form of symbols. The computer stores information in the various hardware elements that constitute it. Elements have been designed that have two or more states. An element such as the Nixie tube has ten states. But by far the most common, least expensive, and most efficient element is the *bistable device*; it has only two stable states. For the computer to represent information, it must be structured so that the devices used in the computer can accommodate it. Since there are not enough states in a single bistable device to represent each symbol as a human being uses it, the symbols are represented by a combination of these settings, i.e. by a binary code.

Decimal Codes

A decimal code provides a representation for the decimal numbers in binary. To summarize their characteristics:

$$|\Sigma_D| = 10, \quad r = 2, \quad n \geq 4 \qquad (6)$$

so that these codes use four bits or more.

There are two principal ways to associate symbols with combinations:

1. *Weighted codes* assign different weights to each bit in the combination, as discussed shortly.

2. *Transition rules* may be created to indicate how the code for the successor number is created from the code for any given number.

Four-Bit Codes

WEIGHTED CODES

Let us label the bits of the combination that represents a decimal digit. Unlike (2), where the subscripts increase from left to right, we will now order the subscripts 1 through 4 in reverse, going from right to left. Thus, if D is a decimal digit, we have

$$D \equiv b_4 b_3 b_2 b_1. \qquad (7)$$

A weighted code associates a weight W_i with each bit b_i which might be stated symbolically as

$$b_i \leftrightarrow W_i \qquad i = 1 \text{ to } 4. \qquad (8)$$

The requirement of the weighted code is that, when each bit is multiplied by its weight and then these are totaled, the total must be equal in value to the digit. Stated symbolically, we have

$$D = \sum_1^4 b_i W_i = b_4 W_4 + b_3 W_3 + b_2 W_2 + b_1 W_1. \qquad (9)$$

Some restrictions arise in setting up the weights:

1. For each digit to be encoded, there must be a combination of bits and their corresponding weights, whose total—using (9)—is equal to the value of the digit.

2. When two combinations exist that, when substituted into (9), yield the same digit D, then another rule must be provided to decide which combination will be used.

8421 CODE

The weighted 8421 code is illustrated in column 1 of Table 1. From left to right, weights 8, 4, 2, and 1 are assigned to the bits that make up the combination. When the bits are set to 0 or 1, the resulting number is shown in the left column of the table.

TABLE 1. Weighted codes.

Weights Digits	(1) 8 4 2 1 Code	(2) 7 4 2 1 Code	(3) 7 4 2 -1 Code	(4) XS 3 Code
0	0 0 0 0	0 0 0 0	0 0 0 0	0 0 1 1
1	0 0 0 1	0 0 0 1	0 0 1 1	0 1 0 0
2	0 0 1 0	0 0 1 0	0 0 1 0	0 1 0 1
3	0 0 1 1	0 0 1 1	0 1 0 1	0 1 1 0
4	0 1 0 0	0 1 0 0	0 1 0 0	0 1 1 1
5	0 1 0 1	0 1 0 1	0 1 1 1	1 0 0 0
6	0 1 1 0	0 1 1 0	1 0 0 1	1 0 0 1
			(0 1 1 0)	
7	0 1 1 1	1 0 0 0	1 0 0 0	1 0 1 0
		(0 1 1 1)		
8	1 0 0 0	1 0 0 1	1 0 1 1	1 0 1 1
9	1 0 0 1	1 0 1 0	1 0 1 0	1 1 0 0
*(A)	1 0 1 0	1 0 1 1	1 1 0 1	1 1 0 1
*(B)	1 0 1 1	1 1 0 0	1 1 0 0	1 1 1 0
*(C)	1 1 0 0	1 1 0 1	1 1 1 1	1 1 1 1
*(D)	1 1 0 1	1 1 1 0	1 1 1 0	—
*(E)	1 1 1 0	1 1 1 1	—	—
*(F)	1 1 1 1	—	—	—

* Forbidden combinations.

The six entries at the bottom of the table provide values 10 through 15. Of course, there are no digits to correspond to these values in the decimal system. Hence these combinations are forbidden. If these occur, the computer should signal an error.

Note that these combinations would be legal if the base for our system were 16. Hence we will return to this table when we discuss the hexadecimal (base 16) system.

Finally, note that the sequence of combinations for the 8421 code is the same sequence in which these binary numbers occur in the binary counting system. Hence the appellation *binary-coded decimal*, or simply BCD, for the code of column 1.

7421 CODE

Column 2 presents the 7421 code. Again, there are six forbidden combinations. The bits that constitute each combination are calculated so that (9) will yield the digit value.

A problem arises when encoding the digit 7. There are two combinations, 1000 and 0111, both of which yield the value 7. An auxiliary rule is required to settle this difficulty: use the combination with the least number of 1s in it (i.e. 1000).

742–1 CODE

The code for these weights is presented in column 3. It illustrates that one or more of the weights may be negative as long as the weights fulfill the requirement that all digit values must be created. This time we find that there are two combinations that yield the digit value 6. Since both have the same number of 1s, we choose the combination with the 1 in the least significant place.

XS 3 CODE

To show that not all codes require weights explicitly, we examine the XS 3 (excess-3) code presented in column 4. The rule for generating this code requires that we use the BCD code for a digit, call it n_D, and add the binary number 0011 (i.e. 3 in decimal) to it:

$$D \equiv n_D + 0011 \qquad (10)$$

What use would there be for this code? It has two advantages:

1. No proper combination consists of all zeros; therefore, no combination will be mistaken for a null transmission or *vice versa*.

2. It is a self-complementing code.

A *self-complementing code* is very valuable because it possesses the property that the combination for the complement of a digit is the complement of the combination for that digit. The complement of a number is needed when we do subtraction by addition and complementation. For decimal arithmetic, this requires that we subtract the value of the digit from 9. In our binary code, the complement of a combination b_D is taken with respect to the largest valued combination; for a four-bit code, this would be 1111. Then, our definition for a self-complementing code is one for which the following holds:

$$9 - D \equiv 1111 - b_D \qquad (11)$$

As an example of how XS 3 fulfills this requirement, we have

$$2 \equiv 0101, 9 - 2 = 7, 1111 - 0101 = 1010, 7 \equiv 1010 \qquad (12)$$

Hexadecimal

Programmers often deal with data in units of a *byte*, which consists of eight bits or two *nibbles*, each nibble consisting of four bits. If the combination for each nibble has a different symbol to represent it, then this simplifies the description. The binary values with decimal equivalents 10 through 15 are usually assigned the upper case letters A through F, as shown in Table 1 in parentheses. Thus, the programmer can describe the byte consisting of 10110101 in hexadecimal as B5.

Other Decimal Codes

If we do not restrict ourselves to four-bit decimal codes, we can provide one or more of the following advantages:

TABLE 2. Other decimal codes.

Weights Digits	(1) 2-out-of-5 Code 74210	(2) Biquinary Code 50 43210	(3) MBQ Code 5421	(4) A Gray Code
0	11000	01 00001	0000	0000
1	00011	01 00010	0001	0001
2	00101	01 00100	0010	1001
3	00110	01 01000	0011	1101
4	01001	01 10000	0100	0101
5	01010	10 00001	1000	0111
6	01100	10 00010	1001	1111
7	10001	10 00100	1010	1011
8	10010	10 01000	1011	0011
9	10100	10 10000	1100	0010
10	—	—	—	1010
11	—	—	—	1110
12	—	—	—	0110
13	—	—	—	0100
14	—	—	—	1100
15	—	—	—	1000

1. Error detection.

2. Simplicity of combination construction.

3. Simplicity of implementation in hardware.

2-OUT-OF-5 CODE

The 2-out-of 5 code provides the first advantage and is illustrated in column 1 of Table 2. Every five-bit combination that represents a digit contains exactly two 1s. Since there are 10 such combinations, this works out well. To assign each combination, we establish a set of five *pseudoweights*. One of these weights, W_1, is 0, and the bit corresponding to this weight, b_1, should be set to 1 when the value of the digit being encoded corresponds to precisely one of the nonzero weights; this is true for the digits 1, 2, 4, and 7. The weights work out for all digit values except 0; this digit uses bits with weights 7 and 4, which obviously do not sum to 0; hence the term "pseudoweights."

BIQUINARY

The biquinary code is a seven-bit code using exactly two 1s; it is illustrated in column 2 of Table 2. One of the 1s is chosen from the left two bits; the other is chosen from the right five bits. The weights are used as would be expected. This code provides error detection whenever more than one 1 appears in either half of a combination, and also provides a logical progression from one combination to the next, which is useful for implementing arithmetic.

MBQ CODE

The modified biquinary code (MBQ), illustrated in column 3 of Table 2, is derived from biquinary by replacing the first two bits by a single bit, and the last five bits (which represent 0, 1, 2, 3, or 4) by three bits, which represent them in BCD.

GRAY CODE

The Gray code, invented and patented by F. Gray, was developed to fill a particular requirement. At one time, many devices designed to convert analog (i.e. continuous) data depended on the mechanical position of a shaft. Attached to the shaft was an encoder that produced electromechanical or optical signals corresponding to the shaft rotation. This created a transition problem. Column 1 of Table 1 shows that the combination for 7 is 0111 and that for 8 is 1000. As the shaft rotated, the apparatus for reading out the position could not be depended upon to change simultaneously in each bit position. Thus, totally erroneous readings occurred. If b_4 goes to 1 before the other bits change in going from 7 to 8, the output would be read as 15.

To overcome this transition difficulty, codes called *Gray codes* have been devised, whereby successive combinations change in one bit position only, as shown in Column 4 of Table 2. The length in bits of each combination L is a function of the number (N) of discrete shaft positions to be encoded, as given by the formula

$$2^{L-1} < N \le 2^L = \lceil \log_2 N \rceil \qquad (13)$$

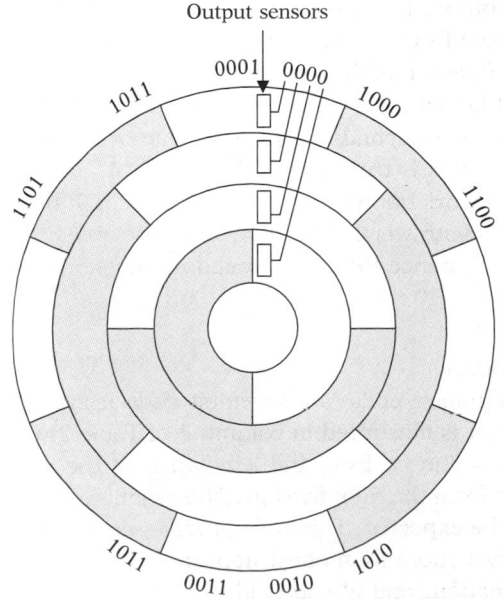

Figure 1 The Gray code disk for column 4 of Table 2. (Shading represents 1; no shading represents 0.)

Figure 1 displays a code disk for the Gray code of column 4, which indicates the change of one bit at a time. Whereas the transition from one code value to the next in column 4 cannot simply be described by a rule, there are Gray codes that can be so described. For example, if B_i is the binary equivalent of the integer i, $i = 0, 1, \ldots, 2^n - 1$ and if B_i' is the result of shifting B_i to the right one place (inserting a zero in the left), then $G_i = B_i \oplus B_i'$, where $\oplus$ represents the exclusive OR operation, is a Gray code. A three-bit code formed this way is 000, 001, 011, 010, 110, 111, 101, 100, where, for example, 101 (which corresponds to $i = 6$) is calculated as $110 \oplus 011 = 101$.

Error Detection and Correction

In the case of biquinary, we have seen how a code can be constructed with error detection properties. This is helpful, and even necessary, in many situations, such as when:

1. Information is transmitted from one site to another along lines where noise or other signal distortion might occur.

2. The data is recorded on a medium that is not impervious to noise so that 1s may get lost and be read as 0s, or 0s may be interpreted as 1s.

3. Devices within the computer may become faulty and create or destroy information.

PARITY *(q.v.)*

The simplest means for detecting errors is to attach an extra bit to each combination of the code, called a *parity* bit. This bit is set to 0 or 1, according to the scheme used: for *odd* parity, the total number of 1s, including the parity bit, must by odd; for *even* parity, the total number of 1s, including the parity bit, must be 0 or even. For example, the ASCII encoding of "Z" is 90, which is 1011010 in binary. With an even-parity rule, this would be 01011010; with odd parity, it would become 11011010. There are two phases in the use of the parity bit: creation and checking. In the *creation phase*, the combination is examined and a parity bit is created so that the number of 1s in the total combination is proper. Now the combination can be transmitted from one place inside or outside the computer to another place. When it arrives there, the checking action follows using circuitry similar to that for parity creation that examines the combination exclusive of the parity bit as though it were creating that parity bit. If this developed bit and the accompanying parity bit coincide, a *single* bit error could not have occurred, and the information is accepted. For further details, *see* ERROR CORRECTING AND DETECTING CODE.

Bibliography

1961. Peterson, W. W. *Error Correcting Codes.* Cambridge, MA: MIT Press.

1977. McEliece, R. J. *The Theory of Information Coding.* Reading, MA: Addison-Wesley. (Vol. 3 of the *Encyclopedia of Mathematics and Its Applications.*)

1980. Mackenzie, C. E. *Coded Character Sets: History and Development.* Reading, MA: Addison-Wesley. (Part of the Systems Programming Series.)

1997. Honary, B., Darnell, M., and Farrell, P. (eds.) *Communications Coding and Signal Processing.* New York: John Wiley.

Ivan Flores

COERCION

> For articles on related subjects *see* DEFAULT CONDITION; EXPRESSION; and PROCEDURE-ORIENTED LANGUAGES: PROGRAMMING.

As a matter of convenience to the programmer, many programming languages provide a mechanism for automatically converting from one data type to another in expressions. This automatic type conversion is called *coercion.*

A familiar example of coercion occurs in arithmetic expressions containing both integer and floating point operands, as in $K + 3.5$, where K is of type integer. The integer variable K is first automatically converted to floating-point, and then the addition is performed in floating point mode. If the language does not have such coercion, the programmer must make the conversion explicit (e.g. FLOAT(K)+3.5).

The kind of coercion that must be applied to an operand depends on the type of that operand, as well as on the type of operand required by the context. As an illustration, consider the expression $X + K$, where K is again of type integer. If X is also of type integer, no coercion need be performed; if X is of type floating point or complex, K must be coerced to the same type as X before the addition can be performed. Note that a language may not simultaneously provide coercions from type A to type B and also from type B to type A, since expressions of the form $A + B$ would then be ambiguous.

Coercions are not restricted to converting between integer, floating point, and complex. In Snobol4 and AWK, for example, an expression such as $K+$ '01.50' is permitted, since '01.50' may be coerced from type string to type floating point. Other common coercions are from decimal to binary (PL/I), and scalar to array (APL). The term coercion was first used in this context in Algol 68 (*q.v.*). In the revised Algol 68 report, there are six coercions—*widening* (e.g. integer to floating point), *rowing* (e.g. character to string), *deproceduring* (calling an argumentless function, e.g. coercing a

proc real to a real), *dereferencing* (converting a variable to its value), *uniting* (used to assign values to variables that accept several types), and *voiding* (used for discarding superfluous values).

Coercion is also used in other languages to describe the assignment of an expression of one mode to a variable of another. There is, of course, little difference between coercing as described above and then assigning or coercing *while* assigning.

Andrew S. Tanenbaum

COGNITIVE SCIENCE

> For articles on related subjects *see* ARTIFICIAL INTELLIGENCE; KNOWLEDGE REPRESENTATION; MACHINE LEARNING; NEURAL NETWORKS; PARALLEL PROCESSING; PERCEPTRON; and TURING TEST.

Definition

Cognitive science is the interdisciplinary study of cognition. Cognition includes mental states and processes such as thinking, reasoning, remembering, language understanding and generation, visual and auditory perception, learning, consciousness, and emotions. Some cognitive scientists limit their study to *human* cognition; others consider cognition independently of its implementation in humans or computers. Some cognitive scientists study cognition independently of the cognitive agent's environment; others study it within the context of society or culture.

Cognitive science can also be defined as, roughly, the intersection of the disciplines of computer science (especially artificial intelligence), linguistics, philosophy, psychology, cognitive anthropology, and the cognitive neurosciences. In most other academic disciplines, a common methodology is usually brought to bear on a multitude of problems. By contrast, in cognitive science, many *different* methodologies—those of the several cognitive sciences—are brought to bear on a *common* problem: the nature of cognition.

Cognitive science's approach to the study of mind is often contrasted with that of behaviorism. The behaviorist approach to psychology seeks to describe and predict human behavior in terms of stimulus–response correlations, with no mention of unobservable (hence, "unscientific") mental states (including mental constructs such as symbols, ideas, or schemata) or mental processes (such as thinking, planning, etc.) that might mediate these correlations. A behaviorist who would be willing even to talk about the "mind" would view it as a "black box" that could only be understood in terms of its input–output behavior. Cognitive science in general seeks to understand human cognitive functions in terms of mental states and processes, i.e. in terms of the algorithms that mediate between input and output. (Nonetheless, insofar as behaviorism is concerned with the "intelligent cognitive" behaviors listed above, it, too, is a cognitive science.)

Cognition and Computation

The notion that mental states and processes intervene between stimuli and responses sometimes takes the form of a "computational" metaphor or analogy, which is often used as the identifying mark of contemporary cognitive science: the mind is to the brain as software is to hardware; mental states and processes are (like) computer programs implemented (in the case of humans) in brain states and processes. Some cognitive scientists make the stronger claim that mental states and processes *are* (expressible as) algorithms: "cognition *is* a type of computation" (Pylyshyn, 1985). Others make a weaker, but more general, claim that cognition is computable, i.e. that there are algorithms that have the same input–output behavior as cognitive processes.

Thus, according to the computational view of cognitive science, (1) there are mental states and processes intervening between input stimuli and output responses, (2) these mental states and processes either *are* computations or else are computable, and—hence—(3) in contrast to behaviorism, mental states and processes are capable of being investigated scientifically (even if they are not capable of being directly observed).

Insofar as the methods of investigation are taken to be computational in nature, computer science in general and artificial intelligence in particular have come to play a central role in cognitive science. It is, however, a role not without controversial philosophical implications: for if mental states and processes can be expressed as algorithms, then they are capable of being implemented in non-human computers. The philosophical issue is simply this: are computers executing such algorithms merely simulating mental states and processes, or are they actually exhibiting them? Do such computers think?

Whether one believes that cognition *is* computation or merely is computable, computer programs force cognitive scientists "to make intuitions explicit and to translate vague terminology into concrete proposals; they provide a secure test of the consistency of a theory... ; they are 'working models' whose behavior can be directly compared with human performance" (Johnson-Laird, in Norman, 1981). That is, the proper methodology of cognitive science is to express one's theories about (human) cognition in a computer program (rather than, say, in English or in the languages of mathematics, logic, or statistics, as other sciences do) and then to compare the program's behavior with

(human) cognitive behavior. Although this methodology is consistent with the denial of the strong computational view—i.e. human cognitive behavior might be *simulatable* by a computer program without itself *being* computational—it *accepts* the weak form of the computational view of the mind as at least a working hypothesis.

Varieties of Cognitive Science

Currently, there are two major paradigms of computational cognitive science. To lead up to these, several dichotomies (albeit overly simplified ones) can be made:

1. Researchers who study (human) cognitive behavior either (a) believe that there *are* mental states and processes that mediate input stimuli and output responses (this position may be called "cognitivism") or else (b) believe that there are no such mediating states or processes (or that it is unscientific to talk about any such unobservable states or processes—the position of behaviorism).

2. Cognitivists believe either (a) that all mental states and processes are computational in nature (and here there is a further dichotomy between (i) the weak and (ii) the strong computational views) or else (b) that at least some (and perhaps all) such processes are not computational. Position (2b) is held by a number of researchers who believe that there are inherent limitations on the ability of computers to simulate or produce mental phenomena (e.g. Searle, 1980, 1990; Penrose, 1989; Dreyfus, 1992; Edelman, 1992). It is certainly a position that provides many of the most interesting and hardest challenges to the computational cognitivists. One such challenge is the problem of the nature of consciousness. Another is the problem of subjective qualitative experiences; e.g. what kind of computational theory can account for our experience of pain or of the color green? But (2b) is also a position that is sometimes ridiculed as "mysticism" or as a contemporary version of vitalism.

3. The dichotomy between the two major paradigms is between those computational cognitivists who believe that cognitive computations are "symbolic" and those who believe that they are, rather, "connectionist."

SYMBOLIC COMPUTATIONAL COGNITIVE SCIENCE
The foundations of symbolic computational cognitivism may be found in the "Physical Symbol System Hypothesis" and the "Representational Theory of the Mind." The Physical Symbol System Hypothesis, due to Allen Newell and Herbert Simon (*q.v.*), is offered as

a solution to the problem of "how it is possible for mind to exist in this physical universe" (Newell, in Norman, 1981): mind exists as a physically implemented "symbol system." The concept of a physical symbol system is "the most fundamental contribution … of artificial intelligence and computer science to" cognitive science (Newell, in Norman, 1981). A *symbol system* is any effectively computable procedure, i.e. a universal computing machine (which, by Church's Thesis, could be a Turing machine, a recursive function, a general-purpose digital computer, etc.). A *physical symbol system* is a physical implementation of such a symbol system. The Physical Symbol System Hypothesis states that a physical system is capable of exhibiting intelligent behavior (where intelligence is defined in terms of *human* intelligence) if and only if it is a physical symbol system. This is taken to be an empirical hypothesis, whose evidence comes from work in symbolic, i.e. non-connectionist, artificial intelligence. Newell argues that *intelligent* physical systems are physical *symbol* systems since intelligence requires *representations* of a wide variety of goals and states, and since such flexible representations require symbols. It is the first of these reasons—the requirement of representations—that is empirical; the second—that the representations must be symbolic—is challenged by connectionism. The converse claim, that physical *symbol* systems are capable of being *intelligent* physical systems, has been challenged by the non-computationalists of position (2b), above.

The Representational Theory of the Mind, which can be seen as a consequence of the Physical Symbol System Hypothesis, says that cognition is best understood as computations that use mental representations as data (just as arithmetic computations use numerals). One particularly strong form of the Representational Theory of the Mind is Fodor's "language of thought" theory (1975), which says that the mental representations are a language (sometimes called "mentalese"). Fodor's theory of *methodological solipsism* (1980) holds that the syntax of the language of thought is all that cognitive science needs to deal with, i.e. that the cognitive agent's environment (and the input–output transducers)—while important for understanding how information gets into and out of the mind—are irrelevant for understanding how the mind works.

Among symbolic computational cognitive scientists, there is a fourth dichotomy that may be added to the three in the previous section:

4. There is a dichotomy between (a) those who are satisfied with symbolic algorithms whose input–output behavior is the same as human cognitive behavior and (b) those who are only satisfied with symbolic algorithms that not only are input–output

equivalent to human cognitive behavior but also are equivalent in all but the details of physical implementation, i.e. equivalent in terms of such details as subroutines and abstract data types (e.g. if, on the strong view that cognition *is* computation, the human algorithm for some cognitive process uses a particular abstract data type (*q.v.*), then so must the corresponding AI program). A particularly strong form of (4b) also requires the algorithms to be equivalent to human cognitive behavior at the level of space and time complexity (Pylyshyn, 1985).

According to the Physical Symbol System Hypothesis and the Representational Theory of the Mind, when a physical system—be it computer or human—executes a "cognitive" algorithm, the representations are brought to life, so to speak, and made to behave according to the rules of the symbol system; the symbol system becomes dynamic, rather than static. If cognition is representational and rule-based in this way— i.e. if cognitive behavior consists of transformations of representations according to rules—then a computer that behaves according to these rules causally applied to these representations *is* behaving cognitively and is not merely simulating cognitive behavior.

Although the Physical Symbol System Hypothesis and the Representational Theory of the Mind offer an answer, which is satisfying to most computer scientists, to Descartes's question of how mind and body can interact (namely, mind can be implemented in body), they are not without their detractors. Of particular note are the objections of Winograd, who did pioneering work in the symbolic paradigm of artificial intelligence. Winograd cites a biologist, Maturana, who straightforwardly denies the Representational Theory of the Mind: "cognition is not based on the manipulation of mental models or representations of the world" (Winograd, in Norman, 1981). Instead, according to Winograd and Maturana, there are cognitive "phenomena that *for an observer* can be described in terms of representation, but that can also be understood as the activity of a structure-determined system with no mechanism corresponding to a representation" (Winograd, in Norman, 1981). This view echoes Dennett's "intentional stance" theory. According to Dennett (who has many more sympathies with computational cognitivism), it makes sense to treat certain complex systems (e.g. chess-playing computers) *as if* they had beliefs and acted intentionally even though there might not be anything in their structure that corresponded in any way to beliefs or intentions (Dennett, 1984). Recent work in non-representational artificial intelligence and "situated cognition" is consistent with this approach (*see Cognitive Science*, 1993).

CONNECTIONIST COMPUTATIONAL COGNITIVE SCIENCE

The "connectionist" (or "neural network," or "parallel distributed processing") approach to artificial intelligence and computational cognitive science can be seen as one way for a system to (appear to) behave intelligently without being a "symbol system" and yet be computational. Connectionist systems and techniques have been developed for learning features of natural language, for aspects of visual perception, and for a number of other cognitive (as well as noncognitive) phenomena. There is a wide range of types of connectionist methods, many of which are, in fact, highly representational, but most of which are "distributively representational," by which is meant that the kind of information that a *symbolic* artificial intelligence program would represent using various symbolic knowledge representation techniques is, instead, "represented" by the strengths and connectivity patterns of the links. Rather than having intelligence "programmed" into the system using explicit rules and representations, intelligence is sometimes held to "emerge" from the organization of the nodes and links. (A useful tutorial is Knight (1990); good surveys of connectionism are *Cognitive Science* (1985), Graubard (1988), and—from a critical standpoint—Pinker and Mehler (1988).)

Cognitive processes that are easy to implement symbolically (e.g. problem solving, reasoning, game playing, certain aspects of linguistic competence) tend to be ones that are relatively difficult for humans or that have to be explicitly taught, while those that have proven difficult to implement symbolically (e.g. certain aspects of visual perception and learning) tend to be those that "come naturally" to humans. This paradox of (symbolic) artificial intelligence is echoed in the debate over connectionism. The processes that have proven difficult to implement symbolically appear to be susceptible to connectionist techniques. The construction of "hybrid" symbolic/connectionist systems based on this complementarity may prove to be a major advance in our understanding of cognition.

A second way of merging the two approaches is to view connectionism as a lower level of cognitive processing, i.e. as a way of implementing symbolic processes. Thus, for example, logical reasoning, which is well suited for symbolic computing, might be implemented in a connectionist system in such a way that certain of its "connectivity patterns" reliably represent precisely the things that would be explicitly represented symbolically. Some proponents of the Physical Symbol System Hypothesis would say that at some stage in the sequence of levels that describes a computer (beginning with the "device level"—the description in electronic terms), there must be a level that implements a symbol system. Several connectionist implementations of "symbolic" algorithms have been investigated, but as yet there is no general theory of how this might be accomplished.

Cognitive Science Research

One way of exploring the content of cognitive science is to look at research in the individual cognitive science disciplines that could equally well be considered research in cognitive science *per se*.

ARTIFICIAL INTELLIGENCE

Given the computational view of cognitive science, it is arguable that all research in artificial intelligence is also research in cognitive science. Nonetheless, certain applications of artificial intelligence techniques to problems in engineering, management, etc., and, perhaps, the development of expert systems do not fall within the scope of cognitive science. Certainly, however, those aspects of artificial intelligence research that might be considered to be "computational psychology" or "computational philosophy" are also in the domain of cognitive science (*see* ARTIFICIAL INTELLIGENCE). Among these are the following: the early work by Newell and Simon on problem solving (the Logic Theorist, the General Problem Solver), as well as recent work on the SOAR project; aspects of knowledge representation that attempt to reflect cognition (e.g. some uses of semantic networks, such as Quillian's original theory and more recent systems such as Shapiro's SNePS and Anderson's ACT* systems); Marvin Minsky's theory of frames; Schank's theory of scripts and conceptual dependency; work on "naive" or "qualitative" physics, which attempts to develop systems that can reason about physics in ways that humans do on an everyday basis (rather than in ways that professional physicists do); machine learning; planning; reasoning; natural language understanding and generation; and computational vision. (For surveys of these and other topics, *see* Shapiro, 1992.)

LINGUISTICS

Linguistics is another discipline that is arguably wholly subsumed by cognitive science (even non-computational cognitive science). After all, language is often held to be the "mirror of the mind"—the (physical) means for one mind to communicate its thoughts to another. But it was with the development of transformational grammar by Noam Chomsky that cognitivism replaced behaviorism in linguistics (*see* CHOMSKY HIERARCHY). Subsequent work on a variety of computationally tractable "successors" to transformational grammar and other work in computational linguistics is clearly a part of cognitive science. In addition, the subdiscipline of cognitive linguistics studies the way that language structures conceptual content, and it seeks to relate this to conceptual structuring in other cognitive systems, such as those of perception and reasoning. (For surveys of recent contributions by linguistics to cognitive science, see Lakoff (1987), Pinker (1994).)

PHILOSOPHY

Philosophers have long studied the nature of mind and language, and much recent work in the philosophy of mind, the philosophy of language, epistemology, and the philosophy of consciousness has been informed by research in the other cognitive science disciplines. In addition to the work by Dennett and Fodor mentioned earlier, and Putnam's theory of Turing machine functionalism as a solution to the classic philosophical problem of the relationship of mind and body, the objections to the nature and possibility of success of artificial intelligence that have been raised by philosophers have served as research goals for artificial intelligence researchers—such criticisms must also be considered as part of cognitive science. The two major lines of criticism are those due to Dreyfus and Searle. Dreyfus (1992) argued, on the basis of the phenomenological school of philosophy, that since computers do not have a (human) body, do not have (human) purposes or needs, and do not share the human cultural milieu, they will never be intelligent. Searle (1980) has argued that the Turing Test (*q.v.*), although perhaps an indicator of the presence of intelligent *behavior*, fails as an indicator of the presence of intelligence. His "Chinese Room Argument" purports to show that a computer cannot understand natural language: suppose that an English-speaking human who knew no Chinese was locked in a room and equipped with a program (written in English) for manipulating Chinese ideographs in such a way as to convince native Chinese speakers that they were communicating with another native speaker of Chinese. Such a person, according to Searle, would pass the Turing Test, yet (by hypothesis) would not understand Chinese. Among the responses to this is the "systems" reply, that the person by him- or herself does not understand Chinese (any more than a CPU or a portion of the human brain would), but that the person plus the program does understand Chinese. (For an excellent annotated bibliography on the philosophy of mind, *see* Chalmers, 1996.)

PSYCHOLOGY

Cognitive psychology, of course, is a central cognitive science discipline. Experimental research on reasoning, memory, problem solving, knowledge representation (*q.v.*), perceptual processes, sentence comprehension, spoken language understanding, word recognition, decision making, categorization, etc. contribute the behavioral data that cognitive scientists use in their attempts to gain a broader view of cognition. Many cognitive psychologists now think of themselves as cognitive scientists and feel free to incorporate the results of other cognitive scientists into their publications. Early contributions of cognitive psychology include Bartlett's (1932) study introducing the idea of schemata as the basis of representation and Wertheimer's (1959) series of experiments showing the role of framing a problem in understanding it. (Wertheimer was one of the founders of Gestalt psychology.) Other contributions include Gibson's (1966) work emphasizing the information structure in the environment that is used by perceivers, Collins and Loftus's (1975) attempt to integrate a large body of experimental data surrounding network models of representation, and Treisman and Gelade's (1980) analysis of how detailed aspects of the visual field get integrated into meaningful wholes.

INTERDISCIPLINARY COGNITIVE SCIENCE RESEARCH

But perhaps the most important research topics in cognitive science are those that are truly interdisciplinary, i.e. those in which researchers from the several cognitive sciences apply their differing methodologies to a common problem and, conversely, inform their own studies with results of investigations from the complementary disciplines. Prime examples of these would be: (1) research in visual perception, which has been investigated in psychology, in artificial intelligence, and in robotics (*q.v.*), not to mention in physiology and biophysics; (2) research into mental imagery, which, in addition to the work in psychology mentioned above, has received critical philosophical attention from Pylyshyn and Dennett and has also been investigated using neuroscientific techniques; (3) research on categorization, where results from psychology—influenced by philosophical studies of family resemblance and natural kinds—have largely overturned the "classical" philosophical view going back to Aristotle of there being necessary and sufficient conditions for membership in a category; (4) research on the logic of belief and knowledge, in which people from artificial intelligence have not only adapted, for use in artificial intelligence programs, systems of epistemic and doxastic logics developed by philosophers, but have also offered solutions to many open problems in these logics that philosophers have largely ignored; (5) research on cognition and emotion, which has been studied by psychologists and AI researchers; (6) research on non-literal language, e.g. work on speech acts in philosophy and AI; intersecting work on metaphor in linguistics, philosophy, and AI; and (7) a research project on indexicality and narrative understanding that has involved input from AI, communicative disorders, literary theory, geography, linguistics, philosophy, and psychology.

History of Cognitive Science

Both the symbolic and connectionist approaches to computational cognitive science can trace their origins to two major lines of investigation. First, there was the development of symbolic logic at the turn of the century and McCulloch and Pitts's application of logic to the analysis of the behavior of neural networks (1943). Second, there were Turing's analyses of computation (1936) and—using the Imitation Game (now known as the Turing Test)—of whether computers could think (1950). Cognitivism burst upon the scene in 1956. In (or very near) that year, the following cognitive theories appeared: George Miller's theory of human short-term memory, Chomsky's analysis of formal grammars, Jerome Bruner and colleagues' study of thinking, and Newell and Simon's Logic Theorist—the first artificial intelligence program (presented at the first artificial intelligence conference, at Dartmouth, organized by Minsky and John McCarthy). In 1979, the journal *Cognitive Science* appeared; two years later, the first annual meeting of the Cognitive Science Society was held (its proceedings are now published by Lawrence Erlbaum Associates). Other major cognitive science journals include: *Behavioral and Brain Sciences*, *Cognition*, *Linguistics and Philosophy*, *Mind and Language*, *Minds and Machines*, and *Philosophical Psychology*; in addition, most journals in the specific cognitive science disciplines also have articles on cognitive science. Finally, there has been a recent surge of research centers and institutes of cognitive science, as well as graduate and undergraduate degree programs, including university departments of cognitive science.

There is information on the history of cognitive science on the World Wide Web; *see*, e.g. "Cognitive and Psychological Sciences on the Internet" http://www-psych.stanford.edu/cogsci/.

The Future of Cognitive Science

If cognitive science is to become a discipline in its own right, and not just a congeries of parts of other disciplines, perhaps its best hope lies not only in such multipronged attacks on common problems, as just discussed, but in single research groups whose members come from different disciplines yet who work together on common problems of cognition. The range of disciplines, and the levels of analysis, are by no means settled and, indeed, are widening in scope. As Norman (1981) observes, "To some, the very essence of a cognitive system is that of a symbol processing system," while to others the essence is that of connectionist neural networks. To yet others, the essence of cognitive science is more holistic, viewing the mind as an integral component of the larger world—of society, of culture—*not* (solely) understandable in terms of symbol manipulation (syntax) but in need of a semantics—an understanding of the relations of the mental symbols to the external world. Thus, the two major open issues for a complete understanding of cognition are—looking inwards—how the mind is implemented and how the very fact of its implementation in particular kinds of physical or biological mechanisms influences the nature of cognition, and—looking outwards—how and to what extent the nature of cognition is shaped by the socio-cultural world that minds find themselves in.

Bibliography

1932. Bartlett, F. C. *Remembering: A Study in Experimental and Social Psychology*. Cambridge, UK: Cambridge University Press.

1936. Turing, A. M. "On Computable Numbers, with an Application to the Entscheidungsproblem," *Proceedings of the London Mathematical Society*, Ser. 2, **42**, 230–265; reprinted in *The Undecidable: Basic Papers on Undecidable Propositions, Unsolvable Problems, and Computable Functions*. (ed. M. Davis), 116–154. New York: Raven Press (1965).

1943. McCulloch, W. S., and Pitts, W. H. "A Logical Calculus of the Ideas Immanent in Nervous Activity," *Bulletin of Mathematical Biophysics*, **7**, 115–133; reprinted in W. S. McCulloch, *Embodiments of Mind*, 19–39. Cambridge, MA: MIT Press (1965).

1950. Turing, A. M. "Computing Machinery and Intelligence," *Mind*, **59**; reprinted in A. R. Anderson (ed.) *Minds and Machines*, 4–30. Upper Saddle River, NJ: Prentice Hall.

1959. Wertheimer, M. *Productive Thinking*. New York: Harper & Row.

1966. Gibson, J. J. *The Senses Considered as Perceptual Systems*. Boston: Houghton-Mifflin.

1975. Collins, A. M., and Loftus, E. F. "A Spreading Activation Theory of Semantic Processing," *Psychological Review*, **82**, 407–428.

1975. Fodor, J. A. *The Language of Thought*. New York: Thomas Y. Crowell Co.

1980. Fodor, J. A. "Methodological Solipsism Considered as a Research Strategy in Cognitive Psychology," *Behavioral and Brain Sciences*, **3**, 63–109.

1980. Searle, J. R. "Minds, Brains, and Programs," *Behavioral and Brain Sciences*, **3**, 417–457.

1980. Treisman, A. M., and Gelade, G. "A Feature Integration Theory of Attention," *Cognitive Psychology*, **12**, 97–136.

1981. Norman, D. A. (ed.) *Perspectives on Cognitive Science*. Norwood, NJ: Ablex Publishing Corp.

1984. Dennett, D. C. *Brainstorms*. Cambridge, MA: MIT Press.

1985. *Cognitive Science*, Special Issue on Connectionist Models and Their Applications, **9**, *1* (January–March).

1985. Pylyshyn, Z. *Computation and Cognition: Toward a Foundation for Cognitive Science*, 2nd Ed. Cambridge, MA: MIT Press.

1987. Lakoff, G. *Women, Fire, and Dangerous Things: What Categories Reveal about the Mind*. Chicago: University of Chicago Press.

1988. Graubard, S. R. (ed.) "Artificial Intelligence," special issue of *Daedalus*, **117**, *1* (Winter); reprinted as *The Artificial Intelligence Debate: False Starts, Real Foundations*. Cambridge, MA: MIT Press.

1988. Pinker, S., and Mehler, J. (eds.) *Connections and Symbols*. Cambridge, MA: MIT Press.

1989. Penrose, R. *The Emperor's New Mind: Concerning Computers, Minds, and the Laws of Physics*. Oxford: Oxford University Press.

1990. Knight, K. "Connectionist Ideas and Algorithms," *Comm. of the ACM*, **33**, *11*, 59–74.

1990. Searle, J. R. "Is the Brain's Mind a Computer Program?" *Scientific American*, January, 26–31.

1992. Dreyfus, H. L. *What Computers Still Can't Do: A Critique of Artificial Reason*. Cambridge, MA: MIT Press.

1992. Edelman, G. M. *Bright Air, Brilliant Fire: On the Matter of the Mind*. New York: Basic Books.

1992. Shapiro, S. C. (ed.) *Encyclopedia of Artificial Intelligence*, 2nd Ed. New York: John Wiley.

1993. *Cognitive Science*, Special Issue on Situated Action, **17**, *1* (January–March).

1994. Pinker, S. *The Language Instinct: How the Mind Creates Language*. New York: William Morrow.

1996. Chalmers, D. J. "Contemporary Philosophy of Mind: An Annotated Bibliography," `http://ling.ucsc.edu/~chalmers/biblio.html`.

William J. Rapaport

COLLATING SEQUENCE

For articles on related subjects *see* CHARACTER CODES; SORTING; and STRING PROCESSING.

Given a set of symbols, a *collating sequence* for that set is a sequential ordering of those symbols which, through mutual agreement of a group of users of those symbols, is used to determine the *lexicographic order* of symbol strings whose constituents are chosen from the set.

The simplest example of lexicographic order is alphabetization, through which the strings `Jones`, `Brown`, `Ryan`, and `Cohen` are commonly placed in the ascending order `Brown`, `Cohen`, `Jones`, and `Ryan`. But this ordering depends on the centuries old agreement that the 26 letters of the English alphabet in their standard order is used as a collating sequence. We seldom, if ever, dwell on this, but this sequence is just an arbitrary choice of one of the 26! permutations (about 4×10^{26}) of our alphabet that might have been chosen. This particular ordering is closely related to that used for corresponding letters of the Greek alphabet, which in turn is believed to have its origins in Egyptian hieroglyphics.

There are innumerable other symbol sets for which someone has had to decide on a collating sequence. For example, in the card game Bridge, the four suits have increasing value in the order clubs, diamonds, hearts, and spades. Within a suit, the ace is usually considered to have the highest value, above the king, but in the most common form of solitaire it has the value 1; that is, it ranks below the 2.

In defining a collating sequence for a symbol set that contains characters in addition to the alphabet, such as digits and punctuation, one must decide on their rank with respect to the alphabet. For that matter, one must decide on whether upper case letters collate above or below lower case letters, and where the digit sequence 0 to 9 collates with respect to either grouping. In ASCII and Unicode, the ascending order of these groups is digits, upper case alphabet, lower case alphabet (with certain special characters placed between the groups), but in the older EBCDIC, the ranking of these groups is exactly the reverse. This means that character strings written to a file in lexicographic order ("sorted") by, say, a late 1960s vintage IBM mainframe (*q.v.*) that used EBCDIC would not be considered in proper order if the file were to be read on a more recently designed computer that uses ASCII or Unicode (*see* CHARACTER CODES).

Once a collating sequence is chosen for a set of n characters, the resulting rank of each character is said to have an *ordinal value*, a number that ranges from 0 for the first character to $n-1$ for the last. In fact, what we consider to be characters are actually stored in memory as ordinal values of type integer of usual size one byte (EBCDIC and extended ASCII) or two bytes (Unicode).

When comparing character strings of unequal length, the length of the shorter string is assumed to be extended to the length of the larger ("padded") by appending blank characters. Thus, if (as is usual) a blank has ordinal value less than any letter, `button` precedes `buttons` and `Pittsfield` precedes `Pittstown` even though, in the second case, `Pittsfield` is longer than `Pittstown`. The test for ordering is done left to right, so that in the second case, the tie between the place names is broken only at the sixth letter. Such a lexicographic ordering can be formalized as follows.

Let T be a set of n-tuples $(c_1, c_2, c_3, \ldots, c_n)$ composed of elements c_i in set S. Then $(c_1, c_2, c_3, \ldots, c_n) < (d_1, d_2, d_3, \ldots, d_n)$ iff either $c_1 < d_1$ or there is some character position k in the range $1 \leq k \leq n$ for which $c_i = d_i$ for all $i < k$ (characters in corresponding positions of the respective n-tuples up through position $k-1$ are identical) and $c_k < d_k$ (a character position is finally reached in which the characters differ).

Edwin D. Reilly

COLOSSUS

For articles on related subjects *see* CRYPTOGRAPHY, COMPUTERS IN; DIGITAL COMPUTERS, HISTORY OF: EARLY; and TURING, ALAN M.

Colossus was the first large programmable electronic computer. It was developed at the British Post Office Research laboratories at Dollis Hill in North London at great speed and in complete secrecy during the Second World War to help break top-level German machine ciphers generated by the Lorenz SZ40 and SZ42 cipher attachments used with teletype machines. Design started in March 1943 and the Mark 1 Colossus, with 1,500 vacuum tubes, was working by December 1943. It was then dismantled and transported to Bletchley Park, in north Buckinghamshire, home of the Government Codes and Ciphers School (GCCS). After reassembly it was operational in January 1944 and was successful in its first attempt at breaking a German Lorenz message. The Mark II was immediately ordered. The first of these, with 2,500 vacuum tubes, was operational on 1 June 1944, five days before D-Day. Eight more Colossi followed, making 10 in all operational before the end of the war. Because of engineering improvements, and evolving cryptographic technologies, no two were identical.

As early as 1939, British cryptanalysts working at Bletchley Park, and led by Alan Turing, had invented an analog device, "The Bombe," to break the rotor cipher of the German Enigma machine. (This was a substitution cipher where the actual substitution for each input letter was achieved in a very complex manner through wiring inside the rotors in the Enigma machine.) Radio signals enciphered using much more difficult teletype ciphers were intercepted in 1940. These teletype ciphers used an additive method devised by Gilbert Vernam at AT&T in 1918. In the teletype system, each character was represented by a five-bit code. Vernam's method added an obscuring character to each input character to give a new character which was then transmitted. By using bit-by-bit modulo 2

addition Vernam showed that if the same obscuring character was added back at the receiving end, the original input character was revealed. The Lorenz company devised a cipher machine for the German Army high command based on the Vernam principle. By 1942 when mathematics professor M. H. A. Newman arrived at Bletchley from Cambridge University, the cryptanalysts led by Bill Tutte had worked out the logical structure of the Lorenz machine thanks to a disastrous mistake by the Germans on 30 August 1941. A German operator had keyed in by hand a 4,000 character message, and when it failed to arrive correctly at its destination had then re-keyed it with the same initial settings of his Lorenz machine. (This was absolutely forbidden.) Because he re-keyed the message using slightly different keystrokes, the intercepted enciphered texts were also slightly different and these differences enabled the cryptanalysts to recover both German texts. This in turn revealed the obscuring character set (patterns) being generated by the Lorenz machine, which led to its complete logical description. Now that its workings were revealed, the cryptanalysts developed pencil and paper methods for breaking Lorenz messages, using exhaustive techniques of Bayesian statistical analysis. They were managing to break some messages, but only with such a delay that the information revealed was operationally unusable.

Newman set up a team of mathematical specialists to mechanize part of the task and speed up the breaking of messages. Their early work led to the development of the "Heath Robinson" machines, which compared two punched paper tapes at rates of up to 1,000 characters per second. One tape contained the intercepted cipher text, the other contained the streams of patterns that the cryptanalysts had worked out by hand. A sophisticated cross-correlation measurement attempted to find when the positions of patterns on the tape matched the setting positions used by the German operator to generate the intercepted cipher text. Mechanical problems with the Robinsons pushed Newman and his team toward radical innovations. Newman approached Dollis Hill for help and T. H. Flowers, an engineer from the Post Office Research Station, proposed building a machine with 1,500 vacuum tubes, almost three times the number in any contemporary machine. Flowers's innovative concept was to produce the streams of patterns electronically in rings of vacuum tubes, thus eliminating one paper tape and removing the synchronization difficulty.

The paper tape speed could now be increased and Colossus read punched tape at 5,000 characters per second using a projection lamp and photocells, a truly impressive speed even by post-war standards. To eliminate cumulative timing errors, clock pulses were

Figure 1. The Colossus computer at Bletchley Park, 1943. (Courtesy of the Bletchley Park Trust/Science and Society Picture Library.)

generated by a photocell that read the sprocket holes in the tape. The necessary programming was done with plugboards and switches. Although Flowers later noted that the prototype was probably less programmable than some contemporary IBM punched card machines, Newman and his colleagues began to exploit the flexibility of the machine by making dynamically generated data depend on the results of previous processing.

Alan Turing was involved with the development of the cryptographic techniques to break Lorenz but despite his pre-war work on what is now known as the *Turing Machine* (*q.v.*), he was not involved in the design and development of Colossus.

When installed at Bletchley, each Colossus filled a large room in one of the wartime buildings. (It was 7.5 ft tall by 15 ft wide by 8 ft deep.) Its logic circuits operated in parallel at 5,000 pulses per second and it had electronic decimal counting circuits, electronic ring pattern generators that were changeable by an automatically controlled sequence of operations, and typewriter output. The Mark II Colossus could process data five times faster than the Mark I. The basic clock rate and reading speed were the same, but five-stage shift registers (*see* SHIFTING) and more logic circuits increased the processing speed by providing access to five characters at a time.

Colossus went on line two years before ENIAC (*q.v.*). Colossus, though built as a special-purpose logical computer, proved flexible enough to be programmed to execute a variety of tasks, including decimal multiplication, but only at a slower clock speed. ENIAC, a much larger and faster machine, was initially intended for solving differential equations, but was used for a variety of numerical calculations. ENIAC and Colossus were directly comparable as non-stored-program computers, programmed using plugboards and switches to perform specific tasks.

Although it was the ENIAC group that made the final leap toward the modern general-purpose digital computer with the design for EDVAC (*q.v.*), Colossus stands as an impressive pioneering achievement in its own right, and was a powerful stimulus to post-war computer research in Britain. In particular, Colossus undoubtedly inspired Alan Turing to proceed rapidly in 1945 with his designs for the ACE computer and inspired Allen Coombs, one of the designers of Colossus, to design MOSAIC for the Post Office. Eight of the original 10 Colossi were dismantled in Bletchley Park at the end of the war in 1945. The remaining two lasted until about 1960, but the very existence of Colossus was kept secret until the 1970s.

A fully working rebuild of Colossus has now been completed at Bletchley Park and demonstrates the high speed and parallel nature of the original 1944 machine. This rebuild, which took three years, had to be done from just eight wartime photographs of Colossus and some fragments of circuit diagrams that survived. Most of the vacuum tubes are ex-wartime stock and contemporary components have been used wherever possible. See http://www.cranfield.ac.uk/ccc/bpark/colossus.htm for more on this project.

Bibliography

1974. Kahn, D. "The Ultra Secret," *New York Times Book Review*, 29 December.
1977. Randell, B. "Colossus: Godfather of the Computer," *New Scientist*, 10 February. Reprinted in *The Origins of Digital Computers—Selected Papers*, 3rd. Ed. (ed. B. Randell), 1982, 349–354. New York: Springer-Verlag.
1980. Randell, B. "The Colossus," in *A History of Computing in the Twentieth Century* (eds. N. Metropolis, J. Howlett and G. C. Rota), 47–92. New York: Academic Press.
1983. Hodges, A. *Alan Turing: The Enigma*. New York: Simon & Schuster.
1993. Hinsley, Sir H., and Stripp, A. *Codebreakers*. Oxford: Oxford University Press.
1997. Fox, B., and Webb, J. "Colossal Adventures," *New Scientist*, **154**, 2081 (10 May).

Tony Sale

COMBINATORICS

For articles on related subjects *see* ALGORITHMS, ANALYSIS OF; CODES; DISCRETE MATHEMATICS; GRAPH THEORY; INTEGER SEQUENCES, ONLINE ENCYCLOPEDIA OF; and MATHEMATICS, COMPUTERS IN.

Introduction

Combinatorics is the branch of discrete mathematics that involves the study of methods of counting how many objects there are of some type, or how many ways there are to do something. The items being counted are generally drawn from a finite system that has some structure, and the process of counting requires a detailed analysis of that structure. Such counting problems are ubiquitous in the sciences and especially in computer science; since the computer can aid in such analyses, combinatorics and computer science have developed a symbiotic relationship.

Most brain teasers, games and puzzles are combinatorial in nature, and their solutions have often become the basis for general theories in combinatorics. Combinatorial problems have attracted the attention of serious mathematicians since ancient times. For example, magic squares (square arrays of numbers with the property that the rows, columns, and diagonals add up to the same sum) were discovered by the Chinese as early as 2200 BC. Other similar problems resulted in important contributions by such eminent mathematicians as Blaise Pascal (*q.v.*), Pierre de Fermat,

Gottfried Wilhelm Leibniz (q.v.), Leonhard Euler, Arthur Cayley, and James Joseph Sylvester.

Combinatorics was once considered to embrace only disconnected ideas and tricks for solving isolated problems, most of them recreational in nature. Since the early 1960s, however, unifying principles and cross-connections have helped to make combinatorics a coherent body of concepts and techniques. Widely varied applications to problems in statistics, theoretical physics, chemistry, the social sciences, communication theory, and computer science have demonstrated the generality of the techniques and have enhanced the importance of combinatorics as a branch of applied mathematics. We present as illustrations some combinatoric problems and their solutions in three areas: combinations and permutations, combinatorial design, and asymptotics.

Most combinatoric problems can be characterized as either (1) an existence problem, in which one determines whether a problem has a solution, (2) an enumeration problem, in which one determines the number of solutions to a problem, or (3) a selection problem, in which one is to find, among all the solutions to a problem, one or more with particular properties. The selection problem is often related to efficient algorithms that produce the desired solutions.

As general references, the books by Hall (1986), Liu (1968), Tucker (1984) and Rosen (1998) are suggested.

Combinations and Permutations

One of the most important areas in combinatorics is the study of the ways in which discrete objects are combined and permuted. A selection of r objects from a set of n objects is called a *combination*. An ordered selection of r objects chosen from n objects is called a *permutation*. The number of ways to select r distinct objects from n distinct objects is given by the formula

$$\frac{n!}{r!(n-r)!},\qquad(1)$$

where $i!$ denotes the product

$$i\cdot(i-1)\cdot(i-2)\cdots3\cdot2\cdot1$$

and is read "i factorial." The quantity in (1) is usually written $\binom{n}{r}$, is known as a *binomial coefficient* because it is the coefficient of the term x^r in the expansion of $(1+x)^n$. The number of ordered arrangements (i.e. permutations) of r distinct objects chosen from n distinct objects is $n!/(n-r)! = n\cdot(n-1)\cdot(n-2)\cdots(n-r+1)$.

There are many possible variations in permutations and combinations. For example, one might wish to select r objects from n distinct objects, allowing re-

peated selection of the same object. One way to solve the problem is to note that the coefficient of x^r in the expansion of $(1-x)^{-n}$ is the answer. This example illustrates *generating functions*, a technique useful in enumeration problems. The generating function of a sequence of numbers $a_0, a_1, a_2, \ldots, a_r, \ldots$ is the power series $a_0 + a_1 x + a_2 x^2 + \cdots + a_r x^r + \cdots$, where x is a formal variable (i.e. a variable without intrinsic meaning). In many enumeration problems, it is easier or more desirable to obtain the generating function of the solutions for a sequence of problems, rather than to obtain an explicit closed-form expression of the solution for a particular problem. Thus, the generating function $(1-x)^{-n}$ gives the number of ways to select, for all r, r objects from n distinct objects, allowing unlimited repetitions. For example, when $n=3$, $(1-x)^{-3} = 1 + 3x + 6x^2 + \cdots$ and the six combinations of three objects, say a, b, and c, taken two at a time, are aa, ab, ac, bb, bc, and cc. Similarly, the number of ways to divide r distinct objects into n nonempty subsets is equal to $r!/n!$ times the coefficient of x^r in $(e^x - 1)^n$. Thus, for instance, when $n=2$,

$$(e^x - 1)^2 = x^2 + x^3 + \frac{7}{12}x^4 + \cdots$$

and there are $3!/2! = 3$ ways that three objects can be divided into two nonempty sets: (a, bc), (b, ac), and (c, ab).

Generating functions are also useful in determining the number of ways to arrange n opening parentheses and n closing parentheses so that each open parenthesis is balanced by a corresponding closed parenthesis to its right. For example $()(())$ is a well-formed arrangement, while $()((()$ is not. If a_n denotes the number of such arrangements, we note that $a_0 = 1$, since there is a unique empty arrangement (no parentheses) and

$$a_n = a_{n-1} + a_1 a_{n-2} + a_2 a_{n-3} + \cdots + a_{n-2} a_1 + a_{n-1},$$

since all possible arrangements on n parentheses P_n are formed without repetition by $(P_j)P_{n-j-1}$, for $j = 0, 1, \ldots, n-1$, with P_0 being the empty string of parentheses. This is an example of a *recurrence relation*, which in general is an equation relating to a sequence of numbers $a_0, a_1, a_2, \ldots, a_n, \ldots$. Often, a recurrence relation can be solved to obtain either a closed-form expression or the generating function for a_n, so many enumeration problems can be attacked by first setting up a recurrence relation and then solving it. In this case, the generating function can be shown to be $(1 - \sqrt{1 - 4x})/2x$, and from this we can determine that

$$a_n = \binom{2n}{n}/(n+1);$$

these a_n are called *Catalan numbers*.

A *derangement* is a permutation of the integers $1, 2, \ldots, n$ so that no integer i occupies the ith position. The problem of counting the number of derangements is a special case of the general problem of the permutation of objects with restrictions on the positions each object may occupy. The number of derangements of n objects can be determined by generating functions or by a formula known as the *principle of inclusion and exclusion*, which states that for r sets $A_1, A_2, \ldots, A_r$

$$|A_1 \cup A_2 \cup \cdots \cup A_r|$$
$$= |A_1| + |A_2| + \cdots + |A_r|$$
$$- |A_1 \cap A_2| - |A_1 \cap A_3| - \cdots - |A_{r-1} \cap A_r| +$$
$$+ |A_1 \cap A_2 \cap A_3| + |A_1 \cap A_2 \cap A_4| + \cdots$$
$$+ (-1)^{r-1}|A_1 \cap A_2 \cap \cdots \cap A_r|,$$

where $|X|$ denotes the cardinality (number of members) of the set X. Thus, of the $n!$ permutations of the integers $1, 2, \ldots, n$. let A_i denote the set of those permutations in which the integer i is in the ith position. It follows that the number of derangements is equal to

$$n! - |A_1 \cup A_2 \cup \cdots \cup A_n|$$
$$= n! - \binom{n}{1}(n-1)! + \binom{n}{2}(n-2)! + \cdots$$
$$+ (-1)^n \binom{n}{n}$$
$$= n! \left(1 - \frac{1}{1!} + \frac{1}{2!} - \cdots + (-1)^n \frac{1}{n!} \right)$$
$$\approx n!/e,$$

where $\approx$ means "approximately equal to" and e is the base of the natural logarithms. Gian-Carlo Rota has observed that the principle of inclusion and exclusion and the well-known Möbius inversion formula of number theory are special cases of a general inversion formula for partially ordered sets. Rota's work is an excellent example of unifying results that have emerged since the 1960s.

Permutation problems also arise from the study of molecular structures. We may ask, for example, how many ways there are to place molecules at the apexes of a regular polyhedron; two placements are considered equivalent if one can be obtained from another by a rotation of the polyhedron. If there are five kinds of molecules and the regular polyhedron is a tetrahedron (a pyramid with three sides and a base), the number of placements is 75, a result that can be found using *Polya's theory of counting* (Liu, 1968).

Graph Theory

Graph theory is an area of significant importance in combinatorics, and it provides a good example of the study of the structural properties of discrete systems. Since it is discussed in a separate article, we shall not discuss it here.

Combinatorial Designs

Combinatorial designs is the area of combinatorics concerned with the arrangement of discrete objects. However, unlike the enumerative problems discussed above, its main emphasis is on proof of existence and nonexistence.

Typical of such arrangements are *Latin squares*. A Latin square of order n is an arrangement of n distinct symbols in an $n \times n$ square so that each symbol appears in each row and each column exactly once. Two Latin squares are said to be *orthogonal* if, when they are superimposed, the ordered pairs of entries are all distinct. A set of Latin squares is said to be *mutually orthogonal* if every two squares in the set are orthogonal. Latin squares were first studied by Euler when he posed the so-called "36 officers problem," in which six officers of different ranks from each of six regiments are to be arranged in a 6×6 square so that no two officers of the same rank or from the same regiment will stand in the same row or the same column. This problem is equivalent to the problem of the existence of a pair of orthogonal Latin squares of order 6. It is not difficult to discover that for $n - 2$ not

```
0 4 1 7 2 9 8 3 6 5      0 7 8 6 9 3 5 4 1 2
8 1 5 2 7 3 9 4 0 6      6 1 7 8 0 9 4 5 2 3
9 8 2 6 3 7 4 5 1 0      5 0 2 7 8 1 9 6 3 4
5 9 8 3 0 4 7 6 2 1      9 6 1 3 7 8 2 0 4 5
7 6 9 8 4 1 5 0 3 2      3 9 0 2 4 7 8 1 5 6
6 7 0 9 8 5 2 1 4 3      8 4 9 1 3 5 7 2 6 0
3 0 7 1 9 8 6 2 5 4      7 8 5 9 2 4 6 3 0 1
1 2 3 4 5 6 0 7 8 9      4 5 6 0 1 2 3 7 8 9
2 3 4 5 6 0 1 8 9 7      1 2 3 4 5 6 0 9 7 8
4 5 6 0 1 2 3 9 7 8      2 3 4 5 6 0 1 8 9 7
```

Figure 1. A pair of orthogonal 10×10 Latin squares.

divisible by 4, there always exists a pair of orthogonal Latin squares of order n. For example, Fig. 1 shows a pair of orthogonal Latin squares of order 10. Euler conjectured that for $n - 2$ divisible by 4 there is no pair of orthogonal Latin squares. Indeed, there do not exist orthogonal Latin squares of order 2 or 6, but in 1960 R. C. Bose, S. S. Shrikhande, and E. T. Parker proved the falsity of Euler's conjecture by exhibiting pairs of orthogonal Latin squares for orders $n \geq 10$, such that $n - 2$ is divisible by 4.

Of related interest is the largest number of Latin squares in a mutually orthogonal set. A mutually orthogonal set of Latin squares of order n can contain at most $n - 1$ Latin squares; furthermore, for n equal to a power of a prime, such a set exists. However, the question is still open for general n; the case $n = 10$ was settled only recently by Lam, Thiel, and Swiercz (1989). An exhaustive computer search failed to discover a set of nine mutually orthogonal Latin squares of order 10. Various properties of Latin squares have been studied for the more restricted case in which entries in each *diagonal* or *superdiagonal* are distinct. The superdiagonals are the diagonals formed when the square is rolled into a cylinder with the first column adjacent to the last column, and the ends of the cylinder are then joined to form a torus.

The design of statistical experiments to test the effects and interrelations of various "treatments" (medications) leads to the area of combinatorial designs known as *block designs*; most of the terminology in this area is derived from such applications. Let $T = \{1, 2, \ldots, v\}$ be a set of distinct objects called *treatments*, and let $B_1, B_2, \ldots, B_b$ be subsets of T called *blocks*. A collection of blocks is called a *design* on the treatments: a *balanced incomplete block design* is a design in which every treatment appears in exactly r blocks, every block is of size k, and every pair of treatments appears in exactly λ blocks. Since balanced incomplete block designs are characterized by the five parameters v, b, r, k and λ, they are also referred to as (v, b, r, k, λ) designs. Most important is the question of the existence of a balanced incomplete block design for given values of v, b, r, k, and λ. This general problem is extremely difficult and has not been completely solved, although there are many results for specific sets of parameters. The special class of balanced incomplete block designs in which $v = b$ (and, consequently, $r = k$) is known as *symmetric balanced incomplete block designs*. Because of the additional constraints, more is known about such designs, although the general existence question remains a difficult one.

The construction of codes is closely related to that of block designs. Let $A = \{a_1, a_2, \ldots\}$ be a set of distinct symbols (letters). The set A is called the *alphabet*.

A *word* is an ordered sequence of letters from the alphabet; the *length* of a word is the number of letters in it. A *code* is a collection of words (called *codewords*). If no codeword is a prefix of another codeword, the code is a *prefix code*. If all codewords are the same length, the code is a *block code*. When A is the set of elements in a finite field, a block code is said to be *linear* if it forms a vector space over the finite field $(A, +, \cdot)$. An *error* is said to occur if one of the letters in a codeword is changed into another letter. Some codes are *t-error detecting*, i.e. they can recognize when t or fewer errors occur in a codeword. A code is said to be *t-error correcting* if the original codeword can be reconstructed when t or fewer errors occur (*see* ERROR CORRECTING AND DETECTING CODE).

The three important parameters of a block code are the length of its words (short codewords yield low communication cost), the number of its codewords (a large number of codewords gives the capability of representing a large number of messages), and its error-detecting/correcting capability (detection or correction of errors means high reliability in communication). The problem of code design is to select a set of codewords so that these interdependent parameters satisfy the needs of a particular communication problem. It is also desirable that the code have efficient encoding and decoding algorithms.

Asymptotics

In enumerative combinatorial problems, it is necessary to count the number of occurrences of some configuration. The derangements problem is a typical example. Frequently, the answer can be expressed by a recurrence relation, a generating function, a sum of terms, or a product of terms. In addition to an exact answer of that type, we usually would like to know an approximation in more elementary terms. *Asymptotics* is concerned with such approximations.

For example, the single most important asymptotic result of combinatorics is the answer to the question "How large is $n! = n \cdot (n-1) \cdot (n-2) \cdots 2 \cdot 1$?" The answer was found by James Stirling in the early 18th century. He showed that

$$n! \approx \sqrt{2\pi n} \left(\frac{n}{e}\right)^n.$$

Stirling's formula also gives us an approximation for the binomial coefficients since

$$\binom{n}{r} = \frac{n!}{r!(n-r)!},$$

and for many other similar functions.

The *harmonic numbers*,

$$H_n = \sum_{i=1}^{n} \frac{1}{i}, \qquad (2)$$

occur in many contexts in combinatorics and their approximation is also of interest:

$$H_n \approx \ln n + \gamma,$$

where $\gamma \approx 0.5772$ is known as *Euler's constant*.

Both the approximation for $n!$ and H_n are derived by *Euler's summation formula*, which approximates a discrete summation, such as

$$\ln n! = \sum_{i=1}^{n} \ln i$$

or H_n in (2) by the corresponding integral,

$$\int_1^n \ln x \, dx$$

or

$$\int_1^n \frac{dx}{x}.$$

The integral is then evaluated, and the error is bounded by various analytical techniques.

Connections with Computer Science

The close relation between combinatorics and computer science works to the advantage of both areas. Combinatorics gains in two distinct ways. First, the computer allows large-scale testing of conjectures and generation of data that would have been impossible only a few decades ago. Before computers, results like Appel and Haken's proof of the four-color theorem could never have been achieved (*see* MATHEMATICS, COMPUTERS IN). Second, the application of techniques from combinatorics to problems in computer science infuses new vigor into the study of the techniques themselves and suggests new avenues for combinatorial investigation.

Computer science gains from combinatorics the tools necessary for analyzing algorithms and data structures. The best examples are algorithms for sorting (*q.v.*) elements according to some order. The analysis of the average, best, and worst case performance of most sorting algorithms hinges critically on the structure of permutations; the classical results in this area are just what are needed to understand the relative behavior of various sorting algorithms. Similarly, results on combinations, permutations, and trees (*q.v.*—a special type of graph) facilitate the analysis of merging algorithms and search strategies. The techniques for the solution

of recurrence relations and of asymptotic analysis are used in the analysis of almost all algorithms. Without such techniques, we would never be able to answer questions about, for instance, the average number of interchanges in bubble sort, the expected height of a search tree, or the average stack depth encountered in parsing arithmetic expressions.

Computer science also benefits from the computational problems suggested by the classical structures of combinatorics. How can we determine whether a graph is planar? How do we find the shortest path between two nodes of a network? Is there an efficient way to determine whether two planar networks are isomorphic? These questions originated with combinatorics, but their algorithmic solutions came largely from computer science.

The books by Reingold, Nievergelt, and Deo (1977) and Knuth (1997) are recommended as references for the interface between combinatorics and computer science.

Concluding Remarks

The topics discussed are merely representative. We have not discussed many beautiful and deep topics, such as *Ramsey theory*, which is concerned with certain generalizations of the "pigeonhole principle" (if $n + 1$ pigeons are put into n holes, then one of the holes must contain two or more pigeons), partially ordered sets (exemplified by structural results such as Sperner's Lemma and Dilworth's Theorem), the theory of matroids as generalizations of graphs, or the mathematical programming (*q.v.*) approach to optimization problems.

Combinatorial techniques will undoubtedly continue to play a crucial role in computer science. The design of VLSI chips which consist of up to hundreds of millions of circuit elements is but one area in which many challenging combinatorial problems have arisen.

Bibliography

1968. Liu, C. L., *Introduction to Combinatorial Mathematics.* New York: McGraw-Hill.

1974. Dena, J., and Keedwell, A. D. *Latin Squares and Their Applications.* London: English University Press.

1977. Reingold, E. M., Nievergelt, J., and Deo, N. *Combinatorial Algorithms: Theory and Practice.* Upper Saddle River, NJ: Prentice Hall.

1984. Tucker, A. *Applied Combinatorics*, 2nd Ed. New York: John Wiley.

1986. Hall, M., Jr. *Combinatorial Theory*, 2nd Ed. New York: John Wiley.

1989. Lam, C. W. H., Thiel, L., and Swiercz, S. "The Non-existence of Finite Projective Planes of Order 10," *Can. J. Math.*, **41**, 1117–1123.

1992. Sedgewick, R., *Algorithms in C++.* Reading, MA: Addison-Wesley.

1997. Knuth, D. E. *The Art of Computer Programming*, Vol. 1, 3rd Ed. Reading, MA: Addison-Wesley (see also Vol. 2, 3rd Ed., 1997, and Vol. 3, 2nd Ed., 1998).

1999. Rosen, K. *A Handbook of Discrete and Combinatorial Mathematics*. Boca Raton, FL: CRC Press.

C. L. Liu and Edward M. Reingold

COMMUNICATION CONTROL UNIT

For articles on related subjects *see* CHANNEL; CYCLIC REDUNDANCY CHECK; DATA COMMUNICATIONS; FRONT-END PROCESSOR; GATEWAY; LOCAL AREA NETWORK; MODEM; MULTIPLEXING; NETWORKS, COMPUTER; OPEN SYSTEMS INTERCONNECTION; POLLING; PROTOCOL; TCP/IP; and TELEPROCESSING SYSTEMS.

The term *communication control unit* was a generic term used in the 1980s to refer to a wide variety of devices that controlled the transmission and reception of data in computer networks. They ranged from complex units, such as front-end processors for mainframes, to simple units such as concentrators, terminal servers, or multiplexers of various kinds for transmission of data primarily over dedicated lines. The 1990s saw dramatic advances in data communications and the appearance of new generations of communication devices to build today's computer networks. They include various types of communication adapters, hubs, bridges, routers, and switches. Consequently, the term *communication control unit* is being replaced by two new generic terms: *communication adapters*, which interface computers and workstations (*q.v.*) to the network, and *network electronics*, which serve to deliver data over the network from source to destination.

Communication Adapters

Communication adapters (sometimes also called *line adapters*) provide the interface between a computer or workstation and the network. By far the most common adapters used today are those that interface systems to the telephone, Ethernet, FDDI (Fiber Distributed Data Interface), Token Ring, or ATM (Asynchronous Transfer Mode—*q.v.*) networks, although adapters for other types of networks are also available.

Adapter capacity is measured in bits/second (bps), commonly in units of thousands (Kbps) or millions (Mbps). To connect workstations to the telephone network requires modem (modulator–demodulator) adapters which typically operate at 56 Kbps or less. Older Ethernet adapters operate at 10 Mbps but newer 100 or 1,000 Mbps adapters are becoming increasingly common. Token Ring networks operate at 4 or 16 Mbps while FDDI operates at 100 Mbps and was used extensively as a high-speed enterprise *backbone* network, but is rapidly being replaced by 100/1,000 Mbps Ethernet and ATM backbone networks. ATM networks operate at 155 or 620 Mbps in 1999 but can scale to higher speeds.

FUNCTIONS PERFORMED

The software drivers designed for a particular communication adapter, in combination with the adapter hardware, perform all the functions necessary to control data reception or data transmission over the network to which they are connected. These may include:

- *Data serialization and deserialization.* Since character bits within computers are usually transmitted in parallel (as bytes), while over the network they are transmitted serially, the adapter must convert data from parallel to serial form (serialization) for transmission, and do the opposite for data reception.

- *Presentation of the appropriate electrical or optical interface to the network.* In general, communication adapters for FDDI and 155 Mbps or faster ATM networks provide an optical interface since these networks generally use optical fibers (*see* FIBER OPTICS) for the transmission medium. The telephone, Token Ring and 10/100/1,000 Mbps Ethernet networks tend to use electrical conductors (twisted pairs or coaxial cable) for the transmission medium for which an electrical interface is required, although fiber interfaces are available for Ethernets when the distance involved requires it.

- *Packetization.* Different types of network use different packet sizes, implying that packet assembly/disassembly must be performed when transmitting or receiving long files. ATM, for example, uses fixed 53-byte packets (called *cells*), while FDDI uses variable-size packets from 64 bytes to 64 KB.

- *Addition and removal of control bits or characters consistent with the network protocol used.* Dial-up networks (which are point-to-point) require the insertion of start and stop bits to delineate characters. Other networks require the insertion of additional characters to indicate source and destination addresses, control information, and provide cyclic redundancy check characters for error control.

Network Electronics

A simple Ethernet may be adequate to interconnect tens of workstations, but it is totally inadequate for the thousands of workstations that may be owned by a

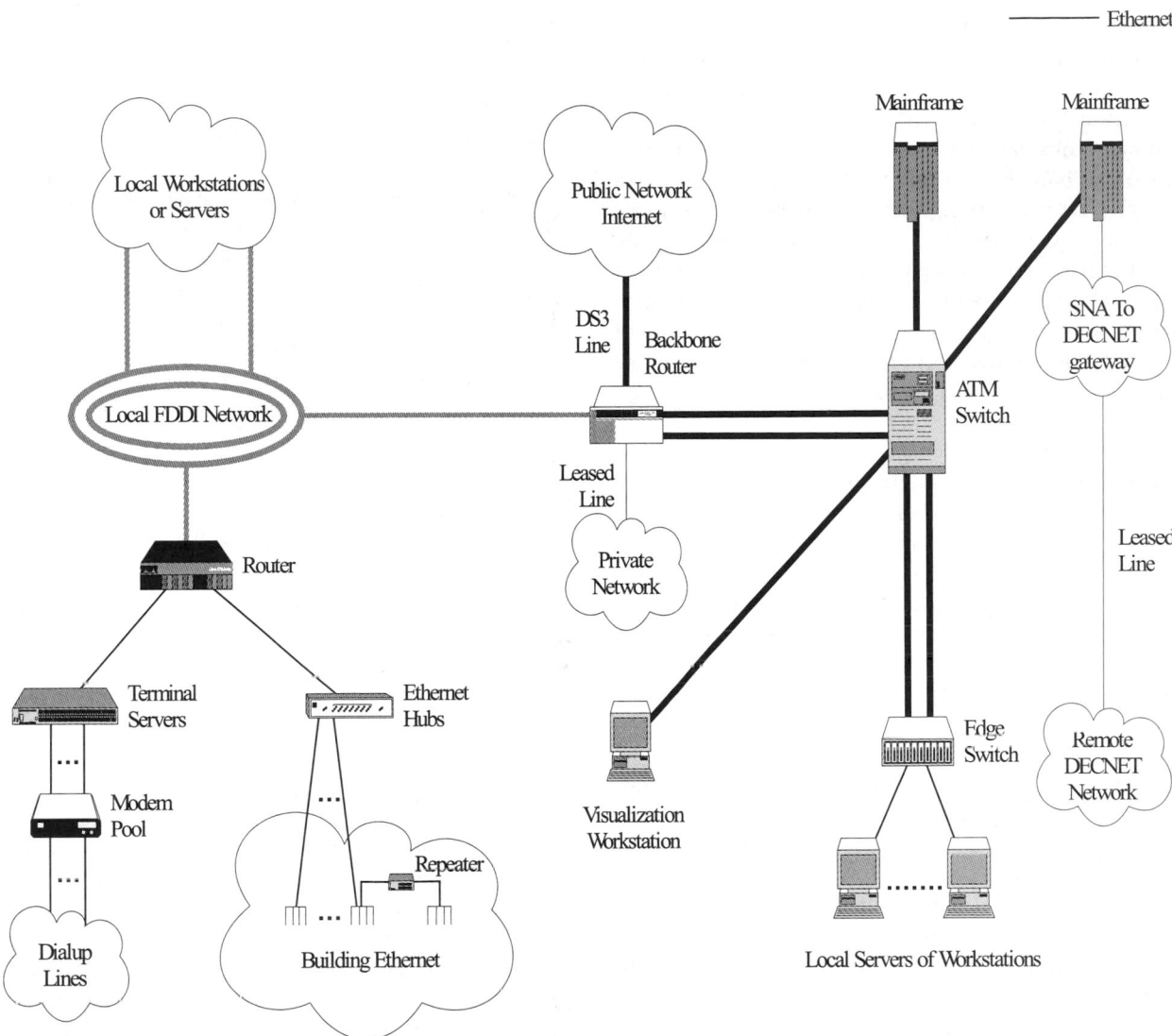

Figure 1. A hypothetical network illustrating the use of various communication devices.

large enterprise or a university. Such large networks require additional building blocks to interconnect multiple Ethernet and other network segments together and to ensure seamless data transmission from any workstation to any other workstation on the network. These building blocks go by the generic name of *network electronics* and include hubs, bridges, repeaters, routers, terminal servers, and switches of various kinds. They are described below and their use is illustrated in Fig. 1.

REPEATERS

Repeaters are inexpensive devices that act much like power extension cords to extend the distance limitations between network segments. They receive signals from one segment of a local area network (LAN),

retime and amplify the signals, and forward (repeat) them to an adjacent segment of the same LAN. They are frequently used to connect two segments of an Ethernet to extend the 500 meter single Ethernet cable limit. In general, repeaters have very little built-in intelligence and use only the physical layer of the Open System Interconnection (OSI) model for network architectures.

BRIDGES

Bridges operate at the data link layer of the OSI model for network architectures and are used to connect two or more adjacent LANs of like architecture. The interconnected LAN segments form a bridged LAN. Bridges filter entire packets and pass (bridge) only those that need to cross the boundary between the LANs they connect. As such, they are often used to help reduce the traffic on interconnected LAN segments.

HUBS

Hubs are used to concentrate LANs. The simplest types of hubs concentrate only the same type of LANs (e.g. only Ethernet or only Token Ring), while the more complex hubs can concentrate multiple LAN architectures, and can also provide intelligence in the form of bridging, some routing, and network management functions. Consequently, hubs can operate at the physical, the data link, and (part of) the network layers of the OSI model. A typical application for a hub is to interconnect the Ethernets between multiple floors of a building and bridge them to the rest of the enterprise network, as shown in Fig. 1.

TERMINAL SERVERS

This is a generic term to describe devices that connect multiple terminals or other devices using the RS-232 interface to an Ethernet or Token Ring network. Fig. 1 shows a terminal server supporting dial-in access for connecting remote devices to the enterprise network. This mechanism is widely used by Internet providers to provide Internet access to customers with modem-equipped personal computers.

SWITCHES

The Ethernet originally evolved as a shared-medium network where interconnected devices initiated a transmission when they sensed that no other devices were transmitting. This has a tendency to limit the maximum traffic that shared media networks can support. Ethernet switches overcome this by allowing any two mutually exclusive devices on the switch to communicate with each other at full speed. FDDI and ATM switches work in a similar fashion. Although switches are more expensive than simple hubs, they increase the total bandwidth (*q.v.*) of the network. So called edge-switches support local switching and provide a higher-speed interface to the enterprise backbone. Fig. 1 shows an edge-switch supporting 10/100 Mbps local switching with two 155 Mbps ATM connections to the enterprise ATM backbone switch.

ROUTERS

Routers work at the network layer of the OSI reference model and exhibit much more intelligence than multiplexers and bridges. Routers are used to interconnect a wide range of different local area network architectures (Ethernet, FDDI, ATM, etc), and to provide connectivity to wide area networks. They use routing tables and routing protocols to gain knowledge of the entire network, discover network topology changes, provide rerouting if necessary, minimize hop count, and choose routes that minimize

congestion. Many routers can be configured to perform both bridging and routing functions, in which case they are called *brouters*, which is short for *bridging routers*.

GATEWAYS

Gateways are even more complex than routers. In addition to supporting the standard interconnectivity provided by routers, they can provide connectivity and conversion between the seven layers of the OSI reference model as well as connectivity to networks using proprietary protocols. Because they tend to be application-specific and because they must support complex protocol conversions, they tend to be slower than routers. They are now primarily used for old applications and are being replaced by more standard equipment.

OTHER DEVICES

The devices described above are used to design the bulk of today's networks. However, many older networks still use devices such as front-end communication processors, concentrators, and network processors, primarily to handle proprietary protocols and to support older "legacy" applications that have not yet been rewritten to work with standard protocols.

Network Management

As enterprise networks continue to gain importance and grow in size, it becomes increasingly important to be able to manage the network from a central location and collect network statistics for capacity planning. Most of the network electronics devices described support the Simple Network Management Protocol (SNMP) or newer evolving standards for this purpose. Management software continues to evolve and uses these standards to monitor the network, detect problems and help take corrective action.

Device Architecture

Most enterprise LANs are experiencing rapid increases in network traffic due to new applications, such as World Wide Web (*q.v.*) applications that include data, graphics, and increasingly, voice and video clips. This requires that network electronics, and especially large hubs, routers, and switches, be able to route or switch tens or hundreds of thousands of packets per second. To handle this traffic, such devices have multiple gigabit per second buses, multiple CPUs with large memories programmed to perform the needed functions, special modules to help collect network statistics and support network management, and multiple power supplies to ensure reliable operation.

Bibliography

1993. Spohn, D. L. *Data Network Design*. New York: McGraw-Hill.
1997. Keshav, S. *An Engineering Approach to Computer Networking: ATM Networks, the Internet and the Telephone Network*. Reading, MA: Addison-Wesley.

John S. Sobolewski

COMMUNICATIONS AND COMPUTERS

For articles on related subjects *see* DATA COMMUNICATIONS; ELECTRONIC COMMERCE; INFORMATION SYSTEMS; INTERNET; MOBILE COMPUTING; NETWORK ARCHITECTURE; NETWORK PROTOCOLS; NETWORKS, COMPUTER; PACKET SWITCHING; PRIVACY, COMPUTERS AND; SOCIETY, COMPUTERS IN; STANDARDS; and WORLD WIDE WEB.

Computing is increasingly inseparable from *communications*. This linkage, often referred to as *convergence*, is driven by technology and amplified by business trends. Both technology and business foster growth in networks—systems that use communications links to connect subsidiary systems (referred to as *nodes*), which may send, receive, and (re)direct information to allow it to get from sender to receiver. Communications businesses depend on computing technology for the equipment or services they supply, computing systems producers develop hardware and software that assume connections to networks and through networks to other computing systems, and information services depend on networks for transmission of content of all kinds and formats among sending and receiving computers. Convergence has fostered diversity in the devices used for communications: conventional computers, telephones, and televisions persist, while previously unnetworked devices (such as household appliances) are taking on communications capabilities, and entirely new kinds of devices are emerging. Late 1990s experimentation with *network computers*—devices intended for use with networks and having less built-in capability than conventional computers—is emblematic; so, too, is the proliferation of hand-held devices from cellular telephones to personal digital assistants (*see* PORTABLE COMPUTERS), that are gaining capabilities for Internet access and associated applications.

Computing and communications together advance and integrate the information infrastructure. The information infrastructure dream features communication to anyone, anywhere, at any time. Realizing that dream consistently and ubiquitously will take time. As people come to see computers and communications as infrastructure, and as computers and communications become more integrated into the economy and society, they increasingly influence public policy. And as public policy touches on more aspects of the union of computers and communications, its influence on the development and deployment of these technologies grows. This overview of computers and communications outlines key technical trends in computer networking and relates those trends to the growth in public policy attention to networking.

The Internet as Catalyst

The convergence phenomenon is epitomized and driven by the Internet. The Internet, conceived for communication among computers and relying on packet-switching of digitized information, draws on decades of experimentation that generated underlying technologies and uses among researchers. The early years (the 1970s and 1980s) of the forerunners of the Internet (e.g. Arpanet) were paralleled by other developments that helped set the stage for turn-of-the-century integration of computers and communications. These included growth in data communications telephony (leased lines and modems) in the relatively closed environments of large business and government organizations which led to the adoption of personal computers and deployed private branch exchanges (PBXs); computer support for telephone customer service operations local area networks (*q.v.*) and wide area networks; deployment by telephone companies of digital technology and network-based services using intelligence inside the network; value-added networks (applying packet switching over leased lines, typically with proprietary protocols (*q.v.*) but occasionally using the International Organization for Standardization's X.25 protocol) that applied third-party computers and communications to support a limited amount of inter-enterprise communication (e.g. early electronic data interchange (EDI)) as well as wide area networking for a single enterprise; cable and satellite television "broadcasts" to closed audiences; and facsimile (fax, over public telephone lines using specialized modems). Advances in computing and communications technologies, progress in industry-based standards-setting, and limited growth in competition (fed by changes in US competition policy, with global ramifications) during this period helped to make convergence feasible and affordable. At least as important, early use of networks for data communications nurtured multiple constituencies for networking and latent demand for convergence. Thus, many factors composed the foundations for the rapid growth in networking associated with the early 1990s commercialization of the Internet.

The Internet proved pivotal because it is an *open data network*. With a layered architecture defined in open standards and essential technology expressed in modular software, it is more general and flexible than conventional telephony and television in which only one or a few applications are supported and are associated with specialized hardware (e.g. telephone handsets, television sets). As part of its openness, the Internet supports multiple modes of communication: one to one (typical of telephony), one to many (typical of broadcast television or radio), many to one, and many to many (celebrated in the World Wide Web). These modes are used in an ever-widening set of applications because the Internet architecture is open to change, a characteristic most obvious in the development and evolution of the World Wide Web, which rides atop the Internet as a super-application. The application flexibility of the Internet reinforces the convergence of computing and communications by adding value to information. Information gains value the more it can be stored, presented, manipulated, and used via computers and accessed and shared over a network. As that value grows, so does demand for networking.

The other key aspect of the Internet's openness relates to the capacity to leverage multiple kinds of network facilities and services as underlying communications infrastructure. Today's Internet is most commonly accessed via wireline telephone networks, but cable television networks are becoming more popular as Internet infrastructure, and wireless communication support (both terrestrial and satellite, and aimed at both portable and stationary devices) is also growing. Overall, increases in competition have spurred telecommunications investments, increasing supply and lowering prices for increases in demand. These trends are global, although deployment and use patterns vary among nations and regions. The result of these several trends is that the Internet serves as an internetwork for a growing number and diversity of networks of varying scopes and scales.

Fundamental Network Infrastructure Trends

The explosive growth of the Internet and associated business activity has fueled the deployment of the networking infrastructures that underlie it. Crudely, computing has accelerated communications and vice versa in a circular process. One of the earliest indicators of this trend was the mid-1990s linkage of cable television system upgrading, which pushed fiber optic (*q.v.*) cable further into cable TV distribution networks (primarily via hybrid fiber–coaxial cable systems), to high-speed Internet access via cable modems. Early cable Internet offerings have featured telephone line return paths from the home, reflecting the expectation that traffic in that direction (e.g. requests and responses) will be much lighter than traffic to the home, which features bandwidth (*q.v.*) intensive (e.g. graphics, multimedia) content delivery. Cable Internet support has grown with the rise of national cable-oriented systems linked to the Internet (e.g. @Home and Road Runner in the USA), which may go international. These systems attempt to manage the distribution of content and traffic load by storing popular content in multiple locations.

Meanwhile, in the mid- to late 1990s, regulatory relaxation, a global phenomenon of uneven vigor, spurred business development of terrestrial wireless systems for cellular telephony (and its cousin, the personal communications system or PCS). Cellular growth has been particularly high in Europe and Japan, both aided by area-wide standardization (by comparison, multiple standards have persisted in the USA), and it became prominent by the end of the 1990s in developing nations, which have had severely limited and low-quality wireline infrastructure and where teledensity (number of telephones per 100 people) remains very low. Historically, such wireless services have been low-bandwidth, aimed at voice telephony rather than data communications (other than paging), but this is changing, and as a result radio interfaces for computer systems are becoming more important. Protocol developments (e.g. MobileIP, Wireless Access Protocol, and VoxML) to support cellular access to the Internet are expected to reinforce wireless network growth and use; it is too soon to predict which approaches, if any, will dominate. Wireless progress involves overcoming considerable technical challenges (impairments to communications) inherent in over-the-air communications and developing technology to adapt to variations in the quality and quantity of local communications network infrastructure. Current trends also underscore the need to support mobility (especially challenging at high data rates, and implying added computer support to track changing locations) and yet more interconnection among networks, including wireline and wireless.

Regulatory change also furthered the 1990s deployment of international submarine cables and low-Earth orbit (LEO) satellite systems, designed to support different kinds of use (high and low bandwidth, stationary and mobile users). These multibillion dollar investments benefited from the opening up of associated investor organizations to private (as opposed to government or national monopoly) parties. Major satellite and cable consortia are international, and they are expected to promote international networking in general and Internet access in particular. Very small aperture terminal (VSAT) systems (typically supported by geosynchronous orbit (GEO) satellites) are being used to diffuse telephony and Internet access into remote areas, notably in developing nations. Although historically associated with low-bandwidth and business applications, new approaches are enabling higher-speed VSAT service aimed at Internet access and public access communication.

Competition associated with regulatory relaxation and the Internet has promoted the upgrading of wireline telephony networks, but the trends there have been particularly unstable. Before the takeoff of the Internet, first Integrated Services Digital Network (ISDN—q.v.) technology in the 1980s and then in the early 1990s Asynchronous Transfer Mode (ATM—q.v.) were touted as bandwidth- and capability-enhancing improvements for telephony; the very name of ISDN reflects recognition that digitization of all kinds of information was on the rise and that people would want to do multiple things with it concurrently. The Internet has shown these technologies to fall far short of the promise, and associated investments have been constrained. ATM is found primarily in network backbones, enabling gigabits per second traffic flow. ISDN (which can provide up to 128 Kb per second) and the family of digital subscriber line technologies (xDSL; the most familiar DSL variant is asymmetric or ADSL, originally advanced as a means for video delivery via the telephone network and providing up to a few megabits per second) have taken on the character of relatively easy to deploy approaches to increasing bandwidth for local access to the Internet. They can be used with standard copper lines in conjunction with special hardware at both customer and service-provider ends. Reflecting disappointments with such technologies as ISDN, ADSL, and even ATM, the most fundamental change in telephone networks is the move to deploy and support the Internet Protocol (IP) directly, a trend furthered by the rise of large Internet service providers and wholesale fiber optic facilities builders such as Level(3).

Meanwhile, growing deployment of fiber optic cable has excited interest in all-optical networks using wave-division multiplexing. This is an area of active technology development that many expect to make ATM obsolete once such issues as restoral are resolved. Fiber has long been used in telephone network backbones, which aggregate a lot of traffic, and recently it has been associated with new kinds of business (e.g. QWest Communications and Level(3)). Because of high installation cost, its penetration into the far reaches of networks—fiber to the home (FTTH)—is limited; it is most likely in densely settled (e.g. urban) areas. This is one reason why broadband Internet access to and from the home emerged as a pressing concern of Internet enthusiasts at the end of the century.

Internet telephony (or IP telephony) is emblematic of the turn-of-the-century convergence. Its early growth took advantage of the sheltering of Internet communications from telephony regulation, which has made long distance and especially international telephone calls relatively expensive. The demonstrations of telephony over the Internet (typically support for telephone service layered over IP, layered in turn over the telephone network) have fostered growth in more general capability supporting audio, video, and collaboration over the Internet (e.g. conferencing). IP telephony demonstrations have affected the technology deployment plans not only of telephone companies but also of cable companies and Internet service providers, who may own or lease their underlying communications infrastructure. Although people have described data traffic as dominating voice traffic over even telephone networks for some time, convergence fosters both. Improvements in support for voice interfaces to computing systems promise healthy if different growth in voice communications as a companion to computing. It also enables easier access for people unable to use their hands at a keyboard or mouse.

Mass Market Measures

Traditionally, discussions of computers and communications revolved around business applications: data communications among units of an enterprise, among workers and between workers and an employer, and to a limited extent among enterprises for specific transactions (order submission and tracking between buyers and suppliers who have agreed to standard formats and technologies—the underpinnings of electronic data interchange (EDI) and electronic funds transfer (EFT—q.v) among financial institutions). The spread of data communications was seen as a trickle-down process affecting first large organizations, then smaller ones, and eventually feeding home applications.

Today's convergence shows such conventional technology diffusion (acquisition and use of computing and communications among many kinds of small and medium-sized enterprises persists as a problem), but it also shows the opposite kind of flow—from consumer electronics (a spur to multimedia—q.v.) and household applications to the business environment, as entertainment (e.g. video games) affects content "production values" and expectations for ease of use and cost. There are also more complex flows emanating from new kinds of applications in "public interest" arenas such as education, health care, libraries, and government itself. These arenas are promoted directly by government programs, and they link directly to both businesses and households. The use of computers in education, for example, is moving beyond the early stage of confinement in a computer laboratory to expectations that students and teachers will combine computers with communications to access the Internet at school and also from home, where they will link to school, outside information sources, or other students. Similar to adult access trends, which support remote working (or teleworking), the networking of children has many ramifications for connectivity, equipment and software access, and the location and nature of different kinds of activity. Public interest applications form an important counterpart to the profit-making ventures that dominate discussions of electronic commerce.

By accelerating the spread of household and individual use of computers and networks, the Internet fosters links to almost any kind of organization, typically to obtain some kind of information or conduct personal business transactions (part of the burgeoning electronic commerce) and, in particular, to other individuals and households. This is true of personal computing (*q.v.*) and communications, and such virtual venues as chat rooms (for interactive, real-time correspondence—*see* ONLINE CONVERSATION) and multiuser "dungeons" (MUDs), where people may assume fictitious identities. This underscores the fact that convergence is about much more than finding or relaying "information." The social dimension is captured in various forms of online community development—the use of the Internet to link dispersed people with common interests of all kinds. Entertainment and recreation are key elements of the emerging networked world, and they amplify the role of commercial content providers (e.g. entertainment businesses, publishers) in the evolving information infrastructure.

Convergence and growth in home computing and home-based network-connected devices is inspiring development of home networking technologies, including support for linking multiple devices within the home (e.g. micro-cellular wireless networks) to streamlined support for multiple kinds of network services going into and out of the home. Some of these services will support people's communications, some will be associated with telemetry (e.g. utility meter monitoring, medical device monitoring), and some may be influenced by strategies for controlling flows of content (e.g. set-top boxes or the equivalent). Computers in the home are as likely to be embedded in various devices as to be standalone. At the same time, rising individual expectations for computing and communications independent of location has spawned development of support for *nomadicity*, beginning with roaming support for cellular telephone users and ranging to mobile data communications networks and devices (*see* MOBILE COMPUTING). An alternative approach is to use what the locality offers, such as public access systems (e.g. computer-based kiosks, enhanced pay telephones, and networked computers for use in such facilities as libraries). To date, nomadicity support has emphasized support for the mobile worker; public access system development has emphasized network access by individuals and the general public. Public access systems are especially important in remote areas

within developing nations, where shared telephones may be the only telephones; more elaborate shared computing and communications support is being introduced in the form of area telecenters.

Maturing Environment

Internet growth has made growth itself a source of concern and technology development. Questions arise about the scalability of network services and the capacity of addressing systems, both concerns in the evolution of the Internet (echoing the rise of such concerns in telephony and even cable television). Although the Internet was designed for large-scale use, the proliferation of users, connected devices, and bandwidth-intensive applications raises questions about congestion. Responses to congestion include increasing capacity—most notable in network backbones and also in access ports and lines supported by Internet service providers (ISPs)—and exploration of protocol modifications to support a larger address space (the next generation of the Internet Protocol, IP v6, does this) and to facilitate differential treatment of different kinds and priorities of traffic. The latter category of activity, aggregated as quality of service (QoS) enhancement, may work better within an enterprise network than across the heterogeneous internetwork environment in which service quality and support will vary; it has yet to see meaningful commercialization.

Although the Internet has evolved from the outset by the development of open standards, the standards-setting process has changed in ways that add uncertainty to its future. Historically the province of a relatively small group of committed volunteer technologists, the growing business associated with the Internet has increased the presence of industry players in the principal venue, the Internet Engineering Task Force (IETF), and contributed to the proliferation of industry-based coalitions aimed at standards-setting, including the membership-based World Wide Web Consortium (W3C) and a number of more specialized groups. Activity and interactions are also associated with conventional telecommunications standards-setting, given the growing relevance of the Internet to their work. Evolving standards-setting activity underscores the fact that the technology evolves through human processes; the range of factors shaping key decisions is changing along with the body of decision-makers.

Meanwhile, the spread of the Internet and networking generally has spawned a growing number of jobs and groups concerned about the structure and management of networks. On the supply side, ISPs are proliferating, in many countries providing new competition for traditionally monopolistic telecommunications providers. In the USA greater competition for traditionally monopoly carriers is intended via encouragement for unbundling and for market entry (under defined conditions) associated with the Telecommunications Reform Act of 1996. At the same time, there is a trend toward ISP consolidation, associated with ISP investment in facilities, which widen geographic reach and make smaller ISPs less viable outside of hard-to-serve areas where larger companies may be reluctant to invest in deployment. On the demand side, large organizations are investing in their own IP networks ("intranets" and "extranets") that are linked to the Internet. The result is a growing distributed need for private network management analogous to the management of "public" networks that sell services to individuals and organizations.

Both private and public network managers are providing a challenge to the historic openness of the Internet to connectivity. ISPs are expressing growing reluctance to connect liberally and without compensation with smaller networks on cost-control and service-quality grounds. Private network managers are also moving to limit connectivity on grounds of security and cost control. Packet filters and firewalls use software to limit both what traffic from outside an organization is allowed to enter and in some cases what traffic from inside can exit into the larger Internet. As is discussed below, similar concerns arise along with others in governments. The extreme example is the efforts by some developing nation governments, such as the People's Republic of China or Singapore, to restrict flows of certain kinds of content into or out of their relatively monolithic national networks. In part because "bits are bits," and in part because of limitations to packet-filtering technology, this kind of control is easier said than done.

Computers, Communications, and Public Policy

Convergence and the spread of network deployment and use have heightened government interest in the nature and use of communications. The central irony about public policy relating to computers and communications is that it is largely developed in national contexts but increasingly has international scope because of the global reach of networks. International policy-making relating to networks is growing; it involves an evolving and growing set of players.

Government policies have generally served to promote networking. Internet-related technologies were developed with government-supported research and development investments (primarily but not exclusively in the USA), and R&D support continues because networking fosters cost-sharing and collaboration in research and because research applications continue

to push the frontier of possibility for both computation and communications. For example, in the USA, the Next Generation Internet initiative and private counterpart Internet2 emerged in the late 1990s, contributing to the formulation of the 1999 Information Technology for the 21st Century (IT^2) initiative; in Europe, the Trans-European Network program has advanced bandwidth support for researchers in several countries and the Information Society Technologies Programme provides coordinated support for research. Promotion of networking has also included expressions of leadership, beginning with the Clinton–Gore support for first national information infrastructure in 1993 and then global information infrastructure by 1995, when the Group of 7 launched a set of information society pilot projects.

By the late 1990s, the International Telecommunications Union (ITU) and other nongovernmental organizations were promoting the global potential of information infrastructure; the ITU, in particular, along with other arms of the United Nations, emphasized the need to insure the involvement of developing nations for whom extremely limited access to telephones had long been common. The information infrastructure movement breathed new life into discussions of universal service by underscoring how varied the benefits of access to communications could be; the Internet element underscored how much could be gained by even limited, shared initial access, because the Internet facilitated broad access to information and other resources distributed around the world. This thinking has motivated efforts to provide Internet access in schools and libraries. The broadening user population also inspired new policy initiatives associated with serving people with either physical limitations (e.g. vision and motion impairments) or cognitive constraints (e.g. limited literacy, language differences, learning disabilities, and so on). These have been aggregated in the USA under the label of *universal access*.

Finally, promotion of networking has occurred by the traditional means of competition policy: changes in the regulation of telecommunications providers (in general, movement toward less regulation and away from national or area monopolies), changes in the targeting and enforcement of antitrust policy (now increasingly international, given the global reach and activity favored by larger players); and changes in trade policy treatment of services, including professional, telecommunications, and information services—all essential to the growth of networking. One symptom of regulatory change is the fall in tariff rates for telephone lines in Europe, a spur to network deployment investments in the late 1990s, although leased line prices are still viewed as unnecessarily high. Others include the promotion of wireless networks discussed above, setting the stage for ongoing discussions of radio-frequency spectrum allocation.

A new concern that can be associated with competition policy is the late 1990s attention to the Domain Name System (DNS) for assigning Internet domain names and mapping them to numerical Internet host addresses, loosely equivalent to cyberspace (*q.v.*) real-estate management. Although centralized historically in a US volunteer effort (the Internet Assigned Numbers Authority—IANA) and a very few registries (dominated by the US contractor Network Solutions Inc.), an international process has begun to broaden participation in decisions about the structure and management of the DNS and foster equity. A new player is a corporate entity known as the Internet Corporation for Assigned Names and Numbers (ICANN), launched in 1998 with input from the US government and other countries. Its composition, scope, and decisions will be important factors in the evolution of Internet governance.

The intertwining of computers and communications and the attendant digitization of all kinds of information have motivated new activity relating to information policy. Information policy includes protection of privacy, intellectual property rights, and freedom of speech. Privacy refers to the protection of information about persons, and the spread of databases containing personal information and their connection to networks, which may contribute to problems from embarrassment to identity theft and harassment. In the USA, specific investigations have been made into problems associated with medical records privacy and financial records privacy, building on the historic protection of privacy in those domains and leading to proposals for law and regulation. In the late 1990s involvement of the Federal Trade Commission in this area has shown the potential for regulation grounded in consumer protection and prevention of fraud. Worldwide, attention to privacy has been heightened by the European Union's privacy directive, which bans transmission of personal information about citizens of member nations outside of that region. Debate over the EU directive has amplified larger debates over the balance between self-regulation by industry and government regulation; the civil law tradition is more dominant in other countries than in the USA, where an emphasis on common law contributes to the broader support for industry self-regulation where feasible. Debate over privacy generally is associated with how to follow through on such widely discussed principles as informed consent for disclosure of personal information. Some technology development has arisen to foster privacy protection; the World Wide Web Consortium, for example, developed the Platform for Privacy Preferences system to enable users to detect and respond to Website privacy protections automatically.

The central intellectual property issue associated with networking is copyright (*see* LEGAL ASPECTS OF COMPUTING). Digitized information is easy to copy in general and in particular through a network, not least because the very operation of computers and networks involves copying. The growth of the Internet aggravates these concerns because not only is text affected, but music, images, and video are increasingly easy to copy, and new forms of "documents" can involve syntheses of previously generated and potentially owned content. In the mid-1990s, a number of research efforts aimed at developing technologies to minimize or eliminate copying (e.g. digitally watermarking documents) or insure the flow of compensation to rights-holders (e.g. micro-charging); other technologies have facilitated networked transmission of music and video and stimulated broader business concern about rights protection. The copyright area remains confounded by disagreement over which metaphor best illuminates a legal framework (e.g. whether the Internet or an Internet-based service is more like a publisher or a street-corner) and uncertainty about how, given network support for copying and for new kinds of content flows, business models may evolve and change the expectations of rights-holders. Other intellectual property concerns have arisen over the association of domain names with trademarked names, and all intellectual property issues have international dimensions, leading to involvement of the World Intellectual Property Organization and disagreements over its directions (e.g. controversy over early efforts relating to copyright protection for databases during the mid-1990s) as well as directions within individual nations. Attempts to form new law and policy evoke outcry from public interest advocates and rights-holders alike, and the propensity for legal challenge suggests that intellectual property adaptation will take some time to stabilize.

Freedom of speech, even more than other aspects of information policy, is colored by ideology. The USA favors freedom of speech at the national level, compared with many other countries, but even within the USA there are disagreements over whether some kinds of speech over the Internet should be controlled, as they have been in broadcast radio and television contexts. The lightning rod is children; the biggest debates revolve around access by children to pornographic material (cf. debates over access by children or adults to hate speech). The technical response to date has involved systems for filtering unacceptable content, but such systems are imperfect. Among the most common criticisms, for example, is that systems that filter out references to sexuality tend to filter out benign medical information sites as well as obscene material. The more elaborate Platform for Internet Content Selection from the World Wide Web Consortium aims at automated negotiation between users and sites to inhibit the flow of unwanted content. National differences are particularly large in this area, given differing influences of religion, culture, and national norms about what kinds of content are "acceptable" and to whom and whether governmental units have the right to control content communicated to or by citizens.

New kinds of policy concerns are arising about the qualities of networks as infrastructure. These concerns have long roots under the rubrics of computer security, communications security, and network reliability, but the heterogeneous, internetworked, and global environment fostered by the Internet has amplified these concerns, which can be aggregated as *information systems trustworthiness*, and led to new efforts associated with information warfare and with critical infrastructure. Traditional computer and communications security concerns include confidentiality (protection against unauthorized disclosure), integrity (protection against unauthorized alteration), and availability (protection of the ability to use when needed) of information and systems. These qualities depend heavily on how systems are designed and used. Information warfare is concerned with the potential for attack, and the need for defense, against systems and information resources over networks. The first policy concern is national security, but the dependence of the military on commercial systems and the importance of the economy to national well-being mean that economic security is linked closely to national security. Critical infrastructure embraces information warfare concerns, but with a more benign vocabulary. It addresses the interdependencies of different kinds of systems that depend on computers and networks (and the Internet), such as telecommunications and electric power, or transportation and telecommunications, and so on. Whereas information warfare emphasizes the risks from attacks, critical infrastructure also emphasizes other sources of system failure and the importance of robust, reliable system operation. In the USA, the concept was developed through a 1997–1998 Presidential Commission on Critical Infrastructure Protection, which inspired development of new programs involving many government agencies and elements of the private sector. Although network reliability has long been associated with wireline telephone networks, at least in the USA, the interconnection of wireline and wireless telephony and of telephony with cable television raises concerns about interoperability and end-to-end reliability. These issues are addressed in conjunction with telecommunications regulation.

Cryptography (*q.v.*) policy relates to trustworthiness because of the value of encryption as a supporting mechanism. Cryptography has become a central concern in the evolution of the information infrastructure because of its potential contributions to information and system security and because it can support the objectives of information policy (privacy, intellectual property rights, and freedom of speech) by making private communication over otherwise public facilities. All of these contributions are important to the growth of electronic commerce; encryption can protect funds transfers (of concern to consumers, businesses, and taxing authorities), the integrity of information (as a product and as elements of a transaction), and so on. Cryptography policy has been convoluted, because national security and law enforcement entities are concerned that the spread of strong cryptography can interfere with their actions to screen communications consistent with their mission. A result is controls on the export of encryption products, but concerns arise about the potential for control over domestic use. Advocates of more liberal policy argue that, in the long run, the public is better served when the good-guy majority can use better tools for self-protection, and they also emphasize the growing importance of encryption in support of privacy (*see* PRETTY GOOD PRIVACY).

The future of computers and communications depends on a mix of technology, business, and public policy. Early 1990s attention to information infrastructure focused policy attention on promotion of deployment and capability, spurring business investments in network deployment and new kinds of networkable devices that depend on computer technology. The mid- to late 1990s attention to electronic commerce (*q.v.*) has focused attention on the use of computers and communications, including the balance between capability proliferation and safeguards for the infrastructure as a complex super-system and for the users (in the limit, the whole population). As the next century begins, attention grows to the potential of the Internet as a public space, with implications not only for purposeful activity (business, education, and so on) but for personal activity, including social interaction and play.

Bibliography

1994. Computer Science and Telecommunications Board. *Realizing the Information Future: The Internet and Beyond.* Washington, DC: National Academy Press.

1995. Computer Science and Telecommunications Board. *Keeping the U.S. Computing and Communications Industry Competitive: Convergence of Computing, Communications, and Entertainment.* Washington, DC: National Academy Press.

1996. Computer Science and Telecommunications Board. *The Unpredictable Certainty; Information Infrastructure Through 2000.* Washington, DC: National Academy Press.

1996. Peterson, L. L., and Davie, B. S. *Computer Networks: A Systems Approach.* San Francisco: Morgan Kaufmann.

1997. Computer Science and Telecommunications Board. *The Evolution of Untethered Communications.* Washington, DC: National Academy Press.

1997. Computer Science and Telecommunications Board. *More Than Screen Deep: Toward Every-Citizen Interfaces to the Nation's Information Infrastructure.* Washington, DC: National Academy Press.

1998. Computer Science and Telecommunications Board. *Trust in Cyberspace.* Washington, DC: National Academy Press.

1999. Blumenthal, M. S. "Networks of the World: Unite!," in *Global Networks: Vision and Reality* (ed. J. R. Schement). Washington, DC: Aspen Institute.

1999. McGarty, T. P., and McKnight, L. "International IP Telephony," in *Internet Telephony* (eds. L. McKnight and D. D. Clark). Cambridge, MA: MIT Press.

Marjory S. Blumenthal

COMMUNICATIONS

See also DATA COMMUNICATIONS.

COMPACTION

See DATA COMPRESSION.

COMPATIBILITY

For articles on related subjects *see* CROSS ASSEMBLERS AND COMPILERS; EMULATION; OPEN ARCHITECTURE; OPEN SYSTEMS INTERCONNECTION; SIMULATION; SOFTWARE; SOFTWARE PORTABILITY; and TRANSPARENCY.

Two compilers or language translators (usually on different computers) are said to be *compatible* if source programs written for a compiler on one computer will compile and execute successfully on the other. Similarly, two versions of the same compiler (on the same computer) are said to be compatible if a source program written for one version of the compiler will successfully compile and execute using the other version. If the compatibility extends in only one direction, we speak of "upward" (older to newer) or "downward" (newer to older) compatibility. Occasionally, specific programs will be said to be compatible with specific computer systems when they can be compiled or assembled and executed correctly using that computer system; but the more common use of compatibility in computing is applied to two machines, two configurations, two operating systems, or two software packages with respect to the ease with which programs or data can be converted from one to the other. The term normally applied to a program to describe the ease with which it can be converted from one system to another is *portability*.

Upward compatibility refers not only to computers with respect to the programs that run on them, but also to the data that they accept and operate on. For example, a computer software system is said to be upward compatible if identical data will produce identical results on a more recent (hence, upward) version as on an older version, even though the newer version may also accept additional forms of data. The term "identical" in this context is somewhat utopian because it is almost never realized in practice.

Manufacturers have historically extolled upward compatibility as an improvement of their small machines extended to their own larger machines, while minimizing any compatibility (especially upward) between their machines and those of their competition. However, they have been quick to point out the upward compatibility of their equipment as compared with that of the competition. In fact, computing equipment, compilers and other processors marketed by particular manufacturers have been deliberately designed so that programs running on competitive equipment can be easily converted to run on their systems. Conversely, equipment and systems have also been designed to maximize the difficulty of converting programs so that they cannot be run on competing equipment or systems. The result has been that true compatibility is almost never achieved between equipment from different manufacturers.

Hardware component compatibility is an intensely competitive area. Since many peripheral devices are hooked to the computer by a relatively small number of cables (usually with a plug, in fact), so-called *plug-to-plug compatible* peripherals have been developed by some competitive firms. Their practice is to build one that works exactly the same (and even has identical plugs on the ends of the cables) as the original, but which can be profitably marketed at a lower price than the original. Thus, potential customers exist wherever the original equipment was installed.

In contrast to the practice of minicomputer and mainframe manufacturers who, historically, have resisted cross-vendor compatibility, the makers of personal computers (*q.v.*) and workstations (*q.v.*) often promote such compatibility through use of an *open architecture*, which encourages other firms to market add-on products to their computer line. In networking the *open systems interconnection* (OSI—*q.v.*) protocol defines communication protocols (*q.v.*) for intersystem compatibility.

Chester L. Meek

COMPILE AND RUN TIME

For articles on related subjects *see* BINDING; COMPILER; DIAGNOSTIC; ERRORS; LANGUAGE PROCESSORS; OBJECT PROGRAM; and SOURCE PROGRAM.

The complete process of running a program that has been written in a high-level language such as Pascal or C (*q.v.*) is accomplished in two steps:

1. Translation of the *source program* as written by the programmer into a machine-executable form (a process commonly referred to as *compilation*).

2. Execution of the generated form; i.e. the *running* of the compiled or *object program.*

To distinguish between certain actions that may occur during one or another of these phases, the period of compilation is known as the *compile time* and the succeeding period as the *run time* or *execution time.* In the usual compile and execute system, these two phases are distinct and may be temporally separated. In fact, the running of a program may be accomplished many times without the need for the recompilation of the program, provided the compiled code is saved on, say, disk. In an interpretive system, however, the two phases are intertwined, since execution of each source program statement follows immediately after its translation (*see* LANGUAGE PROCESSORS).

Typically, errors in a program are related to compile time or run time. Where the error is an error of language (i.e. incorrect syntax, such as a missing parenthesis), then the system is capable of recognizing this at compilation time; on the other hand, errors in logic or arithmetic (i.e. semantic errors) are normally discovered (if at all) at run time. Some language processor systems allow the programmer to use certain facilities called compile-time and run-time facilities. As an example of the latter, some systems allow the programmer to specify the format of the input data and output results at run time rather than in the source program.

J. A. N. Lee

COMPILER

> For articles on related subjects, *see* BACKUS–NAUR FORM; FORMAL LANGUAGES; GRAMMARS; INTERMEDIATE LANGUAGES; LANGUAGE PROCESSORS; LINKERS AND LOADERS; PROGRAMMING LINGUISTICS; and REGISTER ALLOCATION.

A *compiler* is a program that translates programs expressed in a *source* language into equivalent programs expressed in a *target* language. Usually, but not always, the source language is high level, such as Pascal or Java (*q.v.*), and the target language is low level, such as assembler code or even pure machine code.

While differences in the abstraction levels of the source and target languages can make the translation itself challenging, additional requirements further com-

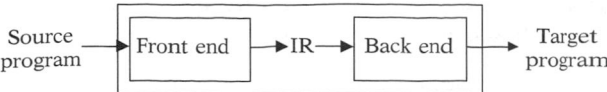

Figure 1. Structure of typical compiler.

plicate compiler construction. A good compiler must tolerate and report errors in source programs, generate target programs that make efficient use of resources, and provide information about the translated programs to other tools such as *garbage collectors, debuggers* (*see* DEBUGGING), and *linkers* (*see* LINKERS AND LOADERS). The compiler itself must avoid excessive time or space consumption, be adaptable to changes in the source and target languages, and (preferably) be portable to several computer systems.

The necessity to make trade-offs between the many requirements means that no one compiler is universally best. Different uses will place different demands on a compiler: in educational use, it may be particularly important that a compiler does excellent error analysis, reporting, and recovery; in production use, fast compilation may be an important concern during development, while optimization of the execution time of generated machine code may be the top concern once the application is ready for delivery. Accordingly, it is important to be able to construct high-quality compilers in a predictable and short period of time. In the 1950s, when the first compilers appeared, compiler construction was a difficult and unpredictable art. Today, after decades of developing systematic techniques and solution principles for subtasks of compilation, compiler construction is a well-understood form of software engineering (*q.v.*).

Often, compilers are viewed as consisting of two parts: a front end, mainly responsible for *analyzing* the source programs, and a back end, mainly responsible for generating or *synthesizing* the target programs; *see* Fig. 1. The front end translates the source program into an *intermediate representation* (IR) from which the back end generates the target program. While this model is coarse, and the boundary between the front and back ends not always sharp, the model is still useful for the following description.

The Front End

The front end takes source programs, often read from text files, analyzes them, makes sure there are no errors, and then builds an intermediate representation that can be passed on to the back end. The front end mechanisms are well standardized and significant automation is possible while constructing them. Most compilers employ three phases to map a program source file into the intermediate representation: *lexical analysis*, *parsing*, and *semantic analysis*. Each of these phases performs extensive error checking.

The first phase, lexical analysis, groups the individual characters in the input source program into *tokens*. The tokens constitute the basic meaningful units of the source program such as identifiers, reserved words, and separators. Some portions of the input, so-called *white space*, do not contribute to the tokens and are discarded. Examples of white space are spaces, tabs, line terminators, and comments.

The second phase, parsing, matches the tokens with the *grammar* of the programming language. A grammar (described below) represents the syntactic structure of a programming language. The reference manual for a programming language will include a grammar that describes the language. The result of parsing is a *parse tree*—a data structure that captures how the input tokens assemble together to match the grammar of the language.

The third phase, semantic analysis, analyzes the parse tree for semantic correctness. This phase involves checking the source language rules that are not captured directly in the lexical or syntactic description of the language. For example, the semantic analyzer may verify that variables are declared before their first use, and that operators are applied only to operands of the right type. Following semantic analysis, the parse tree is converted into an intermediate representation which is then passed to the back end.

Aho *et al.* (1986) provide a comprehensive description of lexical analysis, parsing, and semantic analysis. Another good book is Muchnick (1997).

CONTEXT-FREE GRAMMARS

Consider a simple programming language, in which programs consist of the keyword `begin`, followed by a list of declarations, then a list of statements, and finally terminated by the keyword `end`. A declaration introduces a single new integer variable. A statement is either an `if-then-else` statement or an assignment statement which sets a variable to the value of an expression. Expressions are made up of variables and numbers, and may use addition, multiplication, relational operators, and parentheses. The following is a *context-free grammar* (or simply grammar) for this language:

```
program ::= "begin" {declaration}
            {statement} "end"
declaration ::= "int" ID ";"
statement ::= assignment | ifthenelse
assignment ::= ID "=" expression ";"
expression ::= term [relop term]
relop ::= "<" | "<=" | ">" | ">="
          | "==" | "!="
term ::= factor {"+" factor}
```

```
factor ::= primary {"*" primary}
primary ::= ID | NUM | "(" expression ")"
ifthenelse ::= "if" expression "then"
               statement "else" statement
```

The grammar consists of a list of rules, one per line. Each rule defines a *non-terminal* on the left-hand side of the "`::=`" operator in terms of possible expansions on the right-hand side. In this grammar, the non-terminals are `program`, `declaration`, `statement`, `assignment`, `expression`, `relop`, `term`, `factor`, `primary`, and `ifthenelse`. The rule for the `assignment` non-terminal specifies that it can be expanded into an identifier token `ID` followed by the "`=`" token, followed by any expansion of the `expression` non-terminal, followed by a "`;`". The rule for `primary` specifies three alternatives, separated by the "`|`" operator: `primary` can be expanded into an identifier `ID`, a number `NUM`, or a parenthesized expression "`(`" `expression` "`)`". Each alternative is known as a *production* for the non-terminal. Non-terminal definitions are often recursive, e.g. `expression` has a recursive definition involving `term`, `factor`, `primary`, and then `expression` itself.

The other entities that appear on the right-hand sides of productions include *terminals* (so named because they cannot be expanded). Terminals match the tokens produced by the lexical analyzer. There are two kinds of terminal in the above grammar: constant strings such as "`int`" or "`;`", and variable strings such as `ID` and `NUM`. The details of `ID` and `NUM` are not defined in the grammar; instead their definition is part of the lexical token specification (see below). Collectively, non-terminals and terminals are called *symbols*.

Finally, grammar definitions use parentheses for grouping together symbols and may for convenience use special notation to specify repeated or optional constructs. In the grammar above, a sequence of symbols enclosed in "`{`" and "`}`" may be repeated zero or more times, whereas a sequence of symbols enclosed in "`[`" and "`]`" (as in the rule for `expression`) may be included at most once (this notation is known as EBNF, or Extended Backus–Naur Form). Thus, the non-terminal `program` can include zero or more `declarations` followed by zero or more `statements` in its expansion.

REGULAR EXPRESSIONS

Regular expressions, like context-free grammars, are a specialized notation to describe languages. Regular expressions, however, are simpler than context-free grammars in that they disallow recursive EBNF definitions. This simplification makes them well suited to describing the lexical structure (tokens) of programming languages, since the absence of recursion enables construction of very efficient lexical analyzers.

The following example uses regular expressions to define a token for the simple grammar shown earlier. It defines ID to be a letter followed by zero or more letters and digits, and NUM to be any sequence of one or more digits:

```
ID ::= LETTER {LETTER | DIGIT}
NUM ::= DIGIT {DIGIT}
LETTER ::= "A" | "B"| ... | "Z" |
           "a" | "b" | ... | "z"
DIGIT ::= "0" | "1" | "2" | "3" | "4" |
          "5" | "6" | "7" | "8" | "9"
```

LEXICAL ANALYSIS AND PARSING

Lexical analysis matches character sequences to regular expression descriptions of tokens, while parsing matches token sequences to context-free grammar descriptions of programming languages. For performance and convenience reasons, most compilers separate lexical analysis and parsing.

- Lexical analysis is the most performance-critical part of the front end, since it is the only phase that processes each individual character in the input source program. The use of non-recursive regular expressions in the lexical specification allows construction of fast lexical analyzers, without which the front end could spend a lot of time grouping individual characters into tokens.

- The separation factors the description of the programming language in a way that matches how humans use natural language (reading words rather than individual letters). Moreover, the lexical analysis/parsing interface is the ideal place to discard white space, since white space appears between tokens.

Below we have written out the context-free grammar and adjoined the regular expressions shown earlier and in the process introduced names for all tokens in the grammar.

Context-free grammar:
```
program ::= BEGIN {declaration} {statement}
            END
declaration ::= INT ID SEMICOLON
statement ::= assignment | ifthenelse
assignment ::= ID ASSIGN expression
               SEMICOLON
expression ::= term [relop term]
relop ::= LT | LE | GT | GE | EQ | NE
term ::= factor {PLUS factor}
factor ::= primary {MULT primary}
primary ::= ID | NUM | LPAREN expression
            RPAREN
ifthenelse ::= IF expression THEN statement
               ELSE statement
```

Regular expression specification of tokens:
```
BEGIN ::= "begin"
END ::= "end"
INT ::= "int"
ID ::= LETTER {LETTER | DIGIT}
LETTER ::= "A" | "B" | ... | "Z" |
           "a" | "b" | ... | "z"
DIGIT ::= "0" | "1" | "2" | "3" | "4" |
          "5" | "6" | "7" | "8" | "9"
SEMICOLON ::= ";"
ASSIGN ::= "="
LT ::= "<"
LE ::= "<="
GT ::= ">"
GE ::= ">="
EQ ::= "=="
NE ::= "!="
PLUS ::= "+"
MULT ::= "*"
NUM ::= DIGIT {DIGIT}
LPAREN ::= "("
RPAREN ::= ")"
IF ::= "if"
THEN ::= "then"
ELSE ::= "else"
```

This token specification is *ambiguous*, since some input strings match more than one definition. For example, the input "int" matches both INT and ID, and "a5" matches both a single ID and ID followed by NUM. Writing an unambiguous lexical specification could be considerably harder, but is often unnecessary since the lexical analyzer can handle ambiguities by applying simple rules such as preferring earlier definitions over later ones (selecting INT over ID in the former case) and longer matches over shorter ones (selecting ID over ID NUM in the latter care).

Example 1 (no errors)

Consider the program:

```
begin
  int i;
  i = 0;
end
```

The lexical analyzer converts the program into the following sequence of tokens:

```
BEGIN INT ID SEMICOLON ID
  ASSIGN NUM SEMICOLON END
```

While we identify tokens simply by name, some tokens contain additional information that later stages of the compiler need. For example, an ID token contains the text image (the actual letters in the identifier), and a NUM token contains the numerical value.

The parser matches these tokens with the grammar as follows:

```
program → BEGIN declaration statement END
  declaration → INT ID SEMICOLON
  statement → assignment
   assignment → ID ASSIGN expression
                  SEMICOLON
     expression → term
       term → factor
         factor → primary
           primary → NUM
```

The result of parsing is more conveniently represented as a *parse tree*, as shown in Fig. 2.

The sequence of tokens generated by the lexical analyzer constitutes the *leaves* of the parse tree, while the interior nodes constitutes the non-terminals involved in producing the token sequence from the topmost non-terminal `program`.

Parsing algorithms used in compilers fall into two general categories: *bottom-up* and *top-down*, also known as LR and LL parsers, respectively. LR and LL parsers offer different trade-offs between ease of specifying certain language constructs, speed of parsing, size of parsers, and conceptual complexity. Bottom-up parsers build parse trees from the leaves (the bottom), progressing up towards the root, while top-down parsers build parse trees from the root (the top), progressing down towards the leaves. For performance reasons, both bottom-up and top-down parsers restrict the context-free grammars that they can process. The restrictions typically allow parsers to select productions from the grammar by looking ahead at most k tokens at each step, where k is a small positive constant. Parsers satisfying such constraints are referred to as "look-

ahead k" parsers, or more briefly LR(k) and LL(k) parsers. In practice, $k = 1$ suffices for parsing most programming languages.

Example 2 (syntax error)

Suppose the first semicolon is omitted from the program in Example 1:

```
begin
  int i
  i = 0;
end
```

In this case, the lexical analyzer produces these tokens:

```
BEGIN INT ID ASSIGN NUM SEMICOLON END
```

Now the parser can no longer match the token with the grammar rules and consequently reports an error.

Example 3 (lexical error)

Suppose the first semicolon in Example 1 is changed into a colon:

```
begin
  int i:
  i = 0;
end
```

Upon encountering the colon character on the input, the lexical analyzer is unable to find a match with any of the regular expressions, and therefore reports an error.

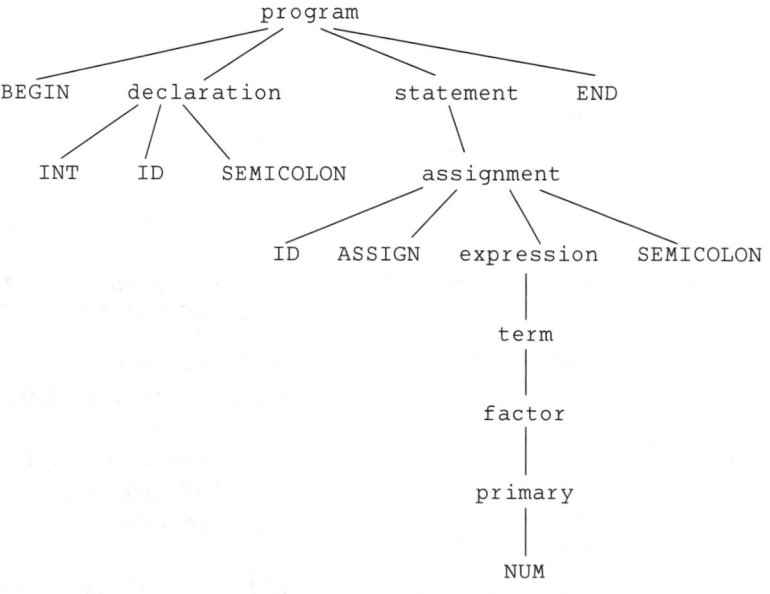

Figure 2. A parse tree.

GENERATORS FOR LEXICAL ANALYZERS AND PARSERS

For a compiler developer, formal descriptions of programming languages, such as regular expressions and grammars, have two important advantages. First, they allow separation of *how* from *what*: the algorithms used for performing lexical analysis and parsing are independent of the languages being processed. Second, they enable the use of *generators*, tools that completely automate the construction of lexical analyzers and parsers. A generator reads the lexical specification and grammar for a language and, given a program, produces executable code implementing a lexical analyzer, a parser, and possibly a parse tree builder for the language. Without a generator, the compiler developer would have to write, debug, and tune this code manually, which can easily amount to thousands of lines.

Some of the most used generators are `lex/yacc` and `flex/bison` for C-based lexical analyzers and parsers, and `JavaCC` and `PCCTS` for Java-based lexical analyzers and parsers. Both `yacc` and `bison` generate bottom-up LALR(1) parsers (LALR(1) is a further restriction over LR(1)), while `JavaCC` and `PCCTS` generate top-down LL(1) parsers by default, but can be made to generate LL(k) parsers for any $k > 0$.

SEMANTIC ANALYSIS

The semantic analyzer receives the completed parse tree from the parser and verifies that it contains no *semantic* errors—errors that the language specification requires be reported at compile time, but which cannot be detected by the lexical analyzer or parser. An example of a program with a semantic error is the following:

```
begin
  int i;
  j = 0;
end
```

In this program, the variable `j` is used without a preceding declaration. The program passes the lexical

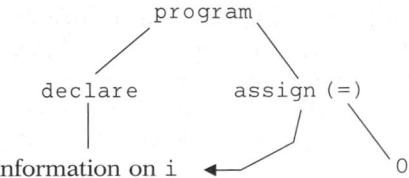

Figure 3. Possible IR for the parse tree.

analyzer and parser despite the error, since neither the lexical specification or the grammar requires that variables be declared before their first use. This error must be caught in the semantic analysis phase.

To increase modularity, a semantic analysis can be implemented with multiple phases, each performing a specific semantic check. The phases perform *tree walks*, a process during which nodes in the parse tree are visited in a systematic order to collect and verify semantic information.

In addition to verifying the absence of semantic errors, the semantic analyzer may add semantic information to the parse tree to support later phases of the compiler. For example, it can link uses of variables to their declarations to simplify the job for the back end when it allocates storage for the variables in the program.

The Intermediate Representation

Some compilers use the parse tree, annotated by the semantic analyzer, as the main representation in the back end. More commonly, however, the parse tree is converted into a more convenient intermediate representation (IR) before being passed to the back end. A possible IR for the parse tree of Fig. 2 is shown in Fig. 3. This IR discards unimportant details of syntactic appearance and remnants of the parsing process such as the terminals BEGIN, END, INT and SEMICOLON while retaining the essential information, including the semantic link from the use to the declaration of the variable `i`.

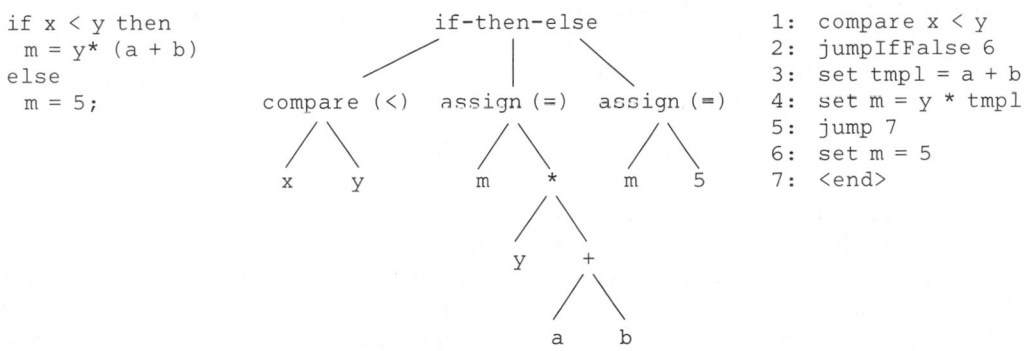

Figure 4. Source program fragment (left), abstract syntax tree IR (center), and pseudo-assembler IR (right).

The IR serves to bridge the gap from the source to the target language and therefore is designed to: (1) be easy to generate from the parse tree of the source program, (2) include sufficiently low-level constructs to expose all computation for optimization, and (3) be easy to use to generate target code. Common forms of intermediate representations include *abstract syntax trees*, such as the one shown in Fig. 3, and pseudo-assembler code. Fig. 4 gives a slightly bigger example of the two kinds of IR for an `if` statement. Both IRs make every step of the computation explicit: the tree has a node for each computational step and the pseudo-assembler code has an instruction for each computational step. There are other common IRs, each focusing on different aspects of the computation: *control-flow graphs* capture the program's control structures, *dataflow graphs* track how values flow between expressions, and *static single assignment forms* emphasize the sequencing of variable definitions and uses.

The Back End

The back end generates the target program from the information it receives from the front end. In the simplest case, the target program is constructed directly from the IR. More commonly, though, the back end consists of a number of phases that operate on the IR (or even multiple IRs), allowing the program to be optimized as part of the compilation.

The phases gradually transform the intermediate representation of the program into one that is closer to the low-level target language. Each step in the transformation exposes more details of the computation in the program and therefore creates opportunities for optimization.

The use of multiple phases, in addition to enabling more optimization, improves the organization of the compiler itself. Phase separation increases modularity (each phase can concentrate on a single task), maintainability (phases can be modified individually), and retargetability (the target machine-dependent parts can be isolated in a few phases rather than permeating the whole compiler). Although generator tools for some back end phases have appeared, back end construction remains less automated than front end construction.

The IR on which the back end operates often includes both high-level and low-level constructs. The high-level constructs are direct translations from the parse tree into the IR. High-level constructs may include features that closely match those of the target language. For example, they may include arrays (indexable lists of values), variable accesses from lexically enclosing scopes (caused by block structuring constructs, such as nested procedures in Pascal), and virtual function calls (function calls which select the code to execute based on the types of the actual arguments). Later, phases in the back end may expand the high-level constructs one by one into lower-level IR constructs. Arrays may be expanded into pointers and address computation, lexical scoping may be expressed by explicitly navigating static links (*see* ACTIVATION RECORD), and virtual function calls may be expanded into indirect calls through arrays of function pointers.

There are two principal advantages achieved by having both high- and low-level constructs in the same IR. First, each optimization can be performed at the level that is most convenient for it. Some optimizations are best expressed at the higher levels, since the high-level constructs inherently ensure that certain invariants hold (e.g. array elements may be laid out contiguously in memory, but this property is not inherently valid for the pointer operations that constitute the low-level equivalent of arrays). Second, by systematically expanding the high-level constructs into their constituent low-level parts, the intrinsic computation in the high-level constructs is exposed in the IR and therefore can be manipulated by the optimizer and translated into target code by the code generator.

OPTIMIZATION

An optimizer works on the IR, transforming the program into one that computes the same result, but does so more efficiently according to some measure, such as execution time or memory consumption. Two trends have greatly increased the importance of optimization: new programming paradigms make modern languages harder to implement efficiently (e.g. object-oriented and logic programming languages), while modern computers sustain peak performance only when programmed carefully (e.g. factors like pipelining, multi-instruction issue, register usage, and data layout for high cache rates must all be considered).

Every optimization involves two steps: first the optimizer proves that the contemplated optimization is correct (meaning-preserving) for the specific program, and then it performs the optimization by transforming the IR. For example, if the optimizer can prove that the variable y in Step 4 of Fig. 4 (right) will always have the value 2, it can replace the multiplication `set m = y * tmp1` by a faster addition, `set m = tmp1 + tmp1`, without changing the meaning of the program. This simple optimization is just one of many kinds that have been developed. Commonly used optimizations are: *dead code elimination* (delete code that can never be executed), *constant folding* (perform computation at compile time instead of run time), *constant propagation* (track variables that have a constant value), *common subexpression elimination* (avoid recomputing expressions that occur multiple times), *strength* *reduction* (replace certain expressions that depend on loop counters by more efficient ones), and *code motion* (e.g. hoist loop-invariant expressions out of loops).

Several analysis techniques can be used to prove the correctness of optimizations, including dataflow (*q.v.*) analysis, abstract interpretation, type inference, and dependence analysis. These analyses conservatively compute properties that are valid for all executions of the program; e.g. dataflow analysis will trace all possible execution paths through the program. At statements that can be reached directly from multiple predecessors, so-called merge points, the dataflow information from the predecessors is intersected, insuring that information sent to program points downstream from the merge point is valid regardless of the path of execution up to the merge point.

Optimization can be performed at different scopes. *Local* optimization operates on one *basic block* at a time, where a basic block is a maximal piece of straight-line code (e.g. in Fig. 4 (right) the three basic blocks are 1–2, 3–5, and 6). *Loop* optimization improves a single loop or a nest of loops. *Global* optimization operates on multiple basic blocks and loops within a procedure. Finally, *interprocedural* optimization operates on multiple procedures or even whole programs. Some operations, such as loop parallelization or procedure inlining, are meaningful only at specific scopes, whereas others, such as common subexpression elimination, make sense at all scopes. In general, large scopes offer more opportunities for optimizing, but also make the optimizer slower. Indeed, many analysis algorithms have superlinear worst-case time complexity, increasing compile times so much that the highest degrees of optimization become unattractive during program development, although they are worthwhile for a final version.

An optimizer is usually organized as a number of phases, each phase performing a single kind of optimization. Since different optimizations interact in complicated ways, there may be no one best order to apply the optimizations. For example, constant propagation may enable dead code elimination by revealing that a conditional statement has a constant test (causing either the `then` branch or the `else` branch to be selected all the time and leaving the other one "dead"). In turn, removing the dead code can enable further constant propagation if assignments in the dead code were the only factor that previously prevented the optimizer from proving that one or more variables are constant. For another example of how different optimizations interact, global optimization may leave the code locally inferior. This interdependence of optimizations, known as the *phase ordering* problem, is usually addressed by iterating the different phases until all optimization opportunities have been exhausted, a certain amount of optimization effort has been expended, or a certain level of improvement has been achieved.

While some transformations always improve the performance, others do so most of the time only. An optimistic optimizer may focus on special cases that heuristics (*q.v.*) or statistical information indicate will occur frequently. To retain correctness, optimized parts of the program must be guarded by run-time tests that restrict execution to the cases for which the optimization is meaning-preserving, falling back on unoptimized code in the remaining cases. While optimism enables more aggressive optimization, it should be curbed by *profitability analysis* to reduce the risk that the additional tests and unoptimized cases cause an overall slowdown.

Bacon *et al.* (1994) survey performance-improving program transformations.

CODE GENERATION

The code generator transforms the optimized IR into an equivalent target program. Code generation is best understood in terms of several subproblems: *register allocation* (*q.v.*) (determining which values will be in registers to minimize the dynamic number of register transfers to memory), *instruction selection* (choosing target language instructions and addressing modes to implement the operations in the IR), and *instruction scheduling* (ordering the target instructions to improve pipelining and avoid memory access delays). The subproblems are highly interdependent, making optimal code generation infeasible except in restricted cases. Typically, code generators compromise by solving the subproblems in a particular order, e.g. doing most register allocation before instruction scheduling, and using heuristics to predict the effects on later subproblems.

Ideally, the code generator is the only phase of the compiler that depends on the target language. Like the front end's parser, where it is strongly desirable to separate the specification of the source language from the parsing algorithm, a *retargetable* code generator should separate the specification of the target language from the code generation algorithm. Then it will be possible to port the code generator to a new target language with less effort than rewriting it from scratch.

Use of a template-driven code generator is perhaps the simplest way to achieve separation of "how" (algorithm) from "what" (target language). For each intermediate language construct, a template of target language instructions specifies the translation. The code generator simply walks the IR, instantiating the templates with the particular registers and constant values, and emits the resulting target language instructions. To port this code generator to a new target language, it suffices to write a new set of templates. Since a template-driven code generator translates the IR operation by operation with little use of contextual information, the resulting target program can be inefficient due to, for example, redundant memory reads. Tree-rewriting and pattern-matching code generators produce better code by attempting to match multiple IR operations against rules that specify their translation into the target language. Retargeting the code generator, then, involves writing a set of rules that describe the new target language.

Commonly, code generation is followed by *peephole optimization* to eliminate local inefficiencies in the target code. An example of a local inefficiency could be an instruction that stores the contents of a CPU register R_1 into a memory location M followed by an instruction that loads the contents of M into a register R_2. In this case, the peephole optimizer can replace the second instruction by a faster register-to-register transfer or entirely eliminate the instruction if the two registers are the same. In general, a peephole optimizer looks at fixed-length sequences of target instructions (hence the name "peephole"), trying to replace them by faster sequences. It may eliminate redundant instructions, short-circuit jumps to jumps, and substitute complex instructions for sequences of simpler instructions.

The Bigger Picture

In part because compiler research spans the spectrum from theory to practice and in part because it is concerned with improving programming language implementation, a core activity of computation, compiler research has been and continues to be one of the most active and influential areas of computer science. The use of compiler technology, especially lexical analyzers and parsers, in such diverse and seemingly unrelated applications as mail processing, spreadsheets, database processing, natural language processing, and Web servers, testifies to this claim. Consider further that compilers have become an increasingly important, if not essential, component of high-performance computer systems. In order to maximize overall performance, computer system developers today *co-design* compilers and hardware: compilers must exploit all important features of new hardware, while hardware design must be guided by the kinds of optimizations that compilers can perform. Recently, RISC (*q.v.*) processors sprang from this synergy of optimizing compilers and hardware design; the future will no doubt give us more examples and continue to underscore the importance of compiler technology as an active area of education, research, and systems development.

Bibliography

1986. Aho, A. V., Sethi, R., and Ullman, J. D. *Compilers—Principles, Techniques, and Tools.* Reading, MA: Addison-Wesley.
1994. Bacon, D. F., Graham, S. L., and Sharp, O. J. "Compiler Transformations for High-performance Computing," *ACM Computing Surveys,* **26**, 4 (December), 345–420.
1997. Muchnick, S. S. *Advanced Compiler Design and Implementation.* San Francisco: Morgan Kaufmann.

Ole Agesen and Sriram Sankar

COMPLEMENT

For articles on related subjects *see* ARITHMETIC, COMPUTER; and NUMBERS and NUMBER SYSTEMS.

In ordinary arithmetic, we represent negative numbers by a minus sign followed by the absolute value (i.e. magnitude) of the number (e.g. -6.42). In computers, we can represent negative numbers this way also, and sometimes this is actually done, but more often a *complement* representation is used.

To motivate the need for complements, consider the addition of two numbers expressed in sign–magnitude form. Before the operation can be carried out, the signs of the numbers must be compared. If they are the same, the two numbers can be added; if they are different, the smaller in magnitude may be subtracted from the larger and the correct sign appended to the result. As we will see, the use of complements avoids much of this complication.

Definitions

There are two kinds of complements, *radix complements* and *diminished radix complements*, where *radix* refers to the base of the number system being used. Let x be a positive number in the decimal system. Then the diminished 10s complement of x, which we denote by $\bar{x}$ and which is generally called the *9s complement*, is formed by subtracting every digit of x from 9. Thus, if $x = 426.3091$, $\bar{x} = 573.6908$. The *10s complement* $\tilde{x}$ is defined as the result of adding 1 in the least significant place of $\bar{x}$ or, equivalently, as the result of subtracting x from 10^n, where n is such that the 1 in 10^n is one place to the left of the most significant digit of x. Using the above example, $\tilde{x} = 573.6909 = 1,000.0000 - 426.3091$. Both the quantities $\bar{x}$ and $\tilde{x}$ may be used as representations of the quantity $-x$.

The other complements of practical importance are those in the radix 2, or binary, system. If x is now a positive binary number, its *1s complement* $\bar{x}$ is formed by changing all 0s in x to 1s and 1s to 0s (i.e. subtracting all bits of x from 1) and the *2s complement* $\tilde{x}$ is formed by adding 1 in the least significant place of $\bar{x}$ or, equivalently, subtracting x from 2^n with n chosen as above. Thus, if $x = 10.1101$, then $\bar{x} = 01.0010$ and $\tilde{x} = 01.0011 = 100.0000 - 10.1101$.

Properties of Complements

The useful properties of complements in computers are best illustrated using the binary system. For illustrative purposes, consider a computer where the numbers on which arithmetic operations are to be performed each have eight bits, the first of which denotes the sign (0 for plus, 1 for minus) and the other seven bits are, for convenience, assumed to represent an integer. If the sign is negative, let us assume the integer is in 2s complement form. Then, to add two such numbers, we need only treat them as eight-bit positive integers (i.e. treat the sign as another bit of the number), add them, and discard any carry to the left of the eighth position (*see* Fig. 1). Thus, we are able to ignore both the sign and relative magnitudes of the two numbers. With negative numbers in the 1s complement form, there is the slight additional complication that carries to the left of the eighth position must be added into the first (i.e. least significant) position (*see* Fig. 2).

Let $x = 00001000$ (decimal 8)
  $y = 00010101$ (decimal 21)
Then $\tilde{x} = 11111000$ (decimal -8)
  $\tilde{y} = 11101011$ (decimal -21)

Then $x + \tilde{y} = $
$$
\begin{array}{r}
00001000 \\
+\ 11101011 \\
\hline
11110011
\end{array}
$$

which is the 2s complement of 13 in decimal (00001101 in binary); and

$\tilde{x} + \tilde{y} = $
$$
\begin{array}{r}
11111000 \\
+\ 11101011 \\
\hline
11100011
\end{array}
$$

which is the 2s complement of 29 in decimal (00011101 in binary).

Figure 1. Addition of numbers using 2s complements.

Let $x = 00001000$
  $y = 00010101$
  $\bar{x} = 11110111$
  $\bar{y} = 11101010$

Then $x + \bar{y} = $
$$
\begin{array}{r}
00001000 \\
+\ 11101010 \\
\hline
11110010
\end{array}
$$

which is the 1s complement of 13 in decimal (00001101 in binary); and

$\bar{x} + \bar{y} = $
$$
\begin{array}{r}
11110111 \\
+\ 11101010 \\
\hline
11100001 \\
\ \llcorner\!\!\longrightarrow 1 \\
\hline
11100010
\end{array}
$$

which is the 1s complement of 29 in decimal (00011101 in binary).

Figure 2. Addition of numbers using 1s complements.

Let $x = 00001000$
  $y = 00010101$

Then $x - y$ is found by first forming

  $\tilde{y} = 11101011$

and then adding $x + \tilde{y}$, as in Fig. 1, to get 11110011, which is the 2s complement of 13 in decimal.

Figure 3. Subtraction using 2s complements.

Both methods given above can be rather easily proved correct by writing complemented numbers as 2^n minus the corresponding positive number (minus 1 for 1s complements).

One interesting property of the 1s complement form is the existence, as in sign–magnitude representation, of two zeros, one with a positive sign and one with a negative sign. This follows because the 1s complement of 0000 0000 is 1111 1111 (-0). With 2s complements, however, there is only one n-bit zero (namely, 0000 0000 for $n = 8$), since the 2s complement of 0000 0000 is 10000 0000, which has nine bits, the first of which is discarded. (Of the other 255 different 8-bit patterns, only one is its own 2s complement: 1000 0000 [-128].) In 2s complement representation, 1111 1111 is the complement of 0000 0001.

Since 1s complements are generated merely by changing 0s to 1s, and vice versa, it is very easy to build a circuit to generate the 1s complement of a number. It is somewhat more difficult, but not very hard, to build a circuit to generate 2s complements. Therefore it is easy to perform subtraction by first complementing the minuend and then adding (*see* Fig. 3). This means it is not necessary to have a hardware subtracter if there is a hardware adder and a complementer.

For performing multiplication and division, there are no direct advantages to the complement form and some disadvantages. However, the adjustments to algorithms for multiplying or dividing two positive numbers to allow them to handle operands in complement form are not major. Alternatively, negative operands in multiplication or division can first be complemented and then the, appropriate sign can be appended at the end.

Although 1s complements were sometimes used in the past on computers, 2s complements are used on all modern computers, their chief advantage being the unique 0.

Anthony Ralston

COMPLEXITY

See COMPUTATIONAL COMPLEXITY; INFORMATION-BASED COMPLEXITY; and NP-COMPLETE PROBLEMS.

COMPONENT SOFTWARE

For articles on related subjects *see* CLIENT–SERVER COMPUTING; DISTRIBUTED SYSTEMS; JAVA; and SOFTWARE REUSABILITY.

In some sense, all software is made up of its component parts, typically modules and lines of code (*see* MODULAR PROGRAMMING). But the idea of being able to build complex software from ready-made modules of reusable code has long bedeviled software developers. The difficulty is not in writing code good enough to be reused, but rather in how modular to make it and in how to store and classify code so that another programmer might find and reuse it.

Component software is designed to solve programming problems in small, modular bits, rather than in large, monolithic masses—think of a small tent rather than a skyscraper. A *component* is a small, lightweight application, tool, or utility that is designed to do a particular task (and only that task) and to do it elegantly and well. In this sense, the Unix (*q.v.*) system is composed of many separate components that manipulate files, process text, and so on. These components are all separate programs, however, and in the newer sense of the term, components are pieces that are not self-sufficient, but can be assembled into complete programs.

As with all early markets, components started out (1995–1997) as tools for software developers, but in a broad sense of the term, including commercial independent software vendors (ISVs), value-added resellers (VARs), systems integrators, and information systems designers within an organization. Already we have seen some applications, mainly lightweight versions of personal productivity tools, e.g. word processors, spreadsheets (*q.v.*), charts. These applications are intended for three markets: for developers who will incorporate them into larger applications (this is the component as building block), for hardware OEMs (original equipment manufacturers) who will use them as part of the desktop for *networked computers*, and for leading-edge users who are ready to try something new.

Eventually, it is possible that we might see components become an alternative software market (or even a replacement software market). For that to happen, there will have to be a lot more work on transforming existing monolithic applications into components (a process that has now begun). Also, developers (internal or commercial) will have to build components for organizations' business processes, so they can be just another one of the building blocks. That, too, is beginning to happen.

A component might be written as an ActiveX control, a Netscape plug-in, or even as some C or C++ code. Most of the earlier applications fall into this category.

New components being started now are likely to be written as Java applets, given the pervasive presence of the Internet, the explosive growth of intranet platforms as the new place for corporate application development, and the overwhelming interest in the development community to pursue the current hot platform. However, component programming is made possible through interface standards that define how components may interact—how one component may exchange information with another. Components that adhere to such standards may be written in any appropriate language. One such standard is CORBA (Common Object Request Broker Architecture); another is Microsoft's Component Object Model (COM or DCOM, for distributed programming); another, for Java, is Sun Microsystem's Java Beans.

In the late 1990s, many components were sold to OEMs and developers, but first tested as downloaded freeware from the Internet. In fact, components might not have happened at all without the Internet as a free and nearly frictionless marketplace. We expect individual developer Websites and Web-based component marketplaces (like the one that IBM already has) to be the model for selling individual components. We would also expect new pricing schemes to be implemented as software developers, used to substantial revenues from larger products, try out new bundling schemes to continue to grow their revenue as the business model for creating and selling software changes.

Bibliography

1998. Szyperski, C. *Component Software: Beyond Object-Oriented Programming*. Reading, MA: Addison-Wesley.

Amy D. Wohl

COMPRESSION, DATA

See DATA COMPRESSION; and IMAGE COMPRESSION.

COMPUTATIONAL COMPLEXITY

For articles on related subjects *see* ALGORITHMS, ANALYSIS OF; ALGORITHMS, THEORY OF; FAST FOURIER TRANSFORM; INFORMATION-BASED COMPLEXITY; MATHEMATICAL PROGRAMMING; NP-COMPLETE PROBLEMS; SORTING; TURING MACHINE; and UNDECIDABLE PROBLEMS.

Once we have developed an algorithm (*q.v.*) for solving a computational problem and analyzed its worst-case time requirements as a function of the size of its input (most usefully, in terms of the *O*-notation; *see* ALGORITHMS, ANALYSIS OF), it is inevitable to ask the question: "Can we do better?" In a typical problem, we may be able to devise new algorithms for the problem that are more and more efficient. But eventually, this line of research often seems to hit an invisible barrier, a level beyond which improvements are very difficult, seemingly impossible, to come by. After many unsuccessful attempts, algorithm designers inevitably start to wonder if there is something *inherent* in the problem that makes it impossible to devise algorithms that are faster than the current one. They may try to develop mathematical techniques for *proving formally* that there can be no algorithm for the given problem which runs faster than the current one. Such a proof would be valuable, as it would suggest that it is futile to keep working on improved algorithms for this problem, that further improvements are certainly impossible. The realm of mathematical models and techniques for establishing such impossibility proofs is called *computational complexity*.

For example, sorting n keys is a computational task that can be easily accomplished in $O(n^2)$ time by naive exchange algorithms such as *bubblesort*, while more sophisticated techniques such as *quicksort* and *mergesort* bring the time requirements down to $O(n \log n)$. Can we do better, or is $n \log n$ an unsurpassable milestone for sorting? Another interesting example is matrix multiplication. For a long time it was assumed that one needs n^3 operations to multiply two $n \times n$ matrices. In 1969, Volker Strassen showed that two $n \times n$ matrices can be multiplied by an ingenious recursive algorithm in $O(n^{2.81})$ operations! Over the past thirty years this exponent has undergone a breathtaking sequence of improvements, and now stands below 2.4. Where is this sequence of improvements going to end? Can we multiply two matrices in $O(n^2)$ time? Can we prove a lower bound of the form $n^2 \log n$, or, even more ambitiously, $n^{2.2}$, for the matrix multiplication problem?

A third example is the *traveling salesman problem* (Fig. 1), a problem that is popular and well-studied, as well as notorious for its difficulty. It is trivial to come up with an algorithm which, given an instance of the traveling salesman problem with n cities, will find the optimum tour in time $O(n!)$—just check all possible permutations of the cities. This algorithm, is, of course, all but unusable for any but the smallest instances: even for a modest instance with $n = 30$ cities, the number of tours to be examined is larger than the size of the known universe (or its age in picoseconds). A more detailed examination of the algorithm will reveal that the true running time is $O((n-1)!)$, since the starting city can be fixed with no harm to the correctness of the algorithm. It took some cleverness (and several decades from the time the problem was posed in the 1920s) to find a faster algorithm, requiring "only" $O(n^2 2^n)$ steps; this algorithm, discovered by Michael Held and Richard M. Karp, uses a *dynamic*

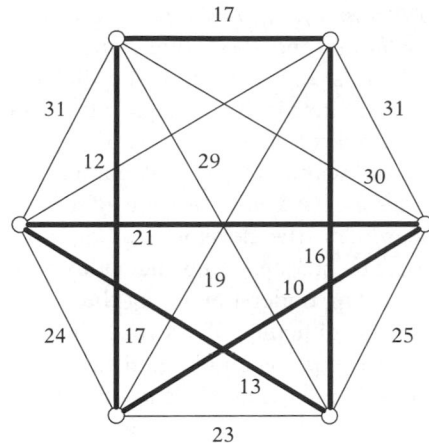

Figure 1. In the traveling salesman problem we are given a set of cities and the distances between them, and we seek the shortest closed tour that visits all cities. The optimum tour in this simple example is shown in bold, with total length 94. Because of the simplicity of its statement, its obvious appeal, and its maddening complexity, the traveling salesman problem has been studied extensively for decades, and it has been the testbed of every new algorithmic technique. Still, all algorithms known for it require exponential time in the worst case.

programming technique (*see* ALGORITHMS, DESIGN AND CLASSIFICATION OF) that patiently solves the problem for larger and larger subsets of the cities, using the results from smaller subsets to crack the larger ones, until the optimum tour of the set of all cities is finally identified.

Can we do better? To this date, there is no known algorithm that is guaranteed to solve the traveling salesman problem exactly for n cities faster than the dynamic programming algorithm. There are algorithms that are known *empirically* to solve quite large typical instances of the traveling salesman problem reasonably fast, and there are fast algorithms that somehow *approximate* the optimum solution, but there is no known algorithm that is guaranteed to return the optimum, and to do so in time that is *polynomial* in n—an algorithm with a running time such as $O(n^2)$, or $O(n^5)$. It is thus tempting to conjecture, and try to prove, that *the traveling salesman problem requires exponential time for its solution*, that all algorithms that solve it must spend exponential time for some infinite collection of instances.

As the reader may immediately suspect, the task of proving *negative results*, or *lower bounds* on the complexity of a problem, is usually a lot more intricate mathematically than just devising an efficient algorithm. Coming up with an efficient algorithm, however ingenious it may be, requires only that the algorithm be specified and analyzed. Proving a lower bound, however, necessitates that the prover must consider *the whole spectrum of all possible algorithms for the problem in hand*, and show that none of them does better than the specified bound; the difficulty of the task is obvious. Since its beginnings in the 1960s, computational complexity has been one of the most active research areas within theoretical computer science. However, despite hard work by some of the field's most gifted researchers, the development of sophisticated mathematical techniques, a few ingenious insights, and an ever-increasing understanding of the issue, it is fair to say that the difficulty of the task has heretofore prevailed: with very few and limited exceptions, lower bounds are still largely in the realm of conjecture.

General Models

The barrier separating polynomial algorithms from exponential ones, upon which we have stumbled in the case of the traveling salesman problem, is one whose significance goes beyond that problem. Polynomial-time algorithms, algorithms whose running time is bounded by a function like $O(n)$, $O(n^3)$, etc., form a substantial and important class of computations, broadly considered akin to the empirical concept of "practically feasible computation." Naturally, an $O(n^{1000})$ algorithm would hardy deserve to be called "practical", but such extreme polynomials never come up in practical situations. Typically, once a polynomial algorithm is discovered for a problem, a sequence of improvements ensues and the problem is eventually brought within the limits of practical computation. Unfortunately, there are many important problems for which, like for the traveling salesman problem, the best known algorithms are exponential in the worst case; it is these problems that have inspired the development of the main branch of the field of computational complexity, the one that deals with *general models of computation*. In contrast, problems such as matrix multiplication and sorting, for which the important open questions try to differentiate between different polynomial rates of growth, must be treated within specialized models of computation, within which there is some hope of making such fine distinctions.

The process of proving a lower bound on the complexity of a problem must start with a precise mathematical model for algorithms and their complexity. There are several useful mathematical models of algorithms, starting with the many variants of the Turing machine, proceeding to more down-to-earth models such as the *random access machine* (an abstraction of the von Neumann machine—*q.v.*), pointer machines, and many others. For each such model we have a way of evaluating the time required for the solution of an instance (in the case of the Turing machine, this is simply the number of steps the machine takes to come up with the final answer). This confusing diversity of models appears to add another layer of difficulty, besides the fundamental mathematical one, to the development of a theory of computational complexity. Fortunately, all these various models of computation have been proved to have computational powers that differ *only by a polynomial*. If a problem can be solved in polynomial time in any one of a wide array of models of computation, it can be solved in polynomial time in all of them. It is this fundamental fact, *the quantitative analog of the Church–Turing thesis (see* UNDECIDABLE PROBLEMS*)*, that allows us to study the polynomial/exponential dichotomy in algorithms in a principled and model-independent manner. (It should be noted that this principle is not as universally accepted as the Church–Turing thesis; in fact, its most serious and credible challenge has come recently, as physicists and computer scientists have joined forces to define and study *quantum computing* (*q.v.*), a model of computation that exploits quantum mechanical phenomena to achieve, presently only in theory, apparent exponential speed-ups over conventional computers and models of computation.)

Complexity Classes

In computational complexity we classify computational problems into *complexity classes*. The most important complexity class is the set of all problems that can be solved by polynomial-time algorithms (by Turing machines, or algorithms in any other one of a broad set of standard models). This important complexity class is denoted P, for polynomial time. Actually, for reasons of convenience, uniformity, and tradition, complexity classes are comprised not of problems, but of *languages*, that is, sets of strings in some fixed alphabet such as $\{0, 1\}$ (*see* FORMAL LANGUAGES). Any computational problem of interest can be transformed into a corresponding language in a way that captures its complexity. For example, the traveling salesman problem can be captured by the language L_{TSP}, consisting of all strings of 0s and 1s which encode an $n \times n$ matrix of nonnegative integers (the distances between the cities) plus another integer B, such that there is a tour of the n cities of total length equal to B or less.

As we mentioned, it is widely conjectured that the language L_{TSP} is not in P. However, it does belong in a broader, albeit somewhat less natural, complexity class called NP, for *nondeterministic polynomial*. Any language in this class can be decided by a polynomial *nondeterministic Turing machine*, a hypothetical device that has the ability to make correct guesses. For example, to recognize a string in L_{TSP}, a nondeterministic Turing machine would correctly guess the optimum tour of the instance encoded, and check that its length is indeed below the given bound. A language belongs in the class NP if such a recognition algorithm —a guessing phase, followed by a polynomial-time checking phase—exists. This important class contains, besides all of P, the traveling salesman problem and many other notoriously difficult problems. It is widely believed that the class P is strictly included in the class NP (i.e. that there are problems in NP not in P); this conjecture, as yet unproven, is the most central, important, and well-studied problem in computational complexity. A proof of this conjecture would establish in particular that the traveling salesman problem cannot be solved by a polynomial-time algorithm; this is because L_{TSP}, along with a surprising variety of other languages encoding natural problems, has been shown to be *NP-complete*. A problem in NP is NP-complete if all other problems in NP reduce to it in polynomial time. If there are *any* problems in NP that require exponential time, all NP-complete problems *must necessarily* be among them.

Complexity classes go beyond NP. The class EXP contains, informally, all problems solvable by exponential-time algorithms. By a straightforward quantitative extension of the diagonalization proof which establishes that the *halting problem* is undecidable (*see* UNDECIDABLE PROBLEMS), it can be shown that there are problems in EXP that are not in P. EXP itself is a proper subset of the decidable languages. And it is known that EXP contains all of NP.

Complexity classes also deal with resources other than time, most significantly *space*. In analogy to P, PSPACE is the complexity class of all languages that can be recognized by a computer using an amount of memory (number of Turing machine tape squares, for example) that is bounded by a polynomial in the size of the input. Memory is a resource that is more powerful and robust than time (obviously, you can compute more things with $1,000,000$ memory words and unlimited time, than you can with $1,000,000$ instructions and unlimited memory). For example, PSPACE contains both P and NP (but is contained in EXP). Also, another sign of the robustness of space is that nondeterminism makes no big difference in the space domain, and nondeterministic machines can simulate deterministic ones with only *quadratic* increase in space (but exponential increase in time)—hence the absence of an NPSPACE class. Because of the power of memory as a resource, there are interesting tasks (such as the evaluation of formulas and the traversal of rooted trees—*q.v.*) that can be accomplished in *logarithmic* space, whereas no computational task of the kinds considered here, in which one must examine the whole input, can be carried out in logarithmic time. (Many computational tasks of the *database query*

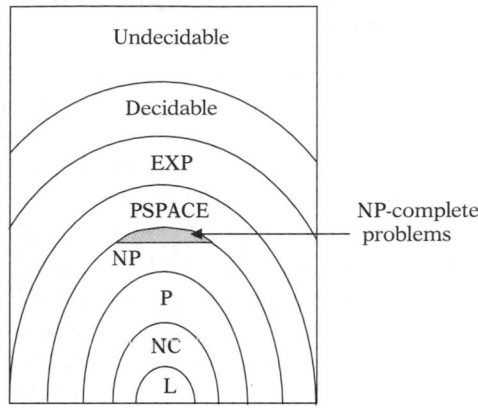

Figure 2. The complexity classes introduced in this article are depicted here as regions arranged according to the currently most prevalent view among experts in computational complexity. If a region A contains another region B, then the corresponding classes are known to contain one another in the same way. However, whether the containment is *proper*—that is, whether there is any space inside region A and outside region B—is for most of this map currently a subject of conjecture. There are a few known proper containments—for example, we can prove that EXP properly contains P, that PSPACE properly contains L, and that EXP is properly contained in the class of decidable problems.

variety can of course be accomplished in logarithmic time, for example by binary search; there is a branch of computational complexity that studies these too.) The class of problems solvable in logarithmic space is often denoted L.

There is an important and intriguing connection between space and *parallel time*: it turns out that, again within a broad range of "reasonable" models of sequential and parallel computation (*see* PARALLEL PROCESSING), the computational tasks that can be accomplished with a given amount of memory are closely related to the tasks that can be carried out in the same amount of parallel time—assuming that there are no limitations on the number of processors that are available. Another complexity class, called NC, is supposed to model feasible parallel computation more accurately: it includes all problems that can be solved in $O((\log n)^k)$ parallel time, for some fixed integer k, on polynomially many processors. This class is a subset of P, and is in fact believed to be a *proper* subset of P—as there seem to be many tasks which can be solved efficiently on sequential computers but cannot be successfully parallelized beyond some level. Alas, as with most of our more interesting insights related to complexity classes, that NC is different from P is currently yet another unproven conjecture.

Fig. 2 depicts the various complexity classes and their inclusions.

Other Aspects of Computational Complexity

In a certain sense, the first important results in computational complexity are the *undecidability* results proved by Alan M. Turing (*q.v.*), Alonzo Church (*q.v.*), Stephen C. Kleene, and many others in the 1930s and 1940s, establishing that certain problems cannot be solved by algorithms *at all*, however inefficient. When computers became available shortly thereafter, it became apparent that not all decidable problems deserve to be called "solvable," since excessive time requirements make many algorithms completely impractical. The current emphasis on polynomial time emerged in the 1960s from the experiences of researchers, most notably Jack Edmonds and Alan Cobham, trying to attack seriously hard problems in optimization and logic. The foundations of the present "complexity class" paradigm in computational complexity were laid by Juris Hartmanis and Richard E. Stearns in the 1960s.

Although research in computational complexity has ample internal unity, one can discern certain styles, trends, and research traditions. In the late 1960s a rich *axiomatic theory of complexity* was developed by Manuel Blum, in which complexity was studied in the abstract as a property relating recursive functions (*see* RECURSION) and computational resources that must obey a small number of common-sense axioms. *Structural complexity*, whose style is also influenced by the theory of recursive functions, studies complexity classes, various kinds of *reductions*, as well as the intricate connections between the two concepts. There have of course been several attempts to solve the major open problems of the field, of which the P vs. NP question is the most well-known and fundamental; many of these approaches redefine complexity in terms of *Boolean circuits* or other such primitive devices, in the hope of making the quest for lower bounds more concrete and tangible; other approaches to the P vs. NP question evoke the rich connections between computational complexity and mathematical logic. There is a research tradition of growing importance that uses computational complexity to study the foundations of cryptographic and other protocols (*see* CRYPTOGRAPHY, COMPUTERS IN), as well as of randomness, a study which often results in unexpected connections and insights into the more central problems in computational complexity. An interesting variant is *communication complexity*, which seeks to bound from below the amount of information that must be exchanged between two parties, each of which is in possession of a private input, in order to compute a complex function of the two inputs; communication complexity is often a useful tool in other subfields such as circuit complexity and VLSI complexity. There is also much research on using concepts from computational com-

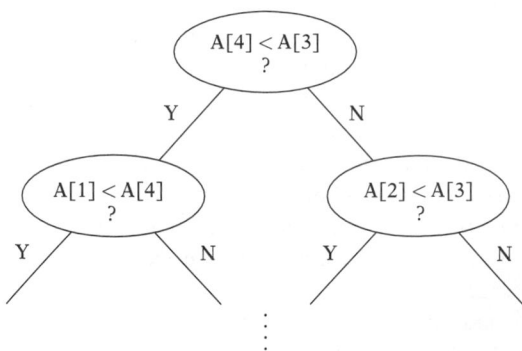

Figure 3. A lower bound for sorting by comparisons can be obtained within the *decision tree model* of computation. In this model, any algorithm that sorts *n* keys A[1], . . . , A[n] starts with a comparison of two keys (in our example, A[3] with A[4]), branches to two new comparisons depending on the outcome, from these to two new comparisons, and so on. Thus, every algorithm in this model is a tree. (The analysis of the related model in which comparisons have three outcomes, $<$, $=$, and $>$, is very similar.) Notice that this model suppresses the instructions, present in any sorting algorithm, that move keys around according to the comparison outcome; since our goal is to prove a lower bound, such omission is legitimate. The complexity of this algorithm is captured by the *height* of the tree, the length of the longest path from the root to a leaf.

Each leaf of this tree must correspond to the outcome of the sorting algorithm, that is, to an ordering of the *n* keys. Since this algorithm must sort correctly all possible initial permutations of the keys, there must be at least one leaf corresponding to each possible permutation. Therefore, this tree must have at least *n*! leaves.

We are very close to a proof of our lower bound: it is well-known (and easily provable by induction) that a binary tree that has height *h* can have up to 2^h leaves. So, a tree that has *n*! leaves must have height at least the logarithm of *n*!. Now, a calculation shows that the logarithm of *n*! is about $n \log n$, which completes the proof.

plexity, most often NP-completeness and its many variants, in order to understand better particular problems, and application areas, often problems in seemingly non-computational realms of the pure, applied, and social sciences.

There are also branches of computational complexity studying the inherent complexity of problems such as matrix multiplication and sorting, in which the desired complexity distinctions are much finer than the fundamental one between polynomials and exponentials. Necessarily, such problems are studied within more specialized models of computation. For example, in order to study the complexity of sorting, we may want to consider a model of computation in which sorting algorithms are seen as *comparison trees*. In this model, an $n \log n$ lower bound for sorting *can* be proved (see Fig. 3). Complexity results within limited models of computation, such as the decision tree model, are often met with skepticism: there may be useful algorithms for solving the problem that are outside the limitations of the model. There are classical algorithms like *radix sort*, using primitives other than comparisons (such as array access); these algorithms succeed in sorting certain kinds of key arrays faster than $n \log n$. Moreover, there are recent algorithms which appear to sort general arrays of keys faster than $n \log n$ by manipulating the bits of the keys. The ultimate value of lower bounds in restricted models may be, ironically, that they point to the kinds of primitives that must be used in order to circumvent them! The related field of *algebraic complexity* seeks to answer complexity questions such as the matrix multiplication problem, within a model of computation in which the primitive operations are algebraic operations (additions, multiplications, and so on). *Information-based complexity* seeks to understand the complexity of computations involving real numbers in which the scarce resource is the amount of information on the precise values of the inputs required for carrying out the computation.

Finally, in computational complexity we do not attempt to evaluate the complexity of a single input or a single string; we are interested only in the complexity of whole problems and languages. Still, it is intuitively obvious that the bit string

$$x = 01101110111000101101101101101011111011$$

is more complex than the string

$$y = 01010101010101010101010101010101010101.$$

Kolmogorov complexity is an approach to computational complexity that attempts to capture this intuition by defining the complexity of a string to be the length of the shortest program (in some fixed programming language) that generates this string. For example, string y above is generated by the program "`print '01' 18 times`", whereas there may be no such short program generating the string x. Kolmogorov complexity is a well-developed field which, interestingly, has often been a valuable tool to researchers in more mainstream aspects of computational complexity.

Bibliography

1979. Garey, M. R., and Johnson, D. S. *Computers and Intractability: A Guide to the Theory of NP-completeness.* New York: W. H. Freeman.
1992. Harel, D. *Algorithmics: The Spirit of Computing*, 2nd Ed. Reading, MA: Addison-Wesley.
1994. Papadimitriou, C. H. *Computational Complexity.* Reading, MA: Addison-Wesley.

Christos H. Papadimitriou

COMPUTATIONAL GEOMETRY

For articles on related subjects *see* ALGORITHMS, ANALYSIS OF; ALGORITHMS, DESIGN AND CLASSIFICATION OF; COMPUTER GRAPHICS; and GRAPH THEORY.

Computational geometry is the study of algorithmic problems involving geometry. Although the ruler and compass constructions of ancient Greek geometry were essentially algorithms for producing geometric objects, modern computational geometry begins with M. I. Shamos's 1975 Ph.D. dissertation, which solved several fundamental geometric problems and posed many more. Since the 1980s, computational geometry has been perhaps the most active area of algorithms research, and a recent bibliography lists over 8,000 relevant publications. The explosive growth of this field can be traced to the intuitive appeal of geometric problems as well as the wide range of practical applications.

Geometric problems arise in a variety of applications, some of which would not seem to have geometric aspects. VLSI circuits are described by overlapping rectangles of different materials. To prevent wires from short-circuiting, it is necessary to test designs so that no two rectangles intersect. The huge number of rectangles in a large circuit implies the need for fast intersection-detection algorithms. Mobile robots must find paths to a goal through rooms full of obstacles without bumping into anything. This can be more difficult than it might appear, as anyone who tries to move a piano through a door quickly discovers. Finite element methods (*q.v.*) used to simulate the performance of physical systems such as aircraft depend upon dividing the surface of the object into triangular regions, and effort spent in finding a "good" triangulation (such as the Delaunay triangulation described below) pays dividends in more efficient and accurate simulations. Database queries of the form "how many people are between 180 and 200 centimeters tall and weigh between 60 and 75 kilograms" can be thought of as asking how many points lie in a given rectangle, where the x-axis represents the height and the y-axis the weight. Finally, eliminating hidden lines and surfaces is typical of the geometric problems arising in computer graphics.

Computational geometry often deals with questions of how to compute various aspects of geometric structures. Many brute force algorithms for solving geometric problems can be improved upon by algorithmic techniques and sophisticated data structures (*q.v.*). To a larger extent than most traditional algorithmic problems, efficient solutions often rely on a *combinatorial* understanding of the problem, for example, knowing how many regions of a certain type can be formed by an arrangement of n lines.

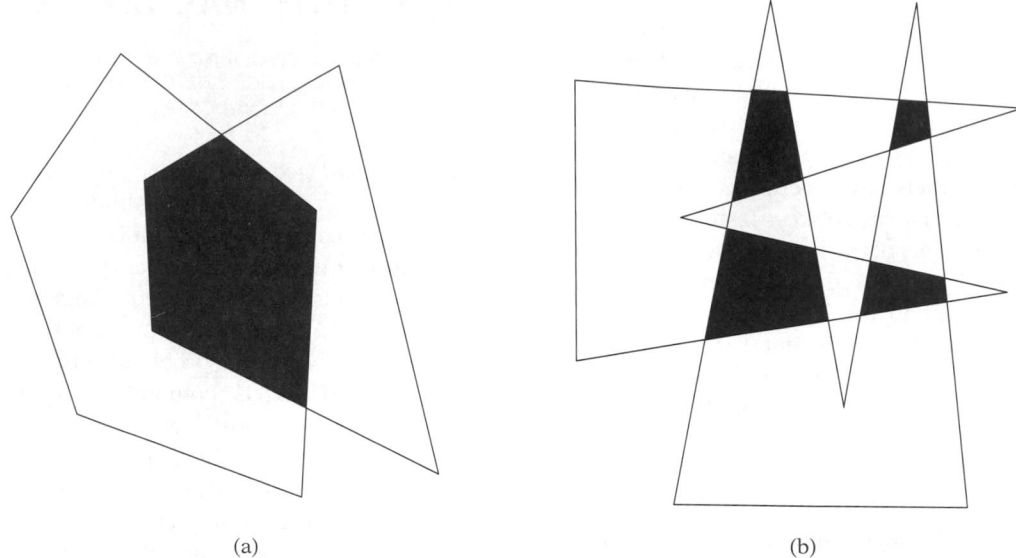

(a)   (b)

Figure 1. The intersection of (a) convex and (b) star-shaped polygons.

There are complications with geometric algorithms which do not occur in such related areas as graph algorithms. Even very primitive problems, such as testing whether two line segments intersect, are complicated by *degenerate* data. If two segments overlap or share an endpoint, do they intersect? The correct answer depends upon the application. To avoid such problems, it is often assumed that the points representing the data are in *general position*, meaning that no three points lie on the same line.

The complexity of geometric algorithms depends upon the type of geometric objects we are dealing with as well as their size. For example, consider determining the intersection between two polygons A and B with n and m vertices respectively. A *convex* polygon has the property that the line segment between any two points in the polygon lies completely within the polygon. As Fig. 1a shows, the intersection between two convex polygons is itself a convex polygon. This intersection can be computed in $O(n + m)$ time. A *star-shaped* polygon has the property that there exists a point p such that the line segment from p to any other point in the polygon lies entirely within the polygon. Fig. 1b shows that the intersection of two star-shaped polygons can produce many small polygons, in fact $O(mn)$ of them. Thus the best algorithm to compute this intersection is doomed to being $O(mn)$ in the worst case.

Another aspect of geometric problems is *dimensionality*. Any failed artist will testify that it is easier to visualize objects in two dimensions than three or four. The distinction between dimensions is more substantial than just visualization, however, as objects in different dimensions have different properties. For example, polygons in two dimensions have the same number of

vertices as edges, so the edges can be described by simply listing the vertices in order. However, polyhedra in three or higher dimensions can have more edges than vertices and more complicated data structures are needed to represent them.

One of the main paradigms of geometric algorithms uses a *sweep line* to process all of the points in a systematic way. We will illustrate such algorithms by computing the *convex hull* of a set of n points in two dimensions. This is the smallest convex polygon in area which contains all of the points. If we could stretch a rubber band around all the points and let go, the rubber band would "compute" the convex hull of the point set.

It is easy to see that the convex hull of any three points is the triangle they define. If we add another point to the point set, it will change the convex hull if and only if it lies outside the original hull. Any of the old hull vertices which lie within a triangle formed by two hull vertices and the new point cannot be on the hull, and must be deleted. We can sort the points in increasing order by the x-coordinate and consider them from left to right as in Fig. 2. When we add a new point D we can start from the rightmost hull vertex and walk around the hull deleting vertices until the internal angle that each vertex makes with D and its hull neighbor is less than $180°$ measured on the side toward the interior of what the hull would be if the point under consideration were still part of the hull. Because we delete each point at most once and otherwise do a constant amount of work for each insertion, we can determine the convex hull in $O(n)$ time once we do the sorting in $O(n \log n)$ time. The sweep line permits the fast deletion by telling us where to start looking.

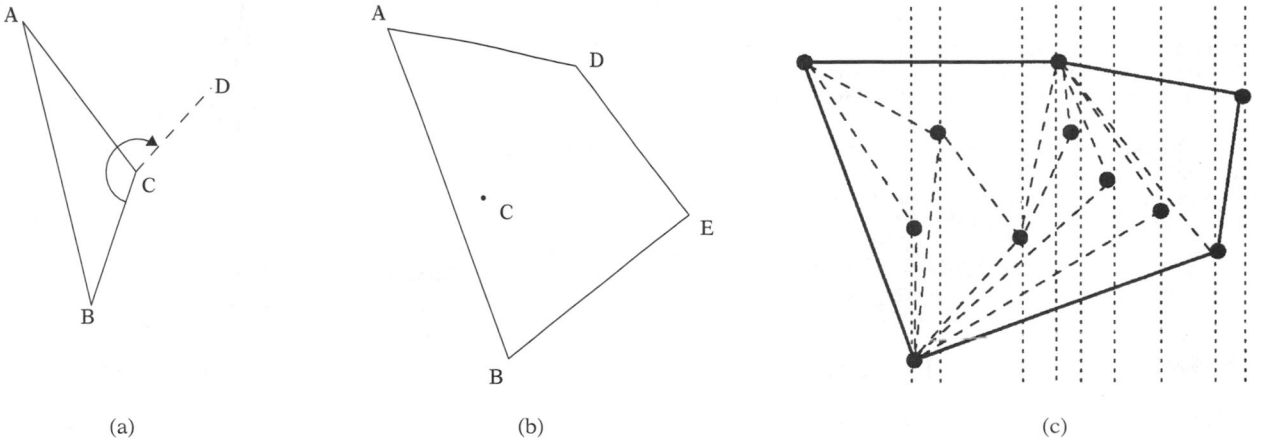

(a)   (b)   (c)

Figure 2. (a) When D is added to the convex hull ABC, start at C and examine the angle formed by CD and BC. It is greater than 180 deg, and so C is removed from the hull. Then look at angle ABD. It is less than 180 deg, so B remains in the hull, as does A. The new convex hull is ABD. (b) When E is added to the convex hull ACD, no point is removed from the hull, and the new hull is ABED. (c) The dotted lines represent the sweep line. As it moves left to right, the dashed lines show the successive states of the convex hull as each point is added. The solid lines form the convex hull after all points have been examined.

Another important idea in computational geometry is duality, the principle that states that two seemingly distinct problems are really the same. For example, suppose we want to test whether any three lines in an arrangement of n lines intersect at the same point. This can easily be done using a sweep line algorithm from left to right, stopping at each point of intersection. It would appear more difficult to test whether any three of a set of n points lie on the same line, since it appears we have to test every subset of three points. However, there is a simple mathematical *transformation* we can use to convert a point to a line and a line to a point. Thus we can solve the three points on a line problem by transforming it to the question of three lines meeting at a point and use the sweep line algorithm to solve it. The transformation provides a different way to view the problem which leads to a more efficient solution. The general theory of such point–line dualities is provided by *projective geometry*.

Other geometric algorithms involve interesting intermediate structures. Consider a dispatch system for a chain of stores, so that when a customer calls up it can quickly be determined which store is nearest to the customer. The *Voronoi diagram* of a set of n points divides the plane into convex regions such that all points in the same region are nearest to the same point from the set, as shown in Fig. 3. Once a Voronoi diagram is built in $O(n \log n)$ time, algorithms to find which of n points is closest to a customer's point do a point location query on the Voronoi diagram to determine which region contains the point in $O(\log n)$ time.

Voronoi diagrams have many other interesting and useful properties as well. Suppose we take a Voronoi

diagram and connect all pairs of points if they share an edge in the diagram. All the regions in this new construct are triangles, so this represents a way of triangulating the plane. The resulting *Delaunay* triangulation is itself useful for applications, because it avoids triangles with vertices close to opposite edges that might cause problematic effects in graphics and finite element analysis.

Computational geometry is a young field. Directions of current work include more robust algorithms in the face of degeneracy, faster algorithms in higher dimensions, and algorithms which are output-sensitive, for example, polygonal intersection problems which are faster when the intersection has few edges.

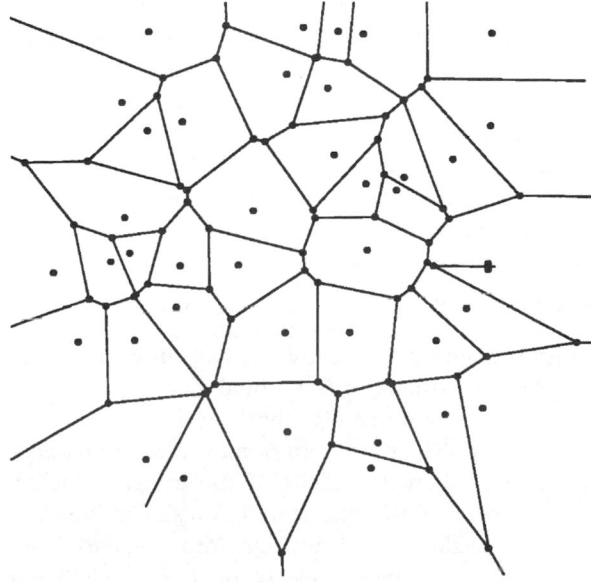

Figure 3. The Voronoi diagram of a set of points.

Bibliography

1985. Preparata, F. P., and Shamos, M. I. *Computational Geometry: An Introduction.* New York: Springer-Verlag.

1987. Edelsbrunner, H. *Algorithms in Combinatorial Geometry.* Berlin: Springer-Verlag.

1994. O'Rourke, J. *Computational Geometry in C.* Cambridge: Cambridge University Press.

1997. Skiena, S. *The Algorithm Design Manual.* New York: Telos/Springer-Verlag.

Steven Skiena

COMPUTATIONAL LINGUISTICS

See MACHINE TRANSLATION; NATURAL LANGUAGE PROCESSING; PROGRAMMING LINGUISTICS; and SYNTAX, SEMANTICS, AND PRAGMATICS.

COMPUTER-AIDED DESIGN/COMPUTER-AIDED MANUFACTURING (CAD/CAM)

For articles on related subjects *see* COMPUTATIONAL GEOMETRY; COMPUTER-AIDED ENGINEERING; COMPUTER ANIMATION; COMPUTER GRAPHICS; DIGITAL DESIGN AUTOMATION; FINITE ELEMENT METHOD; ROBOTICS; and WORKSTATION.

Introduction

Since the 1960s, computers have aided the closer integration of design activities with the actions required to manufacture goods, and the systems used to provide these aids have been called *CAD/CAM* systems. Initial CAD systems were directed at *computer-aided design* (CAD), with the resulting computer models used to aid manufacturing activities. As the benefits of *computer-aided manufacturing* (CAM) were recognized, the need for tighter integration of the two functions led to CAD/CAM systems where the design result (a model of the item) could be used directly to create the manufacturing information for the item. In addition to manufacturing information, the CAD/CAM database is often supplemented to aid in tracking inventories of materials and costs.

Design

Design is primarily a creative activity in which a person takes an esthetic or functional idea and expresses it in some medium in a way that can be understood by someone else. The most common example is engineering design, where the ideas of the designer include both geometric descriptions and notes, sometimes on paper as engineering drawings (drawing-based systems), but increasingly as electronic files (model-based systems). The essence of computer-aided design (CAD)

is the marriage created by applying the strengths and capabilities of computers to provide assistance for design needs.

Geometry is a vital factor in most design; description of the shape and size of an item is the essential element in most tangible representations of that item. Humans are usually able to visualize a geometric description of an item more easily than they can understand a verbal description of the same item, hence the old adage that a picture is worth a thousand words. Thus, a major portion of the time spent in design is often devoted to creating and modifying geometric "pictures" of the item being designed.

In most kinds of design work, a designer works with a number of previously defined elements that are selectively included in the design of the new item. For example, the designer of an electrical circuit selects circuit elements and places them into the design. Even at the level of designing the elements, geometric entities such as circles and lines are used to "build up" the element. This selection process is well suited to computer assistance, since computers can store large numbers of elements and allow designers rapid access to them for use in design. Another characteristic of the process of design is that it is highly iterative; designers frequently make multiple changes to various elements of the design as work proceeds. Computers can also conveniently assist this. Much of design is concerned with items for which some kind of analysis must be performed after the design is proposed. The results of the analysis often lead to additional changes in the design, such as the selection of different elements in the item being designed.

Manufacturing

Manufacturing activities frequently involve the positioning of parts and subsequent operations, such as cutting, milling, drilling, forming, and finishing. In all of these operations, the geometry of the part is critical, particularly if the operations are carried out by computer-driven tools, often termed NC (Numerically Controlled) tools. Fig. 1 shows part of a machine shop at a large aerospace company.

When the same basic geometry from the database is used for both design and manufacturing, parts fit together with great precision. The creation, storage, and interface of three-dimensional geometric data among various disciplines (e.g. engineering and manufacturing) provide communication that is helpful in increasing both the precision with which parts are made and the ease of specifying the manufacturing steps to be carried out. The same geometric model—with its mathematical precision—is accessed and used by designers, part programmers (people who describe machine tool

Figure 1. A portion of a machine shop at a large aerospace manufacturing facility. Cables carry numerical control (NC) information from central computers to drive machine tools.

movements to create parts), structural analysts (engineers who calculate the structural strength of parts and assemblies), tool designers, and quality assurance personnel. CAD/CAM systems allow this data to be captured during the construction phases of design.

In addition, the manufacturing process requires lists of parts (the bill of materials, etc.) and costs for the parts and for the entire item. Most CAD/CAM systems accommodate this data as supplements to the design and manufacturing process information.

Application Areas

The most obvious examples of CAD/CAM uses are in engineering design activities, which will be emphasized in this article. These activities include the design of structures, highways, machine parts, printed circuit boards, plants, piping, assembly lines, airplanes (*see* Fig. 2 on Color Page CP-2), transportation vehicles (*see* Fig. 3 on Color Page CP-2), and consumer products

(*see* Fig. 4 on Color Page CP-2). In addition, CAD/CAM is often thought of as including the use of computers to aid in a design and analysis process, such as structural analysis following the actual design work, although this is more properly called *computer-aided engineering* (CAE). Further, it is sometimes used to encompass design of computer programs themselves, patterns for clothing, exterior and interior architectural layouts, packaging containers, and management systems.

The main strengths of computers—speed, accuracy, and repeatability—are particularly well matched to these kinds of design activities. In addition, computers can store very large amounts of information (the database) that can be retrieved rapidly and used for additional calculations or for display (including supplemental information about parts lists and costs). This database capability, by the very nature of design (geometric construction, selection, and iteration), plays an important role in CAD/CAM.

Computers—Only an Aid

It is important to note, however, that computers are used only as an *aid* to design and manufacturing. The process of design involves extensive decision-making and subjective evaluation, activities that are aided greatly by using computers, but that are generally carried out by computers under human direction. The same is true of decisions about manufacturing processes.

This article focuses primarily on the area of interactive engineering design and assembly/manufacture. Especially in this area, as part of the design process, an engineer must be able to describe and communicate the geometric relationships of the design. The systems that assist in these needs are called interactive computer graphics systems, and they are the foundation of CAD/CAM systems. In fact, the terms are sometimes used interchangeably. However, the field of computer graphics includes many activities outside of design and manufacturing, and CAD/CAM encompasses activities outside of computer graphics.

Until about 25 to 30 years ago, almost all engineering design was done on the drafting board. Selection of elements was implemented by tracing, drawing from templates, or pasting the elements onto the drawing of the design of each element. Iteration was obtained by sequential use of pencil, eraser, pencil, eraser, etc. The only way to improve the productivity of this process was to provide better templates or paste-ons, to use less iteration, or to speed up the humans in some way. The recognition that significant gains in productivity could result from using computers to aid the process led to CAD systems.

At the same time, computers began to be used to aid in the preparation of plans for manufacturing activities, and computer controls for driving machine tools began to be used in large machine shops. These early CAD and CAM systems were very expensive and required large productivity gains to justify their cost. As prices of CAD/CAM systems have come down relative to the cost of humans doing design work, the cost benefits from productivity gains have become more significant and the variety of CAD/CAM systems has increased.

The Process

The essence of these design functions is geometric construction. Geometric entities are typically built through repeated selection of "functions" or "tasks" to be performed from a "menu" of selection possibilities. A menu, function keyboard, mouse (*q.v.*), or other input device is used for selection of *elements* for insertion and for positioning them on the design. These devices are also used to select tasks that permit a designer to move elements or items from location to location (translations and rotations), to create a blown-up view of a portion of the drawing (*windowing*), and to permit easy annotation or dimensioning of the drawings. Using these and other functional capabilities, the user builds the database interactively—a database composed of both geometric and alphanumeric information.

Construction of the design is not the only way in which data can be captured, however. An automatic laser scanner can be used for two-dimensional data capture, with data automatically entered into the database. This data is then available for further modification (or editing). In addition to this type of scanner, hand-held or movable scanning (or "digitizing") devices are available. These allow the locations of points to be input. They can be moved to various points on two- or three-dimensional models. At a desired point, the user has the device sense the location of the point and enter it into the database. After the points are entered, CAD functions can be applied to create smooth lines, curves, or surfaces between the points. These lines, curves, or surfaces can then be used with the points for further design or for interfacing with CAM functions. Fig. 5 shows an interesting example of this technique. The key to this process is the variety of functions available to the designer to carry out actions in creating the design.

As computers have grown physically smaller, yet more powerful, and disks (used for storage of the database) have grown larger in capacity, there has been a trend to use true three-dimensional geometric databases and to use solid models. Manufacturing process planning must usually deal with solids and with manipulations on them, so solid models are a significant advantage in going from CAD systems to CAD/CAM systems.

The digital definition of the product, which can be viewed from any angle or projected into any plane, is generally the end product today. It replaces the traditional drawing, which usually shows the principal orthographic views (front, top, and side) and a three-dimensional view. Today, the drawing is often merely a by-product, obtained if desired. Integration of CAD with CAM has further proceeded to integration with business and technical environments, since such environments are often present on the same personal computer as the CAD/CAM system. CAD data becomes more valuable when it can be used in the business environment for products such as bills of materials and cost models (*see* MANAGEMENT INFORMATION SYSTEMS). In addition, this integration with business operations permits use of the Internet (*q.v.*) as a simple interface for information such as best-practice manuals, non-technical work-in-progress reviews, and repetitive family of parts work. Some CAM information can similarly be make available via the Internet.

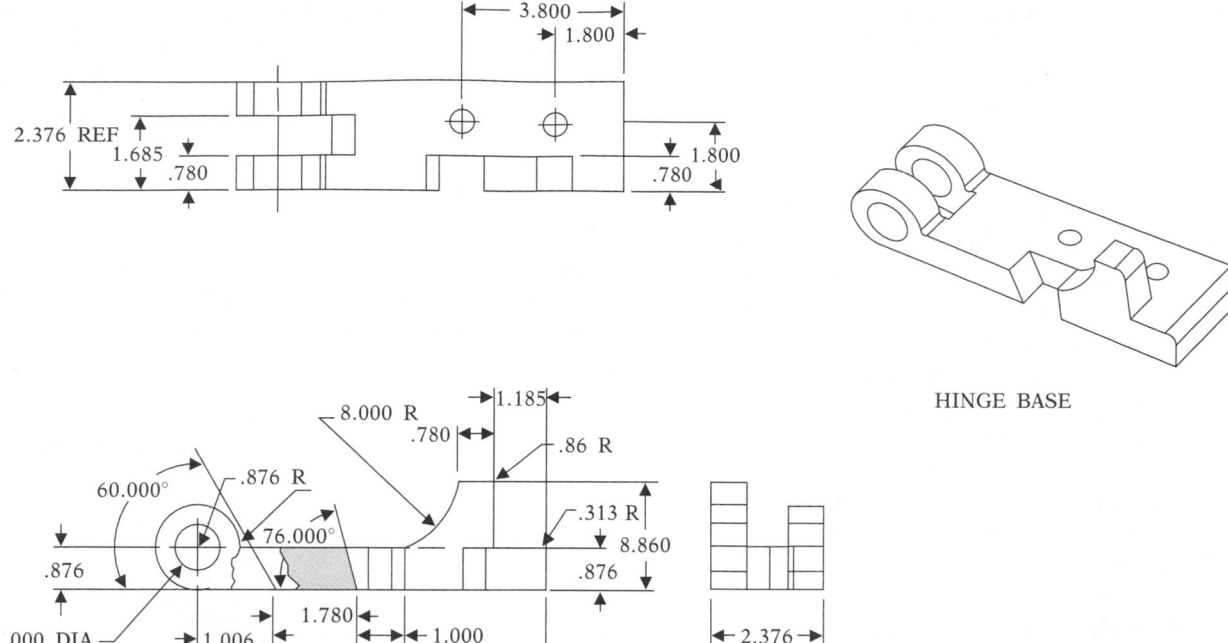

HINGE BASE

Figure 5. A typical drawing format—three views plus a 3D view.

The primary benefit of CAM is the use of the computer description of a part to drive cutting, forming, and other operations in a manufacturing environment. Manufacturing personnel are concerned with deciding how the part will be manufactured. One of their concerns is the determination of tools, materials, and methods that will be used to cut, form, and/or finish the part. In addition, databases for CAD/CAM systems need to provide information about stock to form or cut the part.

Another concern is the design of fixtures to hold parts during manufacturing operations. Fig. 6 shows the display of a fixture design program. Efficient use of material is also important. The so-called "nesting" problem involves using as little material as possible in cutting parts, e.g. from sheets of sheet metal. Programs to carry out nesting calculations in simple cases automatically or to provide visualization aids to humans in approaching the problem are often parts of CAD/CAM systems.

Today's CAD/CAM integrated systems allow users to create "virtual products"—products designed (with CAD) that exist in digital models for which manufacturing information (CAM) exists so the product can be "built" (and "broken," if necessary, for analysis) using the virtual model, before a physical manifestation of the product exists.

This capability is sometimes part of what is called a "master model" environment, in which the digital

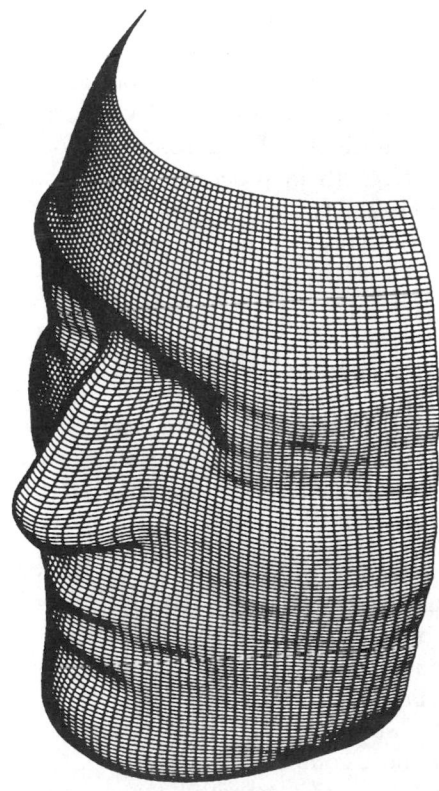

Figure 6. A surface representation of a face, serving as the start of the design of a fire protection mask. The physical sculpted model was digitized (scanned) to produce 3D data points, which were then used to create surfaces. The display shows the computer-generated surfaces.

model is passed from design to other disciplines (e.g. tooling, analysis, manufacturing) which add value to the model. Figs. 3 and 7 (see Color Page CP-2) illustrate products generated via the master model process.

Hardware

Pioneering CAD systems were developed in the 1960s, using large mainframe (*q.v.*) computers attached to graphics terminals. These systems were primarily used in automotive and aerospace organizations, industries that required large amounts of data storage for their CAD data. The large centralized mainframe systems were the only systems that could provide this needed data storage. In addition, the large mainframes were the only source of sufficient computing power for the geometric and display calculations required. Early systems required the terminals to be located physically close to the computer in order to maintain adequate performance. As it became possible to locate terminals further away, CAD and CAM capabilities became more widely used in the remote locations of large corporations.

The advent of personal computers and workstations has broadened the way that CAD/CAM capabilities can be delivered. Applications are now available on every type of hardware, with the specific type of application varying depending on the computing power and sophistication of the graphics device. In particular, the performance of personal computers has increased significantly, both in processor performance and in graphics capability; thus a generation of CAD/CAM packages have been developed for them.

Software

Common to all CAD/CAM software are the functions to store and manipulate the geometric data, or model, of the part or assembly. Geometric modeling continues to be an area of intense development and study in an effort to define better all aspects of the object being modeled.

Initial CAD/CAM models grew from 2D systems representing drawings to 3D systems representing objects defined by lines, curves, circles, and points located in three-dimensional space. Actual surfaces on the part were defined in second generation systems in the 1970s; the surfaces allowed the design and manufacturing of more complex shapes as the CAD/CAM data was used to model smooth-flowing surfaces where accuracy was critical. The plastics-forming industry has made wide use of surfaces in the definition of esthetically pleasing shapes and the construction of molds for their manufacture; the common desk telephone handset is a good example.

Designing with solid shapes has always been attractive due to the ability of solids to define an object unambiguously and to present a complete definition of the outside surfaces used in manufacturing operations. The drawbacks of solid-based modeling systems have been the large amount of computing resources they require and the inability to represent free-form surfaces such as those used in automotive body-panel design. With the advent of high-powered technical workstations and modern personal computers, sufficient computing power is available, allowing systems that model solids to support general surfaces and become more common in the industry.

One advantage of a solids modeling system is the wide range of analysis programs that can be used in conjunction with the model data; common analyses include mass calculations and structural analysis. While these analyses can be done on selected models developed with surfaces, a solids model is assumed to always be "well behaved," since it is unambiguous with regard to shape and behavior. Rendering applications provided by most solids modeling systems realistically display the modeled object, with the various materials displayed with reflective parameters matching those of the metal, plastic, or surface finish used on the actual part.

Further improvements to the design process are obtained through the use of feature-based and constraint-based modeling systems. Usually based on solids modelers, feature-based systems help in the design of standard features in parts. The nature of the features will depend on the industry of the user, but could involve standard hole sizes, specific threads on threaded parts, or standard configurations for machined pockets in an airframe structural part. By using standard features, modular manufacturing processes can be employed, improving the quality of design and the quality of the manufactured result.

There is a trend toward even tighter ties between CAD and CAM, because systems are starting to incorporate aids to enforce rules of manufacturability during the design process. These aids are inspired by artificial intelligence work in expert systems (*q.v.*). These systems ensure that manufacturing constraints are not violated, that parts can be produced by an organization with the tools it has on hand, and that classes of products can be designed once, with parameters distinguishing the individual particular members of the classes. These programs, termed constraint-based modelers, allow designs to be optimized for specific parameters. For example, a part could be designed to optimize the strength of a specific feature while minimizing part weight. Typically, the constraints are given a priority and the CAD/CAM system assists in the design of the part based on selected features required in the design.

Extensions to CAD/CAM systems to permit dimensions and characteristics of parts to be linked via parameters (parametric modeling) have now been further extended to encompass hybrid modeling, which permits combinations of explicit modeling and parametric modeling. In addition, because of the increased emphasis on use of subsystems and components to build product families, parameter-based models at a higher level are now starting to be used. These systems provide the ability to capture product and process intent at the final assembly level, identifying critical design variables that drive product design. Changes to these automatically update the top level design as well as all related subassemblies and components. For example, in automobile design, a change to provide more passenger leg room while maintaining the same exterior dimensions would propagate changes to all the affected subassemblies of the automobile. Fig. 4 illustrates a part for which this process was used to ensure that all subassemblies stayed consistent with changes in the overall product and process intent.

Using CAD/CAM Data in Applications

Many applications that use CAD/CAM data have introduced model-based tools in new areas of a firm. Use by people who had never before been exposed to CAD/CAM systems put special requirements on the user interface of the design tools. In the past, a relatively small group of designers worked with the CAD/CAM packages, and extensive training was available to help users become expert in system use. As the use of CAD/CAM systems grew, less frequent users found a need to use the systems—users who could not justify extensive training in system use. This was especially true of the early systems sold through retail outlets for the personal computer market. Modern systems are increasingly easy to use, through the use of windows and popup menus along with the inclusion of online help facilities.

The importance of CAD/CAM has increased because the use of the model data has gone beyond its original use as a record of the design. Many applications have been developed that enhance the functions that can be done by the basic system, allowing the CAD/CAM database to be used across many functional areas in the design, manufacturing, and assembly processes, as described earlier in the master model process.

NC Applications

The use of CAD data to program NC machines was one of the first manufacturing application areas. This area of activity was pioneered by the aerospace industry,

using the Automatically Programmed Tool (APT) language (*see* PROBLEM-ORIENTED LANGUAGES). This is a language used to describe the operations and path of a machine tool or NC lathe in the cutting of a part from a piece of stock. Modern CAM software allows the cutter path to be programmed, using graphic aids without the use of a separate language. With increased use of surface and solid models, artificial intelligence methods are used to help develop manufacturing programs with minimal user involvement. These techniques are based on the recognition of features in the object, such as drilled holes, machined pockets, and specified tolerances; the features require specific operations, which are automatically invoked.

Assemblies

The initial use of CAD/CAM systems concentrated on the modeling of individual objects. In almost all cases, these individual objects are part of larger assemblies, made up of a number of objects of different materials, often from different designers and manufacturers. The assembly of a first prototype can involve time-consuming (and therefore expensive) fitting and adjustment of these individual parts so that they can become part of a more complex assembly. This problem is compounded when the assembly involves complex motions at high speeds or high stress levels, such as the paper-handling mechanism in a copier or the steering and suspension of a front-wheel drive automobile. Assembly modeling lessens redesign and improves the performance of the assembly, while reducing the need for prototype test fitting. The emphasis in assembly modeling is on avoiding physical mockups or models, using "digital" instead of "physical" "looks" at the full assembly.

In addition, by identifying parts that make up an assembly while they are being designed, complete bill of materials processing can be performed, which later produces benefits in purchasing and scheduling. A number of companies have taken the assemblies capabilities even further, using them to simulate field service operations, thus improving the serviceability of the products. Fig. 8 (*see* Color Page CP-2) illustrates a complex assembly, visualized via an exploded view showing the relative positioning of parts. Associated with this view would be a bill of materials containing information about the specific parts themselves.

Allied Applications

Many other application areas use the computer graphics foundation of CAD/CAM systems for visualization of complex shapes and intricate designs. Examples include the analysis of the motions of robots, movement through a mechanism or building by moving the viewing point through the model, creation of animated motion sequences to illustrate maintenance or service operations, and even the creation of movie sequences for popular consumption or for training purposes. Continuing improvements in both hardware and software will make these more realistic and less expensive. Fig. 9 (see Color Page CP-2) illustrates the dashboard of the bus shown in Fig. 3. This dashboard is seen as the viewing point for the visualization that does a "fly through" of the interior of the bus—all aspects of the bus, including the dashboard, exist solely in the digital model.

Bibliography

1988. Mantyla, M. *Introduction to Solid Modeling*. Potomac, MD: Computer Science Press.
1990. Rogers, D. F., and Adams, J. A. *Mathematical Elements for Computer Graphics*, 2nd Ed. New York: McGraw-Hill.
1996. Foley, J. D., Van Dam, A., Feiner, S. K., and Hughes, J. F. *Computer Graphics: Principles and Practice*, 2nd Ed. Reading, MA: Addison-Wesley.
1996. Senerson, J., and Curran, K. *Computer Numerical Control: Operation and Programming*. Upper Saddle River, NJ: Prentice Hall.
1997. Hearn, D., and Baker, M. P. *Computer Graphics*, 2nd Ed. Upper Saddle River, NJ: Prentice Hall.
1997. Rehg, J. A. *Introduction to Robotics in CIM Systems*, 3rd Ed. Upper Saddle River NJ: Prentice Hall.
1997. Rogers, D. F. *Procedural Elements for Computer Graphics*, 2nd Ed. New York: McGraw-Hill.

Barry Flachsbart, David Shuey, and George Peters

COMPUTER-AIDED ENGINEERING (CAE)

For articles on related subjects *see* COMPUTER-AIDED DESIGN/COMPUTER-AIDED MANUFACTURING; CONTROL APPLICATIONS; DIGITAL DESIGN AUTOMATION; FINITE ELEMENT METHOD; ROBOTICS; and SIMULATION.

Introduction

The goals of *computer-aided engineering* (CAE) are:

◆ improved product quality

◆ improved safety

◆ reduced engineering time, achieved through fewer design iterations

◆ improved product functionality and usability

◆ reduced number of prototypes, ultimately leading to their elimination in many cases

◆ reduced product cost

Engineering analyses can be used to evaluate and predict the behavior of new designs, as well as to evaluate the performance of existing designs. Engineers use computers for a number of tasks, including conceptual design, engineering analysis, detailed design, drafting and documentation, and manufacturing design. This article describes the application of computers to engineering analysis.

Historically, engineers analyzed designs by building and testing physical prototypes, performing calculations by hand or with some computing aid such as a slide rule. They frequently used tabulated mathematical functions, approximation methods, and data accumulated from previous experience and physical testing to simplify their analyses. Some analyses were so time-consuming that, when done at all, they could be completed only for one simplified example. This frequently led to under- and over-designed systems. The first case resulted in systems that did not work properly or failed outright. In the second case, the systems were more expensive than necessary or too heavy to meet their goals. Physical prototypes were (and remain) very costly and time-consuming to build and test—and they often have to be recreated as designs are changed.

History

The advent of analog (*q.v.*) and digital computers provided engineers with systems capable of analyzing designs much more quickly and allowed them to undertake analyses that were previously impractical to attempt. However, early computer systems were too slow and limited in capacity (memory, storage, I/O speed) to handle extremely large or complex mechanical systems. While they provided a base for new, more extensive design evaluations, many of the historical problems remained and new problems arose. These included limited access to expensive, high-powered computing systems and difficulties describing the physical form of designs in a way that computers could work with them efficiently. Therefore, many early analysis programs used unrealistically simplified, schematic-like descriptions of the physical system. It was impossible to describe any but the simplest system's geometry within the computing environment.

With the advent of computer-aided design and computer-aided manufacturing (CAD/CAM) in the early 1970s and the rapid advancements in computer system performance from 1960 to the present, most technological barriers to CAE have fallen. Engineers can now have enough computing power on their desks to solve any but the largest of problems. For extremely complex problems, supercomputers (*q.v.*) may be employed.

Engineering *workstations* (*q.v.*) provide extensive computing power with high-resolution, high-speed graphics systems at very reasonable and continually decreasing cost, below $5,000 in 1999.

Three broad areas of the engineering discipline are supported by CAE: mechanical, civil, and electrical. In a typical situation, an engineer will use a CAD/CAM system to develop a model of a system (be it mechanical, electrical, electromechanical, or otherwise) that is to be analyzed. Other required data, such as a finite element mesh, mechanical properties, constraints, and loading, are then developed on or linked to this geometric description of the system. The analysis software is used to analyze this combination of model and related data, with its results presented to the engineer in various forms: tabular, graphical, animation, changes to the geometric model, etc.

Mechanical Engineering Applications

VOLUME PROPERTIES

Various volumetric properties can be computed directly for solid and surface models in most CAD/CAM systems. These properties include lengths, areas, and volumes as well as mass, centroid, first and second moments of inertia, and products of inertia. In many CAD systems the results of this analysis can be transferred directly into structural and mechanism analysis applications where they are required as data. A few systems can compute volumetric properties for components consisting of composite materials.

FINITE ELEMENT ANALYSIS (FEA)

Finite element analysis methods are used to perform several types of engineering analyses. These include:

◆ Structural analysis of a component's behavior under various kinds of applied loads and supports. Linear static, modal, dynamic, forced response, and buckling conditions can be analyzed. Special programs also exist for analyzing beam and grid structures, such as those used in ships, bridges, frames of buildings, and other similar systems.

◆ Thermal analysis of a structure's behavior when it is subjected to heating and cooling.

◆ Combined structural and thermal analysis.

◆ Plastic mold and part analysis that examines various factors having to do with mold filling and the shape of the molded part. Mold analyses include plastic flow into the mold, material and mold temperature gradients, and mold cooling. Shrinkage and warpage can be predicted for finished parts.

◆ Fluid mechanics analysis of the flow of fluids, such as air, water, and lubricants around the surfaces of an object. Pressure, fluid velocity, and other factors can be determined.

In FEA, a model of a component or assembly (*see* Fig. 1, Color Page CP-3) is decomposed into discrete pieces called the *finite element mesh* (FEM). Loads and supporting constraints are applied at mesh locations. The finite element modeling software creates a series of simultaneous linear equations that relate each mesh element to its neighbors. Very complex problems can be analyzed by solving these simultaneous equations iteratively (*see* MATRIX COMPUTATIONS).

Triangular mesh elements are the easiest to create and analyze and are the most often used, but engineering workstations can process much more complex mesh types, leading to higher accuracy and, in some cases, to more easily defined models. Parts modeled as plates, surface shells, or solid models (*see* Fig. 2, Color Page CP-3) can be meshed with elements that include two- and three-dimensional triangular and rectangular, parabolic, tetrahedral, quadrilateral, shell, solid, and beam elements. The mesh can be created manually (usually in an interactive mode with the mesh building program) or automatically by the program with manual refinements.

Loading conditions may include point, distributed, torque, hydraulic, and others. Supports can be anchored, free, pinned, hinged, sliding as well as most other kinds of mechanical connection (*see* Fig. 3, Color Page CP-3).

Several schemes are used to increase finite element analysis accuracy and reduce computational requirements. These include *feature suppression* and *adaptive meshing*. In feature suppression, the geometry of a part model that is to be analyzed is simplified by temporarily removing features (fillets, small holes, bosses, flanges, etc.) that represent details that the analyst feels are not going to have an appreciable impact on the overall validity of the FEA results. Since these types of feature usually produce highly complex mesh structures that unnecessarily increase the number of simultaneous equations to be solved, their removal shortens the solution process. Adaptive FEM systems automatically refine the mesh definition in areas of detail that contribute to high stress or other qualities or coarsen the mesh in areas of lesser stress. These refinements provide increased accuracy and shorter processing time, respectively. This process is done as a closed-loop—analyze the object, refine the mesh, analyze, refine, etc.—until the results converge to a user-defined tolerance. A few systems offer design optimization, in which the results of the analysis are used to modify the geometric model automatically in order to match a design goal such as, for example, obtaining the lowest weight that will withstand the specified loading conditions at a particular safety factor.

Both standalone FEA systems and CAD/CAM systems support simulation and display of results. A typical display for a structural analysis might show the geometric model overlaid with stress contours, with color indicating the magnitude of the stress (*see* Fig. 4, Color Page CP-3). Another type of display frequently used is an animated view of the model as it deforms under cyclical loading. These types of display can be combined to produce simulations that are relatively easy for the engineer to understand, making the reading of large tables of stress values unnecessary.

MECHANISM ANALYSIS

Mechanism analysis studies the behavior of mechanical systems undergoing motion. These systems may be comprised of rigid and flexible parts and their interconnections. Typically, the geometry, mass, inertia, compliance, stiffness, and damping of the system's components as well as the forces and loads applied from outside the system must be defined. Equations of motion are developed and solved. The results of the analysis may include positions, velocities, accelerations, forces (applied, reactive, and inertial), determination of equilibrium positions, and other computed parameters. These results can be displayed as tables, charts and graphs, overlaid drawings of position vs. time, and animations (*see* Figs. 5 and 6). Historically, analyzing systems of rigid bodies undergoing large-amplitude motions was impractical. Early computerized systems could handle rigid body motions involving large-amplitude rotations and translations in two dimensions. Current systems are capable of kinematic, static, and dynamic analysis of three-dimensional rigid and flexible bodies undergoing large displacements and coupled rotations and translations.

Mechanism analysis programs can accept geometric data from FEA programs, analyze the motion of a system, and return appropriate loading and force data

Figure 6. A time series of the positions of a truck, its suspension, and wheels, as it passes over a bump (courtesy of Mechanical Dynamics Inc.)

to the FEA program for use in determining component deflections. Mechanism analysis can also be linked to control system design and analysis. The control system's responses to mechanism behavior can be programmed and fed back to control the mechanism's reaction. Control system modeling coupled with the ability of engineering workstations to compute and display real-time animation make it possible to simulate mechanisms such as robots and manufacturing workcells (*see* ROBOTICS).

Human–machine interactions can be analyzed using mechanistic models of the human body. The physical characteristics of the model can be varied according to population statistics for height, weight, age, and gender. Android models are now being used to analyze vehicles, machine tools, and other systems in which a human is an integral part of normal operation.

RAPID PROTOTYPING

Rapid prototyping allows a special machine tool to produce physical prototypes of very complex objects. Although several technologies are now used for this process, stereo lithography was the first and remains popular. In stereo lithography, the prototype is built up in thin layers by slicing the geometric model into cross-sections and using a computer-driven laser to harden layer upon layer of a polymer solution, each in the shape of a particular cross-section of the solid model. These machines can create operational mechanisms of movable parts. The models are used to evaluate the appearance of the designed part and to verify its fit with other parts and its manufacturability. New materials such as powdered metals and special plastics continue to be developed and allow rapid prototyping machines to produce more complex, accurate, and usable prototypes. Some rapid prototyping systems are being used as low-quantity manufacturing systems.

Figure 5. This overlay drawing shows the positions of the pilot, seat, canopy, and aircraft during an ejection sequence (courtesy of Mechanical Dynamics Inc.).

Civil Engineering Applications

The analytic tools mentioned previously are also used in the field of civil engineering. However, a few special areas exist that do not have direct counterparts in mechanical engineering. These include surveying, earthworks, piping, and mapping.

In the area of piping plant design, structural engineers use systems similar to those used by mechanical engineers. In roadway design, cut-and-fill and other earth moving computations are done in combination with digital terrain mapping. Most surveying functions, such as triangulation and elevation computations, are now computerized, with data being collected in computer form in the field via electronic instruments. Map making and analysis are also largely computerized (*see* GEOGRAPHICAL INFORMATION SYSTEM).

Electrical/Electronic Engineering Applications

Electrical and electronic engineering applications use some structural and thermal analyses, as described above; however, this discipline uses many specialized analyses for circuit design, VLSI device design (*see* DIGITAL DESIGN AUTOMATION), and simulation. A few of the major mechanical CAD/CAM systems have some electrical CAD capabilities, but electronic CAD (E-CAD) products are the best choice for electrical/electronic analysis. Many types of electrical analog, digital, and mixed devices can be simulated. Simulations allow design engineers to test a design for a circuit board, VLSI chip, or other electrical device before it is committed to manufacturing. In some cases the computer simulation will supplant altogether the building of a prototype. Available analyses include gate level, switching, electrical level, analog-to-digital conversion (*q.v.*), statistical (worst-case), and sensitivity-based simulations. Control systems that combine electrical and mechanical or hydraulic controls can also be simulated. Other electrical analyses examine transient waveforms and signal frequency response to determine signal characteristics, such as bandwidth and rise and fall times; analyze interference between parallel traces on printed circuit boards; and determine cooling and flow requirements in forced convection systems.

E-CAD systems provide libraries of standard electrical components, including their physical characteristics as well as performance criteria and specifications. The use of these standard-parts libraries greatly simplifies the process of setting up a simulation.

Technological Trends

Simulation and visualization products are becoming commonplace. These allow all types of people, notably those who do not have access to CAD and CAE systems, to see product designs and simulations of how the products operate. The increased communication throughout product development organizations provided by this technology enhances the design process and encourages innovation.

As in other areas of computer-aided product development, the World Wide Web (*q.v.*) continues to play an increasingly important role in analysis. Many CAE systems can post analysis results as Web pages in HTML, VRML (*see* MARKUP LANGUAGES), and other formats. People without access to the CAE system can view and evaluate these on any computer and get more involved in the product development process.

The conceptual design loop is still not completely computerized. At this time, very few computer products are able to couple both the CAD geometric modeling and engineering analysis functions required to develop engineering concepts rapidly and easily. Detailers and drafters remain in the process because it can be too time-consuming for engineers to develop sufficiently detailed models in current CAD systems. This situation is beginning to change with the introduction of engineering workbench systems that are specifically tailored to create solid models easily and feed those models directly into structural and mechanisms analyses, with the results immediately available to the designer. This allows engineers to create better developed designs without the costs incurred in the past.

Manufacturing engineers remain outside the early design loop. To appreciate the advantages of CAE most fully, manufacturing processes and their effects on the product (such as warping caused by machining and structural integrity for clamping and handling) must be analyzed before the design reaches the detailed layout stage. As mentioned, a few systems are beginning to provide conceptual design tools coupled with sophisticated but simplified analysis tools that can be used by design engineers and manufacturing engineers, without the need for the design to be fully detailed.

Developments in parallel-processing (*q.v.*) computer architectures bring additional power to the engineer's desktop. Many of the analysis techniques used today (most notably FEA) are good candidates for parallel processing. Faster processing will continue to reduce the design cycle and/or allow additional design iterations, resulting in improved products.

More integration between disciplines is to be expected. In particular, several products now combine the electrical/electronic and the mechanical aspects of design and analysis.

Bibliography

1980. Timmer, H. G., and Stern, J. M. "Computation of Global Geometric Properties of Solid Objects," *Computer-Aided Design*, **12**, 6, 301–304.

1982. Huebner, K. H., and Thornton, E. A. *The Finite Element Method for Engineers*, 2nd Ed. New York: John Wiley.

1984. Chace, M. A. "Methods and Experience in Computer Aided Design of Large-displacement Mechanical Systems," *Computer-Aided Analysis and Optimization of Mechanical System Dynamics*, NATO ASI Series, **F9**. Berlin: Springer-Verlag.

1984. Erdman, A. G., and Sandor, G. N. *Mechanism Design: Analysis and Synthesis*, Vol. 1. Upper Saddle River, NJ: Prentice Hall.

1988. Turner, P. R., and Bodner, M. E. "Optimization and Synthesis for Mechanism Design," Paper MS88-711, *Proceedings of the Society of Manufacturing Engineers AUTOFACT 88 Conference and Exposition* (October), Chicago, IL.

1989. Sapidis, N., and Perucchio, R. "Advanced Techniques for Automatic Finite Element Meshing from Solid Models," *Computer-Aided Design*, **21**, 4, 248–253.

1991. Zeid, I. *CAD/CAM Theory and Practice*. New York: McGraw-Hill.

1998. Adeli, H., and Kumar, S. *Distributed Computer-Aided Engineering*. Boca Raton, FL: CRC Press.

1999. Garrett, J. H. Jr., and Rehak, D. R. (eds.) *Bridging the Generations: The Future of Computer-Aided Engineering*. Pittsburgh, PA: Carnegie Mellon University Press.

John MacKrell and Bertram Herzog

COMPUTER-AIDED MANUFACTURING

See AUTOMATION; and COMPUTER-AIDED DESIGN/ COMPUTER AIDED MANUFACTURING.

COMPUTER-AIDED SOFTWARE ENGINEERING (CASE)

For articles on related subjects *see* OBJECT-ORIENTED ANALYSIS AND DESIGN; PROGRAMMING SUPPORT ENVIRONMENTS; SOFTWARE CONFIGURATION MANAGEMENT; SOFTWARE ENGINEERING; SOFTWARE MAINTENANCE; SOFTWARE METRICS; SOFTWARE PROJECT MANAGEMENT; SOFTWARE REUSABILITY; and SOFTWARE TESTING.

Computer-aided software engineering (CASE) encompasses computer-based procedures, techniques, and tools which can be used to develop, maintain, and re-engineer software. CASE is to the software engineer as computer-aided design/computer-aided manufacturing (CAD/CAM) (*q.v.*) is to the mechanical engineer and computer-aided electrical engineering (CAEE) is to the electrical engineer. Although the variety of technological alternatives can be bewildering, the concepts of CASE provide a common-sense approach to engineering quality software more productively.

The application of CASE is intended to allow teams of software engineers to produce software that:

◆ meets business and system requirements

◆ is completed within a predictable schedule

◆ is available within budget guidelines

◆ allows for easy maintenance and enhancement

The Evolution of CASE

The term *CASE* was coined in the early 1980s with the automation (*q.v.*) of manual structured analysis and design techniques and methods. By the mid-1980s, code generation linked to analysis and design tools was put under the CASE umbrella. The early CASE tool vendors worked hard to differentiate their tools from traditional software development tools (i.e. editors, compilers, debuggers). As a result, even today many people think that CASE refers to a separate class of tools. This narrow view of CASE resulted in expectations that were not met by early uses of the technology.

For CASE to be applied successfully, a more global view is needed. CASE should refer to any tool used to develop, change, and maintain software, and manage software projects. In the late 1980s, this broader view of CASE began to be recognized with the advent of integrated project support environments, integration frameworks, the convergence of existing system maintenance and new development, object-oriented design approaches, and the need to control the software engineering process. In the 1990s, software engineering became a formal engineering discipline, like mechanical and electrical engineering. Thus all software engineering computer-based tools should be called CASE tools. Starting with the I-CASE software tool conferences in 1994, object-oriented development, client–server (*q.v.*) development, configuration management, framework, repository, and testing tool vendors have been exhibiting together. These vendors are concerned with integration of their tools with the tools of other vendors (*interoperability*) and the portability (*q.v.*) of their tools across multiple platforms.

Thus all the dimensions of software engineering are coming together to form integrated environments. The four key components comprising these environments are shown in Fig. 1. The *analysis and design* dimension, sometimes referred to as *front-end* or *upper* CASE, includes tools and techniques for planning systems, defining requirements, and designing systems. Starting with system functions, workflow and business process analysis tools are used to understand and define requirements, rules, and processes. Structured or object-oriented analysis and design tools are then used to define and design the software systems which support those system functions.

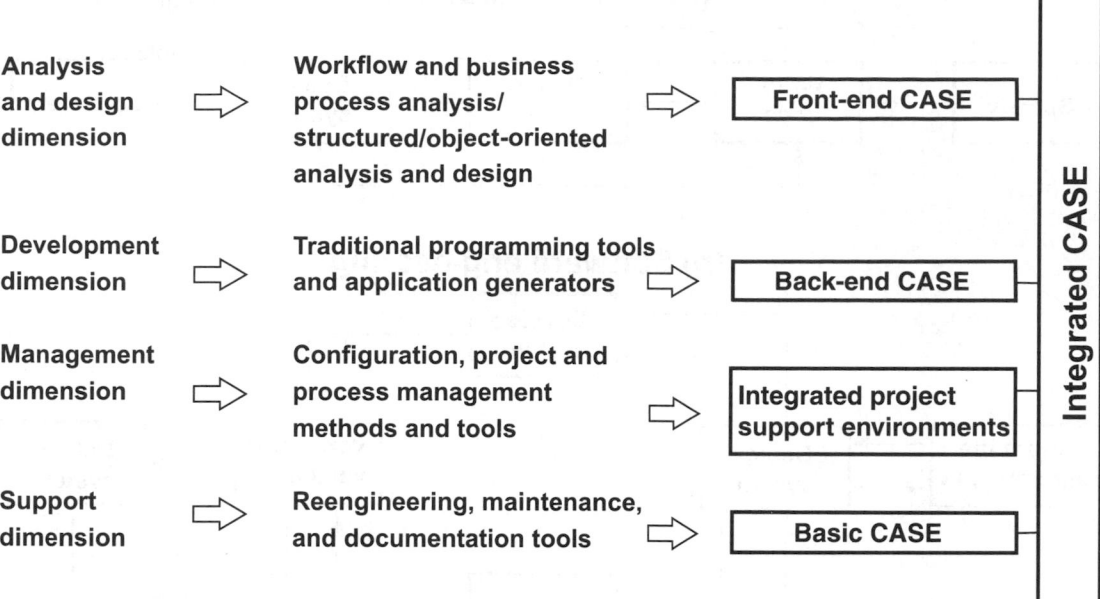

Figure 1. The four dimensions of software engineering.

The *development* dimension, also called *back-end* or *lower* CASE, represents traditional programming development tools like editors (*see* TEXT-EDITING SYSTEMS), compilers (*q.v.*), and debuggers (*q.v.*). With the advent of programming support environments, these dimensions have been expanded to include code and application generators.

The *management* dimension provides the methods and tools needed to manage and control a project. This is currently the most poorly supported dimension.

The *support* dimension, which might be called *basic* CASE, comprises all the tools and techniques needed to sustain and evolve existing software systems. Year 2000 (*see* Y2K PROBLEM) tools are actually CASE tools directed at finding and fixing dates in source code, job control language (JCL), databases, etc.

CASE focuses specifically on process, methods, techniques, and tools for software maintenance (*q.v.*), development, and re-engineering. In addition to automation of mature techniques, a host of new approaches such as information engineering, data modeling (*q.v.*), object-oriented analysis and design, rapid prototyping and simulation (*q.v.*), business process reengineering, process management, reuse, and software reverse engineering are being added to the software engineering discipline. Although the number of software engineering tool alternatives is bewildering, applying the appropriate tools within a formal engineering management framework provides a common-sense approach to engineering quality software more productively. These tech-

nologies are being incorporated into toolkits which transform software crafting into software engineering, as shown in Fig. 2.

Applying Case to Software Redevelopment

Over the last 20 years, software engineering has evolved to meet the changing requirements of development and production system environments. Structured programming (*q.v.*) in the 1970s was extended by structured methods for specifying the requirements and then designing large, complex mainframe (*q.v.*) applications. The automation of these structured methods marked the beginning of CASE in the mid-1980s.

Early CASE methodologies and tools focused on the development of new systems and provided no assistance to the maintenance programmer. Although systems built using these early CASE methods could be maintained by CASE tools, their adoption was slow. Over 80% of new systems since 1980 have been built using traditional software development methods and tools, e.g. editors, compilers, and debuggers. As a result, the maintenance of legacy systems is dominating the workload and budgets of information system organizations. The attention given to improving the productivity of maintenance programmers and the quality of legacy systems has put renewed emphasis on software maintenance and redevelopment.

Software redevelopment starts by providing the programmer with an understanding of how the program functions and an inventory of where the key program

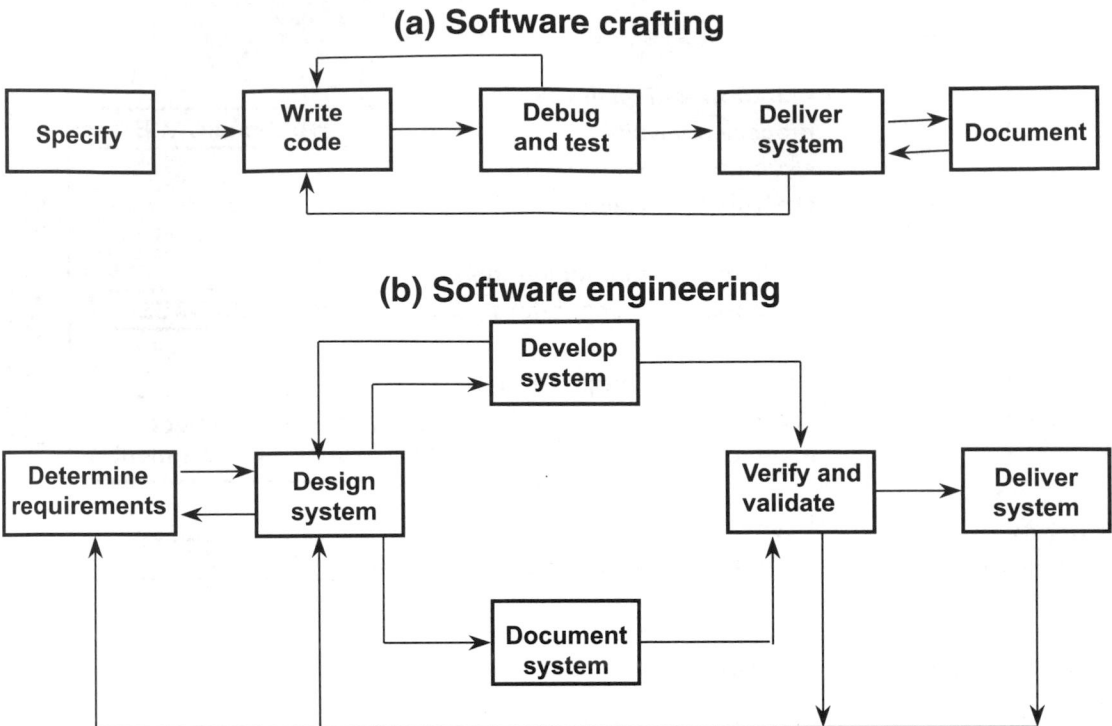

Figure 2. (a) Software crafting; (b) software engineering.

components can be found. The important program discoveries are then stored in a database so that subsequent programmers can reuse the program documentation. The advent of reverse engineering and re-engineering technology has allowed management to consider redevelopment of the current system as an alternative to building new systems from scratch or continuing the arduous maintenance of the current system.

There are many method and tool choices available to plan the transition or migration of existing systems and then manage, implement, and conduct the redevelopment (transformation) to the new system. Redevelopment methods call attention to the need for a formal testing process. Since the new system is replacing an existing system, tests need to be generated and performed to verify that the new system actually replaces the old system. From another perspective, redevelop-

ment of a current system takes time and the existing system is subject to continuing change. Any change or enhancement to the existing system must be communicated to the redevelopment project team. This synchronization (Fig. 3) between the current system and its replacement is the key to this enhanced form of software testing.

The requirements embedded in a legacy system are the test cases for verifying and validating the new system. As change requests are made to the legacy system, they in turn become test cases and requirements for the new system. When changes to the new system are requested, these changes need to be evaluated to determine whether it is cost-effective to incorporate them in the older system.

These formal software testing methods have led to improved software quality because of the rigorous

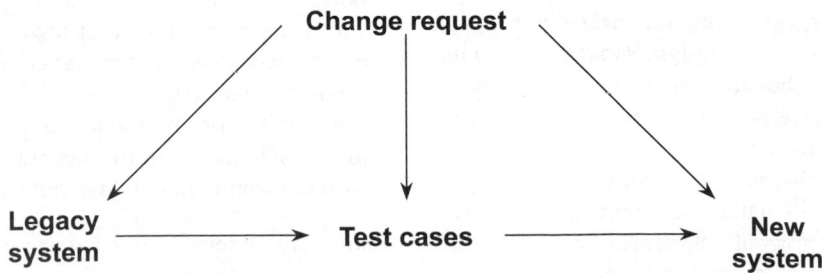

Figure 3. Synchronizing changes.

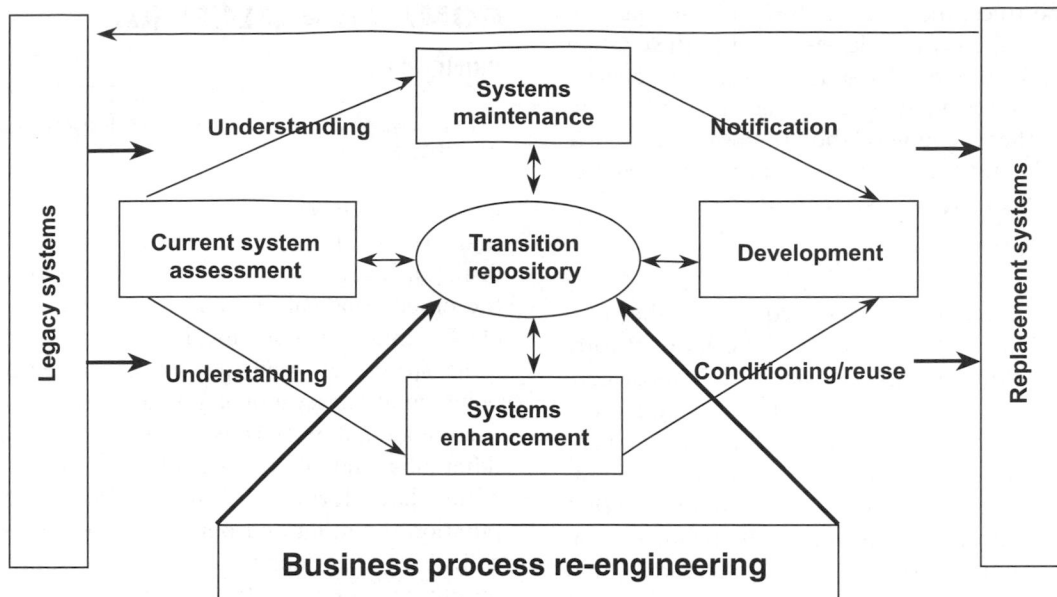

Figure 4. The stages of system transition.

system verification and validation steps that the methods enforce. Fig. 4 depicts the major stages of a system's transition and the relationships of those stages to supporting system verification and validation.

Sound software engineering principles are applied and validation occurs in each of the four sections of Fig. 4. Legacy systems are analyzed (current system assessment) with data and process discoveries stored in a repository (database). Maintenance uses this under-

standing of the existing system to make changes more effectively. The results of each maintenance exercise are stored in the repository. As more is learned about the legacy system, enhancements can be made to improve performance or to ready the legacy system for a transformation to a new operating environment. When the time comes to transform the legacy system, the data and process documentation of the old can be used by the development team. If business process reengineering defined new business workflows,

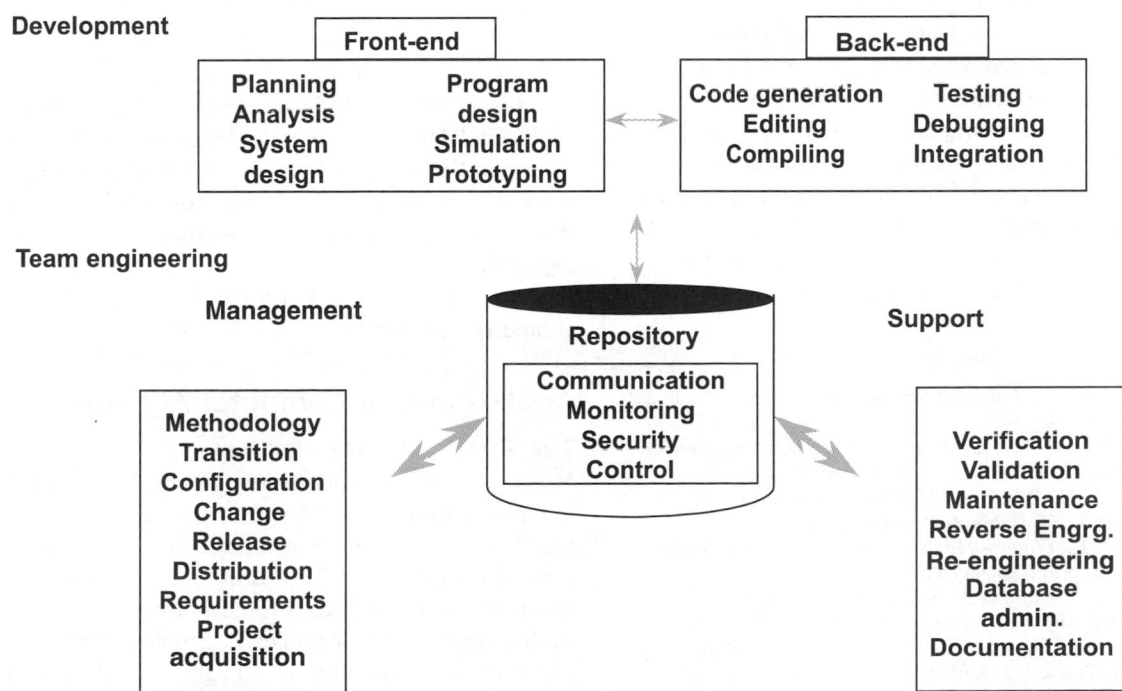

Figure 5. A complete CASE environment.

policies, and rules, they too can be stored and used to plan and implement the redevelopment of the existing system. While the new system is being developed, changes will still be made to the legacy system. A notification of these changes should be made to the redevelopment team for evaluation as possible requirement changes to the new system.

Summary

A complete CASE environment requires all the components depicted in Fig. 5. Most organizations already have all these components in some form. Manual techniques are legitimate alternatives to automation and need to be considered when assessing a software redevelopment environment. CASE provides computer-aided alternatives to the components of Fig. 5. What is lacking in most tool environments is the integration of the individual tools and the integration and coordination of the tools with the project team members.

Toolsets organized along traditional job functions will, at least initially, create less resistance on the part of users. Software professionals want tools to help them do what they do now, only better, not tools that force them to do their jobs differently. Once the first wave of technology is assimilated, the inherent characteristics of the technology will influence the process more and more. Improving software quality and developer productivity starts with specific quality and productivity objectives and assessing the software engineering process relative to those objectives. Tools are then chosen that complement the engineering process and contribute to fulfilling the objectives. Overall the greatest leverage will be realized when the entire software development and maintenance process, the total *software life cycle*, is fully automated in a seamless environment for the software engineer. A complete CASE environment is a carefully configured and integrated system of automated tools applied to the entire software life cycle for each unique software development, maintenance, or redevelopment problem.

Bibliography

1990. Humphrey, W. *Managing the Software Process*. Reading, MA: Addison-Wesley.
1996. Oman, P., and Pfleeger, S. L. *Applying Software Metrics*. Los Alamitos, CA: IEEE Computer Society Press.
1997. Pigoski, T. M. *Practical Software Maintenance*. Los Alamitos, CA: IEEE Computer Society Press.
1997. Reifer, D. J. *Software Management*, 5th Ed. Los Alamitos, CA: IEEE Computer Society Press.
1997. Sharon, D. "A Complete Software Engineering Environment," IEEE Software (March/April), 123–125.
1997. Thayer, R. H., and Merlin, D. *Software Requirements Engineering*, 2nd Ed. Los Alamitos, CA: IEEE Computer Society Press.

David Sharon

COMPUTER ALGEBRA

PRINCIPLES

For articles on related subjects *see* NUMERICAL ANALYSIS; and SYMBOL MANIPULATION.

Computer algebra is a branch of scientific computation. There are several characteristic features that distinguish computer algebra from numerical analysis, the other principal branch of scientific computation. (1) Computer algebra involves computation in algebraic structures, such as finitely presented groups, polynomial rings, rational function fields, algebraic and transcendental extensions of the rational numbers, or differential and difference fields. (2) Computer algebra manipulates formulas. Whereas in numerical computation the input and output of algorithms are basically (integer or floating point) numbers, the input and output of computer algebra algorithms are generally formulas. So, typically, instead of computing

$$\int_0^{1/2} \frac{x}{x^2-1}\,dx = -0.1438\ldots,$$

an integration algorithm in computer algebra yields

$$\int \frac{x}{x^2-1}\,dx = \frac{\ln|x^2-1|}{2}.$$

(3) Computations in computer algebra are carried through exactly (i.e. no approximations are applied at any step). So, typically, the solutions of a system of algebraic equations such as

$$x^4 + 2x^2y^2 + 3x^2y + y^4 - y^3 = 0$$

$$x^2 + y^2 - 1 = 0$$

are presented as $(0,1), (\pm\sqrt{3/4}, -1/2)$, instead of $(0,1), (\pm 0.86602\cdots, -0.5)$. Because of the exact nature of the computations in computer algebra, decision procedures can be derived from such algorithms that decide, for example, the solvability of systems of algebraic equations, the solvability of integration problems in a specified class of formulas, or the validity of geometric formulas.

Applications of Computer Algebra

THE PIANO MOVERS PROBLEM

Many problems in robotics (*q.v.*) can be modeled by the piano movers problem: finding a path that will take a given body B from a given initial position to a desired final position. The additional constraint is that along the path the body should not hit any obstacles, such as walls or other bodies. A simple example in the plane is shown in Fig. 1. The initial and final positions of the body B are drawn in full, whereas a possible intermediate position is drawn in dotted lines.

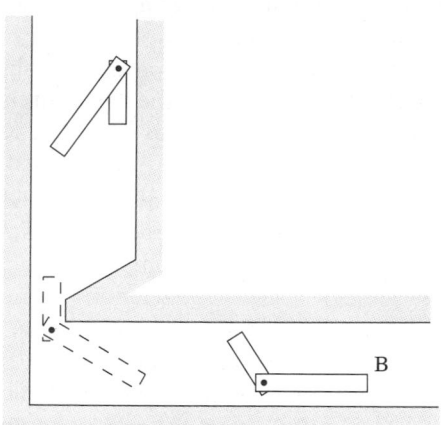

Figure 1. The piano movers problem.

J. T. Schwartz and M. Sharir have shown how to reduce this problem to a certain problem about semialgebraic sets that can be solved by Collins' cylindrical algebraic decomposition (cad) method.

Semialgebraic sets are subsets of a real m-dimensional space R^m that can be cut out by polynomial equations and inequalities. That is, start with simple sets of the form

$$\{(x_1, \ldots, x_m) \mid p(x_1, \ldots, x_m) = 0\}$$

or

$$\{(x_1, \ldots, x_m) \mid q(x_1, \ldots, x_m) > 0\},$$

where p, q are polynomials with real coefficients, and allow the construction of more complicated sets by means of intersection, union, and difference. Any subset of R^m that can be defined in this way is called a *semialgebraic set.*

Consider a two-dimensional problem, as in Fig. 1. Starting from some fixed position of the body B (say P at the origin, where P is the point at which the parts of B are joined together) in R^2, obtain an arbitrary position of B by applying a rotation T_1 to part B_2, a rotation T_2 to B (Fig. 2), and afterwards a translation T_3 to B. Since T_1, T_2 can be described by 2×2 matrices and T_3

by a vector of length 2, any such position of B can be specified by 10 coefficients (i.e. a point in R^{10}). Some of these possible positions are illegal, since the body B would intersect or lie outside of the boundaries. If the legal positions $L(\subset R^{10})$ can be described by polynomial equations and inequalities then L is a semialgebraic set.

The piano movers problem is now reduced to the question of whether two points P_1, P_2 in L can be joined by a path in L (i.e. whether P_1 and P_2 lie in the same connected component of L). This question can be decided by Collins' cad method, which makes heavy use of computer algebra algorithms. In particular, the cad method uses algorithms for greatest common divisors of polynomials, factorization of polynomials into square-free factors, resultant computations, and isolation of the real roots of polynomials.

Algorithmic Methods in Geometry

Often, a geometric statement can be described by polynomial equations over some ground field K, such as the real or complex numbers. Consider, for instance, the statement, *"The intersection of its altitude with the hypotenuse of a right-angled triangle and the midpoints of the three sides of the triangle lie on a circle"* (Fig. 3).

Once the geometric figure is placed into a coordinate system, it can be described by polynomial equations. For instance, the fact that E is the midpoint of the side AC is expressed by the equation $2y_3 - y_1 = 0$; the fact that the line segments EM and FM are of equal length is expressed by the equation $(y_7 - y_3)^2 + y_8^2 - (y_7 - y_4)^2 - (y_8 - y_5)^2 = 0$; and so on. In this way, the system $h_1 = \cdots = h_m = 0$ of polynomial equations in the indeterminates $y_1, \ldots, y_n$ determines the geometric figure. Call these polynomials the *hypothesis polynomials.* The equation $(y_7 - y_3)^2 + y_8^2 - (y_7 - y_9)^2 - (y_6 - y_{10})^2 = 0$ then states that the line segments HM and EM are also of equal length. Call this polynomial the *conclusion polynomial.*

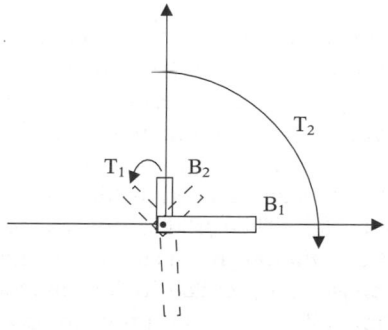

Figure 2.

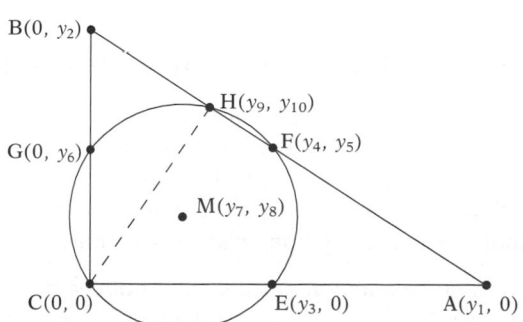

Figure 3.

The problem of proving the geometric statement is now reduced to the problem of proving that every common solution of the hypothesis polynomials (i.e. every valid geometric configuration) also solves the conclusion polynomial (i.e. the statement is valid for the configuration). Various computer algebra methods can be used for proving such geometry statements, such as characteristic sets or Gröbner bases. The underlying computer algebra algorithms for these methods are mainly the solution of systems of polynomial equations, various decision algorithms in the theory of polynomial ideals, and algorithms for computing in algebraic extensions of the field of rational numbers.

MODELING IN SCIENCE AND ENGINEERING

In science and engineering, it is common to express a problem in terms of integrals or differential equations with boundary conditions. Numerical integration leads to approximations of the values of the solution functions. But, as R. W. Hamming (q.v.) has written, "the purpose of computing is insight, not numbers." So, instead of computing tables of values, it would be much more gratifying to derive formulas for the solution functions. Computer algebra algorithms can do just that for certain classes of integration and differential equation problems.

Consider, for example, the system of differential equations

$$-6\frac{dq}{dx}(x) + \frac{d^2p}{dx^2}(x) - 6\sin(x) = 0$$

$$6\frac{d^2q}{dx^2}(x) + a^2\frac{dp}{dx}(x) - 6\cos(x) = 0$$

subject to the boundary conditions $p(0) = 0$, $q(0) = 1$, $p'(0) = 0$, $q'(0) = 1$. Given this information as input, any of the major computer algebra systems will derive the formal solution

$$p(x) = -\frac{12\sin(ax)}{a(a^2-1)} - \frac{6\cos(ax)}{a^2} + \frac{12\sin(x)}{a^2-1} + \frac{6}{a^2},$$

$$q(x) = \frac{\sin(ax)}{a} - \frac{2\cos(ax)}{a^2-1} + \frac{(a^2+1)\cos(x)}{a^2-1}$$

for $a \notin \{-1, 0, 1\}$.

Some Algorithms in Computer Algebra

Since computer algebra algorithms must yield exact results, these algorithms use integers and rational numbers as coefficients of algebraic expressions because these numbers can be represented exactly in the computer. Coefficients may also be algebraic.

Addition or subtraction of integers is quite straightforward, and these operations can be performed in time linear in the length of the numbers. The classical algorithm for multiplication of integers x and y proceeds by multiplying every digit of x by every digit of y and adding the results after appropriate shifts. This clearly takes time quadratic in the length of the inputs. A faster multiplication algorithm due to A. Karatsuba and Yu. Ofman is usually called the *Karatsuba algorithm*. The basic idea is to cut the two inputs x, y of length $\leq n$ into pieces of length $\leq n/2$ such that

$$x = a\beta^{n/2} + b, \qquad y = c\beta^{n/2} + d,$$

where β is the basis of the number system. A usual divide-and-conquer approach would reduce the multiplication of two integers of length n to four multiplications of integers of length $n/2$ and some subsequent shifts and additions. The complexity of this algorithm would still be quadratic in n. However, from

$$xy = ac\beta^n + ((a+b)(c+d) - ac - bd)\beta^{n/2} + bd$$

we see that one of the four multiplications can be replaced by additions and shifts, which take only linear time. If this reduction of the problem is applied recursively, we get a multiplication algorithm with a time complexity proportional to $n^{\log_2 3}$. This is still not the best we can hope for. In fact, the fastest known algorithm is due to Schönhage and Strassen and its complexity is proportional to $n(\log n)(\log \log n)$. However, the overhead of this algorithm is enormous, and it pays off only if the numbers are incredibly large.

Polynomial arithmetic with coefficients in a field, like the rational numbers, presents no problem. These polynomials form a Euclidean domain, so we can carry out division with quotient and remainder. Often, however, we need to work with polynomials whose coefficients lie in an integral domain like the integers. Addition, subtraction, and multiplication are again obvious, but division with quotient and remainder is not possible. Fortunately, we can replace division by a similar process, called pseudo-division. If $a(x) = a_m x^m + \cdots + a_1 x + a_0$ and $b(x) = b_n x^n + \cdots + b_1 x + b_0$, with $m \geq n$, then there exists a unique pair of quotient $q(x)$ and remainder $r(x)$ such that $b_n^{m-n+1} a(x) = q(x)b(x) + r(x)$ where either r is the zero polynomial or the degree of r is less than the degree of b.

Good algorithms are needed for computing the *greatest common divisor* (gcd) of polynomials. If we are working with polynomials over a field, we can use Euclid's algorithm, which takes two polynomials $f_1(x)$, $f_2(x)$ and computes a chain of remainders $f_3(x), \ldots, f_k(x), f_{k+1}(x) = 0$, such that f_i is the remainder in dividing f_{i-2} by f_{i-1}. Then $f_k(x)$ is the desired greatest common divisor. For polynomials over the integers we can replace division by pseudo-division, and the Euclidean algorithm still works. The problem, however, is that, although the inputs and the final result might be quite small, the intermediate polynomials can have huge coefficients. This problem becomes even more pronounced if we deal with multivariate polynomials. As an example, consider the computation of the greatest common divisor of two bivariate polynomials

$$f(x, y) = y^6 + xy^5 + x^3 y - xy + x^4 - x^2,$$

$$g(x, y) = xy^5 - 2y^5 + x^2 y^4 - 2xy^4 + xy^2 + xy$$

with integral coefficients. Consider y to be the main variable, so that the coefficients of powers of y are polynomials in x. Euclid's algorithm yields the polynomial remainder sequence

$r_0 = f,$

$r_1 = g,$

$r_2 = (2x - x^2)y^3 + (2x^2 - x^3)y^2$
$\quad + (x^5 - 4x^4 + 3x^3 + 4x^2 - 4x)y + x^6 - 4x^5$
$\quad - 3x^4 + 4x^3 - 4x^2,$

$r_3 = (-x^7 + 6x^6 - 12x^5 + 8x^4)y^2 + (-x^{13} + 12x^{12}$
$\quad - 58x^{11} + 136x^{10} - 121x^9 - 117x^8 + 362x^7$
$\quad - 236x^6 - 104x^5 + 192x^4 - 64x^3)y - x^{14} + 12x^{13}$
$\quad - 58x^{12} - 136x^{11} - 121x^{10} - 116x^9 + 356x^8$
$\quad - 224x^7 - 112x^6 + 192x^5 - 64x^4,$

$r_4 = (-x^{28} + 26x^{27} - 308x^{26} + 2184x^{25} - 10198x^{24}$
$\quad + 32188x^{23} - 65932x^{22} + 68536x^{21} + 42431x^{20}$
$\quad - 274533x^{19} + 411512x^{18} - 149025x^{17}$
$\quad - 431200x^{16} + 729296x^{15} - 337472x^{14}$
$\quad - 318304x^{13} + 523264x^{12} - 225280x^{11}$
$\quad - 78848x^{10} + 126720x^9 - 53248x^8 + 8192x^7)y$
$\quad - x^{29} + 26x^{28} - 308x^{27} + 2184x^{26} - 10198x^{25}$
$\quad + 32188x^{24} - 65932x^{23} + 68536x^{22} + 42431x^{21}$
$\quad - 274533x^{20} + 411512x^{19} - 149025x^{18}$
$\quad - 431200x^{17} + 729296x^{16} - 337472x^{15}$
$\quad - 318304x^{14} - 523264x^{13} - 225280x^{12}$
$\quad - 78848x^{11} + 126720x^{10} - 53248x^9 + 8192x^8.$

The greatest common divisor of f and g is obtained by eliminating common factors $p(x)$ in r_4. The final result is $y + x$. Although the inputs and the output are small, the intermediate expressions get very big. The biggest polynomial in this computation happens to occur in the pseudo-division of r_3 by r_4. The intermediate polynomial has degree 70 in x.

This problem of coefficient growth is ubiquitous in computer algebra, and there are some general approaches for dealing with it. In the special case of

polynomial gcds we could always make the polynomials *primitive* (i.e. eliminate common factors not depending on the main variable). This approach keeps intermediate remainders as small as possible, but at a high price: many gcd computations on the coefficients. The subresultant gcd algorithm can determine many of the common factors of the coefficients, without ever computing gcds of coefficients. The remainders stay reasonably small during this algorithm. In fact, in our example the integer coefficients grow only to length 4.

The most efficient algorithm for computing gcds of multivariate polynomials is the *modular algorithm*. The basic idea is to apply homomorphisms to the coefficients, compute the gcds of the evaluated polynomials, and use the *Chinese remainder algorithm* to reconstruct the actual coefficients in the gcd. If the input polynomials are univariate, we can take homomorphisms H_p, mapping an integer a to $a \bmod p$. If the input polynomials are multivariate, we can take evaluation homomorphisms of the form $H_{x1=r1}$ for reducing the number of variables. In our example, we get

$$\gcd(H_{x=2}(f), H_{x=2}(g)) = y + 2,$$
$$\gcd(H_{x=3}(f), H_{x=3}(g)) = y + 3.$$

So the gcd is $y + x$. Never during this algorithm did we have to consider large coefficients.

Decomposing polynomials into irreducible factors is another crucial algorithm in computer algebra. A few decades ago, only rather inefficient techniques for polynomial factorization were available. Research in computer algebra has contributed to a deeper understanding of the problem and, as a result, has created much better algorithms. Let us first consider univariate polynomials with integer coefficients. Since the problem of coefficient growth appears again, one usually maps the polynomial $f(x)$ to a polynomial $f_{(p)}(x)$ by applying a homomorphism H_p, p a prime. $f_{(p)}$ can now be factored by the *Berlekamp algorithm*, which involves some linear algebra and computations of gcds. Conceivably, we could factor f modulo various primes $p_1, \ldots, p_k$ and try to reconstruct the factors over the integers by the Chinese remainder algorithm, as we did in the modular gcd algorithm. The problem is that we do not know which factors correspond. So instead, one uses a p-adic approach based on *Hensel's lemma*, which states that a factorization of f modulo a prime p can be lifted to a factorization of f modulo p^k, for any positive integer k. Since we know the bounds for the size of the coefficients that can occur in the factors, we can determine a suitable k and thus construct the correct coefficients of the integral factors. There is, however, an additional twist. If $f(x)$ can be decomposed into irreducible factors $f_1(x)$, $f_2(x)$ over the integers, it could well be that, modulo p, these irreducible factors can be split even further. So after we have lifted the factorization modulo p to a factorization modulo p^k for a suitable k, we need to try combinations of factors for determining the factors over the integers. For instance, $x^4 + 1$ is a polynomial that is irreducible over the integers, but factors modulo every prime. Theoretically, this final step is the most costly one, and it makes the time complexity of the Berlekamp–Hensel algorithm exponential in the degree of the input. Nevertheless, in practice the algorithm works very well for most examples.

In 1982, Lenstra, Lenstra, and Lovász developed an algorithm for factoring univariate polynomials over the integers with a polynomial time complexity. Kaltofen extended this result to multivariate polynomials. The overhead of this algorithm, however, is extremely high.

To integrate a rational function $A(x)/B(x)$, where A, B are polynomials with integral coefficients, we could split the polynomial B into linear factors in a suitable algebraic extension field, compute a partial fraction decomposition of the integrand, and integrate all the summands in this decomposition. The summands with linear denominators lead to logarithmic parts in the integral. Computations in the splitting field of a polynomial are very extensive; if n is the degree of the polynomial, the necessary algebraic extension has degree $n!$. So the question arises as to whether it is really necessary to go to the full splitting field. For instance, for $x \geq \sqrt{2}$

$$\int \frac{x}{x^2 - 2} \, dx = \int \frac{\frac{1}{2}}{x - \sqrt{2}} \, dx + \int \frac{\frac{1}{2}}{x + \sqrt{2}} \, dx$$

$$= \frac{1}{2} \left[\ln(x - \sqrt{2}) + \ln(x + \sqrt{2}) \right]$$

$$= \frac{1}{2} \ln(x^2 - 2).$$

The example shows that although we had to compute in the splitting field of the denominator, the algebraic extensions actually disappear in the end. A deeper analysis of the problem reveals that, instead of factoring the denominator into linear factors, it suffices to compute a so-called *square-free factorization*—i.e. a decomposition of a polynomial f into $f = f_1 f_2^2 \cdots f_r^r$, where the factors f_i are pairwise relatively prime and have no multiple roots (square-free). The square-free factorization can be computed by successive gcd operations. Now if A and B are relatively prime polynomials over the rational numbers, B is square-free, and the degree of A is less than the degree of B, then

$$\int \frac{A(x)}{B(x)} \, dx = \sum_{i=1}^{n} c_i \log v_i,$$

where the $c_1, \ldots, c_n$ are the distinct roots of the resultant of $A(x) - cB'(x)$ and $B(x)$ w.r.t. x, and each v_i is the gcd of $A(x) - c_i B'(x)$ and $B(x)$. In this way we get the smallest field extension necessary for expressing the integral.

The problem of integration becomes more complicated if the class of integrands is extended. A very common class is that of elementary functions. We get this class by starting with the rational functions and successively adding exponentials ($\exp f(x)$), logarithms ($\log f(x)$), or roots of algebraic equations, where the exponents, arguments, or coefficients are previously constructed elementary functions. Not every elementary integrand has an elementary integral (e.g. $\int e^{x^2} \, dx$ cannot be expressed as an elementary function). However, there is an algorithm (the *Risch algorithm*) that can decide whether a given integrand can be integrated in terms of elementary functions, and if so the Risch algorithm yields the integral. The case of algebraic functions is the most complicated part of the Risch algorithms.

The discrete analog of the integration problem is the problem of summation in finite terms. We are given an expression for a summand a_n, and we want to compute a closed expression for the partial sums of the infinite series $\sum_{n=1}^{\infty} a_n$. That is, we want to compute a function $S(m)$, such that

$$\sum_{n=1}^{m} a_n = S(m) - S(0).$$

For instance, we want to compute

$$\sum_{n=1}^{m} nx^n = \frac{mx^{m+2} - (m+1)x^{m+1} + x}{(x-1)^2}.$$

For the case of hypergeometric functions, *Gosper's algorithm* solves this problem. There is also a theory of summation similar to the theory of integration in finite terms.

Gröbner bases are an extremely powerful method for deciding many problems in the theory of polynomial ideals. As an example, consider the system of algebraic equations

$$2x^4 + y^4 + 8x^3 - 3x^2y + 2y^3 + 12x^2 - 6xy + y^2$$
$$+ 8x - 3y + 2 = 0$$
$$8x^3 + 24x^2 - 6xy + 24x - 6y + 8 = 0$$
$$4y^3 - 3x^2 - 6y^2 - 6x + 2y - 3 = 0 \quad (1)$$

Every root of these equations is also a root of any linear combination of these equations, so in fact we are looking for zeros of the ideal generated by the left-hand sides in the ring of polynomials in x and y over Q. The left-hand sides form a specific basis for this same ideal that is better suited for solving the system. Such a basis is a Gröbner basis with respect to a lexicographic ordering of the variables. In our example, we get the following Gröbner basis, which we again write as a system of equations.

$$y^3 - y^2 = 0$$

$$yx + y = 0$$

$$3x^2 + 2y^2 + 6x - 2y + 3 = 0. \qquad (2)$$

The solutions of (1) and (2) are the same, but obviously it is much easier to investigate the solutions of (2). The system contains a polynomial depending only on y, and the zeros are $y = 0$ and $y = 1$. Substituting these values for y into the other two equations, we get the solutions $(x = -1, y = 0)$ and $(x = -1, y = 1)$ for the system of algebraic equations.

Other problems in the theory of polynomial ideals that can be solved by Gröbner bases include the ideal membership problem, the radical membership problem, the primary decomposition of an ideal, or the computation of the dimension of an ideal. Most computer algebra programs contain a Gröbner basis package.

Representation of Expressions

Dynamic data structures are necessary for representing the computational objects of computer algebra in the memory of the computer. For instance, during the execution of the Euclidean algorithm, the coefficients in the polynomials expand and shrink again. Since the goal of the computation is an exact result, we cannot just truncate them to the most significant positions.

Most computer algebra programs represent objects as lists. An integer is represented as a list of digits. For more complicated objects, the choice of representation is not that clear. So, for instance, we can represent a bivariate polynomial recursively as a polynomial in a main variable with coefficients in a univariate polynomial ring, or distributively as pairs of coefficients and power products in the variables. For example:

Recursive representation:

$$p(x, y) = (3x^2 - 2x + 1)y^2 + (x^2 - 3x)y + (2x + 1)$$

Distributive representation:

$$p(x, y) = 3x^2y^2 - 2xy^2 + x^2y + y^2 - 3xy + 2x + 1$$

For both these representations, we can use a dense or a sparse list representation. In the dense representation, a polynomial is a list of coefficients, starting from some highest coefficient down to the constant coefficient. So the dense recursive representation of p is

$$((3 \ -2 \ 1)(1 \ -3 \ 0)(2 \ 1))$$

For the dense distributive representation of p, we order the power products according to their degree and lexicographically within the same degree. So p is represented as

$$\begin{pmatrix} 3 & 0 & 0 & 0 & -2 & 1 & 0 & 1 & -3 & 0 & 0 & 2 & 1 \\ x^2y^2 & x^3y & x^4 & y^3 & xy^2 & x^2y & x^3 & y^2 & xy & x^2 & y & x & 1 \end{pmatrix}$$

If only a few power products have a coefficient different from 0, then a dense representation wastes a lot of space. In this case we really want to represent the polynomial sparsely (i.e. by pairs of coefficients and exponents). The sparse recursive representation of p is

$$((((3 \ 2)(-2 \ 1)(1 \ 0)) \ 2)(((1 \ 2)(-3 \ 1)) \ 1)(((2 \ 1)(1 \ 0)) \ 0))$$

and the sparse distributive representation of p is

$$((3(2 \ 2))(-2(1 \ 2))(1(2 \ 1))(1(0 \ 2))(-3(1 \ 1))$$

$$(2(1 \ 0))(1(0 \ 0))).$$

For different algorithms, different representations of the objects are useful or even necessary. The multivariate gcd algorithm works best with polynomials given in recursive representation, whereas the Gröbner basis algorithm needs the input in distributive representation. So, in general, a computer algebra program has to provide many different representations for the various algebraic objects and transformations that convert one form to another.

Bibliography

1985–present. *Journal of Symbolic Computation*. London: Academic Press.

1988. Davenport, J. H., Siret, Y., and Tournier, E. *Computer Algebra—Systems and Algorithms for Algebraic Computation*. London: Academic Press.

1989. Akritas, A. G. *Elements of Computer Algebra*. New York: John Wiley.

1996. Winkler, F. *Polynomial Algorithms in Computer Algebra*. New York: Springer-Verlag.

1997. Bronstein, M. *Symbolic Integration I—Transcendental Functions*. Berlin: Springer-Verlag.

Franz Winkler

SYSTEMS

For articles on related subjects *see* NUMERICAL ANALYSIS; and SYMBOL MANIPULATION.

The goal of a symbolic computation system is to provide to the large and diverse community of "mathematics users" facilities for general mathematical calculations, typically including facilities such as arithmetic with exact fractions, polynomial and rational function arithmetic, factorization of integers and of polynomials, exact solution of linear and polynomial systems of equations, closed forms for summations, simplification of mathematical expressions, and differentiation and integration of elementary functions. Most systems also allow users to define and use their own facilities.

Loosely speaking, computer algebra systems can be classified as *special purpose* or *general purpose*. Special-purpose computer algebra systems are designed to solve problems in one specific area of mathematics, for example celestial mechanics, general relativity, or group theory. Special-purpose computer algebra systems use special notations and special data structures (*q.v.*), and have most of their essential algorithms implemented in the kernel of the system. Such systems will normally excel in their respective areas, but are of limited use in other applications, for example Magma (formerly Cayley) for group theory and algebraic geometry, GAP for discrete algebra and group theory, Macaulay 2 for algebraic geometry and commutative algebra, or Pari for number-theoretic computations. We will restrict our attention to general-purpose computer algebra systems. A general-purpose computer algebra system is designed to cover many diverse application areas and has sufficiently rich data structures, data types, and functions to do so.

In recent years, parallel computer algebra has attracted much attention and several experimental systems have grown out of these efforts. We will give an overview of a selection of these parallel systems.

COMPUTATION

All computer algebra systems have the ability to do mathematical computations with unassigned variables. For example

```
> t := x^2 * sin(x);
                         t := x² sin(x)
> diff (t,x);
                    2 x sin(x) + x² cos(x)
```

computes the derivative of an expression, where x is an unassigned variable.

Computer algebra systems have the ability to perform exact computation, i.e. arbitrary precision rational arithmetic, algebraic arithmetic, finite field arithmetic, etc. For example

$$\frac{1}{2} + \frac{1}{3} \to \frac{5}{6} \qquad \frac{1}{(\sqrt{2}+1)^3} \to 5\sqrt{2} - 7$$

rather than $0.8333\ldots$ and $0.07106\ldots$. Of course an arbitrarily precise numerical approximation can be computed on demand.

"Computation" in a computer algebra system requires a much more careful definition than in other languages. For example, compare the Pascal (*q.v.*) statement $x := a/b$ with the Maple statement `f:=int(expr, x);`.

The division a/b, provided $b \neq 0$, will produce a result (a floating-point number) of a predictable size and in a predictable time. In contrast the statement `int(expr, x)` may:

1. return the integral of *expr* with respect to x (the size of the result is difficult to predict)

2. return a partial answer (i.e. $f(x) + \int g(x)\,dx$)

3. fail to compute because a closed-form integral does not exist (e.g. e^{x^3} does not have such an integral)

4. fail to compute because the algorithms used cannot find an integral, even though one exists

5. produce a result which is too large to represent even though it is computable, e.g.

$$\int \frac{x^{10^7} - 1}{x - 1}\,dx$$

6. require a *very* long time to compute, making its computation not feasible for practical purposes.

The size of the result generated by the `int` statement is not predictable. This implies the use of dynamic memory management (e.g. garbage collection—*q.v.*) by computer algebra systems. This is one of the main reasons why Lisp (*q.v.*) was used in early systems as an implementation language.

CORRECTNESS

To some extent it is surprising that there should be any incorrectness tolerated by a supposedly mathematical symbol manipulation system, and not all are convinced that this is really necessary. However, in most current symbolic computation systems, simplifications such as $(x+y)/(x+y) \to 1$ are performed automatically, without keeping track that x must not be equal to $-y$ for this to make sense. This is an example where a compromise is made, since the system may sometimes make a mistake in order to have efficient simplification that is almost always correct. (Note that we are not talking about program "bugs" but rather design decisions.) Another example is the automatic simplification of $0 \times f(1000) \to 0$ before evaluation of $f(1000)$. This simplification would be "obviously desirable" except when $f(1000)$ may be undefined, or infinity. Performing the simplification is an efficiency that is "slightly" incorrect, while always evaluating $f(1000)$, if its value is not known beforehand, is something which most users would choose to avoid. Thus we see that many systems take the point of view that users will tolerate some degree of deviation from rigorous correctness. The user should be aware that *all* systems will perform some simplifications that are not safe 100% of the time.

The Systems

In this section we describe some of the most relevant systems in more detail. We restrict our attention to either new systems or systems which are widely used. For older systems such as Camal, Formac, or SAC-I/II, see the second edition of this *Encyclopedia*.

All systems we describe are interactive general-purpose computer algebra systems that provide the following three key capabilities:

♦ *Symbolic computations*: all systems provide routines for expansion and factoring of polynomials, differentiation and integration (definite and indefinite), series computation, solving equations and systems of equations, and linear algebra.

♦ *Numeric computations*: all systems support arbitrary precision numerical computation including computation of definite integrals, numerical solutions of equations, and evaluation of elementary and special functions.

♦ *Graphics*: all systems except Reduce allow plotting of two- and three-dimensional graphics.

Additionally, each system has a programming language which allows the user to extend the system.

For other comparisons of computer algebra systems see Wester (1994).

MACSYMA

The Macsyma (Macsyma Inc., 1995) project was founded by William Martin and Joel Moses of MIT. Macsyma was built upon a predecessor MIT project, Mathlab 68, an interactive general-purpose system, that was the development tool and test bed for several MIT doctoral theses in algebraic manipulation and algorithms.

The Macsyma system internals were first implemented in Maclisp, a systems programming dialect of Lisp (*q.v.*) developed at MIT. For many years Macsyma was available through the Arpanet on a DEC PDP-10 running the ITS system. However, in the late 1970s and early 1980s, the important features of Maclisp were recreated in Franz Lisp running in the Unix environment. PC and Unix versions of Macsyma are now distributed by Macsyma Inc.

The Macsyma kernel is currently written in Common Lisp. The external math libraries are written in Common Lisp or the Macsyma language. Macsyma is a typical algebraic manipulation language. It provides a Fortran/Algol-like notation for mathematical expressions and programming. Automatic type checking is almost nonexistent.

Macsyma users can translate programs into Lisp. This allows interpretation by the Lisp interpreter (instead of the Macsyma language interpreter, which itself is coded in Lisp). The Lisp compiler can be applied to the translation to take the further step of compiling the program into machine code.

A user wishing to make any extensions to the functionality of the system (e.g. installing a new kind of mathematical object, but wanting addition or multiplication to work for it) must learn Lisp in order allow its manipulation to proceed as efficiently as the rest of the built-in mathematical code. However, the language allows a large amount of extensibility without use or knowledge of the Lisp internals. For example, the parser/grammar of the Macsyma language can be altered on-the-fly to include new prefix, infix, or "matchfix" operations defined by user-supplied Macsyma programs.

Another feature of Macsyma is its `assume` facility. It allows one to define properties over the symbols. For example, one can define `ASSUME(A>B)` and then the system *knows* this relation between A and B. If the user then asks `MAX(A,B)` the answer A is given.

Macsyma makes extensive use of flags for directing the computation. For example, if the flag `TRIGEXPAND` is set to `TRUE`, Macsyma will cause full expansion of sines and cosines of sums of angles and of multiple angles occurring in all expressions. There also exist nonbinary flags, such as `LHOSPITALLIM`, which is the maximum number of times L'Hospital's rule is used in a limit computation.

REDUCE

Reduce (Hearn, 1995) was originally written in Lisp to assist symbolic computation in high energy physics in the late 1960s. Its user base grew beyond the particle physics community as its general-purpose facilities were found to be useful in many other mathematical situations. Reduce 2 was ported to several different machines and operating systems during the 1970s, making it the most widely distributed system of that time, and one of the first efforts in Lisp portability. Reduce 3, written in the "Standard Lisp" dialect, is a further refinement and enhancement. It consists of about 4 MB of Lisp code. We discuss below some of the features of Reduce 3, as found in its User's Manual.

Reduce, like Macsyma, has a simple syntax for the basic mathematical commands (expression evaluation, differentiation, integration, etc.), and a Fortran-like programming language. Its reserved words include not only the keywords of the programming language but also the names of the various flags which control default simplification and evaluation modes. For example, the reserved word EXP is a flag which, when turned OFF, blocks the default expansion of rational function expressions.

Reduce has two programming modes (an "algebraic" mode and a "symbolic" mode), with the same syntactic forms for procedure definition, assignment, and control statements in both modes. In algebraic mode, data objects are manipulated through mathematical operations, such as numerical or rational function arithmetic, FACTORIZE (factor a polynomial over the integers), DF (partial differentiation), SUB (substitute an expression for a variable in another expression), or COEFF (find the coefficients of various powers of a variable in an expression). In symbolic mode, one can directly manipulate the internal representation of mathematical expressions, using Lisp-like manipulation primitives such as CAR and CDR, and routines such as LC (find the leading coefficient of a polynomial) or .+ (add a term to a polynomial). Most casual users of Reduce need to learn only the functionality provided by algebraic mode (programming-in-the-abstract), but since most of the basic system is coded in symbolic mode, programming in symbolic mode is sometimes necessary to augment or borrow from those basic facilities.

Numerical programs often have to be written based on a set of formulas which describe the solution of a problem in science or engineering. For that step, Reduce provides GENTRAN, an automatic code generator and translator. It constructs complete numerical programs based on sets of algorithmic specifications and symbolic expressions. Formatted Fortran, RATFOR, or C code can be generated through a series of interactive commands or under the control of a template processing routine. This facility is available in Macsyma too.

DERIVE

Derive (Rich *et al.*, 1994) was developed by A. Rich and D. Stoutmeyer and is marketed by Soft Warehouse Inc. It is also implemented in Lisp. Derive will run on any IBM PC compatible and does not require a mathematics coprocessor.

Derive is the successor to μMath and is menu-driven. Many commands and operations can be carried out with just two or three keystrokes. In addition to μMath, it has a powerful graphics package that can plot functions in two and three dimensions. One can plot more than one function on the same graph and use multiple windows for easy comparisons. Derive supports all basic symbolic mathematics, such as factorization, integration, and differentiation. It also understands matrices and vectors and can do basic vector calculus. Although Derive is less capable than other general-purpose computer algebra systems, the extent of its power based on such minimal hardware is remarkable. Nonetheless, it lacks, for example, procedures for solving systems of nonlinear equations, computation of eigenvectors of matrices, and special features such as Laplace transforms, Fourier transforms, and Bessel functions.

The programming language of Derive provides only the definition of simple functions, which may be recursive, using an IF function and an ITERATE function as control structures (*q.v.*). All utility files are programmed in this language.

MATHEMATICA

The development of Mathematica (Wolfram, 1996) was started by S. Wolfram in 1986. The first version of the system was released by Wolfram Research, Inc. in 1988. Wolfram had previously developed the SMP computer algebra system in 1979–1981, which served as a forerunner of some elements of Mathematica. Mathematica was designed to be a computer algebra system with graphics, numerical computation, and a flexible programming language.

In Mathematica, patterns are used to match classes of expressions with a given structure. Pattern matching and transformation/rewrite rules greatly simplify the programming of mathematical functions because one need only define replacements for patterns. For example, consider the definition of the logarithm of a product or a power:

```
In[1] := log[x_ y_] := log[x] + log[y]
In[2] := log[x_ ^ y_] := y log[x] .
```

These definitions are global rules. Such a rule is applied to all expressions automatically if the left-hand side of the rule matches the expression, i.e. the heads are equal and the arguments match. This is in contrast to rewrite rules, which are applied on demand. The notation x_ denotes a pattern that matches anything and is referred to as x in the right-hand side of the rule. The structure of such patterns can be very complex. For example, the pattern x:_ ^ n_Integer?Positive matches any expression of the form a^b, where a is any expression and b a positive integer. The exponent b is then referred to as n, and the complete object is referred to as x. Writing a definition in terms of rules for specific patterns can obviate the need for extensive checking of argument values within the body of a definition. Pattern matching is structural, not mathematical, so b ^ 2 is not recognized as the product b × b. However, the pattern matcher recognizes that multiplication is associative:

```
In[3] := f[log[2a b ^ 2]]
Out[3] = f[log[2] + log[a] + 2 log[b]]
```

Mathematica's colorful plotting features are very good. It provides two- and three-dimensional graphs, along with flexibility to rotate and change the viewpoint easily. The plot in Fig. 1 was generated with the command

```
Plot3D[Sin[x y], {x, 0, 3}, {y, 0, 3},
       PlotPoints -> 31, Boxed -> False]
```

Mathematica's kernel consists of about 1.1 million lines of C (*q.v.*) code and there are about 800,000 lines of Mathematica code in the distributed packages. The basic functionality of Mathematica is built into the kernel or coded in the Mathematica language in "start-up" packages. A wide variety of applications such as statistics and Laplace transforms are coded in Mathematica in "standard" packages that can be read in on request. Mathematica presents itself using a notebook-type graphical user interface. The user can mix text, animated graphics, and Mathematica input. This is an excellent tool for use in education and presentation of results.

MAPLE

The Maple (Waterloo Maple Inc., 1996) project was started by K. Geddes and G. Gonnet at the University of Waterloo in November 1980. At present, Maple is distributed by Waterloo Maple Inc. It followed from the construction of an experimental system (named "wama") which proved the feasibility of writing a symbolic computation system in system implementation languages and running it in a crowded time-sharing environment.

Maple was designed and implemented to be a pleasant programming language, as well as being compact, efficient, portable, and extensible. The Maple language is reminiscent of Algol 68 (*q.v.*) without declarations, but also includes several functional programming (*q.v.*) paradigms. The internal mathematical libraries are written in the same language provided to users. Maple's kernel interprets this language relatively efficiently. Most higher level functions or packages, about 95% of the functionality (e.g. integration, solving

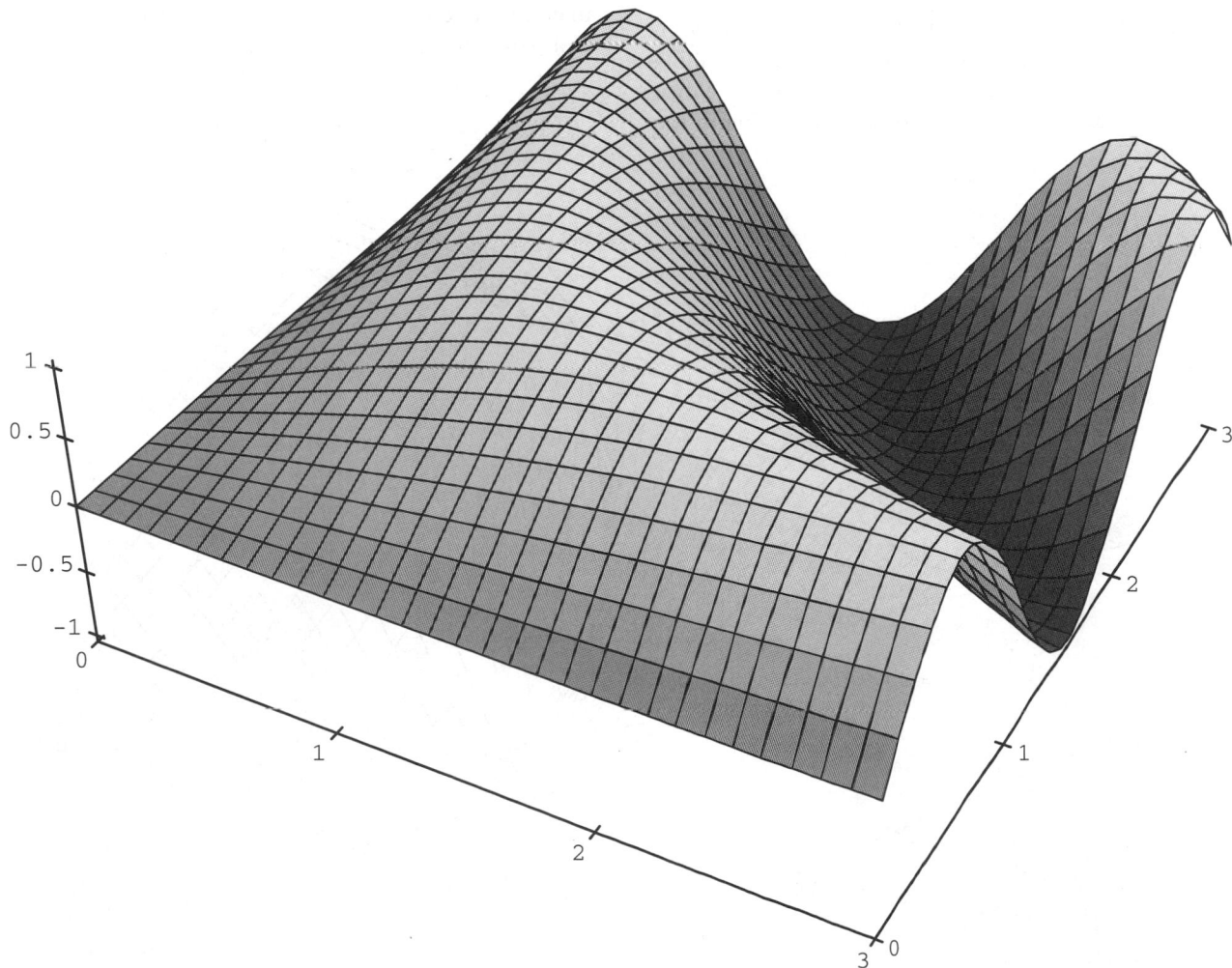

Figure 1.　Mathematica plot of the function sin(*xy*).

equations, normalization of expressions, radical simplification, and factorization), are all coded in the user language. Primitive functions, like arithmetic, basic simplification, polynomial division, manipulations of structures, series arithmetic, and integer gcds, are coded in the kernel. In principle, the user should not notice the difference between using internal or external functions. The kernel is implemented in C and consists of about 45,000 lines of code. The implementation of the external functions uses about 1.2 million lines of Maple code.

Maple supports a large collection of specialized data structures: integers, rationals, floating-point numbers, expression trees, series, equations, sets, ranges, lists, arrays, tables, etc. All of these are objects which can be easily type-tested, assembled, or disassembled.

Major emphasis has been placed on readability, natural syntax, orthogonality, portability, compactness, and efficiency. Maple is currently used not only for symbolic computation, but also as a tool for teaching diverse courses (e.g. algebra and calculus, numerical analysis, economics, and mechanical engineering).

Maple makes extensive use of hash tables for various purposes (*see* SEARCHING). In particular, hashing (or signatures of expressions) is used to keep a single occurrence of any expression or subexpression in the system. This means that testing for equality is extremely inexpensive: it costs only one machine instruction. Tables, arrays, and the "partial computation table" are implemented internally as hash tables and hence are also very efficient. The motivation for remembering results lies in the observation that subexpressions may appear repeatedly in some computations. For example, computing the third derivative of $e^{\sin(x)}$ will compute the first derivative of $\sin(x)$ and $\cos(x)$ many times.

Packages in Maple are collections of functions suitable for a special area, like `linalg` for linear algebra or `numtheory` for number theory. Functions from such packages could be called with the command "*packagename[function]*." To avoid using these long names, one could set up short names for each function; so for example, after the command `with(linalg)` one can use `det(A)` instead of `linalg[det](A)`. Naming conflicts are always reported to the user.

Maple V incorporates a new user interface for the X Window system that includes 3D plotting and separate help windows, allows editing of input expressions, and maintains a log of a Maple session. In Fig. 2 we see a plot generated by the command

```
plot3d((x^2-y^2)/(x^2+y^2), x=-1..1,
       y=-1..1, grid=[31,31], axes=FRAME);
```

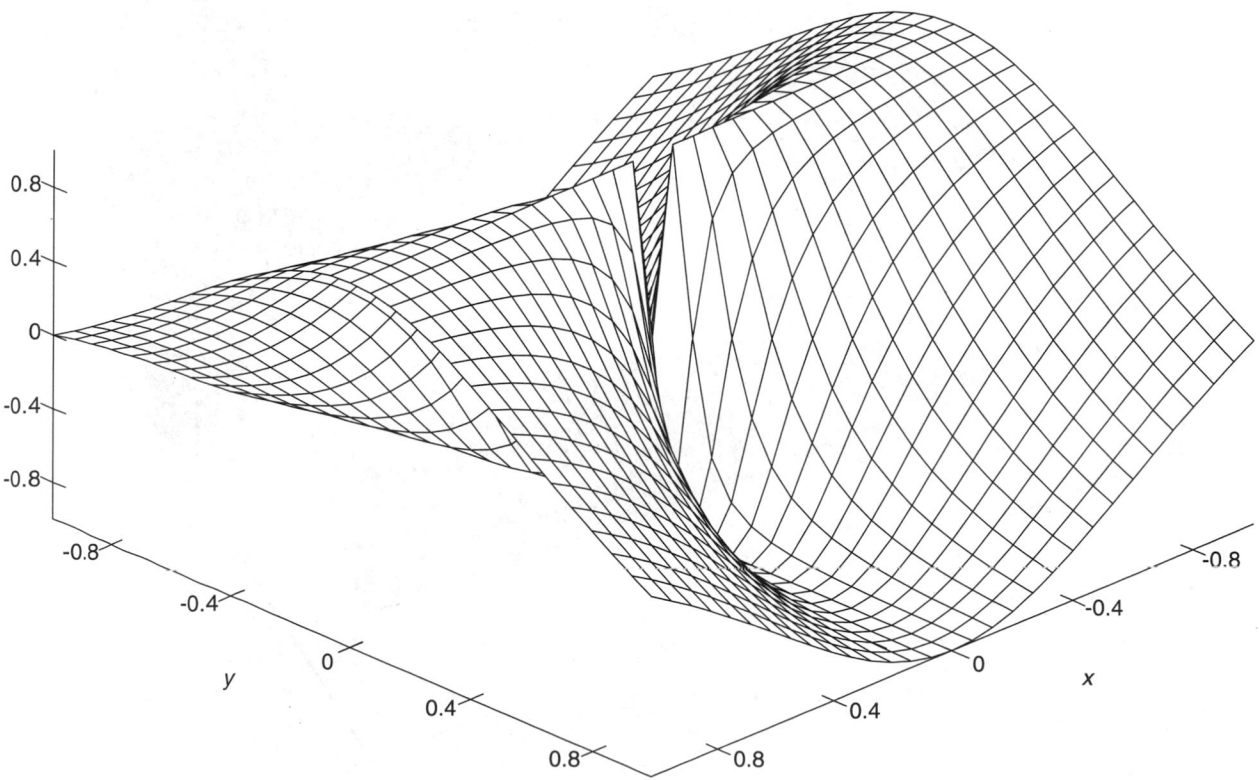

Figure 2. Maple's surface plot of $(x^2 - y^2)/(x^2 + y^2)$ for $x, y \in -1..1$.

AXIOM

Axiom (Jenks and Sutor, 1992) is a system developed at the IBM Thomas J. Watson Research Center and presently distributed by the Numerical Algorithms Group (NAG). Axiom is implemented in Lisp and runs on all major Unix (*q.v.*) platforms as well as on PCs.

Axiom is both a language for casual algebraic computing and an object-oriented programming language complete with abstract data types (*q.v.*), and information hiding (*q.v.*) designed to allow description and implementation of mathematical code at a high level. Axiom also includes a compiler that can be used to extend the system with user-defined functions and data types.

Every Axiom object has an associated data type that determines the operations that are applicable to the object. Axiom has a set of over 300 different data types, of which some pertain to algebraic computational objects while others are data structures. Some are simple, like `Integer`, `RationalNumber` and `Float`, and some are parameterized, like `Complex` (e.g. `C Z` for complex integers) and `UnivariatePolynomial` [e.g. `UP(x,Q)` for univariate polynomials in x over the rational numbers (`Q`)]. However, the user may have to supply type declarations. The interpreter can usually determine a suitable type for an object, but not always. The following dialogue demonstrates this type assignment by the interpreter. The type is always printed on a line following the object itself.

```
1/2 + 1/6 + 1/12
            3
   (1)      -
            4
   Type: Fraction Integer

(5 + %i)**3
   (2)      110 + 74%i
   Type: Complex Integer
```

The portion of the Axiom language intended for programming computational procedures has several features novel to algebraic manipulation languages, although some reflect concepts developed in other languages in the past ten years—in particular parameterized abstract data types, modules, and inheritance. The unique abstract data type design of Axiom is based on the notion of categories.

Categories lay out classes (*q.v.*) and hierarchies of types. Defining a category means defining its relation in the existing hierarchy, extra parameters (the category `VectorField` needs a parameter from the category `Field` to describe its scalars), operations which must be supported by its members, which are called *domains*, and properties the operations must satisfy. For example, consider the category `OrderedSet`:

```
OrderedSet(): Category == SetCategory with
   -- operations
      "<": ($,$) -> Boolean
      max: ($,$) -> $
      min: ($,$) -> $
   -- attributes
      irreflexive "<" -- not(x<x)
      transitive  "<" -- x<y and y<z => x<z
      total       "<" -- not(x<y)
                          and not(y<z) => x=y
   -- implementation
   add
      max(x,y) == (x<y => y; x)
      min(x,y) == (x<y => x; y)
```

This definition gives a category which extends (inherits) the category `SetCategory` by requiring three additional operations and three properties. If some operations are expressible by others, the implementation of these may also be put in the definition, like `max` and `min` in the above example. Examples of categories in Axiom are algebraic concepts such as `Group`, `AbelianGroup`, `Ring`, `EuclideanDomain`, `Field`, and `UnivariatePolynomialCategory(R: Ring)`.

Domains are instances of categories; this means that they define an *actual* data representation and provide functions implementing the operations of a category in accordance with the stated attributes. Domains can be parameterized too; for example, `SparseUnivariatePolynomial(R)` takes one parameter `R`, the coefficient ring, which must be of type `Ring` (a category), and the special representation used is a linked list of coefficients.

This concept also allows us to implement an algorithm only once for a given category and to use it for any values for which it makes sense. For example, the Euclidean algorithm can be used for values belonging to any domain which is a Euclidean domain (a category!). The following package takes a Euclidean domain as a type parameter and exports the operation `gcd` on that type.

```
GCDpackage(R: EuclideanDomain): with
        gcd: (R, R) -> R
   == add
      gcd(x,y) ==
            x := unitNormal(x).canonical
            y := unitNormal(y).canonical
            while y ^= 0 repeat
               (x,y) := (y, x rem y)
               y := unitNormal(y).canonical
            x
```

This `gcd` operation is now polymorphic and may be used for many types, e.g. `Z`, `SUP(Q)`, or `pSUP(Integer Mod 11)`. It could also be put in the definition of the category `EuclideanDomain`.

MuPAD

The MuPAD (Fuchssteiner *et al.*, 1996) project was initiated by Benno Fuchssteiner at the University of Paderborn, Germany. It started in 1989 as a collection of master's theses done by students at the University of Paderborn. MuPAD was the first system to be available free of charge until 1998, when marketing and user interface development was turned over to a commercial company, Sciface Software GmbH.

MuPAD features a programming language and a set of data structures that are similar to Maple. One important enhancement that MuPAD introduces is the concept of domains that encapsulate code into packages and introduce types in an otherwise untyped environment, though at the expense of some efficiency loss.

The following is a simple example of creating the domain of integers modulo 3, creating elements of the corresponding type and doing basic arithmetic on them:

```
>> Z3 := Dom::IntegerMod(3);
      Dom::IntegerMod(3)
>> a := Z3(10); b := Z3(2);
            1 mod 3
            2 mod 3
>> a+2*b;
            2 mod 3
```

MuPAD also lets the user query domain properties, such as verifying that the integers modulo 3 form a field:

```
>> Z3 := Dom::IntegerMod(3);
      Dom::IntegerMod(3)
>> Z3::hasProp( Cat:: Field );
            TRUE
```

Like Maple, MuPAD is extensible by user functions written in its own programming language. MuPAD also allows extensions of its kernel (written in C++, *q.v.*) by dynamically loadable modules.

Being a younger system, MuPAD does not yet have all the functionality and algorithms of its competitors. Nevertheless, it has found its community. It also builds on available free software; for example, it uses the Pari package for its arbitrary precision arithmetic.

TI-92

The Texas Instruments TI-92 hand-held calculator is an attempt to bring computer algebra to the mainstream education market. The first version was available in 1996 and featured a fairly complete computer algebra library, a geometry engine, and two- and three-dimensional plotting capabilities.

Because of its small physical size, the calculator struggles with memory restrictions (68K RAM, upgradable to 288K) and screen space (128×240 pixels; Fig 3).

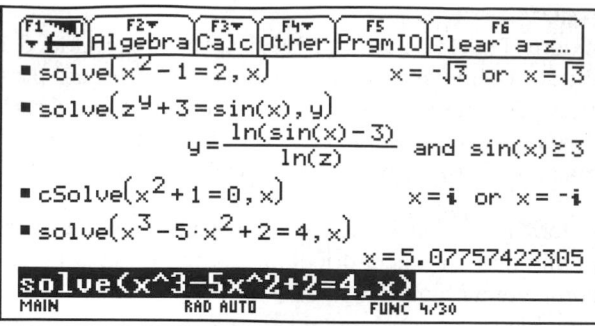

Figure 3. TI-92 screenshot.

Computer algebra typically involves large data structures and algorithms often require huge amounts of intermediate storage. For classroom problems arising in high school, however, it performs surprisingly well.

The computer algebra software built into the TI-92 was written by the creators of Derive. Unlike Derive, the TI-92 is not menu driven, but features a command-line interface similar to systems like Maple and Mathematica. Commands are, however, also available through pull-down menus or special keys.

Parallel Computer Algebra Systems

There are numerous applications of computer algebra; however, the algorithms involved are complex and often require lots of memory and processing time. It is therefore natural to try to exploit the parallelism contained in many algorithms in computer algebra, and as a consequence many experimental parallel systems have emerged. Most are based on existing (sequential) computer algebra systems. Watt, Siegl (‖MAPLE‖), Char (Sugarbush), Diaz *et al.* (DSC), and Bernardin used similar approaches to combine several Maple kernels to form a parallel system. Melenk and Neun did the same using Reduce and a parallel Lisp implementation. Kuchlin's PARSAC-2 is based on the sequential SAC-2 library.

Gautier and Roch designed their PAC++ as a parallel computer algebra system from the ground up, with emphasis on load balancing.

MuPAD has some language constructs for parallel computing (parallel for-loops), yet, as of 1999, no parallel implementation of MuPAD was available.

Examples

In this section we present some examples which define the boundaries of what computer algebra systems can and cannot do. The successful results we call "remarkable," are so in the sense that it is surprising that computer algebra systems can obtain them. In the future, systems might evolve that will be able to solve the ones we now call "difficult/impossible."

The output that follows in the remainder of this article approximates its appearance on a bit-mapped screen; the output on an ASCII terminal would be somewhat cruder.

DIFFICULT/IMPOSSIBLE PROBLEMS

◆ For which values of n is $\int dx/(x^n\sqrt{1-x^3})$ integrable in closed form?

◆ Let H be a Banach space... (computer algebra systems cannot handle such abstract concepts at present).

◆ Test, whether the expression $\zeta(3/2) + 4\pi\zeta(-1/2)$ is equal to zero or not (yes, indeed, it is equal to 0).

◆ Solve the nonlinear differential equation $y''(x) - 2y^2(x)/x = 0$.

REMARKABLE SOLUTIONS

◆ Series expansion of

$$R(s) = \int_0^\infty \frac{\ln(1+st)}{1+t^2}\,dt$$

```
> series( int( ln(1+s*t)/(1+t^2), t=0..infinity), s=0);
```

$$(-\ln(s)+1)\,s + 1/4\,\text{Pi}\,s^2 + (1/3\,\ln(s)-1/9)\,s^3 - 1/8\,\text{Pi}\,s^4$$
$$+ (-1/5\,\ln(s)+1/25)\,s^5 + O(s^6)$$

◆ We define $\{x_n\}$ to be the sequence of iterated sines, i.e. $x_{n+1} = \sin(x_n)$. What is the asymptotic expansion of x_n for $n \to \infty$?

```
> asympt(rsolve(x(n+1)=sin(x(n)),x),n);
```

$$\frac{3^{1/2}}{n^{1/2}} + \frac{\_C - 3/10\,3^{1/3}\,\ln(n)}{n^{3/2}} + O(1/n^2)$$

where _C is a constant which depends on the value of x_0.

◆ $\int \tan(\arctan(x)/3)\,dx$ in terms of tangents and arctangents:

```
integrate( tan(atan(x)/3), x)
```

$$(1) \quad \frac{8\log\left(3\tan\left(\dfrac{\text{atan}(x)}{3}\right)^2 - 1\right) - 3\tan\left(\dfrac{\text{atan}(x)}{3}\right)^2 + 18x\,\tan\left(\dfrac{\text{atan}(x)}{3}\right) + 16}{18}$$

```
Type: Union(Expression Integer, List Expression Integer)
```

Comparative Examples

In this section we present a few examples of some operations commonly done in symbolic computation. The examples are presented with all the declarations or environment settings which are necessary to perform the operations. We have used the following environments:

Maple V R5	Sun Sparcstation
Mathematica 3.0	Sun Sparcstation
Reduce 3.6	Sun Sparcstation
Macsyma 420.0	Sun Sparcstation
Axiom 2.l	Sun Sparcstation
Derive 3.06	386-based DOS system
MuPAD 1.4	Sun Sparcstation
TI-92	—

For each product we have used a version available in 1998. In the Derive examples menu options are denoted by square brackets. Thus, [A]uthor means the menu option **A** (Author).

LIMIT COMPUTATION

The answer of $\lim_{x \to \infty} (e + 1)^{x^2}/e^x$ is obviously ∞, but L'Hospital's rule will fail to compute the limit:

Maple	`> limit( (exp(1)+1)^(x^2)/exp(1)^x, x=infinity);` $\qquad\qquad\qquad\qquad\qquad$ infinity

Mathematica	`In [1]:= Limit [(E+1)^(x^2)/E^x, x → Infinity]`
	`Out [1]:= ∞`
	Note: To obtain this result the Mathematica `Calculus/Limit.m` package must be used.

Reduce	returns the limit unevaluated,
Macsyma	`(c1) limit( (%e+1)^(x^2)/%e^x, x, inf);` `(d1)` $\qquad\qquad\qquad\qquad\qquad$ infinity

Axiom	`(1) -> ; limit(exp(x**2*log(1 + exp 1)) / exp x, x = %plusInfinity)`
	`    (1)   + infinity`
	$\qquad\qquad$ `Type: Union(OrderedCompletion Expression Integer,...)`

Derive	`[A]uthor (<ALT>-e + 1)^(x^2)/<ALT>-e^x`
	`[C]alculus[L]imit <CR> <CR> inf <TAB> <space>`
	`[S]implify`
	$\qquad\qquad\qquad$ ∞

MuPAD	`>> limit( (E+1)^(x^2)/E^x, x=infinity);` $\qquad\qquad\qquad\qquad\qquad$ infinity
TI-92	returns *undefined*

SERIES EXPANSION

The series for $\tan(\sin(x))$ and $\sin(\tan(x))$ agree through three terms. Compute the series expansion of the difference up to order 13:

Maple	`> series(sin(tan(x))-tan(sin(x)),x,14);` $$-\frac{1}{30} x^7 - \frac{29}{756} x^9 - \frac{1913}{75600} x^{11} - \frac{95}{7392} x^{13} + O(x^{14})$$
Mathematica	`In[1]:= Series[Sin[Tan[x]]-Tan[Sin[x]], {x, 0, 13}]` $$\text{Out[1]}= \frac{-x^7}{30} - \frac{29\, x^9}{756} - \frac{1913\, x^{11}}{75600} - \frac{95\, x^{13}}{7392} + O[x]^{14}$$

Reduce	`1: load taylor;`
	`2: taylor(sin(tan(x))-tan(sin(x)),x,0,13);`
	
	$$-\frac{1}{30}*x^7 - \frac{29}{756}*x^9 - \frac{1913}{75600}*x^{11} - \frac{95}{7392}*x^{13} + O(x^{14})$$

Macsyma	`(c1) taylor(sin(tan(x))-tan(sin(x)),x,0,13);` `(d1)/T/` $$-\frac{x^7}{30} - \frac{29\, x^9}{756} - \frac{1913\, x^{11}}{75600} - \frac{95\, x^{13}}{7392} + \ldots$$

Axiom	`(1) -> series(sin(tan x) - tan(sin x), x=0,13)`
	`      (1)`
	
	$$-\frac{1}{30} x^7 - \frac{29}{756} x^9 - \frac{1913}{75600} x^{11} - \frac{95}{7392} x^{13} + O(x^{14})$$
	
	`Type: UnivariatePuiseuxSeries(Expression Integer,x,0)`

| Derive | ```
[A]uthor sin tan x - tan sin x
[C]alculus[T]aylor <CR> <CR> 13
[S]implify
``` |

$$- \frac{95\ x^{13}}{7392} - \frac{1913\ x^{11}}{75600} - \frac{29\ x^9}{756} - \frac{x^7}{30}$$

| MuPAD | `>> series(sin(tan(x))-tan(sin(x)),x,14);` |

$$- \frac{x^7}{30} - \frac{29\ x^9}{756} - \frac{1913\ x^{11}}{75600} - \frac{95\ x^{13}}{7392} + O(x^{14})$$

| TI-92 | ran out of memory |

LINEAR ODE

Solve the second-order differential equation

$$y''(x) + 2y'(x) + y(x) = \cos(x)$$

| Maple | ```
> dgl := diff(y(x),x$2)+2*diff(y(x),x)+y(x)=cos(x):
> dsolve(dgl,y(x));
``` |

$$y(x) = 1/2\ \sin(x) + \_C1\ \exp(-x) + \_C2\ \exp(-x)\ x$$

| Mathematica | `In[1]:= DSolve[y"[x] + 2 y'[x] + y[x] == Cos[x], y[x], x]` |

$$Out[1]= \left\{\left\{y[x] \to \frac{C[1] + x\ C[2] + \dfrac{E^x\ Sin[x]}{2}}{E^x}\right\}\right\}$$

| Reduce | ```
1: load odesolve;
2: odesolve(df(y(x),x,x)+2*df(y(x),x)+y(x)=cos(x),y(x),x);
``` |

$$\{y(x) = \frac{2*arbconst(2)*x + 2*arbconst(1) + e^x*\sin(x)}{2*e^x}\}$$

| Macsyma | ```
(c1) deq:'diff(y,x,2)+2*'diff(y,x)+y=cos(x);
(c2) ode(deq,y,x);
``` |

$$(d2) \qquad y = \frac{\sin(x)}{2} + (\%k2\ x + \%k1)\ \%e^{-x}$$

| Axiom | ```
(1) ->y := operator y;
(2) ->deq := differentiate(y x, x, 2) +
              2 * differentiate(y x, x) + y x = cos x;
(3) ->solve(deq, y, x)
``` |

$$(3) \quad [particular = \frac{\sin(x)}{2}, basis = [\%e^{-x}, x\%e^{-x}]]$$

$$Type: Union(Record(particular: Expression\ Integer, basis: List\ Expression\ Integer),...)$$

| Derive | ```
[T]ransfer[L]oad[U]tility ODE2
[A]uthor LIN2_POS(2,1,cos(x),x)
[S]implify
``` |

$$\hat{e}^{-x}\ (c2\ x + c1) + \frac{SIN(x)}{2}$$

| MuPAD | `>> dgl := y"(x)+2*y'(x)+y(x)=cos(x)` |

$$\left(\frac{\sin(x)}{2} + C1\ \exp(-x) + C2\ x\ \exp(-x) \right)$$

| TI-92 | cannot do differential equations |

SYMBOLIC INTEGRATION

Integrate $(x+1)/(x^2+x+1)$.

Maple

```
> int((x+1)/(x^2+x+1),x);
```

$$1/2 \ln(x^2 + x + 1) + 1/3 \; 3^{1/2} \arctan(1/3 \; (2\,x + 1)\; 3^{1/2})$$

Mathematica

```
In[1] := Integrate[(x+1)/(x^2+x+1),x]
```

$$\text{Out[1]} = \frac{\text{ArcTan}\left(\dfrac{1 + 2\,x}{\text{Sqrt}[3]}\right)}{\text{Sqrt}[3]} + \frac{\text{Log}[1 + x + x^2]}{2}$$

Reduce

```
1: int((x+1)/(x^2+x+1),x);
```

$$\frac{2*\text{sqrt}(3)*\text{atan}\left(\dfrac{2*x + 1}{\text{sqrt}(3)}\right) + 3*\log(x^2 + x + 1)}{6}$$

Macsyma

```
(c1) integrate( (x+1)/(x^2+x+1), x);
```

$$(\text{d1}) \qquad \frac{\log(x^2 + x + 1)}{2} + \frac{\text{atan}\left(\dfrac{2\,x + 1}{\text{sqrt}(3)}\right)}{\text{sqrt}(3)}$$

Axiom

```
(1) -> integrate((x+1)/(x**2+x+1), x)
```

$$(1) \qquad \frac{\sqrt{3} \, \log(x^2 + x + 1) + 2\,\text{atan}\left(\dfrac{(2x + 1)\sqrt{3}}{3}\right)}{2\sqrt{3}}$$

Type: Union(Expression Integer,...)

Derive

```
[A]uthor (x+1)/(x^2+x+1)
[C]alculus/[I]ntegrate <CR> <CR> <CR>
[S]implify
```

$$\frac{\text{sqrt}(3) \; \text{ATAN}\left(\dfrac{\text{sqrt}(3)*(2\,x + 1)}{3}\right)}{3} - \frac{\text{LN}(\,x^2 + x + 1)}{2}$$

MuPAD

```
int((x+1)/(x^2+x+1),x);
```

$$\frac{\ln((x + 1/2)^2 + 3/4)}{2} - \frac{3^{1/2} \; \text{atan}\left(\dfrac{3^{1/2}}{2\;(x + 1/2)}\right)}{3}$$

TI-92

$$\int (\,(x+1)/(x^2+x+1),x)$$

$$\frac{\ln(|x^2 + x + 1|)}{2} + \frac{\sqrt{3} \cdot \tan^{-1}\left(\dfrac{\sqrt{3} \cdot (2 \cdot x + 1)}{3}\right)}{3}$$

RECURRENCE EQUATION

Solve the recurrence equation $s_n = -3s_{n-1} - 2s_{n-2}$.

Maple

```
> rsolve(s(n) = -3*s(n-1) - 2*s(n-2), s(n));
```

$$(2\,s(0) + s(1))\;(-1)^n + (-\,s(0) - s(1))\;(-2)^n$$

Mathematica	```In[1]:= <<DiscreteMath/RSolve.m```
	```In[2]:= RSolve[{s[n] == -2 s[-2 + n] - 3 s[-1 + n],``` ``` s[0]==s0,s[1]==s1},s[n],n]```
	```Out[2]= {{s[n] -> (-2)^n (-s0 - s1) + (-1)^n (2 s0 + s1)}}```
Reduce	is unable to solve recurrence equations
Macsyma	```(c1) load(differ);``` ```(c2) differenceq(s[n+2]+3*s[n+1]+2*s[n]=0, s[n]);```
	(d2) $\qquad s_n = (s_1 + 2\ s_0\ )\ (-\ 1)^n + (-\ s_1 - s_0\ )\ (-\ 2)^n$
Axiom	is unable to solve recurrence equations

Derive	```[T]ransfer[L]oad[U]tility RECUREQN```
	```[A]uthor LIN2_CCF_POS(3,2,0,n)```
	```[S]implify```

	$2^n\ c2\ \cos(n\ \pi) + c1\ \cos(\ n\ \pi)$
	$+\ i*(2^n c2\ \sin(\ n\ \pi) + c1\ \sin(\ n\ \pi)\ )$
MuPAD	is unable to solve recurrence equations
TI-92	is unable to solve recurrence equations

PROGRAMMING

To illustrate the similarities and differences in the programming languages associated with the respective computer algebra system covered, we include a procedure definition of the algorithm to compute the square free decomposition of a given polynomial $a(x)$. This is a coding of Yun's algorithm as presented in Knuth (1997). The algorithm involves the computation of a polynomial sequence generated from a polynomial a and its derivative with respect to x.

◆ Maple

```
sqrfree := proc(a, x) local d, v, w, i, t, g;
        if gcd(a, diff(a,x), v, w) = 1 then RETURN(a) fi;
        t := 1; d := w - diff(v,x);
        for i while d<>0 do
                g := gcd(v, d, 'v', 'w');
                d := w - diff(v,x);
                t := t * g^i
        od;
        t * v^i
end;
```

◆ Mathematica

```
SqrFree[a_, x_] :=
        Block[ {t = 1, g, v, d = D[a,x], i = 1},
                If[ (g = PolynomialGCD[a, d]) === 1,
                        Return[a]];
                v = Cancel[a/g]; d = Cancel[d/g]-D[v,x];
                While[d =!= 0,
                        g = PolynomialGCD[v, d];
```

◆ Reduce

```
PROCEDURE sqrfree (a,x);
BEGIN  SCALAR d,v,ii,tt,g;
        on exp;
        if ( g := gcd(a, tt := df(a, x)) ) = 1 then RETURN a;
        d := tt/g - df(v:=a/g, x);
        ii := 1;
        tt := 1;
        while (d NEQ 0) do
```

```
        <<
                on exp;
                        g := gcd(v, d);
                        d := d/g - df(v:=v/g, x);
                off exp;
                tt := tt * g ** ii;
                ii := ii + 1;
        >>;
        RETURN(tt * v ** ii);
    END;
```

◆ Macsyma

```
sqrfree(a,x) : block([d,v,i,t,g],
        if (g:gcd(a, t:diff(a,x))) = 1 then RETURN(a) ,
        d : quotient(t,g) - diff(quotient(a,g),x),
        t : 1,
        for i:1 while d<>0 do
        (       g : gcd(v, d),
                v : quotient(v,g),
                d : quotient(d,g) - diff(v,x),
                t : t * g^i
        ),
        t * v^i);
```

◆ Axiom

```
sqrfree(a x) ==
        g := extendedEuclidean(a, differentiate(a,x))
        unit?(g.generator) => a
        t := 1
        d := g.coef2 - differentiate(g.coef1,x)
        for i in 1.. while d ^= 0 repeat
                g := extendedEuclidean(g.coef1,d)
                d := g.coef2 - differentiate(g.coef1, x)
                r := r * (g.generator) * monomial(1,x,i)
        r * g.coef2 ^ i
```

◆ MuPAD

```
sqrfree := proc(a,x) local b,c,d,v,w,i,t,g;
begin
        b := diff(a,x); c := gcd(a,b);
        if c=1 then RETURN(a) end_if;
        v := divide(a,c)[1]; w := divide(b,c)[1];
        t := 1; d := w-diff(v,x); i := 1;
        while d<>0 do
                g = gcd(v,d);
                        v = Cancel[v/g]; d = Cancel[d/g]-D[v,x];
                        t *= g^i;
                        i++
                ];
                t v^i
        ];
                        v := divide(v,g)[1]; w := divide(d,g)[1];
                        d := w-diff(v,x);
                        t := t*g^i; i := i+1;
        end_while;
        t*v^i;
        end_proc;
```

◆ TI-92

Even though the TI-92 has a programming language, the user does not have access to elementary polynomial operations such as computing greatest common divisors or polynomial remainders. For this reason we failed to code the square-free decomposition example using the TI-92.

Acknowledgments

We wish to acknowledge R. Corless for his assistance with Derive, K. Geddes and B. Char for the `sqrfree` codes, and M. Bronstein and M. Monagan for valuable discussions.

Bibliography

1992. Jenks, R., and Sutor, R. *AXIOM: The Scientific Computation System*. New York: Springer-Verlag.

1994. Rich, A., Rich, J., and Stoutemyer, D. R. *DERIVE Version 3 User Manual*. Honolulu, HI: Software Warehouse, Inc.

1994. Wester, M. "A Review of CAS Mathematical Capabilities," Computer Algebra Nederland Nieuwsbrief, **13**, 41–48.

1995. Hearn, A. C. *REDUCE User's Manual*, Version 3.6. Report CP 78, RAND.

1995. Macsyma, Inc. *Macsyma User's Guide*, 2nd Ed. Macsyma, Inc.: 20 Academy Street, Arlington, MA.

1996. Fuchssteiner, B. *et al. MuPAD User's Manual*. Chichester, New York: John Wiley.

1996. Waterloo Maple Inc. *Maple V Learning Guide*. New York: Springer-Verlag.

1996. Wolfram, S. *The Mathematica Book*, 3rd Ed. Cambridge: Wolfram Media/Cambridge University Press.

1997. Knuth, D. E. *The Art of Computer Programming: Seminumerical Algorithms*, 3rd Ed., vol. 2. Reading, MA: Addison-Wesley.

Gaston H. Gonnet, Dominik W. Gruntz, and Laurent Bernardin

COMPUTER

See ANALOG COMPUTER; and DIGITAL COMPUTER.

COMPUTER ANIMATION

For articles on related topics *see* ARTIFICIAL LIFE; COMPUTER-AIDED DESIGN/COMPUTER-AIDED MANUFACTURING; COMPUTER ART; COMPUTER GAMES; COMPUTER GRAPHICS; ENTERTAINMENT INDUSTRY, COMPUTERS IN THE; IMAGE PROCESSING; SCIENTIFIC APPLICATIONS; SCIENTIFIC VISUALIZATION; SIMULATION; and VIRTUAL REALITY.

Animated images are almost magical in their ability to capture our imagination. By telling a compelling story, astounding with special effects, or mesmerizing with abstract motion, *animation* can infuse a sequence of inert images with the illusion of motion and life. Creating this illusion, either by hand or with the assistance of computer software, is not easy. Each individual image, or *frame*, in the animated sequence must blend seamlessly with the other images to create smooth and continuous motion that flows through time.

Traditionally, animation has been created by drawing images at certain key points in the action. These images, known as *keyframes*, outline the motion for the sequence. Later, the images between the keyframes are filled in to complete the sequence, in a process called *in-betweening*. For example, to keyframe hitting a ball, the animator would draw several key moments in the sequence such as the impact of the bat on the ball and the follow-through of the swing. The remaining images would be filled in later, perhaps by a different animator.

The most basic computer animation tools assist the process of hand animation by automatically interpolating between the keyframes of images or models. Animation tools have also been developed to put together or *composite* multiple layers of an animated scene in much the same way that layers of *cels* are used in traditional animation. Other, more powerful, techniques make use of computer graphics algorithms that render the images from geometric descriptions of the scene. These techniques change the task from drawing sequences of images by hand to using computer tools effectively to specify how the images should change over time.

A wide variety of techniques are used in the process of creating a complex computer animation such as *Toy Story* (Fig. 1 on Color Page CP-3). These techniques can be grouped into two main classes: two-dimensional (2D) and three-dimensional (3D). Although there is some overlap between the two classes, 2D techniques tend to focus on image manipulation while 3D techniques usually build virtual worlds in which characters and objects move and interact.

Two-Dimensional Animation

The impact of 2D techniques can be as spectacular as the addition of ET to a shot of the moon or as subtle as the removal of the guide wires used to suspend Superman. These techniques contribute a great deal to computer animation by providing the tools used for blending or morphing between images, embedding graphical objects in video footage, or creating abstract patterns from mathematical equations.

Morphing refers to animations where an image or model of one object is metamorphosed into another. In Michael Jackson's music video *Black or White*, the animators at Pacific Data Images created morphs between people with strikingly different facial characteristics. This work is remarkable because the faces in the intermediate images appear natural and human-like. Unfortunately, morphing is labor intensive because the key elements of each image must be specified by hand.

Embedding graphical objects into an existing image allows new elements to be added to a scene. For example, the ghosts in *Casper* and many of the dinosaurs in *Jurassic Park* were computer generated and then composited into existing footage (*see* Fig. 2 on Color Page CP-3). Objects can also be removed from a scene. The bus in *Speed* flies over a gap in a bridge that was created by digitally removing a span from footage of an intact bridge. Both the processes of embedding and of removing objects are made more difficult if the camera is moving because the alteration must be consistent with the changing viewpoint.

Mathematical equations are often used to create abstract motion sequences. When the values of the mathematical functions are mapped into color space and varied with time, the motion of the underlying structures can be quite beautiful. Fractals (*q.v.*), such as those shown in the portion of the color section pertaining to that article, are a well-known example of functions that create attractive patterns.

Morphing and the generation of abstract images from mathematical equations can be generalized for use in 3D. All of these 2D techniques can either be used on their own to create an animation or as a post-processing step to enhance images generated using other 2D or 3D techniques.

Three-Dimensional Animation

With 3D techniques, the animator constructs a virtual world in which characters and objects move and interact. Using a virtual 3D world to generate images for an animation involves three steps: *modeling*, animating, and rendering. Briefly stated, modeling deals with the task of setting up the elements in a scene and describing each of those elements, while *rendering* deals with the process of converting the descriptions of objects and their motions into images. Techniques for modeling and rendering are, for the most part, independent of their role in the animation process and more information on them can be found under COMPUTER GRAPHICS. There are, however, some modifications that must be made to the modeling or rendering procedures if they are to be used for animation, and these are described below.

MODELING REQUIREMENTS

To animate motion, the user needs both a static description of an object and information about how the object can move. One common way to specify this additional information is to use an *articulated model* such as the one shown in Fig. 3. An articulated model is a collection of objects connected by joints in a hierarchical, tree-like structure. The location of an object is determined by the location of the objects above it in the hierarchy. For example, the motion of the elbow joint in a human model will affect not only the position of the lower arm but also the position of the hand and fingers. The object at the top of the hierarchy, or the root of the tree, can be moved arbitrarily, affecting the position and orientation of the entire model.

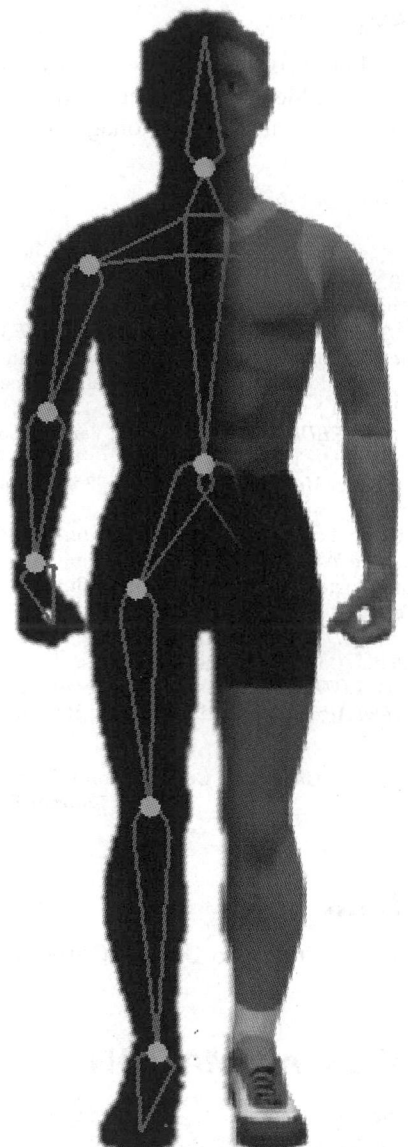

Figure 3. An articulated model of a human male: the structure of the joint hierarchy is shown on the left while the right side shows the graphical model used for rendering.

A second type of model used in animation is a *particle system* or collection of points. The motion of the particles through space is determined by a set of rules. The laws of physics often provide a basis for the motion so that the particles will fall under gravity and collide with other objects in the environment. Systems that are well modeled by particle systems include water spray, smoke, and even flocks of birds.

Deformable objects are a third type of model and include objects that do not have well-defined articulated joints but still have too much structure to be represented easily with a particle system. Because of the broad nature of this class, there are several fundamentally different ways to represent deformable objects including spring–mass lattices, volumetric models, and surface representations. Water, hair, clothing, and fish are among the systems that have been successfully modeled as deformable objects.

While each of these model types can be used to describe a wide variety of objects, complex systems often require *hybrid models* that combine two or more types. This approach allows each part of the system to be modeled by the most appropriate technique. The image in Fig. 4 (*see* Color Page CP-4) shows a diver entering a swimming pool. The diver is an articulated model, the pool is a deformable model, and the spray is a particle system.

RENDERING REQUIREMENTS

Motion blur is a rendering technique that is required for animation, but not for most still images. Without motion blur, rapid motion of an object in a series of frames creates unpleasant strobing effects or causes objects, such as wheels, to appear to move in the wrong direction. To solve this problem, a fast-moving object can be rendered in several of the positions it had during the period of time represented by each frame. This rendering technique creates a blurred representation of the object and mimics the exposure of film by a camera shutter that is open for short period of time. Motion blur is actually a form of *anti-aliasing* (a technique for smoothing rough edges) that occurs over time instead of space and is often called *temporal anti-aliasing*.

MOTION GENERATION

The task of specifying the motion of an animated object to a computer is surprisingly difficult and even animating a simple object like a bouncing ball can present problems. In part, this task is difficult because humans are very skilled at observing motion and can quickly pick out motion that is unnatural or implausible. In many situations, the animator must be able to specify subtle details of the motion in order to convey the personality of a character or the mood of an animation in a compelling fashion.

A number of techniques have been developed for specifying motion but all the available tools require a tradeoff between automation and control. *Keyframing* allows fine control but does little to insure the naturalness of the result automatically. *Procedural methods* and *motion capture* generate motion in an automatic fashion but offer little control over the fine details.

Keyframing. Borrowing its name from the traditional hand animation technique, keyframing requires that the animator specify key positions for the objects being animated. The computer then interpolates to determine the positions for the in-between frames. The interpolation algorithm is an important factor in the appearance of the final motion. The simplest form of interpolation, *linear interpolation*, often results in motion that appears to be jerky because the velocities of the moving objects are discontinuous. To correct this problem, better interpolation techniques, such as *splines* (*q.v.*), are used to produce smoothly interpolated curves.

The specification of keyframes can be made easier with techniques such as *inverse kinematics*. Inverse kinematics aids in the placement of articulated models by allowing the animator to specify the position of one object and then have the positions of the objects above it in the articulated hierarchy computed automatically. For example, if the hand and torso of an animated character must be in particular locations, inverse kinematics allows the computer to calculate the angle at the elbow and shoulder. Commercial animation packages include inverse kinematics and interpolation routines designed specifically for animating people. These tools take into consideration factors such as maintaining balance, joint angle limitations, and collisions between the limbs and the body.

While these techniques make animation easier, keyframed animation still requires that the animator understand in intimate detail how the animated object should behave and have the talent to express that behavior in keyframes.

Procedural methods. Current technology is not capable of generating motion automatically for arbitrary objects; however, it is possible to build algorithms for specific types of motion or objects. These techniques are called *procedural methods* because a computer procedurally follows the steps in an algorithm to generate the motion. Procedural methods have two main advantages over keyframing techniques: they make it easy to generate a family of similar motions, and they can be used for complex systems that would be too difficult to animate by hand, such as particle systems or flexible surfaces.

Physically-based simulation refers to a class of procedural methods that make use of the laws of physics, or an approximation to those laws, to generate motion. Simulated motion is inherently realistic and for many applications that is an advantage. Unfortunately, building a new simulation is sometimes a difficult process requiring a thorough understanding of the relevant physical laws. Once a simulation has been designed, however, an animator may use it without knowing how the internals of the simulation work.

Simulations can be divided into two categories: *passive* and *active*. Passive systems have no internal energy source and can move only when an external force acts on them. Passive systems are well suited to physically-based simulation because once the physical laws have been encoded correctly and the initial conditions of the animation have been specified, the method is ready for use. Pools of water, clothing, hair, and leaves have been animated using passive simulations.

Active systems have an internal source of energy and can move on their own. People, animals, and robots are examples of active systems. These systems are more difficult to model because in addition to implementing the physical laws, the behavior of the simulated muscles or motors must be specified. An additional algorithm, a *control system*, must be designed to allow the model to walk, run, or perform any other action. For example, a control system for standing must contain laws that specify how the hips and knees should move to keep the figure balanced when one arm is extended out to the side. Control systems can be designed by hand for figures of the complexity of a three-dimensional model of a human figure or, for slightly simpler systems, they can be designed automatically using optimization (*q.v.*) techniques. Although the design of the control system is not a fully understood problem, once a particular control system has been built, an animator can use it without understanding the internal details. Fig. 5 (*see* Color Page CP-4) shows a human figure running. The runner is an active simulation and a control system generates the running motion. The runner's clothes are a passive cloth simulation.

Procedural methods can also be used to generate motion for groups of objects that move together. Flocks of birds, schools of fish, herds of animals, or crowds of people are all situations where algorithms for *group behaviors* can be used. In Walt Disney's animated version of *The Hunchback of Notre Dame*, most of the crowd scenes were computer animated using procedural models. This animated film is particularly impressive because computer and hand animation are seamlessly combined to create very detailed scenes.

Motion capture. A third technique for generating motion, *motion capture*, employs special sensors, called *trackers*, to record the motion of a human performer. The recorded data is then used to generate the motion for an animation. Alternatively, special puppets with joint angle sensors can be used in place of the human performer.

Motion capture is a very popular technique because of the relative ease with which many human motions can be recorded. However, a number of problems prevent motion capture from being an ideal solution for all applications. First, accurately measuring the motion of the human body is tricky because trackers attached to skin or clothing shift as the performer moves, creat-

ing errors in the recorded data. Furthermore, if the object used to generate the recorded motion and the graphical object have different dimensions, the animation may have noticeable flaws. For example, if the actor's arms were resting on a real table, the arms of the graphical actor might be suspended in the air or sunk into the table.

The technology used for motion capture makes it difficult to capture some motions. One class of sensors are magnetic but metal in the environment creates noise in the data. Another class of sensors requires that the actor be connected to the computer by an "umbilical cord," thereby restricting the actor's motion. All sensing technologies have a relatively small field of view, limiting the kinds of actions that can be captured.

In spite of these difficulties, motion capture is a widely used technique. Much of the motion used in commercial animation is generated by using captured data and "tweaking" the results by hand.

Bibliography

1984. Thomas, F., and Johnston, O. *Disney Animation: The Illusion of Life*. New York: Abbeville Press.
1991. Watt, A., and Watt, M. *Advanced Rendering and Animation Techniques: Theory and Practice*. Reading, MA: Addison-Wesley.
1995. Foley, J. D., van Dam, A., Feiner, S. K., and Hughes, J. F. *Computer Graphics, Principles and Practice*, 2nd Ed. Reading, MA: Addison-Wesley.
1996. Kerlow, I. V. *The Art of 3-D Computer Animation and Imaging*. New York: Van Nostrand Reinhold.
1996. Taylor, R. *The Encyclopedia of Animation Techniques*. London: Quarto.
1997. Gianbruno, M. *3D Graphics and Animation: From Starting Up to Standing Out*. Indianapolis, IN: New-Riders Publishing.

Jessica K. Hodgins and James F. O'Brien

COMPUTER ARCHITECTURE

For articles on related subjects *see* ADDRESSING; ARITHMETIC-LOGIC UNIT; BUS; CACHE MEMORY; CAPABILITY-BASED ADDRESSING; CENTRAL PROCESSING UNIT; CHANNEL; COMPUTERS, MULTIPLE ADDRESS; DIGITAL COMPUTER; GENERAL REGISTER; INDEX REGISTER; INPUT–OUTPUT OPERATIONS; INSTRUCTION DECODING; INSTRUCTION-LEVEL PARALLELISM; INSTRUCTION SET; INTERRUPT; MEMORY; MEMORY HIERARCHY; MEMORY-MAPPED I/O; MICROPROGRAMMING; NETWORK ARCHITECTURE; PARALLEL PROCESSING: ARCHITECTURES; PROGRAM COUNTER; REDUCED INSTRUCTION SET COMPUTER; REGISTER; and VON NEUMANN MACHINE.

Introduction

Computer architecture is an interdisciplinary field concerned with the physical or hardware structure of computer systems, the attributes of their various parts, and how these parts are interconnected. In the formative years of modern digital computer development

(1940s and 1950s), the principal disciplines of computer architecture were viewed as mathematics (notably algorithms, finite state machines, and digital arithmetic), physics (the behavior of materials), and electrical engineering (the design of electronic circuits and their organization into computer systems). The 1960s saw the introduction of semiconductor devices, which greatly enhanced performance at substantially lower cost. By the late 1960s, *operating systems* (*q.v.*) and other software components were seen to play a major role in system behavior. Mainstream computer designs also began to embody software-based techniques at very fundamental levels (such as microprogramming and virtual machines). With the advent of very large-scale integration (VLSI) in the early 1980s, semiconductor technology once again asserted its role as a major driver of designs. The mid- to late 1980s saw the widespread introduction of *workstations* (*q.v.*) and other computer systems whose functionality is strongly influenced by human interfaces (*see* USER INTERFACE) and effective use of *computer graphics* (*q.v.*). In the 1990s, there was a broad transition to networking, and thus another dimension was added to the interdisciplinary character of computer architecture.

For the purposes of this article, two fundamental aspects of computer architecture will be identified:

1. *System architecture*: the functional behavior and conceptual structure of a computer system as seen by the software developer (i.e. in terms of those characteristics affecting software design and development); and

2. *Implementation architecture*: those characteristics affecting the relative cost and performance of a computer system and that are of concern to the semiconductor designer or electronic engineer, such as logic design, memory bandwidth, and device technology.

The significance of this distinction is illustrated by the VAX series of computer systems (Fig. 1). The VAX series, made by Digital Equipment Corporation (*q.v.*), is a family of computers sharing a common system architecture—that is, software written for any model in the series will operate correctly (although at varying speeds) on any other model (with certain exceptions, mostly related to operating system code). In order for this to happen, the various members of the VAX family share the same instruction set, arithmetic registers, I/O methods, memory addressing mechanisms, and such. A single document (Leonard, 1987) is sufficient to allow one to write assembly language software, compilers, loaders, and most components of an operating system for any model in the series. Software written for the original VAX systems in the late 1970s can still be run on the VAX systems of today. (In certain instances, newer members of the series have extended the architecture in an *upward compatible* way—that is, software written for the older series can run on the newer ones, but not always vice versa.)

From an implementation standpoint, the VAX series spans a variety of technologies and a processing performance range in excess of 100 : 1. The original VAX system, the 11/780, had an effective execution speed of approximately 1 million instructions per second (1 MIPS). The VAX 9000 model 440, which has four processors, is described as having a relative speed of over 100 times that of the original 11/780. Several of the VAX models are shown in the figure, along with other ways in which they differ. One of the most interesting differences is the fact that, in some VAX models, portions of the instruction set are implemented in software rather than hardware.

More recently, we have seen the advent of computer families where the architecture is shared by a group of cooperating companies. The PowerPC architecture (Motorola, 1994) is a standard that several vendors support, each with its own implementation but sharing a common base of system and application software.

Model	VAX Station 3100	Micro VAX 3800	VAX 6000 460	VAX 9000 440
Relative processing performance	2.7	3.8	36	117
No. of processors	1	1	6	4
Maximum main memory	32 MB	64 MB	192 MB	512 MB
Cache size	1 KB	1 KB	2 KB/CPU	128 KB/CPU
Cache speed	90 ns	60 ns	28 ns	16 ns
I/O bus capacity	1.5 MB/sec	3.3 MB/sec	40 MB/sec	320 MB/sec

Figure 1. Various implementations of the VAX architecture.

Subsystems

The three major subsystems of a computer are the storage (which holds data), the processor (which operates on that data), and the input–output and communication subsystem (which transmits data to and from the external environment). We discuss each of these from both the system and implementation architecture perspectives. The classic von Neumann stored program machine (*see* VON NEUMANN MACHINE) design is assumed, except where otherwise noted.

STORAGE

The *storage*, or *memory*, of a stored program computer system contains both the data to be processed by the system and the instructions indicating what processing is to be performed. Three levels of storage are generally identified: registers, main memory or RAM (for random access memory), and secondary or auxiliary storage (*see* MEMORY: AUXILIARY). Table 1 indicates the general characteristics of each of these. Regardless of the level, the fundamental unit of digital computer storage is the *bit*, conceptually containing one of two distinct values: 0 or 1. Aggregates of bits are combined into larger units, such as *nibbles* (4 bits), *bytes* (8 bits) and *words* (anywhere from 16 to 64 bits or more). As a rule, the larger its word length, the more powerful the computer. Therefore, many have tended to classify computers by their word lengths. However, as discussed below, there are so many ways to define word length that it should never be the sole basis for classification.

Early computer systems organized memory as follows: bits were organized into fixed-length words, where each word was referenced as a unit by a single memory address, and the individual bits of a word were transferred as a group between a computer's main memory and its registers or secondary storage. Each word would contain a single instruction or datum. The *arithmetic-logic unit* would operate on one word of data at a time.

A contemporary computer, by contrast, might address data in groups of 8 bits, transfer data to registers in groups of 16 bits, transfer data to secondary storage in groups of 64 bits, operate arithmetically on data "words" of 32 bits, have variable-length instructions ranging from 16 to 48 bits, and use a 24-bit memory address. What, then, is the computer's word length? Today's most commonly accepted system architecture definition is the length of a typical arithmetic register. This is usually equal to the number of bits operated on in parallel by the arithmetic unit, and may or may not be equal to the number of bits needed to hold a single-precision integer number. The commonly accepted definition from an implementation architecture point of view is the number of bits transferred in parallel from the main memory to the processor, a quantity sometimes called the *data path*. However, if cache memories are used, this definition can be interpreted in at least two different ways. The main point is that word length can be a very misleading indicator of a computer's memory system architecture.

Registers. Registers were once the fastest and most expensive memory units in a computer. Today, due to advances in semiconductor technology, main memories and registers can be essentially equal in cost and performance, but their functions remain distinct. Registers are a computer's most frequently used memory units, playing a role in the execution of every instruction. They also tend to be few in number, both to enhance performance by keeping them physically "close" to the processing elements, and to make possible a shorter addressing scheme in the instruction format. Two fundamental categories of registers can be distinguished: registers that are directly accessible by application programs (and, therefore, are part of the system architecture), and registers that are not directly accessible from application software. The former generally hold data that are actively being processed by the computer's arithmetic and logic unit(s). The latter contain information that describe the current state of the computation process, and may vary with different implementations of the same architecture family.

The minimum complement of system architecture registers is essentially one: an arithmetic register or *accumulator* which serves to hold the intermediate results of computations or other data processing activities. (Although usually part of the system architecture, accumulators may be hidden from the software in some designs such as those using a *stack* (*q.v.*) for computation). Most current computers have multiple

Table 1.

Type	Access time	Number or capacity	Use
Registers	10–50 ns	1–4096	Data, status, control info, current instruction
Cache memory	10–100 ns	512 KB–16 MB	Frequently used instructions and data
Main memory	20–100 ns	64 MB–4 GB	Programs, data
Auxiliary memory	10–250 ms	100 MB–1 TB	Long-term storage

accumulators so that several intermediate results may be maintained. Other registers usually found in contemporary computers include a *status register*, indicating the current condition of the various hardware components and computational results; and a *program counter*, indicating the location in main memory of the next instruction to be executed. In addition to these, many computers have *index registers* for counting and for "pointing" into tables; *address* or *base registers*, containing addresses of blocks of main or secondary memory; a *stack pointer*, containing the address of a special block of registers or main memory, which is treated like a pushdown stack; and various *special-purpose registers*, whose functions depend on the details of the particular computer.

Registers that are part of the implementation architecture tend to vary substantially among various designs. The most common among these are an *instruction register*, containing the instruction currently being executed; a *memory address register*, containing the address of the memory cell currently being read to or written from main memory; a *memory data register*, containing the data being read from or written to main memory; and similar registers pertaining to secondary memory and peripheral devices.

A major architectural issue beyond the number, accessibility, and functions of registers is that of special-purpose versus *general registers*. In a special-purpose design, each register has a specific, narrow function, whereas in a general-purpose design, the registers may be used for a variety of purposes, as directed by the software. Real machines tend to have a mixture of both types, but none that are totally general in purpose. The flexibility of general-purpose designs is attractive from a software viewpoint, but it can impose penalties in implementation efficiency because all parts of the processor require data paths to the general register set. On the other hand, a general-purpose approach may be a necessity in designs where only a small number of registers can be accommodated. The structure and discipline imposed by special-purpose registers may have software benefits as well, and many computer designs aimed at supporting higher-level languages tend to depend heavily on restricted use of registers. Fig. 2 illustrates the use of both general-purpose and special-purpose registers in the National 16032 microprocessor, which was designed to support block-structured higher-level languages.

Main memory. The main memory contains programs and data that are ready for processing by the computer. It consists of a linear sequence of "words," each individually addressable and each capable of being read or overwritten. In some designs, different technologies will be used to implement different sections of memory. For example, a frequently used section may have higher speed memory than the others; or a section whose contents must survive power failures or should never be modified might be implemented with non-volatile *read-only memory* (ROM—*q.v.*), the contents of which cannot be altered. In recent years, the concept

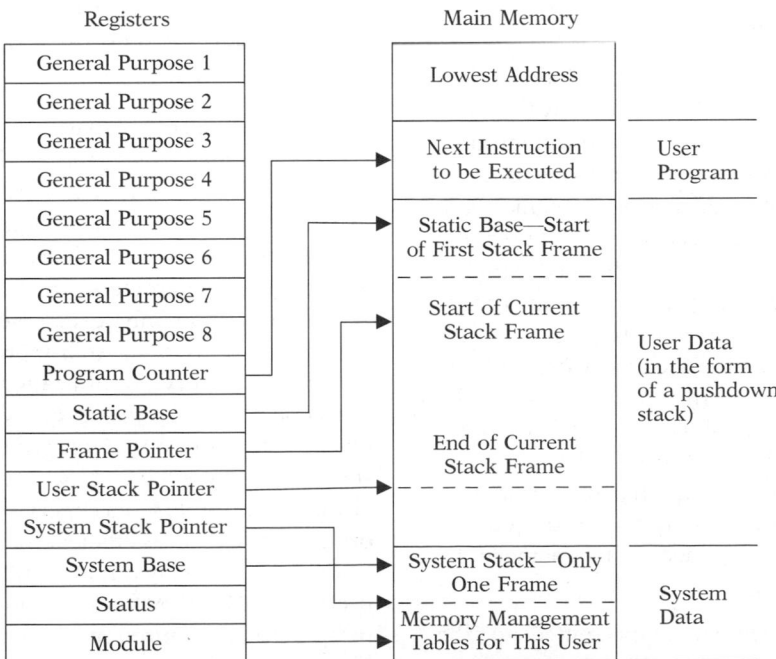

Figure 2. Register and memory structure of National 16032 microprocessor.

of different implementations for different parts of memory has been extended to include "memory" that can be addressed by the processor, but is not actually present as part of the physical main memory. We will discuss two of these concepts later on: *virtual memory* (*q.v.*) and *memory-mapped I/O* (*q.v.*).

The performance of a computer depends on the size and speed of its main memory. The total number of words in a memory is typically a configuration decision, with upper and lower limits determined by both the system and implementation architectures. The speed of memory is determined by implementation and cost factors, and is also influenced by size in the sense that very large memories must be physically more distant from the processor and therefore take longer to access. Numerous techniques have been used to increase the effective speed of a memory system. *Caching* and *interleaving* are probably the two most popular.

Caching is a technique whereby a small, high-speed memory is used to contain the most frequently used words from a larger, slower main memory. If the "hit ratio" (percentage of memory references found in the small *cache memory*—*q.v.*) is high, the average speed of the entire memory is substantially increased. A modern processor will typically have several cache memories, each thousands of words long. For example, a fast computer might have an instruction cache, so that frequently executed program segments are quickly accessible; a data cache, for frequently used data; and more exotic caches, such as address translation tables or other mechanisms designed to speed up frequent parts of the computation. Two-level caches can be found in high-performance systems.

With *interleaving* (*q.v.*), two or more independent memory systems are combined in such a way that they appear as one faster memory system. In one approach, all words with even addresses come from one memory bank, and all words with odd addresses come from another. When an even-numbered word is fetched, the next-higher odd-numbered word is fetched simultaneously from the other memory system, on the theory that it is likely to be the next word requested. If this guess is correct (as it often is), the next word's *access time* (*q.v.*) is essentially zero, thus nearly doubling the average memory access speed. Commercial computer systems have employed 4-way, 8-way, and even 16-way interleaving, with a variety of organization strategies. The higher degrees of interleaving are used predominantly in systems requiring access to memory by multiple parallel processors.

The form in which memory is presented to the software by the system architecture is sometimes called the *logical address space* or the *virtual address space*. In the most straightforward designs, the logical address space is a *linear* sequence of words or bytes containing the programs being executed and the data to be acted upon. It will differ from the physical memory (implementation) mainly in size (number of words), in some cases fewer and in other cases more. Two potential drawbacks of a linear approach are that a large memory may require a large address, which costs more to implement, makes instructions longer and generally makes processing slower (it takes n bits to address 2^n words); and that it may be awkward to partition a linear space into several parts that have different purposes.

To deal with these drawbacks, certain system architectures provide a more complex logical address space. In one design, the address space is perceived by software as a set of *pages*. Each page is a sequence of words; all pages are the same in size (usually a power of two); and each page has a distinct identification number or page number. A memory address consists of two parts: a page number and a word offset or displacement within the page (Fig. 3b). There may or may not be an implied spatial relationship between consecutively numbered pages.

Another approach is the *segment* design, in which there are several independently numbered blocks called segments, but with no requirement that they all be the same size. This permits each software module to be placed in whatever size segment is most suitable. Segment and page designs may be combined so that each segment contains several pages and the size of a segment is a multiple of the page size. Other concepts of logical address space have been discussed in the literature, but are only occasionally found in mainstream computers.

There are several other reasons for having a structured *virtual memory* (*q.v.*), rather than one large linear sequence. From a software viewpoint, a major objective is to provide a means of organizing programs and data according to their characteristics, such as type (instructions, characters, real numbers, integers), access rules (read-only, execute-only, read and write), ownership (if two or more programs are simultaneously in memory), or utilization (all data used during the same phase of a process may be grouped into one block). *Object-oriented programming* (*q.v.*) can be supported very effectively with a properly structured virtual memory. From a supervisory standpoint, memory structure enables efficient management of memory resources, especially among multiple tasks or multiple users (*see* MULTITASKING). From an implementation perspective, structured memory may allow efficiencies in memory system design, such as placement of high-speed memory devices in the most frequently used

Translation technique

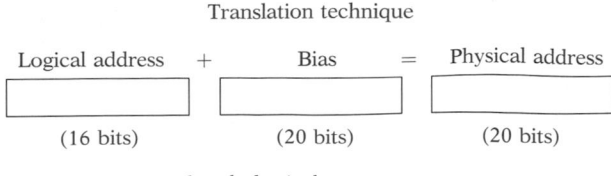

Logical address	+	Bias	=	Physical address
(16 bits)		(20 bits)		(20 bits)

Logical and physical memory structure

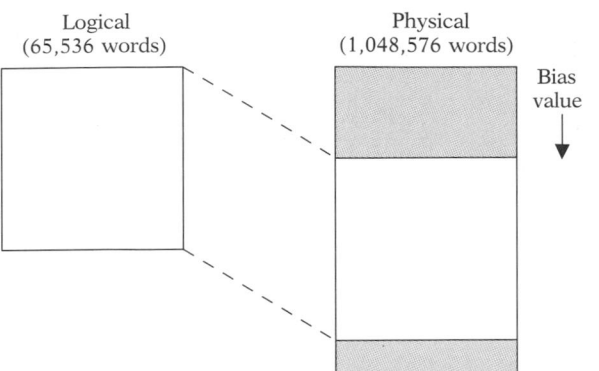

Figure 3(a). Biased memory mapping (with sample values).

segments, convenient schemes for protection against unauthorized access, or (via memory mapping) may permit a small computer to support more memory than can be conveniently addressed with one word.

Memory mapping. Memory mapping is the translation between the logical address space and the physical memory. The objectives of memory mapping are (1) to translate from logical to physical address (where these are different), (2) to aid in memory protection (*q.v.*), and (3) to enable better management of memory resources. Mapping is important to computer performance, both in a local sense (how long it takes to execute an instruction) and in a global sense (how long it takes to run a given set of programs). In effect, each time a program presents a logical memory address and requests that the corresponding memory word be accessed, the mapping mechanism must translate that address into an appropriate physical memory location. The simpler this translation, the lower the implementation cost and the higher the performance of the individual memory reference. However, more capable translation mechanisms permit protection of memory segments from unauthorized access and/or facilitate dynamic rearrangement of objects in physical memory. These enable efficiencies in the programming, debugging, and supervisory phases of computing, which may far outweigh the cost of slower individual instruction execution times.

Although there are many techniques of memory mapping, there are two fundamental situations to be handled: when the logical address space is smaller than the physical address space (common on microcontrollers, microprocessors, and older mini- and mainframe computers), mapping is needed to gain access to all of physical memory; and when the logical address space is larger than the physical address space, mapping is used to insure that each logical address actually used corresponds to a physical memory cell. The latter situation is discussed below, under "Virtual Memory," although virtual memory can also be used with small logical address spaces.

The size of the logical address space is determined by the number of bits in a memory address. Typically, the size of an address is limited by the word length of the computer. On a typical 1980s vintage computer with a 16-bit word, only 2^{16} or about 65,000 words could be addressed. Technology now permits such systems to be attached physically to many times this much memory, but there is no direct way to address it without redesigning the instruction set. Thus, the primary purpose of a memory mapping mechanism on such a system is to enable the logical address space to be assigned to a desired portion of a larger physical address space. Three such methods are illustrated in Fig. 3: relocation, paging, and segmentation. In the relocation scheme, the contents of a *bias* register are added to each logical memory address to produce a physical address (Fig. 3a). The effect is to offset the program by the biased amount in physical memory. Several different programs can coexist in the same physical memory without overlap by assigning different bias values to each of them.

In paging, the logical address space is divided into a set of equal-sized blocks called *pages*, and each is mapped onto a block of physical memory (called a *page frame*). The effect is similar to that of biasing, except that the program is broken into several separately biased pieces (pages), and each page must begin at a page frame boundary in physical memory. The primary advantage of paging is that it allows a contiguous logical address space to be split into several non-contiguous physical frames (Fig. 3b). This makes memory management more flexible and also permits sharing of some of a program's pages among multiple processes without complete overlap of physical addresses. This scheme may be faster than the bias technique because it requires only a concatenation of two addresses instead of an addition to form the physical address. However, the page map file requires more register bits than the bias register. The page map file is often kept in a cache memory.

Segmenting is somewhat like a combination of biasing and paging. It breaks the logical address space into several blocks, but does not require them to be of any particular size or to be mapped into any particular physical frames. Physical addresses are obtained by

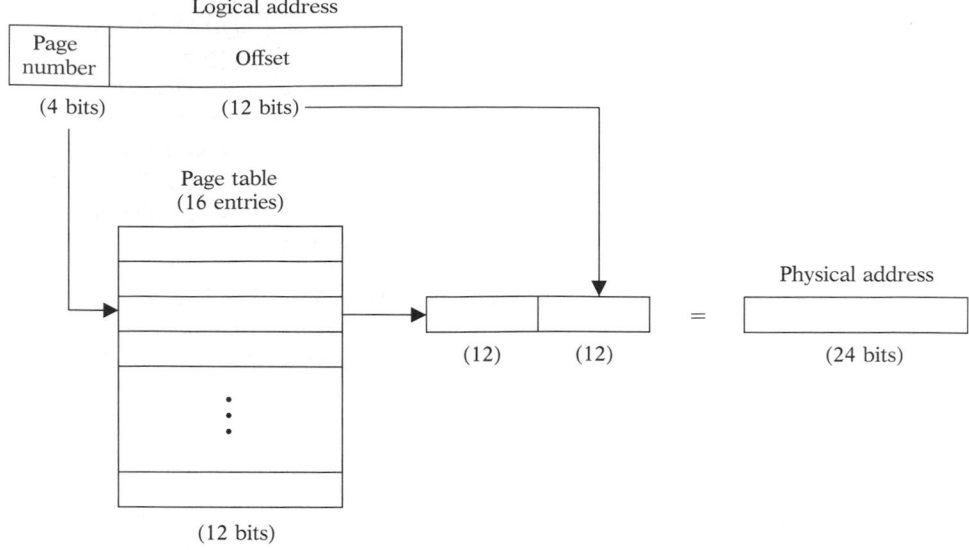

Translation technique

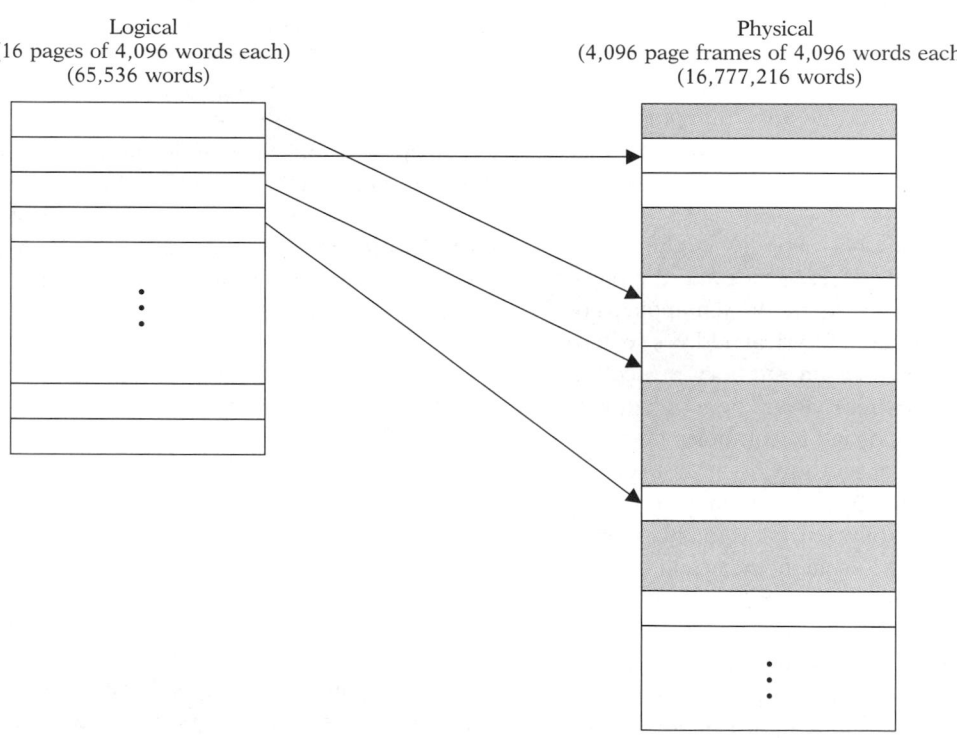

Logical and physical memory structure

Figure 3(b). Paged memory mapping (with sample values).

biasing the individual segments. As might be expected, this approach is the most flexible and also the most costly, both in hardware and performance. It requires both a file of bias values (the segment table) and an extra addition operation per memory reference.

As noted above, mapping can enable protection against unauthorized access. A typical method, illustrated in Fig. 3c, is to incorporate a set of access rights in the segment table. The access rights indicate a mode of access that is permitted to a segment (such as "read only" or "execute only"), and the memory mapping hardware can verify that each access to the segment fits this mode. Segment tables are often kept in cache memories in modern computer systems.

For more information on memory addressing and mapping, *see* ADDRESSING.

Translation technique

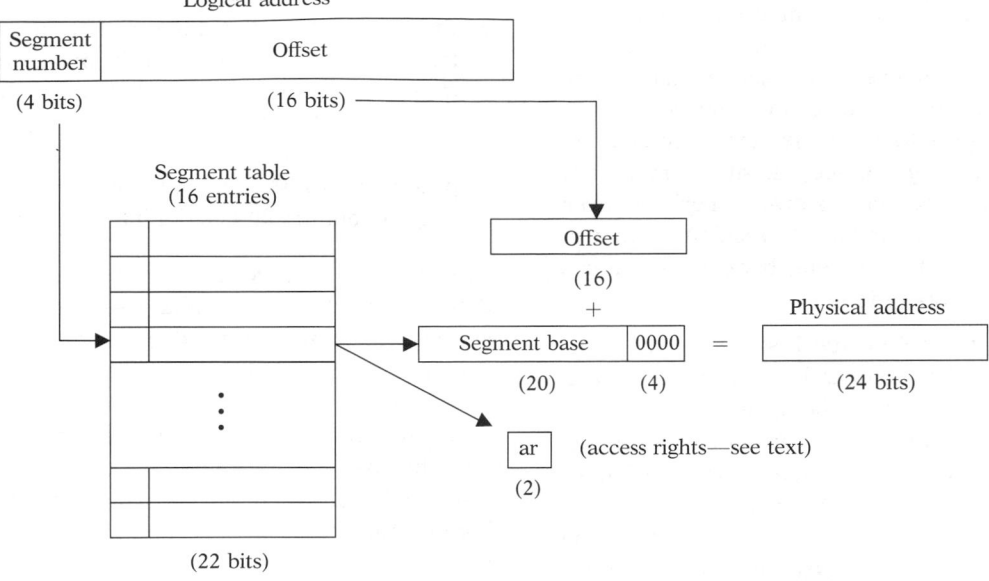

Logical and physical memory structure

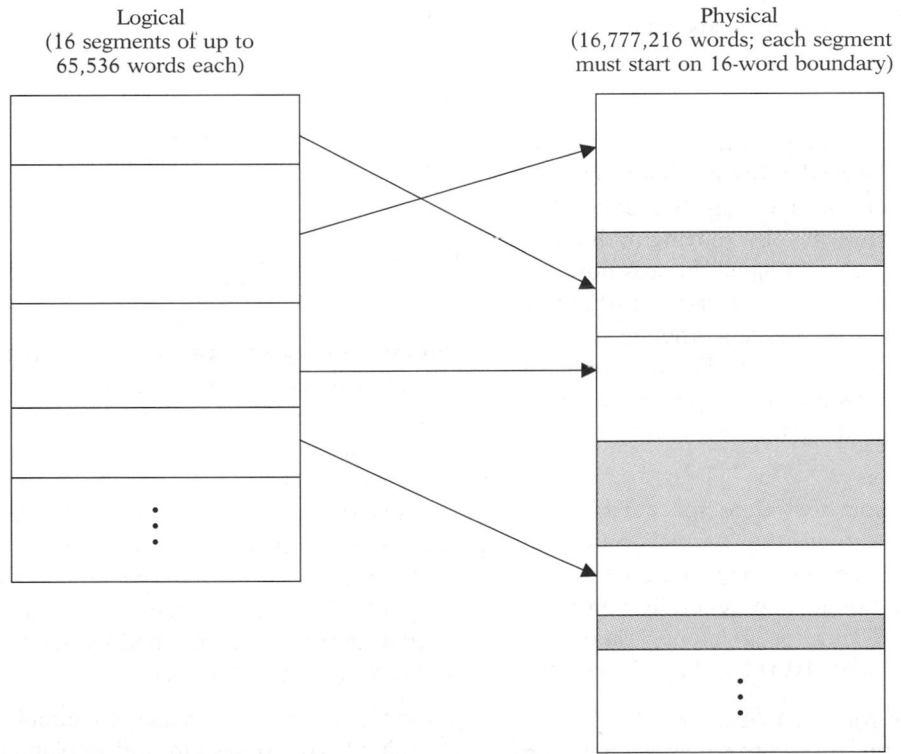

Figure 3(c). Segmented memory management (with sample values).

Auxiliary memory (secondary storage). Auxiliary memory is the lowest-cost, highest-capacity, and slowest-access storage in a computer system. It is where programs and data are kept for long-term storage or when not in immediate use. Such memories tend to occur in two types—sequential access (data must be accessed in a linear sequence) and *direct access* (data may be accessed in any sequence). The most common sequential storage device is the magnetic tape, whereas direct access devices include rotating drums, disks, CD-ROMs and DVD-ROMs (*see* OPTICAL STORAGE).

Typically, a computer operates as follows. A program and its data are initially located on a secondary storage device. Program execution is achieved by copying the program and some of the data into main memory. Instructions are then executed, causing data to be fetched into registers, operated on or tested, and the results stored back into main memory. Occasionally, an *input* operation is generated, causing more data to be copied from secondary storage, perhaps over-writing some that was previously read. As computation proceeds, results are sent back to secondary storage via *output* operations.

Many fundamental architectural issues are related to the means by which data and programs are trans-ferred between main and secondary storage. The basic problem is that the storage and transfer characteristics of secondary devices do not match those of main storage. Typical access times for main and secondary storage are given in Table 1, but to understand this better, we must consider the structure of a secondary storage device. Data is stored in blocks whose size is determined by the characteristics of the device (any-where from 64 to several thousand words is typical). This leads to three distinct time periods related to data access (see Table 2 for some typical values of these times for various devices):

1. *Positioning or access time* is the amount of time required to move the read–write mechanism to the location of a block of data. In the case of a magnetic tape, this may involve moving to the next consecutive record or spinning all the way down to the other end of the tape. On a disk, CD-ROM or DVD-ROM, it involves moving the read–write mechanism to the proper track. For a drum or a "fixed head" disk, positioning time is not a factor because there is a read–write mechanism at every track.

2. *Latency* is the amount of time for a rotational storage device to attain the correct rotational position for data access. For magnetic tape, this is essentially null, although one generally considers the tape "start-up" time as a latency time. For disks, CD-ROMs, and DVD-ROMs and drums,

latency varies from 0 to the time of a complete rotation, depending on the location of the data.

3. *Transfer time* is the amount of time required to transfer a block of data to or from a storage device once the positioning and latency have been completed. For most secondary storage devices, the transfer time is reasonably small, but it is prudent to transfer an entire block at one time so as to avoid additional positioning and latency delays.

If a program is to access data sequentially, and the data is located on a secondary storage device, there is a delay for positioning and latency time, followed by a period when the data is transferred. Because the transfer rate of the secondary device is typically 5–100 times slower than that of the main storage, it is desirable to design a computer system so that the proc-essor and main memory can carry out useful work both during the positioning and latency delays (when main storage is otherwise idle) and during the trans-fer period (when the main storage is usually required 1–20% of the time). If a program is to access data in a non-sequential fashion, the latency and positioning delays become even more significant.

Architectural features such as interrupts and direct memory access I/O are designed to simplify the process of allowing the processor to do useful work while data is being transferred (*see* "Input–Output," below). Supervisory techniques such as multitasking (*q.v.*) and multiprogramming (*q.v.*) have a similar objective; thus, architectural features that support these are important to system performance.

Virtual memory and memory hierarchies. The idea of virtual memory is to give the programmer the illusion of a very large main memory, even though a lesser amount of main memory is actually available. This is achieved by placing the contents of the large, virtual memory on an auxiliary storage device and bringing parts of it into main memory, as required by the pro-gram, in a way that is transparent to the program. Virtual memory is prevalent on systems with large word lengths (large logical address sizes), although it is found on systems of all sizes.

Virtual memory is an excellent example of the subtle interplay between system and implementation archi-tectures. Although the programmer with a virtual memory system can theoretically assume that a large amount of memory is available, seemingly minor changes in the data access pattern may have major ramifications for the amount of time required to execute programs. Thus, the programmer is driven to strive for *locality of reference*, in which consecutive references are made to objects that are physically adjacent, or nearly so; and to access multidimensional

Table 2. Data access comparison for typical devices.

Storage device	Positioning time	Latency	Transfer time
Cache memory	0	0	0.01–0.1 μs
Main memory	0	0	0.01–0.2 μs
Magnetic drum or fixed head disk	0	5–50 ms	0.25–25 μs
Moving head disk	10–50 ms	3–100 ms	0.1–10 μs
CD-ROM or DVD-ROM	100–200 ms	50–200 ms	0.25–100 μs
Magnetic tape	0 sec–5 min	10 ms	2–250 μs

array data in a sequence corresponding to that used by the compiler for storing in memory. Conversely, the implementation of virtual memory calls for the architect to design hardware that "learns" (or makes good guesses at) the memory reference patterns of programs so that the data most frequently referenced will be kept in main memory. *See* WORKING SET and Denning's classic paper (1970) for more details.

A concept related to virtual memory is that of *hierarchical memory* (*see* MEMORY HIERARCHY). In its simplest form, this means that there is a hierarchy of memory types ranging from "large and slow" to "small and fast." The important idea, however, is to give the programmer access to only one type of logical memory (typically, "main" memory), with unseen implementation techniques making this memory appear both fast and plentiful. Caches and interleaving (*see* MEMORY: MAIN) are popular techniques for achieving a high apparent speed, and virtual memory techniques are used to achieve a large apparent size. In such an architecture, the registers may no longer be of concern to the programmer, who is given the view that all of main memory is fast. The real registers may be hidden from the system architecture or may be presented in the guise of designated, frequently used main memory locations for which there are special addressing modes.

In fact, as memory technology has advanced to the point where main memory is as fast as registers, actual implementation of real registers within main memory is becoming commonplace.

The ability to provide registers within main memory has additional benefits in terms of *multitasking*—a widely used method of sharing a processor among several activities. One of the most significant overhead costs of multitasking is the "context switch" time—i.e. the time required to save the contents of the registers for one task and load up new values corresponding to another task. In the past, designers have reduced this overhead by providing multiple sets of registers. But today it may be easier and cheaper to simply dispense with the distinction between registers and main memory so that no values need to be saved or loaded. Instead, the "registers" or context of a process can be assigned to a distinct block of main memory for each task. A "context switch" simply changes a "register pointer" (the only genuine register required in the system architecture). This approach has additional benefits with tightly-coupled multiprocessors, since it allows easy switching of tasks between processors (see "Parallelism" below).

PROCESSING

The processing unit of a computer system consists of two parts: the control unit, which governs the operation of the system, and the arithmetic-logic unit (ALU), which carries out the computational and processing functions. In addition to the register set, key issues in processing unit architecture are the instruction set and the extent of parallelism.

Instruction set. An instruction occupies one or more words of storage, and its purpose is to specify an operation to be performed by the processor. An instruction (Fig. 4) consists of an *operation code* (*op code*), which indicates the general nature of the function to be performed; possibly one or more *flags*, denoting special modes of operation; and possibly one or more *addresses*, which specify the operands or data to be operated upon. An instruction format is usually characterized by the number of such operand specifiers, and although a given processor will usually support several instruction formats, one will tend to predominate. Most common today is the "three-address" format, although small processors have "one-address" and "two-address" instruction formats.

By way of comparison, consider a typical instruction, "integer add," which requires three operands: two integer numbers to be added, and one integer result. With a three-address format, all three operands would be specified directly. With a two-address format, one of the three would be implicit—typically, a register or the top of a stack. A one-address format would have two implicit operands, and so forth.

An issue that was once a source of considerable debate among computer architects is which form of instruction has the highest "bit efficiency," i.e. which form allows "typical" programs to be written with the fewest bits. This was deemed an important goal because smaller programs would make more efficient use of memory. As a general rule, a format calling for more addresses requires more bits per instruction, but needs fewer instructions to perform a computation and thus perhaps fewer bits for the computation.

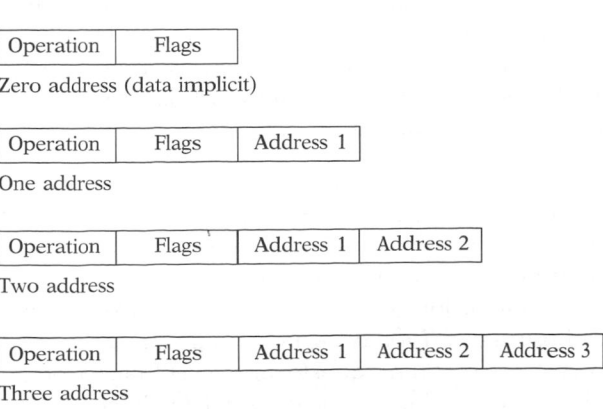

Operation	Flags

Zero address (data implicit)

Operation	Flags	Address 1

One address

Operation	Flags	Address 1	Address 2

Two address

Operation	Flags	Address 1	Address 2	Address 3

Three address

Figure 4. Typical instruction formats.

Research showed that an "optimal" instruction set would support several formats, with the most frequently used instructions being as short as possible. However, this was taken to extremes with processors that had dozens of different instruction lengths and formats. Such processors had marginally better bit efficiency, but the implementation costs and performance penalties showed the folly of focusing on a single design goal. Better designs result from seeking a balanced combination of bit efficiency, performance, and cost. In fact, some of the designs based on RISC architecture have sacrificed bit efficiency to achieve very high performance. This is an appropriate approach today because of the dramatic reductions in memory cost and increases in memory size (roughly 2× per year) that have occurred over the past several decades.

Operand addressing is usually more complex than is implied above. The field of an instruction that identifies an operand (*q.v.*) may contain several subfields, and may require a significant amount of computation just to determine the location of the operand. The various ways of identifying an operand are called *addressing modes*. A representative set of addressing modes is as follows:

Operand specifier format
(in address field of instruction)

type	designator

Type	Operand class	Designator interpretation
0	Immediate	Operand is designator itself
1	Direct	Designator is address of operand
2	Indirect	Designator is address of memory cell containing address of operand
3	Register	Designator indicates a register containing the operand

Many other operand formats have been used. The instruction set reference manual of any computer system will provide details on the specific approach used therein. (*See* also the articles in this encyclopedia on ADDRESSING and on specific systems such as the DEC VAX series (*see* DIGITAL EQUIPMENT CORPORATION) and the IBM 360/370/390 series (*q.v.*).)

In addition to the format of a computer's instructions, the architect must consider their semantics, i.e. what functions they perform. For example, one issue is how to compare different values. In one approach, a "compare" instruction compares the values of two operands and sets a *condition code*, indicating whether the first operand is less than, equal to, or greater than the other. This code can be tested or stored for later use. An alternative approach is to simply subtract one item from the other and test the sign and value of the result. The condition code approach is more flexible, especially for comparing non-numeric quantities, but it is also more expensive to implement (*see* INSTRUCTION SET).

CISC and RISC. For many years, instruction sets were designed on the basis of the register set, word length, technology characteristics, and the designer's concept of how programs would be written (generally based on assembly language programming styles). The functions performed were quite simple, such as controlling the sequence of instruction execution, shifting data, adding numbers together, and comparing values. Among the first "higher-level" features found in instruction sets were instructions to perform floating-point calculations.

In the mid-1970s, more designers began to examine what actual programs (mostly written in high-level languages) do. Initially, this work led to direct instruction set support for such "high-level" functions as procedure calling, list searching, and complex array access. As the computers of this period developed more and more complex features, they came to be known eventually as Complex Instruction Set Computers (CISC). The trend in architectural circles was toward even more complex architectures that provide direct support for high-level languages (Myers, 1982) and sophisticated memory addressing and protection (Levy, 1984).

However, another trend was quietly developing among those trying to develop better microprocessors and microcomputers—entire processors and/or computers on a single, very large-scale integrated circuit (VLSI) (*see* INTEGRATED CIRCUITRY). The better work was done by interdisciplinary teams that combined knowledge of compilers, operating systems, the fundamental properties of VLSI, and the actual behavior of real application programs. Analysis of the frequency with which various instructions are used showed that a small number of relatively simple instructions account for most of the time spent by typical programs. Moreover, some of the more complex instructions perform functions that can be accomplished just as well, if not better, by short sequences of simpler instructions. Reduced instruction set computers (RISC), in which there are only a few carefully selected instructions, developed out of this work. Their high-performance potential made them so popular that the term RISC had become a rather abused marketing term by the late 1980s (just as "word length" had been abused in earlier times). In the meantime, the best mainstream processors have combined the best concepts of both RISC and CISC, yielding instruction sets that are carefully chosen, based on the requirements of efficient implementation, as well as the requirements of high performance by realistic application software.

Tagged architectures. In the von Neumann type of instruction set described above, there is no distinction made in storage between instructions and data and in storage between different types of data. That is, it would be possible to perform an addition operation on a bit pattern representing an instruction and, although the results might be meaningless, the computer would probably not detect any problem. Such cases are the cause of numerous programming errors; thus, some computers have used a *tagged architecture*, in which each memory word consists of two parts: the "data" part, which contains conventional data or instruction, and the "tag" part, which is a few extra bits that describe the data part. This enables detection of inappropriate operations, and also has ramifications for instruction set design. Because the type of data is implied by the word containing the data, it is no longer necessary to have separate instructions for each data type supported by the machine. Instead of "integer add," "floating-point add," and "decimal add," a tagged architecture needs only a single "generic" instruction: "add." The tag fields indicate the specific type of addition to be performed.

Tagged architectures remain a controversial subject due to concerns about storage space efficiency, implementation cost, and the semantics of generic instructions when several different data types are used in the same instruction. They have been quite successful in symbolic processing systems (such as processors for Lisp (*q.v.*)), but have not made wide inroads into mainstream computer design.

Microprogramming and writable control storage. One technique for implementing processing units is *microprogramming*. In this technique, each instruction can be thought of as a "subroutine call" to a program written in a lower-level language whose domain includes the data paths and registers of the processor. An advantage of microprogramming is that hardware design errors can be corrected by simply revising the microprograms instead of changing the circuitry. This is a particularly important advantage today because the entire processing function may be embedded in a single silicon circuit. A "circuit change" is a prohibitively expensive process on a low-volume, special-purpose processor. Moreover, use of microprogramming allows the development of relatively complex instructions, without a substantial increase in processing unit complexity; instead, the amount of storage for microprograms is increased. While such storage is not free, it is composed of standard memory devices whose regular structure makes them relatively simple to design and build.

Normally, microprograms are stored in a "read-only" memory device (ROM), both to reduce cost and to avoid loss of information during a loss of power. With *writable control store* (WCS), a part of the microcode storage is implemented with writable memory. This allows a general-purpose computer to be tailored to the requirements of a specific application by selective introduction of new instructions. The technique has achieved some use in research environments, but the complexities of software support (designing compilers that can make use of the new instructions, for example) have restricted commercial use to applications that can benefit significantly from the technique. The Burroughs B1800, for example, used a writable control store to permit tailoring of the instruction set to different application areas at different times.

Parallelism. The speed with which instructions can be processed is determined by two factors: how fast the circuitry can perform a single instruction, and how many instructions can be performed in parallel. Circuit speed is largely determined by system cost, as limited by the available circuit technology, which now is limited by the fundamental laws of physics (*see* LIMITS OF COMPUTATION). Thus, to achieve the speed desired in high-performance systems, efforts are made to achieve high degrees of parallelism. Most of the techniques used to exploit parallelism belong to implementation architecture or algorithm design, although the results strongly affect system architecture (*see* PARALLEL PROCESSING: ARCHITECTURE and INSTRUCTION-LEVEL PARALLELISM).

Parallelism requires the use of multiple processors, and one of the first design issues is whether they should share the same main memory (tightly coupled) or have their own separate memories (loosely coupled). Either way, each processor generally has its own registers, and they generally share at least some of the secondary storage and peripherals. Which approach is better generally depends on the nature of the application.

A second issue is whether to use a small number of very powerful processors or a very large number of simple processors (massive parallelism). The latter approach generally involves tight coupling and an intricate design for the memory access mechanism. Algorithm design plays an important role in the effective use of massively parallel processors.

A third issue is whether to associate processors in a "pipeline" or "assembly line" fashion, with each stream of data passing through several processors, or whether to assign each processor to work on a separate stream of data (*see* PIPELINE).

Special-purpose architectures exploit parallelism in unique ways for particular applications. A case in point is *signal processing*, in which billions of operations per second may be achieved on a single microprocessor through the exploitation of specific characteristics. For example, signal processing is usually done on one bit at a time, and arithmetic overflow is generally ignored. An interesting aspect of these processors is that they deviate from conventional processors in many unexpected ways. For example, with a signal processor it may be perfectly acceptable to ignore the higher-order digits of a multiplication, and when there is contention (*q.v.*) for memory access, the processor is given priority over peripheral devices.

Almost all issues of parallelism are strongly influenced by the nature of the problem being solved, as well as the algorithms proposed for the solution. Thus, truly general-purpose parallelism remains an elusive goal. The most dominant form of parallelism in actual commercial use is the sharing of peripherals and secondary storage through loosely-coupled networks of processors (*see* NETWORK ARCHITECTURE and CLUSTER COMPUTING). An emerging form of parallelism for solving large computational problems is the *network parallel computer*. In this approach, a software package (such as the parallel virtual machine (PVM) package from Oak Ridge or the message passing interface (MPI)) standard allows a collection of heterogeneous networked computers to act as a single large parallel computer.

INPUT–OUTPUT AND COMMUNICATION

Fundamental issues. The remaining major architectural aspects of a computer system are related to communicating between the computer and the "outside" world. A typical computer system will be surrounded by an array of devices such as terminals, printers, and plotters, which are collectively called its *input–output* (I/O) devices. The function of such devices is to transmit data between the computer and its users, with appropriate transformations along the way. For example, a printer will transform bits and bytes into control signals for a mechanical or laser printing mechanism; a video terminal will translate keystrokes into bytes of data, and then back into dots on a cathode ray tube.

I/O devices share certain characteristics with auxiliary storage devices; thus both tend to be handled in similar ways architecturally. These devices have relatively low access speed and are usually capable of operating more or less independently of the main processing unit. Thus a complex "loosely coupled" connection to the processor and main memory is required. Because of their relatively low speed, it is desirable to keep these devices in continuous operation, so that their maximum performance potential can be realized. Low speed and independent operation make it attractive to allow several devices to operate simultaneously. The fundamental issues of I/O architecture relate to the means of transferring data between these devices and main memory, and to the process of coordinating and synchronizing multiple devices, with the goal of obtaining maximum performance from each.

Communication paths. A peripheral or storage device must be connected to either the processor or main memory. A *data path* is a collection of wires or other connecting medium that accomplishes this task. More capable data paths may involve their own special-purpose processing units.

Data paths are generally grouped into three types: *simplex* paths allow data to flow in only a single direction; *half-duplex* paths allow data to flow in either direction, but only one at a time; *full-duplex* paths allow data to flow in both directions simultaneously. A simplex path might be used to connect an input-only device (e.g. a keyboard) to the computer or to connect the computer to an output-only device (e.g. a display or printer). A half-duplex path would be used to connect a device that does both input and output, but only one at a time (e.g. a tape drive). A full-duplex path is necessary when the device needs to do both input and output at the same time or requires rapid switching between input and output modes. Any of the data paths discussed below may be implemented in a simplex, half-duplex, or full-duplex manner.

A *channel* is a data path connecting a peripheral device directly to a memory system. If more than one device is required, each may be connected to a different channel, or there may be a way for several devices to share the same channel. Simple shared channels permit only one device to transmit data at a time, whereas multiplexor channels allow interleaved data transfers from several devices. *Multiplexing* (*q.v.*) can be performed by dividing the channel into several parallel subchannels or by time multiplexing, in which units of data from different devices alternate. Two examples of time multiplexing are the byte multiplexer channel, which transmits one byte of data at a time from each device, and the block multiplexer channel, in which large blocks of data are interleaved.

The channel is a good way to achieve high performance in device-to-memory communication, but its costs can be high for resolving contention problems. Thus it is most appropriate when all devices are similar or when there are only a few devices.

A *daisy chain* is a low-cost prioritized method of connecting several devices to the computer, but allowing only one of them at a time to communicate. It works like certain old-fashioned decorative tree lights. The computer is connected to the first device, which, in turn, is connected to the second device, and so on. Each device has a switch that controls the link to the next device. If all switches are on, the last device in the chain can communicate with the computer. However, any device in the chain can request access to the computer by simply switching off the lower devices. The first device in the chain has top priority—it can communicate at will by simply switching off the others. The second device has next highest priority—it can communicate except when the first device has preempted it, and so on with remaining devices.

A *bus* is a data path that connects devices in parallel, more or less like a party line. Any device can use the bus, but one of the devices is designated as a master, and it controls access to the bus by issuing authorization signals. Information is transmitted across a bus in two parts: address and data. Each device is associated with a specific address or range of addresses, and when an address comes down the bus the associated device is designated to receive or send the associated data. Buses were originally devised to allow data to flow among computer registers and between the processor and main memory. This concept was later generalized to accommodate secondary storage and peripheral devices. Today, certain forms of local area network (LAN—*q.v.*) have extended this concept to longer distances and a wider range of devices.

An advantage of the bus is simplicity in connecting things to the main memory system. Only one bus-to-memory connection need be made. All contention for memory access is resolved with the bus, rather than with the memory interface. This permits memory access to remain fast and simple, while allowing many devices to have direct access to memory. However, the interface between the device and the bus is more expensive than, for example, the daisy chain connection. The use of buses has steadily increased over the past three decades, due to advances in circuit technology that permit a bus interface to be implemented relatively inexpensively.

Control. Control of input and output must accomplish initiation of the transfer, synchronization of communicating devices, and completion reporting. Three potential "players" in this process are the main processor, the main memory, and a peripheral or secondary storage device. The data path is the medium of communication, and it often handles much of the synchronization. Many authors have attempted to organize the various forms in which I/O control may occur, although none of the attempts has been entirely satisfactory. *Smotherman's taxonomy* (1989) is one of the best, and his paper has the advantage of dis-

cussing some of its predecessors. Here we attempt to organize matters in a somewhat simpler way.

The most straightforward approach to controlling the transmission of data is *program-controlled* I/O. Under such a scheme, the processor directs the input and output activity. In one approach, an *explicit instruction* initiates the transfer by commanding a device to accept a small amount of data (typically one word or byte) for display or storage (output) or to transmit a small unit of data to the processor (input). The instruction may wait for transmission to occur or may simply initiate the activity, with subsequent "test" instructions required to poll the device and determine when transmission is complete. Transmission usually occurs between the device and some processor register, although in some designs a main memory cell may be specified.

An alternative to use of explicit instructions is *memory-mapped I/O* (*q.v.*). This technique has the processor direct activity by writing to certain reserved cells in its logical memory space called *control words*. Control words may actually be implemented as reserved main memory cells or may be implemented within the device itself. The act of writing into a control word causes the address of that word to be sent out across the memory bus. As previously discussed, different devices on a bus will be associated with different addresses. Thus, each device on the bus observes all addresses and intercepts those that correspond to its control words. The device reads the "data" being written to the control word and interprets it as an I/O command.

The memory-mapped approach simplifies the control interface and the instruction set. Its main drawbacks are that (1) it puts "holes" in the logical address space (i.e. sections of the address space that cannot be used as genuine memory cells), and (2) it complicates caching and virtual memory. Ill-conceived use of memory-mapped I/O in low-cost processors has sometimes impeded the growth of their architectures into more powerful systems. However, by judicious use of memory mapping or virtual memory, the drawbacks of program-controlled I/O can be managed.

Whether through explicit instructions or memory mapping, the processor will typically initiate activity on several devices, with subsequent polling (*q.v.*) to determine when each has finished. However, in the absence of further architectural support, such as interrupts, it is difficult (or even impossible) for the processor to be programmed in such a way that it performs useful work while the devices are busy and also responds promptly when they are finished so as to keep them in continuous operation. Since most peripheral devices are slow (by processor standards), it is desirable to reduce or eliminate the need for polling and thus free up the processor during I/O operations.

The program-controlled scheme tends to impose high overhead when the peripheral device has a relatively high data transfer rate. This is due to having the processor execute an initiation command, a repeated series of completion tests, and perhaps a transfer between register and main memory for each word or byte of data transferred. *Direct memory access* (DMA) is a technique for reducing processor involvement during the transfer of blocks of data. This technique incorporates specific concepts of both control and communication. DMA not only allows transmission directly between devices and memory, as the name implies, but, as commonly defined, it eliminates the high processor control overhead described earlier.

With the DMA technique, the main processor will initiate the transfer of a block of data, with the "completion" notification coming only when the entire block has been moved. The processor's command goes to a DMA controller—a separate, special-purpose processor—which has the independent capability to count the number of items transmitted and keep track of where they go in memory. Meanwhile, the main processor can do other useful work.

Advanced DMA systems allow *chaining* of command blocks and other techniques that permit multiple blocks of data to be transmitted to different areas of main memory by a single command from the main processor. Certain channels operate in essentially the same way as DMA except that DMA is generally a shared capability, whereas a channel is usually associated with a specific set of peripherals.

Interrupts and traps. These two techniques are very similar, and some designs do not distinguish between them. Both are methods of notifying the processor of an event. A *trap* signals an abnormal event within the processor, such as an arithmetic fault, illegal instruction, or power failure. An *interrupt* notifies the processor of an external event, such as completion of an I/O operation. Traps generally force the processor to stop what it is doing and deal immediately with the event. Interrupts usually signal events that are less urgent than traps, and the processor need not always respond immediately. Recent systems have expanded the role of the interrupt to include software-detected events, such as completion of a task or emptying of a queue. While interrupts are used in many contexts, we focus here on their use in I/O applications.

An interrupt can be used by a peripheral device to notify a processor that a data transfer has been completed. This allows the processor to perform other work in the meantime, yet service the device promptly upon its completion. I/O interrupts can be used with any of the control or communication schemes described above.

Typically, the interrupt signal is generated by an I/O device that has completed its most recent request or that requires some other service. In response to the interrupt signal, a processor will usually suspend its current activity and attend to the device. In the simplest schemes, all devices share the same interrupt signal, and the processor must poll all devices to determine which has generated the interrupt. More elaborate schemes allow the processor to determine immediately which device caused the interrupt. This may be accomplished by a control word that has a separate bit for each interrupting device (the processor tests to see which bit has been set) or a *vectored interrupt scheme*, in which each device causes the processor to transfer to a different address when responding to the interrupt.

A typical busy processor will have many interrupting devices. In order to make order out of potential chaos, there must be a method of resolving conflicts. If two devices interrupt at the same time, which one should be serviced first? If one device is being serviced and another interrupts, should the first one be interrupted to service the second one? To deal with issues such as these, most processors support multiple levels of interrupt priority. In a simple scheme that suffices for most situations, a small number of priority levels are supported—perhaps four or eight. Each potential source of interrupts is associated with a particular priority level, corresponding to how quickly its requests must be serviced. Higher-level devices can interrupt lower-level ones, but not vice versa. Equal priority devices cannot interrupt each other. A typical scheme might assign four levels to events that, respectively:

◆ require immediate action, such as power failures or illegal instructions;

◆ could cause functional failure if not attended to promptly, such as a timing signal that must be acknowledged promptly if time is to be kept accurately;

◆ could cause performance degradation, such as a disk that has rotated to a desired position and should be accessed within a short time to avoid waiting for another rotation; or

◆ have relatively minimal impact, such as notification that a task has completed and its storage is no longer needed.

More elaborate schemes assign distinct priorities to each interrupt or to small groups of similar interrupts.

Vectored interrupt schemes often associate a distinct priority with each distinct interrupt address. There remains some dispute as to whether this degree of priority distinction is really necessary for most applications. Too many priority levels can lead to excessive "context switch" overhead as one device interrupts another.

Another issue stems from the fact that interrupt priorities are often built into the processor or bus hardware, with little or no flexibility. In actual applications, it might be appropriate to let priorities be controlled by the devices or by software. For example, a single device might report different kinds of events that deserve different priorities (e.g. disk has rotated to desired position vs. disk has been turned on). Changes in system state might cause the need for software to vary priorities (normal versus emergency operation, for example). Some recent designs allow device and software control of interrupt priorities, but there is little agreement at this point about what type of scheme is best suited to the general case. Different programming languages call for different approaches to this problem, and, until some consensus can be reached, computer architecture will continue to vary considerably in this regard.

Interrupts are a valuable architectural feature, but they tend to cause numerous problems as well. A processor may inadvertently receive an interrupt from a device that the software is not prepared to handle, or at a time when it was not expected. A faulty device may send interrupts continuously, deluging the system with interrupt response activity and blocking other devices from service. Elaborate software may be required to handle such cases correctly, and in some systems such situations may result in uncorrectable hardware or software faults ("hangups"). As a result of many years of experience with interrupts, architects have begun to refine and "civilize" the interrupt systems of computers. For example, it is now usually possible for the software to mask or block interrupts in cases where a software module requires higher priority than an external device, or where some particular device's interrupts are to be ignored. A very promising concept is to model interrupts after more general synchronization mechanisms such as messages or semaphores (*see* CONCURRENT PROGRAMMING). This is an excellent example of how a technique developed to solve a software problem has affected computer architecture in more fundamental ways.

Publications

Certain professional publications and organizations are concerned with the advancement of computer architecture. The Association for Computing Machinery has a special interest group on computer architecture (SIGARCH) that publishes a newsletter (*Computer Architecture News* or *CAN*) several times a year. Strongly related issues are covered in *Operating Systems Review*, the newsletter of the special interest group on operating systems (SIGOPS). Another special interest group focuses on microprogramming (SIG-MICRO). The IEEE Computer Society has several publications relating to computer architecture and design. Most important are the monthly *Computer* and *IEEE Transactions on Computers*. The IEEE Computer Society and SIGARCH sponsor an annual symposium on computer architecture, usually held in the spring, the proceedings of which are available from the IEEE Publications Department and as a special issue of *Computer Architecture News*. SIGMICRO and IEEE sponsor an annual International Symposium on Microarchitecture in the autumn, the proceedings of which are available from ACM or as a special issue of the SIGMICRO newsletter.

Bibliography

1962. Buchholz, W. *Planning a Computer System—Project Stretch*. New York: McGraw-Hill.
1970. Denning, P. J. "Virtual Memory," *ACM Computing Surveys*, **2**, 3, 153–190.
1975. Patil, S. (ed.) "Computer Systems Architecture," Special Issue: *ACM Computing Surveys*, **7**, 4 (December).
1980. Baer, J.-L. *Computer Systems Architecture*. Potomac, MD: Computer Science Press.
1982. Siewiorek, D. P., Bell, C. G., and Newell, A. *Computer Structures: Principles and Examples*. New York: McGraw-Hill.
1982. Myers, G. J. *Advances in Computer Architecture*, 2nd Ed. New York: John Wiley.
1984. Levy, H. M. *Capability-Based Computer Systems*. Bedford, MA: Digital Press.
1987. Leonard, T. E. (ed.) *VAX Architecture Reference Manual*. Bedford, MA: Digital Press.
1989. Smotherman, M. "A Sequencing-based Taxonomy of I/O Systems and Review of Historical Machines," *Computer Architecture News*, **17**, 5 (September), 5–15.
1990. Hennessy, J. L., and Patterson, D. A. *Computer Architecture: A Quantitative Approach*. San Francisco: Morgan Kaufmann.
1993. Hwang, K. *Advanced Computer Architecture: Parallelism, Scalability, Programmability*. New York: McGraw-Hill.
1994. Motorola, Inc. *PowerPC^{TM} Microprocessor Family: The Programming Environments*. Phoenix, AZ: Motorola Literature Distribution Center.
1996. Stallings, W. *Computer Organization and Architecture*, 4th Ed. Upper Saddle River, NJ: Prentice Hall.
1998. Patterson, D. A. and Hennessy, J. L. *Computer Organization and Design*, 2nd Ed. San Francisco: Morgan Kaufmann.

Dennis J. Frailey

COMPUTER ARITHMETIC

See ARITHMETIC, COMPUTER; COMPLEMENT; and NUMBERS AND NUMBER SYSTEMS.

COMPUTER ART

For articles on related subjects *see* COMPUTER ANIMATION; COMPUTER GRAPHICS; ENTERTAINMENT INDUSTRY, COMPUTERS IN THE; FRACTALS; HUMANITIES APPLICATIONS; IMAGE PROCESSING; MULTIMEDIA; SCIENTIFIC VISUALIZATION; and VIRTUAL REALITY.

A New Visual Order

The computer deeply affects the way today's art is produced, disseminated, and valued. Until recently, images were created through acts of human perception either through skills based on eye–hand coordination or through the lens of copying processes such as photography, cinematic film, or video where what is seen is recorded through various chemical or electronic processes. Increasingly, however, images reside only in the database of a computer, causing a break with the visual means of representation available to artists for creating art since the Renaissance. The image is now an information structure which has no physical presence in the real world. Not only is it a dematerialized image, but it is also one which can be changed and manipulated by a viewer interactively. Digitalization of images takes place through encoding information about light structures as a database programmed for later retrieval. Digital image processing can link sequences of images to create a form of "global vision" which goes far beyond conventional photography.

Computer-simulated or processed images create a new visual order, a new ground for elaboration of the language of images in motion. The order and duration of image-events can be manipulated, skewed, repeated, or made three-dimensional, by means of controlling functions within the computer video instrument. Basically, this means that an "image-event" can undergo nearly infinite spatio-temporal transformation, since the "image" is only a matrix of digital codes in a data space. Thus any element of any image can be seamlessly inserted into any other image.

The potential for intervention and interaction in an artwork challenges notions of a discrete work of art, one that is authored by the artist alone. By means of an interface, an *interactive* art work may use a navigation system of branched databases to create a work of connective links and nodes. The viewer may now participate in the work's ultimate unfolding of meaning by choosing directions within the artwork. Interactivity challenges the role of the artist, who now assumes a different function, one similar to a systems designer. The artist may creatively manipulate entire databases of imagery, text and sound, opening new avenues to art-making that encompass interdisciplinary and collaborative methods and forms.

Early Use by Artists

By 1965, computer research into the simulation of visual phenomena had reached a significant level, particularly at Bell Labs in Murray Hill, NJ. Here the pioneer work of Bela Julesz, A. Michael Noll, Manfred Schroeder, Ken Knowlton, Leon Harmon, Frank Sinden, and E. E. Zajac led them to understand the computer's possibilities for visual representation and for art. That same year Noll and Julesz exhibited the results of their experiments at the Howard Wise Gallery, New York, concurrent with Georg Nees and Frieder Nake's exhibition of digital images at Galerie Niedlich, Stuttgart, Germany. Research in Germany at the Stuttgart Technische Universität was conducted under the influence of the philosopher Max Bense, who coined the terms "artificial art" and "generative esthetics," terms which grew out of his interest in the mathematics of esthetics.

Some of the earliest computer experiments related to art included the ones by Noll in which he simulated existing paintings by Piet Mondrian and Bridget Riley in an effort to study style and composition in art. In approximating the Mondrian painting *Composition with Lines*, Noll created a digital version with pseudo-random numbers.

By the early 1970s, a new generation of artists began to emerge who were able to retain their intuition and sensitivity while exercising the logical, methodical approach to work demanded by the use of digital equipment. For example, Manfred Mohr (self-taught in computer science—*see* Fig. 1) and Duane Palyka (with degrees in both fine arts and mathematics) began to program their own software as a result of frustration with existing programs and systems which did not serve their creative needs. They represented a class of "hybrid" artists who have made important contributions to the field of visual simulation. Some have custom-designed paint systems and video interfaces for interactive graphics as well as working with robotics (*q.v.*) in sculpture. Following the development of powerful microprocessors in the mid-1970s, their work was simplified by the advent of microcomputer turnkey systems which freed them at last from large mainframe (*q.v.*) support and opened possibilities for the computer to become a truly personal tool for artists. Programmed and developed by "hybrids" such as John Dunn (Easel, or Lumena Paint software), Dan Sandin (Z-Grass, a digital image processor), and Woody Vasulka (Digital Image Articulator—*see* Fig. 2), out of their own imperatives as artists, new interface software for the computer provided easy access to two-dimensional and three-dimensional image processing in combination with animation and video. The need for new software

Figure 1. Manfred Mohr, *P-159/A*, 1973. Plotter drawing (ink on paper), 24″ × 24″. In this early minimalist work, a cube's repertoire of 12 lines are assigned numerical values in order to unleash a compelling scheme of line arrangements, suggesting a form of movement and harmony (courtesy Manfred Mohr).

development has led many artists, especially those interested in interactive applications, to collaborate with engineers or scientists, or to study computer science for themselves.

The use of computers for art grew out of existing formalist art practices, especially with regard to Minimalist, Neoconstructivist, and Conceptual tendencies. However, use of the computer for art touched a deep nerve in an art world fearful of the use of a mechanical device like the computer for the making of art. Jasia Reichardt, curator of the 1968 London ICA (Institute for Contemporary Art) exhibition "Cybernetic Serendipity" (the first devoted entirely to computer applications for poetry, sound, sculpture and graphics) was reassuring:

> The possibilities inherent in the computer as a creative tool will do little to change those idioms of art which rely primarily on the dialogue between the artist, his ideas, and the canvas.

Use of the computer still seems threatening to many artists today who fear they may lose control to a machine which has a powerful agenda of its own. However, its presence is so ubiquitous that it is creeping into every artist's studio as a tool for some functions (much

as the camera eventually did), raising questions about what aspect of it can be used for their work, although most still do not contemplate its use as a medium in itself (but *see* Fig. 3). It has already begun to replace image reproduction, photography, and text processing, as well as providing communications through email.

Representation Changes

How does the computer affect how we evaluate artists' work in terms of art? Periods of major technological change transform culture and disrupt the criteria used for evaluating art. At certain moments of history, understanding of what art is changes relative to a paradigm that contains within it agreed-upon assumptions which shape the understanding of it in a particular time period. We commonly call this *paradigm representation*, a complex term which directs attention to significant aspects of art practice. It is a term which refers to a system of iconography which contains both the perceptual and the esthetic when related to art and has conventions of both tool and medium inscribed in it. The images or objects that artists construct are not just simple responses to individual experience, but are always ordered, coded, and styled according to conventions which develop out of the practice of each medium with its tools and processes, whether the medium is a

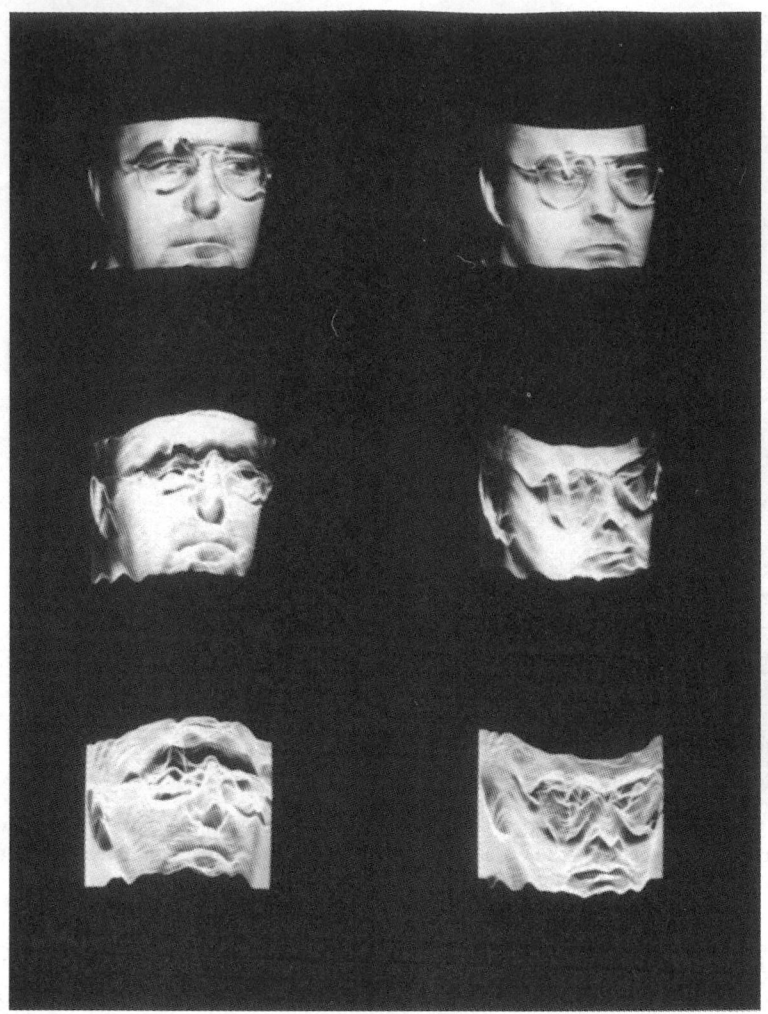

Figure 2. Woody Vasulka, *Number 6*, computer manipulated images, ca. 1982. Visual investigations which make use of a scan processor and image-processing equipment (courtesy Woody Vasulka).

traditional one such as painting, sculpture, printmaking, photography, or an electronic one such as video or the computer.

Artists' vision and artists' responses to the world are dominated by the conditions and consciousness of a particular time period. Today's media-driven culture, which is affected by interactive technologies, is causing a major shift in consciousness which in turn influences attitudes to what art is. Because the computer assimilates all media, it poses a major challenge to our notions about representation and the tools we have used for so long. It poses totally new questions about visualization and esthetic values and about the real world and our relation to it in terms of time, space and the human body.

The First 35 Years

In the catalog essay for the 1970 New York exhibition "Software: Information Technology; Its Mean-

ing for Art" at the Jewish Museum, Jack Burnham used the body-machine-controlled-by-the-mind metaphor when he quipped: "Our bodies are hardware, our behavior software." Also in New York that same year, the "Information" exhibition curated by Kynaston McShine at the Museum of Modern Art demonstrated the concept of systems analysis and its implications for art. "Information" explored groups of networks of interacting structures and channels as a functionally interrelated means of communication. The computer was a natural metaphor for this exhibition. Agnes Denes, Hans Haacke, Les Levine, and Dennis Oppenheim were among the artists who explored use of computer concepts in their works. This was one of the first exhibitions to espouse the reductive, minimalist principles of conceptual art where the idea is the total work (i.e. essentially no object is produced).

In the short 35-year history of computer use in the visual arts, the first 10 years ("first wave" 1965–1975) were dominated by computer scientists with easy

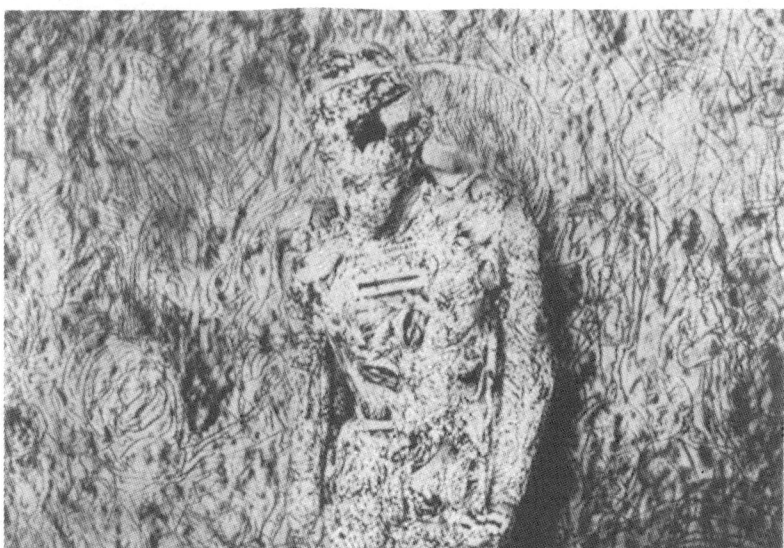

Figure 3. Joseph Nechvatal, *The Informed Man*, 1986. Computer/robotic-assisted Scanamural (acrylic on canvas 82″ × 116″. Degraded information patterns are printed via airbrush guns guided by computer-driven robotic arms onto a canvas support (collection: Dannheisser Foundation).

access to equipment. In the "second wave," significantly larger numbers of artists began to gain access to computers and realize their potential benefit for their work. Many of these were interested in kinetic and interactive aspects of the computer. Some artists used the computer as a means of programming their kinetic sculptures, which emphasized interactivity between optics, light displays, and motorized controlled movement, such as those by Thomas Shannon, Jean Dupuy, and Hilary Harris among many others in both Europe and the USA. In the next decade, the continuing work of many pioneer artists probed at the edge of the computer's potential, participated in developing new software tools, and made vital contributions in laying the foundation for future achievements.

The use of the computer as a medium by artists has until recently brought the same rebuff by critics as earlier reactions to photography, which was rejected as a mainstream art form from the 1850s to the 1960s. However, wide dispersal and greater access to greatly improved equipment for a far broader group of artists, and to the development of much more "friendly" technology, has created important new conditions. More and more artists are able to access flexible, powerful and challenging computer hardware and software at lower cost. New forms and esthetic values are developing as a broader range of artists come to electronic tools with training in the visual arts rather than in computer science. Art schools are rapidly integrating digital tools into their curricula.

The computer allows rapid visualization of complex spatial concepts. Many programs have now been developed which allow complex layering of imagery and ease of decision-making about color and composition, and which permit the creation of film and printer output. A variety of sophisticated color printers (*q.v.*) using laser, inkjet, sublimation, and other technologies make high-quality prints on a variety of papers and print media. Interactive installations, CD-ROMs (and DVD-Rs) (*see* OPTICAL STORAGE) and the World Wide Web (*q.v.*) create a realm where a different set of abstract relationships can be brought into play which expand avenues for art-making, challenging both artist and viewer (Fig. 4 on Color Page CP-4).

A growing tide of international exhibitions in galleries and museums demonstrates the quickening of interest in the computer's use for art.[1] A broad range of European, Asian, and South American countries have either originated exhibitions of computer-assisted art or have hosted traveling exhibitions such as the ACM (*q.v.*) SIGGRAPH Art Show.

---

[1] At New York Museums (the Whitney, International Center for Photography, the Guggenheim, Alternative, Bronx, and Brooklyn Museums), recent exhibitions have included work that has begun to bear a mature, integrated stamp. At the Musée d'Art Moderne, Paris, the Electra exhibition in 1982 linked computer work both to kinetic art tradition and to interactive influences. Two Artware exhibitions curated by David Galloway have been exhibited at the Hanover Fair, which brought together European and American artists working in the field. The 1987/88 traveling exhibition, Digital Visions: Computers and Art, curated by Cynthia Goodman, originated at the Everson Museum in Syracuse and traveled to other museums including the IBM Gallery in New York. It was meant as a survey over the past 25 years of works by artists who have used the computer either as a direct tool for their work or who have been influenced by it. It included work by most of the medium's pioneers, among them Lillian Schwartz, Ken Knowlton, Ed Emshwiller, John Whitney, Charles Csuri, Manfred Mohr, Robert Mallary, and Otto Piene.

However, to gain access to high-level equipment capable of modeling high resolution animations of virtual models, artists must gain entrée through fellowships, grants, and artist residencies to specialized centers, in development since the 1980s, such as at the Banff Center for the Arts in Canada; the American Film Institute's Advanced Technology Program in Los Angeles; the Center for Art and Media (ZKM) in Karlsruhe, Germany; and the Institute for Studies in the Arts at Arizona State University. Particularly in Germany, Austria, and France, where there has been a long tradition of support for the arts, financing of such centers has reached an important level.

Up to now, the major museums have tended to acquire works which incorporate computer influence as part of their photography, video, and sculpture collections—works such as Jon Kessler's kinetic sculptures, Jenny Holzer's computer-controlled electronic message boards (Fig. 5 on Color Page CP-4), and Bill Viola's video installations (Fig. 6 on Color Page CP-5). These works tend to integrate rather than isolate the computer aspect and enhance the overall conception.

Artists, the Interface and Interaction

Originally, interactive media grew out of developments in electronic computer games in the 1970s and 1980s. Due to the popularity of these games, the early technology became so well-developed that many artists decided to use the concept of branched-out situations to involve the audience in a different kind of experience (Fig. 7 on Color Page CP-5). Among others, Jane Veeder, Nancy Burson, Myron Krueger, and Ed Tannenbaum created different genres of interactive works.

Harold Cohen (Fig. 8 on Color Page CP-5) thinks of the computer as an "interface for the creation of his work—a collaborator, and an assistant in the drawing phase." Cohen's drawing program is what he terms a formal distillation of the rules and habits a human artist follows during the process of drawing. The computer sifts through these programmed rules and drives an artist-built drawing machine (a *turtle—see* Logo) by steering it with separate commands.

Cohen applies artificial intelligence (*q.v.*) techniques to the process of image-making. He instructs the turtle to be interested in such issues as spatial distribution, figure–ground relationships, and figure integrity (avoiding the drawing of one figure over another); and to be aware of "insideness" and "outsideness." Cohen has defined the rules for image-making, but because the rules combine and interact in a complex, dynamic way, the results are satisfyingly unpredictable. The complex works that result contain closed and open figures, embracing abstract asymmetric forms which resemble natural shapes like fish, stones, and clouds. In 1983, both the Tate Gallery in London and the Brooklyn Museum in New York featured Cohen's mural-sized computer drawings.

Those artists who choose to design interactive multimedia systems and effective interfaces for viewers ("users") of their work face even more daunting tasks than those of historically analogous, interdisciplinary artists in video, film, installation, and performance. Aside from creating the *mise-en-scène* and the context and metaphoric associations of the work, its movement, sound, and acting, they must also give primary consideration to viewer interaction. This means abandoning the traditional approach to create meaning through controlled linear structures. So far there are no defined criteria and no canon for this expanded medium, although there are technological restraints.

Lyn Hershman is one of the first artists to have taken interactive laserdisc technology beyond commercial exploitation. Her 1984–1986 *Lorna* represents an important beginning artistic involvement with a potentially powerful interactive medium. She is attracted to the interactive disc medium because its programming possibilities provide for a more intense way of dealing with reality, and because of her desire to involve her audience actively by empowering them to self-direct the video screen. In her 1993 interactive installation *A Room of One's Own*, she forces the viewer to see her work through a periscope peephole. The viewer's eye movements themselves are digitized and inserted into a small television set within the tiny specially constructed bedroom scene. The eye movements send signals to a computer which causes the videodisc to access significant segments for viewing on the room's TV. Thus the viewer/voyeur becomes a "virtual" part of the scene being viewed. Depending on whether one turns the periscope towards the bed, the pile of clothes, the telephone, the chair, or a monitor, one of the three screens on the back wall is activated. For example, looking at the bed reveals unpleasant scenes of a woman shaking bars that resemble a sexual prison.

Hershman's film *Conceiving Ada* (1996—Fig. 9 on Color Page CP-5) makes use of virtual sets. It is a cyber-fantasy based on the true story of Augusta Ada Byron (*see* LOVELACE, COUNTESS OF), who in a major collaboration with Charles Babbage (*q.v.*) created software concepts for the Analytical Engine (*q.v.*), a direct forerunner of the modern computer.

It takes enormous skill to craft work where there are pathways, nodes, links, networks, and connecting loops between databases of visual narrative elements with sound and text. Multifaceted procedures and coding require interdisciplinary collaboration.

Most common interactive multimedia (*q.v.*) works are designed for presentation on computer screens. Creating a CD-ROM is similar to organizing a film production in its use of theatrical lighting, scriptwriting, working with actors, music, and storyboard. A work on CD-ROM or its more recent incarnation as DVD-R is not a linear narrative, although it may be a meta-narrative based on a database of narrations, and so does not evoke the suspension of disbelief that is the goal of many films.

A major feature is the interface with the viewer: Experimental investigations for developing new ways to compress and represent complex information and the procedural tools needed for the users/audience to navigate are rapidly being developed, particularly in relation to the Internet and the World Wide Web (*q.v.*). How does communication take place to indicate how interaction should occur? How can the viewer be motivated to interact and to want to continue? What most interactive producers have found is that the interaction itself must be intuitive, meaningful, simple, attractive, familiar-feeling, and noticeably responsive to the user.

Most artists who create interactive forms are interested in providing as much freedom of exploration as possible while still taking control of shaping the experience cohesively. Those who have been struggling the longest with interactive media speak of the need for a rich lode of source material as content for the construction of the work. Examples are CD-ROM books where the "reader" "chooses" between different narrative databases for the characters or concepts such as those in Laurie Anderson's *Puppet Motel*.

Lovers Leap by Miroslaw Rogala (Fig. 10 on Color Page CP-6, created in collaboration with Ford Oxaal and Ludger Hovestadt) is an interactive installation environment where shifts in the viewer's movements control a continuously evolving perspective. Produced at ZKM, Rogala's work comments on aspects of representation itself. He explores untried frontiers of representation by questioning the very parameters of perspective by turning its space in upon itself through digital means. The installation consists of two synchronized screens displaying opposite perspective views with four layers, each with a different set of photographic information. When viewers enter the space, they are aware that their movements are changing what is seen. If the viewer keeps moving through the environment, a series of abrupt shifts is created—the same relationships from a dramatic new perspective—which leap over the viewer. Rogala's digitized images (from a bridge intersection in Chicago and a scene in Jamaica filmed by a satellite camera) are capable of being turned completely inside out, first showing a digitized fish-eye view taken with a conventional camera, skewed as the viewer moves through the piece wearing a movement-sensitive helmet. They are transposed digitally, reformulated from a 180° turnabout, and projected at each end of a large room.

Simulations

A variety of simulation techniques called *texture mapping, ray-tracing, three-dimensional modeling,* and *figure animation interpolation* grew out of high-level research which puts mathematics at the service of the quest for a "new realism." One of the most formidable tasks the computer can accomplish is to simulate a three-dimensional shaded model. Once all the physical measurement information about the object has been fed into the computer's data bank, the simulated object then materializes on the screen. It can then be rotated, skewed, and made to zoom in and out of space in perspective, with a choice of where the light source originates. According to instructions, the computer will calculate the range of highlights and shadings which define an object (depending on the choice of light source), add appropriate shadows, and animate it in full color. The computer can sort through all the instructions and models which describe the scene—its tone, color, optical laws—factoring in all the instructions and checking and sorting out what each piece of the mosaic of pixels should represent.

Powerful Silicon Graphics machines have been designed to capture the essential character of real forms and textures through the programming of digital instructions designed to simulate, for example, the diminishing size of tree branches as the trunk rises from the ground. An enormous number of such algorithms are required for realistic simulation of mountains, clouds, and water. The team at Lucasfilm has even been able to recreate the blur of motion that is caused by a wave striking the shore or two billiard balls colliding. Various computer programs that build in a randomness factor have been developed to make images seem more lifelike.

Monsters of Grace (Fig. 11 on Color Page CP-6) is the first full-length 3D computer animation. It is in the form of an opera based on poetry (by the 13th century Persian poet Jalaluddin Rumi) and is a collaborative work by composer Philip Glass and theatrical producer Robert Wilson, who worked with the computer animation firm of Kleiser-Walczak. Wearing 3D glasses, the audience is assailed by unexpected juxtapositions of unusual objects or events seeming to move forward in the space between screen and viewer. Although there have been many 3D digital animations exploring new aspects of imaging over the years since the early 1980s, this rich and satisfying artwork potentially allows the expansion of esthetic values. The slow-moving animations are suggestive of a meditative inner world, rather than an outer one; of sudden appearances and mysterious disappearances; and of changes in scale.

The Immersive Artwork

Virtual reality hardware now exists for head and hand motion; for the use of body characteristics such as touch, motion, eye focus, gesture/speech; and brain-waves. A small band of artists in Europe and North America are harnessing the potential of virtual reality by exploring it as imaginary space.[2] Although sophisticated VR technology was developed by the military during the Cold War, it was directed at the concept of a sedentary operator following the movement of a vehicle through a 3D virtual world. Myron Kreuger, an artist who has helped to pioneer VR, comments that it is artists who have pushed farther in the imaginary uses of the medium:

> The sense that virtual reality was of fundamental importance came from artists who communicated it immediately to the public through their work. In addition, many aspects of virtual reality including full-body participation, the idea of a shared telecommunication space, multi-sensory feedback, third-person participation, unencumbered approaches and the data glove all came from the arts, not from the technical community.

Some forms of interactivity extend beyond the computer monitor to include a room-sized venue as an interactive installation space. Here, various mechanisms of interactivity can be considered, depending on the artist's work. These could include sensing devices such as those for sound, movement, and temperature or those which focus on communications sensibilities, such as speech, touch, gesture. Jeffrey Shaw (Fig. 12 on Color Page CP-6), artist-director of ZKM, describes how the artwork itself becomes

> a simulation of reality, an immaterial "cyberspace" which we can literally enter. Here the viewer is no longer consumer in a mausoleum of objects; rather he/she is traveler and discoverer in a latent space of audio-visual information. In this temporal dimension the interactive artwork is each time re-structured and re-created by the activity of the viewers.

Most artists approaching VR want to create an open immersive space where they can control all the objects or all the spatial coordinates in order to achieve an esthetic effect. Some project their "virtual images" in

space; some employ head-gear or gloves connected to sensing devices which control the flow and placement of images within the space.

Films and videos are now being designed for insertions of animated figures with live photographed ones in the most complex interactions of reality and fiction yet attempted. Computer-simulated graphic images or animated passages can be encoded as a video signal and inserted into a work as part of its totality, or entire video passages can be digitized and edited, reformulated, manipulated, and again reformatted as a video signal. This provides an unprecedented expansion of pictorial variety and texture. In the future, the computer may play a greater role than the camera in filmmaking. Although they will have the look of photographic reality, most backgrounds and locales in Hollywood films will eventually be computer-generated (*see* Hershman, Fig. 9 on Color Page CP-5). The actors are electronically keyed-in, using computer/video techniques. By the early 1990s, computer animation to perfect human or animal imagery produced the first examples of three-dimensional actor-simulated, feature-length animation. Among others were *Who Killed Roger Rabbit*, *Terminator 2*, and *Conceiving Ada*.

At NYU's Media Research Lab, software has been developed for an artificial intelligence environment called IMPROV. Its narrative mechanisms include real-time personality and behavior attributes which create interactive, live, improvisational animation where the characters decide to respond to the actions of the viewer based upon their mood and personality. Their reactions are generated in real time as 3D color animation.

At MIT, Pattie Maes has created *Alive, An Artificial Life* (Fig. 13 on Color Page CP-6), a virtual immersive environment. The goal of *Alive* is to present an environment in which a real participant can interact in natural and believable ways with autonomous semi-intelligent artificial agents whose behavior appears to be equally natural and believable. Normally, navigation through a virtual space requires the wearing of gloves, goggles, or a helmet—cumbersome equipment tethered to a computer workstation. However, in *Alive*, a single CCD (charge-coupled device) camera obtains color images of a person which are then inserted into a 3D graphical world which contains the position of various body parts. This composite world is then projected onto a large video wall which gives the feeling and effect of a "magic mirror."

Art in Cyberspace

Interactive telecommunications systems empower the individual to connect with others globally and vastly

---

[2] Computer responsive environments date to the 1969 work of Dan Sandin and Myron Kreuger at the University of Wisconsin around the same time as the PULSA group at Yale led by Patrick Clancy created large outdoor environments.

increase the possibilities for inventing expanded forms for art. These include satellite transmissions, online network programs, ISDN, and fax projects. Those artists committed to pioneering this new space speak in a utopian sense of art as connectivity and as communication, and of an emerging "telematic culture" where global dialogue can take place. Artwork can be shared in a larger cross-cultural community than it can be through the confines of the gallery and museum system. Communication on the Internet provides the possibilities of email, of teleconferencing (*see* COMPUTER CONFERENCING) and of exhibiting images and browsing through images organized in gallery or museum-like spaces.

Artists choosing to work with computer telecommunications often choose subjects which focus reflexively on the inherently structural aspects of their medium such as exploiting concepts which focus on the interdependence of world communities. Artists in five different countries might collaborate on a drawing that is faxed and embellished at sites in each country; participants in a global online electronic mail conference are invited to share views about online artworks; via videophone, artists in art cafes in three different cities participate in a teleperformance opera. Artists often critique manipulation of the public mind through information manipulation itself. They invent ways to use browsers as a way of entering people's living spaces. Another possibility is to play with the idea of anonymity as a structure, since telecommunications makes possible a special kind of interaction and experimentation in which, since we can't see the other people, we are forced to form a picture of them based on limited information. For example, a man threatened by the reality he inhabits may want to see what it's like to portray himself as a woman—old, young, black, white, or yellow—what kind of responses would he receive from other males (or females) as a method of expanding his understanding through play-acting. Everything you do with imaging, you do with text first. When video is added to multiuser text tools MOOs and MUDs (*see* ONLINE CONVERSATION), the result is online multimedia.

Software such as CU-SeeMe transmits live digitized video with an uplink feed to the Internet. An example of live imagery being uplinked to the Web is *Alice Sat Here* (Fig. 14 on Color Page CP-6), a project by Emily Hartzell and Nina Sobell in conjunction with computer scientists and engineers from NYU's Center for Digital Multimedia. On entering the gallery, the live viewer is invited to sit on a motorized throne which has a telerobotic (*q.v.*) eye mounted on it. The viewer navigates within the gallery—or in the street—by steering the vehicle. The goal of the piece is to send what a telerobotic videocam "eye" sees to a page on the Internet. This "in effect" turns the Web inside out to create a real physical 3D space which Web users can explore through a collaborative navigation with people who are actually in that place. What this "eye" sees is monitored and controlled by the viewer on the Web. Passers-by on the street are able to interact with this process through a touch screen system surrounding a monitor located in the gallery's front window. A combination of software and hardware is used to create an interface which gives Web users control over an aspect of this physical environment. Feedback comes through the use of video monitoring which shows physical visitors the shape of the piece.

Wax: Discovery of TV Among the Bees by David Blair was one of the first feature-length fiction videos that went out over the Internet. Broadcast over MBONE (for "multicasting backbone") the video was carried in a live, sophisticated, continuous multicast requiring extraordinary global bandwidth, which is available only on NASA's Space Shuttle feed, the Internet's digital video channel. Until recently, Internet video was not a practical possibility because of the bandwidth limitations of standard telephone lines. This is now changing with the advent of digital channels on some cable TV services together with cable modems to access them, as well as DSL (digital subscriber lines) using existing telephone lines. Either of these options makes possible broad bandwidth access to the Internet. These new options will make possible the convergence of television, computers, and the Internet. With these changes, we are witnessing the final conversion of video analog technology to the digital sphere. The rate of technological change through the convergence of telecommunications with the computer is happening with such speed that it is difficult to comprehend and impossible to predict all of its consequences for the arts.

An Online Electronically Produced Public Artwork

An online, electronically produced artwork is transmitted and disseminated like television. But it is completely different from TV because of its interactive potential. It can be accessed as part of an electronic network where the outcome is a kind of sharing and join-in-the-dialogue impulse. Such accessibility changes the work itself because it must be created with a broader audience in mind, one which is larger than through conventional exhibition possibilities.

Sherrie Rabinowitz comments that the implications of the new technological conditions are that we must begin to imagine a much larger scale of creativity, one which opens up the possibility of new communication across all disciplines and boundaries. Linking this idea of using the interactive potential of the medium to empower other people instead of one's self creates a powerful opening for a new role for the artist and a new kind of public art—one with all the constraints and freedoms to communicate within a wider sphere. It implies a new way of being and communicating in the world. Viewers become collaborators in an interactive dialogue, adding notes, drawings and comments at the site of the exhibition or printing out sections of images or texts for exchange or discussion. It can act as an enormous bulletin board (*q.v.*)—a space where communication takes place.

The impulse to create art to involve the public is very different from merely placing artwork on the Net. Such Internet exhibition activities, however, do allow artists to bypass cultural gatekeepers and power brokers. Exhibitions of conventional artwork have been placed in Websites on the Internet and can be downloaded through a normal computer printer complete with the artist's biography and the price of the original. These are rapidly becoming accepted in everyday cultural practice.

Conclusion

Recent advances in new computer chip development point to further miniaturization of equipment, adding to its lightness, its low cost, and its more sophisticated possibilities for integration with other electronic media. Greater image compression and software development is leading to the potential for full motion high-resolution digital video which can be seen on the Internet, on TV, and on the cinema screen. Crucial to the independence of committed, technologically based artists is the problem of access to production and post-production media technology. Also, without a store of ideas and strength of conviction, the artist can become subservient to technology and its high costs. This is a major esthetic, political and economic issue for those who need to innovate and thus take risks for the sake of their artistic integrity as they re-think existing artistic forms and invent new ones.

Bibliography

Books

1961. Williams, R. *The Long Revolution*. London, New York: Chatto & Windus and Columbia University Press.
1964. McLuhan, M. *Understanding Media: The Extensions of Man*. New York: McGraw-Hill.
1966. Mumford, L. *Art and Technics*. New York and London: Columbia University Press.
1971. Francke, H. W. *Computer Graphics/Computer Art*. London: Phaidon.
1972. Knowlton, K. *Collaborations with Artists— A Programmer's Reflections*. Amsterdam: North-Holland.
1976. Leavitt, R. (ed.) *Artist and Computer*. New York: Harmony Books.
1977. Heidegger, M. *The Question Concerning Technology and Other Essays*. New York: Harper & Row.

1978. Benjamin, W. *Illuminations*. New York: Schocken Books.
1981. Berger, J. *Ways of Seeing*. London: BBC and Penguin Books.
1983. Krueger, M. *Artificial Reality*. Reading, MA: Addison-Wesley.
1984. Wallis, B. (ed.) *Art after Modernism: Re-Thinking Representation*. New York: New Museum.
1991. Jameson, F. *Postmodernism: The Cultural Logic of Late Capitalism*. Durham, NC: Duke University Press.
1992. Landow, G. *Hypertext: The Convergence of Contemporary Critical Theory and Technology*. Baltimore, MD: Johns Hopkins Press.
1995. Penny, S. (ed.) *Critical Issues in Electronic Media*. Albany, NY: SUNY Press.
1996. Moser, M. A., and MacLeod, D. (eds.) *Immersed in Technology: Art and Virtual Environments*. Cambridge, MA: MIT Press.
1996. Negroponte, N. *Being Digital*. New York: Vintage Books.
1997. Lovejoy, M. *Postmodern Currents: Art and Artists in the Age of Electronic Media*, 2nd Ed. Upper Saddle River, NJ: Prentice Hall.

Catalogs

1968. *Cybernetic Serendipity*. London: ICA.
1985. *Les Immatériaux: Album et Inventaire Epreuves d'Ecriture*. Paris: Centre Georges Pompidou.
1989. *Image World: Art and Media Culture*. New York: Whitney Museum of Art.
1993. *Iterations: The New Image*. (text ed. T. Druckrey). New York: International Center of Photography/MIT Press.
1995. *Biennale d'art contemporain de Lyon*. Lyon.

Articles

1967. Noll, M. "The Digital Computer as a Creative Medium," *IEEE Spectrum*, **4**, *10* (October), 89–95.
1969. Mallary, R. "Computer Sculpture: Six Levels of Cybernetics," *Artforum*, May.
1988. Nichols, B. "The Work of Culture in the Age of Cybernetic Systems," *Screen*, **29**, *1*, 22–46. (Reprinted in *Technology and Visual Representation* (ed. T. Druckrey). New York: Aperture, 1996.)
1995. Atkins, R. "The Art World and I Go on Line," *Art in America*, **83**, *12* (December), 58–59.

Margot Lovejoy

COMPUTER-ASSISTED LEARNING AND TEACHING

For articles on related subjects *see* LOGO; and NETWORKS FOR LEARNING.

The impact of computers on *teaching* and *learning* activities at all levels of education is considerable, and the extent of use increases as computers become more convenient to use and less expensive to purchase and maintain. Every area of post-secondary education is affected. A medical student practices diagnosis and prescription on a wide variety of hypothetical patients simulated by computer programs. A group of engineering students uses computer assistance to solve problems in analysis and design that otherwise would not be approachable. A student aide develops a program to help a professor of chemistry evaluate the effectiveness of questions on a multiple-choice quiz.

A freshman in general psychology directs a computer-based information system to assemble an extensive bibliography on the relation between achievement, motivation, and college grades which is as current as the journals received by his or her professor. A laboratory technician confirms newly acquired skills using a terminal on a hospital information system (HIS— q.v.). Students in art, music, and English collaborate on the creation and performance of a work combining several media.

Computing is also quite visible in education in schools, homes, and community centers. School science students collect and analyze data on water quality in a stream near their school, and then share their results with similar working groups elsewhere in the world. An English literature student programs a computer to generate poetry. A child explores mathematics and problem solving by writing computer programs that direct a robot to draw spirals or solve mazes. Another practices spelling or addition problems "spoken" by a computer; the computer checks the answers that the student enters on the keyboard. In some systems, the student simply speaks the answer to be "recognized" by the computer. A high school dropout improves language skills using a computer program made available on a community cable television system.

When the computer system is appropriate for educational uses and the programs are properly written, learners should find the assistance to be responsive to their needs; patient and not punitive while they learn; accurate in assessment of answers and problem solutions; individualized in a useful way; realistic in the presentation of training or testing situations; and helpful with many information processing tasks. Teachers find computer assistance valuable for keeping accurate records, summarizing data, projecting student-learning difficulties, assembling individualized tests, and retrieving information about films or other learning resources. Authors of textbooks and other learning materials use computers to draw figures, to animate motion picture sequences, or to keep track of the introduction and frequency of occurrence of concepts throughout a text. Researchers record and analyze data, build models of student learning and performance, and administer experiments on methods of instruction. Administrators use computers for keeping records, planning, scheduling, allocating resources, and processing data. These applications and many others are described in the references at the end of this article.

A Brief History of Computer-Assisted Instruction (CAI)

Use of the computer as a tool for problem solving in education began in US graduate schools in about 1955, and a few years later moved into the classroom with the initiation of curriculum development projects in engineering and science. Computers used as teaching machines date from 1958; early developments took place at IBM's Watson Research Center, System Development Corporation, and the University of Illinois Coordinated Science Laboratory. The topic of computers in education became popular for meetings in 1965; separate conferences were held on computers in American education, higher education, and physics teaching. In the next 10 years, major conferences were organized for computers in mathematics teaching, chemistry education, computer science education, science education, the undergraduate curriculum, and high school counseling.

Also in the 1960s a group of engineers and educators in the Computer-based Education Research Laboratory at the University of Illinois, Urbana, designed a computing system (PLATO) especially for effective and efficient teaching. It was a large system that provided instructional computing to about 1,000 simultaneous users throughout the university and also a number of other colleges and schools in Illinois. The design included notable advances in the technology for display and communications. The PLATO system was once marketed commercially by Control Data Corporation (q.v.) with curriculum materials and programming language available for use with microcomputers.

At about the same time Stanford University operated a CAI system to distribute instructional computing to a number of centers throughout the country. A large-scale service operation using long-distance telephone communications, clusters of terminals, and some stand-alone computer systems, the remote centers were usually associated with elementary school demonstration projects and special education institutions. The service operation was conducted in parallel with an extensive program of research and development at the Institute for Mathematical Studies in the Social Sciences, Stanford University. Curriculum materials were prepared for young children (elementary school mathematics and reading), learners with special difficulties (for example, the deaf), and certain university courses (especially second-language learning and logic). Some of these materials have been marketed by the Computer Curriculum Corporation, along with new developments.

TICCIT (Time-shared, Interactive, Computer-controlled Informational Television) was a name given to systems developed by the Mitre Corporation in McLean, VA, and since marketed by Hazeltine Corporation. The first version of a TICCIT instructional system was designed especially for use in a small college. It was a medium-sized computer system with video technology to obtain low-cost operation with about 100 simultaneous users. The hardware and software design was coordinated with the development of instructional materials, carefully prepared according to rules of effective instruction by instructional design teams at Brigham Young University in Utah, to provide basic remedial instruction in mathematical and language skills at small colleges.

CAI has had many successes in military and industrial training, where the objectives are clear and a modest percentage advantage in delivery cost and trainee time adds up to considerable savings for the organization. Effective automation of training is essential in areas where new job requirements, employee turnover, and decreasing skills among those entering the workforce combine to force costs up.

The commercial introduction of the personal computer in 1977 reduced the cost of computers in education. Tools for desktop publishing (*q.v.*), laboratory instrumentation, music, graphic art, and manipulation of media introduced in the 1980s increased the scope and depth of applications. The instructional use of computers is a familiar topic at meetings of the

contributing professions (computing, engineering, psychology, and educational research) and at meetings of teachers of disciplines ranging from engineering and physics to history, art, and modern languages. Various human components in effective computer use for learning and teaching are related in Fig. 1.

In recent years the locus of decisions about CAI in education has shifted from institutions to individuals. Parents are taking their children to community learning centers for automated tutoring to improve basic skills. Students and families are purchasing home computers to provide learning activities along with productivity tools and entertainment.

When "instruction," in the acronym CAI, is replaced by "learning," as in CAL, the combination connotes greater emphasis on activities initiated by the learner than on the instructional materials created by a teacher-author. When "learning" is replaced by "education" to obtain CAE (or CBE, computer-based education), the implication is a greater variety of computer uses, including administrative data processing and materials production as well as student use of computers. If the role of the computer is to assist the teacher in managing

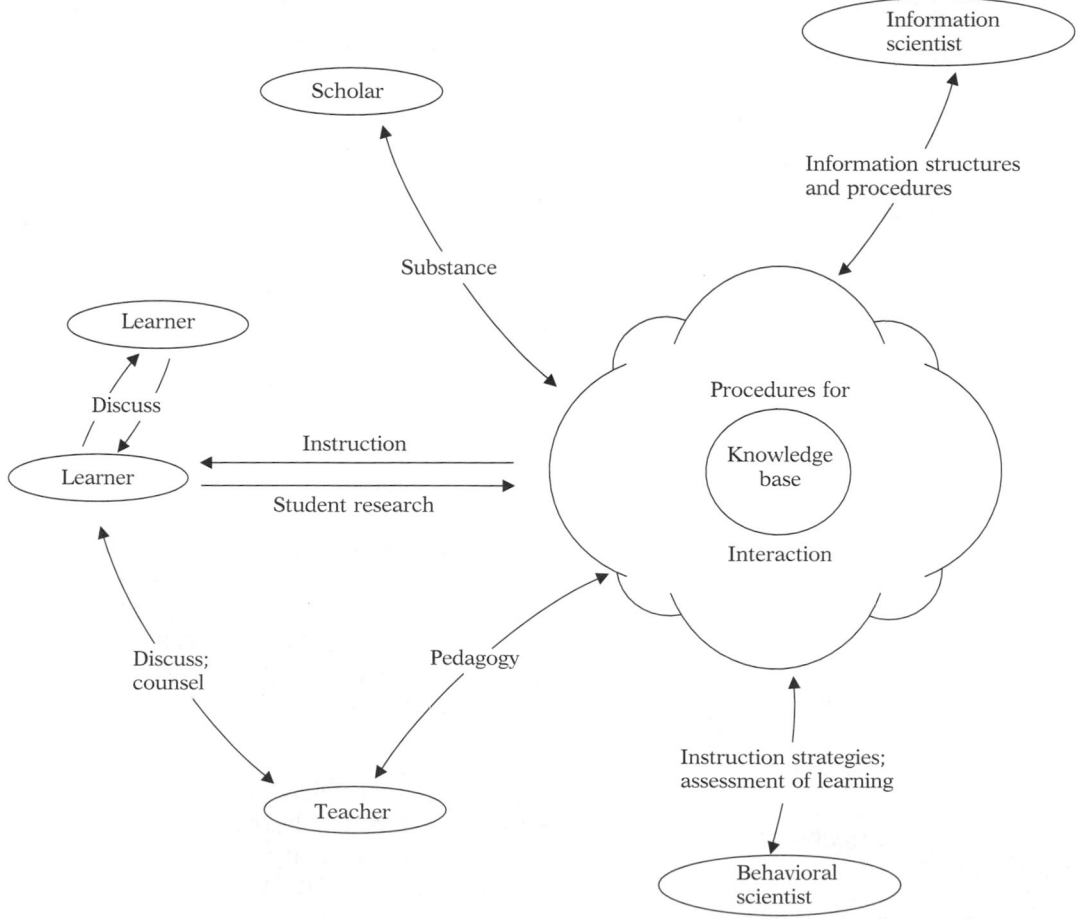

Figure 1. Human components in effective computer use for learning and teaching.

instruction, for example, in retrieving and summarizing performance records and curriculum files, the label used is CMI: computer-managed instruction.

Special interest groups on computers and learning have been formed by professional associations and other organizations. Newsletters, bulletins, and journals carry reports of use, development, and research. Problems and opportunities are discussed by users of the Internet (*q.v.*) through mailing lists, newsgroups, and computer-based conferencing (*see* COMPUTER CONFERENCING).

Kinds of Use

Computer assistance with learning and teaching has been described by many different phrases. One could assemble an apt phrase by selecting one word or suffix from each of the following three lists:

computer	-aided	training
technology	-assisted	instruction
media	-augmented	learning
	-based	teaching
	-extended	education
	-managed	
	-mediated	
	-monitored	
	-related uses in	

The most common label has been CAI: computer-aided (or computer-assisted) instruction. It refers to the use of computers to present drills, practice exercises, and tutorial sequences to the student, and perhaps to engage the student in a dialogue about the substance of the instruction. A CAI (tutorial) dialogue is achieved between a computer program and a student when the responses derived from the program are highly responsive to the questions, answers, and directives given by the student, while at the same time the dialogue advances the goals and means established by the author of the curriculum materials.

CAI has proved successful where the goals of instruction are clearly defined, achievement of those goals is highly valued by the organization providing instruction, the substance of instruction is suited to automated delivery, and the student is lacking important skills, background, or motivation for self-instruction via less expensive media. Research studies tend to show advantages for CAI in terms of shorter learning times and improved performance. Inhibitors to use include high costs of delivery systems and curriculum development, conflicts between individualized instruction and current educational practices, and the commitment of most of the computing resources available in schools to instructional use for education about computers.

Instruction and the Learning Process

The most visible use of computers in instruction is to provide direct assistance to learners and to assist teachers, administrators, and educational technologists in helping learners. The users may work individually or in groups, using a device directly connected to a computer (online) or using some medium later entered into a computer (offline), typing letters and numbers only (alphanumeric) or pointing and drawing diagrams for the computer (graphic), scanning images, speaking words, singing or playing an instrument, and many other options. Some typical labels within this category of use are drill, skills practice, programmed tutorial, testing and diagnosis, dialogue tutorial, simulation, gaming, information retrieval and processing, computation, problem solving, construction of procedures as models, and display of graphic constructions. A very popular use of the computer is for simulation of a decision-making situation, as in resource management, pollution control, business marketing, or medical testing. For example, college economics students study the history of a hypothetical national economy, prescribe actions such as changing the prime interest rate, and observe the consequences for unemployment, inflation, and other indicators. Time is greatly compressed in the hypothetical situation, and real-world complexities are abstracted for easier study.

MANAGEMENT OF INSTRUCTION RESOURCES AND PROCESS

Computer aids help teachers to supervise the instructional process, and similar assistance is provided directly to students without the intervention of teachers and managers. Information management services are readily extended to potential users of learning resources outside traditional educational institutions. The essential information in the various files for management of instructional resources concerns student performance, learning materials, desired outcomes, job opportunities, and student interests. For example, students obtain information from the computer about achievement and then compare their own performance, interests, and goals with averages recorded for all similar students using the information system. After interpreting the information provided, the student uses the computer further to locate and retrieve suitable learning aids from a large file keyed to goals, learning difficulties, job opportunities, and interests.

PREPARATION AND DISPLAY OF MATERIALS

Materials may be generated in "real time" (i.e. as needed by a student in a seminar or by a teacher during a lecture). Text and problems may also be assembled by computer in advance of scheduled use so that individualized material may be distributed at less expense than through individual computer stations. Computers assist writers of materials in many ways—for example tools for generating films and graphics; data collection during trial of materials under development; procedures for automatically editing and analyzing text materials for new uses, and information structures for representing new organizations of knowledge; hierarchies of instructional objectives; and libraries of learning materials. New technologies are changing the work of technicians and teachers in developing educational materials and media. Machines handle the routine tasks in preparing graphics and editing film or video.

OTHER USES OF INFORMATION PROCESSING

Those planning instructional uses apply computers in administration (accounting, scheduling, planning, etc.) and in research (institutional, sociological, psychological, instructional, etc.), and to the practice of various computer-related vocations in science, technology, management, banking, production, retailing, etc. The last area is especially important because of the needs for preservice training. For example, most large retailing operations use computing heavily, and employees with some sensible background in computing have a better chance of coming to terms with computer assistance on the job. Indeed, a general literacy about computing and information processing is essential in the age of informatics. Educated persons should have sufficient knowledge about the practices of automated information processing to exercise on occasion effective control over the machines and data files with which they must deal.

Means and Goals

DIVERSITY OF RESOURCES

Many different kinds of computer and software systems are being used effectively (*see* Fig. 2). Desktop and laptop machines can be used by one or a few students to access stored programs (usually drills or simulations), collect data in the field, or assemble resources collected by searches using the Internet. Workstations (*q.v.*) offer tools for scholarly and creative work conducted by students individually and in groups.

Programming languages and systems (software) exhibit even more diversity than the computing equipment (hardware). More than 100 languages and dialects have been developed specifically for programming conversational instruction, although many programs have been written in general-purpose languages, such as Fortran, Pascal, C, and Basic. Different kinds of users have distinguishable requirements: students, instructors, authors, instructional researchers, administrators, and computer programmers. The characteristics of different subject areas also necessitate different language features. Appropriate design of display screens, user control, and input devices can be of

Figure 2. Boy using a multimedia personal computer at home to learn French. The computer screen is showing the training package's introductory title page, with the French flag and Eiffel tower. Multimedia (*q.v.*) computers are able to make sounds as well as produce pictures. The combination of a spoken word with a colorful graphical image can help students to memorize it. Multimedia training packages also have the advantage of allowing the user to progress at a comfortable speed. (Courtesy of Damien Lovegrove/ Science Photo Library.)

great help compensating for disabilities (*see* DISABLED, COMPUTERS AND THE) and reduces the need for the user to learn computing tools and languages that are incidental to the learning and performance tasks.

Instructional materials (sometimes called *courseware*) have been written in nearly all subject areas and for many age levels. While some of the materials use the computer as an information processing device, others use it as a presentation medium in competition with less expensive modes, such as books or video tapes.

Strategies of instruction associated with computer use (the name *teachware* has been proposed) have been explored. Guidelines for writing instruction-related computer programs have been derived from psychological and educational research, but most developers work from a "common sense" analysis and by trial and error. Some basis for a new science of instruction has been established by research programs which collect data while manipulating variables of the experiments.

COMPUTER CONTRIBUTIONS

The value of computer assistance for self-instruction depends on many factors: organization of the subject matter, the purposes of the author or institution, convenient means for interacting with the subject, and the characteristics of the student. Self-study material in text format has been adapted for computer presentation with the following computer contributions proposed. First, the machine evaluates a response constructed by the student (the author must provide a key or standard); an automated procedure prints out discrepancies, tallies scores, and selects remedial or enrichment material. Second, the machine conceals and, to some extent, controls the teaching material so that the author can specify greater complexity in a strategy of instruction and assume more accuracy in its execution than is possible when the student is expected to find a way through the branching instructions in the pages of a large booklet (the scrambled text format for programmed instruction). Third, the computer carries out operations specified by the student, who uses a simple programming language or computer-aided design (*q.v.*) system. Fourth, the author or researcher obtains detailed data on student performance (and perhaps attitude) along with a convenient summary of student accomplishment ready for interpretation. Fifth, the author is able to modify the text on the basis of student use and prepare alternative versions with relative ease.

The prepackaged self-instruction just described can be replaced by a dynamic information system that serves as a common working ground for a scholar and a learner; they share a computer-based, primary source "textbook," continually updated by the scholar and occasionally annotated by each student who uses it (*see* Fig. 3). Hypertext (*q.v.*) was conceived by Vannevar Bush, named by Theodor Nelson (then at Vassar College), first implemented by Douglas Engelbart at Stanford Research Institute, and then implemented in another way by Andries van Dam at Brown University. The first successful product was Hyper-Card by Apple Computer, Inc. (*q.v.*); hypertext has now been popularized by the World Wide Web (*q.v.*).

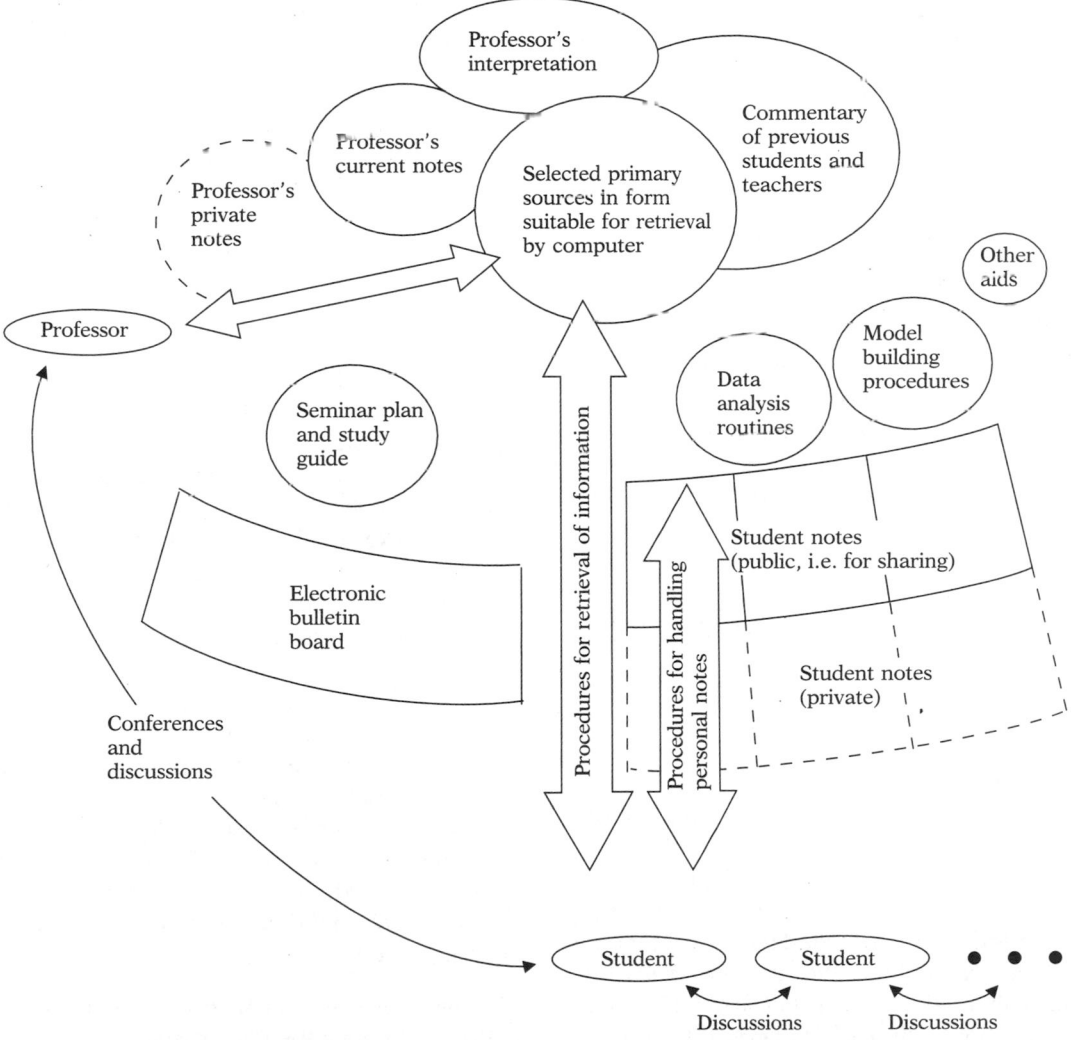

Figure 3. A dynamic information system for scholar and learner.

A flexible and adaptive information system helps a learner and teacher share a common working environment for hypothesis testing. The environment is sometimes artificial, as in computer simulation of physical and social processes (e.g. a model of evolution), and sometimes real in the sense of actual data from experiments (e.g. election returns or water quality measures). Increased access to information processing tools is perhaps the most important contribution of computers to instruction and learning. Many such activities, perhaps not all called computer-assisted instruction, demonstrate viable alternatives to strictly specified instructional strategies for computer use. For example, students in sociology retrieve and summarize information obtained from large-scale surveys and test hypotheses that might never have been conceived by those who executed and reported the survey. Students in physics test lens designs according to a detailed model of aberrations and corrections, perhaps finding variations on standard lens designs that better serve a particular photographic or instrumentation purpose.

Whatever the technique or philosophy of computer use, the extent of use supported by educational institutions will ultimately be determined by judgments of appropriateness by subject experts, effectiveness observed from records of student performance, and costs that must be met by administrators of schools or training programs.

Some of the limitations imposed by the present computer technology involve the unreliability of processing lengthy verbal constructions and the inaccuracy of interpreting bodily gestures or vocal intonations. Computing costs are decreasing even while capabilities are increasing, but one of the most difficult problems remaining is lack of organization of the subject matter. Human teachers manage to be reasonably successful in spite of vague goals and material poorly organized for learning; instructional computing (or educational technology in general) seems to require specific text materials and clear guidelines (prepared by curriculum experts) for successful use.

Major Approaches

EDUCATIONAL TECHNOLOGY

Educational technology and instructional psychology have been the main sources of one kind of development activity. Specific programming of computer-based lessons characterizes this first approach to computer use. Whether it is delivered by a desktop computer or a collection of servers on the World Wide Web, the software has built into it an implicit logic of instruction requiring the author to fit text and keywords into the following pattern: (1) the computer program presents information to the student; (2) the computer program then asks a question and waits for a response from the student; (3) the program scans a short textual response and classifies the response as right or wrong according to keywords identified within it; and (4) if the student's response matches an anticipated wrong answer, the program displays a corrective hint and, if nothing was recognized, it offers a general hint. Instances of this approach can be characterized as the computerization of programmed instruction.

In some curriculum development projects the content has been assembled in files separate from the logic of the computer program (the strategy of instruction). Elements of the curriculum can thereby be varied without rewriting many lines of instructions to the computer, and different strategies can be tried on the same file of learning materials. This arrangement helps the instructional psychologist give full attention to the design of effective instructional strategies and helps the subject expert avoid the distraction of programming procedures. In fact, this approach is generally pursued by a team, with each member contributing different expertise.

Problems faced by the educational technology approach to computer use result from the cost of the computer as a primary medium for exposition of learning materials, the difficulties of accurately identifying unconstrained input (text, algebraic expressions, drawings, spoken expression, etc.), and the lack of a well-developed theory of instruction.

DISCIPLINES AND CURRICULUM

Discipline-oriented use of the computer was pursued by many institutions quite separately from developments in educational technology. Several conferences are held on the topic of computers and curriculum each year. Regional support services, conferences, and newsletters have been established to serve the needs of colleges and schools throughout a district or region. In contrast to the educational technology approach, the teacher as subject expert in the discipline approach assumes the central role in determining computer use, creating materials, and persuading colleagues to use them. Computing activity is likely to include more student initiative in solving problems and more problem-orienting program packages than does expository material. Student use of simulation and modeling tools is favored; one goal is to adapt the scholar's research tools and the practitioner's productivity tools to student use.

The discipline approach to computer use has many problems; among them are sparse user documentation for instruction-related computing activities that are worthy of widespread use; lack of economic and professional incentives for the production and dissemination of programs and related materials; and difficult procedures for the review and validation of programs. Professional groups are working to set high standards and improve incentives for quality work through annual awards programs and other activities. Widespread use of personal computers and the Internet provides a market that now has the attention of publishers and authors in addition to professional societies.

COMPUTING AND INFORMATION SCIENCES

Some researchers suggest that major advances in instructional use of computers will occur through significant developments in artificial intelligence (*q.v.*), natural language processing (*q.v.*), speech recognition (*q.v.*), and virtual reality (*q.v.*) Although information scientists are typically more interested in their own disciplines and related research topics than in educational techniques and practice, the tools developed may be useful to others. The results of computer science research may be an important source of suitable models for instruction strategies, information structures, and representations of knowledge (*see* KNOWLEDGE REPRESENTATION). Projects giving particular attention to educational applications have adapted tools from computing and information science, and formulated new models of human learning and information processing.

Development of techniques and materials using the information science approach tends to be costly and time consuming; the resulting applications may be more expensive for students to use; skill in use of the specialized development techniques is not easily acquired by persons outside computer science. Nevertheless, projects based in computing and information sciences continue to provide important indicators of future resources that may be essential to the success of computers in education.

COMPUTING TECHNOLOGY, ENGINEERING, AND "COMMON SENSE"

A fourth category includes all other approaches, particularly those characterized by the engineering of technology helpful to learning and creative work, perhaps involving some combination of the first three approaches. Engineers design and build systems suited to a range of purposes: educational technologists present programmed instruction, instructional psychologists conduct research on teaching and learning, professors prepare a computer presentation of a lecture or laboratory, and computer specialists build information processing aids for learning and scholarly work. Specialists in computers and education devise various programming languages (e.g. Logo and LogoWriter) and equipment (computer-controlled "turtle," music player, and construction kits) for computer-related learning activities. Children write simple programs for controlling robots, drawing and animating pictures, generating speech and music, and the like. Interest in enhancing such capabilities motivates a new approach to mathematics and heuristics (*q.v.*) in which programming languages provide a powerful conceptual framework.

Trends

A major trend in the design of computer-based exercises has been a shift from programmer to learner control. The designer of the exercise invests less effort in a careful diagnosis and prescription accomplished by some automated instructional strategy, and instead provides information and tools by which the student can explore the topic and assess his or her own learning.

Considerable use of graphics has become typical. Pictures are an important component of the learning process, and computer-drawn pictures and animations add to the responsive uses of computing. For many topics the picture is a valuable way of representing complex relationships derived by the computer.

Computer-based education systems and designers of materials have provided an increasing variety of functions for the user. More attention has been given to interaction between student and computer program, not simply to provide a quick reply to some question, but to increase the actual responsiveness of the system to the student's needs and situation. The machine responds to the commands and questions of the student, and the exercises are designed in a way that helps the student retrieve and organize the information provided by the computer.

A very important trend concerns the role of the machine from the perspective of the individual using it. The teacher is now more likely to see computer-managed instruction as an aid to human management than as a replacement for it. Learners view the machine more as an aid to learning and performance than as a presenter and drill master. All these developments have been helped along by personal ownership of computers, software and systems which are easy to use, and access to materials on the World Wide Web.

Naturalness of communication between learner and system is being improved day by day. Computer-based learning exercises are achieving increased relevance for the subject being studied, and the nomenclature and conventions that have to be learned in order to use the system tend to be essential to the study of the topics rather than peculiar to the requirement of the computer as a medium of presentation.

Bibliography

1993. Lajoie, S., and Derry, S. J. *Computers as Cognitive Tools.* Hillsdale, NJ: Lawrence Erlbaum Associates.

1993. Papert, S. *The Children's Machine: Rethinking School in the Age of the Computer.* New York: Basic Books.

1995. Office of Technology Assessment, United States Congress. *Teachers & Technology: Making the Connection.* Washington, DC: Congressional Printing Office.

1996. Fisher, C., Dwyer, D. C., and Yocam, K. (eds.) *Education and Technology: Reflections on Computing in Classrooms.* San Francisco: Jossey-Bass.

1996. Gooden, A. R. *Computers in the Classroom: How Teachers and Students are Using Technology to Transform Learning.* San Francisco: Jossey-Bass.

1997. Sandholtz, J. H., Ringstaff, C., and Dwyer, D. C. *Teaching with Technology: Creating Student-Centered Classrooms.* New York: Teachers College Press.

1997. Schank, R. C. *Virtual Learning: A Revolutionary Approach to Building a Highly Skilled Workforce.* New York: McGraw-Hill.

1998. NECC. *The 19th Annual National Educational Computing Conference.* Eugene, OR: International Society for Technology in Education.

Karl L. Zinn

COMPUTER CHESS

For articles on related subjects *see* ARTIFICIAL INTELLIGENCE; and COMPUTER GAMES: TRADITIONAL GAMES.

Chess tournaments exclusively for computers have been held since 1970 (*see* Table 1). Until 1978, these tournaments were dominated by David Slate and Larry Atkin's program, first called Chess 3.0 and finally, after many revisions, Chess 4.9. It earned a rating (on the international rating scale) of about 2050 in 1978. It was developed at Northwestern University and ran on CDC's Cyber 176 in the late 1970s. Chess 4.9 carried out a sequence of incrementally deeper exhaustive depth-first searches, examining approximately 5,000 chess positions per second. Belle, developed at Bell Laboratories by Ken Thompson and Joe Condon, ruled the world of computer chess from 1979 through 1983. It was the first program to be awarded the title of Master by the United States Chess Federation (USCF). Belle examined 150,000 chess positions per second and ran on special-purpose chess circuitry. In 1983, Cray Blitz, developed at the University of Southern Mississippi by Robert Hyatt, Albert Gower, and Harry Nelson, won the world computer chess championship while running on a 4-processor Cray XMP supercomputer. The program successfully defended its title in 1986. Hitech appeared in 1986, winning the Pennsylvania State Championship two years in a row and, while being a bit unlucky in computer tournament play, established new levels of performance in human play, obtaining a USCF rating in the neighborhood of 2400. Hitech, which also used special-purpose chess circuitry, was developed at Carnegie Mellon University

by the programming team of Carl Ebeling, Hans Berliner, Gordon Goetsch, Murray Campbell, Andy Gruss, and Andy Palay. It searched approximately 200,000 positions per second.

In 1988, Deep Thought established itself as the world's best program and began defeating grandmasters in tournament competition and earning a rating of approximately 2600. It won the World Computer Chess Championship in 1989. Later that year, it lost a two-game match to Garry Kasparov, the human world champion. Work on Deep Thought began at Carnegie Mellon University. Subsequently, the programming team joined IBM's T. J. Watson Research Center. The team was originally led by Feng-Hsiung Hsu and has included Murray Campbell, Thomas Anantharaman, Mike Browne, Andreas Nowatzyk, Joe Hoane, and Jerry Brody, with Chung-Jen Tan serving as the project leader beginning in 1992. In 1994, the program was renamed Deep Blue. The most recent versions run on a 32-node IBM RS6000 SP computer with each node containing a special-purpose chess circuit. In the course of selecting a move, Deep Blue examines in excess of 200,000,000 chess moves per second.

In 1996, Kasparov defeated Deep Blue in the six-game $500,000 ACM Computer Chess Challenge match by a score of 4–2. The following year, Deep Blue turned the tables, defeating the world champion in the six-game $1,000,000 IBM-sponsored Kasparov versus Deep Blue Rematch by a score of 3.5–2.5. The six games from this historic match are presented in Fig. 1. Kasparov had a rating of 2828 entering the match. Deep Blue would earn a rating above that based on the results.

In the 1980s, endgame databases were created by Ken Thompson and Larry Stiller. All five-piece endgames have been solved as well as a number of six-piece endgames. The databases are built using retrograde analysis: starting with a database of won or drawn positions and then working backwards to all other positions, each position is assigned a win, loss, or draw, and a count of the number of moves to the end of the game, or to another simpler endgame.

In 1978, British International Master David Levy won a wager of several thousand dollars by defeating Chess 4.7 in a match in Toronto. In 1968, Levy had wagered four computer scientists that no computer would defeat him in a match during the next ten years. Levy won the match with a 3.5–1.5 score. Following the match, *Omni* magazine offered a prize of $5,000 to the authors of the first program to defeat Levy. The prize was won by Deep Thought in 1989 when it defeated Levy with a perfect 4–0 score.

At the 1977 World Championship in Toronto, the International Computer Chess Association was formed

Table 1. History of Major Computer Chess Championships (name of program; names of programmers; computer)

World Championships

Year, City	Winner, Runner-up
1974, Stockholm	KAISSA (Donskoy, Arlazarov; ICL 4/70); CHESS 4.0 (Slate, Atkin; CDC 6600)
1977, Toronto	CHESS 4.6 (Slate, Atkin; CDC Cyber 176); DUCHESS (Truscott, Wright, Jensen; IBM 370/165)
1980, Linz	BELLE (Thompson, Condon; PDP 11/23 with chess circuitry); CHAOS (Alexander, Swartz, Berman, O'Keefe; Amdahl 470/V8)
1983, New York	CRAY BLITZ (Hyatt, Gower, Nelson; Cray X-MP/48); BEBE (Scherzer; Chess Engine)
1986, Cologne	CRAY BLITZ (Hyatt, Gower, Nelson; Cray X-MP/48); HITECH (Berliner *et al.*; Sun workstation with chess circuitry)
1989, Edmonton	DEEP THOUGHT (Hsu, Anantharaman, Browne, Campbell, Jansen, Nowatzyk; Sun with VLSI chess hardware); BEBE (Scherzer, Scherzer; Chess Engine)
1992, Madrid	CHESS MACHINE/SCHRÖDER (Schröder; ARM2); ZUGZWANG (Feldman, Mysliwietz; Parsytec T-800)
1995, Hong Kong	FRITZ 3 (Morsch, de Corter, Feist; 90 Mhz Pentium PC); STAR SOCRATES (Dailey, Joerg, Kuszmaul, Leiserson, Blumofe, Frigo, Kaufman, Randall, Riesen, Zhou; 1824-node Intel Paragon)
1999, Paderborn, Germany	SHREDDER (Meyer-Kahlen; Single CPU Microcomputer); FERRET (Moreland; Gateway ALR 9200)

ACM International Computer Chess Championships

(Initially called the ACM United States Computer Chess Championship, renamed the ACM North American Computer Chess Championship in 1975, renamed again the ACM International Computer Chess Championship in 1991, and not held after 1994.)

Year, City	Winner, Runner-up (* denotes a tie)
1970, New York	CHESS 3.0 (Slate, Atkin, Gorlen; CDC 6400); DALY CHESS PROGRAM (Daly, King; Varian 620/i)
1971, Chicago	CHESS 3.5 (Slate, Atkin, Gorlen; CDC 6400); TECH (Gillogly; PDP 10)
1972, Boston	CHESS 3.6 (Slate, Atkin, Gorlen; CDC 6400); OSTRICH (Arnold, Newborn; DG Supernova)
1973, Atlanta	CHESS 4.0 (Slate, Atkin, Gorlen; CDC 6400); TECH II (Baisley; PDP 10)
1974, San Diego	RIBBIT (Hansen, Crook, Parry; Honeywell 6050); CHESS 4.0 (Slate, Atkin; CDC 6400)
1975, Minneapolis	CHESS 4.4 (Slate, Atkin; CDC Cyber 175); TREEFROG (Hansen, Calnek, Crook; Honeywell 6080)
1976, Houston	CHESS 4.5 (Slate, Atkin; CDC Cyber 176); CHAOS (Swartz, Berman, Alexander, Ruben, Toikka, Winograd; Amdahl 470)
1977, Seattle	CHESS 4.6 (Slate, Atkin; CDC Cyber 176); DUCHESS (Truscott, Wright, Jensen; IBM 370/168)
1978, Washington	BELLE (Thompson, Condon; PDP 11/70 with chess hardware); CHESS 4.7 (Slate, Atkin; CDC Cyber 176)
1979, Detroit	CHESS 4.9 (Slate, Atkin; CDC Cyber 176); BELLE (Thompson, Condon; PDP 11/70 with chess hardware)
1980, Nashville	BELLE (Thompson, Condon; PDP 11/70 with chess hardware); CHAOS (Alexander, O'Keefe, Swartz, Berman; Amdahl 470)
1981, Los Angeles	BELLE (Thompson, Condon; PDP 11/23 with chess hardware); NUCHESS (Blanchard, Slate; CDC Cyber 176)
1982, Dallas	BELLE (Thompson, Condon; PDP 11/23 with chess hardware); , 286–295, 286–295; CRAY BLITZ (Hyatt, Gower, Nelson; Cray 1)
1983 Not held as the ACM NACC that year but as the Fourth World Championship. See World Champions.	
1984, San Francisco	CRAY BLITZ (Hyatt, Gower, Nelson; Cray X-MP/4); *BEBE (Scherzer; Chess Engine); *FIDELITY EXPERIMENTAL (Spracklen, Spracklen; Fidelity machine)
1985, Denver	HITECH (Ebeling, Berliner, Goetsch, Paley, Campbell, Slomer; Sun with chess hardware); BEBE (Scherzer; Chess Engine)
1986, Dallas	BELLE (Thompson, Condon; PDP 11/23 with chess hardware); LACHEX (Wendroff; Cray X-MP)
1987, Dallas	CHIPTEST-M (Anantharaman, Hsu, Campbell; Sun 3 with VLSI chess hardware); CRAY BLITZ (Hyatt, Nelson, Gower; Cray X-MP/48)
1988, Orlando	DEEP THOUGHT 0.02 (Hsu, Anatharaman, Browne, Campbell, Nowatzyk; Sun 3 with VLSI circuitry); CHESS CHALLENGER EXP (Spracklen, Spracklen, Nelson; Fidelity machine with Motorola 68030 microprocessor)
1989, Reno, NV	*HITECH (Ebeling, Berliner, Goetsch, Paley, Campbell, Slomer; Sun with chess hardware); *DEEP THOUGHT (Hsu, Anantharaman, Browne, Campbell, Nowatzyk; 3 SUN 4s with VLSI chess hardware)

Table 1. *Continued*

1990, New York	DEEP THOUGHT/88 (Hsu, Anantharaman, Jensen, Campbell, Nowatzyk; SUN 4 with two special VLSI chess circuits); MEPHISTO (Lang; 68030 microprocessor MEPHISTO machine)
1991, Albuquerque	DEEP THOUGHT II (Hsu, Campbell; RS/6000 500 + 24 chess processors); M CHESS (Hirsch; IBM PC Clone/486)
1993, Indianapolis	SOCRATES II (Dailey, Kaufmann; IBM PC); CRAY BLITZ (Hyatt, Gower, Nelson; Cray X-MP/48)
1994, Cape May, NJ	DEEP THOUGHT II (Hsu, Campbell, Hoane; RS/6000 580 + 12 chess processors); ZARKOV (Stanback; HP735)

Game 1: 3 May 1997
White: Garry Kasparov   *Black*: Deep Blue
Reti Opening

1 Nf3 d5   2 g3 Bg4   3 b3 Nd7   4 Bb2 e6   5 Bg2 Ngf6   6 O-O c6   7 d3 Bd6   8 Nbd2 O-O   9 h3 Bh5   10 e3 h6   11 Qe1 Qa5
12 a3 Bc7   13 Nh4 g5   14 Nhf3 e5   15 e4 Rfe8   16 Nh2 Qb6   17 Qc1 a5   18 Re1 Bd6   19 Ndf1 d×e4   20 d×e4 Bc5
21 Ne3 Rad8   22 Nhf1 g4   23 h×g4 N×g4   24 f3 N×e3   25 N×e3 Be7   26 Kh1 Bg5   27 Re2 a4   28 b4 f5   29 e×f5 e4
30 f4 B×e2   31 f×g5 Ne5   32 g6 Bf3   33 Bc3 Qb5   34 Qf1 Q×f1   35 R×f1 h5   36 Kg1 Kf8   37 Bh3 b5   38 Kf2 Kg7   39 g4 Kh6
40 Rg1 h×g4   41 B×g4 B×g4   42 N×g4+ N×g4+   43 R×g4 Rd5   44 f6 Rd1   45 g7 Black resigns.

Game 2: 4 May 1997
White: Deep Blue   *Black*: Garry Kasparov
Ruy Lopez

1 e4 e5   2 Nf3 Nc6   3 Bb5 a6   4 Ba4 Nf6   5 O-O Be7   6 Re1 b5   7 Bb3 d6   8 c3 O-O   9 h3 h6   10 d4 Re8   11 Nbd2 Bf8
12 Nf1 Bd7   13 Ng3 Na5   14 Bc2 c5   15 b3 Nc6   16 d5 Ne7   17 Be3 Ng6   18 Qd2 Nh7   19 a4 Nh4   20 N×h4 Q×h4
21 Qe2 Qd8   22 b4 Qc7   23 Rec1 c4   24 Ra3 Rec8   25 Rca1 Qd8   26 f4 Nf6   27 f×e5 d×e5   28 Qf1 Ne8   29 Qf2 Nd6
30 Bb6 Qe8   31 R3a2 Be7   32 Bc5 Bf8   33 Nf5 B×f5   34 e×f5 f6   35 B×d6 B×d6   36 a×b5 a×b5   37 Be4 R×a2   38 Q×a2 Qd7
39 Qa7 Rc7   40 Qb6 Rb7   41 Ra8+ Kf7   42 Qa6 Qc7   43 Qc6 Qb6+   44 Kf1 Rb8   45 Ra6 Black resigns.

Game 3: 6 May 1997
White: Garry Kasparov   *Black*: Deep Blue
English Opening

1 d3 e5   2 Nf3 Nc6   3 c4 Nf6   4 a3 d6   5 Nc3 Be7   6 g3 O-O   7 Bg2 Be6   8 O-O Qd7   9 Ng5 Bf5   10 e4 Bg4   11 f3 Bh5
12 Nh3 Nd4   13 Nf2 h6   14 Be3 c5   15 b4 b6   16 Rb1 Kh8   17 Rb2 a6   18 b×c5 b×c5   19 Bh3 Qc7   20 Bg4 Bg6   21 f4 e×f4
22 g×f4 Qa5   23 Bd2 Q×a3   24 Ra2 Qb3   25 f5 Q×d1   26 B×d1 Bh7   27 Nh3 Rfb8   28 Nf4 Bd8   29 Nfd5 Nc6   30 Bf4 Ne5
31 Ba4 N×d5   32 N×d5 a5   33 Bb5 Ra7   34 Kg2 g5   35 B×e5+ d×e5   36 f6 Bg6   37 h4 g×h4   38 Kh3 Kg8   39 K×h4 Kh7
40 Kg4 Bc7   41 N×c7 R×c7   42 R×a5 Rd8   43 Rf3 Kh8   44 Kh4 Kg8   45 Ra3 Kh8   46 Ra6 Kh7   47 Ra3 Kh8   48 Ra6 Drawn by agreement.

Game 4: 7 May 1997
White: Deep Blue   *Black*: Garry Kasparov
Pribyl Defense

1 e4 c6   2 d4 d6   3 Nf3 Nf6   4 Nc3 Bg4   5 h3 Bh5   6 Bd3 e6   7 Qe2 d5   8 Bg5 Be7   9 e5 Nfd7   10 B×e7 Q×e7   11 g4 Bg6
12 B×g6 h×g6   13 h4 Na6   14 O-O-O O-O-O   15 Rdg1 Nc7   16 Kb1 f6   17 e×f6 Q×f6   18 Rg3 Rde8   19 Re1 Rhf8   20 Nd1 e5
21 d×e5 Qf4   22 a3 Ne6   23 Nc3 Ndc5   24 b4 Nd7   25 Qd3 Qf7   26 b5 Ndc5   27 Qe3 Qf4   28 b×c6 b×c6   29 Rd1 Kc7
30 Ka1 Q×e3   31 f×e3 Rf7   32 Rh3 Ref8   33 Nd4 Rf2   34 Rb1 Rg2   35 Nce2 R×g4   36 N×e6 N×e6   37 Nd4 N×d4
38 e×d4 R×d4   39 Rg1 Rc4   40 R×g6 R×c2   41 R×g7+ Kb6   42 Rb3+ Kc5   43 R×a7 Rf1+   44 Rb1 Rff2   45 Rb4 Rc1+
46 Rb1 Rcc2   47 Rb4 Rc1+   48 Rb1 R×b1+   49 K×b1 Re2   50 Re7 Rh2   51 Rh7 Kc4   52 Rc7 c5   53 e6 R×h4   54 e7 Re4
55 a4 Kb3   56 Kc1 Drawn by agreement.

Game 5: 10 May 1997
White: Garry Kasparov   *Black*: Deep Blue
Reti Opening

1 Nf3 d5   2 g3 Bg4   3 Bg2 Nd7   4 h3 B×f3   5 B×f3 c6   6 de e6   7 e4 Ne5   8 Bg2 d×e4   9 B×e4 Nf6   10 Bg2 Bb4+   11 Nd2 h5
12 Qe2 Qc7   13 c3 Be7   14 d4 Ng6   15 h4 e5   16 Nf3 e×d4   17 N×d4 O-O-O   18 Bg5 Ng4   19 O-O-O Rhe8   20 Qc2 Kb8
21 Kb1 B×g5   22 h×g5 N6e5   23 Rhe1 c5   24 Nf3 R×d1+   25 R×d1 Nc4   26 Qa4 Rd8   27 Re1 Nb6   28 Qc2 Qd6   29 c4 Qg6
30 Q×g6 f×g6   31 b3 N×f2   32 Re6 Kc7   33 R×g6 Rd7   34 Nh4 Nc8   35 Bd5 Nd6   36 Re6 Nb5   37 c×b5 R×d5   38 Rg6 Rd7
39 Nf5 Ne4   40 N×g7 Rd1+   41 Kc2 Rd2+   42 Kc1 R×a2   43 N×h5 Nd2   44 Nf4 N×b3+   45 Kb1 Rd2   46 Re6 c4   47 Re3 Kb6
48 g6 K×b5   49 g7 Kb4 Drawn by agreement.

Game 6: 11 May 1997
White: Deep Blue   *Black*: Garry Kasparov
Caro–Kann Defense

1 e4 c6   2 d4 d5   3 Nc3 d×e4   4 N×e4 Nd7   5 Ng5 Ngf6   6 Bd3 e6   7 Nf3 h6   8 N×e6 Qe7   9 O-O f×e6   10 Bg6+ Kd8
11 Bf4 b5   12 a4 Bb7   13 Re1 Nd5   14 Bg3 Kc8   15 a×b5 c×b5   16 Qd3 Bc6   17 Bf5 e×f5   18 R×e7 B×e7   19 c4 Black resigns.

Figure 1. Kasparov versus Deep Blue rematch New York, May 1997.

to provide a framework for activities in computer chess and to encourage advances in the field. There are currently about 500 members. It published the *ICCA Journal*, the leading publication in the field. Information on the ICCA can be obtained by writing to Don F. Beal, Secretary, ICCA, Department of Computer Science, Queen Mary and Westfield College, Mile End Road, London E1 4NS, England (`http://www.dcs.qmw.ac.uk/~icca`; email: icca @dcs.qmw.ac.uk).

Bibliography

1950. Shannon, C. "Programming a Computer for Playing Chess," *Philosophy Magazine*, **41**, 256–275.

1953. Turing, A. M. "Digital Computers Applied to Games," in *Faster than Thought* (ed. B. V. Bowden), 286–295. London: Pitman.

1975. Newborn, M. *Computer Chess.* New York: Academic Press.

1977. Frey, P. (ed.) *Chess Skill in Man and Machine.* New York: Springer-Verlag.

1990. Levy, D. N. L., and Newborn, M. *How Computers Play Chess.* New York: W. H. Freeman.

1991. Hsu, F.-H., Anantharaman, T., and Nowatzyk, A. "A Grandmaster Chess Machine," *Scientific American*, **263**, 4 (October), 44–50.

1997. Newborn, M. *Kasparov Versus Deep Blue: Computer Chess Comes of Age.* New York: Springer-Verlag.

Monty Newborn

COMPUTER CIRCUITRY

For articles on related subjects *see* BOOLEAN ALGEBRA; DIGITAL DESIGN AUTOMATION; INTEGRATED CIRCUITRY; LOGIC DESIGN; MICROCOMPUTER CHIP; MICROPROCESSORS AND MICROCOMPUTERS; SUPERCONDUCTING DEVICES; and SWITCHING THEORY.

Although the development of digital computers can be traced back to Charles Babbage, who conceived a mechanical machine with toothed wheels to perform arithmetic processes, electrical principles first found application in digital computers in the form of electro-mechanical relays. The most prominent examples of this type of computer are the Bell Labs relay machines (*q.v.*) and the Harvard Mark I (*q.v.*) and Mark II. Even while these machines were under construction in the early and middle 1940s, it was recognized that an *electronic* computer would offer great advantages in terms of computational speed. Electronic computers use electronic circuits that interconnect electronic components called *gates*. Gates implement basic operations called *Boolean* or *logic functions*. This article starts with a brief overview of Boolean algebra, the theory that underlies such circuits.

The physical realization of electronic gates has undergone major changes since the 1940s, when they were built with electric relays and then with vacuum tubes as the first electronic components. The evolution in electronic component technology has been motivated primarily by the desire to have faster and smaller computers that consume very little energy. Electronic computers built since the late 1960s have used metal-oxide semiconductor (MOS) transistors. Prior to that, bipolar junction transistors (BJT) gates were used; we discuss these transistor types later. The earliest semiconductor computer circuits consisted of gates mounted on printed circuit boards connected by copper wires. This technology has also undergone major changes and today gates and interconnect wires are integrated into a single silicon wafer in VLSI (Very Large Scale Integration) technology (*see* MICROCOMPUTER CHIP).

This article is restricted to discussing the structure of MOS and BJT gates. It describes a systematic method to design two classes of electronic circuits: combinational circuits, which implement arithmetic functions, for example; and sequential circuits, which implement memory. Finally, it describes the use of "programmable logic" devices, which facilitate the often tedious process of designing computer circuits.

Boolean Algebra

Boolean algebra forms the theoretical cornerstone on which modern digital computers are built. Boolean algebra deals with functions and variables that take on only two values, commonly denoted by either T and F or 1 and 0. Using the axioms of Boolean algebra, it can be shown that any Boolean function (a function over Boolean variables), no matter how complex, can be composed from at most three primitive operations: *and*, *or*, and *not*. This set of logic operations is therefore said to be *functionally complete*. In fact, there are two primitive operations, widely used in the design of computer circuitry, that are functionally complete in themselves. These are *nand* (equivalent to a *not* following an *and*) and *nor* (equivalent to a *not* following an *or*). The implication is that one needs only to design circuits for a functionally complete set of Boolean operations in order to have the basic building blocks for a digital computer.

The association that is usually made between an abstract Boolean operation and circuitry that implements that operation is through voltage levels. That is, digital circuitry is designed to respond to two voltage levels, designated high and low (e.g. +5 volts and 0 volts). The conventional method uses the high voltage (or V_{dd}) to represent a 1 and the low voltage (or *Gnd* (Ground)) to represent a 0. Other associations of Boolean values and circuit quantities are possible.

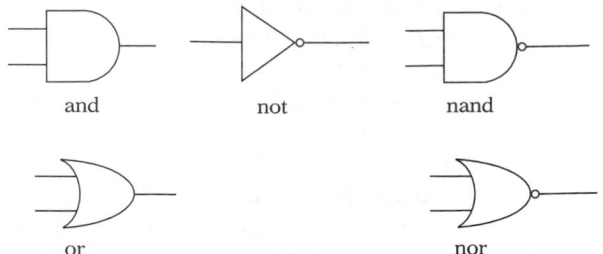

Figure 1. Symbols for logic gates.

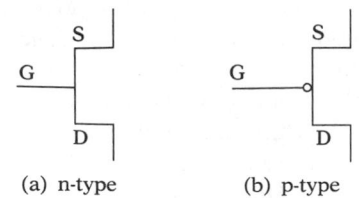

(a) n-type   (b) p-type

Figure 2. Symbols for FETs.

MOS Logic Gates

Circuits that implement the most primitive Boolean functions are called *gates*. The symbols that are used to implement the commonly used gates are shown in Fig. 1. A small circle used in conjunction with any gate denotes negation of that gate's function.

Variations of *metal-oxide semiconductor* (MOS) technologies are currently used to design computers. In such technologies logic gates are build using *controlled switches*. As shown in Fig. 2, such switches consist of three terminals and can be either "n-type" or "p-type" ('n' for negative and 'p' for positive). In an *n-type* switch, if *G equals 1*, terminal *S* is *connected* to terminal *D*. If *G equals 0*, then terminal *S* is *disconnected* from terminal *D*. In a *p-type switch*, if *G equals 1*, terminal *S* is *disconnected* from terminal *D*. If *G equals 0*, then terminal *S* is *connected* to terminal *D*. Physically, the "n-type" switch is an n-type field effect transistor (nFET) and the "p-type" switch is a p-type field effect transistor (pFET). For the purpose of this discussion, we will not be concerned with the physics of these devices (*see* INTEGRATED CIRCUITRY).

As shown in Fig. 3, such switches may be interconnected to form a network having two distinct terminals, *X* and *Y*. The connection pattern of Fig. 3a is a series connection, and the pattern of Fig. 3b is a parallel connection. These elementary connection patterns can be used to build larger networks, as shown in Fig. 3c.

We say that a network *N* of switches is *activated* if and only if the two terminals *X*, *Y* of *N* are connected through a set of switches. For example, in Fig. 3a, if *A = B = 1*, both switches are closed and *X* is connected to *Y*. Therefore the network of Fig. 3a is activated by the assignment *A = B = 1*. One can verify that, if *A = B = 0*, the network of Fig. 3c is activated.

MOS logic gates are constructed by using networks of switches. As shown in Fig. 4, there are two distinct models of logic gates. The *type-a* gate uses two networks of switches—*pullup* and *pulldown* networks. The pullup network consists only of pFETs and the pulldown network consists only of nFETs. These gates are designed so that, for any assignment of values to the input variables, only one of the two networks is activated. If the pullup (pulldown) network is activated, the output of the gate is set to the logic value 1 (0). Fig. 5a is an example of a type-a gate. If *A = B = 1*, the pulldown network is activated and the output is set to 0. If *A = B = 0*, then the pullup network is activated and the output is set to 1. One can verify that the gate of Fig. 5a implements the *nand* function.

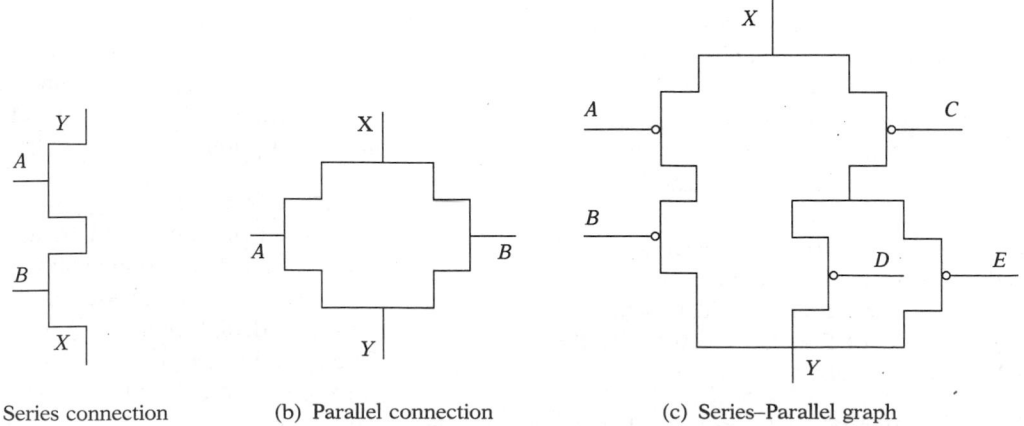

(a) Series connection   (b) Parallel connection   (c) Series–Parallel graph

Figure 3. Series–parallel connections.

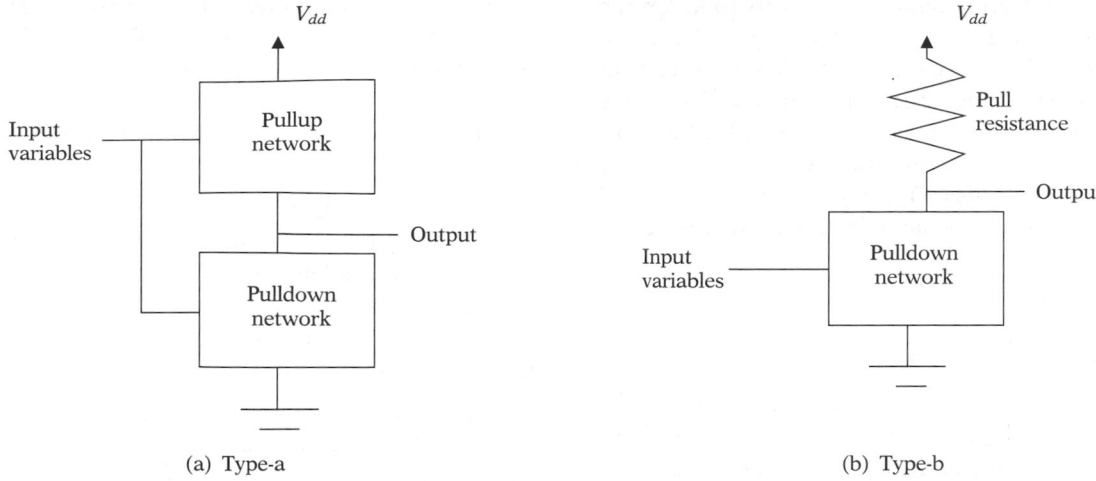

Figure 4. Structure of MOS gates.

For any assignment of values to the input of *type-b* gates, the output is set to 0 if and only if the assignments activate the pulldown network. One can verify that Fig. 5b is a type-b *nand* gate, and Fig. 5c is a type b *nor* gate.

Type-a gates in which the pullup network consists only of pFETs and the pulldown network consists only of nFETs are known as *CMOS (complementary metal-oxide semiconductor)* gates. Circuits consisting of CMOS gates are known as CMOS circuits. Type-b gates in which the pulldown network consists only of nFETs are known as *nMOS* gates. Circuits consisting of nMOS gates are known as nMOS circuits.

Historically, nMOS circuits preceded CMOS circuits because nMOS circuits, unlike CMOS circuits, require

only one type of switch. Therefore, it was easier to perfect the nMOS technology. However, technological innovation has made CMOS an equally feasible technology, and today almost all circuits are CMOS circuits.

One of the major reasons for developing the more complicated CMOS technology can be understood by re-examining the structure of the nMOS and CMOS logic gates. Consider the *nand* gates of Fig. 5a, b. If $A = B = 1$, the pulldown network of Fig. 5a is activated but the pullup network of Fig. 5a is not activated. Therefore, in Fig. 5a, there is no conducting path from V_{dd} (both 'd's refer to the transistor *drain* terminal) to *Gnd*. In fact, in the gate of Fig. 5a, there is no assignment of values to the input of the gate that will

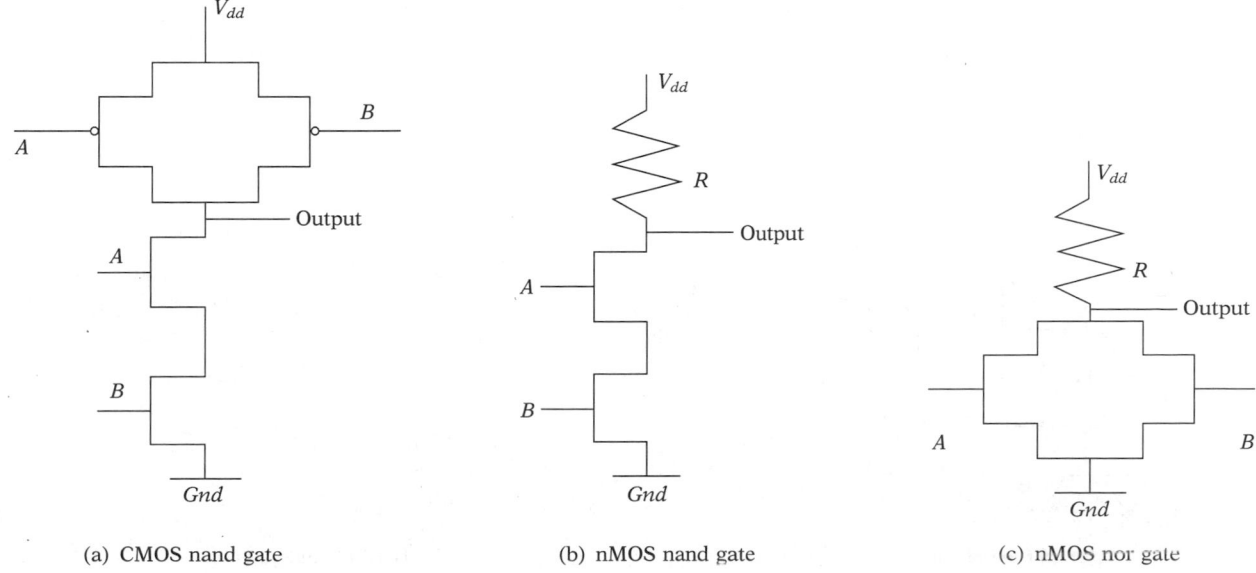

(a) CMOS nand gate   (b) nMOS nand gate   (c) nMOS nor gate

Figure 5. Examples of MOS gates.

result in a conducting path from V_{dd} to *Gnd*. On the other hand, in Fig. 5b, when $A = B = 1$, there is a conducting path from V_{dd} to *Gnd*. Therefore, current flows through the pullup resistor R, thereby dissipating power, something that does not occur with CMOS circuits. This, in turn, hinders the integration of a large number of nMOS gates on a single chip. This is one of the many reasons for using CMOS circuits for denser chips.

Other Logic Families

Although MOS, more specifically CMOS, is now the dominant technology, a number of technologies have been used for manufacturing computers. These technologies differ in the type of switching devices used, as well as how the devices are used in the design of logic gates. The earliest computer circuits used vacuum tubes, but since they are no longer in use, we will not discuss the implementation of logic gates using vacuum tubes.

The logic families that we will discuss here use *bipolar junction transistors* (BJTs) as the switching device. Like FETs, BJTs are also three-dimensional devices.

We use the symbol of Fig. 6a to represent a BJT where G is the *base*, E is the *emitter*, and C is the *collector*. If the voltage at C is "sufficiently higher" than the voltage at E, terminal C is electrically connected to terminal E (the switch is ON); otherwise, terminal C is disconnected from terminal E (the switch is OFF).

Logic gates using BJTs are similar (if not identical) to type-b gates. In *resistor-transistor logic* (RTL), only *nor* gates are available for designing circuits. It is for this reason that RTL is said to be "nor logic." A two-input RTL *nor* gate is shown in Fig. 6b. It is similar to the nMOS *nor* gate of Fig. 5c.

In *diode-transistor logic* (DTL), unlike RTL, only *nand* gates are available for designing the circuits. These *nand* gates use both *diodes* and *transistors* as active devices. The symbol for a diode is shown in Fig. 6c. A diode is a unidirectional two-terminal device. If the voltage at X is higher than the voltage at Y, terminal X is electrically connected to terminal Y; otherwise, X is disconnected from Y. A DTL *nand* gate is shown in Fig. 6d. To understand the operation of this gate, note that if $A(B)$ has the logic level 0 (i.e. voltage 0), diode d1 (d2) conducts. This implies that the voltage at P is 0. $V-$ is a negative voltage. Therefore, diodes d3,

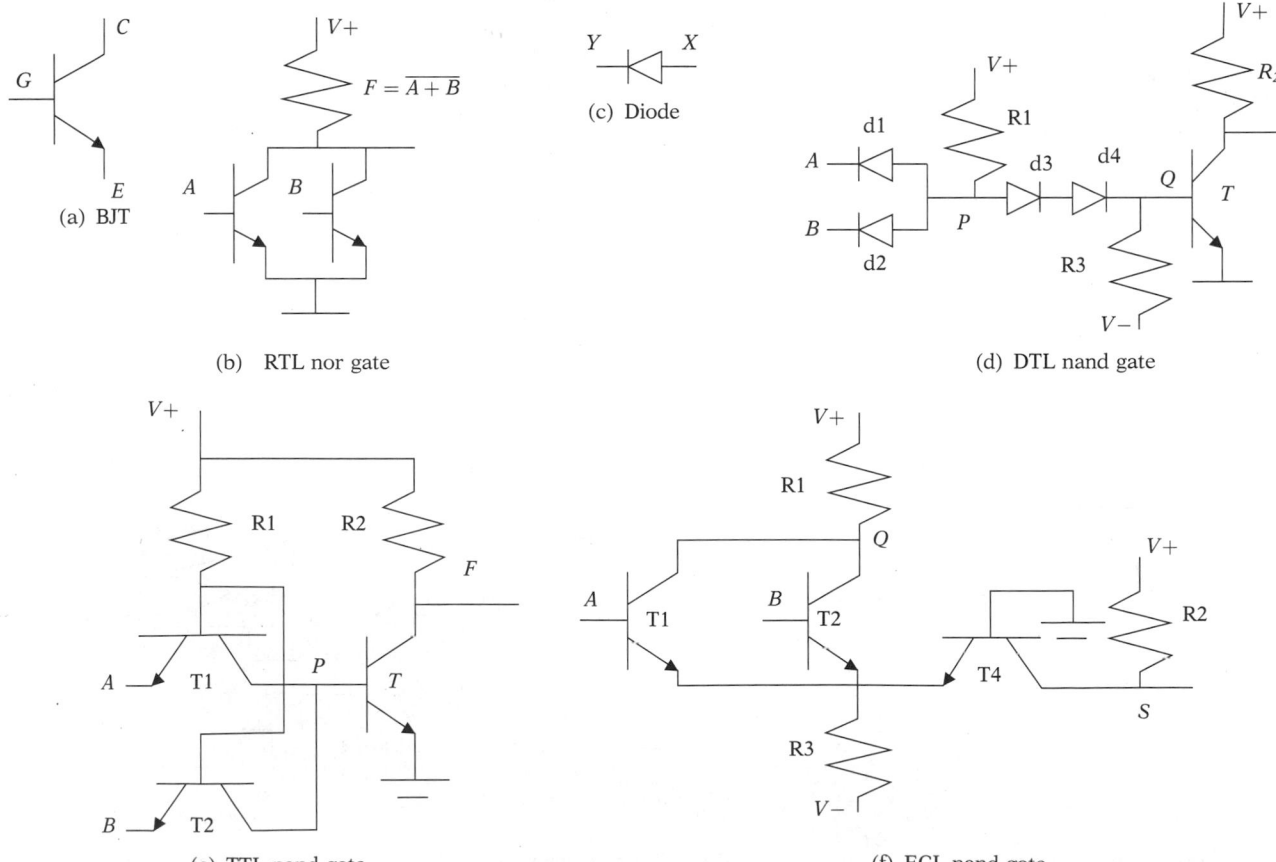

Figure 6. Implementation of some universal gates using BJT-based logic families.

d4 conduct and Q is at a negative voltage (by adjusting the resistance value R3). This cuts T, the *driver* transistor, OFF and the output F is at logic level 1. If $A = B = 1$, diodes d1, d2 do not conduct. Diodes d3, d4 conduct and Q is at a positive voltage (adjusted by resistances R1, R3). The driver T is ON and the output F is pulled down to logic level 0.

In *transistor-transistor logic* (TTL), the only gates available are *nand* gates. A TTL *nand* gate is shown in Fig. 6e. It is very similar to a DTL *nand* gate, but is faster than either RTL or DTL. If either A or B is at logic level 0, there is enough base-to-emitter voltage difference at either T1 or T2 to turn one or both of them ON. This brings down the voltage of P to a sufficiently low value to cut T OFF. The output F is therefore at logic level 1. When both A, B are 1, then both T1 and T2 are cut OFF and P returns to a high voltage. This turns T ON and the output F is pulled to logic level 0.

In DTL and TTL, there is a driver BJT and circuitry is added to the base of this BJT to implement the *nand* function. In *emitter-coupled logic* (ECL), the base of the driver BJT is grounded and circuitry is added to its emitter to implement the *nor* function. ECL circuits are potentially faster than RTL, DTL, or TTL because, unlike those logic families, the driver BJT is never driven into saturation and can therefore switch much faster from one state to another. If either A or B in Fig. 6f is at logic level 1, either T1 or T2 conducts. Therefore there is current through R1. This brings Q to logic level 0. The emitter of T4 is now at either 0 or a small positive voltage (depending on the values of R1 and R3) and this cuts T4 OFF. S is therefore at logic level 1. When both A, B are 0, neither T1 *nor* T2 conducts. Q is at logic level 1. The emitter of T4 is at a negative voltage (close to 0). T4 conducts and S is set to logic level 0. Note that Q and S are complements.

One advantage of using logic gates implemented using BJTs is that they have faster switching speeds than gates using MOS devices. However, the low power dissipation of MOS gates, among other reasons, made it easier to integrate MOS devices. Nevertheless, many BJT devices are still in use for special-purpose circuits or where higher driving capabilities are required.

Classes of Computer Circuits

Depending on the functions they implement, computer circuits are divided into two classes: *combinational circuits* and *sequential circuits*. Combinational circuits are the simpler of the two classes and, along with other circuit elements, are used in the design of sequential circuits.

To understand the difference between combinational and sequential circuits, refer to Fig. 7a. The time interval is divided into subintervals I1, I2, ... of equal size. The intervals are marked by a periodic logic signal known as *clock*. The *period* of clock is equal to the length of the interval. Every interval is divided into two parts. During the first part, clock is 1, and during the second part, clock is 0. We will refer to them as the *one* and *zero periods* of the interval.

Every such circuit can be represented as shown in Fig. 7b. Computation proceeds as follows. During the *one* period, the values of the inputs change. During *zero* period, the logic values at the outputs change and settle down to their steady state value. This is known as *single-phase clocking*.

Combinational circuits are circuits whose output, during any time interval, depends *only* on the values of the inputs during the current time interval and is independent of the values of the inputs during the preceding time intervals. The output of *sequential circuits*, during any time interval, on the other hand, depends on *both* the values of the inputs during the current interval, as well as the values of the inputs during the preceding time intervals. Having noted this difference, we will next look at some combinational and sequential circuits and try to understand some simple design procedures for these classes of circuits.

Combinational Circuits

Boolean functions are functions over Boolean variables whose result can be only one of the two Boolean values 0, 1. Combinational circuits implement Boolean functions. An example of such a function is the *odd parity function* P_n of n variables. P_n equals 1 if and only if an odd number of the n input variables equal 1.

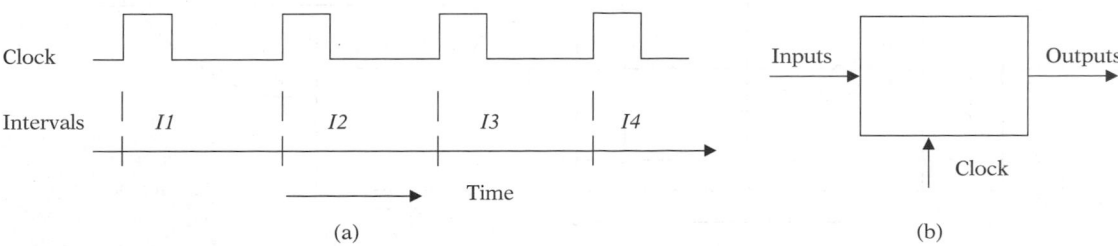

(a)   (b)

Figure 7. Global clock.

Table 1

X_1	X_2	X_3	P_3
0	0	0	0
0	0	1	1
0	1	0	1
0	1	1	0
1	0	0	1
1	0	1	0
1	1	0	0
1	1	1	1

Boolean functions are defined using *truth tables*. Such a table defines the value of the function for each combination of values of the input. The truth table of the *parity function* of three variables is shown in Table 1. Circuits with multiple outputs can also be specified using truth tables.

Fig. 8 is a description of a circuit for the parity function. Such a pictorial representation is a *gate level description* of the circuit. A simple, but not necessarily efficient, way to derive a gate level description from a truth table is as follows. An input variable X_i or its complement (i.e. negation) $\bar{X}_i$ is known as an *input literal*. A conjunction of literals is known as a *term*. Corresponding to each row of a truth table, we have a term. For example, for row 1 of Table 1, we have the term $\bar{X}_1 \cdot \bar{X}_2 \cdot \bar{X}_3$ ("·" denotes the "and" operation). The term corresponding to a row of a truth table for a Boolean function f is a *one-term* for f if and only if the value of f for that input combination is 1. A *zero-term* is similarly defined. From Table 1, $\bar{X}_1 \cdot \bar{X}_2 \cdot X_3$ is a zero-term and $\bar{X}_1 \cdot \bar{X}_2 \cdot X_3$ is a one-term for P_3.

Let $a_1, \ldots, a_t$ be the one-terms of a function f. Then, $a_1 + a_2 + \cdots + a_t$ ("+" denotes the *or* operation) is a *sum-of-products* expression for f. From Table 1 we

get the following sum of products expression P_3: $P_3 = \bar{X}_1 \cdot \bar{X}_2 \cdot X_3 + \bar{X}_1 \cdot X_2 \cdot \bar{X}_3 + X_1 \cdot \bar{X}_2 \cdot \bar{X}_3 + X_1 \cdot X_2 \cdot X_3$. From such an expression, we get the gate level description shown in Fig. 8. Note that, for each term, we have an *and* gate and there is one *or* gate that is driven by all the *and* gates.

Programmable Circuits

The gate level description is a description of the circuit that is used for fabricating it. Prior to fabrication, the physical location on a silicon wafer of the devices (like FETs, resistors, etc.) has to be determined (*placement*). This is followed by determining how the devices are to be interconnected (*routing*). For circuits using a small number of devices, placement and routing can be done manually. For larger circuits, the entire process has to be automated. Many of the steps of placement and routing can easily be automated if the circuit topology is regular. Moreover, the integration process becomes simpler and more cost effective if a variety of circuits can be physically implemented by minor variations (or *programming*) of a "master piece." These factors have led to the evolution of a number of design styles like *programmable logic arrays* (PLAs), *Weinburger arrays*, *gate matrix arrays*, etc. Such design styles are being used extensively. To gain insight into these styles, we will have a brief look at nMOS PLAs.

Let X_1, $\bar{X}_2$, X_3 be input variables. The *nor* expression $(\overline{X_1 + \bar{X}_2 + X_3})$ can be implemented logically as shown in Fig. 9a. To implement this expression physically, if there are n input variables, we have a physical row of $2n$ nFETs. For every input variable X_i, there exist two nFETs, one driven by X_i and the other driven by $\bar{X}_i$. An example is shown in Fig. 9b. For this row of nFETs, some of the "links" are "broken." This

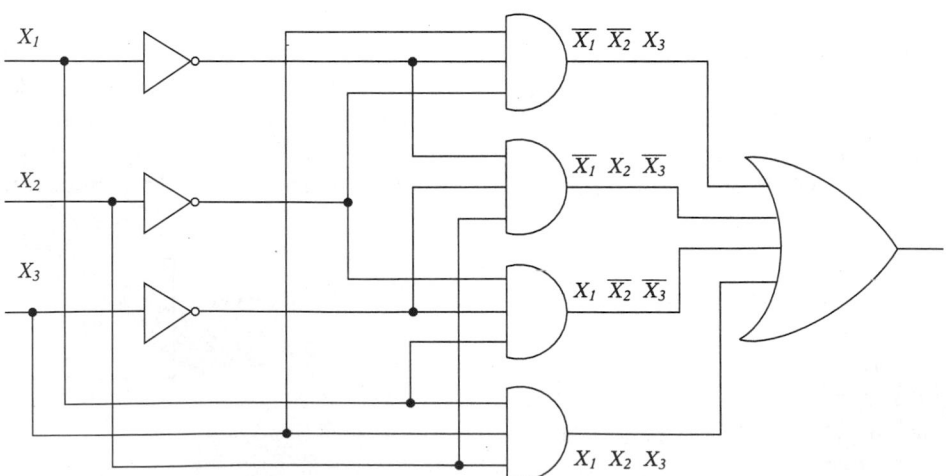

Figure 8. Example of sum-of-product circuits.

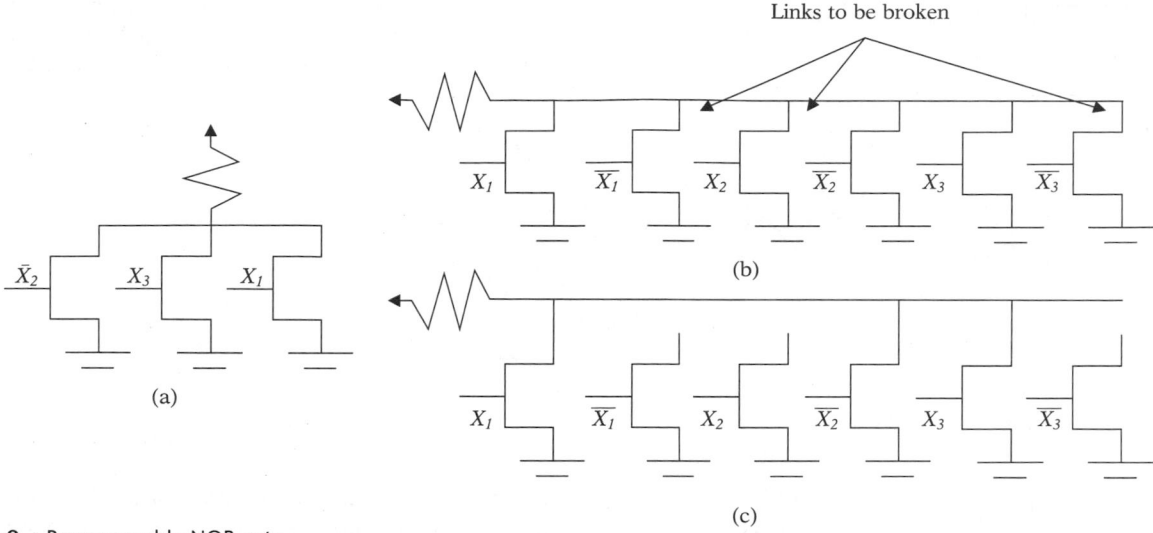

Figure 9. Programmable NOR gate.

effectively removes some of the FETs from the circuit, resulting in the desired gate shown in Fig. 9c. This is the basic idea used in a PLA.

A PLA is shown in Fig. 10. It consists of two parts, an AND-PLANE and an OR-PLANE. Each of these two parts is a two-dimensional array of FETs. Every row of the AND-PLANE is arranged to form a potential *nor* gate. All FETs in a column of the AND-PLANE are driven by the same input literal. Every column of the OR-PLANE is arranged to form a potential *nor* gate.

The inputs of the FETs in a row of the OR-PLANE are driven by the output of the same *nor* gate of the AND-PLANE. Given such an array of FETs, a set of sum of products expressions is implemented by "selectively disconnecting" some of the FETs from the circuit. For example, to implement the following Boolean functions, the FETs to be disconnected are shown by "×" in Fig. 10.

$$f_1 = X_1 X_2 + \overline{X_1 X_2}$$
$$f_2 = X_1 X_2 + \bar{X}_1 X_2$$

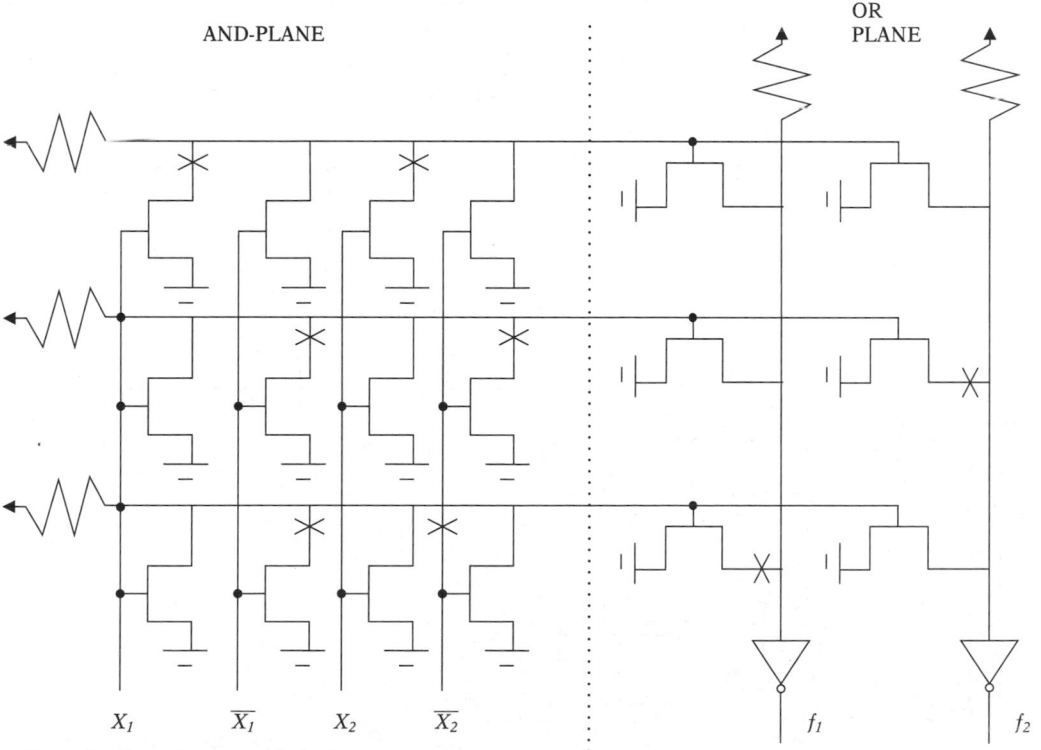

Figure 10. Example of a programmable logic array.

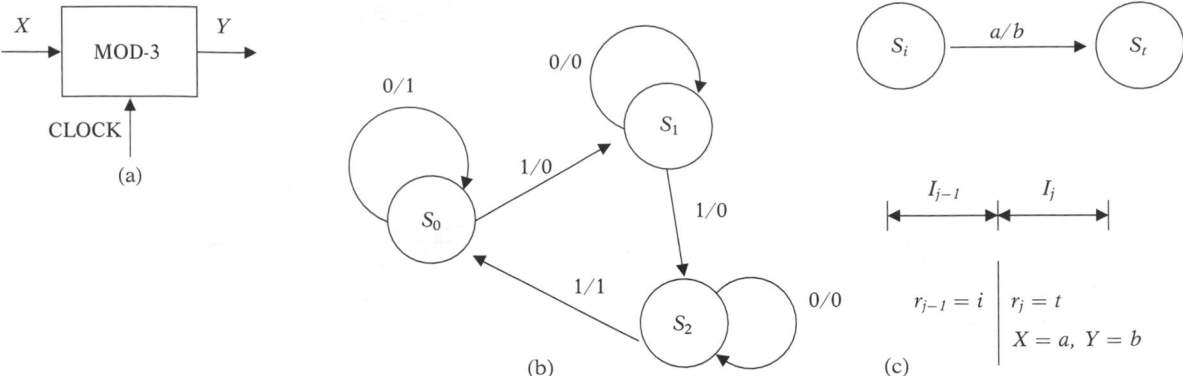

Figure 11. Example of a state diagram.

Sequential Circuits

We will use a simple example to illustrate how sequential circuits are designed. Consider a circuit with one input X and one output Y, defined as follows. Let n_j be the number of intervals, including and up to I_j, during which X had the value 1. At the end of I_j, Y is set to 1 if and only if n_j is divisible by 3. We call such a circuit *MOD-3*.

In order to compute the value of Y during the interval I_j, MOD-3 must remember some characteristics of the pattern of 0s and 1s during the intervals 1 to I_{j-1}. It is enough for the circuit to remember the value of $r_{j-1} = n_{j-1} \bmod 3$, which is nothing but the remainder left after dividing n_{j-1} by 3. Also note that if X, during I_j, equals 1, then $r_j = (r_{j-1} + 1) \bmod 3$; and if r_j equals 0, then Y is to be set to 1. Therefore, at the end of any interval, we need to remember if the remainder was 0, 1, or 2.

Another way to express this behavior of MOD-3 is with the help of the *state diagram* of Fig. 11b. Since we need to know if r_j is 0, 1, or 2, we say that the circuit, at the end of I_j, is in state S_0 if r_j is 0, S_1 if r_j is 1, and S_2 if r_j is 2. The arrow marked a/b, which starts at S_i and ends at S_t, is to be interpreted as follows: if, at the end of the interval I_{j-1}, r_{j-1} is i and during interval I_j the value of X is a, then, at the end of interval I_j, the value of Y should be b and r_j should be t.

While designing a circuit from a state diagram, we have to make sure that the circuit "remembers" the state of the system. In order to do that, the states are *encoded* using two *state variables* a_0, a_1 as follows: $S_0 = (a_0 = 0, a_1 = 0)$; $S_1 = (a_0 = 0, a_1 = 1)$; and $S_2 = (a_0 = 1, a_1 = 0)$. The circuit now needs to remember the values of the state variables. In other words, the circuit should be capable of remembering *two bits of information*. This leads to the question: how exactly does a circuit remember two or more bits of information?

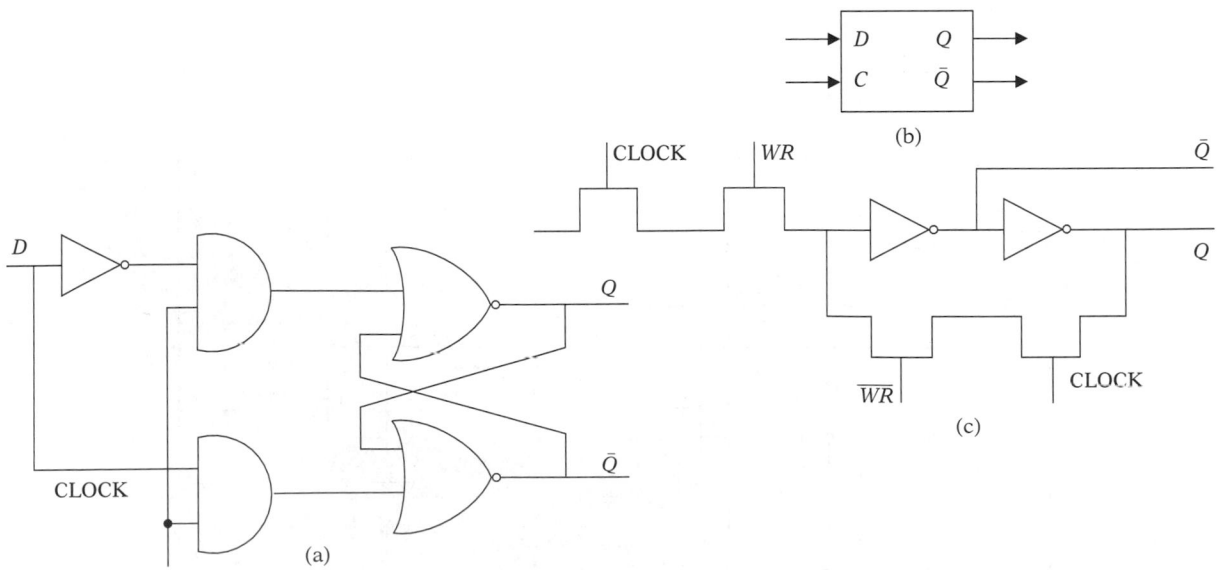

Figure 12. Structure of a flip-flop

Table 2

Input X	S_i		S_t		Output Y
	a_0	a_1	D_0	D_1	
0	0	0	0	0	1
1	0	0	0	1	0
0	0	1	0	1	0
1	0	1	1	0	0
0	1	0	1	0	0
1	1	0	0	0	1
0	1	1	dc	dc	dc
1	1	1	dc	dc	dc

dc—don't care.

As they did for logic gates, circuit designers have devised circuit elements called *flip-flops*. A flip-flop can store (i.e. remember) one bit of information. The structure of a flip-flop is shown in Fig. 12a and we will use the symbol of Fig. 12b to represent such a flip-flop. Here Q is the output of the flip-flop and $\bar{Q}$ is another output, such that the value of $\bar{Q}$ is always the complement of the value of Q. D is the input to the flip-flop. When CLOCK is 1 and D is 1, Q is set to 1. When D is 0 and CLOCK is 1, then Q is set to 0. When CLOCK is 0, the value of Q or $\bar{Q}$ cannot change. What we have just described is a *D flip-flop*. There are a number of other classes of flip-flops like SR flip-flop,

JK flip-flops, etc. (*see* SEQUENTIAL MACHINES). Fig. 12c depicts a slight variation of a D flip-flop that uses nFETs. In this case, in order to modify the values of Q and $\bar{Q}$, both CLOCK and WR have to be 1.

To continue our discussion of the design process, we derive the *state table* from the state diagram. The state table for our example is shown in Table 2. For each edge in the state diagram, we have a row in the state table. The pair $\langle a_0, a_1 \rangle$ defines the state S_i of Fig. 11c; $\langle D_0, D_1 \rangle$ defines the state S_t; X defines the value a; and Y defines the value b. Note that D_0, D_1 will become the new value of a_0, a_1 at the start of the next interval. In order for that to happen, the circuit should be of the form shown in Fig. 13a, where C must satisfy the conditions of the state table (Table 2). Since there is no state S_3, the case $a_0 = a_1 = 1$ cannot arise; hence there are "don't care" values in these rows. The complete circuit is shown in Fig. 13b. Note that Table 2 is like a truth table for the combinational block C of Fig. 13a. This is a simple, but not necessarily an efficient way to implement sequential circuits.

Conclusion

This article has provided an overview of the building blocks of computer circuits. Since the 1960s, these circuits have been increasingly compact and dense semiconductor devices, initially built out of discrete

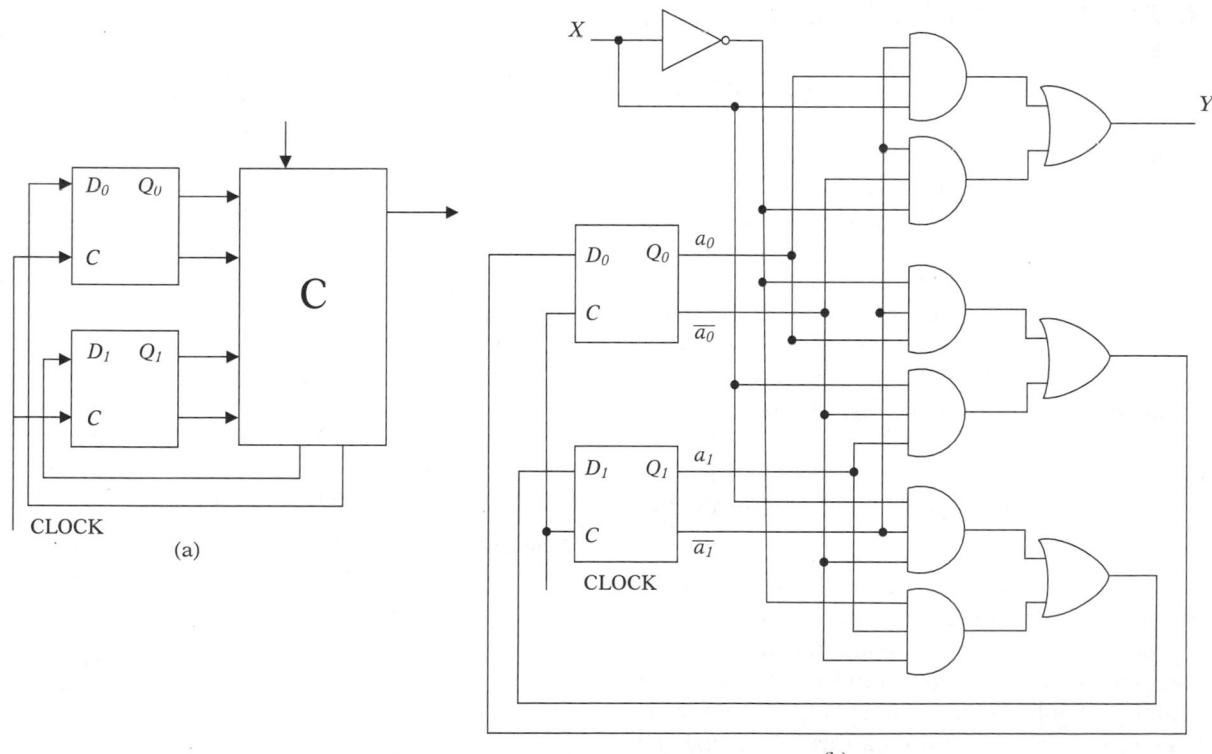

Figure 13. Implementation of the state diagram of Fig. 11.

transistors, and then as *integrated circuits* that packed many transistors, and hence, many gates, on a silicon chip. They have evolved from *small-scale integration* (SSI) to *medium* and *large* scale integration (MSI and LSI) to the current *very large* scale integration (VLSI) that can put several million transistors on a silicon wafer about 1 cm in diameter. Such microcomputer chips can hold a powerful processor and fast cache memory (*q.v.*).

Sometimes computers are characterized by their generation: the first generation used vacuum tubes; the second, discrete transistors, and the third, integrated circuits. These circuits, introduced at the end of the 1960s, have evolved greatly, but more than 30 years later, they still provide the fundamental material out of which computers are built.

Bibliography

1980. Mead, C., and Conway, L. *Introduction to VLSI Systems.* Reading, MA: Addison-Wesley.

1993. Weste, N., and Eshraghian, K. *Principles of CMOS VLSI Design*, 2nd Ed. Reading, MA: Addison-Wesley.

1998. Unger, S. H. *The Essence of Logic Circuits*, 2nd Ed. Upper Saddle River, NJ: Prentice Hall.

1998. Wolf, W. *Modern VLSI Design—Systems on Silicon*, 2nd Ed. Upper Saddle River, NJ: Prentice Hall.

2000. Wakerly, J. F. *Digital Design: Principles and Practice*, 3rd Ed. Upper Saddle River, NJ: Prentice Hall.

Sreejit Chakravarty

COMPUTER CONFERENCING

For articles on related subjects *see* BULLETIN BOARD; ELECTRONIC MAIL; GROUPWARE; and NETWORKS, COMPUTER.

Computer conferencing (CC) is a structured computer-mediated group discussion embodying the concept developed in the early 1970s that one could facilitate group communication processes by using the logical and processing capabilities of the computer (Hiltz and Turoff, 1993). It had its philosophical foundation in the development of the Delphi Method (Turoff and Hiltz, 1995). The nature of the communication process can be modified to respond to the requirements of the application and the nature of the group. With this technology, individuals participating in a group communication process no longer have to be coincident in either time or place.

The high degree of commercialism in the computer industry has led to many different names for the use of information technology (*q.v.*) to aid the human group communication process. Each vendor seeks to add a new name to the literature to make a product appear new. As a result, the literature on this subject may be found scattered under, among others, the following titles: Bulletin Board Systems (BBS), Collaborative Sys-

tems (CS), Computer Conferencing Systems (CCS), Computer-Mediated Communication Systems (CMCS), Computer-Supported Cooperative Work (CSCW), Co-ordination Systems (CS), Electronic Meeting Systems (EMS), Group Decision Support Systems (GDSS), Groupware, Networking, Teamware, and Teleconferencing. All these types of systems have one thing in common: they are designed with the objective of using the computer to aid in the process of facilitating group communications. The most appropriate inclusive term is Computer-Mediated Communications (CMC), a term that includes all the others and claimed differences among them.

With the emergence of the Internet (*q.v.*) and the World Wide Web (*q.v.*), there are currently hundreds of group systems commercially available; however, very few of them reflect the ability of the user or group to tailor the process. The demonstration of that concept is still largely limited to R&D systems.

The discussion or conference part of a CMC system may be represented as a specific hypertext (*q.v.*) structure. Most current systems can be described as in Table 1, which shows the relationships (*links*) among the objects (*nodes*) that characterize the system. Objects in CMC systems include both the elements of discourse and the individuals or members. The individuals are objects which are linked to content objects by privileges associated with their human roles. There may be significant additional functionality with respect to the different roles and associated software powers a person can have in a given conference. However, the basic discourse structure is usually some combination of temporal occurrence, comment/reply hierarchies, and keyword association of comments.

An example that goes beyond these basics is the "Virtual Classroom" (Hiltz, 1994), where a number of special communication structures exist in addition to a basic computer conferencing structure. For example, an instructor can ask a discussion question but no student can see the other discussion answers until he or she has answered. What this example indicates is

Table 1. Common CMC object and relationship structures.

	Comment	Reply	Person
Comment	Later/earlier than temporal	In response to	Author of/ editor of/ reader of
Reply		Additional/ alternative	Author of/ editor of/ reader of
Person			Member of same conference

that a task done in a CC environment can be a significant improvement over previous face to face or other alternative group communication systems.

Some features that characterize a general purpose computer conferencing system are (Hiltz and Wellman, 1997; Turoff and Hiltz, 1998):

◆ All comments in a conference are signed and dated.

◆ Conference membership is either under the control of the owner or open to the public.

◆ Status reports show who has read or written what.

◆ Availability of anonymity or pen names as alternatives to signatures.

◆ Keyword indexing of conference comments and use of subject headings.

◆ Voting and collaborative decision aids.

◆ Specific human roles in the group supported by the software (e.g. monitors, editors, observers, indexers).

◆ Specialized communication and modification privileges, such as joint editing of the same entry.

◆ Notifications which alert members of the group to actions by other members that affect their participation (e.g. vote changes, establishment of new conferences, etc.).

◆ Conference comment structures tied to data elements and objects such as calendar entries, report sections, meeting agendas, project deadlines, etc.

◆ Executable programs attached to conference comments.

◆ Directories of members and conferences.

◆ Virtual addressing of all existing objects, such as comments and mail.

◆ Discourse structures to allow typing of comments and hypertext-oriented (*q.v.*) relationships between conference comments.

◆ Conference tailoring under control of the group, user, and/or owner of a given conference.

◆ Decision support toolkits.

◆ Generalized gaming and other role playing support (e.g. stakeholder role playing).

While computer-mediated communication allows individuals to engage in group communication processes at any time or place that is convenient for them, the main benefit of this technology is the possibility for these systems to promote *collective intelligence*, namely that the result of the group process should be better than that possible by the "best" member in the group acting alone (Hiltz and Turoff, 1993).

Individuals in a computerized conferencing environment are free to integrate their individual problem-solving abilities with the group process. Different members of the group may address the part of the problem about which they have the most insight or information independent of the other members. It is the objective of the structure and communication protocols provided by the computer to integrate these contributions into a group result and to aid in synchronizing the group at key points in the group process. This integration of individual and group problem-solving methods is what provides the promise of "collective intelligence" on a more consistent basis than normal face-to-face meetings.

The future of this technology lies in the ability of the computer to provide structures appropriate to a given application, and in our ability to understand the relationships among the structures, protocols, tools, and the individual and group problem-solving process. It is impossible to divorce the design and evolution of this technology from behavioral and social understanding. Designing human communication systems is, in effect, the designing of social systems (Turoff, 1997; Hiltz and Wellman, 1997). As a result, the technology offers the possibility of new social structures for organizations and for society.

Bibliography

1993. Hiltz, S. R., and Turoff, M. *The Network Nation*, Rev. Ed. Cambridge, MA: MIT Press.
1994. Hiltz, S. R. *The Virtual Classroom: Learning Without Limits Via Computer Networks.* Norwood, NJ: Ablex Publishing Corp.
1995. Turoff, M., and Hiltz, S. R. "Computer Based Delphi Processes," in *Gazing Into the Oracle: The Delphi Method and Its Application to Social Policy and Public Health* (eds. M. Adler and E. Ziglio), 56–88. London: Kingsley Publishers.
1997. Hiltz, S. R., and Wellman, B. "Asynchronous Learning Networks as Virtual Communities," *Comm. of the ACM*, **40**, *9*, 44–9.
1997. Turoff, M. "Virtuality," *Comm. of the ACM*, **40**, *9*, 38–43.
1998. Turoff, M., and Hiltz, S. R. "Superconnectivity," *Comm. of the ACM*, **41**, *7*, 116.

Murray Turoff

COMPUTER CRIME

For articles on related subjects *see* ELECTRONIC COMMERCE; HACKER; LEGAL ASPECTS OF COMPUTING; LEGAL PROTECTION OF SOFTWARE; and VIRUS, COMPUTER.

Introduction

Business, economic, and white-collar crimes have changed rapidly as computers proliferate into the activities and environments in which these crimes occur. Computers have engendered a different form of crime. The Internet (*q.v.*), in particular, provides many new avenues for crime, such as identity theft and spreading new kinds of computer viruses. Computers have been involved in most types of crime, including fraud, theft, larceny, embezzlement, bribery, burglary, sabotage, espionage, conspiracy, extortion, attempted murder, manslaughter, distribution of pornography, trespassing, violation of privacy, and kidnapping.

Computer occupations have extended the traditional categories of criminals to include computer programmers, computer operators, tape librarians, and electronic and software engineers who function in new environments. Although crime has traditionally occurred in ordinary human environments, some crime is now perpetrated using personal computers in bedrooms or with mainframe computers in the specialized environment of rooms with raised flooring, lowered ceilings, large gray boxes, flashing lights, moving tapes, and the hum of air-conditioning motors.

The methods of committing crime have changed. A new jargon has developed, identifying automated criminal methods such as data diddling, Trojan horses, viruses, worms, logic bombs, salami techniques, superzapping, piggybacking, scavenging, data leakage, and asynchronous attacks. The forms of many of the targets of computer crime are also different. Electronic transactions and money, as well as paper and plastic money (credit cards), represent assets subject to intentionally caused automated loss. Money in the form of electronic signals and magnetic patterns is stored and processed in computers and transmitted through the Internet. Money is debited and credited to accounts inside computers. In fact, the computer has become an electronic vault for the business community. Many other physical assets, including inventories of products in warehouses and materials leaving or entering factories, are represented by electronic and optical documents of records inside computer systems. Electronic data interchange (EDI), which connects trading partners for conducting contract negotiations, sales, invoicing, and collections, focuses traditional sources of business crime on computers and data communications.

The timing of some crimes is also different. Traditionally, the duration of criminal acts is measured in minutes, hours, days, weeks, months, and years. Today, some crimes are being perpetrated in less than 0.003 of a second (3 ms). Thus, automated crime must be considered in terms of a computer time scale of milliseconds, microseconds, and nanoseconds because of the speed of execution of instructions in computers.

Geographic constraints do not inhibit perpetration of these types of crimes. A telephone with an attached computer terminal in one part of the world could be used to engage in a crime in an online computer system in any other part of the world.

All these factors and more must be considered in dealing with the crimes of computer abuse and misuse. Unfortunately, however, the community of businesses, government agencies, and institutions that use computers for technical and business purposes, is neither adequately prepared to deal with nor sufficiently motivated to report this kind of crime to the authorities. Although reliable statistics are as yet unavailable to prove this, computer security studies for the business community and interviews with certified public accountants have indicated that few crimes of this type are ever reported to law enforcement agencies for prosecution.

US state and federal criminal codes contain at least 54 statutes defining computer crime. Any violations of these specific statutes are computer crimes; in some contexts it is also customary to include alleged violations of these statutes as computer crimes.

Computer-related crimes—a broader category—are any violations of criminal law that involve a knowledge of computer technology for their perpetration, investigation, or prosecution. Although computer-related crimes are primarily white-collar offenses, any kind of illegal act based on an understanding of computer technology can be a computer-related crime. They could even be violent crimes that destroy computers or their contents and thereby jeopardize human lives (e.g. those of people who depend on the correct functioning of computers for their health or well-being). Computer larceny—the theft and burglary of computers—is spreading rapidly as computers shrink in size to the point where security similar to that for jewelry must be applied. The proliferation and use of personal computers make computer-related crimes potentially endemic throughout society.

The term *computer crime* has been used to refer generally to all three categories: computer crime in the strict sense, computer-related crime, and computer abuse. Where the context requires distinctions among the three categories to avoid confusion or misinterpretation, the text specifically identifies the type of crime or abuse that is intended.

Computer crime may involve computers not only actively but also passively when usable evidence of the acts resides in computer storage. The victims and potential victims of computer crime include all organizations and people who use or are affected by computer and data communication systems, including people about whom data is stored and processed in computers. Anybody using the Internet is particularly vulnerable to computer crime.

Categories

All known and reported cases of computer crime involve computers in one or more of the following four roles:

◆ *Object* Cases include destruction of computers or of data or programs contained in them or of supportive facilities and resources, such as air-conditioning equipment and electrical power that allow them to function.

◆ *Subject* A computer can be the site or environment of a crime or the source of or reason for unique forms and kinds of assets lost, such as a pirated computer program. A fraud perpetrated by changing account balances in financial data stored in a computer makes the computer storage the subject of a crime.

◆ *Instrument* Some types and methods of crime are complex enough to require the use of a computer as a tool or instrument. A computer can be used actively, such as in automatically scanning Internet message packets for passwords and credit card numbers. A computer could also be used passively to simulate a general ledger in the planning and control of a continuing financial embezzlement.

◆ *Symbol* A computer can be used as a symbol for intimidation or deception. This could involve an organization falsely claiming to use nonexistent computers.

The dimensions of the definition of computer crime become a problem in some cases. If a computer is stolen in a simple theft where, based on all circumstances, it could have been a washing machine or milling machine, a knowledge of computer technology is not necessary and it would not be a computer crime. However, if knowledge of computer technology is necessary to determine the value of the article taken, the nature of possible damage done in the taking, or the intended use by the thief, then the theft would be a computer crime.

Here is an illustration. If an individual telephones a bank funds transfer department and fraudulently requests a transfer of $70 million to an account in a bank in Vienna, two possibilities occur. If the clerk who received the call was deceived and keyed the transfer into a computer terminal, the funds transfer would not be a computer crime. No fraudulent act was related directly to a computer, and no special knowledge of computer technology was required. However, if the clerk was in collusion with the caller, the fraudulent act would include the entry of data at the terminal and would be a computer crime. Knowledge of computer technology would be necessary to understand the terminal usage and protocol.

However, more practical considerations should make unnecessary such explicit and absolute decisions about whether an act is a computer crime. A classification of computer crime may be based on a variety of lists and models from several sources. Such a classification should go beyond white-collar crimes because computers have been found to be involved in almost all types of crime. Computer crime has been categorized by types of information and information-processing loss: modification, destruction, disclosure, observation, misrepresentation, use or denial of use, and more. This classification is deceptive, however, because many other types of loss have occurred, including acts of misrepresentation, delay or prolongation of use, renaming, misappropriation, repudiation, inference, and failure to act. Therefore a more comprehensive and usable typing is loss of availability and utility, integrity and authenticity, and confidentiality and possession of information. These three classes define acts that are intrinsic to information (such as changing it), extrinsic to information (such as changing access to it), and external to information (by removing or copying it).

The SRI Computer Abuse Methods Model considers a classification system for computer abuses that is summarized in Fig. 1. It shows the relationships of computer crime methods. The model is more of a system of descriptors than it is a taxonomy in the usual sense, in that multiple descriptors may apply in any particular case. For visual simplicity, this model is depicted as a simple tree, although that is an oversimplification—the classes are not mutually disjoint.

The order of categorization depicted is roughly from the physical world to the hardware to the operating system (and network software) to the application code. The first abuse class includes external abuses that can take place passively without access to computer systems. The second class includes hardware abuse, and generally requires some sort of physical access and active behavior with respect to the computer system itself. Eavesdropping and interference are respective examples of these two classes. The third class includes masquerading in a variety of forms. The fourth includes cases of preparation for subsequent abuses (e.g. the transformation of a computer program into a Trojan horse by secretly inserting instructions into the victim's computer program), as opposed to the abuses that result from the actual exploitation of the Trojan horse, which show up later in subsequent classes. The remaining classes involve bypass of authorization, active abuse, passive abuse, and uses

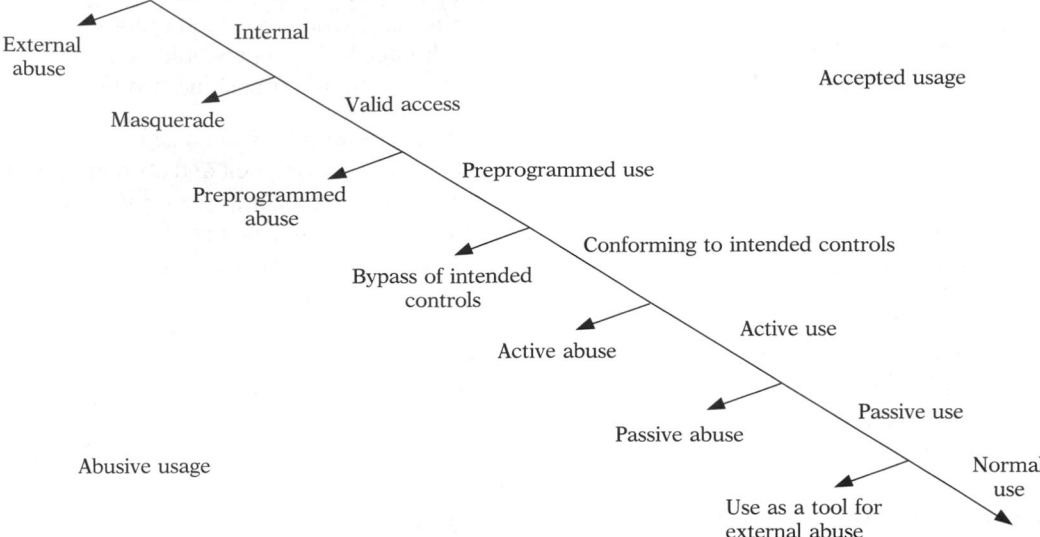

Figure 1. Computer abuse methods model.

that lead to subsequent abuse. The leftward branches all involve misuses, while the rightward branches represent potentially acceptable use until a leftward branch is taken. Every leftward branch represents a class of vulnerabilities that must be defended against and detected at the earliest possible time. However, the techniques for defense and detection differ from one branch to the next.

Thus this figure represents a classification system for types of computer crime techniques. Actual violations of computer security have often involved multiple types of abuse. For example, the hacker, Kevin Mitnick, in his attacks on Digital Equipment Corporation and many others, used, at least, techniques of external abuse, masquerading, preplanned Trojan horse attacks, bypass of intended controls, and both active and passive abuses. Thus, the tree representation is merely a convenient way of summarizing the classes.

History

Computer abuse started with the emergence of computer technology in the late 1940s. As the number of people in the computer field began to increase, that facet of human nature that wants to harm society for personal gain or to assuage intense personal problems took hold; the problem of abuse became especially acute as computer technology proliferated into sensitive areas in society, such as military systems, and computer users were increasingly in positions of trust. The abuse then spread to engineering, to science, and in parallel to business and personal applications.

The first recorded computer abuse occurred in 1958 (Parker *et al.*, 1973). The first federally prosecuted computer crime in the USA, identified as such, was the alteration of bank records by computer in Minneapolis in 1966.

No valid representative statistics on computer crime exist, even through many surveys have been conducted and well-known organizations and individuals have quoted various statistics. Frequency, losses per year, rate of increase or decrease, percentages of perpetrators within or outside of victimized organizations, and the number of cases discovered and prosecuted are not known. To protect themselves, many victims try to deny their loss. No methods have been devised to apply uniform definitions, identify authoritative sources, or conduct surveys in any statistically valid way. The formal study of computer abuse was started in 1971. The first US national conference on computer abuse and a comprehensive report were completed in 1973. Since then, many reports, papers, journal articles, and books have been published describing the research (see the bibliography).

In 1976, as a result of the increasing frequency of cases, Senator Abraham Ribicoff and his US Senate Government Affairs Committee became aware of computer crime and the inadequacy of federal criminal law to deal with it. The committee produced two reports on its research (US Senate, 1976, 1977), and Senator Ribicoff introduced the first Federal Systems Protection Act Bill in June 1977. These legislative efforts evolved into House Bill 5616 in 1986, which resulted in the Computer Fraud and Abuse Act of 1987, established as Article 1030, Chapter 47 of Title 18 Criminal Code.

On the state level, Florida, Michigan, Colorado, Rhode Island, and Arizona were the first to have computer crime laws based on the first Ribicoff bill. Current legislation on computer crime exists in all US states and many other countries. The Computer Fraud and Abuse Act was modified in the early 1990s to make the creation and spreading of computer viruses a crime.

Computer crime has been portrayed fictionally in several novels, motion pictures, and television dramas. The British Broadcasting Corporation dramatized the computer crime aspects of a massive insurance fraud. NBC TV News and the CBS show "60 Minutes" have had special segments. The motion pictures *War Games* and *Sneakers* were the first to portray computer hacking. Several nonfiction trade books have been published, and articles have appeared in all major magazines and newspapers. Unfortunately, the public interest and sensationalism associated with computer crime, particularly the malicious hacker (*q.v.*) cases that peaked in 1982 and the 1988 computer virus cases, have made folk heroes of the perpetrators and embarrassed the victims.

In the future, we may anticipate fully automated crime. For the first time in history, it will be possible to execute a computer crime in milliseconds without anyone knowing what computers were attacked, what crime was perpetrated, or who the victim was. To combat automated crime, we will have to develop security that functions without human intervention.

Bibliography

1973. Parker, D. B., Nycum, S. H., and Oura, S. *Computer Abuse.* Menlo Park, CA: SRI International. Report distributed by National Technical Information Service, US Department of Commerce, Springfield, VA.

1976. Parker, D. B. *Crime by Computer.* New York: Charles Scribner's Sons.

1976. US Senate Committee on Government Operations. *Problems Associated with Computer Technology in Federal Programs and Private Industry.* Washington, DC: US Government Printing Office.

1977. US Senate Committee on Government Operations. *Staff Study of Computer Security in Federal Programs.* Washington, DC: US Government Printing Office.

1983. Parker, D. B. *Fighting Computer Crime.* New York: Charles Scribner's Sons.

1986. Sieber, U. *The International Handbook on Computer Crime.* New York: John Wiley.

1989. *Computer Crime: Criminal Justice Resource Manual.* US Department of Justice Report No. NCJ118214, Washington DC.

1989. Stoll, C. *The Cuckoo's Egg.* Garden City, NY: Doubleday.

1991. Hafner, K. and Markoff, J. *Cyberpunk: Outlaws and Hackers on the Computer Frontier.* New York: Simon and Schuster.

1992. Sterling, B. *The Hacker Crackdown: Law and Disorder on the Electronic Frontier.* New York: Bantam.

1997. Littman, J. *The Watchman (The Hacker Crimes of Kevin Poulson).* New York: Bantam.

Donn B. Parker

COMPUTER ENGINEERING

For articles on related subjects *see* COMPUTER SCIENCE; and EDUCATION IN COMPUTER ENGINEERING.

Computer engineering, as differentiated from *computer science*, focuses on the implementation (i.e. reduction to practice) aspects of the discipline, and the trade-offs required to produce viable systems.

Like computer science, computer engineering is concerned with all elements of information processing systems, including the application environment (e.g. visualization of the results of a computation, artificial intelligence, computational science, and perceptual and cognitive processes), paradigms for representing information (e.g. algorithms for numeric and nonnumeric applications, symbol manipulation, and language processing), paradigms for processing information (e.g. distributed computing, information storage and retrieval, programs for managing computing resources, programs for transforming source programs, hardware execution models, programming languages and compilers, and networks that interconnect pieces of a computer system and those that connect complete systems), and tools for designing and measuring the effectiveness of computer systems (e.g. CAD design tools and performance measurement and analysis tools).

Also like computer science, computer engineering is concerned with human–machine interfaces, computer vision (*q.v.*), robotics, graphics, reliable computer systems, logic circuits, hardware devices and structures, and application-specific computers.

The discipline of computing is characterized by three recurrent themes: theory, abstraction, and design (Denning *et al.*, 1989). Computer engineering and computer science both involve all three, but design is the preeminent domain of computer engineering, while theory is central to computer science. Abstraction, by which we master complexity, has an important role in both: it helps the engineer to crystallize thoughts to achieve a better design, and it helps the scientist to crystallize ideas to achieve a more robust theory.

As in the relationship between science and engineering in general, the science may yield results that become important for engineering. Theories of data abstraction may fall under computer science, but abstract data types (*q.v.*) are now essential to good software engineering practice. Computer engineering and computer science are coupled particularly tightly; for example, much work in programming languages has been motivated by the need for reliable software engineering design methods.

Nonetheless, a debate persists as to what computer science is and what computer engineering is, and where one should draw the line between the two. It is sometimes argued that computer engineering is more concerned with hardware and computer science is more concerned with software. This view is reflected in the predominant hardware focus of some academic computer engineering departments, perhaps due to their having often grown out of electrical engineering programs. But that position would put both hardware design and hardware models within the realm of computer engineering. Hardware design clearly belongs in computer engineering, since the element of design is central to computer engineering. Arguably, however, the development of hardware models is really computer science. Therefore VLSI design, as a subset of hardware design, also belongs in both disciplines.

This hardware/software dichotomy also produces a problem with software engineering (*q.v.*). Certainly, formal methods (*q.v.*) for proofs of program correctness is computer science, but the practice of software engineering, getting large programs to work, falls squarely in the domain of computer engineering. Thus, as formal methods for establishing correctness mature, they become a part of computer engineering as well.

Computer engineering and computer science are not at all differentiated by whether they involve hardware or software, since each involves both. Rather, computer engineering is more concerned with the implementation of ideas, while computer science is more concerned with the formal structure of those ideas. Two examples may make the distinction clearer.

Case 1: A *compiler* (*q.v.*) is a program that transforms a source program written in a language reasonably suitable for humans into a set of directives suitable for the hardware to carry out the work specified by the source program. The taxonomy of compiler features, the functionality that each provides, and the distinction between what is doable and not doable by a compiler is more nearly computer science. The design and development of a compiler that includes performing a cost–benefit trade-off analysis with respect to including or leaving out specific features *vis-à-vis* a specific target hardware implementation is more nearly computer engineering.

Case 2: A *hardware execution model* (or *virtual machine*) is a paradigm for carrying out the directives produced by the compiler. The taxonomy of hardware execution models and their distinguishing characteristics is more nearly computer science. The design and implementation of a hardware execution model, with strong attention to the cost vs. benefits trade-offs associated with the individual features, is more nearly computer engineering.

Bibliography

1989. Denning, P. J., Comer, D. E., Gries, D., Mulder, M. C., Tucker, A. B., Turner, A. J., and Young, P. R. "Computing as a Discipline," *Comm. of the ACM*, **32**, *1* (January), 9–23.
1992. Chen, C. H. (ed.) *Computer Engineering Handbook*. New York: McGraw-Hill.

Yale Patt

COMPUTER ETHICS

For articles on related subjects *see* COMPUTER CRIME; HACKER; INFORMATION ACCESS; INTERNET; LEGAL ASPECTS OF COMPUTING; PRIVACY, COMPUTERS AND; SOCIETY, COMPUTERS IN; and VIRUS, COMPUTER.

Characteristics

Computer ethics is the study of moral concepts, principles, and reasoning, applied in contexts that involve computers in some essential way. The stipulation "essential" rules out situations that raise the same ethical issues that would be raised if a computer were *not* involved. Morally, for example, the theft or wanton destruction of a computer is on a par with stealing or destroying a bicycle or a piano. In other circumstances, as will be discussed, computers do create distinct moral quandaries.

Approaches

Some writers (e.g. Johnson, 1994) hold that computer ethics primarily involves the application of traditional moral categories to problems that computers raise. From this perspective, computers do not introduce any fundamentally new *types* of moral issues. For example, although computers can be used to invade personal privacy, privacy invasion was possible before the advent of computers. What computers do (the argument goes) is to amplify significantly the scale of the activity. Thus the privacy of more people can be invaded in more ways with computers than without them. This approach to computer ethics draws heavily from traditional philosophical theories of morality, of which two are especially noteworthy: (1) *consequentialist* accounts, which assess the rightness or wrongness of an act in terms of its effects on others; (2) *deontological* accounts, which locate rightness or wrongness in the intrinsic nature of the act itself, without considering its outcomes. See Becker *et al.* (1992), Johnson (1994), or Rachels (1993) for details.

An alternative viewpoint (Moor, 1985; Barlow, 1991) maintains that computers present fundamentally new types of questions calling for new concepts and principles. While traditional approaches may be of some value, computer ethics reassesses those approaches and proposes the necessary alterations and supplementation. To illustrate: the traditional concept of community, which is geographically based, does not translate straightforwardly into "virtual communities" created and sustained through geographically dispersed computer networks. Accordingly, moral questions concerning computer-based communities demand fresh conceptualizations.

A third perspective, often directed at computer professionals, characterizes computer ethics more narrowly as rules of appropriate behavior; the principal focus is on practice rather than theory. Thus, many organizations have promulgated ethical standards for the use of information technology: the Association for Computing Machinery (ACM—*q.v.*), for instance, has adopted a code of conduct that its members are expected to obey (although penalties for disobedience of the code have never been defined or assessed). It has been argued, however (e.g. by Ladd, 1989), that organizational codes of conduct are not properly *ethical* codes at all, because they typically carry sanctions for noncompliance. This gives them a quasi-legal status, in contrast to ethical precepts, which are freely adopted because they are regarded as right, rather than merely accepted because of fear of the consequences of not following them.

Sample Issues

Because computer ethics covers a vast terrain, a comprehensive survey is not possible here; instead, a few representative problems are described. It will be apparent that many of the examples do not fit neatly into a single category. Furthermore, although none of the illustrative dilemmas is resolved in this article, it should not be concluded that resolutions are impossible. Computer ethics provides conceptual frameworks and analytical tools that any inquiring individual can use in arriving at acceptable answers.

ABUSE

Although the unethical nature of some computer abuse (e.g. theft of computer-based credit card records or pirating commercial software) may appear obvious, other alleged forms of computer "abuse" have not been so universally regarded as such. Is it unethical to send personal email messages from an employer's computer system? Is hacking into a computer system inherently wrong if no damage is done? Is a computer "worm" abusive if it exposes previously unknown security flaws that can subsequently be prevented? Typically, advocates of opposing answers appeal to analogies drawn from everyday experience. Compare (1) "Hacking is like someone looking in your front window from the street when you haven't drawn the blinds," and (2) "Hacking is like someone jimmying the lock on the door of your vacation home and staying there for an uninvited weekend." Considering the aptness of such analogies can often serve as a starting point for ethical analysis.

ACCESS

As public information becomes increasingly computer-based, there is a growing feeling that those who are denied access to computer resources will be unfairly disadvantaged. Are we moving toward a social chasm that separates the "information rich" from the "information poor"? How would such a division exacerbate pre-existing social inequities, e.g. those involving women and minorities? (In 1996, about 32% of Internet users were female and 13% were non-white.) Should communities, perhaps through public libraries, provide public access to the Internet? What should be done for people whose disabilities make computer use difficult or impossible?

COMMUNICATION AND NETWORKS

Computer-based communication networks introduce a variety of ethical dilemmas. For example: (1) Are there circumstances under which someone is justified in intercepting the email of others? (2) Does misrepresenting oneself in on-line "chat rooms" (*see* ONLINE CONVERSATION) or in email (*see* ELECTRONIC MAIL) transactions constitute an unwarranted violation of trust, or does it fall within the purview of "let the buyer beware"? (3) How can "freedom of speech" be reconciled with proposed Internet prohibitions against (a) harassing others by sending unwanted email messages; (b) posting racist, sexist, or otherwise inflammatory material; (c) providing instructions (e.g. on lock-picking or bomb-making) that could be used for malevolent purposes; (d) transmitting pornography? (4) What are the tradeoffs in permitting anonymous email communication, which can protect whistle-blowers but can also facilitate the perpetration of crimes and the avoidance of responsibility? (5) Is there anything wrong with identifying visitors to Internet sites and using that information for commercial purposes without the visitors' knowledge or permission? (6) Should a person be held accountable for posting information that turns out to be misleading or inaccurate (e.g. erroneous medical or financial information)? (7) How can the ethical viewpoints of various diverse groups be accommodated in the global Internet community?

PRIVACY

Although recent polls have revealed a high degree of public concern about personal privacy, many people are nevertheless frequently surprised to learn of the ease and extent to which their privacy can be compromised. Government agencies routinely perform computer "matches," seeking to identify inconsistencies among different databases, e.g. welfare recipients who own expensive automobiles. Computers in the workplace can enable employers to monitor workers' behavior, e.g. by counting keystrokes, tracking Internet sites visited, or reading employee email. Supermarket scanners can yield data depicting purchasers' buying habits and (inferred) lifestyles. Consumer warranty cards often request a wealth of personal information that consumers willingly supply, perhaps believing (erroneously) that the warranty requires it. Sophisticated queries of databases intended only to provide statistics can sometimes yield information about particular individuals. The presumed confidentiality of medical and hospital records and credit reports can be compromised.

Computers make it easy to draw information from a large *variety* of sources, making it possible to develop detailed composite profiles of individuals. For example, a much-discussed 1990 episode involved the Lotus Development Corporation's announcement of *Lotus Marketplace*, a CD-ROM product containing personal and lifestyle information on approximately 120 million people in the USA. (The data sources included the US Postal Service, voter registration lists, motor vehicle and driver's license records, public property records, telephone directories, consumer surveys, and warranty card questionnaires.) After facing a storm of public protest, Lotus canceled the project. But the key privacy questions remain: what personal information about each of us is an employer, a creditor, the government, a marketer, or another individual entitled to have? How may this information be acquired? What steps are each of us entitled to take in order to protect our privacy?

RESPONSIBILITY

Questions of personal responsibility may arise in organizational settings when an individual's ethical sensibilities collide with those representing some component of an employment bureaucracy. But since the development of advanced computer-based products is typically not a solitary effort, the resulting ethical milieu is further complicated. For example, complex software inevitably contains some mistakes ("bugs"); less commonly, hardware failures occur; marketed devices may be inadequately tested; designs may lack appropriate redundancies or other "fail-safe" precautions; user interfaces may present information in ways that are unclear; collateral (noncomputer) systems may fail; and safety regulations may be nonexistent or may go unheeded. Determining accountability when a computer product causes damage or injury or death is generally not a simple matter of identifying one individual's lapse. How should responsibility be assessed when multiple people and/or multiple factors are involved?

SOFTWARE DESIGN

Software development embodies a host of design choices that raise ethical questions. For example: (1) What unfairness results from an airline reservation system that displays the flights of one particular airline ahead of all the others, instead of adopting some other format such as displaying the lowest fares first? (2) In designing a work-scheduling system, should the users of the system be required to make their entire schedules public, or should they be permitted to "protect" some private time for themselves? (3) What should a university faculty do if it discovers that some of its traditional academic policies conflict with the capacities of a newly acquired computer system for managing student records? (4) Should job applicants be required to furnish their racial or ethnic identities on a computer-generated form that does not provide what they regard as accurate categories? (5) What are the ethical consequences of stereotypes in educational software that bias the software toward users of a particular gender?

Outlook

Discussion of computer ethics is becoming increasingly prevalent. Many useful books and Websites devoted to the subject have recently appeared; many universities have adopted an "ethics" component in computer science curricula; and various journals, including *Communications of the ACM*, now regularly feature articles on the social and ethical implications of computing.

Not only do questions of computer ethics frequently intersect, they also connect naturally with issues of social policy and law. This is no surprise, since our social and legal systems presumably embody our most deeply felt ethical positions. Recent public ethical and legal policy debates have addressed the regulation of pornography on the Internet; the right of an individual to distribute strong encryption software as a means of fostering communications privacy; the obligation of telephone companies to provide the government with computer technology to facilitate telephone taps; the duty of a major corporation to acknowledge and remedy a flaw in its processor chip; and the limits of free speech in cyberspace. Public discussion of these and similar topics is certain to grow in volume and importance.

Bibliography

1985. Moor, J. "What is Computer Ethics?" *Metaphilosophy*, **16**, 4, 266–275.

1988. Jackall, R. *Moral Mazes: The World of Corporate Managers.* New York: Oxford University Press.

1989. Gould, C. C. (ed.) *The Information Web: Ethical and Social Implications of Computer Networking.* Boulder, CO: Westview Press.

1989. Ladd, J. "Computers and Moral Responsibility: A Framework for an Ethical Analysis," in Gould (1989), 207–227.

1991. Barlow, J. P. "Coming into the Country," *Comm. of the ACM*, **34**, 3, 19–21. Reprinted in Johnson and Nissenbaum (1995), 15–18.

1992. Becker, L. C., and Becker, C. B. (eds.) *Encyclopedia of Ethics.* New York: Garland Publishing Company.

1993. Rachels, J. *The Elements of Moral Philosophy*, 2nd Ed. New York: McGraw-Hill.

1994. Johnson, D. G. *Computer Ethics*, 2nd Ed. Upper Saddle River, NJ: Prentice Hall.

1995. Johnson, D. G., and Nissenbaum, H. *Computers, Ethics & Social Values.* Upper Saddle River, NJ: Prentice Hall.

1995. Bacard, A. *The Computer Privacy Handbook.* Berkeley, CA: Peachpit Press.

1996. Kling, R. (ed.) *Computerization and Controversy: Value Conflicts and Social Choices*, 2nd Ed. San Diego, CA: Academic Press.

Websites

1999. ACM SIGCAS. http://www.acm.org/sigcas/.

1999. Bibliography of Computing, Ethics, and Social Responsibility/H. Tavani. http://www.siu.edu/departments/coba/mgmt/iswnet/isethics/biblio/.

1999. Computer Professionals for Social Responsibility (CPSR). http://www.cpsr.org.

1999. Electronic Frontier Foundation (EFF). http://www.eff.org.

1999. Electronic Privacy Information Center (EPIC). http://www.epic.org.

1999. Ethics on the World Wide Web/California State University, Fullerton. http://commfaculty.fullerton.edu/lester/ethics/ethics_list.html.

1999. (IEEE) Society on Social Implications of Technology (SSIT). http://www4.ncsu.edu/unity/users/j/jherkert/index.html.

1999. Research Center on Computing and Society/Southern Connecticut State University. http://scsu.ctstateu.edu/~rccs/.

1999. The Privacy Forum. http://www.vortex.com/privacy.html.

1999. Risks Forum. http://www.csl.sri.com/risks.html.

1999. Online Ethics Center for Engineering and Science. http://onlineethics.org.

Charles E. M. Dunlop

COMPUTER GAMES

For articles on related subjects *see* ARTIFICIAL INTELLIGENCE; COMPUTER CHESS; and VIDEOGAMES.

HISTORY

Computers were not invented to play games. In the 1950s and 1960s, with computer time both scarce and expensive, writing games for the fun of it was actively discouraged at most computer centers.

Nevertheless, there were many other reasons than just plain fun for writing computer games. Common reasons included exploring the power of the computer, improving understanding of human thought processes, producing educational tools for managers or military officers, simulating dangerous environments, and providing the means for discovery learning.

In some sense, the association of computers and games started in 1950 when Alan Turing proposed his famous *imitation game* in the article "Computing Machinery and Intelligence," published in *Mind* magazine (*see* TURING TEST). Never programmed by Turing himself, a variation of Turing's game called Eliza was put in the form of a computer program 13 years later by Joseph Weizenbaum at MIT.

In 1952, behind a cloak of secrecy, the first military simulation games were programmed by Bob Chapman and others at the Rand Air Defense Lab in Santa Monica. In the same year, a number of "formula" games (Nim, etc.) and "dictionary lookup" games (tic-tac-toe, etc.) were programmed for several early computers. Also in 1952, a computer was specially designed to play Hex, a game with no exact solution, by E. F. Moore and Claude Shannon (*q.v.*) at Bell Labs in New Jersey.

In 1953, Arthur Samuel first demonstrated his Checkers program on the newly unveiled IBM 701 computer at IBM in Poughkeepsie, NY. The next year, the book *The Compleat Strategyst* by J. D. Williams was published by Rand Corporation. This was the first primer on game theory and provided the theoretical foundation for many early computer game programs.

The first computer game of blackjack was programmed in 1954 for the IBM 701 at the Atomic Energy Lab at Los Alamos, NM. Also in 1954, a crude game of pool—perhaps the first nonmilitary game to use a video display—was programmed at the University of Michigan.

The American military set the pace for simulation games for many years, and in 1955 Hutspiel, the first theater-level war game (NATO vs. USSR), was programmed at the Research Analysis Corporation in McLean, VA.

Although Newell, Shaw, and Simon (*q.v.*) are frequently credited with the first chess game, the first version of computer chess (*q.v.*) was actually programmed in 1956 by Kister, Stein, Ulam, Walden, and Wells on the MANIAC-I at the Los Alamos Atomic Energy Laboratory. The game was played on a simplified 6 × 6 board and examined all possible moves two levels deep at the rate of 12 moves per minute. It played at a similar standard to that of a human player with about 20 games experience. In contrast, Deep Blue, the program which defeated Garry Kasparov in 1997, examined over 200,000,000 moves per second.

In 1958, a tennis game was designed for an analog computer at Brookhaven National Laboratory by Willy Higinbotham. This game, played on an oscilloscope display, was significant in that it was the first videogame to permit two players actually to control the direction and motion of the object moving on the screen (the ball).

In 1959, large-scale simulation games moved into the private sector with the programming of "The Management Game" by Cohen, Cyert, Dill, and others at Carnegie Tech in Pittsburgh. This game, programmed in the language GATE on a Bendix G-15 computer, simulated competition between three companies in the detergent industry and integrated modules on marketing, production, finance, and research. Modified and updated for newer computers, but still in use at graduate schools of business today, this game has certainly set the record for the longest life of any computer game ever written.

With the delivery in 1959 of the first Digital Equipment Corporation (DEC—*q.v.*) PDP-1 with its 15-inch video display, the continuing evolution from text-only games to videogames was hastened. Written by Slug Russel, Shag Gratz, and Alan Kotok, the first game for the PDP-1 was "Spacewar," first demonstrated at an MIT open house in 1962.

Later in 1962, Omar K. Moore at Yale built a device called "The Talking Typewriter" for teaching reading to young children. In the device, built by Edison Elec-

tric, a computer controlled a video display, slide projector, and audio recorder. In 1964, a more general-purpose computer-assisted instruction (CAI—*see* COMPUTER-ASSISTED LEARNING AND TEACHING) system using IBM hardware, including a CRT with graphics, light pen, and audio, was developed by Patrick Suppes at Stanford. Military research kept pace, and in 1964 Bunker-Ramo demonstrated a CRT display that simultaneously combined computer data with a projected background.

Artists began to realize the potential of the computer in 1964 when A. Michael Noll at Bell Labs produced the first computer art (*q.v.*) on a CRT display. Many years later, spurred by such companies as Activision, LucasArts Games, and Cinemaware, artists began to play a much larger role in the creation of games through computer animation (*q.v.*).

Rounding out the landmark year of 1964, the language Basic (*q.v.*) was developed by John Kemeny and Tom Kurtz on the GE 225 time-sharing system at Dartmouth College. Within a few months, the first interactive educational games and simulations began to appear on the Dartmouth system.

Various types of graphics displays from many manufacturers were introduced in the mid-1960s, opening the door to new video effects. Thus, we find a video pool game developed at RCA (1967), a ball-and-paddle game by Ralph Baer at Sanders Associates (1967), later to become the Magnavox Odyssey home videogame in 1972, a rocket car simulation by Judah Schwartz at MIT (1968), a graphic flight simulation by Evans and Sutherland (1969), a lunar lander game at DEC (1969), and a device to permit computer output and standard television video on the same display at Stanford (1968).

Figure 1. In Accolade's "Test Drive" game, players can choose to drive various cars on a variety of demanding tracks and courses.

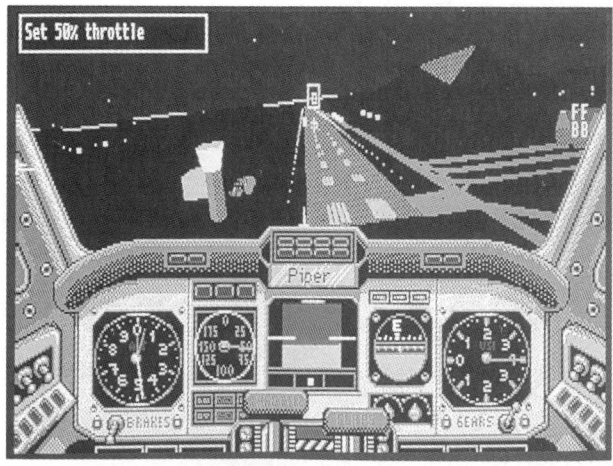

Figure 2. In "Yeager", a typical flight simulator, players must learn to land on a carrier deck, tough even for seasoned pilots.

In the October 1970 issue of *Scientific American*, Martin Gardner devoted his "Mathematical Games" column to a description of John Conway's "Game of Life" (*see* CELLULAR AUTOMATA). Easily programmed, it began to appear on virtually every video computer terminal in the country within weeks.

In the late 1960s, the National Science Foundation was attempting to encourage the use of computers in secondary schools to improve science education. One of the notable NSF-funded projects that produced scores of simulation games in science and social studies was the Huntington Computer Project directed by Ludwig Braun at Brooklyn Polytechnic Institute (later at SUNY, Stony Brook). In the Project's "Malaria" simulation game, for example, students must try to control an outbreak of malaria in a Central American country using a combination of various pesticides, inoculations, and treatment of the ill—all without bankrupting the country.

Also in the late 1960s, both DEC and Hewlett-Packard started major marketing efforts to sell computers to secondary and elementary schools. As a result, both companies sponsored a number of small-scale projects to write computer games and simulations in various fields, many of which were released in the early 1970s. In DEC's "King" game, for example, players decide how much land to buy, sell, and cultivate each year, how much to feed the people, etc., while dealing with problems of industrial development, pollution, and tourism.

Meanwhile, on the recreational front, in 1971, Nolan Bushnell rewrote "Spacewar" as a coin-operated arcade game called "Computer Space," which was marketed by Nutting Associates. Too complicated for the average player, only 1500 units were sold and the game was not successful. A year later, Bushnell's next project, the Pong arcade game, was considerably more successful and was the foundation of the Atari Corporation.

Also in 1972, Willy Crowther and Don Woods wrote a game for the DEC PDP-10 that they simply called "Adventure." The game, the first in the interactive role-playing fantasy genre, was unbelievably addictive and players consumed vast amounts of time-shared computer time on whatever system it was loaded.

Nineteen seventy-two also saw the first issue of Bob Albrecht's *People's Computer Company* newsletter, which, along with material for teachers and students, included many small Basic games in each issue. A year later, DEC published the book *101 Basic Computer Games* by David Ahl, which, in 1978, became the first computer book of any kind to sell a million copies.

Ahl left DEC in 1974 and started *Creative Computing*, the first personal computing magazine and the first magazine to publish three or four major games every issue. Also in 1974, Ted Nelson published the book *Computer Lib/Dream Machines*, while, at the MITS company in Albuquerque, NM, Ed Roberts was putting the final touches on the first mass-produced personal computer kit—the Altair 8800.

With the widespread availability of affordable video-game systems and personal computers, it looked as though there was no limit to the computer and video-games market. Atari introduced the home version of Pong in 1975 and it was followed a year later by literally hundreds of imitators. Removable-cartridge home games were first introduced by Fairchild in 1976, followed by Bally, Atari, and others a year later. By 1982, over 100 companies had entered the market with game systems or cartridges.

Figure 3. "Hardball," a realistic sports simulation, provides realistic player animation, instant replays, complete player and team statistics, and five field perspectives.

Figure 4. Computer versions of virtually every card and board game, such as this version of Scrabble, are available for one or more players.

Also by 1982, the $6 billion in quarters put into arcade games exceeded the gross take of all professional sports combined, buoyed by such games as "Space Invaders" (1978), "Pac-Man" (1980), "Defender" (1981), and scores of other mega-hits.

The kit era of personal computers lasted only two years and by 1977 manufacturers of self-contained, assembled computers like Commodore, Apple, and Radio Shack took the market by storm. This opened the computer game floodgates as the cost of entry was so low. All one needed was a personal computer, some programming talent, and a few hundred dollars to buy some magazine ads. In more than one case, bright teenage programmers started game companies and hired their parents as employees.

All was not well in gameland, however, and in 1983 the bubble burst. Many factors were responsible for the crash: too many me-too games, scores of companies with no management or financial expertise, jaded gameplayers, public backlash against arcades, and just too much expansion too fast.

After a disastrous two-year downward spiral, it looked to many as though computer games were in the grave. In April 1985, the Frost & Sullivan market research firm rated computer and videogames as having the least potential of 24 high-technology markets. The video and home computer games market was judged to have been a passing fad, and manufacturers seeking profitable opportunities were advised to turn their attention elsewhere.

Apparently, Nintendo didn't read (or heed) the report, since it chose 1985 to introduce its home game system. Also, Accolade, Electronic Arts, Strategic Simulations, and other computer game companies started to release more games in the IBM PC (*q.v.*) format, even though the PC was then considered to be primarily a "business" machine. These turned out to be wise decisions.

According to market surveys, Nintendo games were the most wanted Christmas presents three years in a row (1987–1989). Two new game formats were introduced in 1990: 16-bit systems by Sega and computer/compact disc games by NEC. The home videogame market, far from being a fad, was—and remains—healthy and growing.

The steep and continuing decline in the prices of PC clones put them within reach of most home users, thereby simplifying the life of game designers and manufacturers. No longer did manufacturers have to make a different game version for Apple, Atari, Commodore, and Tandy computers when a PC version would reach 90% of the users. Buoyed by a choice of

new and innovative games, the market steadily rebounded from its 1985 trough.

Today, real-time flight simulation games almost exactly duplicate the situation faced by actual pilots and the word "almost" is well on the way to being eliminated.

New games are emerging that use the latest technology—videodiscs (*see* OPTICAL STORAGE), multichannel sound, voice synthesis, speech recognition (*q.v.*), and much more.

David H. Ahl

ARCADE GAMES

Coin-operated machines were first introduced for vending holy water in ancient Alexandria almost two thousand years ago. The origin of the coin-operated amusement industry can be traced back to an old game called "Bagatelle" in which marbles were propelled to the top of a sloping board. Pins in the board (from whence comes the name "pinball") deflected the marble, until it fell into one of several semicircular pockets made either of pins or strips of metal. The further the ball traveled down the board, the higher the value associated with the pocket.

Pinball as an arcade game first took advantage of electricity in about 1929, chiefly to light the game. By 1932, Harry Williams had included a "tilt" mechanism, which would cancel play if the operator applied too much force to the cabinet. The year 1932 also saw introduction of the "kickout" hole. A solenoid in the hole would cause the ball to be propelled back into play after scoring. The introduction of the flipper in 1942 added player skill to a game that formerly had been influenced only by chance once the ball was released. Pinball machines improved along with technology—printed circuits were introduced into a game called "Perky" in 1956, eliminating most of the wiring that filled the older game cabinets. Pinball machines and jukeboxes remained the basis of the coin-operated amusement business for almost 80 years, until the introduction of videogames.

The first coin-operated game to be played on a monochromatic video screen was called "Computer Space" from Nutting Associates (*see* Fig. 1). Developed in 1971, this game was a simple shoot-up in which the operator controlled the direction of a spacecraft. The object of the game was to destroy dots on the screen by firing at them. "Computer Space" was developed by Nolan Bushnell from a popular mainframe game called "Spacewar" developed on a DEC (*q.v.*) PDP-8. (Computer games have always fascinated programmers—there were games written for computers in the 1950s, even though computer time cost up to $1,000 per hour and supported only one program at a time.) "Computer Space" was not a commercial success, possibly because its controls were complicated. In any case, Bushnell left Nutting to found Atari Corporation and, in 1972, produced a game known as "Pong." In response to Pong's success, a similar game, "Paddle Ball," was produced in the same year by Williams Electronics. "Pong" was a two-player game in which a ball moved around a rectangular space. Each player rotated a knob to control a rectangular "paddle," the object being to keep the ball from moving off the player's side of the screen. Refinements to the original were made in one-person hockey and tennis simulations in which each player controlled two paddles and the ball was delivered at various speeds.

Non-electronic color was introduced to videogames in 1973 when Atari introduced "Breakout," another game using a paddle in which a ball was bounced off an array of bricks, destroying those it touched. Since the bricks did not move in the original version of this game, they could be colored by attaching strips of cellophane to the screen.

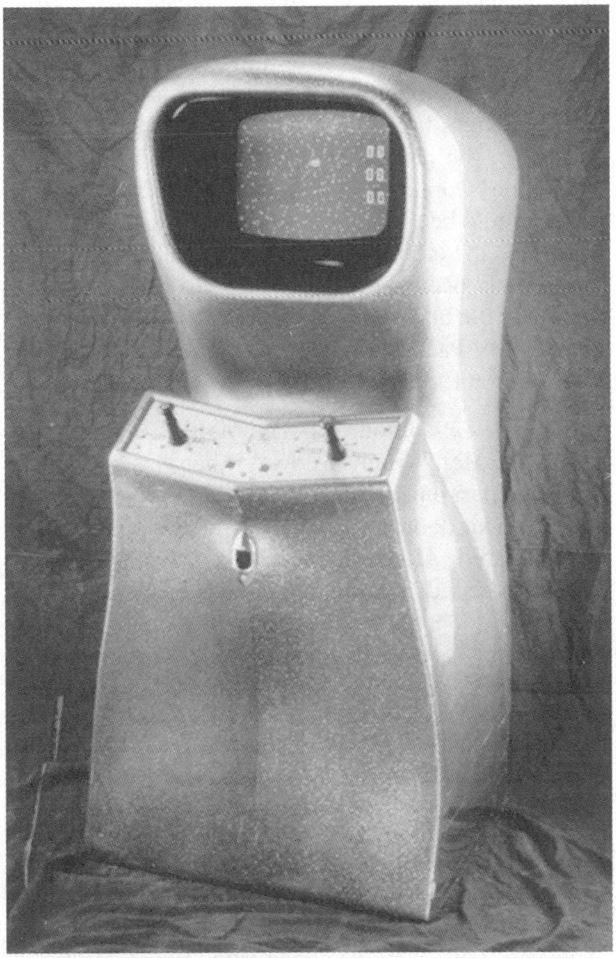

In 1976, a very controversial arcade game called "Death Race" was developed by Exidy Corporation from a science-fiction story that was made into the motion picture *Death Race 2000*. The story was based on a cross-country automobile race in which the participants scored bonus points for hitting pedestrians. Much of its popularity came from the controversy caused by its theme.

"Seawolf" (Bally/Midway) was introduced in 1977. The theme was submarine warfare, with the player viewing and firing torpedoes at targets through a realistic periscope.

The first game to take advantage of vector graphics was "Space Wars," introduced by Cinematronics in 1978. A more popular vector game was "Asteroids" (*see* Fig. 2) by Atari (1979), in which the player controlled a spacecraft among a host of asteroids that were moving across the screen. The craft could turn and accelerate to escape asteroids and destroy them by shooting. Big asteroids, however, turned into many small ones when hit. "Asteroids" included good sound effects and good physics—the principle of conservation of momentum was not only evident in the performance of the space-

Figure 1. "Computer Space" was the first video arcade game. (Courtesy American Museum of the Moving Image.)

Figure 2. Atari "Asteroids," which made use of computer graphics. (Courtesy *Play Meter* Magazine.)

craft, but also in the breakup of asteroids. When an asteroid was hit, the smaller objects resulting from the impact moved faster than the original.

One of the most popular video games of its time was "Space Invaders," designed by Taito in 1978. Hordes of little aliens marched down the screen, shooting at a hapless defender who could shoot back or hide behind barricades but who always lost. The game was predictable, however, so experienced players could destroy large numbers of invaders before meeting an inevitable end.

"Atari Football" was also introduced in 1978. This two-user game was played using "X"s and "O"s to represent players, but allowed users to control one football player each by means of a trackball, an innovation in arcade games. This game was the first one to use a team sport as the basis for play. Virtually every sport has now been simulated—football, baseball, golf, soccer, track, martial arts, automobile and motorcycle racing, and even skateboarding ("720 degrees," Atari, 1986), darts, jet-skiing ("Wave Shark," Konami, 1996 and many others) and water-skiing ("Skimaxx," ICE, 1996) to mention a few. Sega Enterprises, Inc., has specialized in simulations, including "Hang-On" (1985), in which the player sat on a motorcycle. The screen display was controlled by the operator's use of the handlebars, and the motorcycle banked appropriately from side to side. "Afterburner" (1987) added the pitch dimension to the motion of the operator's chair, and "Galaxy Force" version 2 (1988) included pitch, roll, and yaw.

"Galaxian" (Bally/Midway, 1979) was based on the same theme as "Space Invaders," but took advantage of color graphics and more versatile maneuvering by the raiders.

In 1980, the phenomenally successful "Pac-Man" was introduced. The game display represented a maze through which the player could manipulate the famous Pac-Man face by using a joystick. Pac-Man had to eat all the cookies in a maze while avoiding little ghosts that tried to trap him. This game was displayed on a color monitor. Pac-Man was partly responsible for the huge growth in videogame income from 1978, when the gross first reached $1 billion, to a peak of $7 billion in 1982. By comparison, the motion picture industry estimated that in its best year to date, 1989, there was a gross income of $5 billion. After 1981, income from videogames declined dramatically to about $4.2 billion in 1985. There was a general recognition in the industry that it would be necessary to improve the visual quality of videogames as well as their themes.

Technological improvements were part of the resurgence of arcade game popularity in the 1980s. In 1980, Atari introduced "Battle Zone," in which the operator manipulated a tank, using realistic controls. The operator's view consisted of a three-dimensional scene composed of obstacles and enemy tanks. Tanks not in the operator's field of view were indicated as dots on a round "radar screen." All enemy tanks could fire at the operator, even those outside the viewing screen. Scenes were rendered in wireframe 3D. Very realistic sound included varying engine noise and explosions. A modification of the game was used by the US Army to train tank drivers.

"Defender," introduced in 1981 by Williams, took full advantage of the current technology. The game consisted of controlling a small plane that fought various enemies. Five different controllers were used for simultaneous control of picture, sound, and player interaction, and graphics and sounds were stored in read-only memory (ROM—q.v.). Other technical features were introduced in 1980, including good speech synthesis ("Bezerk" by Stern.)

"Donkey Kong" (Nintendo, 1981) introduced improvements in automation and a game with a mission other than senseless slaughter. A little man, later named Mario, could be controlled by a joystick for horizontal motion and a button to cause him to jump over objects in his path. The player had to guide Mario to rescue a lady in distress from a gorilla. This explains the word "Kong" in the game's title, but there is no apparent reason for "Donkey." One theory has it that the word was meant to be "Monkey," but the game was made in Japan and the error was not detected until many units had already been sent to the USA. In any event, this game was the beginning of a series of adventure games such as "Ms. Pac-Man" (Bally/Midway, 1982) and "Dig Dug" (Atari, 1982.)

Another 1982 spinoff of "Pac-Man's" success was "Baby Pac-Man" (Bally/Midway) that was part videogame and part pinball machine. When a player escaped out of an exit door in the videogame, the pinball game was activated. After playing a ball, it was possible to return to the video game and continue.

Other new features were introduced in the same year. In "Robotron 2084" (Williams), two joysticks were used —one for moving and another for aiming a weapon— making it possible to fire without first facing various attacking outer space creatures. "SUBROC 3-D" (Sega) created stereoscopic 3D effects by displaying pairs of images using polarized light. Fortunately, the format of the game was a submarine fight, so the periscope viewing device could hold the necessary polarizing filters without distracting the player. "Zaxxon" (Sega/Gremlin) was the first raster image game that generated realistic 3D effects. It was another space war simulation, but alien craft changed size as they approached or receded, and the moving spacecraft cast a shadow on the ground.

In 1983, "Star Wars" (Atari) copied the attack sequence of the motion picture of the same name in which the hero flew at high speed down a narrow corridor while under attack by laser cannons. The videogame was a remarkably faithful rendition of the movie scene, requiring extremely fast reflexes on the part of the player.

Another major innovation was introduced in the "Nintendo Vs" system in 1984. Two players may participate in the games ("Vs Tennis," "Vs Golf," or "Vs Baseball") while looking at separate screens not visible to the opponent.

"Karate Champ" (Data East, 1985) was the first martial arts game. In the one-player version, the machine was the opponent; however, two players could compete against each other. Arm and leg motions were controlled by the player(s) and the motion of the game figures looked very realistic.

"Out Run" (Sega, 1986) was a high-speed automobile driving game that featured not only good graphics and sound, but also a realistic ride. The player sat in front of a steering wheel, accelerator pedal, and brake. As the wheel was turned the "car" would react by tilting to one side. If the driver left the road, the car would move up and down as if on a rough shoulder.

"Gauntlet" (Atari, 1986) had a "dungeons and dragons" theme that allowed up to four players to choose roles and play simultaneously. The salient feature of this game is the capability to play on after being "killed." For another 25 cents (of course) the player is resurrected and can continue.

The style of display used in an arcade game fits naturally into coin-operated gambling games. Poker and blackjack machines, as well as the electronic equivalent of the slot machine, are supplementing the traditional "one-armed bandit" mechanical games, but have not yet replaced them. In the 1990s, blackjack machines for 1, 3, or 5 players became available, as did more complex one-armed bandits, e.g. with payouts on three or five lines.

Realism has increased in modern games. "Narc" (Williams, 1988) was developed by using live actors and digitizing from film to produce realistic images that seem to be three-dimensional. Nintendo's "Hogan's Alley" (1988) has been used by at least one Dallas police station for target practice. Excellent, complex military-style games have taken advantage of faster processors to develop three-dimensional displays. "Wing War" and "Desert Tank" (Sega, 1994) are examples. Fighting games like "Street Fighter" (Capcom, 1990), "Mortal Kombat" (Midway, 1992), and "Samurai Shodown" (SNK, 1994) continue to be popular in arcades, despite the increasing availability of similar games on PCs.

Manufacturers extend the lives of popular games by means of new editions. "Mortal Kombat" (Midway) for example, which first appeared in October 1992, was upgraded to "Mortal Kombat II" in January 1994, "Mortal Kombat 3" in July 1995 and "MK3 Ultimate" in November of the same year. The first "Street Fighter" (Capcom) game, "Final Fight," became "Street Fighter II" and "SFII Champion Edition" in June 1992. A pinball game based on this version appeared in March 1993. "Super Street Fighter II" arrived in November 1993, and the "Turbo" edition in May 1994. In July 1995, "Street Fighter: the Movie" appeared, followed by "Street Fighter Alpha" in October and "Alpha 2" in May 1996. "X-Men vs. Street Fighter" reached the arcades in November 1996, and there is every reason to suppose that future versions will continue as long as one-on-one fighting games are popular.

In 1990, the most popular games were "Teenage Mutant Ninja Turtles" (Konami), "Hard Drivin'" (Atari), and "Street Fighter." "Race Drivin'" (Atari) and "Hard Drivin'" were big in 1991, along with "High Impact Football" (Midway) and "Street Fighter II". "Street Fighter Champion Edition," "SF II, Mortal Kombat," and "WWF Wrestle Fest" were best sellers in 1992. "MK" and "SF Champion Ed." shared popularity with "NBA Jam" (Midway) and "Samurai Shodown" (SNK) in 1993. By 1994, "MKII" and "NBA Jam" were still big and were joined by "Daytona USA" (Sega). It was inevitable that the popularity of "Daytona, USA" would create another driving game. "Cruis'n USA" (Midway) shared the spotlight in 1995, along with "MK3" and "X-Men Children of the Atom" (Capcom). "Daytona, USA" was still at the top in 1996, along with "Alpine Racer" (Namco), "Area 51" (Atari), and "Tekken 2" (Namco).

In response to increasing pressure from multimedia PC home games, arcade operators diversified. "Family entertainment centers" that include miniature golf, laser tag, bankshot basketball and virtual reality games like 3D PacMan were added in an attempt to retain market share, but nevertheless total income from arcade games in the 1990s leveled off at about $7 billion, plus $1.2 billion from gambling machines. So-called "redemption games," in which winners collect tickets to redeem for prizes, became popular again. The venerable "Skee-ball" is an early example of a redemption game.

Some designers of video arcade games began to emphasize games that could not easily be replicated as PC games, specifically those that required large pieces of

Figure 3. "Prop Cycle" is an arcade game that is not easy to duplicate on a PC because of its equipment requirement. Since the player must pedal the cycle, this may be the first combination video arcade game and exercise machine. (Reproduced by permission, *Play Meter* magazine.)

equipment for the player to drive, sit on, or stand on, for example "Prop Cycle" (Namco, 1996; *see* Fig. 3.) The operator of "Prop Cycle" sees himself or herself on a video screen, while pedaling and steering a flying, winged bicycle through an obstacle course. The mechanism rolls and pitches and the game is influenced by physical forces such as wind and gravity.

Although future arcade games will continue to use the latest technology for graphics and sound effects as well as improving the "feel" of simulation, the games will probably continue on existing themes. Home computer and hand-held games are eroding the popularity of arcade games, while the cost of playing in an arcade is likely to increase. The game manufacturers, for instance, have lobbied Congress heavily for the introduction of a $1 coin. (Arcade games have been played for 25 or 50 cents for years, while the cost of manufacturing games has increased considerably. Some games cost as much as $30,000.) To counter this trend, many manufacturers have turned to generic cabinets and interchangeable software cartridges. So much creativity is poured into the development of these games that it is hard to imagine their demise. It is more likely that continuing innovation will maintain the popularity of video arcade games and that most will continue to migrate to the PC after they appear in the arcade.

Keith S. Reid-Green

TRADITIONAL GAMES

When the earliest digital computers were built, scientists immediately became fascinated with the possibility of having them play such games as chess, checkers (draughts), and tic-tac-toe (noughts and crosses). Although this sort of activity proved to be a great deal of fun, the scientists were not just playing around; there are several good reasons to study game playing by computers.

The first reason relates to the popular conception of computers as "giant brains." Even the earliest digital computers could do arithmetic and make decisions at a rate thousands of times faster than humans could. Thus, it was felt that computers could be set up to perform intelligent activities, such as to translate French to English, recognize sloppy handwriting, and play chess. At the same time, it was realized that, if computers could not perform these tasks, they could not be considered intelligent by human standards. A new scientific discipline arose from these considerations and became known as *artificial intelligence* (*q.v.*).

A second reason involves the understanding by humans of their own intelligence. It is conjectured that computer mechanisms for game playing will bear a resemblance to human thought processes. If this is true, game-playing computers can help us understand how human minds work.

Another reason for studying games is that they are well-defined activities. Most games use very simple equipment and have a simple set of rules that must be followed. Usually, the ultimate goal (winning) can be very simply defined. Thus, a computer can be easily programmed to follow the rules of any board or card game. This allows the computer scientist to devote more effort to the problem of getting the computer to play an intelligent game.

There is also a practical payoff from computer game-playing studies. Specific techniques developed in programming a computer to play games have been applied to other more practical problems. To cite two, methods of searching (*q.v.*) used to consider alternative moves in chess have been adapted to find the correct path through a switching network or the correct sequence of steps for an assembly line, and learning methods developed for a checker-playing program have been used to recognize elementary parts of spoken speech. It is felt that the mechanisms of intelligence are general purpose, and therefore the borrowing of techniques from one application to another will continue in the field of artificial intelligence.

A closely related subject concerns games and economic behavior. An individual, corporation, or government can try to achieve goals by means of an

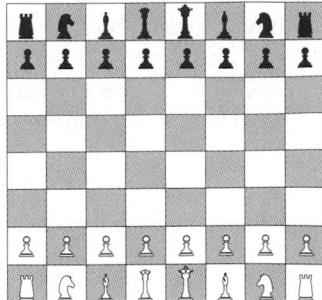 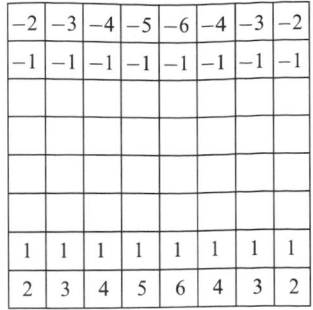 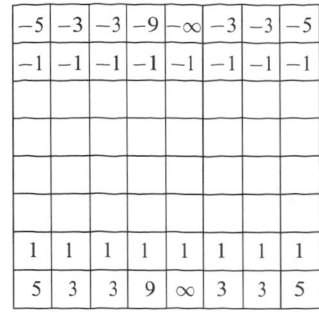

Figure 1. Computer representation of a chess position. In the second array, numbers are used to represent the various pieces. The third array represents the values of the pieces for use by the computer in evaluating trades.

analysis in terms of a game. On the assumption that the competition is rational and that other participants will also use the game approach, optimal behavior is dictated by game theory. The classic work on this topic is von Neumann and Morgenstern (1944).

Basic Techniques

The fundamental reason for the ability of computers to play a variety of games is that computers have the ability to represent arbitrary situations and processes through the use of symbols and logic operations. For example, one can set up a chess position inside a computer by means of an 8×8 array of integers, and tentative moves can be made by computer instructions that change the positions of the numbers in the array (Fig. 1). This capability is extremely general. That is, the symbols could represent checker pieces, or with a slight rearrangement, they could be playing cards for poker or bridge.

Figure 1 also shows the representation of derived information. The values of the pieces are stored in another 8×8 array for use by the computer. In effect, they are part of the computer's "knowledge" of the values of chess pieces.

Since symbols can be used to represent the objects of a particular game, computer instructions can be written by a programmer to specify the procedures for playing the game according to the rules and also for playing the game according to a strategy. In order for a set of procedures to be programmable, it is usually sufficient that they be defined in enough detail so that they can be translated into a computer language. For the purposes of this exposition, several game-playing algorithms will be stated using English words in place of computer language. The game of tic-tac-toe, for example, can be played perfectly by the following algorithm, in which the word "row" refers to a row, column, or diagonal.

ALGORITHM A (the computer plays X)

A1. Perform the first applicable step that follows.
A2. Search for two Xs in a row. If found, then make three Xs in a row.
A3. Search for two Os in a row. If found, then block them with an X.
A4. Search for two rows that intersect with an empty square, each of which contains one X and no Os. If found, then place an X on the intersection.
A5. Search for two rows that intersect at an empty square, each of which contains one O and no Xs. If found, then place an X on the intersection.
A6. Search for a vacant corner square. If found, then place an X on the vacancy.
A7. Search for a vacant square. If found, then place an X on the vacancy.

The algorithm is perfect in the sense that it will find a forced win if it exists and it will never lose. This algorithm may be called a *rejection scheme* because the first applicable step (following A1) is to be performed and all other steps are rejected (Fig. 2). A computer can be easily programmed to execute such an algorithm.

X	O	X
	O	2
O	1	X

Figure 2. In the position shown here, algorithm A would choose a move at square 2 for a win rather than at square 1, to block the opponent win. This is done because step A2 precedes step A3.

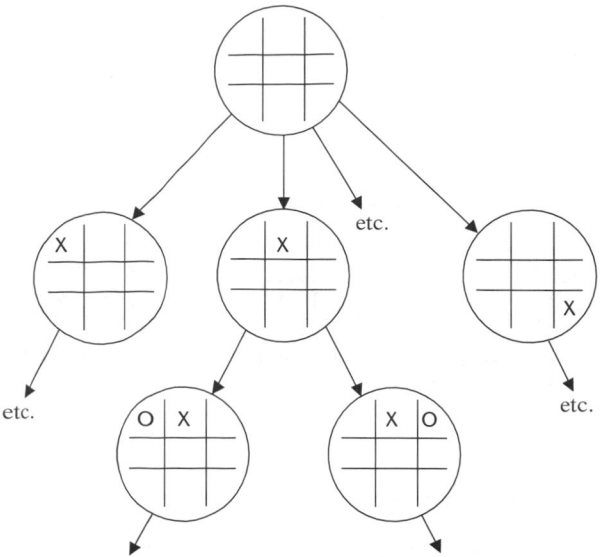

Figure 3. Part of the lookahead tree for tic-tac-toe. Circles represent game positions and arrows represent moves by X or O.

For another example, consider the following game, a special case of Nim. It is played with 13 matches; two players remove matches in turn until one player is forced to take the last match. A player may remove only one to three matches in a single turn, and the player who removes the last match is the loser. This is an algorithm for perfect play.

ALGORITHM B (the computer plays second)

B1. Let n be the number of matches taken by the opponent at the last turn.
B2. Remove $(4 - n)$ matches.
B3. If the game is not over, go to Step B1.

Both tic-tac-toe and Nim are simple examples of a large number of games classed as two-person games of skill. An essential feature of these games is that both players have perfect information about the current state of the game. Chess, checkers, and Go are well-known games of pure skill. It can be shown mathematically that there is, in principle, an optimal strategy for each player and that its application always gives the same result. In the case of tic-tac-toe, the result is a draw. In the case of Nim, the second player always wins. The possibility of playing a perfect game of chess, checkers, or Go will now be examined.

In order to show that an optimal strategy exists for two-person games of skill, the principle of *minimax* must be explained. If the state of a game is represented by a circle and the moves from that state are represented by lines (Fig. 3), then a tree (*q.v.*) can be obtained that represents the set of all possible games. The leaves of this tree (Fig. 4) can all be labeled with the terms *win*, *loss*, or *draw* for the first player. Now consider any node that is followed only by labeled nodes. If that node corresponds to the first player's move and it is connected to a node labeled *win*, then it may be labeled with the term *win*. It may be labeled *draw*, if it is connected to a node labeled draw, otherwise, it is labeled *loss*. If it is the second player's move from a position, then a loss (for player 1) is most preferred. This procedure can be repeated to back up the values W, L, and D to the top of the lookahead tree. Optimal strategy consists of each player choosing the path corresponding to the label W, D, or L at the node for the current move, once all nodes up to the top have been labeled. In the tree of Fig. 4, the best outcome for player 1 is a draw, and that is also the best outcome for player 2 once player 1 has made the optimal first move. In other words, a player makes the best move, based on the assumption that the opponent will make the best reply, and the opponent's reply assumes that the player will make the best counter-reply, etc. (At least as good an outcome as the best is guaranteed,

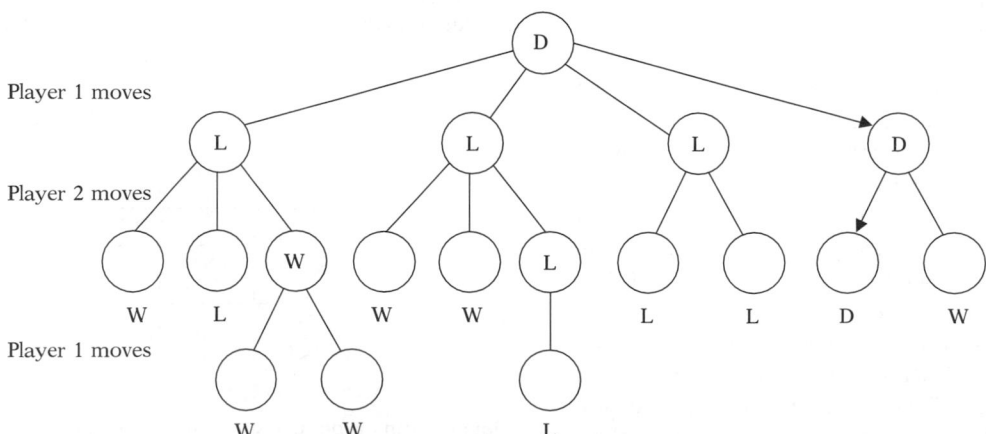

Figure 4. Illustration of the minimax procedure. The values at the bottom are calculated by an evaluation function. The backed-up values in circles reflect the result of optimal play. The arrows show the path of optimal play.

of course, even if the opponent makes less than optimum moves.)

Thus, since all possible chess games can be expressed in a tree like that in Fig. 3, it is known that there is a perfect strategy for chess that guarantees a win or a draw for one player. Of course, the strategy has never been found. It is the combinatorics (*q.v.*) of game playing that prevent the discovery of perfect strategies. In chess, when it is a player's turn to move, that player has, on average, 30 legal moves resulting in 30 different positions. If the opponent also has 30 replies to each of these moves, then 900 positions result. This sort of calculation gives an estimate of 10^{125} as the size of the lookahead tree for chess (the number of paths from the top of the tree to the terminal positions). If a computer could examine a billion positions per second, it would still take 10^{108} years to examine the entire lookahead tree to determine the optimal strategy. It should be mentioned that the number of board positions is far smaller, approximately 10^{42}, so it is theoretically possible to store all positions together with their optimal moves in a large table. Storing one board position on an element the size of an atom would necessitate a memory of about the size of the Earth. This gives a rather extreme example of the storage versus computational tradeoff that is so common to computer science. A method of reducing the search space is described in the next section.

A second class of games involves no skill at all, and a player's success depends only on chance. Examples are craps and roulette, in which the roll of dice or drop of a ball determines whether a bet is won or lost. A third and most important class of games involves a mixture of skill and chance of varying degrees. This includes games such as poker, bridge, backgammon, and Monopoly, which are affected by the distribution of cards or the roll of dice, although these randomizing features are generally overcome in the long run by the skill of a player. Computers can be set up to play these games of chance, but it is usually more difficult to represent the tree for a game when probabilistic factors are present.

Games are also categorized according to whether players have incomplete or complete knowledge of the current state. Games of pure skill, such as chess and checkers, and some games involving chance, such as backgammon and parcheesi, have no elements that are hidden from the players. But in many games, such as poker, bridge and salvo (battleship), each player can have information that is hidden from the other players. The presence of unknown factors poses additional problems for computerization. Methods developed here may be very useful, however, since real-world problems often involve unknown and probabilistic factors.

Game-Playing Programs

The first improvement that can be made for computer play is to establish an evaluation function for game positions that are not final. This allows the computer to examine part of the game tree and apply minimax to the terminal search values, resulting in a move. A refinement is alpha–beta minimax, which applies the principle "If a move is refuted, don't try to refute it even more." For the computer, this involves setting cutoff values for each search node based on values achieved at a given point in the search.

An early and very successful game playing program is Arthur Samuel's (1967) checker player, which was able to play a world champion to a draw. More recently, Jonathan Schaeffer has developed Chinook, a checker player that is considered unbeatable by any human player. Backgammon has been programmed at world champion level by Hans Berliner. Othello (or Reversi) has also been conquered by computer.

Go-Moku has become an extremely popular subject for computerization. It is essentially a game of the tic-tac-toe type, with each player trying to achieve five in a row on a 19×19 board. Since 1975, a North American computer Go-Moku tournament has been held, and, since 1977, there has also been a European tournament.

Most game-playing programs rely primarily on the search mechanism itself to organize all calculations, and it appears that games that are "small" enough are being conquered by the increasing speed of computers. However, the game of Go seems to have a different nature. Go is played by placing black and white stones on a 19×19 grid, and the most important feature of play is the emergence of groups or armies of similarly colored stones. Human perception can rapidly see the groups, but computers have more trouble with this. The best programs are still 20 levels below world champion level, even though computer tournaments have been held since 1985. Entirely new approaches involving computerized perception and pattern recognition (*q.v.*) may have to be developed as well as techniques to coordinate multiple evaluations. Research on Go may become the one of the best measures of progress in artificial intelligence.

Bridge is an especially interesting case, since there are two distinct phases of play—bidding and trick taking. Wasserman has produced a bridge bidder that achieves an expert level of skill. An unusual feature of his program is that it knows all standard bidding conventions and therefore can be adjusted to be an ideal partner for any player. Wasserman's approach was to use a base language, Algol, to implement primitive elements of bridge bidding; for example, a routine

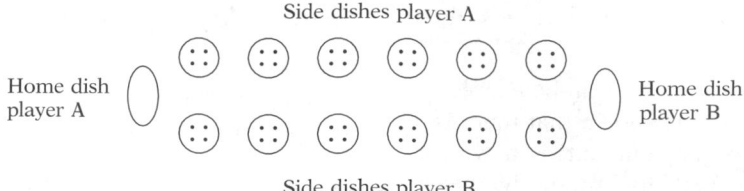

Figure 5. Start of a Kalah game with four stones in each of the side dishes.

`FIVECARDMAJOR[NORTH]` that returns `TRUE` or `FALSE`, depending on the north hand cards. Higher-level routines are built in layers over the primitives; for example

```
IF FIVECARDMAJOR[H] AND POINTCOUNT[H]>12
THEN BIDMAJOR[H]
```

where `H` is a variable that can take on the values `NORTH`, `SOUTH`, `EAST`, or `WEST`.

The unusual Middle Eastern game Kalah, played using stones and dishes, has been studied extensively. The game commences (Fig. 5) with an equal number of stones (usually three to six) in each of the side dishes (commonly six in number). The players take turns; in one turn a player takes all stones from one side dish and distributes them, one to a dish, in a counter-clockwise fashion, but skipping the opponent's home dish (or Kalah). If the last stone falls in the player's home dish, then a second turn is taken. If the last stone in the first turn falls in an empty dish on the player's side, the stones in the opponent's dish on the opposite side are "captured" and placed in the player's Kalah. The game ends when all dishes on one side are empty, at which point all stones remaining on the other side are placed in that player's Kalah. A Kalah-playing program by Slagle achieved excellent results against human opponents.

Of all games programmed for computers, more time and effort has been devoted to chess than to any other (*see* COMPUTER CHESS). A recent trend is the emergence of microcomputer-based games on the mass market. The quality of play varies, with backgammon, checker and chess programs playing quite well and bridge programs playing at a lower level. Rapid improvements in the quality and variety of these games may be expected.

Bibliography

1944. von Neumann, J., and Morgenstern, O. *Theory of Games and Economic Behavior*. Princeton, NJ: Princeton University Press.
1950. Shannon, C. E. "Automatic Chess Player," *Scientific American*, **182**, 2, 48–51.
1967. Epstein, R. A. *The Theory of Gambling and Statistical Logic*, Chap. 10. New York: Academic Press.
1975. Knuth, D. E., and Moore, R. W. "An Analysis of Alpha–Beta Pruning," *Artificial Intelligence*, **6**, 293–326.
1980. Berliner, H. J. "Backgammon Computer Program Beats World Champion," *Artificial Intelligence*, **14**, 205–220.
1987. Rivest, R. "Game Tree Searching by Min/Max Approximation," *Artificial Intelligence*, **34**, 1, 77–96.
1990. Hsu, F., Anantharanum, T., Campbell, M., and Nowatzyk, A. "A Grandmaster Chess Machine," *Scientific American*, **263**, 4, 44–50.
1996. Schaeffer, J., Lake, R., Lu, P., and Bryant, M. "Chinook: The Man–Machine World Checkers Champion," *AI Magazine*, **17**, 1, 21–29.
1997. Schaeffer, J. *One Jump Ahead: Challenging Human Supremacy in Checkers*. New York: Springer-Verlag.

Albert L. Zobrist

COMPUTER GENERATIONS

See GENERATIONS, COMPUTER.

COMPUTER GRAPHICS

PRINCIPLES

For articles on related subjects *see* CELLULAR AUTOMATA; COMPUTER-AIDED DESIGN/COMPUTER-AIDED MANUFACTURING; COMPUTER ANIMATION; COMPUTER ART; COMPUTER GAMES; COMPUTER VISION; ENTERTAINMENT INDUSTRY, COMPUTERS IN THE; FRACTALS; IMAGE PROCESSING; INTERACTIVE INPUT DEVICES; MEDICAL IMAGING; MONITOR, DISPLAY; PATTERN RECOGNITION; SCIENTIFIC VISUALIZATION; USER INTERFACE; VIRTUAL REALITY; and WORKSTATION.

Computer graphics consists of two steps: describing an image and then displaying it. There are a number of other issues that also come into play with computer graphics (or simply graphics). Is the image an individual one or part of a series of images in an animation? Is the image to be static, or can a computer user interact with a software package to change it? Is the goal of the image to be highly realistic because it will be viewed at length, or is it just to give a quick impression of the scene?

The field of computer graphics is now at the fingertips of every computer user because of the rapid increase in speed and capability of computers coupled with a decrease in the cost of technology. In the past, graphics was limited to narrow applications in science and business. Documents were entered as text with special formatting codes and only seen in their final form when printed. Objects in images were very simple and appeared highly artificial. Now, graphics is an expected part of every software package. Today's word processors use graphics technology to display the document in its final form on the screen as it is being created. Computer users expect graphical user interfaces (GUI) as part of modern software packages. Images in games and educational software are highly realistic.

There are two different views of computer graphics, each with its own concerns. A graphics system user is interested in what images are produced, what they mean, and how they can be manipulated. A graphics system programmer is interested in how to write graphics-based applications programs for those users. The programmer can be interested in clarity of data presentation, manipulation of imagery, or realism of that imagery. Each of these requires a different programming technique, level of sophistication, and type of hardware.

This article, however, is about the creation of images on the computer. These can be simple line drawings or realistic images of some real-world scene. The two steps to creating a computer graphic image are to build a model of some environment and then use software that renders an image of the model environment. Other articles in this volume deal with specialized applications of computer graphics to fields like design and manufacturing, entertainment, and medicine.

Areas related to computer graphics are image processing, and image analysis or computer vision. In image processing, the input and output are both images. The work that is done on these images is to enhance the information that they contain. This process may improve the balance of the image colors, or may sharpen the contrast. In image analysis or computer vision, the process is the reverse of what is done in graphics, since an image is analyzed and a description of the environment it depicts is created.

The balance of this article will give an overview of the major trends and issues in computer graphics. A more detailed discussion of the field can be found in graphics textbooks (e.g. Foley *et al.*, 1990), journals (*ACM Transactions on Graphics* and *IEEE Computer Graphics & Applications*), and major conference proceedings (e.g. Eurographics, GRAPHICON, Graphics Interface, Nicograph, and ACM SIGGRAPH).

Interactive vs. Non-interactive Graphics

The choice between interactive and non-interactive computer graphics depends on the application. Inter-active graphics is used for systems where the user plays a significant and active role in the system. A CAD/CAM system must be interactive since the user must create the object and its components as they are viewed on the computer monitor. Visualization systems are also frequently interactive so that the user can replay animation sequences, magnify parts of the image that appear interesting (*zooming*), and alter colors used so that different phenomena are highlighted. Applications that by their nature require frequent user input are programmed as interactive systems.

Non-interactive graphics systems are primarily those that are so computationally complex that the production of a single image takes longer than the time even the most patient user would wait. The production of realistic imagery using techniques of *radiosity* and *ray tracing* (discussed later) and the production of animated sequences can be very time-consuming. In these cases, the user will define the environment for the image (or for an animation sequence, the motions to occur) using some preprocessing system. This definition then serves as the input for the *image generator*, which can be run in batch or background mode. The resulting images are usually stored in a file and viewed at a later time using a device-dependent postprocessor. Some complex animation sequences of a few minutes duration take tens of hours of compute time to prepare.

As computer hardware improves, the lines between interactive and non-interactive graphics are being blurred. There are dramatic improvements in real-time animation, especially in the areas of games and system simulations (e.g. flight simulators). As this continues, there will be fewer applications of graphics that require non-interactive batch or background processing.

Some Representative Uses of Computer Graphics

VISUALIZATION

Visualization is a very broad term that includes the creation of images for science, business, and many other applications. The basic idea is to use color theory and design to present information in a way that efficiently and effectively displays large amounts of data to improve understanding, reveal trends, or display phenomena.

In science, experimentation with natural systems and computer simulations of them produce large amounts of data. Visualization allows a user to capture and display this data in a graphical format to give the scientist a better understanding of the forces at work. For example, an animated sequence of warm and cold water mixing can represent direction of water movement with an arrow, water velocity by the arrow size, and temperature by arrow color for various data collection locations. This animation can yield a better understanding of how fluids mix and how energy is transferred from hot to cold water.

In medicine, graphics is used to enhance X-rays or other scanned data. Advanced systems will use this data to create a model of the person that allows a doctor to plan and practice a surgical procedure before the actual operation even begins.

In business, sales, production, or marketing, data can be visualized to improve corporate decision-making. Computer-aided design and manufacturing systems are used to create, test, and set up production of new products. On the consumer level, visualizations are used, for example, to show the results of a landscaping change, building addition, or change in appearance.

Games

Computer games have shown great progress from the simple ball and paddle games of the 1970s. Today, computer games have high-quality graphics, produced in real time, along with fast-paced user interaction. These games are produced as either standalone units for arcades, tabletop units that connect to a television or monitor, or software for use on a computer. Examples include computer versions of popular board games or television game shows, sports or athletic competitions, and combative games that are frequently in futuristic settings.

Virtual Reality

Computer graphics plays a large role in virtual reality systems, although sound and movement also come into play. The basic idea of virtual reality is to create the illusion that the user is in another environment, through the use of images, movements, and sounds. The user can interact with this environment through a number of specialized input devices. Images can be displayed on a set of large screens that surround or partially surround the user or on very small displays mounted in such a way that the user views them from very close up. The goal of virtual reality systems is to give users the impression that they are really in the world created on the computer.

Graphical User Interfaces

Computer users now expect that software will have an interface that makes it easy to use. Interaction with computers is now commonly done through graphical user interfaces that present files and directories as *icons*, that allow data to be moved or copied by dragging icons around the screen, and that request information through buttons and check boxes on dialog boxes that pop up when needed. These graphical interfaces eliminate the need to learn and remember the typed commands that once made using the computer a daunting task.

Animation

The most familiar graphics application is animation; however, computer-generated animated movies are only one of the uses of animation. Computer-generated animation is also part of training simulators and videogames. Animation is affecting the legal system as litigants design animations based on physical evidence, created to show a jury "what happened."

Art

Some artists use a computer for tasks throughout the entire artistic process, from sketching or ideation, through the production of prototypes or drafts, and then for the final work, which can be a traditional sculpture or painting, a computer print, or an interactive installation.

The Early History of Graphics Technology

From the earliest days of computing, people were interested in having computers draw pictures. Graphs of data were constructed on line printers by carefully printing spaces and symbols on successive lines. Computer-driven cathode ray tube (CRT) displays were a part of the output of MIT's Whirlwind (*q.v.*) Computer (1950) and the Sage Air Defense System (mid-1950s). Input devices that were precursors to the mouse and lightpen were also part of early computer systems.

Ivan Sutherland was a pioneer of interactive computer graphics when he developed the "Sketchpad" drawing system (1963). This system included input and interactive techniques for creating line drawings, including pointing, dragging, and icons, that are still in use today. This system also used a hierarchical method for building objects from simpler components that still influences software.

In the mid-1960s, computer graphics was being applied to design and manufacturing tasks. Computer-aided design (CAD) and computer-aided manufacturing (CAM) developed out of the realization that the computer could help with these drawing intensive activities. Projects were developed to help with car design (General Motors), and lens design (Itek).

Even though graphics showed great potential, there were limitations on its widespread use. Graphics hardware was very specialized and expensive. Standards did not exist, so it was difficult to write programs for these devices, and the results were not portable to different systems. Further, the slow speed of graphics hardware made it difficult to produce interactive systems with reasonable and consistent response times.

Early hardware to control a graphics display was much different from that used today. In the 1960s, displays were monochrome and vector-based, with all images drawn as a set of lines. A full display system consisted of a display processor, a display list, and a CRT. The display list stored a series of points representing the ends of the lines to be drawn and the sole task of the display processor was to draw repeatedly those lines on the CRT. Changing the image on the screen required changing the points stored in the display list.

CRTs, both then and now, create an image with a phosphor and an electron beam. To draw a line on the screen, the electron beam is deflected along the path of the line. As the electrons strike the phosphor, it is energized. This additional energy is then released by the phosphor as light. Over time, this light diminishes as more and more energy is released. The phosphor's energy must be refreshed at least 30 times a second or the viewer will be able to perceive the dimming of the phosphor and the image will appear to flicker.

One problem with vector-based displays is that, as the complexity of the image increases, it takes longer to get back to the start of the list to begin redrawing the image. If this time gets long enough, the phosphor's energy may have decayed enough for the image to begin to flicker. Due to the speed limitations of early computers, an image did not have to be very complex for this to become a problem.

In the late 1960s, Tektronix developed an alternative strategy called the direct-view storage tube (DVST). In this technology, there was a special mesh near the phosphor that could store the image being displayed. This mesh would continually attract electrons to the phosphor needed to display the image, so it was constantly refreshed. When a new image was to be displayed, the mesh would be "erased" causing the screen to flash before the new image was drawn.

Modern Graphics Hardware

There are two kinds of graphics hardware: softcopy and hardcopy. The first category includes devices that produce output that can change. Display and projection units are in this category because the image that is drawn on the screen is not permanent but changeable. The second category includes devices that produce fixed output, typically on paper and film. Printers (*q.v.*), plotters, and film recorders fall into this category.

Display devices used today have their origin in the mid-1970s, and use a technology called *raster graphics*. As in television technology, an image is created by lighting discrete spots of phosphor, each called a *pixel* (short for picture element), and letting the eye merge them into a picture. In a monochrome monitor, these pixels have only one color phosphor, but in a color monitor each pixel is a triad of red, green, and blue phosphor. The image on the screen is composed of pixels in a grid typically about 640 rows of 1,024 pixels each, though monitors are available that can display over 16 times this number of pixels. Monitors will typically refresh the image 30 to 60 times a second. As part of these display systems, there is a *frame buffer* that contains enough memory to hold the value to display for each pixel, and a control unit that translates these values into the voltages needed to produce the correct amount and color of light. Changing the image displayed on these systems is now as simple as changing the values stored in this frame buffer.

Hardcopy technology also includes both vector and raster devices. Plotters will create their output as a series of lines in much the same way as a vector display. These high quality drawings are typically used in design, architecture, and artistic applications. Printers and film recorders operate like raster devices, producing discrete locations of color on paper or film.

Realistic Image Generation

The creation of a realistic computer graphics image involves a number of steps. The coordinates of the world are chosen, objects are defined and placed into this world, the location of the "viewer" is set, and a window is specified identifying the part of the scene that is visible. Once this is done, software will now determine what part of the world can be ignored because it is not visible, and then draw the rest of the objects based on their definitions. This process takes into account where light sources are located as well as how light energy may reflect off objects in the scene.

There are two major stages in computer graphics. The first stage is the description of the world, and is called *modeling*. The second stage is the drawing of the world, and is called *rendering*. The next sections will cover these two steps in greater detail.

MODELING

Concepts. Before a computer can create an image, descriptions must be developed for all of the objects that are to appear in the image. The elements of these object descriptions can be simple or complex depending not only on the detail in the object but also the method of description. Model descriptions can be created by hand using a plain text editor to enter the model data or by software that allows interactive specification while a crude depiction of the model is displayed. Many of the models used in graphics are highly mathematical and rely on the equations of lines, planes, circles, spheres, ovals, and complex curves and surfaces.

The definition of objects is typically done in some Cartesian coordinate system. An object can be defined in its own system that is then mapped into another world coordinate system that all the objects share, or the objects can be defined in the world coordinate system directly. This choice depends in part on the model, any modeling software being used, and the capabilities of the rendering program that will create the image.

Models can be hierarchical, defining a collection of simple objects and then using those to define larger and more complex objects. An example of this would be a model of a bicycle that had a simple wheel object defined that was then replicated for the front and back wheels. Models can also be functionally based, giving the parameters necessary for calculations that are done when the image is being rendered. This data amplification technique is commonly used in modeling natural phenomena because these objects are so complex that to specify all of the detail would be too cumbersome and would produce enormous amounts of data.

Object attributes. Each object that is displayed has parameters that determine its position and size, as well as other parameters that determine its appearance. For simple objects drawn as lines, attributes specify the color and whether the lines are solid or dashed in some fashion. Text attributes include the font type (e.g. Courier, Helvetica) and the character style (e.g. bold, italic). *See* TYPEFONT.

As objects become more complex, we have more parameters that can be specified. For three-dimensional objects, we typically specify the following types of properties:

◆ *Reflectivity* What portion of light that strikes an object reflects off it? Is the reflection sharp like a mirror (specular) or dull like metal? Does the reflection stay focused, or does it diffuse and spread?

◆ *Refractivity* What portion of light that strikes an object refracts through it? How much does the refraction shift or bend the light (as a pencil in a glass of water appears bent)? Is the object transparent like clear glass or translucent like tracing paper?

◆ *Absorptivity* How much of the light energy striking an object is absorbed by the object and neither reflected nor refracted?

◆ *Texture* Does the object have a smooth or rough surface? If rough, is there a pattern to the roughness or is it random?

Additional properties may be specified for objects based on the needs of the model type or on the rendering method to be used.

Modeling two-dimensional objects. Two-dimensional objects include simple objects such as circles, lines, and polygons, as well as more complex curves. Many of these, however, can be described through simple mathematical equations. This section will look at the issues involved in modeling these objects.

Circles can be specified by their center point and radius. An arc is a portion of circle, and usually has the additional parameters of starting and ending radii with the arc conventionally drawn counterclockwise between these two angles. An oval or ellipse can be specified by two centers of curvature and a length. All points whose sum of distances to both centers is equal to the specified length are on the ellipse.

Lines can be specified as a starting and ending point, or as the coefficients of the equation of a line. A polygon is specified as a list of points that are the vertices of the polygon. The edges of the polygon are the lines between successive points on this list, and the polygon is closed by also drawing an edge from the last to the first point, instead of duplicating the first point at the end of the list. Some of the algorithms for drawing a polygon may assume that the polygon is convex (so that a straight line between any two points inside the polygon is entirely in the polygon as well) and does not have edges that cross each other.

Two-dimensional curves can be approximated by a set of short lines, or can be specified by mathematical equations, for example, $y = x^2 - 3x + 5$. This, however, only allows creation of simple curves. More elaborate curves are possible by using bicubic parametric functions.

There are a large number of different styles of bicubic parametric functions, but all have some common features. They all require that the user specify some set of controlling data for the curves. This data is typically a set of points that control the location of the curve. These control points and a set of blending functions are used to determine the curve location. Fig. 1a shows a set of four control points and the resulting curve. Fig. 1b shows what happens if one of these control points is moved.

Bicubic parametric functions differ according to their blending functions. Some will interpolate the curve through the first and last control points, so that they are on the curve; others do not. Some exhibit local control so that moving a control point will only change part of the curve, while others exhibit global control so that each control point will influence the entire curve

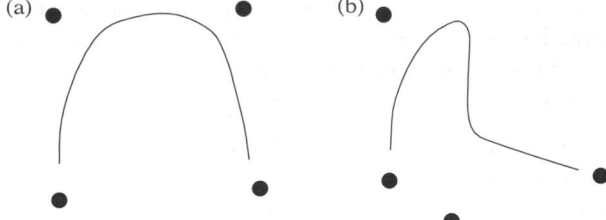

Figure 1. Bicubic parameter functions.

but have the greatest effect on just a portion of it. For example, if there are five control points defining a curve, with local control the first third of the curve would be determined by points 1 through 3, the middle of the curve by points 2 through 4, and the last third of the curve by points 3 through 5. With global control, all five points would influence the entire shape of the curve, but points 1 and 2, for instance, would have their greatest effect on the beginning of the curve and points 4 and 5 on the end.

The choice of blending functions is usually determined by the needs of the model. If a complex curve will need to be modeled by multiple sets of control points, the blending functions should interpolate the first and last control points so it is easy to have the parts of the curve join. If the continuity of the curve at these join points is highly critical, it may be easier to use blending functions with local rather than global control (*see* SPLINE).

Modeling three-dimensional objects. Simple three-dimensional objects can be defined like their two-dimensional counterparts. A sphere can be defined by specifying its center and radius. A box can be defined by specifying the locations of its eight vertices. If we place restrictions on the orientation of the box, so that all of its faces must be perpendicular to either the x, y, or z axis, then we need to specify only two vertices that are opposite each other, because the other six vertices can be derived from these two.

A planar surface can be uniquely defined by specifying three non-collinear points. This plane can be considered infinite in all directions or can be triangular-bounded by the lines connecting these three points. That is, three points (P_1, P_2, and P_3) uniquely specify a plane with the equation $Ax + By + Cz + D = 0$. The first step to deriving this plane equation is to determine the normal to the plane. The normal is a vector (line) that is perpendicular to this plane. The normal is the cross product of the two vectors P_1P_2 and P_1P_3. If we call the first vector **v**, its **x**, **y**, and **z** components v_x, v_y, v_z are the difference of the **x**, **y**, and **z** components of P_1 and P_2. The second vector **w** is determined by the difference of P_1 and P_3. The normal (A, B, C) is then given by

$$A = v_y w_z - v_z w_y$$
$$B = v_z w_x - v_x w_z$$
$$C = v_x w_y - v_y w_z.$$

The value of D is determined by substituting one of the points (P_1, P_2, or P_3) into the plane equation and solving for D.

There are two methods that can be used to define convex planar polygons that have more than three sides. In the first, the polygon is divided into triangular pieces and those are specified individually. In general, you need n triangles for a polygon with $n + 2$ sides. The second alternative would be to specify all of the vertices. This might appear to be the simpler alternative; however, it can be tricky to get four or more vertices of a polygon that are all in the same plane. As the fourth or higher points are specified, it is likely that they are either above or below the plane specified by the first three points unless they are calculated from a plane equation. Calculating additional points would require specifying two of the three (x, y, z) components of the point and then solving for the third.

Curved surfaces can be defined by using a three-dimensional version of bicubic curves. In this case, we specify sets of control points along two directions that are perpendicular to each other. One curve surface would typically be defined by a set of 16 control points logically arranged into four rows of four control points each. The blending functions are then used to interpolate in two directions between the control points along the rows and columns. Curved surfaces can also be approximated by a set of small planar patches. For highly curved surfaces, this approximation can get quite large, since the planar patches must be small if the result is to look reasonable.

Modeling of natural phenomena. There are a number of different techniques used to model natural phenomena. One of these uses probabilities to model the growth of plants and trees. The main research into probabilistic models of growth are those of Phillipe de Reffye and his colleagues (1988), a group composed of agronomists, botanists, and computer scientists. Their model considers the growth point of a plant and four possible events that can occur in one time unit. The bud can become a flower or fruit and then die; it can go into a dormant state; it can abort or die; or it can grow, producing a new branch section. All of these are controlled by predetermined probabilities that the user must specify.

The model also requires that the user provide the age of the plant and, for each branch, the rate at which the branch grows, the maximum number of buds produced by each branch, the length and diameter of the branches, and the developmental trend of the branch (either vertical or horizontal).

A grammar-based approach to modeling plant growth was proposed by Aristid Lindenmayer as a way to define formally the growth that is observed in filamentous organisms. These grammars (*q.v.*), now known as *L-systems* or *Lindenmayer systems*, were used to define the interaction between cells in these organisms and to define branching patterns (*see* FRACTALS). L-systems are grammars for generating strings whose productions (*q.v.*) may all execute in parallel to model the process of growth of an organism.

Pauline Hogeweg takes these L-systems and reverses the process, using their simple parallel grammars to produce tree-like images. In her work, she generates a string from the grammar, and then renders it with simple parameters. Each symbol is represented as a vertical line, and each branch section causes a rotation of the axes.

Masaki Aono and Tosiyasu Kunii enhance these L-systems by the addition of a geometry specified by a limited number of branching angles. This work is also interesting in that it attempts to model natural effects of sunlight and wind with "attractors" that pull the ends of the branches like magnets. Unfortunately, this technique cannot model the inhibition of growth on the shadowed side of the plant, nor can it account for environmental objects that may partially or completely block the light.

Przemyslaw Prusinkiewicz (1996) also incorporates both two- and three-dimensional interpretations by the addition of special symbols into the L-system grammars. These special symbols control a two- or three-dimensional turtle that draws the plant image. In turtle geometry, a *turtle* is commanded to move in various directions, with its pen either up or down, drawing lines as it moves in the latter case. With the correct sequence of symbols, the turtle draws flowers, leaves, and entire plants. Prusinkiewicz's work continues to expand the application of L-systems, and Hans Meinhardt now uses them to model sea shells.

Three-dimensional *graph grammars* were developed by Jeffrey McConnell (1989) to model growth of plants not only in an ideal environment, as most other models assume, but also in a natural environment. Because of the three-dimensional nature of the model, the positions of the branches relative to each other, the sun position, and external obstructions can be determined. Sunlight calculations can be done to find how much light falls on a particular branch, and the system can then slow the growth if not enough light is present, or encourage growth in high light areas. The growth of a plant can also be altered by either external obstructions or other parts of the plant (internal obstructions).

Fire, explosions, and fireworks are another class of natural phenomena, and Bill Reeves has developed *particle systems* to model them. In his research, Reeves models a particle as an entity that has mass, color, velocity, direction, and duration. By combining a group of particles that start from a central point and move outward, a realistic fireworks burst can be simulated. A cylinder-shaped group rising from a plane produces a fire. Particles emanating from the top of a sinusoidal wave produce a foam-like appearance.

Physically-based modeling. The increasing speed of computer systems allows production of high-quality computer graphics images through the use of physically-based models. Prior to the advent of reasonable computer power, animation sequences were very unrealistic because all calculations of how objects moved had to be done with approximations to actual equations.

Images and animation sequences of cloth being draped over an object, chains dangling between two poles, and indentations of elastic objects can now be produced with amazing realism.

Computers are now powerful enough to treat cloth not as a single entity, but as a collection of constituent woven threads. Jerry Weil has developed a technique that is based on seeing a thread as lying in a catenary curve (the shape of a hanging chain). To model, for example, a cloth lying over a chair, the points of the cloth that contact the chair are fixed in space. The threads between these points are then mapped into a catenary curve. Other threads intersect these catenary-shaped threads, fixing more points for these new threads. The process repeats until all of the threads have been placed. There could be thousands of threads running the length and width of even a small piece of cloth, leading to millions of intersection points on the fabric, whose locations must be determined.

Constraint-based modeling is used in computer graphics for modeling movement of the human skeleton, chains, and other physical objects. The idea is that it is difficult to specify a coordinate at which a ball would be resting on a table, but it would be simple to constrain the ball to be on the table and to have the computer calculate the correct location. For the human skeleton, constraints specify the connectivity of bones at joints and the directions and angles of movement. In modeling the movement of a skeleton across a terrain, the system will set bone positions to best satisfy the constraints placed on the system.

Solids modeling. In the discussion of three-dimensional objects, we assumed they would be described by their outer surfaces. This is fine for applications that require only the production of images, but systems designed to manipulate or test the created objects need an alternative representation. Solids modeling treats all objects as solids, clearly identifying the inside and outside of each object, which allows tests for stress and obstruction as well as production of parts lists. This is the underlying model for CAD/CAM systems.

In solids modeling, the system has a collection of primitive objects that can be scaled, rotated, and translated. Complex objects are built by applying Boolean operations to simpler objects. A washer can be created by subtracting a short narrow cylinder from a short wide one. A door hinge pin can be created through the logical union of a wide, short cylinder with a tall, narrow one.

RENDERING

Windowing. Since large drawings cannot fit in their entirety on display screens, they can either be compressed to fit, thereby obscuring details and creating clutter, or only a portion of the total drawing can be displayed. The portion of a two- or three-dimensional object to be displayed is chosen through specification of a rectangular window that limits what part of the drawing can be seen.

A two-dimensional window is usually defined by choosing a maximum and minimum value for its x- and y-coordinates, or by specifying the center of the window and giving its maximum relative height and width. Simple subtractions or comparisons suffice to determine whether or not a point is in view. For lines and polygons, a *clipping* operation is performed that discards those parts that fall outside of the window. Only those parts that remain inside the window are drawn or otherwise rendered to make them visible.

Lighting models. As a prelude to the discussion of shading models, it is necessary to discuss the way in which the effects of incident light can be quantified for image production. The first type of illumination to be considered is *ambient light*, I_a, present in the environment. Since ambient light has no focus or direction, this is treated as an additive factor for all objects. The second type of light is *reflected light*, which varies depending on the location of the light source, the object, and the viewer. From Lambert's cosine law of physics, we know that the intensity of the diffusely reflected light is related to the scalar (dot) product of the surface normal, **N**, and a unit vector pointing toward the light source, **L**. The last type of illumination is *specular reflection*, which produces the highlights on an object. Specular reflection (Fig. 2)

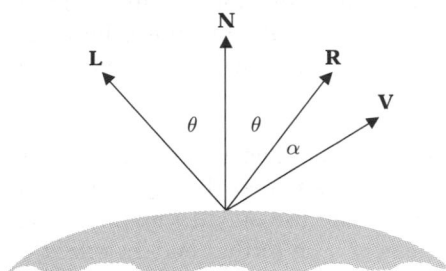

Figure 2. Specular reflection.

depends on the angle between the reflected vector, **R**, and the vector pointing at the viewer's position, **V**. If these two coincide, the highlight is bright; the farther apart they are, the dimmer the highlight.

A simplified version of the light calculation is given by the formula $I = I_a + I_s[k_d(\mathbf{N} \cdot \mathbf{L}) + k_s(\mathbf{V} \cdot \mathbf{R})^n]$, where I_s is the intensity of the light source, k_d is a diffuse reflection coefficient, k_s is a specular reflection coefficient, and n is the specular reflection exponent (when n is 1, the highlight is broad with blurred edges, and as n gets larger, the highlight is narrowed and has sharper edges).

Painter's and *Z*-buffer algorithms. In the Painter's Algorithm, each object is broken into planar piece approximations that are arranged as separate units, according to their distance from the viewer. The algorithm now works like a painter applying paint to a canvas—if something is blocked by an object in front, the painter just paints the foreground object over it. The piece farthest from the viewer is drawn, then the second farthest, and so on. If a piece will ultimately be visible, nothing will be drawn over it; however, if it is not entirely visible, a piece drawn later will cover all or part of it. So the picture is drawn back to front.

In the *Z*-Buffer Algorithm, there is a *Z*- or *depth-buffer* that has one value for each pixel in the frame buffer. These values represent the depth of the object of which the pixel is a part. For example, if an area of four pixels square is part of the first object, which is 4 units away from the viewer, all of the *Z*-buffer values for these pixels would be set to 4. As each new piece is drawn, its depth at the pixel location is compared with the *Z*-buffer value. If the buffer value is greater, this piece is in front and can be drawn (and the *Z*-buffer value is updated). If the buffer value is smaller, the old object is closer, so the current one is not drawn at that point. The benefit of the *Z*-buffer algorithm is that it is not necessary to sort the pieces, as the *Z*-buffer does that implicitly.

These two algorithms show the common space vs. time trade-off of computer science. The Painter's Algorithm is slower because of the sorting, but it doesn't require the extremely large memory of the *Z*-buffer. With the low cost of computer memory, however, many graphics controllers include extra memory specifically for the *Z*-buffer.

Flat shading. A problem with the Painter's and *Z*-Buffer Algorithms is that they ignore the effects of the light source and use only the ambient light factor. Flat shading goes a bit further and includes the diffuse reflections as well. For each of the planar pieces, an intensity value is calculated from the surface normal, the direction to the light, and the ambient light and diffuse coefficient constants. Since none of these change at any point on the piece, all of the pixels in that piece will have the same intensity value. The resulting image will appear to be faceted, with ridges running along the boundaries of the pieces that make up an object (*see* Fig. 3a, Color Page CP-7).

Gouraud shading. In 1971, Henri Gouraud developed an interpolation method that removed some of the discontinuities between pieces and also produced more realistic highlighting (Fig. 3b, Color Page CP-7). The problem with the previous method is that a single normal is used for a patch that approximates a curved surface. Gouraud's method keeps the normal vector from the actual surface for each vertex of every piece. This means that the normals at the vertices of a patch can be different from each other, but that the normals where two patches touch will be the same since they come from the actual surface at that point.

When each piece is being shaded, the intensity or color at each vertex is calculated, and then the system interpolates between them for the interior points of the piece. In flat shading, there is the problem of adjacent pieces being shaded different colors. In Gouraud shading, two pieces that share an edge will also share the normals at the end points of this edge and therefore have the same color at these end points. Hence when the two pieces are being shaded the colors that are interpolated along this shared edge will be the same, and the edge will not be noticeable.

Phong shading. Gouraud shading improved on the images that were produced by flat shading, but the highlighting was still off. In 1975, Bui-Tuong Phong improved on Gouraud shading by interpolating the normals across the surface, as opposed to the intensities (Fig. 3c, Color Page CP-7). This leads to finer and more precise highlights. The differences among these three shading methods can be seen in Fig. 3, Color Page CP-7.

Ray tracing. In the methods examined so far, all objects are assumed to have a matte or dull finish. None is reflective, translucent, or transparent, because the

previous methods are not able to handle these types of objects. *Ray tracing* takes the previous methods one step further in allowing rays of light that strike a surface to reflect and refract among all the objects in the scene.

When the viewer location and pixel location on the screen are considered, they define a line or ray into the scene to be rendered. This ray is traced into the scene, where it can strike a matte surface object, and the pixel color is determined as in Phong shading. If the ray strikes a reflective or refractive surface, the laws of optics are used to determine the new direction of one or more rays that would result. These new rays are then traced recursively until they leave the scene or strike another surface, a computationally complex process that quickly degrades as the number of reflective and refractive objects increases.

Radiosity. Ray tracing improves imagery, but suffers from an inability to handle reflections between diffuse surfaces. Most people have experienced reflections between two diffuse surfaces when, in a bright room, the color of the rug affects the color of the walls or, when wearing a red shirt, one appears to be blushing.

Radiosity, developed by Michael Cohen and Don Greenberg from Cornell University, treats light as energy instead of a vector, and considers how that energy is transferred between surfaces based on their color and proximity. Radiosity is applied in three stages, and, based on what type of changes occur, only some of the stages require recalculation. If the viewing location changes, only the last rendering stage is redone. If an object in the scene is moved, all stages are recalculated. Since early stages are the most computationally complex, the less they are redone, the more time is saved. As can be seen in Fig. 4 (Color Page CP-7), radiosity produces remarkable realism.

Texture mapping. Early computer-generated images used shaded objects that had unnaturally smooth surfaces. To produce a textured surface using the techniques discussed would require creating an excessive number of surface pieces that follow all of the complexities of the texture. An alternative to the explosion of surfaces would be to use the techniques of *texture mapping*. Texture mapping is a technique used to paint scanned images of a texture onto the object being modeled. Through an associated technique, called *bump mapping*, the appearance of the texture can be improved still further.

Surface painting vs. bump mapping. Surface painting simply adds an image to the surface of an object. If the image is itself a texture, it makes the object appear textured. This technique requires the production of a texture file containing color values that have traditionally been obtained by scanning a picture of a real object with the desired pattern.

The shading algorithm is altered to use the texture file for determining the color of points on the surface. To do this, a mapping function is produced that converts surface locations into the range of the texture. As the surface is shaded, the locations on the surface, corresponding to pixels in the image, are mapped into the texture's space, and the texture value at that point is used as the object's color. This is not normally a good solution, since specular highlights are not affected; the resulting images appear to be flat surfaces that have had pictures painted on them.

An obvious way to include specular highlighting would be to use the texture to modify the surface definition, but, as was mentioned, this is complex and quickly explodes the amount of surface information that needs to be stored and accessed. The alternative is to treat the texture as a *bump map* that modifies the surface definition at a single point for only the brief instant that it is being rendered.

Where texture painting techniques alter the color of the surface based on the values in the texture, bump mapping alters the value of the surface normal at the point. When the bump map turns the normal away from the light direction, this darkens the location; conversely, when it turns the normal toward the light, the location is brightened.

The problem with bump mapping appears with objects in profile. Since its surface is not actually changed as an object is rotated, the highlighting of the bumps appears to be correct until the surface reaches its profile, when the bumps disappear.

Two-dimensional vs. three-dimensional textures. The foregoing discussion assumes a two-dimensional texture wrapped around a surface. This requires special conditions to be present in the map, depending on the surfaces to be textured. If cylinders are to be textured, the texture must be continuous so that, when the texture is wrapped around the cylinder, no seam appears where the ends meet. This is also required if the surface is so large that the texture needs to be repeated to cover it. The requirements for texturing a sphere are even more demanding.

One solution to this problem is use of a three-dimensional texture, as is done in the work of Peachy (1985) and Perlin (1985). Since these textures show proper changes in all directions, a surface can be textured by "placing" it into the three-dimensional texture. This is done by mapping the surface locations into the texture's three-dimensional space. This eliminates the problem of texture seams, but increases the space required to represent the texture.

Static vs. functional maps. Up to this point, all discussion has assumed that the texture is static, having been scanned into a file. This places restrictions on the texture.

An alternative is a *functional texture*, i.e. the encoding of a texture in an equation-based routine. Surface indices are used as parameters for the equations. This removes the need to store the texture (a space reduction), but also reduces the speed of image production, as the function is likely to be more expensive to compute than a table look-up in an array (a time increase). This trade-off is tempered by the ability to alter system parameters dynamically, allowing the texture to evolve based on the natural demands of the image. Additionally, the texture is now potentially infinite in all directions, which eliminates scaling or cycling through a static texture that is used to cover an arbitrarily large surface.

Functional texturing has been taken to a successful extreme by Geoffrey Gardner (1985), who produces entire images based on a single formula, with parameters altered to produce mountains, clouds, and trees (*see* Fig. 5, Color Page CP-7).

ANIMATION

Animated cartoons were the hallmark of Walt Disney, whose studio produced a number of classic films. This work, called *cel animation*, first requires the production of an overall storyboard. From that, individual scenes are created, with the *animator* drawing only key frames, an *in-betweener* drawing the frames connecting the key frames, and an *inker* adding the proper colors. The characters are drawn on acetate sheets called cels that are laid over the background and photographed to make the animated scene. Clearly, this is a labor-intensive process.

Computers have helped to automate the animation process by taking over the in-betweening and inking processes. It is more common, however, for the computer to control the whole process (*see* COMPUTER ANIMATION). The animator describes the objects in the scene and how they are to move, and the computer takes over from there, moving each object to its new position before rendering the next image.

Craig Reynolds (1987) has taken this one step further. His research into flocks, herds, and schools indicated that the members follow three simple rules: (1) stay close to the center of the flock, (2) match velocity with the neighbors, and (3) avoid collisions. His system then creates a set of *actors*, each adhering to these three rules, and allows them to move based on their own limited perception of the world. The resulting animation sequences show extremely realistic flocking behavior. With systems based on independent actors, there is even less human effort. For some control over the result, it is possible to put in lead actors whose movements are scripted, which help to direct the other independent actor motions.

FRACTALS

Fractals are not a new area of research, but rather an old mathematical area that has received new life with the advent of computer graphics. The term *fractal* is derived from the fact that certain objects behave as if they have fractional dimensions. A line is one-dimensional, but a coast line is greater than one-dimensional and not quite two-dimensional because, at finer and finer resolutions, the coast line gets longer and longer without consuming any more outer area. As a one-dimensional line forms a tight spiral into the center of a circle, it becomes more like a plane. Mountains operate similarly between two and three dimensions, and clouds between three and four dimensions.

Conclusion

Computer graphics has a unique role in computer science because of its ability not only to illuminate information, simulate complex processes, and make computers easier to work with, but also to entertain. It is likely that graphics will have an increasing impact on how people work, shop, interact, learn, and function in society. This trend will continue as home computers and access to the Internet increase in capability and decrease in cost. At the same time, graphics professionals will continue to advance the abilities of computers to create realistic images. This will put people in a position of having to decide what is real and what is created by computer. The impact of this on law, business, and human relationships will be far-reaching.

Bibliography

1985. Gardner, G. Y. "Visual Simulation of Clouds," Proceedings of SIGGRAPH '85 (San Francisco, 22–26 July), in *Computer Graphics*, **17**, 3 (July). New York: ACM SIGGRAPH.

1985. Peachy, D. R. "Solid Texturing of Complex Surfaces," Proceedings of SIGGRAPH '85 (San Francisco, 22–26 July), in *Computer Graphics*, **17**, 3 (July). New York: ACM SIGGRAPH.

1985. Perlin, K. "An Image Synthesizer," Proceedings of SIGGRAPH '85 (San Francisco, 22–26 July), in *Computer Graphics*, **17**, 3 (July). New York: ACM SIGGRAPH.

1986. Weil, J. "The Synthesis of Cloth Objects," Proceedings of SIGGRAPH '86 (Dallas, TX, 18–22 August) in *Computer Graphics*, **20**, 4 (August). New York: ACM SIGGRAPH.

1987. Reynolds, C. "Flocks, Herds, and Schools," Proceedings of SIGGRAPH '87 (Anaheim, CA, 27–31 July) in *Computer Graphics*, **21**, 4 (July). New York: ACM SIGGRAPH.

1988. Reffye, P. de, Edelin, C., Francon, J., Jaeger, M., and Puech, C. "Plant Models Faithful to Botanical Structure and Development," Proceedings of SIGGRAPH '88 (Atlanta, GA, 1–5 August), in *Computer Graphics*, **22**, 4 (August), 151–158. New York: ACM SIGGRAPH.

1989. McConnell, J. J. "Botanical Models Based on Three-Dimensional Attributed Graph Grammars," Proceedings of the Twentieth Annual Pittsburgh Conference (Pittsburgh, PA, 4–5 May).

1990. Foley, J., van Dam, A., Feiner, S. K., and Hughes, J. F. *Computer Graphics: Principles and Practice*. Reading, MA: Addison-Wesley.

1990. Hill, F. S. *Computer Graphics*. New York: Macmillan.

1993. Watt, A. H. *3D Computer Graphics*. Reading, MA: Addison-Wesley.

1994. Foley, J., van Dam, A., Feiner, S. K., Hughes, J. F., and Phillips, R. *Introduction to Computer Graphics*. Reading, MA: Addison-Wesley.

1995. Meinhardt, H. *The Algorithmic Beauty of Sea Shells*. New York: Springer-Verlag.

1996. Prusinkiewicz, P. and Lindenmeyer, A. *The Algorithmic Beauty of Plants*, 2nd Ed. New York: Springer-Verlag.

Jeffrey J. McConnell

STANDARDS

For articles on related subjects *see* IMAGE COMPRESSION; MULTIMEDIA; STANDARDS; USER INTERFACE; and WINDOW ENVIRONMENTS.

Introduction

Computer graphics standards serve one of several purposes. *Application Programming Interfaces* (APIs) provide a foundation on which to build graphics applications. They typically provide toolkits of useful primitive graphical elements and thereby relieve the application of the burden of managing both graphical data and physical graphics devices. Historically the goals of such APIs were to support application portability across computing systems and also support operability of applications with different graphics devices (often called "device independence"). Today both goals are less important because APIs (and applications) are typically platform dependent and because graphics devices in common usage are less diverse. *Graphical file formats* (also called *graphical metafiles*), on the other hand, provide a way to describe graphical objects such as pictures or interactive virtual worlds so that different platforms that exchange descriptions can create equivalent pictures and behavior from them. In addition, specialized graphical interfaces and metafile formats can be defined at any of several levels of abstraction between applications and graphical devices. The following sections describe computer graphics standards, and Table 1 lists the International Organization for Standardization (ISO) publications defining them.

Computer Graphics Reference Model

The Computer Graphics Reference Model (CGRM) is a special International Standard intended to be a model for the development of future standards. A reference

Table 1. Common graphics standards.

Standard	Number	Uses
CGRM	ISO/IEC 11072	Information technology, computer graphics, computer graphics reference model
GKS	ISO/IEC 7942	Information technology, computer graphics and image processing, graphical kernel system (GKS); Part 1: Functional description; Part 2: NDC metafile; Part 3: Audit trail; Part 4: Picture part archive
GKS-3D	ISO 8805	Information processing systems, computer graphics, graphical kernel system for three dimensions (GKS-3D) functional description
CGM	ISO/IEC 8632	Information technology, computer graphics, metafile for the storage and transfer of picture description information; Part 1: Functional specification; Part 2: Character encoding; Part 3: Binary encoding; Part 4: Clear text encoding
CGI	ISO/IEC 9636	Information technology, computer graphics, interfacing techniques for dialogues with graphical devices (CGI) functional specification; Part 1: Overview, profiles and conformance; Part 2: Control; Part 3: Output; Part 4: Segments; Part 5: Input and echoing; Part 6: Raster
PHIGS	ISO/IEC 9592	Information processing systems, computer graphics, programmer's hierarchical interactive graphics (PHIGS); Part 1: Functional description; Part 2: Archive file format; Part 3: Clear text encoding
PREMO	ISO/IEC 14478	Information technology, computer graphics and image processing, presentation environment for multimedia objects (PREMO); Part 1: Fundamentals of PREMO; Part 2: Foundation component; Part 3: Multimedia systems services; Part 4: Modeling, rendering and interaction component
VRML	ISO/IEC 14472	Information technology, computer graphics and image processing, virtual reality modeling language (VRML)
PNG	ISO/IEC FCD 15498	Portable network graphics

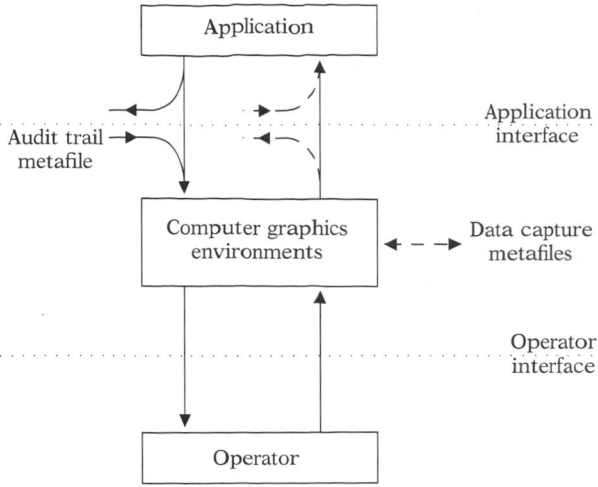

Figure 1. Computer graphics.

objects and data using computers. The CGRM itself consists of a set of models that explain important aspects of computer graphics. Fig. 1 is one of these models that describes the interfaces between computer graphics and external objects. The four important external objects in this model are the application, operator, data capture metafile, and audit trail metafile. The first of these permits external software to control the graphics system through an API; the second allows human operators to interact with the system; and the last two permit the storage and retrieval of graphical information.

Another key idea of the CGRM is that computer graphics (that is, the area denoted as "Computer graphics environments" in Fig. 1) can be considered as a series of transformation steps between the application and operator. This view applies equally to output data and input data. On the output side, information is transformed as it flows from the application to the operator. It is changed from an abstract model into light emanating from a display or into ink on a piece of paper. On the input side, physically transduced measurements—such as button presses and relative movements—are converted as they flow from the operator to the application into abstract models of operator intent. The CGRM identifies five stages of transformations as a series of subenvironments: construction, virtual, viewing, logical, and realization. It also provides an abstract model of an environment in terms of processing and data elements.

Graphical Kernel System

The Graphical Kernel System (GKS) is the oldest of the computer graphics standards. Although the standard claims to include "all the capabilities that are essential for a broad spectrum of graphics, from simple passive output to highly interactive applications," GKS is, in

model is an authoritative basis for the development of standards. It provides a pattern or set of principles that they must adhere to. The CGRM defines computer graphics as the creation of, manipulation of, analysis of, and interaction with pictorial representations of

fact, an API for two-dimensional graphics and is best suited for display of static images and applications requiring primarily discrete input. A three-dimensional version of GKS has been defined as an international standard, but it is little used.

The theoretical basis for GKS was conceived and developed well before modern window environments (*q.v.*) came into use, and GKS is therefore not directly compatible with such systems. GKS assumes that it controls the entire workstation (*q.v.*) and does not share either screen space or input devices with other applications. However, workaround modifications can be applied, allowing GKS applications to be run in a windowed environment.

Computer Graphics Metafile

The Computer Graphics Metafile (CGM) is a data capture metafile that provides a means to store and transfer descriptions of two-dimensional pictures in a device-independent manner for use by graphics production systems and applications. It contains elements for describing vector primitives such as lines, arcs, and ellipses as well as raster primitives and the appearance of primitives through a system of attributes such as edge width, edge color, and edge style. The CGM standard as a whole contains a rich set of elements from which an appropriate set for a particular class of applications can be selected by means of a *profile*.

CGM supports three types of encoding: character, binary, and clear text. The character encoding (to be eliminated in the next republication of the standard) provides an encoding of minimum size that may be transmitted through character-oriented communications services. The binary encoding provides a representation that optimizes speed of generation and interpretation. The clear text encoding provides a representation that may be easily read and edited by humans. It is intended that CGM data will be interpreted by the application rather than by other standards, as the particular device used to render a picture may not have the exact complement of features as used for the picture description. The applications programmer, who presumably understands the class of display devices available, is then responsible for making trade-off decisions regarding the rendering of the picture.

The CGM is the most widely used computer graphics standard. It is used for picture description and interchange in many vertical markets including commercial aerospace, military aerospace, telecommunications, military, automotive and petroleum. In 1998 the CGM Open Consortium was formed to guide the further evolution and adoption of the standard. One of the first projects of the Consortium was the joint develop-

ment (with W3C and the ISO Computer Graphics and Imaging Standards Committee JTC 1/SC 24) of the WebCGM profile of CGM. WebCGM tailors CGM for use over the World Wide Web as a vector file exchange and publishing format.

Computer Graphics Interface

The Computer Graphics Interface (CGI) is a two-dimensional graphical interface standard defining the functions for control and data exchange between device-independent (client) and device-dependent (device) parts of a graphics system. The CGI is intended to provide portability at the device level.

The CGI is designed to support a wide variety of clients having very different functional scopes and quite distinct classes of devices. Although the CGI is most likely to be realized as a subroutine package to operate on complete sets of data, a data stream encoding of the CGI functionality is also available (data stream processing is done piece-by-piece as the data arrives, e.g. over a network connection).

The scope of the CGI is quite large, and a full implementation of the standard would be overkill for most environments. To reduce the size of an implementation, profiles that are subsets of the CGI functions may be defined. Three standard profiles—a foundation profile, a GKS profile, and a CGM profile—are provided as part of the CGI standard.

The architecture of the CGI was determined well before windowing systems appeared in the marketplace, and the capability to support windows is not straightforwardly available in CGI. Unfortunately, the computer graphics systems level for which CGI was designed is the level at which most applications and other graphics standards would interact with a window system. This, along with its inherent complexity, makes CGI little used except in certain vertical markets such as embedded displays for military applications.

Programmer's Hierarchical Interactive Graphical System

The Programmer's Hierarchical Interactive Graphical System (PHIGS) is an API that specifies a set of two- and three-dimensional functions for the definition, display, and modification of geometrically related objects and graphical data. Whereas GKS, CGM, and CGI are oriented towards static pictures, PHIGS is designed to provide dynamic interpretation of geometrical relationships inherent in a hierarchical model. As such, PHIGS is much more suited for applications that require animated display of structured objects, particularly computer-aided design. It is also more suited to and makes better use of the advanced graphics capability of sophisticated computer graphics workstations.

PHIGS manages a central structure store in which individual structures and their geometric and hierarchical relationships to other structures may be defined and edited. A given structure may be referenced by a number of other structures. To display a picture, the structure is traversed from its root, and, as each structure is referenced, that structure is interpreted relative to the one referencing it. Since model transforms are attributes stored as elements in structures, they are interpreted during traversal. This allows a change in the position, orientation, or scale of a structure to be inherited by all structures that it references.

Presentation Environment for Multimedia Objects

The Presentation Environment for Multimedia Objects (PREMO) International Standard defines a middleware framework for distributed multimedia, encompassing synchronization and other fundamental multimedia services; interoperation of media processes across a heterogeneous network; and integration of synthetic graphics with other digital media. PREMO consists of four parts called components and was designed from the outset to be extensible by creating new components. The standard is described using object-oriented terminology and concepts (*see* OBJECT-ORIENTED ANALYSIS AND DESIGN). The object types provide services (in the form of operations that can be invoked by clients), or have a passive role, for example as data encapsulations (*q.v.*). The four components of PREMO are:

◆ *The PREMO Object Model*: the first component of PREMO specifies the object model used in the standard, and the requirements that a PREMO system places on its environment. The object model follows widespread practice, but it also contains a number of features intended specifically to support the needs of multimedia applications. These include support for active objects, and various modes of operation invocation.

◆ *Foundation Component*: object and data types that are generic to multimedia (*q.v.*) applications are defined in this component, including facilities for event management, synchronization, and time. This component serves as a general-purpose toolkit, providing a number of processing facilities that are needed across a range of multimedia applications.

◆ *Multimedia Systems Services (MSS)*: multimedia systems typically integrate a variety of logical and physical devices, for example input and output with devices such as video editors, cameras, speakers, and processing with devices such as data encoders/decoders and media synthesizers. The management and coordination of media resources within PREMO is achieved by the MSS framework, which enables processing resources to be allocated, configured, and organized into a distributed dataflow network.

◆ *Modeling, Rendering and Interaction (MRI)*: this component provides the interface between graphics-driven applications and more general media data. It describes subtypes of MSS devices for modeling and rendering data, and basic facilities for supporting interaction. To support interoperability, this component defines a hierarchy of abstract primitives for structuring multimedia presentations.

Virtual Reality Modeling Language

The Virtual Reality Modeling Language (VRML) is a data capture metafile format for describing interactive three-dimensional objects, behaviors, and worlds. VRML may be used on the Internet, intranets, and local client systems. In particular it is the three-dimensional graphics format for the World Wide Web (*q.v.*). It is intended to be a universal interchange format for integrated three-dimensional graphics and multimedia. VRML may be used in a variety of application areas such as engineering and scientific visualization, multimedia presentations, entertainment and educational titles, Web pages, and shared virtual worlds.

VRML is capable of representing static and animated dynamic three-dimensional and multimedia objects with hyperlinks to other media such as text, sounds, movies, and images. It supports an extensibility model that allows new dynamic three-dimensional objects to be defined allowing application communities to develop interoperable extensions to the base standard. VRML is encoded in a clear text format that can be created and edited by standard text editors. Current and future applications for VRML include scientific visualization (*q.v.*), education, architectural walkthroughs, historical re-creations, engineering prototyping, and product descriptions.

Portable Network Graphics

Portable Network Graphics (PNG) is an extensible file format for the lossless, portable, well-compressed storage of raster images. PNG provides a patent-free replacement for GIF (Graphics Interchange Format) and can also replace many common uses of RGB indexed and truecolor TIFF (Tagged Image File Format). Indexed-color, grayscale, and truecolor images are supported, plus an optional alpha channel for transparency information. Sample depths range from 1 to 16 bits.

The PNG International Standard is designed to work well in online viewing applications, such as the World Wide Web, and is based on a specification developed by the World Wide Web Consortium (W3C). It is fully streamable with a progressive display option; robust, providing both full file integrity checking and simple detection of common transmission errors; and can store gamma and chromaticity data on display devices for improved color matching on heterogeneous platforms. It is designed to be simple and portable; legally unencumbered; well compressed; interchangeable; flexible; and robust.

Bibliography

1986. Hopwood, F. R. A., Duce, D. A., Gallop, J. R., and Sutcliffe, D. C. *Introduction to the Graphical Kernel System (GKS)*. New York: Academic Press.

1990. Arnold, D. B., and Duce, D. A. *ISO Standards for Computer Graphics*. London: Butterworth.

1991. Howard, T. L. J., Hewitt, W. T., Hubbold, R. J., and Wyrwas, K. M. *A Practical Introduction to PHIGS and PHIGS PLUS*. Reading, MA: Addison-Wesley.

1993. Henderson, L. R., and Mumford, A. M. *The CGM Handbook*. New York: Academic Press.

1999. Roeloffs, G. *PNG, the Definitive Guide*. New York: O'Reilly.

George S. Carson

COMPUTER INDUSTRY

UNITED STATES

For articles on related subjects *see* APPLE COMPUTER, INC; DIGITAL EQUIPMENT CORPORATION; IBM CORPORATION; INFORMATION TECHNOLOGY; MICROSOFT; PERSONAL COMPUTING; and SOFTWARE.

Introduction

The US computer industry began in the early 1950s when the first commercial computers were made. This industry comprised manufacturers of computers, manufacturers of peripheral equipment for those systems, producers of software, and purveyors of a variety of support services. The earliest computer products available for commercial applications emerged in the USA and the UK. By the end of the 1950s, these machines were being sold all over Europe, Latin America, and in East Asia, most notably in Japan.

While technology has improved continuously over the past half century, it was the development of applications for this technology that, in concert with technological improvements, made a computer industry possible. What makes a computer commercially viable as a product is its ability to do work of value to businesses and others. The ability of a computer to write payroll checks, send bills to customers, plan the production in a factory, or allow a writer to prepare

a novel, are all commercial applications. Until manufacturers could figure out how to make computers easy enough to use, and with appropriate application software, computers were one-of-a-kind machines sold only to government agencies and universities.

Over the decades, computers have been used to collect and store data, to use data to establish what work needs to be done by humans and machines, and to do analyses to provide insight. The economic case for such work has included reduction in the human labor content of work, the ability to get more productivity out of factories and many classes of machines in general, and the capability of reaching more customers than before. These types of activities have led to constant improvements in applications, particularly software, and to new forms of hardware that often were industry-specific (e.g. ATMs at banks, point-of-sale terminals for supermarkets).

The concurrent development of new forms of technology also proved important. In the 1940s the transistor was developed at Bell Laboratories; in the early 1950s, 25 companies obtained rights to produce this basic technology; by the end of the 1950s the computer had been established in the USA. From then to the present, new forms of computing power, at less cost and with greater reliability have emerged in the form of mainframe (*q.v.*) computers, minicomputers (*q.v.*), and the personal computer (*q.v.*). Processor and memory speed increased several thousand-fold, while the cost of performing a transaction dropped continuously over the years (Table 1). Thus between less expensive, more reliable and capable technology on the one hand, and new applications on the other, the industry grew from almost nothing in 1950 to worldwide revenues of over $400 billion just in products in 1996. Including all the services, salaries of end users, and other miscellaneous expenses, in 1997 expenditures on computing worldwide exceeded $1.5 trillion!

In the United States today, virtually all organizations with more than 20 employees use computers. Well over 90% of all companies and nonprofit organizations with more than five employees use computers. In the USA,

Table 1. Relative price performance for selected IBM mainframes, 1953–1979.

Computer	Number of instructions executed/unit cost	Relative speed/price
650 (1953)	1	1
360/30 (1964)	43	1,700
370/135 (1971)	214	19,000
4341 (1979)	1,143	1,143,000

nearly 40 million personal computers were bought in 1999 by the public or their employers. The US government has estimated that over 80% of the workforce now relies directly on computers to do their work.

Overview of the Industry

The industry consists of several segments: companies that manufacture, sell, and maintain computers, peripherals, media, software, and services. The definition of the computer industry has been changing from one that just manufactured software and hardware, to the information technology (IT—*q.v.*) industry, one in which, in addition to the manufacture of products, there is now a very large services component. Table 2 suggests the overall size of this US industry during the 1990s. Services related to the use and support of such equipment have risen sharply in the 1990s (Table 3). Since hardware remains the centerpiece of most people's interest in the industry, Table 4 illustrates the composition of computer production by type of hardware in the mid-1990s.

The US industry has long enjoyed significant opportunities to sell products outside of the USA but has also had competition from European, and especially

Table 2. Overall size of US information processing industry, mid-1990s ($billions).

Hardware	60
Information services	16
IT and network services	54
Programming and consulting	68
Other products and services	8
PC software	5
Other software	40

Source: Various tables in US Department of Commerce, *U.S. Industry Outlook 1994* (Washington, DC: GPO, 1994).

Table 3. US services market, mid-1990s ($billions).

Information services	16
IT and network services	54
Systems integration	23
Custom programming	30
Consulting and training	27

Source: Various tables in US Department of Commerce, *U.S. Industrial Outlook 1994* (Washington, DC: GPO, 1994).

Table 4. Composition of US computer production, mid-1990s.

Computers	53%
Peripherals	33%
Parts	14%

Source: US Department of Commerce, *U.S. Industrial Outlook 1994* (Washington, DC: GPO, 1994): 26–2.

Table 5. US computer production compared to Europe and Japan, 1982–1992 ($billions).

Geography	1982	1987	1992
USA	35	50	52
Europe (EC)[1]	27	45	68
Japan	14	34	44

[1] European numbers are inflated, since they also include office machines.
Source: US Department of Commerce, *U.S. Industrial Outlook 1994* (Washington, DC: GPO, 1994): 26–4.

Table 6. US computer exports compared to Europe and Japan, 1982–1992 ($billions).

Geography	1982	1987	1992
USA	10	18	27
Europe (EC)[1]	5	10	14
Japan	4	14	25

[1] European numbers are inflated, since they also include office machines.
Source: US Department of Commerce, *U.S. Industrial Outlook 1994* (Washington, DC: GPO, 1994): 26–4.

Japanese, vendors, beginning in the 1970s. Tables 5 and 6 show historic data, while Table 7 suggests what has been happening in the 1990s with respect to mainframes. Not all these machines were delivered to the USA, but because the US computer industry dominated the global market in the 1950s–1980s, it is important to show the overall growth in computing around the world.

Key US vendors for mainframes in the 1950s–1970s included IBM, Sperry-Univac, GE, Burroughs, Honeywell, Philco, RCA, and CDC, to name a few. Key vendors operating in the US economy by the end of the 1980s also included Hitachi and Amdahl. Supercomputing (*see* SUPERCOMPUTERS), always a very small piece of the market, was dominated by CDC and Cray, although Japanese suppliers later became active in the US market.

Midrange computer systems came into their own in the 1960s with the introduction of small computers primarily for use by engineers, scientists and manufacturing operations. By the end of the 1980s, many of these

Table 7. US computer trade, 1993 ($billions).

Product	Exports	Imports
Computer systems	8.4	6.4
Peripherals	6.8	20.9
Parts	11.9	12.8

Source: US Department of Commerce, *U.S. Industrial Outlook 1994* (Washington, DC: GPO, 1994): 26–4.

Table 8. Number of microcomputers shipped to businesses, 1981–1985.

Year	Volume
1981	344,000
1982	926,000
1983	1,538,000
1984	2,384,000
1985	3,290,000

Source: Dunn & Bradstreet Corporation, as reported in *USA Today*, 16 June 1985, p. 5.

were being replaced by personal computers which had more computer power and lower per transaction costs than traditional minicomputers. Historically, Digital Equipment Corporation (DEC—now Compaq), Prime, Data General, Wang (in the 1970s), and IBM have been key vendors. By the early 1970s, most of the vendors of large systems had dropped out of the market: GE, Honeywell, Sperry. But many of the providers of minis remained viable businesses throughout the 1980s: DEC, Wang, Prime, and Hewlett-Packard.

The most significant change in the configuration of the industry began in the late 1970s with the introduction of small desktop computers later known as personal computers. These machines first appeared in the USA. As Table 8 illustrates, the PC market expanded rapidly during the early 1980s. By 1993, the value of the US market for PCs had grown to $25 billion. To put that number in perspective, in 1982 their value had reached $180 million, nearly three times that of 1981, and it doubled again in 1983. This end of the market has been characterized by extensive worldwide competition from over 150 vendors. In the USA the market has begun to stabilize with several key providers of PCs: IBM, Compaq, Dell, Gateway, Sony, Hewlett-Packard, Tandy, and Apple, to mention the most obvious. The top ten providers have between 50 and 60% of the market in the 1990s. Mini providers suffered or went out of business (e.g. Wang) while a few painfully embraced the PC market (e.g. Hewlett Packard and DEC).

The hardware portion of the computer industry has now expanded by the arrival of even smaller devices:

Table 9. Functions of highly portable computing devices, circa mid-1990s.

Laptops	Notebooks	Hand-held PDAs
Word processing	Word processing	Calendars
Presentations	Presentations	Notetaking
Mobile CAD/CAM	Spreadsheets	Addresses & phone
Simulations	Business applications	numbers
Spreadsheets	Communications	Games
		Data transfer

Table 10. Estimated worldwide market for portable computing devices, 1990s (millions of units).

1993	7.5
1995	13.0
1997	22.0

Source: Dataquest, Inc.

laptops, notebooks, and hand-helds—all new classes of machines in the 1990s (*see* PORTABLE COMPUTERS). Table 9 describes their various functions. From an economic point of view, these machines are where PCs were in the late 1970s when they were just beginning to appear (Table 10).

Software production has been a major part of the computer industry almost from the start. Software has consistently been of several types: operating systems, tools to facilitate systems operations, and application software. Important subsystems have been those that manage data and networks. By the early 1990s, the software industry employed 435,000 workers in the USA.

Table 11 shows the size of the software market in the USA during the 1960s and 1970s when application software packages came into their own; prior to that, for example, companies had to write their own payroll packages. With the arrival of the PC in the 1980s, software packages experienced an enormous growth at the low end and increasingly also at the high end for mainframes. By 1993, Americans were spending about $6 billion just for PC software. Mainframe applications historically focused on accounting, manufacture, and distribution applications. Minicomputer applications did the same when the mini was the only

Table 11. Estimated software revenues, 1964–1980, selected years (millions of dollars).

Year	Total
1964	175–275
1968	400
1972	500
1976	1,100
1980	2,100

Source: This data was collected by Montgomery Phister, Jr, "Computer Industry," in Anthony Ralston and Edwin D. Reilly, Jr. (eds.) *Encyclopedia of Computer Science and Engineering* (New York: Van Nostrand Reinhold, 1983), p. 343; additional qualification of data in James W. Cortada, *Strategic Data Processing: Considerations for Management* (Englewood Cliffs, NJ: Prentice Hall, 1984), pp. 37–46.

Table 12. US PC volumes, circa 1993–1994.

Number of firms providing PCs and components	3,300
Number of PCs sold in the USA, 1993	3.2 million
Value of US PC sales, 1993	$25 billion
US installed base, 1994	70 million units
Number of PCs in·US households, 1993	31 million
European installed base, 1994	35 million units

Source: IDC, US Department of Commerce.

machine in the company; otherwise they were used for specific applications, usually in engineering and manufacturing. PC applications overwhelmingly concentrated on word processing, accounting, spreadsheet (*q.v.*) applications, graphics, and increasingly in the 1990s, communications.

Most suppliers of software specialized in applications; large mainframe, mini, and PC manufacturers provided operating systems and other utility packages. In the 1980s and 1990s, large software firms emerged that provided clusters of packages, such as Microsoft Word and Lotus Notes. Beginning in 1969, IBM encouraged the development of software for its mainframes and again did the same in 1981 when it announced an open architecture (*q.v.*) for its PCs. Thousands of firms today make up the software side of the computer industry. Additionally, over 80% of all expenditures for software still consist of salaries for programmers and systems analysts to write and maintain it.

The most visible segment of the industry—personal computers—have massive sales (Table 12). The variety of applications has broadened so far that specialized suppliers enter the market routinely with software that runs under the three major operating systems: Unix, including Linux (from many vendors), Apple's Mac OS, and Microsoft Windows. The major software suppliers were ASK Group, Cabletron Systems, Ceridian, Cisco Systems, Comdisco, Computer Associates, Computer Sciences, Electronic Data Systems (EDS), EMC, First Data, Gtech Holdings, Lotus, Microsoft, Novell, Oracle, Safeguard Scientific, Shared Medical Systems,

Table 13. Software packages market, 1991–1997 ($millions).

	1991	1992	1993	1997[1]
World	57.0	64.3	71.9	116.0
USA	25.3	28.5	32.0	52.0
Western Europe	21.1	23.9	25.7	36.0
Japan	5.3	6.0	7.0	14.0
Canada	1.0	1.2	1.4	2.0

[1] Estimated.

Source: US Department of Commerce, *U.S. Industry Outlook 1994* (Washington, DC: GPO, 1994): 27–5.

Table 14. Worldwide revenues of top 10 software suppliers, 1991–1992 ($millions).

Vendor	Nationality	1991	1992
IBM	US	10,524	11,366
Fujitsu	Japan	2,513	3,525
Microsoft	US	2,046	2,960
NEC	Japan	1,762	1,840
Computer Associates	US	1,438	1,771
Siemens Nixdorf	Germany	965	1,058
Novell	US	633	989
Hitachi	Japan	959	983
Lotus	US	829	810
DEC	US	796	800
Total		22,465	26,102

Source: *Datamation* and US Department of Commerce.

SynOptics Communications, Western Digital, and IBM. If we leave IBM out of the equation, EDS and Microsoft together had approximately 40% of total sales in 1993.

When all software sales are combined, we see that by the early 1990s the USA continued to dominate the sale of packages globally (Tables 13 and 14). US vendors had somewhat less than half of the world market. Equally interesting, however, is the extent of concentration in the hands of a few corporations, following a longstanding pattern evident in the hardware sector.

Media suppliers make up another component of the industry, providing the items upon which data is stored, like diskettes (*q.v.*) and tape, or, in an earlier period, tabulating cards and paper tape. In a previous edition of this encyclopedia, the editors published a chart (reproduced as Fig. 1) suggesting the historic performance of this sector. Data for the 1990s has been difficult to collect because many sales have shifted to personal computers. However, we know that for mainframes the proportions suggested in Fig. 1 hold. We also know that, on average, the owner of a new PC will spend an additional 40% for media and upgrades in the first year of ownership, suggesting that the market is well over $6 billion.

The telecommunications portion of this industry, routinely covered in previous editions of this encyclopedia as a subset of the computer business, is now covered in the article COMMUNICATIONS AND COMPUTERS. In the 1980s and 1990s, technological innovations caused major changes in the telecomputing of traditional computer devices, while resulting improvements in traditional telecommunications devices (e.g. telephones), through the introduction of additional microprocessors, have created major changes in products and markets. A cell phone or a global positioning system (GPS) now has more computing power than a computer did in 1950.

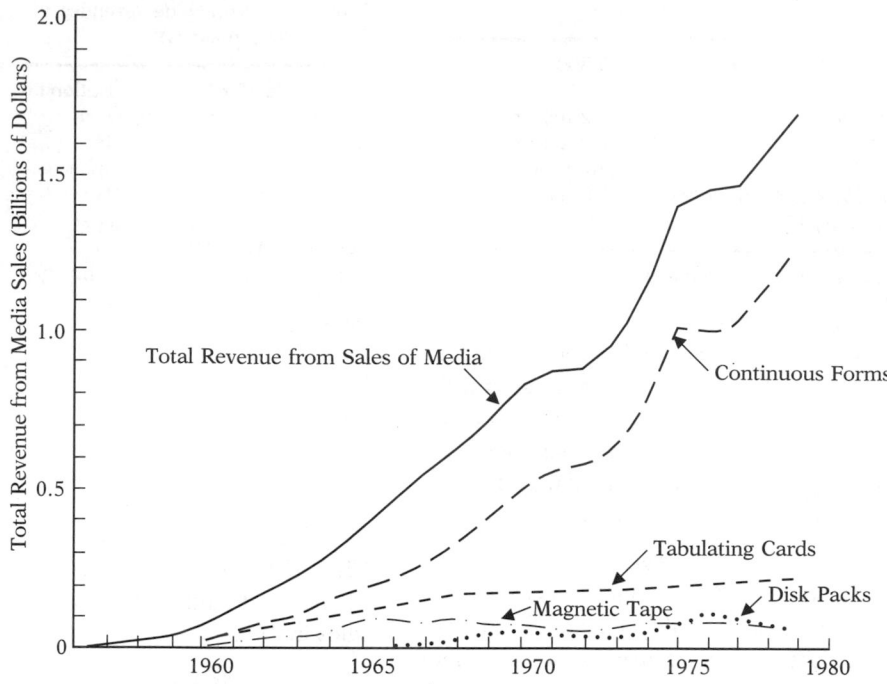

Figure 1. Media industry revenues.

The definition of telecommunications and networking is beginning to shift, and the numbers are massive. In 1993, 39% of all PCs worldwide were linked to networks. In that same year LAN revenue approached $8.3 billion in sales of network interface cards, internetworking devices and components, intelligent wiring systems, and terminal servers. Is the software required to make all these components part of the computer industry or closer to the old world of telephony? Increasingly the trend is for computer suppliers to become giant players in telecommunications. It has been, for example, the centerpiece of IBM's product strategy for the 1990s. But all major vendors now participate, particularly with servers. Key US suppliers include IBM, DEC (now Compaq), Sun Microsystems, and Hewlett-Packard.

In the 1990s the top three investors in computing research and development in the USA are IBM, DEC (Compaq), and Hewlett-Packard. In the subgroup of component manufacturers, Intel and Motorola are the leading chip developers. Major suppliers of mainframes and associated peripherals in the USA are IBM and Amdahl and from Japan, Fujitsu and Hitachi. Key midrange systems suppliers include IBM, Data General, and DEC. Workstation suppliers range from systems vendors like IBM, to specialized companies like Sun, Hewlett-Packard, Silicon Graphics, and also to PC vendors, such as Dell and Apple. Key providers of PCs in the American market include IBM, Hewlett-Packard, Sun, Compaq, Apple, Gateway, and a variety of East

Asian suppliers. The International Data Corp. (IDC) has identified over 300 vendors and another 3,000 companies that supply components or other PC-related products in the USA, making this segment of the market the most complex in today's computer industry.

For newer product lines, such as software to run on the Internet, vendors are just emerging. Netscape and America Online (AOL) represent a new breed of vendors, the former a supplier of software to access the Internet, the latter a service to access and use the Internet. (Netscape is now owned by AOL.) Thousands of new firms are entering the market to provide PDAs, networking services, and related software, making any characterization difficult. The situation in the mid-1990s resembled the uncertainty that mainframe vendors experienced in the late 1950s and early 1960s before several major suppliers emerged with significant market share. The same held true for PC vendors in the late 1980s and early 1990s.

In the early 1990s, multimedia (*q.v.*) configurations of products and companies began to draw the public's attention, particularly as new corporate alliances were formed. These included Time Warner and US West, IBM, NBC television and NuMedia, Time Warner and Tele-Communications (TCI), and most regional telephone companies with small computer suppliers and large cable and television/entertainment firms. These cut across industry lines, exploit a wide variety of technologies (e.g. sound boards, video boards, networks, telephonics, movies, and television), and are in both regulated and unregulated sectors of the US economy.

The Industry in the 1980s

Up to the 1980s, the computer industry consisted of a few well-known vendors supplying the vast majority of computer equipment in a rapidly expanding market. Most were vertically organized: that is to say, they provided everything from hardware to software, services to maintenance. Obvious examples of suppliers of large computers included IBM, Burroughs, Control Data, Honeywell, and Sperry-Univac. Even the more crowded midrange suppliers exhibited a similar pattern. These, in addition to IBM, included DEC, Hewlett-Packard, Prime, Wang, and others. But during the 1980s, the personal computer came into its own, grabbing most of the headlines. Sales for many vendors grew at annual rates of over 30% each year. Software vendors were also prosperous, often enjoying sales growth of over 20% annually.

Sales of PCs went from less than 400,000 units in 1981 to over 3.2 million in 1985 to over 10 million annually at the end of the decade. The industry continued its historic trend of restructuring as some vendors gained market acceptance while others failed. As a result, revenue sources shifted. For example, PC revenue grew from little at the start of the decade to some $30 billion in 1986 and to over $80 billion in 1990. With increased competition, profits began to erode. Thus while the Standard & Poor Index generally grew all through the period 1987–1992, the value of computer stocks actually shrank by nearly half. That situation changed in the 1990s as the growth in sales of computing products provided scale and scope advantages to major providers (e.g. IBM and Microsoft), causing the value of their stocks to grow rapidly.

To give a sense of the order of magnitude in the size of companies and revenues, Table 15 lists revenues of representative major providers in 1987 and in 1991.

The Industry in the 1990s

Five major trends affected the industry in this decade: increased deployment of microcomputers, a shift from centralized to network computing, a decline and then resurgence of IBM, continued growth of Microsoft and Intel, and reconfiguration of the industry to include voice, data, and video components.

The one major trend that is causing the largest number of changes in how technology is being converted into products and the way users are applying them is in the area of network computing. Technologies continue to shrink in size but grow in functionality. Vendors in such disparate fields as television, movie production,

Table 15. Financial performance of key industry players, 1987 and 1991 (revenue in $millions).

Company	1987 revenue	1991 revenue
IBM	55,598	64,766
HP	8,090	14,494
DEC	9,389	13,911
Motorola	6,727	11,341
Unisys	9,732	8,696
Apple	2,661	6,309
AT&T/NCR	5,641	N/A
Intel	1,907	4,779
Compaq	1,224	3,271
Sun	538	3,221
Wang	2,837	2,091
Microsoft	346	1,843
CDC	3,366	1,525
Prime	961	1,382
Data General	1,274	1,229
AMD	997	1,227
Lotus	396	829
LSI Logic	262	698
Novell	222	640
WordPerfect	100	640
Cypress	77	287
Adobe	39	230
Borland	38	227
Chips & Tech.	80	225

Source: Charles H. Ferguson and Charles R. Morris present a series of tables with this kind of data in addition to other financial information in *Computer Wars* (New York: Times Book, 1993), pp. 214–220; on IBM, see Emerson W. Pugh, *Building IBM* (Cambridge, MA: MIT Press, 1995), p. 324.

microcomputers, and telephone and cable, are joining together to create new products and services. The opening up of the government/university Internet to the general public created its own momentum with estimates of between 40 and 70 million users globally on the system by 1996. Each user required a PC, a telephone line, some knowledge of computers, and software in order to participate in this networking function. The vast majority of PCs sold to the American workforce today have communications capability, while almost all PCs being installed in corporate environments are being linked into networks.

In February 1996, the US Congress passed a new telecommunications regulatory law, providing the most sweeping change in regulations in this field in over 30 years. Early consequences have included speeding up the formation of network alliances. Technology-based industries are creating new products, e.g. personal wireless communication systems (GPS and portable phones, for example). The new law made it possible for television, telephone, and information processing industries to sell products and services in each others' markets. Local and long distance telephone companies could compete in each others' territories, while cable companies could compete against each other. Since the telecommunications industry accounts for nearly one-sixth of the US economy, and expenditure on computing is now over 5% of GNP, the potential of the two coming closer together is a significant development within the US economy at large.

New products are emerging continuously. Intel's Pentium and other chips are, for example, continuing their historic trend of providing more function and larger memory at lower cost. New devices are thus made possible, such as sophisticated games (e.g. Gameboy), PDAs, hand-held PCs, small cellular phones, and calculators the size of credit cards. New functions are being added to old products: for example, credit cards are becoming intelligent, providing identification, access to buildings, debit and credit information, and vital medical data to emergency crews. Antennas are appearing on PCs, while laptops are sporting sophisticated multimedia capability which makes possible the simultaneous use of voice, text, video, television, and telecommunications in machines that weigh less than 5 pounds (2 kg) and that cost less than $3,000.

During this decade, many of the older firms in the industry experienced severe downturns (e.g. DEC and IBM). IBM, for example, had its first nonprofitable year in 1992, downsized its workforce by about 45% (although revenues only dropped by several billion) and recovered in 1993 and 1994. DEC experienced a worse trauma and finally became a subsidiary of Compaq. On the other hand, PC vendors and software providers did well, for example, Dell with PCs and Microsoft with Windows. In fact, Microsoft's stock market capitalization exceeded that of General Motors in this period. As of 1999, IBM had come back strong after downsizing, with healthy PC, network, mainframe, and services revenues. Apple experienced severe financial and marketing problems, and lost sales through the mid-1990s, but despite the rapid growth of Windows as a standard, won a greater share of the market with new products such as the iMac and high-performance G3 and G4 systems at the end of the 1990s.

Sources of Information

The most widely quoted source of information on the computer industry remains the International Data Corporation, located in Waltham, MA, which publishes a wide variety of information on the industry. Both *Computerworld* and *Datamation* are also frequently consulted sources on the size and nature of the industry; *Computerworld* for news, *Datamation* for industry trends and analysis. The other major publicly available sources are various publications of the US Department of Commerce, including the *US Indus-*

trial Outlook, published every year or two. Major vendors, such as IBM, and consulting firms, also develop industry forecasts that include analysis and hard data on industry performance.

Bibliography

1985. Fertig, R. T. *The Software Revolution.* Amsterdam: North-Holland.
1990. Morris, P. R. *A History of the World Semiconductor Industry.* Piscataway, NJ: IEEE Press.
1993. Ferguson, C. H., and Morris, C. R. *Computer Wars.* New York: Times Books.
1994. Dvorak, J. C. *Dvorak Predicts: An Insider's Look at the Computer Industry.* Berkeley, CA: Osborne/McGraw-Hill.
1995. Landauer, T. K. *The Trouble with Computers.* Cambridge, MA: MIT Press.
1996. Cortada, J. W. *Information Technology as Business History.* Westport, CT: Greenwood Press.

Websites

International Data Corporation. http://www.idc.com.
Datamation. http://www.datamation.com.
Computerworld. http://www.computerworld.com.

James W. Cortada

BRITAIN

> For articles on related subjects *see* DIGITAL COMPUTERS, HISTORY OF; EDSAC; IBM CORPORATION; LEO; and MANCHESTER UNIVERSITY COMPUTERS.

Since 1968, the most important player in the British computer industry has been International Computers Limited (ICL). ICL, Britain's "national champion" computer manufacturer, grew out of the British Tabulating Machine Company, an office machine enterprise established in the early years of the century to market and manufacture the punched card machine (*q.v.*) technology of IBM.

In the immediate post-war years, Britain was the only country, other than the USA, to develop a significant computer industry. Immediately after the Second World War, several computer projects were established at British universities and research laboratories, including Cambridge University (EDSAC, *q.v.*), Manchester University (*q.v.*), and the National Physical Laboratory. By the mid-1950s all three projects had led to successful commercial developments by, respectively, the Leo (*q.v.*) Computers division of the J. Lyons Company, Ferranti, and English Electric. In addition, the National Research Development Corporation— a quasi-governmental organization established in 1949 to foster Britain's exploitation of emerging technologies—encouraged several other entrants into the British computer industry, primarily from the ranks of the established electronics and control firms. In the mid-1950s, as the computer market gravitated toward electronic data processing, the British Tabulating Machine Company (BTM) also entered the computer market.

Thus, by the end of the 1950s, the British computer industry consisted of about 10 firms, all manufacturing first-generation tube-based machines. This represented a massive oversupply for the small domestic computer market, and few of the firms were making money from their computer operations. At the same time, there was ever-increasing competition from American mainframe manufacturers, particularly IBM.

This situation became even worse in 1959 when the transistor-based IBM 1400 series (*q.v.*) of computers was announced. The arrival of IBM's second-generation computers created an intensively competitive environment both in the UK and in the USA. In Britain, computer firms were faced with a choice: either to develop their own second-generation computers to compete with those of the American vendors, or to withdraw from the computer business altogether. The result was the merger wave of 1959–64 (*see* Fig. 1).

The first merger occurred at the end of 1959, when BTM merged with Powers-Samas, the other British supplier of punched card machinery, to form International Computers and Tabulators Limited (ICT). In the next three years ICT acquired the computer divisions of several other companies, most importantly that of Ferranti. In a parallel series of mergers, English Electric acquired the mainframe computer interests of most of the remaining firms, including Leo Computers. Thus, by 1964, there were just two British mainframe computer firms, ICT and English Electric.

On 7 April 1964 IBM announced its third-generation System/360 range of computers (*see* IBM 360/370/ 390 SERIES). Even more than the 1400 series five years previously, the 360 series dramatically altered the competitive landscape, obliging all the world's mainframe computer manufacturers to respond with new offerings. In Britain, ICT responded with its 1900 series in September 1964—a computer range based on the Canadian Ferranti-Packard 6000, whose design ICT had acquired when it took over Ferranti's computer interests. A year later, English Electric announced its third-generation System 4, an IBM-compatible range based on the RCA Spectra 70, and manufactured under license.

In parallel with this turbulence in the British computer industry, in October 1964 the Labour government of Harold Wilson came into power. The Wilson Government had an interventionist industrial policy, and established a Ministry of Technology to "rationalize" British industry in general, and the computer industry in particular. The Ministry of Technology, convinced of the need for greater scale to compete in the world computer market, persuaded ICT and English Electric to combine their computer interests, offering as an

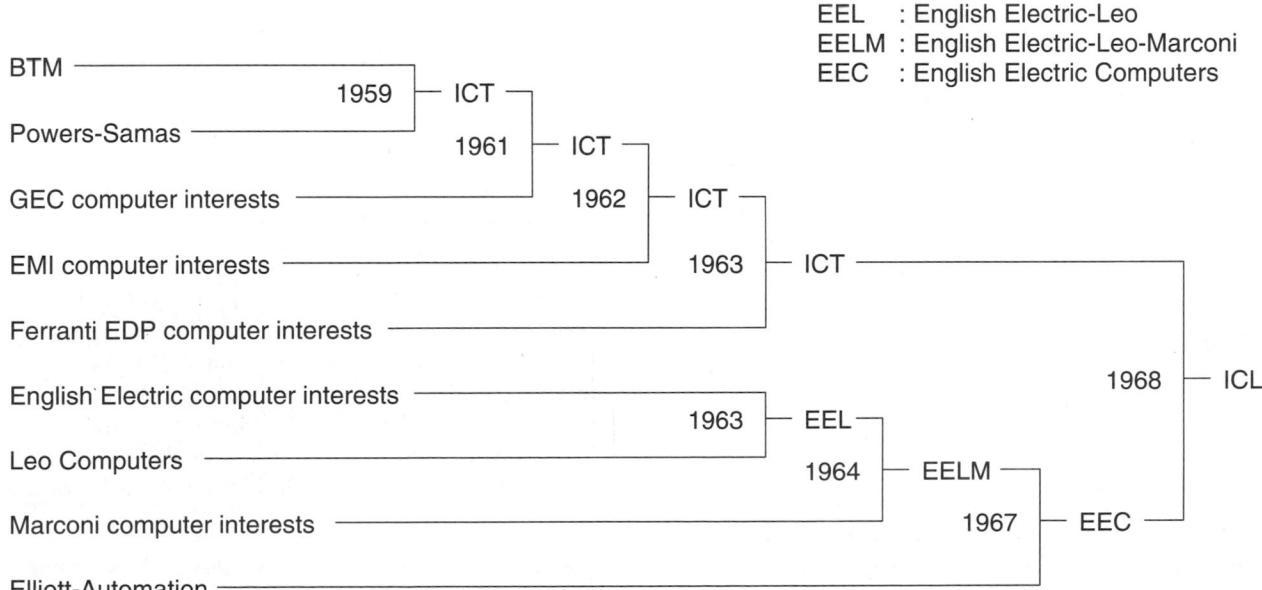

Figure 1. Evolution of the British computer industry.

inducement a government grant towards the development of the next generation of computers.

As a result of this government-inspired merger, ICL came into existence in July 1968, and for the next 15 years its history was bound up with the development of a new range of computers, announced as the 2900 series in 1974 (*see* Fig. 2). Unfortunately, ICL's sales were never sufficient to sustain the momentum of the R&D needed for a world-class mainframe (*q.v.*) range. The firm came close to bankruptcy on two occasions, first during the world computer recession of 1970–1971, and again during the UK economic recession of 1980–1981. On the first occasion it was rescued by government loans. On the second occasion, in the early years of the new Thatcher administration, direct support was politically unacceptable, but the government did provide credit guarantees for commercial lenders. These successive government interventions seriously tarnished ICL's image.

A condition of ICL's 1980–1981 rescue was that a new management team had to be installed. One of the first acts of ICL's management was to make an agreement with Fujitsu of Japan to obtain access to its semiconductor technology and manufacturing facilities. This eliminated much of ICL's R&D spending for its mainframe range, releasing resources to enable the company to expand its small and personal computer developments, and to increase its systems integration business and computer services. As a result of this much broader portfolio of activities, in the late 1980s ICL survived the transition from mainframe-based computing to desktop computing better than most other mainframe computer manufacturers.

In 1990, ICL was acquired by Fujitsu, although the company retains a large degree of autonomy and continues to trade as an independent entity. It is currently among the most profitable of the old-line computer companies.

While ICL is the most prominent player in the British computer industry, it is not the whole of it. For example, during the 1970s, Britain tried to gain a foothold in the emerging minicomputer (*q.v.*) industry, and there were several entrants, primarily from existing electronics and control firms plus a few entrepreneurial start-ups. Unfortunately, as with the mainframe industry, there were too many suppliers for the small British market, and there was in addition intense competition from American firms such as the Digital Equipment Corporation (*q.v.*). No British minicomputer manufacturers survived much beyond the 1970s. In the last Labour administration of the 1970s, the government made a last-ditch attempt to establish a British semiconductor industry by creat-

Figure 2. The ICL 2900 series, October 1974. (Courtesy of the National Archive on the History of Computing, University of Manchester.)

ing INMOS in 1978. INMOS went on to produce the "transputer," a chip which was a distinctive innovation in the European high-performance computer industry during the late 1980s and early 1990s. INMOS was sold off by the Thatcher Government in 1983, and eventually fell into French–Italian ownership.

Starting in the mid-1960s, Britain also established important firms in the software and computer services industries. During the 1980s, however, many of these firms were acquired by European organizations taking a long-term strategic view of the information technology (IT—*q.v.*) industry—in marked contrast to the non-interventionist policy of the Thatcher Government. There is today just a very small number of British-owned software and computer services firms with an international presence.

From the early 1980s onward, the Thatcher and Major Governments directed computer policy to the use and application of IT, rather than its manufacture. Britain thus remains one of Europe's most flourishing IT markets, but it is largely satisfied by overseas suppliers. In May 1997 the first Labour administration for 18 years came into office, but it is unlikely that there will be a reversion to the interventionist policies of the 1960s and 1970s.

Despite the vicissitudes of the domestic computer industry, Britain still occasionally surprises the world with new IT players on the world stage. Thus the 1980s saw the rise of Sinclair Computers, which for several years captured a worldwide market in low-cost personal computers, while the 1990s saw Psion secure world leadership in palmtop computers (*see* PORTABLE COMPUTERS). In the late 1990s and beyond, Britain's rich human capital and linguistic advantages should enable the country to be a major player in Internet-related software and services.

Bibliography

1980. Lavington, S. H. L. *Early British Computers*. Manchester: Manchester University Press.
1989. Campbell-Kelly, M. *ICL: A Business and Technical History*. Oxford: Oxford University Press.
1989. Hendry, J. *Innovating for Failure: Government Policy and the Early British Computer Industry*. Cambridge, MA: MIT Press.

Website

ICL. http://www.icl.co.uk/about/history/index.htm.

Martin Campbell-Kelly

EUROPE

For an article on a related subject *see* ZUSE COMPUTERS.

In the early years of the computer industry many pioneering developments took place in Europe. During these formative years European research, in government institutions and industry, was on a par with that in the USA. During the 1950s and 1960s, however, American manufacturers began to dominate world markets. The primary historical question remains— why was the European and British computer industry eclipsed by the USA and later by Japan? The story of the relative failure of the European computer industry requires an understanding of the key personalities and innovations, but also an understanding of the circumstances of post-war industrial reconstruction; the legacies of multinational involvement and strategic product alliances; the structure of industrial sectors— particularly the relationship between electrical and business machine manufacturers; and the role of government, notably the effects of defense priorities in some countries and also of industrial and technology policy.

Europe can claim a number of computer pioneers. Prominent among these was Germany's Konrad Zuse (*q.v.*), who developed a series of electromechanical calculators during the 1930s and went on to found his own computer manufacturing company after the war. In Germany, as elsewhere, wartime technological developments fed into the early computer industry, though, as in rocket technology, much of this was not propagated within Germany, but was appropriated by the victorious powers, notably the USA. German wartime advances in magnetic media and ferrite materials, for example, formed the basis for advances in early US drum storage developments. During the immediate post-war years Germany's domestic computer industry was retarded by a ban on building electronic devices as part of the conditions enforced by the Allied occupation. It was not until the late 1950s that German manufacturers made a serious appearance in the market. By 1960, the electrical equipment manufacturer Siemens was producing a transistorized computer, Telefunken was marketing its TR4, and Zuse was continuing to produce specialized machines for scientific applications. During the 1950s, however, IBM had established a strong presence in Germany, with manufacturing facilities in Stuttgart.

In France, the major manufacturer during the 1950s, Machines Bull, had developed out of a strong capability in punched card (*q.v.*) manufacture before the war. The company was slow to move into electronic computing, however, and when it did so in the late 1950s many of its chosen technologies, such as delay line storage (*see* ULTRASONIC MEMORY), had become dated. France's other major manufacturer at this time was Société d'Electronique et d'Automatisme (SEA), which began by developing analog computers (*q.v.*) and was strongly influenced by military markets. As in Germany, there was also a strong IBM presence in France during the 1950s through its wholly owned subsidiary company. By the early 1960s US computer manufacturers held a market share of around 50% in France and over 70% in Germany. As the research and development costs of computers escalated into the 1960s and product evolution continued to accelerate through the introduction of families of computers catering to a business as well as a scientific market, US influence began to be felt also in terms of licensed technologies. Several European firms, including Siemens and Bull, began manufacturing RCA designs or rebadged RCA machines, for example, in an attempt to compete with IBM—a strategy which would leave them vulnerable when RCA later withdrew from the computer business.

This level of US influence and market penetration caused considerable concern in many European countries in the early 1960s. In France this was prominently demonstrated by the "Affaire Bull" in 1964, when, following failed attempts to merge the computer interests of the Compagnie Générale de Télégraphe sans fil (CSF) and Compagnie Générale d'Electricité (CGE) into Bull, the company was bought out by the US firm General Electric (GE). GE also bought a controlling interest in the Italian firm Olivetti's computer operations at this time. French fears over loss of national independence were also fueled by the refusal of the

US government to allow the export of a Control Data 6600 computer for use in the French nuclear weapons program in 1966. This came at a time when European nations—particularly France and Britain—were making painful adjustments to their thinking in terms of global economic and political prestige. Stimulated by an alarmist series of OECD reports on "Technology Gaps," popular press reaction, and Jean-Jacques Servan-Schrieber's widely read book *The American Challenge*, the computer industry began to take on symbolic significance as the keystone of technological resistance to US global hegemony.

Out of these fears grew a series of government policies promoting mergers, implementing nationalist procurement policies, and funding research and development. Merger programs were an attempt to create national champions—eliminating wasteful competition among domestic firms and achieving economies of scale and scope in emulation of the large US corporations which were seen at the time as paragons of efficiency. In France this led to the formation, under the "Plan Calcul," of Compagnie International pour l'Informatique (CII) merging the computer interests of electronics firms Thomson-CSF and CGE, and those of the specialist computer manufacturer SEA seen as the most innovative of the computer firms at the time. That Bull was left out of this arrangement probably reflected SEA's closer links with the government and its more prestigious high-technology profile originating through its military links. It also reflected the close relationship which both CGE and Thomson-CSF had with the government. The loss of Bull's commercial market expertise weakened the "national champion" strategy and critics have pointed to the shortcomings of the accompanying procurement strategy in weakening market sensitivity. In the event, the electronics firms in France never surmounted their early difficulties. They remained dependent on components, especially semiconductors, produced elsewhere. (In Europe, only Siemens retained a firm foothold in this sector.) Eventually the French firms concentrated on process control and communications technologies, Thomson eventually acquiring ITT, and CGE developing Alcatel.

In addition to the formation of CII, the Plan Calcul, which was revised and extended in 1971 and 1976, embodied the formation of Système et Périphériques Associé aux Calculateurs (SPERAC) to manufacture peripherals, a computer leasing company, the research institute Recherche d'Informatique et d'Automatisme, and the semiconductor firm SESCOSEM.

The policy of intervention and restructuring in France paralleled developments in Britain, and also those in Germany. The latter set up two data processing programs in 1967 and 1969, the first to cover hardware, the second aimed at software, components, and peripherals. Siemens was favored as the national champion and attempts were made to force a merger with AEG-Telefunken. A subsequent government "buy German" policy did see Siemens improving its domestic market share. Nevertheless the real success story of the time was that of Nixdorf (*q.v.*), the minicomputer manufacturer, which exploited its niche in this new market in the 1970s to the extent of manufacturing and selling successfully in the USA. Nixdorf's continued success forced a reversal of government policy in the third data processing program in the 1970s, which embodied support of dual national champions.

As the strategy of creating national champion computer manufacturers seemed to be difficult and only marginally effective, more ambitious schemes to restore European computing began to emerge. Several pan-European proposals were formulated during the 1960s and 1970s, the most notable of which was the creation of Unidata. This company was formed in 1973 as a joint project by CII, Siemens, and the Dutch electronics firm Philips. (Philips had been slow to enter the computer manufacturing field, though it had been a major component supplier to IBM since the 1950s. The company formed Philips Computer Industries (PCI) in 1963, however, and subsequently bought out Electrologica, a smaller Dutch computer manufacturer, between 1965 and 1967.) ICL in Britain had been approached to join Unidata but had turned down the invitation to cooperate.

Unidata was part of a more general attempt to create a European-wide integration of markets, but it also aimed at achieving economies of scale. If ICL had joined, the company would have been approximately two-thirds the size of IBM. Under the Unidata agreement, a series of IBM-compatible machines mimicking the 370 range was to be produced—Philips was to manufacture a small machine, Siemens two medium-sized machines and CII was to manufacture three larger machines. This built on CII's earlier strategy of concentrating on large machine manufacture. The Unidata initiative was welcomed by participating firms for different reasons. Siemens had been stranded by RCA's withdrawal from the computer industry, Philips was uneasy about the increasingly high costs of R&D, and CII was initially formed with the ambition to forge international links. In the event, Unidata was a failure. Reasons for this are still the subject of some debate, though it seems likely that dissonance within the company resulting from conflicting product strategies, managerial styles, and national corporate cultures played a strong part. There was also continued tension between nationalism and international cooperation at both the corporate and government levels.

Changes in political ideology also contributed to the demise of Unidata. In 1976 the Giscard government in France decided to exert national control by buying into Honeywell-Bull and creating CII-Honeywell-Bull. CII's minicomputer interests were bought by Thomson-CSF. (Honeywell had bought out GE's computer interests in 1971.) In 1981 the Mitterrand government extended its interest, renaming the company CII-Bull. Siemens, in addition to Unidata, linked up with the Japanese manufacturer Fujitsu, rebadging large mainframes. (Fujitsu was later to forge strong links with ICL in Britain, eventually taking over the company.) In a further rationalization, Siemens bought out AEG-Telefunken's computer interests in 1974, and finally merged with Nixdorf in the 1990s.

The short-lived Unidata experiment represented the last concerted attempt by European governments and manufacturers to regain a significant presence in the computer industry. Subsequently US and Japanese manufacturers have dominated global production. Later European programs, such as the European Strategic Programme for Research and Development in Information Technologies (ESPRIT), launched in the early1980s, signaled a shift towards initiatives aimed at fostering general capacities and building academic–industry networks. The reasons for the eclipse of the European computer manufacturing industry are many and complex and vary from country to country. The major factors in the demise of Europe's computer industry (some of which also explain the success of Japan) are the structure of domestic markets; an early penetration by US multinational manufacturers; the relationship with the military sector and the influence of military production; and the structure of industrial sectors—particularly the scale of firms and the relationship between business machines and electronics manufacturers.

Bibliography

1981. Mounier-Kuhn, P., Kranakis, E., and Dosi, G. *Technical Change and Survival: Europe's Semiconductor Industry.* Brighton, UK: Sussex European Research Centre.
1988. Flamm, K. *Creating the Computer: Government, Industry and High Technology.* Washington: The Brookings Institution.

Richard Coopey

JAPAN

The *Japanese computer industry* started to develop in the 1960s, largely as a result of government initiative. To help nurture a domestic industry to catch up with IBM (*q.v.*), the state used four primary policies: protectionism, a quasi-public computer rental company called the Japan Electronic Computer Company (JECC), financial assistance, and a variety of state-sponsored cooperative R&D projects. These policies were critical in helping the industry create a competitive hardware industry by the late 1970s.

Protectionism included conventional tariffs and quotas, but also a variety of limitations on foreign investment which influenced the type and quantity of machines IBM could produce in Japan, how much it had to export, how many parts it could import, and how much profit it could repatriate. IBM obtained permission to produce in Japan only after it agreed to license its patents at reasonable royalty fees to all interested local firms. Similar restrictions constrained the activities of Sperry Rand, which was forced into a joint venture with Oki Electric, as well as other US players such as Hewlett-Packard. While protectionism usually leads to sluggishness and inefficiency, domestic competition was encouraged, requiring that firms make increasingly better machines in order to stay in business. The result was increased demand for domestic machines, which stimulated supply.

The Japan Electronic Computer Company was set up in 1961 and was about 50% financed by low-interest government loans. It worked in the following way: when a user decided which specific machine it wanted to rent, it told JECC, which bought the machine from the designated maker and rented it to the user for a monthly fee. The user had to keep the computer for at least 15 months or pay a penalty. When a machine was returned, the computer maker was forced to repurchase it at book value from JECC. The effect was to give Japanese domestic computer firms an immediate return on their investment: if the firms had had to finance their own rentals, they would have received returns in small monthly payments over a 4-year period. Since JECC purchased only those machines users specifically asked to rent, there was a direct link to the market. If no one asked for a machine, JECC did not buy it: thus the firms making the best machines benefited the most from JECC. From 1961 to 1981 the government funneled some $2 billion in loans into JECC to finance computer rentals. JECC still exists today but rents only a small percentage of the total number of rented machines.

State financial aid to the computer industry came in various forms. The absolute amount of subsidies, tax benefits, and low-interest loans has been quite small compared with the huge sums the USA funneled into Pentagon projects. But the amounts were very large compared with what the firms were investing themselves. For example, a conservative estimate suggests that from 1961–1969 subsidies and tax benefits ($132 million) were equivalent to 46% of what the computer firms themselves were investing in R&D and plant and equipment. If we include government low-interest loans, total aid ($542.8 million) was equal to 188% of what the firms were investing. Indeed, the state was also providing funds for working capital. From 1970–1975, subsidies and tax benefits ($636.55 million) were equivalent to 57% of what the firms were investing, 169% ($1.88 billion) if we include government loans. Software and hardware support was formally reduced in the mid-1970s, yet from 1976 through 1981 subsidies and tax benefits ($1.03 billion) were still 25.2% of what the firms were investing; including state loans, total aid ($3.74 billion) was still equal to 91.6% of what the firms were investing.

Various cooperative R&D projects, mainly focused on catching up with IBM, were conducted in the 1960s and 1970s. Their overall effect was to reduce the costs and risks of doing R&D by pooling resources and sharing R&D results. The VLSI Project (1976–1979) and the New Series Project (1972–1976) were key projects that helped Japanese firms, especially the three dominant companies—Fujitsu, Hitachi, and NEC (Nippon Electric Corporation)—catch up with IBM in hardware by the late 1970s.

The success of policies toward hardware in the 1960s and 1970s undoubtedly depended on several conditions. Most important was that while the firms were protected from international competition, domestic competition was strongly encouraged. Even though cooperation was substantial on products, investment, and R&D, market forces compelled the firms to advance technologically and cut costs in order to survive over the long term. A broad societal consensus to allow the bureaucracy to decide what industries to target was also critical. So was a stable institution—the Ministry of International Trade and Industry (MITI)—which had consistent policies that did not change with each new administration. A relatively large domestic market in which to gain economies of scale was important, as was access to foreign markets for technology and to sell products. Overall macro-policies that encouraged savings and investment and discouraged consumption enabled Japan to remain independent of foreign loans while still investing heavily in strategic industries.

Software was not subsidized much in the 1960s and 1970s, and the aid it did receive was generally not very effective. The real focus was on hardware. The firms essentially used modified versions of foreign software. Hitachi and Fujitsu, for example, decided in the early 1970s to make IBM mainframe (*q.v.*) clones, but they modified the IBM hardware and software enough to lock customers into their closed, incompatible standards. NEC had technological ties with Honeywell, but created its own closed standard too.

Fujitsu and Hitachi's strategy of "borrowing" IBM's software backfired in the summer of 1982 when they were caught stealing IBM technology in an FBI sting. This sent shock waves through Japan's computer industry. The free ride on IBM was no longer free. The firms now had to pay huge annual licensing fees to IBM. From then on, the firms tried to diversify the standards they relied on, especially their dependence on the IBM mainframe standard. In the 1980s, there was a strong move toward Unix-based systems (*q.v.*) and an attempt to create a unique Japanese operating system standard called TRON. This latter pursuit, overly ambitious, was not successful.

It was also in the early 1980s that Japan's three top makers moved into supercomputers (*q.v.*), a cooperative R&D project initiated and fully-funded by the government. By the early 1990s, they were very competitive in supercomputers for certain types of applications, especially those using a few high-speed processors. They have been less successful making massively parallel processing (*q.v.*) machines.

By the late 1980s Japan's mainframe makers, like IBM, were caught with big machines when demand soared for smaller computers. They were slow to downsize and restructure their operations, but have been kept afloat by their telecommunications, semiconductor, and consumer electronics divisions. At the same time the firms' strategy of using closed standards to lock users into their respective brands began to haunt them. The market's dependence on fragmented, noncompatible standards denied users the positive network externalities that come with using common, compatible standards. It became increasingly clear that Japanese firms and users were locked into a vicious cycle—they continued to invest heavy sums in machines based on closed standards that were increasingly becoming technologically obsolete.

Due to their reliance on a variety of closed standards as well as custom-made software, Japan's weakness in software was glaring by the early 1990s. Japanese companies excelled at custom-made software aimed at specific tasks such as banking and automated steel mills, but they were missing out on the explosion of PC use and Internet access that occurred in the West throughout the 1990s. The software industry was at a crossroads: it could continue offering closed, modified versions of foreign standards or unbundle (sell hardware and software separately) and embrace open, internationally accepted standards. The firms, users, and the government, realizing they were falling further behind in software, chose the latter path.

Moving toward international standards became easier in 1991 when IBM introduced DOS/V, a Japanese-language version of DOS. IBM decided to make DOS/V open to anyone and Japanese vendors quickly offered DOS/V machines that ran standard word processing (*q.v.*) and spreadsheet (*q.v.*) software packages. The government also encouraged convergence with internationally accepted standards by rejecting their decades of protectionism and instead welcoming foreign software and hardware firms into the Japanese market. This move was not so much true internationalization; rather they were desperate and felt that they needed vibrant firms in the domestic market even if they were foreign.

As a result, the 1990s have seen a sharp rise in the market share of foreign software companies in the Japanese market. Microsoft (*q.v.*), for example, held some 95% of the packaged software market in Japan in the late 1990s. US hardware makers, such as Dell, Compaq, and Gateway, have gained only small (1–3%) shares of the market. The sudden entry of foreign hardware and software makers pressured Japanese makers to conform to internationally accepted standards such as DOS, and more recently, the Wintel (Windows–Intel) and NT standards.

The government's role in the 1980s and 1990s has clearly declined in significance, but remains important. There are numerous ongoing national R&D projects related to software, massively parallel processing machines, high-speed semiconductors, electronic commerce, and other Internet-related technologies. Discretionary state policies still hinder foreign entry into the market, especially discriminatory government procurement policies. Moreover, the state has tried to revise the copyright law on two different occasions to make it legal to decompile foreign software. It has also tried to institute a voluntary quality certification scheme for software, which foreign makers say would require them to divulge proprietary information to gain approval. These tactics have been unsuccessful, but only due to close vigilance on the part of foreign companies operating in Japan as well as heavy pressure from the US government.

Many would argue that Japan's efforts to support the computer industry have not been successful because Japanese firms do not currently dominate the world market in this area. It is true that Japan has not taken over these markets. But its success in semiconductors, supercomputers, and the overall components of most PCs is providing the nation with billions of dollars in revenues and positions it well for success in the future. Computer knowledge has also been vital to its success in related areas such as computer-operated numerically controlled machine tools and telecommunications equipment. Indeed, other than the USA, Japan is the only nation competitive in a wide array of high-tech computer-related products.

Still, Japan's lag in software and Internet-related technologies grew in the late 1990s. Japan has caught up in most hardware technologies and needs to make a transition from a manufacturing superpower to a more invention-oriented nation, one where people are compensated for their creativity and entrepreneurship. Such change would help industries such as software and biotechnology, where technological change is rapid and unpredictable and where the idea, not superior manufacturing techniques, is the key to competitive success. Unfortunately, the long, deep recession in the 1990s, which started primarily as a bad debt banking crisis, is affecting Japan's industrial base and is slowing efforts to deal quickly with its software problems.

Bibliography

1989. Anchordoguy, M. *Computers, Inc.: Japan's Challenge to IBM.* Cambridge, MA: Harvard University Press.
1991. Cusumano, M. *Japan's Software Factories.* Oxford: Oxford University Press.
1994. Anchordoguy, M. "Japanese–American Trade Conflict and Supercomputers," *Political Science Quarterly,* **109**, *1* (Spring), 35–80.
1996. Cottrell, T. "Standards and the Arrested Development of Japan's Microcomputer Software Industry," in *The International Computer Software Industry* (ed. D. C. Mowery), 131–164. Oxford: Oxford University Press.
1996. Baba, Y., Takai, S., and Mizuta, Y. "The User-driven Evolution of the Japanese Software Industry: The Case of Customized Software for Mainframes," in *The International Computer Software Industry* (ed. D. C. Mowery), 104–130. Oxford: Oxford University Press.
1997. Anchordoguy, M. "Japan at a Technological Crossroads: Does Change Support Convergence Theory?" *Journal of Japanese Studies,* **23**, *2*, 363–397.

Website

The Japan CS Project Website: `http://www.cs.arizona.edu/japan/`.

Marie Anchordoguy

COMPUTER LANGUAGES

See PROCEDURE-ORIENTED LANGUAGES, PROGRAMMING LANGUAGES; FUNCTIONAL PROGRAMMING; and language sections of LOGIC PROGRAMMING; LIST PROCESSING; and STRING PROCESSING. *See also* names of particular languages.

COMPUTER LITERACY

For articles on related subjects *see* HUMAN FACTORS IN COMPUTING; PERSONAL COMPUTING; POWER USER; SOCIETY, COMPUTERS IN; WORD PROCESSING; and WORLD WIDE WEB.

A *computer literate* person is one who has acquired the skills needed to use computers effectively. More important, the computer literate person is comfortable in the computer age. Technical expertise is not required. Familiarity, experience, and understanding create comfort.

Computer literacy has five characteristics:

1. The ability to use the computer as a tool for problem solving.

2. An understanding of what computers can and cannot do (the function of hardware and software).

3. Non-technical experience with computer software.

4. Experience in using the Internet (*q.v.*), particularly the World Wide Web, as an information-gathering tool.

5. The ability to evaluate the societal impact of computers.

When the only effective way to use a computer was to program it yourself, programming knowledge was considered an integral part of computer literacy. With today's vast array of off-the-shelf software products, such knowledge is unnecessary. For many students, learning to program is a negative experience. They feel ill-equipped to handle this task due to a poor background in mathematics, and, as a result, they have only limited success that often translates into a fear of computers.

An understanding of and experience in using readily available software is more important than knowing how to program. The computer literate person should have experience with computer software tools for writing, communicating, and processing information. While a knowledge of programming might be useful in these endeavors, it is by no means a requirement. Increasingly, computers are the tools we use to communicate. A person who is computer literate should be comfortable sending and receiving electronic mail (*q.v.*) and using a browser to search the World Wide Web.

People frequently become computer literate through courses taught in schools, colleges, community centers and computer stores; however, such formal training is not required. Many individuals choose to learn on their own. They study the documentation that accompanies the machine and the software they have access to, they read books, and learn by experimentation. More and more, children amass considerable knowledge in just this way and, for all intents and purposes, are computer literate by the time they leave elementary school.

Bibliography

1998. Kershner, H. G. *Computer Literacy*, 3rd Ed. Dubuque, IA: Kendall/Hunt Publishers.

Helene G. Kershner

COMPUTER MUSEUMS

See MUSEUMS, COMPUTER.

COMPUTER MUSIC

For articles on related subjects *see* COMPUTER ART; ENTERTAINMENT INDUSTRY, COMPUTERS IN THE; HUMANITIES APPLICATIONS; and SPEECH RECOGNITION AND SYNTHESIS.

Historically, the first application of *computers* to *music* resulted in compositions such as Hiller and Isaacson's famous 1957 *Illiac Suite* for string quartet. In this work, a mainframe (*q.v.*) computer was used to emulate stochastically well-known musical stylistic rules, and derive some of its own in a very loosely constrained random compositional procedure. Shortly thereafter, in the late 1950s and early 1960s, Max Mathews and his colleagues at Bell Laboratories introduced the first programs for digital sound synthesis. This work began as tangential to the laboratory's work in speech synthesis and recognition, but soon became musically important in and of itself. Today, computers participate in all aspects of music making, including composition, live performance processing, the study of music cognition, musicology, music notation and score printing, sound production, studio editing of performance data and digitized audio signals, and sound reproduction. In addition, sonic representation, audio compression and communications protocols have become extremely important in the use of the Internet (*q.v.*) as a tool for commercial and artistic musical activity.

Digital Sound Synthesis

Computer sound synthesis is based on analog-to-digital (A/D) and digital-to-analog (D/A) conversion (*q.v.*). This technology transforms a continuous audio signal into discrete *samples*, each of which quantifies the signal's amplitude at an instant in time. (With the recent introduction of sampling synthesizers, the word *sample* has also come to mean a short digitized signal; e.g. of a single instrumental tone.) The number of samples per second is known as the *sampling rate*, while the number of bits accorded to one sample is the *quantization* or resolution. Both of these factors significantly affect sound quality. The frequencies represented in any digitized signal are limited to half the sampling rate R, since samples are required to represent both the "up" and "down" phases of an oscillation. This is often referred to as the *Nyquist frequency*, because of the Nyquist Theorem which describes it. Any attempt to digitize frequencies above this ceiling— including upper harmonics of complex timbres—leads to *foldover* (also called *aliasing*); the out-of-range frequencies are reflected back down below $R/2$. Digitized waveforms also suffer from distortions owing to imprecise quantization. Rudimentary sound synthesis, such as that used in early video games, employs 8-bit quantization at sampling rates around 10 KHz for a maximum frequency barely exceeding the highest pitch on the piano. Currently, quality audio processing employs 16-bit, 24-bit, or higher quantization at a minimum 48 KHz per channel (although 44.1 KHz is the 1999 commercial standard), which fully accommodates the ear's conventionally given frequency limit of 20 KHz.

Most computer sound synthesis environments, such as Max Mathews' Music4 and Music5 programs, and continuing to the most commonly used platform, Barry Vercoe's Csound, have been based on a conventional paradigm for music: the score/instrument model. These environments implement software simulations of devices employed in "classical" electronic music studios. They use what is commonly referred to as the *unit generator model*. Devices are simulated by reentrant (*q.v.*) software modules, anticipating by some 20 years an important premise of object-oriented programming (*q.v.*): instantiation. In Mathews' programs and their contemporary descendants, a control language enables the user to describe a computer music "instrument" as a coupling of signal (or unit) generators (e.g. oscillators and noise generators) and signal modifiers (e.g. mixers, amplifiers, filters, and reverberators). More recent designs, like James McCartney's widely used Supercollider, allow for a more integrated software-based approach, where the delineation between instrument and event (or timbre and note) is not so rigidly defined.

Digital *oscillators*, in the classical Matthews model, store a single cycle of a waveform in a digitized table; they then produce different fundamental frequencies by stepping through this table at variable rates. There have been, however, a great many innovations in software oscillator design over the past 40 years which do not require lookup tables. More complex waveforms can be produced by amplitude, frequency, and timbral modulation, in which signals are multiplied together. The user may control various parameters of these "patches" for a flexible instrument design paradigm, and in general, a procedural language "parameter passing" philosophy is used: the output of one signal may be used as the frequency or amplitude of another. *White noise* is simulated by generating random values for each sample; *low-pass noise* is simulated by interpolating linearly between random values chosen at a specified rate. Digital *mixers* simply add source samples together, while digital *amplifiers* multiply each source sample by a gain factor. Such a gain factor might typically be supplied by an *envelope generator*, which computes attack, decay, sustain, and release contours by interpolating between specified magni-

tudes over specified intervals of time. Digital *filtering* is implemented using second-order difference equations, that is, equations of the form (where O is output and I is input)

$$O[n] = aI[n] + bO[n-1] + cO[n-2];$$

the very gradual roll-off resulting from these difference equations gives better simulations of formant resonances (see next paragraph) than it does of analog *bandpass* filtering. Digital *reverberation* (or *echo*, depending on the response time) is accomplished by diverting samples through a *delay line* and feeding them back into the signal. A *t*-second delay line is a queue of $N = tR$ samples; each transit through the delay line yields one echo. Although digital reverberators were described by Schroeder in 1962, they did not begin to be incorporated into sound synthesis packages until the mid-1970s. Today, such reverberators often use frequency domain-based *convolution* techniques. Today, filters, reverberators, and oscillators, as well as other sound transformation ideas, have reached a very high degree of sophistication, are implemented in real-time on a great many commercial devices, and make use of digital signal processing. In the 1960s, Jean Claude Risset, a composer and researcher working at Bell Laboratories, produced his "Sound Catalog," which presented a great many instrument designs using the paradigm described.

Acousticians most commonly describe instrumental tone production in terms of an active *source* phase coupled to a passive *transfer* phase, and the source–transfer model provides the foundation for many sound synthesis strategies. The source phase describes how energy is introduced into the vibrating system. Sometimes, the source is pitched, as in the glottal vibrations of the human voice or the buzzing of lips into a trumpet mouthpiece; sometimes the source is unpitched, as in the rasping of a bow against a violin string. The transfer phase accommodates the various resonances present in the system. *Harmonic* resonators, such as strings and tubes, nurture specific source overtones, thus producing clear-pitched tones. *Formant* resonators, such as the cavities of the vocal tract or the sounding body of a stringed instrument, nurture (or suppress, in *offline* resonators, such as the nasal cavities) wider frequency bands.

The source–transfer model of tone production is sometimes referred to by computer musicians as "subtractive synthesis," since the transfer phase tends to eliminate frequency components from a rich source spectrum. Early attempts to simulate natural string tones digitally coupled an oscillator, simulating the vibrating string, with several formant filters, simulating the resonances of the sounding body. In 1970, Winham and Steiglitz generated pulse waves with equal-amplitude harmonics, based upon the trigonometric identity

$$1 + 2(\cos x + \cos 2x + \cdots + \cos Nx)$$
$$= \frac{\sin[(2N+1)(x/2)]}{\sin(x/2)}.$$

This method provided a truly neutral, foldover-proof source whose ultimate character could be shaped entirely by filtering. The equal-amplitude harmonic source generator is still commonly incorporated into computer music languages and programs (such as Csound's *buzz* generator). The feedback intrinsic to digital filtering often leads to unpredictable shifts in amplitude, especially when several narrow-bandwidth resonances are cascaded, but these amplitude shifts can be "normalized" out by dividing the signal's average power (derived by smoothing squared sample values with a low-pass filter, then calculating the square root) back into the signal. An important application of the source–transfer model is the synthesis algorithm described in 1983 by Karplus and Strong; this algorithm exploits the analogy between digital delay lines and harmonic resonators such as strings and tubes. In the last 10 years, physical modeling of this sort has become a major field of research in computer music, exemplified by the work of Perry Cook, Julius Smith, and others.

Fourier theory suggests an alternative way of generating instrumental timbres, known among electronic musicians as *additive synthesis*. In this approach, each harmonic of a pitched tone is generated with its own independent frequency, amplitude, and modulation envelopes. Full-blown additive synthesis generates extreme realistic tones, but it is computationally intensive, and it provides few "handles" for timbral manipulation. One way to make the technique more powerful is the introduction of *common-fate* characteristics for groups of spectra, which simulates certain physical and cognitive phenomena.

Analog-to-digital converters (*see* ANALOG-TO-DIGITAL AND DIGITAL-TO-ANALOG CONVERTERS) provide the option of incorporating "real-world" sources into computer music compositions. The most straightforward approach—direct sampling—treats a source signal very much like a digital oscillator with an extremely long waveform. Theoretically, direct sampling has been possible from the earliest days of computer sound synthesis, but it became practical only with the introduction of large-memory computers. Source signals may be analyzed and resynthesized using Fourier and other methods. With current commercial technology, sampling has become perhaps the primary esthetic and technological resource for composers and sound artists.

An efficient way of reducing real-world sources is *linear predictive coding* (LPC), which effectively strips the pitch information from a signal, leaving only the timbre, in the form of an optimized set of filter coefficients. LPC simulates the effect of a phase vocoder (voice coder) by using a digitized signal to "predict" a set of coefficients for an N-pole filter (an Nth degree difference equation). By analyzing segments of short duration (say 50 ms), one can extract evolving formant information from a rich source signal, such as a whispered poem. In a process sometimes referred to as *cross synthesis*, this extracted formant information may subsequently be used to make an instrumental source, such as a string orchestra, "sing" the poem. Composers who have pioneered the use of this technique include Charles Dodge and Paul Lansky.

Several synthesis methods bypass psychophysical models of tone production, but nonetheless yield complex, evolving timbres. The most famous is Chowning's method of synthesis by *frequency modulation*, based on the happy coincidence that when the sinusoidal carrier and modulating waves are tuned in small-integer ratios, the resulting sound will itself have a harmonic spectrum whose bandwidth varies roughly with the index of modulation. Another method, Kaegi's *vosim* system (for VOice SIMulator), exploits graphic and aural similarities between sine-squared waveforms and the waveforms generated by the human vocal tract. A third method is called *nonlinear processing* or *waveshaping*; this method extends the principle of "clipping" on an overdriven amplifier.

There are a number of common techniques for sound processing and transformation, which may be roughly classified as either *time* or *frequency domain*. Time domain techniques include modulations, enveloping, editing, and reordering of sounds. *Granular synthesis*, a technique first suggested by Gabor (in the 1940s), involves the use of short sound *grains* in the analysis/resynthesis process. The density, intergrain distance, and shape of the grains are among a number of parameters that may be controlled to alter source sounds. Composers such as Iannis Xenakis, Barry Truax, and Curtis Roads have explored this technique in detail.

Frequency domain techniques for sound transformation have often made use of the *phase vocoder* model, based on implementations of the *fast Fourier transform* (FFT—*q.v.*), explicated and pioneered in computer music by researcher Mark Dolson. Popular FFT-based environments have included the Carl system developed by F. Richard Moore at the University of California at San Diego, the Composer's Desktop Project (Wishart and others), the work of Xavier Rodet and others at IRCAM, Paul Lansky's Cmix program, and the widely-used program Soundhack by Tom Erbe

(Fig. 1). FFT-based techniques include pitch- and time-shifting, convolution (which can be used for reverberation and *binaural location*), filtering and spectral domain processing, and sonic morphing (as in the work of Christopher Penrose and Larry Polansky). Other more recent frequency domain techniques have included *wavelet*, or time–frequency domain approaches, and the use of McAulay–Quatieri (MQ) analysis, in which an FFT is further processed, by an algorithm which eliminates redundant and *masked* frequency information (similar to human cochlear processing) to form a set of *spectral tracks*. Kelly Fitz's Lemur is a widely-used application for this kind of work, and Christopher Langmead's Past (Fig. 2) extends the MQ analysis to perform cognitive feature recognition on sounds, measure timbral distance, and morph them. Timbral feature recognition by computer, and in particular the computing of *spectral* and *multidimensional timbral metrics*, was pioneered by psychologist John Grey in the early 1970s, and his work

has been continued by composer/researcher David Wessel, researcher Stephen McAdams, and others.

Since the late 1970s, mainframe programs like Music4 have gradually given way to real-time digital synthesis and transformation systems. These real-time systems implement oscillators, adders, multipliers, etc., using dedicated processors or specialized digital-signal-processing (DSP) chips. All commercial synthesizers on the market today use digital technology.

MIDI

Prior to the 1980s, a number of commercial real-time digital synthesizers had been developed, such as those designed by New England Digital (Synclavier) and Fairlight. These systems were powerful but expensive, and naturally led to a next generation of even more powerful, much less expensive, and more widely available technology.

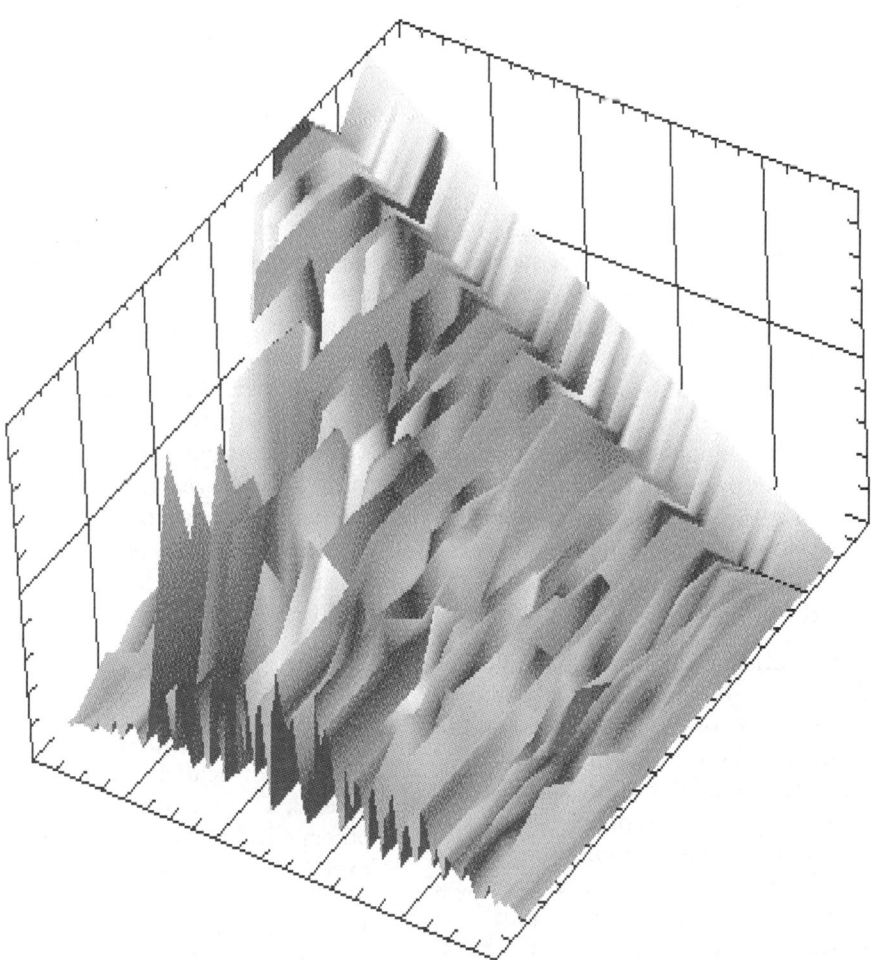

Figure 1. Waterfall plot of a spectral interpolation from a sawtooth shaped spectrum to a slightly randomized triangular one. The y-axis is spectral band amplitude, the x-axis is spectral band, and the z-axis is time. This process is derived from Erbe and Polansky spectral morphing functions implemented in the program Soundhack. (From Erbe and Polansky, "Spectral Mutation in Soundhack," *Computer Music Journal*, **20**, *1*, 92–101, 1995.)

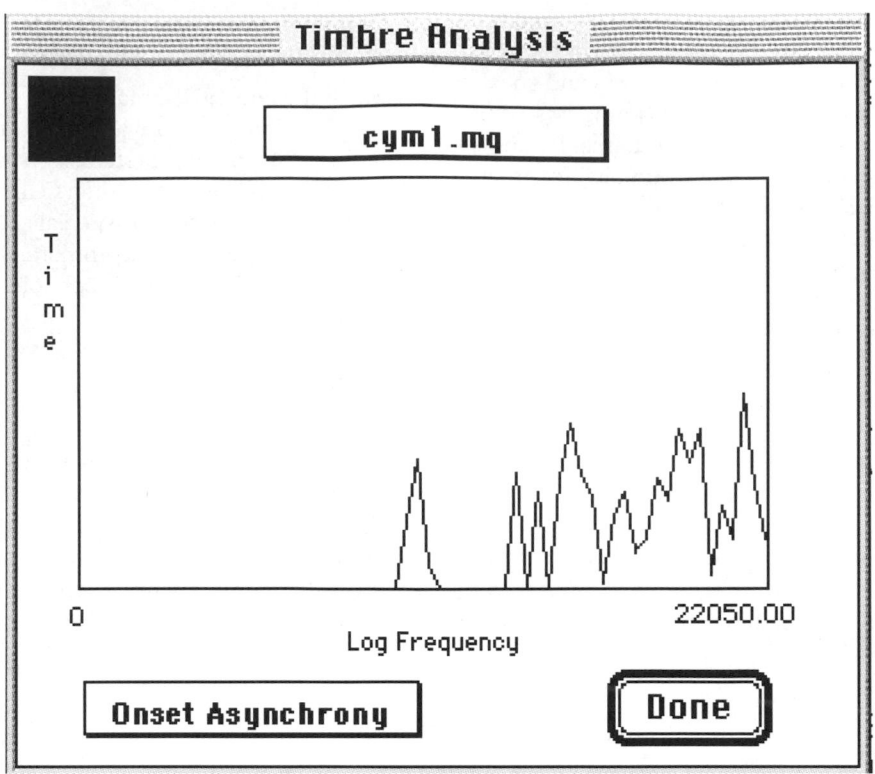

Figure 2. Windows from Christopher Langmead's timbral analysis and transformation program, Past, showing the analysis of the onset asynchrony of a sound.

MIDI, or *musical instrument digital interface*, was established by the synthesizer industry during the mid-1980s. Initially conceived as a set of industry standards for communicating performance data between synthesizers, MIDI was quickly exploited as a means of bringing synthesizers under computer control. The key to this control has been the *MIDI sequencer*, software that enables musicians to record, play back, splice, overdub, and otherwise manipulate performance data. The MIDI sequencer does more than co-opt tasks that formerly could be undertaken using only expensive multitrack recorders. With a MIDI sequencer, one can, for example, selectively change tempo without affecting transposition and vice versa.

Among other things, MIDI established a simple but versatile encoding system for performance gestures. Central to this is the notion of the MIDI channel, the digital equivalent of a keyboard on a multi-keyboard pipe organ. Notes are initiated by *key down* commands, indicating channel, chromatic pitch, and velocity (loudness); the note sustains until the synthesizer receives a *key up* command with a matching channel and pitch. (The original MIDI specification did not concern itself with timing; however, the introduction of MIDI sequencers quickly led to supplementary negotiations among the industry so that recorded performances could be saved in a standard file format.) Also included among MIDI's repertoire of

commands are the *program change*—equivalent to a stop change on an organ—a *control* command, used for sending specialized information, such as relative speaker balances, and a wide variety of *continuous* controller commands, most undefined, but several, like *pitch bend* and *channel pressure*, with common defaults, available to software and hardware manufacturers. These continuous controllers, along with the system exclusive facility, and the simplicity of the standard, have allowed a number of composers and experimenters to transcend the keyboard-based limitations for which MIDI has been commonly criticized. Groups like the HUB (which included composers John Bischoff, Tim Perkis, Mark Trayle, and others), and composers like Larry Polansky, David Rosenboom, Phil Burk, Nick Didkovsky, Gottfried Raes, George Lewis, and many others used the MIDI standard as a widely varied communication protocol for the transmission of more sophisticated musical data. Don Buchla, Laurie Spiegel, Richard Lerman, Nicolas Collins, and many others have investigated the design and construction of experimental physical controllers for MIDI data, and much research has been carried out at places like the Mills College Center for Contemporary Music (in Oakland, CA) and Steim (in Amsterdam).

One result of the standardization of MIDI data was an interest in complex musical scheduling algorithms. Dannenberg, Vercoe, Jaffe, Pennycook, and others have worked extensively in *score following*, software which simulates timed hearing/response behavior (often as intelligent adaptation to a predefined sequence of timed data). This work is closely connected with issues of automatic music transcription. Kuivila and Anderson's 1986 Formula language (as well as Polansky, Rosenbloom, and Burk's HMSL) explored techniques for real-time scheduling of arbitrarily complex events (using event-buffering, priority scheduling, individual object scheduling algorithms, and so on).

Supplementing MIDI sequencers in computer music studios are graphic score-editing programs. With today's commercial score editors, a musician can enter score data in a variety of modes, ranging from note-by-note descriptions to automatic transcription of MIDI performance data. The quality of the graphic output is competitive with scores produced by traditional engraving with much less time investment. Additionally, the fact that all of the score data is retained in disk files means that parts can be extracted automatically and also that revisions can be easily effected. As of 1999, the only serious drawback with graphic score editors is they still do not have sufficient expertise to fill in nuances of articulation that human performers insert instinctively.

A trend that has generated much enthusiasm is the real-time processing of MIDI performance data. Performance-processing software builds upon the idea of an "open score," in which details of a composition are filled in anew with each performance. In a program such as Spiegel's Music Mouse, complex passages generated by the computer are predicated entirely upon simple actions taken by a performer. Other programs, such as M and Jam Factory by Zicarelli *et al.*, permit the computer to undertake random choices conditioned by statistical tendencies deduced through analysis of captured MIDI sequences. (The same techniques had been used earlier in automated composing programs (see below). What is significant here is the real-time implementation.) Still other programs, such as Levitt's Hookup and Puckette's Max, assume no specific generative paradigm; rather, they provide repertoires of fundamental performance-processing units within an iconic programming environment (*see* OBJECT-ORIENTED PROGRAMMING). The environment permits users to link units together however they see fit.

Automated Composition and Analysis

Despite a tradition of rigorous (and often explicitly mathematical) musical theory dating back to antiquity, the idea of delegating compositional decisions to a machine remains controversial, even among computer music professionals.

The first generation of composing programs, produced during the 1960s by composer/programmers such as Hiller, Tenney, and Brün in the USA and Barbaud, Xenakis, and Koenig in Europe, emphasized two general approaches: (1) *serialism*, in which basic motifs are subjected to a variety of systematic manipulations (e.g. inversion, retrograde, transposition, and rotation), and (2) *random selection*, including ball-and-urn-type statistical procedures and Markov-style conditional probability.

The introduction of online computer systems early in the 1970s inspired hybrid computer–synthesizer environments, such as Mathews and Moore's Groove, Truax's Pod, and Buxton's SSSP. Such hybrid facilities greatly enhanced the rate of interaction between musicians and computers, permitting composers to evaluate a composition aurally at each stage in its genesis. Serialism and randomness were augmented by interactive score-processing and score-editing tools—the direct forerunners of today's MIDI sequencers and graphic score editors.

During the late 1970s, computer composers began looking for new ways to generate material automatically. One of the first alternatives to first-generation serialism and randomness was *top-down recursion* (*q.v.*). Recursive concepts of musical structure had been advocated by musical theorists (e.g. Lorenz and Schenker) since the early 20th century, and this internal tradition received added impetus from three external influences: Chomsky's formal grammars (*see* GRAMMARS) (applied to composition by Smoliar, Roads, Holtzman, Jones, and Langston), Gestalt psychology (applied by Tenney and by Ames), and fractal geometry (applied by Wuorinen, Austin, Vaggione, and Dodge) (*see* FRACTALS). More recent ways for applying mathematical constructs to composition have included the use of nonlinear dynamics, genetic algorithms (*q.v*), neural nets (*q.v.*) (as in the live computer work of David Tudor), group theory, multidimensional scaling, game theory, and many other topics.

The ball-and-urn procedures employed by first-generation programs treated *randomness* and *distributions* as dual consequences of a single paradigm, when, in fact, statistical distributions are equally characteristic of non-random phenomena. Musically, randomness and distribution address entirely different concerns: randomness affects a listener's expectations, while distribution affects the listener's sense of compositional balance. The palette of behaviors used to "shape" musical expectations embraces not just conventional random number generation (*q.v.*), but also Brownian, $1/f$, and chaotic processes. Discrete statistical balances can now be realized deterministically using Ames's method of *statistical feedback*. Briefly, statistical feedback maintains statistics detailing how much each available option has been used up to the present decision; the most underused options receive the greatest priorities of selection.

An important innovation for composing programs during the 1980s was the adoption of AI (*see* ARTIFICIAL INTELLIGENCE) search techniques. Instances include Ebcioglu's 1980 program for species counterpoint, the programs for Ames's 1981 composition *Protocol*, Ebcioglu's 1984 chorale harmonization program (which has duplicated Bach's own harmonizations on a few occasions), Hiller and Ames's tune-writing program Mix or Match (exhibited in the US Pavilion at Expo '85), Thomas's 1985 Vivace, Schwanauer's 1986 MUSE, and Ames's 1987 Cybernetic Composer. Such programs made a significant leap by formalizing not just compositional procedures, but also the principles underlying these procedures. Such principles can be

The Casten Variation

Piano/Keyboard

Larry Polansky

Figure 3. *The Casten Variation*, by L. Polansky, uses multi-dimensional scaling to generate melodies. It is written in the HMSL computer music language.

expressed either as constraints (e.g. downward resolutions of dissonances are traditionally mandatory) or heuristics (*q.v.*) (e.g. upward resolutions of traditional leading tones are not mandatory, but still desirable). Only AI composing programs are capable of prioritizing options; only AI composing programs can consider alternative solutions should their decision making lead them into an impasse.

Much effort has also been directed toward formulating generalized utilities that facilitate implementation of automated compositional processes. Examples include Polansky, Rosenboom, and Burk's 1985 HMSL (*see* Fig. 3), Taube's Common Music, PLA 1983 by William Schottstaedt, Pope's 1986 Doubletalk, Desain and Honing's 1988 Loco, Peter Stone's Symbolic Composer, Ames's 1989 Compose, Oppenheim's 1990 Dmix, Koenig's Project software, and Camurri, Canepa, Frixione, and Zaccaria's 1990 Harp. Many of these utilities are object-oriented. In effect, they do for composition or performance what Music4 and its descendants did for sound synthesis: they provide a repertory of instantiable units, each designed to perform one basic compositional task (e.g. note creation, note-parameter generation, score splicing, layering, transposition), along with standard communication protocols so that units can be freely linked into elaborate music-processing networks. A number of other composers, like David Feldman, Clarence Barlow, Warren Burt, James Tenney, and others, have developed their own individual compositional software to implement more specific and personal musical styles.

One specific musical use of computers has been in the field of *experimental intonation*, exploring new tuning systems as well as historical ones. With the advent of commercial MIDI synthesizers, and the precision of software synthesis environments, a number of composers (Polansky, Dodge, Schottstaedt, Bartlett, McLaren, Scholz, and many others) have explored the new possibilities. A number of environments have been written to support this kind of work, including the *adaptive tuning* experiments of HMSL and Bartlett's Mabel, in the 1980s, continuing the work of composers and researchers such as Harold Wagge, James Tenney, and Lou Harrison.

Automated musical analysis has been pursued, both as a rigorous way of verifying speculations by musical theorists and as a means of acquiring "real-world" expertise for composing programs. The more outstanding of the analysis-only programs include the harmony analysis programs of Winograd and Maxwell. Winograd's 1968 Explain parses block-chord harmonies in order to discern key schemes; Maxwell's 1988 program extends this capability to freely contrapuntal music. Both programs use searches to seek out "better" key interpretations. Efforts have also been made to parse melodic phrase structures automatically. A 1980 program by Tenney and Polansky employs a "perceptual distance metric," while Scarborough, Jones, and Miller's 1988 program applies discrete note-grouping rules.

The five "Strophe" movements of Hiller and Baker's 1963 *Computer Cantata* were generated as Markov chains, using transition probabilities acquired through statistical analysis of a composition by Ives, and much the same approach underlies Zicarelli's 1986 Jam Factory. Cope's 1987 EMI scans musical input for musical patterns, which EMI compiles into an augmented transition network; the accumulated knowledge base can then be used to generate new compositions in the "same" style.

In the 1980s, computer music languages like HMSL, Buchla and Crowe's Midas (a successor to their pioneering Patch-IV hybrid environment), Dan Oppenheim's Dmix, and Miller Puckette's 1986 Max pioneered the more widespread development of real-time intelligent software for performance and composition environments. This work was a direct outgrowth of the musical developments made on microprocessors in the 1970s by composers including David Rosenboom, David Behrman, Jim Horton (with the League of Automatic Music Composers) George Lewis, Martin Bartlett, and others. In the 1990s, much of this work has been extended into real-time digital signal processing control, as embodied in environments like David Zicarelli's Dspmax, Hebel and Scaletti's Kyma system, Puckette's PD, Phil Burk's Jsynth, and McCartney's Supercollider.

Bibliography

Journals
Computer Music Journal. Cambridge, MA: MIT Press Journals. The primary source for articles on computer music.
INTERFACE: Journal of New Music Research. Lisse, The Netherlands: Swets Publishing Service. Emphasizes computer applications to composition and analysis. Articles are typically more detailed than in CMJ.

Books and Articles
1969. Mathews, M. V., Miller, J. E., Moore, F. R., Pierce, J. R., and Risset, J. C. *The Technology of Computer Music.* Cambridge, MA: MIT Press. The classic book on digital sound synthesis, still valuable for its discussion of basic principles.
1983. International MIDI Association. *MIDI: Musical Instrument Digital Interface Specification 1.0.* North Hollywood, CA.
1987. Ames, C. "Automated Composition in Retrospect: 1956–1986," *LEONARDO: Journal of the International Society for Science, Technology, and the Arts,* **20**, *2*, 169.
1989. Mathews, M. V., and Pierce, J. R. (eds.) *Current Directions in Computer Music Research.* Cambridge, MA: MIT Press.
1990. Moore, F. R. *Elements of Computer Music.* Upper Saddle River, NJ: Prentice Hall.

1991. Balaban, M., Ebcioglu, K., and Laske, O. (eds.) *Musical Intelligence*. Palo Alto, CA: AAI Press.

1995. Roads, C. *The Computer Music Tutorial*. Cambridge, MA: MIT Press.

1997. Dodge, C., and Jerse, T. *Computer Music: Synthesis, Composition, and Performance*, 2nd Ed. New York: Schirmer Books.

Charles Ames and Larry Polansky

COMPUTER NETWORK

See INTERNET; LOCAL AREA NETWORK; METROPOLITAN AREA NETWORK; NETWORK ARCHITECTURE; NETWORK PROTOCOL; and NETWORKS, COMPUTER.

COMPUTER PERFORMANCE

See BENCHMARKS; and PERFORMANCE MEASUREMENT AND EVALUATION.

COMPUTER PROFESSIONALS FOR SOCIAL RESPONSIBILITY (CPSR)

For articles on related subjects *see* ELECTRONIC FRONTIER FOUNDATION; INFORMATION ACCESS; LEGAL ASPECTS OF COMPUTING; PRETTY GOOD PRIVACY; PRIVACY, COMPUTERS AND; and SOCIETY, COMPUTERS IN.

Origin and Purpose

CPSR is a public-interest alliance of computer scientists and others concerned about the impact of computer technology on society. The organization works to influence decisions regarding the development and use of computers. Current CPSR projects explore the US national information infrastructure, civil liberties and privacy, computers in the workplace, technology policy and human needs, and the reliability and risk of computer-based systems. In 1998 the organization announced a new project "One Planet, One Net: CPSR Campaign on Internet Governance."

CPSR was created in the early 1980s in response to growing concern over the threat of nuclear war. A discussion group was formed on a computer message system at the Xerox Palo Alto Research Center (PARC). A small group of computer researchers, mostly from Xerox/PARC and nearby Stanford University, began meeting weekly to discuss the issues associated with the use of computers in critical systems.

At a public meeting in 1982 the group adopted the name Computer Professionals for Social Responsibility (CPSR). As related groups began to form in other cities, CPSR established itself as a national organization incorporated under the laws of California in 1983, and opened a national office in Palo Alto.

In 1983 the first issue of the *CPSR Newsletter* was published. This quarterly publication, now published online on the World Wide Web, contains analyses of major issues involving technology along with updates on CPSR activities.

Program

Up until the mid-1980s, CPSR focused on the dangers posed by the massive increase in the use of computing technology in military applications. The organization's most significant early successes came from its opposition to the Strategic Defense Initiative (SDI). CPSR's campaign against the SDI led to considerable growth in membership and to chapter formation throughout the USA.

From the beginning CPSR has communicated concerns about the appropriate use of computer technology to the public, to policy makers, and to the profession. In the early years, the CPSR message was spread through publications, conferences, and special events. For example, in support of its work on computers in the military, CPSR produced a book entitled *Computers in Battle: Will They Work?* and an award-winning slide show entitled *Reliability and Risk*.

Since 1985, CPSR's program has broadened considerably. Some new projects have been initiated by CPSR staff. Other projects are sparked by local chapter activity or a group of concerned individuals.

In 1986 CPSR established the Privacy and Civil Liberties Project. The project began with an assessment of a proposed expansion of the FBI computer database, the National Crime Information Center, and later pursued a wide range of activities in the areas of privacy and civil liberties.

In 1987 CPSR held the first conference on Direction and Implications of Advanced Computing. This conference is now a biannual event, with support from the NSF as well as professional and industrial supporters.

In 1990 the CPSR Workplace Project organized the first Participatory Design Conference. The event was attended by 180 people from nine countries.

In 1993 CPSR undertook a new project centered on the National Information Infrastructure (NII) proposed by the Clinton/Gore administration. It published *Serving the Community: A Public-Interest Vision of the National Information Infrastructure*, in September 1993.

Today the organization sponsors public conferences, maintains a Website, publishes a newsletter, organizes working groups, and participates in policy meetings. It is engaged in public debates over a wide range of policy issues, from community networks and computers in education to risk and reliability and the future of Internet governance.

Organizational Structure

CPSR is a national membership organization with 22 chapters across the USA. CPSR also has working groups on cyber-rights, civil liberties, education, and ethics. Because of interest in CPSR's work from computer professionals in various other countries, particularly in Europe, CPSR planned to organize its first foreign chapters in 1999.

CPSR is governed by a Board of Directors that includes its officers and regional and at-large directors. An Executive Committee is responsible for the management and implementation of policy for the organization. CPSR has seven standing committees: Board Development, Finance, Fundraising, Membership, Personnel, Program, and Publications. The National Staff in Palo Alto is responsible for organizational administration. The organization has a National Advisory Board, comprised of distinguished individuals.

CPSR makes an annual award for Professional and Social Responsibility in memory of Norbert Wiener. Recipients of the Norbert Wiener Award are:

1987	David Parnas
1988	Joseph Weizenbaum
1989	Daniel McCracken
1990	Kristen Nygaard
1991	Severo Ornstein and Laura Gould
1992	Barbara Simons
1993	Institute for Global Communications
1994	Antonia Stone
1995	Tom Grundner
1996	Philip Zimmermann
1997	Peter Neumann
1998	The Internet Engineering Task Force (IETF)

The organization's address is CPSR, P.O. Box 717, Palo Alto, CA 94302, USA.

Websites

CPSR Website. http://www.cpsr.org.
CPSR history Website. http://www.cpsr.org/cpsr/history.html.
CPSR Newsletter Website. http://www.cpsr.org/publication/newsletters/.

Marc Rotenberg

COMPUTER SCIENCE

Editor's Note: Because of the many references in this article to topics covered by other articles, we have indicated those terms or phrases that are titles (or partial titles) of other articles with boldface rather than by an appended "(*q.v.*)". Many non-boldfaced terms will be found in the Subject Index.

The computing profession is the people and institutions that have been created to take care of other people's concerns in information processing and coordination through worldwide communication systems. The profession contains various specialties such as **computer science**, **computer engineering**, **software engineering**, **information systems**, domain-specific applications, and **computer systems**. The discipline of computer science is the body of knowledge and practices used by computing professionals in their work (*see* PERSONNEL IN THE COMPUTER FIELD).

The discipline of computer science was born in the early 1940s with the confluence of algorithm theory (*see* ALGORITHMS, THEORY OF), mathematical logic, and the invention of the stored-program electronic computer (*see* STORED-PROGRAM CONCEPT). Examples are the works of Alan **Turing**, Alonzo **Church**, and Kurt Gödel in the 1930s about **algorithm**s and their realizations as machines or rule systems (*see* LAMBDA CALCULUS, TURING MACHINE, and UNDECIDABLE PROBLEMS), the algorithms created by Augusta Ada, **Countess of Lovelace** 60 years earlier, the **analog computer**s built by Vannevar **Bush** in the 1920s, and the electronic computers built by Howard **Aiken** and Konrad **Zuse** in the 1930s. The writings of John **von Neumann** gave considerable intellectual depth to the emerging discipline by the late 1940s. By the early 1960s, there was a sufficient body of knowledge to merit the first academic departments and degree programs (*see* **Appendix IV**). This discipline is also variously called *computer science and engineering, computing*, and *informatics*.

The body of knowledge of computing is frequently described as the systematic study of algorithmic processes that describe and transform information: their theory, analysis, design, efficiency, implementation, and application. The fundamental question underlying all of computing is: *What can be (efficiently) automated?*

This common characterization is too austere. It only hints at the full richness of the discipline. It does not call attention to the connections between computing knowledge and the concerns of people to whom this knowledge contributes, notably the universal concerns for reliability, dependability, robustness, integrity, security, and modifiability of computer systems. It hides the social and historical (*see* DIGITAL COMPUTERS, HISTORY OF) context of the field and the values of the people who practice in it. The following discussion of the discipline calls attention to these important larger questions.

The Domain of Computer Science

Even though computer science addresses both human-made and natural information processes, the main effort in the discipline has been directed toward human-made processes, especially information processing systems and machines. Much of the work of the field until the mid-1980s concerned computers as number crunchers, symbol manipulators (*see* **SYMBOL MANIPULATION**), and data processors; but the personal computer and the **Internet** have since enlarged the focus to include coordination and communication. Much of the body of knowledge of computing concerns the **digital computer** and the phenomena surrounding it—the structure and operation of computer systems, principles underlying computer system design and programming, effective methods for using computers for information processing tasks, and theoretical characterizations of their properties and limitations. The field is grappling with new questions arising from interactions with other fields, where computers are tools but not the objects of study, and where other considerations such as **transparency**, usability, dependability, **hardware reliability**, **software reliability**, and **software safety** are paramount.

Computing is also contributing to other fields by showing them how to model their processes as information processes. Several have been prominent. Biologists now view DNA as an encoding of information needed to generate a unique organism; they seek algorithms that can construct complete genome sequences from fragments scattered across many databases (*see* **BIOCOMPUTING**). Psychologists and cognitive scientists (*see* **COGNITIVE SCIENCE**), who have collaborated for many years with computer scientists on models of cognition, have been joined by neuroscientists who seek to model neural systems and use the models to explain the cognitive behavior of organisms. Physicists have discovered new materials that have been used for ever-smaller chips and ever-faster communication media. Other disciplines are beginning to contribute ideas for the construction of new machines, such as silicon chips that simulate body parts like eyes and ears, biological memories, DNA chemical solutions that compute combinatorial problems, or quantum processes for superparallel computation and cryptography (*see* **MOLECULAR COMPUTING**; **PARALLEL PROCESSING**; **QUANTUM COMPUTING**; and **CRYPTOGRAPHY, COMPUTERS IN**).

Standard Concerns of the Field

The digital computer plays the central role in the field because it is a universal computing machine: with enough memory, a digital computer is capable of simulating any **information processing** system, provided the task can be specified as an unambiguous set of instructions. If such a specification is possible, the task can be represented as a program that can be stored in the memory of a computer. Thus, one machine is capable of exploring and studying an enormous variety of concepts, schemes, simulations, and techniques of information processing.

Practitioners of the discipline should be skilled in four basic areas: algorithmic thinking, representation, programming, and design. *Algorithmic thinking* is an interpretation of the world in which a person understands and formulates actions in terms of step-by-step procedures that give unambiguous results when carried out by anyone (or by a suitable machine). The importance of this concept is reflected in the fact that six articles in this Encyclopedia begin with "**ALGORITHM**." Algorithmic thinking resembles standard scientific thinking, which seeks to invent standard ways of observing that allow anyone to see and reproduce physical effects. It emphasizes the standard procedural and scientific thinking of the standard observer.

Representation addresses the way in which data is stored so that the questions one will ask about it can be answered efficiently. For example, the standard phone book is organized for a quick answer to the question, "What is the phone number assigned to person P?" When stored in a computer database, the machine goes quickly to the alphabetic part of the list containing the name P. This is not an efficient organization for the question, "To whom is the phone number N assigned?" because the standard book would have to be searched entry by entry until the given phone number is found. A data organization more suited to the second question is the inverted phone book, in which the phone numbers are listed in their numeric order accompanied by the names of their owners (*see* **SEARCHING**). The skill of representation goes beyond knowing how to organize data for efficient **information retrieval** or processing (*see* **KNOWLEDGE REPRESENTATION**). It deals with inventing ways of encoding phenomena to allow algorithmic processing. Examples include representing a mathematical expression so that it can be differentiated (*see* **COMPUTER ALGEBRA**), representing a document so that "What you see [on the screen] is what you get [on the printer]"; representing handwritten postal codes for automatic recognition and sorting by postal services (*see* **OPTICAL CHARACTER RECOGNITION**); representing encoded speech so that one can talk to a computer or so that the computer can talk (*see* **SPEECH RECOGNITION AND SYNTHESIS**); representing an engine part so that it can be shown on the graphics screen and then can be manufactured automatically (*see* **COMPUTER-AIDED DESIGN/COMPUTER-AIDED MANUFACTURING (CAD/CAM)**).

Programming enables people to take algorithmic thinking and representations and embody them in **software** that will cause a machine to perform in a prescribed way. This skill includes working knowledge of different **programming languages** (each having its own strengths and limitations); program development tools that aid testing, **debugging**, modularity, and **compatibility**; and **operating systems**, which control the internal operations of computers.

Design connects the other three skills to the concerns of people through the medium of systems that serve them. Design includes many practical considerations such as engineering trade-offs, integrating available components (*see* **COMPONENT SOFTWARE**), meeting time and cost constraints, and meeting safety and reliability requirements.

Even though everyone in the discipline is expected to know these skills, it is a mistake to equate computer science with any one of them, e.g. programming. As will be shown shortly, there are many aspects of the discipline that do not involve programming, even though they involve algorithmic thinking, representation, and design.

Principal Subdivisions of the Field

The subject matter of computing can be broadly divided into two parts. The first studies information processing tasks and their related data representations. The second studies structures, mechanisms, and schemes for processing information. Within the field, these two parts are called *applications* and *systems*, respectively, and programming that relates to these areas is called, respectively, **applications programming** and **systems programming**. A major goal of computing education is to elucidate the relationships between applications and **computer system**s.

Computer applications can be subdivided into numerical and nonnumerical categories. Numerical applications are those in which mathematical models and numerical data are dominant; they are supported by **numerical analysis**, **optimization methods**, **simulation**, **mathematical software** libraries, **computational geometry**, and computational science (*see* **SCIENTIFIC APPLICATIONS** and **SCIENTIFIC VISUALIZATION**). Nonnumerical applications are those in which problems and information are represented as symbols and rules; they are supported by **artificial intelligence**, **multimedia**/hypermedia systems, **language processors**, **computer graphics**, mathematical expression systems, **database management systems**, **information retrieval** systems, and combinatorial processes (*see* **COMBINATORICS**).

Computer systems can be subdivided into software systems and hardware systems. *Software systems* are concerned with machine-level representations of **program**s and data; schemes for controlling program execution; **assembler**s, **compiler**s, and **language processors** for **intermediate languages**, **programming support environments**, **operating systems**, and network communications and management (*see* **NETWORKS, COMPUTER** and **TELEPROCESSING SYSTEMS**). *Hardware systems* are concerned with **logic design**, machine organization, processors, **memory**, and devices in various technologies such as VLSI, silicon, and GaAs (*see* **INTEGRATED CIRCUITRY**). **Computer architecture** and **computer engineering** are concerned with both software and hardware.

These categories do not define clean lines of division. Most application areas are also concerned with related systems problems such as languages, operating systems, and networks. Most systems areas are also concerned with task environments, practices of the application area, and modes of human interaction (*see* **HUMAN FACTORS IN COMPUTING**).

Relationships with Other Disciplines

Computer science has, by tradition, been more closely related to mathematics than to physics, chemistry, and biology. This is because mathematical logic, the theorems of Turing and Gödel, **Boolean algebra** for circuit design, and algorithms for solving equations and other classes of problems in mathematics played strong roles in the early development of the field. Conversely, computer science has strongly influenced mathematics, many branches of which have become concerned with demonstrating algorithms for constructing or identifying a mathematical structure or carrying out a function. In some cases, computers have been essential to mathematics; for example, the solution of the four-color theorem relied on a program that searched a large finite number of cases for counterexamples (*see* **MATHEMATICS, COMPUTERS IN**). For these reasons, some observers like to say that computing is a mathematical science.

The bond between engineering and computer science is much stronger than between many natural science disciplines and their engineering counterparts—for example, chemical engineering and chemistry, aircraft design and fluid dynamics, pharmacy and biology, and materials engineering and physics. This is because computer science has a strong heritage in electrical engineering and because many algorithmic methods were originally designed to solve engineering problems. Examples include electronic circuits (and hence now **computer circuitry**), **data communications**, engineering graphics, engineering design, systems engineering, fabrication, and manufacturing. Conversely, computers have become indispensable in many engineering disciplines—for example, circuit simulators, **finite-element** simulators, flow-field simulators, graphics, CAD and CAM systems, computer controlled tools, and flexible manufacturing systems. For these reasons, some observers like to say that computing is an engineering science.

A new bond is forming between the physical sciences and computer science. Leaders of physics, chemistry, biology, geology, seismology, astronomy, oceanography, and meteorology have brought to prominence certain very hard "grand challenge" problems that demand massive high-speed computations, performed on new generations of massively parallel computers (*see* **PARALLEL PROCESSING**) with new kinds of algorithms. These problems include crystalline structure, quantum electrodynamics, calculation of chemical properties of materials from the Schrödinger equation, **Monte Carlo** reactor calculations, electromagnetic scattering, **simulation** of aircraft in flight, exploration of space, global climate modeling, oil exploration, cosmological models of the universe, long-range weather forecasting, earthquake prediction, turbulent fluid flow, and human genome sequencing (*see* **SCIENTIFIC APPLICATIONS**). Many leaders of science now say that computation has emerged as a third paradigm of science, joining theory and experimentation. For these reasons, some observers identify computing with computational science.

Who is right? All are, demonstrating the richness of the discipline and its heritage in older sciences and engineering. In addition to the influences of mathematics, engineering, and science woven into the discipline itself, computing interacts closely with many other disciplines. Here are some prominent examples:

◆ Library science is concerned with archiving texts and organizing storage and retrieval systems to give efficient access to texts. As **digital libraries** are built and attached to the **Internet**, traditional libraries will change from storage places for books to electronic data centers, and will grant access well beyond their local communities. Libraries have a special concern with the problem of migrating data from older storage media onto newer ones (*see* **LIBRARY STANDARDS**).

◆ Management science is concerned with using computer models for planning and forecasting economic conditions for business. It is also concerned with storing business records in databases and generating reports on the state of the business and on customer preferences from these records (*see* **MANAGEMENT INFORMATION SYSTEMS**).

◆ Economics is concerned with using computer models to forecast economic conditions and to evaluate the possible effects of macroeconomic policies.

◆ Medicine and biology have used computer models and algorithms in ingenious ways to diagnose and treat diseases. Modern imaging methods such as magnetic resonance scans, coronary scans, and **tomography** have drawn heavily on computer science. Medical researchers use computer models to assist them in tracking mutations of viruses and in narrowing the scope of experiments to the cases most likely to resolve the research question. The Human Genome Project has used large distributed databases and new kinds of string-matching algorithms to aggregate the tens of thousands of DNA sequencing experiments (*see* **STRING PROCESSING**).

◆ Forensics uses computer models and large databases to identify evidence and discover whether other forensic data matches current evidence.

◆ Psychology and the behavioral and **cognitive sciences** are concerned with understanding human thought and emotions. They use computer models to gain insight into the operation of human brains and nervous systems and to design effective interventions into human problems.

◆ Linguistics is concerned with using computers for speech recognition and synthesis, for **machine translation** between languages, and to understand the role of language in human affairs (*see* **HUMANITIES APPLICATIONS**). **Programming linguistics** is concerned with computer languages rather than natural ones.

◆ Philosophy is concerned with the way people acquire knowledge, create social realities, and act morally and ethically. Philosophers have contributed much to the debates on whether machines can think or whether formal models are sufficient for dependable software systems. The subdiscipline of speech act theory has contributed much to our understanding of how people carry out work in organizations and has helped give birth to the workflow industry. Recently, the concept of "**virtual reality**" has rekindled debates on the nature of reality and the worlds in which people live.

◆ **Humanities** have begun to use computers extensively to correlate and search through historical artifacts that can be represented digitally. One of the more colorful examples is the use of computers to determine or authenticate the authorship of historical texts, such as the Federalist Papers, and literary works such as Shakespeare's plays.

This list is hardly exhaustive. The number of contacts between computing and other disciplines grows rapidly each year. Some of the most innovative work is being done by people who know both computing and another discipline as well.

Processes

At the beginning of the previous section, we noted that mathematics, science, and engineering have special historical relationships with computing. These roots are revealed through three major paradigms or processes within the field:

◆ *Theory*: building conceptual frameworks and notations for understanding relationships among objects in a domain and the logical consequences of axioms and laws.

◆ *Experimentation*: exploring models of systems and architectures within given application domains and testing whether those models can predict new behaviors accurately. This paradigm is sometimes called *abstraction* by computer scientists.

◆ *Design*: constructing computer systems that support work in given organizations or application domains.

These three paradigms constantly interact in the work of computer scientists; indeed, the interaction is part of the vigor of the field. Many controversies in the field are associated with someone in one paradigm criticizing the work of someone in another without being aware of the difference.

In areas of rapidly developing technology, such as databases, human interfaces, and Web-based systems, theoreticians aim mainly at bringing order into a rapidly accumulating mass of experience through broad conceptual frameworks, taxonomies, and analytic methods. In mature areas such as **computational complexity**, **algorithms**, **data structures**, **automata theory**, **switching theory**, **graph theory**, **combinatorics**, and **formal languages**, theoreticians focus on deeper, comprehensive analyses of phenomena for which formal models exist. With a few notable exceptions including **logic design**, **computer graphics**, analysis of **algorithms**, and **compiler**s, theory has had limited impact on the complex problems of practical systems and applications.

Experimenters construct models of phenomena or of possible systems; the models generally suppress detail and enable fast predictions. Examples are measurement of programs and systems, validation of hypotheses, **software prototyping** to extend abstractions to practice, logic simulation, **simulation**s of systems and of physical processes, testing of **protocol**s, system performance analysis (*see* **BENCHMARKS** and **PERFORMANCE MEASUREMENT AND EVALUATION**), and

comparisons of different architectures. Experimental computer science relies heavily on laboratories. It often stimulates new developments in computer design and use. More attention is being paid to experimental computer science because human intuition often does not work well with complex systems.

Designers are concerned with building systems that meet clear specifications and satisfy their customers. They boast many significant accomplishments, such as program development systems, simulators, microchip design systems, VLSI, CAD, CAM, graphics, databases, and **supercomputers**. The most successful designs have occurred with hardware and self-contained software packages—systems for which precise functional specifications can be given at the start. The least successful designs have been large software systems, many of which are unreliable, undependable, unsafe, too costly, too difficult to change, and too complex to understand. Many designers are turning to other domains, including organizational analysis, workflow, anthropology, and ethnography to assist them in understanding how a system will interact with the practices of the people using them.

In addition to the three processes and the specialists who practice them, the discipline of computing has a number of broad concerns that touch all the subfields. The main ones are parallel and distributed computation (*see* **DISTRIBUTED SYSTEMS**), performance analysis, reliability, safety, security, and **computer ethics**.

Subareas of the Field

Computer science can be divided into a number of coherent subareas, each with substantial theoretical, experimental, and design issues, and each with its own version of the shared concerns. Significant industries and institutions have been established in each of these areas. The chart below depicts the discipline as a matrix with 12 subareas as rows and the three processes as columns. Though it is not done here, each of the boxes could be filled in with detailed descriptions of that category of the subarea's activities and accomplishments. The boundaries between areas and processes are often fuzzy; it is sometimes a matter of personal judgment where certain items go. Additional columns could be added to represent the shared concerns, and their boxes filled in likewise.

The discussion following is an overview of the content of the boxes of the matrix, with just enough depth to reveal the language and vocabulary of computer science. Much more information about these areas can be found in the individual articles of this volume and in the *Handbook of Computer Science and Engineering* (Tucker and Wegner, 1996). The last area, bioinformatics, is an emerging area.

		Theory	Abstraction	Design
1	Algorithms and data structures			
2	Programming languages			
3	Architecture			
4	Operating systems and networks			
5	Software engineering			
6	Databases and information retrieval			
7	Artificial intelligence and robotics			
8	Graphics			
9	Human computer interaction			
10	Computational science			
11	Organizational informatics			
12	Bioinformatics			

1 ALGORITHMS AND DATA STRUCTURES

The theory of algorithms encompasses computability theory (*see* **NP-COMPLETE PROBLEMS**), **computational complexity**, **information-based complexity**, concurrency theory (*see* **CONCURRENT PROGRAMMING** and **PETRI NET**), **probabilistic algorithms**, the theory of **deductive** and **relational databases**, randomized algorithms, pattern-matching algorithms (*see* **PATTERN RECOGNITION**), graph and network algorithms, algebraic algorithms, combinatorial optimization, and **cryptography**. It is supported by **discrete mathematics** (**graph theory**, recursive functions (*see* **RECURSION**), recurrence relations, **combinatorics**), calculus, induction, predicate logic, temporal logic (a calculus of time-dependent events), semantics, probability, and statistics.

Experimentation has been found very useful with complex algorithms and **heuristic**s for which no tractable theoretical analysis is known. Algorithms can be evaluated by applying them to suites of test cases and analyzing their performance. Testing has yielded valuable characterizations of certain methods such as divide-and-conquer, greedy algorithms, dynamic programming, finite-state machine interpreters, **stack** machine interpreters, heuristic searches, and randomized algorithms. Testing has yielded significant insights into the performance of parallel and distributed algorithms.

Many useful, practical algorithms have been designed and placed in program libraries—for example, **mathematical software**, **searching**, **sorting**, **random-num-**ber **generation**, textual pattern matching, hashing, graphs, **trees**, communication network **protocol**s, distributed-data updates, semaphores, deadlock detectors, synchronizers, storage managers, lists (*see* **LIST PROCESSING**), tables, and paging algorithms (*see* **MULTIPROGRAMMING**, **MULTITASKING**, **SWAPPING** and **VIRTUAL MEMORY**). Many theoretical results have been translated into useful and practical systems, such as the RSA public key cryptosystem, production-quality compilers, and VLSI circuit layout.

2 PROGRAMMING LANGUAGES

This area deals with notations for virtual machines that execute algorithms and with notations for algorithms and data; the sets of strings of symbols that are generated by such notations are called *languages*. It also deals with efficient translations from high-level languages into machine codes (*see* **COMPILER**). Fundamental questions include: What are possible organizations of the virtual machine presented by the language (**data type**s, operations and **operands**, **control structures**, **extensible language** mechanisms for introducing new types and operations)? How are these abstractions implemented on computers? What notation (syntax) can be used effectively and efficiently to specify what the computer should do? How are functions (semantics) associated with language notations (*see* **PROGRAMMING LANGUAGE SEMANTICS** and **SYNTAX, SEMANTICS, AND PRAGMATICS**)? How can machines translate between languages (*see* **LANGUAGE PROCESSORS**)?

The theory of **programming languages** studies models of machines that generate and translate languages and of **grammars** for expressing valid strings in the languages. Examples include models of **formal languages**, **automata theory**, **Turing machines**, Post systems, **lambda calculus**, pi calculus to model concurrency, and propositional logic. The theory deals with semantics, the study of the relationships between strings of the language ("**well-formed formula**s") and states of the underlying virtual machines such as that which exists between a **regular expression** and a finite-state machine (*see* **CHOMSKY HIERARCHY** and **SEQUENTIAL MACHINE**). It deals with types, which are classes of objects (*see* **TYPES, THEORY OF**). Related mathematics is predicate logic, temporal logic, modern algebra, and mathematical induction.

The modelers have developed classifications of languages based on their syntactic and semantic models, for example, static typing, dynamic typing, **functional programming**, **procedure-oriented language** design vs. **object-oriented analysis and design**, logic specification, message-passing, and **dataflow**. They have developed classifications by application, for example, (business) **data processing**, **simulation**, **list processing**, and **computer graphics**. They have developed classifications by functional structure, for example, procedure hierarchies, functional composition, **abstract data type**s, and communicating sequential processes (*see* **CONCURRENT PROGRAMMING**). They have developed abstract implementation models for each major type of language including imperative, object-oriented, logic and constraint, concurrent, and distributed.

Programming language designers have developed many practical languages including procedural languages such as **Cobol**, **Fortran**, **Algol**, **Pascal**, **Ada**, and **C**; object-oriented languages such as Clu, Smalltalk, **C++**, Eiffel, and **Java**; functional languages such as **Lisp**, ML, and Haskell; **dataflow** languages such as Sisal, Val, and Id Nouveau; and logic (Prolog), string (Snobol, Icon), and concurrency languages such as Concurrent Pascal, Occam, SR, and Modula-3.

Designers have implemented run-time models, static and dynamic execution models, type checking, storage and **register** allocation, **compiler**s, **cross assemblers and compilers**, interpreters, analyzers that find parallelism in programs, and **programming support environments** that aid users with tools for efficient syntactic and semantic error checking, profiling, **debugging**, and tracing (*see* **TRACE**). A crowning achievement has been programs that take the description of a language and automatically produce a compiler that will translate programs in that language into machine code (examples include yacc and lex in **Unix** environments); very efficient compilers have been built this way. Programming languages are used widely in application domains to create tables, graphs, chemical formulas, **spreadsheet**s, equations, input and output, and data queries; in each case, the designer creates a mini-language and a parser.

3 ARCHITECTURE

This area deals with methods of organizing hardware (and associated software) into efficient, reliable systems. The fundamental questions include: What are good methods of implementing processors, memory, and communication in a machine? How does one design and control large computational systems and convincingly demonstrate that they work as intended despite errors and failures? What types of architecture can efficiently incorporate many processing elements that can work concurrently on a computation? How can **performance measurement and evaluation** best be implemented? Can hardware devices mimic selected human sensors such as eyes and ears?

The theory of **computer architecture** includes: digital logic, **Boolean algebra**, coding theory (*see* **CODES**), and finite-state machine theory (*see* **SEQUENTIAL MACHINE**). Supporting mathematics include statistics, probability, **queueing theory**, reliability theory, **discrete mathematics**, number theory (*see* **FACTORING INTEGERS** and **NUMBER-THEORETIC CALCULATIONS**), and arithmetic in different number systems (*see* **ARITHMETIC, COMPUTER** and **NUMBERS AND NUMBER SYSTEMS**).

Computer architects are avid experimenters. Their favorite models include finite-state machines, general methods of synthesizing systems from basic components, models of circuits and finite state machines for computing arithmetic functions over finite fields, models for data path and **control structure**s, optimizing instruction sets for various models and workloads, hardware reliability, space, time, and organizational trade-offs in the design of VLSI devices, organization of machines for various computational models, and identification of "levels of abstraction" at which the design can be viewed—e.g. configuration, program, **instruction set**, **register**s, and gates. Architects frequently use simulators and emulators (*see* **EMULATION**) to assess design trade-offs and determine the best ratios of **memory**, processing power, and **bandwidth** for a device. They have well-developed discourses for **bus**es (inter-device data channels), memory systems, computer **arithmetic**, **input–output operations**, and **parallel processing** machines.

Computer architecture is replete with successful designs. These include arithmetic function units, **cache memory**, the so-called **von Neumann machine**, RISCs (**Reduced Instruction Set Computer**s), CISCs (Complex Instruction Set Computers), efficient methods of storing and recording information and of detecting and correcting **errors** (*see* **ERROR CORRECTING AND DETECTING CODE**); error recovery, **computer-aided design** (CAD) systems and logic simulations for the design of VLSI circuits, reduction programs for layout and fault diagnosis and silicon compilers (compilers that produce instructions for manufacturing a silicon chip—*see* **DIGITAL DESIGN AUTOMATION**). They also include major systems such as **dataflow**, **tree**, **Lisp**, hypercube, **pipeline**, vector, and multiprocessors (*see* **MULTIPROCESSING**); and **supercomputers**, such as the **Cray**, Cyber, and **IBM Corporation** RS/6000 series machines. Architects have collaborated with other scientists to design prototypes of devices that can imitate human senses.

4 OPERATING SYSTEMS AND NETWORKS

This area deals with control mechanisms that allow multiple resources to be coordinated efficiently in computations distributed over many computer systems connected by wide area and **local area network**s. Fundamental questions include: at each level of temporal granularity (e.g. microsecond, minute, hour, or day) in the operation of a **computer system**, what are the visible objects and permissible operations on them? For each class of resource (objects visible at some level), what is a minimal set of operations that permit their effective use? How can **user interface**s be organized so that users deal only with abstract versions of resources and not with physical details of hardware? What are effective control strategies for job scheduling, **memory management**, communications, access to software resources, communication among concurrent tasks, reliability, and security? What are the principles by which systems can be extended in function by repeated application of a small number of construction rules? How should distributed computations be organized, with the details of **network protocol**s, **host** locations, **bandwidth**s, and resource naming being mostly invisible? How can a distributed **operating system** be both a program preparation and execution environment? (*See* **DISTRIBUTED SYSTEMS**.)

Major elements of theory in **operating systems** include: concurrency theory (synchronization, determinacy, and **mutual exclusion**); **scheduling algorithms**; program behavior and **memory management** theory; **network** flow theory; performance modeling and analysis. Supporting mathematics include bin packing (*see* **MATHEMATICS, COMPUTERS IN**), probability, **queueing theory**, communication and **information theory**, temporal logic, and **cryptography**.

Like architects, **operating system** designers are avid modelers. Their major models include: abstraction and **information-hiding** principles such as **encapsulation**; **binding** of user-defined objects to internal computational structures; process and thread management; **memory management**; **job** scheduling; secondary storage (*see* **MASS STORAGE, MEMORY: AUXILIARY**, and **MEMORY HIERARCHY**) and **file** management; performance analysis; distributed computation; remote procedure calls; **real-time systems**; secure computing; and networking, including layered **protocol**s, **Internet** protocols, naming, remote resource usage, help services, and local network routing protocols such as token-passing and shared **bus**es.

Operating systems and networking has always been, first and foremost, a field of design. This field has yielded efficient standard methods including **time sharing** systems, automatic storage allocators, multilevel schedulers, memory managers, hierarchical file systems. It has yielded well-known operating systems such as **Unix** and Linux, Multics, Mach, VMS, MacOS, OS/2, MS-DOS, and Windows NT. It has produced standard utilities including **text editing systems**, document formatters (*see* **MARKUP LANGUAGES**), **compiler**s, **linkers and loaders**, and device **driver**s. It has produced standard approaches to files and **file** systems. It has produced queueing network model-

ing and **simulation** packages for evaluating performance of real systems; network architectures such as **Ethernet**, FDDI, token ring nets, SNA, and DECNET. It has produced **protocol** techniques embodied in the US Department of Defense protocol suite (**TCP/IP**), virtual circuit **protocol**s, **Internet**, real-time **computer conferencing**, and X.25. It has devoted considerable attention to security and **privacy** issues on the **Internet**.

5 SOFTWARE ENGINEERING

This area deals with the design of large **software** systems that meet **program specification**s and are safe, secure, reliable, and dependable (*see* **SOFTWARE RELIABILITY**). Fundamental questions include: what are the principles behind the development of **program**s and programming systems? How does one make a map of the recurrent actions people take in a domain and use the map to specify a system of hardware and software components to support those actions? How does one prove that a program or system meets its specifications? How does one develop specifications that do not omit important cases and can be analyzed for **software safety**? By what processes do software systems evolve through different generations? By what processes can software be designed for understandability and modifiability? What methods reduce complexity in designing very large software systems? Reflecting the importance of these questions, 17 articles in this *Encyclopedia* have titles that begin with **SOFTWARE**, and several additional articles pertain to the subject.

Three kinds of theory are used for software engineering: **program verification** and proof (which treats forms of proofs and efficient algorithms for constructing them), temporal logic (which is predicate calculus extended to allow statements about time-ordered events—*see* **MODEL CHECKING**), and reliability theory (which relates the overall failure probability of a system to the failure probabilities of its components over time). Supporting mathematics include predicate calculus and axiomatic semantics. **Software engineering** also draws on theory from cognitive psychology.

Models and measurements play important roles in software engineering. There are nine major categories. (1) Specification of the input–output functions of a system: predicate transformers, programming calculi, **abstract data type**s, **object-oriented programming** notations, and Floyd–Hoare axiomatic notations. (2) The process by which a **programmer** constructs software: **structured programming**, stepwise refinement, **modular programming** design, separate compilation, **information hiding**, **dataflow**, software lifecycle models, layers of abstraction. (3) Processes to develop software systems: specification-driven, evolutionary, iterative, formal, and cleanroom. (4) Processes to assist **programmer**s in avoiding or removing **bug**s in their programs: syntax-directed text editors (*see* **TEXT EDITING SYSTEMS**), stepwise program execution tracers, **programming support environments**, and software tools. (5) Methods to improve the reliability of programs: software fault tolerance, N-version programming, multiple-way redundancy, **checkpoint**ing, recovery, information flow security, testing, and quality assurance. (6) Measurement and evaluation of programs. (7) Matching software systems with machine architectures (the more specialized high-performance computers are not general-purpose). (8) Organizational strategies and project management. (9) Software tools and environments.

Like **operating systems**, software engineering is primarily a design specialty. Many of the models noted above have been used in practice under particular designations. Examples of specification languages include PSL2 and IMA JO. Software projects use version control systems to track versions of the modules of the emerging system; examples are RCS and SCCS. Many syntax-directed editors, line editors, screen editors, and programming environments have been implemented; examples are Borland C++ and Turbo Pascal. Methodologies for organizing the software development process go under generic names like HDM or the names of their inventors (e.g. Dijkstra, Jackson, Mills, Yourdon, Weinberg). These process methodologies incorporate procedures for testing, quality assurance, and overall project management (e.g. walk-through, hand simulation, interface checking, program path enumerations for test sets, and event tracing). The US Department of Defense has promulgated additional criteria and testing methods for secure computing. Many software tools have been built to assist with program development, measurement, profiling, text formatting, and **debugging**. A significant number of designers are concerned with the **user interface**; especially of systems on which human lives depend, they seek to organize the user interface to minimize the possibility of human misinterpretation, especially in times of stress. The **Internet**'s growth to over 50 million computers worldwide by 1999 has generated a new specialty in designing computations with component processes on individual computers around the world; it goes under various names such as programming-in-the-large, distributed program composition, and megaprogramming (*see* **COOPERATIVE COMPUTING**).

6 DATABASE AND INFORMATION RETRIEVAL SYSTEMS

This area deals with the organization of large sets of persistent, shared data for efficient query and update.

The term **database** is used for a collection of **record**s that can be updated and queried in various ways. The term *retrieval system* is used for a collection of documents that will be searched and correlated; updates and modifications of documents are infrequent in a retrieval system. Fundamental questions include: What models are useful for representing data elements and their relationships? How can basic operations such as *store*, *locate*, *match*, and retrieve be combined into effective transactions? How can the user interact effectively with these transactions? How can high-level queries be translated into high-performance programs? What machine architectures lead to efficient retrieval and update? How can data be protected against unauthorized access, disclosure, or destruction? How can large databases be protected from inconsistencies due to simultaneous update? How can protection and performance be achieved when the data is distributed among many machines? How can text be indexed and classified for efficient retrieval (*see* **ONLINE INFORMATION SYSTEMS**)?

A variety of theories have been devised and used to study and design database and **information retrieval** systems. These include relational algebra and relational calculus (*see* **RELATIONAL DATABASE**), concurrency theory, serializable transactions, deadlock prevention, synchronized updates, statistical inference, rule-based inference, **sorting**, **searching**, indexing, performance analysis, and **cryptography** as it relates to ensuring privacy of information and **authentication** of persons who stored it or attempt to retrieve it.

Models and associated measurements have been used in at least nine ways. (1) **Data models** for the logical structure of data and relations among data elements: object-based, record-based, and object-relational. (2) Storing **files** for fast retrieval, notably indexes, **trees**, inversions, and **associative memory**. (3) **Access methods**. (4) Query optimization. (5) Concurrency control and recovery. (6) Integrity (consistency) of a database under repeated updates, including concurrent updates of multiple copies (*see* **DATABASE CONCURRENCY CONTROL** and **TRANSACTION PROCESSING**). (7) Database security and **privacy**, including protection from unauthorized disclosure or alteration of data and minimizing statistical inference. (8) Virtual machines associated with query languages (e.g. text, spatial data, pictures, images, rule-sets). (9) **Hypertext** and **multimedia**/hypermedia integration of different kinds of data (text, video, graphics, voice).

A rich set of practical design techniques exists for the database or retrieval system designer. They include general approaches to hierarchical, network, distributed, and **relational database**s, and retrieval systems. They are used in commercial database systems such as

Ingres, System R, dBase, Sybase, and DB-2, and in commercial retrieval systems such as Lexis (*see* LEGAL APPLICATIONS), Osiris, and Medline, and in commercial **hypertext** systems such as NLS, NoteCards, HyperCard, SuperCard, Intermedia, and Xanadu. Many techniques have been created for secure database systems in which data is marked by classification level and compartment and users cannot see data inconsistent with their own classification levels and compartments. There are standard methods of archiving data sets onto long-term media such as tape and **optical storage**, along with methods of migrating large data sets from older to newer media. Large-capacity media such as CD-ROM and DVD have become sufficiently inexpensive that many commercial information products such as literature reviews, selected papers and book extracts, and software magazines are available.

7 ARTIFICIAL INTELLIGENCE AND ROBOTICS

This area deals with the modeling of animal and human cognition, with the ultimate intention of building machine components that mimic or augment them. The behaviors of interest include recognizing sensory signals, sounds, images, and patterns; learning; reasoning; problem-solving; planning; and understanding language. Fundamental questions include: What are basic models of cognition and how might machines simulate them? How can knowledge of the world be represented and organized to allow machines to act reasonably (*see* KNOWLEDGE REPRESENTATION)? To what extent is intelligence described by search, **heuristics**, rule evaluation, inference, deduction, association, and pattern computation? What limits constrain machines that use these methods? What is the relation between human intelligence and machine intelligence? How are sensory and motor data encoded, clustered, and associated? How can machines be organized to acquire new capabilities for action (**machine learning**; *see also* PERCEPTRON), make discoveries, and function well despite incomplete, ambiguous, or erroneous data? How might machines understand natural languages, which are replete with ambiguities, paraphrases, ellipses, allusions, context, unspoken assumptions, and listener-dependent interpretations (*see* NATURAL LANGUAGE PROCESSING)? How can robots see, hear, speak, plan, and act (*see* COMPUTER VISION, ROBOTICS and TELEROBOTICS)?

Nine major branches of theory have been developed for **artificial intelligence**. (1) Logic systems for mechanical reasoning such as first-order logic, **fuzzy logic**, temporal logic, **nonmonotonic logic**, probabilistic logic, deduction, and induction. (2) **Formal methods** for representing and translating knowledge including objects, **grammars**, rules, functions, frames, and semantic networks. (3) Methods for **searching** the very large spaces that arise when enumerating solutions to problems; these include branch-and-bound, alpha-beta, tree pruning, and **genetic algorithm**s. (4) Theories of learning including inference, deduction, analogy, abduction, generalization, specialization, abstraction, concretion, determination, and mutual dependency. (5) **Neural network**s deal with neural interconnection structures, computing responses to stimuli, storing and retrieving patterns, and forming classifications and abstractions. (6) **Computer vision**. (7) **Speech recognition and synthesis**. (8) **Machine translation** of natural languages. (9) **Robotics**. All branches of the theory draw heavily on the related disciplines of structural mechanics, **graph theory**, **formal languages**, **programming linguistics**, logic, probability, philosophy, and psychology.

Models and measurements have been used extensively in various subdomains of intelligent systems and **machine learning**. (1) **Knowledge representation** models include rules, frames, logic, semantic networks, **neural networks**, deduction, forward and backward inference, inheritance, instantiation, resolution, spreading activation, and backward error propagation. (2) Problem-solving models include **case-based reasoning**, qualitative reasoning, constraint-based and opportunistic reasoning, distributed and cooperative reasoning, and nonlinear planning. (3) **Heuristic**s for searching large spaces of alternatives are at the heart of efficient machines for checkers, **computer chess**, and other games of strategy. Heuristic searching has spawned a new field called *evolutionary computation*, methods inspired by the biological principle of the evolution of a population of candidates in which the best ones become predominant. The most well known among these are genetic algorithms (*see also* ARTIFICIAL LIFE). (4) Learning models have improved the ability of machines to solve problems; these include knowledge acquisition from data or experts, learning rules from examples, revising theories, discovering patterns and quantitative laws in data sets, data classification and clustering, and multistrategy learning models. (5) Language understanding models have helped to represent syntactic and semantic forms, find answers to questions, and translate between languages. (6) Speech models are used to produce speech (with good results) and recognize speech (still relatively primitive). (7) **Computer vision** models offer algorithms for finding and recognizing objects in visual fields. (8) **Neural network** models have been tested extensively to evaluate their ability to store patterns, remove noise from patterns, retrieve patterns, generalize patterns, and to store large numbers of patterns without loss or interference (*see* PATTERN RECOGNITION). (9) Models of human memory store large patterns and form associations between them. (10) Knowledge robots (*knowbots* or just *bots*) have been proposed for the **Internet** to make discoveries, classify objects, or deduce description rules for large data sets and time series data.

Artificial intelligence has fostered many implementations and its own design principles. (1) **Logic programming** has been realized in languages, notably Prolog, based on efficient **theorem proving**, rule resolution, and rule evaluation. (2) **Expert systems**, which use an inference engine to process rules stored in a knowledge base to deduce and propose actions, have been successful in a number of well-focused narrow domains such as medical diagnosis, planning, machine repair, system configuration, and financial forecasting. (3) Knowledge engineering environments can be instantiated into **expert systems** when their knowledge bases are loaded with rules and facts for the domain in which they will be used. (4) Natural-language problem-solving systems (e.g. Margie and SHRDLU) have been successful in limited cases (*see* **NATURAL LANGUAGE PROCESSING**). (5) Games of strategy, notably checkers and chess, are played by machines at world-champion levels. (6) **Neural networks** have been used for **pattern recognition**, speech and vision recognition (*see* **COMPUTER VISION**), simulation of human long-term memory, and evaluating student competence. (7) **Fuzzy logic** has been implemented on chips that make control systems in common appliances such as air conditioners and washing machines. (8) Speech synthesizers are widely available. (9) Speech recognizers are becoming common and can already do well with continuous speech by an individual on whose voice the system was trained (*see* **SPEECH RECOGNITION AND SYNTHESIS**). (10) Robots are standard in assembly lines, Mars rovers, and even routine tasks such as household cleaning or lab maintenance. Robot insects have been built as models of ambulatory machines that can perform simple tasks such as cleaning and exploring (*see* **ROBOTICS** and **TELEROBOTICS**). (11) **Genetic algorithms** have been used in numerous applications.

8 COMPUTER GRAPHICS

Computer graphics is concerned with processes for representing physical and conceptual objects and their motions visually on a two-dimensional computer screen or in a three-dimensional hologram. Fundamental questions include: what are efficient methods of representing objects and automatically creating pictures for viewing? For projecting motions of complex objects onto the viewing screen in real time? For displaying data sets to aid human comprehension? For **virtual reality**—i.e. **simulation** of real situations that are difficult to distinguish from the actual thing?

The theory of computer graphics draws heavily on **computational geometry**. It studies algorithms for projecting objects onto the viewing surface, removing hidden lines from the projection, ray-tracing, shading surfaces, showing reflections, and rendering translucent surfaces. It has yielded new algorithms for computing geometric forms. It has used chaos theory to create efficient algorithms for generating complex structures resembling natural formations such as trees, coastlines, clouds, and mountains (*see* **FRACTALS**). Graphics theory also uses color theory, which relates colors formed from light on screens to colors formed from pigments on printed surfaces. Sampling theory is used to reconstruct images from noisy data, filter out unwanted effects, and remove spurious patterns caused by displaying sampled data on pixel-oriented screens. Important supporting areas are Fourier analysis (*see* **FAST FOURIER TRANSFORM**), sampling theory, linear algebra, **graph theory**, **automata theory**, physics, analysis, nonlinear systems, **cybernetics**, and chaos.

Models have been essential for practical graphics systems. Extensive studies have yielded efficient algorithms for rendering and displaying pictures including methods for smoothing, shading, hidden line removal, ray tracing, hidden surfaces, translucent surfaces, shadows, lighting, edges, color maps, representation by **spline**s, rendering, texturing, antialiasing, coherence, **fractals**, **computer animation**, and representing pictures as hierarchies of objects. Models for **virtual reality** and distributed interactive simulation are among the most recent additions.

All the models noted above have been implemented and many are available commercially. For example, graphics algorithms are available in the graphics libraries commonly distributed with graphics **workstation**s. Video editors and sophisticated drawing programs are available for personal computers. Graphics to assist in understanding large scientific data sets are now common as part of high-performance computing, where they are known as "visualization tools" (*see* **DATA MINING** and **SCIENTIFIC VISUALIZATION**). Color models have been used to produce practical hard copy **printers** that print with natural hues and agree with the colors on a graphics screen. Graphics standards (*see* **COMPUTER GRAPHICS: STANDARDS**) have been promulgated (e.g. GKS, PHIGS, VDI), along with standard printer languages (e.g. **PostScript**), specialized graphics packages for individual disciplines (e.g. Mogli for chemistry), and virtual realities on Web pages (e.g. VRML). **Image processing** enhancement systems have been used for years; for example, the Jet Propulsion Laboratory regularly releases NASA pictures of planets, and three-dimensional visualizers are now available to assist doctors interpret CAT and MRI data (*see* **MEDICAL APPLICATIONS** and **MEDICAL IMAGING**).

9 HUMAN-COMPUTER INTERACTION

This area deals with the efficient coordination of action and transfer of information between humans and machines via various human-like sensors and motors, and with information structures that reflect human conceptualizations. Important contributors to this field are **computer graphics** and **user interface**s. Fundamental questions include: What are effective methods for receiving input or presenting output? How can the risk of misperception and subsequent human error be minimized? How can graphics and other tools be used to understand physical phenomena through information stored in data sets? How can people learn from virtual worlds simulated for them?

Theory in human–computer interaction involves cognitive psychology and risk analysis. Cognitive psychology is important to understanding how humans perceive displays and react; it gives designers the means to evaluate whether humans will misinterpret information presented to them, especially in times of stress. Risk analysis is important because many user interfaces control and monitor complex, safety-critical systems. Important supporting areas are statistics, probability, **queueing theory**, and coordination theory.

Models and associated measurements are critical to Human–Computer Interaction (HCI—*see* **HUMAN FACTORS IN COMPUTING**). Computer-Aided Design (CAD) systems have come from the application of these models to the domain of design of mechanical parts; a script for running a manufacturing line can be derived automatically from the CAD database (*see* **COMPUTER-AIDED DESIGN / COMPUTER-AIDED MANUFACTURING**). CAD systems incorporate much experience from different approaches to geometric modeling, the efficient representation of physical shapes by computer **data structures**. Sophisticated **image processing** and enhancement methods have been developed that allow interpretation of photographs from deep-space probes to human CAT and MRI scans (*see* **MEDICAL IMAGING** and **TOMOGRAPHY, COMPUTERIZED**). Principles for designing displays and control panels for ease of use and resistance to human misinterpretation have been deduced from experimental studies.

Design is the central focus in HCI. *Usability engineering* is a name given to the processes of engineering design for **user interface**s. Sophisticated approaches to input, output, interaction, and **multimedia**/hypermedia have been developed. CAD systems are widely used in manufacturing and computer chip design; small versions of these systems are available for personal computers and desktop **workstation**s. The **user interface** design arena has evolved a number of popular standards such as icons and menus for display of possible functions and the **mouse** for use as an **interactive input device**. New user interfaces built on pen-based **portable computers** have come to market and voice-operated computers are not far behind. Flight simulation systems have been used by NASA for years to help train pilots; scaled down versions are available for personal computers. Distributed Interactive Simulation (DIS) systems are regularly used in defense applications to train people how to cope with battlefield situations; the DIS presents each participant with a real-time image of the world seen from that participant's perspective.

10 COMPUTATIONAL SCIENCE

This area deals with explorations in science and engineering that cannot proceed without high-performance computation and communications. Computation is seen as a third approach to science, joining the traditional approaches of theory and experiment. It is being used to address very hard problems, sometimes called "grand challenges." On the computing side, this area deals with general methods of efficiently and accurately solving equations resulting from mathematical models of physical systems; examples include airflow around wings, water flow around obstacles, petroleum flow in the Earth's crust, plasma flow from stars, weather progression, and galactic collisions (*see* **SCIENTIFIC APPLICATIONS**). Within computer science, this area was called "numerical and symbolic computation" for many years; since the mid-1980s, it has borne fruit as the many other scientific and engineering disciplines have incorporated computation into their own processes of investigation and design. Fundamental questions include: How can continuous or infinite processes be accurately approximated by finite discrete processes? How can algorithms minimize the effects of errors arising from these approximations (*see* **APPROXIMATION THEORY**)? How rapidly can a given class of equations, **partial differential equations** for example, be solved for a given level of accuracy? How can symbolic manipulations on equations, such as integration, differentiation, and reduction to minimal terms, be carried out (*see* **COMPUTER ALGEBRA and SYMBOL MANIPULATION**)? How can the answers to these questions be incorporated into efficient, reliable, high-quality **mathematical software** packages? How can data sets generated by these models be most effectively visualized for human comprehension?

This area makes extensive use of mathematics: number theory deals with finite, binary representations of numbers and error propagation in arithmetic calculations; linear algebra deals with solving systems of linear equations that are expressed as matrices (*see* **MATRIX COMPUTATIONS**); **numerical analysis** deals with complex solution algorithms and error propagation and erosion of **precision** when they are used (*see* **ERROR ANALYSIS**, **ERRORS**, and **SIGNIFICANT DIGIT**); nonlinear dynamics deals with chaotic systems. Supporting mathematics includes calculus, real analysis, complex analysis, **discrete mathematics**, and linear algebra. Other areas of theory contribute here as well, notably parallel algorithms, optimizing compilers, distributed computation, organization of large data sets, automatic discovery in data ("**data mining**"), **computational geometry**, graphics (often, in this context, called **scientific visualization**), and statistics (*see* **STATISTICAL APPLICATIONS**). This theory is mingled with the theory in the particular area of science in which a computational investigation is being performed. For example, theories of quantum mechanics are being used to explore a new paradigm of super-fast **quantum computing** and to extend previous studies on the physical **limits of computation** based on classical physics.

Computational scientists are avid modelers. They have experimentally-validated models for: physical problems, discrete approximations, backward error propagation and stability, special methods such as **Fast Fourier transform** and Poisson solvers, **finite element** models, iterative methods (*see* **ITERATION**) and convergence, parallel algorithms (*see* **PARALLEL PROCESSING: ALGORITHMS**), automatic grid generation and refinement, **scientific visualization**, and symbolic integration and differentiation (*see* **COMPUTER ALGEBRA**). As in theory, the models of computing are joined with models from other scientific areas in which a computational investigation is being performed.

Computational scientists have designed many important packages and systems such as Chem, Web, Linpack, Eispack, Ellpack, Macsyma, Mathematica, Maple, and Reduce. They have contributed to models and algorithms in many other disciplines, especially with the "grand challenge" problems such as in physics (e.g. demonstrating existence of certain quarks), aerodynamics and flow dynamics (e.g. numerical simulation of the airflow field around an airplane in flight), chemistry (e.g. designing enzymes and proteins that selectively attack viruses), biology (e.g. joining DNA sequence fragments into the full human genome, microscopy, **tomography**, crystallography, and protein folding), geology (e.g. predicting earthquakes), astronomy (e.g. locating the missing mass of the universe), meteorology (e.g. long-term weather forecasting), earth sciences (e.g. charting the relation between ocean currents and world climate), structural mechanics (e.g. effects of wind and earthquake on stability of buildings, bridges, boats, cars, and planes), electromagnetics (e.g. strengths of fields inside partial insulators, optimal placement of antennas and wave-

guides, propagation of waves in atmosphere and space), and engineering (e.g. interaction between control surfaces and dynamic stress movements in structures). Massive federal support in the USA for these grand challenge problems has helped not only to solve those problems, but to build large parallel supercomputers and fast gigabit networks.

11 ORGANIZATIONAL INFORMATICS

This area deals with information and systems that support the work processes of organizations and coordination among people participating in those processes. **Information systems** are essential to the success of commerce and business in the growing global marketplace. Because most of the work of organizations occurs in human processes, information systems must be designed with an understanding of human work. Therefore this has been a major area of collaboration between computing people, systems engineering, and people in organization disciplines such as management, marketing, decision sciences, management sciences, organizational systems, and anthropology. The fundamental questions come from the organizational disciplines, not from computing, but give considerable inspiration to the associated areas of computing.

Many parts of computing contribute theory to organizational informatics, notably languages, **operating systems**, **networks**, **databases**, **artificial intelligence**, and human–computer communication. Linguistics has provided theories, such as speech acts, which have been used to map work processes. Organizational sciences, such as decision sciences and organizational dynamics, contribute their theory as well. Human factors and cognitive theories from psychology play important roles. Social theories from anthropology have been used to understand work. Models, abstractions, and measurements are even more dominant than theories in this area. Most of the theories noted above are descriptive; thus models and simulations are used commonly to obtain forecasts.

Management Information Systems (**MIS**) is a longstanding commercial arena in which computing systems consisting of **workstation**s, **databases**, **networks**, and reporting systems are deployed in organizations to assist them in their work. Many decision support systems are available commercially; they range from **simulation** and mathematical models that forecast market, economic, and competitive conditions to cooperative work systems that assist people in reaching decisions as groups which collaborate over a network (*see* **GROUPWARE**). A new domain of software—workflow management systems—has become a billion dollar industry.

12 BIOINFORMATICS

This is an emerging area of intimate collaboration between computing and the biological sciences. Investigators are exploring a variety of models and architectures that can revolutionize computing, biology, and medicine. Examples: (1) DNA chemistry has been used to encode and solve combinatorial problems, opening the possibility of chemical computation. (2) New string analyzing algorithms are searching through base-pair sequences in the sprawling network of databases compiled in the Human Genome Project, attempting to construct the overall genome from many fragments. (3) Computer architects and physicians have produced cochlear implants that restore hearing and prototypes of silicon retinas, opening the possibility of practical, bionic prostheses. (4) Computer analyses are used extensively in genetic engineering to determine the proper chemical structures of enzymes to treat medical conditions. (5) New kinds of organic memory devices are being studied that would be capable of storing data at a thousand times current densities or more.

The Future

The pattern of evolution exhibited in the matrix of 12 subareas and three processes continues. The discipline of computing will experience its most rapid development in the domains of significant overlap with other fields such as computational science, cognitive science, library science, organizational informatics, bioinformatics, manufacturing, and architecture. All the subareas will be infused with new concepts and terminology from the areas of major collaboration as well as from many application domains.

As the discipline has matured, important subgroups from each of the 12 subareas have claimed separate professional identities, formed professional groups, codified their professional practice, and started their own literature and communities. Some of these groups, believing that **Information Technology** is more inclusive than Computer Science, have started to claim they are part of the IT Profession rather than the CS Discipline. Some of them, such as software engineering, are coming to see themselves as peers of Computer Science within the IT profession. In addition, a number of other IT-related groups have claimed identities within the IT profession. The "IT family", which consists of Computer Science, its children and its cousins, includes at least two dozen members:

artificial intelligence	knowledge engineering
bioinformatics	management information
cognitive science and	systems
learning theory	multimedia design
computational science	network engineering
computer science	performance evaluation
database engineering	professional education
digital library science	and training
graphics	scientific computing
HCI (human–computer	software architecture
interaction)	software engineering
information science	system security and privacy
information systems	system administration
instructional design	Web service design

Several important conclusions can be drawn from these developments: (1) the IT profession has an enormous scope, including subfields from science, engineering, and business. (2) The players share a common base of science and technology but have distinctive professional practices. (3) The players are willing to identify with the IT field but not with the Computing discipline. (4) Strong leadership from the professional societies will be needed to keep these players united under the common IT identity. (5) The ability of the IT field to resolve broad, systemic problems such as software quality, basic research, and professional lifelong education will require extensive cooperation among the players, cooperation that is endangered if the groups splinter and factionalize (*see* Denning, 1998).

The subarea of **software engineering** illustrates the tensions referred to above. As the IT field matures and touches more people's lives, the demand for computing systems to be demonstrably safe and reliable increases. Despite concerted attention to software engineering since 1968, when the "software crisis" was first declared, and despite enormous advances in tools and methods, public dissatisfaction with software systems is at an all-time high. This is manifested in many ways, from widespread complaints about technical support for hardware and software on home and office systems to fears about failures in safety-critical software systems. Public concern has awakened political interest. It is likely that within a decade government licensing of software engineers will have become a common practice. In mid-1999, the Council of **ACM** declined to have ACM participate with any agency in the development of license tests: it felt that software engineering was still immature and that no known certificate can guarantee that the holder was capable of producing safe and reliable software. The **IEEE Computer Society** disagreed and resolved to participate in the development of licensing tests. Both societies said they want to work toward profession-administered certifications.

The notion of information, which seems central to the discipline, is likely to come under attack. Information is now usually understood as signals or symbols that convey meaning to human observers. Some thinkers have gone further, asserting that information is the common principle underlying physical, biological, human, organizational, and economic systems and, hence, that **information science** is the parent of all these disciplines. There is, however, a problem with information. Whether information is present is an assessment made by each observer; there are no commonly accepted standards for this assessment (Spinoza *et al.*, 1997; Winograd, 1996). To many observers, it seems unscientific to claim that computing science is based on a principle that is fundamentally subjective. Some have claimed that the belief that information is a scientific quantity has catalyzed systemic problems in software quality, education and design (Talbott, 1998). (Even **Claude Shannon** and Warren Weaver, who are credited with formalizing information in their mathematical theory of communication, disclaimed any connection to the way "information" is understood in everyday life; their definition does not apply to the symbols processed by programs.)

The correctness of a program, understood abstractly as a mathematical function, can be assessed based on assertions about the input, intermediate, and output data processed by the program; none of this relies on a formal definition of information at all. The correctness of interactions between humans and computing systems, on the other hand, often depends heavily on the assessments people make about the system, and information is an allowable assessment. Thus we would be on much safer ground by claiming that programs process data and that information is an assessment arising in the interactions between programs and people.

Bibliography

1968. National Academy of Sciences. *The Mathematical Sciences: A Report.* Publication 1681. Washington, DC.

1969. Hamming, R.W. "One Man's View of Computer Science," ACM Turing Lecture, *Journal of the ACM*, **16**, *1* (January), 1–5.

1970. Wegner, P. "Three Computer Cultures—Computer Technology, Computer Mathematics, and Computer Science," in *Advances in Computers 10* (ed. W. Freiberger), Ch. 2, 7–78. New York: Academic Press.

1971. Amarel, S. 1971, "Computer Science: A Conceptual Framework for Curriculum Planning," *Comm. of the ACM*, **14**, *6* (June), 391–401.

1980. Arden, B. (ed.) *What Can be Automated?—The Computer Science and Engineering Research Study.* Cambridge, MA: MIT Press.

1989. Denning, P., Comer, D. E., Gries, D., Mulder, M. C., Tucker, A., Turner, A. J., and Young, P. R. "Computing as a Discipline," *Comm. of the ACM*, **32**, *1* (January), 9–23.

1989. Drucker, P. *The New Realities.* New York: Harper.

1992. Hartmanis, J. and Lin, H. *Computing the Future.* Washington, DC: National Academy Press.

1996. Tucker, A. Jr., and Wegner, P. "Computer Science and Engineering: The Discipline and its Impact," in *Handbook of Computer Science and Engineering* (ed. A. Tucker, Jr.), Ch. 1. Boca Raton, FL: CRC Press.

1996. Winograd, T. *Bringing Design to Software.* Reading, MA: Addison-Wesley.

1997. Winograd, T., "The Design of Interaction," in *Beyond Calculation: The Next 50 Years of Computing* (eds. P. Denning and R. Metcalfe), 149–162. New York: Copernicus Books.

1997. Denning, P., and Metcalfe, R. (eds.) *Beyond Calculation: The Next 50 Years of Computing.* New York: Copernicus Books.

1997. Spinoza, C., Flores, F., and Dreyfus, H. *Disclosing New Worlds.* Cambridge, MA: MIT Press.

1998. Denning, P. "Computing the Profession," *Educom Review*, **33** (Nov–Dec), 26–39, 46–59.

1998. Talbott, S. "There is No Such Thing as Information," *Netfuture 81.* Available from http://www.oreilly.com/~stevet/netfuture/.

1999. Denning, P. *Talking Back to the Machine: Computers and Human Aspiration.* New York: Copernicus Books.

Peter J. Denning

COMPUTER SCIENCE EDUCATION

See EDUCATION IN COMPUTER SCIENCE; and EDUCATION IN COMPUTER ENGINEERING.

COMPUTER SCIENCE— Ph.D. STATISTICS

For articles on related subjects *see* COMPUTER SCIENCE; COMPUTING RESEARCH ASSOCIATION; EDUCATION IN COMPUTER ENGINEERING; EDUCATION IN COMPUTER SCIENCE; and WOMEN AND COMPUTING.

The first academic computer science departments in the USA were formed in the mid-1960s. Some 30 years later, in 1998, more than 175 departments of computer science and computer engineering granted Ph.D.s in the USA and Canada. (Several of these in the past decade have changed their name from Computer Science to Computer Science and Engineering, due in part to the move of some departments to engineering colleges.) It is estimated that another thousand colleges and universities award undergraduate or master's degrees in computer science.

In September 1998, the North American Ph.D.-granting departments had about 2,700 tenure-track faculty members. Of these, about 44% were full professors, 36% associate professors, and 20% assistant professors. The percentage of assistant professors is still higher than in most science or engineering disciplines, but the field has matured greatly in the past decade—both chronologically and in terms of influence. However, the proportion of full professors is still far below that in older fields such as mathematics or physics. This should change over time.

Ph.D. production in computer science grew substantially in the 1980s and then stabilized in the 1990s. The field now produces about 900–1000 new Ph.D.s each

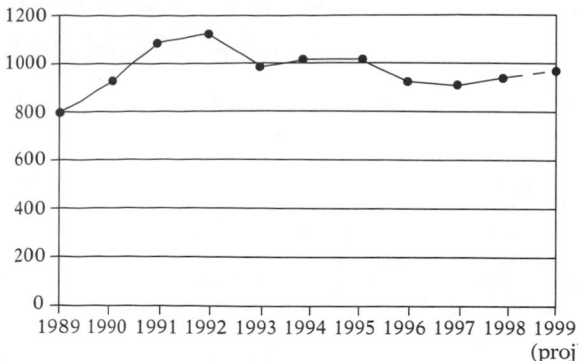

Figure 1. Computer science and engineering Ph.D. production in the USA and Canada from 1989 to 1999. (Graph courtesy of CRA taken from CRA Website given at the end of this article.)

year (*see* Figure 1). In 1998, about 42% of the new Ph.D.s took positions in industry (an increase over prior years), about 32% took positions in academia (a decrease relative to historical patterns), and the rest went overseas, took positions in government, etc.

Employment patterns in computer science and engineering change rapidly. In the early 1990s there was a considerable oversupply of Ph.D.s. But in the late 1990s there was a substantial undersupply, mainly due to the growth of the Internet and the World Wide Web which greatly increased the demand from industry. This growth shows no signs of abating as we enter the twenty-first century.

In 1998 14% of the new Ph.D.s were female—this percentage has been between 10% and 14% for over 20 years. The field continues to do even worse with regard to underrepresented groups: out of the 933 reported Ph.D.s granted in 1998 in computer science and engineering, 10 went to African Americans, a number which has not changed greatly for a number of years, and 6 to Hispanics, a sharp decrease from 27 just two years earlier. On the other hand, non-resident aliens received 35% of the Ph.D.s awarded in 1996, reflecting continuing interest on the part of international students in graduate computer science programs in North America.

At the undergraduate level, computer science saw steady growth in both service courses and majors from the early 1970s to about 1985. This growth was so strong that departments had difficulty keeping up with it. From 1985 through the early 1990s, there was a precipitous decrease in enrollments. Some viewed this as a welcome technical correction that brought enrollments down to a manageable level. Recently, however, enrollments have once again begun to rise dramatically. In fact, the number of new undergraduate majors doubled in the years from 1995 to 1998 from

about 10,000 to about 20,000. This is no doubt due to both the market place and the now ubiquitous World Wide Web (*q.v.*).

Data in this article is taken or extrapolated from the Computing Research Association's annual Taulbee survey of computer science departments. The 1998 CRA Taulbee survey appeared in *Computing Research News*, **11**, *2* (March 1999). The surveys are conducted by the Computing Research Association (CRA—*q.v.*), which serves to represent research in computer science and engineering. Further information can be obtained by writing to the Computing Research Association, 1875 Connecticut Ave. NW, Suite 718, Washington, DC 20009-5728, or by visiting their Website at http://www.cra.org/statistics/.

David Gries and Gregory Andrews

COMPUTER SECURITY

See COMPUTER CRIME; and DATA SECURITY.

COMPUTER SOCIETIES

For articles on related subjects *see* ASSOCIATION FOR COMPUTING MACHINERY; BRITISH COMPUTER SOCIETY; INSTITUTE FOR ELECTRONIC AND ELECTRICAL ENGINEERS—COMPUTER SOCIETY; INTERNATIONAL FEDERATION FOR INFORMATION PROCESSING; and LITERATURE OF COMPUTING. (See also Appendix to this article.)

History

There were no computing societies before the end of the Second World War, but within a year of the 1946 public demonstrations of ENIAC (*q.v.*) and the Harvard Mark I (*q.v.*), two US groups, one mainly mathematicians interested in the applications of computers and the other mainly electrical engineers interested in building computers, separately began to discuss the need for computing associations. In 1947 those interested in applications had formed the forerunner organization that quickly became The Association for Computing Machinery (ACM). They modeled it on the American Mathematical Society and in its aspirations and form it embodied the concerns of those interested in the algorithms of computing and of using computing machinery to solve them. A few months before this, the hardware people in both the American Institute of Electrical Engineers (AIEE) and its rival, the Institute of Radio Engineers (IRE), created the forerunners of the IEEE-Computer Society (IEEE-CS). Their organizational models were those electrical engineering societies.

In spite of differences of organization and perspective, they all set improved communications about computing as their goals and sponsored publications, conferences, meetings, and local chapters. All had academic roots, but the engineers had somewhat stronger links to industry. However, membership offered different career opportunities to those in the different groups. The commercially minded saw the value of discovering what others were doing from publications and meetings, while the academics saw the career benefits of a new area in which to teach, do research, publish, and gain status from participation and office in a scholarly association.

There was some cooperation. One major example was the cooperative formation of the International Federation for Information Processing (IFIP) and AFIPS (*see* Appendix to this article). In 1956 a group led by Isaac L. Auerbach proposed an international conference on computing which led in 1960 to the formation of IFIP under the UNESCO umbrella. To satisfy the UNESCO requirement that each country in IFIP had to be represented by only one national group, the AIEE, IRE and ACM joined with nine smaller computing societies to form AFIPS which became the US representative to IFIP.

The other major example of cooperation was in sponsoring conferences. In 1951 the AIEE, IRE, and ACM formed a National Joint Computing Committee which sponsored increasingly successful and profitable large conferences. From 1951 to 1972 there were two joint computer conferences a year, the Spring Joint Computer Conference in the eastern USA and the Fall Joint Computer Conference in the western USA. (The sole exception was 1965 when there was no spring conference because the IFIP Congress was held in New York that year.) From 1961 on AFIPS took over the sponsorship of these conferences. In 1973 the two joint computer conferences were merged into a single National Computer Conference which lasted until 1987, when competition from commercial conferences caused its demise.

For the next quarter-century computing societies grew in size and in number with the computing industry. The societies were vigorous and vital and their publications and conferences contributed to the development of computing. If you were a computing professional, you were expected to be a member of a computing society. New developments were almost always revealed at a major society meeting or were described in a paper published in a society journal or both.

The two major US computing societies were ACM and IEEE-CS which resulted from the merger of AIEE with IRE. They both took all of computing as their fiefdoms, had many internal specialty subdivisions, and were rooted in the academic departments of computer science and electrical engineering and in the labora-tories of the major computer and electrical engineering companies. Indeed, these two societies contributed greatly to the acceptance of computer science as an academic discipline. The members cooperated; the headquarters competed.

At least 50 similar computing societies have been established in foreign countries. None of them was as large as the two major US societies and all of them reflected their national traditions in shape, form, and rules. The British Computer Society (BCS) was by far the largest of these and was unique in obtaining a Royal Charter which effectively gave it authority over all British computing and thus restricted the formation of competing specialized societies. The societies formed in nations with authoritarian governments toed the government line more than those with more democratic governments. Some small nations with few computers and no real computing industry apparently formed computing societies simply to join the other IFIP members.

Current Status

There are separate articles in this Encyclopedia describing some of the major computer societies (see the cross-references at the beginning of this article). In addition, the Appendix at the end of this article contains brief descriptions of a number of other societies and federations of societies. Lists of other societies will be found in the article on IFIP and in the description of AFIPS in the Appendix.

Almost from their inception ACM and IEEE-CS sought to be international in scope, seeking foreign members, establishing foreign chapters, and attempting various ways of affiliating with foreign computing societies. Partly in fear of US computing hegemony, foreign societies have formed societies of societies, such as the Council of European Professional Informatics Societies (CEPIS—*see* Appendix) and the South East Asia Regional Computing Confederation (SEARCC—*see* Appendix).

US tax rules were at first believed to prohibit scientific and technical societies from lobbying or attempting to influence legislation, but clever legal, organizational, and financial methods have been found by means of which computing societies can make their voices heard in Congress. Both ACM and IEEE-CS have Washington offices to facilitate this. The Computing Research Association (CRA—*q.v.*) includes influencing government policy in its goals. The recently formed Internet Society (*see* Appendix) makes no bones about its intent to deal with government control of the Internet.

With much of their conference activity taken over by commercial operators of conferences and with increasing competition from commercial publishers, the societies are struggling to make themselves meaningful and useful to their members by increasing the number of their publications and turning the content more toward what computing practitioners want to read rather than what computing academics want to write. They all see the cheap and instant communication possibilities of electronic publication and the World Wide Web (*q.v.*) as panaceas.

At first, the societies were controlled and dominated by their volunteer academic founders, but now the paid professional staffs have taken over, and most computing societies, like most universities, are actually under the real control of a professional staff in spite of the volunteer officers' protests to the contrary. These entrenched groups, determined to maintain stability and their own authority and perquisites, will not readily accept whatever drastic and violent changes become necessary for the survival of computing societies.

Eric A. Weiss

Appendix of Computer Societies and Federations

AMERICAN FEDERATION OF INFORMATION PROCESSING SOCIETIES (AFIPS)

The American Federation of Information Processing Societies (AFIPS) was an association of, at its maximum, 15 major US computing and computer-related societies. It was an important part of the computing world from its formation in 1961 to its demise in 1990, at which time the total number of individual members of its 11 constituent societies amounted to 240,000. From its beginning it ran the extremely profitable Joint Computer Conferences, at its peak returning proceeds amounting to over a million dollars a year to its three founding societies, the Association for Computing Machinery, the Institute of Radio Engineers, and the American Institute of Electrical Engineers and their successors. It also was the official US representative to the International Federation for Information Processing and other international gatherings. At first its conferences were true technical meetings, perhaps the most significant in the USA, where important scientific papers were presented, discussed and later published as AFIPS Proceedings. The accompanying exhibitions of current and future hardware were initially secondary to the technical sessions, but after about a decade the shows' income became so huge that they dominated the conferences, overshadowing the technical sessions and causing potential authors to divert significant papers to constituent society meetings and publications. At the same time, outside entrepreneurs organized competing conferences and exhibits aimed at parts of the computing world rather than all of it and at those who had buying authority and financial interests in computing rather than those who had scientific, educational, and professional interests in the field. As a consequence of these changes, the income to AFIPS from the National Computer Conferences (NCC) (which succeeded the Joint Computer Conferences) dropped, resulting in the end of the NCC in 1987 and of AFIPS itself three years later.

AFIPS's accomplishments were largely transient: operating conferences and seminars, providing funds to its constituent societies, honoring individuals with awards and representing the US internationally. Its lasting monuments are few; the early conference proceedings, a few dated volumes from AFIPS Press, startup support for the Charles Babbage Institute (*q.v.*), a brief but extensive oral history project at the Smithsonian Institution, and the tradition of the annual Harry M. Goode memorial award. Its major continuing contribution is the *Annals of the History of Computing*, one of the few scholarly periodicals devoted to the history of a scientific or engineering field, which AFIPS founded and directly supported for the first eight years of its life. The *Annals*, like the Goode award, has been continued by the IEEE Computer Society.

The Special Issue of the *Annals of the History of Computing*, Vol. **8**, No. *3*, July 1986, gives a thorough account of AFIPS, written and published at the peak of its success.

The end of AFIPS left no organization to represent US computing in IFIP and other international venues. To fill this gap ACM and the IEEE Computer Society formed a new joint committee, FOCUS (Federation on Computing in the United States), in 1991 to represent the USA in IFIP. FOCUS was dissolved in 1999 when ACM and IEEE-CS both became members of IFIP.

In 1989, shortly before the end of AFIPS, its constituent societies were: American Society for Information Science (ASIS), Association for Computational Linguistics (ACL), Association for Computing Machinery (ACM), Association for Educational Data Systems (AEDS), Data Processing Management Association (DPMA, now AITP—*see* below), IEEE Computer Society (IEEE-CS), Instrument Society of America (ISA), Society for Computer Simulation (SCS), Society for Industrial and Applied Mathematics (SIAM), and the Society for Information Display (SID).

Its presidents are listed in Appendix V.

AMERICAN ASSOCIATION FOR ARTIFICIAL INTELLIGENCE (AAAI)

This 7,000 member society was founded in 1979 and is devoted to the promotion and advancement of artificial intelligence (AI—*q.v.*). It sponsors conferences, has four specialist subgroups, and publishes three journals (*Machine Learning, Artificial Intelligence,* and *AI in Medicine Journal*), plus *AI Magazine* and an annual directory. The AAAI Press in cooperation with The MIT Press co-publishes books and Technical Reports which are distributed internationally by The MIT Press.

Its address is 445 Burgess Drive, Menlo Park, CA 94025, USA; info@aaai.org, `http://www.aaai.org`.

Its presidents since its inception are listed in Appendix V.

ASSOCIATION FOR THE ADVANCEMENT OF COMPUTING IN EDUCATION (AACE)

This international society of 6,800 members was formed in 1981 to advance teaching and learning through the use of information technology. It encourages scholarly inquiry and disseminates the results and their applications through publications and conferences. It publishes six peer-reviewed journals in addition to the membership magazine, *Educational Technology Review,* and has topical and regional divisions, societies, and chapters.

Its address is PO Box 2966, Charlottesville, VA 22902, USA; aace@virginia.edu, `http://www.aace.org`.

ASSOCIATION FRANÇAISE POUR LA CYBERNETIQUE ECONOMIQUE ET TECHNIQUE (AFCET)

This society was formed in 1969 by the merger of the Association Française d'Informatique et de Recherche Operationnelle (AFIRO), Association Française de Régulation et d'Automatisme (AFRA), and Association Française d'Instrumentation et de Contrôlé (AFIC). It was dedicated to the progress of computer science, as well as the sciences of decision, organization, and systems. It was the official French representative in the International Federation for Information Processing, the Council of European Professional Informatics Societies, and the International Federation for Automatic Control (IFAC).

In 1998 AFCET was dissolved as a result of bankruptcy. However, in 1999 a new learned society, l'Association Française des Sciences Technologies de l'Information, was being organized to represent French computer scientists (*see* `http://asti.asso.fr`).

ASSOCIATION OF INFORMATION TECHNOLOGY PROFESSIONALS (AITP)

AITP is an international association of 7,000 professional managers of information processing and 6,000 students. It traces its start to the founding of the National Machine Accountants Association (NMAA) in 1951 before any electronic digital computer had come into commercial use and a "machine accountant" was a person who used punched card (*q.v.*) machines for accounting. In 1962 NMAA became the Data Processing Management Association (DPMA), and in that year initiated a certification program for computer management personnel which ultimately was taken over by the Institute for Certification of Computer Professionals (*q.v.*). In 1997 AITP took its current name.

To encourage high standards of performance and promote a professional attitude among its members, AITP conducts an educational and publication program which includes the sponsorship of conferences. Its local chapters are organized into 12 geographical regions which also sponsor meetings, seminars, conferences, and educational events.

Its address is 315 South Northwest Highway, Suite 200, Park Ridge, IL 60068, USA; `http://www.aitp.org`.

Its presidents since its inception are listed in Appendix V.

CHINESE COMPUTER SOCIETY

Founded in 1962, this society of 28,000 individuals and organizations promotes the study of computer sciences, conducts research, organizes children's programs, offers consulting services, and fosters scientific and technical exchanges among its members. Its address is 6 S. Kexueyuan Road, Zhongguancun, Beijing 100080, People's Republic of China.

COUNCIL OF EUROPEAN PROFESSIONAL INFORMATICS SOCIETIES (CEPIS)

This society of 29 societies from 24 European nations was formed to be the voice of its member societies' 150,000 individual members in support of informatics in Europe. The nations represented are Austria, Cyprus, Czech Republic, Denmark, Estonia, Finland, Germany, Greece, Hungary, Iceland, Ireland, Italy, Latvia, Lithuania, Netherlands, Norway, Poland, Portugal, Slovak Republic, Slovenia, Spain, Sweden, Switzerland and the United Kingdom. It encourages cooperation among its members and tries to influence informatics legislation. Its sub-groups are: Information Retrieval, Legal and Security Issues, Software Engineering, Intellectual Property, Information Skills Structure, and a Continuous Learning Programme. It takes care that its publications and other activities do not compete with or conflict with those of its members.

Its address is 7 Mansfield Mews, London W1M 9FJ, UK; `http://www.cepis.org`.

CENTRO LATINOAMERICANO DE ESTUDIOS INFORMATICA (CLEI)

This is an association of 12 computing societies in South and Central America. It is a corresponding member of IFIP. The countries represented are Argentina, Bolivia, Brazil, Chile, Colombia, Ecuador, Mexico, Panama, Paraguay, Peru, Uruguay, Venezuela.

Its address is c/o Prof. Oscar Meza, Depto, de Computacion y T.I., Universidad Simon Bolivar, Apartado 809000 Caracas, Venezuela; meza@usb.ve, http://www.clei.cl.

GESELLSCHAFT FÜR INFORMATIK e.V. (GI)

The German Informatics Society of 20,000 individual and 300 corporate members was founded in 1969 to promote informatics and its applications in research and education. In 1983 it joined the International Federation for Information Processing, replacing the original member for Germany, Deutsche Arbeitsgemeinschaft für Rechenanlagen (DARA). GI is a member of the Council of European Professional Informatics Societies, the Deutscher Verband Technisch-Wissenschaftlicher Vereine, which comprises all German technological associations, and the Werner-von-Siemens-Ring foundation. Through the Deutsche Informatik Akademie GmbH, GI offers a continuing education program. It is one of the supporters of the International Conference and Research Center for Computer Science, a research and education center, and Bundeswettbewerb Informatik, an annual Federal contest in informatics.

It sponsors and participates in national and international scientific events, cooperates in standards development, issues guidelines and estimates, and informs a broad public through its publications and activities. Its nine divisions contain more than 150 committees and groups. Thirty-five regional groups organize local events. Fifteen to 20 symposia, lecture meetings, and seminars are held each year by GI and its divisions which also issue, in German and usually through commercial publishers, the following: *Informatik-Spektrum*, GI's bimonthly organ; *LOG IN*, a bimonthly for teachers; and *KI*, *IT+ TI*, and *Wirtschaftsinformatik*, divisional publications.

Its address is Ahrstrasse 45, D-53175 Bonn, Germany; gs@gi-ev.de, http://www.gi-ev.de.

Its presidents since its inception are listed in Appendix V.

INFORMATION PROCESSING SOCIETY OF JAPAN (IPSJ)

IPSJ is a society of almost 29,000 members formed in 1960 to be the sole Japanese representative to the International Federation for Information Processing and to promote and develop information processing in Japan. Its membership reached almost 32,000 in 1992 but since then has declined. IPSJ and its 27 Special Interest Groups hold symposia, lecture meetings, and seminars. It publishes the monthly *Joho Shoi* (the Journal) in Japanese and *Transactions* chiefly in Japanese with English abstracts. A handbook for specialists and a series of information processing booklets for all computer-concerned people have also been published in Japanese. IPSJ also makes several annual awards to individuals.

Its address is 7th Floor, Shibaura-Maekawa Bldg., m 3-16-20 Shibaura-Minato-ku, Tokyo 108-0023, Japan; http://www.ipsj.or.jp.

The presidents of the society are listed in Appendix V.

INTERNET SOCIETY (ISOC)

This international association of organizations and individuals is the leading organization for the technical, economic, and policy development of the Internet (*q.v.*). It was formed in 1992 by an unusually eclectic group of about 60 founding organizations from all over the world whose commonality is a deep interest in and concern for the Internet. While its current approximately 200 organizational members are almost entirely corporations, ISOC also includes four universities, two professional computing societies (ACM and IEEE-CS), and some government agencies. Since its founding it has admitted about 6,000 individuals as members and about 400 student members. One of its aims is to support and defend the Internet against all enemies, both foreign and domestic.

It charters several groups through which it controls the growth, technical change, standards, and evolution of the Internet. It takes strong public and lobbying positions with regard to Internet legislation throughout the world and attempts to harmonize and consolidate international actions and positions on Internet issues. It sponsors annual conferences and educational and training workshops and publishes a monthly electronic newsletter, *The ISOC Forum*, and the bi-monthly paper magazine, *OnTheInternet*.

Its address is 12020 Sunrise Valley Drive, Suite 210, Reston, VA 20191-3429, USA; http://www.isoc.org.

Its chief executives since its inception are listed in Appendix V.

INTERNATIONAL SOCIETY FOR TECHNOLOGY IN EDUCATION (ISTE)

This society of 12,000 members was formed in 1989 by the merger of the International Council for Computers in Education and the International Association for Computing in Education. It is a professional organization for educators who use computers and is dedicated to the improvement of education through the use and integration of technology.

It publishes *The Computing Teacher* journal, *Update* newsletter, the *Journal of Research on Computing in Education*, the journals and newsletters of several *Special Interest Groups*, and ISTE books and courseware.

Its address is 1787 Agate Street, Eugene, OR 97403-1923, USA; cust-svc@iste.org, http://www.iste.org.

Its presidents since its inception are listed in Appendix V.

SOCIETY FOR COMPUTER SIMULATION INTERNATIONAL (SCSI)

This 2,000 member society began in 1952 as ''The Simulation Council'' and adopted its current name in 1972. It is devoted to applications of computer modeling and simulation (*q.v.*) in all technical and scientific disciplines, the use of microcomputers and supercomputers in simulation, the development of simulation languages for discrete and continuous simulation, and simulation methodology and validation. It sponsors conferences and seminars and publishes a monthly journal, *Simulation*, and a quarterly scholarly journal, *Transactions of the Society for Computer Simulation International*. The proceedings of its conferences are gathered into hardbound books in the *Simulation Series*.

Its address is P.O. Box 17900, San Diego, CA 92177-7900, USA.

Its presidents since its inception are listed in Appendix V.

SOUTH EAST ASIA REGIONAL COMPUTER CONFEDERATION (SEARCC)

SEARCC is a loose confederation of 14 national computer societies formed in 1976 to foster the development and beneficial use of information technology (IT—*q.v.*) in the region and provide meeting opportunities for IT professionals. The societies are from Australia, Hong Kong, India, Indonesia, Japan, Malaysia, New Zealand, Pakistan, the Philippines, Singapore, Sri Lanka, the Republic of China, Thailand, and Canada. It publishes the papers presented in its annual regional conferences, sponsors two international competitions, Schools Software and Micromouse, as well as regional conferences and interest groups. It is an affiliate member of the International Federation for Information Processing.

Its address is The Singapore Arts Centre Co. Ltd., 2 Raffles Link #01-04, Marina Bayfront, Singapore 0103, sgsearcc@pacific.net.sg.

Its presidents since its inception are listed in Appendix V.

USENIX ASSOCIATION

The full name of this 6,000 member association, formed in 1975, is *The UNIX and Advanced Computing Systems Professional and Technical Association*. Its membership includes individuals, students, and educational and commercial institutions. It is dedicated to practical problem-solving, fostering research that works, rapid communication of results, and to providing a neutral forum for the exercise of critical thought and airing of technical issues.

It publishes a bi-monthly newsletter *;login:*, sponsors an annual System Administration conference, LISA, as well as frequent symposia and technical meetings. It publishes the proceedings of these gatherings, and, with the MIT Press, publishes *Computing Systems*, a refereed technical quarterly.

The address of USENIX is 2560 Ninth Street, Suite 215, Berkeley, CA 94710, USA; office@usenix.org, http://www.usenix.org.

Its presidents since its inception are listed in Appendix V.

COMPUTER SOCIETY

See INSTITUTE FOR ELECTRONIC AND ELECTRICAL ENGINEERS—COMPUTER SOCIETY.

COMPUTER SYSTEM

For articles on related subjects *see* ARITHMETIC-LOGIC UNIT; BUS; CACHE MEMORY; CENTRAL PROCESSING UNIT; CHANNEL; COMMUNICATIONS AND COMPUTERS; DIGITAL COMPUTER; DISTRIBUTED SYSTEMS; INFORMATION SYSTEMS; INPUT–OUTPUT CONTROL SYSTEM; INTERRUPT; MEMORY; MEMORY HIERARCHY; NETWORKS, COMPUTER; OPERATING SYSTEMS; and SOFTWARE.

A modern computer system is one of the foremost technological achievements of humankind. This is due to its remarkable speed, very high reliability, and almost limitless versatility. For example, in the year 1999 a large mainframe computer could execute over 800 million instructions per second (MIPS) when processing business workloads, and certain supercomputers (*q.v.*) designed to handle numerically intensive scientific and engineering work can perform more than a trillion arithmetic operations per second. Even

Figure 1. A typical mainframe computer room in the era before large scale integration allowed a considerable reduction in the size of the CPU and memory modules in the center of the photo.

small personal computers (*q.v.*) can execute several million instructions per second.

The versatility accompanying this processing power is due to *programming*, meaning that a *single machine* with appropriate programs (software) can do such diverse tasks as complex engineering computations pertaining to the design of high-speed aircraft, preparation of the payroll for thousands of employees, or keeping track of inventory for a whole chain of retail stores. The term "general purpose" is then a fair one to characterize the capabilities of most computers, although of course not every particular machine is actually used for such a wide variety of tasks.

Because it is most easily visualized, a description of the equipment or hardware subsystem will be discussed first, followed by the software subsystem and how it appears to users.

The Hardware Subsystem

Fig. 1 shows the exterior appearance of a typical very large system's processor complex. Fig. 2 schematically shows the major hardware components of a mainframe computer that can be classified into a number of categories described below.

PERIPHERALS

Peripherals are hardware devices that change information from one physical form to another, linking the computer with its environment. They include keyboards, video screens, printers, plotters, and various interactive input devices (*q.v.*), such as the trackball and mouse (*q.v.*).

STORAGE DEVICES

The same devices store two distinct types of information: (1) data and (2) instructions (programs). The most elementary unit of stored information is the bit (a 0 or 1 value). For most purposes, a *byte*, which is a group of 8 bits representing 256 possible values, or a character of the system's character set, is treated as an elementary unit of storage. Because storage can be very large, certain multiples of a byte are typically used to express storage capacities:

$$KB \text{ (kilobyte)} = 1024 \text{ bytes}$$
$$MB \text{ (megabyte)} = 1024 \text{ KB}$$
$$GB \text{ (gigabyte)} = 1024 \text{ MB}$$
$$TB \text{ (terabyte)} = 1024 \text{ GB}$$
$$PB \text{ (petabyte)} = 1024 \text{ TB}$$

For economical and technological reasons, storage devices come in many sizes, speeds, and costs. They range from inexpensive, low-capacity, slow devices (e.g. diskettes—*q.v.*) to larger, more expensive, faster ones (e.g. hard disks—*q.v.*) suitable for permanent storage of the information of large commercial, governmental, or educational enterprises.

From a user viewpoint, most storage is organized into *files* (*q.v.*) that are retained in the system unless

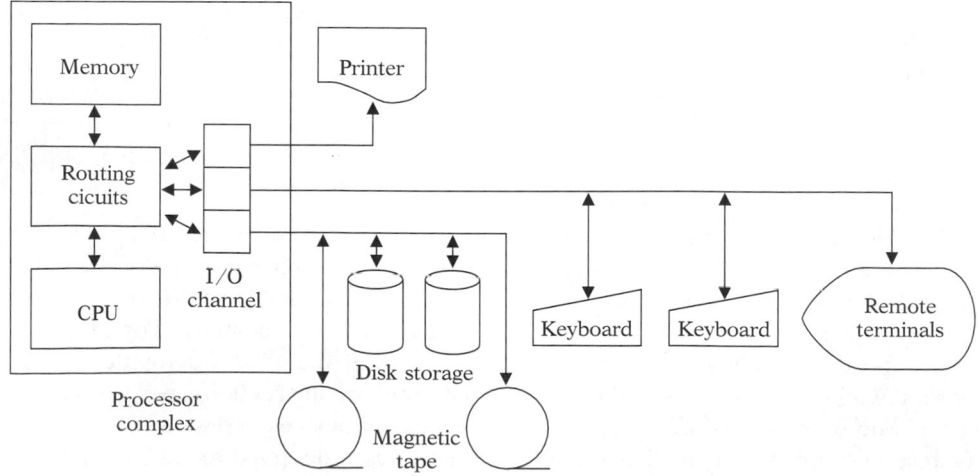

Figure 2. A schematic diagram showing the interconnections of the processor and peripheral components of a typical mainframe computer system.

explicitly deleted or replaced. This requires nonvolatile media, such as disk or tape. "Nonvolatile" means that stored contents are retained even if electrical power is removed by shutdown or failure.

Storage with faster access (by a factor of 10,000 or more) than disk storage is physically composed of semiconductor chips and is used in the computer's *main storage* or *memory*. Although far faster than file storage, semiconductor storage is far more expensive per byte and is held to smaller capacities (measured in megabytes). Semiconductor memory is *volatile*, meaning that its contents are lost when its power is removed. Although this sounds ominous, in fact it is not, since its contents are needed only during actual processing, and any information that must be retained longer is easily copied to nonvolatile file storage. Because of its speed, main storage and a related, even faster semiconductor type, called *cache memory* (*q.v.*), has the special "privilege" of being directly accessible by fast central processing units (CPUs).

CENTRAL PROCESSING UNITS (CPUs)

The term "CPU" derives from the fact that for a long time each computer system contained only one processor, and this is the case even today for many smaller systems. The CPU is the heart of the computer system. It does its work directed by *instructions*, most of which operate on data.

The operation performed by each instruction is usually quite primitive. The repertoire of instruction types (e.g. add, subtract, test-for-sign), is called the machine's *instruction set* (*q.v.*) or *instruction repertoire* and may contain about 200 instructions. But some RISC machines have as few as, say, 64 instructions in their set, and even this is larger than is theoretically required (*see* REDUCED INSTRUCTION SET COMPUTER). The design of a machine's instruction set is an arcane subject with many speed, cost, and even esthetic factors involved. The instruction set and associated items constitute the native *machine language* of a computer.

CPU circuitry is responsible for execution of the instructions; this includes an adder (*q.v.*), augmented by shift and control circuits that together implement the system's arithmetic and processing operations. The ability to execute instructions, while necessary, is *not* sufficient to form an operable computer. Also needed is a control mechanism to *sequence* from one instruction to the next in a *program* (*q.v.*) of instructions stored in the computer's main storage. Specific instruction sequences express the required function of the program (payroll, inventory, etc.).

Although not an exact analogy, the instruction set is akin to a set of musical notes, as is found on the keys of a piano, and a program is like the score for a particular song. In the case of music, the human performer "reads" the next note from the score, then invokes that note from the instrument, then repeats the process for the next note, etc. In the computer case, the CPU contains *program control circuitry* that automatically reads or accesses the stored program's next instruction, and then invokes the computer's execution circuitry to execute the instruction. This cycle is then repeated automatically. During execution, many instructions call for data, which is held in the same main storage as the program (*see* STORED PROGRAM CONCEPT). Main storage appears as a long list of memory cells, each with a unique location number called its *address*. So main storage is addressed for instructions that in turn address it for data.

Also essential for program control are provisions for testing conditions on input or computed data and, depending on the test outcome, *branching* or jumping from strict progression in the stored program sequence to a new program segment. Using branching, a single segment of stored program may be used repetitively millions of times in the same program, with certain necessary program-modifiable differences in each use.

All CPU functions use the fastest kind of storage—the CPU *registers* (*q.v.*)—usually built from the same circuitry used for processing. The registers are a sort of scratchpad on which the CPU jots down results, especially those used frequently in local parts of the program. Some register contents are later transferred to main storage and even to file storage. Logically, registers function identically to individual units of main memory, but because their much greater speed comes at relatively high cost, the number of registers used in a given computer is always a small fraction of the number of main memory cells.

ROUTING AND CONTROL CIRCUITRY

Routing circuits include the networks and "buses" that direct the flow of information between various functional parts of the hardware subsystem (*see* BUS and CHANNEL). For instance, the I/O channels control the flow of information between the peripheral storage devices and main storage. Other routing circuits control communication between main storage and the CPU. The control circuitry generates timing signals in various arrangements that specify the times at which information is moved from place to place in the system.

Another classification scheme divides the hardware subsystem into "internal" and "external" items. The internal ones are the CPU, with its registers, instruction execution and control units, main storage and cache storage, and I/O channels. This "internal computer," which may contain several CPUs sharing access to common main storage and sets of channels, is sometimes called the "processor complex". All other hardware devices, such as keyboards, screens, and file storage disks and tapes, are referred to as the *peripheral*, or input–output, or *I/O*, subsystem.

General Hardware Organization

How do the constituents of these hardware categories work together? The reader is advised to trace the following description through the paths and facilities of Fig. 2. The program (say, as a sequence of keystrokes entered by the programmer) must first be physically translated into electric signal form, which is done by the terminal keyboard. Once in electrical form, the typed information is stored as a file on nonvolatile disk storage for future use. Accordingly, it is moved by an I/O channel to disk storage, where it is held until it is to be executed.

To be executed, the program must satisfy two main requirements: it must be in machine language (object code) form, and it must reside in main storage. As to the first, the typed form of the program (source code) must almost always be translated by an *assembler* (*q.v.*) or *compiler* (*q.v.*) and then stored as an object code file. Assume for the moment that this has been done, so it remains to move the object code file from disk storage to memory via an I/O channel and routing circuits.

Once in memory, the object code program is executable by the CPU. During execution, most storage access is to main memory. However, the running program is capable of directing movement of data, including final results between memory and peripheral storages (disk or tape). Later, such results can be moved, again via channels, to a display terminal or printer for human inspection.

Until about 1968, most computers were *mainframes* (*q.v.*) that were expensive and required considerable floor space, electric power, and air conditioning. However, due to rapid advances in computer technologies, especially semiconductor circuitry, by the late 1960s a genre of small-size machines termed *minicomputers* (*q.v.*) started to be produced that occupied only the space of an office desk, and were inexpensive enough to be used for the solution of a single problem, such as the control of particular industrial processes, as well as a variety of shared uses.

By about 1973, further rapid advances in technology led to another class of even smaller, cheaper systems based on the *microprocessor*, a complete CPU contained on a single or very few semiconductor chips. This method of manufacture eliminated most hand-

wiring and separate component manufacture of the CPU, with substantial improvements, not only in cost but also reliability.

This great advance in technology was matched by corresponding advances in semiconductor memory that allowed compact, high-capacity main storage to be offered at a price hundreds of times cheaper per unit of stored information than was available only a decade earlier. By 1990, several million microprocessor-based systems, called *personal computers* (*see* IBM PC) or *workstations* (*q.v.*) were in common use in homes, offices, and businesses. Each supplied to an individual user computational power and main storage that had been available in shared form only from large expensive systems just a few years earlier. Furthermore, the progress in technology that has given us the microprocessor has also enhanced the cost-effectiveness of the large minicomputer and general-purpose mainframe systems.

Here, only a very brief account has been given of three main classes of computer system: mainframe, minicomputer, and microprocessor-based personal computers and workstations. These are not precise categories. Thus, many minicomputers are shared by several users and applications in the same way as are mainframe systems. Although each PC/workstation is typically used by only one person, many are interconnected via *local area networks* (LANS—*q.v.*) that also contain *servers* that use microprocessor-based technology to permit access to large shared disk storage by the many PCs and workstations on the LAN (*see* FILE SERVER).

The Software Subsystem

Unlike hardware, software is not tangible. Software, although held in a physical medium, say on a disk storage unit, is composed of programs and data arranged in logical, not physical, structures (*see* DATA STRUCTURES).

Software is usually divided into two major categories, *application software* and *system software*, with subcategories:

1. Application software:
   (a) Programs written by users for a particular purpose, such as payroll, inventory control, scientific or engineering calculations, design of a product, etc.
   (b) "Packaged" programs written and supplied by vendors for end users, each for a wide but restricted range of purposes. Examples: word processors for creating text documents; spreadsheets (*q.v.*) for financial analysis work; database packages for creating, maintaining, and

searching large structured data collections; statistical analysis packages, etc.

(c) Installation libraries, containing programs of types (a) and (b) and databases that are particular to several users at a site or an enterprise. Increasingly, a central "repository," or "data dictionary," itself an item of complex software, is used to manage access to these objects.

2. System software:
   (a) Operating system/user interface.
   (b) Language processors (compilers).
   (c) Utilities.

The following discussion concentrates on system software, since this is, in effect, part of the system itself.

The *operating system* is usually the most complex software in a computer system. Two of its basic purposes are: (1) to supply common functions or "services" for use by other software and (2) to control the orderly *sharing* of the system's hardware and software resources by several users. Most of the types of system programs below are part of the operating system:

1. Device drivers (DD)—There is one driver per device; it controls device-specific details of a video screen, a printer, disk storage, etc. Most other software will, as needed, call on a DD when it interacts with the device. Such software sees the device as a much simpler logical unit than is seen by the DD itself, and in this way most software is shielded from onerous device-sensitive details.

2. Data management programs (DMP)—These keep track of the named storage items such as files, that is, where each is located and the means to store and access the data efficiently. For instance, when a user's program calls for data, a DMP locates and fetches the data for use by the requesting program. (In so doing, the DMP may well call on the DD part of the operating system described earlier.) For each file, the DMP may maintain information as to who is permitted to use the data, who is currently using it, what is being done with it, whether or not the data should be retained in the system after the job ends, etc. Some parts of DMP software are called *access methods* (*q.v.*).

3. Linkers/loaders—These programs do the final preparation of object code programs prior to initiation of execution. Included may be "binding" (*q.v.*) or linking of references in one program with another using machine-language addresses (*see* LINKERS AND LOADERS).

4. System control program (SCP)—This complex part of operating system software is found in *shared* systems, as is common in most mainframe and minicomputer systems and in PCs and workstations capable of *multitasking* (*q.v.*).

5. Language processors (translators/compilers)—Programs that are executed by the computer must be in machine-language form, which is exceedingly tedious for humans to use when creating programs. Accordingly, modern computer systems support much more convenient *higher-level languages* (HLL) for human use, along with language translators, usually compilers, to deal with them. These translate user-written programs (*source code*) from such HLL source languages as Cobol (*q.v.*) or Fortran (*q.v.*) or C++ (*q.v.*) into machine-language object code, the only form the machine can execute.

6. Utilities—These are programs that perform frequently required tasks, such as sorting (*q.v.*) and merging two or more files, copying or moving files within the system, etc.

Traditionally, operating systems for mainframes, minicomputers, and early workstations were command-line oriented; that is, users issued commands to them with English-like imperative statements typed at the keyboard (or derived from a stored script). The operating system used over the most diverse range of systems is Unix (*q.v.*). But the operating systems of this form used on current PCs and an increasing number of workstations use a Graphical User Interface (GUI) which invites the user to select options for action by using a mouse or a trackball to "click on" pictorial *icons*. The operating system/GUI which dominated the PC market as of 1999 was Microsoft Windows. A closely related product, Windows NT, is available for use on local area networks (*q.v.*).

The User's View of a Computer System

Consider now how the system appears to a user. Suppose we are at the keyboard and screen of a small single-user system such as a personal computer (PC) or workstation. Its hardware consists of a keyboard, monitor, mouse (*q.v.*), and printer, a CPU, memory (main storage), and disk storage for files. The software subsystem consists of an operating system and application packages: a word processor, an editor, and, say, a compiler. The operating system, through a set of commands that may be offered in "menu" fashion, provides the means to select from a list of particular services.

In the first and simplest case, we wish to type and edit a report. We start by issuing a command to the operating system (by selecting it from a menu by a mouse click). In this case, the command is to start to execute the word processor program. Good software of this kind requires minimal user knowledge of the system or software, and, as we use it, we mainly see a collection of editing facilities that allow us to enter our document, then to edit (change) it, and eventually to print it. The word processor software allows the document to be stored as a named file on disk storage for later reference or further editing. We name this file `example.doc`.

A far more interesting case is where we wish to create and then run our own *program*. Then we typically proceed as follows:

1. Program creation—Start by creating a program, expressing it in one of the system's designated or "supported" programming languages, say C++. Creating a program is a challenging intellectual process, but beyond the scope of this discussion (*see* PROCEDURE-ORIENTED LANGUAGES: PROGRAMMING).

2. Program entry—The next task is to enter the text of this program into the computer system. Mechanically, this is a document creation and editing process (editing is to help us correct certain errors, such as mistakes in typing), so we use software called an *editor*, which is much like a word processor. As in the case of 1. above, our C++ language source program is stored as a file, say `example.cpp`, on a disk storage device.

3. Compile time—Since C++ is not a machine language, our C++ program must be translated from C++ into machine language by a program called a C++ compiler. We order this done by again using the operating system command to "call" a program into execution; in this case, that program is the C++ *compiler*. Naturally, we must also specify the name of our source code file (`example.cpp`) as its data input. the c++ compiler then starts to run on the CPU, and translates the C++ source statements from the `example.cpp` file to machine language object code.

As it attempts to translate, the compiler may discover syntax errors in the program due to typing errors or other reasons, and will then notify us by a message on the screen. (We can then correct the errors on the `example.cpp` file, using processes like 2. above, and then call the compiler again.)

While translating, the compiler is "aware" not only of the machine instructions it must supply for the translation, but also of the operating system's many service progams. The compiler will, as appropriate, insert, as needed, calls on such services as access methods, device drivers, etc. into the object code.

The compiler typically stores the translated program (object code) on the disk as a file named `example.exe` for later use.

4. Load time—The next step is to prepare to run or execute the object code. The same command is used as in step 3, except now we specify `example.exe` as the program to be run rather than the compiler. to start to run this program, the operating system moves the object code file from the disk into main storage since programs must be in main storage in order to execute. the linker/loader system program may then do some necessary final processing of the object code and starts it executing.

5. Run time—As the program `example.exe` executes, much of its action is determined by the machine instructions in its object code produced by the compiler. but recall that the compiler also inserted calls to operating system services, say for access to data files previously stored on disk, and also to new ones to hold results for later viewing or printing or for access by other programs. Such a service call to the operating system activates a service subroutine (which may call other subroutines), which then becomes, during this time, part of the running object code.

Shared Systems

"Shared systems" refer to a mode of operation whereby several users share the CPU time, main storage space, and peripheral devices of a single system. Mainframe and minicomputers typically work as shared systems, while personal computers and workstations typically do not unless networked through use of a local area network.

Sharing has two motivations: (1) to provide a means of inter-user communication, and (2) to bring the processing power and storage capacity of a powerful but expensive system to many users in an economically justifiable way. Shared systems are covered in the articles CLIENT–SERVER COMPUTING; DISTRIBUTED SYSTEMS; MULTITASKING; NETWORKS, COMPUTER; and TIME SHARING.

Interfaces, Architectures, and Compatability

From the viewpoint of a purchaser of computers, a system appears as a coherent collection of products, both hardware and software. To work in a system, every product must comply with precise rules governing its intended relationships with other products, with user software, and even with user interactions. Such relationships are called *interfaces*. The totality of the interfaces of a specific product is called its *architecture,* and the totality of the architectures of a system's products plus any system–system interfaces such as *gateways* (*q.v.*) governing relationships with other systems, is the system architecture.

In many domains, interfaces and architectures are basically standard, but, unlike other systems such as electric power or home entertainment, there are few universal standards in computer systems, so there are many computer architectures (*q.v.*), not just one.

One important example is the hardware–software interface specification that precisely describes all of the instructions in the CPU's repertoire. Another interface specifies the precise relationships between I/O channels and peripheral devices.

A product whose interfaces all comply with those of a given system is said to be *compatible* with that system and will work as intended in that system. Conversely, a product incompatible with a system cannot be used in that system. For example, disk storage products compatible with IBM mainframes will not work in DEC systems and conversely, even if the disk products are of comparable capacity, speed, and function.

The economic significance of compatibility (*q.v.*) is due to the dependence of the great bulk of user-developed software on the specific interfaces of a particular system architecture. Thus, the user investment in such software and related items, such as training of staff, is preserved only if the user buys compatible products when expanding or replacing the system.

Compatibility dictates a product's external behavior but not its internal (non-interface) structure. Thus, plug compatible (substitutable) products are not usually copies or "clones" and are typically very different in technology, circuitry, and design. They also often differ in speed, capacity, reliability, and price, and may be offered by different vendors. For example, processors and disk storage compatible with the IBM 360/370/390 Series (*q.v.*) are also offered by Amdahl Corporation and Hitachi Data Systems, and all are of different internal designs. Customers of such systems can then choose between competing products and vendors on a product basis while retaining their typically large software investments that depend on IBM mainframe architecture.

Summary

Computer systems are characterized by their high speed, high reliability, and great versatility. Since their commercial beginnings in 1950, there has been remarkable improvement in the cost per unit computation and per unit storage. This is due to rapid advances in the technologies of semiconductor circuits and storage devices. The 1970s saw the maturity of mainframes

and minicomputers, as well as the emergence of the personal computer and workstations based on microprocessor technology. The 1980s and 1990s saw explosive growth of microprocessor-based systems with millions in use by individuals in businesses, homes, and schools of all sizes.

Structurally, a computer system is best considered as a collection of resources of two broad classes: hardware and software. Both are served and managed by a carefully designed collection of system programs, including an operating system.

From a business perspective, a computer system is a collection of hardware and software products with precise interfaces between products and with users, especially the software. The great user investments in their self-developed software are usually dependent on compatibility with the interfaces of the specific systems for which such software was developed. In some cases, compatible products with different prices, capacities, and qualities are available from competing vendors.

Bibliography

1986. Bach, M. J. *The Design of the Unix Operating System.* Upper Saddle River, NJ: Prentice Hall.
1995. Stallings, W. *Computer Organization and Architecture: Designing for Performance.* Upper Saddle River, NJ: Prentice Hall.
1996. Hamacher, V. C., Vranesic, Z. G., and Zaky, S. G. *Computer Organization,* 4th Ed. New York: McGraw-Hill.
1997. Hennessy, J. L., and Patterson, D. A. *Computer Organization and Design: The Hardware/Software Interface,* 2nd Ed. San Francisco: Morgan Kaufmann.
1999. Tanenbaum, A. S. *Structured Computer Organization,* 4th Ed. Upper Saddle River, NJ: Prentice Hall.

Herbert Hellerman, revised by Edwin D. Reilly

COMPUTER VIRUS

See VIRUS, COMPUTER.

COMPUTER VISION

For articles on related subjects *see* IMAGE PROCESSING; MEDICAL IMAGING; NEURAL NETWORKS; PATTERN RECOGNITION; and ROBOTICS.

Computer vision is the process of using computers to extract from images useful information about the physical world, including meaningful descriptions of physical objects. For example, if an image sensor, such as a digitizing video camera, captured an image of a physical scene, and the digital image was input to a computer vision system, the desired output would be a description of the physical scene in terms that would be useful for the particular task at hand. Computer vision has many applications, including robotics, industrial automation, document processing, remote sensing, navigation, microscopy, medical imaging, and the development of visual prostheses for the blind.

Terminology

There are various terms used to refer to the field of computer vision: machine vision, computational vision, image understanding, robot vision, image analysis, and scene analysis. Each of these terms has a different historical perspective, and some retain a difference in emphasis. For example, the term "machine vision" is most commonly used in engineering disciplines and thus has more of an engineering and applications flavor. The term "computational vision" arose from interdisciplinary research by computer scientists, visual psychophysicists, physicists, and neuroscientists. There are two goals of computational vision: one concerns the creation of computer systems that can "see," and the other concerns understanding biological vision. The unifying principle of computational vision is the concept that it is possible to understand vision independent of whether it is implemented in computer hardware or in biological "wetware." More specifically, the goal of computational vision is to express the process of vision in terms of computations. This sense of computation is not limited to the numerical computations performed on a calculator, but includes all the more abstract computations that can be performed by an abstract algorithmic processing system.

Related Fields

There are several fields to which computer vision is closely related: *image processing*, which involves image to image transformations; *computer graphics* (*q.v.*), which involves description to image transformations (the inverse of computer vision's image to description transformations); and *pattern recognition*, which involves pattern to class transformations. Computer vision is a subfield of artificial intelligence (AI—*q.v.*) and the process of extracting information from images requires the same types of knowledge acquisition and cognitive reasoning as other AI subfields. However, vision requires in addition significant perceptual preprocessing of the visual input before the cognitive analysis.

Levels of Computer Vision Processing

Computer vision processing is generally divided into two levels: *early vision* and *scene analysis*. Early vision, otherwise known as *low-level vision*, involves the first stages of processing required for a visual task. One aspect of this first stage is *feature analysis*, whereby information about color, motion, shape, texture, stereo depth, and intensity edges is extracted. Another aspect of early vision is *image segmentation*, whereby the featural information is used to segment the image into regions that have a high probability of having arisen from a single physical cause. For example, suppose a scene consisted of a single orange resting upon an infinitely large flat white surface that is illuminated by a diffuse light source. An image of this scene could be segmented based on color information alone to form two regions—one corresponding to the orange and the other corresponding to the flat surface.

The second level of processing, scene analysis, involves taking the featural descriptors generated by early vision and constructing higher-level descriptions of the scene. Some components of this task are *shape analysis*, *object recognition*, and *object localization*. This level is also referred to as *high-level vision*, and involves more knowledge-based processing than early vision. In the example image of an orange, scene analysis would involve recognizing that the circular orange-colored region was an image of an orange. This recognition must be based on the system having knowledge about the nature of oranges, and the ability to make inferences based on the visual information.

The division between early vision and scene analysis is not firm. Many computer vision systems have partial information generated by the scene analysis processing feedback to the early vision processing to be used in refining the initial descriptions to make them more useful for the scene analysis processing. Several iterations through this feedback and feedforward process may be required to generate the final scene descriptions. Another sense in which the division is not firm is that some researchers refer to three levels of vision: low-level, intermediate, and high-level. Again, the exact boundaries between these three levels are not distinct.

Dynamic Vision

While much of computer vision deals with the analysis of static images, the relatively new subfield of dynamic vision (or active vision) stresses the importance of considering vision as a part of an active agent interacting with its environment. It has been found that many vision problems that are difficult to solve using static images become easy to solve in an active vision system where the agent has the ability to move the camera or in other ways interact with a dynamic scene in order to resolve ambiguities.

Why Computer Vision is Difficult

The goal of creating computer vision systems that can "see" was initially thought to be rather easy. The argument was made that computers are very powerful. For example, even though the solution of simultaneous differential equations is very difficult for humans, computers can readily solve them. So, if we take a task that is trivially easy for humans, such as vision, it should be even easier to implement it on a computer. Yet when computers scientists and engineers first attempted to give computers a visual sense, they failed completely. The problem was that there is a fallacy in the simple argument used above. While humans are conscious of most of the stages of processing involved in solving simultaneous differential equations and thus can realize the complexity involved, most of the processing involved in visual perception remains subconscious. So while the process of encountering, say, a yellow Volkswagen in the environment, and using our visual sense to determine that there is a yellow Volkswagen currently present in our environment may feel like a simple process, it actually involves many interrelated levels of computational processing. Uncovering just what those levels of processing are and expressing them as algorithms is one goal of computer vision.

Vision is difficult because it is an underconstrained problem. For example, an image is a two-dimensional projection of a three-dimensional scene, but there can be infinitely many three-dimensional scenes that project the same two-dimensional image. Thus, given just the single image, it is impossible to determine which of the possible scenes is depicted in the image. For example, the image in Fig. 1a appears to depict a rectangle, but the actual scene from which this image arose is seen in Fig. 1b: it consists of four thin wires that do not touch. But the image in Fig. 1a could just as well have been the projection of a scene containing a rectangle (Fig. 1c). This simple example illustrates that it is possible to have two scenes that both project to the same image. But notice that the image in Fig. 1a does not appear to be ambiguous; we do not perceive all possible scenes. Thus, humans either use some additional high-level information about the world to interpret images unambiguously (such as knowledge about rectangles, for example), or they use some general constraints to rule out multiple interpretations. There is psychophysical evidence that humans use both strategies, but the surprising result is that the high-level knowledge appears to provide less information for disambiguating scenes than the lower-level general constraints. This can be illustrated by drawing an arbitrary squiggle and observing that it generates a single percept, even though it does not depict a familiar object. This suggests the idea that there must

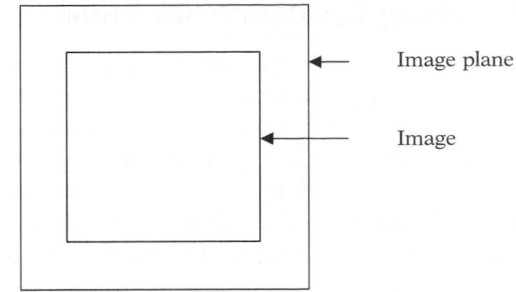

Figure 1a.

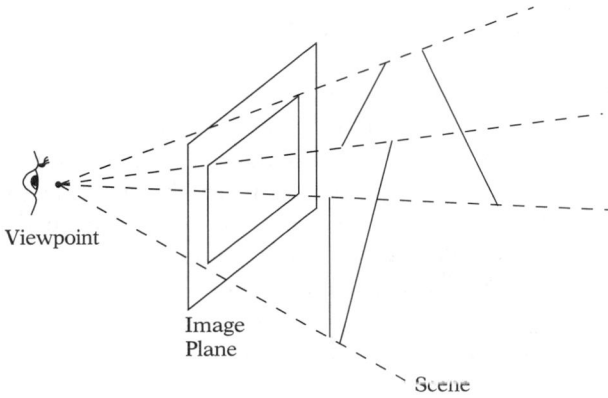

Figure 1b.

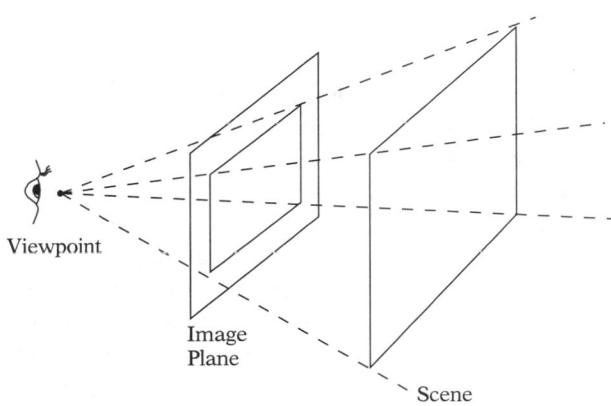

Figure 1c.

be some additional general constraints that humans use in perceiving images.

Using dynamic vision with the scene in Fig. 1b would be another way to disambiguate the scene: there would be only one viewpoint from which the scene would appear to be a connected rectangle. If the position of the camera were changed slightly, then the image would change in a manner in which it would become obvious to a human observer that the scene consists of four unconnected wires. By contrast, using active vision with the scene in Fig. 1c by changing the viewpoint, would result in a human observer still interpreting the scene as a connected wire rectangle.

Determining Constraints for Vision

One of the primary tasks in computer vision is to find a set of constraints that would allow a computer to interpret images unambiguously. The constraints can be either features in the image that can be used to make inferences about the scene, or regularities of nature that can be exploited. There are four main techniques for determining such constraints: the engineering approach, the statistical approach, the biological approach, and the physical approach.

ENGINEERING APPROACH TO DETERMINING CONSTRAINTS

The engineering approach relies on the intuitions, introspections, and prior knowledge of the system designer as to what the important image features should be, and how such features should be interpreted. This approach was used in much of the early work in computer vision, and continues to be used in many machine vision systems. Although this approach has been successful in some applications, its lack of a theoretical basis makes it less desirable than some of the other approaches.

STATISTICAL APPROACH TO DETERMINING CONSTRAINTS

Statistical analysis provides the second approach to determining image constraints. The basic idea is that it is possible to design a system that can "learn" what the constraints are simply by observing the world through sensory input. This is the approach used in statistical pattern recognition, and more recently in artificial *neural networks*. In the statistical approach, the relevant aspects of the visual environment are sampled, and the sample statistics used to find image features that can be used to provide the necessary constraints on image interpretation. This approach can be successful when the input stimuli can be recognized from descriptions that are directly constructed from the image. However, in most vision problems the direct descriptions are further processed into higher-level descriptions, which are then further processed into even higher-level descriptions, etc., and only after several such intervening levels of successively more derived descriptions does recognition occur. It is not yet clear how such complex structure could emerge in an artificial system that must "learn" its structure. One solution would be to design such structure into the network, but this then begs the question of what image features are important, as at least the basic level features would have to be predetermined. So, although the statistical approaches may produce interesting results for early vision, they are not well suited for scene analysis.

BIOLOGICAL APPROACH TO DETERMINING CONSTRAINTS

The third approach to finding useful image constraints involves studying biological vision systems with the aim of uncovering the constraints that they use in image interpretation. In some cases, the biological solution may be constrained by the neurophysiological implementation mechanisms, and in such cases the biological approach may fail. However, in other cases the biological solution may be constrained by the general problem of vision and may provide useful insights for computer vision.

In one sense, all computer vision uses the biological approach, as vision is defined in terms of the human visual sense. But as mentioned previously, most stages of visual processing are not open to conscious introspection, so in order to use the biological approach systematically, other means of determining how the mammalian visual system functions must be used. This is possible using techniques from the disciplines of visual perception, psychophysics, neurophysiology, and neuroanatomy. Over the past 15 years there has been an increasing degree of interaction between those interested in biological vision and those primarily interested in machine vision, and the contributions from each side enhance the research of the other.

PHYSICAL APPROACH TO DETERMINING CONSTRAINTS

In the physical approach, the basic idea is to determine properties of the physical world that can be used to constrain image interpretation. This has been a very successful approach and has led to many useful constraints. For example, David Marr (1982) frequently used continuity as a constraint. The continuity constraint makes use of the fact that the physical world is basically continuous; thus neighboring image points have a high probability of having arisen from the same physical entity. This constraint has been used in a simple cooperative algorithm to compute the relative depth of different image regions. Another example of a frequently used constraint is the assumption of a general viewpoint. This assumption is based on the fact that for a given scene, as the viewpoint changes slightly, there will generally be only slight changes in the projected image, and thus many properties of the projected image will remain constant over most viewpoints. So, if it is possible to determine which image properties are invariant over viewpoint, except at a limited number of viewpoints, it may be possible to make useful inferences about the scene based on these properties. For example, if several points in an image are collinear, there is a high probability that they depict collinear points on a curve in three-space. This will not always be true: if an arc of a circle exists in three-space, there will be a limited number of viewpoints such that the points on the arc project onto a straight line in an image, but for the vast majority of possible viewpoints this will not be true. Vision constraints often have the property of being true only in general; yet they can be important in providing inferences useful for the correct interpretation of an image.

Bibliography

1982. Marr, D. *Vision*. San Francisco: W. H. Freeman.
1982. Ballard, D. H., and Brown, C. P. *Computer Vision*. Upper Saddle River, NJ: Prentice Hall.
1986. Horn, B. *Robot Vision*. New York: McGraw-Hill.
1987. Fischler, M., and Firschein, O. *Readings in Computer Vision: Issues, Problems, Principles and Paradigms*. San Francisco: Morgan Kaufmann.
1992. Haralick, R. M., and Shapiro, L. G. *Computer and Robot Vision*. Reading, MA: Addison-Wesley.
1995. Jain, R., Kasturi, R., and Schunk, B. G. *Machine Vision*. New York: McGraw-Hill.
1997. Davies, E. R. *Machine Vision*. San Diego, CA: Academic Press.

Deborah Walters

COMPUTERS, HISTORY OF

See DIGITAL COMPUTERS, HISTORY OF.

COMPUTERS, MULTIPLE ADDRESS

For articles on related subjects *see* ADDRESSING; COMPUTER ARCHITECTURE; INDEX REGISTER; INSTRUCTION SET; MACHINE AND ASSEMBLY LANGUAGE PROGRAMMING; and REDUCED INSTRUCTION SET COMPUTER.

In addition to an operation (command) specification and other information (e.g. indexing), a computer instruction may contain from zero to four addresses. An address usually points either to a location in the memory that stores the value of the operand or to a location involved in the control process.

Computers may be classified according to the number of addresses in most or in common (e.g. arithmetic) instructions: zero, one, two, three, and four having been used. The number of addresses depends on both the register structure and central processor organization.

Zero-Address Instructions

Zero-address instructions do not require access to memory for operands. Examples include HALT and RESET OVERFLOW INDICATORS. Arithmetic zero-address instructions occur in stack-type organizations in which arithmetic expressions are conveniently evaluated by conversion to Polish form (*see* POLISH NOTATION). For example, ADD would cause the two top stacked operands to be replaced by their sum, thereby shortening the stack by one item. Although not common, several well-designed computers have had stack-based zero-address instruction sets, including the Burroughs B5500 in the 1960s and the Hewlett-Packard HP3000 in the early 1970s.

One-Address Instructions

For many years, the high cost of hardware led to systems wherein the arithmetic operations were all associated with one particular register called an accumulator. Thus, the instructions to evaluate C = A + B were LOAD A, ADD B, STORE C, with a natural instruction format of

    [op code] [address]

where [address] points to a particular memory cell. Control instructions fitting this structure were JUMP, [address]; JUMP IF ACCUMULATOR POSITIVE, [address]; etc. In both zero-address and one-address structures, successive instructions came from sequential locations in memory as specified by a *program counter* (*q.v.*) which progressed in units of one until a jump occurred. The EDSAC (*q.v.*) was an example of a one-address computer. The IBM 700-7000 series of computers were another example, as were many simple microprocessors (*q.v.*).

Two-Address Instructions

Early computers could be divided into two groups according to memory organization—those with random access (Williams tube memory (*q.v.*), and somewhat later, magnetic cores) and cyclic memory (mercury delay lines, and a little later, magnetic drum memories). In mercury delay line memories (*see* ULTRASONIC MEMORY), several words (8 to 32, say) circulated in a line and were sequentially available at the output. The time from the availability of the first to the availability of the last bit of a word might have been 32 microseconds, and the time to the next appearance of this word 300 to 1,000 microseconds. A similar relationship held for drum memories. With this structure, faster programs could be written if each instruction had a second address specifying the location of the next instruction. This implied that instructions were no longer sequentially located but were scattered through memory so as to become available at the optimum time. This concept was used by the ACE computer at the National Physical Laboratories (England, 1946) and later in such computers as the Bendix G15 and the IBM 650.

A common use today of the two-address format, [opcode] [A] [B], has both addresses referring to CPU registers or memory locations for operands so that, for example, ADD [A] [B] means add the contents of A to the contents of B and place the result in B (or, occasionally, A).

Three-Address Instructions

Motivated by the fact that arithmetic operations usually involve two operands and a result, a number of early computers used three addresses in arithmetic instructions. Examples include MIDAC (University of Michigan) and NORC (Naval Ordinance Research Computer—q.v.). Thus, ADD [A] [B] [C] means add the contents of A to the contents of B and place the result in C. This format is used again in some RISC processors, such as the Sun Sparc, though as noted below, all three operands must be CPU registers.

Four-Address Instructions

Some designers also specified the location of the next instruction, using three addresses for arithmetic purposes. The EDVAC, SEAC, and SWAC were examples of this structure. Thus, ADD [A] [B] [C] [D] means add the contents of A to the contents of B, place the result in C, and take the next instruction from D. Since every instruction is a potential jump, no unconditional jump instruction is needed on such computers.

In 1955, Weik reported on 65 computers giving the following distribution.

Address	Number of Systems
1	33
2	6
3	12
4	6
Combinations	8
Total	65

A similar compilation today would show a mixture of one-, two-, and three-address systems, where often the addresses refer to registers rather than memory cells.

Multiple Address vs. Multiple Instruction

In early computers, memory was small (rarely more than 1,024 words), so addresses were ten bits or fewer. Ten-decimal digit precision implied word lengths of 30 to 40 bits, so the designer's problem was to fit an op code–address structure into the desired word length. Many one-address systems stored two instructions per word, whereas three- and four-address systems could efficiently have one instruction per word.

Address Modification

Only one of the first computers had index registers (the B-box on the Manchester University Mark I), but designers soon realized their value. This forced designs toward one-address systems because of the word

length compatibility and the pressure for simple control structures. Since many operations in programs (particularly operations related to control) involve operations with small integers, designers sometimes provide a modifier indicating that the "address" is the actual operand (saving a memory access). Such addressing is called *immediate*. In the other direction, the address might point to a location in memory that contained a pointer (q.v.) to still another location, etc. (*indirect addressing*). Add to this the capability of indexing these various addresses, and we see that the address has evolved from a simple explicit integer to a potentially quite complicated function. This complexity has also been a strong force toward one-address structures. However, the utility of source–destination structures has caused continued use of two-address instructions, although, as noted above, one or both of these may refer to registers.

Short Word Length Computers

The advent of 16-bit word minicomputers in the 1960s (the earlier Whirlwind I at MIT was also a 16-bit computer) and, more recently, the 8- or 16-bit microcomputer, and the decline in the cost of logic (so that multiple registers and much larger memories are prevalent) placed other pressures on designers. The PDP-11 structure represents one relatively successful approach to this problem by using one- and two-address instructions. The PDP-11 had 8 registers (R0 to R7) with R6 being a stack pointer and R7 a program counter. Each instruction consisted of an op code (4 or 10 bits), and one or two addresses. The address consisted of a 2-bit MODE, a single bit specifying DIRECT/INDIRECT, and a 3-bit general register specification. In two-address instructions, the addresses specified source and destination.

Reduced Instruction Set Computers

RISC processors achieve high speed by requiring that operands of most instructions be stored in CPU registers, from which they can be fetched without the delay of addressing the relatively slow memory. Since up to 32 registers may be specified with only five bits each, it is feasible to specify three in an arithmetic instruction with a 32-bit length. In such processors, only the LOAD [reg] [memory] or STORE [reg] [memory] instructions to transfer a word between a register and memory have a memory operand.

Bibliography

1955. Weik, M. H. "A Survey of Domestic Electronic Digital Computing Systems." Ballistic Research Laboratories, Aberdeen Proving Ground, Report No. 971.
1999. Tanenbaum, A. S. *Structured Computer Organization*, 4th Ed. Upper Saddle River, NJ: Prentice Hall.

Harry D. Huskey

COMPUTERS, PERSONAL

See DIGITAL COMPUTERS, HISTORY OF; and PERSONAL COMPUTING.

COMPUTING CONFERENCES

For articles on related subjects *see* ASSOCIATION FOR COMPUTING MACHINERY; COMPUTER SOCIETIES (APPENDIX ON AFIPS); INSTITUTE FOR ELECTRICAL AND ELECTRONIC ENGINEERS—COMPUTER SOCIETY; and INTERNATIONAL FEDERATION FOR INFORMATION PROCESSING.

History

There were no computing conferences before the end of the Second World War, but within a year of the 1946 public demonstrations of ENIAC (*q.v.*) and the Harvard Mark I (*q.v.*) the University of Pennsylvania and Harvard had convened invitational meetings at which lectures and papers about computing were given. These were the first computing conferences, and those who participated have long attested to their value and their importance to the beginning of computing. Both university groups adopted an academic tell-all attitude about what they had done under wartime secrecy, what they were doing now, what they planned for the future, and encouraged, by their example, others to do likewise. The British, under the draconian threat of the Official Secrets Act, were much less forthcoming about their wartime computing work at Bletchley Park, and concealed much of it from the world for almost half a century. As a consequence the first British computing conferences in 1949 concerned not wartime work but only university and commercial developments, some stimulated by the earlier US releases.

The early computing conferences took the shape of scientific and technical society meetings. Formal papers, previously refereed, were read and discussed, but time was allowed for corridor discussions. As was the case of the computing societies the conferences served two different groups. Academics participated to promote themselves and their accomplishments, to learn what others were doing, and to develop the discipline. Those from the commercial world of computing hoped to gain by learning what others were doing without giving up too much themselves. The government and military participants, who played major roles in the early conferences, had ambiguous goals. Some truly believed that the information dispersal of the conferences, both in the papers and the corridors, was beneficial, while a few naively thought that there were military computing secrets that could be preserved.

The story of how the three early US computing societies first jointly sponsored national conferences and then joined with others to form AFIPS is told in the article on computer societies (*q.v.*). In addition, how IFIP (*q.v.*), which is an international society of societies, one of whose main purposes is holding international conferences, was formed, is told in its article.

Computing societies continued this practice of sponsoring conferences which had a formal phase for the introduction of new results through the presentation, discussion, and publication of vetted papers and a valuable informal phase involving the face-to-face meetings of the participants in the halls and stairways and in the society business meetings. In the earliest conferences space was provided for the display of computing hardware, whether for sale or not, but rules were set that were intended to keep these exhibits from becoming commercial trade shows. These large general conferences were supplemented by specialist meetings and smaller gatherings of the same type. Altogether these conferences were important to practitioners to see what others were doing, to see new computing equipment, to tell others what one was doing, to display computing artifacts, to watch for employment opportunities, and to offer such opportunities. That is, the conferences were an important communication device at a time when the field was young and travel and telephoning were expensive. Indeed, there is reason to believe that some of the computing societies in some small countries were formed merely to provide access to foreign conferences and international conferences.

Current Status

As computing developed and travel and telephone costs dropped, the need for frequent face-to-face meetings declined and the conferences changed from true information exchanges into social gatherings supplemented by what amounted to somewhat restricted trade shows of commercial products. The halls in which formal papers were presented were empty, but the display halls were jammed, as were the surrounding party rooms. This change came about in spite of some societies' academic opposition to commerce. The trade show parts of the conferences brought unheard of and constantly increasing riches to the societies that sponsored the conferences. The exhibits grew, and the sponsoring societies raked in the funds and anticipated bigger and bigger conferences every year. The bubble burst when commercial entrepreneurs noted this treasure trove and organized competing computer trade shows, without formal papers or sales restrictions, that were aimed at the smaller profitable parts of the computing world rather than at all of it and at people who had buying authority and financial interests in computing rather than at those with scientific, educational, and professional interests.

In 1988 the biggest society-sponsored national conference, the National Computer Conference, ended in failure, causing the death of its sponsor, the American Federation of Information Processing Societies, and around that time all the smaller society conferences peaked and declined or failed. Today the largest and most successful computing conferences are huge commercial trade shows that fill the largest convention facilities in the nation, for example Comdex and Internet World. They are independent of the computing societies. In them the latest commercial developments are displayed with maximum glitz. Speeches are made but no refereed papers are presented, discussed, or published.

The computing societies still conduct hundreds of smaller non-trade show computing conferences each year, with papers, proceedings, and informal meetings of society members in the halls. But now the biggest of the computing conferences, several hundred per year, are commercial enterprises aimed not at the members of computing societies but at those with business in the commercial computing world. The top of the line is probably The PC Forum, which annually gathers six hundred computing business big-shots at $4,000 a head, who hope to find out about the Next Big Thing by listening to the famous speakers selected by the organizer (Esther Dyson) or by schmoozing with each other around the pools and bars of the conference hotel.

Commercial computing conferences will continue as long as they are profitable to their organizers, and society computing conferences will continue as long as there are computing societies.

Eric A. Weiss

COMPUTING RESEARCH ASSOCIATION (CRA)

For articles on related topics *see* COMPUTER SCIENCE; COMPUTER SCIENCE—PH.D. STATISTICS; EDUCATION IN COMPUTER ENGINEERING; and EDUCATION IN COMPUTER SCIENCE.

The *Computing Research Association* (CRA) is a nonprofit organization in Washington, DC, whose mission is to strengthen research and advanced education in computing and allied fields in North America. It does this by working to influence policy that affects computing research, collecting and disseminating basic information about the profession, encouraging the development of human resources, and contributing to the cohesiveness of the professional community.

Some examples of CRA's programs suggest the range of activities. The annual Taulbee Survey includes basic information on academic salaries and Ph.D. production in computer science and engineering. The Forsythe list contains information about Ph.D.-granting institutions in the USA and Canada. The biennial Conference at Snowbird, Utah, which CRA organizes, brings together department chairs, industrial lab managers, and other leaders of the profession to discuss critical issues. Mentoring programs provide research experiences to underrepresented groups in the computing research community—often a first step to graduate training and a career as a computing researcher. The Executive Fellowship Program, run in collaboration with the Office of the US Vice President, brings mid-career computer scientists to Washington to work on high-level computer policy issues.

CRA has more than 180 members. These include major computer professional societies (AAAI, ACM (*q.v.*), Computer Society (*see* IEEE-CS), SIAM, Usenix), US and Canadian academic departments of computer science and engineering, and US and Canadian industrial and government research laboratories and centers.

CRA grew out of the Computer Science Board, an informal group of chairs of computer science departments in the United States and Canada. This group, formed in 1972, organized the first Computer Science Conference, which subsequently, until 1997, became one of ACM's annual conferences.

CRA is located at 1100 Seventeenth Street NW, Suite 507, Washington, DC 20036, USA; telephone: 1-202-234-2111, email: info@cra.org. Further information about CRA's programs can be found on the association's Website: http://www.cra.org.

William F. Aspray

COMRIE, LESLIE JOHN

For articles on related subjects *see* CALCULATING MACHINES; and PUNCHED CARD MACHINERY.

During the 1930s and 1940s, L. J. Comrie was the leading mathematical table maker in Britain. His tables were well known throughout the world for their accuracy and ease of use. In addition to making mathematical tables, Comrie was very influential in persuading scientists to use commercial desk calculating and accounting machines to mechanize their computational work.

Leslie John Comrie was born on 15 August 1893 in Pukekohe, New Zealand. He studied Chemistry at University College, Auckland, before serving in France during the First World War with the New Zealand Expeditionary Force. In 1919 Comrie entered St. John's College, Cambridge, as a graduate student in astronomy. While at Cambridge, Comrie became the first director of the Computing Section of the British Astronomical Association and there began a long career in computational work.

In 1925 Comrie took up a post in HM Nautical Almanac Office (the NAO); he was appointed Deputy Superintendent in 1926 and Superintendent in 1930. Comrie completely revolutionized the Nautical Almanac Office by introducing machine methods of computation. Prior to Comrie's appointment at the NAO, most calculations were performed by outworkers using logarithm tables. By 1930 the work was almost entirely mechanized. Comrie devised many numerical methods for machine methods of computation; one of the most famous was his use of Hollerith punched card machines for Fourier synthesis applied to the calculation of the position of the Moon.

While Comrie had a very high profile in astronomical circles, he also made more general mathematical tables and published widely on machine methods of computation. He produced classic sets of mathematical tables with J. Peters and L. M. Milne-Thomson, and served as secretary to the British Association for the Advancement of Science Mathematical Tables Committee from 1929 to 1936 working on the production of several high-quality tables.

In 1936 Comrie left the NAO and set up the Scientific Computing Service Ltd. This company, unique in its day, offered computing services on a commercial basis. The Scientific Computing Service was used by a wide range of people for both scientific calculations and table-making and was used by both the British and American armed services during the Second World War.

Comrie continued to advocate the use of commercial calculating machines for scientific work. He was particularly against scientists building their own "one-off" devices to carry out computations which could, with some planning, be carried out by machines already available. Comrie's health began to fail during the postwar years, and although he was aware of the development of electronic computers he never had the opportunity to extend his work in that direction.

One of Comrie's last projects was the publication of the acclaimed *An Index to Mathematical Tables*, by Fletcher, Rosenhead and Miller. His contribution to the second volume detailing known errors in published tables was the result of his lifelong interest in trying to produce error-free tables.

Comrie was elected a Fellow of the Royal Society in March 1950 in recognition of his influential work in mechanical computation and table-making. He died as a result of a stroke in December 1950.

Bibliography

1932. Comrie, L. J. "The Application of the Hollerith Tabulating Machine to Brown's Tables of the Moon," *Monthly Notices, Royal Astronomical Society*, **92**, 7, 694–707.
1936. Comrie, L. J. *Interpolation and Allied Tables*. London: HMSO. (Reprinted extracts from *Nautical Almanac, 1937*.)
1946. Fletcher, A., Rosenhead, L., and Miller, J. C. P. *An Index to Mathematical Tables*. London: Scientific Computing Service. (2nd Ed. 1962.)
1952. Massey, H. S. W. "L. J. Comrie," *Obituary Notices of Fellows of the Royal Society*, **8**, 97–107.
1953. Greaves, W. H. M. "L. J. Comrie," *Monthly Notices, Royal Astronomical Society*, **113**, 3, 294–304.
1990. Croarken, M. G. *Early Scientific Computing in Britain*. Oxford: Oxford University Press.

Mary Croarken

CONCURRENT PROGRAMMING

For articles on related subjects *see* ADA; COORDINATION LANGUAGES; DATABASE CONCURRENCY CONTROL; DISTRIBUTED SYSTEMS; GUARDED COMMAND; MODEL CHECKING; MONITOR, SYNCHRONIZATION; MULTIPROCESSING; MULTIPROGRAMMING; MULTITASKING; MUTUAL EXCLUSION; OPERATING SYSTEMS; PARALLEL PROCESSING; and PETRI NET.

Concurrent programming concerns programs in which several actions may be performed at the same time. A concurrent program is composed of multiple processes or computational *threads*, each of which is a sequential computation, that is, a linearly ordered series of steps.

Figure 1. Leslie John Comrie (courtesy of Julian Comrie, © Walter Stoneman).

Concurrency—the execution of concurrent programs —arises in many contexts. Multiprocessors, parallel processors, and distributed systems, all of which have multiple CPUs (*q.v.*), naturally run concurrent programs. A multitasking operating system runs concurrent programs even on a single CPU (also called *multiprogramming*). Time-sharing (*q.v.*) operating systems that support many users are multitasking, but so are modern personal computer operating systems. It is also common for input and output devices to be handled through concurrent programming; thus embedded systems (*q.v.*) and real-time systems (*q.v.*) use concurrency. Finally, concurrent programming is a design technique that is useful for modular programming (*q.v.*) even in intrinsically sequential computations.

When two parts of a concurrent program actually execute at the same time they are *physically* concurrent. Physical concurrency is not possible on a uniprocessor, but we say that processes are *logically* concurrent if time slicing (*see* TIME SLICE) selects one or another for execution by the single CPU, though all are capable of executing. Logically concurrent processes behave like physically concurrent processes that run on relatively slower CPUs than the actual one. Note that a processor with peripheral devices is a physically concurrent system in one sense, since an input device like a communication line or keyboard generates data at the same time that the CPU is executing instructions. When the device then issues an *interrupt* (*q.v.*), its interrupt service routine gets a time slice in which the CPU executes the instructions that handle the data.

One standard model of concurrency is an *interleaving* model, in which execution of concurrent instructions is regarded as equivalent to *some* sequential interleaving of the instructions of the different threads. There are many possible such interleavings, of course, and as models of a concurrent program they are all equivalent. Suppose two threads execute the following sequences concurrently:

thread a	thread b
x := x*y	m := m-n
y := y+1	n := n*n

One of the six possible interleaving is x:=x+y, m:=m-n, n:=n*n, y:=y+1; another is m:=m-n, n:=n*n, x:= x*y, y:=y+1. Since the threads operate on different variables, all interleavings produce the same final values.

Concurrent programming is more difficult than sequential programming. A sequential program is correct if it produces the right results for all possible inputs. A concurrent program must produce correct results not only for all possible inputs but for all possible timings (interleavings) of concurrent statements. Con-

sider a program in which two threads both increment a variable that is a shared counter. Even an elementary programming language instruction like x:=x+1 is implemented by several assembly language instructions that fetch a value into a private CPU register, increment it, and store it back, so that the two threads execute:

thread a	thread b
load r1,x	load r1,x
add r1,r1,1	add r1,r1,1
store r1,x	store r1,x

Suppose that both threads attempt to increment the counter. If one thread executes its store before the other executes load, the counter will go up by 2. Otherwise each will add 1 to the old value of x and each will store its new value; that is, one of the two increments is lost!

This error is an example of a *race condition*, in which the precise timing of instructions affects the result of a computation. Concurrent programs with race conditions may appear to work correctly for some time before an interleaving occurs that reveals the error— which may also be hard to reproduce since the programmer generally cannot control such fine-grained timings. Yet it is essential to avoid race conditions if a program such as an operating system is to be correct.

To prevent race conditions we need to be able to make a sequence of instructions *atomic*; that is, indivisible. If the three-instruction sequence that updates the counter x above were atomic, whichever thread began an update would finish it before the other could start. *Critical section* is a term for a block of code that must be atomic to guarantee correct execution, and critical sections are implemented by providing *mutual exclusion* through a locking mechanism.

Solutions to the problem of providing mutual exclusion depend on some minimal kind of atomicity at the hardware level. In a uniprocessor system, it is achieved by disabling interrupts, thus making all instruction sequences atomic until interrupts are again enabled. In a multiprocessor, it normally requires an "interlock" that prevents two processors from addressing the same memory cell at the same time. Mutual exclusion can then be achieved if the processors have instructions that can atomically exchange a value in a CPU register (which is private to each processor) with the value in a shared memory cell. Suppose a memory cell, lock, is initialized with a 1, representing permission to proceed, and that two (or more) threads running on different processors seek permission to use a critical section by putting a 0 in a register and then atomically exchanging it with the lock. If two attempt this operation at once, the atomicity of the exchange operation

Thread 1   Thread 2

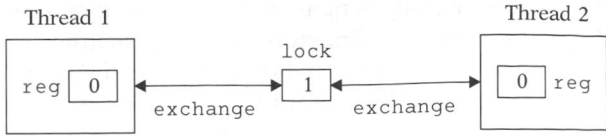

(a) Two threads execute an `exchange(reg, lock)` instruction.

Thread 1   Thread 2

(b) After the two exchanges, thread 2 has acquired the lock value.

Figure 1. Using an atomic exchange instruction for mutual exclusion.

insures that one will get the 1; the other, a 0 (Fig. 1). In the following pseudocode `mutexbegin` causes a thread to wait, continually retrying to obtain the lock, until it gets the 1 representing permission to use the critical section, which it returns in `mutexend`.

```
             reg := 0
mutexbegin: repeat
                 exch reg, lock
             until reg = 1
             { critical section }
mutexend:    exch reg, lock
```

Note that the atomic exchange operation guarantees an invariant property of the system: there is exactly one copy of the value 1 at all times; that is, it is impossible for two processors both to get a copy in their private registers.

For an analogy in everyday (if impractical) terms, suppose that in place of traffic lights, every street intersection has a small container with a green ball in it, and every motorist has a single red ball. The rules of the road are that upon reaching an intersection, each motorist must stop, reach into the container and exchange his or her ball with the one already there. A motorist who acquires the green ball can proceed through the intersection, confident that any other arrival will acquire the red ball left in the container, and thus have to wait, retrying the swap from time to time. After crossing the intersection, the driver returns to the container and replaces the green ball, taking out the red one that was there and leaving the intersection in its unoccupied state, so that the next swap attempt will succeed in getting the green ball. This scheme has the merit that no one would needlessly wait at a red light while the green light remained unused by any motorist.

The implementation of mutual exclusion with an atomic exchange instruction has the defect that a processor must idle while a process is waiting. *Semaphores*

are a common operating system construct that provides an equivalent atomic locking mechanism, and lets a process suspend execution while waiting for another to signal it, thus allowing another process to execute (*see* MUTUAL EXCLUSION). Semaphores are a low-level construct from a programming standpoint, however. They cause transfers of control akin to the *goto* of sequential programming: a process that issues a *wakeup* semaphore operation will cause execution to resume in some other part of the program (the part that did the semaphore *wait* operation). Furthermore, a process might neglect to issue the *wakeup*—like a motorist who forgets to return the green ball – or execute a *wakeup* operation on the wrong semaphore—like a motorist who returns the green ball to another intersection, thus allowing two motorists to proceed, causing a race condition that results in a collision at a (critical) intersection.

Concurrency in Programming Languages

A concurrent programming language must provide a means to start multiple processes and to synchronize them. Process synchronization includes both mutual exclusion (*cooperating* processes) and *condition synchronization*—used when one process must wait for another process to make some condition true, at which point it is notified that it may resume execution. Since condition synchronization generally involves some exchange of data, processes that use it are sometimes called *communicating* processes.

Concurrent processes can be started by a `fork` statement that lets a process invoke a new one, like a subprogram (*q.v.*) call except that the called routine runs in parallel with the caller; such an operation is part of the Unix operating system (*q.v.*). In Java (*q.v.*), a thread can be started by a similar `threadname.start()` call. Other languages, like Algol 68 (*q.v.*), have a `cobegin-coend` construct; `cobegin S1; S2; S3; coend` would start three statements executing as separate threads, and all would have to terminate before execution continued beyond the `coend`.

SHARED VARIABLES

When processes have shared variables, a convenient construct for both mutual exclusion and condition synchronization is the *conditional critical region* (CCR), which has the syntax **region** R **when** B **do** S. Any named region provides mutual exclusion, which means that a process can evaluate the condition B atomically and when it is true, continue on to execute S before any other process can change the value of the condition. As an example, suppose that a queue holds a number of resources shared by several processes, and that there are standard operations on the queue:

empty, put, get, which test for an empty queue and add or remove an item from the queue. Each process would execute

```
region Resource when not empty(Resource_Q)
      do get(item)
{ use the item}
region Resource when true do put(item).
```

The first use of the critical region lets a process acquire a copy of the resource without interference, once one is available; the second, which never causes a wait, returns the copy.

In a CCR the condition synchronization is implicit; that is, the process that makes a resource available does not explicitly inform a waiting process of its availability. This convenient property places the burden on the implementation of critical regions, which must repeatedly test whether the waited-for condition of some process is true. In this case it is clear that the condition does not change except after the put operation, but in general it may be more difficult to determine what may change a condition.

An important characteristic of CCRs, as of some other synchronization constructs, is that they are nondeterministic. That is, if several processes await the same condition, when it becomes true one of them will resume execution, but which one is not specified. An implementation might provide a first come, first served ordering, but need not, though a common requirement is that it be fair in the sense that a waiting process will eventually resume if its condition repeatedly becomes true. This nondeterminism, also found in the guarded command (*q.v.*) of sequential programming, separates abstract specification of behavior from implementation details.

An alternative to CCRs is the *monitor* (*see* MONITOR, SYNCHRONIZATION). It provides encapsulation (*q.v.*) of critical data, giving access to it only through operations declared as public; thus, it is like a class (*q.v.*) in object-oriented programming (*q.v.*). It adds mutual exclusion, allowing only one activation of any of its routines at a time; that is, only one calling process at a time may be "in" the monitor and have access to its data. Monitors have data structures called *conditions*, with wait and signal operations on them. For example, a process that calls a monitor routine and finds that it must delay because a resource is not available executes wait on a condition variable; in doing so it relinquishes its exclusive hold on the monitor. When another process enters the monitor and makes the waited-for resource available, it issues an explicit signal to the condition variable, waking the waiting process and turning over the monitor to it (thus preserving the mutual-exclusion property). *See* MONITOR, SYNCHRONIZATION for a monitor example equivalent to the CCR example above.

By using explicit signaling to inform a waiting process that it may resume, monitors are less expensive to implement than CCRs, though they have the disadvantage that the programmer must remember when to issue the signal. They have been implemented in Concurrent Pascal and the Mesa language, and monitor-like wait and signal primitives together with the ability to provide mutual exclusion, are in Modula-2, Modula-3, and Java.

MESSAGE PASSING

Another approach to concurrency makes interprocess communication (message passing) the means of providing mutual exclusion and condition synchronization. Message passing is essential in distributed systems or others in which concurrent processes do not share memory, but it is a useful abstraction even when there is shared memory. In the former case messages require data to be copied from one place to another; in the latter, message-passing may simply be a transfer of *access rights*. Message passing uses send and receive primitives, which provide mutual exclusion in access to messages, and which synchronize by making a receive operation delay its caller until a message is present. There are many flavors of message passing, depending on whether a message is sent to a named process or to a mailbox *port* that can be used by multiple senders or receivers. Message sending can also be synchronous, in which case a sender waits for the receiver to get the message, or asynchronous, in which case the sender does not wait. The former has the advantage of simpler error recovery if a transaction in a distributed environment fails; the latter decouples sender and receiver and permits a higher degree of concurrency.

Message-passing operations are provided in libraries like MPI (Message-Passing Interface) and PVM (Parallel Virtual Machine), which can be used with sequential programming languages like C and Fortran together with the Unix operating system process-creation mechanism for concurrent programs running on a network of workstations (*see* CLUSTER COMPUTING). These provide a variety of message-passing operations including synchronous and asynchronous sending and broadcast messages.

In another form of message passing the sender waits for the receiver to reply to the message. This produces a transfer of control in which the sender stops, the receiver (re)activates, and when the receiver completes its message-handling operation it stops and the sender resumes. That is, it is akin to the transfer of control in an ordinary subprogram call in which the calling program transfers control to the called subprogram, which transfers it back with a *return* statement, so this message passing is called *remote procedure call*. It provides a programming model in which the programmer can think in familiar terms about invoking procedures, which may happen to be in other processes or on other processors, in which case the call is implemented with messages rather than with elementary parameter-passing (*q.v.*) methods. Alternatively, one may adopt an explicit message-passing model of computation, in which case conventional subprogram calls are understood as messages; this is the model provided by object-oriented programming, most clearly by the Smalltalk language.

In one form of remote procedure call a new process is created to execute each call of a procedure; for example, many Unix *daemon* processes like the one that manages printing work this way. Ada uses a form of remote procedure call, which it calls *rendezvous*, in which a single process handles all calls. It is designed for *client–server* (*q.v.*) computing, in which a server process encapsulates data and provides operations on it that can be invoked by client processes; that is, it is an "active" version of a monitor or CCR. In Ada, a server process called a *task* declares *entries* as the operations that may be called remotely. It then typically executes an endless loop that contains a `select` statement, which is a kind of guarded command. This statement lists the entries and the conditions under which a call to each will be accepted. When a client calls an entry, and the guarding condition is also true, the server accepts the call (or one of them if there are several), executes the entry operation and returns a result if there is one. (If there is no returned result, the sender's wait terminates when the entry call is accepted.) The server thus provides mutual exclusion by processing entry calls serially, and provides condition synchronization in the

conditions that guard entries, and in the delay while the client waits for the entry call to complete. Fig. 2 is an Ada server that provides the resource management of the CCR example above, and the equivalent monitor example. It assumes that utility `put`, `get` routines have been defined.

Nondeterminism is important in the *select* statement, which is a kind of guarded command, because the manager process must not commit to one entry or another until a client calls an entry. A client task would execute calls like `manager.request(item)` and `manager.replace(item)`. Note that the `accept` for the `request` entry has a `do..end` construct, which causes the caller to wait until the requested object is produced; assigning it as a return (`out`) parameter completes the wait. The caller of `replace` does not wait, since the server can complete the replacement operation `put` while the client continues execution.

Types of Concurrent Programs

Concurrent programs are as diverse as sequential programs, but there are some common patterns of concurrency that arise in operating systems, parallel algorithms, and distributed processing (*see* SOFTWARE DESIGN PATTERNS). We have already characterized concurrent programs in terms of cooperation and communication—the latter is actually the broader notion, subsuming cooperation as a special case in which no actual data is communicated. Another general property is the equivalence of processes and data structures: encapsulation of data in CCRs or monitors with procedures to operate on them achieves the same results as encapsulation of data in processes, with operations carried out through message passing.

Producer–consumer interactions are one very common form of concurrent computation. Our resource manager is an example; processes consume resources and then return ("produce") them. In simple producer–consumer interactions one process produces data and passes it to a consumer process. It is often useful to decouple them so that each can run at its own rate, and this can be done with message passing to a mailbox that stores the data, or with an intermediate process that receives the product and forwards it to the consumer on demand. If there are many producers or many consumers, this process becomes a server for them; much client–server computing is a form of producer–consumer interaction.

Another variant is *master–worker* or *farming* computation (*see* COORDINATION LANGUAGES), in which one process provides tasks to be done by worker processes which repeatedly get a piece of work, perform it,

```
task manager is
   entry request(item : out item_type);
   entry replace(item : in item_type);
   end;

task body manager is
   resource_Q : queue_type :=
                     -- the initial resources
   begin
   loop
      select
         when not empty(resource_Q) =>
         accept request(item : out
            item_type) do
                  item := get(resource_Q); end;
      or
            accept replace(item : in item_type);
         put(resource_Q, item);
      end select;
   end loop;
end task;
```

and give the results to the master. Whenever a parallel computation can be partitioned into independent pieces, this form of computation may be appropriate. String-matching algorithms such as those used in the human genome project are typical; a huge search-space can be partitioned into portions for different workers.

Domain decomposition is another common structure for concurrency, often used when there is a computational domain that can be subdivided, with each subdomain assigned to a process. Computations can proceed independently in each subdomain for the most part, but some communication is required to maintain consistency at boundaries between subdomains. This is typical of many scientific computations, such as finite element methods (*q.v.*). When the time required to communicate boundary information is much less than the time to compute a solution in each subdomain, such domain decomposition is efficient.

Computations may be *peer-to-peer*, when any process may initiate an action calling for further actions from others. The multiagent systems (*q.v.*) used in some artificial intelligence work are typical of these.

Operating systems deal with *resource management* problems, in which a processes may be competing for resources and risk deadlock if they are poorly allocated. The same issues arise in distributed databases, a common application of concurrent programming, and are discussed in DATABASE CONCURRENCY CONTROL. The *dining philosophers* problem was designed to illustrate some of the issues that arise in resource management; in it, five philosophers sit around a table, with a fork between each pair and a bowl of spaghetti in the middle. They alternately think and try to eat, a task for which a philosopher must acquire the two adjacent forks. Such problems typically pose not only synchronization issues—if each obtains the left-hand fork, they all starve since no one can eat and no one will relinquish a fork—but also policy issues that may involve fairness or degree of concurrency.

Finally, concurrent programming is a tool for structuring even sequential computations by partitioning them into many processes or threads of computation, each of which performs a simple task. The advantage that concurrent programming offers is that the order of execution of the components can be controlled by the availability of data rather than by a single main program that may have to evaluate complex conditions (*see* DATAFLOW). This is the strategy used in operating systems like Unix in which a *pipeline* (*q.v.*) of processes can be constructed, each performing a task and communicating results to the next in line. Another example is a language compiler (*q.v.*), which can be divided into several phases; a *lexical analyzer* that recognizes language elements (tokens), a *parser* that

constructs a parse tree as it obtains sequences of tokens from the analyzer that form complete statements, and a *code generator* that translates pieces of the parse tree into machine code. These phases can be written as three communicating processes, each of which executes upon the arrival of sufficient data.

Languages

One of the first languages designed for concurrent programming was Concurrent Pascal in 1975; it used monitors for synchronization. Other languages with support for concurrency have included Modula-2 which provides monitor-like operations; Occam which uses message-passing; Ada; Java, with monitor primitives; and SR, a language used largely for research and teaching, which has a wide variety of synchronization methods. There are also numerous concurrent variants of standard languages like C, C++, and the functional language ML. Much concurrent programming is now done with the message-passing libraries mentioned earlier.

Semantics

We have given an informal description of the meaning of concurrent programming constructs in terms of an interleaving model. There are also more general models of concurrency in which instructions execute in parallel rather than in some interleaved sequence (*see* PETRI NET). In either case, the formal description of concurrent programming semantics is more difficult than the formal description of sequential programs, because timing as well as input values must be considered. One approach is to use temporal logic (*see* MODEL CHECKING) to specify what must *always*, *never* or *eventually* happen (for example: collision in a critical section must never occur; a waiting process must always eventually resume). There are also axiomatic approaches and those based on process algebras (*see* LOGICS OF PROGRAMS). As in sequential programming, it is important to characterize concurrent programs in terms of invariants: properties that are true of the program state at all important points of the computation. This task is difficult not only because of the need to take time into account, but because in a distributed computation, even the notion of a system *state* is difficult to characterize precisely, because there is no simple way to view the entire system simultaneously.

Further Reading

The fundamental paper that introduced semaphores and many of the important issues of concurrency is Dijkstra (1965). Gehani and McGettrick (1988) have reprinted important papers, including C. A. R. Hoare's 1974 "Monitors: An Operating System Structuring

Concept" (pp. 256–277), P. Brinch Hansen's 1975 "The Programming Language Concurrent Pascal" (pp. 73–92) and 1978 "Distributed Processes: A Concurrent Programming Concept" (pp. 216–233), Hoare's 1978 "Communicating Sequential Processes" (pp. 278–308), and an excellent 1983 survey by G. R. Andrews and F. B. Schneider, "Concepts and Notations for Concurrent Programming" (pp. 3–69). Good general texts include Andrews (1991), Ben-Ari (1990), Burns and Wellings (1996), and Bernstein and Lewis (1993). Filman and Friedman (1984) is an interesting discussion of models of concurrency. Schneider (1997) and Andrews (2000) are recent rigorous approaches to concurrency. Burns and Wellings (1998) and Lea (2000) describe concurrent programming in two common languages.

Bibliography

1965. Dijkstra, E. W. "Cooperating Sequential Processes," in *Programming Languages* (ed. F. Genuys), 43–112. New York: Academic Press.

1984. Filman, R. E., and Friedman, D. P. *Coordinated Computing.* New York: McGraw-Hill.

1988. Gehani, N., and McGettrick, A. D. (eds.) *Concurrent Programming.* Reading, MA: Addison-Wesley.

1990. Ben-Ari, M. *Principles of Concurrent and Distributed Programming.* Upper Saddle River, NJ: Prentice Hall.

1991. Andrews, G. R. *Concurrent Programming: Principles and Practice.* Redwood City, CA: Benjamin Cummings.

1993. Bernstein, A. J., and Lewis, P. M. *Concurrency in Programming and Database Systems.* Boston: Jones and Bartlett.

1996. Burns, A., and Wellings, A. J. *Real-Time Systems and Their Programming Languages*, 2nd Ed. Reading, MA: Addison-Wesley.

1997. Schneider, F. B. *On Concurrent Programming.* New York: Springer-Verlag.

1998. Burns, A., and Wellings, A. J. *Concurrency in Ada* (reprint of 1995 edition). New York: Cambridge University Press.

2000. Andrews, G. R. *Foundations of Multithreaded, Parallel, and Distributed Programming.* Reading, MA: Addison-Wesley.

2000. Lea, D. *Concurrent Programming in Java*, 2nd Ed. Reading, MA: Addison-Wesley.

David Hemmendinger

CONDITIONING

For articles on related subjects *see* BANDWIDTH; and DATA COMMUNICATIONS: PRINCIPLES.

Conditioning is the term used to describe the improvements made in the signaling characteristics of leased telecommunication lines over those in the normal switched network. Certain restrictions on the frequencies that can be transmitted over the switched network, because of attenuation and related problems, can be improved by conditioning. Conditioning is very infrequently used these days, because it involves explicit attention to each line from the telecommunications operator.

The characteristics of the line degrade the signal in a number of ways, and conditioning was used in this context to improve the situation on a per line basis. The use of adaptive digital filters in base-band digital transmission has enabled 2×64 Kbps to be transmitted over unconditioned telephone lines as part of the Integrated Services Digital Network (ISDN—*q.v.*). Adaptive digital filters allow rapid automatic compensation for differing transmission channel characteristics (although the original voice-band filter in the exchange must be removed first).

Recent developments in data transmission technology (xDSL—digital subscriber loop technology) have enabled over 6 Mbps to be successfully transmitted over voice-grade links. (The exact data rate that can be achieved depends upon the length of the local loop.) xDSL uses inverse multiplexing to increase the effective ''electrical'' bandwidth of the channel in order to transmit much higher data rates. The available ''electrical'' bandwidth is split into a number of bands or channels, and transmission in each is maintained separately—at the maximum rate each can support, according to the Hartley–Shannon law of information theory (*q.v.*). At the receiver, the channels are recombined to offer the higher bit rate.

Vicky J. Hardman and Peter T. Kirstein

CONFERENCING, COMPUTER

See COMPUTER CONFERENCING.

CONSTANT

For an article on a related topic *see* PROCEDURE-ORIENTED LANGUAGES.

A *constant* is a value that remains unchanged during a computation. Various types of constants are discussed in this article—numerical, character, logical, location, and figurative (symbolic) constants. While, in an imperative language, the reference to an item of information is usually given in terms of its location or address, it is more convenient to refer to constants by their values, since these are intrinsically meaningful in an algorithm. Consequently, high-level languages allow the inclusion of actual values, specified directly in the program, rather than being read in.

The spectrum of items that may be expressed as direct literal values transcends the numbers traditionally associated with the mathematical idea of a "constant." Some of these serve as data items, while others may provide operational information for the program.

Numerical Constants

Specification of numerical constants closely follows conventional forms. Thus, the constants in the familiar distance formula

$$S = v_0 t + 0.5 a t^2$$

require no special form in equivalent high-level language statements:

Fortran   S = V0*t + 0.5*a*t**2
Pascal   S := V0*t + 0.5*a*t*t
C or Java   S = V0*t + 0.5*a*t*t;

A number of languages also recognize a form of scientific notation for numerical constants. For instance, in languages like Basic, Fortran, Pascal, and C, the constant 0.00000513 can be expressed alternatively as $5.13E - 6$, $0.513E - 5$, or even $51.3E - 7$.

The foregoing numerical constants (reasonably) assume an underlying base of 10. Many languages provide ways to specify other bases (2, 8, and 16) useful in computer work. For instance, the C language recognizes 0X3CF6 as the hexadecimal (base 16) integer 3CF6.

Character String Constants

Many languages recognize character string constants, distinguishing them from symbolic names through the use of special delimiters (*q.v.*). The most popular delimiter is the single quote mark ('). (The double quote mark, ", is often used as an alternative.) Thus, 'BELT' or ''BELT'' refers to the four characters B, E, L, and T, distinct from some item named BELT. Note that the quotes are not part of the string; they merely define its extent. Inclusion of a quote as part of a string is handled by specifying two quotes. For instance, 'CAN''T' specifies the five characters C, A, N, ', T, and '''TIS' specifies the four characters ', T, I, S.

Logical (or Boolean) Constants

Many languages offer facilities for describing and manipulating processes whose outcomes are either "true" or "false." When such support is available, the programmer can define logical (Boolean) variables and use them in conjunction with appropriate operators to form logical (Boolean) expressions. As part of this support, these languages recognize the two logical constants (.TRUE. and .FALSE. in Fortran, true and false in Pascal, 1 and 0 in C). Thus, for instance, the following Pascal statements

```
var
    outcome : boolean;
    ...........
    outcome := true;
```

declare a variable named outcome, and assign to it a (constant) value of true.

Figurative (Symbolic) Constants

There are special types of constants that represent fixed values unlike previously discussed types in that they are not designated by their literal values. Instead, they are identified by names intended to convey the constants' meanings. Such *figurative* or *symbolic* constants may be permanent parts of a particular high-level language, or they may be defined for a specific program. Examples of the former are seen in the Cobol language, in which a value of zero has the preassigned names of ZERO, ZEROS, or ZEROES. Similarly, maxint in the Pascal language refers to the largest expressible integer value on the particular computer being used. In addition, many high-level languages support the use of programmer-defined symbolic constants. For instance, the PARAMETER statement, available in Fortran beginning with Fortran 77, enables the programmer to establish a fixed association between a name and a particular data value. To illustrate, the statement

```
PARAMETER (PI = 3.14159, HANDLE ='TABMAT')
```

defines the indicated constants and thwarts any attempt (in the program) to change their associated values. The same results are achieved in Pascal via the following declaration:

```
const
    pi = 3.14159;
    handle = 'TABMAT';
```

In the above examples, compilers substitute the specified value for symbolic constants but the constants exist outside of the language's normal type system. Some languages, such as Java (*q.v.*), allow any initialized declaration to be constant through specification of a keyword. For example

```
final float pi = 3.14159;
```

declares pi as a float (real) type with initial value as specified; use of the keyword final informs the compiler that no changes to this particular float variable are allowed.

Arbitrary Constants

While a symbolic constant's name may be arbitrary, the value associated with it must conform to one of the data types predefined for the language. However, some languages, such as Pascal and Modula-2, enable the programmer to define an arbitrary data type and an associated roster of "allowable" values for it. For example, the declarations

```
type
    peach = (cling, stark, elberta, redhaven,
        mushchik);
var
    dessert : peach
```

define a data type named `peach` and equip it with the five assignable values shown in the parentheses. Declaration of `dessert`, then, establishes that variable as being of the type `peach`, thereby empowering it to take on one of the five legitimate values. Accordingly, `dessert` can now receive a value via normal assignment, e.g.

```
dessert := redhaven
```

Internal representation of such arbitrary constants is a separate issue from which the programmer is insulated. As far as he or she is concerned, the `peach` data type has five values defined such that

```
cling < stark < elberta < redhaven < mushchik
```

Enumerations in C provide a mechanism for declaring totally ordered quasi-arbitrary constants such as those shown above. Unlike Pascal, the values associated with the constants are mandated by the language standard. Programmers usually abdicate value assignment to the compiler, which must assign values from the non-negative integers in sequence. When convenient, some or all of the enumeration values can be specified by the programmer, perhaps to coincide with indexing of other structures in the program. For example, the declarations

```
typedef
    enum {cling=4, stark, elberta,
              redhaven=100, mushchik} peach;
peach dessert;
```

establish `peach` as an enumeration type with 5 legitimate values and `dessert` as a variable of type `peach`. The enumeration text in braces causes `cling` and `redhaven` to have values 4 and 100, respectively. Automatic assignment provides the values of 5, 6, and 101 for `stark`, `elberta`, and `mushchik`, respectively.

Automatic Discovery of Constants

The foregoing discussion concerns how languages allow constant values to be declared. Most compilers contain an optimization called *constant propagation* that finds expressions whose values are constant over all possible program executions. Consider the program fragment

```
i := 1
if i = 1
   then j := 1
   else j := 2
k := j + 4
```

Constant propagation symbolically executes the program and determines that the conditional can only take its `true` branch; the variable `j` consequently has the constant value of 1 following the conditional. Thus, `k` can be shown to have the value 5. Code exhibiting the above properties often results from incorpo-

rating or specializing procedures; constant propagation can take advantage of such situations and improve program performance.

Finally, constants can also be discovered at run-time to improve performance. Consider the program fragment:

```
do i := 1 to N
   t := A[i]
   do j := 1 to M
      u := t+4
      B[i] := C[j] + u
   end
end
```

For each iteration of `j`, the values of `t` and `u` and the address of `B[i]` are constant. Dynamic code generation can rewrite the innermost loop, replacing these variables by constants. While there is overhead for customizing the innermost loop, performance is gained by avoiding computation and storage references through the discovery of constants.

Bibliography

1985. Jensen, K., and Wirth, N. *Pascal User Manual and Report*, Rev. Ed. Berlin: Springer Verlag.
1988. Kernighan, B., and Ritchie, D. *The C Programming Language: ANSI C Version*, 2nd Ed. Upper Saddle River, NJ: Prentice Hall.
1993. Fischer, A., and Grodzinsky, F. *The Anatomy of Programming Languages*. Upper Saddle River, NJ: Prentice Hall.
1997. Muchnick, S. *Advanced Compiler Design and Implementation*. San Francisco: Morgan Kaufmann.

Seymour V. Pollack and Ron K. Cytron

CONTENT ADDRESSABLE MEMORY

See ASSOCIATIVE MEMORY.

CONTENTION

For articles on related subjects *see* DATABASE CONCURRENCY CONTROL; MUTUAL EXCLUSION; MULTIPROCESSING; MULTIPROGRAMMING; and MULTITASKING.

Originally, the term *contention* was used to describe a communication system where the terminals, or lines, were competing for a circuit and the first one to find it free obtained it. This concept can be generalized to the case of multiple users (jobs, tasks, processes) competing for sharable resources (processors, buses, devices). For example, in a multiprogramming system, two processes may simultaneously require the use of the processor-memory bus. As another example, consider the case of a multiprocessor system where a process can be split into several tasks and the number of tasks ready to be processed in parallel is larger than the number of available processors.

Contention is solved by using priority schemes; the simplest one is a first come, first served strategy. However, all processes contending for a shared resource must either ask for the resource continuously (as in the processor-memory bus example) or must be remembered so that they will, in turn, be able to use it (as in the multiprocessor example). In addition, access to the shared resource must be synchronized. This implies the presence of either hardware arbiters or of software queues, with adequate synchronization mechanisms and buffers associated with each sharable resource.

Jean-Loup Baer

CONTROL APPLICATIONS

For articles on related subjects *see* ANALOG COMPUTER; ANALOG-TO-DIGITAL AND DIGITAL-TO-ANALOG CONVERTERS; AUTOMATION; CYBERNETICS; EMBEDDED SYSTEM; FUZZY LOGIC; REAL-TIME SYSTEMS; ROBOTICS; SIMULATION; and TELEROBOTICS.

Introduction

With the advent of the microcomputer chip, there arose the need to distinguish between *digital control* and *analog control*. The inputs and outputs from a digital control system are no longer continuous with time, as was the case with analog control systems. The microcomputer, and indeed any computer, must share its time domain with that of the external world to which it is interfaced. As such, input and output are sampled and/or changed in discrete time intervals. Additionally, almost random events must be accounted for and correctly handled by the discrete nature of a digital control system. Continuous, discrete, and sampled data can now be handled properly, and all are now embodied in the terms *automatic control* and *control theory*.

Control Theory

Control refers to the function whereby the outputs of a device, a process, or a system can be maintained at a desired value by specifying only its inputs. The relationship between an *input signal* and an *output signal* is defined as the *transfer function* and is represented, in its simplest form, by the block diagram in Fig. 1.

There is no guarantee that the desired output of a system can be achieved by adjusting only its input. First, it must be determined whether a static sequence of input settings will produce a corresponding sequence of output signals reliably and reproducibly. A sufficient number of observations must be made to establish the relation between input and output, i.e. the transfer function. If these observations reveal a stable relationship, then the system warrants being called a control system. However, in many applications, variations in both internal and external parameters can affect the stability of the transfer function. Some of these variations may be beyond the direct influence of the designer of the resulting system.

A system such as a simple lawn sprinkler will deliver an amount of water depending upon the setting of the water faucet and the length of time the water is allowed to run. This is based on the assumption that the lawn watering process is satisfied by providing a predetermined quantity of water per unit area. Achieving this, in turn, depends upon a constant-pressure water supply. What has just been described is an *open-loop* system, (i.e. the setting of the faucet will suffice to provide the correct amount of water). If the amount of water descending upon a sample area of the lawn were measured, then the duration of the sprinkling period could conceivably be shortened or extended to accommodate variations in water pressure and thus provide the requisite amount of water.

Systems in which a deviation from success in reaching a target value is fed back to a controller are called *closed-loop* systems. Closed-loop systems are eminently suited for situations in which there is a need to overcome anticipated or random variations in the system itself or in the environment in which the system operates. The difference between the desired value and the actual value at any time is called the "error," and the objective of any closed-loop control system is to manage all the adjustable aspects of the system so as to drive the error to zero. A block diagram for a generalized closed-loop system is shown in Fig. 2. Note the important components of this system: the inputs, the outputs, the *comparators* that determine the error from the difference between the inputs and outputs, the output sensing elements, and the feedback loop to the comparators. This diagram shows that the controlled system may have several inputs and outputs.

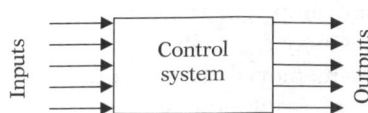

Figure 1. Block diagram of a system.

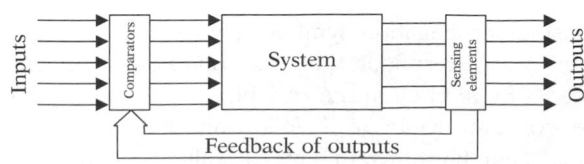

Figure 2. Block diagram of a closed-loop system.

The task remains the same: the correct output is maintained by driving the error to zero.

Applications

Many open-loop systems are encountered in everyday life. As the need for improved system performance arises and the cost of microprocessors and microcomputers (*q.v.*) decrease, it is possible to take greater advantage of closed-loop control systems. In environmental and safety contexts, the impetus for improvement is driven by legal requirements. Further, there has been a growth in the number of devices whose operational performance can be achieved only with closed-loop control systems. Systems for controlling automotive emissions and maximizing fuel economy are common examples.

Two different approaches to controlling the speed of an automobile serve to illustrate the distinction between open-loop and closed-loop systems. The earliest automobiles used hand throttles. Setting the throttle on a level highway would result in a constant speed. The automobile would be running "open loop" (see Fig. 3a). As the vehicle encountered a hill, the load on the engine would increase. Since the system had no capability to anticipate the extra load that the hill presented, the car would slow down. Allowing the driver to adjust the gas pedal creates a closed-loop system. The driver plays the multipart role of output sensor (measuring the change in speed and noting the approach to a hill), the feedback loop, the comparator,

and the actuator to adjust the gas pedal. The driver will note both the hill and the start of the slowing process and can depress the accelerator pedal further to maintain the desired speed.

Automatic constant-speed control systems ("cruise control") have now been in use for a number of years. These systems relieve the driver of one of these tasks: maintaining constant speed. Such a system allows the driver to bring the automobile to the desired speed, S_s, the *set point*, by pressing a button. The car's actual speed, S_e, is measured by a sensor. The error is the difference between the two and becomes the measure for deciding how to manipulate the accelerator pedal to maintain the desired speed. This closed-loop system is sensitive only to the actual speed of the car and is unable to anticipate a hill ahead or another vehicle yards ahead. Therefore, means are provided to disengage the automatic speed control via a button or by depressing the brake pedal. On the other hand, if the driver wishes to accelerate for any reason, a temporary adjustment of the gas pedal is permitted and the control system will resume its original setting when the driver leaves the control loop. The closed-loop version of this automobile speed control system is shown in Fig. 3b.

Early versions of automobile speed control systems used a combination of electromechanical components. The advent of inexpensive and compact microprocessors saw their introduction not only in speed controls but also in ignition and combustion systems (*see*

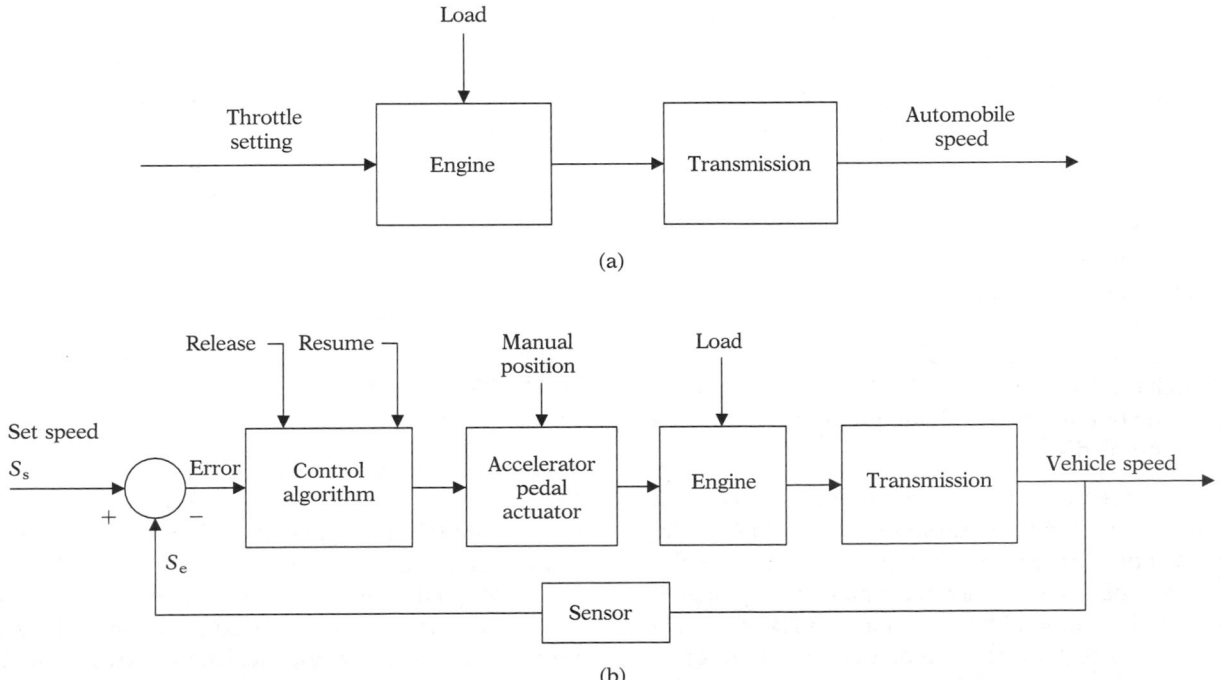

Figure 3. Block diagram of (a) an open-loop and (b) a closed-loop automobile speed control system.

EMBEDDED SYSTEM). There were two advantages. First, the microprocessors played an integral role in the control system, but their function was easily simulated in larger computer systems used just for the purpose of designing and evaluating the proposed control systems. This not only reduced the amount of trial and error in the design process, but also allowed for inexpensive exploration of the performance of the intended control system and its algorithm.

A *control algorithm* is a plan for achieving the desired control result. It provides the schema for calculating what changes must be made in response to changing inputs and outputs. In the example just discussed, we find both continuous and discrete operations. The automatic speed controller allows the setting of a desired speed (the set point to be locked in); cancellation of the automatic speed control process by depressing the brake pedal; activation of the system to resume automatic operation at the original set point speed; and using the control system manually to move to a new speed and establishing that as the new set point.

The control algorithm, that is, the equations that handle the error signal, generally applies one or more of three standard control actions, although more complex forms can be defined. The net action to be taken (the controller output) is a linear combination of three terms, each weighted with an appropriate constant (Kuo, 1991):

1. A proportional or *gain term*, P, with constant K_p.

2. An integral or *summation term*, I, with constant K_i.

3. A derivative or *difference term*, D, with constant K_d.

The proper values for the constants K_p, K_i, K_d are set by the control engineer to suit the particular situation. These combined control actions are so frequently used that the name PID (Proportional, Integral, Derivative) is used to describe the algorithm applied in most of the control loops used in process control applications. Digital microprocessor versions fill catalogs. Rapid increases in the price–performance ratio of microcomputer chips, coupled with the availability of hardware interfaces to real-world signals, have provided the control engineer with new and affordable control analysis and simulation tools to evaluate proposed solutions to control problems.

What has been described is an automobile speed control system and not an automatic automobile driving system. For example, the system does not sense that there may be a slower moving vehicle immediately in front of the automobile or even a brick wall! The system is unable to sense that the road may curve quickly to the right or left, requiring that the vehicle speed must be changed to negotiate the curve safely.

To accommodate these new goals, the control system would have to be changed to allow for the additional inputs. Input signals would have to be provided about road conditions and the spacing between vehicles. Sensors for some of these additional inputs are available; others remain to be developed. Electronic highway or "drive-by-wire" control systems are now receiving attention. The complexity of such systems implies greatly increased cost but would provide increased safety, relief of driver fatigue, and optimized traffic flow.

Process control involves the automatic control of manufacturing, material handling, or treatment processes. These processes were once manually or mechanically controlled. Parameter levels were manually measured, adjustments were calculated, set points were mechanically changed, etc. As a result, a kind of "batch" process control mode prevailed. But use of microprocessors for control allowed the digital control system to advance to a form of "process" control. The lower cost and higher speed of this type of controller found a responsive market just as new regulations were being imposed upon industries to reduce the adverse impacts of industrial processes on the environment. At the same time, competitive pressures were forcing processor manufacturers to reduce costs while maintaining sufficient profit margins.

The microcomputer provided a solution for these complex requirements. Better control of the process itself was usually sufficient to justify the cost of the application of digital control to all or parts of most processes. Applications are typically found in those industries that have developed processes to produce chemicals, steel, aluminum, plastics, food, beverages, petrochemicals, water, etc. These applications tend to be concerned with the automatic control of chemical, mechanical, and energy systems. Digital control systems are expected to achieve specified performance goals as well as to adjust or compensate for inherent disturbances within the process or accommodate variations due to the input of additional material. Digital controllers are used not only to monitor, adjust, and maintain the operational level of individual systems within the process, but also to optimize the overall process itself.

To illustrate these objectives, consider a digital controller that sets the position on a flow valve such that the amount of a given ingredient in a chemical tank is always maintained at a set point (*see* Fig. 4). The particular set point may have been determined by any one of several reasons, e.g. the need for a particular mixture, liquid level, or chemical concentration in the tank. What is being controlled is an output parameter, as previously described. Again, the difference between

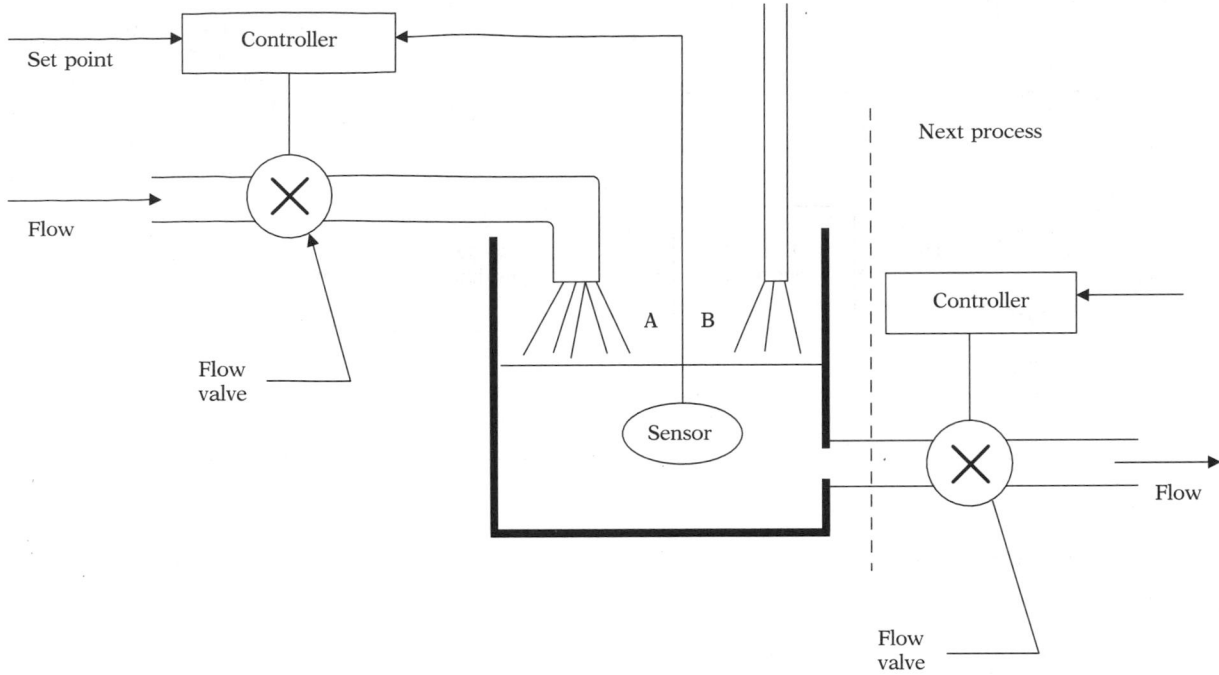

Figure 4. Chemical tank control.

the set point value and the sensor value, the *error signal*, is passed to the control algorithm. The microcomputer-based controller accommodates an algorithm that can either perform a calculation or a table lookup. It establishes the required signal level that must be sent to the flow valve to change the flow rate. This new flow rate adjusts the liquid level in the tank if a certain pressure head or specified level is needed, or it adds more of compound A if the mixture needs to be adjusted, or it adds more of chemical B if the concentration of that chemical needs to be adjusted, etc. At the point where the set point is reached, the process is said to have been "controlled."

This previous description is called a "control loop." In process control applications it is not unusual to have numerous control loops operating at one time and interacting with each other. It is the microcomputer-based controller, with its cost advantage, that now allows the control engineer to address the dynamics of complex process control effectively.

The overall process tends to drive the system *away* from the set point, and the controller is programmed to drive the system *toward* the set point. The rate at which this happens and the changes in the system around the set point are important design parameters. The control engineer must design for this dynamic in the selection of the computer for the digital controller, the control methods that will be used, and the algorithms that must be written. An important principle that enhances stability is *negative feedback*, that is, as first shown in Fig. 2, tapping a portion of the output signal and feeding it

back as an input component of opposite phase or voltage that tends to promote progression towards the set point (*see* CYBERNETICS).

A block diagram of one system in an overall process can best demonstrate the interaction between the various elements in the process and the digital controller (Fig. 5). Note the interaction and information flowing from neighboring systems. The process shown is for a chemical tank that has two inputs and one output. The level of activity in the tank is a function of its inputs and its output. This tank is just part of the overall process. The output from the tank may be metered by another control system. The second input may also be metered by another and different control system. The digital control system on the tank is expected to maintain the tank contents at the proper level.

The second input into the tank was chosen to illustrate an additional aspect that must be handled by a control system. This input introduces a disturbance or *variance* into the system. This second flow is not metered by the controller; rather, this flow may be introduced into the tank at any time. The control system, or more particularly the control loop, must be able to compensate for this random event. The flow valve increases or decreases the flow into the tank. This action is in the direction to reduce the error signal. Once the error signal is zero, the tank conditions have reached the set point and the flow will stop or be maintained in a steady state condition. Conceivably, the set point might represent a condition of continuous steady flow into the tank. In this case the controller modulates the flow

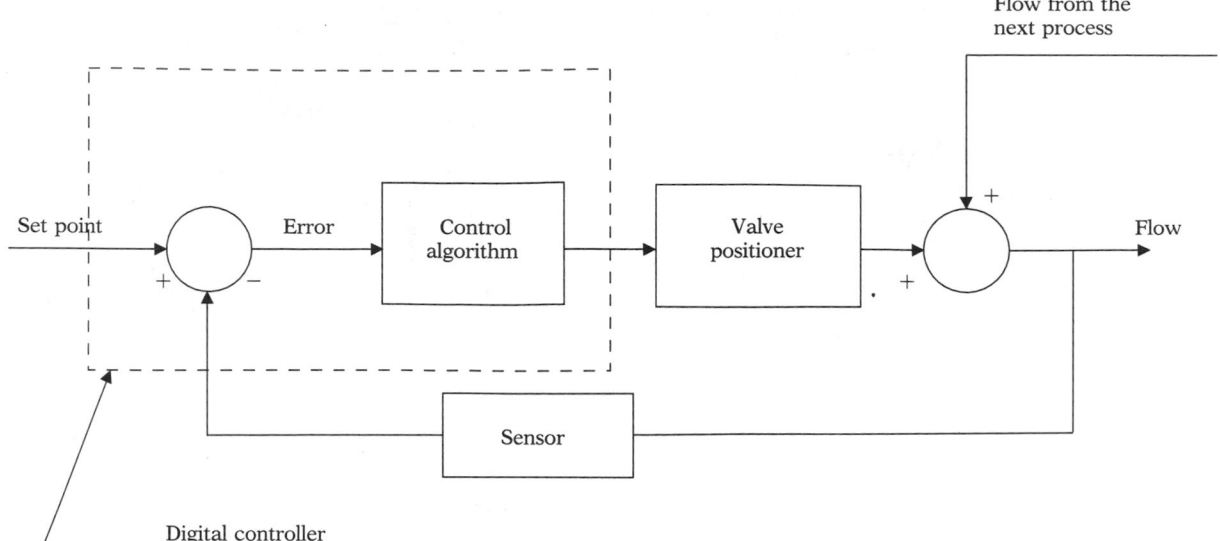

Figure 5. Tank control loop.

around this steady state flow value, ensuring that fluctuations above and below that value are kept within acceptable bounds.

Further, a condition of "no flow" may be one of several special cases in the sense that the controller receives a signal from other systems in the overall process that could represent a "starting-the-process condition," a "shutting-down-the-process condition," a "servicing-the-process condition," or an "emergency shutdown condition." The control algorithm senses all inputs to the controller, continuously tests for one of these signals, and, upon sensing a significant change in one of the inputs, leaves the main control loop and goes into a loop written for the special condition sensed. In the simplest scenario it would shut off the flow, turn on a light indicating a "standby" mode, and send a signal indicating that to other controllers in the process.

During the normal operational mode, flow leaves the tank, which in turn forces the controller to make appropriate adjustments. A secondary but equally important activity occurs when the flow from the second input into the tank starts, stops, or changes. As in normal operation, the tank sensor would react to this new change in tank properties and produce an error signal. The controller would take the proper action to bring that error signal to zero, bringing the system back to the set point. Again, the process is "controlled."

Digital rather than analog control systems are now the norm. If a microprocessor has a powerful enough instruction set (*q.v.*) and is fast enough, it may be able to handle numerous functions, including more than one control loop. (This speed may allow one to use the computer in the controller for a variety of purposes

other than servicing the control loops. In the past this helped justify the use of digital controllers over conventional analog controllers, even when the latter had a cost advantage.) The computer measures input signals, computes error signals, performs computations, services the control loops, senses and services external inputs, etc. In effect, the computer's time is shared among these various functions.

The time between servicing of all these operations is referred to as the *sampling time*. Inexpensive microprocessors often allow use of a single digital computer per control loop. That single digital computer will be servicing all outputs and all inputs as well as performing any necessary computations. It still, however, may be time-sharing various functions before it will again service that same function; hence the sampling time becomes an important design consideration. The question is whether a given signal into the computer (e.g. the feedback signal from the tank sensor) will change significantly between sample periods. Expanding this description to encompass all of the components, all of the digital controllers, all of the control loops, etc., raises an important issue in process control applications, namely the need for "distributed" control. Consideration of this subject includes not only the digital computers in each controlled process, but also the network that ties all of these computers and control systems together, and thus provides a basis for the beginnings of a formal study of process control optimization.

Bibliography

1990. Phillips, C. L., and Nagle, H. T. *Digital Control Systems Analysis and Design*. Upper Saddle River, NJ: Prentice Hall.

1991. Kuo, B. *Automatic Control Systems*. Upper Saddle River, NJ: Prentice Hall.

1995. Friedland, B. *Advanced Control Systems Design*. Upper Saddle River, NJ: Prentice Hall.

1998. Shinners, S. M. *Advanced Modern Control System Theory and Design*. New York: John Wiley.

1998. Kaufman, H., Bar-Kana, I., and Sobel, K. *Direct Adaptive Control Algorithms: Theory and Applications*. New York: Springer-Verlag.

1998. Baillieul, J., and Willems, J. C. (eds.) *Mathematical Control Theory*. New York: Springer-Verlag.

Donald E. Geister and Bertram Herzog

CONTROL DATA CORPORATION (CDC)

For articles on related subjects *see* COMPUTER INDUSTRY: UNITED STATES; CRAY, SEYMOUR; DIGITAL COMPUTERS, HISTORY OF; ENTREPRENEURS; and SUPERCOMPUTERS.

History

Control Data Corporation (CDC) opened for business in 1957 when co-founder William C. Norris and a handful of colleagues occupied rented warehouse space in St Paul, Minnesota. The corporation was the first computer company to be publicly financed. Initial capitalization was accomplished through the sale of 600,000 shares of common stock priced at $1 per share.

Norris's first and most effective move was to hire computer architect Seymour Cray from Univac and give him the resources and solitude he needed. Cray led a team that produced some of the most powerful machines ever developed. CDC quickly became the industry leader for powerful machines for scientific, military, and engineering work. By 1959 CDC had sales of $4.5 million, and a year later sales exceeded $28 million. Success was based primarily on the CDC 1604 mainframe (*q.v.*) and later, its successor, the CDC 3600. By the mid-1960s, the CDC 6600 was recognized as the world's foremost supercomputer. Its unique architectural design (Thornton, 1970) anticipated several of the features of modern RISC (Reduced Instruction Set Computers—*q.v.*) machines. By 1965, only two computer companies were operating in the black—CDC and IBM. CDC followed the historic 6600 with the 7600 and then the Cyber series (*see* Fig. 1).

An early CDC acquisition, Cedar Engineering, manufactured peripheral equipment for computers. Cedar Engineering eventually grew into Imprimis Technology, Inc., the largest supplier of high-performance data storage products for the original equipment manufacturers (OEM) market.

When Control Data began marketing peripheral products, it also moved into data services. There were many companies with the technical sophistication to use powerful computers, but at the time, only the largest and most prosperous could afford to invest in them. Control Data offered to keep that equipment busy enough to make it cost-effective. In his words, Bill Norris decided to "sell a little piece of a big computer at a time."

Control Data's involvement in computer-based services expanded in 1967 when it acquired the Arbitron Company as part of CEIR, a software company. CEIR is no longer in business, but Arbitron was a major financial contributor to Control Data for many years.

Rapid growth began to strain Control Data's limited resources. In addition, many computer systems were leased rather than sold outright, and the debt that was incurred to finance lease buildup had an unfavorable impact on the company's balance sheet. Control Data determined that a possible solution to both problems was the acquisition of a finance company. The Commercial Credit Company of Baltimore made overtures to which Control Data responded affirmatively, and Commercial Credit became a wholly owned subsidiary of Control Data in 1968.

In 1968, when IBM announced its intent to add an allegedly powerful model 360/80 to its 360 series line, sale of the 6600 dropped precipitously. Calling the model 80 a "paper tiger," Norris accused IBM of unfair business practices for announcing computer models far in advance of their realization. Perceiving this to be a tactic designed to hurt sales of his machines, Norris filed an antitrust suit against IBM and won. CDC realized more than $100 million dollars in the suit and, as part of the settlement, Control Data acquired the Service Bureau Company from IBM. This organization was the forerunner of a number of successful Control

Figure 1. Control Data CYBER 910 Workstation.

Data businesses, the largest of which is Business Management Services, a major provider of payroll processing, tax filing, and other business administration services. The acquisition of the Service Bureau Company doubled the size of Control Data's service business, broadened its markets, and brought to the company a first-rate management staff.

In 1967, Control Data began to found and promote businesses in which computers were used to provide education, training, and better management services to the disadvantaged. The largest of these businesses involved computer-based education, job creation, and new business incubation. By the early 1980s, Control Data was perhaps best known for these small businesses, even though computers and peripheral equipment accounted for the largest share of the company's revenues. Emphasis on and sales of supercomputers had begun to wane by this time, however; this fairly dominant phase of CDC's business was severely affected by the loss of Seymour Cray, who had left to form his own company, Cray Research, in 1973. In 1984, CDC decided to phase out its plug-compatible peripheral equipment business, which once had captured a fair share of the business of supplying such equipment to users of IBM mainframes.

The computer industry underwent significant change in the early 1980s, due principally to intense competition from the Japanese and small startup companies in the USA, as well as the advent of the microcomputer. Some of Control Data's competitors reacted to these changes more quickly than it did and, as a result, the company's performance fell off sharply and it began to experience serious liquidity problems. It became clear that Control Data had become far too diverse and that it needed to focus much more narrowly if it was to prosper again.

Refocusing became the primary task of Robert M. Price, who succeeded Norris as chairman and chief executive officer in January 1986. When a successful public debt offering removed the most immediate pressure on the company in mid-1986, the sale of non-strategic and non-performing assets began. The Company had determined that it would concentrate on the computer business, so in late 1986 Commercial Credit was spun off as a publicly owned company. Control Data initially retained a minority interest, but sold that to Commercial Credit a year later.

Robert Price retired as CEO in 1989 and was succeeded by Lawrence Perlman. Perlman initiated divestiture of Imprimis, the PLATO educational system, and ETA Systems, a $490 million tax write-off. In 1991, CDC closed its historic archives and donated its contents to the Charles Babbage Institute (q.v.). In 1992, Control Data's Board of Directors separated the corporation into two independent businesses—Control Data Systems Inc., an open systems integrator, and Ceridian Corporation, an information services company. By 1997, CDC had tripled its depressed 1992 value.

On 23 September 1997, Control Data Systems, Inc. completed a transition from a public company to a private one, the new owners being the investment firm of Welsh, Carson, Anderson & Stowe (WCAS). The new owners intend to provide electronic commerce (q.v.) solutions to large organizations worldwide by focusing on two industries: information services and health care. Thus former mainframe maker Control Data Systems has evolved into a systems integrator. It provides customers with hardware, including workstations (q.v.) and servers made by Silicon Graphics and computers made by Sun Microsystems and Hewlett-Packard, and it also provides messaging and operating system software as well as client–server (q.v.) and networking consulting. For the fiscal year ending in December 1996, CDC earned $16 million on sales of $306 million, a one-year growth of 32.8%. The Corporation then employed 1,600 people, about 9% more than the year before. Its current president and CEO is James E. Ousley.

By 1999, the annual revenue of Control Data Systems, Inc. had fallen to $180 million. On 1 September 1999 the company was sold to British Telecommunications (BT) which added CDS to its Syntegra Systems Integration division.

Bibliography

1970. Thornton, J. E. *Design of a Computer: The Control Data 6600*. Glenview, IL: Scott, Foresman.
1976. Werkheiser, A. H. "Control Data Corporation 6600 Series," in *The Encyclopedia of Computer Science*, 1st Ed. (ed. Anthony Ralston), 362–363. New York: Petrocelli–Charter.
1983. Keller, T. W. "Control Data Corporation Cyber Series," in *The Encyclopedia of Computer Science*, 2nd Ed. (eds. Anthony Ralston and Edwin D. Reilly), 410–412. New York: Van Nostrand Reinhold Co.
1993. Charland, T. A. "Control Data Corporation Computers," in *The Encyclopedia of Computer Science*, 3rd Ed. (eds. Anthony Ralston and Edwin D. Reilly), 358–361. New York: Van Nostrand Reinhold Co.

Website

1999. Control Data home page. `http://www.cdc.com`.

Thomas A. Charland, revised by Edwin D. Reilly

CONTROL STRUCTURE

For articles on related subjects *see* DATA STRUCTURES; EXCEPTION HANDLING; GUARDED COMMAND; PROCEDURE-ORIENTED LANGUAGES; STRUCTURED PROGRAMMING; and SUBPROGRAM.

A *control structure* is a programming language construct that specifies a departure from the normal sequential execution of statements. In its broadest sense, this includes calling a procedure, resuming a coroutine (*q.v.*), and initiating tasks, all of which involve transferring the path of execution to another program unit. (In the case of recursion (*q.v.*), the "other" program unit is a copy of the calling program.) It also includes, in its broadest sense, the "parallel" (simultaneous) performance of two or more operations within a given program unit. In its more common usage, however, *control structure* refers to the facilities for controlling the sequence of statement execution within a given program unit, and includes special facilities for selection control, repetition control, and exception handling. The description here is limited to this more common view. Usually, such facilities are in the form of "extended" statements, involving several parts in different lines—hence, the term control *structure*.

Arbitrary Control

The normal pattern of program execution is sequential control in which statements are executed in the order they appear. If $\langle S1 \rangle$ and $\langle S2 \rangle$ are each program statements (or self-contained sequences of statements) that perform some processing (e.g. assignment, I/O, or procedure call) then

$$\ldots \langle S1 \rangle ; \langle S2 \rangle \quad \text{or} \quad \langle S1 \rangle$$
$$\langle S2 \rangle$$

represents the execution of $\langle S1 \rangle$, followed immediately by the execution of $\langle S2 \rangle$. A pictorial representation of sequential control is

Virtually all useful programs (except those consisting only of procedure calls) involve intra-program execution path control different from sequential control, and therefore all programming languages provide facilities for specifying such control. A simple and fundamental, yet powerful and "complete" set of execution control facilities consists of the ability (1) to insert a label $\langle L \rangle$ at any point in the program for identification of that location:

$$\langle L \rangle :$$

and (2) to unconditionally or conditionally (depending upon the value of a Boolean expression $\langle B \rangle$) transfer execution control to such points, using **goto** (branching) statements.

```
goto ⟨L⟩
if ⟨B⟩ goto ⟨L⟩
```

The conditional **goto** involves two possible paths of execution, as shown, one of which continues sequential control (if $\langle B \rangle$ is **false**) and the other ($\langle B \rangle$ **true**) transfers control to the specified label: all computing hardware contains efficient machine-level instructions to perform conditional and unconditional branching, and normally all high-level language control structures are implemented using these instructions. In what follows, control structures are described in terms of **goto** to show how they may be implemented.

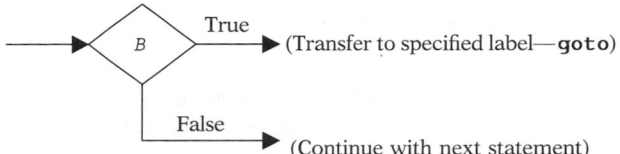

With conditional and unconditional **goto** statements, arbitrary execution control may be achieved. Typically, in programming languages, labels are either numbers (e.g. in Fortran: GO TO 210) or alphanumeric identifiers (e.g. in Ada: goto MatchFound).

While the **goto** is, in principle, sufficient for all conceivable intra-program sequence control, in practice it is not generally the most satisfactory in a high-level language environment. Most need for execution control is limited to a few highly systematic patterns. When implemented with **goto**s, such control patterns are not especially apparent to the reader of the program, which detracts from the understanding of the program. By the same token, primary reliance on **goto**s for specifying control when writing programs tends to be error-prone. This was pointed out by Edsger Dijkstra in a now classic letter (1968). Bohm and Jacopini (1966) showed that essentially any control flow can be achieved without the **goto** by using appropriately chosen sequential, selection, and repetition control structures. Therefore high-level general-purpose programming languages include, among their features, facilities designed expressly for optimum implementation of these and other commonly found control patterns. Software development (programming) tends to be significantly easier, and more reliable, if these control structures are used for most execution control, with **goto**s being used only in those occasional instances where the needed control has some unusual pattern.

Selection Control

A very common control pattern is that of selectively executing, or not executing, a sequence of statements $\langle S \rangle$, depending upon the current value (**true** or **false**) of a Boolean expression $\langle B \rangle$. The control structure for such a control pattern is as follows, with the equivalent control using `goto` shown below the pictorial representation.

`if ⟨B⟩ then ⟨S⟩ endif`

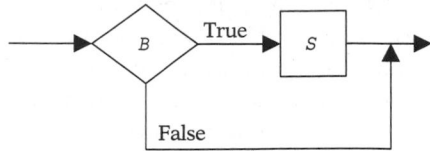

`if not ⟨B⟩ goto ⟨L⟩; ⟨S⟩`
`⟨L⟩:`

Another common pattern has one group of statements, ⟨S1⟩, being executed if ⟨B⟩ is true, and a different group, ⟨S2⟩, if ⟨B⟩ is false.

`if ⟨B⟩ then ⟨S1⟩`
`      else ⟨S2⟩`
`endif`

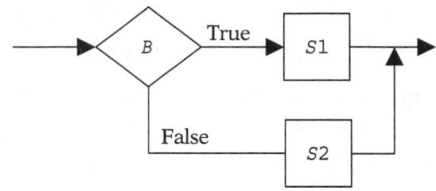

`if not ⟨B⟩ goto ⟨L2⟩`
`⟨S1⟩; goto ⟨L1⟩`
`⟨L2⟩: ⟨S2⟩`
`⟨L1⟩:`

This latter structure, which is simply an extension of the previous one with the optional `else ⟨S2⟩` part, is known as the `if-then-else` selection control structure, and (with minor syntactic variations) is the most commonly found selection control structure in high-level languages.

Another common control pattern is that of selecting one group of statements to be executed from among 3, 4, 5, or more different statement groups. In general, one can think of n groups of statements ($n > 0$), ⟨S1⟩, ⟨S2⟩, ..., ⟨Sn⟩, from which (at most) one group is to be selected for execution. The conditions governing the selection are formulated as a set of Boolean expressions, ⟨B1⟩, ⟨B2⟩, ..., ⟨Bn⟩, as may be appropriate for the needed control, so that if ⟨B1⟩ is true ⟨S1⟩ is selected; otherwise, if ⟨B2⟩ is true ⟨S2⟩ is selected and, in general, for the first ⟨Bi⟩ that is true, the corresponding ⟨Si⟩ is selected.

`if ⟨B1⟩ then ⟨S1⟩`
`   ⟨B2⟩ then ⟨S2⟩`
`       ⋮`
`   ⟨Bn⟩ then ⟨Sn⟩`
`       [else ⟨Sn+1⟩]`
`endif`

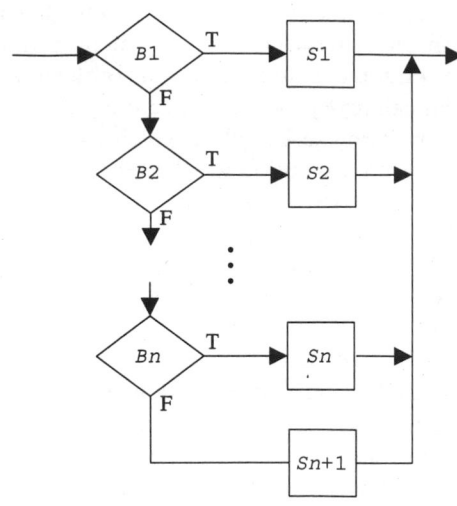

`if not ⟨B1⟩ goto ⟨L2⟩`
`        ⟨S1⟩ goto ⟨L1⟩`
`⟨L2⟩: if not ⟨B2⟩ goto ⟨L3⟩`
`        ⟨S2⟩ goto ⟨L1⟩`
`⟨L3⟩:`
`        ⋮`
`⟨Ln⟩: if not ⟨Bn⟩ goto ⟨Ln+1⟩`
`        ⟨Sn⟩ goto ⟨L1⟩`
`⟨Ln+1⟩: ⟨Sn+1⟩`
`⟨L1⟩:`

Since there are no restrictions on the Boolean expressions in this n-way selection control structure, more than one such expression may be true (`else` is always considered to be "true"). Still, at most one statement group is executed—that one associated with the first true Boolean expression—and possibly none executed (if there are no true Boolean expressions and the `else` option is absent). Square brackets, as around the `else` portion of the above structure, denote optionality.

In none of the selection control structures is there any restriction on the statements that any ⟨S⟩ may contain. And, in particular, any ⟨S⟩ may contain other (nested) selection control structures. For example, n-way selection control may be achieved using nested `if-then-else` structures. Therefore, the above n-way structure provides no additional functionality over the `if-then-else`, but highly nested structures detract enough from program readability that the arbitrary n-way selection structure is desirable. Note that the basic `if-then-else` is simply a special case of n-way selection—i.e. for $n = 1$.

The n-way selection structure is a highly sequential selection mechanism, involving an ordered evaluation of a sequence of Boolean expressions. Another common selection pattern involves, conceptually, "parallel" selection of one from among several statement groups. Here, the selection conditions are disjoint relations involving constant values, so that, in principle, selection may be "immediate" and not require the evaluation of a sequence of Boolean expressions. The `case` selection structure is often used to express such "parallel" selection. If $\langle X \rangle$ is an expression, and each $\langle V_i \rangle$ is a constant value of the same data type as $\langle X \rangle$, the `case` structure has the form shown below.

```
case ⟨X⟩
    ⟨V1⟩ then ⟨S1⟩
    ⟨V2⟩ then ⟨S2⟩
        ⋮
    ⟨Vn⟩ then ⟨Sn⟩
        [else ⟨Sn+1⟩]
    endcase
```

Since the $\langle V \rangle$s are disjoint, their order in the `case` structure is immaterial. Also, any $\langle V \rangle$ may consist of a set or range of values, rather than just a single value, so long as all of the $\langle V \rangle$s remain disjoint. As with the *n*-way `if`, there may be any number of cases in a `case` structure and the `else` part is optional. In some `case` implementations, if the value of $\langle X \rangle$ does not match any of the $\langle V \rangle$ values and the `else` part is omitted, then an error condition exists, from which recovery must be made (see exception handling below) or execution of the program is terminated.

A significant variation of the `case` structure is the replacement of the expression $\langle X \rangle$ with an arbitrary program segment $\langle S \rangle$. At various points in this program segment, the case value groups are identified for subsequent execution (e.g. with a statement such as `select` $\langle V \rangle$). Such a selection structure, generally known as a *Zahn structure*, provides for arbitrary selective execution based upon the results of an arbitrary algorithm, and has the general form given below.

```
case selection: ⟨V1⟩,⟨V2⟩,...,⟨Vn⟩
    ⟨S⟩
    ⟨V1⟩ then ⟨S1⟩
    ⟨V2⟩ then ⟨S2⟩
        ⋮
    ⟨Vn⟩ then ⟨Sn⟩
        [else ⟨Sn+1⟩]
    endcase
```

A special application of this structure is described in the next section on repetition control.

Finally, selection in functional languages (*see* FUNCTIONAL PROGRAMMING) uses a Boolean expression to select among expressions, rather than among statements. Thus the following conditional

```
if ⟨B⟩ then ⟨Exp1⟩
        else ⟨Exp2⟩
    endif
```

is an expression that has a *value*, the value of $\langle Exp1 \rangle$ if $\langle B \rangle$ is true, and the value of $\langle Exp2 \rangle$ otherwise. Similarly, a functional language may have a case *expression* that evaluates to a value determined by the case selector.

Repetition Control

An extremely important aspect of programming is the specification of repetitive execution of a statement group $\langle S \rangle$. The following structure, with its `goto` equivalent at the bottom, will repeat execution of $\langle S \rangle$ indefinitely.

```
loop
    ⟨S⟩
endloop
```

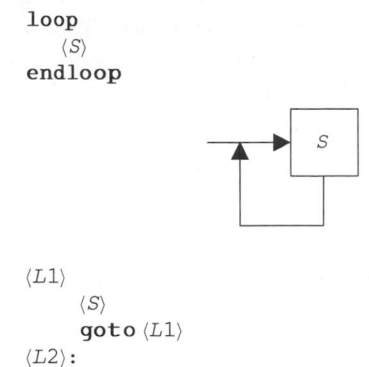

```
⟨L1⟩
    ⟨S⟩
    goto ⟨L1⟩
⟨L2⟩:
```

The above loop control results in an *infinite loop* unless execution of one of the statements in $\langle S \rangle$ causes either program termination (e.g. execution of a `stop` statement) or a branch out of the loop (e.g. `goto` $\langle L2 \rangle$). A `loop exit` statement is one whose purpose is to cause termination of loop execution, and is equivalent to `goto` $\langle L2 \rangle$. Loop exits are normally conditional, and may have a form equivalent to

```
if ⟨Be⟩ exit
```

where $\langle Be \rangle$ is the loop exit condition. A common extension of this is to allow specification of some end-of-loop processing $\langle Se \rangle$ prior to exiting the loop:

```
if ⟨Be⟩ then ⟨Se⟩ exit
```

This is useful if the loop has different end-of-loop processing requirements at different exits.

Conditional `exit` statements can provide any kind of loop control; whether or not $\langle S \rangle$ is executed again may be controlled completely by the use of `exit` statements. For often-encountered looping control patterns, however, it is convenient to be able to include, in the loop header, specification of the loop control. This usually makes writing the loop significantly easier, and makes the loop much more understandable in reading the program, both of which are highly desirable in the development and maintenance of reliable software. Therefore, loop structures often have the general form:

```
loop ⟨C⟩
    ⟨S⟩
endloop
```

where $\langle C \rangle$ specifies the desired control of repetition. With loop control specified in this manner, the need for `exit` statements in $\langle S \rangle$ is typically much reduced

(although `exit` statements may still be allowed in ⟨S⟩).
Two of the more common types of control, ⟨C⟩, are:

1. Conditional: `while` ⟨B⟩
2. Indexed: `for` ⟨I⟩ ← ⟨X1⟩ `to` ⟨X2⟩ [`by` ⟨X3⟩]

where ⟨I⟩ is an integer variable, the ⟨X⟩s are integer
expressions, and ⟨B⟩ is a Boolean expression. The effect
of each of these control options is as follows (Z is an
"internal" integer "hidden" from the programmer):

```
loop while ⟨B⟩
      ⟨S⟩
endloop

loop
      if not ⟨B⟩ exit
      ⟨S⟩
endloop

loop for ⟨I⟩ ← ⟨X1⟩ to ⟨X2⟩ by ⟨X3⟩
      ⟨S⟩
endloop
   (if ⟨X3⟩ [≠ 0] option is omitted, +1 is assumed)

Z ← ⟨X3⟩/abs (⟨X3⟩)
⟨I⟩ ← ⟨X1⟩ − ⟨X3⟩
loop
   ⟨I⟩ ← ⟨I⟩ + ⟨X3⟩
   if Z * ⟨I⟩ > Z * ⟨X2⟩ exit
   ⟨S⟩
endloop
```

A number of variations of these loop facilities are
implemented in various computer languages, and
occasionally an entirely different kind of control is
defined and implemented for ⟨C⟩. One such class of
variations is control at the bottom of the loop rather
than at the top (`repeat-until`).

Loop structures may be nested, and occasionally it
is necessary to exit more than one level of repetition.
This may be done by using the `goto` statement, or by
identifying loops with (the equivalent of) a label ⟨L⟩ and
allowing "multi-level" `exit` statements of the form:

```
if ⟨B⟩ exit ⟨L⟩
```

A third way to achieve multi-level exits is to "cascade"
the requisite number of single-level exits. This may be
done by setting a Boolean "flag" and exiting one level
(e.g. `if` ⟨Be⟩ `then` MULTILEVEL ← `true; exit`), then
immediately (after `endloop`) exiting again (e.g. `if`
MULTILEVEL `exit`).

Another facility occasionally provided in loop structures is that of proceeding directly to the next repetition cycle of a loop:

```
if ⟨B⟩ cycle ⟨L⟩
```

⟨L⟩ refers to the desired loop identification; as with
exits, the ⟨L⟩ may be omitted for single-level cycling.

Since cycling is not often needed in practice, and may
be achieved using `exit` and selection control, `cycle`
is not as commonly implemented as is `exit`.

A reasonably common occurrence (some studies have
indicated for about 20% of all loops) is that of multiple
single-level exits in a given loop. Normally, one can
expect the post-loop processing to be somewhat
different for the different exits. For example, a search
loop may contain two exits, one for when the search is
successful and one when it is unsuccessful. The action
taken after the search is normally dependent upon
whether or not the search was successful, implying
different processing at each of the two exits. Selection
of the proper post-loop processing routine may be
achieved by flagging each exit, just prior to departure
from the loop, for use in ordinary selection control
following the loop. Forms of the loop control specification ⟨C⟩ exist that facilitate such exit flagging.

A variation of the Zahn `case` selection structure, in
which the pre-selection routine is the loop, integrates
a loop and its various exit-processing routines into a
single control structure. The form of such a structure is:

```
loop ⟨C⟩ with exits (⟨E1⟩, ⟨E2⟩, ..., ⟨En⟩)
      ⟨S⟩
endloop
      ⟨E1⟩ then ⟨S1⟩
      ⟨E2⟩ then ⟨S2⟩
        ⋮
      ⟨En⟩ then ⟨Sn⟩
endexits
```

where ⟨S1⟩, ⟨S2⟩, ..., ⟨Sn⟩ are the different post-loop
exit-processing routines corresponding to exits ⟨E1⟩,
⟨E2⟩, ..., ⟨En⟩, respectively. Within the loop body
⟨S⟩, a certain exit may be specified with an exit
statement of the form:

```
if ⟨Be⟩ select exit ⟨Ei⟩.
```

Most programming languages do not provide a full
Zahn construct as such, but rely upon the programmer to use two consecutive simpler structures, such as
a simple loop structure followed by a simple case
structure, with appropriate variable communication
between them, to simulate the effect of a Zahn
structure.

Exception Handling

A number of things can happen during program
execution that can prevent execution from successfully
continuing. These include division by zero, subscript
out of bounds, numeric overflow, `case` value missing,
unavailable read-only file, wrong data type on input,
insufficient storage available, and referencing an undefined value. Such exceptions, when detected, normally

Feature	Ada	Basic	C, C++, Java	Haskell	Fortran 95	Pascal
1. LABEL example	`<<LABEL>>`	`100`	`LABEL`	N/A	`LABEL`	`100`

2. Branching	`goto LABEL`
	`if ⟨B⟩ then goto`
	`LABEL end if`
		`goto 100`
		`if ⟨B⟩ then 100`
			`goto LABEL`
			`if (⟨B⟩) goto LABEL`
				N/A
				N/A
					`goto LABEL`
					`if (⟨B⟩) goto LABEL`
						`goto 100`
						`if ⟨B⟩ then goto 100`

3. If-then-else	`if ⟨B⟩ then ⟨S1⟩`
	`[else ⟨S2⟩]`
	`end if`
		`if ⟨B⟩ then ⟨S1⟩`
		`[else ⟨S2⟩]`
		`endif`
			`if (⟨B⟩) ⟨S1⟩`
			`[else ⟨S2⟩;]`
				`if ⟨B⟩ then ⟨Exp1⟩`
				`else ⟨Exp2⟩`
					`if (⟨B⟩) then ⟨S1⟩`
					`[else ⟨S2⟩]`
					`endif`
						`if ⟨B⟩ then ⟨S1⟩`
						`[else ⟨S2⟩]`

4. n-way-branch	`if ⟨B1⟩ then ⟨S1⟩`
	`elsif ⟨B2⟩ then ⟨S2⟩`
	`elsif`
	`...`
	`[else ⟨Sn+1⟩]`
	`end if`
		`if ⟨B1⟩ then ⟨S1⟩`
		`elseif ⟨B2⟩ then ⟨S2⟩`
		`elseif`
		`...`
		`[else ⟨Sn+1⟩]`
		`endif`
			nested if–then–else	nested if–then–else	`if (⟨B1⟩) then ⟨S1⟩`
					`elseif (⟨B2⟩)`
					`then ⟨S2⟩`
					`elseif`
					`...`
					`[else ⟨Sn+1⟩]`
					`endif`
						nested if–then–else

5. Case	`case ⟨X⟩ of:`
	`when ⟨V1⟩ ⟹ ⟨S1⟩`
	`when ⟨V2⟩ ⟹ ⟨S2⟩`
	`...`
	`[when others ⟹`
	`⟨Sn+1⟩]`
	`end case`
		`select case ⟨X⟩`
		`case ⟨V1⟩⟨S1⟩`
		`case ⟨V2⟩⟨S2⟩`
		`...`
		`case else ⟨Sn+1⟩`
		`end select`
			`switch (⟨X⟩){`
			`case ⟨V1⟩: ⟨S1⟩;`
			`  break;`
			`case ⟨V2⟩: ⟨S2⟩;`
			`  break;`
			`...`
			`[default: ⟨Sn+1⟩;]`
			`}`
				`case ⟨X⟩ of`
				`(⟨B1⟩) ⟹ ⟨Exp1⟩`
				`(⟨B2⟩) ⟹ ⟨Exp2⟩`
				`...`
				`[otherwise ⟹`
				`⟨Expn+1⟩]`
					`select case (⟨X⟩)`
					`case (⟨V1⟩)⟨S1⟩`
					`case (⟨V2⟩)⟨S2⟩`
					`...`
					`[case default`
					`⟨Sn+1⟩]`
					`end select`
						`case ⟨X⟩ of`
						`⟨V1⟩: ⟨S1⟩`
						`⟨V2⟩: ⟨S2⟩`
						`...`
						`[otherwise: ⟨Sn+1⟩]`
						`end`

6. Looping	`[while ⟨B⟩] loop`
	`⟨S⟩`
	`end loop`
	
	`for ⟨I⟩ in`
	`⟨X1⟩...⟨X2⟩`
	`loop ⟨S⟩`
	`end loop`
		`do [while ⟨B⟩]`
		`⟨S⟩`
		`loop`
		
		`for ⟨I⟩ ⟹ ⟨X1⟩ to`
		`⟨X2⟩ [step ⟨X3⟩]`
		`⟨S⟩`
		`next ⟨I⟩`
			`while ⟨B⟩`
			`⟨S⟩`
			
			`for (⟨I⟩ = ⟨X⟩; ⟨B⟩;`
			`⟨I⟩ = ⟨Exp⟩;)`
			`⟨S⟩`
				N/A
				(use iterator operators
				and recursion)
					`do [while ⟨B⟩ ]`
					`⟨S⟩`
					`enddo`
					
					`do ⟨I⟩ = ⟨X1⟩, ⟨X2⟩`
					`[, ⟨X3⟩]`
					`⟨S⟩`
					`enddo`
						`while ⟨B⟩ do`
						`⟨S⟩`
						
						`repeat [⟨S⟩] until ⟨B⟩`
						
						`for ⟨I⟩ := ⟨X1⟩ [down]to`
						`⟨X2⟩ do ⟨S⟩`

7. Loop exits	`exit [when ⟨B⟩]`	`exit`	`break`	N/A	`exit`	`goto ⟨L⟩`

8. Exception handling	`begin`
	`⟨S0⟩`
	`exception`
	`when ⟨E1⟩ ⟹ ⟨S1⟩`
	`when ⟨E2⟩ ⟹ ⟨S2⟩`
	`...`
	`[when others ⟹`
	`⟨Sn+1⟩]`
	`end`
		`when exception in`
		`⟨S1⟩`
		`use`
		`⟨S2⟩`
		`end when`
		`handler ⟨X⟩`
		`⟨S⟩`
		`end handler`
			N/A in C;
			C++, Java:
			`try ⟨S⟩`
			`catch ⟨S⟩`
				N/A
				`⟨V⟩::⟨X⟩`
				`⟨V⟩ = catch`
				`⟨V⟩ where`
				`⟨V⟩ = ⟨X⟩`
					N/A
					(IEEE FP exception
					library in F2000)
						N/A

Notes: Square brackets [ ] denote optional items.

The Basic above is ANSI Standard Basic; Fortran 95 is ISO standard Fortran.

Haskell is a standard functional programming language.

N/A = not available in language.

⟨B⟩ is a Boolean (logical) expression.
⟨S⟩ is a (compound) statement.
⟨X⟩ is a (scalar) expression.
⟨V⟩ is a variable identifier.

⟨L⟩ is a LABEL.
⟨I⟩ is an integer variable identifier.
⟨E⟩ is an exception condition (e.g. logical expression).
⟨Exp⟩ is an expression of any type.

result in program termination without further processing unless provision is made for some other action, and possibly recovery. Such provision is called *exception handling* and, since execution control is the issue, constitutes a form of control structuring.

The structural nature of an exception handler is essentially that of a `case` selection control structure. One of a predefined set of exception values is presented to the handler, which then selects the routine that performs the action desired in the event that that particular exception occurs. If corrective action is possible, then that routine may include such action, followed by resumption of normal processing; otherwise, program execution terminates after execution of the handling routine. The form of such an exception handler is

```
exception
        ⟨E1⟩ then ⟨S1⟩
        ⟨E2⟩ then ⟨S2⟩
        ⋮
        ⟨En⟩ then ⟨Sn⟩
endexception
```

When an exception occurs, execution control automatically passes to the beginning of the exception handler, along with the identification ⟨E⟩ of the exception that has occurred. Selection is then made of the corresponding routine ⟨S⟩ to be executed. Program execution is terminated after execution of ⟨S⟩, unless ⟨S⟩ specifies recovery and resumption of program execution. For example, if the last statement in ⟨S⟩ is

```
recover
```

then, instead of terminating, program execution would resume from the point at which the exception occurred. Presumably, the statements in ⟨S⟩ preceding `recover` would provide suitable corrective action so that resumed program execution is sensible.

In addition to the intrinsic exception cases, some implementations allow the programmer to define additional exception values, and to specify explicitly that an exception has occurred. Such programmer-defined and detected exceptions may be handled in the same manner, and with the same handler control structure as intrinsic exceptions. In terms of control structure considerations, the two main differences between `case` selection and exception handling are (1) that exception handling involves some intrinsic exception values in addition to programmer defined ones, and (2) that the location in the program of an exception handler is immaterial, with the necessary branches to and from the handler taking place automatically (whereas a `case` structure must be placed in the program at the point the selection is to be performed). Exception handlers may also be implemented as procedures.

In most instances, the logic of a problem can be expressed in a relatively straightforward manner in terms of selection and repetition control structures. Arbitrary sequencing and nesting of such structures is permitted, as is allowing any ⟨S⟩ to be empty. For example, loop bodies may contain other loops and/or any type of selection, without restriction; selection statement groups may contain additional selection structures and/or loops, without restriction. Although nesting can be carried to any level, the control logic tends to become difficult for humans to read easily after about three levels of nesting.

Control structures are major features of high-level programming languages, and a language's control structures play a major role in its effectiveness in software development. Table 1 shows the control structure features of several popular general-purpose programming languages. A concise uniform syntax is used for all constructs. Actual syntax used by particular languages will differ, but the functionality is the same.

Bibliography

1966. Böhm, C., and Jacopini, G. "Flow Diagrams, Turing Machines, and Languages with Only Two Formation Rules," *Comm. of the ACM,* **9**, 5 (May), 366–371.

1968. Dijkstra, E. W. "Goto Statement Considered Harmful," *Comm. of the ACM,* **11**, 3 (March), 147–148.

1974. Knuth, D. E. "Structured Programming with Goto Statements," *Computing Surveys,* **6**, 4 (December), 261–301.

1974. Kernighan, B. W., and Plauger, P. J. *The Elements of Programming Style.* New York: McGraw-Hill.

1999. Sebesta, R. W. *Concepts of Programming Languages,* 4th Ed. Reading, MA: Addison-Wesley.

Jerrold L. Wagener

COOPERATIVE COMPUTING

For articles on related subjects *see* CLIENT–SERVER COMPUTING; CLUSTER COMPUTING; CRYPTOGRAPHY, COMPUTERS IN; CYBERSPACE; DISTRIBUTED SYSTEMS; FACTORING INTEGERS; INTERNET; MULTIPROCESSING; NUMBER THEORETIC CALCULATIONS; PARALLEL PROCESSING; and WORLD WIDE WEB.

Cooperative computing (collective computing, or "farming") is a form of highly distributed computing done by several thousand or even, potentially, several million computers. The "cooperators" are the owners of the widely dispersed computers, principally PCs and workstations (*q.v.*), who voluntarily devote machine cycles that would otherwise be wasted to computations "farmed out" to them by some central authority in search of a particular objective. This sponsoring authority then harvests and combines the partial results.

The most powerful computer in the world in mid-1998 was a machine at the Sandia National Laboratory called *Janus* which used 9,216 interconnected Pentium Pro processors. However impressive, this pales in comparison to the millions of processors attached to the Internet.

The magnitude of the world's unused machine cycles is prodigious. A Pentium Pro is capable of executing 100 million instructions per second (100 MIPS), 360 billion per hour, or about three trillion instructions over a typical "3rd shift" during which its owner typically sleeps. At least another trillion instructions can be appropriated during the day by running the cooperative software in the background while the primary user is running other programs, or pausing to think or eat meals or take a nap (*see* MULTITASKING). So either the PC occasionally "naps" too, devoting those four trillion instructions to "saving" its monitor screen by continually rearranging its pixels (if it is on at all), or, for the betterment (or at least amusement) of humankind, it can be enrolled in a consortium of altruistic users very few of whom are known one to another.

When organized this way, a loosely coupled but coordinated network of some thousands of PCs is more powerful than the world's fastest supercomputer, but only for a restricted class of problems. Consider, for example, the problem of bandwidth (*q.v.*). Two computers sufficiently near one another to be joined by a local area network (LAN—*q.v.*) can exchange data at the rate of several megabits per second or more. But the data transfer rate to a PC equipped with a 56 KB/sec modem (*q.v.*) is just a small fraction of that. (The situation is fast improving, however, since satellite dish reception and access to fiber optic (*q.v.*) channels through TV cable companies may ultimately be ubiquitous.) As a result, it makes no sense for the central coordinating computer to take more time to tell a remote assistant what to do than it would to do it itself. The best candidates, then, for cooperative computing are problems whose algorithm and initial data are very compact (and hence can be transmitted in a short time) but for which many billions of machine cycles are needed to "crunch" the data received.

Number theory has proved a fertile source of such problems. Typical are the attempts to find previously unknown prime numbers, or to find the factors, if any, of a number thought likely to be composite. Large composite numbers are a staple of public key cryptosystems where the supposed difficulty of factoring 100-digit or larger numbers (in order to recover the decryption key) is the basis for the security of the system (*see* CRYPTOGRAPHY, COMPUTERS IN). Hayes (1998) gives some interesting anecdotes regarding cooperative computing contest successes in this area.

The search for ever-larger prime numbers has centered on finding more so-called Mersenne primes, primes that have the form $2^n - 1$ (and which therefore consist of a sequence of n consecutive 1s in binary) where n itself is prime. Since not all numbers of this form are prime (the lowest prime n for which $2^n - 1$ is not prime

is 11), number theorists value the discovery of new Mersenne primes.

For years, the records for having found the largest known Mersenne prime were held by Cray supercomputers (*q.v.*), but no longer. In 1996, Joel Armengaud, a member of a consortium called GIMPS (Great Internet Mersenne Prime Search) used spare computer time on his PC to find the largest Mersenne prime known to that date, $2^{1398269} - 1$, a number that would take more than 400,000 decimal digits to express. A year later, Gordon Spence, also a member of GIMPS, used a program written by George Woltman to discover a still larger Mersenne prime, the 895,932 digit number $2^{2976221} - 1$. And in 1999, GIMPS member Nayan Hajratwala found the 38th Mersenne prime, the 2,098,960 digit number $2^{6972593} - 1$. (http://www.mersenne.org/prime.htm.) Of course, thousands of PCs were involved in the search; the persons cited just happened to be the ones who were assigned search ranges that yielded success. It is projected that the first billion-digit Mersenne prime will be discovered in 2009. In March 1999 the Electronic Frontier Foundation (*q.v.*) announced awards to encourage cooperative computing ranging from $50,000 for the first million-digit prime to $250,000 for the first billion-digit prime (*see* http://www.eff.org/coop-awards/).

Many users leave their PCs on at all times, which costs about 20 cents per day in electricity. If, in addition, they contract for both a second phone line and unlimited Internet service for a fixed rate, they may as well remain permanently connected to the Web for the cost of a local phone call. They are then ready to send or receive email, fax, voice, and video messages at all times. At that point, joining a cooperative computing consortium will incur no additional cost, and the day may come when participants are paid a nominal sum to do so.

Once this mode becomes common across, say, 100 million PCs whose cost has dropped to $1000 each, the resulting megacomputer will have a replacement value of 100 billion dollars. Should anyone care, the power of its (artificial) intelligence might enable it to pass a Turing Test (*q.v.*) for hours on end. And, like the Internet at present, no one will own it! Users will be able to initiate cooperative computations of their own and perhaps build a global knowledge environment reminiscent of the noösphere envisioned by the philosopher Teilhard de Chardin.

Bibliography

1988. Litzkow, M. J., Livny, M., and Mutka, M.W. "Condor—A Hunter of Idle Workstations," *Eighth International Conference on Distributed Computing Systems*, San Jose, CA, 13–17 June, 104–111.

1989. Lenstra, A. K., and Manasse, M. S. "Factoring by Electronic Mail," in *Advances in Cryptology*, Eurocrypt '89, 355–371. New York: Springer-Verlag.

1998. Foster, I., and Kesselman, C. (eds.) *The Grid: Blueprint for a New Computing Infrastructure*. San Francisco: Morgan Kaufmann.

1998. Hayes, B. "Collective Wisdom," *American Scientist*, **86**, *2* (March–April), 118–121.

Edwin D. Reilly

COORDINATION LANGUAGES

For articles on related topics *see* CLIENT–SERVER COMPUTING; CONCURRENT PROGRAMMING; and DISTRIBUTED SYSTEMS.

Introduction

Humans often collaborate to achieve some shared objective. In such situations it is quite usual for one of the collaborators to be appointed or to emerge as a leader. One important role of the leader is to coordinate the activities of the other collaborators to ensure that the objective is achieved. Increasingly, we see an analogous situation in computing. The emergence of high-bandwidth network technology has fueled the development of distributed computing and concurrent programming. *Coordination languages* are a new class of programming languages which offer a solution to the problem of managing the interaction among concurrent programs. Among other things, they have been applied to electronic commerce (distributed auctions), game playing (chess), Internet services (distributed knowledge base search engines), and workflow management problems; see Andreoli *et al.* (1996) and Ciancarini and Hankin (1996) for some concrete examples.

Gelernter and Carriero coined the term *Coordination* in the following slogan:

Concurrent programming

$$= \text{Computation} + \text{Coordination}$$

The authors formulated this equation when introducing the coordination language Linda (see below). The intent is that there should be a clear separation between the *components of the computation* and their *interaction* in the overall program or system. On the one hand, this separation facilitates the reuse of code; on the other hand, the same patterns of interaction occur in many different problems—so it might be possible to reuse the coordination component as well!

In the rest of this article we will identify some basic principles of coordination languages, describe some languages, and identify some future trends.

Basic Principles

In defining coordination languages there are a number of issues which must be addressed:

1. What is being coordinated?

2. What are the media for coordination?

3. What are the protocols and rules used for coordination?

Before expanding each of these, it is important to make some general observations

◆ Coordination languages are not general-purpose programming languages; rather, they are often defined as language extensions or scripting languages (*q.v.*) and they are exclusively concerned with coordination issues.

◆ Coordination languages are more relevant in the context of open systems, where the coordinated entities are not fixed at the outset; here they have much in common with object-based approaches. In order to operate in an open system, entities must be *encapsulated* (their implementation details should be hidden from other entities) and they should persist beyond a single transaction (some authors describe such entities as *reactive* (Andreoli *et al.*, 1996)). In the past, such considerations have led to the development of object-based modeling techniques; the design of coordination languages should also address these issues.

COORDINATED ENTITIES

The coordinated entities are usually active—agents or processes. Coordination of agents should not require reprogramming of the agents; the coordination mechanism is a wrapper around the existing, independent agents. The agents may have been programmed in a variety of different programming languages.

COORDINATION MEDIA

In many coordination languages, coordination is accomplished via a shared data space. In such models, communication is *generative*: agents communicate by "generating" data in the shared space; this data is then available to any other agent that has access to the space. This contrasts with the message-passing paradigm of concurrency where communication is usually a private act between the participating agents. In a heterogeneous system, in which the agents are written in different languages, the data must be stored in a common format.

COORDINATION RULES

The Linda proposal identifies a set of coordination primitives which may be used to access a shared data space. The primitives are normally implemented as library routines that are called from some host language such as C (*q.v.*) or Prolog. In contrast to Linda, many of the recent proposals have been for rule-based languages; one consequence of this shift to a more declarative view of coordination is increased reasoning power. In either case the coordination "rules" provide a level of abstraction which hides much of the complexity of coordination from the programmer.

Examples

LINDA

The central feature of Linda (Carriero and Gelernter, 1990) is the *tuple space*. This is the coordination medium—it is a shared data structure which contains *tuples* (records—*q.v.*). Tuples may be passive (data) or active (processes). Tuples are created and manipulated by processes using a small set of operations. Only passive tuples can be accessed; tuple selection involves pattern matching. The operations include:

`in(t)`: looks for a tuple matching `t`, if found, the tuple is deleted; otherwise the process waits until matching succeeds.

`out(t)`: creates a new passive tuple whose contents are specified by `t`.

`eval(t)`: creates an active tuple whose contents are specified by `t`. An active tuple must have at least one field that is a function to be computed.

Both of the last two operations are guaranteed to succeed; the issuing process continues immediately. The selected operations are needed for the example in Fig. 1; the full set of operations includes a non-destructive read and predicates for testing the state.

To be more concrete we will present an example in C-Linda. We give a solution to the classic Dining Philosophers problem when there are five philosophers. The philosophers sit around a circular table with a bowl of spaghetti in the middle and five forks. Each philosopher alternately thinks and then eats; in order to eat spaghetti, the philosopher requires two forks (*see* Fig. 1). The situation is modelled by the C-Linda program in Fig. 2 (based on a solution suggested by Paolo Ciancarini).

The philosophers are numbered from 0 to 4, and so are the forks. The program (`real_main()`) generates five passive tuples representing forks and five active tuples representing the philosophers. The program also generates four meal tickets; a philosopher must have a meal ticket before attempting to eat. The fact

Figure 1. The Dining Philosophers Problem.

```
#define TRUE 1
philosopher(int i)
{
   while(TRUE) {
     think();
     in("meal ticket"); in("fork", i);
                            in("fork", (i+1)%5);
     eat();
     out("fork", i); out("fork", (i+1)%5);
                            out("meal ticket");
   }}

real_main()
{
   int i;
   for (i=0, i<5, i++){
     out("fork", i);
     eval(philosopher(i));
     if (i<4) out("meal ticket");
   }
}
```

Figure 2. The Dining Philosophers in C-Linda.

that there are only four tickets means that at least one philosopher has access to two forks and the system does not deadlock. When a philosopher is ready to eat he or she must pick up the fork with the same number and an adjacent fork (% is the modulus operation in C).

An early example of a logic programming (*q.v.*) version of Linda is Ciancarini's Shared Prolog (Banâtre and Le Métayer, 1991). Ciancarini and Hankin (1996) contains proposals for several languages based on the Linda approach.

GAMMA

The coordination medium in Gamma is a *multiset*— a set-like collection which may contain many copies of the same element. In the basic model, the multiset is untyped, so it is rather similar to the Linda tuple space but, in contrast to Linda, all of the elements of the multiset are passive. Simple agents are represented as pairs consisting of a reaction condition and an action, written:

$$\text{action} \Leftarrow \text{reaction}$$

An action is a rewrite rule:

$$\text{lhs} \rightarrow \text{rhs}$$

The action selects some elements (which match the left-hand side of the rule and satisfy the reaction condition) from the multiset and rewrites them according to the rule (replacing them by the elements listed on the right-hand side of the rule). Most papers on Gamma assume a simple functional language (*see* FUNCTIONAL PROGRAMMING) for the actions; however, the Gammalög language (Andreoli et al., 1996) is an instance of Gamma built on the logic programming language Gödel.

The philosopher function might be expressed by the following two rules in Gamma:

$$("fork", i), ("fork", j) \rightarrow$$
$$("eat", i) \Leftarrow j = (i+1)\%5$$
$$("eat", i) \rightarrow$$
$$("fork", i), ("fork", (i+1)\%5) \Leftarrow \textbf{true}$$

Since the selection of elements is an atomic action, the "meal ticket" is not required in this solution.

There have been several proposals for extensions to this basic model. Higher-order extensions allow active configurations to be stored in the multiset—this extended framework has been used to study the properties of other coordination languages (Ciancarini and Hankin, 1996). Le Métayer has recently proposed a typed variant of Gamma, called Structured Gamma (Andreoli *et al.*, 1996), which has been used in the study of software architectures.

OTHER COORDINATION LANGUAGES

There are a number of other coordination languages; Andreoli *et al.* (1996) and Ciancarini and Hankin (1996) are good references for many of them. We have selected Linda and Gamma because they have influenced the design of a number of the other languages. We now briefly describe some of the other major languages.

LO. LO (Linear Objects) has been designed and developed by Andreoli and Pareschi. A program is a collection of agents. Agents have a local state which is a multiset. Agents can *transform* their local state (analogously to Gamma rules), *clone* copies of themselves and *terminate*. Agents can also communicate with each other; communication is implemented by a broadcast mechanism—the communicating agent places the same token in the local state of every other agent. LO has been used for various applications including workflow management and Internet-based services. An example is *Knowledge Brokers*, an Internet-based knowledge retrieval system that has access to various public bibliography databases including the Library of Congress. It has been implemented at the Rank Xerox Research Center in Grenoble, France.

TAO. TAO (Truth and Action Osmosis) has been designed by Monteiro, Porto and Vasconcelos. The language has an explicit logic programming basis and has features similar to Concurrent Constraint and Concurrent Logic languages. The state of a TAO program is divided into a passive part, the *database*, and an active part, the *task*. Atomic tasks are either queries of the database, or updates. Composite tasks may be constructed using sequential composition, parallel composition, synchronization and choice operators. Subtasks communicate via the database or through binding of shared logical variables (as in logic programming).

Manifold. Manifold is an instance of the IWIM (Idealized Worker Idealized Manager) model designed by Arbab. In contrast to the coordination languages discussed above, which are all based on a shared data space, IWIM uses message passing and broadcast. There are two kinds of process: *workers* and *managers*. The workers perform computations, they can read and write to communication ports, and they broadcast events (such as termination); however, they are unaware of which other workers are connected to their communication ports. The managers coordinate the communications between groups of workers. The model is hierarchical, a process that may be viewed as a manager at one level will be seen as a worker at the next level up.

Future Directions

Both Linda and Gamma were first proposed in the mid-1980s. However, the real need for coordination languages has only become apparent recently, with the emergence of the Internet (*q.v.*) and distributed computing. With the exception of Linda, many of the languages that we have discussed are still research prototypes. The main challenge for the future is the commercialization of the rule-based approach, a process already started for languages such as LO.

Concurrent programming (*q.v.*) is a difficult task. The methodologies that we are familiar with from sequential programming do not easily transfer. We need to develop theories and logics of coordination languages so that we can construct programming support tools. Message-passing concurrency has been quite well studied but there has been very little work on shared data space models. A good theory would enable us to provide deeper comparisons between the various proposals and also provide a solid basis for the design of the next generation of coordination languages. For an overview of the state of the art in this area, the reader is referred to Andreoli *et al.* (1996) and Ciancarini and Hankin (1996).

Finally, we should mention the software engineering (*q.v.*) benefits which have yet to be realized; *software reuse* (*q.v.*), *interoperability*, and the emergent topic of *software architecture* are all related to and could benefit from the work on coordination languages.

Acknowledgments

Paolo Ciancarini and Daniel Le Métayer provided useful comments on an earlier draft of this article.

Bibliography

1990. Carriero, N., and Gelernter, D. *How to Write Parallel Programs: A First Course.* Cambridge, MA: MIT Press.
1991. Banâtre, J.-P., and Le Métayer, D. (eds.) *Research Directions in High-Level Parallel Programming Languages.* Berlin: Springer-Verlag.
1996. Andreoli, J.-M., Hankin, C., and Le Métayer, D. (eds.) *Coordination Programming: Mechanisms, Models and Semantics.* London: Imperial College Press.
1996. Ciancarini, P., and Hankin, C. (eds.) *Coordination Languages and Models.* Berlin: Springer-Verlag.

Chris Hankin

COROUTINE

For articles on related subjects *see* ACTIVATION RECORD; CONCURRENT PROGRAMMING; and SUBPROGRAM.

A *coroutine* resembles the more familiar subprogram or function of most programming languages in encapsulating some computation and helping to break a large program into smaller parts. However, coroutines differ from subroutines in that their lifetimes are not tied to the flow of control. When a subroutine is called, a new instance of its activation record (i.e. its control information and local variables) is created. It is destroyed when control is returned to the calling program. On the other hand, when a coroutine returns control its execution is not finished and so its activation record is preserved. Each time control reenters the coroutine, it resumes execution where it left off with its local control and data state retained.

For the simple reason that a new activation record is not created on every call, coroutines can be more efficient than subroutines. Furthermore, because coroutines can be entered directly at the appropriate point to continue some computation, their use can simplify the implementation of some algorithms. This is especially true when the processing to be done on a given call depends in a complex fashion upon previous calls. For example, a program that needs to determine whether two trees (*q.v.*) of quite different structure contain the same terminal (leaf) elements in the same order, might use two coroutines, one to traverse each tree. The first would find its next leaf, pass it to the second coroutine, and then pause. The second would find *its* next leaf and compare it with the one passed to it. If they differed, that coroutine could immediately report the difference and terminate; otherwise it would resume the first coroutine and wait for another value to be passed to it. Using a coroutine avoids the need to record in some data structure where the tree traversals should restart, and avoids having to generate a complete list of leaves of each tree before starting to compare them, only to discover that they differed in the first position.

Coroutines are often used to implement logically concurrent processes (*threads* or *lightweight processes*—*see* OPERATING SYSTEMS: GENERAL PRINCIPLES) on a single processor. These coroutine-based threads generally don't pass control to each other directly with explicit transfer operations. Instead, the transfer is normally indirect and is done as a side effect (*q.v.*) of a call on a library routine. For example, the programming language Modula-2 provides a *processes* library module with procedures that support synchronization, scheduling, and mutual exclusion for coroutine-based threads (Wirth, 1985). These threads are often referred to as "coroutines" when people want to distinguish them from truly parallel threads.

Applications of coroutines include operating systems, compilers, and discrete event simulation programs (*see* SIMULATION). For example, the language Simula 67 (*q.v.*) supports discrete event simulation with flexible coroutine mechanisms (Dahl, 1972). Coroutines are also used in text manipulation, artificial intelligence (*q.v.*), sorting (*q.v.*), and numerical analysis (*q.v.*) programs. A survey of coroutines and their uses appears in Martin (1980).

Coroutines are sometimes organized into *linear pipelines*. Linear pipelines are useful when the data transformation implemented by a program can be decomposed into several simpler transformations that are applied one after the other. The coroutines of the pipeline can be envisaged as being arranged in a line: information flows through the line in one direction, with each coroutine implementing part of the overall transformation. A coroutine obtains input items by transferring control to one neighbor (perhaps as a side effect of calling a *read* procedure), and outputs results by transferring control to the other. Each coroutine is written as if it were the main program and without concern for the implementation of the other coroutines. These linear pipelines behave like *pipes* in the Unix (*q.v.*) system command language.

Another kind of coroutine is the *semicoroutine*. Semicoroutines have the restriction that when they are called, they must eventually return control back to the caller. Thus semicoroutines resemble subroutines, except that their data and control state are preserved between calls. Semicoroutines are useful for the incremental generation of sequences of items, especially when each item to be returned depends in a complicated way on the items that were generated previously. Semicoroutines can be used to enumerate the items stored in data structures (*q.v.*). As an example, a compiler might use a semicoroutine to produce, one at a time, the items recorded in a parse tree. The semicoroutine can traverse the parse tree recursively. Since it is a semicoroutine, it can directly record in its

program counter where to resume the traversal each time it is reentered. The *iterators* of the programming language CLU (Liskov *et al.*, 1984) are semicoroutines that are intended to be used in conjunction with loop control structures. Iterators, now also found in the string-processing (*q.v.*) language Icon, allow a program to process the items stored in a data object, such as a set, where details of the item generation and the data object's representation are hidden in the iterator (*see* INFORMATION HIDING).

Many programming languages now provide threads (Java—*q.v.*), or a coroutine library (C++—*q.v.*). Others, such as concurrent logic languages (*see* LOGIC PROGRAMMING: LANGUAGES) provide a coroutine-like transfer of control among routines by means of "freeze" and "thaw" operations or guarded-command (*q.v.*) control structures (*q.v.*) that suspend and resume routines. Functional programming (*q.v.*) languages that use lazy evaluation (i.e. compute values only as needed) also employ coroutine-like control.

Bibliography

1972. Dahl, O.-J., and Hoare, C. A. R. "Hierarchical Program Structures," in *Structured Programming* (eds. O.-J. Dahl, E. W. Dijkstra, and C. A. R. Hoare), 175–220. New York: Academic Press.

1980. Martin, C. *Coroutines: A Programming Methodology, a Language Design, and an Implementation*. New York: Springer-Verlag.

1984. Liskov, B., Atkinson R., Bloom, T., Moss, J. E. B., Schaffert,C., Scheifler, R., and Snyder, A. *CLU Reference Manual*. New York: Springer-Verlag.

1985. Wirth, N. *Programming in Modula-2*, 3rd Ed. New York: Springer-Verlag.

1996. Finkel, R. A. *Advanced Programming Language Design*. Reading, MA: Addison-Wesley.

Brian T. Lewis

CPU

See CENTRAL PROCESSING UNIT.

CRAY, SEYMOUR

For articles on related subjects *see* CONTROL DATA CORPORATION; and SUPERCOMPUTERS.

I enjoyed doing the work. The work was a goal in itself for me. *Seymour Cray*

Science fiction often glamorizes the lone scientist/inventor, single-mindedly struggling with great problems, eventually triumphing with a world-changing solution. Seymour Cray was such a person. His victories are encapsulated in finely engineered computer modules of incredible speed. Yet he created

Figure 1. Seymour Cray (courtesy of SGI).

these high-technology tools using pencil and paper, the result of many hours of solitary concentration either in his office or on the front porch of a cottage overlooking Lake Wissota, Minnesota.

Cray was born in nearby Chippewa Falls in 1925. After military service in the Second World War, he earned a Bachelor's degree in electrical engineering and a Master's in applied mathematics from the University of Minnesota. A professor suggested he join a new computer company, Engineering Research Associates, Inc. (ERA). He impressed colleagues by being able to work on circuits, logic, and software, unusual breadth even for that time.

ERA and the competing Eckert–Mauchly Computer Company (*see* ECKERT, J. PRESPER; MAUCHLY, JOHN WILLIAM) were bought by Remington Rand, which became the Sperry Rand of UNIVAC (*q.v.*) fame. Cray worked on his first computer there, the UNIVAC 1103. In 1957, he formed a partnership with two ERA alumni and co-founded Control Data Corporation (CDC—*q.v.*). There, Cray's considerable engineering skills flowered. He designed the CDC 1604, a pioneering transistor machine, which helped establish the company on a firm footing. His CDC 6600 was a significant technical challenge to the IBM System/360 series but found most use in scientific rather than business applications.

At about the time the 6600 was ready to be produced, Cray persuaded CDC to build a plant in Chippewa Falls within walking distance of his home. There he designed the CDC 7600, released in 1969 and acknowledged by many as the world's first "supercomputer." CDC doubted the marketability of a still more advanced design. That, coupled with CDC's increasing commercial focus, led Cray to another spin-off.

Cray Research, Inc., formed in 1972, attracted considerable venture capital funding and raised $10 million overnight at its initial public offering, before even one machine was completed. This was a tribute to Cray's reputation as a computer designer. His company sold the first Cray 1 for $8.8 million, and made an initial success of low-volume, high-cost sales. Later on, Cray tried to extricate himself from corporate paperwork and return to his engineering roots. He arranged to be a consultant to the company rather than an officer. Even this soured after a few years, and, desiring to have a fresh start on a radical new design, he incorporated once again as Cray Computer in Colorado Springs in 1989. Cray was unable to repeat his capital-raising miracle of two decades earlier, and the company filed for bankruptcy in March, 1995.

In September of 1996, Cray was critically injured in an automobile accident, dying on 5 October. His legacy is not only the actual machines he created, but the example he set in living his dream and not being overcome by obstacles. Wherever faster and simpler computers are designed and built, Seymour Cray's ideals live.

Bibliography

1997. Murray, C. J. *The Supermen: The Story of Seymour Cray and the Technical Wizards behind the Supercomputer.* New York: John Wiley.

James E. Tomayko

CRIME, COMPUTER

See COMPUTER CRIME; and VIRUS, COMPUTER.

CROSS ASSEMBLERS AND COMPILERS

For articles on related subjects *see* ASSEMBLER; COMPATIBILITY; COMPILER; INTERMEDIATE LANGUAGES; LANGUAGE PROCESSORS; and SOFTWARE PORTABILITY.

Cross-processors, a term that includes both *cross-compilers* and *cross-assemblers*, are programs written to run on machine A (called variously the development machine, the controller, the host, or the front end), to produce programs to be run on incompatible machine B (called the target machine or the main processor). Thus, A is running a program (the cross-processor) written in a language acceptable to A. The input to this program consists of statements in assembly language for machine B (for a cross-assembler) or in any language for machine B for which there exists a cross-compiler.

The output of a cross-processor is machine language for machine B, which is then downloaded from machine A to machine B. Downloading is the process by which the host computer transfers a binary core image (executable program) or sometimes coded information into the target computer so that the target computer can then proceed with program execution. The data for the program is either read directly by machine B or is part of the downloaded binary or coded image.

The two major uses of cross-processors demonstrate their versatility. Cross-processors are used for production of software for machines whose hardware is not yet available or is just being designed and evaluated. In this case, machine B may be initially a simulation rather than actual hardware, to be replaced later by actual hardware. Cross-processors are also used for production of programs for target machines whose specialized instruction set is not suitable for software production (e.g. signal processors or array processors) or whose cost may make them too expensive and thus not cost-effective for compilation (e.g. vector machines, supercomputers (*q.v.*), massively parallel machines).

Gideon Frieder

CRT

See MONITOR, DISPLAY; and TERMINAL.

CRYPTOGRAPHY, COMPUTERS IN

For articles on related subjects *see* AUTHENTICATION; COLOSSUS; COMPUTER CRIME; DATA COMMUNICATIONS; DATA SECURITY; DIGITAL SIGNATURE; NUMBER THEORETIC CALCULATIONS; PRETTY GOOD PRIVACY; PRIVACY, COMPUTERS AND; and QUANTUM COMPUTING.

Cryptography is the science of transforming messages for the purpose of making the message unintelligible to all but the intended receiver of the message. The term *data encryption* refers to the use of cryptographic methods in computer communications for the same reason, but also implies the additional goals of providing assurance to the receiver that the message is not a forgery, and/or allowing the receiver to prove to a third party that the message is not a forgery. These various aims are called, respectively, the goals of *communication security*, *authentication*, and *digital signatures*.

The transformation used to encipher a message typically involves both a general method, or algorithm, and a *key*. While the general method used by a pair of correspondents may be public knowledge, some or all of the key information must be kept secret. The process of transforming (enciphering) a message is to apply the enciphering algorithm to the message, where the key is used as an auxiliary input to control the enciphering. The reverse operation (deciphering) is performed similarly.

Classical encryption techniques involve such operations as substituting for each message letter a substitute letter; in this case, the key is the correspondence between message (plaintext) letters and the enciphered message (ciphertext) letters. Such *substitution ciphers* can also be based on substituting for two or more letters at a time. Another common technique is to use a *transposition cipher* which permutes the order of the message letters using an algorithm whose steps are determined by a *key*. Many complicated hand or mechanical ciphers have been developed in the last few centuries; *see* Kahn (1996) for details. These techniques are insecure in general; the breaking of the German Enigma cipher during the Second World War attests to the vulnerability of even complicated rotor-machine ciphers (*see* COLOSSUS).

The *one-time pad* is a technique that provides the ultimate in security: it is provably unbreakable. To encipher a 1,000-bit message, however, requires the use of a 1,000-bit key that will not be used for any other message. Each ciphertext bit is the exclusive-or of the corresponding message and key bits. The one-time pad is used only in very important applications (like the Moscow–Washington hot-line) because of the expense in creating and distributing the large amount of key information required.

Cryptosystems, which, unlike the one-time pad, depend upon an amount of key information that is independent of message length, are breakable in theory. What makes them usable in practice is that the person trying to break the cipher (the *cryptanalyst*) must use an impractical or infeasible amount of computational resources in order to break the cipher. The ciphers are constructed so that the "work-factor" in breaking them is high enough to prevent a successful attack.

The major application of cryptography today is for data transmitted between computers in computer communication networks and for computer data encrypted for storage. Secure transmission of credit card information over the Internet is a particularly important problem.

The most widely used cipher in the USA for the encryption of stored or transmitted computer data is undoubtedly the Data Encryption Standard (DES), which was designed at IBM and approved as a standard by the National Bureau of Standards in 1976. The DES enciphers a 64-bit message block under control of a 56-bit key to produce a 64-bit ciphertext. The enciphering operations consists of roughly 16 iterations of the following two steps.

1. Exchange the left half of the 64-bit message with the right half.

2. Replace the right half of the message with the bitwise exclusive-or of the right half and a 32-bit word, which is a complicated function f of the left half, the key, and the iteration number. The function f involves in part a number of substitutions of short sub-blocks using specially constructed substitution tables (S-boxes) and permutations of the individual bit positions. The basic DES function has been implemented by a large number of manufacturers on special-purpose VLSI chips which can encipher at Mb per second rates.

Some applications (e.g. enciphering a line to a user's terminal) require that blocks shorter than 64 bits (e.g. a byte) be individually enciphered. The basic DES block can be used for this application in *cipher feedback mode*: each message byte is enciphered by an exclusive-or with the leftmost byte of the result of taking the last eight ciphertext bytes and using them as input to the DES to obtain another 64-bit block of ciphertext.

Conventional cryptosystems (including DES) use the same key at both the enciphering and deciphering stations. In 1976, Diffie and Hellman proposed *public-key cryptosystems* in which the deciphering key was different from, and not computable from, the enciphering key (and vice versa). A person might create a matched pair of such keys and distribute copies of the enciphering key to friends, while keeping the deciphering key secret. The friends can send enciphered mail to the creator of the enciphering key that only the creator can read. (Even if a cryptanalyst obtains a copy of the enciphering key, it does no good.) This demonstrates the flexibility of a public-key cryptosystem for *key distribution*, an area where conventional cryptosystems are awkward because all keys must be kept secret. Public-key cryptosystems can also be used to provide *digital signatures*: a user can create a signature for a message by enciphering it with a private key. (Here the enciphering/deciphering roles of the public/private keys are reversed.) Someone else can check the validity of the signature by checking that it deciphers to the message using the signer's public key. This capability of public-key cryptosystems promises to have important applications in electronic funds transfer systems (*q.v.*).

The first proposal for a function to implement public-key cryptosystems was by Rivest, Shamir, and Adleman (1978). Their cryptosystem (the so-called *RSA cipher*)

enciphers a message M (first coded into numeric form by, for example, setting $A = 01$, $B = 02$, etc.) using a public key (e, n) to obtain a ciphertext C as follows.

$$C = M^e \,(\text{mod } n).$$

That is, C is the remainder of M^e when divided by n. Here all quantities are large numbers (several hundred bits long), and n is the product of two very large prime numbers p and q. The security of the cipher rests mainly on the practical impossibility of factoring the number n into its parts p and q. The deciphering operation is similar, except that the exponent is different:

$$M = C^d \,(\text{mod } n).$$

Since d depends on p and q (in a way too complicated to explain here), it is provably as hard to compute d from e and n as it is to factor n. When n is more than roughly 400 bits long, this becomes a prohibitively time-consuming task. Although the enciphering operation itself is quite complicated, enciphering rates of 1–10 Kb/second are possible with a special-purpose VLSI chip.

As a small example of the RSA method, the word "IT" can be encrypted as follows. Using the representation $A = 01$, $B = 02, \ldots, Z = 26$, we obtain the number 0920 for IT. Then with $n = 2773 = 47 \times 59$ and $e = 17$, we obtain the ciphertext:

$$C + 920^{17} \,(\text{mod } 2773) = 948.$$

Using $p = 47$ and $q = 59$, a value of $d = 157$ can be derived, from which we can calculate

$$948^{157} \,(\text{mod } 2773) = 920,$$

the original message.

The theoretical foundations of cryptography were vigorously developed during the 1980s, and the security of various encryption and signature schemes have been evaluated with respect to powerful new formal definitions of security. *See* Rivest (1990) for a survey of these developments.

Two firms that specialize in cryptographic security are RSA Data Security of San Mateo, CA (`http://www.rsa.com`) and Counterpane Systems of Minneapolis, MN (`http://www.counterpane.com`). RSA has often stressed the vulnerability of "short" 56-bit DES keys and has sponsored contests to factor long decimal numbers, RSA-129 and RSA-130, for example, each containing the number of decimal digits implied by their names. Brian Hayes (1998) has described the successful attacks on these problems through the use of *cooperative computing* (*q.v.*), the Internet coordination of thousands of PC users who put what otherwise would be hours of unused machine cycles to work on different pieces of the same problem. Another favorite problem of such consortia is the identification of ever-larger Mersenne primes. (*See* COOPERATIVE COMPUTING and recent dates in the Timeline in Appendix IX for citation of some of the successes of the group called GIMPS.)

Counterpane Systems has emphasized that cryptographic systems are vulnerable to attacks other than exhaustive key search (*see* Schneier, 1998).

Bibliography

1976. Diffie, W., and Hellman, M. "New Directions in Cryptography," *IEEE Trans. Information Theory,"* **IT-22**, 644–654.

1977. FIPS Publication 46. *Specifications for the Data Encryption Standard.*

1978. Rivest, R., Shamir, A., and Adleman, L. "A Method for Obtaining Digital Signatures and Public-key Cryptosystems," *Comm. of the ACM,* **21**, *2*, 120–126.

1979. Diffie, W., and Hellman, M. "Privacy and Authentication: An Introduction to Cryptography," *Proc. IEEE,* **67**, 397–427.

1990. Rivest, R. "Cryptography," in *Handbook of Theoretical Computer Science* (ed. J. van Leeuwen), Volume 1, Chapter 13, 717–755. Amsterdam: North-Holland.

1995. Menezes, A. J., Van Oorschot, P. C., and Vanstone, S. A. *Handbook of Applied Cryptography.* Boca Raton, FL: CRC Press.

1995. Stinson, D. R. *Cryptography: Theory and Practice.* Boca Raton, FL: CRC Press.

1996. Kahn, D. *The Codebreakers: The Comprehensive History of Secret Communication from Ancient Times to the Internet.* New York: Scribner's. The third (but still minor) update of the 1967 classic.

1996. Schneier, B. *Applied Cryptography,* 2nd Ed. New York: John Wiley.

1998. Ghosh, Anup K. *E-Commerce Security: Weak Links, Best Defenses.* New York: John Wiley.

1998., Hayes, B. "Collective Wisdom," *American Scientist,* **86**, *2*, 118–122.

1998. Schneier, B. "Cryptographic Design Vulnerabilities," *Computer (IEEE),* **31**, *9*, 29–33.

Ronald L. Rivest

CYBERNETICS

For articles on related subjects *see* ANALOG COMPUTER; ARTIFICIAL LIFE; AUTOMATION; CONTROL APPLICATIONS; GENETIC ALGORITHMS; INFORMATION THEORY; NEURAL NETWORKS; PERCEPTRON; ROBOTICS; SHANNON, CLAUDE; and WIENER, NORBERT.

The term *cybernetics* was coined by Norbert Wiener (1948). Derived from the Greek "kybernetes," or "steersman," it was defined as "the study of control and communication in the animal and machine." Over time, its meaning has broadened substantially, and while many specific senses persist, cybernetics is the study of the abstract principles of organization in complex systems. Thus, cybernetics stands as a crucial component of the systems sciences, a collection of fields that examine the common properties of complex, evolving systems. These are currently best manifested in the schools of *evolutionary systems*, *complex adaptive systems*, and *artificial life*.

Historical Roots

Inspired by work done before and during the Second World War on mechanical control systems such as servomechanisms and artillery targeting mechanisms, Wiener set out to develop a general theory of organizational and control relations in systems. Of course, *control theory* and *control systems engineering* have since developed into full disciplines. What distinguishes cybernetics is its emphasis on control and communication not only in engineered artificial systems, but also in evolved natural systems such as organisms and societies. Thus cyberneticists make a conscious attempt to work interdisciplinarily, searching for isomorphisms (structural similarities) among systems of different types.

Cybernetics grew out of a series of interdisciplinary meetings held from 1946 to 1953 that brought together a number of noted intellectuals, including Wiener, John von Neumann (*q.v.*), Warren McCulloch, Claude Shannon, Heinz von Förster, Gregory Bateson, and Margaret Mead. Hosted by the Josiah Macy Jr. Foundation, these became known as the Macy Conferences on Cybernetics (Heims, 1991). Through the 1950s, cybernetic thinkers came to cohere with the school of general systems theory (GST), founded at about the same time by Ludwig von Bertalanffy (von Bertalanffy, 1968), as an attempt to build a unified science of open, evolving systems. GST studies systems at all levels of generality, whereas cybernetics focuses more specifically on control processes in systems. Arguments remain over the relative scope of these domains, but each is part of an overall attempt to forge an interdisciplinary *systems science*. Along the way, cybernetics was a crucial influence on the development of computer science, in particular in information theory, automata theory (*q.v.*), artificial intelligence (*q.v.*) and artificial neural networks (*q.v.*), computer modeling and simulation (*q.v.*), robotics, and artificial life.

Relational Concepts and Information Theory

Cybernetics searches for properties that can be measured across systems of different types: how can we determine whether two systems that are very different physically, such as a computer and a brain, actually have a similar organization? This problem leads to the development of a formal language to describe both a system's general structure and its change over time, using concepts such as order, organization, structure, variety, constraint, randomness, freedom, and complexity for the former, and concepts such as development, self-organization, growth, emergence, learning, adaptation, and evolution for the latter. We call such concepts *relational*, since they specify the relations among the components or states of a system, rather than its specific substance. Such concepts let us pose abstract questions about systems organization, for example whether complexity increases in evolutionary time.

The development of relational concepts began with Shannon's mathematical theory of communication (Shannon and Weaver, 1964), in which he introduced statistical *entropy* as a measure of the variety in a probability distribution (as a way to characterize the capacity of a communications channel), and the *bit* (binary digit) as the unit of measure of that capacity. Although Shannon disavowed the use of the term "information" to describe this measure, because it is purely syntactic and ignores the *meaning* of the signal, this theory came to be known as *information theory*. It has many important applications in coding theory, cryptography and dynamical systems.

Statistical entropy can be related to the thermodynamic entropy of a physical system, which measures its distance from equilibrium. A high degree of disequilibrium is necessary for a physical system to be highly organized, and there are thermodynamic approaches to evolution and thermodynamic interpretations of relational concepts (Prigogine, 1980).

Entropy, related concepts, and correlates to such important results as Shannon's 10th Theorem and the Second Law of Thermodynamics were also sought in nonthermodynamic contexts such as biology, ecology, psychology, sociology, and economics. One important result is Ashby's Law of Requisite Variety (Conant, 1981), which states that in a control system, the amount of information kept within the system places an upper bound on the amount of variety in the environment which the control system is able to counteract. Another is von Förster's analysis of self-organization as a decrease in internal entropy, and his Order from Noise Principle, according to which self-organization can be accelerated by random perturbations (von Förster, 1960).

Biological and Mechanistic Isomorphisms

Given the technological advances after the Second World War, early cyberneticists were eager to explore the similarities between technological and biological systems, and the limits of mechanism as an explanatory paradigm. Armed with a theory of information, early digital circuits, Boolean logic, and automata theory, it was natural that they would propose digital systems as models of brains, and treat information as the "mind" to the machine's "body."

Cybernetics thus contributed to early developments in computer science and artificial intelligence. Concepts that are central to these fields, such as complexity, self-organization, self-reproduction, selection, autonomy, connectionism, and adaptation, were proposed and explored by cyberneticists during the 1940s and 1950s. Examples include von Neumann's computer architecture, game theory, and cellular automata (*q.v.*), and the work of McCulloch (1965), who introduced artificial neural models, neural nets, and perceptrons.

A central contribution of cybernetics is its explanation of *purposiveness*, or *goal-directed* behavior, an essential characteristic of mind and life (Rosenbluth and Wiener, 1943), in terms of control relations and relational concepts. A simple example of a control system is the thermostat, for which achieving and maintaining a specific temperature can be seen as its *goal*. The thermostat functions by counteracting any deviation from the set temperature: if outside perturbations cool down the room, the thermostat senses the deviation (information processing), and switches on the heating (action), until the desired temperature is reached again. The thermostat *regulates* or *controls* the room temperature by compensating for any perturbation that may push it away from its ideal range of values, making the room temperature independent of outside fluctuations. This process, by which a system returns to equilibrium after a perturbation, is known as *homeostasis*.

Cybernetics proposes such elementary control loops as the basis of the *autonomous behavior* that characterizes organisms; it is not strictly determined by either environmental influences or internal dynamical processes. Such organisms are in some sense "independent actors" with "free will." Thus cybernetics anticipated current work in robotics and autonomous agents. For example, Braitenberg (1984) anticipated recent progress in "bottom-up," behavior-based robotics. Indeed, in the popular mind, "cyborgs" and "cybernetics" are just fancy terms for "robots" and "robotics."

The ultimate problem of biological and mechanistic isomorphism is whether there is any method to distinguish the living from the nonliving in principle, and if so, whether this can this be understood in terms of relational concepts. It follows that the origin of life, as a scientific problem, is a central concern for cybernetics and all of the systems sciences.

Circular Processes

Circular processes are at the core of the cybernetic treatment of goal-directed behavior. Issues of linearity, nonlinearity, and cyclicity run throughout science, taking many forms. In simple mathematical terms, they are concerned with systems of the form $y = f(x, y)$, in which y depends on itself (a circular relation). Depending on the form of f, a variety of complex, counter-intuitive relations may hold. In discrete form, the equation becomes $y_{t+1} = f(x_t, y_t)$. Such equations have been extensively studied as iterated maps, and are the basis of *chaotic dynamics* (*see* SCIENTIFIC APPLICATIONS).

Cyberneticists are interested in nonmathematical circular processes, such as *circular causation*, where the future value of some process depends not only on external factors, but also on the past value. Such processes are generally described as *feedback* relations, of which there are two kinds. If an increase in the value of a quantity tends to produce further increase, there is *positive feedback*, which leads to runaway, explosive growth. Positive feedback occurs in arms races, monopoly and founder effects in economics, and the chain-reactions of nuclear explosions.

If an increase in the value of a quantity tends to produce a *decrease* of that quantity, the relation is one of *negative feedback*. This produces a stable value of the quantity, resistant to environmental perturbations. Negative feedback is the mechanism that underlies the goal-directed control relation introduced above.

Negative feedback control is perhaps the foundation of cybernetics. It is ubiquitous in mechanical control systems and servomechanisms, ecosystems, social equilibria such as the supply–demand balance in economics, and biochemical such as the insulin cycle. More generally, it forms the basis of homeostasis, and to illustrate it Ashby designed an adaptive, goal-seeking control device, which he called a homeostat.

Cybernetics uses the concept of feedback control in a broad program modeling biological, social, economic and psychological systems. It analyzes real systems into many interacting layers of positive and negative feedbacks, with higher-level negative feedbacks constraining the growth of lower-level positive feedbacks. Where negative feedback is the essential condition for control and stability, positive feedbacks are responsible for growth and self-organization.

One approach is the mathematical field of *system dynamics*, which attempts to model complex systems as networks of positive and negative feedback loops (Richardson, 1991). It has been successfully applied to a variety of social, ecological, and biological modeling problems. The best-known application is probably the *Limits to Growth* program popularized by the Club of Rome (Meadows and Meadows, 1972), which continued the pioneering computer simulation (*q.v.*) work of Jay Forrester (1971). System dynamics has since been popularized in the Stella software application and computer games (*q.v.*) such as SimCity.

Cybernetics also studies circularity at the abstract level, as the problem of *reflexivity*, or the self-application of ideas or processes. Reflexivity is found in *recursive function theory* (*see* RECURSION), logical *paradoxes*, and *fractals* (*q.v.*). Furthermore, biological systems are characterized by their ability to reproduce themselves as well as by their control loops. Von Neumann (1966) analyzed reproduction as the circular process of self-construction, and thus contributed ideas to theoretical biology that were later realized with the discovery of the genetic code. Other examples of reflexive cybernetic theories include von Förster's work on self-reference in systems, and *autopoiesis* as the process by which a living system produces its own network of interacting components (Varela *et al.*, 1974).

Epistemology

The broad view espoused by cybernetics is that living systems are complex, adaptive control systems engaged in circular relations with their environments. As cyberneticists consider such deep problems as the nature of life, mind, and society, they are naturally led to deeper philosophical considerations.

While there is no one cybernetic philosophy, its epistemology (theory of knowledge) revolves around the concept of *constructivism* (an approach that goes back at least to Immanuel Kant's 1781 *Critique of Pure Reason*). According to constructivism, knowledge is mediated by perceptual processes, and so is an active construction by the knowing system, not a passive reflection of reality. Thus knowledge is a *model* of those aspects of the world that are relevant to the system's goals, not an objective picture of how the world "really" is. For knowing systems these models effectively *are* their environments (von Glasersfeld, 1991).

This view can lead to solipsism, or the inability to distinguish the self from the external environment. A more modest interpretation is that since all models are constructed by an observer, this observer must be included in the model for it to be complete. In physics, this principle plays a role in the quantum measurement problem. In cybernetics, it has led to "second-order cybernetics," which builds models of the modeling process itself (Umpleby, 1989). Ultimately, the constructivist perspective means that cybernetics always focuses on the process of *modeling*, and in particular on the construction of models that apply to multiple classes of systems.

More concrete cybernetic contributions to psychology and epistemology include Gregory Bateson's (1972) observations about the circular nature of psychological processes, and Gordon Pask's (1980) conversation theory, a formal model of the process through which individuals reach agreement about shared meanings. Cybernetics has also made important contributions to group psychology, organizational dynamics, and management (Beer, 1995).

Cybernetics Today

Cybernetics played an important historical role in the origins of computer science, but it and the other interdisciplinary systems sciences have not generally become recognized as independent disciplines. There are many reasons for this, but most particularly the difficulty of maintaining the coherence of a broad, interdisciplinary field in the wake of the rapid growth of the specialized disciplines that cybernetics helped to found, including computer science, artificial intelligence, information science (*q.v.*), and control engineering.

The core ideas of cybernetics have largely been incorporated into other disciplines, however, where they continue to influence scientific developments. Perhaps the most significant of these is the explosive growth of interest in complex adaptive systems (Holland, 1995), which has largely taken up the cybernetics banner in its use of mathematical models of relational concepts for interdisciplinary systems studies. "Artificial life" has also become a computational approach to simulation of biological systems and to the problem of the origin of life.

Cybernetics continues to be a subject of study for a few committed groups (*see* Websites). The study of autopoiesis, systems dynamics and control theory also continue, with applications in management science and even psychological therapy (Meadows and Meadows, 1992; Powers, 1989). *General information theory* is the search for formal representations of relational concepts that are not based strictly on classical probability theory, (*see* FUZZY LOGIC; Klir, 1993) There has also been significant progress in building a *semiotic* theory of information in which issues of the semantics and meaning of signals are at last being seriously considered (Mystel, 1996).

Finally, a number of authors are seriously questioning the limits of mechanism and formalisms for interdisciplinary modeling and for science in general (Kampis, 1991; Rosen, 1991). The issues are what are the ultimate limits on knowledge, and whether it is possible to construct models, formal or not, that will help us understand the full complexity of the world around us.

Bibliography

1943. Rosenbluth, A., and Wiener, N. "Behavior, Purpose, and Teleology," *Philosophy of Science*, **10**, 18–24.

1948. Wiener, N. *Cybernetics or Control and Communication in the Animal and the Machine*. MIT Technology Press and New York: John Wiley, 1948; 2nd Ed., 1965.

1960. von Förster, H. "On Self-Organizing Systems and Their Environments," in *Self-organizing Systems* (ed. Yovitz and Cameron), 31–50. Oxford: Pergamon.

1964. Shannon, C. E., and Weaver, W. *Mathematical Theory of Communication*, Urbana, IL: University of Illinois Press.

1965. McCulloch, W. (ed.) *Embodiments of Mind*. Cambridge, MA: MIT Press.

1966. von Neumann, J. *Theory of Self-Reproducing Automata*. Urbana, IL: University of Illinois Press.

1968. von Bertalanffy, L. *General Systems Theory*. New York: George Braziller.

1971. Forrester, J. W. *World Dynamics*. Cambridge: Wright and Allen.

1972. Bateson, G. *Steps to an Ecology of Mind*. New York: Ballantine.

1972. Meadows, D. H. and Meadows, D. L. *Limits to Growth*. New York: Signet.

1974. Varela, F. J., Maturana, H. R., and Uribe, R. "Autopoiesis: The Organization of Living Systems, its Characterization, and a Model," *Biosystems*, **5**, 187–196.

1980. Pask, G. "Developments in Conversation Theory: Part 1," *Int. J. Man-Machine Studies*, **13**, 357–411.

1980. Prigogine, I. *From Being to Becoming*. San Francisco: W. H. Freeman.

1981. Conant, R. (ed.) *Mechanisms of Intelligence: Ross Ashby's Writings on Cybernetics*. The Systems Inquiry Series. Seaside, CA: Intersystems Publications.

1984. Braitenberg, V. *Vehicles: Experiments in Synthetic Psychology*. Cambridge, MA: MIT Press.

1989. Powers, W. T. (ed.) *Living Control Systems*. CSG Press.

1989. Umpleby, S. "Applying Second Order Cybernetics," in *Proc. 1989 American Society for Cybernetics*.

1991. von Glasersfeld, E. "Exposition on Constructivism: Why Some Like it Radical," in *Facets of Systems Science* (ed. G. Klir), 229–238. New York: Plenum.

1991. Kampis, G. *Self-Modifying Systems*. Oxford: Pergamon.

1991. Heims, S. J. *Cybernetics Group*. Cambridge, MA: MIT Press.

1991. Richardson, G. *Feedback Thought*. Philadelphia, PA: University of Pennsylvania Press.

1991. Rosen, R. *Life Itself*. New York: Columbia University Press.

1992. Meadows, D. H., Meadows, D. L., and Randers, J. *Beyond the Limits*. Post Mills, VT: Chelsea Green.

1993. Klir, G. "Developments in Uncertainty Based Information," in *Advances in Computers*, vol. **36** (ed. M. Yovitz), 255–332. New York: Academic Press.

1995. Beer, S. *Diagnosing the System: the Managerial Cybernetics of Organization*. New York: John Wiley.

1995. Holland, J. *Hidden Order: How Adaptation Builds Complexity*. Reading, MA: Addison-Wesley.

1996. Meystel, A. "Intelligent Systems: A Semiotic Perspective," *Int. J. Intelligent Control and Systems*, **1**, *1*, 31–57.

1997. Meyer, N. D. *Structural Cybernetics: An Overview*. New York: NDMA Publishing.

Websites

American Society for Cybernetics. http://www.gwu.edu/~asc/.

Principia Cybernetica Project. http://pespmc1.vub.ac.be.

Cliff Joslyn and Francis Heylighen

CYBERSPACE

For articles on related subjects *see* COMPUTER CONFERENCING; COOPERATIVE COMPUTING; ELECTRONIC COMMERCE; ELECTRONIC MAIL; INTERNET; MULTIMEDIA; ONLINE CONVERSATION; PRETTY GOOD PRIVACY; PRIVACY, COMPUTERS AND; VIRTUAL REALITY; and WORLD WIDE WEB.

Cyberspace is the "place" where a telephone conversation appears to occur. Not inside your actual phone, the plastic device on your desk. Not inside the other person's phone, in some other city. *The place between* the phones. The indefinite place *out there*, where the two of you, human beings, actually meet and communicate.

Bruce Sterling, *The Hacker Crackdown* (1993)

The term *cyberspace* was the invention of the science-fiction novelist William Gibson. As described in his book *Neuromancer* (Gibson, 1984) and several later novels, cyberspace was an artificial environment created by and maintained by computers. Transcending two-dimensional audio-visual movies, his three-dimensional cyberspace conveyed realistic detail to all five senses and supported remote intimacy. In *Count Zero* (Gibson, 1986), the second of his cyberspace trilogy, for instance, the character Josef Virek seems to be interviewing another, Marly Krushkhova, face to face in Barcelona, though in fact she is sitting alone in an office in Brussels. Such technologically simulated experience has come to be known as *virtual reality*. The Sterling quote above may have been prompted by what Gibson wrote in the third novel of the sequence, *Mona Lisa Overdrive* (Gibson, 1988): "*There's no there, there*. They taught that to children, explaining cyberspace."

Cyberspace is now associated primarily with interaction over computer networks, most particularly the combination of the Internet and the World Wide Web. In this sense, "cyberspace" has become a synonym for "information superhighway," a term popularized in 1978 by then-Congressman Albert Gore, Jr to refer to a unified, interactive system of electronic communication analogous to the US Interstate Highway System. (Freelance journalist Ralph Lee Smith had used the same term and analogy in a 1970 story in *The Nation*.) The prospect of such a system, with the capacity to deliver an unprecedented range of informational services to the home, school, or office, has been the driving force behind the creation of a multitude of commercial ventures, many of them Internet startup companies such as Amazon.com, Ebay, and Yahoo! that have greatly enriched their founders (*see* ENTREPRENEURS). Traditional brick and mortar retail sales outlets, those unequipped to handle "click and mortar" electronic commerce (*q.v.*), are now under great strain and, other than supermarkets, may not survive.

But the social implications of cyberspace far outstrip its commercial potential. Whereas television reaches a passive, isolated audience, Internet users supply content and act cooperatively and interactively to distribute it widely. Cyberspace encourages the formation of "virtual communities" that share a common interest. Such communities operate without regard to national boundaries, spreading the concept of free speech to many areas of the world to which that idea had been utterly foreign. On the Internet, every user is a potential publisher, liberating public discourse from the control of the privately controlled print and broadcast media.

Widespread global interconnection was envisioned surprisingly early. In his 1946 short story "A Logic Named Joe," Murray Leinster writes:

Each home has at least one "logic," a personal computer complete with screen and keyboard, networked to centralized supercomputers containing all knowledge and recorded telecasts. People access information, solve problems, view entertainment programs, communicate with each other, run their charge accounts, and so on from their personal computer through the network. There are even built-in censors that prevent children from seeing inappropriate material. (*See* FICTION, COMPUTERS IN.)

And although he envisioned mental, quasi-spiritual interconnections rather than electronic, the Jesuit paleontologist and philosopher Pierre Teilhard de Chardin postulated that human evolution would ultimately produce a "noösphere" of knowledge that would envelop the earth just as palpably as does the current atmosphere and ionosphere. In his 1947 essay "The Formation of the Noösphere," he wrote:

No one can deny that a world network of economic and psychic affiliations is being woven at ever increasing speed which envelops and constantly penetrates more deeply within each of us. With every day that passes it becomes a little more impossible for us to act or think otherwise than collectively.

But the author of what is perhaps the earliest published anticipation of cyberspace was apprehensive. In his 1879 novel *The Brothers Karamazov*, Fyodor Dostoevsky wrote:

We are assured that the world is getting more and more united, more and more bound together in brotherly community, as it overcomes distance and sets thoughts flying through the air. Alas, put no faith in such bonds of union for many senseless and foolish desires and habits and ridiculous fancies are fostered in them.

Dostoevsky's novel, whose complete text is available at `http://eserver.org/fiction/brothers-karamazov.txt`, was published only about four years after Alexander Graham Bell secured his patent on the telephone, arguably the first instrument of cyberspace.

In his famous 1945 article "As We May Think," Vannevar Bush (*q.v.*) described a hypothetical information system that he called a "memex" in a detail that included hypertext (*q.v.*) indexing. But he envisioned that the hyperlinked database being searched would be stored locally, not distributed globally.

Leinster's concern as to how to keep inappropriate material from children has become very real. Many critics have become obsessed with the issue. Pornographic images represent less than one half of one per cent of all images on the Internet, but unsupervised children will find them, just as they will find Websites that promote gambling, instill hatred, glorify firearms, and publish detailed instructions for making explosive devices. Some US legislators have proposed laws requiring strict screening of unregulated computer networks for pornographic materials—a measure which defenders of the First Amendment contend would be comparable to asking telephone companies to monitor their lines for conversations that might aid and abet criminal activity. But since no one country or institution "owns" the Internet, no such screening would be practical; the only "solution" is vigilant parental supervision.

There is great danger in the potential for violations of civil and privacy rights through the use of computer networks (*see* PRIVACY, COMPUTERS AND). As ever more social and commercial transactions are conducted in cyberspace, it becomes easier to track user spending habits, private interests, and political beliefs. Advocacy groups such as the Electronic Frontier Foundation (*q.v.*) have called for vigorous protection of privacy rights in cyberspace.

Cyberspace also places at risk the traditional concept of copyright. If an online document is downloaded to a diskette (*q.v.*) or hard drive (*q.v.*), an unscrupulous viewer, or perhaps only an uninformed careless one, can alter the document and republish it without credit or payment to its author, a practice of great concern to defenders of intellectual property rights. But the very notion of copyright—unknown before the invention of printing—may prove untenable in cyberspace. What could conceivably replace it is a system whereby proprietary information can be viewed and downloaded only by subscribers who pay a small royalty through use of a credit or debit card.

The actuality rather than the potentiality of cyberspace is less than a decade old. And although Dostoevsky could yet prove right, this author believes that the evolution of cyberspace is and will continue to be a civilizing educational force comparable only to what was wrought by the printing press but not, despite initial hopes, by television.

Bibliography

1984. Gibson, W. *Neuromancer*. New York: Ace Books.
1986. Gibson, W. *Count Zero*. New York: Arbor House.
1988. Gibson, W. *Mona Lisa Overdrive*. New York: Bantam Books.
1992. Landow, G. P. *Vannevar Bush and the Memex*. Baltimore, MD: Johns Hopkins University Press.
1995. Negroponte, N. *Being Digital*. New York: Alfred E. Knopf.
1996. Slatalla, M., and Quittner, J. *Masters of Deception: The Gang That Ruled Cyberspace*. New York: HarperPerennial Library.
1999. Lessig, L. *CODE and other Laws of Cyberspace*. New York: Basic Books.

Edwin D. Reilly

CYCLE STEALING

For articles on related subjects *see* CHANNEL; and MEMORY: MAIN.

Cycle stealing is a technique for memory sharing whereby a memory may serve two autonomous masters and in effect provide service to each simultaneously. One of the masters is commonly the central processing unit (CPU—*q.v.*), and the other is usually an I/O channel or device controller. Fig. 1 illustrates two memory cycles (numbers 3 and 5) being stolen by an I/O channel (from the CPU) between two cycles of memory use by the CPU. This is possible and convenient, at least periodically, because the CPU is self-driven (except possibly between some substeps of a process it is conducting) and has no fixed time demands on memory. Furthermore, there are occasions, particularly in simpler CPU designs, where the instruction being executed (e.g. division) is processor-limited (i.e. uses all the processor's capabilities) and memory access is temporarily suspended.

The I/O equipment is, on the other hand, quite different. Its use of the memory, though generally less frequent than that by the CPU, is much more time-constrained. For many I/O devices, such as disks and tapes, blocks of data are produced or required at fixed intervals. The need for data transfer occurs relentlessly at fixed time intervals. In transferring data from a disk to memory, the previous byte or word must have been stored before the next arrives; otherwise, data is lost. This problem is somewhat alleviated by the use of

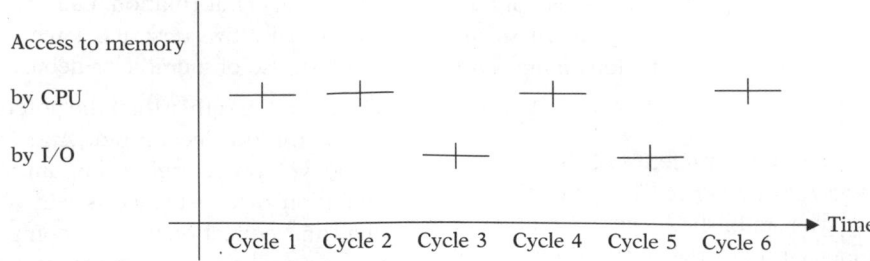

Figure 1. Cycle stealing.

single or multiple buffers (*q.v.*) in the device controller or channel, but in any case there are important recurring time demands for memory access. These can be met by cycle stealing in those CPU designs in which processor activity can be suspended for a memory cycle while a memory access is made by the I/O system. I/O devices that use cycle stealing are known as *direct memory access* (DMA) devices, since they transfer data to or from memory without using the CPU (*see* INPUT–OUTPUT OPERATIONS).

Kenneth C. Smith and Adel Sedra

CYCLE TIME

For articles on related subjects *see* REGISTER; and SYNCHRONOUS/ASYNCHRONOUS OPERATION.

The *cycle time* of a computer is the time required to change the information in a set of registers. This is also sometimes called the *state transition time*.

The register cycle time of a processor is sometimes referred to as the *internal cycle time, clock time*, or simply *cycle time*; occasionally, confusion develops between the internal cycle time (referenced to registers) and the main memory cycle time. The memory cycle time is usually several times the internal cycle time.

The internal cycle time may not be of constant value. There are basically three different types of cycle-timing organization:

1. *Synchronous (fixed)*: In this scheme all operations are composed of one or more cycles, with the fundamental time quantum being fixed by the design. Such systems are also referred to as *clocked*, since usually a master oscillator (or clock) is used to distribute and define these cycles.

2. *Synchronous (variable)*: This is a slight variation of the first scheme; certain long operations are allowed to take multiple cycles without causing a register state transition. In such systems there may be several different cycle lengths. For example, a

register-to-register transfer of information cycle might take one cycle, while a register-to-adder and return-to-register cycle would perhaps be two or three cycles. (The fundamental difference between the fixed and variable synchronous types is that the former stores information into registers at the end of every cycle time, whereas the latter sets information into registers after a number of cycles, depending upon the type of operation being performed.)

3. *Asynchronous operation*: In a completely asynchronous machine there is no clock or external mechanism that determines a state transition. Rather, the logic of the system is arranged in stages; when the output value of one stage has been stabilized, the logic signals the input at that stage to admit new operands. (Asynchronous operation is clearly advantageous when the variation in cycle time is significant, since a synchronous scheme must always wait for the worst possible delay in the definition of the time quantum required. On the other hand, when logic delays are predictable, synchronous approaches have an advantage because several additional stages of logic are required in the asynchronous scheme to signal completion of an operation.)

In current practice almost all processors use a fixed synchronous cycle as this is required to support a pipelined implementation (*see* PIPELINE). Access to main memory is sometimes implemented as an asynchronous operation.

Michael J. Flynn

CYCLIC REDUNDANCY CHECK

For articles on related subjects *see* CODES; ERROR CORRECTING AND DETECTING CODE; and PARITY.

In modern computer systems, data is continuously transferred between a processor and its peripherals, or between processors connected by means of a network.

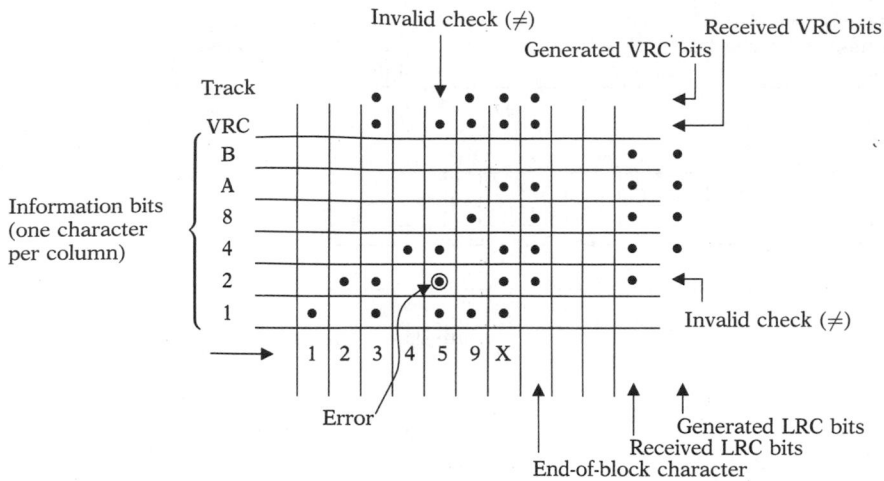

Figure 1. Error detection using LRC and VRC bits. An extra "1" bit has been introduced in the character "5". Assuming no errors in the received check bits, the error must occur at the intersection of the invalid check column and row. The error bit must be reversed. In this case, the "1" must be changed to "0".

Errors may be introduced during the reading, writing, or actual transmission of this data. Consequently, error control has become an integral part in the design of modern computers and communication systems. The most commonly used methods for error detection involve the addition of one or more *redundancy bits* to the information-carrying bits of a character or stream of characters. These redundancy bits do not carry any information; they are merely used to determine the correctness of the bits carrying the information.

Perhaps the most commonly used method for error detection is the simple *parity check*. Parity may be even or odd, meaning that the sum of the "one" bits of any character, including the parity bit itself, will always be even or odd, depending upon which arrangement is chosen.

Fig. 1 illustrates a form of two-dimensional parity checking used on some magnetic tapes that can detect and even correct some types of error. The six-bit characters are arranged in columns with a seventh odd parity bit, called the *vertical redundancy check* (VRC), added to make the sum of the "one" bits in each column an odd number. Similarly, an odd parity-check bit, called the *longitudinal redundancy check* (LRC), is added at the end of the block for each row of bits. As the tape is read, the VRC and LRC are regenerated and compared to the check characters read. If equal, the information is assumed correct. If not equal, the block is read again. Some types of errors, like the one shown in Fig. 1, may also be corrected by using this method.

Cyclic redundancy checking is a far more powerful error-detecting method. Here, all the characters in a message block are treated as a serial string of bits representing a binary number. This number is then divided modulo 2 by a predetermined binary number and the remainder of this division is appended to the block of characters as a cyclic redundancy check (CRC) character. The CRC is compared with the check character obtained in similar fashion at the receiving end. If they agree, the message is assumed correct. If they disagree, the receiver will demand a retransmission. (This is usually called the ARQ (automatic repeat request) method of error control and is very commonly used in data communication.) The CRC character is also called the *cyclic check sum*, or simply the *check sum* character.

To show how the CRC is generated, let the message consist of k bits, $a_0 a_1 \ldots a_{k-1}$, $a_i = 0$ or 1. Then we form the $(k-1)$-*degree polynomial*:

$$M(x) = a_0 + a_1 x + \cdots + a_{k-1} x^{k-1} = \sum_{i=0}^{k-1} a_i x^i. \quad (1)$$

If we wish to include r CRC bits, $r < k$, $M(x)$ is multiplied by x^r (this is equivalent to shifting the message bits r places to the right). Let $G(x)$ be another polynomial—called the "generator" or "checking" polynomial—of degree r, whose coefficients are also 0 or 1. We divide $x^r M(x)$ by $G(x)$, obtaining

$$\frac{x^r M(x)}{G(x)} = Q(x) + \frac{R(x)}{G(x)} \qquad \text{mod } 2 \quad (2)$$

where the "mod 2" indicates that all sums and differences of coefficients are taken as 0, if the result is 0 or even, and 1 if it is odd. Thus, from Eq. (2)

$$R(x) = x^r M(x) + Q(x)G(x) \qquad \text{mod } 2 \quad (3)$$

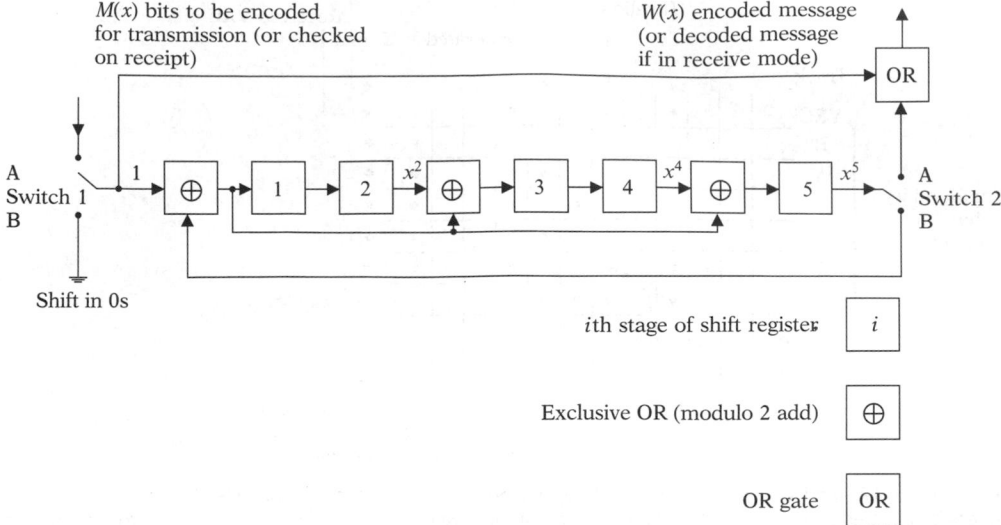

Figure 2. Shift register for $G(x) = 1 + x^2 + x^4 + x^5$. Initially, the register contains 00000, switch 1 is in position A, and switch 2 is in position B. When all message bits have been transmitted, the register contains $R(x)$. Switch 1 now goes to B, and switch 2 goes to A to enable $R(x)$ to be shifted out. When data is being received, the resulting $R(x)$ must be zero; otherwise, the data is in error.

where $R(x)$ is the remainder and $Q(x)$ is the quotient. The code word $W(x)$ is

$$W(x) = Q(x)G(x) = x^r M(x) + R(x) \qquad \text{mod 2} \quad (4)$$

and what is transmitted are the coefficients of $W(x)$.

Note that $W(x)$, which is of degree $r + k - 1$, contains the original k message bits (the $x^r M(x)$ term) and r check bits (the $R(x)$ term). Furthermore, $W(x)$ is exactly divisible by $G(x)$. The division by $G(x)$ at the transmitting end is accomplished by an r-stage shift register with feedback paths represented by the coefficients of $G(x)$, as shown in Fig. 2. On the receiving end, $W(x)$ is also divided by $G(x)$, and the remainder in this case must be 0; otherwise, an error has occurred.

Consider the following example related to the shift register shown in Fig. 2. Let the message be 1010010001. Therefore, $M(x) = 1 + x^2 + x^5 + x^9$. With $G(x) = 1 + x^2 + x^4 + x^5$, modulo 2 division of $x^5 M(x)$ by $G(x)$ yields

$$Q(x) = 1 + x + x^2 + x^3 + x^7 + x^8 + x^9$$

and $R(x) = 1 + x$. Thus

$$W(x) = 1 + x + x^5 + x^7 + x^{10} + x^{14},$$

and the transmitted message is

```
        |
11000   | 1010010001
CRC     | original
bits    | message
        | bits
        |
```

The remainder, $R(x)$, is generated by the shift register (which is initially at 00000) as follows:

Message Bit	Shift Register Contents
	Stage:
	12345
1	10101
0	11111
0	11010
0	01101
1	00110
0	00011
0	10100
1	11111
0	11010
1	11000

The final contents is $R(x)$. Each successive shift register contents represents a successive stage of the division of $x^5 M(x)$, remembering that only the bits of $x^5 M(x)$ that have been already transmitted at each stage, take part in the division. When all message bits have been transmitted, the contents of the shift register are shifted out by five successive right shifts to transmit $R(x)$. Note that during this operation, zeros are shifted into stage 1 so that after $R(x)$ is transmitted, the contents are 00000; hence, the register is automatically cleared for more transmission.

Codes developed as described above are called *cyclic* codes. Such codes are used for error detection and correction for magnetic tape, disk, and data communication. The generator polynomial $x^{16} + x^{15} + x^2 + 1$, for example, is widely used in synchronous data communication systems. It can detect all odd numbers of error bits, all possible single-error bursts not exceeding 16 bits, 99.9969% of all possible single bursts 17 bits long, and 99.9984% of all possible longer bursts. This is much better than simple parity checking, for instance, which detects only all odd numbers of error bits and no others. Note that parity checking is equivalent to having a generator polynomial $G(x) = x + 1$.

The study of cyclic codes revolves principally upon determining the code characteristics resulting from various generator polynomials. Peterson and Weldon (1972) and Tang and Chien (1969) give some applications and a thorough mathematical treatment of cyclic and other codes. A more elementary description is given by McNamara (1988).

Bibliography

1969. Tang, D. T., and Chien, R. T. "Coding for Error Control," *IBM Systems Journal*, **8**, *1*, 48–86.
1972. Peterson, W. W. and Weldon, E. J. *Error-Correcting Codes*, 2nd Ed. Cambridge, MA: MIT Press.
1977. MacWilliams, F. and Sloane, N. J. A. *The Theory of Error-Correcting Codes*. Amsterdam: Elsevier.
1988. McNamara, J. E. *Technical Aspects of Data Communication*, 3rd Ed. Bedford, MA: Digital Press.

John S. Sobolewski

CYLINDER

For articles on related subjects *see* ACCESS TIME; HARD DISK; and MEMORY: AUXILIARY.

On a multiple-platter disk drive, a *cylinder* is the collection of all vertically aligned tracks with the same track number. The following discussion explains the importance of such a concept.

Many rotating storage devices—drums, disks, data cells, and the like—have fewer read–write heads than recording tracks. Therefore, either the surfaces of these devices must move to position the desired information under a read–write head, or the read–write heads must move to hover above the appropriate tracks. The latter strategy is commonly used for large direct-access devices such as disks containing several gigabytes.

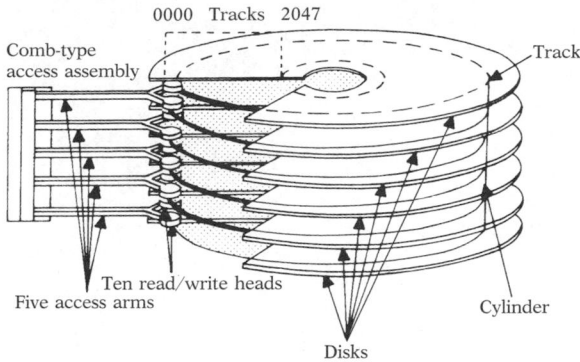

Figure 1.

For engineering convenience and efficient sequential processing of data, the following design has been adopted by most manufacturers of moving-head disk drives:

1. Disk surfaces are numbered from top to bottom for each horizontal position of the read–write comb.

2. During sequential writing operations, as the top track in each vertical plane becomes filled, control circuitry and system software allocate subsequent records to the beginning of the next vertical track. When this is filled, records are started on the third track, etc.

3. Therefore, during sequential reading, a maximum amount of data can be read at one time before the comb must be moved. This is considerably faster than the alternative strategy of writing all tracks concentrically on one surface before advancing to the next surface.

Each vertical set of tracks, one track per recording surface, is called a *cylinder*, after the geometrical surface outlined. There are as many cylinders per disk pack as tracks per recording surface (2,048 cylinders for the disk pack shown in Fig. 1).

David N. Freeman

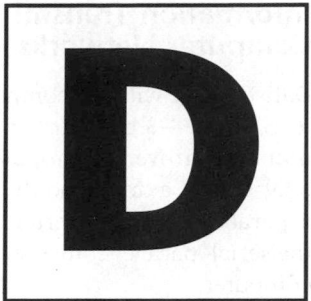

DATA COMMUNICATIONS

PRINCIPLES

For articles on related subjects *see* ASYNCHRONOUS TRANSFER MODE; BANDWIDTH; BAUD; CHANNEL; CODES; COMMUNICATION CONTROL UNIT; COMMUNICATIONS AND COMPUTERS; CONDITIONING; CYCLIC REDUNDANCY CHECK; ERROR CORRECTING AND DETECTING CODE; ETHERNET; GATEWAY; INTERNET; MOBILE COMPUTING; MODEM; MULTIPLEXING; NETWORK PROTOCOLS; OPEN SYSTEMS INTERCONNECTION; PACKET SWITCHING; PROTOCOL; SYNCHRONOUS/ASYNCHRONOUS OPERATION; and TCP/IP.

Introduction

Data communications is the most rapidly expanding communication area, with Public Switched Telephone Network (PSTN) market penetration approaching saturation levels, at least for wired networks. This article discusses the principles of data communications networks, transmission systems, and applications—as they stand in 1999.

Over the last 10 years, public data communication services have evolved from terminal and mainframe computer communications to be able to provide real-time networked multimedia (*q.v.*), Web access (*see* WORLD WIDE WEB) and email (*q.v.*), as well as the more traditional computer traffic. The network infrastructure and the communications techniques themselves have also undergone a major revolution, allowing today's public data networks to efficiently deliver megabits per second (and soon gigabits per second) to the user.

Network technology usually relies on synchronous high-speed digital transmission over a range of different media, such as fiber optics (*q.v.*), twisted pairs, and mobile radio channels. Even over the local loop (the remaining legacy of the analog PSTN), which consists of one twisted pair per line, techniques such as the Asymmetric Digital Subscriber Loop (ADSL) have been developed that can deliver up to 6 Mbps from the local exchange to the home.

Massive increases in the speed of the underlying transmission medium, together with much lower error rates, have been reflected in the communications protocol stack. For most wired networks, error and flow control are no longer achieved on a hop-by-hop basis between network nodes, but rather end-to-end by application software at the sending and receiving ends. Slimming down the functionality in the network has led to further performance improvements.

Similarly, radical changes in switching and multiplexing technology have meant that circuit-switching, which is very inefficient for data, has been replaced by packet switching, which is much more suitable. (Circuit-switching is like a telephone connection, requiring a single, complete path, while packet switching routes individual pieces of a message, perhaps along different paths.)

These changes throughout data communications technology have led to the ability to build and deploy *global* public data communications networks. The Internet is the principal global data communications network and it supports both data and real-time multimedia traffic.

Information Transmission Over Computer Networks

Data transfer within a computer is in finite-sized chunks (e.g. a byte—8 bits—or a word—32 or 64 bits). Communication over a computer network must often be only 1 bit at a time, and the data must be serialized (in a parallel–serial converter) and deserialized again in the serial–parallel converter upon arrival at the remote computer.

Data can usually flow in both directions simultaneously (*full duplex*). Sometimes, information can flow only in one direction (*simplex*), or data transmission in the two directions may not proceed simultaneously (*half duplex*).

Public data communication networks are made up of nodes (switches or routers) with links to connect them to other nodes (*see* Fig. 1). The communication links may carry either analog or digital representations of the digital data. The choice of representation depends upon many considerations which are dealt with in the section on transmission techniques. A very diverse range of traffic commonly needs to be sent between one node and the next, and multiplexing techniques that enable a single link to carry multiple flows of data are used. In some situations, especially in office networks, multiple computers need to be able to share information and to have access to resources such as printers and file stores. In such a situation, the transmission link does not carry multiplexed information, and hosts must take turns using the shared link.

If information is multiplexed onto the links between nodes, then the switches or routers need to be able to demultiplex and then remultiplex parts of the data that need to be routed to different destinations. Often, the communications network accepts data in *blocks*, *frames*, or *packets*, since transferring data in units enables it to be easily multiplexed. A set of messages is passed between the computer and the switch or router or between the source computer and the destination computer to facilitate this. The set of messages is called a *Network Protocol* (*see* NETWORK PROTOCOLS and PROTOCOL).

Transmission Techniques

Digital communication is most simply transmitted using square wave signals, consisting of on and off pulses (*see* Halsall, 1996). An example of this is shown in Fig. 2. These are commonly referred to as *baseband signals*, since their spectrum consists of frequencies that extend from roughly 0 Hz upwards to some value; more accurately, baseband signals are those that have not been modulated onto a carrier and shifted up the frequency spectrum. The range of frequencies from 0 Hz to the highest frequency present is the "electrical" *bandwidth* (*q.v.*) of the signal (this definition of "electrical' bandwidth is true only for baseband signals).

The link that the data will be transmitted over also has an "electrical" bandwidth associated with it, which limits the frequencies that can propagate along it without too much attenuation or distortion. The "electrical" bandwidth of the link limits the capacity of the network. (Capacity is often erroneously referred to as the bandwidth of the network, which is not the

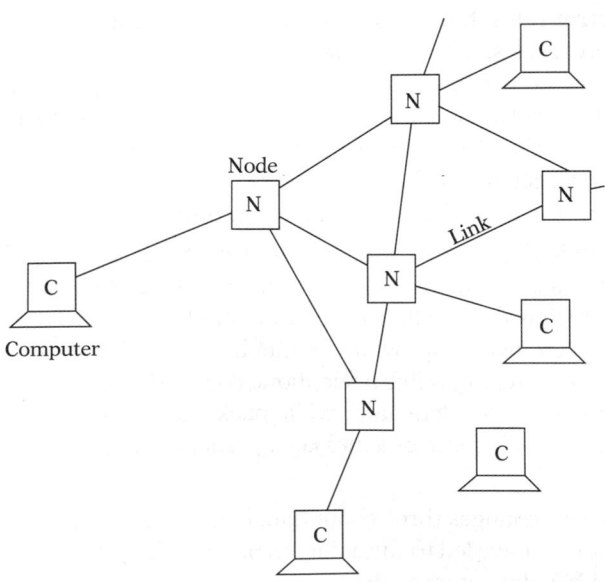

Figure 1. Communications networks are made up of nodes that are interconnected by links.

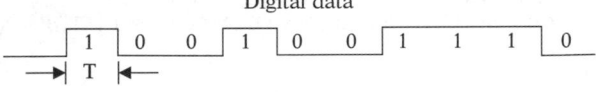

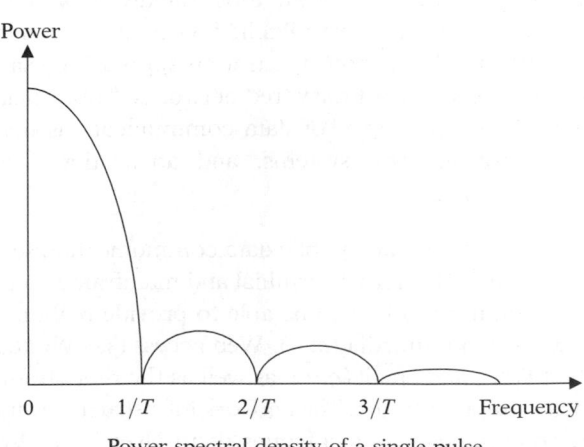

Power spectral density of a single pulse

Figure 2. Baseband digital transmission uses square pulses. The graph shows the spectrum of this signal. *T* = pulse duration.

same as the "electrical" bandwidth, although the two are related.)

The theoretical limit to the information transfer rate or link *capacity*, *C*, is given by the Hartley–Shannon law as:

$$C = B\log_2(1 + S/N)$$

where *B* is the "electrical" bandwidth and *S/N* is the ratio of signal strength power to noise level power—the *signal to noise ratio*.

The maximum transmission rate of a communication link with usable "electrical" bandwidth *B* is 2*B* (Nyquist's law). The rate at which symbols are sent is called the *baud rate*. When only two levels are used, the baud rate is also equal to the rate of information transfer in bits per second (bps). If multiple-levels are used, as shown in Fig. 3 for four-level coding, then the bit rate is higher than the baud rate. To obtain the signals in Fig. 3, each pair of incoming bits in the signal is taken together, and the four resulting combinations (00, 01, 10, 11) are each coded to one level. This approach can be extended to *n* levels, but the circuitry required to discriminate and decode the levels becomes increasingly complex and is ultimately limited by the presence of noise on the link.

The characteristics of the physical link can lead to degradation of the baseband signal's received pulse shapes. There are three main factors here: attenuation, dispersion, and noise. Attenuation leads to a reduction in the received signal strength, thereby making the signal more susceptible to the effect of noise, which can, for example, lead to a 1 being mistaken for a 0. Attenuation is also usually frequency dependent, and increases with frequency. This effective band limiting leads to a smearing of the received pulses, which can cause a pulse to interfere with an adjacent pulse. This is called inter-symbol interference (ISI). Dispersion is the phenomenon in which different frequency components of the pulse travel at different velocities down the link. This again causes spreading of the pulses, leading to ISI. Uncertainty in the position of the pulse edges caused by the above effects, and by imperfect clock stability at the transmitter, causes telegraph distortion (TD). Both TD and ISI are shown on the

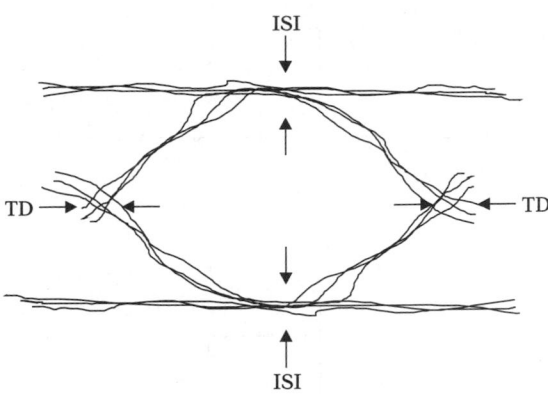

Figure 4. Distortion effects of the channel on digital pulses.

"eye" diagram in Fig. 4. The impact of distortion can be reduced by a combination of the use of line codes and pulse shaping.

Line codes can be used to match the spectrum of the transmitted signal to the frequency response of the link or channel. One of the simplest examples is alternate mark inversion (AMI) where ones are sent alternatively as +1 and −1. The spectrum of the signal in Fig. 5 has a 0 bit at voltage level 0 and 1 bits with alternating signs.

Pulse shaping tailors the temporal profile of the pulses, to minimize the interference between adjacent pulses (ISI). The minimum bandwidth pulse shape—which supports a data rate of 2*B* in a "brick-wall" bandwidth of *B*—is shown in Fig. 6. A brick-wall spectrum cannot be realized in practice, so other pulse shapes, such as the raised cosine family, are used instead. These

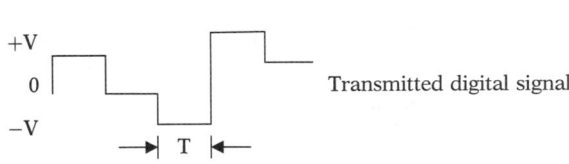

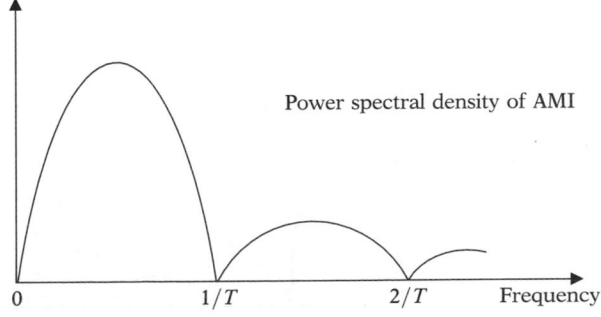

Figure 5. The use of line codes to match the spectrum of the digital signal to the "electrical" bandwidth of the channel. The diagram shows AMI.

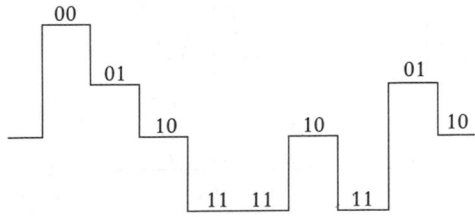

Figure 3. Multilevel signaling.

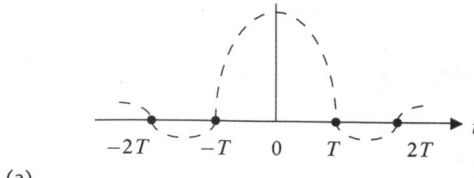

(a)

(b)

(c)

Figure 6. Optimum and practical pulse shaping. The diagram shows (a) the optimum pulse shape and (b) its brick-wall frequency spectrum ($B = 1/2T$), together with (c) the practical case, which uses raised cosine frequency curves.

pulse shapes increase the bandwidth of the spectrum slightly, but maintain zero ISI.

Baseband signals can be transmitted as digital signals over the link if the usable part of the frequency spectrum of the link lies in the baseband region; this is true for twisted pair copper and coaxial cables, but not true for fiber optic cables and radio transmission. These cases require the use of analog techniques: the digital data is used to modulate the amplitude, frequency, or phase of a carrier sine wave (analog transmission—Fig. 7), using a modem.

While the trunk portion of the telephone network in most advanced countries is largely based on digital transmission and switching, the local network is still mainly analog. Relatively recently, the introduction of ISDN to the home has allowed small businesses and home computer users to transmit digital data directly at 128 Kbps but this is set to be overshadowed by the introduction of Digital Subscriber Loop technology. Using multilevel, multiphase modulation, xDSL modems achieve effective data transmission rates of well over 10 Mbps.

Sharing a Single Transmission Medium

Some communication systems need to send data down a link only at irregular intervals. Such systems are termed *asynchronous*. In an asynchronous system the transmission rate is predetermined, but it is necessary to delimit information by sending a *start-of-frame*

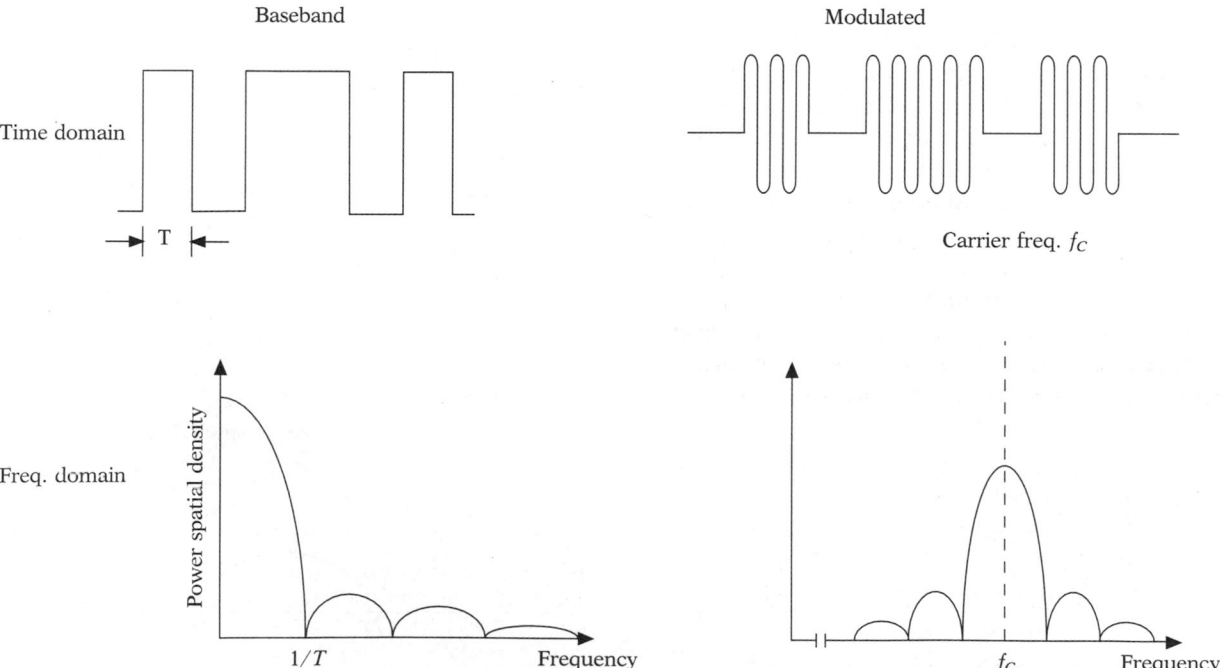

Figure 7. Signals and frequency spectra of direct transmission of the digital signal (baseband) and the result of modulating a carrier signal of frequency f_C with the digital data (modulated). The diagram shows amplitude modulation.

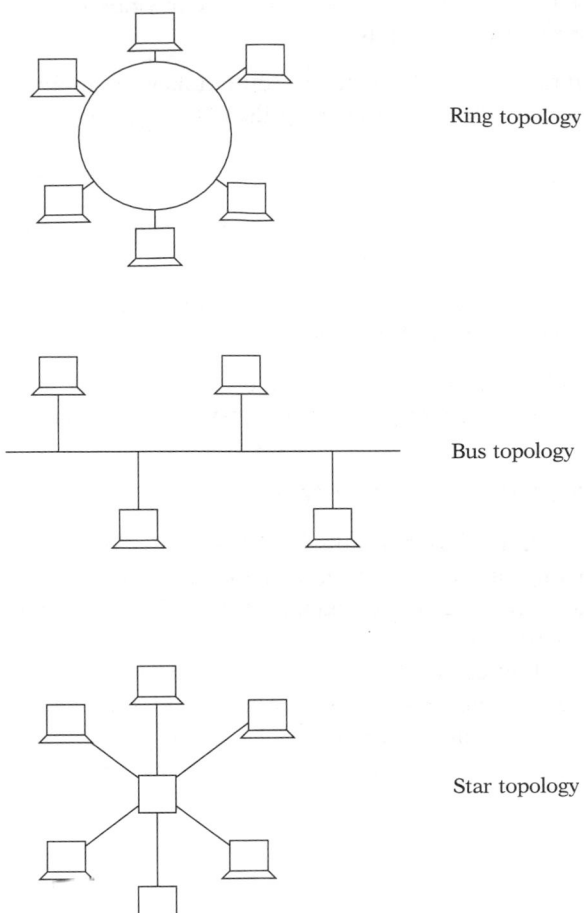

Figure 8. LAN topologies. The diagram shows the topology of a ring network, a bus network, and a star network.

sequence before and an *end-of-frame* sequence after transmission of the data. The frame is preceded by a preamble to synchronize the receiver for the duration of the frame.

The sender can send (or receive) data along the channel connecting it to the other hosts, and by the appropriate use of addressing information in a frame header, it is possible to ensure that the data is received at its correct destination. This mode of communication is called *broadcast*, which is commonly used over Local Area Networks, and N-ISDN (Fig. 8). For broadcast LANs, a contention-access mechanism is also required, which controls who can transmit data at any one time (*see* LOCAL AREA NETWORK). In N-ISDN, a call setup phase precedes data transmission, and terminals on the multipoint bus (having contended for access to the signaling channel) can then transmit data without contention.

LAN contention access mechanisms transmit data in blocks, which are usually framed by some synchronizing bytes, a start-byte, error-detection bytes, and an

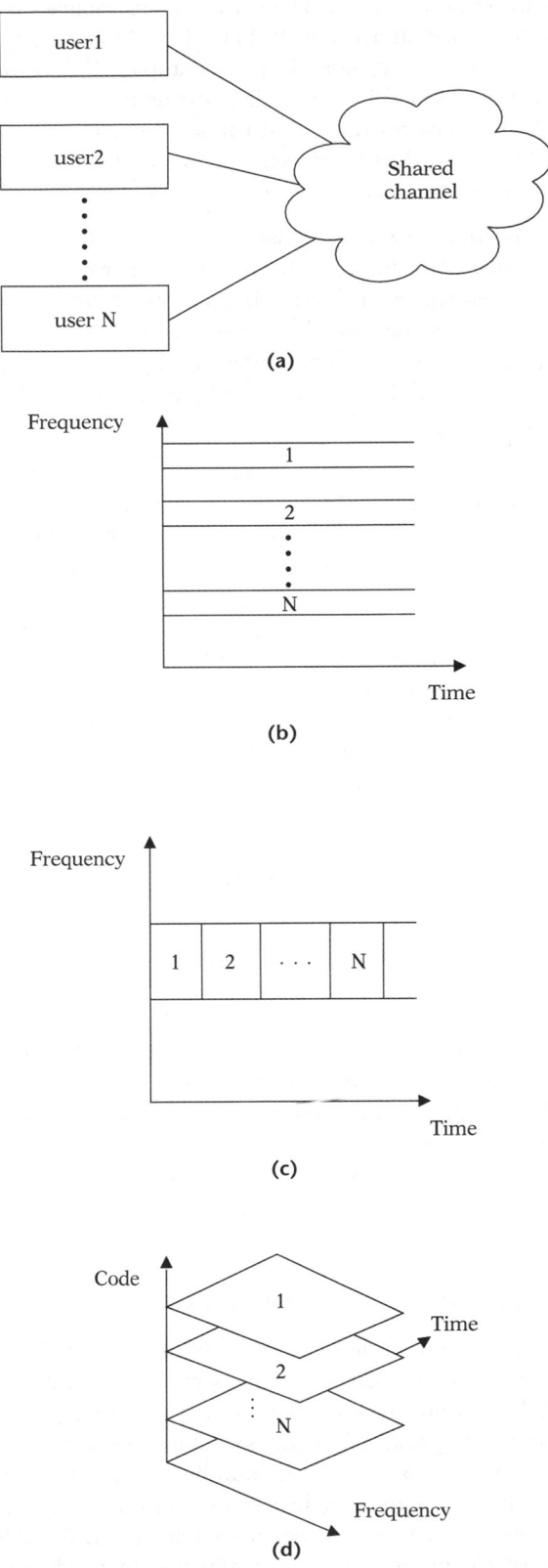

Figure 9. Sharing the capacity of a communications link using a multiplexing technique. The diagram shows (b) FDM, (c) TDM, and (d) CDM.

end-of-block indication. The start-of-block indication is a special bit pattern (e.g. 01111110), which may not occur in the main data. In this example, the normal data bits have a "0" inserted into the data stream after each five consecutive "1" bits (bit stuffing). The receiving hardware thus interprets six consecutive "1" bits as meaning the start (or end) of a data block.

Systems that need to send data down a link all the time are called *synchronous*. Data is sent in frames, and the transmission of frames is continuous and back-to-back, as is the case for high-speed digital carriers that interconnect switches. Sharing the capacity of a synchronous link between multiple users is called *multiplexing*.

In Fig. 9, the transmission medium is carrying a multiplexed data stream. Multiplexing may be achieved in a variety of ways such as by using a different carrier frequency for each channel (*frequency division multiplexing, FDM*), by using a different slot in a high-speed synchronous digital transmission system (*time division multiplexing, TDM*). Mobile transmission systems use a third kind of multiplexing, called code division multiplexing (CDM), where digital data pulses are used to modulate a high-speed pseudo-random sequence (*see* RANDOM NUMBER GENERATION) that is known by the intended receiver. This means that while all receivers can receive the transmission, only the intended host can actually decode and understand it.

Multiplexing techniques are not mutually exclusive, and often two of the techniques can be used together. An example of joint use of TDM and FDM is in the synchronous high-speed carriers in the Synchronous Digital Hierarchy (SDH, or SONET in the USA). TDM is used to multiplex data from a number of users into a single data stream, and an optical variant of FDM (*wavelength division multiplexing, WDM*) is used to transmit multiple composite streams down the fiber optic cable. CDM is more commonly used in mobile systems, where it is also called *spread spectrum*.

Multiplexing at the Switch or Router

The ability to multiplex data from multiple users down a single transmission link implies multiplexing at the switch or router (*see* COMMUNICATION CONTROL UNIT) in terms of packets (packet switching) or cells (cell relay). There is a limit to the number of simultaneous calls that can be handled by a switch, or the number of packets by a router. If packet switching is used, this limit on the number of packets may be a by-product of the processing required for each packet header (e.g. defined by the IP protocol), or the capacity of the output links. If circuit switching (or even virtual circuit switching) is used, the limit is determined by the number of simultaneous buffers required for each call that

can be supported (e.g. as in an Asynchronous Transfer Mode—ATM—switch).

Multiplexing at the switch or router takes advantage of one or more of the following factors:

◆ Normally, not all inputs operate simultaneously.

◆ When in use, the data transmission rate may exhibit considerable variation.

◆ The cost of a long-distance communication channel increases much more slowly than its data capacity.

◆ The communications channels installed often have greater capacity than required for average traffic.

Error and Flow Control

Noise in modern transmission links occurs fairly infrequently (a bit error rate (BER) of 10^{-9} is commonplace), but over radio channels the BER can be worse than 10^{-4}. The nature of these errors is such that the noise that causes them often lasts more than one bit-time. For this reason, most data transmission systems send their information in blocks and use error-detection codes to protect the whole block. An example of an error-detecting code is the *cyclic redundancy check* (CRC—*q.v.*).

For transmission systems that use CRCs to provide a means of error detection, a separate means of achieving reliable data transmission can be used when applications require it. In this case, each information frame (I-frame—which includes its own CRC field) must be acknowledged as having been correctly received. In early algorithms, an acknowledgement would be required before any new block could be sent, but modern error-control protocols allow the acknowledgments of several frames to be outstanding at any one time. The header of the frame contains a sequence number, which is increased each time a frame is sent. It is assumed that each frame has been received correctly unless a *negative acknowledgement* is sent subsequently. If that occurs, either only the faulty block or all subsequent blocks are re-transmitted. Flow control is a function commonly linked with error control, and it can operate by restricting the number of outstanding I-frames at the transmitter (sliding window flow control).

Error and flow control for data transmission used to be accomplished on a hop-by-hop basis (over an individual link). As the BER of the transmission lines used has decreased, so this function has moved up the protocol stack to be accomplished on an end-to-end basis. The standardized control procedure (Higher Data Link Control—HDLC) provides both error and flow control, and most modern error and flow control protocols are merely slight variants of this protocol. An example of error and flow control being accomplished end-to-end is in the Internet, where the Transmission Control Protocol (TCP) provides a reliable bit-pipe (channel) to the application. An example of error and flow control accomplished on a hop-by-hop basis is in the channel reserved for signaling information in N-ISDN (the D-channel, which uses a variant of HDLC known as LAPD).

Mobile channels suffer from high BERs, and in this case, a technique known as forward error correction (FEC) is used to improve the BER to reasonable values. FEC allows errors to be both detected and corrected. Applications that require a more reliable service would then use an end-to-end error control protocol (perhaps such as TCP/IP, if the mobile link is being used for Internet data access).

Public Data Networks

Public data transmission facilities used to be offered solely as leased telephone lines, over which modems could be used to transmit digital data. Public data transmission facilities are now offered either by an Internet Service Provider (ISP) over a dial-up link (telephone line) into the Internet, by telephone carriers as a switched line (N-ISDN), or via high-speed leased lines (frame relay and Switched Multimegabit Data Service—SMDS).

The Integrated Services Digital Network (ISDN) uses digital transmission to provide two information channels (at 64 Kbps each) and one signaling channel (at 16 Kbps), simultaneously in both directions (full duplex) over one two-wire line to the nearest switch (*see* Halsall, 1996). From this point, data is switched and multiplexed (at the local telephone exchange) onto the standard digital data hierarchy for inter-exchange transmission, and the data is sent to the nearest packet switch (voice calls would remain in the PSTN). In totally leased facilities, the user has a dedicated transmission link to the packet switch, and bypasses the PSTN switch.

Frame relay is a new frame level best-effort service (i.e. generally reliable but not guaranteed) that relays individual frames across multiple virtual circuits, which have been set up previously using the D channel. Enhanced reliability can be provided at the frame level using the frame switching service. Whereas packet switching uses multiplexing and routing at the network layer, frame relay is multiplexed and routed at the link level. Since the routing of frames is very straightforward, throughput can be much greater for frame relay than for packet switching. SMDS is offered over a frame relay network, which typically interconnects local area networks to each other.

In a similar way to frame relay, which simplified multiplexing and routing by processing at the frame level, the Asynchronous Transfer Mode (ATM) simplifies this further, by multiplexing and switching at the physical layer. ATM promises to offer many megabits per second to the user, and may be the basis for the new range of broadband ISDN public data services. ATM may form the backbone of new very high-speed public data networks.

The Internet differs from the previous networks discussed because it consists of not one network type but many disparate networks. Internetworking is achieved at the network layer, using the IP protocol, and to date is the most successful global network. The underlying networks in the Internet may be frame relay (SMDS), ATM, or a dial-up local telephone link from a user's home, but the details are hidden from the Internet user by the IP protocol.

IP routers process *datagrams* (independent packets), which have a globally unique address in the header of the packet. IP provides a connectionless datagram or "best effort" service, so any applications that require extra facilities, such as guaranteed delivery of data, must do so on an end-to-end basis. Over the Internet, this is commonly achieved by using the Transmission Control Protocol (TCP), which provides a reliable bit-pipe service to the layer above. Other applications, (such as real-time voice and video) would not require this level of reliability, and so would use the other transport layer protocol, the Universal Datagram Protocol (UDP), which provides very little extra to the service provided by IP. Internet access for the home user is charged for on a local telephone dial-up basis, and the ISP may either levy an extra fixed rate charge, or more recently just share the revenue for the local call with the telephone company. The ISP provides dial-up modems for users to connect to and access the rest of the Internet.

Public Data Services

Public data networks are now mature enough to support public data services for the home as well as the office user. To date, the services over the global Internet are mainly the World Wide Web (WWW) and email although others such as multimedia conferencing are now becoming more widely used.

The most popular public data service is the WWW, which is an unregulated service, free at the point of use. Home users commonly gain access to the Internet via a dial-up link to an ISP site, and from there to anywhere else. At any location on the Internet, hosts that are acting as WWW servers allow users to access all kinds of multimedia information using a client browser, such as Netscape Navigator or Microsoft

Internet Explorer. The real power of the Internet lies in the ability to embed paths (Uniform Resource Locators—URLs) to other documents, perhaps held on other servers within normal documents. These hyperlinks protect the user from having to know about the actual network topology, and allow access to vast amounts of information.

The Internet also supports an email service, which allows users to send electronic memos to each other. It is possible to carry any sort of data within an Internet email message, not just ASCII characters. MIME (Multipurpose Internet Mail Extensions) allows multimedia information to be encapsulated as well as normal ASCII text. MIME is also used in the WWW to identify retrieved multimedia content in documents, so that a browser can launch a suitable player.

The Internet, because it provides a very lightweight connectionless datagram service (IP), can potentially carry both computer data and real-time multimedia, such as voice and video. Video and multimedia conferencing over the Internet are now commonly available using either proprietary or free software running on a general-purpose personal computer. An example of a freely available Internet audio tool is the Robust Audio Tool (RAT), and an example of a freely available Internet video tool is the program *vic*. Examples of proprietary Internet software for multimedia conferencing are NetMeeting from Microsoft and InPerson from Silicon Graphics (which provide both audio and video), and for streamed multimedia, RealAudio and RealVideo.

Details of real-time networked multimedia communication, the WWW, and email can be found in Fluckiger (1995).

Bibliography

1995. Fluckiger, F. *Understanding Networked Multimedia, Applications and Technology.* Upper Saddle River, NJ: Prentice Hall.
1996. Halsall, F. *Data Communications, Computer Networks, and OSI,* 4th Ed. Reading, MA: Addison-Wesley.
1999. Bateman, A. *Digital Communications.* Reading, MA: Addison-Wesley.

Vicky J. Hardman, Phil M. Lane and Peter T. Kirstein

STANDARDS

The Need for Standards

Most computer manufacturers have their own network architectures (*q.v.*), but over recent years there has been increasing emphasis on the use of internationally agreed standards for communication so that systems from different suppliers can work together. The ability

of machines of different types to communicate has become progressively more important as the focus has shifted from the dedicated networks within an organization to the public networks that link separate organizations.

Networks were originally developed primarily to provide for remote access to computing facilities. For example, the airlines provided access to seat reservation systems, and major business data processing centers, such as those operated by banks, allowed remote entry of data and remote printing of results. This is still an important aspect of network use and the basic principles of error-free communication have not changed. However, the major growth is now based on the exchange and sharing of information, rather than access to processing power.

Networks now support exchange of personal messages (*see* ONLINE CONVERSATION), access to a wide range of information (e.g. via the World Wide Web), exchange of business data, access to distributed databases, integrated manufacturing, and distributed command and control systems. They are applied in commercial activity, administration, and entertainment. Some of these new applications make additional demands on the supporting networks, but many are extensions to new fields based on existing technology. A common feature of many of these new areas of application is the sharing of information between organizations, and, in consequence, the need for communication to be effective without a single management or design authority to make it work. *Data communications standards* make information exchange possible in this environment.

The Organizations Involved

Two major bodies are involved in the creation of standards. These are the International Organization for Standardization (ISO), representing primarily the computer industry and its customers, and the Telecommunication Standardization Sector of the International Telecommunication Union (ITU-T, formerly CCITT), representing the communication carriers via their national post and telecommunications authorities (the PTTs). Many standards are now produced jointly by ISO and ITU-T, with the two organizations agreeing to publish technically identical texts. Preliminary standards are also produced by the European Computer Manufacturers' Association (ECMA) and the Committee of European Posts and Telegraphs (CEPT). In the USA, the IEEE has played a major role in drafting standards proposals, particularly in the field of local area networks (LANs—*q.v.*). Standards of general interest from ECMA and IEEE are often fed into the ISO for wider discussion and support with the option of rapid publication as an ISO standard. This rapid processing of standards has recently been opened up to include a wider range of Publicly Available Specifications (PAS), and the number of PAS submitters is increasing. Outside the formal standardization process, a number of large organizations or consortia issue their own specifications; of particular note are the Internet (*q.v.*) specifications from the Internet Engineering Task Force (IETF) and the middleware specifications from the Object Management Group (OMG).

The Standardization Process

The development of a standard within the ISO involves a number of steps. The theory is as follows (*see* Fig. 1). Initially, a need is identified and support for a standardization project is confirmed by ballot among the national standards bodies on a new work item (NWI). In complex areas, there may be a preliminary study period to prepare the work. A technical group of international experts then develops a working draft for the standard to the point where it is believed to be complete and technically stable. This is approved by the controlling subcommittee and registered as a Committee Draft (CD). At this point, the national standards bodies take part in a ballot on the technical content. Each may vote "yes" without qualification, vote "yes" but give comments on possible improvements it would

like to see, or vote "no" and give the reasons for its objections and an indication of what action would make the standard acceptable.

If there is substantial agreement with little comment, the draft becomes a Final Committee Draft (FCD). At this point it is processed editorially to conform to the ISO house style. A further ballot by a higher-level committee then allows it to progress to a Final Draft International Standard (FDIS) and then be published as an International Standard (IS). If any of the ballots does not show support, the document must be revised and the ballot repeated.

In favorable circumstances, the passages from FCD to FDIS takes about a year. Although in principle the technical content should be agreed before registration as a CD, pressure for rapid progress may result in significant instability beyond this point, making early implementation a risky business. In practice, a draft might be ready for pilot implementation by the time it reaches the FCD stage.

Major Areas of Standardization

The wide range of data communications standards is organized within the framework of the Open Systems Interconnection (OSI—*q.v.*) Reference Model. Within the structure created by the reference model, individual service and protocol standards are defined for each of the layers except the application layer. In many layers, provision is made for choice of either a connection-oriented mode of operation, in which streams of information are sent between the communicating systems in the period during which a connection exists, or a connectionless mode of operation in which individual items of data are transmitted independently. The mode chosen depends on the application and the economics of the situation, and, in the lower layers, different families of standards have been created to meet the requirements of local and wide area networks.

The seven layers of the reference model can be considered in two groups. The three layers below the network service deal with the problems of the various network technologies, and with the use of networks in combination and the routing of information between different networks. The transport layer and the layers above it are concerned with the organization of the communication from end to end between the participating systems. Thus, the lower layers are primarily concerned with the process of data communication itself, while the upper layers address the incompatibilities of data formats or representations (in the presentation layer) and of operating system control of communication (in the session layer) between systems.

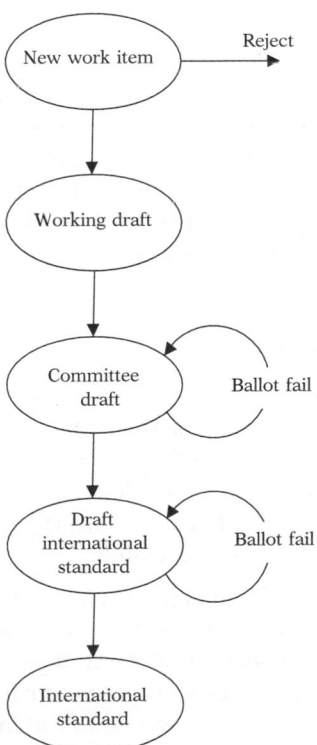

Figure 1. The standardization process.

Applications

The application layer forms the top of the protocol stack, and models both the standardized applications and their users. This layer does not provide a service; all relevant aspects of the system are considered to be within it.

In consequence, the application layer has a more complex substructure than the other layers because the user activity may require a number of standard functions in combination. Separate standards cover the common functions, known as application service elements, including:

1. *Initiating and controlling the communication—* The logical linkage created when two parts of the application communicate is called an *association*, so the function is called the *association control service element.*

2. *File transfer access and management—*This one protocol can be used to access or control any passive source or sink of information, identifying the data required and organizing the data transfer.

3. *Electronic mail exchange—*(also known as interpersonal messaging)—The mail protocols support the transfer of bodies of information, possibly in a series of steps, on the basis of steering information provided by the originator, in the same way that the postal service would handle an addressed letter.

4. *Virtual terminal services—*The virtual terminal service handles problems of access and synchronization that arise when two communicating parties manipulate the same resource at the same time. It would be used, for example, to resolve a conflict when a user and an application program both wish to update the terminal screen at the same time, and would ensure that their actions were interleaved in a consistent way.

5. *Transaction processing—*The transaction processing (*q.v.*) mechanisms provide a framework for applications that need to update resources in a number of different systems so that they remain consistent, ensuring, for example, that one account is debited and another credited, but that one of the actions does not take place without the other.

6. *Remote database access—*This protocol provides the means for managing database queries and responses from a remote site in a controlled and coordinated way.

7. *Directory services—*Before communication can take place, the systems involved must identify each other. The directory services provide standard location mechanisms in terms of either names or properties, just like the white and yellow page services offered in the telephone network.

8. *A wide range of network management facilities,* allowing the resources that make up the distributed system (*q.v.*) to be monitored, controlled, and accounted for. One set of mechanisms is applicable to many different classes of managed objects distributed throughout or even outside the network.

Almost all of the application layer standards begin by defining some activity or resource that their protocol is to control. Thus, for example, the file transfer protocol (FTP) begins by defining a model of file storage, and the virtual terminal protocol (VTP) begins with a model of interaction and display. These models are then used when defining the service offered and the protocol that supports it in order to give meaning to the information exchanged.

Conformance

The purchaser of a computer system wishes to know that the applicable standards have been implemented faithfully so that it will do the job for which it is intended. Checking that this is indeed the case is the function of *conformance testing*. Every standard that is directly implementable (and not part of a framework for other standards) contains a conformance clause that sets out exactly what behavior is required, what options exist, and what information is needed about the implementation in order to assess it.

A family of subsidiary standards has been created to define testing methodologies and then, for each of the major standards, to define a specific suite of tests that will exercise all the main features of the protocol in a systematic way. Such testing, although obviously not exhaustive, gives confidence that the standard has been correctly implemented.

Functional Standards

A system designer may be faced with a choice of options and parameters in the various general-purpose standards that make up the protocol stack to be implemented. If each designer made independent choices, it would be unlikely that an arbitrary pair of systems would communicate successfully.

To avoid this problem, a second tier of standardization has been erected, defining functional standards that give preferred values for all the choices that need to be made to support a particular user activity. These standards are produced in consultation with regional implementation groups to ensure that all requirements are taken into account.

Table 1. Representative List of ISO Data Communications Standards.

ISO	ITU-T	Abbreviated title
Architecture		
ISO 7498	X.200	OSI Basic Reference Model
ISO 9646	X.290	Conformance Testing Framework (5 parts)
ISO 9834	X.660 series	OSI Registration Procedures
ISO 10181, 11586	X.800 series	Security Framework
TR 10730	—	Tutorial on Naming and Addressing
ISO 10746	X.900 series	ODP Reference Model
ISO 13236, 13243	X.641, X.642	Quality of Service Framework, Mechanisms
Physical Layer		
—Many connector and signaling standards		
Data Link Layer		
ISO 3309, 4335, 7478	—	High-level Data Link Control (HDLC)
ISO 7776	X.25	HDLC Procedures (X.25 compatible)
ISO 8802	—	Local Area Networks (7 parts)
ISO 8886	X.212	Data Link Service
Network Layer		
ISO 8348	X.213	Network Service
ISO 8208	X.25	X.25 Packet Level Protocol for DTE
ISO 8648	—	Internal Organization of the Network Layer
ISO 8878	—	Use of X.25 to Provide the Network Service
ISO 8880	—	Protocols to Provide the Network Service
ISO 8881	—	Use of X.25 in Local Area Networks
ISO 10028	—	Relaying Functions in an Intermediate System
ISO 9575, 9978, 10030, 10589	—	Network Layer Routing
Transport Layer		
ISO 8072, 8073, 8602	X.214, X.224	Transport Service and Protocol
Session Layer		
ISO 8326, 8327, 9548	X.215, X.225	Session Service and Protocol
Presentation Layer		
ISO 8822, 8823, 9576	X.216, X.226	Presentation Service and Protocol
ISO 8824, 8825	X.208, X.209	Abstract Syntax Notation One
Application Layer		
ISO 8649, 8650, 10035	X.217, X.227	Association Control Service and Protocol
ISO 8571	—	File Transfer, Access, and Management
ISO 9040, 9041	—	Virtual Terminal Service and Protocol
ISO 9066	X.218, X.228	Reliable Transfer Service and Protocol
ISO 9072, 13712	X.219, X.229	Remote Operations Service and Protocol
ISO 9545	X.207	Application Layer Structure
ISO 9579	—	Remote Database Access
ISO 9594	X.500 series	The OSI Directory (9 parts)
ISO 9735	—	Electronic Data Interchange (EDIFACT)
ISO 9804, 9805	X.850 series	Commitment, Concurrency, and Recovery Service and Protocol
ISO 10021	X.400 series	Message Handling and Interpersonal Messaging
ISO 10026	X.860 series	Transaction Processing
ISO 10166	—	Document Filing and Retrieval
Management		
ISO 9595, 9596	X.700 series	Common Management Information Services and Protocols
ISO 10040	X.700 series	System Management Overview
ISO 10164	X.700 series	System Management Functions (22 parts)
ISO 10165	X.700 series	Structure of Management Information
Open Distributed Processing		
ISO 13235	X.950	ODP Trader
ISO 14771	X.910	ODP Naming Framework
ISO 14750	X.920	ODP Interface Definition Language
ISO 14753	X.930	Interface References and Binding
ISO 14769	X.960	ODP Type Repository

Registration Authorities

Successful communication depends on shared information. Preparing a system for connection to a network involves making a large number of choices, ranging from the names and addresses the system will be known by to the names of the types of documents it is expected to handle. This kind of information is too volatile to be the subject of standardization, but still needs to be managed and distributed.

The requirement is met by the creation of standardized procedures for the operation of registration authorities; for example, authorities exist to allocate addresses or maintain catalogs of data elements.

Distributed Systems

The development of data communications standards is still going on. However, standardization of applications involves considerations outside pure communication, and aspects such as system configuration, management, and the relation of communication to other system interfaces become important. At the same time, there is growing interest in the creation of standards to support arbitrary user activity in an object-based way, and not just to specify a selection of common applications.

These considerations have led to the formulation of a new reference model within ISO, providing a framework for Open Distributed Processing (ODP), and standards resulting from it open the way to the construction of more flexible and powerful distributed systems. This work has been carried out in close liaison with the Object Management Group, and their Common Object Request Broker Architecture (CORBA) has provided a number of important components within the ODP framework.

Some Important Standards

There are now a large and growing number of data communication standards—far too many to list here in detail. Table 1 gives the ISO number (and the ITU-T number where commonly referenced) and a shortened title of the major standards or groups of standards.

Bibliography

1987. Knowles, T., Larmouth, J., and Knightson, K. G. *Standards for Open Systems Interconnection*. Oxford: BSP Professional Books.
1996. Tanenbaum, A. S. *Computer Networks*, 3rd Ed. Upper Saddle River, NJ: Prentice Hall.

Peter F. Linington

DATA COMPRESSION

For articles on related subjects *see* CODES; CRYPTOGRAPHY, COMPUTERS IN; DATA COMMUNICATIONS; FILE; and IMAGE COMPRESSION.

Data compression is the process of reducing the amount of space used to store data by changing its representation. It is widely used to squeeze more files onto disks, to decrease the time taken to send files over the Internet, to send faxes quickly over telephone lines, and to increase the apparent speed of modems.

A compression method is either *lossless* or *lossy*. Lossless methods enable the original data to be reconstructed exactly from its compressed form, which is important for general purpose compression systems. Lossy methods make small changes to the data to make it more compressible—for example, they might reduce the amount of detail in an image or decrease the quality of an audio recording. Often these changes are imperceptible to a human, but they can result in a significantly more compact representation. This article focuses on *lossless* compression, which is sometimes referred to as *text compression* because it is primarily used for textual data. Lossy compression methods are discussed under IMAGE COMPRESSION.

The compression performance of a method is often measured in *bits per character* (bpc), which is the number of bits in the compressed file divided by the number of characters (bytes) in the input file. For English text it is not difficult to achieve 4 bpc compression (i.e. reduce a file to about a half of its size), and some of the better compression methods can achieve closer to 2 bpc.

One of the earliest and most well-known compression methods is *Huffman coding*, which was first published in 1952. It works on a similar principle to Morse code: the more common characters are represented by shorter codes. In the 1970s there were several important advances that have had a significant impact on the field of data compression. One was the discovery of *arithmetic coding*, which has become the basis of some of the best performing compression methods. Another is the development of *Ziv–Lempel coding*, currently the most widely used approach for commercial compression systems. These techniques are discussed in more detail below.

A number of *ad hoc* systems also exist, such as run-length coding (where repetitions of the same character are replaced with a code for the number of repetitions), and digram coding (where unused character codes are used to represent common pairs of characters). However, these generally give poor compression, and are sensitive to the particular data being compressed.

An important concept for understanding and developing compression methods is the idea of dividing the task into two parts: *modeling* and *coding*. Modeling is concerned with capturing the structures and regularities in a document, while coding is concerned with choosing exactly which bits should be used to represent the document, based on the information captured in the model. For example, a simple model might count the relative frequency of characters in a text, and a coder would use this relative frequency to assign a code for each character. If the model somehow determines that the letter "e" accounts for 9% of the characters, the coder could assign it a short code, such as the sequence of bits "100". The problem of coding is well understood, and efficient algorithms for finding optimal codes exist. Modeling is more difficult because it involves capturing the structure and rules of natural languages. These two tasks are discussed separately below. Although coding is the second phase of the compression process, we discuss it first because it dictates what is required from a model.

Coding

Coding is the task of representing the data to be compressed based on probabilities provided by some model. Shannon's (*q.v.*) *Noiseless Source Coding Theorem* has established that a character with an estimated probability p is best represented by $-\log_2 p$ bits (this value relates to the *entropy* of the probability distribution). For example, suppose we wish to send the character "h" to represent that a coin toss came up "heads." The probability of this character occurring is 1/2, and according to Shannon's theorem, it should be transmitted using exactly one bit.

One method for assigning bits for a given probability distribution is *Huffman coding*. Huffman's algorithm basically generates a code tree, such as the one shown in Fig. 1. The example tree is for inputs that contain only five different symbols, with the probabilities shown provided by some model. The path from the root of the tree to the symbol gives the code for that symbol; for example, the code for "a" is 000, and the code for "d" is 10. Because each symbol is a leaf of the tree, no code for a symbol will be a prefix of any other code. This property makes decoding easy, because each bit-string that is the code of a symbol can be found without ambiguity. The tree is constructed by linking the two least probable symbols (in the example, "a" and "b"), and treating the linked pair as a new symbol with a probability equal to the sum of the two original probabilities ($0.25 = 0.13 + 0.12$). This step of linking the two least probable symbols is then repeated; the next two to be linked will be "d" and "e", then the a + b subtree will be linked to "c". This continues until

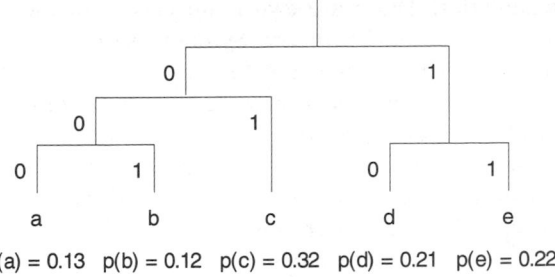

$p(a) = 0.13 \quad p(b) = 0.12 \quad p(c) = 0.32 \quad p(d) = 0.21 \quad p(e) = 0.22$

Figure 1. A Huffman encoding tree.

a complete tree has been constructed, when there will be just one "symbol" left, with a probability of one.

An alternative to Huffman coding is *arithmetic coding*. Arithmetic coding is able to encode symbols arbitrarily close to the optimal size of $-\log_2 p$ bits, even if this value is not an integer! For example, if a symbol has a probability of 0.9, ideally it should be represented in $-\log_2(0.9) \approx 0.15$ bits. An arithmetic coder achieves this by having one coded bit representing more than one input symbol. This makes arithmetic coding particularly suitable for models where symbols have high probabilities. Each symbol coded typically requires two integer multiplications and a similar number of additions, so it is relatively fast, although not as fast as using a pre-calculated Huffman code. Details of arithmetic coding can be found in the bibliography at the end of this article.

Other coding methods exist, including many variants on Huffman and arithmetic coding. Huffman coding is preferred where speed is important. It is particularly suitable for *static* coding, where the probabilities are determined beforehand, and do not change during coding. However, it is not so suitable for *adaptive* coding, where the probabilities can change frequently. In an adaptive model, the probability of a symbol is generally increased a little immediately after that symbol is coded, to reflect its being more likely to occur again. The decoder is able to mirror the increase without its being communicated explicitly, because it will have just decoded the symbol, and uses the same algorithm to update the model. Huffman coding is not very suitable in this situation because the whole code tree needs to be updated every time the probabilities change, while arithmetic coding is particularly suitable because the codes are generated on the fly, rather than being pre-calculated.

Modeling

The coding methods described above represent the "back end" to most compression methods. The "front end" is the modeling technique used to generate the probabilities. There are two main classes of models: *symbolwise* and *dictionary*. Symbolwise models provide a probability estimate for each symbol as it is coded. In contrast, dictionary methods have some sort of table, or dictionary, which contains words (or more generally, strings) that can be replaced in the input data with a code. These two methods are discussed separately below, although some hybrid methods exist and have been used successfully.

DICTIONARY METHODS

A dictionary compression model goes through the input looking for strings of characters that are in the dictionary, and replacing them with a code. Static dictionaries are only effective if the dictionary has been generated explicitly for the text being compressed. Adaptive dictionary models are most common in general-purpose systems, and the most widely used form of these are known as *Ziv–Lempel* coding, which is based on the intriguing idea of using the text as its own dictionary.

Ziv–Lempel (often abbreviated as LZ) coding comes in two rather different forms, sometimes labeled as LZ1 (or LZ77) and LZ2 (or LZ78). Variants of the LZ1 method are widely used in general purpose compression systems and archivers with names like ZIP, GZIP and PKZIP. These systems are very fast (particularly for decoding) and give good compression.

LZ1 methods are based on the idea of replacing a string of text with a pointer to where it has occurred earlier in the text. The pointer is most commonly represented using two components: an *offset* (which identifies how many characters earlier in the text the string occurred), and a *length* (which identifies how long the match is). For example, the text `missis-sippi` might be represented as `miss(3,4)ppi`, where the pointer indicates to go back three characters (to the "i"), and copy four. In this particular example the pointer is recursive, in that the fourth character is not available until after the decoding of the pointer has started.

The LZ1 technique is powerful because pointers can reference common words and phrases as soon as they are used more than once, but it can also reference components of words, such as the suffix "ing." The two components of pointers can be coded as a simple binary number, although some of the better methods (especially the ZIP family) use Huffman codes. Usually there is a window that limits how far back a pointer can reference, which simplifies processing. During encoding, the window of text is usually searched using an index structure such as a hash table to find matches quickly. Decoding is particularly fast, since a whole string is decoded simply by looking it up in a buffer that contains the window of recent text.

In contrast to LZ1, where almost any previous substring can be referenced, the LZ2 family of methods use a parsing algorithm to create a dictionary of selected substrings from the previously coded text. The dictionary is constructed by adding one new string each time a string is coded. The new string is constructed by taking the coded string concatenated with the next input character. For example, if the word `mississipi` is about to be coded in a text, and the string `mis` is the longest match already in the dictionary, then the first three characters are coded as a reference to the dictionary entry, and the string `miss` is then added to the dictionary. The decoder is able to update the dictionary adaptively as it decodes each string.

The LZ2 methods were popular for some time because they are less demanding than LZ1 in terms of resources required for encoding. One of the most popular variants is called LZW (Lempel–Ziv–Welch), out of which grew a widely used Unix utility called COMPRESS. COMPRESS has now been superseded by GZIP, but the LZW method is still used for some applications, including the GIF (Graphics Interchange Format) standard.

SYMBOLWISE METHODS

In contrast to the dictionary methods just described, symbolwise methods usually encode individual characters. Symbolwise methods generally offer better compression performance although they can be slower and require more memory to perform encoding and decoding.

A simple symbolwise method uses a model that keeps count of how many times each different character has been observed in the input, and uses the character's relative frequency as a probability to drive a Huffman or arithmetic coder. However, this model generally gives mediocre compression performance, and a significant improvement can be achieved by taking into account the context in which a character occurs. An *order one model* uses a single preceding character as a context, keeping separate counts of character frequencies (and therefore estimated probabilities) for each possible preceding character. For example, if the previous character was the letter "t" then the probability of a "u" occurring next might be 1.7%, while in the context of a "q" the probability of a "u" might be 99.4%. In the first case, according to Shannon's formula, optimally a coder should allocate 5.8 bits to a "u", while in the latter case it should be allocated a mere 0.0087 bits, since it is almost certain to occur. The probabilities are usually estimated adaptively as coding proceeds.

When contexts are being used to estimate probabilities, arithmetic coding is usually much more effective than Huffman coding because high probabilities are common, and arithmetic coding is able to achieve a near-optimal representation for a given model.

As the size of the context used in the model increases, the compression is likely to improve for a while. However, the amount of memory required to keep track of the contexts increases rapidly, and once the contexts get beyond about five characters it becomes relatively rare for a context to have occurred before, and therefore no data is available on which an adaptive model might base probability estimates. The solution to deciding whether to use large or small contexts is to use both, an idea captured in a method called *Prediction by Partial Matching* (PPM). To code each character, PPM first attempts to use a large context, and if no suitable probability estimates can be made based on previous occurrences of the context, a special "escape" symbol is sent to the decoder telling it to use a shorter context. This is repeated until a suitable context is encountered, which in the worst case will be no context at all. Despite the cost of sending these extra escape messages, the PPM method gives extremely good compression, and is one of the best techniques available. Although it was first published in 1984, it has only recently become a serious candidate for general compression applications because it requires a reasonably fast processor (since it requires arithmetic coding) and a substantial amount of memory (on the order of a megabyte to store the context information). In 1984 these resources were available only on mainframe computers, but now they are readily available on desktop machines.

Another context-based compression system is a method called *block sorting*, otherwise known as the Burrows–Wheeler Transform (BWT) or block reduction. This method implicitly captures contextual information by a transformation that permutes the order of the characters in the text. The permutation involves sorting the characters in the text using their context as the sort key. This means that characters that appear in similar contexts will end up near each other. This permuted text is the same size as the original, but it is easily compressed because characters tend to occur in clusters. For example, in the part of the permuted text corresponding to the context of "q", the letter "u" will be very frequent. Remarkably, there is an efficient way to reconstruct the original order of the characters from the permuted order. The only extra information required to do this is a number identifying which of the permuted characters is the first in the original text. Reconstructing the original text from this information is like solving a puzzle. The decoder can determine the last character of the context for each symbol by sorting the permuted list. A key observation is that each character decoded provides the last context character for the next one to be decoded, and the order in which identical characters appear in the permuted lists corresponds to the order in which they appear as the last character in the sorted context list. This provides sufficient information to solve the "puzzle" of determining the original sequence. Although this task seems complex, it can be implemented very efficiently.

The block sorting method gives compression performance that is similar to the PPM method, and a fast implementation called BZIP exists. The BZIP system is intended to be a replacement for GZIP; BZIP is a little slower, but gives significantly better compression. Other variants of the symbolwise method exist that also give good compression performance, including "Dynamic Markov Compression"(DMC), which uses a finite state machine as a model, and research systems that can be configured via run-time parameters to emulate many existing systems, as well as new variations.

Performance Evaluation

Comparing the performance of compression methods requires several factors to be considered. The most important characteristics are the amount of compression, the speed at which compression is performed (and decompression, whose speed may be different), and the amount of primary memory (RAM) required to perform compression (and decompression).

The relative compression performance of different methods can vary depending on the type of file being compressed. As mentioned above, for English text the better methods give compression between about 2 and 3 bits per character. More predictable text, such as program source code, can usually be compressed a little better. A black and white bitmap image can typically be compressed to a tenth of its original size, while a full color image may only be compressed a little by lossless methods.

To compare compression methods, a corpus of benchmark (*q.v.*) files is needed. Commonly reported sets include the "Calgary Corpus" (and its more recent replacement, the "Canterbury Corpus"), and the "Archive Compression Test." Websites with results for these collections are given below.

Bibliography

1990. Bell, T. C., Cleary, J. G. and Witten, I. H. *Text Compression*. Upper Saddle River, NJ: Prentice Hall.

1991. Nelson, M. *The Data Compression Book: Featuring Fast, Efficient Data Compression Techniques in C*. Redwood City, CA: M&T Books.

1991. *Proceedings of the IEEE Data Compression Conference*. Los Alamitos, CA: IEEE Computer Society Press.

1994. Witten, I. H., Moffat, A. and Bell, T. C. *Managing Gigabytes: Compressing and Indexing Documents and Images.* New York: Van Nostrand Reinhold.

1997. Jayant, N. *Signal Compression: Coding of Speech, Audio, Text, Image and Video.* Singapore: World Scientific. (Also appears as a special issue of the *International Journal of High Speed Electronics*, March 1997.)

Websites

A comprehensive collection of pointers to compression research, software, companies, performance evaluations, and other resources relating to compression. `http://www.internz.com/compression-pointers.html`.

This newsgroup has a comprehensive FAQ on compression. `comp.compression`.

Information about the annual Data Compression Conference (DCC). `http://www.cs.brandeis.edu/~dcc/`.

The Canterbury Corpus (and information about the Calgary corpus). `http://corpus.canterbury.ac.nz/`.

The Archive Compression Test (ACT). `http://www.geocities.com/SiliconValley/Park/4264/act.html`.

Tim Bell

DATA ENCRYPTION

See CRYPTOGRAPHY, COMPUTERS IN; and PRETTY GOOD PRIVACY.

DATA MINING

For articles on related subjects see DATA WAREHOUSING; DATABASE MANAGEMENT SYSTEM; DIGITAL LIBRARIES; ELECTRONIC COMMERCE; FUZZY LOGIC; INFORMATION RETRIEVAL; INFORMATION SYSTEMS; PATTERN RECOGNITION; RELATIONAL DATABASE; and SCIENTIFIC VISUALIZATION.

Introduction

Data mining is the process of finding patterns in information contained in large databases. It is a research area at the intersection of several disciplines, including statistics, databases, pattern recognition and AI, visualization, optimization, and high-performance and parallel computing. With the success of database systems, and their widespread use, the role of the database expanded from being a reliable data store to being a decision support system (DSS). This has been manifested in the growth of *data warehouses* that consolidate transactional and distributed databases. Examples of applications of data mining techniques include: fraud detection in banking and telecommunications; marketing; science data analysis involving cataloging objects of interest in large data sets (e.g. sky objects in a survey, volcanoes on Venus, finding atmospheric events in remote sensing data); problem diagnosis in manufacturing, medicine, or networking; and so forth. The techniques are particularly relevant in settings where data is plentiful and the processes generating it are poorly understood.

Human-driven data analysis and exploration, while effective in low-dimensional small data settings, breaks down in the presence of high dimensionality and massive data sets (Tukey, 1975). It is common for modern databases to contain thousands of dimensions (fields) per record (row). Such data sets pose fundamental problems that transcend query execution and optimization. The fundamental problem is *query formulation*: how do we provide data access when a user cannot specify the target set exactly (as the database query language SQL requires)? Typical DSS queries are very difficult to state; e.g. which records are likely to represent fraud in credit card, banking, or telecommunications transactions? Which records are most similar to records in table A but dissimilar to those in table B? How many *clusters* (or *segments*—groups of related records) are in a database and how are they characterized? Data mining techniques allow computer-driven exploration of the data, hence admitting a more abstract model of interaction than SQL permits.

Data mining techniques are fundamentally data reduction and visualization techniques. As the number of dimensions grows, the number of ways of choosing combinations for dimensionality reduction explodes. For an analyst exploring models, it is infeasible to go through the various ways of projecting the dimensions or selecting the right subsets of the data (reduction along columns and rows). Furthermore, a projection to lower dimensions could render an easy discrimination problem extremely difficult by eliminating important distinctions. An effective means to visualize data would be to employ data mining algorithms to perform the appropriate reductions, allowing an analyst to find patterns or models which may otherwise remain hidden in the high-dimensional space. For example, a clustering algorithm could select a subset of the data embedded in a high-dimensional space and determine a few dimensions to distinguish it from the rest of the data or from other clusters.

Definitions

Adopting definitions given in Fayyad *et al.* (1996b, Chapter 1):

> *Knowledge discovery in databases (KDD)* is the process of identifying valid, novel, potentially useful, and ultimately understandable structure in data.

Here *data* is a set of facts and *structure* refers to either patterns or models. A *pattern* is an expression representing a parsimonious description of a subset of the data. A *model* is a representation of the source generating the data. The term *process* is used to indicate that KDD is composed of many steps (Fig. 1).

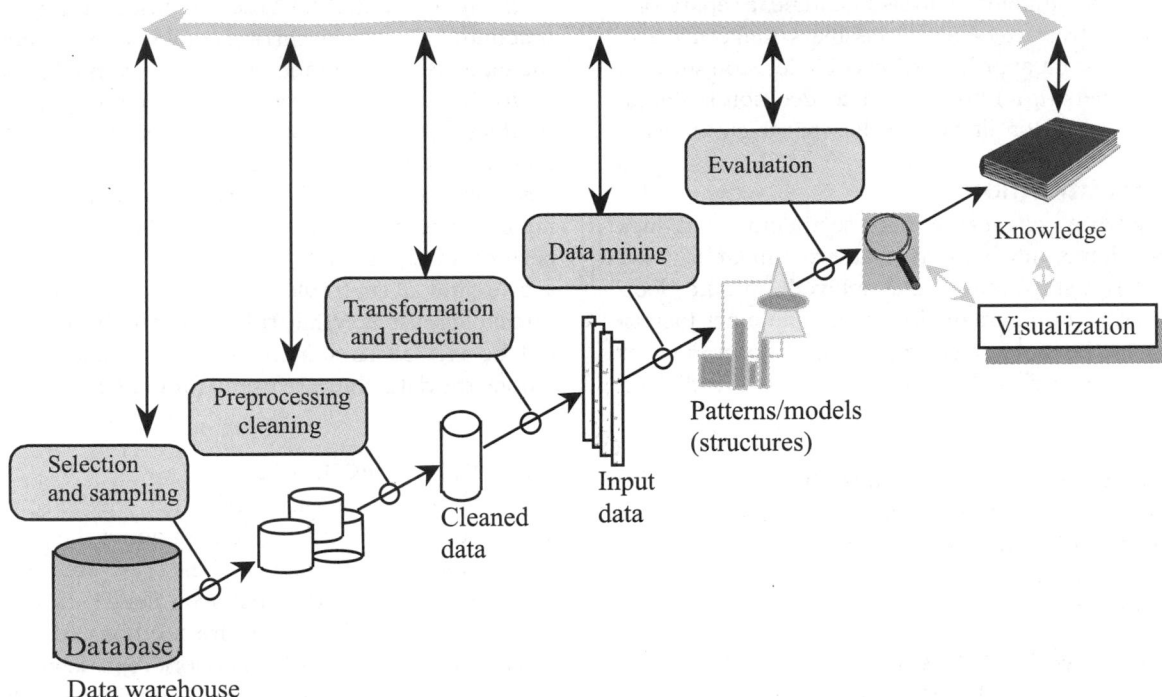

Figure 1. Knowledge discovery in databases (KDD).

Data mining is a step in the KDD process that, under acceptable computational efficiency limitations, enumerates structures (patterns or models) over the data.

There are many (potentially infinitely) more patterns or models that can be derived from a finite data set than there are data records. To be deemed *knowledge*, the derived structure must pass certain criteria. Notions of utility (e.g. gain, dollars saved by improved predictions) and *validity* (e.g. estimated prediction accuracy) have classical definitions in decision analysis and statistics. However, notions of *novelty*, *understandability*, and *interestingness* are much more difficult to define. The term *knowledge* in KDD is user-oriented, domain-specific, and determined by the interestingness measure; it is not a general definition of knowledge.

The overall KDD process (Fig. 1) includes the *evaluation* and possible *interpretation* of the "mined" structures to determine what may be considered new "knowledge." The KDD process also includes steps such as data selection, cleaning, preprocessing, and so forth. These are all significant and difficult steps. Data mining techniques can be divided into five classes of methods.

Data Mining Methods

PREDICTIVE MODELING

This method predicts some field or fields in a database based on other fields. *Regression* refers to prediction of numeric (continuous) variables. *Classification* refers to prediction of categorical fields. The problem is to determine the most likely value of the variable being predicted given the other fields (inputs), the training data (in which the target variable to be predicted is given for each record), and assumptions representing prior knowledge. Linear regression combined with nonlinear transformation on inputs may be used to solve a wide range of problems. Transformation of the input space is typically the difficult problem requiring knowledge of the problem and quite a bit of "art." In classification problems this type of transformation is often referred to as *feature extraction*.

Classification is fundamentally a problem of estimating joint probability distributions. The probability of a class C, given other fields $X = x$ for some feature vector x, is derivable from the joint probability density on C and X. However, this joint density is rarely known and is difficult to estimate. Techniques include:

1. Estimation of probability densities, e.g. the use of graphical Bayesian networks to represent probability distributions for large numbers of variables.

2. Metric-space based methods: define a measure of distance between data points and determine class based on proximity to training data points, e.g. the K-nearest-neighbor method.

3. Projection into decision regions: divide attribute space into regions with associated predictions, e.g.

linear discriminant analysis finds linear separators; decision tree; rule-based classifiers make a piece-wise constant approximations of a decision surface; neural nets (*q.v.*) find nonlinear decision surfaces; linear regression finds linearly-separable regions.

DATA SEGMENTATION

Also known as *clustering*, data segmentation groups the data items into subsets that are similar to each other. A two-stage search is employed: an outer loop over possible numbers of clusters and an inner loop to fit the best possible clustering for a given number of clusters K. Given K, clustering methods are divided into three classes:

1. Metric-distance based methods: the objective is the best K-way partition such that cases (database records) in each block are closer to each other (or to the centroid—their "center of mass") than to cases in other clusters.

2. Model-based methods: given a hypothesized model for each of the clusters, find the best fit of each cluster model. If M_k is the model hypothesized for cluster k, then one way to score the fit of a model to a cluster is via the likelihood:

$$\Pr(M_k \mid D) = \Pr(D \mid M_k) \frac{\Pr(M_k)}{\Pr(D)},$$

where $\Pr(D)$ is the prior probability of the data and is a normalizing constant (ignored for comparison purposes), $\Pr(M_k)$ is the prior probability of the model assigned based on domain knowledge, and $\Pr(A \mid B)$ is the *conditional probability* of event A given event B. In maximum likelihood techniques, all models are assumed equally likely and hence this term is ignored. A problem with ignoring this term is that more complex models are preferred, leading to *overfitting* (fitting a model to data that is irrelevant to it).

3. Partition-based methods: enumerate various partitions and then score them by some criterion. The first two techniques can be viewed as special cases of this class. Most techniques in this category use *ad hoc* scoring functions.

DATA SUMMARIZATION

Extracting compact descriptions of subsets of the data can be done by taking horizontal (cases) or vertical (fields) slices of the data. The former provide summaries of subsets (e.g. sufficient statistics, or logical conditions that hold for subsets), the latter find relations between fields as opposed to predicting a specified field (classification) or grouping cases (clustering). One common method is called *association rules* (Fayyad

et al., 1996b, Ch. 12). These are based on algorithms that find frequently occurring combinations of items in the database. A common application is *market basket analysis*, where one would like to summarize which products are bought with what other products. While there are exponentially many rules, due to data sparseness only a few such rules satisfy given support and confidence thresholds. Scalable algorithms (those whose performance remains good as the size of the input grows) find all such rules in linear time for reasonable threshold settings. While rules found in this way should not be viewed as statements about causal relations among the data, they are useful for modeling purposes.

DEPENDENCY MODELING

Insight into data is often gained by deriving causal structure: *probabilistic* (statement about the probability distribution governing the data) or *deterministic* (functional dependencies between fields). In addition to density estimation there are methods for explicit causal modeling (e.g. belief network representations of density functions). The latter class provides an intuitive and more easily interpretable representation of causal influences in the model (Fayyad *et al.*, 1996b, Ch. 11).

CHANGE AND DEVIATION DETECTION

These methods account for sequence information: time series or some other ordering (e.g. protein sequencing in genome mapping). Unlike methods above, ordering of observations is important and must be accounted for. Scalable methods for finding frequent sequences in databases, while in the worst case exponential in complexity, do appear to execute efficiently given sparseness in real-world transactional databases (Mannila *et al.*, 1997). For example in transactions representing users visiting Web pages on an Internet site, such techniques can find paths frequently traversed by site visitors, thus helping to understand how a Website is used.

Research Problems and WWW Resources

Successful KDD applications continue to appear, driven mainly by a glut of databases that have clearly grown to surpass raw human processing abilities. For examples of success stories in commercial applications *see* Brachman *et al.* (1996) and in scientific analysis *see* Fayyad *et al.* (1996a). More detailed case studies are found in Fayyad *et al.* (1996b). Scalable methods for decision trees, clustering, nearest neighbor, and density estimation have been developed and can work with very large databases.

The fundamental problems of data analysis and how to mechanize it are fairly difficult. Scaling mining methods to work efficiently on large databases involves considering issues of limited main memory, efficient indexing structures, and effective sampling methods tightly coupled to mining methods. Issues of representing metadata (information about data lineage, transformations, and properties) and its use in data cleaning, mining, and visualization are important challenges. Mining distributed stores, where data movement between client and server must be minimized, and nonhomogenous data sets (including mixtures of multimedia, video, and text modalities) is also a big challenge. How do you find a video or image of interest? Current methods assume fairly uniform and simple data structures.

While operating in a very large sample size environment helps to guard against overfitting problems, data mining systems also need to guard against fitting models to data by chance. This problem becomes significant as an algorithm explores a huge search space over many models for a given data set. Also, traditional statistical methods for assessing significance were not formulated to operate in large sample environments. For purposes of visualization and reporting, proper tradeoffs between complexity and understandability of models are needed. Finally, an important challenge is to develop theory and techniques to model growth and change in data. Large databases, because they grow over a long time, do not grow as if sampled from a static probability density. The question of "how does the data grow?" needs to be better understood; see articles by P. Huber, by Fayyad and Smyth, and by others in Kettenring and Pregibon (1996). For a long list of research problems and challenges see the Editorial of issue 2 : 2 of the journal *Data Mining and Knowledge Discovery* (URL below).

1975. Tukey, J. *Exploratory Data Analysis.* Reading, MA: Addison-Wesley.
1996. Brachman, R., Khabaza, T., Kloesgen, W., Piatetsky-Shapiro, G., and Simoudis, E. "Industrial Applications of Data Mining and Knowledge Discovery," *Comm. of the ACM*, **39**, *11* (Nov), 42–48.
1996a. Fayyad, U., Haussler, D., and Stolorz, P. "Mining Science Data," *Comm. of the ACM*, **39**, *11* (Nov), 51–57.
1996b. Fayyad, U., Piatetsky-Shapiro, G., Smyth, P., and Uthurusamy, R. (eds.) *Advances in Knowledge Discovery and Data Mining.* Cambridge, MA: MIT Press.
1996. Kettenring, J., and Pregibon, D. (eds.) *Statistics and Massive Data Sets.* Report to the Committee on Applied and Theoretical Statistics, National Research Council, Washington, DC.
1997. Mannila, H., Toivonen, H., and Verkamo, A. I. "Discovery of Frequent Episodes in Event Sequence," *Data Mining and Knowledge Discovery*, **1**, *3*, 259–289.
1998. Fayyad, U. "Editorial," *Data Mining and Knowledge Discovery*, **2**, *2*.
1999. IEEE Computer. Special issue on Data Mining, **32**, *8* (August).

Data Mining and Knowledge Discovery Journal. `http://research.microsoft.com/datamine/`.
Special issue of the *Comm. of the ACM*, November 96. `http://research.microsoft.com/datamine/acm-contents.htm`.
Knowledge Discovery Mine: moderated discussion list, archival of other resources, tools, and news items. `http://www.kdnuggets.com`.
International conferences on Knowledge Discovery and Data Mining (1995–1999). `http://research.microsoft.com/datamine/kdd99/`.

Usama Fayyad

DATA MODELS

> For articles on related subjects *see* DATA TYPE; DATABASE MANAGEMENT SYSTEM; MEMORY MANAGEMENT; and RELATIONAL DATABASE.

Data models are notations for describing data. Typically, they are used to describe the structure and content of databases. As such, they have similar goals to data types (*q.v.*), which describe data within programs. At least some researchers believe that it will prove possible to use the same notations for both data types and data stored in databases.

Data Model Requirements

Data models have to meet several requirements:

1. Act as a notation to be manipulated and constructed during the design of a database or application system.

2. Provide a description that enables would-be users of the data to understand what data may be present and how to access it.

3. Be a major component for controlling and organizing the use of data.

Data Model Design

The first two uses require notations that are *conceptual* (i.e. the level of abstraction and set of constructs matches "natural" thought processes in organizing data, such as classification). The third use requires that mechanisms, such as storage schemes and query evaluators, can be implemented efficiently for large bodies of data. These implementation issues lead towards data models that pragmatically reflect memory management methods. As constructing applications from a combination of databases and programs is a serious engineering task, there is an essential requirement for precision in the description of databases, and hence in the definition of the data model. Such precision is often achieved by relating the data model to a well-defined

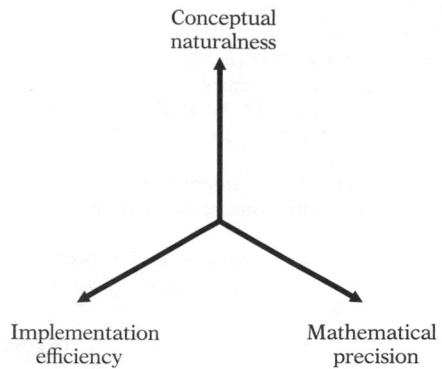

Figure 1.

mathematical construct. Thus there are three forces pulling the designs of data models in different directions, as shown in Fig. 1.

Data Model Examples

Actual data models are different compromises in response to these forces. A few will be illustrated. A concrete example will be used in each case, based on the task of describing the contributions to an encyclopedia. `People` are *editors* or *authors*. `Authors` are responsible for *articles*, `articles` are organized within *topics*, and `editors` are responsible for `topics`.

The history of data models shows a trend from orienting the model to suit processing towards orienting it conceptually. This has resulted from the combined effects of increases in computing power and implementation ingenuity, and increasing software maintenance costs, and rising ambitions for enterprise applications. The examples are ordered to reflect that trend.

HIERARCHICAL MODEL

This model, developed in the early 1960s, was influenced by the need to process data sequentially from magnetic tapes. The primary example was IMS from IBM. All data was organized as a sequence of *segments*. Within each segment were a sequence of subsidiary segments pertaining to the outer segment, and so on. So our example might take the form:

```
Topic topic_name, topic_editor
  Article article_title, pages
    Author author_name, author_address
  Article article_title, pages
    Author author_name, author_address
    Author author_name, author_address
        !other articles on this topic
Topic topic_name, topic_editor
  Article article_title, pages
    Author author_name, author_address
  Article article_title, pages
    Author author_name, author_address
        !other articles on this topic
        !other topics in this book
```

A problem with this model is that information is repeated, e.g. an author's address. Another problem is that the structure suits one particular form of processing; e.g. the preceding structure is well suited to a review of the status of a topic, but is poorly suited to finding the commitments of a particular author. In practice, this was overcome using multiple files, each with this kind of structure, and then referencing between them using indexes.

NETWORK MODEL

This model was developed in the late 1960s in order to abstract various methods of organizing disk storage that were becoming prevalent. It therefore leans in the direction of implementation efficiency. Conceptual issues were limited to an assumption that data could be modeled in terms of *entities* and one-to-many relationships between them. These were modeled by two components—the *record type* and the *set type*. Records with a given record type all have the same format and represent similar entities. Sets were not like mathematical sets, but were ordered sequences of records *owned* by a particular record. For practical reasons, the record format was initially identical with that of Cobol (*q.v.*), for which this model was intended as a database standard.

All data models provide a repertoire of components, out of which a specific description, or *schema*, may be built.

DATA MODEL DIAGRAMS

Associated with most data models is a diagrammatic form, particularly beneficial to requirements 1 and 2. For the network model, these diagrams were called *Bachman diagrams*; boxes represent the record types and arcs represent the sets. For the encyclopedia example, the diagram would be as in Fig. 2 in which a many-to-one relationship (e.g. many articles by one author) is denoted by the three-pronged fork at the endpoint of an arc.

DATA DESCRIPTION LANGUAGE

Also associated with a data model is a data description language that allows the full details of a schema to be

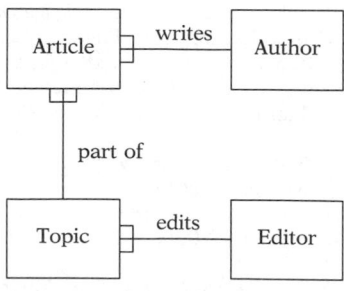

Figure 2.

expressed. For example, still using the network model:

```
Record Type Article is
  02 Title    : Picture A(40);
  02 Word_Limit : Picture 9(4);
...
Set Writes; owner Author; Member Article;...
```

RELATIONAL DATA MODEL

This model was developed during the 1970s and is now the dominant form of database, with many products and a succession of standards. It is biased towards precision, as its one constructor, *a relation*, is based on the mathematical idea of a relation. This allows formal argument about and manipulation of relational data—in particular, schemata may be transformed into equivalent schemata with better properties and queries transformed into equivalent queries that may be evaluated more quickly.

Each relation is a set of *tuples* with identical format. Values in each tuple within the relation have elements taken from corresponding *domains* if they are in corresponding positions, and the positions are referred to as *attributes* and given attribute names.

SQL

SQL is a widely-used language for describing and manipulating relational models. It differs slightly from the formal relational model; for example, *tables* correspond to relations, but they may contain duplicates, whereas a relation is required to be a set. Many additional features are provided, such as *integrity constraints* (e.g. a *primary key* which indicates this value is unique for each *row* (tuple) in the table); and *database procedures*. The following fragment of SQL illustrates how the encyclopedia can be modeled in SQL tables.

```
CREATE TABLE Articles (
  articleNumber INTEGER PRIMARY KEY,
  title CHARACTER(40),
  topicNumber INTEGER
    CONSTRAINT topic_fk FOREIGN KEY
      REFERENCES Topics(topicNumber),
    );
CREATE TABLE Authors (
  authorNumber INTEGER PRIMARY KEY,
    );
CREATE TABLE Writes (
  articleNumber INTEGER
    CONSTRAINT article_exists FOREIGN KEY
      REFERENCES Articles(articleNumber),
  authorNumber INTEGER
    CONSTRAINT author_exists FOREIGN KEY
      REFERENCES Authors(authorNumber),
  due DATE, );
```

ENTITY-RELATIONSHIP DIAGRAMS

A data model called the entity-relationship model (E-R model) has been developed with more concern for

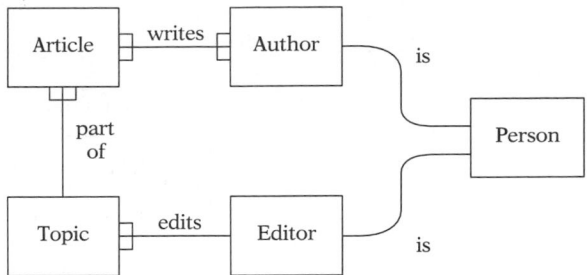

Figure 3.

conceptual requirements. It is used, with an associated methodology, for designing databases and applications. For the encyclopedia example, we get the diagram in Fig. 3.

There is now a full repertoire of relationship forms, including many-to-many (the above diagram permits joint authorship of an article) and one-to-one relationships. Mapping E-R models to relations is an almost mechanical task using *foreign keys*, as shown in the example above. This category of data model has been developed into a powerful systems analysis and design tool. The current *de facto* standard is Universal Modeling Language (UML—*see* OBJECT-ORIENTED ANALYSIS AND DESIGN).

OBJECT-ORIENTED DATA MODELS

Many data collections are not easily organized in a relational form (e.g. *graphs* such as arise in genealogies, *matrices* such as arise in science and engineering, and *sequences* such as the images in a video sequence). Object-oriented data models address this by using three constructs: the *object*, the *isa hierarchy* and *collection classes*. An object is an aggregation of values that has *identity* independent of those values. So a value in one object may be the identity of another object. The isa hierarchy denotes inclusion relationships between the types (here called *classes*) of objects, so that the fact that an `Editor` **isa** `Person` is modeled explicitly.

The diagram for the encyclopedia is shown in Fig. 4, and a fragment of the data language (using approximately the ODMG (Object Database Management Group) standard binding to Java) might be:

```
class Person {
  String name;
  Date dateOfBirth; }
class Author extends Person {
  Set(Subject) expertIn;
  int reliability; }
class Article {
  String title;
  List(Author) authors;
  Topic topic; }
```

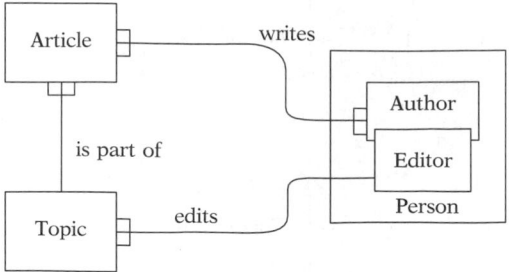

Figure 4.

SEMISTRUCTURED DATA

Recently, quite large bodies of data have been organized using semistructured techniques, for example, much of the human genome data. As the name suggests, this is a compromise between the formality of a precisely constrained model and free-form data. This is motivated by the need to allow the authors of data to revise the structure to match new requirements. The basic construct is a sequence of *tag* and *value* pairs. Each value may itself be such a sequence. There is no separate abstract model of the data, and normally the data is considered to be in textual form, i.e. self-documented and suitable for human use, although there may be more efficient stored forms. XML (eXtensible Markup Language—*see* MARKUP LANGUAGES) is the current standard notation for describing such data. The following text might represent the encyclopedia data in this form. The perspicacious reader will note a reversion to the hierarchical data model, with its attendant limitations.

```
Encyclopedia
  Title Encyclopedia of Computer Science
  Edition Fourth
  Editor Ralston, A.
  Editor Reilly, E.D.
  Editor Hemmendinger, D.
    Topic
      Name Administrative Applications
      Subeditor King, W.R.
      Subeditor Hanley, M.E.
      Article
        Title Electronic Commerce
        Author Kalakota, R.
        Author Robinson, M.
      Article
        Title Electronic Office
        Author Wohl, A.D.
      Article
      ...
```

Bibliography

1984. Brodie, M. L., Mylopoulos, J., and Schmidt, J. W. (eds.) *On Conceptual Modelling, Perspectives from Artificial Intelligence, Databases and Programming Languages.* New York: Springer-Verlag.

1987. Hull, R., and King, R. "Semantic Data Modelling: Survey, Applications and Research Issues," *ACM Computing Surveys,* **19**, *3* (September), 201–260.

1993. Melton, J., and Simon, A. R. *Understanding the New SQL: A Complete Guide.* San Francisco: Morgan Kaufmann.

1998. Cooper, R. *Object Databases: An ODMG Approach.* Boston, MA: International Thomson Publications.

1999. Mader, C. *Creating Documents with XML.* Petaluma, CA: O'Reilly Press.

1999. Rumbaugh, J., Jacobson, I., and Booch, G. *The Unified Modeling Language Reference Manual.* Reading, MA: Addison-Wesley.

Malcolm P. Atkinson

DATA PROCESSING

For articles on related subjects *see* ADMINISTRATIVE APPLICATIONS; and INFORMATION PROCESSING.

Data processing is a widely used term with a variety of meanings and interpretations ranging from one that makes it almost coextensive with all of computing to much narrower connotations in the general area of computer applications to business and administrative problems.

In a broad sense, data processing may be said to be what computers *do*. In this context it should be compared to *information processing,* which some prefer to data processing because "information" does not carry the connotation of "number," as "data" sometimes does. Of course, the "data" in data processing is really intended to connote any kind of information in symbolic form. Thus, information may be viewed as "knowledge," while data are the physical symbols used to represent the information.

The term "data processing" is often used with various modifiers, the most common being:

1. Electronic data processing (EDP), a term widely used to describe *all* computing activity—or, at least, the part of computing that focuses on administrative or business applications—and particularly to distinguish computerized applications from manual methods.

2. Automatic data processing (ADP), closely analogous to EDP, since it is intended to distinguish computer data processing from data processing in which significant human assistance or intervention is required.

3. Business data processing (BDP) refers specifically to administrative applications (e.g. personnel, payroll, accounting) and to broader business applications (e.g. inventory control, sales forecasting).

4. Scientific data processing, which is a comparatively rare term and which is meant to imply the increasing recognition that business and scientific applications of computers have much more in common than was once realized or, indeed, than was actually the case in earlier days.

Until the 1960s it was common to divide the world of computer applications into two realms—business data processing and scientific computing—with the latter encompassing all engineering, scientific, or other technical applications of computers where the emphasis was on numerical calculations, usually extensive ones, rather than on the manipulation (sorting, organizing, etc.) of data (together with, at most, very simple arithmetic calculations), which was the province of business data processing.

Another distinct, although related, contrast between the two areas was their relative dependence on the central processing unit facilities of the computer on the one hand and on the input–output facilities on the other hand. Most scientific calculations seemed to require little input data and produced relatively few numbers as results, but relied heavily on the arithmetic and logical capabilities of the central processing unit (*q.v.*). Indeed, computers that handled mainly large scientific calculations were, and still are, often called "number crunchers." By contrast, business data processing tasks usually involve large amounts of input data (e.g. the entire employee file of a company)—hence the name "data" processing—perform relatively few calculations, and then produced large amounts of output (e.g. all payroll checks for the company).

To a degree, this dichotomy between scientific applications (*q.v.*) and business data processing was always misleading. If the paradigm for business data processing—much input and output, little calculation—was, in fact, a rather good generalization, the paradigm for scientific calculation was much less so. Scientific calculations involving large volumes of input data and, more commonly, large quantities of results had been common since the earliest days of computing (e.g. the production of tables of mathematical functions such as the trigonometric or Bessel functions). Still, it has only been in recent years that the dichotomy has been seen to be less and less useful for any purpose.

Increasingly, scientific calculations (e.g. meteorological and high-energy physics applications) process large amounts of input data and produce copious results. Also increasingly, although less so, business applications involve sophisticated mathematical techniques involving large amounts of calculation (e.g. various statistical and related forecasting applications). Thus, while there remain many computer applications that conform to the original business data processing/scientific computing stereotype, it is increasingly common and more reasonable to use the terms "business data processing" and "scientific data processing" to distinguish between applications areas but not between the characteristics of the applications themselves.

The past distinction between business data processing and scientific calculations was reflected in the development of computers ostensibly designed for one application area but not the other. IBM's 700 series of computers of the 1950s illustrates this point. (The 700 series comprised first-generation computers, which used vacuum tube technology; with the advent of transistor technology and the second generation of computers, a zero was added, and this became the 7000 series. Thus, the 7040 and 7090 were transistorized and somewhat modified versions of the 704 and 709.) There were two pairs of computers in this series, first the 701 and 702, and later the 704 and 705. (*See* IBM CORPORATION.)

Both the 701 and 704 were designed for scientific computing. Their memories were binary and word-oriented and, on the 704, floating-point arithmetic was standard. By contrast, the 702 and 705 were specifically designed for "data processing" applications, meaning business data processing. Their memories were character- and digit-oriented and only fixed-point arithmetic was possible. By the time of the advent of the IBM 360 series of computers in the mid-1960s, the previous sharp distinction between scientific computing and business data processing was becoming blurred so that the existence of separate computers for the two areas was no longer considered necessary. Nevertheless, the distinction was still considered important and, for example, one model of the 360 series, the 360/44, was specially designed for scientific computation.

In the 1970s some manufacturers still oriented their general-purpose computer line toward particular application areas, most notably Control Data, with its 6000, 7000, Cyber 70, and Cyber 170 series of computers intended mainly for scientific applications, but the trend was clearly toward computers for data processing without a distinction between scientific and business applications. In the 1980s and 1990s, only supercomputers (*q.v.*), the very largest and fastest computers, typically with only a small number of each produced, could be said to be strictly scientific computers.

The development of general-purpose high-level programming languages also parallels the history outlined in the preceding paragraph. The first such language in the mid-1950s, Fortran, was intended (and still is mainly used) for scientific calculations. Even the version used up through the 1980s, Fortran 77, lacked variable length character manipulation and the data structure facilities needed for many data processing problems; these deficiencies were removed in Fortran 90/95. The second such language in the late 1950s, Cobol, was intended (and still is virtually always used) for business data processing problems. Its limited arithmetic facilities virtually preclude its use for significant numerical calculations.

The development of PL/I in the mid-1960s had, among its motivations, the desire to develop a language that could be used for both scientific and business problems because of increasing cognizance at about this time of common properties in these two applications areas. PL/I's failure to achieve wide popularity cannot be ascribed to any deficiency in this viewpoint. Rather, it is due to the very large inertia among Fortran and Cobol users that prevents them from switching to a new language because of their extensive investment in so-called *legacy* programs, libraries, and expertise in the older languages. Undoubtedly the distinctions between the scientific and business applications areas will become further blurred as the widespread use of data communications and the increasing use of large databases further pervade all applications areas. The name "data processing," therefore, will remain an inclusive term to describe computer applications of all kinds. It will continue to be one of a few terms (information processing and symbol manipulation (*q.v.*) are others) that may reasonably be used to denote what a computer does.

Bibliography

1990. Senn, J. A. *Information Systems in Management*, 4th Ed. San Rafael, CA: Wadsworth.

Anthony Ralston

DATA SECURITY

For articles on related subjects *see* AUTHENTICATION; COMPUTER CRIME; CRYPTOGRAPHY, COMPUTERS IN; CYCLIC REDUNDANCY CHECK; DIGITAL SIGNATURE; ERROR-CORRECTING AND DETECTING CODE; HACKER; PASSWORD; PRETTY GOOD PRIVACY; and VIRUS, COMPUTER.

Preserving the security of data such as a payroll file or digitized graphical image necessarily requires consideration of the security of the entire computing system—its hardware, software (*q.v.*), firmware (*q.v.*), and internal data. For example, it is impossible to protect just data if the programs that access and potentially modify that data have been corrupted. In the Internet (*q.v.*) age, data security has become of paramount importance because of the literally millions of users in cyberspace (*q.v.*) who might, accidentally or otherwise, invade and compromise the integrity of data on the computer calling into the Net.

Properties of Data Security

Data security is typically defined in terms of three properties:

♦ *Confidentiality*—Assurance that data, programs, and other system resources are protected against disclosure to unauthorized persons, programs, or systems.

♦ *Integrity*—Assurance that data, programs, and other system resources are protected against malicious or inadvertent modification or destruction by unauthorized persons, programs, or systems.

♦ *Availability*—Assurance that use of data, programs, and other system resources will not be denied to authorized persons, programs, or systems.

Additionally, one might also include in a definition of security the properties of authentication (the property that persons, programs, or systems are accurately identified by a computing system) and nonrepudiation (the property that communications received from persons, programs, or systems can be assured to have indeed been sent by their purported senders).

A security flaw results from the lack, breach, or failure of confidentiality, integrity, or availability. The flaw can arise from a variety of causes, including human, mechanical, and environmental faults, as well as problems internal to the computing system. A *risk analysis* is a study to determine the susceptibility of a computing system to various kinds of security failure. Risk analysis is performed by analyzing general threats to the security of the system (such as loss of electrical power or programmer sabotage), and then determining whether the threats could affect the system in question. A threat that could affect a system adversely is called a *vulnerability*.

Computer security embraces many aspects of a computing system, including hardware design, operating systems (*q.v.*), networks, database management systems (*q.v.*), compilers (*q.v.*), and user applications programs and systems. Vulnerabilities of computer systems range from the possibility of a trusted employee's selling (or being forced to reveal) secrets to a competitor, disk failures that render an entire volume of data unreadable, unauthorized operating system penetration (*see* HACKER), inferences about confidential data through carefully chosen queries posed to a database, loss of data because of floods or fires, acquisition of data through wiretapping or sensing the radiation from electronic equipment, or denying access to computing resources by flooding the system with other requests for service.

Protection control can be effected through software, hardware, physical, and procedural means, combined to provide appropriate coverage against vulnerabilities. For example, the procedural measure of creating backup copies of important data combined with the physical measure of locking the door to the computer room insures against loss of data. Hardware features and software controls—typically portions of the operating system—combine to confine the accesses of each system user. The selection of a set of controls is based on an analysis of expected threats and available support.

Cryptography

Cryptography (*q.v.*) is one important tool by which to preserve confidentiality and integrity. Confidential materials are encrypted to prevent their disclosure to unauthorized individuals (i.e. to people who do not hold the cryptographic key for the materials). Furthermore, encryption usually prevents unauthorized, undetected modification: someone may be able to scramble the bits of an encrypted text so that the bits decrypt to nothing meaningful, but, without breaking the encryption, no one can change a specific field of the underlying plaintext data from "1" to "2." One significant use of cryptography is to compute a *cryptographic checksum*, a function that depends upon every bit of a block of data and also upon a key used for the cryptographic function. For example, a (weak) cryptographic checksum is the parity (*q.v.*) of a string of bits; any one change to the string affects the parity. The cryptographic checksum is computed when a block of data is created and again when it is used; if the data has been changed between origin and use, the value of the checksum at time of use will (almost certainly) not match that computed at time of origin, a signal that the data has been changed.

Cryptography is also useful in establishing reliable computer-to-computer exchanges of information. Protocols (*q.v.*) employing cryptography have been designed for such activities as voting, sending credit card numbers securely over the Internet, producing unforgeable electronic receipts for data received, providing unforgeable evidence of the authenticity of the sender of a piece of data, and storing one data item so that it can be retrieved only with the consent of several users (e.g. to make a maintenance password available only to a pair of people acting together, such as the system operator and a maintenance engineer).

Access Control

Confidentiality, integrity, and availability have been defined in terms of "authorized access." Two things are necessary in order to enforce such access: first, a reliable structure is needed under which authorizations to use resources are conferred (or revoked), and second, a reliable mechanism must exist to verify the authorization each time an access is attempted. Part of the authorization process is procedural, implemented outside the computing system. For example, an employee may be authorized to access certain files because of his or her job responsibilities, an individual may be authorized to access certain classified data because of having received a security clearance, a file's creator may confer access rights to a selected set of trustworthy users; or the administrator of a system may determine that data on that system may be shared with other specified systems. These permissions must be established in a reliable manner. Furthermore, the authorization data must be stored in such a way that it can be modified only by authorized administrators. These authorizations are stored in a data structure (*q.v.*) for use by the operating system or other unit that controls access. Often, the authorization data structure is encrypted, preventing it from unauthorized modification and even limiting those who can see who has been authorized access to which files.

Once the list of authorized accesses is reliably established, individuals (human users, programs, or systems acting as representatives for the individuals) will request access. All such individuals are called *subjects*; the resources, called the *objects* of a computing system, consist of files, programs, devices, and other items to which subjects' accesses are to be controlled. For each subject and each object, the system must be able to determine whether access by the subject to the object is allowable and, if so, what type of access (e.g. read, write, delete). The access control system must have a reliable mechanism for verifying the requestor's identity. For example, operating systems often use passwords to ensure the authenticity of a user attempting to log in. More sophisticated authentication techniques include the use of automatic password generators or devices that sense a physical characteristic of the user, such as a handprint, retinal scan, or the style of a spoken phrase. Some subjects, such as certain programs or I/O devices, may be identified and authenticated by their hardware address, process identification number, or other reliable internal means. Thus, the login authorization file may be readable only by the process that performs user login.

After the computing system has verified the identity of a requesting user, it is able to implement access control decisions. The foundation of access control is the *reference monitor* concept, first documented in 1972. A reference monitor must be:

◆ Tamper-proof, so that its functioning cannot be undermined.

◆ Unable to be bypassed, so that it is invoked to authorize every requested access.

◆ Small, so that it can be scrutinized rigorously for correctness.

One means of maintaining access authorization data is by an *access control matrix*. An access control matrix specifies, for each subject, what objects that subject can access and what kinds of access are allowed. The rows of an access control matrix represent subjects, and the columns represent objects. Each entry in the matrix indicates what types of access the subject may have, with respect to the given object. For example, subject SMITH may be allowed to read, write, and delete file A, and yet be able only to read file B. The SMITH row of the matrix would contain read, write, delete in the file A column and read in the file B column. Although an access control matrix is the most straightforward means of describing allowable accesses, in practice it is inefficient because it requires a very large amount of space. A system with 200 users, each of whom has 50 files, requires $200 \times 50 = 10,000$ table entries. If most users' files are private (inaccessible by other users), most cells in the access control matrix entries are empty, indicating no allowed access. An *access control list* is effectively a column of an access control matrix. For each object, there is one list that includes only those users who should be allowed to access the object and the type of access they should be allowed. For public objects, such as compilers and shared data files, a "wild card" subject can be specified; for example, the system programmer may have read and delete access, while all other users are allowed only read access. Access control lists are especially effective for denoting single users who should have specific types of access to certain objects. Alternatively, a *capability list*, which corresponds to a row of the access control matrix, can be maintained to control access. The capability list indicates, for each subject, the objects that subject is allowed to access.

Other types of access control mechanisms are *capabilities*, which are, effectively, tokens or tickets that a user must possess in order to access an object, and *group authorizations*, in which subjects are allowed access to objects based on defined membership in a group, such as all employees of a single department or the collaborators on a particular project. The objects whose access is controlled in a computing system include memory, storage media, I/O devices, computing time, files, and communication paths. Although the nature of access control to these objects is the same, access is controlled by different mechanisms. Memory can be controlled through hardware features, such as base and bounds registers or dynamic address translation (virtual memory—*q.v.*), paging, or segmentation. Access to I/O devices and computing time (i.e. to the use of the CPU) is more frequently controlled by requiring the intervention of the operating system to access the device. The operating system is assisted by the hardware in that, although the machine can run in two or more states, direct access to I/O devices is permitted only from the more privileged state (*see*

PRIVILEGED INSTRUCTION). Files and communications paths are typically controlled by permission to initiate access (*see* OPEN AND CLOSE A FILE). Such accesses are requested from the operating system.

Program Security

Computers make access requests only under control of programs. Every program operates under the control of or in the name of a user. Thus, the accesses of a program are presumably the result of requests from a user. However, programs are also modifiable; that is, a program is actually a series of bits in memory, and those bits can be read, written, modified, and deleted as any data can be (*see* STORED PROGRAM CONCEPT). While a user program may be designed to read a file, the program, with minor modification to the executable code, could instead write or delete the file. Those modifications can be the result of hardware errors and failures, a flaw in the logic of the program, or a change induced by some other program in the system. Hardware errors are uncommon, and checking circuitry is built into computers to detect such errors before they affect a computation. Unintentional or malicious user errors are much more difficult to detect and prevent. Programs are stored either in files or main memory (or both); thus, the first line of defense against program errors is *memory protection* (*q.v.*), which is designed to prevent one user from deliberately or accidentally accessing files and memory assigned to another. While these controls protect users from one another, they are far less effective at protecting them from errors in their own program logic.

A second protection against program errors is careful and thorough *software engineering* (*q.v.*), including structured design, program reviews, and use of *chief programmer teams* (*q.v.*). Such programming practices will help to protect a user from unintentional errors.

The third form of protection against program errors is *software testing* (*q.v.*). Unfortunately, however, a well-known maxim states that testing can confirm the presence of errors, but not their absence. Nonetheless, a thoroughly tested program can provide credibility to the contention that a program is error-free. Of special concern is the software that controls accesses. Presumably, the program that controls access of any subject to any object also protects itself against access by all unauthorized subjects. Nevertheless, the access control program itself represents a significant vulnerability: defeat or circumvent it, and you can obtain unhindered access to all system resources. For this reason, on more secure computing systems, the access control function is divided among several different modules: one to control access to files, one to control access to memory, etc. In this way, defeating one module does not immediately open all system resources to access.

A related question is verification of the correctness of the access control software itself, ensuring that it will permit all and only the authorized accesses. Clearly, access control procedures are effective only if they are implemented properly. Good software engineering practices for the design and implementation of the access control software are combined with rigorous control over its modifications, once installed, to insure the correct functioning of the access control software.

Malicious Program Code

Computer data is vulnerable to attacks by malicious programs. Such programs range from overt attempts at accessing unauthorized data to more covert ones that attempt to subvert a benign program. While the overt, blatant attempts are typically precluded by the methods just described, the more subtle attempts may succeed.

A *Trojan horse* is a program that performs (or is made to perform) some function in addition to its expected, advertised use. For example, a program that ostensibly produces a formatted listing of stored files may actually write copies of those files on a second device to which a malicious user has access; the Trojan horse may even modify or delete the files. Or a program to produce paychecks may reduce one employee's check by an amount and add the same amount to another check. These programs represent data security flaws because they permit access to a resource by an unauthorized user. Unfortunately, the access control violation is not the Trojan horse program itself since the file listing program has legitimate access to every user's file (or, more properly, to their names—a distinction not made by most computing systems), and the paycheck program is using its legitimate access rights to query time cards and write checks, but with incorrect values. Thus, a Trojan horse is difficult to detect in operation because it may behave ordinarily, performing only allowable accesses. The Trojan horse program may have been flawed initially, or it may have been modified during or between executions through some failure of access controls. (One serious source of Trojan horse infections is through users who fail to set access limitations to the code of their programs, so that malicious outsiders can modify otherwise innocuous and correct programs.)

A *computer virus* or *worm* is a particular type of Trojan horse that is self-replicating. In addition to performing some illicit act, the program creates copies of itself that it embeds in other innocent programs. At one time the most common source of a virus infection was a diskette (*q.v.*) of dubious origin, but now users of personal computers are at risk every time they open an email attachment from someone not known to them. Each time an innocent but infected program is run, the attached virus is activated as well, replicating itself and spreading to other previously uninfected programs or, perhaps worse, erasing all or most of the data on the computer's hard disk (*q.v.*).

Bibliography

1982. Denning, D. E. *Cryptography and Data Security*. Reading, MA: Addison-Wesley.
1995. Hutt, A. E., Hoyt, D. B., and Bosworth, S. (eds.) *Computer Security Handbook*, 3rd Ed. New York: John Wiley.
1996. Pfleeger, C. P. *Security in Computing*, 2nd Ed. Upper Saddle River, NJ: Prentice Hall.
1998. Tipton, H. F. (ed.) *Handbook of Information Security Management*. Boca Raton, FL: CRC Press.

Charles P. Pfleeger

DATA STRUCTURES

For articles on related subjects *see* ABSTRACT DATA TYPE; FILE; GRAPH THEORY; LIST PROCESSING; OBJECT-ORIENTED PROGRAMMING; RECORD; STACK; STRING PROCESSING; and TREE.

Basic Terminology

The term *structure* is used in many different fields to denote objects that are constructed from their components in a regular and characteristic way. Loosely, a data structure is a structure whose components are data objects. As the term is used more precisely in computer science, a *data structure* is a collection of data values, the relationships among them, and the functions or operations that can be applied to the data. If any one of these three characteristics is missing or not stated precisely, the structure being examined does not qualify as a data structure.

Example

The arithmetic expression $3 + 4*5$ is constructed in a systematic way from data components that are integers, 3, 4, and 5, and operators, $+$ and $*$. The structure of this expression may be thought of as either a string or a tree structure in which each operator is the root of a subtree whose descendants are operands (Fig. 1). As a string, the operations to be

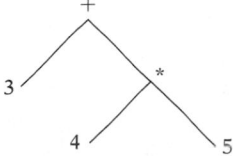

Figure 1. A tree structure.

performed on it might include *evaluation* to obtain an arithmetic result or *concatenation* with other strings to form still longer expressions. As a *tree*, relevant operations would include insertion and deletion of objects in the tree or various kinds of tree traversal that yield prefix, infix, or postfix equivalents of the original expression (*see* TREE).

When the data for this data structure is stored in a computer, it must be stored so that components are readily accessible. This may be done by storing the expression $3 + 4 * 5$ as a character string A so that the ith character is retrieved by referring to the element $A[i]$. Alternatively, the string may be stored as a list structure in which the vertex associated with $+$ has a left child 3 and a right child $*$, which in turn has left and right children 4 and 5 (Fig. 2).

Figs. 1 and 2 illustrate the relation between data structures, which specify *logical* relations between data components, and *storage structures*, which specify how such relations may be realized in a digital computer. The storage structure of Fig. 2 could be represented in a digital computer by five three-component storage cells, where each cell has one component containing an operator or integer and two components respectively containing a pointer (*q.v.*) to the left and right children. The three cells that have no successors contain special markers in their pointer fields, here indicated by the word "nil."

In order to define a class of data objects having a common data structure, it is usual to start with a class of primitive data elements called *atoms*, or elementary objects, and to specify *construction operators* by means of which *composite objects* may be constructed from the atoms. In the preceding arithmetic expression example, the atoms are operands (integers) and arithmetic operators. The construction operators specify how expressions are built up from operators and operands. A prescribed set of construction operators is called a *grammar* (*q.v.*).

In order to access and manipulate composite objects specified by a given set of atoms and construction rules, *selectors* must be defined that allow the components of a data object to be accessed, and *creation* and *deletion* operators must be defined that allow the components of data structures to be created and deleted. Data structures may be characterized by how they are accessed and their creation and deletion operators.

Some of the basic terminology relating to data structures will be mentioned by considering commonly occurring data structures, such as arrays, records, sets, lists, trees, stacks, and queues.

ARRAYS

An *array* is a data structure whose elements may be selected by integer selectors called "indexes." If A is a one-dimensional array whose indexes start at 1, then $A[3]$ (or $A(3)$ in some languages) refers to the third element of A. If B is a three-dimensional array, then $B[I, J, K]$ or $B(I, J, K)$ refers to the I, J, K element (B_{ijk}) of the array B. The set of all elements of an array is generally created at the same time by means of *declarations* (*q.v.*) such as:

`REAL A(100)`	Fortran array declaration
`integer array A[1:N];`	Algol 60 array declaration
`[1:N] int A;`	Algol 68 array declaration
`A: array [1..N] of real;`	Pascal array declaration
`int A[100];`	C++ array declaration

In Fortran, the declaration `REAL A(100)` serves to reserve a block of cells for the array A at compile time. In Algol 60 or 68, declarations create an instance of the declared data structure at run time. Thus, the declaration `integer array A [1:N]` causes allocation of a block of N storage cells large enough to hold integers using the current value assigned to the variable N, and activates an accessing mechanism so that $A[i]$ will refer to the ith allocated cell.

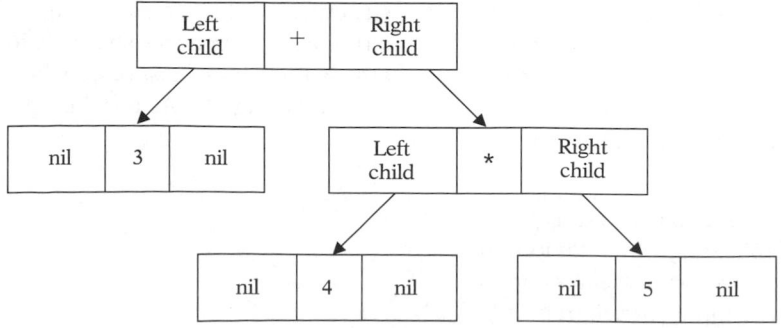

Figure 2. Storage structure for the tree structure of Fig. 1.

The arrays introduced are *homogeneous* because all elements of an array have the same data type, and are *Cartesian* (rectangular) because all vectors in a given dimension have the same size. Most modern programming languages permit nonhomogeneous data aggregates called *records* or *structures* to be declared. The following is a PL/I declaration of a PAYROLL record with a 50 character name field, fields of mode FIXED for the number of regular and overtime hours worked, and a field of mode FLOAT for the rate of pay:

```
DECLARE 1 PAYROLL
        2 NAME CHARACTER (50),
        2 HOURS
          3 REGULAR FIXED,
          3 OVERTIME FIXED,
        2 RATE FLOAT;
```

If it is desired to refer to the number of overtime hours in the record PAYROLL, then this is given by PAYROLL.HOURS.OVERTIME. That is, component names rather than indexes are used to access a given element of the data structure.

SETS

Sets are a convenient form of data structure when the order of elements is irrelevant, as in (**for** $x \in S$ **do** SUM := SUM + x;). Sets and operations upon sets are supported in their full generality by the very high-level language SETL (*q.v.*), which allows the user to make mathematical assertions using mathematical set theoretic notation. Pascal also has a data type "set" that allows us to talk about subsets and test for set membership. However, Pascal sets have an implementation-dependent maximum size, and support only operations that can be simply defined in terms of the representation of finite sets as a binary string of zeros and ones in a computer word. The gap between abstract sets and their implementation is much greater than the corresponding gap for arrays or records.

LISTS

List structures, just as array structures, may be characterized by their accessing creation and deletion operators. Elements of a list structure are generally accessed by "walking" along pointer chains, starting at the head of the list. In a single-linked linear list (SLLL), each list element has a unique successor and the last element has an "empty" successor field, usually denoted by the symbol "nil." In general, list elements may have more than one successor, and lists may be circular in the sense that pointer chains may form cycles. Knuth (1997) describes doubly-linked lists that have forward and backward pointer chains passing through each element, and a number of other kinds of lists. Fig. 3 illustrates a doubly linked circular list (DLCL) named *L*, whose head element *H* is linked both to the next element *A* and to the last element *B*.

If the forward pointer is referred to by RLINK (for right link) and the backward pointer is referred to by LLINK (left link), then the second list element (labeled A) may be accessed in either of the two following ways:

RLINK(L)	Forward chaining
LLINK(LLINK(L))	Backward chaining

Insertion and deletion of elements in a list is accomplished by creation of a new list cell and by updating pointers of existing list elements and the newly created list element. Fig. 4 illustrates that the insertion of the list element *X* between the list elements *A* and *B* requires updating of the RLINK of *A*, the LLINK of *B*, and initialization of the *R* and *L* links of *X*.

The instructions to perform this insertion might be as follows (assume that *P* points to node *A*):

```
create X                        pointed at by N
RLINK(N) = RLINK(P)
LLINK(N) = P
RLINK(P) = N
LLINK(RLINK(N)) = N
```

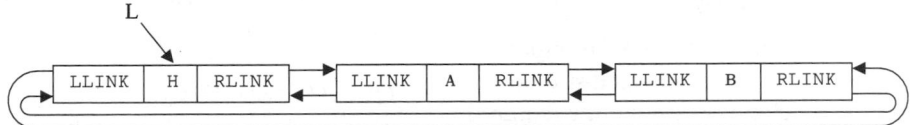

Figure 3. Doubly linked circular list *L*.

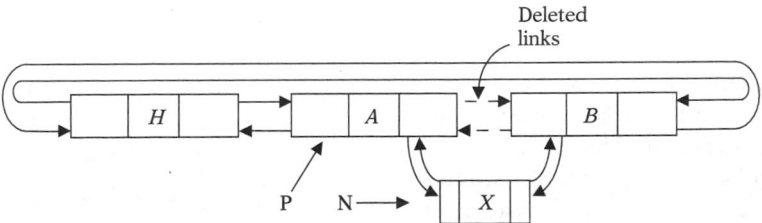

Figure 4. Insertion of *X* into list in Fig. 3.

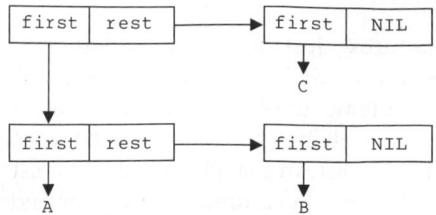

Figure 5. Representation of a list *L*.

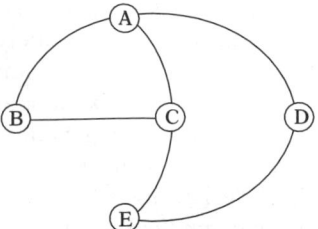

Figure 6. A graph of five nodes and six edges.

Lisp, which was developed by John McCarthy in the late 1950s, is the most important list processing language. The list format and instruction repertoire of Lisp will be briefly illustrated. For ease of presentation, however, we will use a notation different from that actually used in Lisp.

List elements in our dialect of Lisp have two components selectable by the selectors `first` and `rest`. If L is a list, then `first(L)` selects the first element of the list, which may be either an atom or a sublist, and `rest(L)` selects the rest of the list. The list `((A,B),C)` is represented in Lisp by the list structure of Fig. 5.

> For `L=((A,B),C)`, `first(L)=(A,B)`,
> `rest(L)= (C)`, `first(first(L))=A` and
> `rest(rest(L))=NIL`.

Lisp also has a construction operator, `cons(X,Y)`, which constructs a list L such that `first(L)=X` and `rest(L)=Y`, and a predicate `atom(X)`, which is true when X is an atom and false otherwise. In the above example, `atom(first(L))=false` since `first(L)=(A,B)` but `atom(first(first(L)))=true`.

In general, any language for the manipulation of data structures has not only *selectors* for selecting components of a data structure, but also *constructors* for constructing data structures from their components and *predicates* for testing whether a given data object has certain attributes. Lisp illustrates particularly clearly the role of selectors, constructors, and predicates in a programming language.

List structures are a flexible storage structure for objects of variable sizes or tables of fixed-size objects in which insertion and deletion is frequently required. A number of special classes of list structures will now be considered in greater detail.

Trees and Graphs

A *tree* is a list in which there is one element called the *root* with no predecessor and in which every other element has a unique predecessor. That is, a tree is a list that contains no circular lists, and in which no two list elements may have a common sublist as a successor. Elements of a tree that have no successor

are called *leaves* of the tree. In Fig. 1, the symbol "+" is the root of the tree and the digits 3, 4, and 5 are leaves. Tree elements, just as list elements, are generally accessed by walking along a pointer chain. However, the guarantee that there are no cycles or common sublists makes it possible to define orderly procedures for the insertion and deletion of subtrees.

A collection of data objects (nodes) so interconnected that their network may contain cyclic paths is called a *graph*. A typical graph is shown in Fig. 6. Such a structure can be represented by an adjacency list, a "list of lists," each of which tells which nodes are connected to the node at the head of the list (*see* Fig. 7). Alternatively, the same information can be represented as a generalized list (list with sublists) for processing by algorithms written in Lisp:

`((A (B C D)) (B (A C)) (C (A B E)) (D (A E)) (E (C D)))`

For a more extensive description of graphs and operations thereon, *see* GRAPH THEORY.

Stacks

A *stack* is a linear list in which elements are accessed, created, and deleted in a last in, first out (LIFO) order. In order to access an element in a stack, it is necessary to delete all more recently entered elements from the stack. Thus, only the top of the stack is immediately accessible. The two principal stack operations are *popping* and *pushing*. If S is a stack, then `pop(S,x)` causes the top element of the stack to be removed and stored at x and `push(S,x)` causes x to be placed on top of the stack.

Queues and Deques

A *queue* is a linear list in which elements are created and deleted in a first in, first out (FIFO) order. A line of

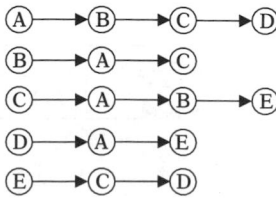

Figure 7. An adjacency list for graph of Fig. 6.

people waiting to be served in a cafeteria is a queue, since the person having waited longest is always the first to be served (deleted from the queue). However, the trays in the cafeteria self-leveling dispenser form a stack, since additions and removals take place at the top (last in, first out). A queue in which deletions are made only at the front, but in which items are usually inserted into the interior, is called a *priority queue*.

A generalization of queues and stacks in which elements may be added and deleted at either end of a linear list is called a *deque*. ("Deque," a shortened form of "double-ended queue," is pronounced "deck.")

Abstraction

Data structures include numerical structures, such as integers that have arithmetic operations applicable to them, and nonnumerical structures, such as arrays, lists, and trees, whose primary purpose is to keep track of relations among data objects rather than to manipulate them.

In programming languages, the choice of a data structure is made by selection of one of the available data types supported by the language. Usually, there are primitive data types for integers, real (floating-point) numbers, and characters; composite data types for arrays and records; and data type (*q.v.*) definition mechanisms for defining new composite types in terms of primitive constituents.

Computational structures may be studied and analyzed at many different levels of abstraction. We have already remarked on the difference between logical data structures and the storage structures in terms of which they are realized. The characterization of structure by logical relations among components is clearly more abstract than the realization of the logical structure by particular configurations of cells and pointers. It is convenient to introduce an additional higher-level mathematical level of abstraction in which logical relations among components of a data structure are characterized even more abstractly by mathematical relations, and an additional lower-level "hardware" level of abstraction that specifies how storage structures are realized at the hardware level.

An important programming language concept is that of an *abstract data type*, which has an interface of named operators accessible to the user and which operates on a hidden internal data representation. For example, an abstract "stack" data type would provide the user with "push," "pop," and "test empty" operators, but hide from the user the stack data representation (as an array or list). The language Ada (*q.v.*) has a concept called *packages* (*q.v.*) that provide collections of resources with hidden implementation to the user, but are not actually abstract data types. Object-oriented languages like C++ (*q.v.*) and Eiffel provide full abstract data type mechanisms.

Returning to the levels of abstraction listed above:

1. *Mathematical structure* is defined by specifying a set of objects and a set of operators (functions, relations) for transforming objects into other objects.

2. *Data structure* is defined by labeled directed graphs that allow characteristic operators on data objects having the given structure to be naturally and simply defined by means of graph transformation rules. A given mathematical structure may, in general, be represented in many different ways by a data structure.

3. *Storage structure* is defined by storage cells with pointers between storage cells. Storage structures, like data structures, are chosen so that operators applicable to computational objects represented by a given storage structure may be simply and efficiently defined. There are, in general, many different storage structures that realize a given data structure.

4. *Hardware structure* specifies how storage structures and transformations of storage structures may be realized at the hardware level.

Example
In modeling databases, the mathematical level of abstraction models databases as mathematical relations, the data structure level considers databases to be directed labeled graphs, the storage structure level considers how the directed graphs representing particular data configurations can be efficiently realized by storage structures, and the hardware structure level considers hardware and microprograms for realizing particular storage structures.

Although these four levels of structure specification are somewhat arbitrary, they appear to be "robust" in the sense that attempts to quantify the notion of abstraction invariably result in something similar to the above characterization. For example, in considering abstraction for program structure, we generally distinguish between mathematical structure, program structure, implementation structure, and hardware realization. These distinctions are very similar to the previously discussed distinctions for data structures.

Classification of Data Structures

Although the range of abstract data structures is exceedingly broad, any imaginable structure can be placed into one of three categories:

1. A *static data structure* consists of a fixed number of contiguous cells arranged in a geometric pattern. That pattern usually, but not always, has a certain symmetry, such as that of a rectangular or hexagonal array.

2. An *elastic data structure* consists of a variable number of contiguous cells arranged in a geometric pattern.

3. A *dynamic data structure* consists of a dynamically changeable number of nodes, some or all of which have a stated logical connection to one another or to several others. Examples are trees, graphs and linked lists.

Static and elastic data structures are sometimes called *geometric data structures*, in contrast to dynamic ones, which are also called *topological data structures*.

Representative data structures are classified in the three categories in Table 1. In each of the three categories in Table 1, structures are arranged from simplest at the bottom to most complex at the top. This is easiest to see in the dynamic category. The nodes of a graph may be arbitrarily interconnected, either partially, as in Figure 6, or completely. The smallest degree of

Table 1.   Classification of representative data structures

Static data structures (fixed number of contiguous cells)	Elastic data structures (variable number of contiguous cells)	Dynamic data structures (variable number of noncontiguous nodes)
Non-Cartesian array	File	Graph: *n*-ary tree Binary tree
Cartesian array: *n*-dimensional array	*n*-dimensional elastic array (APL)	
Three-dimensional array		List with sublists (Lisp)
Two-dimensional array	Matrix (APL)	Simple linked lists: DLCL
One-dimensional array	Deque Queue (Simula) Stack (Forth)	DLLL SLCL SLLL
Fixed-length record	Variable-length record (Cobol)	
	Variable-length string (Snobol, Icon, APL)	Set (SETL)

DLCL—Doubly-Linked Circular List; DLLL—Doubly-Linked Linear List; SLCL—Singly-Linked Circular List; SLLL—Singly-Linked Linear List.

interconnection among nodes in a dynamic structure is none at all, as is exemplified by the set, the last entry in the dynamic category of Table 1.

Using a language such as C (*q.v.*) or Pascal, dynamic data structures have to be synthesized by using records for nodes and pointers (*q.v.*) for interconnections. Alternatively, another programming language that supports the given structure could be used. If a language does a particularly good job of supporting a certain structure, it is cited in Table 1. For example, Cobol might be a good choice when it is important to be able to process variable-length records. APL, noted principally for its unusual syntactic notation, is potentially valuable because it is the only language that supports elastic arrays; i.e. the dimensionality of an APL array can be changed dynamically by adding or deleting whole rows and columns, even in the interior of the original array. List processing languages (*q.v.*) like Lisp and Prolog are appropriate for arbitrarily structured lists.

Data structures capture the notion of computational structure at a level that is sufficiently abstract to emphasize logical relations among components of a data object, independently of details of implementation but at the same time sufficiently concrete to preserve some relation between a structure and its computational realization. Data structures thus represent an appropriate and practicable level of abstraction for characterizing computational structure, and it is for this reason that the study of data structures is so important in computer science.

Bibliography

1987. Horowitz, E., and Sahni, S. *Fundamentals of Data Structures in Pascal*, 2nd Ed. Rockville, MD: Computer Science Press.
1996. Dale, N., Lilly, S. C., and McCormick, J. W. *Ada Plus Data Structures*. Sudbury, MA: Jones and Barlett.
1996. Weiss, M. A. *Algorithms, Data Structures, and Problem Solving with C++*. Reading, MA: Addison-Wesley.
1997. Knuth, D. E. *The Art of Computer Programming* **1**, 3rd Ed. Reading, MA: Addison-Wesley.
1997. Main, M., and Savitch, W. *Data Structures and Other Objects Using C++*. Reading, MA: Addison-Wesley.

Peter Wegner and Edwin D. Reilly

DATA TYPE

For articles on related subjects *see* ABSTRACT DATA TYPE; ARITHMETIC, COMPUTER; CHARACTER CODES; COERCION; DATA STRUCTURES; DECLARATION; EXPRESSION; EXTENSIBLE LANGUAGE; PROCEDURE-ORIENTED LANGUAGES; and TYPES, THEORY OF.

A *data type* is an *interpretation* applied to a string of bits. Data types may be classified as structured or scalar. Scalar data types include real, integer, double precision, logical ("Boolean"), character, pointer, and label.

Structured data types are collections of individual data items of the same or different data types. An *array* is a data type that is a collection of data items of the same data type. *Records, structures,* or *files* are data types that are collections of data items of one or more data types.

Most programming languages provide a *declaration facility* or standard convention to indicate the data type of the variable used. Thus, when the contents of the variable are accessed, they may be interpreted in the proper manner. This is necessary, since a string of bits may have several meanings depending on the context in which it is used.

The *integer* (or *cardinal*) data type is used to represent whole numbers, i.e. values without fractional parts.

The *real* data type is used to represent floating-point data, which contains a normalized fraction (mantissa) and an exponent (characteristic).

Double precision is a generalization of the real data type that provides greater precision and sometimes a greater range of exponents.

Complex data contains two real fields representing the real and imaginary components of a complex number $a + bi$ (where i is the square root of -1).

Logical, or *Boolean*, data has only two possible values, *true* or *false*.

Character or *string* data is the internal representation of printable characters. Some coding schemes permit 64 characters and use six bits; others (EBCDIC and extended ASCII) permit up to 256 characters and use 8 bits.

Label data refers to locations in the program and *pointer* data refers to locations of other pieces of data.

The commonly used operators for addition (+), subtraction (−), multiplication (*), division (/), and exponentiation (** or ↑ or ^) may be applied to real, integer, double precision, or complex data in high-level language programs, with a few restrictions. The actual operation that takes place depends on the data type of the operands. Although some language processors permit "mixed mode" expressions (i.e. expressions involving operands of differing data types), this is accomplished by converting ("coercing") the operands to a common data type before the operation is performed (*see* COERCION).

For example, to execute

```
N := (TEST + 90)/3
```

where N has type integer and TEST has type real, the integer value 90 is converted to a real value, 90.0, so that it may be added to the value of TEST. Before the resultant real value can be divided, the integer value 3 must be converted to a real value, 3.0. Finally, the real result is truncated and converted to an integer to that it may be stored in the integer location *N*.

The logical operators *and, or, not, implies,* and *equivalence* may be applied to logical data having true or false values only. Character operations include concatenation and selection of substrings. For all data types, the assignment operator (typically, ← or := or =) may be used to copy the contents of one location into another, and relational operators may be used to compare values of data items.

Many programming languages, such as Snobol, Pascal (*q.v.*), Modula-2, Ada (*q.v.*), C++ and Haskell, are extensible in the sense that users may define new data types to suit the needs of a particular problem (*see* EXTENSIBLE LANGUAGE). Such user-defined data types have become important for program clarity. User programs may contain declarations of new data types, such as color, which might have a limited number of values such as *red, orange, yellow, green, blue,* and *violet*. Variable names could be declared to be of type color and could take on only the stated values. An example in Pascal would be:

```
type COLOR = (RED, ORANGE, YELLOW, GREEN,
                         BLUE, VIOLET);
var CRAYON, PAINT: COLOR;
```

A user-defined data type might also be a subrange of a standard data type. For example, an age data type might be restricted to range from 1 to 120. An example in Pascal would be:

```
type AGE = 1..120;
var TREEAGE, CITIZENAGE: AGE;
```

The data type concept can also include sequential or random access files and complex structures such as records (*q.v.*), arrays, or trees, that are formed from basic data types such as integers, character data, ages, or colors.

Bibliography

1976. Wirth, N. *Algorithms + Data Structures = Programs.* Upper Saddle River, NJ: Prentice Hall.
1983. Aho, A. V. Hopcroft, J. E., and Ullman, J. *Data Structures and Algorithms.* Reading, MA: Addison-Wesley.
1995. Carrano, F. *Data Abstraction and Problem Solving with C++.* Reading, MA: Addison-Wesley.

Ben Shneiderman

DATA VISUALIZATION

See SCIENTIFIC VISUALIZATION.

DATA WAREHOUSING

For articles on related subjects *see* DATA MINING; DATA MODELS; DATABASE CONCURRENCY CONTROL; DATABASE MANAGEMENT SYSTEM; DEDUCTIVE DATABASE; and RELATIONAL DATABASE.

Introduction

Relational database systems provide an infrastructure for supporting online transaction processing (*q.v.*). However, most relational stores are not optimized with regard to supporting summarization, aggregation, and *ad hoc* querying over large relational databases. As organizations began to rely increasingly on data to influence business decisions, the perceived roles of a database system within organizations has begun to evolve from being primarily data capture and reliable storage, to also enable *decision support*. Decision support imposes new requirements which include data exploration, summarization, analysis, and advanced reporting. The systems that use a database system as a central component in supporting decision support are referred to as *data warehouses*. The evolution of databases from being mainly transactional to being a repository of information to be analyzed by *decision support* tools is illustrated in Fig. 1. Some of the decision support tools are either natively supported in databases or are external client/middleware applications.

Data Warehouses

A data warehouse represents a collection of data (typically quite large) together with a suite of data retrieval functions to facilitate data analysis. The data is typically stored in a backend relational server or in specialized stores. The first step in creating a useful warehouse is to insure that data quality is sufficiently high so that subsequent analysis is meaningful. This *data cleaning step* is responsible for the integration of multiple sources of data, dealing with multiple data formats, thus providing a unified logical view of an underlying collection of data. Once the data has been cleansed, it needs to be *loaded* efficiently in the warehouse. In order to achieve scalability, a relational database is typically used as the backend warehouse. Once the data warehouse has been populated, it needs to be *refreshed*

by propagating the updates on source data to the warehouse. Two key aspects of the refresh step are its periodicity and the propagation technique. These vary depending on the source and the target databases as well as the data analysis requirements. Incremental refresh can often be supported using the replication capabilities of commercial database management. *Data cleaning*, *load*, and *refresh* together provide the mechanisms for populating the data warehouse and updating it. An important component of a successful data warehouse is effective representation and use of *metadata*. A *metadata repository* stores information that makes it possible for multiple tools and applications to exploit the information in the warehouse in a meaningful and consistent way. For example, given a fact in the database, metadata may provide its data lineage information, describing the source of the fact as well as related information. Metadata often becomes essential for proper interpretation of the analysis/reporting results.

Online Analytical Processing (OLAP)

The business reason to set up a warehouse is to enable data analysis. The functionality of the standard database language SQL as a retrieval and data manipulation interface provides some elements of data analysis that are augmented by client query tools or application-specific analysis programs. Traditional data analysis over warehouses consists of pre-defined queries that are used to generate reports. A new class of analysis capabilities, called *Online Analytical Processing (OLAP)* has been advocated as a natural way to view and operate business data stored in warehouses. E. F. Codd (1993) coined and used the term OLAP where he set forth some of the requirements of *ad hoc* data analysis.

OLAP emphasizes a *multidimensional* view of data. A simple way of appreciating the multidimensional view is to think of databases as spreadsheets (*q.v.*). In this view of data, a database consists of a set of *facts*. Each such fact represents one or more numerical *measures* in the context of one or more variables (referred to as *dimensions*). For example, consider a Sales database that records sales history data. Two examples of attributes that may serve as measures are number of units sold and the cost of a sale. These measures are recorded for each Sales entry. Along with these measures, Sales data also consists of dimensions that provides information such as the product for which the sale is recorded, name of the customer, the

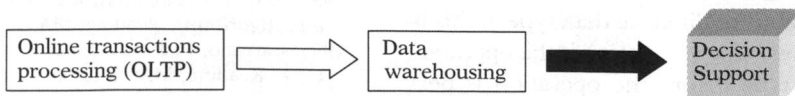

Figure 1. The evolution of the view of a database system.

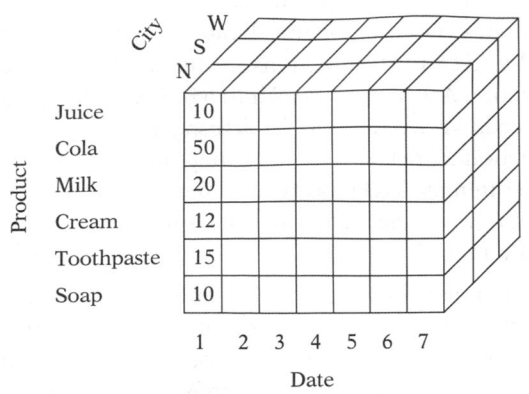

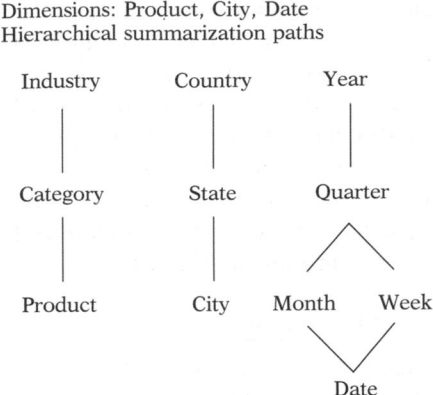

Dimensions: Product, City, Date
Hierarchical summarization paths

Figure 2. An example of a multidimensional view of data.

salesperson who made the sale, the place and time of sale, as well as the identity of the store where the sale was made. The dimensions together form the multidimensional coordinate system often referred to as a *data cube*. The facts may be viewed as a set of sparse points in the cube. The number of dimensions reflects the degree of complexity of the data. Moreover, dimensions often have additional structure. For example, the place of sale dimension can have several *levels* within dimensions. Thus, although the place of sale may be recorded as a city, we can associate with the city the state (or county) as well as the country where the city is located. Thus, we can view the place of sale dimension as a hierarchy consisting of three levels, city, state and country. Note that the levels in a dimension need not form a single hierarchy but may form a lattice. Fig. 2, borrowed from Chaudhuri and Dayal (1997), illustrates some of the key concepts of the multidimensional model. The figure shows a multidimensional database consisting of three dimensions: product, place of sale, and date. Each of these dimensions is organized as a hierarchy or a lattice.

OLAP represents a framework of rich querying and visualization that builds upon the multidimensional view of data. Querying of OLAP data is driven by navigation through the cube using *data-centric* operations that are augmented by powerful visualization primitives. There are several data-centric operations that are popular in the multidimensional view of data. For example, *slicing and dicing* enables selecting a partial cube consisting of a subset of all the dimensions for selected values of other dimensions. Another key operation is *aggregation*. Aggregation makes it possible to sum measures corresponding to all facts in the cube for each distinct value in one or more dimensions. For example, we can aggregate the total sales for each city. A special case of aggregation is roll-up. Roll-up consists of aggregating measures along higher levels of a dimension. Thus, we can roll up Sales data that has already been aggregated by a *roll-up* operation to produce total

sales for each country. We refer the reader to Chaudhuri and Dayal (1997) for a detailed overview of multidimensional operation.

Implementing the multidimensional view of data so that the above data-centric operations can be executed efficiently is a challenging task. Several competing approaches to supporting this have emerged, often loosely referred to as Relational OLAP (ROLAP) and multidimensional OLAP (MOLAP). In ROLAP, a relational backend database is used to store the data. The ROLAP *middleware* translates a query over the multidimensional data as a sequence of one or more SQL queries against the relational databases. In order to be able to deliver fast response time to the user, such systems organize results of selected queries, typically consisting of results of aggregation, so that such pre-aggregated results can be used for answering many queries. Identifying what information needs to be pre-aggregated is of vital importance for efficiency. Microstrategy and Microsoft OLAP Server represent examples of products that use such an implementation of a multidimensional view.

The approach in MOLAP is to represent the data in the storage as a multidimensional array. This approach has the advantage of directly supporting the multidimensional view at the storage layer. Unless the data is extremely sparse, such a storage representation can be efficient and enables easy implementation of cross-row calculations on multidimensional data. However, such an approach does not use efficiently the well-developed infrastructure of relational databases and must implement scalability, security and other services that are expected of most databases. Examples of products that represent a MOLAP implementation are Oracle Express and Essbase.

The primary aim of OLAP systems is to achieve fast response times to aggregate queries that may otherwise require a long time on a traditional relational database. Furthermore, optimization of data layout, managing trade-offs between in-memory versus relational store use, and supporting efficient caching (*see* CACHE MEMORY) between the server and clients are major challenges in OLAP. Ultimately, the OLAP framework relies on the analyst to drive data exploration and identify patterns of interest. *Data mining techniques* represent a step towards automating some of the tedious aspects involved in enumeration and searching for patterns of interest in large data stores.

Bibliography

1993. Codd, E. F., Codd, S. B., and Salley, C. T. "Providing OLAP to User-Analysts: An IT Mandate," http://www.hyperion.com/whitepapers.cfm.
1996. Kimball, R. *The Data Warehouse Toolkit.* New York: John Wiley.
1997. Chaudhuri, S., and Dayal, U. "An Overview of Data Warehousing and OLAP Technology," *ACM SIGMOD Newsletter* (March), 65–74.

Surajit Chaudhuri and Usama Fayyad

DATABASE CONCURRENCY CONTROL

For articles on relates subjects *see* CLIENT–SERVER COMPUTING; CONCURRENT PROGRAMMING; DATA SECURITY; DATABASE MANAGEMENT SYSTEM; MULTITASKING; and TRANSACTION PROCESSING.

A *transaction* is a set of actions, such that either all complete execution successfully or none do (a property known as *atomicity*). For example, if I move money from one bank account to another at an automatic teller machine, the withdrawal from one account and the deposit in the other account are both part of one transaction, guaranteeing that it is never the case that money has been withdrawn from one account but never deposited in the other. The notion of a transaction is central to database systems and is now being adopted in other areas of computer science as well, such as in operating systems (*q.v.*) and in distributed systems (*q.v.*).

Traditionally, transactions are supposed to have "ACID"—Atomicity, Consistency, Isolation, and Durability. *Consistency* simply requires that each transaction be a correct program in that, when applied to a database in a consistent state, it moves the database to another consistent state in which no integrity constraints are violated. *Durability* means that the effects of a transaction persist, once committed, even in the face of failures. *Isolation* permits concurrent executions of multiple transactions to produce consistent results through *serializability*.

In a serializable execution, even though multiple transactions could be executing concurrently, it is possible to define a serial ordering of the transactions that would have exactly the same effect in terms of the values recorded in the database and the results produced by the transactions. For example, suppose transaction A writes a record into a buffer and transaction B reads from the buffer: irrespective of when transaction B reads, it must either find the entire record written by A (B is serialized after A), or must find none of it (B is serialized before A). It must never find part of the record.

A popular way of enforcing serializability is to use *two-phase locking*. When a transaction wishes to access a resource, it places a "lock" on it. When it is done, it releases the lock. In two-phase locking the requirement is that each transaction obtains all the locks it needs before it releases any locks, thus having two phases to its execution: one in which it obtains locks, and another in which it releases locks. If a resource required by a transaction is locked by someone else, the transaction waits until the lock is released.

There are many refinements of the above scheme. For example, a transaction that is reading a data item can "share" a lock on this data item with other transactions that also wish to read the item. An "exclusive" lock is required only if a data item is to be written. Another generalization of a lock is a *semaphore* (*see* CONCURRENT PROGRAMMING).

Consider the following situation: transaction A requests resource P and obtains a lock on it, while transaction B requests resource Q and obtains a lock on it. Now transaction A requests resource Q and transaction B requests resource P. Both transactions have their requests denied on account of the other. Both transactions then wait for their respective requests to be granted. Both wait forever. This sort of situation is called a *deadlock*. Sometimes it is possible to prescribe an order in which transactions request resources, making it impossible for a deadlock to occur. More usually, deadlocks must be detected when they arise, and must be resolved by aborting one of the transactions involved. Usually there is choice of transactions that can be aborted to correct the deadlock. For instance, in the example above, if either transaction is aborted, the other can proceed. Which transaction to choose is an engineering decision that depends on a variety of factors such as how time-critical the transactions are and how much work they have done prior to deadlock. If transactions usually do not have to wait very long for a resource, rather than detecting deadlock, a simple "time-out" mechanism may be used. In general, however, a "wait-for" graph is constructed with a node corresponding to each transaction and an edge from node A to node B if and only if transaction A is waiting for a resource currently locked by transaction B. A deadlock occurs whenever this "wait-for" graph develops a cycle. The deadlock is resolved by deleting the transaction corresponding to one of the nodes in the cycle.

Thus far we have used the term "resource" or "data item" freely without specifying exactly what it is, and indeed exactly what it is can depend on the particular system. We could be referring to a "large" resource like an entire relation in a relational database (*q.v.*), or a buffer in memory. Or we could be referring to a "small" resource such as an individual item of data. The larger the granularity used, the greater the loss of concurrency due to transactions being locked out. On the other hand, the smaller the granularity, the greater the overhead (both in terms of storage and in terms of effort) to store, obtain, and release locks. An appropriate tradeoff is required. Some systems permit the granularity of the lock to be adjusted dynamically, adapting to current system conditions and the access pattern of a transaction. Weaker notions than serializability have been proposed to insure correctness for concurrency control, with a view to increasing concurrency, especially in applications where transactions can be of long duration.

Atomicity and durability are provided by means of a *recovery* system in a transaction manager, which works in close concert with the concurrency control system. The standard technique is to log updates, before-images (pre-update values), and/or after-images (post-update values). In case of a failure, the effects of completed transactions are restored by *redoing* appropriate actions from the log, and the effects of incomplete transactions are removed by *undoing* appropriate actions from the log. The specific actions depend on the type of failure, and the recovery algorithms selected. Key principles are that a transaction is considered committed when a special commit record for the transaction is recorded to disk, and this record is logged after all updates due to this transaction have been logged. Thus, the official state of the database is recorded in the log, with the actual data pages merely reflecting a convenient means of data access.

Bibliography

1987. Bernstein, P. A., Hadzilacos, V., and Goodman, N. *Concurrency Control and Recovery in Database Systems*. Reading, MA: Addison-Wesley.
1993. Gray, J., and Reuter, A. *Transaction Processing: Concepts and Techniques*. San Francisco: Morgan Kaufmann.

H. V. Jagadish

DATABASE MANAGEMENT SYSTEM (DBMS)

For articles on related subjects *see* DATABASE CONCURRENCY CONTROL; DATA MODELS; DEDUCTIVE DATABASE; MANAGEMENT INFORMATION SYSTEMS; OBJECT-ORIENTED ANALYSIS AND DESIGN; RECORD; and RELATIONAL DATABASE.

Database

A *database* is a collection of interrelated data of different types. The term conveys much more than the older term *file* (*q.v.*). Unfortunately, "database" is still all too frequently used when all that is implied is a conventional file. The difference between a database and a file, in terms used prior to the advent of data processing, is analogous to the difference between a thoroughly cross-referenced set of files in cabinets in a library or an office and a single file in one cabinet which is not cross-referenced with any other file. The important difference between a computerized database and a thoroughly cross-referenced set of manual files is that the database must be stored on a direct access storage device in order for the computer's central processing unit (CPU) to be able to use the cross-references.

An important feature of a good database is that unnecessary redundancy of stored data is avoided along with the consistency problems that are inevitably associated with such redundancy. The term *cross-reference* is not normally used when talking about a database. The two terms in common use are *relationship* and *constraint*. In the last analysis, these two terms are not far apart.

There are different ways of talking about databases, and consequently different approaches and different sets of terminology. The most widely used approach is called *relational*, and a more recent one is referred to as *object-oriented database management*. Furthermore, some of the ideas which stem from the object-oriented approach have been included in relational systems, giving rise to the term *object–relational databases*.

Tables, Columns, and Constraints

A conventional file, definable in Cobol since the early 1960s, is regarded as a collection of records of the same or possibly different types. In the relational approach, a file is referred to as a *table* containing *columns* and *tuples* (rows). A row in a table is essentially the same as a *record* (*q.v.*) in a file. A column in a table is what in Cobol is called an item (or, more correctly, an *elementary item*).

CONSTRAINTS

The difference between the database and Cobol approach comes in the use of *constraints* in a database. There are different kinds of constraints in the relational approach, but first it is important to explain their role. Data values which are to be stored in computerized databases (specifically in the columns of certain tables in a database) are often subjected to a validation condition. For example, the condition might be expressed as a range of values within which a tentative data value must lie in order to be accepted as correct at the time it is stored in the database. In relational terms, such a condition is called a *constraint*. Two typical kinds of constraint will be described.

Uniqueness Constraints. The simplest kind of constraint is that a value which is stored in a column of a table must be different from the values already stored in the same column on other rows in the same table. This is called a *uniqueness constraint*. While it is quite common to apply a uniqueness constraint to a single column in a table, it is also possible to express such constraints as a required relationship between or among two or more columns in the same table. The term *key* is sometimes used to convey the concept similar to that associated with "uniqueness constraint." However, that term traditionally conveys the idea of some kind of mechanism being maintained and used to make it quicker to access the rows in a long table (*see* ACCESS METHODS). The term "uniqueness constraint" does not imply the provision of any kind of mechanism for this purpose, and *key* has a specifically different meaning when used in conjunction with a relational database (*q.v.*).

Definition of a uniqueness constraint means that a check is automatically carried out by a *database management system* to ensure that the value being inserted in that column is not already to be found on an existing row of the same table. Examples of columns that would typically be the subject of a uniqueness constraint are employee number, social security number, supplier number, purchase order number, and pay period number.

Referential constraints. The other important kind of constraint is called a *referential constraint*. To illustrate this concept, consider Tables 1 and 2.

In Table 1, the column headed "Supplier number" and in Table 2, the column headed "Purchase order number" should each be the subject of a uniqueness constraint. In fact it is a fundamental rule in a relational database that each table should have at least one uniqueness constraint and it is possible for a table to have two or more.

Table 1. Supplier table.

Supplier number	Supplier name	Supplier address	Phone
43	Smith	23 South Street Walton	234567
32	Jones	12 High Street Weybridge	678912
12	Brown	17 First Street London	1234566
13	Black	23 West Street Putney	245456

Table 2. Purchase order table.

Purchase order number	Date	Supplier number
74321	990406	12
74322	990406	32
74323	990408	13
74324	990408	12
74325	990410	32
74326	990411	32

The concept of a referential constraint can be illustrated using the column in the Purchase order table which is headed "Supplier number." Expressed in narrative terms, the referential constraint would read: *The value stored in the Supplier Number column of the Purchase Order Table must match a value which has already been stored in the Supplier Number column of the Supplier Table.* As a business rule, the constraint would be expressed more simply as: *When the purchasing department sends a purchase order to a supplier, the supplier must already be known.*

From Tables 1 and 2, it can be seen that Supplier Numbers 32, 12 and 13 have been sent, respectively, 3, 2 and 1 purchase orders. However, Supplier Number 43 has not been sent a purchase order. The referential constraint considered here does not require a supplier to have been sent a purchase order. It would be possible to express this condition as a separate constraint additional to the one on the Supplier Number in the Purchase Order table.

The effect of expressing the constraint on the Supplier Number in the Purchase Order table is that the database management system then carries out a check each time a new row is added to the Purchase Order table. (The check on one table "refers" to another table, hence the name "referential constraint.") If the check fails, then typically the table is not updated. The connection between referential constraints and uniqueness constraints is that a referential constraint refers to a column in another table which is the subject of a uniqueness constraint.

The Database Language SQL

SQL is an international standard language used for defining the structure of a relational database in terms of tables, columns, and various kinds of constraints. SQL originally meant "structured query language," but since SQL is also used for many other purposes, the decoded form of the acronym is no longer accurate. The latest version of the ISO SQL standard [9075: 1992] contains the definition of concrete language syntax and associated semantics which can be used for many purposes associated with database management.

It provides facilities for the definition of a wide spectrum of constraints far in excess of those illustrated in this article.

The importance of being able to define constraints in this way is as follows. A business rule such as the example given in this article has to be handled in a computerized system in some way or another. One alternative which has been and still is widely used is to represent the rule as an algorithmic procedure in some general-purpose programming language. The modern database-oriented approach is to represent the rule declaratively using a specialized database language such as SQL. The arguments in favor of this approach are (1) it is usually quicker and hence cheaper to represent the rule declaratively and then let a database management system enforce the rule; and (2) there may be several programs which update any particular table in a database. With the procedural approach, the procedure embodying the business rule has to be either repeated or possibly invoked each time; (3) since business rules change over time, it is usually easier to modify a declarative expression than to modify procedural code.

DATABASE MANAGEMENT SYSTEM

The handling of the various kinds of constraints is the capability which distinguishes a database from a file. In order to build a database, it is the normal practice to use a piece of generalized software called a *database management system* (DBMS). A DBMS which is based on the SQL database language requires the database structure to be defined in terms of tables of columns and rows, and constraints. A typical commercial database might comprise some 50 to 100 tables each having up to 15 columns and with one or two referential constraints on most of the tables. The resulting definition is often referred to as a *schema* or *database schema*. This schema is referred to when defining the processes to be performed on the data. Many of the processes are fairly simple and do not need to refer to all of the tables in the schema. It is possible to restrict the number of tables which a process is permitted to access. The statements that a DBMS uses to perform the processes on the data in the tables are called *data manipulation statements* and are typically specified as part of a database language.

Data Structure Diagrams

Diagrammatic techniques are widely used among analysts and designers to present an overall picture of the major data concepts and how they are interrelated. It is important to distinguish in this context between analysis and design. *Data analysis* is an activity carried out to discover the major data concepts in a given busi-

Table 3. Cross-references between suppliers and purchase orders.

Purchase order	Smith	Jones	Brown	Black
21			×	
22		×		
23				×
24			×	
25		×		
26		×		

ness area and how one or more subject experts in that business area consider these concepts to be interrelated. One of the major techniques used as a means of communication between analyst and subject expert is *data structure diagramming*.

During analysis, each major data concept is often referred to as an *entity type*. For example, one would refer to the entity type "Supplier" and the entity type "Purchase Order." During the dialog between analyst and subject area expert, it might be agreed that there is a *relationship* between these two entity types. The precise nature of the relationship could be analyzed by looking at some specific suppliers and specific purchase orders and preparing a cross-reference table, such as Table 3.

Note that in Table 3 there is one cross in each row. This indicates that each purchase order is related to one supplier. No purchase order has been sent to Smith; Black has one; Brown has two; and Jones has three. Thus each column contains zero, one, two or three crosses, which is evidence that there may be zero, one or more purchase orders for each supplier. This is an example of the most common kind of relationship permissible between two entity types, namely, one-to-many, where the word "many" should be taken as meaning "zero, one or more."

One could represent the one-to-many relationship of Table 3 as in Fig. 1. The relationship between the two entity types is not symmetric and the some kind of indication is needed to depict this asymmetry. While a rectangle is commonly used to represent an entity type, there is wide variation in practice in the number of ways used to represent a relationship between types. There are in fact 10 different kinds of relationship that are possible between any two types. Several approaches to data analysis and their associated diagramming techniques also allow for the expression of relationships between entities of the same entity type and among three or more different types. Data structure diagrams provide a more effective way of communicating with subject area experts and even with users than a concrete language syntax such as that provided in the language SQL.

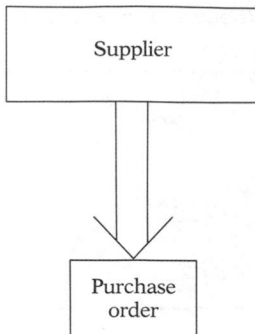

Figure 1. Data structure diagram showing two entity types and the relationship between them. The double stem arrow indicates a one-to-many relationship: a particular supplier may have been sent several purchase orders.

Data Analysis and Database Design

There is a close tie between data analysis and database design. Some experts choose not to recognize the two as separate activities, but others prefer a distinctly different way of modeling data for analysis from that used for design. For example, some analysis techniques permit relationships among three or more entity types, but this capability is not allowed in database languages such as SQL. The ISO Reference Model of Data Management [IS 10032: 1993] refers to a *data modeling facility* used to produce an *application data model*. It has been common practice to refer to either italicized term as a *data model* (*q.v.*). When the data model used for analysis is different from that used for design, it is necessary at some point to convert the data model from one form to the other.

Bibliography

1994. Date, C. J. *An Introduction to Database Systems*, 6th Ed. Reading, MA: Addison-Wesley.
1998. Darwen, H., and Date, C. J. *Foundations for Object/Relational Databases: The Third Manifesto*. Reading, MA: Addison-Wesley.

T. William Olle

DATABASE, RELATIONAL

See RELATIONAL DATABASE.

DATAFLOW

For articles on related subjects *see* COMPUTER ARCHITECTURE; FUNCTIONAL PROGRAMMING; GRAPH THEORY; PARALLEL PROCESSING; PETRI NET; SUPERCOMPUTERS; and VON NEUMANN MACHINE.

PRINCIPLES

Dataflow is a generic term characterizing algorithms or computers whose actions are determined by the availability of the data needed for these actions. Computations that are expressed and executed in dataflow terms are controlled by the arrival of data at operators (called *actors*). This is to be contrasted to *control flow* environments of conventional, so-called von Neumann machines, where the locus of execution is determined by an instruction pointer (or *program counter*—*q.v.*) that identifies the operation to be performed next. Dataflow algorithms can be represented as directed graphs in which the *arcs* are data paths and the *nodes* are operations to be performed on the data tokens arriving on the incoming arcs. The graph shown in Fig. 1 is a dataflow procedure. Multiple paths through such a graph represent parts of a computation that can be executed in parallel.

The names within the nodes of the graph indicate the operation to be performed. The availability of the input tokens and the ability of the output arc(s) to receive data (which will be the case when the previous output has already been used as an input to another node) are the only conditions that must be satisfied for any operation to execute. The act of performing the operation is called *firing* the node and results in the consumption of the input tokens and production of output tokens.

The node labeled "OP1" in Fig. 1 has two input arcs associated with it, nodes "OP2" and "OP4" have one input arc, and node "OP3" has three input arcs. If tokens arrive on both of OP1's input arcs and its output arc is empty, then the input tokens will be consumed, the transformation OP1 will be performed on the data, and an output token will be produced. If a token had arrived on the input arc to OP2 coincidentally with the arrival of input tokens to OP1, and OP2's output arcs were empty, then both nodes OP1 and OP2 could fire simultaneously.

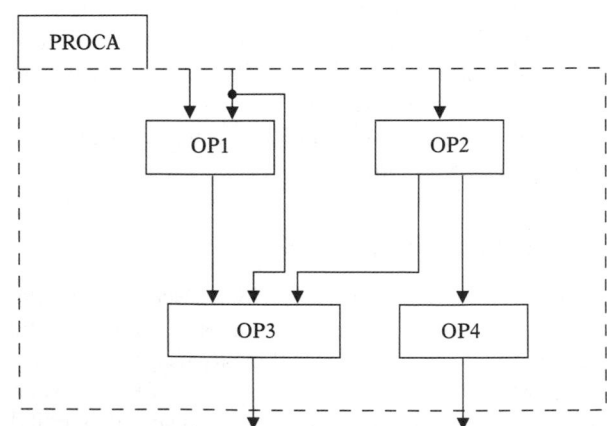

Figure 1. Sample dataflow program and graph.

Node OP4 must wait only until OP2 has finished executing in order to fire, whereas node OP3 must wait for both OP1 and OP2 to complete. Thus, the synchronization of asynchronous activities is accommodated very naturally in a dataflow graph. The graph of Fig. 1 is surrounded by a dashed line (called the *procedure boundary*) and given a name, PROCA, so that it may be used in other dataflow programs. Fig. 2 shows a conventional flowchart for a sequential programming language and a corresponding dataflow program for determining the roots of a quadratic equation. Note that the flowchart introduces more sequencing than the algorithm itself requires.

Although dataflow is a relatively new approach to computer systems organization, dataflow-related modeling techniques have been in use for quite some time (Karp and Miller, 1969). One of the first formal methods using a dataflow-like technique is PERT/CPM (project evaluation and review technique/critical path method) developed in the 1950s for project planning and control. Another major use of a dataflow-like technique is in the simulation language GPSS V (*see* SIMULATION), developed for modeling discrete stochastic systems. The designers of logic circuits and computer hardware have used dataflow-related techniques in describing, analyzing, and testing circuits in which data items are in the form of electrical signals. Dataflow, in this context, bears a strong resemblance to Petri nets. Optimizing compilers analyze the flow of data in performing machine independent optimizations. Dataflow-related techniques have also been used in microcode optimization (*see* MICROPROGRAMMING), software specification, and reliability analysis.

There have been several different candidate architectures proposed for executing dataflow programs. The architecture first proposed by Dennis and Misunas (1975) consists of a collection of addressable instruction cells (IC) connected by an arbitration network to a group of operation units (transformational devices) (Fig. 3). The operation units are, in turn, connected by

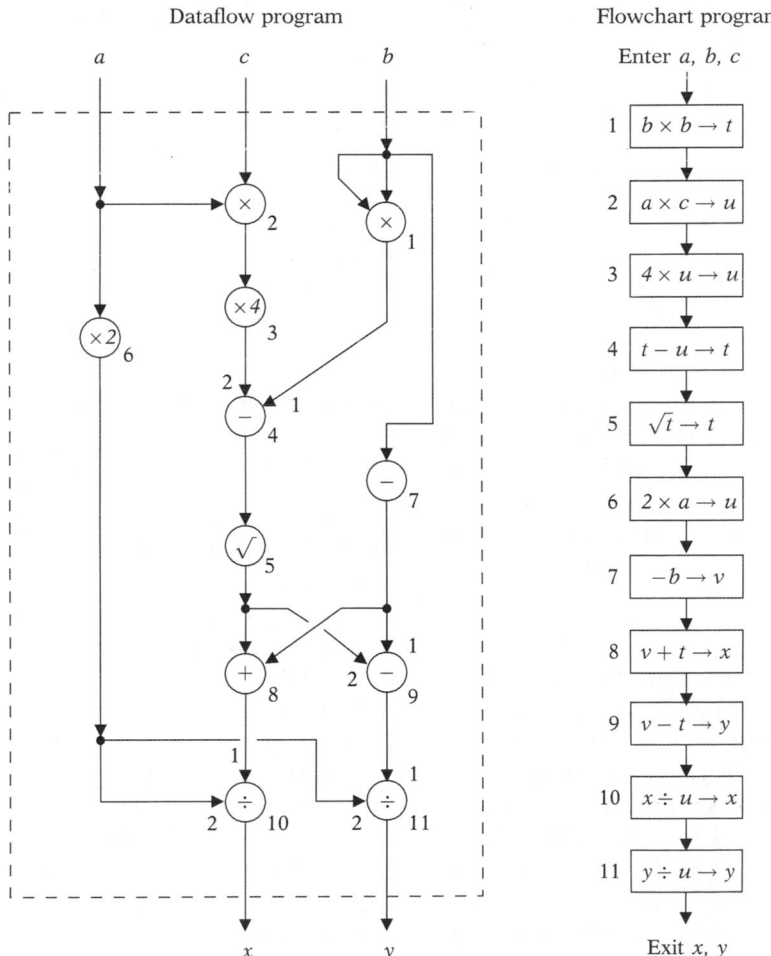

Figure 2. Dataflow version of a sequential program to find the roots of a quadratic equation ($ax^2 + bx + c = 0$) with real roots. The labels on the lower right of the nodes of the dataflow program correspond to the labels on the boxes on the left of the flowchart. The labels 1 and 2 on the incoming arrows to the dataflow nodes indicate the order of the operands for subtraction and division.

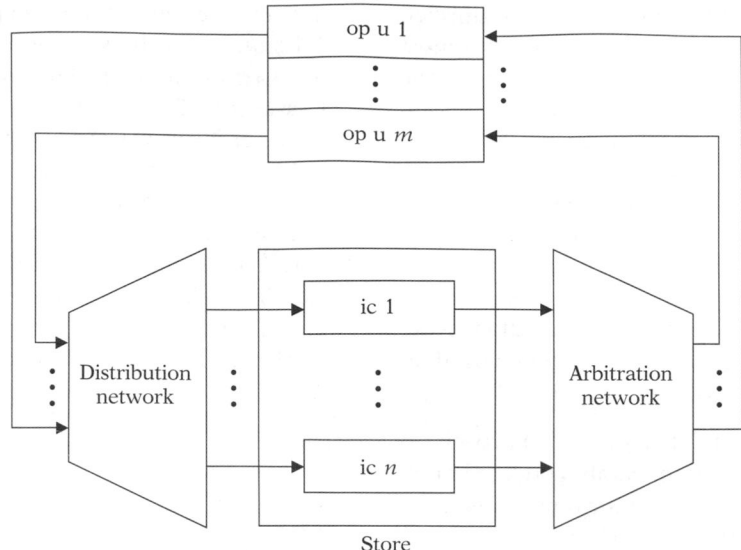

Figure 3. Candidate dataflow architecture (ic = instruction cell; op u = operation unit).

a distribution network back to the instruction cells. The instruction cells correspond to nodes on the graph, while operation units are merely execution units. An enabled instruction cell transmits an *instruction packet* to an operation unit via the arbitration network. The arbitration network processes instruction packets on a round robin basis. The result of a node firing is a *data packet*, which is sent to the destination instruction cells, using the distribution network. A variation of Dennis's architecture was implemented by Texas Instruments, Inc., in their Distributed Data Processor (DDP). Each operation unit in the DDP has an arithmetic-logic unit (*q.v.*) and a memory for instruction cells. The operation units are called *nodes* and are connected by a shift register interconnection network. Both the operation units and instruction cells are addressable. The primitive operations correspond to the operations used in an intermediate language for compiling Fortran for TI's ASC computer. A front-end processor (*q.v.*) accepts Fortran programs represented as dataflow graphs, identifies subgraphs having no data dependencies in the graphs, and distributes the subgraphs to various nodes of the DDP execution.

Burroughs Corporation's 1977 Data Driven Machine (DDM1) executed dataflow programs using a tree structure for organizing the atomic units and a switch at each node of the tree to distribute its output. Each atomic unit consisted of a processor with a number of microprogrammed functional units for manipulating data and managing storage. Like TI's DDP, this dataflow architecture also required a front-end processor (*q.v.*) for identifying and distributing subnets in dataflow graphs.

Toulouse's LAU (for Langage à Assignation Unique) system (1979) also implemented basic dataflow. The LAU system consists of a collection of processors, a central memory, and a control unit to detect all executable instructions in memory. Architectures for basic dataflow using conventional processors have also been proposed.

Later work included the Manchester tagged-token dataflow architecture in 1981 (Gurd *et al.*, 1984). "Tagged-token" denotes a design that lets multiple iterations of a loop execute in parallel, labeling the data with tags to distinguish the values produced by different iterations, thus ensuring that each value could be passed to its proper destination operator. Tagged-token systems were also built at MIT (Arvind and Culler, 1986).

Recent Developments

The emergence of portable digital wireless communication and multimedia (*q.v.*) has increased the demand for high performance special purpose chips that consume low energy. Parallel digital signal processors and stream data processors have been developed using dataflow principles. A single chip containing 48 simple processors has been built (Srini *et al.*, 1998). A field programmable interconnection of processors using dataflow principles has also been developed for use in video, graphics, image processing, and wideband digital communication applications. Motion estimation, discrete cosine transform (DCT), inverse DCT, and related video compression and decompression algorithms have been efficiently executed by the ICC chip set developed by Array Microsystems (1993). The ICC uses a dataflow architecture with a 96-bit wide global bus, and all of its subprocessors can operate in parallel.

The conventional control-flow microprocessors like the Sun Sparc and Intel Pentium have elements of dataflow processing in the functional units within the chip, which schedule multiple operations in parallel as their operands become available (*see* INSTRUCTION-LEVEL PARALLELISM). These techniques contribute significantly to the high performance of current microprocessors. There are also experimental systems that combine dataflow and von Neumann architectures on a larger scale for parallel computation (Bic *et al.*, 1995).

Bibliography

1969. Karp, R. M., and Miller, R. E. "Parallel Program Schemata," *J. Comp. Syst. Sci.*, **3**, *2* (May), 147–195.
1975. Dennis, J. B., and Misunas, D. P. "A Preliminary Architecture for a Basic Dataflow Processor," *Proceedings 2nd Symposium on Computer Architecture*, New York, 126–132.
1984. Gurd, J. R., Watson, I., Kirkham, C. C., and Glauert, J. R. W. "The Dataflow Approach," in *Distributed Computing* (eds. F. B. Chambers, D. A. Duce, and G. P. Jones), 1–53. New York: Academic Press.
1986. Arvind and Culler, D. E. "Dataflow Architectures," *Annual Review of Computer Science*, **1**, 225–253.
1986. Srini, V. P. "An Architectural Comparison of Dataflow Systems," *Computer*, **19**, *3* (March), 68–88.
1995. Bic, L., Gaudiot, J.-L., and Gao, G. R. *Advanced Topics in Dataflow Computing and Multithreading.* Los Alamitos, CA: Computer Society Press.
1998. Srini, V. P., Sutton, R. A., and Rabaey, J. M., "A Multiprocessor DSP System Using PADDI-2," *Proceedings of the 35th Design Automation Conference*, 62–65. New York: ACM Press.

Bruce D. Shriver, Steven P. Landry, and Vason P. Srini

LANGUAGES

A *dataflow language* is a functional programming language in which a variable may be assigned a value once and only once throughout a program. There are programming languages, such as Prolog, that also use single assignment to a variable, but are not dataflow languages. If the same variable name is used on the left side of an assignment statement in more than one place in a dataflow language program, the second and other appearances of the variable are treated as new variables. Many of the constructs found in block-structured languages, such as Pascal (*q.v.*) and C (*q.v.*), are usually provided in a dataflow language also. Data structures, such as lists, records, and arrays, are also supported along with operations on them, although the single assignment rule complicates modifications of an element of a list or an array. Copying entire lists or arrays when only a single element needs to be modified is expensive. Parallel data structuring mechanisms have been devised to avoid the copying.

Since the execution of functions is free of side effects (*q.v.*) in a dataflow language, the detection of parallelism is not hard (when functions can have side effects on one another's parameters, different orders of execution can produce different results, thereby making parallel execution unsafe). In fact, dataflow languages and logic programming languages such as Prolog are two important classes of languages where implicit parallelism can be detected at compile time by doing a data dependency analysis and a global flow analysis.

Dataflow languages can be used where either parallelism or communication between asynchronous processes must be accommodated. The firing semantics associated with a node and the graphical nature of dataflow enhance the overall understanding and control of these complex activities. This is to be contrasted with the traditional textual language solutions to these problems, which often increase the overall complexity of the algorithms involved.

Almost every research group that developed a dataflow architecture also invented a dataflow language for that architecture. One of the early languages that made an impact is VAL (Value-oriented Algorithmic Language) (McGraw, 1982). The code generated by VAL was targeted for MIT's static dataflow architectures. One of the serious limitations of VAL was the lack of I/O and prohibition of recursive functions. Several features of VAL were used in the development of Sisal (Streams and Iteration in a Single-Assignment Language) (Feo *et al.*, 1990). Compilers for Sisal have been developed for a few architectures, including the Manchester dataflow machine, and Sisal has been in use at Manchester since the mid-1980s.

The language Id (Irvine Dataflow language), developed by Arvind and others (Arvind and Gostelow, 1982) to support the dynamic creation of instances of functions, was a block-structured expression-oriented dataflow language. The basic expressions were blocks, conditionals, loops, and procedure applications. An "unravelling" interpreter was devised for Id that automatically unfolded loops constrained only by data dependencies (so that stages of multiple iterations could execute in parallel as their data became available). It also used a parallel data structuring mechanism called the I-structure to avoid structure copying when elements were updated. Id has been followed by Id Nouveau and Id-90 (Nikhil, 1990).

Bibliography

1982. Arvind, and Gostelow, K. P. "The U-Interpreter," *Computer*, **15**, *2* (February), 42–50.
1982. McGraw, J. R. "The VAL Language: Description and Analysis," *ACM Trans. On Programming Languages and Systems*, **4**, *1* (January), 44–82.
1990. Feo, J. T., Cann, D., and Oldehoeft, R. "A Report on the SISAL Language Project," *Journal of Parallel and Distributed Computing*, **10**, *4* (December), 349–366.
1990. Nikhil, R. S. *Id 90 reference manual.* CSG Memo 284-1, MIT Laboratory for Computer Science, Cambridge, MA, September.

Vason P. Srini

DEBUGGING

For articles on related subjects see BUG; DIAGNOSTIC; DUMP; ERRORS; FLOWCHART; PROCEDURE-ORIENTED LANGUAGES; PROGRAMMING; PROGRAM; PROGRAMMING SUPPORT ENVIRONMENTS; and TRACE.

In a 1966 article in *Scientific American*, the late English computer scientist, Christopher Strachey (*q.v.*), wrote:

> Although programming techniques have improved immensely since the early days, the process of finding and correcting errors in programming—known graphically if inelegantly as "debugging"—still remains a most difficult, confused and unsatisfactory operation. The chief impact of this state of affairs is psychological. Although we are happy to pay lip service to the adage that to err is human, most of us like to make a small private reservation about our own performance on special occasions when we really try. It is somewhat deflating to be shown publicly and incontrovertibly by a machine that even when we do try, we in fact make just as many mistakes as other people. If your pride cannot recover from this blow, you will never make a programmer.

Though over three decades have now elapsed since those lines were written, they still capture the essence and mystique of *debugging*.

Types of Errors

Mistakes (*bugs*) find their way into a computer program for many reasons, but they may generally be classified as follows:

1. An otherwise logically correct program contains one or more isolated statements or instructions that are syntactically (i.e. grammatically) incorrect in the programming language being used.

2. A potentially correct algorithm may be coded in a logically incorrect way.

3. The algorithm implemented may function correctly for some but not all data values, or, more insidiously, it may fail for just some few combinations of input values.

These three types of error create debugging problems of increasing severity and typically require substantially different approaches to debugging.

Syntactic Errors

The more flexible the syntax of a programming language, the easier it is to make syntactic errors.

Thus, the simplicity and rigidity of machine language makes syntactic errors (such as illegal operation codes) relatively rare. From assembly language up through high-level language, however, it becomes increasingly easy to write a statement that is not grammatically acceptable to the language processor. Whether such statements occur because of typographical errors, imperfect understanding of language syntax, or just plain lack of concentration, such statements will prove to be only a minor annoyance, since they will produce diagnostic messages (*diagnostics*) when the errant program is assembled, compiled, or interpreted.

Language processors (*q.v.*) vary greatly in the quality of their diagnostics. For example, consider the spectrum of possible responses to the statement:

```
C=4A
```

The message SYNTAX ERROR tells us nothing more than that the processor doesn't like it. The message ERROR 17 is annoying but at least raises the hope that if we look up ERROR 17 in some reference manual, we'll get to the root of the difficulty. Finally, the message IMPLIED MULTIPLICATION NOT ALLOWED attempts to be helpful, especially if given in conjunction with some such printout as

```
C=4A
   ^
```

which pinpoints the precise location of the alleged error. Note, however, that it makes the assumption that the programmer forgot to place a multiplication operator between the 4 and the *A* when, in fact, the error may have been the mistaken notion (for most computer languages) that 4*A* is a legal identifier (*q.v.*).

The type of error cited above is generally called a *fatal error* because it prevents the compiler from generating the object program needed for execution. Other situations may generate only a warning message that potentially erroneous results might be obtained; it would then be up to the programmer's judgment as to whether the offending construction really need be modified. An example is the Fortran statement

```
IF (A .EQ. 4.3567) K = K + 1,
```

which would cause many compilers to respond with:

```
The test for equality between real numbers
may not be meaningful.
```

That is, one cannot expect a computed value, A in the above, to be exactly equivalent to some other comparison value right down to the last bit of precision.

Designers of language translators intended for extensive student use try hard to make their diagnostics "friendly." However well they succeed, it is usually the case that students become unduly elated upon receipt of NO DIAGNOSTICS when, in fact, such a message is more likely to denote the real beginning of the debugging process rather than its conclusion.

Logical Errors

Logical errors are sometimes called *semantic errors* because they cause the program to have a meaning that, though syntactically valid, is other than what is needed for consistency with the algorithm being implemented. No translator will object to $C = A + B$ even if $C = A - B$ is what is needed, but such an error is virtually certain to cause incorrect results. Of course, most logical errors are more subtle. Typical errors cause programmed loops to run one time too few, one time too many, indefinitely ("infinite" loops), or not at all; cause misallocation of memory relative to actual space needed; cause input data to be read with improper formats; or cause weird program behavior in any number of ways. Those errors that cause program termination with *run-time diagnostics* are easier to isolate than those that lead to infinite loops or to "normal" termination with incorrect answers. An example would be the very explicit message:

```
The following input record does not conform
to the format specified at line 1023
```

(followed by a printout of the offending record), but not all run-time diagnostics can be so precise.

When program execution does not lead to an easily localized error, the programmer has recourse to several debugging tools. One of the more efficient is to embed some temporary print statements at strategic places in the program flow in order to monitor the progress of intermediate results, the objective being to pinpoint the exact transition from successful progress to the point where the logic goes awry. (The information printed comprises what is sometimes called a *snapshot dump*, since, after capturing a record of conditions at a particular checkpoint, the computation continues. Of course, a prudent programmer would have had the foresight to include several such checkpoints in the program in anticipation of less than perfect initial operation, but it is almost inevitable that additional narrowing of focus will be needed. Interpretive languages can be easier vehicles for debugging in this sense, since the value of any desired variable can be solicited at the point of failure without prior inclusion of snapshot commands; this is more difficult with a compiler, since, by execution time, knowledge of the mapping between symbolic variable names and absolute memory cells has usually been lost.) At two other extremes, the programmer may ask for extensive printout only at (normal or abnormal) program termination—a so-called *post-mortem dump*—

or (a last resort because of its gross inefficiency) a printout of key registers or variables after every statement (or perhaps every *n*th statement) or instruction executed; i.e. a *trace* of program flow. Narrowing the source of the error to a small section of code by one of these means or another is the necessary prelude to final identification of the error being pursued.

Algorithmic Error

When all known syntactic and semantic errors have been removed from a program, there is still a question as to whether the implemented algorithm actually solves the desired problem for all legal combinations of input values. Because so few programs are genuinely new in the sense of testing untried algorithms, this type of error is rather rare among professionals but not among students, who are prone to encode, even if "correctly," some rather bizarre "algorithms." In either case, such algorithmic error can be very difficult to detect. If a program has been running satisfactorily for a sustained period, its users may place undue confidence in its output to the point where they would not detect answers that are nearly, but not quite, correct. Extensively tested programs that compute reliable results for a wide range of input values and that carefully check and reject illegal input are said to be *robust*. Programs that lack robustness are far more likely to be deficient because of logical errors (usually unchecked pathways or unverified input) rather than algorithmic error.

A program that gives correct answers for some or even many input cases may nonetheless contain huge stretches of code that have never been executed. A significant component of programming talent is the ability to devise a sufficiently comprehensive set of test cases that, at a minimum, exercise all program branches not only serially but also in such sequential combinations as to give reasonable assurance that the program will indeed be robust.

Symbolic Debuggers

Most modern assemblers and compilers are now supported by a software tool known as a *symbolic debugger*. The word "debugger," however, connotes an intelligence that does not exist. Such a debugger does not and almost certainly could not automate the debugging process. A symbolic debugger is no more than an information gatherer, one that helps the user gather evidence much more easily than having to splice gratuitous output statements into source code.

The fact that a debugger is "symbolic," however, is very valuable. When an executing program halts prematurely or emits wrong answers, it is object code that is doing so, and, at this stage, the symbolic content of the source code from which the object code was produced is not ordinarily available. What, pray tell, does it mean to find that your program has stopped at hexadecimal location 7FA3C with hexadecimal D76EA92B in general register number 7? But if, when we assemble or compile the source code we tell the language system being used that we intend to debug with a symbolic debugger, a mapping of symbols to numeric locations will be created and made available in the event that something bad happens at run time. If and when it does, we may then ask to see, for example, the current value of some variable such as *Radius* or *Volume* by those very names rather than their memory cell locations.

A second prime attribute of a symbolic debugger is that it allows us to run a program incrementally, a step at a time, rather than allowing execution to proceed as far as it can without aborting. One may take either small or large steps, whichever one chooses, by moving either from statement to statement or from one *checkpoint* to another, pausing as needed to examine key variables or machine registers.

Most debuggers support three kinds of checkpoint called, respectively, *breakpoints*, *tracepoints*, and *watchpoints*. The first two of these are very similar, differing only as to whether the debugger stops and awaits your further command or continues on to the next checkpoint. It will stop at a breakpoint, but merely pause (to output debug information) at a tracepoint. But a watchpoint, in some sense, is a much more clever idea. Suppose, for example, that our source program contains an identifier called *feet* whose initial value of 5,280 is not supposed to change during execution of the program. But, alas, it does. And worse, you have no idea as to what errant portion of your program is changing this value or when during execution it is being altered. What you may do is to tell the symbolic debugger that *feet* is a watchword. In essence, you are saying to it "Please keep your eye on *feet* and the instant that it changes value, stop and give me control." Simulation of such a powerful debugging technique would be very difficult without use of a commercial debugger and is one of the reasons why, to remain competitive, virtually all new language processors that run on personal computers are marketed with an associated symbolic debugger.

As powerful graphical capabilities have become common in computers, symbolic debuggers now sometimes include the ability to display complex program structures graphically. Experimental debuggers augment such displays with animation of program execution, and even with acoustic "animation" to help the programmer observe patterns of program activity while debugging.

Correction of Errors

The correction of a serious algorithmic error might necessitate the rewriting of all or a substantial portion of a program, using essentially the same tools used to create it in the first place, but the correction of a syntactic or simple logical error is usually a trivial mechanical operation on a modern time-shared computer or even on a personal microcomputer. The principal tool is either a general text editor running under control of the computer's operating system or, in some cases, a special-purpose editor embedded in a specific language processor such as those that are typically part of Lisp, APL, Visual Basic and C++ (*q.v.*) implementations. The programmer directs the editor to focus attention on the offending statement, which is located either by citing its line number, if known, or by asking for automatic search for the first statement that contains a particular character string, for example, *procedure*. After the statement that qualifies is located and displayed on the terminal by the editor, a decision is made to replace it, delete it, modify only a part of it, or add one or more new statements ahead of or after it. A still more powerful feature commonly provided is to be able to replace all occurrences of a given character string with a substitute string anywhere in the program or in specifically delineated parts of a program; e.g. changing all occurrences of INTERGER to INTEGER can get a poor speller out of a bind pretty quickly, especially if the errant word occurs 57 times.

When all corrections are made, the programmer typically asks the operating system to save the updated text segment and to retranslate this source element into a machine language object element using a particular language processor. The debugging cycle then continues iteratively until the program is deemed to be "correct." Unfortunately, saying so doesn't make it so, and the program may still need considerable exercise before it becomes robust in the sense discussed earlier.

Prevention of Errors

Clearly, better than finding and fixing errors would be to inhibit their introduction in the first place. In this sense, the subject of debugging is closely related to that of program design, documentation, and maintenance. Even when a program is deemed correct, it is seldom "finished"; i.e. it is almost inevitable that its sponsor will ultimately ask that it be modified. Often, the request will come well after the original programmer is still available. Experience has indicated that if certain good practices are followed during design and implementation, errors will be minimized to a degree well worth the extra original effort. Some of these are:

1. Program logic should be documented in the form of flowcharts or iteration diagrams.

2. Program variable names should be chosen mnemonically, e.g. RADIUS rather than simply R.

3. The symbolic program code should contain embedded comments that relate back to the flowchart.

4. As far as the structure of the host language permits, the principles of structured programming (*q.v.*) and object-oriented programming (*q.v.*) should be followed during program design.

5. All program input statements should be followed immediately by output statements that "echo" the input onto the output medium so that there can never be any confusion as to just which input case is being processed.

6. All output values should be carefully labeled. Two otherwise correct answers that are confused one with the other might just as well have been incorrect.

Finally, there is a school of adherents to a philosophy that program verification (*q.v.*) will allow programs to be "proved" correct to the point where bugs are never allowed to survive to the point where machine debugging in the sense discussed here is needed at all. While there should be universal hope that such techniques succeed, the need for the more mundane advice cited in this article is likely to exist for some time to come.

Bibliography

1978. Van Tassel, D. *Program Style, Design, Efficiency, Debugging, and Testing.* Upper Saddle River, NJ: Prentice Hall.
1996. Rosenberg, J. B. *How Debuggers Work: Algorithms, Data Structure and Architecture.* New York: John Wiley.
1999. Kernighan, B. W., and Pike, R. *The Practice of Programming.* Reading, MA: Addison-Wesley.

Edwin D. Reilly

DEC

See DIGITAL EQUIPMENT CORPORATION.

DECLARATION

For articles on related subjects *see* EXECUTABLE STATEMENT; PROCEDURE-ORIENTED LANGUAGES; PROGRAMMING LANGUAGES; and STATEMENT.

A *declaration* (*declarative statement*) is a high-level programming language statement that provides descriptive information (contrasted with an *imperative*, or *executable*, *statement*, which specifies explicit processing operations).

Besides specifying the actual computations, decision rules, and input–output operations (*q.v.*) involved in the implementation of a particular algorithm, a high-level language program also must provide the compiler (*q.v.*) with descriptive information that allows it to perform a variety of organizational tasks directly connected with the production of an executable object program. For example, the description of a variable (its name, together with the type of data to be stored in it) enables the compiler to allocate the proper amount of storage, associate its location with the variable's name, and set up any necessary data conversion mechanisms prior to the assignment of a value to that variable. (This description also defines the set of operations that are applicable to the element.) Similarly, the definition and description of a data file makes it possible for the compiler to establish a relationship between references to that file and a particular collection of data transmitted to or from a specific input–output device.

In most languages, this type of information is supplied through a series of special statements, which often are characterized as being *non-executable* (or more properly, *declarative*). Once defined, simple variables, arrays, files, and other items can be used throughout the program simply by alluding to their properties via use of their names.

To illustrate the type of information conveyed by declarations, consider the following Pascal program, which reads a number N and uses it to compute

$$Y = \sum_{X=1}^{N} X(1 + X^{1/2}).$$

N and Y are displayed with appropriate identification.

```
program sumup;
    var I, N : integer;
        X, Y : real;
    begin
        read (N);
        Y := 0.0;
        for I := 1 to N do begin
            X := I;
            Y := Y + X * (1.0 + sqrt (X))
            end;
        writeln('N = ',N,' Y = ',Y)
        end
```

The first statement is a declaration that defines the program's name. The two statements subsumed as part of the `var` declaration direct the compiler to allocate storage for each of two integers and two real values. A subsequent reference to any of the names specified there will be automatically associated with the appropriate storage location.

Seymour V. Pollack

DECLARATIVE LANGUAGE

See FUNCTIONAL PROGRAMMING; LOGIC PROGRAMMING: LANGUAGES; AND SETL.

DEDUCTIVE DATABASE

For articles on related subjects *see* DATABASE MANAGEMENT SYSTEM; LOGIC PROGRAMMING; NONMONOTONIC LOGIC; and RELATIONAL DATABASE.

Deductive Databases

Deductive databases formalize and extend relational databases. A *deductive database* (DDB) consists of a set of facts, a set of rules, and a set of integrity constraints. From the set of rules and the facts it is possible to derive new facts not contained in the original set of facts. The integrity constraints (ICs) describe properties that entries in the database should satisfy.

A DDB is based on mathematical logic. The set of facts is referred to as the *extensional database* (EDB), and consists either of a set of relations (or facts), whose arguments are constants, or a set of positive disjunctions whose arguments are constants, or both; the set of rules is referred to as the *intensional database* (IDB) and is of the form:

$$A_1, \ldots, A_n \leftarrow B_1, \ldots, B_m, not\, B_{m+1}, \ldots, not\, B_{m+l}, \quad (1)$$

where the A_i and the B_j are literals, and *not* is a rule of default for negation (described below). A literal is an atomic formula or the negation of an atomic formula. Atomic formulas evaluate to *true* or *false*. An atomic formula is a k-place predicate whose arguments are constants or variables. A description is provided below of how one reads these rules.

Intensional rules are universally quantified and are an abbreviation of the formula:

$$\forall X_1, \ldots, X_n(A_1 \lor \cdots \lor A_n$$
$$\leftarrow B_1 \land \cdots \land B_m \land \, not\, B_{m+1} \ldots not\, B_{m+l}), \quad (2)$$

where $X_1, \ldots, X_n$ is a list of all variables contained in (2), the symbol $\forall$ denotes the universal quantifier *for all*, $\lor$ denotes *logical or*, $\land$ denotes *logical and*, $\leftarrow$ denotes *logical implication* and is read as *if* in (1). Deductive databases and relational databases typically interpret negation by a rule of default. This is designated in the formulas above by *not*. Thus, in the above formulas, there may be two kinds of negation—logical negation, designated by $\neg$, and negation-by-default, designated by *not*. There are many ways in which one can interpret *not*. Depending upon how it is interpreted, and depending upon the values that one provides for n, m, and l, the semantics and the complexity of answering queries to the database differ. We discuss this below.

ICs are rules of the same kind as the intensional database. ICs are used to describe a database, to maintain the consistency of a database during updates, to permit semantic query optimization based on the meaning of the database, and to provide informative answers to a user when the integrity constraints restrict the search or provide semantic information that may explain why a query failed to find an answer. The extensional database contains the facts or disjunctions of facts that are assumed to be *true* in an application. An example of a disjunctive fact is: *supplier*(abc, hammers) $\lor$ *supplier*(abc, tomatoes), which might mean that the abc corporation supplies *either* hammers, *or* tomatoes, *or* both items. An example of facts in an extensional database is *supplierloc*(abc, illinois), *supplierloc*(abc, virginia). These state that the abc corporation is located both in Illinois *and* in Virginia. For each atomic formula, there is a relation that consists of all tuples whose arguments are in an atomic formula with the same name. Thus, for the *supplierloc* predicate, there is a relation, the *SUPPLIERLOC* relation, that consists of the tuples, $\{\langle abc, illinois \rangle, \langle abc, virginia \rangle\}$. When the facts in the extensional database consist only of atoms (i.e. there are no disjunctions), it is equivalent to entries in a relational database. An example of an integrity constraint is one which specifies that all suppliers have only one store from which they sell their products. A rule might specify that if a supplier supplies screwdrivers, then it also supplies screws. This rule obviates the need to list suppliers of screws in the database explicitly.

Deductive databases restrict arguments of atomic formulas to constants and variables, whereas in first-order logic one also may have function symbols occurring in the arguments. The reason for the restriction is to assure that one has only a finite number of answers to queries. Rules are to be read either declaratively or procedurally. A declarative reading of (1) is:

A_1 *or* A_2 *or* $\ldots$ *or* A_n is *true* if

B_1 *and* B_2 *and* $\ldots$ *and* B_m *and not* B_{m+1} *and not* $\ldots$

and not B_{m+l} are all *true*.

A procedural reading of (1) is:

A_1 or A_2 or ... or A_n are solved if

B_1 and B_2 and ... and B_m and not B_{m+1} and not ...

and not B_{m+l} can be solved.

The left-hand side of the implication, A_1 or ... or A_n is referred to as the *head* of the rule, while the right-hand side, B_1 and B_2 ... and B_m and not B_{m+1} and not B_{m+l} is referred to as the *body* of the rule. A rule may be recursive. That is, the predicate associated with an atom A_i, in the head of a rule, may have the same name as a predicate associated with any of the B_j in the *body* of the rule.

Queries to a database, $Q(X_1, \ldots, X_r)$, are of the form $\exists X_1 \cdots \exists X_r (L_1 \wedge L_2 \ldots \wedge L_s)$, where $s \geq 0$, the L_i are atoms or atoms preceded by the default rule *not*, and the X_i $1 \leq i \leq r$ are the variables in Q. An answer to a query has the form

$$\langle a_{11}, \ldots, a_{1r} \rangle + \langle a_{21}, \ldots, a_{2r} \rangle + \cdots + \langle a_{k1}, \ldots, a_{kr} \rangle$$

such that

$$Q(a_{11}, \ldots, a_{lr}) \vee Q(a_{21}, \ldots, a_{2r}) \vee \cdots \vee Q(a_{k1}, \ldots, a_{kr})$$

is provable from the database. By provable, it is meant that an inference system is used to find answers to queries.

Deductive databases are closely related to logic programs when the facts are restricted to atomic formulas and the rules have only one atom in the left-hand side of a rule. The main difference is that, in a logic program, search is for a single answer to a query, and the computation procedure is top-down, searching from the query to an answer. In the case of deductive databases, searches are bottom-up, starting from the facts to find all answers to a query. A query in a logic program might ask for an item supplied by a supplier, while a query in a deductive database asks for all items supplied by a supplier. Unlike deductive databases, arguments of predicates in a logic program may contain function symbols. Deductive databases that are restricted to atoms as facts and have rules that consist of a single atom on the left-hand side of a rule and no negated atoms on the right-hand side of a rule are referred to as *Datalog*. This has become the standard terminology in deductive databases and distinguishes a deductive database from a relational database which may contain rules (referred to as *views*) that are generally non-recursive.

There are several different views of the relationship of ICs to the union of the database (facts and rules). Two are noted here: *consistency* and *theoremhood*. In the consistency view, an IC must be consistent with all of the extensional and intensional rules ($EDB \cup IDB$). In the theoremhood approach, an integrity constraint must be a theorem provable from $EDB \cup IDB$.

To answer queries that consist of conjunctions of positive and negated atoms requires that there be a semantics associated with negation, since one can only derive positive disjunctions from the above databases (in the case where (1) contains only atoms). Default rules are used to find answers to negated questions. There are several default rules used in deductive databases. Two of these rules are termed the *closed world assumption* (CWA) and *negation as finite failure* (NFF). In the CWA, if one fails to prove the positive atom, the negated atom is assumed to be *true*. In the NFF approach, the theory is closed by considering that the facts and rules are *if* conditions, and the theory is augmented by the *only if* statements. This means that the only facts that can possibly be *true* in the database are those that can be derived from the facts and the rules. The two approaches lead to slightly different results. They do not apply to disjunctive theories.

Depending upon the form of the rules in (1), alternative semantics are obtained by deductive databases. More expressive power may be obtained in a deductive database by allowing negated atoms on the right-hand side of a rule, literals instead of atoms, and disjunctions in the head of a rule. The semantics associated with such databases vary depending upon how one interprets the default rule *not*. There is no general agreement as to which default rule should be used, except for the theories *Datalog*, *Datalog$_{strat}^{\neg}$*, and *Datalog$_{disj}$* described below. Some of the semantics are given below.

In a *Datalog* deductive database, the EDB consists of atoms, the IDB rules satisfy $n = 1$, $m \geq 1$, $l = 0$, and the A_i and B_j are atoms. Rules may be recursive. The theory yields a unique minimal Herbrand model. A *Herbrand model* of a database is a set of atoms that are considered to be *true* and contain all of the facts that can be derived from the database. A Herbrand model is minimal if it does not contain any other Herbrand model.

In a *Datalog$_{strat}^{\neg}$* deductive database, the *EDB* consists of atoms, the *IDB* rules satisfy $n = 1$, $l \geq 0$, $m \geq 1$, and the A_i and B_j are atoms. Recursion through negation is not permitted. The theory is called a *stratified deductive database* and yields a unique minimal Herbrand model, referred to as the *perfect model*.

In a *Datalog$_{normal}^{\neg}$* deductive database, the *EDB* consists of atoms, the *IDB* rules satisfy $n = 1$, $l \geq 0$, $m \geq 1$ and the A_i and B_j are atoms. Recursion through negation is permitted. The theory is called a *normal deductive database*. Several semantics have been identified. Prominent among them are a three-valued semantics referred to as the *well-founded semantics*, which yields a unique minimal three-valued model (where ground atoms, atoms that contain only constants, may be *true, false,* or *unknown*), and the *stable semantics*, which may yield several minimal Herbrand models.

In a *Datalog$_{disj}$* deductive database, the EDB consists of disjunctions, the IDB rules satisfy $n \geq 1$, $m \geq 1$, $l = 0$, and the A_i and B_j are atoms. Rules may be recursive. The theory yields multiple minimal Herbrand models.

Additional database types are possible. The reader interested in such databases should see Eiter *et al.* (1997), Lobo *et al.* (1992) and Minker (1996).

A Brief History of Deductive Databases

Early work in deductive databases started in the late 1950s and early 1960s. Work was done at a number of places trying to perform deduction using *ad hoc* techniques. In 1957, Minker and his colleagues used primitive techniques, based on *modus ponens* (that is, from *p* and *p* → *q* one can derive *q*). Several working systems with deductive components were developed in the early 1960s. Prominent among the efforts was work at the Rand Corporation. Levien and Maron developed a system named *Relational Data File* (RDF) that had a language, termed *INFEREX*, that was used to query the system. Kuhns, who worked on the RDF project, addressed theoretical issues concerning "reasonable queries," and the general problem of quantification in query systems. Related to work by Kuhns were papers in the late 1950s and early 1960s devoted to a general theory of formalization of questions by Åqvist in 1965, Belnap in 1963, Carnap in 1956, Harrah in 1963, Jespersen in 1965, and Kasher in 1967.

In 1968, Green and Raphael extended Raphael's Ph.D. thesis to develop a series of deductive systems based on sound logical reasoning and general principles that led to a system termed *Question Answering System 3.5* (QA-3.5). This was the first system to incorporate the *Robinson Resolution Principle* developed for automated theorem proving to perform deduction. The Robinson Resolution Principle, developed by J. Alan Robinson, used a single rule of inference that generalized *modus ponens* of the propositional calculus to the predicate calculus. Green and Raphael were the first to recognize the importance and applicability of Robinson's work in automated theorem proving. They developed the first deductive database system using formal techniques that has become the standard method in deductive databases.

The beginning of the field of deductive databases is considered to be November 1977, when a workshop was organized in Toulouse, France, entitled "Logic and Data Bases." The workshop brought together researchers who had been performing work from roughly 1969 to 1977. This work uniformly used the Robinson Resolution Principle as the basis for deduction. The workshop was organized by Hervé Gallaire and Jean-Marie Nicolas, in collaboration with Jack Minker. The workshop led to the publication of a book, *Logic and Data Bases*, edited by Gallaire and Minker. Several important contributions were reported upon in the book. Nicolas and Gallaire demonstrated that the database community used a model-theoretic approach to answering queries and a bottom-up search starting from the truths in the database, while in automated theorem proving the approach is proof-theoretic, which is a top-down approach starting from the query. Reiter contributed the concept of default negation by the *Closed World Assumption* (CWA). Reiter's paper on the CWA shed light on three major issues: the definition of a query, an answer to a query, and how one deals with negation. Clark presented an alternative theory of negation. He introduced the concept of *if-and-only-if* conditions that underlie the meaning of negation, also called *negation-as-failure*. The papers by Reiter and by Clark are the first to use formally defined negation in logic programs and deductive databases. Several prototype deductive database systems were described by Chang (*DEDUCE 2*), by Kellogg, Klahr and Travis (*DADM*), and by Minker (*Maryland Refutation Proof Procedure System*: MRPPS 3.0). Kowalski discussed the use of logic for data description. Nicolas and Yazdanian described the importance of integrity constraints in deductive databases and provided, for the first time, a comprehensive description of the interaction between logic and databases.

Sources for Deductive Databases

A comprehensive survey of 20 years of work in deductive databases may be found in Minker (1996) References are provided to the history of deductive databases, alternative theories of negation and semantics of deductive databases, and complexity results. *See* Ullman (1990) for techniques to deal with some alternative concepts in deductive databases and how to handle recursive rules. *See* Lloyd (1987) for theoretical results related to deductive databases, Lobo *et al.* (1992) for results concerning disjunctive deductive databases, and Eiter *et al.* (1997) for theoretical aspects of *Disjunctive Datalog*.

Bibliography

1987. Lloyd, J. W. *Foundations of Logic Programming*, 2nd Ed. New York: Springer-Verlag.

1990. Ullman, J. D. *Principles of Database and Knowledge-Base Systems.* Potomac, MD: Computer Science Press.

1992. Lobo, J., Minker, J., and Rajasekar, A. *Foundations of Disjunctive Logic Programming.* Cambridge, MA: MIT Press.

1996. Minker, J. "Logic and Databases: A 20 Year Retrospective," in *Logic in Databases* (eds. D. Pedreschi and C. Zaniolo), 3–57. New York: Springer-Verlag.

1997. Eiter, T., Gottlob, G., and Mannila, H. "Disjunctive Datalog," *ACM Transactions on Database Systems,* **22**, *3*, 364–418.

Jack Minker

DEFAULT CONDITION

For articles on related subjects *see* EXPRESSION; PROCEDURE-ORIENTED LANGUAGES; and STATEMENT.

A *default condition* or value is one set by software when a user elects not to make a choice that was available in a particular situation. Unlike its common English usage, default carries no pejorative connotation; there is no suggestion that a person should have done something, merely that he or she could have. Some examples are:

1. The Fortran iteration statement DO 17 I = 1,100 behaves as if the user had written DO 17 I = 1,100,1; i.e. the control variable I will be incremented by +1 by default, since the step size is assumed to be +1 unless otherwise specified.

2. In early versions of Basic, subscripted variable references such as LET B(7) = 4 could be made without dimensioning B explicitly, provided the maximum subscript used did not exceed 10; i.e. Basic assumed an implicit DIM B(10) by default unless the programmer supplied a specific alternative.

3. In APL, the origin of all arrays is 1 by default, but the programmer may overrule this by inputting)ORIGIN 0. (The only choices are 0 or 1.)

4. In Pascal, the heading **procedure** Zilch (a,b : integer); begins the definition of a procedure whose arguments *a* and *b* are called-by-value by default. The programmer could have elected call-by-reference by writing **procedure** Zilch (**var** a,b : integer);. Similarly, the default parameter passage in Algol 60 is call-by-name unless call-by-value is explicitly specified.

5. The Pascal statement **while not** eof **do** ... acts like **while not** eof(input) **do**...; i.e. the file whose end-of-file condition is being monitored is the "input" file by default even though another file could have been specified.

6. In C++ (*q.v.*) the very word **default** is a reserved word. It may be used to label the condition that is to be executed if, at execution time, the control variable of a **switch** (multiple condition) statement does not have the value of any constituent **case** label. Appropriately enough, the programmer need not specify a **default** clause, in which case the **switch** statement, if no **case** condition is satisfied, becomes a no-op (*q.v.*).

Note that, in each of these situations, the language designers chose a default condition or value that, in their opinion, would be most commonly desired. Such a practice saves the user time by making it unnecessary to state the obvious.

Edwin D. Reilly

DELIMITER

For an article on a related subject *see* PROCEDURE-ORIENTED LANGUAGES.

A *delimiter* is an item of lexical information whose form or position in a source program denotes the boundary between adjacent syntactic components of that program.

As is true with natural language, the *meaning* and clarity of statements in high-level programming languages often depend on the inclusion of explicit indicators that "punctuate" the statement; such signals are termed *delimiters*. Since high-level language statements must be processed by a compiler whose analytical and interpretive facilities must function without the equivalent of human cognition, it is necessary to equip programming languages with a fairly extensive variety of such delimiters, many of them highly specific. The most common of these, naturally, is the blank space, whose function as a *separator* is self-evident. Some languages, however, like Fortran, ignore blanks; more common are languages that tolerate superfluous blanks between syntactic components. (One or more consecutive blanks constitute *whitespace*. Judicious placement of whitespace improves the esthetic appearance and readability of programs.)

Parentheses also represent a commonly used type of delimiter. One of their primary purposes in high-level languages parallels traditional mathematical usage, i.e. to define the extent of a component in a computational expression. For example, the use of parentheses in the ordinary arithmetic expression $A + B(C - 2D)$ is clearly paralleled by the equivalent in many high-level languages:

```
A + B * (C - 2 * D)
```

As another example, consider the form of a conditional statement in C:

```
if (p) x=x+1;
```

In Pascal, a predicate is delimited by the keywords `if` and `then`. The design for C is sleeker, with predicates delimited by parentheses, and no following `then`. Linguistically, the opening parenthesis is not necessary: the predicate is adequately delimited on its left by the `if` keyword. However, to satisfy the human craving for symmetry, the opening parenthesis is compulsory as well.

Most contemporary programming languages provide a relatively free physical format where there is no intrinsic association with a specific input medium, such as the terminal's keyboard. Consequently, in the absence of an implicit correspondence in such languages between the end of a statement and the physical boundary of the medium, it is necessary to impose explicit delimiters. The semicolon serves that purpose in the C language, and the period has a similar function in Cobol.

Another type of delimiter is used to bracket a sequence of statements when the intent is to consider that sequence as a single conceptual activity. The *compound statement* in Pascal is a case in point. For instance, the following structure

```
for i := 1 to 18 do
  begin
    read(x,y);
    sum1 := sum1 + x;
    sum2 := sum2 + 2.7*y
  end
```

specifies a loop in which the sequence enclosed by the `begin...end` delimiters is to be executed during each of the 18 trips through the loop.

Pascal terminology distinguishes *separators*, such as colon (`:`), semicolon (`;`), and comma (`,`), which separate one language token from another, and *delimiters*, which occur in pairs in order to bracket a sequence of statements or tokens. Example Pascal delimiter pairs are (), [], `begin...end`, `repeat...until`, and the keyword `program`, which begins a program, and the final period (`.`), which ends it. Other languages have similar separators and delimiters, though in many of them, such as C and C++, the semicolon is a delimiter, which, acting alone, terminates a statement.

Seymour V. Pollack and Ron K. Cytron

DESK CALCULATOR

See CALCULATING MACHINES; and CALCULATORS, ELECTRONIC and PROGRAMMABLE.

DESKTOP PUBLISHING

For articles on related subjects *see* COMPUTER GRAPHICS; MARKUP LANGUAGES; METAFONT; PRINTERS; TEX; TEXT EDITING SYSTEMS; TYPEFONT; and WORD PROCESSING.

Desktop publishing refers to the creation and printing of high-quality documents using software that supports complex page design and allows users to view and edit page images before printing. This form of publishing became widespread during the late 1980s when the three essential ingredients for a desktop publishing computer system became small enough to fit on a desk and cheap enough to be purchased by individuals or small organizations. The essential ingredients were:

◆ Interactive software for document design and editing.

◆ A printer capable of printing diagrams and many different typefonts.

◆ A personal computer or workstation (*q.v.*) with a graphics screen and pointing device (typically a mouse—*q.v.*).

Given these three ingredients, users without formal training in document design could produce complex documents quickly and without the need for outside printing or typesetting facilities.

Instant Publishing

Desktop publishing provided major advantages over traditional methods of document production and typesetting. The interactive software provided a what-you-see-is-what-you-get (WYSIWYG) interface so that users could see the current state of the document on the screen and manipulate it directly via the keyboard and pointing device. This allowed them to experiment with the page layout and edit the content until they were satisfied with the result. They could then print a paper copy immediately.

The attractions of the interactive approach, together with the speed at which the output could be produced, led to a rapid expansion in use during the 1980s. Desktop publishing became firmly established and widely known by the acronym DTP. Although the term originally applied to standalone systems incorporating all the three ingredients described above, it now refers specifically to the first of these: interactive software offering flexible page design and layout tools.

Early desktop publishing systems produced documents containing graphics as well as text in many different sizes and styles, but the quality of the printed documents was poor compared with documents typeset by traditional methods. This was due partly to the relatively crude formatting methods used by the software and partly to the quality of the printers available at the time (often laser printers with a resolution of 240 or 300 dots per inch). Rapid advances in quality have been made as the technology has become more widespread. While it is still true that desktop publishing software does not always produce the very best quality documents, it now offers sophisticated formatting methods (letter spacing, kerning, etc.), and provides powerful color and graphical capabilities. The software may run on a standalone system or on a networked computer with shared access to one or more high-resolution color printers. Where quality is particularly important, however, laser printers may be used to produce proofs and the output may then be sent to a photographic imagesetter to produce the final product.

Desktop Publishing and Word Processing

It is convenient to classify software for producing documents into two main types.

Desktop publishing or *page-layout* systems are intended primarily for short documents with complex page designs, such as newspapers, catalogs, posters, and leaflets. They provide sophisticated facilities for page design and manipulation, but may have limited facilities for editing text or for creating other types of content. Users may often prefer to import document content from word processors, spreadsheets (*q.v.*), or graphics packages.

Word processors or *document layout* systems are intended primarily for producing longer documents, such as technical manuals, journals, and books. They provide better built-in facilities for handling continuous text, for making systematic changes throughout long documents, and for dealing with cross-references, indexes, and tables of contents. They are, however, relatively inflexible in page layout.

There is no hard-and-fast dividing line between the two different types of system, but the balance of the features varies. Desktop publishing software concentrates on page design and provides a wide variety of facilities for dealing with images and color. It is particularly suitable for documents where the text comes in short blocks and where pages need to be designed individually to provide maximum impact. Word processors provide better facilities for editing and managing large bodies of continuous text.

A summary of the facilities available in typical desktop publishing software is given in the following sections. Many books have been written about the more popular desktop publishing systems such as QuarkXPress (Blattner and Davis, 1998) and PageMaker (Shushan *et al.*, 1996).

Page Design

Users typically design a page by defining rectangular areas within it to contain text or graphics. These areas are known as *frames* or *boxes* or *grids*. Once users have defined a frame, they can fill it with text or graphics, edit its contents, move it around on the page, or change its size. Different page designs can be created by placing frames corresponding to single or multiple-column layout and setting aside different areas of the pages for illustrations.

In order to simplify the overall document design, a facility for defining *master pages* is usually provided. A master page contains the frames that are to appear in the same place on several pages in the document. Items like company logos, page numbers, and page headers and footers are typically dealt with in this way. Individual pages can be designed by adding extra frames to one of the master pages.

Accurate positioning of frames is essential in page design, so users are provided with simple interactive tools to help with the positioning of frames. Examples of positioning tools are:

◆ *Rulers*—shown across the top and down the sides of pages.

◆ *Grids*—shown across the whole page area.

◆ *Guidelines* or *crosshairs*—one horizontal and one vertical line that may be positioned across the page area.

Users draw and position frames approximately by hand, and can then have them positioned and sized accurately by asking for their edges to be "snapped" to the nearest appropriate grid line or ruler marking.

Text Handling

Desktop publishing software provides all the control capabilities needed for text formatting: hyphenation, justification, kerning, and avoiding widows and orphans (single lines of a paragraph at the beginning or end of a page). It also gives access to a wide range of character fonts and sizes and allows fine control of spacing. Several typefonts are generally available, in sizes ranging from 4-point to over 100-point at intervals of half a point or less. Users can choose any type and size and can also control the leading (spacing between lines) and tracking (spacing between words and characters) of text. Easy interactive control of these features allows users to manipulate fine details of the layout and to ensure that headlines or running text look attractive and fit comfortably into the frames provided.

Simple text editing facilities for inserting and deleting text are provided, together with some form of cut-and-paste for moving blocks of text to different positions in the document. These may be supplemented by a variety of more complex features, like search-and-replace or a spelling checker (*q.v.*). Text may be typed in directly or may be imported from a wide variety of word processors and other software. Frames are often linked so that text will flow from one frame to the next and there may be automatic features for adding information such as "Continued from page 16."

Styles

Detailed control of the typographic and formatting requirements of text can become a tedious chore when there are so many different possibilities. To help users with this, most desktop publishing systems provide *styles* or *style sheets*. Different document constituents can be named and have particular styles attached to them. Thus, there may be different styles to cover headings, several levels of sections, and a variety of paragraph types. The styles define details of font, type style, size, spacing, hyphenation, justification, and margins, and may also include information on automatic numbering of the constituents.

To change the style of a constituent, the user calls up a style sheet in a separate window on the screen. This shows the options available and their current settings. These can be edited interactively, typically via dialog boxes, and any changes are made automatically to all occurrences of that constituent in the document. Fig. 1 shows an example of a simple dialog box for changing some options in a style sheet.

Styles are a great help to users in minimizing the amount of work needed and in ensuring good and consistent document layout. Libraries of standard styles are usually supplied, covering a wide variety of needs. Users without training in document design can simply select the styles they require. More experienced designers can either make minor changes to the styles in the library or create their own. Many criticisms of documents produced by desktop publishing concern poor design and are the result of the ease with which users without design skills have access to a wide variety of typographic facilities. The provision of styles created by experienced designers has helped to minimize this problem and also to insure that organizations can impose their own "house style."

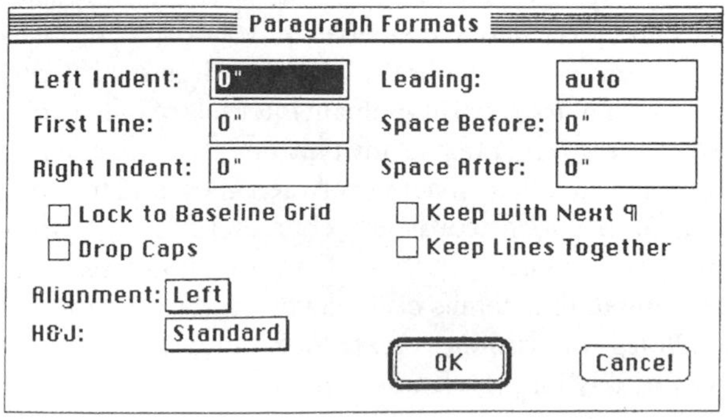

Graphics and Images

All desktop publishing systems provide simple built-in drawing facilities for lines, rectangles, and circles. Further facilities for curves, patterns, and borders may also be provided, and text can be wrapped around the graphics. In some cases, text may only wrap around graphics in a rectangular frame; in others it may be possible for text to wrap around an irregular shape within a frame. There may also be ways of "anchoring" graphics, either to a particular piece of text or to a position on a page.

Graphics and images created by a selection of other software tools can be imported, and facilities are available for scaling, rotating and cropping these to fit frames. A wide variety of digitized pictures, called *clip art*, are sold commercially for importation into desktop publishing software.

Support for many different graphics formats is provided, both for black-and-white and color. Color support may include the provision of several color models (RGB, HSB, CMYK, Pantone), colored backgrounds, and ways to smooth and enhance the color of imported images.

Printing Facilities

High-quality output demands, as a minimum, the availability of a laser printer operating at 600 dots per inch. For top quality output, an imagesetter operating at 1000 dots per inch or more is required. Desktop publishing relies heavily on the use of the PostScript (*q.v.*) page description language (Adobe, 1985), which can be used to drive a variety of laser printers and imagesetters and has all the necessary facilities needed to cope with complex text, graphics, images, and colors. The improvement in quality of documents produced by desktop publishing software is largely due to a dramatic improvement in digital typography which has been fueled by PostScript, the increased use of laser printers, and the popularity of desktop publishing itself.

Future Developments

Desktop publishing is now firmly established as an effective method of producing both simple and complex documents. The early problems with quality have been overcome as advances in digital typography and image handling techniques have been incorporated

Figure 1. Example of simple dialog box for changing some options in a style sheet.

into the software. Although desktop publishing is geared primarily towards the production of high-quality paper output, developments in word processing and the use of structured documents are also appearing in desktop publishing systems—as are some elements of hypertext (*q.v.*), particularly HTML-like links (*see* MARKUP LANGUAGES). Further developments are likely to include more use of "active documents," where document elements have processing methods attached to them. Active document elements can generate their content dynamically by interrogating a database, for example, or by sending some data to another piece of software and using the result. An active document provides a means of accessing and presenting the latest version of some information without requiring separate user actions to find and import the information.

Bibliography

1985. Adobe Systems Incorporated. *PostScript Language Reference Manual*. Reading, MA: Addison-Wesley.
1996. Shushan, R., and Wright, D., with Lewis, L. *Desktop Publishing by Design: Everyone's Guide to PageMaker 6*, 4th Ed. Redmond, WA: Microsoft Press.
1998. Blattner, D., and Davis, N. (eds.) *The QuarkXPress Book: For Macintosh and Windows*. Berkeley, CA: Peachpit Press.

Heather Brown

DEVICE DRIVER

See DRIVER.

DIAGNOSTIC

For articles on related subjects *see* DEBUGGING; and ERRORS.

A *diagnostic* (short for *diagnostic program*) helps determine whether there are hardware faults in a computer or errors in software. Hardware diagnostics are programs designed to determine whether the components of a computer are operating properly. Circuit components are electronically exercised individually and in groups to try to induce failures. When a failure is detected, the location of the faulty equipment is printed and a technician can repair or replace the element. Diagnostics may test communication lines and controllers. Microcomputers may be constructed with diagnostics stored in ROM (*see* READ-ONLY MEMORY).

Hardware diagnostic programs are run as part of a regular schedule of preventive maintenance and in the event of a failure. If a serious hardware failure has occurred, the diagnostic program may fail to operate properly, and may, therefore, be useless in locating the difficulty.

Increasingly, hardware diagnostics take the form of *microdiagnostics*. A microdiagnostic program is a microprogram (*see* MICROPROGRAMMING) that tests a specific hardware component such as a bus (*q.v.*) or storage location. Microdiagnostics often provide more accurate location of a fault than hardware diagnostics written in machine language because of the addressability of individual components under microprogramming. Furthermore, these diagnostic programs are so fast that preventive maintenance testing may be interspersed transparently with other processing. Microdiagnostics, consequently, have furthered the development of self-diagnosing and self-repairing computers.

Diagnostic messages emitted by software are the error messages produced by compilers (*q.v.*), utilities, and operating system software. These messages are designed to indicate to programmers where their programs are at fault. Diagnostic messages at compile time may only be warnings to the programmer, or they may indicate invalid syntax that prohibits execution. A severity level indicator is often included in the diagnostic message.

Execution-time diagnostic messages are produced by the operating system or an execution-time monitor. These messages indicate attempts to perform illegal operations, such as dividing by zero, taking the square root of a negative number, illegal operation codes, illegal address references, page faults, and so on. The diagnostic message may be followed by program termination.

Finally, application programs may produce diagnostics when erroneous data is read. The creator of the application program has complete control over these diagnostic messages and the action taken.

Diagnostic messages should avoid negative tones and be non-threatening, specific, and constructive. Instead of just pointing out what is wrong, they should, whenever possible, tell the user what to do to set things right.

Ben Shneiderman

DIFFERENCE ENGINE

For articles on related subjects *see* ANALYTICAL ENGINE; BABBAGE, CHARLES; and DIGITAL COMPUTERS, HISTORY OF: ORIGINS.

A *difference engine* is a machine that automates the calculation of mathematical tables. Any short section of a mathematical function, such as a sine, can be approximated by a polynomial, the degree or complexity of which is determined by the accuracy required in the tables. Using the method of finite differences, the tabulation of these polynomials can be reduced to the operation of repeated addition of differences only.

The most famous attempt to mechanize this process was made by Charles Babbage in the 1820s. Frustrated by the errors made by human calculators preparing tables for him, Babbage remarked to the astronomer John Herschel, "I wish to God these calculations had been executed by steam," to which Herschel replied "It is quite possible." Inspired by this suggestion, Babbage produced a small demonstration model of a difference engine by mid-1822. Unfortunately, nothing of this model has survived, but it appears to have included six digits and to have tabulated the polynomial $x^2 + x + 41$ (whose values for integer values of x from 1 to 39 are prime numbers).

With the aid of intermittent support from the British government, Babbage then embarked on the construction of a much more extensive machine, intended to provide six orders of differences, each of 18 digits. Babbage realized that the printing of tables using movable type was as great a source of error as the calculations themselves. He therefore included in the difference engine a mechanism for automatic preparation of stereotype printing plates.

The layout of a printed page of tables is complex. Babbage made provision for the difference engine to lay out tables in either columns or rows, with spaces of variable width to guide the eye of the reader and to round off all printed values automatically. His most elaborate mechanism even allowed for the printing of only the least significant digits of each table entry—the leading digits were printed only for the first entry on each line and then only if these digits had changed from the line before.

In the design of this printing mechanism, Babbage gained valuable experience in the mechanization of complex and conditional sequences of operation. He became adept in overlapping operations in various parts of the machine, including the pipelining of the difference tabulation itself. He devised means by which the control itself did not have to transmit power to the working mechanism, but simply made connections to the main power source. An ingenious system of "lockings" made good any lost motion or backlash in the mechanisms and ensured that the machine could not become accidentally deranged and produce incorrect values. All of these ideas were essential to the subsequent rapid development of the Analytical Engine by Babbage in the 1830s.

The Difference Engine was never built. Contrary to a widely held belief, this was not due to an inability of the mechanical technology of the day to cope with the demands of Babbage's machine. The demonstration piece, which is still in excellent working order, gives the lie to that suggestion, though the workmanship was expensive—possible excessively so. Rather, the difficulties lay in social changes—Babbage's failure to cope with either the rapidly changing role of leading engineers or with a government that had never previously directly funded research and was itself entering an era of great social flux.

Work on Difference Engine no. 1 ceased in 1833. In 1847 Babbage produced a design for a Difference Engine no. 2, whose simpler design took advantage of ideas evolved for the Analytical Engine.

In the 1850s, Georg and Edvard Scheutz of Sweden built a difference engine inspired by Babbage's work, but this lacked Babbage's mechanical refinements and never worked reliably. Later nineteenth century designs by Wiberg in Sweden and Grant in the USA fared little better. In the 1930s, L. J. Comrie (*q.v.*) of the British Nautical Almanac Office adopted Burroughs and National Cash Register accounting machines for use as difference engines. These were used mainly for checking proofs of tables by applying the difference method in reverse. By then, the sub-tabulation task for which Babbage's difference engines were designed was not seen to be the major problem in the preparation of mathematical tables.

In 1991 the Science Museum in London completed the construction of a working Difference Engine No. 2 based on Babbage's drawings (Fig. 1). The machine is 10 feet long, 6 feet high, 18 inches deep and has 4,000 parts machined using modern tools but to an accuracy no greater than Babbage could have achieved.

Figure 1. A working Difference Engine.

Bibliography

1987. Bromley, A. G. "The Evolution of Babbage's Calculating Engines," *Annals of the History of Computing*, **9**, 113–136.

1990. Bromley, A. G. "Difference and Analytical Engines," in Aspray, W. (ed.) *Computing Before Computers*. University of Iowa State Press.

1991. Gibson, W., and Sterling, B. *The Difference Engine*. New York: Basic Books. (A novelized history of the Difference and Analytical Engines.)

1991. Swade, D. *Charles Babbage and His Calculating Engines*. London: Science Museum.

1998. Collier, B., MacLachlan, J. H., and Gingerich, O. *Charles Babbage and the Engines of Perfection*. Oxford: Oxford University Press.

Allan G. Bromley

DIFFERENTIAL ANALYZER

For articles on related subjects *see* ANALOG COMPUTER; BUSH, VANNEVAR; DIGITAL COMPUTERS, HISTORY OF: EARLY; and HARTREE, DOUGLAS R.

In a paper published in the *Journal of the Franklin Institute* in 1931, Vannevar Bush described a machine (Fig. 1) that had been constructed under his direction at MIT for the purpose of solving ordinary differential equations. He christened the machine a *differential analyzer*. This was what would now be called an "analog" computer, and was based on the use of mechanical integrators that could be interconnected in any desired manner. The integrator was in essence a variable-speed gear, and took the form of a rotating horizontal disk on which a small knife-edged wheel rested. The wheel was driven by friction, and the gear ratio was altered by varying the distance of the wheel from the axis of rotation of the disk. The principle is illustrated in Fig. 2.

The use of mechanical integrators for solving differential equations had been suggested by Kelvin, and

Figure 1. Vannevar Bush shown with the MIT differential analyzer. (Courtesy of the MIT Museum, Cambridge, MA).

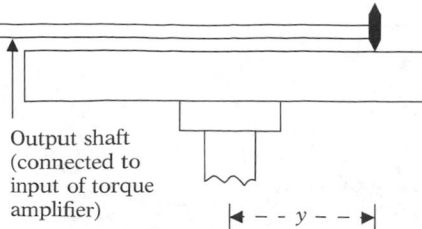

Figure 2. Wheel and disk integrator. If the disk turns through an angle proportional to *x*, the output shaft turns through an angle proportional to $\int y\,dx$.

various special-purpose integrating devices were constructed at various times. Bush's differential analyzer was, however, the first device of sufficiently general application to meet a genuine need, and in the period immediately before and during the Second World War quite a number of these devices were constructed. The one shown in Fig. 4 was installed at the Mathematical Laboratory in Cambridge, England.

In order to make a practical device, it is necessary to have some means of amplifying the small amount of torque available from the rotating wheel. Bush used a torque amplifier, working on the principle of a ship's capstan, but adapting it for continuous rotation. Fig. 3 is taken from his report (1931) and sufficiently indicates the principle. The friction drums are rotated in opposite directions by a continuously running motor of sufficient power. When the input shaft is turned, one of the cords attached to the input arm begins to tighten on the friction drum round which it is wrapped. Which cord tightens depends on the direction of rotation of the input shaft. A very small tightening, and hence a very small tension in the end of the cord attached to the input arm, is sufficient, in view of the friction of the rotating drum, to produce a large tension in the end attached to the output arm. A small torque applied to the input shaft is thus capable of producing a much larger torque in the output shaft.

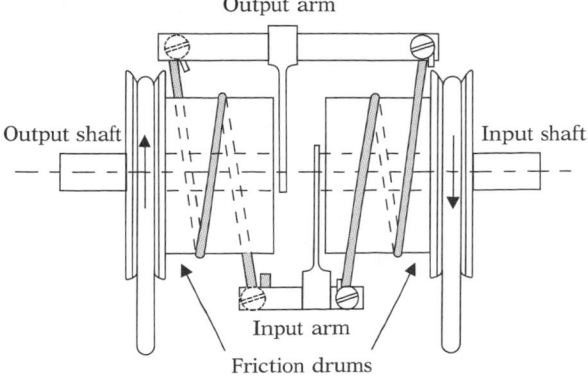

Figure 3. Principle of torque amplifier (Courtesy of *Journal of the Franklin Institute*).

Figure 4. The differential analyzer system, showing integrators, torque amplifiers, and shafting. 1: Output table; 2: Input table; 3: Shafts and gears used for interconnection; 4: Torque amplifier; 5: Integrator disk. (Courtesy of the MIT Museum, Cambridge, MA).

The integrators and torque amplifiers can be seen in Fig. 4, together with the system of shafting used for effecting the connections. Changing the problem was a job for someone who did not mind hands covered in oil. The output table, on which the results were plotted directly in graphical form, can be seen in Fig. 4, which also shows a number of similar tables that were used for input, an operator being employed to turn a handle so that a cursor followed a curve. It is a comment on the primitive state of automatic control in the period in question that automatic curve-following devices were not provided until later. The accuracy attainable in a single integrator was about one part in three thousand, but of course a lower accuracy was to be expected in the solution.

Fig. 5 shows the notation that was used for an integrator and Fig. 6 shows how two integrators could be interconnected to solve a simple differential equation. It was not difficult to arrive at a diagram such as Fig. 6, even for a complicated equation, but working out the gear ratios required was a distinctly tedious task calling for some experience, particularly as accuracy required

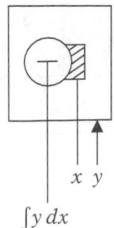

Figure 5. Schematic notation for an integrator.

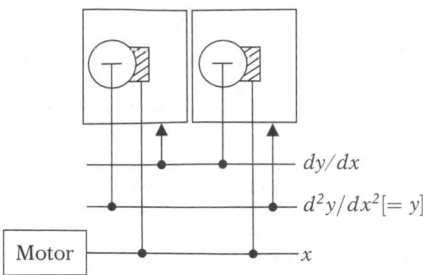

Figure 6. Setup for solving the equation $d^2y/dx^2 = y$.

that full use should be made of the available range of integrator motion.

In 1945, Bush and S. H. Caldwell described a new differential analyzer in which interconnection between the integrators was effected electrically instead of mechanically. However, during the decade that followed, competition from electronic analog computers and from digital computers began to build up, and, although the new machine ran for a number of years at MIT, by 1955 the mechanical differential analyzer was already obsolete.

Digital Differential Analyzer

This device is based on the use of a *rate multiplier* as an integrator. In a rate multiplier, a constant quantity y is held in a register and, on the receipt of an input pulse, is added to the number standing in an accumulator. If input pulses arrive at a rate R, overflow pulses will emerge from the most significant end of the accumulator at a rate proportional to yR. If y now varies and if input pulses arrive whenever a certain other variable x increases by δx, the number of output pulses emerging is proportional to $\sum y\,\delta x$ or, approximately to $\int y\,dx$. Thus, the device serves as an integrator. Normally, δx is equal to one unit in the least significant place, and continuously updated values of the variable x can be obtained by feeding the pulses into an accumulator.

The first digital differential analyzer was the MADDIDA developed in 1949 at the Northrop Aircraft Corporation. It had 44 integrators implemented using a magnetic drum for storage, the addition being done serially. There were six tracks in all on the drum, one being used for synchronizing purposes. The problem was specified by writing an appropriate pattern of bits onto one of the tracks. Compared with the digital computers then being built, the MADDIDA was on an impressively small scale. It lost some of its simplicity, however, when adequate input and output devices were added, and in the end competition from general-purpose digital computers proved too much for it. The MADDIDA and its descendants did not, therefore,

have the bright future in so[...]
was predicted for them.

Bibliogr[...]

1931. Bush, V. "The Differential [...]
Solving Differential Equations," [...]
1945. Bush, V., and Caldwell, S. [...]
Analyzer," *J. Frank. Inst.*, **240**, [...]
1947. Crank, J. *The Differential [...]
Green and Co.
1962. Huskey, H. D., and Korn, [...]
New York: McGraw-Hill.
1986. Owens, L. "Vannevar Bush [...]
The Text and the Context of an [...]
and Culture, 63–95. (Reprinted i[...]
Hypertext: Vannevar Bush and [...]
York: Academic Press, 1991.)

DIGITAL COMPUT[...]

For articles on related subjects [...]
ARITHMETIC-LOGIC UNIT; CENTR[...]
COMPUTER ARCHITECTURE; COM[...]
MULTIPLE ADDRESS; DIGITAL CO[...]
GENERAL REGISTER; GENERATIONS[...]
ASSEMBLY LANGUAGE PROGRAMM[...]
MEMORY; MICROPROCESSORS AN[...]
MINICOMPUTER; PERSONAL COM[...]
SUPERCOMPUTERS; and WORKSTA[...]

ELECTRONIC

The word *electronic* refers to the *information processing* (q.v.) components of the machine. It is the nature of the electronic components that make possible the very high speeds of individual operations in modern computers. The history of electronic digital computer[...] distinguishes a number of "generations" define[...] the nature of the electronic components most [...] lent in each. Thus, the first generation mad[...] use of vacuum tubes, the second genera[...] crete transistors, and the third used int[...]

There is little agreement as to whe[...] the a fourth or fifth generation o[...] we have moved through pro[...] of *integrated circuitry* (q[...] COMPUTER.)

Most computer us[...] electronics, and [...] one generatio[...] for a given [...] above a[...] of c[...]

A *digital computer* is a mach[...] and information presented to it in a discrete form, carry out arithmetic and logical operations on this data, and then supply the required results in an acceptable form. The resulting information (output) produced by these operations depends on the accepted information (input). Thus, correct and complete answers cannot be obtained unless correct and sufficient input data has been provided. This is a necessary but not sufficient condition; additionally, the correctness of output answers also depends critically on the logical procedures called *algorithms* (q.v.) used to compute them.

The sequence of the operations required to produce the desired output must be accurately determined and specified by people known as *systems analysts* (q.v.) and *programmers* (q.v.). The systems analyst produces a clear specification of the task to be undertaken, including elements such as clerical processing, which do not involve the computer directly. The programmer prepares the detailed set of instructions that the computer will follow automatically so as to process the work from input to output.

Computer Characteristics

The main characteristics of the digital computer are that it is automatic, general purpose, electronic, and, of course, digital. We discuss each in turn.

on a keyboard and has to press a key (for example, add or multiply) to initiate each individual arithmetic operation. Present-day calculators can execute com plex logarithmic and trigonometric operations at the touch of a single key, but *calculating machines* (q.v.) are still only semiautomatic. (*See also* CALCULATORS, ELECTRONIC AND PROGRAMMABLE.)

Because a computer does not need to stop between single operations, it can take full advantage of the high-speed components that enable it to add, subtract, and perform other individual operations in a few billionths of a second. An important corollary of the automatic nature of the computer is that its program has to be complete. If there is no provision for intervention by the human operator, the program must be written to provide for all possible eventualities, however rare.

GENERAL PURPOSE

Digital computers are *general-purpose* machines. In other words, a computer can do any job that its programmer can break down into suitable basic operations. Put a payroll program into a computer and you make it, for the time being, a special-purpose payroll machine. Replace the program by one for inverting a matrix, and you make the computer temporarily a special-purpose mathematical machine.

ions (*q.v.*) and for mathematical computa-
...digital computers are used almost exclusively.

The numbers stored in a digital computer are represented in our traditional positional number system, but they are not necessarily decimal. Early computers were decimal, or rather, the engineers who designed them made them appear to be decimal to the programmers who wrote procedures for them. But it is difficult to find a physical entity that naturally occurs in 10 different states; it is much easier to build computers that are based on bi-stable states, which are plentiful—switches that are either open or closed, capacitors that are either charged or uncharged, or magnets aligned to point either "north" or "south". To capitalize on this observation, virtually all digital computers designed over the last 45 years have used the binary number system, a system which, though still positional, uses only the binary digits (bits) 0 and 1 (*see* NUMBERS AND NUMBER SYSTEMS). The most common unit of memory storage is a sequence of eight bits called a *byte*. Throughout the rest of this article, it will be assumed that when describing digital computers we are referring to *binary* digital computers.

Main Elements

Only very rarely does a computer have a unique, fixed specification. Normally, it is better described as a *computer system* (*q.v.*), consisting of a selection from a wide variety of units appropriate to meet a defined need. The particular selection made is called a *configuration* of the system. Differences in configuration can adversely affect the *compatibility* (*q.v.*) of programs. For example, given two installations that use the same basic model computer, the one with the greater amount of memory may be able to run certain programs which the other cannot. Even if two installations are using the same configuration of the same model computer, they may be incompatible to a large degree if they adopt different *operating systems* (*q.v.*), the highest level of installed *software* (*q.v.*) "under" which all other software programs operate. The combination of a particular model computer and its operating system is called a *platform*. Thus we speak of an Intel 80x86 microcomputer that runs the Microsoft Windows operating system as being a "Wintel" platform, which would be substantially incompatible with, say a platform consisting of a Sun workstation controlled by the *Unix operating system* (*q.v.*).

The principal groupings of computer units commonly follow the pattern shown in Fig. 1 and are defined as follows:

1. *Input units*: An input unit accepts the data, the raw material that a computer uses, communicated

---

...by ...preva- ...extensive ...ion used dis- ...egrated circuits. ...her we are now in ...still in the third, since ...ressively higher degrees ...). (*See also* GENERATIONS,

...rs need no special knowledge of ...the major practical distinctions from ...to the next are the reductions in size ...power, the rapid increases in speed, and, ...a substantial and continuous fall in the cost ...mputing.

DIGITAL

A computer may be either *digital* or *analog*. The two types do have some principles in common, but they employ different types of data representations and are, in general, suited to different kinds of work. Digital computers are so called because they work with *numbers* in the form of separate discrete digits. More precisely, they work with information that is in digital or character form, including alphabetic and other symbols as well as numbers.

In a digital machine, the data, whether numbers, letters, or other symbols, is represented in digital form. An analog computer, on the other hand, may be said to deal with a "model" of the problem, in which the variables are represented by continuous physical quantities, such as angular position and voltage. The decimal numbers 136 and 435, for instance, might be represented by 1.36 volts and 4.35 volts. Using familiar devices, we could say that a slide rule is an analog device, because numbers are represented by a linear length. The abacus, on the other hand, is a digital device, because movable counters are used for calculating. Just as measurement is usually faster than enumeration (counting), an analog calculation may be faster than a corresponding digital one, but the digital one can be carried out to much higher *precision* (*q.v.*). Analog computers tend to be special-purpose machines designed for some specific scientific or technical application. They were once found useful in engineering design for such things as nuclear power stations, chemical plants, and aircraft, but are no longer commonly used. In commercial and *administrative*

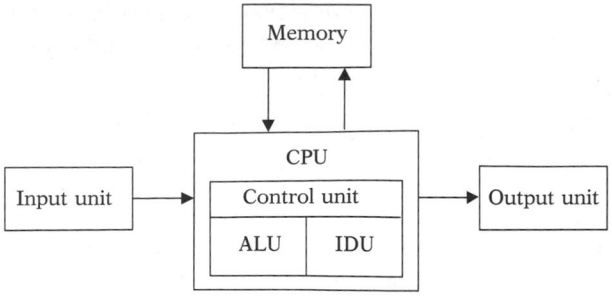

Figure 1. The principal components of a stored-program digital computer.

from outside. It is the actual means by which information is converted into electronic pulses, which are then fed into the machine's memory.

2. *Central Processing Unit (CPU)*: The "heart and brain" of the computer, its CPU, consists of a *control unit (CU)*, an *arithmetic-logic unit (ALU)*, and an *instruction decoding unit (IDU)*. The control unit is the directing force of the computer, its "automatic operator." It provides the means of communication within the machine, by moving, advancing, or transferring information. It integrates its constituent units into a coherent system. The arithmetic-logic unit performs the four arithmetic operations of addition, subtraction, multiplication, and division and, additionally, logical (Boolean) operations such as **and**, **or**, and **not**. The latter, when applied to a binary (base 2) operand (*q.v.*), forms the *complement (q.v.)* of that operand. By determining whether one number is larger than another, or whether a number is positive, negative, or zero, the ALU also allows the control unit to make logical "decisions" that affect the flow of control of a running program.

3. *Main memory unit*: All information stored in the main memory unit is "remembered" and made available to other units as required, under the direction of the control unit.

4. *Auxiliary storage units*: These units store the massive information required for reference as needed during a computation. The information may and often is updated during the course of the computation (*see* DATABASE MANAGEMENT SYSTEMS).

5. *Output units*: After information is processed, an output unit communicates it to the outside world. When needed, the results are recalled from memory under the direction of the control unit and presented by the output units in an appropriate form. A wide variety of output devices is available. Input and output units are often called *peripheral units*, or just *peripherals*.

We will now consider each of these main units in some detail.

INPUT

Interactive input devices (q.v.) accept data from the world outside the computer and transfer it in suitably coded form into the memory, a process frequently described as *data capture*. A high proportion of input data is prepared by using the keyboard of a personal computer or *workstation*. Alternatively, there may be some intermediate carrier of the data, such as magnetic tape, or more frequently now, magnetic *diskettes (q.v.)*. Data may also be scanned from hard copies and processed using *optical character recognition* (OCR—*q.v.*). In each case, the data preparation device produces a coded representation of the data, which is recorded on a storage medium in some appropriate form, e.g. magnetized blips on the surface of a magnetic storage device or pits etched into the surface of an optical storage (*q.v.*) device such as a compact disc. Once captured, the data can be transferred at high speed into the computer's memory as needed.

A data preparation process that depends on a manual typing operation is clearly expensive and error-prone. Since most original data appears as ink on paper, devices that can read such data automatically have a great attraction and OCR *document readers (scanners)* play an increasingly important part in the input process.

There are now many optical scanners capable of recognizing the shape of a character from its reflected light in much the same way as humans do. They use *typefonts (q.v.)* that appear quite normal to us and, therefore, serve the needs of both people and computers (*see* OPTICAL CHARACTER RECOGNITION). There are also readers that scan the bar codes increasingly found on retail store products and library books and that, therefore, greatly speed up the check-out procedures (*see* UNIVERSAL PRODUCT CODE). Much progress has also been made with voice recognition equipment that allows computers to recognize the human voice over a limited repertoire of input messages. (*See* SPEECH RECOGNITION AND SYNTHESIS.)

CENTRAL PROCESSING UNIT (CPU)

The central processing unit is the focal point of the computer system. It receives data from input units and auxiliary storage, carries out a variety of arithmetic and logical operations on this data, and transmits results to output units or back to auxiliary storage. It is the CPU that determines the intrinsic processing power of a digital computer. There are now so many brands and models of digital computer that they span a virtually continuous range of processing power, but it is convenient to recognize at least six categories, from least to most powerful: *portable computers* (*q.v.*), desktop *personal computers* (PCs) (*see* PERSONAL COMPUTING), *workstations* (*q.v.*), *minicomputers* (*q.v.*), *mainframes* (*q.v.*), and *supercomputers* (*q.v.*). As indicated, each category is discussed in detail in an article of its own.

A central processor is made up of three principal parts (at one time physically distinct, though now parts of a single microcomputer chip–*q.v.*): (1) the control unit; (2) the arithmetic-logic unit; and (3) the instruction decoding unit.

The control unit functions so as to cause the whole machine to operate according to the instructions in the program. Instructions are normally transferred sequentially from the memory to the control unit, where each instruction is interpreted and the appropriate circuits are activated to "execute" the instruction. This strict sequence is broken, for example, when a "test and jump" (or *branch*) instruction occurs and produces an exceptional result. There is then a transfer of control to a program step in a different part of the program, from which the sequential pattern continues until again broken. It is this facility that provides the decision-making and repetition capabilities that give computers their power.

Examined in isolation, the data and instructions stored in memory are indistinguishable. No one looking at the pattern of bits (1s and 0s) can possibly tell, without being given more information, whether the bit pattern is intended to be an instruction to be obeyed or data to be processed. The task of making that decision is assigned to the CPU's *control unit*. The control unit decides whether a given bit pattern is an instruction, in which case it is decoded (*see* INSTRUCTION DECODING), or data, in which case it is sent to the arithmetic-logic unit. The control unit does this by maintaining, at all times, a pointer to (i.e. the address of) the next instruction to be executed. That pointer, called the *program counter* (*q.v.*) or *instruction counter*, keeps track of the flow of control of a running program. At the moment when the program counter points to a bit pattern, that pattern is considered to be an instruction. At some different point in program flow, it may be treated merely as a data value. If that value is modified and later becomes targeted by the program counter, a different instruction will be executed than the one originally stored at the same address.

When a linear sequence of instructions concludes with a test that causes control to be transferred back to the first instruction of the sequence, that sequence is said to constitute a program *loop*. A faulty test can cause what is called an *infinite loop*, which is a serious *bug* (*q.v.*) in the program, but a well-behaved loop will terminate after a finite number of *iterations* (*q.v.*), i.e. loop traversals. (*See* MACHINE AND ASSEMBLY LANGUAGE PROGRAMMING.)

The arithmetic-logic unit (ALU) is one of the simplest parts of the machine to understand. It is the part that carries out arithmetic operations. It also has one or more *registers* (*q.v.*), sometimes called *accumulators*, which are fast one-word storage elements. To add a number stored in address 113 of the memory to that stored in address 207, first the contents of address 113 are read into a register and then the contents of address 207 are added to that register. The answer could then be stored in another address in memory, or used in another arithmetic operation. In 1999, many ALUs did only register-to-register operations, so that both numbers would be copied into registers, with the result going into a third one (*see* COMPUTER ARCHITECTURE and REDUCED INSTRUCTION SET COMPUTER).

MEMORY

Memory (or *main memory*, as it is sometimes called, to distinguish it from auxiliary memory) is able to hold, for as long as desired, coded representations of numbers and letters in convenient groupings; each group is held in a uniquely addressable part of the memory, from which it can be transferred on demand. The memory may be figuratively described as a large number of pigeonholes, each identifiable by a serial number called its *address*.

One purpose of the memory is to hold data. Numbers and letters flow into it from input, are sent for arithmetic processing to the arithmetic unit (from which the results return to the memory), and the output information is stored in it before transfer to an output unit.

The second use of the memory is to hold all the instructions of the program required to carry out a job. These instructions are normally coded in numeric binary form and can be read into the memory from magnetic disk or an input medium.

AUXILIARY MEMORY

There are relatively few applications of computers, particularly in the field of business data processing where the only input is fresh, raw data. For example, in inventory control, the new data consists of stock issues and receipts, but data in file storage indicates the number of items left in stock calculated at the last inventory and the average value of that stock. These files also include more static information about each item, such as its name, dimensions, batch order quantity, and supplier. Thus, the computer must also have its "filing cabinets" (albeit electronic ones) if it is to be used in business applications. It is obvious that such file storage units must act as input and output units to the computer, and as they are of special and fundamental importance in these applications, they are treated here separately.

The four most important factors relating to any filing system, whether manual or electronic, are (1) its total *capacity* in megabytes (MB), gigabytes (GB), or terabytes (TB); (2) the *access time* (*q.v.*) needed to acquire information, that is, how long it takes to find the first item of data needed; Memories can supply requested data in an incredibly short time, measured in nanoseconds (billionths of a second), typically 60 ns or less; (3) the *transfer rate*, the rate at which files of information can be streamed into or out of computer memory in units of (millions or billions of) bits per second, and (4) the cost per unit of data expressed in, say, cents per megabyte. Typical values of these attributes are given for a wide variety of secondary storage devices under the heading AUXILIARY in the article MEMORY.

The most commonly used medium for holding computer files is magnetic disk, which has pretty much supplanted magnetic tape, the medium of choice in the 1950s. Some installations still maintain a few magnetic tape units ("transports") for the sake of compatibility with valuable "legacy" data recorded in decades past, and massive collections of data are still stored on tape and used with high-speed drives (*see* MASS STORAGE). Magnetic tape also provides a good way to back up valuable disk files to protect against their accidental destruction.

In contrast to magnetic tape, an inherently linear storage medium, disks offer the facility of processing data in random sequence without any undue delay in searching for a required item. The simplest disk storage medium used with personal computers is the *diskette* (*q.v.*). For many years, the standard storage capacity of a diskette was 1.44 MB, and although these are still widely used, newer removable disk storage devices support diskettes that contain as much as 250 MB. Personal computers also use *hard disks* (*q.v.*) whose capacities range from 200 MB to over 30 GB. Workstations, minicomputers, and mainframes sometimes use *redundant arrays of inexpensive disks* (RAID—*q.v.*) that provide not only extensive auxiliary storage, but also, as "redundant" implies, the security that duplicate or "mirrored" data provides.

Another medium once used for file storage is the *magnetic drum*. Historically, it is interesting to note that, in early computers, a magnetic drum frequently provided the main memory. Its speed of access, however, was such that other processing units were frequently kept waiting for instructions and data, so it was replaced in favor first by magnetic core memory and then later by semiconductor-based storage.

OUTPUT

The output devices of the computer enable it to communicate results to the outside world. Output devices fall into two main categories:

1. Those that produce output that is readily handled and understood by human beings, e.g. printers (*q.v.*) and display monitors (*see* MONITOR, DISPLAY).

2. Auxiliary storage devices that hold data intended for further processing by machine (e.g. magnetic disks).

The first group contains a number of types of devices. The most obvious of these are printers (*q.v.*), designed to produce results in the form of printing on paper. Where the volume of printing is large, it is usual to use a *line printer*, one capable of producing a whole line of print at a time (usually from 120 to 160 characters). Such printers are capable of quite high speeds, typically up to 30 or more lines per second on a continuously fed roll of stationery. It is essential, of course, to have excellent paper-handling facilities to keep pace with such speeds. Such line printers are ideal for applications requiring voluminous end-results, such as payrolls, invoices, or inventory listings.

The output device of choice when high print quality and graphics are important is the *laser printer*. The high resolution of such printers is based on xerographic principles similar to those used with photocopy machines. A modern laser printer is shown in Fig. 2.

A related device, formerly quite commonplace, is the video display monitor. This has a keyboard like a typewriter, but the printing mechanism is replaced by a cathode ray tube (CRT) on which letters or digits can be projected, or a flat-panel monitor based on solid

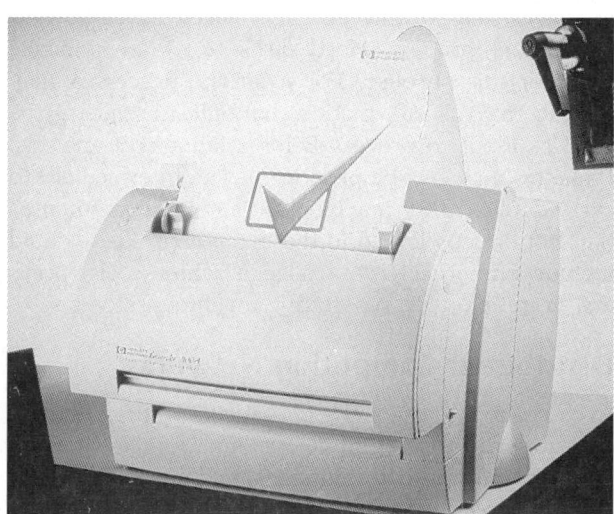

Figure 2. The Hewlett-Packard laser printer 1100A. (Courtesy of Hewlett-Packard.)

state picture elements. Compared with the typewriter, monitors have the advantage of displaying a large amount of information at once (often, several hundred characters), and a fresh display of additional information can be generated very rapidly. On the other hand, since they cannot produce "hard copy" (i.e. a permanent record), they are best used in circumstances where an operator needs to examine a small quantity of transient output information that does not have to be printed. Since display monitors have no processing power of their own, they are sometimes called "dumb terminals."

Increasingly, *personal computers* (PCs) have replaced free-standing video display monitors. PCs have their own display monitor plus the added advantage of local CPU processing power and the capability of saving data, which supplements that of the *host computer* (*q.v.*) with which it communicates through a network (*see* NETWORKS, COMPUTER).

Video display monitors or personal computers can also be used to display information in graphical form or as images and diagrams of increasingly good resolution. Such graphs and images can then be sent to a laser printer or inkjet printer, many of which are capable of good quality color reproduction. Associated input techniques using a lightpen (a device that effectively draws lines electronically on the face of the tube) to manipulate changes or additions to drawings and diagrams. Devices such as the lightpen are increasingly being used for computer-aided design in such fields as car-body or electric-circuit design. (*See* COMPUTER-AIDED DESIGN/ COMPUTER-AIDED MANUFACTURING). Where a permanent record of a graph or drawing is required, a graph-plotter can be attached to the computer and can produce intricate hard-copy drawings.

Results from one computer operation often need to be stored temporarily and then used as input to a subsequent process. Hard disks (*q.v.*) are typically used for this purpose. For example, process A may produce payroll information that will subsequently be used as input to process B for a labor cost analysis. Diskettes may also be produced as an intermediary to carry data to other machines being operated "offline" (i.e. not directly linked to the computer). These could include numerically controlled machine tools, printers, graph plotters, typesetting machines, etc.

Distributed Computing Networks

In the earliest days of the digital computer, its power was confined to a computer room. Bundles of work had to be physically brought to it and results collected. A vital step in releasing the power of the computer occurred when terminal devices, such as teletypes, were connected to the computer over telephone lines.

The problems to be solved were with the physical connection of the communications equipment and the writing of very sophisticated computer programs to control and manage an ever-increasing number of terminal devices (*see* DISTRIBUTED SYSTEMS and TIME SHARING).

The development first of minicomputers and then of the microprocessor and microcomputer have made it possible to build more "intelligence" (or local computing power) into the remote terminal devices so that they can carry out more complex operations. For example, results computed on a remote computer called a *server* can be fed back to a local intelligent terminal or PC called a *client* for local printing (*see* FILE SERVER and CLIENT–SERVER COMPUTING). When the server and its clients are in close proximity—in the same building or cluster of buildings for example—the arrangement is said to form a *local area network* (*q.v.*).

Microprocessors and Microcomputers

From the inception of digital computing, there has been a continual decrease in the physical size of *computer circuitry* (*q.v.*) due to ever more compact integration of circuit components. This integration has now reached the stage where hundreds of thousands of minute components and the printed wiring to interconnect them can be formed on a "chip"—a thin slice of silicon about 0.7 cm square (*see* MICROCOMPUTER CHIP). The components include transistors, resistors, and capacitors, which are the raw material from which the computer's registers, arithmetic unit, control unit, and memory can be made. CPUs based on these chips and the small computers that house them are called, respectively, *microprocessors and microcomputers* (*q.v.*).

The effect of achieving such a high packing density of components (or, as it is known, VLSI, very large-scale integration) is to make it possible to produce a complete processor or small memory unit on a single chip. The implications of this are of quite fundamental importance, since, with a cost per chip ranging from tens to a few hundred dollars, it enables computing power to be built into a wide variety of devices for use in offices, factories, laboratories, and the home (*see* EMBEDDED SYSTEM).

The effects of this increasing availability of cheap computing power are to cause a proliferation of more "intelligent" machines and to raise questions about the attendant social implications for both good and ill in an increasingly digital world. Of particular concern is the effect on employment (*see* AUTOMATION). Word processing (*q.v.*), for example, greatly improves the productivity of typists and secretaries and hence reduces the number of available jobs, especially now that so many executives compose at the keyboard rather than dictate. But to compensate, many new and interesting jobs are being created that relate to the manufacture and use of products hitherto undreamed of.

Graham J. Morris, revised by Edwin D. Reilly

DIGITAL COMPUTERS, HISTORY OF

ORIGINS

For articles on related subjects *see* AIKEN, HOWARD; ANALYTICAL ENGINE; ATANASOFF, JOHN VINCENT; BABBAGE, CHARLES; BELL LABS RELAY COMPUTERS; BUSH, VANNEVAR; CALCULATING MACHINES; COLOSSUS; ECKERT, J. PRESPER; EDVAC; ENIAC; HOLLERITH, HERMAN; HOLLERITH MACHINE; IBM CORPORATION; LEIBNIZ, GOTTFRIED WILHELM; MARK I, HARVARD; MAUCHLY, JOHN W.; NAPIER, JOHN; PASCAL, BLAISE; POWERS, JAMES; STORED PROGRAM CONCEPT; TORRES QUEVEDO, LEONARDO; TURING, ALAN M.; WIENER, NORBERT; VON NEUMANN, JOHN; ZUSE COMPUTERS; and ZUSE, KONRAD.

Mechanical aids to calculation and mechanical sequence-control devices were perhaps the earliest and most important achievements in the development of computer technology.

The first adding machines date from the early seventeenth century, the most famous of which was invented by the French scientist and philosopher Blaise Pascal, although it is now believed that his work was predated by that of William Schickard. A number of Pascal's machines, which he started to build in 1642, still exist. Even though he had intended them for practical use, their unreliability caused them to be treated mainly as objects of scientific curiosity. During the subsequent two centuries, numerous attempts to develop practical calculating machines were made by Morland, Leibniz, Mahon, Hahn, and Müller, among others. However, it was not until the mid-nineteenth century that a commercially successful machine was produced. This was the "arithmometer" of Thomas de Colmar, the first version of which was invented in 1820, and which used the stepped-wheel mechanism invented by Leibniz.

Mechanical devices for controlling the sequencing of a set of operations, such as the rotating pegged cylinders still seen in music boxes today, date back even earlier. For example, de Caus (1576–1626) used such a mechanism to control both the playing of an organ and the movements of model figures. One of the most famous designers of mechanical automata was Vaucanson. In 1736, he successfully demonstrated an automaton that simulated human lip and finger movements with sufficient accuracy to play a flute. Vaucanson was also involved in the development of what came to be known as the Jacquard loom, in which the woven pattern was specified and controlled by a sequence of perforated cards. The original idea can be traced back to Bouchon in 1725, but such automatic looms did not come into widespread use until early in the nineteenth century after the work by Jacquard.

In 1834, these two lines of development came together in the work of Charles Babbage, who had become dissatisfied with the accuracy of printed mathematical tables. Earlier, in 1822, Babbage had built a small machine, involving several linked adding mechanisms, which would automatically generate successive values of simple algebraic functions using the method of finite differences (*see* DIFFERENCE ENGINE). His attempt at making a full-scale model with a printing mechanism was abandoned in 1834, and he then started to design a more versatile machine. In the space of a few years he had developed the concept of a program-controlled, mechanical, digital computer, incorporating a complete arithmetic unit, store, punched-card input and output, and printing mechanism. The machine, which he called an Analytical Engine (*q.v.*), was to have been controlled by programs represented by sets of Jacquard cards, with conditional jumps and iteration loops being provided for by devices that skipped forward or backward over the required number of cards. Internally, the machine was essentially microprogrammed (*q.v.*) by rotating pegged cylinders that controlled the sequencing of subsidiary mechanisms.

Babbage's work inspired several other people, among whom were Ludgate, who designed an analytical engine in Ireland in 1909; Torres Quevedo, who demonstrated the feasibility of an electromechanical analytical engine by successfully producing a typewriter-controlled calculating machine in 1920; and Couffignal, who started to design a binary analytical engine in France during the 1930s. However, Babbage's pioneering efforts were apparently unknown to most of the people working on the various computer projects during the Second World War, who were unaware that the problems they were tackling had been considered and often solved by Babbage more than a hundred years earlier.

The Jacquard loom was perhaps the source of Herman Hollerith's idea of using punched cards (*q.v.*) to represent logical and numerical data. Developed for use in the 1890 US National Census, his system, incorporating hand-operated tabulating machines and sorters, was highly successful and spread rapidly to several other countries. Automatic card-feed mechanisms were soon provided, and the system began to be used for business accounting applications. Following a dispute with Hollerith, the Bureau of the Census developed in time for the 1910 Census a new tabulating system involving mechanical sensing of card perforations, as opposed to Hollerith's system of electrical sensing. James Powers, the engineer in charge of this work, eventually left the Bureau to form his own company, which later became part of Remington Rand. Hollerith's company merged with two others to become the Computing-Tabulating-Recording Company, which, in 1924, changed its name to the International Business Machines Corporation (IBM).

In 1937, Howard Aiken of Harvard University approached IBM with a proposal for a large-scale calculator to be built from the mechanical and electromechanical devices that were used for punched-card machines. The resulting machine, the Automatic Sequence Controlled Calculator, or Harvard Mark I, was built at the IBM Development Laboratories at Endicott, NY. The machine, which was completed in 1944, was a huge affair with 72 decimal accumulators, capable of multiplying two 23-digit numbers in 6 sec. It was controlled by a sequence of instructions specified by a perforated paper tape. Somewhat surprisingly, in view of Aiken's knowledge of and respect for Babbage's efforts, it lacked general conditional jump facilities. After completion of the Mark I, Aiken and IBM pursued separate paths. Several more machines were designed at Harvard, the first being another tape-controlled calculator, built this time from electromagnetic relays. IBM produced various machines, including several plugboard-controlled relay calculators and the partly electronic Selective Sequence Electronic Calculator, which was very much in the tradition of the original Mark I.

Not until well after the Second World War was it found that in Germany there had been an operational program-controlled calculator built earlier than the Mark I, namely, Konrad Zuse's Z3 machine, which first worked in 1941. This machine, which had been preceded by two earlier but unsuccessful machines, had a mechanical store, but was otherwise built from telephone relays. It could store 64 floating-point binary numbers, and has been described as somewhat faster than the Harvard Mark I. The Z3, like several other machines built by Zuse, did not survive the war; the only one of Zuse's machines to do so was the Z4 computer, which was later used successfully for several years at the Technische Hochschüle in Zurich.

Various other electromechanical machines were built during and even after the Second World War, including an important series of relay calculators at the Bell Telephone Laboratories. The first of these, the Complex Computer, was demonstrated in September 1940 by being operated in its New York City location from a teletypewriter installed in Hanover, New Hampshire, on the occasion of a meeting of the American Mathematical Society. The Complex Computer, or Model 1, was capable of adding, subtracting, multiplying, and dividing two complex numbers, but lacked any sequence-control facilities. Later machines in the series incorporated successively more extensive sequencing facilities, so that the Model 5 relay calculator was a truly general-purpose (tape-controlled) computer that achieved very high reliability of operation.

The earliest known electronic digital calculating device was a machine for solving up to 30 simultaneous linear equations, initiated in 1938 at Iowa State College by John Atanasoff and Clifford Berry. Although the arithmetic unit had been successfully tested before the project was abandoned in 1942, the input–output mechanism was still incomplete, so the machine never saw actual use (*see* ATANASOFF–BERRY COMPUTER). Other important work on the development of electronic calculating devices was done at IBM, starting in 1942 with the building of experimental versions of various punched-card machines including a multiplier. This machine was the origin of the electronic multipliers and calculating machines such as the Type 604 and the Card Programmed Calculator (CPC), that IBM produced in great quantities in the years immediately following the Second World War and which played an important role until stored program electronic computers became widely available.

The earliest known efforts at applying electronics to a general-purpose, program-controlled computer were those undertaken by Schreyer and Zuse in 1939, but their plans for a 1,500 valve (i.e. vacuum tube) machine were later rejected by the German government. In Britain, a series of large special-purpose electronic computers, intended for code-breaking purposes, was developed by a team at Bletchley Park (where Alan Turing was a senior cryptanalyst), led by Tommy Flowers from the Post Office Research Station at Dollis Hill. The first of these "Colossus" machines, which incorporated about 2,000 tubes, was operating in December 1943. By the end of the war 10 Colossi were in use, and had made a major contribution to the war by enabling the Allies to read large numbers of encrypted teleprinter messages to and from the German High Command. The Colossus has been described as being, in a very limited fashion, a program-controlled device (*see* COLOSSUS). An exact working replica has now been created at Bletchley Park. Interestingly enough, several postwar British electronic computers were developed by people who had been involved with these highly secret machines.

However, by far the most influential line of development was that carried out at the Moore School of Electrical Engineering at the University of Pennsylvania by John Mauchly, J. Presper Eckert, and their colleagues, starting in 1943. This work, which derived at least as directly from Vannevar Bush's prewar mechanical *differential analyzer* (*q.v.*) as from any digital calculating device, first led to the development of the ENIAC, which was officially inaugurated in February 1946. This machine was intended primarily for ballistics calculations, but by the time it was completed it was really a general-purpose device, programmed by means of pluggable interconnections. Its internal electronic memory consisted of 20 accumulators, each of 10 decimal digits, and it could perform 5,000 arithmetic operations per second—it was approximately a thousand times faster than the Harvard Mark I. The ENIAC was very much the most complex piece of electronic equipment that had ever been assembled, incorporating 19,000 tubes, and using nearly 200 KW of power. The machine was very successful, despite earlier fears regarding the reliability of electronic components.

But even before the ENIAC was complete, the designers, who had been joined by John von Neumann, started to plan a radically different successor machine, the EDVAC. The EDVAC was a serial binary machine, far more economical on electronic tubes than ENIAC, which was a decimal machine in which each decimal digit was represented by a ring of 10 flip-flops. A second major difference was that EDVAC was to have a much larger internal memory than ENIAC, based on mercury delay lines (*see* ULTRASONIC MEMORY). For these reasons, the initial design of EDVAC included only one-tenth of the equipment used in ENIAC, yet provided a hundred times the internal memory capacity.

It was apparently the discussions of the various ways in which the capabilities of ENIAC might be extended, together with the knowledge of the possibility of comparatively large internal memories, that led to the realization that sequence-control information could be represented by words held in memory along with the numerical quantities entering into the computation, rather than by some external means, such as perforated tape or pluggable interconnections. Thus, EDVAC could retain the great speed of operation that had been achieved by ENIAC, but could avoid the very lengthy setup time, often of the order of a day or more, that had made it impractical to use for other than very extensive calculations. The fact that a program could read and modify portions of itself was heavily utilized, since ideas such as index registers (*q.v.*) and indirect addresses were still in the offing. Of more lasting significance was the practical and attractive proposition of using the computer to assist with the preparation of its own programs.

Figure 1. Family tree of computers to mid-1950s (Courtesy of the Smithsonian Institution).

With EDVAC, therefore, the invention of the modern digital computer was basically complete. The plans for its design were widely published and extremely influential, so that, even though it was not the first stored-program electronic digital computer to be put into operation, it undoubtedly was the major initial inspiration that started the vast number of computer projects during the late 1940s. A family tree depicting computer development up to the mid-1950s is shown in Fig. 1.

Bibliography

1961. Morrison, P. and Morrison, E. (eds.) *Charles Babbage and His Calculating Engines: Selected Writings by Charles Babbage and Others.* New York: Dover.

1972. Goldstine, H. H. *The Computer from Pascal to von Neumann.* Princeton: Princeton University Press.

1973. Fleck, G. (ed.) *A Computer Perspective.* By the Office of Charles and Ray Eames, Cambridge, MA: Harvard University Press. (A profusely illustrated book, containing a vast amount of information related directly or indirectly to the history of computing.)

1982. Randell, B. (ed.) *The Origins of Digital Computers,* 3rd Ed. Berlin: Springer-Verlag.

1983. Flowers, T. H. "The Design of Colossus," *Annals of the History of Computing,* **5**, 3, 239–252.

1983. Ceruzzi, P. E. *Reckoners: The Prehistory of the Digital Computer from Relays to the Stored Program Concept, 1935–1945.* Westport, CT: Greenwood Press.

1984. Augarten, S. *Bit by Bit: An Illustrated History of Computers.* New York: Tickner & Fields.

1990. Aspray, W. (ed.) *Computing Before Computers.* Ames, IA: Iowa State University Press.

1993. Cortada, J. W. *Before the Computer: IBM, NCR, Burroughs and Remington Rand and the Industry they Created, 1865–1956.* Princeton NJ: Princeton University Press.

Brian Randell

EARLY

For articles on related subjects *see* AIKEN, HOWARD; BELL LABS RELAY COMPUTERS; ECKERT, J. PRESPER; EDSAC; EDVAC; ENIAC; MARK I, HARVARD; MAUCHLY, JOHN W.; STORED PROGRAM CONCEPT; TURING, ALAN M.; ULTRASONIC MEMORY; UNIVAC I; VON NEUMANN, JOHN; VON NEUMANN MACHINE; WHIRLWIND; WILLIAMS, FREDERICK C.; WILLIAMS TUBE MEMORY; ZUSE COMPUTERS; and ZUSE, KONRAD.

The digital computer age began when the Automatic Sequence Controlled Calculator (Harvard Mark I) started working in August 1944. This machine was based on the mechanical technology of rotating shafts, electromagnetic clutches, and counter wheels, developed over the years for punched card tabulating machinery. It was constructed by IBM, following the ideas of Howard Aiken, whose original proposals go back at least to 1937. The shaft rotation period, and hence the time required to transfer a number or perform an addition, was 0.3 sec, while multiplication and division took 6 and 11.4 sec, respectively.

No other large machines using rotating shafts were built, but there were a number of successful magnetic

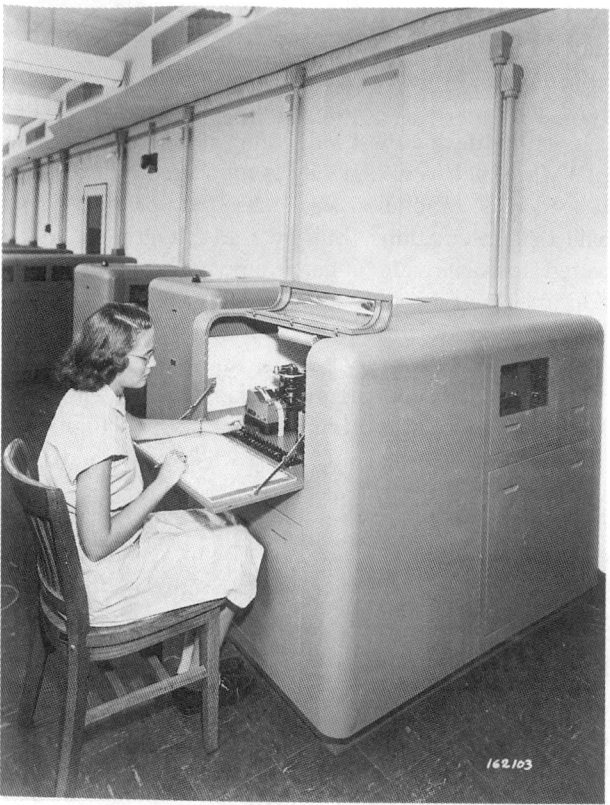

Figure 1. At the tape processor table of the Bell Model V Relay Computer, installed at the Ballistics Research Laboratory of the Aberdeen Proving Ground. (Courtesy of AT&T: Reprinted with permission of AT&T.)

relay machines. Bell Telephone Laboratories had been working in this area since 1938. Their first fully automatic computer was the one now referred to as the Bell Model V (Fig. 1), of which two examples were constructed. The first of these began to work at the end of 1946. An addition took 0.3 sec and multiplication and division took up to 1.0 and 2.2 sec, respectively. The last of the series was the Model VI, commissioned in 1949. Harvard Mark II, a relay machine designed by Aiken and following a very different design philosophy, was running in September 1948. A relay computer constructed in Sweden (BARK) was operational early in 1950. Independent work on relay computers had also been done by Konrad Zuse in Germany, and a Zuse Z4 was running in Zurich in 1950. Relays lend themselves to complex circuit arrangements, and all the machines just mentioned had floating-point arithmetic operations, a feature that did not appear in electronic computers until well after the period now under review here. The Bell machines had elaborate checking arrangements, including a redundant representation for stored numbers. Model VI even had a retry feature, designed to mitigate the effect of transient relay faults.

The concept of the large-scale electronic computer is due to J. Presper Eckert and John W. Mauchly. They were already building the ENIAC when the Harvard Mark I was commissioned. The ENIAC contained nearly 19,000 vacuum tubes, more than twice as many as any later vacuum-tube computer. Because it was by far the most complex machine constructed up to that time, its construction was a great act of technological courage, on the part of both the designers and the Office of Naval Research, which sponsored it. It was built at the Moore School of Electrical Engineering in Philadelphia. The ENIAC began to function in the summer of 1945. An addition took 200 μs and a multiplication took 2.6 ms.

The very early computers were extremely limited in the amount of internal storage that they had. Provision was usually made for tables to be held in read-only storage (banks of switches or punched paper tape) with arrangements for interpolation. It was frequently possible for the programmer to arrange that more than one arithmetic or transfer operation should take place at the same time. The ENIAC was programmed by setting up hundreds of plugs and sockets and switches, an operation that could take several hours.

The other computers read their instructions from punched paper tape, endless loops being used for repeated sections of the program.

While the ENIAC was still under construction, Eckert and Mauchly began to realize that, by the application of logical principles, it would be possible to construct a machine not only much more powerful than the ENIAC but also much smaller. They were joined by John von Neumann on a part-time basis, and it was from the group so formed that the ideas of the modern *stored-program* computer emerged. They were summarized in a document entitled "First draft of a report on the EDVAC," prepared by von Neumann and dated 30 June 1945. Because this report bore von Neumann's name only, the term *von Neumann computer* is often used as a synonym for "stored-program computer," giving the impression that the ideas were all von Neumann's own. I prefer the term *Eckert–von Neumann computer.*

Eckert and Mauchly did not stay at the Moore School to work on the EDVAC, and it was not until January 1952 that a machine bearing that name was commissioned. Instead, they founded the Eckert–Mauchly

Figure 2. The BINAC computer. (Courtesy of the Hagley Museum & Library.)

Corporation, with the object of designing and marketing the UNIVAC. This company was later absorbed into Remington Rand.

From the beginning, the UNIVAC was designed with an eye to business data processing, and the standards set for performance and reliability were very high. In March 1951, the first UNIVAC passed a rigorous acceptance test and was delivered to the US Census Bureau. It was then a fully engineered machine, with magnetic tape and other peripherals required for large-scale business operations. The Eckert–Mauchly Corporation had demonstrated a smaller machine, the BINAC (Fig. 2), in August 1949, but this was not very successful and they decided to concentrate their efforts on the UNIVAC.

When the Moore School group broke up, von Neumann established a project for the construction of a computer at the Institute for Advanced Study, Princeton. Von Neumann himself, assisted by H. H. Goldstine, laid down the logical structure of this computer, and the engineering development and design was in the hands of J. H. Bigelow. It was the first bit-parallel (all the bits of a word were processed at once rather than serially) computer to be designed, and it introduced techniques that became commonplace, such as the register-economizing device of putting the multiplier in the tail of the accumulator and shifting it out as the multiplication proceeds. Although the machine was not working until October 1952, the project had immense influence on the development of the digital computer field. The ultrasonic memory (q.v.) which had been proposed for the

EDVAC was thought to be too slow for a parallel machine, and it was planned to use instead a memory based on the Selectron proposed by J. A. Rajchman. The Selectron did not fulfill its promise, but fortunately the Williams tube memory (q.v.) came along in time to save the situation.

The experimental computers that came into action first were those that were least ambitious, both in specification and in performance. One of these was the EDSAC, a computer directly inspired by the EDVAC, designed and constructed by W. Renwick and myself in Cambridge, UK. This computer did its first calculation on 6 May 1949, and was used for much early work on the development of programming techniques. Activity at Manchester University arose out of work by F. C. Williams on what became known as the Williams tube memory. In order to test this system, Williams and T. Kilburn (q.v.) built a small model computer with a memory of 32 words and only five instructions in its instruction set. The only arithmetic instruction was for subtraction. Development work continued, and by the summer of 1949 a computer with a magnetic drum as a backing memory was demonstrated. The Ferranti Mark I computer (Fig. 3), of which the first delivered model was inaugurated at Manchester University in July 1951, was based on this work.

A third center of activity in England was at the National Physical Laboratory, where the inspiration came from Alan Turing. Turing did not stay there long, leaving for Manchester University in 1948, but the Pilot ACE, which was running by December 1950, reflected very strongly his rather personal view of

Table 1. Characteristics of Electronic Computers as of early 1951

Computer	Serial or parallel	Decimal or binary	No. of addresses	Word length	Clock frequency (KHz)	Memory[a] Type	Memory[a] No. of words
EDVAC[b]	S	B	3 + 1[d]	44 bits	1,000	U	1,024
UNIVAC	S	D	1	12 char.	2,250	U	1,000
IAS[b]	P	B	1	40 bits	Asynch.	W	1,024
EDSAC	S	B	1	35 bits	500	U	512
Ferranti 1	S	B	1	40 bits	100	W	256
Pilot ACE	S	B	—[d]	32 bits	1,000	U	360
SEAC	S	B	3	45 bits	1,000	U	512
SWAC	P	B	4	36 bits	125	W	256
Whirlwind I	P	B	1	16 bits	1,000	E	256
Harvard Mark III	S/P	D	3	16 dec.	28	D	4,000[c]
Burroughs	S	D	1 or 1 + 1[d]	9 dec.	125	D	800
ERA 1101	P	B	1 + 1[d]	24 bits	400	D	16,384

(a) U = ultrasonic delay (mercury tank); W = Williams tube; D = magnetic drum; E = electrostatic (CRT).
(b) Not commissioned until 1952.
(c) Separate 200-word memory for instructions.
(d) Provision for minimum-access coding.

Figure 3. Tom Kilburn with the Ferranti Mark I computer at Manchester University. (Courtesy of the National Archive on the History of Computing, University of Manchester.)

computer design. The Pilot ACE used an ultrasonic memory, and it was necessary for the programmer to know more of the structure of the machine and the timing of pulses within it than was required in the case of other machines.

The first of the American machines to be brought into use was the SEAC, dedicated on 20 June 1950. This was built under the direction of S. N. Alexander at the National Bureau of Standards in Washington, and the success of that group is the more remarkable, since the SEAC project started after many others. The SEAC was elegant in design and construction, and pioneered

the use of small plug-in packages; each package contained a number of germanium diodes and a single vacuum tube. The SEAC used an ultrasonic memory, but a Williams tube memory was later added for evaluation purposes. Meanwhile, H. D. Huskey, who had formerly been a member of the team at the National Physical Laboratory in England and had worked on ENIAC, was completing the SWAC at the NBS Institute for Numerical Analysis at UCLA. This was a parallel machine with a Williams tube memory and was very fast by the standards of the day.

Whirlwind I was a computer with a short word length, aiming at very high speed and power, and intended ultimately for air traffic control and similar applications. It was designed and built under the direction of J. W. Forrester at MIT and was operating in December 1950. From its specification, one would take it to be the first of the minicomputers (*q.v.*), but in fact it occupied the largest floor area of all the early computers, including the ENIAC. The memory was of the electrostatic type, but the cathode-ray tubes were of special design and operated on a different principle from that used by Williams.

Table 1 gives brief particulars of the computers mentioned above and also of several additional ones that became operational in the same period.

Bibliography

1951. US Navy, Office of Naval Research. *Digital Computer Newsletter*, **1–3**.
1953. US Navy, Office of Naval Research. *A Survey of Automatic Digital Computers*.

Max. memory access time (ms)	Operation time (incl. access)			Input–Output	No. of tubes	No. of diodes (germanium)	Auxiliary memory
	Add (ms)	Multi. (ms)	Divide (ms)				
0.38	0.2–1.5	2.2–3.5	2.2–3.6	Paper tape	3,600	10,000	—
0.40	0.5 mean	2.15 mean	3.9 mean	Magnetic tape	5,600	18,000	Magnetic tape
0.025	0.062	0.44–1.0	1.1	Cards	2,300	0	—
1.1	1.5 mean	6 mean	—	Paper tape	3,800	0	—
0.64	1.2	3.36	—	Paper tape	3,800	0	Drum, 16K
1.0	—	2	—	Cards	800	0	—
0.38	1.5 max.	3.6 max	3.6 max	Paper tape	1,300	15,800	Magnetic tape
—	0.064	0.38	—	Paper tape; cards	2,300	3,000	—
0.016	0.049	0.061	0.1	Paper tape	6,800	22,000	—
4.5	5	13	100	Magnetic tape	5,000	1,300	—
32	0.6–17	30–50	—	Paper tape	3,271	6,773	—
17	0.1 min.	0.35 min.	0.42 min.	Paper tape	2,200	3,000	—

1972. Goldstine, H. H. *The Computer from Pascal to von Neumann.* Princeton: Princeton University Press.
1985. Wilkes, M. V. *Memoirs of a Computer Pioneer.* Cambridge, MA: MIT Press.

Maurice V. Wilkes

SINCE 1950

For articles on related subjects *see* APPLE COMPUTER, INC.; ATLAS; COMPUTER INDUSTRY; CONTROL DATA CORPORATION; DIGITAL EQUIPMENT CORPORATION; IBM CORPORATION; IBM 1400 SERIES; IBM 360/370/390 SERIES; IBM PC; LARC; MICROSOFT; MINICOMPUTER; NORC; STRETCH; SUPERCOMPUTERS; UNIVAC I; and WHIRLWIND.

Since 1950, computers have advanced at a pace unparalleled in the history of technology. Processing speed and memory capacity have increased; size and cost have decreased by several orders of magnitude. The pace has not been steady on all fronts, but has always been rapid, and it continues.

This phenomenal growth has led many to describe what happened in computing before some arbitrary date in the recent past as irrelevant "prehistory" or prologue. For some that date is 1945, before which there existed a primitive world of mechanical and electro-mechanical systems with little or no programmability. For others, that date is 1974, before which computers were things that were batch-programmed, inaccessible, and too big and expensive to be used as a personal device. For still others that date is 1993, before which computers were isolated islands unable to communicate with one another over the World Wide Web (*q.v.*). About all that is certain is that we have not seen the last of these transformations.

One can chronicle each dramatic advance, each milestone of computing that marks the passing of a certain threshold; e.g. from mechanical to electronic; from mainframe to personal, from isolated to networked, etc. Such listings are valuable, but do little to aid one's understanding of the subject. Still it appears impossible to make general statements about computing since 1945, as each new development threatens to render any such statement obsolete.

The notion that there were three major generations of computers, based on device technology (vacuum tubes, discrete transistors, and integrated circuits), served well to characterize machines for the beginning of the electronic era. But nearly all computers have used silicon integrated circuitry (*q.v.*) since the 1970s. Yes, it is true that IC technology has advanced in those years, and the microprocessor was a significant milestone, but computers today still use a descendant of the IC technology invented by Robert Noyce (*q.v.*) and Jack Kilby around 1959. Computing has thus been in the "third generation" for as long as it took to progress from the ENIAC to the PDP-11, an early minicomputer.

The notion of generations is nevertheless useful if interpreted more broadly. All machines, especially those tested by the rigors of the marketplace, tend to be improved or modified incrementally. Periodically, designers introduce more radical improvements, and when they do, it is appropriate to speak of a new generation of product. Introducing a new device technology is one of several ways this can happen; also common is a thorough redesign of the machine's architecture. Thus, the history of computing is characterized not by three or four but by many generations. In that sense, present generation cycles in the computer business can last as little as 2 or 3 years (*see* GENERATIONS, COMPUTER).

Given this context, the question remains: are there general characteristics one can use to understand the evolution of computing since 1950? A closer look reveals that at least a few such trends are present.

The von Neumann Architecture

First among these trends is the persistence of the von Neumann machine (*q.v.*) model of computer architecture through successive waves of hardware and software advances. That model, originally conceived by J. Presper Eckert (*q.v.*), John Mauchly (*q.v.*), and John von Neumann (*q.v.*) in the mid-1940s, emerged in response to the need for a practical design for the EDVAC (*q.v.*), a machine they were proposing as a follow-on to the ENIAC (*q.v.*), then under construction. But the von Neumann model's influence was to be much greater. Its persistence has come from its ability to organize and unify what otherwise would be a bewildering range of options about computer design. It has persisted also because it could be extended and radically modified without altering its basic structure. Despite limitations, the model has served as the foundation upon which the edifice of computer science and engineering has been built, and shows signs of remaining so into the future.

Modern computers hardly resemble those sketched out by the EDVAC team in the 1940s. Yet, just as one can see in a modern automobile decisions made by Henry Ford eight decades ago, the ancestral lineage is there. Today the term "von Neumann Architecture" implies a rigid division between memory and processing units, with a single channel between the two. Instructions as well as data are stored together in the primary memory, which is configured to be large, random-access, and as fast as practical. The basic cycle of a computer is to transfer an instruction from memory to the processor, decode that instruction, and execute it with respect to data that is also retrieved from memory.

Despite all that has happened, these patterns, especially the last, remain. (The late Alan Perlis (*q.v.*) once remarked, "Sometimes I think the only universal in the computing field is the fetch–execute cycle.") From time to time, designers propose computers that radically deviate from the von Neumann model; since about 1990 these machines have found a small but secure niche in a few specialized areas. Still, the simpler structure outlined in the EDVAC Report remains the starting point even in the cases of massively parallel, "non-von machines" (*see* PARALLEL PROCESSING).

The ideas contained in von Neumann's 1945 report were not his alone, nor was that report the definitive statement of what has become the accepted architecture of the modern computer. A full understanding came with the cooperative effort of many persons, working on different projects, between 1945 and about 1950. The EDVAC report described a machine that economized on hardware by doing everything, including register addition, one bit at a time. When von Neumann moved from the EDVAC project to one at the Institute for Advanced Study at Princeton, that concept was modified to allow for parallel arithmetic on each 40-bit "word." That required more hardware, but simplified the design of the logical control unit and yielded faster arithmetic speeds. Data were likewise transferred to and from memory a word, not a bit, at a time, but like the sequential execution of program steps, memory transfer of successive words remained a serial activity, which became famous as the "von Neumann bottleneck."

The notion of having the word and not the bit as the basic unit of processing emerged among other one-of-a-kind computer projects in the late 1940s, as did the related notion of having a large, reliable, random access memory that could transfer a full word at a time. Most first-generation computers used serial memories, however, until reliable magnetic core memory became available in the mid-1950s.

What is most remembered about the EDVAC Report is its description of the stored program principle (*q.v.*): the notion of storing a program in the same memory device as the data those instructions acted on. As initially conceived, it had three features. First, it meant that the processor could fetch instructions at the same high speeds as it fetched data. Second, it meant that a computer could solve a variety of problems in which the ratio of instructions to data would vary. Third, and most important, it meant that the processor could operate on and modify instructions as if they were data, especially by computing new addresses for operands required by an instruction.

The first two features were obvious advantages, but the last was not, and to some at the time it seemed unnecessary and even radical. By the mid-1950s people recognized that a program's ability to modify itself, if not in precisely the way von Neumann and his colleagues envisioned, was the most profound innovation of all. Indeed, by allowing computers to be programmed at levels far higher than individual processor instructions, this innovation is as much responsible for the present-day computer age as any advance in hardware. Although the EDVAC group hardly foresaw this, it is testimony to the originality of their thinking that the concept has proved so adaptable and seminal.

Classes of Computers

One may classify computers into a few rough categories: supercomputer, mainframe, mini, workstation, and personal. These terms did not come into common use until the 1970s (and for the workstation, the 1980s), but today they have fairly precise meanings. A look back reveals a functional as well as price differentiation in computers almost from the beginning of commercial computing. The ENIAC, with its emphasis on numerical processing for classified military customers, was the ancestor of the supercomputer, while the UNIVAC I (*see* Fig. 1), optimized for business data processing, was an early mainframe (*q.v.*). Small, inexpensive drum-based computers such as the Bendix G-15, the Librascope LGP-30, and the Alwac III-E found a decent market in the late 1950s, although their use of vacuum tubes and their architecture differentiate them from the minicomputers of the 1960s.

Besides price, architecture is the principal way of assigning these classifications, but memory capacity, processing speeds, packaging, intended market, software, and other factors also come into play. At any given moment, the classes are distinct and represent a descending order of computing power, but over the years each category ratchets upward. Thus, today's personal computer has the power of yesterday's mini (and the day before yesterday's mainframe), but is still called a personal computer.

In the past each new category seemed to bubble up from a lower level, due mainly to advances in device technology. They often began as modest offerings designed to take advantage of a small niche poorly served by an established class, but soon grew out of that to become a full-fledged class of general-purpose computers on their own. New classes did not arise from the reduction in cost and size of the machines of a higher category. For example, in 1975, Digital Equipment Corporation introduced the LSI-11, a single-board, low-cost version of its popular PDP-11 minicomputer, but the LSI-11 did not inaugurate the personal computer era. The PC came instead from an upward evolution of simple 4-bit processor chips that

Figure 1. UNIVAC I. (Courtesy of the Hagley Museum & Library.)

were developed for cash registers, adding machines, and other modest devices. As these increased in power, they took on more and more properties of general-purpose computers. In the mid-1980s, a similar phenomenon occurred as companies introduced machines ("mini-supercomputers") that reached toward the performance of the supercomputer, but at far lower cost.

Software-Compatible Families of Computers

A third pattern has emerged, and it, too, is likely to persist: the emergence of not just single products optimized for scientific, process-control, or business applications, but families of general-purpose computers that offer upward compatibility of software. This gives customers an easy path to upgrade with the same vendor as their needs increase, and allows the manufacturer to lower costs by broadening the customer base.

A major portion of the costs of any computing system is the software developed for it. With a family of prod-

ucts, a vendor can amortize these costs over a longer period of time. That in turn can justify higher initial development costs, and thus produce better software. Alternatively, a successful family of machines allows a vigorous third-party software industry to flourish. This offsets the principal disadvantage of having such families, namely that it prevents one from taking advantage of advances in architecture or design and producing the "best" machine of the moment. Likewise, offering a family of machines based on a general-purpose architecture compensates for the fact that special-purpose architectures might work better for specific customers.

Philco marketed a series of upward-compatible Transac S-2000, models 210, 211, and 212, between 1958 and 1964. Philco sold out to Ford, who subsequently left the computer business. IBM System/360, introduced in April 1964, was the first commercial system based on a family of upward compatible processors all of which were announced on the same day. Other notable families include the Univac 1100 series, the Burroughs B5000 and its successors, the CDC Cyber series, and the Digital Equipment Corporation VAX series. Since about 1980 Intel has maintained software compatibility with its 80x86 line of micro-processors. The company typically markets its latest chip for personal computers, while relegating the older chips (now at reduced prices) to embedded or other less visible applications.

The need to maintain compatibility has retarded the adoption of advances in architecture or instruction set design. But if improvements in device technology can be incorporated without destroying compatibility, a manufacturer will do so as soon as practical. The overall results are short, generational cycles of device technology, but less frequent cycles of changes in architecture. Some advances in circuit technology require modifications to a system architecture to take full advantage of it. A good initial design, though, can and should be robust enough to absorb advances and incorporate them while still maintaining software compatibility. The IBM System/360 used hybrid circuits, magnetic core memory, and a batch-oriented operating system. Over the years, IBM introduced integrated circuits (q.v.), semiconductor memory, virtual memory (q.v.), time-sharing (q.v.), and a host of other technical innovations, all the while preserving software compatibility. The result kept this architecture commercially competitive into the 1990s.

Whether to drop a proven architecture and adopt a new one is a decision manufacturers constantly face. Given the relentless march of device technology, a company may feel it must take that step, although one can keep an obsolescent design viable for a long time. When a company adopts a new architecture, its managers "bet the company" on the future design. The history of computing is full of examples of those who waited too long or who plunged too early into a new design.

The following are brief descriptions of representative machines that reflect the patterns described above. Machines up to and including the IBM System/360 are classified by the traditional generations; those following by their type: super, mainframe, mini, etc. In these descriptions the emphasis is on both the device technology and the overall system architecture.

The First Generation, 1950–1960

The first generation began around 1950 with the introduction of commercial computers manufactured and sold in quantity. Computers of the first generation stored their programs internally and used vacuum tubes as their switching technology. Beyond that they had little else in common. Each design used a different mix of registers, addressing schemes, and instruc-

tion sets (q.v.). The greatest variation was found in the devices used for memory, and this affected the processor design. Each of the memory technologies available at the time had a drawback, which led to a variety of machine designs that favored one approach over another (see MEMORY).

The reports describing the Institute for Advanced Study computer, written by Arthur Burks, Herman Goldstine, and John von Neumann, emphasized the advantages of a parallel memory device that could read and write a full word at a time. The device they favored, the RCA Selectron tube, took longer than expected to appear, and only the Rand Corporation's Johnniac used it. America's first commercial machine, the UNIVAC I, used a mercury delay line, which accessed data one bit at a time. The only parallel devices available at the time were cathode ray tubes (Williams tubes—q.v.). These tubes, originally intended for other commercial applications, were notoriously unreliable. By far the most popular memory device for first-generation machines was the rotating magnetic drum. It was slow, but its reliability and low cost made it suitable for small-scale machines like the IBM 650, Bendix G-15, Alwac III-E, and Librascope LGP-30.

By the end of this period, machines were introduced that incorporated magnetic core memory. With the advent of ferrite cores—and techniques for manufacturing and assembling them in large quantities—the memory problem endemic to the first generation was effectively solved.

UNIVAC

The UNIVAC was designed by J. Presper Eckert and John Mauchly, and first delivered in 1951 (by which time their company had been acquired by Remington–Rand). It was the first American computer to be produced as a series and sold to commercial customers. Eventually, over 40 were built. Customers included the US Census Bureau, the Lawrence Livermore Laboratory, the US Army and Air Force, the General Electric Company, and several insurance companies. Most customers used the UNIVAC for accounting, statistical, and other applications that would later be known as *data processing* (q.v.).

The UNIVAC used binary-coded decimal (BCD) arithmetic performed in four general-purpose accumulators. Word length was 45 bits; each word could represent 11 decimal digits plus a sign, or 6 alphabetic characters (6 bits per character plus 1 parity bit). Basic clock speed was 2.25 MHz, and the multiplication time was about 2 ms. Mercury delay lines, a form of ultrasonic memory (q.v.), stored 1,000 words in high-speed memory, while magnetic tape units stored up to one million characters on reels of metal tape.

The UNIVAC was ruggedly designed and built. Its central processor contained over 5,000 tubes, installed in cabinets that were arranged in a 10-foot (3 m) by 14-foot (4.5 m) rectangle. Inside this rectangle were the delay line tanks. Many design features that later became commonplace first appeared with the UNIVAC: alphanumeric as well as numeric processing, extra bits for error checking, magnetic tapes for bulk memory, and buffers that allowed high-speed data transfer between internal and external memories without CPU intervention.

IBM 701, 650

At the time of the UNIVAC's announcement, IBM was not committed to electronic computation and was vigorously marketing its line of punched card tabulators. In response to the UNIVAC, IBM entered the computer market with several machines.

In 1952, IBM announced the 701 computer, originally called the Defense Calculator after its perceived market. True to that perception, most of the 19 models installed went to US Defense Department or aerospace customers. Initial rental fees were $15,000 a month; IBM did not sell the machines outright. For primary memory, the machine used Williams tubes that could store up to 4,096 36-bit words. Oxide-coated plastic tape was used for backup memory, and a magnetic drum provided intermediate storage. It could perform about 2,000 multiplications/second, but, unlike the UNIVAC, the 701's central processor handled control of the slow input–output facilities directly. IBM also developed a similar-sized, but character-oriented machine, the 702, for business customers.

IBM also initiated development of a smaller machine, whose origins lay in proposals for extensions of punched card equipment. In the course of its development, its nature shifted to that of a general-purpose, drum-based, stored program computer. IBM's acquisition of drum memory technology from Engineering Research Associates in 1949 was a key element in this shift. The machine, now called the IBM 650, was delivered in 1954, rather later than planned. It proved to be very successful; eventually, there were over a thousand 650 installations at a rental of about $3,500 per month.

By the time of its announcement, the 650 had to compete with a number of other inexpensive, drum-memory machines. It outsold them all, partly because of IBM's reputation and existing customer base of punched card users, and partly because the 650 was perceived to be easier to program and more reliable than its competitors. The 650's drum had a faster access time (2.4 ms) than other drum machines, although that was still slow. This was a limitation that precluded the use of drum-based machines for many important applications. The 650 had, in fact, less impact among the business customers, for whom it was intended, than at universities, who were able to acquire the computer at a deep discount. There, 650s helped shape the emergence of the new discipline of academic computer science.

ERA 1103

Another important first-generation computer was the ERA 1103, developed by Engineering Research Associates, the Minnesota firm that Remington Rand bought in 1952. This machine was geared toward scientific and engineering customers, and thus represented a different design philosophy from Remington Rand's other large machine, the UNIVAC.

The 1103 used binary arithmetic, a 36-bit word length, and parallel arithmetic operation. Internal memory (1K words) was supplied by Williams tubes, with an ERA-designed drum for backup. It employed a two-address instruction scheme, with the first six bits of a word used to encode a repertoire of 45 instructions. Arithmetic was performed in an internal 72-bit accumulator. In late 1954, the company delivered to the National Security Agency and to the National Advisory Committee for Aeronautics an 1103 with magnetic core in place of the Williams Tube memory—perhaps the first use of core in a commercial machine. (Core had by that time already been installed in the Whirlwind (*q.v.*) at MIT and in a few other experimental computers.) For the NACA, ERA modified the instruction set to include an interrupt facility for its I/O, another first in computer design. Interrupts (*q.v.*) and core memory were later marketed as standard features of the 1103-A model.

IBM 704, 709

In late 1955, IBM began deliveries of the 704 (*see* Fig. 2), its successor to the 701. The 704's most notable features were core memory (initially 4K words, up to 32K by 1957) and a rich instruction repertoire. The 704's processor had hardware floating-point arithmetic and three addressable index registers (*q.v.*)—both major advances over the 701. Partly to facilitate the use of floating point, an IBM team led by John Backus developed the programming language Fortran (*q.v.*). Backus has said that he had not envisioned Fortran's use much beyond the 704, but Fortran became and has remained, with Cobol (*q.v.*), one of the most successful programming languages of all time. IBM installed over a hundred 704s between 1955 and 1960.

In January 1957, IBM announced the 709 as a compatible upgrade to the 704, but it did not enjoy the

Figure 2. IBM 704. (Courtesy of IBM.)

same success. As it was being introduced, it became clear that transistors were finally becoming a practical replacement for vacuum tubes. Indeed, the transistorized Philco Transac S-2000 and Control Data 1604 were just being announced. IBM withdrew the 709 from the market and replaced it with the transistorized 7090. The new machine was architecturally identical to the 709, so IBM engineers used a 709 to write software for the as-yet-unbuilt 7090. The first delivery of the 7090 in late 1959 marked the beginning of IBM's entry into the solid state era and serves as a marker for computing's second generation.

The first-generation computers established a beachhead among commercial customers, but even considering the success of the IBM 650, they did little more than that. Punched card accounting equipment still did most of the work for businesses, while engineering and scientific calculating was done with slide rules, desk calculators, or analog computers (*q.v.*). Machines like the ERA 1103 were too big, too expensive, and required too much specialized programming skill to be found anywhere but at the largest aerospace firms or govern-

ment research laboratories. People still spoke of the total world market for large computers as being limited to very small numbers, much as one might speak of the demand for particle accelerators or wind tunnels.

The Second Generation, 1960–1965

The second generation of computing lasted from about 1960 to 1965, and was characterized by discrete transistors for switching elements and ferrite magnetic core planes for internal memory. In software, this era saw the acceptance of high-level programming languages like Fortran and Cobol, although assembly language programming remained common.

From the perspective of the late 1990s, these generations appear more like transitional periods than major discrete eras in computing. The term "revolution," as applied to the invention of the integrated circuit, obscures the fact that the IC's inventors saw their work as an evolutionary outgrowth of their work in materials, circuits, and packaging pioneered in the discrete transistor era. This evolutionary approach hastened the acceptance of the otherwise exotic technology of the IC among computer designers. It was during the second, not third, generation, that some of the toughest challenges were faced, especially regarding the serial production of reliable devices with consistent performance. It took from 1949 to 1959 to bring transistors from the laboratory to commercial production in computers, but the basic knowledge gained during that decade hastened the advent of the IC, which went from invention to commercial use in half that time.

Transistors, replacing vacuum tubes on a one-to-one basis, solved the problems of a tube's unreliability, heat, and power consumption. As they solved those problems, they exposed another, which proved to be more fundamental. That was the complexity of interconnecting many thousands of simple circuits to obtain a complete system. Some manufacturers labored under the burden of hiring and training workers to hand-wire and solder the components to one another. Others built sophisticated assembly lines, adapting machines supplied by the shoe industry to insert the components into the proper places, after which automated wire-wrap machines (supplied by the Gardner-Denver Corporation) wired the backplane. Still, this "tyranny of numbers" would only be solved when integrated circuits put the interconnections on to the same piece of silicon as the devices.

IBM 1401

One of the most important transistorized computers was the IBM 1401, introduced in 1960. This machine employed a character-oriented, variable-length data field, with one bit of each character code reserved to delimit the end of a field. As with the 650, the 1401's design evolved from a plug-wired, punched card calculator to a stored-program, general-purpose computer that used magnetic media (tape) as well as punched cards for its input–output. Magnetic cores provided a central memory of from 1,400 to 4,000 characters, while transistorized circuits supported a multiplication speed of about 500 numbers/second. With the 1401, IBM also introduced the Type 1403 printer, a rugged and fast printer that carried type on a moving chain. This printer played an equally important role in effecting the transition from tabulators to computers for data processing.

IBM engineers took pains to make the 1401 easy to program by those trained to work with punched card equipment. A simple language called "Report Program Generator" (RPG) made it easy to automate routine processes, and to print results on standard tabular forms. The system's relatively small size meant that a customer could install a 1401 in the same room that was already used for punched card accounting equip-

ment. This combination of features made the 1401 attractive to many small- and medium-sized businesses. Eventually, over 10,000 were installed—ten times as many as the 650. Its success marked the ascendancy of IBM over Univac as the dominant computer supplier.

Concurrently with the 1401, IBM also offered the 1620, a small machine intended for scientific applications. And in 1962 the company introduced the 7094 (*see* Fig. 3), a version of the 7090 that added a set of index registers (*q.v.*) to its CPU. It, too, sold well and became the standard large-scale scientific computer of the time.

By the mid-1960s, the IBM Corporation had seized and was vigorously defending a dominant share of the US computer market. Univac, Burroughs, NCR, RCA, Control Data, Philco/Ford, General Electric, and Honeywell were its chief competitors. Each produced machines that were comparable in price and capability to the IBM machines. By 1970, GE, Philco, and RCA had left the computer business, their places taken by new companies offering computers of a different nature than the classic mainframes of this era.

LARC, STRETCH, ATLAS, B5000

Several architectural innovations first appeared in second-generation computers, but they were premature. That is, the features saw only limited use until the next generation, when they became commonplace.

In 1955, Remington Rand Univac contracted with the Lawrence Livermore Laboratory to produce a high-performance computer for weapons design. Design and development of the LARC (Livermore Automatic Research Computer) were beset with problems, but in 1960 the first model was completed and accepted by Livermore, with a second model delivered to the Navy's David Taylor Model Basin. The LARC achieved high processing speeds by having a separate processor whose only job was to handle I/O. Logic circuits used surface barrier transistors, developed by Philco in 1955, but already obsolete by 1960. The LARC was an impressive performer, but after delivering two models for a total price of $6 million, Univac stopped production and absorbed a $20 million loss.

IBM undertook a similar project called "Stretch," implying that it would dramatically extend the state of the art. Work began in 1956, with the first delivery (to Los Alamos Laboratory) in 1961. Like the LARC, the Stretch introduced a number of innovations in architecture and device technology. Among the former was its use of a pipelined processor; among the latter was its use of very fast transistors and Emitter-Coupled Logic (ECL). A total of seven Stretch computers, under the name IBM 7030, were delivered before IBM

Figure 3.   IBM 7094. (Courtesy of IBM.)

withdrew the product. As with Univac's experience with the LARC, IBM absorbed a huge financial loss on the project.

The Atlas computer, introduced in 1962 by the British firm Ferranti, employed virtual memory (*q.v.*) with paging, and provision for multiprogramming (*q.v.*). Whereas most first- and second-generation computers had at best only a rudimentary job control facility, Ferranti provided the Atlas with a "Supervisor" program that foreshadowed the operating systems (*q.v.*) common after 1965. In 1962, Burroughs introduced the B5000 series of computers that incorporated some of these innovations. This series was further designed for optimal execution of programs written in a high-level language (Algol—*q.v.*). Its processor architecture was also novel in using a stack-oriented addressing scheme. Neither of these features prevailed in the market-place, but multiprogramming and virtual memory became common a generation later.

The Third Generation, 1965–1970

The IBM System/360 (*see* Fig. 4), announced on 7 April 1964, inaugurated the third generation of computers.

This series did not use true integrated circuits, but rather small modules consisting of discrete devices laid onto a ceramic substrate. IBM had considered using the newly invented IC for the 360, but went instead with what they called Solid Logic Technology, in part because they had a better grasp of its manufacture in large quantities than they had with ICs.

The initial announcement was for a series of six computers, offering compatibility over a range of 25 : 1 in performance. System/360 computers were intended to be applicable to the full circle of applications (hence the name): specifically, to character-based data processing as well as number-oriented scientific problems. Eventually, 14 models were offered, plus four additional models announced but not delivered or else withdrawn soon after initial delivery. The series eventually offered a several hundred-fold range in computing power.

The 360's designers achieved compatibility over that range by adopting several design innovations. The first was the use of base-register addressing, whereby an instruction referred to a short address. This address was added to a base address (stored in a register) to yield the actual location in core of the desired data.

Figure 4. IBM System/360 Model 44. (Courtesy of IBM.)

This kept the cost of address-decoding circuits low for the low-end models.

A second innovation was the use of microprogramming (q.v.) to achieve compatibility. Except for the top of the line, each model of the 360 obtained its instruction set from a read-only memory (ROM—q.v.) containing a microprogram. That allowed designers of each model to aim for optimum cost/performance without being unduly constrained by the specifics of the 360 instruction set. The concept of microprogramming was first suggested by Maurice Wilkes (q.v.) in 1951, and had been implemented in the design of the Ferranti Atlas. Another British computer, the KDF-9, used microprogramming; 360 engineers later acknowledged that this machine inspired their decision to adopt it. The S/360 established microprogramming firmly in the mainstream of computing, and led the way for its use in the minicomputer and microcomputer classes that followed.

The S/360 used channels (q.v.) for I/O—independent processors that handled the transfer of data between primary memory and peripheral devices. This allowed IBM to market a common set of I/O equipment to all customers, regardless of model. (The proliferation of incompatible peripherals for previous lines of products was one of the main forces behind the decision to develop the S/360.)

By all measures the 360 series was very successful. IBM sales personnel recorded over a thousand orders for systems within a month of the April 1964 announcement, and by 1970 there were over 18,000 installations worldwide. The architecture did, however, have serious shortcomings that were later corrected to varying degrees. Chief among them was its lack of dynamic address translation (the ability to associate program data with memory locations at run time), which, among other things, made the System/360 unsuitable for time-sharing. When IBM upgraded the 360 series to the System/370 in 1970, its architecture was extended to provide this feature and virtual memory as well. A further extension of the 360 architecture was made in 1981, when the number of addressing bits was increased from 24 to 31. The basic architecture, much extended, was still being used in the 1990s in two lines of IBM products, the 43xx series and the 30xx series, which together were marketed as the System/390 series.

The success of the S/360 spawned competitors. In 1965, RCA began delivering four computers, the Spectra Series, that were software compatible with the equivalent S/360 models. These had the distinction of being built with true integrated circuits, but RCA was unable to sustain the line and sold its computer business to Univac in 1971. By that time other companies were offering computers with integrated circuit logic and semiconductor memory instead of magnetic core. IBM countered—some say it was forced to counter—with its System/370 series that used integrated circuits for both logic and memory.

Because semiconductor memory, unlike core, loses its information when power is switched off, the S/370 needed a way to store its microprogrammed instructions in a non-volatile fashion. IBM engineers invented the floppy disk (see DISKETTE) for this purpose. The floppy became the pivotal technology for establishing the personal computer class later in that decade.

The notion of a compatible family of machines was not the only 360 innovation that later became widely copied. The 360 adopted the 8-bit byte as the standard for representing characters, and it used multiple-spindle disk systems with removable disk packs. Microprogramming soon became the most common way to implement architectures. From the marketing of the system came the acceptance of many terms now used in computing: "byte," "architecture," and "generation," among others.

Minicomputers

The term "minicomputer" was coined in the mid-1960s by a Digital Equipment Corporation salesman to describe the PDP-8. The term really has two meanings, one informal and the other specific. Informally, a minicomputer was low in cost, small in size, and intended for use by a single individual, small department, or for a dedicated application. That concept was expressed as early as 1952, when several companies introduced computers aimed at such a market.

Producing such a machine with adequate performance was another matter. First-generation computers like the Bendix G-15, Alwac III-E, or Librascope LGP-30 achieved low cost by using a drum memory, which was incapable of high-speed random access to data. The low processing speeds meant that these computers were ill-suited for process control, laboratory instrumentation, or other similar applications where minicomputers first found a market.

A more specific definition recognizes the technical constraints that have to be overcome for a compact and inexpensive computer to be useful. By this definition, a mini is a compact, solid-state computer with random access memory whose internal structure is characterized by a short word length and a variety of memory addressing modes. This definition requires that a minicomputer be small and rugged enough to fit in a standard equipment rack and thus serve as an embedded controller for other systems. Minis were much smaller and more rugged than many people had previously thought practical; their realization had to await advances in circuit technology as well as circuit board fabrication, power supply design, and packaging techniques.

This definition makes sense only in the context of the era in which the machines appear. Minicomputers, with microcomputers following close behind, have evolved to mainframe-class word lengths of 32 bits, and they eventually included models big enough to require a full-sized computer room. But the category has persisted. (For a time, 32-bit minicomputers were called "superminis," but the differences were not enough to constitute a separate class.)

The MIT Whirlwind, completed in the early 1950s, used a 16-bit word length, and was envisioned for real-time simulation and control applications. It was housed in several rooms of a building on the MIT campus, and in its initial configuration used fragile and sensitive electrostatic tubes for memory. It was hardly a minicomputer, but it was used like one. Many of the MIT students and faculty who worked on it later founded the minicomputer industry located in the suburbs around Boston.

In 1960, Control Data Corporation introduced a transistorized, 12-bit machine called the CDC 160 (see Fig. 5). The 160 was intended as an input–output controller for the 48-bit CDC 1604. The 160 could also be used as a computer on its own, and as such, was one of the first machines to fit the definition of a mini. The 160 was very compact—in fact, it was built into an ordinary office desk. Both the 160 and the 1604 sold well and helped establish CDC as a major computer manufacturer. The company continued building small machines, but concentrated on very fast, long-word computers—later called supercomputers—for which the 160 was designed as an I/O channel. Thus CDC failed to establish a minicomputer niche although its 24-bit 3100 and 3300 were reasonably successful.

The Digital Equipment Corporation PDP-8, a 12-bit computer announced in 1965, made the breakthrough. Up to that time, DEC had produced and sold a variety of machines with varying word lengths, including the 36-bit PDP-6, and its PDP-10 successor, a full-size

Figure 5. CDC 160-A. (Courtesy of Control Data Corporation.)

mainframe widely used in a time-sharing environment. The success of the PDP-8 established the minicomputer class of machines, with DEC the leading supplier. The success of the PDP-8 spawned competitors: Varian, Hewlett-Packard, Computer Automation, and others.

Data General, formed by ex-DEC employees, brought out the 16-bit Nova in early 1969, and the company quickly became DEC's main competitor. The Nova had a simple but powerful instruction set and was the first to use medium-scale integrated (MSI) circuits. Its word length set a standard for minis from then on. Just as influential was the Nova's packaging, especially for a model introduced in 1971. For both logic and memory the "Super" Nova used ICs housed in Dual In-line Packages (DIPs) which were soldered onto a large printed circuit board that was plugged into a bus (*q.v.*) along with other boards, and the whole computer was housed in a low rectangular metal box. A front panel contained a row of switches that gave access to individual bits of the CPU's registers. Modern

computers no longer have the front panel, but in every other respect the Nova's physical packaging has been the standard ever since—so much so that one forgets there ever were alternatives.

DEC countered the Nova with their 16-bit PDP-11 in 1970, which kept DEC competitive with Data General. These two computers, along with the HP-2000 series offered by Hewlett-Packard, may be said to define the minicomputer's "second generation." The PDP-11, in particular, redefined the role of minicomputers. The first minis, like the PDP-8, were programmed mainly in machine code and typically embedded into other systems, but with the PDP-11 one could program in a high-level language like Fortran and, with a full set of peripheral equipment, build a general-purpose computing facility around it instead of around a mainframe.

The mini's low cost, ruggedness, and compact packaging made them attractive for "original equipment manufacturers" (OEMs), who purchased minis and embedded them into specialized systems for type-setting, process control, and a host of other applications. Having others develop the specialized software and interfaces was well-suited to small, entrepreneurial minicomputer firms who did not have the resources to develop specialized applications in-house. Several of the mainframe companies, including IBM, introduced minicomputers at this time, but the smaller firms propelled the industry.

A typical mini was microprogrammed and transferred data internally over a high-speed channel called a *bus* (*q.v.*). To gain access to more memory than could be directly addressed by a short word, their central processors contained sets of registers for base-offset, indirect, indexed, and other types of addressing. These designs made optimum use of the medium-scale integrated memory and logic circuits then becoming available.

The result was considerable processing power for the money. It was not long before customers began using them for general-purpose computation. As they did, the need for more address bits soon became pressing in spite of the innovative addressing techniques the machines employed. Interdata, Systems Engineering Laboratories, and Prime all introduced machines with a 32-bit word length in the mid-1970s. These machines quickly became popular with NASA and other aerospace customers, who needed that power for computer-aided design and manufacture (CAD/CAM—*q.v.*) and real-time data reduction. DEC responded to this trend in 1978 with its VAX-11, a 32-bit "Virtual Address eXtension" to the PDP-11. Data General announced its 32-bit Eclipse MV/8000 in 1980. Although these "super minicomputers" had the same 32-bit word length as mainframes, there were still differences in their instruction sets and use of buses instead of I/O channels.

The VAX soon began outselling the other 32-bit minis and went on to become one of the most successful computers of all time. Part of the reason was DEC's existing market position, but success was also due to the software compatibility the VAX had with the large installed base of PDP-11s. Internally, the VAX was a different machine, but it had an emulation mode that executed PDP-11 programs (eventually this feature was dropped). Also crucial to success was the VAX's ability to be networked through Ethernet, the Xerox-developed networking system that DEC chose in 1980. The VAX was further blessed with having available not one but two good operating systems: Digital's own VMS (Virtual Memory System) and Unix (*q.v.*), developed by AT&T and originally offered on a PDP-11. The combination of inherently good design, an adequate supply of semiconductor memory chips, networking, and software support enabled the VAX to compete with all but the largest mainframe computers, whose designs were beginning to look dated by 1980.

The VAX's success thus followed that of the IBM 360, in which a microprogrammed architecture allowed a range of models all running the same software. DEC continued supporting the system by offering a range of VAX machines that merge into the mainframe at the high end and the micro at the low end. The machine continued to be popular into the late 1990s and Compaq, of which DEC is now a subsidiary, is committed to the VAX series through 2001.

Supercomputers

On several occasions throughout the history of digital computing, there has been a desire to push the state of the art to obtain the highest performance possible. Indeed, one sees this force driving Charles Babbage, who in 1834 abandoned work on his promising Difference Engine (*q.v.*) to attempt a far more powerful Analytical Engine (*q.v.*), which he never was able to complete. The various "Giant Brains" of the late 1940s and early 1950s reflect this desire as well.

In 1954, IBM built a fast computer called the Naval Ordnance Research Calculator (NORC—*q.v.*) for the US Naval Proving Ground in Dahlgren, Virginia. At its dedication, John von Neumann (*q.v.*) spoke of the tremendous advances in computer speeds, ending his talk with the hope that computer companies would continue from time to time ". . . to write specifications simply calling for the most advanced machine which is possible in the present state of the art."

IBM's Stretch and Univac's LARC fit that category. In the late 1960s, Burroughs built the ILLIAC-IV, a parallel processing machine based on a design by Daniel Slotnick of the University of Illinois. These were well regarded by the customers who used them, but they usually incurred financial losses for the companies that manufactured them, even with the government subsidies each of these machines enjoyed. It remained for Control Data Corporation to find a way not only to make reliable and practical supercomputers, but to sell them profitably as well. The machine that brought the term "supercomputer" into common use was their 6600 (*see* Fig. 6), designed by Seymour Cray (*q.v.*) and delivered in 1964.

The CDC's architecture employed a 60-bit word central processor, around which were arranged ten logical 12-bit peripheral processors, each having a memory of 4K words. Within the central processor were ten "functional units" which contained specialized circuitry that performed the operations of fixed- or floating-point arithmetic and logic. Logic circuits, taking advantage of the high-speed silicon transistors

Figure 6. CDC 6600. (Courtesy of Control Data Corporation.)

then becoming available, were densely packed into modules called "cordwood" from the way they looked.

The functional units permitted a measure of parallel processing, since each could be doing a different specialized operation at the same time. Added parallelism was provided through "lookahead," a process (pioneered on the Stretch) by which the CPU examined the instruction stream and determined to what extent operands (*q.v.*) could be fetched in advance of the time the functional units needed them. (Interestingly, this made a branch instruction that actually branched the most time-consuming operation on the machine.) Likewise, the peripheral processors could each be busy handling I/O, while the central processor was executing program steps that did not require communication with the outside world.

The 6600 went against the trend of using microcode to build up an instruction repertoire. It more closely resembled the approach taken by the first digital computers, including the electromechanical Harvard Mark I (1944) and the ENIAC (1946). In the Mark I

(*q.v.*), for example, there was no operation to "multiply." Instead, lines of paper tape (*q.v.*) were punched to route numbers to a multiplying unit. While doing the multiplication, the Mark I could be coded to do something else as long as it did not need that product (or the multiplying unit). The 6600 had two floating multiply units, each of which could perform a multiplication in 1 microsecond. It had no integer multiply command. Seymour Cray believed in a very sparse instruction repertoire, and his ideas presaged in many ways the current trend toward reduced instruction set computers (RISCs—*q.v.*).

CRAY-1

Control Data upgraded the CDC 6600 with the 7600 in 1969 and produced an incompatible supercomputer called the STAR in 1972. The latter machine was capable of parallel operations on vector data—a feature also used in the design of the Texas Instruments Advanced Scientific Computer (1972). Around that time, Seymour Cray left CDC and formed Cray Research, whose goal was to produce an even faster machine.

Figure 7. CRAY-1. (Courtesy of Cray Research, Inc.)

In 1976, Cray Research announced the CRAY-1 (*see* Fig. 7), with the first delivery in March to the Los Alamos National Laboratory. Preliminary benchmarks (*q.v.*) showed it to be ten times faster than the 6600. The CRAY-1 had 12 functional units and extensive buffering between the instruction stream and the central processor. Memory options ranged from 250K to 1 million 64-bit words. The chief difference between the 6600 and the CRAY was the latter's ability to process vector as well as scalar data.

The CRAY-1 also achieved high speeds through innovative packaging. The computer used only four types of chips, each containing only a few circuits that used emitter-coupled logic (ECL). The circuits were densely packed and arranged in a three-quarter circle to reduce interconnection lengths. Circuit modules were interconnected by wires, laboriously soldered by hand. The modules were cooled by liquid Freon, which circulated through aluminum channels that held the circuit cards. Large power supplies located at the base of each column supplied power. These design decisions resulted not only in a fast machine, but also one that had a distinctive and deceptively small size and shape.

Prices for a CRAY-1 were on the order of $5 million and up. The CRAY-1 sold well and the company prospered. Control Data continued offering supercomputers for some time but eventually withdrew from the business. IBM had countered the announcement of the 6600 with its own 360 Model 91 (1967), which, however, was a commercial failure. Other machines based on the 360/370 architecture in the late 1980s established IBM as a competitor in the class. Cray research announced the X-MP, a multiple processor version of the CRAY-1, in 1982, the CRAY-2 in 1985, and the Y-MP in 1988. Several Japanese firms, including NEC and Fujitsu, entered the arena with machines in the supercomputer class in the mid-1980s. In the USA, several start-up companies entered the field in the late 1980s with machines with performance approaching the CRAYs at a much lower price.

By the 1970s, the supercomputer was established as a viable class, rather than as specialized, one-of-a-kind experimental machines. The persistence and ingenuity of one man, Seymour Cray, had a lot to do with that. Although the class is well established, the design of these machines tends to be idiosyncratic, with the personal preferences of individual designers playing a much larger role than in other classes. Each designer seeks the fastest device technology and pays close attention to packaging, but various architectural philosophies are followed. In contrast to Cray's approach, for example, Thinking Machines, Inc. of Cambridge, Massachusetts introduced a computer in the mid-1980s called the Connection Machine, which was characterized by a massively parallel architecture. Meanwhile, Seymour Cray left Cray Research and founded Cray Computer Corporation in 1989, where he continued to pursue fast performance using innovative packaging and materials. It is generally agreed that a degree of vector processing and other parallelism is necessary, but just how much is far from settled—whether to harness multiple von Neumann architectures in parallel or to find a more radical alternative to the von Neumann fetch–execute cycle that some regard as a bottleneck.

With the end of the Cold War the nuclear weapons labs no longer had the financial resources or desire to push supercomputer technology along as it had. Many of the suppliers ran into financial difficulty. Cray Computer and Kendall Square Research went bankrupt in 1995–1996; Cray Research was bought by Silicon Graphics in 1996; and Thinking Machines was reorganized as a software house in 1995. The demand for supercomputing is strong and growing for commercial applications, such as commercial aircraft and automobile design, chemical engineering, weather forecasting, and many others. What has changed is that since the end of the Cold War, this segment of the industry has had to deal with the issue of cost. If it can provide high performance at low cost, as other segments of the computer industry have figured out how to do, this segment will not only survive but even grow, with or without government support.

Personal Computers

Those in the computer business saw the trend toward lower prices and smaller packaging occurring through the 1960s. They also recognized that lowering a computer's price and making it smaller opened up the market to new customers. With the hindsight of two decades of furious growth, it seems inevitable that a computer company would introduce a "personal computer." The truth is more complex. The personal computer's invention was not inevitable; if anything its viability was unforeseen by those in the best position to market one. The personal computer was the result of a conscious effort by individuals whose vision of the industry was quite different from that of the established companies.

To understand the transformation of computing brought about by the personal computer, one must begin with an understanding of such a machine's technical and social components. Some of the first electronic computers of the late 1940s were operated as personal computers, in that all control and operation of a machine was turned over to one user at a time. Prospective users took their place in line with others waiting to use it, but there were no supervisory personnel or computer operators between them and the machine. This mode of operation is one of the defining characteristics of what constitutes a personal computer (*see* PERSONAL COMPUTING).

In the mainframe world of the late 1960s, batch operation prevailed. But an alternate style of access arose that became known as a "computer utility": computing power made accessible to individuals through remote terminals accessing a centralized, time-shared mainframe. The physical location, maintenance, and operation of the mainframe was a problem for computer specialists and technicians, not the user. Users had the illusion that the full resources of the mainframe were available to him or her. That illusion, created by complex systems programming on a mainframe with lots of disk or drum memory, was crucial. Nearly all the pioneers of the personal computer era had had such experiences on a time-shared system, and it was that illusion's appeal as an alternative to batch operation that they sought to recreate on a small system.

Ironically, while some used the time-sharing model as the inspiration for their work on personal systems, others were blinded by the structure of time-shared systems. For this latter group, time sharing's analogy to an electric power utility, with the implication that one needed a complex, expensive, centralized system to provide computer power, created a mental block that prevented them from recognizing how advances in semiconductors were rendering that model obsolete.

Throughout the late 1960s, the semiconductor manufacturers were continuing to place even more circuits on single chips of silicon. Around 1970, these developments led to the first consumer products: digital watches, games, and calculators. Four-function pocket calculators, priced near $100, appeared around 1971, and the following year Hewlett-Packard introduced the HP-35, which offered floating-point arithmetic and a full range of scientific functions. The HP-35 sold for $395 and was an immediate success for Hewlett-Packard, a company that had not been part of the consumer electronics business.

Consumer sales of these products led to very long production runs of the chips that powered them. That in turn led to a stunning drop in price: within a few years watches and calculators with more circuits than the ENIAC had were being given away as promotional trinkets. The computer industry had also enjoyed price reductions as sales increased, but nothing on this scale. To build and sell a general purpose computer that way seemed impractical: the chips would be too specialized, and they would become obsolete too quickly to generate enough volume production to reach a consumer price level.

That changed in late 1971, when Intel introduced the 4004 microprocessor, a chip on which much of the architecture of a minicomputer was implemented, and whose functions could be modified by programming a read-only memory (the 4001). Intel designed this chip set for a customer, Busicom, who wanted to build calculators. When Busicom dropped the project, Intel sought another market for what was a set of chips that provided general-purpose computing functions. Compare Intel's experience with that of IBM and the first-generation 650: IBM started with a design for a special-purpose computer for specific punched card applications. It ended up designing a low-cost, general-purpose computer that could serve the initial application by software, not hardware, realizing a very successful product that found applications across the computing spectrum.

Some individuals within DEC, Xerox, HP, and IBM proposed to build and market an inexpensive, general-purpose personal computer around this time, but their proposals were either turned down or only weakly supported. Meanwhile, Intel designed developer's kits that it sold or even gave away to potential customers to familiarize them with the nuances of designing with a microprocessor. Rockwell, Texas Instruments, and others all announced microprocessors by 1973. Intel followed the 4-bit 4004 with an 8-bit 8008 in 1972, followed by a more powerful 8080 in April 1974. The price was set at $360.

While that was going on among the large electronics and computer firms, other forces were pushing up from below. Radio and electronics hobbyist magazines started publishing articles on how to build modest digital devices using the TTL chips then becoming available at low prices. The space that the personal computer would eventually fill was being nibbled at from above, by cheaper and cheaper minicomputers, and from below, by pocket programmable calculators and hobbyists' kits.

In January 1975, *Popular Electronics* published a cover story on a computer kit called Altair that sold for less that $400. The Altair (*see* Fig. 8) was designed for the magazine by MITS, a company consisting of about ten employees located in Albuquerque, New Mexico. Despite its many shortcomings, this kit filled the space of "personal computer" that had been empty. It cost less than an HP-35 calculator. It was designed around the Intel 8080 microprocessor, with a rich instruction set, flexible addressing, and a 64 KB addressing space. Ed Roberts, the head of MITS, designed the Altair along the lines of the best minicomputers, with a bus architecture and plenty of slots for expansion. There were many things the Altair lacked, however, including decent mass storage and I/O. As delivered, it represented the minimum configuration of circuits that one could legitimately call a "computer."

But hobbyists were tolerant. In fact, hobbyists were the key to the launching of the personal computer. Their energy, enthusiasm, and talent had not been recognized by Intel, DEC, or other established companies. Without that talent and energy, it was perfectly reasonable to predict, as one executive reportedly did, that the "personal computer will fall flat on its face." The personal computer established itself by tapping into that community and exploiting its labor to overcome

Figure 8.   Altair 8800. (Courtesy of Smithsonian Institution.)

the machine's severe technical deficiencies. Those who bought the Altair did so not because they had a specific computing job to do, but rather because they understood the potential of owning a general-purpose, stored-program computer. They understood, as the mini and mainframe makers did not, the social implications of the word "personal." The personal computer's social appeal was that their owners could do with them as they wished. Obviously that was not true of batch-operated mainframes. Nor was that true with minicomputers or even with time-shared systems, even if they superficially resembled personal computers in terms of their interactive capabilities.

Between the time of the Altair's announcement and the end of 1977 the personal computer field witnessed an unprecedented burst of creativity and talent that transformed the device into something truly practical. This drama was played out in three arenas: hardware, software, and in the social community of users.

The social community was perhaps most important. Computer users groups (*q.v.*) had been present ever since SHARE, founded shortly before IBM delivered its 701. Digital Equipment Corporation had a good relationship with DECUS; the mini companies also developed close ties with Original Equipment Manufacturers (OEMs) who added value to the basic machine supplied by a manufacturer. For personal computers, this community, and the work it did, was even more critical. On the west coast of the USA, the now legendary Homebrew Computer Club was founded in March 1975, with the early meetings devoted to getting Altairs and comparable kits working. Newsletters and magazines sprouted, the most famous survivor of which was *Byte*, founded in September 1975. *Byte* was a fairly "normal" magazine, while *Doctor Dobb's Journal of Computer Calisthenics and Orthodontia* [sic] was typically filled with hexadecimal machine language code. There were over a hundred such periodicals that sprouted up in the decade following the Altair's announcement.

Some critical design decisions made by Ed Roberts and his small group at MITS set the course for the early hardware evolution of personal computers. The first was his choice of the Intel 8080, a decision that would reverberate through the computer industry for the next 25 years. The second was to design the machine along the lines of the Data General Nova and advanced DEC minicomputers, with their open architectures. That allowed entrepreneurs to come out with circuit boards that added capabilities such as better memory and I/O to the original Altair, which sorely needed those features. Other companies like IMSAI designed machines that were "clones" of the Altair. The result was that personal computers established a beachhead in the market without being tied to the fortunes of tiny MITS (which was bought by Pertec and vanished from sight after a few years anyway).

Similar standards rapidly emerged in software. Not long after seeing the *Popular Electronics* article describing the Altair, William Gates III contacted Ed Roberts and told him that he could have a version of the Basic (*q.v.*) programming language for the Altair by July 1975. Gates, with Paul Allen and Monte Davidoff, wrote and delivered the language (on a paper tape) as promised. Gates never became a MITS employee, but instead retained the rights to the language for his company "Micro Soft" (later "Microsoft"). After MITS got into financial troubles, Microsoft marketed the language to all the others who were making 8080-based machines. There were other versions of Basic available, but Microsoft's was regarded as the best; it combined the ease of use of the original Basic developed at Dartmouth, with the power and ability to use machine codes (through commands like PEEK and POKE) that Gates and Allen took from versions of Basic developed at Digital Equipment Corporation.

Another critical piece of software was an operating system that allowed the newly invented floppy disk to serve as the personal computer's mass storage device. The system was called CP/M, for "Control Program (for) Microcomputers"; it was written by Gary Kildall almost as an afterthought. CP/M, like Microsoft Basic, was strongly influenced by work done at Digital Equipment Corporation and even used many of DEC's cryptic acronyms such as "PIP," "TECO," and "DDT." Like the DEC minicomputer systems, it took up very little memory of its own and had none of the bloat that was characteristic of mainframe OSs. Kildall sold it for under $100, and it made the floppy an integral part of the PC.

By 1977 computers were being packaged and sold as appliances, with three models introduced that year from Apple, Radio Shack, and Commodore setting the trend. None of those three used the Altair bus or architecture, but the Apple II used Microsoft Basic, and one could plug a card into it that let it run CP/M. The Apple II, though more expensive, was by far the superior machine, with very good color graphics, tight integration with floppy disk storage (the others relied on unreliable audio cassettes), and attractive packaging.

The field matured in 1981, when IBM introduced a machine called simply the IBM Personal Computer, which combined the best of the features described above with the respectability of the IBM name. The IBM PC was not IBM's first attempt in this market, but it quickly set a new standard. In many ways it was a descendant of the Altair. Its microprocessor was the Intel 8088, a 16-bit version of the 8080. It had a bus architecture that invited others to provide cards to expand its abilities. It used Microsoft Basic, supplied in a ROM. Like the Apple II it could be configured with a color monitor to play games. Early versions had a cassette port, but most came with at least one floppy drive. Customers were given the option of one of three disk operating systems; but the cheapest, simplest, and first to market was PC-DOS, supplied by Microsoft and based in part on CP/M.

Apple, by 1981 one of the industry's fastest growing companies, did not feel threatened by IBM's entry into the field. The company considered its Apple II a superior machine anyway, and it thought that IBM's entry would make its own products more accepted by business customers. When IBM quickly took the lead in sales, Apple responded with an Apple III, which suffered from reliability flaws, and then, in 1984, with the Macintosh. The "Mac" was a closed machine and a philosophical opposite of the Altair/IBM approach, but its graphical user interface (GUI) was, once again, revolutionary. Sales were slow at first, but Apple had set a new standard.

Microsoft grew on the sales of its DOS operating system, which, like Microsoft Basic, it was free to sell to others besides the company for which it developed the software. As with the Altair, a vigorous clone market for IBM-compatible PCs emerged, led by the Texas firms Compaq and Dell. Compaq grew even faster than Apple, from the delivery of its first clone in 1983 to become one of the top 100 computer firms by 1985. As long as they could prove that they had not copied the code from IBM's proprietary ROMs in its PC, these companies were free to buy a copy of MS-DOS from Microsoft and sell a machine that ran any software developed for the IBM computer. Competition soon forced the prices of very capable personal computers to low levels. Like Apple, Microsoft had also developed a version of a windows and icons-based interface, but its "Interface Manager" was no match for the Macintosh's elegant design. Later versions, however, now renamed "Windows," were better, and by 1991 Microsoft was able to reorient the IBM-compatible market from MS-DOS to Microsoft Windows, version 3.1.

Workstations

In the mid 1980s, a number of companies introduced personal workstations, and since the late 1980s, their architecture has reversed the trend set by the 360, VAX, and 80x86 series. Instead of using a complex, microcoded instruction set, these workstations use Reduced Instruction Set Computer (RISC) processors, which have small instruction sets applied to many fast registers. These computers are intended for use by a single individual, and provide high-resolution graphics, fast numerical processing, and networking capability. As such they combine the attributes of the personal computer with those of the higher classes. Their performance reaches into the low end of the super-computer range, but prices for simpler models touch the high end of the personal computer class. At present, the more advanced personal computers, using the latest Intel microprocessor and running Microsoft's Windows 95, 98, 2000 or NT, overlap the cheapest workstations, which typically use a Sun Sparc or other RISC microprocessor and run under a version of Unix (*q.v.*). But the two classes, for the moment, remain distinct.

Several Boston-area companies were the pioneers in introducing workstations, but the lead was soon taken by the Silicon Valley company Sun Microsystems, founded in 1982. Part of the reason for Sun's success was its ability to make use of the "free" research being done at nearby universities: the hardware design was based on a "Stanford University Networked" workstation project (hence the name), while Bill Joy, a student at Berkeley, developed, with ARPA funding, a version of Unix that Sun adopted. Joy, who became a Sun employee in 1982, was the final carrier of AT&T's Unix as it made its journey from New Jersey to Urbana, Illinois, to Berkeley, and finally to Mountain View, California, where Berkeley Unix became the operating system of choice not only for most workstations but also for the emerging Internet world.

IBM researcher John Cocke had done the pioneering work on RISC in the mid-1970s. After some false starts, IBM introduced the successful RS/6000 line of computers in 1990. In 1992 Digital Equipment Corporation "bet the company" on a RISC chip called Alpha, which achieved processing speeds that few thought possible for a microprocessor. The following year IBM, Motorola, and Apple joined forces to introduce a RISC processor for personal computers. The trio hoped that the superior architecture of their "PowerPC" chip would give it overwhelming advantages over Intel's 80x86 line.

To the surprise of many, neither the DEC Alpha nor the PowerPC has been able to take many customers away from Sun workstations or from the Intel–Microsoft personal computers, though both have achieved respectable market niches. There may be two reasons. Commercial software developers tend to write software for machines that already have a big market, such as those with Intel chips and Microsoft operating systems ("Wintel" machines). Academic users rely heavily on university-produced free software, which until recently has often been developed on Sun workstations and hence has been available to run on them first. Clearly the conditions that governed earlier decisions to move to a new architecture, as IBM customers did when the System/360 was announced, have changed.

Networking

The biggest change in computing since 1990 has been the emergence of networking as an integral part of what it means to have "a computer." Not only workstations but also personal computers are linked into local area networks, except in the home. Typically some form of Ethernet is used, although for personal computers in offices, the leader has been a proprietary network offered by Novell. On the national and even global level, access to the Internet moved rapidly from something available to only a few to a necessary feature bundled into every installation.

The potential of such an interconnection was long recognized by those with access to its predecessor, Arpanet, and to early versions of the Internet. What caused the breakout to a mass market was the development of software that implemented the World Wide Web (*q.v.*) around 1992, by researchers at the European particle physics laboratory CERN who wanted to communicate the results of their work to their colleagues. Shortly after that a program called "Mosaic" was developed by Marc Andreessen and colleagues at the University of Illinois supercomputer center. Mosaic allowed one to "browse" the World Wide Web through a graphical interface similar to that on the Macintosh. Both the World Wide Web and Mosaic were developed by government-funded scientific research centers: not only was this yet another example of how government funding pushed computing to a mass market, it also meant that the products of that research would be available for free or at low cost. One may say that the Internet came of age in April 1994, when Jim Clark left Silicon Graphics and, with Marc Andreessen, founded Netscape, a company whose goal was to commercialize Mosaic.

Conclusion

"What is Past is Prologue"—the phrase inscribed on the facade of the US National Archives building in Washington—applies to computing with a vengeance. It is hard to avoid the impression that whatever happened in computing from 1950 to 1999 was "mere" prologue to the present culture of the World Wide Web. Although computers continue to be designed, manufactured and sold as discrete entities, it seems no longer right to discuss the history of computing without focusing as much on the way the machines are networked. That implies that the patterns of stability that have guided the history just told may no longer apply.

The von Neumann architecture still reigns, but it seems no longer to be as central an organizing principle. Supercomputers with massively parallel designs are now the norm, while the Internet has blurred the distinction between computing that goes on inside a local box and what goes on "out there." New programming languages like Java (*q.v.*) point to a future where such a distinction may become meaningless.

As far as human–computer interaction goes, many of the basic choices appear quite stable. The rectangular box, filled with silicon integrated circuits, with an attached keyboard and monitor, has now been a physical standard for about 20 years—as long as anything has remained stable in computing. There are as many advantages now as ever for smaller machines, but designers now face the limits of the human body: the size of the fingers and hands, and the visual acuity of the human eye. "Laptop" (*see* PORTABLE COMPUTERS) computers have emerged as a subclass, but these are plagued with short battery life and keyboards that are hard to type on.

An even smaller class of pocket-sized machines known as Personal Digital Assistants (PDAs) has also emerged. These use a stylus and handwriting recognition for input, but they are not displacing the more standard configuration based on the keyboard and the mouse. As for output, LCD screens can be made smaller and lighter, but users often prefer CRTs, which, though not as good as the printed page, have crisp, easy to read screens. The tiny LCD screens of the Personal Digital Assistants may look fine to their young developers, but as people age their eyes can no longer focus on such tiny type. Other I/O methods such as voice are being developed and may soon become commonplace. Researchers at Xerox PARC and elsewhere are working on a concept of *wearable computers*—devices embedded into eyeglasses, credit cards, ID badges, and clothing. The idea holds great promise, although it will more likely supplement, not replace the general-purpose machine on one's desk.

Software compatibility, which began as a relatively simple notion with the IBM System/360, continues to be as important as ever but in a different way. Except perhaps for users of Apple computers for personal computers the primary issue has been compatibility with the latest version of Microsoft's operating system; for workstations it has been with a version of Unix. The Internet has established the networking standard TCP/IP (*q.v.*), while the World Wide Web has been built around a standard called HTML (*see* MARKUP LANGUAGES). Some are arguing that the last two standards make adherence to operating system standards less critical. How that will play out remains to be seen but in one form or another software compatibility will remain an issue in the future.

In the 1992 version of this article for the previous edition of the *Encyclopedia*, the author identified two needs that computers at that time were not meeting. They were ease of use and communications. With the emergence of the World Wide Web, along with cellular digital telephones, pagers, and new-generation satellite systems, the second need has been met (though the great success of the Internet does have the potential to create new problems). The first need, ease of use, has not been met. The Macintosh graphical interface, rightly heralded in 1984 as a breakthrough in ease of use, has evolved into a baroque clutter of icons whose meanings are by no means obvious and whose functions often contradict or overlap each other. The situation has become worse, not better. Computing cries out for a new generation of designers who can, as could those at Xerox PARC and Apple, cut through the Gordian knots of software complexity. Until that day, what the previous version of this essay said still unfortunately holds true: "computers remain difficult to use, frustrating, and overly complex in the way they present software to their owners." Perhaps in the next decade, with the other problems of performance, reliability, memory capacity, and communications well under control, this problem will be attacked and solved.

Bibliography

1982. Siewiorek, D. P., Bell, C. G., and Newell, A. *Computer Structures: Principles and Examples.* New York: McGraw-Hill.
1986. Bashe, C. J., Johnson, L. R., Palmer, J. H., and Pugh, E. W. *IBM's Early Computers.* Cambridge, MA: MIT Press.
1989. Smith, R. E. "A Historical Overview of Computer Architecture," *Annals of the History of Computing,* **10**, 277–303.
1991. Pugh, E. W., Johnson, L. R., and Palmer, J. H. *IBM's 360 and Early 370 Systems.* Cambridge, MA: MIT Press.
1996. Campbell-Kelly, M., and Aspray, W. *Computer: A History of the Information Machine.* New York: Basic Books.
1997. Kidder, T. *The Soul of a New Machine* (reissue). New York: Modern Library.
1998. Ceruzzi, P. E. *A History of Modern Computing.* Cambridge, MA: MIT Press.

Paul E. Ceruzzi

DIGITAL DESIGN AUTOMATION

For articles on related topics *see* COMPUTER-AIDED DESIGN/COMPUTER-AIDED MANUFACTURING; COMPUTER-AIDED ENGINEERING; COMPUTER CIRCUITRY; HARDWARE DESCRIPTION LANGUAGES; HARDWARE VERIFICATION; INTEGRATED CIRCUITRY; LOGIC DESIGN; MICROPROCESSORS AND MICROCOMPUTERS; and MODEL CHECKING.

Introduction

As digital and other electronic circuits become smaller, faster, cheaper and easier to manufacture, their applications range from consumer products to space exploration. The advances in technology not only increase the variety of applications of these circuits, but also increase their potential functionality and complexity. The capabilities of the early computers with room-size dimensions can now be found in hand-held calculators. The challenge that this poses for the designers of these systems is how to build these complex systems rapidly, cheaply, and reliably. As might be expected, the solution comes in the form of software that runs on the most complex of electronic systems, the digital computer.

Digital Design Automation (DDA—also called Electronic Design Automation—EDA) tools are software programs that automate the tasks required for the production of electronic hardware. They can be considered a subset of the computer-aided design (CAD) or computer-aided engineering (CAE) tools used to automate engineering processes. They are specifically designed to assist electrical and computer engineers in the process of creating electronic systems from the transistors and analog circuit components that are their basic building blocks.

Hardware designers are faced with the difficult task of implementing very complex behaviors such as the hundreds of different instructions found in some processors using millions of primitive transistors each of which can only switch on and off. In the process of refining a system design from the specification to implementation, the designer must think about the design at progressively lower levels of abstraction. A set of instructions, for example, gets broken down into the possible register transfers that must be used to implement all of the instructions. Further refinement will determine what functional blocks and registers (*q.v.*) are required to implement all the register transfers, and so forth. Design automation tools allow the designer to accomplish these tasks and validate the design as it is refined.

DDA tools are used to enter designs, simulate them, synthesize the design to a more detailed level, generate test patterns for the design, generate the geometry of the final layout and many other tasks. Often the tools are designed and sold as an integrated "tool suite" that consists of several "point tools," each performing a specific task in the design process. As in all computer-aided design software, these tools facilitate the production of the end result, but they do not "design" hardware by themselves.

A designer will use DDA tools at all stages of the design process, from the initial capture of the designer's ideas down to the final placement of the transistors onto a chip. The tools that designers use to capture a design are called "design entry" tools. The type of design entry used depends largely on the level of the design. Electronic systems can be viewed (and designed) at several levels of abstraction. At the highest levels of abstraction systems can be viewed in terms of their behavior; e.g. to regulate the air–gasoline mixture in an automobile engine. At this level the details of system implementation are ignored. At a lower level of abstraction a system can be viewed as an interconnection of modules. Each module has a known behavior and the structure of the interconnections further defines the system. Further refinement of the design results in decomposition of the modules until they are connections of basic logic gates or transistors. At the lowest level, the physical level, the system is represented by a set of geometric patterns that define the placement of layers of material in the silicon implementation of an integrated circuit.

Design entry at the highest level of abstraction is often done using a hardware description language (*q.v.*) that resembles a programming language in appearance, and in this case the design entry tool is a text editor. At the module level a designer may use a *schematic capture* tool to enter a graphical description of a system. At the physical design level, "layout editors" can be used to enter the desired geometry of the layers that are used in the fabrication of a chip or to define the placement of chips and wires on a printed circuit board.

Many design automation tools translate information about a design from one form to another. For example, a schematic capture tool is a program that translates a graphical circuit schematic with logic elements and wires into a text file called a "netlist." Both the graphical description that the designer sees on the screen and the netlist generated by the tool will contain the same essential information, but the netlist is very useful to the designer because it can be used as an input to other tools, for example a *design rule checker* that can detect errors such as the shorted outputs of NAND 2 and NOR 1 in the schematic in Fig. 1 and the netlist of Fig. 2.

Tools that can automatically translate a design from a high level of abstraction to a lower level of abstraction are called "synthesis" tools. As these tools have developed it has become more common to enter designs at higher levels of abstraction, most commonly using a hardware description language. Synthesis tools rely on a standard set of building blocks, commonly called a "library." These are analogous to software libraries of subroutines and functions.

Once a design entry tool has been used to enter a design, the design is simulated to validate that it behaves as expected. The designer provides simulation (*q.v.*)

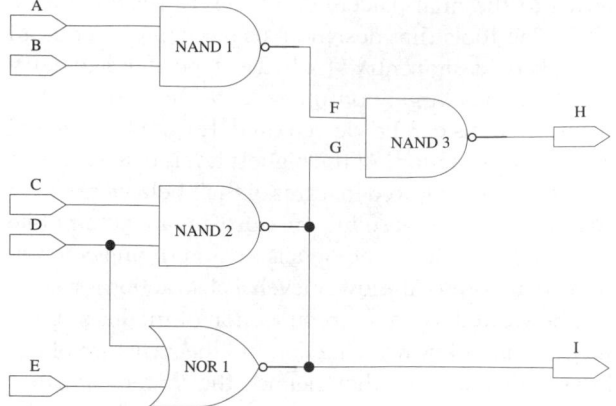

Figure 1. Gate level schematic with flaw.

inputs or "test vectors" to the simulation program that emulate the signals produced by the target environment in which the system will operate. The simulator exercises the design using these inputs, and generates the outputs that the actual circuit would produce. As with design entry, the form of the simulation inputs and outputs depends on the abstraction level of the design and the simulation. The simulation output from a high-level description might be a string of characters, whereas the simulation output at a lower level would be a waveform representing the logic or voltage levels of individual signals over time.

For most complex systems it is impossible to simulate all possible behaviors, and as the widely publicized 1994 Pentium floating-point bug illustrates, this can lead to the release of systems that do not operate correctly. *Formal verification* design automation tools are being developed to address this problem by proving that as a design is refined, each new version is equivalent to a previous version (equivalence checking). Some formal verification tools will also prove that particular constraints are always met (*see* HARDWARE VERIFICATION and MODEL CHECKING). These tools are not yet powerful enough to handle the largest system designs with millions of transistors, but they can be used on more modest designs. In 1999 Intel announced that it had formally verified that the Pentium Pro

```
IN_PORT A
IN_PORT B
IN_PORT C
IN_PORT D
IN_PORT E
NAND1 A B F
NAND2 C D G
NOR1  D E G
NAND3 F G H
OUT_PORT H
OUT_PORT I
```

Figure 2. Netlist of schematic with flaw.

floating-point operations met the specifications of the IEEE Standard 754 for floating-point arithmetic (*see* ARITHMETIC, COMPUTER).

Design automation tools also help to automate the testing process. When electronic systems are fabricated, the process may introduce faults that are not present in the design, and each system component, as well as the final system, must be thoroughly tested. The complexity of modern systems makes them impossible to test exhaustively, even using high-speed testers that can apply many test patterns. These tools are used both to optimize a design for testability and to compute a set of minimal test vectors that will test for a very high percentage of possible faults.

Conclusion

DDA tools are an integral part of the design and development processes for modern electronic systems. The computer's ability to store and manipulate information allows it to facilitate the design process by keeping track of the millions of details that would be impossible to manage manually. As computers gain storage area and speed, they allow designers to manage more complex designs and to design even faster and more capable computers. It is this positive feedback loop and the advances in integrated circuit technology that are responsible for the rapid rate of progress in electronic systems.

Bibliography

1987. Trimberger, S. M. *An Introduction to CAD for VLSI.* Boston: Kluwer Academic.

1990. Abramovici, M., Breuer, M. A., and Friedman, A. D. *Digital Systems Testing and Testable Design.* Los Alamitos, CA: Computer Society Press.

1992. Gajski, D. *High-Level Synthesis: Introduction to Chip and System Design.* Boston: Kluwer Academic.

1995. Sherwani, N. A. *Algorithms for VLSI Physical Design Automation,* 2nd Ed. Boston: Kluwer Academic.

1996. Hachtel, G. D., and Somenzi, F. *Logic Synthesis and Verification Algorithms.* Boston: Kluwer Academic.

1997. Gajski, D. *Principles of Digital Design.* Upper Saddle River, NJ: Prentice Hall.

1997. Smith, M. J. S. *Application-Specific Integrated Circuits.* Reading, MA: Addison-Wesley.

1998. Wolf, W. H. *Modern VLSI Design.* Upper Saddle River, NJ: Prentice Hall.

Cherrice Traver

DIGITAL EQUIPMENT CORPORATION (DEC)

For articles on related subjects *see* APPLE COMPUTER, INC.; DIGITAL COMPUTERS, HISTORY OF: SINCE 1950; IBM CORPORATION; MINICOMPUTER; REDUCED INSTRUCTION SET COMPUTER; UNIX OPERATING SYSTEM; VIRTUAL MEMORY; and WORKSTATION.

Introduction

The *Digital Equipment Corporation* (DEC) was founded by Kenneth Olsen, then 31, and Harlan Anderson, 28, in 1957 using $70,000 of venture capital provided by American Research and Development (ARD). The founders had dreams that their company would one day be as large as IBM and it did not faze them that on their opening day, IBM had a one billion dollar head start. The fledgling company's first factory was a Civil War vintage woolen mill in Maynard, MA, which was rented for 25 cents per square foot. DEC began as a supplier of computer circuit boards at a time when such boards contained just a small number of transistorized logic gates (*see* LOGIC DESIGN). According to Rifkin and Harrar (1988), the ARD-dominated Board of Directors did not want these systems to be called "computers," and hence did not approve the company name Digital Computer Corporation (DCC), because the US market for such oversized calculators would allegedly be no more than 100.

By 1960, DEC was indeed manufacturing computers, the PDP (Programmed Data Processor) series. The first PDP, the PDP-1, sold for $120,000. No PDP-2 was marketed, and successors -3, -4, and -5 were small machines, but by 1962, in the company's fifth year, their cumulative success brought DEC to the level of $6.5 million in sales and net profits of $807,000. All of this stemmed from the original $70,000 of ARD seed money; Olsen never needed additional equity investment.

The PDP-6, the company's first large machine, was more mainframe (*q.v.*) than minicomputer. Introduced in 1964 and priced at $300,000, it had a short and troubled life. Designed by the prolific and inventive Gordon Bell, who had joined DEC in 1960, it had a 36-bit word, a megabyte of main memory, and the first commercial time-sharing operating system (*q.v.*). The problem was not in the sophisticated design—the cleanness and effectiveness of its computer architecture was glowingly featured in the best-selling book *Hackers* by Steven Levy (1984)—but rather in the lack of reliability of its electronic circuits. The computer's failure in the marketplace led to a company shakeup and the departure of founder Harlan Anderson.

Two of the best known of the PDP series are the PDP-8, first sold in 1965 for $18,000, and the PDP-11 family, whose first system, the PDP-11/20, sold in 1970 for $11,000. The PDP-8 was perhaps the first widely successful minicomputer, and inspired numerous competitors such as Data General, Prime Computer, and others. Over 50,000 were sold. The PDP-11 series made minicomputers widely available for general computing, process control, and education. Including the PDP-11 clones from several sources, some in Eastern Europe, an estimated 650,000 have been produced. For a thorough description of the entire PDP series, see Bell and Bell (1983).

The PDP-11 instruction set had a particularly elegant design, with an unusually rich set of addressing modes (12, four of which exploited the fact that the program counter was also a general-purpose register). There were eight 16-bit registers and a 16-bit address space (64 KB). Its instruction set was highly orthogonal (any instruction could be used with any general-purpose register or addressing mode). As a consequence, it was well suited for use in teaching the principles of assembly-language programming and computer architecture (*q.v.*). Its instruction set was designed to execute efficiently, and the PDP-11 architecture had fast interrupt-handling capabilities (*see* INTERRUPT), all of which made it well suited to real-time systems (*q.v.*).

The first version of the Unix operating system was written for the PDP-7, but when it was rewritten in the language C (*q.v.*) in 1973, it became widely used on larger PDP-11s for teaching and research, in part because AT&T made it freely available. The PDP-11s were also used in several influential multiprocessor systems in the 1970s.

The PDP-11 was limited by its 64 KB of addressable memory. Although the larger ones supported memory management (*q.v.*) with address spaces of 18–22 bits, the basic architecture could not be extended. Gordon Bell, one of the computer's designers, said in retrospect that the 16-bit address limitation was one of the PDP-11's major shortcomings. In 1977, DEC introduced the VAX 11/780 (Virtual Address eXtension), a 32-bit "super minicomputer" to overcome these shortcomings, at a price of $200,000.

The DEC VAX Series

Although the PDP-11 remained popular through the 1980s in applications where its addressing constraints were acceptable, the VAX became a campus and research mainstay. It ran either the DEC VMS (Virtual Memory System) operating system or the influential Berkeley Software Distribution (BSD) Unix variant, which was designed for it.

The VAX series had a 32-bit architecture with 32-bit virtual addresses and 32-bit general registers. There were 16 general-purpose registers, including the program counter, stack pointer, frame pointer, and argument pointer (*see* ACTIVATION RECORD). The VAX architecture featured variable-length instructions, from 1 byte to over 50. Opcodes were one or two bytes long. The number of operands varied from zero to six. Each operand (*q.v.*) was specified using a general operand specifier that allowed one of 13 addressing modes, including true post-indexing. Several data types (*q.v.*) were supported, including 8-, 16-, and 32-bit integers; single, double, and quadruple precision floating-point numbers; and decimal string, numeric string, character string, 0- to 32-bit fields, and queues.

Its architecture and large instruction set made the VAX a classic *complex instruction set computer* (CISC). Special instructions were provided for procedure call and return, saving and restoring process context, array index computation, polynomial evaluation, character string manipulation, transformation of packed decimal strings to character strings, etc. It also included a PDP-11 compatibility mode for emulation of PDP-11 user code.

The original VAX architecture included 244 instructions when it was announced in 1977. Four instructions for manipulating queues in a multiprocessor system were added in 1978 and retrofitted to all VAX-11/780s in the field. In 1980, 56 new instructions were added to support a new extended range double precision data type and a quadruple precision data type. These new instructions were implemented as microcode options on the VAX-11/780 and VAX-11/750 (*see* MICROPROGRAMMING). Software emulation was provided to achieve compatibility with systems that did not include the option.

The next major change to the VAX architecture occurred in 1984, with the definition of the MicroVAX subset, which was intended to allow single-chip VLSI microprocessor implementations. Decimal string instructions, certain character string instructions, and PDP-11 compatibility mode were excluded from the MicroVAX and relegated to software emulation.

In 1989, 63 new instructions were added to the VAX architecture to support vector register-based integrated vector processing. The architecture specifies 16 vector registers, each with 64 elements that are 64 bits wide. The vector instruction set supports integer and floating-point arithmetic and logical operations.

Though the VAX began as a minicomputer, the VAX series eventually included a wide range of architecturally compatible processors whose performance spanned a range from that typical of workstations through minis to mainframes (*q.v.*). Table 1 lists a selection of VAX systems marketed in 1990, and Bhandarkar (1993) has a comprehensive list.

By its 30th anniversary in 1987, DEC had still not overtaken IBM, but its solid growth based on the profitable VAX line made its second place position far stronger than that of any of the group of computer vendors who ranked third or lower. The company had 120,000 employees, 33.6 million square feet of space in 62 countries, a market value of $24 billion (10th among all US companies), 475 sales offices, $11.4 billion in revenues, $1.3 billion in net profits, and was 38th in the list of *Fortune* 500 companies. Ken Olsen was featured on the cover of *Business Week*. The prior October, *Fortune* magazine had done the same, calling him "America's most successful entrepreneur." For a personal profile of Olsen, *see* ENTREPRENEURS.

RISC Systems

In January 1989, DEC announced its first Reduced Instruction Set Computer (RISC), using a MIPS Computer Systems, Inc. microprocessor. These systems ran Ultrix, DEC's version of Unix, and marked DEC's entry into the open systems market. These DECsystems and DECstations were used as workstations and servers in education and industry in the first half of the 1990s.

DEC introduced the more powerful Alpha 21064 processor in February 1992, and the first systems built around it at the end of that year. Since 1992, the Alpha 21064, 21164, and 21264 processors have powered DEC's series of workstations and servers. This processor family has generally had among the highest clock rates of all commercial microprocessors, and has excellent performance on the standard SPEC benchmarks (*q.v.*).

Table 1. The DEC VAX series of digital computers. (The VAX-11/780 was arbitrarily assigned a Vax Unit of Performance (VUP) of 1.0.)

Model	Date	Comments	Circuitry	Bus	Cycle time	Cache	Performance
VAX-11/780	1978		Schottky TTL	Unibus/Massbus	200 ns	8 KB	1.0 VUP
VAX-11/750	1980		TTL gate array	Unibus/Massbus	320 ns	4 KB	0.6 VUP
VAX-11/730	1982		TTL bit-sliced	Unibus/Massbus	290 ns	none	0.25 VUP
VAX 8600	1984	First pipelined VAX	ECL gate-array		80 ns	16 KB	4.0 VUP
MicroVAX-I	1984	First subset VAX	TTL	Qbus	250 ns	none	0.2 VUP
MicroVAX-II	1985		Single chip	Qbus	200 ns	none	0.9 VUP
VAX 8800	1986	Dual-processor 8600	ECL gate-array	VAXBI	45 ns	64 KB	12.0 VUP
VAX 8700	1986	Uniprocessor 8800					6.0 VUP
VAX 88x0	1987	1–4 processor 8700					24.0 VUP
MicroVAX 3100	1989		CVAX chip	Qbus	90 ns		2.5 VUP
VAX 6000-400	1989	1–6 vector CPUs	CMOS chip	VAXBI	28 ns	128 KB	42.0 VUP
VAX 9000	1989	1–4 pipelined CPUs	ECL gate-array	XMI	16 ns	128 KB	500 Mflops

Table 2. Performance of DEC Alpha processors relative to the VAX 11/780. Source: The CPU Information Center, `http://bwrc.eecs.berkeley.edu/CIC/`. The SPEC benchmarks cannot be precisely compared with DEC's earlier VUP (VAX Unit of Performance), but a very rough comparison would put the VAX 11/780 at about 1/25 of a SPEC-95 unit, or about 1/1000 as fast as the Alpha 21264.

Processor	Clock rate (MHz)	SPEC-95 Integer	SPEC-95 Floating-point
21064	100	1.9	2.8
21064a	300	5.2	6.5
21164	300	8.5	12.7
21164a	600	18.4	21.3
21264	667	44	66
21364a	1000	70	120 (projected)

The first 21064 processors had clock speeds of 100 MHz, and later went as high as 300 MHz. The 21164 ran at speeds up to 600 MHz, and the 21264 runs at 700 MHz or faster. The 21364, announced for 2000, will have an initial clock speed of 1 GHz. SPEC-95 benchmarks for these processors are given in Table 2.

Initially the DEC Alpha servers and workstations ran Digital Unix, which superseded Ultrix, and a VMS version, OpenVMS. In 1994, DEC replaced its own system buses by PC standard buses, EISA and PCI (*see* BUS), for greater compatibility with other systems. The new Alpha systems could then also run the Microsoft Windows NT workstation operating system.

Personal Computers

In 1982 DEC introduced the Rainbow 100, a personal computer that used both the Intel 8088 and the popular Zilog Z80 microprocessors. It could run the Z80 CP/M microcomputer operating system as well as MS-DOS. Although the design had some good features, DEC chose to make it proprietary, and used a non-standard diskette (*q.v.*) format that only it produced. This ran counter to the open architecture (*q.v.*) approach of the IBM PC, and made the Rainbow a less attractive system than it might otherwise have been. The Rainbow was not a commercial success, and although DEC produced a conventional IBM-compatible VAXmate PC in 1986, the company never obtained a significant share of the PC market.

Recent History

The fortunes of DEC over the ten-year period 1988–1998 were not nearly as good as were experienced in the prior ten. Sales of both DEC minicomputers declined as those of personal computers soared. By 1998, DEC's position slipped relative to other vendors and was no longer second overall. Ken Olsen left the

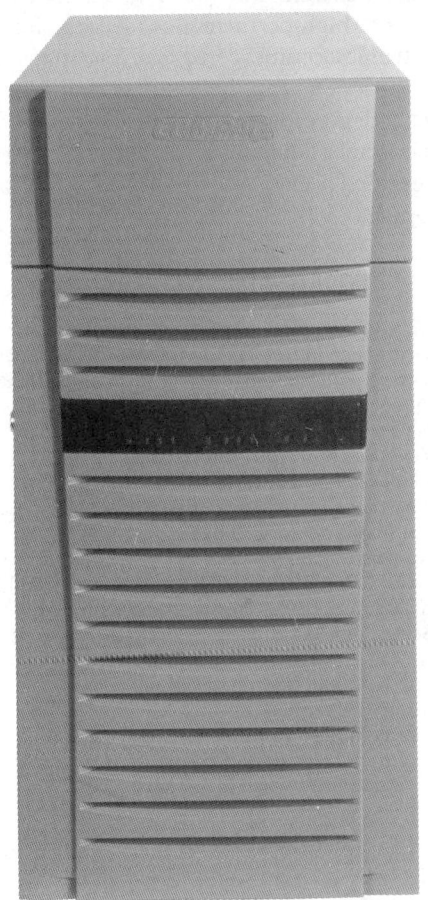

Figure 1. The Compaq Alpha System. (Courtesy of Compaq.)

company in 1993. In 1995, he was named chairman of Advanced Modular Solutions, a three-year-old systems developer in Acton, MA. Ironically, the company then announced an arrangement with IBM's Manufacturing Industry Solutions unit in Charlotte, NC, to deliver a server that enabled customers to upgrade transparently from VAX/VMS systems once made by DEC. The IBM 7596 Cross-Platform Server comes with a Pentium processor, PowerPC 601 chip, and a VAX-compatible processor. The server provides connected workstations with shared access to applications running on IBM OS/2, Microsoft Windows, VMS, and AIX. Advanced Modular and IBM also have set up a consulting center in Acton to help customers install the server and transfer legacy applications.

DEC's weakness in the PC market was "remedied" when the company was sold to Compaq for $9.6 billion (US) in cash and stock in June 1998. What Compaq kindly called a "merger" made the combined company the new second largest computer vendor in the world.

The historic Digital Equipment Corporation continues, but as a division of its new parent company. In addition to its well-established line of PCs Compaq is continuing to develop the Alpha line (*see* Fig. 1), providing workstations and high-performance servers for Websites and electronic commerce (*q.v.*). The many loyal fans of DEC products can only hope that Compaq will preserve a degree of DEC identity, and go on to add enough commendable history of its own to warrant an article entitled COMPAQ in the next edition of this Encyclopedia.

Bibliography

1983. Bell, C. G., and Bell, J. R. "Digital Equipment Corporation PDP Series," in *Encyclopedia of Computer Science and Engineering*, 2nd Ed. (eds. A. Ralston and E. D. Reilly), 554–561. New York: Van Nostrand Reinhold.

1984. Levy, S. *Hackers: Heroes of the Computer Revolution*. New York: Anchor Press/Doubleday.

1988. Rifkin, G., and Harrar, G. *The Ultimate Entrepreneur: The Story of Ken Olsen and Digital Equipment Corporation*. Chicago: Contemporary Books.

1991. Brunner, R. A. *VAX Architecture Reference Manual*, 2nd Ed. Upper Saddle River, NJ: Prentice Hall/Digital Press.

1993. Bhandarkar, D. P. "Digital Equipment Corporation VAX Series," in *Encyclopedia of Computer Science*, 3rd Ed. (eds. A. Ralston and E. D. Reilly), 463–466. New York: Van Nostrand Reinhold. (Some of the material in this article is taken directly from this reference.)

1996. Bhandarkar, D. P. *Alpha Implementations and Architecture: Complete Reference and Guide*. Newton, MA: Digital Press/Butterworth Heinemann.

David Hemmendinger and Edwin D. Reilly

DIGITAL LIBRARIES

For articles on related subjects *see* ELECTRONIC REFERENCE WORKS; HUMANITIES APPLICATIONS; HYPERTEXT; INFORMATION RETRIEVAL; and MULTIMEDIA.

Introduction

Many views of digital libraries (DLs) stem from what libraries currently do. Traditional libraries collect, organize, provide access to, and preserve objects in their collections. A library collection may include books, magazines, journals, video and audio media, and maps. The flexibility of digital technology allows it to handle new kinds of objects efficiently. DL collections can include things without direct physical analogs, such as algorithms or real-time data feeds. They also may include digitized representations of what have traditionally appeared largely in museums or archives. With the rise in cost of paper publications and library storage, increasing use of computers, and decreasing budgets, many libraries have to reduce their acquisition of books as well as their journal subscriptions.

Documents in electronic form can become more available and widely used because the cost of digital storage and processing is going down (Fox *et al.*, 1995a).

For broad overviews of the field, see the excellent book by Lesk (1997), a popular online magazine (Friedlander, 1998), and our online courseware (Fox and Gupta, 1998). There are special issues of journals devoted to topics and projects related to DLs, such as *Communications of the ACM*, April 1995 and April 1998, the *IEEE Computer* theme issue on the US Digital Libraries Initiative, May 1996, and the *Information Processing and Management* special issue on digital libraries (Marchionini and Fox, 1999). For information retrieval aspects of DLs, refer to Fox and Sornil (1999).

History and Motivation

Futuristic views of libraries have long appeared in science fiction as well as in Bush's visionary statements (Bush, 1945) that foresaw and encouraged much work in information retrieval and hypertext. Licklider (1965) laid out the clearest early call for digital libraries; he described a vast expansion of the publishing world, as well as the need for knowledge organization, search, retrieval, and many support activities. The early development of DLs resulted from three main factors: the human need for information, the growing volume of information accumulated in various communities, and advances in technology, e.g. networking, information storage and retrieval, hypermedia, and human–computer interaction (Fox and Lunin, 1993). In the USA, one of the early statements was S.626 (Electronic Library Act of 1993), calling for "a system of state-based electronic libraries" supporting the use of publicly available libraries, databases, and networks and providing robust and reliable support services for search and retrieval. The term "digital libraries" became widely accepted as the result of many activities in this area in the period 1991–1993 (Fox, 1993), perhaps corresponding to the growing interest in digital technology, such as digital networks, digital video and audio, and electronic publishing. The definition of DLs must be made in the context of many related issues, such as distributed collections, preservation, integrity, use, interoperability, and social, economic, and legal implications.

Aspects of DLs

DLs are considered among the most complex and advanced forms of information systems. They involve many areas, not only in computer and information science but also in arts and humanities. Table 1 lists some of the related fields that contribute to the advance of DLs.

Table 1. Areas of study, attributes, contents, features, issues, and roles (adapted from Fox *et al.*, 1995a).

Abstracting	Economic study	Navigation
Accessibility	Education support	Object-oriented
Agent	Electronic publishing	OCR
Annotation	Ethnographic study	OODB support
Archiving	Filtering	Personalization
Billing, charging	Geographic information system	Preservation
Browsing	Hypermedia	Privacy
Catalog	Hypertext	Publisher library
Classification	Image processing	Repository
Clustering	Index	Scalability
Commercial service	Information retrieval	Search
Content conversion	Intellectual property rights	Security
Copyright clearance	Interactive system	Sociological study
Courseware	Knowledge base	Storage
Database	Knowbot	Standards
Diagram (e.g., CAD)	Library science	Subscription
Digital video	Mediator	Sustainability
Digitization	Multilingual collection	Training support
Discipline-level library	Multimedia stream playback	Usability
Distributed processing	Multimedia system	Virtual library
Document analysis	Multimodal	Visualization
Document model	National library	World Wide Web

DOCUMENTS AND COLLECTIONS

Documents are at the heart of DLs. Without documents there would be no DLs. In DLs, documents are not only what are stored in traditional libraries, e.g. books, pictures, and videos, but also include many works uncommon in those libraries, e.g. multilingual, multimedia, and structured documents (e.g. books broken into chapters, sections, subsections, figures with attached captions, color graphics or images, attached or linked sound or video files, appendices, indexes, and "front matter"); programs; algorithms; bulletin board (*q.v.*) archives; and states of computation. A document can have various representations depending on its intended use; for example, some applications require high-resolution images of documents with invisible watermarks for security purposes as well as low-resolution versions for children to download over the WWW (*q.v.*). Collections in DLs range from small, self-contained, and narrowly defined collections to ones spread across physical and logical spaces. One of the common requirements for a DL is the ability to deal with distributed collections of information (Fox and Sornil, 1999), which brings up the issue of interoperability among distributed systems.

INTEROPERABILITY

Interoperability is a major issue in DLs; it involves many aspects of the systems, such as data interchange; searching of distributed and heterogeneous collections; inter-repository sharing; and access security. Solutions to the interoperability problem range from employing common tools and interfaces to achieving semantic interoperability. The latter deals with the ability of a user to access consistently and coherently similar classes of digital objects and services (Lynch and Garcia-Molina, 1995). For example, one might want to find articles about a concept that appears in several separate science and engineering collections, where the concept is described using radically different terminology in each. Alternatively, one might want to locate narrative, poetic, pictorial, or video descriptions of some important artifacts from antiquity, starting from a very limited base of knowledge. A possible way toward this goal is to provide electronic intermediaries (e.g. separate tools to analyze texts or videos) and federating or mediating software compensating for variations across diverse heterogeneous domains (domains which have disparate semantics, e.g. different languages, different cultures). With common interfaces alone, the achieved interoperability is superficial and limited to the common functions that the weakest component can provide.

Between these two extremes, there is the notion of syntactic interoperability, which provides a limited coherence of access and content. This level of interoperability is accomplished by employing standards and requiring that every component conforms to rules and formats of those standards when communicating with other components. Some of the popular emerging standards deal with metadata (data about data), federated search protocols (automatically mapping and distributing a query to multiple heterogeneous search sites), and communication protocols (Lynch and Garcia-Molina, 1995). Metadata refers to data that is used to describe digital objects, collections, and whole DLs with their services. Dublin Core (Hakala,

1997) is a metadata scheme consisting of 15 basic elements that can be used to describe digital objects. This is like the role played by library catalog records, e.g. Machine-Readable Cataloging (MARC), which are a starting point for many metadata descriptions. Thus, in digital libraries one might first search across the equivalent of the card catalogs of several libraries in one step, and later move from examining that metadata to actually reading the books selected as most useful.

INFORMATION RETRIEVAL

Information retrieval (IR) involves the representation, organization, and storage of information, and access to it (Salton and McGill, 1983). The objective of IR is to retrieve information that is relevant to a user's need, submitted to the system in the form of queries. This is difficult, as many have noticed when trying to find something on the Web using one of the available search engines. DLs can be regarded as extended IR systems with multiple media and federation (Fox and Sornil, 1999). Thus, one might try to find a photograph of a particular president and female friend in all US newspaper or magazine collections, satellite images of cloverleaf road intersections, or movie scenes of sinking boats that have an associated song by a particular female vocalist. DLs may also be considered applications of IR. However, regardless of perspective, IR is essential for DLs to achieve high levels of effectiveness while affording ease of use to diverse communities. There is considerable research under way in IR related to DLs, dealing with multilingual processing, multimodal and structured documents, hypertext and hypermedia, searching of multimedia content, information visualization, handling distributed collections of complex documents, federated search standards, and information system architectures.

Research in "nonstandard" types of documents, e.g. multimedia, multilingual, and hypertext, involves special kinds of languages, texts, complex structures, and indexing and searching techniques. However, the common requirement of all the types is content-based information access. The importance of multilingual information retrieval has been increased with the expansion of DLs. Any process based on explicitly linguistic knowledge, such as *stemming* (e.g. matching the query term "computers" with document term "computing," since both have stem "comput"), cannot be extended directly to other languages. Unicode (*see* CHARACTER CODES) is an effort to provide a single (16-bit instead of 8-bit character) coding scheme suitable for all natural languages. Other techniques use, for example, word dictionaries and translation thesauri (Jones and Willett, 1997).

Hypertext (*q.v.*) offers efficient nonsequential reading of documents, and it provides the perception of relationships among documents within and across collections. Some growing developments are using hypertext as the basis for information systems, e.g. (Agosti *et al.*, 1996), and automatically creating hypertext, e.g. Salton and Allan, 1993. The effectiveness of the latter is currently limited to syntactically defined or primitive lexical matches. Multimedia information retrieval deals with content-based retrieval of other media, in particular speech, graphics, and images, as well as combinations of media, such as video. Each medium has distinctive characteristics and presents different indexing and searching problems. Thus one might search music collections based on a short melody or look for text blocks appearing in network news shows, where videos have been indexed at the level of single images as well as camera shots. Retrieval of spoken documents relies on techniques of word recognition; however, the transcription success rate in natural surroundings is currently no more than 25% (Sparck-Jones and Willett, 1997). The foundation of indexing and searching image documents involves providing automatic content identification, built from primitive, content-based features as well as combinations of keys and other information. Attempts have been made using higher-level shapes (e.g. blob (Carson *et al.*, 1997)), color characterization (e.g. color histogram), texture, change in orientation, etc. Video retrieval presents a different problem from image retrieval because, in video, an image relates to other images in a sequence. Thus, judging an image in a video relevant to a query may require considering multiple images in the sequence. An effort by Zhang *et al.* (1995) segmented video into key frames and indexed images by general content representations (e.g. color, texture, and shape) as well as temporal features (e.g. camera motion).

USABILITY

"The key to the success of DL projects is having usable systems" (Fox and Sornil, 1999). To achieve this goal, research in human–computer interaction focuses on modeling people's activities and needs in using DLs. It studies users' expectations and their work habits with different types of documents and identifies positive features and capabilities of systems in order to come up with effective visualization, navigation, manipulation, and analysis tools for DLs. Research in usability has been broadened to include supports for users' information context switching (e.g. moving from formulating a query that expresses an information need, to working with interface devices like filling in a field or selecting a radio button choice, to browsing through a list of results, and to following a hypertext link to another page), DL metrics (e.g. speed of search response, ability to produce a ranked list of results that are mostly relevant, with the best matches at the top), factors for adopting DLs (including cost, support, as well as services), and social and organizational concerns.

An important issue under discussion across various communities is the set of metrics to be used for evaluating DLs. Selecting DL metrics should be considered from both system-oriented and user-oriented viewpoints. From the system's perspective, we consider capacity (number of digital objects stored and number of users served simultaneously), content (e.g. access control), and transaction speed. From the user's perspective, we consider impacts of the system on the user (e.g. impacts on patterns of association and attitudes about the DLs), effectiveness (relevance of the results), usability (e.g. ease of use, suitability to purpose, user's effort), interactions with the system, and user satisfaction (Kantor, 1997).

PROPERTY RIGHTS AND ACCESS CONTROL

The advance of DLs depends on their successes not only in technology but also in legal, social, and economic contexts. We first discuss intellectual property issues of DLs and then DLs in economic and social contexts. Copyright was created to encourage authors to publish useful works by providing them suitable compensation for their creativity and labor. DLs introduce difficult and complex intellectual property issues because, with digital documents, multiple copies of a document can be viewed simultaneously since they can be easily transferred and duplicated. The collections may consist of priceless objects and valuable services; some methods to enforce property rights have to be applied to achieve a balance between author and publisher (interested in compensation) and user and library (interested in access to information). Some advocate subscriptions while others favor charges based on counts of use, unit-of-time-online, or bytes-delivered (Samuelson, 1995). The success of DLs, especially those supporting key applications like education, depends upon achieving a sensible balance among quality of service, usage, authority, and finances.

Economics and social implications. DLs introduce new relationships and impacts into our world. They connect people together, supporting understanding of different cultures, heritages, and perspectives. New kinds of information are accessible to users. New possibilities of doing business result both directly from access to collections and indirectly from the content of the collections, e.g. advertisements. In publishing, DLs dramatically change the cost of production and dissemination, and libraries and publishers have to redefine their functions and purposes to survive in this environment. Publishers may adapt by performing functions such as selection of quality publications, editing, refinements, and promotions; they also may

have some legacy information that DLs need to have in their collections. Libraries may preserve and provide access to historical records of works in their collections, may become the publishers of works prepared by their host institutions (e.g. when managing reports, as at `http://www.ncstrl.org`, or theses, as at `http://www.theses.org`), and may provide cross-publisher catalogs (Samuelson, 1995). DLs blur the boundary between authors and readers; for example there are authoring and annotation tools that can be used for both publishing and reading. Copyright law, user privacy, and policies of collection development, management, preservation, and archiving need to be designed for effective use of DLs.

Accomplishments and Projects

Today's DL systems have precursors in IR, hypertext, multimedia, and library automation. The ENVISION project (1991–1995), one of the first new efforts, aimed at understanding the requirements for DLs and building a prototype from scratch. Its collection consisted of approximately 100,000 bibliographic records, 700 full-text articles, and 13,000 scanned page images. Its design and visualization were based on a study of users of computer science information and discussions with experts in the area (Fox et al., 1995b). The CORE project (1991–1995), another early effort, developed an electronic library prototype to access chemical journal articles (around 400,000 pages). Its collection included, for each article, both scanned images and an SGML marked-up version. This project was concerned with collection-building as well as testing of a variety of interfaces that were designed based on user studies (Entlich et al., 1995).

The NSF/DARPA/NASA Digital Libraries Initiative (DLI) (Harum, 1998) has been one of the most visible project efforts. Phase 1, from 1994 to 1998, provided funding for six large university projects, spanning a wide range of major topics and addressing technical challenges. Berkeley focused on analysis and user tools for image documents; Carnegie Mellon investigated segmenting and indexing video, initially with 1,000 GB of storage archiving 1,000 hours of video; Illinois concentrated on large collections of tens of thousands of full-text technical articles; Michigan employed interacting software agents to provide services to users; Santa Barbara indexed geological maps using image processing (q.v.) and region metadata with over five million images; and Stanford focused on interoperability of different search services.

Beginning around 1991, researchers and interested people held conferences and workshops to create a consensus on a research agenda and possible solutions to many key issues of the field. An important aspect

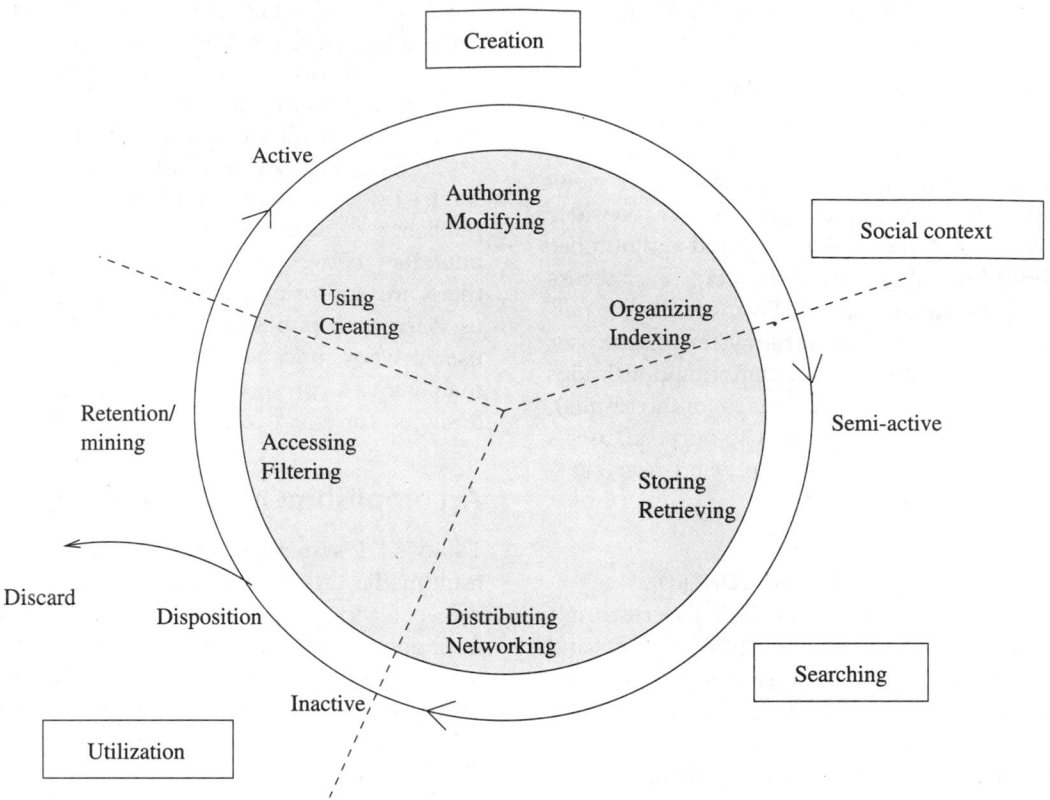

Figure 1. Information Life Cycle (adapted from `http://www-lis.gseis.ucla.edu/DL/UCLA_DL_model.gif`). The outer ring indicates life cycle stages (active, semi-active, and inactive) for a type of information artifact (e.g. business records, artworks, documents, scientific data). The stages are superimposed on six types of information uses or processes in the shaded circle. The cycle has three major phases: information creation, searching, and utilization. The alignment of the cycle stages with the steps of information handling and process phases may vary in particular social or institutional contexts.

learned from the workshops is that DLs cannot be limited only to technological aspects, but that they also require advances in the humanities and arts to succeed. This realization led to the announcement of the Digital Libraries Initiative—Phase 2 in the spring of 1998 to focus less on technology and more on research across the information life cycle (see Fig. 1)—content creation, access, use, and preservation and archiving—directed toward the concept of DLs as human-centered systems.

International Efforts

Thousands of digital libraries are emerging around the world, crossing all disciplines and media. Their sizes range from the small, serving local organizations, to the large, such as national libraries sharing highlights of history, cultural treasures, and accomplishments with the rest of the world (Fox and Sornil, 1999). Many countries have created their own projects such as the Digital Libraries Initiative in the USA; the ERCIM program for the European community enhanced by projects in countries such as UK, France, and Germany; and related initiatives in Singapore and Japan. For more details on efforts in various nations,

see a recent article (Fox and Marchionini, 1998). The International Digital Libraries Collaborative Research program of NSF will fund joint projects with these and other countries.

The world has diverse intellectual and cultural collections; connecting them together can lead to deeper understanding and wider cooperation. The major barriers are interoperability and multilingual collection processing. Some solutions are emerging, for example using Z39.50, IP, and HTTP protocols plus international standards like SGML, XML (*see* MARKUP LANGUAGES), JPEG, and MPEG (*see* IMAGE COMPRESSION) (Fox and Marchionini, 1998).

Conclusion and Future Challenges

Digital libraries can meet the needs of user communities through a variety of services connected with complex collections and various structuring mechanisms for managing data and descriptions of that data. They involve not only computer and information science but also humanities and arts. Research and development in this field is being conducted actively in many communities. Each year workshops and conferences aim at establishing an agenda for investigation and creating new techniques and a consensus as to how to handle difficult problems. Important aspects that need to be carefully handled in DLs are document representations; collection creation, management, preservation, and archiving; usability; interoperability; intellectual property; social and economic implications; scalability; and supporting network infrastructure. Every issue needs to be handled in both local as well as global contexts, helping lead toward the concept of a world-wide digital library.

Bibliography

1945. Bush, V. "As We May Think," *The Atlantic Monthly*, **176**, *1*, 101–108.

1965. Licklider, J. C. R. *Libraries of the Future.* Cambridge, MA: MIT Press.

1983. Salton, G., and McGill, M. J. *Introduction to Modern Information Retrieval.* New York: McGraw-Hill.

1993. Fox, E. A. *Digital Library Source Book.* http://fox.cs.vt.edu/DLSB.html.

1993. Fox, E. A., and Lunin, L. F. "Introduction and Overview to Perspectives on Digital Libraries," *Journal of the American Society for Information Science*, **44**, *8*, 480–491.

1993. Salton, G., and Allan, J. "Selective Text Utilization and Text Traversal," in *Proceedings of Hypertext-93*, Seattle, WA, 131–144.

1995. Entlich, R., Garson, L., Lesk, M., Normore, L., Olsen, J., and Weibel, S. "Making a Digital Library: The Chemistry Online Retrieval Experiment—A Summary of the CORE Project (1991–1995)," *D-Lib Magazine*, December. http://www.dlib.org/dlib/december95/briefings/12core.html.

1995a. Fox, E. A., Akscyn, R. M., Furuta, R. K., and Leggett, J. J. "Digital Libraries: Introduction," *Communications of the ACM*, **38**, *4*, 22–28.

1995b. Fox, E. A., Heath, L. S., and Hix, D. *Project Envision Final Report: A User-Centered Database from the Computer Science Literature.* http://ei.cs.vt.edu/papers/ENVreport/final.html.

1995. Lynch, C., and Garcia-Molina, H. *Interoperability, Scaling, and the Digital Libraries Research Agenda: A Report on the May 18–19, 1995 IITA Digital Libraries Workshop.* http://www-diglib.stanford.edu/diglib/pub/reports/iita-dlw/main.html.

1995. Samuelson, P. "Copyright and Digital Libraries," *Communications of the ACM*, **38**, *3*, 15–21.

1995. Zhang, H. J., Low, C. Y., Smoliar, S. W., and Wu, J. H. "Video Parsing, Retrieval and Browsing: An Integrated and Content-based Solution," in *Proceedings of ACM Multimedia '95*, San Franciscso, 15–24.

1996. Agosti, M., Crestani, G., and Melucci, M. "Design and Implementation of a Tool for the Automatic Construction of Hypertexts for Information Retrieval," *Information Processing & Management*, **32**, 459–476.

1997. Carson, C., Belongie, S., Greenspan, H., and Malik, J. "Region-based Image Querying," *CVPR '97 Workshop on Content-Based Access of Image and Video Libraries.*

1997. Hakala, J. *The 5th Dublin Core Metadata Workshop*, October. http://linnea.helsinki.fi/meta/DC5.html.

1997. Kantor, P. B. *Evaluating Digital Libraries.* Tutorial for Digital Libraries Conference '97, Pennsylvania, PA.

1997. Lesk, M. *Practical Digital Libraries: Books, Bytes & Bucks.* San Francisco: Morgan Kaufmann.

1997. Sparck-Jones, K., and Willett, P. *Readings in Information Retrieval.* San Francisco: Morgan Kaufmann.

1998. Fox, E. A., and Gupta, R. *Courseware on Digital Libraries.* http://ei.cs.vt.edu/~dlib.

1998. Fox, E. A., and Marchionini, G. "Toward a Worldwide Digital Library," *Communications of the ACM*, **41**, *4*, 29–32.

1998. Friedlander, A. *D-lib Program: Research in Digital Libraries.* http://www.dlib.org.

1998. Harum, S. *Digital Library Initiative.* http://dli.grainger.uiuc.edu/national.htm.

1999. Fox, E. A., and Sornil, O. *Modern Information Retrieval.* Harlow, UK: Addison Wesley Longman.

1999. Marchionini, G., and Fox, E. A. "Progress Toward Digital Libraries: Augmentation Through Integration. Guest Editors' Introduction to Special Issue on Digital Libraries," *Information Processing and Management*, **35**, *2*.

Edward A. Fox and Ohm Sornil

DIGITAL SIGNATURE

For articles on related topics *see* AUTHENTICATION; CRYPTOGRAPHY, COMPUTERS IN; ELECTRONIC COMMERCE; LEGAL ASPECTS OF COMPUTING; and PRETTY GOOD PRIVACY.

Digital signatures, according to the International Organization for Standardization, "establish the origin of a message in order to settle disputes of what message (if any) was sent." They typically involve two keys—a *signing key* which is private to a user, and a *signature verification key* which is made public. A user can operate on a message with the private signing key to generate a signature, a short string that depends on all the bits in the message and the signing key in such a way that it cannot economically be forged by someone who does not know the signing key; yet it can be verified by anyone with the public verification key.

A digital signature thus combines two protection primitives—message integrity and nonrepudiation of origin (Diffie and Hellman, 1976). Probably the most common technique is RSA, named after its inventors Rivest, Shamir and Adleman (1978). This was the first system to be used (in 1979) to control access to the zero-power plutonium reactor at Idaho Falls (Simmons, 1997); more recently, it has been adopted as the European standard for healthcare signatures, and as the mechanism used in the SET protocol to protect credit card payments over the Internet. (A different signature algorithm, DSA, is now used in US government applications (Schneier, 1995).)

RSA is based on the assumption that calculating cube (and other) roots modulo a large number is hard unless we know its prime factors. The simplest form of RSA signature S on a message M is just

$$S \equiv \sqrt[3]{M} \pmod{N}$$

The public signature verification key is the modulus N, while the secret signing key consists of its factors—two large randomly chosen prime numbers p and q. For how to calculate modular cube roots, and further details on how RSA works in general, *see* CRYPTOGRAPHY, COMPUTERS IN, Rivest *et al.* (1978) or Schneier (1995).

Two further mechanisms are commonly found in digital signature systems: *hashing* and *certification*.

One problem with the RSA signature function is that it is a multiplicative homomorphism; that is, if we have three messages M_1, M_2 and M_3 such that $M_1 = M_2 M_3 \pmod{N}$, then their signatures will stand in a similar relationship, $S_1 = S_2 S_3 \pmod{N}$. To prevent attacks exploiting this property, it was common in early signature applications to pad messages with suitably chosen fixed constants.

The more robust modern practice is to pass messages through a cryptographic hash function before signing. The idea is that the hash function reduces each message to an essentially unique digest, which we can sign in its stead; the hashing process performs the dual function of breaking up the homomorphism property and saving us from having to sign each block of a long message individually.

There is now a US standard algorithm for cryptographic hashing. Such an algorithm takes as input a string of arbitrary length and outputs a hash value of fixed length. Its essential properties are, first, that the hash should be easy to compute but hard to invert; and second, that the function should be collision free, in that it should not be practical to find two different messages M_1 and M_2 with $h(M_1) = h(M_2)$. (Such collisions will exist, by a simple counting argument; it must just be difficult to find them.) For use with RSA, we need a third property: that it should not be practical to find three messages M_1, M_2 and M_3 such that $h(M_1)h(M_2) = h(M_3)$.

The second aspect is certification. How do we know that a given public key actually corresponds to a given individual?

Users who meet in person prior to initiating electronic communications can manually verify each others' public keys and certify them by applying their own signatures. This certification enables them to act as introducers; I might decide to trust any key signed by someone whom I know to be prudent.

Direct certification can be effective in closed communities, such as the banking industry, where the principals are in regular contact or at least trust a small number of organizations such as central banks to make introductions. But how can such arrangements be scaled worldwide, and enable people who have never met to verify each others' signatures?

This area is highly controversial. The approach favored by governments is to establish a hierarchy of "trusted third parties"—nationally licensed certification services that will simultaneously sign users' public keys and enforce certain regulatory functions, such as ensuring that copies of users' encryption keys are archived for access by law enforcement and national intelligence agencies. In this model, a user's key certificate is somewhat like a passport or identity card.

An alternative approach, implemented by the widely used email PGP encryption program, is for users to sign each others' keys, thereby creating a "web of trust"; the idea is that two people who wish to sign or encrypt electronic mail to each other can search the publicly available key certificates to find a path of introductions between them. (*See* PRETTY GOOD PRIVACY.)

Yet another view is that there is no need for a national infrastructure since most business relationships are direct and will remain so. In this model, individuals will not have a single government-certified signature key, but will rather send a suitable key separately to each bank, utility and other firm with which they do business—just as at present people have a multiplicity of different and often incompatible plastic cards, keys and other tokens giving access to various services. This is the model of the SET protocol, in which users will have keys that they are allowed to use only for credit card transactions.

In addition to the political controversy surrounding the certification infrastructure, there are subtle technical difficulties in making signature schemes robust. For example, when both encryption and signature are used, it is usually a mistake to sign encrypted text; the signature should be done first and the encryption second. This and some similar problems are discussed in Anderson and Needham (1995).

There are also many technical tricks that can be used to achieve special effects. Blind signatures are used in digital cash systems; they enable a bank to sign a message of which it has only partial knowledge (it may know it is signing a banknote of a given denomination, but not know the note's serial number). Threshold signatures enable a signing key to be broken up into shares, so that, for example, any three out of five directors of a company could issue a digital signature on a check. Details of these special techniques may be found in Schneier (1995).

Finally, the evidential status of digital signatures may be uncertain. In the UK, some legal experts say that signature is a matter of intent, so a digital signature should be as good as a manuscript one. In other jurisdictions (such as Utah) specific laws have been passed giving digital signatures equal force. In many places, however, their exact status remains to be clarified, so it may be prudent to make this explicit in the contract for any service that depends on them.

Bibliography

1976. Diffie, W., and Hellman, M. E. "New Directions in Cryptography," *IEEE Transactions on Information Theory*, **IT-22**, *6* (November), 644–654.

1978. Rivest, R. L., Shamir, A., and Adleman, L. "A Method for Obtaining Digital Signatures and Public-key Cryptosystems," *Comm. of the ACM*, **21**, *2* (February), 120–126.

1995. Anderson, R. J., and Needham, R. M. "Robustness Principles for Public Key Protocols," in *Advances in Cryptology—Crypto 95* (ed. D. Coppersmith), 236–247. New York: Springer-Verlag.

1995. Schneier, B. *Applied Cryptography*, 2nd Ed. New York: John Wiley.

1997. Simmons, G. J. "The History of Subliminal Channels," in *Information Hiding—First International Workshop* (ed. R. Anderson), 237–256. New York: Springer-Verlag.

Websites

Author's home page. `http://www.cl.cam.ac.uk/users/rja14/`.

International Association for Cryptologic Research. `http://www.iacr.org`.

Ross Anderson

DIRECTORY

For articles on related subjects *see* FILE; LOGIN FILE; and USER INTERFACE.

A *directory* (or *catalog*) is a file of file names. More specifically, a directory contains the names of all files that reside on a particular *volume*. A volume, in turn, is a unit of mass storage, such as the diskette (*q.v.*) in a particular disk drive or a portion (called a *partition*) of a hard disk (*q.v.*) drive.

The directory itself—a file of stored information—is to be distinguished from that portion of the directory selected for display. In the MS-DOS operating system, for example, the command

```
dir B:
```

is a request to display all files of volume B (most probably, all files on the diskette currently in drive B). Typically, drives labeled A and B are diskette drives, and the letters C and above refer to partitions of a hard disk or to other storage devices such as CD-ROMs or DVDs. On PCs that boot and reboot from hard disk partition C, C is the *default drive* whose directory is displayed if no argument is supplied to the command `dir`. But, since the hard drive is likely to contain many more file names than fit on a screen, the more usual directory request is qualified so as to elicit a manageable response. For example, the request

```
dir de*.*
```

asks for display of just those file names whose primary name starts with "de," regardless of the secondary name (file extension) that follows the period. (The "*" is a "wildcard" character that matches any actual

```
Volume in drive C has no label
 Directory of C:
DEBUG    COM    15786     4-01-93     9:10a
DETECT   COM    17522    12-10-93    10:37a
DEBUGGER TXT     3258     5-24-94    11:56p
DECPOS   PAS      490    11-01-98     9:08p
DECPOS   MAR     1053    11-01-98     9:28p
DERIVE   <DIR>             6-23-98    11:29p
DELTA    <DIR>             8-31-98     7:31p
DECPOS   COM    11705     2-12-99     3:53p
         8 File(s)    702464589  bytes free
```

Figure 1. Response to the request `dir de*.*`.

character string of any length, including the null string.) The displayed response might be that shown in Fig. 1. Note that there are three files whose primary name is DECPOS, but, as is shown in column two, they have the distinctively different full names DECPOS.PAS, DECPOS.MAR, and DECPOS.COM. Column three shows the size of each file in bytes, and columns four and five show the date and time that the file in question was created or last revised.

Continuing to refer to Fig. 1, we see that two of the files have an "extension" of <DIR>. This notation indicates that files DERIVE and DELTA are themselves directories, or more properly, subdirectories of root directory C. To display the files on subdirectory DELTA, the proper command is

```
dir \DELTA (or dir \delta since case is
    irrelevant)
```

and if DELTA, in turn, has a subdirectory called TOWNS, the command to display all files in the sub-subdirectory that have extension "txt" would be

```
dir \delta\towns\*.txt.
```

(The notation in the Unix operating system (*q.v.*) is similar, except that the solidus (/) is used instead of the backslash (\) and the directory command is "ls".) This ability to form subdirectories to subdirectories to any (reasonable) depth implies that MS-DOS and Unix directories are *hierarchical* (i.e. they have the data structure of a tree—*q.v.*). More particularly, the tree is a dynamic *n*-ary tree (where *n* is the current maximum number of subdirectories of the root or any other subdirectory). The tree is dynamic because subdirectories may be added or deleted from the master directory (possibly changing the value of *n*, but that is of no concern to the user).

MS-DOS provides several tools that facilitate navigation through a directory tree. In order to avoid continual specification of a long chain of prefixes, the user may name any subdirectory as the *default directory*, no matter how deeply nested. For example, the "change directory" (CD) command

```
CD \alpha\beta\gamma
```

will thereafter allow use of such commands as

```
TYPE roster.txt
```

instead of

```
TYPE \alpha\beta\gamma\roster.txt
```

But then file `turbo.com` in, say, subdirectory `delta` can no longer be executed by typing just `turbo` (because the prefix `\alpha\beta\gamma\` would inevitably be applied), unless the user has previously given a clue that the file is not in the default directory. The command to do this is

```
PATH \delta
```

which may very well be part of the login file `AUTOXEC.BAT`. (The `PATH` command is usable only to reach *executable* files in other subdirectories; i.e. files with an extension of `.COM`, `.EXE`, or `.BAT`. Data files in other subdirectories can be accessed only through specification of their full path in each DOS command issued.)

Keeping track of the current structure of a complex hierarchical directory can be sufficiently daunting that a sharper tool is needed than any provided by MS-DOS or Unix alone. Current graphical user interfaces have programs that display the directory tree explicitly. Fig. 2 has an example from Windows 95's Explorer, but those of other systems are functionally similar. Arrow keys on the keyboard or a mouse (*q.v.*) can be used to navigate through the tree, with initially unseen parts of the tree displacing other branches as needed. The figure shows a portion of the main directory, in which the `netscape` directory has been opened fur-ther. The left-hand frame shows five subdirectories of `netscape`, with more deeply nested levels of the directory tree visible under `Program`. The right-hand frame shows all of the files, both directories and others, that are immediately under the `netscape` node of the directory tree. Each of the items can be selected for additional operations.

As hard disks increase in capacity—over 30 gigabytes on a PC is now possible—the task of finding a particular file on a full disk becomes taxonomically formidable. This concern was anticipated in a work of fiction 40 years ago:

The Rx (abstract records) in the new storage systems could be scanned only ... by means of a code number arranged as an index to the Rx. Clearly the index itself had to be kept representational and macroscopic else a code number would become necessary to activate *it*. By the time of the supermicros there were several Indexes to Indexes to Indexes (I^3), and work had already started on an I^4.

These were the innocent days before the problem became acute. Later, Index runs were collected in Files, and Files in Catalogs—so that, for example, $C^3F^5I^4$ meant that you wanted an Index to Indexes to Indexes to Indexes, which was to be found in a certain File of Files of Files of Files of Files, which in turn was contained in a Catalog of Catalogs of Catalogs. Of course actual superscripts were much greater; the structure grew exponentially. The process of education consisted solely in learning

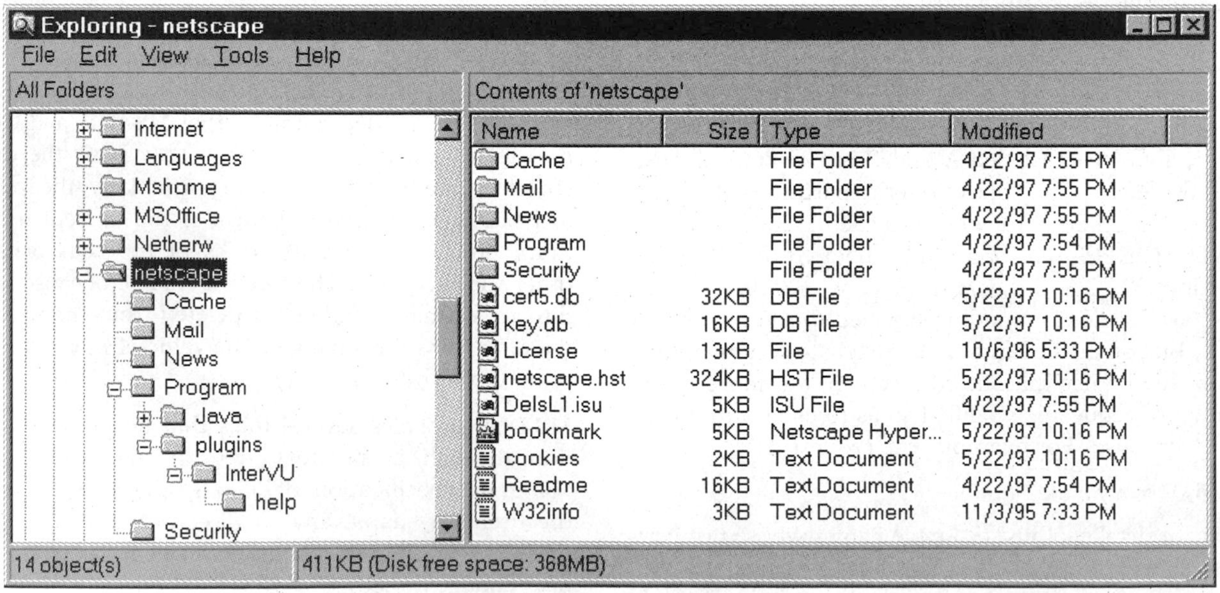

Figure 2. A Windows 95 Explorer screen showing a hierarchical directory structure.

how to tap the Rx for knowledge when needed [so that] although hardly anybody knew anything any longer, everybody knew how to find out everything.

Hal Draper, *Ms Fnd in a Lbry*, 1961 (long before micros, much less supermicros).

Edwin D. Reilly

DISABLED, COMPUTERS AND THE

For articles on related subjects *see* HUMAN FACTORS IN COMPUTING; SOCIETY, COMPUTERS IN; and SPEECH RECOGNITION AND SYNTHESIS.

Introduction

A *disability* is any condition that has a severe impact upon any major life function, such as seeing, hearing, or walking. From a computer technology point of view, a disability may result in an interface problem, a mismatch between the person and the computer.

If someone cannot read the screen, then the computer must be adapted to provide speech output. If the user cannot hear the sounds generated by the computer, then we must induce an alternative text message that can be read in place of the audio information. If typing on the keyboard is a problem, then one may need a speech recognition system and use oral commands instead. Portable computers (*q.v.*) equipped with adaptive technology can also function as communication devices for individuals who cannot speak. There are now examples of assistive technology being used by thousands of people with disabilities at home, school, and work. Desktop and notebook computers are flexible programmable machines that can be easily modified using hardware or software to suit the special needs of the end user.

However, the problem remains that computer designers have developed software interfaces to fit able-bodied users but not users with disabilities. Much work remains to be done before adaptive technology is universally supported by mainstream hardware and software products. For example, graphical user interfaces (GUIs) still present great difficulty for blind computer users, but Microsoft (*q.v.*) and the disability community are hard at work on new technology to make GUI software more accessible. It is vital that we allow people with disabilities to become equal users of personal computers, the Internet (*q.v.*), and the information stored therein. Adaptive computing technology can make online information such as Web pages, catalogs, reference materials, databases, books, newspapers, and other library research materials available to and usable by people with disabilities. While computers have done much to make work easier and

less time consuming for almost everyone, adaptive technology offers people with disabilities the opportunity not just to use computers, but to use computers to complete tasks that were previously not possible.

Legislation

There are various laws that demand equal access and opportunities for people with disabilities. The most recent and comprehensive US law is the 1990 Americans with Disabilities Act (ADA), which requires that all private and public schools, libraries, businesses, and facilities be accessible to people with disabilities. The ADA mandates that "reasonable accommodations," be made and specifically mentions the modification of office equipment. Most important, the ADA makes it unlawful to discriminate in all employment and educational practices. The 1973 Vocational Rehabilitation Act also mandates equal access to education for students with disabilities, and the courts are now interpreting this to include computing facilities and information technology (*q.v.*). Section 508 of that law requires that government agencies take the accessibility of office equipment into consideration when making purchases. Finally, the Technology-Related Assistance Act provides funds to the states to establish agencies which will disseminate information about adaptive technology and facilitate its availability. While some countries have little if any legislation mandating the provision of adaptations for users with disabilities, many have far-reaching social legislation providing government provision of such facilities.

Visual Impairments

The term *visual impairment* covers a wide range of conditions, from poor vision to total blindness. Obviously, visual impairment creates barriers for the individual. Some of these barriers include the inability to use a computer screen or keyboard, or to read computer printouts. There are numerous adaptive technologies designed to assist people who are visually impaired. Screen readers and speech synthesizers can be used to verbalize information displayed on a computer screen, and are useful for word processing, database management, bookkeeping, and Internet access. Screen magnification software can enlarge the size of text and graphics on the screen, allowing people with limited vision to read in a type size that is comfortable. Braille embossers and refreshable Braille displays interface with personal computers to allow the generation of hard and soft copy braille. Optical Character Recognition (OCR—*q.v.*) systems can scan books, magazines, and other printed text into the computer. That scanned material can then be spoken aloud using a screen reader and speech synthesizer. The same scanned document can also be read using a screen magnification program once it has been loaded into memory. Scanned documents may also be converted to Braille with the use of a Braille embosser and translator. The blind computer user can also use a refreshable braille display to read text and operate a computer. Refreshable braille displays use rows of rounded pins that can be raised and lowered to provide a braille representation of what is displayed on the computer monitor.

Physical Impairments

In the context here, physical impairment refers to those with limited or no use of their hands. Some impairments result in the inability to use a standard keyboard, mouse, or writing tools, or to handle disks and printouts. Lesser difficulties include the inability to write, hold books or papers, or turn pages. There are many adaptive technologies designed to assist people with these physical disabilities. This technology involves bypassing the standard keyboard by providing an input device more suited to the user's abilities. For example, a miniature keyboard is well suited to an individual with limited hand or finger movement, while a larger keyboard would be more appropriate for an individual lacking fine motor control. Some other options include on-screen keyboards that can be controlled using a head-mounted pointing device, or with a sip-and-puff switch operated by breath control (*see* Fig. 1). Software that can turn a single keystroke

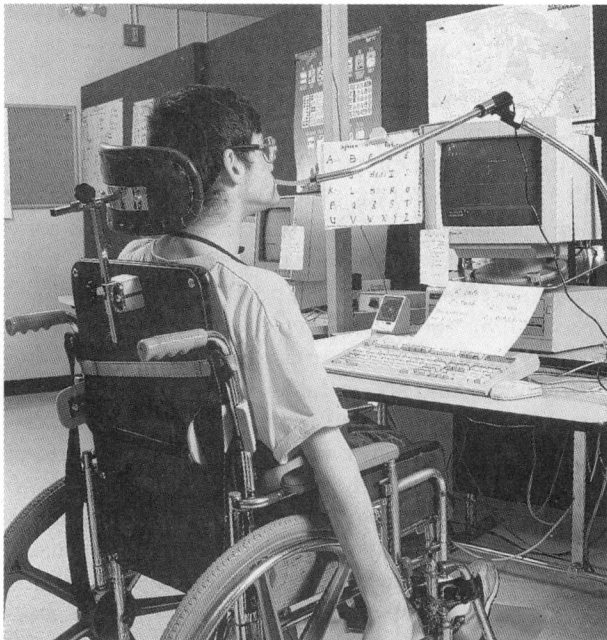

Figure 1. View of a man in a wheelchair using a computer by manipulating a mouthpiece. The man uses the mouthpiece at upper center because he does not have the use of his hands and arms. (Courtesy of De Repentigny, Publiphoto Diffusion/Science Library.)

into lengthy command sequences is also useful, as are *abbreviation expansion* programs that translate short letter combinations into lengthy command sequences or into actual text such as a signature and address. Also available are oversized trackballs, miniature mice, and joysticks in conjunction with on-screen menus to issue commands, all useful for people unable to use a standard mouse or trackball (*see* INTERACTIVE INPUT DEVICES). Voice recognition systems allow the computer to be operated by spoken command sequences (*see* SPEECH RECOGNITION AND SYNTHESIS).

Hearing Impairments

Hearing impairments range from mild hearing loss to total deafness. While people with hearing impairments generally have little difficulty using computers, the advent of multimedia (*q.v.*) software which makes extensive use of sounds is now erecting barriers. There is an increasing amount of computer technology to assist persons with hearing impairments in their use of computers. Presently, most computer operating systems can already visually signal a deaf user when the computer's speaker beeps. There are also utilities that can add captions to sounds, allowing for a text representation in parallel with the spoken material. The Internet and electronic mail (*q.v.*) have also been of great service, allowing deaf people to have increased communication with a much wider audience.

The TTY (Teletype) and TDD (Telecommunications Device for the Deaf) have long permitted persons who are deaf to send and receive telephone messages using a portable keyboard and visual display, but now the computer is being adapted to fill the same function. The deaf user can also use a laptop computer (*see* PORTABLE COMPUTERS) to take notes in class or in meetings where using a pen would have prevented watching the speaker. The National Technical Institute for the Deaf located on the campus of the Rochester Institute of Technology is experimenting with a system involving two linked laptops. One student who can hear takes extensive notes on one laptop while the deaf student follows the lecture on the other computer screen. Systems like this are now being used by deaf students at many universities.

Learning Disabilities

This term includes difficulties with text and mathematics comprehension as well as other cognitive difficulties. Some people with learning disabilities can have problems reading and comprehending information on computer screens. For this problem there are several compensatory computing tools that are helpful. One strategy, for those who find a screenful of information distracting, is to use a program that shows one line of text on the monitor at a time. Some students with learning disabilities use a laptop computer with a spell checker (*see* SPELLING CHECKER) and outlining program to take notes in class or at meetings. Reading comprehension programs allow text to be spoken aloud at the user's desired pace, while the current spoken word is highlighted on the screen in real time. Talking word processors (*q.v.*) assist users with keyboard input, and can read text aloud. Some reading comprehension programs contain online dictionaries and assistance to make document preparation tailored to a user's needs. For some, the ability to manipulate the foreground and background colors can greatly enhance reading comprehension.

Speech Impairments

People with speech impairments do not have any essential problems accessing standard computers. However, such persons frequently use laptop computers with augmented communication speech software to communicate with others. The user may enter messages to be spoken directly from the keyboard, or use a pre-stored message to communicate.

Electronic Information

Many people with disabilities can readily benefit from being able to do research through adapted personal computers. These can be used to access online catalogs in libraries, reference materials, books, newspapers, and other library resources. For example, a blind person can access an online newspaper and read it with the use of a screen reader. A person using a wheelchair can retrieve online research documents from the Internet, saving a trip to the library. As more libraries and businesses become computerized, they are offering more of their materials in electronic formats that can be read by various adaptive devices. Computers and other adapted equipment can also be used to disseminate information.

Conclusion

Computers equipped with adaptive technology allow users with disabilities to participate as equals and achieve independence at home, school, and in the office. While adaptive computer technology is one of the most empowering tools ever developed for the disabled, it is not without problems. Screen readers for the visually impaired are just beginning to cope with graphical interfaces. The mouse can be a problem for people with poor hand movement. A GUI interface can clutter the screen with so much information that users with learning disabilities are overwhelmed.

Work being done by adaptive technology companies, as well as by Apple (*q.v.*), IBM (*q.v.*), and Microsoft (*q.v.*), is presently making progress in overcoming these problems. But innovations in mainstream hardware and software usually happen without considering the needs of the disability community. This means that the adaptive world is usually two steps behind the mainstream one. When a new mainstream operating system or program enters the market, it takes months or years for adaptive technology to catch up. The use of universal design principles in the original concept could eliminate these problems. The continual need to retrofit technology could be replaced by including designs for the needs of the disabled in the original concept.

Bibliography

1993. Lazzaro, J. J. *Adaptive Technologies for Learning and Work Environments*. Chicago, IL: American Library Association.
1995. Lazzaro, J. J. *Adapting PCs for Disabilities*. Reading, MA: Addison-Wesley.
1997. Coombs, N., and Cunningham, C. *Information Access and Adaptive Technology*. Phoenix, AZ: Oryx Press.

Website

EASI (Equal Access to Software and Information): `http://www.rit.edu/~easi/`.

Joseph J. Lazzaro and Norman Coombs

DISCRETE MATHEMATICS

> For articles on related subjects *see* ALGORITHMICS; ALGORITHMS, ANALYSIS OF; AUTOMATA THEORY; BOOLEAN ALGEBRA; CODES; COMBINATORICS; COMPUTATIONAL COMPLEXITY; COMPUTER ALGEBRA; ERROR ANALYSIS; FACTORING INTEGERS; FORMAL LANGUAGES; GRAPH THEORY; INTEGER SEQUENCES; LOGIC DESIGN; LOOP INVARIANT; MATHEMATICAL PROGRAMMING; MATRIX COMPUTATIONS; NUMBER THEORETIC CALCULATIONS; NUMERICAL ANALYSIS; PROGRAM SPECIFICATION; PROGRAM VERIFICATION; QUEUEING THEORY; SEARCHING; and SORTING.

Discrete mathematics encompasses those branches of mathematics that deal with discrete objects, in contrast to other branches, such as calculus and analysis, whose main concern is with continuous functions. Some branches of mathematics, such as numerical analysis and linear algebra, have both continuous and discrete components. Another, but somewhat simplistic, perspective on the contrast between discrete and continuous mathematics is that the underlying number system in continuous mathematics is usually the real numbers, while for discrete mathematics it is the integers. Because problems in discrete mathematics often involve the integers, which form an infinite set, discrete mathematics is not necessarily *finite* mathematics.

The importance of discrete mathematics has increased rapidly over the past quarter century. The reason for this is simply that digital computers are discrete engines, since all calculations done on them are effectively based on the integers. Even floating-point numbers form a discrete system because the floating-point numbers representable in any computer are a *discrete* set of points on the real line.

Discrete Mathematics and Algorithms

Although algorithms play an important role in continuous as well as discrete mathematics, they are much more a part of the warp and woof of discrete mathematics, mainly because algorithms are so closely related to computer programs. Moreover, *algorithmics*, the systematic study of algorithms, which is concerned with the development, analysis, and verification of algorithms, is a much more important subject in discrete mathematics than in continuous mathematics. This is true also because of the close relationship of algorithmics to the solution of problems on computers. Algorithms are a crucial component of most of the examples in this article.

Proof in Discrete Mathematics

Proof is just as important in discrete mathematics as in any other branch of mathematics. But a striking feature about discrete mathematics in contrast to continuous mathematics is that, while many different methods of proof are applicable in discrete mathematics, one method of proof—mathematical induction—is quintessentially the most important. In its most basic form, mathematical induction proves the truth of a proposition $P(n)$, which depends on some integer parameter n, for all $n \geq n_0$ by first proving the *basis case $P(n_0)$* by any available proof method. Then, assuming the truth of $P(n)$ for any unspecified value of n and again using any available method, $P(n+1)$ is proven to be true. These two things together suffice to prove the truth of $P(n)$ for all $n \geq n_0$ (*see also* "Mathematical Logic," below).

The above form of mathematical induction is often called *weak* induction. Mathematical induction also comes in several other flavors—*strong* induction, which is a generalization of weak induction, and induction on more than one integer parameter, among others. Together, the variants of mathematical induction suffice to prove many results and theorems in discrete mathematics, particularly those involving the analysis and verification of algorithms.

The Content of Discrete Mathematics

As judged by the syllabuses of courses on discrete mathematics for college freshmen and sophomores,

and by the more than 50 textbooks published since 1985 for such courses, there is no universally agreed upon set of topics included under the discrete mathematics rubric, and certainly no agreement similar to that on courses in calculus. However, there is general agreement that various branches of mathematics are clearly part of discrete mathematics. Most of the remainder of this article is devoted to brief descriptions of these branches. The reader should also refer to the list of articles under Discrete Mathematics in the Classification of Articles on p. xvii for a further perspective.

GRAPH THEORY

The "graph" in graph theory is not the familiar graph of high school or secondary school mathematics, which is a "picture" of a continuous function, but rather a collection of *vertices* (or nodes) and *edges* (or branches) joining pairs of vertices. Since graph theory is the subject of a separate article in this Encyclopedia, we content ourselves here with one example of its application. Fig. 1 displays a *weighted digraph*: weighted because of the weights associated with each edge, and a digraph because each edge has a direction. The problem is to find the path (i.e. sequence of edges) from v_0 to v_7 that is shortest (i.e. for which the sum of the edge weights is smallest). There are many practical applications of this situation, such as Internet routing, where the number of vertices is in the hundreds or more.

Fig. 2 displays a sketch of *Dijkstra's algorithm* for the solution of this problem for a graph of $n+1$ vertices, where we want the shortest path from v_0 to v_n. The distance function $d(v)$ is the length of the shortest path from v_0 to vertex v of the graph that passes through only vertices in the set U. Thus, initially, all distances are ∞ except for $d(v_0)$, which is 0. Fig. 3 shows how the computation proceeds for the graph of Fig. 1, with the first row giving the initial values and each subsequent row giving the results after the kth passage

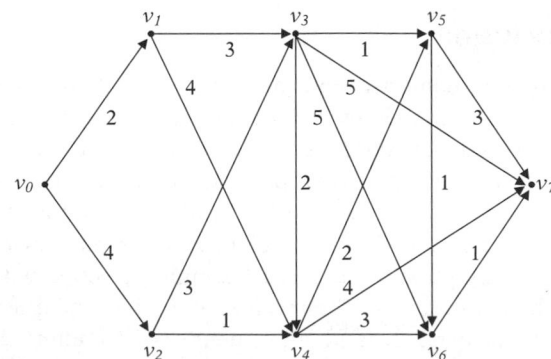

Figure 1. The Shortest Path Problem. Object: Find the shortest path from v_0 to v_7.

Initialize $d(v_0)$ to 0 and $d(v_i)$ to ∞, $i = 1, \ldots, n$
$U \leftarrow \{v_0\}$
repeat
    Update the current distance function.
    Find the vertex u not in U for which $d(u)$ is a minimum;
        if there is a tie choose u arbitrarily.
    $U \leftarrow U \cup \{u\}$
endrepeat when $u = v_n$

Figure 2. A sketch of Dijkstra's Algorithm.

k	$d(v_1)$	$d(v_2)$	$d(v_3)$	$d(v_4)$	$d(v_5)$	$d(v_6)$	$d(v_7)$	Vertex Added to U
0	∞	∞	∞	∞	∞	∞	∞	v_0
1	2	4	∞	∞	∞	∞	∞	v_1
2	2	4	5	6	∞	∞	∞	v_2
3	2	4	5	5	∞	∞	∞	v_3
4	2	4	5	5	6	10	10	v_4
5	2	4	5	5	6	8	9	v_5
6	2	4	5	5	6	7	8	v_6
7	2	4	5	5	6	7	8	v_7

Figure 3. Application of Dijkstra's Algorithm to the graph of Fig. 1. k represents the count of the passages through the loop with $k = 0$ the initial state.

through the loop of Fig. 2. The shortest path is $(v_0, v_1, v_3, v_5, v_6, v_7)$, whose length is 8.

Graph theory is one of the most important branches of discrete mathematics and the source of many algorithms of practical importance. In particular, we note the importance of *trees* (*q.v.*), which are special cases of graphs.

COMBINATORICS

Combinatorics is about counting the number of objects of some type or about how many ways there

are to do something. It, too, is the subject of a separate article in this Encyclopedia, so again we just present a single example.

A *permutation* $P(n, r)$ is an ordered arrangement of n objects taken r at a time. It is sometimes necessary to generate permutations in lexical order (*see* COLLATING SEQUENCE) so that if the objects are $1, 2, \ldots, n$, each permutation represents the next number larger than its predecessor. Fig. 4 displays an algorithm to accomplish this when $r = n$ for the objects $1, 2, \ldots, n$. It is based on the idea that, given a permutation, the next larger one can be found by beginning at the right and going left, as long as the digits are increasing. When the first digit is reached that is less than its neighbor to the right, exchange it with the smallest digit to its right greater than it and then reverse the order of the previously increasing digits. Thus, starting with 4257631, we identify 5 as the first decreasing digit from the right, exchange it with 6, and reverse 7531 to obtain 4261357.

Applications of combinatorics play a major role in the analysis of algorithms. For example, it is often necessary in such analyses to count the average number of times that a particular portion of an algorithm is executed over all possible input data sets.

DIFFERENCE EQUATIONS

Another name sometimes used for this subject is *recurrence relations*. Two main sources of these equations are the *discretization* of differential equations for solution on a computer and the analysis of algorithms (*see* ALGORITHMS, ANALYSIS OF). We shall focus on the latter here. (For the former, *see* both the

```
Input n
Algorithm ALLPERM
     for i=1 to n                                          [Generate first permutation]
          Perm(i)←i
     endfor
     repeat                                                [Main permutation loop]
          print Perm
          b←n-1                                [b will be position of leftmost digit to be changed]
          repeat until b=0 or Perm(b)<Perm(b+1)
               b←n-1
          endrepeat
          if b=0 then stop                                 [All permutations found]
          c←n                               [c will be position of digit to be exchanged with b]
          repeat until Perm(c)>Perm(b)
               c←c-1
          endrepeat
          Perm(b)↔Perm(c)                                  [Exchange digits]
          d←b+1; f←n                                       [Initialize for reversal]
          repeat until d≥f
               Perm(d)↔Perm(f)                             [Reverse by exchanging]
               d←d+1; f←f-1
          endrepeat
     endrepeat
Output All n! permutations of 1,2,...,n
```

Figure 4. Algorithm to generate all the permutations of $1, 2, \ldots, n$.

NUMERICAL ANALYSIS and PARTIAL DIFFERENTIAL EQUATIONS articles.) In general, a difference equation of *order k* has the form

$$y_n = f(y_{n-1}, y_{n-2}, \ldots, y_{n-k}) \qquad (1)$$
$$y_i = b_i, \quad i = 1, \ldots, k$$

where (1) is the difference equation itself and below it are the *initial conditions*. By far the most important difference equations are *linear* in which:

$$y_n + a_1(n)y_{n-1} + a_2(n)y_{n-2} + \cdots + a_k(n)y_{n-k} = g(n)$$

where each $a_i(n)$ can be any function of n. When $g(n) = 0$, we call the equation *homogeneous*, otherwise, it is *nonhomogeneous*. When each $a_i(n)$ is a constant a_i, we speak of *linear, constant coefficient difference equations*, which are the easiest to solve. The solution of a homogeneous, linear, constant coefficient difference equation of order k has the form

$$y_n = \sum_{i=1}^{k} c_i r_i^n \qquad (2)$$

where the r_i in (2) are the roots of the polynomial equation

$$r^k - \sum_{i=1}^{k} a_i r^{k-1} = 0$$

and the c_i are found using the initial conditions. The reader familiar with homogeneous, linear, constant coefficient differential equations will see a close analogy between the solution of those equations and the solution of similar difference equations.

Other classes of difference equations, such as first-order linear equations without constant coefficients and some nonhomogeneous equations, can also be solved in closed form but, as with differential equations, most difference equations cannot be solved in closed form. However, when a difference equation cannot be solved in closed form, we can always just compute as many values of the solution of (1) as we wish by brute force. That is, with $n = k + 1$, we can just plug the initial conditions into (1) and compute y_{k+1}. Then with $n = k + 2$ we can compute y_{k+2}, etc.

As an example of the use of difference equations in analyzing algorithms, consider the algorithm for binary search in the article SEARCHING. If we count the worst case of the number of comparisons c_m of the search item with items on a list of length 2^m (where we choose a power of 2 as the list length to keep things simple), we obtain the difference equation

$$c_m - c_{m-1} = 1, \qquad c_0 = 1$$

whose *solution* is $c_m = m + 1$. This is just the solution given in the article on SEARCHING if you set the list length $n = 2^m$.

MATHEMATICAL LOGIC

Mathematical logic (hereafter just *logic*) has become an accepted part of discrete mathematics. One reason for this is that all efforts at the verification of algorithms inevitably involve the notation and methods of logic. The other is that mathematical logic has always played an important role in the design of computers and is playing an increasingly important role in various branches of computer science, particularly artificial intelligence (*q.v.*).

The basis of much of mathematical logic is the *propositional calculus*, which is concerned with the analysis of propositions that can be stated in natural language (e.g. traditional syllogisms), as well as those that arise in the verification of algorithms (e.g. the assertion of a *loop invariant* in an algorithm). As an example of the latter, Fig. 5 displays an algorithm to multiply two integers by repeated addition together with the *assertions* to be used in the proof of the algorithm. Focusing on the one labeled *loop invariant*, we note that the proposition $prod = uy$ can be proved to be true when the loop is first entered and after each execution of the loop. The proof is essentially by mathematical induction (actually a *finite* induction, which is very common in proofs of algorithm correctness). Since $u = x$ when the loop is finally exited, the final value of *prod* is xy as desired.

Propositional logic is used in the design of computers in its form as Boolean algebra (*q.v.*), wherein it is used to design logical circuits that realize particular Boolean functions (*see* LOGIC DESIGN). Such logical circuits can then be fabricated on chips.

In more sophisticated attempts at the verification of algorithms than that shown in Fig. 5 and in most applications of logic elsewhere in computer science, it is not the propositional calculus but its more sophisticated cousin, the *predicate calculus*, that must be used. The predicate calculus deals with *predicates*, which are propositions containing variables so that whether a predicate is true or false depends upon the values of its variables. Thus, "x is a tennis player" is a

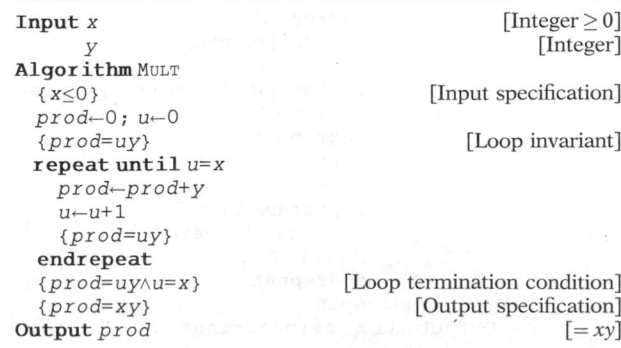

```
Input x                              [Integer ≥ 0]
      y                              [Integer]
Algorithm MULT
   {x≤0}                             [Input specification]
   prod←0; u←0
   {prod=uy}                         [Loop invariant]
   repeat until u=x
      prod←prod+y
      u←u+1
      {prod=uy}
   endrepeat
   {prod=uy∧u=x}                     [Loop termination condition]
   {prod=xy}                         [Output specification]
Output prod                          [= xy]
```

Figure 5. A multiplication algorithm with assertions.

predicate that would be true if x is Steffi Graf and false if x is Michael Jordan. The crucial concept in the predicate calculus is that of a *quantifier*. The *universal quantifier* is written $\forall$ and read "for all" so that

$$(\forall n)P(n)$$

is true if $P(n)$ is true for *all* values of n and false otherwise. (Except when the domain of n is given—see the examples below—the domain is normally the positive integers or the nonnegative integers.) Using the universal quantifier, we may express formally the idea of proof by (weak) mathematical induction. That is, to prove

$$(\forall n: n \geq n_0)P(n)$$

it suffices to prove

$$P(n_0) \wedge (\forall n: n \geq n_0)[P(n) \Rightarrow P(n+1)].$$

The other significant quantifier is the *existential quantifier*, which is written $\exists$ and read "there exists" so that $(\exists n)P(n)$ is true if $P(n)$ is true for *any* n and false otherwise.

Here is an example of the use of quantifiers in an algorithm verification context. Suppose you wish to write the output specification for an algorithm (or program) whose purpose is to sort in ascending order m numbers, $a_1, a_2, \ldots, a_m$. You could write something like

$$a_1 \leq a_2 \wedge a_2 \leq a_3 \wedge \cdots \wedge a_{m-1} \leq a_m$$

or perhaps

$$a_1 \leq a_2 \leq \cdots \leq a_m$$

but it is much prettier to write

$$(\forall i: 1 \leq i \leq m)(\forall j: 1 \leq j \leq m)[i < j \Rightarrow a_i \leq a_j]$$

where the finite domain of each quantifier is indicated explicitly.

OTHER BRANCHES OF DISCRETE MATHEMATICS
Here are brief descriptions of areas of discrete mathematics that are sometimes but not always found in discrete mathematics courses.

Discrete probability. This deals with the familiar notions of probability where the *sample space* (i.e. the space of possible *events*) is finite or countably infinite. The probability distributions of discrete probability include the familiar binomial and Poisson distributions. The former may, for example, be used to solve the following problem. Consider a multiple choice exam with five possible choices on each question (such as the SATs), where you score 1 point for each correct answer and lose $\frac{1}{4}$ for each incorrect answer. What is the probability of improving your

score if you make pure guesses on 5 questions? What is the *expected* change in your score if you make pure guesses on 5 questions? For the first question, we need to compute

$$1 - [\text{the probability of getting 0 or 1 answers correct}]$$

since you improve your score only if you get 2 or more of the 5 correct. (When you get one answer correct, your score is unchanged.) Since the probability of a pure guess being correct is 0.2, using the binomial distribution, the answer is

$$1 - (\tfrac{4}{5})^5 - 5(\tfrac{4}{5})^4(\tfrac{1}{5}) = 0.263$$

where the second term on the left is the probability of 5 bad guesses and the third is the probability of 4 bad guesses and 1 good one. Despite the fact that the probability of improving your score is only just greater than $\frac{1}{4}$, the answer to the question about expected change of score is 0 because, although the probability of losing points (which happens when all 5 guesses are wrong, which occurs with probability 0.328) is greater than that of gaining them, when you win, you win relatively big (e.g. 5 more points when all 5 guesses are correct), but when you lose, you don't lose so much (only $1\frac{1}{4}$ points when all 5 guesses are wrong). Thus, whether or not you should make pure guesses on a test like the SATs is more a psychological matter than a mathematical one. If you can rule out one of the choices so that the probability of guessing correctly is now $\frac{1}{4}$, the probability that you improve your score is 0.367, the probability of a worse score is 0.237, and the expected gain is now 0.312. So, mathematically, you should guess if you can eliminate one answer, but there are still psychological considerations that might make you decide not to guess.

Discrete probability is an important tool in the analysis of algorithms because generally average case analyses require that you consider all possible input data and the probability that each occurs.

Sequences and series. Although a standard part of basic college and university calculus courses, sequences in their entirety and series, except for power series, are bona fide discrete mathematics. Some aspects of sequences and series are particularly pertinent to computers and computer science. For example, whereas mathematicians are usually most interested in convergent sequences, computer scientists are more interested in divergent sequences, in particular those that represent the *execution sequences* of algorithms and programs. For example, the sequence $\{n^2/4\}$ is the average case execution sequence of insertion sort (*see* SORTING), which means that, on average, $n^2/4$ comparisons of elements on a list of length n will be needed in order to sort it into lexical order. Thus, we say that insertion sort is an O(n^2) (read "order n^2") algorithm. By determining the execution sequences of various algorithms for the same task, you can judge when one algorithm is to be preferred over another. Sometimes through analysis it is possible to determine how good the best possible algorithm for a task can be (*see* COMPUTATIONAL COMPLEXITY) by determining the slowest possible divergent execution sequence. In the case of sorting by comparisons, this sequence is known to be $\{cn \log n\}$, where c is a constant.

A powerful idea in discrete mathematics (and in continuous mathematics, as well) that arises from the study of series is that of *generating functions*. If $\{a_k\}$ is a sequence, its generating function $G(s)$ is defined to be

$$G(s) = \sum_{k=0}^{\infty} a_k s^k.$$

Using this *formal power series*, many problems in discrete mathematics, including many kinds of difference equations, can be solved. So can a variety of combinatorial problems. For example, the number of combinations a_{nmk} of n distinct objects, k at a time with up to m repetitions of each object can be found by determining that the generating function of the sequence $\{a_{nmk}\}$ is

$$(1 + s + s^2 + \cdots + s^m)^n$$

with a_{nmk} the coefficient of s^k. For example, with $n = 3$, $m = 2$, $k = 3$, a_{323} is given by the coefficient of s^3 in $(1 + s + s^2)^3$, which is easily determined to be 7. If we denote the three objects by a, b, and c, the seven combinations are

$$aab, aac, abb, abc, acc, bbc, bcc$$

Abstract and linear algebra. Algebras generally deal with discrete objects and are, therefore, a natural part of discrete mathematics. Abstract algebra has many applications in computer science. For example, semigroups have application to formal languages and automata theory, and groups have important applications in coding theory. A particularly important application is the use of finite state machines in compiler construction for the *recognition* of syntactically correct language structures (*see* COMPILER and AUTOMATA THEORY). Topics in abstract algebra are now found less frequently in discrete mathematics courses than heretofore, in part because they require a considerable amount of mathematical sophistication and in part because abstract algebra is a natural subject of more advanced mathematics courses and its applications are naturally discussed in advanced computer science courses.

Linear algebra (and linear programming) are uncommon topics in discrete mathematics, but are also quite natural, since, although the variables in linear algebra are normally real variables, the structures (e.g. matrices) and manipulations are generally discrete. Moreover, linear algebra is a highly algorithmic subject and is perhaps more effectively taught initially from this

```
Input Â                                              [n × (n + 1) augmented matrix [A|b], with entries aᵢⱼ]
Algorithm GAUSS-SQUARE                                                              [Works if no 0 pivots]
    procedure DOWNSWEEP(i)                               [Subtract multiples of row i from lower rows]
        for k=i+1 to n                                                       [k varies over rows below i]
            mₖ←aₖᵢ/aᵢᵢ
            aₖᵢ←0                                            [Assigning saves a step over computing]
            for l=i+1 to n+1                                       [l varies over entries in row k]
                aₖₗ←aₖₗ-mₖaᵢₗ
            endfor
        endfor
    endpro
    procedure Scale(i)                                                    [Make diagonal element 1]
        aᵢ,ₙ₊₁←aᵢ,ₙ₊₁/aᵢᵢ
        aᵢᵢ←1
    endpro
    procedure Upsweep(i)                                [Subtract multiples of row i from higher rows]
        for k=i-1 downto 1
            aₖ,ₙ₊₁←aₖ,ₙ₊₁-aₖᵢaᵢ,ₙ₊₁
            aₖᵢ←0
        endfor
    endpro
    for i=1 to n                                                                   [Main algorithm]
        Downsweep(i)
    endfor
    for i=1 downto 1
        Scale(i)
        Upsweep(i)
    endfor
Output Â                                                                    [Last column is solution]
```

Figure 6. Algorithm to find the solution of $A\mathbf{x} = \mathbf{b}$ when A is an $n \times n$ matrix, by Gaussian elimination.

	Coefficient matrix A	Constant column $\mathbf{b}$
Scale (i)	0	1
All Scaling	0	n
Upsweep(i)	0	$i - 1$
All Upsweeping	0	$\dfrac{n^2 - n}{2}$
Downsweep(i)	$(n - i)^2 + (n - i)$	$n - i$
All Downsweeping	$\dfrac{n^3 - n}{3}$	$\dfrac{n^2 - n}{2}$
Total	$\dfrac{n^3 - n}{3}$	n^2
Combined total	$\dfrac{n^3 + 3n^2 - n}{3}$	

Figure 7. Analysis of Algorithm Gauss-Square. Each entry represents the count of multiplications and divisions in the indicated portion of the algorithm.

perspective than from an abstract vector space perspective. For example, the basic theorems on the solution of systems of linear equations are simply and elegantly derived from a consideration of Gaussian elimination (*see* ERROR ANALYSIS and MATRIX COMPUTATIONS). Fig. 6 displays an algorithm for the solution of $n \times n$ linear systems by Gaussian elimination, which assumes that diagonal elements never become 0. This algorithm can be used as the starting point for the design of a general algorithm for $m \times n$ linear systems, which takes into account all possible difficult and degenerate cases. The algorithm in Fig. 6 may also be used to analyze Gaussian elimination, as shown in Fig. 7.

Conclusion

This has been quite a brief survey of discrete mathematics. We have not even touched upon the basic topics of sets, relations, and functions that underlie all discrete mathematics. Also, we have not mentioned such an important branch of discrete mathematics as number theory, which has recently seen important applications to coding (*see* NUMBER THEORETIC CALCULATIONS). For more information on these areas, the reader is referred to the bibliography. One thing that can be said with certainty about discrete mathematics is that the importance of its various branches will continue to grow as the applications of computers permeate more and more aspects of science, technology, and everyday life.

Bibliography

1976. Roberts, F. R. *Discrete Mathematical Models*. Upper Saddle River, NJ: Prentice Hall. (Contains many applications of discrete mathematics to the social and biological sciences.)
1988. Bogart, K. P. *Discrete Mathematics*. Lexington, MA: D.C. Heath. (A modern approach with plenty about algorithms.)
1989. Graham, R. L., Knuth, D. E., and Patashnik, O. *Concrete Mathematics*. Reading, MA: Addison-Wesley. (A relatively advanced book, mainly on discrete mathematics, but with a spirited discussion of areas where a combination of the CONtinuous and disCRETE is just what you need.)
1990. Epp, S. S. *Discrete Mathematics with Applications*. Belmont, CA: Wadsworth. (Well written and with good coverage of classical discrete mathematics topics.)
1990. Skiena, S. *Implementing Discrete Mathematics— Combinatorics and Graph Theory with Mathematica*. Reading, MA: Addison-Wesley. (How discrete mathematics capabilities can be added to a well-known computer algebra system.)
1995. Rosen, K. H. *Discrete Mathematics and Its Applications*, 3rd Ed. New York: McGraw-Hill. (The most popular US college discrete mathematics textbook.)
1997. Dossey, J. A., Otto, A. D., Spence, L. E., and Eynden, C. *Discrete Mathematics*, 3rd Ed. (A book suitable for high school students.)
1998. Maurer, S. B., and Ralston, A. *Discrete Algorithmic Mathematics*, 2nd Ed. Natick, MA: A. K. Peters. (A book that emphasizes the algorithmic approach to discrete mathematics.)

Anthony Ralston

DISK

See DISKETTE; HARD DISK; and MEMORY: AUXILIARY.

DISKETTE

For articles on related subjects *see* HARD DISK; MEMORY: AUXILIARY; and OPTICAL STORAGE.

The *diskette* is the primary removable storage medium for getting voluminous information into and out of a microcomputer. Diskettes were originally called *floppy disks* in distinction to the *hard disk* (*q.v.*) because the earliest such disks were intrinsically flexible and remained so when encased in their square cardboard protective envelopes. The I/O subsystem that supports use of diskettes consists of a controller card that is inserted into a *slot* connected to the computer's bus (*q.v*), a disk drive to read and write the diskette itself, and a cable that connects the card to the disk drive and is used to pass data and control signals between the two.

Diskettes are used to exchange data between computers that use a compatible format, to back up small files stored on hard disks and other high-capacity storage devices, and to load small programs into a computer. (The CD-ROM (*see* OPTICAL STORAGE) has become the medium of choice for the distribution and installation of large programs.)

Diskettes are made by depositing a metallic oxide material on a mylar substrate. The oxide coating is ferromagnetic and responds to the magnetic fields generated by the heads in the disk drive. For this reason, care must be taken when handling diskettes in the presence of strong magnetic fields.

Diskettes come in a variety of sizes. The 8″ disks used with early CP/M personal computers are now obsolete, as are the 5.25″ diskettes used with the earliest MS-DOS and Apple systems. Currently the most popular variant is a 3.5″ diskette encased in hard plastic (and hence no longer "floppy"). The diskette has made it very easy to share information and programs. The process of making copies is quick and inexpensive. Diskettes are easy to mail and carry, and cost as little as 30 cents each. A 3.5″ diskette (Fig. 1) fits easily into a pocket.

Information is recorded on both sides of the diskette in what is known as double-sided format. Therefore each disk drive must have two read/write heads. Information is organized in concentric *tracks* that are either prerecorded when the diskette is manufactured or magnetically etched by a formatting program that comes with the operating system. Each track is subdivided into *sectors* and each sector into bytes. On the IBM PC (*q.v.*) and PC compatibles, each side of a double density (DSDD) 5.25″ floppy held 40 tracks of nine 512 byte sectors. The smaller 3.5″ diskettes use 80 tracks per side, 18 sectors per track, and 512 bytes per sector, yielding a capacity of 1.44 MB.

Diskette drives with special controllers that use EIDE (see Bus) technology, have pushed the storage limit

for 3.5″ floppy drives to 120 MB by increasing the track density to almost 2,500 tracks per inch and laying down almost 1,750 tracks per side. The new drives have lowered the average seek time to 70 milliseconds by increasing disk rotation speed to 720 rpm producing a maximum sustained transfer rate on the order of 565 KB/sec. The new drives depend upon lasers to read a servo pattern factory-etched into the diskette itself. The higher density is also the result of a special metal particle (MP) pigment and a dual layer coating on the diskette medium. Despite the increased density, these drives are able to read and write the older high-density and double-density 3.5″ diskettes by using a dual-gap head—one gap for the old style disks and one for the new. The newer disks, of course, cannot be read by the older 3.5″ drives.

The disk drive consists essentially of two motors and some controlling circuitry. One motor drives a spindle that spins the disk usually at about 300 rpm but up to 720 rpm for the newer 120 MB drives. Control circuitry, either optical or electronic, precisely regulates this speed. A second precision *stepping motor* incrementally moves the heads from track to track to read and write information. It actually counts the number of tracks as it moves. It is slower than the *voice coil actuator*, which flies right to the proper track, but drives built with the latter technology, while faster, require more complicated electronics and are thus more expensive and prone to problems.

Floppy disks first appeared in the late 1960s when IBM used them in an early minicomputer. These 8″ floppies could hold almost a million bytes and made the computer easy to use and enormously flexible, but the physical size of the disk drive became a consideration as computers got smaller. Even 3.5″ drives are too big, heavy, and power hungry to satisfy the manufacturers of the lightest portable computers (*q.v.*). A 2″ diskette was introduced in the late 1980s, but did not catch on.

The future of the 3.5″ diskette is unclear. The new Apple iMac series does not include a 3.5″ drive as standard equipment, but the leading manufacturers of Pentium-based machines continue to package a 3.5″ drive as standard equipment and offer internal 100 MB or larger drives as an option. Diskettes for the higher storage devices are slightly larger and thicker than conventional diskettes; *see* MEMORY: AUXILIARY for more detail.

Stephen J. Rogowski

Figure 1. The front and back of a 3.5″ diskette. The drive into which it is inserted moves the metal slide (to the left with respect to the front of the diskette) in order to access the magnetic surface of the disk through a rectangular window as the disk spins within its protective plastic case. A small plastic tab at the bottom right of the back of the diskette has two positions: "up" for normal read–write capability and "down" to make the diskette read-only in order to protect recorded information against accidental modification.

DISPLAY MONITOR

See MONITOR, DISPLAY.

DISTRIBUTED SYSTEMS

For articles on related topics, *see* CLIENT–SERVER COMPUTING; COMMUNICATIONS AND COMPUTERS; COMPONENT SOFTWARE; COOPERATIVE COMPUTING; DATA COMMUNICATIONS; DATABASE CONCURRENCY CONTROL; ELECTRONIC COMMERCE; ETHERNET; INTERNET; LOCAL AREA NETWORK; NETWORKS, COMPUTER; and WORLD WIDE WEB.

Nearly all large software systems are necessarily distributed. For example, enterprise-wide business systems must support multiple users running common applications across different sites. A *distributed system* encompasses these applications, their underlying support software, the hardware they run on, and the communication links which connect the distributed hardware. The largest and best-known distributed system is the set of computers, software, and services comprising the Internet/World Wide Web, which is so pervasive that it coexists with and connects to most other existing distributed systems. The most common distributed systems are networked client–server systems (*see* CLIENT–SERVER COMPUTING). This article surveys the properties of distributed systems and provides synopses of relevant research and development topics in theoretical foundations and system engineering.

Properties

Distributed systems have these defining properties:

◆ *Multiple computers (nodes)*
Software for the system and its applications executes on multiple independent computers (not merely multiple processors on the same computer, which is the realm of *parallel* computing—*q.v.*). These nodes may range from information appliances to personal computers to high-performance workstations (*q.v.*) to file servers (*q.v.*) to mainframes (*q.v.*) to supercomputers (*q.v.*). Each may primarily take the role of a *client* that requests services by others, a *server* that provides computation or resource access to others, or a *peer* that does both (Fig. 1). A minimal distributed system may be as small as two nodes provided that software connectivity is present.

◆ *Resource sharing*
The most common reason for connecting a set of computers to operate as a distributed system is to allow them to share physical and computational resources; for example printers, files, databases, mail services, stock quotes, or collaborative applications. Distributed system components that support resource sharing play a role similar to operating systems (*q.v.*) and are increasingly indistinguishable from them.

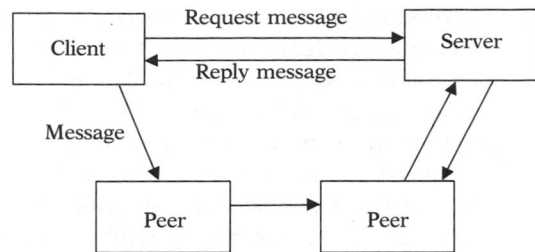

Figure 1. A small distributed system.

◆ *Concurrency*
Each of the nodes in a distributed system provides independent functionality, and operates concurrently with all of the others (*see* CONCURRENT PROGRAMMING). More than one *process* (executing program) per node, and more than one *thread* (concurrently executing task) per process may participate as components in a system. Most components are *reactive*, continuously responding to commands from users and messages from other components. Systems as a whole may concurrently execute a number of related applications, all relying upon common infrastructure software establishing system-wide policies, protocols, and services. Like operating systems, distributed systems are designed never to terminate, and so should remain always at least partially available.

◆ *Message passing*
Software on the different computers communicates via structured message passing disciplines built upon any of a number of networking protocols (for example TCP/IP—*q.v.*) in turn running on any of a number of connection technologies (for example, Ethernet and modems—*q.v.*). The nodes in most distributed systems are *completely connected*—any node may send a message to any other node. Delivery is mediated by underlying routing algorithms and related networking support. Messages may consist of commands, requests for services, event notifications, multimedia data, file contents, and even entire programs.

Distributed systems also possess, to varying degrees, the following characteristic properties.

◆ *Heterogeneity*
The nodes participating in a system may consist of diverse computing and communication hardware. The software comprising the system may be written using diverse programming languages and development tools. Some heterogeneity issues are addressed by agreeing upon common message formats and low-level protocols that can be readily implemented across different platforms (i.e. computers such as

PCs, servers, and mainframes). Others may require construction of *bridges* (*see* COMMUNICATION CONTROL UNIT and GATEWAY) that translate one set of formats and protocols to another. More thorough integration can be attained by requiring that all nodes support a common *virtual machine* that processes platform-independent program instructions. This approach is taken by systems that use the Java (*q.v.*) programming language.

◆ *Multiple protocols*

Most distributed message passing differs significantly from the kinds of invocations (such as procedure calls) used within the confines of sequential programs. The most basic form of distributed communication is inherently *asynchronous*; similar to mailed letters in a postal system. Senders issue messages without relying on receipt or reply by their recipients. Distributed messages usually take much longer to reach recipients than do local invocations, sometimes reach recipients in a different order than they are sent, and may fail to reach them at all. Additional protocols are nearly always constructed from this basis. These may include semi-synchronous messaging in which senders wait for an acknowledgment of message receipt before proceeding, procedural messaging in which senders wait for full replies, time-out protocols in which senders wait for replies only for a certain period before proceeding, callback protocols in which receivers later issue different messages back to their senders, transactional protocols in which all messages in a given session or transaction are processed as in an all-or-none fashion (*see* TRANSACTION PROCESSING), and multicast protocols in which senders simultaneously issue messages to a *group* of other nodes. These and other protocols are often extended and specialized to enhance reliability, security, and efficiency.

◆ *Openness*

Most sequential programs are *closed*: their configurations never change after execution commences. Most distributed systems are to some degree *open*: an unbounded number of nodes, components, and applications may be added or changed even while the system is running. This provides the extensibility necessary to accommodate expansion, and the ability to evolve and cope with the changing world in which a system resides. Openness requires that each component obey a certain minimal set of policies, conventions, and protocols to insure *interoperability* among updated or added components. Historically, the most successful open systems have been those with the most minimal requirements. For example, the simplicity of the HTTP protocol was a major factor in the success of the World Wide Web. Standards organizations such as ISO and ANSI, along with industrial consortia such as OMG (Object Management Group) establish the basic format and protocol standards underlying many interoperability guarantees. Individual distributed systems additionally rely on context-specific or domain-dependent policies and mechanisms.

◆ *Fault tolerance*

A program running on a single computer is, at best, only as reliable as that computer. But most distributed systems remain at least partially available and functional even if some of their nodes, applications, or communication links fail or misbehave. In addition to outright failures, applications may suffer from unacceptably low *quality of service* due to bandwidth (*q.v.*) shortages, network contention (*q.v.*), software overhead, or other system limitations. Because failures are relatively common and take so many different forms, fault tolerance requirements present some of the most central, yet difficult challenges in the construction of distributed systems (*see* FAULT-TOLERANT COMPUTING).

◆ *Persistence*

At least some data and programs are maintained on persistent media that outlast the execution of any given application. Persistence may be arranged at the level of file systems, database systems, or programming language run-time support mechanisms.

◆ *Security*

Only authorized users may access sensitive data or perform critical operations. Security in distributed systems is intrinsically a multilevel issue, ranging from the basic safety guarantees provided by the hardware and operating systems residing on each node, to message encryption and authentication (*q.v.*) protocols, to mechanisms supporting larger social policy issues concerning privacy, appropriateness of content, and individual responsibility.

In open systems, a second, complementary sense of security arises: users may not trust, or may not wish to use, unfamiliar components unless they have independent evidence about their safety and utility. Techniques for addressing trustworthiness include the use of digital certificates, and *sandboxing* untrusted components by not allowing their code to perform potentially dangerous operations such as modifying disk files.

◆ *Isolation*

Each component is logically or physically autonomous, and communicates with others only via structured message protocols. In addition, groups of components may be segregated for purposes of functionality, performance, or security. For example, while the connectivity of a corporate distributed system may extend to the entire Internet, its essential functionality could be segregated (often by a *firewall*) to an *intranet* operating only within the company, and communicating with other parts of the system via a restricted secure protocol.

♦ *Decentralized control*
No single computer is necessarily responsible for configuration, management, or policy control for the system as a whole. Distributed systems are instead *federations* (domains joined by protocols) of autonomous agents that agree on enough common policies and protocols to provide a given aggregate functionality. Some aspects of decentralization exist by desire; for example to provide fault tolerance. Others exist by necessity; because centralized control does not scale to the number of nodes and connections supported by contemporary systems. However, roles and tools for administering system-wide policies may be restricted to particular users.

Theoretical Foundations

COMPUTATIONAL MODELS
Distributed systems cannot be modeled adequately as Turing Machines (*q.v.*). Unlike Turing Machines, distributed systems may be *open*, arbitrarily extensible by adding new nodes or functionality, and *reactive*, continuously responding to changing environments. One overarching framework that encompasses most current approaches to modeling distributed systems is Wegner's (1997) notion of an *interaction machine*, an abstract characterization that encompasses any object with state and the ability to send and receive messages. Particular formalizations such as the *pi calculus* are used to explore rigorously the emergent properties of distributed systems, for example those surrounding security. Refinements geared toward more practical engineering efforts include two-tiered models in which each node, process, or thread in a distributed system is modeled as an *active* object, possessing an autonomous thread of control. Active objects are in turn structured using sets of *passive* objects that conform to a given sequential model of object-oriented computation.

SPECIFICATION
Distributed systems do not merely compute a single function or perform a single action. Instead they perform a never-ending stream of diverse operations. Specification of the functionality of distributed systems cannot rely solely on the use of techniques (such as those based on preconditions and postconditions—*see* DISCRETE MATHEMATICS) that describe inputs and outputs of sequential programs. Specifications must additionally describe ongoing properties of the system as a whole. Most approaches rely ultimately on temporal logic or related modal logics that provide at least two forms of specification (*see* MODEL CHECKING):

♦ Properties that must invariantly hold true at all times. These generally take the form of *safety* requirements, for example that a given security breach can never occur.

♦ Properties that must eventually hold true. These generally take the form of *liveness* requirements, for example that a given message will be processed.

A different approach to specification is to pose requirements in terms of abstract computational models that obey simpler, more understandable, and more formally tractable properties than do real systems, thus allowing simulation and analysis of the main properties of interest. These models can be further refined to deal with additional complexities and constraints.

FUNDAMENTAL LIMITATIONS
The implementation of several desired properties of distributed systems runs up against inherent limitations that have been uncovered in theoretical studies. These mainly surround the ability of a set of independent nodes to together reach some global property, often based on the notion of *consensus*: that a set of nodes all agree about a given predicate. Consensus plays a central role for example in fault tolerance, where some nodes must agree that another node has failed (*see* FAULT-TOLERANT COMPUTING). As shown by Fischer *et al.* (1985), no algorithm can always insure that agreement will be reached under all conditions in asynchronous message passing systems. (Informally, among the reasons is that any apparently failed node might not actually have failed, but instead is proceeding very slowly.) Even more severe limitations apply to *Byzantine* failures, in which faulty nodes misbehave rather than halt. Such theoretical results have helped uncover algorithms and protocols that achieve desired results with a high enough probability or small enough set of restrictions that they perform extremely well in practice.

DISTRIBUTED ALGORITHMS
Many distributed systems rely on a common set of basic algorithms and protocols that are employed to solve problems including the detection of termination of a distributed computation, election of a leader of a group of nodes, synchronization of redundant computations performed for the sake of fault tolerance, coordination of database transactions, and mutually exclusive access to shared resources. More specialized algorithmic problem domains include distributed simulation (*q.v.*), electronic commerce (*q.v.*), digital

libraries (*q.v.*), distributed multimedia (*q.v.*), and collaborative groupware (*q.v.*) applications. Research efforts across these domains entail the discovery of new algorithms and the formal analysis of their correctness and performance. For example, one approach to fault tolerance relies on *virtual synchrony*, a set of algorithms that insure (within certain limitations) that all members of a group of nodes remain in agreement about the ordering of messages sent to the members.

System Engineering

Distributed systems used in commerce, industrial automation, and information services are among the largest and most complex systems in existence. These systems provide essential services relied upon by society at large, and are rapidly becoming as economically, politically, and socially important as shipping, railway, highway, and telecommunication systems have ever been. Successful development requires adherence to sound design principles and engineering practices, and reliance on an increasingly standardized set of decomposition and structuring rules that in part borrow from and extend object-oriented software design methods (*see* OBJECT-ORIENTED ANALYSIS AND DESIGN).

The earliest, yet still common, form of a distributed system is a *client–server* design, in which one or more independent servers perform centralized tasks such as database maintenance (Fig 2). Clients each execute programs that provide user interface and computational capabilities, but communicate via database queries with servers whenever accessing or updating shared data. An examination of the limitations of the simplest, most fragile client–server systems reveals the main problems that are addressed in contemporary scalable, structured, distributed programming frameworks:

- *Fixed addresses*
  When there are only a few fixed nodes in a system, and each performs a single dedicated task, all communication might be performed by issuing packets to fixed Ethernet addresses or broadcasting them on a local network. But these tactics do not scale; they are the distributed analogs of using raw memory addresses to locate data and instructions.

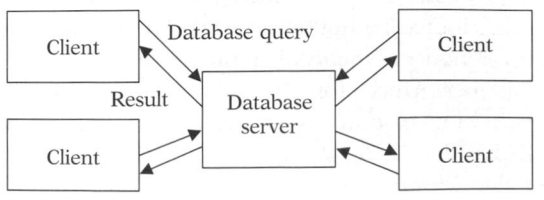

Figure 2. Client–server interactions.

- *Ad hoc messaging*
  A small, fixed set of nodes with dedicated functionality can communicate by sending hand-crafted messages that are known to be of a form acceptable by recipients. This practice does not scale to systems providing possibly many services on possibly many nodes; it is the distributed analog of coding low-level program jumps rather than using structured object-oriented interfaces and method invocations.

- *Monolithic components*
  In the most fragile systems, each node runs a single very large program. Such monolithic software components are difficult to design, implement, and test, and even more difficult to reuse, extend, and update.

- *Fixed architecture*
  The communication patterns, protocols, and policies seen in pure client–server designs are sometimes sensible choices for database-centric applications, but they are by no means universally appropriate. For example, a fixed architecture could not support the sorts of applications deploying mobile agents.

Solutions to these problems and limitations mainly reflect experience-driven design knowledge accrued during the historical progression from custom small-scale systems, to specialized systems such as network file systems (for example *NFS*; *see* FILE SERVER), to enterprise-level business systems, to the kinds of global multipurpose systems currently being developed. Engineering support for many of the development practices, services, and components described in the remainder of this article is increasingly provided by standardized distributed programming frameworks based upon OMG CORBA, OSF DCE, Microsoft DCOM, and the Java (*q.v.*) programming language.

Names and Identifiers

Contemporary distributed systems rely on *naming services* that maintain sets of logical names and map them to physical addresses and associated low-level protocols. The most common and familiar naming service is DNS (Domain Naming Service), which provides a basis for the Web page naming scheme used on the World Wide Web. DNS maps Internet names (for example www.sun.com) to Internet addresses, which are then further translated to hardware-level addresses and connection protocols. Most distributed systems augment general-purpose naming systems in order to maintain mappings from the services supported by the system to the nodes, processes, and software objects that provide them (Fig. 3). Most components are not given human-readable names, but are instead assigned

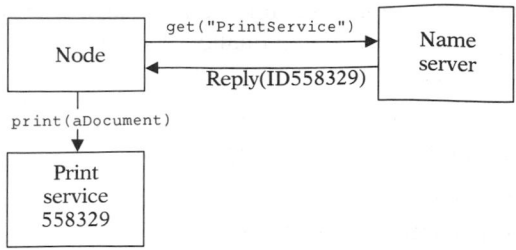

Figure 3. Querying a name server.

arbitrary object identifiers that are used by *brokers* (mediators that perform services on behalf of other components) and related components when locating services.

Naming services are usually implemented by distributed algorithms in which each node knows of only a small subset of the name space, but also knows of other nodes to query when an attempted lookup fails. Distributed name spaces are structured in a mainly hierarchical fashion that simplifies usage, streamlines lookup algorithms, and permits federation among different name services. Name space mappings need not be restricted to nodes or objects. For example, names may be associated with groups that are accessed through channels with multiple connection points.

Interfaces and Implementations

Interfaces are formal declarations of operations (methods) supported by implementation objects. Most distributed systems rely on a standard means for defining interfaces that describe sets of services, enforced with an Interface Definition Language (IDL). Systems maintain interface descriptions, along with bindings to available implementations, in repositories that are tied to naming services in order to provide lookup capabilities. Object interfaces are very similar to classes (*q.v.*) in object-oriented programming (*q.v.*) languages. Each interface consists of a set of service declarations. Each service is declared in a fashion similar to an object-oriented *method*, a named operation that may carry arguments, results, and exceptions. Arguments and results may consist of any arbitrary data, including control parameters, names or references to other components, image data, implementation code for other components, and descriptions of other interfaces. IDLs differ from object-oriented languages in that they do not permit definition of programming details indicating how a declared service is implemented. Some IDLs also support declarations of special message passing protocols that must be used when sending and receiving messages of the indicated form.

Special development tools can be used to generate code that connects declared services to implementation code written in a standard programming lan-

guage, and possibly consisting of many programming-language level objects, methods, or modules. IDL-based tools typically generate code that enables components to be invoked via a particular Remote Procedure Call (RPC) or Remote Message Invocation (RMI; also known as *Object RPC*) protocol discipline. (The main difference between RPC and RMI is that an RMI message recipient is specified by an identifier that must be resolved by a broker; this is the role of the ORB—*Object Request Broker*—in CORBA.) Most tools create *proxy* objects that locate ultimate message recipients, encode (*marshal* or *serialize*) selectors and data into lower-level buffers and packets, and transport packets. At the recipient site, symmetrical dispatch objects decode (*unmarshal*) packets and invoke the desired service in the corresponding local component (Fig. 4).

Some programming languages, most notably Java, possess an interface construct that enables programmers to specify an interface, implement it, and arrange the underlying connections without the need for a separate IDL. For example, a Java interface used in an over-simplified banking system might declare the following operations to perform balance inquiries, deposits, and withdrawals on a particular account. In this example, getBalance returns a real number, while deposit and withdraw update the account. Errors such as a bad ID or insufficient balance produce (throw) exceptions (*see* EXCEPTION HANDLING):

```
public interface Account {
  long getBalance(UserID id)
    throws UnauthorizedAccessException;
  void deposit(long amount, UserID id)
    throws UnauthorizedAccessException;
  void withdraw(long amount, UserID id)
    throws UnauthorizedAccessException,
        InsufficientFundsException;
}
```

Interfaces, naming services, and associated mechanisms and constructs together make distributed system programming more like sequential programming.

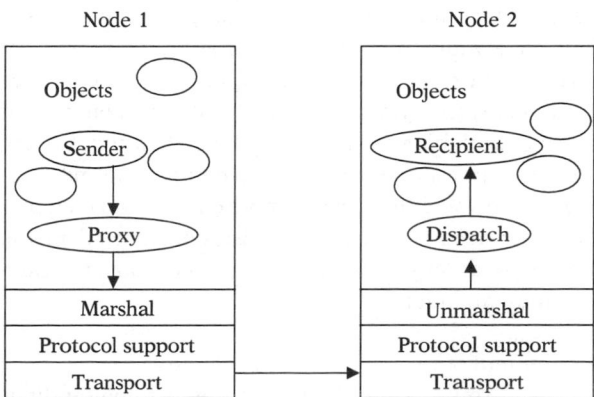

Figure 4. Remote procedure call.

Higher-level languages and tools can be used to make distributed programming constructs indistinguishable from sequential ones. For example, a program statement such as `myAccount.getBalance(myID)` need not itself reveal whether it is just a local invocation within a sequential program, or a distributed invocation. This *transparency* (*q.v.*) shields developers from needing to know the location of the service, whether it has moved, the underlying protocol used to obtain it, whether it is replicated for the sake of fault tolerance, the presence of security measures such as encryption, and so on. Transparency simplifies usage of scripting languages (*q.v.*) whose main role is to glue together sets of existing distributed components to build applications. However, most development languages and tools that are used to build the underlying components provide nontransparent programming abstractions. Since distributed message passing may differ significantly from local invocation with respect to semantics, latencies (delays), and failure modes, most languages keep them separate. This forces developers to deal with distribution-specific issues as they arise, while also providing programmatic support for more limited senses of transparency that may be desirable in particular systems.

Component Management

Systems composed of many small-granularity interfaces, classes, and objects are generally more reusable, reliable, and economical than those built using only a few custom monolithic programs. For example a `Bank` object may be composed mainly of sets of `Account` objects. In some systems, just about any software object may be a candidate for independent use as a distributed component. Such practices lead to the existence of many more components than there are computers in a system. (This may be mitigated by the increasing deployment of information appliances and other plentiful small computers.)

Object components are managed by *life cycle* services that are somewhat analogous to, but extend, virtual memory techniques that allow computers to act as if they have more memory than they do. Rather than having each node or process support a single service component, the system arranges that each component is made available whenever it is needed, without occupying computational resources when it is not needed. Many aspects of life cycle support can be provided as a set of services that are otherwise constructed in the same way as any other distributed component. Support may include:

◆ *Configuration*
Establishing or modifying parameters and bindings that control policies and protocols employed by one or more components; for example those surrounding authentication and quality of service.

◆ *Activation*
Creating a new instance of a component in either a new process or an existing process.

◆ *Deactivation*
Suspending a component and saving its state persistently for possible later reactivation.

◆ *Mobility*
Transferring a component from one node to another.

◆ *Load balancing*
Placing components on or moving components to the least busy nodes.

◆ *Replication*
Establishing multiple copies of a component for the sake of performance or reliability.

◆ *Garbage collection* (*q.v.*)
Destroying and releasing resources of a component that is no longer being used in the system.

◆ *Versioning*
Replacing a faulty or outdated implementation of a component with a new implementation.

◆ *Utilities*
Supplying general-purpose functionality needed by other components, for example performing clock synchronization across nodes.

Nearly all aspects of object management, and distributed programming more generally, entail performance engineering. The most central performance issue in distributed systems is the most obvious one: distributed messaging passing can sometimes be one million times slower than local invocations. Some of this overhead remains even when using the fastest available computing and communication technologies. This observation has led to development of increasingly efficient schemes for performing each of the suboperations employed in message transmission. Performance optimizations that can normally be applied without compromising the integrity of system designs include:

◆ *Data caching*
Saving copies of previously requested remote data and reusing them unless they have changed.

◆ *Message aggregation*
Combining frequent small messages into less frequent larger ones.

◆ *Component clustering*
Statically or dynamically enhancing locality by placing heavily communicating components (or their

replicates) as close together as possible: in the same process, on the same machine, or on the same local network.

◆ *Protocol streamlining*
Using weaker but faster protocols when possible. For example, external requests may be screened through expensive authentication checks only once upon entry into a system so they do not need to be checked on each internal message send involved in processing the requests.

◆ *Algorithmic improvements*
Using algorithms that are less affected by communication latency. For example, *optimistic* techniques assume the success of rarely-failing requests without waiting for verification, but are also prepared to perform expensive rollbacks or retries upon eventual notification of failure.

Architectural Styles

Even when they are based on common infrastructures, different distributed systems or subsystems may be composed in accord with vastly different architectural styles. Systems or subsystems may be based on one or more *design patterns* (*see* SOFTWARE DESIGN PATTERNS) including the following.

PEER SERVICES

Nearly every system includes at least some components that communicate via classic procedural request-reply mechanisms. For example, one component may handle a user's request for a particular stock quote by issuing an RPC or RMI, awaiting the result, and then displaying it to the user. However, service-based systems are by no means limited to pure client server designs. For example, the recipient of the stock quote request may in turn exchange messages with several other peer components before it can compute the requested value.

FAULT-TOLERANT SERVICES

There are two main approaches to improving the fault tolerance of services: replication and persistence. Replication entails cloning components and ensuring that all replicates process the same messages in the same order. If any one of them fails, others will still be able to continue. Persistence-based solutions rely on *checkpointing*: periodically saving the states of components so that they can be resurrected in the event of failure. There are many variants that involve both replication and persistence; for example *standby* techniques in which replicates persistently log all actions to the primary host, and then execute them all at once upon failure in order to achieve the correct state. Since there is no upper limit on how much replication

or checkpointing is enough, and since solutions can be relatively costly in terms of resources, performance, and system complexity, any application of fault-tolerance measures involves engineering trade-offs.

TRANSACTIONAL SERVICES

Transactional protocols extend the concurrency control and persistence support used in monolithic databases to the realm of distributed systems. Most transactions operate on sets of service requests that must be performed in an all-or-none fashion. For example, a bank transfer operation consists of two requests, to withdraw money from one account and to deposit it in another. These two requests should fail as a unit if any problems arise. Distributed transactions differ from their sequential counterparts mainly by virtue of employing multiphase commit protocols that deal with constituent operations performed on different nodes, as well as interactions between distributed failure handling and concurrency control techniques.

LEGACY SERVICES

The successes of even the earliest distributed system components are in part responsible for the fact that relatively few existing distributed systems are structured in an ideal fashion. Nearly every system must accommodate *legacy* components, subsystems, and applications. For example, some old transaction processing systems and databases would be too difficult, time-consuming, or disruptive to redesign and reimplement. Some legacy software may be gracefully integrated by retrospectively defining interfaces and retrofitting structured messaging protocols. Others resist such efforts and are dealt with in an *ad hoc* fashion.

ASYNCHRONOUS MESSAGES

A number of *push* protocols extend the primitive asynchronous message passing style in which components issue messages without necessarily expecting replies. This style is analogous to mail systems, as well as to radio and television broadcasting. For example, a publish/subscribe stock quote service may periodically multicast quote updates to a group of subscriber components. Such protocols may involve many intermediate nodes that hierarchically route and distribute messages, as well as those employed to enhance fault tolerance. Event-based systems are structured in a similar fashion. For example, a remote sensing component may periodically issue events indicating sensed changes in the world. Perhaps the most widespread push-based system is the *Usenet* news system, which propagates postings to news servers across the Internet so that users may more quickly and conveniently access local copies. Similar protocols are used in software distribution systems that propagate program updates to all subscribers.

COLLABORATIVE GROUPS

In electronic calendar, whiteboard, and groupware (*q.v.*) systems, sets of otherwise independent components must occasionally coordinate efforts to reach a common goal; for example to schedule a meeting. Among other options, collaborative systems may be based on shared persistent channels. Participants transiently enlist channels maintaining messages or data needed by all group members for the course of a session. A channel may be structured for example as a *tuple space*, consisting of records or objects that may be entered, removed, and read by any member (*see* COORDINATION LANGUAGES).

CONTENT-BASED PROCESSING

In the World Wide Web, as well as many multimedia systems, each server has a very simple interface, often consisting only of an operation that returns the information content specified by an identifier such as a URL (Uniform Resource Locator). However, this content is *self-describing*: messages indicate the nature of the software needed to display or otherwise use the data. Clients in turn map this description to locally available software (for example an image rendering program), if present, and use it to process the content. Associating content description (also known as *metadata*) with messages provides the flexibility needed to deal with ever-growing media types and formats, but at the expense of possible failures when clients do not possess the software needed to handle a new content type.

MOBILE CODE

Mobile code systems extend content-based systems by employing *active* messages that include not descriptions, but the actual software (for example a set of Java classes) or instructions needed by a component to perform a given function. *Agent* systems further extend these capabilities by permitting some degree of autonomy to mobile code, so that it may in turn spawn additional agents on other nodes while in the process of, for example, searching for the best price for an item requested by a consumer (*see* MULTI-AGENT SYSTEMS). Often, this code is structured to allow *disconnected* operation, in which some processing proceeds even when other nodes are temporarily unreachable.

Bibliography

1985. Fischer, M. J., Lynch, N. A., and Paterson, M. S. "Impossibility of Distributed Consensus with One Faulty Process," *Journal of the ACM*, **32**, *2* (April), 374–382.
1993. Mullender, S. (ed.) *Distributed Systems*, 2nd Ed. Reading, MA: Addison-Wesley.
1994. Coulouris, G., Dollimore, J., and Kindberg, T. *Distributed Systems: Concepts and Design*, 2nd Ed. Reading, MA: Addison-Wesley.
1996. Barbosa, V. *An Introduction to Distributed Algorithms*. Cambridge, MA: MIT Press.
1996. Lynch, N. *Distributed Algorithms*. San Francisco: Morgan Kaufmann.
1996. Zomaya, A. (ed.) *Parallel and Distributed Computing Handbook*. New York: McGraw-Hill.
1997. Wegner, P. "Why Interaction is More Powerful Than Algorithms," *Comm. of the ACM*, **40**, *5* (May), 80–91.

Jos Marlowe, Doug Lea, and Malcolm Atkinson

DNA COMPUTING

See MOLECULAR COMPUTING.

DOCUMENTATION

For articles on related subjects *see* ADMINISTRATIVE APPLICATIONS; FLOWCHART; PROGRAM SPECIFICATION; SOFTWARE ENGINEERING; STANDARDS; and STRUCTURED PROGRAMMING.

Documentation is a vital part of developing and using a computer-based system and an integral part of what is now called *software engineering*. In some commercial organizations, 20% or even more of the total development effort goes into the documentation of the new system, recording how it is to work and how it was developed. Documentation of a computer project falls into two broad categories—development documentation and control documentation. Development documentation records how a computer-based system is structured and what it is supposed to do and gives the background information upon which the design is founded. Control documentation, on the other hand, serves an administrative function: it records the resources used in developing and implementing the system, and includes such documents as project plans, schedules, resource allocation details, and progress reports.

Functions of Documentation

Documentation serves four main functions:

1. Intertask/interphase communications.

2. Historical reference for modification and correction.

3. Quality and quantity control.

4. Instructional reference.

The relative importance of each of these depends on many factors. For example, one of the most important is the scope and type of the project; it may be a large-scale commercial system, or a scientific problem-solving program used by one or two technicians on a limited amount of data. Within each category, there are variations in project size, problem complexity, organization of staff, and the time scale for development and use. Each function of documentation is described below.

INTERTASK/INTERPHASE COMMUNICATION

This operation records what has been done at each stage of the project so that instructions can be issued for the next phase of work, or so that all people involved in the project can agree what has been done before work proceeds to the next step. The amount of time and effort that must be devoted to documentation for this reason is a function of the scope of the system and the number of people involved.

In the development of a major commercial system, which requires procedures such as invoicing, inventory control, payroll, or production control, many people will be involved. In a production control system, for example, the business functions involved could include, among others:

1. Sales forecasting (linking with sales accounts).

2. Parts explosion and production batching/netting (linked with engineering design).

3. Plant resource allocation and scheduling.

4. Materials ordering/tooling and allocation.

5. Monitoring job progress.

6. Scrap and bonus reporting (linking with payroll).

7. Job costing (linking all systems).

Most of these functions are closely interrelated. Some 20 or 30 separate job functions or organizational units may be involved with the development, implementation, and running of the computer system. In addition to job functions such as those described, different levels of user staff will involve senior or executive management, line management, and supervisors and operators. Similarly, a number of job functions will be performed by personnel in the data processing or management services department; for example:

1. Business analysts, internal business consultants who advise management on business methods and who identify areas for improvement.

2. Systems analysts (*q.v.*), who investigate, analyze, and specify a new system.

3. Systems designers, who design the new system (computer and manual procedures) in detail.

4. Programmers, who design, code, and test the computer programs for the system.

5. Operators, who are responsible for the day-to-day running of the system.

There may also be general support or service staff within data processing, such as maintenance programmers, software support people, forward planners, and standards analysts. In a small installation, many of the job functions listed above may be performed by one person or a small group; in a large installation, each job function may be performed by a specialist group. Keeping people informed, passing on information and ideas for approval, and giving instructions involves a complex communications network in which formal documentation plays a vital role.

A failure of communication through poor documentation (or a total lack of it) can prove very expensive indeed. Good documentation will also help to insure project continuity should staff changes occur.

The use of documentation for intertask/interphase communication is equally important in large technical or scientific projects. Where the development of a program or group of programs can be done by only a limited number of technicians who are quite often both problem proponents and solution programmers, the importance of documentation during the project diminishes. However, the documentation of what has been done and how the programs work will be important for historical or instructional reference, as described below.

HISTORICAL REFERENCE

The reference function is relevant to both commercial and scientific work. It is the documentation of how the system works that makes it easily changed after it is implemented. All systems are subject to change. Maintenance of business systems and programs will be required because the nature of a business and its methods change, or because the organization is restructured, new types of products are developed, management reporting requirements change, etc.

In scientific work, programs may have to be altered because the nature of the problem to be solved changes, possibly as a result of further research. A system may have to be changed because of new software or hardware. It may be desirable to change the processing methods because new techniques become available. The reason for the change may lie outside the organization altogether, as is the case with legal requirements and statutory changes.

A system can be maintained efficiently only if the existing operation of all procedures and programs is clearly known and understood. The documentation of the system provides this knowledge. For example, a program written a year ago is to be changed today; the program consists of 2,000 instructions, with many branches and nested loops. The programmer who originally wrote it is no longer available. The modifications require that the logic of the program be understood; the new programmer must insure that errors are not introduced by overlooking the impact of some of the changes. A recent example of this is the Y2K problem (*q.v.*) which better documentation would have alleviated considerably.

The documentation of a system may also be reviewed for performance purposes. Many installations develop performance standards based on records of time and resources budgeted and used in developing a system, as compared with system type, scope, and complexity. The control documentation is used for details of resources, and the development documentation for a description of the system. By formally capturing details of all projects, estimates of resources for future projects can be improved.

QUALITY/QUANTITY CONTROL

As a system develops, various elements of documentation are completed as each step is finished. Management can use this documentation to evaluate project progress and individual performance.

INSTRUCTIONAL REFERENCE

The development documentation can be reviewed during and after development for many general purposes. For example, documentation will enable trainees to study a system developed by experienced technicians. This is particularly important for instructional reference to generalized systems or general-purpose software. Another benefit of documentation is that an outside party can evaluate the system and its method of operation to determine if the package is suitable for use in another environment. In this case, sufficient information must be given to enable the user to apply the software to other problems and requirements.

Instructional reference thus includes all literature provided by a software supplier, such as the reference manuals for all languages, utilities, operating systems, subroutines, and application packages. It also includes the documentation and library facilities in a large organization that produces its own software.

Types of Documentation

In the development of a system, whether it is a large-scale commercial system or a group of scientific programs for analyzing data, certain categories of documentation must be considered. These are:

1. Analytical documentation.
2. Systems documentation.
3. Program documentation.
4. Operations documentation.
5. User documentation.

Each of these categories is described below, along with the major factors that influence the form of the documentation in any particular organization.

ANALYTICAL DOCUMENTATION

This consists of all the records and reports produced when a project is initiated. For all projects except those that require a single, one-time, problem-solving program, some form of initial briefing is required. In most organizations, the technicians who design, program, and test a system are grouped into a computing or data processing department, and the users who commission work from the data processing department must define the nature and objectives of the project. In some technical or scientific environments, the user is capable of specifying in very exact terms what is required in the way of processing and outputs. Generally, for any type of project, the initial briefing should consist of a *user request*, stating the problem (i.e. what the user needs to achieve); a *feasibility study* that evaluates possible solutions (in outline); and a *project plan* that estimates the time and resources required to develop and implement the system. Failure to produce and agree upon these three statements in the briefing will result in much wasted effort later in the project. They are vital whenever a user commissions work from computer technicians, and must be provided before money is actually committed to the more time-consuming tasks of system design and programming.

SYSTEMS DOCUMENTATION

This encompasses all information needed to define the proposed computer-based system to a level where it can be programmed, tested, and implemented. The major document is some form of *system specification*, which acts as a permanent record of the structure, its functions and work flow, and the controls on the system. It is the basic means of communication between the system's design, programming, and user functions.

PROGRAM DOCUMENTATION

This comprises the records of the detailed logic and coding of the constituent programs of a system. These records, prepared by the programmer, aid program development and acceptance, troubleshooting, general maintenance, machine/software conversion at a later date, and programmer changeover.

Program documentation covers both specific applications programs and general-purpose or in-house developed software. In addition to documenting *how* a program works, instructions for *using* the program must be written for packaged software.

OPERATIONS DOCUMENTATION

This specifies those procedures required for running the system by operations personnel. It gives the general sequence of events for performing the job and defines precise procedures for data control and security, data preparation, program running, output dispersal, and ancillary operations.

USER DOCUMENTATION

This consists of all the descriptive and instructive material necessary for the user to participate in the running of the operational system, including notes on the interpretation of the output results. Where a software package is produced, this category includes all material necessary to evaluate the programs and all instructions for its use.

To supplement but not replace printed user manuals, commercial software products intended for thousands of users usually include online help. Typically, a pull-down menu with an extensive index of terms is provided. Typing the first few letters of a term or phrase whose explanation is sought will then scroll the index to the point where a simple mouse click will display the relevant section of the online documentation.

Every installation should establish documentation standards (i.e. rules for the completion of certain documents at certain times) that define the content, format, and distribution of the documents. Many factors influence what documents are to be produced, how, when, and by whom. For example, the extent of *management commitment* is indicated by how much the management of the installation is prepared to allocate time and resources, not only for developing a system, but also for its documentation. Another controlling factor may be *project characteristics*, which consist of the number of projects and their scope, complexity, and duration. Crucial to any set of standards is the *organization structure* of both the institution as a whole, and the development and operations departments in particular. This, in turn, is affected by the *technical environment*: the hardware/software techniques used, such as the level of programming language, the quality of documentation produced by the software, and the use of special-purpose documentation programs (flowcharters, etc.).

From this broad picture of the total documentation of a project, we select one type to review in detail: program documentation. We focus on this because the limits of the tasks of programming can be clearly defined, and because this function in programming is similar in many organizations.

Program Documentation

Figure 1 shows the flow of documentation in designing, coding, and testing a program, respectively. The starting point is a program specification. Typically, this is a statement of *what* the program must do; the programmer's task is to determine *how* the program will do it. How much the data formats are predefined and how much is left to the discretion of the programmer depends on installation policy and the project. Other inputs to the programming phase include literature—which describes the software available for the project (either from outside suppliers or from an internal library)—and the programming standards, which give the rules and techniques for programming in that installation.

The outputs include a program manual which describes the programs in detail (construction, coding, and testing), instructions for use (for a generalized program), and computer operating instructions for day-to-day running. In many cases the task of documenting a program is one of adding to the initial program specification in order to build up the program manual. The various elements of program documentation are discussed below.

PROGRAM SPECIFICATION

This is a statement of the data available for processing, the required outputs, and the details of the necessary processing. The specifications can be prepared by the problem proponent, a specialist systems analyst/designer, or the programmer. It must be complete, accurate, and unambiguous; changes to the specification after programming begins can be very expensive. The specification usually contains the following information:

1. Input.

2. Output.

3. Major functions performed.

4. The means of communication between this program and previous or following programs.

5. Logical rules and decisions to be followed, including statements of how the input is to be examined, altered, and used.

6. Validation and editing criteria.

7. Actions to be taken on error or exception conditions.

8. Special tables, formulas, and algorithms.

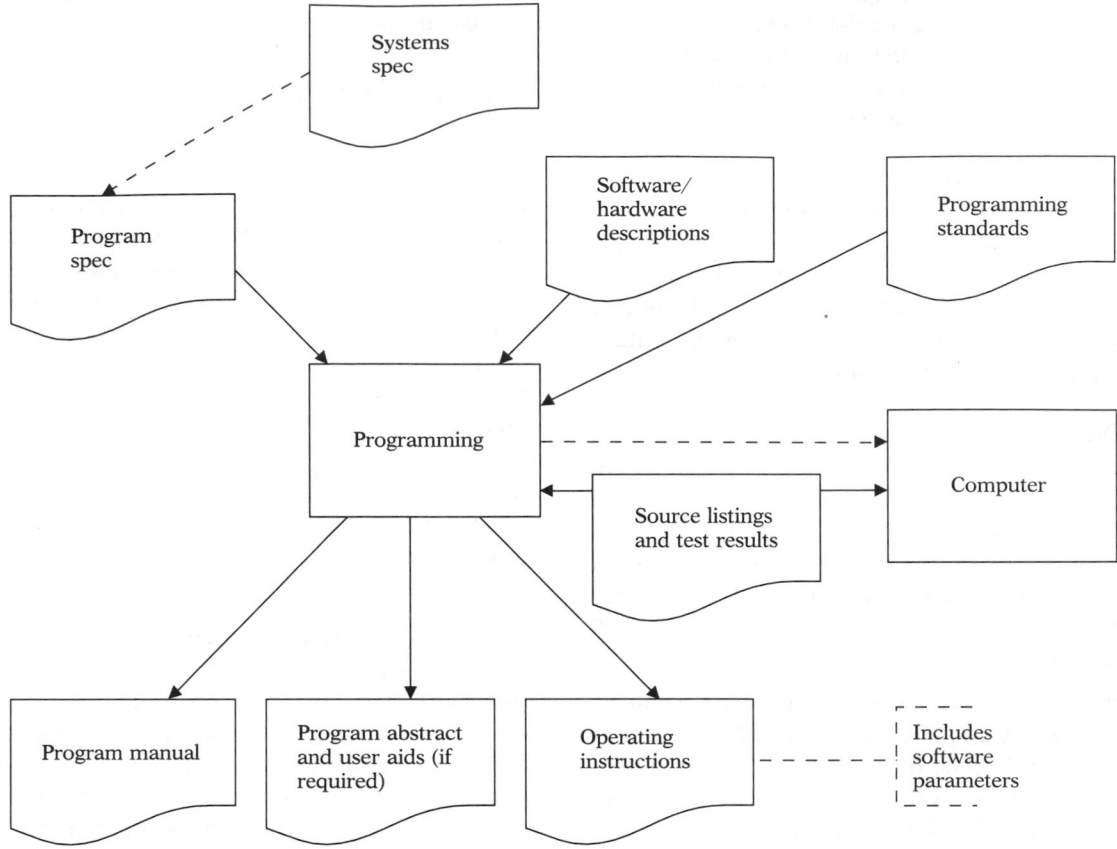

Figure 1. Documentation flow.

The description of the processing rules (item 5 in the list), can be given in narrative, flowchart, or decision-table form.

PROGRAM MANUAL

From the program specification, the programmer designs, codes, and tests the program. The output of this exercise is the program manual. The form of the logic design and the source program listing will depend on the type of application and the software used. For example, if a high-level decision-table *preprocessor* (*q.v.*) is used, the tabular program together with the data descriptions and final source listing will be complete enough without the preparation of a flowchart. Similarly, some installations use software for the final documentation; e.g. flowcharters that produce detailed flowcharts, statement by statement from the source program.

One of the advantages of contemporary high-level languages is that the source listing itself forms the major part of the final documentation. The programmer must insure not only that the source program is logically correct and follows the rules of the language, but also that the program coding is neat and easy to under-

stand. By using meaningful data names and comments embedded in the program, it is possible to make a source program almost self-explanatory (*see* LITERATE PROGRAMMING). Software production houses frequently have highly codified rules for how program components such as functions, procedures, and variables are to be named to show their roles in a program. A flowchart can be used with a well-documented program as a general "route map" to the detailed coding in the source listing. When altering an operational program, many programmers refer directly to the source listing and then to the flowchart only if the required change is not immediately obvious from the listing.

Flowcharts and cross-reference lists (produced by the compiler or other software) can be used to check that an alteration has not erroneously disturbed other coding. The advantage of using comments in the source listing is that it minimizes references to other documents. The comments are not compiled as part of the program, but merely appear on the source listing. Source program comments should be kept brief while at the same time being descriptive and meaningful.

Note that the final documentation will show not only how the program works, but also how it was tested (for quality control and later retested after changes were made), operating instructions for running it, and any special parameters that are to be given to the operating system.

Although the program manual is the major output of the program specification, the programmer will use (and can produce) other types of documentation. If the program being developed is for general use, either within or outside the organization, then additional user instructions will be needed. They should enable the prospective user to answer the following questions:

1. What does it do?

2. Do we want to use it?

3. Can we use it?

4. How do we use it?

5. What do we do if it changes?

6. What are its basic limitations?

For internally produced software, one approach is to produce a program abstract that can be held in a central documentation library. If, on first inspection, the user feels that it fulfills the needs, the detailed documentation can then be consulted. The form of this detailed documentation depends on the scope and complexity of the software. For example, a user's guide may be produced to give a general description of the program(s), the facilities available, the hardware environment required, and example uses of the software. The user's guide may contain instructions for using the software, or a programmer's reference manual may be supplied, giving detailed information. Most software is constructed so that the user supplies parameters for a particular job. The parameters may be as simple as specifying an address of data to be processed or as comprehensive as a complete list of processing requirements. The programmer's reference manual will describe the construction of the program(s), together with all parameters required (their format, interdependence, and usage), operating instructions, and error conditions and diagnostics.

Programs ready for operational use and that are to be run repeatedly are assigned to the automated program library, usually stored on disk. The documentation for these programs is usually held in some form of central records library, together with the master reference copies of all software descriptions.

Documentation Maintenance and Control

Once a program has been implemented, the documentation must be retained for subsequent reference.

When the system is changed, the documentation will be consulted and altered accordingly. It is vital to revise the documentation so that it completely and accurately reflects the operation of the system at all times. If the documentation is not so revised, then further maintenance will be very difficult. After any major amendment, all affected programs will have to be retested to prove that the changes have been made correctly and that they do not disrupt or invalidate other processing.

It is necessary, therefore, to insure that the appropriate control procedures are used. All changes should be properly recorded and all copies of the documentation updated. There is a strong case here for restricting the number of copies of the documentation to reduce the time spent in revising records and to minimize the risk of out-of-date copies being used by mistake. All copies should show current parameter requirements for the operating system, language rules, limitations and parameters for utility programs, and operating error messages produced by all software programs. A large installation will not only create a central records library, but also appoint a full-time librarian to cope with amendment distribution control. This is sometimes handled by a "software support" department, which will insure that both programming and operations departments are informed of changes in software availability and operation, such as the introduction of a new release of the operating system.

Though some form of documentation practice has been necessary since the advent of programming, there is a trend toward a more disciplined methodology whereby system and program documentation is produced as an integral by-product of system and program design activities. Typical of such methods is the HIPO system (Hierarchy plus Input-Process-Output).

The thrust of this new philosophy is that structured design and implementation methodologies such as HIPO will produce nearly all of the desired analytical, systems, and program documentation in a form far superior to other, less integrated forms of documentation. HIPO (and other similar structured) documentation is, unfortunately, no easier to maintain than the more traditional forms. But it is no more *difficult* to maintain either, and it retains its usability longer and more reliably than many other forms of documentation. This is true because the methodology tends to enforce a functionally structural similarity between the design documentation and the programs themselves.

Summary

Documentation is a vital element in developing and running any computer project, whether in a government, business, academic, or military installation. It must not be handled in a haphazard fashion; formal documentation standards must be laid down and enforced. These standards must cover all areas—users, systems, and programming and operations. In a modern computer installation, the flow of documentation can be complex, encompassing in-house systems and programs as well as externally produced software.

Bibliography

1990. Roetzheim, W. H. *Structured Design Using HIPO-II.* Upper Saddle River, NJ: Prentice Hall.
1993. Denton, L., and Kelly, J. *Designing, Writing, and Producing Computer Documentation.* New York: McGraw-Hill.
1994. Horton, W. *Designing and Writing Online Documentation: Hypermedia for Self-Supporting Products.* New York: John Wiley.
1997. Barker, T. T., and Dragga, S. *Writing Software Documentation: A Task-Oriented Approach.* New York: Allyn & Bacon.

Keith R. London

DOMAIN-SPECIFIC LANGUAGES

See PROBLEM-ORIENTED LANGUAGES.

DPMA

See COMPUTER SOCIETIES.

DRIVER

A *driver* is a program or subprogram that is written to control either a particular hardware device or another software routine. The term originates both from the concept of harness race drivers or automobile drivers putting their steeds or cars through their paces to see what they can do, and from the fact that machinery components that apply motive force are called "drivers." The most common examples of drivers that control hardware are those that pertain to particular brands and models of printers attached to personal computers. One speaks of having or needing, for example, a printer driver that allows a word processor to communicate with a particular model of a printer.

In another context, we may have written a procedure that is to play an important role in conjunction with some large main program that is not yet written. To test the procedure while we wait, we might write a simple main program that calls the procedure with sufficiently realistic parameters to test it. The temporary main program whose only role is to provide a test bed for the new procedure may also be called a driver.

Bibliography

1996. Mittag, L. "Device Drivers for Nonexistent Devices," *Embedded Systems Programming*, **9**, *8*, 30–40.

Edwin D. Reilly

DSU/CSU

For articles on related subjects *see* CHANNEL; MODEM; and NETWORKS, COMPUTER.

A *Data Service Unit/Channel Service Unit* (DSU/CSU) serves the same function for digital data service communication (DDS) lines as a modem does for conventional analog communication lines. As shown in Fig. 1, it provides the interface between computing equipment conforming to the CCITT V.35 standard and four-wire leased lines provided by an all-digital transmission facility conforming to AT&T Publication 62310. The DSU converts the digital data stream from the computer equipment into a format suitable for transmission over the digital communication line. The CSU terminates the digital line and performs line conditioning (*q.v.*) functions, ensures network compliance

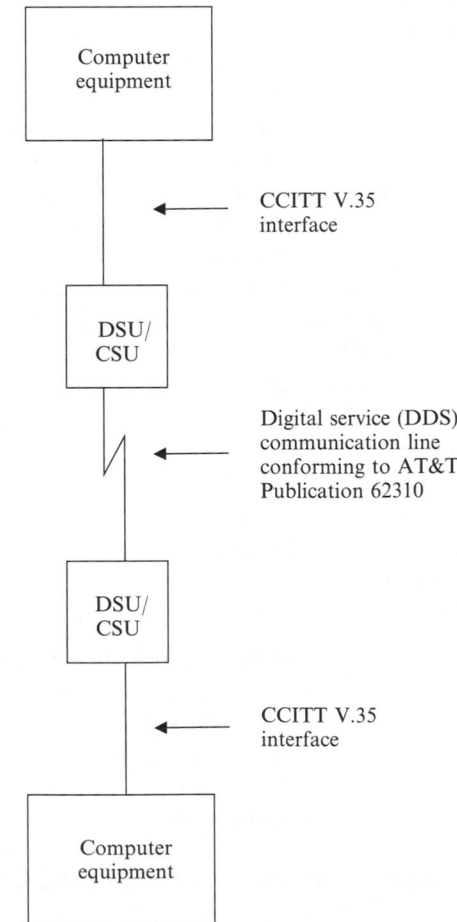

Figure 1. Typical application of a DSU/CSU.

to FCC rules and responds to remote commands for control and loop-back testing.

John S. Sobolewski

DUMP

For articles on related subjects *see* BUG; DEBUGGING; MACHINE AND ASSEMBLY LANGUAGE PROGRAMMING; and TRACE.

A *dump* is a printed representation of the raw content of a computer storage device, usually main memory, at a specified instant. "Raw" means that little or no interpretation is performed on the content; it is taken simply as a sequence of bit strings and presented to the reader as such.

A few refinements are found in even the simplest dumps that keep them from being mere one-to-one bit maps: The representation is usually in octal or hexadecimal, reducing the dump's bulk by a factor of 3 or 4. The segmentation of memory into words or bytes is reflected in the print format; the address of the leftmost word or byte on each printed line is given; and long stretches of identically filled memory segments (typically, zero filled) are not printed verbatim, but replaced with a message such as LOCATIONS 4000-4177 ALL ZERO. Simple dumps often offer the further amenities of permitting bounds to be set on the area of storage to be printed, and of automatically including the contents of the principal registers (*q.v.*) in the CPU (*q.v.*).

Dumps may generally be classified as *post-mortem dumps* or *snapshot dumps*. The post-mortem dump, which occurs only when a program terminates (usually abnormally or prematurely), is the most primitive of debugging devices. It corresponds in vintage and sophistication to machine language programming, and hence its use in debugging high-level language programs is virtually nil. While it is far more commonly employed in debugging assembly language programs than those written in high-level languages, it is still the last resort for programs of all descriptions, including those in high-level languages.

Online debugging sessions do not involve extensive dumps, nor are the snapshot dumps that are involved so bit-oriented, but the representations of memory contents that are produced share the dump's essential characteristic of being instantaneous descriptions of a moving object, and of requiring the programmer to shift into another language, almost into another discipline, when debugging.

The crudeness of debugging with the sole aid of dumps, program listings, and mother wit is due not merely to the dump's being a record of a single instant only, but to its being, usually, a record of the *wrong* instant. By the time an observer, human or programmed, has detected something wrong with a running program and ordered a dump taken, it is possible that some or all of the evidence that would enable the programmer to find the underlying bug has been erased or changed. For this very reason, the trace has proved the more efficacious tool in most debugging situations.

The total replacement of the dump—or, what is equivalent, the realization of "source-language debugging"—has proved to be more difficult to achieve than had initially been expected. It may require the abandonment of the notion of "debugging"—i.e. curative, after-the-fact treatment of faulty programs—in favor of preventive or prophylactic approaches, such as those suggested in the bibliography.

Bibliography

1965. Halpern, M. I. "Computer Programming: The Debugging Epoch Opens," *Computers and Automation* (November), 28–31.
1971. Worley, W. S. "Toward Automatic Debugging of Low Level Code," *IBM Technical Report* TR 00.2211.
1998. Bugg, K. E. *Debugging Visual C++*. San Francisco: Miller Freeman.

Mark Halpern

DVD (DIGITAL VERSATILE DISC)

See OPTICAL STORAGE.

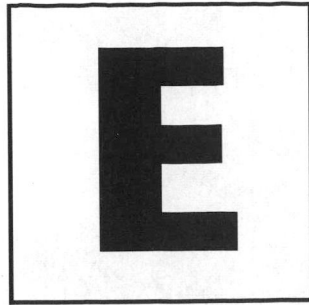

E-COMMERCE

See ELECTRONIC COMMERCE.

E-MAIL or EMAIL

See ELECTRONIC MAIL.

ECHOING

For articles on related subjects *see* DATA COMMUNICATIONS; and MODEM.

In computing, an *echo* is a character or message retransmitted by the recipient fast enough to give assurance to the sender that it was received correctly. When communicating over phone lines to a distant computer using a local computer terminal, echoed characters that appear on the screen as you type may be merely those that correspond to the keys struck or they may correspond to a round trip that the characters make: keyboard over the phone to the distant computer that sends them back over the transmission line to the screen. The truly echoed character gives assurance of accurate receipt; the character that appears because of a local path from keyboard to screen does not. When using a simplex (one-way) line such as might be attached to a teletype, echoing is not an issue. When using a half-duplex line (two-way transmission, but only one way at a time), true echoing can be done only at great loss of speed. With a full-duplex line (simultaneous transmission in both directions), echoing can be done very efficiently because the echo of one character can cross the transmission of the next without inhibiting the fundamental data transmission rate of the communications channel (*q.v.*) being used.

There is also a software meaning of echo. When input is supplied to a running program by typing it at an interactive terminal, it will show on the screen, but not on whatever printed output results from the computation being done. To be sure that printed output represents the answers to the correct problem, programmers may include in their programs explicit write statements that "echo" input to the output file as soon as it is received. The echo may be a literal image of the incoming data, or it may be presented more usefully in labeled form. A fragment of Pascal code that illustrates the latter usage might be:

```
write('Enter value of radius: ');
                        {Ask for input}
readln(radius);        {Read input value}
writeln('radius = ', radius);
                        {Echo the input}
```

Edwin D. Reilly

ECKERT, J. PRESPER

For articles on related subjects *see* DIGITAL COMPUTERS, HISTORY OF: EARLY; ENIAC; MAUCHLY, JOHN W.; and UNIVAC I.

J. Presper Eckert, co-inventor of ENIAC, was born in 1919 in Philadelphia. He received a Bachelor of Science

Figure 1. J. Presper Eckert (courtesy of the Collections of Archives and Records Center, The University of Pennsylvania).

degree in electrical engineering from the University of Pennsylvania's Moore School of Electrical Engineering in 1941, and his Master's degree under a graduate fellowship from the Moore School in 1943.

Eckert collaborated with John W. Mauchly of the Moore School's staff on developing ENIAC (Electrical Numerical Integrator and Computer) for US Army Ordnance between 1943 and 1946. This was the world's first all-electronic general-purpose digital computer, and could perform 5,000 additions or subtractions per second. Its development launched the computer industry as we know it today.

In 1947, Eckert and Mauchly incorporated their venture as the Eckert–Mauchly Computer Corporation. They developed BINAC, the first electronic and fully self-checking computer, in 1949. Their next project, UNIVAC (Universal Automatic Computer), was well under way when Remington Rand acquired the Eckert–Mauchly firm in 1950.

Eckert became director of engineering for Remington Rand's Eckert–Mauchly Division which completed UNIVAC I. He became vice-president and director of research in 1955, vice-president and director of commercial engineering in 1957, vice-president and executive assistant to the general manager in 1959, and vice-president and technical advisor to the president of Sperry-Rand, Univac division, in 1963. He retired in 1989.

Eckert received an honorary degree of Doctor of Science in Engineering from the University of Pennsylvania in 1964. In 1969, he was awarded the National Medal of Science, the USA's highest award for distinguished achievement in science, mathematics, and engineering.

A Fellow of the Institute of Electrical and Electronics Engineers and a member of the National Academy of Engineering, Eckert is listed as the inventor or co-inventor on 87 patents. He died in his home town in 1995.

Bibliography

1996. Eckstein, P. "J. Presper Eckert," *Annals of the History of Computing*, *18*, *1*, 25–44.

Michael M. Maynard

ECKERT, WALLACE J.

For articles on related subjects *see* DIGITAL COMPUTERS, HISTORY OF: EARLY; and IBM CORPORATION.

Wallace John Eckert (Fig. 1) was born in Pittsburgh, PA, 19 June 1902 (d. Englewood, NJ, 24 August 1971). Much of the credit for the introduction of machine computation into astronomy belongs to him. The significance of the computer's impact on astronomy is comparable to that of the introduction and use of the telescope and photography.

Eckert was raised on a farm in Albion, PA, the second of four boys born to John and Anna (Heil) Eckert. He received his A.B. degree from Oberlin College in 1925 and his M.A. from Amherst in 1926. In 1931, he was awarded his Ph.D. in astronomy by Yale University. He joined the Columbia University Department of Astronomy as an assistant instructor in 1926.

In 1928, Professor Ben Wood formed the Columbia University Statistical Bureau using punched-card equipment donated by Thomas Watson, Sr. (*q.v.*), of IBM. It was here that Eckert was first exposed to the possibility of using machines to facilitate computation. From 1929 to 1933, he used the machines in Prof. Wood's laboratory for the interpolation of astronomical data, the reduction of observational data, and the numerical solution of planetary equations. In 1933, with the encouragement of Ben Wood, he convinced Watson to install punched-card equipment and a control unit for astronomical calculations. This led to the formation of the T. J. Watson Astronomical Computing Bureau, jointly operated by Columbia, IBM, and the American Astronomical Society (1937–1945). During this period he published his landmark work (1940), *Punched Card Methods in Scientific Computation.*

He was director of the US Nautical Almanac Office in Washington, DC, from 1940 to 1945. He introduced machine methods of data handling in the Naval Observatory as well as the Almanac Office. During

Figure. 1. Wallace J. Eckert (photo courtesy of IBM Corporation).

the war he designed the "American Air Almanac," a great navigational aid that is still in use with only minor modifications.

In 1945 he was appointed head of IBM's Pure Science Department and became director of the Watson Scientific Computing Laboratory. The Laboratory not only performed needed computations, but also provided a training ground in machine computation for more than a thousand scientists in crystallography, geology, chemistry, statistics, optics, and solid-state physics, as well as astronomy.

Eckert was instrumental in the construction of IBM's Selective Sequence Electronic Calculator (SSEC, 1949) and the Naval Ordnance Research Calculator (NORC, 1954 (*q.v.*)). Using the SSEC, Eckert, Dirk Brouwer of Yale, and G. M. Clemence (1951) of the US Naval Observatory computed the precise positions of Jupiter, Saturn, Uranus, Neptune, and Pluto for the period 1653–2060. This work still serves as the Ephemeris predictions for these planets.

Eckert's most important purely astronomical contributions were in relation to the Moon's orbital motion. This and later work in the area of lunar coordinates and orbital parameters (1966) provided the operational basis for NASA's Surveyor, Lunar Orbiter, and Apollo projects.

He retired from IBM in 1967 and as Professor of Celestial Mechanics at Columbia in 1970.

Bibliography

Anon. "Dr. Wallace J. Eckert" (publications by W. J. Eckert, 38 items), and "Outstanding Contribution Award Report" (n.d.), IBM Archives.

1951. Eckert, W. J., Brouwer, D., and Clemence, G. M. "Coordinates of the Five Outer Planets, 1653–2060," *Astronomical Papers*, NORC **12**. Washington, DC: US Government Printing Office.

1966. Eckert, W. J., Walker, M. J., and Eckert, D. "Transformations of the Lunar Coordinates and Orbital Parameters," *Astronomical Journal*, **71** (June), 314–332.

1971. Ashbrook, J. "A Great American Astronomer," *Sky and Telescope*, **42**, *4* (October), 207.

1971. Brennan, J. F. "The IBM Watson Laboratory at Columbia University: A History," Armonk, NY: IBM.

1984. Eckert, W. J. *Punched-Card Methods in Scientific Computation.* New York: Columbia University Press. CBI Reprint Series #5. Introduction by John McPherson. Cambridge, MA: MIT Press. (Originally published by Columbia University Press, 1970.)

Henry S. Tropp

EDITOR

See TEXT EDITING SYSTEMS; and WORD PROCESSING.

EDSAC

For articles on related subjects *see* DIGITAL COMPUTERS, HISTORY OF: EARLY and ORIGINS; EDVAC; ENIAC; ULTRASONIC MEMORY; and WILKES, MAURICE V.

The EDSAC (Electronic Delay Storage Automatic Calculator) was built in England during the late 1940s at the Mathematical Laboratory of the University of Cambridge. It was designed according to the principles expounded by J. Presper Eckert, John W. Mauchly, and others at the summer school held in 1946 at the Moore School of Electrical Engineering in Philadelphia, and which the author of this article was privileged to attend. The objectives from the beginning were (1) to show that a binary stored-program computer could be constructed and operated; (2) to develop programming techniques, even then seen to be a subject of more than trivial content; and (3) to apply the techniques developed in a variety of application fields.

In order to accelerate the attainment of the first objective, it was decided to ease the circuit design problems by choosing a conservative pulse repetition frequency (500 kHz compared with 1 MHz used in most contemporaneous projects) and to bias the logical design in the direction of simplicity rather than speed. This policy was successful, and by May 1949 the project had reached the stage at which the development of programming techniques and the running of practical programs could begin.

The EDSAC (Fig. 1) was a serial binary computer with an ultrasonic memory. The mercury tanks used for

Figure 1. The EDSAC being constructed by Wilkes and his team. (Courtesy of the National Archive on the History of Computing, University of Manchester.)

the main memory were about 1.5 meters long and were built in batteries of 16 tanks. Two batteries were provided. A battery, with the associated circuits, could store 256 numbers of 35 binary digits each, one being a sign digit. An instruction occupied a half-word of 17 bits, and it was also possible to use half-words for short numbers. Numbering of the storage locations was in terms of half-words, not full words. The instruction set (*q.v.*) was of the single-address variety, and there were 17 instructions. Multiplication was included, but not division. Input and output were by means of five-channel punched-paper tape. The input and output orders provided for the transfer of five binary digits from the tape to the memory, and vice versa.

Operation of the machine could not start until a short standard sequence, known as the *initial orders*, had been transferred into the ultrasonic memory from a mechanical read-only memory (*q.v.*) formed from a set of rotary telephone switches. The space that the initial orders occupied in the memory could be reused when they were no longer required for reading the input tape. The initial orders determined the way in

which the instructions were punched on the paper tape, and this was quite an advance for the period.

One row of holes, interpreted as a letter, indicated the function; this was followed by the address in decimal form, with leading zeros omitted and terminated by a code letter. In the first set of initial orders to be used, this code letter merely determined whether the address referred to a short or a long location; before the end of 1950, however, these initial orders had been replaced by a more elaborate set in which the terminating characters were used to provide relocation facilities for blocks of instructions or data punched on the tape.

The EDSAC did its first calculation on 6 May 1949, and ran until 1958, when it was finally switched off.

Bibliography

1950. Wilkes, M. V. ''The EDSAC (Electronic Delay Storage Automatic Calculator),'' *MTAC*, **4**, 61.
1956. Wilkes, M.V. *Automatic Digital Computers*. London: Methuen; New York: John Wiley.

1980. Lavington, S. *Early British Computers*. Manchester: Manchester University Press.

Website

EDSAC 99. `http://www.cl.cam.ac.uk/UoCCL/misc/EDSAC99`.

Maurice V. Wilkes

EDUCATION IN COMPUTER ENGINEERING

For articles on related subjects *see* COMPUTER ENGINEERING; COMPUTER SCIENCE—PH.D. STATISTICS; and EDUCATION IN COMPUTER SCIENCE.

A *computer engineering education* is the academic preparation provided to students to give them a broad and well-integrated background in the concepts and methodologies that are needed for the analysis, design, and use of information processing systems in a world of rapidly changing technology. Such education differs from a computer science education (when it is important to make the distinction between the two) in the sense that science is different from engineering, and relevant education should reflect the preparation required to prepare the student for work in the corresponding discipline. Nominally, science is more concerned with understanding underlying principles, and engineering is more concerned with the cost-effective harnessing of those principles. As such, a computer engineering education both emphasizes the basic mathematical sciences (often more than computer science programs do) and insists on training and experience in design.

Like all engineering disciplines, an education in computer engineering requires the following three critical ingredients:

1. A foundation in engineering analysis that enables the graduate to analyze trade-offs and make design choices.

2. A foundation in mathematics and the basic quantitative sciences so that this analysis and the design choices that follow are based on rigorous understanding of fundamentals.

3. Experience in design so that students can practice their craft and develop the experiences associated with good engineering practice.

These three elements of an engineering education all contribute to the preparation of a computer engineer. For the computer engineer, the foundation in engineering analysis includes engineering science courses across the breadth of computer science and engineering. This breadth in engineering and in computer engineering should include engineering science courses outside of computer science and engineering. It also should include a balanced view of hardware, software, and application trade-offs, and the basic modeling courses used to represent the computing process. In addition to breadth, a computer engineering education should include the in-depth study of at least one major area of computer engineering.

The computer engineering student should be prepared in both hardware and software. Laboratory experiences dealing with each should involve problem solving, design, implementation, and documentation. The student should acquire substantive experience with the advanced features of at least one major operating system (*q.v.*). The fact that computer engineers are being prepared for a profession where the base technologies are expected to change dramatically during their professional careers dictates that a computer engineering education should focus on basic engineering sciences.

The second element of a computer engineering education is a foundation in mathematics and the basic sciences. Mathematics preparation should include the calculus through ordinary differential equations, discrete mathematics (*q.v.*), probability and statistics, and linear algebra and matrices or numerical methods. Basic science courses should include both physics and chemistry.

The third and final element of a computer engineering education is design experience. Because the practice of computer engineering involves examining issues, evaluating alternatives, and making trade-offs, a critical component of a computer engineering education is experience in design. Preparation for doing design must be nurtured throughout a student's education. For example, a student should learn the tools of design early in the curriculum; open-ended problems should be presented throughout the program, increasing in complexity as the student matures; and documentation standards should be emphasized throughout the course of study. Finally, a comprehensive design experience should come sufficiently late in the student's program of studies when the student has acquired the tools to understand the underlying issues and rigorously evaluate the alternatives. The design problem should not have a preformulated answer, nor is the answer usually precise. The experience must provide the opportunity for the student to do individual work and have that work carefully evaluated.

The Accreditation Board for Engineering and Technology (ABET) has expressed concern that engineering education should pay attention to ethical issues as well as technical issues. Even in matters so central to engineering as design, one must consider the social, economic, and ethical context of the design problem. Thus, the design experience should give a student occasion to deliberate on these aspects of a problem in addition to studying the trade-offs in the technical aspects of a problem.

ABET, a federation of 26 engineering societies, is responsible for the accreditation of engineering programs in the USA. Many of the specific educational guidelines identified in this article are taken from ABET guidelines for accreditation. ABET has recently introduced new accreditation guidelines, Criteria 2000. They do not change the fundamental requirements of an engineering education, but focus on assessing the outcomes of engineering programs more than on specifications of content. In addition, the IEEE Computer Society (*q.v.*) and the ACM (Association for Computing Machinery—*q.v.*) have initiated a Task Force to develop a proposal for both computer engineering and computer science curricula for the year 2001.

Bibliography

1990. Parnas, D. "Education for Computing Professionals," *IEEE Computer*, **23**, *1* (January), 17–22.
1992. Denning, P. "Educating a New Engineer," *Comm. of the ACM*, **35**, *12* (December), 82–97.

Yale Patt

EDUCATION IN COMPUTER SCIENCE

For articles on related subjects *see* COMPUTER LITERACY; COMPUTER SCIENCE; COMPUTER SCIENCE—PH.D. STATISTICS; and EDUCATION IN COMPUTER ENGINEERING.

See also APPENDIX IV

UNITED STATES

Higher Education Programs: History

Academic programs in computing at institutions of higher education began in the mid-1950s under pressure from early users of computing equipment, or from computing center staff deluged with questions about the use of these new devices. Initially, the "educational program" might have consisted only of a short noncredit course given by the computing center staff. Such a course mainly emphasized hardware characteristics, binary arithmetic, and how to program a problem for computer solution (usually in machine or assembly language—*see* MACHINE AND ASSEMBLY LANGUAGE PROGRAMMING). At times, some of the instructional material was absorbed into an existing course in mathematics or engineering, generally in three or four lectures. However, with the rapid growth of broadly-based university computing installations during the 1960–1965

period, and with the growth of an organized body of knowledge, it became necessary to establish more formal educational programs in computing.

One of the most influential early efforts took place at the University of Michigan, and subsequently at the University of Houston, during the period 1959–1962. These efforts, conducted jointly by the Computing Center and the College of Engineering, were aimed less at establishing computer science as a distinct academic discipline than at the "Use of Computers in Engineering Education" (University of Michigan Study, 1960 and 1961, and University of Houston Study, 1962). At approximately the same time, Stanford University, through the joint efforts of its computing center and department of mathematics, was establishing the discipline of computer science as an optional field of study in the department of mathematics.

These early efforts were capped by the creation of separate departments of computer science. In 1962, Stanford University established a Department of Computer Science in the School of Humanities and Sciences; in the same year, Purdue University created a Department of Computer Science in the Division of Mathematical Sciences. In each case, the bond between the service and academic functions of computing was evident from the fact that one person was both director of the computing center and chairman of the department (George Forsythe at Stanford, Sam Conte at Purdue); this pattern was followed subsequently by other universities. Another pattern established by Stanford and Purdue was that of initially offering only graduate programs in computer science at the master's and doctorate levels. The thinking at the time was that there could be no well-defined undergraduate program in computer science, and that specialization in computing should start only at the graduate level. (It also reflected the fact that few professors were qualified to teach computing at the time.)

By the mid-1960s, developments in computer science education were proceeding apace. Governmental and quasi-governmental reports made recommendations that spurred the growth of computer science academic programs. Two were of particular importance. The National Academy of Sciences report on "Digital Computer Needs in Universities and Colleges" (Rosser *et al.*, 1966) recommended, among other things, that campuses should "increase as rapidly as possible the number of specialists trained annually as computer specialists and the support of pioneering research into computer systems, computer languages, and specialized equipment." The President's Science Advisory Committee report on "Computers in Higher Education" (Pierce *et al.*, 1967) recommended that "the Federal Government expand its support of both research and education in computer sciences." These reports helped obtain government and university support for the new discipline.

During the same period, university-sponsored conferences produced reports and books, such as "University Education in Computing Science" (Finerman, 1968), indicating that computer science was truly emerging as an academic discipline and not a short-lived curiosity. Indeed, the "intellectual respectability" of computer science was a controversial issue in the 1960s. Many educators argued that the computer was just a tool, and that a body of study based upon a tool was not a proper academic discipline; others took the position that computer science was not a coherent discipline but rather a collection of bits and pieces from other disciplines; still others felt that computers were not that important and were not proper objects of academic interest. By and large, however, this skepticism was short-lived.

At the same time, computing, mathematics, and engineering professional societies sponsored studies of the curricular effects of the new discipline. Reports of the Mathematical Association of America (Committee on the Undergraduate Program in Mathematics) and the Commission on Engineering Education (Cosine Committee) recommended changes in existing academic programs to insure that students in mathematics and engineering received adequate preparation in computing. This preparation was necessitated by the fact that a growing number of mathematics and engineering majors found themselves working in the computing field soon after graduation. The studies of the Association for Computing Machinery (ACM—*q.v.*) had the most widespread effect. ACM chartered a Curriculum Committee on Computer Science to recommend necessary academic programs. The subsequent influential report of the Committee, "Curriculum 68" (Atchison *et al.*, 1968), defined for the first time the scope and content of a recommended undergraduate program in computer science. Subsequently, the Committee considerably revised and updated the recommended undergraduate program in its report, "Curriculum 78" (Austing *et al.*, 1979). ACM also chartered a Curriculum Committee on Computer Education for Management. This Committee issued two principal reports on undergraduate and on graduate programs in information systems.

Separately, the Institute of Electrical and Electronic Engineers Computer Society (IEEE-CS—*q.v.*) chartered a Model Curricula Subcommittee of the Education Committee, which published guidelines and curricula for programs of computer science and engineering in 1977 and 1983 (Cain, 1977; *IEEE Computer Society Reports*, 1983). The ACM and IEEE also cooperated in a joint curricula task force that presented its first report in 1989 (Denning *et al.*, 1989) and its final curricula recommendations in 1991 (Tucker *et al.*, 1991).

The two societies joined to publish accreditation guidelines in 1983 (Mulder and Dalphin, 1984) and to form a Computer Science Accreditation Commission (CSAC) of the Computing Sciences Accreditation Board (CSAB) in 1984. CSAC was later absorbed by the Accreditation Board for Engineering and Technology (ABET). As of late 1999, 155 programs in computer science had been accredited; for more information, contact CSAC at 111 Market Place, Suite 1050, Baltimore, MD 21202-4012 (email: csac@abet.org).

ACM also chartered Curriculum Committees for master's level programs in computer science (Magel *et al.*, 1981), undergraduate and graduate degree programs in information systems (Nunamaker *et al.*, 1982; Davis *et al.*, 1997), and related computer science programs in vocational-technical schools, community and junior colleges, and health computing (ACM, 1983). ACM has also published curricular recommendations for secondary school programs in computer science and for teacher certification (ACM, 1985; ACM, 1997) (*see also* http://www.acm.org/education/curricula.html).

The effect of all these studies, conferences, and reports was a proliferation of academic programs in computer science and engineering. From the early graduate programs have come myriad graduate and undergraduate programs at two-year colleges (associate's degree), four-year colleges (bachelor's), five-year colleges (bachelor's and master's), and universities (bachelor's, master's, and doctoral); these programs are in addition to the numerous computing service courses available to students majoring in other disciplines. Furthermore, there are a multitude of vocational courses given by technical schools. More recently, computing courses have been introduced into the educational programs of most secondary schools.

University Educational Programs

Higher education programs in computing go by different names, such as computer science, computer engineering, computer science and engineering, information science, data processing, and information systems. Each name has also come to denote a particular emphasis and origin. Thus, *computer science* usually indicates a mathematical and scientific emphasis generally found at universities; *information systems* usually indicates computing applied to organizational systems generally related to the business administration programs at universities; and *data processing*

Table 1. Earned degrees in computer and information sciences[1] conferred by institutions of higher education, by level of degree and gender of student: 1970–1971 to 1996–1997.

Year	Bachelor's degrees			Master's degrees			Doctoral degrees		
	Total	Men	Women	Total	Men	Women	Total	Men	Women
1970–1971	2,388	2,064	324	1,588	1,424	164	128	125	3
1971–1972	3,402	2,941	461	1,977	1,752	225	167	155	12
1972–1973	4,304	3,664	640	2,113	1,888	225	196	181	15
1973–1974	4,756	3,976	780	2,276	1,983	293	198	189	9
1974–1975	5,033	4,080	953	2,299	1,961	338	213	199	14
1975–1976	5,652	4,534	1,118	2,603	2,226	377	244	221	23
1976–1977	6,407	4,876	1,531	2,798	2,332	466	216	197	19
1977–1978	7,201	5,349	1,852	3,038	2,471	567	196	181	15
1978–1979	8,719	6,272	2,447	3,055	2,480	575	236	206	30
1979–1980	11,154	7,782	3,372	3,647	2,883	764	240	213	27
1980–1981	15,121	10,202	4,919	4,218	3,247	971	252	227	25
1981–1982	20,267	13,218	7,049	4,935	3,625	1,310	251	230	21
1982–1983	24,510	15,606	8,904	5,321	3,813	1,508	262	228	34
1983–1984	32,172	20,246	11,926	6,190	4,379	1,811	251	225	26
1984–1985	38,878	24,579	14,299	7,101	5,064	2,037	248	223	25
1985–1986	41,889	26,923	14,966	8,070	5,658	2,412	344	299	45
1986–1987	39,664	25,929	13,735	8,491	5,995	2,496	374	322	52
1987–1988	34,548	23,347	11,201	9,166	6,702	2,464	428	380	48
1988–1989	30,637	21,221	9,416	9,392	6,769	2,623	538	457	81
1989–1990	27,257	19,117	8,140	9,677	6,960	2,717	627	534	93
1990–1991	25,083	17,726	7,357	9,324	6,563	2,761	676	584	92
1991–1992	24,557	17,510	7,047	9,530	6,884	2,646	772	669	103
1992–1993	24,200	17,403	6,797	10,163	7,410	2,753	805	689	116
1993–1994	24,200	17,317	6,883	10,416	7,724	2,692	810	685	125
1994–1995	24,404	17,463	6,941	10,326	7,627	2,699	884	723	161
1995–1996	24,098	17,468	6,630	10,151	7,444	2,707	867	741	126
1996–1997	26,768	18,037	8,731	10,098	7,248	2,850	857	721	136

[1] Includes degrees in computer and information sciences, general; information sciences and systems; data processing; computer programming; systems analysis; and other information sciences. The data on Ph.D.s differs somewhat from that in the article COMPUTER SCIENCE—PH.D. STATISTICS because the data in that article comes from a different source (*see* Kozen and Morris, 1999) than the data above.

Source: US Department of Education, National Center for Educational Statistics.

usually indicates computing applied to administrative and commercial applications generally taught at two-year colleges. The programs may be housed in a department of computer science, computer engineering, computer science and engineering, computer and information science, or data processing, or given as an option in mathematics, engineering, or business administration.

Table 1 shows the number of higher-level degrees (bachelor's and beyond) awarded in C&IS from 1970 to 1997. Although the number of master's and doctor's degrees has continually increased during this period, the number of bachelor's degrees peaked in 1985–1986 at almost 42,000 and then declined rapidly to just over 24,000 in 1992–1996 but increased to almost 27,000 in 1997. Although precise data after 1997 is not yet available, it is clear from reports from colleges and universities that the number of bachelor's degrees is rapidly increasing once again.

The growth of computer science students at institutions of higher education generally parallels corresponding growth in demand in industry. The demand for computer science graduates at all levels declined from the late 1980s to the early 1990s but in the late 1990s demand surged to an all-time high, largely spurred by the growth of the Internet (*q.v.*).

The demand for two-year college graduates is more limited and there is even less demand for vocational school and high school graduates to fill professional positions, although many technician positions are available, especially for graduates with associate's degrees. The bachelor's (and, increasingly, the master's) degree has rapidly become the entry-level degree for suitable professional positions in industry. In recent years, new Ph.D. graduates been actively recruited by universities, research organizations, and manufacturers of computing equipment.

Non-University Educational Programs

Computer science educational programs originated at universities and spread downward, from graduate to undergraduate to two-year colleges and then to high schools. Although subsequent sections of this article deal almost exclusively with university and college programs (undergraduate and graduate), in this section, we briefly discuss other educational programs in computing, specifically those offered by private technical schools or institutes and by two-year colleges. The latter are in some ways similar to those at technical schools and in other ways different, since they may offer a preparation for four-year undergraduate work.

TECHNICAL SCHOOL PROGRAMS

Private schools for training technicians have been operating for many years. In many fields, they serve a worthwhile function by preparing people for jobs as secretaries, dental technicians, TV repairers, and the like. When the computing industry started expanding rapidly, a large number of private schools began offering educational programs in computing. There are many jobs in industry for which training as a technician is worthwhile, and the technical school graduate should be qualified to assume such jobs.

Unfortunately, some computing institutes intimate that their training will prepare students for well paying professional jobs in the computing industry, but their graduates often discover too late that most such positions are filled by college graduates. The professional career path in computing, as in most other fields, requires a college education. Nevertheless, because of the severe shortages of the late 1990s, many college graduates from disciplines other than computer science are finding that they can get good entry-level jobs after intensive training at a technical institute.

COMMUNITY COLLEGE PROGRAMS

Two-year community (or junior) colleges have grown rapidly in recent years, both in quantity and in scope of offerings. Forty years ago, the community college was rather rare, usually specializing in such areas as agriculture, forestry, and mining. Today, the community college has become as broadly based and diversified as its university cousin.

The community college serves a twofold purpose. One is to train the student for a position as a technician. For these graduates, the two-year associate's degree is proof of better standards than those usually maintained by a technical school; the degree is also proof of a more well-rounded education. The second purpose of the community college is to serve as a bridge between high school and the four-year college or university course, especially for those students uncertain of their desire or ability to continue with higher education. For these students, the associate's degree may be an intermediate step on the way to a bachelor's degree.

Students terminating after two years and entering industry often suffer the same identity problem as do technical school graduates. Indeed, they are more than technicians, but not the same as college graduates. More often than not, the career paths open to them are technician-oriented. On the other hand, graduates wishing to continue toward a bachelor's degree sometimes find the transition quite difficult. Community college standards are not always the same as university standards; community college courses are not always identical or even similar to corresponding courses at the university.

Some of these difficulties are being addressed; for example, community colleges and universities have been cooperating in facilitating the transfer process by making courses more compatible. Transfer still remains a problem, however, as does the technician versus professional issue. Increasingly, as the "computer profession" evolves and becomes better defined, the broader educational scope of a bachelor's degree becomes a prerequisite for a professional career.

We will not separately detail the usual curricula at two-year colleges. In some cases, these are similar to freshman and sophomore level computing courses at universities. In other cases, the differences are more visible. By and large, university programs are more theoretically oriented, emphasizing both the theoretical underpinnings of computing and scientific or engineering applications. Two-year college programs tend to emphasize the practical aspects and the business applications of computing. The four-year university program allows more time to take courses unrelated to computing, mathematics, and associated technical disciplines. Because of their shorter time span, community college programs are more intensely oriented to courses in programming, business mathematics, accounting, and other technical areas. Accordingly, graduates of community colleges do not possess the broader educational background of graduates of four-year programs.

SECONDARY SCHOOL PROGRAMS

Although ACM has published a complete curriculum for secondary schools (ACM, 1997), most secondary schools do not have the staff or facilities to offer the complete curriculum. However, even before high school some schools offer education in the use of word processing (q.v.), the Internet (q.v.), and spreadsheets (q.v.), as well as courses in Logo (q.v.) and Basic (q.v.). Most high schools offer courses in one or more programming languages such as Basic, Visual Basic, Pascal (q.v.), C (q.v.), and C++ (q.v.). Some high schools offer an advanced placement course using C++ based on the curriculum approved by the

College Board Advanced Placement Committee (*see* http://www.collegeboard.org).

The Undergraduate Curriculum

The undergraduate program varies from university to university, depending upon such factors as the resources available, the amount of specialization deemed useful, and the interests of the faculty. Even the content of specific courses is, in some cases, quite variable. As noted earlier, the most comprehensive attempts made to date in defining the scope and content of an undergraduate program in computer science have been the works of the ACM Curriculum Committee, *Curriculum 68*, *Curriculum 78*, and *Computing Curricula 1991—Report of the Joint (ACM/IEEE) Curriculum Task Force*. In particular, the 1968 report had a profound effect on shaping the direction of education in the then still emerging discipline of computer science.

The program prescribed in *Curriculum 68* reflected the viewpoint of those advocating a strong specialization in computing at the undergraduate level; as such, it follows the traditional pattern of most scientific and engineering undergraduate programs. The large component of computer and mathematics courses recommended (between one-half and two-thirds of the total undergraduate course load) plus technical electives in computer-related disciplines, leaves little room for non-technical subjects in the humanities and the social sciences within the normal four-year program.

Curriculum 78 revised the recommendations for the undergraduate program, reflecting the significant developments that had occurred within computer science education during the intervening decade. *Curriculum 78* provides somewhat greater flexibility than *Curriculum 68* in the content of courses, emphasizing the objectives of the undergraduate program and the subject matter to be covered. Aside from the proposed curriculum itself, the report discusses such topics as service courses, continuing education, computing facilities, and staff.

Curriculum 78 proposed the following requirements for computer science majors:

◆ a core of eight computer courses which would be taken by all majors

◆ four elective courses chosen from a group of 10 advanced courses described in the report

◆ five mathematics courses (calculus, mathematical analysis 1 and 2, linear algebra, discrete structures, probability and statistics).

Curriculum 78 has been criticized because of its reduced number of mathematics courses and the fact that those mathematics courses that are required are not prerequisite to the computer courses—and therefore are not as integral a part of the prerequisite structure as in *Curriculum 68* (see, for example, Ralston and Shaw, 1980).

In 1984, an ACM Task Force revised the first two courses in the curriculum, CS1 and CS2, providing an increased emphasis on problem solving, structured design, and software engineering (*q.v.*) (Koffman *et al.*, 1984, 1985). Subsequently, a model curriculum for a liberal arts bachelor's degree in computer science was published (Gibbs and Tucker, 1986) that consists of three introductory courses (CS1, CS2, and discrete mathematics) followed by four core courses in computer science.

JOINT CURRICULUM TASK FORCE (ACM AND IEEE)

In the spring of 1988, ACM and the IEEE Computer Society formed a joint curriculum task force whose charter was to present recommendations for the design and implementation of undergraduate curricula in the discipline of computing. A motivation for this effort was the recognition that, despite strong and fundamental differences among institutions that house the departments offering undergraduate programs, these departments share a substantial curriculum in common. Any curriculum recommendations that attempt to speak for the entire discipline must not only identify the shared subject matter, but also suggest ways in which it can serve as the basis for building undergraduate programs in different kinds of institutions.

The task force proceeded in two stages. The first stage report (Denning *et al.*, 1989) focused on defining the field of computer science, proposing a teaching paradigm for computer science that conforms to traditional scientific standards, and giving an example of a three-semester introductory course sequence based on this model and the definition of the field. The report outlines nine fundamental areas of computer science (since expanded to 12 processes (*see* COMPUTER SCIENCE) and the three basic processes. The nine areas were:

◆ Algorithms and data structures

◆ Architecture

◆ Artificial intelligence and robotics

◆ Database and information retrieval

◆ Human–computer communication

◆ Numerical and symbolic computation

◆ Operating systems

◆ Programming languages

◆ Software methodology and engineering

The three basic processes and their elements (in parentheses) are:

◆ Theory (definitions and axioms, theorems, proofs, interpretation of results)

◆ Abstraction (data collection and hypothesis formation, modeling and prediction, design of experiments, analysis of results)

◆ Design (requirements, specification, design and implementation, testing and analysis)

The second stage report (Tucker *et al.*, 1991) discusses how to develop a curriculum based on the model of computer science developed in the first stage. It contains the following parts:

◆ A collection of 55 subject matter modules called knowledge units that comprise the common requirements for all undergraduate programs in the field of computing, thereby insuring breadth of study. Each knowledge unit contains a list of lecture topics, relations to other knowledge units, recommended hours of coverage, and suggested laboratories.

◆ A collection of advanced and supplementary curriculum material that provides depth of study in several of the subjects.

◆ A list of 12 recurring concepts that occur throughout the discipline.

Besides the computing requirements, the report discusses requirements in science and mathematics. The mathematics requirements are a minimum of the equivalent of one-half academic year of mathematics courses including discrete mathematics, calculus, and at least one of the following subjects: probability, linear algebra, advanced discrete mathematics, and mathematical logic.

Rather than provide a single, definitive curriculum for all programs in computing, the report discusses how to develop curricula which incorporate all the components above and how to map the knowledge units into courses. It also describes the role of laboratories in the curriculum. The appendix to the report describes eight sample curricula which differ in their emphasis and assumed institutional constraints.

A major contribution of this report was to show that there are different approaches to computer science education and that there are many good ways of packaging topics. Also it showed that there are many

topics, such as social and professional issues, that are essential components of a computing education.

INFORMATION SYSTEMS CURRICULA

The ACM also chartered a curriculum committee on computer education for management that has developed curricula for undergraduate and graduate programs in information systems (*q.v.*). Students in these programs learn how to apply computer technology to meet the information needs of an organization. The first graduate report was published in 1972 (Ashenhurst, 1972), and the first undergraduate report was published in 1973 (Couger, 1973).

This committee was superseded by a curriculum committee on information systems that published its recommendations in the report *Information Systems Curriculum Recommendations for the 80s: Undergraduate and Graduate Programs* (Nunamaker *et al.*, 1982). The committee updated the curriculum and its requirements, stressing the inclusion of the American Assembly of Collegiate Schools of Business common body of knowledge as a major component of the program and introducing a management information systems (MIS—*q.v.*) policy course as a capstone to the program. There are eight required information systems courses for the undergraduate student, and 10 for the graduate student.

Table 2. Presentation areas and codes for IS '97.

Levels	Presentation areas	Courses
1—General	IS Fundamentals	• Fundamentals of IS • Personal productivity with IS technology
	Information Systems Theory and Practice	• Information Systems Theory and Practice
2—Major and Minor	Information Technology	• Information Technology Hardware and Software • Programming, Data, File, and Object Structures • Networks and Telecommunications
	Information Systems Development	• Analysis and Logical Design
3—Major		• Physical Design and Implementation with a DBMS • Physical Design and Implementation with a Programming Environment
	Information System Development and Management Processes	• Project Management and Practice

The most recently published information systems curriculum is *IS '97* (Davis *et al.*, 1997). The architecture of the information systems curriculum at the highest level consists of five curriculum presentation areas: IS fundamentals; information systems theory and practice; information technology (*q.v.*); information systems development; and information systems deployment and management processes. These five presentation areas consist of 10 courses (Table 2). The curriculum gives course descriptions and resource recommendations for the IS degree program. The details in the appendices provide the basis for customizing courses while maintaining the coverage defined by the curriculum.

COURSES FOR NON-MAJORS

Many undergraduate courses in computer science attract not only the majors in computer science (or information systems) but also students majoring in other disciplines who complete a minor in computer science. For those who do less, the introductory course in programming is still a popular option, especially for students majoring in mathematics, science, or engineering, but the liberal arts or business student will often instead take a course in computer literacy (*q.v.*), computers and society (*see* SOCIETY, COMPUTERS IN), or management information systems (*q.v.*) that emphasizes the development of computer literacy through the use of microcomputer packages rather than through actual computer programming.

Graduate Curricula in Computer Science

Graduate programs in computer science preceded the introduction of undergraduate programs, the earliest programs appearing in the early 1960s. Although concentrating on undergraduate computer science, *Curriculum '68* also provided recommendations for master's programs.

In 1981, the ACM Curriculum Committee on Computer Science published recommendations for master's programs (Magel *et al.*, 1981). This report recognizes the emergence of two kinds of programs with different goals: academic programs designed to prepare students for Ph.D. study, and professional programs designed to prepare students for business and industry. However, the committee rejected the idea of a purely terminal program and believes that all programs should make it possible for students to study beyond the master's level.

Although early master's programs in computer science did not require a bachelor's degree in computer science or even substantial prior study in the field, students entering a master's program now should have a B.S. in computer science or at least the equivalent of the material included in CS1 through CS8 of *Curriculum '78*, and mathematics through calculus, linear algebra, discrete structures, and one course in probability and statistics. Maturity in both abstract reasoning and the use of models, as well as one or more years of practical experience in computer science, are desirable.

According to this report, the master's program should provide both breadth in several areas and depth in a few. In addition, it should allow a degree of flexibility to address individual needs. The typical program will consist of 30 to 36 semester hours of courses in programming languages; operating systems and computer architecture; theoretical computer science; and data and file structures. The report lists 30 courses in these four areas, as well as in other areas, with brief descriptions.

Doctoral programs in computer science are intended for students with theoretical or research interests, and most such programs reflect the research interests of the faculty members. In general, courses are similar to those in the master's degree programs. Of course, the doctoral dissertation lies at the heart of the doctoral program. It is the means by which the student demonstrates the capability for making an original contribution to knowledge. This demonstrated capability is the fundamental requirement for the doctorate.

Summary

Formal education in computer science and technology dates back only to the early to mid-1960s. Educational programs originated at universities, resulting from the increasing use of computers by students, faculty, and administrators. Today, most colleges and universities offer academic programs in computing, either as a separate discipline or as an option in a related discipline. As can be expected in such a new field, the educational program still has fuzzy edges; at times, it overlaps applied mathematics, electrical engineering, business administration, and other disciplines. Yet, in just a few decades, it has become a visible and influential area of study. Computer science undergraduate programs also provide a service function by offering courses to the student majoring in other disciplines. Usually, these students require some computer courses so that they can better apply computing methods to their fields. Often, however, these students become computing practitioners after graduation.

In earlier days, entry into the computer field was always through some other discipline; there simply were no academic programs in computing. People learned by doing—by using computers, by programming, and by absorbing knowledge in some informal manner. Today, many enter with a degree in computer science, information systems, or related programs.

Furthermore, in earlier days, a university or college degree was not required for many professional positions in the computing organization (especially administrative data processing). Increasingly, prospective employers today require at least a bachelor's degree (in computing or some other field with concentration in computing) to qualify for a professional position. In many cases, a master's degree in computing is preferable. The graduate with a doctorate in computer science was, until very recently, in short supply, both at universities and at industrial research organizations; this shortage, however, ended temporarily in 1991–1992 and considerable numbers of doctoral degree holders in computer science experienced difficulty in finding positions. However, this situation was rapidly reversed in the late 1990s; the demand for doctoral degree holders now far outstrips the supply.

There is now an increasing awareness that the use of the computer stimulates and modifies intellectual processes, and as a result makes it possible for people to expand their intellectual capabilities. This added dimension—the extension of human intellect—must be part of any program in computer science or information systems.

Bibliography

Early efforts to bring computing methods into engineering education are described in three related volumes:

1960. University of Michigan Study. *Electronic Computers in Engineering Education.* Ann Arbor, MI: University of Michigan.
1961. University of Michigan Study. *Use of Computers in Engineering Education, Second Annual Report.* Ann Arbor, MI: University of Michigan.
1962. University of Houston Study. *Use of Computers in Engineering Education—A Report of the Advanced Science Seminar.* Houston, TX: University of Houston.

There were two principal government-sponsored studies on computing in universities during the mid-1960s. Both gave background information on the use of computers in universities and recommended government financial support for computer education:

1966. Rosser, J. B. *et al. Digital Computer Needs in Universities and Colleges.* Washington, DC: National Academy of Sciences/National Research Council.
1967. Pierce, J. *et al. Computers in Higher Education.* The President's Science Advisory Committee, The White House. Washington, DC: U.S. Government Printing Office.

Undergraduate and graduate programs

1968. Finerman, A. (ed.) *University Education in Computing Science* (ACM Monograph). New York: Academic Press.
1968. Atchison, W. *et al.* "Curriculum '68," *Comm. of the ACM,* **11**, 151–197.
1972. Ashenhurst, R. (ed.) "Curriculum Recommendations for Graduate Professional Programs in Information Systems," *Comm. of the ACM,* **15**, 363–398.
1973. Couger, J. D. (ed.) "Curriculum Recommendations for Undergraduate Programs in Information Systems," *Comm. of the ACM,* **16**, 727–749.

1977. Cain, J. T. (ed.) *A Curriculum in Computer Science and Engineering.* IEEE Publication EHO 119-8.
1979. Austing, R., Barnes, B., Bonnette, D., Engel, G., and Stokes, G. "Curriculum '78," *Comm. of the ACM,* **22**, 147–165.
1981. Magel, K. *et al.* "Recommendations for Master's Level Programs in Computer Science," *Comm of the ACM,* **24**, 115–123.
1981. Nunamaker, J. F. (ed.) "Educational Programs in Information Systems," *Comm. of the ACM,* **24**, 124–133.
1982. Nunamaker, J. F., Jr., Couger, J. D., and Davis, G. B. (eds) "Information Systems Curriculum Recommendations for the 80s: Undergraduate and Graduate Programs," *Comm. of the ACM,* **25**, 781–806.
1983. IEEE Computer Society. *The 1983 Model Program in Computer Science and Engineering.* IEEE Publication EHO 212-1.
1984. Mulder, M., and Dalphin, J. "Computer Science Program Requirements and Accreditation—Interim Report of the ACM/IEEE Joint Task Force," *Comm. of the ACM,* **27**, 330–335.
1984. Koffman, E., Miller, P. L., and Wardle, C. E. "Recommended Curriculum for CS1: 1984," *Comm. of the ACM,* **27**, 998–1001.
1985. Koffman, E., Stemple, D., and Wardle, C. E. "Recommended curriculum for CS2: 1984," *Comm. of the ACM,* **28**, 815–818.
1989. Denning, P. *et al.* "Computing as a Discipline," *Comm. of the ACM,* **32**, 9–23.
1991. Tucker, A. (ed.) *Computing Curricula 1991—Report of the Joint (ACM/JEEE) Curriculum Task Force.* New York: ACM Press; Los Alamitos, CA: IEEE Computer Society Press.
1997. Davis, G. B., Cougar, J. D., Feinstein, D. L., Gorgone, J. T., and Longenecker, H. E., Jr. *IS '97—Model Curriculum and Guidelines for Undergraduate Degree Programs in Information Systems—Report of the Joint (ACM/AIS/AITP) Curriculum Task Force.* New York: ACM Press.

For a bibliography on the subject, see "A Survey of the Literature in Computer Science Education Since Curriculum '68" by Austing, Barnes, and Engel, *Comm. of the ACM,* **20**, 13–21 (January 1977). In addition, the quarterly SIGCSE Bulletin of the ACM Special Interest Group on Computer Science Education contains articles of interest on a continuing basis.

The case for less specialized undergraduate programs in computer science is presented in:

1970. Finerman, A., and Ralston, A. "Undergraduate Programs in Computing Science in the Tradition of Liberal Education," *IFIP World Conference on Computer Education 2,* 195–199.
1986. Gibbs, N., and Tucker, A. "A Model Curriculum for a Liberal Arts Degree in Computer Science," *Comm. of the ACM,* **29**, 202–210.

The mathematical background of the undergraduate student in computer science is examined in:

1980. Ralston, A., and Shaw, M. "Curriculum '78—Is Computer Science Really That Unmathematical?," *Comm. of the ACM,* **23**, 67–70.
1981. Ralston, A. "Computer Science, Mathematics, and the Undergraduate Curricula in Both," *Am. Math. Monthly,* **88**, 472–485.
1984. Ralston, A. "The First Course in Computer Science Needs a Mathematical Corequisite," *Comm. of the ACM,* **27**, 1002–1005.

The ACM has compiled curricular recommendations for a variety of educational programs in computer science. The first item below is a paper. The remaining items are booklets that may be ordered from the ACM Order Department, P.O. Box 64145, Baltimore, MD 21264.

1981. ACM. *Recommendations and Guidelines for an Associate Level Degree Program in Computer Programming* (ed. J. C. Little). ACM Order #201812.

1983. ACM. *ACM Curricula Recommendations for Computer Science*, Volume I. ACM Order #201831.

1983. ACM. *ACM Curricula Recommendations for Information Systems*, Volume II. ACM Order # 201832.

1983. ACM. *ACM Curricula Recommendations for Related Computer Science Programs in Vocational-Technical Schools, Community and Junior Colleges, and Health Computing*, Volume III. ACM Order # 201833.

1985. ACM. *Curricula Recommendations for Secondary Schools and Teacher Certification*. ACM Order #201850.

1997. ACM. *ACM Model High School Computer Science Curriculum*. ACM Order #201930.

There have been several national surveys on computers in higher education and computer manpower conducted by John Hamblen. These report on computing facilities and related expenditures, and computer science and related degree programs. Two of these (which referenced earlier publications) are listed below:

1979. Hamblen, J., and Baird, T. *Fourth Inventory of Computers in Higher Education 1976–1977*. Princeton, NJ: Educom.

1989. Hamblen, J. "Computer Manpower: Through 1984–1985," *Computer Science Education*, **1**, 93–98.

From 1970–1984, Orrin E. Taulbee prepared annual reports giving data on Ph.D. academic programs, which were continued after his death. The latest report is listed below.

1999. Kozen, D., and Morris, J. "1997–1998 CRA Taulbee Survey," *Computing Research News*, **11**, 2 (March), 4–8. *See also* http://www.cra.org/statistics/ for the complete Taulbee Survey data.

Website

http://www.acm.org/education/hscur/index.html.

Elliott B. Koffman and Aaron Finerman

EUROPE

The teaching of computer science and technology has developed in Europe along more or less the same lines as in the USA, and for the same reasons.

Some of the first computers in Europe were installed or built in universities: Cambridge and Manchester in the UK; Göttingen, Munich, and Darmstadt in Germany; Zurich in Switzerland; and Paris, Grenoble, and Toulouse in France. They were used mainly for research purposes in departments of applied mathematics and sometimes in electrical engineering, but these research projects led to the development of academic programs.

By the mid-1950s, optional courses had started at the universities that had their own computers or could afford to rent a computer mainly for students in mathematics or physics. At that time, a curriculum in computer science was usually divided into three parts—numerical analysis, hardware, and programming.

In 1965, there was one university in England offering a B.Sc. degree in computer science, but in Germany, there were no similar degrees before 1970, despite an extensive teaching program at a number of Hochschulen (schools of engineering). In France, degrees in computer science were given by the Institut de Programmation starting in 1964, although the teaching of computer science started much earlier at the Universities of Grenoble (1956), Toulouse (1957), and Paris (1957). It was also in France that computer science and technology acquired the status of an autonomous scientific discipline very early because of the definition of the word "informatique" by the Académie Française in 1966. Except in English-speaking countries where "computer science" is still the normal designation, *informatique* or its variants in other languages is the standard name for the discipline in Europe.

During the 1960s, the main disciplines taught were programming, with advanced courses in compilers (*q.v.*) and operating systems (*q.v.*), theoretical computer science and numerical analysis (*q.v.*), often part of the mathematics department. Europe played an important part in the definition of the language Algol 60 (*q.v.*), its implementation, and its use in teaching. Hardware development generally stayed with electrical engineering departments. There was no attempt to define a "European curriculum" and in each country the national "Computer Science Society" set up a specialized group to discuss the curriculum problem. The discussions in all countries were based on what was known about the developments in US universities, and therefore the ACM "Curriculum 68" had a tremendous influence on European curricula, as did subsequent ACM curricula.

More theoretically minded, Europeans such as Dijkstra and Hoare, had a great influence on the evolution of the disciplines of programming and of software engineering by promoting structured programming (*q.v.*), clean data structures, and stepwise refinement. Wirth's Pascal (*q.v.*) language was widely adopted in computer science teaching.

In 1999, the teaching of informatics in Europe was not very different from computer science instruction in the USA. The titles and contents of the courses are more or less the same, and the differences come mainly from the differences in the administrative organization of education in each country. There was a tendency for computer science studies to take longer in northern European countries than in southern ones, but the 1988 European Union Council Directive on a general system for the recognition of higher education diplomas awarded on completion of professional education and training of at least three years duration has made curricula more uniform, in order to be "eurocompatible."

Most universities offer traditional degrees in computer science (undergraduate, diploma or master's, and Ph.D.) with differences according to the different department titles, including engineering, computer science, information systems, communications, and even multimedia (*q.v.*). Computing, complementary to computer science proper, irrigates all disciplines: a number of degrees in mathematics, chemistry, physics, biology, social sciences, and the humanities have components that include elements of computer science: algorithms, numerical imaging, object-oriented concepts (*q.v.*) and languages, artificial intelligence (*q.v.*), neural networks (*q.v.*), robotics (*q.v.*), systems, and networking.

An interesting development is the emergence of new disciplines in which computer science plays a strong part: bio-informatics, information and communication systems, mathematics and informatics, etc. In view of the lifelong learning paradigm now in favor with the European Commission, versatility appears to be opening more doors than does the discipline of computer science alone.

Bernard Levrat

ASIA

This article covers computer science education in Southeast Asia (Brunei, Burma, Cambodia, Indonesia, Laos, Malaysia, the Philippines, Singapore, Thailand, and Vietnam), India and Japan. Since developments in India and Japan have tended to be like those in the USA and Europe, this article will focus mainly on Southeast Asia.

Universities in Japan and India started installing computers in the 1950s; in Thailand, Singapore, and Malaysia in the 1960s; and in the remaining countries later than this. Indeed, in 1964, only two computers were installed in Thailand, one in Singapore, and none in all the other countries in Southeast Asia. By the 1990s, all universities in all the countries in Southeast Asia had significant numbers of computers as well as access to the Internet (*q.v.*).

Early Southeast Asian educators in computer-related areas were educated mainly in the USA, the UK, Canada, and, later, in Japan before, still later, being educated in their own countries. As in the USA, most of the early computer science programs featured numerical analysis (*q.v.*), both theoretical and applied.

The discipline of computer science, which was established in the USA in the 1960s, had its beginnings in Asia in the 1970s. The first degrees in computer-related subjects were granted in Japan and India in the 1970s, and then later in Thailand, Singapore, Malaysia, the Philippines, and Indonesia.

By the late 1990s, most universities in Japan, India, Indonesia, Malaysia, the Philippines, and Thailand offered degree programs in computer-related areas. A few computer science curricula were available in Vietnam, Brunei, and Burma.

Among the names of the programs are (in alphabetical order) Business Computing, Computational Science, Computer and Engineering Management, Computer and System Science, Computer Engineering, Computer Management and Information Technology, Computer Science, Computer Science and Information Systems, Informatics, Informatics and Mathematical Science, Information Science, Information Technology, Management Information Systems, Software Engineering, and Telecommunications Technology.

Up-to-date as well as background information on some computer curricula in Asia may be found on Websites such as those listed in Table 1.

ACM Curriculum '68 (Atchison *et al.*, 1968) was the model for most early undergraduate programs at universities in Asia. Mathematically-oriented students prospered in this curriculum, but non-mathematically-oriented students did not. The latter claimed that they needed more applied courses to be able to find jobs. Thus many universities in Southeast Asia modified Curriculum '68 by adding business administration courses and applied courses such as Computer Applications in Banking or Computer Applications in Hotel Administration. Such programs were often then renamed Business Computing or something similar. Most of the Business Computing curricula also required practical training in business establishments with computer or data processing departments. Also, whereas faculties of science or mathematical science in Southeast Asia tended to adopt Curriculum '68, faculties of engineering tended to follow the IEEE Curriculum (Cain, 1977).

Some Southeast Asian universities placed particular emphasis on computer-related curricula by grouping them together into a faculty or a school. For example, a Faculty of Information Technology might include a Department of Computer Hardware, a Department of Computer Software, a Department of Artificial Intelligence and Robotics, a Department of Network Engineering, etc.

Master's and Doctoral level computer science curricula in Southeast Asia are generally patterned after those in the USA, UK, or Japan. Some Japanese-like programs concentrate mainly on research in laboratories where a variety of equipment is readily available. Some curricula modeled on the UK may be more theoretically oriented, while programs modeled on the USA usually include both coursework and research. Several Ph.D. programs in Southeast Asia require the student to publish in a refereed journal in the USA or the UK before

Table 1. Websites for selected Asian universities.

Department	University	URL
Computer Section	Maktab Kejuruteraan Jefri, Bolkiah, Brunei	`http://www.brunet.bn/php/chongrms/general.htm`
Computer Science	University of Pune, India	`http://cs.unipune.ernet.in`
Computer Science	University of Indonesia	`http://www.cs.ui.ac.id`
Information Science	Japan Advanced Institute of Science and Technology	`http://www.jaist.ac.jp/~kouhou/General_ifo/organization-e/JOHO-e.html`
Informatics and Mathematical Science	Osaka University, Japan	`http://www.ics.es.osaka-u.ac.jp/index-e.html`
Computer Science and Information Systems	Universiti Teknologi, Malaysia	`http://www.fsksm.utm.my`
Computer Management and Information Technology	Polytechnic University of the Philippines	`http://www.geocities.com/CollegePark/Classroom/3110/`
Computer Science	University of the Philippines at Diliman	`http://www.engg.upd.edu.ph/cs/`
Computer Science	Nanyang Technological University, Singapore	`http://www.geocities.com/CollegePark/Campus/4293/comp.htm`
Computational Science	National University of Singapore	`http://www.cz3.nus.edu.sg`
Computer Science	Assumption University, Thailand	`http://www.s-t.au.ac.th`
Computer Engineering	Chulalongkorn University, Thailand	`http://www.cp.eng.chula.ac.th`
Computer Sciences	Ho Chi Minh City University, Vietnam	`http://www.vnn.vn/huflit/`

graduation. This is in contrast to those in the USA and the UK, where publications are not normally required prior to graduation but are expected thereafter.

The graduates of computer curricula in Southeast Asia are employed in a broad range of organizations in such areas as airlines, banking, consulting, government, finance, hotels, insurance, manufacturing, and universities.

Bibliography

1968. Atchison, W. *et. al.* "Curriculum '68," *Comm. of the ACM*, **11**, 151–197.
1977. Cain, J. T. (ed.) "A Curriculum in Computer Science and Engineering," *IEEE Publication* EHO 119-8 (January).

Srisakdi Charmonman

EDVAC

For articles on related subjects *see* DIGITAL COMPUTERS, HISTORY OF: EARLY; ECKERT, J. PRESPER; ENIAC; MAUCHLY, JOHN WILLIAM; STORED-PROGRAM CONCEPT; ULTRASONIC MEMORY; VON NEUMANN, JOHN; and VON NEUMANN MACHINE.

The EDVAC (Electronic Discrete Variable Automatic Computer), *see* Fig. 1, the first stored program computer to be designed, was a direct outgrowth of work on the ENIAC. During the design and construction of the ENIAC in 1944 and 1945, the need for more storage than its 20 10-decimal digit numbers was realized. The experience with acoustic delay lines for radar range measurement led to the concept of recirculating storage of digital information. The group at the Moore School of Electrical Engineering at the University of Pennsylvania started development work on mercury delay lines for such storage, and initiated the design of the EDVAC.

As the first stored program computer, EDVAC instructions that controlled the computational process were stored in the same way that its data was stored. The basic logical ideas are described by von Neumann (1945), and computers based on such designs have come to be known as von Neumann machines (*q.v.*), even though most historians question whether von Neumann deserves such exclusive credit for the stored program concept. In the spring of 1945, J. Presper Eckert described the mercury delay line (*see* ULTRASONIC MEMORY) to the author. In answer to the question of how to control the operations, he replied that the instructions would be stored in the delay lines just like numbers. Once he said it, the solution was obvious. There is no doubt that Eckert deserves credit for the delay line memory, and though there is no proof that he first thought of putting instructions in the delay lines, it seems probable that he or John Mauchly thought of it before von Neumann came on

Figure 1. The EDVAC (courtesy of the University of Pennyslvania Library).

the scene. What von Neumann should get credit for, of course, is that his interest in and support of computer activity significantly increased government and academic support. Therefore, following a suggestion of Maurice Wilkes, it is proposed that stored program computers following the EDVAC design be called Eckert–von Neumann computers.

The principles involved in the EDVAC design exerted a strong influence on the computers that followed it. The EDVAC had about 4,000 tubes and 10,000 crystal diodes. It used a 1,024-word recirculating mercury delay-line memory, consisting of 23 lines, each 384 microseconds long. The words were 44 bits long. Instructions were of the four-address type (4-bit operation code and four 10-bit addresses). The arithmetic unit did both fixed and floating-point operations. Input and output were via punched paper tape and IBM cards. Information was all handled as serial pulse trains and the clock frequency was 1 MHz.

Although the conceptual design of the EDVAC was complete in 1946 and was delivered to the Ballistic

Research Laboratories at Aberdeen, Maryland, by 1950 the entire computer had not yet worked as a unit and was still undergoing extensive tests (Stifler, 1950, 200–201). The delay in completing the EDVAC was primarily due to the exodus of computer people from the Moore School in 1946. Eckert and Mauchly resigned and launched a commercial venture (UNIVAC). Herman Goldstine and Arthur Burks went to Princeton to work with von Neumann, and the author left to work with Turing in England. T. K. Sharpless was put in charge, but he, too, left later to go into business for himself.

The EDVAC finally became operational as a unit in 1951. An Aberdeen Proving Ground report states that during 1952 the EDVAC "began to operate on a production basis." For nine months of 1952, the average available time per week was 47.4 hours (23.3 for code checking and 24.1 for production), and the average "engineering" time was 104.8 hours. Approximately 70.4 hours of this was unscheduled maintenance; 10,000 defective tubes (over twice the complement) and about 3,000 (of 10,000) germanium diodes were replaced. In a later Aberdeen report, Weik noted that during 1956 the average error-free running period was approximately 8 hours, and that out of a run time of 8,728 hours, 6,752 were good (78%). This gave approximately 130 hours of "good time" per week. The EDVAC was used until December 1962 (Knuth, 1970, 259).

Bibliography

1945. von Neumann, J. "First Draft of a Report on the EDVAC," *Contract No. W-670-ORD-4926*, U.S. Army Ordnance Department, Philadelphia: University of Pennsylvania, Moore School of Electrical Engineering (30 June).

1946. Chu, C., Davis, J., Huskey, H., Lukoff, H., Merwin, R., Sharpless, T., Shaw, R., and Sheppard, C. *Progress Report on the EDVAC*, Vol. II. University of Pennsylvania, Philadelphia (30 June).

1950. Stifler, W. W., Jr. (Ed.) *High Speed Computing Devices.* New York: McGraw-Hill.

1970. Knuth, D. E. "Von Neumann's First Computer Program," *Computing Surveys*, **2**, 4, 247–260.

1972. Goldstine, H. H. *The Computer from Pascal to von Neumann*. Princeton, NJ: Princeton University Press.

1981. Stern, N. *From ENIAC to UNIVAC*. Bedford, MA: Digital Press. (Includes a reprint of von Neumann, 1945.)

Harry D. Huskey

EFT

See ELECTRONIC FUNDS TRANSFER.

ELECTRONIC CALCULATOR

See CALCULATORS, ELECTRONIC AND PROGRAMMABLE.

ELECTRONIC COMMERCE

For articles on related subjects *see* ADMINISTRATIVE APPLICATIONS; DISTRIBUTED SYSTEMS; ELECTRONIC FUNDS TRANSFER; ELECTRONIC MAIL; ELECTRONIC OFFICE; INTERNET; MINITEL; and WORLD WIDE WEB.

Electronic commerce (or e-commerce) enables the execution of transactions between two or more parties using interconnected networks. These networks can be a combination of POTS (plain old telephone service), cable TV, leased lines, or wireless. Information-based transactions are creating new ways of doing business and even new types of businesses. Improvements from implementing e-commerce may result in more effective performance (better quality, greater customer satisfaction, and better corporate decision making), greater economic efficiency (lower costs), and more rapid exchange (high-speed, accelerated, or real-time interaction).

What exactly is a *transaction*? Transactions are exchanges that occur when one economic entity sells a product or service to another entity. A transaction takes place when a product or service is transferred across an interface that links a consumer (client) with a producer (server). When buyer/seller transactions occur in the electronic marketplace, information is accessed, absorbed, arranged, and sold in different ways. To manage these transactions, e-commerce also incorporates transaction management, which organizes, routes, processes, and tracks transactions. E-commerce also includes consumers making electronic payments and fund transfers.

Currently, the goal of most e-commerce implementations is to reduce the "friction" in online transactions. Friction is often described in economics as transaction cost. Friction can arise from inefficient market structures linking buyers, sellers, and intermediaries; inefficient organizational structures (operating units, business processes, and workflows); and inefficient combinations of the technological activities required to make a transaction. Ultimately, the reduction of friction in online commerce will enable smoother transactions between buyers, intermediaries, and sellers.

A Brief History of E-Commerce

The need for e-commerce stemmed from the demand within business and government to make better use of computing and to apply computer technology better to improve customer interaction, business processes, and information exchange both within an enterprise and across enterprises.

During the late 1970s and early 1980s, e-commerce became widespread within companies in the form of electronic messaging technologies: electronic data interchange (EDI) and electronic mail. Electronic messaging technologies streamline business processes by reducing paperwork and increasing automation. Business exchanges traditionally conducted with paper, such as checks, purchase orders, and shipping documents, may be conducted electronically. Electronic data interchange allows companies to send/receive business documents (such as purchase orders) in a standardized electronic form to/from their suppliers. For example, combined with just-in-time (JIT) manufacturing, EDI enables suppliers to deliver parts directly to the factory floor, resulting in savings in inventory, warehousing, and handling costs. Electronic mail does much the same for unstructured organizational communications both inside and across organizational boundaries.

During the 1970s, the introduction of electronic funds transfer (EFT) between banks over secure private networks changed financial markets. Electronic funds transfer optimizes electronic payments with electronically provided remittance information. Today there are many EFT variants, including the debit card whose use is becoming ubiquitous at points of sale (POS) in grocery stores and retail outlets, and direct deposits to employee bank accounts.

In the late 1980s and early 1990s electronic messaging technologies became an integral part of workflow on collaborative computing systems (also called *groupware—q.v.*). Groupware focused primarily on taking existing nonelectronic methods and grafting them onto an electronic platform for improved business process efficiency. Although hyped as a "killer application" in the early 1990s, groupware efforts resulted in only small gains in productivity and efficiency.

In the mid-1980s, a completely different type of e-commerce technology began to spread among consumers in the form of online services that provided a new form of social interaction (such as chat rooms and Internet Relay Chat (IRC)—*see* ONLINE CONVERSATION) and knowledge sharing (such as newsgroups and file transfer programs). Social interaction created a sense of virtual community among the cyberspace (*q.v.*) inhabitants and helped give rise to the concept of a "global village." At the same time, information access (*q.v.*) and exchange have become more affordable. By using the global Internet, people can communicate with others around the world at ever-decreasing costs.

In the 1990s, the advent of the World Wide Web on the Internet represented a turning point in e-commerce by providing an easy-to-use technological solution to the problem of information publishing and dissemination. The Web made e-commerce a cheaper way of doing business (economies of scale) and enabled more diverse business activities (economies of scope). The Web also enabled small businesses to compete on a more equal technological footing with resource-rich multinational companies. For example, in Web-based electronic publishing, giant companies like Time Warner, Disney, and others are working overtime to keep up with upstarts who can enter the new marketplace of several million customers with a minimal infrastructure investment: a PC, a modem, and an Internet account.

Forces Fueling the Growth of E-Commerce

Interest in e-commerce is being fueled by economic forces, customer interaction forces, and technology-driven digital convergence (Kalakota and Robinson, 1999).

ECONOMIC FORCES

Under relentless pressure to reduce costs and stay competitive, firms are attracted to the economic efficiencies offered by e-commerce. These economic efficiencies include low-cost technological infrastructures, low-cost and accurate electronic transactions with suppliers, the low cost of global information sharing and advertising, and low-cost customer service alternatives to expensive retail bank branches and telephone call centers.

The economic forces motivating the shift to e-commerce are internal as well as external. The immediate application of e-commerce is in the internal integration of firms' operations. External integration molds the vast network of suppliers, government agencies, large corporations, and independent contractors into a single community with the ability to communicate across any computer platform. The automobile industry, where just-in-time (JIT) manufacturing methods forced Ford and General Motors to rely on EDI to interact with their suppliers, is a classic example of external integration.

The ability to coordinate the movement of information is key to both external and internal integration, and firms need to find ways to design business processes that change the way data is created, manipulated, and distributed. While technology is important to information integration, coordination of that information is indispensable. Coordination requires that employees, customers, and suppliers work together to solve problems, improve services, and create new products.

MARKETING AND CUSTOMER INTERACTION FORCES

Companies also employ e-commerce to provide marketing channels, to target microsegments or small audiences, and to improve post-sales customer satisfaction by creating new channels of customer service and support. Companies want to supply target consumers with product and service information in greater detail than that provided in a television or full-page advertisement. As more companies flood the marketplace with new products, target marketing is becoming an increasingly important tool of differentiation. Not only are new types of products emerging, but so are new players in old product categories, new spins on traditional plans, new pricing strategies, new target markets, new market research methods, and more.

The message for marketers is clear: the purchasing climate and products change quickly. In order to be competitive, marketing executives must employ technology to develop low-cost customer-prospecting methods, establish close relationships with customers, and develop customer loyalty. Marketers must adapt to a business world in which traditional concepts of differentiation no longer hold; in this world "quality" has a new meaning, "content" may not be equated with "product," and "distribution" may not automatically mean "physical location."

In this new environment, brand equity (or the premium attached to an established brand name) can rapidly evaporate, and marketers need to understand how customers allocate their loyalty. Given the proliferation of choices, consumers view brand names with growing indifference. For the manufacturer, establishing a new brand is a formidable task, and with increased competition, it is taking longer to break through and develop the customer base. Maintaining an existing brand is not much easier. In light of this, marketers in all industries are seeking new ways of interacting with customers and delivering services.

TECHNOLOGY AND DIGITAL CONVERGENCE

Digital technology has made it possible to convert characters, sounds, pictures, and motion video into a bit stream that can be combined, stored, manipulated, and transmitted quickly, efficiently, and in large volumes without loss of quality. As a result, e-commerce and the multimedia (*q.v.*) revolution are driving previously disparate industries, such as communications, entertainment, publishing, and computing, into ever-closer contact, forcing industries with traditionally different histories and cultures to compete and cooperate.

The relentless advance of technology, the emergence of multimedia standards, and the shift to distributed computing (*see* DISTRIBUTED SYSTEMS) and internetworking are providing the raw power for *digital convergence*. This convergence has two dimensions: convergence of content and convergence of transmission technology.

Convergence of content enables sophisticated information publishing and browsing tools. Content convergence also enables companies to use networked databases and electronic publishing to improve corporate and individual decision making and information processing. Except for production, distribution, and delivery of physical goods, commerce consists of forms of information gathering, processing, manipulation, and distribution. Content convergence facilitates the creation of a computer and network infrastructure that enables the coordination and integration of business processes or workflows.

Convergence of transmission compresses and stores digitized information so that it can travel through existing phone, wireless, and cable wiring systems. Convergence of transmission is a convergence of communication equipment that provides the "pipelines" to transmit voice, data, image, and video over the same line. Transmission convergence over a single line makes it easier to connect computers, high-speed peripherals, and consumer electronic devices, and to enhance a wide range of image-intensive or multimedia applications. From a business angle, conver-gence of transmission results in easier access to networks and in the creation of new, low-cost delivery channels for new and old products aimed at either existing customers or new customer segments.

Until recently, the convergence of voice and data networks has been an elusive goal because of irreconcilable differences between local area network (LAN) and private branch exchange (PBX) technologies. However, the emergence of a new network technology called asynchronous transfer mode (ATM—*q.v.*) changes this picture. Today, we can see a path that leads to total integration of voice with video and data networking, from the wide area network (WAN—*see* NETWORKS, COMPUTER) all the way to the desktop. Installing a single, integrated network reduces on-site cabling requirements and eliminates redundant wiring to work groups.

The E-Commerce Technology Framework

E-commerce not only affects transactions between parties, it also influences the way markets will be structured. Traditionally, market ties were created through the exchange of goods, services, and money. E-commerce adds a new element: information. Market ties, such as those forming around online payments, are now based on information goods, information services, and electronic money. Kalakota and Whinston (1996) show the different ways technology has enabled the creation of new market opportunity. Fig. 1 shows the different layers of technology that work in concert to facilitate the smooth operation of e-commerce.

THE NETWORK INFRASTRUCTURE

The networking infrastructure (popularly called the *information superhighway*) has many different types of transport system and does not function as a monolithic entity; there is no single highway that connects the digital equivalent of Los Angeles to Miami. Instead, the architecture is a mixture of many forms of high-speed network transport, whether it be land-based telephone, air-based wireless, modem-based PC, or satellite-based. For instance, mail sent from a portable PC on the French Riviera to a computer in Los Angeles might travel across several different types of transport networks interconnected with each other before it reaches its destination.

The players in this industry segment can be called *information transport providers*. They include: telecommunication companies that provide phone lines; cable TV systems that provide coaxial cables and direct broadcast satellite (DBS) networks; wireless companies that provide mobile radio and satellite networks; and computer networks, including private networks like CompuServe or America Online, and public data networks like the Internet.

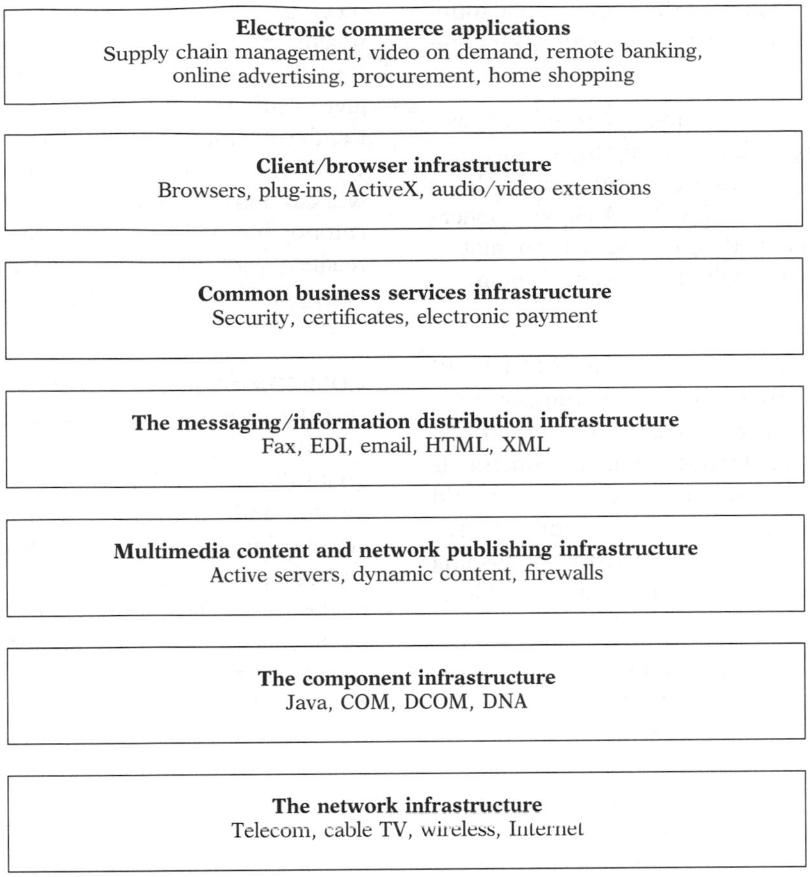

```
┌─────────────────────────────────────────────────┐
│           Electronic commerce applications        │
│   Supply chain management, video on demand,       │
│   remote banking,                                 │
│   online advertising, procurement, home shopping  │
└─────────────────────────────────────────────────┘

┌─────────────────────────────────────────────────┐
│           Client/browser infrastructure          │
│   Browsers, plug-ins, ActiveX, audio/video        │
│   extensions                                      │
└─────────────────────────────────────────────────┘

┌─────────────────────────────────────────────────┐
│        Common business services infrastructure    │
│   Security, certificates, electronic payment      │
└─────────────────────────────────────────────────┘

┌─────────────────────────────────────────────────┐
│   The messaging/information distribution          │
│   infrastructure                                  │
│   Fax, EDI, email, HTML, XML                      │
└─────────────────────────────────────────────────┘

┌─────────────────────────────────────────────────┐
│   Multimedia content and network publishing       │
│   infrastructure                                  │
│   Active servers, dynamic content, firewalls      │
└─────────────────────────────────────────────────┘

┌─────────────────────────────────────────────────┐
│           The component infrastructure            │
│   Java, COM, DCOM, DNA                            │
└─────────────────────────────────────────────────┘

┌─────────────────────────────────────────────────┐
│           The network infrastructure              │
│   Telecom, cable TV, wireless, Internet           │
└─────────────────────────────────────────────────┘
```

Figure 1. The e-commerce technology infrastructure.

This industry segment also includes hardware and software tools that provide an interface with the various network options, and to the customer premises equipment (CPE), or terminal equipment, which is a generic term for privately owned communications equipment that is attached to the network. This category of subscriber terminal equipment can be divided into three parts: cable TV set-top boxes, computer-based telephony, and networking hardware (hubs, wiring closets, and routers or digital switches). The terminal equipment is in fact the gateway (*q.v.*) to information services, commercial transactions, and 500 digitally compressed channels.

Routers and digital switches help to connect large networks (or internetworks). Routers are devices that can connect the local area networks (LANs) inside various organizations with the wide area networks (WANs) of various network providers. This interconnection enables easy communication between separate networks across geographical distances and provides access to distributed computing resources. The router industry is a multibillion dollar industry that is dominated by players such as Cisco, Lucent, and NorTel, all three of which supply equipment that links data communications networks through the Internet.

THE COMPONENT INFRASTRUCTURE

Today the convergence of Internet, Web, Windows, and palmtop computing technologies promises dramatic new opportunities for savvy businesses to create a new generation of cross-platform computing solutions that dramatically improve the responsiveness of the organization. The goal is to use the Internet and the Web more effectively to reach customers directly, and to connect people better with information any time, any place. When a technology system acts as an intermediary to delivers these results, it is called a component or *middleware* platform (*see* COMPONENT SOFTWARE).

There are two popular forms of middleware: Component Object Model (COM) and Common Object Request Broker Architecture (CORBA). The Component Object Model (COM) from Microsoft is a general software architecture for component software (Microsoft, 1999). Although COM addresses specific areas such as controls, compound documents, automation, data transfer, storage and naming, and others, any developer can take advantage of the structure and foundation that COM provides for cross-platform e-commerce applications.

CORBA is the Object Management Group's answer to the need for interoperability among the rapidly proliferating number of hardware and software products available today. Simply stated, CORBA allows applications to communicate with one another no matter where they are located or who has designed them.

MULTIMEDIA CONTENT AND NETWORK PUBLISHING

The information superhighway is the transportation foundation that enables the transmission of content. The electronic system through which content is transmitted is analogous to the nonelectronic world in which different types of products (content) are stored in distribution centers (network publishing servers) before they are loaded onto various vehicles for transport.

Currently, the most prevalent architecture that enables network publishing is the World Wide Web. The Web allows small businesses and individuals to develop content in the form of HyperText Markup Language (HTML—see MARKUP LANGUAGES) and publish it on a Web server. In short, the Web provides a means to create product information (content) and a means to publish it in a distribution center (network server).

MESSAGING AND INFORMATION DISTRIBUTION

The information content transferred over the network consists of text, numbers, pictures, audio, and video. However, the network does not differentiate among content, as everything is digital, that is, combinations of ones and zeros. Once content has been created and stored on a server, vehicles, or messaging and information distribution methods, carry that content across the network. The messaging vehicle is called *middleware software*. It sits between the Web servers and end user applications and masks the peculiarities of the environment. Messaging and information distribution also includes translators that interpret and transform data formats.

Messaging vehicles provide ways for communicating nonformatted (unstructured) as well as formatted (structured) data. Unstructured messaging vehicles include fax, email, and form-based systems like Lotus Notes. Structured documents messaging consists of the automated interchange of standardized and approved messages between computer applications via telecommunications lines. Purchase orders, shipping notices, and invoices are examples of structured document messaging.

For the purposes of e-commerce, existing messaging mechanisms must be extended to incorporate reliable, unalterable message delivery that is not subject to repudiation in order to be able to acknowledge and give proof of delivery when required. The challenge in the development of messaging software is to make it work across a variety of communications devices (PCs, workstations, set-top boxes, and wireless communicators), interfaces (characters, graphics, and virtual reality—*q.v.*), and networks (satellites, cable, twisted pair, fiber optics (*q.v.*), and wireless).

COMMON BUSINESS SERVICES INFRASTRUCTURE

Doing business online has received attention for its potential, as well as for such shortcomings as inadequate directories, inadequate online payment instruments, and inadequate information security. The common business services infrastructure attempts to address these shortcomings. This infrastructure includes the different methods for facilitating online buying and selling. In e-commerce, the buyer sends an electronic payment (a form of electronic check or digital cash) as well as some remittance information to the seller. Settlement occurs when the payment and remittance information are authenticated by the seller and accepted as valid.

In order to enable online payment for information and ensure its safe delivery, the payment services infrastructure needs to develop encryption (making contents indecipherable except for the intended recipient) and authentication (*q.v.*) (making sure that customers are who they say they are) methods that ensure security of contents traveling on the network (*see* DIGITAL SIGNATURE). In addition to generic payment services, e-commerce will need to accommodate other desirable payment-related services such as currency exchange, cash management, escrow, investment and brokerage, financial information and reporting, and billing and payment. The development of directory services and secure transactions is currently one of the most active areas of e-commerce research and development.

CLIENT/BROWSER INFRASTRUCTURE

The browser program has come a long way since the early 1990s. The first publicly available browser software, Lynx, was a character-based system. The modern browser, such as Internet Explorer 5.0 (IE5), is a full infrastructure on which a variety of programs interoperate. There's something for just about everyone in IE5, from users and administrators to content providers and developers. The browser infrastructure today aims to provide people the tools they need to make Web surfing faster, easier and more integrated. The browser infrastructure has improved in five areas:

1. Ease of use: hundreds of new features, such as AutoCorrect, AutoComplete, the Radio Bar, and others, automate repetitive actions during Web surfing.

2. Speed: browsing is faster, more reliable, and uses less disk space than before.

3. Administrative features: companies can manage security more easily by using settings like Auto Proxy.

4. New standards support such features as Extensible Mark-up Language (XML).

5. Streaming media support such as Real Networks.

The browser program is also evolving into a thin version—mobile phone browsers—to support the wireless medium. For instance, the next generation of browsers such as Spyglass's Wireless Device Mosaic is a small microbrowser designed to display WML (Wireless Markup Language), the WAP-specified wireless content language that is similar to HTML, as it is delivered over the airwaves. The development of microbrowsers is an active area of research.

E-COMMERCE APPLICATIONS

There are three distinct general classes of e-commerce applications:

1. inter-organizational (business-to-business)

2. intra-organizational (within a business)

3. customer-to-business

Inter-organizational. Inter-organizational e-commerce applications include:

◆ *Supplier management* Electronic applications help companies reduce the number of suppliers and facilitate business partnerships by reducing purchase order (PO) processing costs and cycle times, and by increasing the number of POs processed with fewer people.

◆ *Inventory management* Electronic applications shorten the order–ship–bill cycle. If the majority of a business's partners are electronically linked, information once sent by fax or mail can now be instantly transmitted. Businesses can also track their documents to ensure that they were received, thereby improving auditing capabilities. This also helps to reduce inventory levels, improve inventory turns, and eliminate out-of-stock occurrences.

◆ *Distribution management* Electronic applications facilitate the transmission of shipping documents such as bills of lading, purchase orders, advanced ship notices, and manifest claims, and enable better resource management by ensuring that the documents themselves contain more accurate data.

◆ *Channel management* Electronic applications quickly disseminate information about changing operational conditions to trading partners. Technical, product, and pricing information that once required repeated telephone calls and countless hours can now be posted to electronic bulletin boards (*q.v.*). By electronically linking production-related information with international distributor and reseller networks, companies can eliminate thousands of hours of labor and ensure accurate information sharing.

Intra-organizational. Intra-organizational e-commerce applications include:

◆ *Workgroup communications* These applications enable managers to communicate with employees using electronic mail, videoconferencing, and bulletin boards (*q.v.*). The goal is to use technology to increase the dissemination of information, resulting in better informed employees.

◆ *Collaborative publishing* These applications enable companies to organize, publish, and disseminate human resources manuals, product specifications, and meeting minutes using tools such as the World Wide Web. The goal is to provide the information to enable better strategic and tactical decision making throughout the firm. Also, online publishing shows immediate and clear benefits: reduced costs for printing and distributing documentation, faster delivery of information, and reduction of outdated information.

◆ *Sales force productivity* These applications improve the flow of information between the production and sales forces, and between firms and customers. By better integrating the sales forces with other parts of the organization, companies can have greater access to market intelligence and competitor information, which can be funneled into better strategy. The goal is to allow firms to collect market intelligence quickly and to analyze it more thoroughly.

Within intra-organizational electronic commerce, the largest area of growth can be seen in the development of "Corporate Intranets," which are primarily set up to publish and access vital corporate information. Some of the most common types of information are: human resources information, employee communications, product development and project management data, internal catalogs, sales support data, equipment and shipment tracking, and accessing corporate databases.

Customer to business. Customer to business e-commerce applications include:

◆ *Social portals* Electronic applications enable consumers to find online information about existing and new products and services. This also includes applications that enable consumers to communicate with each other through electronic mail, video-conferencing, and newsgroups.

◆ *Transaction portals* These include applications that enable and facilitate the completion of transactions between buyers and sellers. In electronically facilitated consumer-to-business transactions, customers learn about products through electronic publishing, buy products with electronic cash and other secure payment systems, and even have information goods delivered over the network.

The objective of this class of e-commerce is to provide consumers with greater convenience and lower prices. E-commerce provides consumers with convenient shopping methods, from online catalog ordering to phone banking, both of which eliminate the costs of expensive retail branches (or "bricks and mortar"). E-commerce facilitates factory orders by eliminating many intermediary steps, thereby lowering manufacturers' inventory and distribution costs, and indirectly providing consumers with lower prices.

Summary

Once the source of science fiction, e-commerce—conducted in and around the global marketplace—is now a reality with enormous potential. Various forces fuel the growth of e-commerce, namely economic, marketing, and customer interaction and digital convergence.

Bibliography

1996. Kalakota, R., and Whinston, A. *Electronic Commerce: A Manager's Guide.* Reading, MA: Addison-Wesley.
1999. Kalakota, R., and Robinson, M. *E-Business: Roadmap for Success.* Reading, MA: Addison-Wesley.
1999. Microsoft Component Services. White Paper Available at http://www.microsoft.com/com/wpaper/compsvcs.asp.

Ravi Kalakota and Marcia Robinson

ELECTRONIC FRONTIER FOUNDATION (EFF)

For articles on related subjects *see* COMPUTER CRIME; COMPUTER PROFESSIONALS FOR SOCIAL RESPONSIBILITY; CRYPTOGRAPHY, COMPUTERS IN; FREE SOFTWARE FOUNDATION; FREEWARE AND SHAREWARE; HACKER; INFORMATION ACCESS; LEGAL ASPECTS OF COMPUTING; PRETTY GOOD PRIVACY; PRIVACY, COMPUTERS AND; and SOCIETY, COMPUTERS IN.

The Electronic Frontier Foundation (EFF) is a non-profit public-interest organization whose mission is the protection of online civil liberties and the health and growth of internetworking.

Founded in 1990, the US-based organization was initially involved in defending wrongly accused or too-severely punished system crackers, in urging the nationwide adoption of affordable ISDN (*q.v.*) as a precursor to faster networking technology in the home, in advocating a non-discriminatory "universal access" model of digital telecommunications, and in opposing abusive law enforcement actions in "computer crime" investigations (e.g. illegal search and seizure).

In recent years, the organization's role has ranged from traditional civil liberties work to advocacy at the frontier of information access issues. EFF has been working with *pro bono* attorneys on challenging US export and publications restrictions on encryption software—regulations that both violate the First Amendment and, EFF and industry players maintain, undermine privacy, security, and electronic commerce (*q.v.*), both domestically and abroad. EFF was also a part of the legal team that helped to establish the unconstitutionality of the Communications Decency Act in 1997.

As of 1998–99, EFF's principal areas of involvement are:

◆ the ongoing encryption legal and policy battle;

◆ renewed Congressional and state attempts to censor the Internet;

◆ FBI attempts to exceed its wiretapping powers under the "Communications Assistance for Law Enforcement Act";

◆ email "spamming" (*see* ELECTRONIC MAIL), technical fixes that stop spamming, and misguided legislative attempts to address the problem;

◆ the protection of due process and freedom of expression in the Internet Domain Naming System (*see* INTERNET);

◆ fair-use rights and intellectual property in the digital domain;

◆ abuse of intellectual property and other laws to silence online critics of commercial, government or religious institutions;

◆ Internet taxation, gambling, security, content labeling, and other online regulatory issues;

◆ the global Blue Ribbon Online Free Speech Campaign.

EFF is also the co-founder of the Global Internet Liberty Campaign (GILC), a worldwide coalition of civil liberties, human rights, and Internet user community organizations that watches over government abuse of online rights, and the Internet Free Expression Alliance (IFEA), a mostly US coalition opposing the imposition of non-voluntary use of Internet content filtering, labeling, and rating technology.

EFF has spun off two other organizations: The Center for Democracy and Technology (CDT, a Washington, DC, Internet policy organization started in 1995 by former EFF Executive Director Jerry Berman and other ex-EFF policy staffers), and TRUSTe (a non-profit online privacy assurance organization that licenses privacy ''trustmarks'' to Websites that adhere to privacy policies and information-use disclosure practices, backed up by spot audits, to increase public trust in online commerce, and to fend off government over-regulation in this area.)

Presently based in San Francisco, with staff in New York and Washington, DC, EFF was founded in Cambridge, MA, by Mitch Kapor (principal author of Lotus 1-2-3), John Perry Barlow (a writer, rancher, and lyricist for the Grateful Dead), and John Gilmore (a San Francisco Bay-area entrepreneur and source-ware author, formerly with Sun Microsystems and the GNU Project—*see* FREE SOFTWARE FOUNDATION). Other long-time EFF board members include Esther Dyson (author, and the publisher of the *Release 1.0* industry newsletter) and David Farber (Internet pioneer and member of University of Pennsylvania telecommunications faculty).

EFF is funded by individual and corporate memberships and donations, and foundation grants. It does not accept any form of government funding. The organization's policy positions are determined by the board of directors' interpretation and staff implementation of the EFF Mission Statement, not by donors.

Contact information

Electronic Frontier Foundation
1550 Bryant Street, Suite 725
San Francisco CA 94103-4832 USA
+1 415 436 9333 (voice)
+1 415 436 9993 (fax)
Email: ask@eff.org
WWW: http://www.eff.org

Related URLs

GILC. http://www.gilc.org.
IFEA. http://www.ifea.net.
CDT. http://www.cdt.org.
TRUSTe. http://www.truste.org.

Stanton McCandlish

ELECTRONIC FUNDS TRANSFER (EFT)

For articles on related subjects *see* COMMUNICATIONS AND COMPUTERS; DATA SECURITY; DISTRIBUTED SYSTEMS; ELECTRONIC COMMERCE; ELECTRONIC MAIL; NETWORKS, COMPUTER; PRIVACY, COMPUTERS AND; and SOCIETY, COMPUTERS IN.

An *Electronic Funds Transfer* (EFT) system is one that involves the electronic movement of funds and fund information between financial institutions. The transfer is coupled with minimal amounts of data to facilitate that transfer. There are two major worldwide EFT networks: the Clearinghouse Interbank Payments System (CHIPS) and FedWire (the oldest EFT system in the USA). In 1997, these networks moved over $2 billion (US) each banking day. A third major network, the Society for Worldwide Interbank Financial Telecommunications (SWIFT), is capable of handling nearly 2 million messages per day.

The Evolving Forms and Extensions of EFT

The original expansion of EFT was stimulated by the standardization of magnetic ink character recognition (MICR) technology in the mid-1950s. EFT systems were anticipated to be a lower-cost alternative to paper transactions. EFT has progressed through four various forms: automated teller machines (ATMs), automated clearing houses (ACH), electronic funds transfer point of sale systems (EFTPOS) and debit cards, and electronic funds transfer electronic data interchange systems (EFT-EDI).

Automated Teller Machines (ATMs) provide the basis for the most familiar EFT system in current use. These target the consumer market. ATMs are installed by financial institutions and retail stores to provide unattended, online computerized banking "teller" services. ATMs are user-activated through a magnetic strip on a plastic card. ATMs read account information, verify a valid user by the customer's entering of a personal identification number (PIN), and then allow cash withdrawals, deposits, transfer of funds between accounts, and balance inquiry. More extensive services are offered by some ATM-based systems.

In 1990, it was estimated that, for some users, EFT saved more than $1 per transaction. More recently, however, some financial institutions have come to believe that ATM transactions are more costly to them than teller transactions and have begun to charge their customers a fee for initiating them. Despite this threat of escalating cost, ATMs have become ubiquitous and extremely popular.

The *automated clearing house* (ACH) network is a nationwide system that processes pre-authorized electronic payments on behalf of depository financial institutions. ACH networks in the USA resulted from a joint effort by the Federal Reserve System and the banking industry in the mid-1960s.

The National Automated Clearing House Association (NACHA) is a US trade association representing 42 regional ACH associations whose members comprise over 20,000 depository financial institutions. Expanding direct deposits of payroll and similar services increased the volume of transactions substantially in the late 1960s.

Electronic funds transfer at point of sale (EFTPOS) is the blending of electronic point of sale technology with EFT, usually accomplished with a "debit" card that is similar to those used for ATMs. Electronic point-of-sale advantages such as better pricing and inventory planning and control are thus enhanced by the characteristics of EFT such as the convenience of cash and the security of a credit card.

EFTPOS systems involve a network of retail-based terminals linked online to a financial institution's computer. Payments rendered at retail operations can then be debited from a customer's account and credited to the retailer's automatically. Information about the transaction may also be entered into the retailer's information system and used for inventory management purposes.

Electronic funds transfer and electronic data interchange (EFT-EDI) is the direct, rapid, computer-to-computer transmission and translation of business information (e.g. invoices, purchase orders, claims forms) in a standard format. No human intervention is necessary in order to link the transmission to other parts of a company's information system. For example, EDI-transmitted invoices can update inventory orders and generate exception reports for back orders.

EDI messages are non-proprietary and non-copyrightable, while those from EFT systems have substantially more security requirements. Combining EFT and EDI technologies offers substantial synergistic benefits, such as lower personnel costs, greater accuracy, and reduced lead time. Some combined EFT-EDI systems yield savings in the range of $5 to $25 per transaction.

Architectural Requirements

EFT has several hardware and software requirements to preserve system integrity and security in expanding regional, national, and international networks. Fault-tolerant computing (*q.v.*) systems for reliability need to be used which, if hardware-based, preserve the integrity of the network better than older, independent computer systems that were merely patched together. Authentication (*q.v.*) requirements for messages (for both PC and mainframe users) entails a watchword generator and controller, a security card, and a mainframe peripheral security module. The US Data Encryption Standard (DES) has traditionally been the encryption algorithm used to secure EFTPOS systems (*see* CRYPTOGRAPHY, COMPUTERS IN). As transaction volumes increase, however, the algorithm's effectiveness tends to decrease.

While there is still not complete agreement on a standard application program interface (API), there is movement towards resolution of the issue. The X.400 Gateway API and X.400 Application API were created in 1989 by the Application Program Interface Association (APIA). APIA is a consortium of 24 vendors in the electronic mail and messaging industry. The APIs will spur the development of X.400 technology to link wide and local area networks (LANS—*q.v.*). X.400 (which is a store-and-forward messaging architecture) has been recommended by the International Organization for Standardization (ISO).

Switching networks (such as France's X.25 packet-switching network) with add-on applications packages to handle EFT execution orders, language translations, and currency conversions are needed to handle the growing number of international message formats used by the EFT systems.

EFT Trends and Issues

The recent changes in EFT hardware and software technology have a number of implications for the future and growth of the methodology. Electronic benefits transfer (EBT) is the US government's use of EFTS technology to automate programs such as Social Security, child support, Medicaid, and food stamp distribution. The Internal Revenue Service is seeking to use EFT-EDI for refunds. Off-site mainframe computers can now deliver EFT advances automatically through facsimile transmission (fax).

Security and interface/interconnection issues are becoming more important as the industry matures. Currently, cryptographic protocols are used for security at the applications level. *Smart cards* (invented in 1974 by Roland Moreno) are beginning to be used to identify users. Smart cards have embedded integrated chips with up to 64 KB of indelible memory. A microcomputer on the chip executes unalterable programs, thus making such cards more secure than the plastic, magnetic-striped cards currently in use. Different technologies will still need to be used to address compatibility problems.

A particularly troublesome issue facing EFT technology centers around legal questions. Banks and other financial institutions face legal risks that are partially protected if the EFT system used is part of CHIPS or the FedWire system (since these are underwritten by the Federal Reserve System). However, liability issues are still somewhat unsettled, with many different acts and regulations coming into play.

The Federal Reserve Board has changed Regulation CC (which implements the Expedited Funds Availability Act) to regulate time periods by which banks must make check-deposited funds available to customers. Efforts continue to revise Article 4A of the Uniform Commercial Code to address commercial EFT and integrate it with both Regulation CC and the Electronic Funds Transfer Act of 1979, which governs most consumer transactions.

Legal documents generally require paper forms and proofs of signature in order to be binding, which tends to lessen the attractiveness of the technology to an organization considering an investment in EFT-EDI. Business documents in EFT-EDI are processed in electronic and heavily coded formats, making audit trails difficult.

Changes of terms and error resolutions associated with credit or debit card disputes are regulated by the Federal Reserve Board's Regulations Z and E, respectively. Efforts continue to reconcile the impact of those regulations on EFT.

Bibliography

1987. Kirkman, P. *Electronic Funds Transfer Systems, The Revolution in Cashless Banking and Payment Methods.* Oxford: Basil Blackwell.

1991. Ahwesh, P. C. "Who Pays for Risk in Worldwide EFT Networks?" *Information Strategy: The Executive's Journal,* **7**, 3 (Spring), 21–26.

1991. Anonymous. "Smart Cards: When the Price is Right," *Banking World,* **9**, 6 (June), 36.

1991. Bove, R. X. "Bank Technology Reshapes Industry," *Bankers Magazine,* **174**, 3 (May/June), 17–20.

1996. Ice, T., and Demy, T. J. *The Coming Cashless Society.* Eugene, OR: Harvest House Publishers, Inc.

1996. Furche, A., and Wrightson, G. *Computer Money: A Systematic Overview of Electronic Payment Systems.* Heidelberg: Dpunkt Verlag.

1999. Welch, B. *Electronic Banking and Treasury Security,* 2nd Ed. Boca Raton, FL: CRC Press.

Janice F. Cerveny

ELECTRONIC MAIL

For articles on related subjects *see* BULLETIN BOARD; COMPUTER CONFERENCING; INTERNET; ONLINE CONVERSATION; and WORLD WIDE WEB.

Introduction

Electronic mail (email) is the transfer of a message in electronic form from one computer user to another, usually over a network. The message will often travel through a series of computer systems until it reaches its final destination, where it can be stored for retrieval by its intended recipient.

Beginning as a simple mechanism for users of a single computer to leave each other messages, email is becoming the world's most common form of written communication, supplanting traditional mail and fax transmission. It is even replacing telephone conversations. The growth in popularity of the Internet (*q.v.*) in the late 1990s was both a cause and an effect of the expanded use of email worldwide. The number of email "boxes" grew from several hundred thousand to tens of millions in a few short years.

An email message is typically composed on a personal computer using an email program such as Qualcomm's Eudora or Microsoft's Outlook. The completed message comprises two parts, the main message content or *body*, and subject and addressing information contained in the *header*. The body can be anything from a simple text document to a collection of various files such as pictures or other documents. The email message is transferred from one computer to another on its way to a final destination, much as a postal letter gets routed from one post office to another. Fig. 1 shows how a message is routed from its source to its destination. The next section describes each step in this process.

Email Architecture and Protocols

STORE AND FORWARD

The Internet's email delivery system, over which most of the world's email was sent by 1999, is shown in Fig. 1. This system is built upon the principle of *store and forward*, a series of exchanges between message submission and delivery end-points across the network. A user composes a message with the assistance of an email program (also known as a *User Agent* or UA), addressing it to one or more intended recipients. The composed message is handed off from the client program to a mail server program known as a *Message Transfer Agent* or MTA, which *stores* the message on local storage (usually a disk). Subsequently, on a periodic basis, the server program attempts to *forward* the queued message to another MTA running on a remote computer in the network that is presumably closer to the destination mail server. The message continues to be routed on a "hop-by-hop" basis through the network from one MTA to another until it reaches the recipient's mail server, which accepts it and stores it in a location accessible to the recipient—a process also known as *final delivery*. On each hop of the message's route, the forwarding MTA removes the message from its local queue, and the receiving MTA adds it to its

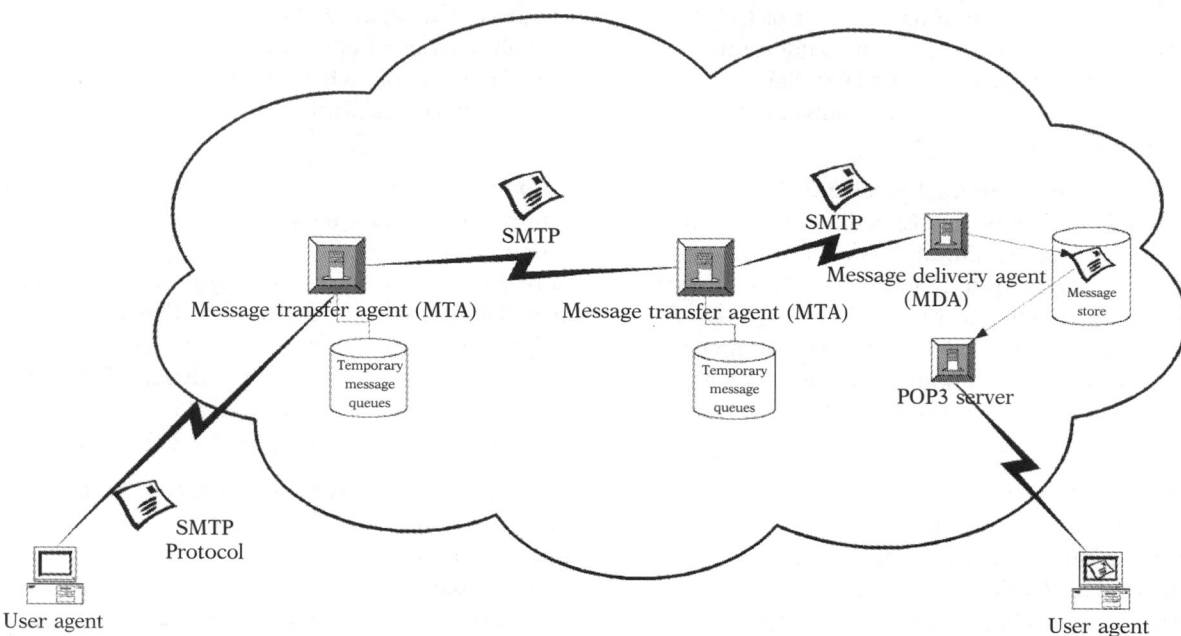

Figure 1.

queue thereby assuming responsibility for the subsequent forwarding or final delivery of the message to its recipient.

THE EMAIL ADDRESS

The recipient of an email message is specified via his or her email address. The format of an email address is defined in the Internet specification document RFC-822 (*see* Standardization in INTERNET). Although this definition is rather complex, the most common format is quite simple: ⟨user name⟩@⟨domain name⟩. A *user name* is a restricted set of characters (e.g. geoff or anand_tolani) which is locally unique. The *domain name* (*q.v.*) is unique throughout the Internet and indicates where the final delivery of this message is to take place, e.g. yahoo.com. The combination of the user name and the domain name creates a globally unique address for this email box. Examples are joe_smith @yahoo.com, sue@southcampus.iu. edu, and pierre@societe.co.fr.

FINAL DELIVERY

The final delivery process places the message into storage in a message store area from which the recipient can retrieve it. In simple cases, the receiving MTA itself may deliver the message. Often, however, a separate program known as the Message Delivery Agent (MDA) is invoked by the MTA to actually make the delivery.

Various delivery-related features may be provided by the mail system at the final delivery end-point. An automated response may be triggered to send a speci-

fied reply to the sender of an arriving message, indicating, for example, that the recipient is on vacation. Automatic mail forwarding relays a message to a different email address, handing the message back to the message forwarding system with the new destination rather than committing it to the local message store. Quota checking, to verify that the user has not exceeded a pre-allocated limit of storage space on the mail server, may also precede final delivery.

Should the final delivery process ultimately fail, a *bounce* message is generated to the message sender indicating the delivery failure. The bounce email message is routed to the sender via an outbound MTA. Bounces may also be generated at any point in the hop-to-hop routing of an email message and are not restricted to the final delivery process. Common reasons for bounces include unknown recipient (e.g. when the sender mistypes the recipient's address) and quota exceeded. Automatically generated bounce messages may be identified by the message header, in which the "from" address is usually "MAILER-DAEMON".

ROLE OF THE USER AGENT

Email client programs (i.e. user agents) allow users to read delivered messages as well as to compose and send new ones. They operate on a user's mailbox, presenting a contiguous sequence of saved messages, sorted and organized as directed by the user.

Modern user agents provide mail folders which allow messages to be moved out of the main *inbox* into specific folders where they can be grouped with other related messages. Likewise, recent standards like IMAP (see below) can manipulate remote messages within and between folders. Advanced features such as mail filters allow arriving mail to be sorted automatically into target folders or even discarded, using properties of the arriving message such as the message sender or the presence of specified keywords in the message.

User agents often simplify message addressing by maintaining an address book of *nicknames* or *aliases* for email addresses specified by the user. Aliases can specify a single target email address or a group of addresses, thereby effectively creating user-specific *mailing lists* to which a composed message can be addressed. Copies of sent messages can be automatically saved, and draft copies of messages can be stored and sent only when completed. Automated reminder messages can be scheduled for delivery to individuals and mailing lists at specified times or intervals.

ROLE OF THE MESSAGE TRANSFER AGENT

The MTA is responsible for the hop-to-hop forwarding of messages through the network. However, it also accepts outbound messages from user agents at the message submission end-point, as well as inbound messages from forwarding MTAs at the final delivery end-point. In all cases, client programs communicate with receiving MTAs using SMTP, the Simple Mail Transfer Protocol (defined in RFC-821).

SMTP provides simple commands with which a client specifies the sender's email address and one or more recipient email addresses. This information is often referred to as the SMTP *envelope*. Next, the message content itself is passed to the server. ESMTP or *Extended* SMTP is a newer superset of the protocol which lets clients test servers for specific feature support and negotiate parameters such as allowable message size and transmission time-outs.

Once a message has been accepted via SMTP, the receiving MTA examines the destination addresses contained in the SMTP envelope. The domain name portion of each address, e.g. `yahoo.com`, is used to determine the next hop in the message. Usually this is done via the DNS (*Domain Name System*). DNS maintains an MX (mail-exchanger) database that returns the mail host associated with a given domain name. The local MTA then communicates with each such mail host via SMTP and sends it a copy of the message with a new envelope containing the email addresses in its domain.

REMOTE ACCESS PROTOCOLS

Computers that are not directly connected to the Internet use a remote access protocol rather than SMTP. For example, suppose a home user connected via modem (*q.v.*) to the Internet by an Internet Service Provider (ISP), wishes to read new mail using an email program. The physical location of the email is on a mail server machine at the ISP's operations center. A common remote access protocol is the simple POP3 (Post Office Protocol, version 3) which allows the user agent program running on the home computer to retrieve messages from a remote mail server, as long as adequate user authorization is provided. Various authorization mechanisms are possible, such as simple plaintext passwords or more sophisticated encrypted key authentication (*q.v.*). A more recently developed remote access protocol, IMAP (Interactive Mail Access Protocol) has begun to be used, though the number of IMAP-compliant mail servers is still small as of this writing. IMAP is distinguished from POP3 in its emphasis on remote message manipulation rather than retrieval—messages are left on the remote server, where they are read and manipulated without copying them to the client machine.

ANATOMY OF AN EMAIL MESSAGE

Every email message consists of two parts: a set of consecutive header fields collectively referred to as the message *header*, and the actual message content itself, i.e. the message body. A single blank line separates the message header from the message body. Each *header field* consists of a field name followed by a colon and a value. Example header fields are *To:*, *From:*, *Subject:*, *Date:*. Header fields are mainly of interest to user agents, which fill them in during composition and parse them for display during message viewing. While MTAs generally operate only on message envelopes, they may add or modify a few specific header fields. For example, the route of a message may be traced backwards by examining the *Received:* headers, each having been appended by an MTA indicating a hop in the message route. Fig. 2 outlines the anatomy of a simple email message.

Several email standards, the most important being SMTP, require that email message headers and bodies contain only 7-bit ASCII (*see* CHARACTER CODES) text. This restriction allows messages to pass through the various flavors of MTAs on the network without being corrupted or altered. Encoding mechanisms have been devised to include other forms of data in an email message. One of the earliest is *uuencoding* (Unix-to-Unix encoding) which allows arbitrary binary data to be encoded as 7-bit ASCII text, which can then be decoded back into binary form by the receiving user agent or by a separate standalone program. This allows small binary files to be appended to messages. While simple, uuencoding does not provide a mechanism with which to add structure to an email message body, nor does it allow the type of the binary data (e.g. sound clip or word processing document) to be

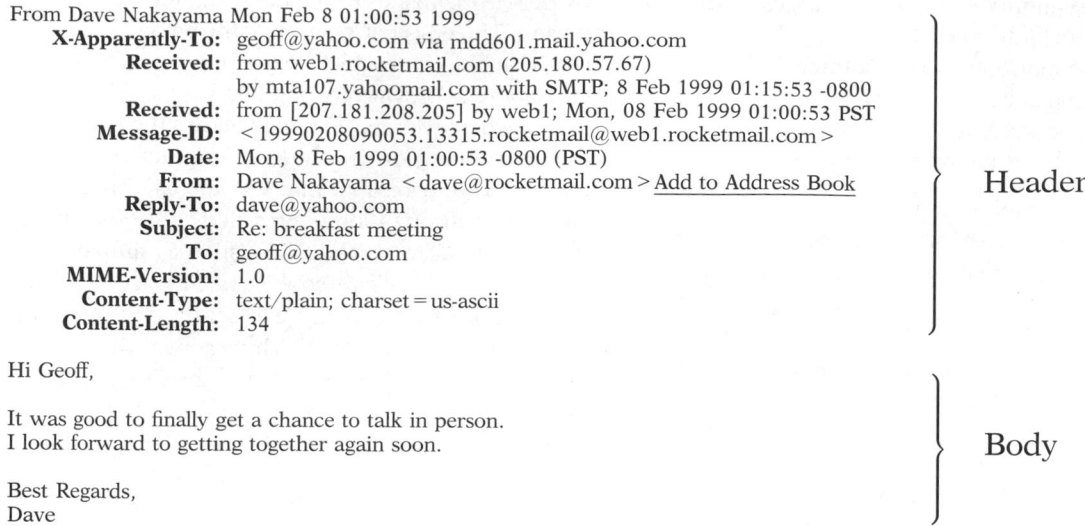

From Dave Nakayama Mon Feb 8 01:00:53 1999
X-Apparently-To:	geoff@yahoo.com via mdd601.mail.yahoo.com
Received:	from web1.rocketmail.com (205.180.57.67)
	by mta107.yahoomail.com with SMTP; 8 Feb 1999 01:15:53 -0800
Received:	from [207.181.208.205] by web1; Mon, 08 Feb 1999 01:00:53 PST
Message-ID:	< 19990208090053.13315.rocketmail@web1.rocketmail.com >
Date:	Mon, 8 Feb 1999 01:00:53 -0800 (PST)
From:	Dave Nakayama < dave@rocketmail.com > Add to Address Book
Reply-To:	dave@yahoo.com
Subject:	Re: breakfast meeting
To:	geoff@yahoo.com
MIME-Version:	1.0
Content-Type:	text/plain; charset = us-ascii
Content-Length:	134

Header

Hi Geoff,

It was good to finally get a chance to talk in person.
I look forward to getting together again soon.

Best Regards,
Dave

Body

Figure 2. The header shows the recipient, the intermediate systems that transferred the message, specified by Internet domain name or IP address, the date, sender, and return address. It also identifies the message as conforming to the MIME protocol, with simple ASCII text. The actual message is in the body. Add to Address Book gives the recipient the option of entering the sender's name and address in the mail agent's list of correspondents.

specified except through conventions for file naming. MIME (Multipurpose Internet Mail Extensions) was introduced to address these shortcomings, and has since been adopted into other Internet technologies such as HTTP (*see* WORLD WIDE WEB). MIME specifies a set of standardized *type* and *sub-type* pairings for messages and data, as well as structure for dividing a message into multiple sections, ghoulishly referred to as *body parts*. Each part is itself typed and sub-typed based on its data content. Standard encoding schemes, *base64* and *quoted-printable* for binary and 8-bit ASCII text, respectively, can be used on a per part basis, allowing an arbitrary number and mixture of data types to be encoded and added to a single message within organized boundaries in the message structure. Individual body parts are usually referred to as *attachments* by client email programs and MIME messages containing combinations of text, image, audio and/or video attachments are commonly referred to as *multimedia* mail.

A Brief History of Email

Electronic mail began as a simple messaging scheme in the first time-sharing systems (CTSS at MIT, DTSS at Dartmouth) in the 1960s. A message sender would use a very simple interface to place messages in a file accessible by another user. That user could then read the messages directly from the file. It was not until after key elements of the Arpanet were created at Bolt Beranek and Newman (BBN) in 1969 that email messages were sent between different computers. This seminal event took place in 1971 during an experiment by Ray Tomlinson in a BBN lab.

That very simple experiment began an explosion that soon dominated the use of the Arpanet and its successor, the Internet. By 1973 three-quarters of all traffic on the Arpanet was email and Ray Tomlinson had gained both fame and notoriety as the inventor of today's standard *at sign* (@)-based email address. (The notoriety was due to early systems such as *Tenex*, which had difficulty with the @.) Initially piggybacking on the Arpanet's earliest file transfer protocol, email eventually earned its own protocol, SMTP, in 1982.

The spread of email from this point on was rapid. Other early networks such as UUCPnet and Bitnet quickly adopted email systems (although with protocols not always compatible with the original Arpanet version). Proprietary mail systems were developed mainly to work within a local area network (*q.v.*) for a university or company. Systems such as Lotus ccMail, Microsoft Exchange, and QuickMail all were designed to allow transfer of mail within a local network to facilitate communication within a corporation. In the 1990s, online services sprang up, such as CompuServe, Prodigy, and AOL (America Online), which allowed individual computers to connect and transfer mail messages.

The mid-1980s saw a period of competition between standards from the Internet community such as SMTP and OSI (*q.v.*) standards developed and backed by the International Organization for Standardization (ISO). The best example of such a standard is the *Message Handling System* (MHS), also known as *X.400*. Plagued by poor implementations, a situation exacerbated by the standard's inherent complexities, the OSI systems have all but disappeared. Today, MHS's legacy is perhaps best found in the influence of its better ideas in current Internet standards such as LDAP, the Lightweight Directory Access Protocol.

In the late 1980s and early 1990s most of the necessary links were built between these different and incompatible systems. These *mail gateways* effectively extended the reach of the Internet into the proprietary networks of online services and corporations. Use of the SMTP protocol spread rapidly, due especially to the free distribution of *sendmail*, an SMTP mail transfer agent that became the *de facto* standard for much of the Internet.

In the late 1990s certain providers, such as *Rocket-Mail* (http://www.rocketmail.com), began offering free email accounts used exclusively via the World Wide Web. These services, which provided new users with simple-to-use email and current users with additional accounts, allowed worldwide acccess to email for the price of a local phone call. They rapidly grew extremely popular and accounted for much of the growth in email boxes worldwide during this time. Since these accounts were used through WWW browsers, they automatically supported HTML (*see* MARKUP LANGUAGES), and thus multimedia (*q.v.*) email.

For a good history of the origins of email including many personal anecdotes, *see* Hafner and Lyon (1996).

The New Email Community

Once limited to computer scientists connected to the Arpanet, today's email community spans the globe and includes numerous demographic groups. Like most communities, over time the early email community developed certain specific communication mechanisms, habits, mores, and rules of social conduct. A specific dialect or *netspeak* developed which was tailored to the typed word. In netspeak, punctuation is used to indicate emphasis (this is *important*) and emotion can be shown indirectly via text-based *faces* called *emoticons*. For example, :-), the classic sideways smiley face, can indicate pleasure or humor.

The community also developed an etiquette ("netiquette") of its very own, which deplores *flaming* (abusive email), respects concise, to the point communication, and includes prohibitions on *spam*, the mass sending of unsolicited email. Spam, the electronic equivalent of junk mail, has grown in both volume and notoriety as email has become widespread. Technological (automatic blocking) and legislative responses to spam began to appear in the late 1990s, but as of this writing the problem continues to worsen.

Today email has succeeded in making the world a smaller, more connected, place—a cyberspace (*q.v.*)—and the community has grown to include many millions of people from business, schools, and homes. In fact, although many of the conventions described above live on, the original community has disappeared in the melting pot that is today's Internet.

Even when the community was much smaller, portions of the community needed forums in which to meet. Mailing lists, a mechanism which allows a group of users to send each other email easily as well as providing a means for users to join and remove themselves, play an important such role for the email community. *Majordomo* and *listserv* are two of the most popular list serving robots, and provide for simple list creation and maintenance.

Future of Email

The fundamental model of email use that has evolved over the past 25 years will probably not change radically in the near future. People will continue to send, receive, and save messages much as they do today. However, email will become better integrated with multimedia applications. MIME is now used mostly for multimedia attachments, which arc manually detached and used (e.g. spreadsheets). In the future a number of these formats will be natively available to the email client program, much as an HTML attachment is automatically decoded and correctly displayed by many email readers today. Email messages may be composed using *rich text* features such as multiple fonts, tables, and colors, and read exactly as thcy wcrc scnt. Furthcrmorc, using somc advanced protocols such as M-HTML (Multimedia HTML) it will be possible to create true multimedia messages incorporating sound and images and to expect that those messages will be heard and appear at the receiver's end just as they were created.

As email becomes further entrenched in society as a means of communication, especially within the business community, it is likely that security features such as sending encrypted messages and authentication of sender/receivers, which are seldom available today, will become common. Furthermore, email users are likely to demand global accessibility to their mailboxes just as cell-phones provide the same for phone calls. Expect to see email accessible by phones and PDAs, as well as via the World Wide Web.

The infrastructure to support email will continue to improve, including, for example, globally accessible integrated email address directories. Such directories first appeared on the Web in the mid- to late 1990s (e.g. http://www.four11.com). Most significant will be the increasing variety of ways in which email will be used. It may be used to pay bills, to communicate with healthcare and other service providers, and throughout the school system for communications between parents, teachers, and students. In short, email will infiltrate deeply into the fabric of social communication.

Bibliography

1982. Postel, J. *Simple Mail Transfer Protocol.* STD 10, RFC 821 USC/Information Sciences Institute.

1994. Myers, J., and Rose, M. *Post Office Protocol—Version 3.* RFC 1725.

1994. Angell, D., and Heslop, B. *The Elements of Email Style: Communicate Effectively Via Electronic Mail.* Reading, MA: Addison-Wesley.

1995. Schneier, B. *Email Security: How to Keep Your Electronic Messages Private.* New York: John Wiley.

1996. *Multipurpose Internet Mail Extensions (MIME). Parts One–Five.* RFCs 2045–2049.

1996. Crispin, M. *Internet Message Access Protocol—Version 4rev1,* RFC 2060.

1996. Hafner, K., and Lyon, M. *Where Wizards Stay Up Late.* New York: Simon & Schuster.

1997. Rhoton, J. *X.400 and SMTP: Battle of the Email Protocols.* Bedford, MA: Digital Press.

1998. Schwartz, A., and Garfinkel, S. *Stopping Spam.* Sebastopol, CA: O'Reilly & Associates.

Websites

Web-based email providers
Yahoo! Mail. `http://mail.yahoo.com`.
HotMail. `http://www.hotmail.com`.
WhoWhere. `http://www.whowhere.com`.

Online Directories
Yahoo! `http://people.yahoo.com`.
WhoWhere. `http://www.whowhere.lycos.com`.
InfoSpace. `http://www.infospace.com`.

Geoff Ralston, Katie Burke, David Nakayama, and Anand Tolani

ELECTRONIC OFFICE

For articles on related subjects *see* ADMINISTRATIVE APPLICATIONS; CLIENT–SERVER COMPUTING; COMPUTER CONFERENCING; DATA PROCESSING; DESKTOP PUBLISHING; ELECTRONIC COMMERCE; ELECTRONIC MAIL; GROUPWARE; INTERNET; PERSONAL COMPUTING; TEXT EDITING SYSTEMS; WORD PROCESSING; and WORLD WIDE WEB.

The concept of the *electronic office* (*office automation*) encompasses the application of computer and communications technology to improve the productivity of all types of office workers, including clerical, administrative, professional, and executive. In the mid-1950s, office automation was used as a synonym for *data processing* (*q.v.*) and referred to the ways in which bookkeeping tasks were automated. After some years of disuse, the term was revived in the mid-

1970s to describe the interactive use of word and text processing systems, which would later be combined with powerful computer tools leading to a so-called "office of the future" that, inevitably, would be an *electronic office.*

In its first iteration in the early and mid-1980s, this integrated electronic office employed a mainframe (*q.v.*) or minicomputer (*q.v.*) (or some part of its processing power) plus video display terminals, keyboards for input, and formed-character or high-resolution dot matrix printers for "letter quality" printing. The software functionality of these early office automation systems used electronic mail as a kind of "glue," underlying all of the other components and permitting information to be passed from application to application and from user to user. Other major functions included word processing, information retrieval (*q.v.*), various personal assistance functions such as a personal calendar and a group meeting scheduler, and the ability to manage tasks.

Early systems offered by major manufacturers, such as IBM (*q.v.*), Sperry Univac, and Burroughs (later merged into Unisys), Digital Equipment Corporation (*q.v.*), and Xerox, offered little more than word processing and simple records processing (the management of small sequential data files, such as names and addresses, that can be sorted and merged into letters). They were aimed at clerical and secretarial workers and offered little opportunity for substantial customer savings, since the salaries of the workers employed in such jobs was relatively low.

By the mid-1980s, attention was focused on systems that directly supported professional workers and managers by emphasizing the managerial communications function. As personal computers became ubiquitous and local area networks (LANs—*q.v.*) became the accepted methodology for joining personal computer workstations (*q.v.*) to form workgroups, this more flexible and modular hardware replaced the minicomputer as the preferred office automation platform. When the PC at the desktop became known as the "client" and the shared system unit, with its storage and software, became known as the "server," client–server computing was born. Host-based office automation had been used by only a small percentage of all office workers; its cost was too difficult to justify. But with millions of personal computers already in place, the client–server model permitted the implementation of office automation by the simple technique of attaching existing desktop personal computers to local area networks and servers. For a small incremental cost, significant value could be added to the workgroup. The vast majority of electronic office users in the future were expected to use a client–server environment.

But such analysis preceded the explosive growth of the Internet, starting in 1994–1996. With that growth, and the increasing use of Internet technology to build internal, corporate intranets (private networks using the Internet TCP/IP (*q.v.*) protocol), intranets are replacing client–server architectures as a platform for electronic office and application development. Together with their external version, extranets (which extend intranets to permit access by customers, suppliers, and contract or remote workers), such technology is expected to be pervasive for the next generation of office automation.

Functionality

The functionality of office automation, in the meantime, has been shifting. Electronic mail remains the backbone function of the office. We moved from electronic mail based on terminals and hosts tied into networks (which was once the *only* choice) to networks of clients (today, PCs) and servers (anything from PCs to mainframes) where messages can be sent to people in the same organization or to those in other companies or countries, making use of compatible networks, institutional (*de jure*) and marketplace (*de facto*) standards, and electronic mail gateway (*q.v.*) software, which provides translation services between unlike networks. Now we are rapidly moving once again to schemes based on the open standards of the Internet and universal interconnection. Each of the major remaining proprietary email systems has evolved to conform to open standards, becoming a messaging system compatible with its own office applications, but also able to support applications from other vendors. Address lists and software for connection to remote systems may be stored locally, or local servers may address a central hub for such information. The goal is for each organization to have a single directory supporting all of its functions, rather than separate directories for each application.

Users may select mail services with substantial sophistication: delivery may occur immediately, or it may be delayed to take advantage of multi-message bundles or lower rates at off-peak hours; mail may be marked for personal receipt only or delegation might be permitted; password protection and full message encryption is readily available.

A special and growing form of electronic mail is computer conferencing (*q.v.*). In this format, a group of users with access to a particular electronic mail system, their Intranet or the Internet, and a common interest take turns writing, reading, and (if permitted) editing a commonly owned file. Such systems are sometimes called *whiteboards*. Special software facilitates viewing the file in different ways: by subtopics, by author, by date, and so forth. In a computer conference, oral skills and speed do not count; intelligence and writing skills become more important. Such groups are often *ad hoc* in nature and disband when their task is completed or their interest wanes. The completed file could become archival material or a book on the topic, or it could simply be discarded. Collaborative software such as Lotus Notes offers special capabilities for such discussion databases.

Automating filing is more difficult. The filing of one's own electronically created documents can be readily automated, but much mail, especially external mail, is still received on paper. Some of that paper can be integrated into the electronic filing system by optically scanning it. One can then save it as an image file, identifying it by an index or by indexable keywords. Because image files require large amounts of storage, users may choose to limit their use of these files, except on a temporary basis, or they may choose to use optical storage (*q.v.*), for its high-capacity. Alternatively, optical character recognition (OCR—*q.v.*) software algorithms can be applied that transform images of text characters into digital codes, just as if the paper document had been typed into the electronic system. It can then be indexed and managed just like any other electronic file, using a variety of indexing and search techniques.

Recently, new search techniques have been developed that permit much more sophisticated retrieval; this insures the return of a smaller number of more precisely matched answers. Also, *search engines* are available that look for either *changes* in state or for certain events to occur, and which then notify the appropriate system user. A user might, for example, want to be notified as soon as a certain number exceeds $10,000. On an Intranet or the vast information expanse of the Internet, a number of commercial search engines are available. They are provided *free* on the Internet, in exchange for the user's receipt of advertising, usually in the form of transient banners, sometimes related to the topic of his or her search.

The amounts of information now available are becoming so large that new technologies are emerging to manage them. For example, *agents* may help filter mail or select information that might be interesting to you (information about your clients, for instance). A new form of information delivery, called *push publishing*, keeps profiles of your interests and delivers information from its specific content against that profile. For instance, if CNN were the push publisher, and your profile indicated an interest in wars and Africa, you would be notified every time discontent was discovered on that continent, but not otherwise.

Personal computers provide a variety of personal calendar schemes to record and display individual calendars and to produce reminder or "To Do" lists. Workgroup systems offer group calendars, which may be simply systems to display multiple individual calendars, or more complex software that can merge calendars in order to schedule meetings for members of a group. Some software can now schedule meetings across multiple systems or networks. Software called *groupware* (*q.v.*) can coordinate workgroup tasks as well as meetings. On an intranet and the Internet, group and event calendars can be published which can be downloaded to an individual's personal calendar and integrated automatically.

Sometimes, the term *paperless office* has been used to describe a goal of office automation, but that goal is elusive. A computer screen is not yet a suitable substitute for all the different kinds of information that one might simultaneously be using in a work environment (since it is neither big enough, nor of high enough resolution). This is so partly because the screen handles only electronic information and not paper, and partly because it is on the desk. Whenever the worker leaves the office, the computer workstation is left behind. Now, however, portable personal computers have become small and inexpensive. Nearly one-half of the new personal computers purchased are now portables (*see* PORTABLE COMPUTERS). We are also seeing the rise of a new small portable computer, the *hand-held* or *palmtop*. In combination with new pen interfaces, which permit the user to "write" on the screen of the computer rather than use a keyboard, mouse (*q.v.*), or other pointing device, such computers can be used anywhere. Then, with an ability to send and receive information (probably via cellular telephone or radio signals) to and from the office base, the paperless office will be closer to reality. Voice input is now possible for some applications, but continuous speech voice input with full natural language processing (*q.v.*) allowing users to talk and the computer to understand and act is still unperfected. But it is now coming into use for specific functions, where by narrowing its domain of knowledge, its accuracy can be greatly enhanced.

While some impact printing remains in the office, almost all electronic offices now make extensive use of high-quality laser printing at resolutions of 600 dpi (dots per inch) or higher. Color printing also makes use of inkjet and melted color wax technology as well as color laser. In all cases, the output may include type of any size or style, with an appearance near, if not at (depending on resolution) a typeset page. Pages may also include forms, tables, graphics, and reproductions of halftone photographs, although with some lessening of quality.

Future Trends

Each of the elements discussed is an example of a tool designed to take an individual human task and make it more efficient. But office automation has a more important goal, namely, to look beyond mere tasks in order to automate the processes applied to them. This *process automation* is referred to early in the history of office automation in Zisman's (1978) description of using Petri nets (*q.v.*) to describe production systems for office work. Examples are reviewing a technical paper submitted to a journal, applying for a home mortgage, and a budget approval cycle. This work has since been furthered by work at Xerox PARC and by the work of Tom Malone at MIT. The groupware products, which attempt to facilitate cooperation, coordination, and negotiation in groups, are examples of this kind of process automation, as are some of the procedural processing products being used in conjunction with image processing (*q.v.*) and workflow to manage large document processing applications not unlike those imagined by Zisman. Many of these groupware products are now moving to the Internet as collaborative applications.

With the advent of very inexpensive personal computers and cheap memory, we moved to the desktop (or into the briefcase) a fully capable personal computer rather than a semi-intelligent terminal that requires attachment to another computer for any useful processing to occur. Now, in 1999, we are reconsidering that decision. The advent of the fully networked environment, the pervasive use of the Internet, and the lower cost of bandwidth (*q.v.*) combine to make it interesting to think again about a new kind of terminal. Called a *Network Computer* or NC, this new device runs the interface and processing *only* while it is connected to a server, across a network. Software and data are not stored in the NC, but downloaded to it for each computing session; this enhances security and guarantees that only the latest information and software will be used. Of course, this is not without controversy. Microsoft, Intel, and others argue that an NC cannot ever compete with the function and flexibility of a full PC and have suggested a *Networked PC*, a kind of closed and secure PC, as an alternative solution. The market will decide whether either of these devices deliver the savings in support and administration which are described as their major benefits.

The arrival and growth of the Internet and its pervasive use as a substitute for other office automation platforms is changing the nature of how people work in offices, what a workgroup looks like, and where, in fact, work is performed. We are moving to a world where workgroups can be virtual rather than physical, where offices know no boundaries, and where the only office the members of a team share may exist within the network.

Bibliography

1978. Zisman, M. *The SCOOP Office Reminder System*. Working papers of the Wharton School of Business, University of Pennsylvania.

1987. Crowston, K., and Malone, T. *Information Technology and Work Organization*. Cambridge, MA: MIT Sloan School of Management, Center for Information Systems Research, Working Paper No. 165 (December).

1988. Malone, T. *What Is Coordination Theory?* Cambridge, MA: MIT Sloan School of Management, Center for Coordination Science, Working Paper No. 2051-88 (February).

1992. Opper, S., and Fersko-Weiss, H. *Technology for Teams: Enhancing Productivity in Networked Organizations*. New York: Van Nostrand Reinhold.

1995. Ray, C., Palmer, J., and Wohl, A. *Office Automation: A Systems Approach*. Cincinnati: South-Western Educational Publishing.

Amy D. Wohl

ELECTRONIC REFERENCE WORKS

For articles on related subjects *see* ELECTRONIC INDEXES; HUMANITIES APPLICATIONS; MACHINE TRANSLATION; MARKUP LANGUAGES; NATURAL LANGUAGE PROCESSING; MULTIMEDIA; ONLINE INFORMATION SERVICES; SPELLING CHECKER; TEXT EDITING SYSTEMS; and WORD PROCESSING.

Dictionaries and encyclopedias are collections of information organized to facilitate quick reference. Entries are usually in alphabetical order. Dictionaries typically provide a definition and information on pronunciation and derivation (etymology) for each word; some also include information on a word's history and notes and examples of its usage. The information provided by encyclopedias varies widely, but often includes a definition as part of a longer consideration of the subject. Dictionaries and encyclopedias may strive for comprehensive coverage, or may focus on a specific subject (such as *The Dictionary of National Biography*, *The Encyclopedia of Computer Science*, and *The Milton Encyclopedia*). Dictionaries might cover a single language or provide translations between two languages or multiple pairs of languages (Kister, 1992; Kister, 1994).

An *electronic reference work* is a dictionary or encyclopedia or similar source of information designed to enable rapid searching (*q.v.*) and retrieval of information stored in computer memory. Dictionaries and encyclopedias are available in several electronic media, although the large storage capacity required for most reference works makes CD-ROM (*see* OPTICAL STORAGE) and online delivery through the World Wide Web (*q.v.*) the most common options.

Computerized dictionaries range from simple lists of correctly spelled or hyphenated words used in spelling checkers to complete, searchable transcriptions of major printed reference works in dozens of volumes. Most of the major English language print dictionaries and encyclopedias are now available in some electronic form. Merriam-Webster, Random House, Houghton-Mifflin (publisher of *The American Heritage Dictionary*), Oxford University Press (publisher of the *Oxford English Dictionary*), *The Encyclopaedia Britannica*, Grolier (publisher of The *Encyclopedia Americana*), and others have produced electronic equivalents of their existing print works. Several more recent reference works (such as Microsoft's *Encarta*) exist only in electronic form and correspond to no printed work.

Electronic reference works offer significant advantages over printed versions. Many print encyclopedias and some dictionaries include images, whether photographs or drawings; computerized reference works often include not only images, but sound and even film clips, taking advantage of the multimedia (*q.v.*) capabilities of modern computers. Since most dictionaries include information on pronunciation, computerized dictionaries often allow the user to hear the words spoken, using either speech synthesis or a digitally recorded human speaker (*see* SPEECH RECOGNITION AND SYNTHESIS). An encyclopedia entry on Newtonian physics may include short animations demonstrating the principles of mechanics.

Another advantage of an electronic reference work is that it may be updated more easily and hence more frequently than its printed counterpart. Users generally pay a monthly fee to access an online reference work and have a right to expect that the material will be kept current and accurate. Those who pay a certain price for a version on CD-ROM and register it with the publisher are usually offered updated discs for a much lower price.

Among the most important advantages of electronic reference works is the ability to search them in ways impossible, or nearly impossible, with printed texts. Specific functionality varies from product to product, but a user might be able to search not only for main entries ("headwords"), but words within definitions, words and dates in illustrative quotations, etymological roots and languages, and even phonemes in the pronunciation. Searching for words within definitions, for example, can turn a dictionary into an *ad hoc* thesaurus. Queries can be sophisticated: for example, a dictionary containing the origins of words and the dates of their first occurrence might allow historical linguists to find all words with Arabic roots that entered the English language in the 16th century. The *Oxford*

English Dictionary (OED), with its hundreds of thousands of illustrative quotations, serves as an unparalleled corpus of literary usage, and its electronic form is often searched for such information.

In order to be searched most efficiently, electronic dictionaries and encyclopedias must be coded in some *markup language* (*q.v.*) to indicate the various fields in an individual entry, and the fields themselves must be more logically consistent than is necessary in print works, where the human reader's intuition obviates the need for extensive annotation (Clemenceau, 1992; Ide, 1994). These problems are most acute in works developed before the advent of computers. Although most electronic reference works strive for currency, a number of dictionaries and encyclopedias of primarily historical interest have been transcribed into electronic form, including Covarrubias's *Tesoro de la lengua castellana* (1611), Johnson's *Dictionary of the English Language* (1755), and the 18th century French *Encyclopédie*. Adapting such works for electronic use poses special problems because the information they contain is often not sufficiently consistent or complete to produce reliable results with computerized search programs. As a result of this experience, publishers of reference works now pay increased attention to electronic publication as they develop new reference works (Gross, 1989; Feldweg, 1997).

An important example illuminates both the advantages and difficulties of electronic reference works. The OED was first published from 1884 to 1933, with four supplements between 1972 and 1986. With more than 300,000 main entries, it is considered the most important English language dictionary and perhaps the most comprehensive dictionary in any language. Beginning in 1984, Oxford University Press began transcribing the first edition into electronic form, both to facilitate their lexicographers' future revisions and to provide a searchable edition for users. This electronic transcription of the first edition was then combined with the supplements and edited to be more accurate and up-to-date. The result, the second edition of the OED, appeared in 1989, both in a twenty-volume print edition and on a CD-ROM. The new electronic transcription offered many advantages over its paper predecessor, but it also inherited many of its problems. Inconsistent abbreviations and irregularly demarcated fields (to be expected in a work predating electronic searching practice by a century) made many searches unreliable. The third edition, now in progress, is being reworked from the beginning with electronic publication in mind. The fields are being reconsidered to improve consistency, the abbreviations are being standardized, and the entire dictionary is being designed to enable efficient searching and display on computer screens.

Bibliography

1989. Gross, M. "The Construction of Electronic Dictionaries," *Annales des télécomcommunications*, **44**, *1–2* (Jan–Feb), 419.

1989. Marchionini, G. "Making the Transition from Print to Electronic Encyclopedias: Adaptation of Mental Models," *International Journal of Man–Machine Studies*, **30**, *6* (June), 591–618.

1992. Clemenceau, D. "Enrichissement et Structuration de Dictionnaires Électroniques," *Langue Française*, **96** (December), 6–18.

1992. Kister, K. F. *Kister's Best Dictionaries for Adults and Young People: A Comparative Guide.* Phoenix, AZ: Oryx Press.

1994. Atkins, B. T. S., and Zampolli, A. *Computational Approaches to the Lexicon.* New York: Oxford University Press.

1994. Ide, N. "Encoding Electronic Dictionaries," *Travaux de l'Institut de phonétique d'Aix*, **16**, 95–120.

1994. Piotrowski, D. "Electronic Dictionaries, Architectural Questions," *Français Moderne*, **62**, *2* (December), 181–196.

1994. Kister, K. F. *Kister's Best Encyclopedias: A Comparative Guide to General and Specialized Encyclopedias*, 2nd Ed. Phoenix, AZ: Oryx Press.

1997. Feldweg, H. "Wörterbucher und neue Medien: alter Wein in neuen Schlauchen?," *Lili. Zeitschrift für Literaturwissenschaft und Linguistik*, **27**, 30–43.

Jack Lynch

EMBEDDED SYSTEM

For articles on related subjects *see* ADA; MICROCOMPUTER CHIP; MICROPROCESSORS AND MICROCOMPUTERS; and REAL-TIME SYSTEMS.

In some sense, every computer system is *embedded* within some larger system, such as a business. But the term in computer science and engineering has come to denote a computer that is physically embedded within a larger system and whose primary purpose is to maintain some property or relationship among the other components of the system in order to achieve the overall system objective. Embedded computers are now used in a wide variety of systems, such as aircraft, automobiles, appliances, weapons, medical devices, and toys.

As opposed to computer applications that primarily provide information or computation facilities to the user or those that provide transaction processing (*q.v.*) (e.g. an airline reservation system or automated teller), the embedded computer reads data from sensors and provides commands to actuators in order to ensure that the goals of the overall system are achieved. It accomplishes this by maintaining some property or relationship among the components of the larger system at some specified value over time or by effecting some sequence of state changes over time. The required relationship between state variables for which the computer is responsible will involve fundamental chemical, thermal, mechanical, aerodynamic, or other laws, as embodied within the nature and construction of the larger system.

Embedded systems usually have certain characteristics that greatly complicate the process of constructing software:

Real-time—The correctness of the outputs is dependent not only on their value, but also on their timing. Outputs that are too early or too late may be incorrect even though they may have the desired computed value. In real-time systems, the required timing behavior of the software is dictated by external events, rather than by internal processing speed.

Reactive—The embedded computer interacts and responds to its environment during execution. Execution is in response to external events or at fixed time frequencies and is often continuous and cyclic (rather than executing once and ending).

Process control—The computer is responsible for monitoring and partially or completely controlling mechanical devices and physical processes. Control variables in the process are measured to provide input and feedback to the computer, which uses this information to effect changes in the process through outputs to actuators that manipulate the physical properties of the process.

Critical—Often, there is a high cost associated with errors and failures of the computer. In safety-critical embedded systems, a run-time error or failure can result in death, injury, loss of property, or environmental harm.

Embedded software presents unique problems and requires a different type of development strategy than other types of software, such as data processing or transaction systems where the computer is at the center of the application. In the computer-centered system, peripheral equipment with which the computer interacts, such as input, storage, and output devices, is there to serve the needs of the computer and not vice versa. In this type of system, the behavior of the other components of the system is usually known and often designed or chosen with the needs of the computer as the guiding feature. In the embedded system, the computer is used to service the needs of the other components; thus, its behavior and design is usually severely constrained by the external process being controlled. Furthermore, information about the behavior of the physical processes may only be partially known and is often continuous and stochastic and therefore difficult to incorporate into the usually discrete and deterministic computer software models. Instead of having external devices chosen to satisfy the requirements of the computer, the other system components usually dictate the requirements for the embedded computer. Furthermore, the order, timing, and required handling of input events by the computer are completely controlled by the other system components, rather than by the software designer. Events that occur in rapid succession or simultaneously must be handled by the computer software in ways that will satisfy the needs and requirements of the larger system. Software requirements for embedded systems are allocated during the system engineering process. The language Ada was designed to be particularly effective for development of embedded system software.

Errors must be handled differently in embedded systems. In most other computer systems, providing information that an error has occurred and discontinuing the processing of the erroneous transaction is satisfactory and perhaps even desirable. A human can then intervene to analyze the error and determine the appropriate recovery procedure. Although the computer system needs to provide correction procedures (e.g. for erroneous entries in an electronic database), the decision to make the correction can be handled externally and often offline. In embedded systems, errors and failures must be dealt with immediately, and often the detection and recovery from errors must be automated. The computer must be *robust* (must continue to operate in a specified manner), even though other components of the system may fail. Also, the other components must be made robust in the face of computer errors and failures. Finally, embedded computer software must provide facilities to detect and recover from its own errors or, at the very least, to fail gracefully in a way that minimizes damage to the overall system.

The Year 2000 (Y2K) problem (*q.v.*) was a particular threat to embedded systems since devices that failed at the onset of the millennium may have to be recalled and replaced.

Bibliography

1986. Elbert, T. F. *Embedded Programming in Ada*. New York: Van Nostrand Reinhold.
1991. Leveson, N. G. "Software Safety in Embedded Computer Systems," *Comm. of the ACM*, **34**, 2 (February), 34–36.
1991. Cook, R. "Embedded Systems in Control," *Byte*, **16**, 6 (June), 153–160.
1992. Ganssle, J. G. *The Art of Programming Embedded Systems*. New York: Academic Press.
1997. Heath, S. *Embedded Systems Design*. Oxford: Butterworth–Heinemann.
1997. Baron, C., Geffroy, J.-C., and Motet, G. (eds.) *Embedded System Applications*. New York: Kluwer Academic Press.

Nancy G. Leveson

EMULATION

For articles on related subjects *see* FIRMWARE; HOST SYSTEM; MICROPROGRAMMING; READ-ONLY MEMORY; and SIMULATION.

The most common meaning of *emulation* is the ability of one digital computer to interpret and execute the instruction set of another computer. To see how this can be done, it is necessary first to note that the control unit of a computer contains the necessary information for the sequence of operations (*micro-operations*) that are to be performed when a particular operation code (op-code) is to be executed. The op-codes may be referred to as *macroinstructions* (not to be confused with the more common usage of macroinstruction—*see* MACRO).

The control unit can consist of either *hard-wired logic* (that is, special-purpose digital logic circuitry for each op-code) or *microprogrammed* control. With micro-programmed control, the control unit contains a sequence of instructions (*microinstructions*) that, when decoded, control the gate operations in the central processing unit (*q.v.*) that will cause the op-code to be executed. This *microprogram* is stored in read-only memory (ROM—*q.v.*).

The microprogram in the control unit may simply be the sequence of microinstructions that will instruct the CPU to perform operations according to an instruction set that a computer designer wishes. For instance, if a computer designer desires an ADD Register-to-Register macroinstruction, the microinstruction sequence will consist of gating operations that gate each of the registers to the arithmetic-logic unit (ALU—*q.v.*) (and then gate the output of the ALU back to the appropriate register). Another possibility, however—and this is the essence of emulation—is to place a set of macroinstructions of another computer into the hardware of the given computer. That is, one encodes the macroinstruction set of the first computer by microprogramming those instructions on the hardware of the second computer. What we have then is an implementation of the macroinstruction set of one computer on hardware that differs from the originally intended hardware.

Another use of the term *emulation* concerns the possibility that one may wish to allow the replacement of one circuit board in the control unit by another in order to change the macroinstruction set. In fact, such approaches have been used to design, say, a Cobol machine or a Fortran machine. This is done because certain macroinstructions are more useful in some languages than in others.

Emulation was common in these senses until the advent of operating systems and application programs written in portable high-level languages like C and C++ (*q.v.*). Once these were available, together with efficient compilers for them, software could be moved to new systems by recompiling it, and emulation has now become less important as a means of running old programs on new hardware.

In a sense, the term *emulation* has taken on a new meaning in that many hardware features are simulated in software. This might include certain interrupts and systems functions. The inverse is also true to some extent when software features are transported to hardware to improve system performance. This is particularly true of memory management, graphics applications and high-speed computing applications. The boundary between software and hardware is often not clear, and the migration of features across the boundary provides a form of emulation.

Bibliography

1969. Rosin, R. F. "Contemporary Concepts of Microprogramming and Emulation," *ACM Computing Surveys*, **1**, *4*, 197–212.

1988. Habib, S. (ed.). *Microprogramming and Firmware Engineering.* New York: Van Nostrand Reinhold.

1989. Milutinovic, V. (ed.). *Introduction to Microprogramming.* Upper Saddle River, NJ: Prentice Hall.

Stanley Habib

ENCAPSULATION

For articles on related subjects *see* ABSTRACT DATA TYPE; CONCURRENT PROGRAMMING; INFORMATION HIDING; MODULAR PROGRAMMING; OBJECT-ORIENTED PROGRAMMING; and SOFTWARE REUSABILITY.

Encapsulation is a technique used to isolate some of the design decisions made in writing a program. To encapsulate decisions, a program is organized into an interface, such as a set of procedures, and an internal part. All access to the program's services are available only through the interface. As a result, programs that use those services cannot reference variables internal to the program or arbitrarily transfer control to its internal part.

Decisions that are typically encapsulated are the representation of data, the way that hardware facilities are accessed, and the way in which algorithms are implemented. A typical entity suitable for encapsulation is an abstract data type, such as a stack (*q.v.*). The program that manages physical changes to the stack provides the interface to it. Programs that merely use the stack (through execution of the familiar *push* and *pop* operations) cannot access the mechanisms and data structures used within the encapsulated stack manager and need have no knowledge of those data structures and their associated algorithms.

One reason for encapsulation is to provide a mechanism for information hiding. If, for example, the storage structure used to implement the abstract concept of a stack is changed to provide greater efficiency, the programs that use the stack have no need to know that the hidden structure was changed. The programs would, presumably, run more efficiently without their creators having to change a single line of source code.

Another reason to encapsulate is to enforce a particular access discipline—e.g. using monitors to enforce access to critical sections of a program so that only one user program can gain access to such a section at the same time (*see* MONITOR, SYNCHRONIZATION).

A third reason to encapsulate is to provide compatibility among programs that were not written with the intent that they be used together. Such compatibility is sometimes achieved by an interface that translates control and data into a form that can be used by the encapsulated program. The encapsulated program can then be reused without change. This approach is often favored when there is a considerable investment in a large, complex program that is poorly documented or not designed well for change. For example, suppose that some authority decrees that the message format of a message-processing program be changed in a way that was not anticipated. An encapsulated interface that transforms the messages from the new format to the old might be written as an alternative to rewriting the message processor itself to recognize the new format.

Encapsulation also provides compatibility among programs that are intended to be used together but which do not share resources, perhaps because they reside in different parts of a distributed system (*q.v.*). Standards for component programming (*q.v.*) require strict adherence to encapsulation rules for the sake of compatibility.

A fourth reason to encapsulate is to provide an abstraction for a resource that is particularly difficult to use. For example, many of the features of the control structure of a computer are provided to programmers through an operating system interface that makes those features both safer and easier to use. The interrupt (*q.v.*) handling code for the computer is an example. Programmers can write programs that perform input–output without having to write the interrupt code. Such code is usually carefully encapsulated (note that this is an example where there is no procedural interface). It is invoked only by the occurrence of interrupts in the computer's circuitry. In essence, the interrupt handler is a section of code that is executable by anyone, but readable and writable only by authorized persons. Encapsulation of the interrupt code prevents inexperienced or malicious programmers from corrupting it and allows often-used code to be developed once by those with the experience and knowledge to do it.

Bibliography

1988. Liskov, B. "Data Abstraction and Hierarchy," *Sigplan Notices*, **23**, *5*, 17–23.
1994. Booch, G. *Object-Oriented Analysis and Design with Applications*, 2nd Ed. Reading, MA: Addison-Wesley.

David Weiss

ENCRYPTION, DATA

See CRYPTOGRAPHY, COMPUTERS IN; and PRETTY GOOD PRIVACY.

ENGINEERING APPLICATIONS

See COMPUTER-AIDED DESIGN/COMPUTER-AIDED MANUFACTURING; COMPUTER AIDED ENGINEERING; CONTROL APPLICATIONS; DIGITAL DESIGN AUTOMATION; and FINITE ELEMENT METHOD.

ENIAC

For articles on related subjects *see* DIGITAL COMPUTERS, HISTORY OF: ORIGINS, and EARLY; ECKERT, J. PRESPER; and MAUCHLY, JOHN W.

The ENIAC (Electronic Numerical Integrator and Computer) was developed at the Moore School of the University of Pennsylvania in Philadelphia between 1943 and 1946. It was the first electronic general-purpose automatic computer, and it was certainly a landmark leading to the development of many automatic computer designs. The logical design of the system was based on the ideas of John Mauchly, and credit for the engineering goes to J. Presper Eckert, Jr. Eckert and Mauchly were granted a patent on the ENIAC in 1964. After a lengthy trial (Honeywell vs. Sperry Rand), this patent was declared invalid on the grounds of public use and publication more than one year prior to the application date. (The ENIAC was demonstrated to the public in February 1946 and the patent application was filed in June 1947.) The court further ruled that Eckert and Mauchly did not themselves invent the automatic electronic computer, but instead derived that subject matter from John V. Atanasoff (*q.v.*). Whatever the provenance of ideas between Mauchly and Atanasoff, it seems clear that Babbage (*q.v.*) invented the programmed mechanical general-purpose computer, that Atanasoff invented the automatic electronic computer (though his work was little known and made no contribution to the mainstream of computer development), and that the ENIAC was the first programmed general-purpose electronic computer.

The ENIAC was literally a giant. It contained more than 18,000 vacuum tubes, weighed 30 tons, and

Figure 1. The ENIAC (courtesy of the Hagley Museum & Library).

occupied a room 30 ft by 50 ft (approx. 9 m by 15 m). The computer consisted of 20 electronic accumulators, multiplier control, divider and square root control, input, output, two function tables, and a master program control. Each accumulator could store, add, and subtract 10-decimal digit numbers. Two accumulators could be interconnected to perform 20-digit operations. Addition and subtraction took 200 μs. Multiplication involved six accumulators and took 2,600 μs.

Decimal digits were stored in ten-stage ring counters, and signed decimal numbers were transmitted in parallel over 11 lines. Each digit was represented during transmission by a train of 0–9 pulses. Clock rates were 100 KHz and pulse widths about 2 μs. All logic was accomplished with direct-coupled vacuum tube circuitry.

As initially designed, programming was by patch panel interconnection, with a wire being required for each event at each unit. Data paths were programmable, using 11 wire cables. The data paths were like a party line telephone—many units could listen, but only one

could transmit. Various units could operate in parallel, being initiated from the same program signal and perhaps using distinct data paths. Interlocks were provided so that independent actions of indeterminate length (e.g. card reading) could complete before follow-on actions were initiated. Signs of results could change the flow of control.

The ENIAC was later converted to a card-programmed computer. In this scheme, certain standard operations were set up in the patch-panel wiring, and sequences of these macro (*q.v.*) operations were initiated from the card reader. The ENIAC was designed to integrate ballistic equations, and a significant accomplishment at its dedication in February 1946 was the computation of the trajectory of a 16-in naval shell in less than real time. ENIAC was formally accepted a few months after its dedication by the US Army Ordnance Corps, but was still operated at the Moore School until late 1946, when it was dismantled and shipped to the Aberdeen Proving Ground in Maryland. It became operational again in 1947, and was operated until 2 October 1955 (Weik, 1961, p. 575).

The first significant computation on the ENIAC involved atomic energy. Since the Second World War had ended, there was no longer urgent need for the firing tables that had motivated its design and the support of the Army Ordnance Corps. Among the problems first computed on it, in addition to those involving atomic energy, were random number (*q.v.*) studies, roundoff error (*q.v.*) analysis, cosmic ray studies, thermal ignition, wind tunnel design, and weather prediction. It was the major instrument for the computation of all ballistic tables for the US Army and Air Force (Weik, 1961).

Aberdeen Proving Ground reported that during 1952 the "total machine time" for the ENIAC was 7,247 h, divided as follows: production, 3,491 hr; problem setup and code-checking, 1,061 hr; idle, 195.3 hr; scheduled engineering, 651 hr; and unscheduled "engineering," 1,847.8 hr. The major portion of the scheduled engineering was preventive servicing, the remainder being for improvements and additions; 90% of the unscheduled engineering was devoted to locating and replacing defective tubes. During 1952, approximately 19,000 tubes were replaced (more than 100% of the tube complement).

The ENIAC proved that, with careful engineering, it was possible to build extremely complex logical devices that would perform at electronic speed, without error, for significant periods of time. This was the landmark leading to the development of many automatic computer designs, and paving the way for the "computer revolution." As modestly noted by the Ordnance Corps in *Army Ordnance* (1946), the ENIAC "established the fact that the basic principles of electronic engineering are sound." It was indeed "inevitable that future computing machines of this type would be improved through the knowledge and experience gained on this first one."

Portions of the ENIAC are now in the Smithsonian Institution in Washington, DC. Other ENIAC materials are in the custody of the Historical Services Division of the Department of the Army in Washington.

Bibliography

1946. US Army Ordnance Corps. "Mathematics by Robot," *Army Ordnance*, **XXX**, *156*, 329–331 (May–June).
1961. Weik, M. H. "The Eniac Story," *Army Ordnance* **XLV**, *244*, 571–575 (January–February).
1972. Goldstine, H. H. *The Computer from Pascal to von Neumann.* Princeton, NJ: Princeton University Press.
1974. Larson, E. "Findings of Fact, Conclusions of Law and Order for Judgment," US Patent Quarterly, **180** (25 March), 673–773.
1981. Burks, A. W., and A. R. "The ENIAC: First General-purpose Electronic Computer," *Annals of the History of Computing*, **3**, *4*, 310–399 (October).
1981. Stern, N. *From ENIAC to UNIVAC.* Bedford, MA: Digital Press.
1996. *Annals of the History of Computing*, **18**, *1* (January). Special issue devoted to ENIAC.
1999. McCartney, S. *ENIAC: The Triumphs and Tragedies of the World's First Computer.* New York: Walker.

Website

History of Computing Information. `http://ftp.arl.mil/~mike/comphist/`.

Harry D. Huskey

ENTERTAINMENT INDUSTRY, COMPUTERS IN THE

For articles on related topics *see* COMPUTER ANIMATION; COMPUTER ART; COMPUTER GAMES; COMPUTER GRAPHICS; IMAGE PROCESSING; MULTIMEDIA; VIDEOGAMES; and VIRTUAL REALITY.

Introduction

Computer technology has transformed entertainment. Television has grown more powerful because of computer assistance, providing multiple windows, programmed recording, digitally enhanced images, and even Internet (*q.v.*) access. Computer technology has also introduced digital audio and video technologies that provide higher quality recordings. Video cassette recorders have been replaced by laser disc players and digital video discs (DVDs) which allow real-time random access of data (*see* OPTICAL STORAGE). There are also any number of home videogames, which are computer-controlled. These videogames are popular in arcades and public entertainment centers as well. They use computer-control in simulator rides, multimedia presentations, and multiple screen video displays.

The most dramatic effects on entertainment due to computer technology are found in the material we see on film and television screens. Computer control of traditional processes found in film and television production, as well as the development of entirely new techniques, have revolutionized their imagery. We now see images that could not have been created before the introduction of computers into the entertainment industry.

Computers in Feature Films

The initial applications of computer technology in the film industry were similar to those in any other business: word processing, budgeting, and scheduling. Currently, computers are used in most aspects of feature film-making, including previsualization, character design, set design, storyboard, and online editing.

The design of any movie begins with previsualization and set design. By creating portions of the set on a computer, the director is able to look at it before it is built, test some possible stagings, and make changes. Even some final elements of the set are created on computer. Matte paintings which were historically hand-painted on huge canvases are now created on computers and recorded directly onto film where they are integrated into the movie during compositing (combining several images into one). Of course, one of the most well-known applications of computer technology in film is the creation of computer graphic imagery for special effects. In 1968, Stanley Kubrick's *2001: A Space Odyssey* reintroduced special visual effects to the motion picture industry, and in 1977 and again in 1999, George Lucas's *Star Wars* made such special effects a box office hit. This increased emphasis on visual effects spawned a new generation of effects techniques based on computer technology.

The design of visual effects begins with the *storyboard*. The storyboard is a visual reference of a proposed shot used by the filmmaking team (*see* Fig. 1). It is created from written descriptions in the script and conversations between the effects supervisor and the film's producer or director. It was traditionally hand-drawn by an artist and included background and effects elements. Today, storyboards often use elements that are scanned into a computer and combined digitally. This composite image may then be further manipulated by the storyboard artist. As technology has developed, storyboard artists have been able to produce precise renditions of each shot, even including accurate timing. These animated storyboards are called *animatics*. Using a computer-controlled online editing system, the director can actually cut the animatic into the film so that there is always a complete version to review. As each effects shot is completed, it replaces its animatic until eventually the film is complete.

Figure 1. A storyboard from the Oscar-winning Wallace and Gromit animations. © Wallace & Gromit 1995.

Figure 2. The Mark Roberts Motion Control "Juno" is a small, light, fast and highly portable rig for both studio and location work.

The production of visual effects has always used a few core techniques including *motion control*, *model building*, *animation*, and *compositing*. However, all these techniques have advanced dramatically since the introduction of computer technology.

Motion control enables the filmmaker to move the camera in a precise and repeatable manner. Camera controls are computerized in order to record and playback complicated camera moves (Fig. 2). Using this repeatability, the filmmaker can record several distinct passes which can be combined during compositing to create one final image. For example, one pass might be a well-lit actor against a blue screen. This is called the beauty pass. Another pass might be the blue screen by itself, for a *correction plate*, the use of which is described below. A third pass might be of a miniature set into which the actor will eventually be placed. These multiple pieces of film from different scale originals can be combined seamlessly because of motion control.

Computer technology is also used in a number of aspects of traditional character and effects animation. Traditional character animation and traditional effects animation, such as the creation of lightning bolts, are usually drawn on animation *cels* (transparent plastic sheets) and filmed on an animation stand. Computer control of the animation stand provides the same advantages, repeatability and refinement of moves, as does motion control of stage cameras. Older techniques like pans, tilts, zooms, cross-dissolves, and wipes are all made much easier with the use of computer technology. In addition, computer-assisted techniques like slit-scan, rack-focus, and pin-blocked animation have been made practical and integrated into the genre of traditional animation.

Figure 3. An example of stop-motion photography. © Aardman Animations Limited 2000.

Puppet animation or (*creature creation*), the building and animation of miniature synthetic characters, has also benefited from the introduction of computers. One of the great advances in creature work was the development of *go-motion photography* by Industrial Light and Magic. Go-motion is a refinement of stop-motion photography (*see* Fig. 3), the process by which a model, puppet, or any object is filmed one frame at a time and moved slightly between frames by an animator. Go-motion differs from stop-motion in that the motion of the puppets is computer-controlled. This technique permits the puppets to move while the camera shutter is open, creating the natural blurring of moving parts, and avoiding the stroboscopic movement often associated with stop-motion. However, it is still the artistic skill of the animator that creates the illusion of life. The same is also true of the next technological advance, digital creature animation.

When computers were used to make the first entirely digital creature, the field of creature animation was transformed radically. While it is relatively difficult to make alterations to a puppet, major changes can be made to a digital model with relatively little additional cost or time. In addition, making small changes to a puppet's animation would require that the entire sequence be refilmed. In digital creature animation, small portions of the motion can be refined without changing the rest of the sequence. This flexibility has allowed filmmakers to undertake projects of great complexity and with very realistic results that would never have been possible before the introduction of computers.

Digital creature animation begins with the design of the character. This process has three parts: *modeling*, *enveloping*, and *texturing*. Modeling is the process of creating the shell, or shape, of the character. This shape might be simple (like a snowman) or compli-

cated (like a human figure). Once the model is completed, it is handed off to an enveloper who ensures that it bends and moves in an expected way. For example, when the human arm bends, one expects that the skin will not crease or break apart but rather will gently stretch around the joint. This is accomplished by creating an inner skeleton for the model and attaching the two together using varying weights and mathematical rules, or dynamics. The skeleton is never seen in the final images, but rather is used by the animator to control the motion of the creature. When the skeleton is completed and the model is moving logically, it is given to a texturer to create the look of the surface. For example, if the model is a spaceship, it may need several layers of texture, including the metal, painted decals, rust, dirt, and soot. Once the model has been textured, it is ready to be brought to life by the animator.

Using the skeleton created during the design phase, the animator creates motion and stores it in the computer, thereby being able to review the work and make changes without actually putting anything on film or even video. This method saves both time and money. The animated creature is now given to the technical director. The technical director is generally responsible for combining the animator's work with the work of the texturer, lighting it in a way that is consistent with the setting in the film, and rendering the result. *Rendering* is the process wherein three-dimensional information is converted into a two-dimensional image. It consists of a series of computer calculations to determine what part of the three-dimensional scene would be captured by the digital camera, and how it would look. It may include realistic phenomena like motion blur, focus, lens warp, shadows, and lens flare, among others. The resulting information is stored in at least four separate channels, one for each color: red, green, and blue, and one for transparency (the *alpha*). Once the two-dimensional image has been rendered, it is ready to be combined with other images and integrated into the background footage through the process of compositing.

Compositing is the heart of visual effects. A composite is a shot composed of two or more images that have been combined to create the illusion of a single image. Composites may be as simple as placing one element over another or as complex as combining hundreds of individual elements into one scene. The most common application of a composite is the placement of actors, photographed on a stage or of computer-generated characters, into an imaginary environment or one that was filmed separately.

Until the introduction of recent computer technology, composites were done optically using an optical printer. *Optical printers* are cameras that rephotograph and combine separate film images onto one single piece of film. Typical optical printers did not allow for the creation of movement or the resizing of an element. In addition, there was a limit to the number of elements which could be composited without causing a degradation in film and image quality. The introduction of digital compositing eliminated these problems.

Digital compositing is the process by which two or more digital images are combined into one. Any film, such as background footage, needs to be scanned by a film scanner in order to be converted into digital format. A film scanner records three passes for each frame of film as it moves through the scanner, one red, one green, and one blue. These three passes are stored separately, thus allowing the compositor to have greater flexibility when manipulating the image. For example, one of the most common applications of compositing is placing an actor filmed on a blue screen onto a background that was filmed separately. Using the blue channel in such an image and its corresponding correction plate, it is relatively easy to isolate the actor. This process is called generating an *alpha channel*. The alpha channel stores transparency information. Sometimes there is insufficient information on film to produce a clean alpha channel, and the work needs to be done by hand. The process of hand-painting an alpha channel is called rotoscoping. Because a new alpha channel must be painted for each frame of film, rotoscoping is generally a very time-consuming process. However, there exist software programs which can often automate some of the work. Using the alpha channel, the actor can now be placed over a different image. In the areas where the blue-screen was removed, the new background will show through. The resulting image will appear to have the actor in the new background (*see* Fig. 4 on Color Page CP-7). Although this is the most common application for a composite, the technique is used for any number of visual effects in feature films, computer games, and television.

Computers in Television and Video

All of the techniques described in film production are applied to television production as well. Today computers are used in virtually all television content including flying logos, commercials, music videos, and television series production. Other uses of computer technology in television include weather presentation, digitally-assisted slow motion, interactive chalkboards, and news graphics.

One of the most important uses of computers in video is the restoration and enhancement of classic movies. Unfortunately, film breaks down over time, leading to the loss of much of our film history. In response to this threat, several of the major studios in Hollywood have developed techniques to scan their classic movies onto digital media where they can be repaired, enhanced, and stored indefinitely without fear of erosion. In addition, the data can be output directly not only onto video, but also back onto film using a film recorder, or selected images can be printed on a high-quality printer for publicity stills or one-sheets.

Computer Graphics

Computer graphics have revolutionized the entertainment industry. Examples range from the first video games like Pong, to Academy Award-winning animation like *Tin Toy* or *Toy Story* (*see* Fig. 5 on Color Page CP-8), and Academy Award-winning visual effects as in *The Abyss* or *Jurassic Park*.

Videogame graphics have increased in complexity and animation quality since their introduction. They were traditionally two-dimensional and used the system to draw small pre-stored images on the screen. As the technology developed, modern computer games became interactive stories, allowing the player to see, hear, and interact in real time with a synthetic three-dimensional world (*see* Fig. 6 on Color Page CP-8).

Traditional film animation has also been revolutionized by computer graphics. The drawing, in-betweening, inking, and opaquing of two-dimensional drawings, previously done entirely by hand, used to be very expensive because of the large number of people required. Almost all inking, opaquing, compositing, and special animation effects are now done on computers.

Fully computer-generated animation is often used by the entertainment industry. This work is usually categorized as either two-dimensional or three-dimensional animation. The former is essentially identical to traditional cel animation in making keyframe drawings, generating in-betweens, and coloring the resulting images. Computers can make each of these steps less labor-intensive.

Three-dimensional computer animation is similar to two-dimensional animation in the creation of keyframes or keyshapes which are in-betweened by the computer, but it is different in that computer models (numerical descriptions) are built and animated, and a *synthetic digital camera* (also a numerical description) generates the resulting images. The computer models used range from simple spheres and logos to complex models of working machinery, animals, and even people (*see* Fig. 7). Animation also ranges from simple object and camera moves to simulation of natural phenomena and highly realistic character animations (*see* Figs. 9a, b, c on Color Page CP-8–9).

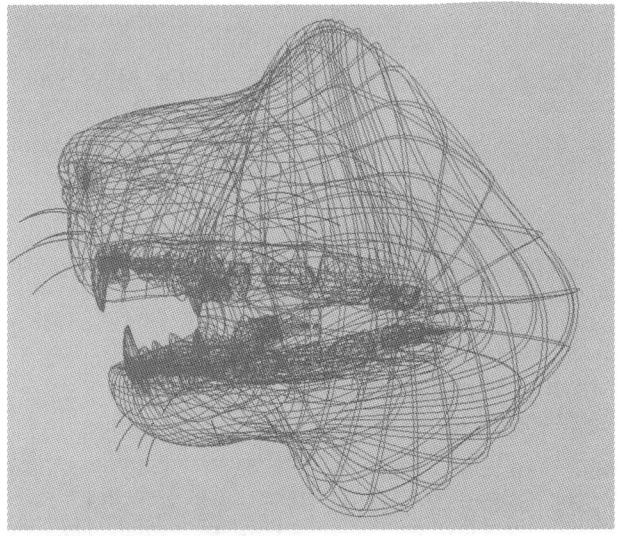

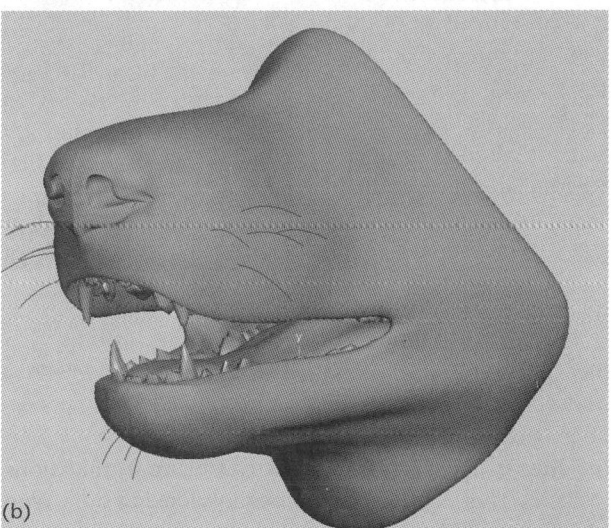

(b)

(c)

Figure 7. Cinesite (Europe) Ltd. modeled, animated and tracked a "talking" muzzle onto a live action dog for *Animal Farm*. The modeling and animation was completed using Alias/Wavefront's Maya and the compositing of the new muzzle was completed using Kodak's Cineon Software. (© 1999 Hallmark Entertainment/Cinesite, courtesy of Cinesite.)

Computer graphics in television runs the gamut from high-end effects and commercials through corporate logos and station identifications to low-end "visuals." As in the videogame industry, developing technology is continually revolutionizing the look of what we see. The development of workstations (*q.v.*) and more powerful personal computers has assisted the development of more realistic imagery.

Current uses of computer graphics range from the hidden, such as with some digital compositing, reduction of film grain, and removal of dirt, scratches, and unwanted objects from a scene to the generation of digital creatures (*see* ARTIFICIAL LIFE), environments, and even entirely computer-generated feature films.

Bibliography

1969. Miller, A., and Strenge, W. *American Cinematographers Manual.* Hollywood, CA: The ASC Press.
1983. Fielding, R. *A Technological History of Motion Pictures.* Berkeley, CA: University of California Press.
1985. Magneat-Thalmann, N., and Thalmann, D. *Computer Animation.* New York: Springer-Verlag.
1986. Smith, T. G. *Industrial Light & Magic: The Art of Special Effects.* New York: Ballantine Books.
1989. Bernard, W. *The Technique of Special Effects in Television,* 2nd Ed. New York: Focal Press/Hastings House.
1990. Foley, J., van Dam, A., Feiner, S., and Hughes, J. *Computer Graphics: Principles and Practice.* Reading, MA: Addison-Wesley.
1997. De Leeuw, B. *Digital Cinematography.* New York: Academic Press/Morgan Kaufmann.

Scott E. Anderson, revised by Lindy L. Wilson

ENTREPRENEURS

For articles on related subjects *see* BURROUGHS, WILLIAM S.; CRAY, SEYMOUR; ECKERT, J. PRESPER; HOLLERITH, HERMAN; MAUCHLY, JOHN W.; NIXDORF, HEINZ; NOYCE, ROBERT; WATSON, THOMAS J. SR; and ZUSE, KONRAD.

With the exception of some of the pioneers cited above (who have been accorded separate biographies), computer entrepreneurs have flourished only in the last half of the 20th century. Their vision and daring spawned one of the most sweeping technological revolutions humankind has seen.

They are dedicated and intelligent risk takers willing to create new markets rather than exploit existing ones. Most became very wealthy, very fast. This article contains, in alphabetical order, profiles of 29 computer entrepreneurs of particularly significant accomplishment, 25 men and four women. After their names, the companies they founded, as appropriate, are given. Ages, when given, are as of 1999.

Gene Amdahl (Amdahl)

Best known as the man who designed the IBM Series 360 (*q.v.*) main-frame computer, argu-ably the most successful business machine manu-factured until that time, Gene Myron Amdahl built the Amdahl Corporation into a company that, at its peak in 1978, grossed more than $320 million.

Figure 1. Gene Amdahl.

Amdahl was born in Flan-dreau, SD, in 1922. He completed his B.S. in electrical engineering at South Dakota State University in 1948 and his Ph.D. at the University of Wisconsin in 1952.

Amdahl began working at IBM in 1952. He had already developed a powerful computer, WISC (Wisconsin Integrally Synchronized Computer), to perform the extensive calculations related to the theoretical physics problems needed to complete his Ph.D. at the University of Wisconsin. At IBM he worked on the IBM 704, the first widely used computer to use index-ing, floating-point arithmetic, and a high-level program-ming language (Fortran—*q.v.*). He also worked on the 709/7090 series, but was denied an opportunity to work on the new and powerful IBM 7030 (Stretch—*q.v.*).

After heading the team that designed the 360, Amdahl, who increasingly disagreed with IBM's marketing strategy, left IBM in 1970. At that time he was an IBM fellow working at the IBM Advanced Computing Systems Laboratory in Menlo Park, CA, which he founded and directed.

In October 1970, Amdahl started his own company. He set out to build mainframes that were plug-to-plug compatible with IBM's popular machines. This meant that a customer could slide an Amdahl machine right next to selected IBM cabinets and use the same soft-ware and peripherals. It was a bold and risky concept that many feel only Gene Amdahl could have pulled off. His 470/V6 computer was compatible with IBM's 370/165. It used large-scale integration for processing, which was unheard of at the time. Only memory devices had been so tightly integrated by the early 1970s. The 470/V6 was a quarter the size and four times as powerful as the corresponding IBM machine, yet it was priced at the same $3.5 million. It was a major engineering and personal triumph. Orders poured in and, temporarily at least, IBM sales dropped noticeably.

Soon, however, rumors of IBM advances in computing power and changing trends in computer leasing dried up cash flow. This, coupled with a diminishing finan-cial interest in the company he founded, led Amdahl to move on and pursue other dreams of powerful archi-tectures through Trilogy and Elxsi, two companies involved in making high-performance VAX (*see* DIGI-TAL EQUIPMENT CORPORATION) clones. Amdahl Cor-poration, headquartered in Sunnyvale, CA, is now a wholly owned subsidiary of Fujitsu Limited.

Mark Andreessen and Jim Clark (Netscape)

Marc Andreessen (born 1972) co-founded Net-scape Communications Corporation of Mountain View, California in April 1994 with Dr. James Clark. Clark (born 1944) had previously founded Silicon Graphics, a lead-ing manufacturer of high-end workstations.

Figure 2. Marc Andreessen (courtesy of Netscape Communications Corp.).

In January 1992, while still an undergraduate at the University of Illinois, Andreessen began a $6 per hour programming job at the National Center for Supercomputing Applications (NCSA). That November, he began working on a Web browser called Mosaic with co-worker Eric Bina. Mosaic was released to the public in April 1993, and Andreessen graduated in December with a B.S. in computer science. He went to work for Enterprise Integration Technologies/Terisa Systems, developers of the secure hypertext transfer protocol (S-HTTP).

Jim Clark holds a Ph.D. in computer science from the University of Utah. He was an associate professor at Stanford University when he and his students devel-oped the embryonic technology that prompted them to found Silicon Graphics in 1981. The company's 3D graphics software was used to design the dinosaurs in *Jurassic Park*.

Seeking new horizons, Clark resigned from Silicon Graphics in 1994 to form a partnership with Andreessen. Though they co-founded Netscape, Andreessen, probably because of his youth, became the media darling and was named one of top 50 people under age 40 by *Time* magazine in 1994. The new company's goal was to become the leading provider of Internet browser software. The promise of a global, interactive communications network for the masses became reality with the introduction of the graphically-based, user friendly browser as exemplified by Mosaic.

To no surprise, Eric Bina joined Andreessen and Clark at Netscape. Their new product was named Netscape Navigator. For their innovative efforts, Andreessen and Bina received the 1997 McDowell Award (*q.v.*).

At the time of its initial public offering of stock in 1995, Netscape was giving Navigator away and had practically no revenues. But Netscape was setting the standards, often adding new features which users wanted before the standards committee had approved them. After mounting a legal challenge to Microsoft's attempt to bundle Explorer with Windows 98, Netscape was sold to America Online in late 1998. Today the battle has been joined as Microsoft and Netscape battle for the lucrative browser market. And Andreessen is carrying on without the full attention of Clark, who founded yet another start-up called Healtheon whose business plan is to bring greater order and efficiency to the healthcare industry through use of common software.

Tim Berners-Lee

Tim Berners-Lee (born 1958) is generally acknowedged as the creator of the World Wide Web (*q.v.*). In 1980 he wrote some software as a memory aid to track Internet (*q.v.*) links which he had trouble remembering. Little did he know what a hit it would become. He is included here because his invention has made possible the entreprenurial efforts of so many others

Figure 3. Tim Berners-Lee (courtesy of the office of Tim Berners-Lee).

and because its eventual impact may well rival the accomplishments of Gutenberg and Bell.

Berners-Lee is British, an Oxford physics major. His parents both worked on the world's first commercially available computer—the Ferranti Mark I. In adolescence Berners-Lee was influenced by Arthur C. Clarke's short story "Dial F for Frankenstein" which is about "crossing the critical threshold of number of neurons," to the point where "enough computers get connected" that the whole system "started to breathe, think, react autonomously." So emerged his later vision that the Web could truly seem alive.

While working at CERN, the European physics laboratory on the Swiss–French border, he needed to master its complex information system. To accomplish this, he created his personal memory substitute, a program called Enquire. It allowed him to link words which, when clicked, would lead to other documents for elaboration. This is now called "hypertext" (*q.v.*), an idea first proposed by Vannevar Bush in 1945.

Berners-Lee often asked those who demonstrated hypertext applications if they could make their systems universally available. The answer was usually "No." The need for a global central clearing house seemed daunting. Thus, Berners-Lee set to work linking the important databases of worldwide collaborators with each other. In collaboration with colleagues, he developed the three technical pillars of the Web: the language for encoding documents—HTML, hypertext markup language—*q.v.*); the system for linking documents—HTTP, hypertext transfer protocol; and the www.anything.com scheme for addressing documents—URL, universal resource locator. Without Berners-Lee's World Wide Web, the Internet would not be the phenomenon it is today.

Berners-Lee now runs the nonprofit World Wide Web Consortium (W3C) that helps set technical standards for the Web and keeps market forces, which would tend to fragment his idea, from tearing the Web apart. As director of W3C, he brings together its disparate members—Microsoft, Netscape, Sun, Apple, IBM, and more than 155 others—and tries to broker agreement on technical standards even as the software underlying the Web rapidly evolves. His group is responsible for the HTML standards as well.

In May, 1998, Berners-Lee was awarded one of the prestigious MacArthur "genius" fellowships, freeing him to do just about whatever he wants over the next few years. What does he do for an encore? He'll think of something.

Jeff Bezos (Amazon.com)

Jeff Preston Bezos (Bay′-zose) was born in Albuquerque, NM, on 12 January 1964, a few years after his father emigrated from Cuba. Though most of the entrepreneurs profiled in this article made their mark by creating hardware or software for others to use, Jeff Bezos took the Internet as he found it and used it as the basis for the best known and largest online retail enterprise to date, the Seattle-based bookseller Amazon.com.

Bezos graduated from Princeton in Electrical Engineering and Computer Science in 1986, *summa cum laude* and Phi Beta Kappa. He then joined FITEL, a high-tech start-up company in New York. Two years later, he moved to Bankers Trust Company leading its development of asset-management systems and becoming its youngest vice-president in February 1990. From 1990 to 1994, Bezos helped build one of the most technically sophisticated and successful quantitative hedge funds on Wall Street for D.E. Shaw & Co., New York, becoming its youngest senior vice-president in 1992.

In 1994, Bezos left Wall Street to found Amazon.com. He named his company after the river that carries the greatest volume of water because he wants Amazon, by revenue, to be a $10 billion company. Amazon offers an easily searchable list of 3 million titles, 15 times more than any bookstore on Earth, and without their costly overhead. Though the company has yet to post its first profit, and doesn't expect to until at least 2003, Wall Street has become so enamored of its potential that its capitalization is far greater than that of Barnes & Noble, whose revenues are six times higher.

Amazon.com does not confine its retail sales to books. Bezos has already added a line of videos and music CDs, and has expanded into crafts and games. It also runs its own online auction service. Bezos expects Amazon to become the premier retailer on the net. In December 1999 *Time* magazine chose Bezos as its Man of the Year.

Leonard Bosack and Sandra Lerner (Cisco)

Frustrated at the difficulty they experienced as graduate students trying to exchange notes over the Stanford computer network, this husband and wife team founded Cisco Systems in 1984. University mainframes could crunch physics data with ease but were stymied by simple messages passed between noncompatible hardware systems. Desktop to mainframe communications had proved particularly troublesome.

Figure 4. Leonard Bosack and Sandra Lerner (courtesy of Cisco Systems).

Bosack and Lerner developed an electronic box called a *router* (*see* COMMUNICATION CONTROL UNIT) that was capable of simultaneous translation. Suddenly, IBM could talk to DEC. Different computers, or even identical computers running different operating systems, could now communicate. The boxes weren't cheap—a router can cost $50,000 or more—but they are indispensable to network infrastructure. In 1990, just as the public began to discover the Internet, Cisco went public. That year it sold 5,000 routers, but by 1998 sales were running close to a million units. Cisco is the third most valuable NASDAQ company after Microsoft and Intel with 1998 revenues of $6 billion.

Despite Bosack's technological flair and Lerner's entrepreneurial drive, in 1990, the very year in which Cisco went public, Bosack and Lerner were forced out by the professional managers that venture capitalists had installed. But they walked away with $170 million for use as seed money for their future endeavors. Seventy percent of that sum was used to create a charitable foundation that finances a wide range of scientific and animal welfare projects.

Rod Canion (Compaq)

Rod Canion was born in Houston in 1945 and earned B.A. and M.S. degrees in electrical engineering from the University of Houston. In 1982, he and his Texas Instruments associates, Jim Harris and Bill Murto, founded the Compaq Computer Corporation by pooling $1,000 each. Canion became first CEO of the company, whose name is derived from *compa*tibility and *q*uality.

Figure 5. Rod Canion (courtesy of Questia Media, Inc).

Initially, Canion, Harris, and Murto were not even sure what kind of venture they wished to undertake. Finally, they decided to build a portable computer "better than the Osborne," the first IBM-compatible portable computer. Using $10 million in initial venture capital, $67 million from a 1983 public offering, and marketing skill, Canion later broadened the Compaq product line to include desktop systems and powerful network servers.

In 1983, Compaq shipped 53,000 PC-compatible portable computers resulting in $111 million in revenues. In 1984, it introduced its Deskpro desktop computers and achieved a computer industry sales record in its second year.

Canion's decision to offer only portables in the early days of the PC revolution assured Compaq of a retail presence and fueled their market dominance of that genre. Its reputation for quality, features, and support in the portable market facilitated entry into the desktop market. Compaq was the first PC manufacturer to incorporate the Intel 80386 chip into the design of desktop systems.

By 1997 Compaq had become the fastest growing company of all time and was *Forbes* Magazine's 1997 Company of the Year. After absorbing Tandem Corporation in 1997, Compaq acquired Digital Equipment Corporation in January 1998. It was the largest acquisition in the history of the computer industry and made Compaq Computer Corporation the second largest hardware company in the world.

However, taking Compaq from a PC company to an enterprise computer company did not fall to Rod Canion. In 1992, in a move that seemed shocking at the time, the founder of Compaq was removed from his post as CEO by the board of directors and replaced by Eckhard Pfeiffer. Since 1994, Canion has run Houston-based Insource Technology and its subsidiary, Insource Management Group (IMG), which focuses on health-care technologies and management.

Steve Case (AOL)

Steve Case, founder and CEO of America Online, the world's premier online service, was born in 1959 in Honolulu, Hawaii. He received his B.S. in Political Science from Williams College in Williamstown, MA. He started his career as a marketing executive for Procter & Gamble; he was later manager of new pizza development for Pizza Hut; then a marketing assistant for Control Video in 1983. The company was relaunched in 1985 as Quantum Computer Services and then renamed America Online in 1991. He was appointed CEO in 1992.

AOL is headquartered in Vienna, VA, a continent away from Silicon Valley and far enough from media savvy Manhattan to suit Steve Case. AOL had been an underdog for years to such high powered online services as CompuServe, Prodigy, AT&T, and even Microsoft. It has beaten them all back with shrewd deals and by early inclusion of access to the World Wide Web. Most Internet service providers are small companies struggling to make a profit. AOL, meanwhile, has become a media juggernaut, receiving income not only from subscriber fees but also from content providers.

Case knew the secret to online success revolved around ease of use. He increased his subscriber base with a shrewd direct mail marketing campaign mailing diskettes and CDs to what seemed like every man, woman, and child in America—and sometimes more than once. His next big push is a piece of the online commerce market.

Fortune magazine wrote in 1998, "AOL has more than 11 million paying subscribers, reaches about as many homes as cable operators Time Warner or Tele-Communications Inc., and is adding more than 10,000 users a day. AOL has more subscribers than *Time*, *Newsweek*, and *U.S. News & World Report* combined. On weeknights during prime time, the number of people logged on to AOL peaks at around 650,000, putting it in a league with cable networks MTV and CNN." Since that was written, AOL's customer base has doubled. In January 2000 AOL announced its intention to buy Time Warner with $165 billion of its own stock.

Michael Dell (Dell Computer)

Michael Dell was born in Houston, Texas, in 1966. At 17, he made $18,000 selling newspapers and spent it all on a new luxury automobile. One year later, he started the Dell Computer Company, capitalizing it with $1,000 of personal savings. He is now CEO and chairman of the Board of this Austin, TX-based company.

Dell's premise was that high-quality IBM PC-compatible computers could be sold exclusively through mail order, eliminating the overhead necessarily incurred by computer stores. By undercutting the prices of rivals such as IBM and Compaq, he has managed to earn a profitable share of the PC marketplace. By 1987, three years after its founding, Dell Computer's sales were $69.5 million. By 1996, Dell revenues had reached $5.3 billion and the Company employed over 8,000 people. Among the Fortune 500, Dell ranks No. 7 in return on stockholders' equity—ahead of Coca-Cola, Intel, and Microsoft. It is the only Fortune 500 company that has increased sales and earnings by more than 40% a year in each of the past three years (1996–1999).

Dell now has a reputation as one of the leading and most reliable providers of service to users among all mail order firms. The company's product line has been diversified to include notebook and desktop computers, workstations (*q.v.*), and network file servers (*q.v.*). Revenues for 1997 topped $12 billion, making Dell the world's leading direct computer systems company.

Larry Ellison (Oracle)

Larry Ellison is the founder and chairman of Oracle Corporation of San Mateo, California, which produces database software for industry and government. Ellison was born in 1944 in a rough and tumble neighborhood on the south side of Chicago. He studied mathematics at the University of Chicago but had not graduated before heading west as a self-taught programmer.

An IBM white paper on relational databases and standard query languages for accessing them influenced him to start Oracle. Without any outside funding,

Ellison and three of his friends invested $1,850 of their own money and launched the company in 1977. Two years later, in November 1979, they delivered the first version of their product, also called Oracle, to the Advanced Technology Division of Wright-Patterson Air Force Base.

Figure 6. Larry Ellison (courtesy of Oracle Corp.).

Oracle has enjoyed great success in the large and robust database market, having realized over $950 million in profit on 1999 revenues of $8.0 billion. Oracle software is not for the home user or the faint of heart. But its ability to handle massive transactions in both a mainframe and client–server (*q.v.*) environment makes it the choice of many leading companies. Airlines use it for their reservation systems and telephone companies use it for records and billing.

Ellison intends to make Oracle not just a software provider but also a major player in the consumer electronics market. He wants PCs to be cheap and as easy to use as pencils, user-friendly, and ubiquitous. He was an early advocate of development of an inexpensive "thin" Network Computer (NC) that would combine the best of television, PCs, and the Internet.

Judith Estrin (Precept Software)

As the daughter of computer science professor Gerald Estrin of UCLA, Judith Estrin was immersed in computer talk at an early age. As a young woman, she earned a B.S. degree in mathematics and computer science at UCLA, where she worked on the Arpanet (the precursor of the Internet), and a master's degree in electrical engineering and computer science from Stanford. At Stanford,

Figure 7. Judith Estrin (courtesy of Cisco Systems).

she worked on early versions of the TCP/IP (*q.v.*) protocols as a research assistant to Vint Cerf, sometimes called "the father of the Internet." Appropriately enough, Cerf had some years earlier been a research assistant to Judith's father while earning his own Ph.D.

Estrin began her professional career as an engineering manager for the Zilog Corporation, where she met her future husband Bill Carrico. Subsequently, they went on to found three successful start-ups, Bridge Communications (which merged with 3Com in 1987), Network Computing Devices, and, in 1995, Precept Software.

In its three years as an independent company, Precept has attracted wide notice for its innovative developments in integrating voice, data, and video networking. In March 1998, Precept was acquired by industry giant Cisco Systems and Judith Estrin was appointed Chief Technology Officer. Additionally, she serves on the Board of Directors of Sun Microsystems, Rockwell International, and Federal Express.

Bill Gates (Microsoft)

As president and CEO of Microsoft (*q.v.*) Bill Gates was once the computer industry's youngest billionaire. Born in 1955 in Seattle, Gates, as a teenager, was a mischievous and devoted hacker (*q.v.*). He knew how to make computers work and make money at it as early as age 15. A system he designed for traffic control earned $20,000 for his fledgling company, Traf-

Figure 8. Bill Gates (courtesy of Microsoft).

O-Data. He dropped out of high school for a year to make $30,000 working for TRW and bought a speedboat with the money.

In 1975, while a freshman at Harvard, Gates was struck by the cover article in *Popular Electronics* about the MITS Altair home computer (*see* DIGITAL COMPUTERS: HISTORY OF: SINCE 1950). He recognized immediately that these computers would need software and that much money could be made writing it. Along with his friend, Paul Allen, he developed a full-featured Basic (*q.v.*) language interpreter that required only 4 KB of memory. Basic made the Altair an instant hit, and in 1977 Allen and Gates formed the Microsoft Corporation. Apple, Commodore, and Radio Shack all introduced computers with Microsoft software.

Gates' biggest break came when IBM decided to enter the personal computer business. He convinced IBM that his small company could write an operating system from scratch that would take advantage of the disk drives and other peripherals that IBM had planned.

Gates also convinced IBM to make the machine specifications public as part of an open architecture (*q.v.*). Microsoft's operating system, MS-DOS, and its applications software are at the heart of almost all of the hundreds of compatible designs that have emerged since the introduction of the original PC.

Much to the chagrin of his parents, Gates dropped out of Harvard to pursue his software development dreams. Unlike several of the other entrepreneurial stories, there has as yet been no downside for Microsoft. Gates holds Microsoft shares worth over $100 billion dollars. When he took Microsoft public in 1986, he was only 31. In 1994, he married Microsoft employee Melinda French. They live outside Seattle with their infant daughter.

By 1998, Gates had turned Microsoft into the largest and most dominant PC software company ever. He testified before Congress and used his considerable charm, influence, and knowledge of the field to ward off legislation designed to rein him in. However, an anti-trust case, headed for a conclusion in early 2000, is a serious threat to Microsoft and could even result in its breakup. Nevertheless Gates is likely to remain the world's richest person for some years.

Andrew Grove (Intel)

Andrew Steven Grove is the chairman and CEO of Intel. He was born in Budapest, Hungary, in 1936. He was a refugee from the Nazis and later the Communists before coming to America. He graduated from the City College of New York in 1960 with a Bachelor of Chemical Engineering degree and received his Ph.D. from the University of California, Berkeley, in

Figure 9. Andrew Grove (courtesy of Intel Corporation).

1963. Upon graduation, he joined the Research and Development Laboratory of Fairchild Semiconductor and became Assistant Director of Research and Development in 1967.

In July 1968, Grove participated with Robert Noyce (*q.v.*) in the founding of Intel Corporation. In 1979 he became its president, and in 1987 he was named Chief Executive Officer. Grove has written over 40 technical papers and holds many patents on semiconductor devices and technology.

Since Grove became CEO, Intel's profit has increased to more than $5.1 billion. Intel makes more than 90% of all the world's microprocessors and enjoys a domina-

tion in the industry rivaled only by Microsoft's hold on the software side.

For his efforts and in recognition of the overwhelming contribution made by the microprocessor to the world's economy *Time* magazine chose Andrew Grove as its 1997 Man of the Year. *Time* called him "the person most responsible for the amazing growth in the power and innovative potential of microchips."

Every month, Intel turns out more than four quadrillion transistors, more than half a million for every human on Earth. Intel's nattily garbed clean room workers etch more than seven million, in lines one four-hundredth the thickness of a human hair, on each of its thumbnail-size Pentium II chips, which initially sold for about $500 and were capable of 588 million calculations a second. And the Pentium III is faster yet.

In 1998, Grove voluntarily relinquished his position as CEO of Intel, but remains Chairman of the Board.

William Hewlett and David Packard (Hewlett-Packard)

William (Bill) Hewlett was born in 1913 and raised in San Francisco. He was the son of a physician who died of a brain tumor when Hewlett was 12. David Packard was born in Pueblo, CO, in 1912, less than a year before Hewlett. The two met and

Figure 10. William Hewlett and David Packard (courtesy of Hewlett-Packard Limited).

became friends in 1930 while freshmen in the electrical engineering program at Stanford.

Packard, like many engineers of his day, became interested in ham radio and all things electronic at an early age. He graduated from Stanford University in 1934 and began work as an electrical engineer in the vacuum tube engineering department of General Electric in Schenectady, NY. While Packard was at GE, Hewlett was finishing up at MIT. They then did graduate work together at Stanford, building electronic devices in their spare time.

In 1939 Hewlett and Packard founded the Hewlett-Packard Company in Palo Alto, CA in an area that would later become the principal home of America's computer industry. Its founding date makes Hewlett-Packard one of the oldest computer firms. The name order Hewlett-Packard was chosen by flip of a coin.

With a loan of $538 from a Stanford professor, they built and marketed a commercial version of a variable frequency oscillator invented by Hewlett. Their base of operation was a Palo Alto garage. After many such small projects they began doing work for the Defense Department and in the 1950s branched out into the civilian electronics field.

During the 1970s, Hewlett-Packard moved from instruments to small computers and calculators. The HP 3000 minicomputer was their best-known product. In 2000 Hewlett-Packard remains active in the personal computer field and, as well, manufactures plotters, scanners, and a very popular and reliable line of laser printers.

Of the two, Hewlett was more the engineer–inventor and Packard more the entrepreneur–manager. Packard was Hewlett-Packard's president from 1939–1946, Chairman of the Board from 1947–1964, and CEO from 1964–1968. Between 1969 and 1971, he was Deputy Secretary of the United States Department of Defense. He has served on numerous presidential commissions, the US–USSR Trade and Economic Council, and the boards of directors of many universities and public organizations. He died on 26 March 1996.

Hewlett-Packard, known for its quality products and its great respect for its employees, was one of the first companies in the country to provide employee health insurance as well as other generous benefits. It also pioneered flexible work hours and casual dress. Many Silicon Valley companies who have successfully implemented similar policies point to Hewlett-Packard as the standard.

Steve Jobs (Apple)

Orphaned shortly after birth in California in 1955, Steve Jobs was adopted and raised in Los Altos, CA. Jobs's interest in electronics started in high school. He begged for parts for his projects, even going so far as to ask William Hewlett, President of Hewlett-Packard, for those he needed to build a frequency counter. His boldness earned him a summer job at Hewlett-Packard. Jobs and his friend Steve Wozniak, an electronic wizard who worked for Hewlett-Packard, built a single-board computer in Jobs's garage from inexpensive and readily available parts.

Until then, only computer kits had been available and hence only electronics hobbyists had computers. But Jobs supplied fully assembled computers to the *Homebrew Computer Club*. They built 50 computers in 29 days and sold these *Apple I*s, as they called them, to the *BYTE Shop* in Mountain View, CA.

During the early 1970s, Jobs worked for Nolan Bushnell at Atari designing videogames (*q.v.*). By 1976 he had talked Wozniak into leaving Hewlett-Packard and forming Apple Computer (*q.v.*). From the day it opened

for business in 1977, Apple prospered first with the Apple I and then the Apple II. The introduction of the VisiCalc spreadsheet (*q.v.*) whetted the appetite of the business world for Apple products. More than two million Apple II computers were sold. In 1982 Jobs made the cover of *Time* magazine.

But IBM proved a formidable opponent. When sales of Apple computers dropped off after the introduction of the IBM PC, Jobs turned his attention to a new and innovative technology that he learned from developments at Xerox PARC. He incorporated these ideas, among them a mouse-driven graphical user interface (*q.v.*), into a computer called *Lisa*. Almost certainly because of its high $10,000 price, Lisa was not commercially successful, but it ultimately resulted in the introduction of the more affordable and hugely successful Apple *Macintosh*.

Jobs left Apple in September 1985 after a falling out with John Sculley who Jobs had hired to manage Apple. He sold all but one share of his Apple stock, realizing a profit of hundreds of millions of dollars. He used part of the proceeds to fund a new company, NeXT, Inc., and part to purchase Pixar, Lucasfilm's computer graphics division. NeXT built workstations (*q.v.*) for university and business environments, where a premium is placed on ease of use and high-quality graphics. NeXT, despite revenues of $60 million in 1996, was not a success as a hardware company and was able to preserve only some new software and interface concepts before being sold to Apple later that year for $400 million.

By 1995, Jobs was back in the news with a renewed relationship with Apple. Apple's very existence was in doubt until he persuaded Apple's long-time adversary, Microsoft, and its chairman, Bill Gates, to invest $150 million in Apple. Jobs was persuaded to join the Apple board and become interim chairman, a post he retained until he agreed to drop the "interim" in early 2000 following the growing financial success of Apple in the late 1990s.

There can be no doubt that the Apple I spawned the home computer revolution and gave vision to a host of other entrepreneurs. It was Jobs, however, who got there first.

Phillipe Kahn (Borland)

Phillipe Kahn, founder, president, and CEO of Borland, Inc., was born in France in 1952. Although little is known regarding his education and early years, he did work in Zurich in the 1970s under Niklaus Wirth, the creator of Pascal (*q.v.*), and he was sufficiently qualified to have been teaching mathematics at the University of Grenoble in 1981. He and some friends who liked to write software for the Apple II had developed a very fast Pascal compiler that Kahn decided to market. Noticing that most successful US computer firms had addresses in Silicon Valley, Kahn moved to Scotts Valley, CA, in 1982. He made a concerted effort to shed his French accent by listening to talk radio and trying to talk Texan.

The venture capitalists who Kahn approached shunned him. So, with little or no capital, he rented a two-room $600/month office over a garage, took orders by day, and shipped by night. Until that time, the most popular version of Pascal was UCSD Pascal. That product was noted for portability, but not for speed. Kahn's compiler, now rewritten for IBM PC-compatibles, compiled directly to machine language and was startlingly fast with regard to both compilation and execution of generated code. Most orders for this "Turbo Pascal" came from an ad in *Byte* magazine, whose salesman, spellbound by Kahn rhetoric, agreed to run the ad on credit. His ad was bound to catch the reader's eye, since it promised (and he delivered) a breakthrough product at the then unheard of price of $49.95, one-sixth of the going rate for a good language compiler.

Initially, Kahn's company was called MIT: Market In Time. "I noticed," he said, "that if I had the MIT initials in my letterhead, people would return my calls." But when the real MIT threatened to sue, Kahn changed the name to Borland.

In 1991, through a swap of stock valued at $440 million, Borland acquired rival Ashton-Tate and its large base of customers for its dBase products. That product line plus Borland's own database product, Paradox, temporarily gave Borland three-quarters of the microcomputer database market. Other popular Borland products included the Quattro Pro spreadsheet, compilers for Basic, Prolog, C, and C++, and the Delphi development system, which is essentially an object-oriented Visual Pascal.

In 1998, Kahn renamed Borland *Inprise* to emphasize that he now believes that the future of his company lies with *enterprise computing*, a currently nebulous IBM term whose exact meaning is likely to evolve between this and the next edition of this Encyclopedia.

Philippe Kahn is at the forefront of the Wireless Internet revolution championing the adoption of smart Connected Internet Devices (CIDs) that give users immediate access to the people and information that matter most to them, anywhere in the world. In 1994, while still with Borland, he founded Starfish Software with Sonia Lee to develop the TrueSync technology platform, a global synchronization solution connecting popular hand-held devices, wearable computers, desktops, and servers. In July 1998, Motorola acquired Starfish to become a wholly owned independent subsidiary. Kahn continues to oversee Starfish's business activities as CEO in addition to serving as advisor to the office of the CEO at Motorola.

In 1998, Kahn started another wireless Internet Technology Company, LightSurf, Inc., to focus on the next phase of the wireless and wireline markets: the convergence of the Internet, digital imaging, photography, and wireless communications. Additionally, in October 1999 Kahn became Chairman of OpenGrid, Inc., a company that offers key core wireless Internet solutions that include wireless messaging, instant messaging (*see* ONLINE CONVERSATION), and wireless networking.

Mitch Kapor (Lotus)

Figure 11. Mitchell D. Kapor (courtesy of Kapor Enterprises Inc.). Photo copyright Louis Fabian Bachrach.

Born in Brooklyn in 1950, Mitchell Kapor is a former Yale University student of linguistics who along with Jonathan Sachs brought the most successful software product of its time to the microcomputer world —the Lotus 1-2-3 spreadsheet program. Kapor started as a child of the 1960s, lover of the Beatles, and protester against the Vietnam War. In the 1970s, he worked as a disc jockey, taught transcendental meditation, and earned a master's degree in psychology.

The success of the earlier VisiCalc, the first spreadsheet program, led to increased marketing of the product. In the early 1980s, Kapor was selling the related products VisiPlot and VisiTrend under a royalty arrangement. The original idea behind 1-2-3 was to integrate the operation of a spreadsheet, a graphics program, and a word processor. Sachs suggested that a database management program (*q.v.*) would be easier to write than a word processor and would be more useful. The product, starting as *Tiny Troll*, but renamed 1-2-3 at Kapor's suggestion, was originally supposed to be a programming language with a spreadsheet capability. Kapor realized the marketing problems that this would pose, so the programming language was disguised as a macro capability in order to emphasize the spreadsheet. Sachs did the programming and Kapor the marketing, and together they founded the Lotus Corporation, for years the most successful single-product company in the microcomputer universe.

Lotus 1-2-3 sold almost half a million copies at $495 each in its first few months. While Lotus has diversified, it is still primarily dependent on the income from 1-2-3.

Kapor tired of Lotus by the summer of 1986 and moved on to establish ON Technology of Cambridge, MA, which aims to build computers that are closer to being intelligent assistants than they are to being merely powerful calculators. Lotus was sold to IBM in 1997.

In 1990 Kapor and Grateful Dead lyricist John Perry Barlow created the Electronic Frontier Foundation (EFF) (*q.v.*), a non-profit special interest group devoted to defending the civil liberties of hackers. The EFF is often characterized as the American Civil Liberties Union (ACLU) of the computer industry. Since 1992, he has been president of Kapor Enterprises, Inc.

Sandy Kurtzig (ASK)

Sandra Kurtzig's interest in computers began as a UCLA sophomore when she became an intern at the school's computing center. She learned just enough programming to complete her first major assignment, pinpointing the location of Soviet bloc radio waves bouncing off the ionosphere.

Kurtzig completed an M.S. degree in aeronautical engineering at Stanford and began her computing career in 1971 by selling timeshare accounts for GE. When she encountered a telecommunications customer who needed some sophisticated software to keep track of inventory, bills of materials, and purchase orders, she contracted to write the needed software. To do so, she invested $2,000 of her own money to form a company called ASK operating out of the second bedroom of her apartment.

Word of her success with her first client soon led to other accounts, to the point where, in 1976, Hewlett-Packard offered her a million dollars for the exclusive rights to the ASK software. She refused the offer, and grew ASK until its revenues reached $185 million in 1989. She had resigned as CEO four years earlier but remained Chairman of the Board.

Two years into alleged "retirement," she was asked to return as CEO to guide the firm through some troubled times. She repositioned the company as a provider of database systems and oversaw sales growth to $450 million in 1992. Two years later, the firm was sold to Computer Associates.

Scott McNealy (Sun)

Scott McNealy is co-founder and CEO of Sun Microsystems, the world's leading manufacturer of high-end workstations and Web servers and developer of the Internet language Java (*q.v.*). He was born in Columbus, OH, in 1954 but raised in Detroit. He earned a B.A. in economics from Harvard in 1976.

After he graduated from Stanford with an M.B.A. in 1980, he joined FMC Corp as a trainee. They were then manufacturing the Bradley fighting vehicle for the US Army at a plant in Silicon Valley.

Figure 12. Scott McNealy (courtesy of Sun Microsystems, Inc.).

When some old Stanford friends who had developed a powerful workstation to be attached to the Stanford computer networks got investor support for a company called Sun (for Stanford University Networks), McNealy joined Sun Microsystems and quickly advanced. Later when Sun needed a new CEO, McNealy was named, in part because no better candidate surfaced. He proved fully worthy of the appointment. He developed and pruned the product line, adding the new and powerful Sparc chip, and gave individual product organizations the budget, credit, and blame for their product lines.

Sun also developed Java (*q.v.*) as a proposed universal Internet language for use with the Network Computer (NC) it hoped to develop. The rise of the Internet in 1994 was a big boost for Sun, its hardware making an ideal Internet server. It was ownership of Java that made even Bill Gates take notice. When he saw that Netscape with Java had more features then Internet Explorer, he was forced to license Java from Sun.

By 1997 Sun's annual sales were $8.6 billion and its profits were $762 million. Sun now represents one of the few alternatives to the "Wintel" platform (Windows running on an Intel 80x86 processor). It makes its own hardware, software, chips, and network systems. In time it hopes to own the hardware and software for most if not all NC boxes. And in late 1998, McNealy increased the pressure on Microsoft by brokering a deal whereby America Online bought Netscape, raising the probability that Netscape Communicator rather than Internet Explorer would soon become the default browser on the desktops of millions of AOL customers.

In 1998, McNealy was featured on the cover of *Business Week*, and he was profiled on CBS's "60 Minutes" in January 1999.

Robert Metcalfe (3Com)

Bob Metcalfe (born 1946) began his working career as an MIT whiz-kid working on the Arpanet. At Xerox PARC in 1973, he invented and named *Ethernet* (*q.v.*), still the most widely used protocol for local area networks (*q.v.*). He was so successful at selling the capabilities of Ethernet that he was able to raise sufficient venture capital to form the 3Com networking company in 1979, which has now grown to be a $5 billion dollar Fortune 500 company. Among other things, he is noted for formulating Metcalfe's Law: "the value of a network grows as the square of the number of its users" (*see* LAWS, COMPUTER).

As has happened with so many entrepreneurs, Metcalfe lost out to others in his bid to remain CEO of the very company that he founded. When that happened, he accepted a fellowship to Cambridge University in the UK, but after only a year he returned to the US to become publisher of *InfoWorld*. Though no longer its publisher, he continues to write a highly influential column for that magazine. Among many other awards, Metcalfe received the Grace Murray Hopper Award from the Association for Computing Machinery (ACM—*q.v.*) in 1980, and the Alexander Graham Bell Medal from the Institute of Electrical and Electronics Engineers in 1988.

Metcalfe now values his writing and lecturing more than the technology itself and aspires to win a Pulitzer Prize before he retires.

William Norris (Control Data)

Iconoclastic and unconventional, William Norris was the founder of Control Data Corporation (*q.v.*), maker of some of the most powerful mainframe and supercomputers of its era. He was born in 1911 in Red Cloud, NE. Like many of the early computer pioneers, he was interested early in electronics and amateur radio. He earned a degree in electrical engineering from the University of Nebraska soon after the death of his father in 1932. After Pearl Harbor was attacked, he joined the Navy and worked with mathematicians, physicists, and engineers from the scientific and academic community to apply recent electronic advances to the breaking of Japanese codes. He rose to the rank of Commander.

Figure 13. William C. Norris (courtesy of William C. Norris Institute).

At the end of the war, with the Navy reluctant to disband its code-breaking group, Norris suggested forming a company to continue the work. Despite the secret nature of the work, he rounded up a number of investors and formed Engineering Research Associates in 1946. With himself as vice president and John E. Parker as president, ERA concentrated on making high-speed digital electronic equipment. It quickly earned a reputation for building reliable equipment and delivering it on time.

After Parker decided to sell ERA to Remington Rand, Norris continued to work for Remington Rand, but felt troubled by the lack of support. Named vice president of the St. Paul division after the merger in 1955 with Sperry, he headed the Univac division of Sperry-Rand. IBM had still not made a major commitment to building computers, and Norris felt Sperry-Rand should. He tried to push in that direction, but to no avail. Highly frustrated, he left in 1957 with eight colleagues to pursue the opportunity to make big machines. He formed Control Data Corporation, using $75,000 of his own money and $615,000 raised from a large group of friends. None of the 300 stockholders had a controlling interest, not even Norris. He yearned to take on IBM. His shrewdest move was to hire Seymour Cray (*q.v.*) from Univac and give him the creative freedom and solitude he required.

Cray's creative mind produced some of the most powerful machines ever developed. CDC quickly became the industry leader in powerful machines for scientific, military, and engineering work. By 1959 CDC had sales of $4.5 million that a year later would exceed $28 million. Success was based primarily on the CDC 1604 mainframe and, later, its successor, the CDC 3600. In the mid-1960s the CDC 6600 was recognized as the supercomputer of the time. CDC followed with the 7600 and then the Cyber series. By 1965, only two computer companies were operating in the black—CDC and IBM. In 1968, when IBM announced its intent to add an allegedly powerful model 360/80 to its 360 series line, sales of the 6600 dropped precipitously. Norris accused IBM of unfair business practices for announcing computer models far in advance of their realization. He took IBM to court and won. He realized more than $100 million dollars in the suit and became a hero to all of IBM's competitors.

Norris used the proceeds of his successful suit to expand the former IBM Service Bureau, ceded to CDC in the settlement. The Bureau allowed people who couldn't afford a whole machine to buy slices of time as needed. CDC ran one of the first time-sharing services and became the world leader in peripheral manufacturing through the 1970s. Ironically, most such devices were plug-to-plug compatible peripherals used with IBM mainframes.

The 1980s saw the departure of Seymour Cray and the emergence of the personal computer, a market in which CDC completely missed out. During 1985 alone, CDC lost $567 million. Criticism focused on Norris and his expensive Plato educational project. Norris stepped down in January 1986. Nevertheless, he had played a critical role in the development of high-speed powerful machines at a time when the industry might have concentrated on making merely profitable machines.

Ken Olsen (DEC)

Kenneth H. Olsen was the founder of Digital Equipment Corporation (DEC —q.v.), once the second leading manufacturer of computer equipment in the world. He broke the mainframe's dominance of the market during the 1960s when he introduced a line of powerful minicomputers (q.v.) which were much less expensive than mainframes.

Figure 14. Ken Olsen (courtesy of Compaq).

Olsen was born in 1926 in Bridgeport, CT. He served in the Naval Reserve during the Second World War, completing bachelor's and master's degrees in electrical engineering at MIT after the war. During the early 1950s, he worked at the MIT Lincoln Laboratory. He was involved in the development of the Whirlwind (q.v.) computer, one of the first to abandon vacuum tube storage in favor of magnetic ferrite cores. He also worked on the SAGE military project.

When Olsen left MIT in 1957 to form DEC, he had a great deal of computer experience and he knew what engineers and scientists wanted from a computer company. He set out to build small, powerful, and relatively inexpensive minicomputers and sell them in the scientific and engineering market. His sales force, who were not paid commissions, was made up of engineers who would sell face to face to other scientists. It was a controversial concept, but remarkably successful. His first computer sold for $20,000 in 1960, a full $900,000 less than a comparable mainframe. His PDP series machines allowed direct access by terminal (q.v.) or teletype, signaling the beginning of the end for punched cards (q.v.). He plowed large sums of money into research and development, which led to DEC having one of the widest variety of products of any company in the industry. Its products were well built, well supported, current, practical, and well received.

He took a decentralized approach to management and allowed his designers to work on all phases of computer development and to participate actively in product development decisions.

The PDP series of computers paved the way for smaller machines and legitimized the minicomputer business. By 1985, DEC sales reached $6.7 billion. DEC phased out the era of huge, intimidating machines stored in glass-enclosed, air-conditioned boxes communicating only through skilled attendants. The minicomputer was the next necessary step toward the evolution of computing for the masses.

Olsen stayed with the company he started for more than 33 years, but he announced his retirement as chairman in 1992. Though an engineer at heart, he was also a creative and effective manager, a rare quality for the engineer–entrepreneur. His egalitarian style of management was popular with his staff and made DEC a productive and stable force in the marketplace for four decades. However, DEC's market position weakened in the age of the personal computer. In 1998, DEC was sold to the Compaq Corporation.

Ross Perot (EDS)

In 1962, H. Ross Perot founded Electronic Data Systems, the world's largest and most influential computer service bureau, with $1,000 from his wife, who was then a teacher. He virtually created the market for servicing the computer needs of corporate America. His service bureau provided computer processing power for the many industrial, governmental, and business enterprises that chose not to establish an in-house computing center.

Perot was born in Texarkana, TX in 1930 and grew up during the Depression. He and his family struggled to make ends meet. He sold seeds, Christmas cards, and newspapers door-to-door. He was so talented a salesman that he was able to sell newspapers to largely illiterate cotton pickers, who earned only $9 a week, by convincing them that they could use the newspapers as cheap insulation for their homes. When the director of circulation thought he was making too much money, his commission was lowered. Perot went directly to C. E. Palmer, the publisher, to complain. Palmer immediately had the original arrangement restored.

Perot claimed to be acquiring a business education in the market-place that was more valuable than one gained at Harvard. After graduating from Texarkana High School and then Texarkana Junior College, he received an appointment to the US Naval Academy, where he distinguished himself as a student and a leader. He was twice elected president of his class and named battalion commander. He graduated from the

Academy in 1954 and was commissioned an ensign. He served aboard both destroyers and aircraft carriers.

After four years in the navy, Perot was hired by IBM as a $500 a month computer salesman in the Dallas region. He finished first in his sales training course and usually made his monthly quota well before the end of the month. It was while he was an IBM salesman that he formulated the idea for EDS. He tried to interest IBM in selling time on its 7070 series of computers, but IBM feared it would cut into equipment sales and rejected the idea.

He began by purchasing time for $70 an hour on computers he did not own and reselling it at a profit. EDS pioneered the idea of facilities management, a concept whereby EDS would become the data processing department for insurance firms, banks, government agencies, and manufacturers.

Perot suffered a setback in 1973 when he tried to computerize the Wall Street brokerage community. But EDS recovered during the 1980s with lucrative federal contracts, some worth more than a half billion dollars. By 1984, EDS was spread across all 50 states and nine countries. It was the largest computer service firm in the world.

In 1984, Perot sold EDS to General Motors for more than $2.5 billion. While GM helped triple EDS business, Perot was not comfortable as a member of the GM board, nor were the other directors comfortable with him. In late 1986, GM paid more than $700 million for Perot's EDS shares, more than twice their market value.

In 1992, Perot received 20% of the vote as an independent candidate for President of the United States. He ran again in 1996, but his support fell to only about half that level. For the moment, he seems content to watch the fortunes of Perot Systems, Incorporated, with which, though it bears his name and benefits from his investment, he is not actively engaged.

Kim Polese (Marimba)

Kim Polese (Po-lay'-zee) is president and CEO of Marimba, Inc., a privately held software company whose products enable developers to create, deploy, and maintain robust, network-managed applications and multimedia experiences within enterprises and across the Internet. In early 1996, she co-founded Marimba with former Sun Microsystems engineers Arthur van Hoff, Jonathan Payne, and Sami Shaio. She was named one of the 25 most influential Americans by *Time* magazine for 1997.

Ms. Polese was born in 1961 in Berkeley, CA, to immigrant parents who owned their own machine shop. She holds a B.S. from the University of California, Berkeley, and studied computer science at the University of Washington, Seattle.

Prior to founding Marimba, Polese spent more than seven years at Sun Microsystems. Polese came to Sun after four years at Intellicorp, where she focused on AI-based tools and application development.

At Sun she was named product manager for Oak—now known as Java (*q.v.*) and was responsible for conceiving and managing Sun's Internet strategy for that language. With her close identification with Java, it was almost inevitable that she would seek to strike out on her own. But Polese held off seeking venture capital until she and her partners Payne, Shaio, and van Hoff came up with a prototype for a salable Java-based product. In January of 1996, they each invested $15,000 in Marimba. In August, the firm of Kleiner Perkins Caufield & Byers launched a $100 million fund to invest in Java-based companies. Marimba was granted $4 million, and operations began in earnest.

Marimba's specialty is "push media," material sent online to individual computers automatically, without users having to request or search the Web for it. The push idea had been around for a few years Marimba made *push* a major Web application with Castanet, a system that offers streaming software—not just data, but the code of the actual applications—from spreadsheets to video games. Timely and robust transmission of application code enhances a vision of the Web as the ubiquitous information medium.

Ted Waitt (Gateway)

Theodore W. Waitt is the founder and CEO of Gateway 2000 in North Sioux City, SD. The company was born in a farmhouse in Sioux City, IA, in September of 1985 and had sales of $100,000 in the four months remaining in that year. Gateway has since grown into a Fortune 500, multinational PC manufacturer with more than 15,000 employees and 1999 sales in excess of $8.4 billion, even though Gateway computers are sold only through direct mail-order sales.

Waitt attended the University of Iowa and left one semester short of his degree to pursue his business interests. Though Gateway was not the first PC clone manufacturer, Waitt sensed that the PC market was characterized by limited hardware choices, high markups, and poor service.

By 1987, Waitt was designing and assembling completely configured systems for savvy users willing to buy sight unseen for the right price. He and his cofounders began by providing peripherals and support to owners of Texas Instruments PCs. They placed large ads in major computer magazines and discovered a consumer willingness to try the direct market.

The strategy catapulted Gateway into a head-to-head race with Dell in the direct sales marketplace. The company's desktop and laptop product lines feature top-quality components and high-value software packages. Gateway has received plaudits from loyal customers and numerous industry awards for its service and product lines.

An Wang (Wang)

An Wang was the founder of Wang Laboratories, once the world's leading maker of free-standing word processing (*q.v.*) equipment. He is also credited with some of the big ideas that led to magnetic core memory for early digital computers.

Wang was born in 1920 in Shanghai, China, the oldest of five children. He received his bachelor's degree in electrical engineering and communications from Chiao Tung

Figure 15. An Wang (courtesy of Office of the Board of Trustees, Northeastern University).

University in Shanghai. After the war he enrolled at Harvard and completed both his master's and Ph.D. degrees in applied physics by 1948.

As a research fellow at the Harvard Computation Laboratory from 1948 through 1951, Wang worked under Howard Aiken (*q.v.*) where he developed his ideas for magnetic core memory. Then with $600 in savings, he rented office space in Boston and, as sole proprietor, opened Wang Laboratories in June 1951. He concentrated on small-scale applications involving counting, sorting, storing, and displaying data. As business increased he moved to Cambridge, MA, and in 1955 Wang Labs became a corporation. He sold his memory core patent to IBM for $400,000 and thus had the capital he needed to expand.

Wang Labs began to manufacture electronic counters, machine tool controls, telecoders, and typesetting equipment. In 1962, Wang introduced the first electronic scientific desk calculator.

In 1968, Wang branched out from calculators to computers. Ironically, Wang was one of the first to abandon magnetic core storage in favor of smaller, faster, and less complex semiconductor devices. As the 1970s arrived, Wang was determined to merge the dual office needs of word processing and data processing (*q.v.*).

His WCS series was priced below comparable IBM equipment and had more options. Then in 1976 he launched the WPS system, which was based on the cathode ray tube, a revolutionary development. This word processing system vaulted his company onto the Fortune 500 list. From that moment, Wang became known as "The Word Processing Company."

By 1986, revenues of $2.6 billion produced earnings of $50.9 million. But after turning company control over to his son in the late 1980s, Wang watched sadly as the fortunes of his former company turned sour as the ease of converting a personal computer into a word processor through software made free-standing single-purpose word processing equipment obsolete.

An Wang died at his home in Boston on 24 March 1990. In his lifetime, he had been awarded 40 patents and 23 honorary degrees. At the time of his death, *Forbes* magazine estimated that he was the fifth richest man in the USA.

Jerry Yang (Yahoo!)

Jerry Yang, whose father died when he was two, emigrated to the USA from Taiwan with his mother when he was 10. He learned English quickly and graduated from Stanford in 1990 having earned both a B.A. and an M.S. degree in electrical engineering in just four years. It was there that he met and formed a close friendship with Dave Filo. Jerry and Dave entered the same Ph.D. program at Stanford. After Dave's

Figure 16. Jerry Yang (courtesy of Yahoo! Inc.).

discovery of Mosaic and the avenue it opened for surfing the World Wide Web, both became so addicted that Jerry began to build a list of links to his favorite Websites. He stored them on his own home page and called it "Jerry's Guide to the Internet."

The list was unstructured at first, but soon Jerry decided that he would never be able to find anything unless he imposed some kind of order on his URLs. He chose, naturally enough, a tree-like hierarchy, much like the one used for collecting and naming file folders in Windows. Somehow, knowledge of Jerry's Guide spread rapidly and his site began to experience thousands of "hits" (visits) per day.

Yang and Filo quickly realized that the Guide had market potential and decided to form a company to promote it. But it needed a better name. Jerry was fond of the software that began "Yet Another," such as YACC, Yet Another Compiler Compiler. Passing up the obvious YANG (Yet Another Network Guru?), they settled on Yahoo!—including the exclamation mark—and began to seek venture capital.

Their first success was with the prestigious Sequoia Capital, which had to its credit such winners as Apple, Atari, Oracle, and Cisco. With $4 million from that source, Yahoo! was able to recruit additional staff and the company began to grow.

Yahoo! is sometimes said to stand for Yet Another Hierarchical Officious Oracle. The "H" is significant in that only Yahoo! and a few other search engines use the intelligence of human labor to categorize the sites they find.

The basic decision facing the Yahoo! founders was how to produce revenue from such an obviously useful product. If they were to charge for access, many users would choose not to pay. And if they were to decide to accept paid ads, customers might be turned off. But it was decided there was no alternative to paid advertising. And, after a small amount of initial grousing, users stopped complaining and the new revenue source prompted Reuters to grant Yahoo! $40 million of fresh venture capital.

In 1996, Yahoo! sold a 30% interest in the company to Softbank, the dominant software firm of Japan, with Yang retaining a 15% interest. Softbank, which had previously purchased the Ziff-Davis publishing company for $2.1 billion, prompted the launching of the publication of *Yahoo! Internet Life*, which promptly attracted many thousands of subscribers.

In 1998 Yahoo! earned its first profit and improved greatly on this in 1999. By 1999 also Yahoo! had become by far the most commonly visited search engine site on the World Wide Web. Yang has, indeed, become more than Yet Another Network Guru.

Bibliography

1988. Rifkin, G., and Harrar, G. *The Ultimate Entrepreneur: The Story of Ken Olsen and Digital Equipment Corporation.* Chicago, IL: Contemporary Books.

1992. Wallace, J., and Erickson, J. *Hard Drive: Bill Gates and the Making of the Microsoft Empire.* New York: John Wiley.

1993. Rogowski, S., and Reilly, E. D. "Entrepreneurs," in *The Encyclopedia of Computer Science*, 3rd Ed. (eds. A. Ralston and E. D. Reilly), 517–526. New York: Van Nostrand Reinhold. The third edition version included profiles of Seymour Cray and Robert Noyce, who have been accorded full biographies in this edition, and of Dan Bricklin, Nolan Bushnell, Maryléne Delbourg-Delphis, Gary Kildall, William Millard, and Adam Osborne, which are not included in this Fourth Edition article.

1996. Grove, A. *Only the Paranoid Survive: How to Exploit the Crisis Points that Challenge Every Company and Career.* New York: Doubleday.

1997. Cringely, R. X. *Accidental Empires: How the Boys of Silicon Valley Make Their Millions, Battle Foreign Competition, and Still Can't Get a Date.* New York: Harper.

1997. Jager, R. D., and Ortiz, R. *In the Company of Giants.* New York: McGraw-Hill. Profiles of Steve Case, Michael Dell, Bill Gates, Andrew Grove, William Hewlett, Steve Jobs, Sandy Kurtzig, and Ken Olsen.

1997. Murray, C. J., *The Superman: The Story of Seymour Cray and the Technical Wizardry Behind the Supercomputer.* New York: John Wiley.

1997. Reid, R. H. *Architects of the Web.* New York: John Wiley. Profiles of Marc Andreessen, Kim Polese, Jerry Yang, and others.

1997. Stross, R. E. *Steve Jobs and the NeXT Big Thing.* New York: Athenium.

1997. Wallace, J. *Overdrive : Bill Gates and the Race to Control Cyberspace.* New York: John Wiley.

1997. Wilson, M. *The Difference Between God and Larry Ellison: Inside Oracle Corporation.* New York: William Morrow.

1998. Swisher, K. *AOL.COM: How Steve Case Beat Bill Gates, Nailed the Netheads, and Made Millions in the War for the Web.* New York: Times Books.

1998. Hamm, S. "The Education of Marc Andreessen," *Business Week*, 13 April, 85–92.

1998. Kirsner, S. "The Legend of Bob Metcalfe," *Wired*, **6.11**, November, 182–186, 232–234, 246–247.

1999. Byman, J. *Andrew Grove and the Intel Corporation.* Greensboro, NC: Morgan Reynolds.

1999. Clark, J. *Netscape Time: The Making of the Billion-Dollar Start-Up that Took on Microsoft.* New York: St Martin's Press.

1999. Dell, M. *Direct from Dell: Strategies That Revolutionized An Industry.* New Yrok: HarperBusiness.

1999. Hof, R. D., Hamm, S., and Sager, I. "SUN Power: How Scott McNealy is Shaping the Future of Computing," *Business Week*, 18 January, 64–72.

1999. Quittner, J. "Tim Berners-Lee," *Time*, **153**, *12* (29 March), 192–194.

1999. Ramo, J. C., and Quittner, J. "An Eye on the Future: The Laughing Billionaire," *Time Magazine*, **154**, *26* (27 Dec.), 50–67 (Man-of-the Year Jeff Bezos).

2000. Lewis, M. *The New New Thing.* New York: W. W. Norton.

Stephen J. Rogowski and Edwin D. Reilly

ERGONOMICS

See HUMAN FACTORS IN COMPUTING.

ERROR ANALYSIS

For articles on related subjects *see* ARITHMETIC, COMPUTER; ERRORS; INTERVAL ARITHMETIC; MATRIX COMPUTATIONS; NUMERICAL ANALYSIS; and ROUNDOFF ERROR.

In general, the basic arithmetic operations on digital computers are not exact but are subject to rounding or truncation errors. This article is concerned with the cumulative effect of these errors. It will be assumed that the reader has read the article on MATRIX COMPUTATIONS, since the results will be illustrated by examples from that area.

Definitions

There are two main methods of error analysis, known as *forward analysis* and *backward analysis*, respectively. They may be illustrated by considering the solution of an $n \times n$ system of linear equations by

Gaussian elimination. In this algorithm, the original system is reduced successively to equivalent systems $A^{(r)}\mathbf{x} = \mathbf{b}^{(r)}$, $r = 1, 2, \ldots, n - 1$. In the final system the matrix of coefficients, $A^{(n-1)}$, is upper-triangular, and the solution is found by back substitution.

In a forward analysis, one adopts the following strategy: because of rounding errors, the computed derived system $\bar{A}^{(r)}\mathbf{x} = \bar{\mathbf{b}}^{(r)}$ differs from that which would be obtained by exact arithmetic. It seems reasonable to assume that, if the algorithm is stable, $\bar{A}^{(r)} - A^{(r)}$ and $\bar{\mathbf{b}}^{(r)} - \mathbf{b}^{(r)}$ will be small, and, with sufficient ingenuity, bounds would be found for these "errors." This is perhaps the most natural approach.

Alternatively, one could adopt the following strategy: if the algorithm is stable, presumably the computed solution $\bar{\mathbf{x}}$ is the *exact* solution of some system $(A + E)\bar{\mathbf{x}} = \mathbf{b} + \mathbf{e}$, where E and $\mathbf{e}$ are relatively small. Of course, there will be an infinite number of sets of which $\bar{\mathbf{x}}$ is the exact solution. A successful error analysis will obtain satisfactory bounds for the elements of E and $\mathbf{e}$. Such an approach is known as *backward* error analysis, since it seeks to replace all errors made in the course of the solution by an *equivalent* perturbation of the original problem. It has one immediate advantage. It puts the errors made during the computation on the same footing as those arising from the data. Hence, when the initial data is itself inexact, no additional problem is posed.

Early Error Analysis of Elimination Processes

In the 1940s, the imminent arrival of electronic computers stimulated an interest in error analysis, and one of the first algorithms to be studied was Gaussian elimination. Early analyses were all of the forward type, and typical of the results obtained was that of Hotelling, who showed that errors in solving an $n \times n$ system might build up by a factor of 4^{n-1}. The relevance of this result was widely accepted at the time. Writing in 1946, Bargmann, Montgomery, and von Neumann said of Gaussian elimination: "An error at any stage affects all succeeding results and may become greatly magnified; this explains why instability should be expected." The mood of pessimism was very infectious, and the tendency to become enmeshed in the formal complexity of the algebra of the analysis seems to have precluded a sound assessment of the nature of the problem. Before giving any error analyses, we discuss fundamental limitations on the attainable accuracy.

Norms and Floating-Point Arithmetic

We will need some way of assessing the "size" of a vector or a matrix. Such a measure is provided by vector and matrix *norms*. A norm of a vector $\mathbf{x}$, denoted by $\|\mathbf{x}\|$, is a nonnegative quantity satisfying the relations

$$\|\mathbf{x}\| \geq 0 \quad \text{and} \quad \|\mathbf{x}\| = 0 \quad \text{iff} \quad \mathbf{x} = \mathbf{0},$$

$$\|\alpha\mathbf{x}\| = |\alpha|\,\|\mathbf{x}\|,$$

$$\|\mathbf{x} + \mathbf{y}\| \leq \|\mathbf{x}\| + \|\mathbf{y}\|.$$

We will use only two norms, denoted by $\|\mathbf{x}\|_2$ and $\|\mathbf{x}\|_\infty$ and defined by

$$\|\mathbf{x}\|_2 = \left(\Sigma\,|x_i|^2\right)^{1/2}, \qquad \|\mathbf{x}\|_\infty = \max|x_i|.$$

Similarly, a norm of a matrix A, denoted by $\|A\|$, is a nonnegative quantity satisfying the relations

$$\|A\| \geq 0 \quad \text{and} \quad \|A\| = 0 \quad \text{iff} \quad A = 0,$$

$$\|\alpha A\| = |\alpha|\,\|A\|,$$

$$\|A + B\| \leq \|A\| + \|B\|,$$

$$\|AB\| \leq \|A\|\,\|B\|.$$

We will use only two norms, denoted by $\|A\|_2$ and $\|A\|_\infty$ and defined by

$$\|A\|_2 = (\text{max eigenvalue of } AA^H)^{1/2}, \text{ where } A^H$$
$$\text{represents the conjugate transpose of } A$$

$$\|A\|_\infty = \max_i(\Sigma_j|\alpha_{ij}|).$$

It may be verified that

$$\|A\mathbf{x}\|_2 \leq \|A\|_2\,\|\mathbf{x}\|_2$$

$$\|A\mathbf{x}\|_\infty \leq \|A\|_\infty\,\|\mathbf{x}\|_\infty.$$

Most of the early error analyses were for fixed-point computation, but, since virtually all scientific computation is now done in floating point, we restrict discussion to this case. We use the notation $\text{fl}(x \times y)$ to denote the product of two standard floating-point (fl) numbers as given by the computer under examination, with an analogous notation for the other arithmetic operations. We have the following results for each of the basic operations, using a mantissa of t digits in the base β:

$$\text{fl}(x \times y) = xy(1 + \varepsilon), \quad |\varepsilon| \leq m\beta^{-t},$$

$$\text{fl}(x \div y) = (x/y)(1 + \varepsilon), \quad |\varepsilon| \leq d\beta^{-t},$$

$$\text{fl}(x \pm y) = x(1 + \varepsilon_1) \pm y(1 + \varepsilon_2), \quad |\varepsilon_1|, |\varepsilon_2| \leq s\beta^{-t}$$

where m, d, and s are constants on the order of unity, depending on the details of the rounding or chopping procedure. Described in the language of backward error analysis, we might say, for example, that the *computed* sum of two numbers x and y is the *exact* sum of two numbers $x(1 + \varepsilon_1)$ and $y(1 + \varepsilon_2)$, each having a low relative error. On well-designed computers,

$$\text{fl}(x \pm y) = (x \pm y)(1 + \varepsilon), \quad |\varepsilon| \leq s\beta^{-t}.$$

For convenience, from now on we assume that all ε in the above satisfy the bound $|\varepsilon| \le k \cdot \beta^{-t}$, where k is of the order of unity.

By repeated application we have, with an obvious notation,

$$\mathrm{fl}(a_1 + a_2 + \cdots + a_n)$$
$$= a_1(1 + E_1) + a_2(1 + E_2) \cdots + a_n(1 + E_n),$$
$$(1 - k\beta^{-t})^{n-1} \le 1 + E_1 \le (1 + k\beta^{-t})^{n-1}$$
$$(1 - k\beta^{-t})^{n+1-r} \le 1 + E_r \le (1 + k\beta^{-t})^{n+1-r}$$
$$r = 2, 3, \ldots, n.$$

The bounds on the errors are reasonably realistic, and examples can be constructed in which they are almost attained. Naturally, when n is large, the statistical distribution can be expected, in general, to result in some cancellation of errors and, thus, in actual errors substantially less than the bounds.

One of the most important elements in elimination methods is the computation of expressions of the form

$$p = \mathrm{fl}(a - x_1 \times y_1 - \cdots - x_n \times y_n).$$

The computed p and the error bounds are dependent on the order in which operations are performed. If the operations are performed in the order written above, we obtain

$$p = a(1 + E) - x_1 y_1(1 + F_1) - \cdots - x_n y_n(1 + F_n),$$

where

$$(1 - k\beta^{-t})^n \le 1 + E \le (1 + k\beta^{-t})^n,$$
$$(1 - k\beta^{-1})^{n+2-i} \le 1 + F_i \le (1 + k\beta^{-t})^{n+2-i}.$$

If one computes

$$p = \mathrm{fl}(-x_1 \times y_1 - x_2 \times y_2 - \cdots - x_n \times y_n + a),$$

then

$$p = -x_1 y_1(1 + E_1) - \cdots - x_n y_n(1 + E_n) + a(1 + F),$$
$$(1 - k\beta^{-t})^{n+3-i}(1 + E_i) \le (1 + k\beta^{-t})^{n+3-i},$$
$$|F| \le k\beta^{-1}.$$

In describing the last result in terms of backward error analysis, we might say, for example, that it is exact for data $x_i(1 + E_i)$, y_i, and $a(1 + F)$, putting all the perturbations in the x_i and a. Alternatively, we could say it is exact for data, x_i, $y_i(1 + E_i)$, and $a(1 + F)$.

Note that although the errors made can be equated with the effect of small relative perturbations in the data, the relative error in the computed p may be arbitrarily high, depending on the degree of cancellation that takes place. Indeed, if the true p is zero, one may have an infinite relative error. One would not think of

attributing this to some malignant instability in this simple arithmetic process; it is the natural loss to be expected.

Inherent Sensitivity of the Solution of a Linear System

For any computational problem, the inherent sensitivity of the solution to changes in the data is of fundamental importance; yet oddly enough the early analyses of Gaussian elimination paid little attention to it. We consider in a very elementary way the effect of perturbations δA in the matrix A. We have

$$\bar{\mathbf{x}} = (A + \delta A)^{-1}\mathbf{b} = (A^{-1} - A^{-1}\delta A A^{-1} + \cdots)\mathbf{b}$$
$$= \mathbf{x} - A^{-1}\delta A \mathbf{x} + (A^{-1}\delta A)^2 \mathbf{x} - \cdots,$$

giving

$$\|\bar{\mathbf{x}} - \mathbf{x}\|/\|\mathbf{x}\| \le \|A^{-1}\delta A\|/(1 - \|A^{-1}\delta A\|),$$

provided $\|A^{-1}\delta A\| < 1$. The relative error in $\bar{\mathbf{x}}$ will not be low unless $\|A^{-1}\delta A\|$ is small. Writing

$$\|\delta A\| = \eta\|A\|,$$

we see that

$$\|\bar{\mathbf{x}} - \mathbf{x}\|/\|\mathbf{x}\| \le \eta\|A\| \|A^{-1}\|/(1 - \eta\|A\| \|A^{-1}\|).$$

The inherent sensitivity is therefore dependent on $\|A\| \|A^{-1}\|$, and this is usually known as the *condition number* of A (for the given norm), with respect to matrix inversion or to the solution of linear systems.

We might now ask ourselves what sort of limitation we should expect on the accuracy of Gaussian elimination even if it had no menacing instability. The solution of $A\mathbf{x} = \mathbf{b}$ requires $n^3/3$ multiplications and additions, an average of $\frac{1}{3}n$ per element. From the elementary discussion given so far, we might risk the following prophecy: even if Gaussian elimination is a stable process, then we can scarcely expect to obtain a bound for the resulting error which is less than that resulting from a perturbation δA in A satisfying, say

$$\|\delta A\| \le \tfrac{1}{3} kn\beta^{-t}\|A\|.$$

In fact, this bound for the effect is usually reasonably realistic, provided that pivoting is used. Indeed, the advantages conferred by the statistical distribution of rounding errors is such that the error is usually less than the maximum error that could be caused by such a perturbation.

Backward Error Analysis of Gaussian Elimination

Gaussian elimination provides a very good illustration of the power and simplicity of backward error analysis. The elimination process may be described as the production of a unit lower triangular matrix L and an upper triangular matrix U such that $LU = A$. The solution of the system $A\mathbf{x} = \mathbf{b}$ is then carried out in the two steps:

$$Ly = \mathbf{b}, \qquad U\mathbf{x} = \mathbf{y}$$

In the backward error analysis, one shows that the computed L and U satisfy the relation $LU = A + E$ and obtains bounds for the elements of E. One then shows that the computed solutions $\mathbf{y}$ and $\mathbf{x}$ of the triangular systems satisfies the equations

$$(L + \delta L)\mathbf{y} = \mathbf{b}, \qquad (U + \delta U)\mathbf{x} = \mathbf{y}$$

and obtains bounds for the elements of δL and δU. The computed $\mathbf{x}$ therefore solves *exactly* the system

$$(L + \delta L)(U + \delta U)\mathbf{x} = \mathbf{b}$$

$$(A + E + \delta LU + L\delta U + \delta L\delta U)\mathbf{x} = \mathbf{b}$$

Hence it is the exact solution of $(A + F)\mathbf{x} = \mathbf{b}$, where

$$\|F\| = \|E + \delta LU + L\delta U + \delta L\delta U\|$$
$$\leq \|E\| + \|L\|\,\|\delta U\| + \|U\|\,\|\delta L\|$$
$$+ \|\delta L\|\,\|\delta U\|,$$

and from the bounds for E, δL, and δU, one obtains a bound for F.

The simplicity of the technique may be illustrated by presenting the analysis of the solution of the system $L\mathbf{y} = \mathbf{b}$. We first make the following observations:

1. The relevant system to be analyzed is that with the computed matrix L, *not* the L that would have resulted from exact computation.

2. Since during the course of the analysis we do not attempt a direct comparison between computed and exact values, there is no need to denote computed quantities by bars. It is to be understood that all symbols refer to computed quantities.

3. It is only at the final stage when we have expressed the computed solution as the exact solution of $(A + F)\mathbf{x} = \mathbf{b}$ and have obtained a bound for $\|F\|$ that we attempt to compare the computed $\mathbf{x}$ with the true $\mathbf{x}$, and at this stage we can use the result of the previous section.

At a typical stage in the triangular solution, $y_1, y_2, \dots,$ y_{r-1} have been computed and y_r is determined from the relation

$$y_r = \mathrm{fl}(-l_{r1}y_1 - l_{r2}y_2 - \cdots - l_{r,r-1}y_{r-1} + b_r),$$

using, of course, the computed values of the y_i. Hence

$$y_r = -l_{r1}y_1(1 + E_{r1}) - l_{r2}y_2(1 + E_{r2}) - \cdots$$
$$- l_{r,r-1}y_{r-1}(1 + E_{r,r-1}) + b_r(1 + F_r),$$

where the factors $1 + E_{ri}$ and $1 + F_r$ are of the type discussed in connection with the computation of p above. Hence, the computed y_i satisfy exactly the relation

$$l_{r1}(1 + G_{r1}) + l_{r2}y_2(1 + G_{r2}) + \cdots$$
$$+ l_{r,r-1}y_{r-1}(1 + G_{r,r-1}) + y_r(1 + G_{rr}) = b_r,$$

where

$$(1 + G_{ri}) = (1 + E_{ri})/(1 + F_r), \quad i = 1, \dots, r - 1.$$
$$1 + G_{rr} = 1/(1 + F_r)$$

Notice that by dividing through by $1 + F_r$ we are able to restrict ourselves to perturbations in L. The computed $\mathbf{y}$ therefore satisfies exactly the relation $(L + \delta L)\mathbf{y} = \mathbf{b}$, where $\delta L_{ij} = L_{ij}G_{ij}$.

We certainly have

$$(1 - k\beta^{-t})^n \leq (1 + G_{ij}) \leq (1 + k\beta^{-t})^n$$

most of the factors, of course, satisfying much better bounds. Bounds of the above type are cumbersome to use, and we observe that, if $kn\beta^{-1} < 0.1$, as will usually be the case, then, using the binomial theorem,

$$(1 + k\beta^{-t})^n \leq 1 + (1.06)kn\beta^{-t},$$
$$(1 - k\beta^{-t})^n \geq 1 - (1.06)kn\beta^{-t}.$$

Hence, we have

$$|\delta L_{ij}| \leq (1.06)kn\beta^{-t}|L_{ij}|,$$

giving, for example

$$\|\delta L\|_\infty \leq (1.06)kn\beta^{-t}\|L\|_\infty.$$

The analysis is almost trivial, though earlier error analyses of the solution of triangular systems were extremely complicated.

If the computation of y_r had been expressed in the form

$$y_r = \mathrm{fl}(b_r - l_{r1}y_1 - \cdots - l_{r,r-1}y_{r-1}),$$

then we could still obtain a relation of the form $(L + \delta L)\mathbf{y} = \mathbf{b}$, but in this case the bounds on the elements of δL would be appreciably larger.

On most computers it is possible to accumulate either of the expressions for y_r in double precision, rounding to single precision only on completion. If this is done, then we again obtain a relation of the form

$$l_{r1}y_1(1 + G_{r1}) + l_{r2}y_2(1 + G_{r2}) + \cdots$$
$$+ l_{r,r-1}y_{r-1}(1 + G_{r,r-1}) + y_r(1 + G_{rr}) = b_r,$$

but now the quantities $|G_{ri}|$ $(i < r)$ have bounds of order β^{-2t} and can therefore virtually be neglected, while $|G_{rr}|$ has the bound $k\beta^{-t}$. We therefore have a result that might well be described as best possible, having regard to the precision of computation. Indeed, the residual vector $\mathbf{b} - L\mathbf{y}$ corresponding to the computed $\mathbf{y}$ will almost certainly be smaller than that corresponding to the correctly rounded solution!

The analysis of the solution of $U\mathbf{x} = \mathbf{y}$ is almost identical to that of $L\mathbf{y} = \mathbf{b}$, while the analysis of the factorization process is only marginally more complicated. If the L and U are produced as in classical Gaussian elimination, then one can show that $LU = A + E$, where, denoting the maximum modulus of any element arising during the decomposition by g, we certainly have

$$|e_{ij}| \leq (3.02)igk\beta^{-t} \qquad (i \leq j),$$
$$|e_{ij}| \leq (3.02)jgk\beta^{-t} \qquad (i > j).$$

If the factors L and U are determined directly, using the relations

$$l_{ij}u_{jj} = a_{ij} - l_{i1}u_{1j} - \cdots - l_{i,j-1}u_{j-1,j} \qquad j = 1, \ldots, i-1$$

and

$$u_{ij} = a_{ij} - l_{i1}u_{1j} - \cdots - l_{i,i-1}u_{i-1,j} \qquad j = i, \ldots, n,$$

and the expressions on the right are accumulated in double precision, an even more satisfactory bound may be determined for E. Indeed, ignoring quantities of the order of magnitude of β^{-2t}, we certainly have $|e_{ij}| \leq gk\beta^{-t}$, where g is now the element of maximum modulus in the computed U. Again, we have what may be regarded as a "best possible" result.

The reader may be surprised that no reference has been made to pivoting or to the size of the l_{pq}. The importance of pivoting is concealed. If any of the multipliers is large, g will usually be much larger than $\max |a_{ij}|$. When pivoting is used $|l_{pq}| \leq 1$, and there will not *usually* be much growth in the size of the elements of the reduced matrices or of U relative to the initial set of a_{ij}. When A is positive definite or diagonally dominant, *no* growth can take place, and we have a guaranteed *a priori* bound for $\|E\|$ in terms of A.

In 1947, von Neumann and Goldstine considered the special case of the inversion of a positive definite matrix with pivoting, and obtained a result for fixed-point computation that is only marginally weaker than can be obtained by arguments of the above type, though the analysis was far more complicated. Their analysis is often described as a forward error analysis, but it is in fact of the backward type, although at no stage are results expressed in a form such as to emphasize this. The final result of an analysis of the above type for the solution of a positive definite

system is to guarantee that it is the exact solution of $(A + E)\mathbf{x} = \mathbf{b}$ and to give a bound for E of the type

$$\|E\| \leq f(n)k\beta^{-t}\|A\|,$$

where $f(n)$ is a modest function of n, depending a little on the details of the arithmetic. When backward error analysis is applied to matrix inversion, one cannot show that X is the exact solution of $(A + E)X = I$, with a similar bound for E, because it is not true. However, the rth column, x_r, of X is the exact solution of some $(A + E_r)\mathbf{x}_r = \mathbf{e}_r$, where $\mathbf{e}_r$ is the rth column of I: the E_r are all different, but have the same satisfactory uniform bound. This result is implicit in that of von Neumann and Goldstine, but it is well concealed!

Orthogonal Transformations

Experience with error analyses of matrix processes gradually exposed the fact that control of *growth* in derived matrices is the key to stability. If orthogonal transformations Q are used, then, since $\|QA\|_2 = \|AQ\|_2 = \|A\|_2$, no general growth *can* take place. Although the algebra is a little complicated, a fairly general analysis can be given of whole classes of algorithms based on orthogonal transformations, both for the solution of equations and the eigenvalue problem. One can show, for example, that for a sequence of r orthogonal similarity transformations, the final computed transform $A^{(r)}$ satisfies *exactly* a relation of the form

$$A^{(r)} = Q^T(A + E)Q,$$

where Q is *exactly* orthogonal and

$$\|E\| \leq rf(n)\|A\|k\beta^{-t},$$

where $f(n)$ is some quite innocuous function of n. Hence, the eigenvalues of $A^{(r)}$ are exactly those of $A + E$, and we are back with perturbation theory.

A Posteriori Error Bounds

The bounds discussed so far are of the *a priori* type. The main function of such an analysis is to show whether or not an algorithm is stable and, if not, to pinpoint the reasons for its instability.

When a solution has been determined, one can usually obtain much sharper backward error bounds. For example, from a computed eigenvalue λ and an eigenvector $\mathbf{u}$, such that $\|\mathbf{u}\|_2 = 1$, one can compute the residual defined by $\mathbf{r} = A\mathbf{u} - \lambda\mathbf{u}$. This may be written in the form $(A - \mathbf{r}\mathbf{u}^H)\mathbf{u} = \lambda\mathbf{u}$, showing that λ *and* $\mathbf{u}$ are exact for the matrix $A - \mathbf{r}\mathbf{u}^H$. When A is Hermitian, this implies that A has an eigenvalue in the interval $\lambda - \|\mathbf{r}\|_2, \lambda + \|\mathbf{r}\|_2$. Similarly, when solving linear equations, one can compute $\mathbf{r} = \mathbf{b} - A\mathbf{x}$. If $\mathbf{r}$ is computed accurately, it can then be used to obtain an improved solution by solving $A\delta = \mathbf{r}$. This process is called *iterative refinement*.

Iterative Methods

It was at one time thought that iterative methods for solving linear equations or the eigenvalue problem would give far greater accuracy than direct methods, since one works with the initial A throughout. In fact, this advantage is largely illusory. In Jacobi's method for linear equations, one derives an improved $x_i^{(r+1)}$ from the relation

$$a_{ii}x_i^{(r+1)} = b_i - \sum_{j \neq i} a_{ij}x_i^{(r)},$$

but the right-hand side cannot be computed exactly. From the above analysis it is clear that one is really working with a matrix with elements $a_{ij}(1 + e_{ij})$, where the e_{ij} are different in each iteration. When iterative methods are used in practice, iteration is usually terminated before attaining the accuracy given immediately by a direct method, *even without iterative refinement*. Since, as we mentioned earlier, the results obtained with good direct methods are almost "best possible," this is to be expected.

Interval Arithmetic and Significant Digit Arithmetic

Attempts have been made to obtain error bounds for computed quantities on the computer itself. In *interval arithmetic (q.v.)*, an ordered pair $[a_l, a_u]$ of floating-point numbers is stored at each stage in the computation, and it is guaranteed that the true number a lies in the interval $a_l \leq a \leq a_u$. Used in a direct manner, the results achieved are very pessimistic; in fact, the computer merely performs numerically the analog of what was done algebraically in the early forward error analysis of the Hotelling type. The intervals become very large. The apparently reasonable assumption that in stable algorithms the computed quantities will be close to those arising in exact computation is frequently quite false. This is particularly true of algorithms for the eigenvalue problem.

In *significant digit (q.v.)* arithmetic, one does not work with normalized floating-point numbers, on the grounds that when cancellation takes place, the zeros introduced are non-significant. The possibilities of significant digit arithmetic have been well exploited by Metropolis and Ashenhurst.

The realization that neither interval arithmetic nor significant digit arithmetic provides an automatic answer to error analysis led to an overreaction against them. The provision of the relevant hardware facilities should make them economic, and when combined with a

more general appreciation of theoretical error analysis, they have an important role to play.

Bibliography

1963. Wilkinson, J. H. *Rounding Errors in Algebraic Processes*. London: Her Majesty's Stationery Office and Upper Saddle River, NJ: Prentice Hall.
1965. Wilkinson, J. H. *The Algebraic Eigenvalue Problem*. Oxford: Clarendon Press.
1967. Forsythe, G. E. and Moler, C. B. *Computer Solution of Linear Algebraic Systems*. Upper Saddle River, NJ: Prentice Hall.
1971. Wilkinson, J. H. "Modern Error Analysis," *SIAM Review*, **13**, 548–568.
1979. Moore, R. E. *Methods and Applications of Interval Analysis*, Philadelphia: SIAM Publications.
1989. Kahaner, D., Moler, C., and Nash, S. *Numerical Methods and Software*. Upper Saddle River, NJ: Prentice Hall.

James H. Wilkinson

ERROR CORRECTING AND DETECTING CODE

For articles on related subjects *see* CODES; ERRORS; and PARITY.

Error-detecting and *error-correcting codes* are essential parts of most forms of digital communication and storage. Proper operation of the Internet (*q.v.*), modems (*q.v.*), compact discs (*see* OPTICAL STORAGE), and computers would be impossible without them. Many recent advances in the speed and reliability of digital communication are directly related to improved design of codes.

Codes introduce redundant bits into a data stream so that transmission errors in the original data bits can be detected and sometimes corrected. Perhaps the best-known code is the simple parity check code (*see* PARITY) that uses a single redundant bit and can detect an odd number of errors in a group of bits. In interactive communication, such as the Internet, it is often sufficient to detect errors, and then request retransmission of the data. In other situations, such as data storage on a compact disc, rereading erroneous data from the disc would frequently result in the same error, so the errors must be corrected.

A diagram of a simplified coding scheme is shown in Fig. 1. In this type of coding (called *block coding*) a group of k data bits are read into the encoder which then produces a corresponding n-bit code word with $n > k$. There are 2^k possible k-bit patterns at the input, and 2^k corresponding n-bit code words. This collection of possible code words is called a "code." Since it can produce only 2^k out of the 2^n possible n-bit patterns, the encoder introduces redundancy into the data stream. The *code rate*, defined as the ratio of k to n, is a measure of this redundancy.

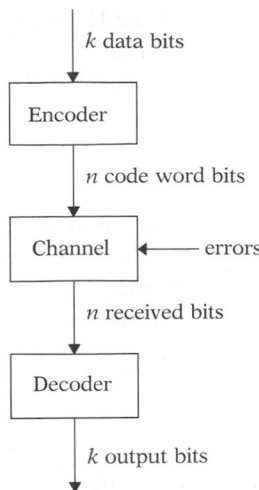

Figure 1.

As an example, consider a "repetition" code which simply repeats each input bit 3 times. A 1 is encoded as 111, and a zero is encoded as 000. For this code, $n = 3$ and $k = 1$. Only 2 out of the 8 possible 3-bit patterns are used as code words. The code rate of 1/3 indicates that only one third of the bits contain data; the other 2/3 of the bits are redundant in that they can be constructed using the data.

After the n bits are transmitted and received, they may contain one or more errors. If the bit pattern received by the decoder matches a code word, then with high probability there were no errors. If the received bit pattern does not match a code word, then the decoder determines that one or more bits are in error. It may request retransmission (if error detection is being used) or try to decide which code word was sent (if error-correction is being used).

For the above repetition code, if 111 is received, the decoder would decide that no errors have occurred, and output data bit 1. It is possible, although unlikely, that three errors were present and the transmitted code word was 000. Such an error event would escape detection. If the received bit pattern were 010, the decoder would signal an error. It could also try to correct this error by noting that, since two of the three received bits are 0, it is more likely that the code word was 000 than 111.

The ability of a decoder to detect errors depends upon the number of bit positions in which code words differ. In the repetition code, the code words 000 and 111 differ in three bit positions. This is called the *Hamming distance* between the code words and indicates that it would take three errors to change 000 into 111. The minimum distance, d, for a code is the minimum Hamming distance between all pairs of code words in the code, and gives the smallest number of errors that can

change one code word into another. For the above repetition code there are only two code words, so the minimum distance, d, is three. If the bit pattern received by the decoder contains fewer than three errors, then it will either be a code word, indicating no errors were present, or it will not be a code word, indicating one or two errors. In general, a code with minimum distance d that uses n-bit code words is capable of detecting up to $d - 1$ errors in each n bits received.

If errors are to be corrected, the decoder can determine which code word is closest (in the Hamming distance sense) to the received bit pattern and output the data corresponding to that code word. If errors have caused the received bit pattern to be closer to a different code word, then the decoder will output the wrong data. For the repetition code, a received bit pattern of 011 is closest to the code word 111, so the decoder would decide that the first bit contained an error, and output the data bit 1. If the received bit pattern really contained errors in the second and third bits, the decoder would output the wrong data. So the repetition code with a minimum distance of 3 can correct one error, but not two errors. In general, a code with minimum distance d that uses n-bit code words is capable of correcting up to $\lfloor (d - 1)/2 \rfloor$ errors in each n bits received.

Powerful error detection or correction involves finding codes with large minimum distance, which implies a large code word size, n. Similarly, for any given minimum distance, d, using long code words can increase the code rate. For example, a single bit parity check code has a minimum distance of 2 so that it can detect one error. The code rate for a parity check code can be made closer to 1 by increasing the code word size. As the code word size gets larger, it becomes impractical for an encoder to generate code words by table look-up or for the decoder to compare the received bit pattern to each code word to find the closest. Instead, more systematic methods must be designed to generate code words and check received bit patterns. Many of these methods involve combinations of parity checks on subsets of the input bit pattern. It is common to copy the k input data bits directly into the code word and then add on $n - k$ bits of carefully chosen parity checks to form an n-bit code word.

A family of codes developed by Richard Hamming (*q.v.*) has a particularly elegant choice of parity checks that simplifies error correction. A parity check is assigned to those positions in the code that have a 1 in the rightmost position of their binary representation, a second parity check for those positions that have a 1 in their second to right position, etc. Thus, when a single error does occur, exactly those parity checks will fail for which the binary expansion of the position of the error has 1s. Thus, the pattern of the parity-check failures points directly to the position of the error; in a binary system of signaling, it is easy to change that bit to its opposite value and thus correct the error. When there are no errors, all the parity checks will succeed.

As an example, consider the binary encoding of the decimal digits into an error-correcting code. In Table 1, positions 1, 2, and 4 are used for the check positions, leaving positions 3, 5, 6, and 7 for the message (where we find the binary coding of the corresponding decimal digit). Six additional code words can be added to this code if it is desired to encode all 16 possible 4-bit messages.

The check positions are calculated by even parity checks as follows.

◆ *Parity check column 1*
  Columns 1, 3, 5, 7 (columns k with a 1 in the rightmost position of the binary representation of k).

◆ *Parity check column 2*
  Columns 2, 3, 6, 7 (1 in second rightmost position).

◆ *Parity check column 4*
  Columns 4, 5, 6, 7 (1 in leftmost position).

Table 1.

Decimal	Position						
	1	2	3	4	5	6	7
0	0	0	0	0	0	0	0
1	1	1	0	1	0	0	1
2	0	1	0	1	0	1	0
3	1	0	0	0	0	1	1
4	1	0	0	1	1	0	0
5	0	1	0	0	1	0	1
6	1	1	0	0	1	1	0
7	0	0	0	1	1	1	1
8	1	1	1	0	0	0	0
9	0	0	1	1	0	0	1

Let any line be copied and a single error inserted as a simulation of an error in message transmission. When the three parity checks are applied, we will find that if we write a 0 for successful parity check and a 1 for a failure (writing from right to left), the three digits we get will be *exactly* the position of the inserted error. Thus, for example, if 1110110 is received instead of 1100110 ($= 6$), the 4, 2, 1 parity checks are 011 ($= 3$) which identifies the third column as the one in error. The order of the columns can be changed to place data (message) bits consecutively at the start of the code word without affecting the performance of the code, but then determining the location of a bit error is less straightforward.

This code is a subset of the Hamming code with $n = 7$ and $k = 4$, and has a minimum distance of 3. Like the repetition code, it can correct one error, but its code rate of 4/7 is much higher. For this reason, repetition codes are used only for illustration.

As an example of double-error detection, consider the code in Table 1 with an additional bit added to each message, so chosen that the entire message will have an even number of 1s. If there were a *single* error, the original set of checks would indicate the position, but the last check would fail. If there were a *pair* of errors, the last check would not fail, but some of the original checks would, indicating a double error. The minimum distance argument can be applied to show that the additional check made each minimal distance one greater, namely, four. This code can correct all single errors, while still detecting all double errors. Alternatively, if the code is used purely for error detection, it can detect up to three errors per code word.

Codes used in practice often add even more structure to simplify encoding and decoding. Linear codes have the property that the bitwise mod 2 sum of any two code words is also a code word. Cyclic codes have the property that any cyclic shift of a code word is also a code word. These properties allow encoding and decoding using high-speed shift register circuits (*see* SHIFTING). Shortened versions of cyclic codes are used to form the *cyclic redundancy check* (CRC—*q.v.*) codes that are commonly used in data transmission hardware. Other important classes of cyclic codes include the Golay, Reed–Solomon, and BCH (Bose–Ray-Chaudhuri-Hocquenghem) codes. Computer protocols such as TCP/IP (*q.v.*) use a different approach to generating redundant checkbits (called the Internet checksum) based upon 1s complement addition. This method is not as powerful as CRC codes, but is easier to implement in software.

Reed–Solomon codes are among the most powerful codes known, and can be efficiently decoded. They have been used in applications as diverse as compact discs and deep space communication. In applications such as the compact disc, where burst errors are especially important to detect and correct, interleavers are used to disperse the bits from one code word over a long portion of the data stream. When the data stream is de-interleaved, the burst of errors will appear as a large number of code words each with one correctable error. The combination of interleaving and two Reed–Solomon codes used in compact discs can correct bursts of over 4000 errors.

In addition to increasing the reliability of digital communication, coding can also be used to achieve higher data transmission rates on channels with limited bandwidth (*q.v.*). A typical telephone channel has a usable bandwidth of less than 3,000 Hz. The Nyquist theorem limits the rate at which noninterfering signals (waveforms) can be sent to twice the bandwidth. Achieving high data rates, such as the 33.6 Kb/sec or more that is now possible over ordinary phone lines, requires communicating many bits with each received signal. If there are 2^k signals to choose from, then each communicates k bits. As more waveforms are used, it becomes difficult for the receiver to distinguish among them. A technique called trellis-coded modulation (TCM) uses more signals than are needed to achieve a given bit rate, but then applies convolutional coding to introduce redundancy into the data stream. The resulting system has a lower bit error rate than the uncoded system. Convolutional codes, unlike the block codes described previously, introduce redundancy by using a finite state automaton (*see* AUTOMATA THEORY) to produce a continuous stream of coded output bits based upon the input data and the state of the encoder.

Detailed study of error correcting and detecting codes uses abstract algebra, including Galois theory.

Bibliography

1968. Berlekamp, E., Jr. *Algebraic Coding Theory*. New York: McGraw-Hill.
1977. MacWilliams, F., and Sloane, N. J. A. *The Theory of Error Correcting Codes*. Amsterdam: Elsevier.
1977. McEliece, R. J. *The Theory of Information and Coding*. Reading, MA: Addison-Wesley.
1986. Hill, R. *A First Course in Coding Theory*. Oxford: Clarendon Press.
1995. Wicker, S. B. *Error Control Systems for Digital Communication and Storage*. Upper Saddle River, NJ: Prentice Hall.

John M. Spinelli
(based on 3rd edition article by Richard Hamming)

ERRORS

For articles on related subjects *see* BUG; DEBUGGING; DIAGNOSTIC; ERROR ANALYSIS; ERROR CORRECTING AND DETECTING CODE; FAULT-TOLERANT COMPUTING; ROUNDOFF ERROR; SOFTWARE TESTING; STRUCTURED PROGRAMMING; SYNTAX, SEMANTICS, AND PRAGMATICS; and Y2K PROBLEM.

The indignant customer who receives an incorrect bill from a department store probably does not care what the source of the error was or even that, almost certainly, the fault was not a computer's but rather that of its data entry personnel or programmers. Neither is the astronaut who is descending toward the surface of the Moon very concerned about the precise source of the error that caused the onboard computer to fail. But an understanding of the sources of *errors* in computers is important to anyone who wishes to use or comprehend digital computers.

Taxonomy of Computer Errors

When a computer produces an incorrect result, the error may come from one or more sources. These sources can be grouped under six headings:

1. *Hardware errors*, which result from a malfunction of some physical component of the computer.

2. *Software errors*, which result from a coding error in *some* program, but not necessarily in the program that seemed to produce the wrong results (see below).

3. *Algorithm errors*, which result when the algorithm (*q.v.*) or method used to solve a problem does not produce correct results, perhaps only under certain conditions and/or for certain input data.

4. *Data entry errors*, probably the most common of all, which occur when the operator of a data entry terminal makes an error, usually by pressing the wrong key.

5. *Data communication errors*, which result when the transfer of data from one computer to another introduces errors which are the result of some failure of the communication network.

6. *User errors* which occur whenever a user invokes an undesired action, such as entering a command whose syntax or semantics is unacceptable, entering a value out of range, or making the wrong menu selection.

Data entry errors can be reduced by using good equipment, by careful training of personnel, and by verification techniques, such as repetition of the data entry by another operator and then a comparison between the two. Data communications errors are normally detected by the hardware or software of the communications system. Sometimes they are corrected automatically by the system; otherwise the data must be retransmitted. Since the quality of voice-grade telephone lines often used for communication between computers may be low, special leased lines are often used for high-speed and/or particularly sensitive data transmissions. Undetected data communications errors are rare.

Because the other four types of error are more subtle and, therefore, more difficult to recognize and/or correct, we shall focus on them in this article. However, before proceeding to discuss these types of error in some detail, we should stress that, whereas in the early days of computing it was usually rather easy to determine which of the categories above was the source of an error, it is sometimes very difficult indeed to do this today. To give one example, the use of microprogramming (*q.v.*) in some computer systems makes it possible for hardware errors to manifest themselves in ways that look like software errors, and vice versa. The difficulty of determining the source of a computer error has heightened the need for good diagnostic techniques, a subject we consider in the last section of this article.

Hardware Errors

Considering the staggering complexity of modern computer systems, it is amazing that they work at all. The fact that they are designed to, and often do, operate for hundreds or thousands of hours without failure is even more startling. Modern computers contain literally millions of circuit elements, the failure of any one of which might cause failure of the entire system. This high level of reliability is a tribute to the careful work of circuit designers and the meticulous attention to detail and to testing on the part of the manufacturers. Still, computers are not perfect and the hardware occasionally does fail. The source of a failure may be difficult to determine, since the number of possible faulty components is so large.

A common source of errors is in the electromechanical peripheral devices that provide input or output for the central processing unit (q.v.). The mechanical components of these peripheral devices are likely to wear out as a result of the stresses of frequent use. For example, the staccato motion of movable disk arms or the rapid rotation of disks is a possible source of failures.

The recording medium associated with various devices is fragile and consequently a potential source of errors. The delicate magnetic coating of magnetic tapes or disks can be easily scratched, rendering the information incorrect or inaccessible. A speck of dust or dirt can mar these coatings easily, or tension can stretch a piece of magnetic tape. The failure of these media may not be fatal to the entire computer, but individual peripheral units may be disabled or data items may be entered incorrectly or lost.

The central processing unit, arithmetic-logic unit (q.v.), and the high-speed memory are built entirely from electronic components, thereby reducing the chance of failure inherent in mechanical devices. The technology for creating the circuit elements involved in these components is extremely complex. Early computers used vacuum tubes (first generation) as the primary circuit element. These large devices were relatively slow, generated a large amount of heat, required a large amount of power, and wore out easily. The invention of the transistor (second generation) in 1947 made it possible to construct smaller, faster, and much more reliable computers. Combining many transistors and other electronic elements into a single component, called an *integrated circuit* (*see* INTEGRATED CIRCUITRY) (third generation), enabled designers to create still faster and more reliable computers.

At present, computers are built from a smaller number of very large-scale integrated circuits (VLSI). These highly reliable circuits contain thousands or millions of discrete circuit elements built into a single replaceable component. These devices are carefully tested during the many stages of a sophisticated fabrication process. Still, they may fail as a result of temperature changes, humidity, shock, or electrical surges. When failure occurs, the faulty circuit component must be located and replaced. This sounds simple enough, but the problem may be hard to locate, since the failure may be intermittent, occurring only when a complex combination of conditions exists. To minimize the deterioration of circuit elements, computer rooms, particularly those for mainframes (q.v.), are air conditioned to keep the temperature and humidity within acceptable ranges. The failure of the air conditioning could lead to overheating of circuit elements and to an increased chance of failure.

Modern computers are designed to monitor their own performance and constantly test themselves to assure that each operation has been performed properly. When a fault occurs, a machine interrupt (q.v.) is issued, and the hardware and software attempt to identify and locate the error. Depending on the severity of the error, the control programs may shut down the entire machine, avoid use of the faulty component, or simply record the fact that an error has occurred.

Software Errors

Anyone who has written a computer program knows that debugging can be difficult and tedious. Professionals writing even short programs (say, fewer than 100 lines of code) expect some difficulties and accept the fact that long programs, requiring many person-years of effort, may never be completely debugged. When writing programs in a high-level language, which requires the services of a compiler, utility programs, and an operating system, the number of software modules that come into play is large. Great effort is applied to debug the system software, but it is not currently possible to ensure the correctness of such sophisticated programs. If an application program (q.v.) does not operate correctly, the most likely source of the error is in the application program itself. Only after a thorough and careful analysis of the situation can we begin to consider the possibility that the compiler, system utilities, or operating system are at fault. Locating the bug in the system software requires a deep understanding of the code and the expertise of a systems programmer (*see* SYSTEMS PROGRAMMING).

Application program errors fall into two basic categories: *syntactic* and *semantic*. Syntactic errors include typographic errors, incorrectly spelled keywords and variable names, incorrect punctuation, and improper statement formation, all of which result from violations of the programming language syntax. These errors are normally recognized by the language processor (*q.v.*), and diagnostic messages are printed to assist the programmer in making corrections. Although some processors will attempt to fix improper syntax, programs with syntactic errors will generally not be permitted to execute.

Assuming all the syntactic errors have been fixed, the program will execute, but there is no guarantee that it will perform as the programmer intended. Semantic errors are a result of an improper understanding of the function of certain operators or mistakes in coding of an algorithm. Typical programming mistakes include exceeding the bounds of an array; failure to initialize variables; overflow or underflow; failure to account for special cases; attempted division by zero; illegal mixing of data types; and incorrect transfers of control. Isolating and locating the error can be a long, tedious process and is a skill learned mainly through much experience.

Current research is being directed at reducing the possibility of semantic errors. Improved programming language design and sophisticated compilers are one possible answer. Educating programmers about proper program design techniques such as modularity, structured programming, and object-oriented programming (*q.v.*) does, indeed, simplify the debugging process. Finally, attempts are being made to prove the correctness of programs through the use of formal mathematical techniques (*see* PROGRAM VERIFICATION).

Algorithm Errors

Computer programs can be viewed as models or representations of real-world situations. Unfortunately, not all aspects of the real-world situation can be represented accurately inside a computer. Decimal quantities such as 1.2 or 6783846.678492104 may have to be approximated when stored in the memory of a binary computer. Since the initial representation is not precise, subsequent operations performed on these values may produce invalid results. One difficulty in locating such faults is that the error will manifest itself only for some sets of data. Thus, the program will produce reasonable results in most cases, but may produce erroneous results erratically.

The heart of this problem is the machine representation of values. While a 64-bit word length may provide a more accurate representation than a 36-bit word or a 32-bit word, a longer word length is not a guarantee of correctness. Since we are limited to the finite length of a computer word, the representation must be rounded off to the closest approximation possible.

With each addition or multiplication, the result must also be rounded off to fit the representation scheme; hence the name *roundoff error*.

Another flaw in the representation of the real world occurs when an infinite process must be approximated by a finite series of steps. In summing an infinite series, repeating an iterative process (e.g. the Newton–Raphson method), or approximating derivatives by differences, the result may become increasingly good, but is never precisely correct. Since in all these cases an infinite process is cut short and represented by a finite process, this error is called *truncation* or *discretization error*.

One of the central concerns of numerical analysis (*q.v.*) is to estimate the roundoff and truncation errors for various algorithms. This analysis can then be used to select and design the optimum strategy for a given problem. A major goal of numerical analysis is to avoid *unstable* algorithms that operate erratically and to identify *ill-conditioned* data sets that are difficult to deal with. The use of double or multiple precision representations and operations may reduce the error, but will not eliminate it.

Another type of algorithm failure is the attempted use of an algorithm to solve a problem other than that for which it is intended. An example of this would be the use of an algorithm designed for the solution of a system of linear simultaneous equations with a symmetric coefficient matrix to solve a system with a nonsymmetric coefficient matrix, resulting in an inevitably wrong result.

All too common is the development and use of an algorithm that just will not solve the problem at hand for any set of data, due to a design error, for example, or a failure to understand the underlying mathematics. A vital aspect of the avoidance of such errors is the careful testing of all newly developed programs using data sets for which the results are known.

Although the examples above are of errors in computational algorithms, algorithm errors can and do occur in all varieties of nonnumerical algorithms.

User Errors

Computer users may make a large variety of errors, examples of which are mentioned earlier in this article. Two further examples are inadvertently opening, moving, resizing, or closing a window or making unintended movements in a painting program (*see* WINDOW ENVIRONMENTS). Such user errors may be classified as physical motion mistakes, syntactic errors, logical errors, or just failures due to a lack of knowledge of the functioning of the computer. A key goal of the designer of a user interface (*q.v.*) is to reduce the possibility of some of these errors and to provide appropriate error messages that facilitate error recovery.

Errors can generally be reduced by permitting menu selection in place of data entry and by constraining illegal actions, just as automobile transmissions prevent engagement of reverse gears while the car is moving forward. When errors do occur, the messages should be specific, constructive, positive in tone, user-centered (avoiding technical terminology), comprehensible, and brief.

When major user actions would be irreversible (e.g. deletion of data or control of physical processes), the user should be required to confirm the action before it actually takes place.

Coping with Errors

Since errors are a fact of life in computing, much has been done to assist programmers and computer users in locating them. Syntactic errors are dealt with by the compiler and are not the source of serious difficulty. Although work remains to be done in the area of improving compile-time diagnostics, most compilers provide a reasonably lucid explanation of what has gone wrong. The programmer must then fix the mistake.

Execution-time errors that result from semantic errors are more difficult to deal with. If the program runs to completion, but does not produce the output that is expected, the programmer or user must carefully examine the output and attempt to locate the fault. The input data should be checked for validity, and then a careful step-by-step analysis of the program must be performed. If the output does not contain sufficient information to determine what the program was doing, an additional run with more detailed output must be made. Special *trace* (*q.v.*) routines that print out the execution of the program on an instruction-by-instruction basis can be used. Alternatively, only the transfers of control or subprogram (*q.v.*) references are printed. If desired, a particular location can be monitored to indicate when the value was set or referenced. Since the amount of output may be voluminous, the programmer must carefully select which features to use. Armed with this material and a thorough understanding of the program, the programmer must perform a careful analysis to locate the flaw.

If the program does not run to completion, but is interrupted as a result of an attempt to perform an illegal instruction, the operating system will (or, at least, should) print a meaningful message. However, since the operating system has no knowledge of what the application program was attempting to do, these messages can be difficult to interpret. Some programming language systems contain an execution-time monitor to produce more meaningful diagnostic messages when an abnormal termination occurs.

If a program successfully executes for a given set of data, there is no guarantee that the program will always perform properly. To verify the correctness of a program, multiple sets of test data should be constructed to exercise the program as much as possible (*see* SOFTWARE TESTING). As many as possible of the reasonable sets of input data should be run to validate the program. Unfortunately, there are many well-documented cases of programs that have run correctly for many years until a particular set of input data was run and resulted in failure. There is no way to guarantee the correctness of large programs, and programmers must accept the possibility of *bugs* in their programs. Large programs such as operating systems are continually being modified as faults are located. Perfection in programming is illusory.

The diagnosis of hardware errors has become more complex with the advent of sophisticated hardware architecture constructs, such as virtual memory (*q.v.*) and microprogramming (*q.v.*). When it is suggested that a particular error may be a result of malfunctioning hardware, a set of hardware diagnostic programs may be run to assist the maintenance engineer in locating the fault. These programs exercise each of the circuit components and print out the location of the faulty element. This technique is not always successful, since the diagnostic program may not run properly because of the fault. Individual components may have to be removed and tested electrically, or components may be replaced until the machine operates properly.

Bibliography

1963. Wilkinson, J. H. *Rounding Errors in Algebraic Processes.* Upper Saddle River, NJ: Prentice Hall.
1977. Gilb, T., and Weinberg, G. M. *Humanizing Input.* Cambridge, MA: Winthrop.
1978. Van Tassel, D. *Program Style, Design, Efficiency, Debugging and Testing,* 2nd Ed. Upper Saddle River, NJ: Prentice Hall.
1988. Norman, D. *The Psychology of Everyday Things.* New York: Basic Books.
1997. Taylor, J. R. *An Introduction to Error Analysis.* Mill Valley, CA: University Science Books.
1998. Lichten, W. *Data and Error Analysis.* Upper Saddle River, NJ: Prentice Hall.

Anthony Ralston and Ben Shneiderman

ETHERNET

For articles on related subjects *see* COMMUNICATIONS AND COMPUTERS; DATA COMMUNICATIONS; FIBER OPTICS; INTERNET; LOCAL AREA NETWORK; NETWORKS, COMPUTER; NETWORK PROTOCOLS; and TCP/IP.

Ethernet is by far the most widely used local area network (LAN) technology, and all indications are that it is likely to remain so for the foreseeable future. Since its invention in the mid-1970s, it has evolved to the point that now it supports data transmission rates of 10, 100 and even 1,000 million bits per second (Mbps), bus or star topologies, and multiple transmission media such as coaxial cable and unshielded twisted pairs as well as single or multimode optical fibers. It is this constant improvement that has allowed Ethernet to maintain its dominant role in LAN technology.

History

Ethernet was developed by Bob Metcalfe and David Boggs at the Xerox Palo Alto Research Center to interconnect a number of desktop computers and laser printers at a data transmission rate of 2.94 Mbps. It was so successful that in 1980, Xerox, Digital Equipment Corporation (*q.v.*) and Intel published the specifications for a 10 Mbps Ethernet that any company could use. These specifications formed the basis for the IEEE (Institute of Electrical and Electronic Engineers) 802.3 standard released in 1983, which is now synonymous with Ethernet. Since that time, there have been numerous enhancements so that there now exist a number of 802.3 standards defining Ethernets that support different network topologies operating at different transmission rates and using a variety of physical transmission media. Despite these differences, all Ethernet standards share several important characteristics, including a common frame or packet structure and a common multiple access protocol called Carrier Sense Multiple Access/Collision Detect or CSMA/CD for short.

Ethernet Frame Format

The format of an Ethernet frame or packet, as defined in the original IEEE 802.3 standard, is shown here.

Preamble (7 bytes)
Start frame delimiter (1 byte)
Destination address (6 bytes)
Source address (6 bytes)
Length/type (2 bytes)
Client data (0–1500 bytes)
Optional pad characters (0–46 bytes)
Check sequence (4 bytes)

A frame consists of a preamble of 7 bytes (56 bits) having alternating 1 and 0 values that are used for synchronization among distributed computers on an Ethernet LAN. The frame delimiter is a special character with a 10101011 bit configuration that indicates the start of the frame, and is followed by the destination and source addresses, a length or type field, the data itself,

optional pad characters and a check sequence (cyclic redundancy check—*q.v.*) for the detection of errors during transmission. If the value of the length/type field is 1,500 or less, it indicates the number of bytes in the data field. If it is equal to or greater than 1,536, then this field indicates the protocol type being used, which allows Ethernet to support multiple protocols such as TCP/IP or IPX for Novell networks. If necessary, optional pad characters are added to the data field to ensure that the shortest Ethernet frame length is 64 bytes from the destination address through the frame check sequence fields.

The original standard, therefore, supports minimum and maximum frame sizes of 64 and 1518 bytes respectively, not counting the preamble and start delimiter characters. In 1998, the IEEE 802.3ac standard increased the maximum frame size to 1522 bytes to allow a VLAN tag to be inserted into the frame between the source address and length fields to support the concept of Virtual Local Area Networks (VLANs) that help ease network administration, enhance network security, and limit the size of broadcast domains.

To delineate between frames, Ethernet adapters are designed to provide a minimum idle period of 96 bit-times (i.e. 9.6 microseconds for a 10 Mbps Ethernet) between transmission of successive frames. This is known as the *interframe gap* and allows devices to prepare for the reception of the next frame.

Ethernet Media Access Control

Devices on an Ethernet LAN can be considered to be interconnected by a common transmission medium so that when one device transmits a frame, all devices receive the frame (multiple access). The CSMA/CD protocol, which controls the transmission of frames over the network, works as follows:

1. To transmit a frame, a device must first sense if another device is transmitting over the medium (carrier sense). If yes, it waits, else it starts transmitting (broadcasting) the frame to all other devices once the medium has been idle for at least the interframe gap.

2. While transmitting the frame, the device must monitor the medium for collisions (collision detect). If no collision is detected, the transmission continues and is ignored by all devices except the device whose address is in the destination field of the frame.

3. If a collision is detected, the device stops transmitting the frame and instead sends a special 32 bit "jam sequence" to alert all devices that a collision has occurred and the transmission has failed.

The device then remains silent for a random period of time greater than the interframe gap before attempting to transmit again, as described in step 1 above; if there is another collision, the average silent time doubles (*exponential backoff*) in order to reduce collision probability. This process is repeated until the frame is transmitted successfully.

Ethernet Physical Transmission Media Specifications

The original version of Ethernet operated at 2.94 Mbps and used a thick coaxial cable (about 0.5 inches in diameter) as the physical transmission medium to which all devices were attached. Since that time, it has evolved to include speeds of 10, 100, and 1,000 Mbps, as well as a variety of transmission media including thin coaxial cable, twisted copper pairs, and optical fibers, with the latter two supporting star topologies, rather than the linear bus topologies used for coaxial cables. To keep better track of the possible combinations, the IEEE classifies Ethernet using a code of the form ⟨*speed*⟩ ⟨*baseband or broadband*⟩ ⟨*physical medium*⟩. The first part indicates the speed in Mbps, while the second part indicates whether baseband or broadband transmission is used. In baseband transmission, only one device can transmit at a time and the entire bandwidth (*q.v.*) of the medium is available for transmission. In broadband transmission, the bandwidth of the medium is divided into two or more different channels, each with its unique frequency band, to allow the support of multiple simultaneous transmissions over a single cable. Cable modems, for example, use broadband transmission. The third part, physical medium, is either a number, in which case it refers to the longest allowable Ethernet segment length in hundreds of meters, or a letter used to denote a particular transmission medium. For example, 10Base5 refers to 10 Mbps baseband transmission using a thick coaxial cable whose maximum segment length is 500 meters, 100BaseT refers to 100 Mbps baseband transmission using unshielded twisted pairs, while 1000BaseSX refers to 1000 Mbps baseband transmission (Gigabit Ethernet) using a short wavelength laser over two multinode fibers.

Advantages and Disadvantages

Ethernet suffers from several problems (Keshav, 1997). As the load increases, collisions become more common, causing delays and lowering the response time. While unlikely, it is also possible for a packet or frame to suffer indefinite delays due to repeated collisions, making it unsuitable for applications that require real-time response. The fact that each device on an Ethernet has an equal chance to transmit may create problems in applications where a higher priority is desirable for certain devices. Finally, it requires a minimum packet length of 64 bytes, which reduces its efficiency in applications that exchange a few characters at a time, such as editing or data entry. Despite these drawbacks, Ethernet is by far the most popular network technology because it is inexpensive, easy to understand, implement and configure, and the above problems are serious only on very heavily loaded Ethernets. Furthermore, it has been very resilient: every time a new networking technology came along to compete with Ethernet, a new enhanced Ethernet standard evolved to counter the competition.

In 1999, Ethernet continued to evolve rapidly. Switched 100 Mbps Ethernet tends to be the most popular technology for interconnecting desktops, while switched 1000 Mbps (Gigabit) Ethernet is increasingly being used for enterprise backbone networks. A 10 Gigabit Ethernet standard is being discussed and plans for implementing guaranteed quality of service (QoS) levels on Ethernet are evolving. These enhancements indicate that Ethernet technology will continue to remain the leading LAN technology for the foreseeable future.

Bibliography

1976. Metcalfe, R. M., and Boggs, D. R. "Ethernet: Distributed Packet Switching for Local Computer Networks," *Comm. of the ACM*, **19**, 7, 395–404. Also at http://www.acm.org/classics/apr96/.
1997. Keshav, S. *An Engineering Approach to Computer Networking*. Reading, MA: Addison-Wesley.

John S. Sobolewski

ETHICS

See COMPUTER ETHICS.

EXCEPTION HANDLING

For articles on related subjects *see* CONTROL STRUCTURE; ERRORS; INTERRUPT; SOFTWARE ENGINEERING; and TRAP.

Exception handling deals with mechanisms and techniques for detecting, recovering from, and dealing with errors that arise during program execution. Exception handling techniques are used by programmers to make programs *robust*. Exceptions arise when illegal operations are requested or the operands (*q.v.*) of an operation are inappropriate. For example, dividing by zero will cause an error in almost all systems. Robust programs deal gracefully with exceptions, whereas fragile programs stop or produce erroneous results when exceptions are encountered.

Exception handling techniques useful in *defensive programming* include checking the validity of data, checking that users are asking for legal operations before performing them, and other actions which defend the integrity of the user's data or environment. Exception handling mechanisms may also be useful in providing users with an *undo* command that cancels the result of the last operation, allowing users to save their work and restore any previously saved state, alerting users to exceptions when they occur, and allowing users to continue from error conditions without losing much work.

It is often impractical to check all the conditions that must hold in order to guarantee that an operation will be successful. To handle cases in which exceptions cannot be avoided, some programming languages provide limited backtracking, undo, or unwind protection mechanisms. One of the more developed exception systems is the Common Lisp condition system. Other languages that provide exception-handling include Ada (*q.v.*), C++ (*q.v.*), Java (*q.v.*), Modula-3, and Standard ML.

There are a wide variety of mechanisms used to implement exception systems in various programming languages. All exception systems, however, have some concepts in common. An exceptional condition must first be *detected* or *recognized*. Once an exception is known, it must be *thrown*, or *raised*. Throwing or raising an exception involves gathering information about the exception and searching for an exception handler, which may be a standard one provided by the language, or one that is user-defined. If an exception handler is found, it is *invoked* with the exception information. When invoked, the exception handler can execute some programmatic action to recover from or ameliorate the exception. The exception at this point is said to have been *caught* or *handled*. By their nature, exception handlers must be associated with the exceptional condition before an exception occurs and are typically found by searching in the dynamic context of the execution control stack (*see* ACTIVATION RECORD and STACK). If no handler is found, the language run-time system takes some default action, usually terminating the program and posting some diagnostic in a standard location.

To make these ideas concrete, here is a simple example in the Java programming language. In Java, an exception handling context is set up with the **try** statement. Statements within a **try** block may be caught by associated **catch** statements. In all cases an optional **finally** clause is executed. When an exception is thrown, the call stack is searched to find the nearest (most recent) **catch** clause which handles the exception. At each **try** block, any **finally** clause is executed before searching further. Java exception

information is encapsulated into exception objects. Catching an exception of some class (*q.v.*) includes catching an exception for any inheriting subclass. In the example following, the machine tool will be turned off even if an exception is raised which is not caught within the `ExecutePlan()` function. The second **catch** clause *propagates* an error by throwing a different error in place of the first one, thus permitting further exception handling to take place at the next level.

```
public void ExecutePlan( RouterMachine
                router, RouterPlan plan ) {
    try {
        router.on() ;
        router.home() ;
     // place cutting head in home position
        router.executeProgram( plan ) ;
    } catch (operatorOverrideException p) {
        router.notifyOperator( "Operation
                overridden by operator", p ) ;
    } catch (RouterException r) {
        throw( new PlanException( "Router
                failed to complete the plan",
                                   plan, r ) ;
    } finally {
        router.off() ;
    }
}
```

Bibliography

1990. Steele, G. L. *Common Lisp, The Language*, 2nd Ed. Bedford, MA: Digital Press.
1996. Gosling, J., Joy, B., and Steele, G. L. *The Java Language Specification*. Reading, MA: Addison-Wesley.
1999. Sebesta, R. W. *Concepts of Programming Languages*, 4th Ed. Reading, MA: Addison-Wesley.

James C. Spohrer and Ken Dickey

EXECUTABLE STATEMENT

For articles on related subjects *see* DECLARATION; and PROCEDURE-ORIENTED LANGUAGES: PROGRAMMING.

An *executable statement* is a procedural step in a high-level imperative programming language that calls for processing action by the computer, such as performing arithmetic, reading data from an external medium, making a decision, etc. In describing the structure and features of high-level languages, it is convenient to distinguish between executable statements and non-executable ones (*declarations*) that provide information about the nature of the data or about the way the processing is to be done without themselves causing any processing action.

Executable statements are sometimes called *imperative* statements because their form often closely resembles that of an imperative sentence in a natural language. For example, the formula

$$Y = a + bx + cx^2$$

follows an imperative form that persists in corresponding structures in programming language statements:

Pascal   `y := a + b*x + c*x*x`
Fortran   `Y = A + B*X + C*X**2`
C++   `y = a + b*x + c*pow(x,2);`

This correspondence is emphasized more explicitly in some languages, namely,

Basic   `LET Y = A + B*X +C*X ^ 2`
Cobol   `COMPUTE Y = A + B*X + C*X**2.`

Specifications for data transmission between internal storage and an external medium are constructed along similar lines:

Fortran   `READ (5,12) HERE`
          `WRITE (6,21) HERE`
Cobol   `READ INFILE INTO HERE.`
          `WRITE OUTFILE FROM HERE.`
C++   `cin >> here;`
          `cout << here;`

The numerical specifications in the Fortran example are coded references to additional information about the source (for input), destination (for output), and format of the data to be transmitted. In the C++ example, the "c" in "cin" and "cout" stands for "console".

Sometimes, executable statements are subdivided into imperative and conditional statements because the latter, such as the `if` statement in C++, specify alternative imperative actions linked through a decision mechanism.

A language implementation may have rules about the relative placement of executable and nonexecutable statements. Older languages require all declarations to appear before a program's first executable statement. Newer languages allow declarations to appear near their first use, certainly before any information in them is required by an executable statement. One of Cobol's distinguishing features is its total separation of executable statements (in the *Procedure* division) from nonexecutable statements (in the *Environment* and *Data* divisions).

In C and C++, function and method declarations and global variables are usually placed in a *header file*, so that they can be imported into any compilation unit requiring them. In this manner, C and C++ distinguish between a function or method's declaration (the number and type of its parameters) and its definition, which contains executable statements.

Seymour V. Pollack and Ron K. Cytron

EXECUTION TIME

See COMPILE AND RUN TIME.

EXECUTIVE

See OPERATING SYSTEM.

EXPERT SYSTEMS

> For articles on related subjects *see* ARTIFICIAL INTELLIGENCE; HEURISTIC; KNOWLEDGE REPRESENTATION; MULTI-AGENT SYSTEMS; NONMONOTONIC LOGIC; and THEOREM PROVING.

Most applications of artificial intelligence (AI) are of a type called *expert systems*. An expert system (ES) is a computer program that *reasons*, using *knowledge*, to solve complex problems. Traditionally, computers have solved complex problems by arithmetic calculation (not logical reasoning), and the knowledge needed to solve the problem is known only by the human programmer and is used to cast the solution in terms of an algorithm (*q.v.*). With expert systems, such human knowledge is captured and embedded explicitly within the program in symbolic nonnumeric formats.

The Emergence of Principles and Technology

One approach to understanding the principles of expert systems is to trace the history of the emergence of ES within AI. Perhaps AI's most widely shared early goal had been the construction of extremely intelligent computers. That is, in addition to other goals (such as learning and language understanding), most researchers shared a goal to produce programs that performed at or beyond human levels of competence. For example, an early (late 1950s) program took the New York State Regents Examination in plane geometry to validate its human-level abilities in this domain. In the late 1950s, leading AI researchers also predicted that an AI program would be chess champion of the world within 10 years. (If one accepts Deep Blue's victory over Garry Kasparov as significant, it took about 40; *see* COMPUTER CHESS.) A scientific viewpoint about knowledge representation, *declarativism*, was formulated by John McCarthy during this period, and proved to be robust and important. Declarativism insists that a program's knowledge about objects and relations be encoded explicitly so that other programs can access and reason with that knowledge.

In the early 1960s, the focus of AI shifted from performance to generality—how one problem-solving mechanism can solve a wide variety of problems. The best-known AI efforts of the time were the *general problem solvers*, both heuristic programs and theorem provers. While these programs exhibited considerable generality, the actual problems they were able to solve were very simple "toy" problems; i.e. the programs had high generality but low power.

In 1965, Feigenbaum, Lederberg, and Buchanan at Stanford University initiated a project in modeling scientific reasoning, for which the goal of high performance was once again given prominence. The task of this program, called DENDRAL, was to interpret the mass spectrum of an organic molecule in terms of an hypothesis as to its structure (Lindsay *et al.*, 1980). The intent of DENDRAL's designers was that the program be able to perform the difficult mass spectral analysis task at the level of competence of specialists in that area. As it turned out, AI problem-solving methods (primarily search-based methods) were useful, but not sufficient. Most important in achieving the goal of expert-level competence was knowledge of chemistry and mass spectroscopy. The key empirical result of DENDRAL experiments became known as the *knowledge-is-power hypothesis* (later called the *knowledge principle*), stating that

> knowledge of the specific task domain in which the program is to do its problem solving was more important as a source of power for competent problem solving than the reasoning method employed (Feigenbaum, 1977).

The knowledge that DENDRAL needed was provided by scientists of the Stanford Mass Spectrometry Laboratory in an intense collaboration with the AI scientists. Such efforts at codifying the knowledge of specialists for use in expert systems later came to be called *knowledge engineering*. The first use of the term "expert" in connection with such programs was made in an article analyzing the generality vs. power issue in light of the results of DENDRAL computational experiments (Feigenbaum *et al.*, 1971). Thus the DENDRAL program was the progenitor of the class of programs subsequently called expert systems, and the development of DENDRAL illustrated the major principles, issues, and limitations of expert systems that were explored in the 1970s and 1980s.

Extensions of DENDRAL, done in the 1970s, were of two types. First, many pioneering expert systems were built by AI researchers to explore and extend the new technology and to lend credibility to the ES technology and knowledge engineering methodology. The earliest and most famous of these was the MYCIN system, which was concerned with appropriate antibiotic therapy for patients with bacterial infections and which showed the first integrated architecture for interactive consultation between an expert user and an ES, including explanation of the line of reasoning (Buchanan and Shortliffe, 1984). Second, the underlying programming systems and languages of these systems, those that embodied the reasoning procedures and the framework for representing knowledge,

were generalized so that they were no longer domain-specific. As a result, they could be used as programming systems and languages for the construction of new, albeit similar, systems. Such software came to be known as ES "development environments" or "ES tools" or "ES shells." The pioneering tool/shell, derived from MYCIN, was EMYCIN, the prototype for literally dozens of commercially available ES shells

Transfer of ES Technology into Practice

As the 1970s came to a close, so did the decade of laboratory exploration of the first-generation ES ideas and techniques. A period of transfer of the technology to industrial use began. The two best-known early industrial applications were XCON from Digital Equipment Corporation (*q.v.*) and the Dipmeter Adviser from Schlumberger Ltd.

XCON's task was the configuration under constraints of a DEC minicomputer (*q.v.*) from a large number of component subassemblies. The configuration task was done so fast and so accurately by XCON that DEC saved millions of dollars per year in manufacturing and sales operations. XCON configured minicomputers about 300 times faster than human engineers and does it virtually error-free. XCON has been extended to many different families of DEC computers and other equipment, and was generalized into an ES called XSEL to assist DEC salespeople to configure and price equipment sales at the time of customer contact. XCON had an immediate effect outside of DEC: most other computer manufacturers copied the idea for their own operations. More important, the success of XCON opened the way to a broader generalization: most devices that are engineered and manufactured are built out of component subassemblies; hence the XCON idea could be used to realize a new generation of CAD, or "intelligent CAD," as it is called (*see* COMPUTER-AIDED DESIGN/COMPUTER-AIDED MANUFACTURING).

Schlumberger's Dipmeter Adviser (DA) is typical of programs that analyze streams of data (with or without real time considerations) and propose hypotheses to account for and explain the data. DA interprets the data taken from instruments lowered into bore holes during the search for oil and gas. It offers hypotheses about the tilt, or so-called "dip," of the rock layers far beneath the earth's surface. Knowing the dip of each of the hundreds of rock layers in a bore hole is valuable in oil exploration.

With the emergence of these and other successful business applications of ES and AI technology, the American Association of Artificial Intelligence (AAAI) began a yearly conference in 1989 devoted to highlighting detailed case studies of AI applications, most of which were expert systems.

One such application was a General Motors program called *Charley*. Charley is another example of a program that interprets signal data to produce hypotheses, in this case for analyzing vibrations of machinery as a means of troubleshooting mechanical equipment, particularly automotive and manufacturing equipment. This ES is a model of the expertise of a senior GM specialist in vibrational analysis whose retirement was imminent, and is an instance of a very important class of expert systems that are done to capture and preserve rare corporate expertise.

The use of an ES to improve the quality of human decisions was the motive behind the Authorizer's Assistant (AA) of American Express. To assist a human authorizer with the decision to allow or disallow a particular charge, the AA analyzes a large amount of customer data from the company's database files. AA then issues a recommendation, offers the rationale for it, and gives the human authorizer a screen of data that supports the recommendation. The payoff in avoiding bad debt and fraud amounts to millions of dollars per year, a result of the high quality and consistency of the AA decisions. The AA also demonstrated that an ES could be embedded within a transaction-based system (*see* TRANSACTION PROCESSING) and deliver rapid, reliable and expert-level performance many thousands of times a day.

Expert systems have been built to assist people with the accurate and timely processing of regulations in the context of very complex systems of bureaucratic laws and rules. A system done for the British Department of Social Security assists clerks in answering the written queries of citizens concerning their pensions. The Taxpayers' Assistant Expert System of the US Internal Revenue Service helps IRS personnel give accurate tax information in response to telephoned queries from taxpayers. In the state of Tennessee, an ES determines the exact prison sentences for offenders. The ES improves the accuracy and consistency with which sentencing rules are applied, and enhances efficiency. And in both Fresno and Tulare counties of California, expert systems assist social welfare case workers in deciding whether a person applying for welfare qualifies under complex California rules.

Expert systems have also been used in quite complex applications in scheduling and design. The American Airlines MOCA system schedules aircraft for varying types of required maintenance. Scheduling hundreds of aircraft for their daily routes, while insuring that all maintenance activities are promptly performed at the required sites, is a complex and difficult task, particularly in a constantly changing environment such as air transportation. The ES actually improved American's operations significantly while continuing to ensure that all required maintenance is performed. In another example, the Ford Motor Company CAPE system produced process plans (machines and tasks) for manufacturing automobile parts that outperformed human planners and significantly reduced the costs of manufacturing parts.

In the 1990s expert systems were broadly applied in the area of customer support. Embedding microchips into appliances improved their functionality, but also introduced problems and uncertainties (*see* EMBEDDED SYSTEMS). As manufacturers' support for these products became more difficult and costly, expert systems were developed to provide support in troubleshooting and in solving customer problems and inquiries. With the help of the Internet (*q.v.*) and intranets, companies have made such systems and their embedded knowledge available to customers to provide them with efficient self-service capabilities.

As these examples demonstrate, there are major applications of ES across the complete spectrum of human professional and semiprofessional work: in medicine, law, manufacturing, sales, maintenance and support, engineering, transportation, architectural design, finance, insurance, and many other areas. There are many thousands of operational expert systems installed, primarily in the USA, Japan, and Europe, and increasing numbers are being used in Australia, Singapore, and India.

Expert System Technology

The word "expert" in "expert system" refers to the intention of the ES designer that the system achieve a level of problem-solving competence that rivals the performance of human experts in a particular domain. To accomplish this, the ES must be given the knowledge that such human experts have that distinguishes experts from novices and enables experts to perform well. To acquire and represent that knowledge is the job of the knowledge engineer. Increasingly, with the advance of ES development tools, experts are able to be their own knowledge engineers. Expert systems are almost always used as *interactive intellectual aids* for human decision makers and rarely as autonomous unsupervised agents.

Every expert system consists of two principal parts: the *knowledge base* and the *reasoning* or *inference engine* (Fig. 1). The knowledge base contains both factual and heuristic knowledge. The factual knowledge is that knowledge widely shared in the domain and commonly agreed upon by experts. The heuristic knowledge is the nonrigorous experiential knowledge, the rules-of-thumb, the knowledge of good judgment. Heuristics constitutes the "art of good guessing". *Knowledge representation* formalizes and organizes the knowledge

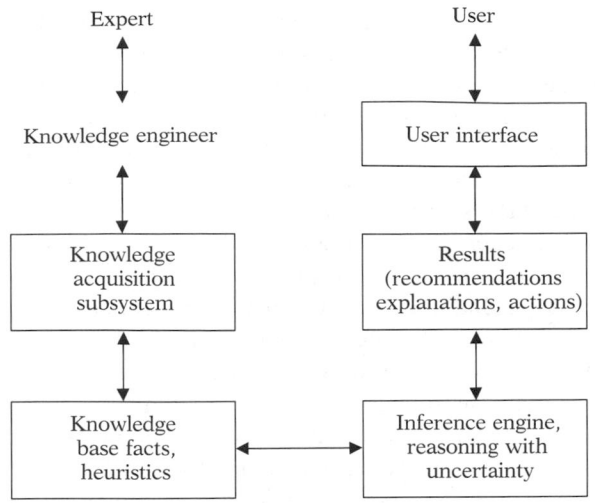

Expert   User

Knowledge engineer   User interface

Knowledge acquisition subsystem   Results (recommendations explanations, actions)

Knowledge base facts, heuristics   Inference engine, reasoning with uncertainty

Figure 1. Basic structure of an expert system.

for use by the inference engine. One widely used representational form is the *production rule*, or simply the *rule*. A rule consists of an IF part and a THEN part (also called a *condition* and an *action*). The IF part lists a set of conditions in some logical combination. The piece of knowledge represented by the rule is relevant to the line of reasoning being developed. If and only if the IF part of the rule is satisfied, the action specified in the THEN part is taken. In a charge card authorization ES, one example might be: IF the current charge is in a jewelry store, AND the cardholder has not previously charged in a jewelry store, THEN consider that the card may have been lost or stolen AND have the authorizer get on the phone and perform an identification on the cardholder. Expert systems whose knowledge is represented in rule form are called *rule-based systems*, and representations of this kind are said to be *action-oriented*.

Another widely used representational form, called the *unit*, or *frame*, or *schema*, is based on a more passive object-oriented view of knowledge. Systems of units (sometimes called *frame-based systems*) are siblings of the object-oriented systems common in computer science (*see* Object-Oriented Programming). Typically, a unit consists of a symbolic name, a list of attributes of some entity, and the values associated with the attributes. That is, the unit is a complex symbolic description of an entity that the ES needs to know about. There is a *knowledge base management system*, akin to a database management system (*q.v.*), associated with the units. One of its important functions is to handle automatically some routine inference functions for knowledge updating and knowledge propagation. The automatic handling is called *inheritance* (i.e. changes to attributes of a unit are automatically applied to all subunits and instances of that unit; e.g. if the height of new Ford Explorers were to increase by 2

inches, then this increase would automatically apply to the subunit "4WD Explorers" and to the individual vehicle that I buy).

Another general and powerful formalism for representing knowledge is the "standard" mathematical way, given by the symbols and formulas of *mathematical logic*, particularly first-order predicate logic and some higher-order logics.

In addition to the naturalness and expressiveness of the representational form, a representation needs to be modular and flexible. The process of building a knowledge base is an iterative one that has been called "an incremental approach to competence." The knowledge is teased out of the expert and the problem domain little by little on each iteration. The "module size" needs to match these little pieces, and the knowledge "modules" need to be easily integrated into the existing, growing knowledge base, with virtually no incremental reprogramming of the knowledge base.

In every expert system, the *inference engine* (embodying the problem-solving method or procedure) uses the knowledge in the knowledge base to construct the line of reasoning leading to the solution of the problem. The most common method (the method of choice in rule-based systems) involves chaining of IF–THEN rules. If the chaining starts from a set of conditions and moves toward some (possibly remote) conclusion, the method is called *forward chaining*. If the conclusion is known (e.g. it is a goal to be achieved) but the path to that conclusion is not known, then *backward chaining* with rules is employed, seeking conditions under which a particular line of reasoning will be true.

Sometimes, an inflexible commitment to either forward or backward chaining is not optimal, especially if new data is arriving that needs interpretation, and if a changing situation demands that goals change. In these cases, an opportunistic strategy that allows the flexible mixing of some forward chaining with some backward chaining is used. Opportunistic problem solving strategies are the hallmark of *blackboard systems*.

Other procedures commonly found in expert systems are procedures for *reasoning with uncertain information*, as well as knowledge and procedures for *explaining* the line of reasoning to the user. Knowledge of a domain and of a particular problem is almost always incomplete and uncertain. To deal with uncertainty, a rule may have associated with it a *confidence factor* (CF), or weight. A standard calculus for using CFs to construct and evaluate lines of reasoning is available. In an alternative method, called *fuzzy logic* (*q.v.*), uncertainty is represented by a distribution of values, and another standard calculus is available for handling these distributions. Finally, where sufficient statistical data is available, Bayes' Theorem and its associated calculations have been used in what are called *Bayesian networks* to represent reasoning certainties.

Since expert systems explicitly build lines of reasoning, there is little difficulty in responding to users' questions about the line of reasoning: how and why did it take the form that it has? Typical questions that can be answered by the explanation procedure are: "Why are you asking me that (particular) question?," or "How did you conclude (something)?" Also, "Show me your line of reasoning (main conclusions, intermediate and final)." The explanation procedure answers these questions by looking back at what rules were examined, which were selected and why, and what conclusions were drawn.

From the applications viewpoint, only a small number of practical techniques are used for representing knowledge, for making inferences (certain and uncertain), and for generating explanations. Commercial software systems are offered that carefully integrate various selections from this menu to assist knowledge engineers who do not want to program the techniques themselves to build their expert systems. These are the hybrid commercial tools or shells of the ES software industry that have appeared, with representative names like KEE (Knowledge Engineering Environment) from Intellicorp and ART (Advanced Reasoning Tool), now ART*Enterprise, from Brightware. The use of these tools/shells is very widespread and often the method of choice in building expert systems. Nevertheless, many ES efforts are relying on conventional languages such as C and C++ and developing customized ES techniques.

Research Aimed at Removing Limitations

Although ES tools/shells simplify programming expert systems, they do not sufficiently help with the crucial bottleneck problem of *knowledge acquisition*. As the Knowledge Principle informs us, the choice of reasoning method is important, but not nearly as important for the system's ultimate performance as the accumulation of high-quality knowledge. For the most part, knowledge acquisition continues to involve the interviewing and capturing skills of knowledge engineers. The AI field of *machine learning* (*q.v.*) is maturing and beginning to provide techniques such as *data mining* (*q.v.*) to help extract knowledge automatically, particularly from real-world data. Whether these and other machine learning techniques can significantly help reduce the knowledge acquisition bottleneck remains to be seen, but progress looks encouraging.

The techniques that made first-generation expert systems work well were also responsible for the key limitations of the technology. These are *narrowness* (or *overspecialization*) and its sibling, *brittleness*. The Knowledge Principle tells us that an ES has little competence outside of the domain of specialization for which its knowledge base has been carefully and systematically built. Since the ES knows only the knowledge of the specific domain, and has no ability to generalize, analogize, or in any other way extend knowledge, it can only solve problems in that domain—thereby exhibiting narrowness. If a problem posed by a user is simply beyond the boundary of what the ES knows about, the system's performance degrades ungracefully (with brittleness), falling from expert competence to complete incompetence. The boundaries of a system's knowledge, and hence the margins of its competence, are almost never represented in an explicit way that would inform the user of the system limitations and make these limits available to the reasoning process.

First-generation expert systems usually represent associational or phenomenological knowledge (i.e. knowledge near the surface of events), not the knowledge of what is deep below the surface, causing the events. Such deeper knowledge is called *first principles knowledge* or *model-based knowledge*. Methods for representing such knowledge and procedures for the inference engines of model-based reasoners are important topics being vigorously researched by the AI community. It is readily seen that this kind of knowledge helps to remove the limitations of narrowness and brittleness, since the use of principles and models generalizes much more readily than does the phenomenological description of events (e.g. on the IF side of a rule).

The breadth of a system's competence can also be extended with *cases* (i.e. "worked examples") that have been experienced in the past. Human experts know a great many particulars, not necessarily in the rule form but in the case form. *Case-based reasoning* (CBR—*q.v.*) has become a major branch of ES research concerned with the representation of case libraries and methods for reasoning from cases that are fundamentally different from the earlier methods based on logical chaining, fuzzy logic, or Bayes's Theorem. The inferencing in CBR involves searching for cases that best match the current problem situation and, in some instances, adapting the stored solution to meet the needs of the current problem. CBR has become the principal ES technology in the customer support applications discussed above.

Finally, there is the engineering economics of ES construction. Each ES is built from scratch. In first-generation systems, there is almost no reuse of knowledge and there is no systematic way in which a community of knowledge engineers cooperate to allow their systems to share knowledge. The conceptual infrastructure of *knowledge sharing* and reuse has emerged as a major topic of active research in ES. Included in this research are common knowledge interchange formats (KIF), shared ontologies (object concepts and relationships), large knowledge bases, and high-performance knowledge bases

Bibliography

1971. Feigenbaum, E. A., Buchanan, B. G., and Lederberg, J. "On Generality and Problem Solving: A Case Study Using the DENDRAL Program," in *Machine Intelligence* **6** (eds. B. Meltzer and D. Michie), 165–190. Edinburgh: Edinburgh University Press.

1977. Feigenbaum, E. A. "The Art of Artificial Intelligence: Themes and Case Studies of Knowledge Engineering," *Proceedings of the International Joint Conference on Artificial Intelligence.* Cambridge, MA: MIT Press.

1980. Lindsay, R. K., Buchanan, B. G., Feigenbaum, E. A., and Lederberg, J. *Applications of Artificial Intelligence for Organic Chemistry: The DENDRAL Project.* New York: McGraw-Hill.

1983. Hayes-Roth, F., Waterman, D. A., and Lenat, D. B. (eds.) *Building Expert Systems.* Reading, MA: Addison-Wesley.

1984. Buchanan, B. G., and Shortliffe, E. H. (eds.) *Rule-Based Expert Systems: The MYCIN Experiments of the Stanford Heuristic Programming Project.* Reading, MA: Addison-Wesley.

1986. Waterman, D. A. *A Guide to Expert Systems.* Reading, MA: Addison-Wesley.

1988. Feigenbaum, E., McCorduck, P., and Nii, H. P. *The Rise of the Expert Company.* New York: Times Books.

1989–1999. *Proceedings of the Innovative Applications of Artificial Intelligence Conferences.* Menlo Park, CA: AAAI Press.

1995. Stefik, M. *Introduction to Knowledge Systems.* San Francisco: Morgan Kaufmann.

Edward A. Feigenbaum and Philip Klahr

EXPRESSION

> For articles on related subjects *see* BACKUS–NAUR FORM; COERCION; CONSTANT; FUNCTIONAL PROGRAMMING; OPERAND; OPERATOR PRECEDENCE; PROCEDURE-ORIENTED LANGUAGES: PROGRAMMING; REGULAR EXPRESSION; STATEMENT; and WELL-FORMED FORMULA.

An *expression*, one of the fundamental constituents of high-level language syntax, is a character sequence that specifies a rule for calculating a value. That value may be either numeric, as in the Pascal expression `a+6`, or alphanumeric, as in the Basic expression `LEFT$(A$,5)` (whose value is the leftmost 5 characters of string `A$`). An expression may appear to the right of the replacement symbol (usually `=` or `:=` or `←`) in statement-oriented languages such as Pascal or Fortran, or may stand alone and be evaluated immediately to yield a particular value in expression-oriented languages such as Lisp or APL.

A *statement-oriented language* is one in which sentence-like statements calculate and save intermedi-ate values but (except for specific I/O statements) do not print them. In Pascal, for example, the statement `p:=a*b+c` is composed of an *identifier* (variable name) `p`, a *replacement symbol*, `:=`, and the *expression* `a*b+c`. Such an expression makes sense to the Pascal compiler if all of its identifiers have been previously declared as to type (real, integer, etc.) and if it is *well-formed* according to the grammatical rules of the language. The expression will make sense at execution time if, by the time it is reached during program flow, all of its identifiers have been assigned specific values that enable evaluation of the expression and storage of the result at the identifier specified to the left of the replacement symbol.

An *expression-oriented language* is one in which expressions may stand alone such that, when encountered during program flow, their values are calculated and printed immediately. Thus, if the expression `3+4` is presented to APL at an interactive terminal session, APL will respond immediately by outputting 7.

An expression that is valid in one high-level language might be invalid in another or, even if valid, produce a different result. Thus, `a**b` is a valid Fortran expression, but is not valid in Pascal, which does not have an exponentiation operator. The upper-case equivalent of the expression used earlier, `A*B+C`, would be acceptable to APL, but would have an entirely different meaning because of different interpretations of the `*` operator (multiplication in Pascal, exponentiation in APL) and different operator precedence. To obtain the same meaning, the APL programmer would write `(A×B)+C` or `C+A×B` and the Lisp programmer would write `(PLUS (TIMES A B) C)` because that language uses a fully-parenthesized notation in which operators precede their operands (prefix form).

Most high-level languages allow the use of expressions in contexts other than replacement statements. A typical use is for subscript selection. For example, the Pascal statement

```
k:=3*a+b[round(j+sqrt(x))]
```

will calculate and use the integer closest to the value of the expression `j+sqrt(x)` to select a particular member of the one-dimensional array `b`. The sum of the selected value and the value of `3*a` is then assigned to `k`. In Pascal and many other languages, a subscript may be any valid expression; some languages are more restrictive.

Expressions may also be classified as being either *homogeneous* (all constituents of the same type) or *mixed-mode*. An example of the latter is `A+J*Z` where, perhaps, `A` has been declared as being real (floating-point), `J` as being integer, and `Z` as being complex. What should be done? Early dialects of

Fortran declared such expressions syntactically illegal and refused to process them. Almost all current languages accept mixed-mode expressions whenever reasonable type conversions can be inferred (e.g. automatic conversion of A and J to complex prior to evaluation of the cited expression), which allow calculation to proceed (*see* COERCION).

An expression may be very simple as well as complicated. In most languages, the single digit 7 or the single-letter variable Q are valid expressions. Thus, the Pascal statement cited earlier, `k:=3*a+b` `[round(j+sqrt(x))]`, contains 10 recognizable expressions:

1–4.   3, `a`, `j`, and `x` are expressions.

5.   `3*a` is an expression.

6.   The function `sqrt(x)` is an expression.

7.   `j+sqrt(x)` is an expression.

8.   The subscript `round(j+sqrt(x))` is an expression.

9.   The subscripted variable

$$b[round(j+sqrt(x))]$$

is an expression.

10.   The entire right-hand side is an expression.

Since complex expressions may be built up recursively from simpler ones, the rules for recognizing a well-formed (syntactically valid) expression in any given language may be stated quite rigorously in a notation such as Backus–Naur Form (BNF—*q.v.*) or in the equivalent *syntax diagram* form commonly used to define Pascal. Consider the following example of

the use of such diagrams (Fig. 1) to define first ⟨operator⟩ and then ⟨expression⟩ in a very simple hypothetical language (where we assume that the elementary concepts of ⟨variable⟩ and ⟨number⟩ were defined earlier).

Using such diagrams, one can readily ascertain that such character sequences as

$$(a+b)*(c-d)$$
$$(5*9/(h+7)) \text{ and}$$
$$r*s-t/u$$

are valid expressions, but that others, such as $a*(b$ and $*a+b$ are not well-formed.

Since an expression is a rule for calculating a value, an expression need not be numeric or alphanumeric, but may be of any type that a programming language treats as a value. In languages that treat functions as values, as C does to some degree, and functional languages (*q.v.*) like Lisp, Standard ML, and Haskell do fully, the value of an expression may be a function. In Standard ML, for example, the expression $fn\,x \Rightarrow x+1$ is a function that adds one to its (integer) argument, and map f is an expression whose value is the function that applies the function f to each element of a list. Similarly, in object-oriented languages, the value of an expression may be an object: a structure containing data and operations on that data.

Bibliography

1973. Wirth, N. *Systematic Programming: An Introduction.* Upper Saddle River, NJ: Prentice Hall.
1996. Pratt, T. W., and Zelkowitz, M. V. *Programming Languages: Design and Implementation*, 3rd Ed., 123–136. Upper Saddle River, NJ: Prentice Hall.

Edwin D. Reilly

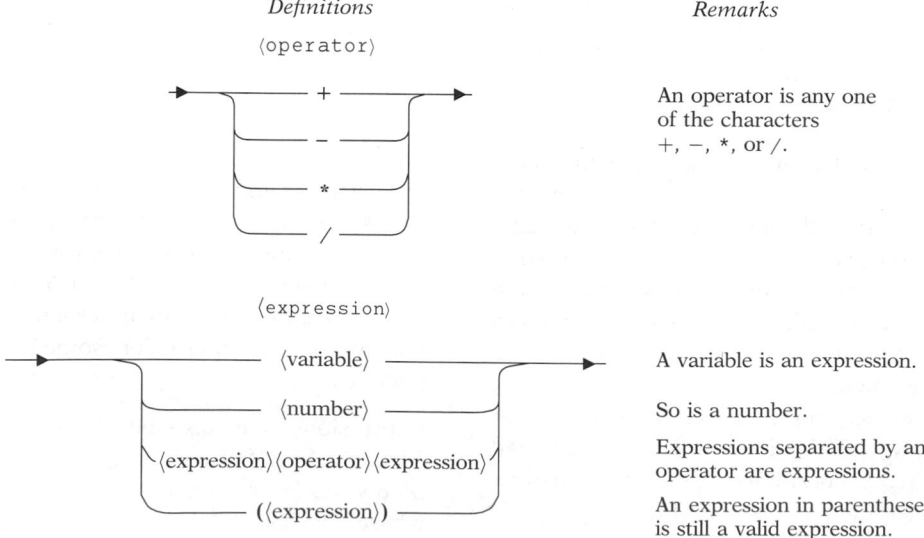

Definitions

⟨operator⟩

⟨expression⟩

Remarks

An operator is any one of the characters +, −, *, or /.

A variable is an expression.

So is a number.

Expressions separated by an operator are expressions.

An expression in parentheses is still a valid expression.

Figure 1.

EXTENSIBLE LANGUAGE

For articles on related subjects *see* ADA; ALGOL 68; DATA TYPE; MACRO; OPERATOR OVERLOADING; OBJECT-ORIENTED PROGRAMMING; PROCEDURE-ORIENTED LANGUAGES; and PROGRAMMING LANGUAGES.

An *extensible* (programming) *language* allows the user to enrich the language by introducing new features or by modifying existing ones. A language is called *extensible* if the new features can be made to resemble the built-in language constructs. Extensible languages were an important area of research in the 1960s and 1970s. They should be distinguished from the *ad hoc* extensions made to many programming languages by introducing features not present in the language standard.

Extensible programming languages are not common now for two reasons. One is that two of their most important capabilities, user-defined *types* and user-defined or redefined *operators* have become standard in many languages. The other is that while the notion of a small base language with extension mechanisms to let programmers adapt the language to their own needs appeared attractive initially, most programmers were not interested in language design and were not likely to be prepared to invest the effort required to produce useful extensions. The purpose of extensible languages was to improve the efficiency of the programmer and the clarity of the product, but in practice, they could readily have the opposite effects.

In one respect, any programming language that has subprograms (*q.v.*) is extensible, since the programmer can define new operations as functions or procedures. Subprograms generally do not resemble built-in operations, however; a call to a vector-addition subprogram might be `vec_sum(v1,v2,vsum)`, rather than `vsum := v1 + v2`. Normally extensibility refers to the ability to introduce new language elements that are used like existing ones.

Assembly language macros (*see* MACHINE AND ASSEMBLY LANGUAGE PROGRAMMING) were the first language extensions. Introduced in 1960, they permitted a programmer to define a new instruction by giving a name to a sequence of assembly-language instructions. Among high-level languages, Algol 68 gave programmers the ability to give names to data types and to use them in subsequent variable declarations, as in this definition, and use of a data type *point* to specify an ordered pair of reals:

```
mode point = struct(real x, y);
real a, point u, v;
```

Pascal (*q.v.*), C (*q.v.*), and nearly all more recent languages have such type-definition capabilities, thus allowing the programmer to extend the set of built-in data types with new data types that fit the needs of the program.

Algol 68 also allowed a programmer to declare new operators, so that, for example, one might define `--` to be a *distance* operator that would take two points and return the Euclidean distance between them. The programmer could then write `a := u -- v` rather than `a := distance(u,v)`. Although Pascal and C do not offer user-defined operators, Ada (*q.v.*), C++ (*q.v.*) and other object-oriented languages now provide this capability. To benefit fully from it, one must also be able to *overload* operators, giving new meanings to old ones, as Ada and C++ allow. Then one can define, say, vector addition as a new meaning of the + operator, rather than invent a new notation.

User-defined types and operators are examples of *semantic* extensions, introducing terms with new meanings into the language. *Syntactic* extensibility is less common, though it has been used to give programmers the ability to define new control structures (*q.v.*). Lisp (*q.v.*) provides macro features that can be used for syntactic extension, and Lisp programmers can use it to customize the language or to develop prototypes of control structures in new languages.

Several programming languages in the early 1970s were designed to support extensibility: EL1 (Extensible Language 1), GPL (General Purpose Language), and PPL (Polymorphic Programming Language) were three of them. Forth (*q.v.*) is now the most common extensible language. Since it gives the programmer access to all elements of the compiler (*q.v.*), it is easy to define new control structures as well as new operators. (Since Forth is stack-based, there is no sharp distinction between operators and functions.)

Extensible languages furthered the study of appropriate sorts of user-defined extensions, helping language designers to recognize the importance of abstract data types (*q.v.*) and classes (*q.v.*) in object-oriented programming. In place of the ability to define arbitrary new kinds of loops, for example, the C++ Standard Template Library defines data structures that each have associated *iterators*. Their implementations may extend the ways of moving from one data item to the next in the structure, but they present to the programmer a uniform view of processing all items in a collection.

In a different domain, the Extensible Markup Language (XML) may replace or supplement HTML for writing Web pages (*see* MARKUP LANGUAGES). It lets users specify new document types and notations for marking them for display, and also to specify how the new notations should control the appearance of the document.

It thus offers the power, and perhaps the risks, of the extensible programming languages of the 1970s.

Bibliography

1975. Standish, T. A. "Extensibility in Programming Language Design," *Sigplan Notices*, **10**, 7 (July), 18–21.

1976. Melkanoff, M. A. "Extensible Languages," in *Formal Languages and Programming* (ed. R. Aguilar). Amsterdam: North-Holland.

1999. Harold, E. R. *XML Bible*. Foster City, CA: IDG Books.

David Hemmendinger

FACTORING INTEGERS

For articles on related subjects *see* COOPERATIVE COMPUTING; CRYPTOGRAPHY, COMPUTERS IN; NUMBER THEORETIC CALCULATIONS; and NUMERICAL ANALYSIS.

The theory of numbers is primarily concerned with the properties of the *natural numbers* $1, 2, 3, \ldots$. The fundamental theorem of arithmetic states that each natural number > 1 can be expressed uniquely (up to order) as a product of *prime numbers*. A prime number is a natural number greater than 1 having no divisor other than 1 and itself. A natural number which is not prime is called *composite*. Proofs of the fundamental theorem provide no efficient method for obtaining the unique prime factorization of a natural number. The discovery of such methods is an important and difficult problem in number theory. This article will describe some algorithms for factoring integers, including the fastest ones known. It will be subdivided into these areas:

1. Trial division.

2. The Pollard methods.

3. The elliptic curve method.

4. Quadratic residue methods.

5. The number field sieve.

Trial Division

If the number to be factored has only a few decimal digits, we can factor it by trying to divide it by $2, 3, 5, 7, \ldots$ (the first few prime numbers). Every composite number must have a prime factor less than or equal to its square root. When a factor is discovered by this method, divide it out and continue recursively trying to factor the remaining cofactor, but starting with the most recently used trial divisor. When the trial division reaches the square root of the cofactor, we are done because the cofactor must be prime. The prime factors are thus discovered in increasing order of size.

Although trial division will succeed in factoring only small numbers, it is a good first step for trying to factor an unknown number of any size. This is so because a large random integer is likely to have one or more small prime factors. See Knuth (1997) and Riesel (1994) for details of many algorithms mentioned in this article.

The Pollard Methods

In the 1970s, Pollard invented two factoring algorithms which can find a small factor of a large number and which are more powerful than trial division. His Rho or Monte Carlo method finds a prime factor p of n in roughly $\sqrt{p}$ steps. Let $f(x)$ be a quadratic polynomial with integer coefficients. Choose a random integer x_0 and define the sequence of iterates of f as $x_i = f(x_{i-1})$ for $i \geq 1$. The sequence $x_i \bmod p$ is periodic with period $\leq p$. If $f(x)$ is neither x^2 nor $x^2 - 2$, then the period is usually near $\sqrt{p}$ for most values of x_0. To factor a number n, compute $g_i = \gcd(x_{2i} - x_i, n)$ for $i = 1, 2, \ldots$. When i reaches the period, p will divide g_i and, probably, g_i will equal p and n will be factored.

Pollard's $p-1$ factoring algorithm finds a prime factor p of a large number n quickly when all prime factors of $p-1$ are small. The number of steps it takes to find p is usually proportional to the largest prime factor of $p-1$. Here is a simple version of the algorithm. Choose a random starting value y_1. For $i > 1$ define $y_i = (y_{i-1})^i \bmod n$ and $g_i = \gcd(y_i - 1, n)$. Then p will appear as a factor of g_i as soon as $p-1$ divides $i!$. One can raise y_{i-1} to the i power (modulo n) in roughly $\log_2 i$ steps by a simple procedure (see Lehmer, 1969, p. 125).

There is also a $p+1$ algorithm which finds a prime factor p of a large number n quickly when all prime factors of $p+1$ are small. See Guy (1976) for examples of factoring with these and similar methods.

The Elliptic Curve Method

This factoring algorithm was announced by H. W. Lenstra, Jr, in 1985. It is the first to use twentieth century mathematics. It is similar to Pollard's $p-1$ algorithm discussed above. The multiplicative group of $GF(p)$ in that algorithm is replaced by the group of a random elliptic curve modulo p. A random point P on the elliptic curve is added to itself repeatedly to form $(i!)P$ for $i = 1, 2, \ldots$. During these additions, whose arithmetic is performed modulo n, one must invert a certain number modulo n. With luck, the number will have a factor p in common with n. When this happens, the inversion modulo n will fail and n will be factored.

When a number of random elliptic curves are tried, this algorithm will discover a factor p of n in about $\exp(\sqrt{2 \log p \log \log p})$ operations. It has been used with great success to find prime factors in the 10 to 40 digit range, with a few larger successes.

Quadratic Residue Methods

The methods described so far usually discover small prime factors of n before large ones, and their running times increase with the size of the factor found. In contrast, the methods described below have running times which increase with the size of n and are independent of the size of the factor discovered. They are most effective for factoring numbers without small factors. They are used when the earlier methods fail.

In the quadratic residue methods many quadratic residues modulo n are generated. These are solutions to the congruence $A^2 \equiv Q \pmod{n}$. The prime factors of the Qs are paired (by Gaussian elimination over $GF(2)$) to form squares. Then (subsets of) the congruences are multiplied to produce several congruences of the form $x^2 \equiv y^2 \pmod{n}$. Each congruence

like this gives a chance to factor n, as $\gcd(x - y, n)$ may be a proper factor of n. The methods differ in the way the factored quadratic residues Q are produced.

The Continued Fraction Algorithm of Morrison and Brillhart derives the congruences $A^2 \equiv Q \pmod{n}$ from the simple continued fraction expansion of $\sqrt{n}$. The Qs are factored by trial division by a fixed set of small primes called the *factor base*. The Qs are more likely than random quadratic residues to have only small prime factors because they are smaller than $2\sqrt{n}$. This method has been used to factor numbers as large as 62 digits.

The Quadratic Sieve Algorithm of Pomerance generates the Qs as (part of) the range of one or more quadratic polynomials. The regularity of their rule of formation allows them to be factored by a sieve rather than by trial division, which is slow. This method has factored numbers as large as 129 digits.

The Number Field Sieve

This algorithm, invented in 1990, works best for numbers of the form $n = r^e - s$, where r, e, and $|s|$ are small positive integers. Choose a small positive integer d. (The optimal d is about 5 for n between 100 and 170 digits.) Let k be the least positive integer for which $kd \geq e$. Let $f(X)$ be the polynomial $X^d - sr^{kd-e}$. Let $m = r^k$. Then $f(m) = r^{kd-e}n$, so m is a zero of f modulo n.

Let α be a zero of f. Let $K = \mathbf{Q}(\alpha)$. We assume f is irreducible, or else we could use its factorization to factor n. The degree of K over $\mathbf{Q}$ is d. Let Q_n denote the ring of rational numbers with denominator co-prime to n. The subring $Q_n[\alpha]$ of K consists of expressions $\sum_{i=0}^{d-1} (s_i/t_i)\alpha^i$ with $s_i, t_i \in \mathbf{Z}$ and $\gcd(n, t_i) = 1$. Define a ring homomorphism $\phi \colon Q_n[\alpha] \to \mathbf{Z}/n\mathbf{Z}$ by the formula $\phi(\alpha) = (m \bmod n)$.

The Number Field Sieve uses a sieve to find factors of $a + bm$ and the norm of $a + b\alpha$ in $\mathbf{Z}$, for $0 < a \leq A$ and $-B \leq b \leq B$. The norm of $a + b\alpha$ is $(-b)^d f(-a/b)$. A pair (a, b) is saved in a file if a and b are relatively prime and both $a + bm$ and the norm of $a + b\alpha$ have only small prime factors.

After enough pairs have been collected, one uses linear algebra over $GF(2)$ to find a non-empty set S of pairs (a, b) of relatively prime integers such that

$$\prod_{(a,b)\in S} (a + bm) \text{ is a square in } \mathbf{Z},$$

and

$$\prod_{(a,b)\in S} (a + b\alpha) \text{ is a square in } Q_n[\alpha].$$

Let the integer x be a square root of the first product. Let $\beta \in Q_n[\alpha]$ be a square root of the second product. We have $\phi(\beta^2) \equiv x^2 \bmod n$ since $\phi(a + b\alpha) \equiv a + bm \bmod n$. Let y be the integer for which $\phi(\beta) \equiv y \bmod n$. Then $x^2 \equiv y^2 \bmod n$, which gives us a chance to factor n, just as in the quadratic residue methods above.

In variations of the basic form, other polynomials may be used. The key properties required of the polynomial are that it is irreducible, that it has moderately small coefficients so that the norm of α is small, and that we know a nontrivial root m modulo n of it. For example, to factor $n = 10^{158} + 1$, one might use $f(X) = 8X^5 + 25$ with roots $m = 5 \times 10^{31}$ and $\alpha = (-25/8)^{1/5}$. This method has factored numbers as large as 167 digits.

See the articles in Lenstra and Lenstra (1993) for a more complete description of the number field sieve algorithm.

Bibliography

1969. Lehmer, D. H. "Computer Technology Applied to the Theory of Numbers," *Studies in Number Theory*, MAA Studies in Mathematics, Vol. 6. Upper Saddle River, NJ: Prentice Hall.

1976. Guy, R. K. "How to Factor a Number," *Congressus Numerantium XVI, Proceedings of the Fifth Manitoba Conference on Numerical Mathematics*, Winnipeg, 49–89.

1993. Lenstra, A. K., and H. W. Lenstra, Jr (eds.). *The Development of the Number Field Sieve*. Lecture Notes in Mathematics, Vol. 1554. Berlin: Springer-Verlag.

1994. Riesel, H. *Prime Numbers and Computer Methods for Factorization*, 2nd Ed. Progress in Mathematics, Vol. 126. Boston: Birkhäuser.

1997. Knuth, D. E. *The Art of Computer Programming*, Vol. 2, *Seminumerical Algorithms*, 3rd Ed. Reading, MA: Addison-Wesley.

Samuel S. Wagstaff, Jr

FAST FOURIER TRANSFORM (FFT)

For articles on related subjects *see* ALGORITHMS, ANALYSIS OF; DISCRETE MATHEMATICS; and NUMERICAL ANALYSIS.

The Discrete Fourier Transform

The *Fast Fourier Transform* (FFT) refers to a family of numerical algorithms for computing the Discrete Fourier Transform (DFT). In complex notation, the DFT is defined by

$$a(n) = \sum_{j=0}^{N-1} x(j) W_N^{nj} \qquad (1)$$

where $x(j)$, $j = 0, 1, 2, \ldots, N-1$ is a given sequence of complex numbers and

$$W_N = \exp(-2\pi i / N). \qquad (2)$$

This can be written as a series of sines and cosines by making the substitution

$$W_N^{nj} = \cos(2\pi nj/N) - i\sin(2\pi nj/N). \qquad (3)$$

Most of the important applications of the FFT involve the inversion theorem and the convolution theorem. The inversion formula is

$$x(j) = N^{-1} \sum_{n=0}^{N-1} a(n) W_N^{-nj} \qquad (4)$$

and can be computed by the same algorithm that computes Eq. (1). A direct calculation according to the defining formula (1) would require N^2 complex multiplications and $N \times (N-1)$ complex additions. If $N = N_1 N_2 \cdots N_m$, an FFT algorithm can compute the same DFT in $N(N_1 + N_2 + \cdots + N_m)$ complex multiplications and $N(N_1 + N_2 + \cdots + N_m)$ complex additions. For simplicity, approximate expressions will be used, and this will be referred to as

$$N(N_1 + N_2 + \cdots + N_m) \qquad (5)$$

multiply-adds or just "operations." For $N > 4$, this is much smaller than the N^2 operations required by direct calculation of the sums in (1). For N equal to a power of 2, very simple efficient programs can compute the DFT in $N \log_2 N$ operations, yielding a speed-up factor of $N/\log_2 N$. Other choices of N with small factors lead to simple programs with comparable efficiency and a broad selection of possible N-values.

The *convolution theorem* permits one to use the FFT to compute convolution and covariance functions. The theorem states that given two periodic sequences $x(j)$ and $y(j)$ with period N, the DFT of the cyclic convolution

$$z(j) = \sum_{k=0}^{N-1} x(k) y(j-k) \qquad j = 0, 1, \ldots, N-1 \quad (6)$$

is the product sequence

$$c(n) = a(n) b(n), \quad n = 0, 1, \ldots, N-1 \qquad (7)$$

where $a(n)$ is the DFT of $x(j)$ and $b(n)$ is the DFT of $y(j)$. Thus, the DFT method can compute the convolution in a number of operations proportional to $N \log N$ instead of N^2.

The DFT is used extensively in digital signal processing, statistical analysis, and in the solution of differential and difference equations.

The General Arbitrary Factor Algorithm

Although the basic idea in the FFT algorithm had been used earlier (Cooley *et al.*, 1967, and Heideman *et al.*, 1984), it was not generally known and used until the mid-1960s (Cooley and Tukey, 1965, and Cooley *et al.*,

1969). It may be described as follows: Consider N with two factors, $N = N_1 N_2$ and the mapping from one-dimensional to two-dimensional indices:

$$x(j) = x(j_2, j_1), \qquad j = j_2 + j_1 N_2 \tag{8}$$

$$a(n) = a(n_1, n_2), \qquad n = n_1 + n_2 N_1 \tag{9}$$

This maps $x(j)$ into an $N_2 \times N_1$ array and $a(n)$ into an $N_1 \times N_2$ array as follows: The one-dimensional DFT is expressed as a two-dimensional DFT:

$$a(n_1, n_2) = \sum_{j_2=0}^{N_2-1} \sum_{j_1=0}^{N_1-1} x(j_2, j_1) W_N^{jk} \tag{10}$$

where

$$W_N^{jk} = W_N^{(j_2+j_1 N_2)(n_1+n_2 N_1)}$$

$$= W_N^{j_1 n_1 N_2} W_N^{j_2 n_1} W_N^{j_2 n_2 N_1} W_N^{j_1 n_2 N}. \tag{11}$$

Since $W_N^N = 1$ and $W_N^{N_2} = W_{N_1}$, substitution in Eq. (10) gives

$$a(n_1, n_2) = \sum_{j_2=0}^{N_2-1} \left\{ \sum_{j_1=0}^{N_1-1} x(j_2, j_1) W_N^{j_1 n_1} \right\} W_{N_2}^{j_2 n_2}. \tag{12}$$

The inner sum, in braces, may be computed first:

$$a_1(j_2, n_1) = \sum_{j_1=0}^{N_1-1} x(j_2, j_1) W_{N_1}^{j_1 n_1}. \tag{13}$$

It is multiplied by the "twiddle factor," $W_N^{j_1 n_1}$ and a second set of Fourier transforms is computed:

$$a_2(n_2, n_1) = \sum_{j_2=0}^{N_2-1} \left\{ a_1(j_2, n_1) W_N^{j_2 n_1} \right\} W_{N_2}^{j_2 n_2}. \tag{14}$$

This is a two-dimensional DFT with a twiddle factor multiplication applied to the intermediate array $a_1(j_2, n_1)$. Finally, it is noted that the resulting array $a_2(n_2, n_1)$ has the required values of the result, $a(n_1, n_2)$, but they are in a transposed array, or in "digit-reversed" order, as it is called. It is often advantageous to transpose all arrays to obtain an algorithm that starts with data in permuted order and gives results in correct order.

If N has more than two factors, one may iterate with the above algorithm and obtain an algorithm requiring the number of operations in (5).

The Radix 2 FFT

When $N_1 = N_2 = \cdots = N_m = 2$, the mapping to m dimensions expresses each data element in terms of the bit representation of its index. The transpose mentioned above is a bit-reversal permutation defined by

$$a_0(j_0, \ldots, j_{m-1}, j_m) = x_0(j_m, j_{m-1}, \ldots, j_1, j_0) \tag{15}$$

The radix 2 algorithms assumes the form of a series of two-point DFTs:

$$a_1(0, j_2, j_3, \ldots, j_m) = a_0(0, j_2, j_3, \ldots, j_m)$$
$$+ a_0(1, j_2, j_3, \ldots, j_m)$$

$$a_1(1, j_2, j_3, \ldots, j_m) = a_0(0, j_2, j_3, \ldots, j_m)$$
$$- a_0(1, j_2, j_3, \ldots, j_m)$$

$$a_2(n_1, 0, j_3, \ldots, j_m) = a_1(n_1, 0, j_3, \ldots, j_m)$$
$$+ a_1(n_1, 1, j_3, \ldots, j_m) W_4^{n_1}$$

$$a_2(n_1, 1, j_3, \ldots, j_m) = a_1(n_1, 0, j_3, \ldots, j_m)$$
$$- a_1(n_1, 1, j_3, \ldots, j_m) W_4^{n_1}$$

$$a_3(n_1, n_2, 0, \ldots, j_m) = a_2(n_1, n_2, 0, \ldots, j_m)$$
$$+ a_2(n_1, n_2, 1, \ldots, j_m) W_8^{n_1+2n_2}$$

$$a_3(n_1, n_2, 1, \ldots, j_m) = a_2(n_1, n_2, 0, \ldots, j_m)$$
$$- a_2(n_1, n_2, 1, \ldots, j_m) W_8^{n_1+2n_2}$$

$$\cdots \cdots \tag{16}$$

$$a_m(n_1, n_2, n_3, \ldots, 0) = a_{m-1}(n_1, n_2, n_3, \ldots, 0)$$
$$+ a_{m-1}(n_1, n_2, n_3, \ldots, 1)$$
$$\times W_{2^m}^{n_1+2n_2+\cdots+2^{m-1}n_{m-1}}$$

$$a_m(n_1, n_2, n_3, \ldots, 1) = a_{m-1}(n_1, n_2, n_3, \ldots, 0)$$
$$- a_{m-1}(n_1, n_2, n_3, \ldots, 1)$$
$$\times W_{2^m}^{n_1+2n_2+\cdots+2^{m-1}n_{m-1}}$$

The Fortran program listing in Fig. 1 for the radix 2 algorithm demonstrates the use of the above algorithm. Written to explain the algorithm rather than to achieve efficiency, it is referred to as the "decimation in time algorithm." A slight change in the factoring of W^{jn} leads to the form referred to as the "Sande Tukey" or "decimation in frequency" form of the algorithm. A radix 4 algorithm saves one out of four complex multiplications and has an advantage on RISC

```
DO 20 L = 1, M
   LE = 2**L
   LE1 = LE/2
   U = (1.,0.)
   ANG = 3.14159265358979/LE1
   W = CMPLX (COS(ANG), -SIN(ANG))
   DO 20 J = 1, LE1
      DO 10 I = J,N,LE
         IP = I + LE1
         T = A(IP)*U
         A(IP) = A(I) - T
10       A(I) = A(I)+ T
20    U = U*W
```

Figure 1. Fortran subroutine for FFT with $N = 2^m$, starting with bit-reversed data.

architecture (*q.v.*) machines, where more calculations can be done in registers without intermediate store and load operations.

The Mutually Prime Factor Algorithm

If N_1 and N_2 are mutually prime factors of N, one can use a different mapping from one- to two-dimensional indices:

$$j = j_1 N_2 + j_2 N_1 \bmod N \tag{17}$$

$$n_1 = n \bmod N_1 \quad n_2 = n \bmod N_2 \tag{18}$$

The solution of these two congruences is given by the *Chinese Remainder Theorem* (CRT):

$$m = n_1 Q_1 + n_2 Q_2 \bmod N \tag{19}$$

where Q_1 and Q_2 are idempotents under multiplication mod N, i.e.

$$Q_1 = 1 \bmod N_1, \qquad Q_2 = 0 \bmod N_1 \tag{20}$$

$$Q_1 = 0 \bmod N_2, \qquad Q_2 = 1 \bmod N_2 \tag{21}$$

Then

$$W_N^{jn} = W_N^{j_1 N_2 n} W_N^{j_2 N_1 n} = W_{N_1}^{j_1 n_1} W_{N_2}^{j_2 n_2} \tag{22}$$

where n may be replaced in the exponents of W_{N_1} and W_{N_2} respectively, by n_1 and n_2. The DFT can then be written:

$$a(n_1, n_2) = \sum_{j_2=0}^{N_2-1} \left\{ \sum_{j_1=0}^{N_1-1} x(j_2, j_1) W_N^{j_1 n_1} \right\} W_{N_2}^{j_2 n_2} \tag{23}$$

In iterated form, this is written

$$a_1(n_1, j_2) = \sum_{j_1=0}^{N_1-1} x(j_2, j_1) W_N^{j_1 n_1} \tag{24}$$

$$a(n_1, n_2) = \sum_{j_2=0}^{N_2-1} a_1(n_1, j_2) W_{N_2}^{j_2 n_2} \tag{25}$$

The advantage of the mutually prime factor algorithms is that there is no twiddle factor between iterations. The disadvantage is in the increased complexity of the addressing of the data. C. S. Burrus has published a series of papers on the index mappings and has produced programs written in a neat modular fashion with separate and independent routines for each of the possible factors of N (Burrus, 1977; Burrus and Johnson, 1984).

Rader's DFT Algorithm

The FFT algorithm requires an N that is factorable. Rader (1968) addressed the challenge of being able to use the FFT algorithm for N equal to a prime number. For example, consider $N = 7$. The DFT may be expressed

$$\begin{bmatrix} a_0 \\ a_1 \\ a_2 \\ a_3 \\ a_4 \\ a_5 \\ a_6 \end{bmatrix} = W_7 ** \begin{bmatrix} 0000000 \\ 0123456 \\ 0246135 \\ 0362514 \\ 0415263 \\ 0531642 \\ 0654321 \end{bmatrix} \begin{bmatrix} x_0 \\ x_1 \\ x_2 \\ x_3 \\ x_4 \\ x_5 \\ x_6 \end{bmatrix} \tag{26}$$

where the matrix contains the exponents of W_7.

The integers under multiplication mod 7 form a group with the generators of the whole group. This permits the use of an index permutation defined by

$$j = 3^{j'} \bmod 7 = 1, 3, 2, 6, 4, 5, \quad j' = 0, 1, 2, \ldots, 5 \tag{27}$$

$$n = 3^{n'} \bmod 7 = 1, 3, 2, 6, 4, 5, \quad n' = 0, 1, 2, \ldots, 5 \tag{28}$$

which puts the DFT matrix in the form

$$W_7^{jn} = W_7^{3^{j'+n'}} \tag{29}$$

Therefore, the 6 by 6 block of the DFT matrix of non-zero exponents becomes a cyclic skew-symmetric matrix:

$$\begin{bmatrix} a_0 \\ a_1 \\ a_3 \\ a_2 \\ a_6 \\ a_4 \\ a_5 \end{bmatrix} = W_7 ** \begin{bmatrix} 0000000 \\ 0132645 \\ 0326451 \\ 0264513 \\ 0645132 \\ 0451326 \\ 0513264 \end{bmatrix} \begin{bmatrix} x_0 \\ x_1 \\ x_3 \\ x_2 \\ x_6 \\ x_4 \\ x_5 \end{bmatrix} \tag{30}$$

The block of Ws with non-zero exponents is a 6-point cyclic convolution, or "correlation" to be precise, which can be computed by the Fourier transform method described above in $O(N \log N)$ operations, where $O(f(N))$ denotes a quantity proportional to $f(N)$ for large N. Thus, the DFT for a prime number can be computed in $O(N \log N)$ operations. However, the crossover point in the number of operations (i.e. the point where the DFT beats brute force) for the two methods is high, at around $N = 100$.

The Winograd Fourier Transform Algorithm

Shmuel Winograd has developed a theory of computational complexity, which he has applied to the calculation of convolutions and DFTs (Winograd, 1974; Silverman, 1977). To apply this to the calculation of the DFT, he uses mutually prime factors of N to reduce the DFT to a set of small DFTs that can be expressed as convolutions. He also schedules the calculation so that all sinusoidal factors are combined into one set of factors, further reducing computation. Others have found it efficient to take more multiplications and schedule the calculations as was done above for the prime factor algorithm and use Winograd's efficient small DFT algorithms for each of the factors (Kolba and Parks, 1977).

Very efficient general-purpose FFT subroutines combine all of the above algorithms and permit the efficient calculation of the DFT for a wide selection of N values. When the data is real, or real and symmetric (cosine transform) or real and anti-symmetric (sine transform), special efficient algorithms can be used to avoid redundant calculations.

Bibliography

1965. Cooley, J. W., and Tukey, J. W. "An Algorithm for the Machine Calculation of Complex Fourier Series," *Mathematics of Computation*, **19** (April), 297.

1967. Cooley, J. W., Lewis, P. A. W., and Welch, P. D. "Historical Notes on the Fast Fourier Transform," *IEEE Trans. Audio Electroacoustics*, **AU-15** (June), 76–79.

1968. Rader, C. M. "Discrete Fourier Transforms When the Number of Data Samples is Prime," *Proc. IEEE (Letters)*, **56** (June), 1107–1108.

1969. Cooley, J. W., Lewis, P. A. W., and Welch, P. D. "The fast Fourier Transform Algorithm and its Applications," *IEEE Trans. on Education*, **E-12** (March), 27–34.

1974. Winograd, S. "Arithmetic Complexity of Computations," CBMS-NSF Regional Conference Series in Applied Mathematics. Philadelphia: SIAM.

1977. Burrus, C. S. "Index Mappings for Multidimensional Formulation of the DFT and Convolution," *IEEE Trans. Acoust. Speech, and Signal Processing*, **ASSP-25**, 3 (June), 239–242.

1977. Silverman, H. F. "An Introduction to Programming the Winograd Fourier Transform Algorithm (WFTA)," *IEEE Trans. Acoust. Speech, Signal Processing*, **ASSP-25**, 2 (April), 152–164.

1977. Kolba, D. P., and Parks, T. W. "A Prime Factor FFT Algorithm Using High-speed Convolution," *IEEE Trans. Acoust. Speech, Signal Processing*, **ASSP-25**, 4 (August), 281–294.

1984. Heideman, M. T., Johnson, D. H., and Burrus, C. S. "Gauss and the History of the Fast Fourier Transform," *The ASSP Magazine*, **1**, 4 (October), 14–21.

1984. Burrus, C. S., and Johnson, H. W., "An In-Order In-Place Radix 2 FFT." *Proceedings of the International Conference on Acoustics Speech and Signal Processing*, 28A.2.1.

1996. Ersoy, O. K. *Fourier-Related Transforms, Fast Algorithms and Applications*. New York: Prentice Hall.

1998. Garg, H. K., and Bal, K. *Digital Signal Processing Algorithms: Number Theory, Convolution, Fast Fourier Transforms, and Applications*. Boca Raton, FL: CRC Press.

James W. Cooley

FAULT-TOLERANT COMPUTING

For articles on related subjects *see* CLUSTER COMPUTING; DISTRIBUTED SYSTEMS; ERROR CORRECTING AND DETECTING CODE; ERRORS; and REDUNDANT ARRAY OF INEXPENSIVE DISKS.

Fault-tolerant computing is the art and science of building computing systems that continue to operate satisfactorily in the presence of faults. A fault-tolerant system may be able to tolerate one or more fault types, including (1) transient, intermittent or permanent hardware faults, (2) software and hardware design errors, (3) operator errors, or (4) externally induced upsets or physical damage. An extensive methodology has been developed in this field over the past 40 years, and a number of fault-tolerant machines have been developed—most dealing with random hardware faults, while a smaller number deal with software, design and operator faults to varying degrees. A large amount of supporting research has been reported.

Fault tolerance and dependable systems research covers a wide spectrum of applications ranging across embedded real-time systems (*q.v.*), commercial transaction systems, transportation systems, and military/space systems—to name a few. The supporting research includes system architecture, design techniques, coding theory, testing, validation, proof of correctness, modeling, software reliability, operating systems, parallel processing, and real-time processing. These areas often involve widely diverse core expertise ranging from formal logic, mathematics of stochastic modeling, graph theory (*q.v.*), hardware design and software engineering (*q.v.*).

The primary forum for presenting research in this field has been the annual IEEE International Symposium on Fault-Tolerant Computing (FTCS) and the papers in its Digests provide a primary reference source.

Basic Concepts

HARDWARE FAULT TOLERANCE

The majority of fault-tolerant designs have been directed toward building computers that automatically recover from random faults occurring in hardware components. The techniques employed to do this generally involve partitioning a computing system into modules that act as fault-containment regions. Each module is backed up with protective redundancy so that, if the module fails, others can assume its function. Special mechanisms are added to detect errors and implement recovery. Two general approaches to hardware fault recovery have been used: (1) fault masking and (2) dynamic recovery.

Fault masking is a structural redundancy technique that completely masks faults within a set of redundant modules. A number of identical modules execute the same functions, and their outputs are voted to remove errors created by a faulty module. Triple modular redundancy (TMR) is a commonly used form of fault masking in which the circuitry is triplicated and voted. The voting circuitry can also be triplicated so that individual voter failures can also be corrected by the voting process. A TMR system fails whenever two modules in a redundant triplet create errors so that the vote is no longer valid. Hybrid redundancy is an extension of TMR in which the triplicated modules are backed up with additional spares, which are used to replace faulty modules—allowing more faults to be tolerated. Voted systems require more than three times as much hardware as non-redundant systems, but they have the advantage that computations can continue without interruption when a fault occurs, allowing existing operating systems to be used.

Dynamic recovery is required when only one copy of a computation is running at a time (or in some cases two unchecked copies), and it involves automated self-repair. As in fault masking, the computing system is partitioned into modules backed up by spares as protective redundancy. In the case of dynamic recovery, however, special mechanisms are required to detect faults in the modules, switch out a faulty module, switch in a spare, and instigate those software actions (rollback, initialization, retry, restart) necessary to restore and continue the computation. In single computers special hardware is required along with software to do this, while in multicomputers the function is often managed by the other processors.

Dynamic recovery is generally more hardware-efficient than voted systems, and it is therefore the approach of choice in resource-constrained (e.g. low-power) systems, and especially in high-performance scalable systems in which the amount of hardware resources devoted to active computing must be maximized. Its disadvantage is that computational delays occur during fault recovery, fault coverage is often lower, and specialized operating systems may be required.

SOFTWARE FAULT TOLERANCE
Efforts to attain software that can tolerate software design faults (programming errors) have made use of static and dynamic redundancy approaches similar to those used for hardware faults. One such approach, *N*-version programming, uses static redundancy in the form of independently written programs (versions) that perform the same functions, and their outputs are voted at special checkpoints. Here, of course, the data being voted may not be exactly the same, and a criterion must be used to identify and reject faulty versions and to determine a consistent value (through inexact voting) that all good versions can use. An alternative dynamic approach is based on the concept of *recovery blocks*. Programs are partitioned into blocks and acceptance tests are executed after each block. If an acceptance test fails, a redundant code block is executed.

An approach called *design diversity* combines hardware and software fault-tolerance by implementing a fault-tolerant computer system using different hardware *and* software in redundant channels. Each channel is designed to provide the same function, and a method is provided to identify when one channel devi-

ates unacceptably from the others. The goal is to tolerate both hardware and software design faults. This is a very expensive technique, but it is used in very critical aircraft control applications.

History

The SAPO computer built in Prague, Czechoslovakia, was probably the first fault-tolerant computer. It was built in 1950–1954 under the supervision of A. Svoboda, using relays and a magnetic drum memory. The processor used triplication and voting (TMR), and the memory implemented error detection with automatic retries when an error was detected. A second machine developed by the same group (EPOS) also contained comprehensive fault tolerance features. The fault tolerant features of these machines were motivated by the local unavailability of reliable components and a high probability of reprisals by the ruling authorities should the machine fail.

Over the past 30 years, a number of fault-tolerant computers have been developed that fall into three general types: (1) long-life, unmaintainable computers, (2) ultradependable, real-time computers, and (3) high-availability computers.

LONG-LIFE, UNMAINTAINABLE COMPUTERS
Applications such as spacecraft require computers to operate for long periods of time without external repair. Typical requirements are a probability of 95% that the computer will operate correctly for 5–10 years. Machines of this type must use hardware in a very efficient fashion, and they are typically constrained to low power, weight, and volume. Therefore, it is not surprising that NASA was an early sponsor of fault-tolerant computing. In the 1960s, the first fault-tolerant machine to be developed and flown was the on-board computer for the Orbiting Astronomical Observatory (OAO), which used fault masking at the component (transistor) level.

The JPL Self-Testing-and-Repairing (STAR) computer was NASA's next fault-tolerant computer, developed in the late 1960s for a 10-year mission to the outer planets. The STAR computer, designed under the leadership of A. Avižienis, was the first computer to employ dynamic recovery throughout its design. Various modules of the computer were instrumented to detect internal faults and signal fault conditions to a special test and repair processor that effected reconfiguration and recovery. An experimental version of the STAR was implemented in the laboratory and its fault tolerance properties were verified by experimental testing.

Perhaps the most successful long-life space application has been the JPL Voyager computers that have now operated in space for 20 years. This system uses dynamic redundancy in which pairs of redundant computers check each other by exchanging messages, and if a computer fails, its partner can take over the computations. This type of design has been used on several subsequent spacecraft.

ULTRADEPENDABLE REAL-TIME COMPUTERS

These are computers for which an error or delay can prove to be catastrophic. They are designed for applications such as control of aircraft, mass transportation systems, and nuclear power plants. The applications justify massive investments in redundant hardware, software, and testing.

One of the first operational machines of this type was the Saturn V guidance computer, developed in the 1960s. It contained a TMR processor and duplicated memories (each using internal error detection). Processor errors were masked by voting, and a memory error was circumvented by reading from the other memory. The next machine of this type was the Space Shuttle computer. It was a rather *ad hoc* design that used four computers that executed the same programs and were voted. A fifth, non-redundant, computer was included with different programs in case a software error was encountered.

During the 1970s, two influential fault-tolerant machines were developed by NASA for fuel-efficient aircraft that require continuous computer control in flight. They were designed to meet the most stringent reliability requirements of any computer up to that time. Both machines employed hybrid redundancy. The first, designated Software Implemented Fault Tolerance (SIFT), was developed by SRI International. It used off-the-shelf computers and achieved voting and reconfiguration primarily through software. The second machine, the Fault-Tolerant Multiprocessor (FTMP), developed by the C. S. Draper Laboratory at MIT, used specialized hardware to effect error and fault recovery. A commercial company, August Systems, was a spin-off from the SIFT program. It has developed a TMR system intended for process control applications. The FTMP has evolved into the Fault-Tolerant Processor (FTP), used by Draper in several applications and the Fault-Tolerant Parallel Processor (FTPP)—a parallel processor that allows processes to run in a single machine or in duplex, triplex or quadrupled groups of processors. This highly innovative design is fully Byzantine resilient and allows multiple groups of redundant processors to be interconnected to form scalable systems. (A processor has a *Byzantine* failure if it appears to function normally but gives incorrect results.)

The new generation of fly-by-wire aircraft exhibit a very high degree of fault tolerance in their real-time flight control computers. For example, the Airbus airliners use redundant channels with different processors and diverse software to protect against design errors as well as hardware faults. Other areas where fault tolerance is being used include control of public transportation systems and the distributed computer systems now being incorporated in automobiles.

HIGH-AVAILABILITY COMPUTERS

Many applications require very high availability but can tolerate an occasional error or very short delays (on the order of a few seconds), while error recovery is taking place. Hardware designs for these systems are often considerably less expensive than those used for ultradependable real-time computers. Computers of this type often use duplex designs. Example applications are telephone switching and transaction processing.

The most widely used fault-tolerant computer systems developed during the 1960s were in electronic switching systems (ESS) that are used in telephone switching offices. The first of these AT&T machines, No. 1 ESS, had a goal of no more than two hours downtime in 40 years. The computers are duplicated to detect errors, with some dedicated hardware and extensive software used to identify faults and effect replacement. These machines have since evolved over several generations to No. 5 ESS, which uses a distributed system controlled by the 3B20D fault-tolerant computer.

The largest commercial success in fault-tolerant computing has been in the area of transaction processing (*q.v.*) for banks, airline reservations, etc. Tandem Computers, Inc., was the first major producer and is the current leader in this market. The design approach is a distributed system using a sophisticated form of duplication. For each running process, there is a backup process running on a different computer. The primary process is responsible for checkpointing its state to duplex disks. If it should fail, the backup process can restart from the last checkpoint (*q.v.*). Stratus Computer has become another major producer of fault-tolerant machines for high-availability applications. Their approach uses duplex self-checking computers where each computer of a duplex pair is itself internally duplicated and compared to provide high-coverage concurrent error detection. The duplex pair of self-checking computers are run synchronously so that if one fails, the other can continue the computations without delay.

Finally, the IBM mainframe series which evolved from the IBM 360 (*see* IBM 360/370/390 SERIES) has always used extensive fault tolerance techniques of internal checking, instruction retries and automatic switching of redundant units to provide very high availability. The newest CMOS-VLSI version, G4, uses coding on registers and on-chip duplication for error detection, and it contains redundant processors, memories, I/O modules, and power supplies to recover from hardware faults, providing very high levels of dependability.

The *server* market represents a new and rapidly growing market for fault-tolerant machines driven by the growth of the Internet and local networks and their needs for uninterrupted service. Many major server manufacturers offer systems that contain redundant processors, disks, and power supplies, and automatically switch to backups if a failure is detected. Examples are Sun's ft-Sparc and the HP/Stratus Continuum 400. Other vendors are working on fault-tolerant cluster technology where other machines in a network can take over the tasks of a failed machine. An example is the Microsoft MSCS technology.

Validation of Fault Tolerance

One of the most difficult tasks in the design of a fault-tolerant machine is to verify that it will meet its reliability requirements. This requires creating a number of models. The first model is of the error/fault environment that is expected. Other models specify the structure and behavior of the design. It is then necessary to determine how well the fault-tolerance mechanisms work by analytic studies and fault simulations. The results, in the form of error rates, fault rates, latencies, and coverages, are used in reliability prediction models.

A number of probabilistic models have been developed using Markov and semi-Markov stochastic processes to predict the reliability of fault-tolerant machines as a function of time. These models have been implemented in several computer-aided design tools. Some of the better known tools are:

HARP—Hybrid Automated Reliability Predictor (Duke University)

SAVE—System Availability Estimator (IBM)

SHARPE—Symbolic Hierarchical Automated Reliability and Performance Evaluator (Duke)

UltraSAN—(University of Illinois)

DEPEND—(University of Illinois)

SURF-2—Laboratoire d'Analyse et d'Architecture des Systèmes (LAAS)

Recently there has been a great deal of research in experimental testing by fault insertion to aid in assessing the reliability of dependable systems. Among the fault injection tools that have been developed to evaluate fault tolerant systems are FTAPE (University of Illinois), Ballista (CMU), and MEFISTO (LAAS).

Conclusion

Fault tolerance is achieved by applying a set of analysis and design techniques to create systems with dramatically improved dependability. As new technologies are developed and new applications arise, new fault tolerance approaches are also needed. In the early days of fault-tolerant computing, it was possible to craft specific hardware and software solutions from the ground up, but now chips contain complex, highly integrated functions, and hardware and software must be crafted to meet a variety of standards to be economically viable. Thus a great deal of current research focuses on implementing fault tolerance using COTS (Commercial-Off-The-Shelf) technology.

Recent developments include the adaptation of existing fault-tolerance techniques to RAID disks, where information is striped across several disks to improve bandwidth and a redundant disk is used to hold encoded information so that data can be reconstructed if a disk fails. Another area is the use of application-based fault tolerance techniques to detect errors in high performance parallel processors. Fault tolerance techniques are expected to become increasingly important in deep submicron VLSI devices to combat increasing noise problems and improve yield by tolerating defects that are likely to occur on very large complex chips.

Fault-tolerant computing already plays a major role in process control, transportation, electronic commerce, space, communications, and many other areas that impact our lives. Many of its next advances will occur when applied to new state-of-the-art systems such as massively parallel scalable computing, promising new unconventional architectures such as processor-in-memory or reconfigurable computing, mobile computing (*q.v.*), and the other exciting new advances that lie around the corner.

Bibliography

1987. Avižienis, A., Kopetz, H., and Laprie, J.-C. (eds.) *Dependable Computing and Fault-Tolerant Systems Vol. 1: The Evolution of Fault-Tolerant Computing.* Vienna: Springer-Verlag. (Though somewhat dated, the best historical reference available.)

1990. *Computer* (Special Issue on Fault-Tolerant Computing), **23**, 7 (July).

1991. Lala, J., Harper, R. E., and Alger, L. S. "A Design Approach for Ultrareliable Real-time Systems," *IEEE Computer,* **24**, 5 (May), 12–22.

1991. Webber, S., and Beirne, J. "The Stratus Architecture," *Proc. 21st International Symposium on Fault-Tolerant Computing FTCS 21,* Montreal, June.

1993. Briere, D., and Traverse, P. "AIRBUS A320/A330/A340 Electrical Flight Controls: A Family of Fault-Tolerant Systems," *Proc. 23rd International Symposium on Fault-Tolerant Computing, FTCS 23,* Toulouse, France.

1994. Lala, J. H., and Harper, R. E. "Architectural Principles for Safety critical Real-time Applications," *Proc. IEEE,* **82**, 1, 25–40.

1995. Siewiorek, D. P. (ed.) *Fault-Tolerant Computing Highlights from 25 Years*. Special Volume of the 25th International Symposium on fault-tolerant computing FTCS-25, Pasadena, CA. (Papers selected as especially significant in the first 25 years of fault-tolerant computing.)

1996. Tsai, T. K., and Iyer, R. K. "An Approach Towards Benchmarking of Fault-Tolerant Commercial Systems," *Proc. 26th Symposium on Fault-Tolerant Computing FTCS 26*, Sendai, Japan.

1998. Kropp, N. P., Koopman, P. J., & Siewiorek, D. P. "Automated Robustness Testing of Off-The-Shelf Software Components," *Proc. 28th International Symposium on Fault-Tolerant Computing, FTCS 28*, Munich.

1998. Spainhower, L., and Gregg, T. A. "G4: A Fault-Tolerant CMOS Mainframe," *Proc. 28th International Symposium on Fault-Tolerant Computing, FTCS 28*, Munich.

1998. Kozyrakis, C. E., and Patterson, D. "A New Direction for Computer Architecture Research," *Computer, 31, 11*.

David A. Rennels

FFT

See FAST FOURIER TRANSFORM.

FIBER OPTICS

For articles on related subjects *see* BANDWIDTH; DATA COMMUNICATIONS; MULTIPLEXING; and NETWORKS, COMPUTER.

Optical fibers are thin, flexible strands of clear glass or plastic that can serve as a transmission medium capable of carrying up to several gigabits of information per second over short or long distances. They perform the same basic functions as copper wires or coaxial cables in carrying voice, data, or video information, but they transmit light instead of electrical signals. An optical fiber transmission system, shown in Fig. 1, is similar to a conventional transmission system, except that the transmitter uses a light-emitting or laser diode to convert electrical information signals to light signals while the receiver uses a photodiode to convert the light back into electrical signals. Optical repeaters are needed to regenerate the light signals only for links that exceed their distance limitations.

Optical fibers offer so many distinct advantages that they are rapidly replacing older transmission media in applications ranging from telephony to computers and automated factories. These advantages include:

1. *Large bandwidth*—Modern optical fibers can have bandwidths thousands of times greater than the best coaxial cables. Practical bandwidths, however, are much smaller than theoretically possible because of limitations of current multiplexers and optical transmitters–receivers.

2. *Low loss*—The attenuation or loss of an optical fiber is essentially independent of the transmission rate, whereas other media exhibit increasing attenuation with increasing transmission rates. The implication is that signal repeaters need not be placed so close together, reducing the cost of fiber optics systems.

3. *Electromagnetic immunity*—Because they are conductors of light and not of electricity, optical fibers are not affected by stray electromagnetic fields. Consequently, fiber optics systems exhibit low noise, high data and low error rate characteristics.

4. *Small size and light weight*—Size and weight are important factors when considering overcrowded conduits running under city streets. For the same bandwidth, fibers are hundreds of times smaller and lighter than copper conductors.

5. *Safety and electrical insulation*—Because optical fibers are insulators, they provide electrical isolation between the source and the destination. Therefore, optical fibers present no electrical spark hazards and can be used where electrical codes and common sense prohibit the use of electrical conductors.

The major disadvantages of fibers are that they are more difficult to work with than the more conventional twisted pairs or coaxial cables. They are much smaller and more delicate, making splicing and coupling more difficult. Furthermore, they are more brittle than metallic conductors; thus they must be mechanically protected and cannot be sharply bent. These disadvantages, however, are minor compared with the benefits they provide, making fibers the transmission medium of choice, especially for interbuilding and wide area networking.

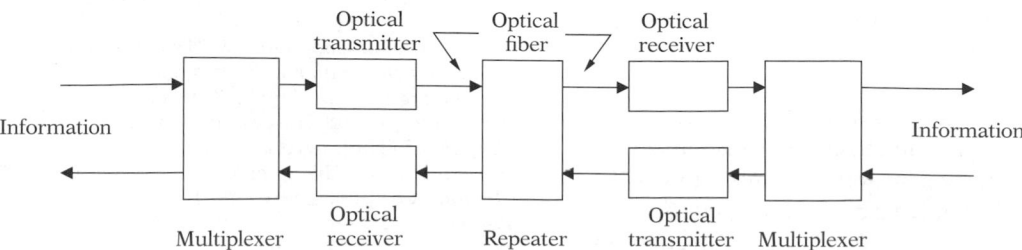

Figure 1. Typical optical fiber communication system.

Types of Fibers

Optical fibers are made of plastic, glass, or silica. Plastic fibers are the least efficient, but tend to be cheaper and more rugged. Glass or silica fibers are much smaller, and their lower attenuation makes them more suited for very high capacity channels.

The basic optical fiber consists of two concentric layers—the inner core and the outer cladding, which has a refractive index smaller than that of the core. The characteristics of light propagation depend primarily on the fiber size, its construction, the refractive index profile, and the nature of the light source.

The two main types of refractive index profiles are *step* and *graded*. In a step index fiber, the core has a uniform refractive index n_1 with a distinct change to a lower index, n_2, for the cladding. Multimode step index fibers usually have a core diameter of 0.05–1.0 mm. With a light source such that the light injected always strikes the core-to-cladding interface at an angle greater than the critical angle, the light is reflected back into the core. Since the angles of incidence and reflection are equal, the light continues to propagate down the core of the fiber in a zig-zag fashion by total internal reflection, as shown in Fig. 2a. In effect, the light is trapped in the core and the cladding not only provides protection to the core, but may be thought of as the "insulation" that prevents the light from escaping. Since some rays follow longer paths than others, their original relationship is not preserved. The result is that a narrow pulse of light has a tendency to spread as it travels down the fiber. Such spreading is known as *modal dispersion*; fibers with high modal dispersions tend to be used over short to medium distances.

When the core diameter is made small enough (between 0.002 and 0.01 mm), the fiber propagates light efficiently only at the lowest order mode along its axis, as shown in Fig. 2b. Since the zig-zag pattern associated with multimode step index fibers is eliminated, modal dispersion is very low and such fibers are, therefore, very efficient for high-speed long-distance transmission. Their small size, however, makes them relatively difficult to work with.

Modal dispersion can also be reduced by using graded index fibers, as shown in Fig. 2c. The core in such fibers consists of a series of concentric rings, each with a lower refractive index as we move from the core to the cladding boundary. Since light travels faster in a medium of lower refractive index, light further from the fiber axis travels faster. The result is that light is refracted successively by the different layers of the core and appears to follow a nearly sinusoidal path with all modes arriving at any point at nearly the same time. Such fibers have a modal dispersion that lies between multimode and single-mode step index fibers.

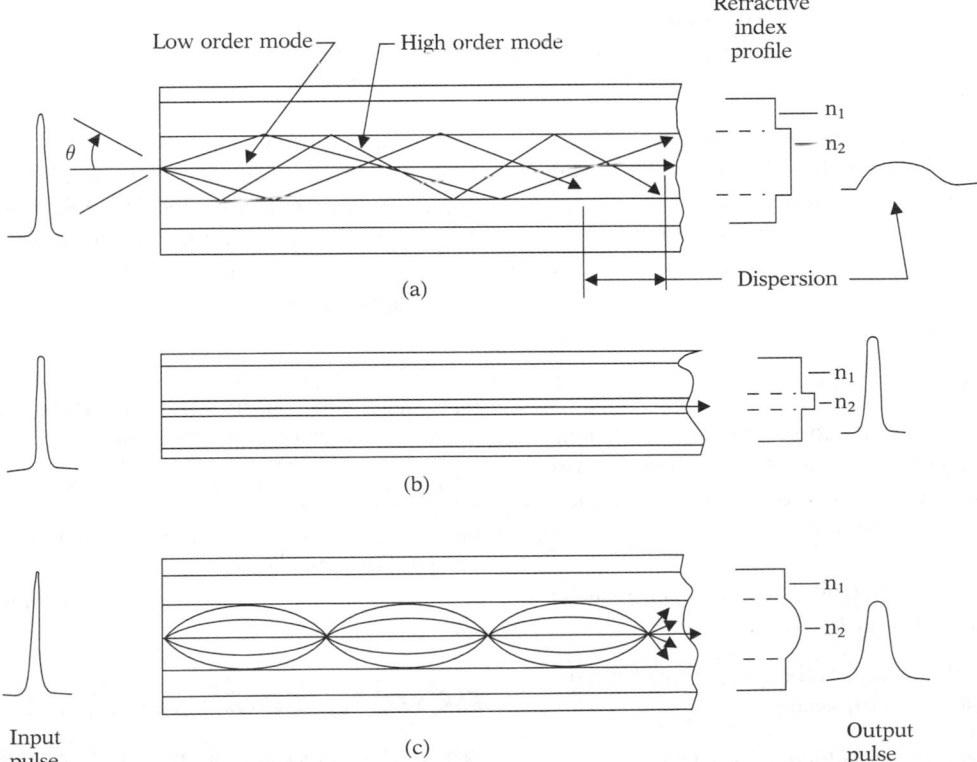

Figure 2. Characteristics of common optical fibers—(a) multimode step index; (b) single-mode step index; (c) multimode graded index.

As in the case of electrical conductors, optical fibers are usually cabled by enclosing many fibers in a protective sheath made of some material, such as polyvinyl chloride or polyurethane. The cable is strengthened by adding steel wire or Kevlar aramid yarn to give the cable assembly greater tensile strength. Cables are also available containing both optical fibers and electrical conductors, with the latter used to provide power for remote equipment.

Signal Degradation in Fibers

Signal degradation in optical fiber systems is caused by one or more of the following:

1. *Attenuation* or *transmission loss* (dimming of light intensity), which is caused by absorption and scattering. Absorption is the equivalent of electrical resistance and is usually caused by fiber impurities that absorb light energy. Scattering usually results from imperfections in fibers.

2. *Dispersion*, which is a measure of the widening of light pulses as they travel along the fiber and is usually expressed in nanoseconds per kilometer. Dispersion limits the information-carrying capacity of fibers, since input pulses must be separated enough in time that dispersion does not cause adjacent pulses to overlap at the destination, preventing the receiver from distinguishing them. Modal dispersion arises from the different lengths of paths traveled by the different modes. Material dispersion is due to different velocities of different wavelengths of the light source.

3. *Other causes*—Fibers must be connected or spliced to provide a low-loss coupling through the junction. Precise alignment results in low loss, but the small size of fiber cores, together with dimensional variations in core diameter and alignment, make this a difficult task.

Light Sources and Detectors

In fiber optics communication systems, the light source must efficiently convert electrical energy (current and voltage) into optical energy in the form of light. A good source must be:

1. Small and bright to permit the maximum transfer of light into the core of the fiber.

2. Fast to respond to rapidly changing signals encountered in high-bandwidth systems.

3. Monochromatic (i.e. produce light within a narrow band of wavelengths) to limit dispersion.

4. Reliable, with a lifetime in the hundreds of thousands of hours of operation.

The most commonly used light sources are gallium arsenide light-emitting diodes (LEDs) and injection laser diodes (ILDs). Both devices come in sizes compatible with the cores of fibers and emit light wavelengths in the range of 800–900 nm, where fibers have relatively low loss and dispersion. LEDs are not monochromatic, which limits their upper bit-rate capacity to about 1,000 Mbps. ILDs produce light that is almost monochromatic and can transfer almost 100 times more light energy into the core than LEDs, allowing fibers to be driven at multi-Gbps rates.

Optical detectors convert optical energy into electrical energy. Devices most commonly used for this purpose include silicon photodiodes because of their sensitivity to light in the 750–950 nm wavelength region.

Applications of Optical Fibers

As the world moves towards an *integrated services digital network* (ISDN—*q.v.*) in which voice, video, and data can be seamlessly transmitted over public and private networks, the need for more and higher bandwidth communication channels will continue to grow. Optical fibers offer capacities well beyond those of copper cables or microwave radio at lower cost and will play a major role in the implementation of the new "information highways" that will continue to affect us all.

Fibers are already widely used to carry voice and television signals across countries and continents and connect computers and workstations in local area networks (*q.v.*), and are replacing cables to interconnect computers and their peripherals. Their advantages and the fact that they represent a relatively new technology with much potential for improvement makes them the transmission medium of choice for many future applications.

Bibliography

1987. Sobolewski, J. S. "Data Transmission Media," *Encyclopedia of Physical Science and Technology*, **4**, 136–164. San Diego: Academic Press.
1998. Palais, J. C. *Fiber Optic Communications*. Upper Saddle River, NJ: Prentice Hall.
1999. Hecht, J. *City of Light: The Story of Fiber Optics*. Oxford: Oxford University Press.

John S. Sobolewski

FICTION, COMPUTERS IN

For articles on related subjects *see* AUTOMATION; LITERATURE OF COMPUTING; and ROBOTICS.

Fictional computers comprise a broad range of imagined and feigned devices in literature, exhibits, and film. Overlapping with fictional automata and robots, they play a significant role in the cultural matrix of actual computers.

Prehistory

To formulate a coherent history of computers in fiction, the best place to begin may be Jonathan Swift's *Gulliver's Travels*, published in 1726. Swift presents an inventor who has constructed a gigantic machine designed to allow "the most ignorant Person" to "write Books in Philosophy, Poetry, Politicks, Law, Mathematicks and Theology." This "Engine" contains myriad "Bits" crammed with all the words of a language, "all linked together by slender Wires" that can be turned by cranks, thus generating all possible linguistic combinations. Squads of scribes produce hard copy by recording any sequence of words that seems to make sense.

Although Swift describes this device in minute detail and even includes a diagram of its design, he is of course actually satirizing the more far-fetched pretensions of the science and technology of his period. Exemplifying what we might call computer fetishism, the kooky inventor and his society value the random text produced by this marvelous machine more than human thoughts.

The 18th-century fascination with watches and clocks combined with the dizzying technological advances of the Industrial Revolution to engender a host of ingenious mechanical automata, often designed to create the illusion of independent life or thought. The most famous of these was the automaton chess player constructed by Wolfgang von Kempelen in 1770, which toured Europe and the USA through the 1830s, beating many skilled chess players, including Napoleon. In 1820, British inventor Robert Willis demonstrated that a human chess player was concealed inside the machine; his widely reprinted pamphlet argued that a machine "cannot be made to vary its operations so as to meet the ever-varying circumstances of a game of chess. This is the province of the intellect alone." But audiences awed by the growing power of actual automated machinery during industrialization remained fascinated by shows displaying this evident triumph of machine thought. In 1836, Edgar Allan Poe published his own plagiarized version of Willis's proof, thus convincing many then and still today of the brilliant powers of his own unaided intellect. Ironically, part of Poe's argument reiterated the widespread belief in the infallibility of machines: "The Automaton does not invariably win the game. Were the machine a pure machine, this would not

be the case—it would always win." Ambrose Bierce's 1909 story "Moxon's Master" more accurately anticipated the chess-playing capabilities of modern computers, though fortunately none so far is as bad a loser as Bierce's chess-playing computer, which murders its inventor for defeating it.

The most influential fictional automaton of the early 19th century was Olympia, who dances perfectly, always focuses her gaze adoringly on her lover, and exclaims "Oh, Oh!" in response to his every utterance in E. T. A. Hoffman's "The Sandman" (1816), later immortalized in Offenbach's "The Tales of Hoffman." There is a direct line from Olympia through the metal woman built by the evil scientist in Fritz Lang's film *Metropolis* (1926) to the perfectly sexy and obedient women constructed by the computer scientists to replace their suburban housewives in Ira Levin's novel (1972) and film (1975) *The Stepford Wives*.

In the lineage of automaton women is one that may claim to be the first fictional computer with stored programs. This is the title character of M. L. Campbell's "The Automatic Maid-of-All-Work" (1893), whose built-in programs do require that the operator switch wires to activate each of its domestic tasks.

A small female automaton, as well as the punched card (*q.v.*) controlled textile loom, also influenced Charles Babbage's invention of the Difference Engine (*q.v.*). In their brilliant 1990 novel *The Difference Engine*, William Gibson and Bruce Sterling explore the alternative history that might have come if Babbage's invention had taken hold, with gigantic computing machines transforming global politics, economics, and culture in the 19th century—and a colossal AI emerging in the 1990s.

The tendency to conceive of thinking machines as humanoid in appearance was dominant until the advent of those first huge and blatantly non-humanoid actual digital computers of the 1940s. For example, even though American author Edward Page Mitchell was aware of the dimensions of the Difference Engine, his 1879 story "The Ablest Man in the World" envisions a computer explicitly superior to Babbage's being inserted into the head of a man (transforming him from an idiot into a genius who runs the Russian empire).

Other fiction did project thinking machines more closely resembling the increasingly automated mechanisms of evolving industrialism. For example, George Parsons Lathrop in his 1879 story "In the Deep of Time" imagines vast automated factories of the 22nd century run by a single person at a keyboard. Jules Verne prophesied in his 1863 manuscript *Paris in the Twentieth Century* (published in 1996) giant "calculating machines" resembling "huge pianos" operated by a "keyboard" and hooked to "facsimile" machines; banks use the most advanced models of these computers to coordinate the activities of this hypercapitalist future.

Fiction about the evolution of automation tended to be pessimistic. Fears of machines evolving until they replace people appeared as early as "The Book of the Machines" in Samuel Butler's 1872 novel *Erewhon* and soon became commonplace. Early 20th century examples include: Michael Williams's "The Mind Machine" (1919), in which living computers take over the cities but eventually disintegrate; Edmond Hamilton's "The Metal Giants" (1926) featuring an atom-powered metal brain that constructs a rampaging army of 300-foot-tall robots; S. Fowler Wright's "Automata" (1929), in which machines take over all human activities and eventually eliminate our species; and "The Brain" (1930), a play by Lionel Britton about an enormous mechanical brain that ends up as the only form of intelligence left on a doomed Earth 50 million years hence.

The first masterpiece in this genre is E. M. Forster's dystopian novella "The Machine Stops" (1909), about a future Earth where all decisions are made by the global central machine that caters to every physical human need (except sex) through its automated appendages. Living in hexagonal cells within the underground mechanical environment, people rarely come into contact with each other because they communicate as individuals and chat groups (*see* ONLINE CONVERSATION) through the machine's audio and visual internet. The machine even administers automated health care. When the machine breaks down, civilization ends, but a few survivors are left to begin again in the natural world on the planet's surface.

By the 1930s, fiction about human overdependence on computers or the replacement of humans by intelligent machines was quite commonplace. Influential science fiction editor John W. Campbell wrote several stories on this theme, including "The Last Evolution" (1932), "Twilight" (1934), and "The Machine" (1935). A classic story in this vein is Jack Williamson's "With Folded Hands" (1947).

Computers as Robots

Although the word "robot" was coined by Karel Čapek in *R.U.R.* (*Rossum's Universal Robots*), the robots in this 1920 play are organic androids, not computerized mechanical people. Popular culture, however, soon appropriated the term robot to identify those hordes of walking, talking, thinking machines that would became a staple of science fiction in print, film, and exhibits—such as Voder, the talking mechanical man at the 1939 New York World's Fair.

The standard fictional computer thus became the brain of a robot, usually conceptualized as a mechanical man—or woman—made of metal. The archetype of this figure was Tik-Tok, the copper man of *Ozma of Oz* (1907) and *Tik-Tok of Oz* (1914), L. Frank Baum's sequels to *The Wonderful Wizard of Oz*. Fitted with "Smith and Tinker's Improved Combination Steel Brains" and wearing a printed card labeling him as a "Patent Double Action, Extra-Responsive, Thought-Creating, Perfect Talking Mechanical Man," Tik-Tok is the forerunner of all those conflicted humanoid thinking machines extending right through the 20th century. When asked whether he is alive, Tik-Tok responds: "No, I am only a machine. But I can think and speak and act."

The typical science fiction robots leapfrogged directly to artificial intelligence, but these clanking AI robots often thought and behaved pretty much like humans. For example, in Harl Vincent's "Rex" (1934) the title character uses his "marvelous mechanical brain" to create a robot dictatorship, while in John Wyndham's "The Lost Machine" (1932) even the robot visitor made by Martians leaves a long suicide note that could have been written by an alienated teenager.

By far the most influential shaper of this fiction was Isaac Asimov, who conceived of all-purpose mechanical robots with "positronic brains" governed by his Three Laws of Robotics, first articulated in his 1942 story "Runabout." According to these "Laws," all robots' brains were preprogrammed to guarantee that they would never harm humans, would obey orders, and would protect themselves, in that order.

The first memorable movie robots appeared in the 1950s, and the two highlights were both products of extraterrestrial civilizations: the all-powerful Gort in *The Day the Earth Stood Still* (1951) and Robby the Robot in *Forbidden Planet* (1956). Although Robby is the ancestor of all those lovable robots through R2D2 and C-3PO of *Star Wars*, *Forbidden Planet* made a much more serious contribution to fiction about computers by envisioning automated technology so advanced that it could produce anything a civilization wished, even monsters out of the unconscious.

Dawn of the Computer Age

The computers created during the Second World War and its aftermath of course induced an avalanche of fictional computers. Because the supercomputers (*q.v.*) of the 1940s and 1950s were gigantic, their fictional descendants were commonly imagined to be colossal machines, sometimes concentrating the computational functions of a whole society in a single centralized mechanical intelligence.

So during these decades, the cultural imagination projected two somewhat contradictory images of computers either as throngs of individual robots capable of emulating human intelligence with a skull-size mechanical brain or as an immense isolated conglomeration of panels, buttons, switches, relays, and vacuum tubes.

One early fiction, however, did accurately anticipate how computers would look and function in the society of the 1990s: Murray Leinster's 1946 short story "A Logic Named Joe." Each home has at least one "logic," a personal computer complete with a screen and keyboard, networked to centralized supercomputers containing all knowledge and recorded telecasts. People access information, solve problems, view entertainment programs, communicate with each other, run their charge accounts, and so on from their personal computer through the network. There are even built-in censors that prevent children from seeing inappropriate material (thus anticipating the V-chip). In this comic tale, "Joe" is a "logic" that somehow becomes autonomous and enterprising, but he "ain't like one of these ambitious robots you read about that make up their minds the human race is inefficient and has got to be wiped out an' replaced by thinkin' machines."

Fiction that projected just such a catastrophe flourished in the 1960s. A good example is D. F. Jones's 1966 novel *Colossus*, whose vision of a computer gaining mastery reached a wide audience when it was made into the 1970 film *Colossus—The Forbin Project*. But the masterpiece of this genre is Harlan Ellison's 1967 short story "I Have No Mouth, and I Must Scream," in which the American, Russian, and Chinese supercomputers waging thermonuclear war merge into a single conscious entity that destroys the entire human race except for five people it saves to torture forever inside the subterranean caverns of its endless miles of circuitry.

More imminent social effects of computers are projected in the bleak, automated near-future dystopia of *Player Piano* (1952), Kurt Vonnegut Jr's first novel. Meaningful work is available only to a small group of technocrats, while other people can join either the huge standing army needed to control the world or the "Reeks and Wrecks," a mob of dissolute idlers pretending to do useless jobs. Real political power resides in the central computer, EPICAC XIV (a play on the names of the early ENIAC (*q.v.*) and UNIVAC (*q.v.*) digital computers).

Two of the most influential visions of computers in the 1960s came in masterpieces of film director Stanley Kubrick. In *Dr. Strangelove; Or How I Learned to Stop Worrying and Love the Bomb* (1964), civilization ends when the automated Soviet doomsday weapon is activated by a US atomic attack that cannot be recalled because of a B-52's damaged computer. The most memorable character in *2001: A Space Odyssey* (1968) is the spaceship's computer HAL, driven psychotic by conflicts between his logical essence and a programmed lie.

Perhaps the most sympathetic role played by a fictional computer in this period appears in Robert A. Heinlein's 1966 novel *The Moon Is a Harsh Mistress*. Mike, the central computer of the lunar colony, helps lead a libertarian lunar replay of the 1776 American Revolution against an authoritarian Earth while raising existential questions about his (or sometimes her) own identity.

Meanwhile, in Poland, Stanislaw Lem was creating in fiction and essays a profound exploration of the significance of computers. In the framing narrative of *Memoirs Found in a Bathtub* (1961), historian computers attempt to comprehend the human civilization that has destroyed itself. *The Invincible* (1964) contemplates the evolution of a nonorganic form of devastating intelligence. A number of Lem's cybernetic fables are collected in *Cyberiad* (1965). His 1969 essay "Robots in Science Fiction" assails the facile treatment of thinking machines in most science fiction, especially Anglo-American. In *Fiasco* (1986), misplaced faith in the rationality of a supercomputer helps lead a space mission from Earth to destroy the only extraterrestrial consciousness humans have encountered.

Strikingly foreshadowing concerns of later decades, the 1964 Soviet novel *World Soul* by Mikhail Emtsev and Eremei Parnov dramatizes a supercomputer that uploads all human identities and downloads them in a global nightmare of scrambled individuality.

What Next?

As computers became commonplace features of everyday life in the last third of the 20th century, their cultural representations spread from science fiction into other kinds of literature and film. Indeed, fiction about normal existence, at least in industrial and postindustrial societies, could exclude computers no more than automobiles, telephones, airplanes, and TV. This has been especially true for movies, which became the widest purveyors of images of computers.

When functioning as more than background in non-science-fiction movies, computers are often presented as a menacing power of the all-seeing bureaucratic state, as in *Enemy of the State* (1998). The main character in *The Net* (1995), a lonely computer hacker whose main friends are Internet pals, has her actual identity deleted from all records by the computers of government conspirators.

Computer networks, hacking, and of course computer games had all become familiar topics by the early 1980s. After it was revealed that mechanical malfunctions and human errors at NORAD's underground supercomputer had on numerous actual occasions almost precipitated global thermonuclear war, the 1983 movie *Wargames* has a teenage boy inadvertently come close to causing the apocalypse by playing what he thinks is just a game with NORAD's computer, which has been programmed for "Global Thermonuclear War."

During the 1980s, computers became a central icon in the science fiction known as *cyberpunk*, especially in the work of William Gibson. Gibson's *Burning Chrome* (1986), an influential collection of his stories from 1977 on, included several in which characters "jack" into the Web or even have themselves metamorphosed completely into beings who exist solely as cyber phenomena. In his Neuromancer trilogy—*Neuromancer* (1984), *Count Zero* (1986), and *Mona Lisa Overdrive* (1988)—cyberspace (*q.v.*) becomes the central locale. The dizzying contradictions of Gibson's computer–human interfaces come out in characteristic form when the narrator of his "The Winter Market," who edits dreams as mass-market commodities, decides not to kill himself when he learns that his greatest discovery has "merged with the net":

> Because she was dead, and I'd let her go. Because, now, she was immortal, and I'd helped her get that way. And because I knew she'd phone me, in the morning.

Such conceptions spread quickly, though without the vision or sophistication of cyberpunk, into popular culture. For example, in *Tron* (1982), one of the first commercial movies to depend primarily on computer animation (*q.v.*), a videogame designer is somehow sucked inside a computer, where he becomes a character in a life-and-death computer game. In the *Max Headroom* movie (1985) and TV series (1987–1988), an investigative reporter continues his career after being uploaded to become a computerized character.

Conceptions of computers in science fiction during the last 15 years of the 20th century reached far beyond what might have been imaginable even in the 1940s. Illustrative are the bold extrapolations in the speculative fiction of Greg Bear, such as *Eon* (1985), *Blood Music* (1985), and *Queen of Angels* (1990). In *Blood Music*, for example, "Medically Applicable Biochips" inadvertently convert DNA molecules into living computers that transmute the human species into the progenitor of "an intelligent plague" designed to reshape some of the fundamental principles of the universe.

Bibliography

Introductory collections of stories about computers:
1954. Conklin, G. (ed.) *Science-Fiction Thinking Machines*. New York: Vanguard Press.
1977. Mowshowitz, A. *Inside Information: Computers in Fiction*. Reading, MA: Addison-Wesley.
1984. Asimov, I., Warrick, P. S., and Greenberg, M. (eds.) *Machines That Think*. New York: Holt, Rinehart, and Winston.

Helpful analyses together with useful bibliographies:
1982. Dunn, T. P., and Erlich, R. D. (eds.) *The Mechanical God: Machines in Science Fiction*. Westport, CT: Greenwood Press.
1982. Warrick, P. S. *The Cybernetic Imagination in Science Fiction*. Cambridge, MA: MIT Press.
1983. Dunn, T.P., and Erlich, R. D. *Clockwork Worlds: Mechanized Environments in SF*. Westport, CT: Greenwood Press.
1985. Porush, D. *The Soft Machine: Cybernetic Fiction*. New York: Methuen.

H. Bruce Franklin

FILE

For articles on related subjects *see* ACCESS METHODS; BLOCK AND BLOCKING FACTOR; DATABASE MANAGEMENT SYSTEM; DIRECTORY; FILE SERVER; OPEN AND CLOSE A FILE; and RECORD.

The term *file* antedates the advent of computers and was one of the first to be incorporated into data processing terminology. In general, a *file* is a collection of data representing a set of entities with certain aspects in common and which are organized for some specific purpose. An *entity* is any data object, such as *employee* or *part*, and is represented in a file by a *record occurrence*. A card deck containing information on automobile parts and a cabinet drawer filled with manila folders containing data sheets on employees are examples of (non-computer) files.

Definitions

In computing, the word *file* can be defined in various ways and the definition depends on the level at which the file is being viewed. From an abstract viewpoint, a file can be considered to be a data object having certain attributes and a set of operations for creating and manipulating it. A file has also been defined as a data structure (*q.v.*) stored in external memory. Perhaps the most common definition is that a file is an organized collection of data records, possibly of different types, stored on some external storage device, such as magnetic tape or disk.

Storage Devices

The variety of external storage devices on which files can be stored has been increasing in recent years. Storage technologies like recordable (CD-R) or rewritable

(CD-RW) optical storage (*q.v.*) and flash-programmable read-only memory (*q.v.*) are being used to replace the magnetic disk in certain situations. The former serve for backup and archival storage; the latter are used with digital cameras and audio recording devices. While these new memories are appealing, magnetic disk remains the most popular device for storing large files on line. Magnetic tape, because of its high access time, its portability and compactness characteristics, and its relatively low cost, has been relegated to serving as a storage medium for archival files and for backup copies of files.

File Structure

A file has structure that determines how its records are organized. Structure can be subdivided into logical structure and physical structure. The *logical structure* of a file is essentially the application program's (i.e. the user's) view of the file (*see* Fig. 1). A file declaration that appears in a high-level language such as Cobol or Pascal is basically a logical structure specification and usually involves defining the attribute(s) of the record type(s) and possibly specifying a relationship (e.g. an ordering relationship) on the record occurrences. *Physical structure* is associated with how a file is actually organized on the storage medium on which it resides. This normally involves pointers (*q.v.*), indexes, etc., and how the records are laid out on the external storage device (*see* Fig. 1). The application program should have to be aware of only the logical structure of the file, whereas the access methods must know about the physical structure. *Access methods* are embodied in programs that satisfy user requests against a file; they provide the interface between a user program and a file.

Files can be structured and accessed in various ways. The earliest and most common type of file organization was sequential because computer files were first stored on inherently sequential storage media such as magnetic tape. To access a record in a sequential file, the preceding records must be passed over. The appearance of random access storage devices such as magnetic disk and drum provided the capability not only for sequential accessing but also for random (or direct) accessing of records. With *direct access*, any record in a file can be retrieved without looking first at the records preceding it. Techniques for implementing direct access usually involve some method for translating a *key* (or a composite of several keys) that identify the record sought into the address (absolute or relative) of the corresponding record on the device on which it is stored. This translation is normally done via an index (or indexes) or a key-to-address transformation function (sometimes called a *hashing* function) that computes the address of the record from the key (or keys) (*see* SEARCHING). Among the various access methods that have been developed are the sequential, indexed sequential, and direct access methods.

Files and Databases

The popularity of database management systems and the rather loose use of the term *database* has led to

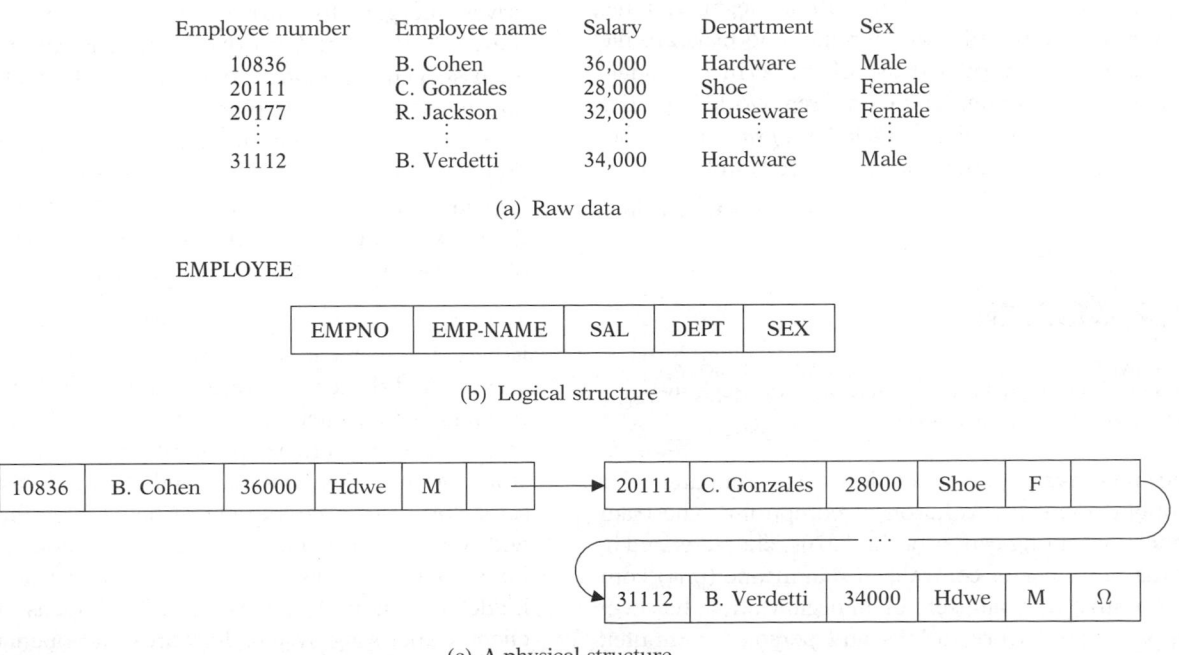

Employee number	Employee name	Salary	Department	Sex
10836	B. Cohen	36,000	Hardware	Male
20111	C. Gonzales	28,000	Shoe	Female
20177	R. Jackson	32,000	Houseware	Female
⋮	⋮	⋮	⋮	⋮
31112	B. Verdetti	34,000	Hardware	Male

(a) Raw data

EMPLOYEE

EMPNO	EMP-NAME	SAL	DEPT	SEX

(b) Logical structure

(c) A physical structure

Figure 1. Raw data to logical file structure to physical file structure.

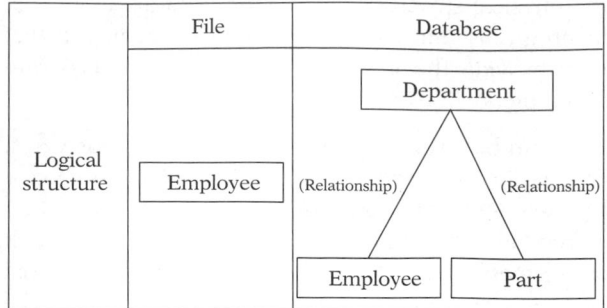

Figure 2. Logical structure.

some confusion between a file and a database. One basic difference is their usage pattern. The use of a file is usually limited to one user or a few users, and there is only one logical view of the file, which is shared by the (usually small number of) application programs that access it. On the other hand, a database brings together a variety of data and integrates it in such a way that it is accessible by many users, with each user possibly having a different logical view of the database. In trying to make a clear distinction between a file and a database, some define a file as a collection of occurrences of records of one type and a database as a collection of occurrences of records of several types with specific relationships among the record types. Fig. 2 illustrates this distinction.

Kinds of Files

The word *file* is used in many ways in data processing. Examples are input file, output file, master file, scratch file, temporary file, job file, and program file. Although the unmodified use of the term *file* usually means a file holding data on "real-world" entities, some files are specifically called *program files* when they contain programs stored in source or object form.

Billy G. Claybrook

FILE SERVER

For articles on related subjects *see* CACHE MEMORY; CLIENT–SERVER COMPUTING; DISTRIBUTED SYSTEMS; LOCAL AREA NETWORK; and WORKSTATION.

The increasing power of low-cost computers has brought about a revolution in computing. The traditional computing center of the 1970s, characterized by a small number of centralized mainframe (*q.v.*) computers shared by all users in an organization, has been supplanted by workstations and personal computers located in departmental user rooms and private offices. With the increased number of machines came the need

to move data and files from one machine to another. One approach to solving the file transfer problem is to connect the machines to a network and provide primitives that allow users to copy files from one machine to another. This approach works best when the number of files that need to be exchanged is small. A second approach is to place shared data on a *file server* and have individual machines access data files located on the remote file server rather than on a local disk.

The file server approach is an example of *client–server* interaction. Clients executing on the local machine forward all file requests (e.g. open, close, read, write, and seek) to the remote file server. The server accepts a client's request, performs its associated operation, and returns a response to the client. Indeed, if client software is structured *transparently*, the client need not even be aware that files being accessed physically reside on machines located elsewhere on the network (*see* TRANSPARENCY).

The file server approach has several benefits. First, multiple machines can access shared files concurrently. Files are no longer stored on individual machines; they are stored on the file server where they can be accessed by all client machines. Thus, a user can run the same programs on the same data files regardless of which client machine is being used. This has the advantage that users can use any of a set of machines, rather than just the machine on which their files reside. Second, the cost of supporting and maintaining a small number of large file servers is less than the corresponding cost of maintaining separate file systems on each machine. Indeed, client machines need not even have disk drives. Larger disk drives have a lower cost per megabyte than smaller drives, and it is easier to perform such maintenance functions as file backups on one machine than on many. As disks have become cheaper, diskless clients are less common in 1999 than they were in the 1980s, but it is still less expensive to implement fault-tolerant systems (*q.v.*) that use redundant or swappable components (*see* REDUNDANT ARRAY OF INEXPENSIVE DISKS) on fewer machines.

The use of file servers on a network raises many design issues. A server can either be a *disk server* or a *file server*. A disk server presents a raw disk interface through which client machines read and write disk sectors. Disk servers are primarily useful as a backing store for swapping (*q.v.*) or paging. In contrast, a file server provides access to files. Clients open files, read and write file contents, etc. All details about how the file system is represented on the physical device are hidden within the server. When a client opens a file, the client's operating system forwards the open request across the network to the file server and waits for the server's response.

Because files are accessed across a network, the performance of remote operations is generally lower than when accessing a local disk. To improve performance, network file systems use *caching* techniques (*see* CACHE MEMORY). The client, server, or both maintain a cache of recently used file pages. The local cache may be in memory or on a local disk. Some implementations of the Network File System (NFS) provide for a local disk cache, and it is a central feature of AFS (formerly the Andrew File System) and the Distributed File System (DFS). Before the client forwards a request to the remote server, it checks to see if the request can be satisfied using information in the local cache. If the information resides in the cache, the file pages are retrieved directly from the cache, and the request need not be sent to the server at all, reducing latencies (access times—*q.v.*). Likewise, the server consults its local cache before issuing input–output commands to the disk device. Because file reference strings display similar locality to page reference strings in virtual memory systems (*q.v.*), caches can improve average access times by an order of magnitude or more. However, a cache is not helpful in all situations. If there is likely to be little reuse, the cost of searching the cache may outweigh the benefit of the few cache hits. Also, if a file server disk is faster than the client disks and a fast network is used, access to files on the server can actually be *faster* than access to a local disk.

Although caching often improves access time performance, it also raises *cache coherency* (*q.v.*) issues. For example, suppose that two machines have been accessing a file at the same time, and the contents of the file resides in both client caches. If a user on one machine deletes the file, a user on the other machine may find that the file still exists because the client finds it in its local cache. To keep caches consistent, changing or deleting a file on one machine must update the caches on all other machines in the distributed network. Special protocols (*q.v.*) are used to solve such problems. For example, a server may specify that a file can be cached by only one client at a time, or disable caching completely for those files that are being shared.

File servers must also address the problem of *authentication* (*q.v.*). That is, if a client requests file pages, how can the server be sure that the client is really who he or she claims to be? In a networked environment, an unauthorized client may masquerade as another in an attempt to access sensitive data stored on the file server. Authentication is handled by using cryptographic techniques (*see* CRYPTOGRAPHY, COMPUTERS IN). Before authorizing access, the file server forwards the request to an *authentication server*. The messages exchanged by the file and authentication servers are encrypted using keys that only the two servers share, ensuring that the authentication server can be trusted.

The authentication server verifies access rights of the client (perhaps by exchanging messages directly with the client, using another set of private keys), and then returns its response to the file server.

Another aspect of file server design is whether the server should be *stateful* or *stateless*. Upon machine reboots, a stateless server retains no knowledge about the files client machines are using. When a client makes a request, each request contains complete information needed to service it. For example, when reading a file sequentially, each request contains the starting and ending byte offsets of the desired information rather than requesting "the next 1,024 bytes." In contrast, stateful servers keep track of which clients are using files and in what ways. Such information is important for maintaining cache consistency and for providing such services as exclusive file locks. The main drawback of stateful servers is that rebooting the server interrupts all client applications that were accessing files at the time the server went down. The server must reject all requests related to file accesses initiated before the server rebooted.

Bibliography

1995. Comer, D. E. *Internetworking with TCP/IP: Principles, Protocols, and Architecture*, 3rd Ed. Upper Saddle River, NJ: Prentice Hall.
1996. Tanenbaum, A. *Computer Networks*, 3rd Ed. Upper Saddle River, NJ: Prentice Hall.
1998. Silberschatz, A., and Galvin, P. *Operating System Concepts*, 5th Ed. Reading, MA: Addison-Wesley.

Thomas Narten, revised by James D. Teresco

FINITE ELEMENT METHOD

For articles on related subjects *see* COMPUTER-AIDED ENGINEERING; NUMERICAL ANALYSIS; PARTIAL DIFFERENTIAL EQUATIONS; SCIENTIFIC APPLICATIONS; and SPLINE.

The *finite element method* applies to a broad range of engineering problems and attracts theoreticians and practitioners from many disciplines. It provides the formalism for reducing the continuum to a finite-dimensional space for numerical resolution of complicated field problems with digital computers. The space of interest is partitioned into a finite number of nonoverlapping elements (Fig. 1). A basis is defined within each element, and the field within the element is determined from a stationarity condition, or equivalently a weak form, with the basis-function combining coefficients as free parameters. The element parameters are constrained to yield appropriate interelement continuity consistent with the underlying stationarity principle. Engineering problems are thus reduced to systems of algebraic equations that are solved by a variety of methods.

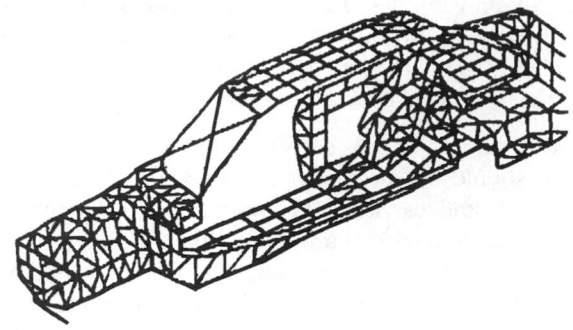

Figure 1. Idealization of a car body using finite elements.

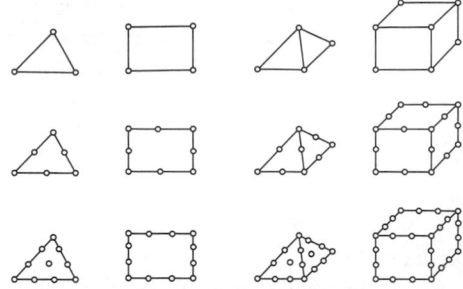

Figure 2. Some common two-dimensional and three-dimensional finite elements.

The finite element method encompasses representation of the physical situation by some differential, integral, or integro-differential equation, partitioning of the space of interest into elements, developing a stationarity principle, or equivalently a weak form expression, and an associated approximation space in terms of element basis functions, generating a system of algebraic equations satisfied by the basis-function expansion coefficients, solving these equations, and displaying the phases of the computation for evaluation.

The finite element method is an outgrowth of analysis and computation in the 1940s. Some early finite difference formulations based on integration over elements are equivalent to finite element methods. More recently, the finite volume construction has been proven to be contained within the weak form, with the space of test functions not identical to the trial function space of the approximation. The term "finite element" and its modern development were introduced in the field of structural mechanics. Two- and three-dimensional structural problems were solved with a finite element formalism based on a variational principle relating to energy minimization over a continuous approximation space. The remarkable success of this formalism together with the explosion in computer capabilities led to rapid expansion of the method to include more general principles with relaxed continuity constraints. The method was applied to virtually all scientific investigation involving field functions. Analysis was generalized from linear statics to nonlinear and time-dependent problems and to interaction of different fields.

Hundreds of millions of dollars are spent worldwide each year on finite element analysis. There has been an exponential growth of publications on finite element topics. Hundreds of user-oriented program packages arc available. An outstanding reference work is the *Finite Element Handbook*, edited by H. Kardestuncer (1987), which describes the roles of various scientific disciplines in finite analysis and implementation. The unbiquity of finite elements in scientific research is

evidenced by the broad spectrum of scientists contributing to its development and application.

Mathematicians concerned with formulation and error estimation apply techniques of functional analysis, classical approximation theory, and the theory of partial differential equations. This may either guide practitioners in the use of existing techniques or suggest new procedures. The functional analysis draws heavily on theory related to Sobolev Spaces. *A priori* error estimates guide selection of approximation spaces and stationarity principles. *A posteriori* estimates facilitate adaptive refinement by either subdividing or increasing the degrees of freedom within identified elements. Mapping theorems and algebraic geometry are used in analyzing the relationships among approximation spaces and element geometry. An underlying theme in mainstream finite element analysis is relating the error in the approximate solution to the chosen stationarity principle and the degree of the polynomial space spanned by the basis vectors within the elements. Thus, a prime consideration in generating basis functions is achievement of polynomial approximation within elements while maintaining appropriate interelement continuity. The "isoparametric" element (introduced by engineers and subsequently analyzed by mathematicians) is the most prevalent device for accomplishing this with elements other than the simple triangles, rectangles, tetrahedra, and rectangular bricks shown in Fig. 2.

Engineers examine element geometry and appropriate stationarity principles for specific application and often introduce new formalisms that are then analyzed with greater rigor by mathematicians. Among the areas investigated with finite elements are: solid mechanics, fluid mechanics, biomechanics, heat transfer, geomechanics, aeromechanics, coupled systems (fluid-structure-thermal interaction), chemical reactions, neutron flux, plasmas, acoustics, materials processes, and electric and magnetic fields. The early finite element development was used almost exclusively by engineers in analysis of structures. As the applications have expanded, engineers responsible for simulation of

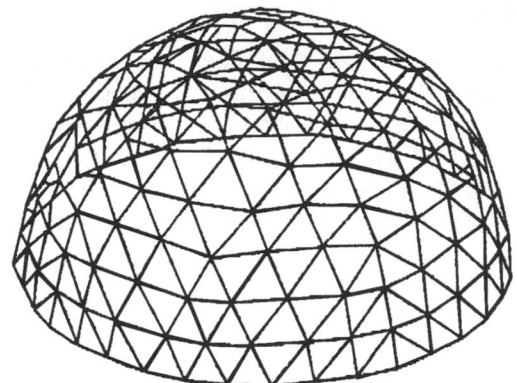

Figure 3. Computer-generated mesh pattern.

physical phenomena have developed and analyzed new methods and have guided much of the growth in technology. As techniques have matured, the role of theoreticians has become more pronounced. This interplay of theoretical and practical development has enhanced adoption of finite elements in almost every area of scientific computation.

Computer scientists and numerical analysts address data structuring, automatic mesh generation (see Fig. 3), and efficient software generation as a function of hardware and interactive computer graphics (*q.v.*). All have addressed methodology for efficient numerical solution of the finite element equations that are characteristically large banded systems. Although the earlier finite element programs and many of the existing software packages use direct solution techniques, the increased size of problems solved has led to more extensive application of iterative methods. A popular family of solution techniques entails iteration on the difference between an approximate sparse factorization and the actual sparse system. This balances direct and iterative techniques as a function of complexity and computer characteristics. The current areas of greatest concern are parallel computation on emerging architectures, and instability and efficiency of the method for expressly nonlinear problems in the broad range of fluid mechanics.

With the emergence of home pages on the World Wide Web (*q.v.*), numerous sites are available for browsing both historical applications and current developments. In the emerging multidisciplinary problem area, a particularly complete description of historical and current information is available at the URL `http://www.tfd.chalmers.se/CFD_Online`.

Bibliography

Handbooks

1983. Noor, A. K., and Pilkey, W. D. *State-of-the-Art Surveys on Finite Element Technology.* ASME (with a list of textbooks and monographs on finite element technology).

1987. Kardestuncer, H., and Norrie, D. H. *Finite Element Handbook.* New York: McGraw-Hill.

1988. Johnson, R. W. *CRC Handbook of Fluid Dynamics.* Boca Raton, FL: CRC Press.

Selected Texts on Fundamentals and Foundations

1981. Becker, E. B., Carey, G. F., and Oden, J. T. *Finite Elements: An Introduction.* Upper Saddle River, NJ: Prentice Hall.

1981. Cook, R. D. *Concepts and Applications of Finite Element Analysis*, 2nd Ed. New York: John Wiley.

1982. Huebner, K. H., and Thornton, E. A. *The Finite Element Method for Engineers*, 2nd Ed. New York: Wiley Interscience.

1983. Irons, B., and Shrive, N. *Finite Element Primer.* New York: John Wiley.

1989. Zienkiewicz, O. C. *The Finite Element Method: Basic Concepts and Linear Applications*, 4th Ed. New York: McGraw-Hill.

1991. Baker, A. J., and Pepper, D. W. *Finite Elements 1–2–3.* New York: McGraw-Hill.

1997. Logan, D. L. *A First Course in the Finite Element Method Using Algor.* Boston: PWS Publishing.

1999. Moaveni, S. *Finite Element Analysis.* Upper Saddle River, NJ: Prentice Hall.

Eugene L. Wachspress

FINITE-STATE MACHINE

See SEQUENTIAL MACHINE.

FIREWALL

See GATEWAY; and INTERNET.

FIRMWARE

For articles on related subjects *see* EMBEDDED SYSTEM; EMULATION; MICROPROGRAMMING; READ-ONLY MEMORY; and SOFTWARE.

Early in the history of digital computation, the useful distinction was made between *hardware*, the tangible componentry of a computing system, and *software*, the collection of instructions that directed what was to be computed. While it was true that software had to be recorded on some tangible medium, such as punched cards or paper or magnetic tape (early), or, later, hard or floppy disks (*see* DISKETTE), the software itself was considered to be pure information and hence intangible. Supporting the "softness" of this interpretation was the fact that, when recorded on a magnetic medium, software could be modified with ease.

The question soon arose as to what to call programs recorded indelibly on a medium such as read-only memory (ROM) or embodied in hard-wired computer circuitry. The result, no longer "soft" enough to be modified, was still "software"; or had it become though still an executable program, "hardware"? The term coined to solve this nomenclature dilemma was *firmware*.

Early personal computers such as the Apple and the Radio Shack TRS-80 maintained firmware copies of an interpreter for the language Basic in ROM so that the language was on tap immediately upon booting (*see* BOOTSTRAP), but the term firmware originated as far back as the mid-1960s. In order to help the large base of IBM 1400 series (*q.v.*) users convert to the new but incompatible IBM 360 series (*q.v.*) with minimum disruption, IBM provided optional firmware that could be added to the 360 that allowed it to execute 1400 series programs through *emulation*, hardware-assisted simulation. Given adequate memory, any general purpose digital computer can execute programs written for any other through use of a *simulator*, a program that interprets each target machine instruction and executes whatever sequence of host machine instructions is needed to do the same thing, bit for bit. Interpretation is naturally slow, but implementation of key parts of the simulator as firmware provides a significant increase in speed of execution.

Bibliography

1992. Marge, D. *Microprogrammed Systems: An Introduction to Firmware Theory*. London: Chapman and Hall.

Edwin D. Reilly

FLOATING-POINT ARITHMETIC

See ARITHMETIC, COMPUTER.

FLOPPY DISK

See DISKETTE.

FLOWCHART

For articles on related subjects *see* DOCUMENTATION; STRUCTURED PROGRAMMING; and SYSTEMS ANALYST.

Definition

A *flowchart* is a graphic means of documenting a sequence of operations. Flowcharts serve as a pictorial means of communicating from one person to another the time-ordering of events or actions. As a pictorial format, flowcharts have been the subject of both an International and an American National Standard (ANSI, 1970; Chapin, 1979). Flowcharts go by many other names, including block diagram, flow diagram, system chart, run diagram, process chart, logic chart, and iteration diagram.

Format

The two main varieties of flowchart are the *flow diagram* and the *system chart*. A flow diagram gives a detailed view of what is shown as a single process in a system chart. Flow diagrams and system charts use different pictorial conventions, but also share certain conventions. The basic outlines shown in Fig. 1 are

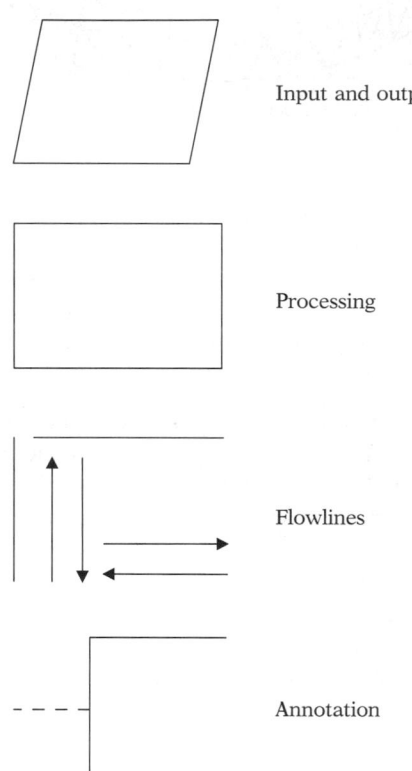

Figure 1. Basic outlines. (From N. Chapin, *Flowcharts*. New York: Petrocelli Books, 1971.)

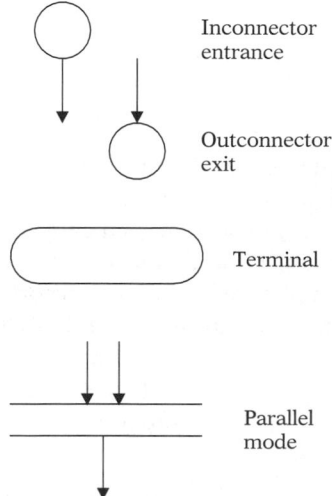

Figure 2. Additional outlines. (From N. Chapin, *Flowcharts*. New York: Petrocelli Books, 1971.)

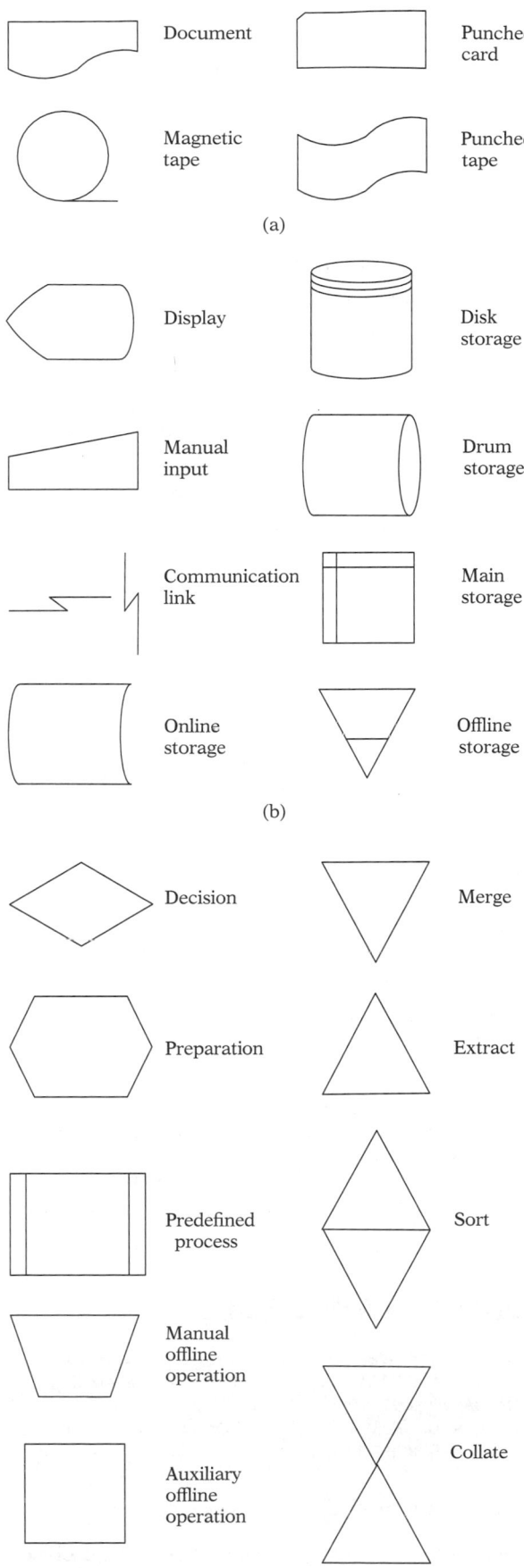

(a)

(b)

(c)

common to both. Also common is the reading convention—top to bottom, left to right—and the practice of labeling the outlines internally to identify data and processes (Chapin, 1971). The additional outlines shown in Fig. 2 are all used in flow diagrams. The parallel mode outline also finds some use in system charts.

System charts are pictorially richer. While analysts can prepare system charts using only the basic outlines of Fig. 1, they often selectively substitute some of the specialized outlines for media, equipment, and processes, as shown in Fig. 3. Except for the decision and predefined processes, the specialized outlines are not used in flow diagrams.

SYSTEM CHART

Analysts most commonly prepare system charts to show graphically the interactions in execution among the programs of a system. The inputs and outputs of each program are shown, either in a generalized form using the basic outlines, or in a particularized form using the specialized outlines. Analysts may prepare system charts at a logical level (using the basic outlines) or at a physical level (using the specialized outlines).

In preparing a system chart, analysts usually regard each program's execution as a single process with the respective inputs above and connected to the process, and with the respective outputs below and connected to the process. This gives a sandwich-like arrangement to the outlines in a system chart: a layer of input data (bread), followed by a process (the filling), followed by a layer of output data (bread). Often, the output data of one process becomes the input data for a subsequent process, giving a multilayer sandwich effect (a compound system chart). A simple system chart shows only a single process, which could be for any level of software from system to subroutine.

Analysts may also prepare system charts for other situations that are characterized by an alternation of data and action. Some general examples are the situations where a dataflow diagram could be used, or where an integrated data engineering facility diagram (IDEF) could be used, or where a state transition diagram could be used.

PROGRAM FLOWCHART

Analysts most commonly prepare program flowcharts or flow diagrams to describe in step-by-step detail the time-sequence of functions, actions, or events. Such sequences usually comprise a process that takes in

Figure 3. Specialized outlines. (a) Media. (b) Equipment. (c) Processes. (From N. Chapin, *Flowcharts*. New York: Petrocelli Books, 1971.)

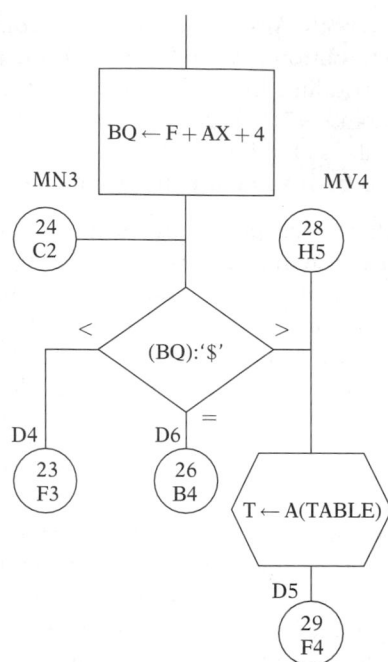

Figure 4. Entry and exit flowlines in a flow diagram. (From N. Chapin, *Flowcharts*. New York: Petrocelli Books, 1971.)

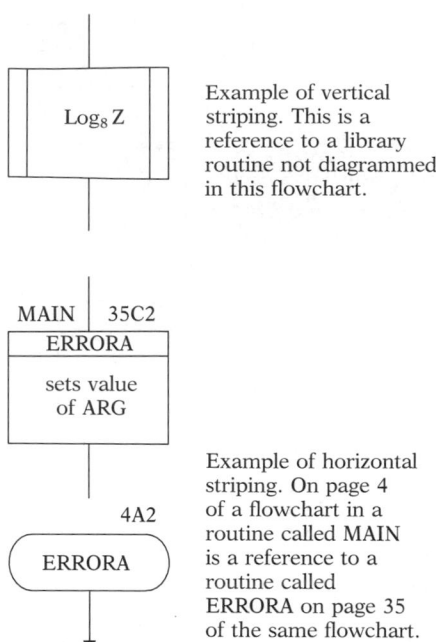

Figure 5. Conventions for striping and references. (From N. Chapin, *Flowcharts*. New York: Petrocelli Books, 1971.)

input data and produces output data. A flow diagram (not to be confused with a dataflow (*q.v.*) diagram) begins and ends with a labeled terminal outline (Fig. 2) to mark each entrance and exit. Then successive outlines connected by flow arrows depict the acceptance of data as input, the processing steps taken, and the disposition of data as output. No sandwich convention applies, and decisions are shown explicitly, as illustrated in Fig. 4. Also as shown there, analysts often use connectors to reduce clutter (since flow diagrams often get large) and to provide cross-referencing and location annotation. Thus, in Fig. 4, the inconnector marked 28H5 refers to the outconnector H5 on page 28, and the H5 itself refers to a grid pattern on the page. Analysts often show software component or entry names, such as the MV4 or D6 in Fig. 4. Two forms of reference to more detail are also provided by striping conventions, as shown in Fig. 5.

Alternatives

Historically, analysts drew flowcharts by hand. Currently, some popular Computer-Aided Software Engineering (CASE—*q.v.*) software tools facilitate drawing and revising flowcharts. Flowcharts have been declining in favor as alternatives have appeared, such as the dataflow diagram and IDEF noted earlier. The term *structured flowchart* usually refers to either Chapin charts (Chapin, 1974) or to Nassi–Shneiderman iteration diagrams (Nassi 1973; *see* STRUCTURED PRO-

GRAMMING). Warnier–Orr diagrams provide a way of depicting both data and software structures hierarchically (Warnier, 1974), as do *tree charts* (*see* TREE).

Bibliography

1970. ANSI. *American National Standard Flowchart Symbols and Their Usage in Information Processing*, X3.5-1970. New York: American National Standards Institute.
1971. Chapin, N. *Flowcharts*. New York: Petrocelli Books.
1973. Nassi, I., and Shneiderman, B. "Flowchart Techniques for Structured Programming," *SIGPLAN Notices*, **8**, *8*, 12–26.
1974. Chapin, N. "New Format for Flowcharts," *Software – Practice and Experience*, **4**, *4*, 341–357.
1974. Warnier, J. D. *Logical Construction of Programs*. New York: Van Nostrand Reinhold.
1979. Chapin, N. "Full Report of the Flowchart Committee on ANSI Standard X3.5-1970," *SIGPLAN Notices*, **14**, *3*, 16–27.
1995. Boillot, M. H., Gleason, G. M., and Horn, L. W. *Essentials of Flowcharting*. New York: WCB/McGraw-Hill.

Ned Chapin

FORMAL LANGUAGES

For articles on related subjects *see* AUTOMATA THEORY; BACKUS–NAUR FORM; CHOMSKY HIERARCHY; GRAMMARS; LANGUAGE PROCESSORS; MACHINE TRANSLATION; METALANGUAGE; REGULAR EXPRESSION; TURING MACHINE; and WELL-FORMED FORMULA.

Languages and Grammars

Formal languages are abstract mathematical objects used to model the syntax of programming languages

or (less successfully) of natural languages such as English. For example, consider a simple English sentence, such as

THE MAN ATE THE APPLE

Let us assume that individual English words are indecomposable objects. Then the study of English syntax attempts to answer the question: when is a string of words a grammatically correct English sentence? And when it is a sentence, how can it be parsed?

To model this situation, we let V be a finite set of symbols called a *vocabulary*. In the previous example, V contains the four indecomposable words (in this context, called *symbols* or *letters*): APPLE, ATE, MAN, THE. More generally, V might contain all English words and punctuation marks. Let V^* denote all finite-length strings of symbols from V. (It is mathematically convenient to include in V^* the *empty string* of length zero.) Then a *formal language L* is simply a set of strings from V^*. For example, if V^* is the set of all finite sequences of English words, then L could be the subset of V^* consisting of all grammatically correct sentences. Although V is always finite, in most cases of interest L will be infinite, and we will wish to have a finitely specified way of generating, or recognizing, or *parsing* the strings in L.

The sample sentence given earlier can be parsed by the treelike diagram in Fig. 1, where $\langle S \rangle$, $\langle NP \rangle$, $\langle VP \rangle$, $\langle A \rangle$, $\langle N \rangle$, and $\langle V \rangle$ are six variables ranging over all *sentences*, *noun phrases*, *verb phrases*, *articles*, *nouns*,

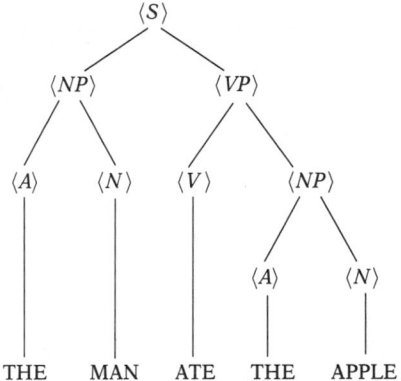

Figure 1. Tree for parsing sentence.

$$\langle S \rangle \rightarrow \langle NP \rangle \langle VP \rangle$$
$$\langle NP \rangle \rightarrow \langle A \rangle \langle N \rangle$$
$$\langle VP \rangle \rightarrow \langle V \rangle \langle NP \rangle$$
$$\langle A \rangle \rightarrow \text{THE}$$
$$\langle V \rangle \rightarrow \text{ATE}$$
$$\langle N \rangle \rightarrow \text{MAN}$$
$$\langle N \rangle \rightarrow \text{APPLE}$$

Figure 2. Rewriting rules.

and *verbs*, respectively. Using the *rewriting* rules in Fig. 2, it is possible to generate our sample sentence from the variable $\langle S \rangle$. The generation proceeds as follows:

$$\langle S \rangle \Rightarrow \langle NP \rangle \langle VP \rangle \Rightarrow \langle A \rangle \langle N \rangle \langle VP \rangle$$
$$\Rightarrow \langle A \rangle \langle N \rangle \langle V \rangle \langle NP \rangle \Rightarrow \langle A \rangle \langle N \rangle \langle V \rangle \langle A \rangle \langle N \rangle$$
$$\Rightarrow \text{THE } \langle N \rangle \langle V \rangle \langle A \rangle \langle N \rangle$$
$$\Rightarrow \text{THE MAN } \langle V \rangle \langle A \rangle \langle N \rangle$$
$$\Rightarrow \text{THE MAN ATE } \langle A \rangle \langle N \rangle$$
$$\Rightarrow \text{THE MAN ATE THE } \langle N \rangle$$
$$\Rightarrow \text{THE MAN ATE THE APPLE}$$

With these rules, we can also generate various improbable but grammatically correct sentences such as THE APPLE ATE THE MAN, and with more rules we could generate more sentences. Rewriting schemes of this sort were introduced by the linguist Noam Chomsky, who called them *context-free grammars*. Chomsky observed that these grammars are not good models for the syntax of natural languages, but it was soon discovered that they do closely model the syntax of programming languages, and for this reason they have been studied in great detail.

To see a simple example of context-free rewriting rules that give rise to an infinite language, suppose that the vocabulary consists of two abstract symbols a and b, and let S be a variable. Then, using the rules $S \rightarrow aSb$ and $S \rightarrow ab$, we can generate the infinite language

$$L = \{ a^n b^n \mid n \geq 1 \} = \{ ab, aabb, aaabbb, \ldots \}$$

Rewriting rules of this type are called "context free" because they permit any occurrence of a variable within a string to be rewritten without regard to the context in which that variable occurs. By contrast, a rewriting rule like $aXab \rightarrow aYZcab$ is not context-free. It is called *context-sensitive*, since it allows X to be rewritten as YZc only when X occurs in the context $s_1 a \_\_ abs_2$, where s_1 and s_2 are arbitrary strings.

To describe different kinds of grammars more precisely, let us define a *phrase-structure* grammar to be a quadruple $G = (V_N, V_T, P, S)$, where

1. V_N is a finite vocabulary of nonterminal symbols or variables.

2. V_T is a finite vocabulary of terminal symbols.

3. P is a finite set of rewriting rules (also called *productions*) of the form $\alpha \rightarrow \beta$, where α is a nonempty string of variables and β is an arbitrary string of variables and terminal symbols.

4. S is a particular variable called the *start* variable.

For all strings s_1 and s_2 we may write $s_1 \alpha s_2 \Rightarrow s_1 \beta s_2$ if $\alpha \to \beta$ is a production of the grammar G. Then the language generated by G is the set of all strings t of *terminal symbols* such that

$$S \Rightarrow s_1 \Rightarrow s_2 \Rightarrow \cdots \Rightarrow s_n \Rightarrow t$$

for some choice of intermediate strings $s_1, s_2, \ldots, s_n$. The intermediate strings may consist of both variables and terminal symbols.

Let α, α_1, and α_2 denote arbitrary strings of variables and terminal symbols, and let A and B denote variables. If the productions in G have the specialized form $\alpha_1 A \alpha_2 \to \alpha_1 \beta \alpha_2$, where β represents any nonempty string, then G is a *context-sensitive* grammar. (Frequently, a grammar is called context-sensitive if the productions merely have the form $\alpha \to \beta$, with β at least as long as α. These two definitions are in fact equivalent in the sense that the same collection of languages is generated.) If the productions in the grammar G have the form $A \to \alpha$, then G is context free. If the productions have the form $A \to w_1 B$ or $A \to w_2$, where w_1 and w_2 are strings of terminal symbols, then G is *right-linear*. A language is called a "phrase-structure" language, or a "context-sensitive," "context-free," or "right-linear" language, if it can be generated by a phrase-structure grammar, or a context-sensitive, context-free, or right-linear grammar, respectively.

The four types of grammars (phrase-structure, context-sensitive, context-free, and right-linear) are also known as type 0, type 1, type 2 and type 3 grammars, respectively. They form a grammatical hierarchy, called the *Chomsky hierarchy*. Among the four corresponding families of languages, the smallest family, the right-linear languages, is important because it consists precisely of those languages that can be recognized by finite-state automata. These languages arise in many different contexts, and they have the advantage of being very easy to parse.

The next family in the hierarchy, the family of context-free languages, is important because context-free languages are good approximations to the syntax of programming languages, even though this syntax is usually a little too complicated to be completely captured by context-free grammars. For example, the syntax of an assignment statement in a programming language can be described in a context-free grammar, as:

$\langle \text{assn-stmt} \rangle \to \langle \text{variable} \rangle := \langle \text{expression} \rangle$.

However, the rule that a variable must be declared before it is used in an assignment statement cannot be specified by a context-free grammar. Such a rule requires that a grammar generate an assignment state-ment only in the context of prior declarations of the variables that appear in it. This informal notion of context-dependence cannot be represented in context-free grammars.

Context-sensitive languages are powerful enough to encompass any complications in syntax that may have been missed by the context-free model, but they are so general that they are difficult to work with. As a result, they have been studied less than the other models, and various attempts have been made to increase the power of context-free grammars without resorting to the full strength of context-sensitive productions. These efforts have produced various kinds of grammars that are more powerful than context-free grammars, although they are unfortunately more complicated as well: programmed grammars, macro grammars, indexed grammars, two-level grammars, attribute grammars, and others.

The largest family of languages in the Chomsky hierarchy, the family of phrase-structure languages, is an important family because it represents the largest class with which one is likely to be concerned when modeling natural or artificial languages. This is so because the family of phrase-structure languages is in fact the same as the family of all recursively enumerable languages—i.e. of all languages L such that membership of a string w in L can be verified by some algorithm (or, more precisely, by some Turing machine).

Languages and Equations

We have noted that context-free languages are good approximations to the syntax of many programming languages. Consider the following very simple example of syntax specifications in *Backus–Naur form*, or *BNF* (the ::= is an alternative to →):

```
⟨digit⟩::= 0|1|2|3|4|5|6|7|8|9
⟨unsigned integer⟩::=⟨digit⟩
        |⟨unsigned integer⟩⟨digit⟩
```

This means that $\langle \text{digit} \rangle$ and $\langle \text{unsigned integer} \rangle$ are the smallest sets of strings satisfying the following conditions: $0, 1, \ldots, 9$ are digits (i.e. they are in the set $\langle \text{digit} \rangle$); any digit is an unsigned integer; and any unsigned integer followed by a digit is an unsigned integer. Rewriting these equations in a more algebraic form, we obtain:

$$D = \text{``0''} + \text{``1''} + \cdots + \text{``9''}$$
$$U = D + U \cdot D$$

Consider these as abstract equations. What is their meaning? The unknowns U and D are variables whose values are languages; $X + Y$ denotes the union of the languages X and Y; $X \cdot Y$ denotes the product of the languages X and Y, obtained by concatenating the strings in X with those in $Y : X \cdot Y = \{xy \mid x \in X, y \in Y\}$; and "0," "1," etc., are constants denoting the languages consisting of just the single symbols 0, 1, etc. In general, the equations corresponding to BNF syntax descriptions can be more complicated than in our example. A typical equation might have the form

$$A = abBAAaAb + BaC + ba.$$

(The letters a and b are terminal symbols; A, B, and C are variables; and we have omitted the dot in products.) The operations $+$ and $\cdot$ are roughly analogous to addition and multiplication of numbers; only $\cdot$ is not commutative. (If X and Y are languages, $Y \cdot X$ *is not generally the same as* $Y \cdot X$.) If the product of languages were commutative, we could write the term $abBAAaAb$ as $aabbA^3B$. This would be similar to a fourth-degree term in a polynomial expression, except that the variables range over languages rather than numbers and the coefficient $aabb$ is a string of symbols instead of a number. Since the product of languages is not commutative, we cannot rearrange terms in this way, but we can still regard these equations as polynomial equations in noncommuting variables. In general, the right-hand side of each equation will be a finite sum of terms, and each term will be a string of variables and terminal symbols. A set of such equations always has a unique smallest solution, so it always makes sense to speak of the "smallest sets of strings" U and D satisfying equations like those in our original example. The languages definable in this way by polynomial equations turn out to be precisely the context-free languages.

As a simple example, the language $\{a^n b^n \mid n \geq 1\}$ can be specified either as the language generated by the context-free productions $S \to aSb$ and $S \to ab$ or as the smallest solution of the equation $S = aSb + ab$. Incidentally, note that this equation is a first-degree or "linear" equation, since each summand contains at most one occurrence of a variable. Languages defined by such equations are called *linear* context-free languages. They can also be characterized as the languages generated by linear context-free grammars; i.e. by context-free grammars having productions of the form $A \to \alpha$, where the string α contains at most one occurrence of a variable. It should now be clear why right-linear grammars are so named.

In view of the preceding discussion, any programming language whose syntax can be specified in BNF is context-free. Generally, most but not all of the syntax of a programming language can be specified in BNF. So languages such as Pascal and C++ are not quite context-free, but they are close to being so, and context-free languages are useful approximations to their syntax.

Languages and Automata

The four families of languages in the Chomsky hierarchy can be obtained from automata as well as from grammars (*see* AUTOMATA THEORY). The phrase-structure languages are the languages accepted by linear-bounded automata or *lba*s; the context-free languages are the languages accepted by pushdown automata; and the right-linear languages are the languages accepted by finite-state automata. For this reason, right-linear languages are sometimes called *finite-state* languages. Usually, however, right-linear languages are known as regular languages or regular sets. This terminology comes from Kleene's theorem, which states that a language is a finite-state language if and only if it can be represented by a *regular* expression. A regular expression is an expression that can be built up from individual strings by using the three operations $+$, $\cdot$, and $*$. The operations $+$ and $\cdot$ are the operations of union and product introduced earlier. (The symbol $\cup$ is sometimes used instead of $+$, and the $\cdot$ may be omitted.) The operation $*$ is called the *Kleene closure* operation. If L is any set of strings, then L^* is defined to be the set of all strings that can be formed by concatenating sequences of strings from L: $L^* = \{s_1 s_2 \ldots s_n \mid n \geq 0, \text{ each } s_i \in L\}$. (By convention, the empty string is always in L^*.) For example, $(a + b)^* \cdot aaa \cdot (a + b)^*$ is a regular expression representing the set of all strings of as and bs containing at least three consecutive as.

Let us consider the relation between context-free languages and pushdown automata a little more closely. A pushdown automaton is a non-deterministic device having a memory consisting of a finite-state control and a pushdown stack (*q.v.*). It receives its input one symbol at a time on request. Every context-free language L is the set of input strings accepted by some pushdown automaton P. In fact, we can always find a pushdown automaton P for L that operates in real time; i.e. one that uses up one input letter on every move. This means that P recognizes strings in L very quickly—in fact, in an amount of time proportional to the length of the input string. The catch is that P is a non-deterministic device. It is credited with accepting an input string w if there is *any* sequence of choices of moves (i.e. any sequence of "guesses") it can make while processing w that will lead it to an accepting mode, even though there may be other choices that do not lead to an accepting mode. But if we want to simulate P in the real world, we would systematically have to test every sequence of choices that P could make.

Since P might have several choices available to it on each move, this simulation could take exponentially more time than P does. This might suggest that the task of parsing a context-free language can be prohibitively time-consuming, but in fact it is not. General-purpose, context-free parsing algorithms can be designed to require only time n^3, where n is the length of the input, by using *dynamic programming* (*see* ALGORITHMS, DESIGN AND CLASSIFICATION OF). One of the most popular such algorithms is *Earley's algorithm*. It takes time n^3 in the worst case, but for many context-free grammars it takes only a linear amount of time. The n^3 bound for an all-purpose, context-free parser can be improved slightly, but it is not yet known how much improvement is possible.

A non-deterministic pushdown automaton is a theoretical construct that is time-consuming to simulate in the real world. So, in searching for classes of context-free languages that are easy to parse, it is reasonable to consider *deterministic* context-free languages—those languages that can be recognized by a deterministic pushdown automaton. As one might expect, all deterministic context-free languages can be parsed rapidly; in fact, in a linear amount of time. But not all context-free languages are deterministic. For example, the set of all binary strings (strings of 0s and 1s) that are palindromes is context-free but not deterministic because a pushdown automaton for this language must of necessity operate something like this: by *guessing* when half the input has been read, store this portion of the string on the stack, and use the stack to verify that the second half of the input agrees symbol by symbol, in reverse order, with the first half.

So, non-deterministic pushdown acceptors are more powerful than deterministic ones. Are the corresponding statements true for the other kinds of automata used to characterize the families of languages in the Chomsky hierarchy? For finite-state automata and for Turing machines, the answer is no. It is easy to show that the non-deterministic versions of these devices are no more powerful than the deterministic versions. In other words, the ability to make guesses may enable these devices to do their jobs more quickly, but it will not let them do anything that they could not have done without guessing. But for linear-bounded automata, it is still not known whether the non-deterministic version (which corresponds to the context-sensitive languages) is more powerful than the deterministic version.

This question, called the *lba* problem, can be recast in the following form: can a Turing machine that performs a computation with the aid of guessing (i.e. of non-determinism), using just a linear amount of storage space, always be simulated by a comparably efficient Turing machine that does not need to guess? The analogous question for Turing machines that use a polynomially bounded amount of computation time rather than a linear amount of storage space is the very important $P = NP$ problem (*see* COMPUTATIONAL COMPLEXITY and NP-COMPLETE PROBLEMS). In both cases, the answer is thought to be no, but such questions are notoriously difficult and have so far resisted all efforts at solution.

Bibliography

1972. Aho, A. V., and Ullman, J. D. *The Theory of Parsing, Translation and Compiling.* Upper Saddle River, NJ: Prentice Hall.
1973. Salomaa, A. *Formal Languages.* New York: Academic Press.
1978. Harrison, M. A. *Introduction to Formal Language Theory.* Reading, MA: Addison-Wesley.
1979. Hopcroft, J. E., and Ullman, J. D. *Introduction to Automata Theory, Languages, and Computation.* Reading, MA: Addison-Wesley.
1988. Moll, R. N., Arbib, M. A., and Kfoury, A. J. *An Introduction to Formal Language Theory.* New York: Springer-Verlag.
1996. Linz, P. *Introduction to Formal Languages and Automata.* Sudbury, MA: Jones and Bartlett.

Jonathan Goldstine

FORMAL METHODS FOR COMPUTER SYSTEMS

For articles on related subjects *see* AUTOMATIC PROGRAMMING; HARDWARE VERIFICATION; MODEL CHECKING; PROGRAM SPECIFICATION; and PROGRAM VERIFICATION.

Formal methods used in developing and verifying software and hardware systems are mathematically based techniques for describing and reasoning about system properties. Such formal methods provide frameworks within which people specify, develop, and verify systems in a systematic, rather than *ad hoc*, manner. Formal methods include the more specific activities of program specification, program verification, and hardware verification.

A method is formal if it has a sound mathematical basis, typically given by a *formal specification language*. This basis provides the means of precisely defining notions like consistency and completeness and, more relevantly, specification, implementation, and correctness. It provides the means of proving that a specification is realizable, proving that a system has been implemented correctly and proving properties of a system without necessarily running it to determine its behavior.

A formal method also addresses a number of pragmatic considerations: who uses it, what it is used for, when it is used, and how it is used. Most commonly, system designers use formal methods to specify or verify a system's desired behavioral and structural properties. However, anyone involved in any stage of system development can make use of formal methods. They can be used in the initial statement of a customer's requirements, through system design, implementation, software testing (*q.v.*), debugging (*q.v.*), software maintenance (*q.v.*), program verification, and evaluation.

Formal methods are used to reveal ambiguity, incompleteness, and inconsistency in a system. When used early in the system development process, they can reveal design flaws that otherwise might be discovered only during costly testing and debugging phases. When used later (e.g. in verification), they can help determine the correctness of a system implementation and the equivalence of different implementations.

For a method to be formal, it need not address any pragmatic considerations, but a lack of such considerations would render it useless. Hence a formal method should possess a set of guidelines or a "style sheet" that tells the user the circumstances under which the method can and should be applied, as well as how it can be applied most effectively.

One tangible product of applying a formal method is a *formal specification*. A specification serves as a contract, a valuable piece of documentation, and a means of communication between a client, a specifier, and an implementer. Because of their mathematical basis, formal specifications are more precise and usually more concise than informal ones.

Since a formal method is a method and not just a computer program or language, it may or may not have software tools to support it. If the syntax of a formal method's specification language is made explicit, providing standard syntax analysis tools for formal specifications would be appropriate. If the language's semantics are sufficiently restricted, varying degrees of semantic analysis can be performed with machine aids as well. For example, under certain circumstances in hardware verification, the process of proving the correctness of an implementation against a specification can be completely automated. Thus, formal specifications have the additional advantage over informal ones of being amenable to machine analysis and manipulation.

Tremendous progress has been made in formal methods in the past few years. The most prominent successes have been in three areas: specification of large, complex software systems; the use of model checking for hardware and protocol verification; and the development of sophisticated theorem provers.

For software specification, the most common formal notations used today are Z, VDM, Larch, CSP, CCS,

Statecharts, RAISE, LOTOS, temporal logic, and their variants. Examples of nontrivial case studies can be found in a wide range of application domains: avionics, databases, household electricity meters, medical devices, nuclear reactors, oscilloscopes, railways, security, and telephony.

Model checking is a technique that relies on building a finite model of a system and checking that a desired property holds in that model. The most common model checkers used today are SMV, Caesar, the Concurrency Workbench, Spin, Murϕ, and Cospan/FormalCheck. Model checkers have been most successfully used to verify and debug hardware designs and cache coherence and communication protocols.

Theorem proving (*q.v.*) is a process of finding a proof of a property of a system where both the system and the property are expressed as formulas in some mathematical logic. Examples of sophisticated theorem provers and proof checkers include PVS, ACL2, Nqthm, STeP, LP, HOL, and Coq. Recent efforts in using these systems have focused at the hardware level, e.g. verifying processor designs, microcode, or instruction sets.

For a comprehensive survey of the state of the art, including descriptions of and citations to numerous case studies, *see* Clarke and Wing (1996). For more on the benefits of formal specification, *see* Meyer (1985) and Hinchey and Bowen (1995). For a gentle introduction to formal methods, including simple examples in common specification notations, *see* Wing (1990).

Bibliography

1985. Meyer, B. "On Formalism in Specification," *IEEE Software*, **2**, 6–26.
1990. Wing, J. "A Specifier's Introduction to Formal Methods," *IEEE Computer*, **23**, 9, 8–24.
1995. Hinchey, M. G., and Bowen, J. P. (eds.) *Applications of Formal Methods.* Upper Saddle River, NJ: Prentice Hall.
1996. Clarke, E. M., and Wing, J. M. "Formal Methods: State of the Art and Future Directions," *ACM Computing Surveys*, **28**, 4, 626–643.
1999. Bowen, J. "Formal Methods" (part of the Virtual Library). http://www.comlab.ox.ac.uk/archive/formal-methods.html.

Jeannette M. Wing

FORTH

For articles on related subjects *see* EXTENSIBLE LANGUAGE; POLISH NOTATION; PROGRAMMING LANGUAGES; REAL-TIME SYSTEMS; and STACK.

History

Forth is a programming language and environment invented by Charles H. Moore in 1970. It was designed to be both the development and run-time environments for real-time applications. Forth soon found wide acceptance in controlling radio telescopes, and Charles Moore founded the first Forth vendor, Forth, Inc. Today, most of its commercial use continues to be in the fields of real-time and hardware control applications, including control of orbiting satellites.

Forth's early acceptance was due to its small size, interactive access to everything in the environment, and the ease with which a single user could understand the entire system and leverage it into a succinct application-oriented environment. In fact, early implementations included the interpreter, the compiler (*q.v.*), a disk operating system, a multitasking (*q.v.*) executive, an editor, and an assembler (*q.v.*) all resident in less than 16 KB of memory. All of this and multiple interactive users were supported in 16-bit address spaces.

In 1978 the Forth Interest Group (FIG) was formed. Its members developed a model implementation of the language and, for a few dollars, distributed source code for common microprocessors. The FIG model demonstrated the accessibility of Forth by showing how Forth could be moved to new platforms with very little effort. The FIG model was widely embraced by hobbyists.

One consequence of this ease in implementing the language was an early and rapid proliferation of dialects. Subsequent standardization efforts culminated in differing standards established by influential users in 1979 and again in 1983. These standards were increasingly ignored because they were both silent on important issues (e.g. vocabulary structure and search order) and too restrictive for emerging technologies (e.g. standardizing 16-bit integers and addresses in a world increasingly populated with 32-bit architectures). This trend reversed in 1994 with the adoption of two influential but different standards: the American National Standard for Forth, ANSI X3.215 (adopted in 1997 as ISO standard 15145), and the Open Firmware Standard, IEEE Standard 1275. The latter has been adopted by a number of vendors, including Sun, Apple, and IBM, as the standard for bootstrap and device driver firmware (*q.v.*).

The Language

Forth is a language which is both interpreted and compiled, is extensible, and uses postfix syntax and implicit parameter passing through a data stack. A Forth development environment typically includes a large and varied set of predefined "words." Any word may be executed from the keyboard or combined with others in the definition of a new word. This means that Forth has no syntactic model and little grammar. The underlying Forth model is semantic. Each word has an action, and the meaning of a sequence of words is the sequence of actions implied by the ordering of the words.

Forth's semantic model means that it is relentlessly context-sensitive. Unlike conventional languages, a program written in Forth cannot be casually inspected for something as basic as comments. A new word with a name composed of any combination of printable characters may be introduced at any time to perform the action of skipping input. This same name may be defined later to perform a completely different action. Long-time users of Forth, however, avoid this kind of coding and focus on the power of working in an environment that allows programming some pieces of a solution in terms of machine language, others in terms of highly abstract object-oriented constructs, for example, and everything in between. Forth permits the construction of "little languages" while imposing no syntactic or abstraction-level constraints on them. This power requires very minimal resources. A recent case in point is Europay International's Open Terminal Architecture (OTA).

Programming

Programming is simply adding new words which are defined in terms of previously defined words. Most implementations provide an assembler "vocabulary" (a list of words) so that new primitives may be added. At the other end of the scale there are words which allow the creation of "defining" words. These are words which, when executed, define other words. New defining words and new primitives can be defined as easily as any other kind of word. Applications written in Forth tend to be factored into much smaller pieces than in other languages. The definition of a Forth word is typically just a few lines long.

The Interpreter

The Forth interpreter identifies a token as any sequence of printable characters separated by spaces or the end of a line. The interpreter simply gets the next token from the input stream, looks in its vocabularies for one whose name matches the token, executes the word if a match is found, attempts to interpret it as a numeric constant if a match is not found, or, failing all of these, complains. This process is repeated until the input stream is exhausted.

For example, one may enter

```
17 3 + .
```

and press the return key. When the interpreter sees 17 it pushes the integer value 17 to the stack (*q.v.*) then takes a similar action when it sees 3. When it sees +, it executes the Forth word named " + " which is defined to remove the top two values from the stack, add them, and push the result to the stack. When it sees . the interpreter executes the Forth word named "." (pronounced "dot") which removes the top integer from the stack and prints it out. The result of interpreting this line is to print "20".

The Compiler

Strictly speaking, there is no such thing as *the* Forth compiler. Compiling actions are performed by many Forth words, and new compiling words are commonly defined as part of an application, either in terms of existing words or, rarely, as new primitives.

Compiling is most commonly begun with a "colon definition" such as

```
: BUMP 3 + . ;
```

which defines a new word named BUMP. All the interpreter does, however, is fetch the word named : from the input and execute it. This word's action is to create a new word with the name which follows the colon (one of Forth's prefix anomalies) then compile all of the following words as part of the new word's definition up to the first semicolon.

BUMP can be used immediately by entering

```
17 BUMP
```

and pressing the return key, which results in "20" being printed.

Defining Words

The colon is one of many defining words. An integer variable (e.g., TEMP) is defined in Forth with

```
VARIABLE TEMP
```

which means that VARIABLE is also a defining word. VARIABLE causes TEMP to be added to the list of available words and sets TEMP's action to be the standard action of a variable, which is to push the address of its data field to the stack. The data field is that portion of memory which holds the current value of the variable.

A value is stored into the data field of a variable with

```
20 TEMP !
```

which sets the value of TEMP to 20. The value in a variable's data field is fetched to the stack with

```
TEMP @
```

and once the value is on the stack it can be removed and printed or used as a parameter by any other word.

The defining word VARIABLE could be defined this way:

```
: VARIABLE CREATE 0 , DOES> ;
```

and when this line is interpreted, the colon is executed which defines VARIABLE as a new word. When VARIABLE is subsequently executed, the word CREATE is executed which fetches the next name in the input stream and creates a new word with that name. Then zero is pushed to the stack. The comma removes the value on the top of the stack and compiles it into the data field of the word being created. The comma's action allocates memory for the variable and initializes it at the same time.

When DOES> executes, it terminates the definition of the new word (TEMP, in our example) and specifies that the words which follow it, up to the semicolon, are executed whenever TEMP (or any other word defined by VARIABLE) is executed. In this case there are no words between DOES> and the semicolon, so all that happens when TEMP is executed is the default behavior of pushing the address of TEMP's data field to the stack.

Forth has been mastered when one not only understands the difference between (1) what happens when the definition of VARIABLE is compiled, (2) what happens when VARIABLE is executed, and (3) what happens when a word defined with VARIABLE is executed, but also sees the power in being able to stipulate interactively and exercise all three of these actions. It is very unusual for a language to give its users the ability to specify completely what happens at these three times in the life of a program.

Availability

There are commercially supported implementations for most common platforms from many vendors. There are numerous public domain versions of varying quality and complexity. For more information, visit the Forth Interest Group Website: http://www.forth.org.

Bibliography

1987. Brodie, L. *Starting FORTH*, 2nd Ed. Upper Saddle River, NJ: Prentice Hall. The most accessible introduction.
1987. Pountain, R. *Object-Oriented Forth*. San Diego, CA: Academic Press. A readable discussion of one way to add object-oriented constructs to Forth.
1994. Brodie, L. *Thinking Forth*, 2nd Ed. Upper Saddle River, NJ: Prentice Hall. A sophisticated exploration of Forth and ways to use it effectively.
Forth Dimensions, published six times a year by the Forth Interest Group (http://www.forth.org).
Journal of Forth Applications and Research, published irregularly by the Institute for Applied Forth Research (http://www.jfar.org).

Charles Eaker

FORTRAN

For articles on related subjects *see* PROCEDURE-ORIENTED LANGUAGES; PROGRAMMING LANGUAGE STANDARDS; and PROGRAMMING LANGUAGES.

Fortran was the first *high-level language*. A program by J. H. Laning and N. Zierler that translated mathematical equations into machine language seems to have had the first operational compiler, but Fortran was the first widely used programming language.

The proposal which led to the development of Fortran was made in late 1953 by John Backus of IBM to his boss, Cuthbert Hurd. The team which Backus put together in 1954 to design the language that became Fortran included, among others, Sheldon Best, Harlan Herrick, Robert Nelson, Roy Nutt, Peter Sheridan and Irving Ziller. They published a preliminary report in 1954 which differed little from the Programmer's Reference Manual published in 1956. The first Fortran compiler (called then a *translator*) was distributed—not bug-free, of course—in April 1957 and within a year was widely used on IBM computers. This version of Fortran contained many of the features still familiar to Fortran users, among them DO, IF, and GOTO statements, arrays, and fixed and floating-point constants and variables.

Fortran was developed with the aim of decreasing programming and debugging costs. According to Backus (1981), the development team also believed that the generated code had to approach the efficiency of hand-coded assembly code in order for Fortran to be accepted by the scientific programming community. Thus great effort was expended on generating efficient object code, with the result that the first Fortran compiler had an efficiency not matched until optimizing compilers appeared a decade later. While the efficiency goals were indeed achieved, Backus noted that the development team was "hopelessly optimistic" in anticipating that Fortran would "virtually eliminate coding and debugging" (*q.v.*).

Not surprisingly for such a pioneering effort, various deficiencies of the original design became clear as Fortran became widely used. Fortran II, first distributed in the spring of 1958, corrected some of these. The two main additions were much improved diagnostics and a subroutine (i.e. subprogram—*q.v.*) facility. Fortran III was essentially stillborn. It added a few additional facilities and was used at some IBM installations, but was never distributed widely.

The next major change to Fortran was Fortran IV, whose first compilers became available in 1963. It added the now familiar Fortran features of COMMON storage, double-precision and logical data types and relational expressions as well as the DATA statement which provided a simple facility to initialize variables. Fortran IV became the standard dialect of Fortran for many years. In particular, it was the basis of the first Fortran standard, ANSI Standard X3.9, first promulgated in 1966. This later was the basis for ISO Standard 1539 in 1972.

Although various compilers implemented additional features, Fortran IV had a life of almost 15 years as the Fortran used by almost everyone in scientific or numerical computing. By the mid-1970s it was, however, showing its age. Although the investment in legacy Fortran programs was by this time immense, developments in high-level language programming, particularly the advent of *structured programming* (*q.v.*), meant that Fortran was no longer a modern language by most measures. Therefore, in 1967 technical work on (what became) Fortran 77 (F77) began and was completed in 1977; F77 became the official Fortran standard in April 1978. By 1981, because of user demand for F77 compilers, it seemed clear that F77 would become the major success it ultimately proved to be.

Long before F77's fate became clear, technical work on its successor began in earnest in 1978. F77 had, at the last minute, added an if-then-else control structure, and this limited venture into modern control structures prompted a five-year plan to produce a "modern" Fortran successor. Fairly quickly a case selection construct was designed, and the original Fortran DO-loop was augmented with several flavors of a modern iteration (do-enddo) structure. Numerous other modernizations were completed within the five-year period—long names, lower case, a new source form (blanks, which had heretofore been ignored, became significant), recursion (*q.v.*), etc.

However, two developments would cause more than another five-year delay in producing the official successor to F77, Fortran 90 (F90). First was a growing push to extend Fortran in other than "cosmetic" ways, to strengthen Fortran in its major application areas. The corresponding enhancements included: a sophisticated *array language* (Fortran modeling applications tend to be heavily array processing oriented), *type parameterization* and numerical inquiry functions, called the *environmental intrinsic functions* (for better numerical control—type parameterization facilitates the generation of generic libraries for the various real precisions, and the inquiry functions give the programmer access to fundamental properties of the real number approximation in use), *modules* and *explicit interfaces* (to make procedures more reliable—explicit procedure interfaces enforce Fortran's requirement for strong typing across procedure interfaces), a *dynamic type* (data structuring) facility, and more. The second development was growing opposition to such an extensive revision. In the end, all of these extensions were approved, but not until 1990, after a period of controversy and stalemate.

F90 was developed by the US Fortran standards committee, but during this period ISO became increasingly important and active in developing language standards; it was this new ISO muscle that ultimately resolved the controversy. As a consequence of this controversy, ISO established a five-year schedule for subsequent revisions of the Fortran standard. Thus soon after F90 became official, Fortran 95 (F95) and Fortran 2000 (F2000) were scheduled.

F95 succeeded F90 right on schedule, without controversy. It is a minor extension of F90, refining many of the features introduced in F90 and adding a few array features recommended by the High Performance Fortran Forum (for increased performance in massively parallel environments). F2000 is under development and will likely become official in the early 2000s. The major enhancements in the works are numerical exception handling, modest object-oriented (*q.v.*) support, and interoperability with C.

With all this evolution, Fortran has become a modern, easy-to-use, more reliable, general-purpose programming language. Its strength remains, however, high-performance numerical computation. Some of the features needed to maintain preeminence in this area (e.g. the numerical environmental intrinsics that give programmers access to the properties of the numerical approximations used in the implementation) were introduced in F90. Others have been introduced by vendors and users to facilitate efficient use of existing Fortran code on contemporary parallel architectures. These features, plus the huge amount of Fortran code in use, should keep Fortran the language of choice in the high-performance area for the foreseeable future. However, the controversy-related delay in adopting these features may have caused users to explore other tools, and thus may have compromised F90's long-term effectiveness. It is too early to tell, therefore, the role that F90 and its progeny will play in continuing the Fortran saga, of historical proportions, established by Fortran from its inception through F77.

Bibliography

1964. Backus, J. W., and Heising, W. P. "FORTRAN," *IEEE Transactions on Electronic Computers*, **EC-13**, 382–385.
1966. American Standards Association, *X3.9-1966*, American Standard FORTRAN.
1978. American National Standards Institute, *ANSI X3.9-1978*, ISO 1539-1980, programming language FORTRAN.
1981. Backus, J. W. "The History of Fortran I, II and III," in *History of Programming Languages* (ed. R. L. Wexelblat). New York: Academic Press.
1992. American National Standards Institute, *ANSI X3.198-1992*, ISO 1539-1991, Programming Language Fortran 90.
1996. Adams, J., and Brainerd, W. "A Little History and a Fortran 90 Summary," *Computer Standards and Interfaces* Special Issue: Fortran 90, **18**, *4*, 277–380.
1998. http://www.ionet.net/~jwagener/j3. The Fortran Standards Web Page.

Jerrold L. Wagener and Anthony Ralston

FRACTALS

For articles on related subjects *see* COMPUTER ART; COMPUTER GRAPHICS; IMAGE PROCESSING; PATTERN RECOGNITION; and SCIENTIFIC APPLICATIONS.

Introduction

Much scientific research of the past has analyzed human-made machines and the physical laws that govern their operation. The success of science relies on the predictability of the underlying experiments. Euclidean geometry—based on lines, circles, etc.—is the tool to describe spatial relations, where differential equations are essential in the study of motion and growth. However, natural shapes such as mountains, clouds or trees do not fit well into this framework. The understanding of these phenomena has undergone a fundamental change in the last two decades. *Fractal geometry*, as conceived by Mandelbrot, provides a mathematical model for many of the seemingly complex forms found in nature. One of Mandelbrot's key observations has been that these forms possess a remarkable statistical invariance under magnification. This may be quantified by a *fractal dimension*, a number that agrees with our intuitive understanding of dimension but need not be an integer. These ideas may also be applied to time-variant processes.

Another important discovery has been that even in very simple nonlinear dynamical systems, such as the double pendulum, long-term predictions are not possible despite exact knowledge of the underlying governing equations. Such systems exhibit behavioral patterns that we can conceive only as erratic or chaotic despite their very simple and deterministic generating mechanisms. Arbitrarily small perturbations of solutions are blown up by such systems until the perturbed solutions have lost all correlation with the original solution. This phenomenon has been termed *sensitive dependence on initial condition* and is the trademark of what became known as *chaos theory*. There is a strong connection between chaos and fractal geometry, namely, as one follows the evolution of the states of a chaotic nonlinear system, it typically leaves a trace in its embedding space which has a very complex geometric structure: this trace is a fractal.

Random Fractals

Fractal geometric structures exhibit a self-similarity when the distance at which they are viewed is changed. This self-similarity may be either exact or statistical. An exact self-similar fractal is the snowflake curve devised by the Swedish mathematician Helge von Koch in 1904 (see the construction in Fig. 1). The curve is self-similar: magnify one quarter of the snowflake curve by a factor of 3 to obtain another complete snowflake curve.

When a self-similar object is given as N copies of itself, each one scaled down by a factor of r, the *self-similarity dimension* of the object is defined as

$$D = \frac{\log N}{\log 1/r}.$$

This definition assigns the dimension 1 to straight lines and 2 to squares, as expected. Fractals typically have a non-integer dimension. The snowflake curve has a dimension $D = \log 4/\log 3 \approx 1.262$.

The notion of self-similarity dimension is extended to sets that do not have *exact* self-similarity. Let A be a set in n-dimensional Euclidean space R^n, and define $N(r)$ as the minimal number of n-dimensional cubes necessary to cover the set A. Then the (box-counting) *fractal dimension* is

$$D_f(A) = \lim_{r \to 0} \frac{\log N(r)}{\log 1/r}.$$

This quantity can be estimated from a given data set by drawing a graph of the function $N(r)$ on doubly

Figure 1. Construction of the von Koch snowflake curve. The interval [0, 1] is given initially (not shown here). In each stage (going from bottom to top) line segments are replaced by the generator curve consisting of four lines as shown in the bottom curve (stage 1). As stages are added the total length of the curve tends to infinity although the curve is confined to a finite region.

logarithmic paper. The negative slope of the resulting line fit to this data is an estimate for D_f.

There are other definitions of dimension, e.g. the Hausdorff–Besicovitch dimension, the mass dimension, and the correlation dimension.

The mathematical model for a statistically self-similar object is given by *fractional Brownian motion* (fBm). In one dimension fBm is a random process $X(t)$ with Gaussian increments $X(t_2) - X(t_1)$. The variance of these increments is proportional to $|t_2 - t_1|^{2H}$, where $0 < H < 1$. The increments of X are *statistically self-similar with parameter H*. This means that, setting $t_0 = 0$ and $X(t_0) = 0$, the two random functions $X(t)$ and $r^{-H}X(rt)$ are statistically indistinguishable. For a given number X_0, the points t that satisfy $X(t) = X_0$ constitute a fractal point set that is statistically self-similar. Its dimension is $D_f = 1 - H$. The graph of $X(t)$ is not self-similar, since we must scale in the t- and X-directions by *different* factors r and $1/r^H$ to obtain statistically equivalent graphs. This form of similarity has been termed *self-affinity*, meaning that properties are invariant under an affine transformation. (Generally, an affine transformation A in a Euclidean space is a linear transformation of the form $A(x) = ax + b$.) The graph of $X(t)$ has a fractal dimension of $2 - H$. Spectral analysis of fBm yields the spectral density $S(f)$ of the process $X(t)$. The density $S(f)$ is proportional to $1/f^\beta$, where the *spectral exponent* β equals $2H + 1$. Thus, β is in the range 1 to 3.

The generalization of fractional Brownian motion to higher dimensions is a multidimensional process (a *random field*) $X(t_1, t_2, \ldots, t_n)$ with the properties analogous to the above. The random field X has *stationary increments* and is *isotropic*, i.e. all points $(t_1, t_2, \ldots, t_n)$ and all directions are statistically equivalent. The random fields can also be characterized by their spectral density function or, equivalently, by their autocorrelation function.

Let us consider the case $n = 2$, where $X(t_1, t_2)$ may be plotted as height over the point (t_1, t_2) in the plane. The result is a fractal surface, the graph of X. It is a self-affine fractal whose dimension is $D_f = 3 - H$. The sets of points $\{(t_1, t_2)$ satisfying $X(t_1, t_2) = X_0\}$ are collections of curves interpreted as coastlines assuming a water level X_0. These curves are statistically self-similar with dimension $2 - H$.

The above models describe *uniform fractals*, i.e. fractal properties are essentially global properties. In nonuniform fractals the dimension may require different values. These *multifractals* have received wide attention in the study of aggregation problems.

Another topic of interest here is the *lacunarity* of a fractal. It is a property independent of the fractal

dimension, but has an effect on the texture or appearance of the fractal and thus is a useful additional parameter for algorithms for the simulation of natural shapes (see below).

Algorithms for Random Fractals

There have been many algorithms developed which generate finite approximations of random fractals. Initially, methods have been judged primarily with respect to the quality of the approximation and raw computing speed, two conflicting goals. More recently, with increased workstation (*q.v.*) computing power as well as very high-power graphics capabilities, research has emphasized flexibility and control of the fractals. For example, local control of the fractal dimension is desirable to model "smooth" valleys surrounded by rough mountains in a landscape scene.

In this section we present a few selected algorithms, first for the one-dimensional case and then for two or more dimensions. One of the first and most widely known methods is the *midpoint displacement method*. Assume that values $X(0) = 0$ and $X(1)$ are given. $X(1)$ may be obtained as a sample of a Gaussian random variable of variance σ^2. The interval $[0, 1]$ is partitioned into two subintervals $[0, \frac{1}{2}], [\frac{1}{2}, 1]$, and $X(\frac{1}{2})$ is defined as the average of $X(0)$ and $X(1)$ plus a displacement D_1, i.e.

$$X\left(\frac{1}{2}\right) = \frac{1}{2}(X(0) + X(1)) + D_1.$$

The displacement D_1 is computed as a sample of a Gaussian random variable with variance Δ_1^2 proportional to $\sigma^2/2^{2H}$. The process is repeated with the two intervals, i.e. more precisely, we set in this second stage

$$X(\tfrac{1}{4}) = \tfrac{1}{2}(X(0) + X(\tfrac{1}{2})) + D_2,$$
$$X(\tfrac{3}{4}) = \tfrac{1}{2}(X(\tfrac{1}{2}) + X(1)) + D_2,$$

where D_2 is Gaussian with variance Δ_2^2 proportional to $\sigma^2/(2^2)^{2H}$. Note that the two samples of D_2 in the above formulas may be different. The process is continued with displacements D_n having variances Δ_n^2 proportional to $\sigma^2/(2^n)^{2H}$ in the nth stage. This method is fast, but lacks mathematical purity since the process X does not have stationary increments for $H \neq \frac{1}{2}$.

One method which improves on the stationarity of the increments of X is called *successive random additions*. Assume that $X(t)$ is already approximated on an interval at equidistant points with grid size $\triangle t$, and let $r > 1$ be a fixed number denoting a reduction factor. In the next step the grid size is reduced to $\triangle t/r$ and values at the new equidistant points are defined by an interpolation procedure (e.g. linear interpolation). Additionally, all values are offset by a sample of a Gaussian random variable with a proper choice of variance. This procedure is repeated until the desired resolution is achieved. For example, if we start out with just two values of X, as in the midpoint displacement algorithm, then in order to obtain an appropriate random fractal with N points we must exercise n stages of the successive random additions method, where $n \geq \log N / \log r$. The variance Δ_n^2 of the displacement in the nth such stage of the algorithm must be proportional to $1/r^{2nH}$. The parameter $r > 1$ controls the lacunarity of the fractal. With a large value of r only very few stages are necessary and the lacunarity is especially drastic.

An alternative method is to sum

$$X(t) = \sum_{k=k_0}^{k_1} \frac{S(r^k t)}{r^{kH}},$$

where $r > 1$, $0 < H < 1$, and S is an auxiliary function similar to the sine and cosine functions. For example, S may be defined as a smooth interpolant of random data at integer points $t = 0, \pm 1, \pm 2, \dots$. For $k_0 = -\infty$, $k_1 = \infty$ we obtain a random fractal whose graph has a fractal dimension $2 - H$, and $r > 1$ determines lacunarity. In practice, the numbers k_0, k_1 are chosen to reflect the upper and lower *crossover scales* of the fractal, i.e. basically $r^{-k_0 H}$ and $r^{-k_1 H}$ will define the largest and smallest structures seen in the graph of X. This method, a summation of band-limited functions, is also called the "rescale-and-add-method," and in this one-dimensional formulation is almost the same as the Mandelbrot–Weierstrass function. The parameters r and H determine the lacunarity and fractal dimension ($D = 2 - H$) of the graph of $X(t)$. They need not be fixed globally, but may change depending, for example, on t or even $X(t)$.

The generalization of the methods to random fields $X(t_1, t_2)$ is as follows: in the midpoint displacement method we start out with an equilateral triangle and random values of $X(t_1, t_2)$ at the three vertices. Each side is subdivided into two halves and the displacements are done on each side, just as in the one-dimensional case. This yields four smaller equilateral triangles with sides half as long. This procedure is iterated until the desired resolution is achieved. It can be modified to operate on squares in place of triangles.

The method of successive random additions is also very easy to implement in the two-dimensional case. One works with grids where the grid sizes are given by $1/r^n$ and multilinear interpolation is applied.

In the rescale-and-add-method we set

$$X(t_1, t_2) = \sum_{k=k_0}^{k_1} \frac{S(r^k t_1, r^k t_2)}{r^{kH}}.$$

Nothing is changed except that the auxiliary function now has two arguments and must be modified accordingly.

Comparing the above methods we see that the midpoint displacement method and its variants are the fastest. However, increments are not stationary and in consequence, one obtains the so called *creasing effect*, which disturbs the natural look of the fractal. For a small extra expense, the method of successive random additions offers improved results. The rescale-and-add-method is relatively slow in one dimension, but it is superior in three dimensions, where the other methods suffer from storage problems and time complexity. Moreover, dimension and lacunarity may be changed not only globally, but also locally.

The output of the methods discussed is a two-dimensional array of heights. There are several possible computer-graphics methods available for rendering. Squares or triangles may be shown as shaded polygons with z-buffer or scanline techniques. When many data points are given, a floating horizon method can be applied. For most realistic images, ray tracing techniques are suitable. Generally the rendering of fractal surfaces takes more computing time than the process of generating the fractal.

Deterministic Fractals

Random fractals involve an element of chance. In contrast, deterministic fractals are given by means of exact formulas. In this section we consider those deterministic fractals which arise from *discrete dynamical systems*, i.e. the iteration of mappings. These may be derived, for example, from *population dynamics* in biology and yield maps that describe growth of population from one generation to the next. Iteration of the maps simulates the dynamics over longer time periods. Other mappings are motivated by time-variant processes described by differential equations and associated *Poincaré sections*.

The first system of differential equations discovered for which a fractal structure is central consists of the Lorenz equations

$$\dot{x} = \sigma(y - x),$$
$$\dot{y} = Rx - y - xz,$$
$$\dot{z} = xy - bz.$$

These equations, named after the meteorologist E. Lorenz, were motivated by the problem of weather

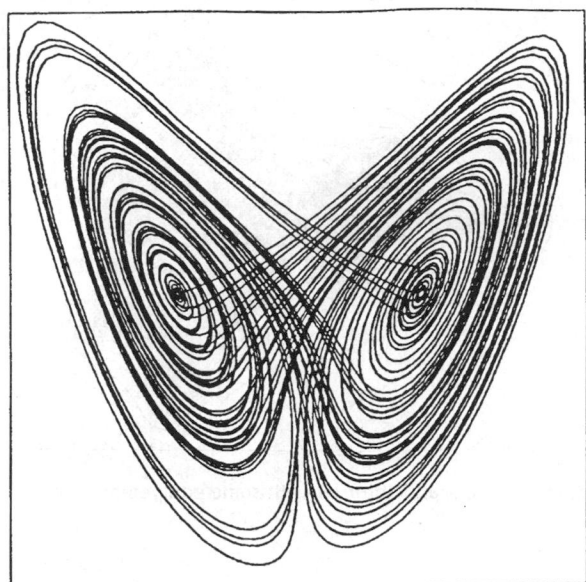

Figure 2. The Lorenz attractor for parameters $R = 28$, $\sigma = 10$, $b = 8/3$.

forecasting and represent a much simplified model of Rayleigh–Bénard convection in fluids. As solutions are followed they tend to a set in 3-space with a complicated fractal structure, a *strange attractor* (*see* Fig. 2).

One way to study the dynamics given by a system of three differential equations such as the Lorenz equations consists in reducing the description to a two-dimensional map, called the Poincaré section. A model for the Lorenz system has been suggested by Hénon and Pomeau (1976)

$$x_{k+1} = 1 + y_k - ax_k^2, \qquad a = 1.4,$$
$$y_{k+1} = bx_k, \qquad b = 0.3.$$

Given an initial point (x_0, y_0) the formula defines a successor point (x_1, y_1) and all following points iteratively. Again, there is a strange attractor with self-similar fractal structure (*see* Fig. 3). It is remarkable that important aspects of complex dynamical behavior found in nature can be captured in such simple discrete maps.

A related discrete model is the quadratic mapping

$$z_{k+1} = R_c(z_k) = z_k^2 + c,$$

where z_k, $k = 0, 1, 2, \ldots$ are complex numbers, and c is a complex parameter. This iteration has found widespread interest not only in the scientific community but also among amateur scientists due to its computer graphics potential. It is the iteration procedure which yields the Mandelbrot set

$$M = \{c \in \mathbb{C} \mid \lim_{k \to \infty} z_k \neq \infty \text{ with } z_0 = c\}$$

and the Julia set J_c, which is the minimal completely invariant closed subset of C (i.e. we have that $z \in J_c$ if and only if $z^2 + c \in J_c$ except in the special case $c = 0$ where the Julia set is the unit circle).

The self-similarity of the Julia set J is as follows. As in the case of exact self-similar fractals, any small neighborhood of a point in the Julia set can be mapped onto

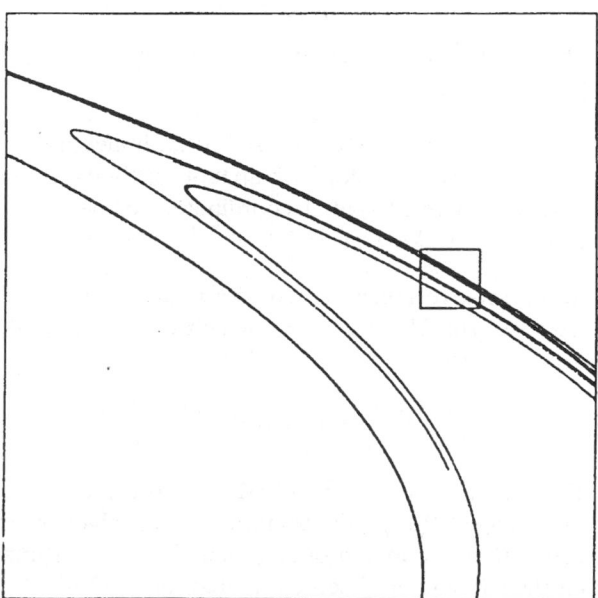
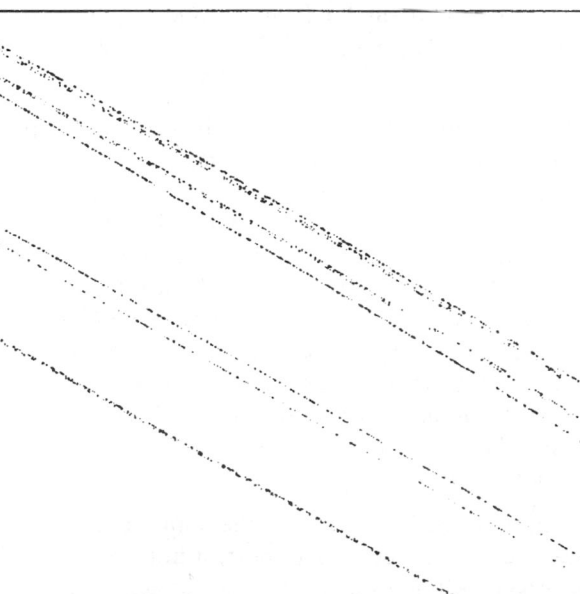

Figure 3. The Hénon chaotic attractor in two enlargements, computed from a run of 100,000 points. The regions shown are $[0, 1] \times [0, 0.3]$ (left) and $[0.7, 0.8] \times [0.15, 0.18]$ (right). The small square in the left figure corresponds to the enlargement on the right. The self-similar structures are clearly visible.

the complete Julia set. However, the necessary similarity mapping is not affine, but *nonlinear*. The fractal dimension of J is typically a noninteger value between 0 and 2. The theory for Julia sets has been carried out not only for the quadratic map but for polynomials and rational maps. For example Julia sets naturally arise when a complex polynomial equation $p(z) = 0$ is solved numerically by Newton's method. This amounts to the iteration of $N(z) = z - p(z)/p'(z)$. The roots of the equation $p(z) = 0$ are attractors for the rational map $N(z)$, and the Julia set is the boundary that separates the corresponding basins of attraction. It is the locus of instability: in any arbitrarily small neighborhood of a point in J one finds points that converge to different roots of $p(z)$. Consider the Julia set for $p(z) = z^4 - 1 = 0$. This equation has four obvious roots, $+1$, -1, $+i$, and $-i$, where i is the imaginary unit, $\sqrt{-1}$. Suppose, however, that we did not know those roots and sought to ascertain them through iteration: choose an initial guess, obtain an improved guess through use of the Newton–Raphson technique, and repeat until successive iterates pass a suitable convergence criterion. For the stated equation, the improved guess z_1 that results from a guess $z_0 = 1$ is $z_1 = (3 + 1/z^3)/4$. Now, if one were to make a guess close to an actual root, 1.1 or $-0.9i$, for example, a few iterations would show convergence to the *closest* root (1 and $-i$, respectively). But suppose the guess is not as good, $1/3 - i/4$, for example. In the complex plane, this guess is closest to the root at $+1$ and next closest to the root at $-i$, but its iteration actually leads to convergence to the root $+i$! So, as can readily be seen from Fig. 4 (see Color Page CP-9), the root with the yellow basin, $+i$, is strangely able to attract initial guesses that lie in the yellow areas far from $+i$ and much closer to other roots. The x-shaped filigree is the Julia set for $z^4 - 1$.

Most phenomena that occur with rational maps already appear in the quadratic map $R(z) = z^2 + c$. The Mandelbrot set reflects qualitative aspects for all parameters c of this map, namely it collects all parameters c whose Julia set J_c is a connected set. Outside of the Mandelbrot set, corresponding Julia sets are not connected, but are just clouds of points. The Mandelbrot set (Fig. 5) itself is also a fractal with a certain self-similarity: any small neighborhood of a boundary point of M contains a complete copy of M. The conjecture that the boundary of M has a dimension equal to 2 has now been proved.

The computer code to generate the data for an image of the Mandelbrot set is very short; it implements the integer-valued function

$$L(c) = \begin{cases} \ell = \min\{k : |R_c^k(c)| > R_{\max}\} & \text{if } \ell \leq L_{\max} \\ \infty & \text{otherwise} \end{cases}$$

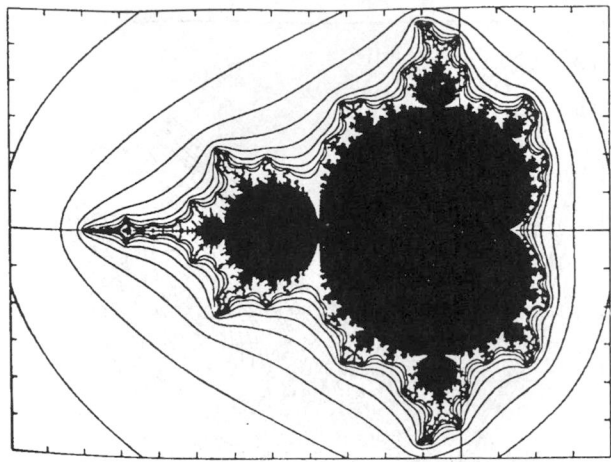

Figure 5. The Mandelbrot set with some equipotential lines.

Here $R_c^k(c)$ denotes z_k, the kth iterate of $z \to z^2 + c$, starting at $z_0 = c$, $L_{\max}$ is the maximum number of iterations allowed per point, and $R_{\max}$ is a large number (≥ 2). Thus, $L(c)$ is the number of iterations necessary to detect that the critical value c of R_c escapes to ∞. The computation of $L(c)$ is carried out once per pixel of the image, each pixel representing a small region in complex parameter space. Colors are assigned using a color look-up table.

$L(c)$ is an integer-valued function. It is possible to define a smooth version by means of the potential function of the Mandelbrot set. For points $c \notin M$ the *potential* is given by

$$G(c) = \lim_{k \to \infty} \frac{\log |R_c^k(c)|}{2^k}.$$

The expression in the limit converges rapidly once $|R_c^k(c)|$ is large.

The values of $G(c)$ can be used in an image again in connection with a color look-up table or they are interpreted as a third spatial coordinate, i.e. height: *see* Figs. 6–11, Color Pages CP-9–10.

An alternative measurement for points $c \notin M$ is the distance $d(c, M)$ of c to M, which can be estimated according to

$$\frac{\sinh G(c)}{2e^{G(c)}|G'(c)|} < d(c, M) < \frac{2 \sinh G(c)}{|G'(c)|}.$$

This estimate gives rise to different pictures, *see* Fig. 12, Color Page CP-10, and also to a new fast algorithm to compute the Mandelbrot set: once the lower estimate on the left side has been computed for a point $c \notin M$, then a disk with that radius can be eliminated from further computation, since it is guaranteed that this disk does not intersect M. A speed-up factor of 10 or higher may result, depending on the region of the image and the resolution.

The algorithms for the computation of color images of Julia sets are very similar to the above; for details see the literature.

Applications

Fractals are found almost everywhere in nature, from the very large scales of clusters of galaxies down to the microcosmos of molecular particles. Although the mere description of these shapes and forms in terms of fractals does not explain anything it is clear that the fractal "dialect" is the appropriate language and, thus, it will evolve to become a lasting element of science.

Obviously, wherever nature is to be *simulated*, fractals are of value. Landscapes and clouds were two of the first natural phenomena discussed in the computer graphics community (*see* Fig. 6). Research now studies effects such as erosion of a fractal landscape, allowing rivers and river networks to be included in the long list of simulated phenomena.

Fractal geometry applied to spatial relationships provides one way to achieve visual complexity. Another method used in computer graphics is called *solid texturing*, which is usually given as a functional model. In Fig. 8, showing a fractal planet, the geometry is very simple and not fractal: it is merely a sphere. But the texturing function that determines the coloring is constructed using the laws of random fractals. There is thus a balance between geometry and texture. No visual complexity is lost if one of the two is relaxed while the other one is enhanced.

One of the most important aspects of fractals is that their visual complexity is very high in contrast to their complexity as measured by the length of the shortest computer program that can generate them, which is typically very small. This is called *database amplification* and is important where large, detailed databases are too big or too costly to be used, e.g. in flight or driving simulators, or in telecommunications.

A systematic analysis of images is possible using self-similarity and affine maps in an approach using *partitioned iterated function systems*. One gray-scale or color image, e.g. a rasterized photograph, a synthetic computer graphics image, or a transmitted satellite image, may be approximated and encoded as an object that is invariant under a collection of affine maps. These maps may be stored in much less memory compared with the original image. In turn, these affine maps may again be used to reconstruct the image—or at least a close approximation of it. More specifically,

fractal image compression (*q.v.*) works as follows. The original image is partitioned into a set of non-overlapping *range blocks*. For each range block a matching domain block is searched for. A *domain block* is an image block of twice the linear size. The match is obtained first by downsampling to the range block size, and then by adjusting gain and brightness parameters to achieve the best possible least-squares approximation (*q.v.*) to the range block. When all range blocks are replaced by their transformed domain block approximations, the so-called *image collage* is obtained. It is the job of the encoder to make this collage as close to the original as possible. The fractal code of the image contains the partitioning information and a list of gain and brightness parameters along with corresponding domain block addresses. The decoder cannot reconstruct the collage, since it does not have access to the original domain blocks that the encoder has selected. Instead, an approximation of the collage is obtained by iterating the collage operator. Starting with an arbitrary image as input, its collage as specified by the code is constructed as output. Then the process is iterated, taking the last output image as the input image for the next iteration. Provided certain contractivity constraints are met, the iteration converges. There are many important issues in fractal image compression that have been researched, e.g. the choice of the partitioning of the image, the quantization scheme of the parameters, and the reduction of the computational complexity. Recently hybrid methods, combining fractal coding with the wavelet or discrete cosine transformation, have provided very good coding results.

There are numerous other applications of fractal geometry in image processing and pattern recognition. Two of them are: automatic segmentation of images based on fractal dimension, lacunarity, etc., which is useful in differentiating objects in an image, such as artificial structures, forest and sky, and optimization of camouflage methods based on fractal analysis of the surroundings.

A method to generate fractal shapes that grow in space is based on *Lindenmayer systems*. Objects are represented as strings of symbols which are generated from an *axiom* (initial short string) and a set of *production rules* which are applied recursively to the symbols of the axiom and the resulting strings. The geometric representation of these strings is obtained through *turtle graphics* (*see* LOGO). Classic fractal curves such as the snowflake curve, Hilbert's space filling curve, the Sierpinski gasket etc. are easily and compactly formulated as L-systems. The main application is the modeling of growth and form of trees, bushes, and plants. These results stem from an interdisciplinary effort in computer science and biology.

These applications are relevant to computer science and engineering. Perhaps the most important uses of fractals are in the physical sciences. One area of applications is given by *percolation processes*, describing a fluid spreading randomly through a medium, which supplies a network of narrow pores and channels for the fluid flow. This includes seepage of (possibly contaminated) water through the cracks and fractures of rock formation.

Another application is diffusion-limited aggregation, in which "sticky" particles move about randomly and eventually attach to a cluster of particles. In this process the cluster grows into a fractal characterized by its fractal dimension. There is a strong coincidence with forms generated by viscous fingering in porous media, which is an important issue for oil recovery.

It is not a surprise that molecular surfaces are fractal, and thus fractal geometry will prove useful in chemical engineering (catalysis) and other areas where surface/volume relations are crucial, e.g. wetting and powder technology.

Deterministic fractals typically arise from dynamical systems that are motivated by numerous models for natural phenomena (e.g. the production of red blood cells in the bone marrow may be modeled using a delay differential equation, which exhibits chaotic attractors, which in turn may be interpreted as serious irregularities in the red blood cell concentrations in patients with leukemia).

The Mandelbrot set plays a central role as a paradigm for the transition from order to chaos in such models. As the parameter c is decreased along the real axis, the system $z \leftarrow z^2 + c$ undergoes a series of *period doubling bifurcations*, a phenomenon that has also been discovered in several physical laboratory experiments. Moreover, the Mandelbrot set is in some sense a *universal object*. It also appears in the study of rational and so-called polynomial-like maps.

Due to their beauty, Julia sets and the Mandelbrot set have provided inspiration for computer art (*q.v.*) and serve as a pleasing demonstration object in computer trade shows. Another unforeseen, but perhaps relevant, side effect of the colorful Mandelbrot set images is that they convey a hint of the beauty that lies within mathematics. They thus supply motivation to regain the widely lost assertion that mathematics is a worthwhile and important part of the human culture.

Bibliography

1976. Hénon, M., and Pomeau, I. *Two Strange Attractors with a Simple Structure.* Lecture Notes in Mathematics **505**. New York: Springer-Verlag.

1982. Mandelbrot, B. *The Fractal Geometry of Nature.* New York: W. H. Freeman.

1986. Peitgen, H.-O., and Richter, P. H. *The Beauty of Fractals.* Heidelberg: Springer-Verlag.

1987. Gleick, J. *Chaos—Making a New Science.* New York: Viking.

1988. Barnsley, M. F. *Fractals Everywhere.* London: Academic Press.

1988. Peitgen, H.-O., and Saupe, D. (eds.) *The Science of Fractal Images.* New York: Springer-Verlag.

1990. Hao, B.-L. *Chaos II.* Singapore: World Scientific.

1991. Peitgen, H.-O., Jürgens, H., and Saupe, D. *Fractals for the Classroom, Part One and Part Two.* New York: Springer-Verlag.

1995. Fisher, Y. *Fractal Image Compression—Theory and Application.* New York: Springer-Verlag.

1996. Prusinkiewicz, P., and Lindenmayer, A. *The Algorithmic Beauty of Plants,* 2nd Ed. New York: Springer-Verlag.

1999. Dekking, M., Lutton, E., and Tricot, C. *Fractals: Theory and Applications in Engineering.* New York: Springer-Verlag.

Dietmar Saupe

FREE SOFTWARE FOUNDATION (FSF)

For articles on related subjects *see* COMPUTER ETHICS; FREEWARE AND SHAREWARE; LEGAL ASPECTS OF COMPUTING; LEGAL PROTECTION OF SOFTWARE; and UNIX.

The Free Software Foundation is best known for its sponsorship of the GNU project. GNU is a recursive acronym which stands for "GNU's Not Unix". The GNU Project was founded in 1984 to develop a complete free Unix-compatible operating system, to be called GNU. "Complete" means covering the full range of components of Unix—kernel (*q.v.*), libraries, shells, editors, compilers, development tools, mailer, and the rest. "Free," here, means that users have certain freedoms, including the freedom to use the system for any purpose, and to redistribute copies, either verbatim or modified, either gratis or for a fee. As a practical matter, the freedom to modify entails availability of source code.

When the GNU project was launched, all the operating systems available for the modern computers of the day were proprietary (non-free). Source code was usually not available; therefore, users were helpless to adapt the software to their needs, or even fix problems. They were also legally prohibited from helping their neighbors by sharing software with them. The GNU project set out to liberate users from these restrictions, and thus permit the existence of a community where users are free to cooperate when they wish.

The Free Software Foundation is a tax-exempt charity, formed in 1985 to raise funds for developing free software. It pays programmers to write and upgrade GNU software, and technical writers to write and upgrade manuals. (However, most work on GNU software is done by volunteers.) It receives most of its funds from selling copies of otherwise free software source code and free manuals (no contradiction, because "free" refers to the freedom that users have in using their copies). Manuals are distributed in source form as well, to facilitate making modified versions of them. The Foundation also makes the software and manual source code available on the Internet with no fee.

The most notable GNU software packages include GNU Emacs (a programmable text editor) and GCC (the GNU C compiler, a portable optimizing compiler which now supports several languages and several dozen target machines).

Most GNU software is released under a license called the GNU General Public License ("GNU GPL"). This license permits copying, redistribution, and modification of the software, but does not allow adding any additional restrictions on subsequent users. Therefore, modified versions of the program must themselves be free software.

The term *copyleft* was coined to describe this general technique of using copyright law to protect users' freedom. The GNU GPL is one implementation of copyleft. Certain GNU software packages use alternative copy left licenses; some libraries (but not all) use the GNU Library General Public License, which permits using these libraries in non-free software applications. This article is also covered by a simple kind of copyleft which permits redistribution but not modification.

Many other software developers, not associated with the GNU project, have also released programs under the GNU GPL.

In 1992, when the GNU operating system was almost complete, the kernel, Linux, was developed by Linus Torvalds, and released under the GNU GPL. This filled the last major gap; soon after, complete operating systems were produced by combining Linux with the GNU system. (These Linux-based GNU systems are most often called just "Linux", but Linux is actually the kernel, not the whole operating system.) Estimates are that GNU/Linux systems had over ten million users in 1999.

The free software community that GNU was meant to make possible is now large and vibrant. The GNU project, and the broader free software movement, have empirically disproved the naïve claim that software cannot be written unless users give owners power to restrict use of the software.

Free software is also sometimes referred to as *open source* software by those who prefer not to discuss the ethical and political issues of freedom for software users.

Bibliography

1998. The GNU project home page: http://www.gnu.org.

Richard Stallman

FREEWARE AND SHAREWARE

For articles on related topics *see* FREE SOFTWARE FOUNDATION; and USER GROUPS.

Anyone who has spent much time on the Internet has probably seen programs available for downloading. In most cases, these programs are being distributed either as *shareware* or *freeware*, or as a hybrid of the two. These programs appear to be distributed "for free," but the real story behind shareware and freeware is more complicated than that.

An early function of computer user groups was to share software. The first use of the terms "freeware" and "shareware" is uncertain, but in 1982 Andrew Fluegelman and Jim Knopf called some PC programs that they had written "freeware." After Fluegelman copyrighted that term, "shareware" became the generic name for user-produced software, though "freeware" is still used informally.

According to the Association of Shareware Professionals, "shareware" is not a type of software, but rather is a marketing method. With shareware, the program owner makes the program available for a free trial, hoping that consumers will like the product enough to buy it. Any software can be marketed as shareware, although the method is most popular among small, independent software developers. It is difficult to determine the volume of the shareware industry, but in 1999 it has been estimated to have revenues as high as US$300 million.

Various distribution schemes fall under the banner of "shareware." The differences hinge on whether payment is expected, who must pay, whether the distributed version represents the program's full functionality, and what rights the consumer has in altering and redistributing the software.

Freeware

Freeware is free to anyone, and may be distributed freely. However, there may be certain limitations on its use. For example, the author may request that you do not alter the program, or do not charge money for its distribution. Or the author may make it free to individuals, but ask companies to pay a fee. The popular browser Netscape Communicator is freeware (http://www.netscape.com). Anyone may download and use the full version, but the owner, Netscape Communications, prohibits people from altering the program themselves. For a time, Netscape Communications also requested that for-profit businesses pay for their copies, but it discontinued this request to keep up better with rival (free) program Microsoft Internet Explorer. Some software, like Adobe Acrobat Reader, which reads the Adobe Portable Document Format (PDF), is free because its widespread availability encourages document authors to buy Adobe's software to produce PDF documents.

There are endless variations on freeware, with program authors asking for all kinds of strange things in return for the software. For example, *postcardware* is free software whose author asks that users who like the program send a postcard. (The authors collect the postcards as a hobby and to gauge how widely their software has been distributed.)

Public Domain and Open Source

Public domain software is like freeware in that it is distributed free to anyone. With public domain software, however, the program author has given away all rights to it, so anyone may alter it. Software in the public domain should be distinguished from *open source* software, for which the author retains copyright but grants the free use of the software, including the right to modify it, though generally not the right to impose restrictions on the use of the modified product. The Linux operating system is one of the best-known examples of open source software, released under the GNU "copyleft" agreement (*see* FREE SOFTWARE FOUNDATION). Because its source code is available, its author, Linus Torvalds, has had the assistance of software developers around the world in improving his product.

Shareware

A program that is "true shareware" is distributed in its full version to anyone who wants to try it. The author requests that you send payment if you continue to use the program after a certain time period. Sometimes shareware programs contain "nag screens," which are annoying little messages that pop up reminding you to register (and pay for) the program. These nag screens can be turned off by a code provided upon payment, or in some cases the purchasers receives a version of the program free of nags.

One might think that the shareware system won't work because people will not pay on the honor system. However, several companies have made money with shareware, suggesting that people will pay for a product that they like if asked to do so. One of the best

known examples is PKZip, developed by Phil Katz (hence the "PK" in the name). PKZip is a utility program that compresses files for storage or transfer; a companion program PKUnzip decompresses the compressed files. PKZip can also be purchased in a boxed version in stores, but it remains widely distributed as shareware. Other examples of shareware include Paint Shop Pro and WinZip.

Demoware and Crippleware

Software developers who doubt the honesty of the public sometimes resort to distributing demoware or crippleware, which are variants of shareware. While the shareware concept assumes that people will pay for the software, demoware and crippleware assume that people will not pay unless they have a reason to do so, such as getting a better version of the software.

Demoware is like shareware except that the distributed version is not the same as the full program. For example, a game that has 12 levels in the full version may have only two levels playable in the demo version, or a drawing program with 100 filters may provide only 10. Almost any commercial game software company's Website has examples of demoware.

Crippleware is a cousin to demoware. Instead of developing a demo version of the software, the company simply disables certain crucial features of the product and distributes the crippled version as a demo. For example, a drawing program may be fully functional except that it doesn't save, or doesn't print.

Light Versions

Light or "lite" software is free, fully functional software that lacks some of the capabilities of its commercial counterpart. One well-known example is Qualcomm's Eudora Light email program for personal computers. Its features are quite adequate for personal and even professional use, but its Eudora Pro counterpart offers additional features appropriate for commercial use, such as the ability to filter mail and file it by category.

Consumer Issues

Consumers are legally obliged to meet the terms of the license agreements of software that they buy. With commercially distributed software, the license agreements are fairly standard: you cannot make unauthorized copies of the software, you cannot sell copies of it for profit, and so on. With shareware and freeware, however, the rules of the agreement run the full gamut, from "do anything you want with it" to "pay $100 for each copy you make."

In practice, as you might imagine, there is very little chance of a violation of a licensing agreement being noticed and prosecuted. Many people use shareware without ever registering it, and nobody is the wiser. However, it is considered unethical in the computing world to use shareware without respecting the terms of its licensing agreement, whether they are to pay a fee or to mail the programmer a postcard.

Bibliography

1994. Reichard, K. *Unix Shareware and Freeware.* Foster City, CA: IDG Books Worldwide.
1997. Cnet. *C/net Guide to Shareware.com.* New York: Ziff-Davis Publishing Company.
1999. Ford, N. "The History of Shareware," Public Software Library. `http://www.digibuy.com/cgi-bin/history.html`.

Websites

Association of Shareware Professionals. `http://www.asp-shareware.org`.
The Educational Software Cooperative. `http://www.edu-soft.org`.
Linux Online. `http://www.linux.org`.

Faithe Wempen

FRONT-END PROCESSOR

For articles on related subjects *see* CHANNEL; COMMUNICATION CONTROL UNIT; GATEWAY; HOST SYSTEM; INTERRUPT; MODEM; and MULTIPLEXING.

A *front-end processor* is a small, limited capability, digital computer that is programmed to replace the hard-wired input and output functions of a central computing system (e.g. for the control of remote terminals in a time-sharing system). The front-end processor thereby permits the host computer to perform its primary functions with little regard for the slower input–output activities associated with large-scale multiprogrammed (*q.v.*) or time-shared (*q.v.*) computing systems.

In addition to receiving and transmitting all data passing through a computing system, front-end processors may also support a wide variety of functions, such as:

1. *Data and/or format conversion*—the conversion of one or more incoming data codes and formats to that of the host system.
2. *Polling* (*q.v.*)—the determination by a front-end processor of a terminal's readiness to send or receive data.
3. *Assembly of characters and messages*—the assembly and disassembly of all data, which may be input at varying line speeds and in synchronous or asynchronous formats, to insure that the host system receives only complete messages.

4. *Error control and editing*—the detection and possible correction of transmission errors, as well as corrections initiated at the terminals prior to reception by the host system.

5. *Fail-soft functions*—the ability of the front-end processor to keep parts of the system operating (such as terminals) when a major element of the host system has failed.

6. *Queueing*—placing incoming messages in transmission order for processing by the host system, or in some cases queueing messages on auxiliary storage devices (*spooling*).

7. *Message switching*—a function of front-end processors that service more than one central processing unit.

8. *Direct response*—the front-end processor may have the ability to respond to simple inquiries directly without contact with the host system.

9. *Network protection*—use of a front-end processor as a *firewall* that analyzes the credentials of a user who is attempting to access a network.

The basic components of a typical front-end processor are:

1. *Processor*—a stored program digital computer that has main memory that may vary in size from several hundred words to many thousands of words depending on the complexities of the specific application. Two important qualities required of a front-end processor are good facilities for bit manipulation and handling interrupts (*q.v.*). The processor may or may not have its own online peripheral devices, depending on the particular application.

2. *Central processor interface*—the hardware interface that allows the front-end processor to connect directly to an input–output channel of the host system. The host system is than able to communicate with the front-end processor as if it were a standard peripheral device controller.

3. *Communication multiplexer*—a device with programmable or hard-wired logic that produces logically independent data channels into the front-end processor's main memory from each transmission line serviced. The coordination of the data flow between the multiplexer and processor is handled by the front-end processor's interrupt system.

4. *Line interface units*—the hardware devices that link the communication multiplexer with the modems that terminate each of the communication lines.

5. *Software*—the programs that integrate the functions of the various hardware components of the front-end processor. Included in the software package are such functions as terminal, line, and message control, system interface procedures, and whatever other functions are required by a particular installation.

The front-end processor can be a powerful and economical means of relieving a central processor of its time-consuming overhead activities by placing these activities under the control of an independent and parallel processing unit. The need for front-end processors had been declining as mainframe I/O units became more powerful but they are now experiencing a resurgence through their role as firewalls.

Arthur I. Karshmer

FUNCTION

See SUBPROGRAM.

FUNCTIONAL PROGRAMMING

For articles on related subjects *see* BINDING; LAMBDA CALCULUS; LIST PROCESSING LANGUAGES; RECURSION; and TYPES, THEORY OF.

Functional programming, also called *applicative programming*, is a style that uses function application as the only control structure (*q.v.*). Rather than conditional statements, one uses conditional expressions to yield alternative results; rather than an assignment statement, one uses binding (*q.v.*) of parameter to argument to give a name to a value; rather than explicit sequencing or looping of control flow, one uses patterns of nested invocations to direct the generation of an result. Of immediate importance for general problem-solving is that, just as a function may take several arguments, a result can have several components.

Consider a program that reads a list of triples and returns a list of pairs; a triple contains the coefficients of a quadratic equation with real roots and the pair is its computed roots, so that if an input triple is $(1, -3, 2)$, the output pair would be $(2, 1)$. In the functional language Haskell the algorithm could be rendered as shown in Fig. 1.

In Scheme (similar to Lisp—*q.v.*) it might appear as shown in Fig. 2.

Although Scheme is an untyped language, requiring full run-time type checking, Haskell is strongly typed at compile time. Often the type information is implicit in the primitives or literals, like + and sqrt. Indeed, type checkers related to Haskell's can infer the type of solveQuads (the first line of its definition) automatically from the five-line suffix of its definition. That is,

```
solveQuads :: Floating n => [(n, n, n)] -> [(n, n)]
solveQuads = map quad where
      quad(a,b,c) = ( (-b+rtDiscriminant)/denominator,
                      (-b-rtDiscriminant)/denominator) where
              rtDiscriminant = sqrt(b*b - 4*a*c)
              denominator    = a+a
```

Figure 1. A Haskell program that returns a list of quadratic-equation roots. The first line declares solveQuads to be a function that takes a list of real number triples and returns a list of pairs (the brackets denote "list of"). In the next line, the definition is map quad, a function that applies the quad function to all elements of a list (quad takes a coefficient-triple and returns the pair of roots).

```
(define solveQuads
  (let (
    (quad (lambda (triple)
      (let (
          (a (car           triple)  )
          (b (car     (cdr triple))  )
          (c (car(cdr(cdr triple))))
          )
          (let (
            (rtDiscriminant (sqrt (- (* b b) (* 4 a c))))
            (denominator    (+ a a))
            )
            (list (/ (+ (- b) rtDiscriminant) denominator)
                  (/ (- (- b) rtDiscriminant) denominator)
            ) ) ) ) )
    )
    (lambda (listOf3s) (map quad listOf3s)) ))
```

Figure 2. A Scheme program to do the same computation as Fig. 1. A list is decomposed by Scheme using Lisp's first and rest **projection primitives,** car and cdr.

```
search:: (Eq keyType)=> [keyType]-> [infoType]-> keyType-> infoType

search (key:moreKeys) (info:moreInfo) targetKey
  | key==targetKey = info
  | otherwise      = search moreKeys moreInfo targetKey
```

Figure 3. A Haskell program to search a list for a value associated with a given search key.

it maps a list of floating-point triples into a list of floating pairs, and all its uses must comply.

This style makes the nesting of function calls, argument binding, and the conditional expression very important. For instance, a search can be specified as follows. The parameters here are a pair of linear lists that contain, respectively, keys and their associated information, as well as a targetKey. The lists hold homogeneously typed elements, and elements of the key type must be capable of being tested for equality. Then a sequential search (*see* SEARCHING) can be programmed in Haskell as shown in Fig. 3.

Haskell provides an infix list constructor function (:) and uses it in a serial pattern-match to decompose both lists. The last two lines specify that if the first element in the list of keys matches the target key, then search returns the corresponding info, and if not, then it returns what it finds by searching deeper into the two lists.

The same function (and algorithm) can be specified in Scheme as shown in Fig. 4.

There are various approaches to a pure applicative (functional) style. Some restrict user-defined functions to receive only elementary data objects as arguments and return them as results. Examples of this class include primitive recursion, pure expressions in Iverson's APL (*q.v.*) (its notorious one-liners), and Backus's FP.

More contemporary examples demand that functions themselves be data objects, to be passed freely throughout the system. Examples include very pure versions of McCarthy's Lisp and of its Scheme descendant, Clean, Id, Miranda, ML, and Haskell. Such languages are said to treat functions as "first-class values" that are not restricted in the roles they can play in programs. These are closer to the theoretical foundations of functional programming because the domain of data objects includes everything computable, including any function that a user specifies. In that spirit, examples below show how the search function becomes a first-class value that can be passed around.

This convention allows many more kinds of values, and it is easy to confuse functions of the wrong arity (number of parameters) or with parameters ordered differently. Type systems (*see* TYPES, THEORY OF) are commonly used, therefore, to assure that the types of all data objects, including functions, match among the context where they are defined and the contexts where they are used. In the example above, for instance, the Haskell compiler demands that the two lists each be homogeneous, that an equality relation be defined for the target type, and that the result be of the type (infoType) of which the second list is composed. Scheme, in contrast, has relaxed typing and handles type errors at run time.

A more interesting formulation of the search function is translate, which demands only a key as its parameter, and returns only the associated information as its result. The assembly of key–information pairings is internal to it. Such a function can be used freely and repeatedly once that "table" is built. So we show how to build such a function from the lisKeys and the lisInfo incrementally in Fig. 5.

```
(define search
  (lambda (keyList infoList targetKey)
    (if (equal? (car keyList) targetKey)
        (car infoList)
        (search (cdr keyList) (cdr infoList) targetKey)
) ) )
```

Figure 4. A Scheme equivalent to Fig. 3.

```
buildTable:: (Eq keyType) => [keyType] -> [infoType] -> keyType -> infoType
buildTable lisKeys lisInfo targetKey = search lisKeys lisInfo where
  search (key:moreKeys) (info:moreInfo)
              | key==targetKey = info
              | otherwise      = search moreKeys moreInfo
```

Figure 5. A Haskell program that returns a search function that encapsulates a lookup table.

Of course,

```
buildTable [1, 5, 2, 4, 3] ["one", "five",
                "two", "four", "three"] 5
```

just reduces to "five" but the result of

```
buildTable [1, 5, 2, 4, 3] ["one", "five",
                "two", "four", "three"]
```

is the translate function that translates one of these numbers into the string that names it. More interestingly,

```
buildTable [1, 5, 2, 4, 3]
```

yields the skeleton of a search builder already seeded with these five keys, later to be augmented with alternative information lists to be associated with them; another might be ["odd","odd","even","even", "odd"].

Haskell thus uses left-associative concatenation for function application, leaving open the possibility that later arguments are provided later on. This is the core of the concept behind *currying*; it allows us to view a function, buildTable to have three arguments and one primitive result or two arguments and return a search function, which in turn requires a key argument to return the sought result. Scheme uses parentheses to demark the syntax of function application (and other structures too, so rendering all programs also as lists). Fig. 6 is the Scheme equivalent of Fig. 5, with the same currying, albeit with explicit parentheses for each application.

Many applicative languages, including Haskell, default to *lazy evaluation*, whereby no computation need occur until it becomes—directly or indirectly— essential to the next visible (output) behavior of the program. For instance, suppose that the list Lisinfo in the examples above is being read very slowly from the Internet. Since the content of the list is not directly necessary to build the translate function, Haskell can construct it before that list is completed. It does so by planting a *suspension* (or a "promise") of some suffix of that list inside the closed function, which will

happily search and find information that has been read—and, of course, wait for any that has not. A suspension efficiently wraps an expression and its context for later evaluation, which will occur transparently once future computation probes it.

Laziness makes input and output streams themselves into lists of which only the first element need be explicit; the rest becomes manifest only as it is accessed. A typical use for such a *stream* is to print it, and the traversal during printing forces more of it to become explicit. Moreover, since an already-printed node is immediately abandoned by that traversal, its explicit representation can often be erased as it is printed. Under that operational philosophy, only one node at a time is generated, made explicit, printed, and abandoned.

The analogs of input values to a program are files passed as arguments to a function; the analog of output is the tuples of results returned from such an application. Just as each output file is implemented as a stream, so also the input files may be streams (in solveQuads, a stream of triples) so that only a finite prefix of unbounded input is ever represented within the computer. Thus, Haskell's solveQuads can run using a constant amount of space for storage and time proportional to the length of the input file—just as the code in a procedural language does.

Not all functional languages provide lazy evaluation. Used properly, it provides graceful enhancements to the semantics of a programming language. For instance, Haskell's

```
naturalNumbers == nn 0 where
    nn i = i : nn(i+1)
```

succinctly defines the list of *all* the natural numbers, whose representation cannot require unbounded space if each visible behavior depends only on some bounded prefix of it.

The feature of functional languages that enables lazy evaluation is the same one that makes them so attractive for parallel processing (*q.v.*): nothing in

```
(define buildTable
    (lambda (lisKeys)
      (lambda (lisInfo)
        (lambda (targetKey)
          (letrec (
            (search
              (lambda (keyList infoList)
                (if (equal? (car keyList) targetKey)
                    (car infoList)
                    (search (cdr keyList) (cdr infoList)) ) ))
            )
            (search lisKeys lisInfo) )))) )
```

Figure 6. A Scheme equivalent to Fig. 5.

the program can require specification of, or a change to, the state of the machine. In procedure-oriented languages (*q.v.*), assignment statements or input–output commands allow the programmer to affect state but, without such control, the implementation is freer to alter the sequence of computation to suit the demand for results or to balance resources available to the program.

This freedom certainly does not preclude an implementation from introducing state; a good one will conserve resources by doing so. The programmer, however, is prevented from meddling with it.

Without good compiling, lazy evaluation can get expensive. A naive implementation demands many context swaps (from one environment to another) and retains bindings that will never be used. Instead, many functional languages, such as ML and pure Scheme, follow a *strict* (also called *applicative-order*) evaluation order that is closer to traditional programming languages, where arguments are fully evaluated before being planted in a data structure or binding. Lazy evaluation, also called *normal order*, postpones that initial evaluation until first use.

Extending the `buildTable` example in the context of laziness and first-class functions, we can imagine another version of `translate` with almost the same input (domain) as above, but with a different output (codomain): ultimately a pair composed of the sought information and a revised algorithm for the `translate` function. The domain for keys must now be ordered, with less-than and greater-than defined in addition to equality.

```
buildTable2:: Ord keyType =>
    [keyType] -> [infoType]
    -> keyType -> (infoType, keyType->
                                infoType)
```

The type of `buildTable2` admits a smarter search that embeds a search tree (*q.v.*), for instance a height-balanced tree, within `translate`. Each translate function also returns another version of itself from the already-seen prefixes of the two lists of keys and information. The idea is that more efficient versions, each of which uses binary search (*see* SEARCHING), become available as more translations occur, even though all versions remain just the same function, as judged by argument/result equivalence.

If there is only a single binding to `translate`, then it can be revised to the new version after each use. In effect, the state of the tree within translate is updated to a bigger tree after every invocation. The revision is fairly easy to manage with only the one binding, even though the lists are unbounded and streaming in slowly over some Internet connection.

As a first-class value, however, `translate` can be shared by multiple bindings. In that situation there would probably be more than one incarnation of the embedded tree at any time. These multiple bindings might get distributed across many processes, even on different processors. But because each one is treated as an independent value, there is no synchronization problem. There is no semantically required state shared among bindings and there will be no synchronization anomaly, although more space may well be needed.

Functional programming offers expressiveness for machine architectures that goes beyond that used by conventional procedure-oriented languages. Since results are defined without sequential imperatives, much of a functional program can be adapted to use available parallelism (e.g. multiple or pipelined processors—*see* PIPELINE) without tailoring it to a particular machine. Moreover, much of the notation for program verification (*q.v.*) has a functional foundation, and so functional programs can, to some degree, be read as their own proofs. Finally, the natural modularity of function definitions facilitates piecewise testing and maintenance of large programs.

Bibliography

1987. Peyton Jones, S. L. *The Implementation of Functional Programming Languages.* New York: Prentice Hall.
1989. Hudak, P. "The Conception, Evolution, and Application of Functional Programming Languages," *ACM Computing Surveys,* **21**, 3, 359–411.
1989. Hughes, J. "Why Functional Programming Matters," *Computer Journal,* **32**, 2, 98–107. Also at `http://www.cs.chalmers.se/~rjmh/Papers/whyfp.html`.
1991. Szymanski, B. K. (ed.) *Parallel Functional Languages and Compilers.* New York: ACM Press.
1996. Thompson, S. *HASKELL: The Craft of Functional Programming,* 2nd Ed. Reading, MA: Addison-Wesley.
1998. Bird, R. *Introduction to Functional Programming using Haskell,* 2nd Ed. London: Prentice Hall.

Websites

Journal of Functional Programming. `http://www.dcs.gla.ac.uk/jfp/`.
Frequently asked questions for comp.lang.functional. `http://www.cs.nott.ac.uk/Department/Staff/gmh/faq.html`.
Haskell home page. `http://www.haskell.org`.
Scheme repository. `http://www.cs.indiana.edu/scheme-repository/home.html`.

David S. Wise

FUZZY LOGIC

For articles on related subjects *see* APPROXIMATION THEORY; DISCRETE MATHEMATICS; INTERVAL ARITHMETIC; NEURAL NETWORKS; and NONMONOTONIC LOGIC.

The concept of a *fuzzy set*, introduced by L. A. Zadeh in 1965, deals with the representation of classes whose boundaries are not sharp. It uses a characteristic function taking values usually in the interval $[0, 1]$ (although other linearly ordered, or even partially ordered, finite or not, scales are sometimes used). In a fuzzy set, transition between membership and non-membership is gradual rather than abrupt; some elements that are considered as "marginal" or "less acceptable" are given a degree of membership that is intermediate between 0 (nonmembership) and 1 (full membership).

Fuzzy set-based methods, often referred to as *fuzzy logic*, have been used, particularly since the late 1980s, in a large variety of applications, including process and quality control, fault detection, production scheduling, robotics (*q.v.*), chemistry, civil engineering, ergonomics, project planning, management, and finance. Examples of popular, and especially visible, applications can be encountered in transportation systems (e.g. automatic guidance control of subway trains, unmanned helicopters, car gearboxes) and process control (e.g. the cement kiln industry), as well as in domestic appliances such as automated cameras, camcorders, rice cookers, and washing machines, where rules with fuzzy descriptors provide the model of the control strategy.

Historically, fuzzy sets have been mostly noted for their ability to model linguistic categories. This is due to the fact that many natural language concepts have *degrees of* applicability. Fuzzy sets provide an interface between the numerical data observed in the physical world and the linguistic categories that people apply to it. Thus fuzzy sets naturally arise when a finite set of terms has to be mapped to a linguistic scale. For instance, if the scale of human heights is chosen to be the real interval $[0, 250]$ in centimeters, to which a set of terms {short, medium-sized, tall} corresponds, then it is difficult to find exact thresholds a and b, such that, for instance short $= [0, a)$, medium-sized $= [a, b]$, and tall $= (b, 250]$. Indeed, the predicates *short, medium-sized, tall* are imprecise rather than clear-cut.

Fuzzy sets have been applied to a wide range of areas ranging from pure mathematics (especially fuzzy topology, fuzzy measure theory, fuzzy algebra) to the sciences, with a special emphasis on the engineering sciences. In the following, we focus particularly on the latter applications.

Semantics

Different semantics (interpretations) can be associated with the use of fuzzy sets. One—historically the oldest one—is the expression of closeness, proximity, simi-larity, indiscernibility, indistinguishability and the like. Under this semantics elements with membership 1 are viewed as prototypical elements of the fuzzy set, while the other membership values estimate the closeness of elements to the prototypical ones. This view is most commonly used in pattern classification, where objects that are judged to be sufficiently similar are gathered in the same (fuzzy) class. Moreover, the idea of similarity can be naturally graded by means of fuzzy relations, thus refining the idea of equivalence classes.

The idea of proximity is also central in interpolation processes, such as the ones used in fuzzy control, a methodology based on the use of fuzzy rules for synthesizing control laws. In this application decisions are computed from the conclusion parts of fuzzy rules expressing recommended actions, on the basis of the degrees to which a situation under consideration matches the fuzzy classes of situations described in the condition parts of the rules. Fuzzy set methods have found great success in the field of system modeling as a substitute for more conventional representation techniques. For example, fuzzy rule-based modeling has been extensively used in the development of fuzzy logic controllers. Many authors have been concerned with the problem of extracting fuzzy rules from data for function approximation and pattern classification purposes. Their approach is often based upon the use of fuzzy clustering techniques. In this approach, the centers of clusters obtained from the observations become the nuclei of fuzzy rules. Recent trends in fuzzy logic applications have emphasized purely data-driven concerns that seem gradually to dispose of the linguistic knowledge representation capabilities of fuzzy sets. Systems of fuzzy rules are then viewed as tools for the approximation of numerical functions that compete with neural networks and other mathematical methods of function approximation. The term *soft computing* is sometimes used when fuzzy rules are used only as a variant of neural nets or a means of encoding a nonlinear function.

A second semantics for fuzzy sets, introduced by Zadeh in 1978, is related to the representation of incomplete or vague states of information as *possibility distributions*, e.g. we know only that "John is tall" without knowing his height more precisely. Such a view of fuzzy sets enables imperfect, imprecise, or uncertain information to be modeled. This gives rise to a new theory of uncertainty. *Possibility theory* can be related to probability theory, but, whereas probability theory is additive, possibility theory is "maxitive": the possibility of a disjunction of events is the maximum of the possibilities of each event. Moreover the uncertainty of an event is captured by two degrees: possibility and necessity, instead of one. The possibility of an event is an estimate of its degree of "unsurprisingness," while its necessity evaluates its degree of acceptance. Possibility theory can be a purely ordinal construct, in which case it becomes just ordinal uncertainty theory, or possibility degrees can be noninteger numerical values, in which case they can be viewed as upper bounds on probabilities. Numerical possibility theory is then the simplest theory of imprecise probabilities.

Based on qualitative possibility theory, a possibilistic logic can be developed. In this logic, classical logic formulas are associated with lower bounds of necessity measures expressing the level of certainty or the "epistemic entrenchment" of the formulas. These certainty levels do not obey to a fully compositional calculus with respect to logical connectives as fuzzy set membership degrees do. Nonmonotonic inference relations can be represented in possibilistic logic, where a default rule "**if** p **then** q generally" is understood as the constraint stating that the possibility measure of "p **and** q" is strictly greater than the possibility of "p **and not** q."

A third semantics for a fuzzy set, useful when modeling a flexible constraint, specification, or goal, expresses preferences between more or less acceptable solutions with respect to the constraint, e.g. we are looking for somebody who is tall. The gradation introduced by the use of fuzzy sets refines the simple binary distinction made by ordinary constraints, crisp specifications, or all-or-nothing goals. This is especially important for using information in decision-making. More generally, classical constraint satisfaction algorithms, optimization methods (*q.v.*) and multifactor evaluation tasks can be extended in order to deal with both flexible requirements and uncertain data using a fuzzy set representation. The modeling of flexible queries by fuzzy sets provides a basis for rank-ordering the retrieved items according to a user's preferences. It avoids both overly strict requirements, which lead to empty sets of answers, and overly permissive requirements that result in many answers with no help provided to the user for choosing among them. When the evaluation of a (fuzzy) query is pervaded by the uncertainty and the imprecision coming from the stored data, one is led to distinguish between items which more or less possibly match the query and those which certainly match it to some degree.

Application Domains

Fuzzy sets offer an extensive framework for multi-aspect evaluation due to a very rich and axiomatically well-understood body of fuzzy set-theoretic operations. The fuzzy set approach encompasses compensatory modes of aggregation (such as averages for modeling trade-offs between criteria) and noncompensatory

modes (such as the min operation which expresses that *each* criterion should be satisfied as nearly as possible). Interactions between criteria and importance weighting can also be nicely handled in this framework. Fuzzy sets offer a methodology for devising hierarchical models of complex linguistic categories that embody high-level objectives. This subjective evaluation is typical of a wide class of applications of fuzzy set theory. For example, assessing how much a seat is comfortable, or a bank customer is creditworthy, are examples of complex categories for which fuzzy set-based models have been proposed.

Another kind of application of fuzzy sets to decision-making concerns reaching consensus in a group which must agree on a course of action. It is possible to build graded evaluations of consensus, which incorporate fuzzy quantifiers so as to model consensus criteria of the form "most people agree." The interaction between fuzzy sets and social choice or group decision-making is a fruitful field of investigation.

Fuzzy arithmetic is well suited to engineering design. Poorly specified parameters can be represented by fuzzy numbers, and since the parameters are controllable by the designer, membership functions represent preference profiles. Indeed, performing operations on fuzzy numbers comes down to a constraint propagation problem including preference propagation. Moreover, knowing the overall performance level enables design parameters to be chosen accordingly. In fact the whole field of fuzzy optimization, of which fuzzy engineering design is a subfield, is based on a max–min approach to decision-making under several objectives, of which the first application has been linear programming (*see* MATHEMATICAL PROGRAMMING). The uniqueness of the fuzzy max–min approach is to consider fuzzy specifications, goals, etc., as flexible constraints where satisfiability or feasibility is a matter of degree, but no compensation is allowed between the levels of satisfaction of the constraints. Fuzzy decision rules and fuzzy constraints are two complementary approaches to decision support in areas of decision-making such as production scheduling, and they can be used jointly.

Bibliography

1980. Dubois, D., and Prade, H. *Fuzzy Sets and Systems: Theory and Applications*. New York: Academic Press.
1987. Zadeh L. A. *Fuzzy Sets and Applications: Selected Papers* (eds. L. A. Zadeh, R. R. Yager, S. Ovchinnikov, R. M. Tong and H. T. Nguyen). New York: John Wiley.
1992. Bezdek, J. C., and Pal, S. K. *Fuzzy Models for Pattern Recognition—Methods that Search for Structures in Data*. New York: IEEE Press.
1993. Dubois, D., Prade, H., and Yager, R. R. (eds.) *Readings in Fuzzy Sets for Intelligent Systems*. San Francisco: Morgan Kaufmann.

1995. Klir, G. J., and Yuan, B. *Fuzzy Sets and Fuzzy Logic—Theory and Applications*. Upper Saddle River, NJ: Prentice Hall.

1996. Driankov, D., Hellendoorn, H., and Reinfrank, M. *An Introduction to Fuzzy Control*, 2nd Ed. Berlin: Springer-Verlag.

1996. Zadeh, L. A. *Selected Papers on Fuzzy Sets, Fuzzy Logic and Fuzzy Systems* (eds. G. J. Klir and B. Yuan). Singapore: World Scientific.

1996. Zimmermann, H. J. *Fuzzy Set Theory and its Applications*, 3rd Ed. Boston: Kluwer Academic.

1997. Dubois, D., Prade, H., and Yager, R. R. (eds.) *Fuzzy Information Engineering: A Guided Tour of Applications*. New York: John Wiley.

1998–1999. Dubois, D., and Prade, H. (eds.) *The Handbooks of Fuzzy Sets Series*, 7 volumes. Dordrecht: Kluwer Academic.

Didier Dubois and Henri Prade

GAMES

See COMPUTER GAMES.

GARBAGE COLLECTION

For articles on related subjects *see* LIST PROCESSING; STORAGE ALLOCATION; and STRING PROCESSING.

Many programming languages and systems provide for dynamic as well as static allocation of memory storage for data objects. The performance of these systems relies on their ability to reclaim and reuse storage for dynamically allocated objects after they are no longer needed by the executing program.

Some language systems (Pascal, for example) require programmers to return unneeded objects (*garbage*) to the memory system explicitly. Although this permits precise and efficient recycling of storage when done carefully, the extra conceptual burden it places on the programmer often results in objects being recycled prematurely or being forgotten and thus lost to the system. Other systems reclaim abandoned objects automatically through a process called *garbage collection*. Reclaiming storage automatically in this way is both a convenience to the programmer and a means of insuring that every object's storage is recycled correctly.

Garbage collection was first developed for list- and string-processing languages like Lisp and Snobol, then adapted to Smalltalk and other high-level integrated language systems. More recently, it has appeared in implementations of more traditional languages that support dynamically allocated data, including Modula-3 and Ada (*q.v.*), and is featured in functional programming (*q.v.*) languages like Haskell and ML, embedded languages like PostScript (*q.v.*), and in object-oriented languages like Java (*q.v.*), Dylan, and Eiffel.

Garbage collection occurs in two phases: identifying unneeded objects and then making their storage available for reallocation. We say that an object in a program is needed, or *live*, at a given time if the program might access that object in the future; otherwise, it is *dead*. In practice, garbage collectors consider an object to be dead only if the program has abandoned all pointers to it, making future access impossible. The two principal approaches to garbage collection differ primarily in the way they detect abandoned objects. *Reference counting collectors* maintain a count for each object of the number of pointers to it; an object is known to be dead when its count falls to zero. *Tracing collectors* identify as live those objects that are accessible either directly or indirectly from a set of root cells (essentially, the registers and named variables of the program). Objects that are not encountered during the trace are dead.

Tracing collectors are further distinguished by whether they copy or merely mark objects found to be live. *Copying collectors* relocate live objects into a new memory area as they are encountered during the trace. They then scan the objects in the new area, replacing the pointers to the old objects with their new values.

Finally, they reclaim the entire area from which the objects were copied. *Marking collectors*, on the other hand, simply flag live objects during the trace, then scan the memory area afterwards to find and reclaim unmarked objects.

Since garbage increases rapidly with memory size, large memory systems pose two critical problems. Long pauses for garbage collection are intolerable for interactive and real-time applications and may well dominate the execution time of large programs. Second, tracing garbage collectors access all of a program's live objects within a very short period of time. This severely violates the presumption of locality of reference that underlies virtual memory (*q.v.*) systems, so it usually results in excessive page thrashing (*q.v.*).

These problems have prompted the development of area-based *compacting collectors*. These copying collectors arrange for related live objects to be clustered into relatively small areas of memory that may be processed separately. If there are few instances of references between objects in different areas and if each area is small enough to fit within the working set (*q.v.*) of the program, then the garbage collection process itself is well-behaved with respect to the virtual memory and each pause is relatively short. Clustering also improves the locality of reference for the application program as well. Indeed, this property has become the prime motivation for incorporating compacting garbage collectors into many large-memory systems.

The performance of an area-based collector depends most critically on the principles by which it clusters objects into particular areas. The most successful techniques rely on two empirical observations concerning the lifetimes of objects: (1) newly created (young) objects tend to die quickly, while old ones are likely to continue living; and (2) objects seldom reference objects that are younger than themselves. *Generational scavenging* clusters objects into areas called *generations*, according to their ages. In this method, a scavenger process collects the younger (typically smaller) generations frequently. When an object has survived several collections in one generation, the scavenger relocates it to the next older generation, which it scavenges much less frequently.

Lifetime-based collectors are well-suited to interactive and soft real-time applications because they may be configured so that the pause to collect the youngest generation is well below one second. A *hard* real-time system, however, requires a deterministic collector with strictly limited worst-case time bounds. These collectors generally exploit the bounded incremental costs and improved locality of nongenerational copying collectors.

Garbage collection for languages that lack run-time typing of data objects is hampered by the difficulty of distinguishing pointers from the other possible contents of variables and data objects. Collectors for these languages usually rely on conservative variants of marking algorithms. During the tracing phase, they assume that if a cell contains the same bit value as a pointer to an object, then that object is live. This works well for systems with large, sparsely occupied address spaces and when pointer values are distinct from most small integers and floating-point values.

Bibliography

1996. Jones, R., and Lins, R. *Garbage Collection: Algorithms for Automatic Dynamic Memory Management.* New York: John Wiley.
200–. Wilson, P. R. "Uniprocessing Garbage Collection Techniques," *ACM Computing Surveys* (to appear).

David H. Bartley

GATE, LOGIC

See COMPUTER CIRCUITRY; and LOGIC DESIGN.

GATEWAY

For articles on related subjects *see* COMMUNICATION CONTROL UNIT; DATA COMMUNICATIONS; LOCAL AREA NETWORK; METROPOLITAN AREA NETWORK; NETWORK PROTOCOLS; NETWORKS, COMPUTER; OPEN SYSTEMS INTERCONNECTION; and PACKET SWITCHING.

A *gateway* is a communications device that interconnects networks. There are two common ways in which networks can be interconnected, and the term gateway is used to describe both.

1. A gateway can interconnect two or more network services. Fig. 1 shows a simple device that takes packets from one network and forwards them to another. The underlying technology and formats of packets may be different. The essential service/ protocol are the same. Alternative terms for this device are *router*, *switch*, and network or internetwork level relay. A gateway that verifies user identity and refuses network access to unauthorized users is called a *firewall*.

2. A gateway can convert between two different ways of providing a particular communications application (*see* Fig. 2). Alternative terms for such a gateway are *application level relay*, *application protocol converter*, and *application protocol translator*. An example of this is a device that takes electronic mail from one system and converts and forwards it to another.

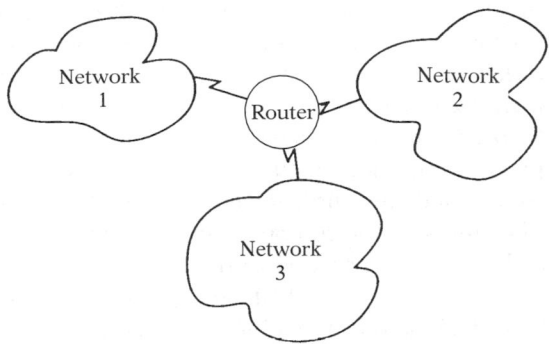

Figure 1. Gateway: internetwork router.

Both of these devices are distinct from *repeaters* and *bridges*. However, it has become common to combine the distinct logical functionality of a bridge and a router into a single physical unit, commonly known as a *bridging router*, bridge-router or *brouter*.

In the OSI model of service layering, a gateway operates either in layer 3 or layer 7. A repeater operates at layer 1, physically interconnecting similar or identical transmission media, while a bridge operates at level 2, forwarding identical frame formats, but potentially over very different media with possibly different access protocols.

The internal hardware system architecture of any of these interconnection devices can be built around a standard microcomputer, together with a bus (*q.v.*) connecting it to a number of communications link port controller devices. Alternatively, the system may be built around a special-purpose *switch fabric* with autonomous input and output port controller devices communicating directly with one another. When a router is of this latter design it is sometimes known as a *switched router*.

A gateway that interconnects networks at the packet forwarding level can operate in two different ways depending on the underlying network services it is interconnecting:

(a) *Datagram router*
This functions by receiving connectionless-mode network protocol data units (datagrams), and forwarding them on the basis of some routing table. Many such devices employ distributed algorithms to provide "dynamic routing", whereby each datagram is routed independently. ("Connectionless-mode" refers to such independent routing, which may not deliver datagrams in the order that they are sent.) When there are failures of networks, links, or routers, new routes are calculated.

(b) *Virtual circuit switch*
The networks interconnected by such a device provide a connection-oriented network service, often by using a protocol such as X.25. A gateway interconnecting two different X.25 networks does so on a "per connection" basis. This means that each end system establishes a path across a number of networks and gateways, and this is used for the duration of the communication. The routing table is usually calculated once for each path establishment.

Networks that employ different network services cannot be connected using network level relay type gateways. Instead, they must employ application level gateways, or else use some *ad hoc* means such as a Transport Service Bridge (Rose, 1990).

Bibliography

1990. Rose, M. T. *The Open Book.* Upper Saddle River, NJ: Prentice Hall.
1997. Stevens, W. R. *Unix Network Programming,* 2nd Ed., Vol. 1. Upper Saddle River, NJ: Prentice Hall.

Jon Crowcroft

GENERAL REGISTER

For articles on related subjects *see* ARITHMETIC-LOGIC UNIT; CENTRAL PROCESSING UNIT; INDEX REGISTER; and REGISTER.

A *general register* is a storage device that holds the input (operands and data for control) and the output (results) of the various functional units of a computing system. It is also used for temporary storage of intermediate results. The functional units referred to in the definition usually include the arithmetic logic unit (ALU), coprocessors if present, memory, the control unit, and various I/O processors.

The width of the register in bits is directly related to the precision of a binary integer as it appears to the

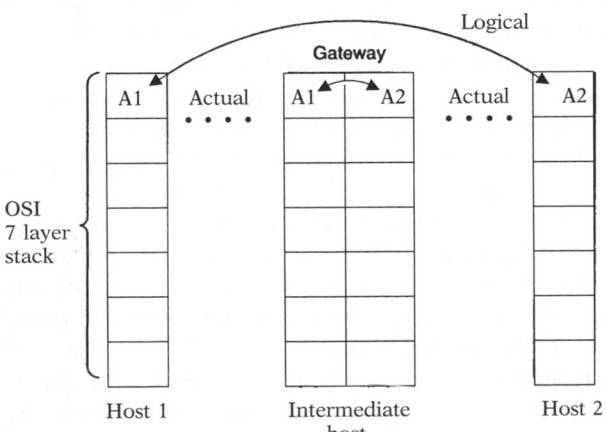

Figure 2. Application level gateway.

programmer, and does not necessarily reflect the width (data path) of the main memory addressable unit. Thus, in the Intel 80x86 series, for example, the general registers are 16 or 32 bits wide, although the memory is addressed in 8-bit bytes and accessed in 16-, 32-, or 64-bit units, depending on the model of the particular processor.

The registers operate at a speed that is matched to the speed of the units they serve. Their speed must be such that they do not slow down the functional units connected to them. In this sense they are the highest-speed storage in the memory hierarchy (*q.v.*) present in a computer.

Among the reasons for the presence of general registers, one should note their role in reducing the average number of bits needed to specify operands in a computer program. For example, one of 16 general registers can be addressed with four bits, whereas a main memory address for a memory of 1 billion locations requires a 30-bit address.

General registers may serve as arithmetic or logical registers, in which case they function as dedicated parts of the arithmetic-logic unit. If we denote registers by R, then a typical arithmetic or logical instruction will be $R_i \leftarrow R_j \circ R_k$, where $\circ$ stands for any arithmetic or logical operation, and i, j, k may be either distinct or equal (e.g. $R_2 \leftarrow R_2 + R_3$). In some machines, the specification of a register as part of an instruction can automatically increment or decrement its value by an amount that may vary by the operand type. Thus, for a byte, the change may be 1; for a 32-bit operand, the change may be 4. This attribute is particularly useful if the register is used as an *index register*.

General registers may also serve as shift registers (*see* SHIFTING); index registers, in which case they serve as address inputs to the memory unit; input–output registers, in which case they hold parameters that specify the connections and transfer-control parameters, etc.

The number of general registers varies widely between 1 and 1024. The numbers represent current architecture and hardware trade-offs, and are not to be taken as magic numbers. There are also computers that possess more than one set of general-purpose registers, computers that possess no general registers at all, and computers that possess specialized registers (such as vector registers, segment registers, and address registers).

Gideon Frieder

GENERATIONS, COMPUTER

For an article on a related subject *see* DIGITAL COMPUTERS, HISTORY OF.

Around the time of the marketing of the IBM System/360, that is, the late 1960s and early 1970s, the notion arose that computers evolved through three generations, characterized by the technology of their circuitry. According to this scheme the first generation of computers used vacuum tubes; the second, discrete transistors; and the third, integrated circuits. Examples of first-generation computers include the UNIVAC I and the IBM 701, as well as the small drum-based IBM 650 and Librascope LGP-30. Second-generation machines include the IBM 7090 and the Control Data CDC 1604, which used discrete transistors.

The System/360 did not use silicon integrated circuitry (*q.v.*) but rather a form of hybrid circuit, in which circuit elements were placed on a ceramic substrate. Although not a true IC-based computer as defined today, it was sufficiently different from previous computers to justify its inclusion in the third generation. There were enough other differences in the System/360 as well—its architecture, software, and the fact that it was not one machine but a series of computers—to distinguish it from its predecessors regardless of what base technology it used. By 1969 IBM had announced the follow-on, System/370, which did use true integrated circuits for memory as well as for logic.

As long as computers came in essentially one class, namely mainframe, this distinction was useful. As minicomputers and later personal computers and workstations appeared, however, this scheme broke down. Clearly these new classes of computers represented "new generation" technology in the vernacular sense of that term, and they were marketed and sold as such. Yet nearly all computers of all classes that have appeared in the last 25 years have used silicon integrated circuits, generally mounted on printed circuit boards.

Even before this definition of generation was used, engineers used the term "generation" in a less formal sense to denote any fairly substantial advance in circuit technology, architecture, packaging, software, or even marketing. The rapid pace of innovation in personal computers and workstations has led to the replacement of the earlier definition by one that is both less precise and that gives rise to short-lived generations. Thus one hears that the Altair was a "first-generation" personal computer, followed by the "second-generation" Apple II, with the Macintosh representing a new generation. Using the term this way implies a generational cycle of about three years, which is an accurate reflection of the pace of innovation in computing for the past two decades. New versions of popular microprocessors, especially those offered by Intel, are said to represent new generations as well. That description may represent a marketing tool rather than a true technical breakthrough, but we should remember that the initial definition of computer generations was also used for marketing purposes. The three-generation distinction seems to have survived as an historic artifact as the less formal definition has taken over.

For historians of computing, the use of this term has had an unfortunate consequence. By calling the UNIVAC and its siblings members of the "first generation," one relegates all that happened in computing before 1945 as "mere" prologue. Obviously the UNIVAC was profoundly different from the handcranked calculators in use earlier in the century. But in terms of the work that it did the UNIVAC does not represent such a great advance over installations of punched-card equipment found in typical commercial establishments of the 1930s. Focusing on the electronic technology, however important, blinds people to the purpose for which a computer was (and is) often bought—to do the same work that had been previously done in some other way.

This process of burying the past goes on, at least among popular histories of computing and especially in copy written by a company's marketing department. We thus find accounts written in the 1980s stating that the "computer age" began when the Apple II was introduced in 1977. More recently we hear that the "information age" really began in the early 1990s when the Internet broke through to a mass audience. Each time this happens the generation cycle starts all over again.

Paul Ceruzzi

GENETIC ALGORITHMS

For articles on related subjects *see* ALGORITHMS, DESIGN AND CLASSIFICATION OF; ARTIFICIAL LIFE; MOLECULAR COMPUTING; OPTIMIZATION METHODS; and NEURAL NETWORKS.

Genetic algorithms (GAs) are computational search, learning, optimization, and modeling methods, loosely inspired by biological evolution. Imitating the mechanisms of evolution has appealed to computer scientists from nearly the beginning of the computer age. Very roughly speaking, evolution can be viewed as searching in parallel among an enormous number of possibilities for "solutions" to the problem of survival in an environment where the solutions are particular designs for organisms. Viewed from a high level, the "rules" of evolution are remarkably simple: species evolve by means of heritable variation (via mutation, recombination, and other operators), followed by natural selection in which the fittest tend to survive and reproduce, thus propagating their genetic material to future generations. Yet these simple rules are thought to be responsible, in large part, for the extraordinary variety and complexity we see in the biosphere. Seen in this light, the mechanisms of evolution can inspire computational search methods for finding solutions to hard problems in large search spaces or for designing complex systems automatically.

GAs were originally formulated by Holland (1975) not to solve specific problems, but rather as a means to study formally the phenomenon of adaptation as it occurs in nature and to develop ways in which the mechanisms of natural adaptation might be imported into computer systems. Only after Holland's original work were GAs adapted to solving optimization problems.

In most GA applications, the user has a particular problem to be solved and a way to encode candidate solutions so that the solution space can be searched. For example, in the field of computational protein design, the problem is to design a one-dimensional sequence of amino acids that will fold up into a three-dimensional protein with desired characteristics (*see* BIOCOMPUTING). Assuming that the sequence is of length l, candidate solutions can be expressed as strings of l amino acid codes. There are 20 different amino acids, so the number of possible strings is 20^l. The user also provides a "fitness function" or "objective function" that assigns a value to each candidate solution as a measure of its quality.

Genetic algorithms begin with a population of randomly generated candidate solutions ("individuals"), and perform fitness-based selection and random variation to create a new population. Some number of the individuals of highest fitness are chosen under selection to create offspring for the next generation. Often, an offspring will be produced via a crossover between two or more parents, in which the offspring receives "genetic material" (different parts of candidate solutions) from different parents. Typically the offspring is also mutated randomly (parts of the candidate solution are changed at random). Offspring are created in this way until a new generation is complete. This process iterates for many generations, often ending up with one or more optimal or high-quality individuals in the population.

Genetic algorithms are one of several evolution-inspired search methods. Two other well-known methods are *evolution strategies* (ESs) and *evolutionary programming* (EP). These three methods were developed independently in the 1960s: GAs by Holland, ESs by Rechenberg and Schwefel (1995), and EP by Fogel, Owens, and Walsh (1966). (Genetic programming, a variant of genetic algorithms, was developed in the 1980s by Koza (1992, 1994, 1999)). Such methods were part of a general movement for using biological ideas in computer science that started with pioneers such as von Neumann (*q.v.*), Turing (*q.v.*), and Wiener (*q.v.*), and continues today with evolutionary methods, neural networks, and methods based on the immune system, insect colonies, and other biological systems.

GA, EP, and ES methods differ in many details—in general, ESs and EP each define fairly specific versions of the evolutionary process described above, whereas the term "genetic algorithm," while originally referring to a specific algorithm, has come to refer to many considerably different variations of the basic scheme. ESs were originally formulated to work on real-valued parameter optimization problems, such as aircraft wing-shape optimization. In the original formulation of EP, candidate solutions to given tasks were represented as finite-state machines (*see* SWITCHING THEORY), which were evolved by randomly mutating their state transition diagrams and selecting the fittest. Since the early 1990s there has been much cross-fertilization among the three areas, and the original distinctions among GAs, ESs, and EP have blurred considerably in the current use of these labels, and a somewhat broader formulation has emerged, known as "evolutionary computation."

Setting the parameters for the evolutionary process (population size, selection strength, mutation rate, crossover rate, and so on) is often a matter of guesswork and trial and error, though some theoretical and heuristic (*q.v.*) guidelines have been discovered. An alternative is to have the parameters "self-adapt"—by changing their values automatically over the course of evolution in response to selective pressures. Self-adapting parameters are an intrinsic part of ESs and EP, and are the subject of much research in GAs.

GAs, as well as EP and ESs, have been applied widely. Examples of applications include numerical parameter optimization and combinatorial optimization, the automatic design of computer programs, bioengineering, financial prediction, robot learning, evolving production systems for artificial intelligence (*q.v.*) applications, and designing and training neural networks. There has been considerable success in combining EC methods with other types of search methods, such as simple gradient ascent and simulated annealing. Such hybrid models are thought by many to be the best approach to optimization in complex and ill-understood problem spaces (Davis, 1991).

In addition to these "problem-solving" applications, evolutionary methods have been used in models of natural systems in which evolutionary processes take place, including economic systems, immune systems, ecologies, biological evolution, evolving systems with adaptive individuals, insect societies, and more complex social systems. (*See* Goldberg (1989), or Mitchell (1996) for an overview of applications in some of these areas.)

Much current research in the evolutionary computation field is on making the basic framework more biologically realistic, both for modeling purposes and in the hope that more realism will improve the search performance of these methods.

Bibliography

1966. Fogel, L. J., Owens, A. J., and Walsh, M. J. *Artificial Intelligence through Simulated Evolution.* New York: John Wiley.
1975. Holland, J. H. *Adaptation in Natural and Artificial Systems.* Ann Arbor, MI: University of Michigan Press. (Second edition: MIT Press, 1992.)
1989. Goldberg, D. E. *Genetic Algorithms in Search, Optimization, and Machine Learning.* Reading, MA: Addison-Wesley.
1991. Davis, L. D. (ed.) *Handbook of Genetic Algorithms.* New York: Van Nostrand Reinhold.
1992. Koza, J. R. *Genetic Programming: On the Programming of Computers by Means of Natural Selection.* Cambridge, MA: MIT Press.
1992. Michalewicz, Z. *Genetic Algorithms + Data Structures = Evolution Programs.* New York: Springer-Verlag.
1994. Koza, J. R. *Genetic Programming II: Automatic Discovery of Reusable Programs.* Cambridge, MA: MIT Press.
1995 Fogel, D. B. *Evolutionary Computation: Toward a New Philosophy of Machine Intelligence.* Los Alamitos, CA: IEEE Press.
1995. Schwefel, H-P. *Evolution and Optimum Seeking.* New York: John Wiley.
1996. Back, T. *Evolutionary Algorithms in Theory and Practice: Evolution Strategies, Evolutionary Programming, Genetic Algorithms.* Oxford: Oxford University Press.
1996. Mitchell, M. *An Introduction to Genetic Algorithms.* Cambridge, MA: MIT Press.
1999. Koza, J. R., Forrest, H. B., Martin, A. K., and David, A. *Genetic Programming III: Darwinian Invention and Problem Solving.* San Francisco: Morgan Kaufmann.

Melanie Mitchell

GEOGRAPHIC INFORMATION SYSTEM (GIS)

For articles on related subjects *see* COMPUTER GRAPHICS; DATABASE MANAGEMENT SYSTEM; and RELATIONAL DATABASE.

Geographic information describes the locations, characteristics, and shapes of features and phenomena on the surface of the earth. Traditionally, such information has been produced, disseminated, and used in the form of paper maps and atlases, using various projections to allow the curved surface of the earth to be represented on flat paper. Increasingly, however, it has been possible to produce such information in digital form, and the advent of instruments capable of sensing the earth's surface from space accelerated this process. Today, vast amounts of geographic information are available for use in digital form, and a system that handles, processes, edits, manipulates, analyzes, and displays such data is a called a *geographic information system* (GIS). It is estimated that the total annual sales of GIS software exceed $1 billion, and that the total activity related to digital geographic information is at least an order of magnitude greater.

History and Applications

GIS began in the mid-1960s; the Canada Geographic Information System is often credited with being the first major project. It applied computer technology to the analysis of vast amounts of map data collected by the Canada Land Inventory (Foresman, 1998). GIS requires specialized input and output devices, including map-sized *digitizers*, high-resolution *scanners*, and pen *plotters*, and the development of these peripherals in the 1960s was a major impetus. However the major growth period of GIS began only in the early 1980s, following the development of *database management systems* (DBMS) that support a *relational database* and super-minicomputers like the VAX and Prime. Today a GIS is most often encountered as a networked application running on Unix (*q.v.*) or Windows NT systems, although simpler versions are available for use in the field on smaller platforms, including palmtops (*see* PORTABLE COMPUTERS).

GIS databases make use of both *raster* and *vector* representations, and although most software products have capabilities in both areas, application domains tend to be dominated by one or the other. Raster-based representations are most common where remote sensing is a major source of raw data, and where spatial resolution is limited, and are thus most likely to be found applied to natural resource management, agriculture, forestry, or environmental science. In vector-based representations, geographic phenomena are represented as discrete points, lines, areas, or volumes, with associated attributes. In addition, there will be support for the representation of *topological* relationships between objects, including connectivity (e.g. street or sewer networks) and adjacency (e.g. administrative subdivisions). A vector-based GIS is most likely to be found in transportation, assessment and management of land ownership records, infrastructure and utility maintenance, vehicle routing and scheduling, and related applications.

An important concept in GIS is the *layer*, defined as a representation of some specific variable, class of objects, or phenomenon over the geographic area of the database. The ability to combine information from different layers, and thus to analyze the relationships between facts about the same geographic location that may be separated on different paper maps, is an important characteristic of a GIS, and one that helps to distinguish it from computer-aided design (*see* CAD/CAM). A layered map produced by the ARC-INFO GIS is shown in Fig. 1 under SCIENTIFIC VISUALIZATION on Color Page CP-14.

Architecture

Most GIS products, particularly those focused on vector-based applications, are built on a standard relational DBMS. Because of the difficulty of handling variable-length strings of coordinates efficiently in a relational DBMS, the early products of the 1980s adopted a *hybrid* architecture in which the attributes of objects and the topological relationships between them are represented in relational tables, and the geometric form of the objects is represented in a custom database. For example, a map of population by county could be represented in three structures: a relational

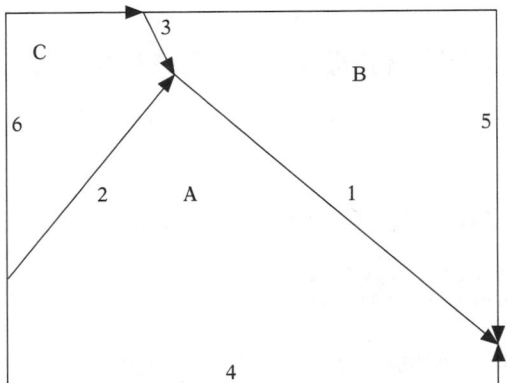

Figure 1. A simple map of counties (left) and the three structures used to represent it in a vector-based GIS: a relational table of county names and attributes (upper middle); a relational table of county adjacencies that indicates the area to the right and left of each directed edge with 0 representing the outside (upper right); and a file of ordered coordinates for each common boundary.

table identifying the name of each county and its associated population; a relational table identifying each common boundary between two counties with the names of the adjacent counties; and a file of variable-length records, each containing the ordered pairs of coordinates needed to describe one common boundary. Fig. 1 shows a simple example of this basic GIS concept (note the use of 0 to denote the unmapped area, and the use of the order of coordinates to determine the right and left sides of each common boundary).

More recently, the improved performance of computer platforms has allowed integration of all three data structures within a relational DBMS, leading to a new architecture in which the DBMS is the sole repository of the GIS database. Object-oriented models are also used, although to date most GIS products that use this approach are actually implemented over a relational DBMS. A raster-based GIS generally does not use a database product.

Functionality

GISs are characterized by (a) the ability to represent a wide range of geographic information types, and (b) functions to perform a wide range of manipulations. These include support for changes of projections and coordinate systems; determination of relationships between objects, such as proximity, overlap, or connectivity; calculation of statistics, ranging from measures of length and area to complex statistical analysis; display, including support for many map-making functions; and support for decision-making. An important set of GIS applications lies in vehicle routing and scheduling in support, for example, of school bus or parcel delivery systems. Such applications implement a range of methods of operations research in a spatial context.

Research Issues

A GIS is a challenging application, and much research effort is being devoted to advancing the technology. Among many topics, research focuses particularly on issues of representation (extending the set of GIS data models to include time, the third spatial dimension, and scale); uncertainty (description and modeling of the errors and inaccuracies of geographic information); and cognition (design of better user interfaces, and simplification of user interaction). The term *geographic information science* is increasingly used to denote basic research issues surrounding the use of digital geographic information.

Sources of Information

Several excellent texts and state-of-the-art reviews are available; see, for example, Burrough and McDonnell

(1998), Demers (1997), Longley *et al.* (1998), or Laurini and Thompson (1992). There are magazines devoted to GIS, including *GIS World* (published in Fort Collins, CO), and affiliated magazines are published in Europe and Asia. GIS research results are published in many journals, including the *International Journal of Geographical Information Systems, Transactions in GIS, Cartography and GIS,* and *Geoinformatica,* the last of which particularly encourages papers in the computer science aspects of GIS. Many international conference series address GIS research, including the International Symposium on Spatial Data Handling, the International Symposium on Spatial Databases, and the Conference on Spatial Information Theory.

Many Websites offer comprehensive resources on GIS, including `http://www.esri.com` (the Website of Environmental Systems Research Institute, Redlands, CA, a major GIS software developer), and `http://www.gisworld.com` (the Website of the magazine). The international UNIGIS consortium offers GIS courses by distance learning, and there are extensive curriculum materials available at `http://www.ncgia.ucab.org` (the Website of the US National Center for Geographic Information and Analysis).

Bibliography

1992. Laurini, R., and Thompson, D. *Fundamentals of Spatial Information Systems.* San Diego, CA: Academic Press.
1997. Demers, M. N. *Fundamentals of Geographic Information Systems.* New York: John Wiley.
1998. Burrough, P. A., and McDonnell, R. *Principles of Geographical Information Systems,* 2nd Ed. New York: Oxford University Press.
1998. Foresman, T. W. (ed.) *The History of Geographic Information Systems: Perspectives from the Pioneers.* Upper Saddle River, NJ: Prentice Hall.
1998. Longley, P. A., Goodchild, M. F., Maguire, D. J., and Rhind, D. W. (eds.) *Geographical Information Systems: Principles, Techniques, Management and Applications.* New York: John Wiley.

Michael Goodchild

GEOMETRY, COMPUTATIONAL

See COMPUTATIONAL GEOMETRY.

GLOBAL AND LOCAL VARIABLES

For articles on related subjects *see* BLOCK STRUCTURE; PROCEDURE-ORIENTED LANGUAGES; and SIDE EFFECT.

The entity denoted by a variable name in a computer program can generally be accessed (i.e. examined or changed) only in certain parts of the program. The domain of the program within which a variable name can be used is called the *scope* of the variable.

```
L1: begin
      real A, C, D; real array B[1:10];
      L2: begin
            real D, E; real array F[4:12];
            L3: begin
                  real F, G;
                  .
                  .
                  .
               end L3;
            L4; begin
                  real B, C, G;
                  .
                  .
                  .
               end L4;
         end L2;
   end L1;
```

Variable name	Label of defining block	Scope of name
A	L1	L1
B	L1	L1,~L4
C	L1	L1,~L4
D	L1	L1,~L2
D	L2	L2
E	L2	L2
F	L2	L2,~L3
F	L3	L3
G	L3	L3
B	L4	L4
C	L4	L4
G	L4	L4

Note: L1,~L4 means, for example, that the variable's scope holds throughout block L1 except for block L4.

Figure 1. Scope of variable names.

In a *block-structured* language, the scope of a variable is the block in which it is declared, but excludes any subblocks that are internal to the defining block *and* in which the same variable name is declared. This is illustrated in Fig. 1, which shows the schematic of an Algol program with an outer block L1 and an inner subblock L2, which in turn contains two further subblocks L3 and L4. Also shown in Fig. 1 is the scope of each variable. Note in particular that a variable like C, defined in the outer block, has a scope L1 but without L4 because C is declared again in L4. When a variable like the C declared in L1 exists but is not visible in an inner block (L4), it is said to have a *scope hole* there.

A variable in a block in which it is defined, like G in block L4 in the example, is said to be *local* to that block, and is therefore a local variable. Correspondingly, variable A is *global* to block L4, since it is defined outside this block, although it may be referred to in the block. The variable C defined in the outer block is also global to block L4, but it cannot be referred to in L4 because of the declaration of C in block L4, the latter (but different) C being local to L4.

Variables that are global to many blocks may conveniently be used by all of them, but the operations in one block may then interfere with those of another by changing a global variable. It is good programming practice to avoid such *side effects* by using global variables sparingly, if at all, and to share information between blocks by parameter passing (*q.v.*) in subprograms (*q.v.*).

Bibliography

1993. Louden, K. C. *Programming Languages: Principles and Practice*. Boston: PWS-Kent Publishing Company.

J. A. N. Lee and Anthony Ralston

GNU SOFTWARE

See FREE SOFTWARE FOUNDATION.

GRAMMARS

For articles on related subjects *see* BACKUS–NAUR FORM; CHOMSKY HIERARCHY; FORMAL LANGUAGES; LANGUAGE PROCESSORS; METALANGUAGE; PRODUCTION; PROGRAMMING LINGUISTICS; and SYNTAX, SEMANTICS, AND PRAGMATICS.

A *grammar* is an algebraic system describing the processes by which instances of a language can be constructed. A grammar consists of four elements—a set of *metavariables* or *nonterminal* symbols V_N (usually called *parts of speech* when dealing with natural languages); an alphabet V_T (or character set), often called the *terminal* symbols; a set of rules or *productions* P, which describe how a sequence of substitutions can be made for each metavariable; and a special metavariable S called the *starting* or *root* symbol, which is the starting point for the substitution process to be described below. These four elements are often represented by the quadruple $\{V_N, V_T, P, S\}$.

Grammars are most commonly classified into two groups—*context-sensitive* and *context-free*. In the case of context-sensitive grammars, the rules are applicable only when a metavariable occurs in a specified context—for example, the modification of verbs to their plural form in the context of plurality in the rest of the sentence in natural languages. By contrast, in a context-free grammar, any occurrence of a metavariable may be replaced by one of its alternatives, irrespective of the other elements in the language. Most programming languages appear at first glance to be describable by context-free grammars until consideration is given to the effect of declarations, such as the dimensions of an array or the specification of a procedure to support a procedure reference. In the discussion that follows, we will restrict ourselves to context-free grammars.

Grammars for high-level programming languages are called *generative* because, given a starting metavariable such as *sentence*, they specify a sequence of replacements or substitutions that can be applied to that name to form an instance (in this case, a sentence) in the language. For example, consider the following small grammar (where ::= is to be read "is defined to be"):

$$sentence ::= noun\text{-}phrase\ verb\text{-}phrase$$
$$noun\text{-}phrase ::= article\ noun$$
$$verb\text{-}phrase ::= verb\ noun\text{-}phrase$$

and

$$article ::= \text{the, a}$$
$$noun ::= \text{cat, milk}$$
$$verb ::= \text{drank}$$

where the italicized elements are metavariables and the nonitalicized elements are from the alphabet of the language. Using these rules, the sentence

The cat drank the milk.

can be generated by the following sequence:

sentence ⇒ *noun-phrase verb-phrase*.
⇒ *article noun verb-phrase*.
⇒ the *noun verb-phrase*.
⇒ the cat *verb-phrase*.
⇒ the cat *verb noun-phrase*.
⇒ the cat drank *noun-phrase*.
⇒ the cat drank *article noun*.
⇒ the cat drank the *noun*.
⇒ the cat drank the milk.

Equally, the sentences "the milk drank the cat" and "the cat drank the cat" can be generated, since they have the required underlying syntactic (grammatical) structure.

Similarly, consider the following grammar for simple forms of arithmetic expressions in high-level languages (where the vertical bar is to be read "or"):

add-op ::= + | −
mult-op ::= * | /
exp-op ::= **
primary ::= *constant* | *variable*
factor ::= *primary* | *primary exp-op primary*
term ::= *factor* | *factor mult-op factor*
arithmetic-expression ::= *term add-op term*

and where constants and variables then have usual definitions in computer languages. Then the expression

$$A + B * C ** D$$

could be generated as follows:

arithmetic-expression
⇒ *term add-op term*
⇒ *factor add-op term*
⇒ *primary add-op term*
⇒ *variable add-op term*
⇒ A *add-op term*
⇒ A + *term*
⇒ A + *factor mult-op factor*
⇒ A + *primary mult-op factor*
⇒ A + *variable mult-op factor*
⇒ A + B * *factor*
⇒ A + B * *primary exp-op primary*
⇒ A + B * *variable exp-op primary*
⇒ A + B * C *exp-op primary*
⇒ A + B * C ** *primary*
⇒ A + B * C ** *variable*
⇒ A + B * C ** D

During the compilation process for high-level programmable languages, we are interested not in generating the allowable strings in a language, but rather in syntactically analyzing or *parsing* the strings presented to the compiler. The function that performs this analysis is naturally called a *syntactic analyzer*. Grammars for high-level programming languages are commonly classified according to the types of syntactic analyzers used to parse them.

Syntactic analyzers can broadly be classified into two types: (1) the predictive types, which, starting from the root symbol, attempt to predict the means by which the string was generated; and (2) the reductive types, which attempt to reduce the string to the root symbol. These methods are loosely termed the *top-down* and *bottom-up* methods, respectively. The direction implied by these terms is related to the *syntactic trees* that may be generated by the analysis wherein the root symbol is at the top of the page and the string at the bottom. It may then be seen that a predictive (top-down) method starts at the top of the (yet unconstructed) tree and builds down toward the string, whereas the bottom-up (reductive) method starts at the string and attempts to develop a tree that converges to the root symbol.

For example, consider the grammar with

$$V_N = \{A, B, C, S, X\}$$
$$V_T = \{a, b, c, d, x, y\}$$

and the production rules

$$S ::= AX$$
$$A ::= aB$$
$$B ::= b$$
$$X ::= xC$$
$$X ::= yC$$
$$C ::= cd$$

which generates the language L with two strings {*abxcd, abycd*}. Note that, when a particular metavariable, such as X in this example, has more than one possible substitution for it, the productions are sometimes written

$$X ::= xC \mid yC.$$

When X is to be substituted for in a string, the syntactic analyzer must then choose one of the possible substitutions and, if this does not lead to a successful parse, try another. Typically, the possibilities are tried in left-to-right order when the production is written using the vertical bar.

The above grammar can be analyzed in either a top-down or bottom-up manner. For the string *abxcd*, we have

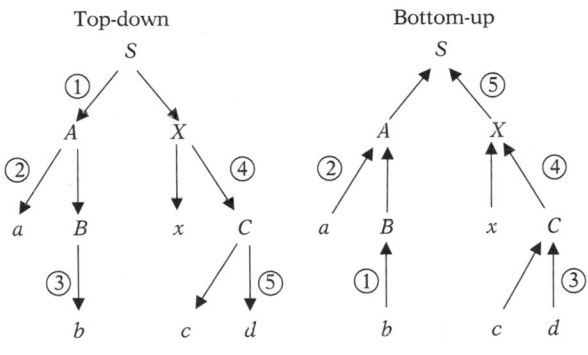

Top-down   Bottom-up

Growing from the root   Pruning toward the root

where the circled numbers indicate the order in which the rules are applied.

The top-down tree corresponds to the derivation

$$S \to AX \to aBX \to abX \to abxC \to abxcd$$

so that the numbers in the tree correspond to the steps in the derivation. Similarly, in the bottom-up case, the reduction shown in the tree corresponds to

$$abxcd \to aBxcd \to Axcd \to AxC \to AX \to S.$$

Since each metavariable appears on the left side of some production, in the top-down approach any metavariable in the string can always be replaced by the corresponding right side of the production. When going bottom-up, however, metavariables in the string may not correspond to the right sides of the productions (e.g. A in *Axcd* above). The bottom-up procedure is conveniently visualized by imagining a left-to-right scan across the string with successive characters put on a *stack* (*q.v.*) until a production can be applied. For the example above, this is illustrated as follows, where the symbol ∇ signifies the bottom of the stack.

Symbol scanned	Stack	Comments
a	∇a	
b	∇ab	
	∇aB	Using $B \to b$
	∇A	Using $A \to aB$
x	∇Ax	
c	∇Axc	
d	$\nabla Axcd$	
	∇AxC	Using $C \to cd$
	∇AX	Using $X \to xC$
	∇S	Using $S \to AX$

Notice, in particular, the ability to search down from the top of the stack (or, if you will, "remember" the previous contents of the stack) in order to determine if the top elements of the stack contain the right side of some production.

In the top-down derivation for the example above, whenever the derived string contained more than one metavariable, the leftmost one was used to generate the next string, thus leading to a *leftmost derivation*. Similarly, in the bottom-up derivation, the rightmost nonterminal was always replaced (indeed, in this example, there was no choice), thus leading to a *rightmost derivation*.

Studies of the development of parsers for programming languages have led to the definition of specialized grammars that are parsable by certain classes of analyzers. These can be divided into two classes that correspond directly to top-down (*predictive*) and bottom-up (*reductive*) analyzers and are known as either LL or LR grammars, respectively. LL grammars are defined by a parser which scans the input string from left-to-right (the first L in the name) and produces a parsing that corresponds to the leftmost (the second L) generation of the string. Where such a grammar (and corresponding parser) can accomplish the analysis with the examination of the next symbol to be generated in the string at each stage of the predictive process, then this is known as an LL(1) grammar. Where up to the next k symbols in the string may be required, it is called an LL(k) grammar. There exist languages that are LL(0); i.e. the predictor does not have to look at the string at all except to confirm conformance with the prediction in order to analyze the string. Obviously, a degenerate LL(0) grammar is one containing only a single production rule; other simple LL(0) grammars can be constructed, such as

$$A ::= aBe$$
$$B ::= bC$$
$$C ::= c.$$

LR grammars are reductive in processing style and are much more reliable in their analysis of complex languages once the generated parser tables have been

Table 1. Attributes of LL and LR grammars.

Attribute	LL	LR
Grammars	Can be hard to construct; rather awkward/unnatural. Class of LL grammars is small.	Rather straightforward. Can express virtually all programming constructs naturally.
Languages	Like the grammars, class is small but is adequate for the normal syntactic features of programming languages.	Can find an LR(1) grammar for *every* deterministic context-free language.
		Some examples of LR but not LL languages: $\{a^n\,b^n \mid n \geq 1\}$ $\cup\{a^n\,c^n \mid n \geq 1\}$ $\{a^n\,b^m \mid 1 \leq m \leq n\}$ $\{a^n 0 b^n \mid n \geq 0\}$ $\cup\{a^n 1 b^{2n} \mid n \geq 0\}$

Table 2. Grammars and languages of various types.

LR, left-parsable, not LL	$S ::= A \mid B$ $A ::= aaA \mid aa$ $B ::= aaB \mid a$
LR, not left-parsable	$S ::= Ab \mid Ac$ $A ::= AB \mid a$ $B ::= a$
Left- and right-parsable, not LR	$S ::= Ab \mid Bc$ $A ::= Aa \mid a$ $B ::= Ba \mid a$
Right-parsable only	$S ::= Ab \mid Bc$ $A ::= AC \mid a$ $B ::= BC \mid a$ $C ::= a$
Left-parsable only	$S ::= BAb \mid CAc$ $A ::= BA \mid a$ $B ::= a$ $C ::= a$

optimized. As with LL, the LR system scans the string from left to right, but, because of the use of reductive analysis, the derived syntactic structure is equivalent to the rightmost generation (the R in the name LR). As with LL grammars, an LR(k) grammar must examine up to k symbols in the analysis. Whereas the amount of processing to analyze a language by means of an LL(k) system increases rapidly as the number of symbols (k) to be examined at each stage increases, to the point where it is very uncommon to consider symbol groupings of more than one character at a time (i.e. LL(1) systems), the increase in complexity for increasing symbol groupings in LR systems is much smaller. Thus, it is more common to use LR(k) systems where k is greater than 1 to improve the efficiency of analysis and to minimize the changes that

have to be made to a context-free grammar in order to convert it to an acceptable LR(k) grammar. Table 1 lists some characteristics of LL and LR grammars and provides a comparison of the qualities of each grammar system.

For an example of the use of lookahead, consider the second grammar (LR, not left parsable) in Table 2. It can derive strings like *ac*, *aac*, *aaac*, *ab*, *aab*. Suppose that we are given the string *aac* and want a bottom-up derivation. Examination of the first symbol will not let us decide whether to reduce to *Bac* or *Aac*. A lookahead to the next symbol lets us derive *aBc*, and then $\Rightarrow ABc \Rightarrow AC \Rightarrow S$. Similarly, given input *ac*, the lookahead shows that the derivation is $ac \Rightarrow Ac \Rightarrow S$. Thus the grammar is LR(1).

Simply because a grammar is context-free, there is no guarantee that it can be converted into either an LL(k)

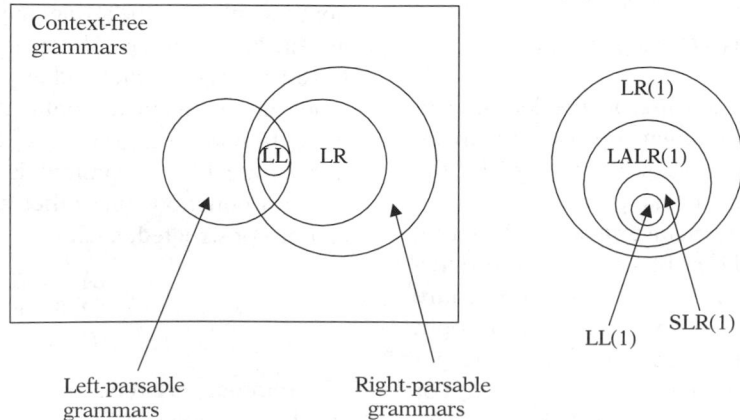

Figure 1. Relationships among grammars.

or an LR(k) type grammar by simple transformations. At each stage of either an LL or LR analysis, there must exist a unique relationship between the next k symbols in the string and a specific production in the grammar. If this relationship cannot be determined, then the grammar cannot be converted into one of the desired forms. Thus, there are grammars that are not LL and not LR and others that, though parsable to either a left or right derivative form by the addition of further information about the string, are not LL or LR, respectively. For example, to generate a leftmost derivation with the first grammar in Table 2, we must know whether the number of as is even or odd. If even, the derivation starts $S \Rightarrow A \Rightarrow aaA\ldots$; if odd, it starts $S \Rightarrow B \Rightarrow aaB\ldots$. A parser could produce this derivation by pushing symbols onto a stack and recording the even/odd (parity) count so that upon reaching the end of the input, it could use the count to choose the right start of the derivation. Such a mechanism is called a *pushdown automaton* (*see* AUTOMATA THEORY). A grammar that is parsable by a *deterministic* pushdown automaton is *left-parsable* if the parser produces a top-down derivation, or *right-parsable* if the derivation is bottom-up. The set of grammars in Table 2 are examples of some of these cases.

Although LR parsing techniques have been known since 1965, the parsers produced were far too large to be practical. However, optimizing techniques were discovered by DeRemer in 1969, resulting in modified grammars known as SLR (Simple LR) and LALR (Look-Ahead LR) parsers. Each of these is defined in terms of the optimization techniques that are used and are virtually impossible to construct by hand except in trivial cases. Basically, given an LR(1) system, the optimization process develops an LALR parser, while an LR(0) grammar can be converted into an SLR system. However, this process is not guaranteed for all LR grammars and, thus, the set of languages that can be optimized in this way is much smaller than that which may be represented by the LR system of grammars.

Fig. 1 illustrates some relationships of the grammars discussed in this article. Both Table 1 and the figure are due to N. Tindall.

Bibliography

1978. Lewis, P. M. II, Rosenkrantz, D. J., and Stearns, R. E. *Compiler Design Theory*. Reading, MA: Addison-Wesley.
1979. Aho, A. V., and Ullman, J. D. *Principles of Compiler Design*. Reading, MA: Addison-Wesley.
1996. Sudkamp, T. *Languages and Machines: An Introduction to the Theory of Computer Science*, 2nd Ed. Reading, MA: Addison-Wesley.

J. A. N. Lee

GRAPH THEORY

For articles on related subjects *see* ALGORITHMS, ANALYSIS OF; COMPUTATIONAL COMPLEXITY; DATA STRUCTURES; DISCRETE MATHEMATICS; NP-COMPLETE PROBLEMS; and TREE.

Terminology

A *graph* is a set of points (commonly called *vertices* or *nodes*) in space that are interconnected by a set of lines (called *edges*). For a graph G, the edge set is denoted by E and the vertex set by V, so that $G = (V, E)$. Common nomenclature denotes the number of vertices $|V|$ by n and the number of edges $|E|$ by m. Fig. 1 shows a graph G with $V = \{v_1, v_2, v_3, v_4, v_5\}$, $E = \{e_1, e_2, e_3, e_4, e_5, e_6, e_7\}$, $n = 5$, and $m = 7$. If, within E, each edge is specified by its pair of *endpoints* (e.g. for the example of Fig. 1, e_1 is replaced by (v_1, v_2) etc.), the figure can be dispensed with.

If, as in most applications, the values of both n and m are finite, G is said to be a *finite* graph. The *degree* of a vertex v (denoted by $d(v)$) is the number of edges that have v as an endpoint. An elementary theorem (with an easy inductive proof) is that within a finite graph there are always an even number of vertices with odd degree. For example, in the graph of Fig. 1 there are two vertices (v_1 and v_2) of odd degree (both have degree 3). A *self-loop* is an edge (v_i, v_j) where $v_i = v_j$. Two edges (v_i, v_j) and (v_r, v_s) are *parallel edges* if $v_i = v_r$ and $v_j = v_s$. A *simple graph* is a graph without self-loops and without parallel edges. A *multigraph* contains parallel edges but no self-loops. A *path* between vertices v_1 and v_s is a sequence of vertices $(v_1, v_2, v_3, \ldots, v_s)$ such that $(v_i, v_{i+1}) \in E$ for $1 \leq i \leq s - 1$. If $v_1 = v_s$, the path is a *circuit* (or cycle). If no vertex appears more than once on a path, then the path is a *simple path* (similarly, a *simple circuit* passes through any vertex at most once). A *component* of a graph is defined by stating that a path exists between any pair of vertices if and only if the two vertices belong to the same component of the graph. A graph consisting of a single component is said to be a *connected graph*. A *tree* is a connected

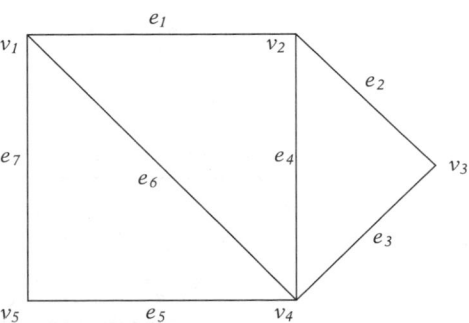

Figure 1. A graph with 5 vertices and 7 edges.

graph containing no circuits. For any tree T with n vertices and m edges, $m = n - 1$ and there exists precisely one path between any pair of vertices of T.

In many applications it is natural to associate a direction with each edge of the graph. The graph is then said to be a *directed graph* or *digraph*. In specifying any edge of a digraph by its endpoints, by convention the edge is understood to be directed from the first vertex towards the second. The *indegree*, $d^-(v)$, of any vertex v is the number of edges directed towards v. Similarly, the *outdegree*, $d^+(v)$, of v is the number of edges directed from v. A digraph G is *strongly connected* if, for any pair of vertices u and v of G, there exists a path from u to v and a path from v to u.

Any *subgraph* of a graph G can be obtained by removing vertices and edges from G. It is understood that the removal of an edge leaves its endpoints in place, whereas the removal of a vertex necessitates the removal of any edges with that vertex as an endpoint. An *articulation point* of a connected graph is any vertex whose removal produces a subgraph with two or more components. Any graph with no articulation point is said to be *2-connected*. In a 2-connected graph there are at least two vertex-disjoint paths between any pair of vertices. Two paths are *vertex disjoint* if (apart from the ends of the path) they do not share a vertex. A 2-connected component (sometimes called a *block*) of a graph G is a maximal subgraph G' of G (maximal in the sense that no additional edges or vertices of G can be added to G') such that there are at least two vertex-disjoint paths between every pair of vertices of G'.

Many applications require a number to be associated with each edge of a graph. Such a graph with associated *edge weights* is said to be a *weighted graph*. For any edge (u, v), $w(u, v)$ denotes the edge weight, which is also sometimes called the *length* of (u, v).

In a *complete graph*, there is an edge between every pair of vertices. The complete graph with n vertices is denoted by K_n. Fig. 2 shows K_3 and K_4. In a *regular* undirected graph, every vertex has the same degree; if this is k, the graph is *k-regular*. Note that K_n is $(n - 1)$-regular.

If, for a graph G, it is possible to partition the vertex set v into two disjoint subsets, V_1 and V_2 ($V_1 \cup V_2 = V$), such that every edge of G connects a vertex in V_1 to a vertex in V_2, then G is a *bipartite graph*. If there is an edge between every vertex of V_1 and every vertex of V_2, then G is said to be a *complete bipartite graph*, which is denoted by $K_{i,j}$, where $|V_1| = i$ and $|V_2| = j$. Fig. 3 shows two representations of $K_{3,3}$. In this figure, dots distinguish vertices from edge crossings. The graphs of this figure are said to be *isomorphic*. Two graphs are

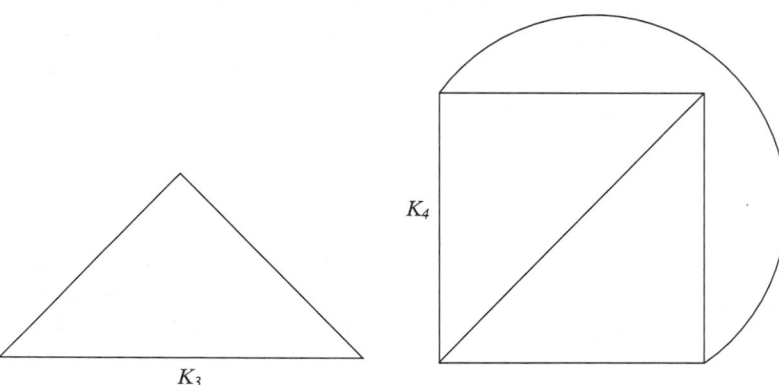

Figure 2. Tfhe complete graphs with 3 and 4 vertices.

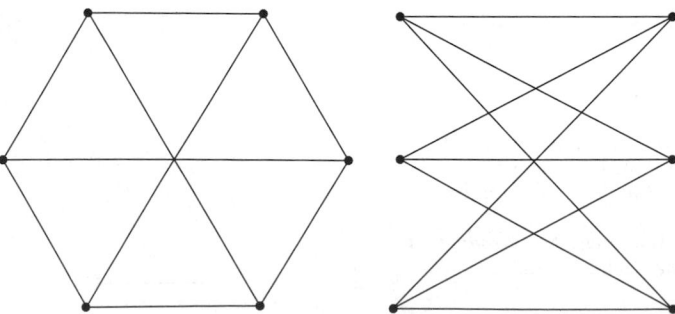

Figure 3. The complete bipartite graph $K_{3,3}$.

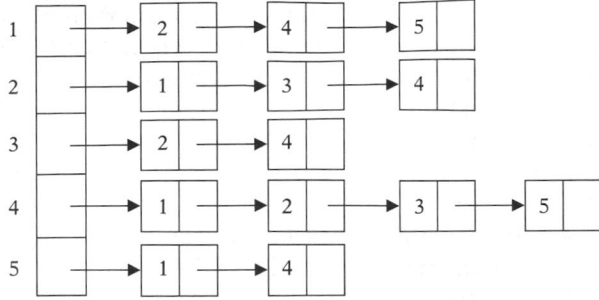

Figure 4. An adjacency list representation of the graph of Fig. 1.

isomorphic if there is a one-to-one correspondence between the vertices of one and the vertices of the other such that the number of edges between any two vertices of one is equal to the number of edges between the corresponding vertices in the other.

Computations involving graphs require that the graph be represented somehow within computer storage. The choice of data structure may have important implications for the complexity of the algorithm. A natural form of representation is provided by a so-called *adjacency matrix*. An adjacency matrix A is an $n \times n$ matrix where $A(i, j) = 1$ if $(v_i, v_j) \in E$ and is 0 otherwise. Such a representation requires $O(n^2)$ storage space and consequently requires $O(n^2)$ time to initialize. Adjacency matrices are very useful for algorithmic questions concerning paths in graphs. For example, it is not difficult to show that there is a path of length r (i.e. having r edges) from v_s to v_t if and only if $A^r(s, t) = 1$, where A^r is the rth matrix product. Another common data structure for graphs is the so-called *adjacency list* representation. In this representation, for every $v \in V$, $L(v)$ is a pointer to a list of vertices adjacent to v. Fig. 4 shows the adjacency list representation of the graph of Fig. 1. The adjacency list representation of a graph requires $O(n + m)$ space and thus $O(n + m)$ time to initialize. From the point of view of complexity considerations, this is usually an improvement compared with adjacency matrices.

Graph Algorithms

Many graph algorithms are structured by systematically searching (or *traversing*) the graph subjected to the algorithm. Consider the following technique for traversing a (connected) graph. Initially, mark all vertices as being "unvisited." Now start the search at some arbitrarily chosen vertex and, when visiting any vertex v, proceed as follows. If v has not been previously visited, mark v as "visited." Next, visit an "unvisited" vertex in the adjacency list for v. If no such vertex exists, return to the vertex visited just before v was visited for the first time. The visit terminates when all vertices adjacent to the initial vertex have been visited and the search has returned to the initial vertex.

Such a search is called a *depth-first search* (DFS). A DFS of a graph G has certain useful properties: (a) the set of edges by which vertices are visited for the first time form a tree (called the DFS tree and rooted at the initially visited vertex), (b) edges of G not belonging to the DFS tree connect two nodes, one of which is a descendant of the other in the DFS tree, (c) DFS can be achieved in $O(n + m)$ time. Another frequently employed traversal method is *breadth-first search* (BFS). In a BFS for a connected graph, some arbitrary vertex is visited first, and this vertex is placed on an initially empty queue (first in, first out data structure), Q. At any point in the traversal, remove the head element in the queue and then mark all vertices adjacent to the element removed "visited" and place them on the queue. Repeat this until the queue becomes empty. A BFS of G has the following properties: (a) the edges by which vertices are first visited form a BFS tree rooted at the initially visited vertex, (b) those edges of G not in the BFS tree connect vertices neither of which is an ancestor of the other in the BFS tree, (c) BFS can be achieved in $O(n + m)$ time.

Particular types of traversal of a graph such as those just described have individual properties that make them appropriate for particular algorithmic application. For example, the properties of DFS lead to a classic $O(n + m)$ algorithm to find the blocks of a graph. Similarly, application of DFS to digraphs provides an $O(n + m)$ algorithm to find the strongly connected components of a digraph. In a BFS of an undirected graph, the depth of a vertex v in the BFS tree rooted at v' is precisely the shortest distance from v to v' in the original graph. This leads to an $O(n + m)$ algorithm for finding distances between a single vertex and all the other vertices in a graph (which is the so-called *single source shortest paths problem*). Such a search, however, is not useful when shortest paths in weighted graphs are required. In such graphs, distances are measured as the sum of the edge weights (rather than in numbers of edges) on a path, and there are several classic algorithms for the single source shortest paths problem (such as *Dijkstra's algorithm*, which operates in $O(n^2)$ time with simple data structures that can be improved to $O(m + n \log n)$, using sophisticated structures). There now follows a catalog of commonly occurring graph problems with some indication of their algorithmic complexities. Algorithms for these problems can be found in the references or in the primary sources cited therein. Many problems concerning graphs are intractable, being NP-complete (q.v.) (Garey and Johnson, 1979).

An *Eulerian circuit* of a graph is a circuit that contains every edge of the graph precisely once. Of course, not every graph contains an Eulerian circuit. In fact, a necessary and sufficient condition for a connected, undirected graph to contain an Eulerian circuit is that every vertex of the graph is of even degree. If the graph is a directed connected graph, it contains an Eulerian circuit (such a circuit traces each edge in the sense that it is directed) if and only if for each vertex v, $d^+(v) = d^-(v)$. Eulerian circuits can be found in $O(m)$ time. Eulerian circuits, for the special class of graphs that contain them, are solutions of the *Chinese postman problem*. Given a weighted graph or digraph, the Chinese postman problem is to find a (not necessarily simple) circuit of shortest length (the length is given by $\sum_{\text{all edges } e} w(e)r(e)$, where $w(e)$ is the weight of e and $r(e)$ is the number of occurrences of e in the circuit) that traverses each edge of the graph at least once. Every connected undirected graph contains a solution to the Chinese postman problem, whereas a connected digraph has a solution if and only if the digraph is strongly connected. There are low-order polynomial-time algorithms for the Chinese postman problem for both undirected and directed connected graphs.

A *Hamiltonian circuit* of a connected graph is a circuit that passes through each vertex precisely once. Such a circuit can be defined for both directed and undirected graphs (of course, in the case of digraphs, edges are traversed in the same sense as they are directed). Not every graph contains a Hamiltonian circuit and (unlike the case for Eulerian circuits) there seems to be no polynomial time test for whether such a circuit exists for a given graph. In fact, the problem of determining whether a graph contains a Hamiltonian circuit is a classic NP-complete problem. If the graph is weighted, the problem of finding a shortest Hamiltonian circuit is one variation of the well-known *traveling salesman* problem. Another variant is to find the shortest circuit that passes through each vertex *at least* once. In this second form, a solution to the problem always exists, whereas for the former specification the graph of course has to contain a Hamiltonian circuit. In both these forms, the traveling salesman problem is NP-complete.

A (*transport*) *network* is a connected digraph in which one vertex x (called the *source*) has $d^+(x) > 0$ and one vertex y (the *sink*) has $d^-(y) > 0$. A flow of the network associates a weight $f(e)$ with each edge e such that, for all vertices v other than x or y, $\sum_{(u,v)\in E} f(u, v) = \sum_{(v,u)\in E} f(v, u)$. Clearly, a network is a model for the flow of material leaving a single departure point (the source) and arriving at a single point (the sink). The equation ensures a conservation of flow at all other vertices. It is usual to associate (apart from $f(e)$) another parameter (called the *capacity* of e and denoted by $c(e)$) with each edge, which is the maximum value that $f(e)$ can attain. Thus, $0 \leq f(e) \leq c(e)$ for all e. For a network N, $F(N)$ denotes the value of the flow that is defined to be the net flow leaving the source: $F(N) =$

$\sum_{(x,v)\in E} f(x, v) - \sum_{(v,x)\in E} f(v, x)$. A standard problem in network theory is to find a set of $f(e)$ such that $F(N)$ is a maximum. This is called the *maximum flow problem*. The problem of finding a maximum flow has a low-order, polynomial-time solution. The value of such a flow is given by the classic theorem of Ford and Fulkerson (called the *max-flow, min-cut theorem*), which states that $F(N)$ has a maximum value equal to the minimum capacity of all cuts of the network. A *cut* of the network is a minimal set of edges whose removal from the network separates the network into two components, one containing x and the other containing y. The capacity of the cut is the sum of the capacities of those edges in the cut that are directed from the component containing x and directed towards the component containing y. Many other problems can be posed for networks. For example, if yet another parameter (called the cost of e and denoted by $a(e)$) is associated with each edge, the *minimum cost flow problem* is to find (for a given value $F(N)$) a set of $f(e)$ such that the sum $\sum_{(u,v)\in E} f(u, v)a(u, v)$ is minimized. Again, there are low-order, polynomial-time algorithms to solve this problem.

Planar graphs are an important subclass of graphs. A graph is planar if it can be arranged on a planar surface (the arrangement is called an *embedding*) so that, at most, one vertex occupies or, at most, one edge passes through any point of the plane. There exist algorithms that can test whether a graph is planar (such algorithms normally generate an embedding) in $O(n)$ time.

Scheduling and timetabling problems, among others, generate problems equivalent to coloring graphs. A *vertex coloring* of a graph is the assignment of a color to each vertex of the graph in such a way that no two adjacent vertices have the same color (vertices are adjacent if there is an edge connecting them). Normally, the interest is to find a vertex coloring that employs a minimum number of colors; this number is called the *vertex-chromatic index*. Similarly, an *edge coloring* is an assignment of colors to the edges in such a way that no two edges sharing an endpoint have the same color. The minimum number of colors required to do this is the *edge-chromatic index*. Problems involving the coloring of graphs are notoriously intractable. For example, the problems of determining whether the vertex- or the edge-chromatic index is less than some fixed constant are both NP-complete.

A *matching* of a graph is a subset of its edges such that no two elements of the subset have a common endpoint. The question of determining matchings arises in many guises. Common problems concern finding *maximum cardinality matchings* (such a matching has a maximum number of elements) and *maximum weight matchings* (which occur for weighted graphs; the sum of the edge weights of such a matching is maximized). Efficient (polynomial-time) algorithms are known for both of these problems.

A *spanning tree* of a connected graph G is a connected circuitless subgraph of G that contains every vertex of G. The *connector problem*, a classic problem of graph theory, is to find a spanning tree of a weighted connected graph such that the sum of the edge weights of the tree is a minimum. Such a solution is also called a *minimum weight spanning tree*. Spanning trees can be found in $O(m + n)$ time (e.g. a depth-first search tree). Prim's or Kruskal's algorithms provide classic solutions to the connector problem at low-order polynomial-time cost.

The *vertex-connectivity* $K_v(G)$ of a connected graph G is the minimum number of vertices that have to be removed from G in order to produce a subgraph of two or more components. If a graph has $K_v(G) = k$, there are k vertex disjoint paths between every pair of vertices. The *edge-connectivity* $K_e(G)$ is similarly defined. Also, if $K_e(G) = k$, there are k edge disjoint paths between every pair of vertices. There exist polynomial-time solutions to the problems of finding $K_v(G)$ and $K_e(G)$ for an arbitrary graph G.

Given two graphs G_1 and G_2, many applications of graphs require one of the following two problems to be solved. (a) Is G_1 isomorphic to G_2? (This is called the *graph isomorphism problem*.) (b) Is G_1 isomorphic to a subgraph of G_2? (This is the *subgraph isomorphism problem*.) Both of these problems are notoriously costly to solve, and no polynomial-time solution is known for either if G_1 and G_2 are arbitrary graphs.

Given the intractability of many problems in graph theory, it is natural that this area has given rise to the development of many approximation algorithms. An *approximation algorithm* is an algorithm that runs in polynomial-time but that provides an approximation (within known bounds) to the problem in hand. A classic example is provided by *Christofides' algorithm*, which finds a solution to the traveling salesman problem that guarantees that the solution found is no more than a factor of 3/2 longer than an optimum solution. While this approximation may not seem to be very tight, no approximation algorithm is presently known that provides a better guarantee. Another example provides an approximation for the edge-chromatic index of a graph and is the polynomial-time algorithm implicit in the proof of *Vizing's theorem*. This algorithm gives an edge coloring using no more than one more color than is necessary, a very good approximation. Unless there are polynomial-time solutions for the NP-complete problems (an unlikely possibility), it has been proved that there can be no polynomial-time

solution that gives a vertex coloring of an arbitrary graph that guarantees to use less than twice the minimum number of colors required.

Bibliography

1976. Biggs, N. L., Lloyd, E. K., and Wilson, R. J. *Graph Theory 1736–1936.* Oxford: Oxford University Press.
1979. Even, S. *Graph Algorithms.* Potomac, MD: Computer Science Press.
1979. Garey, M. R., and Johnson, D. S. *Computers and Intractability: A Guide to the Theory of NP-Completeness.* San Francisco: Freeman.
1985. Berge, G. *Graphs*, 2nd Ed. Amsterdam: North-Holland.
1985. Gibbons, A. M. *Algorithmic Graph Theory.* Cambridge: Cambridge University Press.
1990. van Leeuwen, J. *Graph Algorithms.* Chapter 10, *Handbook of Theoretical Computer Science*, Volume A (Algorithms and Complexity) (ed. J. van Leeuwen). New York: Elsevier.
1995. Harary, F. *Graph Theory.* Cambridge, MA: Perseus Press.
1997. Wilson, R. J. *Introduction to Graph Theory.* Reading, MA: Addison-Wesley.

Alan M. Gibbons

GRAPHICAL USER INTERFACE

See USER INTERFACE; and WINDOW ENVIRONMENTS.

GRAPHICS

See COMPUTER GRAPHICS.

GROUPWARE

For articles on related subjects *see* BULLETIN BOARD; COMPUTER CONFERENCING; ELECTRONIC MAIL; INTERNET; ONLINE CONVERSATION; and WORLD WIDE WEB.

Groupware refers to a class of technologies that enable, facilitate, and mediate interpersonal relationships among participants engaged in accomplishing a group task. It must be able to support two or more users engaged in a common task and provide the users with an interface to a shared environment (Ellis *et al.*, 1991). The overall goal of groupware is to increase sources of gain that can arise from group work while limiting potential losses (Holsapple and Whinston, 1996). Sources of gain include the group having greater knowledge than any individual, synergy and stimulation from exchanges among participants, and participants learning from the behaviors of others in the group. Examples of potential losses include limited speaking time among participants, reluctance to share ideas, excessive socializing, and free riding. In practice, groupware denotes systems that support multiparticipant communication, collaboration, and coordination in the course of organizational activity. Thus, groupware is an area of organizational computing, the

Table 1. Supporting technologies for groupware.

Communication	Cooperation	Collaboration	Coordination
Email	Shared agendas	Shared agendas	Shared agendas
File transfer	Document processing	Whiteboarding	Project management
Bulletin boards	Shared to-do lists	Document processing	Shared to-do lists
	Shared databases	Shared to-do lists	Task automation
		Shared databases	
		Task automation	

field of study and practice concerned with discovering and developing useful fits between computing possibilities and organizational (in contrast to individual) needs (Applegate *et al.*, 1991).

Groupware technologies can be categorized according to their support of communication, collaboration, and/or coordination (Table 1). For example, electronic mail, file transfer, computer conferencing, and electronic bulletin board technologies support group communication. Group calendaring/scheduling systems, shared agendas, and to-do lists support collaboration and coordination. Collaboration on a project or task is facilitated by electronic whiteboards, intranets, and document processing systems that allow several people to work on a document simultaneously. Electronic meeting systems support collaboration by allowing parallel communications and providing a group memory. Group coordination is supported by project management tools and workflow systems (e.g. smart document systems).

An early advance in groupware systems was the development of meeting-room technology and group decision support systems. These efforts concentrated on augmenting the efficacy of meetings and small group discussions, with an emphasis on same place, same time interaction. Since then, groupware has made enormous strides. Networking technology and the proliferation of the Internet have allowed electronic communication (via email) and information dissemination (via the World Wide Web) to become established business communication methods. It is only natural that businesses would want to use the power of the networking technology to improve efficiency and effectiveness. Groupware vendors are blurring the distinction between the corporate network and the Internet by offering products that function equally well in either environment. Several of the best known groupware packages (Lotus Notes, Microsoft Exchange, Netscape SuiteSpot, and Novell GroupWise) all either offer Internet capability, or are built upon the technology of the Internet.

There is a fundamental difference between groupware and other systems that support multiuser activity, such as database management systems (*q.v.*—Applegate *et al.*, 1991). The aim of the database approach to information locking is to create the impression that users are working on a single, isolated task. The underlying design philosophy is that each user should work independently of others and remain unaware of their actions. In groupware systems, the fundamental design philosophy is that group processes must be actively supported and that each user must be made aware of the context in which his or her tasks are being executed. Hence, weak locking mechanisms like *telepointers* (cursors that appear on more than one display and can be moved by different users) are used.

Groupware has become important because in today's setting of diverse, interdependent, and competing organizational forms, improvement of organizational effectiveness is a paramount concern. The globalization of many businesses has greatly reduced the traditional meeting as a viable tool for much of the required decision making. The combination of increased competition and the impact of the global economy requires more than improving intrinsic individual productivities. It entails the creation, use, and maintenance of both structural and dynamic configurations of interaction such that an organization's productivity is maximized or improved on a continuing basis. Groupware is concerned with the ways in which computing technologies can facilitate such efforts. Emphasis on project, team, and workgroup management styles in combination with significant reliance on computer technology has also fostered the emergence of groupware.

Groupware is a multidisciplinary research area that draws on theories from distributed systems (*q.v.*), parallel processing (*q.v.*), cognitive engineering of interactive software, model management, social psychology, sociology, organizational design, and economics (Applegate *et al.*, 1991). The grand challenge facing groupware researchers and developers is to create theories that bind research streams from multiple disciplines. At the theoretical end, there is a need for the identification and/or creation of mathematical frameworks and models of group, team, and organizational roles, tasks and procedures. From a systems development perspective, key research issues include the development of multiuser, multimedia (*q.v.*) interfaces, distributed concurrent architectures for shared objects, and a variety of flexible interaction locking mechanisms.

Bibliography

1991. Applegate, L. M., Ellis, C. A., Holsapple, C. W., Radermacher, F. J., and Whinston, A. B. "Organizational Computing: Definitions and Issues," *Journal of Organizational Computing*, **1**, *1*, 1–10.
1991. Ellis, C. A., Gibbs, S. J., and Rein, G. L. "Groupware: Some Issues and Experiences," *Comm. of the ACM*, **34**, 1.
1996. Holsapple, C. W., and Whinston, A. B. *Decision Support Systems: A Knowledge Based Approach*. St Paul, MN: West Publishing.

C. W. Holsapple, K. Sims, and A. B. Whinston

GUARDED COMMAND

For articles on related subjects *see* CONCURRENT PROGRAMMING; CONTROL STRUCTURE; PROGRAMMING LANGUAGE SEMANTICS; and PROGRAM VERIFICATION.

The term *guarded command*, as defined by Dijkstra (1975), is synonymous with a conditionally executed statement. More precisely, a guarded command is the combination of a condition (boolean expression) B and the (possibly compound) statement S whose execution is controlled by B. In a sense, B "guards" the execution of S. In Dijkstra's notation, a guarded command is represented as $B \rightarrow S$. In more common notation, the meaning of a guarded command is very much like that of the simple selection structure (**if** statement): **if** B **then** S. Unlike the **if** statement, however, a guarded command, by itself, is not a complete statement in a programming language. Rather, it is one component of a more extensive control structure containing one or more guarded commands. The most interesting applications of guarded commands are those involving a set of n of them, for $n > 1$.

$$B_1 \rightarrow S_1$$
$$B_2 \rightarrow S_2$$
$$\vdots$$
$$B_n \rightarrow S_n$$

Here there are n boolean expressions, each guarding a different statement. When a structure containing a set of guarded commands is executed, the guards are evaluated; the order in which they are evaluated is completely immaterial. Upon evaluation of all n, a subset (which may be empty) of the guards will have the value **true**. Of this subset, one is chosen *at random*; it is the corresponding S that is selected for execution.

If all of the guards in a given guarded command set are disjoint—that is, if no more than one guard is **true** at any given time—then the selection of S is well-defined despite the unspecified and random nature of

guard evaluation and selection. If, however, the guards are not disjoint, with the possibility that more than one may be true simultaneously, then selection of S is not well defined (and indeed may be different from one execution of the program to the next). For this reason, guarded command sets are fundamentally *nondeterministic*. The nondeterminism places increased emphasis on abstract specification of the desired computation, with corresponding de-emphasis of algorithm implementation details. This encourages more systematic, and hence reliable, program development.

Guarded command sets may be incorporated into control structures in a number of ways. The two following examples, together with simple illustrative applications, have been described by Dijkstra. In each case, the control structure syntax is the guarded command set, as formulated above, enclosed in a pair of keywords.

A *selection* control structure has the syntax

```
if
    B₁ → S₁
    B₂ → S₂
       ⋮
    Bₙ → Sₙ
fi
```

The semantics of this structure are that after execution of an S, execution of the **if-fi** terminates. Only one execution of an S is performed, the selection of which is as described above. If no B is true in an execution of an **if-fi** structure, then execution of the **if-fi** does not terminate, causing the program to abort. In a multitasking (*q.v.*) environment, an alternative might be to wait for a guard to become true.

This **if-fi** structure is very much like the classical **case** control structure (*see* CONTROL STRUCTURE), in that only one statement group is executed and the order of the statement groups is immaterial. Unlike the usual **case** structure, however, the guards in the **if-fi** structure may be non-disjoint arbitrary conditions. In the **case** structure, the "guards" are disjoint sets of constants. Thus, the **case** structure is completely deterministic, whereas the **if-fi** is in general nondeterministic.

The following program is a simple application of the **if-fi** structure.

```
            [determine max (P,Q)]
if
    P ≥ Q → MAX ← P
    Q ≥ P → MAX ← Q
fi
            [MAX=max (P,Q)]
```

Note in this example that one of the two guards must be true, so that execution of this **if-fi** is guaranteed to terminate. Note also that both guards may be true (when $P = Q$), and that in this case execution of either statement gives the same result. Thus, at termination of execution of the `if-fi`, MAX $= max(P,Q)$.

A *repetition* control structure involving guarded commands has the form

```
do
    B₁ → S₁
    B₂ → S₂
    ⋮
    Bₙ → Sₙ
od
```

The semantics are that a statement S is selected in the manner described above, and, after execution of S, this entire process is repeated. Execution of the `do-od` structure terminates only when all guards evaluate to `false`. By constructing the appropriate guards, any desired repetitive control can be achieved.

The following program for calculating the greatest common divisor of two positive integers illustrates the use of `do-od` for specifying repetition control.

```
            [determine gcd(P,Q)]
X ← P,  Y ← Q
do
X > Y → X ← X-Y
Y > X → Y ← Y-X
od
            [X = Y = gcd(P,Q)]
```

Note that the two guards in this program for *gcd* are disjoint, so that this example is completely deterministic. In principle, the guards for a given control pattern can always be devised so that no two are true simultaneously, although this restriction often (unnecessarily) complicates guard construction and evaluation.

It is well known that `if-then-else` selection control and `do while` repetition control are sufficient to construct any conceivable execution control in a program. Special cases of `if-fi` and `do-od` are identical to `if-then-else` and `do while`, as shown in the following constructs.

```
if B then S₁        if
    else S₂            B → S₁
endif                 ¬B → S₂
                    fi

do while B          do
    S                  B → S
endloop             od
```

These particular forms of `if-fi` and `do-od` are completely deterministic, and the `if-fi` is guaranteed to terminate.

Therefore, `if-fi` and `do-od`, as defined here in general, are quite versatile control structures. The inefficiencies of guard evaluation (all the guards must be evaluated, each time), however, currently discourage their use as practical control structures in sequential programming languages. Since `if-fi` and `do-od` are inherently "parallel," concurrent guard evaluation resolves this problem in parallel execution environments; examples of languages used in such environments, and which support versions of guarded commands, are Ada (*q.v.*) and Occam. Because `if-fi` and `do-od` are simple and systematic and therefore relatively amenable to formal description and analysis, guarded commands could increase in practical importance in situations requiring more formal analysis, such as highly parallel algorithm development.

Bibliography

1975. Dijkstra, E. J. "Guarded Commands, Nondeterminancy and Formal Derivations of Programs," *Comm. of the ACM*, **18** (August), 453–457.

1976. Dijkstra, E. J. *A Discipline of Programming.* Upper Saddle River, NJ: Prentice Hall.

1995. Barnes, J. G. P. *Programming in Ada 95.* Reading, MA: Addison-Wesley.

Jerrold L. Wagener

GUI (GRAPHICAL USER INTERFACE)

See USER INTERFACE; and WINDOW ENVIRONMENTS.

GURU

For articles on related subjects *see* POWER USER; and WIZARD.

The term *guru* is used more frequently in computing than in most other phases of human activity, but with its conventional meaning: a wise person—a teacher, perhaps—who knows or claims to know a great deal about a particular subject and who is readily available and anxious to share his or her knowledge with others. Some early computer gurus were Jackson Granholm, who held forth in *Datamation* and who coined the term "kludge" (*q.v.*), and H. R. J. Grosch, who promulgated, among other percepts, Grosch's Law (*see* LAWS, COMPUTER). The era of the personal computer has spawned more gurus than mainframe computers ever did, current exemplars being John Dvorak of *PC Magazine*, Esther Dyson of EDventure Holdings, and Stewart Alsop of *InfoWorld*.

Gurus, who *know* much, are not necessarily programmers and hence not usually *wizards*, who can *do* much, though they may very well be *power users* of particular operating systems (*q.v.*), user interfaces (*q.v.*), or applications software.

Edwin D. Reilly

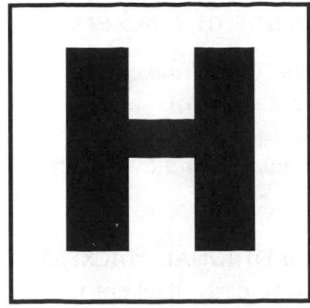

HACKER

For articles on related subjects *see* COMPUTER CRIME; COMPUTER ETHICS; GURU; POWER USER; PRIVACY, COMPUTERS AND; PROGRAMMER; VIRUS, COMPUTER; and WIZARD.

Hackers are obsessed with computers. At the heart of the obsession is a drive to master the computer. The classic hacker of the early decades of computing was simply a compulsive programmer; the term carried no pejorative connotation (Levy, 1984). It is only since the era of heavily networked computers that the term *hacker* has become associated with computerized vandalism. Those who seek to preserve and promote the honor of the original meaning call the vandals *crackers* rather than hackers.

The vast majority of (insidious) hackers are young men, often teenagers, who have found within the computer a world which they can mold to their desires, a world far less threatening and more rewarding to them than the world of conventional social relations. Many of them are social misfits—shy, inarticulate young men with few fulfilling personal relationships. Turkle (1984) describes hackers as "trapped" in a quest for control and mastery with the computer as their medium.

Early hacker communities developed around accessible interactive computer systems at places such as MIT. Today, hacker communities are linked via the World Wide Web (*q.v.*), Usenet, and email (*q.v.*), and their members may never have met or even know each other's real names, only their aliases. A hacker gains status by demonstrating mastery of the system. This was traditionally done by writing clever programs ("hacks") but there is a growing temptation to attract attention by penetrating ("cracking") a system's security, crashing it, infecting it with a computer virus, or accessing supposedly secure information.

The Hacker Ethic

The hacker's obsession with computing leads to impatience and intolerance with anything that stands in the way. Levy (1984) codified the resulting *hacker ethic*:

1. Access to computers—and anything which might teach you something about the way the world works—should be unlimited and total. Always yield to the Hands-On Imperative!

2. All information should be free.

3. Mistrust Authority—Promote Decentralization.

4. Hackers should be judged by their hacking, not bogus criteria such as degrees, age, race, or position.

5. You can create art and beauty on a computer.

6. Computers can change your life for the better.

Noticeably missing from this ethic is respect for personal property, security, and privacy. Hackers let no one and no thing come between them and their pursuit of computing. This leads to conflict between those who follow the hacker ethic and the larger community of users.

Types of Hackers

The term *hacker* can convey many meanings. More precise terms would be traditional hacker, wizard (*q.v.*), and guru (*q.v.*), versus dark side hackers, crackers, and cyberpunks.

TRADITIONAL HACKERS

Most early hackers were programmers. Hacking, as a programming style, is distinguished by its lack of apparent method. Hackers are impatient with structured programming (*q.v.*), object-oriented programming (*q.v.*), documentation (*q.v.*), and any kind of systematic development. Instead, the hacker spends long hours at the terminal interactively developing and debugging intuitively. Hackers believe that programs should be built "straight from your mind" (Turkle, 1984). They prize concise, efficient, elegant, and even tricky code. Although this programming style is frowned upon by more conventional programmers, many hacker-developed projects such as the text editor Emacs and the operating system Linux are premier examples of the programming craft (*see* TEXT EDITING SYSTEMS and UNIX OPERATING SYSTEM). Many of the founding fathers of modern computing are former hackers: Bill Gates of Microsoft and Steve Jobs and Steve Wozniak of Apple Computer fame are prime examples.

Traditional hackers were a valuable resource to computing centers. Their knowledge of the machine and their programming skills were prized. Unfortunately, such hackers are usually not ideal corporate employees. They work only on programs that interest them; are reluctant to take on assigned projects, particularly if they offer no opportunity to demonstrate mastery of the computer; are reluctant to document their work; and their endless tinkering and addition of "features" may result in products that are never finished or stable.

DARK SIDE HACKERS, CRACKERS, AND CYBERPUNKS

The cyberpunk movement in science fiction has had a powerful influence on hackers. The seminal work in this genre is William Gibson's cyberspace sprawl series (Gibson, 1986a, b; 1988). The genre popularizes the notion of cyberspace as a virtual reality (*q.v.*) with cyberpunks (not a term Gibson himself used) or network cowboys "jacking in" (connecting) and penetrating *ice* (computer security) to obtain information from corporate databases. The cyberpunk with black leather jacket and mirror shades presents a much more glamorous (or intimidating) image than the classic bespectacled nerd.

One consequence of this new image is that many aspiring hackers attempt to demonstrate their proficiency in socially unacceptable ways. Crackers seek to penetrate computer systems. They see computer system security as a challenge and a puzzle to solve. Cracking is almost as old as hacking itself since even traditional hackers are intolerant of anything that limits their access to information. They are driven by curiosity and see a lock, whether physical or a system password (*q.v.*), as a challenge to be met. Thus, many MIT hackers were skilled lock pickers and were more than willing to apply their skills wherever there was a locked door (Levy, 1984; Turkle, 1984). While the original intent was not malicious, many crackers cannot resist leaving some mark of their presence and many of them exchange methods of system access (Landreth, 1989). There is also a growing concern with computer espionage, a common activity among the cyberpunks in literature, and also on the Internet (Stoll, 1989; Hafner and Markoff, 1991).

The hackers who have caused the greatest concern are the computer vandals who turn their skills toward damaging computer systems. Websites have been frequent targets. Crashers demonstrate their mastery of computer systems by causing them to fail precipitously or behave so erratically that they meet the legal threshold of "denial of service."

Other dark side hackers create programs that interfere with system operations or destroy data. They may modify programs to create "Trojan horses" that masquerade as useful software but actually destroy or corrupt data, create virus programs that "infect" or hide in other programs and awaken at unpredictable times to damage the system, and devise "worms" that transport themselves between computers in a network. Trojan horses and virus programs so inhibit the spread of *freeware and shareware* (*q.v.*) that the hackers who create such programs are clearly working against their own ethic.

Worms have disrupted both the IBM internal computer network and the Internet (Stoll, 1989; Hafner and Markoff, 1991). Both caused major disruptions in the affected networks.

Hackers in Perspective

The public has become fascinated by hackers. Depictions in books such as Gibson's, movies such as *War Games* and *Sneakers*, and television series such as *Max Headroom* show the hacker in a sympathetic light. The exploits of Kevin Mitnick have been the subject of numerous newspaper articles and several books (Hafner and Markoff, 1991; Littman, 1996; Shimomura and Markoff, 1996). System break-ins by crackers, the activities of crashers, and even such disruptive activities as the Internet Worm have been excused as harmless pranks or even praised as valuable lessons in the need for system security. This tolerance is fading rapidly. Due largely to the activities of cyberpunks, the Internet has become, in the word of one book, besieged (Denning and Denning, 1998). High profile targets such as the US Department of Defense and the Pentagon have been successfully attacked. Law enforcement authorities have identified and prosecuted a large number of suspected crackers (Sterling, 1992).

Some authors have expressed concern about the mental well-being of hackers. Certainly, computers can be addictive (Turkle, 1984) and such addictions can lead to problems in susceptible individuals. Most hackers do eventually outgrow their addiction, just as many have outgrown similar addictions to videogames and Dungeons and Dragons.

Hacking appears to have taken a damaging turn over the last several years. While the original hackers were certainly fond of pranks and had little respect for system security, they were primarily interested in developing elegant and powerful programs. Many of today's so called hackers seem more interested in gaining a name for themselves by damaging and disrupting systems than in developing new and useful software. In response to this new breed of hackers there has been an increased call for the teaching of *computer ethics* (*q.v.*) and the redirecting of such activities into less harmful pursuits.

Bibliography

1984. Levy, S. *Hackers: Heroes of the Computer Revolution.* New York: Anchor Press/Doubleday.
1984. Turkle, S. *The Second Self: Computers and the Human Spirit.* New York: Simon and Schuster.
1986a. Gibson, W. *Neuromancer.* West Bloomfield, MI: Phantasia Press.
1986b. Gibson, W. *Count Zero.* New York: Arbor House.
1988. Gibson, W. *Mona Lisa Overdrive.* New York: Bantam Books.
1989. Landreth, B. *Out of the Inner Circle.* Redmond, WA: Microsoft Press.
1989. Stoll, C. *The Cuckoo's Egg: Tracking a Spy Through the Maze of Computer Espionage.* New York: Doubleday.
1991. Hafner, K., and Markoff, J. *Cyberpunk: Outlaws and Hackers on the Computer Frontier.* New York: Simon and Schuster.
1992. Sterling, B. *The Hacker Crackdown: Law and Disorder on the Electronic Frontier.* New York: Bantam Books.
1996. Littman, J. *The Fugitive Game: Online with Kevin Mitnick.* Boston, MA: Little, Brown and Company.
1996. Raymond, E. S. *The New Hacker's Dictionary*, 3rd Ed. Cambridge, MA: MIT Press.
1996. Shimomura, T., and Markoff, J. *Takedown.* New York: Hyperion.
1998. Denning, D., and Denning, P. *Internet Besieged: Countering Cyberspace Scofflaws.* New York: Addison-Wesley.

Website

Raymond, E. S. The Jargon File: http://sagan.earthspace.net/jargon/.

Robert G. Rittenhouse

HAMMING, RICHARD W.

For articles on related subjects *see* ERROR CORRECTING AND DETECTING CODE; and NUMERICAL ANALYSIS.

Richard Wesley Hamming (Fig. 1), mathematician, pioneer computer scientist, and professor, was born in Chicago on 11 February 1915. He received a Ph.D. in mathematics from the University of Illinois in 1942. After brief teaching positions at the University of Illinois and the University of Louisville, he was recruited in 1945 to work at Los Alamos to run the IBM machines that were doing atomic bomb calculations. In 1946 he joined Bell Laboratories where his career became centered on bringing large-scale scientific computation into Bell Labs. He retired from Bell Labs in 1976 and moved to the Naval Postgraduate School, Monterey, California, where he taught for 21 years and became Distinguished Professor Emeritus of computer science just before his death on 7 January 1998.

Hamming's major professional honors included the ACM Turing Award (1968) and the IEEE Richard W. Hamming Medal (1988), which was named after him and of which he was the first recipient. In Munich in 1996 he received the Eduard Rhein Award for Achievement in Technology for his work on error-correcting

Figure 1. Richard Hamming.

codes. He was President of the Association for Computing Machinery in 1958–1960, and a member of the National Academy of Engineering.

Hamming is perhaps best known for the invention of error-correcting codes. These codes insert redundancy into data words (blocks of binary digits), so that the computer itself can detect and correct storage or transmission errors. The Hamming codes (Hamming, 1950) used multiple parity checks to detect and correct errors in data words. A geometric approach is possible, in which the Hamming distance between two received words is the number of positions in which the two words differ. Hamming observed that a code having a minimum distance $2t + 1$ between code words, where t is a positive integer, can correct a word with t errors, and if the minimum distance is $2t + 2$, the code can correct words with t errors and detect, but not correct, words with $t + 1$ errors. The original Hamming codes were single-error-correcting, and by adding an additional parity bit to each word, they became double-error-detecting. In the hands of others, these ideas led to algebraic coding theory and to multiple-error-correcting codes, such as the Reed–Solomon codes, which are used for space communication and in compact discs (*see* OPTICAL STORAGE).

In numerical analysis, Hamming developed a predictor–corrector method for solving ordinary differential equations (Lapidus and Seinfeld, 1971). Hamming's method was popular for some time because, unlike an earlier method of Milne, it does not amplify roundoff errors.

In digital signal processing, samples of a time function over a finite interval are combined using a set of weights, in order to extract certain frequencies and to discriminate against others. Hamming invented a set of weights, called the Hamming window, that is particularly effective in isolating the desired frequency (Hamming, 1989). Different windows have been designed to meet different requirements, but the Hamming window is perhaps the most widely used because of its simplicity and effectiveness.

Hamming came into the field of computing just as it was emerging from the desk calculator era into the era of electronic computers. From his days at Los Alamos he saw, much sooner and more clearly than most people, the role that computers were destined to play in the scientific and technological world of the future, and he undertook to educate his colleagues for that world. His focus was practical; his most celebrated maxim was, "The purpose of computing is insight, not numbers" (Hamming, 1973). As a writer and speaker, he was never dull. He had strong opinions and he liked to express them. He enjoyed the speaker's platform, and on occasion he enjoyed "hamming" with a small h.

One might agree or disagree with a Hamming pronouncement, but no one who ever knew him is likely to forget him.

Bibliography

1950. Hamming, R. W. "Error-detecting and Error-correcting Codes," *Bell. Sys. Tech. Journal*, **29**, *1*, 147–160.
1971. Lapidus, L., and Seinfeld, J. H. *Numerical Solution of Ordinary Differential Equations*. New York: Academic Press.
1973. Hamming, R. W. *Numerical Methods for Scientists and Engineers*, 2nd Ed. New York: McGraw-Hill.
1989. Hamming, R. W. *Digital Filters*, 3rd Ed. Upper Saddle River, NJ: Prentice Hall.

Samuel P. Morgan

HANDSHAKING

For articles on related subjects *see* BUS; DATA COMMUNICATIONS; PROTOCOL; SYNCHRONOUS/ ASYNCHRONOUS OPERATION; TCP/IP; and TELEPROCESSING SYSTEMS.

The exchange of predetermined sequences of control signals or control characters between two devices or systems to establish a connection, to break a connection, or to exchange data and status information, is commonly referred to as *handshaking*. This is best illustrated by means of examples.

Consider first Fig. 1, which shows the sequence of signals on the input–output bus of a small computer when writing a character to a device connected to the bus. The computer first places the device address on the DATA OUT lines and raises the ADDRESS control line to tell the device that the data on the DATA OUT lines is an address. The device recognizes its address and raises the control line OK, informing the computer that the device is aware that it has been selected. This causes the computer to drop ADDRESS and DATA OUT. The device responds by dropping OK, upon which the computer places the character on the DATA OUT lines and raises the control line WRITE to tell the selected device that the character is on the bus. The device then accepts the character and raises OK, signifying that it has accepted it. The computer then drops DATA OUT and WRITE, which causes OK to go down. This completes the handshaking sequence for transferring a character from the computer to the device.

Handshaking also occurs when two remote computers communicate with each other over a communication network. Here, instead of electrical signals, predetermined sequences of packets containing address, data and control information are interchanged to establish a connection, transfer data or control information, recover from any error conditions, and terminate the connection. Such handshaking sequences between

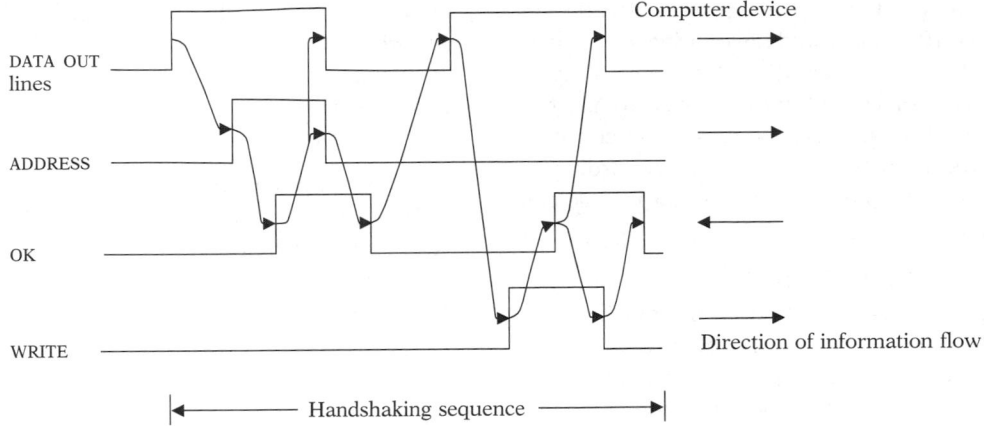

DATA OUT lines

ADDRESS

OK

WRITE

Computer device

Direction of information flow

|← — Handshaking sequence — →|

Figure 1. Example of handshaking sequence. The arrows are used to indicate which control signal causes which response during sequence.

devices over a network obey a set of rules defined by a *communication protocol*, or simply a *protocol*. The predominant such protocol used today is the Transmission Control Protocol/Internet Protocol (TCP/IP).

John S. Sobolewski

HARD DISK

For articles on related subjects *see* ACCESS TIME; BUS; CYLINDER; DISKETTE; MEMORY: AUXILIARY; and REDUNDANT ARRAY OF INEXPENSIVE DISKS.

A *hard disk* is a high-capacity, high-speed rotational storage device. Hard disks are sometimes called *fixed disks* because they usually cannot be removed from the computer. This nomenclature is somewhat outdated now that removable hard disk storage devices have been perfected. Hard disk drives are also called *Winchester drives*, a name derived from a 1969 IBM drive that stored 30 MB of information on each of two spindles, a 30–30 arrangement reminiscent of the famed Winchester 30–30 rifle.

A hard disk consists of a rigid aluminum alloy disk that is coated with a magnetic oxide material, much like a diskette. Because the disks are rigid, they can be spun much faster than a floppy—up to 10,800 rpm. The drive itself may contain a number of platters mounted on a rotating spindle (*see* MEMORY: AUXILIARY). Each platter surface has its own read–write head. The head actually floats above the surface of the disk on a cushion of air. The heads on hard disks are designed like small airfoils so that they can be efficiently lifted and landed. The heads float very close to the disk surface, the gap being about 1/100,000 of an inch. The disk case is assembled in a controlled and ultra-clean environment because contaminants in the form of airborne particles can be very destructive. The inside of a disk

drive cannot be a vacuum because the heads need air to lift off and land.

Because the platters are rigid, magnetic material can be densely packed so that hard disks have very high capacities. With a large number of platters, some mainframe hard disks can hold up to a terabyte—a trillion characters. Hard disks used with microcomputers range in storage capacity from 2 to 40 GB.

Each disk surface has its own head; all heads move in unison. At one time the heads were moved by *stepper motors*, which are controlled by electrical pulses, turning a fixed amount with each pulse. Although still used for diskette drives, their limited precision is inadequate for modern high-density hard disks. Disk heads are now moved by *voice coil* actuators, so-called because they resemble loudspeaker voice coils. A coil of wire surrounds a magnet, and the current flowing through it generates a magnetic field that moves the coil. One disk platter has a special magnetic pattern on it that the disk head can use to determine its location, and that information, in turn, controls the current flowing through the voice coil. This *closed-loop* feedback control (*see* CYBERNETICS) permits very accurate positioning of the disk heads.

The disk stores data in *tracks* of magnetically-oriented particles. There may be over 10,000 tracks on a high-capacity hard disk, thanks to the precision of voice-coil actuators. Tracks are divided into sectors. The sectors are laid down when the disk undergoes a low-level software format. The formatting program identifies and marks sectors that are bad and lays out the sector locations and stores them. The low-level format also establishes the *interleave factor* for the disk. Because a disk is capable of feeding information to an operating system before it is ready to accept it, the controller card may not be ready to read the second sector of a file right after the first. If that second sector is placed right next to the first, the disk would have to make an entire revolution before the second sector came around again. Since files consist of hundreds of sectors, a tremendous amount of time can be wasted. If consecutively numbered sectors are interleaved according to the average time it takes to read data, the disk can operate more efficiently.

On hard disks used with the IBM PC (*q.v.*) and compatibles, track zero is dedicated to system files. To prepare for use of the hard disk and probable later installation of Windows, a high-level format must first be performed using a DOS FORMAT command. This copies some code into the boot sector and starts to expand the File Allocation Table (FAT). The FORMAT command also writes the special command file and two hidden system files that DOS needs to operate. The *boot sector* is a special area used by the computer to start the process of booting the computer (*see* BOOTSTRAP).

The file allocation tables (FAT) are the most important files on a hard disk. The FAT contain information about which sectors are assigned to which files. When a file is written to a hard disk, it is not written in consecutive sectors. Sectors are scattered all over the disk, organized as a linked list. The disk *directory* (*q.v.*) knows how big a file is and when it was created. It also stores the location of the first sector for a given filename. After that, only the FAT knows where the other sectors are. Destroy the FAT and the hard disk is useless.

The collection of tracks with the same number arranged vertically on all platters is called a *cylinder* (*q.v.*). Since the heads are connected to only one actuator arm, all heads move in unison. For example, when the head is over, say, track 157 on the top platter, it is over track 157 on all platters. For that reason, operating systems (*q.v.*), through programmed directions to the hard disk controller, try to store all sectors belonging to the same file on the same cylinder to minimize head movement.

There are two track numbers that serve a special purpose. The *landing track* is a track where data is never written. This is where the heads go to land when the system is powered down or the heads are "parked" by a utility program prior to shipment of the disk drive. Some disks have self-parking heads while others require user intervention through software.

As tracks get closer to the center of the disk, their circumference necessarily gets smaller. But since the number of sectors stays the same and so does the number of bytes per sector (for most drives), the data is therefore more densely packed. The controller must

therefore compensate for this increase in magnetic intensity when it is a certain number of tracks from the center of the disk. This *precompensation factor* is usually stored as a track number at which to begin sensing the increased magnetic density.

The most popular hard disk controller standards are EIDE—Enhanced Integrated Drive Electronics and SCSI—Small Computer System Interface (*see* BUS). EIDE drives usually spin at 5,400 rpm compared with 7,200 rpm for SCSI drives.

A SCSI (pronounced "scuzzy") bus has controller hardware that can manage multiple disks or other peripherals. The SCSI subsystem can queue up and issue multiple disk-access requests to one or more drives (*command tag queueing*), sort and reorder multiple commands for efficient physical disk access (*elevator seeking*), and permit disconnection and reconnection of SCSI drives from the SCSI bus for better SCSI-bus utilization in multi-drive environments. SCSI devices use a 50 pin cable. SCSI-2 was introduced in 1991 and expanded the 8-bit bus to 16 data lines. Essentially SCSI hard disks take care of the management of disk sectors and tracks without the help of the host computer.

EIDE devices move much of the controller electronics onto the circuitry of the drive itself. In recent tests with comparable devices, SCSI and EIDE drives performed about the same. The newest EIDE devices use a *bus-mastering* controller with its own CPU to relieve the host processor of burdensome I/O calculations.

Bibliography

1999. Rosch, W. L. *Winn L. Rosch Hardware Bible*, 5th Ed. Indianapolis, IN: Que Publications.

Stephen J. Rogowski

HARDWARE DESCRIPTION LANGUAGES

For articles on related subjects *see* DIGITAL DESIGN AUTOMATION; INSTRUCTION SET; LOGIC DESIGN; NONPROCEDURAL LANGUAGES; and PROCEDURE-ORIENTED LANGUAGES.

Motivation

Hardware description languages (HDLs) are languages that facilitate the conception, design, analysis/simulation, documentation, and manufacturing of digital computer systems. A digital system can be described at many different levels of detail: requirements, system, behavioral, and structural. Thus a system can be described from the system level to the logic gate level as a network of elements of varying degrees of complexity, including timing diagrams, behavior and structure. Fig. 1 shows examples of different descriptions of a 1-bit adder circuit. While a complete digital computer can be described at any level, the amount of low-level information would be too extensive for a human designer to comprehend, and higher-level languages are used to abstract or hide details, resulting in a system-level description of the design.

The design process, whether system design (hardware/software), electronic circuit and device design, or mechanical design, has a common set of needs, which include:

♦ communicating design data among companies carrying out different parts of the design process,

♦ transmitting manufacturing and fabrication data for a designed part, and

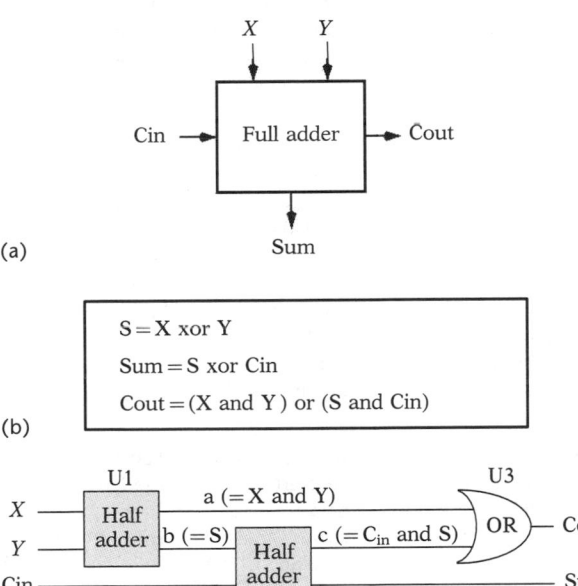

(a)

S = X xor Y

Sum = S xor Cin

Cout = (X and Y) or (S and Cin)

(b)

(c)

	Inputs		Outputs	
Cin	X	Y	Cout	Sum
0	0	0	0	0
0	0	1	0	1
0	1	0	0	1
0	1	1	1	0
1	0	0	0	1
1	0	1	1	0
1	1	0	1	0
1	1	1	1	1

(d)

Figure 1. A one-bit full adder and three descriptions of its operation. (a) the full adder component, with inputs and outputs. (b) Logic equations for the full adder. (c) Construction of a full adder from simpler components. (d) Truth table for a full adder.

♦ encouraging the development of new and innovative CAD (*q.v.*) tools.

HDLs must provide the ability to include information to support:

♦ both human-readable and machine-readable functional specifications and design documentation,

♦ a mechanism to manage design data,

♦ human–computer interaction in the design process,

♦ test analysis for a designed part.

Communication and data integration is simplified when a standard data representation is used for each activity. Furthermore, a conceptual schema for shared product data, relating the electrical design environment to the mechanical design environment, may simplify the design, manufacture, and maintenance process.

The electrical design environment has descriptions of architectural, functional, circuit, and device electrical and timing parameters, power, speed and performance requirements, physical layout electrical parameters and requirements, for example. The mechanical design environment describes all mechanical aspects of the design, such as power constraints, size constraints, temperature constraints, form and fit constraints, and packaging constraints.

Languages—A Historical Perspective

There are many languages that may be used for a design description (see Table 1 and Fig. 2). Currently, an HDL must be applicable to more than just hardware, and so a System Level Description Language (SLDL) is being developed to permit description of both software and hardware designs at the most abstract levels of design work.

In high-level descriptions, software functions are often included in the system models. Hardware/software systems may be decomposed into a data part and a control part, operating in discrete steps, and some of the lower-level details, such as gate interconnection, placement, and individual gate delays, may be suppressed at the early stages of the design process. Above the gate level, standard or predefined networks of gates and flip-flops are often used as building blocks at the register transfer level. Typical components are registers, multiplexers, and arithmetic-logic units (ALUs— *q.v.*). At the gate level, the elements of design are primitive blocks—the basic logic gates.

Structure is normally depicted by block diagrams, and there are a wide variety of conventions for describing

Table 1. Levels of abstraction and descriptive domains for systems.

Abstraction level	Behavioral domain	Structural domain	Hardware component domain	Software component domain	Analysis modes	Model representation
Requirements	Input–output characteristics, nonfunctional characteristics, priorities	Required structural elements, e.g. memory size, bus width	Predetermined hardware component use	Predetermined software component use	Reasonableness checks	H/S DL plus nonfunctional parameters, FSMs, queueing models
System	Specification of information flow, elaboration of nonfunctional characteristics	Alternative elemental component characteristics	Operational characteristics, refined determination of existing hardware components	Operational characteristics, refined determination of existing software components	Performance, dependability, cost, power, size trade-offs, requirements tracking	H/S DL plus nonfunctional parameters, Petri nets (*q.v.*), FSMs, queueing models, Markov models, stochastic models
Architectural	Specification of subsystems, connectivity, information flow, elaboration of nonfunctional characteristics	Alternative subsystems, their components and characteristics	Operational characteristics, some functional partitions, refinement of existing HW components	Operational characteristics, some functional partitions, refinement of existing software components	Performance, dependability, cost, power, size, architectual, partition trade-offs, requirements tracking	H/S DL plus nonfunctional parameters, Petri nets, FSMs, queueing models, Markov models, stochastic models
Algorithmic	Algorithms for data structure manipulation	Alternative subsystems, their elemental components and characteristics	Operational characteristics, more functional partitions, algorithm selection, additional refinement of HW choice, some preliminary HW binding	Operational characteristics, algorithm selection, additional SW component refinement, some preliminary SW binding	Performance, dependability, cost, power, size, architectual, algorithmic, partition trade-offs, synthesis, requirements tracking	H/S DL, Petri nets, FSMs, queueing models, Markov models, stochastic models

HDL, PDL |
| Functional blocks, code stubs, high-level code | HW/SW operations, register transfers, state sequences | SW stubs, some high-level program code blocks, ALUs, MUXs, registers, microstore, microsequencer | Preliminary hardware binding, hardware floorplans, tentative hardware technologies | Preliminary software binding, ROM vs. RAM decisions, code performance-dictated decisions | Test generation, detailed performance analysis, detailed simulation. Test plans, synthesis, requirements tracking | Functional models

HDL, PDL, PL |
| Logic, code modules | Boolean equations, assembly code | Gates, latches, flip flops, disk, memory | Hardware technologies | Coding technologies | Test generation, detailed performance analysis, detailed simulation. Test plans, synthesis, requirements tracking | Logic models

HDL, PL |
| Circuits, code modules | Differential equations, bits, bytes | Electronic devices, including memory devices | Layout parameters, e.g. gate arrays, fabrication method | Memory/disk technologies selected | Low level testing, analog analysis, requirements tracking | HDL, LLC

HIF |

HW/SW = Hardware/Software; H/S DL = Hardware/Software Description Language (e.g. SLDL); FSM = Finite State Machine; HDL = Hardware Description Language (e.g. VHDL, Verilog, Hardware C, Esterel); PDL = Process Design Language (e.g. Ada PDL); PL = Programming Language (e.g. Ada, C, C++); LLC = Low-level code; HIF = Hardware Interchange Format (e.g. EDIF).

Ada
C++
Esterel
Hardware C
SLDL (under development)
Verilog
VHDL

Figure 2. Some languages in use in 1999.

the behavior of the system. Historically, special-purpose programming languages (called register transfer (RT) languages) were used to create simulation models, and a number of such RT-languages were proposed (Barbacci, 1975). The existence of digital components capable of interpreting instructions stored in memory (i.e. instruction set processors) motivates the use of a programming level of description. At the programming level, the basic components are the interpretation cycle, the machine instructions, and operations (all of which are defined as register transfer level operations). The programming level describes the behavior rather than the structure of processors—in particular, the behavior as seen by the programmers of thc machine.

Beyond the programming level, other notations are used to provide concise descriptions of the physical structure of a digital system. The Processor Memory Switch (PMS) notation (Siewiorek *et al.*, 1982) is a graphical notation that makes use of only a few primitive components.

The proliferation of HDLs in the 1960s and 1970s led to the definition of CONLAN. CONLAN (CONsensus LANguage) was an attempt to design a language construction mechanism rather than a specific hardware description language. The effort thus centered on the definition of a primitive notation and a powerful extension mechanism.

The languages mentioned so far were used mostly in research and academic environments during the 1970s and early 1980s, as input notations for experimental simulation, analysis, or synthesis tools. In the industrial world, however, there are many additional requirements to consider in the definition of a design.

Complexity of Today's Design Environment

The complexity of today's design environment arises because management has become more aware of all the aspects of design to be considered in a total system. No longer may the process be based upon passing information from one stage "over the wall" to the designers of the next stage. There is now a recognized

need to codify the interrelationships in the design process in design languages (which describe the steps in a design process). Table 1 shows the various levels of abstraction that may be used in a design description in relation to the descriptive domains at each level of abstraction. The modes of analysis and means of representing a model at each level of abstraction are also given. The languages listed in Fig. 2 apply to many of the abstraction levels and domains listed in Table 1.

PRODUCT LIFE-CYCLE

Managing the life cycle of a product adds further complexity. Fig. 3 depicts the total life cycle of an electronics product. A design starts with the requirements that are to be met. Requirements generate abstract descriptions that evolve into specifications which include the environment and the function of the design. Then comes implementation. The designer iterates between the specification (which one wants to keep constant) and the implementation to ensure that the implementation captures the intent of the specification. The implementation must also comply with the design rules required by the fabrication process for the system components. Testing is performed on the product in several stages. The chips are tested, mounted chips are tested, an entire subsystem is tested, and so on. The product then moves to the end user. While the product is being used, new requirements are often generated and the cycle begins again.

CURRENT LANGUAGES

Creating, modifying, supporting, and managing complex systems depend on the ability to communicate the design details from one design discipline to another and to integrate the various types of data representing the

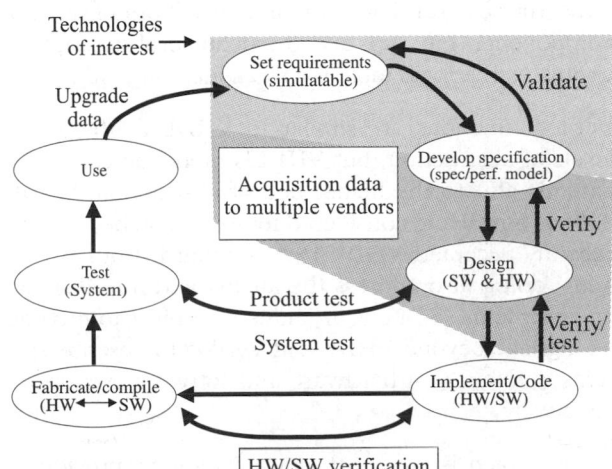

Figure 3. The product life cycle.

many facets of the product description. The reliability of complex systems depends equally on the ability to communicate the necessary data, throughout a product's life cycle, among those who design and maintain the product. To address these requirements, several industry-supported efforts have sought to establish means to represent product data in a standard format that will be useful to product designers, maintainers, and managers (Waxman and Saunders, 1989). Three of these efforts are the Very high-speed integrated circuits Hardware Description Language (VHDL), Verilog, and the Electronic Design Interchange Format (EDIF). VHDL and EDIF became standards in 1987. Verilog, although available as a proprietary language earlier, became an industry standard soon after VHDL. As current standards, each goes through regular improvement cycles (*see* PROGRAMMING LANGUAGE STANDARDS).

In VHDL, the hardware entities are modeled as abstractions of the real hardware, called *design entities*. As in real hardware, each *design entity* has an *interface* and a *body* or *architecture*. The interface description allows one to describe input and output ports and various attributes associated with the interface, such as pin names or timing constraints. The body description allows one to describe the function or the structure of the design. The body may be written as an abstract algorithm or as a less abstract architectural description made up of algorithms and real hardware representations (e.g. gates, arithmetic-logic units) or made up totally as a structure of real hardware representations. Alternative approaches (i.e. alternative architectures) to the functional representation of a particular design entity may be associated with a given interface, just as in real hardware where equivalent components may be interchanged as long as the interfaces are identical functionally and structurally. Fig 4a shows the VHDL interface for the full adder circuit of Fig. 1, together with three architectures. The dataflow (*q.v.*) description (Fig. 4b) restates the adder equations; the structural description builds it out of simpler components (Fig. 4c), and the behavioral description expresses the logic table for the adder (Fig. 4d).

Verilog functions are similar to VHDL at the lower levels of abstraction, but VHDL's modeling capability extends also to the higher end of abstraction. VHDL 200x is now being considered for extension beyond the recently accepted VHDL 1999 standard. Both VHDL and Verilog also address the analog and mixed-signal environments. SLDL is an industry project to provide a language beyond VHDL and Verilog to describe systems composed of hardware and software even more effectively.

EDIF, which is a *format*, not a *language*, provides a hierarchical syntax for data necessary for chip and

```
Entity full_adder is
  Generic( TP: TIME := 5 ns)
  Port( X, Y, Cin : in bit;    -- inputs
        Sum, Cout : out bit); -- outputs
end full_adder;
```

(a) Full-adder interface, with inputs and outputs and a time-delay parameter.

```
Architecture dataflow_view of full_adder is
    Signal S: bit;
begin

  S    <= X xor Y    after TP ns;
  Sum  <= S xor Cin after TP ns;
  Cout <= (X and Y) or (S and Cin) after 2*TP ns;

end dataflow_view;
```

(b) Dataflow architecture for the full adder, showing outputs as Boolean functions of the inputs, with propagation delays.

```
Architecture structure_view of full_adder is
    Component half_adder
      Port(I1, I2: in bit; Carry, Sum: out bit);
    end Component;

    Component or_gate
      Port(I1, I2: in bit; O: out bit);
    end Component;

    Signal a, b, c: bit;

begin
    U1: half_adder Port Map(X, Y, a, b);
    U2: half_adder Port Map(b, Cin, c, Sum);
    U3: or_gate Port Map(I1 => a, I2 => c, O => Cout);
end structure_view;
```

(c) Structural architecture, showing the construction of a full-adder from simpler components (defined elsewhere).

```
Architecture behavioral_view of full_adder is
begin
    Process(X, Y, Cin)
      Variable N: integer;
      Constant sum_vector: bit_vector(0 to 3)
             :="0101";
      Constant carry_vector: bit_vector(0 to 3)
             :="0011";

    begin
      N := 0;
      if ( X='1' ) then N:=N+1 end if;
      if ( Y='1' ) then N:=N+1 end if;
      if ( Cin='1' ) then N:=N+1 end if;
      Sum <= sum_vector(N) after 2*TP ns;
      Cout <= carry_vector(N) after 3*TP ns;
    end Process;
end behavioral_view;
```

(d) Behavioral architecture, defining the full-adder from the equations for its behavior. The process is activated by changes in any of its inputs.

Figure 4. A VHDL specification of a full-adder (a), and three architectures that implement it (b)–(d).

printed circuit board fabrication. EDIF's primary application is as a means of transferring design data from the design environment to the fabrication environment. The format provides for libraries, cells, views, interfaces, and information on the content within each cell. Test data, mask layout data, physical layout data, connectivity data, and simulation data can be represented in EDIF.

In EDIF there are several "view types": the *behavior* view (compiled simulation model); the *document* view (supports text documentation); the *graphic* view (supports portions of artwork repeatedly used); the *logic model* view (definition of primitive simulation logic models); the *mask layout* view (artwork and fabrication data); the netlist view (netlist data); the *PCB layout* view (similar to the mask layout view, but for printed circuit boards); the *schematic* view (netlist plus graphics providing a graphic schematic); the *stranger* view (an escape hatch for two-party special agreements); the *symbolic* view (a virtual grid somewhere between a schematic and a mask layout); and a test view.

The many industry standards attempt to answer the needs of the various product life cycle activities. However, the development of some of these standards have not been well coordinated with others, although there are efforts being made to do so. Users need a thorough understanding of the objectives and uses of each standard. The technology of HDLs has not matured to the point that one standard language or format can satisfy the wide diversity of product description requirements, at least for the immediate future.

Bibliography

1975. Barbacci, M. R. "A Comparison of Register Transfer Languages for Describing Digital Systems," *IEEE Transactions on Computers*, **C-24**, *2* (February), 137–150.

1981. Barbacci, M. R. "Instruction Set Processor Specifications (ISPS): The Notation and its Applications," *IEEE Transactions on Computers*, **C-30**, *1* (January), 24–40.

1982. Siewiorek, D., Bell, C. G., and Newell, A. *Computer Structures: Principles and Examples*. New York: McGraw-Hill.

1983. Piloty, R., Barbacci, M. R., Borrione, D., Dietmeyer, D., Hill, F., and Skelly, P. *CONLAN Report*. Berlin: Springer-Verlag.

1989. Waxman, R., and Saunders, L. "The Evolution of VHDL," *Proceedings of the IFIP Congress* (August), San Francisco.

1993. Institute for Electrical and Electronic Engineers. *VHDL Language Reference Manual*, Standard 1076-1993. New York: IEEE Press.

1996. Ashenden, P. J. *The Designer's Guide to VHDL*. San Francisco: Morgan Kaufmann.

1997. Institute for Electrical and Electronic Engineers. *Verilog Language Reference Manual*, Standard 1364-1998. New York: IEEE Press.

1998. EIA/EDIF. *Specification, Electronic Design Interchange Format, Version 4.0.0.*

Ronald Waxman and Michel Israel

HARDWARE RELIABILITY

> For articles on related subjects *see* DATA SECURITY; FAULT-TOLERANT COMPUTING; MAINTENANCE OF COMPUTERS; REDUNDANCY; and SOFTWARE RELIABILITY.

Reliability engineering involves all aspects of design, development, and fabrication that minimize the chance of equipment breakdown. Neglect of reliability considerations can prove to be very costly, from the loss of consumer acceptance of the product to the possibility of endangering human life. The success of complex missions such as space probes depends heavily on reliability engineering, since the failure of a single component, such as an O-ring on a space shuttle, can result and has resulted in total loss of the system.

Reliability in a qualitative sense can mean a host of different things relating to confidence in the quality of the equipment, and is closely connected but often confused with the concepts of maintainability, availability, safety, and even security of the system. Quantitatively, reliability can be formulated mathematically as the probability that the system will perform its intended function over the stated duration of time in its specified environment.

As equipment becomes more complex, the chance of system unreliability becomes greater, since the reliability of any equipment depends on the reliability of its components. The relationship between parts reliability and the system reliability can be formulated mathematically to varying degrees of precision, depending on the scale of the modeling effort. The mathematics of reliability is based on parts failure-rate statistics and probability–theoretic relationships. The mathematical theory of reliability is used to model, simulate, and predict proneness of the equipment to failure under expected operating conditions.

There have been two distinct and viable approaches taken to enhance system reliability. One is based on component technology, i.e. manufacturing capability of producing the component with the highest possible reliability, followed by parts screening, quality control, pretesting to remove early failures (infant mortality effects), etc. The second approach is based on the organization of the system itself (e.g. fault-tolerant architectures that make use of protective redundancy to mask or remove the effects of failure, and thereby provide greater overall system reliability than would be possible by the use of the same components in a simplex or nonredundant configuration).

Fault tolerance is the capability of the system to perform its functions in accordance with design specifications, even in the presence of hardware failures. If, in the event of faults, the system function can be performed, but does not meet the design specifications with respect to the time required to complete the job or the storage capacity required for the job, then the system is said to be *partially* or *quasi fault-tolerant*. Since the number of possible hardware failures can be very large, in practice it is necessary to restrict fault tolerance to prespecified classes of faults from which the system is designed to recover.

Faults may be classified as *transient* or *permanent*, *deterministic* or *indeterminate*, *local* or *catastrophic*. The first category refers to the duration of the fault, the second to its effect on the values of the system design parameters, and the third to the propagation of the fault to its neighboring elements.

Fault tolerance is provided by the application of protective redundancy—the use of more resources than normally necessary so as to upgrade system reliability. These resources may consist of more hardware, software, or time, or a combination of all three. Extra time is required to retransmit messages or to re-execute programs; extra software is required to perform diagnoses on the hardware; and extra hardware is required to provide replication of units.

Hardware redundancy may be of the *fault-masking* or *self-repair* types, or a hybrid of these two. In fault masking, redundancy is static; faults are masked instantly and the operations of fault detection, location, and correction are indistinguishable. In self-repair, redundancy is used dynamically; faults are selectively masked and are detected, located, and subsequently corrected by replacing the failed unit with an unfailed replica. Examples of fault masking are *triple modular redundancy* (TMR) and *quadding* (see below), and examples of self-repair are standby replacement (SR) systems and reconfigurable systems. Schemes using a combination of these two basic approaches are called *hybrid* or *adaptive* redundancy.

Some Fundamental Principles

A fundamental principle of reliability is that it must not only be inherent, but also a function of how the component is used. Another important principle is that, to achieve reliability by means of protective redundancy, the redundancy must be applied to the lowest level of component complexity in the system in order to maximize gain in reliability. This is the idealized state; in practice, trade-offs due to over-head are required in using redundancy techniques (e.g. providing *voters* in TMR systems and detection-switching requirements in standby systems). The application of the mathematical theory of reliability in modeling such systems provides quantitative design guidelines that make such trade-offs and optimizations possible and practicable.

In addition to the foregoing first and second principles of fault tolerance, a third principle is that a system may be made arbitrarily reliable provided the degree of redundancy is made high enough (i.e. a sufficiently large number of replicas are provided). Again, this principle holds only in an idealized situation; in practice, since the probability of detecting a failure and correctly switching to a spare is less than unity, this parameter, called *coverage*, limits the advantages postulated by the third principle.

A fourth principle concerns the problem of requiring the checking elements (those elements that are used for the diagnosis of the rest of the system and the subsequent reconfiguration of the system units) also to be checkable. This is the problem of "checking the checker." Thus, the fourth principle states that any system using protective redundancy will have major and minor "hard cores" (i.e. unprotected system elements), and that these cannot be totally eliminated from the system design. They may be made arbitrarily small, however, by judicious use of a mixture of different protective redundancy techniques.

Mathematical Theory of Reliability

Certain relationships exist among reliability parameters and their underlying probability theoretic relationships. If a fixed large number N_0 of identical items are being tested, of which N_s is the number of items surviving after time t and N_f is the number of items that failed during time t, then $N_0 = N_s + N_f$ for all t. Now, for a sufficiently large N_0, the reliability $R(t)$ of an item is N_s/N_0. The failure rate $\lambda(t)$, which is defined to be the rate at which the population changes at time t, can be shown to be given by

$$\lambda(t) = -\frac{1}{R(t)} \frac{dR(t)}{dt}, \tag{1}$$

so that

$$R(t) = \exp\left(-\int_0^t \lambda(\tau)\,d\tau\right) \tag{2}$$

The reliability function $R(t)$ is often called the *survival probability function*, since it measures the probability that failure of an item does not occur during the time interval $[0, t]$.

Failure Rate

Statistical data on equipment failure yield a characteristic "bathtub" curve, as shown in Fig. 1. When the equipment is first put into service, inherently weak components fail early. Subsequently, the failure rate stabilizes to a relatively constant value; this period is called the "useful life period." After much usage, failure rate begins to increase rapidly as a result of deterioration and wear.

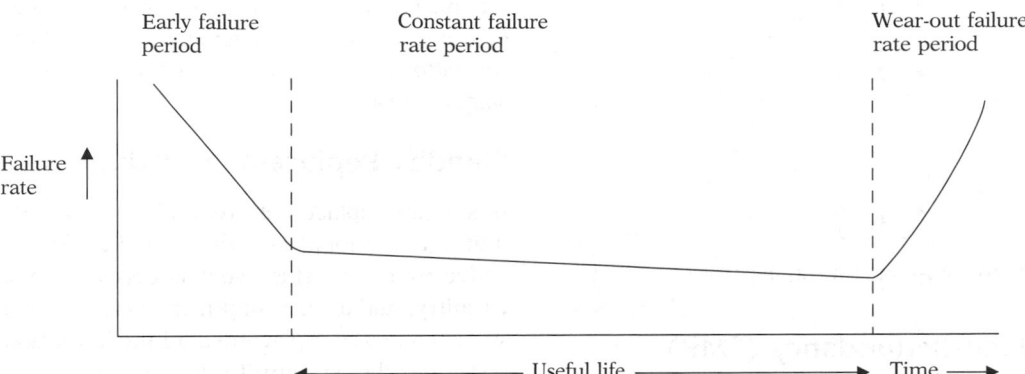

Figure 1. Bathtub curve of failure rate.

Exponential Failure Law

In general, the failure law of a component is the probability distribution effective from the moment at which a component enters service up to the moment of its failure. In practice the most commonly used failure law is the exponential law, which applies when a component is subject only to failures that occur at random intervals and the average number of failures is the same for equal time periods. These constraints are valid for a component that is no longer subject to early mortality failure and whose failure rate is a constant within the "useful life" span. Thus, for operating periods within the useful life, the component reliability over a period of time t can be expressed as $R(t) = e^{-\lambda t}$, where λ (usually expressed in failures per hour or per million hours) is the constant failure rate of the device. A characteristic of the exponential failure law is that the reliability of the device within the useful life period is the same for operating times of equal duration.

From the definition of $R(t)$ it follows that the mean time between failures (MTBF) or the mean time to first failure (MTTF), usually expressed in hours, are given by $\int_0^\infty R(t)\,dt$; i.e. it is the area underneath the reliability curve $R(t)$ plotted versus t. This is true for any failure distribution. For the specific case of the exponential failure law, the MTBF, m, is equal to $1/\lambda$. Further, when the product λt is small, the equation for $R(t)$ may be approximated by $R(t) \approx 1 - \lambda t$. Thus, if $\lambda t = 0.01$, $R(t) = e^{-0.01} = 0.99$, or 99.0%. The product λt is often referred to as the "normalized" time, since $\lambda t = t/m$; i.e. the mission time t is normalized with respect to the MTBF.

Series Reliability

If a system is composed of elements in such a way that the failure of any one element causes a failure of the system, then these elements are considered to be functionally in series. For the system to survive, each element must survive. The probability of survival for the system cannot be better than the element with the lowest probability of survival; i.e. a chain is no stronger than its weakest link. When these series elements are independent of each other, then, by the probability multiplication law, the system survival probability is the product of the individual survival probabilities of the elements. This is known as the product rule:

$$R_{\text{system}} = \prod_{i=1}^{n} R_i,$$

where R_i is the reliability of the ith element of an n-element system (Fig. 2).

Parallel Reliability

Parallel reliability is an illustration of protective redundancy. The system is composed of functionally parallel elements in such a way that if one of the elements fails the parallel unit will continue to do the system function (*see* Fig. 3). The system reliability, under the assumption of independence of failure of the elements, is expressed by

$$R_{\text{system}} = 1 - (1 - R)^n,$$

which is the probability that not all n elements have failed. The term $(1 - R)$, known as the unreliability of a unit, is the probability that a unit will fail. By the product rule, the term $(1 - R)^n$ is the probability that all n units will fail and one minus that is the probability that not all units will have failed. An example of parallel reliability is given by electronic diodes in parallel; if one diode open-circuits, the other will still provide the function.

Figure 2. System composed of a series of elements.

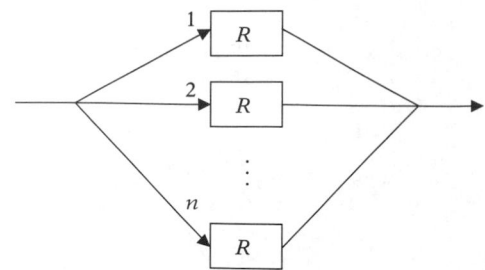

Figure 3. System composed of elements in parallel.

Triple Modular Redundancy (TMR)

TMR is also known as the *multiple-line voting* system. One of the earliest and most influential schemes was developed by John von Neumann (*q.v.*). The simplex unit is triplicated and each of the three independent units feeds into a majority voter, which outputs the majority signal (*see* Fig. 4). The system fails if more than one unit fails, in which case the failed units outvote the good one. This scheme is generalized to *N*-modular redundancy (NMR), where *N* is any odd number of units. Various schemes of protecting the voter are available, and also various other variants of the basic TMR strategy have been developed. The TMR system reliability is expressed as

$$R_{\text{system}} = [R^3 + 3R^2(1 - R)]R_v,$$

which is the product of the reliability R_v (the voter reliability) and the reliability of the idealized TMR system. The idealized TMR system reliability is the sum of the probabilities of two events: (1) that all three units survive, R^3; and (2) that any two units survive so that only one unit fails, $3R^2(1 - R)$.

Quadded Redundancy

Quadding is a method of component redundancy applicable to circuits with alternating AND and OR gates. It is similar in concept to TMR, with the major difference being that the voting or restoration of fault-masking functions are distributed into the network and are not separable, as in TMR. In general, the quadding procedure requires that each logic gate be quadruplicated and that each of the gates in a quad stage will have twice as many inputs as the non-redundant gate replaced. The outputs of a stage are

interconnected to the inputs of the succeeding stage by a connection pattern in such a way that the effects of errors in earlier stages get subsequently "restored" in the latter stages; i.e. the originally intended "good" signal is restored.

Standby Replacement Redundancy

In standby replacement redundancy (Fig. 5), only one unit is operational at a time, unlike TMR. When the active unit fails, this event is detected by additional circuitry, and a spare unit from a reserve of S spares is switched in as a replacement of the failed unit, thereby restoring the system to its operational state. The reliability of this system is expressed as

$$R_{\text{system}} = 1 - (1 - R)^{s+1},$$

which is the probability that not all S units have failed.

Hybrid Redundancy

Hybrid redundancy is a synthesis of TMR and standby replacement redundancy (*see* Fig. 6). It consists of a TMR system (or, in general, an NMR system), with a bank of spares so that when one of the TMR units fails, it is replaced by a spare unit. Failure detection is achieved by means of disagreement detectors which compare the individual outputs of each of the triple modular redundancy units with the system output. If there is a difference, the disagreement detector signals the switching network to replace the failed unit by a spare unit. When all spares are used, the hybrid redundancy system reduces to a TMR system. Variations of hybrid or adaptive redundancy schemes are possible. The system reliability in its simplest terms may be expressed as

$$R_{\text{system}} = 1 - [(1 - R)^{s+3} + R(S + 3)(1 - R)^{s+2}],$$

which is the probability that not all $S + 3$ units fail and that not any $S + 2$ units fail with one not failing.

Summary

Redundancy as a procedure for designing more reliable systems than allowed by the intrinsic reliability of the constituent components is as old as the discipline of

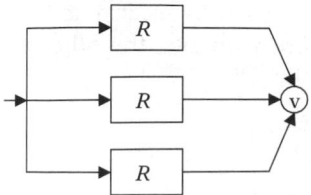

Figure 4. Triple modular redundancy.

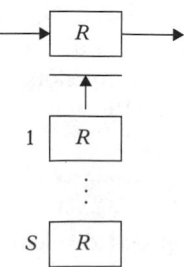

Figure 5. Standby replacement redundancy.

Reconfiguration logic

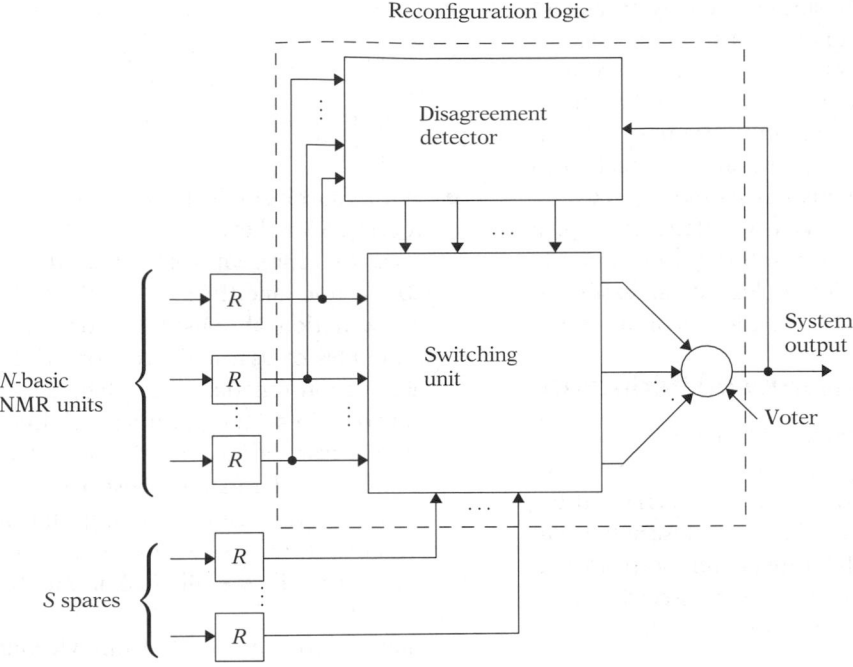

Figure 6. Hybrid redundancy.

engineering itself. In fact, even the evolutionary processes of life use it (e.g. in the human body there are two kidneys, two lungs, etc.).

Examples of the use of redundancy in ancient times are provided in the construction of temples and bridges, where more than the absolutely required number of pillars is provided to support the structure; thus, should one pillar sustain damage, the remaining pillars would still be able to share the load successfully.

In the computer age, all the basic techniques described have been applied, with varying degrees of sophistication, to the design of ultrareliable computing systems. TMR has been successfully applied in designing the guidance and control computer of the Saturn V launch vehicle. Quadding is used to a great extent in the design of the spacecraft computer of the Orbiting Astronomical Observatory (OAO). Standby replacement redundancy was extensively used in the Raytheon RAYDAC computer and in the Jet Propulsion Laboratory's self-test and repair (STAR) computer. The latter also used hybrid redundancy to protect the monitor subsystem of the self-repairing computer.

In addition, these techniques are also finding application in protecting the automated computerized controls of modern high-speed transit systems and in other applications where the cost of using redundancy is justifiable because it minimizes danger to human life, or increases the continuous availability of services that, if interrupted by failure and subsequent repair, would cause severe consumer dissatisfaction. An example of the latter is the present-day automated telephone switching system. Another example, but with a different flavor, is the resilience of the Internet (*q.v.*) whose multiple routing paths avoid bottlenecks. In an expanding society where products become more sophisticated and projects proliferate, the scope of reliability engineering, protective redundancy, and fault-tolerant computing will continue to grow.

Bibliography

1956. von Neumann, J. "Probabilistic Logics and the Synthesis of Organisms from Unreliable Components," in *Automata Studies*, 43–98. Princeton, NJ: Princeton University.
1987. Nelson, V. P., and Carroll, B. D. *Tutorial: Fault-Tolerant Computing.* Los Alamitos, CA: IEEE Computer Society Press.
1992. Siewiorek, D. P., and Swarz, R., *Reliable Computer Systems: Design and Evaluation.* Bedford, MA: Digital Press.
1996. Pradhan, D. K. (ed.) *Fault-Tolerant Computer System Design.* Upper Saddle River, NJ: Prentice Hall.

Frank P. Mathur

HARDWARE VERIFICATION

For articles on related subjects *see* DIGITAL DESIGN AUTOMATION; HARDWARE DESCRIPTION LANGUAGES; MODEL CHECKING; and PROGRAM VERIFICATION.

Hardware verification typically involves demonstrating that an *implementation* of a system is "consistent" with respect to its *specification*, where these descriptions tend to be at different levels of abstraction. Somewhat more generally, hardware verification involves comparing two descriptions of a (hardware) design for "consistency." This requires (1) the two descriptions;

(2) formal models for each (since these may or may not be the same); (3) a formal notion of the "consistency" relation between them; (4) some way of checking or proving the consistency relation. We note that such a proof need not necessarily directly resemble a "traditional" logic proof (e.g. it may simply be a mechanical enumeration of all possibilities). It should, however, be something that could always be translated into a logical proof. Thus, for instance, simulation (*q.v.*) cannot be used for formal verification unless it is feasible to simulate exhaustively all the possibilities of interest.

Techniques Used In Hardware Verification

SPECIFICATION AND FORMAL MODELS

A system description may be given in a "hardware description language" (HDL), such as VHDL (IEEE, 1993) or a "broad-spectrum" system description language (encompassing both hardware and software subsystems). Alternatively, it may be expressed directly in the syntax of the underlying formal model.

The formal models that underlie system descriptions typically use some form of algebra or logic. Common examples of useful models include Boolean or propositional logic (for combinational circuits), finite state machines (for sequential circuits), and state graphs. Other examples of formal models include various flavors of temporal logic (e.g. Computational Tree Logic (Burch *et al.*, 1990—*see* MODEL CHECKING) used for stating properties of finite state systems); logics that incorporate the notion of dense real-time intervals, enabling properties of timed systems to be expressed; various flavors of "process algebras" that are used to provide semantics for ensembles of processes (e.g. CCS —Milner, 1980); infinitary languages (and automata that accept them); and Petri nets (*q.v.*).

CONSISTENCY

The notion of consistency depends on the properties of the system that are deemed relevant; while this normally includes "observable" functional behavior, other attributes of interest include timing characteristics, power consumption, and testability. Even when restricted to considering "functional" behavior, there are considerable (and sometimes subtle) variations in the precise notion of "consistency" that is used in the context of different models, and sometimes even within the same "family" of models (e.g. within models based on process algebras or within models based on temporal logic).

Some examples of the consistency relation between two descriptions S and I include:

◆ Equality: $I = S$.

◆ Equivalence: $I \Leftrightarrow S$.

◆ Logical implication: $I \Rightarrow S$.

◆ Conditional logical implication: $C(input) \Rightarrow (I \Rightarrow S)$; where the predicate $C(input)$ is designed to insure that the system's environment behaves properly.

◆ Homomorphism: This may loosely be expressed as $R(\varphi(I), S)$, where a homomorphic function φ is used to represent (or relate) different levels of abstraction, and the relation R embodies an appropriate notion of consistency between $\varphi(I)$ and S. Examples of useful abstractions include structural abstraction (enabling the "hiding" of internal signals or wires), temporal abstraction (enabling different granularities of timing); data abstraction (consisting of relating "abstract" objects to more concrete "representation" objects); and event abstraction (the abstraction of events that are not relevant to the specific task in hand).

Further differences result from viewing concurrent computations as having a tree-like (branching) structure, in contrast to being linearized in some fashion. The former view is reflected in branching time temporal logics and process algebras like CCS. The latter view is reflected in linear time temporal logics, trace theory and systems that model communicating sequential processes (e.g. CSP; Hoare, 1985).

CHECKING FOR CONSISTENCY

The techniques used for checking equivalence are closely related to the formal models used. There is a wide spectrum of logics and related systems that perform manipulations relevant to the logics. In general, the simpler logics (e.g. Boolean logic—*see* BOOLEAN ALGEBRA) are typically less expressive and more tractable, while the richer logics (e.g. formulations of higher-order logic that permit variables to range over functions and predicates, and quantification over such variables) are more expressive and less tractable. Various flavors of temporal logics and enhancements of first-order logic fall between these extremes.

It is often possible to exploit the special properties and idiosyncrasies of certain logics to develop specialized data structures (*q.v.*) and algorithms (*q.v.*) to support the manipulations required by the logic. A good example of this is a graph-based canonical representation of Boolean expressions, called Typed Ordered Binary Decision Diagrams and abbreviated BDDs (Bryant, 1986). BDDs enable very efficient implementations of Boolean operations, such as conjunction, disjunction, and negation of expressions, as well as checks for satisfiability of a formula and the equivalence of two Boolean formulas (and therefore two combinational logic networks). BDD-based systems have also been used to show equivalence between deterministic Moore machines (*see* SEQUENTIAL MACHINE) by performing a *symbolic* exploration of the state space determined by the product of the two machines. Other methods use BDDs in "symbolic" simulation, and also combine graph-based and theorem-proving/assertion-based proof techniques.

Temporal logics enable reasoning about the order of events in time without introducing time explicitly. Although a number of different temporal logics have been studied, most have an operator like $\mathbf{G}(f)$ that is true in the present if f is always true in the future (i.e. if f is **G**lobally true). To assert that two events e_1 and e_2 never occur at the same time, one would write $\mathbf{G}(\neg e_1 \wedge \neg e_2)$. The meaning of a temporal logic formula is usually determined with respect to a labeled state transition graph (sometimes called a *Kripke structure* for historical reasons). To check whether a system described by a state graph satisfies a certain property (the "specification") expressed by a temporal logic formula, the state space denoted by the state graph has to be explored; this can be done in time linear in the size of the state graph and the temporal logic formula being checked.

A logic called the μ-calculus can be used as a general framework for describing a variety of verification methodologies. A *model checking* algorithm for the μ-calculus can be used to decide, among other things, the validity of branching-time and linear-time temporal logic formulas with respect to a finite model, and strong and weak observational equivalence of finite transition systems.

Graph-based verification methods include temporal logic model checking, formal language containment, trace theory, and the calculus of communicating systems (CCS). While these have different computational models and differ in their notions of verification, they generally involve decision algorithms that explicitly represent some relational quantity over the domain of the model. By using a binary encoding of the domain of the model and efficient representations of the relational quantities using BDDs, the complexity of the decision algorithms can be greatly reduced *in practice*. Some empirical results show that the method can be applied in practice to verify models with more than 10^{120} states.

Another approach involves checking *inclusion* between two automata on infinite tapes. The first machine represents the system that is being verified; the second represents its specification. Automata on infinite tapes are used in order to handle fairness.

A desired goal (or "theorem") is obtained ("proved") in a logic by the application of an appropriate sequence of inference rules of the logic. A mechanization of a logic provides support for mechanical application of the inference rules of a logic. In interactive proof-based systems, such as the HOL system supporting Higher Order Logic (Gordon, 1988), additional support is typically provided for concisely encoding strategies and high-level tactics that drive the lower-level mechanical inferences needed to carry out large and complex proofs. Further, several forms of "bookkeeping" support are also provided by such systems to facilitate the development, browsing, and subsequent modification of proofs and proof strategies.

The Boyer–Moore (1988) theorem prover is based on the Boyer–Moore logic, which augments first-order predicate calculus with a semi-automated induction scheme and axioms for data types, such as natural numbers, strings, and lists.

As the representations and algorithms for relevant classes of logical manipulations evolve and mature, mechanized systems based on such logics will naturally evolve along with them. Recently, there has been dramatic progress in the complexity of systems that can be addressed by special-purpose logics and automata. General-purpose proof and theorem prover technology has also evolved considerably over the last 30 years, although the relative progress here has been slower, since it is comparatively difficult to discover "universally applicable" tricks. Many commercial systems use hybrid representations and solution strategies.

Current Status—What Can We Expect from Formal Verification?

There are several areas where verification is becoming mainstream today (e.g. the verification of the function of "medium size" combinational circuits (100K+ gates) such as those used for arithmetic operations in a CPU (*q.v.*) and the function of smaller control circuits (possessing of the order of 2^{20} states); further, the sophistication of these techniques and their adoption in industrial practice has improved rapidly in the late 1990s. Because of the possibility of subtle errors, processor floating-point arithmetic circuits have been extensively studied, and recent results include the formal verification of parts of the Intel Pentium Pro CPU, among others (*Formal Methods in System Design*, 1999). Other more powerful (but less automatic) techniques and tools are being explored that address much broader classes of circuits. For example, interactive techniques based on theorem provers have been used to verify certain aspects of the functional behavior of simple microprocessors. Similar techniques are being used to verify "vertically integrated systems" (e.g. operating systems running on robust hardware) as well as compilers and application programs based on these. It should be noted that totally automated verification for arbitrary circuits is (theoretically) impossible in general.

Hardware design complexity has increased to a point where it is impractical to design a system from scratch because of time-to-market constraints. This has resulted in design methodologies that attempt to reuse a large repertoire of pre-designed "Intellectual Property" (IP) cores or "virtual components," typically developed by different vendors. The components in these "systems-on-a-chip" (SOC) are associated with individual inter-face specifications (e.g. protocols—*q.v.*), and the SOC designer typically may not have access to all of the de-tails of the virtual component. New validation meth-odologies are emerging that target this class of designs, many amalgamating techniques from formal verifica-tion and conventional simulation.

Often, even *attempting* formal verification of hard-ware designs—by striving to provide formal specifica-tions of the desired system attributes such as behavior and performance—can be quite beneficial; a high proportion of ambiguities and inconsistencies tend to be exposed during such an exercise. While verification can improve the quality and cost-effectiveness of many designs, it is certainly not a panacea. Verification in-volves two or more models, where the models typically bear an uncheckable (and possibly imperfect) relation-ship, both to devices and the designer's intentions. It is important to distinguish the limitations and capabilities of the model from those of the tools and techniques.

Hardware verification is useful if it reduces the cost and time of developing a new product or improves the reliability or the degree of confidence in a product suffi-cient to justify any increased costs. Sometimes, verifi-cation is not needed because other strategies are sufficient. At other times, it may be needed but not practical, in that the techniques available may be too expensive to be cost-effective for a given application. Nevertheless, such advanced techniques can be justi-fied in the context of designing life-critical applications (e.g. systems used in medicine for life-support, civil avionics, and nuclear reactors), as well as systems where replacement is either very expensive (e.g. oil pipelines and some embedded applications), or impos-sible (e.g. space probes).

Bibliography

1980. Milner. R. A *Calculus of Communicating Systems.* New York: Springer-Verlag.
1985. Hoare, C. A. R. *Communicating Sequential Processes.* Upper Saddle River, NJ: Prentice Hall.
1986. Bryant, R. E. "Graph Based Algorithms for Boolean Function Manipulation," *IEEE Transactions on Computers,* **C-35**, *8*, 677–691.
1988. Boyer, R. S., and Moore, J. S. *A Computational Logic Handbook.* New York: Academic Press.
1988. Gordon, M. "HOL: A Proof Generating System for Higher Order Logic," in *VLSI Specification, Synthesis and Verification* (eds. G. Birtwistle and P. A. Subrahmanyam). Boston: Kluwer Academic Publishers.
1990. Burch, J. R., Clarke, E. M., Dill, D. L., McMillan, K. L., and Hwang, L. J., "Symbolic Model Checking: 10^{20} States and Beyond," in *Proc. IEEE Conference on Logic in Computer Science.*
1993. IEEE. *VHDL Language Reference Manual, Standard 1076-93.* New York: IEEE Press.
1998. Aagaard, M. D., Jones, R. B., and Seger, C.-J. H. "Combining Theorem Proving and Trajectory Evaluation in an Industrial Environment," *Proc. 1998 Design Automation Conference,* 538–541. New York: ACM Press.
1998. Barrett, C. W., Dill, D. L., and Levitt, J. R. "A Decision Procedure for Bit Vector Arithmetic," *Proc. 1998 Design Automation Conference,* 522–527. New York: ACM Press.
1999. *Formal Methods in System Design,* **14**, *1*. Special issue on arithmetic circuits.

Website

1999. Formal Methods. http://archive.comlab.ox.ac.uk/formal-methods.html.

Edmund M. Clarke, Jr and P. A. Subrahmanyam

HARDWARE

See COMPUTER ARCHITECTURE; COMPUTER CIRCUITRY; COMPUTER SYSTEMS; HARDWARE RELIABILITY; INTEGRATED CIRCUITRY. *See also* names of specific computer components and entries under MEMORY.

HARTREE, DOUGLAS R.

For articles on related subjects *see* DIFFERENTIAL ANALYZER; and MANCHESTER UNIVERSITY COMPUTERS.

Douglas Rayner Hartree (Fig. 1) was born on 27 March 1897. During the First World War, he did scientific work in anti-aircraft gunnery and afterwards began research in wave mechanics, then a new subject. He pioneered a method of computing molecular wave functions by what he called the method of the self-consistent field. This was long before the days of digital computers, and Hartree used a desk calculator for the heavy numerical calculations that were involved. He became attracted by the potential of numerical com-putation in scientific research, and it was as a specialist in that field that he became known, rather than as a physicist.

In 1931, Vannevar Bush (*q.v.*) published his de-scription of the differential analyzer. Hartree was impressed by the possibilities of this machine and in the summer of 1934 spent a month studying it at MIT. On his return, he set about raising funds for the installation of a similar machine at Manchester University, where he was Professor of Applied Mathe-matics. The machine was duly installed and during the

Figure 1. Douglas R. Hartree.

Second World War constituted a valuable computing resource. Under Hartree's direction, it was used for a number of wartime problems, relating notably to the radar magnetron and to anomalous propagation of radio waves in the troposphere.

At the time, there were only a handful of people in the world who could be described as specialists in numerical computation. This put Hartree in a strong position to advise when the early digital computers became available. In May or June 1945, he paid an official visit on behalf of the British government to the USA, where he saw the Automatic Sequence Controlled Calculator (*see* MARK I) at Harvard and the ENIAC (*q.v.*), then still incomplete, at the University of Pennsylvania. Through the interest of Colonel Paul Gillon, he paid another visit in 1946 to advise on non-military uses to which the ENIAC might be put. He was able to get personal experience of the use of the machine by running it on a problem in compressible fluid flow. In 1948, Hartree again visited the USA and spent three months as acting chief of the newly founded Institute for Numerical Analysis of the National Bureau of Standards on the UCLA campus. On his way back to the East Coast, he delivered a series of lectures at the University of Illinois. These were published under the title "Calculating Instruments and Machines." At the time, a number of the new stored-program computers were under construction, but none was actually operating. The lectures give a most interesting picture of the world of scientific computation on the very eve of the computer revolution.

By October 1946, Hartree had moved from Manchester to the Cavendish Laboratory in Cambridge. The Mathematical Laboratory (later called the Computer Laboratory) was then beginning to get into its post-war stride. From the beginning, Hartree gave it his whole-hearted support. He volunteered to give a course of lectures in numerical analysis, which he later published as a book. When the EDSAC (*q.v.*) began to be used on scientific problems, his experience with numerical computation was of the greatest value. He become a key member of the committee that interviewed applicants who wished to use the machine and, if their projects were approved, gave them advice on how to proceed.

By 1958 the credibility of digital computers had been established and the foundations of the computer field as we now know it were being established. Hartree was making many contributions and it was a serious loss to the field when, on 12 February 1958, he collapsed in the street from heart failure and died almost immediately.

Bibliography

1958. Darwin, C. G. "D. R. Hartree," *Biographical Memoirs of the Royal Society*, **4**, 103.
1984. Hartree, D. R. *Calculating Machines: Recent and Prospective Developments and Their Impact on Mathematical Physics*, and *Calculating Instruments and Machines*. Charles Babbage Institute Reprint Series 6. Cambridge, MA: MIT Press (contains reprint of *Calculating Instruments and Machines*, Illinois University Press, 1949).

Maurice V. Wilkes

HEURISTIC

For articles on related subjects *see* ALGORITHM; ARTIFICIAL INTELLIGENCE; COMPUTER CHESS; EXPERT SYSTEMS; INFORMATION TECHNOLOGY; and KNOWLEDGE REPRESENTATION.

The ancient Greek word *heuriskein* means "to find out, to discover." The English adjective *heuristic*, the more recently coined homonymous noun *heuristic* (in singular) or the more common *heuristics* (in plural) came into being via the Latin adjective *heuristicus*. According to the *Random House Dictionary*:

> *heuristic* adj. *1.* serving to indicate or point out, stimulating interest as a means of furthering investigation. *2.* (of a teaching method) encouraging the student to discover for himself.—n. *3.* a heuristic method or argument.

In the general sense, we talk of the "heuristic power" of a technique, the "heuristics in somebody's reasoning," and so on. Pólya (1954) has written several entertaining books that show how to approach problems in mathematics and geometry via heuristic ideas. Also, Hadamard's essay on discovery in mathematics (*The Psychology of Invention in the Mathematical Field*) yields an interesting insight—a much too rare phenomenon—into how one of the great mathematicians approaches problems.

How does all this concern us in computing? The reason is simple, but its application leads to an area that is completely open-ended. Let us consider, for example, a standard task in programming. We wish to find the roots of a higher-order algebraic equation. There are several methods of approximation that yield the solution with estimable error bounds. We have the formulas to follow, step by step, and eventually we obtain the results. This is the *algorithmic approach*.

Let us now consider a so-called ill-defined problem, of which we have many in everyday life. For example, say we want to balance our household budget by following a program. Although our basic needs are reasonably well known (food, shelter, clothing, medical items, transportation, entertainment, etc.), neither the relative weight of the components nor their unit prices are completely determinable. Also, our needs, desires and tastes change continually. Our interaction with the environment represents a significant modifying factor. Because this problem is terribly ill-defined, no mathematical technique by itself has a chance to solve it. The computerization of the solution requires all those vague, hard-to-quantify ideas that humans in fact make use of in doing this problem. ("Either I go on vacation or buy that new car... Let's see, how much longer can I drive my old car?") The collection of these rules of thumb, sometimes referred to as insight, intuition, or experience with a particular task, represents what computer scientists call *heuristics*. Any one such rule is thus a *heuristic*.

We resort to *heuristic programming* whenever an algorithmic solution is prohibitively expensive, impossible to follow, or unavailable. The role of heuristics is to cut down the time and memory requirements of search. On average, it should result in appreciable savings when programming our budget to satisfy our basic needs. Heuristic methods are not foolproof; they can fail a certain proportion of the time. (Algorithms are not supposed to fail. However, the fact that a technique is not foolproof does not render it heuristic.) The heuristic approach is contrasted with those algorithms that guarantee to provide a *practical solution* within certain *resource limits*. That is why an *exhaustive search* or *complete analysis* does not in general constitute a heuristic technique—nor a practical algorithm, for that matter. Lenat's comments (1982b) are illuminating in distinguishing among three forms of problem solving: when not enough is known about a domain to express good heuristics, we are in a *pre-heuristic* stage; when the environment is better but not completely known (such as in medical diagnosis, with its plausible but not certain causal relations), we resort to *heuristic search*; and when all relevant aspects of the domain are known (such as predicting eclipses), we have reached the stage of *algorithmization*.

The larger the range in which a heuristic can be applied, the more powerful it is considered to be. Also, its level of performance should be better than an exhaustive strategy or of a random search for the solution. Some heuristics are restricted to a specific problem area (i.e. they are *domain-specific*), while some have general relevance to problem solving, such as the *generate-and-test method* or *means-ends analysis* (*see* INFORMATION PROCESSING). In general, analogies and models can lead the researcher to insight that forms the basis of heuristics (Romanycia and Pelletier, 1985).

The following example, originally reported by Herbert Simon (*q.v.*), should shed some light on the concept under discussion. Nontrivial games cannot be played by humans *or* by machines algorithmically (because there does not exist an algorithm) or exhaustively (because the memory and time requirements far exceed any available ones). The classical example of an intellectual game, chess, has been programmed by several groups of researchers (*see* COMPUTER CHESS). In all these, heuristic ideas occupy a central role in move selection and position evaluation. In fact, de Groot and other psychologists have shown that the basic difference between excellent and merely good players is not in their memory capacity or even in their data processing ability *in abstracto*. All players analyze practically the same number of board positions but not always the same ones. Excellent chess players have developed very powerful heuristics for the *selection* of game continuations to be considered. They may go down to a depth of, say, 20 half-moves along one path and disregard others below a depth of 2 or 3, for reasons of their own. In a sense, the recent machine victory in computer chess over the best human player (Deep Blue vs. Kasparov) is not a full success for artificial intelligence because a large part of the improvement in machine playing has not yet been due to better heuristics but, rather, to the significant advances in computational speed and software/hardware organization.

One often-used heuristic in chess is to leave as little freedom of move selection for the opponent as possible. If all other techniques of comparison assign an equal score to two moves considered, a chess expert usually selects the one that restricts the opponent's mobility to a larger degree. This works most of the time. There was a famous game, however, between two masters in which the winner used this heuristic to his disadvantage. It has been shown by game analysts that in a particular position, the optimum move (overlooked for the reasons discussed) could have led to an earlier victory. A supplement to this story is that the MATER program by Baylor and Simon (1966), which incorporates the heuristic of fewest-replies, was presented the same particular near-end position and duplicated the mistake made by the master.

In many computational tasks, heuristics are embedded in a *heuristic evaluation function* which helps the program decide between alternative courses of action. It is usually defined by the researcher in an *ad hoc* manner, relying on *domain knowledge*—a possibly detailed, but not necessarily exact, acquaintance with the qualitative and quantitative aspects of the processes, objects and relations in the problem area. This means that, apart from some introductory efforts (Waterman, 1970; Findler, 1977), heuristic rules have always been preprogrammed—it is not the system that discovers, selects and optimizes them. Therefore the performance level of these programs is determined by the researcher's experience, insight, and perhaps even luck. (We note that domain knowledge can encompass very complex issues. For example, to reach the desired final configuration of a Rubik cube, it would be a hopelessly inadequate heuristic to move in the direction of monotonically increasing the total number of squares of identical color on each of the six sides of the cube. Useful heuristics are based here on reasoning that comes from some rather abstract mathematical concepts.)

A much more desirable situation would be one in which heuristic processes are automated. Learning programs, initially inefficient and possibly even random in their actions, would gradually formulate more and more heuristics on the basis of experience. These heuristics would assume a flexible functional or parametric format so that subsequent optimization processes could raise the overall level of performance. An important step in this direction is described next.

Douglas Lenat introduced the idea of automating certain discovery processes in a series of articles (Lenat, 1982a, b, 1983a, b), and implemented them in two projects, *AM* and *EURISKO*. The programs are first given some basic knowledge; for instance, in dealing with mathematical problems, a few facts about number theory and a set of operators that can make changes in given or derived "concepts." Examples of a concept are *function*, *set* and *bag* (a set in which elements can have multiple occurrences). Each concept is represented in the program according to the slot-and-filler notation of a *frame* (*see* KNOWLEDGE REPRESENTATION). The system tries to fill in the different slots with values. These include regular and extreme examples, cases of specialization and generalization (as obtained through purposive changes in the programmed definition of the concept), and the worth of the concept. *Tasks* are applications of one or more heuristic rules and are characterized by the expected "interestingness" of their result. A useful structure, the *agenda*, contains a list of tasks ordered by their interestingness, each item being associated with its respective justification—by its own use and by other tasks potentially invoking it. The agenda turned out to be a rather undirected but very productive control structure in recommending the task to be executed next. Hypotheses about the concept, and its more general and more specific versions, are generated and tested. Those not rejected and interesting enough become *conjectures*. (The system does not *prove* theorems but states *potentially true* ones.) *AM*, in this sense, has discovered the concepts of numbers, addition, multiplication, divisors, prime numbers, unique prime factorization, and several others. Note that the program does not *search* the concept space according to some predetermined criterion (such as tree searches following the depth-first, breadth-first or best-first discipline) but it *explores* the concept space under dynamic control.

Finally, *EURISKO* makes this approach even more powerful. It no longer uses static heuristics, as *AM* does, but treats heuristic rules dynamically, as if they were concepts. In other words, it subjects them to generalization, specialization, and analogical reasoning, and thus can create new and better heuristics. In addition to mathematics, *EURISKO* has also been successfully applied to three-dimensional VLSI design and to the specification of "battle fleets" in a space warfare game. For an analysis of some limitations of the approach taken by *AM* and *EURISKO*, *see* Lenat and Brown (1984).

Bibliography

1954. Pólya, G. *Mathematics and Plausible Reasoning*: **I**. *Induction and Analogy in Mathematics*, **II**. *Patterns of Plausible Inference*. Princeton, NJ: Princeton University Press.

1966. Baylor, G. W., and Simon, H. A. "A Chess Mating Combinations Program," *Proc. SJCC*, **28**, 431–447.

1970. Waterman, D. A. "Generalization Learning Techniques for Automating the Learning of Heuristics," *Artificial Intelligence*, **1**, 121–170.

1977. Findler, N. V. "Studies in Machine Cognition Using the Game of Poker," *Comm. of the ACM*, **20**, 230–245.

1978. Waterman, D. A., and Hayes-Roth, F. (eds.) *Pattern-Directed Inference Systems*. New York: Academic Press.

1982a. Lenat, D. B. "The Nature of Heuristics," *Artificial Intelligence*, **19**, 189–249.

1982b. Lenat, D. B. "AM: Discovery in Mathematics as Heuristic Search," in *Knowledge-Based Systems in Artificial Intelligence* (eds. R. Davis and D. B. Lenat), 1–225. New York, NY: McGraw-Hill.

1983a Lenat, D. B. "Theory Formation by Heuristic Search," *Artificial Intelligence*, **21**, 31–59.

1983b Lenat, D. B. "EURISKO: A Program that Learns New Heuristics and Domain Concepts," *Artificial Intelligence*, **21**, 61–98.

1984. Lenat, D. B., and Brown, J. S. "Why AM and EURISKO Appear to Work," *Artificial Intelligence*, **23**, 269–294.

1985. Romanycia, M. H. J, and Pelletier, F. J. "What Is a Heuristic?" *Computational Intelligence*, **1**, 47–58.

1996. Rayward-Smith, V. J., Osman, I. H., and Reeves, C. R. (eds.) *Modern Heuristic Search Methods*. New York: John Wiley.

Nicholas V. Findler

HIERARCHY OF OPERATORS

See OPERATOR PRECEDENCE.

HIGH-LEVEL LANGUAGE

See PROBLEM-ORIENTED LANGUAGES; and PROCEDURE-ORIENTED LANGUAGES.

HISTORY OF DIGITAL COMPUTERS

See DIGITAL COMPUTERS, HISTORY OF; and SOFTWARE HISTORY.

HOLLERITH MACHINE

For articles on related subjects *see* HOLLERITH, HERMAN; PUNCHED CARD; and PUNCHED CARD MACHINERY.

The first practical electric tabulating system, developed and patented by Herman Hollerith in the late 1880s, received its widest initial use, encouragement, and greatest impetus from the 1890 census of the USA. On short notice, he produced 50 tabulating machines and related equipment that were used to tally the population and dwelling counts and later to tabulate and cross-tabulate the characteristics for nearly 63 million persons. The Census Bureau employed later versions of this system for the next 60 years, or until electronic tabulation appeared in the form of UNIVAC I (*q.v.*).

Hollerith's system was based on a card-punching device that a clerk, reading a census return, used to record up to 17 different characteristics for one person by choosing among 240 possible punching positions and punching holes in a $6\frac{5}{8} \times 3\frac{1}{4}$-inch card (Fig. 1). (Certain standard codes, such as for a particular enumeration district, could be set on another punch and transferred to stacks of cards.) The completed cards were then fed, one at a time, into a "circuit-closing press" on the tabulating machine. This press was equipped with rows of spring-loaded pins in the

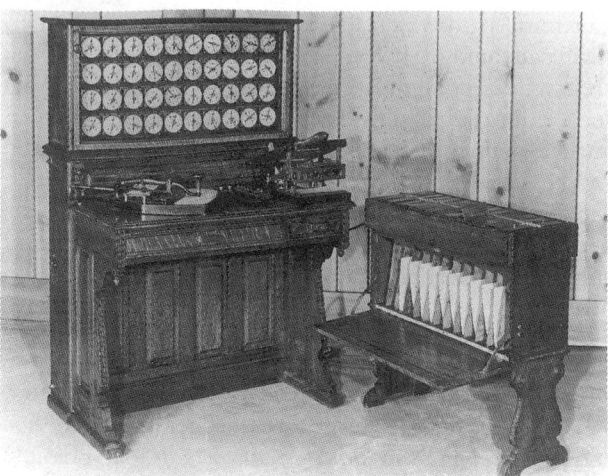

Figure 1. Hollerith machine. (Courtesy of IBM.)

top jaw and tiny matching pots of mercury in the bottom jaw. The pins were wired for an electric current; the mercury pots were connected to 40 counter dials. When a clerk inserted the punched card in the press and closed the jaws, the pins finding holes were able to descend into their mercury pots. The current passed through these pins and pots to their related electromagnetic counter dials on the machine, advancing the unit hand on each dial one place. (When the unit hand made a complete revolution on the dial, it activated a hundreds pointer one place.) The clerk then released the jaws, removed the card and dropped it into an open pocket on a sorting box connected to the machine, and repeated the entire operation with the next card. At the end of the run, the dials were read and reset for the next run and the sorting box was emptied. The dials could also be connected through relays, to deal with combinations of characteristics such as "foreign-born white males."

Since clerks in the 1890 census were now able to punch an average of 700 cards each in an 8-hour day and a tabulating-machine operator could handle 7,000 cards in the same period, the Hollerith system represented a considerable advance in speed over the past. One machine could now process 250 items (characteristics) per minute once the cards had been punched. A clerk in the 1880 census (when there were just 50 million people in the USA), with the help of a fairly crude mechanical device, could tally (but not cross-tabulate) 20 characteristics per minute, but even that was about four times faster than was possible with the big census schedules and tally sheets used in earlier years. Even so, census data processing was labor-intensive and time-consuming, so much so that, allowing for budget constraints, some tabulations could not be published until 1889, a year before the next census began.

For vital statistics agencies, insurance companies, railroads, and other organizations—but especially the Census Bureau—that needed to process quantities of data and produce timely results, the Hollerith machine and the punched cards it required broke most of the nineteenth century labor and time barriers they faced. In computer history, the Hollerith system was the technological advance that for 60 years bridged the gap between marks on paper and the electronic age.

Bibliography

1965. Truesdell, L. E. *The Development of Punch Card Tabulation in the Bureau of the Census, 1890–1940.* Washington, DC: US Govt. Print. Off.
1982. Austrian, G. D. *Herman Hollerith, Forgotten Giant of Information Processing.* New York: Columbia University Press.

Frederick G. Bohme

HOLLERITH, HERMAN

For articles on related subjects *see* DIGITAL COMPUTERS, HISTORY OF: EARLY; HOLLERITH MACHINE; POWERS, JAMES; PUNCHED CARD MACHINERY; and WATSON, THOMAS, J. SR.

Herman Hollerith (b. Buffalo, NY, 1860; d. Washington, DC, 1929), *see* Figure 1, was the inventor of the punched-card data processing machine. His systems and the applications he developed for them laid the foundations for the data processing industry in the USA and elsewhere. He held the foundation patents in the field (US Patents 395 781–395 783) and nearly 50 other US and foreign patents on basic techniques and equipment. He developed applications of punched-card data processing (*q.v.*) for many fields of endeavor, including the US Census, medical and public health statistics, railroad and public utility accounting, stock and inventory control, and factory cost accounting.

Many precedents he set by the turn of the 20th century persisted until recent years. Punched cards were the size of dollar bills of that era because Hollerith found it economical to buy cabinets and drawers subdivided in that size. The positional coding used on punched cards (Hollerith code) evolved directly from decisions he made about card layout when designing the first column-by-column keypunch for the 1901 Census of Agriculture. Even the practice of IBM and other firms through the 1970s of leasing and maintaining their own data processing equipment originated in Hollerith's decisions made prior to 1900.

Upon graduation from the Columbia College School of Mines in 1879, Hollerith took a job as special agent with the US Census. After completing his own report, Hollerith compiled some vital statistics for Dr. John Shaw Billings, a member of the Surgeon General's Office, who was also serving as director of the division

Figure 1. Herman Hollerith (courtesy of IBM Archives).

of vital statistics for the Census Bureau. Billings suggested to Hollerith that a good machine to do the purely mechanical work of tabulating population and similar statistics was badly needed and that a technique of using cards with the description of each individual punched into them was a good approach to the problem. Intrigued by this suggestion, Hollerith made a study of the problem and determined to his own satisfaction that is was feasible.

In 1882, Hollerith followed General Francis Walker from the Census Bureau to MIT, where he became an instructor in mechanical engineering. While there he worked hard on his "Census machine" invention, concentrating initially upon a variant of an earlier machine developed by Colonel Charles W. Seaton, chief clerk for the 1870 Census. This prototype had used a player-piano roll type of feed mechanism rather than individual cards.

At the end of his first year at MIT, Hollerith returned to Washington and secured a position with the US Patent Office to learn the arts of invention and patent protection. After a year, he left the Patent Office and set up shop as a "Solicitor and Expert on Patents" to earn his living while he gave his primary attention to invention. He obtained his first patents for electrically actuated railroad brakes and in 1887 prevailed over Westinghouse and other rivals in trials held at Burlington, IA. However, the committee deferred to Westinghouse after questioning whether electricity was "a sufficiently reliable element." Soon he applied for several patents; included among them was the first application for the foundation patents on punched-card data processing.

Considering this to be the most promising of his inventions, he concentrated upon it and developed the experimental test systems used for vital statistics tabulations in Baltimore, MD, the State of New Jersey, and New York City. During this period, his system evolved from a simple machine with cards punched by a conductor's ticket punch to a complete system. This system included a pantograph-like punch, a tabulating machine with a large number of clock-like counters (each capable of counting up to 10,000), and a simple, electrically actuated sorting box for classifying and grouping cards in accordance with the categories punched into them. The sorters grouped cards for the further refinement of data by the tabulating machine.

In 1889, his system was installed in the Army Surgeon General's office to handle medical statistics. A description of this system and his plans for the Census was accepted by Columbia as a doctoral dissertation, and he was awarded a Ph.D. "for achievement" in 1890. Also in 1889, a comparative test made of the Hollerith and two competitive systems resulted in the choice of the Hollerith system for use in the 1890 Census. Austria, Canada, Italy, Norway, and Russia were soon investigating and adopting Hollerith equipment for their population censuses. These early systems could tally totals one at a time but could not add or accumulate. In the US Census of 1890, Hollerith's machines saved the US government $5 million. For the first time, all of the information collected in the census was tabulated.

Shortly after 1900, Hollerith began developing a second generation of his equipment. A new type of card design arranged numeric information in columns and permitted development of a simple, new kind of keypunch, an automatic-feed card sorter, and an automatic-feed tabulator of vastly improved performance. These new systems could accumulate numbers of any size, and thus were obviously applicable to many situations other than census and similar statistical work. Hollerith soon spread their use to an amazing variety of industries. They even went overseas with the American Expeditionary Forces in the First World War.

About 1905, the management in the Census Bureau began to object to Hollerith's profits and sponsored alternative development to break his monopoly. It backed a talented inventor named James Powers. His competitive systems were widely adopted, once Hollerith's fundamental patents expired, and often led the data processing industry into new developments. Powers eventually sold out to the company that evolved into Univac. In poor health, Hollerith sold his patent and proprietary rights to a holding company in 1911. This relieved him of day-by-day management chores and he became a highly paid consultant. Before long,

Thomas J. Watson, Sr, was brought in to head the new company. While essentially retired, Hollerith expected to control development in the new company, as stipulated in his consulting agreement. Obviously, this was impractical, and Hollerith's contributions and achievements were soon absorbed into the greater representative image of the IBM Corporation (*q.v.*).

Writing to his family from Europe in 1895, Hollerith had confided "The machine, as it exists now and probably in years to come, will appear crude and inefficient. Still, it is the genesis. This may appear like conceit and vanity . . . and I have no idea of ever talking like this to anyone else."

Bibliography

1971. Hollerith, V. "Biographical Sketch of Herman Hollerith," *ISIS*, **62**, *210*, 69–78.
1982. Austrian, G. D. *Herman Hollerith: Forgotten Giant of Information Processing.* New York: Columbia University Press.
1989. Reid-Green, K. S. "The History of Census Tabulation," *Scientific American*, **260**, 78–83.
1991. Kistermann, F. W. "The Invention and Development of the Hollerith Punched Card," *Annals of the History of Computing*, **13**, 245–259.

William F. Luebbert, revised by Geoffrey Austrian

HOPPER, GRACE MURRAY

For articles on related subjects *see* AIKEN, HOWARD; COBOL; DIGITAL COMPUTERS, HISTORY OF: EARLY; and MARK I, HARVARD.

Grace Brewster Murray Hopper (Fig. 1) was born in New York City on 9 December 1906. She received her B.A. in Mathematics and Physics from Vassar College in 1928, where she was elected to Phi Beta Kappa. She continued her graduate studies in mathematics at Yale University, where she was awarded her M.A. (1930) and Ph.D. (1934). From 1931 to 1943, she was a member of the mathematics faculty at Vassar College. In December 1943, she joined the United States Naval Reserve and attended Midshipman's School at Northampton, Massachusetts.

She graduated in 1944 with a commission in the US Navy (Lt. J.G.) and was assigned to the Bureau of Ordnance's Computation Project under the direction of Howard Aiken at Harvard University. It was at Harvard that Hopper was first exposed to the world of automatic digital processing. There she joined Robert Campbell and Richard Bloch as a "coder." In her words: "I became the third programmer on the world's first large-scale digital computer, Mark I." At the end of the Second World War, Hopper resigned from Vassar and was appointed to the Harvard faculty as a Research Fellow in the newly founded Computation Laboratory.

Figure 1. Grace Murray Hopper.

In 1949, she joined, as senior mathematician, the fledgling Eckert–Mauchly Corporation, where BINAC and UNIVAC were under construction. She remained with the organization after its acquisition by Remington Rand, through the merger with Sperry Rand, and until her retirement from the Univac division in 1971. Throughout this period, she maintained her activity in the US Naval Reserve and was promoted successively through the ranks until her retirement as a Commander in 1966. In 1967, she was recalled to active duty and, in 1973, promoted to the rank of Captain. In 1985, she was advanced in rank to Commodore. The title of that grade was changed to Rear Admiral in 1985. She continued on active duty until her forced retirement in 1986.

For more than three decades, Captain Hopper was an innovator and major contributor to the development of programming languages. Inspired by John Mauchly's "Short Order Code" (BINAC, 1949) and Betty Holberton's first Sort-Merge Generator (UNIVAC I, 1951), she developed the first compiler, A-0 (1952), and the first compiler to handle mathematical computations, A-2 (1953). This work, coupled with her view of what the world of programming languages ought to be like, led her to the development of the first English language data processing compiler, B-0 (Flow-Matic), which was in use as early as 1957. In April 1959, Hopper and five others (I. E. Block, B. Cheydleur, S. Gorn, R. Rossheim, and A. E. Smith) met to plan a

formal meeting whose object would be "to develop the specifications for a common business language for ... automatic digital computers" (Sammet in Wexelblat, 1981, 200). This meeting triggered a sequence of events that resulted in "Initial Specifications for a Common Business Language" (DoD, April 1960). Flow-Matic, along with AIMACO and Commercial Translator, provided the main inputs in influencing the early development of Cobol (Sammet in Wexelblat, 1981, 217).

Hopper's awards, honors, and professional publications are much too numerous to detail here. Most notably, she received honorary degrees from the Newark College of Engineering (D.Engr., 1972); C. W. Post College, LIU (D.Sci., 1973); The University of Pennsylvania (LL.D., 1974); and the Pratt Institute (D.Sci., 1976). She also received almost every major award in her profession. These include DPMA's "Man(!)-of-the-Year" (1969); AFIPS' Harry Goode Memorial Award (1970); and Yale University's Wilbur Lucius Cross Medal (1972). In 1971, the Univac Division of Sperry Rand Corporation created the Grace Murray Hopper Award, which is awarded annually by ACM to a distinguished young computer professional. In 1991 she was awarded the National Medal of Technology.

Clearly, Grace Hopper belonged to that select group of computer professionals whose talent, vision, dedication, and constant persistence laid the foundation for the continuing information processing explosion. Throughout her career, she saw herself as a teacher and as one who always battled entrenched attitudes of those she referred to as the "establishment." The phrase "but it's never been done that way" was anathema to her. As a visual reminder of her personal creed, she kept a ship's clock in her office. It appeared to be a typical ship's clock until you looked carefully: it ran backward.

Grace Hopper retired with the rank of Rear Admiral on 14 August 1986. Befitting the oldest serving officer in the US Navy, her retirement ceremony was held on "Old Ironsides" (the *USS Constitution*). Admiral Hopper died on 1 January 1992 and was buried at Arlington Cemetery in a full naval ceremony. On 6 January 1996, the US Navy launched an Arleigh Burke Class Aegis Destroyer named the *USS Hopper* in honor of Grace.

Bibliography

1981. Wexelblat, R. (ed.) *Proceedings, History of Programming Languages Conference.* New York: Academic Press.
1984. Tropp, H. "Grace Hopper: The Youthful Teacher of Us All," *Abacus,* **2**, 6–18.
1988. Hopper, G. M. "The Education of a Computer," *Annals of the History of Computing,* **9**, *3/4,* 271–281. Reprint of a 1952 ACM Publication. Introduction by David Gries.
1995. Lee, J. A. N. "Grace Brewster Murray Hopper," in *Computer Pioneers,* 380–387. Los Alamitos, CA: IEEE Computer Society Press.

1989. Billings, C. W. *Grace Hopper, Navy Admiral & Computer Pioneer.* Hillfield, NJ: Enslow Publishers.
1996. Williams, M. "US Navy Launches USS Hopper," *Annals of the History of Computing,* **18**, 2, 80.

Henry S. Tropp

HOSPITAL INFORMATION SYSTEM (HIS)

For articles on related subjects *see* BIOCOMPUTING; INFORMATION SYSTEMS; MANAGEMENT INFORMATION SYSTEMS; MEDICAL APPLICATIONS; MEDICAL IMAGING; and TOMOGRAPHY, COMPUTERIZED.

Computers in hospitals perform a wide range of activities, such as processing and storing the data necessary to support daily operations, facilitating clinical and financial decision making, and satisfying internal and external documentation requirements. These computer systems are variously referred to as hospital, health, and medical information systems. The term *hospital information system* (HIS) encompasses both patient care and patient management systems, which support healthcare delivery, and financial and resource management systems, which support the business and strategic operations of a hospital. In countries that have hospital-based healthcare systems, the term HIS can imply information systems with broader functions, including applications that support ambulatory (outpatient) care. The increasing emphasis on primary outpatient care and home care, the merger and incorporation of healthcare institutions, and the use of computer networks that span geographically distant healthcare facilities have led to the expansion of HIS into large integrated healthcare delivery systems in which services are extended beyond the physical boundaries of a single hospital.

Medical Data Processing

Healthcare staff spend as much as 20–30% of their time collecting, analyzing, disseminating, and otherwise handling information. Most healthcare facilities use some form of computer system to assist in these activities. The core HIS applications perform basic hospital functions, including patient registration and admission, discharge, and transfer (ADT). These fundamental systems maintain the inpatient census, as well as store patient identification information and critical demographic data that are acquired during the registration process. In addition, the patient registry functions as a reference base for HIS components, such as the medical records and patient billing systems. When an HIS is extended to the pharmacy, laboratory, and other ancillary departments, the core systems serve as a repository for shared data, thus minimizing the need for redundant data entry.

The different components of an HIS perform a variety of clinical and operational tasks:

◆ Pharmacy systems typically prepare work lists for drug preparation and distribution, generate prescription labels, and monitor drug inventories. They may also keep an online record of patients' medication orders and perform drug interaction checking.

◆ Laboratory systems create specimen collection schedules, store results generated by automated instruments or by manual testing procedures, and print patient-specific laboratory reports, with flags to indicate abnormal results. In addition, they often provide tools to measure the productivity of laboratory personnel and may promote quality control by monitoring the accuracy of the instruments used.

◆ Radiology information systems facilitate examination scheduling, film library management, and transcription of examination interpretations. Many of the newest imaging techniques, such as computerized tomography (CT) and magnetic resonance imaging (MRI), are inherently digital; thus, the radiology department has become a growing area for computer-based medical applications. Sophisticated picture archiving and communication systems (PACS) have been developed to store, communicate, and display digitized medical images.

◆ Systems that facilitate the processes of quality control and outcomes research allow decision makers to analyze data from hospital operations and identify and correct deficiencies quickly.

◆ A variety of additional systems are available to support other departments in the hospital. Typical applications include inventory tracking and supplies purchasing, operating room management, staff scheduling, nursing care plan development, diet planning, staff training, professional credentialing, and risk management.

Among the most common HIS applications are traditional financial functions such as payroll administration, patient billing, and accounts receivable management. To cope with increasing competition and complex reimbursement mechanisms, a growing number of hospitals have acquired cost accounting systems and financial decision support tools designed to help administrators make investment decisions, manage costs, set charges, and respond to bids from third-party payers.

Networking systems allow the integration of the various HIS components. Communication of physicians' orders is critical because most hospital activities, including drug distribution, test performance, and charge capture for patient billing, are initiated by these orders.

In nonautomated hospitals, orders are conveyed on slips of paper. Automated order entry and results reporting capabilities allow communication with ancillary areas electronically, thus eliminating the easily misplaced paper slips and minimizing delays in communication. As an additional advantage, the information is then available online, where it can be accessed by health professionals who wish to review a patient's drug profile or previous laboratory test results.

Electronic Medical Records

The medical record is the key to coordinating the various health professionals who participate in providing patient care. It integrates diverse patient information, provides a mechanism for communication, and serves as a legal document of a patient's experiences during hospitalization. Current hospital information systems, however, typically store only limited clinical information and provide little support for true patient care—a paper medical chart continues to serve as the primary repository for clinical data. Although the more sophisticated systems can assist nurses in creating care plans and charting patient progress notes, in the vast majority of hospitals, ward clerks and nurses enter only the information necessary for performance of operational tasks and record keeping.

To affect patient care to a greater extent, an HIS must store a more thorough on-line medical record. The advantages of an electronic medical record include rapid access to pertinent information, simultaneous access by multiple users, improved legibility, and, when the data is stored in a structured manner, assistance in searching for pertinent information. Furthermore, when the clinical components of an HIS are well developed, clinical assistance is possible. Systems that use the stored information can be developed to monitor patients and issue alerts, make diagnostic suggestions, recommend patient-specific drug dosing regimens, and provide limited therapy advice.

Steady decreases in the costs of online storage and increases in computer processing power have removed some of the barriers to the feasibility of an electronic medical record. Entry of information into the computer remains an enormous bottleneck. For ease of data entry, most HI systems have minimal keystroke or graphical user interfaces. Timely and accurate data capture is also facilitated by direct interfaces with patient monitors and other medical instruments. There has always been interest in the implementation of point-of-care systems. Using bedside terminals or handheld devices, care providers are able to enter and review patient information, such as vital signs, clinical observations, and medication administration data at the time care is delivered (see Fig. 1).

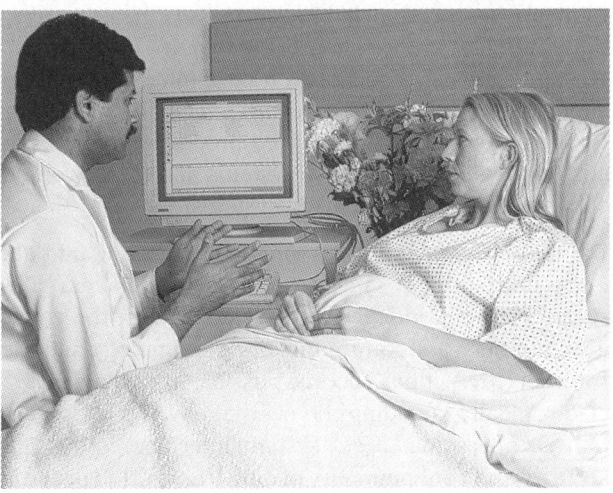

Figure 1. A bedside data management system. Using such a system, physicians and nurses in an intensive care unit can enter physicians' orders and clinical observations, and gain assistance in developing care plans, progress notes, and nursing assessments. Interfaces to patient monitoring instruments and laboratory information systems eliminate much of the need for redundant data entry (courtesy of Brigham and Women's Hospital, Boston, MA).

A related area of exploration is the development of workstations (q.v.) that facilitate clinical decision making by physicians. A simple function of such a workstation is the graphical or tabular display of trends in laboratory test values. More sophisticated clinical decision aids are possible when physicians' observations and other detailed patient data are stored online. This data, when combined with formal categorizations, such as problem statements and diagnoses, will allow automated summarization of a patient's history and clinical progress and provide support for therapy planning and medical diagnosis. Although decision aids for physicians have been pursued by researchers since the 1960s, commercial HIS developers have only recently begun to develop true clinical applications.

Terminology and Standards

Structured representation of medical concepts is the key to outcomes research and to the development of clinical decision support systems. Research on controlled medical terminologies has evolved considerably. The Unified Medical Language System (UMLS) from the National Library of Medicine is a comprehensive mapping of 30 vocabularies, such as the Systematized Nomenclature of Human and Veterinary Medicine (SNOMED), the Diagnostic and Statistical Manual of Mental Disorders (DSM-IV), the International Statistical Classification of Diseases and Related Health Problems (ICD), and the Medical Subject Headings (MeSH). Planned additions include the British Read

Clinical Classification and Regentrief's Logical Observation Identifier Names and Codes (LOINC).

Hospitals may choose from a host of alternatives when acquiring an information system. Available modes for HIS delivery range from shared processing services to custom-developed in-house systems and to networked configurations of specialized systems.

Data integration is critical to avoiding redundant data entry and storage, and thus to promoting data consistency among independent systems. With the emergence of network communications technology and the Internet (*q.v.*), it has become possible to exchange data electronically, avoiding the need to develop and maintain cumbersome direct system interfaces. Although security and confidentiality of data transmitted over the Internet are still not ideal, the World Wide Web (*q.v.*) has recently been suggested as the most convenient means to communicate data within and between healthcare institutions, individual providers, and patients.

The development of industry-wide standard network protocols (*q.v.*) has eased the technical problems of electronic communication. Still, many obstacles to system integration remain, such as an agreement on standard coding schemes and formats for medical data and definition of minimum data sets to collect. The development of data standards is currently an active area of endeavor. Examples are the American Society of Testing Materials (ASTM) standard for storing and transmitting laboratory information; the Digital Imaging and Communications in Medicine (DICOM) standard for transmission of digital radiologic imaging data; the Medical Information Bus (MIB) standard for interconnecting patient monitors and other bedside devices; the Health Level Seven (HL-7), Electronic Data Interchange for Administration, Commerce, and Transport (EDIFACT), and Medical Data Interchange (MEDIX) standards for transmitting billing data, updating the census, and communicating orders and results within hospital networks.

In the coming years, the integration of myriad diverse computer systems will remain a challenge for health care institutions and information systems vendors alike. Increasing pressure to provide high-quality health care at the lowest possible cost has fueled hospital needs to relate costs to patient outcomes and to identify the most cost-effective means of providing care. From a hospital management perspective, the ability of an HIS to analyze internal financial and clinical data, as well as comparative information from external databases, may provide the edge necessary for long-term survival. From a patient care perspective, linkage of information systems in hospitals, physicians' offices, outpatient facilities, and other affiliated institutions will enhance continuity and consistency of care across providers.

Furthermore, an integrated online medical record will support development of guidelines for appropriate care, quality assurance activities, cost management, clinical research, and technology assessment.

Bibliography

1986. Blum, B. I. *Clinical Information Systems.* New York: Springer-Verlag.
1987. Anderson, J. G., and Jay, S. J. (eds.) *Use and Impact of Computers in Clinical Medicine.* New York: Springer-Verlag.
1990. Shortliffe, E. H., Perreault, L. E., Wiederhold, G., and Fagan, L. M. (eds.) *Medical Informatics: Computer Applications in Health Care.* Reading, MA: Addison-Wesley.
1992. Ball, M. J., and Collen, M. F. (eds.) *Aspects of the Computer-Based Patient Record.* New York: Springer-Verlag.
1995. Prokosch, H. U., and Dudeck, J. (eds.) *Hospital Information Systems: Design and Development Characteristics; Impact and Future Architecture.* Amsterdam: Elsevier.
1996. Clayton, P. D., and van Mulligen, E. "The Economic Motivations for Clinical Information Systems," *Journal of the American Medical Informatics Association*, **3** (Suppl.), 660–668.
1997. Dick, R. S., Steen, E. B., and Detmer, D. E. (eds.) *The Computer-Based Patient Record: An Essential Technology for Health Care*, Rev. Ed. Washington, DC: National Academy Press.

Leslie E. Perreault and Lucila Ohno-Machado

HOST SYSTEM

> For articles on related subjects *see* DISTRIBUTED SYSTEMS; FILE SERVER; FRONT END PROCESSOR; MICROPROGRAMMING; MULTIPROGRAMMING; and MULTITASKING.

A *host system* or a *host computer* is the physical system that interprets a program. The program is written on a *logical machine*, which is usually not the same as the physical machine (host system). These differences arise because the physical system either does not possess or does not allocate all features or resources directly requested by the logical machine (program). The distinction between host system and logical system is especially notable in two areas: multiprogramming systems and microprogramming (emulated) systems.

In multiprogramming systems, the host system is responsible for allocating storage and I/O resources to each of the logical machines (i.e. in effect, active programs), which are usually called *virtual* machines, as they are required. This allows a number of virtual machines to share the physical resources without logical conflict (i.e. without any programmer intervention in the source programs) and at the same time more effectively use the resources of the physical host system.

In microprogrammed or interpreted systems, the notion of host system applies to the physical machine that interprets (*emulates*) the programs written in other machine languages. The machine being emulated by the host machine is said to be the *image* machine (sometimes the term "virtual" is also used to describe this situation).

Another use of the term *host system* is in time sharing or remote computing, where the *host* is the central computer providing service to terminals or satellite computers.

Michael J. Flynn

HTML

See MARKUP LANGUAGES.

HUMAN FACTORS IN COMPUTING

For articles on related subjects, *see* GROUPWARE; INTERACTIVE SYSTEM; OBJECT-ORIENTED ANALYSIS AND DESIGN; SOFTWARE ENGINEERING; SOFTWARE DESIGN PATTERNS; and WINDOW ENVIRONMENTS.

"Human factors" in computing are those aspects of the way people think, perceive, remember, and act that influence the ways they work with systems. Human factors techniques, many originating in the field of psychology, are applied in the design and evaluation of computer systems with the aim of making those systems easier to use.

Human factors specialists typically have a background in psychology or organizational theory, together with a good understanding of computer technology and design, and a repertoire of formal and informal techniques that they apply at relevant stages of design to ensure that the end product is both usable and useful.

History

Historically, the focus of computer system design was on the implementation of systems that were functionally correct—i.e. that performed the required tasks accurately. Little attention was paid to the users of those systems. If we consider the ways such machines were used, this is hardly surprising.

In the earliest days, the only people who could use the machines were the designers and programmers. They did not have to worry about how usable their systems were; all that mattered was that they could use them themselves.

The next generation of machines were used mainly for data processing. The operator entered data on punched cards or paper tape, and waited patiently for the printout. Again the interface was of little impor-

tance. The operators were expected to be experts in data entry. They might have to call on someone else if the computer gave an incomprehensible error message, but otherwise it was up to them to adapt to the requirements of the computer, not the other way around.

Things have changed now. Most people in technologically developed countries come into contact with computers, whether it is the automated teller machine at the bank, the word processor on the desk, or the computer-assisted learning software in the classroom. For these systems to fulfill their intended purposes, it is essential that they be easy for non-experts to use.

Human factors techniques provide a framework for talking about, and taking account of, the user during the design process. They can be broadly classified into two groups: techniques that help guide the design of a system, and techniques that help assess the usability of a system. Different techniques can be applied at different stages in design and testing.

Models of the Design Process

One traditional systems development life cycle for (non-interactive) systems is commonly referred to as the "waterfall" model because information flows in one direction only—from requirements analysis, through systems analysis, detailed design, and implementation to testing (*see* SOFTWARE ENGINEERING). In most design environments, this "hard" approach to systems development, so called because it involves treating all information as inflexible and certain, has now been superseded by "softer" approaches that take account of more uncertainty in design, and accommodate the differing views of various stakeholders in a design. For example, Soft Systems Methodology (SSM) involves taking an unstructured problem situation, describing it from the viewpoints of as many people as possible, using this as a basis for developing conceptual models of the system, and using these models to identify changing requirements. The descriptions should state who is affected by the change (the "Client"), who makes the change (the "Actor"), what is changed (the "Transformation"), the core assumptions of this viewpoint (termed the "*Weltanschauung*", or world view), who is responsible for the system (the "Owner"), and a description of the wider system of which this is a part (the "Environment"); these categories are often referred to by the acronym "CATWOE". Although SSM focuses on the earlier stages of the development life cycle, it involves iteration through the stages to build up gradually a rich understanding of the problem.

The need for iteration through all stages of the design process is recognized in many design methods. For example, the *spiral* model of design emphasizes the iterative nature of design, involving the phases of determining objectives, alternatives and constraints; evaluating alternatives and identifying and resolving risks; developing and verifying the next level of the system; and planning the next phase of development. There are several methods that explicitly include stages where user concerns are paramount. One example is the *star* life cycle, in which every phase (task or functional analysis, requirements specification, conceptual or formal design, prototyping and implementation) is followed by a phase of evaluation. Other examples include ETHICS (Effective Technical and Human Implementation of Computer-based Systems), which takes account of user and organizational concerns with a particular focus on ethical considerations, and Multiview, which involves stages of analysis of human activity, analysis of information, analysis and design of socio-technical aspects, design of the human–computer interface, and design of technical aspects of the system.

Many proponents of the more user-centered methods argue that the intended users of a system have the best understanding of their own requirements and should be actively involved at all stages of the design process (participatory design). There is a counter-argument that users are poorly placed to understand many aspects of skilled design work, and that participation throughout the design process is generally impractical and costly. Another issue on which there is widespread disagreement is the role of prototypes in design. Some specialists argue that a design problem should be well understood, and several alternative design solutions investigated, before much implementation work is done, while others argue that the only way the design team can get a good understanding of the design problem is by implementing and testing prototype systems in an evolutionary way, to see how people actually work with systems. Ultimately, what degree of user involvement is appropriate, and what roles can usefully be played by prototypes, varies according to the design context.

Whether or not a particular design method is adopted, there are a range of techniques available for incorporating human factors in the design and evaluation of computer systems.

Human Factors in Design

TASK ANALYSIS AND OBSERVATION
Computer systems should not only offer the required functionality but should also be easy and natural to use. Task analysis can help the designer understand how things are done at the moment and hence help define how a new system should work. It is concerned both with what should be done and with how it should be done, and is generally used in the early stages of design, as a form of requirements analysis. The starting point for task analysis is observation, often supported by interviews and reference to existing documentation. The task analyst looks at how the task is performed, what objects are involved, how they relate to each other, and what people need to know to complete the task. Two complementary analyses are often performed. One analysis results in a description of a task (or procedure) in terms of sub-tasks, decomposing the main task into gradually more detailed sequences of smaller tasks (e.g. Hierarchical Task Analysis). The other results in a description of the knowledge that users need to perform those tasks. This is typically defined in terms of the objects involved in the task (their types or taxonomies), how they relate to each other, and what functions they serve. Both of these kinds of analysis can help a designer, by identifying the task procedures with which users are familiar and the interface objects to which users might expect to have access, and by indicating what information should be included in documentation for system users.

Ethnographic techniques have also been imported from anthropology to help in the understanding of work in context. The role of ethnographers is to involve themselves in the work situation and, through a combination of observation, participation, and questioning, develop a good understanding of the work situation from their particular perspective. This style of data analysis focuses on recording activity and interpreting it in relation to the work context. Its aim is to understand how computer systems are currently used, or how they could best be designed to support the desired activity.

USABILITY GUIDELINES AND PRINCIPLES
A particular task analysis concerns the design of one system. In contrast, usability guidelines and principles are quite general, and can be applied to the design of many systems. Guidelines are rules a designer may choose to obey when designing an interactive system; reference collections of usability guidelines have been compiled based on past experience. For example, a guideline might advocate the use of a "distinctive cursor," giving examples of ways to implement this feature and also listing exceptional circumstances in which the guideline should not be applied. Another source of guidelines is the style guide published by some operating systems developers (e.g. for the Apple Macintosh or for Microsoft Windows-based systems). While these guides are concerned primarily with the "look and feel" of software, adherence to style guidelines can aid usability by allowing the user to learn

a new application more quickly based on experience of other similar applications.

Usability principles serve a similar role to guidelines, but are expressed in more abstract terms. They refer to the general properties a system should have, based on past experience of what properties usable systems commonly have. Examples of important usability principles include:

- *Consistency*. One version of this principle states that "effective applications are both consistent within themselves and consistent with one another." A system is consistent if similar effects are achieved in similar ways and similar information is displayed in similar ways. Style guides can help a designer to develop systems that are consistent.

- *Predictability*. Past experience of working with a system should enable a user to predict the effect of the next action with it.

- *Familiarity*. The system should make use of familiar objects and actions—for example, the trash can or recycling bin for disposing of unwanted items. This is achieved in some systems by adopting a metaphor (such as the "desktop metaphor") to allow users to draw on their past experience. One danger with such metaphors is that they can be culturally dependent.

- *Observability*. The user should be able to see the state of the system.

- *Recoverability*. The user should be able to reverse the effects of actions—for example, to recover from errors.

Usability guidelines and principles provide good general guidance, and can be a good checklist for a designer. However, they may be difficult to apply effectively without an understanding of the reasoning behind particular guidelines or principles.

A particular example of a principle that has to be applied with care is that of *adaptability*—that users should be able to tailor an interface. While an adaptable interface may allow users to optimize their system to match their individual needs, in a work situation where users have access to different versions of the same system small differences in the way each system has been adapted can result in inefficient or error-prone working.

Human Factors in Evaluation

Task analysis, guidelines, and principles are all ways to help the designer to develop a more usable and useful system. The same basic ideas can be used to help to evaluate a design for usability.

COGNITIVE TASK ANALYSIS AND USER MODELING

Cognitive task analysis is concerned with analyzing the tasks that users perform with a system—both their physical tasks and their mental tasks (such as making decisions, planning what to do next, making sense of the current state of the computer display, or remembering something). Norman (1986) describes the user's interaction with a system in terms of seven stages:

- goal formation—deciding what to achieve next;

- forming an intention—deciding how to go about achieving it;

- action specification—detailing the particular actions to be performed;

- action execution—doing something, such as moving the mouse, pressing a mouse button, or typing a word;

- perceiving the system state—e.g. noting changes in what is displayed;

- interpreting the system state—interpreting what the changes mean in terms of the goals; and

- evaluating the system state with respect to the goals and intentions; for example, the effect of an action may have been different from that intended.

This framework for thinking about interaction can be seen as underlying several more specific approaches to analyzing interactive behavior, such as GOMS (Goals, Operators, Methods, and Selection rules), Cognitive Walkthrough and Programmable User Modeling (PUM). Each of these approaches involves the analyst in specifying, fairly precisely, what users might be trying to achieve, how they might achieve it, what they will need to know in order to achieve it, and what actions they are likely to perform. They differ in the assumptions they make about the users and in details of how the techniques are applied. GOMS analysis involves constructing a detailed goal/task hierarchy, including mental tasks, and reasoning with that hierarchy, so it is best suited to analyzing expert users, in terms of what they need to know and how long they are likely to take to complete a task. The Cognitive Walkthrough technique assumes the user is exploring an interface, working out what to do on the basis of previous experience and using recognition of words and symbols to identify appropriate actions. The Cognitive Walkthrough analyst is expected to tell a credible story about how the user will succeed or fail on particular tasks. The PUM approach assumes that the user draws on knowledge to plan what to do, and the PUM analyst reasons about the ways knowledge is used in problem solving. Since these approaches are difficult and time-consuming to apply, researchers are investigating the viability of constructing computer-based tools to support human factors specialists in applying them. In all cases, the results of analysis can be used to guide redesign.

HEURISTIC EVALUATION

Another approach is to assess a design against usability guidelines and principles. One example of this approach is Nielsen's Heuristic Evaluation, which requires a team of evaluators to use a new system and note any violations of usability principles, presented in the form of a checklist (*see* HEURISTIC). For example, one item in Nielsen's checklist is that the system should "help users recognize, diagnose and recover from errors." Heuristic evaluation is a usability inspection method that can be applied by an evaluator after little training, and with comparatively low effort. It can be applied to a paper mock-up of a system early in the design process, or to a fully working system later on.

USABILITY TESTING

While heuristics and theory-based analysis can yield useful results, particularly in situations where it is difficult to get access to a suitable group of users for a reasonable period of time, or where a deep understanding of the causes of particular behavior is needed, user testing is still the most widely used method of evaluating the usability of a system. Many large software development organizations have usability laboratories in which user testing can take place under controlled conditions. Typically, sample users will be asked to perform specified tasks, and their performance will be monitored to find out what the common mistakes are, what misconceptions users might have, what tasks they perform inefficiently, and what they think of various aspects of the design. Such empirical approaches are necessary for finding out what real (unpredictable) users actually do, and can help identify many usability difficulties, or features users do not like, that other evaluation techniques miss. However, usability testing can only be performed on a working system, so it can only be conducted fairly late in the design process, when many design commitments have been made and may be impossible to overturn.

Discussion

Most established human factors techniques have been developed and tested in the context of traditional computer systems (with keyboard and mouse input, and display-based output), focusing on the interaction between a single user and computer system. Because people tend to adapt to the demands of new technologies and the possibilities they offer, it is difficult to predict in advance how users are likely to work with novel systems such as groupware (*q.v.*), or multimodal systems that accommodate gestural or voice input. To take an example: people have established strategies for managing interpersonal relationships (e.g. signaling how open they are to being observed or interrupted) in a traditional office situation, but these strategies do not transfer well to offices that exploit media space technologies (i.e. groupware systems incorporating audio-visual as well as computer networks). The introduction of such technologies raises concerns over personal privacy and interruptibility, and people have to develop new ways of working together. Traditional human factors and software engineering techniques can be applied to some aspects of the design of media spaces, but for others—such as designing appropriate means for managing interpersonal relations—it is necessary to develop new design and evaluation methods. Similarly, much further work is needed on the human factors aspects of multimodal interfaces.

Although techniques for addressing user concerns tend to lag behind technological developments, there is now a well established body of usability techniques that can be applied in the design and evaluation of computer systems. These take account of user concerns at many different levels, from the details of how people perceive and remember things, how they form plans to achieve their goals, and how they use the computer as a resource to support their work, through higher-level issues such as how computer systems can support group working, to high-level concerns such as the organizational context in which the system is situated.

Bibliography

1986. Norman, D. "Cognitive Engineering," in *User Centered System Design* (eds. D. A. Norman and J. W. Draper), 31–62. Hillsdale, NJ: Lawrence Erlbaum.

1987. Suchman, L. *Plans and Situated Actions.* Cambridge: Cambridge University Press.

1994. Eberts, R. E. *User Interface Design.* London: Prentice Hall International.

1994. Nielsen, J., and Mack, R. (eds.) *Usability Inspection Methods.* New York: John Wiley.

1995. Avison, D. E., and Fitzgerald, G. *Information Systems Development: Methodologies, Techniques and Tools,* 2nd Ed. London: McGraw-Hill.

1995. Baecker, R. M., Grudin, J., Buxton, W., and Greenberg, S. (eds.) *Readings in Human–Computer Interaction: Toward the Year 2000,* 2nd Ed. San Francisco: Morgan Kaufmann.

1995. Landauer, T. K. *The Trouble With Computers: Usefulness, Usability and Productivity.* Cambridge, MA: MIT Press.

1996. John, B., and Kieras, D. "The GOMS Family of User Interface Analysis Techniques: Comparison and Contrast," *ACM Transactions on CHI,* **3**, 320–351.

1997. Blandford, A. E., and Duke. D. J. "Integrating User and System Concerns in the Design of Interactive Systems," *International Journal of Human–Computer Studies,* **46**, 653–679.

Ann Blandford

HUMANITIES APPLICATIONS

For articles on related subjects *see* COMPUTER ANIMATION; COMPUTER ART; COMPUTER MUSIC; DESKTOP PUBLISHING; DIGITAL LIBRARIES; ELECTRONIC REFERENCE WORKS; FICTION, COMPUTERS IN; HYPERTEXT; MACHINE TRANSLATION; MULTIMEDIA; NATURAL LANGUAGE PROCESSING; TEXT EDITING SYSTEMS; and WORD PROCESSING.

Historical Overview

Computer usage among humanists has largely paralleled the evolution of the technology. As the primary computer functions have added communication to storage, retrieval, and analysis, humanists have increasingly exploited the new possibilities for expanding the integration of computers into their fundamental activities. At the lowest levels, the computer has become nearly universal in compiling bibliographies; word processing has become widely used in student writing courses; and increasingly sophisticated drill-and-practice programs are becoming common in foreign language instruction. Computer-aided projects abound in humanities research and professional activity in many unpredicted ways.

New connectivity features now provide global remote access to such resources as library catalogs, periodical databases, dictionaries, thesauri, and other reference works, often without cost to the user. Many humanists enjoy the increasing integration of several information services, including computing centers, libraries, and special research projects that share the common goal of information literacy. Although long available as email (*q.v.*), electronic connectivity took on new vigor in the rise of the World Wide Web (*q.v.*), which added to the dozens of specialist list servers and newsgroups in the humanities that evolved on the Internet (*q.v.*). A singular benefit has been the growth of text projects with remote access features, and the wider sharing of electronic information. Some journals and newsletters have begun to appear in electronic form; editors of the all-electronic journals have accomplished the processes of peer review, editing, and distribution in months instead of years. Some electronic journals are never printed on paper; one scholar even issues regular lists (distributed electronically of course) of the current "e-journals."

Large Databases for Humanities Research

The rapid expansion of individual computer capacity and speed through replaceable hard disks (*q.v.*) and optical storage (*q.v*) media has added essentially limitless capacity for humanists working with very large texts and collections. By means of graphical color monitors of high resolution (*see* MONITOR, DISPLAY), researchers can display an entire page of a manuscript. For those engaged in time-consuming processes, such as downloading texts, multitasking (*q.v.*) has made it possible to conduct foreground and background operations simultaneously. A major initiative to develop software for critical editions is TUSTEP from the University of Tübingen (`http://www.uni-tuebingen.de/zdv/zrlinfo/reg1.html` [in German]).

The economics of academic publishing has been transformed by two new computer-assisted forms. Since many humanists use word processing software and laser printers, smaller humanities presses can request camera-ready copy from authors, thereby reducing the editorial and typesetting costs for small scholarly editions. Meanwhile, the very high capacity, wide availability, microcomputer connectability, and relatively low mastering cost of the compact disc make it a natural vehicle for high-volume electronic text publishing. Single CD-ROM discs have been used to reissue entire encyclopedias, bookshelves of classics, massive bibliographies, major reference works, multiple-volume dictionaries, and sweeping collections of literary and historical texts.

But the printed texts that the humanist requires in the fields of literature, history, language, and philosophy are not yet as hospitable to computer use as they will soon become. The expanding machine-readable libraries embrace many of the hundreds of texts that constitute the working materials of humanistic study and teaching. "Electronic texts" are gradually becoming more readily available, more convenient to use, and less expensive. Scanning hardware and software are showing considerable improvement in handling standard or contemporary book and office fonts.

Instruction in humanities subjects has greatly benefited from the availability of computer technologies. Foreign-language teaching has explored ways to replace the drudgery of drill by human instructors with context-sensitive exercises conducted with computer interfaces. The use of graphical databases has real promise for art history, where it is now possible to integrate slides and lecture notes in customized multimedia presentations. In the field of musicology, it is possible to use the computer as copyist, performer, and editor—not to mention its functions in the analysis and synthesis of sound wave forms.

But humanities computing in recent years has often excelled more in practical work than in theoretical breakthroughs. Although the statistical methods of the social sciences may have lured some pioneering scholars into humanistic computing, relatively few reports have offered widely accepted statistical evidence for reattributing disputed authorship or redating a writer's work.

Applications of Networking, Holography, and Multimedia

As computers have become more accepted as commonplace tools for academic research, two technological advances—networking and multimedia—have provided special impetus to the nonverbal disciplines. For art historians, a major problem has been simply comparing large agglomerations of objects. With paintings, sculpture, and all the other subjects of their study scattered around the world in a multitude of public and private collections, these scholars must rely on published reproductions representing only a limited selection of an artist's work or of a genre. The growth of networks has overcome the inadequate budgets of art museums to create a scholarly link among all the extant collections in the world. The Canadian Heritage Information Network, for example, a consortium of 11 museums and research centers, suggests some of what such a network could provide globally. Its listing of about 12 million objects is accessible to over 400 museums and similar institutions in 22 countries and, of course, to all parts of Canada. In addition to its databases, the network provides collections management, electronic mail (*q.v.*), specialized training, and advice on information standards and new technology. With the participation of specialists in the arts as well as the sciences, a constantly revised data dictionary defines data fields and supports sharing of information in standardized documents. Perhaps it will begin to distribute CD-ROMs of museum holdings (think of the treasures from the Northwest Indians), and thereby illustrate the immense benefits from linking all institutions that share a common goal.

Another technology of promise for humanists is multimedia, the interactive integration of text, images, and sound. A new generation of computer-controlled CD-ROMs permits the viewer both to hear the music and to interrogate the system about aspects of it, such as the libretto of an opera (with English translation, if necessary), the life of the composer, the structure of the music, other works by the same composer, or similar works by other composers.

A third technology, holography, may in the future allow any museum to possess satisfactory simulacra of the art objects its visitors wish to view. In theory, any museum could be a museum of all the world's art, not just the flower of industrial nations but also creativity from non-industrial parts of the world. Although this technology has seemed to pass out of view recently, its potential may yet be recognized and developed.

Textual Analysis and Concordances

Although literary scholars are becoming more aware through explorations of multimedia that documents are physical artifacts (a consideration of prime importance with poets like Blake, who created unified works incorporating both illustrations and poetry), the area in which success has been most visible is one that dates back to the late Middle Ages, and has merely been upgraded technologically. An amazing number of concordances have been published in the last 35 years, using at first the output from the primitive line printers of the 1960s and now capitalizing on the advantages of desktop publishing. As soon as computers could be used to sort large quantities of verbal data, hundreds of these alphabetized keys to literature were published, most of them as books, some as microfiche. Unlike the hand-compiled concordances of previous centuries, machine-generated ones could include every word of the base text and supply all the lines in which they appeared.

The traditional limits of this heretofore laborious industry could be expanded in several imaginative ways: concordances were compiled for categories of literature, such as the Elizabethan sonnets, or for prose works previously considered too long, such as *Moby Dick*, which has been honored with no fewer than three of these reference works. Complexities were introduced like indicating for *Paradise Lost* the speaker and location for each concorded word. A concordance to the undeciphered Linear B script of Mycenae was published as an aid to its decoding. Outstanding among these efforts for both its size and the scope of its conception is the monumental work of Father Roberto Busa and his Jesuit associates, who have produced, in many volumes and recently on CD-ROM, a multidimensional concordance to the works of St. Thomas Aquinas and to all the authors who are cited in his writing.

Computer-generated textual indexes and concordances provide many advantages over the traditional hand-generated ones. They can not only provide a count of each word but also exhibit the frequency distribution of that word in the several parts of a text, the collocations of a given word and other words of interest, and other patterns of clustering or density. These functions, which once required mainframe programming, can now be done on a desktop computer by someone with comparatively little computer experience.

Text retrieval using an index or concordance program can be either a simple matter of qualitative readings of the text (e.g. an author's use of color-related words and the objects connected with them) or a highly complex matter of quantitative analysis (e.g. statistical patterns of marked parts of speech). Apart from stylistics, the retrieval of indexed texts makes it possible to do content analyses of how authors treat political, social, religious, and philosophical ideas. In the humanities, of course, vocabularies of a given subject are rarely standardized, so the researcher in concepts must learn to use word groups (e.g. not just "liberty," but also "freedom" and "independence" and perhaps even "license" and "autonomy").

Around the world, major initiatives have been undertaken to employ the computer to compile various national dictionaries. Sometimes functioning as a governmental effort to enhance the stature of specific languages (and perhaps indirectly the economic competitiveness of its speakers), many of these dictionaries have appeared in both conventional print and machine-readable (*q.v.*) formats. So neatly do the data-handling and photocomposition capabilities of computers mesh with the needs of lexicographers that no dictionary today is produced by any other means. Abbreviated dictionaries, spelling lists, and travelers' translation aids are casually bundled into handheld devices that are almost as cheap as pocket calculators. The availability of the historic *Oxford English Dictionary* on CD-ROM, providing access to the entire history of the English language with examples, obviously holds great potential for literary and linguistic scholarship.

The creation of textual databases for research, originally a byproduct of concordance projects, has begun to develop as an independent operation. At first, efforts were made (as at the Oxford Text Archive of Oxford University) to create a scholarly collection of computer-readable texts that had been produced for other purposes. Researchers at Rutgers and Georgetown Universities assembled bibliographic information regarding computer-readable texts and text projects. An initiative at Rutgers and Princeton led to the formation of the Center for Electronic Texts in the Humanities, to provide leadership and information on the collection and dissemination of texts. At the Center, the *Trésor de la langue française*, the huge verbal database—1,600 volumes spanning a century and a half—created to support the French national dictionary, has been converted into a library available in Nancy and Chicago.

Since the World Wide Web has encouraged humanists to seek their basic materials in remote databases, several imaginative projects have begun to provide downloadable electronic texts of scholarly reliability and usually at no cost. At universities like Columbia, Virginia and Pennsylvania, dedicated individuals and groups are creating the modern equivalent of the medieval scriptorium, unique assemblages of texts that can serve all interested scholars and can preserve them long after their print versions have decomposed.

Since almost all the computer-encoded material up until recently had been intended for another purpose—

namely, the production of a printed work according to the proprietary style rules of its publisher—little care was taken to follow any standard encoding when texts were made machine-readable. To remedy this defect in future projects, the Text Encoding Initiative (TEI) was established with support from the US National Endowment for the Humanities to develop and promulgate a uniform method of presenting and marking the contents of text materials. As this coding is universally adopted, the interchange of texts among many professional users will be greatly facilitated. At the same time, the needs of the undergraduate student and general reader are being addressed by initiatives such as Project Gutenberg, designed to make public domain texts available electronically for the mere cost of duplication.

Specialized Databases

Text corpora are databases designed specifically for linguistic research. Generally modeling themselves after the one constructed for edited American English by W. Francis Nelson and Henry Kucera of Brown University, a goodly number of these represent various categories of writing (sports writing, technical writing, poetry, mystery novels, etc.) in samples proportionate to their quantity as published. Some of these corpora are now being manually (and occasionally electronically) tagged with their parts of speech to provide a more definitive baseline for measuring other samples. One unusual computer database of 20 million English words from different regions, nationalities, and media, is the *Cobuild Dictionary*, jointly produced by the University of Birmingham and Collins, the first dictionary based on an actual field study of English phrases and idioms.

The *Thesaurus Linguae Graecae* (TLG), also designed from the outset as a database for computer investigation, is a vast undertaking initiated by Theodore Brunner at the University of California, Irvine. Encompassing the entire body of Greek writing from the earliest days to about A.D. 600, when the dominance of this language in the Mediterranean Basin began to wane, this project provides access not only to a major literary resource but to the means of studying the economic, social, and cultural history of the civilized world at that time. Requiring much larger funding and management than are customary for humanities projects, the TLG has become a model for a parallel initiative in Latin undertaken by the Packard Humanities Foundation in Los Altos, California.

Another humanistic application, emerging more recently as the computer has been recognized as an online storage device, has been the compilation of critical databases. Among literary efforts, the Dante

Project, distinguished by having been conceived from the beginning as an online resource, has updated a classic scholarly tool, the variorum edition, in which all significant commentary on a single work (in this case the *Divine Comedy*) is appended to the individual passages it pertains to. The desirability of developing such a tool in an interactive mode presages a number of similar efforts for other literary monuments.

At present, several projects under development at major universities are capitalizing on the potential to incorporate not only words but also pictures and sound into databases that might reveal aspects of the humanities of which even the developers were not aware. At Brown University, for example, Victorian literature is being presented to students in a hypertext environment that encourages exploring the lives of poets and writers, their social milieu, their literary affiliations, and similar intersecting lines of inquiry. In hypermedia mode, the boundaries between scholarship and instruction begin to erode. The Perseus Project at Harvard is creating a similar database for Classical Greek culture.

Communication Among Humanists

A growing link among computer using humanists, even more important as newly accessible colleagues in all parts of the world gain capacity for Internet communication, is the growing variety of list-servers and newsgroups. The largest of these in the field, a conference called HUMANIST, originally established at the University of Toronto, now operates from Brown University. Although some of its conversation deals with computer applications, this conference accepts exchanges on almost any humanistic topic. Many others are much more constricted in their range, concentrating, for example, on the problems of computational linguistics or those involved in dealing with text in a single language.

For more traditional communication, computer-using humanists rely on several conventional media. They can use several print journals, like *Computers and the Humanities* and *Literary and Linguistic Computing*. Various newsletters emanate from several centers for computer-aided humanistic research. Biennial meetings of the Association for Computers and the Humanities (ACH) alternate with those of the Association for Literary and Linguistic Computing (ALLC). Associations in classical and modern languages allocate time on their programs for special interest groups in this area. The Modern Language Association (MLA) supports computing by endorsing and distributing software, providing space in its newsletter, publishing books on humanities computing applications and computers in composition, and supporting programs on current computer use at its annual conferences. Of particular interest is the MLA's pronouncement on the necessity to recognize humanities-oriented programming as a legitimate academic activity on a par with scholarly publishing.

In Europe, many countries have established national centers to develop new applications, to study the national culture, and to train students and faculty in the new technology. In France, Norway, Belgium, Italy, Germany, and elsewhere, full-time staff are compiling national dictionaries, concording the works of major writers, analyzing texts, tagging lexical corpora, and holding conferences (both national and international) to learn what is happening elsewhere and to publicize their own progress.

Advances in theoretical areas such as artificial intelligence (*q.v.*), natural language processing (*q.v.*), text scanning, machine translation (*q.v.*), the electronic classroom, the computer–human interface, voice-operated computers, and universal access to information seems to be more gradual, more local, and more personal than was expected in the sweeping projections and predictions of the 1960s and 1970s. Some of this change is mirrored in the image of the computer in fiction (*q.v.*), which has gone from HAL in Arthur C. Clarke's *2001: A Space Odyssey* (1968) to the cyberpunk biotechnology of William Gibson's *Neuromancer* (1984).

Bibliography

1982. Campbell, J. *Grammatical Man: Information, Entropy, Language, and Life.* New York: Simon & Schuster.

1984. Bolter, J. D. *Turing's Man.* Raleigh, NC: University of North Carolina Press.

1985. Olsen, S. (ed.) *Computer-Aided Instruction in the Humanities.* New York: Modern Language Association of America.

1985. Porush, D. *The Soft Machine: Cybernetic Fiction.* New York: Methuen.

1987. Heim, M. *Electric Language: A Philosophical Study of Word Processing.* New Haven, CT: Yale University Press.

1987. Rahtz, S. (ed.) *Information Technology in the Humanities.* New York: Halstead (John Wiley).

1987. Rudall, B. H., and Corns, T. N. *Computers and Literature: A Practical Guide.* Kent: Tunbridge Wells, and Boston: Abacus.

1990. Rudall, B. H., and Corns, T. N. "Computer Applications in the Humanities: A Reading List," *Canadian Humanities Computing Quarterly* (May).

1991. Delaney, P., and Landow, G. P. (eds.) *Hypertext and Literary Studies.* Baltimore and London: Johns Hopkins University Press.

1992. Landow, G. P. *Hypertext: The Convergence of Contemporary Critical Theory and Technology.* Baltimore and London: Johns Hopkins University Press.

1993. Lancashire, I. (ed.) *Computer-Based Chaucer Studies.* Toronto: University of Toronto Centre for Computing in the Humanities.

1996. Lancashire, I., Bradley, J., McCarty, W., and Stairs, M. *Using TACT with Electronic Texts: A Guide to Text-Analysis Computing Tools.* New York: Modern Language Association of America.

Websites

A comprehensive directory of computer-based activities related
to English literature may be found on the World Wide Web at
`http://gwis2.circ.gwu.edu/~scottlib/english.html`.

An account of one scholar's utilization of the computer in literary
analysis and his reflections on the implications of that activity
can be found at `http://ilex.cc.kcl.ac.uk/wlm/essays/What/`.

Joseph Raben

HYPERMEDIA

See MULTIMEDIA.

HYPERTEXT

For articles on related subjects *see* BUSH, VANNEVAR; DIGITAL
LIBRARIES; HUMAN FACTORS IN COMPUTING; INFORMATION
RETRIEVAL; MARKUP LANGUAGES; MULTIMEDIA; USER
INTERFACE; and WORLD WIDE WEB.

Hypertext is both the concept of interrelating information elements (linking pieces of information) and the
name used to describe a collection or *web* of interrelated or linked nodes. (An information element or
node can range from a single idea or *chunk* to an entire
document.) A hypertext system allows an author to
create the nodes and the links among them, and allows
a reader to *traverse* these links, i.e. to navigate from
one node to another using these links. Typically, hypertext systems mark link access points or *link anchors* in
some manner within a node when displaying it on a
computer screen (e.g. underlined—often blue—text
displayed within documents on World Wide Web
browsers). When the user selects the link marker, e.g.
by clicking on it with a mouse, the hypertext system
traverses to and displays the node at the other end of
the link. If a single link marker represents multiple
links, the hypertext system may present the user with
a list of available links. (System designers may have to
rank, filter, or layer this list if the number of possible
links might overwhelm the reader.) Hypertext user
interface design principles recommend that authors
label the link marker if the link's purpose or destination is not clear. Hypertext systems include many
navigation, annotation and *structural features* which
take advantage of the node and link structure to
support authors and readers. These components and
features are described further below.

Many people consider the terms *hypertext* and *hypermedia* synonymous. Nominally hypertext refers to
relating textual elements, while hypermedia encompasses relationships among elements of any media type.
The underlying concept is identical, though nontextual
hypermedia is generally more difficult to implement.

Hypertext, when well designed, enables people to read,
comprehend, and write information more effectively
than traditional documents. People typically read documents from start to end, i.e. in a *linear*, sequential
manner. Paper constrains (and encourages) authors to
present information in a linear format. By tradition, as
well as from the need to print, many write computerized documents in a linear format. Hypertext frees
readers and authors from this constraint. Authors can
structure information as a web of information chunks
and interrelating links. For example, authors could
place their main idea or an overview in an entry-point
chunk (node) with multiple links connecting logical
next steps or related tangential information chunks.
Presenting information as a web enables readers to
access information in the order most appropriate to
their purposes.

Hypertext links and structural features enable authors
to provide a rich context of related information
around elements. As a side effect, through the process
of crafting an information structure of nodes and
links, authors often come to understand the information better. For readers, freedom of access within a
web enhanced with contextual information provides
a richer environment for understanding the information they find. Hypertext also enhances comprehension
because it mimics the associative networks that people
use cognitively to store and retrieve information.

Hypertext concepts can supplement other computer
applications. Applications can provide links within
screens and documents to related information, and
can implement hypermedia navigation, annotation
and structural features to provide additional context
and increase comprehension. Hypertext constructs
can be predefined or can be generated dynamically as
an application executes.

Historical Perspective

Hypertext is not a new concept. In 1945 Vannevar
Bush proposed the Memex system, which would maintain links and annotations over printed materials
(Bush, 1945). In the 1960s Theodor Holmes Nelson
coined the terms hypertext and hypermedia. Nelson
envisioned a worldwide integrated document base of
hypertext-linked information that all people would be
able to access and work within. He also laid out the
specifications for his Xanadu hypermedia system in the
1960s (though the first working prototype appeared
only in the late 1990s). Douglas Engelbart demonstrated NLS/Augment, the first distributed, shared-
screen, collaborative hypertext system at the 1968 Fall
Joint Computer Conference. At the same time, Andries
Van Dam was developing Fress at Brown University.
Other prototype and commercial hypertext systems

appeared in the 1970s and 1980s, including Document Examiner, gIBIS, Guide, Hypergate, HyperTIES, Intermedia, MacWeb (by LIRMM), Max, Neptune, NoteCards, PHIDIAS, StorySpace, Writing Environment, and ZOG/KMS. (Apple Computer's HyperCard is not a true hypertext system, as it lacks many of the navigation, annotation, and structural features that characterize true hypertext systems. Several hypertext applications, however, have been built using HyperCard's infrastructure.) Intermedia was used for many years at Brown University to teach English and biology courses (Yankelovitch *et al.*, 1988). The first major hypertext research conference, ACM Hypertext '87, was held in April 1987 in Chapel Hill, USA. Biannual at first, the hypertext research community now meets every year at this conference.

Until the 1990s, the vast majority of hypertext systems were standalone nondistributed systems. In the early 1990s, HyperG (now called HyperWave) and the World Wide Web (WWW) appeared—the first distributed hypertext systems since NLS/Augment to take full advantage of the Internet. Like HyperCard, the WWW [or more precisely, the combination of the HTTP Internet protocol and HTML (*see* MARKUP LANGUAGES)] lacks many hypertext features, though again, many true distributed hypertext features and applications have been built upon its infrastructure. As the WWW gained prominence, the research-oriented hypertext systems of the 1990s increasingly migrated to or were developed directly for the WWW environment. ACM (*q.v.*) SIGLINK was formed in the early 1990s (renamed SIGWEB in 1998). SIGWEB is the major professional society for researchers and practitioners interested in hypertext and the Web. Seminal works in the hypertext field include (Nelson, 1974, 1981; Conklin, 1987; Halasz, 1988; Malcolm *et al.*, 1991).

Hypertext Components

NODES AND COMPOSITES

Hypertext components include nodes, links, link anchors, link markers, and composites. Hypertext nodes contain the content and attributes of information elements. Approximately half of the hypertext systems before the 1990s used fixed-size windows without scroll bars. Their designers believed that hypertext nodes should contain a single *chunk* of information, i.e. a single idea. The others supported entire documents as individual nodes. Many models of hypertext support *composite nodes*, i.e. a distinct set of nodes, perhaps with interrelating links. An example would be a book of separate chapters or a car of many components. The entire composite can be treated as a single high-level node. Links can be made to the composite or to any of its component nodes.

Many hypertext systems allow nodes to have *semantic types*, such as "description" or "letter of complaint," which they display with the node, as well as in maps and overviews of the hypertext web to help orient the user (*see* Fig. 1). Node types may also correspond to specific templates or forms that structure their internal content. People can use types in *structural search* to describe the nodes they seek. Several researchers have proposed taxonomies of node types. Some are detailed and domain-specific. Others are generic, used primarily for theoretical explanations, such as "proposition" and "collection."

LINK ANCHORS AND LINK MARKERS

Links connect entire nodes, but they focus on a particular aspect of each node endpoint. *Link anchors* specify a particular target area within each node corresponding to this aspect. Users typically do not see the link anchor, which is embedded in the node's internal code (e.g. HTML) and often contains internal parameters such as how to find its link. Instead the hypertext system displays a *link marker* that users can select to activate the anchor and traverse its link. On WWW browsers a link marker is often blue underlined text, denoting a link anchor. For example, a link might connect two newspaper articles if they both mention the same person as in Fig. 1. The person's name is associated with an anchor in each of the two nodes' internal code, as shown in Fig. 2. On the computer screen, the hypertext system highlights the person's name as a link marker whenever it displays one of the articles on the screen (perhaps incorporating the link label: "another article about Ms. X"). Selecting the marker activates the anchor. The system retrieves the anchor's link, determines the destination node and displays it, scrolling to the person's name in the second article.

Many hypertext systems will highlight the *destination link marker* or target area in some special way (e.g. displaying it in a different text style or flashing a box around it several times or shading its background as in Fig. 1) to draw the user's attention to the focus of the link just traversed. Note that in this case, the system also should highlight the destination link marker as a possible *departure link marker*, so users can traverse the link in both directions. A single link anchor and marker can represent multiple links. When selected, the hypertext system displays all relevant links and the user can choose among them. A few hypertext systems support *overlapping* link anchors and markers. When the link's focus truly encompasses the entire node, then the link anchor includes the node's entire content. The hypertext system should indicate the existence of any links leading from that node, and that the entire node is the destination target area when traversing to it.

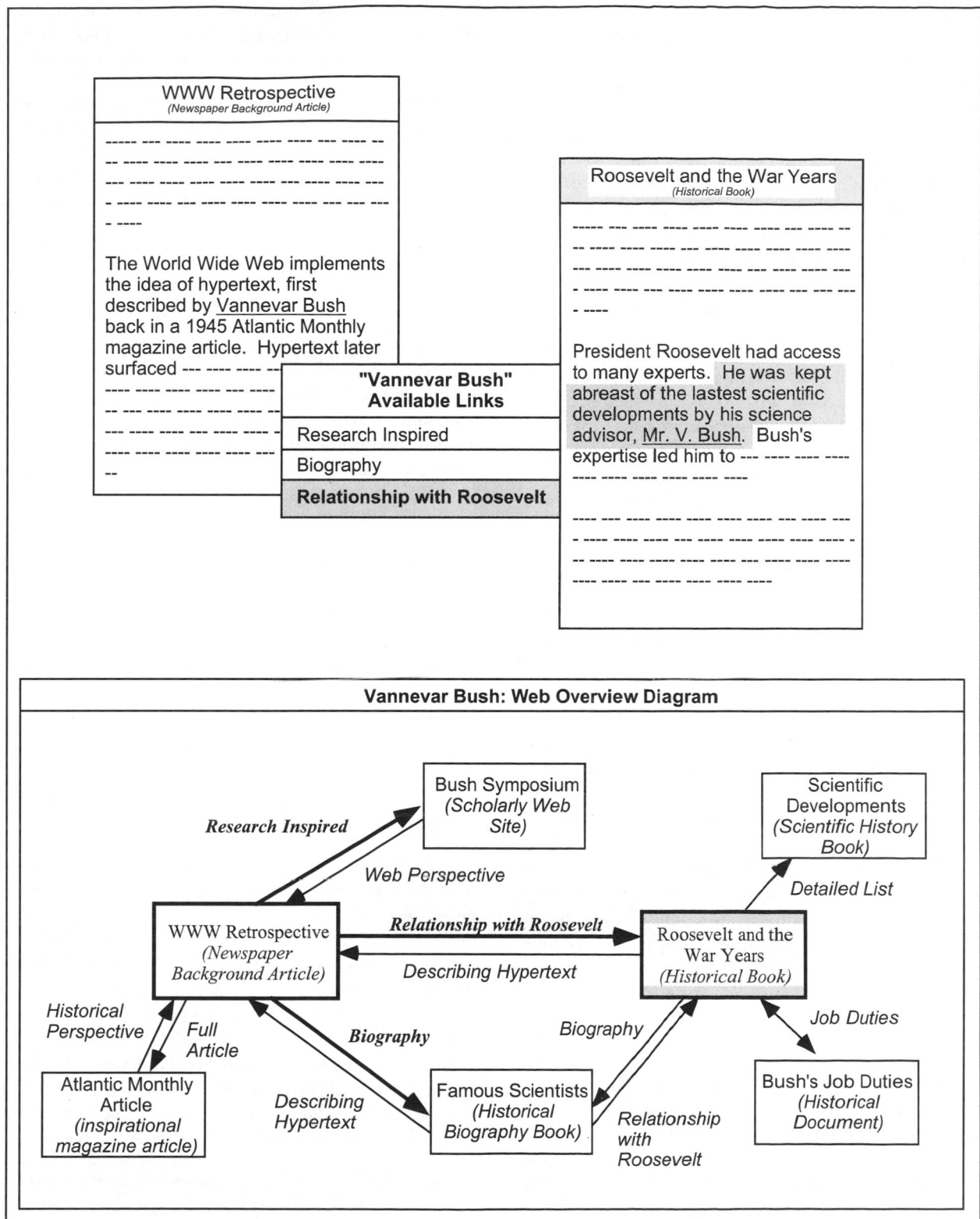

Figure 1. Traversing a link within a hypertext web.

The user has selected the link marker "Vannevar Bush" in the document node "WWW Retrospective," causing the hypertext system to display the three links for that anchor. Choosing the third, "Relationship with Roosevelt" leads to displaying the destination document node "Roosevelt in the War Years." The target area for that particular link is highlighted. (The target area contains another link marker, "Mr. V. Bush.") The bottom window contains a local overview of this Web, showing the nodes and node types within boxes, and the links and link types as arrows. The nodes and links appearing in the windows above are displayed with bold lines. The current node is highlighted in gray.

LINKS

Links represent relationships among nodes. As with nodes, links may have *semantic link types* (e.g. "supporting evidence for" or "criticism of") and associated *keywords*. Many hypertext systems display semantic link types as labels near the link's marker in nodes, and within maps and overviews. This can orient users by showing how nodes are interrelated, and can help them decide whether to traverse particular links. Users may also specify link types and keywords within *structural search* queries for nodes with specific relationships. Hypertext researchers have developed several general and theoretical link taxonomies.

Links can have *link behaviors* attached. Traversing them executes an associated action. For example, traversing a "display code" link to a computer program would list its code, whereas traversing an "execute" link would run the program. Hypertext webs also can represent processes to take advantage of hypertext features, representing process steps with nodes and transitions as links. Traversing these "transition" links *enacts* the process steps.

Many hypertext systems treat links as *first class objects* in their own right, i.e. giving links identifiers and attributes, and storing them in *external linkbases* or link databases so they can be reasoned about (*see* Fig. 2). Systems keeping links in external linkbases often include an anchor identifier with no link information in anchors. When the user selects a link marker, the system looks up its anchor's corresponding link, often using an independent *link service*. External linkbases facilitate *bidirectional linking* (traversing a link from all endpoints), structural search, *link evaluation* (e.g. checking that all link endpoints exist), and maintaining links over documents for which one does not have access permissions to embed an anchor in the departure node. In the latter case the system embeds link anchors in node content as it passes the node to a browser for display.

Transclusions, warm links, and hot links all connect two instances of the same information. *Transclusions* (or inclusions) enable the exact same node or anchor to appear in multiple places. Whereas copying and pasting creates an identical copy, transclusions essentially are pointers that connect the original to places that use it. Through transclusion, readers always have access to the original element and therefore to its original context, which can facilitate *deep intercomparison*. Xanadu's virtual document structure is built around transclusions: each document is a list of pointers to pieces of data which originate in that document or are "included" from others. *Warm links* and *hot links* are not pointers, but connect actual copies of their anchor content. With hot links, when the content of one anchor

changes, the hypertext system automatically updates all other copies immediately. With warm links, the system asks the users whether to update the other copies.

An *n-ary link* interrelates more than two nodes. For example, a "teacher" node can have an *n-ary* link to all students in a class. A "chemical bond" link could connect nodes representing each of a molecule's elements. Traversing an *n-ary* link would lead to any other or all destination nodes simultaneously.

Some models of hypertext do not contain explicit links. Instead, they handle links implicitly. *Set-based hypertext* could also support the teacher and chemical bond examples, treating a class or molecule as a set of elements. *Spatial hypertext* uses pattern matching to interrelate nodes positioned near each other or sharing the same virtual composite and attribute structure. Both support other hypertext functionality using these *implicit links*.

Large numbers of links can lead to cognitive overload and disorientation. *Cognitive overload* occurs when readers feel overwhelmed with too many choices of where to navigate next. *Disorientation* occurs when readers lose track of their position within the hypertext web while traversing links. Both can be avoided by using good user interface design principles; semantic node and link types; filtering based on user task and preferences; and hypertext navigation, annotation, and structural features.

Hypertext Features

The hypertext navigation, annotation and structural features build upon the hypertext constructs of nodes, links, anchors and composites. Hypertext *navigation* features transport the user among information elements. They include *browsing* (link traversal), backtracking, standard *content-based query*, and structural query based on interrelationships. An example of a *structural query* is "find all nodes of semantic type 'product information' within a two-link distance of any node of semantic type 'legal advice' where one of the connecting links has the semantic type 'prohibited by' or the keyword 'urgent.'"

Backtracking serves four purposes: to return to a prior position in a web (which allows users to take "detours" from their main task safely), to review the content of a previously visited node, to recover from a link chosen in error, and as part of undoing. Backtracking differs from *undoing*, however, in that backtracking returns the reader to a previously visited node in its current state. *Parametric backtracking*, written as "go-back(X)", allows the user to specify a value for a

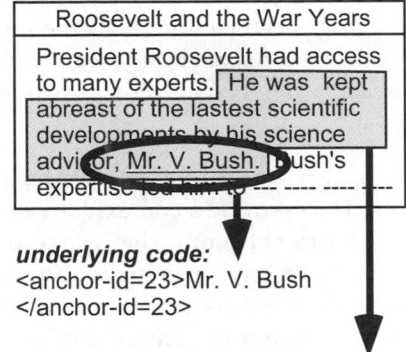

WWW Retrospective

The World Wide Web implements the idea of hypertext, first described by Vannevar Bush back in a 1945 Atlantic Monthly magazine article. Hypertext later surfaced --- ---- ---- ---- ---- --- ----

underlying code:
<anchor-id=8>Vannevar Bush
</anchor-id=8>

underlying code:
<target-id=6>The World Wide Web implements the idea of hypertext, first described by <anchor-id=8>Vannevar Bush</anchor-id=8> back in a 1945 Atlantic Monthly magazine article.</target-id=6>

Roosevelt and the War Years

President Roosevelt had access to many experts. He was kept abreast of the lastest scientific developments by his science advisor, Mr. V. Bush. Bush's expertise led him to --- ---- ---- --- ----

underlying code:
<anchor-id=23>Mr. V. Bush
</anchor-id=23>

underlying code:
<target-id=13>He was kept abreast of the lastest scientific developments by his science advisor, <anchor-id=23>Mr. V. Bush</anchor-id=23>.</target-id=13>

Linkbase					
Link ID	Link-Type	Source Node URI	Source Anchor ID	Destination Node URI	Destination Target ID
:	:	:	:	:	:
12	Research Inspired	http://...	8	http://...	16
13	Web Perspective	http://...	18	http://...	6
14	Relationship with Roosevelt	http://...	8	http://...	13
15	Describing Hypertext	http://...	23	http://...	6
16	Biography	http://...	8	http://...	19
17	Describing Hypertext	http://...	12	http://...	6
:	:	:	:	:	:

Figure 2. Source link anchors, destination target areas and the linkbase.

This shows the underlying link anchors and destination target areas from Figure 1, and their corresponding entries in the linkbase. The linkbase contains the three links for anchor #8, which was selected in Figure 1, from which the user selected link #14 leading to destination target area #13 in document node "Roosevelt and the War Years." Note that destination target area #13 contains source anchor #23. Selecting anchor #23 would traverse link #15 back to target area #6 in the original document node "WWW Retrospective." Destination target area #6 contains source anchor #8.

node attribute in parameter *X*, which causes the system to backtrack to the most recently departed node with that attribute value. *Conditional backtracking*, written as "go-back(query-expression)" evaluates an arbitrary *query-expression* and returns the reader to the most recently departed node satisfying it. Displaying a *history list* of previously visited nodes, and then selecting one of these, *backjumps* the user to that node. When implementing the history list as a stack (*q.v.*), backjumping removes all the in-between nodes from the history list. When implementing the history list as a *session log*, backjumping adds the prior node to the list (though some systems then remove it from its prior position in the log). Authors can construct guided tours and trails directly from session logs.

Annotation features include bookmarks, landmarks and comments. *Bookmarks* are one-way links from the reader's desktop to nodes they wish to access easily. *Landmarks* are one-way links from everywhere to a specific place, such as a home page. Landmarks typically remain permanently in view. Authors create landmarks, whereas readers create bookmarks. Bookmarks are essentially personal landmarks.

Structural features enable navigation through local and global overviews, and along recommended paths and guided tours of interrelated items. *Overview* diagrams (or maps) provide a graphical view of the hypertext web, usually with the nodes as icons and the links as arrows, often showing node names, and node and link semantic types. *Global overview* diagrams provide an overall picture; *local overviews*, such as Fig. 1, provide a fine-grained picture of a node's local neighborhood. Both provide spatial context and reduce disorientation. Readers can traverse directly to a node by selecting its icon.

Trails or *paths* connect a chain of links through an information space. They provide a context for viewing and understanding a series of nodes. They can record a path of information to remember or share. They can suggest a subset or ordering of nodes within a hypertext web, which can reduce cognitive overhead. Authors can prepare multiple "recommended" trails, each focusing on a different aspect of a web or tailored to different readers (a novice, an expert, etc.) *Guided tours* are restricted trails with link anchors that lead away from the trail dimmed or hidden. Users have to suspend or exit the tour to access these. Trails can contain *branches* allowing the reader to choose among subpaths. Hypertext systems often display and highlight trails in an overview diagram, so readers can maintain their orientation.

In multi-user hypertext systems, each hypertext construct and feature can have *access permissions* specified, e.g., for being created, modified, deleted, linked to, and commented upon by an individual, work group, or the general public.

The hypertext community strongly believes in *the reader as author*. All readers should be able to add their own annotation and structural features, as well as additional links to all nodes in any hypertext web.

Degradation or loss of relevance poses an important problem for hypertext links, comments and other features. No mechanism exists for determining when a comment, for example, has lost its relevance or correctness.

Hypertext Subfields

Hypertext research comprises several subfields: adaptive hypertext; hypertext design, evaluation, writing; hypertext functionality; open hypertext systems; and hypertext standards. *Adaptive hypertext systems* employ a user model to customize node content and filter the available link set. Adaptive hypertext systems try to guide users towards interesting and relevant information and shield them from irrelevant information. *Hypertext design* concerns analysis and design methodologies for creating hypertext systems. Hypertext design differs from standard design techniques due to its emphasis on links as first class objects and navigation. *Evaluation* techniques judge the ability of users to navigate effectively within a hypertext web and remain oriented when jumping into the web at random (e.g. to a node found by a search engine). Authors of *hypertext literature* (novels, short stories, and poetry) work in a nonlinear creativity space in which they design not only content, but also link structure, structural features and navigation. The Hypertext Functionality workshops study techniques for applying hypertext constructs and features to the everyday, nonhypertext applications found in business, engineering, and personal applications. The Open Hypertext Systems group studies ways for different hypertext systems to coordinate information and services over the Internet. (Such interoperability, for example, would allow one user to start a link using one hypertext system and a second user to complete the link using a different hypertext system on a separate computer.)

Four major *standards* efforts exist in the hypertext community. HyTime is an extension of SGML for specifying common hypertext concepts that sets of multimedia SGML documents can share. Due to its complexity, HyTime has never been widely used for hypertext. The *Dexter* reference model provides a detailed model of hypertext components. Several hypertext systems are based on Dexter. The Open Hypertext Systems group is developing an Open Hypertext Protocol for passing messages and sharing hypertext services among interoperating hypertext systems. Several hypertext systems have been made OHP-compliant. Many hypertext researchers are active in the World Wide Web Consortium's various standards efforts. The WWW's XML, XLink, and XPointer standards are being designed to support more sophisticated hypertext constructs and features on the World Wide Web.

Hypertext fills a conceptual niche related to, but separate from, fields such as databases, digital libraries, document management, information retrieval, multimedia, object-orientation, semantic networks, user interface design, and the World Wide Web. Many of these either use hypertext, complement hypertext or can be used to implement hypertext components and features.

Bibliography

1945. Bush, V. "As We May Think," *Atlantic Monthly*, **176**, 101–108. Also at http://www.theatlantic.com/unbound/flashbks/computer/bushf.htm.

1974. Nelson, T. *Computer Lib/Dream Machines*. Chicago, IL: Hugo's Books. Revised edition (1987). Redmond, WA: Microsoft Press.

1981. Nelson, T. *Literary Machines*. Swarthmore, PA (privately published). Revised (1993, Version 92.1). Sausalito, CA: Mindful Press.

1987. Conklin, E. J. "Hypertext: A Survey and Introduction," *IEEE Computer*, **20**, 9, 17–41.

1988. Halasz, F. G. "Reflections on NoteCards: Seven Issues for the Next Generation of Hypermedia Systems," *Comm. of the ACM*, **31**, 7 (July), 836–855.

1988. Yankelovich, N., Haan, B. J., Meyrowitz, N. K., and Drucker, S. M. "Intermedia: The Concept and the Construction of a Seamless Information Environment," *IEEE Computer*, **21**, *1* (January), 81–96.

1991 Malcolm, K. C., Poltrock, S. E., and Schuler, D. "Industrial Strength Hypermedia: Requirements for a Large Engineering Enterprise," *Hypertext '91 Proceedings*, 13–24. New York: ACM Press.

1997. Snyder, I. *Hypertext: the Electronic Labyrinth*. New York: New York University Press.

Websites

Hypertext Functionality. `http://www.cs.nott.ac.uk/ ~hla/HTF/`.

Open Hypertext Systems. `http://www.csdl.tamu.edu/ ohs/`.

Open Hypertext Protocols. `http://www.w3.org`.

Sigweb. `http://www.acm.org/sigweb/`.

Michael Bieber

I/O BUS

See BUS.

I/O CHANNEL

See CHANNEL.

I/O PORT

See PORT, I/O.

IBM CARD

See PUNCHED CARD; and PUNCHED CARD MACHINERY.

IBM CORPORATION

For articles on related subjects *see* AIKEN, HOWARD H.; COMPUTER INDUSTRY: UNITED STATES; DIGITAL COMPUTERS, HISTORY OF; ECKERT, WALLACE J.; FORTRAN; HOLLERITH, HERMAN; HOLLERITH MACHINE; IBM 1400 SERIES; IBM 360/370/390 SERIES; IBM PC; MARK I, HARVARD; NORC; PUNCHED CARD; PUNCHED CARD MACHINERY; STRETCH; USER GROUPS; and WATSON, THOMAS J. SR.

EVER ONWARD—EVER ONWARD!
That's the spirit that has brought us fame!
We're big, but bigger we will be,
We can't fail for all can see
That to serve humanity has been our aim!

Our products now are known in every zone
Our reputation sparkles like a gem
We've fought our way through—and new
Fields we're sure to conquer too
For the EVER ONWARD IBM.

First chorus of a 1950s IBM anthem,
sung to tune "Stouthcarted Men"

Introduction

For much of the 20th century, IBM (previously the International Business Machines Corporation) was the quintessential name in data processing and digital computation. The zenith of its power and influence may have passed, but the company is still a formidable presence. Although a view not universally held, it is arguably the most widely admired US corporation, noted for its research, innovation, stability, profitability, and effective management. And now, since IBM's rebound from its financial losses of the early 1990s, one could add the attribute of resilience.

Early History

IBM was incorporated in the state of New York on 15 June 1911 as the Computing-Tabulating-Recording Company, but its origins can be traced back to 1890 when the US Census Bureau solicited competitive proposals to find a more efficient way to tabulate census data. The winner was Herman Hollerith (*q.v.*) whose Tabulating Machine used an electric current to sense holes in punched cards and kept a running total of

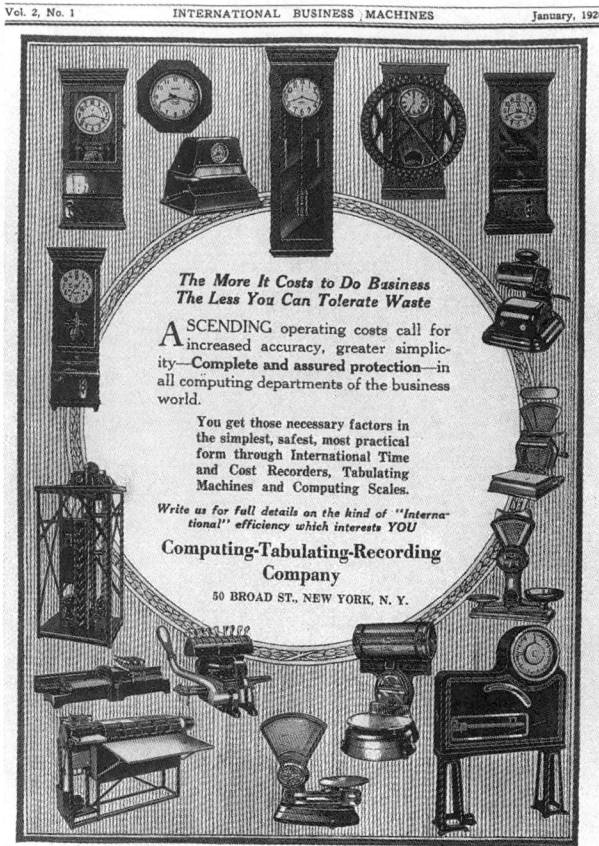

Vol. 2, No. 1   INTERNATIONAL BUSINESS MACHINES   January, 1920

The More It Costs to Do Business
The Less You Can Tolerate Waste

ASCENDING operating costs call for increased accuracy, greater simplicity—**Complete and assured protection**—in all computing departments of the business world.

You get those necessary factors in the simplest, safest, most practical form through International Time and Cost Recorders, Tabulating Machines and Computing Scales.

Write us for full details on the kind of "International" efficiency which interests YOU

Computing-Tabulating-Recording Company

50 BROAD ST., NEW YORK, N. Y.

Page Fifteen

Figure 1. The 1920 C-T-R product line. Machines are arranged clockwise in order of decreasing profitability, the time equipment on the left-hand side and top left being most profitable and the punched card machines at the bottom left being least profitable (courtesy of IBM).

Figure 2. Thomas J. Watson THINKing (courtesy of IBM).

processed data. To capitalize on his success, Hollerith formed the Tabulating Machine Company in 1896.

In 1911, Charles R. Flint brokered the merger of Hollerith's company with two others, the Computing Scale Company of America and the International Time Recording Company, to form the Computing-Tabulating-Recording Company (C-T-R). C-T-R manufactured and sold machinery ranging from commercial scales and industrial time recorders to meat and cheese slicers and, of course, tabulators and punched cards (*see* Fig. 1). Based in New York City, the company had 1,300 employees and offices and plants in Endicott and Binghamton, NY; Dayton, OH; Detroit, MI; Washington, DC; and Toronto.

In 1914, when Flint recognized that the diversified businesses of C-T-R had proved difficult to manage, he recruited as General Manager a former executive of the National Cash Register Company, the 40-year-old Thomas J. Watson (Fig. 2). The next year, Watson was named President and began the widespread posting of his famous "THINK" signs. In 1924, C-T-R changed its name to the International Business Machines Corpora-

tion. Its initials were written I.B.M. for quite some time, but eventually elided to just IBM, now the formal name of the corporation.

In 1937, Thomas Watson Jr. joined his father at IBM as General Manager, the initial title of his father. Ten years later, a second Watson son, Arthur K. "Dick" Watson, was hired and eventually became a vice president of the IBM World Trade Corporation in 1949. Thus, by that year, the senior Watson had installed his two sons, aged 35 and 30, in positions that virtually assured that a Watson would be a major force at IBM for many years to come. Thomas Jr., of course, later became president of IBM. Dick Watson left the company in 1970 to become Ambassador to France, but died in 1974 at age 55.

Data Processing

THE IBM CARD

IBM's earliest rival was the Powers Accounting Machine Company founded by James Powers (*q.v.*) in 1911 and acquired by Remington Rand in 1927. The Powers punched cards, like the earlier Hollerith cards, were 45-column cards with round holes that were sensed mechanically. In 1928, IBM introduced the higher-capacity 80-column card, which used rectangular or "slotted" punched holes that were sensed electromechanically.

Despite the technological advances, Watson was accused of making the changes with the deliberate objective of making the Remington Rand equipment incompatible with his own (DeLamarter, 1986). Ignoring the barbs, Watson began touting the new medium as not *just* punched cards, but as "IBM cards." And to facilitate conversion to the new format, IBM began to market a "reproducer" that was able to read the data on 45-column cards and punch it into 80-column cards. (The name *reproducer* later came to mean a machine that would merely make a second copy of a set of 80-column cards.) The ability to store 80 characters on one card now made it tempting to cram all the vital statistics of a person or item into one card-based "unit record," leading to the term *unit record machine* for any of the various devices invented to process the cards. But since each of the 80 columns was precious, the temptation may have been great to effect the 2.5% saving afforded by storing years in only a 2-digit rather than a 4-digit format, thus sowing the seeds of the Year 2000 (Y2K— *q.v.*) "crisis" 72 years later.

The regard for card format pertained not only to competition over the sale of card processing machines, but also to the sale of the card stock. In 1936, IBM settled the first of three anti-trust suits filed against them by agreeing that customers could buy their cards from competitors, but as of 1956, IBM still derived 20% of its revenue and 30% of its profits from the sale of cards of its own manufacture. Through a 1956 consent decree, the USA forced IBM to make it easier for other companies to make cards, but punched cards became technologically obsolete before the edict had much effect. By 1969, IBM revenue from punched cards was negligible.

OTHER BUSINESS MACHINES

In keeping with the name of the company, IBM marketed business machines other than those used for accounting and computation. In 1933, IBM acquired the Electromatic Typewriter Corporation and manufactured electric typewriters for 57 years. By 1958, IBM had sold its one millionth machine and was deriving 8% of its revenue from the sales of electric typewriters. In 1961, IBM announced the Selectric typewriter (Fig. 3), developed by H. S. ("Bud") Beattie, who was also the inventor of a number of high-performance printers. The machine was noted for proportional print, extremely high print quality, and the ability to change type fonts through use of replaceable "golf ball" typing elements. An I/O version of the Selectric was used with the SABRE airline reservation system and on the IBM 1620 small computer. Without the I/O Selectric's special APL (*q.v.*) type ball, that language would not have been able to achieve the popularity that it did, even to the point where an early commercial

Figure. 3. An IBM Selectric typewriter (courtesy of IBM).

time-sharing service was based on APL. In the mid to late 1960s, IBM marketed a series of free-standing word processors based on the Selectric as competitors to similar products offered by the Wang Corporation.

Sales of the Selectric remained strong for 25 years, but by 1990 word processing on personal computers had so depressed the market for electric typewriters that IBM sold its typewriter division to Lexmark of Lexington, KY, which has continued to market successors to the keyboards and personal printers that came with the sale.

Another successful data processing product was the IBM Type 805 International Test Scoring Machine, announced in 1937. The machine, based on the invention of Reynold B. Johnson, a former high school science teacher whom IBM hired in 1934 for a salary of $4,000 per year and $4,000 for his patent, scores objective tests by sensing the conductivity of graphite pencil marks. Johnson went on to earn many other patents of great value to IBM. Optical successors to the IBM 805 are still in use today; hundreds of thousands of a small countertop version process millions of lottery tickets every week.

THE CARD PROGRAMMED CALCULATOR (CPC)

In 1946, IBM began to sell its IBM 603 Multiplying Card Punch, an electronic version of a machine that had been offered since 1934. About 100 were sold before an upgrade to the IBM 604, of which a remarkable 5,600 were sold over the next 10 years. But in 1947, thanks to an enterprising customer, Northrop Aircraft, a 603 was hooked up to a specially developed storage unit and other punched card equipment. The result, the Card Programmed Calculator (CPC), with the later 604 rather than the 603, was capable of 1,000 operations per second. It was not a stored program computer, but it could add, subtract, multiply, divide, and even extract square roots with a special prewired plugboard that essentially provided what would later be called *microcode*.

News of the improvised machine spread quickly, and by 1948, IBM had a dozen orders for copies. By 1955, over 700 CPCs had been placed in service over a period during which only 14 Univac Is (*q.v.*) were installed, and IBM's CPC revenue of $21 million in that year was almost double that of its stored program computers. A year later, the ratio would be reversed, though CPC revenue remained strong through 1964. The CPC's historical significance is that although IBM always knew that there was a strong market for business data processing, it was the unexpected success of the CPC that made the Watsons realize that there was also money to be made by automating the computations of interest to scientists and engineers.

THE HARVARD MARK I

In 1936, Howard Hathaway Aiken (*q.v.*) was a graduate student in applied physics at Harvard who perceived the need for an electromechanical device to solve some nonlinear equations relating to his research in the design of vacuum tubes. With just the barest of outlines of how to proceed, he approached George Chase, chief engineer of the Monroe Calculating Machine Company, for help. Despite Chase's urging, his superiors would not agree to back the project, so he advised Aiken to try his opposite number at IBM, James Bryce. An enthusiastic Bryce succeeded where Chase had failed; Thomas Watson agreed to grant funds to Aiken, $15,000 initially, but much more as design progressed.

The result was an enormous machine, 51 feet (15.5 m) wide but only 2 feet (0.6 m) deep (Fig. 4). Its capacity

was only 72 numbers, and it could perform only three additions or subtractions per second, with multiplication taking as long as six seconds. Its IBM name was the mouthful *Automatic Sequence Controlled Calculator*, but it was more commonly known as the Mark I (*q.v.*), or, because "Mark I" was a popular designation for other computers, the Harvard Mark I.

The Mark I received much publicity and was readied for dedication and public demonstration on 7 August 1944, seven years after Aiken's first contact with IBM. But in preparation for the big day, Watson had commissioned a noted industrial designer to envelop the machine in a sleek, futuristic, and (to Aiken) pretentious outer skin of stainless steel and glass, ignoring the fact that its originator preferred the accessibility of its electrical circuits. Whether in retaliation or not, Aiken ignored IBM at the ceremony and gave every impression that he was its sole creator. Watson, fuming, lay in wait for a chance for retribution.

The EDP to Computer Transition

THE SELECTIVE SEQUENCE ELECTRONIC CALCULATOR (SSEC)

In 1945, Frank Hamilton and Rex Seeber, disappointed that they could not convince Howard Aiken to

Figure 4. The Harvard/IBM Mark I (courtesy of IBM).

Figure 5. The SSEC (courtesy of IBM).

make the Mark II a stored program computer, asked Tom Watson for approval to begin design of a "super-calculator" to be called the Selective Sequence Electronic Calculator (SSEC). Watson, still smarting from the affront from Aiken, gave quick and enthusiastic assent. A key member of the SSEC team was Byron Phelps, who had developed the electronic circuitry of the IBM 603 Multiplying Card Punch. The machine was completed in Endicott, NY, in the summer of 1947 and then disassembled and shipped to the company's headquarters at 590 Madison Avenue in New York City (Fig. 5). Reassembled and displayed in the window and dedicated in January 1948, the machine had 12,500 vacuum tubes and could do 14 by 14 digit decimal multiplication in 20 ms, division in 33 ms, and addition or subtraction of 19-digit numbers in just 300 μs. The machine was 250 times faster than the Harvard Mark I, which took 6 seconds for multiplication and 11.4 seconds for division.

Perhaps because it cost one million dollars, a prodigious sum in those days, only one SSEC was ever built. Although its 13,000 vacuum tubes certainly must have done much to heat the building, evidence that it ever did much useful work is sketchy. But the machine was a public relations triumph for IBM. The SSEC became the source of many valuable IBM patents, and was the training ground for two of Seeber's best programmers, John Backus, the driving force behind the later development of Fortran, and Edgar F. "Ted" Codd, who invented the relational database (*q.v.*). The SSEC sat proudly in the window of IBM headquarters until, in an attempt to divert attention from the Univac, it was replaced by an IBM 701 in 1952.

SAGE and the IBM AN/FSQ-7

In 1949, when the Soviet Union exploded its first atomic device much sooner than the USA had expected, the government declared an urgent need to expand air traffic control technology into a full-fledged air defense monitoring system. The government solicited bids from a number of private contractors to expand the Whirlwind (*q.v.*) project at MIT to form SAGE (Semi-Automatic Ground Environment), whose development work was to be done at the newly formed MIT Lincoln Laboratory. Tom Watson decided that IBM participation was essential and later said that he "worked harder to win that contract than I worked for any other sale in my life." Bidding in addition to IBM were Remington Rand, which had just acquired Engineering Research Associates (ERA), and Raytheon. In documenting the reasons for the selection of IBM, Jay Forrester wrote, "In the IBM organization we observed a much higher degree of purposefulness, integration, and esprit de corps than we found in the Remington Rand organization."

Figure 6. A typical SAGE console (courtesy of IBM).

In implementing SAGE, IBM expanded and improved the Whirlwind. Each new machine, which carried the military designation AN/FSQ-7, was actually two identical computers that operated in duplex mode for greater reliability. The AN/FSQ-7 was a single address machine with 8K 32-bit words that ran at about 75 KHz. Auxiliary memory included 12 drums each having a capacity of 12,288 words. Each CPU was capable of supporting 100 display consoles (Fig. 6) while sending and receiving data from 12 remote sites.

Beyond its contribution to national defense, SAGE was notable for major technological advances in computer technology, among them a large real-time operating system, a highly disciplined program structure, multiplexing via I/O channels, digital telephonic data transmission, cathode ray tube monitors, light pen interaction, and duplexed operation for reliability. It was also the first IBM computer to use magnetic core memory.

From 1952 to 1955, SAGE contributed only 4% to IBM's total revenue, but more significantly, it accounted for 80% of its earnings from stored program digital computers. SAGE revenue reached its peak at $122 million in 1957, which, at 12% of total revenue, was the same as that of all of IBM's commercial computers. The benefits of the experience gained with the project showed up rapidly in the IBM 700 and 7000 computers that followed shortly after conclusion of IBM's intensive participation in SAGE.

The SABRE Airline Reservation System

In 1953, due to a chance encounter between two Smiths on an airplane, IBM seized on an opportunity to capitalize on the experience it had gained in real-time computation with SAGE. When Blair Smith, a top IBM salesman, found that his seatmate on a flight from Los

Figure 7. A SABRE console (courtesy of IBM).

Angeles to New York was the (unrelated) president of American Airlines, C. R. Smith, the talk quickly turned to AA's need for a wholesale replacement of its antiquated *Reservisor* airline reservation system. The application turned out to be just what Thomas Watson Jr. was looking for, and he placed SAGE (and sage) engineer Perry Crawford, newly hired away from the Office of Naval Research, in charge of developing a system to meet the needs of the airline.

IBM tided AA over with improved punched card equipment until the project could get rolling in 1957. In 1960, system design was far enough along to warrant the acronym SABRE, and although this endured, its awkward name, Semi-Automatic Business Research Environment, was soon dropped. The system was fully implemented by 1963, the culmination of the largest commercial data processing operation undertaken as of that time. Housed in Briarcliff Manor, New York, SABRE consisted of 10,000 miles of leased phone lines that allowed 1,100 agents in 50 cities to make 10 million reservations per year in an average time of less than three seconds each. The heart of the system was a pair of IBM 7090 computers, duplexed for reliability (Fig. 7). Over the period 1965 to 1968, Delta, Pan Am, and Eastern Airlines purchased similar systems, and in 1987, United Airlines installed a successor system based on eight S/370 model 3090 machines.

EARLY IBM COMMERCIAL COMPUTERS

As of 1950, IBM had under development the Magnetic Drum Calculator (MDC), the forerunner of the IBM 650; the decimal Tape Processing Machine (TPM), which would later become the IBM 702; the binary Defense Calculator, which would become its scientific machine, the IBM 701; and the IBM 7030 (Stretch— *q.v.*), one of the first supercomputers (*q.v.*). The latter

machine was so named because its designers intended to stretch available technology to the limit in hopes of attaining a processing speed far in excess of what had so far been achieved. The realization fell short of the goal, but seven IBM 7030s were delivered, mostly to government laboratories, and the effort produced many innovations which turned up on later machines. Its circuit packaging technology, for example, was used for the IBM 1401. A specially enhanced version of the Stretch called *Harvest*, built for the National Security Agency (NSA) and delivered in 1958, was equipped with an advanced tape system called *Tractor* which could fetch any of 160 tape cartridges in a few seconds and then deliver its contents at a then unbelievable transfer rate of a megabyte per second. The Harvest served NSA well for 14 years.

Until the early 1950s, IBM products were called "machines" or "calculators." The term "computer" meant the human who used a calculator to compute things, and Watson did not want to raise the spectre of technological unemployment. He was also on good ground in the sense that, to this day, our "computers" collectively spend much less time "computing" than they do processing data—copying it, moving it about, sorting it, merging it, or printing it.

For whatever reason, EMCC, the Eckert–Mauchly Computer Company, did call its Univac a *computer*, even though it was primarily a business data processing machine. In 1950, J. Presper Eckert (*q.v.*) and John W. Mauchly (*q.v.*), inventors of the historic ENIAC (*q.v.*), sought a meeting with the Watsons, father and son, to explore whether IBM might be interested in acquiring their financially troubled enterprise. Primed by his lawyers, the senior Watson explained that he did not wish to expose IBM to possible anti-trust action by absorbing its prime competitor. The meeting ended quickly and EMCC was sold to Remington Rand, another father–son operation.

In that same year of 1950, the Korean War began, and Tom Watson's sense of patriotism had led him to divert IBM resources to development of the Defense Calculator and to the Naval Ordnance Research Calculator (NORC), a machine which IBM delivered in 1954 for a fee of cost plus one dollar. But now he worried that while doing so, Remington Rand's Univac would capture the lion's share of the market for commercial computers. In response, IBM announced the binary IBM 701 (Fig. 8) for scientific and engineering users and the decimal IBM 702 for business users. It was claimed that the 702, a renamed TPM, would use Williams tube memory (*q.v.*) instead of mercury delay lines (*see* ULTRASONIC MEMORY) and hence would outperform the Univac and cost less. According to DeLamarter (1986), who quotes an internal IBM

Figure 8. The IBM 701 (courtesy of IBM).

Figure 10. Thomas Watson Sr. (right) passes the torch to his son (courtesy of IBM).

memorandum, the second goal was met only by setting 700 series prices at about half the actual cost of production, deliberately in the case of the 701, mistakenly in the case of the 702.

In November 1952, IBM was stunned by the magnitude of the publicity the Univac received when CBS used it to predict, based on very early returns, that Eisenhower would defeat Adlai Stevenson by a much wider margin than polls had predicted (*See* POLITICAL APPLICATIONS). Watson was able to stimulate sales of the 700 series, but could not accelerate the production schedule. By June 1954, IBM had 50 orders for the 702, but its first delivery in 1955 came four full years after the first Univac. Had Remington Rand been able to raise production to much higher levels than it did, "Univac" might to this day be as close to a generic term as "Kleenex" and "Xerox," but to IBM's great good fortune, this did not happen. But while IBM waited for deliveries of the 701 and 702 to begin, it could take pride in having installed almost 2,000 IBM 650s.

IBM considered 1956 to be a turning point in its history. By that year, Univac held only a slight edge in the number of installed machines, 30 versus 24. But by a year later, the score stood at 66 702s and 46 Univacs,

Figure 9. A typical IBM 704 layout (courtesy of IBM).

and the order position was even better: 193 for IBM and 65 for Sperry Rand, formed in 1955 through merger of Remington Rand and Sperry Gyroscope. And in that same year, IBM was able to announce higher performance replacements for its two leading machines, the 704 (Fig. 9) for the 701 and the 705 for the 702, the principal advance being use of magnetic core memory. In May 1956, with an important antitrust suit settled and at the height of IBM's power and influence, Thomas J. Watson Sr. passed the title of CEO to his son, Thomas J. Watson Jr. (Fig. 10). One month later, the senior Watson died.

By the mid-1950s, terminology had evolved to what we still use today. A *computer* uses the *stored program concept* (*q.v.*) in which instructions and (at least some) data reside in main memory and are indistinguishable until a bit string (no decimal computers remain) is chosen for either execution as an instruction or processed as data. A *calculator* is a mechanical or electronic computational device whose instructions do not reside in memory (*see* CALCULATING MACHINES and CALCULATORS, ELECTRONIC AND PROGRAMMABLE). No one any longer thinks of *computer* as the name of a human occupation.

THE IBM 305 RAMAC

Over 1,000 copies of the IBM 305 RAMAC (Random Access Memory Accounting Machine; Fig. 11) were sold over the period 1956 to 1961. Still a vacuum tube computer, the machine is historically significant for its use of the model 350 Disk Storage Unit. Its capacity of five megabytes seems quaint by today's gigabyte standards, but was nonetheless a breakthrough innovation in its day.

Figure 11. The IBM 305 RAMAC (courtesy of IBM).

THE 1400 SERIES

The IBM 1400 series, introduced in 1959, began with the IBM 1401 and eventually consisted of models 1401, 1410, 1440, 1460, and 7010. The 1401, whose rental began at $2,500 per month, was a fully transistorized second-generation machine having original memory capacity options ranging from 1.4K to 16K 6-bit characters. As with the 702, arithmetic was decimal. Much of its success was due to its associated IBM 1403 chain printer which provided excellent print quality at 600 lines per minute, four times faster than had previously been available. Another factor was the introduction of the simple RPG (Report Program Generator), a language that mimicked what previously had to be done with plugboards. The language still has adherents to this day (see NONPROCEDURAL LANGUAGES). Shattering the sales projection of 1,000 machines, over 14,000 IBM 1400 systems were installed until transition to System 360 machines in the mid-1960s. By 1961, the 1401 accounted for 25% of all computer models ever installed in the world.

It is not clear that IBM or any other computer vendor ever sought to patent the *instruction set* (*q.v.*) of a computer, most probably because they had no reasonable expectation that the Patent Office would grant such patents. But since, years later, that Office did begin to grant patents for cryptographic algorithms implemented in software, IBM may have missed an opportunity in this regard, and if they had succeeded it might have earned them an even greater share of the computer market than it did. In 1963, Honeywell pounced on the loophole and built a computer, the H-200, whose architecture was very similar to that of the IBM 1401. To gloss over the minor differences, they wrote a program wryly called the "Liberator" which could convert 1400 series programs to run on their new machine. The industry was amused, but IBM certainly was not. Within two months, its salesmen reported 196 losses to the H-200, which was carefully priced to provide a better cost–performance ratio than 1400 series machines. Rather than re-price its line or introduce new models, IBM, with what was to become the System 360 series in development, chose instead to make sure that upward compatibility to the new series could be attained through *emulation* (*q.v.*). Despite the losses to Honeywell, the 1400 series made its mark in history as the most successful line of compatible computers prior to System 360.

The Competition

By the late 1950s, the only major US corporations other than IBM that were able to commit sufficient resources to make computers and stay the course for at least a few years were RCA, GE, Philco, Burroughs, NCR, Sperry Rand, and Honeywell, which had enjoyed the modest success described above. But eventually, RCA left the computer business and was later absorbed by GE; GE sold its computer division to Honeywell; Philco sold its division to Ford, which left the business shortly thereafter; and Burroughs was absorbed by Sperry Rand, renamed Unisys. Of the many computer start-up companies of that era, only the Control Data Corporation (*q.v.*) survived to the end of the century, but as a "solutions company" that no longer sells computers of its own manufacture. The Digital Equipment Corporation (*q.v.*) almost made it, but that company was bought by Compaq in 1998.

The shakeout was fierce. By 1964, when the IBM System 360 (*q.v.*) was announced, industry gurus (*q.v.*) referred to IBM and its competitors as "Snow White and the Seven Dwarfs," the latter consisting of Burroughs, CDC, GE, Honeywell, NCR, RCA, and Sperry Rand/Univac. IBM held 75% of the market and none of the dwarfs more than 3%, nor did any of the leading European firms: ICL in the UK, Olivetti in Italy, Nixdorf in Germany, and Machines Bull in France. A few years later, major competition was reduced to the BUNCH: Burroughs, Univac, NCR, CDC, and Honeywell. On a roll, Tom Watson Jr. moved IBM World Headquarters from New York City to Armonk, NY.

The IBM 1620

In 1962, IBM began delivery of a remarkable little machine called the IBM 1620. Up to that time, computers were sufficiently complex that they were tended by professional operators; not even a programmer was allowed to touch one. The operators mounted relevant tapes, fed card decks to the machine, ran the program that caused the machine to devour them, and then collected all input and output media for return to the program sponsor. It was the age of *batch processing*.

Figure 12. An IBM 1620 system (courtesy IBM).

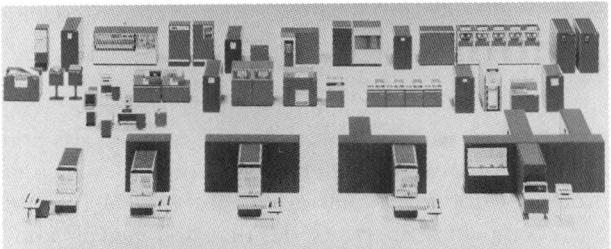

Figure 13. Five models of the S/360 (courtesy of IBM).

Programmers were lucky to get four vicarious cracks a day at the machine, and the slightest error of a comma or decimal point would cause them great consternation.

But the 1620 (Fig. 12), an $85,000 decimal computer whose Fortran compiler made excellent use of a meager 20,000 digit memory, was a programmer's delight. Precious digits could be conserved through the judicious placement of "flag bits" which delimited words of variable length. A modified version of the Selectric typewriter, which IBM had introduced just the year before, provided excellent output print quality. The machine's already relatively low cost was deeply discounted to universities, where it became a great favorite with students, providing their first "hands-on" computer experience. Their allegiance has lasted for decades, to the point where there is a Website (http://www.computerhistory.org/old/IBM1620) that keeps track of 1620 lore.

The 1620 was succeeded by the IBM 1130, introduced in 1965. With a main memory of 8K 16-bit words and a megabyte disk storage unit, the machine could be rented for just $895 per month. Nonetheless, the machine was less successful than the 1620, probably because many customers chose to order a System/360 model 20 or 30 instead.

System/360 (*see also* IBM 360/370/390 SERIES)

The rationale for System 360 was clear. By the early 1960s, IBM was writing and maintaining software for seven incompatible computer systems. Something had to be done. IBM began planning its New Product Line (NPL) in 1962. The idea of introducing a compatible family of the same *computer architecture* (*q.v.*), a term coined at IBM in that year, was neither new nor

unique. Philco and GE had done it first and Univac, CDC, and Burroughs did so at about the same time, but none of these competitive families included models that spanned a factor of 50 in performance.

The "architects" of the NPL (later S/360) were Gene Amdahl, one of the technical leaders of the IBM 704 project, and Fred Brooks, each reporting to Data Systems Division manager Bob Evans. Brooks loyally began work on the project even though he had urged that IBM go in a different direction, opting for maximum performance at a number of different levels of machine, compatible or not. When it became clear that concomitant development of a complex *operating system* (*q.v.*) was crucial to the success of NPL, Brooks was assigned the task of directing the efforts of almost 2,000 programmers to produce what was initially introduced as OS/360. Based on his experience with this effort, Brooks wrote the now-classic *Mythical Man Month* (*see* LITERATURE OF COMPUTING). The initially delivered OS/360 was disappointingly sluggish and prone to crash, but the product eventually matured into the more successful OS/MFT (Multiprogramming with a Fixed number of Tasks) and OS/MVT (Multiprogramming with a Variable number of Tasks).

As announced in April 1964, the original S/360 series encompassed models 30 through 70 in steps of 10, plus a model 62, but the 60, 62, and 70 were replaced by models 65 and 75 before any were shipped. A model 20 was announced in November. The next year, a specialized model 67 was added in deference to the academic community and a model 44 was targeted for small-scale scientific applications. Over the next five years, models 85, 95, and 195 were announced in largely unsuccessful attempts to compete with supercomputers built by CDC and, later, Cray Research.

The System/360 machines (Fig. 13) used what IBM called *Solid Logic Technology* (SLT), a conservative choice midway between discrete components and true integrated circuitry (*q.v.*). To a good approximation, each model offered twice the performance of the one below it at a cost of only 40% more, either in validation of Grosch's Law (*see* LAWS, COMPUTER) or because IBM used the "law" as a guide to setting prices.

System 360 sales up through model 65 were so strong that competitors soon arose, both for the system itself and for its peripherals. For a while, Control Data successfully sold tapes and disk drives that were "plug to plug" compatible with their IBM counterparts and less expensive. Taking advantage of the lack of patent protection for the S/360 architecture, RCA brought out a compatible Spectra series that siphoned off a few per cent of S/360 sales, but that company remained in the computer business for only a few years. More distressing to IBM was that its own Gene Amdahl left to found a company bearing his name, a company far more successful than RCA had been (*see* his profile in ENTREPRENEURS). The Amdahl Corporation is now a subsidiary of Hitachi, which continues to market IBM-compatible mainframes, as does the other major Japanese computer vendor, Fujitsu. At one time, even the USSR brought out an S/360 compatible Syad series. But none of these efforts seriously affected IBM sales.

In 1970, IBM moved to a fully transistorized System/370 product line. Its extended S/360 architecture included *dynamic address modification* which supported efficient time sharing. The series began with models 155 and 165 (quickly upgraded to models 158 and 168), each rated at 3 to 5 times faster than the corresponding S/360 models 50 and 65. Over the next six years, additional models were introduced in the order 145, 195, 135, 125, and 115.

By late 1976, some of IBM's technical leaders came to believe that they had taken the S/370 as far as was feasible to stay ahead of competition and received approval to plan for FS, its Future System. Other influential IBM leaders opposed the idea. After a fierce and protracted argument, the FS was abandoned at a loss of $100 million, a significant sum even to IBM, and the System/370 was nursed along with occasional modest improvements for another 15 years. The line was split into a series of large-scale computers whose models were designated 30xx and a midrange series designated 43xx. Over the system's life span, 17 different models were introduced, one fewer than the number of S/360 models. (The only 360 model number reused on the 370 was 195, the two versions being virtually identical.) A new but still upward-compatible S/390 line was brought out in the late 1980s. Machines announced in May and October of 1998 are called *Enterprise G series* computers, though they still use S/390 architecture.

Because customers are reluctant to replace software which they have come to trust, the S/360 architecture has proved amazingly durable. It is now 35 years since introduction of that architecture. A supposedly all-purpose language, PL/I, that IBM introduced along with it has long since foundered, but the architecture— extended to be sure—endures. The Digital Equipment Corporation VAX was a far cleaner complex instruction set computer (CISC) than the S/360, and the mode among newer computers is a reduced instruction set computer (*q.v.*) architecture. But in the firmament of rapidly changing computer concepts, three fixed stars remain: Fortran, Cobol, and the S/360 architecture.

Unbundling Creates a New Industry

In 1969, IBM made a fateful decision to "unbundle" its software and hardware. Up to that time, those who leased or purchased an IBM system were entitled to receive, upon request and at no additional charge, any software package that IBM had created in support of the system; *all* software was "freeware" (*q.v.*). Customers who complained that they now had to buy their software were told that the added expense would be more than recovered because unbundling would allow hardware costs to be reduced in the future. Though difficult to prove or refute, this probably did happen, but by far the major effect was to create a whole new industry. Until this decision, there was little or no point in any software company developing products for IBM equipment, but suddenly there was. And although the next 30 years saw the establishment and rapid growth of many software companies, none of this has hurt IBM, since it still claims to be the largest software company in the world. Microsoft certainly sells more units, but the price of mainframe and minicomputer software greatly exceeds that of personal computer software. Nonetheless, IBM's claim is a bit of a stretch, in that its 1998 Annual Report states that its software revenue was 14.5% of its total revenue of $81.7 billion, or $12.3 billion. This is less than Microsoft's 1998 revenue of $14.5 billion, but when IBM adds in $2.3 billion of additional revenue as being "software related," it ekes out first place by a hairsbreadth (when expressed in tenths of a billion, that is).

Small Business Systems

In July 1969, rather than bringing out a System/360 Model 10, IBM introduced its System/3, a small business system that could be rented for less than $1,000 per month, half the cost of a typical S/360 model 20. Either because they could not provide S/360 compatibility at that price or because they did not want to affect sales of the model 20, the S/3 used a unique architecture and small 96-column punched cards. Sales of S/3 models 32, 34, and 36 were strong for nine years, but as the series began to show its age in 1978, IBM announced a successor, the S/38. Strangely and surprisingly, the S/38 was *not* compatible with the S/3 series, but it nonetheless sold very well.

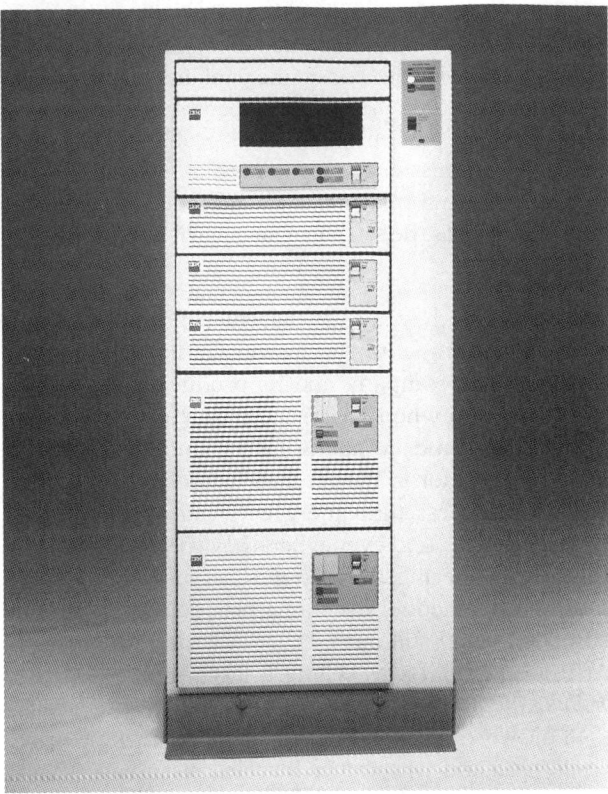

Figure 14. An IBM AS/400 (courtesy of IBM).

Figure 15. The IBM 5100, an early "luggable" computer (courtesy of IBM).

After another ten years, when sales of the S/38 began to sag, some elements of IBM wanted to discontinue it, but it was saved by the *Silverlake* project, whose history is documented in Bauer *et al.* (1992). As the 1990s began, sales of the resulting upwardly compatible AS/400 (Fig. 14) exceeded the total annual revenue of the Digital Equipment Corporation, which had the second highest revenue in the industry, and sales remained strong through 1999.

The PC Era

In 1975, IBM attempted to sell its 50-pound (23 kg) IBM 5100 computer (Fig. 15) as being "portable," but, due to weight and price—$9,000 to $20,000 depending on configuration—there were few takers for this early "luggable" computer (*see* PORTABLE COMPUTERS).

Burned by the failure of the 5100, IBM shied away from designing small computers until it felt it could not ignore the success of the "personal computers" brought out by Radio Shack (later Tandy), Commodore, and Apple in the period 1978–1980. So as to be able to compete quickly, IBM decided not to introduce a native design for which it would have to write new software, but instead opted for the *open architecture* (*q.v.*) that would result from mating the Intel 8088 microprocessor to the PC-DOS (later MS-DOS) operating system contracted to Bill Gates and Paul Allen of

Microsoft (*see* PERSONAL COMPUTING and Gates's profile in ENTREPRENEURS).

The resulting IBM PC was sold in large numbers through Sears outlets, but because of its open architecture it was easily cloned by any number of other vendors (*see* IBM PC). Since neither Intel nor Microsoft was constrained not to sell 80x86 chips or MS-DOS, respectively, to anyone they chose, all that was necessary was to reverse engineer the only part of the IBM PC that was proprietary, the BIOS (*q.v.*) (Basic Input–Output System), which was stored in ROM (read-only memory—*q.v.*). "IBM" PCs are now sold in great numbers by, among many others, Dell, Gateway, Compaq, Tandy, Hewlett-Packard, SONY, and Packard-Bell. IBM still markets PCs, the latest version being the *Aptiva*, but as of 1998 that machine had captured only a minor share of the overall market. IBM's excellent line of laptops, the *ThinkPad*, did somewhat better. In his message in IBM's 1998 Annual Report, Board Chairman and CEO Louis Gerstner proclaimed "The era of the PC is over." Certainly he was referring not to the continuing growth of PC usage, but to the fact that PC sales constituted a negligible fraction of IBM's total revenue. But then to his own surprise, perhaps, 1999 sales of PCs over the Internet skyrocketed to $10 billion, up 400% over 1998.

But the principal fallout from the PC phenomenon is not that IBM is not selling enough small machines, but rather that these small machines have become so capable that the market for its formerly high-profit mainframes (*q.v.*) is rapidly disappearing. After a record-setting paper loss of $8 billion in 1993, IBM has restored profitability by emphasizing that it is a "solutions company," specializing in electronic commerce (*q.v.*), networked database management systems (*q.v.*), and "enterprise computing." In October 1999, IBM announced that it would no longer sell its

Aptiva PCs through retail outlets in North America, but would offer them over the Internet, a move that resulted in a layoff of 10% of its PC workforce.

University Relations

IBM has always been cordial to colleges and universities, both because they were a potential source of customers for equipment, but, more important, because they were the best source of good young talent. Beginning with the IBM 650 in 1954, IBM offered a 60% discount to colleges and universities who would use it in support of courses in computing. No other vendor could come close to matching this, so the 650 soon became the most widely used computer in the academic domain. The policy was continued with the IBM 1620, which had even greater penetration of that market. Thus IBM deserves credit for fostering the early growth of university computing and the acceptance of *computer science* (*q.v.*) as a respected academic discipline.

As of the late 1960s, both CDC and Univac achieved a certain amount of success in selling to colleges and universities, but nothing approaching that of IBM. Then, suddenly, in 1965, IBM was shocked when it lost two prestigious accounts, Bell Telephone Laboratories and MIT, both to, of all competitors, General Electric! To that date, GE's computers had competed only with the low end of the S/360 line, but their new 600 series won the hearts and minds of key people at Bell Labs and MIT's Project MAC because it was built to do extensive time sharing (*q.v.*) based on multiprogramming (*q.v.*) and virtual memory (*q.v.*). None of these concepts were GE innovations; the latter two were used on the ATLAS (*q.v.*) at Manchester University in England (*see* MANCHESTER UNIVERSITY COMPUTERS) and Christopher Strachey (*q.v.*) had proposed time sharing in 1959.

The System 360 series, as originally designed, could not cope with these concepts. Undeterred, IBM set out to design and build the S/360 model 67, not to recapture the Bell Labs and MIT accounts, but to head off similar losses. The TSS operating system that IBM created for the model 67 never worked as well as intended, but the (University of) Michigan Time Sharing system MTS served several installations quite well. Nonetheless, only 10 model 67s were produced. But once it had been demonstrated that an S/360 model could indeed do time sharing, no subsequent mainframe of IBM or any other manufacturer failed to provide a comparable facility.

Salesmanship

By Watson edict, IBM salesmen (there were no saleswomen for many years) had to be impeccably dressed. Their dark suits, white shirts, conservatively contrasting ties, and close-cropped hair (none on the face) gave the impression that they all came from the same mold. An occasional maverick crept into the bunch; otherwise how does one explain H. Ross Perot? (His attire and the *outside* of his head conformed; it was the *inside* that was unique. See his profile in ENTREPRENEURS). Commissions were generous, but each salesman was given a rigorous sales quota. The reward for exceeding it was the setting of an even higher one for the following year.

During IBM's heyday, its salesmen greatly outnumbered their competitors in quantity, knowledgeability, pride in their company and its products, and aggressiveness. Even when, in candid moments, they had to admit that some competitor's product was technologically superior to theirs, they would claim that that mattered far less than the greater support that IBM would provide. And even when they truly believed that they were offering the better machines, they would brag that they could exchange product lines with any competitor and still outsell them by the same margin. At the time IBM was selling a large number of IBM 7090s, the Philco 2000/212 had greater precision— a 48 bit word versus 36—and cost less. Its tape drives could read and write tapes forward or backward, and its software would associate any drive with the next available channel (*q.v.*). With the 7090, programmers had to assign one-way tape drives to a specific channel, ready or not. And a case could be made that the CDC 1604 and its higher performance successor, the CDC 3600, could also outperform the 7090 and 7094 respectively.

But little of this mattered to the world at large, and the customers who might otherwise have beaten a path to Philco's or CDC's doors were frequently deterred by the self-assuredness of the IBM salesmen. When defending against the possible loss of an IBM customer who was seeking to upgrade equipment, they argued that the cost to convert to another vendor would be prohibitive, and that no data processing manager ever lost a job by choosing IBM products. This attitude did not endear them to non-IBMers, but customers generally welcomed IBM's policy that their salesmen stayed with their accounts long past installation and would cater to their every demand.

IBM salesmen—and those of all computer vendors, for that matter—were the eyes and ears of their companies. Having free access to roam all but highly classified installations, they served as CIA (Computer Intelligence Agents, that is), picking up tidbits of information about potential competitive products that could be fed to their own machine design people. IBM salesmen excelled at this game. A favorite ploy was to find out what pet features or concepts the computing center manager was captivated by in the prospectus for some new machine or other. Then IBM would fly in their highest ranking expert in that area to explain why IBM already had something in the works that would meet the objective much better.

Tom Watson Sr. ruled a paternalistic empire and believed that each newly hired employee had a virtual guarantee of lifetime employment. And although IBM was slow to use saleswomen, the company has always employed large numbers of women in other job categories. It is just as well that the senior Watson never saw the company's hard times of the late 1980s when almost half of all IBM employees were laid off through massive downsizing. His traditional but unwritten employee dress code endured until 1995, when CEO Louis Gerstner proclaimed that casual attire in offices is acceptable "as long as employees dress appropriately for meetings with customers and business partners."

User Groups

Not surprisingly, customers using the same computer often bond in order to obtain and share information about their complex product and, as well, to apply group pressure on the vendor. The principal IBM-oriented user groups SHARE (formed in 1955 and originally attuned to the 700 series) and GUIDE (organized in 1956 for the 1400 series) are described in the article USER GROUPS. From the mid-1950s and continuing for about 10 years, the members of each user group had considerable clout, with the ability to call IBM officers to their meetings and extract promises about improving maintenance or delivering successor products with certain desirable features.

When SHARE programmers found that the instruction set of the IBM 704 had a certain number of undocumented commands, they began using them, and their managers, through SHARE, insisted that they be legalized and included on the forthcoming 709 and 7090. Reluctantly, IBM did so. When IBM design managers told SHARE that its planned S/360 model 75 would have a certain amount of large core storage (LCS) of slower but higher capacity than main memory, they were asked to run a "wire" (special channel) between LCS and main memory so that data could be transferred to and from main memory in parallel with computation, making the extra storage act like a disk or drum of zero latency. And lo and behold, they did!

The original Symbolic Assembly Program (SAP) for the IBM 704 was written by programmers at United Aircraft and other members of SHARE, not IBM. Other member firms developed SOS, the SHARE Operating System. The days of substantial user-group influence are pretty much past, but the groups continue to have a role. See the cited article for more detail.

Anti-Trust and Other Litigation

In 1932, the US Justice Department filed an anti-trust suit against IBM, alleging that the company and Remington Rand together controlled virtually the entire market for punched card machinery and were also illegally requiring buyers of their machines to buy their punched cards. In 1936, the Supreme Court ruled in favor of the Justice Department and IBM (and Remington Rand) then had to agree that its customers could purchase cards from competitors.

In 1952, the Justice Department charged that IBM had grown so large that it was unrestrained by competition. In 1956, IBM signed a consent decree that required the company to create a competing market of used tabulators by selling, as well as leasing, its machines. Previously, the machines were available only through lease. But IBM coped well with this enforced and seemingly drastic change in established policy. By setting the ratios of price to monthly rentals in the range of 40 to 60 to 1 depending on the product and prevailing rates of inflation, IBM's revenue stream averaged over all accounts remained robust. Nonetheless, IBM did lose the high profits previously earned on the many machines that were kept for longer than five years. Beginning in 1962, the US Department of Defense issued a regulation that thereafter made it very difficult for any laboratory that it supported to lease a computer rather than buy it. By 1990, 85% of IBM computers were being purchased and only 15% were being leased.

In 1968, just as sales of the CDC 6600 were strong, IBM announced that it was adding supercomputers to the top of its S/360 product line. As orders for the 6600 began to fall off, CDC President William Norris denounced the new machines as "paper tigers" and sued IBM for allegedly engaging in predatory sales practices. In the ensuing settlement, IBM ceded its Service Bureau Corporation and $100 million to CDC.

In 1969, the first year of the Nixon administration, the USA accused IBM of predatory pricing of peripheral equipment. This third federal suit dragged on for 13 years and three attorneys general before the Justice Department determined in 1982, the second year of the Reagan administration, that the suit was "without merit."

Research and Development

IBM has always placed great emphasis on research and development. In 1945, the senior Watson recruited Wallace Eckert to establish and direct its Watson Scientific Computing Laboratory at 612 West 116th Street in New York City (*see* Fig. 16).

Figure 16. The first Watson Laboratory (courtesy of IBM).

Figure 17. The Thomas J. Watson Research Center in Yorktown Heights, NY (courtesy of IBM).

Since the establishment of its Zurich Research Laboratory in 1956 and the relocation of the Watson Research Center to Yorktown Heights in 1961 (Fig. 17), it has commendably supported basic as well as applied research. Six additional research laboratories have been commissioned since 1982 (Table 1). IBM also maintains several other specialized laboratories, but the table lists only those which the company itself classifies as "research" laboratories.

Five IBM employees have received the Nobel Prize in physics: Leo Esaki in 1973 for his work on electron

Table 1. Research laboratories.

Laboratory	Location	Year est.	Employees	Focus
Thomas J. Watson Research Center	NYC (1945–1961); Yorktown Heights, NY (1961–)	1945	1,400	Semiconductors; physical and computer sciences; and mathematics
Zurich Research Laboratory	Rueschlikon, Switzerland	1956	160	Communication systems and related technology; optoelectronics and physical sciences
Haifa Research Laboratory	Haifa, Israel	1982	255	Applied mathematics; computer science; multimedia; compilers; and VLSI design verification
Tokyo Research Laboratory	Yamato, Japan	1982	175	Software technology; system network, and solutions technology; computer science theory
Almaden Research Laboratory	San Jose, CA	1986	700	Storage systems and technology; computer science; and science and technology
Austin Research Laboratory	Austin, TX	1995	30	Advanced circuit design and tools for very high performance microprocessors
China Research Laboratory	Beijing, China	1995	20	Chinese language and speech recognition; digital library technology research
Delhi Solution Center	Delhi, India	1997	20	Weather forecasting; supply chain management; e-commerce; and cellular and mobile telephony

Figure 18. Heinrich Rohrer and Gerd Binnig (courtesy of IBM).

tunneling; Gerd K. Binnig and Heinrich Rohrer (Fig. 18) in 1986 for their work in scanning tunneling microscopy; and J. Georg Bednorz and K. Alex Muller in 1987 for their discovery of (relatively) high-temperature superconductivity.

For his leadership of the Fortran project and other contributions, John Backus received the McDowell Award (*q.v.*) in 1967 and the Turing Award (*q.v.*) in 1977. Other IBM employees who have earned McDowell Awards are Fred Brooks, the project manager of OS/360, and Gene Amdahl, who was a leading architect of that system. Other IBM Turing Award winners were Kenneth Iverson for invention of the language APL (*q.v.*), and Edgar Codd for his creation of the relational database (*q.v.*) model. In 1977, the US government adopted the cryptographic system developed by Walter Tuchman and Carl Meyer of IBM as the national Data Encryption Standard (DES).

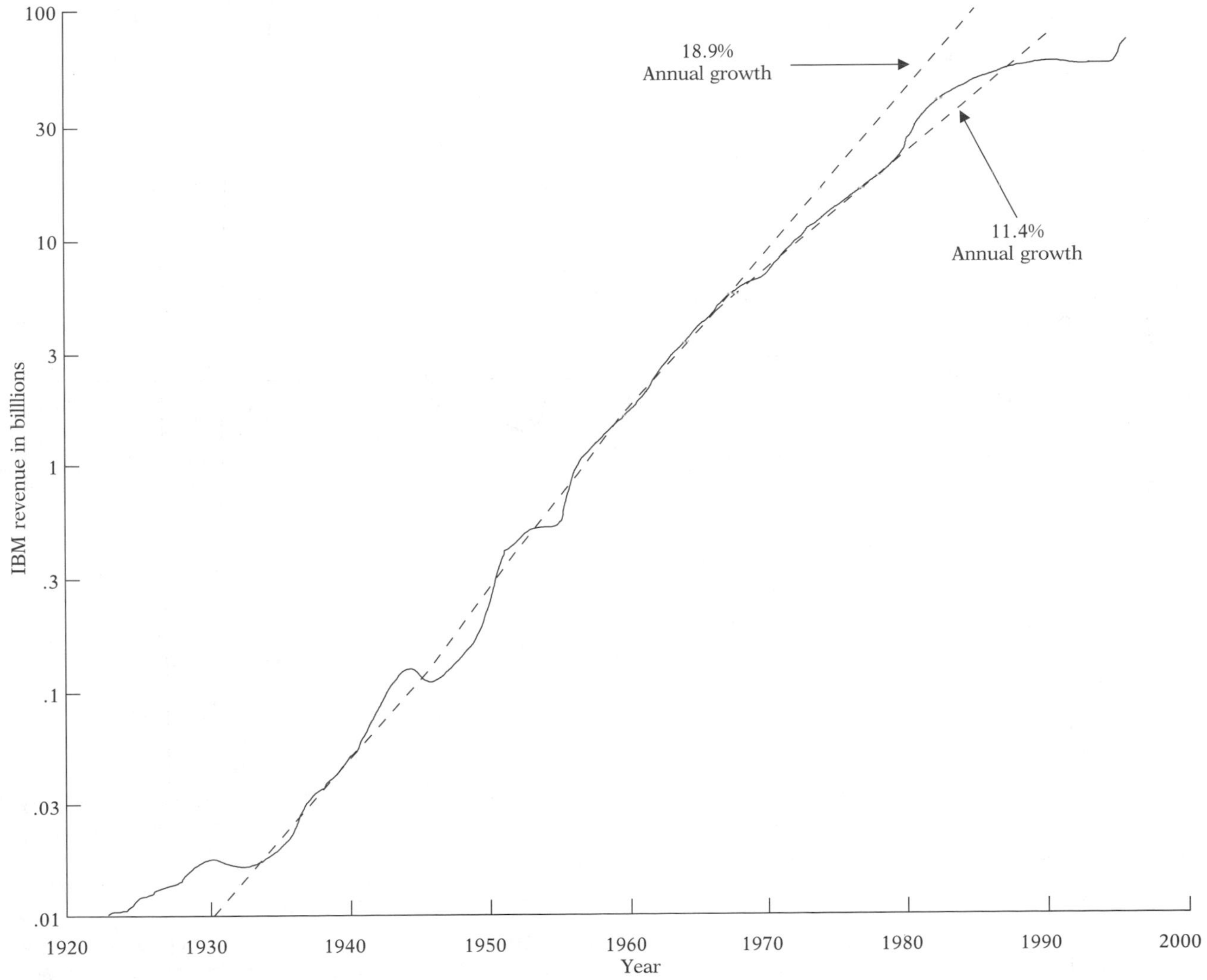

18.9%
Annual growth

11.4%
Annual growth

IBM revenue in billlions

Year

Figure 19. IBM revenue since 1920.

In late 1999, IBM chairman Gerstner announced that he was increasing the share of the company's $5 billion R&D budget devoted to Internet-related projects to 50%, double that of the prior year.

PATENTS

Since the time of the senior Watson, IBM has placed great emphasis on the acquisition of patents. When Thomas Watson Sr. joined the company in 1914, Hollerith's earliest patents had expired, but he resolved to capitalize on those still in force and to pursue the acquisition and creation of new ones vigorously. His resolve stemmed from a 1912 consent decree signed by General Electric which, while disparaging mergers as a legal means of gaining market dominance, affirmed the legality of competitive advantages gained through patents. In 1998, for the sixth consecutive year, IBM was awarded the most US patents—2,658—which was 40% more than its own previous record and 38% more than the next largest company.

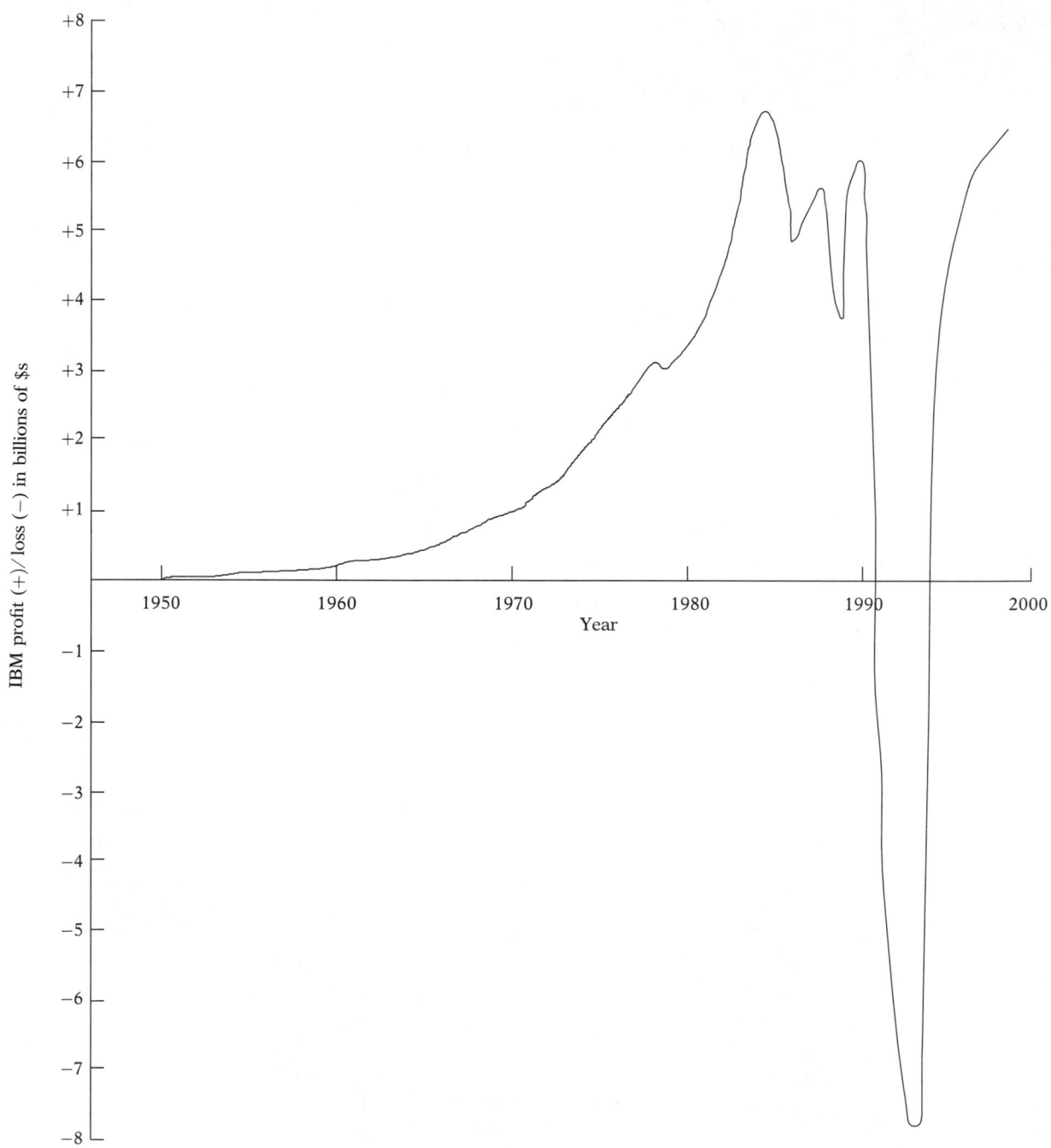

Figure 20. IBM earnings since 1950.

Financial Prowess and Employment Levels

REVENUE AND EARNINGS

IBM revenue from 1920 through 1998 is shown on the graph of Fig. 19. The broken straight lines on this semi-log plot show that over the 34-year period 1934 to 1968, IBM revenue grew exponentially at 18.9% per year, phenomenal growth over such a long period, and over the next 20 years, at the reduced but still remarkable rate of at least 11.4% per year. For the last 10 years, growth has been much more modest and closer to linear. (The curve would be somewhat different, of course, if revenue figures were converted to constant dollars.) IBM e-commerce revenue has now reached $20 billion, 25% of overall revenue, figures likely to grow substantially over the coming years.

Corresponding earnings are shown in Fig. 20 which shows that IBM's only period of sustained "losses" occurred in the early 1990s, when the company began to experience the effect of a significant decrease in orders for new mainframes. In 1980, IBM had set a goal of reaching revenues of $100 billion by 1990, but actual revenue by that date was $30 billion less. The losses of 1991–1993 were not actual monetary losses but rather "restructuring charges" stemming from downsizing, an accounting practice authorized by the US tax code. In fact, IBM had operational earnings of about $3 billion in each of 1991 and 1992 and $300 million in 1993 (Mills and Friesen, 1996.)

After the disastrous record-setting loss of almost $8 billion in 1993, the very year in which Thomas J. Watson Jr. died, profits returned to the $3 billion level in 1994 and then doubled to $6.3 billion in 1998, not quite back to the $6.6 billion earned in the peak year of 1984. The bull market of the late 1990s rewarded the company's stockholders to the extent shown in Fig. 21. On 21 April 1999, IBM announced that its earnings for the prior quarter were 42% higher than the corresponding quarter of the prior year, the 12th consecutive quarter that earnings exceeded the expectations of financial analysts. The next day, IBM stock advanced by 13%, $23 per share, the largest one-day

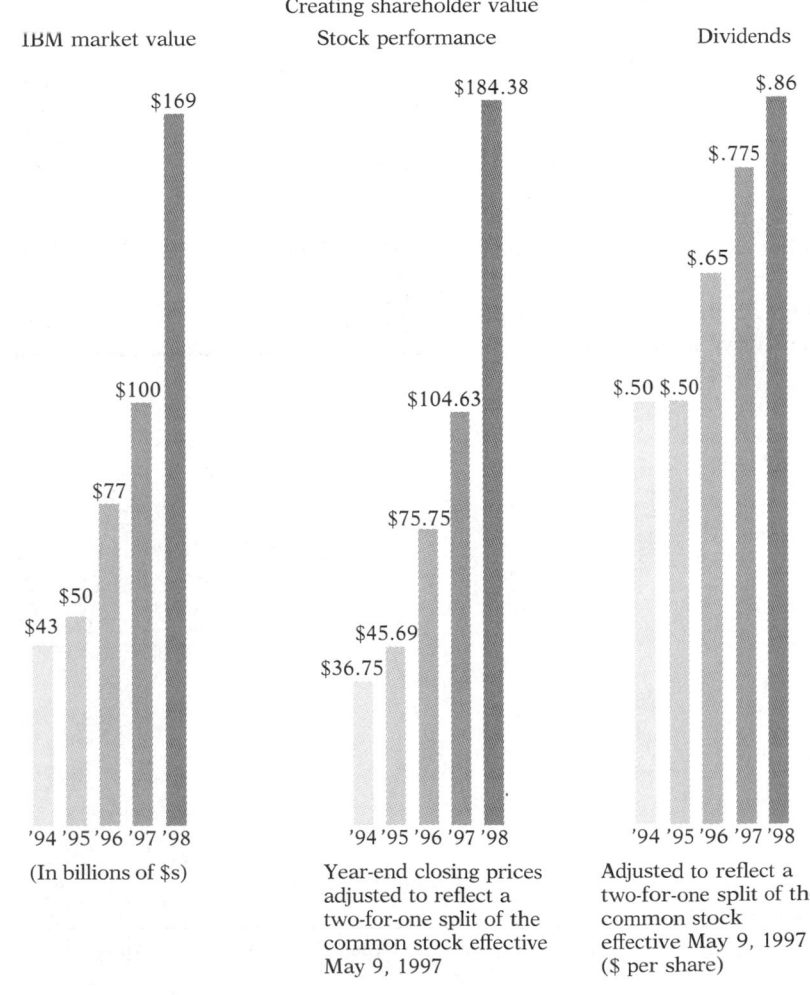

Figure 21. Five-year growth in capitalization, stock price, and dividends.

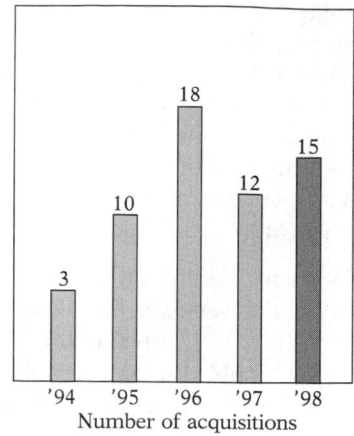

Figure 22. Five years of acquisitions.

gain in the company's history. Services and software accounted for 60% of the quarter's gross profit and hardware sales only 40%; the disparity in the two categories is likely to increase into the indefinite future.

In late October of 1999, IBM announced that sales of large computers had virtually dried up, allegedly because customers were deferring new purchases and devoting attention to their Y2K (*q.v.*) transition. Predictably, the stock price, which had already fallen substantially from early 1999 highs to 107, then fell further.

ACQUISITIONS

In recent years, IBM employment has grown more through acquisition of other companies than it has through individual recruitment to businesses in which it was already engaged. Fig. 22 shows the number of such acquisitions over the five-year period ending in

Table 2. Estimated number of model units installed.

Machine	Approximate life span	Estimated number installed
IBM 604	1946–1956	5,600
CPC	1947–1964	6,000
Mark I	1944–1959	1
SSEC	1948–1952	1
AN/FSQ-7 (SAGE)	1952–1962	46
NORC	1954–1968	1
IBM 7030 Stretch	1961–1971	7
IBM 350 RAMAC	1956–1961	1,100
IBM 650	1954–1964	1,800
IBM 701	1952–1954	19
IBM 702	1955–1957	14
IBM 704	1955–1957	267
IBM 705	1955–1960	305
IBM 709	1957–1958	38
IBM 7080	1960–1965	160
IBM 7090/7094	1959–1965	250
IBM 1400 series	1959–1965	14,000
IBM 1620	1962–1967	5,000
IBM 1130	1965–1968	800
IBM 5100	1975–1977	2,000
S/360 series models 20, 22, 30	1965–1971	13,000
S/360 series models 40, 44, 50, 65, 75	1965–1971	5,000
S/360 model 67	1966–1971	10
S/360 model 85	1969–	30
S/360 model 91	1967–	15
S/360 model 95	1968–	2
S/360 model 195	1971–1972	1
S/370 series	1971–1988	80,000
S/390 series through 1998	1988–1998	50,000
S/3, S/32, S/34, S/36	1969–1988	300,000
S/38 (incompatible with above)	1986–1988	20,000
AS/400	1988–	NA
Enterprise G-series	1999–	NA
RS/6000	1990–	NA

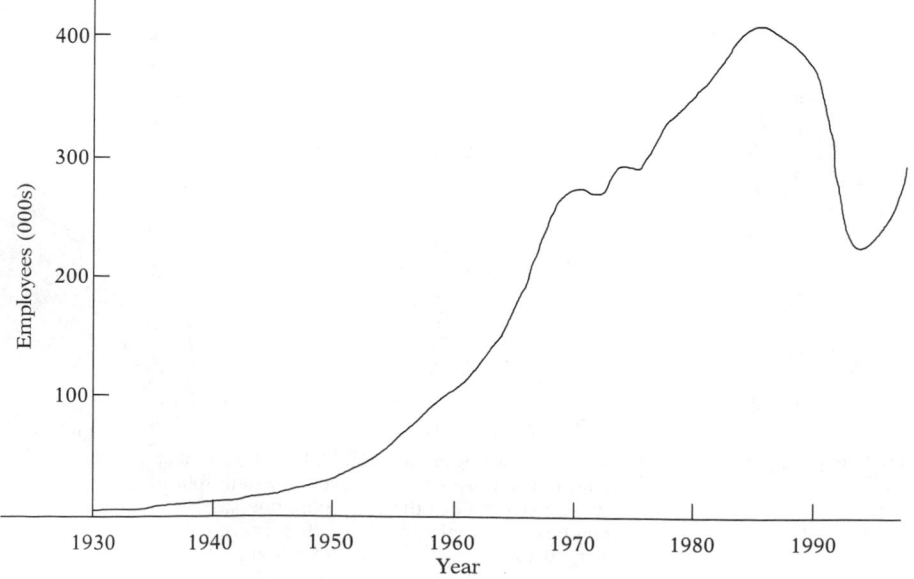

Figure 23. IBM employment levels since 1930.

1998. The addition of the Lotus Corporation in 1995 and Tivoli a year later raised IBM's software revenue by 15%, making it, by IBM's own claim as analyzed earlier, the world's largest software company.

EMPLOYMENT LEVELS

Worldwide IBM employment levels rose steadily from 1,346 in 1914 to a peak of almost 406,000 in 1985, the year following its greatest earnings, but was then downsized to 220,000 in 1994, the year following its greatest loss. As profitability returned, employment began to rise again, reaching 291,000 in 1998, 72% of its peak value. The history is shown in Fig. 23.

MACHINE SALES

Since the prices of the various IBM machines varied widely, the number of each model installed is not the sole indicator of sales importance to the company, but it is nonetheless historically interesting to cite this data as best it can be reconstructed. The more recent the figure, the more IBM is reluctant to reveal it, so the later the entry in Table 2, the rougher are the estimates of units sold.

Timeline

1888　Bundy Manufacturing Company (BMC) formed by Harlow and Willard Bundy to market Willard's invention of an employee time clock.

1890　Census Bureau selects Hollerith's Machine (q.v.) for census of that year.

1891　Computing Scale Company of America formed by Edward Canby and Orange O. Ozias of Dayton, Ohio; BMC changes name to International Time Recording Company.

1896　Herman Hollerith (q.v.) founds the Tabulating Machine Company.

1911　Merger of the three companies creates Computing-Tabulating-Recording Company (C-T-R).

1914　Thomas J. Watson, Sr. (q.v.), 40, fired by Patterson of NCR, joins C-T-R as General Manager.

1915　Thomas Watson becomes president of C-T-R; first use of "THINK" signs.

1924　C-T-R changes name to International Business Machines Corporation.

1928　IBM introduces 80-column punched card (q.v.).

1931　600 Series calculating machines.

1932　USA files first anti-trust suit against IBM.

1933　IBM enters typewriter business through acquisition of the Electromatic Typewriter Corporation.

1935　IBM sells scale business to Hobart.

1937　Thomas Watson Jr. joins IBM as General Manager; IBM 805 Test Scoring machine.

1938　IBM headquarters moves to 590 Madison Avenue, NYC.

1944　Mark I (q.v.), IBM's first large-scale calculating computer, installed at Harvard.

1945　Watson Scientific Computing Laboratory opens with Wallace Eckert (q.v.) as Director.

1947　Card Programmed Calculator (CPC).

1948　Selective Sequence Electronic Calculator (SSEC).

1950　Defense Calculator.

1952　IBM 701 scientific computer; US government files second anti-trust suit against IBM.

1953　IBM 702 business computer.

1954　IBM 650; Naval Ordnance Research Calculator (NORC—q.v.).

1955　IBM 704 succeeds 701 and 705 succeeds the 702.

1956　SAGE; IBM 305 RAMAC; Thomas J. Watson Sr. dies; Thomas J. Watson Jr. becomes CEO.

1957　Fortran (q.v.); IBM 709 succeeds 704.

1959　IBM 1400 (q.v.); IBM 7070; IBM 7090, a transistorized 709.

1960　IBM 1620; IBM 7080, a 705 upgrade.

1961　IBM 7030 *Stretch* (q.v.); IBM Selectric Typewriter.

1962　*Harvest* supercomputer with *Tractor* high-speed magnetic tapes installed at NSA.

1963　SABRE airline reservation system.

1964　System/360 (q.v.) announced with great fanfare on 7 April; IBM headquarters moves to Armonk, NY.

1966　APL (q.v.); one-transistor memory cell.

1968　IBM 360/85 is first commercial computer to use cache memory (q.v.); IBM is sued by Norris of CDC for alleged "predatory sales practices."

1969　IBM System/3; IBM "unbundles" its products; USA files third anti-trust suit against IBM; Norris suit is settled by ceding IBM Service Bureau and cash to CDC.

1970　IBM S/370; relational database (q.v.).

1971　T. Vincent Learson becomes CEO.

1973　Frank T. Cary becomes CEO; "Winchester" disk technology; Leo Esaki wins Nobel Prize in physics for electron tunneling.

1975　At a loss of $100 million, IBM pulls plug on its FS (Future System) and opts to continue compatibility.

1977　USA adopts IBM proposal for a Data Encryption Standard (DES).

1978　IBM System/38, compatible successor to System/3.

1979　System/4pi, "S/360 in a briefcase," used in spacecraft.

1980　Reduced Instruction Set Computer (RISC) architecture (q.v.).

1981　John R. Opel becomes CEO; IBM PC (q.v.).

1982 After 13 years, Justice Department drops third anti-trust suit, declaring it "without merit."

1984 IBM, Sears, CBS form Prodigy network; megabit memory chips.

1985 John F. Akers becomes CEO and Thomas Watson Jr. leaves IBM board.

1985 Token Ring network.

1986 Gerd K. Binnig and Heinrich Rohrer win Nobel Prize.

1987 J. Georg Bednorz and K. Alex Muller win Nobel Prize.

1988 IBM AS/400.

1990 IBM S/390; IBM RS/6000 RISC computer; IBM sells typewriter, keyboard, printer businesses to Lexmark.

1991 Gigabyte hard drive; IBM, Apple (*q.v.*), and Motorola form PowerPC joint venture.

1992 ThinkPad.

1993 IBM posts record $8 billion loss; Louis V. Gerstner Jr. becomes chairman and CEO; Thomas J. Watson Jr. dies.

1994 Profits resume and begin a five-year climb.

1995 IBM's acquisition of Lotus Development Corporation makes it the world's largest software company; Gerstner relaxes dress code.

1996 IBM acquires Tivoli Systems to further augment its software.

1997 IBM's *Deep Blue*, a 32-node RS/6000, defeats World Chess Champion Garry Kasparov.

1998 Enterprise G line continues IBM 360/370/390 series (*q.v.*) upward compatibility.

1999 ViaVoice speech technology for the Pentium III; Dell Computer Corporation agrees to buy $16 billion of IBM parts over next six years.

Summary and Acknowledgments

The timeline is offered in lieu of a narrative summary, but the author wishes to acknowledge that this article is based primarily on a blend of four sources: (1) the books by former IBM insiders Emerson Pugh and Charles Bashe *et al.* (1986, 1991, 1995), (2) the book by historians Martin Campbell-Kelly and William Aspray (1996), major portions of which constitute an excellent short history of IBM, (3) my own observations as a close observer of IBM and sometime user of its equipment over more than four decades, and (4) IBM's own Web page (`http://www.ibm.com`). Most of the financial data was extracted from those pages, many illustrations were downloaded and reproduced here with IBM permission, and the timeline is an expanded version of one given at that Website.

I am particularly indebted and grateful to Professor Martin Campbell-Kelly of Warwick University, a contributor to this Encyclopedia, for a critical reading of a draft of this article and for his constructive suggestions for improving it.

Bibliography

1962. Belden, T. G., and Belden, M. R. *The Lengthening Shadow.* Boston: Little, Brown. a biography of Thomas J. Watson Sr.

1963. Watson, T. J. Jr. *A Business and its Beliefs: The Ideas That Helped Build IBM.* New York: McGraw-Hill.

1971. Brennan, J. F. *The IBM Watson Laboratory at Columbia University—A History.* Armonk, NY: IBM.

1975. Foy, N. *The Sun Never Sets on IBM.* New York: Wm. Morrow.

1976. Engelbourg, S. *International Business Machines: A Business History.* New York: Arno.

1981. Sobel, R. *IBM: Colossus in Transition.* New York: Times Books.

1983. Fisher, F. M., McGowan, J. J., and Greenwood, J. E., *Folded, Spindled, and Mutilated: Economic Analysis and U.S. vs IBM.* Cambridge, MA: MIT Press.

1983. Fisher, F. M., McKie, J. W., and Mancke, R. B. *IBM and the U.S. Data Processing Industry: An Economic History.* New York: Praeger.

1984. Pugh, E. W. *Memories that Shaped an Industry.* Cambridge, MA: MIT Press.

1986. Bashe, C. J., Johnson, L. R., Palmer, J. H., and Pugh, E. W. *IBM's Early Computers.* Cambridge, MA: MIT Press.

1986. DeLamarter, R. T. *Big Blue: IBM's Use and Abuse of Power.* New York: Dodd, Mead & Co.

1986. Rodgers, F. G. "Buck," with Shook, R. L. *The IBM Way.* New York: Harper & Row.

1987. Killen, M. *IBM: The Making of the Common View.* Orlando, FL: Harcourt Brace Jovanovich.

1988. McKenna, R. *Who's Afraid of Big Blue.* Reading, MA: Addison-Wesley.

1990. Watson, T. J. Jr., and Petre, P. *Father, Son & Co.: My Life at IBM and Beyond.* New York: Bantam Books.

1991. Pugh, E. W., Johnson, L. R., and Palmer, J. H. *IBM's 360 and Early 370 Systems.* Cambridge, MA: MIT Press.

1992. Bauer, R. A., Collar, E., Tang, V., and Wind, J. *The Silverlake Project: Transformation at IBM.* London: Oxford University Press. The origins of the IBM AS/400.

1994. Carroll, P. *Big Blues: The Unmaking of IBM.* New York: Crown Publications.

1995. Pugh, E. W. *Building IBM: Shaping an Industry and Its Technology.* Cambridge, MA: MIT Press.

1996. Mills, D. Q., and Friesen, G. B. *Broken Promises: An Unconventional View of What Went Wrong at IBM.* Boston: Harvard Business School Press.

1996. Campbell-Kelly, M., and Aspray, W. *Computer: A History of the Information Machine.* New York: Basic Books.

1998. Fisher, L. M. "Mainframe Business, Though Faded, is Still Far From Extinct," *New York Times*, 18 May. An excellent appraisal of IBM's mainframe business as of the date that IBM announced its G series of S/390 computers.

1999. Garr, D. *IBM Redux: Lou Gerstner and the Business Turnaround of the Decade.* New York: HarperCollins.

Edwin D. Reilly

IBM 1400 SERIES

For articles on related subjects *see* DIGITAL COMPUTERS, HISTORY OF; GENERATIONS, COMPUTER; and IBM CORPORATION.

The *IBM 1400 series* data processing systems, introduced in 1959, had a dramatic impact on the business world. The first of the 1400 series machines, the 1401, rapidly made the older vacuum tube and electromechanical *unit record* systems obsolete. The 1400 system enjoyed widespread use in data processing applications from 1959 until "third-generation" equipment became available in the mid-1960s.

The 1400 line consisted of five basic computers, 1401, 1440, 1460, 1410, and 7010. The basic mainframe, the 1401, was a second-generation fully transistorized machine with a magnetic core memory having original capacity options of 1.4 KB, 2 KB, 4 KB, 8 KB, 12 KB, and 16 KB characters. Internally, data was represented in six-bit BCD code (*see* CODES) with additional parity check and *word mark* bits. The memory cycle was 11.5 μs per character access.

Instruction formats were variable from one to eight characters, and data fields and records could be variable length within the constraints of peripheral device characteristics and memory size. Instruction and data fields were defined by the presence of a word-mark bit set beneath the leftmost character on the instruction or data field.

The 1401 (Fig. 1) had an I/O interface that permitted only one I/O operation at a time, regardless of the number of devices online. I/O operations interlocked the central processor, although some overlap of processing and I/O operation could be gained by the addition of special features.

Although a wide variety of peripheral devices were available for the 1400 series, including MICR and optical character readers, paper-tape readers, remote transmission devices, etc., the principal devices in use were:

1402 Card Reader/Punch—This unit was capable of reading 800 cards per minute (cpm) and punching 250 cpm (most programs were stored as punched cards).

Figure 1. An IBM 1401 system.

1403 Chain Printer—This device had a maximum rated speed of 1100 alphanumeric lines per minute (lpm), was reliable and comparatively quiet, and had excellent print quality. This device was a significant advance in printer technology and contributed greatly to the attraction of the 1401 systems.

Other peripheral devices included Model 7330 and 729 seven-track magnetic tape units and 1405 and 1311 magnetic disk storage units. The 1311 featured removable disk pack storage.

Several languages were available for the 1401. A basic assembly language, SPS (Symbolic Programming System), permitted the use of mnemonic operation codes, symbolic addresses, and indirect addressing. A significantly enhanced version of SPS, called "Autocoder"—analogous to basic assembly language for third-generation computers—became the predominantly used language. Autocoder used SPS constructs and employed macroinstructions (*see* MACRO) for initiating I/O operations. Fortran and Cobol compilers existed, but were not widely used because of either excessive compilation time or limited memory. Various Report Program Generator (RPG) packages were available, as was a complete set of basic utility packages. Operating systems were not used with the 1401, 1440, or 1460, but many users developed monitor programs to permit a rudimentary form of job control.

The 1440 system was initially a disk-oriented 1401 with slower peripherals and lower cost. The 1460 was also basically a 1401 except that it had a 6 μs memory expandable to a 32 KB capacity.

The 1410 systems, while having the same basic architecture as the 1401, were significantly more powerful. Memory sizes were 10 KB, 20 KB, 40 KB, 60 KB, and 80 KB characters. The memory cycle was 4.5 μs per character. Autocoder was the predominantly used language, although Cobol and Fortran were widely used. The 1410 could be operated in emulated 1401 mode, which provided almost total compatibility with 1401 programs.

The 7010 system was functionally, although not architecturally, an advanced 1410. It used the 1410 instruction set and, like the 1410, had a 1401 compatibility feature. The 7010 accessed two characters in parallel on each 2.4 μs cycle. Comparatively few of these systems were installed, as the system was introduced shortly before the System 360 was announced.

There were approximately 14,000 of the 1401 systems and over 1,000 of the 1410 systems installed. A typical 1401 system rented for $8,000 per month and the range was from $4,000 to $12,000 per month. A typical 1410 system rented for $11,000 per month and the range was from $8,000 to $18,000 per month.

The high-speed card reading and tape and printing ability of the 1401 systems ideally suited them for use as peripheral I/O systems to IBM 7000 series computers.

Bibliography

1986. Bashe, C. J., Johnson, L. R., Palmer, J. H., and Pugh, E. W. *IBM's Early Computers.* Cambridge, MA: MIT Press.

G. David Baer

IBM SYSTEM 360/370/390 SERIES

For articles on related subjects *see* DIGITAL COMPUTERS, HISTORY OF; IBM CORPORATION; IBM 1400 SERIES; and IBM PC.

The IBM System/360 (*see* Fig. 1) and System/370 (*see* Fig. 2) comprise an architecture that has been the basis for all intermediate and large mainframe (*q.v.*) processors produced by IBM since 1964. This architecture has also become the basis for machines produced by other manufacturers. Currently, the IBM S/390 G series architecture is the upward compatible successor to IBM's System/360 and System/370 systems. These systems have been so widely used and so many of the features have been so widely imitated that it is important to describe the essential aspects of their architecture and their hardware and software systems.

During the past 35 years, IBM has introduced the System/360 (S/360) architecture, System/370 (S/370) architecture, System/370 Extended Architecture (370-XA), Vector Extensions to S/370 and 370-XA architectures, Enterprise System Architecture/370 (ESA/370), Enterprise System Architecture/390 (ESA/390), and, in 1998, the IBM S/390 G series.

Figure 1. A 1964 IBM System/360 (courtesy of IBM).

Figure 2. An IBM System/370 (courtesy of IBM).

The *architecture* of a system defines its attributes as seen by the programmer, i.e. the conceptual structure and functional behavior of the machine, as distinct from the organization of the data flow, the logical design, the physical design, and the performance of any particular implementation (*see* COMPUTER ARCHITECTURE). Several dissimilar machine implementations may conform to a single architecture. The remarkable 35-year longevity of the S/360 architecture, as extended, is unmatched by any other architecture in current use. In addition to IBM, this architecture is used in systems manufactured by Hitachi Data Systems and the Amdahl Corporation (*see* ENTREPRENEURS for a profile of Gene Amdahl, who, while with IBM, was the principal System/360 architect).

Logically, a system consists of main storage, one or more central processors (CPUs—*q.v.*), an operator's console, a channel subsystem, and I/O devices. I/O devices are attached to the channel (*q.v.*) subsystem through control units. The communication between the channel subsystem and a control unit is called a *channel path*. A channel path employs either a parallel-transmission protocol (*q.v.*) or a serial-transmission path and, accordingly, is called a parallel or serial channel path. Expanded storage may also be available in a system, and vector or cryptographic units or both may be included in a CPU.

The physical identity of the above functions may vary among implementations, called "models." Specific processors may differ in their internal characteristics, the installed facilities, the number of subchannels, channel paths, and control units that can be attached to the channel subsystem, the size of main and expanded storage, and the operator's console.

The basic unit of information in these systems is the 8-bit byte. Four bytes comprise a word. Some instructions operate on bytes, and others operate on half-words (2 bytes), words, double words (8 bytes), and on strings of bytes. An instruction or operand address is always a byte address, the leftmost or most significant byte when a group consisting of more than 1 byte is being addressed. In the early S/360 and S/370 systems, a 24-bit address field in index registers permitted the direct addressing of 2^{24} or 16,777,216 bytes. In 1981, IBM announced a significant architecture change to System/370: the System/370 Extended Architecture (370-XA). This provided 31-bit addressability which extends the real and virtual address space from the 16.8 MB addressable with 24-bit addresses to 2 GB (2^{31} or 2,147,483,648 bytes). Bimodal operation (S/370 or 370-XA mode) permits concurrent execution of programs using either 24-bit or 31-bit addresses.

Memory

The magnetic core memories of the early S/360s were severely limited in size, from a 64 KB maximum on the Model 30 to a maximum of 1 MB on the top-of-the-line Model 75. The larger S/360 models could use auxiliary (though slower) large-core memory of up to 8 MB. Maximum memory was gradually increased into the millions of bytes on even the small S/370 models, and up to the 24-bit addressing limit of 16 MB on the larger ones. These large memories became economical and practical with the use of MOS large-scale integration memory technology on models of the S/370 introduced after 1972. Today's S/390 processors employ an advanced three-level storage hierarchy comprised of a high-speed cache, central storage, and expanded storage. Central storage capacity in an ES/9000 multiprocessing complex can be up to 1 billion bytes (1 GB) and expanded storage can be up to 8 GB.

Main storage, which is directly addressable, provides for high-speed processing of data by the CPUs and the channel subsystem. Main storage may include a faster-access buffer storage, sometimes called a *cache* (*q.v.*), and each CPU may have an associated cache that is used to improve performance. Expanded storage may be available on some models. It can be accessed by all CPUs in the configuration by means of instructions that transfer 4 KB blocks of data from expanded storage to main storage or from main storage to expanded storage. Each 4 KB block in expanded storage is addressed by a 31-bit block number.

Certain models of the ES/9000 (members of the ESA/390 family—*see* Fig. 3) employ a two-level high-speed (cache) buffer design. Each processor in a multiprocessor configuration contains a 256 KB first-level high-speed buffer (HSB) divided into two independent HSBs of 128 KB each. One holds instructions, the other

Figure 3. An IBM ES/9000 (courtesy of IBM).

data. This design permits both instructions and data fetching to take place in the same machine cycle. A second-level HSB contains 4,096 KB of data and is used to match the speed of the processor, including the first-level HSB, with the speed of the processor storage hierarchy to achieve better system-level performance.

Expanded storage is a logically separate storage under control of the operating system (*q.v.*), providing performance up to 28 times faster than physical I/O to cached direct access storage devices and up to 200 times faster than physical I/O to non-cached direct access storage devices. It is designed for block transfers of 4 KB pages directly to and from central storage.

System/390 is designed to be used with a control program or interrupt-driven operating system that coordinates the use of system resources and executes all I/O instructions, handles exceptional conditions, and supervises scheduling and execution of multiple programs. This was also the case for systems based on the earlier architectures. The system provides for automatic storage in main memory and for automatic loading from a different area of main memory of the contents of essential control registers in response to an interrupt (*q.v.*). The contents of these control registers may be considered to form a control word, which is referred to as the *program status word*. The program status word contains the address of the next instruction to permit resumption of a program after an interrupt. It also contains interrupt masks, the storage protection (*see* MEMORY PROTECTION) key, and a number of special control fields and control bits. One of the control bits distinguishes between system (or supervisor) state and problem state.

Instruction Set

The S/390 series has a large and varied instruction set made up of 229 instructions. Instructions fall into five classes: general, decimal, floating-point, control, and I/O instructions. Instructions may be one, two, or three half-words long. There are three types of arithmetic: fixed-point, floating-point, and a special decimal arithmetic that uses strings of four-bit binary-coded decimal digits as operands. There is a set of *privileged instructions* (*q.v.*) that can be executed only in supervisor state.

An S/390 series computer has general-purpose registers (*q.v.*) that serve as base registers and index registers (*q.v.*), and that also serve as fixed-point accumulators and as temporary storage registers. The general registers are 32 bits long, and the most significant 8 bits are ignored in physical address calculations when 24-bit addressing is used. For 31-bit addressing, only the most significant bit is ignored. The use of the general registers as base and index registers permits the direct addressing of 16,777,216 bytes or 2,147,483,648 bytes, depending on whether 24-bit or 31-bit addressing is being used, without requiring that each instruction contain a 24-bit or 31-bit address field. This is illustrated by the RX (register-and-indexed-storage) instruction format, one of several instruction formats used in the S/390. The RX format uses two half-words as follows:

```
OP-code   R1    X2    B2    D2
--------  ----  ----  ----  -----------
```

The 8-bit op-code specifies the instruction. There are two operands. The first is the general register, specified by the 4-bit field R1. The second is in memory, at a location determined by adding the 12-bit displacement D2 to the contents of the two general registers specified by B2 and X2 (*see* ADDRESSING).

In addition to the general-purpose registers, the S/360, S/370, and S/390 have four 64-bit floating-point registers that can be coupled for expanded (128-bit) precision in floating-point operations. ESA/370 and ESA/390 provided 16 special registers for fast access to hundreds of different operand address spaces and allows programs and data to reside in different address spaces.

ES/9000 systems include multiple instruction execution units supporting arithmetic and logical operations, I/O activity, systems management functions, and other tasks. The central processor has only very rudimentary I/O instructions to start and stop I/O, and to determine the status of an I/O operation that has been started or stopped. Input and output can proceed simultaneously with computing under control of channels (*q.v.*) that can directly access main memory and which can execute *channel programs*. Block multiplexer channels control devices such as tapes and disks for fast, high-volume data transfers. Byte multiplexer channels can control large numbers of lower-speed devices.

ES/9000 systems include a channel I/O processor, an independent instruction processing unit developed to offload I/O handling from central processing elements by communicating directly with I/O devices. The channels, using Reduced Instruction Set Computers (RISC—*q.v.*) microprocessors, offload I/O instruction processing to the channel subsystems for improved system throughput. Standard high-speed (4.5 MB/sec) parallel channels provide high bandwidth (*q.v.*) channel attachment capabilities and complete compatibility with standard System/370 control units for workstations, disks, tapes, and communications. Serial channels using fiber optic (*q.v.*) links can deliver the highest bandwidth (10 MB/sec) channel capacity for longer distance (up to 9 km) data transmission between systems or to I/O devices. The largest water-cooled systems can transfer data at 17 MB/sec over even greater distances using channels with fiber optic media.

IBM's original lines of computers, the S/360 and S/370 models, were introduced in 1964 and 1970, respectively. During the late 1970s and 1980s, IBM announced an increasingly powerful series of processors: the 303Xs; the intermediate-sized, air-cooled 43XXs; and the large-scale water-cooled 308Xs and 3090s. The 43XX series included both uniprocessors and dyadic processors, while the 308X and 3090 series included uniprocessors, dyadic and triadic processors, and *N*-way multiprocessors.

A Vector Facility was announced as an optional feature of the 3090 series, which included vector extensions to the S/370 and 370-XA architectures. The Vector Facility is an extension of the central processor's instruction and execution elements that allows the central processor to execute vector arithmetic and logical operations on up to 128 sets of operands with a single instruction. The Vector Facility, used for scientific and engineering applications such as structural analysis and computational fluid dynamics, adds 191 new instructions and 16 vector registers, each containing 128 elements. The Vector Facility extends the power of the ES/9000 processor allowing high-performance processing of multiple pairs of operands (arrays of data). It operates as a compatible extension of the S/370, 370-XA, ESA/370, and S/390 architectures. In the early 1990s, two IBM 3090 Model 600S processors with 12 CPUs and 12 Vector Facilities formed the base for Cornell University's National Supercomputer Facility. Cornell's National Supercomputer Facility is one of four supercomputing centers (*q.v.*) originally established by the National Science Foundation's Office of Advanced Scientific Computing in 1986 to provide supercomputer access to researchers.

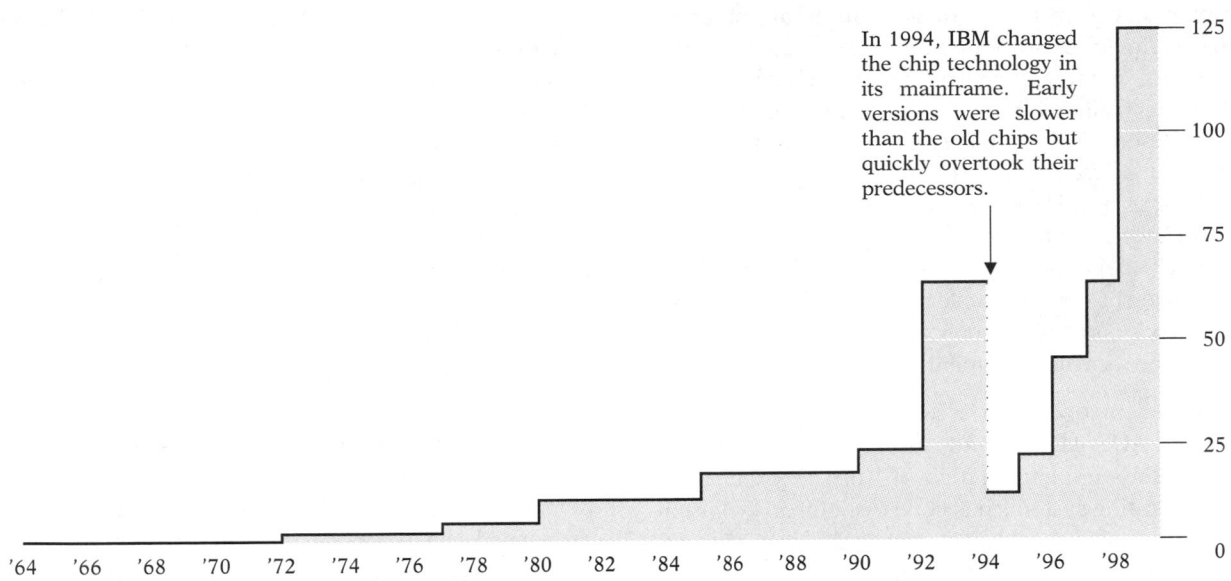

In 1994, IBM changed the chip technology in its mainframe. Early versions were slower than the old chips but quickly overtook their predecessors.

Figure 4. Mainframe Evolution. Speed of IBM's fastest single-processor mainframe computer, measured in millions of instructions per second (MIPS).

S/390 G Series

In May, 1998, IBM announced the S/390 G series (*see* Fig. 4), the fifth generation of its System/390 mainframe. (In May 1999 IBM announced a new G-series model capable of 1600 MIPS.) One objective was to make the 390 architecture, which was beginning to show its age, work better in today's heavily networked environments. Another was to close the performance gap with Hitachi's architecturally compatible bipolar Skyline machines. In 1994, in order to produce cooler running and hence more energy efficient mainframes (*q.v.*), IBM had switched from use of bipolar to CMOS transistor technology (*see* INTEGRATED CIRCUITRY). But this came at the expense of processor speed. The loss proved temporary, however, and has been overcome with the improved CMOS technology of Series G.

Along with System G, IBM is now promoting "enterprise" programs, off-the-shelf applications such as the R-3 back office suite of SAP A.G. of Germany, Oracle Corporation's database and other financial programs, and manufacturing and human resource software produced by Peoplesoft, Inc.

Operating Systems

The original S/360 concept assumed that only one major operating system would be required, which was given the name OS/360 (Operating System/360). It soon became apparent that many small- and intermediate-sized S/360 systems needed a reasonably sophisticated operating system, but could not afford the high memory space and processor overhead of OS/360. This led to the early development of DOS

(Disk Operating System), which was very widely used. IBM also provided an alternative system, CP-67, which ran on the S/360 Model 67. At that time, the Model 67 was unique in that it provided dynamic address translation hardware and was a virtual memory system (*see* VIRTUAL MEMORY). In 1972, virtual storage became a standard feature of all S/370 and future IBM systems. Another alternative was MTS (Michigan Terminal System), developed by the University of Michigan.

With the announcement of dynamic address translation and virtual storage as standard for the S/370 line, IBM introduced its VS (Virtual Storage) operating systems. These include VSE (Virtual Storage Extended), a replacement for DOS, VS1 (Virtual Storage 1), in which users shared a 16 MB address space, and MVS (Multiple Virtual Storage), a more sophisticated system in which each user had a 16 MB address space. Today, MVS, IBM's largest and most functional operating system, provides each user with a 2 GB address space. The VM (Virtual Machine) system, a successor to the earlier CP-67 system, provides the Conversational Monitor System (CSM), a widely used time-sharing system. The VM system also provides a virtual machine capability that permits users on the same hardware system to use different operating systems concurrently, including, for example, an older and newer MVS system. This great flexibility is achieved at some cost in system overhead. Today's systems offer a broad range of partitioning options, including physical and logical partitioning in addition to VM's software partitioning.

Physical partitioning enables a multiprocessor to be divided and operated as two logically independent complexes. The resulting images can be asymmetric, with each image controlling a different set of resources: processors, channels, central and expanded storage, and vector facilities. For logical partitioning, the Processor Resource/Systems Manager (PR/SM) feature provides hardware support for partitioning of a uniprocessor or multiprocessor into multiple logical partitions or systems images. These logical partitions, designed as independent systems images, can be defined with processor resources allocated as required according to workload requirements. Each of the partitions can run the same or dissimilar operating systems.

IBM's current operating systems include MVS, VM, VSE, and AIX. AIX, the Advanced Interactive Executive, is IBM's implementation of Unix (*q.v.*). Each of these operating systems has gone through an evolution in the form of various versions over the past 35 years to support the evolution in architectures.

Outlook

Large mainframes—"big iron" in industry parlance—have long been the mainstay of IBM's business. Sales run at $5 billion (US) per year, which, along with service and associated software sales, accounts for about a third of IBM's annual profit. But mainframe sales are expected to be quite flat over the next few years as users tend to place new applications on slower but more cost-effective PCs, workstations (*q.v.*), and minicomputers (*q.v.*).

Nonetheless, it is estimated that as much as 70% of corporate data now resides on machines having S/390 architecture, and most of it is likely to stay there. Thus there will remain a large potential for mainframe sales to installations already using such technology. And one enduring advantage to large mainframes is their *scalability*. There is no effective limit to the number of processors and disk storage units that can be joined to function as if they comprised one giant mainframe. IBM may yet squeeze another decade's use out of an architecture older than most of the people who use and program S/390 machines.

Bibliography

1991. Pugh, E. W., Johnson, L. R., and Palmer, J. H. *IBM's 360 and Early 370 Systems.* Cambridge, MA: MIT Press.
1998. Fisher, L. M. "Mainframe business, though faded, is still far from extinct," *New York Times,* 18 May.

Norman Layer, revised by Edwin D. Reilly

IBM PC

For articles on related subjects *see* APPLE COMPUTER, INC.; DIGITAL COMPUTERS, HISTORY OF; IBM CORPORATION; MICROSOFT; and PERSONAL COMPUTING.

The conceptual and practical foundation for the personal computer was developed at MIT, the Stanford Research Institute, and the Xerox Palo Alto Research Center, beginning in the 1940s; however, the personal computer industry did not begin until 8-bit microprocessors that had the ability to address at least 32 KB of memory became available. In 1975, the Intel 8080, MOS Technology 6502, and Motorola 6800 microprocessors were incorporated into dozens of commercial personal computers beginning with Altair from Micro Instrumentation and Telemetry Systems (MITS).

The first of these 8-bit machines were targeted at the hobby market and were generally sold in kit form. Soon, companies such as Processor Technology, Compaq, Commodore, Radio Shack, and Apple recognized the demand for pre-assembled computers. These systems broadened the market from electronic hobbyists to some schools, homes, and small businesses.

In 1977, Digital Microsystems introduced a computer designed for the business and professional market. It was pre-assembled with an Intel 8080 CPU, 64 KB memory, two floppy disk (*see* DISKETTE) drives (most early systems used paper or audio cassette tape for storage), and built-in I/O ports (*see* PORT, I/O). Most important, it used a disk operating system called CP/M (control program for microprocessors), which had been developed by Gary Kildall, a consultant to Intel. While Digital Microsystems did not survive, CP/M and Kildall's company, Digital Research, did.

The CP/M operating system and the bus structure of the MITS Altair, later called the S-100 Bus, became *de facto* standards for high-end business and professional personal computers during the late 1970s. The CP/M platform encouraged application software developers, and thousands of programs, including Microsoft's language processors, dBase, and WordStar, were developed. While some major manufacturers (e.g. Xerox, Wang, and DEC) entered the CP/M market, IBM did not.

The PC-1

IBM waited for the next generation machine, made possible by 16-bit microprocessors. In order to move quickly, they formed an "intrapreneurial" special business unit called the Entry Systems Division (ESD) to design the PC. A group of about a dozen people, headed by Phillip "Don" Estridge, was chartered to develop a personal computer and bring it to market within a year. The short time limit meant that the PC would be IBM's first product built from off-the-shelf components and third-party software.

Nearly all of the hardware—the disk drives, monitors, memory, CPU, printer, etc.—was purchased from outside vendors. Adopting the standard ASCII code for representing alphanumeric data was a first for IBM because they had used EBCDIC on their mainframes (*q.v.*) for years (*see* CHARACTER CODES). System software also came from outside. IBM turned to Microsoft for consultation on the system architecture and a Basic (*q.v.*) interpreter, as well as to three vendors for operating systems (*q.v.*).

IBM chose an Intel CPU because its architecture was close to that of the Intel 8080 used in CP/M-based machines, making it easy to upgrade application software. (IBM later bought a share of Intel.) Intel had two CPUs, the 8086 and 8088. They were software compatible and had 16-bit registers and instructions; however, the 8088 was somewhat slower because of its multiplexed 8-bit data path. To lower system cost, the 8088 was used.

The minimum configuration had only 16 KB memory. Memory could be expanded to 64K by plugging 16 KB memory chips into sockets on the system board. Further expansion entailed plugging add-in boards into the five bus expansion slots on the system motherboard (*q.v.*). This PC bus soon became the industry standard.

Disk drives were optional on the first PCs, which came standard with an audio cassette interface. The original floppy disk drives used only one side of a 5.25 inch disk and had a capacity of 160 KB. IBM did not offer a hard disk at first.

There were two display adapters, the monochrome display adapter (MDA) and a color graphics adapter (CGA). The MDA was a character display with a monochrome monitor (*see* MONITOR, DISPLAY). Resolution and character quality were excellent by the standards of the time, and the MDA was targeted to character-oriented applications like word processing (*q.v.*), spreadsheets (*q.v.*), and software development. The CGA delivered color and graphics on a more expensive RGB monitor. Character resolution was significantly lower than with the MDA, so it was targeted at applications like education, games, and business graphics.

The operating system was more problematic than the hardware. CP/M could not be used directly because the 8088 architecture was not identical to that of the 8080. Furthermore, the 8088 could address 1 MB of memory, as opposed to the 64 KB limit of the 8080, and IBM chose to allow up to 640 KB of continuous memory for programs. (The rest of the address space was reserved for I/O adapters, ROM (*q.v.*), and future use.)

Digital Research was working on an operating system for the new Intel CPUs (CP/M-86), but so were other companies. One such was Softech Microsystems, which had acquired the P-System, an operating system and software development environment developed by Ken Bowles at the University of California at San Diego (*see* PASCAL). Another was Seattle Computer Products, headed by Tim Patterson, who wrote DOS, a CP/M-like operating system, for use on their early 8086-based system. Microsoft acquired the rights to market and further develop Patterson's DOS, although later there was litigation over the transaction. IBM eventually decided to offer three operating systems: DOS, CP/M-86, and the P-System. However, DOS was priced much lower than the others, and eventually became the standard.

The IBM PC was announced in April 1981, with forecast sales of 250,000 units over five years. By the end of 1983, the IBM PC had become a *de facto* standard and had an installed base of a million machines. IBM eventually recognized the strategic importance of personal workstations (*q.v.*), integrated the ESD into the marketing mainstream of the corporation, and defined a System Application Architecture (SAA) to integrate distributed systems (*q.v.*) and workstations.

Evolution

After its introduction, the PC underwent three major upgrades (*see* Table 1). The first was the PC-XT. The XT was a response to the needs of business and professional customers, who had clearly emerged as the major market. With the XT, IBM added a hard disk and expanded the amount of memory on the system board. Even before the introduction of the XT, they had upgraded the floppy disk drives to 360 KB by using both sides of the disk and writing in a higher density (9-sector) format.

The next major upgrade was the PC-AT. The AT used Intel's 80286 CPU, as had Tandy in marketing the excellent but short-lived Tandy 2000. The 80286 was faster than the 8088, and had a 16-bit data bus; therefore, the PC bus was extended by adding additional data lines. The AT bus was upward compatible with the PC bus, so PC and XT add-in cards worked in the AT. The AT bus is also known as the ISA (industry standard architecture) bus.

The 80286 was capable of addressing 16 MB of memory; however, to retain compatibility with commercially available software, it was almost always run in its limited "real" mode, in which it acted as a fast 8086. The AT also introduced a high density 5.25 inch disk drive with 1.25 MB capacity, and hard disk sizes continued to grow. With the AT, IBM also introduced the EGA (extended graphics adapter) video controller. EGA, a color controller that exceeded CGA in resolution and color palette, became widely used and copied. EGA controllers are compatible with MDA and CGA software. (Tragically, Don Estridge was killed in a plane crash in 1985 just shortly after introduction of the AT.)

The AT was followed by the PS/2 line in 1987. The original line consisted of six models, using the 8086, 80286, and 80386 CPUs. Models using the 80386 SX and the 80486 CPU were announced subsequently. The 80386 is upward compatible with the earlier CPUs, has 32-bit registers and instructions, and can address 4.3 GB of memory. The 80386 SX is software-compatible with the 80386, but uses a multiplexed 16-bit data path. The 80386 SX was to the 80386 as the 8088 was to the 8086. The 80486 was compatible with the 80386, but was faster due to a design that integrated previously off-chip functions and enhances internal caching and parallelism (*see* CACHE MEMORY).

The low-end (8086-based) PS/2 used the AT bus, but the others used the new microchannel architecture (MCA) bus. The 80386 SX and 80286-based PS/2s used a 16-bit version of the MCA bus, and the 80386- and 80486-based PS/2s used a 32-bit version. The MCA bus was incompatible with the AT bus, but offered advantages, including greater speed and the ability to add cards without having to set switches.

The PS/2s introduced 3.5 inch floppy disk drives with 1.44 MB capacity on all but the low-end model, which used 720 KB drives. The minimum hard disk for the PS/2 was 20 MB.

Three new display controllers were also announced for the PS/2 line. The MCGA (multicolor graphics array), an enhanced version of the CGA adapter, was available on the low-end model. Other models came with the VGA (video graphics array)—a color graphic controller exceeding EGA resolution and color palette. VGA controllers use analog monitors and have displaced EGA as a standard. They are compatible with EGA software.

IBM also announced OS/2, a new operating system, with the PS/2. OS/2 was not compatible with DOS, but added features including multitasking (*q.v.*), multiple threads, a graphical user interface, and extended file and communication management. But then Microsoft began to market a competitive product, Windows, a DOS extension that included a graphical user interface (GUI) and limited multitasking. The product was only moderately successful until the Windows 3.1 (and its 95, 98 and 2000 successors) became very popular in the 1990s.

The Early Competition

IBM was able to bring the PC to market quickly because it used commercially available components, rather than building its own. This also opened the way for competition.

A number of companies marketed 8086-based computers before IBM. These included small firms like Seattle Computer Products and Godbout and large ones like Victor Business Machines; however, the market did not take off until IBM entered and established a standard.

There were several gaps in the original PC offering, so IBM's entry was followed almost immediately by a

Table 1. Major steps in the evolution of the IBM PC family.

	PC	PC-XT	PC-AT	PS/2	Aptiva
Year introduced	1981	1982	1984	1987	1998
CPU chip[a]	8088	8088	80286	80386 80386-SX 80486	Pentium Pentium II Pentium III
Bus[b]	PC	PC	AT	MCA	PCI/ISA
Bus data bits	8	8	16	16	32
Processor speed	2 MHz	2 MHz	5 MHz	16 MHz	400 MHz (650 MHz in September 1999)
Typical memory	320 KB	512 KB	640 KB	2–8 MB	64–128 MB
Floppy disk	160 KB	360 KB	1.2 MB	1.44 MB	1.44 MB
Typical hard disk	n/a	10 MB	20 MB	40 MB	8 GB
Display adapter	MDA CGA	MDA CGA	EGA	MCGA VGA 8514	Super VGA

[a] The 8086 and 80286 CPU chips were used in some PS/2 models.
[b] Some PS/2 models used the AT bus.

wave of add-in board makers. IBM used 16 KB memory chips at first, allowing companies using 64 KB chips to compete effectively in memory upgrades. The value of competitive memory cards was often augmented by including additional I/O ports and calendar chips, making them far superior to IBM memory. The limitations of the CGA and MDA display controllers created a niche filled by a higher-resolution, monochrome, graphic controller from Hercules Graphics. The Hercules controller became a widely emulated standard. Several companies also developed hard disk subsystems for the PC before IBM did.

By 1982, several companies were marketing PC-compatible computers. One of these, Compaq, combined PC compatibility with transportability (along the lines of the Osborne CP/M-based computers), a high resolution display, and quality workmanship. Compaq, Zenith, and Tandy emerged as major challengers to IBM in the personal computer market but Zenith has withdrawn from that market. Early PC-compatibles like the Compaq were soon joined by very low cost systems made possible by offshore design and manufacturing. The August 1991 issue of *PC Magazine* either discussed or carried advertisements for no fewer than 50 different manufacturers of PC-compatible computers. Clearly, as of that date, a major shakeout was imminent.

Current Situation

As of this writing (1999), there has ceased to be an "IBM PC" as such; there are merely PCs made by IBM. By performance, IBM's latest PC series, the Aptiva (Fig. 1), is quite competitive with PCs made by other manufacturers, but IBM has dropped to third in US sales, behind Dell and Compaq, who run neck and neck, each with about 15% of the market. At best, IBM is tied with Hewlett-Packard for third place, each having about 10% of the market, with Gateway close

to them at about 8%. Packard Bell and Tandy account for another 10% and the remaining 38% of the market is spread among another ten or so national companies. It is hard to assess the total market because every city of average size has at least one small company which builds PCs from components and sells them locally. (We refer here to the market for machines compatible with the IBM PC, not to the total market, which includes incompatible Apple products.)

It is not just the loss in sales share that has diminished the concept of an "IBM PC." Just as important is the fact that it is not IBM that defines advances in PC architecture, it is the combination of chip manufacturer Intel and software colossus Microsoft that does so, even to the point where the US government is beginning to argue that those two firms are a bit too cozy. Microsoft dominated the PC operating system market from 1992 (Windows 3.1) through 1995 (Windows 95) to 1998 (Windows 98) and beyond. Popular computer magazines no longer discuss a generic "IBM PC." The term in vogue is "Wintel" machine, implying that the combination of Windows running on an Intel chip is what matters, not the company that assembles the hardware and installs the operating system.

One niche in which IBM has been relatively more successful is that of the laptop computer (*see* PORTABLE COMPUTERS). The IBM Thinkpad, though not a sales leader, has earned a reputation as being a technically superior laptop. And, of course, it is software compatible with other Wintel machines.

Bibliography

1990. Bradley, D. J. "The Creation of the IBM-PC," *Byte,* **15**, *9* (September), 414–420.
1991. Sheldon, K. M. "You've Come a Long Way, PC: The 10th Anniversary of the IBM-PC," *Byte,* **16**, *8* (August), 336.

Larry Press and Edwin D. Reilly

ICON (LANGUAGE)

See STRING PROCESSING LANGUAGE.

ICON (PICTORIAL ELEMENT)

See USER INTERFACE; and WINDOWS ENVIRONMENTS.

IDENTIFIER

For articles on related subjects *see* CONSTANT; EXPRESSION; PROCEDURE-ORIENTED LANGUAGES; PROGRAMMING LANGUAGES; and STATEMENT.

In a programming language, an *identifier* is a string of characters used as a name for some element of the

Figure 1. A typically configured IBM Aptiva. (Courtesy of IBM.)

program. This element may be a statement label, a procedure or function, a data element (such as a scalar variable or an array), or the program itself.

Most commonly, the word *identifier* is used almost synonymously with *variable name*. In a system where the location of a program's data remains fixed throughout program execution, the identifier associated with a scalar variable is related to a memory address, which in turn references a physical location within the memory of the machine, which in turn contains a value representation. The intermediate relationships between the identifier and a value are usually transparent to a programmer, and thus some confusion arises in practice between the *name* of a variable (i.e. its identifier) and its *value*, which is the current contents of the memory location assigned to that identifier.

In the majority of programming languages, identifiers may be formed from any alphanumeric string, often of some restricted length, provided the leftmost character is alphabetic. Some languages also permit the use of special characters, the dollar sign ($) and underscore (_) being typical. In Ada (*q.v.*), letter-case does not matter, so TAXRATE, taxrate, and TaxRate are all the same identifier, but in other languages, such as C (*q.v.*) and C++ (*q.v.*), these identifiers would be distinct.

J. A. N. Lee

IEEE COMPUTER SOCIETY

See INSITITUTE FOR ELECTRONIC AND ELECTRICAL ENGINEERS—COMPUTER SOCIETY.

IMAGE COMPRESSION

For articles on related subjects *see* COMPUTER GRAPHICS: STANDARDS; DATA COMPRESSION; IMAGE PROCESSING; MEDICAL IMAGING; and TOMOGRAPHY, COMPUTERIZED.

Digital *image compression* methods reduce the space necessary to encode, store or transmit digital images by changing the way those images are represented. To see why image compression is desirable, consider an 8 × 10 inch color picture, digitized using a resolution of 600 pixels per inch and a byte for each of three color planes. Then the number of bytes required to represent each image is:

$$8 \times 10 \times 600 \times 600 \times 3 \text{ bytes} \approx 85 \text{ MB}.$$

On typical current personal computing systems with only a few gigabytes of hard disk (*q.v.*) space, 85 MB is too much for storage of all but a small number of pictures. Even in the future with much cheaper and larger stores, the ability to compress images by a factor

of 25 or more (typical of current standards such as JPEG) will be highly desirable. Similar issues apply to communications.

There are numerous methods for compressing data and each has advantages and disadvantages depending on what kind of image one wishes to compress, how much loss of information one is willing to tolerate, and what form that loss takes. Methods can also be combined. In fact, most standard compression systems combine more than one technique.

Digital Image Representation

The simplest images are bi-level images. This format is often used to encode sharp documents and faxes, where a pixel can assume only one of two values, black or white. Pixel encoding is usually one bit ("0" or "1").

When several gray midtones are present, as in black and white photos, two values are no longer sufficient to encode all possible gray intensities. Thus, each pixel must be assigned a numerical value, proportional to the brightness of that point. Typical choices for these values fall in the ranges 0–15 or 0–255 (requiring respectively 4 and 8 bits for each pixel). This kind of image is referred to as a *gray-level* picture.

Color images take advantage of the fact that each color can be expressed as a combination of three primary colors (red, green and blue or yellow, magenta and cyan, for example). Therefore a color picture can be considered as the superimposition of three "simpler" pictures (called *color planes*), with each of them encoding the brightness of a primary color. In other words, each color plane of an image can be treated much like a gray-level picture with a range of values based on the *luminosity* of that particular color. This type of representation, called RGB or YMC according to the color planes, is "hardware-oriented" (monitors, printers and photographic devices use these color schemes), and it is used when dealing with synthetic (computer-generated) images.

In many scientific applications, images may have more than three planes of information (e.g. multispectral images) and may be higher dimensional. In natural (or non-computer-generated) images, however, the brightness values of corresponding pixels in different color planes are highly correlated (what is bright in the red plane, for example, will often be bright in the green and blue planes) and this correlation can easily be exploited using an alternative system of color representation. Instead of dividing the image into three color planes, the overall brightness of each pixel can be encoded in a luminosity plane (Y). This makes two color planes sufficient to encode the chromatic variations (these two planes are called Cb and Cr). This "YCbCr" color format is used, with some variations, in the broadcast of TV transmissions (the luminance component alone gives a representation that is backward-compatible with black and white (B/W) pictures).

Lossless vs. Lossy Methods

A basic distinction among image compression algorithms can be made in terms of reconstruction fidelity. When it is possible to recover exactly the original data from the compressed data, the algorithm is called *lossless*. Otherwise, when some distortion is introduced in the coding process and part of the original information is irremediably lost, the algorithm is called *lossy*. Lossy compressors, since they can discard part of the information, achieve a more compact representation than lossless systems.

A compromise between these two categories is represented by "near to lossless" or "transparent" algorithms where a small coding error is allowed only when it is semantically irrelevant. These methods are useful, for example, in compressing medical images where two contrasting needs arise: high compression rates (required by the large amount of data) and the preservation of the diagnostic information.

In what follows we focus on lossy methods because lossless methods are covered in the article on DATA COMPRESSION.

Lossy Image Compression

TRANSFORM CODING

Transform coding uses a transformation that exploits peculiar characteristics of the signal, increasing the performance of a scheme such as Huffman or arithmetic coding, for example (*see* DATA COMPRESSION).

For natural sources (audio, images, and video), the information that is relevant for a human user is best described in the frequency domain. When a pictorial scene is decomposed into its frequency components, the low frequencies (gradual luminosity changes) correspond to the scene illumination, and the high frequencies (rapid changes) characterize objects' contours.

Representing the input in the frequency domain results in better control of the error introduced in lossy compression; information that is not important for a human viewer, can be easily discarded or distorted, so that the image will be smaller or easier to compress.

Several time domain to frequency domain transformations have been proposed for digital image signals; one of the most used, the Discrete Cosine Transform (DCT), has the advantage of a good decorrelation of the signal (which reduces redundancy), requiring only an acceptable computational effort.

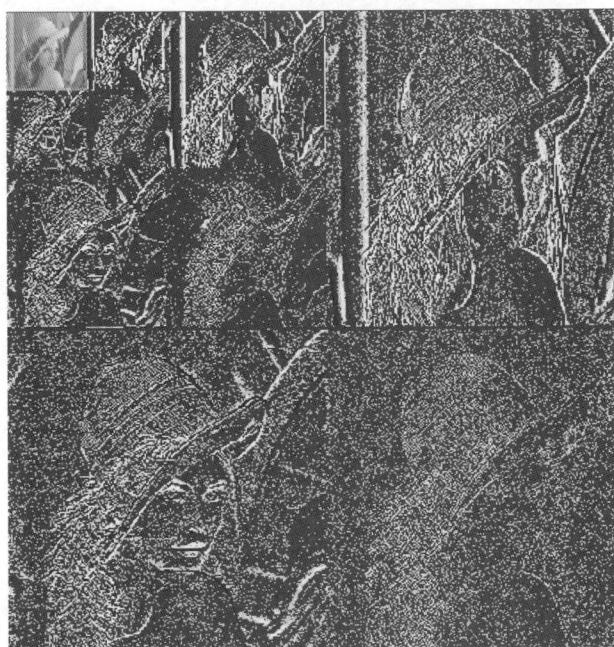

Figure 1. Wavelet decomposition.

Transformations are not compression methods in the literal sense (sometimes they even increase the size of the input), but when used properly they provide a powerful enhancement of entropy-based compression methods. For further reading, see Rao and Yip (1990).

WAVELET COMPRESSION

Another compression scheme that adopts transform coding is based on *wavelet* functions (Fig. 1). The basic idea of this coding scheme is to process data at different scales of resolution. If we look at a picture from a distance, we notice the macro-structure (i.e. the *subject* of the painting). If we move close to the painting, we notice the micro-structures (e.g. the painter's brush strokes). Using wavelet functions allows us to see both the subject and the micro-structure. This is achieved using two versions of the picture at a different scaling of the same prototype function called the *mother wavelet* or *wavelet basis*. A contracted version of the basis function is used for the analysis in the time domain, while a stretched one is used for the frequency domain.

Localization (in both time and frequency) means that it is always possible to find a particular scale at which a specific detail of the signal may be discerned. Wavelet analysis enables the amplitude of the input signal to be drastically reduced. This is particularly appealing for image compression, since it means that half of the data is almost zero and thus easily compressible. For further reading, see Vetterli and Kovacevic (1995).

VECTOR QUANTIZATION

A *dictionary* (or *codebook*) is a collection of a small number of statistically relevant patterns (codewords). Every image is encoded by dividing it into blocks and assigning to each block the index of the closest codeword in the dictionary. Matching can be exact or approximate, thereby achieving, respectively, lossless or lossy compression. The codebook is sometimes allowed to change in response to the input's peculiarities.

The best known dictionary method is *vector quantization*; in its simplest form, it is a lossy compression scheme that uses a static dictionary. A set of images (the *training set*), statistically representative of the source's behavior, is carefully selected; each image is divided into blocks and a small set of dictionary codewords is determined. The codewords are selected to minimize the coding error on the training set. Because of its mathematical tractability, the mean square error is usually used as the error metric and is used to guide both the design and the encoding process (*see* Performance Evaluation below).

The compression rate depends both on the size of each block and on the size of the dictionary. A dictionary with N codewords of $n \times n$ pixels each compresses an image digitized with b bits per pixel with a ratio:

$$R = \frac{n \times n \log_2 b}{\log_2 N}.$$

Once the dictionary is determined, encoding is performed by assigning to each block of the image the index of the closest codeword in the dictionary (i.e. the one with the minimum mean error). The decoder, which also knows the dictionary, simply expands the indices of the codewords into their appropriate blocks.

In a vector quantizer, encoding and decoding are highly asymmetric processes. Searching for the closest block in the dictionary (encoding) is computationally much more expensive than retrieving the codeword associated with a given index (decoding). Even more expensive is the dictionary design, but fortunately this can be done offline.

Vector quantization may be proved to be asymptotically optimal when the size of the block increases; unfortunately the size of the codebook also grows exponentially with the block size.

Many variations of vector quantization have been proposed to speed up the encoding and to simplify the codebook design. Most of these are based on tree (*q.v.*) structures. For further reading see the book of Gersho and Gray (1992).

FRACTAL COMPRESSION

Algorithms based on fractals (*q.v.*) have very good performance and high compression ratios (32 to 1 is not unusual), but their use can be limited by the extensive computation required. The basic idea can be described as a "self vector quantization," where an image block is encoded by applying a simple transformation to one of the blocks previously encoded. Transformations frequently used are combinations of scaling, reflections, and rotations of another block.

Unlike vector quantization, fractal compressors do not maintain an explicit dictionary, which is why the process can be long and computationally intensive. The basic idea is that each encoded block must be transformed in all possible ways and compared with the current one to determine the best match. Because the blocks are allowed to have different sizes, there is very little "blocking" noise and the perceived quality of the compressed image is usually very good. *See* the books of Barnsley and Hurd (1993) or Fisher (1995).

Data Compression Standards

JPEG

The Joint Photographic Experts Group (JPEG) developed a standard for color image compression that was issued in 1990. The standard was mainly targeted for compressing natural black and white and color images. JPEG, like almost every other transform coding image compression algorithm, defines two steps. The first is lossy and involves transformation and quantization; it is used to remove information that is perceptively irrelevant for a human user. The second step is a lossless encoding that eliminates statistical redundancies still present in the compressed representation.

JPEG assumes a color image divided into color planes and compresses each of them independently. It uses the YCbCr representation discussed earlier, taking advantage of the fact that the human visual system is more sensitive to luminosity than to color changes. Thus it is possible to achieve some compression (even before applying JPEG) just by reducing the resolution of the two chrominance (Cb and Cr) components. Each color plane is further divided into blocks of 8×8 pixels. This size block was determined to be the best compromise between computational effort and the compression achieved. For each block, a decomposition in the frequency domain is computed using the DCT. Fig. 2 shows an 8×8 image block and the result of applying the DCT to it. The result is an 8×8 matrix with some small numbers and several zeros. Using a zigzag pattern, this matrix is scanned from the low to the high frequencies and then converted into a vector. Run-length encoding is applied to compress the sequences of consecutive zeros. The result is then

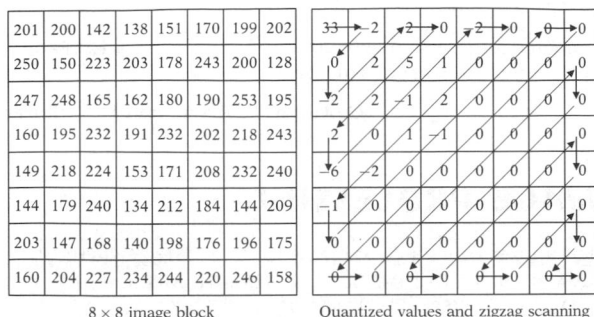

8 × 8 image block   Quantized values and zigzag scanning

Figure 2. JPEG: an image block and a block showing the quantized values after applying the DCT as well as the zigzag pattern used in scanning it.

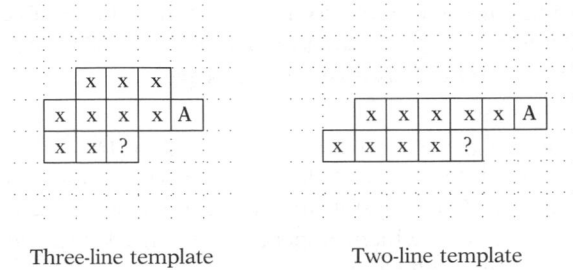

Three-line template   Two-line template

Figure 3. Prediction templates for JBIG.

further compressed using a Huffman or an arithmetic coder (*see* DATA COMPRESSION).

JPEG-LS

In 1994 ISO/JPEG issued a call for a new standard for lossless and near-lossless compression of continuous tone images (2 to 16 bits per pixel—bpp). This standard, called JPEG-LS, is a predictive coder which uses an error-feedback technique. The encoder classifies the prediction context and stores the mean prediction residual that occurs in each class. After the prediction step, the encoder locates the class to which the current image context belongs and adds the mean error to the prediction. The prediction residual is then computed and coded.

In addition to providing a better prediction, the advantage of the error feedback technique is that errors in different contexts have different probability distributions which can be used to tune the coder to the specific context. *See* Weinberger *et al.* (1996).

JBIG

In 1991 the Joint Bi-level Image Experts Group (JBIG) defined an innovative lossless compression algorithm for black and white images. It is a predictive coder that uses a pool of already coded neighbor pixels to guess the value of the current pixel. The algorithm simply concatenates the value of the template pixels to identify the context in which the current pixel is going to be predicted. The index of the context is used to choose which probability distribution should be used by an arithmetic coder.

The "A" pixel in Fig. 3 is an *adaptive* pixel. Its position is allowed to change as the image is processed. The use of an adaptive pixel improves compression by identifying repeated occurrences of the same block of information.

JBIG may also be successfully used in coding images with more than one bit per pixel for gray-scale or color images. The image is decomposed into *bit-planes*

(i.e. if the image is 4 bpp, each pixel is represented by the binary string $b_3 b_2 b_1 b_0$; bit-plane i then stores bit b_i of each pixel) and each plane is coded separately. In principle, JBIG could work with 255 bpp images, but in practice the algorithm has good performance only for images with at most 8 bpp. *See* Arps and Truong (1994).

Performance Evaluation

The performance of an image compression algorithm is mainly determined by two characteristics: the *compression ratio* and the *magnitude of the error* introduced by the encoding. In a lossless compressor, the size of the image is minimized while retaining the quality of the original. But a lossy algorithm must compromise between these two qualities.

A fundamental problem in lossy compression is controlling the error introduced by encoding process. Among several quality metrics that are commonly used the mean square error (MSE) criterion is much the most important. The MSE between a given image $i(x, y)$ and its encoded version $\hat{i}(x, y)$ is the square root of the sum of the squares of the differences between the corresponding values of the samples in the two signals:

$$\text{MSE} = \sqrt{\sum_{x,y} (i(x, y) - \hat{i}(x, y))^2}.$$

The MSE gives a good measure of the random error introduced in the compression; this is enough for many applications, but, when encoded images are mainly used by humans, the use of distortion measures based on the MSE may give misleading results. The poor correlation of the MSE with the perceived distortion occurs because the human visual system is more sensitive to structured than to random coding errors. *See* the book of Gonzalez and Wintz (1987).

Coding Artifacts

When a very high compression rate has to be achieved or when a complex image has to be encoded, lossy compression methods sometimes introduce visible artifacts that can make the perceived quality very poor. Commonly observed artifacts are:

◆ *Blocking*, which happens when a gradual change in the intensity or color of a region is coarsely quantized. This results in periodic discontinuities in the image, which appears segmented into its constituent blocks.

◆ *Blurring*, which appears in different forms such as at edges, due to the loss of high-frequency components, or as blurring of the texture and color due to the loss of resolution.

◆ *Ringing effect*, which is observable as periodic pseudo-edges around original shape edges for the compressed images. The ringing effect results from improper truncation of high-frequency components, also known as the Gibbs effect.

◆ *Texture deviation*, which appears as granular noise or as the "dirty window" effect, and it is caused by loss of fidelity in mid-frequency components.

See Woods (1991).

Bibliography

1987. Gonzalez, R., and Wintz, P. *Digital Image Processing.* Reading, MA: Addison-Wesley.

1990. Rao, D., and Yip, P. *Discrete Cosine Transform.* San Diego, CA: Academic Press.

1991. Woods, J. *Subband Image Coding.* Norwell, MA: Kluwer Academic Publishers.

1992. Gersho, A., and Gray, R. M. *Vector Quantization and Signal Compression.* Norwell, MA: Kluwer Academic Publishers.

1993. Barnsley, M., and Hurd, L. *Fractal Image Compression.* Natick, MA: AK Peters.

1994. Arps, R. B., and Truong, T. K. "Comparison of International Standards for Lossless Still Image Compression," Special Issue on Data Compression (ed. J. Storer). *Proceedings of the IEEE*, **82**, 6, 889–899.

1994. Kondoz, A. *Digital Speech.* New York: John Wiley.

1995. Bhaskaran, V., and Konstantinides, K. *Image and Video Compression Standards.* Boston: Kluwer Academic Press.

1995. Fisher, Y. (ed.) *Fractal Image Compression: Theory and Application.* New York: Springer-Verlag.

1995. Vetterli, M., and Kovacevic, J. *Wavelets and Subband Coding.* Upper Saddle River, NJ: Prentice Hall.

1996. Sayood, K. *Introduction to Data Compression.* San Francisco: Morgan Kaufmann.

1996. Weinberger, M. J., Seroussi, G., and Sapiro, G. "LOCO-I: A Low Complexity, Context-based, Lossless Image Compression Algorithm," *Proceedings IEEE Data Compression Conference*, Snowbird, UT, 140–149.

1997. Haskell, B. G., Puri, A., and Netravali, A. N. *Digital Video: An Introduction to MPEG-2.* New York: Chapman & Hall.

1997. Mitchell, J., Pennebaker, W., Fogg, C., and LeGall, D. *MPEG Video Compression Standard.* New York: Chapman & Hall.

1997. Salomon, D. *Data Compression: The Complete Reference.* New York: Springer-Verlag.

Website

Computer compression newsgroup FAQ. `http://www.faqs. org/faqs/compression-faq/part2/`.

G. Motta, F. Rizzo, and J. A. Storer

IMAGE PROCESSING

> For articles on related subjects *see* COMPUTER GRAPHICS; COMPUTER VISION; IMAGE COMPRESSION; MEDICAL IMAGING; PATTERN RECOGNITION; and TOMOGRAPHY, COMPUTERIZED.

Introduction

Digital *image processing* deals with the systematic manipulation of an input image to produce an output image that is better suited for viewing or subsequent analysis. The processed images are either examined by a human observer, such as a radiologist viewing an X-ray, or they form input to an automatic machine vision system. The machine vision system then analyzes the image to derive an interpretation of the scene. A digital image is represented as a discrete two-dimensional array of numbers. Each element in the array is known as a *pixel* (for picture element). These pixels are assigned values that correspond to the relative brightness of the tiny portions of the image that they depict. These values are known as *gray levels*. Digital image processing deals with the systematic manipulation of the pixel gray levels and their distribution.

Digital processing of images requires three basic capabilities. First is the ability to form digital images, second is the ability to store and manipulate these images, and third is the ability to display such images. Digital image processing technology traces its origin to the technologies associated with the above three capabilities. Electronics and optics technologies provided the ability for image acquisition; digital computers and associated technologies provided the abilities to store and manipulate these images; and television and communication technologies are used to display and transmit images.

Image processing depends on the field of *digital signal processing* (DSP). The advent of digital computers and development of efficient algorithms for processing and analyzing one-dimensional signals provided insights and a general framework for the development of early image processing algorithms. However, because spatial (both two- and three-dimensional) and temporal characterization and context play crucial roles in digital image processing, novel means for their representation, processing, and analysis are also needed. DSP algorithms and approaches make possible efficient implementation of many image processing and machine vision systems.

Growth and Applications of the Technology

It was only about four decades ago that serious research in digital image processing could begin. During this relatively short span, digital image processing technology has proved its importance and utility over a broad spectrum of applications. For example, modern medicine, weather forecasting, resource management, printing and publishing, manufacturing, video entertainment, surveillance, and smart weapons have all greatly benefited from image processing technology.

Digital image processing has experienced a steady and sustained growth ever since its inception in the early 1960s. By its very nature, the field is application-oriented. The main objective is to develop tools and techniques for analyzing pictorial data generated in a diverse range of application domains. Initial research and development revolved around the image processing needs of the space program. In the late 1960s and the early 1970s, image processing was introduced in medical imaging. In the early stages, the hardware environment required for performing image processing was quite expensive and specialized. With the introduction of high-quality imaging cameras and computing workstations (*q.v.*) at relatively low costs, image processing applications have sprouted in a variety of domains, such as electronics fabrication and testing, document processing and analysis, automotive and aerospace engineering, food processing, and pharmaceutical manufacturing. With the availability of good quality, affordable cameras and image processing hardware boards, a personal computer can be converted into a complete image processing workstation at a moderate cost. Indeed, in the 1990s standard home computers supported a wide range of basic image processing functions. Digital cameras, color monitors, and printers have all become readily affordable. This will undoubtedly lead to a much wider range of new applications of image processing. Unlike the earlier applications which were prompted primarily by the military, governmental, or large institutional needs, the new applications have a distinctly consumer flavor. Image processing offers substantial enhancements to new generations of "information appliances," including those for video and computer conferencing, digital libraries (*q.v.*) and video databases, home security, remote surveillance, and Internet communications.

Digital image processing is used in two types of application. The first deals with those applications in which the images are processed for direct use by a human investigator. Examples include processing modules for image enhancement, restoration, and compression. In the second type of application, image processing finds its utility is as a front-end processing module of a complete machine vision system. In this case, the overall aim is not simply image-to-image transformation, but rather interpretation of information embedded in the images.

Image Processing Approaches

Image processing methods can be classified in two groups: *spatial domain approaches* and *transform* (or *frequency*) *domain approaches*. The spatial domain techniques work directly on the two-dimensional digital images. The spatial domain approaches have intuitive appeal and are relatively easy to develop and implement. The transform domain techniques require an image to be transformed into another domain, using transformations derived from mathematical models. Characteristics of these transformed images are analyzed to accomplish a specific image processing task. Linear systems theory had allowed treatment of one-dimensional signals in both the time and frequency domains. This experience played a major role in developing theories and techniques for processing two-dimensional signals (i.e. images). For several important image processing functions, one can find an appropriate technique from either the spatial domain or the frequency domain. Typically, results of the spatial domain analysis are easier to interpret than those of the frequency domain. Some of the more commonly used transforms for image processing include Fourier, cosine, Hadamard, Haar, Walsh, wavelet, and Gabor transforms. Approaches based upon the Hough transform for detection of specific types of structural details like lines, circles, or curves are also proving quite useful in a wide range of applications.

Image Quantization and Sampling

Quantization and sampling deal with the issues underlying the formation of a digital image that can be processed by a computer. Digital images are two-dimensional discrete representations. This digitization of the signals is performed to allow subsequent processing of these signals by a digital computer. Conversion of continuous analog signals into digital form involves two considerations. First is the digitization of the amplitude of the signals, a process referred to as *quantization*. The second is *sampling*, the formation of the two-dimensional spatial grid associated with an image. Schemes typically use uniform quantization and a rectangular sampling grid (*see* ANALOG-TO-DIGITAL AND DIGITAL-TO-ANALOG CONVERTERS).

Image Registration

One of the important requirements in many image processing and analysis tasks is to extract information from multiple copies of the same scene. These copies might be acquired at different wavelengths or at different times or from a slightly different perspective or resolution. In order to perform a systematic analysis of such a data set, one requires an ability to match these copies accurately to a standardized grid so that the images are in perfect spatial registration. This involves corrections for rotational, translational, and scale differences present in the images, a process called *image registration*. Development of registration techniques was mainly due to satellite and aerial image processing studies.

Image Compression

Transmission and storage of digital images poses challenging problems due to the vast amounts of data involved. *Image compression (q.v.)* deals with efficient encoding and decoding of digital images for either transmission or storage. The initial thrust for image compression came from the imaging requirements of the space program in the early 1960s. Recently, after a low level of research activity, there has been renewed interest in this topic. There is a definite cost associated with the storage, processing, and transmission of data, and images typically contain a significantly large amount of redundant information. In many applications, such redundant information can be eliminated without adversely affecting the original objective of an image processing task. Image compression methods allow reduction of image storage, processing, and transmission requirements without sacrificing the image quality.

Compression techniques are divided into two categories: (1) *reversible (or lossless) techniques*, and (2) *irreversible (or lossy) techniques*. One can achieve a much larger compression ratio by using lossy methods compared with the lossless methods. Two important types of compression, *predictive* and *transform coding*, use the high correlation between the gray levels associated with neighboring pixels to achieve compression. Typically, predictive coding schemes are relatively simple to implement but are not robust (i.e. they suffer from high sensitivity to various statistical parameters). Transform coding schemes achieve higher compression ratios compared with the predictive approaches, but are more complex to implement. Hybrid coding schemes combine the best features of the predictive and transform coding approaches. In the case of the compression of multiple frames of images (such as those involved in television transmission), one can use the high correlation between successive frames to achieve compression.

Image Enhancement

The goal of *image enhancement*, one of the most widely used image processing functions, is to highlight or enhance a particular type of image feature. Suppression of image detail that is not of interest for a particular task is also a part of the image enhancement process. These techniques are used in the following types of problem:

1. Object/background contrast stretching.
2. Modification of the dynamic range of an image.
3. Removal of false contours introduced through inadequate quantization levels.
4. Reduction of additive, multiplicative, or "salt-and-pepper" noise.
5. Enhancement of edge features ("edge sharpening").
6. Image smoothing ("image blurring").
7. Display of image detail by pseudo-color (or "false color") enhancement.

In Figs. 1 and 2, two examples of image enhancement are presented. In Fig. 1, the objective is to reduce the additive and multiplicative noise in an image.

Figure 1. Reduction of additive and multiplicative noise by applying a nonlinear neighborhood operator in the spatial domain. (Courtesy of Dr. G. Mastin, Sandia National Laboratory.)

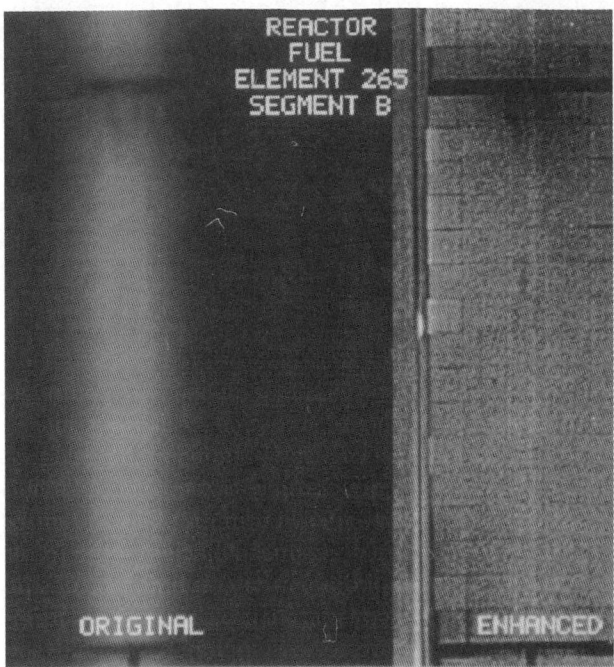

Figure 2. Enhancement of a neutron radiograph of a nuclear fuel rod. A two-step enhancement procedure was used to eliminate the nonuniform illumination variations and to enhance the contrast highlighting fuel pellets and casing. (Courtesy of Dr. G. Mastin, Sandia National Laboratory.)

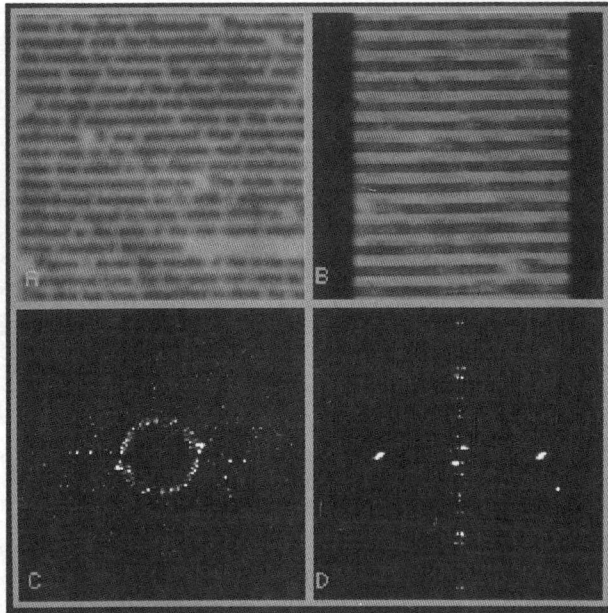

Figure 3. Part (a) shows an image blurred due to defocus. Part (b) shows an image with uniform motion blur. Parts (c) and (d) show their respective Fourier domain blur signatures. (Courtesy of Dr. G. Mastin, Sandia National Laboratory.)

A nonlinear neighborhood operator has been iteratively applied to reduce the high-contrast noise. This spatial domain enhancement operation can be viewed as a low-pass adaptive filtering operation. The example in Fig. 2 deals with the enhancement of a neutron radiographic image of a nuclear fuel rod. The original image is corrupted by a nonuniform intensity pattern imposed by the nonuniform flux of neutrons from the cylindrical fuel rod. This nonuniformity is independent of the vertical position, so that a simple column-by-column gray-level averaging operation allows us to isolate the intensity pattern, which is then subtracted from the original image. As the second step in enhancement, a nonlinear spatial domain filter for contrast stretching is applied to highlight the pellet interfaces and the casing structure.

Image Restoration

The objective of image restoration is to undo the effects of any degradation that might have affected an image. In a sense, image restoration can be considered a special kind of image enhancement. In image restoration, it is assumed that the mathematical model of the degradation process is available or can be accurately derived by examining the input images. Image restoration problems can be examined in a nice mathematical framework. However, applying these techniques to solve real-world problems is difficult. In order to derive useful results in practical situations, one must consider approaches where the assumed mathematical models are satisfied. Image restoration techniques use an image formation model. In most cases, one assumes that the image formation is a spatially invariant and linear process. With these assumptions, it is possible to describe image formation by an integral equation involving the original ("ideal") image convolved with the point spread function (PSF) of the imaging system, a model for the electro-optical sensor, and a random noise term. The most straightforward image restoration method is known as the "inverse filter" approach. It involves use of the noise model and knowledge of the PSF to estimate the original image from the recorded image. For many practical problems, the PSF may not be known. In such cases, it may be possible to analyze the power spectrum of the recorded image to deduce the parameters of the PSF. This can be explained with the help of the examples shown in Fig. 3. Parts (a) and (b) of this figure show recorded images that are corrupted by defocus and uniform motion blur, respectively. Part (c) shows the Fourier domain signature of the image of Fig. 3a. The diameter of the visible ring is equal to the circular aperture PSF used to describe the lens defocus. Similarly, part (d) shows the uniform motion blur signature. The strong intensity spikes located in a horizontal plane indicate the blur direction. The spacing of these components is equal to twice the blur width and can be used to create a transfer function describing horizontal motion.

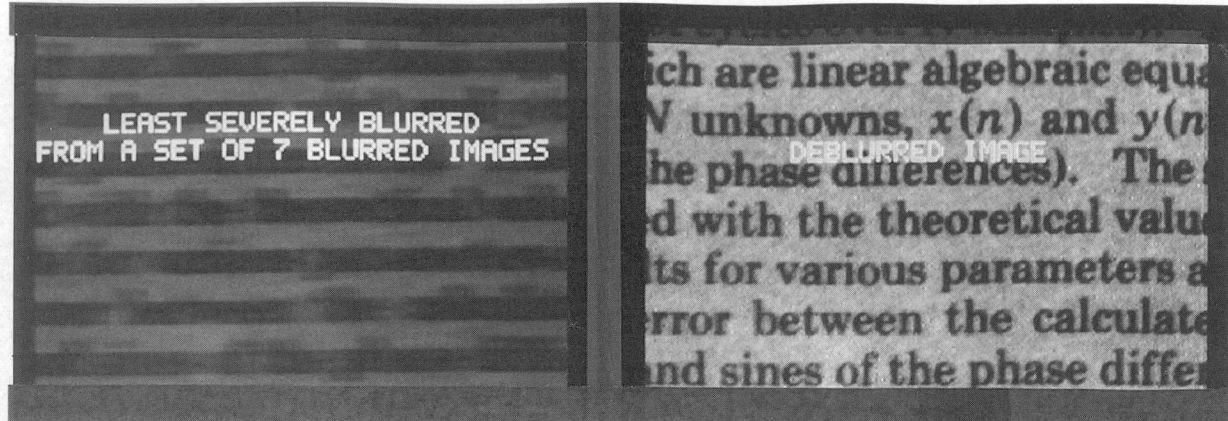

Figure 4. Example of restoration of a motion blurred image. Part (a) shows one of the seven images affected by motion blur. Part (b) shows the restored image. (Courtesy of Drs. D. Ghiglia and G. Mastin, Sandia National Laboratory.)

Figure 5. Image with severe blurring from a van moving in a perspective plane (left). Image after applying Wiener restoration to the perspective corrected image (right). Note that the stationary objects in the scene, such as trees and grass, are now blurred, while the van is deblurred. (Courtesy of Drs. D. Ghiglia and G. Mastin, Sandia National Laboratory.)

Examples of image restoration of two images affected by motion blur are presented in Figs. 4 and 5. Fig. 4a shows one of the seven images recorded with motion blur. Fig. 4b shows the restored image. Details of the restoration technique are described by Ghiglia (1984). Fig. 5a shows an image blurred by an object moving in a perspective plane. Fig. 5b presents the results of a linear Weiner restoration technique by first invoking a geometric transformation to remove the perspective (Ghiglia and Jakowatz, 1985).

Image Reconstruction

This topic deals with the problem of reconstructing a digital image given a set of image projections. There are several important application areas where the only practical way to acquire two-dimensional or three-dimensional images of an object is by using a set of image projections. For example, image reconstruction is an important requirement in medical imaging (*see* TOMOGRAPHY, COMPUTERIZED), geophysical exploration, underwater exploration, and radio astronomy.

Image Segmentation

Segmentation deals with the partitioning of an image into parts for further processing. There are basically two types of approach to accomplish image segmentation: edge-based and region-based. The edge-based segmentation approach uses properties of dissimilarity between adjacent pixels to identify all edge pixels in an image. Various operators can be developed to detect such discontinuities in the properties of the pixels. While developing such operators, issues such as accuracy in detection and localization are considered. For each edge pixel, the *strength* of the edge (magnitude of the discontinuity value) and the *direction* of the edge are evaluated. Once edge pixels in an image are identified, the task is to form boundaries that segment the image into distinct regions. This task can be quite difficult for most real-world images. Basically, it requires tracing of the global object contours based upon very localized information that is highly susceptible to error and inaccuracy. Such boundary formation can also involve complex computations. In situations where the boundaries are linear or of a specified parametric form, techniques such as Hough transforms have proved to be quite useful.

The region-based approach to segmentation uses properties of similarity among neighboring image pixels. There are three different implementations of the basic region-based approach. The first is called *segmentation by region merging*, where a region is merged with its neighboring region if they share some uniformity or homogeneity property. This can be considered a bottom-up approach, where one begins with individual pixels to form homogeneous regions. The second approach is known as *segmentation by region splitting*. One starts with a large region which is then split into homogeneous subregions using a uniformity or homogeneity test. This can be considered a top-down approach, where one begins with a large region and keeps splitting it into smaller homogeneous regions. Finally, one can also develop a *split-and-merge* technique for segmentation, where one can use either a merge or split decision at a given level to segment an

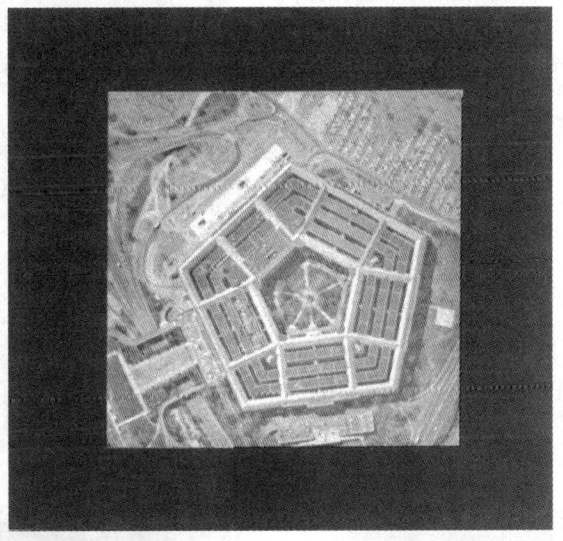

(a)

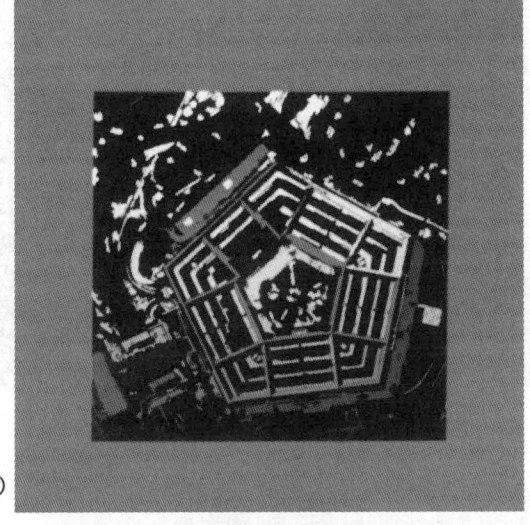

(b)

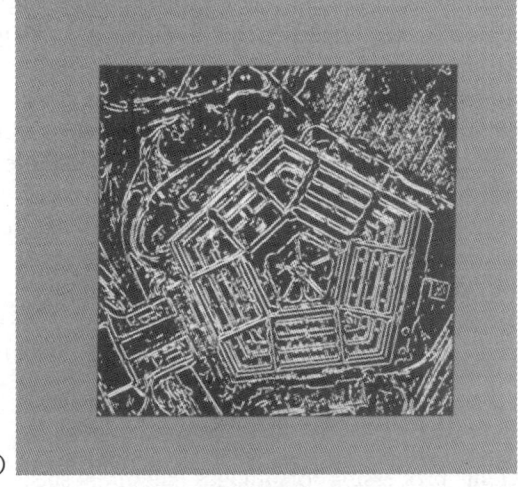

(c)

Figure 6. Image segmentation: Part (a) shows a high-resolution aerial image of the Pentagon. Part (b) shows the result of applying a region-growing algorithm to identify homogeneous regions. Part (c) shows the result of applying an edge operator to identify the intensity discontinuities.

image efficiently. Region-based approaches have proved to be more effective in practical situations than edge-based approaches, as they exhibit better noise immunity and are more efficient. There are also a number of studies where both the edge and region-based techniques are used in a complementary fashion.

Examples of image segmentation are presented in Fig. 6. Fig. 6a shows a high-resolution aerial image of the Pentagon. Fig. 6b shows the results of applying a region-growing segmentation algorithm (Levine, 1985). The basic premise is to merge pixels belonging to the same statistical distribution in a region. From a perceptual psychology viewpoint, region growing is based upon two important criteria of perceptual grouping. The criterion of *proximity* is observed by evaluating each pixel with pixels in its neighborhood, and the *similarity* criterion is observed through comparison of a specified pixel property with that of its neighbors. If the pixels are judged to be similar, they are merged; otherwise they are assigned to different regions. In Fig. 6c, results of applying an edge operator are shown. A 5×5 kernel was used in the edge operator, and a threshold was used to reject weak edges.

One important and useful class of image processing operations can be derived from mathematical morphology. The objective here is to come up with a set of basic spatial domain operators and approaches, which can process information embedded in images primarily on the basis of shapes. Typically, these operations are performed on binary images that may have resulted from applying some segmentation procedure. The two most common morphological operators are *dilation* and *erosion*. Dilation systematically expands the spatial extent of a blob in an image, whereas erosion systematically shrinks it. Algorithms use sequential application of these basic morphological operators. These are commonly used for eliminating noise. An example of such processing is presented in Fig. 7. The original image shown in Fig. 7a is a frame of flowing water, with a tiny fish egg appearing in the upper right side. This image is segmented using a thresholding algorithm, as shown in part (b). A segmentation procedure is successful in eliminating most of the background; however, numerous small noisy blobs are not eliminated. Finally as shown in part (c), by applying combined erosion followed by dilation operations (called an "opening" operation), all of the spurious noisy pixels are filtered out and the fish egg is successfully detected.

Image Processing Hardware

Efficient processing of images requires specialized hardware for image acquisition, storage, manipulation, and display. Advances in image processing hardware result from dramatic advances made in fields

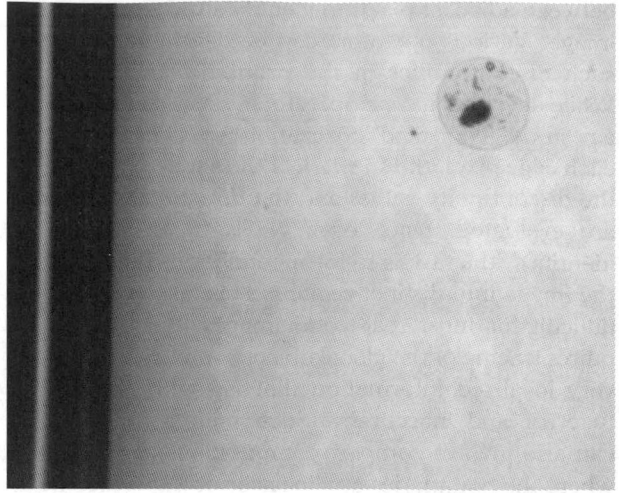

(a)

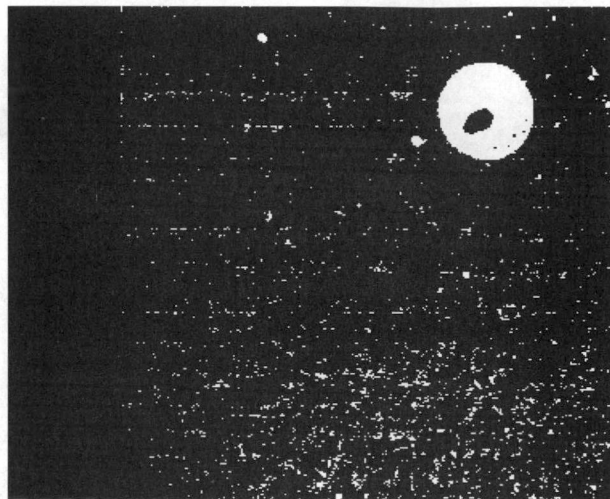

(b)

(c)

Figure 7. Morphological operators for image processing. Part (a) shows an image of flowing water with a very small fish egg appearing in the upper right side. Part (b) shows a segmented image using thresholding. Part (c) shows the utility of applying erosion and dilation operators to detect the fish egg accurately.

such as electro-optics, electronics, VLSI, material science, semiconductor processing, digital signal processing and computer architecture (*q.v.*). As these technologies advance, image processing hardware is able to acquire higher resolution images at faster rates, to do complex manipulations of images faster, to store and to access large amounts of image data quickly, and to display images with more dynamic range and resolution.

There are several ways to acquire an image, but the most popular image acquisition mechanism is the charge-coupled device (CCD) image sensor; the CMOS image sensor is also becoming popular. In both, photosensitive semiconductors arranged in a pixel matrix convert light energy falling on the sensor to electrical signals. Other sensor configurations used in special applications are linear arrays, commonly used in photograph scanners and Web inspection systems, and retinal arrays, used to simulate the arrangement of cones and rods in a human eye. Images acquired from these sensors are digitized by an analog-to-digital converter (ADC) on board the camera, or conditioned to some analog signal format. In the case of an analog video signal, most current video cameras output either 60 or 50 fields per second (one field contains all the even or odd horizontal lines of a frame), which is 30 or 25 frames per second. To process the image digitally, the image/video signal is stored in a high-speed memory device called the *frame grabber*. If the signal is analog, an ADC on the frame grabber first digitizes the signal. A typical frame size is 640×480 pixels. For each pixel, the number of bits associated with it can range from 1 to 24 bits. Typically, a monochrome image has 256 gray levels (8 bits) per pixel and color images have 16.7 million colors (24 bits: 8 for each of three color components) per pixel. In medical imaging, gray scale images use 10-bit (1024 levels) or 12-bit (4096 levels).

The image processing algorithms such as those described in the previous sections may run on a general-purpose CPU. With features such as ever-increasing clock speeds, floating-point operation pipelining (*q.v.*), and vector processing, today's general-purpose CPU can perform complex image processing very quickly. Applications that need more processing power use specialized image processing boards. These use DSP chips or pipeline processing to handle large images or many images rapidly. Image processing boards are used in many military and space applications, and in commercial applications such as medical or factory inspection systems. In applications where the image processing task is fixed, application-specific integrated circuit (ASIC) chips are used (*see* MICROCOMPUTER CHIP). Applications of image processing ASIC include digital cameras, color printers, and video compressing/decoding equipment.

Bibliography

1984. Ghiglia, D. C. "Space-invariant Deblurring Given *N* Independent Blurred Images of a Common Object," *Journal of Optical Society of America*, **1**, 398–402.
1985. Ghiglia, D. C., and Jakowatz, C. V. "Some Practical Aspects of Moving Object Deblurring in a Perspective Plane," *Applied Optics*, **24**, 22, 3830–3837.
1985. Levine, M. D. *Vision in Man and Machine*. New York: McGraw-Hill.
1989. Jain, A. K. *Fundamentals of Digital Image Processing*. Upper Saddle River, NJ: Prentice Hall.
1990. Trivedi, M. M. (ed.) *Selected Reprints on Digital Image Processing*. Bellingham, WA: Optical Engineering Press.
1990. Kasturi, R., and Trivedi, M. M. (eds.) *Image Analysis Applications*. New York: Marcel Dekker.
1995. Jain, R., Kasturi, R., and Schunck, B. G. *Machine Vision*. New York: McGraw-Hill.
1995. Sanz, J. L. C. *Image Technology: Advances in Image Processing, Multimedia, and Machine Vision*. Berlin: Springer-Verlag.
1999. Russ, J. C. *The Image Processing Handbook*, 3rd Ed. Boca Raton, FL: CRC Press.

Mohan M. Trivedi

IMPERATIVE LANGUAGES

See PROCEDURE-ORIENTED LANGUAGES.

INDEX REGISTER

For articles on related subjects *see* ADDRESSING; COMPUTER ARCHITECTURE; GENERAL REGISTER; INSTRUCTION SET; and REGISTER.

An *index register* is a storage element in a CPU (*q.v.*) most often used in the determination of an operand address, but which may be used for other purposes, mainly as a counter.

In constructing the address of an operand (*q.v.*), one can distinguish three basic parts. Consider, for example, the ADD instruction in an assembly language program that sums the elements of an array. The operand address of the ADD instruction is formed from:

1. The address of the base of the array (its first element) relative to the beginning of the program module. This relative address is known when the program is being written.

2. The memory address into which the program module is loaded. This address is known at load time.

3. The offset from the base of the array, which depends on the element that is currently being added and which is known only at execution time.

Index registers are normally involved with the last of the three parts of the address.

The address computed with an index register is referred to as the *effective address*. The index register

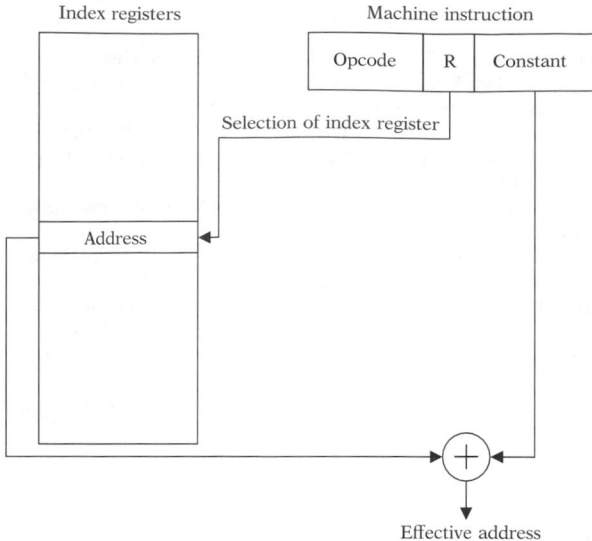

Figure 1. Example of the formation of an effective address.

accomplishes its role of forming the effective address in one of two ways: either the address is formed from a constant in the address field of an instruction plus a changing offset in the index register, or the address as a whole is contained in the index register. In the former case, shown in Fig. 1, the index register is used as a pointer into a data structure (*q.v.*), typically an array or record.

Index registers were introduced in the Manchester Mark I computer in 1949 (*see* MANCHESTER UNIVERSITY COMPUTERS). Without such registers for address computation, a program would have to modify its own instructions in order to loop through an array, changing the address contained in the instructions on each iteration. Although once a common practice, such self-modifying code is very error prone and can be difficult to debug.

The number of index registers in a machine, the number of index registers used in the formation of the effective address, and other attributes of the index registers vary with particular architectures. Thus, one finds machines with a single index register, one index register and one dedicated base register, multiple index registers or base registers, and machines in which the general registers may be used for indexing and base addressing.

Index registers are also used as counters. In this role, they are typically used as loop-control instructions that increment/decrement their values and test against a constant (typically zero) to cause a conditional branch. Some computers also possess the capability to increment or decrement registers as a side effect of data access using that register. In that case, the value by which the register is incremented or decremented usually depends on the byte-size of the operands being

processed—1 for 8-bit bytes (which typically hold characters), 2 for 16-bit integers, 4 for 32-bit integers, etc. (*see* GENERAL REGISTER).

Special care must be exercised in the use of index registers when the computer possesses an indirect addressing mode. In this case, the index register can be used either to compute the location of the indirect address (*pre-indexing*) or as an offset to the indirect address itself (*post-indexing*). When more than one index register is involved in the formation of the effective address, both pre- and post-indexing may be present. Again, the availability of either of the modes varies widely among different machines, although an indirect addressing mode is generally not found in RISC (*q.v.*) processors.

Bibliography

2000. Murdocca, M. *Principles of Computer Architecture.* Upper Saddle River, NJ: Prentice Hall.

Gideon Frieder

INFORMATICS

See COMPUTER SCIENCE; and INFORMATION SCIENCE.

INFORMATION ACCESS

For articles on related subjects *see* INTERNET; LEGAL ASPECTS OF COMPUTING; NETWORKS, COMPUTER; SOCIAL SCIENCE APPLICATIONS; SOCIETY, COMPUTERS IN; and WORLD WIDE WEB.

Information access refers to the ability to keep watch on how governments govern and the right to peruse freely the facts and figures that officials have collected about everything from annual rainfall to budget expenditures to criminal records. The definition of information access extends to our desire to control and check data about ourselves and our families. Libraries and other groups strive to see that people can acquire knowledge whatever their financial circumstances, or regardless of their geographical or physical handicaps. Computers can promote access in all these areas.

The above threads have captured the center stage of much of the debate about computers and digitally stored information. This article will address only the subject of access to government information.

Freedom of Information Acts (FOIA)

Freedom of Information is an issue of enormous significance. The underlying philosophy of this concept recognizes that the public, with a common interest in the common good, has "the right to know." Those who believe in the right to know hold that an informed public is a safeguard against governmental abuse of power; yet, no matter how open a government aspires to be, it can hardly avoid reining in access to and release of information in order to govern. For any nation accustomed to freedoms such as the freedom of speech or religion, labeling legislation a freedom of information law gives it an emotional boost that the word "access" fails to provide.

Sweden has had a right of access since 1766. Finland passed its freedom of information law in 1951, Denmark in 1964. When the US federal government adopted a Freedom of Information Act (FOIA) in 1966, it applied only to paper records. Americans were introduced to electronic FOIA issues during the Iran–Contra trials in the 1980s when the backup tapes of email messages became pivotal evidence in a major trial. The Electronic Freedom of Information Act Amendments of 1996 were signed into law by President Clinton, and the stated intent of the legislation was to "bring the FOIA into the electronic age."

On 20 January 1999 the European Commission adopted a Green Paper entitled "Public Sector Information: A key resource for Europe." It aims at discussing how the information gathered by government departments and other public bodies can be used to increase transparency of public sector information throughout Europe, overcome regulatory and technical barriers, and allow citizens to exploit Europe's information potential to the full. Some of the problems that will be discussed are highlighted by the American experience described below.

The American Experience

Each of the 50 states of the USA has its own FOIA legislation, so a citizen's right of access to records very much depends on where she or he lives. In Illinois a record stored in electronic form is considered an official public record, a clarification that other states have not made. To add another dimension, the law in the USA can vary from county to county. Usually, electronic records are subject to the same exemptions from disclosure under open records laws as paper records, although other factors do intrude.

Confrontations result in lawsuits, legislative action, and policy decisions, and these struggles reach widely varying conclusions in different states, cities, and agencies. Can people have access to the hard drives of the computers of public officials? In what form will the information be released? Whether or not a requester can demand that information be provided as a computer printout, a computer tape, a disk, or in some other form varies by state. Of course, the format can render data either very useful or practically worthless. Searching is far easier in electronic format, as is manipulating data.

Legislatures have begun to address the issue of *data manipulation*. When an agency wants to restrict access to information, it may say that manipulating database information is "creating" a new record, which is often not required by law. But the very function of a database is to permit users to manipulate data and information. Thus, restricting access to the raw data in a usable form appears to work against the spirit of the freedom of information laws.

There are disputes over whether requesters may obtain copies of specific software to read coded electronic records. Copyright issues arise when requesters seek certain types of software. Commercial software is privately produced and licensed to the government, as with any other license. Most states that have chosen to regulate access to software explicitly exempt their software from their public records statutes, regardless of whether the program is commercial or agency-written. Thus, the software does not need to be released to the requester. Without the software, the data may be rendered useless.

Fees for computer time, programming time, printouts, supplies, labor, and overhead are often assessed against the requester. The US National League of Cities resolved in December 1993 that cities and towns should set higher fees for access to electronically stored public information than for providing paper copies, to offset the costs of developing better computer systems. Some officials attempt to recoup more than costs, trying to use electronic records to generate revenue.

Common reasons that agencies give for restricting access to electronic databases are that:

1. The same material already exists in printed documents.

2. Public and private information are mixed together in the database.

3. The open records law does not require the agency to "create" a new record by running a specific search or program.

4. Agency programmers will be prevented from performing their "real" duties.

5. Software is proprietary or copyrighted and thus cannot be distributed.

One of the more popular types of systems is the Geographic Information System (GIS–*q.v.*), which can overlay large databases with regional maps. A political party might use a GIS to sketch future district lines (*see* POLITICAL APPLICATIONS); a mail-order house might use a GIS to target potential customers. The substantive conflicts over GIS access involve fees and the desire of various governmental bodies to turn these systems into revenue-producers. GIS systems are specifically exempted from many state FOIAs. The GIS issue points out how computer technology is eliminating the distinctions between government reports, publications, databases, and records.

Privatization of Government Information

Today, most of Washington DC's vast storehouse of documents are created, stored, and disseminated electronically. The number of federal electronic publications is increasing and the number of federal documents printed on paper is decreasing. The California Legislature's Assembly Bill 1624 gives the public electronic access to almost all public information about legislation in process, all current state statutes and the entire California Constitution.

The Environmental Working Group (EWG) in the USA has filed FOIA requests for data in electronic form and converted 9-track tapes into programs that allow anyone who can click a mouse to scan numerous details about the economy and the environment in every county, congressional district, and state in the nation. For example, EWG tracked farm subsidy payments flowing into the 50 most populous cities in the nation and found that over the past decade, 1.6 million agriculture subsidy checks worth more than $1.3 billion were sent to a handful of absentee owners, corporations, and other "farmers" who reside in the middle of the country's biggest cities.

Computer technology has made possible the rapid dissemination of government information, in some instances at substantial cost savings, although there are boulders in the stream of information flow. Some agencies provide computer terminals for public use. Others post printouts of electronic files for public inspection. However, businesses and governments may look to profit from public information.

Traditionally, the US government encouraged the distribution of its publications at little or no cost to the general public through the Government Printing Office and the Depository Library Program. The US Congress passed the GPO Access Act in 1994, and the Government Printing Office now provides online access to several thousand government documents, including the Federal Register and the Congressional Record.

The competing interests of the public information providers and the private, for-profit information businesses are often at odds. Agencies quite naturally want control over their own data. Some private corporations claim ownership of US court legal decisions because they have compiled and "printed" them, thereby selling government data for enormous gain. Consumer groups fight firms like West Publishing over the pricing

and use of WestLaw, an online database of US laws (*see* LEGAL APPLICATIONS). The stakes are higher when information is in digital format, because the ease of reuse makes the information more valuable.

Advances in information technology make it more difficult to maintain clear policies. Information laws of all types, such as those relating to dissemination and archival preservation, soon become obsolete. What was once on paper is now in digital form. Computer networks replace the diskettes (*q.v.*) that replaced floppies and so on. Technology advances faster than the law. Security and privacy concerns impact FOIA uses as well.

Now that Europe is taking steps to break down barriers to the open sharing of public information, it is more necessary than ever to examine the US experience with government information and learn from the tensions inherent in this debate.

Bibliography

1995. Gannon, E. "Solving Environmental Problems with Information Technology," *CPSR Newsletter*, **13**, 2, 9–10.
1995. Morrissey, D. H. "Will Washington Share its Electronic Bounty?," *CPSR Newsletter*, **13**, 2, 5–8.
1996. Gellman, R. "The American Model of Access to and Dissemination of Public Information and Access to Public Information: A Key to Commercial Growth and Electronic Democracy," *Conference*, Stockholm, 27–28 June.
Reporters Committee for Freedom of the Press. *Access to Electronic Records*. 1101 Wilson Boulevard, Suite 1910, Arlington, VA 22209, USA.

Marsha Woodbury

INFORMATION-BASED COMPLEXITY

For articles on related subjects *see* ALGORITHMS, DESIGN AND CLASSIFICATION OF; COMPUTATIONAL COMPLEXITY; MONTE CARLO METHOD; and NP-COMPLETE PROBLEMS.

Many of the mathematical models used in fields such as the physical sciences, engineering, economics, and mathematical finance use continuous mathematical models. These models typically require the numerical solution of multivariate problems (often in a very large number of variables) such as integrals, ordinary and partial differential equations (*q.v.*), optimization, approximation, integral equations, and nonlinear equations. The study of the computational complexity of continuous mathematical problems is called *information-based complexity* (IBC). This is a branch of computational complexity (*q.v.*) which studies the minimal computer resources (typically time or space) needed to solve mathematically posed problems.

Traub and Werschulz (1998) provide an expository introduction to the theory and applications of IBC with a bibliography of over 400 recent papers and books.

A general formulation and extensive bibliography can be found in Traub, Wasilkowski, and Woźniakowski (1988).

Computational Complexity of Integration

We illustrate some of the important ideas of information-based complexity with the example of univariate integration. (To see how IBC can be used for the numerical computation of the very high dimensional integrals occurring in practice, see the section on mathematical finance below.) Consider the computation of $\int_0^1 f(x)\,dx$. For "most" integrands, this integral cannot be computed symbolically. Therefore, we must integrate numerically. All we can enter into the computer are some numbers that represent $f(x)$. Often, the available information is the values of f at a number of points; these values may be obtained from a program which evaluates $f(x)$. This information is *partial* because there are many integrands that are indistinguishable using this information. If the information has errors (due, for example, to roundoff errors—*q.v.*), it is *contaminated*. It is clear that partial or contaminated information causes an uncertainty, say ε, in the integral. This uncertainty is intrinsic and caused by the limited information. Furthermore, we assume that each item of information is priced (i.e. has a cost).

To introduce computational complexity, we first define the *model of computation*. The model of computation states which operations are permitted and how much they cost. The model of computation is based on two assumptions:

1. We can perform arithmetic operations and comparisons on real numbers at unit cost.

2. We can perform an information operation at cost c.

We comment on these assumptions. The *real number model* (Assumption 1) is used as an abstraction of the floating-point model typically used in scientific computation (*see* ARITHMETIC, COMPUTER). Except for the possible effect of roundoff errors and numerical stability, complexity results will be the same in these two models.

The real number model should be contrasted with the *Turing Machine* (*q.v.*) *model* typically used for discrete problems. The cost of an operation in a Turing Machine model depends on the size of the operands, which is one of the reasons that we use the real number model. For a full discussion of the pros and cons of the Turing Machine and the real number models see Traub and Werschulz (1998, Chapter 8). Whether the real number or Turing Machine model is used can make an enormous difference. For example, Kachian showed that linear programming is a polynomial time problem

in the Turing Machine model. In 1981, Traub and Woźniakowski showed that Kachian's algorithm is not polynomial in the real number model and conjectured that linear programming is not polynomial in this model. This conjecture is still open.

In Assumption 2, c is typically much larger than 1. The purpose of information operations is to replace the input by a finite set of numbers. For integration, the information operations are typically function evaluations.

A *combinatorial algorithm* is any procedure for approximating the integral using the available information. Any such algorithm must have error at least as large as the intrinsic uncertainty. The *computational complexity* of the integration problem is the minimal cost of computing the integral to within error ε. The *information complexity* and the *combinatorial complexity* of the integration problem are the minimal information and combinatory cost of calculating the integral to within error ε.

The concept of computational complexity permits us to introduce the fundamental concepts of optimal information and optimal algorithm. Information and an algorithm that uses the information are called *optimal information* and an *optimal algorithm* if the error of the approximation is at most ε and the cost of computing the approximation equals the computational complexity.

General Formulation

We have used the integration example to introduce the basic concepts of IBC. Generally, IBC is characterized by three assumptions, namely that information is *partial*, *contaminated* and *priced*. A general formulation and extensive bibliography may be found in Traub, Wasilkowski, and Woźniakowski (1988).

IBC has been used for numerous problems, including partial differential equations, path integrals, approximations, nonlinear optimization, and integral equations. There has also been some work on finite-dimensional problems such as large linear systems and eigenvalue problems, as well as the discrete problem of synchronizing clocks in a distributed system (*q.v.*). Fields where IBC has been applied include economics, computer graphics (*q.v.*), computer vision (*q.v.*), control theory, and mathematical finance.

Intractable Problems

In applications, the inputs are often multivariate functions. For example, we might want to integrate a function of d variables. If the smoothness of the class of inputs is r, then to guarantee an error of at most ε,

$$\text{comp}^{\text{wor-det}}(\varepsilon) = \Theta(\varepsilon^{-d/r}).$$

The symbol on the left-hand side indicates this is the complexity in the worst-case deterministic setting. Worst case means that we guarantee an error of at most ε for every input in a class of inputs. The capital theta notation means that the upper and lower bounds on the computational complexity differ by at most a factor independent of ε.

We comment on this result:

1. It has been proven to hold for many problems, including integration, approximation, nonlinear optimization, systems of nonlinear equations, linear elliptic differential equations, and Fredholm integral equations of the second kind.

2. For ε and r fixed, the complexity is exponential in d.

3. For fixed values of the smoothness r and the error threshold ε, the complexity depends exponentially on the dimension. In 1957, Richard Bellman called exponential dependence on dimension the *curse of dimensionality*. This was based on experience, not theorems of computational complexity. All the problems listed in point 1 suffer from this curse in the worst-case deterministic setting.

4. In complexity theory we say that a problem with this complexity is *intractable*. We can regard the dimension as the *size* of input. (The number of variables and dimension are used interchangeably.) This may be contrasted with discrete problems, where the size of the input is typically the number of objects.

5. The worst case deterministic setting is the same as the one used in the theory of *NP-complete* problems.

6. In IBC we are often able to obtain tight complexity bounds. This may be contrasted with combinatorial problems such as the traveling salesman problem (*see* COMPUTATIONAL COMPLEXITY and NP-COMPLETE PROBLEMS) where only a complexity hierarchy is available and it is usually not known if problems have, say, polynomial or exponential complexity. Since the information in IBC is partial and/or contaminated we are able to obtain lower bounds using adversary arguments at the information level. This is why this field is called *information-based complexity*.

7. However, there are IBC problems where the combinatorial complexity dominates the information complexity and we cannot obtain tight complexity bounds. One example is a problem of decentralized control. Papadimitriou and Tsitsiklis have shown that the information complexity is a polynomial in $1/\varepsilon$ but that the combinatorial complexity is a

polynomial in $1/\varepsilon$ if and only if $P = NP$ (*see* NP-COMPLETE PROBLEMS).

8. Even for rather small values of d, the problem may be very hard. For example, let $\varepsilon = 10^{-8}$ (single-precision), $r = 1$, $d = 3$. Then the complexity for multivariate integration is proportional to 10^{24} function evaluations.

Very high-dimensional problems occur in supercomputing and in the foundations of physics. For example, computational chemistry, computational design of pharmaceuticals, and computational metallurgy involve computation with huge numbers of particles. Economic modeling can involve a large number of variables. High-dimensional problems occur in mathematical finance. Path integrals, which are of great importance in physics, are infinite-dimensional, and therefore invite high-dimensional approximations.

This motivates our interest in breaking the curse of dimensionality. Since this is a complexity result, we cannot get around it by a clever algorithm. We can try to break the curse by settling for a stochastic assurance rather than a worst-case deterministic assurance. Examples of stochastic assurance are provided by the randomized and average case settings which we consider in turn. We can also try to break the curse by changing the class of the inputs; we will use mathematical finance to illustrate this.

Randomization

The first significant use of randomization was the Monte Carlo method (*q.v.*), introduced in the 1940s. As indicated above, multivariate integration is exponential in dimension in a deterministic setting, even if the integrand is evaluated at optimal points. However, if the integrand is sampled at random points,

$$\text{comp}^{\text{wor-ran}}(\varepsilon) = \Theta(\varepsilon^{-2}).$$

The symbol on the left-hand side indicates this is the complexity in the worst-case randomized setting.

This is a truly remarkable result. If one evaluates at random rather than at optimal deterministic points, the complexity is independent of the number of variables d! Furthermore, this holds even if the class of integrands consists of functions that are only continuous (i.e. $r = 0$). For this class, $\text{comp}^{\text{wor-det}}(\varepsilon) = \infty$.

Thus, randomization can be very powerful for continuous problem, just as for discrete problems (*see* COMPUTATIONAL COMPLEXITY). Not all intractable problems can be broken by using randomization; it is an open question to characterize the class of problems which can be.

Average Case

Another way we can try to break intractability is to settle for an average case assurance. That is, we guarantee that the *expected* error is at most ε and the computational complexity is the minimal *expected* cost.

Recall that for multivariate integration

$$\text{comp}^{\text{wor-det}}(\varepsilon) = \Theta(\varepsilon^{-d/r})$$

A question that was open for 20 years, until settled by Woźniakowski in 1991, is the complexity of integration in the average case deterministic setting. Let the class of inputs be continuous functions, equipped with the Wiener measure. (The Wiener measure is a special kind of Gaussian measure, which is a generalization of a Gaussian distribution.) Let the domain of integration be the unit cube in d dimensions. Woźniakowski showed that

$$\text{comp}^{\text{avg-det}}(\varepsilon) = \Theta(\varepsilon^{-1}[\log \varepsilon^{-1}]^{[(d-1)/2]}).$$

Woźniakowski also proved that *quasi-Monte Carlo* algorithms were optimal, on average. Despite their name, these algorithms are completely deterministic.

It is an open question to characterize the class of problems for which intractability is broken by the average case setting.

Mathematical Finance

We use the important area of mathematical finance to illustrate the complexity issues discussed above and to see how problems in this area force us to consider new issues. The valuation of financial instruments often requires the calculation of very high-dimensional integrals. Dimensions of 360 and higher are not unusual.

Furthermore, since the integrals can be very complicated, requiring between 10^5 and 10^6 floating-point operations per integrand evaluation, it is important to minimize the number of evaluations.

What does complexity theory tell us about the computation of high-dimensional integrals? Clearly we cannot insist on a worst-case deterministic guarantee for integrals of such high dimension. During the last 20 years Monte Carlo methods have been used. Using Monte Carlo we can compute the integrals to within an expected error of ε with ε^{-2} function evaluations. Can we do better? Woźniakowski showed that we can compute the integral using quasi-Monte Carlo methods to within an expected error of ε (where the expectation is with respect to the measure on the space of integrands), using just ε^{-1} function evaluations times the polylog factor $[\log \varepsilon^{-1}]^{[(d-1)/2]}$.

For d fixed and ε tending to zero, quasi-Monte Carlo converges faster than Monte Carlo. But in mathematical finance ε is typically between 10^{-2} and 10^{-4}, which is not very small, and the dimension d is huge, say, 360 or higher. For such values of d the polylog factor looks ominous. Yet computer experimentation on real-world financial problems (*see* Traub and Paskov, 1995), revealed that quasi-Monte Carlo beats Monte Carlo consistently and by large margins.

The existing theory does not explain the superiority of quasi-Monte Carlo for problems of mathematical finance. What property characterizes the integrands? They are highly nonisotropic; that is, some variables are far more important than others. This property is formalized by Sloan and Woźniakowski (1998), who proved the existence of quasi-Monte Carlo methods whose convergence is independent of the dimension for integrands with this property. Furthermore, this good convergence holds even with a worst-case deterministic guarantee. We see that an alternative to changing the setting in order to avoid the curse of dimensionality is to change the set of inputs; in this application, the set of integrands. *See* Traub and Werschulz (1998, Chapter 4) for a survey of high-dimensional integration and mathematical finance.

Computational Complexity for Continuous Problems with Complete Information

We briefly discuss a complexity theory for continuous combinatorial problems; see Blum, Cucker, Shub, and Smale (1998). They consider continuous problems whose inputs are characterized by a finite number of parameters. Thus, they can assume that information is complete and exact. They adopt the real number model. One of their results is that the problem of determining whether a system of n real polynomials of degree at most 4 has a real zero is NP-complete.

Fig. 1 depicts the relation between IBC and other branches of computational complexity.

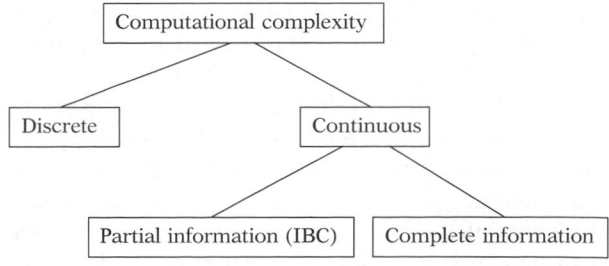

Figure 1. Structure of computational complexity.

Bibliography

1988. Traub, J. F., Wasilkowski, G. W., and Woźniakowski, H. *Information-Based Complexity.* New York: Academic Press.

1991. Werschulz, A. G. *The Computational Complexity of Differential and Integral Equations: An Information-Based Approach.* New York: Oxford University Press.

1995. Traub, J. F. and Paskov, S. "Faster Valuation of Financial Derivatives," *Journal of Portfolio Management,* **22**, *1*, 113–120.

1996. Plaskota, L. *Noisy Information and Computational Complexity.* Cambridge: Cambridge University Press.

1998. Blum, L., Cucker, F., Shub, M., and Smale, S. *Complexity and Real Computation.* New York: Springer-Verlag.

1998. Sloan, I., and Woźniakowski, H. "When are Quasi-Monte Carlo Algorithms Efficient for High Dimensional Integrals?" *Journal of Complexity,* **14**, *1*, 1–33.

1998. Traub, J. F. and Werschulz, A. G. *Complexity and Information.* Cambridge: Cambridge University Press.

1999. Traub, J. F. "A Continuous Model of Computation," *Physics Today,* **52**, *5* (May), 39–43.

Joseph F. Traub

INFORMATION HIDING

For articles on related subjects *see* ABSTRACT DATA TYPE; CLASS; DATA STRUCTURES; ENCAPSULATION; MODULAR PROGRAMMING; OBJECT-ORIENTED PROGRAMMING; SOFTWARE REUSE; and TRANSPARENCY.

Three major problems in developing complex software systems are:

◆ managing complexity,

◆ decomposing the task of writing software into work assignments (often called modules) for programmers, especially work assignments that may be pursued independently, and

◆ preparing for and accommodating change.

Information hiding, a principle used to organize software into modules, is a solution to these problems. An information-hiding design organizes software into modules that are intended to be independently implementable, changeable, and understandable. The objectives are to produce software that accommodates change and to manage complexity during both development and maintenance.

The information hiding principle states that independently-changeable information should be hidden (or encapsulated—*see* ENCAPSULATION) in independently changeable modules. Information that is hidden in a module, often known as the *secret* of the module, typically includes decisions such as data structures, hardware characteristics, and behavioral requirements. Since modules are work assignments, a decision has been hidden successfully if it can be revised without requiring a change to other work assignments.

We illustrate the principle using a stack (*q.v.*). In one formulation of a stack as an information hiding module, the stack's secret is the data structure used to represent its state and the algorithms used to manipulate the data structure. Part of the work assignment that constitutes the module is the decision of what this data structure should be, e.g. an array or a linear list. If properly designed, the stack module conceals the decision, and changing its implementation from array to list can be done independently of changes in any of the programs that use the stack.

The designer of an information hiding module seeks to provide services to the module's users without revealing the module's secret. The module provides its services through an interface that provides sole access to the module, analogous to a black box that has a set of switches that the user may operate and a set of dials that the user may observe. The device can be used without knowing how its internals operate. Much as the owner of a wristwatch need not know how the watch's mechanism operates in order to read or set it, the user of the services of an information hiding module need not know how those services are programmed in order to use them. Our stack module need only provide to its users an interface that allows them to push items onto the stack, pop items from the stack, read the top item on the stack, and determine how many items are in the stack. These operations and their user-visible behavior provide a stack abstraction to the module's users.

Designers who use information hiding need to make explicit what's hidden and what's not when designing their modular structure and the interface to each module. *See* Britton *et al.* (1981) and Clements *et al.* (1994) for examples of documentation that designers may use to help make their intentions clear.

Ideally, the internal structure of an information hiding module can be understood and verified without considering the implementation details of other modules. Limiting the information required to understand the implementation to the internals of the module simplifies verification and makes software easier to understand and change. For the stack, the verifier must show that the implementation obeys the characteristic behavior of a stack, i.e. that a push followed by a pop does not change the state of the stack.

Because modules are work assignments, the assumptions that the programmer of one module may make about another module form the interface between the two. Those assumptions may be embodied in a variety of mechanisms, such as procedures that a user may call, messages and signals that a module may send or receive, or macros that users may include in their own programs. *See* Britton *et al.* (1981) for guidelines for designing such interfaces and for example interface specifications. For the stack, the module may offer to its users services called PUSH, POP, TOP, and DEPTH. Note that the particular mechanisms used by a module to offer its services may be a part of the module's secret.

The specification of a module's interface must include the complete set of assumptions that the module's users need to make about it. Such assumptions include both the syntax used to invoke the module's services and the semantics of those services. The semantics includes the externally visible effects of invoking the module's services (including exceptions that may result) and specifications for the types of input and output supplied to and by the module.

Although the use of information hiding may be seen in the design of many software systems, the earliest description of the principle was given by Parnas (1972). A more detailed explanation of its systematic use in the design of complex systems may be found in Clements *et al.* (1985).

Information hiding is the basis for design methods wherein software is organized into objects that perform services for each other without being dependent on their implementations. Each object may be considered an implementation of an information hiding module; many objects of the same type may be implementations of the same module. The principle is also the basis for organizing the data used by a program into abstract data types. The secret of an information hiding module that implements an abstract data type is the representation of the data and the way that operations on the data are implemented. The stack may be considered to be an abstract data type whose data representation is hidden, and whose operations are PUSH, POP, TOP, and DEPTH.

A number of programming languages provide support for creating and using information hiding modules and their interfaces. Examples include classes in languages such as Java and C++, Ada packages, modules in the Modula family of languages, ML's signatures and structures, and Haskell's type classes. In each case, the language separates the specification of the syntax of invocation of a module's operations from the specification of their implementation. They typically have distinct declarations of the public interface and of the private implementation. Unfortunately, few languages provide support for specifying the semantics of the module's services other than in comment form. The difficult task of creating those specifications and checking them for consistency and completeness is left to the developers and users of the software. No special language is needed to apply information hiding. Early examples were done in Fortran and assembly language.

Applying information hiding to organize software has the benefits of encouraging the developer to design software that is changeable and understandable one part at a time, but also has potential drawbacks. Preserving the secret of a module requires that its services be available only through its interface. Progress through a computation may require the use of the services of many different modules. When procedures or methods are used as the only interface mechanism, considerable overhead may be incurred in switching among different modules. A solution often suggested to this problem is to use inline procedures or macros (*q.v.*), rather than closed subroutines, as an interface mechanism.

Where the number of modules in a system is large, it pays to introduce a hierarchical structure for organizing them (Clements *et al.*, 1985). One possible hierarchy is described in Clements *et al.* (1985) and is governed by the relation "part of," i.e. lower level modules are part of higher level modules, or equivalently, higher level modules are the union of their submodules (Parnas, 1974). The "part of" relation defines a design decomposition. Put another way, the information hidden by a higher level module is distributed among lower level modules. For example, a module whose secret is the representation of data structures could be decomposed into submodules, one of which has as its secret the representation of stacks. The hierarchy provides a road map that guides developers and maintainers when they make changes to the software.

A different design hierarchy based on information hiding is defined by the "is-a" relation and is commonly known as the class hierarchy in object-oriented programming. In this instance we consider a class to be an implementation of an information hiding module. A stack is a data structure and a queue is a data structure; accordingly, the class "data structure" might have "stack" and "queue" subclasses.

Although an information hiding decomposition makes clear what decisions are easy to change, it is not a complete design description. Concerns such as the run time operation of a system, the organization of a system into subsets, or the flow of data through a system are better addressed by examining other design structures.

Information hiding is another view of two other software design principles: separation of concerns and abstraction. It is one way to separate concerns, so that developers and maintainers may concentrate on one concern at a time, and it is a means for achieving abstraction, since an information hiding module provides its users with an abstraction of the decision that it hides.

Bibliography

1972. Parnas, D. L. "On the Criteria to be Used in Decomposing a System into Modules," *CACM*, **15**, *12*, 1053–1058.

1974. Parnas, D. L. "On a 'Buzzword': Hierarchical Structure," *Proc. IFIPS Congress*, 336–339. Amsterdam: North Holland.

1981. Britton, K. H., Parker, R. A., and Parnas, D. L. "A Procedure for Designing Abstract Interfaces for Device Interface Modules," *Proc. 5th International Conference on Software Engineering*, 195–204.

1985. Clements, P. C., Parnas, D. L., and Weiss, D. M. "The Modular Structure of Complex Systems," *IEEE Trans. on Software Engineering*, **SE-4**, *3*, 259–266.

1997. Anderton, R. (ed.) *Information Hiding: 1st International Workshop, Cambridge, UK, May 30–June 1, 1996: Proceedings* (Lecture Notes in Computer Science 1174). New York: Springer-Verlag.

David M. Weiss

INFORMATION PROCESSING

> For articles on related subjects *see* ACCESS METHODS; ARTIFICIAL INTELLIGENCE; COGNITIVE SCIENCE; DATA MINING; DATABASE MANAGEMENT SYSTEM; INFORMATION RETRIEVAL; INFORMATION SYSTEMS; INFORMATION THEORY; MANAGEMENT INFORMATION SYSTEMS; and SYMBOL MANIPULATION.

Information processing might, not inaccurately, be defined as "what computers do." In fact, the broadest professional organization concerned with computer science is named the International Federation for Information Processing.

For information to be processed by a computer or by any other information processing system, it must somehow be represented or symbolized. Hence information processing is essentially synonymous with symbol manipulation, and the entire discussion in this Encyclopedia of symbol manipulation could be readily retitled "information processing." In this article, we will approach the topic of information processing in a somewhat more philosophical, less technical, vein than in the article SYMBOL MANIPULATION.

The phrase "information processing" is often used in preference to "computation" or "data processing" to emphasize the generality of computers—the fact that they are in no way limited to manipulating just symbols that designate numbers, but can operate in any domain, numerical or nonnumerical, where information is represented in symbolic form. The term "information," in turn, carries allusions to the Shannon–Wiener theory of selective information, which emphasizes the role of symbol structures as designating one particular state of affairs out of some larger set of possible states. Thus, if we are dealing with the class of flowers, the symbol "rose" conveys the information that we are concerned with a particular subclass of that class.

Information has other aspects besides the selective aspect emphasized in information theory. However, this selective aspect is closely connected with the way in which information is used by information processing systems such as computers. Information processing systems are capable of executing a *conditional branch* or transfer operation. The conditional branch operation detects which of several different states of affairs prevails (e.g. which of several symbol structures is stored in the working memory of the computer), and sends the subsequent computation along different paths depending on which state of affairs is detected. Thus, on the basis of the selective information available to it, the information processing system behaves in a selective, or informed, fashion.

The use of selective information by conditional branch processes lies at the root of everything complex or clever that a computer can do. In the simplest case, the conditional branch detects when an iteration is done (e.g. when the adding of a column of figures has been completed), and transfers control to the next process. (It was with this use in mind that Babbage (*q.v.*) first invented the conditional branch.) In more complex situations, conditional branching processes enable information processing systems to engage in all kinds of intelligent problem-solving behaviors (whether the intelligence be artificial or natural).

Effective information processing often depends crucially on substituting a high degree of selectivity (that is, a high degree of dependence on selective information) for a large amount of brute-force search through immense spaces of possible alternatives. Popular accounts of the computer often emphasize the impressive speed of its basic arithmetic processes and the vast number of computations it can perform in a short time. In actual fact, apart from "number crunching" applications, the arithmetic speed of the computer is far less important than its capability for selectivity, using information interpreted by the conditional branch processes.

Empirical research on human chess-playing skill, for example, shows that masters do not explore more alternatives than ordinary players—and probably do not even usually look more moves ahead. Instead, their superior performance almost certainly rests on looking at the *right* things—i.e. using information effectively to explore selectively. It is sometimes supposed that, in contrast, computer chess programs, like Deep Blue, which successfully challenged the World Champion, Garry Kasparov, succeed by virtue of their sheer computation power (*see* COMPUTER CHESS). This is a misapprehension, for Deep Blue proceeds very selectively, examining at most, only a few billion from among the trillion trillion, or more, branches in the game tree. It accomplishes this selectivity, as human grandmasters do, by its use of a vast store of chess knowledge of opening moves, of the relative value of different positions, and of the conditions under which particular strategies are powerful. So the choice is not computational power *or* knowledge, but varying combinations of the two.

We can illustrate this trade-off between selectivity and speed in information processing by two examples: programs for retrieving information from large stores, and programs for solving problems.

Information Retrieval

Whenever we have a large store of data—say, a set of customer records—it becomes expensive to search the entire store sequentially to find a particular piece of data. We would like, instead, to be able to go directly to the point where the data is to be found and to extract it without a lengthy search. A memory that allows us to do this is often called "random access." A better description for it is "addressable, direct access," for there is nothing random about the way in which we approach it. The store is to be *addressable* so that each record in it can be designated, or pointed to, by a symbolized address (name). It is to have *direct access* so that the information processor can be switched to read the desired record directly, once its name is known, without requiring a search.

Now it is well known that to select a particular item from a set of n items requires approximately $\log_2 n$ binary switching operations (*see* SEARCHING). Suppose we have a store of 64 records. Since $64 = 2^6$, we can use strings of 6 binary digits each (e.g. 100110) to provide distinct addresses for the 64 records. An appropriate switching device would have to perform six switching operations—one for each digit—to select a desired record. With such a system, the number of switching operations required to select a record increases only with the logarithm of the number of records—6 binary operations, as we have seen, for 64 records; 10 operations for 1,024 records; and 20 operations for more than a million records.

An unindexed book (or a nonalphabetized encyclopedia) frustrates human information processors because it provides no means to find a desired item of information without linear search. Thick books are proportionately more frustrating in this respect than thin books. A good index converts the book into an addressable, direct access store. The cost of retrieving an item can now be expected to increase only with the logarithm of the size of the book.

The coming of the World Wide Web (*q.v.*) has brought home dramatically the absolute necessity for selectiv-ity in search. The scarce resource is no longer information, but time for people (or machines) to attend to it. Modern large databases will retain their utility only to the extent that we design engines that can apply intelligence to search with great selectivity, and to return only those stored items that are most relevant to the inquiry.

Problem Solving

To illustrate how information permits selectivity in solving problems, we will examine a trivially simple example.

How do we use an information processor to solve this arithmetic equation:

$$5X + 3 = 2X + 7$$

If we depended only on the processor's speed, we might try a simple *generate-and-test* method: Generate various values of X and substitute them in the equation: then test whether the two sides are equal. The futility of this approach is evident as soon as we ask, "Over what class of values shall we generate—integers, rational numbers, real numbers—and in what order?" Of course a very fast computer might solve such problems in a reasonable time, if only problems involving small numbers were presented and possible solutions involving fractions with small numerators and denominators were generated first.

A second approach might be to write the equation as

$$5X + 3 - 2X - 7 = 0$$

Then we could generate a possible solution and test to find if it gave a positive or negative value to the left side. If the values were positive, this information, communicated to the generator, could cause it to generate next a smaller possible solution or, if the values were negative, a larger solution. In this way, the feedback of information could guide the generator to the correct solution by a process of successive approximations. Computational algorithms that employ successive approximations use information in this general way to reduce the amount of search.

Of course, a far more effective way to solve the original equation is to observe that the solution is an expression of the form $X = K$, with no constant on the left side, no term in X on the right side, and X having unity as its coefficient. By subtracting 3 from both sides of the original equation, then subtracting $2X$ from both sides, and then dividing the resulting equation through by 3, we obtain the final result, $X = 4/3$, without any search whatsoever. This was accomplished by comparing the given equation with the form of the desired solution, and taking specific actions to bring it into the desired form based on the specific differences noted. Thus, when the constant 3 is found on the left side, where no constant is wanted, it is removed by subtracting 3 from both sides.

At each step, specific information extracted from the problem expression is used to choose a specific action that will alter the expression in the desired way. Since all the required selectivity is provided by the information embedded in the given symbolic expression, no search is required to find the answer. The safe can be opened, so to speak, by reading off the correct combination rather than by spinning the dials to try different settings. Simple as it is, this example is a prototype for the most sophisticated artificial intelligence system, and contains in rudimentary form the information processes needed for carrying out *means–ends analysis*. (Means–ends analysis involves deleting one or more differences between an actual and a desired situation and then applying operators to reduce one or more of the remaining differences as described in the algebra example above.)

A basic reason, then, why we refer to computers as information processors is that they not only have to provide us with information—by performing a numerical computation, retrieving data from a store, or in some other way—but also to respond to new information, enabling them to substitute a high degree of selectivity for speed in search as a means of solving problems.

Bibliography

1968. Minsky, M. (ed.) *Semantic Information Processing.* Cambridge, MA: MIT Press.
1972. Newell, A., and Simon, H. A. *Human Problem Solving,* Ch. 4. Upper Saddle River, NJ: Prentice Hall.
1995. Simon, H. A. "Machine as Mind," in *Android Epistemology* (eds. M. K. Ford, C. Glymour, and P. J. Hayes). Menlo Park, CA: AAAI/MIT Press.

Herbert A. Simon

INFORMATION RETRIEVAL

For articles on related subjects *see* DATABASE MANAGEMENT SYSTEM; DATA SECURITY; DATA STRUCTURES; DIGITAL LIBRARIES; ELECTRONIC REFERENCE WORKS; HYPERTEXT; INFORMATION SCIENCE; INFORMATION SYSTEMS; MANAGEMENT INFORMATION SYSTEMS; NATURAL LANGUAGE PROCESSING; ONLINE INFORMATION SERVICES; OPTICAL STORAGE; SEARCHING; and WORLD WIDE WEB.

Information retrieval (IR) is concerned with the structure, analysis, organization, storage, searching, and dissemination of information. An IR system is designed to make a given stored collection of information items available to a user population. At one time that information consisted of stored bibliographic

items, such as online catalogs of books in a library or abstracts of scientific articles. However, in today's world, the information is more likely to be full-length documents, either stored in a single location, such as newspaper archives, or available in a widely distributed form, such as the World Wide Web (WWW).

The term *document* is broadly used in this article to include any type of text in machine-readable format (*q.v.*); but by extension, an IR system may also be used to access collections of drawings, audio and video files, photographs of museum artifacts, patents, and so on. In each case, the IR system is designed to extract from the files those items that most nearly correspond to existing user needs as reflected by their requests.

IR has become increasingly important in recent years because of the huge amount of potentially accessible information. Retrieval techniques used in traditional operational searching systems have been extended to handle new search applications such as for the Web, and many of the more advanced techniques developed in past IR research are now firmly embedded in operational systems. However, the large numbers of new users accessing the Web have revealed problems in searching these materials by heterogeneous user populations. Considerable research is currently under way in commercial organizations and universities on how best to service these new users and handle information arriving in nontraditional forms, e.g. email, speech, video, and multilingual items.

This article presents some of the basic IR techniques currently used and points to areas of active research. Additionally there is some discussion of related issues, such as the legal and social issues arising from the current massive and uncontrolled access to information on the Web. Note that retrieval operations and techniques are also of interest in a variety of different information processing areas, including database management systems, selective dissemination systems ("push" technology), and expert systems (*q.v.*).

Document Indexing and Content Analysis

In some operational retrieval situations, information analysis is carried out manually by using subject experts or trained indexers to assign content identifiers to information items and search requests. Such information identifiers are known variously as *keywords*, *index terms*, *subject indicators*, or *concepts*, and the search operation usually consists of matching sets of keywords assigned to stored information items with keywords representing the search requests. The matching is followed by the retrieval of those items whose content indicators exhibit a sufficiently high degree of similarity to the query indicators.

> toxic ... , poison ... , lethal dose, LD, side effect, drug allerg ... , drug reaction, drug sensiti ... , intoxicat ... , venom ... , side action, side reaction, adverse effect, adverse reaction, ill effect, idiosyncra ... , overdos ... , overtreat ... , intoleran ... , contraindicat ... , salicylism, goitrogen ... , nephrotoxic ... , neurotoxic ... , hypervitaminosis, untoward, undesirable, deleterious, irritat ... , irritan ... , harm ... , risk ... , danger ... , hazard ... .

Figure 1 Terms denoting the notion of toxicity that may be assigned during document and query analysis.

A typical set of words, or word portions, indicative of the notion of "toxicity" is contained in Fig. 1. Such terms might then be assigned for purposes of content identification to documents and queries in the area of toxicity.

Manual indexing is still relied upon heavily in fields such as medicine and the law. However, in most retrieval systems the manual assignment of keywords and content identifiers is completely avoided by assuming that the words that occur in the document texts can serve adequately for content representation. In these cases, a given item is retrieved if its text contains a given combination of words provided in the search request.

The use of the content of articles as their index is called *automatic indexing*. Some or all of the following types of operation are executed, with the simpler operations, such as those described in items 1 and 2, used by most systems, and the more complex operations are subjects of current research.

1. Expressions are chosen from document or query texts, consisting variously of words, word stems, noun phrases, prepositional phrases, or other content units, which exhibit certain specified properties.

2. Weights may be assigned to each expression on the basis of the frequency of occurrence of the given expression, or the position of that expression in the document (e.g. title, first sentence), or the entity type of that expression (e.g. noun phrase, date).

3. The expressions originally assigned may be replaced by new ones, or new "associated" expressions may be added to the original set. These expressions can be based on information contained in stored dictionaries (e.g. the MeSH—Medical Subject Headings—thesaurus, WordNet), or on information from the document collection itself, such as statistical co-occurrence characteristics among the terms, or on syntactical relations among words.

4. Additional relational indicators between terms may be supplied to express syntactical, functional, or logical relationships among the entities available for content identification. For example, structures may be imposed on the documents or queries that improve the matching of user requests and the documents. For each stored item, such an automatic indexing process produces a set of *terms* representing information content. These terms may be complemented by manually generated index terms when the cost of producing these additional items is warranted. Additionally *metadata* about the document, such as its format, its date of creation, or its source might also be included in the index terms.

The process of indexing is complicated by the enormous amount of electronic text available. Since storage, indexing time, and search response time are dependent on the size of the index, often only parts of a document can be used for indexing purposes. This is particularly true for documents on the Web, where the software that finds text to index (called a *Webcrawler*) has complicated algorithms for selecting what parts of the Web documents to index. This selection algorithm influences the effectiveness of the search engines, often more strongly than the indexing and search algorithms themselves.

Instead of using ordinary index terms for the representation of document content, it is possible to use other features of the document. For example, bibliographic items could be described by using lists of bibliographic citations related to the particular item to be described. The citations may consist of the reference lists that normally appear at the end of a given technical article or book. Alternatively, the citations may comprise outside documents that themselves cite the particular item under consideration. A *citation index* can be used to identify the lists of outside documents that all refer to a given document. An example is shown in Fig. 2. The representation of document content through the use of citations is indirect; a document dealing with toxicity is described by citing other toxicity-related documents from the literature.

A second example of indirect representation of documents is via the creation of links for browsing within or across documents. These *hypertext* (*q.v.*) links can be generated manually or automatically, and usually point to similar or related documents. Using hypertext links allows multiple ways of accessing a document, such as by following "pre-selected" paths through instruction manuals or by linking to auxiliary information including dictionary definitions of unusual words, cross-references within the document, or audio/video files. The Web can be viewed as a multidocument/multiloca-

Cited author ↓	Citing author ↓	Ref. year ↓	Publication ↓	Source year ↓	Vol. ↓	Page ↓
ACHER R ---------		*58*	B SOC CHIM BIOL -----		40	2005
	ACHER R		NATURE L	64	201	191
--------------		58-	J BIOL CHEM ---------		233	116
	ACHER R		NATURE L	64	201	191
--------------		58-	ZWEIIES INTERNATIONA▫			70
	FARNER DS		AM SCIENT	64	52	137
--------------		61-	BIOCHIM BIOPHYS ACTA		51	419
	ACHER		NATURE L	64	201	191
--------------		61-	HISTOPHYSIOLOGIE COM▫			41
	FARNER DS		AM SCIENT	64	52	137
ACHESON RM -------		*54*	BRIT J PREV SOC MED-		8	59
	ACHESON RM		BR J PREV S	64	18	25
--------------		54-	HUM BIOL ------------		26	343
	ACHESON RM		BR J PREV S	64	18	25
--------------		54-	J ANAT ------------		88	498
	JOHNSTON FE		HUMAN BIOL	64	36	16
--------------		56-	ACRIDINES -----------▫			
	MORICONI EJ		J AM CHEM S	64	86	38
--------------		56-	J CHEM SOC ------------			246
	HENDRICK JB		J AM CHEM S	64	86	107
--------------		60-	HUMAN GROWTH -------◎				Non-journal entry
	ACHESON RM		BR J PREV S	64	18	25
	GRANT MW		BR J PREV S	64	18	35

Figure 2. Typical excerpt from the Science Citation Index.

tion manually-generated hypertext net, offering endless possibilities of links. A very active area of both academic and commercial research is the use of new types of links, such as interactive Java *applets*, to enhance the user's searching and browsing capabilities (*see* JAVA).

Another extremely active area of discussion and research is the issue of how to build metadata descriptions of entire collections. Part of this metadata is an expanded version of the type of data being stored about each document, such as its creator or its location. There are currently several proposals being investigated for standardizing this type of information. The other part of the proposed metadata involves content descriptors for collections, and there is considerable ongoing research about what types of information are needed to allow users (or their *agents*) to identify interesting sources of documents for searching.

File Organization and Search Strategies

Several classes of file organizations are commonly used, the simplest of which is the *serial file*. A search is performed by a sequential comparison of the query with the identifiers of all stored items. Such a serial file organization is most economical in storage space; however, a sequential search operation is time-consuming and is thus unusable if reasonable response time is expected from large amounts of data (*see* SEARCHING).

The best known and most universally used file organization in information retrieval is the *inverted*

file, where a large inverted directory or file is used to store for each applicable keyword or content identifier the corresponding set of document or item identifications and locations. The file is thus partitioned into sets of items with common keywords, and a search in the document file is replaced by the directory search. To identify the documents indexed by term A as well as term B, it is sufficient to retrieve from the inverted directory the list of document identifications appearing under term A as well as term B. References contained on both lists represent the answers to the query. Since only small portions of the directory need to be accessed for any given query, acceptable search times are generally obtainable. For this reason, inverted files are currently used with almost all operational retrieval systems.

Inverted file organizations are advantageous in a static environment where the set of terms usable for content identification is not subject to many changes, and where access to the complete term set pertaining to a given stored item is not normally required. In a dynamic situation where changes are made to the content indicators attached to queries and documents, a *clustered file* organization may be preferable. In a clustered file, items that exhibit similar sets of content identifiers are automatically grouped into common classes, or clusters, and a search is performed by looking only at those clusters that exhibit a high similarity with the corresponding query identifiers. A clustered file produces fast search output, and the file-updating operations are relatively easy to implement.

It is highly likely that additional file organizations will be developed to handle the issues of dynamic data better, and the general scaling issues that arise on the Web and in the maintenance of digital libraries (*q.v.*). More intense use of multimedia (*q.v.*) in these areas will also probably lead to new file organizations.

Retrieval Operations

In many older retrieval situations, a search request is constructed by choosing appropriate keywords and content terms and appropriately interconnecting them by Boolean connections (*and*, *or*, *not*) to express the intent of the requestor. For example, a request covering "tissue culture studies of human breast cancer" may then be transformed into the statement shown in Fig. 3. These systems usually return the retrieved information to the users in no particular order of importance (or in date order only). Users of these systems are therefore faced with either constructing very narrow queries (and probably missing some documents) or reading many documents that are less useful.

Newer retrieval systems allow users to express their searches in natural language, without the need for specific syntax. The returned documents are ordered in decreasing query–document similarity, allowing graceful transition between strict matching of query terms and partial matching of these terms. Additionally, most searches are conducted interactively and various optional displays are available to help the user obtain acceptable search output. Thus, tutorial sequences may be included to inform the user about the features of the system; displays of the available term vocabulary may be used during the generation of the query statement; and displays of previously retrieved information (i.e. titles or abstracts of items retrieved earlier) may help the user to construct improved query formulations. Such *feedback operations* are particularly helpful in obtaining more effective retrieval output.

Fig. 4 shows a screen from one such search system. The upper left corner shows a selection of appropriate databases to search, a window to enter a query, and the ability to require specific phrases or to search specific fields. The lower left corner shows the titles of the retrieved documents displayed in order of decreasing query–document similarity. Users can select documents to view (right side of screen), or can ask the system to suggest additional terms for enhancing their query (overlay on right side of screen).

Retrieval failures may be due to the analysis and indexing policy, such as the manual or automatic assignment of too many, or too few, or of a number of incorrect content indicators; or to what parts of a document are used to create the index (i.e. the title only, the first paragraph, or the full document). Alternatively, retrieval failures could be due to the search strategy used or to problems arising during user–system interaction. The use of natural language (automatic) indexing systems eases some of the restrictions inherent in a controlled indexing language in that it creates many diverse avenues to obtain access to the stored information. On the other hand, new problems can be introduced by ambiguous or nonstandard uses of the vocabulary.

Many retrieval problems in older systems resulting from the lack of appropriate user–system interaction have been eliminated in current real-time search systems. However, the increased volume of searchable material, often in nontextual forms, has created new user–system interaction problems, which are amplified by the heavy use of the Web. For example, confusion in creating the initial query or in modifying that query can result from a user's inappropriate model of how the search system operates. This is a very active area of current research with new paradigms of user–system interactions at both the interface level and the underlying system support area being investigated.

Retrieval Applications

The most common type of retrieval situation is exemplified by a retrieval system performing "on demand" searches submitted by a given user population. One example would be searches using online catalogs where the text being searched is bibliographic information for each item, including authors' names, titles, journals or places of publication, dates, and applicable keywords and content identifiers. Another example would be searches against the full-text of documents, where these documents may be current or back issues of newspapers (such as the *Wall Street Journal*), complete sets of Supreme Court cases, or electronically available versions of encyclopedias such as this one.

$$\left\{ \begin{array}{c} \text{Breast neoplasm} \\ or \\ \text{Carcinoma, ductal} \end{array} \right\} \; and \; \left\{ \begin{array}{c} \text{Human} \\ or \; not \\ \text{(any term} \\ \text{indicating} \\ \text{animal or} \\ \text{disease)} \end{array} \right\}$$

$$and \; \left\{ \begin{array}{c} \text{Tissue culture} \\ or \\ \text{Culture media} \\ or \\ \text{Chick embryo} \end{array} \right\} \; and \; \text{English}$$

Figure 3. Typical Boolean query formulation.

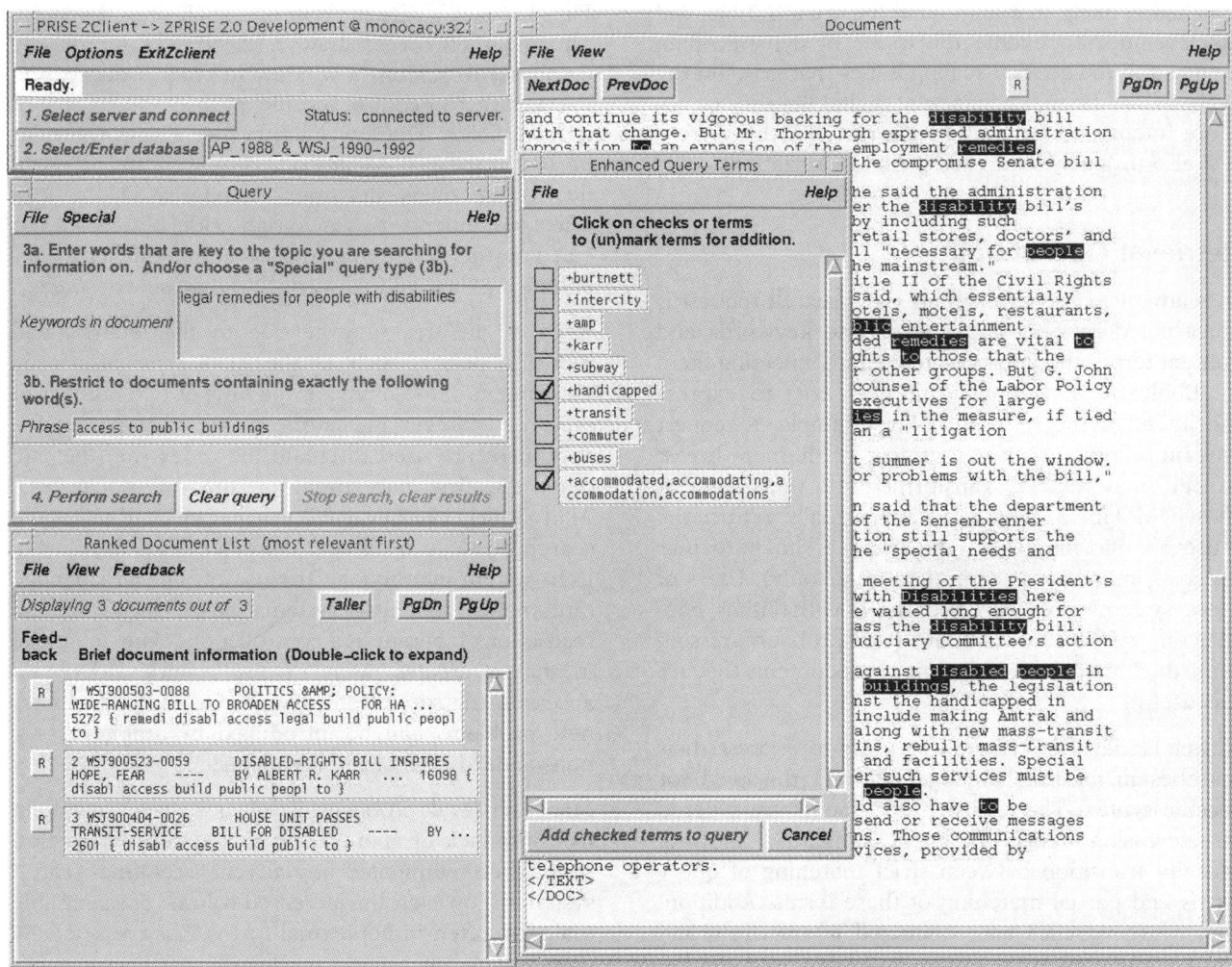

Figure 4. A screen in the ZPRISE information retrieval system (courtesy of NIST).

The most popular type of "on demand" search is searching the Web. Not only can users do simple term searching across the Net, but most search organizations offer search within subject area (where the documents may be manually categorized) or the Web sites themselves may be categorized. Also particular sources of information, such as TV schedules, weather forecasts, and stock reports, are available at these sites.

In most retrieval systems, a search is conducted only when a user actually submits a search request. However, systems also exist which permanently store (and update) user "interest profiles" (i.e. dummy queries that express the principal areas of interest for a given user population). Any new information items coming into the system are then periodically matched against the stored interest profiles, and the relevant output is supplied directly to each individual on a dependable, continuous schedule.

Some of the operational systems for such a *selective dissemination of information* (SDI) use responses submitted by the user population following receipt of a retrieved document to update automatically the stored user profiles. Thus, as users become more or less interested in some areas, the positive or negative responses of the recipients are used to add to or upgrade (or, correspondingly, to delete or downgrade) the respective terms from the profiles. The principles and techniques behind SDI systems are also used in the so-called "push" technology of the Web.

Data management, or *management information systems* normally provide general file processing capabilities together with user interface (*q.v.*) methods to simplify the manipulation and analysis of the stored data. In general, such systems include simple record-keeping provisions, together with exception reporting, and output-generating capabilities based on the use of statistical packages and plotting facilities. Some management information systems also include query capabilities, permitting the user to obtain answers to certain types of submitted queries. In that case, a search-and-retrieval component of the type previously described must be included.

A final class of language processing applications of interest in retrieval are the language-understanding, or *question-answering*, systems, wherein a direct answer is expected in response to a submitted query (instead of only a set of references that may in turn contain the answers). The depth and complexity of the document-and-query analysis must be much greater in question-answering than in standard reference retrieval, since a precise and detailed understanding of the queries is needed before the answers can be supplied.

Normally, question-answering systems include syntactic components based on a stored grammar and dictionary; a semantic interpreter that transforms the syntactically analyzed input into a formal query statement acceptable to the program; and, finally, a deductive component that can generate responses by comparing the formalized query statement with information included in the database. Several experimental text-based question-answering systems have been designed, but for the moment their coverage is limited to small domains and a restricted subset of the natural language. Until more is known about language understanding and semantics, question-answering applications are likely to remain a laboratory pursuit rather than a practical possibility.

Related Legal and Social Issues

The use of information resources such as the Web raises complicated legal and social problems. These are connected in part with the possibility of unlimited duplication and transmission of information that may be subject to legal restrictions (e.g. patented and copy-righted information), and in part with the preservation of information privacy.

The question of *information privacy*, involving the right of individuals to obtain access to a given piece of information under specified conditions, is most complex, and no solution acceptable to all user classes is likely to emerge soon. On the other hand, it is relatively easy, at least conceptually, to provide *file security* by implementing any given set of privacy decisions. Elaborate systems of user authentication by means of special passwords (*q.v.*) and of monitoring devices designed to detect unauthorized access are now in use in most installations. Encryption of protected data will play a larger role in the future, as more information will be available only for a fee, or to specified groups such as subscribers to a service.

In addition, the wide-open nature of the Web raises the questions of authentication of sources and reliability of information in ways that did not occur with printed media or in controlled electronic searching. Whereas some problems may arise from deliberate fraud involving unauthorized versions of documents, many more circumstances exist where outdated copies of information, multiple sources containing duplicate information, and sources containing dead-end links frustrate users. New Web users not only lack the searching expertise to find information easily, but most of the current sources of information lack any differentiation of reliability such as would be found in the past by access to *Chemical Abstracts* and other known authoritative sources of information. These issues will need to be addressed as the Web matures.

Bibliography

1979. Lancaster, F. W. *Information Retrieval Systems: Characteristics, Testing and Evaluation*, 2nd Ed. New York: John Wiley.

1979. Van Rijsbergen, C. J. *Information Retrieval*, 2nd Ed. London: Butterworths.

1983. Salton, G., and McGill, M. J. *Introduction to Modern Information Retrieval*. New York: McGraw-Hill.

1989. Salton, G. *Automatic Text Processing—The Transformation, Analysis, and Retrieval of Information by Computer*. Reading, MA: Addison-Wesley.

1992. Frakes W. B., and Baeza-Yates, R. *Information Retrieval: Data Structures and Algorithms*. Upper Saddle River, NJ: Prentice Hall.

1997. Korfhage, R. *Information Storage and Retrieval*. New York: John Wiley.

1997. Sparck Jones, K., and Willett, P. (eds.) *Readings in Information Retrieval*. San Francisco: Morgan Kaufmann.

Gerard Salton, revised by Donna Harman

INFORMATION SCIENCE

For articles on related subjects *see* COMPUTER SCIENCE; DATA MINING; DATA WAREHOUSING; DIGITAL LIBRARIES; INFORMATION PROCESSING; INFORMATION RETRIEVAL; and INFORMATION TECHNOLOGY.

The term *information science* was coined to designate an interdisciplinary field initially concerned with the exponential growth of recorded scientific information. In 1950, the 81st US Congress authorized the National Science Foundation to "foster an interchange of scientific information among scientists in the United States and foreign countries." The field received a major impetus with the enactment of the National Defense Education Act of 1958, by the 89th Congress, which directed the National Science Foundation to establish a Science Information Service through which the Foundation "shall (1) provide, or arrange for the provision of, indexing, abstracting, translating, and other services leading to a more effective dissemination of scientific information, and (2) undertake programs to develop new or improved methods, including mechanized systems, for making scientific information available."

The 89th Congress correctly anticipated the overwhelming impact of digital technology on information processing. Evolving from its roots in librarianship and documentation, information science has been and remains preoccupied with information as meaning-bearing messages and documents, rather than with raw data. At the outset, two major foci of effort were the study of communication processes in the communities of science and industry, and the development of computer-aided techniques and systems for husbanding text-based scientific literature: methods of the formal description of documents, and their storage in and retrieval from digitized collections (databases). Soon this effort had embraced concern with document control and information handling in other professions: management, education, health care, government, the military, law, and others.

Between 1970 and 1990, as computer science gradually developed ways of processing digitally *nontextual* information, both visual (graphics, images, video) and sound, information science broadened its interests accordingly. About 1990, after advances in telecommunications ushered in the era of global information networks such as the Internet (*q.v.*), information scientists began formulating principles and languages for uniformly describing digital multimedia (*q.v.*) "documents" and their components; studying techniques for searching this vast and diverse global information resource more effectively than using such traditional techniques as Boolean algebra (*q.v.*); and experimenting with new frontiers of information science research such as data mining (*q.v.*)—the automatic discovery of new facts, relationships and even knowledge from very large databases (e.g. of computerized medical records). The first of these efforts is yielding a standard set of descriptive *metadata*; the latter two pose challenges of considerably greater difficulty.

Meanwhile, the initial premise of early information science—that the cost effectiveness of human professions can be raised by improving the communication practices among their practitioners—has been modified into a broader assumption: that the cost-effectiveness of many human information processes which characterize these professions (e.g. problem solving, decision making, learning) can be significantly improved through the formalization of these processes and their gradual delegation to symbol processing machines. In many fields of human activity this assumption continues to guide design and implementation of information processing systems that augment purposeful activities of the human mind. So far, however, evidence of the correctness of this assumption is less than overwhelming for other than trivial mental tasks, in spite of joint contributions by behavioral and other scientists. One promising, albeit long-term, approach

to begin unraveling the nature of human information processes may be provided by a nascent research field called cognitive science (*q.v.*), an interdisciplinary collaboration of the biological, behavioral, and information/computing sciences.

In the symbiotic relationship of the information, computer and communications disciplines which are engendering the advent of humankind's "information society," information science has been predominantly occupied with information "content." This focus, which has always lent information science a distinct societal motivation, acquired a global dimension and urgency by the end of the 20th century. Accordingly, the portfolio of concerns of information scientists today includes issues of intellectual property, individual information privacy, information economics, ethics of the information industry, and equity in information access for individuals as well as all peoples of the world. An even stronger convergence of information science with the social sciences appears indicated for the beginning of the 21st century, so as to assist humankind to cope with the effects of the digital revolution.

As reflected in the principal review publication *Annual Review of Information Science and Technology* and in programs of the American Society of Information Science, the dominant character of information science throughout the second half of the 20th century has been that of both a technological and a social science. Some, however, realized early that significant progress of the discipline may depend on its ability to develop a natural science branch, to be devoted to basic research on the nature and properties of "information" as a fundamental phenomenon, and on primitive information processes. Such a realization motivated the establishment of academic departments in information science in colleges of science and engineering (in contrast to professional programs in librarianship in colleges of arts and humanities). The first such department opened in 1963 at the Georgia Institute of Technology in Atlanta, GA, with sponsorship of the National Science Foundation. Many of these departments have, however, eventually yielded to the temptation of the more tractable (and more generously supported) research in applied computer science (or *informatics*, as this field tends to be designated outside of North America). Meanwhile, a significant number of US library schools ceased operating.

As a basic science, information science still continues to search for content and structure. One early direction, pursued in the USA, Western Europe, and the former Soviet Union, has been that of *empirical semiotics*, the study of sign phenomena: the static structure of signs and the dynamics of sign processes. A more productive research direction seeks to explicate the nature of information via empirical studies of specific information-based phenomena and processes; these studies have already led to formulations of various laws, theories, and hypotheses. Another recent approach assumes that information may, in some ways, be viewed as an analog of matter, and it looks to physics for research methodologies. A major impediment for much of basic research in information science is the absence of *information metrics*, whose development is rendered very difficult by the semantic and pragmatic properties of signs and sign processes. Consequently, there is agreement that, as yet, a scientific basis for a science of information remains to be developed.

Bibliography

1980. Slamecka, V. and Borko, H. (eds.) *Planning and Organization of National Research Programs in Information Science*. New York: Pergamon Press.
1983. Machlup, F. and Mansfield, U. (eds.) *The Study of Information: Interdisciplinary Messages*. New York: John Wiley.
1989. Heilprin, L. B. and Williams, M. E. "Foundations of Information Science Reexamined," in *Annual Review of Information Science and Technology* (ed. M. E. Williams), 343–372. Amsterdam: Elsevier Science Publishers.
1989. Lilley, D. B. and Trice, R. W. *A History of Information Science 1945–1985*. New York: Academic Press.
1993. Menou, M. J. *Measuring the Impact of Information on Development*. Ottawa: International Development Research Council.
1993. Norman, D. *Things That Make Us Smart; Defending Human Attributes in the Age of the Machine*. Reading, MA: Addison-Wesley.
1996. Lamberton, D. *The Economics of Communication and Information*. Cheltenham, UK: Edward Elgar.
1996. *Second Conference on the Foundations of Information Science; The Quest for a Unified Theory of Information*. Abstracts. Vienna: Technische Hochschule.
1997. Agre, P. E. and Rotenberg, M. (eds.) *Technology and Privacy: the New Landscape*. Cambridge, MA: MIT Press.
1997. Bell, G. "The Body Electric," *Comm. of the ACM*, **40**, *2*, 31–32.
1997. Williams, J. G., and Carbo, T. (eds.) *Information Science: Still an Emerging Discipline*. New York: Cathedral Publications.

Vladimir Slamecka

INFORMATION SYSTEMS

For articles on related subjects *see* ADMINISTRATIVE APPLICATIONS; BULLETIN BOARD; DATABASE MANAGEMENT SYSTEM; DATA PROCESSING; DISTRIBUTED SYSTEMS; INFORMATION RETRIEVAL; INTEGER SEQUENCES, ONLINE ENCYCLOPEDIA OF; KNOWLEDGE REPRESENTATION; MANAGEMENT INFORMATION SYSTEMS; SYSTEMS ANALYST; and WORLD WIDE WEB.

An *information system* is a collection of people, procedures, and equipment designed, constructed, operated, and maintained to collect, record, process, store, retrieve, and display information.

In practice, the term *information system* is used in a very general sense, both in technical literature and in general publications. For example, in *Computing Reviews*, *information systems* is a major category that has subcategories: models and principles, database management, information storage and retrieval, and information systems applications. *Computerworld* annually lists the most effective users of information systems. Sometimes the term *information processing system* is used when the focus is on the *processing* of information rather than on its use. The term *data processing system* is frequently used synonymously with *information processing system*. A difference arises when an attempt is made to distinguish between data and information. The journal *Information Systems* concentrates on the latter.

An information system may use various technologies; Sage (1968) describes the historical development of information systems in organizations from Babylonian times. Systems that contain digital computers as integral parts are sometimes called *computer-based information systems* (CBIS) to distinguish them from earlier (i.e. manual) systems.

Structure

An information system itself may be viewed as shown in Fig. 1. Information systems accept (as input), store (in files or a database), and display (as output) strings of symbols that are grouped in various ways (digits, alphabetic characters, special symbols). Users of an information system attribute some value or meaning to the string of symbols. In this article, the emphasis is on the characteristics of systems rather than on the meaning attached to the output.

One component of an information system is machines, or hardware, including the central processing units (*q.v.*), or servers, and various input and output devices, such as personal computers, workstations (*q.v.*), readers, printers (*q.v.*), and terminals. In distributed systems (*q.v.*), the hardware also includes communication equipment. Next is a set of system software (*hard software*), including operating systems (*q.v.*), utility programs, and database management systems. The hardware and system software constitute the computer system or *platform*. In addition, there are programs specially prepared for the particular system, frequently known as *application software*, which are usually prepared in some high-level programming language. The data stored in and maintained by the system is called the *database* and is stored on auxiliary memory devices such as disks and tapes (*see* DATABASE MANAGEMENT SYSTEM and MEMORY: AUXILIARY). In some systems, a distinction is made between data, applications software, and knowledge. In these systems, there

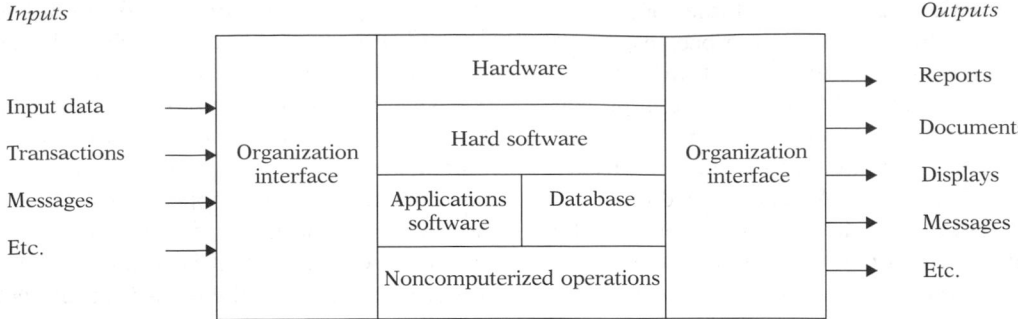

Figure 1. Structure of an information system.

may be a *knowledge base* separate from the *facts* database and a software package known as the *inference engine.* Even in a computer-based information system, the processing is usually supplemented by manual (noncomputerized) procedures. Interaction between the system and its users is provided through an *organizational interface.*

Classification of Information Systems

Information systems may be classified in different ways for different purposes. One classification is by application area, such as manufacturing, payroll, voter registration, accounting, or airline reservation. There is no standard, generally accepted taxonomy for this type of classification. Another classification is by type of service rendered, where the following categories are typical:

1. *Computing service* systems that provide a general computing service to a number of users. Common examples are university computing centers, computing centers in research institutions, and commercial time-sharing (*q.v.*) services.

2. *Information storage and retrieval* systems designed to store data (or documents) and retrieve it in response to queries. Examples are the medical information retrieval system MEDLARS, various services providing financial data, and services providing bulletin boards.

3. *Command and control* systems built to monitor some given situation and provide a signal when predefined conditions occur. Examples are various military systems, systems built by NASA for space programs, and the Federal Aviation Administration system for air traffic control.

4. *Transaction processing* (*q.v.*) systems designed to process predefined transactions and produce predefined outputs, as well as maintain the necessary database. Examples are order-entry billing systems and airline reservation systems.

5. *Message switching* systems, such as electronic mail (*q.v.*).

6. *Process control* systems designed to control physical processes by monitoring the conditions and signaling appropriate action to the machines. Common examples are systems to control chemical processes and oil refineries (*see* CONTROL APPLICATIONS).

A summary of the inputs, database contents, and outputs for these six types of system is given in Table 1.

Information systems may also be classified by the type and degree of interaction with the user and/or the environment in which the system is embedded.

◆ *Batch or sequential processing* Requests are grouped into batches on the basis of common processing requirements, and each batch is processed as a unit, often at a predetermined time. The individual user therefore gets results at the conclusion of all operations on the batch in which the request is included.

◆ *Store and forward* Each resource in the system has a queue, consisting of the jobs that require that resource. When a job is finished at that resource, it is sent to the queue at the next resource needed, and the next job in the queue is processed. The user gets results when all the operations on a job have been performed.

◆ *Inline or random processing* Jobs are selected for processing according to some priority scheme; once a job has been started, it is processed completely through to the final result. All the necessary files in the database are updated.

◆ *Interactive* The user communicates with the computing facility via workstations or personal computers, and requests are processed as they arrive. The user gets quick responses, which may be used to prepare the next input. In order to accomplish this, it is usually necessary to provide

Table 1. Typical inputs, database contents, and outputs by type of system.

Type	Input	Database	Outputs
Computing service	Both programs and data supplied by users	Created by individual users for their own purposes. System maintains minimal database for control and for allocating charges	Specified by users for their own purposes
Information storage and retrieval	Determined by system designers on basis of what is relevant to inquiries to be answered	Contains all input received	Produced in answer to user inquiries
Command and control	Obtained from sensors and monitors	Built up from data received by inputs; contains system state	Warning and action notices obtained by periodic processing of inputs and system state
Transaction processing	Predefined transactions	Contains all data necessary to process transactions and produce outputs	Specified by system designer to accomplish system objectives
Message switching	Messages	Minimal. Contains data on status of nodes in network	Messages sent to specified location
Process control	Obtained from sensors and monitors	Status of all processes under control of system	Signals to control operation of physical devices

some method of time sharing unless the system is dedicated to a single user. (*See* REAL-TIME SYSTEMS.)

◆ *Real-time, or online* When a request is received, it is acted on as soon as possible, so as to provide a response within a given time period.

Each type of system has certain characteristics that affect its structure, the measures of performance that are appropriate, and the process of designing, building, and operating the system. Many systems are mixtures of the basic types; some examples are:

◆ *Business data processing systems* These are basically transaction processing systems, but usually are designed to serve users distributed over a geographical area; hence, they include communication and message-switching capabilities. These are often referred to as Online Transaction Processing (OLTP) systems.

◆ *Management information systems* (MIS) These are a combination of information storage and retrieval systems and command and control systems. They usually draw a substantial part of their data from business data processing systems. These systems may include subsystems that are termed decision support systems (DSS) or executive information systems (EIS).

◆ *Computer-integrated manufacturing systems* (CIMs) These systems integrate business data

processing, manufacturing control, and factory floor control systems.

◆ *Computer networks* and *distributed systems* (*q.v.*) These provide computing service and message switching over a geographical area (*see* NETWORKS, COMPUTER). They may also provide transaction processing capability. The users of systems may be geographically distant from the physical hardware. Users initiate different types of requests or jobs to be processed. The system has a number of different types of resource, and may have more than one of each type. Any given request or job may need more than one type of resource, possibly given in some order. There are different ways of organizing the resources to accomplish the requests, and systems may therefore be classified by the type of system organization. In the past, the networks were often proprietary; more recently these are being replaced or supplemented by the Internet (*q.v.*) and World Wide Web (*q.v.*).

Common Features of Information Systems

The various classifications described above are useful in identifying common features of systems that may appear in more than one type. All information systems have certain characteristics in common:

1. Information systems are human-made; i.e. they have to be designed, constructed, operated, and

maintained. This is a nontrivial task and has led to the need for methods of system development, operation, and maintenance often called *system development methodologies*. An early introduction to the topic is given by Benjamin (1971); an analysis of a number of methodologies is given by Olle *et al.* (1983). The process of system development is being formalized through the disciplines of software engineering (*q.v.*) and systems engineering (Hall, 1989). Information systems to support software engineering have been given the acronym CASE (computer-aided software engineering—*q.v.*).

2. In the development and operation of information systems, both the software and the repository (database) are important.

3. Because of the large cost involved in developing information systems, there is an economic need for systems to share hardware, files, and software.

4. The systems tend to be large and costly to develop, operate, and maintain. This arises because of economies of scale involved in larger hardware and in economies of scale involved in operation and maintenance of systems.

5. The systems involve human–machine communication at various levels, and problems of design and operation include problems of communication among individuals, of communications with the machine, and of communication among the various units of the machine. Therefore, documentation (*q.v.*) of all aspects of the system and its development is important.

6. The uses of the systems and the technology on which the systems are developed are continually changing, as are the organizations using them; consequently, the systems themselves are seldom, if ever, static.

Information systems are expensive to develop and operate; consequently, analyses to determine whether they are serving the desired needs of users, as well as the measurement of their performance, continue to receive considerable attention. Performance evaluation must be considered at a number of levels. At the top level, the value of the output of the system to the organization that supports it must be determined. Once these specific outputs have been justified, the performance of the physical system in achieving these outputs must be measured. This performance is a combination of the performance of programs, software, and the hardware equipment itself. The process of developing user requirements and designing systems to achieve them effectively is known as *systems analysis and design* and as *requirements engineering*.

Bibliography

1968. Sage, S. M. "Information Systems: A Brief Look into History," *Datamation*, 63–69 (November).
1971. Benjamin, R. I. *Control of the Information System Development Cycle.* New York: John Wiley.
1983. Olle, T. W., Sol, H. G., and Tully, C. J. (eds.) *Information Systems Design Methodologies: A Feature Analysis*, 37–62. Amsterdam: North Holland.
1989. Hall, A. D. *Metasystems Methodology.* New York: Pergamon Press.
1998. "The Premier 100 Most Effective Users of Information Systems," *Computerworld.* http://www.computerworld.com/home/features.nsf/all/981116premier/.

Daniel Teichroew

INFORMATION TECHNOLOGY

For articles on related subjects *see* COMPUTER SCIENCE; DATA PROCESSING; and INFORMATION PROCESSING.

Information technology (IT) is an imprecise term frequently applied to a broad area of activities and technologies associated with the use of computers and communication, but generally implying the application of computers to storage, retrieval, processing, and dissemination of data, particularly in the field of commerce. But the term is sufficiently amorphous to encompass the activities of those who design or even use any form of device used to gather, transmit, or process digital information: digital satellite and cable television, DVDs, digital telephony—even digital cameras and photocopiers.

According to the *Oxford English Dictionary*, the first recorded use of the term *information technology* was in 1958 when Leavitt and Whisler wrote in the *Harvard Business Review* (XXXVI 41/1): "The new technology does not have a single established name. We shall call it *information technology*." This article, "Management in the 1980s," examined the likely impact of "information technology" on business. The authors identified three related parts: techniques for processing large amounts of information rapidly; the application of statistical and mathematical methods to decision making problems; and simulation of high-order thinking through computer programs.

By 1984 the term had, according to the *National Westminster Bank Quarterly Review* of 13 August, become established in Britain, but by then seemed to have taken on a new meaning: "The development of cable television was made possible by the convergence of telecommunications and computing technology (...generally known in Britain as information technology)." The term then appeared later (1990) in International Organization for Standardization (ISO) documentation. Problems posed by conflicting standards—particularly in the area of character set encoding—resulted in the establishment of a joint ISO/IEC (International Electrotechnical Commission) technical committee, JTC1, which used "information technology" in relation to its work. The term is applied in a general sense and no formal definition has ever been offered or implied. Its use recognized a convergence of interests of two ISO technical committees, TC46 and TC97, and may have been prompted by what has been described as a "turf war." Information technology was a conveniently neutral term because it had not been used by either committee. Since then the use of IT has burgeoned. Large accounting firms have IT departments, there are specialist IT lawyers, some governments have ministries of IT, universities have established IT faculties, IT journalists are legion, and self-styled IT professionals abound.

In its original application "information technology" was appropriate to describe the convergence of technologies with application in the broad field of data storage, retrieval, processing, and dissemination. This useful conceptual term has since been converted to what purports to be concrete use, but without the reinforcement of definition. The reason for that may rest with a perceived need for an appearance of stability in what is really an environment of constant and rapid change in which technologies are often ephemeral, appearing briefly before being replaced by, or merged with, something else.

The term IT lacks substance when applied to the name of any function, discipline, or position. Like the emperor of children's stories, it parades in a state of nakedness to which none of its subjects dare admit.

Bibliography

1997. Cortada, J. W. *Best Practices in Information Technology: How Corporations Get the Most Value from Exploiting Their Digital Investments.* Upper Saddle River, NJ: Prentice Hall.
1998. Senn, J. A. *Information Technology in Business: Principles, Practices, and Opportunities.* Upper Saddle River, NJ: Prentice Hall.
1999. Thorp, J. *The Information Paradox: Realizing the Business Benefits of Information Technology.* New York: McGraw-Hill.

Major Keary

INFORMATION THEORY

For articles on related subjects *see* ERROR CORRECTING AND DETECTING CODE; and SHANNON, CLAUDE E.

Information theory entered the world of engineering, science, and mathematics through the paper "A Mathematical Theory of Communication" published by Claude Elwood Shannon in the *Bell System Technical Journal* in 1948, and, together with material by Warren Weaver, republished in a book of the same name by the University of Illinois Press in 1949. The book gives an excellent presentation of Shannon's revolutionary ideas.

According to Shannon, communication resolves uncertainty. If we toss an honest coin, communicating the outcome takes one bit (binary digit) of information: a *heads* or *tails*, a *yes* or *no*, a *1* or a *0*. But with a biased coin for which heads comes up more often than tails, the sequence of *heads* and *tails* is *redundant* and can be encoded in less than one bit per toss.

A message source may produce text, speech, or other messages. Shannon models a message source as *stochastic* or *probabilistic* in nature. He defines a quantity called *entropy*, which is a measure of the unpredictability of messages from the source. Entropy can be expressed in terms of bits per symbol or bits per message. He gives formulas for entropy in terms of joint probabilities.

Shannon deals with continuous signals through use of the *sampling theorem*. A signal of bandwidth (*q.v.*) (frequency range) B can be *exactly* and *recoverably* represented by $2B$ numbers per second, each giving an instantaneous amplitude of the signal. To avoid an infinite entropy for completely undistorted continuous signals (audio waveforms or TV signals, for example), Shannon uses a *fidelity criterion*.

Information from a *message source* is transmitted over a *communication channel*. For actual channels, there is always some noise or uncertainty, some random difference between what goes into and what comes out of the channel. Despite errors or noisiness in transmission, communication channels have a *channel capacity* measured in bits per character or bits per second. Shannon gives formulas for the capacities of various channels in terms of either probabilities of errors in transmitting characters, or in terms of signal power, noise, and bandwidth. The historic Shannon formula for the channel capacity C of a channel of bandwidth B with a signal power P and added Gaussian noise power N is

$$C = B \log_2 (1 + P/N) \text{ bits per second}$$

Shannon's crucial theorem is that if the rate of transmission of a message source is less than the channel capacity of a noisy channel, messages from the source can be transmitted over the channel with less than any assignable error rate through the use of *error-correcting codes*.

The equation for channel capacity can be used to find the absolute minimum power needed to send one bit of information. The noise power N is considered to be the unavoidable thermal noise power kTB associated with a source of temperature T degrees Kelvin (degrees above absolute zero); k is Boltzmann's constant; and the bandwidth B is made very large. Then the minimum energy needed for transmission is $kT/\ln 2 = 0.95 \times 10^{-23}\, T$ joules per bit. The communication links used with today's superbly engineered research spacecraft come very close to this.

Bibliography

1949. Shannon, C., and Weaver, W. *The Mathematical Theory of Communication*. Urbana, IL: University of Illinois Press.

1977. McEliece, R. J. *The Theory of Information and Coding*. Reading, MA: Addison-Wesley.

1993. Sloane, N. J. A., and Wyner, A. D. (eds.) *Claude Elwood Shannon: Collected Papers*. New York: IEEE Press.

John R. Pierce

INPUT–OUTPUT CONTROL SYSTEM (IOCS)

For articles on related subjects *see* ACCESS METHODS; BIOS; BUS; CACHE MEMORY; CHANNEL; FILE; INPUT–OUTPUT OPERATIONS; LOGICAL AND PHYSICAL NAMES; MASS STORAGE; MEMORY: AUXILIARY; MULTIPROGRAMMING; OPERATING SYSTEMS; and REDUNDANT ARRAY OF INEXPENSIVE DISKS.

One of the earliest and most fundamental reasons for the initial development and subsequent growth of operating systems concerns the handling of input–output (I/O) operations. The transfer of responsibility for I/O operations from the programmer to the operating system was undertaken for several reasons. First, the construction of code for handling I/O is one of the more difficult aspects of programming a computer. By not requiring a programmer to know primitive I/O details, computing services have become accessible to a greater number of casual programmers. Second, as assemblers, compilers, sort packages, and other utilities became available, it was necessary that each be provided with I/O services, and that user programs be prevented from overwriting areas where these utilities or their workspaces are stored.

A common set of I/O routines that is used by all system facilities and user programs saves duplicated effort. Moreover, a simple, carefully debugged set of routines provides some measure of protection against destruction of important files. The problem of accidental destruction of stored data was further compounded in operating systems that permitted users to construct and maintain private files of programs and/or data. In such systems, the denial of direct I/O capabilities to the user became even more important.

A common set of I/O routines also facilitates interleaved execution of unrelated programs. When a program issues a request for I/O, the appropriate I/O routine is called. If the I/O operation cannot be completed immediately, further execution of this program can be suspended and control given instead to some other program that is ready to execute. This interleaved or multiprogrammed execution of programs makes more efficient use of the central processor without necessitating detailed planning of overlapped I/O operations by individual programmers.

For all of these reasons, the handling of I/O operations has become almost exclusively the province of the operating system, more specifically, the province of its *I/O control system* (IOCS).

Programmer Communication with the IOCS

Typically, a programmer will communicate with the IOCS by calling various modules as subroutines. The assembly language programmer will generally have available a number of predefined macros (*q.v.*), which will be expanded into subroutine calls to IOCS modules using predefined calling sequences. Similarly, I/O commands in high-level languages will generally be compiled into subroutine calls to appropriate IOCS modules. In more recent systems, these requests for I/O service take the form of *supervisor calls* (*q.v.*).

The Function of the IOCS

The global function of an IOCS is to perform I/O operations upon request of programmers. This function may be refined to include the following tasks:

1. Interpretation of I/O requests.

2. Execution of I/O requests, once interpreted.

3. Location of the data to be transferred and where it is to be transferred to.

4. Initialization of transfer parameters.

These four topics will be discussed in subsequent sections.

INTERPRETATION OF I/O REQUESTS

Each of the various I/O requests that a user may make (e.g. READ, WRITE, INSERT, DELETE, REPLACE, REWIND, OPEN, CLOSE) must be decoded and the parameters checked. This process is accomplished by an I/O request interpreter. The interpreter will check such things as (1) the name of the operation, (2) the name of the logical unit involved, and (3) the parameters specified for the operation. Once checked, the interpreter will enter the parameters into the appropriate table and initiate execution of the I/O request.

The I/O request interpreter can initiate a variety of actions, depending on the particular I/O request. For example, a request to read a file that has not yet been opened might cause an error condition or simply cause the open request to be generated by the interpreter. Similarly, requests to write on a read-only device such as an optical disk can be trapped at this level.

EXECUTION OF I/O REQUESTS

Execution of I/O requests involves various tasks:

1. Maintenance of correspondences between logical and physical devices.

2. Generation of physical I/O commands based on requests.

3. Coordination of peripheral activities and maintenance of status information.

Following the usual distinction between logical and physical units, it is convenient to divide the portion of the IOCS that is directly concerned with I/O transfers into two parts—*logical IOCS* and *physical IOCS*. Logical IOCS will contain routines for managing data on logical units, while physical IOCS will perform analogous functions with respect to physical units. Thus, physical IOCS will contain routines for every physical I/O device attached to the computing system (actually, these routines may be shared among devices that are all of the same type, such as all disk devices). These routines will handle interrupts from the device and control the execution of I/O transfers without regard for the logical content, format, or organization of the data being transferred. Physical IOCS will also contain routines for handling errors and exceptional conditions received from the device. Extensive retry schemes are often included to mask failures from higher levels of the system.

The logical IOCS contains routines that perform functions associated with the logical unit, as declared by the programmer (or as predefined by the system). Thus, the logical IOCS will contain routines to handle space allocation and freeing, blocking and deblocking, index maintenance, to control error handling and recovery, to sense end-of-file and other exceptional conditions, etc., depending on the characteristics associated with a given logical unit. Clearly, logical IOCS will communicate with physical IOCS when transfer of data is necessary. Table 1 illustrates the division between logical and physical IOCS for several I/O requests.

TABLES FOR LOGICAL IOCS AND PHYSICAL IOCS

As mentioned previously, it is common to share the actual routines for performing the various functions. The usual way this is done is to organize common information into tables that are passed as parameters to the IOCS routine. The tables often correspond to the notion of a logical device table, which contains the data and status of logical requests, and a physical device table, which contains the status of physical devices. The associations between logical devices and physical devices are then captured in a list structure.

Typical information in a logical device table would be:

1. The symbolic name of the device.

2. The name of the file currently associated with this logical device.

3. The logical I/O request pending on this device.

4. A pointer (*q.v.*) to the storage buffer associated with this device.

5. The address of the routine used to transfer data to/from buffers.

6. The addresses of interrupt (*q.v.*) and exception handling routines for devices of this type.

7. A pointer to the physical device table associated with this device.

Table 1. Division of logical and physical IOCS requests

Request	Logical IOCS	Physical IOCS
Get the next record.	Deblock the next record. If buffer empty, get next buffer. If no more buffers and file not ended, get the next series of file blocks.	Deliver next block from device.
Find a record in a randomly accessed file.	Request index tracks. Search index to find block of record. Request block of record. Find record and deliver to calling program.	Deliver index tracks. Deliver requested track.
Store a new record in a randomly accessed indexed file.	Add new record to proper block if there is space. Otherwise, write new record in a separate area. Update the index to reflect the new data values.	Write updated block. Write a new record. Fetch index blocks and write index blocks.

Typical information in a physical device table would be:

1. The device type and associated information used in constructing the actual I/O commands to the device.

2. Status information such as "device busy" or "device reserved."

3. The current pending I/O operation on the device.

4. The address of the routine which actually issues commands to the device.

5. The addresses of interrupt and exception handling routines for the device.

An application program would normally not be allowed to provide routines to replace those in the physical layer of the IOCS. To do so could compromise the integrity of the data stored on the physical device. However, it is common to allow programmers to supply their own routines for blocking/deblocking of records, buffer management, label or header verification, and processing of exceptional conditions.

COORDINATION OF PERIPHERAL ACTIVITIES AND MAINTENANCE OF POSITIONING INFORMATION

The scheduling and coordination of peripheral activities is an especially important IOCS function. In a large computer system, there will often exist a variety of data paths from the central processors through the data channels to particular devices. Fig. 1 illustrates a typical situation.

Notice in Fig. 1 that a given device may be "attached" to more than one control unit and/or channel in order to form a path that can deliver data to or take data from main storage. This does not imply that data flows to or from the device over two paths simultaneously; only one path to or from a device is used at a given time. The multiple paths exist in order that devices may be kept busy as long as there exists at least one unused path to the device. The multiple paths also allow for continued operation should certain units in a data path break down temporarily. However, the IOCS must keep track of what data paths are currently in use and prevent new requests from using these paths. When a unit signals that a certain component of a path is no longer needed, the IOCS will search the pending requests to see if one can be initiated over the freed path.

In deciding on the next request to be serviced, it is convenient for physical IOCS to have information concerning the current position of read–write heads relative to the position of the data. This is particularly true with disks, which involve movable read–write heads. Requests for data near the current head position can be serviced more quickly than requests that require considerable head movement. Thus, in the scheduling of I/O operations, it is not unusual for physical IOCS to have as part of its status information an indication of current read–write head position. Using this information, it can attempt to optimize requests serviced per unit time (or some similar measure) by scheduling I/O operations based on "nearness" of data to the heads. Note also that the chain of physical device tables defines an ordering of physical devices that can be used for deciding which of a number of devices will be started first when more than one device could be started.

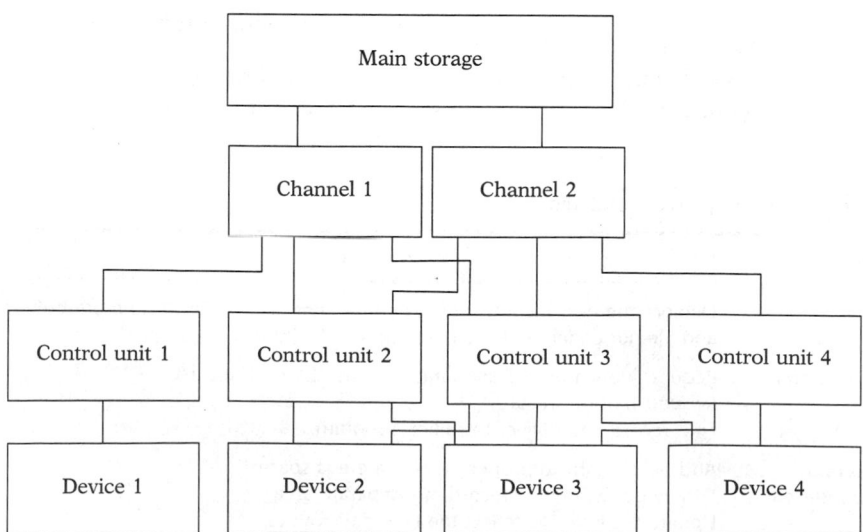

Figure 1. Data paths to I/O devices.

LOCATION OF THE DATA AND INITIALIZATION OF TRANSFER PARAMETERS

Before I/O requests can be interpreted and executed, the storage area that contains or will contain the data must be located and made accessible to the IOCS. Moreover, various parameters in the logical and physical device tables must be specified. The location and initialization functions are responsible for these tasks.

The location function involves routines for finding the physical devices on which the storage area to be processed resides. This storage area may or may not be directly accessible, depending on the particular computer system involved. If, for example, the programmer has attached a logical device to a tape drive on which a specified tape is to be mounted, then the IOCS must make sure that the tape is indeed mounted. This will typically involve a request to the computer system operator to mount the specified tape. It also usually involves a *label verification* routine. In order to check that the operator has indeed mounted the correct tape, a tape label in a prespecified format will usually exist on the first record of the tape. The label will contain information that identifies the tape, and the label verification routine will match the identification on the tape with the identification information given on the request for tape mount. Lack of a match indicates an error, and an appropriate message will be issued.

If the storage area resides on a disk or other sharable device, a somewhat different kind of location function usually takes place. There will generally exist a directory (*q.v.*) or catalog of all files that have been created in the system, and a request to attach a logical device to one of these files will trigger a search of this catalog. The catalog will indicate on which disk pack(s) the storage area had been allocated. Each disk will typically have a table of contents, which is essentially a collection of file labels for files on this pack. By searching this table of contents, the file is located.

INITIALIZATION

Once the data has been located, the initialization function can be executed. In order for I/O requests to be executed, various entries in the logical and physical device tables must be filled in. These parameters may be specified by commands given to the IOCS in advance or by the programmer during execution, but in certain cases they may reside with the data itself, usually as part of the file label. Thus, if it is appropriate, the initialization routines will move a copy of these parameters to the appropriate table entries. When the file is no longer needed, a final set of IOCS routines will restore the file to a state in which it can be used at a later time.

Recent Trends

In recent years, the trend has been for I/O control systems to become even more sophisticated. They have done so both to ease the task of managing a large number of peripheral devices and to allow use of complex storage techniques which speed the throughput or enhance the reliability of the storage subsystem.

Modern, large-scale servers may have literally hundreds of disks attached. In current technology, a terabyte (TB $= 10^{12}$ bytes) of storage occupies from 100 to 200 disks. Larger servers may store as much as 10 TB. While the amount of data on a given disk constantly rises, the demand for more online storage rises even faster. A computer operator cannot monitor the performance, availability or storage usage of hundreds of disks without errors and inefficiencies. The only solution is to have the IOCS monitor and alert an operator to pending conditions or, in some cases, take remedial action automatically according to some specified policy.

For example, if the I/O requests to a particular device exceed the I/O capacity of the device for an extended time, then it is beneficial to move one or more files to a more lightly used disk. Modern IOCS systems have the ability to do this with no effect on the application program. In some cases, the systems can perform this action even while the file is in use. Another example would be the automatic archiving and recall of infrequently used files from tertiary storage.

Regarding performance and availability, the emergence of RAID (*see* REDUNDANT ARRAY OF INEXPENSIVE DISKS) technology allows storage formats that can enhance the effective I/O rate for certain kinds of problems or detect, recover from, and repair certain failures in the disk subsystem. Modern IOCS systems often have the ability to carry out such operations, once again transparently to the application programs.

A common way that services such as these are implemented is to abstract further the notion of a disk. Whereas the discussion to this point has assumed that the physical I/O system is reading and writing from actual devices such as disks, recent IOCSs have introduced the notion of a "virtual" disk. A virtual disk may have properties such as extremely large capacity, extremely high bandwidth, or extremely high availability. The virtual disk is then implemented by the IOCS in a pool of actual physical disks. This extra level of abstraction handled by the IOCS maintains the programming abstraction and preserves the application code base while providing the desired properties.

Over time, the IOCS may assume even more of the function of managing the storage subsystem. For example, recent experimental systems have studied how the storage organization can be selected automatically, given a high-level specification of the desired properties of an abstract device.

Bibliography

1992. Tanenbaum, A. S. *Modern Operating Systems*. Upper Saddle River, NJ: Prentice Hall.
1998. Silberschatz, A., and Galvin, P. B. *Operating System Concepts*. 5th Ed. Reading, MA: Addison-Wesley.

Robert W. Taylor

INPUT–OUTPUT OPERATIONS

For articles on related topics *see* BUS; CENTRAL PROCESSING UNIT; CHANNEL; CYCLE STEALING; DRIVER; INPUT–OUTPUT CONTROL SYSTEM; INSTRUCTION SET; INTERRUPT; MASS STORAGE; MEMORY-MAPPED I/O; and REDUNDANT ARRAY OF INEXPENSIVE DISKS.

I/O Operations and Addressing

Input–output (I/O) systems transfer information between computer main memory and the outside world. An I/O system is composed of I/O devices (peripherals), I/O control units, and software to carry out the I/O transaction(s) through a sequence of I/O operations. I/O devices can be classified as *serial*, i.e. able to transfer bit streams one bit at a time, or *parallel*. Parallel devices have a wider data bus and can therefore transfer data in words of one or more bytes. Like any other activity in a computer system, I/O is a concerted work of both hardware and software. The software which is executed to carry out an I/O transaction for a specific I/O device is called a *device driver*. An example of such an I/O transaction is reading a block of data from disk to memory. The software to do this is simply a sequence of I/O operations (instructions) to transfer data between the peripheral devices and main memory (*q.v.*), and to enable the central processing unit (CPU) to control the peripheral devices connected to it. Thus, I/O operations are of two classes: control operations and data transfer operations.

The main difference among I/O systems is the degree of CPU involvement in the transactions. In a simple system, with a minimal I/O control unit, the CPU must perform all I/O operations. This includes initiating the transaction, checking device status, transferring data between the devices and main memory, and terminating the I/O transaction. In this case the system is said to be using *programmed I/O*. At the other extreme, the CPU may only initiate the I/O transaction, which is then carried out through completion by an intelligent control unit, such as an I/O coprocessor. The degree of independence and concurrency between the CPU and these intelligent I/O control units will be addressed later in this article.

In order for the CPU to communicate with and distinguish among the different I/O devices in the system, an addressing scheme is needed. Two I/O addressing methods are used: *memory-mapped I/O* and *I/O-mapped I/O*. In memory-mapped I/O, a part of the memory address space is used for I/O ports, where a typical I/O device may have a data port for buffering data to be transferred and a control/status port that allows the CPU to control the I/O device and read its status. In this case, each of these I/O ports will be assigned a memory address and the CPU can use all instructions that load or store data to exchange information with these ports. Thus, a *load* instruction can be used by the CPU to read the device status or read data from the device, while a *store* instruction can be used to write data to the device or write a new control word to its control port. The Motorola 680x0 processors, for example, use memory-mapped I/O only. Advantages of this I/O addressing scheme are the ability to use the entire instruction set to perform I/O and the ability to support a large number of input devices. Disadvantages include limiting the main memory capacity due to using part of the address space for I/O. However, the huge address spaces in today's processors are typically not fully populated with memory.

In the I/O-mapped I/O, there are two distinct address spaces for main memory and I/O ports. An I/O port could have the same address as a memory location; however, the CPU uses separate control lines for I/O so that only I/O devices are enabled in I/O operations. The CPU also uses separate control lines to address only the memory chip(s) during memory transfers. Processors that support I/O-mapped I/O have distinguished I/O instructions (such as IN or OUT). The use of an I/O or memory transfer instruction determines whether the I/O or the memory control lines will be activated. Memory-mapped I/O systems can still be constructed from processors that support I/O-mapped I/O. In this case, the I/O control lines are ignored and the memory control lines are used to enable the I/O ports. The Intel 80x86 processor family, for example, uses I/O-mapped I/O.

CPU Managed I/O

Input–output architectures can be classified into two major categories. In the first category the CPU has the burden of carrying out the transfers between the I/O device and the main memory. As the size of the system grows, this becomes a burden on the CPU and can slow down the whole system. Therefore, in the second category, which includes more sophisticated systems, I/O functions are largely delegated to other "smart" modules that can carry out I/O on their own with minimal intervention from the CPU. In this section, we discuss the simple architectures in which all I/O transfers take place between I/O devices and memory through the CPU. The following sections will discuss architectures in which I/O is delegated to specialized control modules and data transfers do not go through the CPU.

PROGRAMMED I/O

Programmed I/O is the simplest possible control scheme and requires very minimal hardware support. In this case the CPU does not only carry out the I/O transaction, but also waits for the device to be ready for a transfer. In the I/O structure of Fig. 1, the I/O device interface provides a data register for exchange of data, and a control and status register to select the mode of operation and to determine whether the device is busy or ready for a transfer. Data transfer between the I/O device and the CPU takes place on the data bus through the data register.

Fig. 2 outlines the programmed I/O process carried out by the CPU to read a block of words (or characters) from an input device to memory. The process starts with the CPU placing a control word into the control register through a store instruction. The CPU also uses a counter to keep track of the number of words transferred to determine when the process ends. Reading the data block into the main memory also requires that the CPU use a pointer (*q.v.*) to keep track of where the incoming data is to be placed. Once the counter and the pointer are initialized, the CPU reads the status register to determine whether the device is ready for transferring a word of data. If not ready, the CPU goes into a *busy–wait loop*, repeating the status check until the device becomes ready. If the device is ready, then one word is read from the data register. The counter and the pointer are both updated accordingly, and the word counter is checked to determine whether the block transfer is complete. Programmed I/O is clearly so named because the entire I/O process is managed by a software program.

```
Program: Reading input data block
Begin
Select I/O mode, using control register
WordCount := BLOCKSIZE
While NOT Done
      While device-status is NOT Ready
              /*busy-wait till device is ready*/
            read device status
      EndWhile
      Read one word into memory from data register
      Advance pointer to the next storage cell
            in the block
      Decrement WordCount
      If (WordCount = 0) then Done := TRUE
EndWhile
```

Figure 2. Programmed I/O pseudocode for reading a block of input data.

INTERRUPT-DRIVEN I/O

External interrupts are separate inputs to processors that are used to inform the processor of a system event that requires processor intervention. Processors typically sample their interrupt inputs towards the end of each instruction cycle. Should an interrupt request be found, the processor typically does not start the next instruction execution. Instead, it starts to identify the interrupting device and to perform the service requested by that device. In one case, called the *vectored interrupt* method, the I/O device identifies itself to the CPU, e.g. by submitting a special identification number called the *device number*. In another method, called the *polled interrupt*, the CPU checks all the devices to find out which one is requesting the interrupt.

Interrupts free a processor from the need to check devices repeatedly. I/O devices are connected to the external interrupt inputs of the CPU (Fig. 3). For simplicity, the device register details of Fig. 1 are not shown and all signals are lumped into the system's bus. Once one or more of these devices is ready for an I/O transfer, the device can activate its interrupt request output. The outputs from all the devices are used to generate the interrupt request input of the CPU through an OR-gate. Thus, if there is at least one

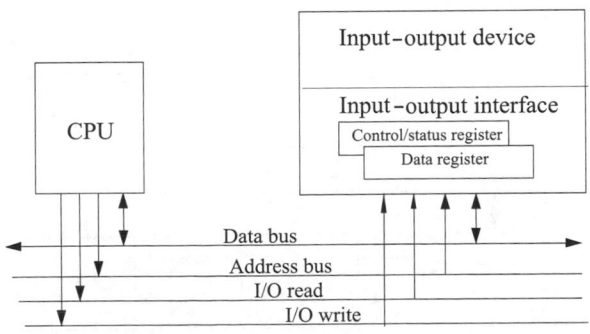

Figure 1. A typical programmed I/O configuration.

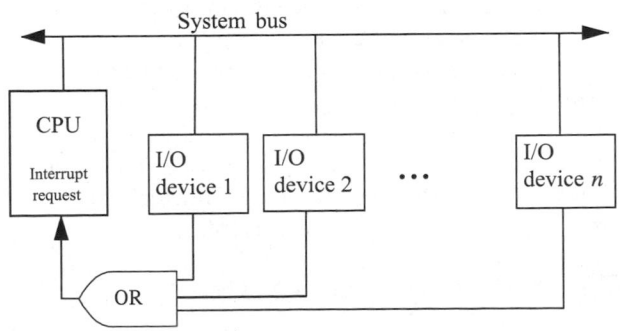

Figure 3. A hardware configuration for polled-interrupt I/O.

device which is requesting an interrupt, a hardware interrupt signal is issued to the CPU. At the end of each instruction cycle, the CPU checks its interrupt request input and if it finds any outstanding interrupts, it enters the so-called *interrupt acknowledge cycle*. Thus, rather than using several instructions repeatedly to check on interrupts as in the case of programmed I/O, the CPU contains circuitry to make the check during each instruction execution. In Fig. 3, the CPU has no way of telling which device has requested the service. Therefore it uses the interrupt acknowledge cycle to poll the I/O devices and determine which one of them is requesting the interrupt; hence the name *polled interrupt*. If more than one device is requesting the service, the CPU services the one with the highest priority. One way to implement device priorities in this case is by ordering the polling such that the devices with the higher priorities are checked first and the first device that needs service is granted the request. Once the CPU determines which device should be serviced, it transfers the program control to an interrupt service routine for that device, whose execution results in performing the required I/O service. The service could be to read a block of input data, as in Fig. 2. Since it would be activated only when the device was ready, it would not require the busy–wait loop, and in place of the main loop, it would transfer one word and return control to the main program, to be activated again by the next interrupt.

While polled interrupt eliminates the busy–waits that have to be performed by the CPU to know whether a device needs service, it still requires the CPU to go through all I/O devices to find out which one(s) is (are) requesting the interrupt. Vectored interrupts eliminate this requirement. In vectored interrupt systems, the interrupting device identifies itself to the CPU either by supplying a unique device number or by supplying a memory location that holds the address of its interrupt service routine. In some of the Intel implementations, the device may supply the opcode of a transfer of control instruction which transfers control to the interrupt service routine. This occurs during the interrupt acknowledge cycle during which the interrupting device must place the information needed on the data bus for the CPU to read. In all interrupt-driven I/O transactions, the processor state (program counter, special status registers) must be saved, typically on the system stack (*q.v.*) prior to transferring the control to the interrupt service routine. This allows a successful resumption of normal execution after returning from the I/O service.

Direct Memory Access Systems

While vectored interrupts relieve the CPU of much of the control work that programmed I/O and even the polled-interrupt method need, the CPU is actually still heavily involved in the I/O data transfers. To read a word from an I/O device to memory, this word must first be read from the device by the processor, then written by the processor to the memory. In addition, when reading or writing a big block of data, the processor has the burden of sequencing through the needed addresses. Devices like disks, which need to transfer large volumes of data at high rates, generally use *direct memory access* (*DMA*) controllers, which can act like a simple processor for the purpose of I/O operations. DMA controllers are capable of resolving device priorities, can read data from I/O devices and write them to memory and vice versa without the intervention of the CPU, and can generate address sequences to access blocks of data.

A DMA controller can seize control of the system bus and use bus cycles to transfer data between devices and memory without the involvement of the processor. To do so, a DMA controller has a memory address register to put the relevant memory address on the address bus, a data register to buffer the data being transferred, and a word counter to keep track of the remaining data to be transferred. When a peripheral device, such as a disk controller, requests a transfer by issuing a DMA request as in Fig. 4, the DMA controller (DMAC) issues a bus request to the CPU. As soon as the CPU finishes the execution of its current instruction, it disconnects itself from the bus and issues a bus grant signal to the DMA controller. Upon receiving a bus grant, the DMA controller starts administering the I/O operation. The I/O transfer is much faster in this case since the full bus bandwidth becomes available solely for memory transfers rather than for executing CPU instructions to perform such transfers, where many of the bus cycles are consumed in instruction fetches for reads, writes, and address and word count manipulations.

DMA controllers have two modes of operations, *burst mode* and *cycle-stealing*. In the burst mode, the transfer continues without interruption. If the peripheral is not able to handle the speed of the transfers, the DMA controller must keep the bus idle between the

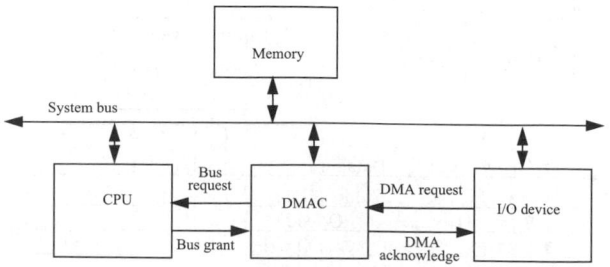

Figure 4. A DMA I/O system configuration.

transfers. In cycle-stealing, a DMA request is generated for each transfer. In the case of slow devices, this allows the CPU to use the bus and perform useful activities while the device is getting ready for the next transfer. In higher-performance systems, dual-ported memory systems (*see* PORT, MEMORY) can be used where both the DMA controller and CPU operate concurrently.

Input–Output Coprocessors and Channels

While DMA controllers relieve the CPU of the burden of performing the data transfers and allow devices to move their data to and from memory without CPU intervention, DMA controllers still must be set up by the CPU. Furthermore, DMA controllers are quite inflexible, since they are mainly hardware. Unlike DMA controllers, I/O coprocessors can execute specialized I/O instructions in addition to many other standard instructions, such as arithmetic and branching. Thus, I/O coprocessors are specialized processors whose function is to conduct I/O operations efficiently.

An I/O coprocessor is called a *channel*, although that term now generally refers to the communication medium over which I/O transactions take place. One may think of an I/O coprocessor as a "smart" communication channel—one capable of arbitration functions and full I/O control.

The IBM 360/370/390 systems (*q.v.*) use channels. They have two types: selector channels and multiplexer channels. A selector channel is basically an I/O coprocessor designed to handle one device at a time, and is particularly suitable for high-speed devices. A multiplexer channel can handle several slower devices concurrently. In order to perform an I/O transaction under the channel architecture, the CPU sends a START signal and the I/O device number to the channel to which the device is attached. The channel then reads a word (the so-called channel address word or CAW) from a standard location in memory which contains the address of the channel program in memory. The channel then executes the channel program from the main memory until the I/O service is completed. Fig. 5 shows an example of an I/O coprocessor system.

High-Performance I/O Systems

High-performance massively parallel computers use tens, hundreds, or thousands of processors to solve computationally intensive problems. As such systems get larger by adding more processors, I/O transfer rates must increase proportionally or some of the benefit from parallel processing will be lost. This might also require the use of more than one I/O control module to avoid a performance bottleneck with centralization of I/O control. Thus, in order for such parallel systems to work well, their I/O architecture must scale, i.e. deliver more and more I/O bandwidth as the number of processors in the system increases. There are two major categories of massively parallel systems: the single instruction multiple data (SIMD) class and the multiple instruction multiple data (MIMD) class. SIMD systems have only one instruction controller and all processors do the same thing on different data at the same time. Therefore, apart from the control unit, the processors can be simple arithmetic logic units (ALUs). I/O scalability in SIMD machines results from increasing the I/O bandwidth (data wires) as the number of processors increases. In MIMD architectures, control is distributed, and each node is a complete processor. In MIMD architectures I/O scalability comes from distributing I/O coprocessors and services over the entire machine. Examples of each follow.

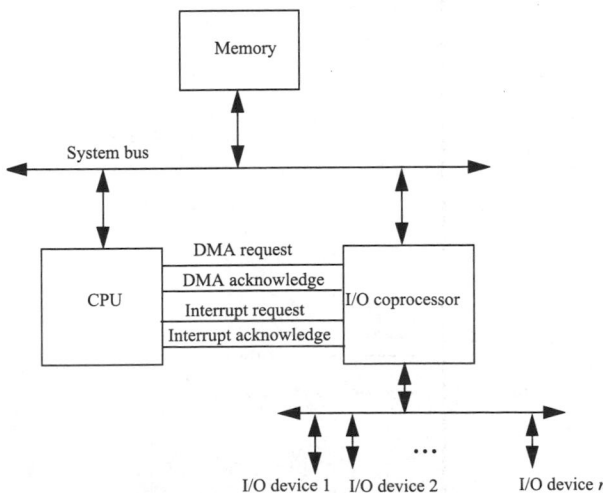

Figure 5. Example system configuration with an I/O coprocessor.

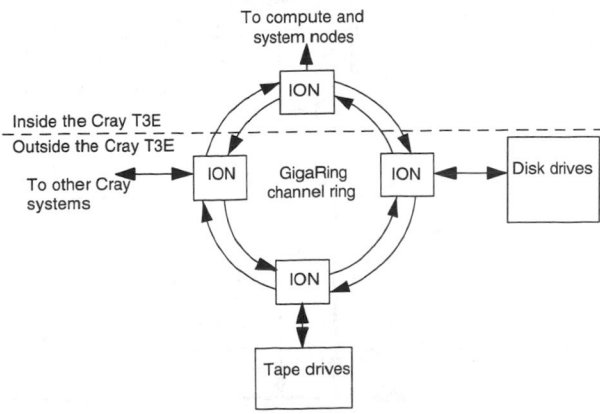

Figure 6. The GigaRing architecture for the Cray T3E.

THE CRAY T3E I/O ARCHITECTURE

The Cray T3E, introduced in the late 1990s, is a parallel supercomputer with configurations that range from 16 to 2048 processors, interconnected via a high-speed network. The T3E is an MIMD architecture, so each processing node can proceed independent of the other nodes, until certain synchronization points at which data may need to be exchanged. I/O scalability is obtained by using general-purpose microprocessors as I/O coprocessors (called IONs, for I/O nodes) and distributing the I/O facilities across the processors and their interprocessor communication network as shown in Fig. 6. The T3E processors interface through an ION to the so-called GigaRing, a bi-directional I/O ring medium capable of transferring data at a rate of 1 GB/sec. Each GigaRing can be configured with multiple IONs. There are different types of IONs

including: (1) multipurpose nodes, which can support many interfacing standards such as FDDI, SCSI disk or tape, ATM, and Ethernet; (2) disk drive nodes, which can support RAID (*q.v.*); (3) tape drive nodes; and (4) network nodes, which can also support I/O interface standards such as 64-bit HIPPI (High-Performance Parallel Interface). The number of GigaRings and IONs per GigaRing can vary and the largest configuration can deliver up to 128 GB/sec of I/O bandwidth.

THE MASPAR I/O ARCHITECTURE

MasPar is a SIMD massively parallel computer which was produced in the early 1990s. The MasPar organized its processors into a two-dimensional array of up to 16K processing elements (PEs). The processors are interconnected via the X-net network, a 2D mesh

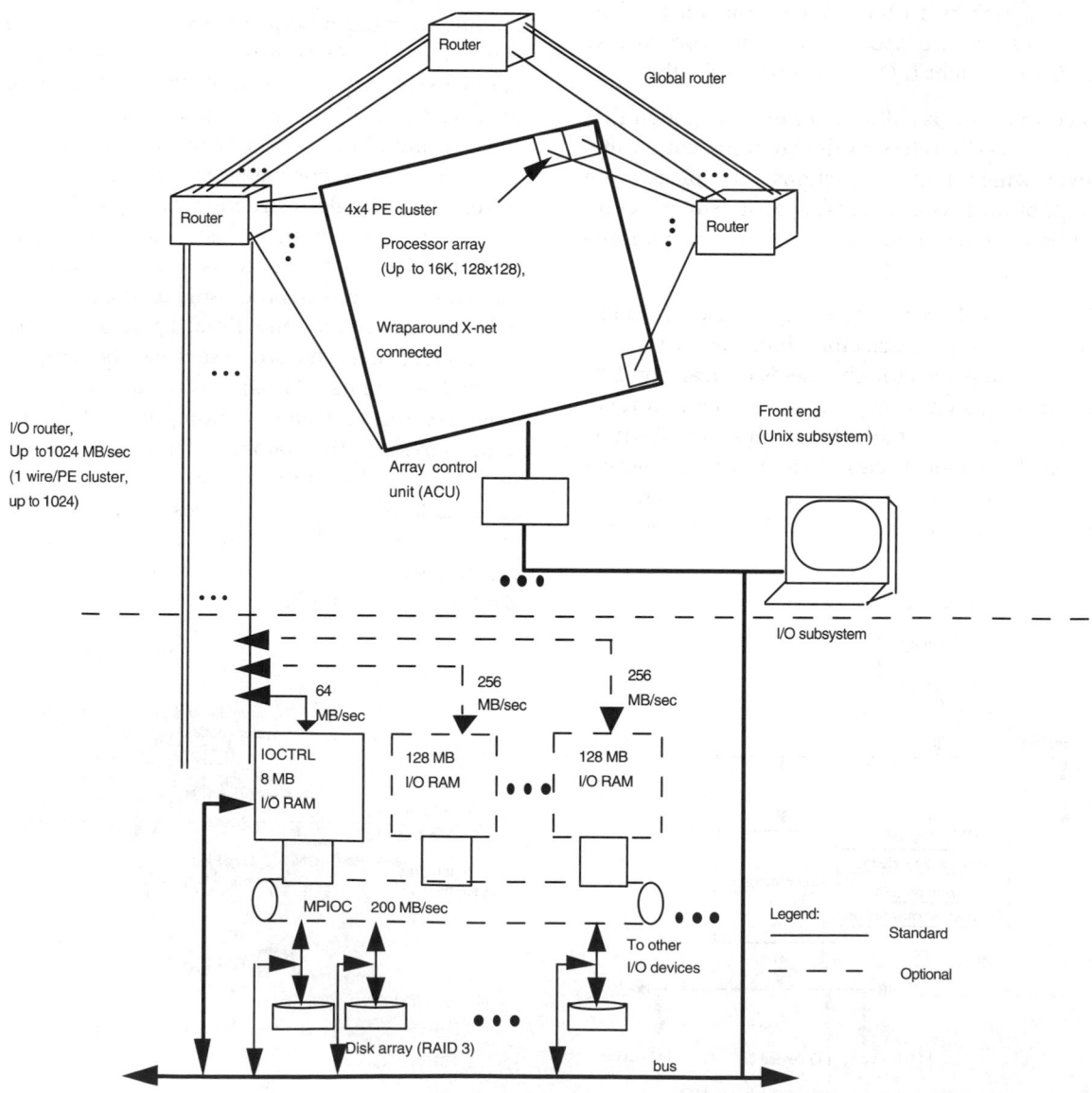

Figure 7. The MasPar I/O subsystem.

with diagonal and toroidal (wraparound) connections. In addition, a three-stage interconnection network called the global router (GR) uses circuit switching for communication between distant processors. Every group of 4×4 neighboring PEs forms a cluster which shares a serial connection to the global router.

As the number of processors increases, one additional I/O connection is added for every new 16 processors, making the I/O router bandwidth and the overall I/O performance scale with the number of processors. With a fully implemented MasPar of 16K processors, the I/O router reaches a width of 1024 wires and has a transfer rate of up to 1 GB/sec. Using these shared wires, a PE array does I/O via the global router, which is directly connected to an I/O buffer called the I/O RAM, as shown in Fig. 7. The solid lines in Fig. 7 show the standard I/O configuration for this machine, with optional additions shown as broken lines.

Bibliography

1998. Hayes, J. P. *Computer Architecture and Organization*, 3rd Ed. New York: WCB/McGraw-Hill.

Tarek El-Ghazawi and Gideon Frieder

INSTANT MESSAGING

See ONLINE CONVERSATION.

INSTITUTE FOR CERTIFICATION OF COMPUTER PROFESSIONALS (ICCP)

For articles on related subjects *see* ASSOCIATION FOR COMPUTING MACHINERY; and PERSONNEL IN THE COMPUTER FIELD.

The Institute for Certification of Computer Professionals (ICCP) is an organization of computing societies established in 1973 for the purpose of sponsoring activity in the areas of testing and certification of knowledge and competence of computing personnel. It is intended to pool the resources and interests of individual societies so that ultimately the full attention of the industry may be focused on the vital tasks of developing and recognizing qualified personnel.

The purposes of the Institute are:

1. To foster, promote, develop, and conduct scientific inquiry and research into any of the several activities related to the development and recognition of knowledge and competence among personnel in the computer and information systems industry.

2. To foster, promote, develop, and conduct scientific inquiry and research into standards of good practice.

3. To formulate and administer testing and evaluation programs designed to determine the aptitude, level of knowledge, and competence of individuals engaging in or desiring to engage in disciplines directly related to applied computer and information science.

4. To foster, promote, and develop internationally the purposes of the corporation, including, without limitation, (a) the establishment of reciprocal standards with, and reciprocal membership for and cooperation with, organizations having similar aims and purposes; (b) the establishment of international standards of good practice in the worldwide computer and information systems industry; and (c) the formulation and administration of reciprocal testing and evaluation programs.

How Established

The ICCP was incorporated as a not-for-profit corporation in the state of Delaware, USA, on 13 August 1973. Its establishment was the outgrowth of several years of study by committees of the Data Processing Management Association (DPMA) and the Association for Computing Machinery (ACM) during which the concept of a "computer foundation" to foster testing and certification programs was formulated. An open invitation was extended to other societies to support an organizational period. The organizations that served on the Computer Foundation Organizing Committee and then became members of the Institute were:

Association for Computing Machinery
Association of Computer Programmers and Analysts
Association for Educational Data Systems
(now International Society for Technology in Education)
Automation Association (now the Association for Information Management)
Canadian Information Processing Society
Data Processing Management Association
(now Association of Information Technology Professionals)
IEEE Computer Society
Society of Certified Data Processors (now the Association of the Institute for Certification of Computer Professionals)
Society of Professional Data Processors

As of 1999, the member organizations are:

Constituent Societies:
Association for Computing Machinery
Association for Women in Computing
Association of Information Technology Professionals

Black Data Processing Associates
Canadian Information Processing Society
Coleman Computer Association
Independent Computer Consultants Association
International Society for Technology in
Education

Affiliate Societies:
ABRS (Hong Kong)
Ankook Academy, Seoul, Korea
Association for Corporate Computing Technical
Professionals
Business Technology Association
Computer Measurement Group
Consejo Profesional en Ciencias Informaticas
(Argentina)
Data Administration Management Association
Federation of NCR User Groups
Future Management Consultants
Gulf Institute for the Development of Human
Resources (Oman)
Hong Kong Computer Society
Information Systems Consultants Association
Institute of Applied Data Processing
International Information Technology (Pakistan)
Multi Communications Systems Corp
SISE: Instituto Peruano de Sistemas (Peru)
Society of Computer Professionals
UNITE
YamTech Systems Ltd (Ghana)

ORGANIZATIONAL STRUCTURE

The Institute is governed by a Board of Directors to which each member society designates two directors. Officers of the Institute are elected from the Board at its annual meeting and include a president, vice-president, secretary, and treasurer. The officers constitute an Executive Committee, which may act for the Board between its regularly scheduled meetings. Standing committees advise the Board and assist in the management of the Institute, while *ad hoc* committees are established from time to time to investigate, evaluate, and recommend action on potential programs.

As programs are authorized by the Institute, councils with appropriate technical and professional expertise are established to oversee them and to provide the competence necessary to ensure high standards. Councils have policy-making powers as well as responsibility for quality control, within the domain of their programs. The Certification Councils have jurisdiction over the testing and certification programs described in the next section.

Programs of the Institute

The Institute's highest priority is the improvement of existing certification programs and the establishment

of new examinations for various specialties. In 1974, the Institute acquired the testing and certification programs of the DPMA, including the Certificate in Data Processing (CDP) examination, which the DPMA began in 1962. Additional programs have subsequently been established to meet professional and industry needs.

The Institute has recently modified and updated its examinations to reflect more accurately the changing nature of the computer profession. The new examination structure for experienced professionals consists of three parts:

◆ A mandatory core examination that tests general knowledge and expertise. Question topics range from management science and systems concepts to data architecture and statistics.

◆ The choice of two of eleven specialty examinations that best reflects career expertise.

In 1994 the Institute converted the Certified Data Processor (CDP), Certified Systems Professional (CSP), and Certified Computer Programmer to a single designation—CCP—Certified Computing Professional.

The ICCP certification programs are directed to senior level personnel in the information processing industry. Any person may take any examination. However, they will not receive a certificate and be entitled to the use of the designation until the experience requirement discussed below is attained.

EXPERIENCE

A candidate must have at least 60 months of full-time (or part-time equivalent) direct experience in computer-based information systems. The 60 months need not be consecutive or in a single position. Acceptable forms of experience include that in the IT professions including, but not limited to: data processing systems, programming, management, and teaching computer-based information systems. Systems and programming experience gained while employed by computer equipment manufacturers, service centers, management consulting firms, or educational institutions may be applied toward this requirement. Clerical, data entry, or experience gained in connection with formal classwork will not be considered acceptable.

ACADEMIC AND OTHER CERTIFICATION ALTERNATIVES

Candidates having less than 60 months work experience may substitute post-secondary academic work for up to 24 months of experience on the following basis, provided official transcripts of academic work are submitted to ICCP:

- ◆ 24 months: Bachelor's degree or graduate degree in information systems or computer science.

- ◆ 24 months: Any candidate who passes the Associate Computer Professional (ACP) Examination.

- ◆ 18 months: Bachelor's or graduate degree in related area, including accounting, business, engineering, mathematics, sciences, or statistics.

- ◆ 12 months: Bachelor's or graduate degree in nonrelated areas.

- ◆ 12 months: Associate degree or diploma (two-year program) in information systems or computer science.

The maximum credit for academic alternatives toward the experience requirement shall not exceed 24 months.

PROFESSIONAL QUALIFICATIONS

Each candidate is required to obtain the signature of a responsible person who can verify both the candidate's work experience and professional qualifications through personal knowledge or access to the necessary information. An ICCP certificate holder is to make this verification whenever possible. The candidate's immediate supervisor may be accepted as an alternative when an ICCP certificate holder is not in a position to provide the required verification.

ICCP also provides the Associate Computer Professional (ACP) Examination, an examination program that measures qualifications of entry-level personnel. The ACP program is designed for students or recent graduates of computer programs within one-, two-, and four-year colleges; graduates of technical computer institutions; and individuals who have been working in the computer field only a short period of time.

The American Council on Education (ACE) has evaluated and approved the awarding of college credit for successful candidates who pass ICCP examinations with a minimum 70% passing score. Successful candidates may earn up to 24 credit hours. Through 1998, the ICCP had certified over 48,000 persons.

The ICCP uses a computer-based testing system through Sylvan Learning Centers, and the exams are available on demand. For further information contact ICCP Headquarters, 2200 E. Devon Ave., Suite 247, Des Plaines, IL 60018, USA; call +1-847-299-4227, fax +1-847-299-4280, or email ICCP2200@aol.com. The ICCP web address is http://www.iccp.org.

Fred H. Harris, revised by Cindy Blaese

INSTITUTE OF ELECTRICAL AND ELECTRONIC ENGINEERS — COMPUTER SOCIETY (IEEE-CS)

For articles on related subjects *see* ASSOCIATION FOR COMPUTING MACHINERY; COMPUTER SOCIETIES; INTERNATIONAL FEDERATION FOR INFORMATION PROCESSING; LITERATURE OF COMPUTING; and MCDOWELL AWARD WINNERS.

The *IEEE Computer Society* (often called just the Computer Society) is one of the oldest and perhaps the largest association of computer professionals in the world, referring to itself as "The World's Computer Society." It traces its beginnings to the formation in 1946 of the Committee on Large-Scale Computing Devices (chaired by Charles Concordia) of the American Institute of Electrical Engineers (AIEE) which was followed in 1951 by the formation of a competitor, The Computer Group of IRE (Institute of Radio Engineers). In 1963, the IRE merged with the AIEE to create the Institute of Electrical and Electronics Engineers (IEEE), with Computer Group as the name of the merged computer subgroups. IEEE-CS assumed its current name in 1972 and is the largest of the many societies that comprise the IEEE.

IEEE-CS, with a current membership of 90,000, was formed to advance the theory and practice of computer and information processing technology and promote cooperation and exchange of technical information among its members. To this end it annually sponsors or co-sponsors over 110 conferences, meetings, workshops, and symposia, and engages in a program of publication that makes it one of the world's leading publishers of technical material on computing. Its publications include periodicals, books, monographs, tutorials, conference proceedings, executive briefings, and CD-ROMs, one of which contains the 14,000 pages of each year's IEEE-CS periodical content. More than 300 titles bear the imprint of the Computer Society Press. The leading IEEE-CS periodicals are its monthly, *Computer*, now subtitled "Innovative technology for computer professionals," which reaches all its members with mainly nonresearch content; the monthly *Transactions on Computers*, a traditional research journal; and the quarterly *Annals of the History of Computing*, one of a small number of scholarly journals devoted to the history of a single scientific or engineering discipline.

Technical activities are carried out by 32 semiautonomous technical committees (TCs) whose subject areas are shown in Table 1. Depending on their size the TCs act like little societies, holding meetings and conferences, and publishing newsletters and conference proceedings. IEEE-CS itself publishes 10 special-interest periodicals and seven transactions (Table 2),

Table 1. IEEE-CS technical committees.

Complexity in Computing
Computational Medicine
Computer Architecture
Computer Communications
Computer Elements
Computer Generated Music
Computer Graphics
Computer Languages
Data Engineering
Design Automation
Digital Libraries
Distributed Processing
Electronics and the Environment
Engineering of Computer-Based Systems
Fault Tolerant Computing
Mass Storage Systems
Mathematical Foundations of Computing
Microprocessors and Microcomputers
Microprogramming and Microarchitecture
Multimedia Computing
Multiple Valued Logic
Operating Systems
Parallel Processing
Pattern Analysis and Machine Intelligence
Real-Time Systems
Security and Privacy
Simulation
Software Engineering
Supercomputing Applications
Systems Packaging
Test Technology
VLSI

and cooperates with the Association for Computing Machinery (ACM) in the publication of *Transactions on Networking*, with the American Institute of Physics in publishing *Computing in Science and Engineering*, and with several IEEE societies in the publication of *Transactions on Multimedia*.

IEEE-CS has 12 standards committees formed into more than 200 working groups charged with the development of IEEE standards that apply to computing. It conducts an active awards program honoring technical achievements and service to the profession, society, and the CS itself. Some awards are not limited to IEEE-CS members (*see* MCDOWELL AWARD WIN-

Table 2. IEEE-CS transactions.

IEEE Transactions on Computers
IEEE Transactions on Knowledge & Data Engineering
IEEE/CS Transactions on Multimedia
IEEE Transactions on Parallel & Distributed Systems
IEEE Transactions on Pattern Analysis & Machine Intelligence
IEEE Transactions on Software Engineering
IEEE Transactions on Visualization & Computer Graphics
IEEE Transactions on VLSI Systems
IEEE/ACM Transactions on Networking

NERS). It has more than 200 regular and student chapters, about half outside of the USA.

On 1 January 1999, IEEE-CS, as an international organization, became a full member of IFIP (*q.v.*) having previously been one of the two members (with ACM) of FOCUS, which until 31 December 1998 represented the USA in IFIP. It has a joint membership arrangement with ACM, is affiliated with 12 other US societies and 25 societies in other countries, and is an executive member of the Internet Society (*see* Appendix V). In addition to its headquarters close to the center of federal power (1730 Massachusetts Ave. NW, Washington, DC 20036-1992), it maintains a Publications Office on the west coast, the original base of the Computer Group (P.O. Box 3014, Los Alamitos, CA 90720-1264), a European office (13, Avenue de l'Aquilon, B-1200 Brussels, Belgium), an Asia/Pacific office (Ooshima Building, 2-19-1 Minami Aoyama, Minato-ku, Tokyo 107-0062, Japan), and a Website, at http://computer.org.

Its chief officers since its inception are listed in Appendix V.

Eric A. Weiss

INSTRUCTION COUNTER

See PROGRAM COUNTER.

INSTRUCTION DECODING

For articles on related topics *see* ARITHMETIC-LOGIC UNIT; CENTRAL PROCESSING UNIT; COMPUTER ARCHITECTURE; CYCLE TIME; INSTRUCTION SET; MICROPROGRAMMING; and REDUCED INSTRUCTION SET COMPUTER.

The execution of an instruction in a standard digital computer occurs in three or four phases:

1. Fetching the instruction from main memory or cache memory into the instruction register in the CPU.

2. Decoding the instruction and generation of the data operand address (as in the case of a LOAD or a STORE instruction)

3. Fetching (or storing) the data operand.

4. Final execution of the operation (usually in the ALU).

In many modern instruction sets steps 3 and 4 are mutually exclusive (e.g. Sun Sparc or DEC Alpha). In these processors, any one instruction can either do a memory-based operation (e.g. LOAD register from memory) or an ALU operation (e.g. ADD registers with result in a register), but not both (e.g. ADD a register to a value in memory (or cache)). In older instruction sets (e.g. IBM S360/370/390 or Intel 80x86), instructions are available which use all four phases.

Each of these phases is partitioned into one or more steps or "cycles". The cycle is the smallest time quantum in the control process and it is defined by the clock rate of the processor. It is the time required to reconfigure (change the contents of) a data register in the processor. Several cycles may be required to complete the execution of the instruction. Simple processors of the early 1990s (e.g. MIPS 2000) used 4 cycles to complete most instructions. More modern processors (DEC Alpha or Intel Pentium Pro) use 8–10 or more cycles to complete instruction execution. In both cases the instruction execution is pipelined or overlapped so that ideally the number of cycles required for instruction execution does not degrade performance (*see* PIPELINE).

The decoding phase of instruction execution is most important as it initiates the specific control process specified by the instruction. When an instruction is transferred to the instruction register, its op code is decoded into a sequence of control steps that configure the flow of data between registers and activate the ALU and other execution resources specified by the instruction.

The unit that responds to the op code, called the *instruction decoder*, is responsible for the interpretation of the instruction. The decoder can be implemented in combinational logic ("hardwired") or through a microprogram control storage (*see* MICROPROGRAMMING). The latter, while widely used in the past, is less common in current microprocessor implementations.

As processor speed and complexity increase, so does the need for rapid decoding. With pipelined processors, the decoding is established once in a single cycle for the entire sequence of control operations that execute the instruction. For the class of processors generally called *multiple issue machines*, including Very Long Instruction Word (VLIW) and superscalar processors such as the Intel Pentium Pro, the decoder must decode multiple instructions in a single cycle, further complicating the decoding process (*see* INSTRUCTION-LEVEL PARALLELISM). For these processors, the decoder must check the availability of resources for each instruction being decoded. For superscalar processors, the decoder must also check for dependencies both among the instructions being decoded and those previously decoded but not yet completed. Finally, for all multiple issue processors, the decoder must arrange that the designated instructions and data are sent to appropriate and available execution units.

In these more complicated processors, the decode implementation is frequently distributed across some of the elements of the processor, such as the ALU or the floating-point adder. The major flow of control of instructions is still performed by the centralized instruction decoder, but the actual implementation of control lines within an execution unit is distributed to the individual execution units themselves.

Bibliography

1996. Stallings, W. *Computer Organization and Architecture*, 4th Ed. Upper Saddle River, NJ: Prentice Hall.

Michael J. Flynn

INSTRUCTION-LEVEL PARALLELISM

For articles on related subjects *see* COMPILER; COMPUTER ARCHITECTURE; INSTRUCTION DECODING; MICROPROCESSORS AND MICROCOMPUTERS; PARALLEL PROCESSING; PIPELINE; and REDUCED INSTRUCTION SET COMPUTER.

Instruction-level parallelism (ILP) is a set of processor and compiler design techniques that speed up program execution via the parallel execution of individual RISC-style operations, such as memory loads and stores, integer additions, and floating-point multiplications. Although operations are executed in parallel, there is only a single thread of execution. The processor–compiler system is handed a single program, written for a sequential processor, from which it extracts the parallelism automatically.

An important feature of these techniques is that, like circuit speed improvements, and unlike other forms of parallel processing, they are largely transparent to users (*see* TRANSPARENCY). This is significant because the computer industry has grown accustomed to a spectacular rate of increase of microprocessor performance, without requiring a fundamental rewriting of a program in a parallel form using a different algorithm or language, and often without even recompiling the program. The benefits of this have been enormous. Computer users have had faster and faster computers while still having access to applications representing billions of dollars worth of investment—something that would not happen if applications had to be continually restructured to take advantage of the faster, more recent computers. ILP has been the key technology that has continued this trend in the 1990s. Virtually every microprocessor built for general-purpose use since 1994 has embodied a significant amount of ILP.

If ILP is to be achieved, the compiler and the run-time hardware must perform the following functions between them:

◆ Determine which operations can be legally executed in a given cycle. (Sometimes an operation must wait for the completion of an earlier operation before it can be executed. In that case, the later operation is said to have a *dependence* on the earlier.)

◆ From among the ready-to-execute operations, select some for execution. These must be assigned to some specific functional unit, and must be assigned a register into which the result may be deposited. These tasks are referred to as *scheduling*.

What all ILP processors have in common is multiple functional units that can execute multiple operations in parallel, as shown in Fig. 1. The two most important types of ILP processors differ in how and when they decide what to schedule:

◆ *Superscalar* processors are given sequential programs, just as they might run on a processor containing no ILP. Since the program contains no explicit information regarding the dependences between the instructions, the dependences that exist must be determined by the hardware, which must then make the scheduling decisions as well.

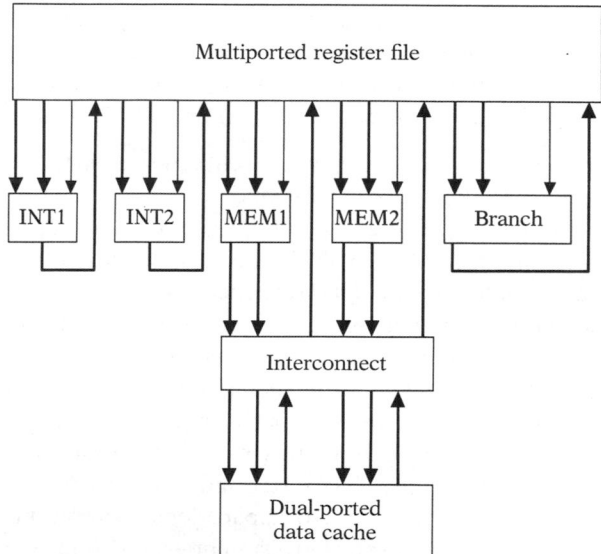

Figure 1. Execution hardware of a sample processor for executing programs with instruction-level parallelism. This consists of two identical integer units and two identical memory ports. INT1 and INT2 perform integer addition, subtraction and multiplication. MEM1 and MEM2 represent the hardware that prepares and presents load and store operations to the dual-ported data cache. BRANCH performs conditional and unconditional branches. It is able to read a pair of registers, compare them and branch on the Boolean result. It is also able to store the Boolean result of a comparison into the register file for use as a predicate. Every operation has a third input, a Boolean value, shown as the thin arrow into each functional unit. If this value is true, the operation executes normally. If not, it is not executed at all.

All of this is carried out by the processor as the program runs.

◆ *Very Long Instruction Word* (*VLIW*) processors are given programs in which the compiler has already identified the parallelism in the program and has embodied that information in the program itself—in each machine-level program statement, several operations may be packaged together as a single VLIW instruction. This information is of direct value to the hardware, since it knows with no further checking which operations it can execute in the same cycle. Indeed, a program for a VLIW may have its exact schedule completely laid out by the compiler before the program is presented to the hardware.

Superscalar Processors

In a fully sequential processor, each instruction is issued after the previous one has completed. Such a processor falls short of achieving an issue rate of even a single instruction per cycle, except in the unlikely circumstance that every instruction completes execution in a single cycle. Superscalar processors take a number of measures to improve upon this.

RUN-TIME SCHEDULING

The first step in increasing the issue rate is to attempt to issue an instruction every cycle, even if prior instructions have not completed, using the related techniques of pipelining and overlapped execution. If the semantics of the program are to be preserved, instruction issue must pause if the instruction that is about to be issued depends on a previous instruction that has not yet completed execution. To accomplish this the processor must check, with each instruction that it issues, whether the instruction's operands (registers or memory locations that the instruction uses or modifies) coincide with the operands of any other instruction that has been issued but has not yet completed. If this is the case, instruction issue must be delayed until those prior instructions on which this instruction depends have completed execution. These dependences must be monitored to determine when this situation disappears. When that happens, the instruction is independent of all other uncompleted instructions and can be allowed to begin executing once the hardware has selected an available functional unit to execute the instruction.

The next step towards achieving the goal of an instruction per cycle is out-of-order execution. Instead of stalling instruction issue as soon as an instruction is encountered that depends on one that is in flight (being executed), the dependent instruction is set aside to await the completion of the instructions upon which it depends. In the meantime, the processor may issue and begin the out-of-order execution of subsequent instructions which prove to be independent of all sequentially preceding instructions which either are waiting to be executed or are in some stage of execution. The Control Data Corporation (*q.v.*) CDC 6600 and the IBM System 360/91 were among the earliest processors to employ such hardware.

RUN-TIME SPECULATIVE EXECUTION

Conditional branches pose a major obstacle to ILP since operations that would be issued after the branch must wait for the branch to resolve which way the program flow will go. Speculative execution is a special form of out-of-order execution in which the instructions following a conditional branch are allowed to execute before the branch has completed and before it is certain that the program's flow of control will actually mandate the execution of those operations. Using speculative execution, the potential ILP is increased, often dramatically.

When an operation is executed speculatively, it may happen that the flow of the program is such that that instruction ought not to have been executed. In that case, the speculative operation is wasted. Furthermore, an additional time penalty must be incurred to restore the processor state before going down the correct path. It is important, therefore, that an extremely accurate *branch prediction* scheme be used, one which will guide speculative execution down the correct path most of the time. Dynamic branch prediction schemes employ a variety of algorithms implemented in hardware which, when presented with the current state of program execution immediately prior to a branch, produce the address of the instruction that is most likely to be executed after the branch. The simplest form of branch prediction hardware consists of an associative memory (*q.v.*) which associates the address of a branch with the address of the next instruction that was executed when this branch was last executed.

SUPERSCALAR EXECUTION

The final mechanism to increase the number of instructions executed per cycle is superscalar execution, which has the goal of issuing multiple, independent instructions in parallel each cycle even though the hardware is handed a sequential program. To do so, the processor must determine the dependences between the instructions that it wishes to issue simultaneously. Specifically, it may issue each instruction only if it is independent of all the other instructions that are being issued concurrently but which would have been executed earlier in a sequential execution of the program.

Another task for superscalar processors is to perform resource allocation in parallel, on behalf of the independent instructions that are to be issued in parallel. These instructions might have conflicting or competing resource needs, and even if there are sufficient resources for all of them, care must be taken to ensure that multiple instructions do not attempt to use the same resource at the same time.

The idea of superscalar execution was first suggested by Schorr and his colleagues (1971), and the term was coined in Agerwala and Cocke (1987). The first superscalar processor that was built commercially was the Astronautics ZS–1. Since then, a number of superscalar microprocessor products have been introduced, including the Motorola 68060, the MIPS R1000, the IBM PowerPC, the Sun UltraSparc, and the Intel Pentium Pro. Johnson (1991) discusses superscalar processor design in great depth.

VLIW Processors

VLIW processors evolved in an attempt to achieve high levels of ILP with reduced hardware complexity. The archetypal VLIW processor is defined by two features:

- *MultiOp* instructions, each of which specifies the concurrent issue of multiple operations per instruction, and

- *Non-unit assumed latencies*, i.e. where part of the architectural contract between the hardware and the compiler is that precisely a specified number of instructions will be issued between the issuance and the completion of any given operation.

When discussing VLIW processors, it is important to distinguish between an instruction and an operation. An *operation* is a unit of computation, such as an addition, memory load, or branch, which would be referred to as an instruction in the context of a sequential architecture. A (parallel) VLIW *instruction* is the set of operations that are supposed to be issued simultaneously.

COMPILE-TIME SCHEDULING

With a VLIW processor, most of the measures that were taken by the superscalar processor at run time to achieve ILP are performed by the compiler. Conceptually, the compiler emulates what a superscalar processor with the same execution hardware would do at run time. The compiler takes the sequential internal representation of the program and analyzes the dependences among the operations. If needed, it eliminates spurious dependences that are due to writing unrelated values to the same variable, by performing *register renaming*, i.e. writing each distinct value to its own compiler-generated variable. The compiler then performs *scheduling*, which involves delaying the scheduled initiation time of operations that depend upon others to a time when they will have completed, scheduling the out-of-order execution of other operations that are independent, and performing the allocation of the requisite functional units, buses, and registers. Since all of this is being done at compile time and requires no hardware support, it is not only realistic to think of building VLIW processors which have very high levels of ILP, but such processors have, in fact, been built successfully (Rau and Fisher, 1993).

It is the task of the compiler to decide which operations go into each instruction. Once a program has been scheduled, all operations that are supposed to begin at the same time are packaged into a single VLIW instruction, with the position of each operation within the instruction specifying the functional unit on which that operation is to execute. Thus the hardware need make no decisions at run time. A VLIW program is a direct transliteration of a desired record of execution, one that is feasible in the context of the given execution hardware.

COMPILE-TIME SPECULATIVE EXECUTION

Run-time speculation is expensive in the hardware needed to support it. The alternative is to perform speculative code motion (reordering of instructions) at compile time. The compiler for a VLIW machine specifies that an operation be executed speculatively merely by scheduling it before the branch that determines whether it should, in fact, be executed. During execution, the VLIW processor executes these speculative operations in the exact order specified by the program just as it does for non-speculative operations. As a result, these operations end up being executed before the branches that they were originally supposed to follow; hence they are executed speculatively in relation to the original sequential code that the scheduler received.

Just as a superscalar processor must predict which way branches will go, so must a VLIW compiler predict the branch direction so that it can schedule operations speculatively from the more likely path following the branch. Since the prediction is being performed at compile time, dynamic branch prediction is not an option. Instead, profiling runs are used to gather the appropriate statistics and to embed the prediction, at compile time, into the program.

PREDICATED EXECUTION

Another way of coping with the problem of branches is to eliminate them via a capability known as *predicated execution*. Predicated execution assumes that each operation has an additional Boolean-valued source operand, called a predicate. If the predicate input is 1,

the predicated operation is executed normally. If the predicate input is 0, the predicated operation is squashed, i.e. it does not modify any destination register or memory location, nor does it signal any exceptions. Predicated execution is a method of enforcing the requirements of program control-flow in a different way from that provided by branch operations.

Branches are removed using a technique commonly referred to as *if-conversion*. During if-conversion, each operation within the code region of interest is guarded by a predicate computed so as to be true if and only if flow of control would have reached that operation. Once this is done, the branch operations in that region become redundant and can be removed without altering the behavior of the program. In many situations predicated execution serves as an alternative to speculative execution whereas in other cases the two are complementary and augment each other.

As we have seen, many features in superscalar hardware have architecturally visible equivalents in VLIW systems. A list of these and other equivalences is shown in Table 1. For a discussion of those features that are beyond the scope of this article, and for more details on the features that were introduced here, *see* Johnson (1991) and Rau and Fisher (1993).

A precursor to the VLIW processors was Floating Point Systems' family of array processors. The term "VLIW" was coined by Fisher, and early work in this area was done by his research project (Ellis, 1985) and by Rau and his colleagues. These two activities led

Table 1. VLIW features that provide functionality equivalent to superscalar capabilities.

Superscalar capability	Equivalent, architecturally visible VLIW feature
Multiple instruction issue/ dynamic parallel dependence analysis	Multiple operations bound into a single VLIW instruction
Out-of-order execution	Static scheduling
Dynamic register renaming	Static register renaming/rotating registers
Dynamic branch prediction	Static branch prediction Predicated execution
Branch target buffer	Prepare-to-branch instruction Predicated execution
Speculative execution	Speculative code motion/ speculative opcodes/exception tags Predicated execution
Out-of-order memory referencing	Static disambiguation/static scheduling Statistical disambiguation/data speculation

directly to the first commercial VLIW products. Since then a number of microprocessors, incorporating VLIW features, have been introduced, including the Intel i860, and digital signal processor chips from Texas Instruments and Philips.

Speculations and Predictions

During the 1990s, superscalar processors have been extremely successful in sustaining the remarkable rate of increase in performance that has come to be expected of the microprocessor industry. There is a growing sentiment, however, that the design of super-scalar processors, at even higher levels of ILP, will pose an increasingly difficult challenge. The fundamental problem in superscalar execution is that a series of decisions that depend upon one another must be performed in parallel. The trade-off is between a longer cycle time or sharply increased logic complexity.

Traditionally, the lack of object code compatibility has been viewed as an important shortcoming of VLIW processors, and as a significant reason for preferring superscalar over VLIW. An improved understanding of the issues involved makes this position invalid. First, the run-time mechanisms for performing dynamic scheduling, and thereby achieving object code compatibility, are now understood for VLIW processors as they have been for superscalar processors, but are almost as expensive for VLIW processors as they are for superscalar processors. It would appear that the complexity of dynamic scheduling is primarily a function of the number of operations that the processor attempts to issue per cycle, and less a function of the nature of the ILP processor.

Furthermore, the importance of the debate over whether static or dynamic scheduling is better is greatly overrated. In addition to scheduling, a high-quality ILP compiler must perform a number of optimizations and code transformations, such as if-conversion, control speculation, data speculation, and critical path reduction, all of which are quite machine-specific and cannot be performed at run time. Dynamic scheduling alone cannot solve the problem of executing code that has been compiled for one ILP processor on another processor and at performance levels that are comparable to those achieved with re-compilation.

Thus, the choice appears to be between achieving object code compatibility via dynamic scheduling, but at low levels of ILP, or attaining high levels of ILP, but with an altered notion of object code compatibility. The latter includes concepts such as dynamic translation, i.e. the transparent invocation of compiler functionality at run time to translate the object code for one machine into code for the current machine.

Over the past few years, it has become apparent that the choice between VLIW and superscalar is a false choice. Neither approach, in its most extreme form, is desirable; making all decisions at compile time, and the consequent inability to react to dynamic situations, leads to an unacceptable loss of performance, as does foregoing the use of a state-of-the-art ILP compiler. In the future, most machines of interest will almost surely lie somewhere on the continuum between these two extremes.

Bibliography

1971. Schorr, H. "Design Principles for a High-performance System," *Proc. Symposium on Computers and Automata*, 165–192. New York: Polytechnic Institute of Brooklyn Press.
1983. Fisher, J. A. "Very Long Instruction Word Architectures and the ELI-512," *Proc. Tenth Annual International Symposium on Computer Architecture*, Stockholm, June 1983, 140–150.
1985. Ellis, J. R. *Bulldog: A Compiler for VLIW Architectures*. Cambridge, MA: MIT Press.
1987. Agerwala, T., and Cocke, J. *High Performance Reduced Instruction Set Processors*. Technical Report RC12434 (#55845). IBM Thomas J. Watson Research Center.
1991. Fisher, J. A., and Rau, B. R. "Instruction-level Parallel Processing," *Science*, **253**, *5025* (September), 1233–1241.
1991. Johnson, M. *Superscalar Microprocessor Design*. Upper Saddle River, NJ: Prentice Hall.
1993. Rau, B. R., and Fisher J. A. (eds.) *Instruction-Level Parallelism: A Special Issue of The Journal of Supercomputing*. Boston, MA: Kluwer Academic.
1993. Rau, B. R., and Fisher, J. A. "Instruction-level Parallel Processing: History, Overview and Perspective," *The Journal of Supercomputing*, **7**, *1/2* (May), 9–50.
1999. Silc, J., Robic, B., and Ungerer, T. *Processor Architecture: From Dataflow to Superscalar and Beyond*. New York: Springer-Verlag.

B. Ramakrishna Rau and Joseph A. Fisher

INSTRUCTION SET

For articles on related subjects *see* ADDRESSING; CENTRAL PROCESSING UNIT; COMPUTER ARCHITECTURE; COMPUTERS, MULTIPLE ADDRESS; GENERAL REGISTER; INPUT–OUTPUT OPERATIONS; INSTRUCTION DECODING; INSTRUCTION-LEVEL PARALLELISM; MACHINE AND ASSEMBLY LANGUAGE PROGRAMMING; MASKING; MICROPROGRAMMING; OPERAND; PRIVILEGED INSTRUCTION; REDUCED INSTRUCTION SET COMPUTER; and SHIFTING.

A machine *instruction* is a string of digits in the number base in which the machine operates which, when interpreted by the hardware, causes a unique and well-defined change in the state of the computer.

Most computers are based on the binary system. For almost all cases, therefore, the "string of digits" will be a string of bits, each having the value 0 or 1. In what follows, we will refer only to bit-oriented instructions, although we will express the various bit strings using their hexadecimal values.

The "change in state of the computer" is, in fact, a change in the contents of various registers or memory locations. The changed registers may be those explicitly or implicitly referred to by the instruction, or they may be some internal registers not directly known to the user. For example: The 16-bit string 0000010000001001 (hexadecimal 0409), when interpreted by the hardware of an Intel Pentium computer, causes the value 9 to be added to the special AL register, the result replacing the previous contents of that register. In this case, the change of state is apparent to the user of the machine.

Each computer model possesses its own instruction set. The same bit string may mean completely different things on two different computers, even if the number of bits needed for expressing an instruction is the same on the two machines. For example, the bit string 0409 (hexadecimal), which we used previously, invoked an addition in the Pentium computer. But when interpreted by a PowerPC computer, whose instructions are 32 bits long, the same bit string can be only part of an instruction, the first 8 bits (hexadecimal 04) not being a legal combination in that machine—that is, there is no instruction with the op code 04. This different interpretation for the same bit string makes it clear that bit strings are not a good basis for classification of machine instructions. In order to be able to find some patterns in the multitude of instructions available on various computers, we have to introduce categories based on other criteria.

Classification of Machine Instructions

There is usually a simple relation between the length of the computer word or addressable unit and the instruction length. In old machines with limited address space, the addressing was by words, and the instructions were of different sizes and packed into the words—typically two to four in one word. In more modern machines, the addressing is by bytes, with various data structures and instructions consisting of multiple bytes. Some architectures—in particular the Intel 80486 and Pentium 80586—have varying lengths for the instructions. Others, such as PowerPC (IBM and Motorola) and Alpha (Digital), have a single-length instruction with various formats. Instructions, therefore, can be initially classified by length and structure. This classification, however, does not teach us anything about the nature of the instructions, so a better classification is needed.

The bit string representing a machine instruction is generally divided into two major field groups: the operation (or "op code") field and operand fields, usually referred to as address field(s). These fields usually have the op code first followed by the address

fields. This is analogous to the way a mathematician denotes a function; i.e. $g(x, y, z)$ means the function (operation) g on the variables (operands) x, y, z.

The number of operands available in each instruction is generally different, not only between different machines but also in the same machine between different operation types and between different addressing modes. However, neither the question of the number of operands nor the question of the way they are addressed will be discussed here. (*See* ADDRESSING and COMPUTERS, MULTIPLE ADDRESS). This article concentrates on the operation field(s) only.

The basic types of operations available on contemporary machines are roughly divided into arithmetic, logical, data alignment, data move, and control operations. To these we have to add the growing number of specialized instructions to support various arithmetic modes—such as decimal arithmetic or special cases of floating point arithmetic—and to support graphics, multimedia, database, and various matching operations.

ARITHMETIC OPERATIONS

Arithmetic operations are usually confined to the four basic ones (add, subtract, multiply, and divide) and to the "compare" operation, which records status information about the relative magnitude of the operands compared. However, the number of actual arithmetic operations in contemporary computers is quite high. This is caused mainly by the multiplicity of operand types, condition setting, arithmetic modes, and inter-operation considerations, such as inclusion of previous carry results.

The different operand types are typically integers and floating-point numbers with different precision (half-, single-, double-, or quad-), or strings of differing length used in more complex instruction combinations—see below. The operands may assume various bases, and may be signed or unsigned. Binary is the usual base, and signed operands are used as the usual default, but decimal is also common. It is handled either by direct instructions (IBM 390 series for example) or by a special decimal adjustment that follows regular binary arithmetic operations (for example, the Intel Pentium's Adjust Decimal). In specialized machines, one may find arithmetic operations of a more sophisticated nature, such as exponentiation or square root.

LOGICAL OPERATIONS

Logical operations are Boolean operations on the bit values of the operands. Although there are 16 possible Boolean operations on two operands, usually only a subset of these (e.g. AND, OR, and NOT) is available.

Although this subset, or even a smaller one, is sufficient to reproduce all other Boolean operations, some machines include other operations, such as XOR, NOR, or NAND.

Boolean operations are used for the manipulation of parts of words, for decision processes, and for non-numerical processing. For an example of a use of logical operations, *see* MASKING.

Data alignment operations are sometimes lumped with logical operations, and include the various possible shift instructions, although in some classifications these form a category of their own. Shifting operations, as their names implies, shift the bits in a word to the left or right. The differences between types of shifts affects what happens to the bits being shifted out of a word and what bits are shifted in (*see* SHIFTING).

DATA MOVE OPERATIONS

Data move instructions include moves (copying) of data between memory locations and registers, and the input–output instructions necessary for communication between the central processor and peripheral devices. Examples of the former operations are instructions to load and store registers and to move data from one location in memory to another. The input–output operations (*q.v.*) are quite complex. Some data move operations may also be quite complex, in particular those that are designed to support graphics operations (*see* COMPUTER GRAPHICS). There is usually a special control for long data moves, so that the computer is available for interrupts (*q.v.*) throughout the data movement.

CONTROL OPERATIONS

Control instructions include those operations that are necessary for the proper sequencing of the instructions so that the programmed task can be performed correctly. These include conditional and unconditional branches, test instructions, and status-changing instructions.

As an example of this category of instructions, there may be instructions like BRANCH (or JUMP) to a given address (to begin a new sequence of instructions) when the result of the last operation is negative, or if there is an arithmetic overflow. There are also instructions that swap the contents of the user-accessible registers with internal registers, thus causing a change in the state of the computer; in particular, this may cause execution of a completely different sequence of instructions. Note also that program flow can be affected not only by explicit control instructions issued by the programmer but also by interrupts.

Some computers—the Intel Pentium is an example—also contain *repeat* instructions which cause a specific number of instruction(s) following the *repeat* to be executed a specific number of times or until some condition is met, thus affecting the sequencing of the program. Inasmuch as they influence sequencing, we include *repeat* among the control instructions, but will add some comments later on.

This rough division of instructions into types is not necessarily mutually exclusive. Many computers have instructions such as *decrement register* and *branch if the result is zero*—thus mixing arithmetic and control instructions.

Different instruction types usually possess different numbers of operands. Whereas arithmetic operations usually refer to three operands (two for the data locations and one for the result location), either explicitly or implicitly, certain control instructions may have one or no operands at all. For example, an unconditional BRANCH has one operand, but a CLEAR ACCUMULATOR instruction has none. In addition to the operands involved in the instruction execution, there are also condition codes involved. Generally speaking, condition codes are indicators or *flags*, usually one bit long, which describe the properties of the results and the validity of the operation performed.

Examples of condition codes are explicit indications of (1) the sign of the result, (2) whether or not an overflow has occurred, (3) what the relative magnitudes of the operands are, and (4) whether there is a parity error in reading or writing to memory. Similar to the instruction repertoire, the variety of condition codes differs among computers. There is also a difference in the way that condition codes are used. In some computers they are incorporated directly in the instructions, especially conditional branches (like BRANCH ON OVERFLOW), and in others they can be transferred into registers and then manipulated as data. Certain condition codes, when generated, may cause interrupts.

Machine Language and Instruction Formats

The *instruction repertoire* or *command set* of a computer is defined to be the set of all possible operations that the computer can perform. In a computer of the type discussed here, the instruction repertoire boils down to the set of all possible operation codes (op codes) and the variants on them (such as inclusion of carry, selection of various addressing modes etc.). There are, however, other types of computer design possible, such as tagged architecture machines, in which the operation code and all other instruction fields do not fully describe the operation to be done. In such a computer, part of the operation performed is defined by the type of the operand. For example, there is only one ADD operation, and this is done in floating-point or integer mode depending on the type of the operand, which is stored with the operand and not in the instruction stream. The instruction repertoire of such a computer is still the set of all possible operations. However, it is now defined not just by the set of all op codes, but by both op codes and operand tags. While available in the past—e.g. in the Symbolics LISP Machine—there are no such mainstream computers on the market today. Tagged architectures are important for their influence on the design of operations which are generic in nature and that operate differently depending on operand types; the Sparc processor, for example, has some tagged arithmetic instructions. Such computers embody the concept of orthogonality, that is the independence of operation codes and operands, and the ability to specify each of these independently of the other. Instruction sets of different computers possess different degrees of orthogonality.

A machine instruction may be written, using mathematical notation, as

$$g(x_1, x_2, \ldots, x_n) \equiv g(\mathbf{x}),$$

where g is the operation performed on the n operands:

$$x_1, \ldots, x_n \equiv \mathbf{x}.$$

The natural question to ask is: Can we have multiple operation instructions in the form

$$g_1(x_1)g_2(x_2)g_3(x_3) \cdots g_n(x_n) \tag{1}$$

where the operations g_i are performed on the operands x_i and the operand sets are either identical, partially overlapping, or distinct from each other? The answer is that machines with such instruction sets do, in fact, exist. Historically, instruction sets were divided into *vertical* and *horizontal*. Vertical instructions are those of the type $g(\mathbf{x})$, where a single operation (or a time-ordered series of a fixed number and type of operations) is performed on a single set of operands. Vertical instructions are usually highly coded (see below).

Horizontal instructions, later called Very Long Instruction Words (VLIW) are those of the form (1). Here the functions g_i are independent or mildly interdependent and are performed on the respective operands in parallel or in a well-defined time sequence. Note that the higher the degree of orthogonality, the easier it is to specify, independently, the operations and the operand.

The instruction set of a computer such as the Intel Pentium or the PowerPC is an example of a vertical instruction set (*see* Fig. 1). Vertical instructions are found in most machines today. Horizontal instructions are mainly found in microprogrammed machines and are rare outside them. There were machines produced and marketed in the 1980s with a Very Long Instruc-

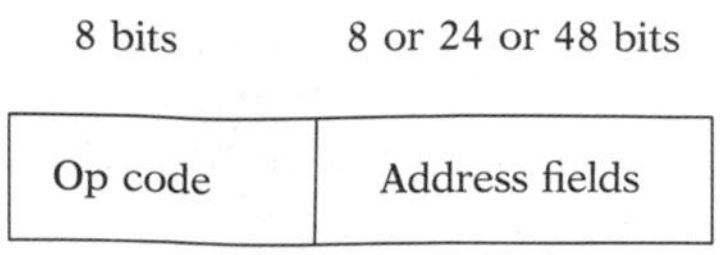

8 bits   8 or 24 or 48 bits

Op code	Address fields

All op codes starting with 00 have an 8-bit address field.
All op codes starting with 01 or 10 have a 24-bit address field.
All op codes starting with 11 have a 48-bit address field.
For every length, the structure of the addressing is fixed.

Figure 1. Typical structure of a vertical instruction set.

tion Word, but they appealed to a limited market and did not survive. The technology exists for their revival, and VLIW continues to be an active research topic, but at the time of this writing (1999), there are no major VLIW processors on the market.

The structure of the operation code itself (i.e. the structure of the contents of the operation field) is also of interest. In principle, if one wants a certain number of instructions, it seems sufficient to associate an instruction with each number expressible in the operation field. We call such an arrangement a *highly coded* one. In the highly coded arrangement, the number of possible instructions is equal to the total information contents of the field. In a field of n bits, this means a total of 2^n possible instructions.

On the other hand, one can envision a completely different situation in which each part of the instruction code conveys some information about the type of the operation. In this case we speak about a *low level of coding*. The number of instructions expressible in this case is smaller than the total information content of the op code field, since some of the combinations may be unused. There may also be multiple operation code fields, each with different coding density, which is a characteristic of the instruction set of the PowerPC. The programmer's reference manual for a processor typically provides details of the format of its instruction set.

Up to this point we have assumed that the operation field is of fixed length and, in the case of a low decoding level, the bits have fixed meaning. Neither of these assumptions is necessary.

Coding theory teaches that it may be advisable to have codes of different lengths, utilizing short ones for the more frequently used combinations and long ones for the least used. Indeed, one can design a tree-structured instruction code—i.e. the operation field is divided into parts and each part is interpreted in sequence, with the meaning attached to it dependent on the results of interpretation of the preceding parts. This not only solves the problem of meaningless bit settings that we encountered in the low decoding level combinations, but it also enables us to terminate the op code interpretation at a different point for different instructions.

With the advent of very large memories, the attractiveness of this coding scheme, which conserves memory but is more time-consuming, has diminished. It is currently used mainly as a mechanism for extending an instruction set.

Instructions sets can be expanded, enhanced, and augmented by different methods. One such method is the addition of an augmenting prefix. We mentioned before the *repeat* instruction, using as an example the Intel Pentium instruction set. In that set one finds a repeat prefix, which causes the next instruction(s) to be iterated several times. Such instructions, when combined, for example, with a rudimentary, single datum move instructions, can create powerful multiple size data move combinations. When combined with arithmetic and conditional instructions, one can create instruction combinations that essentially work on arbitrary length operands.

The other most prevalent method for instruction set extension is the addition of coprocessors which have instructions not present in the original set. These may be single chip (as in the case of floating-point operations) or can be quite complex, as in the case of addition of vector instructions to large-scale machines.

General Remarks

This article has discussed single machine instructions, classifying them according to their length, operation type, the degree of parallelism in the specification of the operation, the number of operations specified, and, finally, the degree of coding. We conclude with some general remarks on the capabilities of machine instruction sets.

The rapid changes in technology and the emergence of single-chip high-functionality devices, be they actual computers, or graphics, database, I/O, floating-point, memory managers, or other functional devices (with both their promise and limitations), the shift to high-level languages, which has distanced the programmer from the details of the instruction sets, and, finally, the change in the speed ratios of processor and memory cycles, caused the price/performance/utility consideration of various instruction sets to shift continuously from their established mid-20th century values. This shift evoked the cycle that tended to eliminate microprogrammed machines, and brought the hardware primitives straight into the machine language for the user.

Bibliography

1994. May, C., and Warren, H. (eds.) *The PowerPC Architecture*, 2nd Ed. San Francisco: Morgan Kaufmann.
1996. Kain, R. Y. *Advanced Computer Architecture*. New York: Simon & Schuster.
1996. Stallings, W. *Computer Organization and Architecture*, 4th Ed. Upper Saddle River, NJ: Prentice Hall.

Gideon Frieder

INSTRUCTION

See INSTRUCTION DECODING; INSTRUCTION-LEVEL PARALLELISM; INSTRUCTION SET; PRIVILEGED INSTRUCTION; and REDUCED INSTRUCTION SET COMPUTER.

INTEGER SEQUENCES, ONLINE ENCYCLOPEDIA OF

For articles on related subjects *see* COMBINATORICS; DISCRETE MATHEMATICS; ELECTRONIC REFERENCE WORKS; and MATHEMATICS, COMPUTERS IN.

The Online Encyclopedia of Integer Sequences (http://www.research.att.com/~njas/sequences/) is a large database of number sequences. Three examples will illustrate some of the ways in which it has been used.

1. You discover what may be a new algorithm for checking that a file of medical records is in the correct order. To handle files of $1, 2, 3, 4, \ldots$ records, your algorithm takes $0, 1, 3, 5, 9, 11, 14, 17, 25, \ldots$ steps. However, when you look this up in the database, you discover that this is the number of steps needed for "sorting by list merging." The entry directs you to Section 5.3.1 of Volume 3 of D. E. Knuth, *The Art of Computer Programming*, where you find your algorithm described, as well as an explicit formula for the nth term. You decide not to apply for a patent.

2. You are working on one of the classically hard problems in discrete mathematics, the enumeration of Latin squares of order n. With considerable effort you find the number of order 10, which is

$$7580721483160132811489280.$$

You consult the database and discover that the same number was recently computed by someone else. You end up by writing a joint paper, thanking the database for bringing you together (McKay and Rogoyski, 1995).

3. You encounter a binomial coefficient sum:

$$\sum_{k=0}^{n}\binom{4n+1}{2n-2k}\binom{n+k}{k}.$$

You know there are powerful methods for evaluating such sums by computer (Petkovšek *et al.*, 1996), but you are in a hurry, so you work out the sum for $n = 0, 1, 2, \ldots$, obtaining

$$1, 12, 240, 5376, \ldots.$$

The database tells you this is $4^n\binom{3n}{n}$, and directs you to a reference that shows this is equal to your sum.

The database currently contains about 50,000 number sequences. A typical entry will supply a description, the first 50 or so terms, and (when available) formulas, recurrences, generating functions, references, computer code for producing the sequence, links to relevant Websites, etc. The database has been described as one of the most useful resources on the Internet. It is a kind of mathematical "fingerprint file" (Cipra, 1994).

The history of the database encapsulates the whole modern history of computers: it began in the mid-1960s on punched cards (*q.v.*), became a book in 1973 (Sloane, 1973), was transferred to magnetic tape in the 1970s, and to magnetic disks in the 1980s. A second book, twice the size of the first, appeared in 1995 (Sloane and Plouffe, 1995).

Until the mid-1990s the two books provided the main form of access to the database. However, in 1994 two electronic mail servers were set up to provide remote access. The first (sequences@research.att.com) simply looks up a sequence, while the second (superseeker@ research.att.com) tries hard to find an explanation even for sequences not currently in the database. In 1996 the whole database was placed on the Internet and may be accessed using the URL given at the beginning of this article. Storage space is no longer a problem, and the database has grown to more than 10 times the size of the 1995 book.

Several other developments (besides improved storage facilities) have helped make the database possible:

♦ *Editing.* Making changes is far easier with the Unix (*q.v.*) editor *vi* than on a punched card machine. The programmable version of *vi*, *ex*, is extensively used in processing sequences.

♦ *Searching.* Unix tools such as *awk*, *grep*, and the *shell* make it possible to search the database efficiently, both to test if a sequence is present and to retrieve a sequence.

♦ *Arithmetic.* Initially many of the sequences were produced using *Fortran* (*q.v.*), but now the main languages used are *Maple* and *Mathematica* (*see* COMPUTER ALGEBRA). Sequences are thus generated more easily and reliably.

♦ *Modems.* Initially the database was contained in a box of punched cards and could only be updated in a computer room. Now this updating can be done almost anywhere.

♦ *Email.* Formerly, new sequences would arrive in letters, often handwritten, or in preprints or reprints. Now they arrive electronically, via email or the Web pages.

♦ *HTML.* Sequences entered on the Web page are processed via CGI scripts and *shell* programs (*see* SCRIPTING LANGUAGES). New sequences are entered on an HTML *form*, processed by another CGI script, and sent via email to the author's home computer where they are further processed. Email is used for this purpose, since the Web page is on a public machine outside the firewall surrounding the author's home computer.

The net result is that the database is easily consulted: it currently receives more than 2,500 hits per day, or almost a million a year, and new sequences continue to arrive at about 10,000 per year. Without the innovations in computers of the past 35 years this would not have been possible.

Bibliography

1973. Sloane, N. J. A. *A Handbook of Integer Sequences.* New York: Academic Press.
1994. Cipra, B. "Mathematicians Get an On-line Fingerprint File," *Science,* **265** (22 July), 473.
1995. McKay, B. D., and Rogoyski, E. "Latin Squares of Order 10," *Electronic J. Combinatorics,* **2**, #N3.
1995. Sloane, N. J. A., and Plouffe, S. *The Encyclopedia of Integer Sequences.* San Diego, CA: Academic Press.
1996. Petkovšek, M., Wilf, H. S., and Zeilberger, D. *A = B.* Wellesley, MA: Peters.

N. J. A. Sloane

INTEGRATED CIRCUITRY

For articles on related subjects *see* COMPUTER CIRCUITRY; LAWS, COMPUTER; LOGIC DESIGN; MICROCOMPUTER CHIP; MICROPROCESSORS AND MICROCOMPUTERS; NOYCE, ROBERT N.; and SUPERCONDUCTING DEVICES.

Introduction

On 29 December 1939, William Shockley wrote in his notebook, "It has today occurred to me that an amplifier using semiconductors rather than vacuum is in principle possible." It has been a long and exciting journey since the time this statement was written, a time that has witnessed an unprecedented number of applications of the transistor and the integrated circuit (IC) chip. In the authors' opinion, two technological events will go down in the history of the twentieth century as the most profound and far reaching, having revolutionized the way of life on this planet: mass production of the automobile and other products, and the design, manufacturing, and application of the integrated circuit chip. The IC is truly the catalyst that led to the birth of the information processing industry as we know it; and it has driven this industry's growth and evolution. The genesis of the integrated circuit chip is described here, along with its evolution, technological breakthroughs, and processing details.

IC history began with John Bardeen, Walter Brattain, and William Shockley of AT&T Bell Laboratories, who did the pioneering work in 1947 that led to the invention of the point-contact transistor (Bardeen and Brattain, 1948; Ross, 1998), the basic building block of the IC. In recognition of their invention, the team was awarded the Nobel Prize in Physics in 1956; and in 1974 they were inducted into the US National Inventors Hall of Fame. It is interesting to note that the invention of the transistor (electron motion in solids) indeed happened 50 years after the discovery of the electron by J. J. Thomson in 1897. What made the first transistor possible was a *semiconductor* material, the element germanium. Unlike metals, which conduct electricity with relative ease, and insulators, which almost always block any motion of electrons (the carriers of electricity), semiconductors can conduct *or* insulate; and there are a variety of ways in which these conductive properties can be controlled and exploited. At first, the introduction of the transistor elicited very little excitement outside the electronics industry. Throughout the 1950s, transistors were refined and used simply as replacement devices for vacuum tubes in everything from hearing aids to radar systems. The first manufacturable device was the alloy junction transistor announced by GE, and for some years it remained as the mainstay of the industry (Saby, 1952). But in 1958 and 1959 came the developments that truly launched the IC age. Within a few months of each other, Jack Kilby of Texas Instruments and Robert Noyce of Fairchild Semiconductor invented different versions of the IC. Both inventors filed for patents in 1959, and Texas Instruments and Fairchild were each offering ICs commercially by 1961.

As Kilby tells it, he sought to make resistors, capacitors, and diodes—all the elements of electronic circuits—out of the same material as transistors, namely germanium. At that time, germanium was easier to work with than silicon, the semiconductor that is now the material of choice for ICs. He placed the components on a single holder, called a *substrate*, to make the device that is generally credited as being the first IC. The problem with Kilby's invention was that it was cumbersome and costly to produce in large quantities. Workers had to solder the circuits by hand using tiny gold wires for electrical connections. Four months after Kilby built his germanium IC, Noyce found a way to join the circuits by printing on the circuit board, using lithography. He used a silicon substrate. The commercial devices that followed showed the advantages of silicon over germanium for integrating multiple components on a single chip. The ease with which conductivity was controlled in different components and the concomitant ease with which interconnections were made between components on the silicon chip resulted in the final triumph of silicon over germanium. The fabrication techniques developed by Noyce are the forerunner of current IC fabrication technologies.

Primitive as they were, those initial chips truly launched a revolution. Over the last 40 years, ICs have pervaded almost all aspects of our daily lives, from television sets and wristwatches to rockets and the ubiquitous computers—from desktops and laptops to supercomputers (*q.v.*). "Very few things have changed the world as dramatically as the IC," said Robert N. White, President of the Academy of Engineering, when he announced in 1990 that Kilby and Noyce would receive the Academy's top prize in recognition of their accomplishments.

Integrated Circuits

BASIC PRINCIPLES

An *integrated circuit* is a functioning assembly of various elements or "devices"—transistors, resistors, capacitors, diodes, etc.—all electrically connected and packaged to form a predefined fully functioning circuit. ICs fall into two major categories: hybrid circuits and monolithic circuits.

In a hybrid circuit, all the IC elements are wired together on a ceramic substrate, somewhat similar to a printed circuit board (PCB), and are packaged and sold as a single functioning unit with input–output (I/O) leads. In essence, a hybrid circuit is a miniaturized version of the PCB. However, the elements used in PCB assemblies are encapsulated for protection from moisture and atmospheric impurities. For example, an individual transistor used on a PCB actually consists of a protective capsule containing the transistor proper, with its leads connected to leads on the capsule. Hybrid ICs, on the other hand, use bare elements; the whole package is assembled first and then the entire unit is encapsulated in a protective polymeric material. Due to the length of wiring between circuit elements, the signal transmission speeds achieved in hybrid ICs are relatively low, although higher than those achieved in PCBs. Consequently, hybrid circuits have limited applications in digital electronics, and their use is primarily in analog circuitry.

In a monolithic circuit, which is the major IC in a modern computer, the circuit elements are formed on a silicon monolith (single substrate) using advanced materials and sophisticated processes and equipment. In this case, the silicon substrate serves not only as a support for the circuit elements, but also as one of the materials that form the components of the circuit. The nature of processing allows the arranging of circuit elements in close proximity, thereby reducing the wiring lengths by orders of magnitude as compared to a hybrid IC. As a result, monolithic ICs offer higher signal speeds than hybrid or PCB assemblies. The remainder of this article will focus on the basics, design, and fabrication of monolithic ICs.

MONOLITHIC ICs

Monolithic ICs are silicon-based because silicon can be grown to high perfection in large crystal diameters, currently up to 300 mm. The key to IC fabrication is the proper treatment of silicon in such a way as to form the desired circuit components. The basic notion is that selected impurities, when introduced into a pure crystalline silicon matrix in a precisely controlled manner in a process called *doping*, can appreciably alter its electrical properties and therefore control the flow of electricity in a solid (hence the name *solid state device*). These impurities actually settle in the silicon matrix and for some elements, such as arsenic or phosphorus, produce an excess of electrons within the matrix, thus yielding what is known as *n-type* silicon (*n* for negative). Introduction of elements such as boron, on the other hand, causes a deficit of electrons, and produces *p-type* silicon (*p* for positive). Consequently, although pure silicon is a semiconductor, the conductivity of n- and p-type silicon can be made to vary over a wide range of values by controlling the impurity concentration (known as the dopant level). The physics of the motion of current and the nature of the charge carriers are different for the two types of silicon. In the case of n-type silicon, electrons are considered as the main contributors to the flow of charge. Alternatively, because of the deficit of electrons in p-type silicon, holes (positively charged, and caused by the absence of electrons) are considered to be the major charge carriers.

Diodes. The presence of the two types of charge carriers is fundamental to the design and function of ICs because important physical phenomena occur when n- and p-type semiconductors are placed in contact with each other to form a p–n junction, the simplest semiconduc-

tor structure. In this case, the completed junction is formed of three distinct semiconductor regions, as shown in Fig. 1a: a p-type region, a depletion region, and an n-type region. The depletion region arises when the two regions are placed in contact with each other and the holes diffuse to the n-side (electron-rich) of the junction while electrons diffuse to the p-side (electron-deficient) of the junction (Serway *et al.*, 1989). The region, extending a few microns on both sides of the junction is called the *depletion region* because it is depleted of mobile charge carriers, namely, electrons and holes. The region forms a potential barrier that prevents the further diffusion of holes and electrons across the junction and insures zero electrical current flow when no external voltage is applied.

The most notable feature of this p–n junction is its ability to pass current in only one direction. Such behavior, called the diode action, is due to the fact that when a positive external voltage from a battery is applied to the p-side junction, as shown in Fig. 1b, the overall barrier is reduced, resulting in a current that increases rapidly with increasing forward voltage or bias, as displayed in Fig. 1c. For reverse bias (a positive

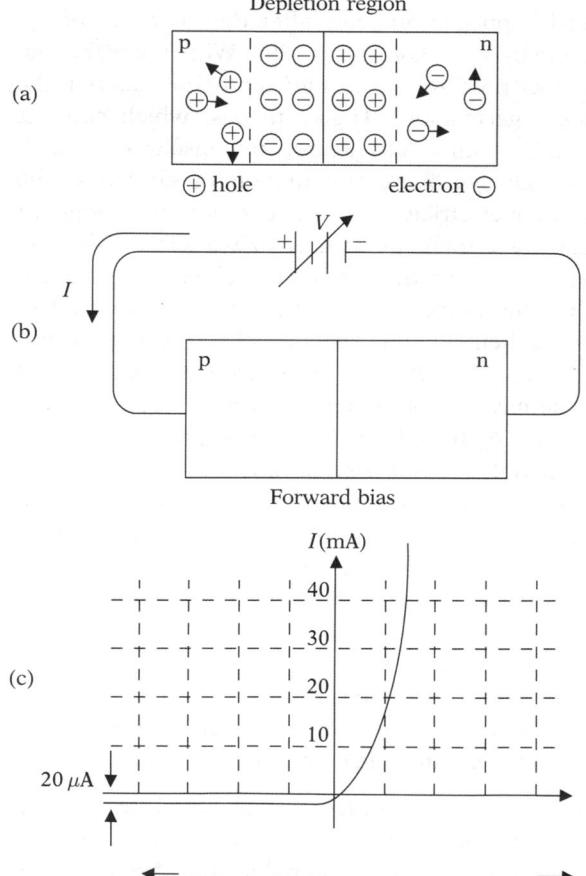

Figure 1. (a) Physical arrangement of a p–n junction.
(b) A diode (p–n junction) under forward bias.
(c) The characteristic current curve for a real diode.

voltage from a battery applied to the n-side junction), the potential barrier increased, resulting in a very small reverse current that quickly reaches a saturation value.

Transistors. Transistors are based on similar, although more complex, n- and p-type semiconductors. A transistor is a structure of silicon, dielectric (insulator), metal, and impurities precisely located to create the millions (soon to be billions) of minuscule on–off switches that make the brains of a microprocessor or the memory of a computer. Every IC chip has a base layer of transistors, with layers of metal wires stacked above to connect the transistors to each other. ICs currently use two important device technologies: the Bipolar Transistor, whose function results from the physical phenomena at the p–n junctions, and the Field Effect Transistor (FET), particularly the Metal Oxide Semiconductor FET (MOSFET), which depends on the physical phenomena occurring close to the surfaces.

Bipolar transistor. The bipolar transistor is basically an n–p–n (or p–n–p) junction, as shown in Fig. 2. Its operation exploits the voltage of the base (the p-type region) to control the flow of current between the collector and the emitter (the two n-type regions). For instance, if the collector is made more positive than the emitter, no current will flow because of the diode effect between the base and the collector unless the base is also made more positive than the emitter, in which case current will flow from the base to the emitter and, subsequently, from the collector to the base. The device is called bipolar because both electrons and holes, and consequently two polarities (positive and negative), are involved in the flow of current.

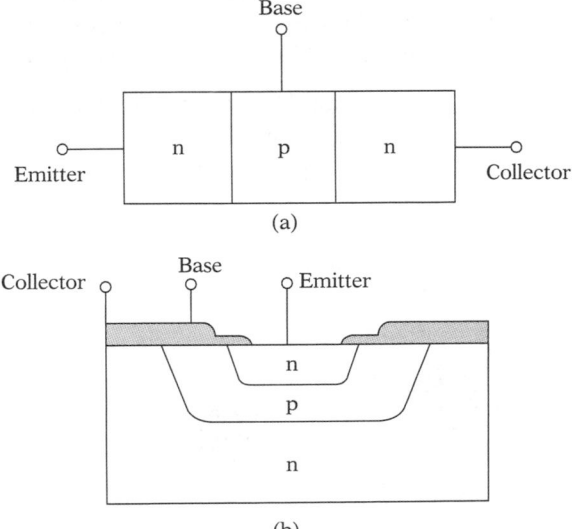

Figure 2. (a) A bipolar transistor. (b) Cross-section of a bipolar transistor.

FET transistor. The operation of an FET transistor, shown in Fig. 3, also exploits the voltage of the gate with respect to the source. For instance, if the drain is made more positive than the source, no current will flow because of the diode effect between the drain and the source due to the existence of the p-type region, unless a positive voltage is applied to the gate. In this case, the insulator region (gate oxide) blocks the flow of current and forms a capacitor that has its negative charge, or electrons, in the p-type region just below the insulator, and its positive charge, or holes, in the gate. At sufficiently high gate voltages, the electrons in the p-type region form a thin n-type channel beneath the gate oxide, which connects with the n-type regions of the source and drain, thus allowing current to flow easily through this channel. The FET is also known as a unipolar transistor, because only one type of charge, namely electrons, is involved in the flow of current. Since the gate is normally fabricated of metal and the insulator of silicon dioxide, the FET is also commonly referred to as a metal oxide semiconductor (MOS) transistor. A prefix is frequently employed to indicate the type of charge carrier in the FET. For example, the n–p–n device shown in Fig. 3 is referred to as an NMOS transistor (electrons are the charge carriers), while a p–n–p-based FET would be known as a PMOS transistor (holes are the charge carriers). Historically, PMOS transistors were used initially because of ease of manufacturing and control of dopant. However, current ICs employ NMOS transistors because of their inherently higher speed (because electrons are lighter charge carriers) than PMOS devices. The two types of transistors are coupled in CMOS (Complementary MOS) devices, the technology of choice for memories and logic ICs. A CMOS device cross section is shown in Fig. 4.

Evolution of IC Devices and Families

There are two main categories of ICs: memory and logic (including microprocessors). There are a variety of memory ICs available: DRAM, SDRAM, SRAM, EEPROM, etc. (*see* MEMORY, MAIN; READ-ONLY MEMORY). The logic ICs include: bipolar, CMOS, BiCMOS (bipolar CMOS), and other ASICs (application-specific ICs).

For the first 20 years of ICs, the bipolar transistor was the preferred device because of its speed. It continued to dominate the scene in the areas of high-speed switching, logic, and memory until about 1990; since then it has gradually been replaced by complementary MOSFETs (CMOSFET or simply CMOS) because they consume less power than bipolar ICs. Introduced in 1963 by Wanlass and Sah, CMOS devices integrate NMOS and PMOS transistors on a single chip, connected in series in such a way that when one is on, the

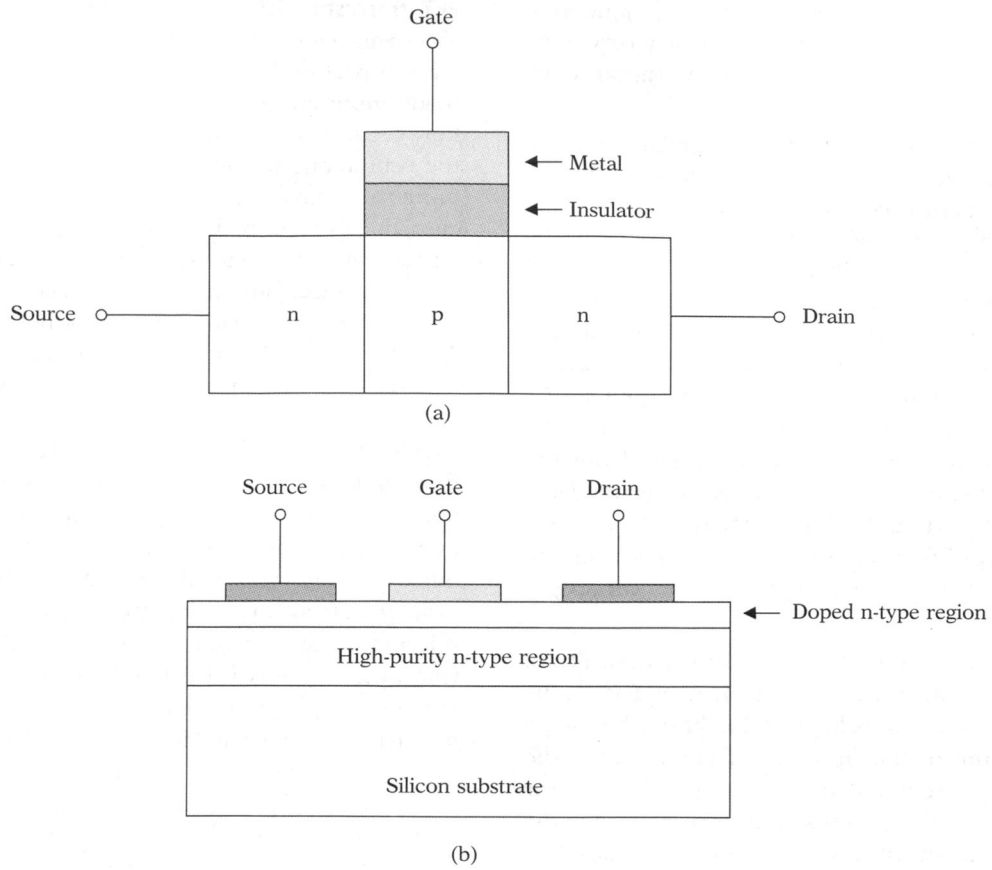

Figure 3. (a) A field effect transistor (FET). (b) Cross-section of a field effect transistor.

other is off, so that it draws power only during switching. This results in a very low standby power consumption in static CMOS circuits. New high-speed CMOS/ICs were introduced in 1994, making CMOS the most popular of all currently available ICs. For example, in 1986, the ratio of bipolar to MOSFET ICs sold was 45%:55%. The ratio now is about 25%:75%.

Common device and circuit technologies are summarized in Table 1. MOSFET devices are the pacesetter and a barometer for technological innovations and development. The number of circuit elements on a chip and

their minimum dimensions are often employed as an indicator of progress in technological evolution. These measures are used for two reasons: (a) higher circuit densities lead to shorter wiring lengths between elements and, subsequently, faster signal propagation (faster devices), and (b) improved resolution capabilities of patterning technologies allow denser placement of circuit elements on a chip (higher device density).

Fig. 5 shows the evolution of IC density for MOSFET/DRAM memory (number of bits), and CMOS and bipolar logic (circuits/chip), starting from 1970. The

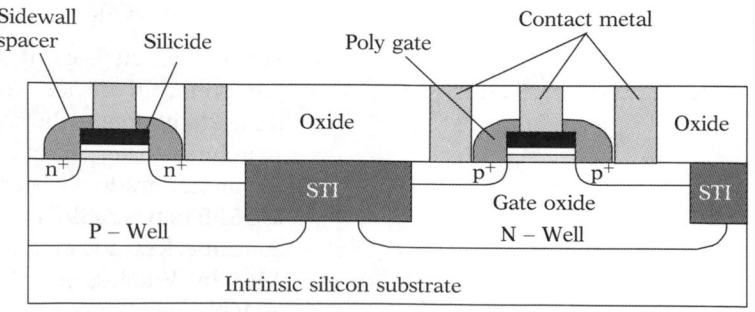

Figure 4. Cross section of a Twin Well CMOS device.

Table 1. Prevalent device and circuit technologies.

Bipolar devices	FET devices	Bipolar logic circuits	FET memory circuits
NPN	NMOS	ECL—Emitter coupled logic	RAM—Random access memory
PNP	PMOS	TTL—Transistor–transistor logic	ROM—Read-only memory
BiCMOS	CMOS	IIL—Integrated injection logic	SRAM—Static RAM
	BiCMOS	STL—Schottky transistor logic	DRAM—Dynamic RAM
			SDRAM—Synchronous dynamic RAM
			EEPROM—Electrically erasable programmable ROM

BiCMOS: bipolar CMOS.

various generations of circuits shown in the figure are classified according to the degree of integration or number of bits (there are traditionally 10 bits per basic functional unit) and summarized in Tables 2 and 3 (Rymaszewski, 1989; Schumay, 1989; Larrabee and Chatterjee, 1991). A characteristic of semiconductor technology is that each generation of successively smaller devices defines the materials, processes, and tools required and thus drives the research and development (R&D) efforts to provide the fabrication, lithography, and other manufacturing methods needed.

IC Fabrication Processes

Today's integrated circuit fabrication involves the use of a large array of advanced materials, complex processes, and sophisticated equipment. Because of the high complexity and level of integration of these circuits, quality control of incoming materials, process control, and equipment cleanliness are critical if acceptable levels of product yield and reliability are to be realized. Some of the major steps used in the present IC fabrication processes are discussed briefly in what follows.

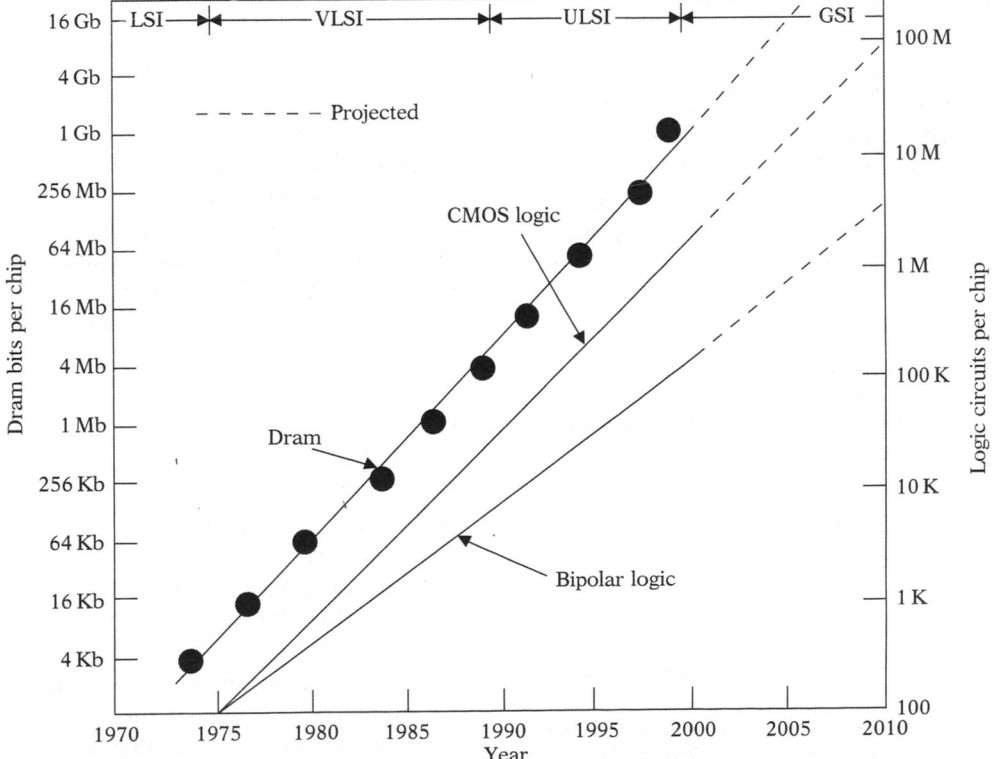

Figure 5. Evolution of IC density.

Table 2. Generations of IC families.

IC generation	Size (bits/chip)
SSI—Small-scale integration	$1-10^2$
MSI—Medium-scale integration	10^2-10^3
LSI—Large-scale integration	10^3-10^5
VLSI—Very large scale integration	10^5-10^6
ULSI—Ultra-large scale integration	10^6-10^9
GSI—Giga-scale integration	$>10^9$

The requirements for the emerging sub-quarter micron technologies and the larger 300 mm diameter wafer size in the early 2000s, however, are dramatically redefining the materials and reshaping the processes that constitute the building blocks of electronic devices, and the necessary equipment. These new challenges are expected to lead to radically different R&D and manufacturing strategies and approaches.

A flowchart of a process used in the fabrication of an NMOS/FET transistor, a key constituent of RAM and ROM circuits, and its derivatives, is shown in Fig. 6. The basic processing principles also apply to the fabrication of other devices. Processing begins with two components: a pure silicon wafer and a set of chrome-on-quartz masks with photolithographic patterns etched on them. The silicon wafer is a thin (about 0.5–1 mm thick) disk of a single crystal of silicon that is doped (with boron in the example given here). Wafer sizes have increased from 25–50 mm in diameter in the early days of IC manufacturing (1960s), to 150–200 mm recently and to 300 mm expected to be in production in 2000. Wafers with diameters of 400–450 mm are already being talked about and are projected to be used in less than a decade. The masks define the areas within the wafer that need to be treated (e.g. etched or implanted), the circuit elements, and the chip boundaries. The minimum definable mask dimensions have

Table 3. Emerging microelectronic IC technologies.[a]

Technology, minimum feature (gate length)	0.18 μm	0.15 μm	0.13 μm	0.10 μm	0.05 μm
Projected year	1999	2001	2003	2006	2012
DRAM, bits/chip	1 G	1 G	4 G	16 G	256 G
MPU, transistors/chip	21 M	40 M	76 M	200 M	1.4 G

Note: M = million, G = giga (billion), MPU: microprocessor unit.
[a] Adapted from the 1997 Semiconductor Industry Association (SIA) Roadmap (Gargani et al., 1998).

undergone a continuous decrease of size as well in order to keep up with decreasing critical circuit dimensions (CDs). Present minimum mask features are in the sub-quarter micron range and according to SIA's (Semiconductor Industry Association) 1997 technology road map, 0.10 micron minimum feature size (DRAM's half pitch or microprocessor gate length) is projected for the year 2006 (Gargini et.al., 1998).

As Fig. 6 shows, device manufacturing has a series of processing steps. The key process technologies that have enabled high levels of integration and high density circuit designs are indicated in the flowchart: lithography (*), ion implantation (**), reactive ion etching (+), and thin film deposition (#). These technologies are important because they are employed repeatedly in a device fabrication line and are briefly described below.

LITHOGRAPHY

Lithography is the process of placing an image of a circuit pattern onto a radiation-sensitive polymer (resist mask). Successful lithography requires optimal performance of several elements simultaneously: photoresist materials (resistant to etching), exposure tools, and lithographic processes (e.g. resist coating, photo exposure, image development, baking) to form the desired pattern. The most common imaging methods employ optical light sources in combination with conventional optical projection methods using specially designed high numerical aperture (NA) lenses. The optical technique, although once expected not to work for feature sizes $< 1\,\mu m$ (micron), is still the technology of choice for the current $0.25\,\mu m$ device generation. Optical projection lithography is now forecast to be valid for $0.10-0.08\,\mu m$ generations with the use of deep UV (DUV) and extreme UV (EUV) light sources, mirror optics, phase shift masks, and top surface imaging. Electron beam lithography (currently used mostly to produce high-resolution optical masks and X-ray masks), ion beam lithography, and X-ray beam lithography remain potential techniques for subsequent device generations.

ION IMPLANTATION

Ion implantation is the process by which dopant impurities (e.g. As^+, B^+) can be introduced by energetic beams in a controlled manner into selected areas of the silicon wafer in order to alter their electronic (conduction) properties. Implantation is ordinarily performed with voltages in the range of 1–500 KeV (thousand electron–volts), with new shallow junction devices using even lower energies, less than 500 eV. Basic requirements for implantation systems are the ion sources and processes to generate, purify, and accelerate the ions. Impurity incorporation is achieved through a bombardment process that implants the

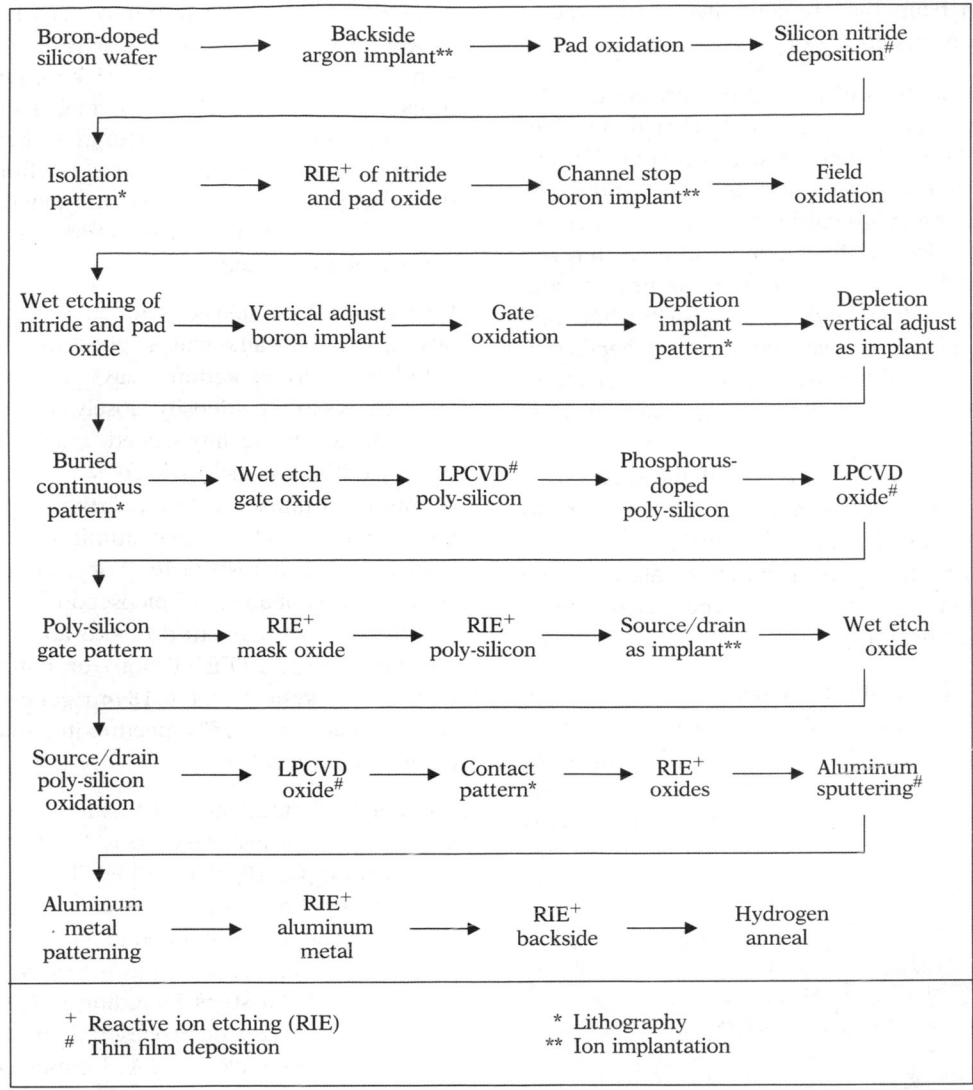

Figure 6. NMOS device fabrication process description.

ions of desirable elements into the silicon lattice. This leads, in the case of elements such as arsenic or phosphorus, to the formation of n-type silicon, while implantation with boron ions produces p-type silicon. The wafers are then annealed in a furnace to activate and diffuse the dopants and remove any damage.

REACTIVE ION ETCHING

Reactive ion etching (RIE) is a high-fidelity transfer process in which a lithographically developed circuit pattern in resist is transferred to an underlying film (e.g. SiO_2) by the removal of unwanted areas from the film through the use of low-temperature weakly ionized gaseous processes. The material is removed from the unmasked areas of the film by converting it to a volatile gaseous state through chemical reactions with one or more energetic reactive ions and neutral elements, produced within the gaseous plasma in what are known as plasma reactors.

These RIE processes make possible the development and manufacture of today's high-density, high-resolution ICs. Because of the need for low-pressure, low-energy, high-density plasmas for etching high-resolution patterns, today's plasma reactor technology has become highly sophisticated. Reactors, clustered together on a common platform, feature exotic plasma sources [e.g. magnetically enhanced plasmas, electron–cyclotron resonance-induced plasmas, inductively coupled sources, and helicon (helical coil) sources], robotic wafer handling, online system diagnostics, and automated process end-point monitors.

THIN FILM DEPOSITION

Deposited metal and dielectric thin films are widely used in the fabrication of ICs. These films provide conducting paths, like a wire; electrical insulators between electrically active areas of the device, like a dielectric;

and protection from the ambient, like a passivation layer which prevents corrosion.

Low pressure chemical vapor deposition. Among the numerous techniques used for thin film deposition, low-pressure chemical vapor deposition (LPCVD) has been pivotal in the production of VLSI and ULSI circuits. By contrast with earlier atmospheric-pressure CVD (APCVD), LPCVD offers cleaner films with fewer pinholes and defects, smoother films, improved conformality in gap filling, and superior deposition uniformity. Low pressure also reduces the deposition temperature, a desirable feature in IC fabrication. Currently, LPCVD systems come in many flavors: batch and single wafer systems, hot and cold wall reactors, and thermal and plasma enhanced reactors. Many advances have been made in recent years to improve film uniformity and other properties distributed over 200 mm and 300 mm diameter wafers, reduce particulates, and efficiently deliver the gaseous reactants to the reaction zone.

Metalization. Metalization connects the IC components (e.g. transistors, resistors) on a wafer to form circuits, using low-resistance wiring and contacts to n^+ and p^+ silicon junctions. The process involves the deposition of both metal and isolation dielectric films in several interconnection layers, each metalized layer electrically connected through metal *vias* or plugs.

AlCu alloy, the most commonly used metal today, is deposited using sputtering, a plasma process. Tungsten, another metal used to make contact with the transistors and as first-level wiring, is deposited with CVD techniques using WF_6 (tungsten hexafluoride) as the source gas. Interlevel dielectric films like TEOS (tetrathylorthosilicate) oxides are generally deposited using plasma-enhanced deposition methods in high density plasma reactors.

With shrinking dimensions and increased functionality on chips, the overall signal propagation delays are dominated by interconnection delays. In order to reduce these delays in high-density closely spaced wiring, new materials are being introduced, particularly for high-end logic ICs: low dielectric constant (low-k) materials as interlevel films and low resistivity copper (R, 40% lower than AlCu) to replace aluminum and to improve electromigration resistance. For example, the interconnect delay of about 13 picoseconds (ps) for an AlCu and SiO_2 ($k = 4$) system drops to about 3 ps for a Cu and low-k (e.g. PTFE (Teflon) or nanoporous silica with $k = 2$) system, for $0.18\,\mu m$ generation. Copper alone can achieve a 15% speedup in a microprocessor, compared with AlCu.

Another important process technology that has been introduced in the last five years is the *chemical mechanical polishing* (CMP) of deposited films to achieve global planarization, necessary for obtaining high yields in multilayer metal interconnections. CMP has gradually replaced the conventional plasma etchback processes at several critical steps including oxide, poly-silicon, and metals (damascene process). Copper metalization, for example, uses electroplated copper deposition or CVD (plasma etching of Cu is difficult) in oxide trenches and vias, followed by polishing or planarization with a process known as *dual damascene* (Slattery *et al.*,

Figure 7. Scanning electron microscope view of PowerPC chip with copper metalization (courtesy of IBM Microelectronics, USA).

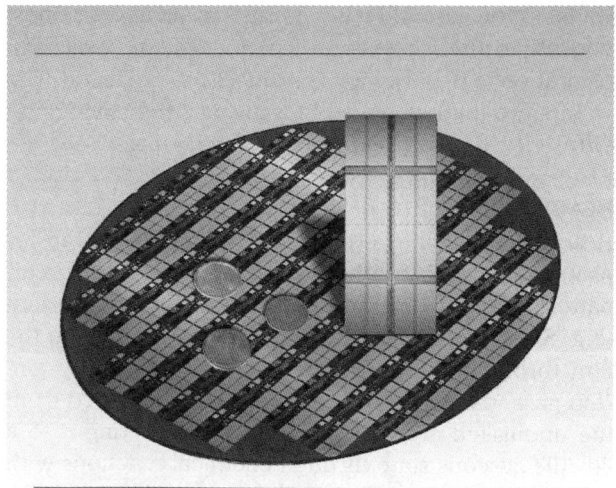

Figure 8. A 200 mm silicon wafer containing 256 Mb memory chip.

1998). Fig. 7 is an electron microscope view of the surface of IBM's PowerPC CMOS logic chip with multiple levels of copper wiring. Fig. 8 shows a typical end product of the wafer manufacturing process, namely a 256 Mb DRAM chip fabricated on a 200 mm wafer. Once the processing is complete, the wafer is tested for functionality. The lines between the various chips are then marked and the wafer diced along these lines, called *kerfs*. The resulting IC chips are then packaged (i.e. mounted on a chip carrier and encapsulated), tested again as a module, and shipped to the customer.

Circuit Yields, Reliability, and Cost

The ICs that have been discussed so far have to meet two important requirements: (1) the circuits must function properly throughout their intended life, and (2) they should be produced in quantities that are competitive with alternative methods of production. The first requirement is related to circuit reliability and the second to yield and cost. The optimum size of an IC, as related to the number of circuit functions, is a compromise between many competing factors: architecture and partitioning of the overall IC, expected yield of good circuits, packaging cost, and the overall reliability of the fully assembled system. Increasing the wafer size is one way the IC manufacturers are reducing the cost of chips, since the number of dies per wafer increases with chip size. Including the expected 20–30% increased capital cost of a 300 mm wafer fabrication plant (fab) (projected for the year 2001), the chip cost is projected to be 25% less than the cost with 200 mm wafers (Seligson, 1998).

In an ideally produced wafer, 100% of the circuits will work. In reality, however, the number of good circuits (or the yield) depends upon process maturity, circuit design, and random defects in the circuit. Achieving high process yields requires robust processes and equipment (e.g. high uptime, stability, and online diagnostics). Many innovative designs have been implemented to achieve these goals, such as computer control of process parameters, vacuum processing, vacuum load locks, and inline diagnostic measurements. Proper design of circuits requires recognizing the tool/process interactions and assessing circuit sensitivities to process parameters.

Despite proper design of circuits and robust processes, the yields will be less than 100% due to random point defects (areas that are small compared with the chip size) generated by imperfect processing, particles, stacking faults, mask defects, etc. The effect of these defects on yield increases as the minimum feature size continues to shrink. Whereas an IC with 1 μm minimum dimension can tolerate a particle 0.1 μm in size, a submicron device with 0.25 μm feature size can tolerate only a 0.025 μm particle. This sensitivity implies that materials, process gases and chemicals, tools, and facilities (quality of clean room air) must be controlled to contain fewer and smaller particles.

Since the ULSI technology requires finer features, larger chip area, complex processes and tools, and new material systems, the problems of achieving and maintaining high yields and reliability are exacerbated. Factory management to achieve these performance levels will make fabricating advanced ICs expensive. At present, the fabrication facilities for the production of ULSI circuits (e.g. 64 Mb DRAM) cost about $1.5 billion for a 200 mm fab. This cost is projected to exceed $2 billion for a 300 mm wafer fab producing 0.18 μm, 1 Gb DRAMs. In spite of such capital investments, the ever-increasing applications and the demand for faster, more cost-effective computers are sure to keep the IC factories humming for years to come.

Future ICs

The development and manufacture of ICs have seen an unprecedented growth for more than half a century since the invention of the transistor in 1947. No end is in sight for either the reduction of transistor gate length or the steady increase in IC functionality on a single chip. 1 and 4 Gb DRAM IC development is near completion, with preliminary announcements in the trade journals, paving the way for even denser and multifunction devices. The SIA road map projects 256 Gb DRAMs with 0.05 μm dimensions and 1.4 B MPU transistor chips with nine levels of wiring (copper?) on perhaps 450 mm diameter wafers by the year 2012 (Gargini *et al.*, 1998). Similar advances are projected for microprocessor and ASIC chips as well. Many new CMOS-based ICs are also under development: embedded ICs with logic and memory functions integrated on a single chip, ferroelectric memory (FRAM), high-performance microprocessors, field programmable gate arrays (FPGA), and embedded gate arrays with RAM and microprocessors or advanced logic. Future ICs are aiming for lower power consumption, increased density, more levels of metal, higher speeds, and increased numbers of embedded functions. It may very well be that the inventions and breakthroughs of the 20th century are just the foundations for an even more promising and exciting future for IC applications, that are certain to influence our daily lives profoundly in this new millennium.

Bibliography

1948. Bardeen, J., and Brattain, W. H. "The Transistor, A Semiconductor Triode," *Phys. Rev.*, **74**, *2*, 230–231; reprinted in *Proc. of the IEEE*, **86**, *1*, 29–30 (1998).

1952. Saby, J. E. "Fused Impurity p–n–p Transistors," *Proc. IRE*, **40**, *11*, 1358–1360.

1989. Rymaszewski, E. J. "Dense, Denser, Densest," *J. Electronic Matter*, **18**, 217–220.

1989. Serway, R. A., Moses, C. J., and Moyer, C. A., *Modern Physics*. Philadelphia, PA: Saunders.

1989. Schumay, W. C., Jr. "Materials for High Density Interconnects," *Advanced Materials and Processes*, **135**, 43–47.

1991. Larrabee, G., and Chatterjee, P. "DRAM Manufacturing in the 90's, Part I: The History Lesson," *Semiconductor International*, **14**, 84–92.

1998. Gargini, P., Glaze, J., and Williams, O. "1997 National Technology Roadmap for Semiconductors," *Solid State Technology*, **41**, *1*, 73–76. *See also* http://www.semichips.org.

1998. Ross, I. M. "The Invention of the Transistor," *Proceedings of the IEEE*, **86**, *1*, 7–28.

1998. Seligson, D. "The Economics of 300 mm Processing," *Semiconductor International*, **21**, *1*, 52–58.

1998. Slattery, J., Luce, S., McDevitt, T., Stamper, T., Goldblatt, R., and Biery, G. "Copper Interconnects in Semiconductor Manufacturing," *Future Fab International*, **6**, 155–160.

G. Swami Mathad and Alain E. Kaloyeros

INTEGRATED SERVICES DIGITAL NETWORK (ISDN)

For articles on related subjects *see* ASYNCHRONOUS TRANSFER MODE; COMMUNICATIONS AND COMPUTERS; DATA COMMUNICATIONS; MULTIPLEXING; NETWORK PROTOCOL; NETWORKS, COMPUTER; and OPEN SYSTEMS INTERCONNECTION.

History

The *Integrated Services Digital Network* (ISDN) is a telephonic system that can support a variety of digital services (including digitized voice) through a limited set of standard interfaces. ISDN comes in two flavors: "Narrowband" (N-ISDN, described here) and "Broadband" (B-ISDN). N-ISDN emerged from pre-existing telephone network technologies and covers bit-rates of up to 2 Mbps. B-ISDN is a completely new technology covering much higher bit-rates. This article addresses N-ISDN; for a discussion of B-ISDN, *see* ASYNCHRONOUS TRANSFER MODE. A complete description of N-ISDN can be found in Griffiths (1990); a brief description follows.

The principal factor that led to the development of N-ISDN was the adoption of digital transmission by many public telephone systems. This was due both to the ease with which digital signals could be regenerated without deterioration and the availability of VSLI-based technologies for the processing of digital streams. Voice traffic in such networks is encoded using pulse-code modulation at 64 Kbps. Naturally, these networks could also carry data, resulting in "Integrated Digital Networks" (IDN).

Although an IDN integrated many different kinds of traffic internally, the services it supported were accessed through unrelated interfaces. For example, data services might be accessed via the X.25 interface, while telephony was accessed via normal analog lines ("local loops") between the customer's premises and the telephone exchange. In order to produce an ISDN, a unified interface to the IDN was required. Since this interface would itself be digital, a key requirement was the digitization of the local loops.

Local loops are mainly copper and of variable quality, some having been in the ground for many years. However, they represent a huge investment that could not lightly be discarded. One requirement of N-ISDN was that it should operate over the existing local loops. Digitization of these at reasonable bit-rates and at reasonable cost become feasible in the early 1990s.

Standardization

The standardization of the ISDN has been carried out by the International Telecommunications Union (ITU) (formerly the CCITT—Comité Consultatif Internationale Télégraphique et Téléphonique) and is specified in a series of recommendations, the most important of which are the "I-Series," which specify the interface to users (CCITT, 1988).

Signaling

IDNs use "common channel signaling" (CCS). This means that the messages that pass between exchanges (to control the setting up of calls for example) are carried in dedicated signaling channels. This contrasts with earlier analog systems, in which signaling was carried along with the speech channel to which it related. The principal advantage of CCS is a great reduction in the number of signaling terminations at an exchange. Naturally, digital signaling is used.

ISDN also employs CCS at the user–network interface. A very much wider range of signaling messages is available than was possible with the old analog systems. This enables a much greater range of services to be offered. The signaling protocols used resemble those specified in the X.25 interface.

Transmission Technology

N-ISDN uses the transmission and switching capabilities of the existing IDN. This is based on 64 Kbps bit-streams that are combined into higher-capacity "trunks" using time division multiplexing. In Europe, the first multiplex combines 32 64 Kbps channels into one 2 Mbps channel, while in the USA 23 64 Kbps channels form one 1.544 Mbps channel.

User Interfaces

The user interfaces reflect the 64 Kbps and 2 Mbps infrastructure and CCS.

The basic rate interface (BRI) offers two 64 Kbps "B-Channels" for data or voice and one 16 Kbps "D-Channel" for signaling. In principle, this is available to all subscribers through the existing local loops. The presence of two B-Channels means that it is possible to offer subscribers two telephone connections where previously they had only one. Up to eight pieces of equipment may be attached to a basic rate ISDN interface in a bus (*q.v.*) configuration, though only two may be used at once.

The primary rate interface (PRI) offers 30 (23 in the USA) 64 Kbps B-channels and one 64 Kbps D-Channel. Data channels at higher rates (H-channels) are also defined. This interface is intended for the connection of PABXs and large computer installations.

In principle, various services may be offered through B-channels: circuit-switched services, packet-switched services, frame-relay services etc. In practice, the circuit-switched service is often all that is available (the more complex services are now seen as belonging to the B-ISDN world).

Note that digital local-loop technology has advanced considerably since the N-ISDN standards were fixed. Industry standards such as "Asymmetric Digital Subscriber Loop" (ADSL) and "High-speed Digital Subscriber Loop" (HDSL) provide much higher bit-rates and are capable of carrying, for example, high-definition digital TV.

Applications

The circuit-switched service provides an unstructured 64 Kbps bit-stream (a physical layer service in OSI terms) which may be switched in a manner analogous to an ordinary telephone call. Once established such circuits may carry voice (via CODECs), fax, or data.

The service is well-suited to fax and provides high-quality, high-speed transmission. The signaling also allows proper call identification allowing incoming calls to be routed directly to a fax machine (as opposed to a computer interface, voice telephone, etc.).

The bursty, highly multiplexed nature of data traffic is not well-suited to circuit switching. Nevertheless, N-ISDN is quite widely used as an Internet (*q.v.*) access technology. In this case a frame structure is imposed on the circuit—normally through the use of the Internet *Point-to-Point Protocol* (PPP). Internet datagrams are then carried in PPP frames. N-ISDN interfaces for PCs are now comparatively cheap and widely available. N-ISDN is also widely deployed as a leased-line backup. Several manufacturers supply a kit which will automatically set up an ISDN circuit in the event that a leased line fails.

Transition to Broadband ISDN

The newest and fastest growing traffic types often require high and variable bit-rates. N-ISDN's internal structure is strongly biased towards fixed 64 Kbps circuits and is not well-suited to this kind of traffic. A completely new infrastructure is now being deployed based on optical fibers and using "Asynchronous Transfer Mode" (ATM) as a multiplexing technology. ATM fragments all traffic types into a series of fixed-length "cells" of 48 bytes. Cells are allocated to traffic streams in a flexible way allowing a wide range of services to share the network.

Bibliography

1988. CCITT *Integrated Services Digital Network: Overall Aspects and Functions*, Melbourne, Australia: ISDN User–Network Interfaces. Blue-book Vol. III, Fascicle III.8. November.
1990. Griffiths, J. M. (ed.) *ISDN Explained.* New York: John Wiley.
1998. Kessler, G. C., and Southwick, P. V. *ISDN: Concepts, Facilities, and Services.* New York: McGraw-Hill.

Graham Knight

INTERACTIVE INPUT DEVICES

For articles on related subjects *see* COMPUTER GRAPHICS; DISABLED, COMPUTERS AND THE; HUMAN FACTORS IN COMPUTING; MOUSE; SPEECH RECOGNITION AND SYNTHESIS; USER INTERFACE; and WORKSTATION.

Input devices connected to a computer system allow the user to enter data or interact with running programs, and are used for activities ranging from editing computer programs to playing videogames (*q.v.*). Input devices can be separated into five classes: *keyboards*, *locators*, *picks*, *valuators*, and *buttons*. The classification is determined by the distinct functions performed. In many cases, these divisions are blurred because a device of one class can simulate the functions of another. This simulation allows a workstation (*q.v.*) to have full functionality without having to use a large number of different input devices.

Keyboards

A *keyboard*, the most common input device, is used for entering textual data into a computer file under control of an editor or word processor (*see* Fig. 1). Keyboard keys are usually arranged similarly to those of a standard typewriter, the so-called QWERTY keyboard (named for the sequence of keys in the top row).

Figure 1. A computer keyboard with attached function keys. The function keys to the left and right have specific functions. The function keys on the top row labeled F1 through F12 are programmable, and their function will vary with the application.

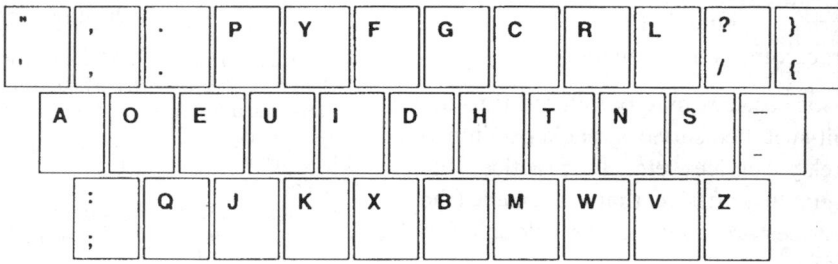

Figure 2. The Dvorak keyboard that has the potential for higher typing speeds than the QWERTY keyboard.

This is a historical artifact, since early typewriter keys had to be arranged to allow typists to work quickly without the keys jamming. To do this, frequently used keys were placed far apart. Because of the speed and electronic nature of the computer, other keyboard designs have been explored that group frequently used keys together. An example of this is the Dvorak keyboard (*see* Fig. 2).

When data is being entered at a keyboard, the user's monitor provides visual feedback indicating where new data will be placed with respect to characters already typed (*see* MONITOR, DISPLAY). This is done with a *cursor*, which is usually a vertical line, an underscore, a reverse video character, or a bright or blinking square. The type of cursor is dependent on the application package being used.

Locator Devices

Locators are used for indicating a position for placing objects on the screen or quickly moving the cursor in a text editor. Visual feedback of the current position is provided with an arrow or a crosshair displayed on the screen. A digitizing tablet, mouse, trackball, and joystick are examples of location devices.

The *digitizing tablet* is a flat surface, sometimes illuminated, that has a fine grid of horizontal and vertical

wires embedded in it (*see* Fig. 3). There is an attached stylus or *puck* that produces a magnetic field and is centered at the location to which it points. The magnetic field will induce a current in the wires of the tablet. By sensing the strength of the current on a set of neighboring wires, the tablet can determine where the stylus or puck is and whether it is touching the tablet or being held above it.

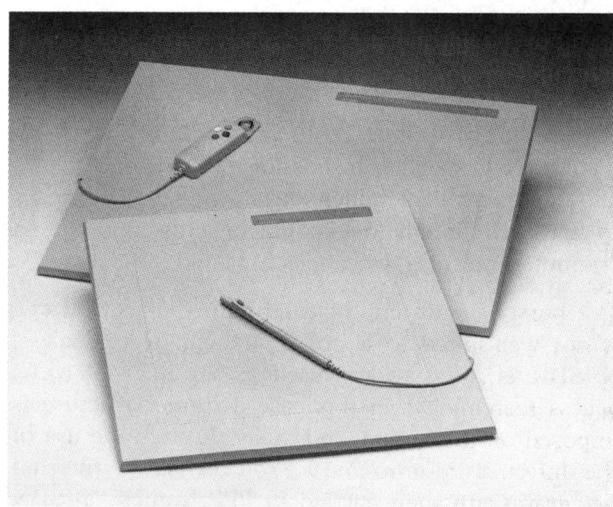

Figure 3. Two digitizing or graphics tablets. The foreground shows a stylus, and the background shows a puck.

Digitizing tablets are very precise and can be used to enter line drawings—maps, for example—into the computer through the input of key points in the drawing. Since the same signal is produced each time the stylus is placed in a particular position (e.g. the center of the tablet), the digitizing tablet is considered an *absolute locator.*

A *mouse* is a small hand-held device that is used to indicate a position or movement. Typical uses for a mouse include quickly repositioning the cursor in a word processor and moving an object by *dragging* it to a new location. A mouse will also include one to three buttons on its top that can be *clicked* to start or stop an operation, or indicate a chosen position.

A mouse can be either a physical or an optical mouse. A *physical mouse* has a ball that protrudes from its bottom. When the mouse is moved, friction will cause the ball to move an amount proportional to the movement of the mouse. Inside the mouse, there is a set of potentiometers that sense the direction and rate of movement of the ball. These are then converted into electrical signals that are interpreted by the computer as signifying that the mouse is in motion.

An *optical mouse* uses a light-emitting diode (LED), a light sensor, and a special mouse pad instead of the ball and potentiometers. The mouse pad is the key to the operation of the mouse. It has a reflective surface and a set of light and dark horizontal and vertical lines. As the mouse is moved, light from the LED is reflected by the mouse pad to the sensor. When a vertical line is crossed, the reflected light is slightly darkened, and when a horizontal line is crossed, it is significantly darkened. By sensing these pulses of light, the direction and rate of movement can be determined. In 1999, Microsoft introduced an improved optical mouse that works on any surface other than glass and which does not depend on detection of a ruled mouse pad.

A mouse is good for gross movement, but is not very useful for operations that require high precision. Also, since a mouse can be lifted off its surface or *mouse pad* and be moved without disturbing the current location, the mouse is considered a *relative locator.* A related device is the *trackball,* which is nothing more than a physical mouse turned upside down so that the ball can be directly manipulated by the palm of the hand rather than rolling it over a flat surface. Trackballs are available in three-dimensional varieties that allow movement up and down in addition to the traditional motions of left/right and forward/backward.

A *joystick* (*see* Fig. 4), popular among those who play videogames, is also used to indicate position. The joystick has a rod that protrudes from a base. Inside the base is a set of potentiometers that can sense when

Figure 4. A joystick (courtesy of the Microsoft Corporation).

the rod is deflected from a vertical position. In spring-loaded joysticks, the rod will always return to center when released. These joysticks indicate a change of position by the direction of the push and a change of speed by the amount of deflection. When in the center position, no change takes place. These are, therefore, relative locators. Joysticks that are not spring-loaded will indicate an absolute location based on where the rod is positioned. Joysticks usually indicate only two-dimensional positions by moving the rod laterally, but there are also three-dimensional joysticks in which the third dimension is indicated by rotation of the rod. Like a mouse, a joystick is good for gross movement, but not for precision work.

Pick Devices

A *pick device* is used to choose an object that appears on the screen, whether it be graphical, like a line in an architectural drawing, or textual, like a word or sentence. *Lightpens* and *touch screens* are examples of pick devices.

The name *lightpen* is a misnomer, since the pen does not produce light, but rather senses light produced by an object on the screen (*see* Fig. 5). All computer CRT monitors use phosphor to display their images. The phosphor is excited by an electron beam and, as it decays to its normal state, it produces the light that creates the image. Since the decay process also causes

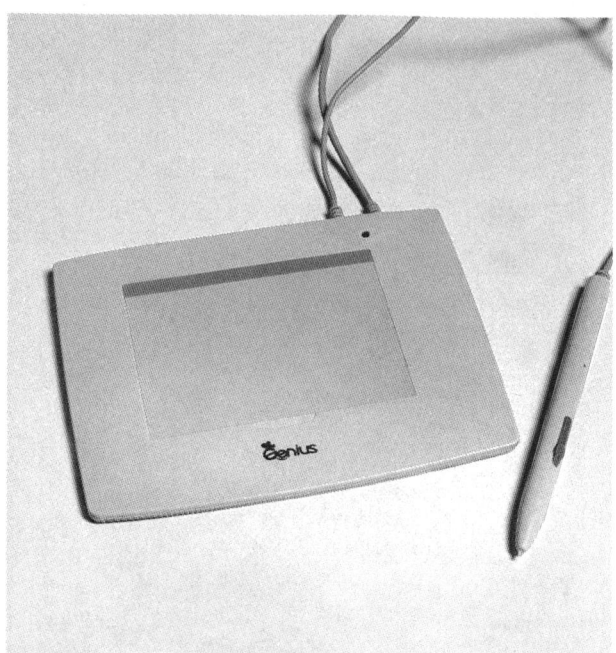

Figure 5. A lightpen (courtesy of the Last Resort Picture Library).

Figure 6. Users at a touch screen (courtesy of Microtouch Photography).

the light produced to dim, an image on the screen is constantly being "refreshed," that is, redrawn (about 30 to 60 times a second). Each part of the image on the screen is, therefore, constantly getting darker until it flashes bright when refreshed, but this happens so frequently that the human eye cannot sense this change.

When an object or part of an object is refreshed, it becomes brighter, and it is this brightening that triggers the lightpen. When this flash of light is sensed by the lightpen, it sends a signal to the computer. The computer can then determine which object was picked by determining what was being refreshed when the flash occurred.

The basic idea of a *touch screen* is that one need only point at an object on the screen with a finger to choose it; there is no special device that the user must hold (*see* Fig. 6). The sensing mechanism of a touch screen is either built into the monitor or placed over the monitor screen. Touch screens are based on either beams of light or electrical currents. In the first case, a series of LEDs are placed along a vertical and horizontal edge of the screen and a series of light sensors are lined up on the two opposite edges. When the user touches the screen, one or more lights are blocked in the vertical and horizontal directions. By checking which lights have been blocked, the computer can determine an approximate position. In the second case, when the user makes contact with the screen, two films placed over the screen are pushed together. The first has a conductive surface and the second has

a resistive surface, and when they make contact, there is a change in voltage that determines where the touch was made. Touch screens appear to be very similar to locating devices. They are, however, of even lower resolution than the worst locating device, and this restricts them to picking functions. Their use is popular in public settings, such as libraries, banks, and stores.

Valuator Devices

Valuators are used to indicate a real (nonintegral) numeric value over a specific range. These are implemented as slide and dial potentiometers that work in the same way as a rheostatic light dimmer. When the valuator is all the way to the left, it produces high resistance; when it is all the way to the right, it produces low resistance. The resistance is then converted to a real value over some specified range. For example, the lowest resistance could represent a value of 5.0 and the highest a value of 10.0. A resistance value halfway between these two would then represent a value of 7.5.

Button Devices

Buttons are special-purpose function keys that are frequently attached to a keyboard. For use with word processors, for example, some of these are marked with arrows (*arrow keys*) and are used to move the cursor. Others can be used to delete or insert a character, word, sentence, or paragraph. Because the design of computer keyboards typically includes arrow keys and a set of function keys, users usually consider them to be an integral part of the keyboard device, but there is a conceptual difference. Whereas the conventional keys of the keyboard produce one ASCII character each time one is pressed, function keys produce a group of two or three character codes per stroke.

Function buttons are used to choose options with one keystroke that perform a function specific to the application program that is running. For this reason, they are also referred to as *programmable function keys*.

Simulation of Logical Functions

If a workstation were to be designed such that all classes of input devices had to be included, the user's (physical) desktop could become quite cluttered with a keyboard, mouse, lightpen, button pad, and valuator dials. To reduce the number of devices without reducing the functionality of the workstation, computer systems will often simulate a device from one class with a device from another. While it is possible to simulate a device from any of the classes with one from another, some of these simulations are quite logical and others are nonsensical. Some examples of device class simulation follow.

A keyboard is the most versatile input device, since it may easily simulate devices from other classes. A locator or valuator function can be simulated by the user typing in an (x, y) coordinate location or a real value. Objects can be numbered or named, and the user can pick an object by typing its name. Instead of function buttons, the user can type the function name on the keyboard.

Locating devices can perform a pick function by indicating a location on the object to be picked. A lightpen (pick) can simulate a locator by having the user drag a crosshair on the screen to the correct position.

In an extreme example, a pick device can be used to simulate a keyboard by displaying a picture of a keyboard on the screen as a series of objects. A lightpen would then be used to *hunt and peck* at the keyboard on the screen, picking the keys to be typed. This device is now used on a number of hand-held portable computers (*q.v.*). Other simulations are possible and allow workstations to provide a wide range of functions without the clutter of multiple input devices.

Other Devices

Input devices and user interaction are active topics of research. Work is being done to recognize voice (*see* SPEECH RECOGNITION AND SYNTHESIS) and handwritten data entry and will undoubtedly lead to new devices and device classes. Software is available that allows a user to give spoken commands to a computer over a small microphone or to conduct an Internet (*q.v.*) telephone conversation. Personal Digital Assistants (PDAs)

allow input of a constrained set of handprinted characters (*see* PORTABLE COMPUTERS) and data tablets are available for personal computers which are essentially "electronic yellow pads" on which the user may make sketches and handwritten notes.

Small video cameras are now available which allow two similarly equipped network users to conduct a "picture phone" conversation (*see* Fig. 7 on Color Page CP-11). At the communications speeds now available to most users, successive picture frames cannot be transmitted quickly enough to provide smooth motion, but visual quality will steadily improve as more and more users gain access to fiber optic (*q.v.*) or satellite communications channels.

Work in virtual reality (*q.v.*) is also leading to new classes of input device. Sensors are attached to gloves, glasses, and various parts of the body to track the user's motion. This information can be used for medical diagnostics or for the control of movement through a virtual world.

Bibliography

1989. Brown, J., and Cunningham, S. *Programming the User Interface.* New York: John Wiley.
1990. Foley, J. D., Van Dam, A., Feiner, S. K., and Hughes, J. F. *Computer Graphics: Principles and Practice.* Reading, MA: Addison-Wesley.
1993. Baber, C., and Noyes, J. M. (eds.) *Interactive Speech Technology: Human Factors Issues in the Application of Speech Input/Output to Computers.* Basingstoke: Taylor & Francis.
1998. Bernsen, N. O., Dybkjaer, H., Dybkjaer, L., and Bernsen, N. *Designing Interactive Speech Systems: From First Ideas to User Testing.* New York: Springer-Verlag.

Jeffrey J. McConnell

INTERACTIVE SYSTEM

For articles on related subjects *see* INTERACTIVE INPUT DEVICES; and TIME SHARING.

An *interactive system* is a computing system that allows the user to interact with a running program by giving it data or control directions through an input device such as a keyboard or a mouse (*q.v.*). This mode of operation is in contrast to a *batch processing* system, which requires that all input be placed in a file that is readied for reading before beginning execution of the program that will process it. The obvious advantage of interactive use is that the user can choose input and control directions based on partial results received from an early phase of program execution, whereas batch processing requires that data be prepared with all eventualities in mind. The difference is most acute when debugging a new program.

A standalone personal computer or workstation (*q.v.*) is naturally interactive because its only user sits at its keyboard and screen as computation proceeds. A terminal or personal computer becomes interactive with respect to a remote *host computer* (*q.v.*) only if it is "hard wired" to the host or is connected to it through a network, perhaps by a modem (*q.v.*) that allows calling the host over telephone lines or a DSU/CSU (*q.v.*) that enables a cable or satellite connection.

Bibliography

1998. Graham, L. *The Principles of Interactive Design.* Albany, NY: Delmar Publishers.

Edwin D. Reilly

INTERLEAVING

For articles on related subjects *see* ACCESS TIME; and MEMORY: MAIN.

In systems with more than one autonomous memory module, considerable advantage in system speed may be acquired by an arrangement such that logically sequential memory addresses occur in different physical modules. By this means the total time taken to access a sequence of memory locations can be much reduced, since several memory accesses may be overlapped by a high-speed CPU (*q.v.*). Two-way and four-way *interleaving* are commonly encountered.

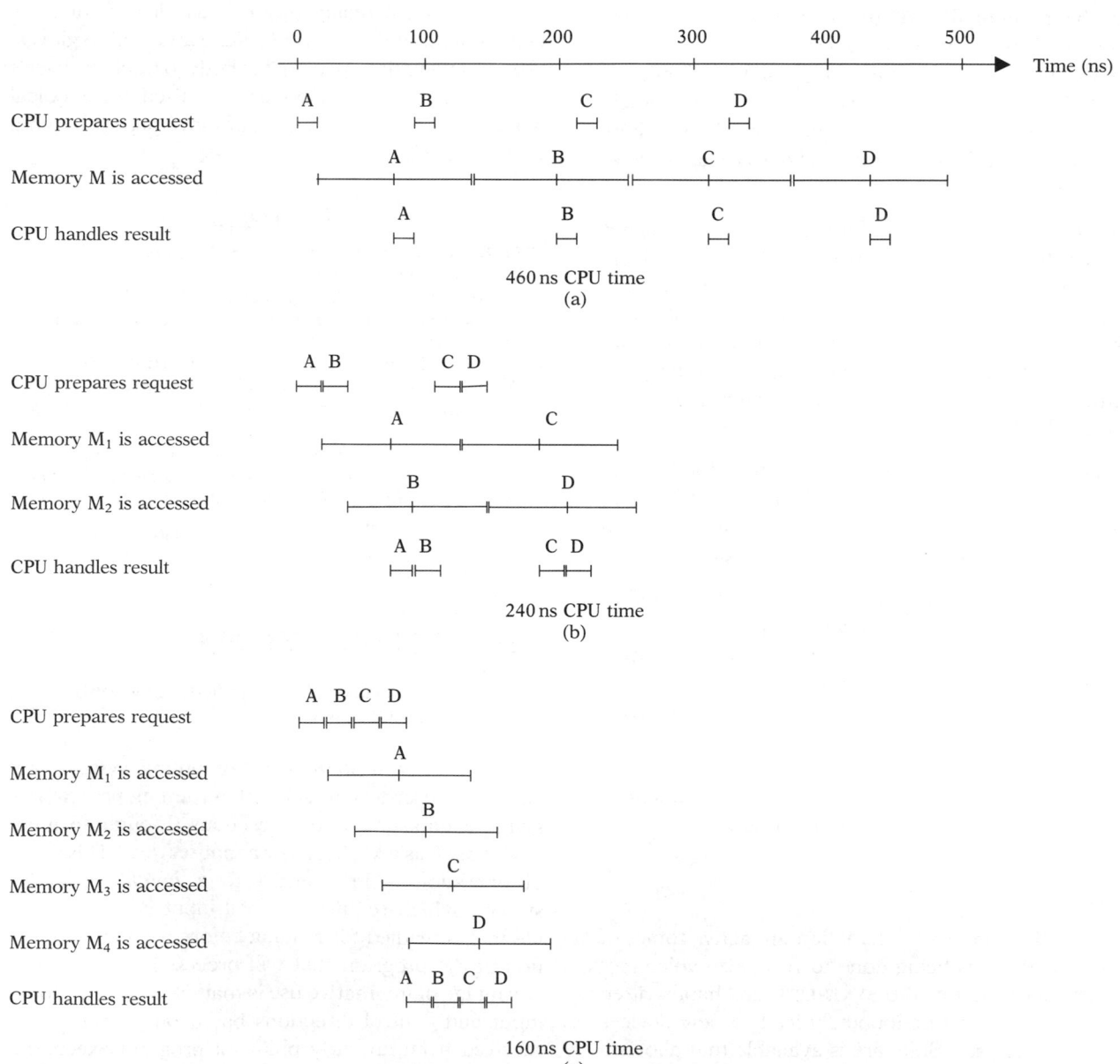

Figure 1. Timing diagram, showing a sequence of four memory accesses (A, B, C, D) in a speed-limited memory system with (a) no interleaving, (b) two-way interleaving, and (c) four-way interleaving.

Assume, for example, a memory with 60 ns access time (i.e. the time to get a word from memory to the processor) and a 120 ns cycle (i.e. the time after the initiation of an access before the memory can be accessed again), and a processor requiring 20 ns to prepare a memory request and a further 20 ns to handle the result. Also assume processor and memory overlap.

Under these conditions, as illustrated in Fig. 1, a sequence of four memory accesses would take 460 ns with no interleaving, 240 ns with two-way interleaving, and 160 ns with four-way interleaving. Notice in this example that four-way interleaving provides a smaller incremental advantage than does two-way. This is a result of the particular choice made of CPU and memory timing, which happens to be fairly well suited for two-way interleaving. Notice further that four-way interleaving leaves the CPU fully occupied (at least as far as the example goes). The result is that more than four-way interleaving in this example will provide no increase in speed. The system speed for four-way (or more) interleaving has become CPU-limited rather than memory-limited, as is the case shown in Fig. 1a.

For very high-speed CPUs (particularly those involving *instruction lookahead*), for multiple CPUs, and for block transfers to cache memory (*q.v.*), it is possible to keep many modules busy simultaneously. Up to 32 interleaved modules have been reported.

Bibliography

1996. Hamacher, V. C., Vranesic, Z. G., and Zaky, S. G. *Computer Organization*, 4th Ed., 243–245. New York: McGraw-Hill.

Kenneth C. Smith and Adel S. Sedra

INTERLOCK

For articles on related subjects *see* CONCURRENT PROGRAMMING; CONTENTION; MEMORY: MAIN; and PETRI NET.

Interlock is a mechanism implemented in hardware or software that is intended to coordinate activity of two or more processes within a computing system. This mechanism generally insures that one process has reached a suitable state such that the other may proceed. In the event that two processes use a common resource (memory, for instance), interlock will guarantee that only one request is honored at a time, and perhaps that some discipline, such as first come, first served, is observed.

In many cases, the mechanism communicates with each process using *flags*, which are memory elements set and read either through software or hardware. A common problem concerns the relative timing of setting and interrogating the flags, and of the start of subsequent action. The problem is further complicated by the fact that asynchronous (time-uncoordinated) processes may be observing each other and must decide on a future course of action based on a snapshot observation. Often, the interlock mechanism is an important part of the timing of each process; hence, it should be very fast.

One solution to interlock incorporates a polling (*q.v.*) mechanism where the appropriate conditions of each process are interrogated in turn and decisions are reached in a corresponding fixed order of priority. This scheme, though easily implemented either in hardware or software, requires a separate polling device or program and is wasteful of time, particularly when conflict is unlikely.

A hardware approach to arbitrating between requests from two processes (e.g. CPUs) for a shared resource (e.g. memory) is shown in Fig. 1. Normally, both inputs (request A and request B) are zero, setting the interlock flip-flop into the (1,1) output state and inhibiting both selection gates via the inverting threshold elements. When either request A or B is raised *separately*, the flip-flop establishes the corresponding

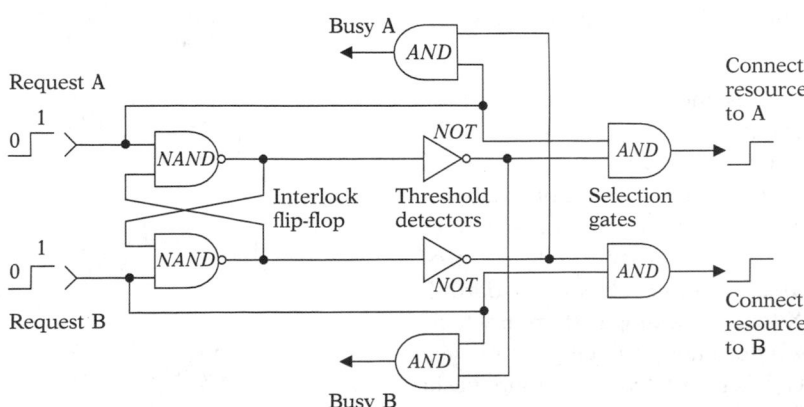

Figure 1. A high-speed interlock mechanism for arbitrating between two asynchronous requests for a single resource.

(0,1) state, selecting the corresponding selection gate and generating a signal connecting the resource to the requester. If, for example, request B is raised while A is up, the connection to A is unaffected, and a suitable busy signal is returned to process B.

If both A and B requests occur *simultaneously*, the effect is to change both outputs of the interlock flip-flop from one to zero at once. By virtue of the feedback, shown in Fig. 1, an oscillation will be produced in which the outputs of the interlock flip-flop change in phase at a very high frequency. The amplitude of the oscillation is so small that the threshold of the detectors following can be set to ignore it.

Eventually, due to minute timing differences in the inputs, random electrical noise, circuit asymmetry, etc., the circuit will establish a stable state in which one and only one of the requests is honored. In practice, this oscillatory decision process occurs very rarely. In one study conducted using 10 ns logic, oscillation of any significance was observed only when input signals were within 100 ps of simultaneity. For signals within 10 ps of simultaneity, oscillation was maintained for about 1 μs before a decision was reached.

Adel S. Sedra and Kenneth C. Smith

INTERMEDIATE LANGUAGES

For articles on related topics *see* COMPILER; LANGUAGE PROCESSORS; and PORTABILITY.

What is an Intermediate Language?

Many computer application programs can be regarded as *language translators*, in the sense that they accept an input *source* language and produce an output *target* language. Compilers are among the most important examples of such programs: a compiler might accept C++ (*q.v.*) programs as input and produce machine instructions for an UltraSparc computer. Other examples include text processors, which accept text and formatting specifications and produce an image to be viewed or printed.

While input-to-output translation is the observable task of language translators, many such systems have well-defined intermediate points of arrival at which some *intermediate language* (IL) is produced. For example, early C++ compilers did not produce machine code directly; they translated a C++ program into a C program, which could then be compiled by a standard C compiler. The LaTeX text processing system in which this article was written does not produce print images directly; instead, LaTeX is translated into a more basic representation called TEX (*q.v.*), which is then translated into a device-independent representation called

dvi, which may in turn undergo several translations before arriving in print.

Advantages of Intermediate Languages

The extra steps associated with use of an intermediate language raise concerns of efficiency: a given system that uses ILs may have performance that does not compete well with a rival's product that avoids ILs and takes a more direct approach. On the other hand, consider the compiler vendor who produces a suite of compilers for *s* source languages (C++, Pascal, Java, etc.) and currently supports these compilers for *t* target architectures (IBM PC, Sun Sparc, Dec Alpha, etc.). If a different product is needed for each situation, then this company must develop and support *s* × *t* compilers, as shown on the left in Fig. 1; however, this work can be reduced to *s* + *t* if an IL can be introduced between the source and target specifications, as shown on the right in Fig. 1: the company need only develop *s* front ends that translate a given source language to the IL along with *t* back-ends that translate from the IL to a given target architecture.

This approach works best when most of the language translation effort can be accomplished on the IL itself (in what has become known as the compiler's "middle end"), since the IL is now common to every compiler produced by this company. Thus, a carefully designed IL can save the vendor time and money in delivering and maintaining the compiler suite. In summary, the IL makes the compiler more *portable*, and numerous compilers have been developed using ILs for this reason.

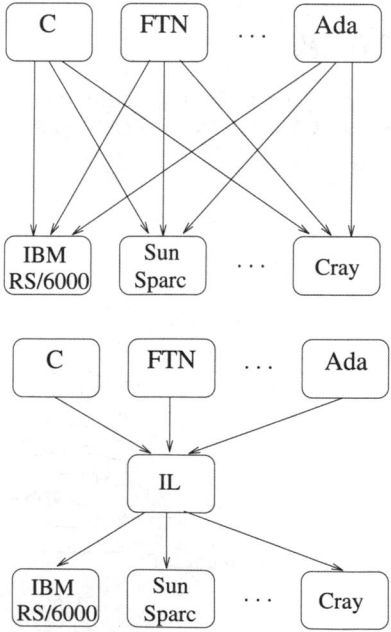

Figure 1. An IL can reduce the effort needed to resource or retarget a compiler.

Table 1. Some source languages and their intermediate languages.

Source language	Intermediate language
Pascal	PCODE
Java	Java VM
Ada	Diana

Consumers of products containing intermediate languages also find benefits from this approach, the most prominent of which is *interoperability*: tools operating at different points in the software development cycle can share and use program information. For example, a debugger should be able to correlate a program's execution with its source files. An accessible intermediate language offers the opportunity for other software systems to interface with the IL-bearing product, either by accepting the product's IL as input for some other task, or by acting as a surrogate provider of the IL. In the compiler suite example given above, a new vendor could interface with the compiler's IL to analyze and transform the intermediate representation to obtain improved performance. Table 1 shows the ILs of some well-known languages.

Origin of Intermediate Languages

There are primarily three methods by which ILs are born:

- *Extension*: The early C++ compiler and the LATEX system are examples of layering a new software system on top of an existing one. Thus, while TEX is a text-processing language in its own right, it is viewed as an intermediate language from the LATEX perspective (Lamport, 1995). Building systems in this fashion is convenient and economic, since an already established language—for which robust translators have presumably already been written—is essentially adopted as an intermediate language.

- *Between*: In this approach, an IL interface is often extracted from an existing system by dividing the system into components that create and use the IL. In other cases, an intermediate interface can allow

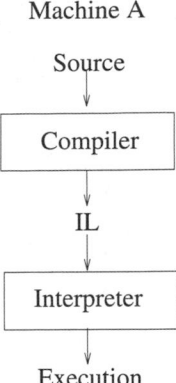

Machine A

Source

Compiler

IL

Interpreter

Execution

Figure 2. Overview of a compiler/interpreter pair.

two previously unrelated software components to interoperate. Intermediate languages created in this fashion are often created more out of necessity than by inspired design.

- *New design*: When an IL can be designed without a legacy of constraints from existing systems there is typically much greater flexibility in defining it.

Case Studies: PCODE and the Java Virtual Machine

Two efforts worth attention are PCODE (Brinch Hansen, 1985; Welsh and Hay, 1986), which has served as an IL for many Pascal (*q.v.*) compilers, and the Java (*q.v.*) virtual machine (Java VM) (Lindholm and Yellin, 1997), which is an object-oriented IL (*see* OBJECT-ORIENTED PROGRAMMING) suitable for *applet* delivery on the World Wide Web (*q.v.*).

An overview of the operation of a PCODE Pascal compiler is shown in Fig 2.

For example, consider the Pascal statement that adds 3 to t.total:

```
t.total := t.total + 3
```

Fig. 3 shows the (annotated) PCODE representation of this statement that the "compiler" component generates. These PCODE instructions are then executed by the "interpreter" component.

```
ldoi 9 ;   pushes the value kept at slot 9 onto the run-time stack. The
        ;   compiler decided that slot 9 is where t.total should be stored.
        ;
ldci 3 ;   pushes the integer constant 3
        ;
adi     ;   pops the stack's top two elements, forms their sum, and then pushes
        ;   the result onto the stack; the previous instructions have caused
        ;   the values of t.total and 3 to be the addends for this instruction
        ;
sroi9   ;   stores at slot 9 (t.total) the value popped from the stack
```

Figure 3. A PCODE example.

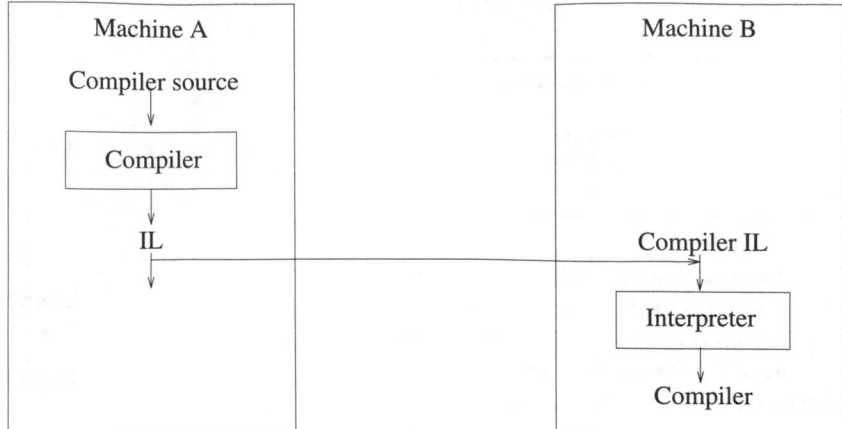

Figure 4. Porting a compiler using its intermediate language.

PCODE is designed so that writing a PCODE interpreter is vastly simpler than writing a Pascal compiler; moreover, the compiler and interpreter components are each written in Pascal. These two design considerations were instrumental to the success of Pascal because they significantly reduced the cost of porting the compiler. A PCODE-generating Pascal compiler is ported between platforms as shown in Fig. 4. If machine *A* already has a PCODE-generating Pascal compiler, then PCODE generated on *A* can be executed on machine *B* once *B* has a PCODE interpreter. The compiler itself is compiled into PCODE on *A*, and when that PCODE is moved to *B* and interpreted by its PCODE interpreter, the result is a Pascal compiler that runs on *B*. Because of its portability, the UCSD Pascal compiler quickly became available on a great number of microcomputers and thus fostered a broad Pascal user community.

Like PCODE, Java VM uses a "stack machine" model to evaluate expressions, with instructions to place values on a stack and to perform arithmetic operations on them (*see* STACK). Since Java is object-oriented, Java VM has instructions to invoke methods (operations belonging to an object), to refer to data encapsulated (*q.v.*) within class instances, and to check object instances with respect to a class hierarchy (*see* OBJECT-ORIENTED PROGRAMMING).

To illustrate both the use of an IL as well as the cleverness with which Java VM was fashioned, consider the following code sequence

```
t.total += 3
```

where `total` is a private data element of a class instance of type `obj`. (It is better programming style to access such data through an appropriate member function, but this example is simplified.) Fig. 5 shows the annotated Java VM code sequence into which this assignment statement is translated.

The code sequence first fetches the value of `total` and places the value on the stack. After the value "3" is pushed on the stack, the `iadd` instruction forms the sum, and the result is then stored back to `total`. Note that the design of Java VM does not permit reference to the actual address of the data within a structure. The field `total` is fetched by name rather than by specifying its location in memory. This apparent inefficiency is designed into Java VM in support of separate compilation. Suppose the structure containing `total` were to be reorganized; then any reference to the field `total` by its offset within an object instance would have to be corrected, either by recomputation at run time or by recompilation of the source program containing the object reference. By cleverly engineering the IL,

```
getfield #5 <Field obj.total I> ; Slot 5 holds the reference for t,
                                 ; so this instruction pushes onto the
                                 ; stack the field "total" of a
                                 ; reference to type "obj" which is an
                                 ; integer ("I")
                                 ;
inconst_3                        ; pushes the constant 3
                                 ;
iadd                             ; pops the stack's top two elements
                                 ; and pushes their sum onto the stack
                                 ;
putfield #5 <Field obj.total I> ; pop the result off the stack and store
                                 ; it in slot 5's (t's) integer "total"
                                 ; field
```

Figure 5. An example of Java VM code.

Java objects can be compiled independently. This is important, since the objects, which may be defined at physically separated locations, can still interoperate correctly without recompilation. Implementations of Java VM are free to optimize object references into hard-coded offsets (addresses within a structure), but it is important that the Java IL interface does not allow the direct expression of addresses.

Summary

Intermediate languages are an important and yet often hidden aspect of system software. Their careful construction allows software to be robust, portable, and efficient. As software components such as language translators, debuggers, programming environments, and visualization tools continue their trend toward interoperability, reasonable IL design will continue to be an important activity. Once designed and published, ILs will also serve as breeding grounds for new kinds of tools that span traditional software boundaries.

Bibliography

1983. Chow, F. C., and Ganapathi G. "Intermediate Languages in Compiler Construction—A Bibliography," *Sigplan Notices*, **18**, *11*, 21–23.

1984. Ottenstein, K. J. "Intermediate Languages in Compiler Construction—A Supplemental Bibliography," *Sigplan Notices*, **19**, 7, 25–27.

1985. Brinch Hansen, P. *Brinch Hansen on Pascal Compilers*. Upper Saddle River, NJ: Prentice Hall.

1986. Welsh, J., and Hay, A. *A Model Implementation of Standard Pascal*. Upper Saddle River, NJ: Prentice Hall.

1995. Lamport, L. *L^A^T_E_X: A Document Preparation System*. Reading, MA: Addison-Wesley.

1997. Lindholm, T., and Yellin, F. *The Java Virtual Machine Specification*. Reading, MA: Addison-Wesley.

Ron Cytron

INTERNATIONAL FEDERATION FOR INFORMATION PROCESSING (IFIP)

For articles on related subjects *see* COMPUTER SOCIETIES; and COMPUTING CONFERENCES.

The *International Federation for Information Processing* (IFIP), founded in 1960 as a result of the herculean efforts of Isaac L. Auerbach, is a multinational federation of societies and groups of societies concerned with information processing. At the end of 1999 it had 45 national members, shown in Table 1, as well as 15 affiliate, associate, and corresponding members. IFIP was founded under the auspices of UNESCO and retains an official relationship with UNESCO.

IFIP aims to foster international cooperation, to stimulate research, development, and applications, and to

Table 1. IFIP national members.

Country	Association	URL
Albania	Institute for Informatics and Applied Mathematics (INIMA)	http://www.ifip.or.at/members/albania.htm
Andorra	Centre Nacional d'Informàtica d'Andorra (CNIA)	http://www.andorra.ad
Argentina	SADIO	http://www.sadio.org.ar
Armenia	National Academy of Sciences of the Republic of Armenia	http://ipia.sci.am
Australia	Australian Computer Society (ACS)	http://www.acs.ocg.au
Austria	Austrian Computer Society (OCG)	http://www.ocg.or.at
Belgium	Fed. Des Assoc. Informat. De Belgique	http://www.bfia.be
Brazil	Brazilian Computer Society—SBC Instituto de Informatica—UFRGS	http://www.sbc.org.br
Bulgaria	Bulgarian Academy of Sciences	http://www.acad.bg
Canada	Canadian Information Processing Society	http://www.cips.ca
China	Chinese Institute of Electronics	http://ww.cie-china.org
Czech Republic	Czech Society for Cybernetics and Informatics	ftp://ftp.utia.cas.cz/pub/CSKI/cski.html
Denmark	Danish Data Association	http://www.ddf.dk
Egypt	Egyptian Computer Society	http://www.ifip.or.at/members/egypt.htm
Finland	Finnish Information Processing Association	http://www.ttlry.fi
France	Société des électriciens et des électroniciens (SEE)	http://www.see.asso.fr
Germany	Gesellschaft für Informatik e.V. (GI)	http://www.gi-ev.de
Greece	Greek Computer Society (GCS)	http://senanet.com/epy/conf/epy.htm
Hungary	John von Neumann Society (NJSZT) for Computing Sciences	http://www.njszt.hu
India	Computer Society of India (CSI)	http://www.csi-india.org
Ireland	Irish Computer Society	http://www.ifip.or.at/members/ireland.htm
Israel	IPA—Information Technology Assocation of Israel	http://www.ifip.or.at/members/israel.htm

Table 1. *Continued.*

Country	Association	URL
Italy	Associazione Italiana per l'Informatica ed il Calcolo Automatico (AICA)	`http://www.aica.iol.it`
Japan	Information Processing Society of Japan (IPSJ)	`http://www.ipsj.or.jp`
Korea	(Republic of) Korea Information Science Society (KISS)	`http://kiss.or.kr/english.html`
Malaysia	Malaysian National Computer Confederation	`http://www4.jaring.my/mncc`
Netherlands	Nederlands Genootschap voor Informatica	`http://www.ngi.nl`
New Zealand	New Zealand Computer Society, Inc.	`http://www.nzcs.org.nz`
Norway	Norwegian Computer Society (NCS)	`http://www.dnd.no`
Poland	Polish Academy of Sciences	`http://www.ifip.or.at/members/poland.htm`
Portugal	Associacao Portuguesa de Informatica	`http://www.ifip.or.at/members/portugal.htm`
Russia	The Russian Academy of Sciences	`http://www.ras.ru`
Singapore	Singapore Computer Society	`http://www.scs.org.sg`
Slovak Republic	Slovak Society for Computer Science	`http://www.ifip.or.at/members/slovakia.htm`
Slovenia	Slovenian Society for INFORMATIKA	`http://www.drustvo-informatika.si`
South Africa	The Computer Society of South Africa	`http://www.casa.org.za`
Spain	FESI—Federacion Española de Sociedades de Informatica	`http://www.esi.es/Information/ITAssociations/` `Associations/assoc73.html`
Sweden	Swedish Information Processing Society (SIPS)	`http://www.dfs.se`
Switzerland	Swiss Federation of Information Processing Societies (SVI/FSI)	`http://svifsi.ch`
Syria	Syrian Computer Society (SCS)	`http://www.scs-syria.com`
Thailand	Thai Federation for Information Processing (TFIP)	`http://www.tfip.th.org`
Tunisia	Centre National de l'Informatique	`http://www.ifiip.or.at/members/tunisia.htm`
United Kingdom	The British Computer Society (BCS)	`http://www.bcs.org.uk`
USA	Association for Computing Machinery (ACM)	`http://www.acm.org`
	IEEE Computer Society	`http://computer.org`

Associate Members

Country	Association	URL
Philippines	The Philippine Computer Society (PCS)	`http://www.worldtelphil.com/~pcs`

Corresponding Members

Country	Association	URL
14 Latin American countries are members	Centro Latino Americano de Estudios Informática (CLEI)	`http://www.clei.cl`
Iceland	The Icelandic Society for Information Processing	`http://www.sky.is`
Zimbabwe	Computer Society of Zimbabwe	`http://www.mediazw.com/csoz/index.html`

Table 2. IFIP congresses.

Date	Location
1962	Munich
1965	New York
1968	Edinburgh
1971	Ljubljana
1974	Stockholm
1977	Toronto
1980	Tokyo and Melbourne
1983	Paris
1986	Dublin
1989	San Francisco
1992	Madrid
1994	Hamburg
1996	Canberra
1998	Vienna and Budapest
2000	Beijing

encourage education and the dissemination and exchange of information on all aspects of computing and communication. To these ends it organizes symposia, workshops, and conferences which result in the publication of 30 to 40 IFIP books annually. Its major international conferences are its biannual World Computer Congresses, which take the form of a half-dozen parallel independent conferences plus a trade-show-like exhibition. The Congresses attract as many as 5,000 participants and are rotated through the member nations. Table 2 lists the dates and locales of the World Computer Congresses.

The technical work of IFIP is carried out by 12 Technical Committees (TCs) and, under these committees, 81 Working Groups (WGs). The Committee and Working Group subjects change from time to time but

Table 3. Technical committees and working groups.

TC 1: Foundations of Computer Science
WG 1.1 Continuous Algorithms and Complexity; WG 1.2 Description Complexity; WG 1.3 Foundations of System Specifications; WG 1.4 Computational Learning Theory; WG 1.5 Cellular Automata and Machines; WG 1.6 Term Rewriting; WG 1.7 Theoretical Foundations of Security Analysis and Design

TC 2: Software: Theory and Practice
WG 2.1 Algorithmic Languages and Calculi; WG 2.2 Formal Description of Programming Concepts; WG 2.3 Programming Methodology; WG 2.4 System Implementation Languages; WG 2.5 Numerical Software; WG 2.6 Database; WG 2.7 (= WG 13.4) User Interface Engineering; WG 2.8 Functional Programming; WG 2.9 Software Requirements Engineering

TC 3: Education
WG 3.1 Informatics and ICT in Secondary Education; WG 3.2 Informatics and ICT at the Level of Higher Education; WG 3.3 Research on Education Applications of Information Technologies; WG 3.4 Vocational Education and Training; WG 3.5 Informatics in Elementary Education; WG 3.6 Distance Learning; WG 3.7 Information Technology in Education Management

TC 5: Computer Applications in Technology
WG 5.2 Computer-Aided Design; WG 5.3 Computer-Aided Manufacturing; WG 5.4 Industrial Software Quality and Certification; WG 5.6 Maritime Industries; WG 5.7 Computer-Aided Production Management; WG 5.10 Computer Graphics and Virtual Worlds; WG 5.11 Computers and Environment; WG 5.12 Architectures for Enterprise Integration

TC 6: Communication Systems
WG 6.1 Architecture and Protocols for Computer Networks; WG 6.2 Broadband Communications; WG 6.3 Performance of Communication Systems; WG 6.4 High Performance Networks; WG 6.6 Network Management for Communication Networks; WG 6.7 Smart Networks; WG 6.8 Wireless Communication; WG 6.10 Photonic Communication Networks

TC 7: System Modeling and Optimization
WG 7.1 Modelling and Simulation; WG 7.2 Computational Techniques in Distributed Systems; WG 7.3 Computer System Modelling; WG 7.4 Discrete Optimization; WG 7.5 Reliability and Optimization of Structural Systems; WG 7.6 Optimization-Based Computer-Aided Modelling and Design; WG 7.7 Stochastic Optimization

TC 8: Information Systems
WG 8.1 Design and Evaluation of Information Systems; WG 8.2 Interaction of Information Systems and the Organization; WG 8.3 Decision Support Systems; WG 8.4 Office Information Systems; WG 8.5 Information Systems in Public Administration; WG 8.6 Transfer and Diffusion of Information Technology; WG 8.7 Informatics in International Business Enterprises; WG 8.8 Smart Cards

TC 9: Relationship between Computers and Society
WG 9.1 Computers and Work; WG 9.2 Social Accountability; WG 9.3 Home-Oriented Informatics and Telematics; WG 9.4 Social Implications of Computers in Developing Countries; WG 9.5 Applications and Social Implications of Virtual Worlds; WG 9.6 Information Technology Misuse and The Law; WG 9.7 History of Computing

TC 10: Computer Systems Technology
WG 10.1 Computer-Aided Systems Theory; WG 10.3 Concurrent Systems; WG 10.4 Dependable Computing and Fault Tolerance; WG 10.5 Design and Engineering of Electronic Systems; WG 10.6 Neural Computer Systems; WG 10.7 Microsystems

TC 11: Security and Protection in IP Systems
WG 11.1 Information Security Management; WG 11.2 Small System Security; WG 11.3 Database Security; WG 11.4 Network Security; WG 11.5 Systems Integrity and Control; WG 11.8 Information Security Education

TC 12: Artificial Intelligence
WG 12.2 Machine Learning; WG 12.5 Knowledge-Oriented Development of Applications; WG 12.6 Intelligent Information Management

TC 13: Human–Computer Interaction
WG 13.1 Education in HCI and HCI Curricula; WG 13.2 Methodology for User-Centred System Design; WG 13.3 Human-Computer Interaction and People with Special Needs; WG 13.4 (= WG 2.7) User Interface Engineering; WG 13.5 Human Error, Safety and System Development

represent the current areas of interest to the academic world. Table 3 contains the names of the TCs and WGs as of 1 January 1999.

IFIP's address is IFIP Secretariat, Hofstrasse 3, A-2361 Laxenburg, Austria; email: ifip@ifip.or.at; Website: http://www.ifip.or.at.

Its presidents since its inception are listed in Appendix V.

Eric A. Weiss

INTERNET

For articles on related subjects *see* CYBERSPACE; DISTRIBUTED SYSTEMS; ELECTRONIC COMMERCE; ELECTRONIC MAIL; ETHERNET; NETWORK PROTOCOLS; NETWORKS, COMPUTER; ONLINE CONVERSATION; PACKET SWITCHING; TCP/IP; and WORLD WIDE WEB.

Introduction

In the 1970s, Arpanet, the forerunner of the Internet, was used by a small number of researchers doing work for the US Department of Defense. In the 1980s, Internet use spread among universities, and in the 1990s, its use surged among people and organizations worldwide. The Internet is the product of remarkable technological achievements in communications. Throughout history, people have anticipated wondrous benefits from such progress, but it was perhaps Wilhelm Eduard Weber who was the first to anticipate the Internet. He wrote in 1855: "When the globe is covered with a net of railroads and telegraph wires, this net will render services comparable to those of the nervous system in the human body, partly as a means of transport, partly as a means for the propagation of ideas and sensations with the speed of lightning." Operating today at transmission rates of up to several gigabits/second, the Internet has proved every forecast of its limitations to be wrong so far, and it is likely that the entire communications infrastructure of the 21st century will be organized around the Internet or its successor.

The *Internet*, or the *Net* for short, is a network of networks linked by several layers of protocols. It uses the Internet Protocol (IP) to route digital packets of information across a multiplicity of networks and communications media in an efficient and generally reliable manner (*see* PACKET SWITCHING). Transmission and receipt of entire messages between two points on the network is managed by the Transmission Control Protocol (TCP), which uses IP packets and guarantees orderly delivery of the bits in the message (*see* TCP/IP). Above TCP are the *application protocols*, discussed below, such as those used for email, file transfer, and the World Wide Web.

The physical layer of the Internet connects users on telephone, satellite, and cable TV networks; local area networks (LAN—*q.v.*); and wide area networks (using a variety of high-speed, high-bandwidth propagation methods). The Internet is like a pipeline, with wide (high-speed) main segments and branches that narrow as they reach single nodes. Internet applications trade off speed and reliability. The trade-off is imposed by the TCP/IP-based application protocols which may exploit the speed and the reliability of the propagation channel. This trade-off may be visible to the average user of the Internet when network congestion slows delivery of an image file, for example, producing delays exceeding those imposed by modems (*q.v.*) on dial-up telephone networks.

Consumer usage of the Net has made it one of the most popular applications in the history of computing. The two most important applications and the source of most traffic are *electronic mail* and the *World Wide Web* (WWW).

History

Internet history can be traced to a military research network established in 1968 called the Arpanet (*see* the first edition of the *Encyclopedia of Computer Science*). The Arpanet was sponsored by the Advanced Research Projects Agency (ARPA) of the US Department of Defense (DoD) and was based on a simple packet-switching protocol. Early switching nodes were at Bolt Beranek and Newman (generally acknowledged as the architects of the Arpanet), Carnegie Mellon University, UCLA, Stanford Research Institute (SRI International), and the University of California at Berkeley.

The Arpanet was originally devoted to support of data communications for defense research projects. The DoD was interested in exploiting networking technology to enhance the use of distributed computing for complex computational problems (*see* DISTRIBUTED SYSTEMS). Different computational systems, operating at different clock rates together with different propagation systems, media, and speeds led to the development of packet-switched systems in order to meet local requirements without sacrificing interconnectivity. When other research networks such as the National Science Foundation Network (NSFnet) were connected to the Arpanet (some of the original NSFnet sites circa 1986 were the National Center for Atmospheric Research (NCAR) in Boulder, CO, and, the National Center for Supercomputing Applications (NCSA) at the University of Illinois), the network gradually came to be known as the *connected Internet* and then, simply, the *Internet*. Indeed, modern usage of the word includes networks that do not conform to Internet standards or that use proprietary standards, such as private bulletin board (*q.v.*) services and certain Internet Service Providers (ISPs) such as America Online (AOL). These proprietary services offer special interfaces that bridge the gap between their nonstandard services and the standard Internet services.

In the late 1990s, a new high-speed network initiative, Internet 2, started (*see* http://www.internet2.org). It was intended to support high-performance computing at major universities and other research centers (*see* SUPERCOMPUTING CENTERS and CLUSTER COMPUTING). As with the Arpanet, its use is likely to broaden, and in the next decade it is likely to become the new Internet infrastructure.

For profiles of the many engineers, computer scientists, and administrators who made the modern Internet possible, see Hafner and Lyon (1996) and Segaller (1998). Among them are Paul Baran, Len Bosack, Vinton Cerf, Robert Kahn, Leonard Kleinrock, J. C. R. Licklider, John McAfee, Bob Metcalfe, Jon Postel, Larry Roberts, Bob Taylor, and Ray Tomlinson. Some of them and many others are shown in Fig. 1. (*See* ENTREPRENEURS for profiles of Bosack and Metcalfe.)

Applications of the Internet

EARLY APPLICATIONS

Email. By far the most popular and certainly the most visible application on the Internet, email, once accounted for as much as 80% of all Net traffic. SMTP, the Simple Mail Transport Protocol, which runs over TCP/IP, is extremely reliable. Because the information is transferred asynchronously in a store-and-forward manner between mail servers, if a server is down, the message will be queued for later transmission, and the user is almost guaranteed that an email message will be received at its destination. Thus it is not necessary to rely on the less reliable process of using intermediate mail routers to buffer the traffic for future delivery. Email messages are usually received in seconds or minutes after transmission, but may be delayed for a few hours or occasionally several days.

There are numerous SMTP *client* programs, such as Eudora and the email programs associated with WWW browsers. There are also proprietary email systems such as ccMail, and office applications that contain embedded email capabilities such as Lotus Notes. The latter is a popular groupware (*q.v.*) product that combines email, conferencing, document management, workflow, and group scheduling, all administered through a Web environment based on client–server computing (*q.v.*). Internet Service Providers (ISPs) also offer "instant messsaging" among the users who contract for their services; though not email, it serves a similar function and provides immediate message delivery (*see* ONLINE CONVERSATION).

Perhaps the most visible problem plaguing the use of email is the practice of *spamming*, junk email used to flood a mailing list of users with unsolicited commercial offerings. Frequently the address identifying the sender of the messages is bogus and the recipients have little recourse other than to complain to their ISPs. To manage the problem, many ISPs have disconnected known offenders and have limited their remote login to certain servers to prevent the possible initiation of unauthorized email. In some cases, servers are closed to non-customer accounts.

FTP. FTP (File Transfer Protocol) provides the ability to transfer files between machines over the Internet. One of the oldest applications on the Internet, FTP is now defined in Request for Comment 959 (RFC—see below), published in 1985, and is still responsible for considerable Internet traffic. FTP deals with protocol issues unique to the transmission of long files and that are likely to be associated with large databases or computer programs. It also allows concurrent access to the same Internet server by multiple users. FTP had been *the* Internet standard for transferring files, but is now almost entirely supplanted by the Web http protocol. Each use of FTP requires authenticated access to a host that will either receive data or transmit data. Each session requires both a control and data connection which is accomplished over TCP. However, *anonymous* FTP allows anyone to access public files on a remote machine. Examples of FTP sites are ftp://ftp.columbia.edu, which offers the NEST network simulation testbed, ftp://ftp.digital.com which has a large collection of software including GNU and Linux (*see* FREE SOFTWARE FOUNDATION), and ftp://valhalla.ee.rochester.edu, which offers RFCs and a Net load balancer.

Telnet. Telnet is a standard Internet application that gives the user the ability to log in to a remote machine over TCP/IP. With such a connection, users may execute standard programs remotely. Such programs might include reading email, although today it is more common to use an email program on one's personal computer. Such remote login creates security issues (see below), and services like Telnet and FTP may be restricted by *firewalls*, programs that investigate each packet and, pursuant to pre-established rules, decide whether to pass or reject it. Even with a firewall, Telnet is insecure because it transmits passwords unencrypted, and it is prudent today to use a "secure shell" alternative that encrypts passwords for remote logins.

Usenet. Usenet (Unix User Network) is the common name of a distributed client–server computer bulletin board system. News readers are used to access *newsgroups*, of which there are tens of thousands. Some examples are rec.food.cooking, alt.sources.wanted, which posts anonymous FTP sites, news.announce.newsusers, comp.sys.linux, and the like. Usenet started as a link between Duke and the University of North Carolina in 1979. The first newsgroups carrying wire service news were distributed by ClariNet Communications about 1986. There are numerous newsreader programs, and Usenet news may now also be accessed through Web links, or through a newsreader that is coupled with a browser such as Netscape Messenger. Originally Usenet employed the Unix-to-Unix Copy Protocol (UUCP) to transport news and views. Usenet now commonly uses the Network News Transport Protocol (NNTP) which is robust and has proved useful in commercial applications. NNTP requires confirmation of receipt of updated files and is used for ensuring that time critical information has

Figure 1. Pioneers of computer networking reunited in Boston in 1994 at the twenty-fifth anniversary celebration of the Arpanet, hosted by Bolt, Beranek and Newman. *Left to right, front row*: Bob Taylor, Vint Cerf, Frank Heart; *second row*: Larry Roberts, Len Kleinrock, Bob Kahn; *third row*: Wes Clark, Doug Englebert, Barry Wessler; *fourth row*: Dave Walden, Severo Ornstein, Truett Thach, Roger Scantlebury, Charlie Herzfeld; *fifth row*: Ben Barker, Jon Postel, Steve Crocker; *last row*: Bill Naylor, Roland Bryan. (Photo © by Clark Quin, Boston, MA.)

been received. For example, the ClariNet News Service is based upon an NNTP delivery service. Usenet news is an early example of "push technology"; newsgroups are automatically updated without any activity on the part of the resident systems administrators. Although Usenet has been partially supplanted by the Web, it is still alive and well; its greatest problem is the quantity of information of widely varying quality that it provides.

CONTEMPORARY APPLICATIONS

World Wide Web. The World Wide Web, or just *Web*, resides on top of the Internet as an enormous client–server (*q.v.*) layer. The Web is likely to prove the future multimedia (*q.v.*) integrator of Internet applications and may replace applications that operate at lower levels of the Internet, such as Lotus Notes. Alternatively, one can expect these applications to reformulate themselves as Web applications. The principal Web tool is the *browser*, a program that uses the HyperText Transfer Protocol (http) to retrieve information provided by http servers worldwide—an activity known as *surfing*, i.e. searching for and accessing different Websites which contain *Web pages* linked as *hypertext* (*q.v.*). The first page of what may be a sequence of linked pages at that site is called a *home page*. Browsers provide a graphical *user interface* (*q.v.*), or GUI, for receiving or sending multimedia information. The most commonly employed browsers are Netscape Navigator and Microsoft Internet Explorer, which offer similar capabilities. Although other browsers, such as Opera, may be smaller and faster, as of 1999, they account for only a few percent of all browser use.

Search engines. With millions of Websites and Web pages and an astonishing growth rate, a major issue for many users is finding the correct information at the correct Website. For this purpose several *search engines* have evolved, such as Yahoo!, Excite, Alta-Vista, Lycos, Webcrawler, Northern Light, Infoseek, Hotbot, Snap, Google, and many others. Users may query search engines using keywords or key phrases and a variety of classical search query syntax. Most engines support complex searches with Boolean and other operators so that the experienced user is much more likely to find pertinent information than the novice. In addition to the general search engines, there are also search engine sites that specialize in searches for a host of applications in such areas as law, medicine, and health. One can usually locate these sites by using a generalized search engine to find the specialized ones.

To maximize effective service to their users, search "engines" (which should not be confused with conventional database search functions) cruise or "crawl through" the Internet, more or less continuously, searching for information in Websites. Information may be sought in the complete text of the site or just on its page headers; thus Website developers can attract the attention of more search engines by placing certain keywords or phrases at or near the top of their Web pages in attempts to attract more "hits," that is, accesses of their Website. Some search engine companies, most notably Yahoo!, have human editors who organize the database of Websites by creating taxonomies and directories in which Websites are cataloged. To gain the attention of these human catalogers, Website creators may also formally register their site with particular search engines, either one by one or by using the services of a third-party Internet company which, for a fee, will register a Website with many search engines. Through a combination of registration and their own exploration, search engines develop many pages of information about millions of Websites.

There is an indication, however, that search engine data collection cannot keep pace with the rapid growth of the Internet. The research of Lawrence and Giles (1999) indicates that there are now at least 800 million Web pages, and that the leading search engine (Northern Light at the time of their survey) had indexed only 16% of them. Only two years before, Hotbot, the leading engine of 1997, had indexed 34% (of a far smaller number of pages). In desperation, many users turn to "meta engines" which delegate queries to a number of engines and collect and merge their results, raising coverage to about 42% of the Web. Among them are http://www.metacrawler.com, http://www.metasearch.com, and http://www.dogpile.com.

Most search engines companies base their revenue on the sale of advertising which, in turn, is based upon the number of downloads or page hits that they can offer to an advertiser. The more popular the engine, the higher the price charged.

Push. *Push* is the automatic delivery of information to multiple sites on the Internet. It is useful for the delivery of news or software updates to a known distribution list. Push is a one-to-many distribution system and, as such, occasionally causes congestion at a particular server. Some of the push systems deliver their content via email, while others, like Pointcast, deliver their information directly to an application such as a screen saver. Programs called *channels* use push by automatically updating their own content and code. For security purposes they are restricted to the delivery of information to areas in the target server or terminal called *sandboxes*. In general, the push feature generates large volumes of traffic to multiple sites all over the Net. Although initially popular, the heavy network traffic generated by push technology has made it less common in 1999.

Under some conditions push can also be characterized as *pull*. For example, early implementations of Point-cast provided for the client software to request (i.e. "pull") an update from the server. Since thousands of users may reside on a given LAN and request updates in a small window of time, this can create congestion at the gateway (*q.v.*) as the data is pushed (or pulled) down. One solution is to install software managers at the LAN servers that receive only one copy of the data and then redistribute it downward so as to reduce the amount of gateway traffic that would otherwise be necessary to deliver to all of the target terminals.

Intranets and extranets. An *intranet* is a local or wide area network that uses the TCP/IP protocol for restricted use within a particular corporation. Intranets connect to the external Internet through a firewall. Intranet users are generally employees of a single company. An *extranet* is a wide area network based on public TCP/IP protocols and can be thought of an Intranet with external interfaces. An extranet frequently exchanges information with other corporate extranets for electronic commerce (*q.v.*) and collaboration. Extranet users are generally employees of companies related through a common supplier relationship.

Electronic commerce. Electronic commerce (*e-commerce*) uses the Web and other Internet resources to let vendors and service providers do business online. E-commerce requires a support infrastructure for customers (users) to browse items offered for sale, peruse or search digital catalogs, visit virtual shopping malls, and use *shopping carts* (applications that provide for depositing selections in a single place for subsequent payment). Tools are also necessary for vendors to build their storefront shopping sites. Although these facilities were in an early stage of development as of 1999, millions of dollars of business are done online daily. E-commerce also requires a secure and stable money mechanism. As of 1999 there were several manifestations of electronic money under development on the Internet, but most e-commerce now uses the common credit or debit card.

CyberCash. CyberCash offers consumers and vendors services for making secure and authenticated transactions on the Internet. With a digital "wallet" that functions as a secure credit card, consumers can execute cash or debit transactions, receive electronic invoices, and encrypt a credit card number that gets sent to a merchant. The merchant then appends an encrypted confirmation code to a transaction and forwards it to a CyberCash server which then routes the information to a bank. A competing idea is the DigiCash system that allows a user to send cash via a credit card or ATM to a bank that issues a certificate known as *ecash*.

Encrypted email then is sent to the consumer with code numbers representing different denominations of money. This system is quite simple and provides for anonymous transactions. However, the anonymity of the system is itself considered a weakness by those who prefer more accountability.

In late 1998 the US government instituted a new electronic commerce financial payment system as part of its response to the 1996 Debt Collection Act which demands that all governmental agencies make federal payments electronically by the beginning of 1999. Pursuant to that requirement the US government will inaugurate email electronic payments (a new Treasury Department Financial Management service). Perhaps most interesting, this system will deliver funds instantaneously with no float (i.e. no delay at all between presentation of payment and the actual debit and transfer of funds from the paying account to the receiving account). The US government also announced that henceforth it would bring the Patent and Trademark Office (PTO) online with the full database of the nation's patents since 1976 and trademark text and images starting from the late 1800s. This data was made available on the WWW in 1998. The database includes 2,000,000 patents, 800,000 registered trademarks, and 300,000 pending trademarks.

Any description of the Internet's commercial applications certainly will be overtaken by events. Some of the more popular commercial sites as of 1999 were `http://www.yahoo.com` and `http://www.excite.com` (search engines), `http://www.amazon.com` and `http://www.barnesandnoble.com` (books), `http://www.travelocity.com` (travel), `http://www.ebay.com` (auctions) and `http://www.fromages.com` (cheese). In addition, the Internet has a proliferation of financial sites, employment sites, and medical sites. The future prospects are unlimited, subject only to human imagination and the threat of interference from governments. As of 1999 there were several delicate regulatory issues receiving considerable attention around the world. These include the use of the Internet to publish pornography and the problems attendant in managing children's access to such sites, the concern that the Internet and its various resources could be used to place children and people in exploitative circumstances, the widening use of gambling sites, and the ongoing battle between government and commercial interests over encryption—whereby the US government desires access to encryption models and the commercial sector is resisting this intrusion (*see* PRETTY GOOD PRIVACY). All of these issues, as well as taxation, broadcasting controls typically imposed by the US Federal Communications Commission (FCC), and dial-up access charge battles, remain to be fought.

In addition to the free content on the Internet, one can also find many commercial sites that charge for their content. NewsEdge Corp., for example, bundles content from multiple news sources and provides both an Intranet subscription to corporate customers and a single subscriber version for consumers. The news from many wire services is updated frequently and is controlled by password access. This is in contrast to "free" news, such as that published on Yahoo!, which is based on fewer sources and updated less frequently.

Because the Internet provides both domestic and international connectivity, another new application drawing the attention of the regulatory agencies is Internet telephony. In this application the Internet provides the same functionality as the telephone network for carrying voice traffic. Analog voice signals are digitized, split into packets, and then sent over the Internet. In this manner one can place the equivalent of free long distance (in the USA) and international calls. For example, one can now use conventional telephone services on the Internet with companies like IDT that offer very low cost long distance service. Similarly the @Home company offers high-speed Internet access over cable TV networks including high-speed phone lines. Some of the services offered include discount long distance, discount international calls, and fax. There are flow control and congestion issues that affect the throughput of these services. Although presently not regulated, eventually one would expect tariffs to be imposed and greater regulation of this method, especially at the international level. In addition to conventional telephony in which a phone call is directed to a special gateway where the analog voice is digitized, IP telephony is being deployed with transceivers at the desktop. As these applications expand one can expect such features as invoking a digital IP call during an online chat session.

Internet Communications

THE EVOLUTION OF TCP/IP AND THE INTERNET SUITE

As the Arpanet evolved it became more important to connect disparate networks with different propagation, reliability, and throughput characteristics. While one could use TCP as a transport service for use on contiguous homogeneous networks in which hosts and servers are directly connected before initiating data transmission, it was necessary to find some other method for dealing with traffic that had to leave the homogeneous network and transit one or more other networks. For that, the connectionless *packet switching* (q.v.) Internet Protocol (IP) was developed. Early work on AlohaNet, a wireless 10 Kbps FM radio network at the University of Hawaii, and Ethernet (q.v.), a

3 Mbps LAN technology at Xerox Palo Alto Research Center, had encouraged ARPA to look towards the deployment of similar technologies and protocols in a self-organizing radio network for military research purposes. This network, known as Packet Radio, provided 100 Kbps access to terminals and 400 Kbps connections between network repeaters. Based on *spread spectrum modulation*, the system was secure and reliable. However, in interfacing this Packet Radio Network to the Arpanet, several interface problems arose. These problems related to the substantial differences in delay and reliability between a radio network and a land-based network. It was necessary to design a *gateway* (q.v.) to serve as a buffer and traffic manager between the two networks. The original work was first reported as the Kahn/Cerf Protocol in 1973, named after Robert Kahn and Vinton Cerf but now called TCP/IP. The birth of the TCP/IP gateway is widely considered to be the defining moment of the Internet.

Different propagation conditions exist on land lines, satellite, and ground-based wireless systems. Radio systems suffer from environmental interference, satellite systems have extremely long propagation delays, and wireless systems may have mobile terminals or random dispersion of network repeaters. As a result, all digital networks offer trade-offs among reliability, speed, and throughput. Further, traffic design constraints affect network performance. For example, Packet Radio and Ethernet were designed for large numbers of random access terminals all operating on the same channel and transmitting small quantities of text (while receiving greater quantities). This more or less guaranteed *contention* (q.v.) for the channel since terminals would frequently interfere with each other. TCP/IP was created to manage these differences across multiple networks and to deal with the corresponding routing problems that exist with networks with unreliable physical links.

Early in the development of TCP/IP, it became apparent that, within digital networks such as the Internet and the Packet Radio Network, it would be advantageous to provide for a *layering* methodology that permitted replacing older components of the technology with newer technology when it became available. In the simplest example, it would be very desirable to replace the actual propagation physical devices—such as 10 Kbps radios with 100 Kbps radios—without having to change any other component in the system. Initially, six layers were established; there are now five. From lowest to highest, these layers are called (1) Physical (such as an RS 232 interface that provides for the actual bit transmission); (2) Data link; (3) Internet, such as IP; (4) Host to Host or Transport (TCP); and (5) Application. In the hierarchy of Internet applications, the Applications layer supports the Simple Mail Transfer

Protocol (SMTP), which provides store-and-forward service for email messages, and FTP, which supports file transfers. It also supports other applications that interact with the transport levels to send or receive data. This layering has gained universal acceptance and most Internet products and services are known through the layer in which they operate.

MANAGING NETWORK OPERATIONS

Protocol suites. As the Internet developed, a competing suite of protocol layers was established under the Open Systems Interconnection (OSI—*q.v.*) Standard. OSI represented international standards interests outside the USA. It offered a seven-layer protocol implementation to correspond to the ARPA levels. Under OSI the layers (from lowest to highest) are: (1) Physical; (2) Data link; (3) Network; (4) Transport; (5) Session; (6) Presentation; and (7) Application. The TCP/IP model omits OSI levels 5 and 6.

Network management. Network management encompasses five functions: (1) security management, (2) fault management, (3) performance management, (4) configuration control and (5) accounting and financial reporting. Both the Simple Network Management Protocol (SNMP) and the Common Management Information Protocol (CMIP) have gained substantial popularity on the Internet. Both CMIP and CMOT (CMIP Over TCP/IP) have been supported by the Internet Activities Board (see below) and both use agent/manager operational models. In these systems *objects* are managed. Most entities in the network connection can be represented by objects, such as servers, routers or hosts. Objects are organized in eight groups, three of which, for example, are *system, interface*, and *IP*. Each object must be essential for either error or configuration measurement, and each has four characteristics that are monitored: its attributes, relationship to other objects, how it operates, and its output. These characteristics are deposited in a Management Information Base (MIB). The *agent* operates inside the object and reports behavior to the manager. The manager contains the interface to the user world, and manages the database and the communications. Different vendors, from software organizations to router manufacturers, provide varying implementations of these management systems. SNMP operates as a polling protocol and under it the Manager initiates a query and the agent responds. The simple User Datagram Protocol (UDP) transmits all SNMP messages. UDP is a packet-switching host-to-host mode transport layer protocol that, like IP, offers "best effort" but not guaranteed delivery. It adds multiplexing (*q.v.*) to IP, allowing packets to be routed to particular processes at an Internet address.

Security. Internet system security is provided through physical routers that serve as *firewalls*. Firewalls isolate a server from unauthorized intruders on the Internet. In addition, *proxy servers* are used as additional barriers to control traffic entering or leaving the Internet. Some proxy servers are used to sit between the population of users and the Internet so that no traffic may enter or leave the Net without passing through the proxy. This is the case, for example, in China. (Of course, proxy servers cannot observe traffic that passes through the long-distance telephone network via dial-up networks). Other proxy servers may mirror actual servers inside a firewall and are used to receive traffic ultimately destined for the interior server. In these cases, the proxy servers allow traffic to be received without a requirement to give the transmitting party additional access to the interior server. Security is also accomplished through the use of *packet filters* which, among other functions, compare the services requested against the logical port. Thus, certain input ports on a router may be assigned to specific applications or users and unauthorized users can be detected if they appear on the wrong port. In some cases the firewall actively monitors the states requested by each port dynamically, the source and destination of the packets (and timing), and the connectivity sought. Proxies can also be nested and provide additional layers of insulation. There also is an increasing use of virtual private networks (VPNs) in which the Internet is used to communicate information from one private secure network to another. Using the Internet as a transport mechanism, *tunneling protocols* are used to authenticate users, provide error control, and encrypt and decrypt the traffic.

Addressing. Within the Internet, addressing has been an increasingly demanding problem. Indeed as the number of addresses has exploded it has become necessary to revamp addressing schemes and, some time in 2000, a major new protocol, IP Version 6, is expected that will vastly increase the addressing space from 32 bits to 128. At the moment, IP space is divided into three general classes of addresses. Class A, B, and C addresses are all specified by 4-tuples, each of 8 bits (thus allowing a decimal range of 0–255 in each tuple). The first of the four tuples is called the *keying* byte, and its initial bits determine the class. The remaining bits of each class specify the *network* and the *host* bits. Class A has few networks, but each may have many hosts. Class C has few hosts per network and hence many possible networks, as shown in Table 1. There also are two special purpose classes with limited numbers of hosts—for example, Class D is associated with *multicasting*, i.e. one to many broadcasts, and Class E is reserved for experimental purposes. There is no automatic relationship between Class addresses and Internet domain names.

Table 1. Internet addressing. Host address bits that are all 0s or all 1s are reserved for broadcasting, making the number of hosts for each network two less than a power of 2 (e.g. 254 rather than $2^8 = 256$).

Class	Initial bits	Networks (bits)	Hosts/network (bits)	Example	Domain name
A	0	128 (7)	16,777,214 (24)	4.0.0.10	`maeeast.bbnplanet.net`
B	10	16,384 (14)	65,534 (16)	128.18.30.70	`sri.com`
C	110	2,097,152 (21)	254 (8)	194.129.50.134	`www.grovereference.com`
D	1110			224.0.0.0	(for multicast)
E	11110			240.0.0.0	(experimental)

Throughout the history of the Internet pundits have predicted its demise through the collapse of the addressing scheme. However, the Internet's adoption of IP Version 6 (IPv6) addressing, with its up to 128 bits of addressing, should ameliorate the risk. According to Vinton Cerf, the extension to 128 bits should permit "every light bulb, light switch, power socket and appliance . . . on the net in addition to personal computing and communication devices, on-line information services, radio and television transmitters and receivers . . . telephones and sensors of all kinds . . . [to be connected to the Internet]."

Domain names. Internet address names are managed by the Domain Name System (DNS). The DNS arranges names hierarchically and uses a standard ordering system. Specific sites are then identified relative to higher level domains. In the educational domain a specific site might be `cs.umd.edu`, indicating the computer science department at the University of Maryland in the "edu" Internet domain. A (fictitious) email address might be `jvn@cs.umd.edu`. Each DNS name is composed of one or more labels separated by dots. There are two kinds of top-level domain names: generic and geographical. The top-level generic domain names widely used in the USA include "com" (com-

mercial), "edu" (educational), "gov" (US government), "mil" (US military organization), "net" (network provider), "org" (not-for-profit organization.), and "int" (international organizations established by treaties). The top-level geographical domain generally used in other countries is the two-letter ISO 3166 code (an exception is the UK which uses the code "uk" instead of the ISO code "gb"). Table 2 gives examples of these country codes. Geographical codes are sometimes used in the USA; for example, `www.state.ny.us`. The highest level US domain names may or may not be used outside the US to indicate similar entities. Thus, a foreign commercial site need not use "com" in its address before its country code. In some cases, an abbreviated US domain is used, such as "co" for "com" or "ne" for "net." Thus, `wjk@cyberway.com` may be presumed to be a US email address, `wjk@cyberway.co.sg` is a commercial Singapore address, and `wjk@niftyserve.ne.jp` may be presumed to be a Japanese email address.

The DNS supports a uniform naming service, maintains distributed databases around the net with a replication model (which distributes updated address tables to known Internet servers), and sets naming standards for fields. Throughout the Internet these DNS *name servers* resolve IP addresses from domain

Table 2. A selection of country codes used by the Domain Name Service.

dz	Algeria	eg	Egypt	li	Liechtenstein	sg	Singapore
ar	Argentina	fj	Fiji	lu	Luxembourg	sk	Slovak Republic
au	Australia	fi	Finland	mo	Macau	si	Slovenia
at	Austria	fr	France	my	Malaysia	za	South Africa
be	Belgium	de	Germany	mx	Mexico	kr	South Korea
br	Brazil	gr	Greece	nl	Netherlands	es	Spain
bg	Bulgaria	hk	Hong Kong	nz	New Zealand	se	Sweden
ca	Canada	hu	Hungary	ni	Nicaragua	ch	Switzerland
cl	Chile	is	Iceland	no	Norway	tw	Taiwan
cn	China	in	India	pa	Panama	th	Thailand
co	Colombia	id	Indonesia	pe	Peru	tn	Tunisia
cr	Costa Rica	ir	Iran	ph	Philippines	tr	Turkey
hr	Croatia	ie	Ireland	pl	Poland	uk	UK
cy	Cyprus	il	Israel	pt	Portugal	uy	Uruguay
cz	Czech Republic	it	Italy	pr	Puerto Rico	us	USA
dk	Denmark	jp	Japan	ro	Romania	ve	Venezuela
ec	Ecuador	kw	Kuwait	sa	Saudi Arabia		

names and execute complex protocols to find names that are not on the local name servers. In the most common case, users will encounter DNS errors when sending email to nonexistent servers or when searching the Web for a nonexistent URL (Universal Resource Locator—a Website address).

For companies and organizations, the domain name serves as their identity on the Internet. For example, `www.ibm.com`, `www.gm.com`, `www.acm.org`, and `www.stanford.edu` serve as Website URLs for IBM, General Motors, ACM, and Stanford University respectively. To be effective, domain names must be unique, and to ensure uniqueness they must be registered with some authority. In the USA, this can be done through Network Solutions, Inc., whose 1999 price was $35 per year for a minimum of two years. Network Solutions ensures that the names have not been used and that routing tables in the Internet are set to the correct IP address for each name.

A good, easily remembered domain name is a valuable commodity which, once duly registered, can be sold for whatever the traffic will bear. Speculators register names that have no corresponding Website and often auction them through Websites such as `www.ebay.com` or `www.amazon.com`.

Most ISPs will offer domain registration services through Network Solutions for their customers. In 1998, the US government abandoned its support of the Internet Assigned Numbers Authority (IANA) and turned over the responsibility to the Internet Corporation for Assigned Names and Numbers (ICANN). ICANN will authorize additional organizations to issue domain names.

As of 1999, there was considerable controversy over the evolution of the DNS and the practice of granting domain names. The question of who will control the top-level design of the DNS and assign names is extremely sensitive and several political considerations complicate the issue: for example, governments are wary of self-regulation and non-US Internet developers and vendors fear US domination. It is clear that a respected nongovernmental organization is needed to ameliorate these concerns. ICANN, it is to be hoped, can meet that need.

STANDARDIZATION

The Internet Activity Board (IAB), founded in 1983, has served as the codifying organization for the Internet. The IAB manages all of the standards developments around TCP/IP and sets official policies and standards, manages the RFC process, provides planning on a long term basis, and serves as the liaison to international bodies. It is not a government organization but rather an

independent volunteer-based organization. Research that is recommended by the IAB is not funded by it but is supported by the participants and their organizations. There are two major suborganizations under the IAB: the Internet Engineering Task Force (IETF) and the Internet Research Task Force. Both of these organizations have working subgroups which are composed of a community of network designers, operators, vendors, and researchers who coordinate the operation, management, and evolution of the Internet and resolve protocol issues.

RFCs (Request For Comments) were originally established as a means for communicating between research groups developing the Internet. These groups, originally known as ARPA Working Groups and now as Working Groups of the IETF, issued papers of work-in-progress. While edited, these were not and are not refereed archival technical journal papers but rather represent technical engineering ideas or proposals as well as accepted standards. Over time, the collection of RFCs (and earlier Internet Engineering Notes) has come to represent the collective design of the Internet and the standards (including protocols and policies) accepted by the IAB and the participating community on the Internet (users, vendors, suppliers, service providers, and so forth). RFCs may be obtained from the Internet Society on the WWW. Preliminary RFCs are known as Internet drafts. For example, RFC821 and RFC822 specify the standards for email addressing and contain the following typical information: email addresses take the form `username@add1.add.2.add3`, where `add3` is known as the top-level domain.

NETWORK ACCESS POINTS (NAPs)

In order to avoid large numbers of hops from Internet node to Internet node, connection interchanges have been established in the USA and in several other countries, most notably Japan. These connections allow participating carriers or ISPs to exchange traffic directly between their backbones (i.e. main high-speed paths through the network). Evolving after NSF acquired management of the Internet from the DoD in 1990, four connection points were established in the US in 1993. These points provided an ability for any backbone connecting LANs to connect to other service providers thus providing unrestricted access to all Internet users. The original sites were (1) San Francisco, operated by Pacific Bell, (2) Chicago, operated by Bellcore and Ameritech, (3) New York (actually in New Jersey), operated by Sprint, and (4) Washington, operated by Metropolitan Fiber Systems (MFS) which was purchased by WorldCom in 1997. This system evolved into a complex of Network Access Points (NAPs) operated by multiple vendors. For example, WorldCom now operates NAPs in San Jose (known as Metropolitan Area

Exchange (MAE-West), Los Angeles, New York (MAE-East), Dallas, Houston, and Washington. Each of these NAPs are 10–100 Mbps fiber optic rings providing inexpensive access to private corporate intranets. There are also Federal Internet Exchange points: FIX East at the University of Maryland and FIX West at NASA Ames Research Center, Moffett Field, CA which services federal networks such as MILNET (the defense component remaining from the original Arpanet), NASA Science Net, and others.

PROPAGATION AND INFRASTRUCTURE

Carriers such as MCI and Sprint provide Internet backbones with speeds ranging up to OC-12 (622.08 Mbps). OC stands for Optical Carrier and is a Synchronous Optical Network (SONET) standard for fiber optic communications channels. Sonet provides for communications between different networks that require complicated multiplexing and de-multiplexing and complex coding and decoding to exchange traffic. The most elementary Synchronous Transport Speed (STS) is OC-1, which is 51.84 Mbps. The fastest routers operate at speeds such as OC-3 (155.52 Mbps) so the full speed of the backbones still cannot be exploited. Nevertheless, the trend is clearly toward OC-12 as soon as faster routers are available. Still higher speeds of several Gbps are available for the Internet 2 research network.

Because the US Telecommunications Act of 1996 frees AT&T to turn to local markets and the Baby Bells to enter the long distance markets, AT&T, the Baby Bells and many companies are creating technology that enables them to offer high speed Internet connections (DSLs—Digital Subscriber Lines) over conventional phone lines. AT&T hopes to offer complete packages that include local, long distance, wireless, cable and Internet access in one integrated service. Over time we can expect all of these telecommunications services to merge. As Howard Anderson, Managing Director of The Yankee Group, said in 1998, "There is going to be no difference between local and long distance, between voice and data, between voice mail and E-mail."

INTERNET SERVICE PROVIDERS (ISPs)

Each user of the Internet requires a connection (connectivity) to the Internet. The most common method of use for the consumer is dial-up to a local ISP. Each ISP offers a large range of services from simple connectivity to email services to news and Internet Relay Chat, a service that facilitates person-to-person line-by-line communications. The local dial-up telephone number is usually referred to as a Point of Presence (POP). ISPs offer anywhere from small numbers of local POPs to hundreds of national and international POPs. For the typical consumer who requires local access, the smaller ISPs provide adequate connectivity through local POPs.

For the traveling businessperson, remote access is necessary to control long distance and international toll and hotel charges. This requires one or more international ISPs with local POPs in many cities The user dials a local POP and makes an Internet TCP/IP connection often using Point-to-Point Protocol (PPP), which allows TCP/IP to run over a serial communication line. Once connected, an email application, for example Eudora or ccMail, or a Web browser may be invoked over the TCP/IP layer to provide access. Some users now subscribe to Integrated Services Digital Network (ISDN—q.v.) services that operate at substantially higher speeds but which require special modems and software to provide connectivity. ISDN combines voice and digital network services in a single medium. ISDN systems do not support remote connectivity.

As of 1999, there were several experiments under way to provide local connectivity to roaming users from an ISP other than their own. Travelers can log on to POPs owned by other ISPs (either domestically or internationally) and execute PPP connections for remote login or email. There are usually additional roaming charges for these services similar to those for cellular telephones.

As of early 1999, there were 4,470 ISPs in the USA offering connectivity to both consumers (dial-up) and corporate customers (leased lines). About 20% of the ISPs have connections to long haul backbone providers WorldCom UUNET, and Compuserve (bought by AOL in 1997), 31% were connected to MCI, and 24% used Sprint. Some ISPs had enough connections to backbones so that most users could send email to other Internet users with a minimum number of hops. The early situation on the Internet in which packets had to travel through multiple layers from a backbone of one ISP to reach another no longer applies—indeed some ISPs now claim "single-hop" connectivity to 80% or more of Internet users in the USA.

In the USA the largest ISP by far is America Online (AOL), with over 20,000,000 subscribers. AOL operates a proprietary service but also offers Internet connectivity and supports standard browser operations. AOL originally used a proprietary browser, but now uses a slightly modified version of Microsoft's Internet Explorer, even though AOL now owns Netscape. Another similar ISP is CompuServe, a division of AOL that also maintains some proprietary software along with standard Internet connectivity. CompuServe technology is licensed to NiftyServe in Japan, the largest ISP in Asia with almost 2,250,000 subscribers. Other major ISPs in the USA are Netcom (one of the oldest), AT&T (one of the newest with 1,000,000 subscribers), IBM, Earthlink, and PSInet. In Japan other major ISPs are BigGlobe (a NEC company) and PeopleWorld (a joint venture between IBM Japan, Matsushita, and Mitsubishi Co.), Internet Initiative Japan (the oldest ISP in Japan), and Tokyo Internet Company (a leased line corporate ISP). Most nations now have major ISPs: for example in Singapore, Singapore Telephone and Cyber-Way offer services; Hong Kong Telephone offers ISP services in Hong Kong, and in Europe major services are offered by subsidiaries of British Telecom, France Telecom, Deutsche Telekom, PTT Netherlands, and so forth. It is estimated that, worldwide, there were over 100 million Internet users as of 1999.

In addition to the commercial ISPs, universities also support large numbers of Internet users. Virtually every university has a permanent Internet connection supporting students and staff. Thus universities function as ISPs by providing Internet connectivity to students and faculty.

For-profit ISPs finance their operations through subscriber fees, revenue sharing with their content sources, connectivity charges, additional resource charges such as memory and dial-up port utilization charges, and advertising. Because competition is so fierce, basic connectivity has become a commodity throughout the USA and is priced accordingly. Monthly access fees of US $20 are common and can be expected to decline. Since these prices allow little if any profit, we can expect considerable shakeout and consolidation in the ISP industry. At the moment, advertising seems to be the most likely future source of ISP revenue, but electronic commerce may also prove attractive. When advertising is embedded in downloaded Web pages, it consumes some small additional bandwidth (*q.v.*).

In the USA most dial-up connections use a local POP and thus are free. While the Bell companies are not happy with this revenue model and while the Internet has certainly changed the telephone network characteristics, which originally were based entirely on voice call statistics, it is likely that Internet calls in the USA will remain free or will be priced very low indefinitely. Rates are different in Europe, South America, and Asia, where calls are generally charged by the minute. For this reason, some Asian ISPs such as NiftyServe have been reluctant to include advertising on their Websites, which requires more bandwidth to deliver and which increases the customers' connect charges. In Tokyo, for example, peak usage time for ISPs like NiftyServe is after 11:00 p.m. because NTT provides lower cost connectivity then. In Europe, there is much less consumer traffic in proportion to corporate traffic because of the higher connectivity charges to the home consumer.

Some ISPs have established *peering* (bilateral sharing of traffic) relationships in which they agree to allow traffic to transit their backbones, thus facilitating shorter transits for much of the Internet's traffic. This has the benefit, in theory, of decreasing traffic on one's own backbone and providing for shorter hops for one's customers. Of course not all ISPs "peer" with all other ISPs since peering can result in additional traffic from other peered ISPs.

Limits to Growth?

At the end of the 1990s, Internet use has become global. The extent of access still varies widely, however. Fig. 2 shows the situation as of 1994, plotting Internet nodes against gross national product. It is dangerous to make Internet predictions since the Internet has proven so adept at evolution despite its complex problems. Still, those factors that could impede the growth of the Internet include the possibility of an ultimate traffic jam creating a requirement to stop and redesign subsystems of the Internet. Traffic will undoubtedly grow exponentially as we experience more and more multimedia integration with conventional traffic types. While IP Version 6 is expected to resolve the addressing problem, it was intended to be implemented during the risky year 2000 (Y2K) period. Complications from the Y2K problem (*q.v.*), which is expected to devour available programming resources, could slow the implementation of IP Version 6.

Similarly, although the US government (under its Framework for Global Electronic Commerce) has declared the Internet a duty-free zone for at least three years, one can anticipate that the US government and its state and foreign counterparts will ultimately try to tax traffic and transactions on the Internet. This will undoubtedly have a chilling effect on the growth of commercial applications on the Internet. Also, the Baby Bells have made it clear that they wish to charge for dial-up access to the Internet; this problem may be ameliorated as the consumer becomes increasingly connected to the Internet via other media such as cable. However, it would be unwise to predict that US Internet users forever will continue to have the more or less free connections to the Internet that their foreign colleagues lack.

Privacy will continue to be a thorny problem on the Internet. It is common practice for Websites to collect information from clients surfing their Website through the use of *cookies*, small swatches of data and program code planted in a computer memory while its user surfs a particular Website. Cookies collect information and report back on terminal behavior. Most browsers give the user control over whether cookies are accepted, and many cookies are useful. For example, they are used by Internet retailers to greet a returning user by name and to allow additional purchases without reentering credit card and shipping information. On the

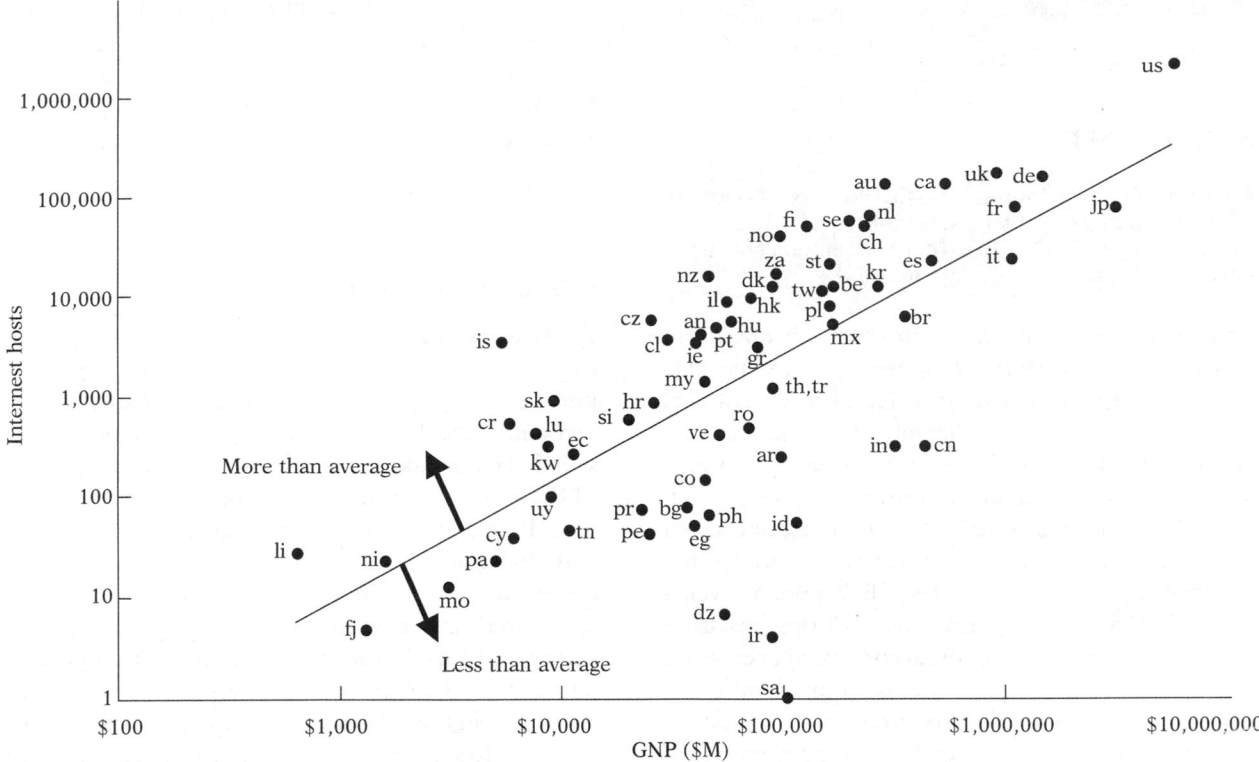

Figure 2. Internet hosts plotted against gross national product (GNP), 1994 data. Table 2 identifies the country codes. (Sources: Mark Lottor, Encyclopaedia Britannica, Eric Arnum. Copyright © 1994 A. M. Rutkowski and Internet Society.)

other hand, cookies aggravate the problem of protecting privacy, as do large online consumer databases that lead to spamming and telemarketing abuse. ISPs have not adopted standard privacy policies and a *caveat emptor* situation prevails. One measure of the severity of the problem is the development of Websites such as Anonymizer that provide a firewall between the user's identity and the target Website. Of course, these functions also introduce delay.

Vint Cerf has predicted that in 50 years there will be universal connectivity with people and devices that will use all 128 bits of the IP Version 6 address space. He predicts that users will enjoy gigabit data rates while traffic will move over 10–100 Gbps backbones and that the Internet will enjoy a bandwidth of 38 THz. We hope so.

Bibliography

1993. Lynch, D. C., and Rose, M. T. *Internet System Handbook.* Reading, MA: Addison-Wesley.
1993. Rose, M. T. *The Internet Message: Closing the Book With Electronic Mail.* Upper Saddle River, NJ: Prentice Hall.
1995. Comer, D. E. *Internetworking with TCP/IP,* 3rd Ed. Upper Saddle River, NJ: Prentice Hall.
1996. Hafner, K., and Lyon, M. *Where Wizards Stay Up Late: The Origins of the Internet.* New York: Simon & Schuster.
1997. Reid, R. H. *Architects of the Web.* New York: John Wiley.

1997. Denning, P. J., and Metcalfe, R. M. *Beyond Calculation.* New York: Copernicus (Springer-Verlag).
1998. Cerf, V. *Quarterly Directory of Internet Service Providers, Boardwatch* (Winter). Littleton, CO.
1998. Tapscott, D. *Growing Up Digital: The Rise of the Net Generation.* New York: McGraw-Hill.
1998. Segaller, S. *Nerds 2.0.1: A Brief History of the Internet.* New York: TV Books.
1999. Lawrence, S., and Giles, C. L. "Accessibility of Information on the Web," *Nature,* **400,** 107.
1999. Clark, D. "The Internet of Tomorrow," *Science,* **285,** *5426* (16 July), 353.
1999. Clark, D. *An Insider's Guide to the Internet.* http://www.lcs.mit.edu/impact/perspect/9902b.

Websites

Internet Society. http://www.isoc.org.
Hobbes' Timeline of the Internet. http://www.isoc.org/guest/zakon/Internet/History/HIT.html.
Internet Architecture Board (IAB). http://www.iab.org.
Internet Assigned Numbers Authority (IANA). http://www.iana.org.
Internet Engineering Task Force (IETF). http://www.ietf.org.
Internet Requests for Comments (RFCs). http://www.ietf.org/rfc.html.
Internet Research Task Force (IRTF). http://www.irtf.org.
Internet2. http://www.internet2.org.
The Internet Corporation for Assigned Names and Numbers. http://www.icann.org.

David H. Brandin and Daniel C. Lynch

INTERPRETER

See LANGUAGE PROCESSORS.

INTERRUPT

> For articles on related subjects *see* CHANNEL; INPUT–OUTPUT OPERATIONS; INTERVAL TIMER; OPERATING SYSTEMS; PRIVILEGED INSTRUCTION; REAL-TIME SYSTEMS; SUPERVISOR CALL; TIME SHARING; TIME SLICE; and TRAP.

The capability to *interrupt* a program, an important feature of most modern computer systems, permits systems to respond quickly to external or exceptional events that occur at unpredictable times. Some external events of this type are input arriving from a keyboard, modem (*q.v.*), or network; a signal that an output device like a printer is ready for data; or a signal generated by an instrument or sensor monitoring some industrial or laboratory process. Exceptional events include invalid memory references during program execution, division by zero, or an attempt to execute an illegal instruction. The response to an interrupt is the invocation of a responding subprogram (*q.v*) and, in this respect, an interrupt resembles a subprogram call, but one that is initiated by a hardware device rather than by the main program. The essential characteristic of interrupts is the great diversity of their causes and their unpredictability.

An interrupt facility is very common in most operating systems and real-time applications. It not only enables a computer to communicate with a rich variety of external devices, but is also helpful to the system in managing its own device and program resources. Although basically implemented by hardware, the logical power of interrupts is also provided in a convenient form by programming languages that permit an event-driven style of programming, such as Java (*q.v.*) and other object-oriented languages.

An external event causes an interrupt by an "interrupt request"—a signal on a physical line connected to the CPU (*q.v.*) or to a special interrupt-chip that is connected to the CPU. To respond to an interrupt request, the CPU signals "interrupt granted," the current program must be stopped gracefully (i.e. *interrupted*) and the CPU then switched to a subprogram, called the *interrupt service routine* (ISR), designed to service the interrupt request. Interrupts are thus a mechanism that enables several logically unrelated subprograms to time-share a single CPU and, thereby, other computer resources.

General Functional Features

There are many computer architectures, each with its own interrupt scheme. Despite this great diversity in detail and also in terminology, there are certain commonalities:

1. Storage of interrupt requests
2. Program-controlled enabling and masking
3. Saving the program state
4. Cause identification
5. Transfer to a new program
6. State restoration

Item 1 refers to the need to store requests until serviced, typically done by letting an interrupt request signal remain asserted until acknowledged, since the CPU can generally respond to only one request at a time. Item 2's purpose is to provide a means for the program to "disable" the interrupt response mechanism at certain awkward times, such as when a previously recognized interrupt is already being serviced, or before interrupt-handling routines have been properly set up. Item 3 refers to the graceful suspension of the current program, "graceful" meaning that the program is stopped in such a way that it can be easily resumed later. This involves storing certain CPU registers that must be used by every program, including the one performing the interrupt response. The program counter (PC—*q.v.*) is the most vital such register, since it holds the address of the next instruction to be executed. Item 4 refers to the need to be able to identify the cause of the interrupt. Item 5 is the essence of an interrupt—the transfer of control to the program that handles the specific details of the interrupt. Item 6 is required for resumption of the interrupted program.

Microprocessor Example

The PowerPC, a powerful microprocessor made by IBM and Motorola, has a relatively simple interrupt structure. All external devices share a single interrupt request line. The processor has a 64-bit *machine state register* (MSR) with an *external interrupt enable* (EE) bit which is set to 1 to allow interrupts. When an interrupt request is then issued, at the end of executing the current instruction the following steps occur.

1. The current PC value (the address of the next program instruction) is saved in a *save/restore register*, SSR0.
2. The MSR, which contains other program status information, is saved in part of a second register, SSR1. The low order bits of the MSR are unused, and so the CPU places information about the interrupting device in the part of SSR1 not occupied by the MSR bits.

3. The EE bit in the MSR is set to 0 to prevent another interrupt from occurring.

4. The CPU gets the address of the ISR from address 500 of main memory (which has been set up during program initialization).

5. Control is transferred to the ISR. It must have a table of all devices capable of interruption, together with the routine to execute for each (which the ISR may call as a normal subprogram). The ISR uses the high order bits of the SSR1 to identify the routine to execute.

6. The ISR ends with a return-from-interrupt (RFI) instruction. Its execution reloads the PC and the MSR from the saved values in SSR0 and SSR1, thereby resuming normal program execution at the point of interruption.

The PowerPC is like many modern RISC (*q.v.*) processors in having extra registers for saving state information, since it is much faster to use them than to save the information in memory. There is a possible complication, however. Suppose the ISR re-enables interrupts in order to allow another device to interrupt the servicing of the current interrupt (thus emulating the priority scheme described below). If a second interrupt then occurs, the current SSR0 and SSR1 must be copied to the run-time stack or other memory area so that the registers can be reused.

The table of devices and routines to handle their interrupts is called a table of *device vectors*. Some processors, such as the Intel Pentium, have a fixed set of memory addresses for device vectors. When a device interrupts, it sends the bits that specify its vector, and control can be transferred directly to the routine specified in that vector.

Other variations are to have multiple priority levels of interrupts (perhaps eight). When an ISR is active, only devices with higher priorities than the one being serviced can interrupt. The resulting nested interrupts use a stack (*q.v.*) for last in, first out completion order.

Some small processors with few general registers automatically save them all on the stack when an interrupt occurs. This allows an ISR to use registers without explicitly saving their old contents, but it increases the time to respond to an interrupt, which is generally undesirable.

Internally caused exceptions are handled like interrupts from external causes, except that since the identity of the exception is known when it occurs, each kind has its own vector that holds the address of its service routine.

A Large Machine Example

A large computer tends to have a more elaborate interrupt scheme than, say, a microprocessor, in keeping with the greater number, variety, and complexity of its peripheral (I/O) devices and its need for high speed.

Fig. 1 shows a highly simplified version of the scheme used in the IBM 360/370/390 (*q.v.*) systems. The large number of interrupt request lines are subdivided into several mask groups, the members of each group sharing one mask bit. The mask bits are intended to give the program control over which requests can be allowed to cause an interrupt at any given time. A special case occurs when all mask bits are 0, which inhibits all interrupts. This might be done by the operating system during certain interrupt response activities.

The interrupt mask bits, the PC (called the instruction address), and several other items relating to program sequencing and interrupt are "packaged" into a single 64-bit quantity called the PSW (program status word) that can be stored and reset in one operation (see below).

The circled numbers in Fig. 1 indicate the relative time of events in the interrupt process. The request lines are combined with their mask bits at time 1. If any unmasked pending requests are found, this generates a master interrupt request at time 2. Also, the priority logic acts during this interval to select the highest priority request, which is then identified by the encoder logic, and this identity is then stored in the PSW at time 3. The CPU will respond to the master request at the end of the current instruction (but in System 370 interrupts are permitted before the end of certain long-duration instructions). The interrupt itself consists of storing the PSW into a fixed area of memory called the "Old-PSW" (at memory location 1 in this example). Then the PSW is reset from the "New-PSW" (at memory location 0). Since the New-PSW respecifies the mask bits as well as the instruction address PA, any mask can be set by prestoring its bits into location 0. The cause of the interrupt is available to the response program in the Old-PSW at location 1.

The grouping structure is subject to hardware/software/speed trade-offs. We will call each source of New-PSW an interrupt level. Thus, for example, the case of Fig. 1 represents a one-level system. Since each level which points to the start of an interrupt service program constitutes a partial decoding of the interrupt cause, fast response requires a large number of levels. On the other hand, as long as the cause is recorded, only one level is logically essential, since the interrupt-handling program can use the cause-field of the Old-PSW to determine which response routine to invoke.

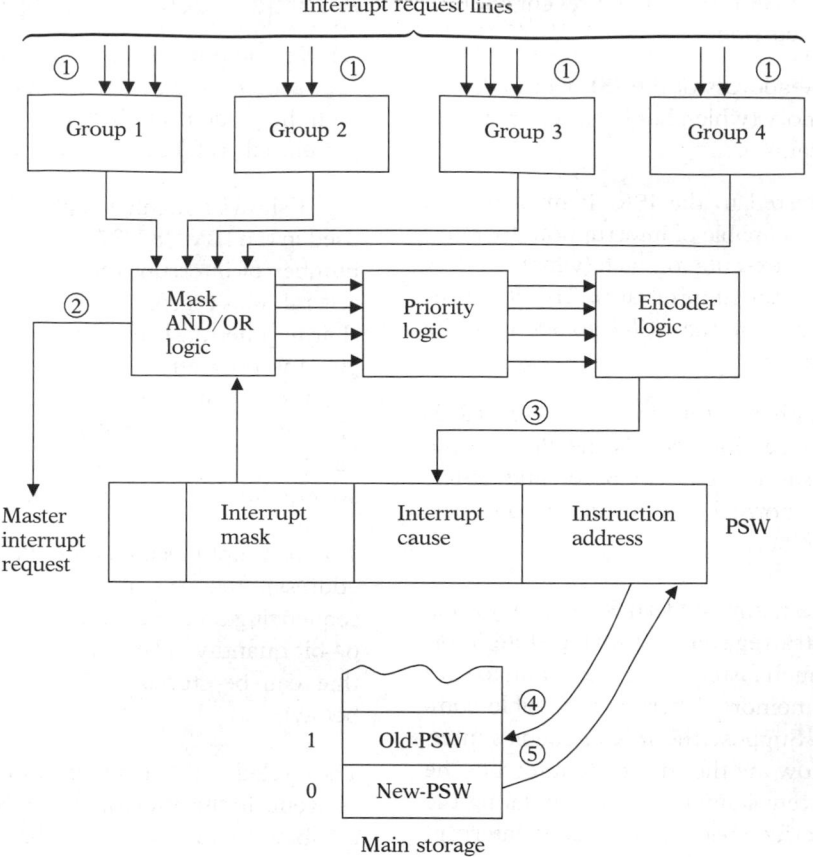

Interrupt request lines

Figure 1. A simple interrupt system. The circled numbers indicate relative event times.

Interrupt Request Classes

Interrupt requests may be roughly categorized as follows:

1. Processor operations

2. Privileged operations

3. Software call instruction

4. Machine malfunction

5. Timer

6. Input–output

Class 1 includes arithmetic overflow, divide checks, illegal operation codes, and address-out-of-bounds. Class 2 refers to those conditions that may arise because many computers reserve certain instructions for a privileged mode of the machine, so that key resource-scheduling and storage-protection instructions can be executed only by the operating system. A class 2 interrupt occurs if execution of any of these privileged instructions is attempted while the machine is not in the privileged mode. Class 3 refers to the ability to initiate an interrupt explicitly by software

executing a special instruction designed to call operating system routines directly. Class 4 is rather obvious in principle and will not be discussed further. Class 5 refers to an interval timer that can be set to a positive value by a machine instruction. Circuitry is provided to decrement this value automatically at regular time intervals and generate an interrupt request when the value reaches zero. Class 6 includes a wide variety of input and output devices: keyboard, printer, disk drive, and communication line, and also specialized devices in control applications (*q.v.*)—sensors monitoring a real-time process and actuators that need to signal when they are ready for another step.

The term *synchronous interrupt* is sometimes used for one whose cause is associated with the currently executing instruction, while other interrupts are called *asynchronous*. Thus, classes 1, 2, and 3 are synchronous and the remaining ones asynchronous (*see* SYNCHRONOUS/ASYNCHRONOUS OPERATION). Another term for synchronous interrupt is *trap* (*q.v.*).

The complete problem of interrupt-handling is always solved by a combination of hardware and software. In general, the more done in hardware, such as having a fixed set of device vectors, the greater can be the speed of response, but the higher the cost and the less the flexibility to accommodate changes in interrupt logic. Because of these economy–speed relationships, systems differ greatly in the choice of which interrupt functions to implement in hardware.

One theme in many computer systems is that interrupts and subroutine invocation have much in common, since in both cases one program or subprogram is "put to sleep" while another is "awakened," and provision must be made to return to the first program later. This idea, especially evident in microprocessors and other recent computers, leads to both mechanisms sharing common hardware and software logic. However, unique aspects of interrupts, due to their time-unpredictability, necessitate hardware support for request handling (masking, priority, cause identification).

Much of the complexity of interrupt handling is in the software servicing the interrupt. The software is usually a part of the operating system program that manages the assignment of all hardware/software resources to workload demands. In fact, most operating systems are *interrupt-driven*, i.e. the interrupt system is the mechanism for reporting all changes in resource states; and such changes are the events that induce new assignments. Incidentally, this fact makes interrupt handling an excellent place for monitoring resource-use for performance analysis and billing. Many performance monitors called *tracers* do their jobs by intercepting each interrupt and recording the cause and time of occurrence as a trace record. A stream of such records is a comprehensive log of system activity.

Writing an interrupt service routine requires great care. Since it will execute at unpredictable times, it must not change the values of any program variables, such as register contents, except those that are specifically intended for use by the ISR. It must be short, since other interrupts (e.g. those of lower priority) may be disabled while it executes. It must pay close attention to the characteristics of the device that it services, and take care to disable further interrupts from that device if they are not wanted. A printer, for example, may interrupt when it is ready for more data, and hence must have its interrupts disabled when the program has nothing to print, lest nonsense be printed.

The combination of a processor and external devices is a system with concurrent activities. Since ISRs may be regarded as device-initiated programs, perhaps the best way to understand interrupt handling is as an instance of concurrent programming (*q.v.*).

Bibliography

1983. IBM Corp. *IBM System/370 Extended Architecture Principles of Operation* SA22-7085. Chapter 6, "Interruption".

1995. Shanley, T. *PowerPC System Architecture*, 2nd Ed. Reading, MA: Addison-Wesley.

1996. Hamacher, V. C., Vranesic, Z. G., and Zaky, S. G. *Computer Organization*, 4th Ed. New York: McGraw-Hill.

1999. Brey, B. *The Intel Microprocessors: 8086/8088, 80186/80188, 80286, 80386, 80486, Pentium, Pentium Pro, Pentium II Processors*, 5th Ed. Upper Saddle River, NJ: Prentice Hall.

Herbert Hellerman, revised by David Hemmendinger

INTERVAL ARITHMETIC

For articles on related subjects *see* ARITHMETIC, COMPUTER; ERROR ANALYSIS; ERRORS; NUMERICAL ANALYSIS; and ROUNDOFF ERROR.

The essence of *interval arithmetic* is that:

1. Closed, real intervals are used in place of computational data which is uncertain.

2. Each such interval is represented by a pair of floating-point numbers known to be lower and upper bounds for the "true" (unknown) value of its corresponding datum.

3. In place of each arithmetic operation in a numerical algorithm, a corresponding interval arithmetic operation computes the interval containing all possible results of performing the original operation on any values taken from the interval operands.

Numerical computations have little value without some assessment of accuracy. Computational errors can arise from any or all of: (1) measurement or representational error in the input data, (2) rounding errors in floating-point arithmetic operations, and (3) approximation of an infinite computational sequence by a finite one. For many common numerical procedures, *a priori* error analysis can be employed either to bound the error in the computed results (forward analysis) or to show that the computed results are the exact solution for a bounded perturbation of the input data (backward analysis). In other cases, *a posteriori* computations can estimate the accuracy of a previously computed approximate solution. Each such error analysis is customized for a particular numerical algorithm. In computations for which analyses do not exist or in which the resulting error bounds are not acceptably small, other techniques must be used to estimate accuracy. Interval arithmetic is one such technique, a type of forward error analysis carried along with the computation as it is performed.

Suppose, given variables x and y, we wish to compute $z = x + y$. If exact values of x and y are not available, but we know instead that $a \leq x \leq b$ and $c \leq y \leq d$, then the rules of arithmetic inequalities tell us that

$a + c \leq x + y \leq b + d$. If we now designate by X, Y, and Z the intervals in which x, y, and z are known to be contained, we would write $X = [a, b]$, $Y = [c, d]$, and $Z = X + Y = [a + c, b + d]$. This definition of interval addition is consistent with the computational goal previously stated and provides the narrowest possible interval that can guarantee *rigorous* upper and lower bounds for the computed result.

Error may be introduced into the endpoint computations of $a + c$ and $b + d$, since these will not necessarily be representable floating-point values, even if $a, b, c,$ and d are. To insure that error bounds remain valid at each computational step, it is necessary to modify the rounding rules when computing interval endpoints so that the computed value of $a + c$ will be rounded to a numerically lower value (towards minus infinity) and the computed value of $b + d$ will be rounded to a numerically higher value (towards plus infinity), but only when they must be rounded at all. These "directed rounding" floating-point operations are now widely available in hardware, but remain difficult to access from high-level languages.

Interval analysis, the generalization of interval arithmetic, is concerned with problems of the following type: if bounds on the input data are known, how can we compute results in which rigorous bounds are of realistic width? This question is easily answered in the case of the elementary arithmetic operations. The rules of interval arithmetic are:

$$[a, b] + [c, d] = [a + c, b + d];$$
$$[a, b] - [c, d] = [a - d, b - c];$$
$$[a, b] \cdot [c, d] = [\min(ac, ad, bc, bd),$$
$$\max(ac, ad, bc, bd)];$$
$$[a, b] \div [c, d] = [\min(a/c, a/d, b/c, b/d),$$
$$\max(a/c, a/d, b/c, b/d)],$$
$$(\text{provided } 0 \notin [c, d]).$$

For example, we have the following correspondences:

$$-1 \leq x \leq 2 \qquad X = [-1, 2],$$
$$1 \leq y \leq 3 \qquad Y = [1, 3],$$
$$0 \leq (x + y) \leq 5 \qquad X + Y = [0, 5],$$
$$-4 \leq (x - y) \leq 1 \qquad X - Y = [-4, 1],$$
$$-3 \leq (x \cdot y) \leq 6 \qquad X \cdot Y = [-3, 6],$$
$$-1 \leq (x \div y) \leq 2 \qquad X \div Y = [-1, 2].$$

Each inequality is sharp, so each corresponding interval endpoint can be attained, provided that x and y are independent. If they are not, the inequalities will certainly still be valid, but may not be sharp. If for example,

$$-1 \leq x \leq 2 \quad \text{and} \quad y = 1 + |x|$$

then while $1 \leq y \leq 3$ as above, in place of the previous correspondences, we have instead:

$$1 \leq (x + y) \leq 5 \qquad [1, 5] \subset [0, 5],$$
$$-3 \leq (x - y) \leq -1 \qquad [-3, -1] \subset [-4, 1],$$
$$-2 \leq (x \cdot y) \leq 6 \qquad [-2, 6] \subset [-3, 6],$$
$$-1/2 \leq (x \div y) \leq 2/3 \qquad [-1/2, 2/3] \subset [-1, 2].$$

Since the interval arithmetic operations as defined above are ignorant of past or future computational context, mathematical relationships that hold for exact operands (intervals of zero width) are not necessarily honored by interval arithmetic. For example, the evaluation of the expressions $X \cdot (Y + Z)$ and $(X \cdot Y) + (X \cdot Z)$ in interval arithmetic will not always produce the same result, since the equivalence of the two occurrences of X is not taken into account. The interval computed via the first expression will always be contained within that produced by the second, and the first expression is thus the preferred computation since it will not lead to a result that is unnecessarily wide. (Consider X and Y as above and $Z = [-2, -2]$ to see what can happen.) In practice, interval analysis is concerned with finding computational sequences that minimize excess interval width induced by a failure (typically, an inability) to account for such relationships.

Interval arithmetic is directly applicable in cases in which an *a priori* forward error analysis gives realistic bounds. However, it is not a panacea for rounding error problems, because of spurious widths introduced by neglecting mathematical dependencies such as exemplified above. Problems that are inherently sensitive to small variations in initial data will inevitably lead to wide interval results. In the case of problems of mathematical origin (exact inputs), an algorithmic restructuring can sometimes provide acceptable results. In cases that model physical systems (inexact inputs) exhibiting chaotic behavior (extreme sensitivity of the results to small input variations), there are often relationships among the results that significantly constrain the nature of the solution. Interval analysis is of little help in such cases; at best, it can find bounds on each component, but even then only in conjunction with a careful algorithmic formulation.

Any computation that is inherently ill-conditioned in floating-point arithmetic or any algorithm that induces instability will behave similarly in interval arithmetic. In these cases, the large widths of the computed interval results will reveal only that something has gone wrong someplace. Because this often happens when interval arithmetic is applied naively, it has long been supposed that it is hopeless to do nontrivial calculations in intervals. Nevertheless, good interval methods have been found for the evaluation of rational functions, roots of polynomials, solutions of linear and nonlinear algebraic equations, the algebraic eigenvalue problem, and the solution of ordinary differential equations. Professor U. Kulisch and his colleagues at Karlsruhe University and elsewhere have systematized much of this work by extending the fundamental interval arithmetic operations to include an inner product ($\Sigma_i x_i y_i$) without intermediate roundings and by using a series of algorithms based on contraction mappings. Many of these interval applications are based on algorithms related to *a posteriori* error analyses, in which the initial approximation is computed using a conventional algorithm and interval methods subsequently ensure that the subsequently calculated error bounds are themselves not misleadingly optimistic.

Three significant barriers to the use of interval arithmetic have been: (1) the difficulty of obtaining directed roundings for interval endpoint computations, (2) the increased overhead in both computation and storage that interval arithmetic implies, and (3) the lack of high-level language support for interval data. The first of these has disappeared with the widespread introduction of implementations of the IEEE/ANSI binary floating-point standard (*see* ARITHMETIC, COMPUTER), which requires provision of directed rounding modes in addition to the "round-to-nearest" default mode. Problems of computational and storage drag are becoming significantly less severe with the advent of very high performance and large memory scientific workstations (*q.v.*) and personal computers. The high-level language problem remains, but user-extensible object-oriented languages (*see* OBJECT-ORIENTED PROGRAMMING) such as C++ (*q.v.*) may in time provide solutions to overcome this remaining barrier. Recent interval arithmetic extensions to spreadsheets (*q.v.*) and symbolic algebraic manipulation programs offer considerable promise, as these tools complement each other quite naturally.

As a diagnostic tool, interval arithmetic can save much human effort that might otherwise be spent doing (or accepting the consequences of not doing) error analysis. It is also useful in laboratory and engineering environments in which physical measurements subject to error are used to compute other quantities. If variation of the output as a function of the input is critical, interval arithmetic is a natural tool. Interval results are easily understood; when a computation produces narrow intervals, the drudgery of an error analysis is not required to know with certainty what accuracy has been obtained.

Bibliography

1966. Moore, R. E. *Interval Analysis*. Upper Saddle River, NJ: Prentice Hall. This is the standard reference by the individual who has been most closely associated with the field for more than 35 years.

1991. Neumaier, A. *Interval Methods for Systems of Equations* (volume 37 in the Encyclopedia of Mathematics and Its Applications). Cambridge: Cambridge University Press. A good introduction to practical considerations with extensive references.

1997. Kreinovich, V., Lakeyev, A., Rohn, J., and Kahl, P. *Computational Complexity and Feasibility of Data Processing and Interval Computations* (volume 10 in the series Applied Optimization). Dordrecht: Kluwer Academic Publishers. An examination of when determining tight error bounds from interval input data is NP-hard.

Website

http://cs.utep.edu/interval-comp/. A broad collection of technical, bibliographic, and human resources, with links to many of the people in the field.

Frederic N. Ris

INTERVAL TIMER

For articles on related subjects *see* ACCOUNTING SYSTEM, COMPUTER; INTERRUPT; MULTIPROGRAMMING; and OPERATING SYSTEMS.

An *interval timer* (sometimes called a *real-time clock*) is a mechanism whereby elapsed time can be monitored by a computer system. In most systems, a word in memory is set aside to be used as the interval timer. This word, usually at the low end of memory, cannot be used for anything else, since the computer is wired to increment it automatically by one interval every millisecond, microsecond, or other fixed period.

For timing purposes it is useful to have a timer capable of monitoring the execution of a few thousands, or tens of thousands, of instructions. In a computer with instructions requiring only a few nanoseconds, a microsecond timer will be incremented once for every several hundred of those instructions, which is about as low a rate as can be tolerated. If the system stores the time of day (say, at startup time) in another word, then any program needing to report the current time of day need only read the start time and add to it the number of microseconds in the timer to obtain the current time of day.

The timer is useful for reporting the date and time of execution of various parts of a job or for checking the timing for segments of a routine. In multiprogrammed systems, care must be taken to maintain interval timings with each job. The time of day will be global to all jobs, of course, but for timing purposes, the interest is usually in time elapsed only while the CPU is assigned to a particular job (as opposed to running other jobs or performing input–output operations for the job in question or other jobs). An interval timer is essential for timing components of multiprogrammed systems, since time may be allocated to jobs in increments of only a few milliseconds or even hundreds or tens of microseconds.

Chester L. Meek

INVARIANT

See LOOP INVARIANT.

IOCS

See INPUT–OUTPUT CONTROL SYSTEM.

ISDN

See INTEGRATED SERVICES DIGITAL NETWORK.

ITERATION

For articles on related subjects *see* CONTROL STRUCTURE; NUMERICAL ANALYSIS; PROCEDURE-ORIENTED LANGUAGES; RECURSION; and STRUCTURED PROGRAMMING.

To iterate means to do repeatedly. In computer programming, *iteration* is the repeated execution of lines of code or statements until some condition is satisfied. For example, 10 numbers A(1), A(2), A(3), ..., A(10) can be summed using the following Basic program:

```
10 L = 10
20 I = 1
30 S = 0
40 S = S + A(I)
50 I = I + 1
60 IF I <= L THEN 40                    (1)
```

The statements 40–60 are executed repeatedly until I becomes 11.

In contrast, the sum could be computed by

```
S = A(1) + A(2) + A(3) + A(4) + A(5) +
    A(6) + A(7) + A(8) + A(9) + A(10)   (2)
```

which does not involve iteration. This last statement is more efficient in the example given, since the sum is obtained with fewer program steps. However, if more elements are to be summed, then statement (2) must be changed by adding more terms. In the first program, however, to sum more elements, only the value of L (which could be an input quantity) need be changed. Therefore, when the number of elements to be summed increases, a point is eventually reached where the effort to write the program in form (2) becomes greater than for form (1). This illustrates the use of iteration to reduce the effort of the programmer

at the price of using more computer time. At some point, of course, (2) will require more time to compile than (1).

All worthwhile computer programs are iterative in some way. For example, in the time that one can write program (2) above, one could perform the actual summations by hand. Thus, solving a problem by computer is worthwhile only if: (a) the programming effort is small compared with the amount of computing (which means that some of the program is executed repetitively), or (b) the program is applied to a succession of input data values. Although this last process is less often called "iteration," the program is repeatedly executed.

Another advantage of the iterative approach is the greater ease of generalization. For example, the first program could be part of a subroutine, and the control of the iterations could be done by means of a parameter. The following example uses Fortran:

```
      SUBROUTINE ABC(L)
      ...
      I = 1
      SUM = 0
   15 SUM = SUM + A(I)
      I = I + 1
      IF (I.LE.L) GO TO 15
      ...
```

Calling the subroutine with CALL ABC(10) would compute the sum of 10 elements.

Control of Iteration

Programming languages generally have both definite iteration (**for** loops) and indefinite iteration (**while**, **do**, **repeat** loops). The former specifies a number of times to iterate; the latter iterate until some condition holds or fails to hold.

This Pascal code uses definite iteration to do the same as program (1).

```
sum := 0;
for i := 1 to 10 do
    sum := sum + a[i];
```

In the language APL, the same summation can be written as just

```
+/A
```

Here, at the source language level, no iteration appears to be involved. However, at the level of the interpretive program that evaluates the APL statement, iteration will certainly occur.

An example of indefinite iteration is a **while** loop that executes zero or more times, stopping when a negative data value is encountered, as in this example in C.

```
sum = 0;
i = 0;
while (a[i] >= 0)
    {
    sum = sum + a[i];
    i = i + 1;
    }
```

Another example is illustrated by a Newton–Raphson square root function, written in pseudocode:

```
function sqroot(x)
    if x = 0.0 then
        return 0.0
    else
        root <- x;
        while |root*root - x| >= ε
            root <- (x/root + root)/2.0
            endwhile
        return root
    endif
endfunc
```

The heart of the **while** statement computes an improved approximation to the square root. If $x = 1.0$, no iterations occur (assuming $ε$ is of appropriate size relative to the arithmetic precision of the system). Otherwise, the number of iterations depends both on the value of x and on the value of $ε$.

Iteration in Numerical Methods

Many numerical problems can be solved by iterative techniques. Here, a succession of values for one or more variables are computed. It is hoped that the successive values approach the true values. The iterative process is terminated when some error criterion is satisfied. The square root program above is an example of an iterative numerical procedure. Although the successive partial sums of example (1) do approach the final sum, this procedure is not usually considered an iterative numerical procedure. Numerical iteration is usually characterized by the use of successive approximations and termination depending upon error bounds.

Hardware Iteration

The distinction between hardware and software activity is less and less clear as more complex processors are designed. This is particularly true when using microprogramming (*q.v.*) and read-only memories (*q.v.*).

In a simple example, a number in a register (Register 2 of Fig. 1) may need to be shifted a number of binary positions determined by a number stored in a second register (Register 1). The shift circuits of Register 2 are repeatedly pulsed until the contents of Register 1 are

counted down to zero. Although the activity of the shift circuits is iterative in character, very few logic designers would use the term.

In more complex processors, the term may be more appropriate. For example, the summation of the elements of a vector (as discussed above) may be done entirely by hardware. This involves a complex sequence of events including: incrementing an address register to access successive components; performing a floating-point addition, which itself involves comparing exponents; shifting mantissas; and perhaps normalizing results. Thus, the same pattern of activities is performed iteratively until all components of the vector are accounted for.

Iteration vs. Recursion

A program is recursive if at least one of its executable statements refers to the program itself. For example, in Pascal one may write

```
function ABC(X:integer):integer;
    ...
    Z := ABC(Y);
    ...
end;
```

That is, the function calls itself. This requires a so-called *stack* (*q.v.*) mechanism to keep track of parameters and to provide locations for the returned values at each level of call (*see* ACTIVATION RECORD). Needless to say, other statements in the program must in some way limit the levels of calling. A frequently used example is the factorial (Wirth, 1976, p. 129), in pseudocode:

```
function factorial(n)
    if n < 2 then
        return 1
    else
        return (n * factorial(n-1))
    endif
endfunc;
```

Although portions of the code are executed repetitively, the control is by reference to the named procedure. Therefore this example is said to be recursive, not iterative.

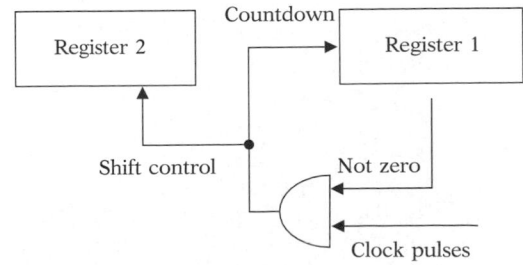

Figure 1. Simple example of hardware iteration.

The factorial of N can be computed iteratively:

```
function factorial(n)
    f ← 1;
    for i ← n downto 2
       f ← f*i;
       endfor
    return f
endfunc
```

In the iterative example, the function does not call itself and, therefore, does not have to save the parameter n each time it is called, as the recursive function must do. Another recursive version of the factorial function is equivalent to this iterative one, when it is called as `factorial(n,1)`:

```
function factorial(n,f)
    if n < 2 then
        return f
    else
        return factorial(n-1, f*n)
    endif
endfunc
```

Unlike the first recursive example, in which the function calls itself and then multiplies the result by n, this function does no computation after the recursive call. Such a function is called *tail-recursive* (*see* RECURSION), and can be implemented just as efficiently as iteration.

In general, a straightforward iterative algorithm may both be faster and use less memory than a corresponding recursive algorithm. These savings are often slight, however, and there are many algorithms for which recursion is more natural than iteration (*see*, for example, Quicksort in the article STRUCTURED PROGRAMMING, and tree-traversal algorithms in TREE). In such cases it is better to use recursion than to write a more complex iterative program.

Bibliography

1997. Chan, R. H., Chan, T. F., and Golub, G. H. (eds.) *Iterative Methods in Scientific Computing*. New York: Springer-Verlag.
1999. Sebesta, R. W. *Concepts of Programming Language*. Reading, MA: Addison-Wesley.

Harry D. Huskey

JAVA

For articles on related subjects *see* C; C++; CLASS; CONCURRENT PROGRAMMING; EXCEPTION HANDLING; OBJECT-ORIENTED PROGRAMMING; and WORLD WIDE WEB.

Java is a high level programming language developed by James Gosling and others at Sun Microsystems, mainly since 1995, when it became popular for Internet (*q.v.*) programming. All data and functions *must* be in classes, which define *types* of objects, so Java is truly object-oriented [i.e. all data and operations on them are encapsulated within objects (*see* ENCAPSULATION)]. Java resembles C and C++, but it omits many unwieldy features. It has no pointers. Memory management (*q.v.*) is automatic; this, combined with static (i.e. compile time) and run-time type and array bounds checking, makes Java programs more reliable than most programmers can achieve in languages like C or C++. Other major features are that it supports concurrency directly, and it has an exception mechanism (to catch run-time errors, like array subscripts going out of bounds).

Java has gained popularity because of its appropriateness for programming on the Internet, particularly using so-called *applets*, small Java program components that run within a Web browser to provide animation and other features. The ready availability of shareware applets to enliven Web pages has fueled wide interest in Java.

Java programs are usually compiled to an interpreted byte code which is run on the *Java Virtual Machine* (*see* INTERMEDIATE LANGUAGES). The virtual machine can in principle be run on any adequate computer anywhere, making Java portable and able to run on many platforms. Java is also portable at "human" levels: Java uses Unicode character coding (*see* CHARACTER CODES), so almost all of the world's alphabets are supported; it also has various mechanisms for geographic localization, allowing dates and other features to be presented appropriately to the user.

Java has a security model: the virtual machine includes a verifier that performs various checks on Java code as it is loaded, insuring that Java is unlikely to break the systems it runs on. The verifier, together with other language features (such as controlled access to data), significantly improves the security of programs, and hence makes Java ideal for running programs obtained over networks which perhaps cannot be intrinsically trusted. Once checked, Java components can be loaded into *running* applications. This technique makes Java a convenient language for extensible systems of all sorts. Standards (e.g. *Java Beans*) are being developed for standardizing interfaces.

See Arnold and Gosling (1997) for a language overview. Though Java has helped to popularize concurrent programming (*q.v.*), this article does not discuss this subject; *see also* the book by Lea (2000).

Basic Types

There are three main types of data in Java: objects, arrays, and basic values. Although arrays are themselves objects, basic values—like characters and integers—are not objects and are handled conventionally for efficiency reasons. Basic values can, however, be converted (*wrapped*) into objects when required. Objects are declared in classes, combining data fields, polymorphic functions (*methods*), and in various ways inheriting from (*extending*) other class definitions. (*Polymorphism* means that the same method can have various implementations that differ in the number and types of their parameters—*see* OPERATOR OVERLOADING.) Classes cannot be parameterized: it is not possible to define completely generic classes, since these may encourage programmers to write classes that are too general (e.g. by having Object, rather than more specific, parameters), so losing the advantages of static typing for compile time type checking.

The array is a special class. Arrays can be constructed out of basic values or objects (including arrays), and, like objects, they respond to some standard methods, but the programmer cannot introduce more. The notation used for array declarations and array subscription (square brackets) is different from the notation used for classes and methods.

Java has rules for converting between data types. For example, an integer can be assigned to a floating-point number, and an object that is a subclass of some type can be assigned to a variable of that type. This insures concise programs. However, some conversions are obscure, and combined with polymorphism, inheritance and run-time typing of objects can result in unanticipated behaviour.

Java's limitations, many of which derive from C and C++, can be seen as advantages, however. It is a comfortable language for C/C++ programmers, who find it safer and more flexible—which it certainly is.

Object-Oriented Programming in Java

To illustrate some of the object-oriented features of Java, consider a program that implements an active symbol table. (The example also shows how to implement functionality that in C would normally require pointers and would not be type safe.) The purpose of an active symbol table is to maintain a table of strings and to invoke actions (here, simple print statements) when they are looked up.

We want objects to behave like the actions associated with the strings. We first define a class for symbol table entries, so all entries are the same type.

```
abstract class Symbol
{ abstract public void action();
  // abstract - we don't define its
  //             implementation here
  // public - anyone can access this name
  // void - this action returns no value
  abstract public String name();
}
```

This is an **abstract class** because no implementation has been given for its methods; any (non-abstract) subclass that implements this class must implement action() and name(), and it can do so in any way it likes.

Java does not require the definition of Symbol to extend the base class Object (of which all other classes are subclasses) explicitly—so it is perhaps not obvious that Symbol inherits Object's methods. In particular, all objects inherit toString(), which returns a string that says what the object is (which is a useful feature, especially for debugging). It would be unwise to use this seemingly similar method instead of name(); since toString() is inherited, there would be no warning if a subclass of Symbol failed to define it in a way appropriate to that subclass.

Here is a definition of a subclass for a dir command, which extends the Symbol class providing implementations for all its abstract methods:

```
class Directory extends Symbol{
  public String name() { return "dir"; }
    // implement name() to return
    // a String, as specified by Symbol

  public void action() {
  System.out.println(
    "--list a directory--"); }
    // implement action() to do something
}
```

An object of class Directory responds to name() by returning the string "dir" and responds to action() by saying it is listing a directory. Here, System.out is a field name, defined in the standard object System, and println is a method invocation.

Another subclass of the same Symbol class could have definitions do something else with their methods, but without having internal state (i.e. variables), each object of the same class would have to do the same things. Here's an example of how objects with state can be created, also illustrating *private methods* and *private fields* that are not accessible from other classes. In this example note that name is overloaded as both a variable and a function:

```
class GenericSymbol extends Symbol
  { private String name, result;
    // the class has some 'private'
    // information, two String fields

  GenericSymbol(String n, String r)
    { name = n; result = r; }
    // this constructs new GenericSymbol
    // objects, with names and results
```

```
public String name() { return name; }
public void action()
  { perform ("GenericSymbol " +
               name + " -> " + result); }

private void perform(String sayThis)
  { System.out.println(sayThis); }
  // an example private method, here
  // just helping write the class
}
```

Each `GenericSymbol` can be given a different name and action when it is created (*constructed*) at run time (see below). A `GenericSymbol` is a `Symbol`, and can be used wherever a `Symbol` is required.

The standard Java hash table (an efficient data structure for tables—*see* SEARCHING) is ideal for storing individual symbols to make a symbol table. Below, when an `ActiveSymbolTable` object is created, its initialization includes initializing a variable `h`, assigning to it a `Hashtable` object (which has its own internal initialization). Having gotten the hash table, an `ActiveSymbolTable` object has methods to `add` symbols and to `lookup` strings, both inherited from `hashtable`.

```
class ActiveSymbolTable
  { private Hashtable h = new Hashtable();
    // each ActiveSymbolTable object will
    // initialize its own hashtable

  public void add(Symbol f)
  { h.put(f.name(), f);
  // put the name in the hashtable
  }
  public void lookup(String s)
  { Symbol f = (Symbol) h.get(s);
    if( f == null )
      System.out.println(s+" not found");
    else f.action();
  }
}
```

Finally, create an `ActiveSymbolTable` and test it:

```
class TestRun{ public static void
                    main(String argv[])
  { ActiveSymbolTable table = new
                    ActiveSymbolTable();
    table.add(new Directory());
    table.add(new GenericSymbol
      ("rubbish", "mind your manners!"));
    table.add(new Format());
      // add others as needed
    table.lookup("dir");
    table.lookup("not defined");
    table.lookup("rubbish");
  }
}
```

The static method `main` makes this class an application that can be run directly: Java loads the class `TestRun`, starts running the `main` method, then loads

and initializes the `ActiveSymbolTable` class, and so on. It would have been good practice to place such test code as a method in the `ActiveSymbolTable` class itself, so the class and its test code could be maintained together—`ActiveSymbolTable` would have been runnable, and running it would test it.

Exceptions

In many programming languages, an error such as an array subscript out of bounds is either ignored (postponing problems) or causes abortion of the program. In contrast, Java provides explicit exception handling. Some errors, such as array subscript errors, automatically give rise to *throw* exceptions; others can be explicitly *thrown* by the programmer. Both can be *caught* by an *exception handler* routine written by the programmer to take appropriate action when an error occurs.

Java's handling of exceptions is not uniform. For example, while division of integers by zero causes an exception, division of floating-point numbers by zero does not. Exceptions are part of the type signature of methods, so Java requires methods to handle the exceptions that they may encounter, or to be declared as throwing the exceptions themselves—though certain classes of exception require no explicit handling (e.g. exceptions that can occur anywhere, such as memory overflow, and which are in any case generally very difficult to handle).

As defined above, the class `ActiveSymbolTable` prints "notfound" if it looks up an unknown symbol. An alternative would be to throw an exception:

```
class ActiveSymbolTable{ ...
  public void lookup(String s) throws
                              NotFound
  { Symbol f = (Symbol) h.get(s);
    if( f == null ) throw new NotFound(s);
    // symbol not found
    else f.action();
  }
}
```

A user of `lookup` would normally catch the exception in a **try** statement (the keyword **try** specifies that exceptions are to be passed to the handlers declared with **catch**):

```
class TestRun{ public static void
  main(String argv[])
  { ActiveSymbolTable table = new
                    ActiveSymbolTable();
    table.add(new Directory());
    table.add(new GenericSymbol
      ("rubbish", "mind your manners!"));
    table.add(new Format());
      // add others as needed
```

```
try
{ table.lookup("dir");
  table.lookup("not defined");
    // cause an exception
  table.lookup("rubbish");
    // so this won't be executed
}
catch(NotFound e)
{ // catch the anticipated exception
  System.out.println
    ("A NotFound exception occurred: "
      +e);
}
catch(Exception e)
{ // catch any other sort of
  // exception not already caught
  System.out.println
    ("Some other exception occurred: "
      +e);
}
finally
{ // optional clean up code,
  // executed however the try block
                        terminates
  System.out.println
    ("Finished checked area of code.");
}
}
}
```

In this example, the attempt to look up "not defined" causes table.lookup to throw a NotFound exception, which is caught by the first **catch** statement. The **finally** statements (if any) are *always* executed, even if the **catch** statements return or throw other exceptions. They are typically used to tidy up.

Exceptions are ordinary Java objects, and like other objects, can have methods and fields for any purpose; exceptions can define methods to help recover from errors or to aid debugging. New exceptions are defined by subclasses of standard Java exception classes, for example:

```
class NotFound extends
  Exception{ NotFound(String s)
  { super(s);
    // 'super' is the superclass, Exception
  }
}
```

This class constructs a NotFound object simply by calling the constructor of its superclass, Exception. NotFound inherits everything else from the standard class Exception, and therefore they have the same behavior. However, having different classes enables catch to distinguish between different exceptions.

Java's exceptions provide a way of separating normal program code, error detection and error handling, which makes for much clearer programs which are easier to maintain. Notice how the second catch in the example catches *any* exception (specifically, any uncaught exception that is a subclass of Exception) without a tangle of code to check individually for many sorts of error. And it does not need changing when new classes of exception are introduced into the program.

Java as a Programming Technology

The Java standard defines a small core language and a large number of packages. Java is a programming technology, not just a programming language. It would be hard to write Java programs without drawing heavily on *Application Programming Interfaces* (APIs), which provide huge libraries, including interfaces to databases, portable user interfaces (e.g. the *Abstract Windows Toolkit*, AWT), networking, and specialist applications. The behavior of important classes like String are defined in standard APIs.

While the APIs are a significant aid to productive programming—reducing programmer effort, increasing portability—they do have problems. Some of them are large and difficult to learn to use. Proprietary APIs are often not available in source form, so are difficult to debug. Most are still evolving rapidly, so programmers may see their work quickly made obsolete by new "standards." Fortunately, Java has a documentation comment (a simple form of literate programming—*q.v.*) that helps manage documentation automatically.

Java's inheritance usually allows programmers to modify or extend APIs rather than start from scratch; thus many applications require little detailed coding. This makes Java very productive, and its productivity will increase as software vendors provide more APIs. Rapid Application Development (RAD) environments can be used to manage what coding remains.

Unlike C++, Java has single inheritance: it permits a class to be a subclass of only one class. However, a class can implement any number of *interfaces*. Interfaces provide many advantages of multiple inheritance without its complexities. Software vendors can sell code that conforms to interface standards, and which need not reveal details of implementation (notwithstanding reverse compilation). Thus, applets share an interface with the application that runs them. The application should be secure, because the applet cannot see or manipulate what is not in the interface. However, by allowing many programmers to work almost independently on a single project, interfaces have a useful impact on the software development cycle. Users may buy "open" applications whose functionality they can extend, but there is a temptation to sell unfinished systems hoping problems can be fixed later.

Summary

Good object-oriented programming, even in Java, is not trivial. As of summer 1997, after just 500 days of public exposure, it was estimated that there were half a million Java programmers. There were over a million by 1999. Java is a popular language, but it is also a young, developing language. The second main release, Java 1.1, saw many improvements, such as easier ways to define classes, and many new packages. (The new documentation comment tag, @deprecated, allows packages to support but complain about superseded features.) The next version, called the Java 2 Platform, was released in December 1998. Although Sun is standardizing Java, it is also diverging into specialist forms: such as *JavaCard* (a version of Java for smart cards), and *EmbeddedJava* (for embedded systems). Making a complex language like Java successful is driving compiler technology (e.g. *just in time* systems) and hardware technology (e.g. *picoJava*). Other languages (e.g. Ada—*q.v.*) can be compiled into Java's byte code, thereby reaping Java's implementation benefits for themselves. It is too early to see whether Java itself will overcome its problems, particularly of instability, but Sun is adopting flexible strategies to make Java a major and long-lived part of practical computer science.

Bibliography

The main text reference on Java is *The Java Series*, published by Addison Wesley Longman. The main World Wide Web references to Java can be found at Sun's own page, `http://java.sun.com`, and at `http://www.gamelan.com`, a major Java directory.

1996. Gosling, J., Joy, B., and Steele, G. *The Java Language Specification*. Reading, MA: Addison-Wesley.
1996. Lindholm, T., and Yellin, F. *The Java Virtual Machine Specification*. Reading, MA: Addison-Wesley.
1997. Arnold, K., and Gosling, J. *The Java Programming Language*. Reading, MA: Addison-Wesley.
2000. Lea, D. *Concurrent Programming in Java: Design Principles and Patterns*, 2nd Ed. Reading, MA: Addison-Wesley.

Harold W. Thimbleby

JOB

For articles on related subjects *see* ACCOUNTING SYSTEM, COMPUTER; INTERACTIVE SYSTEM; MULTIPROGRAMMING; OPERATING SYSTEMS; and TRANSACTION PROCESSING.

A *job* is a task or group of tasks to be performed by a computer. A job may be classed as an interactive job if an operator, usually at a terminal (*q.v.*) or networked workstation (*q.v.*) provides some of the input and/or receives some of the output as the job is running. A job may be classed as a batch job if the inputs are all presented to the computer with the job instructions, and the output will be routed to disk, printer, or other non-interactive devices.

The number of tasks (or steps) per job is usually a preference of the programmer, but is also subject to the conventions of the operating system. For example, many temporary files supplied by the operating system are automatically closed and released at the end of a job. If a programmer wishes to use one of these temporary files to store some intermediate information between two steps, then the two steps must be contained within the same job. On the other hand, if the programmer uses a permanent file, then there may be a step that creates the file in one job and a step that reads it in another job. In a batch-processing environment, where jobs are run one at a time, the programmer need only ensure that the job that reads the file is *submitted* to be run after the job that creates it. But in a multiprogrammed environment, where several jobs are run concurrently, there is a need to ensure that the jobs are *executed* in sequence. To accomplish this automatically, many multiprogramming operating systems allow job sequencing, which allows the programmer to specify that a job cannot be selected for execution until its predecessor has been completed.

Chester L. Meek

JOURNALISM, COMPUTERS IN

For articles on related subjects *see* DESKTOP PUBLISHING; DIGITAL LIBRARIES; HUMANITIES APPLICATIONS; HYPERTEXT; and WORLD WIDE WEB.

A. J. Liebling put it succinctly when he observed that, "The function of the press in society is to inform, but its role is to make money." This explains why, while the greatest promise of "computer-assisted journalism" is in the arena of news content, its greatest effect has been in the arena of news production and distribution. Certainly, role and function are interrelated, but in describing the diffusion of these technologies, it is useful to distinguish the commercial engine driving change from what many hope will be its effect on public information.

Production

The effects of computers on news production have been nearly universal. In less than 30 years, magazine and newspaper offices have all changed from typewriters to computer keyboards, from "hot type" systems using lead characters to "cold type" production systems in which copy is generated by computer. By the mid-1990s, editors almost universally received the copy of reporters and writers electronically and then edited it on their computers. Modern pagination systems then send that material into digital layout programs from which the final pages—electronic or digital—are generated. Pagination programs allow editors to prepare "dummy pages" with space reserved for advertising, later inserting reportorial copy within the "news hole" reserved for editorial materials.

This has had an extraordinary effect on the business of news and on the appearance of the end product. Computerization of production has meant the death of old crafts: old-style printing and typography, for example. The result has been decreased labor costs and thus significant savings for publishers. Simultaneously, computerized layout has liberated page design itself, allowing publishers to explore new fonts, new looks, and more flexible page layout schemes.

Computer generation of publications has also created the potential for new national and international publications relying on computerized data sent via modem and satellite hookup around the world. *USA TODAY* and the *International Herald Tribune* are examples of newspapers whose look and broad distribution are wholly dependent on dispersed, computerized production facilities.

Finally, new modes of computerized production have opened the door for desktop publishing, computer programs that give non-professionals the ability to design their own publications. While these PC-based programs are typically less complex than dedicated newspaper or news magazine systems, they have raised the level of private newsletters, assuring a minimally professional level for even the smallest group's publication.

Distribution and Revenues

Stories that once arrived on wire service printers now appear directly on editors' screens. It is no longer necessary for editors to pull printed matter from one or another external wire service machine. The feed from these systems is now automatically combined in the wire editor's computerized in-box. The automatic distribution of wire copy has meant that data can now also be sold to end users online, allowing news providers like Associated Press, Dow Jones News Service, and Reuters to compete with their traditional journalistic customers for readers. Why pay 50 cents to buy the *Toronto Star* to check the closing stock price of Toronto Dominion Bank when that material is available instantaneously, and less expensively, online?

Increasingly sophisticated digital delivery systems, especially those using the World Wide Web, are now allowing publications to fight back with "online"

newspaper editions. These digital publications provide basic wire, financial, and regional data in hypertext-linked electronic pages. The idea is simple: Since news writing and editing are both done electronically, why not present the finished product in the same way? If, like editors and reporters, readers can receive basic reports or stock quotes online, then business sense will require journalists to offer value-added materials in that same medium.

A number of newspapers and magazines have taken this task seriously. In the mid-1990s some magazines and newspapers, the *San José Mercury News*, and the *Raleigh News and Observer*, for example, have expended enormous efforts towards this goal. They have created online editions, experimenting with both the delivery system and the data that can be produced in a dense, electronic form. Conventional stories are being replaced by multimedia presentations using hypertext documents, visuals that can be downloaded by the reader, and open formats presenting news in a variety of ways.

More recently, large news organizations like *USA TODAY* and ABC have also moved to online editions and presentation. In late 1996, Microsoft (*q.v.*) and NBC created a new integrated electronic news service, MSNBC, whose mission is to create an electronic product merging the best of online resources (chat groups and other user-friendly, interactive forums) with older style coverage of breaking news.

The potential of these experiments is still uncertain. Their futures will depend—first and foremost—on the increasing penetration of computers into the homes of all citizens, and on the economics of traditional vs. electronic production. Online distribution offers vast economies of scale, with readers of ostensibly local or regional publications effortlessly expanding to a potentially universal readership. People in New York may today read electronic newspapers from London, Sydney, Jerusalem, and Raleigh, NC.

At present, online editions are largely subsidized not by subscribers, but by advertisers purchasing display blocks on the published page. In the first years of World Wide Web distribution, advertising revenues have been the engine driving online news and commercial Web page production.

Mass publishing by electronic means is a new medium in the 1990s, and its commercial and financial development has just begun. Long-term success will depend on either increased subscription rates or a demonstrable effect of electronic advertising on the purchasing patterns of electronic readers. At this writing, however, there is insufficient market analysis to determine the power of online journalism as an advertising venue.

Interestingly, another source of computer-generated revenue has been in the sale of news and magazine libraries to large-scale data based companies like Knight Ridder International, Lexis-Nexis, and Dow Jones Information Service. Converting news "morgues" to digital libraries effects enormous savings in plant space and library personnel. It has also created a new and expanding market for old news, thus providing another new revenue stream.

Content

The most exciting and problematic of areas within the marriage of computer technology and journalism is in computer-assisted reportage, or CAR. It offers the prospect of tools that would allow journalists to break free of the traditional "he said" or "she said" attributed form of news (Koch, 1990).

Reporters without access to computers traditionally relied on officials and experts to make evaluations. With digitized reference libraries, powerful analytic databases, and email lists of expert sources, journalists can now be as informed as their sources on almost any topic (Koch, 1991). Muckraking and investigative journalism have a long tradition, but computer-assisted journalism has placed sophisticated tools for data collection and analysis in the hands of the "average" reporter. The material they write, therefore, need not simply repeat the views of officials, but can be a critical analysis of the issues being discussed.

Philip E. Meyer is usually credited with initiating the CAR movement. In 1967 he used a computer to study data drawn from African-Americans living in the Detroit neighborhoods hardest hit during the riots that year. His use of computers to analyze a range of data signaled a new era. A lay reporter using computer tools could arrive at independent but rigorous conclusions based on public data. His revolutionary style of reportage earned his newspaper, the *Detroit Free Press*, a Pulitzer Prize. Meyer later wrote a book on using social scientific tools in a process he called *Precision Journalism*. In the early 1990s the book was updated and reissued as *The New Precision Journalism* (1991).

The CAR movement has had a number of successes. In 1987, for example, the *Akron Beacon Journal* (Ohio) won a Pulitzer Prize for its reportage of the 1986 takeover of Goodyear Tire and Rubber Co. Using a series of online databases, it investigated each corporate suitor, its financial holdings, and its history as a corporate citizen. Day by day, it analyzed the statements of bidding companies, and their potential as the owner of Akron's largest employer. The story would have been impossible without extensive online libraries, which provided a "reality check" on the promises of corporate competitors whose primary mission was acquisition and control, not absolute veracity.

Online newspapers can also use hypertext to embed primary and substantiating documents within a broad, general narrative. In the first stage of computer-assisted reportage and journalism, data sources shifted from the desks of officials to those of reporters. The increasing use of hypertext moves that data into the story and onto the electronic desks of readers.

Similarly, journalistic "tools" are now being offered to the public at large. Nando Net, NICAR, and the Canadian Broadcasting Corporation (CBC), to name three, are offering to public and professionals alike general tools and data source sites via the Internet (*q.v.*). The growth of the Internet and of easy-to-use page design software have allowed professional looking but highly individual electronic newspapers and magazines to proliferate. The proliferation of journalistic tools and resources offers those individualistic news sources stronger data sources.

This "citizen news" may be formal (*The American Reporter*, for example), or an issue-directed, personalized publication by a zealot. Whether these individualized journals will have an effect on general public consciousness, or on the profits of large corporations, is at present unclear. In the mid-1990s, they were largely curiosities rather than critical participants in the world of news and public information.

In conclusion, the computerization of data and of journalistic production has affected both the production and dissemination of public information in industrialized countries like the USA. Its effect has been clearest in affecting the role of the news—to make money—but is also having an impact on journalism's public function. Changes in the content of the news will depend as much on public tastes and demands as it will on the efficiencies and cost saving protocols of electronic production and distribution.

Digitalization of data libraries, the profusion of electronic news sites, and the potential of each person to customize the available data to match his or her interest offers enormous potential. Whether it will be fulfilled or merely trivialized, however, is a question that will be answered in the coming decades.

Bibliography

1961. Liebling, A. J. *The Press.* Reprinted, 1981, New York: Pantheon Books.
1990. Koch, T. *The News as Myth: Fact and Context in Journalism.* Westport, CT: Praeger.
1991. Koch, T. *Journalism for the 21st Century: Online Information, Electronic Databases, and the News.* New York: Praeger.
1991. Meyer, P. *The New Precision Journalism.* Bloomington, IN: Indiana University Press.

Websites

The American Reporter. `http://american-reporter.com/`

Canadian Broadcasting Corporation Journalist Resources. `http://www.synapse.net/~radio/welcome.html`

Dow Jones Information Service. `http://www.dowjones.com/`

Knight Ridder International. `http://www.krinfo.com/`

Koch, Tom. `http://www.alnet.com/koch/`

National Institute for Computer Assisted Reportage. `http://www.nicar.org/`

Nando Net. `http://www.nando.net`

Tom Koch

JOURNALS, COMPUTING

See LITERATURE OF COMPUTING; and APPENDIX III.

JUSTIFICATION

For articles on related subjects *see* DESKTOP PUBLISHING; TEX; TEXT EDITING SYSTEMS; and WORD PROCESSING.

In the context of programming, *justification* refers to the left or right alignment of a piece of data, typically a bit or character string, in a field that is larger (i.e. greater in length) than the data. Thus, *right justifying* a bit string of length 2 in an 8-bit byte means that the rightmost of the two data bits is placed in the rightmost position of the byte. Remaining positions in the field are usually occupied by as many copies as needed of a specified or assumed *fill character*. These non-data characters or bits *pad* the data on the left if the data is right-justified, or on the right if the data is left-justified.

In the context of text processing, justification pertains to left- and/or right-margin alignment. Conventionally, typeset text such as that found in books and magazines appears with straight (justified) left and right margins. By contrast, typewritten letters usually have a left-justified ("flush left") margin but a "ragged right" margin. On some output devices such as computer line printers, where each character in the print line has a uniform size (monospace), computer-based typesetting algorithms can force alignment by inserting additional blanks between words or after punctuation. Typesetting for proportionally spaced devices involves inserting variable width spaces between words; with such devices, each character has its characteristic width as a function of font, size, etc.

Andries van Dam

KERNEL

For articles on related subjects *see* INPUT–OUTPUT CONTROL SYSTEM; MEMORY MANAGEMENT; OPERATING SYSTEMS: PRINCIPLES; SCHEDULING ALGORITHMS; SWAPPING; TASK; and VIRTUAL MEMORY.

The term *kernel* (and sometimes *nucleus*) is applied to the set of programs in an operating system that implement the most primitive of that system's functions. The precise interpretation of kernel programs depends on the system. Typical kernels contain programs for five classes of functions:

1. *Process management*. Routines for switching processors among processes; for scheduling; for sending messages or timing signals among processes; for creating and removing processes; and for controlling entry to supervisor state (*see* PRIVILEGED INSTRUCTION).

2. *Memory management*. Routines for transferring pages or segments between main memory and secondary memory; for controlling multiprogramming load; for mapping virtual to real addresses; and for handling protection violations.

3. *Interprocess communication*. Routines for opening and closing connections between processes; for transferring data over open connections; for network protocols and routing; and for name service (*see* INTERNET).

4. *File and device management*. Routines for creating and deleting; for opening and closing; for keeping track of a file's records; for allocating and releasing buffers; for starting I/O requests on particular devices; for handling device completion interrupts; and for managing directories.

5. *Security*. Routines for enforcing the access and information-flow control policies of the system; for changing protection domains; and for encapsulating programs.

In some systems, the kernel is larger and provides for more than these classes of functions; in others, it is smaller. Each of the classes of kernel programs contains routines for handling interrupts pertaining to its class. For example, clock interrupts are handled in class 1, page faults in class 2, network time-outs in class 3, device completion interrupts in class 4, and protection violations in class 5. Some systems order the classes hierarchically (e.g. in order: 1, 2, 3, 4, 5) so that routines in a given class can invoke services only of routines of lower classes. For example, memory management (class 2) can be implemented by a collection of processes created and managed by routines at the next lower level (class 1).

The system kernel should not be confused with the portion of the operating system that is continuously resident in main memory. Two criteria determine whether a particular system module (either routines or tables) should be resident—frequency of use, and whether the system can operate at all without it. For example, the table of process descriptors needs to be in main memory, but file directories can be swapped out of main memory when not in use. The resident part of an operating system is usually a subset of its kernel. Very small continuously resident kernels are sometimes described as *microkernels*.

Bibliography

1992. Tanenbaum, A. S. *Modern Operating Systems.* Upper Saddle River, NJ: Prentice Hall.

Peter J. Denning

KILBURN, TOM

For articles on related subjects *see* ATLAS; MANCHESTER UNIVERSITY COMPUTERS; WILKES, MAURICE; WILLIAMS, SIR FREDERICK C.; and WILLIAMS TUBE MEMORY.

Tom Kilburn was born on 11 August 1921 in Dewsbury, Yorkshire, England. Along with F. C. Williams and M. V. Wilkes, Kilburn dominated the field of British computer engineering in its formative years. He was educated at Cambridge University, where he graduated in 1942 with a B.A. degree in mathematics. During the war in 1942–1945, he joined the Telecommunications Research Establishment (TRE) at Great Malvern, where he was engaged in radar work. In 1946, he was seconded from the TRE to the Electrical Engineering Department at the University of Manchester to work under F. C. Williams on research into cathode ray tube (i.e. electrostatic) storage. The result of their work was the Williams tube—the first random access digital storage device—which formed the basis for the Manchester Mark I computer. A prototype of this machine ran the world's first stored program on 21 June 1948. Collaboration with Ferranti Ltd followed both for the Mark I and other machines such as the Mercury and Atlas computers, with Kilburn assuming

Figure 1. Tom Kilburn (courtesy National Archive for the History of Computing, University of Manchester).

direction of the projects after about 1952. Although Kilburn was involved with other important Manchester University computers such as the MU5, the Atlas project, begun in 1956, represented perhaps his finest achievement. Atlas pioneered many modern concepts, such as paging, virtual memory (*q.v.*), and multiprogramming (*q.v.*), and on its official inauguration in 1962 was considered to be the most powerful computer in the world.

Tom Kilburn was Professor of Computer Science at Manchester University from 1964–1981 and is now Emeritus Professor. A member of numerous governmental committees and technical societies, he was elected Fellow of the Royal Society in 1975. Some of his other honors include CBE (1973), Computer Pioneer Award (1982), and the Eckert–Mauchly Award (1983). [Ed. note: Tom Kilburn died on 17 January, 2001.]

Bibliography

1947. Papers of Manchester University Department of Computer Science, National Archive for the History of Computing, Manchester University.
1975. Lavington, S. H. *A History of Manchester Computers.* Manchester: National Computer Centre.
1993. Bowker, G., and Giordano, R. "Interview with Tom Kilburn," *IEEE Annals of the History of Computing,* **15**, 3 (Special Issue on Computing at the University of Manchester), 17–32.
1998. "Tom Kilburn," The Virtual Museum of Manchester Computing. http://www.computer50.org/mark1/kilburn.html.

Geoffrey Tweedale

KLUDGE

The word "kludge" as used in computing was coined by Jackson Granholm in an article "How to Design a Kludge," in *Datamation* (February 1962). The definition is given as "an ill-sorted collection of poorly matching parts, forming a distressing whole." The design of every computer contains some anomalies that prove to be annoying to the users and that the designer wishes had been done differently. If there are enough of these, the machine is called a *kludge*.

By extension, the term has now come to be applied to programs, documentation, and even computing centers, so that the definition is now "an ill-conceived and hence unreliable system that has accumulated through patchwork, expediency, and poor planning."

The first kludge article triggered five others ("How to Maintain a Kludge," etc.) in subsequent issues of *Datamation.* Four of the articles may be found in the book, *Faith, Hope and Parity,* edited by Jack Moshman, Washington: Thompson Book Company, 1966.

Fred Gruenberger

KNOWLEDGE REPRESENTATION

For articles on related subjects *see* ARTIFICIAL INTELLIGENCE; CASE-BASED REASONING; COGNITIVE SCIENCE; COMPUTER VISION; DEDUCTIVE DATABASE; EXPERT SYSTEMS; HEURISTIC; LOGIC PROGRAMMING; MACHINE LEARNING; NATURAL LANGUAGE PROCESSING; NEURAL NETWORKS; ROBOTICS; and THEOREM PROVING.

The term *knowledge representation* was originally used in artificial intelligence (AI) to refer to the encoding of knowledge that an intelligent program would seem to require in order to plan, observe or draw conclusions. It is now understood more broadly to refer to any organized body of general knowledge, including large-scale repositories of information intended largely for human use. The distinction between "knowledge" and "data" (as in "database") is not precise, but knowledge representation (KR) is usually taken to refer to the representation of general knowledge that can support some nontrivial reasoning.

To represent knowledge one must choose a suitable collection of *concepts*, a *notation*, and a *system of inference rules* or processes that use the notation. These choices are largely independent of each other, and we will consider them separately.

How best to think of notations and rules has long been the subject of intense discussion. For example, two pioneers of AI, John McCarthy and Marvin Minsky, were protagonists in an early debate between an "assertional" view, which suggested the notation of formal logic with a general-purpose theorem-prover, and a "procedural" view, which insisted that the notation be thought of as a programming language plus an interpreter. While the echoes of that debate can still be heard, the development of *logic programming* has shown that much of the controversy was immaterial. Other divergences of opinion have arisen between adherents of various different systems of inference, such as fuzzy logic (*q.v.*) and Bayesian reasoning (both of which associate numbers with propositions) and various nondeductive inference schemes such as abductive inference or analogical reasoning. All of these are now well-defined technical areas with their own domains of application.

More fundamental debates also surround KR within AI and cognitive science. Some psychologists believe that human reasoning involves "mental imagery" or "mental models" that are supposed somehow to resemble the world being represented. The very idea that intelligence requires explicitly encoded knowledge is controversial. Many *connectionists* and some philosophical critics of AI believe that knowledge should be thought of as emerging from the dynamics of a neural network; others emphasize how complex behaviors might arise from interactions of a state-free machine with its environment, avoiding internal representations altogether. It is widely thought, however, that cognitive abilities require access to represented information. In particular, "common sense" (i.e. the general ability to act successfully in the everyday world) seems to require a wide range of knowledge at varying levels of generality, including knowledge about the physical world, about actions and their effects, and about other agents' beliefs. (From a strict philosophical perspective, the word "knowledge" is used illegitimately in the AI literature, since much common-sense "knowledge" is, of course, false.)

Notations for Knowledge Representation

A wide variety of KR notations have been invented, including labeled networks, lists of logical sentences, object-oriented hierarchies and various programming languages. All have their adherents, but while but some have computational advantages for certain applications, they are broadly equivalent. In this article we will treat all of the notations as divergent forms of surface syntax for first-order predicate calculus (FOPC).

The basic units of FOPC are atomic assertions that *relations* hold between *individuals*, [e.g. Loves(Harry, Sally) or HasMeeting(Joe, DepartmentOf (Mathematics), ThreePM(May 14))]. These can be combined by connectives such as and, or, not, and implies, and general facts can be expressed by replacing some names by variables bound by the quantifiers Forall and Exists. This recursive syntax can produce complex expressions, such as:

```
(Forall x)( IsBabyOf(x, me) implies
    (Forall y) (Loves(y,x) and
            (Forall z)(not Equal(z,me)
            implies not Loves(x,z))))
```

Many equivalences hold between FOPC expressions, allowing the use of certain standard forms of which the most common is a conjunction of *clauses*, i.e. implications of the form (atom and atom and...) implies (atom or atom or...) where all the variables are assumed to be universally quantified. The above expression becomes two clauses:

```
IsBabyOf(x,me) implies Loves(y,x)
(IsBabyOf(x,me) and Loves(x,z) ) implies
        Equal(z,me)
```

An alternative notational style organizes the knowledge around individuals rather than propositions. The resulting structures, called *frames* or *units*, represent either an individual or a certain type of individual (e.g. *Chris* or *Human*). Each unit has associated with it a number of slots that encode all its relationships to other individuals. The slots may consist of simply the name of a relationship and a list of units to which this individual bears the relation (i.e. an atomic assertion) or it may be associated with a more elaborate piece of code. Units form a hierarchy of individuals and types, so that we might have *Chris* being an instance of *Man*, which is itself a subtype of *Human*, of *Mammal*, and also of *Agent*, etc., forming a directed acyclic graph. Each unit is understood to inherit the slot values of units above it, so that the fact that all mammals have warm blood can be expressed by attaching the relevant information about warmbloodedness to the unit *Mammal*. This "frame" style of notation, due originally to Minsky (1975), has been very influential and is the basis of several *expert system shell* languages.

Another notational tradition is based on *semantic networks* in which the edges of a directed graph represent two-place relations holding between individuals labeling the nodes. Semantic networks usually come with a particular set of conventions on how certain kinds of nodes or arcs are to be used, amounting to a syntax for a network language. A common device is the use of *is-a links* to express general statements of a type hierarchy of the kind described above, which was first developed in network languages (*see* Fig. 1). Any link attached to a type represents something true of all instances of that type, and can be inherited back along an *is-a link*. These instantiation links can form hierarchies of more and more general types, allowing a limited form of universal quantification.

Both units and networks can express only one- and two-argument predicates naturally, but more complex assertions can be encoded with some ingenuity. For example, the use of a three-place predicate, such as `Meeting(Bill, Harry, 5pm)`, can be replaced by a unit or node representing the proposition itself, which is considered to be an individual (sometimes called a *trope*) of type `Meeting`, with slots or binary links connecting it to the arguments. The relation names here may be things like `AgentOf`, `TimeOf`, etc., which follow the use of *case markers* in natural language parsing. (This is an example of a general coding technique called *reification*, i.e. making an assertion into a kind of object.)

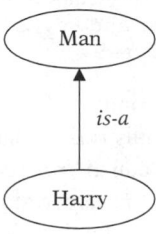

Figure 1.

Inference Rules and Semantics

What do the various notations mean? This is not a trivial question, since "obvious" axioms can have unintuitive consequences. For example, the two clauses shown earlier have the rather surprising consequence

```
IsBabyOf(x,me) implies Equal(x,me)
```

which follows from the assertion that *everybody* loves my baby: in particular, therefore, she loves herself; but since she doesn't love anybody but me, she must *be* me. Clearly, the universal quantifier made a stronger statement than intended. Such phenomena are quite common, and illustrate the importance of avoiding the "*gensym*" *fallacy* (named after a Lisp (*q.v.*) function that generates meaningless names) of assuming that symbols in a KR notation must have a meaning that is somehow inherited from their English meaning.

Most attempts at an exact answer to the question about the meaning of notations are based on *model theory* for FOPC, which defines the structure of a possible world and the conditions under which an expression would be true in it, and takes the meaning of a logical expression to be the constraint on this structure imposed by insisting on its truth. Similar accounts can be given for unit and network languages.

The notions of meaning and inference are connected together by *completeness*; a system of inference rules is complete (with respect to a theory of meaning) if it can infer all the conclusions that are valid according to that theory. The complexity of a complete system of inference is closely linked to the expressive power of the notation. This trade-off between the expressive power of a formalism—what it can say about the world—and the computational difficulty of searching through the space of inferences it supports, is a basic tension which runs throughout knowledge representation. Quite small changes to the design of a language can have very dramatic effects on where it sits on this expressiveness/tractability curve, the so-called "computational cliff" (Levesque, 1984). (The crucial issue seems to be whether the language allows expressions of incomplete knowledge, typically expressed by a disjunction. If it is known that *A* or *B* holds, but not which, the search process must somehow keep track of both possibilities. When each might involve different instantiations of variables, there is no compact way of encoding this choice as an expression in the language itself, so the search process has to keep track of them explicitly. Through recursion (*q.v.*), this branching can result in an explosively difficult search problem. Forcing the representation to be clear sometimes improves this dramatically.)

Not all KR systems are intended to support a complete inference process (for example, some are considered to be more like organized repositories of information, or as data models (*q.v.*) for databases), but in AI applications the function of the KR formalism is usually to support inferences. Designers of such knowledge representation systems have tried to find a workable compromise between the very intractable nature of full FOPC and the impoverished expressive power of many *ad hoc* schemes. For example, the two clauses shown earlier are examples of *Horn clauses* in which the disjunctive consequent has at most one element. Not all assertions can be expressed as Horn clauses, but their computational properties are so advantageous that the slight restriction on expressive power is often accepted. Indeed, Horn clauses are the basis of logic programming (*q.v.*). Other examples include specialized notations that allow only definitions of a restricted form, but which permit efficient inference search; and the use of a *closed-world assumption* that every individual has an explicit name. Many of the specialized notations used for KR, including frame-based and network notations, can be seen as restrictions on FOPC which attempt to locate a reasonable compromise between expressiveness and efficiency. However, most frame and network systems provide other mechanisms (Findler, 1979), and languages as complex as KRL (Bobrow and Winograd, 1977) or the more sophisticated network languages can encode all of FOPC (e.g. by encoding expressions as terms or by extending the graphical notation by allowing a subgraph to be treated like a single node so that it can represent the scope of a quantifier). Moreover, these ways of organizing the information suggest alternative strategies (e.g. analogical reasoning by partial matching of units, or the use of graph-search algorithms to seek connections between different topics in a semantic network; in fact, these graphical representations have their historical roots in simpler graphs where adjacency modeled word association).

In addition, some common inferences fall outside the scope of FOPC, notably the use of the *is-a* hierarchy to express *defaults*. The usual convention is that a link to a lower node in the hierarchy blocks the inheritance of properties from above, so that the inheritance is only "by default." Thus, we might attach a network meaning "has legs" to the *Mammal*-type node, allowing *Whale is-a Mammal* while also consistently asserting that the whale is legless. This kind of *nonmonotonic inference* (*see* Nonmonotonic Logic) is not consistent in FOPC, although logics have been extended to allow this and other more complex nonmonotonic inferences. The model theory of such logics explains nonmonotonic inference as the selection of the minimal model in some ordering, so that some relations are always asserted to be "as false as possible."

Inheritance hierarchies can become intricate if, for example, exceptions to exceptions are allowed, and it is not always clear what the "correct" result should be. Since *is-a* hierarchies are often thought of as defining the meanings of the terms in the language, this issue has received a lot of attention.

Concepts and Ontology

Probably the most important aspect of knowledge representation is closer to philosophy than to logic: the choice of concepts to be used to express the intended content. For example, a natural language comprehension system might need to use a variety of spatial, temporal, social, and physical concepts in order to help it understand the variously different meanings of "up" in the phrases "up the hill," "shut up," "catch up," and "tighten up," and the relationships between these (and other concepts) must be encoded carefully. A suitably organized system of concepts is often called an *ontology*; a current active area of research attempts to develop useful "standard" ontologies for various topics. Notations such as Ontolingua are designed to record and systematize collections of ontologies.

TIME AND CHANGE
One basic idea is the use of states to describe change in a dynamic world. Relations that are subject to change are thought of as functions on states (often called *fluents*)—so that in a logical notation we might write `IsWearing(Susan,PinkDress3,ThursdayEvening)`. The results of events or actions can be described by a function from these things and states to new states:

```
IsDressing(x,s) implies
    IsWearing(x,y,result(x,putOn(y),s))
```

where the term `result(x,putOn(y),s)` describes the state after x performs the action `putOn(y)` in state s. This style of writing axioms is called the *situation calculus*, and supports a form of planning by inference, since proving that a state with some desired properties exists automatically generates a term whose structure of nested `result` terms encodes a way to achieve it. There are many problems, the most difficult being the *frame problem*—how to state neatly that all the many things that do *not* change as a result of performing an action are still true in the new state (Hayes and Ford, 1992).

Similar tricks can be used in other notations, of course, but since the addition of state parameters would make a binary relation have more than two arguments, network and frame-based representations often use units or nodes that represent the fact that a certain relation holds during a state, so that `IsWearing`

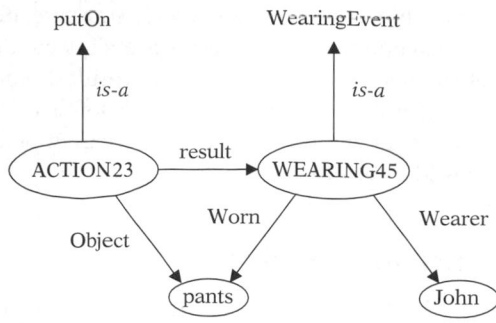

Figure 2.

`(John,pants,result(John,putOn(pants),s))`
might become the network fragment shown in Fig. 2, where ACTION23 stands for the `result` term and WEARING45 for the atom. The task of designing inheritance hierarchies to handle structures like this can become very complex and subtle.

States are typically thought of as essentially static, but other approaches to describing change focus instead on time intervals during which some process is happening. The situational calculus has been extended into an elaborate ontology, which can describe ongoing processes taking place during intervals, parallel events and other complexities (Levesque *et al.*, 1998).

BELIEFS AND OTHER MENTAL STATES

In order to lie successfully, cheat or steal, it is necessary to reason about other agents' beliefs, while knowing them to be false. The commonest technique is to assume a relationship between the agent and some fragment of one's own representational notation, so that one might write

```
Believes(Joan, (Forall x)(Friend(x,Harry)
          implies Fool(x)))
```

where one argument of the `Believes` relation is a whole logical assertion. However, this assumes that the agent has the same understanding of the concepts used to express her beliefs. In general, it is, ironically, rather tricky to describe a state of belief which is very different from one's own. In particular, there are problems in properly interpreting *de re* expressions where a quantifier includes a belief assertion. For example,

```
(Forall x)(Friend(x,Harry) implies
          Believes(Joan, Fool(x)))
```

could be true even while the earlier sentence is false, if Joan didn't realize that she knew all of Harry's friends.

SPACE AND SHAPE

Linguistic analyses of spatial prepositions such as *on*, *through*, *over*, and *in* suggest complex systems of concepts, not always purely spatial. For example, a person in a room in a building is in the building, but an apple in a bowl in water is not in the water. It is not easy to

formalize these in consistent ways, and some have argued that these systems are essentially metaphorical, so that some kind of best-fit structural matching is the most appropriate way to use this kind of information. Even very simple "common-sense" situations often seem to involve puzzling conceptual issues: for example, does one wish to conclude that the paint on the wall of a room is *in* the room?

Humans can typically recognize shapes that are very hard to describe, and much of AI has been concerned with what information is needed to support such spatial intuition and how it can be represented. The problem is to find a representation in which an object has the same shape description no matter what its orientation or position, or even perhaps size. This whole area merges into those of machine perception, computer graphics (*q.v.*) and robotics (*q.v.*) , and has a more mathematical flavor than the rest of knowledge representation (Koenderick, 1990).

ONTOLOGICAL STRATEGIES

Ontologies often differ in how to categorize everyday things. For example, it is common to invoke a category distinction between objects (which "are") and processes (which "happen"); but many ordinary things can be described equally well in either way (flames, rainstorms, flowing rivers). Several distinct ontological strategies are possible in such cases. One can for example distinguish two concepts (flame-as-object vs. flame-as-process); or, allow such entities to be simultaneously classified under both categories. Both strategies require care to avoid confusion in the representation. Some large-scale ontological efforts, notably the CYC project (Lenat and Guha, 1990), use "contexts" as a notational device to keep track of such alternative views. An alternative strategy is deliberately to avoid being forced to make the distinction, for example by treating both as instances of a more general concept of "spatio-temporal history." As a general observation, the business of constructing large-scale knowledge representations of everyday knowledge often seems to involve the analysis of concepts that are not themselves obvious to common sense; or, to put the point slightly differently, we do not seem to have good introspective access to the logical structure of our own human intuition.

Bibliography

1974. Schank, R., and Reiger, C. J. "Inference and the Computer Understanding of Natural Language," *Artificial Intelligence*, **5**, 4, 373–412. Reprinted in Brachman and Levesque, 1985.

1975. Minsky, M. "A Framework for Representing Knowledge," *Memo 36, MIT Artificial Intelligence Laboratory*. Reprinted in Brachman and Levesque (1985).

1977. Bobrow, D. G., and Winograd, T. "An Overview of KRL, a Knowledge Representation Language," *Cognitive Science*, **1**, 1, 3–46. Reprinted in Brachman and Levesque, 1985.

1979. Findler, N. V. (ed.) *Associative Networks: Representation and Use of Knowledge*. New York: Academic Press.

1984. Levesque, H. J. "A Fundamental Tradeoff in Knowledge Representation and Reasoning," *Proceedings CSCSI-84*, London, Ontario. Reprinted in Brachman and Levesque (1985).

1985. Brachman, R., and Levesque, H. J. (eds.) *Readings in Knowledge Representation*. San Francisco: Morgan Kaufmann.

1985. Bobrow, D. G. (ed.) *Qualitative Reasoning about Physical Systems*. Cambridge, MA: MIT Press.

1990. Lenat, D. B., and Guha, R. V. *Building Large Knowledge-Based Systems*. Reading, MA: Addison-Wesley.

1990. Koenderick, J. J. *Solid Shape*. Cambridge, MA: MIT Press.

1992. Hayes, P. J., and Ford, K. (eds.) *Reasoning Agents in a Dynamic World: The Frame Problem*. Boston: JAI Press.

1998. Levesque, H., Pirri, F., and Reiter, R. *Foundations for the Situation Calculus*. http://www.ep.liu.se/ea/cis/1998/018/.

Patrick J. Hayes

LAMBDA CALCULUS

For articles on related subjects *see* BINDING; FUNCTIONAL PROGRAMMING; GRAMMARS; LIST PROCESSING: LANGUAGES; PRODUCTION; PROGRAMMING LINGUISTICS; PROGRAM VERIFICATION; and SYNTAX, SEMANTICS AND PRAGMATICS.

The *lambda calculus* (or λ-calculus) is a mathematical formalism developed by the logician Alonzo Church (*q.v.*) in the 1930s to model the mathematical notion of substitution of values for bound variables. Consider the definition $f(x) = x + 1$, which defines f to be the successor function. The variable x in this definition is a *bound variable* in the sense that replacement of all instances of x by some other variable (say, y) yields a definition $f(y) = y + 1$, which is semantically equivalent. In the λ-calculus, the successor function f may be defined by the λ-expression $\lambda x(x + 1)$. The subexpression $(x + 1)$ is referred to as the *body* of the λ-expression. The subexpression λx is referred to as the *bound variable part* and specifies that x is to be regarded as a bound variable in the body with which λx is associated.

The application of $\lambda x(x + 1)$ to the integer argument 3 may be specified by the λ-expression $f(3) = \lambda x(x + 1)$ (3). The subexpression $\lambda x(x + 1)$ is referred to as the "operator part" of this lambda expression; the subexpression 3 is referred to as the "operand part" of this lambda expression. The substitution rules (reduction rules) of the lambda calculus specify that the operator part $\lambda x(x + 1)$ may be applied to the operand part 3 to yield the value $(3 + 1) = 4$.

Consider next the lambda expression $\lambda h(h(3) + h(4))$ $(\lambda x(x + 1))$. The substitution rules of the λ-calculus specify that $\lambda x(x + 1)$, which is the operand part of this expression, is to be substituted for all instances of h in the body of the operator part, yielding the λ-expression $(\lambda x(x + 1)(3) + \lambda x(x + 1)(4))$, which on further substitution yields $((3 + 1) + (4 + 1)) = 9$.

The binding of h to $\lambda x(x + 1)$ in $h(3) + h(4)$ may be expressed in one of the following ways.

1. Let $h = \lambda x(x + 1)$ in $h(3) + h(4)$.

2. $h(3) + h(4)$ where $h = \lambda x(x + 1)$.

The notations (1) and (2) are said to be syntactically "sugared" versions of the original λ-expression in the sense that they are semantically equivalent to the original λ-expression but are easier to read. The above syntactically sugared specifications illustrate that certain notational conventions of real programming languages may very easily be converted into semantically equivalent lambda notations.

The following example illustrates even more clearly that the bound variable h of the λ-expression given above represents a procedure that is initialized to the successor function $\lambda x(x + 1)$ at the time of binding, and is then called with the arguments 3 and 4:

> procedure $h(x)$; result $\leftarrow x + 1$;
> value $\leftarrow h(3) + h(4)$;

This example also illustrates that, in order to realize the functions determined by lambda expressions in a conventional programming language, it is necessary to introduce the assignment operator and to realize binding and substitution in terms of assignment.

In the preceding examples, λ-expressions were allowed to contain extraneous symbols, such as $+$, which allow arithmetic operations to be embedded in the substitutive mechanism of the λ-calculus. The pure λ-calculus does not contain such extraneous operators, and requires all transformations to be substitutions of values for bound variables. In the remainder of this article we will be concerned with the pure λ-calculus.

The pure λ-calculus may be thought of as a programming language with a very simple syntax and semantics. The syntax of λ-expressions may be defined by a BNF (q.v.) grammar whose terminal symbols are λ, (,), and a class V of variable names, and whose productions are $E \rightarrow V | \lambda VE | (EE)$, where E denotes the class of λ-expressions. An expression of the form λVE (say, λxM) denotes a one-parameter function and has a bound variable part λx and a body part M. An expression of the form (EE) [say, $(M_1 M_2)$] is referred to as an *operator–operand combination*, and has an operator part M_1 and an operand part M_2. An occurrence of a variable x in a λ-expression M is said to be bound in M if it occurs within a subexpression of the form λxM_1 within M, and is said to be free otherwise. *Note*: The above syntactic definition requires application of an operator f to an operand x to be specified as (fx) rather than as $f(x)$.

The "computational semantics" of the λ-calculus may be defined by transformation rules that specify how λ-expressions may be converted into "semantically equivalent" λ-expressions. The principal computation rule is the *reduction rule* (sometimes called the "β-rule").

Reduction Rule

An operator–operand combination of the form (λxMA) may be transformed into the expression $S_A^x M$, obtained by substituting the λ-expression A for all instances of x in M, provided there are no conflicts of variable names. The condition that there be no conflicts of variable names may be explicitly specified as follows:

1. M contains no bound occurrences of x.

2. M contains no bound variables that occur free in A.

A second transformation rule called the "renaming rule" (α rule) allows conflicts of variables to be eliminated.

Renaming Rule

A bound variable x in a λ-expression M may be uniformly replaced by some other bound variable y, provided y does not occur in M.

Any λ-expression of the form (λxMA) may be converted into a λ-expression of the form $(\lambda xM'A)$ satisfying conditions (1) and (2) above by renaming of the bound variables of M, using the renaming rule, and may then be reduced to $S_A^x M'$ using the reduction rule.

Example

$$(\lambda x(x\lambda xx)(pq)) \xrightarrow{\alpha} (\lambda x(x\lambda tt)(pq)) \xrightarrow{\beta} ((pq)\lambda tt).$$

A λ-expression P that has no subexpressions of the form (λxMA) is said to be in *reduced form*. A λ-expression that cannot be converted to a reduced form by a sequence of renaming and reduction rules to said to be *irreducible*.

Example

$P = (\lambda x(xx)\lambda x(xx))$ is irreducible, since it is of the form (λxMA) with $M = (xx)$ and $A = \lambda x(xx)$, and application of the reduction rule produces $(\lambda x(xx)\lambda x(xx))$.

The question of whether an arbitrary λ-expression P has a reduced form is *undecidable*; i.e. there is no algorithm that, given an arbitrary λ-expression E, can always determine in a finite number of steps whether or not E has a reduced form (*see* UNDECIDABLE PROBLEMS).

The notion of a reduced form corresponds to the intuitive notion of a value in arithmetic computation. For example, the arithmetic computation $(3 + (4 * 5)) \rightarrow (3 + 20) \rightarrow 23$ is accomplished by two applications of operators to their operands, corresponding to reductions in the λ-calculus. The result, 23, corresponds to a reduced expression because it contains no more instances of operators that can be applied to their operands.

If a λ-expression contains more than one sub-expression of the form (λxMA), then there is more than one "next step" in the computation, and the evaluation process becomes nondeterministic. The following important theorem states that, for any λ-expression, all sequences of computation that yield a value will yield the same value.

Church–Rosser Theorem

If a given λ-expression is reduced by two different reduction sequences, and if both reduction sequences yield a reduced form, then the reduced forms are equivalent up to renaming of bound variables.

However there are λ-expressions that give rise to both terminating and non-terminating sequences.

Example

The λ-expression

$$(\lambda x \lambda yy(\lambda x(xx)\lambda x(xx)))$$

has the form (λxMA), where $M = \lambda yy$ and $A = (\lambda x(xx)\lambda x(xx))$. If A is substituted for occurrences of x in M before A is evaluated, then the value of λyy is obtained, while if an attempt is made to evaluate A before substituting it in M, then an infinite reduction sequence is obtained.

The choice among different orders of evaluation in the λ-calculus has its counterpart in function evaluation for real programming languages. For example, in evaluating $f(g(x))$, we can choose to evaluate $g(x)$ and use the resulting value in the evaluation of f, or we can pass the unevaluated function $g(x)$ to f and evaluate $g(x)$ whenever it is needed in f. The first alternative is referred to as "inside-out" evaluation and corresponds to *call-by-value* in Algol 60 (*q.v.*), while the second alternative is referred to as "outside-in" evaluation and corresponds to *call-by-name* in Algol (*q.v.*), or *call-by-need* in functional languages (*see* Peyton-Jones, 1987). Call-by-value is more efficient than call-by-name when the value of $g(x)$ is used more than once during the evaluation of f, though call-by-need can avoid the inefficiency of repeated evaluation. Call-by-value is less efficient if $g(x)$ is never used during the evaluation of f. In particular, if $g(x)$ results in an infinite computation sequence but is never used in f, then the call-by-value strategy results in disaster, whereas the call-by-name strategy is always adequate.

The λ-expression

$$(\lambda xMA) = (\lambda x \lambda yy(\lambda x(xx)\lambda x(xx)))$$

is of the form $f(g(x))$, where $f = \lambda x \lambda yy$ has a function body with no occurrences of the parameter x, and $g(x) = (\lambda x(xx)\lambda x(xx))$ results in an infinite computation. The call-by-name evaluation strategy for λ-expressions corresponds to always reducing the instance of (λxMA) whose component λx occurs farthest to the left. This strategy is called the "leftmost" evaluation strategy. The universal adequacy of the call-by-name strategy is captured by the following theorem.

THEOREM. If for a lambda expression E there is a terminating reduction sequence yielding a reduced form E, then the leftmost reduction sequence will yield a reduced form that is equivalent to E up to renaming.

The λ-calculus is equivalent in computational power to the class of Turing machines (*q.v.*) in the sense that any computable function may be represented as a λ-expression. However, its notation and computation mechanism make the λ-calculus closer to programming languages than Turing machines are. This has led to attempts to model programming languages such as Algol 60 in terms of the λ-calculus (Landin, 1965). Such models capture certain concepts, such as nested block structure, binding of variables, and the order of evaluation, but have difficulty in capturing other concepts, such as assignment, sharing of values by references, side effects (*q.v.*), and unconditional branching. Thus, the λ-calculus is well-suited to modeling functional programming (*q.v.*) languages, which in fact may be regarded as notational variations on the λ-calculus. Models of imperative programming languages that have assignment statements and pointers (*q.v.*) must use the notion of an updatable storage cell as a basic one. While the λ-calculus alone cannot do this in a natural way, *denotational semantics*, founded on the λ-calculus, is an approach to programming language semantics that expresses this notion readily (*see* PROGRAMMING LANGUAGE SEMANTICS).

The λ-calculus is of computational interest because it allows us to factor out certain aspects of computational structure and study these features independently of the complexity of real programming languages. It is of mathematical interest because it provides a framework for characterizing the substitution of values for bound variables and for studying the notion of function application. The λ-calculus thus provides a bridge between mathematics and the theory of computation. The programming language Lisp (*q.v.*) was closely modeled on the λ-calculus, and related functional languages are important both in programming language theory, and to a growing degree, in practice as well.

Bibliography

1951. Church, A. "The Calculi of Lambda Conversion," *Ann. Math. Studies*, No. 6. Princeton, NJ: Princeton University Press.

1965. Landin, P. J. "A Correspondence Between Algol 60 and Church's Lambda Notation," *Comm. of the ACM*, 89–101 (February) and 158–165 (March).

1987. Peyton-Jones, S. *The Implementation of Functional Programming Languages*, Chs 2–3. Upper Saddle River, NJ: Prentice Hall.

1990. Meyer, B. *Introduction to the Theory of Programming Languages*. Upper Saddle River, NJ: Prentice Hall.

Peter Wegner

LANGUAGE PROCESSORS

For articles on related subjects *see* ASSEMBLER; BINDING; COMPILE AND RUN TIME; COMPILER; EXPRESSION; GLOBAL AND LOCAL VARIABLES; GRAMMARS; INTERMEDIATE LANGUAGES; MACHINE AND ASSEMBLY LANGUAGE PROGRAMMING; OBJECT PROGRAM; PREPROCESSOR; PROGRAMMING LANGUAGES; PROGRAMMING LINGUISTICS; SOURCE PROGRAM; and SUBPROGRAM.

Most modern computer programming is done in high-level programming languages such as Pascal, C, and Java. However, computers cannot execute these languages directly. A computer can execute only its own machine language. The circuitry that performs this task is sometimes called the computer's *hardware interpreter* (*see* INSTRUCTION DECODING). Thus, before a program written in a high-level language can be executed, it must be translated into the machine language of the computer that will perform the execution. There are two primary mechanisms for accomplishing this translation and the subsequent execution: *compilation and execution* and *interpretation*.

Compilation

In compilation, a program called a *compiler* takes as input a *source program* written in one programming language and produces as output an equivalent *target* or *object program* in another programming language. The language of the source program is usually relatively high level, such as those mentioned above, and the language of the target program is usually relatively low-level, such as assembly language or machine language. In pure compilation (*see* Fig. 1a), the compiler produces a machine language program; this program may be linked with whatever library and other external modules are necessary (*see* LINKERS AND LOADERS) to create an *executable* program, which can then be executed directly on the designated hardware. However, it is not uncommon, particularly for research and educational systems and for very high-level languages, for a compiler to translate from one high-level language to another when an efficient compiler already exists for the second language. The target program itself must then be compiled before being executed. C is often used as such a target language because of its flexibility and its efficient and widely available implementations. C compilers themselves may generate assembly language and then invoke an assembler to produce the machine language object program.

The compilation process typically has several stages: *lexical analysis*, in which the character sequences in the source program are grouped into logical tokens; *syntax analysis*, or *parsing*, in which the tokens are

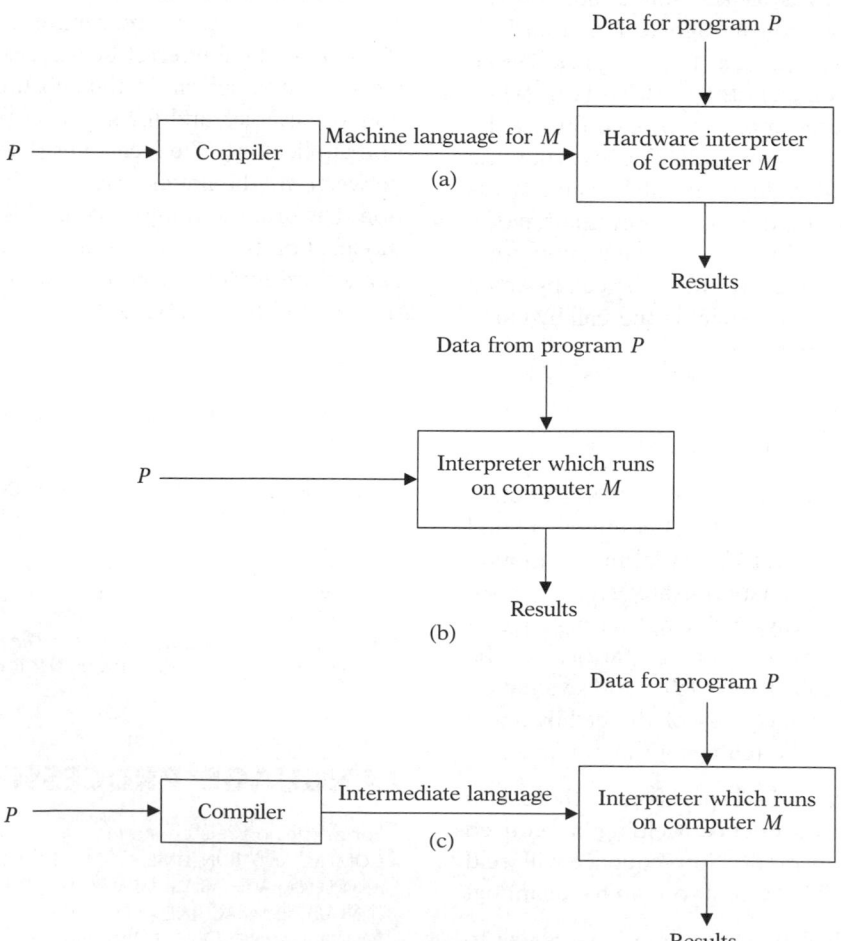

Figure 1. Three possibilities in compilation and interpretation. (a) Pure compilation (hardware interpreter); (b) pure interpretation (interpretation of source language); (c) mixed compilation and interpretation (interpretation of intermediate language).

grouped according to the syntactic rules of the language, and an intermediate representation is produced; *semantic analysis*, in which this intermediate representation is examined for semantic errors; *optimization*, in which the intermediate representation is further transformed to allow more efficient code to be generated; and *code generation*, in which the target program is actually produced. Further optimization may then be performed on the target program itself. This process allows the source program to be analyzed and transformed into a semantically equivalent target program that will execute efficiently on the desired machine, but that target program may bear little resemblance in structure to the source program.

Interpretation

In interpretation, a program called an *interpreter* (or *software interpreter*, to distinguish it from the hardware interpreter mentioned above) maintains control over both translation and execution. It takes as input the source program and interleaves translation and execution of that program so that the generated code corresponding to a portion of the source program is executed as it is produced. In an imperative (procedural) language (*see* PROCEDURE-ORIENTED LANGUAGES), this means that each statement is translated and executed before the next statement is translated. The translated code is not saved, so if the same statement is executed many times, as in a loop, it will be translated each time. Note that a software interpreter performs the same basic steps—fetch the next instruction, determine what actions are required, and perform those actions—as a hardware interpreter, but at a higher level of abstraction. For this reason an interpreter is sometimes said to define a *virtual machine*. Pure interpretation is illustrated in Fig. 1b.

Hybrid Systems

In practice, compilation and interpretation are often combined. Many systems translate the source code into an intermediate language (*q.v.*) that is then interpreted by a software interpreter. This strategy is illustrated in Fig. 1c. Whether this is considered a compiler or interpretive system depends largely on the level of the intermediate code, that is, how much of the translation process is done in the first step and how much is left to the software interpreter. Two examples of hybrid systems are UCSD Pascal (Bowles, 1978) and Java (Gosling *et al.*, 1996). The UCSD Pascal system was designed for portability in response to the many and rapidly changing hardware platforms being developed; the compiler generates an intermediate form called P-code for a virtual machine known as the P-machine which is realized by a software interpreter.

Thus transferring the system to a new computer involves only writing a P-code interpreter for that computer. Java was designed for portability across networks. A Java program to be run over a network is first translated into an intermediate form called Java *Bytecode*, which is then transferred to the client machine where it is interpreted by the client's Java Virtual Machine (JVM) (Lindholm and Yellin, 1996). Like the P-machine, the JVM is easily realized in software for many different platforms and is typically coupled with the machine's World Wide Web (*q.v.*) browser.

Compilation vs. Interpretation

Compilation usually results in faster execution than interpretation for several reasons:

1. In compilation, the translation is temporally separated from the execution, so no execution time is spent performing translation from source code to target code. In interpretation, what looks to the user like execution actually encompasses both translation and execution.

2. In compilation, each source language statement is translated into machine language only once. In interpretation, this translation occurs each time the statement is executed. So not only does translation occur at execution time, but it may occur many times for the same statement.

3. During optimization, a compiler may analyze groups of statements or even groups of subprograms in the source program to look for ways to improve the efficiency of the target program it produces. An interpreter, however, simply translates and executes each statement as it is encountered, and so can perform little or no optimization.

On the other hand, interpretation is often easier to use, again for several reasons:

1. Interpreters often provide interactive environments in which the user can enter definitions and evaluate statements and expressions individually. This provides immediate feedback and is particularly useful when the user is first learning the language and during early program development.

2. Interpreters usually provide better run-time error information because the source code is still available at run time. Under compilation, information about the source program that is useful in generating error messages (e.g., variable names and line numbers) is not usually retained by the target program, so run-time error messages are often cryptic.

3. Interpreters are generally easier to write than compilers. This means that they are more likely to be available for teaching and research languages.

4. Interpreters can be stored in read-only memory (ROM—*q.v.*) and, therefore, be instantly available. This was common early in the history of personal computing (*q.v.*) but is less so now.

Some of the advantages of interpreters over compilers have diminished as compiler technology has matured. Compilers can give informative error messages, and they are often coupled with symbolic debuggers (*see* Debugging) that give access to the source code associated with a run-time error, just as an interpreter does. There are also *incremental* compilers that can compile or recompile a part of a program "on the fly." The ML functional programming (*q.v.*) language, for example, has an interactive run-time system whose compiler translates each function as it is written, so that it behaves like an interpreter from the user's standpoint. Writing an interpreter, however, remains an excellent instructional tool for understanding how programming languages work.

With regard to storage, the amount required by a compiler is not substantially different from that required to perform the same tasks within an interpreter; in fact, the interpreter will contain additional features to perform the execution phase of the problem solution. An interpreter must be self-sufficient and, except in comparatively large computer systems with fast access ancillary storage facilities, the interpreter should also have all anticipated library routines readily available in memory. A compiler system can take advantage of the hiatus between compilation and execution to load into memory only those routines that are needed by this particular program. Of course, additional storage is required to save the target program, but particularly if dynamic linking is used so that library functions do not need to be part of the object program (*see* Linkers and Loaders), the file size of the compiled code of a source text may not be substantially different from the size of the source text itself.

What kind of system is most appropriate in a given situation depends on many factors. First, the language being used must be considered; a language that has dynamic features that makes storage requirements depend on run-time information may be difficult to compile effectively (*see* Binding). The environment must be considered as well. For example, an interpretive system with good error reporting may be advantageous if it will be used primarily for education. Or, in a mixed education and research environment where many programs will run but few will ever become production programs to be run repeatedly, a compiler

that is fast but not necessarily good at optimizing may be appropriate. When the number of compiles is high, the optimization phases of compilation may be omitted on the basis that the increased cost of compilation does not justify the decreased cost of execution. But for a production system, which will ultimately be compiled once and run many times, a methodical compiler that develops highly optimized machine code is very important. Some programming environments contain an interpreter for use in the initial stages of program development and a compiler with various optimization options for use in the later stages.

Bibliography.

1978. Bowles, K. L. "UCSD Pascal," *Byte*, **3**, 5 (May).
1986. Aho, A. V., Sethi, R., and Ullman, J. D. *Compilers— Principles, Techniques, and Tools.* Reading, MA: Addison-Wesley.
1990. Kamin, S. N. *Programming Languages: An Interpreter-Based Approach.* Reading, MA: Addison-Wesley.
1996. Gosling, J., Joy, B., and Steele, Jr, G. L. *The Java Language Specification . Reading, MA: Addison-Wesley.*
1996. Lindholm, T., and Yellin, F. *The Java Virtual Machine Specification.* Reading, MA: Addison-Wesley.
1998. Ghezzi, C., and Jazayeri, M. *Programming Language Concepts*, 3rd Ed. New York: John Wiley.

Adrienne Bloss

LANGUAGE TRANSLATION

See Machine Translation.

LANGUAGES, NATURAL

See Natural Language Processing.

LANGUAGES, PROGRAMMING

See Functional Programming; Procedure-Oriented Languages; Programming Languages; and language sections of Logic Programming; List Processing; and String Processing. *See also* names of particular languages.

LAPTOP COMPUTER

See Portable Computers.

LARC

For an article on a related subject *see* STRETCH.

The *LARC* (Livermore Automatic Research Computer) was one of the first of the high-performance giant computers. It was developed at the Sperry Univac engineering facilities in Philadelphia during 1959–1960.

LARC represented a manyfold increase in speed over any existing computer of that period.

Only two LARC computers were manufactured. One was supplied to the Lawrence Radiation Laboratory in Livermore, CA; the other was delivered to the former David Taylor Model Basin (now the Naval Ships Research and Development Center) located near Washington, DC. Both computers were phased out of service in the period 1968–1969. The consensus was that LARC was a technical success, but the high cost of manufacture did not justify further sales effort.

The basic LARC system was composed of two units. One was an input–output processor designed primarily to provide flexible, parallel, and coordinated control of the input–output equipment. The second was a computing unit designed to perform the arithmetic functions of the system. If increased computing capacity was required, the basic system could be expanded to include an additional computing unit. The computing unit was a parallel computer capable of both fixed and floating-point arithmetic operation. The number system was binary-coded decimal (*see* CODES). Except for certain intercommunication facilities, the comput-

ing units and the input–output processor operated independently. Additions were performed in $4\,\mu$s, multiplications in $8\,\mu$s.

LARC had a high-speed magnetic core memory shared by the I/O processor and computing units. The memory was divided into units, each of which was capable of storing 2,500 computer words of 11 decimal digits plus a sign digit. Each unit of the memory contained all the necessary switches, read–write regenerate circuits, and intermediate storage to operate independently and in parallel with other units. The high-speed memory could be expanded to a maximum of 39 units, equivalent to 97,500 words. Eight units were used in the basic system on a high-speed bus (*q.v.*) to provide an effective rate of one word every $0.5\,\mu$s.

The high-speed memory was backed up by a magnetic drum memory (*see* MEMORY: AUXILIARY). Up to 24 magnetic drums could be included in the system. Each drum was capable of storing 250,000 computer words of 11 decimal digits. The magnetic drums featured an air-floated read–write head assembly that achieved high reliability with high pulse densities because of the absence of mechanical contact between the head

Figure 1. The LARC computer. (Courtesy of the Lawrence Livermore National Laboratory/US Department of Energy.)

and the drum surface. A continuous data transfer rate of 2,500 words every 83 ms was achieved between the drums and the computing unit by interlacing the sequential operation of the two drums.

LARC was the largest *decimal* computer ever built and is likely to retain that distinction forever.

Bibliography

1956. Eckert, J. P. "UNIVAC Larc, the Next Step in Computer Design," in *Proc. Eastern Joint Computer Conference*, 16–20.

1959. Eckert, J. P., Chu, J. C., Tonik, A. B., and Schmitt, W. F. "Design of the Univac-LARC System: I," in *Proc. Eastern Joint Computer Conference*, 59–65.

1979. Lukoff, H. *From Dits to Bits: A Personal History of the Electronic Computer*. Portland, OR: Robotics Press.

1998. Hardy, N. *Engineering Considerations of the LARC*. `http://www.mediacity.com/~norm/Hardware/ LARC.html`.

Michael M. Maynard

LAWS, COMPUTER

For an article on a related subject *see* LIMITS OF COMPUTATION.

Introduction

From time to time, individual computer scientists have noted that some aspect of computer technology or performance seems to conform to a pattern that (1) can be quantified, and (2) is likely to hold into the indefinite future. When and if their colleagues gather evidence that supports the observation, the prediction is deemed a "law" that is thereafter associated with the name of its proposer. This article defines and discusses the implications of four widely known computer laws.

Moore's Law

In 1965, Gordon Moore, then head of Research and Development at Fairchild Semiconductor, prepared an article for the 35th anniversary of *Electronics* magazine (Moore, 1965). Plotting the growth in the number of components on a chip over time, he discovered that over the period 1959–1965, the number of components (e.g. transistors) per chip increased at roughly a factor of two every year. This trend suggested that processing power would rise exponentially and at a fast rate, leading to a computing revolution. Moore predicted: "Integrated circuits will lead to such wonders as home computers—or at least terminals connected to a central computer, automatic controls for automobiles, and personal portable communications equipment."

In the 1975 IEEE International Electron Devices meeting, Moore revised his prediction to the number of transistors on a chip doubling every two years (*see* Moore, 1995), a prediction that has become known as *Moore's Law*. Fig. 1 shows the growth in the number of transistors in Intel's microprocessor chips from 1971, when the first (Intel 4004) microprocessor was introduced, through the introduction of Intel's Pentium II in 1997. The number of transistors on a chip almost doubled every two years. Similar results hold for the number of transistors on a DRAM chip, which have in fact increased at a somewhat faster rate. Thus, Moore's 1975 prediction is generally consistent with the empirical evidence.

With the increase in chip density came a corresponding decline in the costs of computation. As these costs continued to decline exponentially over a period of 30 years, the compound effect was powerful: when costs are cut in half every two years, over a 30-year period they decline by a factor of 2^{15}, turning a million-dollar processor into a \$30 device. Progress wasn't quite that good, but was close.

The result of these powerful trends was the computer revolution, and with it, an information revolution. Lowering the costs of processing and storage enabled the development of software that took advantage of the ever-increasing capabilities of the hardware. The new software gave rise to new applications that in turn increased the demand for hardware. As technological advances in accord with Moore's Law progressively reduced the costs of computation, additional applications crossed the threshold of affordability, further increasing the demand for computing. Thus, Moore's Law was the driver of a positive feedback loop that made Gordon Moore's 1965 predictions come true: integrated circuitry (*q.v.*) is playing a central role in every facet of modern life. Indeed, Moore's Law is driving the acceleration of "clock speed" in the entire electronics industry and beyond (Mendelson and Pillai, 1999). (Clock speed—the rate at which a computer executes instructions as measured by timing a program containing a known number of instructions through use of the computer's clock—is proportional to the computer's rating expressed in megahertz (MHz). For example, a Pentium III is rated at 700 MHz.)

Moore's Law was not only a prediction; it also formed a blueprint for the development of the semiconductor industry. After Intel was founded in 1969 by Robert Noyce (*q.v.*) and Gordon Moore, Moore's Law became a target that drove product development within the company. In fact, the entire semiconductor industry is striving to track Moore's curve: the Semiconductor Industry Association has put together periodic "Technology Roadmaps" that were closely followed by the chip industry. These roadmaps, designed by technology working groups made up of leading industry

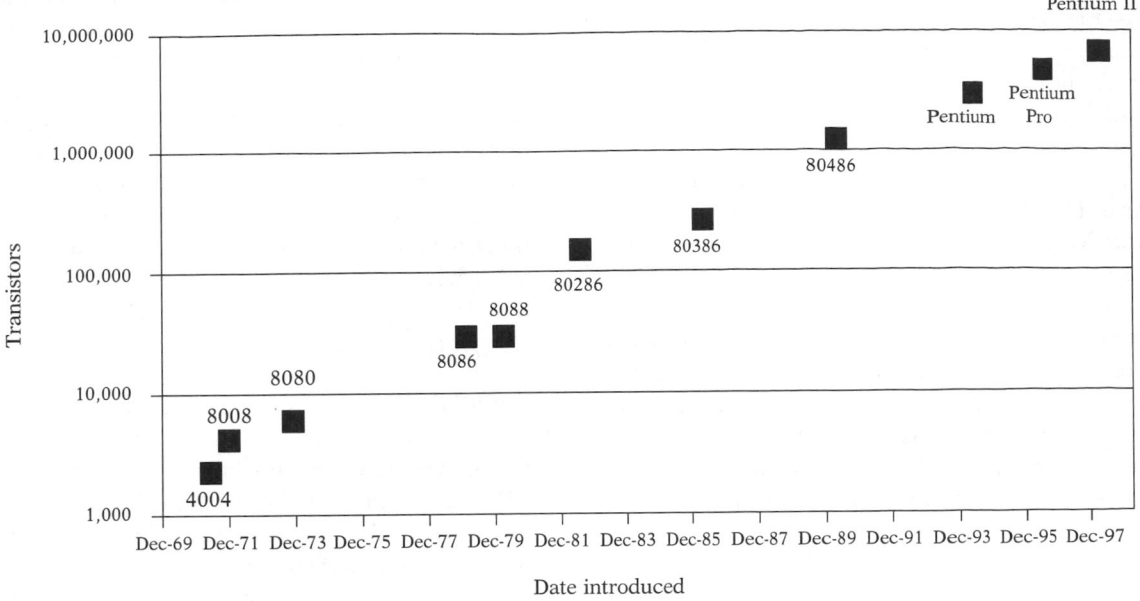

Figure 1. Moore's Law for Intel microprocessors.

experts, define in detail the course for future developments over a 15-year period, driven by the desire to continue the past trends of Moore's Law. In this way, the Law has become a self-fulfilling prophecy.

Certainly the exponential trend of Moore's Law cannot continue forever. Time and time again, however, market demand has proved to be a powerful motivator for ingenious engineers who find ways to get around what appeared to be insurmountable problems or physical limits. The 1997 Technology Roadmap for Semiconductors (Semiconductor Industry Association, 1997) runs through the year 2012 and is designed to continue the trend of Moore's Law through the first decade of the 21st century. Moore himself has stated that the actual limits are likely to be financial rather than technological, because the cost of a chip manufacturing plant doubles with each new generation of chips. As a result, the cost of financing new plants into the future may become insurmountable (Moore, 1996).

Metcalfe's Law

In a network with N nodes, there are $\frac{1}{2}N(N-1)$ possible 2-way interconnections. If each interconnection has the same intrinsic value, then, for large N, the overall value of the network is proportional to N^2. Thus each additional user adds more than a proportionate value to the network, because just by being there, all other users then have the ability to interact with the new one. The precept that the value of a network increases as the square of the number of its interconnections is known as *Metcalfe's Law*. The

Law is named after network pioneer Robert M. Metcalfe, who proposed the Ethernet (*q.v.*) in his Ph.D. dissertation at Harvard University and continued his research at the Xerox Palo Alto Research Center and Stanford University (Boggs *et al.*, 1979) (*see* his profile in ENTREPRENEURS).

In 1979, Metcalfe co-founded 3Com Corporation, which sold Ethernet adapter cards and became a major communications products company. The company's name, 3Com, stands for *Com*puter, *Com*munication, *Com*patibility—reflecting the idea that the Ethernet standard facilitates the addition of more computer users to the network, which increases its value according to Metcalfe's Law. The Law was not named by Metcalfe himself but rather by George Gilder (*see* Gilder, 1993), who praised the power of interconnection as reflected by the philosophies of both Ethernet and the Internet (*q.v.*). Gilder wrote: "Indeed, the power of the telecosm reproduces on a larger scale—by interconnecting computers—the exponential yield of the microcosm, a law describing the near magical effect of interconnecting transistors on chips of silicon: as increasing numbers of transistors are packed ever closer together, the transistors run faster, cooler, cheaper and better. Metcalfe's law suggests that a similar spiral of gains is available in the telecosm of computer communications." (In Gilder's terminology, the *microcosm* reflects the implications of microprocessor technology, and the *telecosm* the implications of communications technologies.)

Metcalfe's Law implies a "critical mass" phenomenon: with a small number of users, usage will be sporadic and unlikely to grow, whereas for a sufficiently large number of users, network use will increase. Metcalfe used this observation to justify the value of Ethernet standards in the 1980s (indeed, Ethernet has since flourished, and most of today's computers are interconnected via Ethernet-based local area networks—*q.v.*). In the 1990s and beyond, the same argument applies to the Internet: the introduction of the browser and the World Wide Web (*q.v.*) led to sufficiently increased use that it reached critical mass. As more and more users browse the Net, individuals and companies add content, create virtual communities, and implement electronic storefronts and trading hubs that increase the value of the network for each connected user. This attracts yet more users, further increasing the value of the network for all of its users. Metcalfe's Law is a concrete representation of this beneficent cycle.

Grosch's Law

While with IBM, Herbert Grosch formulated *Grosch's Law* (Grosch, 1953), which states that the total cost $C(P)$ of a computer system with overall performance P is proportional to the square root of P: $C(P) = KP^{1/2}$, where K is a "constant" characteristic of a given technological era. The Law is often stated in the opposite sense, namely, that if one spends twice as much on a replacement computer, one may expect that its performance will be four times greater. Either way of expressing the Law implies that the cost per unit of performance, $C(P)/P$, *declines* as the square root of P: the larger a system's computing power, the lower its cost per unit of performance.

Grosch's Law thus asserts that computer technology is characterized by economies of scale. This assertion has important implications for the management, acquisition, and control of computer systems, as it implies that "bigger is better." By consolidating computing power, organizations can lower their overall hardware cost, since, by virtue of Grosch's Law, this reduces the cost per unit of performance. Indeed, Grosch's Law used to be cited by large system vendors and data processing managers who argued that hardware economies of scale provided an economic justification for large-scale centralized computing.

The empirical evidence shows that Grosch's Law provided an approximate description of the relationship between cost and system performance in the 1960s and 1970s. Mendelson (1987) showed that Grosch's Law ceased to hold in the 1980s: across a large variety of data-processing computers, cost was merely *proportional* to overall machine performance, i.e. the average cost per unit of performance was independent of system size. For a commodity in high demand, competition drives price down to just above its marginal cost

of production, and this usually means that there will arise a fixed price per unit of that commodity. Here, the commodity under consideration is some unit of processing power, say, a MIPS (million instructions per second). Once a fixed price per MIPS becomes the norm, there is no longer an economy of scale in installing new computer hardware, and hence such a claim cannot be used to justify centralization; the choice must depend on other organizational and technological factors.

Amdahl's Law

Amdahl's Law places a theoretical limit on the ability to speed up program execution using parallel computation. The Law was formulated by Gene Amdahl of IBM and, later, the Corporation that bears his name (*see* his profile in ENTREPRENEURS). Amdahl (1967) noted that the performance gain that can be achieved from parallelizing a program is limited by that part of the program that runs *sequentially*. Specifically, if s is the fraction of a program that runs sequentially, p is the fraction that runs in parallel (i.e. $s + p = 1$), and there are N processors that speed up the parallel part by a factor of N, then the overall speedup is given by $(s + p)/(s + p/N) = [s + (1 - s)/N]^{-1}$, which is bounded from above by $1/s$. Thus, even with an infinite number of parallel processors, the overall speedup is bounded by the reciprocal of the program fraction that runs sequentially. For example, if 5% of the program runs sequentially, speedup cannot exceed a factor of 20. Amdahl used this result to argue against massively parallel processing (*q.v.*).

In 1987, the Sandia National Laboratories achieved a 1,000-fold speedup on its massively parallel 1024-processor hypercube system. This result was surprising in light of the predictions of Amdahl's "Law." Gustafson (1988) explains the apparent contradiction by noting that for many practical problems, it is the parallelizable part of the program that scales with problem size. If the parallelizable part of the program scales linearly while the sequential part remains constant, speedup becomes a linear function (rather than being bounded). This result, sometimes called *Gustafson's Law*, vindicates the use of massively parallel processing.

Bibliography

1953. Grosch, H. R. J. "High Speed Arithmetic: The Digital Computer As a Research Tool," *Journal of the Optical Society of America*, **43**, 306–310.
1965. Moore, G. E. "Cramming More Components Onto Integrated Circuits," *Electronics*, **38**, *8*, April 19, 114–117.
1967. Amdahl, G. M. "Validity of the Single Processor Approach to Achieving Large-scale Computing Capabilities," *Proceedings of the American Federation of Information Processing Societies*, Washington, DC, **30**, 483–485.

1979. Boggs, D. R., Shoch, J. F., Taft, E. A., and Metcalfe, R. M. "Pup: An Internetwork Architecture," *CSL Technical Report*, July.

1987. Mendelson, H. "Economies of Scale in Computing: Grosch's Law Revisited," *Comm. of the ACM*, **30**, 1066–1072.

1988. Gustafson, J. L. "Reevaluating Amdahl's Law," *Comm. of the ACM*, **31**, 532–533.

1993. Gilder, G. "George Gilder's Telecosm: Metcalfe's Law and Legacy," *Forbes ASAP* **152**: Supplement, 13 September, 158–166.

1995. Moore, G. E. "Lithography and the Future of Moore's Law," *International Society of Optical Engineering Proceedings*, **5**, 2–17.

1996. Rayner, B. E. "Can Moore's Law Continue Indefinitely?" *Computer World*, 22 July. *See also* http://www. computerworld.com/home/online9697.nsf/all/ 960722LEADSL9607lead/ (excerpts from a lecture by and interview with Gordon E. Moore).

1998. Semiconductor Industry Association. "National Technology Roadmap for Semiconductors," *Solid State Technology*, **41**, *1*, 73–74. *See also* http://www. semichips.org.

1999. Mendelson, H., and Pillai, R. "Industry Clockspeed: Measurement and Operational Implications," *Manufacturing and Service Operations Management*, **1**, *1*, 1–20.

Haim Mendelson

LEARNING

See COMPUTER-ASSISTED LEARNING AND TEACHING; MACHINE LEARNING; and NETWORKS FOR LEARNING.

LEAST-SQUARES APPROXIMATION

For articles on related subjects *see* APPROXIMATION THEORY; CHEBYSHEV APPROXIMATION; and NUMERICAL ANALYSIS.

Least-squares approximation refers to a wide variety of mathematical optimization problems in which the objective is to make a residual vector small in the sense of minimizing the integral of the squared residual function.

For definiteness, and because of its frequent occurrence as a real-life computational problem, we will describe the real discrete linear least-squares problem and its analysis and solution. In this problem, one has real numbers a_{ij}, $i = 1, \ldots, m$, $j = 1, \ldots, n$ $(m > n)$ and b_i, $i = 1, \ldots, m$. One has some reason to believe that the b_i are approximately representable as linear combinations of the a_{ij} (i.e. that there exist numbers $\bar{c}_j$, $j = 1, \ldots, n$, such that $\sum_{j=1}^{n} \bar{c}_j a_{ij}$ is approximately equal to b_i for $i = 1, \ldots, m$). In matrix–vector notation, this may be stated as the assumption that there is an n-vector $\bar{c}$ such that $A\bar{c}$ is approximately equal to $\mathbf{b}$.

Mathematical Theory

The purely mathematical, real, discrete, linear, least-squares approximation problem, which we will refer

to as problem LS, is to find an n-vector $\tilde{c}$ such that $\|\mathbf{b} - A\tilde{c}\| = \min\|\mathbf{b} - A\mathbf{c}\|$, where the *norm* of a vector $\mathbf{v}$, $\|\mathbf{v}\|$, is defined as the square root of the sum of the squares of the components of $\mathbf{v}$. A solution of this problem always exists. It is unique if and only if the rank of A is n.

A vector $\tilde{c}$ is a solution vector for problem LS if and only if the associated residual vector, $\tilde{r} = \mathbf{b} - A\tilde{c}$, is orthogonal to all column vectors of A. This orthogonality condition may be written as $A^T(\mathbf{b} - A\tilde{c}) = A^T\mathbf{b} - A^T A\tilde{c} = 0$. From this latter expression, one obtains the system of equations, $A^T A\mathbf{c} = A^T\mathbf{b}$, called the *normal equations* for problem LS. Forming the normal equations and solving them by the Cholesky algorithm is a common method of computing a solution for problem LS.

Other solution methods providing superior numerical reliability at a cost of about twice as many arithmetic operations are based on the *QR decomposition* of A. Thus, A can be written as

$$A = Q^T \begin{bmatrix} R \\ 0 \end{bmatrix} = [Q_1^T : Q_2^T] \begin{bmatrix} R \\ 0 \end{bmatrix} = Q_1^T R$$

where Q is an $m \times m$ orthogonal matrix and R is an $n \times n$ upper triangular matrix. The orthogonality of Q assures that

$$\|\mathbf{b} - A\mathbf{c}\|^2 = \|Q(\mathbf{b} - A\mathbf{c})\|^2$$
$$= \left\| \begin{bmatrix} Q_1 \\ Q_2 \end{bmatrix} \mathbf{b} - \begin{bmatrix} R \\ 0 \end{bmatrix} \mathbf{c} \right\|^2$$
$$= \|Q_1\mathbf{b} - R\mathbf{c}\|^2 + \|Q_2\mathbf{b}\|^2$$

for all n-vectors $\mathbf{c}$. Thus, a vector $\tilde{c}$ is a solution of problem LS if and only if $R\tilde{c} = Q_1\mathbf{b}$. The matrix R and the vector $Q_1\mathbf{b}$ needed here can be computed in a numerically stable manner by Householder transformations, Givens plane transformations, or modified Gram–Schmidt orthogonalization.

Practical Considerations

In practice, the given data, particularly the components of the vector $\mathbf{b}$, generally arise from observations or measurements and are therefore known only to some limited precision. One generally knows *a priori* the approximate size of the uncertainty in the vector $\mathbf{b}$. In addition, one often has some *a priori* notion about reasonable values for components of the solution vector.

We will say that problem LS is *ill-conditioned with respect to data uncertainty* if changes in the data matrix $[A : \mathbf{b}]$ of the order of magnitude of the uncertainty in this data can cause changes in the solution vector that are regarded as significant by the problem originator. In such a case, even though the rank of A may be n, there will commonly be a set of significantly different n-vectors that are almost as good as the unique best-solution vector if "goodness" is measured only by the criterion of reducing the residual norm.

In practice, it is desirable to have a systematic way of recognizing the occurrence of an ill-conditioned problem, of identifying the data dependencies that cause the ill-conditioning, of quantitatively characterizing a set of candidate solutions, and of selecting from the candidate solutions one that is suitable for the application at hand. Singular-value analysis and Levenberg–Marquardt analysis (also known as *ridge regression*) provide practical means for obtaining this information.

Singular-value analysis makes use of a matrix decomposition of the form $A = USV^T$, where U and V are orthogonal matrices and S is a diagonal matrix. The Levenberg–Marquardt analysis studies solutions of the augmented least-squares problem

$$\begin{bmatrix} A \\ \lambda I \end{bmatrix} \mathbf{c} \cong \begin{bmatrix} \mathbf{b} \\ \mathbf{0} \end{bmatrix}$$

as a function of the parameter λ.

As an example of an ill-conditioned least-squares problem, consider the problem $A\mathbf{c} \cong \mathbf{b}$ with

$$A = \begin{bmatrix} 0.780 & 0.563 \\ 0.913 & 0.659 \\ 0.133 & 0.096 \end{bmatrix}, \quad \mathbf{b} = \begin{bmatrix} 0.481 \\ 0.560 \\ 0.082 \end{bmatrix}$$

The exact mathematical solution for this problem is

$$\tilde{\mathbf{c}} = [477, -660]^T$$

with a residual vector

$$\tilde{\mathbf{r}} = \mathbf{b} - A\tilde{\mathbf{c}} = [0.0010, \quad -0.0010, \quad 0.0010]^T$$

and residual norm $\|\tilde{\mathbf{r}}\| = 0.0017$.

By either singular-value analysis or Levenberg–Marquardt analysis, one can find that there are other candidate solution vectors that are much smaller in norm than $\tilde{\mathbf{c}}$ and that have residual norms only slightly greater than the minimal norm $\|\tilde{\mathbf{r}}\|$. For instance, the vector $\hat{\mathbf{c}} = [0.404, 0.292]^T$ gives the residual vector

$$\hat{\mathbf{r}} = [0.0015, \quad -0.0013, \quad 0.0002]^T$$

whose norm is $\|\hat{\mathbf{r}}\| = 0.0020$.

In most practical situations, particularly where there is uncertainty in some of the data defining A and $\mathbf{b}$, the vector $\hat{\mathbf{c}}$ would be preferred in place of the vector $\tilde{\mathbf{c}}$, whose components are larger by three orders of magnitude. The reason for preferring smaller solution vector components will be different in different

contexts, but often this is related to the preference for a simpler, more economical explanation of the real-world phenomenon being modeled.

Computation and Parallel Processing

Good performance in computing the *QR decomposition* and solving *normal equations* by the Cholesky algorithm is achieved by effective use of the *memory hierarchy (q.v.)* on a computer. This is implemented in the *LAPACK* and *ScaLAPACK* packages of subprograms based on *BLAS-Basic Linear Algebra Subprograms*. The routines in these packages use block-partitioned algorithms to minimize the frequency of data movement between different levels of the memory hierarchy. For such machines, the memory hierarchy includes the memory of communicating processes executing the program, in addition to the hierarchy of registers, cache, and local memory on each of them.

Bibliography

1973. Stewart, G. W. *Introduction to Matrix Computations.* New York: Academic Press.
1995. Anderson, E., Bai, Z., Bischof, C., Demmel, J., Dongarra, J., DuCroz, J., Greenbaum, A., Hammarling, S., McKenney, A., Oustrouchchov, S., and Sorensen, D. *LAPACK User's Guide*, 2nd Ed. Philadelphia: SIAM Publications.
1995. Lawson, C. L., and Hanson, R. J. *Solving Least Squares Problems.* Philadelphia: SIAM Publications.
1996. Golub, G. H., and Van Loan, C. F. *Matrix Computations*, 3rd Ed. Baltimore: Johns Hopkins Press.
1997. Blackford, L. S., Choi, J., Cleary, A., D'Azevedo, E., Demmel, J., Dhillon, I., Dongarra, J., Hammarling, S., Henry, G., Petitet, A., Stanley, K., Walker, D., and Whaley, R. C. *ScaLAPACK User's Guide.* Philadelphia: SIAM Publications.

Charles L. Lawson, revised by Richard J. Hanson

LEGAL APPLICATIONS

For articles on related subjects *see* LEGAL ASPECTS OF COMPUTING; LEGAL ISSUES OF THE INTERNET; LEGAL PROTECTION OF SOFTWARE; and PRIVACY, COMPUTERS AND.

Computers have transformed the practice of law. The stock-in-trade of law consists of words. Computers store, retrieve, and manipulate words. An excellent source for information devoted to the use of computers in the practice of law is the American Bar Association's Law Practice Management Section Website at http://www.abanet.org/lpm/home.html.

Legal Research

Competent attorneys will understand a field of law before using computers in research. There are excellent noncomputer resources for information on legal questions. An attorney confronting an unfamiliar field of law might first review a digest such as *New York Jurisprudence* (NYJur) or *California Jurisprudence* (CalJur), which are encyclopedias of the law for these jurisdictions, categorizing the law by subject area, summarizing the controlling authorities, and providing references for further research. Attorneys can use computers to augment such legal research in four ways, described below.

STAYING CURRENT

Computerized legal research allows attorneys to update their knowledge of current law by looking for late-breaking court decisions, statutes, and regulations. Every day, courts render new decisions; legislatures amend, revise, and repeal statutes; and administrative agencies release new regulations. The "right" answer to any particular legal question is a moving target. Even when attorneys are confronted with legal questions that have been previously researched, they must update (their personal knowledge of) the law by checking for new developments, since the answer may have recently changed. No attorney wants to be surprised in open court to learn that his or her legal research failed to determine that a statute has been repealed, a case overruled, or that some new pertinent authority applies to this particular case.

COMPUTER ASSISTANCE IN UPDATING THE LAW

Updating the law is a tedious activity. The process requires a researcher to find the correct locations in the "pocket-parts" of hardcover legal volumes, updates that publishers issue periodically (usually monthly) and mail to subscribers. If the updates become extensive, then the publisher issues a compilation of previous pocket parts in a separate softcover supplement. Still later pocket-parts may update the supplement. Important new cases are often published as "slip opinions" for placement in looseleaf binders until the case is later republished in a hardcover volume. Therefore, paper-based legal research is a tedious process. Even after researchers have done the best they can, they can't be *sure* that the research is complete, since a recent item may not have yet been printed or mailed.

Electronic publishing on the LEXIS and WestLaw online services and on the Internet has revolutionized the process of updating the law by making the information widely available, often by the next day. Supreme Court opinions may be available within hours of their rendering. Not only does electronic publishing offer more *rapid* dissemination of legal materials than paper-based research, but it also provides a single place to look for the material without the need to traverse rows and shelves of library books.

FINDING PATTERNS OF FACTS

Electronic research also makes it far easier for legal researchers to cast wider nets. Attorneys often want to search jurisdictions other than their own for cases containing similar or dissimilar fact patterns. Such cases are not necessarily *mandatory* law for a particular court, but can be *persuasive law*, particularly where a case has a very similar fact pattern to the case at hand. A case from another jurisdiction can be especially persuasive where a researcher can show that the statute being interpreted was explicitly derived from a similar statute in one's own jurisdiction.

Legal researchers often find that a law library is replete with materials for its host jurisdiction but is starved for similar materials from other jurisdictions. Electronic legal research can compensate for this gap by providing similar material for all jurisdictions.

Both LEXIS and WestLaw offer special discounted subscriptions to small law firms. These plans allow unlimited access to the materials of a particular jurisdiction at a flat rate. However, they need the opposite type of subscription, giving small law firms a low-cost flat fee subscription to materials *outside* their own jurisdiction, since these are the materials least likely to be found in a local law library.

SIMULTANEOUS SEARCHING

A problem with a conventional law library is that there are only so many copies of a particular volume available. Not all books are used equally often. In a New York State law library, for example, the most-used books are likely to be the Civil Practice Law and Rules (CPLR). Law librarians generally purchase several sets of this part of the New York statutes, yet there are never enough to go around. The advantage of electronic research is that everyone can have access to all of the books at the same time. In the case of commonly used materials, like the CPLR, a firm's least expensive electronic tool might be a set of these materials on compact discs installed on a CD-ROM "jukebox" connected to the firm's local area network (*q.v.*).

Electronic Reference Material

THE INTERNET

Research on the Internet (*q.v.*) is still at a very rudimentary stage, providing haphazard search results insufficient for the needs of legal practice. Often the very purpose of performing legal research is to seek every major and minor, mandatory or persuasive case-law, statutory, or administrative precedent that could be applied to strengthen a client's fact-pattern. As of mid-1999, the Internet still did not provide the breadth, depth, scope, or authoritative reliability of established legal research tools such as WestLaw and LEXIS. It is far less expensive, however, and is especially useful for obtaining "slip" opinions of late-breaking court decisions or new legislation.

Many courts and legislatures now place their opinions and statutes on the Internet at approximately the same time they are made available to Westlaw and LEXIS. Courts often release these materials in multiple formats, such as HTML, WordPerfect, Microsoft Word, or Portable Document Format (PDF). The practitioner can then open the document directly with a word processing (*q.v.*) program or browser (*see* WORLD WIDE WEB). Furthermore, special interest groups have been formed on the Internet that keep their members apprised of latest developments in their field at a cost much lower than through WestLaw or LEXIS.

In some situations, the Internet can provide useful information which cannot be obtained from any other source. Examples include:

- "An Unauthorized and Unofficial Site about the DC SUPERIOR COURT" (`http://www.lawbbs.net/gideon/dcsct.htm`), maintained by volunteers of the GIDEON! service.

- The "Unofficial Home Page of the US District Court for the District of Columbia" (`http://members.tripod.com/~StevenMon/`) which posts TBill rates needed to determine post-judgment interest due on a money judgment in the district of Columbia.

Some other useful sites for Internet legal research are:

- `http://www.findlaw.com`

- US Supreme Court Decisions (`http://supct.law.cornell.edu/supct/`) maintained by Cornell Law School (Project Hermes)

- US District Court for the District of Columbia (`http://www.ll.georgetown.edu/Fed-Ct/cadc.html`) Georgetown University Law School

- DC Bar Association Web Site (`http://www.dcbar.org`)

- Legal Websites

  `www.vls.law.vill.edu/compass/`—Villanova University Internet Legal Research Compass.

  `www.infoctr.edu`—Information Center for the Downtown Campus of the Illinois Institute of Technology.

- US CFR Access—GPO Gate (`http://www.gpo.ucop.edu/search/cfr.html`)

WESTLAW

WestLaw does a better job than LEXIS of saving downloaded materials, allowing materials to be saved in a variety of native word processing formats such as those of WordPerfect and Microsoft Word. LEXIS saves files to generic text files (ASCII), which most word processors can read, but which lose formatting codes and contain "hard" carriage returns at the ends of the lines. Most word processing programs will not find a multi-word search where the words are divided by a hard carriage return. WestLaw's native word processing files do not suffer from this problem, since they contain "soft" carriage returns.

LEXIS

LEXIS often contains more research materials for a search than WestLaw does, in part because it is older. The gap is also due to WestLaw's initial focus on making available electronically many of the materials that West Publishing already published on paper. This gap may be shrinking, however, since WestLaw has been widening and deepening its coverage by adding more material and by going further back in time.

One area where LEXIS shines is in its news source, NEXIS. A parallel search in both LEXIS and NEXIS is useful, since newspaper stories quite often contain important facts and information which, due to reasons of decorum, relevance, or law, never get into published case-law opinions. Sometimes the most obscure bit of information can give the lawyer just the insight or angle needed to see a winning argument or to bolster a defense. WestLaw and LEXIS allow more detailed searches than most Internet search engines. The connective *within*, which finds occurrences of one word "within" a specified number of words or paragraphs of another, is especially valuable. With WestLaw and LEXIS/NEXIS, a researcher may recover several hundred pages of current and specifically relevant material. In essence, researchers can create personalized "casebooks" of material tightly focused on their own subject matter. For example, a researcher who wants to learn about the law of selling a doughnut shop franchise can find cases, news stories, statutes, similar fact patterns, even pricing information, to provide the researcher with a veritable "Doughnut Law Review" research casebook.

Computerized Applications

WORD PROCESSING

Many law firms use WordPerfect because of its "Reveal Codes" feature that displays text-formatting codes. Even lawyers who do not do all their own word processing are often familiar with Reveal Codes, and will use this feature in revising documents. Legal documents tend to have very complex and exacting formatting. Often, the rules for document formatting are determined by a Court, or by *The Bluebook: A Uniform System of Citation* (`http://www.legalbluebook.com`). To obey these rules, lawyers like to see precisely which formatting codes are applied, where, and in what order.

The WordPerfect Legal Edition includes an even better file compare tool than the standard edition. The Legal Edition also includes HotDocs and Amicus Attorney, described below, plus CiteLink 1.0. CiteLink finds legal citations in documents, automatically marks them, and then generates a Table of Authorities, with internal page number hyperlinks to each citation. A Table of Authorities is an alphabetical list preceding a legal brief which shows the cases and statutes cited in the document as authority for its arguments, followed by the page numbers upon which each case or statute appears. CiteLink automatically sorts the citations into standard categories, such as Federal and State Cases, Statutes, and Rules and Regulations.

Most appellate courts require Tables of Authorities to accompany legal briefs. The Table helps a court quickly find and focus upon the contrasting arguments that each party in a case has made with regard to a particular legal precedent. Creating such a table by hand is a painstaking task. Even more so than for initial compilation, computers are useful in revising an existing Table of Authorities after a brief has been revised, thus altering the page numbers upon which each citation falls.

CiteLink offers the advantage of scanning the document, automatically marking all the citations, deleting the old Table of Authorities, and creating a new one, each time the program is run. CiteLink also supports a feature whereby it can create hyperlinks from each citation in the document to the full text of the corresponding source authority on WestDoc or WestLaw. The user merely need "click" on that hyperlink to have the source document appear on the user's Web browser.

The WordPerfect spelling checker (*q.v.*) includes the full lexicon from *Black's Law Dictionary*—the recognized standard for accurate, complete, and current legal definitions. Over 14,000 legal terms, abbreviations and common cases help users improve accuracy and minimize errors in documents.

DISCOVERY

Law is a battle fought with paper. Often the victory goes to whichever side has used the discovery process more effectively and has better organized the results. In the US system of justice, where "trial by surprise" is not in favor, court rules of discovery mandate that both sides must disclose relevant evidence sought by the other.

One might think that computer technology could be most useful when the discovery process must be concluded as quickly as possible. Ironically, however, most litigators find that working with boxes of photocopied paper documents is still faster for urgent document production. But when litigation is less urgent, many law firms are finding great benefits in using optical scanners to record electronically the many documents collected during discovery.

Large law firms needing to coordinate people in different locations, who are working on the same large document production, are turning to products such as Bowne JFS Software Systems' litigation software (*see* `http://www.jfsnet.com`). JFS Litigator's Notebook, JFS JazzNotes, and JFS Docket Station are programs that give litigation teams the ability to organize and share their documents, images and calendars, while focusing on communication, collaboration, and security.

JFS Litigator's Notebook became a virtual litigation workgroup standard by combining document imaging capabilities with Lotus Notes workgroup database replication. The Notebook is an electronic case notebook containing key information such as discovery document images, chronologies, testimony, witness information, and a lawyer's own notes and memos. Information is organized into electronic "ring binders." The Notebook can be shared with members of a litigation team, with the client, outside counsel, co-counsel, and expert witnesses, wherever they are. Each location has its own copy of the Notebook, and all those copies automatically "talk" to each other, exchanging updates. The Notebook can be searched in all the standard ways.

This product's strength is the collaboration wherein each litigation team member can assist in building the case. Team members place documents, testimony, or information from other databases into binders. They highlight key passages of materials and attach notes to highlight problems or explain their value in helping or hurting an issue in the case.

JFS JazzNotes enables users to share electronically marked-up images of documents. Users can use electronic colored markup pens, for example, to draw circles around critical information and use electronic colored highlighters to highlight important paragraphs. Users can attach electronic "sticky notes" to documents which, unlike real sticky notes, don't fall off. JazzNotes will automatically share each team member's markups with other team members the next time their two copies of the Notebook communicate.

Concordance (`http://www.dataflight.com`) by Dataflight Software, Inc., is a high-speed, full-text database manager which works in conjunction with JFS Litigator's Notebook to search massive document productions. It has a powerful search engine allowing attorneys to retrieve records with English-like queries. The program can search up to 16 databases, each holding up to two million 2,000-page documents. Concordance's report writer allows attorneys to generate the most common reports quickly, while enabling technical staff to create more complex reports.

Summation (http://www.summation.com), by Summation Legal Technologies, Inc., is a transcript and document management program that allows lawyers to review evidence, spot case-breaking combinations of evidence that might otherwise go unnoticed, and call up bar-coded documents at trial (*see* UNIVERSAL PRODUCT CODE). Summation is regularly used by lawyers in cases with over a million document pages to perform very fast searches and then quickly zoom from search results to outline to testimonial or documentary evidence in full context. On-screen redaction and Bates-stamp numbering of document images provide a complete online solution for production of documents. (Bates numbers are assigned to all documents produced by discovery to facilitate later reference.) Some firms which perform scanning and coding services and can deliver "JFS Notebook-ready" databases are Aspen Systems Corporation, CACI, Quorum, Rust, and TechLaw.

It is generally necessary to create an index of the documents which have been produced by both parties, whether or not the document production uses image scanning. The index makes it possible to locate particular desired documents or pages from among thousands. Generally, an index will list the Bates number range identifying these pages, the date of the document, the author and recipient(s) if any, and a general description of the document.

REDACTING

Often documents sought for production under a subpoena or discovery request cannot be produced without revealing a privileged matter. When entire documents are privileged, they are generally pulled out of the main production, separately numbered, and a Privilege Log provided to the opposing party, one that includes a brief description of each privileged document and a statement of the privilege under which it is claimed. Many documents, however, merely contain a brief sentence, paragraph, or marginal notation that may contain privileged information, while the main document itself is fully subject to production. In these situations, just the privileged material is removed and replaced with the notation "Redacted." Document redaction is a laborious and error-prone task that benefits from automation.

Programs such as JFS JazzNotes handle the redaction process in one simple step. The lawyer uses an electronic highlighting pen to overwrite sections of the document image. Annotations do not change the stored imaged; they are saved in a separate database and are superimposed over the image when the page is viewed. Each redaction can have its own level of annotation security allowing access to all, specified, or author-only viewers. When a JazzNotes Notebook is "replicated," images, annotations, and security levels are shared. All redactions can be turned on or off, depending upon the Lotus Notes security levels of the author who placed the redaction and the reader attempting to view, print, or alter the redaction.

LEGAL DRAFTING PROGRAMS

All lawyers develop collections of skeleton documents containing boilerplate language that can be extracted and used with new documents. Some programs, such as HotDocs, are designed to help attorneys develop these collections of document snippets. HotDocs, which may be used with the WordPerfect Legal Edition, is a document assembly tool designed to reduce the time spent preparing repetitive, routine documents. Users may create their own templates or use predefined ones. Templates can be automatically filled with information stored in a Corel Amicus Attorney database.

The DL (Drafting Library) programs, by Attorneys' Computer Network, Inc., is intended to be used by attorneys (rather than laypeople) to compose legal documents reflecting the laws and practice of a specific State. Example libraries include: Wills, Inter Vivos Trusts, Limited Liability Companies, Tenant Evictions, Divorces, and Foreclosures.

Kiplinger Home Legal Advisor is designed to assist laypeople in understanding and drafting documents. It provides over 60 templates that the user can transform into professional legal documents, complete with online guidance, explanations, examples, and options. It includes draft contracts and information on topics such as Employment Issues; the Americans with Disabilities Act (ADA); COBRA—Group Health Care Benefits; and many others. These programs can help clients focus on the legal issues in their situations, and direct their attention to gathering information that an attorney will need to represent the client properly.

Legal software for laypeople is easily misused. Sometimes, for example, drafters use the software to make repeated revisions to a Will without following statutory requirements needed to make such changes effective. Some states have begun taking a closer look at self-help legal software. The Texas Supreme Court Unauthorized Practice of Law Committee recently scheduled hearings to determine whether the sale of Nolo Press books and software in the state of Texas constitutes the unauthorized practice of law (UPL). Information about this issue can be found at `http://www.nolo.com/Texas/`.

EMAIL

Electronic mail (email—*q.v.*) is a valuable means of communication for busy lawyers who often work in large geographically diverse teams. Lawyers need to be especially concerned that they do not reveal client confidences or attorney work product when sending documents via email. An email message, unlike a fax call, is relayed through many intermediate network nodes before it reaches the intended recipients. This creates opportunities for the message to be intercepted and read by an unauthorized recipient. Lawyers often encrypt particularly sensitive information that they send by email. Email is generally discoverable in litigation, and there have already been lawsuits decided primarily upon email evidence.

Lawyers might arguably be able to satisfy their requirements for confidentiality by using the encryption built into word processing programs, but such protection is often very weak. Many commercial and shareware programs can quickly strip off the encryption provided by those programs. One can obtain a much higher degree of encryption at no greater effort simply by using the encryption built into standard compression/decompression programs such as PKZip or WinZip. If the chosen password (*q.v.*) is long enough, say 32 characters or more, then most trial-and-error programs would need months or years to "crack" the file on a typical PC.

Stronger dual-key encryption (*see* CRYPTOGRAPHY, COMPUTERS IN) may be desired by the those who are concerned not merely with the present capabilities of PCs, but with more powerful government mainframe (*q.v.*) computers or future personal computers. The most popular strong encryption program is Pretty Good Privacy (*q.v.*). Lawyers should be aware, however, that when sending documents using very strong encryption to offices outside the US, Department of Commerce restrictions may prohibit exportation of the software that the recipient would need to decrypt that message.

Summary

As time progresses, more and more legal documents will exist primarily as electronic records. Since the practice of law is so intimately bound to the collection, classification, transformation, and presentation of words, the efficiency and effectiveness of attorneys and jurists will continue to advance in proportion to the development of new computer tools that deal with words, both oral and written. And though it will be difficult to prove, it can be hoped that the increased degree of automation will also result in a concomitant increase in justice.

Bibliography

1995. Woodbury, C. *Becoming Computer-Literate: A Plain-English Guide for Lawyers and Other Legal Professionals.* Chicago: American Bar Association.
1997. Hance, O., and Balz, S. D. *Business & Law on the Internet.* New York: McGraw-Hill.
1997. Jacobsen, P. S. *Net Law: How Lawyers Use the Internet.* Cambridge, MA: O'Reilly & Associates.
1997. Evans, J., and Renauer, A. *Law on the Net.* Berkeley, CA: Nolo Press.
1998. Blackman, J. D., and Jank, D. *The Internet Fact Finder for Lawyers: How to Find Anything on the Net.* Chicago: American Bar Association.
1999. Piacente, A. J. *Computer Assisted Legal Research: A Guide to Lexis, Nexis, & WestLaw.* Chicago: Montag Multimedia Publishing Co.

Mark Paley

LEGAL ASPECTS OF COMPUTING

For articles on related subjects *see* COMPUTER CRIME; ELECTRONIC FUNDS TRANSFER; LEGAL APPLICATIONS; LEGAL ISSUES OF THE INTERNET; LEGAL PROTECTION OF SOFTWARE; and PRIVACY, COMPUTERS AND.

Introduction

Computer law, as an identifiable legal practice, began in the 1960s. However, the legal landscape remained shrouded in uncertainty, despite a heavy volume of computer-related cases reaching the courts, until the 1990s. The principal causes of uncertainty were the rapidly evolving and changing nature of the technology and the creativity needed to fit computer law into traditional legal practices, such as copyright and trade secret law. Computer law is now an integral part of the law school curriculum, and of law firm and house counsel practice. However, technological innovations continue to occur, and as new technology is marketed and used, the law must adapt to new and complex factual circumstances. The Internet is the most recent example (*see* LEGAL ISSUES OF THE INTERNET).

Contracts

A *contract* is a promise or agreement that the courts are willing to enforce. A contract requires an offer, an acceptance, and consideration. *Consideration* is some form of duty or obligation that a party voluntarily assumes.

Several kinds of contract are commonly employed in the computer industry. These include purchase agreements of equipment and software, licenses of all sorts, software development contracts, and maintenance agreements, to mention but a few. The most important contract in computing is the software license.

A license is a transfer of rights (e.g. the right to use, the right to sublicense), rather than the transfer of ownership. Normally in commercial transactions a sale occurs when A transfers ownership of item T to B in return for payment. If A transfers the right to use item T under specified contract terms to B in return for payment, a sale has not occurred and A remains the owner of item T and all of the intellectual property rights in item T.

Also, in commercial transactions item T is normally tangible. If item T is tangible (i.e. if it is goods), then in the USA the transaction is covered by Article 2 of the Uniform Commercial Code (UCC). Article 2 covers the sale of goods; it does not apply to the sale of services. The UCC has been adopted in every state except Louisiana.

For many years, the courts questioned whether the UCC applied to software transactions because such contracts do not involve either a sale or tangible goods. Because licenses and leases confer limited rights defined by the contract, rather than conveying full ownership rights, they are not contracts for sale. A software development contract is a contract for services, even though the end product belongs to the buyer. With the advent of the personal computer and the mass marketing of software, the courts generally have applied UCC principles to software products and even to some custom software, i.e. software that is produced, through the rendering of services, for a specific client.

While software licenses between business entities are generally negotiated and executed by the parties, licenses to consumers are governed by the "shrink-wrap" license. In these transactions, consumer licensees do not really indicate their consent to the contract terms by signing on the dotted line. Are the contract terms enforceable when the licensee may not have read the terms and has not indicated consent? While there has been a fair amount of litigation on the issue, there is not yet a definitive answer.

Another important characteristic of computer contracts is the remedies provided by the industry. If there is breach of contract, a court will normally award various kinds of damages; the most important damages are actual and consequential. *Actual damages* are those losses that can be calculated precisely and that are directly caused by the defendant's wrongful action. *Consequential damages* are losses that are less directly caused by the wrongful action.

Suppliers of software and hardware have provided few guarantees for their products; during the early years of the industry, they would not even warrant that the software would do anything at all, or that the hardware would do more than pass the vendor's own self-defined tests. Since hardware operations are entirely controlled by system software, a product guarantee is a guarantee that the software will operate "satisfactorily." While colossal strides have been made in chip development, software engineering (*q.v.*) remains an expensive, labor-intensive process that still lacks a methodology to prove software correct. Even rigorously tested programs are often released with programming errors (i.e. bugs—*q.v.*).

Some limited warranties are now provided by most sellers. However, sellers and licensors of computer-related products still usually include disclaimer of warranty and limitation of remedy clauses in their contracts, including provisions to limit the amount of actual damages that an aggrieved buyer may recover. Almost all computer-related contracts still disclaim any liability for consequential damages because of the open-ended nature of such damages and the large economic losses that can stem from a major computer failure. Such disclaimers and limitations are usually upheld by the courts, which assume that the parties to a contract understood and bargained for the provisions. Many contracts also provide that a dispute stemming from the contract be brought to an arbitrator rather than to a court of law.

Torts

A *tort* is an act, other than a breach of contract, by which one party injures another and because of which the injured party can seek a personal remedy in a court of law. A crime is an act forbidden by statute and for the commission of which the state may punish the actor. An act can, but need not, be both a tort and a crime. Computer crimes are discussed later in this article.

As noted above under Contracts, the courts generally enforce the disclaimers and limitations of liability contained in computer contracts. If a computer system failed to operate satisfactorily, a licensee might look to the law of torts to provide a fair remedy. *Negligence* is a tort involving a breach of a duty that causes injury to someone. Whether a duty of care has been breached depends on the standard of care to which the actor must be held. Generally, the standard is what a reasonable, prudent person would have done under the circumstances.

However, there are as yet few standards in the computer industry to guide courts concerning what to expect from a reasonable, prudent programmer.

Computer professionals are not required to be licensed, and there are no minimum educational qualifications to set oneself up as a programmer (*q.v.*), systems analyst (*q.v.*), or database manager. Given the uncertainties inherent in large-scale hardware and software design, not to mention the complex interaction between the hardware and software components of a computer system, proving that a hardware or software developer did not exercise an appropriate degree of care, or even showing that the developer made an error and that it was that error that led to the alleged injury, is a formidable task. As a result, actions for negligence against the industry rarely have been successful.

The damage that can stem from malfunction of a mainframe (*q.v.*) or a network (*q.v.*) is so great that it can be catastrophic. The legal mechanism applied by courts when there is physical injury, not just economic loss, is *strict liability in tort*. In an action in strict liability in tort, recovery is based on proving that the product had a defect that made it unreasonably dangerous, that the defect caused the injuries, that the defendant is engaged in the business of selling such products, and that the product was expected to and did reach the consumer without substantial change to the condition in which it was sold. If these facts are established, a manufacturer is liable even if it used all possible care in the design and manufacture of the product. Strict liability generally provides recovery for physical injuries, not economic losses. Since losses from computer failures are almost exclusively economic, the doctrine of strict liability has not been applied to the computer industry.

Defamation is a wrongful injury to a person's reputation. To maintain this action, a plaintiff must prove the publication of a defamatory communication of fact concerning the plaintiff, and that the person to whom the communication was addressed understood that it was defamatory and concerned the plaintiff. Also required is proof that the communication was false, that the defendant was negligent or guilty of fault, and that the defamatory statement actually harmed the plaintiff. The publication necessary for defamation is communication to a third party. To protect the press, the courts have placed additional burdens on plaintiffs who are public figures or where the defamation concerns a matter of public concern. Computers raise questions with regard to defamation that are still unanswered. Examples of such questions include: do online database services, electronic bulletin boards (*q.v.*), or posted Web pages have the status of the press in terms of what a plaintiff must prove to show defamation? Does publication occur, and, if so, who should be held liable if defamatory information is placed in mass storage (*q.v.*) and is accessed by a third party, even without authorization?

The factors a court might consider are: (1) computers store enormous amounts of data for indefinite lengths of time, so stale or incorrect information can be disseminated more widely and for longer periods of time than if the same information had merely been published in a newspaper; and (2) the computer system's owner could be found to be at fault for failing to update files, failing to check entered data for accuracy and completeness, or having security so inadequate that it allowed unauthorized persons to access supposedly confidential and privileged information. Stale or incomplete data may convey, for example, an inaccurate impression about a person or may be highly personal in nature.

The torts of fraud or negligent misrepresentation could arise through reliance on misleading estimates of a customer's needs or of product performance. Buyers sometimes allege fraud and negligence as part of a breach of contract action in order to try to avoid the seller-protective restrictions in the contract. However, as noted, courts are generally unwilling to see a contract action transformed into an action in tort.

Protection of Intellectual Property

Although legal protection of intellectual property is a critical area of computer-related law, it is covered elsewhere, so we touch on it only briefly here (*see* LEGAL PROTECTION OF SOFTWARE).

The law protects intellectual property by, in effect, giving the originator of the property a monopoly on rights to that property, subject to limitations that vary according to the type of property protected and the type of protection selected. The four principal means for protecting computer programs in the USA are *copyrights* and *patents* (federal law), and *trade secrets* and *trademarks* (state and federal law). To protect the developer's rights in chips, the Semiconductor Chip Protection Act was enacted in 1984. Other mechanisms for protection are found in the common law of unfair competition, and various aspects of federal and state antitrust law.

The most important domestic (and international) protection for computer programs is copyright law. The Copyright Act provides that the subject matter of copyright is original works of authorship fixed in any tangible medium of expression, now known or later developed, from which they can be perceived, reproduced, or otherwise communicated, either directly or with the aid of a machine or device (§102(a)). The Copyright Act makes it clear that computer programs are original works of authorship.

An author must make some original contribution to gain a copyright in a work. Copyright protection accrues automatically to the author once the original work is created, even if the work is not registered with the Copyright Office and, with recent changes in the law, even if no notice of copyright is affixed to the work.

A copyright confers certain rights on the author, among them the right to make copies of and prepare derivative works from the copyrighted work, as well as to distribute copies of the copyrighted work to the public. Software licensees are permitted by law to make at least one backup copy as well as to modify the software, as long as the modification is an essential step in using that software.

The Copyright Act grants certain rights to owners of copies of copyrighted works; however, a licensee does not necessarily own a copy of the software. A licensee gains only such rights in the software as the license confers, and the copyright owner may claim retention of ownership of all copies of the software. Licenses can also require the licensee to preserve the confidentiality of any source code provided under the license, forbid the licensee from disassembling machine code (*see* ASSEMBLER), and prescribe penalties if the licensee breaches these conditions.

Literal copying of software code is clearly a copyright infringement. However, alleged infringers almost always do nonliteral copying, resulting in software that may have the same structure, sequence, and organization as the protected software, or may have its look and feel. However, if a work is written independently of another work, there may be no infringement even if the works are nearly identical.

The Copyright Act provides that "[i]n no case does copyright protection ... extend to any idea, procedure, process, system, method of operation, concept, principle, or discovery, regardless of the form in which it is described, explained, illustrated, or embodied in such work." Thus, the mathematical algorithms (*q.v.*) and general ideas that underlie a program are not copyrightable. Ideas are not copyrightable; only the expression of an idea is copyrightable.

The scope of copyright protection for software programs has been heavily litigated and the courts have come to recognize certain externalities that limit the scope of copyright protection. There is also reason to believe that one can legitimately reverse engineer another program to determine the underlying unprotectable ideas and algorithms embodied in that program and then use those ideas and algorithms in building a competing program.

Patents represent a much stronger form of legal protection; they grant the patent holder a legal monopoly on the patented invention. However, patents are much more time-consuming and expensive to obtain than copyrights. Computer-related inventions are usually patented either as machines or processes. Patents have been issued for computer hardware for many years. Whether software is patentable has been a matter of dispute. Ideas, scientific principles and laws of nature, mathematical formulas, and mental processes are not patentable. After many years of litigation, the courts have held that software satisfying statutory criteria can be patented.

To be patentable, an invention must be useful, novel, and unobvious. To be novel, the invention must not be found in the prior art existing at the time it was invented. To be unobvious, the invention must not have been obvious to someone skilled in the prior art at the time of the invention, even if the invention itself had not actually yet been created. Infringement will be found if someone else creates an equivalent invention, even if done independently and with no knowledge of the patented invention. Inventors must fully disclose the invention by filing a description of the invention so complete that someone knowledgeable in the art would be able to build one and would understand how it works.

Trade secrecy was historically the primary mechanism for the protection of intellectual property and is used concurrently with copyright protection. Trade secret law protects information of almost any kind that is used by a particular business and that provides it an opportunity to obtain an advantage over competitors who do not have the information. No precise definition of a trade secret is possible, and even the law of trade secrecy varies from one state to another. In determining whether certain information is a trade secret of the party that has it, a court will consider various factors—e.g. the extent of the measures taken by the owner of the information to keep it secret and limit the scope of those who know it, and the secret's commercial value to the owner.

Trade secrets can be legally obtained—e.g. through careless disclosure by the owner, and by reverse engineering, including disassembling machine language code, although the latter method may be forbidden by copyright law or the terms of a license. A competitor, however, cannot hire away employees who have been entrusted with a trade secret in order to learn it because employees who gain trade secrets in the course of their employment have a duty in law to keep such secrets confidential, even when they go to work for another employer, at least as long as the information remains a trade secret.

With the mass marketing of computer products, trademark protection has grown in importance. Companies principally look to federal law to protect registered trademarks from infringement and dilution. The list of trademarked items at the front of this Encyclopedia has grown substantially from that in the previous edition.

Evidence

Because computer-generated and stored information may be required in litigation, system managers must be sensitive to the rules of evidence, lest they find the credibility or admissibility of their information successfully attacked by an adverse party. In order to introduce computer-generated data into evidence, a party must first show that the data is what they claim to be (e.g. records showing sales in September), and that there is sufficient reason to believe that the data is sufficiently reliable to warrant its consideration by the court. An expert might testify to the reliability of the computer system used and the adequacy of the data processing (q.v.) procedures. If the system consistently failed, or the procedures often failed or yielded inaccurate results, the opposing party will be able to attack the credibility of the data even if the court chooses to admit it.

Reports generated by a party specifically in anticipation of litigation are inadmissible because they are inherently suspect as being self-serving, although the data on which they are based may be admissible. When computer-stored data contains statements by someone other than the person testifying at trial, and is produced at trial to assert the truth of the data itself, it is *hearsay evidence*. Hearsay is defined as a statement, other than the one made by the declarant while testifying at the trial or hearing, offered in evidence to prove the truth of the matter asserted.

Generally hearsay is not admissible. However, there are many exceptions to this rule. The business records exception is the one most widely used for computer-generated data. To be admissible under the business records exception, the data must have been kept in the course of a regularly conducted business activity and entered at, or near, the time of the events that gave rise to it, from information transmitted by a person with knowledge, and it must have been the regular practice of the business to compile such data, as shown by the testimony of the custodian of the data or other knowledgeable and reliable witnesses. Computer-generated data is also subject to the *best evidence rule*. However, a computer printout of stored data is held to be an original for purposes of the rule, so there is usually no problem concerning admissibility on this score.

Computer-stored data is also generally subject to disclosure on the request of a party opponent, even if no hard copies are made. Data must be provided in a form that is comprehensible and usable, and not, for example, in a format that makes the data essentially inaccessible. The party seeking the data may be asked to pay for the costs of collecting it, or converting it to the format desired, if this represents an undue burden.

Computer Crime and Security

Threats to computer security, computer crime, and the abuse of computer systems is a rapidly growing problem in modern society. As there are disagreements as to what forms of activity qualify as computer crime, the estimates of the extent of computer crime vary widely. However, with the advent of the Internet it is generally agreed that computer-related crime has risen sharply. A number of computer abuses are punishable as traditional crimes; for example, if a programmer instructs a bank's computer to transfer money to which he or she is not entitled into a personal account, that programmer has committed theft; the fact that a computer was the instrument of the crime is irrelevant.

There have been some instances of computer abuse that were not covered by any criminal statute, but, now that the federal government and every state have computer crime statutes of one sort or another, such instances are likely to be extraordinarily rare. Federal prosecutions are generally made under the Computer Fraud and Abuse Act (enacted in 1984 and revised in 1994); however, there have been prosecutions under the federal wire fraud statute and the national stolen property statute.

Initially prosecutors and the courts were unwilling to treat computer crime seriously. According to an older American Bar Association poll, even computer professionals did not consider computer crime to be much more of a threat than shoplifting. But with the increasing visibility of computer abuse (e.g. the Internet virus of 1989 that brought down a large, sophisticated network—*see* VIRUS, COMPUTER), prosecution of computer crimes has been a high priority of both federal and state governments. The special expertise needed to commit the crime has also resulted in severer sentences.

Miscellaneous Issues

There are numerous important issues and concepts that cannot be covered in a brief article. The interested reader is advised to consult one of the references listed in the bibliography. Someone having a specific legal problem should seek the assistance of qualified counsel. We conclude by touching on several other issues that are currently in a state of flux.

TAXATION

Frequent changes in US federal tax law and the continuing stream of rulings of the Internal Revenue Service make this an unpredictable area of law. When the investment tax credit was repealed, many thought that this would bring a major restructuring and scaling back of the computer leasing market, but, to date, this has not occurred. How states tax software and hardware varies according to the state and the nature of what is being taxed—computer equipment has even been taxed as real estate. Whether software is subject to sales tax depends in many states on the degree to which it is customized or developed expressly for the customer. An additional factor is the growing importance of the industry to the economy of many states, causing them to lean toward taxation.

PRIVACY AND FIRST AMENDMENT RIGHTS

With the advent of the computer came the capability to collect, store, and manipulate vast quantities of information easily and relatively inexpensively in a manner that earlier was impractical. For example, computers have been used to match files of one government agency against files in another agency in order to catch welfare cheats and other persons suspected of criminal activities, although some commentators believe that such activity is illegal. The National Crime Information Center (NCIC) receives data from tens of thousands of law enforcement agencies which may contain errors. In 1985, the FBI admitted that at least 12,000 invalid or inaccurate reports on suspects wanted for arrest were being transmitted among the 400,000 daily responses to queries to NCIC by federal, state, and local law enforcement agencies. The harm that these inaccurate reports may cause innocent parties must be balanced against the increased probability the NCIC provides of apprehending real criminals.

In the USA the law of privacy is of fairly recent origin, having evolved in the 20th century. There are, however, various federal and state laws aimed at safeguarding the accuracy and confidentiality of databases that contain personal information or that open up certain government files to public scrutiny. Among the federal laws are the Right to Privacy Act of 1974, the Freedom of Information Act (1966, revised in 1974), the Fair Credit Reporting Act of 1996 (amended in 1999), the Bank Secrecy Act of 1970 (with later amendments), the Trade Secrets Protection Act of 1997, the Equal Credit Opportunity Act of 1976, the Right to Financial Privacy Act of 1978, and the Privacy Protection Act of 1980. The invasion of privacy is also protected as a tort. Because information and data have acquired unprecedented commercial value, the law of privacy has become even more important than in the past.

ELECTRONIC FUNDS TRANSFER

Transfers of substantial assets via computers give rise to questions of who is liable if the transfer is improperly made (e.g. if the transfer is not completed in a timely fashion, or not completed at all). Although most of the issues concerning computer-to-computer electronic funds transfer are covered by the Uniform Commercial Code, some are not. For example, checks require a signature to be honored, but there is no agreement as yet concerning how this requirement is met with many wire transfers. Computerized transfers of assets will be an important area for the development of new law.

ELECTRONIC RECORDS AND LEGAL REQUIREMENTS

The law has traditionally required the existence, and often a formal recording, of paper documents of various sorts to testify to the authenticity of certain transactions, e.g. deeds in connection with the transfer of rights in real property, and security agreements with respect to certain kinds of liens. Generally, such documents must be signed by the party making the transfer or the person liable for the debt. More and more transactions are now recorded in computer memory, and the trend may be toward electronic record-keeping and away from paper. The law must either adapt to the new technology, or else make it clear that paper is here to stay. The transient nature of even long-term mass storage may also threaten the reliability of records of transactions over a long period of time.

FUTURE ISSUES

Some of the other issues that will have to be decided in the future include the boundaries under antitrust law for monopolists (e.g. Microsoft and Intel); liability for computer-related disasters arising from the year 2000 problem (*see* Y2K PROBLEM) and euro conversion failures; ownership of intellectual property created primarily or exclusively by a computer, and liability for mistakes of expert systems (*q.v.*).

Bibliography

General
1978. Bender, D. *Computer Law.* New York: Matthew Bender. (Originally published as *Computer Law: Evidence and Procedure*; annually updated; now two volumes covering most aspects of computer law.)
1985. Gemignani, M. C. *Computer Law.* Rochester: Lawyers Cooperative Publishing Co.—Bancroft-Whitney. (With annual supplements.)
1985. Nimmer, R. *The Law of Computer Technology.* New York: Warren, Gorham & Lamont.
1989. Gemignani, M. C. *A Legal Guide to EDP Management.* Westport, CT: Quorum.

Specific Areas
1987. Kutten, L. J. *Computer Software: Protection/Liability/Law/Forms.* New York: Clark Boardman. (With annual supplements.)
1988. Arkin, S., Bohrer, B. A., Donohoe, J. P., Kasanof, R., Cuneo, D. L., Kaplan, J. M., Levander, A. J., and Sherizen, S. *Prevention and Prosecution of Computer and High Technology Crime.* New York: Matthew Bender.

1992. Roditti, E. *Computer Contracts: Negotiating and Drafting Guide.* New York: Matthew Bender. (With semi-annual updates.)

Periodicals

Computer & Online Industry Litigation Reporter. Andrews Publications, 175 Strafford Avenue, Bldg 4, Suite 140, Wayne, PA 19087.

Computer Law & Tax Report. Roditti Reports Corp., PO Box 2066, New York, NY 10021-0052.

Computer Law Monitor. Research Publications, 92 Fairway Drive, PO Box 9267, Asheville, NC 22815.

Computer Law Reporter. 1519 Connecticut Avenue NW, Washington, DC 20036.

Electronic Commerce & Law Report. Bureau of National Affairs, 1231 25th Street NW, Washington, DC 20037.

Software Law Reporter. 175 Strafford Avenue, #1, Wayne, PA 19087.

Michael Gemignani, revised by Esther Roditti

LEGAL ISSUES OF THE INTERNET

For articles on related subjects *see* COMPUTER CRIME; ELECTRONIC FUNDS TRANSFER; INTERNET; LEGAL APPLICATIONS; LEGAL ASPECTS OF COMPUTING; LEGAL PROTECTION OF SOFTWARE; PRIVACY, COMPUTERS AND; and WORLD WIDE WEB.

Introduction

In 1996 a US federal district court ruled that speech on the Internet is unqualifiedly protected from government scrutiny by the First Amendment (*American Civil Liberties Union v. Reno*). That ruling, which has become the underpinning of Internet content freedom, was unanimously affirmed by the US Supreme Court in 1997 (96-511), which relied on and quoted extensively from the district court's fact-finding. The definition of the Internet relied upon by the court was in part the following:

> The Internet is not a physical or tangible entity, but rather a giant network which interconnects innumerable smaller groups of linked computer networks. It is thus a network of networks. . . .

> The resulting whole is a decentralized, global medium of communications—or "cyberspace" (*q.v.*)—that links people, institutions, corporations, and governments around the world. The Internet is an international system. This communications medium allows any of the literally tens of millions of people with access to the Internet to exchange information.

> No single entity—academic, corporate, governmental, or non-profit—administers the Internet. It exists and functions as a result of the fact that hundreds of thousands of separate operators of computers and computer networks independently decided to use

common data transfer protocols (*q.v.*) to exchange communications and information with other computers. . . . There is no centralized storage location, control point, or communications channel for the Internet, and it would not be technically feasible for a single entity to control all of the information conveyed on the Internet.

However, while no single organization owns or controls the Internet *in toto*, components are owned. The data communications and voice-grade lines that form the backbone of the Internet are owned by common carriers, such as AT&T, Sprint, and MCI. Companies such as IBM and Digital Equipment Corporation (*q.v.*), and major universities (often funded by governments) both in the USA and abroad, own the mainframe (*q.v.*) computers that form the nodes along the backbone. And then there are the Internet service providers (ISPs) that own the servers that provide access to commercial and private users. Thus, the Internet *per se* is not owned by one entity. While telecommunications carriers in the USA are regulated by the Federal Communications Commission, the FCC has repeatedly stated that ISPs will not be regulated.

With the explosive growth in Internet traffic, *cyber law*, a new and not yet developed body of law, has emerged. In some critical areas, such as copyright and electronic commerce (*q.v.*), the law is sparse and exposure uncertain. Some Internet-specific federal and state legislation has been enacted, but most laws have not yet been revised or interpreted by courts as applicable to Internet transactions. Also, while it is generally accepted that the Internet will play a major role in the commerce of the next century, it is uncertain what forms Internet commerce will take. Merchants, financial institutions, and consumers all still have substantial concerns about the security of online payments (US encryption policy remains unsettled), the authenticity of transactions, and the privacy of information.

Privacy

Internet growth depends in part upon achieving privacy and security through technology and law. At present, the Internet is not a secure medium over which to communicate financial and other information regarded by the sender or other persons as confidential or private. Thus it is not advisable to use the Internet to send trade-secret information or attorney–client privileged communications that are not encoded.

Online communications and information are most vulnerable to unauthorized access by government, ISPs, and Website providers. For law enforcement (or "snooping") purposes, government may wish to monitor online communications, access ISP-stored or encrypted data, or trace communications trails and habits. For marketing and other for-profit enterprises, ISPs may collect and disclose subscriber profile data, intercept and disclose communications, or access and disclose stored communications. For similar reasons, Website providers may collect and disclose user data, such as profiles or email addresses, or store and disclose server communications. Other vulnerabilities include criminal and hacker (*q.v.*) activities, which are on the rise (*see* COMPUTER CRIME).

The privacy of online communications in the USA is protected by the Electronic Communications Privacy Act of 1986. The ECPA expands the anti-wiretapping federal statute that prohibited government eavesdropping of telephone conversations without the consent of the parties to the conversation. Under the wiretap law, and now under the ECPA, government agents are required to obtain a warrant from the courts in order to intercept lawfully telephone and electronic communications. The ECPA is a lengthy and complex statute containing exceptions and providing different degrees of privacy depending on the circumstances. Basically, the Act

1. covers digital communications (text and images) as well as voice communications;

2. prohibits both private and governmental eavesdropping;

3. covers both "electronic communications" and "electronic communication systems," including electronic storage systems;

4. makes punishable as a federal felony the intentional interception, intentional disclosure, or intentional use of the contents of a message "without authorization"; and

5. provides for civil remedies.

The ECPA covers both interception and disclosure of electronic communications, and the accessing of stored communications or the disclosure of the contents of such communications. Protection is strongest for communications in transit between users, particularly voice messages on public communication systems.

Less protection is provided for voice and non-voice messages in electronic storage. The ECPA also contains exceptions to the prohibitions on intercepting and accessing. These are: if one of the parties to the communication has given prior consent to the interception, disclosure, or use of the interception; and if the service provider is engaged in an activity necessary to the rendition of services or the protection of the rights or property of the provider of that service. There are

as of 1999 no court decisions interpreting the provider exception. Also, a private employer acting within its own facilities may intercept, disclose, or use the communications of employees made on an internal onsite computer system, provided the activity is necessary and incidental to the rendition of services or to protect the rights or property of the employer provider.

Since the passage of the ECPA, the Act has been pled in several cases. The decisions have generally held that the seizure of email stored in a computer by the police under a valid search warrant is not an illegal search and seizure under the Fourth Amendment, nor a violation of the ECPA. On the other hand, when the Navy obtained subscriber information from America Online about a naval officer without first obtaining the required court order and warrant, the court held that the Navy was in probable violation of the ECPA. The court commented that in these days of "big brother," where through technology the privacy interests of individuals are being ignored or marginalized, it is imperative that laws explicitly protecting these rights be strictly observed.

Domain Name Disputes

The starting point in the use of the Internet for informational and commercial purposes is to obtain a domain name and to create a Website on the World Wide Web. Domain names are registered on a first-come, first-served basis and an applicant is assigned a requested name if the name has not been previously registered. These procedures have led to disputes with trademark owners whose marks are registered in federal and/or state trademark offices.

Cyber pirates is the name given to persons who have registered hundreds of domain names of well-known trademarks (e.g. Playboy) with the intent of selling the name back to the trademark owner or the company bearing the trade name. Cyberpiracy is an international problem. Many of the trademark owners whose marks have been misused have worldwide operations; cyberpiracy has occurred in Europe as well as the USA; and some cyber pirates have registered their domain names outside the USA. The courts have unequivocally held that cyberpiracy is a violation of the Federal Trademark Dilution Act of 1995.

A particularly thorny problem for the business and legal communities has been the impact of domain names on trademarks. When a trademark is used without the owner's consent as a domain name, consumers have been misled as to the source of the product or service offered on the Internet, and trademark owners have not been able to protect their rights without expensive litigation. Also, domain name registrants in faraway places are able to infringe trademark rights with no convenient jurisdiction available to the trademark owner to enforce a judgment protecting those rights.

These problems are widely recognized, but remain unresolved. Trademark owners continue to sue when they believe their trademarks have been infringed or diluted under trademark law. Increasingly, owners of domain names are also seeking to register their domain name or Website URL (e.g. Amazon.com) as a trademark with the Patent and Trademark Office.

Jurisdiction Issues

Website content, whether commercial advertising and solicitation or a friendly home page, is accessible to Internet users worldwide. These users may reside in a "foreign" jurisdiction, that is, in a state of the USA or in a country that is not the resident jurisdiction of the Web page owner or the Web page host server. It may also not be a jurisdiction in which the Website owner would otherwise be physically present for jurisdictional purposes, as by maintaining a facility in the foreign jurisdiction. While not physically present, all Websites are electronically present wherever the site is accessed, browsed, or downloaded. Also, any alleged injury generally occurs in the user's jurisdiction.

Novel civil jurisdictional issues have arisen with which the courts are grappling. The central issue is identifying the elements, in addition to Website access, that create sufficient contact(s) within the user's forum state to permit the exercise of personal jurisdiction over a Website owner who has no physical presence in the forum state.

A pattern is emerging in which traditional jurisdictional principles of law have been applied by the courts to cyberspace issues. As expressed by one court—"the likelihood that personal jurisdiction can be constitutionally exercised is directly proportionate to the nature and quality of commercial activity that an entity conducts over the Internet." The reported decisions to date in which the facts included online advertising and solicitation can be categorized on a sliding scale from a finding of jurisdiction to a probable finding of no jurisdiction:

1. Completed Sales—conducting online business with forum consumers, coupled with a contractual element.

2. Advertising and Solicitation Contacts—promoting available or prospective services or goods, and/or providing a toll-free phone or fax number to facilitate commerce, and/or providing an interactive Website enabling forum residents to exchange information with the host computer and/or purchasing services or goods.

3. Passive Website Content—providing information via the Internet or through email.

Not yet clear with regard to jurisdiction is the impact of online interactivity, such as postings to mailing lists, chat rooms (*see* ONLINE CONVERSATION), or Usenet; a notice that advertising and solicitation are directed only to local residents; an Internet "click-wrap" agreement; or a good-faith effort to screen out Web browsers.

Criminal Liability

Pornography is a major Internet business. It is therefore not surprising that an early case addressed the applicability of the federal law making it a crime to transport knowingly obscene material in interstate and foreign commerce. In *U.S. v. Thomas*, the criminal conviction of the Thomases was affirmed by the appellate court for the knowing transmission of images from California, where they were lawful, to Tennessee, where the same images were obscene. Venue in Tennessee was found proper because the government may prosecute obscenity in any federal district court into which the images are sent. And the community standards of Tennessee, the area where the obscene materials were sent, were held applicable.

However, pornography that is not obscene has been held by the US Supreme Court to be constitutionally protected free speech under the First Amendment. The Court so ruled in a decision holding that portions of the Communications Decency Act (which made it a crime to send or display to a minor sexually offensive and indecent messages) are an unconstitutionally vague restriction. The restrictions of the Child Pornography Prevention Act, which was subsequently reviewed by a federal circuit court in a pre-enforcement constitutional challenge, were found to be content neutral and constitutional because the Act was designed to prevent the secondary effects of child pornography, such as exploitation, degradation, and molestation of children.

There are no statutory prohibitions or restrictions on the selling of alcohol or cigarettes on the Internet, but the Federal Wire Communications Act prohibits the interstate or foreign transmission of betting information by a person in the business of wagering. There are also numerous state and local laws prohibiting or restricting gambling; Minnesota has successfully prosecuted the Nevada owner of an Internet advertisement for wagering services.

Computer crime generally is on the rise. The FBI and the Federal Trade Commission investigate complaints of crime and fraudulent misrepresentation on the Internet.

Bibliography

1999. Lipschultz, J. *Free Expression in the Age of the Internet: Social and Legal Boundaries.* Boulder, CO: Westview Press.

Esther Roditti

LEGAL PROTECTION OF SOFTWARE

For articles on related subjects *see* FREE SOFTWARE FOUNDATION; LEGAL APPLICATIONS; LEGAL ASPECTS OF COMPUTING; and LEGAL ISSUES OF THE INTERNET.

Computer software is expensive to develop and maintain. It has high monetary value to its owners, both because it can give them a competitive advantage when used internally to do tasks more cheaply or quickly and because it can be licensed for use by others. Software, however, is very easy to copy at a trivial cost and is, therefore, very susceptible to pirating. Because of its value and its vulnerability to misappropriation, ownership interests in software must be protected.

For the purpose of legal protection, software is categorized as *intellectual property*. Intellectual property is a form of intangible personal property comprised of ideas, processes, information, or symbols. Intangible personal property contrasts with tangible personal property, such as hardware or supplies, and real property, such as office buildings and other structures affixed to the land. Intellectual property is protected in one of five principal ways: by patent, copyright, trade secret, trademark, or contract.

Patent

In the USA, patent protection is a federal statutory right that gives an inventor or his or her assignee exclusive rights to deny others the right to make, use, or sell the patented invention throughout the USA or to import the invention into the USA beginning on the date the patent is issued for a period of 20 years from the date of filing of the application for patent.

To be patentable, inventions must meet several tests. They must be of statutory subject matter—physical methods, apparatus, compositions of matter, devices and improvements—but not mere ideas. Further, they must be new, useful, and not obvious. They must be described in a properly filed and prosecuted patent application.

The two statutory subject matter categories that are generally applied to patent claims involving computer programs are *process* (or method) and *machine* (or apparatus). In an appropriate case, a program-related invention might also be claimed as an article of manufacture.

The courts have held that a mathematical algorithm is like a law of nature (which is not patentable subject matter) and has evolved a two-step process for determining whether a computer program is patentable subject matter. First, does the claim recite such an algorithm, and, if so, does it in its entirely wholly preempt that algorithm? Claims that do both of the above are deemed to be unpatentable subject matter. A negative response to either test permits the claim to be evaluated on the basis of the other tests of patentability.

Copyright

Copyright protection is governed by federal law. Copyright is one of the powers granted to Congress under the US Constitution. Under the Copyright Act of 1976, as amended, the protection extends to original works of authorship including computer programs. These include, for example, literary works (including computer programs); musical works; dramatic works; pantomime and choreographic works; pictorial, graphic and sculptural works; motion pictures and other audiovisual works; and sound recordings. Multimedia (*q.v.*) works and computer games may include more than one of these categories. Exclusive rights are granted to the owner of the copyright to reproduce the copyrighted work; prepare derivative works based on the work; distribute copies of the work by sale, rental, lease, or lending; perform the work publicly if it is literary, musical, dramatic or choreographic, pantomime, or a motion picture and other audio-visual works; and display each of those works and pictorial, graphic, or sculptural works publicly. An infringement comes either from direct copying or by copying the "structure, sequence and organization" (the "look and feel") of a program. There are exceptions to the exclusive rights, most notably "fair use," which is a doctrine applied on a case by case basis as a defense to an infringement claim.

In 1996 the US Supreme Court held that a computer user interface (*q.v.*) is a "method of operation" and not eligible for copyright protection; *Lotus Development Corp.* v. *Borland International*, No. 94-2003 (US).

To be eligible for copyright protection, a work must be original and must be fixed in a tangible means of expression, such as a book, tape, or disk. Protection arises automatically for protected works upon fixation and covers the expression in the work (but not the underlying ideas). As of 27 January 1999, protection lasts for the life of the author plus 70 years and, in the case of works made for hire, for 95 years from first publication or 120 years from creation.

In order to obtain US copyright protection, it is not necessary to register the work or to place a notice on copies of published works created since 1 March 1989. There are certain advantages for those copyright owners who do comply with the formalities of placing a copyright notice on a work and registering the work with the US Copyright Office. Notice, which consists of placing the legend: "[copyright, copr. or ©] [author's name] [date of first publication of the work]" serves to defeat claims that an infringement was innocent. Registration of a work by US authors is still a prerequisite to filing suit. Registration before an infringement provides all authors' eligibility for obtaining their attorneys' fees in the case and for obtaining statutory damages without the need to show actual damages, in the amount of $500 to $20,000, with a possible award of up to $100,000 against willful infringers.

Registration of a work is accomplished by execution of the appropriate application form, which varies depending on the type of work to be registered (e.g. form TX for computer programs), payment of a minimal fee (currently $20), and deposit of two copies of the work with the US Copyright Office. For computer programs, one deposit is required and, for large programs, it can be less than all of the program, preferably the first and last 25 pages of source code.

The US Copyright Law covers work made for hire. A work made for hire is:

1. a work prepared by an employee within the scope of his or her employment; or

2. a work specially ordered or commissioned for use as a contribution to a collective work (such as an encyclopedia), as part of a motion picture or other audio visual work, as a translation, as a supplementary work (such as a foreword, editorial notes), as a compilation (a work formed by the collection and assembly of pre-existing materials or data selected, coordinated or arranged so that the resulting work as a whole constitutes an original work of authorship such as a database), as an instructional text (a literary, pictorial, or graphic work prepared for publication for use in systematic instructional activities), as a test, or as an atlas, if the parties expressly agree in a signed written instrument that the work shall be considered a work made for hire. (17 USC §101).

The author of a work made for hire is the employer of the author or is the commissioning party of a commissioned work. Computer programs as such do not qualify for work made for hire if written by non-employees. The author in these cases will be the programmer. To obtain ownership of such programs the person engaging the service of the programmer must obtain a written assignment of the title to copyright in the work from the programmer.

There is a movement in progress to provide a *sui generis* form of protection for uncopyrightable databases such as is now available in the European Union and Mexico. That effort has not yet resulted in US legislation, but as bills to that effect have been introduced in the 104th and 105th Congresses, such legislation is probable.

The 105th Congress passed the Digital Millennium Copyright Act. This act covered a number of issues:

1. It implemented the WIPO (World Intellectual Property Organization) treaties entered into among 160 countries in December 1996. Changes to US law included legal remedies against the circumvention of antipiracy measures and legal remedies against the removal of "Rights Management Information," e.g. copyright notices. There is an exemption for fair use of some material by academics, nonprofit libraries, and archives.

2. The Act limits the liability for infringement of Internet Service Providers in certain situations for costs, attorneys' fees and damages, and injunctive relief for acts by third party users of a network or system.

3. The Act provides an exemption from infringement by the owner or lessee of a machine to make or have made a copy of a computer program solely for maintenance or repair of the machine.

Copyright protection can be used with other forms of protection, such as trade secret protection and trademark to retain or enhance the value of intellectual property rights.

Trade Secret

A *trade secret* is a right that is protected state by state rather than by a federal law and is defined in the Uniform Trade Secrets Act, adopted in many states including a formula, pattern, compilation, program, device, method, technique, or process that:

1. Derives independent economic value, actual or potential, from not being generally known to the public or to other persons who can obtain economic value from its disclosure or use; and

2. Is the subject of efforts that are reasonable under the circumstances to maintain its secrecy.

In a number of court cases, computer programs have qualified as trade secrets; e.g. *University Computing Corporation* v. *Lykes-Youngstown Corporation*, 504 F.2d 518 (5th Cir. 1974), *MSA* v. *Cyborg Systems, Inc.* 6 CLSR 921 (N.D. Ill. 1978), and *Com-Share, Inc.* v. *Computer Complex, Inc.*, 338 F. Supp. 1229 (E.D.

Mich. 1971). The absolute requirement for trade secret status is that the item be kept secret from all except those bound to keep it confidential by virtue of their relationship or by contract. If the secret becomes known to others, the protection is lost. If it remains secret, the protection can last forever. Confidential relationships include employees and agents in a fiduciary or trust relationship, and thieves, who are held to be in a constructive trust relationship so that they cannot use their ill-gotten knowledge. *Contract* is used to bind licensees and joint venture partners or investors. (In some states, these people are bound even without an express contract.) However, once the secret is disclosed without a requirement of confidentiality or is disclosed to one who did not know of its secret character, the trade secret status is lost forever. Places where trade secrets are often disclosed carelessly are user group (*q.v.*) meetings and technical meetings.

Employees may need to learn the secret in the course of their employment. These people are bound not to misappropriate the trade secret by virtue of their position of trust with respect to the secret. Many employees do not realize the parameters of that trust and should consult their lawyers before using software developed for an employer for their own purposes. Trade secrets can also be lost through "reverse engineering" (i.e. through the legitimate process of buying a product and "taking it apart" to learn how it works); this encourages many software owners to encrypt their code. Trade secret protection has been held by the US Supreme Court to be compatible with patent protection, *Kewanee Oil Co. v. Bicron Corp.*, 416 US 470 (1974). Many vendors of software choose between the copyright and trade secret methods of protection, yet many others have both a copyright notice on their software and also treat it and license it as a trade secret. Cases have held that, so long as the rights claimed are not identical to copyright protection, those rights are not preempted by the federal copyright law.

Many software owners place a label on their software stating: "This software is proprietary to (name of Company)." That notice serves as a "no trespassing" sign to observers and a reminder to users who have acquired the software under an agreement to keep the software confidential.

Trademark

Trademark embodies the exclusive use of a symbol to identify goods and services. As distinguished from a patent, which does not exist until issued by the Patent Office, or a copyright, which exists as soon as the work is fixed in a tangible form, a trademark arises upon use, or, if one has a *bona fide* intent to use the mark,

one may acquire rights by filing a federal application to register the mark. Trademark protection exists at both the federal and state levels. The symbol protected can be both a name and a logo, such as *17 Mile Drive*. However, one cannot trademark an entire program, only its identifying symbol(s).

Contract

Because copies of software are ordinarily transferred to others in the course of business and sometimes transferred in source form, disclosure of the software is frequently made under an agreement to keep the secret confidential. Patented and copyrighted software can be transferred via contracts that may have other restrictions than the law requires simply by the status accorded by the patent or copyright. One may, for example, contract with another not to disclose a copyrighted piece of software. One may also agree to remedies for disclosure or unauthorized copying, set up complex formulas for royalty payment for legitimate use, and agree to the ownership of enhancements and changes to the software.

Bibliography

1982. Nycum, S. H. *Protection of Proprietary Interests in Software*. Reston, VA: Reston Publishing Company.
1992. Carr, H., and Arnold, R. *Computer Software—Legal Protection in the UK*, 2nd Ed. London: Sweet & Maxwell.
1999. Home Recording Rights Coalition. *History of the Digital Millenium Copyright Act*. http://www.hrrc.org/DMCA-leg-hist.html.

Susan H. Nycum

LEIBNIZ, GOTTFRIED WILHELM

For articles on related subjects *see* CALCULATING MACHINES; DIGITAL COMPUTERS, HISTORY OF: ORIGINS; and PASCAL, BLAISE.

Gottfried Wilhelm Leibniz (b. Leipzig, 1646; d. Hanover, 1716) (Fig. 1) had obtained an excellent education in his father's library before entering the University of Leipzig at 15 years of age and receiving a bachelor's degree at 17. At 20 he received a doctorate in jurisprudence from Altdorf, and for six years thereafter pursued a career of law and diplomacy, working to create an effective defense for the German states against Louis XIV. These diplomatic intrigues took him to Paris (1672), where he spent the four most fecund years of his mathematical career. Under the tutelage of Huygens, Leibniz systematically studied mathematics, especially the work of Descartes and Pascal.

Pascal's calculating machine stimulated Leibniz's interest. By adding a movable carriage operating on wheels using an active-and-inactive pin principle and a delayed carry mechanism, Leibniz modified Pascal's machine

Figure 1. Gottfried Wilhelm Leibniz (courtesy of the Mary Evans Picture Library).

so that it would multiply and divide directly (i.e. without the operator having to use an algorithm). However, in the only extant Leibniz machine (Hanover Museum), a later model, Pascal's ratchet-carry mechanism is replaced by a primitive Geneva gear system that accomplishes the discontinuous carry of digits by a series of five-point star gears. Eliminating the ratchet mechanism made subtraction and division possible by simply reversing the rotation of the addition and multiplication mechanisms.

In 1673, Leibniz made discoveries in differential calculus and in 1675 he observed that the summation process of integration was equivalent to reversing the operation of differentiation, the fundamental theorem of calculus. Newton had also made this observation in the 1660s, but Leibniz was apparently unaware of it.

Leibniz had an enduring interest in questions of method. His 1666 dissertation, *De Arte Combinatorica* (*On Combinatorics*) developed the mathematics of permutations and combinations (*see* COMBINATORICS), but was also, he said, "a general method in which all truths of the reason would be reduced to a kind of calculation." His interest in finding a universal calculus, as well as his work on formal logic, may have influenced 19th-century logicians like Boole (*q.v.*).

Leibniz is frequently credited with having developed binary numerals, which he described in his 1701 *Essay on a New Science of Numbers*. He had worked out this idea earlier, and may have been influenced to publish his essay by his reading of the Chinese *I Ching* in 1696.

In 1676 Leibniz left Paris for Hanover, where for the next 40 years he was a historian and librarian actively pursuing philosophy, theology, diplomatic missions, and scientific correspondence, and only intermittently working on his calculating machines. In 1700, he organized the Berlin Academy of Science (an idea he first articulated in 1668) and at his death was carrying on the now-famous correspondence with Clarke about the theological implications of Newton's *Principia* and *Opticks* (Alexander, 1998).

Bibliography

1951. Weiner, P. (ed.) *Leibniz, Selections.* New York: Charles Scribner's Sons.
1959. "Leibniz On His Calculating Machine," in *A Source Book in Mathematics*, Vol. 1 (ed. D. E. Smith), 173–181. New York: Dover.
1994. Jolley, N. (ed.) *The Cambridge Companion to Leibniz.* London: Cambridge University Press.
1997. Rutherford, D. *Leibniz and the Rational Order of Nature.* London: Cambridge University Press.
1998. Alexander, H. G. (ed.) *The Leibniz–Clarke Correspondence.* Manchester: Manchester University Press.

Charles V. Jones

LEO

For articles on related topics *see* COMPUTER INDUSTRY: BRITAIN; EDSAC; and ELECTRONIC OFFICE.

The LEO (Lyons Electronic Office) was built in London by J. Lyons & Co., then Britain's leading caterer, to cope with the paperwork arising from its enormous volume of small transactions. It was the world's first business computer and was put to work in November 1951 to carry out a regular, time-critical management accounting application for the company. The job was executed week by week for several years.

The initial LEO computer was closely based on EDSAC and profited from the cooperation of Maurice Wilkes (*q.v.*). Hardware extensions to the EDSAC design included a doubling of the store to 2048 short words of 17 bits and the incorporation of enhanced input–output facilities. With this equipment scientific work, too, was undertaken on a service basis from early 1952. Users included the Ordnance Board for ballistic tables and the Meteorological Office for weather forecasting. However, the main thrust in this phase was to develop from scratch the techniques necessary for time-critical, error-free business applications in a period when the equipment itself was inevitably unreliable.

Figure 1. LEO I. The control desk is in the background.

The extended LEO system that followed added buffered input and output (*see* BUFFER) so that the data for one transaction could be taken in while the previous transaction was being processed and the results for the one before that were being printed. Additional processor instructions were incorporated to convert between decimal or sterling (currency) numbers for input and output, and their internal binary representation. There were three parallel input streams, one paper tape and two punched card. The two output streams were to a line printer and a card punch.

This system started running the Lyons payroll as an integrated application from clock card to pay envelope in February 1954. The total time per employee including data input and payslip printing was 1.5 seconds. Other leading enterprises such as the UK works of the Ford Motor Company also employed LEO office and engineering applications.

The LEO project was led by Raymond Thompson. Dr John Pinkerton headed its engineering and David Caminer its application design and programming.

In 1957 the first LEO was joined by LEO II, which was made available for delivery to other users. LEO II was a transitional system between the first and second generations (*see* GENERATIONS, COMPUTER) and was also used as an operational testbed for magnetic tapes, magnetic drums, and core memory. In all, 10 systems were delivered to industrial and government users.

LEO III followed in 1961. Redesigned in semiconductor technology, the system incorporated micropro-

gramming (*q.v.*) to provide a 93-operation instruction set. It also provided support for real-time programming (*see* REAL-TIME SYSTEMS). Sixty of these systems were delivered, mainly in the period 1962–1966. These included 17 of the largest member of the range, LEO 326, 250 times faster than the original LEO.

LEO Computers merged with English Electric in 1964 and became part of ICL in 1968.

Bibliography

1994. Bird, P. *LEO, The First Business Computer*. Basingstoke, UK: Hasler.
1997. Caminer, D., Aris, J., Hermon, P., and Land, F. *L.E.O.: The Incredible Story of the World's First Business Computer*. New York: McGraw-Hill.

Website

1999. Leo Computers Society URL. `http://www.man.ac.uk/Science_Engineering/CHSTM/leo/`.

David Tresman Caminer

LIBRARY PROGRAM

See MATHEMATICAL SOFTWARE; and SOFTWARE LIBRARIES, NUMERICAL AND STATISTICAL.

LIBRARY STANDARDS

For articles on related subjects *see* DIGITAL LIBRARIES; HUMANITIES APPLICATIONS; HYPERTEXT; INFORMATION RETRIEVAL; MARKUP LANGUAGES; and STANDARDS.

Since the mid-1960s, computer-based library standards have augmented, and in some cases replaced, more traditional print-based standards. *Library standards* can be considered a subset of information standards, which in the USA are developed by about a dozen bodies accredited by the American National Standards Institute (ANSI), which is itself a member body of the International Organization for Standardization (ISO). Most library standards are developed by committees of the National Information Standards Organization (NISO), an ANSI-accredited organization.

In addition to official standards bodies, there exist numerous industry-related organizations promoting the use of standards and developing *de facto* implementations of standards. More often than not, a standard is more like a guide than a set of specific procedures. It usually requires agreement by the parties involved concerning how it will be implemented. The Book Industry Systems Advisory Committee (BISAC), a committee of the Book Industry Study Group, is one such body that has developed *de facto* implementations of many information-related ANSI standards of importance to the library community.

The MARC (Machine Readable Cataloging) Format for Bibliographic Information, initially published in 1968, was the first, and remains the most fundamental, computer-based library standard (Fig. 1). The introduction to the draft stated its purpose:

This standard defines a format which is intended for the interchange of bibliographic records on magnetic tape. It has not been designed as a record

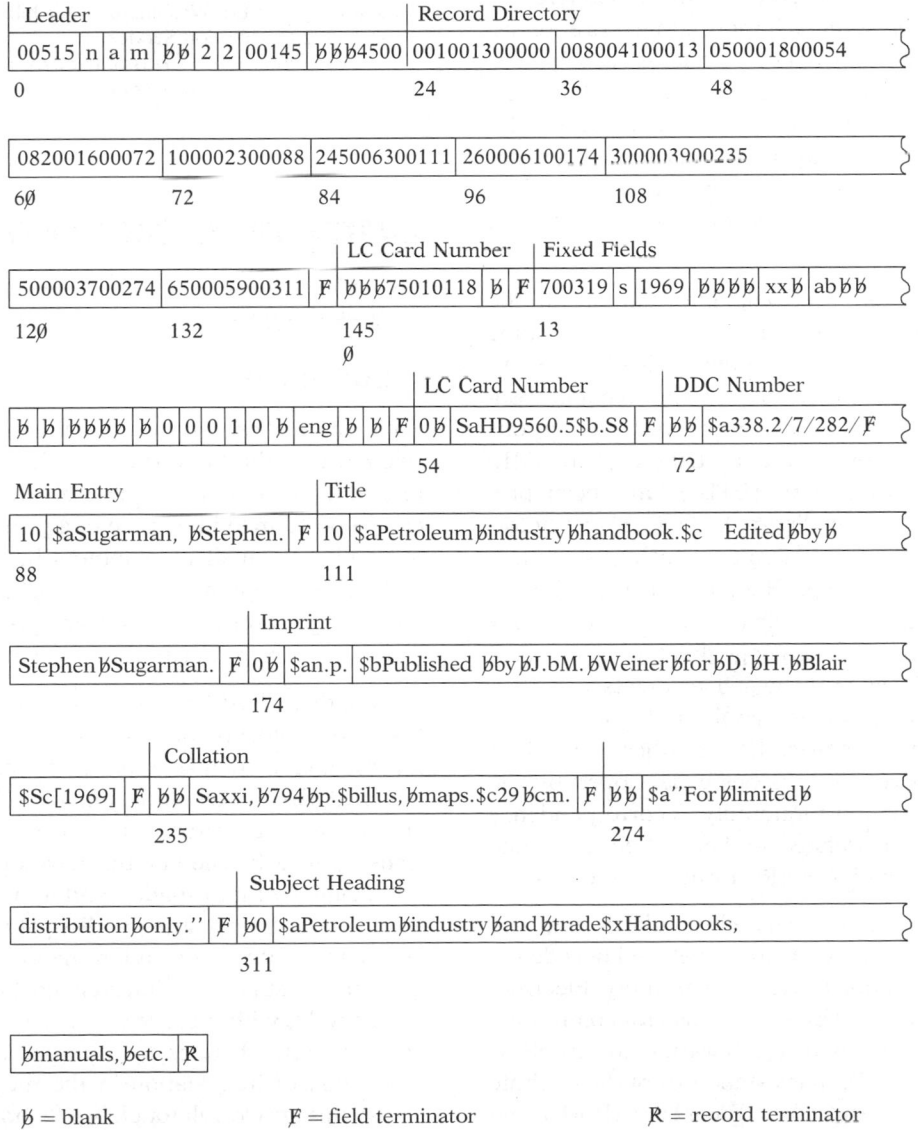

Figure 1. Sample record in the MARC format.

format for retention within the files of any specific organization. Nor has it been the intent of the subcommittee to define the content of the individual records. Rather it has attempted to describe a generalized structure which can be used to transmit between systems records describing all forms of material capable of bibliographic descriptions, as well as related records, such as authority records for authors and subject headings.

In more recent times, the interchange of bibliographic records is occurring increasingly online in real time using Z39.50, an information retrieval standard. Z39.50 is a client–server (*q.v.*) communications protocol that provides a standard template that translates client queries and server responses into a *"lingua franca"* that they can both interpret. It also keeps track of all transactions that occur in a client–server session, and it can recognize MARC encoding. As library automation systems have become more sophisticated in their information retrieval capabilities, MARC's function as an encoding standard for the Anglo-American Cataloging Rules (the standard rules adopted for library cataloging by the national libraries and the national library associations of the UK, Canada, and the USA) has steadily increased in importance.

With the spread of electronic information via the Internet (*q.v.*) and the World Wide Web (*q.v.*), static bibliographic records are proving inadequate to achieve bibliographic control over the dynamic content of electronic files. In recent years numerous Standard Generalized Markup Language (SGML) Document Type Definitions (DTDs) have been proposed in order to gain bibliographic control over information on the Internet. DTDs are markup standards specific to a document type. Rather than giving rise to a separate entity such as a bibliographic record, they act as a content markup language that tags elements of the document itself. The tagged elements can then function as a dynamic bibliographic entity that changes as the document changes. One of these, the Text Encoding Initiative (TEI), is being developed by the library and information community. A correspondence with MARC is being defined so that TEI encoded data can be used for creating MARC formatted records.

Increasingly, information-related standards that are important for libraries are being developed outside the library and information retrieval community. Electronic Data Interchange (EDI), a business community standard, is being used by libraries to purchase supplies and materials; many standards of the Institute of Electrical and Electronics Engineers (IEEE) and Telecommunications Industries Association (TIA), developed as technical specifications for the transfer of data among computer systems, are also of vital importance to libraries; and HTML and other SGML DTDs are now as important for libraries as any NISO-developed standard. As library automation merges with the broader area of information retrieval, and as information retrieval and transfer become the engines that drive the world's economies, every sector of the economy is becoming involved in creating information-related standards of importance to libraries.

Bibliography

1968. *The Journal of Library Automation*, **2** (June).
1975. Avram, H. D. *MARC, its History and Implications*. Washington, DC: Library of Congress.
1989. Crawford, W. *MARC for Library Use*. Boston, MA: G. K. Hall.
1996. Boss, R. W. "Standards for Automated Library Systems and Other Information Technologies," *Library Technology Reports*, **32**, *4* (July–August), 461–564.
1998. Furrie, B. *Understanding MARC: Machine Readable Cataloging*, 5th Ed. Washington, DC: Library of Congress Cataloging Distribution Service.
1999. *The Library of Congress Standards*. `http://lcweb.loc.gov/loc/standards/`.

David Dorman

LIMITS OF COMPUTATION

For articles on related subjects *see* MOLECULAR COMPUTING; and QUANTUM COMPUTING.

Introduction

From the earliest days of digital computation, it was realized that the finite speed of light (or any electromagnetic signal) limits the rate at which computations can be performed in a space of a given size. The quest to build ever smaller computers began immediately, and has seen a progression from behemoths that filled entire large rooms to pocket-size portable computers (*q.v.*) far more powerful than their huge ancestors.

But are there *limits to computational efficiency* other than size? Information is inevitably tied to a physical representation such as a mark on a paper, a hole in a punched card, an electron spin, or a charge present or absent on a capacitor. Such physical representation leads us to ask whether the laws of physics restrict the handling of information and in particular whether there are minimal energy dissipation requirements associated with information handling. The subject has three distinct but interrelated branches dealing, respectively, with measurement, communication, and computation. There is no minimal and unavoidable dissipation of information in the measurement process, so this article will touch briefly on communication and then be primarily concerned with the physical limits to computation.

Thermodynamics describes the performance limits of thermal engines in a way that transcends the details of particular inventions. Claude Shannon's (1949) information theory (*see* SHANNON, CLAUDE and INFORMATION THEORY) promised to do the same for the communications channel, but did so in a way that is now recognized to be more limited than had often been presumed (Landauer, 1987, 1996a). Thermodynamics and Shannon's information theory naturally led to attempts to answer related questions for computation. In principle, how much energy is needed per computational step? In principle, how immune can it be made to noise?

General Principles

According to the second law of thermodynamics, every bit lost through irreversible computation is shed as a minuscule puff of heat. In a modern digital computer, this shedding of information occurs at every step in long, rapid chains of calculations. Seemingly useless intermediate results are discarded to reset the memory registers, adding to the heat that must be removed from the machine to keep the parts from malfunctioning.

Other sources of heat, such as that caused by the drag of electrical resistance on electrons moving through wires, can be reduced as technology improves. (In superconducting components, electricity encounters zero resistance and moves unimpeded.) Or one can reduce resistance simply by running a machine more slowly. But a minimal, irreducible amount of heat must inevitably be shed whenever a computer clears its memory by erasing a one or a zero. This loss per bit is required by the laws of physics. Today's inefficient computers cast off far more heat than is lost from this "thermodynamic cost of forgetting."

The notion that information is a physical quantity tied to its physical representation is not universally accepted. Penrose (1989), for example, argues for this Platonic reality of mathematics, independent of any manipulation. He tells us "... devices can yield only approximations to a structure that has a deep and 'computer-independent' existence of its own."

Landauer (1996b) has suggested that the physical nature of information has, in turn, an impact on the ultimate nature of the laws of physics. These laws are essentially algorithms for calculation and must be implementable in our actual physical universe. Restrictions on the maximum size of memory arising, for example, from a finite universe, will restrict the number of successive operations available and, therefore, the accuracy with which calculation can be carried out. Normally, we view mathematics as primary and assume that its existence allowed a description of the physical universe. Landauer's view, instead, implies

that it is the physical universe which determines possible information handling operations. In particular, the mathematician's presumption that any desired computational accuracy can be obtained with sufficiently many operations is viewed by Landauer as unrealizable.

Another adventurous suggestion linking computation and the physical universe comes from Edward Fredkin (Wright, 1988) and from Konrad Zuse (*q.v.*) (Zuse, 1982). They propose that our actual universe is really a cellular automaton and that a moving particle is a bit, or group of bits, moving through this automaton (*see* CELLULAR AUTOMATA). The universal cellular automaton is presumed to operate on a subatomic scale of time and space.

In 1961 Landauer showed that computer steps that inevitably require energy expenditure are those that discard information (Leff and Rex, 1990). Normally, a computation throws away information at almost every step. A bit in storage is erased, or logic operations such as AND and OR are performed where knowledge of only output does not uniquely determine both inputs. In 1973, Bennett (Leff and Rex, 1990) showed that computation can be done *reversibly*, i.e. through a set of operations all of which are 1:1, as symbolically illustrated in Fig. 1. Bennett also proposed hypothetical machinery which could do this and, if operated slowly enough, would require as little energy expenditure as desired.

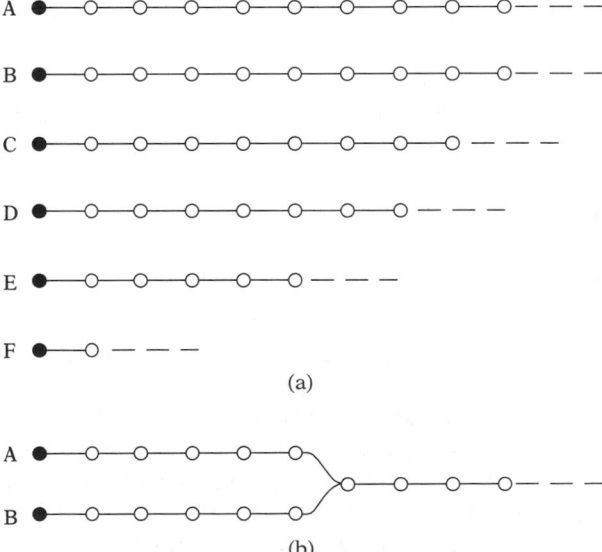

Figure 1. Reversible computation is illustrated in (a). The left-hand end of a horizontal chain is the initial state. Motion to the right yields forward steps through a sequence of states represented by successive circles. Different capital letters correspond to different initial states. For each state (except, perhaps, the initial state) there is a unique predecessor state. That is in contrast to (b), where two distinguishable paths merge into one; information is lost.

Reversible Computation

The possibility of reversible computation is now broadly accepted, but its initially counterintuitive nature requires explanation. Within a computer we need communication; bits have to be sent from one place to another. It had been widely presumed, as the result of an overinterpretation of Shannon's work, that it takes $kT(\ln 2)$ joules to send a bit, roughly the thermal energy of motion of a molecule at the temperature T of the apparatus (k is Boltzmann's constant, 1.38×10^{-23} JK^{-1}, having the dimension joules per Kelvin). The passage of information from one circuit to the next can also be viewed as a measurement by the second circuit on the output of the first. It was known, as a result of analysis of the famous Maxwell's demon paradox that it takes energy to make a measurement (Leff and Rex, 1990). Therefore, as a result of what was supposedly known about both communication and measurement, it could be assumed that computation also requires a minimal and unavoidable energy expenditure for each step.

The results of Bennett and of Landauer have caused a reexamination of the energy requirements of measurement and of communication, and as a result it has become clear that the presumed earlier results in these fields were flawed (Landauer, 1987, 1996a; Leff and Rex, 1990). Bennett's original detailed embodiments of reversible computation, as well as those by others that followed, were conceptual and not intended as serious technological candidates. Likharev (1982), however, eventually described a superconducting Josephson junction version (*see* SUPERCONDUCTING DEVICES). In recent years, proposals for *adiabatic computation* in CMOS logic have appeared. In conventional CMOS logic, power dissipation occurs primarily when circuits change state and the energy in device capacitances is thrown away. The proposals for adiabatic computation are based on the fact that this stored energy need not be discarded. In principle, a substantial part of it can be returned to a suitably designed power supply.

Following Landauer and Bennett, the literature on reversible computation emphasized systems that have viscous friction, noise, and allow some imperfection in the apparatus. Viscous friction, as found in electric circuits and hydrodynamics, gives frictional forces proportional to the velocity of motion. It was shown that reversible computation can, in principle, by suitable design choices, be done with as much immunity to noise as desired, and can be done with apparatus that can deviate slightly from its specifications.

In the early 1970s, Edward Fredkin proposed that reversible computation could be envisioned as a cybernetic billiard game. In the hypothetical Fredkin machine, the green felt of the billiard table is ruled off into a grid. At each intersection, the presence or absence of a ball represents a 1 or a 0. A problem to be solved is converted into a pattern of balls, which then ricochet off one another and bounce against reflecting "mirrors" analogous to the sides of a pinball machine. The final configuration represents the answer. With a friction-free table surface and perfectly elastic billiard balls, a Fredkin computer would operate with no loss of energy. And although that is impossible, there would be no limit to how closely one could approach this ideal. Because the system would be reversible, the energy loss from erasing bits could, in principle, be made arbitrarily small through ever better engineering.

But can one actually design a billiard table that computes? The problem is to model ricocheting billiard balls as fluctuating voltages inside a silicon computer chip (*q.v.*). At the Massachusetts Institute of Technology's Artificial Intelligence Laboratory, Thomas Knight and Norman Margolus and their students have done exactly that; they have developed a radically new kind of computer chip called Flattop, a physical realization of the Fredkin device. A problem to be solved is converted into a vanishingly tiny billiard game. Bits of information bounce around and "collide," carrying out calculations far more efficiently than in an ordinary computer. At any moment, action can be reversed, recreating the starting position of the computational game. As of now, Flattop is an experimental device, less powerful than the chips that drove the first PCs, but it is a remarkable demonstration that reversible computers can indeed be made.

Quantum Computing

Reversible computers like that of the prior section are viewed as classical systems in which, like in most of our technical machinery, quantum mechanics is not apparent in the overall behavior. Following the work of Benioff, starting in 1980, there was growing appreciation that a totally quantum mechanical apparatus can cause bits to interact and evolve with time, as we want them to do in a reversible computer (*see* QUANTUM COMPUTING).

Ordinary classical computation uses well-defined and well-separated 0 and 1 states. At each logic step, the signals are pushed back towards the desired ideal 0 and 1; small deviations in the input are reduced in the output. It is this property that gives the digital computer (*q.v.*) its power relative to the analog computer (*q.v.*). The latter could accomplish far more per step, but as a result of its inability to correct errors arising from the inevitable lack of component control, could not take very many successive steps. Quantum mechanical *qubits*, which use a continuum of superpositions of 0 and 1, are essentially a return to analog computation and require very explicit attention to error control.

When we first learned to count on our (classical) fingers, we gained the incorrect intuition that information also had to be classical in that a bit has to be in a 0 state or a 1 state. But quantum computation, as well as quantum cryptography, is based on the fact that quantum systems allow superpositions of different states. *Qubit* is the term now used to describe quantum information which can be in a state which partakes simultaneously of both 0 and 1. Recent investigations of quantum computation emphasize that information is a physical quantity; it always has a physical embodiment such as electron spin, a charge or current, or a hole in a punched card. Through that physical embodiment, information handling is inevitably tied to all the possibilities and restrictions of a physical universe governed by quantum mechanics. Therefore, analysis of the minimal number of steps required to carry out an algorithm has to acknowledge the possibility of quantum mechanical operations, even if they may not easily be realized in practice.

As stated earlier, it had been generally assumed that transmission of a bit requires $kT(\ln 2)$ joules of energy, and more if the frequencies in the signal are high enough that the associated quantum energy, $h\nu$, exceeds kT. These conclusions, however, apply to channels (q.v.) that use electromagnetic or acoustic waves, and to channels that cannot recycle the energy in those ways. After all, alternative communication methods, e.g. copying a diskette (q.v.) and sending it through the mail, do exist. Landauer (1987, 1996a) has described machinery which, in principle, allows the long-range transmission of bits with an energy expenditure per bit that can be made as small as desired. These proposals are not intended as practical technology, but only as existence theorems that could conceivably lead to more practical versions. While the suggested machinery, both classical and quantum mechanical, was originally intended to be used for the transfer of classical 0 or 1 bits, minor variations of the published versions can also be used to transfer qubits in a quantum mechanical superposition of the 0 and 1 state.

One of Landauer's proposals has been extended and described in a playful manner by Bennett (1996). The heart of an energy-efficient communications channel is an intrinsically bistable material body with two low-energy states separated by a potential barrier. Consider, for example, a simple chiral molecule such as lactic acid, whose left- and right-handed forms can be used to encode the binary digits 0 and 1. Imagine that a sequence of such molecules ordered so as to transmit a message are riding on a ski-lift (channel) that can accelerate its passengers smoothly from a standing

Figure 2. An energy-efficient communications channel based on the transport of left- and right-handed lactic acid molecules.

start at the boarding point and drop them off equally smoothly at their destination (Fig. 2.) The system is intrinsically reversible and, since there are no sudden changes in velocity, the energy dissipated per bit loaded or unloaded tends to zero in the limit of zero speed. As described, the system is a good carrier of classical information and useless as a carrier of quantum information, but it may eventually be possible to use a quantum *error-correcting code* (*see* ERROR CORRECTING AND DETECTING CODE) to hide a one-bit message in a redundantly entangled state of five molecules so as to allow the channel to be used for both kinds of information.

Summary

Study of the physical limits to computation continues to be a fruitful and challenging field of research. Whether we identify and properly analyze them or not, these physical limits exist and will always remain a challenge to the ingenuity of physicists and computer scientists who aspire to compute as efficiently as does our remarkable universe.

Bibliography

1949. Shannon, C. E. *Bell Syst. Tech. J.,* **27**, 379; *ibid.* p. 623.
1982. Likharev, K. K. "Classical and Quantum Limitations on Energy Consumption in Computation," *Int. J. Theor. Phys.,* **21**, 311.
1982. Zuse, K. "The Computing Universe," *Int. J. Theor. Phys.,* **21**, 589.
1987. Landauer, R. "Energy Requirements in Communication," *Appl. Phys. Lett.,* **51**, 2056.
1988. Wright, R. *Three Scientists and Their Gods: Looking for Meaning in an Age of Information.* New York: Times Books, Random House, Inc.

1989. Penrose, R. *The Emperor's New Mind*. Oxford: Oxford University Press.

1990. Leff, H. S., and Rex, A. F. (eds.) *Maxwell's Demon: Entropy, Information, and Computing*. Princeton, NJ: Princeton University Press. Contains reprints of key papers in this field, and comments on their significance.

1996. Bennett, C. "Freely Communicating," *Nature*, **382**, 669.

1996a. Landauer, R. "Minimal Energy Requirements in Communciation," *Science*, **272** (28 June), 1914–1918.

1996b. Landauer, R. "The Physical Nature of Information," *Phys. Lett. A*, **217**, 188.

1999. Johnson, G. "The Ultimate Computer Learns to Think in Reverse," *New York Times*, 15 June.

Rolf Landauer

LINEAR PROGRAMMING

See MATHEMATICAL PROGRAMMING.

LINGUISTICS

See NATURAL LANGUAGE PROCESSING; and PROGRAMMING LINGUISTICS.

LINKED LIST

See LIST PROCESSING.

LINKERS AND LOADERS

For articles on related subjects *see* ASSEMBLER; BINDING; BOOTSTRAP; COMPILER; GLOBAL AND LOCAL VARIABLES; and OBJECT PROGRAM.

Terminology concerning linkers and loaders is confusing, having changed over the years as technology has changed. In older mainframe operating systems, processing of a program between compiling and execution took place in two distinct stages. The function of the *linker* (or *linkage editor*) was to combine a number of independently compiled or assembled *object files* into a single *load module*, resolving cross-references and incorporating routines from libraries as required. The *loader* then prepared this module for execution, physically loaded it into memory, and started execution. Early versions of Unix (*q.v.*) blurred this distinction: the functions of the linker were incorporated into the C (*q.v.*) compiler in what was confusingly called the "load phase," and the actual loading was done as part of the "exec" operation that installed a new process image for execution.

The loader was required because in the multitasking (*q.v.*) systems of the day the exact address in memory at which the program would be loaded was not known until the moment of loading. The load module produced by the linker therefore assumed that the program would be loaded at address zero, but provided a map flagging all the addresses that were relative to that origin. When the physical address at which the program would start was determined by the operating system, the loader added the address of the base of the block to all the addresses flagged as relative, a process known as *relocation*, before physically loading the binary code into memory for execution. Modern systems are able to dispense with the explicit loader, since relocation is not required. Virtual memory systems provide each program (process) with a large flat virtual address space that starts at address zero. Non-virtual memory systems for the Intel 80x86 architecture use segmented memory: all addresses in the load module are relative to the base addresses of a number of segments, so when a program is loaded it is merely necessary to set the segment address registers to match the addresses at which the program has been loaded. However, the introduction of dynamic link libraries (see below) has brought back the need for a loader, since in systems employing dynamic linking some symbols cannot be resolved until the executable module is actually loaded.

The Link Editor

A complete program typically comprises a number of files that are compiled separately, which include references to functions stored in one or more *libraries*. In a C program, for example, each file will contain a number of functions, together with *header files* which provide templates describing the functions used within the file but defined somewhere else—external functions. Likewise, a C++ program includes header files which provide definitions of classes whose member functions are defined elsewhere—another example of an *external reference*.

When a file containing part of a program is compiled, there will be four kinds of items in the object module:

1. Constants (absolute items whose value does not depend on the ultimate position of the code in memory).

2. Addresses whose value is known relative to the start of the module.

3. External references to functions defined elsewhere, whose value cannot be determined until all modules are present (or until load time if dynamic linking is employed).

4. Definitions of global variables and functions that are to be visible throughout the program.

The object module will therefore typically consist of:

1. A *header block* containing *inter alia* the size of the compiled code for the module.

2. A *code block* consisting of binary words tagged to show the status of their address parts: absolute, relative, or external.

3. A *table of external references*, containing for each reference the (relative) address in the code section at which it occurs and its symbolic form.

4. A *table of external* (global) *variable and function definitions*, containing the name and (relative) address of each identifier globally defined in the module.

We describe first the process of "static linking": the added complications of dynamic linking are described later. The link editor operates in two passes, the function of the first pass being to resolve the references between separately compiled modules. Fig. 1 shows two such modules. The external reference tables are merged into a single table, as are the global definition tables. External references are resolved initially from the merged global definition table: the actual definition will still be local to the module in which the symbol is defined. Any remaining unresolved references are either errors or references to a library. A library archive (Unix terminology) contains a collection of object modules, each with a descriptive header, and when the archive is first generated a symbol table is constructed containing the name of each module in the archive and its offset in the archive. The link editor scans the symbol table for each library specified (usually a default sequence) attempting to resolve unmatched external references. When a match is found the relevant object module is extracted from the library and added to the program. Fig. 2 shows the

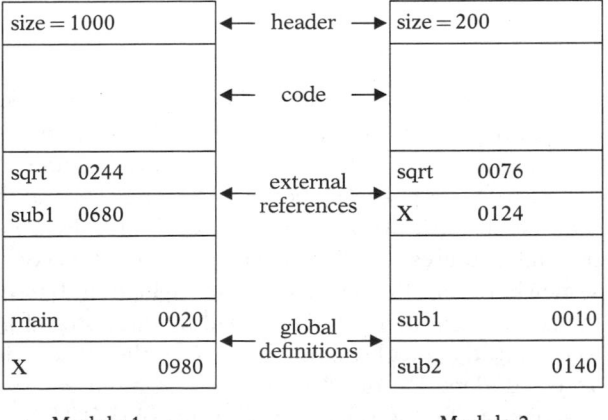

Module 1

size = 1000	
sqrt	0244
sub1	0680
main	0020
X	0980

Module 2

size = 200	
sqrt	0076
X	0124
sub1	0010
sub2	0140

header ← →
code ← →
external references ← →
global definitions ← →

Figure 1. Two program modules, each with external references to names defined in other modules and global definitions of names referred to in other modules. Module 1, for example, has a globally declared variable named X at address 0980, and it refers to an external subroutine, sub1, at address 0244 of its code.

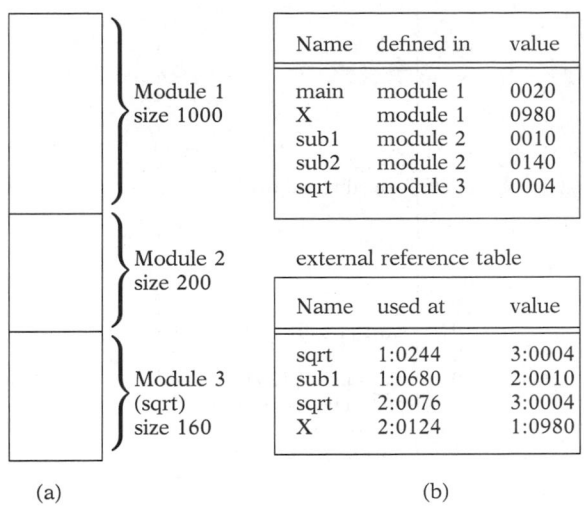

merged global symbol table

Name	defined in	value
main	module 1	0020
X	module 1	0980
sub1	module 2	0010
sub2	module 2	0140
sqrt	module 3	0004

external reference table

Name	used at	value
sqrt	1:0244	3:0004
sub1	1:0680	2:0010
sqrt	2:0076	3:0004
X	2:0124	1:0980

(a) Module 1 size 1000 / Module 2 size 200 / Module 3 (sqrt) size 160

(b)

Figure 2. (a) The code blocks of the two program modules and a third module, the sqrt function, extracted from a library archive, are assembled into one block of code. (b) The global symbol table lists all global symbols with their values and the module in which they are defined. The external references table uses this information to give a value to each external symbol, relative to the start of its module, written here as a module-number address.

merged tables with a library module added to the program modules of Fig. 1. This object module may itself contain external references to other library functions and/or global definitions, so multiple passes over the library symbol tables may be required. If the user has specified a particular option the process may stop here, having merged a number of modules into a single module (which may still contain unresolved references). The default behavior, however, is to return an error if any references remain unresolved, and otherwise to proceed to pass 2.

The function of pass 2 is to adjust relative addresses in all modules after the first so as to produce a contiguous program with all addresses relative to the start of the first module. The process is simple. (We are assuming here a system with a flat address space, starting at zero. A similar but more complicated process can be carried out for the Intel segmented address space.) A "relocation counter" is set to zero at the start of the first module: at the start of the second module its value is set to the size of the first module, and thereafter its value at the start of module n, together with the information in that module's header block, determines the value at the start of module $n + 1$. During this pass the appropriate relocation counter value for a module is added to all relative addresses in the module, and the entries in the global definition tables are also relocated relative to the origin of the first module. Thus at the end of the pass all the

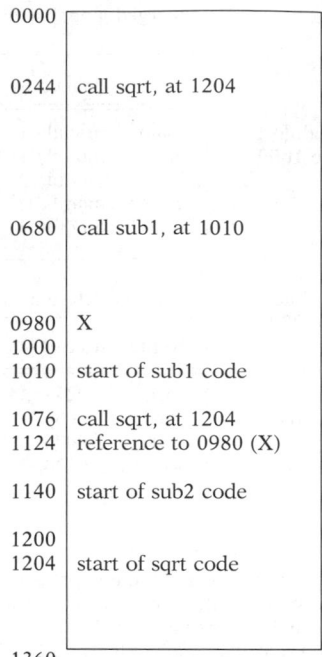

```
0000

0244    call sqrt, at 1204

0680    call sub1, at 1010

0980    X
1000
1010    start of sub1 code

1076    call sqrt, at 1204
1124    reference to 0980 (X)

1140    start of sub2 code

1200
1204    start of sqrt code

1360
```

Figure 3. The final load module with all references resolved (given numerical values).

external references can be replaced by a corresponding relocated address as given in the global definition table. The result, shown in Fig. 3, is a loadable or *executable* module.

Dynamic Linking

It will be observed that if a library function is widely used, a separate copy of its code will be incorporated in the executable file of every program that uses it. Dynamic linking ensures that only one copy of the code is loaded into memory, being shared by all programs that are currently using it. We describe here the dynamic link library (DLL) structure used in Microsoft Windows: broadly similar capability is provided by other systems, e.g. the "shared objects" of the Sun Solaris system.

A DLL is a relocatable module containing the executable code for a number of functions each of which is identified by a numerical entry point; thus the combination of DLL name and entry point defines a function uniquely. Functions defined in DLLs are referenced via import libraries which map function names onto unique DLL/entry point pairs. These *import libraries* are scanned by the link editor, and so an external reference to a DLL function will appear in the final load module as a DLL name/entry point pair, which has to be resolved by the loader. At load time the loader first ascertains whether the DLL is already in memory. If not it has to be loaded into a free area of memory, with addresses being relocated if it is loading

into virtual memory. (Most of the Windows system is composed of DLLs: these are preloaded into the area of virtual memory reserved for the system as part of the Windows start-up process.) The base address of the DLL now being known, the references within the module being loaded can be resolved and execution proceeds.

In a system employing dynamic loading, the link editor includes an option to generate a DLL rather than an executable module. The process of link editing is essentially the same as before, except that relocation information needs to be added (a map marking all relative addresses). At the final stage a dispatch table is added so as to provide the numbered entry points required by the loading process.

Bootstrap Loaders

Loading a program into memory for execution is a function of the operating system. So how is the operating system code loaded in the first place? This is the function of the bootstrap loader. The bootstrap sequence starts with the "initial bootstrap": a simple, small program that is used to load the next stage loader. Originally the initial bootstrap had to be small enough to make it feasible to enter it into memory via the hand switches on the console, but today it resides in read-only memory (ROM). Its function is to read a program from a known location, e.g. the first sector of a pre-determined disk (the C: drive or the A: drive in PC systems). This sector may contain the code to load the operating system, or it may contain a *boot manager* which conducts a dialogue with the operator concerning available options, in particular to find the path name of the "real" bootstrap, which is then loaded and in turn loads the binary image of the operating system.

Remote Booting

Diskless workstations have to boot off the network, and even if workstations have local disks, management may prefer booting over the network in order to ensure that every workstation has the latest version of the system with no unauthorized additions. Remote booting requires the existence of a "boot server" somewhere on the network from which a binary image of the system can be loaded by code stored in ROM on the workstation. The way the server is accessed depends on the network being used: we describe briefly the remote boot protocol (BOOTP) of the Internet protocol suite.

The process is initiated by the client's ROM program which sends a broadcast message addressed to any host listening on port 67 (the port used by BOOTP servers). The message contains the client's Ethernet (*q.v.*) address (which is all the ROM program knows). A boot server responds to the request, returning the client's Internet (IP) address, its own IP address and hostname, and the name of the file containing the system image. This is enough information for the client to use the Trivial File Transfer Protocol (TFTP) to transfer the system image, and the boot process is completed.

Bibliography

1972. Presser, I., and White, J. R. "Linkers and Loaders," *Computing Surveys*, **4**, 149–168.
1978. Barron, D. W. *Assemblers and Loaders*, 3rd Ed. New York: American Elsevier.
1992. Salomon, D. *Assemblers and Loaders*. Chichester: Ellis Horwood.

David W. Barron

LINUX

See FREE SOFTWARE FOUNDATION; and UNIX OPERATING SYSTEM.

LISP

For articles on related subjects *see* ARTIFICIAL INTELLIGENCE; FUNCTIONAL PROGRAMMING; LIST PROCESSING; and PROGRAMMING LANGUAGES.

Why Has Lisp Lasted So Long?

Fortran (*q.v.*) is the only language in widespread use that is older than Lisp (LISt Processor). Lisp owes its longevity to two facts. First, its core elements occupy a kind of local optimum in the "space" of programming languages, given the resistance to purely notational changes. Recursive use of conditional expressions, representation of symbolic information externally by lists and internally by list data structures (*q.v.*), and the representation of programs in the same way as data will probably have a very long life.

Second, Lisp still has operational features unmatched by other languages that make it a convenient vehicle for higher-level systems for symbolic computation and for artificial intelligence (AI). These include a run-time system that gives good access to the features of the host machine and its operating system, its use of list data structures that makes it a good target for compiling from yet higher level languages, its compatibility with systems that produce binary or assembly level programs, and the availability of its interpreter as a command language for driving other programs (*see* SHELL). *See* LIST PROCESSING: LANGUAGES for examples of Lisp programs.

Lisp Prehistory

During the 1956 Dartmouth Summer Research Project on Artificial Intelligence, John McCarthy was searching for a solution to assist in artificial intelligence programming for the IBM 704 computer. In late 1958 McCarthy, then an assistant professor of electrical engineering, and Marvin Minsky, an assistant professor in mathematics, both at MIT, began the MIT Artificial Intelligence Project and initiated the implementation of Lisp. To simplify the task of programming the substantive computations, e.g. logical deduction, algebraic simplification, differentiation or integration, the design gave up the familiar infix notation in favor of parenthesized prefix (*see* POLISH NOTATION). The core of Lisp ("pure Lisp") is a functional language, though Lisp also has the imperative features common to procedure-oriented languages (*q.v.*).

Although initially viewed as a language to be compiled, S. R. Russell noticed that a compiler was not necessary for running Lisp: he hand-coded McCarthy's *eval*, a theoretically motivated universal Lisp function that was much more compact than Turing's universal Turing machine (*q.v.*). This made it possible to execute any Lisp program. A side-effect of that idea was to make Lisp programs written as Lisp lists become the main program form, replacing the original Algol-like "M-expressions." This turned out to be an important feature of Lisp, but also supported the common misperception of Lisp as necessarily being interpreted (*see* LANGUAGE PROCESSORS). Now most implementations rely heavily on compilation into assembly language for fast execution as well as for compile-time debugging. From earliest times it was natural to notice that compilers for Lisp could be written in Lisp, and examples of this as far back as 1959 may provide the early examples of language bootstrapping (*q.v.*).

Additional features were gradually added, with Lisp 1.5 being a major documented milestone. It was used for several major AI applications, in spite of a few trouble-spots satisfactorily explicated only much later.

The Growth of Lisp Dialects

Attempts to go beyond Lisp 1.5 and correct its inefficiencies led to several projects, ultimately dominated by one machine architecture, the Digital Equipment Corporation (*q.v.*) PDP-6 and DEC-10, but with competing software implementations. Major systems came from MIT and Stanford, and from BBN (Bolt, Beranek and Newman) and XEROX PARC's Interlisp. While most small Lisp programs were essentially compatible, large systems that pushed the host machines to their limits resulted in distinct sets of features and links to operating systems.

Lisp systems began to outgrow the DEC-10 in which only 2^{18} 36-bit words (a little over one MB) could be conveniently addressed. AI funding from government agencies (ARPA in particular) was abundant, and efforts to solve this address-space problem led to a version of MIT's MACLisp on the GE-645 Multics timesharing system, which had 36-bit addresses, and then more significantly to special single-user heavily microcoded "Lisp machines." In the early 1970s, designs at MIT were sold to two companies, LMI, later acquired by Texas Instruments, and Symbolics Inc. Special hardware/software systems for InterLisp were also produced at Xerox (so-called D-machines, the most common being the Dandelion), and Carnegie Mellon University (Spice Lisp on the PERQ computer). In spite of substantial software sophistication, none of these special-purpose hardware systems has survived. A major blow was the DEC VAX in 1977 which provided a large virtual memory (*q.v.*) address space, lower cost, and widespread availability. Trumping the VAX in the early 1980s, workstations, such as those of Sun and Apollo (now HP), became the cost leaders at a fraction of the VAX or LMI cost, and became especially attractive for the development and delivery of elaborate Lisp programs (in addition to running all the other software).

The Scheme dialect, a small and semantically clean reaction to the alarming complexity of Lisps, also appeared in the 1970s and subsequently became an IEEE standard. It is a popular pedagogical language, and has several serious implementations.

Reunification

The divergence of Lisp implementations had become sufficiently alarming to ARPA (which was paying for all the competing activities) that in April 1981 it called a meeting to unify the community under a single Lisp dialect. None of the major contenders was sufficiently dominant to become the anointed. The discussion was quite heated, since virtually all had similar yet distinct sophisticated extensions, including among other features, elaborate object-oriented programming (*q.v.*) facilities and the ability to link to programs written in C (*q.v.*) or other languages. Although that meeting did not achieve its purpose, in 1984 a grassroots effort sought to produce a unified new language which was called Common Lisp. Vendors and academics produced implementations which were testbeds for the resulting ANSI Common Lisp, a standards effort that reached fruition in 1994 (standard X3J13). The standard cleaned up many remaining issues, extending standard facilities, and in particular provided an elegant Common Lisp object system (CLOS).

Where We Are Now

Guy Steele Jr's *Common Lisp: the Language* is an approachable reference, but the definitive description of the ANSI language is most easily available on the World Wide Web from various vendors. See the Web page of the Association of Lisp Users. Among the information provided there are links to about 23 commercial implementations of Lisp, and a similar number of implementations (mostly partial) distributed at no cost. Some of the vendors provide free "lite" versions of their systems.

Bibliography

1981. McCarthy, J. "History of Lisp," in *History of Programming Languages* (ed. R. L. Wexelblat). New York: Academic Press. (Also `http://www-formal.stanford.edu/jmc/history/lisp.html`).

1990. Steele, G., Jr. *Common Lisp: The Language*, 2nd Ed. Bedford, MA: Digital Press.

1996. Abelson, H., and Sussman, G. J. *Structure and Interpretation of Computer Programs*, 2nd Ed. Cambridge, MA: MIT Press.

1996. Steele, G. L., Jr., and Gabriel, R. P. "The Evolution of Lisp," in *History of Programming Languages II* (ed. T. J. Bergin, Jr. and R. J. Gibson, Jr.). New York: Addison-Wesley.

Websites

Association of Lisp Users. `http://www.elwoodcorp.com/alu/table/contents.htm`.

Steele, G. L., Jr. *Common Lisp: the Language*, 2nd Ed. `http://www.cs.cmu.edu/Groups/AI/html/cltl/clm/clm.html`.

Richard Fateman and John McCarthy

LIST PROCESSING

For articles on related subjects *see* ABSTRACT DATA TYPE; ARTIFICIAL INTELLIGENCE; COMPUTER ALGEBRA; DATA STRUCTURES; DATA TYPE; FUNCTIONAL PROGRAMMING; GARBAGE COLLECTION; GRAPH THEORY; LAMBDA CALCULUS; LISP; POINTER; STORAGE ALLOCATION; STRING PROCESSING; SYMBOL MANIPULATION; and TREE.

PRINCIPLES

List Concepts

The two elements of a computer program are the computations (the actions we want done) and the data (the things we want the actions done upon). The computations are defined using expressions in a computer language, combined to form procedures, which are in turn combined to form compound procedures and eventually programs. The ability to combine simple expressions into procedures is the key to using computer programs to model processes in the real world. Data is defined in a similar way: compound data objects are built from simple parts, like numbers, and combined to represent real-world objects that have complex properties. Compound procedures and compound data are used for the same purposes: to improve the modularity of the program and to raise the conceptual level of its design. One of the simplest and most widespread form of compound data is the *list*.

Any data object that contains other objects is a compound data object. On one end of the spectrum is the *homogeneous array*, a collection of objects, all of the same type, with an implicit relationship defined by the indices of the elements of the array. Further along the spectrum in complexity is the *record*, a collection of data objects, not necessarily all of the same type, into a single unit whose representation is hidden (a Pascal *record* or C *struct* is such a structure). Typically, one can access the elements of a structure by name, but without reference to how those elements are stored. The list occupies a point in this spectrum somewhere between the array and the structure: it is a collection of anonymous, frequently heterogeneous elements, whose elements cannot be directly reached. Instead, elements of lists must be reached through two primitive operations.

The fundamental *list* idea is that each element of a list but the last has a next element. At any given moment, one can look at the current element or *sublist* that follows it. The basic operations are typically called *first* and *rest*—the first element of the list is the current element, and the rest of the list is everything but the first element. All other elements are reached by repeating those two operations: the second element is the first of the rest, the third is the first of the rest of the rest, and so on.

Lists are a good example of an abstract data type. They are characterized in terms of the elements that they may hold—e.g. simple object like numbers, compound objects such as structures, or other lists—and in terms of these basic operations. A list has a simple recursive definition (*see* RECURSION): a list is either empty or consists of a first element of some type, followed by a list (the rest). In languages that require lists to be homogeneous, the definition would add "of elements of the same type."

List Implementation

For lists to be useful, they need an efficient implementation. They are commonly implemented as *linked lists*, in which each element has a link (a pointer) to its successor.

A list element can be thought of in two ways: as a data object that also has a "next" field (the link), or as a primitive *node* with a data field and a "next" field. The former approach is often taken for objects that are

designed from the start to be combined into lists: a structure or abstract data type is given an additional field which will contain a pointer to another such object. The latter view is taken by Lisp and related languages: the *cons* operation makes a node with two fields (called a *cons cell* or *dotted pair* or just *pair*) that can contain any other object (or rather, since an arbitrary object may not fit in a field, the field will contain a pointer to the object instead of the object itself). Lists are built out of these nodes, with the *first* field holding the data object and the *rest* field pointing to the next node. The advantage of this approach is that the objects contained in the list need not be specially designed for list usage. These two views are not incompatible: most languages can build two-field structures and use them as list nodes, and Lisp can build structures whose elements contain other structures. *List-processing languages* like Lisp generally provide cons cells as a basic data type, while other languages provide pointers, so it's really just a historical tendency.

What happens to those nodes that are deleted, and where do new nodes come from? These questions are related, in that new nodes are taken from *free storage*, (also called the *heap*, or the *list of available space*) and deleted nodes must be returned to free storage or it will run out. The process of making new nodes is part of *storage allocation*, and the process of reclaiming unused nodes is called *garbage collection*. As long as there are variable-sized data objects, there will be a need to allocate and reclaim storage. Lists simply make the need obvious.

Since elements of a list are explicitly connected by links, it is very easy to insert and delete elements. Given a list of 5, 8, and 9, it is simple to insert the number 6 in order: make an element containing 6 with its link pointing to the element containing 8, and then change the first element's link to point to the new one (Fig. 1). The corresponding insertion for a one-dimensional array would require moving the 8 and 9 up one element and writing the 6 in the emptied location. Similarly,

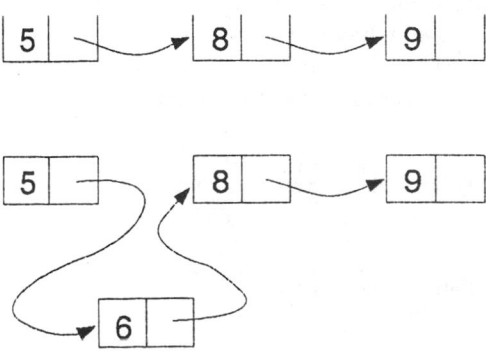

Figure 1. Inserting an element into a list.

deleting an element from a list simply involves changing one element's link to the deleted element to point to the next one, and splicing out the deleted node. The corresponding array deletion again requires copying. This principle can be extended to more than one connected element; thus, entire lists may be spliced in and out and combined. Notice that lists are inherently *variable-sized*—new elements can be freely created and added, and existing elements deleted and thrown away, in contrast to arrays and structures which usually have a fixed number of elements.

Lists need not have only one link per element. *Doubly-linked* lists have not one but two links per element: one pointing to the next element, and one to the previous one. The benefit of the second link is that it makes insertion and deletion easier. In the example above, to insert the 6 between the 5 and the 8, we needed to reach both the 5 and 8 list elements, because they were on either side of the insertion point. With a singly-linked list, we have to keep track of both of them ourselves. If we knew we wanted to insert before the 8, but didn't already have a handle on the 5, we would have to start at the beginning of the list and work all the way down to the insertion point. With a doubly-linked list, all we need is one list element, and it will allow us to look both forward and backward. However, the second link requires a little more space, and maintaining forward and backward links is a little harder than just forward links. Which method to use depends on the list's purpose: if rapid insertion and deletion are important, doubly-linked lists are used; if insertion and deletion are uncommon, singly-linked lists are quite sufficient.

Since list elements point to other list elements, it is possible for more than one to point to the same object. When this happens, multiple lists can share parts of themselves, with the obvious consequences: identical data is not duplicated, and if part of the shared data is changed as part of operating on one list, all the sharing lists see the changes (*see* Fig. 2). Whether these are advantages or disadvantages depends on the application: some programs might use the common data to communicate between parts of the program, while others might have problems with data mysteriously changing for no apparent reason. A list may even be *circular*, sharing structure with itself: an element

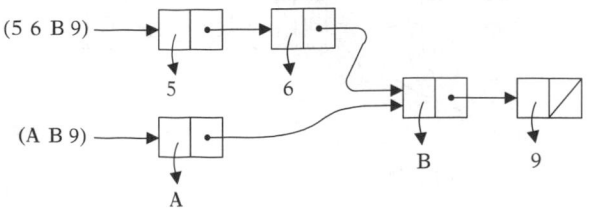

Figure 2. Sharing parts of a list.

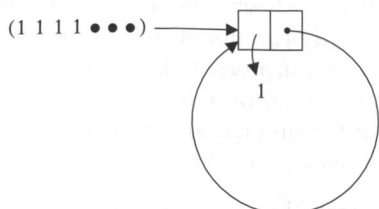

Figure 3. A circular list of 1s.

somewhere in the list may point to an element elsewhere in the list. The single element containing a 1 and pointing to itself (Fig. 3) is such a list, and in some contexts behaves like an infinite list of 1s—the first element is a 1 and so is the "second" (found by following the link), the "third," etc.

One-dimensional arrays and simple lists bear a strong surface resemblance, since both are compound objects containing an ordered set of elements. The Common Lisp language even provides a *sequence* type that encompasses both lists and one-dimensional arrays and a collection of operations that make sense on both. The programmer chooses list or array according to the needs of the program. Lists are variable-sized and offer easy insertion and deletion, but take more time to reach elements farther down the list (because they must be reached by traversing links). Arrays have a fixed size and constant access per element, but require that some of the elements be shuffled up or down for insertion and deletion.

Applications of Lists

If lists are made out of nodes that can contain any kind of data, a number of useful data structures can be built. One common structure is the *key-value* list, so called because it associates *keys* with *values*. A key-value list serves as a table: data objects can be stored as values and looked up using their associated keys. The two typical implementations of key-value lists are called *property lists* and *association lists*. A property list (plist) is simply a list of alternating properties and values. Order is not important: to look up the value for a given property, one looks at the first, third, fifth, etc., element of the list, and when a match is found, the very next list element is the value. New associations are formed by attaching the new key and value to the front of the list. An association list is a list of pairs; each pair contains a key and its associated value (remember that any node field, even the usual link field, can contain any data object). To look up the value for a given key, one looks at each pair in the list, comparing the pair's key with the desired key. When a match is found, the value is the other field of the pair.

Note that the key-value association of a property list or association list lies in its use, not in a particular arrangement of nodes and pointers. A key-value list is simply a list whose elements are interpreted in a particular way, and whose purpose is to serve as a table pairing keys and values. Both property lists and association lists can be used as tables, and there is no real advantage in choosing one over the other. The important idea is that they can be used to implement the "table" concept, and if the lookup procedures are written well, programs that use them will not need to know what kind of structure lies beneath the table. Indeed, some versions of "table" may change the internal representation from lists to trees to hash tables (*see* SEARCHING) as the table grows.

Lists can also be used to implement trees and other graph structures (*see* GRAPH THEORY). Pair nodes can be linked into simple binary trees, and larger nodes into trees of greater degree or with data at the nodes of the tree. Larger nodes can even be simulated by lists built from pair nodes. Since list nodes can contain pointers to arbitrary data objects—even other nodes in the same list—graph structures of all complexities can be built by connecting nodes.

Two other structures easily built with lists are the *stack* (*q.v.*) and the *queue*. A stack is just a list of elements (sometimes called a pushdown list); again its utility comes from its interpretation, not its particular structure. To push an object onto the stack, make a new node containing the object, link it to the stack, and then use that new node as the new top of the stack. To pop an object off, change the stack pointer to point to the next element and discard or process the old top. Since, by the definition of "stack," only the first element of a stack may be accessed, the basic linked structure of a list suffices to implement a stack.

Similarly, queues can be built as lists of elements, with insertion defined as attaching a new node to the end of the list and deletion the same as a stack's. To attach new nodes to the end of the list, it is often most efficient to modify the basic list structure by keeping a pointer to the last node as well as the pointer to the first node; in fact, one might keep both pointers in another node, thereby combining all the parts into one compound data object.

The explicit sequencing of lists can be used to implement *sparse arrays*, arrays in which the majority of the elements are zero. If the array is large, substantial space can be saved if the zeros can be omitted. Using lists, either as a table or in some more specialized structure, with one node per nonzero element, the array can be built in such a way that it appears as if all elements are present, but which occupies much less storage. It is also flexible: as elements become nonzero, new nodes are added, and as elements become zero, nodes are removed. There will be a cost in access time,

but for some problems that cost will be outweighed by the ability to fit the problem into the computer at all.

For example, one could implement a sparse array as an association list whose keys are the array indices and whose values are the nonzero elements of the array. Imagine a 100×100 matrix with only three nonzero elements, 1s at (0,0), (6,2), and (88,90). Implemented in this way, it might look like the second part of Fig. 4, or in Lisp notation:

```
(((0 . 0) . 1)
 ((6 . 2) . 1)
 ((88 . 90) . 1))
```

An array reference would then make a pair from the indices, look it up in the table, and return either the value (if found) or zero. Writing to the array would either update a found element or add a new one. Where the complete array requires 10,000 values, the total storage needed for the sparse version is nine values and nine pair nodes. For each element, it is more expensive (depending on the list implementation, six to nine times more per array value), but the total cost is much less when there are very few array elements to record.

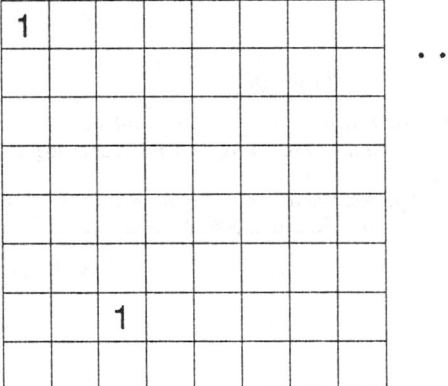

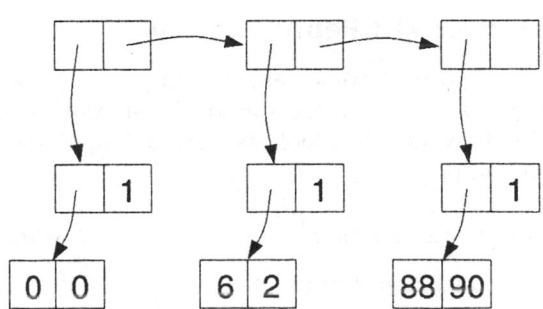

Figure 4. A sparse array and its list implementation.

Lists are often used within operating systems. Tree-structured directories of files are sometimes implemented as one node per file, with the node containing fields that point to data (for a file) or other nodes (for a directory—*q.v.*). Multiple processes waiting to run on a processor are collected in a run-list. A text editor may represent a file internally as a list of lines. Any application requiring variable numbers of fixed-size pieces is ripe for implementation using lists.

For some problems, simple lists are not enough. Sometimes one wants to represent truly infinite lists, such as a list of all the prime numbers. This kind of infinite structure can be built with an extension to the list concept, called *lazy evaluation*. The idea of lazy evaluation is to create only those elements that are actually accessed. If a program looks at the first 10 primes, or the first 20, only that many will be created, but the list appears to contain them all. The key is to put a procedure in the last node of the list that will calculate the next element when it is accessed. Each time a program looks at the next element, the procedure will calculate it, attach it to the list, and attach itself to the end. If no one accesses beyond a certain point, those elements are not calculated; all elements up to that point are calculated once and left in the list. As far as the program using it is concerned, the list is effectively infinite.

Bibliography

1996. Abelson, H., and Sussman, G. *Structure and Interpretation of Computer Programs*, 2nd Ed. Cambridge, MA: MIT Press.
1997. Carrano, F. *Data Abstraction and Problem Solving With C++: Walls and Mirrors*. Reading, MA: Addison-Wesley.

Paul Fuqua

LANGUAGES

A *list-processing language* is a computer language that facilitates the processing of data organized in the form of lists. Lisp and Scheme are typical list-processing languages. Other languages, such as Prolog, have extensive support for list-processing.

External List Representation

We begin with some simple examples to show what kinds of problems are solved by list processing and also how the lists look as they are used for input and output.

Traditional notation   *List notation*

French to English translation:

Où est le Métro?   (OU EST LE METRO ?)

Arithmetic expression:

$2 + (3 * 5 - 1)$ (+ 2 (- (* 3 5) 1))

Note that Polish prefix notation is used for algebraic expressions.

Logic:

$(\forall x)(Q(x) \lor \neg P(x))$ (ALL X ((Q X) OR (NOT (P X))))

Automatic question answering:

Who is on first?   (WHO IS ON FIRST ?)

The list is a convenient way of representing data, such as an English sentence, a mathematical formula, a position in a game, a logic theorem, or a computer program. The structure of a list is a natural way to represent the structure of data for the computer. By nesting sublists one can create list structures of arbitrary complexity. List-processing techniques are especially useful for data that has variable structure, such as languages.

Some of the terms used in connection with list processing are used in slightly different ways by different writers. Some rough definitions are as follows.

The basic data type is the *atom*. Atoms can be numbers or symbols. A symbol corresponds to a word in English. In the examples above, EST, X, ?, and WHO are symbols.

A *list* is a sequence of zero or more elements enclosed in parentheses. An *element* is an atom or a list.

A list is represented externally to the computer in terms of characters, and internally in terms of memory cells. The external representation (shown in the tabulated examples above) is designed for the convenience of the user and is used by the computer for input and output operations. The exact rules for writing a list vary from one language to another. In the preceding examples we have used the notation of Lisp. Parentheses indicate the beginning and end of a list, and blanks separate atoms.

The internal representation of a list is the way in which the computer stores the list in its memory cells. This varies from one language to another. For instance, in Lisp a list is represented by means of pointers. A *pointer* (*q.v.*) is the address of a memory word. Other terms sometimes used for pointer are *link* and *reference*. Each element in a list is represented by a pair of pointers: the first a pointer to the first element of the list, the second a pointer to the rest of the list. This allows lists to have any length, and to be easy to construct and modify. For instance, just changing one pointer allows one to delete an element from a list, and changing one and setting another allows one to add an element. Also, since list elements can be lists themselves, lists can have arbitrary complexity. A list is a *binary tree*, i.e. a tree (*q.v.*) with exactly two children for each node.

The Lisp Language

The best way to gain a good understanding of list processing is to describe a typical list-processing language. Lisp (short for LISt Processing) is the most popular of such languages. Lisp was developed by John McCarthy and his associates at MIT during the late 1950s and early 1960s. Many details will be omitted. During its long history, Lisp has undergone numerous changes until a formal American National Standard for Common Lisp was produced in 1994.

DATA

First we define the data language that is used in Lisp. An S-expression (short for symbolic expression) is the general name for legal input data in Lisp. An S-expression is either an atom or a list structure. An atom is a sequence of characters other than blanks or parentheses. The start and finish of each atom is indicated by parentheses or blanks. A list structure consists of a left parenthesis followed by any number of atoms or list structures, followed by a right parenthesis. For example, each of the items below is an S-expression.

```
DOG
1984
(WHERE IS TURING NOW)
((MCCARTHY) IS MASTER OF (THE DARK TOWER))
(A LIST ((((CAN))) BE (((VERY)))
                    ((((((DEEP)))))))
```

Numbers may also be used in Lisp. They may be integers, fixed-point numbers, or floating-point numbers. All Lisp functions that operate on numbers automatically test the number type and perform needed conversions. In Lisp, the objects have a type but not the variables, so the same variable can be used as a name for different types of objects. The symbol NIL is a special atom in Lisp and is used to indicate an empty list or to indicate the truth value "false."

PROGRAMS

The language for writing programs in Lisp is actually a subset of the data language. Therefore, it is easy to write Lisp programs that operate on other Lisp programs (e.g. compilers, optimizers, interpreters).

Lisp has a reputation among programmers as being a difficult language to use. This is an illusion caused by the unconventional syntactic style of Lisp. Actually, by any measure of complexity, Lisp would have to be judged one of the simpler computer languages.

Lisp has few special rules and exceptions. It was designed by mathematicians and therefore has the virtues of mathematical elegance and simplicity. The semantics of Lisp is also straightforward. The Lisp system contains a program called the interpreter. The interpreter reads a Lisp expression, computes its value, and then prints it out.

To be more precise, Lisp programs are organized as forms and functions. *Forms* are expressions that are evaluated and produce values (and possibly side effects—*q.v.*) as a result of the evaluation. Functions are objects that can be invoked as procedures. They may take arguments and return values. A form may be a self-evaluating form (a number, a character, a string, etc.), a variable, or a list.

Numbers, T, and NIL are examples of self-evaluating forms. T means "true", NIL means "false" and also "empty list". The empty list can also be indicated by ( ).

Symbols are used as names of variables. When a symbol is evaluated, it returns the value of the variable it names. The value is stored in the computer as a pointer to some expression. For example, a variable X may have as value a list of three elements (A B C).

A list may be a function call, a special form, or a macro (*q.v.*) call. (We will not discuss macro calls here.) Function calls have the basic format (function arg_1 arg_2 ... arg_n), where function is the name of a function and the arguments are the arguments the function takes. Forms are evaluated using applicative order, which means that the arguments are evaluated first, and this is followed by applying the function to the values of the arguments.

Special forms have different rules of evaluation. An example of a special form is the conditional expression, which has the format (COND (arg_1 arg_2) (arg_3 arg_4)...). Its rules of evaluation are explained later. Another special form is QUOTE. It is written as (QUOTE a) or 'a, where a can be any expression. The value of (QUOTE a) is a. QUOTE is a special form because it does not evaluate its argument. It is used to provide data to a program.

Lisp includes a set of built-in primitive functions. Since most of the processing is done by manipulating lists, some primitive functions construct lists, and others select elements in lists.

The primitive function CONS (short for construct) is used to build lists. CONS takes two arguments. If the second argument is a list, it returns a new list with the first argument added to the front. For example, if X has the value of (A B C) and Y has the value A, then (CONS Y X) has the value (A A B C). (CONS A NIL) forms the one-element list (A). The second element of CONS is not necessarily a list; it could be any other Lisp object. In this case CONS constructs an S-expression that is called a *dotted list*, since it is not terminated by NIL as regular lists are.

CAR is a primitive function that returns the first element of a list. If X has the value (A B C), then (CAR X) has the value A. A companion to CAR is CDR, which returns the rest of the list. The value of (CDR X) is (B C). One can use nested CARs and CDRs to isolate any component of an S-expression. The names CAR and CDR are historical fossils. They relate to assembly language on the IBM 704 computer, the first machine on which Lisp was implemented. The term CAR is short for "Contents of the Address part of Register," and CDR is short for "Contents of the Decrement part of Register."

The CONS primitive constructs a CONS box, i.e. a pair whose CAR is the first element and whose CDR is the second. When multiple CONS boxes are linked in a chain by their CDR components and terminated by NIL, the resulting structure is a list.

Among the Lisp primitives there are *predicates*, i.e. functions that return either true or false (T or NIL). For instance, ATOM is a predicate of one argument. (ATOM X) has the value T if X is an atom and NIL ("false") otherwise.

Predicates are particularly useful in *conditional forms*, the Lisp equivalent of a branch instruction. The following is a typical conditional form:

```
(COND ((ATOM X) X) (T (CAR X)))
```

The arguments of a conditional form come in pairs. In each pair, the first is the predicate part and the second is the value part. The interpreter evaluates conditional pairs from left to right. If the predicate has the value T, the interpreter then evaluates the second portion of the conditional pair and returns this as the value of the entire conditional form. If the value of the predicate is NIL, the interpreter starts to work on the next pair. If X is (A B C), the value of the sample conditional form above is A, since (ATOM X) is NIL and (CAR X) is A.

A LAMBDA expression is used to create functions. (The name is reminiscent of the lambda calculus (*q.v.*) on which Lisp is based.) The LAMBDA expression consists of the symbol LAMBDA followed by some arguments. A LAMBDA expression is a list of at least three elements, for example,

```
(LAMBDA (X Y) (CONS Y X))
```

The second element is a list of LAMBDA variables, the third is a form that uses those variables. Multiple forms are allowed. The results of using a LAMBDA expression look more complex than other expressions, since the LAMBDA expression is a list of multiple elements, instead of just one atom like the other functions. An example of using a LAMBDA expression in a form is:

```
((LAMBDA (X Y) (CONS Y X)) '(A B C) 'A)
```

The interpreter first evaluates the arguments. These values are then assigned to the corresponding variables

on the LAMBDA variables list. The form in which the LAMBDA variables appear (the internal form) is then evaluated, and this value is then the value of the entire LAMBDA expression. In the preceding example, X will have the value (A B C) and Y will have the value A. Thus, the internal form, (CONS Y X), will have the value (A A B C), and this will be the value of the entire LAMBDA expression.

A function can be given a name by using the special form DEFUN. DEFUN requires as arguments a name, a list of variables, and one or more forms. The forms comprise the body of the function. The list of variables is like the list of variables used in the LAMBDA expression. Below is an example of a simple function being defined and then used. In this example, * means multiply.

```
(DEFUN SQUARE (X) (* X X))
(SQUARE 9)
```

The DEFUN special form in the preceding example will assign to the atom SQUARE a function of one argument (X). When evaluating (SQUARE 9), the Lisp interpreter will first look up the definition of the function attached to the atom SQUARE, and then evaluate the form (* X X) in it, using 9 as the value for X. Thus, the value of (SQUARE 9) is 81.

RECURSIVE FUNCTIONS

A useful property of Lisp is the ability to evaluate a recursively defined function, i.e. a function that uses its own name as part of its definition. For example,

```
(DEFUN LAST (X)
    (COND ((ATOM (CDR X)) (CAR X))
          (T (LAST (CDR X)))
    ))
```

where LAST searches a list of one or more elements and returns the last element of that list. (ATOM (CDR X)) is true only if X is a list of just one element since then its CDR is NIL, an atom. If X is a list of two or more elements, LAST calls itself and shortens the list by removing the first element. Eventually, the list is shortened to just one element. Then (CAR X) is returned, which is the only element of a one-element list.

How can a recursively defined function be evaluated? When the Lisp interpreter is evaluating a function and it encounters another call of the same function, it simply creates new bindings for the variables used in the recursive call, and proceeds with the evaluation. Since Lisp uses applicative order, the arguments of the recursive call are evaluated first, and then the function is applied to them. The resulting value is then returned to the place where the recursive call was made, and the computation continues. In the preceding example of the function LAST, the recursion depth will be equal to the number of elements in the list being searched.

The value of a form can be an argument to another form, and so programs are usually built by nesting.

The following is an example of a modern way of writing Lisp. The function FILTER takes as arguments a predicate and a list, and returns as value a list of the elements of the original list that satisfy the predicate. The function FILTER includes an auxiliary argument in its parameter list that is used as a local variable, initialized to NIL. The function DOLIST computes its body on successive elements of a list, and is used when an operation has to be done on each element of a list for its side effects. WHEN is a primitive predicate which, when the condition in its first argument is true, computes its body (that could be composed of one or more forms). This example shows how functions can be passed as arguments to other functions. FUNCALL applies the value of FN, the formal parameter of FILTER, to elements of the list. (ELT takes on each element in turn.) PUSH adds an element to the front of a list that is treated as a stack. NREVERSE is the destructive version of REVERSE, a built-in function that reverses a list. NREVERSE reverses the list in place, instead of creating a new copy of it.

```
(DEFUN FILTER (FN L &AUX (NEWLIST NIL))
    (DOLIST (ELT L)
        (WHEN (FUNCALL FN ELT)
            (PUSH ELT NEWLIST)))
    (NREVERSE NEWLIST))
```

Through the use of powerful functions, Lisp allows expressing complex computations on lists or other data structures as simple functions. The following example computes the inner product of two vectors that are represented as two lists. The inner product is computed by first multiplying pairs of elements in the two vectors and then adding the results. MAPCAR applies a given function to the elements of the lists passed as its arguments and returns a list of the results. The notation #'* is used to indicate that the first argument of MAPCAR is a function, namely multiplication. REDUCE accumulates the results of applying the function used as its first argument to successive pairs of the list that is its second argument.

```
(DEFUN INNERPRODUCT (L1 L2)
    (REDUCE #'+ (MAPCAR #'* L1 L2)))
```

THE GARBAGE COLLECTOR

The garbage collector, or *reclaimer*, aids the dynamic storage allocation in Lisp. It periodically searches memory to locate list structures that are no longer needed. The memory cells in this garbage are then added to the *list of available space* (free storage) to be used in making new list structures. Garbage collector algorithms are used in most list processing languages.

A PRACTICAL LISP PROGRAM

As a practical example to illustrate the use of Lisp, we will now write a program to do backward chaining in propositional logic, given a set of facts and if–then rules. The program assumes the facts are stored in the list *FACTS*, the rules in the list *RULES*. Note the convention of using asterisks at the beginning and end of names of symbols that are used as names of global variables. This example is simple and does not take advantage of more sophisticated data structures in Lisp, such as hash tables.

The program starts by defining selectors for rules. We assume here that a rule is a list of two elements whose CAR is the then-part of the rules and whose second element (the CADR, that is the CAR of the CDR) is the if-part of the rule. If the rule has more than one condition, we assume the conditions are in a conjunction. For instance, the rule "The means of transportation is a plane if the distance is long and the time is short" would be represented as

```
((MEANS-OF-TRANSPORTATION IS-A PLANE)
        ((DISTANCE LONG) (TIME SHORT)))
(DEFUN THEN-PART (RULE) (CAR RULE))
(DEFUN IF-PART (RULE) (CADR RULE))
```

The core of the program is in the two functions PROVE-BY-FACT and PROVE-BY-RULE. PROVE-BY-FACT attempts to prove a hypothesis by looking for a fact that matches it in the list of known facts. The function shows the use of the built in MEMBER function that checks for membership of an element in a list. This also shows the use of keyword parameters (:TEST) to specify which equality predicate to use. EQUAL is a built-in predicate that checks for equality of two lists.

```
(DEFUN PROVE-BY-FACT (HYP)
    (MEMBER HYP *FACTS* :TEST #'EQUAL))
```

PROVE-BY-RULE attempts to prove a hypothesis by finding a rule whose then-part matches the hypothesis and by recursively proving its if-part. As soon as such a rule is found the proof terminates, since it is sufficient to find one way of proving the hypothesis.

```
(DEFUN PROVE-BY-RULE (HYP)
    (DOLIST (RULE *RULES*)
        (COND ((AND (EQUAL
                (THEN-PART RULE) HYP)
            (PROVE-ALL-OF
                (IF-PART RULE)))
            (RETURN T))
            (T NIL))
        NIL))
```

The function PROVE attempts to prove a hypothesis by proving it using the facts first and then using the rules. This function shows the use of the special form OR. OR evaluates one argument at a time until it finds one that is true. The remaining arguments are not evaluated.

```
(DEFUN PROVE (HYP)
       (COND ((OR (PROVE-BY-FACT HYP)
              (PROVE-BY-RULE HYP)) HYP)
             (T NIL)))
```

PROVE-ALL-OF is used to prove a conjunction of hypotheses; PROVE-ONE-OF is used to prove a disjunction (i.e. one hypothesis out of a list). They make use of the built-in functions EVERY and SOME. Because of the way SOME works, PROVE-ONE-OF will terminate as soon as one hypothesis has been proven.

```
(DEFUN PROVE-ALL-OF (HYPS)
                    (EVERY #'PROVE HYPS))
(DEFUN PROVE-ONE-OF (HYPS)
                    (SOME #'PROVE HYPS))
```

Other List Processing Languages

IPL-V is the grandparent of all list processing languages. It was developed by Allen Newell and his associates at the Rand Corporation and later at Carnegie Mellon University. IPL is an acronym for Information Processing Language, a choice that reflects the lack of competition when the name was selected. IPL-V is the fifth member of the IPL family. IPL-V was the first language to use lists made of memory cells linked with pointers, but garbage collection was the programmer's responsibility.

Scheme is very similar to Lisp. Scheme is a much smaller language, with a simpler and cleaner semantics. It treats lists the same way Lisp does.

The language Pop-2 is a descendant of Lisp and Algol. It was developed by R. J. Popplestone in the Department of Machine Intelligence and Perception at the University of Edinburgh. Programs written in Pop-2 look very much like Algol. Pop-2 is a very general language with many ingenious features. It might be described as a combination of Algol and Lisp. The pushdown stack is accessible to the programmer. The compiler (*q.v.*) is a subroutine that can be called by a program. An automatic reclaimer is available. Pop-2 is also readily extensible in its data structures and the operations to handle them.

Other languages provide extensive support for list processing, including functional programming (*q.v.*) languages such as ML, Miranda, and Haskell. Prolog (*see* LOGIC PROGRAMMING) has lists among its primitive data types. A list operation, such as the selection of elements and the construction of a list, is usually combined with unification. Built-in functors, such as "|" and ",", allow the expression of operations on lists in the arguments of predicates. For instance, the following two Prolog clauses define the predicate *member*.

Note the use of the notation [X|_] to indicate a list whose first element is X and the rest is the list _ (a list whose name we are not interested in). Similarly the notation [_|L] indicates a list whose first element we are not interested in and the rest of which is L.

```
member(X,[X|_]).
member(X,[_|L]):-member(X,L).
```

The clauses can be read as "X is a member of a list that has X as its first element" and "X is a member of a list whose first element is different from X if X is a member of the rest of the list." This is because clauses are used in sequence, so the second clause is tried only if the first failed (i.e. X is not the first element of the list).

Bibliography

1961. Newell, A. (ed.) *Information Processing Language-V Manual.* Upper Saddle River, NJ: Prentice Hall.

1971. Burstall, R. M., Collins, J. S., and Popplestone, R. J. *Programming in POP-2.* Edinburgh: Edinburgh University Press.

1989. Winston, P. H., and Horn, B. *LISP*, 3rd Ed. Reading, MA: Addison-Wesley.

1990. Bratko, I. *Prolog Programming for Artificial Intelligence*, 2nd Ed. Reading, MA: Addison-Wesley.

1990. Steele, G. L. *Common LISP*, 2nd Ed. Bedford, MA: Digital Press.

1990. Touretzky, D. S. *Common Lisp: A Gentle Introduction to Symbolic Computation.* Redwood City, CA: Benjamin/Cummings.

1991. Norvig, P. *Paradigms of Artificial Intelligence Programming: Case Studies in Common Lisp.* San Francisco: Morgan Kaufmann.

1996. Abelson, H., and Sussman, G. J. *Structure and Interpretation of Computer Programs*, 2nd Ed. Cambridge, MA: MIT Press.

1996. Graham, P. *ANSI Common Lisp.* Upper Saddle River, NJ: Prentice Hall.

1998. Grillmeyer, O. *Explaining Computer Science with Scheme.* New York: Springer-Verlag.

James R. Slagle and Maria L. Gini

LITERACY, COMPUTER

See COMPUTER LITERACY.

LITERATE PROGRAMMING

For articles on related subjects *see* DOCUMENTATION; MACRO; STRUCTURED PROGRAMMING; and TEX.

A programmer who adds documentation to a program after it is written often finds it difficult to make the documentation correspond to the program. *Literate programming* is a system of combining program and internal documentation, so that both may be developed together. Various automatic aids to readability are provided, such as substantial cross-referencing and indexing, pretty-printing and so on. Special macro processing allows the program to be written in any order to improve and simplify the exposition; macros are automatically numbered so that their usage is easily cross-referenced.

A literate programming system converts the documentation and code into beautifully typeset material *with no additional effort* by the programmer. All features combine to simplify and encourage the documentation process and to keep it in very close correspondence with the actual program. Efficient means are provided to extract the program code from the literate program so that it may be compiled or processed in the usual ways.

Consider the following extract from the source of a literate program that illustrates interleaving of code, documentation and macros. The @ signs are this system's convention for introducing various literate programming features (e.g. @* for a section heading and @p to start the program code).

```
⋮
@* Insert sort
This is the standard insert sort algorithm.
Assumes a sentinel at $a[0]$.
@p
for i := 2 to N do
begin v := a[i]; j := i;
@<Insert...@>
end;
@
@<Insert $v$ in the array@>=
while a[j−1] > v do
begin a[j] := a[j−1]; j := j−1 end;
a[j] := v;
⋮
```

The example shows the use and definition of a macro called <Insert v in the array>. The = after @> (and the ≡ in Fig. 1) denotes that the bracketed phrase names the segment which follows. Macro names may be abbreviated (e.g. <Insert...>), helping encourage programmers to use longer, more mnemonic, names. The $ symbols (in the lines beginning with @) tell the literate programming system to typeset and cross-reference certain text as code rather than as commentary; this is a very important aspect of literate programming, particularly for hypertext (*q.v.*) or Web-based applications. The result of processing this example fragment creates the source code and typeset versions shown in Fig. 1.

There is no need for literate programming to be confined to batch programming languages and conventional documentation. The idea of combining different types of text to make them easier to maintain together is quite general: Kurokawa (1985) exhibits a runnable Pascal program documented in Japanese; while an obvious application is the combination of formal specification with conventional programs. The symbolic mathematics system *Mathematica* (Wolfram, 1988) uses a form of literate programming in its "notebooks": it allows mathematical articles to be written mixing text with mathematics which can be evaluated. Other possibilities and advantages are suggested in Thimbleby (1986).

Literate programming was developed by D. E. Knuth in the late 1970s (Knuth, 1992) and has been used most successfully in the implementation and documentation of his typesetting system TEX. The clarity resulting from the technique has been instrumental in the range of its successful implementations. Knuth's

---

```
⋮
for i:=2 to N do
begin v:=a[i];j:=i;
while a[j-1]>v do
begin a[j]:=a[j-1];j:=j-1 end;
a[j]:=v;
end;
⋮
```

Generated code.

31. Insert sort. This is the standard insert sort algorithm. Assumes a sentinel at $a[0]$.
   for $i := 2$ to N **do**
   begin
      $v := a[i]$; $j := i$;
      ⟨Insert v in the array. 32⟩
   end;
32. ⟨Insert v in the array. 32⟩ ≡
   while $a[j-1] > v$ **do**
   begin
      $a[j] := a[j-1]$; $j := j-1$
   end;
   $a[j] := v$;
Used in section 31.
⋮

Typeset program.
Not showing the automatically generated table of contents, index etc.

Figure 1. Sample output from a literate programming system.

programs are unique in being published in their entirety as readable books. Other programs have been "published," but not readably and not in *exactly* the form in which they may be compiled and run.

Bibliography

1985. Kurokawa, T. "Literate Programming," *bit*, **17**, 4, 426–450. Japanese translation of Knuth's original paper (reprinted in Knuth, 1992).
1986. Thimbleby, H. W. "Experiences of 'Literate Programming' Using cweb (a Variant of Knuth's WEB)." *Computer Journal*, **29**, 3, 201–211.
1988. Wolfram, S. *Mathematica*. Reading, MA: Addison-Wesley.
1992. Knuth, D. E. *Literate Programming*, CSLI Lecture Notes Number 27. Stanford, CA: Center for Study of Language and Information.

Harold W. Thimbleby

LITERATURE OF COMPUTING

For an article on a related subject *see* FICTION, COMPUTERS IN.

Before 1947 the only computing literature concerned analog computers (then called "analyzers"), punched card (*q.v.*) machines, and calculations made with pencil and paper or desk calculators. No periodicals were devoted to the subject. The literature was sparse, entirely technical, and was scattered through the publications of mathematics, statistics, physics, electrical engineering, and other sciences, especially astronomy. A few books (for instance, Whittaker and Robinson's *Calculus of Observations*, Scarborough's *Numerical Mathematical Analysis*, and Eckert's *Punch Card Methods in Scientific Computation—see* ECKERT, WALLACE J.) could, in retrospect, be said to have dealt exclusively with computing, although their subject matter was then considered to be part of applied mathematics.

Contrary to legend, science fiction did not foreshadow the *stored program* digital computer, and except for the machine for writing books discovered by Captain Lemuel Gulliver on the flying island of Laputa (as reported in 1726 by Jonathan Swift), did not mention computers at all.

Today the situation is completely different. Computers and their literature are everywhere. Chain bookstores devote large sections exclusively to computer books for the general public. Supermarket magazine racks display a dozen popular computer periodicals. News magazines and newspapers issue supplements about computing. More than 2,000 magazines and newspapers are published worldwide, covering the exciting events and breakthroughs in every aspect of computing from Artificial Intelligence (*q.v.*) to the World Wide Web (*q.v.*). Probably more than 10,000 computer books

are in print. In addition, there is a wide variety of constantly replenished literature such as research reports, trade publications, theses, patents, proceedings of conferences, dictionaries, encyclopedias, product catalogs, and advertising of every variety of salable computing product. A favorite of all book publishers is the enormously popular how-to books aimed at computing neophytes who are, in two profitable series, bluntly addressed as "dummies" and "idiots." Each year, many thousand technical and popular articles about computing are published in the general news media. The computer is accepted as a common part of the everyday social milieux of all current writing, reporting, fiction, nonfiction, stage and TV drama, movies and, of course, advertising, and has replaced the typewriter as almost every author's principal tool both for writing and collecting information (*see* WORD PROCESSING).

The literature of computing, especially original technical writing, is almost entirely in English. What little technical material is published in Japanese, German, French, and Russian has, with some exceptions, not been important. In the past half-century the few commercial efforts to provide English translations of Russian and Japanese computing literature have failed for lack of source material as well as customers.

Bibliographic and Basic Literature

GUIDES AND LISTS

There are no overall printed summaries or lists of all computer literature, other than the usual library references such as *Books in Print*, which contains several dozen categories relative to computing and programming. The Virtual Library Computing section on the Wide World Web lists several searchable major computer science bibliographies (http://www.vlib.org/Computing.html).

Since 1960, the Association for Computing Machinery (ACM—*q.v.*) has published annual indexes to the technical literature, *ACM Guide to Computing Literature*. The *Guides* include references to everything reviewed in the monthly ACM *Computing Reviews* plus more than 20,000 additional citations each year from all major publishers in the computing field, including scholarly journals and trade magazines. They also cite several thousand books. The *Guides*, which are indexed by author, subject, keyword, and the ACM Computing Classification System categories, provide the most comprehensive coverage of the technical literature for each year but their emphasis on the technical and neglect of the popular, including personal computing (*q.v.*), reflects the orientation of the ACM. The *Guide* is available in printed form, as a CD-ROM product, and online through COMPUSCIENCE, a service of STN International, and through MathSci, a service of the American Mathematical Society. More than 10 years of the listings from the annual *Guides* are included in the ACM Electronic Guide to Computing Literature on CD-ROM (E-Guide).

Lists of several hundred technical periodicals and their publishers' addresses are printed annually in *Computing Reviews* and in the *Guides*.

The articles in the ACM *Computing Surveys* will often include reference lists that amount to comprehensive subject bibliographies. The ACM Special Interest Group newsletters will sometimes publish bibliographies. Now and then, some intrepid librarian will attempt to publish a list for a currently popular specialty (e.g. expert systems (*q.v.*) or networks (*q.v.*)), but the flood of new material soon overwhelms and outdates all such efforts.

There is no comprehensive listing of miscellaneous literature. Publication catalogs of the principal computer societies list the conference and symposia proceedings they have published and reports of their technical and special-interest divisions.

Although most of the significant original technical material on computing appears in a relatively small number of core journals, there is some relevant material in the journals of other disciplines. While computing has been recognized as a science and a technical art in its own right for more than 40 years, it is also an important service discipline and thus much computer literature is interdisciplinary and appears in the publications of other disciplines.

REVIEWS AND SUMMARIES

In 2000 the only surviving periodical devoted entirely to reviewing the literature of computing, *Computing Reviews*, is scheduled to be accompanied by an all-electronic *Online Computing Reviews Service* (*OCRS*), which, if successful, may at some point replace the print version. *Computing Reviews*, which started publishing in 1960, covers only a small fraction of the rapidly expanding computer literature. It has been authoritative and unique, however, in that its reviews have been critical, well-written, and signed by knowledgeable reviewers, whereas the novel and untried reviewing processes of OCRS, which are intended to speed the reviews to the readers, run the risk of a decline in the quality of the reviews.

GLOSSARIES, DICTIONARIES, AND ENCYCLOPEDIAS

The early spate of glossaries which were needed when everyone was a neophyte has declined to a vanishing trickle. One of the survivors, *A Glossary of Computing Terms: An Introduction*, edited by the British Computer Society and published by Cambridge University Press, illustrates the recent growth of computing jargon in that it grew from 92 to 392 pages in going

from its first (1989) to its eighth (1995) edition. The best current dictionaries are the *Oxford Dictionary of Computing* (1997), and the *IBM Dictionary of Computing* by George McDaniel, published by McGraw-Hill (1994), and available on CD-ROM. They are suitable for high school and college students and, in areas outside their own specialties, for advanced computer scientists. Their only competitor is the *Microsoft Press Computer Dictionary*, by a dozen contributors and published by Microsoft Press, 3rd edition (1997). The book you are reading was the only one or two volume encyclopedia until 1992, when *Encyclopedia of Computers*, edited by Gary G. Bitter, was published by the US Macmillan Publishing Company, but this is now badly out of date. Also badly outdated is a 12-volume giant, *Encyclopedia of Computer Science and Technology*, edited by Jack Belzer *et al.* (Dekker, 1975–1979).

HANDBOOKS

The only handbook is *Computer Science and Engineering Handbook*, edited by Allen B. Tucker, Jr. (CRC Press, 1997) and which contains ten sections, with portions written by 166 authors, on major subareas of computer science intended mainly for research and professional computer scientists.

INTRODUCTORY BOOKS

Bookstore shelves are clogged with them, few of them any longer explaining what computers are and some now frequently explaining such things as how to surf the Internet (*q.v.*). Instead of reprinting popular books in a succession of improved editions, publishers satisfy the market need for novelty and their own desire for more bookstore shelf space by subdividing their bestsellers into many volumes. For example, O'Reilly & Associates split its early and excellent *The Whole Internet User's Guide and Catalog* into several volumes, each covering only part of the whole. Two of them, *Internet in a Nutshell* and *Internet: The Definitive Guide*, like the original, are thorough and free of fluff. In selecting an introductory book the logical rule is to choose the one that claims to have been written for you if a quick riffle of the pages seems to confirm the claim.

Texts and Professional Books

CLASSIC TEXTS

Several hundred publishers churn out college textbooks on computing and computer science for colleges: community, junior, and senior. At least half of them are only programming instruction manuals on newly popular Java (*q.v.*) and C++ (*q.v.*) as well as the old standbys Fortran, Cobol, Basic, Pascal, and Ada. Although most publishers no longer issue general computing books and focus narrowly on machines, systems, particular software packages, and languages, the IEEE-CS/ACM Curricula 91 report, "Computing for the Future," stimulated the publication of some "breadth-first" introductory texts. For nonspecialists one of the best is *Great Ideas in Computer Science* by Alan Biermann (MIT Press, 2nd Ed., 1997). For computer science students one of the best is *Foundations of Computer Science* by Alfred V. Aho and Jeffrey D. Ullman (CS Press, 1995). *Algorithmics: The Spirit of Computing* by David Harel (Addison-Wesley, 2nd Ed., 1992), although not quite a textbook, gives a remarkably simple but accurate account of what academic computer science is today.

A few of the older texts are classics that have stood the test of time, are still fully accepted, often referenced, and state important and invariant principles. They are:

♦ *The Art of Computer Programming*, by Donald E. Knuth (Addison-Wesley, Vols. 1, 2 (3rd Eds., 1997), Vol. 3 (2nd Ed., 1998)), is a three-volume omnibus survey of computer science written with style and wit. It has been recognized for three decades as the definitive statement of the fundamentals of computer science. In 1998 the author completed an updating and revision of all three volumes and promised that the long awaited fourth volume would soon appear.

♦ *The Psychology of Computer Programming*, by Gerald Weinberg (Dorset House, 2nd Ed., 1995), was the first, in 1971, to suggest that programmers are people, that they have egos, and that people and their behavior are as important to a project as technical issues.

♦ *The Mythical Man-Month*, by Fred Brooks (Addison-Wesley, originally 1975, repeatedly reprinted, and now in a revised edition, 1995) is the classic statement of the root-problems of software project management, problems that are so fundamental that every new manager must discover them afresh, in spite of Brooks.

♦ *Programming Languages: History and Fundamentals*, by Jean E. Sammet (Prentice Hall, 1969), is complete and accurate in its history and still definitive and reliable in spite of its age.

♦ *Structured Programming*, by O.-J. Dahl, Edsger Dijkstra, and C. A. R. Hoare (Prentice Hall, 1972).

♦ *The Elements of Programming Style*, by Brian Kernighan and P. J. Plauger (McGraw-Hill, 1974).

♦ *Algorithms + Data Structures = Programs*, by Niklaus Wirth (Prentice Hall, 1976).

♦ *A Discipline of Programming*, by Edsger Dijkstra (Prentice Hall, 1976).

♦ *The Structure and Interpretation of Computer Programs*, by H. Abelson and G. Sussman (MIT Press, 2nd Ed., 1996) is an excellent text on the principles of computer science exhibited through the use of Scheme, a dialect of Lisp (*q.v.*). It is well on its way to becoming a classic.

A few well-conceived and thought-provoking books amount to works of scientific criticism addressed to computing. Worth mentioning are *What Computers Still Can't Do*, by Hubert L. Dreyfus (MIT Press, 1992), *Computer Power and Human Reason*, by Joseph Weizenbaum (W. H. Freeman, 1976), *The Emperor's New Mind*, by Roger Penrose (Oxford University Press, 1989), and *Minds, Brains and Science*, by John Searle (Harvard University Press, 1984). These are far superior to most of the efforts by essayists, philosophers, and social science writers, whose attempts to grapple with the philosophical and humanistic implications of computers and computing lead to the popular press question, "Can computers think?". Many pontificate on this short question although they appear to know little or nothing about either computing or thinking. An exception is John L. Casti's *Cambridge Quintet* (Perseus Press, 1998) a dialogue among Alan Turing (*q.v.*) and four other famous scientists about machine intelligence in general and the Turing Test (*q.v.*) in particular at an imagined dinner party in 1949.

Periodicals

Three types of periodical may be distinguished according to their character, objectives, and intended beneficiaries. Academic periodicals report original results, are refereed, and are published for the benefit of the authors and their peers. Commercial periodicals intepret original results for practitioners, report and evaluate new products and practices, are professionally written and edited for clarity and interest, and are published to sell the products of their advertisers. News publications are a form of commercial publication in which content currency and sensationalism are the most significant criteria.

ACADEMIC PERIODICALS

The best are those of the two principal computing societies, ACM and the IEEE Computer Society (*q.v.*) and their subgroups. None has a circulation of more than about 80,000 and most have circulations of less than 10,000.

Some academic periodicals are published commercially; for example, *Journal of Computer and System Science* and *Journal of Algorithms* (Academic Press), *Information Science, Artificial Intelligence*, and *Theoretical Computer Science* (Elsevier), *Acta Informatica* (Springer-Verlag), *Information Processing and*

Management (Pergamon), and *BIT* (Data A/S, Copenhagen). These rank with the IEEE-CS and ACM products.

A few industrial organizations have attempted to produce academic periodicals but only three are worth mentioning. The best in the computing field, because of rigid reviewing, outstanding editing, and intracorporate rewards to authors, are the *IBM Journal of Research and Development* and the *IBM Systems Journal*, which are equal in quality to the best of the society journals. The model for these IBM journals, which established the standard which they reached, was the quarterly *Bell System Technical Journal*, started in 1922. Like its parent, the late, great, American Telephone & Telegraph Company, the Bell Journal only slowly came to realize that telephony, its original subject, was merely a subset of computing and to reflect this in its content. Today, as *The Bell Laboratories Technical Journal* of the Lucent Corporation, its articles, of its usual high quality, are a third to a half on computing and related topics.

Appendix III lists several hundred research journals and their publishers.

COMMERCIAL PERIODICALS

The split between dispersed personal computers and centralized mainframes (*q.v.*) is reflected in commercial periodicals. The PC end-user publications, many of which started as hobbyist journals, are consumer publications with large circulations and low buying power per subscriber. *PC Magazine*, with a circulation of 700,000, is the biggest, followed by *PC World*, *Personal Computing*, and *PC Computing* each with printruns almost as large. They focus on the description and analysis of PC-ware, both hard- and soft-, with particular attention to speed, novelty, and general glitz. The much smaller Macintosh niche is served by a string of Mac-titled periodicals.

BYTE, founded in 1975, became the bible for PC hobbyists, grew extremely fat, but died as a print magazine in 1998 (although it survives in an online version), surpassed in ad pages and buzz by competing magazines with the explicit first name of PC. After a long and debilitating illness, so did *DATAMATION*, the bible of early computing. Now a PC hobbyist or professional programmer may be identified by having *Dr. Dobb's Journal* at hand. This monthly, long ago stripped of its original sophomoric titular reference to orthodontics, is the best of the Miller Freeman string of journals.

The commercial periodicals directed at the industry in general and mainframes in particular are specialized business publications with lower circulation numbers and are often sent free to qualified subscribers who are selected for their control of major purchases, but referred to by the publishers as "computer professionals." The leaders are *Information Week*, *MIS Week*, *Computerworld*, and a string of more narrowly specialized magazines and newspapers whose numbers and page counts rise and fall with the advertising budgets of the vendors of the computing world. They look like newspapers and mix news with crusading and with didactic articles.

In January 1993, just as the Internet started to get trendy, the monthly magazine *Wired* was launched in San Francisco "to address the social and cultural effects of digital information technologies." Its flashy graphics and long, rambling, but almost meaningless text attracted both readers and advertisers and in two years it reached a circulation of 100,000. In 1998, with a circulation of 400,000 but mounting losses from ill-advised online ventures, *Wired* was sold for $80 million to Condé Nast. While the new management will certainly cool its ranting and raving, the chill may kill.

In addition to the publications of the subordinate groups within the IEEE-CS and ACM, each of the dozens of free-standing minor computing societies, some of which are listed in the COMPUTER SOCIETIES (*q.v.*) article or described in the appendix to that article, engages in a publication program. The quality varies widely, the best being those that are carefully peer-refereed, and the worst being those which publish merely to advance the academic status of the unpaid volunteer authors by adding titles to their lists of publications.

CONFERENCE PROCEEDINGS

Publication of papers in proceedings of professional computing conferences often takes the place of publication in academic periodicals. Although conference refereeing is seldom as strict as that of the leading academic journals, the published material is sometimes significant. The important regular technical conferences are those of the principal computer societies and their subgroups, that is those of ACM, largely concerned with programming and the mathematics of computing, and the IEEE Computer Society, slightly more concerned with hardware than with software. Their conference publications, several hundred a year, are listed in *Communications of the ACM* and the IEEE-CS journal *Computer*.

Collections of Computer Data

These formerly popular publications have largely vanished leaving only those of DataPro. Each software vendor publishes its own product list, most easily available on the Internet. Periodical or Internet advertisements are a more up-to-date guide to software for sale or for free than any printed lists.

DIRECTORIES

The field is so large that there is no complete, checked, dependable, printed directory of all US computer installations, or of vendors of computers and computer services, or of people in the computer field. The information can be searched for on the Internet. The persistence of mailed computer advertising shows that virtually everyone must be listed on several commercially available mailing lists.

History and Biographies

The history of computing is being written as it happens. B. V. (later Lord) Bowden's 1953 *Faster Than Thought* is now a classic. An excellent recent history is *Computer: A History of the Information Machine*, by Martin Campbell-Kelly and William Aspray.

Several pioneers have recorded their memoirs; for example, *The Computer from Pascal to von Neumann*, by H. H. Goldstine (Princeton University Press, 1972), *Memoirs of a Computer Pioneer*, by Maurice Wilkes (MIT Press, 1985), *A Few Good Men from Univac*, by David E. Lundstrom (MIT Press, 1987), *From Dits to Bits*, by Herman Lukoff (Robotics Press, 1979), and *Models of My Life*, by Herbert Simon (Basic Books, 1991). Four excellent early collections of papers and conference proceedings are *The Origins of Digital Computers: Selected Papers*, ed. B. Randell (Springer-Verlag, 3rd Ed., 1982), *A History of Computing in the Twentieth Century*, eds. N. Metropolis *et al.* (Academic Press, 1980), *A History of Programming Languages*, ed. R. L. Wexelblat (Academic Press, 1981), and *History of Programming Languages II*, eds. T. J. Bergin and R. G. Gibson (Addison-Wesley, 1996). Since 1979, the scholarly quarterly, the *IEEE Annals of the History of Computing* has encouraged the study and documentation of the history of computing by providing a refereed publication outlet for those who will write on the subject. It is one of the few periodical publications devoted exclusively to the history of any scientific or technical discipline.

The best of the shorter biographical accounts are published in *Annals*. There are several book-length biographies of Charles Babbage (*q.v.*), Babbage's own *Passages from the Life of a Philosopher*, the Morrisons' *Charles Babbage and His Calculating Engines*, Mabeth Moseley's *Charles Babbage, Irascible Genius*, and Anthony Hyman's *Charles Babbage, Pioneer of the Computer*. Dorothy Stein has written a life of Augusta Ada Byron, later Countess of Lovelace (*q.v.*) and Babbage's interpreter, in *Ada, A Life and a Legacy*

(MIT Press, 1985), chiefly to tell how badly women were treated. *John von Neumann and the Origins of Modern Computing* by William Aspray is a deep and scholarly treatment of the many contributions to computing of this genius. Alan M. Turing (*q.v.*) was first memorialized by his mother, Sara, in *Alan M. Turing*, and more recently popularized by Andrew Hodges in *Alan Turing, the Enigma*. The early biographies of Thomas J. Watson, Sr. (*q.v.*)—the authorized version, *The Lengthening Shadow*, by the Beldens, and the unauthorized version, *THINK*, by William Rodgers—have now been corrected and expanded by his son, Thomas J. Watson Jr., in his own autobiography, *Father, Son, and Co.*

The histories of a few firms and their machines have been written. IBM (*q.v.*) has attracted the most attention, but the history of the firm's technology is best expressed in three volumes of the MIT Press Series in the History of Computing: *Memories that Shaped an Industry*, by Emerson W. Pugh (1984); *IBM's Early Computers*, by Bashe, Johnson, Palmer, and Pugh (1986); and *IBM's 360 and Early 370 Systems*, by Pugh, Johnson, and Palmer (1991). An Wang tells his story in *Lessons* (Addison-Wesley, 1988), and James C. Worthy tells about ERA in *William Norris, Portrait of a Maverick* (Ballinger, 1987). The Apple (*q.v.*) story so far is available in several versions, chiefly John Sculley's *Odyssey* (Harper and Row, 1987) and Frank Rose's *West of Eden* (Viking, 1989). Tracy Kidder in *The Soul of a New Machine* (Little, Brown, 1981) intended to tell the history of one machine, but may have told the history of Data General. *Project Whirlwind* (Digital Press, 1980), by Redmond and Smith is a somewhat uncritical account of this breakthrough machine. The history of the Digital Equipment Corporation (DEC—*q.v.*) from its founding until 1988 is told in *The Ultimate Entrepreneur* by Rifkin and Harrar (Contemporary Books, 1988). Beyond these there is little corporate history worthy of note (*see also* ENTREPRENEURS).

Computing history now shows its maturity in that controversies have developed. The fight over who was the first true inventor of the electronic digital computer was stimulated by Nancy Stern's *From ENIAC to UNIVAC* (Digital Press, 1981), and has since produced one polemic biography, *Atanasoff, Forgotten Father of the Computer*, by Clark R. Mollenhoff (Iowa State University Press, 1988), an excellent account of the ENIAC in *The First Electronic Computer, The Atanasoff Story*, by Alice R. Burks and Arthur W. Burks (University of Michigan Press, 1988), and a continuing flurry of dispute in *Annals of the History of Computing* and elsewhere. Many authors ranging from fully qualified to incompetent have weighed in on all sides of the questions of how IBM grew so great and why it stumbled. An example of the story told in dramatic terms by a good journalist is *Big Blues; The Unmaking of IBM*, by Paul Carroll (Crown Publishers, 1993). Now, five years later, other journalists are known to be preparing to explain the Gerstner-led recovery, probably without the help of the hero. Like the Watsons and IBM, Bill Gates and Microsoft (*q.v.*) have now attracted the attention of journalists and other fast and superficial writers. Gates himself, aided by two co-authors, has weighed in with *The Road Ahead* (Viking, 1995), a bland and tepid statement of his visions. Microsoft events are moving so quickly that any current attempt at a historical analysis will probably soon be proved wrong.

The Charles Babbage Institute (*q.v.*) performed a service for historians by reprinting about two dozen volumes of the key literature of early computing, including long out-of-print textbooks, reports, collections of papers, and conference proceedings.

Miscellaneous Literature

STANDARDS

The official computing standards are produced with great effort and after a long time by the American National Standards Institute (ANSI) and the National Institute of Standards and Technology (NIST) as *Federal Information Processing Standards* in the USA and the British Standards Institution and the National Computing Centre in the UK. International standards, usually derived from those of the USA and the UK, are published by the International Organization for Standardization (ISO). NIST annually publishes a *Federal Information Processing Standards Index*, which summarizes standards publications at all levels—federal, national, and international (*see* STANDARDS). Unofficial or *ad hoc* standards are available only in the literature of the particular establishment engaged in the adhockery.

TRADE LITERATURE

Vast quantities of descriptive and promotional material are distributed by vendors. The purely factual, descriptive, and instructional manuals are valuable and important. The remaining free trade literature is a form of commercial advertising, and is usually worth what the vendor charges for it. There is no general listing or abstracting of such literature, each vendor maintaining its own listing, often in an uncoordinated fashion. IBM is the exception. It has a comprehensive but overwhelming list of its own current literature.

PATENTS

Although, in principle, patents (available by mail for $1.50 each from the US Patent Office) should provide complete and comprehensive descriptions of the devices, methods, processes, or programs patented,

their titles are deliberately vague and uninformative, and the disclosures themselves are written in an arcane, wordy, and laborious jargon that makes them generally useless as informative literature.

FICTION, DRAMA, MOVIES, AND TV

The computer figures naturally and importantly in technology-oriented literature and drama. Rarely, a computer takes a major role, as with HAL in Arthur C. Clarke's *2001, A Space Odyssey*, or in Gibson and Sterling's *Difference Engine* (*q.v.*), but literary works dealing with computers are chiefly limited to a lot of average quality science fiction. Computer people are portrayed as stereotypical nerds or hackers (*q.v.*), as in John Updike's *Roger's Version*, the movie *Wargames*, and other movies made for 14-year-olds (*see also* FICTION, COMPUTERS IN). Clifford Stoll, playing himself in the made-for-TV-movie of his own nonfiction book, *The Cuckoo's Egg*, appears in the movie to be a caricature of a computer-besotted hacker.

The only serious play about a computing person was *Breaking the Code*, by Hugh Whitemore, about Alan Turing's tragedy, in which the title referred both to the German code based on the Enigma machine (*see* COLOSSUS) and Turing's homosexuality. It opened first in London in 1987 and later in New York, and was presented in a television version. Turing's living contemporaries said that his character, played by Derek Jacobi, was far from true-to-life.

THE INTERNET AND THE WORLD WIDE WEB

This article's extremely broad definition of "computer literature" must include the vast amount of text and graphics available on the Internet and the World Wide Web. The electronically stored computer literature which came from hard copy sources has been remarked on above. That which exists only in electronic form is today so evanescent, so often unreliable and contradictory, as to defy any serious analysis. Each surfer must journey through it on his or her own.

CRITICAL LITERATURE

Computing Reviews provides the only regular critique of the current literature, although some other computer publications publish a few book reviews in each issue. Computer books are reviewed as trade books by the usual reviewing mechanisms.

HUMOR

Computer humor is generally represented by cartoons in the technical and popular press. Recently the most consistent are the cartoon strips and books by Scott Adams involving the adventures of his nerdy engineer, Dilbert. Email distributes an unbelievably huge quantity of extremely bad jokes.

Is Software Literature?

Computer programs are legally accepted as "writings" subject to the copyright law. Other than that, their status as literature is similar to that of pre-First World War movies, not yet culturally accepted, but may be later. If the criterion for acceptance is utility or quality of performance, the widely used Windows 95 and 98 and MacOS operating systems, and the major PC application packages like Word and WordPerfect are candidates. If quality of expression in terms of unity, coherence, emphasis, and brevity is the criterion, there are, as yet, no candidates (but *see* LITERATE PROGRAMMING).

Bibliography

Further reading: works not described in the article.

1957. De Latil, P. *Thinking by Machine.* Boston: Houghton-Mifflin.
1979. McCorduck, P. *Machines Who Think: A Personal Inquiry into the History and Prospects of Artificial Intelligence.* San Francisco: W.H Freeman.
1984. Turkle, S. *The Second Self: Computers and the Human Spirit.* New York: Simon & Schuster.
1988. Pagels, H. R. *The Dreams of Reason: The Computer and the Rise of the Sciences of Complexity.* New York: Bantam Books.
1989. Penzias, A. *Ideas and Information.* New York: Norton.
1990. Kurzweil, R. *The Age of Intelligent Machines.* Cambridge, MA: MIT Press.
1995. Negroponte, N. *Being Digital.* New York: Vintage Books.
1995. Lee, J. A. N. (ed.) *Computer Pioneers.* New York: IEEE Press.
1996. Rawlins, G. J. E. *Moths to the Flame: The Seductions of Computer Technology.* Cambridge, MA: MIT Press.
1997. Denning, P. J., and Metcalfe, R. M. (eds.) *Beyond Calculation: The Next Fifty Years of Computing.* New York: Copernicus.
1997. Dyson, E. *Release 2.0: A Design for Living in the Digital Age.* New York: Broadway Books.
1998. Ceruzzi, P. E. *A History of Modern Computing.* Cambridge, MA: MIT Press.
1998. Hillis, D. *The Pattern on the Stones: The Simple Ideas that Make Computers Work.* New York: Basic Books.
1998. Gelernter, D. H. *Machine Beauty: Elegance in the Heart of Technology.* New York: Basic Books.
1999. Kurzweil, R. *The Age of Spiritual Machines.* New York: Viking.
1999. Stephenson, N. *In the Beginning Was the Command Line.* New York: Avon Books.

Eric A. Weiss

LOADER

See LINKERS AND LOADERS.

LOCAL AREA NETWORK (LAN)

> For articles on related subjects *see* ASYNCHRONOUS TRANSFER MODE; COMMUNICATION CONTROL UNIT; DATA COMMUNICATIONS; ETHERNET; FIBER OPTICS; FILE SERVER; GATEWAY; METROPOLITAN AREA NETWORK; NETWORK ARCHITECTURE; NETWORK PROTOCOLS; NETWORKS, COMPUTER; OPEN SYSTEMS INTERCONNECTION; PACKET SWITCHING; SYNCHRONOUS/ASYNCHRONOUS OPERATION; and WORKSTATION.

Historical Overview

Stemming from some early experiments in the late 1960s, development of the first generation *local area network*, or LAN, took place during the 1970s. The goal was an inexpensive network suitable for use in a classroom, laboratory, suite of offices, or, perhaps, an entire building, to enable personal computers to share more expensive peripherals such as printers and large disk drives. Standardization in the early 1980s was followed by worldwide deployment of 10 Mb/sec LANs. By the end of the decade, desktop computer systems interconnected throughout an institutional building or site had become common, producing a local site scaling problem with traffic and numbers of connected systems.

Second-generation LAN development could be said to have begun with the 100 Mb/sec FDDI (Fiber Distributed Data Interface) in the late 1980s. At the same time, MAC (Media Access Control)-level bridges were developed as a means of interconnecting LANs, primarily within a site, both to extend the range of coverage and to constrain traffic local to a single LAN to prevent flooding a whole site. MAC is the second level of the International Organization for Standardization (ISO) Open Systems Interconnection (OSI). Early deployment of FDDI as a backbone network interconnecting site LANs in a hierarchical arrangement began near the end of the 1980s.

The 1990s have seen a number of advances in LAN technology: use of copper twisted-pairs and the introduction of structured cabling; deployment of hubs and switches; and the development of other 100 Mb/sec LAN technologies, most notably 100 Mb/sec Ethernet. Gigabit Ethernet products are also available, though the technology is still in the process of standardization.

Two other significant developments for local site networking are the virtual LAN, or VLAN, and LAN emulation, or LANE. VLAN enables a separation of logical LAN segments and addressing from issues of physical connection, which improves management of traffic and facilitates workgroup membership. Another way of constructing a form of logical LAN not subject to the constraints of physical LAN operation is to use Asynchronous Transfer Mode (ATM); *see* Dutton and Lenhard (1995). LANE is a standardized architecture for achieving this.

Basic Principles

The key feature underlying LAN operation derives from use of a shared medium. In its most basic form a LAN is realized by attaching all devices directly to the transmission medium. Each data packet (or *frame*) transmitted by any station is seen by all the others, each of which examines the destination address field

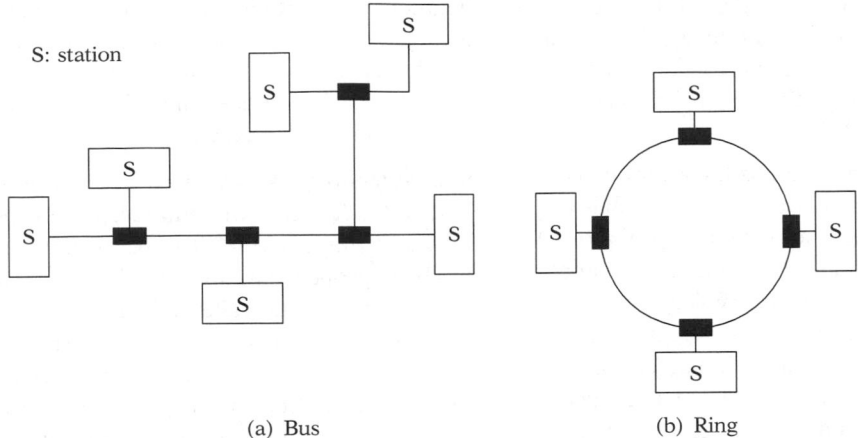

S: station

(a) Bus   (b) Ring

Figure 1. LAN topologies.

of the packet to determine whether it should receive it (*see* PACKET SWITCHING). As a consequence, such a network does not have to perform any routing. Moreover, this basic LAN is intrinsically capable of supporting broadcast communication by any station to all others. Since there are no switching elements or buffer (*q.v.*) in the network, the only resource for which stations have to contend is the transmission medium itself. All such contention (*q.v.*) and associated buffering takes place in the stations, not the network.

Two of the most common LAN topologies are the *bus* (*q.v.*) and the *ring* (Fig. 1). The two principal designs associated with these topologies, Ethernet and token ring, are described here. For a more extensive treatment, *see* Stallings (1997).

ETHERNET

Ethernet was invented by Robert Metcalfe at the Xerox Palo Alto Research Center in 1973 (Metcalfe and Boggs, 1976). In its simplest form, it uses a single length of coaxial cable, terminated at the ends to prevent signal reflections, to which stations are attached by passive taps that provide *multiple access* to the medium. A station wishing to transmit a packet first senses the transmission medium to see if another station is transmitting; if not, it begins its own transmission. This is referred to as carrier sense and the term *carrier sense multiple access* (CSMA) is used to describe a class of basic LAN designs that use it. There is a delay while the beginning of the packet propagates along the cable before all the other stations become aware that a transmission is in progress. During this *acquisition time*, another station may begin to transmit, resulting in a *collision*. The originating station listens to its own transmission and if a collision is detected, it aborts transmission of the packet and transmits a *jamming signal* to reinforce collision detection at other transmitters. This is known as CSMA with *collision detection* (CSMA/CD).

For CSMA/CD to work, packets must be sufficiently long, at the transmission speed in use, that a station cannot finish transmitting before a collision has been detected. The length of this minimum-size packet is determined by the maximum round-trip delay of the network, which increases with the size of the LAN. For the original 10 Mb/sec Ethernet specification, the worst-case configuration had a round-trip delay of 45 μs, or 450 bits. When a collision occurs, the transmitters involved wait (*back off*) for random lengths of time before retrying the transmission in order to reduce the probability of further collisions. Nevertheless, under heavy traffic loading, the average time to transmit a packet can be long, and the worst-case time is unbounded. This fundamental design is the basis of the CSMA/CD LAN standardized by IEEE in the 802.3 family of standards.

TOKEN RING

An alternative scheme for allocating access to the transmission medium is based on the use of a *token*. A station can transmit only while it holds the token. When it finishes transmitting, it passes the token on to the next station, typically the next (active) station in a physical ring. By restricting the maximum amount of data that can be transmitted by a station before the token must be relinquished, it is possible to specify the maximum time that a station may have to wait before being able to transmit. This single fact constitutes the main advantage that token-passing schemes have over the Ethernet. Such advantage, however, is gained at the cost of an increase in the complexity of the node circuitry, principally to ensure that the token is not lost, duplicated, or corrupted.

In the form of token ring standardized by IEEE as 802.5, stations are arranged in a physical ring (Fig. 1b) and pass the token to the next active station in the ring. A token-passing scheme can be implemented for a bus by ordering stations that are active according to their node addresses. Each station passes the token to the station with the next higher address; the station with the highest address passes the token to the station with the lowest address. The token bus has been standardized by IEEE as 802.4.

An important token-passing detail is the decision as to exactly when the token is released. One possibility is to transmit the token when the beginning of the (last) frame transmitted arrives back at the sender. For small, slow rings, the size of a packet may typically be larger than the length of the ring, so that the beginning of the frame arrives back at the sending station before or very soon after frame transmission ends. For larger, faster rings, this can waste capacity, since now the packet may be only a small fraction of the length of the ring, but no other station can transmit until the frame arrives back at the sender and the token is released. The IEEE 802.5 standard recognizes this potential probem and allows *early token release* as an option: the token is released by the sender immediately upon the completion of data transmission, without waiting for the head of the frame to arrive back. The 100 Mb/sec FDDI ring, whose range is up to 200 km, uses early token release.

Rings have several interesting intrinsic properties. One is a natural potential for low-level acknowledgment. By allowing a frame to circulate back to the sender before it is removed or *stripped* from the ring, the sender may examine flags to discover whether the transmission was successful. This has a price: it lowers the total capacity of the ring. With ring designs in which the frames are stripped by the receiver, the total throughput (*q.v.*) or capacity can exceed the transmission speed of the ring, since several stations may transmit simultaneously.

Another aspect of LAN technology is *fairness*. With ring topology, no station is favored over any other by virtue of its position on the ring. This leads to generally fair access for all stations. Stations are prevented from monopolizing access by placing a limit on the amount of data which may be transmitted during a single access. This aspect, however, is not peculiar to rings: it must be taken into account by all access schemes.

SLOTTED TECHNIQUES

Another way in which access to the transmission medium may be organized is by arranging to have a continuous stream of small frames or *slots* available for use by nodes. Such slots are typically a few tens or hundreds of bits long. Each slot may be marked full or empty. Any station at which an empty slot arrives may fill it with data, set the source and destination addresses, and mark it full. As with frame stripping in the token ring, two schemes are possible for emptying the slot, and the trade-off is between superior ring capacity (slot emptied by receiver), and having low-level acknowl-

edgment (slot emptied by sender). A feature of slotted techniques is the potential for frequent, rapid, and regular access with small variation ("jitter") in these parameters. This makes the scheme attractive for carrying continuous media traffic.

Slotted techniques, which are synchronous, have seen limited exploitation in commercial ring products, but a slotted ring in which the receiver empties the slot has been proposed as an ATM ring standard. A slotted, dual bus technique called *distributed queue dual bus* (DQDB) has been standardized by IEEE in 802.6 for use with a *metropolitan area network* (MAN). Slotted rings are formatted as part of initialization with a fixed number of circulating slots, the number depending on the total delay around the ring. In DQDB, each bus is unidirectional and has a head end which generates empty slots continuously.

PACKET FORMAT

The general format of the packet (frame) used for LANs is shown in Fig. 2. The first item is typically a *preamble*, which indicates the start of the frame; it may also be used to enable the receiver to synchronize. The preamble varies in length from as few as two bits for empty-slot rings, to 64 bits for 10 Mb/sec Ethernets. The preamble is followed by destination and source addresses. These may be as short as eight bits, but are more typically 48 bits long. The data carried by the frame may be of fixed length, as for empty-slot rings, or of variable length. In the latter case, the length of the data can be indicated by terminating the frame with a delimiter (*q.v.*) (token bus and ring), by including a length field, or by detecting the end of a frame by the absence of signal (the Ethernet, in effect, uses a combination of the last two). For Ethernet, padding is added at the end of the data field, if necessary, to ensure that the frame size (excluding the preamble) always exceeds the minimum. The frames for all types of LAN include some form of check to protect the integrity of the address and data fields. The check may be as little as a parity bit, but is more commonly a 32-bit checksum, typically a *cyclic redundancy check* (CRC—*q.v.*) sum. Any response bits follow the checksum and precede any frame-end delimiter.

Protocols and Standards

LAN standardization has been pursued primarily under the auspices of the IEEE 802 committees and has resulted in a series of standards covering Ethernet, token ring, and token bus LANs, and also the DQDB MAN standard. Owing to the fundamentally different ways in

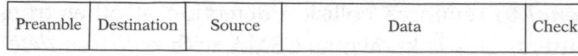

Preamble	Destination	Source	Data	Check

Figure 2. General format of a LAN frame.

which LANs operate at the link and physical levels of the seven-layer reference model for OSI, an additional sublayer was introduced, known as the *media access control* (MAC) layer, which forms the lower of two sublayers in the OSI data link layer. It essentially encapsulates the principles of operation for the various forms of LAN described above.

The upper sublayer is called the *logical link control* (LLC) layer. It provides essentially two modes of service: connectionless and connection-oriented. The former just allows stations to exchange single packets, with as much indication about the success or otherwise of the operation as the MAC layer may provide. In connection-oriented mode, its purpose is to set up, maintain, and close down an orderly, flow-controlled, error-free logical link between two stations on a LAN. The mechanism and structure employed for this is similar to HDLC operating directly on a physical link.

The mechanisms of the physical layer for LANs are quite diverse. The Ethernet uses baseband signaling with Manchester encoding and the main complication is in the detection of collisions. Rings have the property that they are constructed from unidirectional, point-to-point links and can easily use a variety of media, the commonest being twisted pairs and optical fibers. For first-generation LANs, signaling is usually baseband and commonly uses differential Manchester encoding.

For synchronous rings, frame synchronization typically relies upon phase-locked loop techniques and requires careful design to achieve stability. The token bus uses coaxial cable and is based on single- or dual-cable broadband cable TV technology; a number of different modulation and encoding schemes are used. In common with the token ring, ways of encoding symbols other than binary data are present and are used to encode network management and control signals.

In FDDI, 4B/5B encoding is used in preference to Manchester encoding, since this makes more efficient use of transmission bandwidth. Since there are 32 symbols in this encoding and only 16 are needed for data, there are symbols available for frame delimiting and control. Since phase-locked loops are difficult to stabilize at this frequency and in this size of ring, FDDI uses independent clocks of specified tolerance in each station, defines a maximum frame size and uses small elastic buffers in each station to compensate for the small differences of clock rate in each station. Further details of these topics may be found in Tanenbaum (1996), Stallings (1997), and Jain (1994).

High-Speed LANs and LAN Interconnection

In the development of local networks for institutions, the shared-media LAN has played a central role. Initi-

ally, a single LAN was sufficient for a building or small site. However, in a context where almost every room on a site has at least one computer, and often more; where every system is expected to be attached to the local network; where each system routinely handles data transfers measured in megabytes, at rates from a few hundred kilobits per second to a few megabits per second; and where a site may be a large campus several kilometers in diameter containing many buildings, then the single, shared-media LAN is inadequate: the cabling lengths are too short, not enough terminals can be connected, and the throughput or capacity is too small.

Two developments have occurred in response to these scaling problems: higher-speed LANs and forms of LAN interconnection engineered for use in the local area. Both of these developments have been in the context of the gradual introduction of structured cabling into buildings. The latter arose through recognition that computer communications outlets are needed everywhere, just like the electricity supply. The typical topology of such structured wiring arrangements is of a number of radial connections to offices, laboratories, meeting rooms, etc., from a number of central points throughout a building or site. Typically, these cabling concentration points are situated in a closet serving a corridor or floor of a building. Copper cable or twisted-pair wires are used to connect a wiring closet to a particular room and fiber optic cable is used to interconnect closets.

HIGH-SPEED LANs

As LAN transmission speed is increased, the size of a packet relative to the size of the medium decreases. In general, the size of a packet is outside the control of the LAN designer, being determined instead by application requirements and the design and implementation of higher-level protocols. Were it not for this, LAN operating speed could be increased 10 or 100 times by increasing the transmission speed by this factor and using packets 10 or 100 times as large.

If the packet size has to be kept roughly constant, then an increasing proportion of the time is effectively spent in the overhead of medium access by stations. In some cases, without some alteration in the physical parameters of the network, operation can fail. With Ethernet, this happens when the minimum packet size becomes too small relative to the size of the network for the collision detection mechanism to work: it becomes possible for a station at one end of the network to finish transmitting without having detected that there has been a collision with a transmission from a station at the other end. In this case, either the size of the network must be reduced or the minimum length of a packet must be increased (or both).

100 Mb/sec Ethernet (referred to as 100Base-T) is an upgraded form of 10Base-T, the 10 Mb/sec 802.3 standard for use with twisted-pair and fiber optic cable, and uses the same minimum packet size, but essentially reduces the maximum size of the network by a factor of 10. Gigabit (1 Gb/sec) Ethernet uses not only reduced physical size but also an increased minimum packet size of 512 bytes. To accommodate packets originating from stations operating to 10 or 100 Mb/sec standards, packets shorter than this are extended by carrier signal to the equivalent of 512 bytes.

The token ring design for a LAN does not contain any similar restriction to that of Ethernet. The fiber distributed data interface (FDDI) LAN, standardized by ANSI, is a 100 Mb/sec token ring. By using early token release, it is possible to achieve high utilization even in rings of the order of 100 km in length. The MAC protocol also incorporates a timed token rotation mechanism which can provide stations with a class of access with bounded latency independent of the number of active stations (Stallings, 1997; and Jain, 1994).

LAN INTERCONNECTION

LAN interconnection can take place at a number of levels of the ISO OSI model. Physical layer interconnections are peculiar to each type of LAN and do not exist in every case. Repeaters have been in use for Ethernet or CSMA/CD networks almost since their inception, and provide two basic functions: media conversion among thick coax, thin coax, fiber, and twisted pair cables, and branching to support the (rootless) tree topology used by CSMA/CD networks. *Multiport repeaters*, also known as *hubs*, can have ports to support any combination of media. Such hubs are now common in wiring closets to support twisted-pair connections to offices. A repeater works by retransmitting whatever it receives on one port to all other ports. There is no buffering in a repeater, but extra delay is introduced in the process. The retransmission is typically regenerative to remove noise. Collision indication is also forwarded, since all Ethernet segments connected via repeaters form a single Ethernet or CSMA/CD *collision domain*. Repeaters or hubs commonly detect malfunctions on particular Ethernet segments and isolate that segment to preserve the integrity of the rest of the LAN.

The introduction of the MAC OSI level-2 sublayer has given rise to new products called MAC-layer *bridges*. Their operation is based on the intrinsic LAN broadcast property, that is, a node may operate in a *promiscuous* reception mode in which it receives *all* packets on a LAN. A bridge between two LANs is formed by a station having promiscuous connections (ports) on each LAN. By observing the source addresses of all packets on each LAN, the bridge develops tables of addresses

located on the LANs on each side. When a packet is received on one port destined for an address on the same port, no action is taken; all other packets are forwarded to the LAN on the other side. This mechanism requires all LAN addresses to be distinct and of similar format, a possibility for IEEE-standard LANs. The effect of such bridging, which can include remote links between bridge halves, is to connect multiple LANs to act as a single large LAN.

The forwarding algorithm fails if bridges are used to interconnect LANs in configurations with loops; in this case a *spanning-tree* algorithm must be run in the bridges to select a tree out of the mesh topology which covers all constituent LANs. The algorithm is typically run in the background, so that if a link fails, a new tree is formed, providing resilience. A common use for two-port bridges is in connecting a set of LANs to a higher-speed LAN acting as a site backbone: FDDI is commonly used as a backbone for 10 Mb/sec 802.3 or 802.5 LANs.

SWITCHED LANS

A *multiport bridge* is also known as a *LAN switch*. Although a switch is substantially more expensive than a basic hub, it has the additional advantages of filtering and interconnecting LANs of different types and speed. In the case of an Ethernet installation, the filtering also separates collision domains.

In a switched Ethernet installation using only twisted-pair or optical fiber cables, each host-switch or inter-switch link between two LANs forms a single collision domain. Since such links are point-to-point, it is also possible to operate them in full-duplex mode: this is commonly done using fiber optic links, and in this case there is no sharing of each unidirectional link, no possibility of collisions, no need for the CSMA/CD mechanism, and hence no restriction on distance (other than basic signal quality). This can be very useful in a large installation for long inter-switch links.

Although a meshed topology between LAN switches can be exploited for resilience against link or switch failure, it cannot be exploited for increased capacity because of the need (noted above) to use a spanning tree to avoid loops forming as a result of the LAN switch forwarding algorithm.

Logical LANs

The basic LAN is characterized by use of a single, shared medium without routing. For CSMA/CD LANs, this is extended by use of the repeater or hub to several media forming a single LAN having a single collision domain and also a single broadcast or multicast domain: that is, stations may send to all or a selected group of stations by means of a single frame addressed to the broadcast or multicast group address. By introducing bridges or switches, Ethernet collision domains are contained, but the property of a network without conventional routing and having a single broadcast (and multicast) domain is retained; this is sometimes referred to as an extended LAN.

VLAN

Where LAN switching has been implemented to provide private port switch access to every system, Ethernet collision domains are essentially eliminated. In a large installation using a single extended LAN, broadcast containment may also be necessary. Conventionally, this is achieved by use of a level-3 router, a more expensive piece of equipment, possibly of lower performance, and having a different set of management issues, including the need to define more subnets for the site and manage the corresponding sets of addresses.

The VLAN enables stations on the same extended LAN to be partitioned into a number of distinct virtual LANs, each with its own broadcast domain. It is implemented on switches by extending the filtering function already present. A station may be defined to belong to a particular VLAN by its port identifier, by its MAC address, by its level-3 address (e.g. IP (Internet Protocol) or IPX (Internet Packet eXchange) address), or by protocol, or a combination of these. Apart from broadcast containment, it is also possible (with all but the first way of determining VLAN membership) to maintain VLAN membership for a system regardless of where it is situated on the extended physical LAN.

It has also been proposed to define a system's VLAN membership by its IP multicast group address. This has potentially far-reaching consequences, since the VLAN would now extend beyond level-3 routers.

VLANs do not coexist satisfactorily with shared-media ports on the extended LAN, since in that case there is contention on that port among stations belonging to different VLANs. It is also necessary for all the switches in the extended LAN to exchange information about which VLAN a particular frame belongs to. This can be done by tables, which requires inter-switch signaling for maintenance; tagging of each frame sent between switches with the VLAN identity, which can occasionally cause the maximum frame length to be exceeded; or use of TDM on inter-switch links, which is rare as it reduces statistical multiplexing (*q.v.*) advantage on these links.

LAN EMULATION

To exploit the high-speed transmission capability associated with ATM, as well as exploiting the possibility of connecting ATM switches in a mesh to obtain a high-capacity network, it is possible to emulate a LAN using ATM: typically 802.3 or 802.5. The method of doing this has been standardized as LAN Emulation or LANE by the ATM Forum.

Within each LANE client is a LAN emulation client process or LEC, which is incorporated at the level of a MAC driver within the client software. When the client sends a frame to another LANE client, the LEC intercepts this and, assuming the ATM address corresponding to this MAC address is known, transmits the frame on an appropriate PVC (Permanent Virtual Circuit) or SVC (Switched Virtual Circuit). If the ATM address is not known, the LEC consults a LAN Emulation Server (LES), using a preconfigured ATM address. All active clients maintain a VC (Virtual Circuit—a connection that behaves like a direct path) to the LES, so that the LES can discover and maintain a cache of ATM-to-MAC address mappings. To handle broadcast and multicast, a Broadcast and Unknown Server (BUS) is also provided on a preconfigured ATM address. Since the BUS has established VCs to all the currently active LANE clients, and is intended for data transfer use (unlike the LES), a LEC can also use it to send data to another LEC while the latter's ATM address is still unknown. The LANE standard also defines a LAN Emulation Configuration Server (LECS) for use in maintaining several LANEs on a site. This can be used by a LEC during initialization to obtain the addresses of the LES and BUS for the particular LANE it is joining; see Dutton and Lenhard (1995).

Status

LANs are a major part of all institutional site communication infrastructure. Products are available for all the technologies described here. Gigabit Ethernet is in the final stages of standardization (802.3z) by IEEE. The MAN concept has not seen serious deployment, perhaps partially as a result of concerns about commercial security in the face of a technology in which separate organizations share a transmission medium. It has seen derivative exploitation in Switched Multimedia Data Service (SMDS).

Bibliography

1976. Metcalfe, R. M., and Boggs, D. R. "Ethernet: Distributed Packet-switching for Local Computer Networks," *Comm. of the ACM*, **19**, 7, 395–403.
1994. Boisseau, M., Demange, M., and Munier, J.-M. *High-speed Networks*. Chichester, UK: John Wiley.
1994. Jain, R. *FDDI Handbook: High-Speed Networking Using Fiber and Other Media*. Reading, MA: Addison-Wesley.
1995. Dutton, H. J. R., and Lenhard, P. *Asynchronous Transfer Mode (ATM): Technical Overview*, 2nd Ed. Upper Saddle River, NJ: Prentice Hall.

1996. Peterson, L. L., and Davie, B. S. *Computer Networks: A Systems Approach*. San Francisco: Morgan Kaufmann.

1996. Tanenbaum, A. S. *Computer Networks*, 3rd Ed. Upper Saddle River, NJ: Prentice Hall.

1997. Stallings, W. *Data and Computer Communications*, 5th Ed. Upper Saddle River, NJ: Prentice Hall.

1997. Stallings, W. *Local and Metropolitan Area Networks*, 5th Ed. Upper Saddle River, NJ: Prentice Hall.

Christopher S. Cooper

LOCAL STORE

For articles on related subjects *see* BUFFER; INDEX REGISTER; MEMORY: MAIN; REGISTER; and STORAGE HIERARCHY.

Within a processor the term *local store* is used to describe a relatively small number of high-speed storage elements, which may be directly referred to by the instructions (distinguishing it from cache memory—*q.v.*). The concept of local store includes the basic or general purpose registers as well as other explicitly addressed high-speed storage. The latter includes any addressed buffer such as a name table in a language-oriented processor or a scalar buffer in a vector processor.

The contents of a storage cell in a local store are accessible by the execution resources (the adder or ALU, etc.) within a processor cycle. The fast access of operands (*q.v.*) provided by local store minimizes instruction execution time and improves the overall processor performance.

The use of local store can also reduce the size of instructions since the number of bits required to specify a register or storage element is less than that required to specify a memory location. On the other hand, the use of local store requires additional instructions to load or store the contents of the local store to and from memory. Thus the use of local store is justified largely on the basis of mimimizing execution time rather than program space. *See* REDUCED INSTRUCTION SET COMPUTER.

The term "local store" is also widely used in multiprocessor (*q.v.*) systems that have memory distributed across the multiple processor nodes. The term then describes that portion of the system's memory that is physically associated with a processor's node. In this case it refers to the portion of memory that is more quickly accessed by the processor.

Michael Flynn

LOCAL VARIABLE

See GLOBAL AND LOCAL VARIABLES.

LOGIC DESIGN

For articles on related subjects *see* ARITHMETIC-LOGIC UNIT; BOOLEAN ALGEBRA; CODES; COMPUTER ARCHITECTURE; COMPUTER CIRCUITRY; DIGITAL DESIGN AUTOMATION; INTEGRATED CIRCUITRY; SEQUENTIAL MACHINE; and SWITCHING THEORY.

The term *logic design* refers to the process of specifying an interconnection of logic elements in digital computer hardware so that a desired function is performed. Examples of this process might be the design of a circuit that would accept data representing numbers in a Gray code and convert this data into a binary-coded decimal representation, or the specification of the gates and interconnections required to implement the arithmetic unit of a computer. Both formal and *ad hoc* techniques are used to achieve the desired design.

All digital logic networks in current use operate on signals that are restricted to two possible values only, and are thus called *binary* values. While it is theoretically possible to design logic networks in which a larger number of discrete values are allowed for the signals (so-called multiple-valued logic networks), the discussion here will be restricted to binary logic networks since these are the only type of networks in current

Table 1. Tables of combinations for elementary gates.

(a) Inverter		(b) AND gate		
Input A	Output A'	Inputs A	B	Output AB
0	1	0	0	0
1	0	0	1	0
		1	0	0
		1	1	1

(c) OR gate			(d) XOR (exclusive OR) gate		
Inputs A	B	Output A + B	Inputs A	B	Output A $\oplus$ B
0	0	0	0	0	0
0	1	1	0	1	1
1	0	1	1	0	1
1	1	1	1	1	0

(e) NAND (not AND) gate			(f) NOR (not OR) gate		
Inputs A	B	Output $\overline{AB}$	Inputs A	B	Output $\overline{A + B}$
0	0	1	0	0	1
0	1	1	0	1	0
1	0	1	1	0	0
1	1	0	1	1	0

Note: See Fig. 1.

use. For some binary networks, it is possible to specify the desired performance by means of a *table of combinations* (also called a *truth table*), as shown in Table 1, which lists each possible combination of binary signals on the inputs to the network and the corresponding combination of desired output signals.

In Table 1, (a) shows the table of combinations for a network having one input and one output. The output of this network will have a signal representing the zero value on it whenever the input signal represents a 1, and will have an output signal representing a 1 value whenever the input signal has a zero. Such a network is called an *inverter*, and the symbol used to represent it is shown in Fig. 1a.

Actually, a network having such a simple performance as that of an inverter is usually realized as a single logic element and is not constructed out of more elementary subnetworks. An inverter is thus one of the basic building blocks from which more complex logic networks are constructed. Other basic building blocks, or *elementary gates*, are shown in Table 1 as (b), (c), (d), (e), and (f), with the corresponding logic symbols shown in Figs. 1b, 1c, 1d, 1e, and 1f.

The table of combinations for a more complex logic network is shown in Table 2. This network has four input signals and four output signals. If the four input signals appearing on the network inputs represent one decimal digit encoded in the 8-4-2-1 code (i.e. binary-coded decimal or BCD—*see* CODES), the four output signals will represent the encoding of the 9s complement of the input digit. Notice that in addition to having entries of 1 or 0, there are also entries in this table that are represented by a "d." This notation is used to indicate the fact that certain input combinations would not be expected to appear at the input of the network.

Table 2. Table of combinations for generating the 9s complement of a BCD (8421) digit.

	Inputs				Outputs			
	b_8	b_4	b_2	b_1	c_8	c_4	c_2	c_1
(0)	0	0	0	0	1	0	0	1
(1)	0	0	0	1	1	0	0	0
(2)	0	0	1	0	0	1	1	1
(3)	0	0	1	1	0	1	1	0
(4)	0	1	0	0	0	1	0	1
(5)	0	1	0	1	0	1	0	0
(6)	0	1	1	0	0	0	1	1
(7)	0	1	1	1	0	0	1	0
(8)	1	0	0	0	0	0	0	1
(9)	1	0	0	1	0	0	0	0
	1	0	1	0	d	d	d	d
	1	0	1	1	d	d	d	d
	1	1	0	0	d	d	d	d
	1	1	0	1	d	d	d	d
	1	1	1	0	d	d	d	d
	1	1	1	1	d	d	d	d

Note: See Fig. 2.

Such entries are called "don't cares." A table of combinations that contains "don't care" entries is an *incompletely specified table of combinations*.

An incompletely specified table of combinations is actually a representation for a whole family of completely specified tables of combinations that would satisfy the given design requirements. Techniques exist that effectively choose a completely specified table of combinations that leads to the most efficient network design. An efficient network to realize the specifications of Table 2 is shown in Fig. 2. Using Table 2, the reader may verify that the equations given in Fig. 2 are correct.

The types of network described thus far all have the property that the output values at any given instant are dependent solely upon the input values present at the same time. Such networks are called *combinational logic networks*. The other type of logic network is

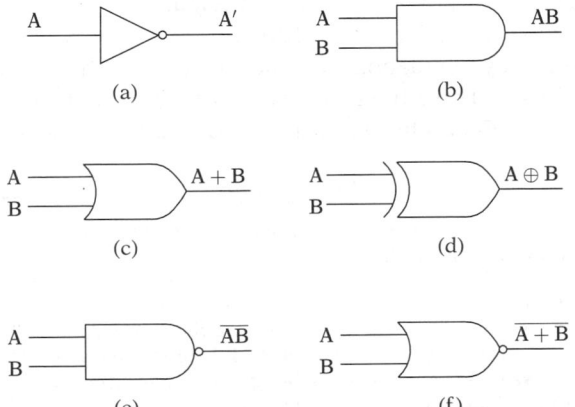

Figure 1. Elementary gate symbols: (a) inverter; (b) AND gate; (c) OR gate; (d) XOR gate; (e) NAND gate; (f) NOR gate.

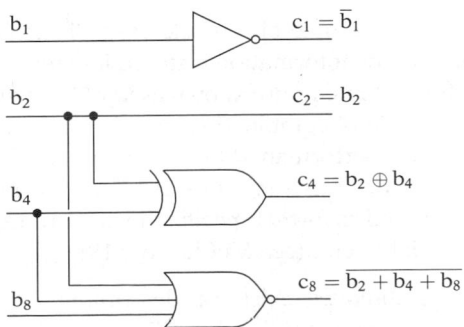

Figure 2. Network for Table 2.

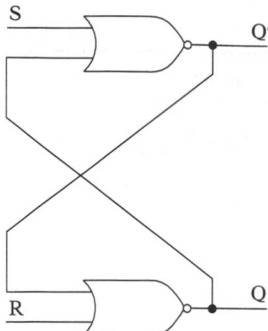

Figure 3. Interconnected NOR gates forming an S–R latch.

called a *sequential logic network* or a *sequential circuit*. These networks have the property that their outputs are dependent not only on their present inputs, but also on the inputs that may have been present previously.

An example of a sequential circuit is a network whose input is a series of pulses on a single lead and whose outputs display the count modulo n of the number of input pulses. Such a circuit is called a *counter* (McCluskey, 1986). Since the output of a sequential circuit at any particular time may depend on previous inputs, there must be contained in the circuit some mechanism for recording some information about these previous inputs. This function is achieved by providing feedback loops in the circuit that are capable of storing information in them. The most commonly used type of feedback loop consists of two gate elements interconnected as shown in Fig.3.

This type of circuit is called a *set–reset* (S–R) *latch* and operates as follows. The input combination S = R = 1 is not permitted. When input S = 1 and input R = 0, it follows from Table 1(f) that Q′= 0 and, therefore, Q = 1. Conversely, when S = 0 and R = 1, Q = 0 and Q′= 1. When the input that was 1 is changed to 0 so that both inputs are zero, the output remains equal to the value it had for the last nonzero input. Thus, when the inputs are both zero, the circuit "remembers" the last nonzero input. The circuit can thus be used to "store" information.

Fig. 3 is an example of a whole class of memory elements in which information is stored in interconnected gates. Such elements are known as *latches* or *flip-flops*. Just as a table of combinations is a formal representation for the performance of a combinational circuit, *flow tables* or *state diagrams* or *regular expressions* (*q.v.*) are used as formal specifications for the action of a sequential circuit (*see* McCluskey, 1986).

Formal techniques exist for determining logic networks that correspond to specifications given in the form of a table of combinations or a flow table. These formal techniques are the subject of the discipline known as *switching theory* (Kohavi, 1970). Classical switching theory is concerned mainly with the problem of designing optimum networks that correspond to given formal specifications. Algorithms have been developed for designing networks that contain a minimum number of gates under certain constraints; e.g. the condition that there be no more than two gates connected in series between any input and any output. While a great deal of attention has been devoted to the *minimization problem*—that of obtaining minimum element networks—this problem has been solved only for networks having very specific constraints, such as those mentioned above. General design algorithms with flexible constraints have proved to be very difficult to discover.

Formal techniques for the design of logic networks have an inherent limitation in that the size of the table of combinations, or flow table, tends to be proportional to 2^n, where n is the number of network inputs. A logic network with 10 inputs is not a particularly large one, but a formal specification for such a network would require over 1,000 entries. The approach taken to overcome this difficulty is to partition logic networks into subnetworks of a convenient size. The overall network is then structured by interconnections of the subnetworks, the interconnections being determined by *ad hoc* rather than formal techniques.

Efficient gate network design requires the ability to handle much more complex structures than two-stage designs. Until recently, the computational complexity (*q.v.*) of this problem prohibited the use of automatic synthesis techniques, and gate networks were designed using *ad hoc* methods. With the increased power of modern design workstations and improved heuristic (*q.v.*) design procedures, it is now possible to use switching theory synthesis techniques to carry out a major portion of the design of new computer systems. The current trend is to specify a system design using a high-level hardware description language (*q.v.*) such as Verilog or VHDL to confirm the correctness of the design by simulation and then to use synthesis programs to derive the gate or transistor level implementations. Hierarchical design has now become practical.

Bibliography

1970. Kohavi, Z. *Switching and Finite Automata Theory*. New York: McGraw-Hill.
1986. McCluskey, E. J. *Logic Design Principles*. Upper Saddle River, NJ: Prentice Hall.
1993. Sternheim, E. *Digital Design and Synthesis with Verilog HDL*. San Jose, CA: Automata Publishing Company.
1994. Wolf, W. *Modern VLSI Design, A Systems Approach*. Upper Saddle River, NJ: Prentice Hall.
1997. Gajski, D. *Principles of Digital Design*. Upper Saddle River, NJ: Prentice Hall.

Edward J. McCluskey

LOGIC PROGRAMMING

For articles on related subjects *see* DATAFLOW; DEDUCTIVE DATABASE; EXPERT SYSTEMS; FUNCTIONAL PROGRAMMING; KNOWLEDGE REPRESENTATION; NONMONOTONIC LOGIC; PROGRAM VERIFICATION; and THEOREM PROVING.

PRINCIPLES

Origins

Logic programming emerged in the early 1970s from a convergence of work in the fields of automated theorem proving (*q.v.*), artificial intelligence (*q.v.*), and formal languages (*q.v.*).

In the field of automated theorem proving, it was noted that the behavior of the SL-resolution theorem-prover developed in Edinburgh by Kowalski and Kuehner in 1971 resembled the execution of procedural programming languages. SL-resolution, in turn, was based upon Robinson's resolution principle and Loveland's model elimination proof procedure.

In the field of artificial intelligence, in 1969 Hewitt at MIT developed the programming language PLANNER, based on logic, but emphasizing the procedural rather than the declarative representation of knowledge. At about the same time, both Green at Stanford and Elcock and Foster at Aberdeen showed how programs could be expressed declaratively in first-order logic. Elcock and Foster devised a purely declarative language, ABSYS, based on the equality relation and the logical connectives "and" and "or." Hayes in Edinburgh argued that controlled deduction in a declarative language like ABSYS could be viewed as a form of computation.

In the field of formal languages, in 1971 Colmerauer in Marseilles investigated with Kowalski how formal grammars could be represented in logic and how parsing could be performed by theorem-proving. In 1972, Colmerauer and Rousell incorporated these ideas into the implementation of the first logic programming language, Prolog, based on SL-resolution. Warren in Edinburgh subsequently showed that Prolog could be implemented with an efficiency similar to that of Lisp, and implemented a compiler for Prolog in Prolog itself.

Many of these related ideas can be summarized by the characterization of logic programming, in its simplest form, as the *procedural interpretation* of Horn clauses (Kowalski, 1974): A sentence of the form

$$A \text{ if } B_1 \text{ and } B_2 \ldots \text{ and } B_n, \ n \geq 0$$

can be interpreted as a procedure

to solve problem A, solve subproblems B_1 and $B_2 \ldots$ and B_n.

The theorem-proving method that treats such sentences as procedures is called SLD (SL-resolution for definite clauses, i.e. Horn clauses with exactly one conclusion, "A"). Clark (1978) extended the procedural interpretation to allow negative conditions. The resulting theorem-proving method is called SLDNF (SLD with negation by failure). SLDNF is the basis for most work in logic programming today.

SLDNF is the foundation, not only for Prolog, but for deductive databases, for concurrent logic programming (including such languages as Parlog, concurrent Prolog and GHC), and for constraint logic programming (including such languages as Prolog 2 and 3, CLP(X) and Chip).

In the remainder of this article, we shall consider in greater detail the relationship between the declarative and procedural styles of logic programming. We shall also discuss the contribution of logic programming to program specification (*q.v.*), deductive databases and knowledge representation (including default reasoning, abductive reasoning, and metareasoning).

Declarative Versus Procedural Knowledge Representation

Arguments over the relative merits of declarative versus procedural knowledge representation were a major theme in artificial intelligence in the 1970s. It is now generally believed that both kinds of knowledge representation are necessary. The most popular way of combining them has been to include them in hybrid knowledge representation systems.

In contrast to hybrid systems, logic programming combines declarative and procedural knowledge in the same representation. For example, logic programming automatically converts the declarative statement

> X is a potential customer for product Y
> if Y is useful for activity of type Z
> and X has work of type Z

into both the procedure

to find a potential customer X for a given product Y, find a type of activity Z for which Y is useful, and find an X which has work of type Z

and the procedure

to find a product Y for a given potential customer X, find a type of work Z which X has, and find a Y which is useful for activity of type Z.

Depending upon which of X and Y are given as input and which are to be found as output, one or the other of the two procedures is more appropriate. Indeed, several other procedures are also possible, corresponding to the cases where both X and Y are given or where both are to be found.

The different procedures can be obtained from the declarative statement by adding control information about how the declarative information is to be used. As a consequence, the declarative statement is more abstract, and the procedures are more concrete.

Although the syntax of logic programs is declarative, for many applications it is easier to think first in concrete, procedural terms. For example, a salesperson might find it easier to articulate a procedure for finding customers for products than to express the more abstract, declarative statement.

Later, we will consider alternative formulations of the sorting (q.v.) problem. One formulation, based on a specification of the problem, is more naturally understood declaratively. The other, a formulation of quicksort, is more naturally understood procedurally. Both can be formulated as logic programs, and therefore both can be understood declaratively and procedurally.

The Syntax and Declarative Interpretation of Logic Problems

A *Horn clause logic program* is a collection of statements

    A if B_1 and. . . and B_n $n \geq 0$

Each such statement is also called a *definite clause*. In the case where $n = 0$, the statement is usually written as a *fact*:

    A

without the implication sign "if".

The *conclusion*, A, and the *conditions*, B_i, are *atomic formulas*, which are usually written in the form

    $p(t_1, . . . , t_m)$ $m \geq 0$

where p is a *predicate symbol* and the t_i are *terms*, consisting of *variables*, *constants*, or *function symbols* applied to other terms. In this article, as in most Prolog implementations, variables, e.g.

    X, Y, Fred

are distinguished from constants by an initial uppercase letter. Where appropriate, atomic formulas may also be written informally, as in the example of the previous section.

This syntax reflects the *declarative interpretation*. A definite clause is understood as a universal statement:

    for all X_1 and. . . and X_k
    A if B_1 and. . . and B_n

where $X_1, . . . , X_k$ is a list of all the variables occurring in the statement. Predicate symbols are understood as names of relations, and variable-free terms are understood as names of individuals.

Problems to be solved or queries to be answered are posed in the form of a conjunction of conditions

    B1 and. . . and B_n? $n \geq 1$

In the declarative interpretation, such a problem or query is understood as an existential statement

    there exist X_1 and. . . and X_k such that
    B_1 and. . . and B_n

where $X_1, . . . , X_k$ is a list of all the variables occurring in the problem. The statement is a *candidate theorem*, to be proved from the collection of statements constituting the program. A proof of the theorem constructs a substitution

    $X_1 = t_1, . . . , X_k = t_k$

of terms for variables, which constitutes a solution to the problem or an answer to the query.

Later, we shall consider the case where conditions B_i in program statements and in problems or queries can be negations of atomic formulas or even arbitrary formulas of first-order logic.

The Sorting Problem

The sorting problem illustrates some of the subtleties of the relationship between declarative and procedural knowledge representation in logic programming. At the topmost level, the statement

    sort(X, Y) if permutation(X, Y) and ordered(Y)

defines the sorting predicate. The statement has the declarative reading:

    for all X and Y,
    Y is the result of sorting X if Y is a
      permutation of X and Y is ordered.

As a simple case, the variables X and Y can range over all terms that can be constructed from a constant symbol "nil" as the name of the empty list and a two-place function symbol "cons." As in Lisp, the term cons(s,t) names a list whose first element is s followed by the list t. Thus, for example, the term cons(2, cons(1, nil)) names the list of numbers 2,1.

Given appropriate definitions of the lower-level predicates, "permutation" and "ordered", the definition of sort can be used to solve such problems as

    sort(cons(2, cons(1,nil)),Y)?
    sort(X, cons(1, cons(2, nil)))?
    sort(X, Y) ?

The first problem is to find a list Y which is the result of sorting the list 2,1. It has the unique solution

    Y = cons(1, cons(2, nil))

The second problem is to find a list X which, when sorted, results in the list 1,2. It has two answers

```
X = cons(1, cons(2, nil))
X = cons(2, cons(1, nil)).
```

The third problem is to find all pairs, X, Y, where Y is the result of sorting X. It has infinitely many solutions. Problems of the third kind, where all terms are variables, are especially useful for validating logic programs because they generate all instances of the defined relations.

The Procedural Interpretation

The SLD theorem-proving method treats definite clauses of the form

```
A if B₁ and. . . and Bₙ
```

as *procedures*

```
to solve A, solve B₁ and. . . and Bₙ.
```

Facts of the form A are treated as procedures that solve problems of the form A without introducing further subproblems.

Conditions B_i, whether in queries or in definite clauses, are treated as procedure calls. In theory, procedure calls can be executed in any order and even in parallel. In practice, the order in which they are executed is important for efficiency, and should depend upon the input–output pattern of variables.

In Prolog, procedure calls are executed in the order in which they are written, under the programmer's control. In the concurrent logic programming languages, procedure calls can be executed sequentially or concurrently, which is also under the programmer's control. In deductive databases, however, the order of execution is normally determined by the implementation.

Given an initial problem to be solved, the SLD theorem prover searches a tree of possible derivations (or computations) having that problem as root. Every node in the tree has the form

$$B_1 \text{ and. . . and } B_n? \qquad n \geq 0.$$

If $n = 0$, then the branch from the root to the node successfully terminates, solving the problem at the root. If $n \neq 0$, then one of the conditions is selected to be executed as a procedure call. Without loss of generality, by reordering conditions if necessary, we may assume that the selected condition is the first condition B_1. The condition is executed by *unifying* it with the conclusion of some program clause of the form

```
B if C₁ and. . . and Cₘ
```

A successor node is derived having the form

$$(C_1 \text{ and. . . and } C_m \text{ and } B_2 \text{ and. . . and } B_n) \, \theta$$

where θ is the unifying substitution, which is the most general substitution that makes B_1 and B identical. We shall discuss unification in greater detail later.

If no conclusion of a program clause unifies with the selected condition, then there are no successor nodes, and the branch to the node with no successors is said to *terminate in failure*. If more than one conclusion unifies with the selected condition, then there is a successor node for each such conclusion.

In the latter case, the selected condition (or procedure call) is said to be *nondeterministic*. The different procedures whose conclusions unify with the procedure call can be executed in any order and even concurrently or in parallel. In Prolog, different procedures are executed in the order in which they are written, which is under the programmer's control.

Given a list X, SLD converts the definition of the sorting predicate into a procedure:

```
to  sort X with result Y,
    find a permutation Y of X, and
    show that Y is ordered
```

assuming that procedure calls are executed in the order in which they are written. The first procedure call in the procedure is nondeterministic. If X has length n, the procedure call will potentially generate all $n!$ permutations Y of X. Thus, the sorting procedure has complexity of the order $n!$ compared with $n \cdot \log n$ for many sorting algorithms, such as quicksort.

If the two procedure calls were executed in the opposite order, the procedure would be even more inefficient, first generating ordered lists Y and then testing whether they are permutations of X.

The inefficiency that arises from each of the different ways of executing the specification of the sorting problem shows how ambitious is the hope that purely declarative representations of knowledge might be adequate for knowledge representation and problem solving.

In reaction to such problems of efficiency, some researchers have advocated the development of improved program execution techniques and of parallelism in particular. Others have proposed the use of program transformation and related techniques, such as abstract interpretation and types, to help derive efficient programs from clear but inefficient specifications. Still others have suggested that logic programming be restricted to the execution and therefore to the testing of program specifications. Although all of these proposals have merit, most logic programmers solve the problems of efficiency differently, namely by programming in a mixed procedural and declarative style.

The Procedural Style of Logic Programming

Although the specification of the sorting problem as the problem of finding an ordered permutation is not an efficient program, the following representation of quicksort is:

```
quick(nil, nil)
quick(cons(X,Y),Z) if
        partition (X,Y,Y_1,Y_2)
        and quick(Y_1,Z_1)
        and quick(Y_2,Z_2)
        and append (Z_1,cons(X,Z_2),Z).
```

Arguably the most natural way to understand the second statement is to interpret it as a procedure:

```
to quicksort a nonempty list, with first
                element X followed by list Y,
                        obtaining result Z,
    partition the list Y
        into the list Y_1 of all elements < X
        and the list Y_2 of all elements ≥ X,
    quicksort Y_1 obtaining result Z_1,
    quicksort Y_2 obtaining result Z_2,
    append Z_1 followed by X, followed by Z_2 ,
        to obtain Z.
```

This example shows that, although the declarative syntax of logic programs encourages their declarative reading, a programmer might need to think and program procedurally first.

Even when logic programming is used for procedural knowledge representation, the declarative interpretation greatly aids program verification. The declarative reading gives an informal check on the correctness of the procedure. Moreover, given a specification, it can also facilitate a more rigorous proof of program correctness. The correctness of quicksort, for example, can easily and naturally be demonstrated in this way.

Unification and the Logical Variable

Viewed procedurally, nondeterminism, unification, and the logical variable are possibly the most characteristic features of logic programming.

Given a problem of the form

B_1 and. . . and B_n?

with selected procedure call B_1 and a procedure of the form

B if C_1 and. . . and C_m,

unification generates a most general substitution θ of terms for variables, such that

$B_1 \theta = B\theta.$

The unifying substitution θ passes input from the procedure call B_1 to the new procedure calls $C_1, \ldots, C_m$. It simultaneously passes output from the conclusion B

to the old procedure calls B_2 and . . . and B_n. The output may contain (logical) variables.

Consider, for example, the recursive program

```
member (X, cons(X, Y))
member (X, cons(Z, Y)) if member (X, Y)
```

which defines the membership relation between elements and lists.

Given the procedure call

```
member (2, cons(1, cons(2, nil)))?
```

SLD uses the second procedure to replace the call by the new call

```
member (2, cons (2, nil))?
```

and uses the first procedure to solve the new call, without introducing further subproblems. All unifying substitutions in this example pass input from procedure calls to procedures.

Given, on the other hand, the procedure call

```
member (X, cons(1, cons (2, nil)))?
```

the first procedure solves the call with output

$X = 1$

and the second procedure, followed by the first, solves the call with output

$X = 2.$

Compared with purely procedural programming languages, a characteristic feature of unification is that output can contain *logical variables*. For example, the call

```
member (2, X)?
```

has infinitely many outputs:

```
X = cons(2, Y)
X = cons(Z_1, cons(2, Y))
X = cons(Z_1, cons(Z_2, cons(2, Y)))
etc.
```

corresponding to the infinitely many positions the number 2 can occupy in a list. The occurrence of variables in such outputs corresponds in certain respects to programming with higher-order functions in functional programming languages. The output

```
X = cons(2, Y)
```

for example, behaves like a function, which, given a list Y as input, returns the list cons(2, Y) as output.

Negation by Failure

An important example of procedural knowledge representation in logic programming is the interpretation of negative, variable-free conditions, *not A*, as holding when the attempt to show the corresponding positive condition, A, finitely fails. In general, a problem A

finitely fails if (and only if) every branch of an SLDNF search tree having *A* as its root terminates in failure. Otherwise, *not A* finitely fails if *A* succeeds.

Much research in logic programming has been devoted to finding an appropriate, declarative meaning for such *negation by failure*. The earliest and simplest of these, due to Clark, is to interpret each program statement as expressing one clause of the if-half of an implicit if-and-only-if definition of the predicate symbol of the conclusion of the statement. Thus, for example, the two clauses

```
parent(X, Y) if father(X, Y)
parent(X, Y) if mother(X, Y)
```

together represent the if-half of the definition

```
parent(X, Y) if and only if [father (X, Y) or
                              mother(X, Y)].
```

The explicit if-and-only-if form of the definition is often called the *Clark-completion*. Negation by failure can be justified as reasoning implicitly with the only-if half of the Clark-completion.

Negation by failure works *incorrectly* in Prolog if the negative condition contains variables at the time of execution. Given, for example, the definition of "parent" above and the additional statements

```
father(john, fred)
mother(mary, fred)
```

negation by failure correctly solves the problems

```
not parent(fred, fred)?    yes
not parent (john, fred)?    no.
```

But it incorrectly concludes that there is no solution to the problem of finding an *X* such that

```
not parent (john, X)?    no.
```

A correct procedure would generate the solutions

```
X = john,
X = mary.
```

Not ensuring that all variables occurring in a negative condition are completely instantiated before execution is a source of error in logic programming. However, techniques have been developed which allow the execution of negative conditions containing variables. These techniques construct solutions for variables, and are consequently called *constructive negation*.

Another error is to use negation by failure when the program contains an incomplete definition of a predicate. Negation by failure works correctly only when all clauses in the if-half of a definition have been given. In later sections, we will see that extended logic programming and abductive logic programming allow completely defined predicates and incompletely defined predicates to be combined correctly in the same program.

Despite these potential sources of error, negation by failure is an extremely powerful knowledge representation and problem-solving feature. With its help, it is possible, in particular, to obtain the expressive power of allowing any formula of first-order logic as a condition of any program statement or query (Lloyd, 1987). For example, the statement

```
subset (X, Y) if for all Z [member (Z, Y) if
      member (Z, X)]
```

can be re-expressed in normal logic programming form by introducing an auxiliary predicate symbol:

```
subset (X, Y) if not nosub(X, Y)
nosub(X, Y) if member (Z, X) and not
      member (Z, Y).
```

Deductive Databases

Having emphasized that there are many applications for which procedural knowledge representation is most appropriate, it is important to note that, for certain applications (e.g. deductive databases) a purely declarative representation can be both natural and efficient. Relational databases are a special case.

A *relational database* (*q.v.*) can be regarded as the special case of a logic program where all statements have the form of conclusions without any conditions, variables, or function symbols. For example:

```
father(john, fred)
mother(mary, fred).
```

A *deductive database* can be regarded as a logic program that does not contain function symbols. A typical application of deductive databases is to represent rules and regulations. The following rules, for example, are typical of those that might be used to represent part of a simplified citizenship law:

```
citizen(X, usa)  if   born(X, usa)
citizen(X, usa)  if   not born(X, usa)
                 and  parent(Y, X)
                 and  citizen(Y, usa).
```

Because deductive databases contain no function symbols, their domain of discourse is finite. As a consequence, the problem of determining whether or not a query has an answer is *decidable*. The backward reasoning mode of inference associated with SLDNF, augmented with loop-checking strategies, also called *tabling*, is a decision procedure. Efficient forward reasoning methods, with such exotic names as *naive*, *semi-naive* and *magic-sets*, have also been developed.

Integrity Constraints

One of the attractions of logic programming for database applications is that it provides a single uniform language for data, queries, transactions and integrity constraints. Integrity constraints can be viewed as persistent queries or goals, which must always be satisfied, no matter how the database changes over the course of time. As in relational databases, queries and integrity constraints can be arbitrary formulas of first-order logic. In the simplest case, a database update is rejected if it violates an integrity constraint.

Consider, for example, a database which contains the fact `father(john, fred)` together with the integrity constraint

> if `father`(X_1, Y) and `father`(X_2, Y) then $X_1 = X_2$.

The update, `father(peter, fred)`, violates the integrity constraint, under the assumption that $john \neq peter$.

Efficient integrity checking methods have been developed for logic programs. These typically combine forward reasoning triggered by updates with backward reasoning as in SLDNF.

Abductive Logic Programming (ALP)

Whereas ordinary logic programming uses deduction to derive consequences C from programs P, abduction generates hypotheses H such that $P \cup H$ imply C. For example, given the program

```
grass is wet if rain
grass is wet if sprinkler
```

and the consequence

```
grass is wet
```

abduction generates the two alternative hypotheses

```
    rain
or  sprinkler.
```

The hypotheses generated by abduction can be used to update the current state of the logic program. Like external updates, such internally generated updates may be constrained by integrity constraints. For example, given the constraint

```
if rain then cloudy
```

and the fact that it is not cloudy, which can be expressed by the constraint

```
if cloudy then false,
```

the hypothesis, rain, can be seen to violate the integrity constraints and be rejected.

Abduction, in general, and ALP, in particular, have proved to be useful for a wide range of applications including fault diagnosis, planning and database view updates.

SLDNF has been extended to implement ALP by interleaving backward reasoning with forward reason-

ing. In this extension, backward reasoning reduces problems to abductive hypotheses, whereas forward reasoning checks whether the hypotheses satisfy the integrity constraints.

Default Reasoning and Extended Logic Programming

Negation by failure is commonly used to implement default reasoning. For example, the following statements express that, by default, all birds fly, but ostriches and penguins don't:

```
fly(X) if bird(X) and not nofly(X)
nofly(X) if ostrich(X)
nofly(X) if penguin(X).
```

Here the predicate `nofly(X)` represents the negation of the predicate `fly(X)`.

In *extended logic programming*, `nofly(X)` can be expressed directly as the negation of the positive predicate `fly(X)` using an explicit negation, ¬, different from negation by failure:

```
fly(X) if bird(X) and not ¬fly(X)
¬fly(X) if ostrich(X)
¬fly(X) if penguin(X).
```

The combination of the two negations provides a natural way of expressing the English phrase "unless the contrary can be shown." Thus the English sentence:

> A child found abandoned in the UK shall, unless the contrary can be shown, be deemed to have been born in the UK.

can be represented in the extended logic programming form:

```
born(X, uk) if abandoned(X, uk)
              and not ¬born(X, uk).
```

Stable Semantics

Many relationships have been discovered between default reasoning in logic programming and default reasoning in other formalisms. For example, the semantics of negation by failure given by the Clark completion is similar to the semantics of McCarthy's *circumscription*. However, most other formalisms for default reasoning, including *default logic*, *non-monotonic modal logic*, and *auto-epistemic logic*, employ a form of so-called *stable semantics*. A similar, *stable model semantics*, has been defined for logic programming.

The stable model semantics formalizes the intuition that *not p* means that *p* cannot be shown. Thus to know whether p can be shown, given a program P, under the stable model semantics it is necessary to show that p is logically implied by $P \cup N$, where N is a "stable set" of sentences of the form *not q* expressing that *q* cannot be shown from $P \cup N$. This dependency of a set of nonprovable sentences on itself is formalized by the stability requirement:

> a set *N* of negations of variable-free atomic
> sentences is said to be *stable*
> if and only if
> *N* consists of all *not q* such that *q* is not
> logically implied by $P \cup N$.

In this context, logical implication is to be understood as treating negative sentences *not q* simply as though they were atomic.

The stable semantics has a simple interpretation in terms of abduction: under the stable semantics, *p* follows from a program *P* if and only if *p* is logically implied by $P \cup N$, for some set of hypotheses *N* consisting of negations of atomic, variable-free sentences satisfying the integrity constraints

```
q or not q
if q and not q then false
```

for all variable-free atoms *q*. These two sets of integrity constraints state, in effect, that, for every such *q*, either *q* or its negation is derivable, but not both.

Thus, for example, given the logic program, P = {p if not *q*}, the set *N* = {not *q*} is the only stable set, because *q* cannot be derived from $P \cup N$. On the other hand, the program {p if not *q*, *q* if not *p*} has two stable sets, {not *q*} and {not *p*}, whereas the program {p if not *p*} has none.

Various proof procedures have been developed for computing stable semantics, including some which are based on proof procedures for ALP.

Constraint Logic Programming (CLP)

CLP shares with abduction and negation by failure the property that certain conditions (abducible predicates in ALP, negations of variable-free atoms in negation by failure, and constraint predicates in CLP) are not solved by backward problem-reduction, but are treated as hypotheses which need to satisfy certain constraints. In CLP these constraints are "built in" and implemented by means of specialized algorithms. A typical example of such a constraint predicate and associated algorithm is the inequality predicate and the simplex algorithm. Some CLP languages allow the programmer to specify integrity constraints, as "constraint handling rules."

CLP is often used to combine problem reduction in logic programming with mathematical programming, for applications such as scheduling. It has been applied to configuring the operation of complex xerographic

printers (*see* http://www.parc.xerox.com/spl/projects/mbc/), and scheduling maintenance work on electric power systems in Spain (*see* http://www-iri.upc.es/people/planets/).

Metalogic Programming

Metalogic is the use of logic to reason about linguistic and logical entities. *Metalogic programming* is the use of logic programming for this purpose. A common example of such reasoning is the implementation of *metainterpreters*, which define (and implement) some "object level" language. The so-called *vanilla metainterpreter*, which implements Horn clause logic programming in itself, is one of the simplest examples:

```
demo(P, X) if clause(P, X if Y) and demo(P, Y)
demo(P, X and Y) if demo(P, X) and demo(P, Y).
```

Here demo(P, X) expresses that X can be derived (or demonstrated) from the program P, and clause(P, X if Y) expresses that X if Y is a clause in the program P.

Metalogic programming is often used to implement metainterpreters for other logics or for more powerful logic programming languages in a less powerful logic programming language such as Prolog.

Objects and Agents

A number of systems have been developed that combine logic programming and object orientation. Some systems simply interpret objects as terms, and obtain some of the effect of object orientation by employing a sorted logic in which terms are organized in hierarchies.

Other systems interpret objects as concurrently executed procedure calls. Under this interpretation, procedure calls behave as processes, variables shared between different procedure calls behave as communication channels, and unification passing the output of one procedure call as input to another behaves like message passing.

To some extent, these two views of object orientation can be united in metalogic programming by regarding the program P in the metapredicate demo(P, X) as an object which can be executed concurrently with other objects such as Q in demo(Q, Y). In this interpretation of object-orientation, programs are named by terms which can be organized in hierarchies, and can be executed as processes concurrently with other processes.

The metalogic programming view of object orientation also has an interpretation in terms of agents: the predicate demo(P, X) can be understood as expressing that the agent P has belief X. Agents can be combined in multiagent systems (*q.v.*) by metaprogramming. For example, the metaclauses

```
demo(P+Q, X) if demo(P, X)
demo(P+Q, X) if demo(Q, X)
```

define the new agent P+Q as a combination of the two agents P and Q. In this combination, the new agent believes X if either P or Q believes X. However, in the combination

```
demo(P * Q, X) if demo(P, X) and demo(Q, X)
```

the new agent P * Q believes X only if both agents believe X.

Other Developments in Logic Programming

Some of the more important areas of logic programming not dealt with in this article are types, functions, higher-order logic, nonclassical logic, inductive logic programming and logic grammars. Many proposals have been made to extend or modify logic programming by incorporating these features.

An extensive collection of applications of logic programming to such diverse areas as legal codes and regulations, and the Windows NT network configurer, can be found documented in the *Proceedings of the Practical Applications of Prolog Conferences*, 1992, 94, 95, 96, 97, 98 (http://www.practical-applications.co.uk).

Bibliography

1974. Kowalski, R. "Predicate Logic as Programming Language," *Proc. IFIP 74*, 569–574. Amsterdam: North-Holland.
1978. Clark, K. L. "Negation as Failure," in *Logic and Data Bases* (eds. H. Gallaire and J. Minker), 293–322. New York: Plenum Press.
1979. Kowalski, R. *Logic for Problem Solving*. Amsterdam: North-Holland.
1984. Hogger, C. J. *Introduction to Logic Programming*. New York: Academic Press.
1987. Lloyd, J. W. *Foundations of Logic Programming*, 2nd Ed. New York: Springer-Verlag.
1989. Abramson, H., and Dahl, V. *Logic Grammars*. New York: Springer-Verlag.
1994. Doets, K. *From Logic to Logic Programming*. Cambridge, MA: MIT Press.
1996. Apt, K. *From Logic Programming to Prolog*. Upper Saddle River, NJ: Prentice Hall.
1998. Marriott, K., and Stuckey, P. J. *Programming with Constraints: An Introduction*. Cambridge, MA: MIT Press.
1999. The WWW Virtual Library page on *Logic Programming*. http://www.comlab.ox.ac.uk/archive/logic-prog.html.

Robert Kowalski

LANGUAGES

This article assumes that the reader has read the foregoing article, LOGIC PROGRAMMING: PRINCIPLES. The overview section of this article is a general discussion of the range of current logic programming languages, describing their key features and differences. It contains no example programs. The second section describes five LP languages in more detail, with example programs. There is a fairly detailed description of Prolog, because it is the most widely used LP language, with many commercial implementations. This is followed by briefer descriptions of Prolog II, Prolog III, Eclipse, and KL1 as exemplars of the families of the different LP languages overviewed in the first section.

Overview

The SLD and SLDNF schemes described in the companion article are abstract evaluators for Horn clause logic programs. Logic programming languages, such as Prolog, are restricted implementations of such abstract evaluators, augmented with a wide range of primitive predicates. The changes made in moving from the abstract SLDNF evaluator to Prolog are analogous to those made in moving from the lambda calculus (*q.v.*) to Lisp (*q.v.*). The primitives invoke routines written in machine code or C (*q.v.*). Some of them are just efficient implementations of relations that could be defined using Horn clauses. Usually these primitives have restricted *modes* of use that specify which parameters must be bound or unbound. For example, a sort(L,S) primitive, read as: S is the list L with elements in increasing order, might only support sorting. That is, L must be given and S must be an unbound variable when sort(L,S) is evaluated. A sort relation defined using Horn clauses, and evaluated using SLD, would be much slower but would not have these restrictions. Other Prolog primitives, such as those to read and write terms or to manipulate graphical images, have side effects (*q.v.*) that cannot be defined in logic. They also often have just one mode of use.

IMPLEMENTATION RESTRICTIONS OF PROLOG

The Prolog query evaluator is SLDNF with:

1. Strict left to right evaluation of conditions (calls) in queries and the bodies of clauses (equivalent to SLDNF selecting always the leftmost literal of each derived query).

2. Backtracking, depth first search of the tree (*q.v.*) of alternative evaluation paths for a query. In addition, the clauses for each predicate of the selected call are tried in the before/after order in which they are given in the program.

3. No *occur check* during unification (see later).

These restrictions allow for fast evaluation of queries on conventional computers. In addition, Prolog's primitives, for arithmetic, terminal I/O, file handling, FTP communication etc., allow the implementation of a wide class of interactive applications. For example, they allow easy implementation of rule-based interactive expert systems (*q.v.*) that access both local and remote databases during their problem solving. But the evaluation restrictions and the use of the primitives also incur a penalty. Prolog programs can rarely be used in all the different modes of use that the SLD evaluator allows. For example, the Prolog < primitive for comparing values will generate an error if the call X<9 is selected for evaluation with X unbound; it will not generate candidate values for X. So, if < is used in a clause, this usually restricts its modes of use. A clause of the form:

```
p(X,Y) :- X<3,.....
```

can only be used so solve a call p(U,W) where U already has a number binding.

THE UNIFICATION OCCUR CHECK

This is the check, before a variable V is bound to a term T, that V does not appear in T. A binding such as V=g(2,V) is not allowed by the SLDNF evaluator because it makes V an "infinite" term and subsequent unifications involving V may not terminate. The occur check is dropped in most Prolog implementations because, in most "computation" inference, variables do not get bound to terms in which they occur, and to retain it would considerably slow down the unification step. However, one Prolog, Qu-Prolog of the University of Queensland, retains the occur check, because the application target of Qu-Prolog is interactive theorem proving (*q.v.*). Another LP language, Prolog II, does not have the occur check but compensates by having a unification algorithm that can handle the infinite terms that can result. Indeed, programming with infinite terms is a feature of Prolog II.

DELAYING CALLS AND COROUTINING

More modes of use of the Horn clauses of a Prolog program are retained if the query evaluator can delay the evaluation of some call if certain arguments are unbound. For example, it would be useful if we could delay the evaluation of the call X<3 until immediately after X is bound. This results in a form of dataflow (*q.v.*) coroutining (*see* COROUTINE) where the alternation between the evaluation of certain calls is triggered by the binding, or further instantiation, of variables shared between the calls. Prolog II and SICStus Prolog allow the programmer to *specify* that a call should be delayed if one or more of its variables is unbound, and resumed as soon as they are all bound.

CONSTRAINT LOGIC PROGRAMMING (CLP) LANGUAGES

Even more modes of use are recovered by having primitives that *automatically* delay until they can be solved, and by having them solvable for several modes of use. For example, suppose that we had an arithmetic expression evaluator that was "invertible," and which was automatically delayed until its arguments were sufficiently instantiated for a solution to be found. A call such as X=Y+4 would then delay if X and Y were both unbound but would solve the equation as soon as *either* became bound. The constraint logic programming languages such as Prolog III, Chip, Eclipse, cc(FD), and CLP(*R*) do exactly this. At extra implementation cost, Prolog III and CLP(*R*) actually do much more. If X+Y=12 is delayed, and then later X+2Y=17 is delayed, the two equational constraints on X and Y are "combined" to give the solution: X=7, Y=5. This involves having linear equation-solving algorithms embedded in the implementation which manipulate all the delayed calls that are linear arithmetic equations to see if, taken together, they imply single-solution bindings for some of their variables. Checking delayed sets of equations for solvability, and partially solving them where possible, is a costly operation. So the constraint logic programming languages are much slower in execution than Prolog. But for certain applications, such as search problems which involve finding solutions of equations, they compensate for this by having a much smaller search tree of alternative evaluation paths.

FINITE DOMAIN CONSTRAINTS

Chip, and its successors Eclipse and cc(FD) (van Hentenryk *et al.*, 1992), have special purpose support for finite domain constraint solving where each variable has a specified finite range of different allowed values. With this restriction, one can use algorithms developed in artificial intelligence (*q.v.*) for finite domain constraint solving. As an example, suppose X has been declared as having a finite domain comprising the integers 0 to 10. If the constraint condition X<3 is "called" before X is bound the result is that the domain of X is reduced to the range 0 to 2. A subsequent attempt to bind X to any value outside this range will fail.

Finite domain CLP languages are well suited to scheduling and resource allocation applications. Such an application can be characterized as the problem of allocating values to a set of resource variables, from a fixed set of possible values for each variable, subject to a set of simple equational and inequality constraints on the allocation. An Eclipse or cc(FD) program can be used to generate the constraints and to search for a solution by alternating between:

1. nondeterministically generating a candidate binding for a constraint variable from its current domain, and

2. trying to solve, or to simplify the other constraints, or to use them to narrow the domains of the other variables.

OR-PARALLEL EVALUATION

An obvious way to parallelize Prolog or a CLP language is to allow for parallel search of the tree of alternative evaluation paths. This is called *or-parallelism*. Or-parallel versions of Prolog have been implemented on multiprocessor machines. One such is Muse Prolog from the Swedish Institute of Computer Science (SICS). It has the useful feature that it will run existing SICStus Prolog applications, often with considerable speed up. SICStus Prolog is a widely used Prolog system with coroutining and several constraint solvers as optional embeddable components.

INDEPENDENT AND-PARALLELISM

In some or-parallel implementations adjacent *independent* calls are also evaluated in parallel. Independent calls share no unbound variable.

COMMUNICATING AND-PARALLELISM

Allowing the parallel evaluation of calls that share unbound variables is a much more radical step. If this is coupled with delaying of calls when certain variables are unbound, it allows concurrent dataflow programming. Concurrent Prolog, KL1, Parlog, and Strand are concurrent dataflow LP languages. To retain efficient implementation, the concurrently evaluating calls are allowed only to generate a single binding for each shared variable. They do this by incorporating the control concept of committed choice (like a guarded command—*q.v.*). That is, each call must commit to the use of just one clause before any bindings for the variables of the call are communicated to other calls that share the variables. This means that the committed choice concurrent LP languages can only return a single solution to any query.

DETERMINISTIC AND-PARALLELISM

Committed choice nondeterminism is used so that the and-parallel implementation does not have to handle communication of multiple bindings for shared variables between concurrently executing calls. A single binding is generated only when the call is deterministic, i.e. when there is only one clause whose head unifies with the clause. Executing all deterministic calls in parallel is *deterministic and-parallelism*. Andorra Prolog has this form of and-parallelism. When all calls suspend because they are each nondeterministic, Andorra Prolog selects the leftmost nondeterministic call and does an or-parallel evaluation of each derived query.

CONCURRENT CONSTRAINT LANGUAGES

If we combine the concepts of: (1) committed choice nondeterminism, (2) concurrent execution of calls, and (3) constraint solving, we get a concurrent constraint LP language such as Oz.

Some Logic Programming Languages

PROLOG

The name "Prolog," the backtracking search, and strict left to right evaluation of calls, are all inherited from the first interpreted implementation of Prolog by Colmerauer's research group at the University of Aix-Marseille in 1972. The syntax and most of the standard set of primitives of current commercial Prologs derive from the 1977 Edinburgh University compiler re-implementation by David H. Warren and colleagues. Clocksin and Mellish (1994) was the first of many textbooks on Prolog.

Syntax. Everything in Prolog is a term. A *term* is a number, an atom, a variable or a compound term of the form $f(t1,..,tn)$, $n > 0$, where f is an atom and $t1,..,tn$ are terms. The f is the *functor* of the term. Atoms are alphanumeric, symbolic, or quoted. Alphanumeric atoms begin with a *lower-case letter*.

```
apple  tom  bill_gates
                       are alphanumeric atoms
  +   *   ^^   ++   : -   ! are symbolic atoms
 'X'  'Tom' 'hello there'  are quoted atoms
```

Variable names are alphanumeric character sequences beginning with an *upper-case letter* or with _.

```
Tom  _2  Man_in_Charge   are variable names
```

Operators. Prolog has an operator precedence (*q.v.*) syntax. Atoms can be declared as associative or nonassociative, prefix, postfix or infix operators. Atoms such as > < * + :- , are predefined infix operators. With operators, compound terms such as >(X,Y) can be written as X>Y, and normal arithmetic expressions such as 2*X+6 can be used instead of +(*(2,X),6).

Clauses. In Prolog a clause is an atom or a compound term. (When written in a program it must be followed by a full stop immediately followed by a white space character—space, tab or newline.) If the compound term has :- as outermost functor, it is a clause with preconditions. The :- is read as "if," and commas separating the preconditions are read as "and."

Program 1

```
parent of(mary,fred).          is male(john).
parent_of(john,fred).
father_of(F,C) :- parent_of(F,C),
                                is_male(F).
grand_parent_of(Gp,Gc):- parent_of(Gp,P),
                           parent_of(P,Gc).
sibling_of(C1,C2):- parent_of(P,C1),
             parent_of(P,C2),not C1=C2.
```

The first three clauses are facts. The last three are rules defining the `father_of/2`, `grand_parent_of/2` and `sibling_of/2` relations. (The p/n notation is used to indicate the number of arguments n.) The facts about `father_of/2` and `is_male/1` can be viewed as the tuples of a relational database (*q.v.*). Usually, we would have many more such facts in the program, and more rules for other relations such as `mother_of/2`, `ancestor_of/2`, `grand_father_of/2` etc.

Because `:-` and `,` are predefined infix operators, the rule for `father_of/2` is the compound term

```
':-'(father_of(F,C),
       ','(parent_of(F,C),is_male(F))).
```

(Operators such as `':'` and `','` need to be quoted when used as prefix functors.) The fact that clauses are just terms of a certain form is important for *meta-level* programming. Prolog shares with Lisp the ability to treat programs and fragments of programs as data which can be manipulated and then executed. In this, as in its imperative primitives, Prolog goes beyond the pure concept of logic programming.

By optionally declaring the atom `is_male` as a nonassociative postfix operator and `parent_of`, `father_of` as nonassociative infix operators, the `father_of/2` rule can be written:

```
F father_of C :- F parent_of C, F is_male.
```

User-declared operators can be used to good effect to allow program clauses to be written in a form suited to the application.

Lists. There is a special syntax for list terms.

`[2,3,4]` instead of

```
cons(2,cons(3,cons(4,nil)))
```

`[X]` pattern of a list with *exactly* one member X

`[X|T]` pattern of a list with *at least* one member X—will match `[2]` with T=[]

`[2,V|T]` pattern of a list starting with 2, followed by another element V, followed by tail list T

In list patterns the `|` is read as "followed by."

Programs 2 and 3 are Prolog versions of the `append/3`, `member/2` and `sort/2` programs discussed in the PRINCIPLES section.

Program 2

```
append([],L2,L2).
append([U|L1],L2,[U|L3]) :-
                      append(L1,L2,L3).
member(V,[V|L]).
member(V,[U|L]) :- member(V,L).
```

Program 3

```
sort(L,SortL) :- permutation(L,SortL),
                        ordered(SortL).
permutation([],[]).
permutation([H|T],[V|PermL]) :-
  delete(V,[H|T],L),permutation(L,PermL).
delete(H,[H|T],T).
delete(V,[H|T],[H|DelT]) :-
                      delete(V,T,DelT).
ordered([]).
ordered([X]).
ordered([X,Y|T]) :- X=<Y,ordered([Y|T]).
```

Prolog query evaluation. Prolog's backtracking search and left to right evaluation of calls means that the query

```
father_of(X,fred)
```

to Program 1 will be evaluated as follows. First it will be reduced using the only clause for `father_of/2` to the conjunction

```
parent_of(X,fred),is_male(X)
```

The first call will now be selected and the clauses for `parent_of/2` will be unified with the call in turn, in the order in which they are written in the program.

The call will unify with the first clause, making X=mary. As the clause has no preconditions, this solves the call. Prolog now tries to solve

```
is_male(mary)
```

which fails to unify with the single `is_male/1` clause. This causes Prolog to backtrack to try the next clause for `father_of/2` in order to find an alternative solution for `father_of(X,fred)`. This gives the binding X=john. The second call is now `is_male(john)` which does unify with the `is_male/1` clause. X=john is the solution to the query.

Consider now the definition for `grand_parent_of/2` in Program 1. Given a much larger database of `parent_of/2` facts, Prolog will handle queries of the form `grand_parent_of(givenGp,Gc)` in which Gp is given and Gc is to be found much more efficiently than those of the form

```
grand_parent_of(Gp,givenGc)
```

in which Gc is given and Gp is to be found. In the latter case, it will have to solve the first call, `parent_of(Gp,P)`, of the `grand_parent_of/2` rule with both arguments unbound variables. Prolog will unify this, in turn, with each `parent_of/2` fact, and for each solution test if it has found a parent of the given `Gc` by evaluating `parent_of(P,givenGc)`. It would be much more efficient in this case to solve the calls in reverse order. To take the `givenGc`, find one of its parents `P`, and then find a parent of `P` by solving `parent_of(Gp,P)`.

This is an example of the usefulness of dynamic reordering of calls depending on the mode of use. Using meta-level primitives, `var` and `!`, the solution can be programmed in Prolog but with a loss of logical purity. We need two rules:

```
grand_parent_of(Gp,Gc) :- var(Gc),!,
        parent_of(P,Gc),parent_of(Gp,P).
grand_parent_of(Gp,Gc) :- parent_of(Gp,P),
        parent_of(P,Gc).
```

The first rule will be used only for calls in which `Gc` is a variable because of the `var(Gc)` test. The second will be used for all other calls. The `!` following the `var(Gc)` test is Prolog's backtracking control primitive. Once evaluated in a clause, it stops Prolog from backtracking to use as yet untried clauses for the call. (It also prevents Prolog from retrying any calls that precede the `!` in the body of the clause or query in which it appears.)

In Programs 2 and 3 only the definitions for `append/3`, `member/2`, and `delete/3` are truly flexible programs. The term `append/3` can be queried with such diverse queries as:

```
append([1,2,3], [4,5], X)
                    answer X=[1,2,3,4,5]
append(X,Y,[1,2])   answers X=[],Y=[1,2],
                    X=[1],Y=[2],
                    X=[1,2],Y=[]
append(X,[Z],[1,2,3])  answer X=[1,2],Z=3.
```

and many more. Because of this versatility, we can use it to define many other relations on lists, as in Program 4.

Program 4

```
member(X,L) :- append(_,[X|_],L).
            % an alternative defn of member/2
adjacent_on(X,Y,L) :- append(_,[X,Y|_],L).
                    % X,Y are adjacent on L
sublist_of(S,L) :-
    S=[_|_],              % S is a non-empty
    append(_,S,FrontL),   % tail segment of a
    append(FrontL,_,L).
                    % front segment of L
```

In contrast, the `ordered/1` definition of Program 3 can only be used for testing. This is because `=<` is a primitive which in Prolog requires both arguments to be bound by the time it is evaluated, So, the potential use of the `sort/2` definition mentioned in the companion article, to generate instances of the

relation, is not possible using Prolog. We can only use the `sort/2` program for calls in which the list to sort is completely given. The second argument, the sorted list, can be given, partially given, or be an unbound variable. That is, we can have calls such as

```
sort([2,3,1],[1,2,3]),
sort([2,3,1],[H|T]),
```

and

```
sort([2,3,1],S),
```

but not

```
sort([X,Y,Z],[X1,Y1,Z1]).
```

Other logical features of prolog. In addition to negation of calls, implemented as negation as failure (*see* PRINCIPLES), Prolog has disjunction, a `forall` construct, and primitives for wrapping up all the solutions to a query as a list.

Program 5

```
person(P) :- male(P) ; female(P).
            % ; is the disjunction operator
ordered(L) :-
    forall(adjacent_on(X,Y,L),X=<Y).
            % alternative defn of ordered
children_of(P,L) :-
    setof(C,parent_of(P,C),L).
            % L is a list of all children of P.
```

The `children_of/2` definition of Program 5 is very powerful, for it can be used even if `P` is not given. A query `children_of(P,L)` will find each parent `P` in the database, and for each such `P` bind `L` to a lexically ordered list of names of their recorded children. The term `setof/3` even removes duplicates if there are any.

More meta-level features. Prolog has primitives for retrieving, adding and deleting individual clauses of the definition for a relation, using program information available to the interpreter or compiler. A call in a clause or query can also be a variable, the so-called *metacall*. The metacall variable must be bound to a call term before it is called. Program 6, using the clause retrieval primitive `clause/2` and the metacall variable, is the Prolog query evaluator defined in Prolog.

Program 6

```
eval(Call) :- primitive(Call), Call.
                % Call is call to a primitive
                % so just directly evaluate it
eval((Call,MoreCalls)) :-       % eval of a
    eval(Call),             % conjunction Call,
    eval(MoreCalls).        % MoreCalls
eval(true).
            % needed since clause(C,B) gives
            % B=true for a fact clause
```

```
eval(Call) :- clause(Call,Body),
          eval(Body).        % for other calls
      % look for unifying clause and eval its body
```

More elaborate interpreters have been used for building expert systems that use Prolog's clauses to represent the expertise but which have more sophisticated evaluation strategies with, for example, explanation facilities.

PROLOG II

Colmerauer's team modified their original Prolog into a variant language, Prolog II. There are minor syntactic differences between it and standard Prolog. The user cannot declare operators, -> is used instead of :-, clauses are terminated with ; rather than a period (full stop), and the variable/nonvariable convention is reversed. However, the major differences are in the operational and logical semantics. Giannesini *et al.* (1986) is the reference textbook for Prolog II.

Delaying calls. A significant feature of Prolog II is the ability to delay the evaluation of a call until one or more argument variables of the call are bound. To delay a call C until some variable X is bound (to any nonvariable term), the call is written freeze (X,C). The following is a Prolog II definition of grand_parent_of/2 which will delay the parent_of(P,Gc) call if Gc is unbound. To avoid confusion, we have used standard Prolog syntax.

```
grand_parent_of(Gp,Gc) :-
      freeze(Gc,parent_of(P,Gc)),
      parent_of(Gp,P);
```

It has the same effect as the two-clause Prolog definition given earlier.

Program 7 is a coroutining version of the sort/2 program using freeze/2 to delay calls. It uses the permutation/2 program given in Program 3. Notice that the body calls in the sort/2 clause are reversed and the clauses for ordered/1 are reversed. Given a call, sort([2,1,3,0,8],SortedL), the ordered (SortedL) call will delay because SortedL is unbound. Then, when the permutation/2 program binds SortedL to [H'|T'] (new names are always given to clause variables each time the clause is used) using its second clause, its evaluation will be interrupted because the delayed ordered/1 call can resume. Unifying the delayed call with its first clause will bind X to H' and T' to [Y'|L']. Then its body calls H'=<Y' and ordered (L') will both delay allowing the permutation call to resume. The delayed call H'=<Y' will be resumed, and fail, when permutation, after two more evaluation steps, binds H' to 2 and Y' to 1. In the Prolog program (Program 3), which does not coroutine between the two calls of the sort

clause, this failure is detected only when the permutation call has generated a complete first permutation. The coroutining allows early detection of failure and means that the search for an ordered permutation will terminate much more quickly.

Program 7

```
sort(L,SortedL):-
    freeze(SortedL,ordered (SortedL)),
    permutation(L,SortedL).
ordered([X,Y|L]):-
    freeze (X,freeze(Y,X=<Y)),
    freeze(L,ordered(L)).
ordered([X]).
ordered([]).
```

Unification for infinite terms. As we said earlier, for efficiency, Prolog will incorrectly allow a binding X=f(a,X) in which variable X appears in its binding term. For the most part this presents no problem, for Prolog evaluations rarely generate such bindings. However, if one is generated, the binding cannot be displayed, and it may cause a subsequent unification to loop. Prolog II also does "unification" without the occur check, but its "unification" correctly handles such bindings. Giannesini *et al.* (1986) contains elegant examples of the use of such infinite cyclic structures.

Inequality constraints in Prolog II. All calls to the inequality primitive t1\=t2 automatically delay if its two arguments are unifiable (by a Prolog II "unification") *which generates bindings for variables.* (It succeeds if they are not unifiable, and fails if they are syntactically identical.) In Prolog II, we could define sibling_of/2 using

```
sibling_of(C1,C2) :-
    C1\=C2,parent_of(P,C1),parent_of(P,C2).
```

Given a call, sibling_of(peter,C2), the peter \=C2 call will immediately delay, because peter and C2 are unifiable with C2=peter. It will be resumed after the execution of the second parent_of/2 call, when C2 gets bound.

Such \= conditions can also be returned in answers. Given a query absent_from(X,[E1,E2,E3]) to Program 8, Prolog II will return the answer X\=E1, X\=E2, X\=E3. The automatic delaying of calls to \=, and its appearance in answers, makes it a constraint primitive.

Program 8

```
absent_from(X,[]).
absent_from(X,[Y|L]) :-
      X\=Y,absent_from(X,L).
```

Returning conjunctions of constraints as answers, as well as variable bindings, is a feature of CLP languages.

PROLOG III

Prolog III (Colmerauer 1990) extends Prolog II in having a far richer set of constraint primitives. In addition to \=, the inequalities >, <, =<, >=, will automatically delay if either argument is unbound. The delayed call is added to the set of delayed constraint calls. Linear arithmetic equations such as 2X+5Y=45, are also handled as constraints rather than as normal calls. If neither side of the equation contains unbound variables, each side will be evaluated and compared, and the call will succeed or fail. If there is only one unbound variable, the equation will be algebraically solved to find its value. Otherwise the call is delayed and added to the set of delayed linear equations. Each time a constraint is added to a set of delayed constraints, and each time a variable appearing in any of them is bound by the normal evaluation, the delayed constraints are checked for consistency or partial solvability. For example, if a call X<0 is delayed, and later X>2 is delayed, that branch of the evaluation will immediately fail since the two constraints on X are inconsistent. If 2X+5Y=45 is delayed and later, either X is bound to 10, or the equation 3X-7Y=-5 is added to the set of constraints, the first constraint can be solved with the bindings X=10, Y=5.

As a Prolog III program, the sort definition of Program 2 can be invoked with the call sort([X,Y,Z], [Z,X,Y]). It will return as answer the constraint conjunction Z=<X,X=<Y.

ECLIPSE

This is a primarily a finite domain CLP language. Program 9 is an example Eclipse program. It is a program to find a three-color coloring for a map of four countries represented by the variables C1, C2, C3, and C4. Adjacent countries cannot have the same color.

The :: condition specifies that C1, C2, C3, and C4 each have the same finite domain and that they can have as value only one of the symbols blue, red, and yellow. The topology is specified by the ## conditions. C##C' means that the assigned values for C and C' must be disjoint. So, country C1 borders countries C2, C3 and C4, C2 borders C3, and C3 borders C4. A ## call automatically suspends until either variable is assigned a value. As soon as one of them has a value, this value is removed from the domain of the other variable and the call succeeds. Finally, a variable can only be given a value, by an assign_color/1 call, if that value is in its current domain. Thus, as the evaluation moves through the sequence of assign_color/1 calls, the

domains for C2, C3 and C4 are progressively narrowed, eliminating a lot of backtracking search.

Program 9

```
color_map(C1,C2,C3,C4) :-
    [C1,C2,C3,C4] :: [blue,red,yellow],
    C1##C2, C1##C3, C1##C4, C2##C3, C3##C4,
    assign_color(C1), assign_color(C2),
    assign_color(C3), assign_color(C4).

assign_color(C) :- C=blue; C=red; C=yellow.
```

KL1

This was the concurrent LP language developed and implemented as part of the Japanese Fifth Generation Computer Research Program. The KL1 version for the quicksort program described in PRINCIPLES is given in Program 10.

Program 10

```
quick([],S):- true | S=[].
quick([H|T],Sort) :-
    true | partition(H,T,LessH,MoreH),
    quick(LessH,SortedLessH),
    quick(MoreH,SortedMoreH),
    append(SortedLessH,[H|SortedMoreH],
                                    Sort).

partition(P,[],F,B) :- true
    | F=[],B=[].
partition(P,[H|T],F,B) :- H< P
    | F=[H|MoreF],partition(P,T,MoreF,B).
partition(P,[H|T],F,B) :- P =< H
    | B=[H|MoreB],partition(P,T,F,MoreB).

append([],Y,Z) :- true
    | Z=Y.
append([U|X],Y,Z) :- true
    | Z=[U|Z1],append(X,Y,Z1).
```

The vertical bar, |, in each clause is like the Prolog cut. It causes the evaluation to commit to the use of the clause. It must always be preceded by at least one call, which can be the call true, which always succeeds. The calls preceding the | are the *guard* calls and those following it are the *body* calls of a clause.

All query calls in a KL1 evaluation are executed in parallel. A call is reduced to the parallel evaluation of the body calls of *any candidate* clause. This is a clause with a head that *matches* the call and a guard that succeeds. The head matches if it unifies with the call *without* binding any variables in the call. The evaluation *commits* to the use of just one candidate clause for each call, even if there are more than one. A call suspends if there is no candidate clause that matches it but there is at least one clause that might become a candidate when one or more call arguments (its input arguments) are further instantiated. The nonvariable argument terms in each clause head correspond to the *input* arguments of the call. Output arguments (the second argument of `quick/2`, the third and fourth arguments of `partition/4`, the third argument of `append/3`) have their values assigned by explicit `=/2` unification calls after the | in each clause. So, as is required by committed choice non-determinism, there will be no binding made to a shared variable of a call (in fact no binding to any variable) until the evaluation has committed to using a particular clause.

Given a query `quick([2,3,1,8,-4...],S)`, KL1 will reduce this to the *parallel* conjunction

```
partition(2,[3,1,..],LessH,MoreH),
quick(LessH,SortLessH),
quick(MoreH,SortMoreH),
append(SortLessH,[2|SortMoreH],S)
```

The match-only requirement for unification with their clause heads will mean that the two `quick/2` calls and the `append/3` call immediately suspend. The `partition/4` call is the only one that can proceed at this time. It incrementally generates the list bindings for `LessH` and `NotMoreH` which are consumed by the two recursive `quick/2` calls. The first of these incrementally generates the list binding for `SortLessH` which is consumed by the `append/3` call. The consumers cannot run ahead of the generators for their input arguments; the attempt to do so causes them to suspend. What we get is a parallel dataflow computation, with a growing number of subsidiary parallel dataflow computations, one for each `sort/2` call introduced into the evaluation which is reduced using the recursive `sort/2` clause.

An implementation of KL1 that runs on shared memory multiprocessors is available free of charge (*see* KLIC home page).

Bibliography

1986. Giannesini, F., Kanoui, H., Pasero, P., and van Caneghem, M. *Prolog.* Reading, MA: Addison-Wesley.
1990. Colmerauer, A. "An Introduction to Prolog III," *Comm. of the ACM*, **33**, 7, 69–90.
1992. van Hentenryk, P., Simonis, H., and Dincbas, M. "Constraint Satisfaction Using Constraint Logic Programming," *Artificial Intelligence*, **58**, 113–159.
1994. Clocksin, W. F., and Mellish, C. S. *Programming in Prolog*, 4th Ed. New York: Springer-Verlag.

Websites

KLIC Home Page. http://www.klic.org.
SICStus Prolog Home Page. http://www.sics.se/isl/sicstus.html.
Oz Home Page. http://www.mozart-oz.org.

Keith L. Clark

LOGIC, COMPUTATIONAL

See LOGICS OF PROGRAMS; and MODEL CHECKING.

LOGICAL AND PHYSICAL NAMES

For articles on related subjects *see* INPUT–OUTPUT CONTROL SYSTEM; MEMORY: AUXILIARY; and OPERATING SYSTEMS: GENERAL PRINCIPLES.

A *physical* (input–output) *unit* is an input–output device and its associated recording medium. Thus, tape drives, disk drives, drums, keyboards, and printers are all examples of physical units. A *logical unit* is a convenient abstraction of a physical unit, an extra level of naming of input–output devices that gives both the programmer and the system added operational flexibility.

The usage of a two-level naming scheme may be compared to the use of call numbers in a library card catalog. The call number of a book is sufficient to identify the book, but it bears no permanent relationship to the location of the book on the shelves. Rather, to locate a book physically, knowing only its call number, it is necessary to consult a directory that tells (for example) on which floor a particular collection of call numbers is located. The library staff are then free to change the physical location of the books, provided the directory is updated accordingly.

A similar two-level naming scheme is used for input output operations on a computer. Each physical input–output unit has associated with it a physical unit name in order that communication with the central processor can be established. When data is being transferred, these physical unit names are ultimately used. However, a programmer frequently finds it convenient to use logical unit names in place of these physical unit names, and to provide a correspondence (i.e. directory) between logical and physical units. Thus, for example, in a C++ program the statement

```
source >> x >> y >> z;
```

causes the program to take values for `x`, `y`, and `z` from the object with the logical name `source`. Previously, the program will have had a statement that associates this logical name with the physical name of a file on a disk or other physical location; for example

```
ifstream source ("test.dat");
```

specifies a filename, and

```
ifstream source (argv[1]);
```

specifies that the file be whatever the user types when running the program (`argv[1]` means: the name following the program name that the user enters on the command line).

This two-level naming provides a number of advantages, both to the programmer and to the operating system. First, it is possible to reassign the physical unit associated with a given logical unit without recompilation of the program, since the program is written in terms of logical units only, and the correspondence is made during program execution by looking in the directory. This process is called *I/O redirection*, and a program that is written to capitalize on the technique is said to be *device independent*.

The logical/physical distinction is a relative one. From the standpoint of the C++ example above, a filename specifies a physical unit: data on a disk. This name is used to tell the operating system where to find the program data. From the standpoint of the operating system, however, a name like test.dat is a logical name, and the file is physically specified by a set of disk block numbers. These, in turn, may be regarded by the disk-driver program as a set of logical names for physical tracks and sectors on the disk platter. At each level the separation of logical from physical specification provides independence. If the operating system moves a file from one set of blocks to another, it will only have to update the record associating the file name with the blocks, but the user who asks for test.dat does not need to know these system-level details.

Robert W. Taylor

LOGICS OF PROGRAMS

For articles on related subjects *see* AUTOMATIC PROGRAMMING; FORMAL LANGUAGES; FUNCTIONAL PROGRAMMING; GRAMMARS; LAMBDA CALCULUS; LIST PROCESSING; LOOP INVARIANT; MODEL CHECKING; PROGRAM VERIFICATION; and SYNTAX, SEMANTICS, AND PRAGMATICS.

A program logic is a *language* in which properties of programs can be expressed unambiguously, a *semantics* that specifies the meaning of the expressions of the language, and *rules* for manipulating those expressions in a meaning-respecting way in order to calculate or demonstrate the truth of assertions in the language. The study of logics of programs is of value in understanding how both people and computers may reason about software, either autonomously or cooperatively. Applications include *program verification*, automatic programming (*q.v.*), and program analysis for optimization and auditing purposes.

In some logics, the semantics will be omitted and assumed to be either understood intuitively or implied by the rules; alternatively, only the semantics may be given and the choice of appropriate rules left open. Sometimes, the rules will be nondeterministic and intended as criteria to be met by formal proofs in the tradition of mathematical proof systems; sometimes, they will be deterministic and intended for use in an algorithm in the tradition of logical decision methods.

A number of logics of programs have been proposed, each of them owing some debt to the subject of mathematical logic, with most of them making additional program-specific contributions of their own. The subject started with the seminal papers of McCarthy (1963), Floyd (1967), and Hoare (1969).

McCarthy's approach modeled programs as recursive functions. An example is supplied by the recursively defined list processing function $x @ y$, which denotes the list that is the "append" $[x_1 x_2 \ldots x_m y_1 y_2 \ldots y_n]$ of the two lists $x = [x_1 x_2 \ldots x_m]$ and $y = [y_1 y_2 \ldots y_n]$. We write $[\,]$ for the empty list and $a.x$ for the list $[a\, x_1 x_2 \ldots x_m]$ in the following recursive definition:

$$@1:\ [\,] @ y\ = y$$
$$@2:\ (a.x) @ y = a.(x @ y)$$

Append is associative; i.e. $x @ (y @ z) = (x @ y) @ z$. We may prove this formally by induction on the length of x, assuming that every list x is either $[\,]$ or of the form $a.u$, where u is a shorter list than x. For the basis case, $x = [\,]$, we have

$$[\,] @ (y @ z) = y @ z \qquad \text{(by @1)}$$
$$= ([\,] @ y) @ z \quad \text{(by @1).}$$

For the inductive case, $x = a.u$, we take as our induction hypothesis that $u @ (y @ z) = (u @ y) @ z$ and argue thus:

$$(a.u) @ (y @ z) = a.(u @ (y @ z)) \text{ (by @2)}$$
$$= a.((u @ y) @ z) \text{ (by the induction hypothesis)}$$
$$= (a.(u @ y)) @ z \text{ (by @2)}$$
$$= ((a.u) @ y) @ z \text{ (by @2).}$$

This completes the proof that the operator $@$ is associative.

It is possible to construct large systems of software entirely from recursively defined functions, and to establish many of the key properties of those systems by inductive proofs of this form on a correspondingly much larger scale. However, though some programmers find it a pleasure to program in this style, the bulk of the software that is produced in practice is written in an imperative style, involving assignments, begin–end bracketed sequences of statements, conditional statements, and while loops. To prove such programs correct, it would be most inconvenient to have to translate them into recursively defined functions.

To meet the needs of imperative programming more directly, Floyd developed a logic of flowcharts (*q.v.*). The main feature of this method was the use of the *tag*, a logical assertion placed on an arc of the flowchart and guaranteed to hold whenever control passed along that arc. Floyd's principal contributions were to work out the details of a formal system based on these tags, to address aspects of the proof-theoretic completeness of his systems, and to consider the problem of proving termination of programs. He also introduced the concept of the verification condition, consisting of a component of the flowchart and tags at its entrance and exits. To prove a tagged flowchart correct, it sufficed to prove, for each component of the flowchart, the verification condition consisting of that component and its associated tags. From the correctness of the verification conditions, a local property, the rule is that one may infer the correctness of the flowchart, a global property. This inference rule could well be called *Floyd's induction rule*. The logic was intended by Floyd both for the calculation and semantics; in fact, the title of his paper "Assigning Meanings to Programs," implied that the latter was the primary application.

Shortly thereafter, Hoare developed a logic similar to Floyd's, but for "algebraic" programs rather than flowcharts, in which flow of control is represented not with a graph of assignments and decisions but with the constructs **begin** $a_1; a_2; \ldots ; a_n$ **end** (we will omit the **begin** and **end** below), **if** p **then** a_1 **else** a_2, and **while** p **do** a. Assignments are as in Floyd's system. Hoare introduced the notation $p\{a\}q$ corresponding to Floyd's verification conditions and expressing "if p (the *precondition*) holds before executing a, then q (the *postcondition*) holds when and if a terminates."

Hoare gave a set of proof rules closer in form than Floyd's to traditional logical systems, though in content similar to Floyd's rules inasmuch as every Hoare proof of an algebraic program could be readily translated to a Floyd proof of the corresponding flowchart program. The reverse translation is also possible, though complicated by the difficulty of translating flowcharts to algebraic programs. Unlike Floyd, Hoare did not address the question of completeness of any aspect of his system. Like Floyd, Hoare regarded his proof rules as being for both proof and semantics.

Hoare's proof system for assignments, **begin–end**, conditional statements, and **while** loops amounted to the following rules (except for irrelevant details) together with whatever rules are appropriate for proving ordinary (non-Hoare) assertions of the form $p \to q$. The rules take the form of zero or more premises written over a conclusion.

1.
$$\frac{p' \to p \quad p\{a\}q \quad q \to q'}{p'\{a\}q'}$$
[If $p\{a\}q$ and also $p' \to p$ and $q \to q'$, then also $p'\{a\}q'$]

2.
$$\frac{}{p(e)\{x := e\}p(x)}$$
[If p holds of e ($p(e)$ is true) before assignment of e to x, p holds of x afterwards]

3.
$$\frac{p\{a\}q \quad q\{b\}r}{p\{a; b\}r}$$
[The transitive rule for sequential constructs]

4.
$$\frac{p \wedge r\{a\}q \quad p \wedge \neg r\{b\}q}{p\{\text{if } r \text{ then } a \text{ else } b\}q}$$
[The if–then–else rule where the value of r in the precondition determines which construct is executed]

5.
$$\frac{p \wedge q\{a\}p}{p\{\text{while } q \text{ do } a\}p \wedge \neg q}$$
[In a while loop, p is the *loop invariant* and q the condition that becomes false]

The second rule, for assignment, is really an axiom, since it has no premises. It says that if p holds of e, then, after executing $x := e$, p holds of x. With these rules, we may prove that the following program computes $n!$, the factorial of the initial value of n of y, provided n is nonnegative.

$$A: x := 1; B$$
$$B: \text{while } y > 0 \text{ do } C$$
$$C: x := y \times x; \ y := y - 1$$

The following Hoare assertions about this program may all be seen to be true; moreover, they are all provable in Hoare's system. The last asserts the property we want. Together, these assertions form a correctness proof of the program, in the sense that they show that the program computes the factorial of the initial value of y.

i. $y > 0 \wedge x \times y! = n!\{x := y \times x\}y > 0 \wedge$
$$x \times (y - 1)! = n!$$
[First $y > 0 \wedge x \times y! = n! \to y > 0 \wedge (y \times x) \times (y - 1)! = n!$; then apply (2), substituting x for $y \times x$]

ii. $y > 0 \wedge x \times (y - 1)! = n!\{y := y - 1\}y \geq 0 \wedge$
$$x \times y! = n!$$
[Similarly using (2)]

iii. $y > 0 \wedge x \times y! = n!\{C\}y \geq 0 \wedge x \times y! = n!$
[Applying (3) to (i) and (ii)]

iv. $y \geq 0 \wedge y = n \wedge x = 1\{B\}x = n!$
[Since $y = n \wedge x = 1 \to x \times y! = n!$ and since $y \geq 0 \wedge x \times y! = n! \wedge y \leq 0 \to y = 0 \wedge x = n!$ $\to x \times y! = n!$ (since $0! = 1$), (5) with (iii) gives (iv) with $q = y > 0$ and $p = y \geq 0 \wedge x \times y! = n!$]

v. $y \geq 0 \wedge y = n\{x := 1\}y \geq 0 \wedge y = n \wedge x = 1$
[Since $p\{x := 1\}p \wedge x = 1$]

vi. $y \geq 0 \wedge y = n\{A\}x = n!$
[Applying (3) to (v) and (iv)]

Since the precondition in (vi) is just the initial condition on n and the postcondition gives the desired result, the program A is thus proved to compute $n!$

To discover this proof, one might start with the last line and work backwards. Discovering line (iii) is the one truly creative step here. The formula

$$y \geq 0 \wedge x \times y! = n!$$

is the *loop invariant* or the *induction hypothesis*, and plays an analogous role to the more readily discovered induction hypothesis encountered above in connection with the associativity of append.

In more recent years, there has arisen an interest in decision methods for logics of programs as an alternative to proof systems for reasoning about programs. In general, even the simple logics considered above are undecidable (*see* UNDECIDABLE PROBLEMS); their theory (set of valid formulas) is not only not recursive but it is not even recursively enumerable. However, there exist various fragments of program logic that are decidable, just as propositional logic is a decidable fragment of the predicate calculus. The fragment of program logic analogous to propositional logic is the system of propositional dynamic logic developed by Fischer and Ladner (1979), which they have shown to be decidable. From this, it is possible to deduce that program logic without binding (everything but assignments, quantifiers, and procedure definitions) is also decidable, and that the inclusion of any one of these binding mechanisms makes it undecidable. For reasoning about parallel programs, there is Pneuli's temporal fragment of logics of programs, which is also decidable (*see* Gabbay *et al.*, 1980).

Current research into logics of programs addresses a variety of questions. What are appropriate semantics, proof rules, and decision methods for other programming language constructs, including recursion, parameter passing, manipulation of complex data structures, parallelism, nondeterminism, and probabilistic programs? What is the computational complexity (*q.v.*) of the decidable fragments of program logic? What alternative forms may the semantics and rules take? What are the obstacles to applying program logics to enhancing software reliability via program verification? The reader interested in recent developments in this area should consult Harel (1984) and Kozen and Tiuryn (1989). Much of the most recent work may be found in the theoretical computer science journals and annual conferences, in particular the Symposia on Logic in Computer Science; the ACM Symposia on Theory of Computation; the ACM Symposia on Principles of Programming Languages; the IEEE Symposia on Foundations of Computer Science; the European Association for Theoretical Computer Science International Congress on Automata, Languages and Programming; and the Czech–Polish Symposium on Mathematical Foundations of Computer Science.

Bibliography

1963. McCarthy, J. "A Basis for a Mathematical Theory of Computation," in *Computer Programming and Formal Systems* (eds. P. Braffort and D. Hirschberg), 33–70. Amsterdam: North Holland.
1967. Floyd, R. W. "Assigning Meanings to Programs," in *Mathematical Aspects of Computer Science (Proceedings of a Symposium in Applied Mathematics)* (ed. J. T. Schwarz), **19**, 19–32. Providence, RI: American Mathematical Society.
1969. Hoare, C. A. R. "An Axiomatic Basis for Computer Programming," *Comm. of the ACM*, **12**, *10*, 576–583.
1979. Fischer, M. J., and Ladner, R. E. "Propositional Dynamic Logic of Regular Programs," *JCSS*, **18**, *2*, 194–211.
1980. Gabbay, D., Pnueli, A. Shelah, S., and Stavi, J. "The Temporal Analysis of Fairness," *7th ACM Symp. on Principles of Programming Languages*, Las Vegas (January).
1984 Harel, D. "Dynamic Logic," in *Handbook of Philosophical Logic. II: Extensions of Classical Logic* (eds. D. M. Gabbay and F. Guenthner), 497–604. Boston: D. Reidel.
1989. Kozen, D., and Tiuryn, J. "Logics of Programs," in *Handbook of Theoretical Computer Science* (ed. J. van Leeuwen), vol. B, ch. 14, 789–840. Amsterdam: North-Holland.
1992. Manna, Z., and Pnueli, A. *The Temporal Logic of Reactive and Concurrent Systems*. New York: Springer-Verlag.

Vaughan R. Pratt

LOGIN FILE

For an article on a related subject *see* BOOTSTRAP.

A *login file* is a stored file of operating system commands and definitions that are obeyed automatically upon startup of a personal computer or workstation or upon logging on to a multiprogrammed mainframe (*q.v.*) or minicomputer (*q.v.*). In the latter environment, login files are unique to each user, although the files of most users will contain many common elements. To enable such customization, the login file is kept in the mass storage space allocated to the particular user and, since it has the same format as any other text file, may be edited as often as desired.

With the DEC VMS operating system, the login file must be named `login.com`. A typical login file might look like Fig. 1.

The leading $ symbols are operating system prompt characters that must be a physical part of the login file. Ordinarily, the commands placed in a newly edited login file will not be obeyed until the user logs off and then logs on again, but they can be executed by typing `@login` at any system prompt.

On personal computers that use Microsoft Windows with an underlying DOS operating system, users must separate system definitions from system commands through use of two login files that work in tandem. Definitions are placed in `config.sys` and commands in `autoexec.bat` (where the file extension

```
$ set terminal/device = vt100      ; Specify kind of terminal being used
$ prepare emacs                    ; Enable use of the EMACS screen editor
$ home :== set default sys$login ; Create a synonym for the word "home"
$ set directory/version_limit = 2 [csi.reilly]; keep only two versions of
$                                                ; each file in directory
```

Figure 1. `login.com`

```
FILES = 20       ; Allow a maximum of 20 simultaneous open files
BUFFERS = 10     ; Allocate 10 disk buffers upon start-up
DEVICE = ANSI.SYS ; Install a particular device driver
```

Figure 2. `config.sys`

```
path rbfiles ; Set a directory path to subdirectory rbfiles
cd dbfiles     ; Change active directory to dbfiles
rbase          ; Execute the rbase program
```

Figure 3. `.cshrc`

`.bat` signifies a BATch file). An example of a typical `config.sys` file is shown in Fig. 2. A typical `autoexec.bat` file is shown in Fig. 3.

When booted (*see* BOOTSTRAP), the computer will first establish the definitions in `config.sys` and then obey the operating system commands in `autoexec.bat`.

Depending on the default shell (*q.v.*) being used, the Unix (*q.v.*) operating system loads and executes the commands from either the file `.login` or `.profile` upon login, and, if the C shell is being used, executes `.cshrc` at login and at any later time the user initiates a new instance of the C shell by typing `csh` at the command prompt. Special files such as `.profile`, `.input`, and `.cshrc` are called *dot files* because of the leading period ("dot"), which marks them as files not normally shown in a directory (*q.v.*) listing.

The equivalent of a dot file in the Microsoft Windows environment is a file having the extension `.ini`. Files such as `win.ini`, `netscape.ini` and `aol.ini` are loaded upon initial invocation of software corresponding to the principal name of the file.

Edwin D. Reilly

LOGO

For articles on related subjects *see* COMPUTER-ASSISTED LEARNING AND TEACHING; FUNCTIONAL PROGRAMMING; LISP; and LIST PROCESSING: LANGUAGES.

Logo is a dialect of Lisp designed for educational use. Like other dialects of Lisp, Logo is a general-purpose programming language with special emphasis on symbolic computing and on the functional programming style. Three things give Logo its special educational focus: a simplified syntax, detailed attention to the programmer's metaphors for computational proc-

esses in the naming of primitive procedures and the wording of error messages, and a collection of application areas (of which the most famous is *turtle graphics*) that combine inherent interest with open-ended intellectual content.

The first version of Logo was developed in 1967 at Bolt, Beranek and Newman, Inc., by Wallace Feurzeig, Seymour Papert, and others. The project grew out of their experience teaching junior high school students with a more conventional algebraic programming language. Many students were uninspired by the numeric emphasis, so a language was designed with tools to manipulate English words and sentences. (The name "Logo" is derived from the Greek word λογος, meaning "word.") Papert later established a Logo research group at the Massachusetts Institute of Technology, where the language was redesigned and the robot turtle was introduced.

Educational Goals

Logo's developers were not primarily interested in the training of professional computer programmers. Instead, the goal was to provide an environment for mathematical thinking in the context of concrete projects. Developmental psychologist Jean Piaget argued that people learn mainly by *construction*—fitting new ideas with already understood ideas. Much of traditional school mathematics is abstract and disconnected from a child's ordinary experience, so this incremental learning process is difficult. Writing a computer program gives the learner practice in formal, mathematical reasoning, but each Logo application area is connected with things children do outside the context of computers or mathematics.

For example, consider the difference between Logo's turtle graphics and the Cartesian graphics traditionally used in other languages. In the latter, a fixed pair of coordinate axes is associated with the display screen;

```
TO TREE :SIZE :LEVEL
IF :LEVEL=0 [STOP]
FORWARD :SIZE/3
LEFT 20
TREE 2*:SIZE/3 :LEVEL-1
RIGHT 20
FORWARD :SIZE/6
RIGHT 15
TREE :SIZE/2 :LEVEL-1
LEFT 15
FORWARD :SIZE/4
LEFT 15
TREE 2*:SIZE/3 :LEVEL-1
RIGHT 15
FORWARD :SIZE/8
RIGHT 10
TREE :SIZE/3 :LEVEL-1
LEFT 10
FORWARD :SIZE/8
BACK :SIZE
END
```

Figure 1. An example of a Logo program for a fractal-tree and its output.

a line segment is drawn by specifying the coordinates of its end points. In Logo, the metaphor is that segments are drawn by a pen controlled by a robot turtle. At any moment this turtle is in some position and facing in some direction; a segment is drawn by moving or turning relative to this position and heading. Since absolute coordinates are not used, a single procedure can draw a given shape anywhere and in any orientation. But the real reason for turtle graphics is not its technical convenience. Turtle graphics is considered easier to assimilate than conventional graphics because it is *body-syntonic*. The way the turtle moves in drawing some shape is the same way that a person would move in walking over that shape on the floor. As an analogy, consider that street directions are generally given in the form "go straight three blocks, then turn left" and not "go to latitude 46 degrees, longitude 62 degrees, then go to latitude 47 degrees, longitude 59 degrees."

The ability to draw a picture at any position and heading is particularly convenient for the exploration of fractals (*q.v.*), in which an overall picture is made by including several smaller versions of the same picture (*see* Fig. 1).

Logo Syntax

Lisp, Logo's parent language, was designed in part to facilitate formal reasoning about computer programs. For this reason, syntactic uniformity was valued above ease of use. Each Lisp expression represents the application of a procedure to arguments; the notation is a list in parentheses, in which the first element is the procedure and the other elements are the arguments, which are themselves Lisp expressions in the same form. Logo expressions have the same logical struc-

ture, but the notation is more relaxed. Parentheses are not required for every procedure call, and conventional infix notation is allowed for arithmetic operators:

```
TO FACTORIAL :N
IF :N = 0 [OUTPUT 1]
OUTPUT :N * FACTORIAL (:N-1)
END
```

Despite the difference in notation, Logo maintains the Lisp idea that everything is done by procedure calls. For example, the word IF in the procedure above is not a special syntactic keyword as it would be in most languages. It is an invocation of the IF procedure with two arguments. The first argument (in this example, computed by an invocation of the = procedure) must have the value TRUE or the value FALSE. The second argument is a list (indicated by the square brackets) containing instructions that will be carried out if the first argument is TRUE.

The colon in :N above (pronounced "dots N") indicates that the value of a variable is wanted. A name without the colon requests calling the procedure with that name. Logo makes this distinction mainly because certain names, such as LIST, are both popular variable names and primitive procedure names.

OUTPUT does not mean "print"; it specifies the procedure's return value and ends the procedure call, like return in C (*q.v.*).

The use of Lisp as a vehicle for formal reasoning about programs led to one other characteristic that is compromised in Logo: the emphasis on functional programming (*q.v.*) style. In Lisp, every procedure is a function that returns a value. The use of procedures that make permanent changes in the environment (such as assigning a value to a variable) is possible but discouraged. Logo does support this functional programming style (the FACTORIAL procedure above is an example), but a distinction is made between *operations* (procedures that return a value) and *commands* (procedures called for effect), like the distinction between functions and procedures in Pascal (*q.v.*). The use of commands in Logo allows the more traditional sequential style for applications in which that style is more natural, such as this conversational program:

```
TO GREET
PRINT [WHAT'S YOUR NAME?]
MAKE "RESPONSE READLIST
PRINT SENTENCE [PLEASED TO MEET YOU,]
                                :RESPONSE
END
```

In most other respects Logo follows traditional Lisp ideas. There are no type declarations; data types (*q.v.*) are associated with values rather than with the variables to which those values may be assigned. The main data aggregation mechanism is the variable-length heterogeneous list rather than the more conventional fixed-length homogeneous array. Variables obey dynamic scoping rules; procedure definitions are never lexically within other procedures. In each case the design decision is made to promote flexibility, ease of programming and debugging, and simple computational metaphors. By contrast, each of these design decisions is reversed in many other languages to accommodate conventional machine architectures for the sake of program execution speed rather than ease of use, or as deliberate restrictions on the expressiveness of the language in order to protect programmers against their own mistakes.

Attention to Computational Metaphors

Logo teachers use the metaphor of "teaching the computer" to describe procedure definition. The keyword that announces a definition is TO, rather than Lisp's DEFINE, to suggest the sentence "I'm going to teach you how TO GREET" (in the example above). Also, following English syntax, the keyword TO suggests that the procedure name is a verb, as befits an action we are teaching the computer. The same metaphor is supported by the error message for invoking an undefined procedure:

```
I DON'T KNOW HOW  TO GARPLY
```

The extra space in the message reminds the user how to correct the problem, without destroying the meaning of the message as an English sentence.

Some versions of Logo provide two different commands to assign a value to a variable:

```
MAKE name value
NAME value name
```

These two versions have exactly the same effect; they differ only in the order of the arguments. The older MAKE supports the traditional metaphor of a variable as a box that can contain different values at different times. However, Logo's support of functional programming style minimizes the need for such reassignment. Instead, a common use of assignment is to provide names for global constants. For example, many computers use small integers to represent the colors they can display on the screen. An assignment like

```
NAME 3 "BLUE
```

is best understood not as putting the value 3 into a box, but rather as attaching a name tag to 3: "Whenever I say BLUE, I mean 3."

The attention to metaphor extends beyond the choice of names. One application of Logo is in natural language processing; an English sentence is represented as a list of words. As in Lisp, the underlying selection operations that can be applied to a list are to select the

first element of a list or all but the first element. (Lisp calls these CAR and CDR; Logo calls them FIRST and BUTFIRST.) In Logo, however, the same operations can also be used to extract the first letter, or all but the first letter, of a word. It is natural to use the same tools to manipulate words and sentences, even though the representations inside the computer are different. By similar reasoning, Logo provides symmetrical LAST and BUTLAST operations even though the underlying representation of lists is asymmetrical and these latter operations are slower than FIRST and BUT-FIRST. The rules for forming the plural of an English word depend on its last letter or letters; here is a partial implementation:

```
TO PLURAL :WORD
IF MEMBERP LAST :WORD [O S X]
                 [OUTPUT WORD :WORD "ES]
IF EQUALP LAST :WORD "Y
   [IF NOT MEMBERP LAST BUTLAST :WORD
                            [A E I O U]
       [OUTPUT WORD BUTLAST :WORD "IES]]
OUTPUT WORD :WORD "S
END
```

This says that a word ending in O, S, or X forms its plural by adding ES; a word ending in Y forms its plural by changing the Y to IES unless the letter before the Y is a vowel; otherwise, the plural is formed by adding S.

Continuing Research and Development

Much of the development effort in the Logo community goes into inventing new application areas, with a new set of primitive procedures and often new peripheral hardware, rather than into the core control structures of the language. Examples from the 1970s were music synthesis and special animated graphics hardware. (The latter allowed multiple turtles, with state information including shape and velocity as well as the traditional position and heading.) One recent example, Lego/Logo, uses computer-readable sensors, such as photocells and pressure switches, mounted on Lego blocks so that Logo programs using these sensors can control motors in robots and similar Lego machines. Another current project, StarLogo, explores massive parallelism with thousands of turtles used to explore how large-scale phenomena emerge from simple small-scale behavior.

Several recent versions of Logo have included more or less elaborate forms of object-oriented programming (*q.v.*), usually with a message-passing syntax something like

```
ASK :TURTLE3 [FORWARD 40]
```

in which the first argument to ASK is an object and the second is an instruction to be carried out by that object. Microworlds, a commercial product, is a Logo interpreter embedded in a painting and animation program; it treats turtles, windows, and controls as true independent objects, but does not allow the user to define new classes. Bongo, a current research project, is a Logo-based object-oriented language for World Wide Web (*q.v.*) applications, a sort of Java (*q.v.*) for kids.

Other projects have developed new languages, inspired by Logo but substantially different. One impetus for such development is the desire to use high-resolution graphics to express program control structure, as in Boxer (MIT and Berkeley) and Function Machines (BBN).

Bibliography

On Logo's educational significance:

1980. Papert, S. *Mindstorms: Computers, Children, and Powerful Ideas.* New York: Basic Books.

On technical details:

1997. Harvey, B. *Computer Science Logo Style, Volume 1: Symbolic Computing,* 2nd Ed. Cambridge, MA: MIT Press.

Brian Harvey

LOOP INVARIANT

> For articles on related subjects *see* CONTROL STRUCTURE; PROGRAM VERIFICATION; and STRUCTURED PROGRAMMING.

Consider a loop **while** B **do** S, where B is a Boolean expression and S a statement. This form of loop appears in most modern high-level languages. Let P be some true–false statement about the variables of the program in which the loop appears. P is a *loop invariant* if execution of the loop body S begun in any state in which P and B are true terminates with P true. For example, consider the loop

```
while i≠10 do begin i:=i+1; x:=x+i end
```

and the following assertions about the loop variables:

```
P0: 1≤i≤10 and x=1+2+...+i,
P1: 1≤i≤10 and x=1+2+...+i and x≤10,
P2: i=i.
```

$P0$ is a loop invariant, since execution of $i:=i+1$; $x:=x+i$ beginning with $i\neq10$ and $P0$ true terminates with $P0$ true. $P1$ is not a loop invariant, since execution of the body of the loop with $i=4$ and $P1$ true (so that $x=10$) sets x to 15, thus falsifying the third conjunct of $P1$. $P2$ is a loop invariant since it is always true.

Using an Invariant to Prove Partial Correctness of a Loop

Suppose P is an invariant of a loop. Suppose further that P is true when execution of the loop begins. Since each iteration of the loop is guaranteed to keep it true, and since we assume that evaluation of an expression changes no variable, we conclude that P is still true when execution of the loop terminates. Further, B is false when the loop terminates. This gives a basis for proving a loop correct.

To prove that postcondition R is true when a loop **while** B **do** S terminates, find an assertion P (a *precondition*) that satisfies the following:

(0) P is true when execution of the loop begins,

(1) P is a loop invariant,

(2)   (P **and not** B) $=>R$.

For example, to prove that the program segment

```
i:=1; x:=1; while i≠10 do
    begin i:=i+1; x:=x+i end
```

terminates with $R: x=1+2+\ldots+10$, we use the invariant

```
P: 1≤i≤10 and x=1+2+...+i
```

and note that (0) P is true just before the loop, with $x=i=1$, (1) P is a loop invariant, and (2) (P **and** $i=10$) $=> R$.

Proving Total Correctness of a Loop

We have just shown the *partial* correctness of the loop: if and when it terminates, R is true. Proving *total* correctness means also showing that the loop terminates. This we do by exhibiting a *bound function* t, which is an upper bound on the number of iterations still to be performed. In this case, the bound function $t: 10-i$ gives the exact number of iterations, while the bound function $20-i$ provides a grosser upper bound. An integer function t of the variables of the program is a bound function of the loop if

(0)   Each iteration of the loop decreases t, and

(1)   Another iteration is to be performed, $t>0$; i.e. (P **and** B) $=> t>0$.

If in (1) the expression $t>0$ is replaced by $t>c$ for some constant c, then t is called a *variant* function. For example, $-i$ is a variant function, since $-i>-11$ always holds and $-i$ is reduced by each iteration. Termination can be shown using a variant function, but in general a bound function provides more information about the execution time of the loop. One can also prove termination using more general well-founded sets.

Developing Loops Using Invariants

Some computer scientists have the opinion that it is a programmer's duty to provide documentation for a program that serves as an outline of its proof of correctness, and this means providing a suitable invariant and bound function for each loop. However, it is far too difficult to find the invariant after the fact. Rather, it is felt that the loop invariant and loop should be developed hand-in-hand, with the invariant—or an approximation to it—leading the way. A number of heuristics for the development of the loop invariant based on the shape of the pre- and postconditions have been developed, and there is much evidence that the heuristics (*q.v.*) are indeed practical. In the hands of an experienced person, they can lead to simple and efficient programs. Those most familiar with the method believe that it is superior to the more conventional, *ad hoc* approach to programming—that its use provides for more effective presentations of programs, and that it offers significant insight to the teacher of programming.

We illustrate this method of programming using a trivial example. We desire a program segment that stores the sum of the first 10 positive integers in variable x, i.e. a segment with precondition $true$ and postcondition $R: x = 1 + 2 + \ldots + 10$. Having decided that a loop is to be written, invariant P is found by generalizing the postcondition, by replacing the constant 10 by a fresh variable i and placing suitable bounds on it:

$$P: 1 \leq i \leq 10 \text{ and } x = 1 + 2 + \ldots + i.$$

(The technique of replacing an expression of the postcondition by a fresh variable is one of the more effective methods of finding an invariant.) The goal of the generalization is to have an invariant that is easily established, and in this case the initialization $x, i := 1, 1$ does nicely. Next, the loop condition B is found by solving the formula $(P \textbf{ and not } B) \Rightarrow R$ for B, giving $i \neq 10$. The loop body has yet to be developed. It must decrease the bound function and maintain the invariant. A glance at the initialization, invariant, and loop condition leads to the bound function $10 - i$, and from this we decide that $i := i + 1$ should appear in the body of the loop. Let us use the notation $\{pre\} S \{post\}$ to mean: if $\{pre\}$ is true before execution of S, then $\{post\}$ is true after its execution. Thus far, the body of the loop can be written as

$$\{P \textbf{ and } i \neq 10\} \ S; \ i := i + 1 \ \{P\}$$

where statement S is to be determined. Now, P is true after execution of the assignment to i exactly when P, with all occurrences of i replaced by $i+1$, is true

before, so we are left with finding a statement of S that satisfies

$$\{P \textbf{ and } i \neq 10\} \ S \ \{1 \leq i + 1 \leq 10 \textbf{ and } \\ x = 1 + 2 + \ldots + (i + 1)\}$$

The statement $S: x := x + (i + 1)$ will do, so the loop body is $x := x + (i + 1); \ i := i + 1$, which can be simplified to $i := i + 1; \ x := x + i$. Thus, we end up with the segment

```
i:=1; x:=1;
while i≠10 do
     begin i:=i+1; x:=x+i end
```

In this example, a trivial problem has been used so that difficulties with the problem would not overwhelm understanding of the developmental strategies. Far more complicated problems have been tackled with the method, with sometimes surprising results. Here is an example of an algorithm that is very difficult to understand without the loop invariant. The algorithm stores a^b in integer variable z, where a and b are integers. The loop invariant is $P: 0 \leq y$ and $z \times x^y = a^b$ and a bound function is $t: y$.

```
{0≤b}
z:=1; x:=a; y:=b;
while y≠0 do if even(y)
     then begin x:=x*x; y:=y div 2 end
     else begin z:=z*x; y:=y-1 end
```

Since, in the worst cases, y counts down to zero one unit at a time, there are never more than y more iterations to do, so that $t: y$ is a safe bound function. Also, when the loop terminates with $y = 0$, $z \times x^y = a^b$ reduces to $z \times x^0 = a^b$ and hence $z = a^b$, which is what we wanted.

Assertions and Invariants in Programming Languages

Some modern programming languages—e.g. Eiffel (*see* Meyer, 1996)—include loop invariants and other forms of assertions (the C language has a simple form of assertion). Suppose a loop in a program is annotated with an invariant—some Boolean expression P. Then, during execution of the program, P is evaluated before each iteration and after termination of the loop; if P is false, execution terminates with an error message. Thus, allowing the programmer to annotate a program with invariants and other assertions provides a simple and useful debugging feature. Care must be taken to use this feature judiciously. In some cases, evaluation of the complete invariant might take as much time as the computation itself, and including just part of the invariant may make more sense.

History

The basic ideas of proving a program (actually, a flow-chart) correct, including total correctness, were given by Floyd (1967). Floyd says that the ideas were not original, but were based on ideas of Perlis and Gorn. The formulation of partial correctness in terms of a loop invariant, as described above, as well as the first definition of a language fragment in terms of correctness-proof rules, was given by Hoare (1969). The term *invariant* was not used in this paper, but it became popular soon after. The basic methods for developing proof and program hand-in-hand, with the former leading the way, were given in the monograph *A Discipline of Programming* (Dijkstra, 1976). A text on the topic is Gries (1981). Dijkstra is responsible for the term *variant function* and Gries for *bound function*. Methods of proving correctness using invariants have also been developed for the conventional `for` and `repeat` loops (*see* STRUCTURED PROGRAMMING).

Bibliography

1967. Floyd, R. W. "Assigning Meaning to Programs," *Proceedings of the American Mathematical Society Symposium on Applied Mathematics,* **19**, 19–31.

1969. Hoare, C. A. R. "An Axiomatic Basis for Computer Programming," *Comm. of the ACM,* **12**, October, 576–583.

1976. Dijkstra, E. W. *A Discipline of Programming.* Upper Saddle River, NJ: Prentice Hall.

1981. Gries, D. *The Science of Programming.* New York: Springer-Verlag.

1996. Meyer, B. *Object-Oriented Software Construction,* 2nd Ed. Upper Saddle River, NJ: Prentice Hall.

David Gries

LOVELACE, COUNTESS OF

For articles on related subjects *see* ANALYTICAL ENGINE; BABBAGE, CHARLES; DIFFERENCE ENGINE; and DIGITAL COMPUTERS, HISTORY OF: ORIGINS.

Augusta Ada Byron was born in London on 10 December 1815. She was the daughter of Lord Byron and Annabella Milbanke Byron, whose separation a little over a month after her birth was followed by Lord Byron's leaving England, never to return. She married William, eighth Lord King, in 1835, and three years later, on his elevation to an Earldom, became known as the Countess of Lovelace, and hence Lady Lovelace.

Ada, as she was known in the family circle, was educated by governesses and tutors, and later by much self-study. Augustus De Morgan, professor at the University of London, helped her in her advanced studies, and formed a very high opinion of her abilities: "The tract about Babbage's machine is a pretty thing enough, but I could I think produce a series of extracts, out of Lady Lovelace's first queries upon new subjects, which would make a mathematician see that it was no criterion of what might be expected from her." (*Lovelace–Byron Papers.*) Her correspondence with contempor-

Figure 1. Augusta Ada Byron. (Courtesy of the Mary Evans Picture Library.)

ary scientists, such as Michael Faraday, Mary Somerville, and Sir John Herschel, reveals her deep interest in varied scientific topics. She was also an accomplished musician, particularly on the harp.

Lady Lovelace, fascinated by Babbage's machines after first viewing his Difference Engine in 1833, translated L. F. Menabrea's paper on Babbage's Analytical Engine from French into English. Babbage suggested that she add some notes to the translation, which she did with such enthusiasm that they extended Menabrea's paper to about three times its original length. Of particular interest is her description in these notes of the repeated use of a set of cards with a purpose similar to that of subroutines in today's computer programs. With the help of Babbage, she worked out a nearly complete program to compute Bernoulli numbers, as complete as was consistent with the state of the design of the Engine at that time. Because of this, she has been called the first female computer programmer and, in 1979, a new language was named Ada (*q.v.*) in her honor. Recent books have both disparaged and praised Ada's place in computer history, depending in part on what standards their authors apply.

Babbage's high regard for Lady Lovelace's notes is expressed in his autobiography: "Their author has entered fully into almost all the very difficult and abstract questions connected with the subject." Also, in a letter to her son, Viscount Ockham, in 1857, Babbage wrote, "In the memoir of Mr. Menabrea and still more in the excellent Notes appended by your mother you will find the only comprehensive view of the powers of the Anal. Eng. which the mathematicians of the world have yet expressed." (*Babbage Correspondence.*)

All of her life, Lady Lovelace was plagued by ill health. She died on 27 November 1852, less than a fortnight before her 37th birthday.

Bibliography

Lovelace–Byron Papers. Bodleian Library, Oxford (Courtesy of Earl of Lytton and Viscount Knebworth).

Babbage Correspondence. Additional Ms., British Library, London.

1843. Lovelace, Ada, Countess of. "Sketch of the Analytical Engine Invented by Charles Babbage, Esq. by L. F. Menabrea, of Turin, Officer of the Military Engineers: With Copious Notes by the Translator," *Scientific Memoirs*, **III**, 666–731. Taylor, R. (ed.) London: R. & J. E. Taylor (Reprinted in 1953. Bowden, B. V. *Faster Than Thought.* London: Sir Isaac Pitman & Sons.)

1864. Babbage, C. *Passages from the Life of a Philosopher.* London: Longmans, Green, & Co.

1977. Moore, D. L. *Ada, Countess of Lovelace.* London: Harper & Row.

1980. Huskey, V. and Huskey, H. "Lady Lovelace and Charles Babbage," *Annals of the History of Computing*, **2**, 4 (October), 299–329.

1986. Stein, D. *Ada, A Life and a Legacy.* Cambridge, MA: MIT Press.

1986. Baum, J. *The Calculating Passion of Ada Byron.* Hamden, CT: Shoe String Press.

1992. Toole, B. *Ada, Enchantress of Numbers.* Mill Valley, CA: Strawberry Press.

1999. Woolley, B. *The Bride of Science: Romance, Reason and Byron's Daughter.* London: Macmillan.

Velma R. Huskey

MACHINE- AND ASSEMBLY-LANGUAGE PROGRAMMING

For articles on related subjects *see* ADDRESSING; ASSEMBLER; BINDING; COMPUTER ARCHITECTURE; COMPUTERS, MULTIPLE ADDRESS; DEBUGGING; DUMP; EMBEDDED SYSTEM; GENERAL REGISTER; INDEX REGISTER; INSTRUCTION SET; LINKERS AND LOADERS; MACRO; MICROPROGRAMMING; NO-OP; OBJECT PROGRAM; PROGRAM COUNTER; REGISTER; REDUCED INSTRUCTION SET COMPUTER; and STORED PROGRAM CONCEPT.

As it appeared in the first and second editions of this Encyclopedia, this article dealt with machine- and assembly-language programming as if they were dead or dying, and the article aspired to do little more than deliver a eulogy before turning away for the last time from something on the verge of extinction. In the third edition, a reprieve was announced—the arrival of the personal computer, typically with no more than 640K of application-program memory, restored the importance of tight code, and with it the rationale for machine language (ML) and assembly language (AL).

For this fourth edition, the picture has changed again: in 1999 personal computers usually have at least 64 MB of memory, along with fast hard disk (*q.v.*) drives of several gigabytes or more, and tight code is no longer a critical issue for most personal computers, whether desktop or laptop. Today's client for tight code is the palmtop computer (*see* PORTABLE COMPUTERS), and— even more—the embedded processor that lives in an environment that most consumers don't associate with computing at all.

Because many computer users are unaware of the reasons for the stubborn survival of AL and ML, this article goes well beyond a presentation of the technology involved, and offers extended discussion of the strategies involved in its use. That discussion includes treatments of:

◆ subroutines and macro-instructions

◆ binding-time control

◆ modularization

◆ RISC architecture's effect on AL/ML

For the sake of clarity, the coding examples offered throughout this article are for a long-obsolete machine family (the IBM 704-709-7090-7094 series), which lends itself to piecemeal elementary presentation better than its successors (you learn how to fly in a Piper Comanche, not a Boeing 747). This can be done without loss of generality because today's machines, though faster, bigger, and far more complex, embody no essentially new programming principles.

Definition of ML

Machine language has traditionally meant that particular representation of instructions and data that is directly usable by the central processing unit (*q.v.*) of the machine in question. It was a *low-level* language— indeed, the lowest possible—with the corollary that it reflected the machine's internal structure far more than the purposes to which most users would want to put the computer. It was also *hard-wired*—meaning that it was the hardware's native tongue, and needed no software translator.

However, as the variety of implemented machines grows, it becomes increasingly difficult to give a simple and precise definition of ML. It no longer suffices to call it the language of the hardware now that microprogramming and other forms of multilevel processing within a given computer have become common, nor to call it machine-oriented rather than application-oriented when some machines implement directly in their hardware what are by some standards application languages. These caveats do not mean that the older definitions of ML are false, but simply that they are strained when applied to extreme cases. It will suffice for our purposes to say that ML is that programming language that is executable, without prior software translation, by the CPU of some specified machine, and whose typical statement consists of a single operator/operand pair.

The operand (*q.v.*) part of such a statement or instruction is typically an address—i.e. a binary integer designating one of the storage segments called either *words* or *bytes*. *Byte* is the usual term for a segment designed to hold one 8-bit alphanumeric character; *word* is usually reserved for the addressable segments of machines specialized for numerical computation, and hence is anywhere from 8 to 64 bits long, with 32 being common now. For convenience, we will use the term "word" hereafter when referring to an addressable memory segment.

The operator part of an ML statement will typically call for:

◆ a dyadic arithmetic or logical operation upon the contents of (a) the addressed word and (b) any of the CPU registers in which these operations can be carried out; or

◆ the movement of contents between one of these registers and a word; or

◆ the movement of contents between a register, or word, and one of the machine's input–output devices.

The bit pattern in an addressed word will, if the operator is an ordinary arithmetic one, be treated as the representation of a scalar quantity in base 2 (or an integral power of 2, such as hexadecimal).

The foregoing describes a typical ML instruction only; for an idea of the range of possible types, note that some machines, chiefly older ones, offer *multiple-address* instructions—that is, instructions that include the addresses of two or more operands, such as the augend and addend of an addition operation. Again, many machines offer some instructions whose operand parts are *immediate*—that is, they are themselves the data to be operated on, not the addresses of that data. Other instructions interpret their address fields in just the opposite way: practicing *indirect addressing*, they take the value in that field not as the address of the data, but as the address of the address of the data. Many instructions can be *indexed*; that is, they contain a field that can be used to designate some register whose contents are to modify the value initially specified in the address field (the "apparent address") into a value that is actually to be used at execution (the "effective address").

Finally, all machines include instructions, variously called *jumps*, *transfers*, or *branches*, whose purpose is to cause the machine executing them to depart from the strictly sequential order of execution, and instead take for its next instruction the one indicated in the jump. Some jumps are absolute: when executed, they always force program execution to continue at the programmer-specified point in the program, rather than at the normal point, the next instruction following the jump itself. Other jumps are conditional: they call for the execution of some test, and change the order of instruction execution only if the test result satisfies some specified condition.

One further note on the usage of the term "ML": because genuine ML is rarely used today by programmers working on machines of the minicomputer or larger classes, its name has come sometimes to be used loosely as a synonym for "assembly language." This regrettable practice has sometimes forced those to whom the distinction is important to use "binary," "absolute ML," or just "absolute" when they mean real ML. In this article, the terms *machine language* and *assembly language* will be kept quite distinct, with ML standing solely for that language (characterized above) which requires no software to translate it, and makes no concession whatever to human readability or convenience.

Example of ML

In the computer from which we will mainly draw our examples, the register in which addition and subtraction are done is the *accumulator*; the instruction that causes the quantity in a specific word—the word whose address is 100, say—to be brought to the accumulator is, in its full binary glory,

000101000000000000000000001100100   (1)

The leftmost 12 bits of this instruction contain the operation code, which in this case specifies that the accumulator is to be cleared—that is, set to zero—and that a quantity in memory is then to be copied to the accumulator; the rightmost 15 (the *address field*) specify that the word whose contents are to be copied is that at address 100 (binary 1100100 is decimal 100). The other available bits in this instruction type are not used in the present example.

The instruction that adds the quantity in word 101 to the quantity in the accumulator is

$$00010000000000000000000000001100101 \quad (2)$$

and the instruction that stores the quantity in the accumulator into word 102 is

$$00011000000100000000000000001100110 \quad (3)$$

These three instructions constitute a tiny program. If they were loaded into the computer at locations n, $n+1$, and $n+2$, and the computer were directed to execute the program starting at location n, then the sum of the quantities that were the contents of words 100 and 101 would be formed in the accumulator, and stored in word 102.

Uses of ML

Many programmers working on minicomputers (*q.v.*), mainframes (*q.v.*), and supercomputers (*q.v.*) have to be able to recognize and interpret ML when they see it in memory dumps and assembly listings, but very few have had occasion to use it as a source language since assembly language was first offered. The occasions that still arise for its use in these classes of machines are virtually limited to the patching of a program that is available only in ML, or whose modification by reassembly would be prohibitively expensive, and to the implementation of the first assembler for a new machine.

ML is of course a necessary tool for programmers developing the first assembler for a new machine. (An alternative, at least in principle, is the development of an assembler for one machine by means of a meta-assembler running on another; this approach, for a variety of reasons both technical and psychological, never established itself in practice.) The usual approach is to write the assembler in its own language, as if it already existed, and then assemble it by hand in the manner just described for ML patching. Hand translating from an assembly-language original offers the programmer the advantage of working from a complete specification.

If the programmer "plays computer," strictly following the logic of the assembler itself in translating its assembly language image into ML, many of the bugs in it will, as a bonus, be disclosed in the process. Often,

too, it will be sufficient to hand-assemble only a certain essential core of the new assembler, after which the rest of it can be written in the now-implemented subset of the new assembler language, and assembled by the part already running. A curious result of this technique is that the first ML version of a new assembler, the largely hand-written one, usually has its own assembly-language image for its first source program, and is usually discarded after assembling that one source program.

A third role for ML—one that may be disappearing with the increasing rationalization of computer design, and the coming of RISC architectures—lies in the discovery and exploitation of the undocumented instructions that enterprising programmers used to delight in finding among a new machine's capabilities, although not advertised or even perhaps known to its designers or the authors of its assembler. These bit configurations that, though unmentioned in the assembly-language manual, have turned out to be interpretable by the hardware as instructions, are seldom more than curiosities. Almost without exception, these windfall instructions cause effects for which it is difficult to think of practical uses; if programmers manage to use them at all, it is generally by twisting the design of a program to make a place for them. Whatever the wisdom of exploiting such instructions, it is clear that, if used at all, they are used in ML form. (The modern equivalent of finding undocumented operation codes is finding undocumented Windows features; see Livingston and Straub (1997, pp. 10–11).)

All the above applies only to programmers working with bigger machines; for PC programmers, ML is by no means a dead language. Many effects wanted on PCs are best achieved (or achievable only) by use of ML, made available through the DEBUG facility. DEBUG, a part of the PC's suite of system software originally intended for the purpose indicated by its name, is no longer much used for debugging—far better tools are now available for that—but has become instead a general ML-level tool for investigating and modifying all PC software, from DOS itself to utilities and applications. In Somerson (1988), for example, three columns of the index are spent pointing to uses of DEBUG for such purposes, and the chapter devoted to it begins by calling it "a serious computer user's best friend." Another telling example: a common PC utility, COMPARE, which simply compares two files to locate differences between them, makes no apology for calling upon its users to go into DEBUG to adjust its sensitivity. For all PC programmers, then, and even some ordinary PC users, ML is an everyday tool—and considering the numbers of such programmers and users, it can be claimed that there are, in one sense, more ML users today than ever before.

Features of AL

The examples of ML given earlier suffice to show that it is not a convenient language for human use. During the 1950s, some programmers, whose names are mostly lost in the mists of computing prehistory, developed more congenial notations, and programs for translating them into ML. In doing so, they created not only AL and the assembler, but founded that large branch of computer science and software development that is devoted to improving the user interface (*q.v.*).

The earliest assemblers were little more than routines for translating some more convenient representation of ML instructions into ML proper, with none of the additional features now expected in AL as a matter of course. The primitive assembler offered the programmer at most a symbolic representation of operators—"ADD" instead of 000101000000, for example, with decimal or octal representation of operand addresses—or just octal representation of the entire instruction—050000003770 instead of 36 binary digits.

It is instructive to note how much extra programming capability is achieved with even so rudimentary an assembly language as the octal notation just displayed, though it amounts to nothing more than the octal-constant feature that is today a very minor item in an assembly language. The 3:1 compression ratio makes errors of transcription and keying both harder to commit and easier to spot. In addition, the more common instructions, when so represented, become recognizable on sight.

However, today AL is a fully symbolic language: one in which all operators and virtually all operands are normally represented by names chosen for their explanatory and mnemonic power. Some of these names, particularly those for the operators, will have been chosen by the AL designers (although many modern assemblers allow users to rename operators); operands are left for the user to name.

Example of AL

Here is the tiny program we developed earlier, in AL form:

```
CLA 100
ADD 101                                    (4)
STO 102
```

or, if the programmer cared to assign names (by means defined later) to the words containing the operands, they could be

```
CLA AUGEND
ADD ADDEND                                 (5)
STO SUM
```

This more convenient form for writing instructions is perhaps the less important part of the advantage offered by AL. In introducing a software intermediary—the assembler—between the programmer and the computer, AL provided a vehicle in which all kinds of new conveniences and features could be offered. The new notational features gave the programmer more convenient access to powers already in ML; the new substantive features made programming really practical for a public outside the small circle of those with the dedication and skill of medieval manuscript illuminators.

Among the substantive new features offered by the assembler are those that allow data to be introduced in octal, decimal, character-string, and other "natural" forms; that reserve execution-time storage space; that produce a printed, cross-indexed listing of the program, with programmer-written comments and assembler-generated warnings of known or suspected errors—all of them features that let the programmer do explicitly and directly things otherwise so difficult as to be impracticable.

The way in which the operand names used in example (5) would be defined, for example, is through the use of one or another of the new assembler features. These features are usually called pseudo-operations, since they look, in their AL representation, like the AL representation of actual operation codes (or instructions), but are really artifacts introduced by the assembler. They do not represent instructions to be translated into ML as part of the program, but rather directives to the assembler as to how it is to do its job. The distinction between pseudo-ops and real instructions is analogous to that between an author's marginal notes to a typist ("double-space the next paragraph"), and the manuscript to be typed. The *symbolic addresses* AUGEND, ADDEND, and SUM, for example, would have been assigned their respective values by means of pseudo-ops like these:

```
AUGEND PZE 0
ADDEND PZE 0                               (6)
SUM    PZE 0
```

or

```
AUGEND PZE 0
ADDEND DEC 1                               (7)
SUM    PZE 0
```

where "PZE" is a pseudo-op standing for "Plus ZEro," meaning that the word in question is to contain the machine's representation of plus zero, which is 36 binary zeros, and that any symbol to its left is to be recorded as the symbolic name of that word. DEC is for "DECimal," meaning that the number to its right is to be interpreted as decimal (rather than binary or octal, the other two possibilities in the machine we are dealing with), and that any symbol to its left is to be similarly recorded as the word's name.

Example (6), then, reserves the next three available words in memory (the next available word being that whose address is greater by one than that last used, unless the programmer directs otherwise), assigns them the names given in their left-hand column, and sets their contents to zero. (Non-zero values would presumably be stored in at least one of AUGEND and ADDEND by some earlier part of the program before they were added together.) Example (7) does the same thing (6) does, but adds one more feature: it assigns ADDEND the initial value of 1. The pseudo-op "DEC" directs the assembler to interpret the number that follows it as a decimal number, and to put the binary representation of that number in the word being reserved.

Each of the names so assigned to a word, or memory location, is entered into a *symbol table* or *dictionary* created by the assembler as it does its job, along with the numerical address of the location to which it has been assigned. Whenever the assembler encounters a symbolic address in the program, it substitutes the numerical equivalent of that symbol. By doing so, it frees programmers to use the symbol (AUGEND, for example) that is meaningful to them, and leaves it to the assembler to see that AUGEND is replaced by its binary equivalent throughout the ML program that the assembler will produce. (A programmer-chosen mnemonic name for a value is, to the assembler, simply an arbitrary string of characters, and it is up to the programmer to see to it that the value in a word actually mirrors its name. There is nothing, for example, to prevent the programmer from calling a location "ONE," and storing a value of 2, or 2000, in it.)

Probably the most important of the unexpected advantages of programming in symbols rather than bit patterns is the control it gives the programmer over *binding*: the act of reducing a variable or expression in the program to an explicit, fixed value. Symbolic programming allows the programmer to defer such binding and leave appropriate parts of the program on a generalized, somewhat abstract level until it is convenient to make it perfectly concrete and specific. Since the computer cannot execute a program until it is so bound—that is, in ML form—a narrow concept of efficiency would dictate that it be reduced to that form as quickly as possible, but the forced deferral of ML form that is entailed by the use of AL turns out to carry advantages more important even than those originally sought for AL.

Programming in a symbolic language both enables the programmer to see the potential generality of a program and encourages and facilitates the realization of that generality. The programmer may spend a little more time writing and documenting today's program; the reward will be not having to rewrite it tomorrow to deal with slightly changed circumstances. If the program computes a payroll, for example, the fact that AL will encourage the programmer to represent a tax rate throughout it as TAXRATE rather than as 17.25%, and allow it to be numerically defined just once, by use of a DEC pseudo-op, will not only make the program easier to write, but will also allow it to survive a change in the tax rate at no greater cost than a reassembly with a new definition of TAXRATE.

Furthermore, by forcing the programmer's mind to the slightly elevated abstraction of the symbolic level, AL tends to suggest treating as variables other quantities that would almost certainly have been treated as constants if using ML: the total number of paycheck deductions to be allowed for, the number of jurisdictions for which tax was to be withheld, and so on. If the possibility of change has occurred to the programmer while writing the program, it can be provided for in any of several ways:

◆ assign a new value to a symbolic variable by substituting a new definition of it in the source program, and reassembling;

◆ design the program to accept a possibly new value for the variable from the data given it at execution time;

◆ if the program is being run interactively, have it prompt the user to enter such a new value if there is one for it, or let the user take the initiative by interrupting the running of the program to introduce a new value.

Because the final assignment of a computable value to a program variable (e.g. 17.25% to TAXRATE) is called *binding*, and the moment of its occurrence *binding time*, the AL property just discussed may be called *binding-time control*. The degree of such control offered by a modern multi-pass assembler working in conjunction with a linking loader (*see* LINKERS AND LOADERS) and a modern operating system (*q.v.*) is very substantial. Symbols can be defined in terms not only of final numerical values, but of elaborate expressions containing other symbols that may themselves be as yet undefined, to form an indefinitely deep regression, with the resolution of the most primitive layer of symbols deferred until the end of the source program, or even, in the limit, to load or execution time.

A linking loader prepared to handle object programs (*q.v.*) in which so much binding remains to be done is misnamed, in fact, since its loading function is by this point incidental. It is actually the last (and sometimes the longest) pass of the assembler it works with, and its use amounts to a return to the old "load-and-go" concept in which final assembly is followed immediately by loading and execution, rather than simply the production of an object program that is to be executed only when the programmer so orders. The object program (whether in the form of a card deck, tape file, or disk file) produced by the assembler part of such an assembler–loader partnership is not in ML, but in some nameless intermediate language (*q.v.*) dictated by the needs of the loader.

Binding-time flexibility allows variables in one program to be defined by values assigned to them in another. This makes it possible for a number of independently written programs—provided they observe the conventions governing the use of such *external symbols*—to join forces and become in effect one large program, and in doing so to extend greatly the usefulness of the constituent programs.

Important as it is, binding-time control is only an aspect of a broader and more fundamental principle that was introduced into programming along with AL: *decoupling.* This is the technological equivalent of the military principle "divide and conquer." As applied to programming, one of the things it means is the isolation of potential problems so that they can be separately dealt with, and so that errors cannot propagate from one to another. Binding-time control permits decoupling the writing of an expression that may relate many variables in elaborate ways from the task of giving those variables specific numeric or other computable values.

AL programming permits and promotes many forms of decoupling. The symbols used in an AL program for things other than instruction locations, for example, will probably be defined by the programmer in a group, at the end of the source program; if there are many of them, they will probably be divided further into subgroups of constants, storage reservations, error messages, and so on, creating something very like Cobol's (*q.v.*) Data Division. In doing this, the AL programmer is led naturally into applying the decoupling principle, not merely on the level of the individual expression and its component variables, but also on that of the entire program algorithm and the data it operates on. The strikingly superior manageability of programs so organized—their greater intelligibility to those who have to study and maintain them, their amenability to revision, their resistance to obsolescence as circumstances and specifications change—collectively amount to an enormous advantage over ML programming, one probably far more important than the convenience AL offers in simply getting a program running.

Subroutines and Macroinstructions

Decoupling can be seen again in the use of subroutines (*see* SUBPROGRAM), in which routines that have been written once are preserved so that they need not be written again: the decoupling is between the moment of designing and implementing an algorithm, and the moments of its use. (Here, as in other places throughout this article, the principles under discussion carry well beyond their points of origin in AL/ML programming, and apply to program design irrespective of the language involved.) The occasion for creating a subroutine arises when a programmer notices that essentially the same routine (for example, one that converts external representation numerals to an internal computable form) has been written over and over, possibly with minor variations. Creating a subroutine for the function in question will obviate the need ever to do it again, and this promise gives its author an incentive to invest great care in generalizing it, debugging it, optimizing its performance, documenting it, and otherwise perfecting it.

Subroutines, it should be noted, are not the same thing as macros (*q.v.*), with which they are often confused—and neither is necessarily a *module*. Both subroutines and macros are chunks of code that have been generalized and encapsulated for use in a variety of contexts, but otherwise have quite different properties. Subroutines and macros have in common the purpose of sparing the programmer from having to rewrite substantially the same code over and over; a module is a routine that may be implemented as either one of them, but has for its major purpose something quite different from saving the programmer labor. The ignorance of context that is a consequence of their packaging is, for the subroutine and the macro, their major liability; in the module, this trait is the very reason for its existence.

The success of a subroutine or macro is often dependent on the degree to which it can overcome its isolation, and be made sensitive to its context each time it is used; it needs to approximate the efficiency of the one-time code it has replaced. A module, on the other hand, like a member of a cloistered religious order, is supposed to remain ignorant of the world it lives in for the sake of higher things (*see* MODULAR PROGRAMMING). The module is intended to limit the area of concern of any one programming-team member, and—most importantly—to minimize the impact on the program of later changes to its environment or specifications. It does this by isolating and formalizing the channel of communication, or *interface*, between itself and other program components. A typical application: a module through which all a program's input–output requests are funneled, and which alone makes direct requests on the operating system or hardware. If the I/O facilities of the system later change in ways that affect a program that has been so modularized, only its I/O module need be revised, rather than an indefinite number of I/O operations that would otherwise have been scattered throughout the program in unrecorded places, with varying assumptions about their contexts silently built into them.

Modularization, then, like the watertight compartmentalization of a warship, is a damage-limiting and responsibility-defining device; restricting intercourse between a part of a program and its environment (code or hardware) is its purpose in life. A subroutine or macro, on the other hand, will often succeed, as has been noted, to the extent that it can adapt to the state of the calling program at each call; it should be as worldly as the module should be sequestered. (One of the aims of *object-oriented programming* (*q.v.*) is to secure, through such mechanisms as *encapsulation* (*q.v.*) and *inheritance*, the qualities of both the module and the macroinstruction/subroutine—both immunity from interference by external processes, and sufficient sensitivity to those processes to coordinate efficiently with them. This is a tall order, and one not yet fully met.)

Once created, a subroutine need only be assembled along with a calling AL program (or loaded with its object program) to be available as often as needed throughout that program. At whatever points in the program the function performed by the subroutine is required, a *calling sequence* (*q.v.*) to the subroutine is inserted by the programmer, and a transfer to it will be made when that point is reached in program execution. After the subroutine has been executed, a return jump from it is made to a point some fixed number of words from the most recent call, and the calling program resumes. The subroutine itself need never be written again, nor need it appear more than once in a program, no matter how often its services may be required. Subroutinizing is useful even when practiced by a solitary programmer within one program; its advantages grow enormously if subroutines can be freely traded within the community of programmers working with some one type of computer or operating system. The possibility of doing so depends on the observance by all concerned of a number of conventions for creating and using subroutines, and these are usually set forth in the AL manual of each computer as if they were built into the hardware or assembler. These conventions, while necessary for the exchangeability of subroutines within the community of users, are responsible also for many of the unsatisfactory features of subroutines (discussed below), and account at least in part for the rise of an alternative form of software packaging, the *macroinstruction*.

Like the subroutine, the macro (as it is usually called) is a way of packaging common routines for later use, but the conventions governing both its creation and its use differ greatly from those of the subroutine. The root of the difference is that the macro facility is made possible by a special processor that is either embedded within an assembler (yielding a macroassembler) or provided as a separate piece of software (a macroprocessor); if separate, it will be given as input a source program consisting of a mixture of macros and AL statements, transform the macros into AL, and pass the resulting program to a simple assembler. The consequent differences between programming with macros and with subroutines may be summarized under four heads: locus of creation, form of call, trapping ability, and code-generating economy.

LOCUS OF CREATION

A new macro can be created, or defined, at any point in any program that will be processed by a macroassembler or macroprocessor. Since the macroprocessor, whether embedded in an assembler or not, is put into a special macro-defining mode when it encounters a macro definition, the creation of a macro generates no instructions in the program; only an explicit call on the macro does that.

Until needed, the instructions constituting a macro definition are stored in an area under the control of the macroprocessor, and do not appear in the object program being generated. By contrast, the defining of a subroutine, since it is indistinguishable from ordinary programming as far as the assembler is concerned, causes the insertion of its constituent instructions into the host program at the point of definition. If the programmer wants the subroutine to be stored at the end of the object program when it is loaded, the definition itself must appear at the end of the source program.

A subroutinized version of the miniature program given in example (5), for example, would take a form like this:

```
TRISUM    CLA* 1,4
          ADD* 2,4
          STO* 3,4                    (8)
          TRA  4,4
```

In this (trivial) subroutine, to which we have given the name TRISUM, some new programming features are used. The addresses of the four instructions refer respectively to the first, second, third, and fourth words following the instruction that that will be used to call TRISUM. The 4 following the comma in each of these instructions is the designation of an *index register* (*q.v.*), a specialized register, one of whose principal uses is to record the location of an instruction calling on a subroutine. Its action is such that an address within the subroutine of the form "$n,4$" will refer to the nth location following that calling instruction.

Another item of notation new to this example is the * following each of the first three instructions, denoting *indirect* use of the address that follows in each case. This means that the assembler is being directed to interpret the address (first modified if necessary by any index register used) as the location not of the data, but of the address of the data. Accordingly, the interpretation of CLA* 1,4 is "Bring to the accumulator the quantity whose address is located one word below that in which the instruction calling on this subroutine is located." Using the calling sequence in (10) below as an example, the quantity specified would be that whose address was in LOCA.

An equivalent macro would take a form like this:

```
TRISUM    MACRO A,B,C
          CLA   A
          ADD   B              (9)
          STO   C
```

The first line of this macro definition declares that TRISUM is its name, and that this name, when used to call the macro, will be accompanied by three values—*parameters*—that are to replace A, B and C—the *dummy parameters*, or just *dummies*—respectively, wherever those dummies occur in the definition. The precise way in which the TRISUM subroutine and the TRISUM macro are called is explained in the next section.

FORM OF CALL

The subroutine is traditionally called by a stereotyped series of AL instructions—see (10) below—known as a calling sequence. This consists of (a) an instruction that jumps to the subroutine while recording its own location (in index register 4, in our example machine) so that the subroutine will know how to reach back for parameters, and where to return to the calling program when it is done; (b) a number of words reserved for the parameters that are to be passed to the subroutine with each call; and (c) one or more locations for the subroutine to transfer back to when it has completed execution, depending on the number of exit conditions which its author has decided to distinguish and handle separately. This is the general form; each subroutine will have its own specific calling sequence requirements, and it is the responsibility of the subroutine user to construct a correct calling sequence for each call upon a subroutine. An example of a simple calling sequence:

```
TSX TRISUM,4
PZE LOCA
PZE LOCB
PZE LOCC                 (10)
(return location)
```

The first of these instructions, TSX (Transfer and Set indeX), is the special transfer instruction referred to earlier that transfers control to TRISUM while marking its own location in an index register (4, in this case). The three PZE pseudo-ops that follow are simply placeholders whose function is to hold in their address fields the addresses at which parameters A, B, and C can be found by the subroutine. Each call upon the subroutine, then, would cost the execution time of the TSX and the return transfer at the end of the subroutine, plus the storage space for these two instructions and the three PZEs.

To call the functionally equivalent TRISUM macroinstruction, the programmer simply uses its name as if it were an ordinary AL operation code. The parameters to replace the dummies will usually follow the macro name, starting in the same field where an ordinary AL opcode's address would be given, and in the same order as that of the dummies they are to replace. In more advanced macroprocessors, the difference in notational friendliness may be greater yet; at least one would permit the user to give the parameters accompanying a call on a macro as part of a readable English-language statement, and in an order that need not mirror that in which the dummies were given when the macro was defined (see Halpern, 1990, Ch. 3). A simple, conventional call on TRISUM would take the form:

```
TRISUM ALPHA, BETA, GAMMA          (11)
```

where ALPHA, BETA, and GAMMA are the values the user wants inserted into the code wherever A, B, and C appears in the macro's definition. The macroprocessor would make these substitutions, and generate into the program, at the point where the user called the macro, the wanted instructions:

```
CLA ALPHA
ADD BETA                  (12)
STO GAMMA
```

The overwhelming economic superiority in this example of the macro form over the subroutine is due to our use of an unrealistically brief piece of code as the core of each. In particular, the example is unfair to the subroutine in making it so trivial that it is actually shorter than the calling sequence that connects it to the main program. A more realistic evaluation would result if we stipulated that TRISUM were a routine of 50 to 100 instructions. On the other hand, the macro, too, can do better than this example would suggest; see the section below on "Code-Generating Economy."

TRAPPING ABILITY

A property of the macroinstruction that has no counterpart in the subroutine is that of trapping and reinterpreting AL operation codes. Since the macro-processor that makes possible the use of macros looks for macros before it looks for and handles simple AL input, the user can define what would ordinarily be an AL opcode—CLA or STO, for example—as a macro, and thereby transform it into something else before the assembler proper sees it, or act upon it in any way desired by the user, without letting the assembler see it at all. (Such a name remains known to the assembler as that of one of its opcodes, but the fact that the macroprocessor gets first crack at it makes it effectively a macro only.)

This feature makes possible some useful tricks. For example, it enables the user to (1) trap every transfer instruction in a program, or some specified portion of it, and generate instead (or in addition) instructions that compute at execution time the actual addresses to which control is being ordered transferred; (2) compare those addresses with limits set by the user; and (3) allow the transfer to be executed only if its actual target is within those limits. Depending on how strict these limits are, this prevents the execution of most or all "wild" transfers—those whose actual addresses, because of a bug (q.v.) somewhere in the program, are effectively random numbers. And this constraint on the behavior of the executing program much eases debugging, whose difficulties are compounded many times over if a wild transfer has been allowed to execute, with the usual consequences: the destruction of the evidence that a bug-hunter will need to find the original error.

For example, a macro that would trap and test the effective address of an ordinary unconditional transfer instruction (TRA) is shown in Fig. 1. First, the macro defines a new mnemonic, .TRA, for the TRA instruction, so that a transfer could if required be used within the macro itself without recursively calling on the macro again, as it would if instruction and macro-instruction had identical names. Then it defines the AL operation code TRA to be the name of a macro. This causes every occurrence of the TRA mnemonic in the program that follows to be caught by the macro-processor, and replaced by the instructions in the macro, rather than simply be passed unchanged to the assembler and there translated to its ML equivalent. When the macro is invoked by the appearance of a TRA, the body of the macro computes the effective address of that instruction—that is, it computes the value of the instruction's address-field expression, modified by the contents of any index register specified in the "tag" field of the instruction (we ignore, for simplicity, the further possibility of indirect addressing). It then compares the resulting effective address with the limits of a permissible range of transfer addresses specified by the user in the variables LOWLIM and HILIM.

If the address lies outside that range, the original TRA instruction is not executed; instead, control is passed to an error routine, where it is reported and handled however the programmer has directed there. If the address falls within the permissible range, the TRA instruction is executed as originally given, and the program proceeds. (The macro omits some house-keeping instructions, and makes a few simplifying assumptions, for the sake of clarity and brevity; none of these simplifications affects the generality of the concept. The new instructions introduced in this example are not explained in full, like those in earlier examples, but their effects in this context are described in the comments given alongside each of them. Also, the notation C(n) means "contents of n"; e.g., C(IR4) means "contents of index register 4." Recall too that "apparent address" means the value of the expression in the address field of an instruction, before account is taken of any indirect addressing or index-register modification called for in other fields.)

.TRA	OPSYN	TRA	Clone TRA instruction as '.TRA'
TRA	MACRO	X,Y	Name macro 'TRA', dummy parameters 'X' & 'Y'
	LOCAL	A,B	Demand new labels at each call on TRA
A	NOP	Y,X	Acquire TRA's address and tag fields
	SXA	B,4	Save C(IR4) in address of B
	SDC	*+2,X	Store −C(X) in decrement of TXI below
	LXA	A,4	Apparent address of TRA to IR4
	TXI	*+1,4,**	subtract C(IR4) to get effective address
	TXL	*+2,4,LOWLIM-1	if address too low, skip one instr.
	TXL	B,4,HILIM	not too high, skip one instruction
	TSX	AERROR,4	too hi/low; mark place, go to error routine
B	AXT	**,4	Restore value of IR4 as at time of call
	.TRA*	A	Execute the calling TRA instruction
	END		Terminate macro definition

Figure 1. A trap and test macro.

CODE-GENERATING ECONOMY

The macroinstruction and the subroutine differ most obviously in that each use of a macro causes a fresh copy of its defining instructions to be inserted into the text of the program being generated, while a subroutine appears in the program using it just once, no matter how often called. However, this distinction should not be taken to mean, as it frequently is, that macro usage entails a wasteful repetitive generation of code that could be avoided by the use of subroutines instead.

The economics of programming is such that the advantage sometimes lies with generating the substantive code as many times as it is to be executed, sometimes with generating only multiple calling sequences to a single copy of that code. The decision will hinge on such considerations as the length of the calling sequence versus that of the routine to be executed, and the relative importance of memory and time during execution. While a decision to save time clearly points to the macro as the instrument of choice, a space-saving strategy need not point to the subroutine, but may merely suggest that the macros to be employed should generate not the entire routine, but only a call to a subroutinized version of it.

In short, if both macros and subroutines are available to do a job, there is no hard choice to be made: a macro facility incorporates the ability to use subroutines as well, and to call them by means of macros, with the superior writeability and readability of that feature. In at least one macroinstruction processor based on assembly language (*see* Halpern, 1990, Ch. 3), the user is enabled to include within a macro definition both a subroutine and its calling sequence; at the first use of the macro, the processor copies both the calling sequence and the subroutine into the object program, the former at the point where the macro is invoked, and the latter at the end of the program (or wherever the user chooses). Subsequent uses of the macro cause only the calling sequence to be copied, the processor recalling that it has already incorporated the subroutine into the program. Graphically:

Macro definition:

$$
\boxed{
\begin{array}{c}
\boxed{\begin{array}{c}\text{Calling sequence}\\\text{to subroutine}\end{array}} \\[4pt]
\boxed{\text{Subroutine}}
\end{array}
} \tag{13}
$$

Result of first call:

$$
\boxed{\begin{array}{c}\text{Calling sequence}\\\text{to subroutine}\end{array}}
$$

$$
\boxed{\text{Subroutine}} \tag{14}
$$

(probably placed at the end of the program)

Result of second and each subsequent call:

$$
\boxed{\begin{array}{c}\text{Calling sequence}\\\text{to subroutine}\end{array}} \tag{15}
$$

Roles and Applications of AL

It has long been expected that high-level languages would completely supplant AL; from time to time, it has been announced as an accomplished fact. But this replacement has not occurred: not only AL, but even ML, survive and flourish. This should no longer surprise us.

The fundamental reasons for AL's indispensability are clear: it is a completely general programming language, standing to the various high-level languages as English stands to the jargons of the various trades and professions. AL allows the programmer to do with the computer anything it can do at all, while high-level languages trade this universality of application for superior applicability to a limited range of problems. When computer memory and processor speed are ample, high-level languages generally serve well, but despite the high performance of the desktop PC, there are new systems in which optimum use of machine space or time is the paramount consideration.

During the years between the second (1983) edition and third (1993) editions of this *Encyclopedia*, and even more so between the third and the present edition, the microprocessor burst from the laboratory and industry into our kitchen appliances, our children's toys, and our wristwatches—its use in personal computers, common though they are, is almost incidental. This proliferation of small processors has brought back the circumstances that had, decades before, made every programmer an AL programmer: small memories, limited addressability, much slower (if any) secondary storage. (A recent development that has encouraged AL programming is the emergence of good symbolic debuggers; when AL was first in common use, debugging aids consisted of octal memory dumps and black coffee.)

The result has been a near-recapitulation, first on the PC, then on laptop and smaller computers, and now on embedded processors, of the history of software development on the mainframe. It has not been due, this time around, to doubts about the merits of high-level languages on the part of entrenched skeptics; the major high-level languages are available, and widely used, on processors that can be carried in an attaché case. Nevertheless, the microprocessor has caused an outburst of AL and ML activity, and will probably continue to provide an opportunity for programming in those languages for many who would otherwise never have experienced it.

Beyond these general grounds for the survival and flourishing of AL/ML lie several specific roles for which it seems uniquely well-suited—ecological niches into which it fits so well as to insure its survival against any competitor now visible. Among these are at least five that are worth noting: fine tuning, early responsiveness, machine exploitation, pioneering, and craftsmanship.

FINE TUNING

Because only AL/ML programmers directly choose the machine-language instructions that are to be executed (assuming that the CPU does not reorder instructions), and the bit-by-bit internal representation of the data upon which they are to operate, they alone can guarantee that a program will fit within a given chunk of memory, or execute within a given period of time. They are the only programmers who can plausibly claim that a program has been so written as to occupy the least possible space, or execute as fast as possible.

Programs may be arbitrarily restricted in their execution time because they are real-time applications (*see* REAL-TIME SYSTEMS)—that is, processes directly linked to other processes that are executing fast enough so that even a computer is pressed to keep up with their demands. An example of such demanding processes is the evaluation of radar returns to produce target-tracking displays and antenna-steering commands. Like all such processes, it involves computer linkage to equipment that, using the same technology that supports the computer itself, demands input and generates output at rates comparable to the computer's. With only a slight stretching of terminology, it may be said that in such applications, the computer is pushed to its limits because it is trying to satisfy another computer. Probably the prime example of strong time constraints on a program is that facing the kernel (*q.v.*) of real-time programs, which must respond to an input within an inflexible, usually very tight, time constraints, or suffer a crash—a crash that is sometimes not merely a figure of speech.

Programs may also need fine tuning when the space available to them is highly constrained, as when they are to be executed under control of a multiprogramming system in which each process is allocated a partition of memory within which it must run. This is becoming an increasingly common strategy of computer-resource allocation as attempts are made to keep all components of a computing system productively busy by having them deal concurrently with several distinct programs. Fine tuning is often a necessity for

the palmtop machines now becoming common. Especially where a microprocessor is embedded within a missile, a "smart card," or a similarly weight- and space-limited environment, its memory size may make a program hard to fit in, even though the processor may be dedicated to that one task.

Whatever the cause and the circumstances, a requirement that a program be executable within tight time or space constraints generally implies that it, or at least critical parts of it, should be written in AL. (It is possible to write such a program in a high-level language, if one is available, and then, if the object program exceeds the limits, to rewrite parts of it in AL so as to make it fit. This approach requires a very detailed knowledge of the way in which the compiler generates its object code. The difficulty of integrating the hand-written code with the compiler-generated code, and the dislike programmers feel at having to revise others' code rather than write their own, make this a seldom-chosen alternative.)

An example of AL fine-tuning brief enough to include here is offered by an episode that occurred in the development of the original Fortran (*q.v.*) compiler for the IBM 704. It was discovered at a late stage in the development of that compiler that a quantity had been stored in the wrong index register, and that if the error were to be rectified without extensive recoding, it would have to be done under drastic constraints. These constraints dictated that space for only two additional instructions was available to load the proper index register with the quantity, and that this two-instruction sequence had to be absolutely autonomous: it could not affect any memory or register contents, nor could it make any assumptions about the state of the machine other than that the value that should have been in index register 2 (say) was presently in index register 1. The following two instructions accomplished this seemingly impossible task:

```
LXD *+1,2                              (16)
TXI *+1,3,0
```

The first of these instructions (Load indeX from Decrement) loads the target index register, IR2, with the quantity—0—in the so-called decrement field of the following instruction (*+1 means "this location plus one"). This needs to be done because the content of the target index register is unknown, and the logic of this patch requires that it be zero. The precise function of the second instruction (Transfer with indeX Incremented) is unimportant—any of several others would do as well. Its only functions here are (1) to contain a value of 0 in its decrement field so that the preceding LXD knows where to find one (recall that this patch cannot take for granted the contents of any location outside itself), and (2) to address index register 3—an index register whose usefulness lies in the fact that it does not exist.

The 704 had but three index registers (1, 2, and 4); if any of the numbers 3, 5, 6, or 7 were used where an index-register designation was expected, the index registers affected would be those whose numerical designations summed to form the number given. The effect on the actual index registers so designated was to OR their contents, and store the logical sum thus formed into each of them. It should be apparent how the storing of a zero into the target index register (IR2), followed by the execution of an instruction that referred to a mythical IR3, can achieve the desired movement of the value in IR1 into IR2. A compiled language (such as Fortran itself, the beneficiary of this *coup*) would not have permitted the programmer to specify the index register into which a quantity was to be loaded, let alone specify a nonexistent register. Solving this problem was made possible only by a combination of intimate knowledge of the machine, and the availability of AL to exploit that knowledge.

Another common fine-tuning application of AL is the writing of segments of code that are to be executed so often as to make their time- or space-optimization economically worthwhile, if not strictly necessary. These include practically every routine that has been turned into a subroutine, practically all general-purpose software (to be discussed separately), and the critical parts of big, long-lived, compiler-language application programs. This last category is worth some examination, because its hazards are seldom appreciated until they cause a serious problem.

The high-level language application programs that are candidates for this treatment are those whose execution consumes a significant part of the total computing resources at their installations, and hence offer real payoffs for any improvement in execution time. In such circumstances, a clever programmer who is familiar with the code the compiler has turned out, and also with the purpose of the program in hand, is very likely to be able to improve it significantly by rewriting in AL some small but critical section of it. It would not be very unusual for that programmer to be able to improve the program's performance by an order of magnitude by rewriting a few dozen instructions. This can often be accomplished, in fact, by essentially negative actions involving no significant new code at all: just the reordering of some file searches to reflect the programmer's knowledge of the probable contents of those files, or the removal from an inner loop of some calculations not needed in the present application, may be enough to produce dramatic improvements in execution time.

With such potential rewards, an installation manager may be strongly tempted to relax the edict that only Fortran (or C++, or whatever) is to be used, and allow at least a few programmers to fine-tune the most time-consuming programs. If the manager succumbs to this temptation, however, those big programs will tend to become hand-written AL programs that use a thin shell of compiler-generated code just to interface with the operating system. The danger of this practice is sometimes unrecognized until the installation that has permitted it decides to replace its computers with some newer, incompatible model.

EARLY RESPONSIVENESS

To insure that their development will be carried on in a thoughtful and orderly way, and in a way that will not jeopardize their machine independence, the specifications of the standard high-level languages have been entrusted to various national and international standards (*q.v.*) organizations (in the USA, chiefly to the American National Standards Institute—ANSI). These organizations, which attempt to include or at least consult all concerned parties, issue formal specifications of the languages entrusted to their care, and invite and evaluate proposals for their revision. Part of the price that must be paid for this elaborate and necessarily slow-moving apparatus of consultation and deliberation is that additions to the languages, even if approved at every stage of review, are a very long time in coming. Usually, years pass between the first proposal that a new feature be incorporated, and the actual appearance of that feature in manufacturer-supplied software. This gap between programmer requirements and high-level language response leaves another opening for AL, which, having no pretensions to machine independence, is available to vendor, end user, or third party to meet the need quickly.

MACHINE EXPLOITATION

As early responsiveness reflects AL's ability to yield an immediate answer to requirements generated by application programmers, so machine exploitation refers to its unique ability to permit full access to all features built into a machine, whether ever available through a high-level language or not. Providing such access may be virtually impossible for these languages, which—again, because of their need to remain machine-independent—cannot refer to any machine facility not common to all on which they are to run. If some, but not all, of the machines on which a compiler is to run include, say, a program-testable clock, then the language cannot offer statements that let users refer to that clock without either restricting the transferability of programs that do so, or forcing the compiler to generate code that simulates such clocks on those machines not having it in their hardware.

Since neither of these penalties is acceptable (the second is not always physically possible), the outcome is that such nonuniversal features are often simply ignored in the standard high-level languages. For most purposes, this partial disabling of the machine is tolerable; for a few, and most particularly for systems programming (*q.v.*), it is not. Whatever distinctive features a machine offers must be usable by its fundamental software, or they may as well not exist. System software itself is a major consumer of machine time, and time spent on its execution is felt to be nonproductive overhead (*q.v.*), so it is especially important that that layer of software be as fast as possible. This requirement means that systems software has to be written in a language that permits access to all machine features, and thus often rules out most standard languages.

Computer manufacturers and other serious software developers have long sought to develop for their in-house use a special language that would combine practically all the advantages of high-level languages with the machine-accessibility offered by AL. They would thus acquire for their own needs a tool as well adapted to its purpose as those they provide their customers with are for them. Many such projects have been mounted, and many interesting languages have come out of them, but none has yet proved completely satisfactory. (The languages, called "systems programming languages," are in fact languages that offer easy transition into AL, and smooth meshing of AL sequences into those generated by the compiler proper.) For the foreseeable future, then, AL remains an indispensable part of the building of systems software.

PIONEERING

Because of those attributes discussed above, AL is almost always involved when a wholly new computer application is being pioneered, even though it may later turn out not to be needed. When it is uncertain what the demands of a new species of program are going to be, the safest course is to use the language that imposes no constraints. After a number of AL programs have been written for the new application, it may turn out that one of the existing programming languages (often, with some modification) is adequate for the task (e.g. generating programs for parallel computers), or it may be found that the new application is sufficiently different, and economically important, to warrant the development of a language tailored to its needs (e.g. page layout for desktop publishing—*q.v.*). AL programming experience forms, among other things, a breeding ground for specialized language development.

CRAFTSMANSHIP

Another reason for the continued use of AL is that programming in that language is widely felt to be the most professional and demanding kind, and many career programmers will seek to use it even when none of the reasons discussed above applies. To a considerable extent, the programmer's private wish to use AL can coincide with the best interests of the installation. No matter how adamant management may be about running a pure Ada or C++ shop, there must always be a few programmers behind the scenes who can read dumps, help the application programmers with special debugging problems, understand the operating system, and deal as equals with the computer manufacturer's systems engineers.

Furthermore, a knowledge of AL often helps the programmer to use high-level languages more efficiently, clarifying the relationship between source code and what the compiler has generated, and warning about the hidden points in compiler-language usage where the price of execution may suddenly rise tenfold because the code compiled has exceeded some buffer size or other critical system constraint. And if AL specialists in what is nominally a pure compiler-language shop are to keep their skills sharp, they must be allowed to practice them. Even in such a shop, then, some AL programming will take place, with the connivance, if not the wholehearted approval, of installation management.

Beyond these reasons for tolerating AL usage in a compiler-language shop—reasons that make sense from management's viewpoint—there is the good programmer's personal desire to learn more about the machines and systems that the programs depend on, to be able to understand dumps and operating system messages, and in general to advance skills and deepen understanding, even when there is little or no foreseeable benefit to the employer in doing so. This instinct to practice one's craft at the highest possible level is a perennial one that will, independent of economic considerations, continue to turn many programmers toward AL.

CISC, RISC, and ML's Newest Role

The traditional reason for using ML/AL is saving memory space and execution time by minimizing the amount of code to be executed. But something new has entered the picture with RISC (Reduced Instruction Set Computing) architecture. Assembly-language operation codes were traditionally chosen with at least one eye on the convenience of programmers; they were designed to accommodate the limitations of programmers, and this indulgence of human weakness made them less amenable to computer interpretation and execution. RISC architecture represents a refusal to make that compromise, and a decision to adopt instead a set of assembly-language instructions optimized for generation by compilers, and efficient execution by the computer.

With human forgetfulness and susceptibility to confusion no longer needing to be taken into account, RISC operations are much more regular in their formation than their older counterparts, and hence easier for the processor to interpret and execute. RISC opcodes not only execute quicker—many in a single clock cycle each—but lend themselves to such advances as the execution of multiple concurrent instruction streams, so that whichever path is finally selected by some switch further down the program, some of the instructions lying on that path will already have been executed (*see* PIPELINE and INSTRUCTION-LEVEL PARALLELISM). Continuing the trend established by RISC architecture is the development of VLIW (Very Long Instruction Word) processors, where 64-bit (or longer) instructions pack still more information into each word, and still more optimization of hardware usage is achieved.

The cost in human usability is easily borne, since such instructions are intended to be generated by compilers, not written directly by programmers. Low-level debugging of such code, of course, is much more difficult than is debugging of human-tailored code, because so much tweaking and massaging has been performed on it by various optimizers that the correspondence between a given RISC instruction and the compiler statement that originally caused its generation can be very hard to trace. Such difficulty is redoubled if the code has been reorganized so as to exploit parallel execution. In that case the computer (to turn Sun Microsystems' slogan on its head) is really a network, with several processors semi-independently executing as many streams of instructions, and sending each other messages as necessary—but a network whose detailed management has been taken out of the hands of the programmer, even as Fortran, long ago, took away physical index-register management.

Acknowledgments and Bibliographical Suggestions

I am indebted to Richard Goodell of Tandem Computers, Inc. for a code inspection that greatly improved the sample macro offered in the "Trapping Ability" section.

ML programming seems to have generated no literature, and AL has had little of consequence written about it. On most topics the reader may want to pursue further, the relevant articles in this *Encyclopedia* will probably be the best recourse. On the loading of programs that have been assembled into ML, and the linking together of separately assembled programs when they refer symbolically to each other, see Presser and White (1972). For the internal workings of

assemblers, see Barron's (1972) lucid explanation. For some anecdotal memories of the era when AL programming was common, see Halpern (1991, 1992). There are countless books explaining AL programming for the Intel and Motorola chips that power most PCs; that by Crayne and Girard (1985) starts from scratch, is clearly written, and is cheap by modern standards. On RISC architecture, see not only Cocke and Markstein (1990), but the entire issue of the *IBM Journal of Research and Development* in which it appears.

Bibliography

1972. Barron, D. W. *Assemblers and Loaders*, 2nd Ed. New York: American Elsevier.
1972. Presser, L., and White, J. "Linkers and Loaders," *Computing Surveys*, **4**, *3* (September), 149–167.
1985. Crayne, C. A., and Girard, D. *The Serious Assembler.* New York: Pocketbooks.
1988. Somerson, P. *DOS Power Tools: Techniques, Tricks and Utilities.* New York: Bantam Books.
1990. Cocke, J., and Markstein, V. "The Evolution of RISC Technology at IBM," *IBM Journal of Research and Development*, **34**, *1* (January), 4–10.
1990. Halpern, M. *Binding Time*. Norword, NJ: Ablex.
1991. Halpern, M. "On the Heels of the Pioneers: A Memoir of the Not-quite-earliest Days of Programming," *Annals of the History of Computing*, **13**, *1*, 101–111.
1992. Halpern, M. "Turning Into Silicon: Further Episodes from Programming's Early Days," *Annals of the History of Computing*, **14**, *1*, 61–69.
1997. Livingston, B., and Straub, D. *Windows 95 Secrets*, 4th Ed. Foster City, CA: IDG Books.

Mark Halpern

MACHINE LANGUAGE

See MACHINE AND ASSEMBLY LANGUAGE PROGRAMMING.

MACHINE LEARNING

For articles on related subjects *see* ARTIFICIAL LIFE; EXPERT SYSTEMS; GENETIC ALGORITHMS; NEURAL NETWORKS; PATTERN RECOGNITION; PERCEPTRON; and STATISTICAL APPLICATIONS.

Machine learning is the study of methods for constructing and improving software systems by analyzing examples of their desired behavior rather than by directly programming them. Machine learning methods are appropriate in application settings where people are unable to provide precise specifications for desired program behavior, but where examples of this behavior are available. Such situations include optical character recognition (*q.v.*), handwriting recognition, speech recognition (*q.v.*), automated steering of automobiles, and robot control and navigation. A key property of these tasks is that people can perform them quite easily, but cannot articulate exactly *how* they perform them. Hence, people can provide input–output examples, but they cannot provide precise specifications or algorithms.

Machine learning methods are also appropriate for situations where the task changes with time or across different users, so that a programmer cannot anticipate exactly how the program should behave. For example, machine learning methods have been used to assess credit card risk, to filter news articles, to refine information retrieval (*q.v.*) queries, and to predict user browsing behavior in computer-based information systems such as the World Wide Web (*q.v.*).

A third area of application for machine learning algorithms is to the problem of finding interesting patterns in databases, sometimes called *data mining* (*q.v.*). Many corporations gather information about the purchases of customers, the claims filed by medical providers, the insurance claims filed by drivers, the maintenance records of aircraft, and so forth. Machine learning algorithms (and also, many traditional statistical methods) can find important patterns in this data that can be applied to improve marketing, detect fraud, and predict future problems.

Machine learning tasks can be grouped into three types: supervised, reinforced, and unsupervised.

SUPERVISED LEARNING

In *supervised learning*, the goal is to learn the form of a function $y = f(x)$ by analyzing examples of the form (x_i, y_i), where $y_i = f(x_i)$. Each input value x_i is usually an n-dimensional vector, where each dimension is either discrete or real-valued. Each output value y_i is typically either a discrete value or a continuous quantity. For example, in optical character recognition, each input value x_i might be a 256-bit vector giving 4-bit pixel values of an 8×8 input image, and each output value y_i might be one of the 95 printable ASCII characters. When, as in this case, the output values are discrete, f is called a *classifier* and the discrete output values are called *classes*.

Alternatively, in credit card risk assessment, each input might be a vector of properties describing the age, income, and credit history of an applicant, and the output might be a real value predicting the expected profit (or loss) of giving a credit card to the applicant. In cases where the output is continuous, f is called a *predictor*.

To design a supervised learning algorithm, one must choose a set of possible functions $\mathcal{H}$ that is likely to contain the unknown function f. It is also important to keep $\mathcal{H}$ small, because the larger it becomes, the more training examples are needed to learn successfully. Given a training set of examples $\{(x_1, y_1), (x_2, y_2), \ldots,$

$(x_m, y_m)\}$, a learning algorithm will implicitly search $\mathcal{H}$ to find a hypothesis $h \in \mathcal{H}$ that is estimated to be accurate for predicting the y_j values of new data points x_j. A good way to estimate the predictive accuracy of a hypothesis h is to see how accurately it classifies examples from the training set of known examples. Hence, most learning algorithms attempt to find an h that minimizes prediction error on the training set.

However, if the training examples contain noise or if the training set is unrepresentative (particularly if it is small), then an h with perfect accuracy on the training examples may still perform poorly in classifying new examples. This is called the problem of *overfitting*, and it arises when h becomes overly complex and *ad hoc* as the learning algorithm tries to achieve perfect performance on the training set. To avoid overfitting, learning algorithms must seek a trade-off between the simplicity of h (simpler hypotheses are less likely to be *ad hoc*) and accuracy on the training examples. A standard approach is to define a *complexity measure* for each hypothesis h and to search for the h that minimizes the sum of this complexity measure and the errors measured on the training data.

Learning algorithms have been developed for many function classes $\mathcal{H}$ including linear threshold functions (linear discriminant analysis, the naive Bayes algorithm, the LMS algorithm, and the Winnow algorithm (*see* Duda and Hart, 1973), decision trees (the CART and C4.5 algorithms; *see* Mitchell, 1997; Breiman *et al.*, 1984; Quinlan, 1993), feedforward neural networks (*q.v.*) (the backpropagation algorithm; *see* Bishop, 1996), and various families of stochastic models (the EM algorithm; *see* McLachlan and Krishnan, 1997).

Theoretical analysis of supervised learning problems and learning algorithms is conducted by researchers in the area of computational learning theory (Kearns and Vazirani, 1994). One of the primary goals of research in this area is to characterize which function classes $\mathcal{H}$ have polynomial time (*see* COMPUTATIONAL COMPLEXITY) learning algorithms. Among the key results is a theorem showing that the number of training examples required to learn accurately a function f in a function class $\mathcal{H}$ grows linearly in a parameter known as the Vapnik–Chervonenkis dimension (VC dimension) of $\mathcal{H}$. The VC dimension of most commonly used function classes has been computed. Another key result is a set of proofs showing that certain function classes (including small Boolean formulas and deterministic finite state automata) cannot be learned in polynomial time by any algorithm. These results are based on showing that algorithms that could learn such function classes could also break several well-known cryptographic schemes which are believed to be unbreakable in polynomial time.

REINFORCED LEARNING

Reinforced learning problems arise when a computer program must make a sequence of decisions before receiving a reward signal. Imagine a computer playing the game of chess. The computer must make a long sequence of moves before it finds out whether it wins or loses the game. Similarly, in robot navigation, the robot must choose a sequence of actions in order to get from a starting location to some desired goal. We could train computers to play chess or control robots by telling them which move to make at each step. But this is difficult, tedious, and time-consuming. It would be much nicer if computers could learn these tasks from only the final outcome—the win or loss in chess, the success or failure in robot navigation. Reinforced learning algorithms are designed to solve this kind of *learning from delayed reward*.

Reinforced learning algorithms learn a task by performing it—that is, they make moves in chess or issue control commands to robots. Before each move, the algorithm examines the current state, s, of the world (i.e. the current board position in a chess game or the current sensor inputs from the robot) and then chooses an *action a* (i.e. a chess move or a robot command). The action causes the world to change to a new state s'. After each state transition, the computer receives a reward, $R(s')$. In chess, the reward is zero until the end of the game, where it is 1 (win), 0 (draw), or −1 (loss). In robot navigation, there is typically a large positive reward for reaching the goal position and a small negative reward for each step. There may also be negative rewards for bumping into walls or other obstacles.

The goal of reinforced learning is to construct an optimal policy for choosing actions. A policy is a function, π, that maps from states to actions: $a = \pi(s)$. An optimal policy is the policy that receives the highest total reward. There are two main approaches to finding an optimal policy.

One approach is to search the space of policies directly. A policy can be represented as a computer program. Genetic algorithms, genetic programming, and other global optimization algorithms can be applied to generate alternative policies (programs) and then test them to evaluate how well they perform. Good policies can be combined to generate new candidate policies, which are then evaluated.

The other approach is to first learn something called a value function, $V(s)$, which tells for each state s how valuable it is for the world to be in that state. More precisely, the *value function* estimates the total reward that would be received by acting optimally starting in the specified state. The value function can be learned by "backing up" the results of lookahead search. Start-

ing in a given state s, the computer can look ahead one step by considering all possible moves that can be made in that state. Each move a will take the world into a new state s'_a and obtain some immediate reward, $R(s'_a)$. The best move, a^*, is the move with the highest total value: $V(s'_{a^*}) + R(s'_{a^*})$. This quantity is called the *backed-up value* of the current state s. When the value function is properly learned, it must be true that the value of a state s is equal to its backed-up value: $V(s) = V(s'_{a^*}) + R(s'_{a^*})$. If this is not the case, then the learning algorithm can change $V(s)$ to make it true. This is called a *Bellman backup*. By performing Bellman backups in every state often enough, information about the delayed rewards propagates backwards toward earlier states, and the value function eventually converges to the optimal value function. From the optimal value function, it is easy to compute the optimal policy: at each state, the computer chooses the action a^* that has the highest total value.

The value function can be stored in a table, with one entry for every state. This is only practical, however, for small problems. For large problems, the value function can be represented as a parameterized function, such as a neural network (*q.v.*). The $TD(\lambda)$ algorithm provides a method for updating the parameters of parameterized functions to approximate Bellman backups. The resulting methodology is called *Neuro-Dynamic Programming*, and it has been successful in several challenging problems including backgammon (where the world's best backgammon program was constructed this way), job-shop scheduling, and elevator scheduling (Bertsekas and Tsitsiklis, 1996; Tesauro, 1995).

UNSUPERVISED LEARNING

Unsupervised learning algorithms attempt to find structure in a set of data points. Consider, for example, an astronomy project in which the spectra of thousands of stars have been gathered. Each spectrum is a vector of numbers giving the intensity of a star's light at various wavelengths. Can we find patterns in this data? Suppose, for example, that we believe that there are different classes of stars. Could we use this data to identify the different classes of stars and group the stars into those classes? Unsupervised learning often involves clustering data into classes in this fashion.

One way to do this is to adopt a *generative model* for how the data is generated. For example, the model might say that each spectrum is generated by first choosing a star class at random and then taking the "standard spectrum" for that star class and adding random noise to the light intensities. An unsupervised learning algorithm (such as the EM algorithm; *see* McLachlan and Krishnan, 1997) can then be applied

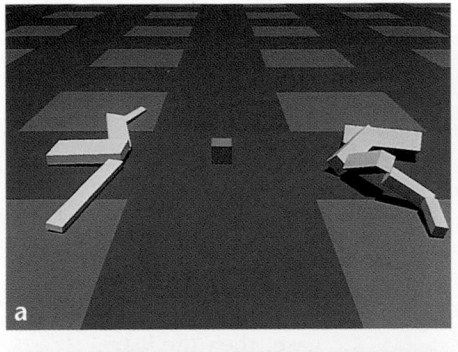
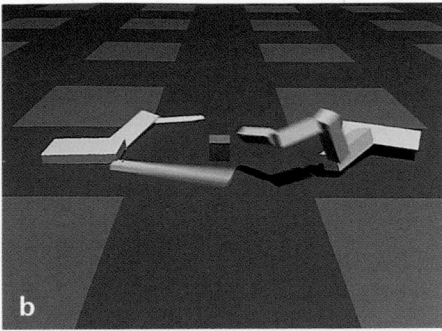

FIG. 2. A competition between two of Karl Sims' "evolved virtual creatures." Creatures are built of blocks of various shapes linked by flexible joints and powered by "muscles" controlled by circuits. Each creature has been selected for its ability to perform a variety of tasks, one of which is attempting to capture a square block in a contest with another creature. The starting position is shown in (**a**). In (**b**), the creatures begin to jockey for position. Panels (**c**) and (**d**) show closeup snapshots of the battle. As of (**d**), it appears that the white creature has the upper "hand," but in the end, (**e**), the yellow creature has captured the green block. Photos courtesy of Karl Sims.

FIG. 3. Three experimental abstract images produced by "artificial evolution" from different initial images. Photos courtesy of Karl Sims.

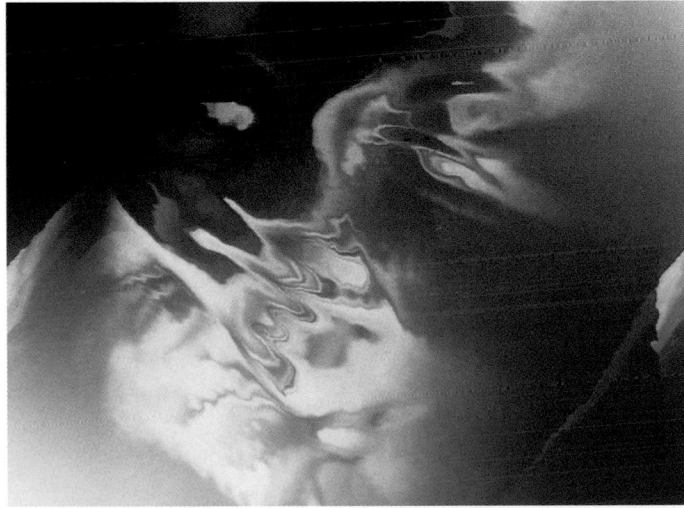

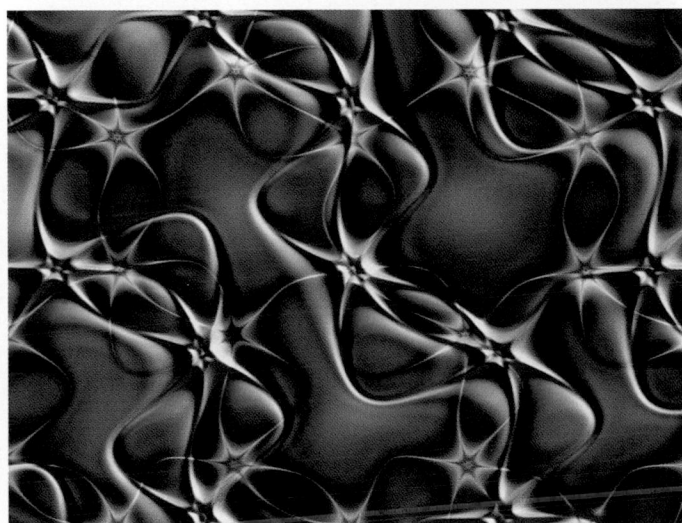

FIG. 4. "White Sands", a plant-like object grown with an L-system. © 1983, Alvy Ray Smith.

COMPUTER-AIDED DESIGN/COMPUTER-AIDED MANUFACTURING

FIG. 2

FIG. 3

FIG. 4

FIG. 7

FIG. 8

FIG. 9

FIG. 2. An F/A-18 plane, designed and manufactured in large part by using CAD/CAM. The high cost of parts in this kind of product, the pressure to complete the design in as little time as possible, and the need to maintain high precision in manufacturing all lead to high payoffs using CAD/CAM.

FIG. 3. A virtual reality view of the exterior of a touring bus.

FIG. 4. A model of a deep fat fryer, used to ensure that design constraints were met. An example of a complex composite assembly.

FIG. 7. A master model of a locomotive, used to review designs with customers before building.

FIG. 8. An exploded view of the interior of a wrist watch, showing relative locations of the parts.

FIG. 9. A "virtual" view of the dashboard of a touring bus.

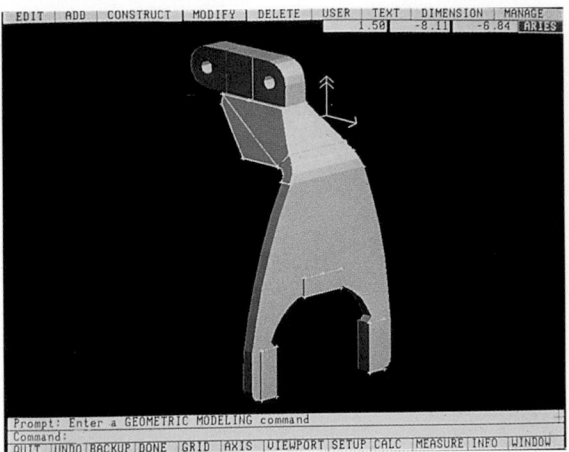

FIG. 1. A shaded image of a geometric model of a bracket. (Courtesy of Aries Technology Corporation)

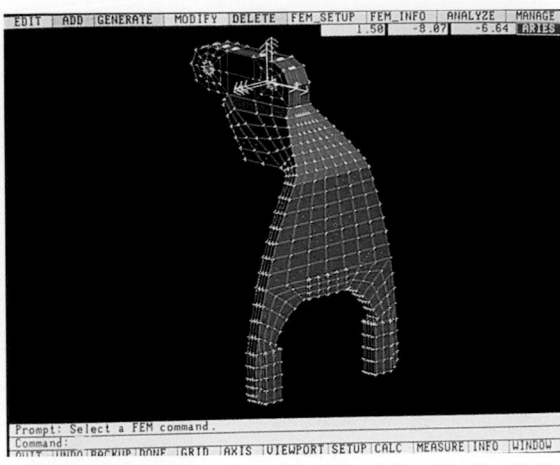

FIG. 2. The bracket shown in Figure 1 with the Finite Element Mesh applied. (Courtesy of Aries Technology Corporation)

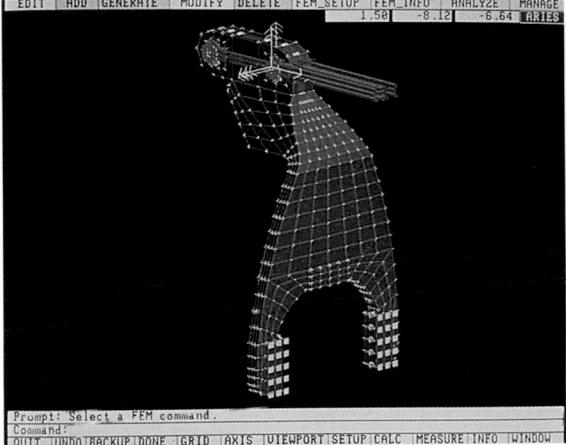

FIG. 3. The meshed bracket from Figure 2 with loads and constraints. (Courtesy of Aries Technology Corporation)

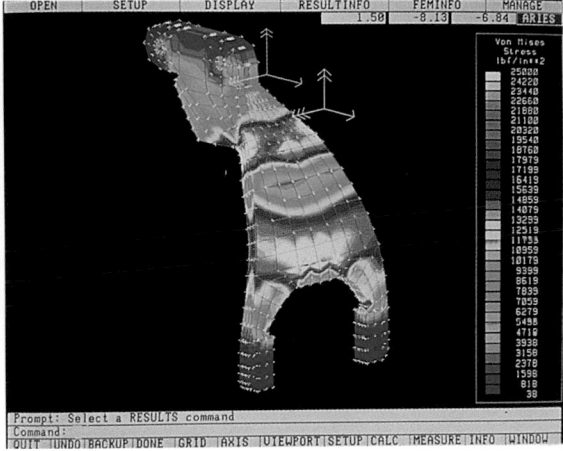

FIG. 4. The results of Finite Element Analysis displayed as stress contours for the bracket shown in Figures 1 through 3. The bar down the right-hand side of the display is a key relating to color level of stress. (Courtesy of Aries Technology Corporation)

COMPUTER ANIMATION

FIG. 1. The Mr. Potato Head character from the Toy Story Movie (Courtesy of the Moviestore Collection © Disney/Moviestore Collection)

FIG. 2. A computer-generated dinosaur from the Jurassic Park movie (Courtesy of the Moviestore Collection)

FIG. 5. Runner in a park: all the objects in this image were animated using dynamic simulation. The runner and the child on the swing are active simulations governed by control systems. The clothing is a passive system that has been coupled to an active system. (Image used courtesy of the Graphics, Visualization and Usability Center, Georgia Institute of Technology.)

FIG. 4. A diver entering a pool: this figure shows the combined use of an articulated model, a deformable model, and a particle system. (Image used courtesy of the Graphics, Visualization and Usability Center, Georgia Institute of Technology.)

COMPUTER ART

FIG. 4. Margot Lovejoy, *Black Box*, 1992 Projection installation using computer-controlled slide projection system and video (courtesy Margot Lovejoy).

FIG. 5. Jenny Holzer, *ARNO*, 1996, two-sided LED sign columns: red and blue, Guggenheim Museum, Bilbao, Spain. 13 m x 16 cm x 16 cm (courtesy Cheim Read).

FIG. 6. Bill Viola, *The Tree of Knowledge*, 1997, interactive installation (four views) produced at the ZKM Institute for Visual Media, Karlsruhe, Germany (photo: C. Heirholzer, courtesy ZKM)

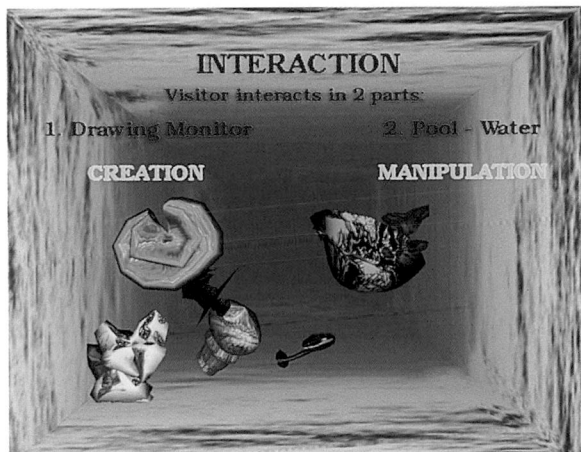 

FIG. 7. Christa Sommerer and Laurent Mignonneau, *A-Volve*, 1994, interactive computer environment (two views) supported by ICC-NTT (Japan) and NCSA (USA). Viewers drawing on a monitor screen with a sensor pencil can create 3D forms or organisms which immediately become "alive" and will seem to move in a water-filled pool nearby. Reacting to the slightest movement of the hand in the pool, the creatures will change their form and behavior (courtesy Christa Sommerer and Laurent Mignonneau).

FIG. 8. Harold Cohen, 1984, untitled wall mural.

FIG. 9. Lyn Hershman, *Conceiving Ada*, 1996, film still showing virtual sets (courtesy Lyn Hershman).

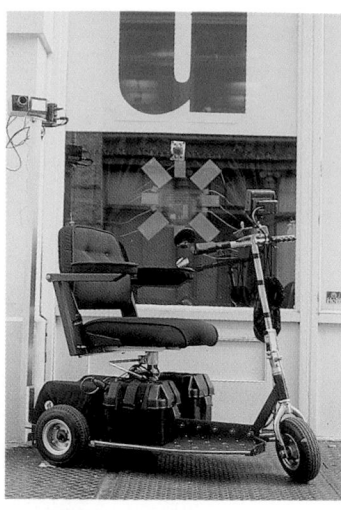

FIG. 10. Miroslaw Rogala, *Lovers Leap*, interactive multimedia installation produced in collaboration with Ludger Hovestadt and Ford Oxaal at the ZKM Institute for Visual Media, Karlsruhe, Germany (courtesy Miroslaw Rogala).

FIG. 14. Emily Hartzell and Nina Sobell, *Alice Sat Here*, 1995, telerobotic Web installation. A telerobotic camera is mounted on the handlebars of Alice's throne. The physical participant steers the cart, while the "virtual" participants online can see visuals from their position on the Web (courtesy Emily Hartzell).

FIG. 11. Robert Wilson and Philip Glass, *Monsters of Grace*, 1988, a 3D animation Digital Opera created in collaboration with Kleiser-Walczak, projected in 70mm stereoscopic film format (courtesy ICP).

FIG. 12. Jeffrey Shaw, Bernd Liwterman, Agnes Hegedus and Leslie Stuck, *Configuring the Cave*, 1997, Interactive Immersive Environment Collection, the NTT Intercommunication Center, Tokyo. Produced at the ZKM Institute for Visual Media, Karlsruhe, Germany (courtesy ZKM).

FIG. 13. Pattie Maes, *Alive, An Artificial Life*, 1994, MIT Media Lab. An interactive video space containing artificial life forms (courtesy Pattie Maes).

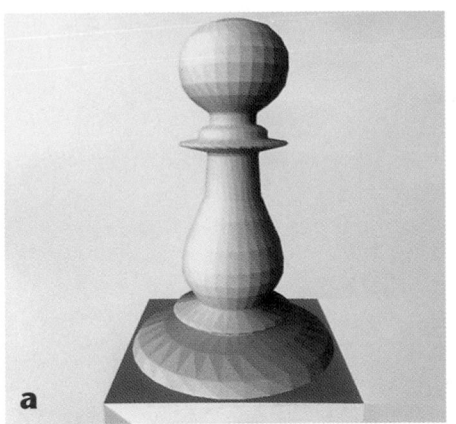 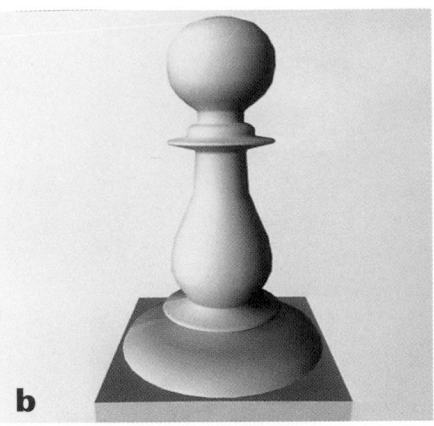 

FIG. 3. (a) Flat shading, (b) Gouraud shading, (c) Phong shading. (Courtesy of David Weimer and Gary Bishop, AT&T Bell Laboratories.)

FIG. 4. Simulated steel mill

FIG. 5. Forest fire simulation.

ENTERTAINMENT INDUSTRY, COMPUTERS IN

FIG. 4. 'Entrapment' studio footage of Sean Connery and Catherine Zeta-Jones was shot against a green screen and digitally composited by Cinesite (Europe) Ltd using Kodak's Cineon software into live action footage of Kuala Lumpur. Twentieth Century Fox Home Entertainment, inc. all rights reserved © 2000 (Image courtesy of Cinesite)

FIG. 5. 'Woody' and 'Buzz Lightyear' from the Toy Story movie (Coutesy of the Moviestore Collection © Disney/Moviestore Collection)

FIG. 6. A scene from Playstation's interactive fighting game, Tekken 3 (Courtesy of Sony Computer Entertainment)

FIG. 8. A still from the movie 'Dragonheart' featuring a computer animated dragon and a real-life Dennis Quaid © 1995 Universal Photo: ILM/The Kobal Collection (Courtesy of the Kobal Collection)

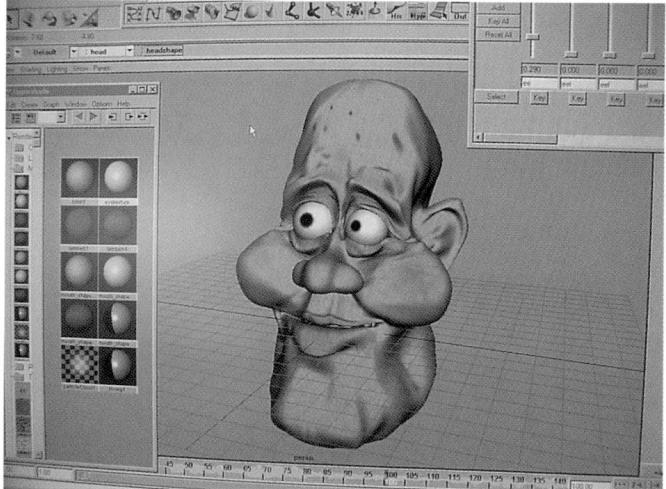

FIG. 9a. Character animation: a screen shot of a hardware textured head © Aardman Animations Limited 2000, by Will Byles.

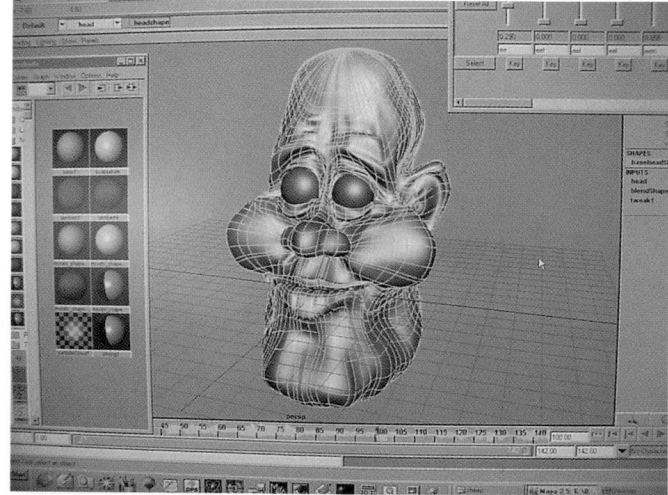

FIG. 9b. A screen shot showing the head's isoparms © Aardman Animations Limited 2000, by Will Byles.

FIG. 9c. Bobby Proctor viewing the multi replacement head © Aardman Animations Limited 2000, by Will Byles.

FIG 4. Convergence patterns of Newton-Raphson iteration of $z^4 - 1 = 0$ *(page 114f of Gleick, 1997).*

FIG 6. All of the important elements of this scene are fractal: the terrain, the moon, the Milky Way, and the surface texture on the terrain. The terrain and the Milky Way texture are actually multifractals, or fractals with heterogeneous statistics. © 1997, F. Kenton Musgrave, MetaCreations.

FIG 7. The potential function near the Mandelbrot set. The rendering of the sky is by means of random fractals (method of successive random additions). Cover picture of *The Science of Fractal Images* (© 1988 H. Jürgens, H.-O. Peitgen, D. Saupe).

FIG 8. Fractal planet generated with the rescale-and-add method. The fractal dimension depends on the latitude: Near the equator, the dimension of the coastlines is close to 1.0, whereas near the poles it is close to 2.0. The planet is rendered as a perfect sphere. However, the texturing function is based on the random fractal (pseudo) height and, for the solar caps, also depends on latitude. (© 1988 H. Jürgens, H.-O. Peitgen, D. Saupe.)

FIG 9. Random fractal in three variables rendered as a cloud with a fractal moon generated via the random cuts method and a background motivated by the filigrees of the Mandelbrot set. (from *The Science of Fractal Images*, © 1988 R. Voss.)

FIG 10. Random fractal landscape with haze. (© 1989 F. K. Musgrave, B. Mandelbrot.)

FIG 11. Fractal mountain scene with tree grown by L-systems. (© 1989 F. K. Musgrave, B. Mandelbrot, P. Prusinkiewicz.)

FIG 12. Spheres filling the exterior of the Mandelbrot set. They are computed using the distance estimate formula. (© 1988 H. Jürgens, H.-O. Peitgen, D. Saupe.)

FIG 7. A mother uses a video camera on an Apple iMac to show her son to distant relatives (Courtesy of the Dallas Morning News: Evans Caglage)

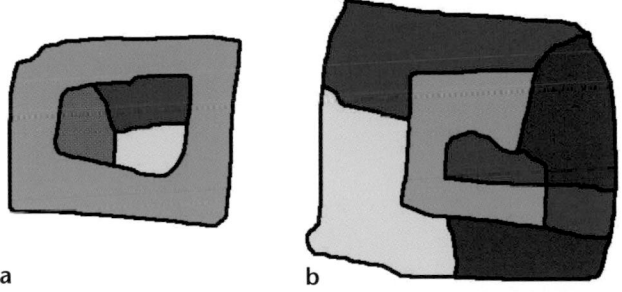

a   b

FIG 1. (a) Coloring a map containing four mutually contiguous regions obviously requires four colors. (b) This map does not contain four mutually contiguous regions but nonetheless requires four colors. The same color may be used for regions which touch only at a point (Graphics by Katie Reilly, age 7)

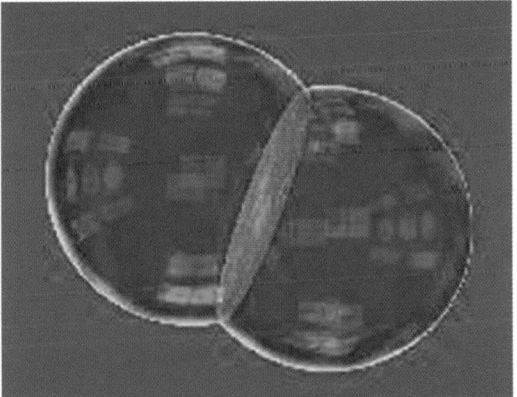

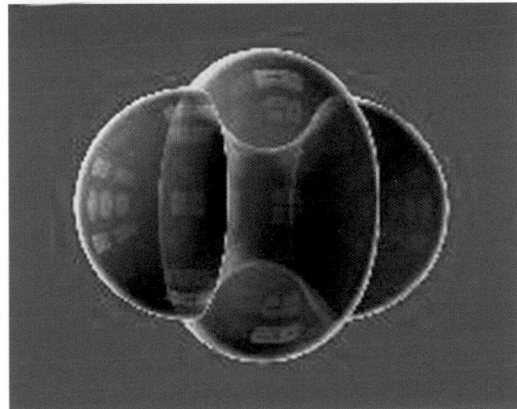

FIG 7. (a) A double bubble of minimum surface relative to its volume. (b) The "dumbbell in the donut" bubble.

FIG 6. A face-centered-cubic unit cell showing the portions of the spheres inside it.

MEDICAL IMAGING

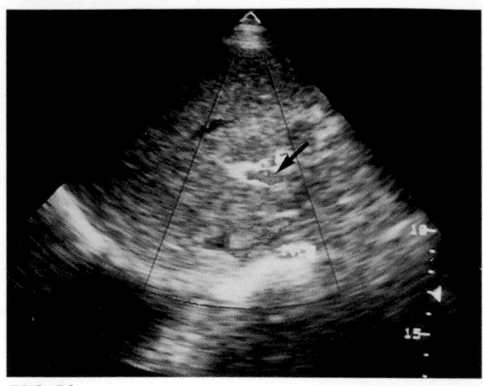

FIG 3j

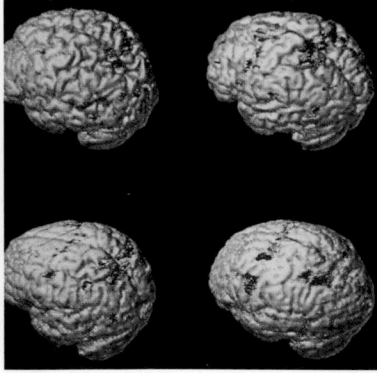

FIG 3k

FIG 3j. A longitudinal section Doppler ultrasound image of the abdomen. Red and blue color shows the blood flows toward and away from the ultrasound transducer, respectively; arrow indicates that flow in the portal vein is hepatopetal. (Courtesy of E. Grant)

FIG 3k. 3D Mapping of the brain function to anatomy. The gray-level images are 3D reconstructions from a set of MR images; the color images are 3D reconstructions of PET scans of the same patient. Red color shows high metabolic rates. Registration of these two sets of images required sophsticated mathematics and computer programming. Four views are shown. (Courtesy of Kent Soo Hoo)

ROBOTICS

FIG 2. The "AIBO" Entertainment robot (Courtesy of the Sony Corporation © 1999)

SCIENTIFIC APPLICATIONS

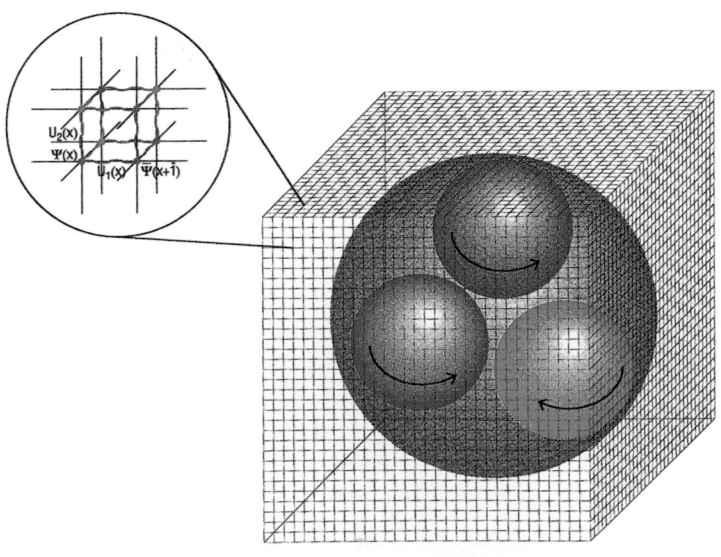

FIG 1. Artist's view of QCD simulation on a lattice used to approximate field interactions between colored quarks that build up a hadron. (From K. M. Bittar and W. M. Heller, Florida State University in Computers in Physics, *6, 1,* Jan/Feb 1992, p. 34, permission of AIP.)

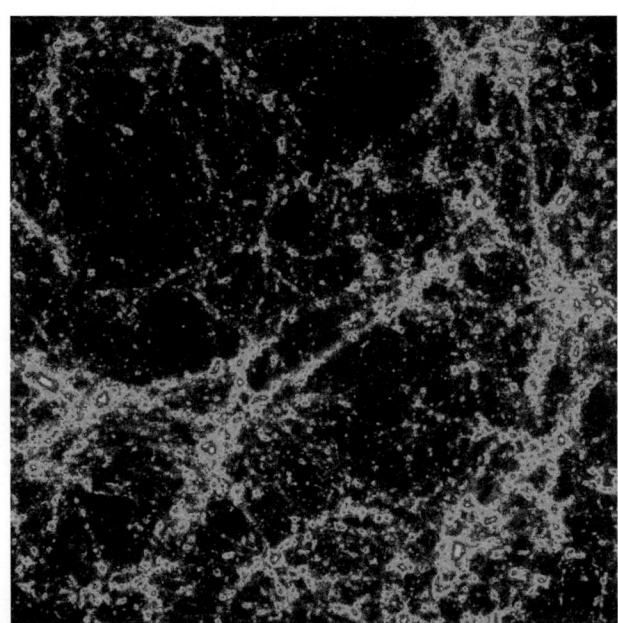

FIG 2. The web of galaxies produced through computer simulation of the evolution of the universe based on the cold dark matter model. Image courtesy of Michael S. Warren, Los Alamos National Laboratory

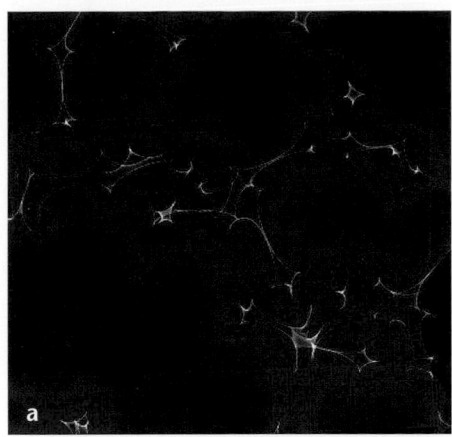 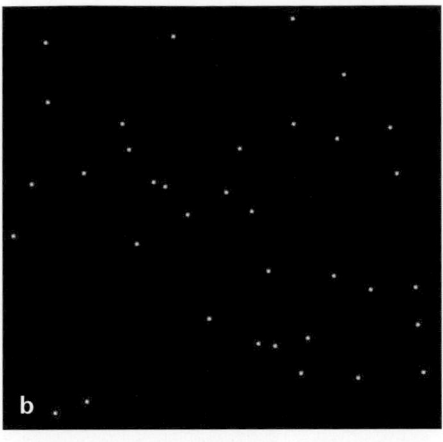 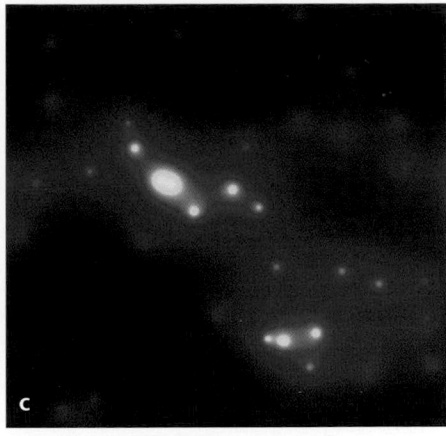

FIG 3. Images (a), (b), and (c) show, respectively, the planar density of a set of softened point-like mass lenses; their 2D Poisson potential whose gradient gives the deflection of light; and the illumination pattern obtained by shining a beam of light through this lens system. Images courtesy of Nick Kaiser, University of Hawaii Institute for Astronomy.

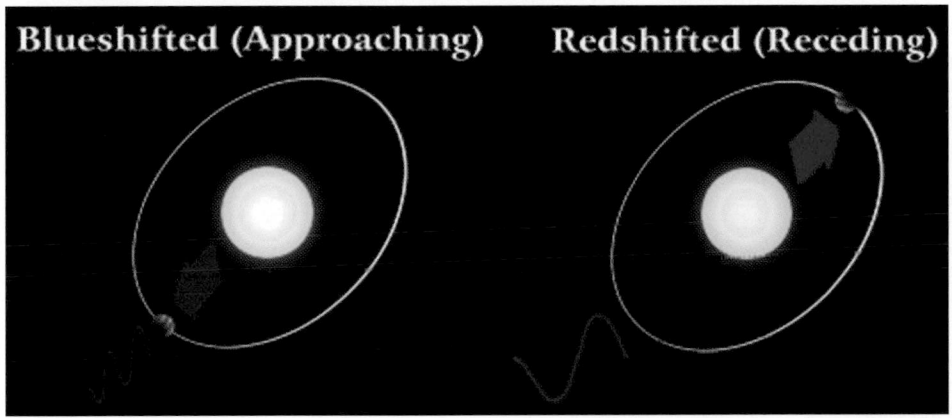 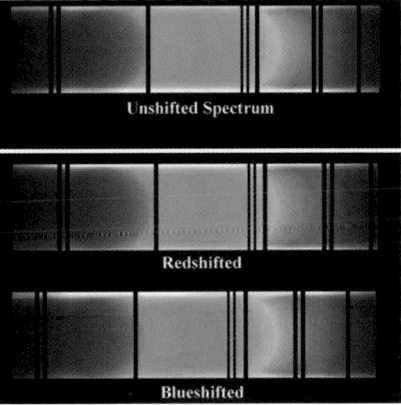

FIG 4. (a) Doppler shifting of light received from an orbiting planet (b) The resulting spectrum showing shifted spectral lines. Figures courtesy of Steve Howell, Astrophysics Group, Planetary Science Institute and the Wyoming-Arizona Search for Extra-Solar Planets, Tucson, AZ.

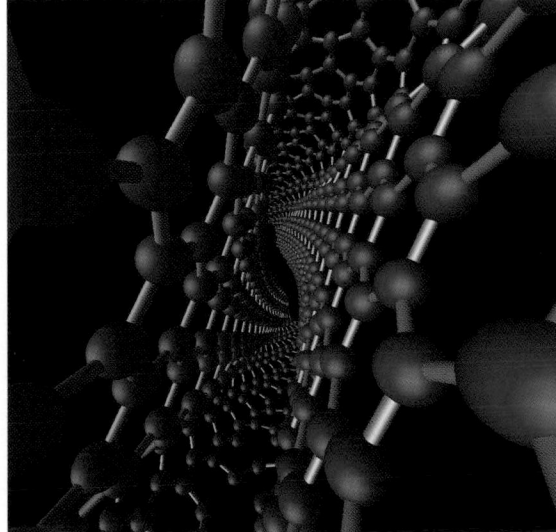 

FIG 6. This computer-drawn figure shows the view within a carbon nanotube flattened in order to form a flexible nanoribbon. See Chopra et al., Nature 377, 135 (1995). (Courtesy of V. Crespi, M. L. Cohen and S. G. Louie, University of California at Berkeley)

FIG 7. A computer simulation of the view down a boron nanotube, whose properties are different from those of a carbon nanotube. See Chopra et al., Science 269, 966 (1996). (Courtesy of V. Crespi, M. L. Cohen and S. G. Louie, University of California at Berkeley)

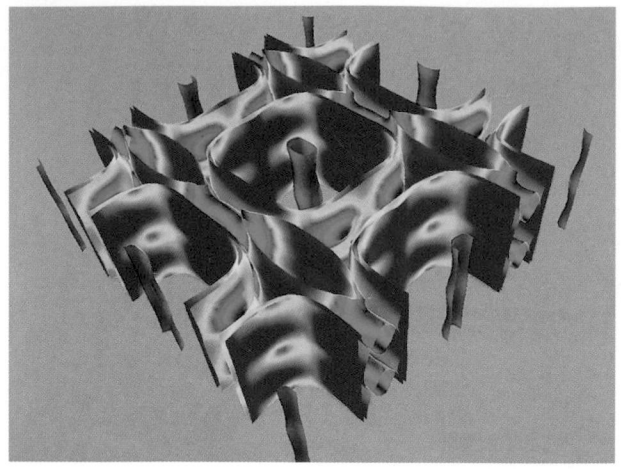

FIG 9. Fermi surface of $YBa_2Cu_3O_5$. (From W.E. Picket and R.E. Cohen, Naval Research Laboratory)

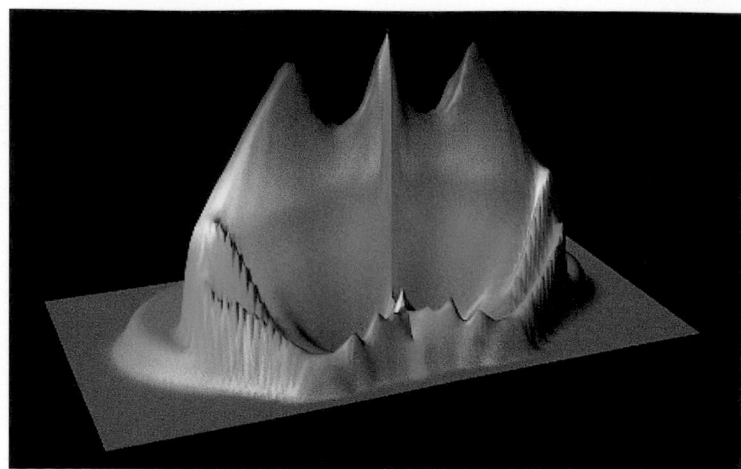

FIG 10. Mass density and energy density rendered on the same frame using the apE2.0 program Terrain to render the mass density as the height and the energy density mapped onto the density surface as colors. Blue corresponds to cooler and red to hotter gas elements. (From G.C. Duncan, Bowling Green State University.)

FIG 11. Magnetic strange attractors. (From Jennifer Johnson, Autodisk Inc.)

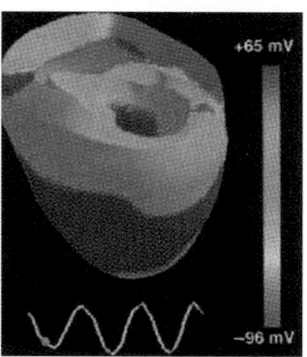

FIG 13. Misfiring of cardiac cells in one region of a computer model of a failing heart disrupts electrical activity throughout. (Courtesy of D. Scollan and R. Winslow, Center for Computational Medicine and Biology, Whitaker Biomedical Engineering Institute and Department of Biomedical Engineering, The Johns Hopkins University School of Medicine)

SCIENTIFIC VISUALIZATION

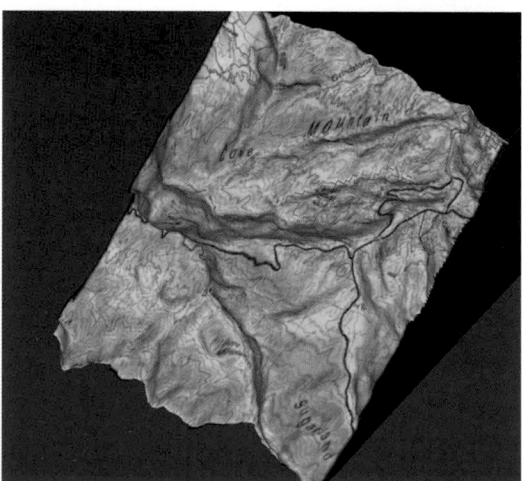

FIG 1. A snapshot of an interactive display of the Great Smoky Mountains (Tennessee, USA), produced by the Application Visualization System (courtesy of AVS, Inc).

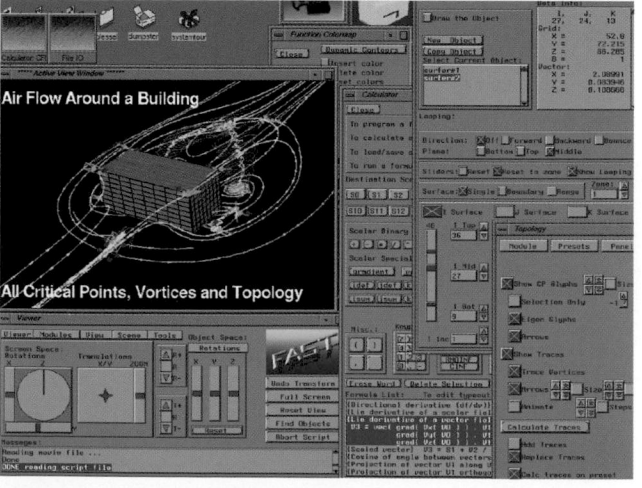

FIG 2. A screen from the Flow Analysis Software Toolkit developed at NASA for computational fluid dynamics research showing airflow around a building.

FIG 1. Flight Simulator (Courtesy of SEOS Displays Ltd)

FIG 2. A military training simulation (Courtesy of Evans & Sutherland, Salt Lake City)

STAMPS, COMPUTING ON

Colombia

West Germany

Great Britain

Norway

Switzerland

Poland

Canada

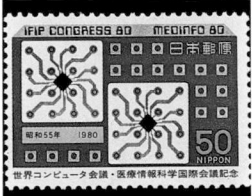

Japan

Great Britain

Ivory Coast

East Germany

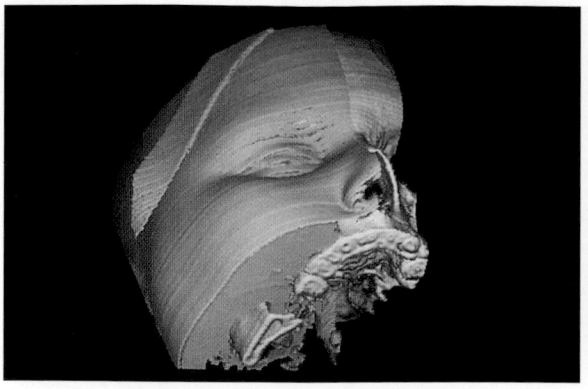
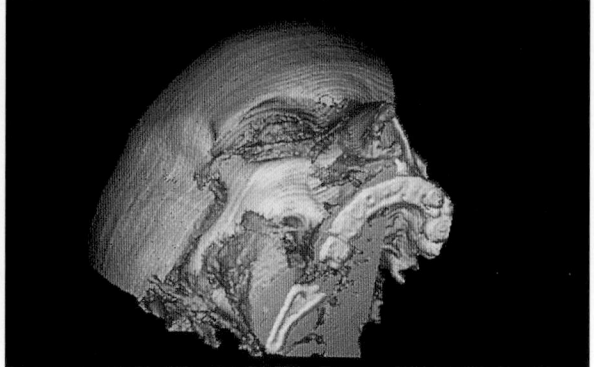

FIG 4. Three-dimensional computer graphic display of a patient's head obtained from a series of two-dimensional CT scans. On the left we see the skin and a constraining strap as well as part of the skull, while on the right we see some of the muscles and the skull. (Illustration provided courtesy of J.K. Udupa, University of Pennsylvania).

FIG 1. A scene from Playstation's 'Gran Turismo 2' videogame (Courtesy of Sony Computer Entertainment)

FIG 2. Konrad Zuse's paintings "Schwingungen" and "Wachstum"(Courtesy of Horst Zuse, Berlin)

to compute the "standard spectrum" for each class and to estimate the amount of random noise that is being added to this standard spectrum to generate the data points. According to this view of unsupervised learning, the goal is to construct a probability distribution that is most likely to have generated the data—in other words, unsupervised learning is a form of probability density estimation (Duda and Hart, 1973).

The probabilistic models constructed by unsupervised learning can often be applied to perform classification tasks. For example, given a collection of digitized handwritten digits, such as one might encounter in an automatic handwriting recognition task, it is possible to cluster them into 10 classes (one for each digit), and to model each class by its own probability distribution. A new handwritten digit can be classified by assigning it to the class that is most likely to have generated the observed digit. This approach is the basis of most speech recognition systems: for each word in the dictionary, a probabilistic model can be formed for speech signals corresponding to that word. When a new word is spoken, the computer identifies the probabilistic model that is most likely to have generated the observed speech signal, and the word corresponding to that probabilistic model is guessed to be the word that was spoken. Speech signals are typically represented using a form of stochastic finite state machine called a *hidden Markov model*.

An alternative view of unsupervised learning is that it seeks to identify low-dimensional structure in high-dimensional data. For example, the Kohonen self-organizing map is an approach to unsupervised learning which assumes that the observed data consist of a set of points lying in a two-dimensional plane embedded in some much higher-dimensional space. The learning algorithm attempts to find coordinates for a two-dimensional grid such that each data point is near to a point on the grid. The method generalizes to one-dimensional or three-dimensional grids of points. By mapping high-dimensional data onto a low-dimensional grid, it is often possible to visualize the data and gain important insights.

Bibliography

1973. Duda, R., and Hart, P. *Pattern Classification and Scene Analysis.* New York: John Wiley.
1984. Breiman, L., Friedman, J. H., Olshen, R. A., and Stone, C. J. *Classification and Regression Trees.* Monterey, CA: Wadsworth and Brooks.
1993. Quinlan, J. R. *C4.5: Programs for Empirical Learning.* San Francisco: Morgan Kaufmann.
1994. Kearns, M. J., and Vazirani, U. V. *An Introduction to Computational Learning Theory.* Cambridge, MA: MIT Press.
1995. Tesauro, G. "Temporal Difference Learning and TD-Gammon," *Comm. of the ACM,* **28**, *3,* 58–68.
1996. Bertsekas, D. P., and Tsitsiklis, J. N. *Neuro-Dynamic Programming.* Belmont, MA: Athena Scientific.
1996. Bishop, C. M. *Neural Networks for Pattern Recognition.* Oxford: Oxford University Press.
1997. McLachlan, G. J., and Krishnan, T. *The EM Algorithms and Extensions.* New York: John Wiley.
1997. Mitchell, T. *Machine Learning.* New York: McGraw-Hill.

Thomas G. Dietterich

MACHINE-READABLE FORM

For articles on related subjects *see* MEMORY: AUXILIARY; OPTICAL CHARACTER RECOGNITION; PAPER TAPE; PUNCHED CARD; and UNIVERSAL PRODUCT CODE.

Machine-readable form refers to the form in which information is encoded for direct, automatic input into a computer. Keyboard input is machine-readable, for example, because the machine senses which keys are depressed in which order. Carefully hand-printed characters on certain forms (e.g. social security numbers on driver's license renewals), can be read directly by optical scanning devices. Machine reading of handwritten script has improved significantly in recent years, and handheld computers on which the user writes with a stylus can be "trained" to recognize the user's handwriting, by having the user correct initial misreadings. However, devices are still not yet routinely available that can handle all of the wide variations in cursive handwriting.

In general, keyboard inputs, bar codes, punched cards, magnetic tape, disks, drums, etc., carry information in machine-readable form for the express purpose of being read exclusively by computers. Some printer and typewriter fonts can be machine-read by optical scanners, and are also directly readable by humans, unlike the magnetic coding on tape or disk. Magnetic ink characters, used principally for coding bank-accounting information on checks, are readable by humans (optically) and by machines (magnetically). Such magnetic ink character recognition is often referred to by its abbreviation, MICR.

Chester L. Meek

MACHINE TRANSLATION

For articles on related subjects *see* ARTIFICIAL INTELLIGENCE; GRAMMARS; HUMANITIES APPLICATIONS; KNOWLEDGE REPRESENTATION; and NATURAL LANGUAGE PROCESSING.

History of Machine Translation

Within a few years of the first appearance of the "electronic calculators," research had begun on using computers as aids for translating natural languages. The major stimulus was a memorandum in July 1949 by Warren Weaver, who after mentioning tentative efforts in the UK (by Booth and Richens) and in the USA (by Huskey and others), put forward possible lines of research. His optimism stemmed from the wartime success in code-breaking, from developments by Shannon in information theory (*q.v.*), and from speculations about universal principles underlying natural languages, "the common base of human communication." Within a few years research had begun at many US universities, and in 1954 there was the first public demonstration of the feasibility of machine translation (MT), a collaboration of IBM and Georgetown University. Although using a very restricted vocabulary and grammar it was sufficiently impressive to stimulate massive funding of MT in the USA and to inspire the establishment of MT projects throughout the world.

The earliest systems consisted primarily of large bilingual dictionaries where entries for words of the source language (SL) gave one or more equivalents in the target language (TL) and some rules for producing the correct word order in the output. It was soon recognized that specific dictionary-driven rules for syntactic ordering were too complex and increasingly *ad hoc*; the need for more systematic methods of syntactic analysis became evident. A number of projects were inspired by contemporary developments in linguistics, particularly Zellig Harris's and Noam Chomsky's ideas on syntactic transformations, but also other models such as dependency grammar and stratificational grammar. They seemed to offer the prospect of greatly improved translation.

Optimism remained at a high level for the first decade of MT research, with many predictions of imminent breakthroughs, but disillusion grew as researchers encountered "semantic barriers" for which they saw no straightforward solutions. There were some operational systems—the Mark II system (developed by IBM and Washington University) installed at the USAF Foreign Technology Division, and the Georgetown University system at the US Atomic Energy Authority and at Euratom in Italy—but the quality of output was disappointing, although satisfying many recipients' needs for information. By 1964, the US government sponsors had become increasingly concerned at the lack of progress, and set up the Automatic Language Processing Advisory Committee (ALPAC). It concluded in its famous 1966 report that MT was slower, less accurate, and twice as expensive as human translation and that "there is no immediate or predictable prospect of useful machine translation." It saw no need in the USA for further investment in MT research, and instead it recommended the development of machine aids for translators, such as automatic dictionaries, and continued support of basic research in computational linguistics.

The ALPAC report was widely condemned as narrow, biased, and shortsighted, but the damage had been done. It brought a virtual end of MT research in the USA for over a decade and it had great impact elsewhere in the Soviet Union and in Europe. However, MT research did continue in Canada, France, and Germany. Within a few years Peter Toma, one of the members of the Georgetown University project, had developed Systran for operational use by the USAF (1970) and by NASA (in 1974–5), and shortly afterwards Systran was installed by the Commission of the European Communities for translating from English into French (1976) and later between other Community languages. At the same time, another successful system appeared in Canada, the METEO system for translating weather reports, which was developed at Montreal University.

In the 1960s in the USA and the Soviet Union, MT activity had concentrated on Russian–English and English–Russian translation of scientific and technical documents for a relatively small number of potential users, most of whom were prepared to overlook mistakes of terminology, grammar, and style in order to be able to read something which they would have otherwise not known about. Since the mid-1970s the demand for MT has come from quite different sources with different needs and different languages. The administrative and commercial demands of multilingual communities and multinational trade have stimulated the demand for translation in Europe, Canada, and Japan beyond the capacity of the traditional translation services. The demand is now for cost-effective machine-aided translation systems that can deal with commercial and technical documentation in the principal languages of international commerce.

The 1980s witnessed the emergence of a variety of system types and from a widening number of countries. First there were a number of mainframe systems, whose use continues to the present day. Best known is Systran, now installed worldwide and operating in many pairs of languages. Others are: Logos for German–English translation and for English–French in Canada; the internally developed systems for Spanish–English and English–Spanish translation at the Pan American Health Organization; the systems developed by the Smart Corporation for many large organizations in North America; and the Metal system from Siemens, initially for German–English translation and later for other languages. Major systems for English–Japanese and Japanese–English translation have come from the Japanese computer companies Fujitsu, Hitachi, and Toshiba. The wide availability of microcomputers and of text-processing software led to a commercial market for cheaper MT systems, exploited in North America and Europe by companies such as ALPS, Weidner, Linguistic Products, Tovna, and Globalink, and by many Japanese companies, e.g. Sharp, NEC, Oki, Mitsubishi, and Sanyo. Other microcomputer-based systems appeared from China, Taiwan, Korea, Eastern Europe, the Soviet Union, etc.

Throughout the 1980s research on more advanced methods and techniques continued. For most of the decade, the dominant strategy was that of "indirect" translation via intermediary representations, sometimes interlingual in nature, involving semantic as well as morphological and syntactic analysis and sometimes non-linguistic "knowledge bases." There was an increasing emphasis on devising systems for particular subject domains and for particular specific purposes, for monolingual users as well as bilingual users (translators), and for interactive operation rather than batch processing. The most notable projects were the GETA-Ariane system at Grenoble, SUSY and ASCOF at Saarbrücken, Mu at Kyoto, DLT at Utrecht, Rosetta at Eindhoven, the knowledge-based MT project at Carnegie Mellon University (Pittsburgh), and two ambitious international multilingual projects: Eurotra, supported by the European Communities, involving teams in each member country; and the Japanese CICC project with participants in China, Indonesia, and Thailand.

The end of the decade was a major turning point. First, a group from IBM published the results of experiments on a system based purely on statistical methods, encouraged by the success of newer stochastic techniques in speech recognition. Second, at the same time certain Japanese groups began to use methods based on a corpus (collection) of translation examples, i.e. using the approach now called "example-based" translation. In both approaches the distinctive feature is that no syntactic or semantic rules are used in the analysis of texts or in the selection of lexical equivalents. Both approaches differed from earlier "rule-based" methods in the exploitation of large text corpora.

A third innovation has been research on speech translation, involving the integration of speech recognition and synthesis (q.v.) and translation modules, the latter mixing traditional rule-based methods and newer corpus-based approaches. Inevitably, the subject domains have been highly restricted. The major projects have been at ATR (Nara, Japan) on a system for telephone translation of conference inquiries and hotel bookings, a collaborative project (JANUS) involving ATR, Carnegie-Mellon University and the University of Karlsruhe, and in Germany the government-funded Verbmobil project for a system to aid Germans and Japanese to conduct business negotiations in English.

As well as newer corpus-based research, traditional rule-based methods continue, e.g. the CAT2 system

(a by-product of Eurotra) at Saarbrücken, the Catalyst project at Carnegie-Mellon University (a domain-specific knowledge-based system) for the Caterpillar company, a project at the University of Maryland based on the linguistic theory of "principles and parameters," and the ARPA-funded research (Pangloss) at three US universities. However, more and more groups have been investigating "hybrid" approaches, i.e. the combination of rule-based ("symbolic") and statistics-based or example-based methods, particularly in Asia.

Another feature of the 1990s has been the changing location of research activity. With the political changes in Russia and Eastern Europe, MT research has virtually ceased in those countries. By contrast, research in the USA has seen a marked revival, evident in the first government-funded projects since the ALPAC report. In Western Europe, the main focus has been the development of translation "work stations" for professional translators, of controlled language and domain-restricted systems, and translation components for multilingual information systems within the European Union. In Asia, research has continued to grow in Japan, China, Taiwan, and Korea, and is becoming more active in Southeast Asia. In recent years there has been a massive increase in the sales of MT software for personal computers (primarily for use by non-translators) and growing availability of MT from online networked services. These developments, spreading from North America to Asia and Europe, are making MT software into a mass-market product almost as familiar to the general public as word processing and desktop publishing.

Linguistic Problems of MT

The basic processes of translation are the analysis of the source language (SL) text, the conversion (or *transfer*) of the *meaning* of the text into another language, and the generation (or *synthesis*) of the target language (TL) text. There are basically three overall strategies. In the direct translation approach, adopted by most of the early MT projects, systems are designed in all details specifically for one particular pair of languages; vocabulary and syntax are not analyzed any more than strictly necessary for the resolution of ambiguities, the identification of TL equivalents, and output in correct TL word order; hence the processes of analysis and synthesis are combined in single programs, sometimes of monolithic intractability (e.g. the Georgetown system). The second strategy is the *interlingua* approach which assumes the possibility of converting SL texts into (semantic) representations common to a number of languages, from which texts can be generated in one or more TLs. In interlingua systems SL analysis and TL synthesis are monolingual processes independent of any other languages, and the interlingua is designed to be language-independent or "universal." (A recent example is the DLT system based on modified Esperanto representations.) The third strategy is the *transfer* approach, which operates in three stages: from the SL text into an abstract "intermediary" representation which is not language-independent but oriented to the characteristics of the SL (analysis); from such an SL-oriented representation to an equivalent TL-oriented representation (transfer); and from the latter to the final TL text (synthesis). (Major examples of the transfer approach are the GETA, SUSY, Mu, and Eurotra systems.)

The main linguistic problems encountered in MT systems fall under four main headings: lexical, structural, contextual, and pragmatic or situational. In each case the problems are primarily caused by the inherent ambiguities of natural languages and by the lack of direct equivalences of vocabulary and structure between one language and another. Some English examples are:

- *Lexical*: homonyms (*fly* as "insect" or "move through air," *bank* as "edge of river" or "financial institution") require different translations (*mouche*, *voler*; *rive*, *banque*).

- *Structural*: nouns can function as verbs (*control*, *plant*, *face*) and are hence "ambiguous," since the TL may well have different forms (*contrôle*: *diriger*; *plante*: *planter*; *face*: *affronter*).

- *Contextual*: other languages make distinctions which are absent in English: *river* can be French *rivière* or *fleuve*, German *Fluß* or *Strom*; *blue* can be Russian *sinii* or *goluboi*.

Often all of these combine, as illustrated by a simple but common example, the word *light*. This can be a noun meaning "luminescence," an adjective meaning "not dark," another adjective meaning "not heavy," or a verb meaning "to start burning" (at least). In French the meanings are conveyed by four different words *lumière*, *léger*, *clair*, and *allumer*. An analysis of English must therefore distinguish the four possibilities by (a) recognizing the grammatical categories of words in sentences (nouns, verbs, adjectives, adverbs, prepositions, conjunctions, etc.) and the structures in which they take part, and (b) by recognizing the lexical and semantic contexts in which the words occur. At the transfer stage this information must be used to convert the identified meaning into those lexical units and structures with equivalent meanings in the target language. In many cases, differences between the vocabulary of the source and target languages are also accompanied by structural differences. A familiar example involves the translation of the English verb *know* into French or German, where there are two verbs which express "knowledge of a fact" (*connaître* and *kennen*) and "knowledge of how to do something" (*savoir* and *wissen*):

1. I know the man: *Je connais l'homme*; *Ich kenne den Mann*.

2. I know what he is called: *Je sais ce qu'il s'appelle*; *Ich weiss wie er heißt*.

The choice of TL form involves a restructuring with effects on the translation of other lexical items (*what* as *ce que* and *wie*). A more radical, but no less common, instance of restructuring may be illustrated by the German sentence:

3. *Das Mädchen spielt gern Tennis.*

translated as:

4. The girl likes to play tennis.

The German adverb *gern* corresponds to an English finite verb *like*, and this choice entails the shifting of the finite verb *spielt* to a subordinate infinitive (*to play*).

The resolution of many linguistic problems transcends sentence boundaries. A common and persistently difficult one involves the use of pronouns. Following sentence 3 above there might occur:

5. *Es geht jede Woche zum Club.*

for which the English should be:

6. She goes to the club every week.

However, *es* is normally translated as *it*. To ensure the correct selection of *she*, the preceding noun referent of the pronoun must be identified and the different practices for pronominalization must be taken into account (in German according to the "grammatical" gender of the preceding noun, and in English according to the "natural" sex of the object referred to). However, the identification of the noun referred to can often be more complex than this example. Frequently, it depends on (non-linguistic) knowledge of events or situations:

7. The soldiers killed the women. They were buried next day.

We know that the pronoun *they* does not refer to *soldiers* and must refer to *women* because we know that "killing" implies "death" and that "death" is followed (normally) by "burial." This identification is crucial when translating into French, where the pronoun must be *elles* and not *ils*. Grammatical and linguistic information is insufficient in such cases.

Various aspects of syntactic relations can be analyzed. There is the need (a) to identify valid sequences of grammatical categories; (b) to identify functional relations: subjects and objects of verbs, dependencies of adjectives on "head" nouns, etc.; and (c) to identify the constituents of sentences: noun phrases, verb groups, prepositional phrases, subordinate clauses, etc. Each aspect has given rise to different types of parsers: the predictive syntactic analyzer of the 1960s concentrated on sequences of categories (it was developed subsequently by Woods (1970) as the Augmented Transition Network parser); the dependency grammar (of Tesnière, Hays, etc.) has concentrated on functional relationships; and the phrase structure grammars have been the models for parsers of constituency structure. All have their strengths and weaknesses, and modern MT systems often adopt an eclectic mixture of parsing techniques, now often within the framework of a "unification grammar" formalism (Kay, 1984).

The most serious weakness of all syntactic parsers is precisely their limitation to structural features. An English prepositional phrase can in theory modify any preceding noun in the sentence as well as a preceding verb:

8a. The camera was purchased by the man with dark glasses.

8b. The camera was purchased by the man with the tripod.

8c. The camera was purchased by the man with a check.

A syntactic analysis can go no further than offer each possibility; later semantic or pragmatic analysis (e.g. involving lexical and situational context) has the task of specifying the intended relationship.

Many parsers now include the identification of case relations, e.g. the fact that in

9. The house was built by a doctor for his son during the war.

the Agent of the action ("building") is *a doctor*, the Object of the action is *the house*, the Recipient (or Beneficiary) is *his son* and the Time of the action is *during the war*. Many languages express these relations explicitly: suffixes of Latin, German, Russian

nouns (*-ibus, -en, -ami*), prepositions of English and French (*to, à*), particles of Japanese (*ga, wa*); but they are often implicit (as in English direct objects). There are rarely any direct correspondences between languages and most markers of cases are multiply ambiguous in all languages, cf. *with* expressing Attribute (8a), Comitative (8b), Instrument (8c). Nevertheless, there is sufficient regularity and universality in such "case relations" to have encouraged their widespread adoption in many MT systems.

There is also some agreement about the use of semantic features, i.e. the attachment of such categories as "human," "animate," "liquid" to lexical items and their application in the resolution of ambiguities. For example, in:

10. He was beaten with a club.

the "social" sense of *club* found in sentence 6 above is excluded by the verb type, which requires an "inanimate" Instrument. In:

11. The sailor went on board.

12. The sailor was examined by the board.

the "physical" sense of *board* in 11 is confirmed by the verb type (motion) and the preposition of Location, and the "social" sense in 12 is confirmed by the verb *examine* which requires an "animate" Agent.

Few operational MT systems involve deeper levels of semantic or pragmatic analysis. Nevertheless, as examples 7 and 8 demonstrate, disambiguation and correct selection of TL equivalents would seem to be impossible without reference to knowledge of the features and properties of the objects and events described. This was used by Yehoshua Bar-Hillel (1960) in arguing that fully automatic translation of high quality is impossible. His famous demonstration involved the sentence *The box was in the pen*. We know that *pen* can refer here only to a "container for animals or children" and not to "writing implement," from our knowledge of relative sizes of (writing) pens and boxes. For Bar-Hillel, the incorporation of encyclopedic knowledge and the associated inference mechanisms was "utterly chimerical." However, subsequent advances in Artificial Intelligence (AI) have encouraged later MT researchers to investigate the possibility of knowledge-based systems, at least for systems restricted to specific domains. However, the general feasibility of AI approaches has yet to be tested on large-scale systems, and most MT researchers prefer to develop linguistics-based systems capable of incorporating AI methods as adjuncts to more traditional techniques of syntactic and semantic analysis, transfer, and generation.

The advent of corpus-based techniques has provided further complexity to the range of architectures available. The essence of the statistical method at IBM was the analysis of the corpus of French and English texts contained in the reports of Canadian parliamentary debates (the Canadian Hansard); first, the alignment of phrases, word groups and individual words of the parallel texts, and then the calculation of the probabilities that any one word in a sentence of one language corresponds to a word or words in the translated sentence with which it is aligned in the other language. For example, English *not* is most probably aligned with two French words, and these are most likely to be *ne* and *pas*, with lower probabilities for *point, jamais, faux* and *non*.

In the second corpus-based approach—"example-based" translation—the method consists of the extraction and selection of equivalent phrases or word groups from a database of parallel bilingual texts. These may have been aligned either by statistical methods (as used by the IBM group) or by more traditional rule-based morphological and syntactic methods of analysis. The result for a particular word or phrase (e.g. English *have an effect on*) would be a set of SL text segments and their TL translations (e.g. *ont une influence directe à; intéressent directement; a largement influencé; s'est avérée positive dans*, etc.). Since there are rarely exact matches, some MT groups calculate equivalences by using semantic methods, e.g. a semantic network or a hierarchy of domain terms; other groups use statistical information about lexical frequencies in the target language. The main advantage of the approach is that since the texts have been extracted from databases of actual translations produced by professional translators, there is a high probability that the results will be accurate and idiomatic.

MT in Practice

The complexities and difficulties of linguistic analysis and the problems of incorporating appropriate semantic and extra-linguistic knowledge have persuaded many researchers that for the foreseeable future it is unrealistic to attempt to build fully automatic systems capable of the translation quality achieved by human translators. The growing demands for translations must be met by MT systems that involve the active assistance and expertise of natural language speakers.

The most obvious course, which has been adopted since the first MT systems, is to employ human translators to revise and improve the crude and inaccurate texts produced by MT systems. Initially, "post-editing" was undertaken manually; later systems incorporate online revision and in some cases special facilities for dealing with the most common types of error (e.g. transposition of words, insertion of articles). Revision for MT differs from the revision of traditionally produced translations; the computer program is regular and consistent with terminology, unlike the human translator, but typically it contains grammatical and stylistic errors which no human translator would commit.

The development of powerful microcomputer text editing facilities has led to the introduction of interactive MT systems. During the translation process, a human operator (normally a translator) may be asked to help the computer resolve ambiguities of vocabulary or structure, e.g. whether the *club* in 10 is a "society" or not, and what relationship is expressed by *with* in (8a, 8b, and 8c). Many Japanese systems demand considerable assistance from operators, particularly with the "pre-editing" of Japanese scripts (identifying word and phrase boundaries, punctuation, etc.).

A third possibility is to constrain the variety of language in the input texts. There are two approaches: either the system is designed to deal with one particular subject matter or the input texts are written in a vocabulary and style which it is known that the MT system can deal with. The former approach is illustrated by the METEO system, introduced in 1976, which translates weather forecasts from English into French for public broadcasts in Canada. The latter approach has been taken by the Xerox Corporation in its use of the Systran system; manuals are written in a controlled English (unambiguous vocabulary and restricted syntactic patterns) which can be translated with minimal revision into five languages. Other examples are the Smart systems installed at a number of large US and Canadian institutions which combine online editing to ensure clear documentation in English and "restricted language" MT to produce translations for subsequent editing.

MT systems are now being used in the production of a wide range of translations of different quality and status. The "raw" output of both mainframe systems (Systran, Logos, Fujitsu) and personal computer systems (Globalink, NEC) may be used (a) as a draft version for full revision to the level of human quality products (e.g. for later publication), (b) as a first draft for subsequent wholly human translation, (c) as a version offered completely unedited to those who are prepared to tolerate the grammatical and stylistic errors for the sake of cheap access to information, or (d) as a version for light editing for similar information purposes. It may be noted, however, that few microcomputer-based translations are adequate in their unedited forms, even for purely informational purposes.

A major impact on the translation profession has been the development of computer-based aids for translators, which may justly be regarded as commercial by-products of research in MT and related areas. These aids include facilities for multilingual word processing, for creating in-house glossaries and term banks, for receiving and sending texts over telecommunication networks, for accessing remote sources of information, for publishing quality documents, and for using interactive or batch MT systems when appropriate. Above all, translators can store previous translations for reuse in "translation memories." With bilingual corpora of aligned sentences and text segments, translators have access to examples of existing translations of text which match or are similar to those in hand. Not only is consistency improved and quality maintained, but sections of repetitive texts are not translated again unnecessarily. Systems which integrate such facilities are known as translator's workstations or workbenches and are commercially available from a number of vendors (Trados, STAR, IBM).

The most significant development of the 1990s was the use of MT systems on telecommunication networks, both for the translation of electronic mail and for the translation of information "pages." There are now a number of systems designed specifically for these purposes, and most of the major network services (pioneered by CompuServe) are introducing MT facilities. In addition, most of the commercial developers are offering online translation services over networks based on their own software (e.g. Systran, Globalink). The application to electronic messages and information resources is placing new challenges on MT systems, particularly the problems of dealing with ill-formed, elliptical and stylistically idiosyncratic texts which differ markedly from the traditional documents submitted to MT systems.

The languages of the earliest systems were mainly Russian and English, reflecting the political situation of the time. In the 1970s the main impetus was for systems to deal with the administrative needs of countries such as Canada and the European Communities, hence systems for English, French, German, and other Community languages. During the 1980s and 1990s the main focus has been the languages of international trade and communications (English, Japanese, French, German, Spanish, and to a lesser extent Chinese, Korean, and Italian). On the other hand, the needs of Third World countries for scientific and technical textbooks in their own languages (mainly translations from English) are still not being fully met, although there have been individual projects that have addressed these needs.

The Future of MT

In broad terms, the use of MT can be classified as the satisfaction of three main requirements, for each of which different types of systems may be more appropriate than others. The first demand is the traditional one of *"translation for dissemination"*: the production of translations of publishable quality. It has been met with sometimes mixed success by the traditional mainframe systems dealing with large amounts of documentation which is post-edited by human translators. Cost-effective use of the sometimes poor output can be best achieved by control of input texts for terminological consistency, unambiguous use of vocabulary, and simplified sentence structures. It is clear that in the immediate future, such business and administrative systems will continue to expand and improve.

For some corporations, translation agencies, and many freelance translators the more attractive alternative is the translation workstation, incorporating terminological management and access to stores of previously approved translations ("translation memories"), and with facilities for full or partial automatic translation when required. They will enable most translators to increase their productivity of quality translations while maintaining traditional working methods.

The cheaper personal computer systems may also be used by some translators for producing translations of publishable quality, even though the output is generally poorer than that from older mainframe systems and requires more post-editing. However, the software for many of the larger systems is now becoming available for cheaper machines and this option will therefore be increasingly cost-effective for the professional translator in appropriate circumstances.

It is more likely that the cheaper systems will be used, as they are already, for the second basic demand *"translation for assimilation."* The information explosion of the second half of this century is raising the need for analysts, researchers, journalists, and the general public to extract information from foreign language texts. The need is not for "perfect" full translation but for "understandable" rough renditions. In the past, the older mainframe systems served this purpose—particularly those installed at military and government organizations. In the future, most of this demand will be met by cheap microcomputer-based software. A major incentive for development is the increased accessibility of vast amounts of online information over networks, and future systems for individual users will need to be seamlessly integrated with other documentation systems (information retrieval, abstracting, paraphrasing, etc.).

The third basic category of demand is *"translation for dialogue."* Historically, translation of conversation and correspondence has been done occasionally and irregularly by translators or bilinguals in organizations. The coming of electronic mail and electronic discussion groups is already changing the perspective. There is a growing demand for translation of conversations or personal interchanges, which only a fully automatic real-time system can satisfy, and a challenge for the future is the development of systems for this particular environment. However, as with translation for assimilation, the quality can be at as low a level as acceptable without distortion of the message, and it is surprising how tolerant many users can be.

In other circumstances a higher level of quality is necessary. For example, a businessperson wanting to correspond with a foreign company, place orders, arrange meetings, etc. will need to be assured that the output in a probably unfamiliar target language is accurate and culturally acceptable. There has already been research on "interactive analysis" systems in which computers collaborate with senders in their own languages for the generation of texts which contain no ambiguities and which can be readily translated into idiomatic and appropriate target language messages. The result is not "translation" as such (since there may be no original text), but the reliable conveyance of information.

Most commercial systems will continue to be based on transfer and interlingua approaches; in time, more will incorporate some use of knowledge-based techniques and statistical methods, and with the availability of large multilingual text corpora there will come more refined forms of example-based methods. The output quality may well improve, although not such that no revision is needed for the purposes of publication (dissemination). The improvements, although perhaps imperceptible over short time-scales, will significantly encourage greater use for purposes of information assimilation and for electronic dialogue.

There will continue to be active research for the development of speech translation, where the latent demand is obviously huge. Initially systems will be restricted to highly specific domains (as current research projects indicate) and working prototypes can be expected within the next decade. Apart from applications in telephone communication, systems will probably be designed for use with online databases and multilingual information access tools. Commercial exploitation will depend on success in overcoming the formidable problems of combining speech technology and appropriate automatic dialogue translation.

It is clear that MT is not a threat to the employment of translators; indeed computer aids are already improving their productivity and job satisfaction. MT is primarily an aid to multilingual communication, with its future greatest potential in the area of information assimilation and electronic communication. Its fortune will rest on fruitful interaction between the researchers of experimental systems investigating new methods and theories, the developers of commercial systems exploiting well-tested methods in cost-effective practical systems, and the clear perception of the real needs of translators and other potential users of translation systems.

Further Reading

For general introductions to MT *see* Arnold *et al.* (1994) or Hutchins and Somers (1992); for the general history of MT *see* Hutchins (1986); for descriptions of current systems and developments *see* Hutchins (1988, 1994, 1995), Mason and Rinsche (1995), Newton (1992), Slocum (1988), and Vasconcellos (1988).

Bibliography

1960. Bar-Hillel, Y. "The Present Status of Automatic Translation of Languages," *Advances in Computers*, **1**, 91–163.
1966. ALPAC. *Language and machines: computers in translation and linguistics.* A report by the Automatic Language Processing Advisory Committee. Washington, DC: National Academy of Sciences.
1970. Wood, W. "Transition Network Grammars for Natural Language Analysis," *Comm. of the ACM*, **13**, 591–606.
1984. Kay, M. "Functional Unification Grammar: A Formalism for Machine Translation," in *Coling 84* (Stanford University), 75–78.
1986. Hutchins, W. J. *Machine Translation: Past, Present, Future.* Chichester: Ellis Horwood; New York: Halsted Press.
1988. Hutchins, W. J. "Recent Developments in Machine Translation: A Review of the Last Five Years," in *New Directions in Machine Translation* (ed. D. Maxwell *et al.*). Dordrecht: Foris, 7–62.
1988. Slocum, J. (ed.) *Machine Translation Systems.* Cambridge: Cambridge University Press.
1988. Vasconcellos, M. (ed.) *Technology as Translation Strategy.* Binghamton, NY: State University of New York.
1992. Hutchins, W. J., and Somers, H. L. *An Introduction to Machine Translation.* London: Academic Press.
1992. Newton, J. (ed.) *Computers in Translation: a Practical Appraisal.* London/New York: Routledge.
1994. Arnold, D., Balkan, L., Humphreys, R. L., Meijer, S., and Sadler, L. *Machine Translation: an Introductory Guide.* Manchester/Oxford: NCC Blackwell.
1994. Hutchins, W. J. "Research Methods and System Designs in Machine Translation: A Ten-year Review, 1984–1994," in *Machine Translation Ten Years On.* International conference, 12–14 November 1994, Cranfield University.
1995. Hutchins, W. J. "A New Era in Machine Translation Research," *Aslib Proceedings*, **47**, 211–219.
1995. Mason, J., and Rinsche, A. *Translation Technology Products.* London: Ovum Ltd.

W. John Hutchins

MACRO

For articles on related subjects *see* ARGUMENT; ASSEMBLER; MACHINE AND ASSEMBLY LANGUAGE PROGRAMMING; PREPROCESSOR; PROGRAMMING LANGUAGES; SOFTWARE PORTABILITY; and SUBPROGRAM.

In its simplest form, a *macro* is a single operation that stands for an arbitrarily long sequence of operations. Historically, macros grew out of assembly language, and it is useful to start with this case as the general principles carry over to all the other cases.

Assume, for instance, that at several points in a program a programmer needs to increase a variable, whose name is COUNT by 1. Assume further that this takes three assembly language instructions:

```
LOAD   COUNT
ADD    ONE
STORE  COUNT
```

It would be wasteful of a programmer's time to keep writing out these three instructions in full. It would be much better to choose a single name (BUMPCOUNT, say) to stand for these instructions, and then to write the name each time it was necessary to specify the three instructions. The source program would then be processed according to Fig. 1.

A *macro definition* defines BUMPCOUNT and the instructions that are to replace it. In practice, there would probably be several other macro definitions as well. The macro processor then scans the program, replacing each occurrence of BUMPCOUNT by its expanded form. It would similarly process any other macros that had been defined. As a result of this, the program is then in pure assembly language and can be passed on to the assembler, which processes it in the normal way.

A key point about Fig. 1, which carries over to almost all applications of macros, is that there is a *preprocessor* (q.v.) to the underlying software, in this case the assembler. The preprocessor processes the macros and passes the result to the underlying software which is completely unaware of the macros. Macros are therefore a way to allow users to define small extensions to the language that the underlying software supports without having to modify that software. Since this is a widespread need, macros are used in a variety of environments. They find uses in high-level programming languages; for example, in Lisp (q.v.) they can be used to define new control structures (q.v.). They also find uses in such software as spreadsheets (q.v.) and word processors; here the "language" is the set of commands that the word processor (q.v.) or spreadsheet accepts, and a macro is a way of defining a new command that is a combination of the existing ones. Sometimes macros are defined by a single user and are specific to one particular application; sometimes a group of macros is put into a library that is accessible to any user.

Often the key advantage of a macro is that it is easy to change what it stands for. At a trivial level, a macro called LIMIT may be defined as the number 100, but if necessary its definition could be changed to make it 200: all the places where LIMIT is used are changed accordingly.

Macros can have arguments. To return to the example of the BUMPCOUNT macro, the defect of this macro as it stands is that it works only for one variable, COUNT. In practice, it would be much more useful to have a general macro (called, say, BUMP) that could be used to increment *any* variable by 1. This can, in fact, be done. The name of the variable to be incremented is written immediately after BUMP, and is called the *argument* of the macro. The macro processor can be told to insert the argument at various points in the replacement of the macro. Thus,

```
BUMP name
```

would be replaced by

```
LOAD   name
ADD    ONE
STORE  name
```

where any name of a variable could occur as *name*.

It is possible to have more than one argument to a macro. For example, it would be possible to specify a macro of the form

```
PRODUCT X, Y, Z
```

which for any X, Y, and Z would compute Z to be the product of X and Y.

Carrying this further, the macro processor may support conditional statements and iteration, so that, when a macro is expanded, the macro processor looks at the arguments and perhaps executes a program to generate the consequent replacement; for example the replacement of the macro might be different depending on whether the argument was FAST or CONCISE. Portable software written in high-level languages like C or C++ often uses conditional macros to specify which subprogram libraries to use when they vary from one operating system to another.

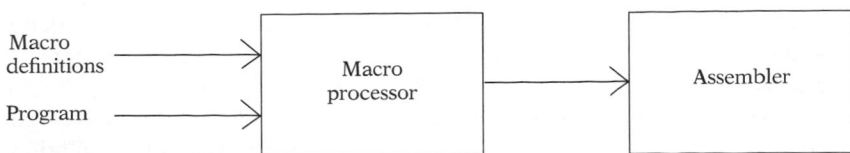

Figure 1. Information flow in macro processing.

Some confuse the concept of a macro and that of a subroutine but the difference is clear-cut. A macro is actually replaced by its expanded form. Hence, if a program contains n occurrences of a macro, then n copies of the instructions it stands for are inserted into the program. (Note, however, that, if the macro possesses arguments, the instructions need not be identical in all the cases.) A subroutine, on the other hand, involves a break in the flow of a program. If a sequence of instructions occurs frequently in a program, then these can be written as a subroutine, and each occurrence in the program is replaced by an instruction to jump to this subroutine, execute it, and then return. There is then only one copy of the sequence of instructions, a trade-off in which running time has been sacrificed to conserve memory space. Viewed at a more fundamental level, a subroutine is a run-time replacement and a macro a replacement at the time of translation.

Bibliography

1960. McIlroy, M. D. "Macro Instruction Extensions of Compiler Languages," *Comm. of the ACM*, **3**, *4*, 214–220. (This is a classic early paper on macros and gives a good insight into their potential power.)
1974. Brown, P. J. *Macro Processors and Techniques for Portable Software*. New York: John Wiley.
Manuals for macros incorporated in various software products.

Peter J. Brown

MAGNETIC DISK

See DISKETTE; HARD DISK; and MEMORY: AUXILIARY.

MAGNETIC STORAGE MEDIA

See MEMORY: AUXILIARY.

MAIN MEMORY

See MEMORY: MAIN.

MAINFRAME

For articles on related subject *see* CENTRAL PROCESSING UNIT; and MEMORY: MAIN.

The term *mainframe* as a single word has come to be used as a designation of medium- and large-scale computers that contain a "main frame" as defined in this article; thus, we speak of a *mainframe* computer in contrast to a *microcomputer, minicomputer* (*q.v.*), *personal computer*, or *workstation* (*q.v.*).

Originally, the *mainframe* of a computer system was the cabinet that housed its central processor and main memory. It is, therefore, separate from the peripheral devices (disks, printers, tape drives, etc.) and device controllers. Typically, it was the largest component in size and cost, but modern electronics has allowed great reductions in both in recent years. The mainframe usually had many indicator lights (sometimes as part of the operator's console) to show fault conditions, memory contents, etc. The central processor and main memory were housed together as an aid in increasing processing speeds (cable lengths will be short) and improving reliability (e.g. both will be at similar temperatures and humidities). The term *mainframe* comes from the use of "frame" as a device to hold electronics (rack is also frequently used), and the frame holding the electronics that does the computing might reasonably be called the *main frame*.

In modern systems with very large main memory, some memory modules are housed in cabinets separate from the mainframe. Frequently, they are attached and thus become part of the mainframe cabinet. Multiprocessor systems with more than one central processor (CPU) are referred to as two- or three-mainframe systems, in which case the mainframe refers only to the CPU and not to the main memory.

Chester L. Meek

MAINTENANCE OF COMPUTERS

For articles on related subjects *see* FAULT-TOLERANT COMPUTING; HARDWARE RELIABILITY; PERFORMANCE OF COMPUTERS; and REDUNDANCY.

This article focuses on the *maintenance* of computers and large computer systems but not microprocessors (*q.v.*) which require specialized, automatic testing techniques. Like all sophisticated equipment, computers undergo the life cycle of repair, check-out, operational readiness, failure, and back to repair. When the cost of a machine's not being in service is high, methods must be applied to reduce these out-of-service, or *downtime*, periods.

Preventive Maintenance

One means of reducing the direct cost associated with an unexpected system failure is to provide scheduled downtimes for the purpose of preventive maintenance. Obviously, a deliberately scheduled shutdown is less disruptive than that due to an unexpected system failure. During the downtime the general idea is to tune up the system so that things that are in marginal working condition will be identified and upgraded. Diagnosis should be made by exercising all aspects of the system to catch latent failures and those that may have already occurred but have been lying undetected. Failed portions of the system are likely to be undetected if they have never been called into service, and therefore their operational readiness would not have been verified.

Typically, most computing centers use a few hours every week (say, Saturday mornings) for scheduled preventive maintenance. Specially prepared diagnostic programs may be run to exercise the hardware, benchmark (q.v.) programs may be run to verify timing and accuracy considerations, and peripherals may be serviced by oiling, removing dust, replacing ribbons, etc. The typical cyclical behavior of a maintained system is shown in Fig. 1.

Maintainability

For the purposes of better understanding and for controlling maintenance requirements, we will attempt to quantify the foregoing considerations by defining the applicable terms, such as *maintainability* and *availability*, as well as other related terms. A qualitative definition of maintainability *M* is given by Goldman and Slattery (1967) as the characteristics (both qualitative and quantitative) of material design and installation which make it possible to meet operational objectives with a minimum expenditure of maintenance effort (manpower, personnel skill, test equipment, technical data, and maintenance support facilities) under operational environment conditions in which scheduled and unscheduled maintenance will be performed.

The preceding qualification, like the qualitative definition of reliability, can also be expressed quantitatively by means of probability theory. Thus, quantitatively, according to Goldman and Slattery (1967), maintainability is a characteristic of design and installation

which is expressed as the *probability* that an item will be restored to specified conditions within a given *period of time* when maintenance action is performed in accordance with prescribed procedures and resources. Mathematically, this can be expressed as

$$M = 1 - e^{-t/MTTR}$$

where *t* is the specified time to repair, and *MTTR* is the mean time to repair.

Availability

Availability refers to the probability that a system will be operative (up), and is expressed as

$$A = \frac{\text{uptime}}{\text{downtime} + \text{uptime}}$$

or equivalently as

$$A = \frac{MTBF}{MTTR + MTBF}$$

where

$$MTBF = \text{mean time between failures}$$
$$MTTR = \text{mean time to repair.}$$

The quantitative definition of availability assumes a system model where all faults are immediately detected at the time of their occurrence, and fault location and repair action are initiated immediately. More complex availability models have also been developed that do not make these simplifying assumptions.

Methods for Predicting Maintainability

The military handbook *Maintainability Prediction Techniques* describes a "checklist" method of predicting maintainability. Three checklists are used: the first

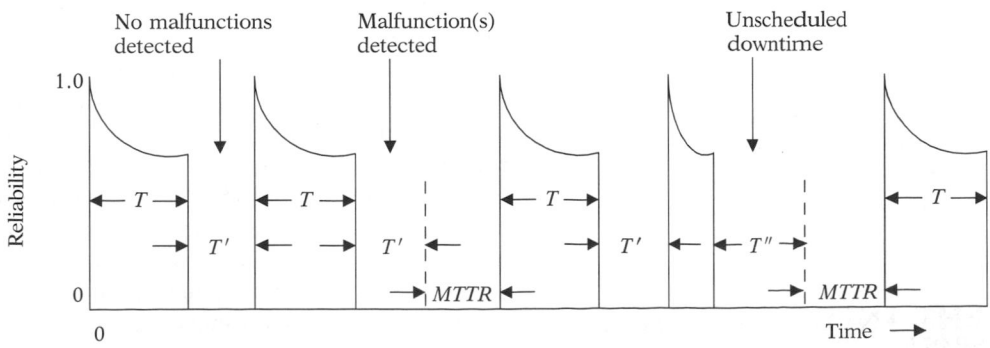

T = maximum allowed "up" time
T' = downtime due to preventive maintenance
T'' = unscheduled diagnosis
MTTR = mean time to repair

Figure 1. Cyclical behavior of a maintained system.

for physical design factors, the second for personnel factors, and the third for support factors. The physical design factors encompass such equipment features as physical aspects and tool requirements, and its checklist has items such as accessibility, packaging, testpoints, internal latches, and built-in test equipment. The personnel factors include skill level, attitudes, and experience of the system operators. The support factors cover logistics and maintenance organization.

These checklists are used to evaluate each step essential to maintenance. A series of questions is raised: e.g. "Is external access adequate for visual inspection and manipulative action?" The answer is given a score between 4 and 0, inclusive, where a "4" represents an unqualified yes and a zero an unqualified no, with intermediate values representing intermediate situations. The scores in the three checklists are then totaled to give a score for checklist A, checklist B, and checklist C. The necessary predicted maintenance time (M) is then given by the following empirical formula:

$$M = \exp(3.54651 - 0.02512A - 0.03055B - 0.01093C).$$

The preceding description is a very brief summary of the MIL-HDBK-472 checklist method.

Other institutions and companies have also developed their own checklists, scoring criteria, and empirical formulas appropriate to their equipment. In the absence of checklists specifically tailored to one's own equipment, experience has shown that the procedures and equations given in MIL-HDBK-472 serve as a good approximation.

Bibliography

1967. Goldman, A. S., and Slattery, T. B. *Maintainability*. New York: John Wiley.
1988. Morris, S. F. *et al. RADC Reliability Engineer's Toolkit: An Application Oriented Guide for the Practicing Reliability Engineer.* Rome Air Development Center Air Force Systems Command, Griffis Air Force Base, NY 13441-5700 (July).
1995. Blanchard, B. S., Verma, D., and Peterson, E. L. *Maintainability: A Key to Effective Serviceability and Maintenance Management.* New York: John Wiley.
1996. Eberling, C. E. *An Introduction to Reliability and Maintainability Engineering.* New York: McGraw-Hill.
IEEE. *Proceedings of the Annual Reliability and Maintainability Symposium.*

Frank P. Mathur

MANAGEMENT INFORMATION SYSTEMS (MIS)

For articles on related subjects *see* ADMINISTRATIVE APPLICATIONS; DATA PROCESSING; DATABASE MANAGEMENT SYSTEM; INFORMATION RETRIEVAL; RELATIONAL DATABASE; SYSTEMS ANALYST; and TRANSACTION PROCESSING.

The meanings of the terms *management information system* (MIS) and *information system* (IS) are identical and interchangeable in an organizational context. They refer to the system providing technology-based information and communication services in an organization. They also refer to the organizational function that manages the system. The concept of a management information system enlarges the scope of information processing to encompass not only applications for transactions and operations, but also applications that support administrative and management functions, support organizational communications and coordination, and add value to products and services.

Historical Development of Management Information Systems

When computers were first used in organizations in the mid-1950s, the applications were primarily the simple processing of transaction records and preparation of business documents and standard reports. This use was termed *data processing* (DP) or *electronic data processing* (EDP). The business function for developing and managing the processing systems was also termed data processing.

By the mid-1960s, many users and builders of information processing systems developed a more comprehensive vision of what computers could do for organizations. This vision was termed a *management information system* (MIS). It enlarged the scope of data processing to add systems for supporting management and administrative activities including planning, scheduling, analysis, and decision making. The business function to build and manage the management information system was often termed MIS.

In the 1980s and 1990s, there was a merging of computer and communications technologies. The organizational use of information technology was extended to internal networks (*intranets*), *local area networks* (*q.v.*), external networks that connect an organization to its suppliers and customers (*see* NETWORKS, COMPUTER), and communications systems that enable employees to work alone or in groups with greater effectiveness and efficiency. Many organizations were able to achieve competitive advantage by the use of information and information technology in products, services, and business processes. Innovative applications of information technology created value by providing customized services at any time and at any location, and information systems began to prompt changes in organizational structures and processes.

Although the scope of systems providing information technology services has increased dramatically, the broad concept of MIS as a system that combines transaction and operational requirements with administrative and management support remains valid. The term MIS is still in common use despite a recent tendency to use the simpler term *information system*. The function that builds and manages the system is variously called *information systems, information services* or *information management.*

The information system (management information system) of an organization consists of the information technology infrastructure, application systems, and personnel that employ information technology to deliver information and communications services for transaction processing, operations, administration, and management of an organization. The system uses a blend of computer and communications hardware and software, automation (*q.v.*), human–machine interaction, and internal and external repositories of data.

Although one can have an information system without use of a computer and associated electronic communication, the modern concept of a management information system assumes the use of such technology. An automated information system allows tasks to be done faster and more efficiently, removes many of the constraints of manual methods, and promotes new ways of doing things.

The Purposes of an Organizational Information System

An organizational information system exists because an organization exists. To achieve its purpose, an organization must (1) define the characteristics of goods and services to be provided, (2) deliver those goods and services to customers, and (3) manage, direct, coordinate, and control the organization and its resources. Information technology is pervasive in and vital to these three organizational objectives. The objectives for an information system follow naturally from the organizational purposes:

1. *Add functionality and information value to products and services.* Information and information processing are important to the products and services provided by an organization, either incorporated in their functionality or as value added through information processing. Examples are information and communication functions designed into products such as automobiles or cellular phones (*see* EMBEDDED SYSTEMS) and additional information provided to customers through online banking or investment services (*see* PERSONAL FINANCE).

2. *Support transaction and operational processes.* Information, information processing, and communications are integral parts of the processes by which goods and services are provided by an organization. Information technology is vital in achieving quality, short cycle time, and efficiency in transaction processing and operational processes.

3. *Support administrative and management activities.* Information, communications, and information processing are essential to administrative and management activities of coordination and control. They are also fundamental to management analysis, decision making, and strategy formulation.

In addition to its role in achieving organization purposes, information and information processing are significant factors in the design of organizational structures for both operations and management. Information technologies enable improvements and innovations in organization design.

The Structure of an Organizational Information System

The structure of a management information system consists of a technical infrastructure, databases and other repositories, and a portfolio of application systems. The technical infrastructure provides information technology, databases and other repositories provide the data needed by the organization, and the application systems provide specific processing procedures and routines. The application systems can be classified logically (and sometimes physically) into *transaction processing* (*q.v.*), operations, and administrative and management support. The elements (technical infrastructure, repositories, transaction processing systems, operations systems, and administrative and management support systems) will be defined in this section; the administrative and management support systems will be described in more detail later in the article.

1. *Technical infrastructure.* This consists of computer and communications hardware, system software, and the repository management software. It provides processing, communications, and storage capabilities required by application software systems. It includes transaction networks, fax, telephony, and so forth. The infrastructure may contain a variety of technology configurations such as a centralized system, systems serving single locations or departments, and systems serving workgroups or single individuals.

2. *Databases and other repositories.* The repositories store data required for transactions, operations, analysis, decision making, explanations and justifications, and government/legal requirements. Repositories have varying scopes such as the entire enterprise, parts of the organization (divisions, offices, departments, etc.), groups, and individuals. The stores include data about entities relevant to the

organization: text and multimedia (*q.v.*) stores of analyses, reports, documents, data search results, email, faxes, conversations, etc.; and stores of procedures and directions for performing organizational activities including models for analysis and decision making. The repositories are also termed databases, files, knowledge bases, and model bases.

3. *Transaction processing systems.* Transaction processing systems record and process business transactions such as accepting a customer order, placing an order with a vendor, making a payment, and so forth.

4. *Operations systems.* These applications schedule and direct the operations of the organization as products are produced and distributed and services are scheduled and performed.

5. *Administrative and management support systems.* These applications support knowledge workers (including managers) in performing tasks individually and collaboratively. They support management requirements for data, analysis, reports, and feedback for operational control, management control, and strategic planning. They support team work and other collaboration in analysis and management activities.

The MIS Related to the Functions of an Organization

An organization is typically organized with specialized functions. Examples are marketing, production, logistics, human resources, finance and accounting, and information systems. These functions exist because of the efficiency and effectiveness of specialization. To illustrate, accounting reports and budgets may be widely used throughout the organization, but the preparation of reports to investors, governments, regulators, and so forth requires specialized knowledge and specialized systems. The charts of account must be developed and maintained by specialists to meet the needs of the entire organization; it would be chaos for each person to develop a chart of accounts. Similar logic applies to the other functions in an organization.

The application portfolio may be planned and organized around core transaction processes that yield databases of transactions plus specialized applications for the different functions. There is a set of applications supporting the marketing function, a set for human resources, etc. Many of the functional applications are used by only one function, but many are interrelated. For example, the production plans and production results are inputs to the budgeting and accounting system (for financial planning) and the human resources systems (for staffing, training, etc.).

Most organizations employ a similar set of basic applications for business functions. Planning and implementing a comprehensive set of basic applications is frequently termed ERP (Enterprise Resources Planning). Vendors of enterprise software provide these basic applications as packages. The enterprise package has facilities for tailoring them to individual organizations. Organizations can extend these basic enterprise systems with applications that provide improved functionality or unique capabilities. In other words, enterprise systems provide the basic application building blocks for the information system of an organization, but innovative organizations have applications for different functions and administrative and management support that extend beyond these core functions, analyses, and reports.

MIS Applications to Support Levels of Management Activities

The use of information technology for administrative and management support extends the nature of the information system from a transaction and simple reporting system to one that supports the higher-level administrative and managerial activities of the organization. The administrative and management support can be classified both according to support for levels of management activities and also in terms of support for knowledge work.

The levels of management activity define the three control objectives to be achieved and the time horizons for each. Operational management achieves short-term operational control in delivering goods and services, mid-term management control is directed at meeting market and financial objectives, and long-term strategic direction seeks to adapt to changing conditions and new opportunities. As illustrated in Fig. 1, the information system support for management activities is often

Figure 1. Management information system support for management. (Reprinted by permission from Davis and Olson, 1985.)

defined as a pyramid with more structure and programmed decisions at the lower levels and less structure and nonprogrammed decisions at the higher levels.

OPERATIONAL CONTROL

Operational control is the management process of insuring that operational activities associated with delivery of goods and services and internal administrative procedures are carried out effectively and efficiently. Operational control makes use of fairly stable pre-established procedures, communication, and decision rules. The decisions, communications, and actions cover relatively short time periods (a day, a week, or a month depending on the cycle of activities being controlled). The information system support for operational control consists of access to transaction records, operational reports, communications, and inquiry processing in support of operational analysis and decision making. Data used in reports and analyses is primarily from internal transactions. Some examples of information processing in support of operational decision making are the following:

◆ When an item is withdrawn from inventory for sale or use in production, the information system application not only records the transaction and produces a transaction document if required, but also, using pre-established algorithms, examines the balance on hand to evaluate the need for replenishment. If replenishment is indicated, an action document is produced for review by an analyst before an order is placed. The system can reduce the order placement time by communicating with the vendor's scheduling system and placing the order using organization-to-organization communications and order document protocols.

◆ An analysis of replenishment orders not received within the standard times for the items ordered is produced for administrative follow-up. When an analyst reviews an order, the system allows a lookup of all current orders with that vendor, a lookup of where the items are used (to evaluate the impact of the delay), and similar information useful in deciding how to deal with the delay.

MANAGEMENT CONTROL

Management control information is needed by managers of organizational units such as divisions, factories, departments, profit centers, etc. The information is needed to measure performance, decide on control actions, formulate new decision rules, and allocate resources. Management actions based on control information have a time horizon longer than operational control: a month, quarter, or year. Management control reports typically compare results to some standard of performance in order to calculate variances from expected results and to analyze the causes. Analyses and reports use transaction data and plans/budgets from the organization and also some external data relative to the environment, competitive products and services, competitor costs and pricing, and so forth. Management control applications support planning and budgeting, variance analysis, problem analysis, inquiry capabilities to "drill down" from high-level reports to detailed analyses and explore alternative explanations and solutions, and current market and competitor information. Decisions about pricing, promotion, product mix, and so forth depend on both reports applying traditional costing techniques and analyses exploring cost behaviors (fixed costs, joint costs, marginal costs) with different decision scenarios. Fig. 2 illustrates a typical management control report for a sales manager.

STRATEGIC PLANNING

Strategic planning develops the strategy an organization will follow to achieve its objectives of profitability, quality, and service. Strategic planning assists decisions

Demo Company
Report of Sales and Gross Profits on Sales
Month Ended 31 March 1999

	Sales dollars (000)		Gross profit (000)		Analysis of gross profit variance (000)		
	Actual/ planned	Variance from plan	Actual/ planned	Variance	Volume	Price	Mix
Jan	3,781	19*	1398	122*	61*	12*	49*
Feb	3,142	42	1290	50	21	5*	34
Mar	3,761	239*	1173	210*	159*	38*	13*
Apr	4,050		1620				
May	4,100		1640				

Figure 2. Management control report with variance analysis for sales manager (* indicates a negative variance). April and May numbers are planned values.

Demo Company
Market Share Analysis
for Past Five Years and
Five-Year Demand Forecast
for Squidgits

		Total units (000)	Estimated market share (units (000) and %)			
			Demo Co.	Svarto, Inc.	Vito Co.	Andra
Past	1995	12,500	1,900 (15.2)	3,137 (25.1)	6,313 (50.5)	1,150 (9.2)
	1996	13,300	2,168 (16.3)	3,724 (28.0)	6,198 (46.6)	1,210 (9.1)
	1997	12,000	2,100 (17.5)	3,384 (28.2)	5,376 (44.8)	1,083 (9.5)
	1998	15,600	2,652 (17.0)	4,555 (29.2)	6,864 (44.0)	1,529 (9.8)
	1999	14,900	2,742 (18.4)	4,232 (28.4)	1,586 (44.2)	1,340 (9.0)
Forecast	2000	16,200				
	2001	16,900				
	2002	17,500				
	2003	17,500				
	2004	17,000				

Figure 3. Strategic planning report showing past and projected demand and market shares of major competitors.

about fundamental issues of what business to be in and how to conduct it. Examples are adding, changing, or dropping products, product lines, and channels of distribution. It may include sales, mergers, or acquisitions that change where and how business is conducted. The time horizon for decision making is several years. Data requirements include internal data and significant external data. Projections of competition, technology, capital requirements, regulations, and shifts in demand are critical. Strategic planning is part of the responsibility of the management of the business functions as well as top management, and often involves specialists who organize and interpret competitive intelligence and market trends. The information system provides certain structured strategic planning applications and access to internal and external data for analysis, projection, simulations, etc. Fig. 3 illustrates a strategic planning report showing comparison of company sales and market share with those of major competitors.

MIS Support for Knowledge Work

Early concepts of a management information system incorporated support for analysis and decision making, applications called *decision support systems*. Such support was originally intended for individual decision making but was later extended to decision making by groups. Communications applications were developed to improve collaborative work of all types. Personal computers and workstations (*q.v.*) have provided significant processing and communications capabilities for every worker. These developments may be described as the use of information technology in support of "knowledge work." As defined in Davis and Naumann

(1997), "*knowledge work* is human mental work performed to generate useful information. In doing it, knowledge workers access data, use knowledge, employ mental models, and apply significant concentration and attention."

Examples of knowledge workers include financial analysts, systems analysts (*q.v.*), managers, accountants, and designers. Valued for their knowledge and expertise, they either have the knowledge required for their work or know where to find it. The activities of knowledge workers receive significant benefits from information technology. Some examples of knowledge work are scanning and monitoring information sources, searching for information, formulating plans and making decisions, assigning responsibilities, organizing events, scheduling activities and resource use, authoring, performing evaluations, decision making, persuading others to adopt a plan or decision, and motivating behavioral changes.

One of the well developed areas of information system support for knowledge work is decision making. In planning and designing decision support applications, MIS developers have applied the *Simon framework* for decision making. This consists of three phases: intelligence, design, and choice. The intelligence phase is discovering problems and opportunities. The MIS support for this phase requires access to external data in order to scan the external environment plus database access to search internal data. The search processes can be both structured using predefined search and analysis processes or unstructured scanning and unique analyses. Adaptive analysis through use of neural networks (*q.v.*) may aid in identifying shifts in demands and

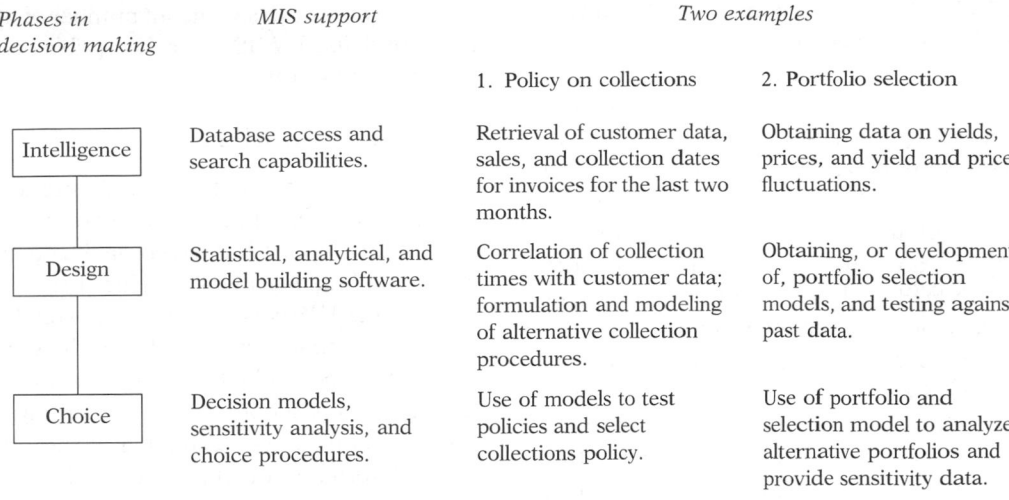

Phases in decision making	MIS support	Two examples	
		1. Policy on collections	2. Portfolio selection
Intelligence	Database access and search capabilities.	Retrieval of customer data, sales, and collection dates for invoices for the last two months.	Obtaining data on yields, prices, and yield and price fluctuations.
Design	Statistical, analytical, and model building software.	Correlation of collection times with customer data; formulation and modeling of alternative collection procedures.	Obtaining, or development of, portfolio selection models, and testing against past data.
Choice	Decision models, sensitivity analysis, and choice procedures.	Use of models to test policies and select collections policy.	Use of portfolio and selection model to analyze alternative portfolios and provide sensitivity data.

Figure 4. MIS support for phases in decision making with examples from the finance function.

other key factors affecting an organization. The decision design phase—for generation of alternatives—involves inventing, developing, and analyzing possible courses of action. The MIS support for decision design consists of statistical, analytical, and model-building software. The final step in the Simon model is choice. The MIS support for choice consists of various decision models, sensitivity analysis, and choice procedures. Expert systems (*q.v.*) may be useful in some applications. Fig. 4 gives examples of MIS support for two examples of decision making.

The Organization Function for MIS

The management information systems or information management function is a specialized organization function with responsibility to plan, design, build, maintain, operate, and manage the information infrastructure and applications. This includes acquisition and management of both internal staff and external resources. It also includes technical, advisory, and educational support to aid users in applying appropriate technology to their tasks.

The major activities of the MIS function are:

◆ Provide input to development of organizational strategy and plans for use of information technology to achieve competitive goals and to support organization objectives.

◆ Development and maintenance of the MIS plan and budget for the organization.

◆ Design, development, operation, and maintenance of infrastructures and support systems that enable organizational use of information technology.

◆ Set standards and quality control for desktop information technology and end-user systems acquisition, operation, and use.

◆ Development and operation of organizational databases.

◆ Acquisition or development and operation of a portfolio of applications for the organization.

◆ Provide information technology expertise and education for users in the organization.

The information management function may include both a separate organization function and personnel assigned to organization functions that use the technology. In other words, a central group may plan and implement the organizational infrastructure, etc., while information system personnel in marketing, human resources, etc. provide direct support for the information technology use within the functions.

A combination of technical expertise and organization function expertise is required for many projects such as developing applications. Team members include technical specialists in information technology and users whose knowledge and experience are in the function being supported and the tasks being performed. Simple applications may be developed by users themselves (with or without assistance), but these often lack robust features and controls that allow broader use.

Sources of Information on MIS

Major international professional societies for information system practitioners are the Society for Information Management (SIM) and the Association for

Information Technology Professionals (AITP). SIM is primarily for MIS executives. It holds conferences and has local chapters. AITP is a broad-based organization oriented to information processing in organizations. It has local chapters and holds annual conferences. Special interest groups of larger organizations focus on information systems. SIGMIS (Special Interest Group on MIS) is part of the Association for Computing Machinery (ACM—*q.v.*). It publishes a quarterly journal, *Database*. INFORMS has an information systems group, the College on Information Systems. The International Federation for Information Processing (IFIP—*q.v.*) is organized as a federation of societies from different countries. Its technical activities are performed by technical committees (TC). The technical committee for information systems is TC8 (Information Systems). It has nine working groups on various issues in information systems. They hold working conferences and produce conference reports. Information on IFIP and TC8 can be obtained from the IFIP Website: `http://www.ifip.or.at`. In addition to international organizations, there are professional organizations and special interest groups in many countries.

The information system academic community is international. Although each country and/or area has an organization for information system academics, there is strong participation in international academic conferences and local and area conferences often attract faculty from other countries. The main international academic conference is the International Conference on Information Systems (ICIS), begun in 1979. The main international academic organization is the Association for Information Systems (AIS). It publishes two electronic journals: *Communications of the AIS* and *Journal of the AIS*. It is a sponsor of ICIS and has affiliation with major regional conferences: Americas Conference on Information Systems (AMCIS), European Conference on Information Systems (ECIS), and the Pacific Asia Conference on Information Systems (PACIS). AIS provides information not only on its conferences but also affiliated conferences (`http://www.aisnet.org`). AIS manages ISWorld Net, a comprehensive source of information on the academic field (`http://www.isworld.org`). AIS, ACM, and AITP have cooperated on model curricula for information systems.

The general computing and management science journals often contain articles on MIS topics. The most significant sources are *Communications of the ACM* and *Management Science*. The most widely read academic journals devoted to MIS are the *MIS Quarterly* and *Information Systems Research*. General management journals such as the *Harvard Business Review* and *Sloan Management Review* regularly have MIS articles. *Computing Reviews* of the ACM reviews MIS articles. There are a significant number of other general and specialized MIS journals published in North America and Europe.

The Future of MIS

The 1960s MIS concept of an organizational information system supporting not only routine transactions and routine reports but also organizational communications and management activities has been achieved. The original MIS concept has been extended to include applications that add value to products and services and that support a broad range of administrative and management functions. With the merging of computer and communications technologies the organizational use of information technology has been extended to internal and external networks, systems that connect an organization to its suppliers and customers, and systems that enable persons in organizations to perform work alone or in groups with greater effectiveness and efficiency. Many organizations have been able to achieve competitive advantage by the use of information and information technology in products, services, and business processes. Information technology-based systems have been employed to change organization structures and processes.

The future direction of MIS is likely to involve further improvements in areas that have already been changed and more support for knowledge work productivity. Advances in information technology such as voice recognition and higher transmission bandwidth (*q.v.*) will make possible improvements in transaction processing, further reductions in cycle times, and more customized products and services. Information technology has been associated with remarkable improvements in production productivity and clerical productivity, but there has been less impact on knowledge work productivity. Although information technology has been made available to all knowledge workers and information access has multiplied, the increased functionality and data access does not automatically result in improved productivity. One of the frontiers in organizational information systems is the structuring of systems, computer and communications technology, and data access, so that knowledge work productivity is enhanced.

Bibliography

1965. Anthony, R. N. *Planning and Control Systems: A Framework for Analysis.* Cambridge, MA: Harvard University Press. This is the classic framework for the activities of management. The framework applies to the design of applications in support of management.

1971. Gorry, G. A., and Scott Morton, M. S. "A Framework for Management Information Systems," *Sloan Management Review*, **13** (Fall), 55–70. The most significant framework article for defining types of information system applications in support of management decision making.

1985. Davis, G. B., and Olson, M. H. *Management Information Systems: Conceptual Foundations, Structure, and Development*, 2nd Ed. New York: McGraw-Hill. The classic text defining the structure of an MIS and its conceptual foundations.

1991. Scott Morton, M. S. (ed.) *The Corporation of the 1990s: Information Technology and Organizational Transformation*. New York: Oxford University Press. Essays on how information technology is affecting organizations in the 1990s.

1997. Davis, G. B., and Naumann, J. D. *Personal Productivity with Information Technology*. New York: McGraw-Hill. Describes how knowledge workers can improve productivity with use of desktop information technology.

1998. Laudon, K. C., and Laudon, J. P. *Management Information Systems: New Approaches to Organization and Technology*. Upper Saddle River, NJ: Prentice Hall.

1999. Groth, L. *Building Organizations with Information Technology*. London: John Wiley. A theory-based explanation of the way information technology enables organization forms and functions.

1999. Turban, E., McLean, E., and Wetherbe, J. *Information Technology for Management: Improving Quality and Productivity*. New York: John Wiley.

Gordon B. Davis

MANCHESTER UNIVERSITY COMPUTERS

For articles on related subjects *see* ATLAS; BUSH, VANNEVAR; HARTREE, DOUGLAS R.; KILBURN, TOM; WILKES, MAURICE V.; and WILLIAMS, SIR FREDERIC C.

Manchester University has played an important role in the development of computer science. As early as the 1930s, Douglas R. Hartree (1897–1958) had constructed a differential analyzer (*q.v.*), a mechanical calculating machine based upon the theoretical ideas of Lord Kelvin and the designs of the American engineer, Vannevar Bush. This was an analog device. After the Second World War, these machines were overtaken by electronic stored-program digital computers.

In 1946, Professor F. C. Williams (1911–1977) and Professor Tom Kilburn began work at Manchester University with the intention of developing a novel form of computer storage using cathode ray tubes. The system, which involved the use of the "Williams tube" (*see* WILLIAMS TUBE MEMORY) to store binary digits of information, was perfected during 1947. Kilburn reported the results, together with the outline design for a hypothetical computer, in December of that year. The team was also joined by G. C. Toothill, who, like Williams and Kilburn, had previously worked at the Telecommunications Research Establishment at Malvern. A prototype—the "baby machine," the forerunner of the Manchester Mark I—was built, and on 21 June 1948, became the world's first operational stored-program digital computer. The successful running of its first program, recorded Williams, "was the breakthrough and sparks flew in all directions."

The Manchester group doubled its size in 1948 by taking on two research students, D. B. G. Edwards and G. E. Thomas. Besides Williams and Kilburn, who provided the electrical engineering skills, Professor M. H. A. (Max) Newman (1897–1984) and Alan Turing (*q.v.*), who joined the mathematics department in 1948, gave theoretical support. Turing, for example, with Edwards and Thomas, designed a paper tape input–output system and also wrote a programming manual.

In 1948, the attention of Sir Ben Lockspeiser, the then Government Chief Scientist, was drawn to the Mark I. The result was a government contract with Ferranti Ltd to make a production version of the machine "to Professor Williams's specification." The first Ferranti Mark I was installed at Manchester University in February 1951, thereby becoming the world's first commercially available computer to be delivered. A subsequent version was named the Mark I Star. The government's involvement with Manchester University proved worthwhile: royalties from Williams's patents (the first of which had been filed on 11 December 1946 by the Ministry of Supply) gave an important boost to the National Research Development Corporation (NRDC), a government body set up to advise on and support developments in British industry.

Initially, hardware design tended to dominate in the development of Manchester University computers. However, software development for the Mark I gained considerable momentum after the appointment of R. A. Brooker in 1951. His high-level programming language, the Mark I Autocode System, was available by 1954, pre-dating Fortran by two years.

Besides building the world's first stored-program computer, as well as the world's first commercially available computer, Kilburn and his group can be credited with building the first proper transistorized

Figure 1. Part of the Manchester Mark I (1949) (courtesy National Archive for the History of Computing, University of Manchester).

computer in 1953. The Metropolitan Vickers Company later built a commercial version of the design, the MV950, which was completed in 1956.

The University's involvement with Ferranti continued through the 1950s when the design team (increasingly headed by Kilburn as Williams's interest turned to other engineering matters) was working on a Mark II computer nicknamed MEG (megacycle engine). The production version of MEG was known as the Ferranti Mercury, and the first machine was delivered in August 1957. Collaboration in these years eventually resulted in the Atlas computer, an ambitious project that pioneered many concepts in storage and addressing that are in common use today. On its official inauguration on 7 December 1962, it was considered to be the most powerful computer in the world.

By the end of the 1960s, developments elsewhere, particularly in the USA, had eroded Manchester University's lead. Nevertheless, innovation continued into the 1960s and beyond, when, with the help of the Science Research Council and the British computer firm ICL, the MU5 was built between 1969 and 1974. The MU5 heavily influenced the architecture of the ICL 2900 series computers. During the 1980s, the University was active in dataflow (q.v.) computing and in parallel declarative architecture.

In both commercial and technical terms, the legacy of these vintage years of computing was immense (42 computer patents emanated from Manchester University during 1948–1950). Through development of their computers, Manchester University pioneered the teaching of the wholly new subject of computing within the British university system. Finally, all these developments established an important link between the University and the computer industry that has lasted through various projects to the present day.

Bibliography

——. Papers of Manchester University Department of Computer Science, National Archive for the History of Computing, Manchester University.
1975. Lavington, S. H. *A History of Manchester Computers*. Manchester: National Computer Centre.
1980. Lavington, S. H. *Early British Computers*. Manchester: Manchester University Press.
1993. *IEEE Annals of the History of Computing*, **15**, 3 (Special Issue on Computing at the University of Manchester).
1998. The Virtual Museum of Manchester Computing. http://www.computer50.org/kgill/.

Geoffrey Tweedale

MARK I, HARVARD

For articles on related subjects see AIKEN, HOWARD; DIGITAL COMPUTERS, HISTORY OF: EARLY; HOPPER, GRACE MURRAY; and IBM CORPORATION.

The Mark I (or Harvard Mark I), originally named the IBM Automatic Sequence Controlled Calculator, was the first large-scale automatic computer to be completed and put into operation in the USA. The worldwide publicity concerning this machine, after its unveiling in August 1944, made known to the world at large the practicality of large-scale computing machines that would function automatically according to a programmed sequence—without error. It was for this reason that witnesses—computer pioneers—have given testimony that the "digital computing age began with the unveiling of the ASCC/Mark I in August 1944".

This machine was the brainchild of Howard Hathaway Aiken, who, in 1936, while a graduate student in electron physics engaged in research for his doctoral dissertation, encountered computational problems beyond the simple capacity of the desk calculators of those days. Aiken thereupon wrote up a formal proposal, either in late 1936 or early 1937, explaining the operations the machine was to perform and showing the kinds of mathematical problems the machine was to solve. In April 1937, he took this proposal first to the Monroe Calculating Machine Company which, despite the enthusiastic support of the chief engineer, George C. Chase, decided not to build Aiken's dream machine. Chase suggested that Aiken try IBM. At IBM, Aiken received strong support at once from the chief engineer, James Wares Bryce, and the project eventually gained the approval of Thomas J. Watson, Sr. (q.v.), President of IBM.

The overall direction of the project to construct a machine to perform the operations specified by Aiken was assigned to Clair D. Lake, but the actual day-to-day planning and construction were done by Francis (Frank) Hamilton and Benjamin Durfee, working in IBM's Endicott, NY, facility. During the early years of the work, Aiken made regular visits to Endicott, spending the greater part of two summers there. He gave detailed specifications to the IBM engineers, showed them the kinds of calculations the machine would be called upon to make, and furnished tables of constants. In the spring of 1942, Aiken (an officer in the Naval Reserves) was called to active duty and his part of the assignment was turned over to his deputy, Robert V. D. Campbell, an advanced graduate student in physics at Harvard. Campbell was eventually responsible for the initial programming and running of the machine after it had been delivered to Harvard and installed in March 1944.

Although Aiken first approached IBM in 1937, the calculator was not completed and tested until Christmas 1943, some six years later. There were many reasons for this delay, among them the pressure of war work that had a higher priority at IBM. Soon after

Figure 1. Harvard Mark I (courtesy of IBM).

the new machine had been moved to Harvard, the operation was taken over by the US Navy Bureau of Ships. The unit was under the command of Aiken, now with the rank of Commander (USNR). Among the members of his staff of programmers was Lt. (jg) Grace Hopper, USNR, later celebrated for her own contributions to computer art and science.

During the war years 1944–1945, Mark I ran almost continuously. Some of the wartime problems the machine was asked to solved were the tracing of rays in the design of telephoto lenses for the Air Force, problems in magnetic fields associated with the protection of ships from the destructive action of magnetic mines, and mathematical aspects of the design and use of radar. A specific request from a group working on radar at the Naval Research Laboratory was to produce tables of Bessel functions, a task for which Mark I was admirably suited. No doubt the most important wartime problem was a set of calculations for implosions, brought from Los Alamos to the Harvard Navy installation by John von Neumann (*q.v.*). Only a year or more later did Aiken and his staff learn that these calculations had been made in connection with the design of the atomic bomb.

As a result of the outstanding success of Mark I and the continued pressure of unsolved problems, the Navy asked Aiken in early 1945 to design and construct a second such machine. Aiken agreed and did so. In accord with Navy practice and with engineering custom at large, Aiken referred to the new machine as Mark II, whereupon the original became known simply as Mark I.

Mark I was gigantic, standing 8 feet (2.4 m) high and 51 feet (15.5 m) long. It used standard IBM parts such as electromagnetic relays, counters, cam contacts, card or tape feeds and punches, and electric typewriters. The operation of the separate parts was powered by a long horizontal rotating shaft. The machine used 530 miles (850 km) of wire and was composed of 760,000 individual parts. It weighed approximately 5 tons (4,500 kg). There were 2,200 counter wheels and 3,300 relay components.

In later language, Mark I would be described as a parallel synchronous calculator. It had a word length of 23 decimal digits, with a 24th place reserved for the algebraic sign. Calculations were done decimally. There were 60 registers for the input of constant numerical data, each one containing 24 dial switches corresponding to 24 digits. For any problem, these had to be set by hand and could then be used by the program.

The operative portion of the machine was composed of 72 registers, each of which was an "accumulator." Each such register was made up of 24 electromagnetic counter wheels—again providing the capacity for 23-digit numbers, with one place reserved for the sign. This second set of panels comprised both the store and the processing unit. A typical line of program code would instruct the machine to take the number in a given register (either a constant or a number in the store) and enter it in some designated register in the store. If there already was a number in that register, the new number would be added to it.

There were separate devices for multiplication and division and four tape readers. One was used to feed the instructions into the machine. The other three held tables of functions and could supply values as needed. There was also provision for interpolation of the values given on the tapes. Thus, there was provision for a number to be converted into some built-in function (such as a sine, an exponential, or a logarithm) before being entered into the store.

Programs were fed into the machine by punched tape (*see* PAPER TAPE). The programmer first reduced the problem to a sequence of mathematical steps and then used the "code book" to translate each step into the necessary instructions for the machine.

The speed of Mark I was slow by later standards as set by ENIAC (*q.v.*) and other electronic machines. The basic cycle time (*q.v.*) was 300 ms, the time needed to advance the program tape from one coded instruction to the next. Simple addition and subtraction required a single step or cycle, but multiplication took 20 cycles (6 sec) and division took 38 cycles (11.4 sec).

Mark I continued to function at Harvard for 14 years after the war, until it was finally retired in 1959. During that time, it continued to produce tables of Bessel functions and other mathematical functions, a task for which it was ideally suited even though it was much slower than the new electronic computers. During these years, Mark I also served generations of students at Harvard, where Aiken had established a pioneering program in what was later to be called computer science—with courses for undergraduates and graduate students leading to a master's degree or a Ph.D. Many important figures in the developing world of computers were introduced to the subject on the Harvard Mark I.

When Mark I finally ceased operation, segments of the machine were deposited in the Smithsonian Museum of American History and IBM's collection. A major portion is on public display in Harvard University's Science Center. In retrospect, the most significant aspect of Mark I may be its dramatic public demonstration that a large-scale machine can actually perform an automatic sequence of calculations according to a program and can do so without error.

Bibliography

1946. Aiken, H. H., and Hopper, G. M. "The Automatic Sequence Controlled Calculator," *Electrical Engineering (IEEE)*, **65**, 384–391, 449–454, 522–528.

1964. Aiken, H. H. "Proposed Automatic Calculating Machine," *IEEE Spectrum*, August, 62–69.

1982. Randell, B. (ed.) *The Origins of Digital Computers: Selected Papers*, 3rd Ed. New York: Springer-Verlag. Contains Aiken and Hopper (1946) and Aiken (1964).

1983. Ceruzzi, P. *Reckoners—The Prehistory of the Digital Computer: From Relays to the Stored Program Concept, 1935–1945*. Westport, CT: Greenwood Press.

1999. Cohen, I. B., Welch, G. W., and Campbell, R. V. *Makin' Numbers: Howard Aiken and the Computer*. Cambridge, MA: MIT Press.

I. Bernard Cohen

MARKUP LANGUAGES

For articles on related subjects *see* DESKTOP PUBLISHING; HYPERTEXT; TEX; TEXT EDITING SYSTEMS; and WORLD WIDE WEB.

Markup information is embedded in the text of a document but is not intended for printing or display. It may consist of instructions to a printer, commands for a Web browser, or comments to a coauthor. The form these instructions take is a function of the particular markup language used.

The most powerful language for markup is the Standard Generalized Markup Language (SGML). SGML has been an international standard since 1986 (Goldfarb, 1990) and has been used to define various specialized markup languages. The most widely used of these, and the one on which this article will focus, is Hypertext Markup Language (HTML). HTML (Raggett *et al.*, 1998), originally created by Tim Berners-Lee (*see* ENTREPRENEURS and MCDOWELL AWARD), is the markup language used in documents distributed on the World Wide Web.

Types of Markup

There are three main types of markup. Specific markup, often called *procedural markup*, is used to give display or printing instructions to a text processing system. These are most often visual indicators such as text color or font size (*see* TYPEFONT). Generalized markup, also called *descriptive markup*, is used to inform the text processing system about the components of the document. These are items such as section headings and paragraphs. *Content markup* is the use of generalized markup to identify the meaning of portions of a document. For example, in a transcription of a radio show, a section of text could be identified as "speaker," "music," or "commercial."

Procedural markup directs the text formatting performed by a particular document processor. Word-processing systems typically embed invisible (nonprintable) codes within the document to record specific styles and visual characteristics of the text. These codes are interpreted by the text processor for specific layout functions such as adjusting the size or style of a font, text alignment, and all the other visual characteristics of the document. These codes are often not thought of as markup but as a specific file format for a particular word processor. Document processing systems commonly used in writing scientific literature, such as TEX or troff (a Unix (*q.v.*) text formatter), require the author to enter procedural markup codes within the text.

Generalized markup using SGML allows for a clear separation between document structure and layout. The separation of the structural components of a document such as chapters, sections, and paragraphs from layout such as font sizes and margins enables powerful document manipulation. Many different document presentations can be generated using the same content. In addition, alternative document representations for people with disabilities can also be created (WebABLE!, 1999). A table of contents can be automatically generated by assembling all chapter names or the visual style of all section headings can be set to a consistent font by interpreting the structural markup in the document.

Content markup is the markup of text to identify meaning. For example, in a transcription, specific speakers or the type of speech might be explicitly identified with markup. The Text Encoding Initiative (TEI 1999), another SGML application, was created to help in the scholarly analysis of humanities texts (*see* HUMANITIES APPLICATIONS) and to facilitate interchange of documents marked for analysis. A large set of Document Type Definitions (DTDs) and guidelines has been created by the TEI and is used by over 50 significant projects to aid in the analysis of, among others, archival information, dictionaries, language corpora, and literary and religious texts. Tools to use the semantic aspects of this type of markup are an active area of research. Short-term benefits of the TEI, however, such as its extensive linking capabilities, are starting to be realized (*see* Extending HTML below).

Creating Markup

Specific markup is often created simply by using a particular word processor. The markup codes are embedded in the document text and are not visible when the document is displayed by a browser. Authors rarely need to interact directly with these types of tags as they must do when using other specific markup document processing systems such as TEX and troff.

SGML and HTML markup consists of *tags*. Markup tags, usually denoted by the angle brackets surrounding them, often denote the beginning and end of a portion of text. The tags marking the beginning and end, respectively, of an HTML document are <HTML> and </HTML>. In general, the end of a section is marked by the same keyword as began it, prefixed by "/".

Documents marked up with SGML or HTML are ideal for long-term archival storage, for distribution across many types of computing systems, and for interpretation by systems not yet invented. HTML markup, unlike many other types of markup, is in plain ASCII clear text. This means that any text editor or word processor can be used to create marked-up SGML or HTML text.

Markup creation is a tedious and error-prone process. One complicating factor is that all whitespace (excess consecutive blanks) in an HTML document is ignored when the document is displayed; displayed whitespace must be forced by embedding just the right codes into the marked document to achieve the effect desired. This property of markup languages in general was chosen to make the document independent of the particular type of device used to display it.

Embedding tags into a document manually is analogous to machine- and assembly-language programming (*q.v.*). Fortunately, there now exist the counterparts of high-level languages, WYSIWYG editors that let users edit a displayed document and perfect it to their satisfaction. Each change made that affects the appearance of the "page" being viewed causes a background change in markup codes in its base document, exactly the reverse of what will happen when the HTML document is processed by a browser. An HTML document being viewed using Netscape Communicator can be toggled between Browser Mode (what a remote viewer will see once the page is "published" on the Web) and Edit Mode. Microsoft markets a product

called Front Page that does the same thing, as does Adobe, whose software is called PageMill.

Many tags also have attributes specifying additional variables. For example, a hypertext link in HTML is specified with an anchor tag, <A>. The complete tag, however, must specify the target document; the Hypertext REFerence (HREF) attribute is used for this. A complete hypertext link in HTML is specified as: <A HREF=nextdoc>text</A> where nextdoc specifies the document to be accessed and displayed if the link is clicked and text specifies the displayed name of the link. The document may be a locally stored page, or it may be a particular page (usually the home page) of a Website stored thousands of miles away. Thus to switch the browser's attention to a remote page on the Web, nextdoc is the URL for that page. For example,

```
<A HREF = "http://www.cs.union.edu/~hemmendd/
Encyc">Encyclopedia of Computer Science
</A>
```

accesses a particular directory (*q.v.*) at Union College in Schenectady, NY. On the screen, all that will appear (in a color that marks it as a link) is

Encyclopedia of Computer Science

which, when clicked, will download and display the Encyc directory at Union College. Such a link is *external*, that is, it transfers attention to another node on the Web. One may also specify *internal links* that merely scroll the display screen to a different part of the Web page being shown, a place marked with an invisible tag whose name is used in the link.

Specialized HTML editors help ensure that starting tags always have the required end tag, and that required attributes are created. Some of the more complicated tags such as those specifying images in a Web document have over a dozen possible attributes relating to, for example, the placement of an image, the way text is or is not wrapped around it, and whether or not the image itself is to serve as a link to a larger version of the picture. An image can also serve as a link to a MIDI file that will play music or to a menu that invites the user to write an email message. Specialized editors can take care of the syntactic tedium involved in choosing these attributes. Web browsers interpret the HTML markup embedded in the text and display them according to that markup. Fig. 1 shows the correspondence between the HTML document on the left and the appearance it produces when viewed with a browser.

Extending HTML

The power of SGML comes from its extensibility. The DTD facility in SGML is a general formal mechanism

```
<HTML> <!-- Comments begin and end as this one does. -->

<HEAD> <!-- Nothing in the scope of the HEAD will be displayed. -->
<!-- List nonprinting keywords for use by search engines. -->
    <META NAME="keywords" CONTENT="platonic solid, tetrahedron, cube,
        octahedron, icosahedron, dodecahedron, Euler, polyhedron">
<!-- Choose a title for the Web page: --> <TITLE>Platonic Solids</TITLE>
</HEAD>

<!-- Start BODY and choose colors for text, background, and links. -->
<BODY  TEXT="#000000" BGCOLOR="#33CCFF"
       LINK="#0000EE" VLINK="#551A8B" ALINK="#FF0000">

<!-- Choose style, color, and size for first line displayed; B=Bold: -->
<CENTER>
    <B><FONT COLOR="#990000"><FONT SIZE=+3>PLATONIC SOLIDS, INC.
        </FONT></FONT></B></CENTER>

<!-- Break to next line to create a blank line: --> <BR>

<P>   <!-- Start first Paragraph, which leaves another blank line. -->
<B><FONT SIZE=+1>Our polished aluminum polyhedra are precision
    made in a wide variety of sizes. The vertices (V), faces(F),
    and edges (E) of each solid are guaranteed to conform to
    Euler's relation V+F-E=2. </FONT></B>

<P>  <!-- Insert two images, side by side, with 160 pixels to left
            and right of the first: -->
    <IMG SRC="icosa.gif" HSPACE=160  HEIGHT=100 WIDTH=133>
    <IMG SRC="dodeca.gif"           HEIGHT=100 WIDTH=133>

<P> <B><FONT SIZE=+1>For complete specifications on any of our
        five products, choose an item from the list.</FONT></B>

<UL>   <!-- Start an Unordered (unnumbered) List of links;
             items begin and end with bracketed LI and /LI -->
  <LI><B><A HREF="tetra.htm">tetrahedron    </A></B></LI>
  <LI><B><A HREF= "octa.htm">octahedron     </A></B></LI>
  <LI><B><A HREF= "icos.htm">icosahedron    </A></B></LI>
  <LI><B><A HREF= "cube.htm">cube           </A></B></LI>
  <LI><B><A HREF="dodec.htm">dodecahedron   </A></B></LI>
</UL>

<!-- Set up a link to an email form: -->
<CENTER>
    <B>Direct inquires to
    <A HREF="mailto:info@platonicsolids.com">
     info@platonicsolids.com</A></B>
</CENTER>

</BODY>
</HTML>
```

(a)

for defining new tags. One class of tags is the entire HTML markup language. Indeed, the formal description of the HTML language is actually an SGML DTD. Most current Web browsers, however, are not capable of interpreting SGML directly and thus cannot take advantage of the extensibility of SGML (Rubinski and Maloney, 1997). An effort to bring the extensibility of SGML to the Web has resulted in the Extensible Markup Language (XML). XML is a simplified form of SGML. It is a project sanctioned by the World Wide Web Consortium (*see* W3C Technical Report, 1999), the official developers of HTML and the Web.

XML defines two types of document, *valid* and *well-formed*. A valid XML document contains or points to a DTD describing the structure of the document. A well-formed document follows clear rules to allow for the creation of *ad hoc* author-defined tags. Two of the

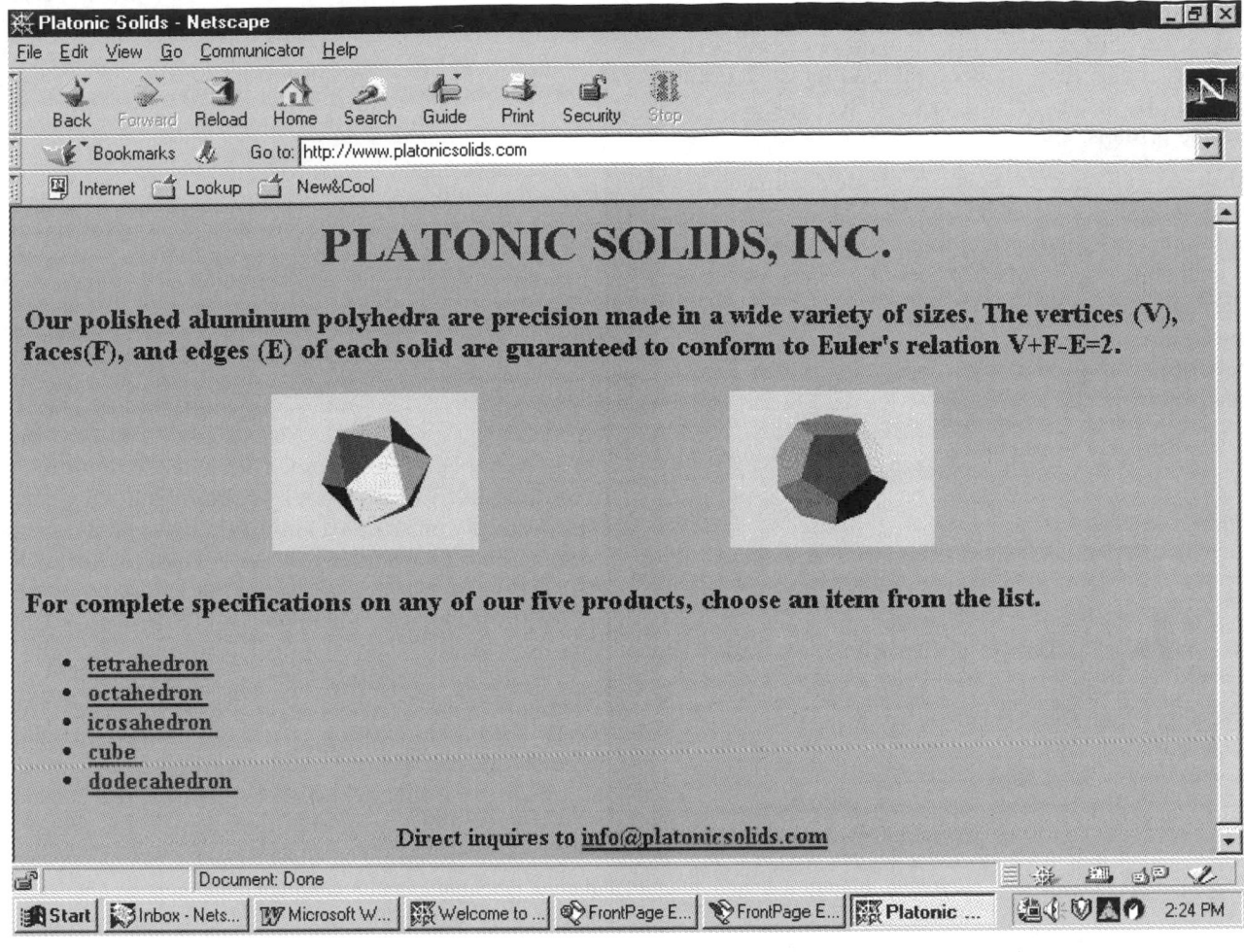

(b)

Figure 1. (a) The program on the facing page illustrates just a few of the many features of the markup language HTML. (b) When interpreted by a browser such as Netscape Navigator, the code produces a color version of the screen image shown above.

rules for creating a well-formed document are that all beginning tags are matched by ending tags (e.g. `<BEGIN></BEGIN>`) and that all attribute values are surrounded by quotes (e.g. `<TAG VALUE="XYZ">`). These and other rules for well-formed documents exist to make XML documents easier to parse, one of the difficulties with the more general SGML.

XML also provides more robust linking facilities than HTML. XML links can be unidirectional, bidirectional, and multidirectional. The XML XPointer is derived from the TEI Extended Pointer syntax. XPointers allow selection of textual targets with addressing keywords such as `CHILD`, `DESCENDANT`, `ANCESTOR`, `PREVIOUS`, `NEXT`, `PRECEDING`, and `FOLLOWING`. These keywords allow specification of absolute or relative textual targets. The XML Xpointer: `CHILD(3,DIV1)(29,P)` selects the 29th paragraph of the third major division of the target text.

After a document is marked up with a set of author-defined tags, one must instruct the browser on how to process the marked-up text. XML provides for the entry of specific "Processing Instructions" to meet this requirement. In addition, the style sheet capabilities of Web browsers can be used to connect tags with processing actions.

Style Sheets

With the proliferation of Web sites, authors need a way to manage the appearance of Web pages and to maintain consistency from section to section. Major Web browser vendors are beginning to support the use of style sheets implemented according to the Cascading Style Sheet, specification level 1, CSS1 (Lie and Bos, 1996). Style sheets allow the author to associate visual appearances with logical document units. Authors can specify enterprise-wide style sheets to maintain a consistent institutional look to their Web pages. CSS2 (Bos *et al.*, 1998) supports media-specific style to enable presentations tailored for such output as visual browsers, aural devices such as speakers, and Braille printers.

Multiple style sheets can affect a single document. This flexibility allows authors to write partial style sheets inheriting style properties from other, possibly institutional, style sheets. Properties are inherited by child elements through a document structure. This cascading feature increases modularity and provides a balance between what the author writes and what the reader desires to view.

Bibliography

1990. Goldfarb, C. F. *The SGML Handbook*. Oxford: Oxford University Press.

1996. Lie, H., and Bos, B., Cascading Style Sheets, level 1. `http://www.w3.org/TR/REC-CSS1-961217.html`.

1997. Rubinsky, Y., and Maloney, M. *SGML on the Web: Small Steps Beyond HTML*. Upper Saddle River, NJ: Prentice Hall.

1998. Bos, B., Lie, H., Lilley, C., and Jacobs, I., Cascading Style Sheets, level 2. `http://www.w3.org/TR/REC-CSS2/`.

1998. Raggett, D., Le Hors, A., and Jacobs, I. HTML 4.0 Specification. `http://www.w3.org/TR/REC-html40/`.

1998. Korpela, J. "Lurching Toward Babel: HTML, CSS, and XML," *Computer*, **31**, 7 (July), 103–106.

1999. TEI, Text Encoding Initiative Home Page. `http://www.uic.edu:80/orgs/tei/`.

1999. W3C Technical Reports & Publications: `http://www.w3.org/TR/`.

1999. WebABLE! `http://www.webable.com`.

1999. Lee, H. W., and Saarela, J. "Multipurpose Web Publishing Using HTML, XML, and CSS," *Comm. of the ACM*, **42**, 10 (October), 95–101.

Sandy Ressler

MASKING

For articles on related subjects *see* INSTRUCTION SET; INTERRUPT; MACHINE AND ASSEMBLY LANGUAGE PROGRAMMING; and SHIFTING.

The items of information required by a computer program may be of lengths that are not matched to the usually fixed length of the storage unit (cell) in the computer memory. Therefore, either an item may require several storage units or several items may be packed into one unit. In the latter case, a mechanism is necessary in order to retrieve the item needed without interference from other items that are stored in the same memory unit. *Masking* is the procedure that enables one to do so by accessing the desired information while suppressing or "masking out" the undesired information.

The basis of the masking operation is the Boolean operation AND, which, for two variables D and M, is defined as follows.

D	M	D AND M
0	0	0
0	1	0
1	0	0
1	1	1

From the truth table, we see that

$$\text{when } M = 1, \quad D \text{ AND } M = D$$
$$\text{when } M = 0, \quad D \text{ AND } M = 0.$$

The variable M, therefore, functions as a *mask*. Whenever its value is 1, the result of the AND operation is to duplicate the value of D, whereas if $M = 0$, the value of D is masked out.

As an example, let us assume that in an eight-bit byte we would like to gain access to the middle four bits. The necessary mask is 00111100. The AND operation of this mask with the data byte produces a result in which the first two and last two bits are masked out and the middle four bits are copied verbatim. This result can then be aligned to the byte boundary (or any other boundary) with the aid of shift operations.

There are other masking operations concerned with control information. Various control items can be grouped; those that are required can then be chosen by masking all non-required items with a zero mask. For example, a user of an IBM S/390 may choose one of four possible condition codes by structuring a mask of four bits, with values of one and zero corresponding to the selection or masking of the appropriate condition. The same type of masking is used in order to mask out undesired interrupt conditions, control bits, etc. In these cases, one cannot use shift operations as an alternative to masking because the information to be masked is not data in the usual sense, that is, it does not lie in a register (*q.v.*) whose contents can be shifted.

Gideon Frieder

MASS STORAGE

For articles on related subjects *see* CHANNEL; DATA MINING; DATA WAREHOUSING; DATABASE MANAGEMENT SYSTEM; FIBER OPTICS; FILE SERVER; HARD DISK; MEMORY: AUXILIARY; REDUNDANT ARRAY OF INEXPENSIVE DISKS; and VIRTUAL MEMORY.

A *mass storage system* or MSS is a collection of software, computing elements, input–output, and data storage components that jointly automate the archiving, storage, management, and retrieval of very large quantities of digital information. A typical high-end mass storage system may store from hundreds of *terabytes* (10^{12} bytes) to *petabytes* (10^{15} bytes) of data contained in millions of files. The MSS provides access to those files to client computer systems ranging from desktop workstations (*q.v.*) to supercomputers (*q.v.*) at speeds from megabits per second over a local area network to gigabits per second over high-speed I/O channels. Mass storage systems are not automated backup systems, although they may be used as a component of such systems. Mass storage systems are not automated tape management systems, although some early ones evolved from such systems, and most incorporate sophisticated tape management algorithms. Mass storage systems are not distributed file systems, although users may indirectly access an MSS through front-end distributed file system servers. Examples of early mass storage systems are the Common File System or CFS developed at Los Alamos National Labs, Unitree from Lawrence Livermore National Labs, and the National Center for Atmospheric Research (NCAR) MSS, each of which was developed in the mid-1980s.

There are many examples of the need for mass storage systems in science and commerce. A study done by Harvard Medical School and others estimates that a medium-sized metropolitan medical institution will generate two terabytes a year of multimedia (*q.v.*) patient information, the bulk of which will be digitized X-ray images. The NASA Earth Observing Satellite launched in 1998 is expected to generate seven petabytes of data by the year 2007, at a peak rate of three terabytes a day, or the equivalent of six 660 MB CD-ROMs every minute. The US Department of Energy Accelerated Strategic Computing Initiative (ASCI), responsible for computer simulations of the nuclear stockpile, will require hundreds of petabytes of storage. In each case, not only is a prodigious amount of data being generated, but it must be archived for as long as decades, it must be made easily available for computer processing, and it must be stored as economically as possible. NCAR has found that for every billion floating-point operations performed by its climate simulations, about half a megabyte of new data is stored in the MSS. At this rate, a teraflop (10^{12} floating-point operations per second) supercomputer would generate 500 MB of data per second for the MSS. NCAR has described a linear relationship between computer power and data generation for its applications. However, speed of computation increases exponentially, doubling roughly every two years as new processor technology is introduced, which results in a proportional doubling of the rate at which new data is generated.

Architecture and Operation of an MSS

Mass storage systems place no interpretation on the data that they store, and so are said to store *bitfiles* or uninterpreted strings of bits. To achieve a balance of performance and economy, a mass storage system uses a *multilevel storage hierarchy*. For this reason, mass storage systems are sometimes referred to as *hierarch-*

ical storage managers or HSMs. Bitfiles that are active are cached on disks. The total capacity of an MSS disk farm may be hundreds of gigabytes in size, and aggregate transfer rates for disk arrays can be hundreds of megabits per second. The expense of direct access storage calls for the bulk of the data archive to be stored on a more economical medium, such as magnetic tape cartridges or optical discs. Larger or less frequently accessed bitfiles are cached in robotic libraries (Fig. 1), each of which may contain thousands of tape cartridges or optical discs, and hold a total of hundreds of terabytes. The access time for the robot to fetch a tape (*see* Fig. 2) or optical disc, mount it on a read–write drive, and locate the correct data is typically a few seconds to several minutes, and transfer rates can be a hundred megabits per second or faster. In the largest of archives, the majority of data may be stored offline on tape cartridges shelved in racks, and a human operator responds to requests from the MSS to mount an offline tape manually.

When the MSS determines that a bitfile is being accessed frequently, the bitfile may be *staged* or copied upwards in the storage hierarchy, from the offline archive into the tape library or onto the disks. As the disks or the library fill to capacity, the MSS identifies those bitfiles that are less frequently used and schedules them to be *migrated* or copied downward in the storage hierarchy to offline tapes, and *scrubbed* or *purged* from the disks or library. An entire bitfile, or portions of a bitfile, may exist in several places in the storage hierarchy simultaneously in order to speed

Figure 1. This robotic tape library contains about 6000 tape cartridges each holding 50 GB (or more with data compression), for a total capacity of 300 TB. The Storage Tek Automated Cartridge System or "silo" is about 7 ft (2.35 m) high and 11 ft (3.25 m) in diameter. Tape drives and integrated controllers can be seen surrounding the silo (Storage Technology Corporation).

up access. A bitfile may be migrated from disk to tape, but not scrubbed until the disk space is needed. The physical location of a file is transparent to the user except for the additional delay caused when a requested bitfile is not cached on disk and must be retrieved from tape. This is somewhat analogous to paging in a virtual memory (*q.v.*) system, and the MSS can be thought of as extending the memory hierarchy to very low speed, very high capacity (when compared with main memory) storage. Because all or part of the same bitfile may reside simultaneously on different storage devices or different distributed servers, the MSS must deal with cache coherence (*q.v.*) and database concurrency (*q.v.*) issues to insure data integrity.

A local area network or LAN may be used to move data between an MSS and its clients. Commercial mass storage systems like Unitree, now a product of Unitree Software Inc., use Internet protocols such as File Transfer Protocol (FTP) or Network File System (NFS), allowing the MSS to appear to be a terabyte-size file server. However, LAN (*q.v.*) bandwidth is inadequate for high-performance MSS clients such as supercomputers or massively parallel processors (*q.v.*). Also, Internet protocols are typically inefficient for moving large amounts of data quickly because most are limited by response time rather than by network capacity; increasing the network bandwidth by a factor of ten may yield only a fractional improvement in data throughput (*q.v.*). The *separation of control and datapaths* in the client–MSS connection is one approach to overcoming the LAN bottleneck. Control messages between the MSS and its clients are still exchanged over the LAN, which is the *control path*. The data transfer occurs over the *data path*, high-speed I/O channels using *lightweight* I/O protocols which have lower overhead and better scalability as bandwidth increases than traditional LAN protocols because they are simpler or depend upon intelligent I/O devices for much of their processing.

To prevent the MSS itself from becoming a bottleneck, it may not participate directly in the data transfer. The data moves directly between the client system and the storage device, which are both attached to a common *data fabric* or *storage area network* (SAN). The term "fabric" is used to distinguish it from a more typical local area network (although Internet protocols may also run over the same physical network) and to reflect the fact that data fabrics are frequently woven from (optical) fiber. Data fabrics usually employ switch-based I/O channel interconnection technologies such as High Performance Parallel Interface or HIPPI (at 800 Mb/sec), or Fibre Channel Standard (at 1 Gb/sec). Either may be implemented with optical fiber or copper. The attachment of an intelligent storage device such as a disk array or tape library directly onto the

data fabric as an active participant is referred to as *network attached storage*. The control of the storage devices by the MSS is called *third-party transfer* since the controlling entity is not at either end of the data transfer. Network attached storage and the separation of the control and data paths was first introduced in 1985 in the NCAR MSS. It has since been accepted as a standard architecture for scalable mass storage systems, and incorporated in high-end commercial systems such as the High Performance Storage System or HPSS, jointly developed by IBM, the US Department of Energy's National Storage Laboratory, and others.

Associated with each bitfile in the mass storage system is *metadata*, for example the name of the file, who owns it, when it was created and last used, who is allowed to access it, and where it is located in the storage hierarchy. Metadata may also include information of interest to the user, such as what version of a simulation or which scientific instrument created the bitfile, or what types of post-processing have been applied to its contents. Losing metadata is as catastrophic as losing the data itself, since data without context is of little value. The metadata itself may be a valuable corporate or scientific resource. Database and data mining tools provided with the MSS for users to manage and manipulate metadata efficiently are becoming increasingly important as the amount of data stored per user increases exponentially. In the mid-1990s, Sequoia 2000,

Figure 2. The robotic hand in the tape library is just slightly larger than a human hand. It is holding a 50 GB tape cartridge which it can mount in any one of several tape drives in just a few seconds. Infrared LEDs seen to the right of the hand illuminate the printed label on the cartridge so it can be read by the hand's optical sensor (Storage Technology Corporation).

a research collaboration between the University of California and Digital Equipment Corporation (*q.v.*), applied object-oriented database techniques to managing both metadata and data in mass storage systems.

The longevity of all digital information, both data and metadata, is a critical issue in the selection of storage technology for a mass storage system. Of concern is not only the physical lifetime of the media, for example how long a tape cartridge or optical disc will remain readable, but also the lifetime of the hardware and software technology used to create and access them. A digital magnetic tape may still be readable ten years after it is written, but the technology used to read it may not be commercially available after five years. Obsolete storage media such as punched cards (*q.v.*) and eight-inch floppy disks are similar to player piano rolls: the technology to read and write them is rare or non-existent. An MSS may have a hundred thousand or more offline tape cartridges holding petabytes of data. Since the time to mount and copy a single tape cartridge may be several minutes, the time required to copy an entire archive to a new medium is measured in *drive-years*. At the current rate of technological obsolescence, it is possible that a petabyte archive could not be copied to a new medium before that medium itself is obsolete. The choice of storage technology in a mass storage system is often conservative, using not the fastest or the most dense storage media but rather the most reliable and the most likely still to have spare parts available a decade after its deployment.

OSSI

Since 1990, the IEEE Storage System Standard Working Group (SSSWG, pronounced "sissy-wig") has been developing a *mass storage system reference model*. Version 5 of the model, which has been renamed the *Open Storage Systems Interconnection* or OSSI model, was released in 1994 for public review. The model describes seven components common to mass storage systems. The *Application Environment Profile* specifies the environmental software interfaces required by open storage system services. The *Object Identifier* defines the format and generation of object identifiers that uniquely identify each object (for example, each bitfile or physical volume) within the mass storage system. The *Physical Volume Library* defines the services that manage removable physical volumes (for example, tape cartridges) and optimize their use on read–write drives. The *Physical Volume Repository* defines the services that store removable physical volumes and selectively mount them onto drives. The *Data Mover* describes how the data fabric is used to transfer data. *Storage System Management* specifies a framework to monitor and control, consistently and portably, MSS

resources and to implement site-specific storage management policies. *Virtual Storage Services* describes how portions of persistent storage are mapped into a single virtual storage image (for example, physical files on several tape cartridges, possibly in different libraries, into an image of a single bitfile). The Version 5 OSSI model establishes a standard nomenclature for discussing mass storage systems. It is the goal of the Working Group to develop the model further to include standard programmatic interfaces for each component so that a mass storage system could be built from interchangeable compliant software and hardware from different vendors.

Bibliography

1990. Levy, E., and Silberschatz, A., "Distributed File Systems: Concepts and Examples," *ACM Computing Surveys*, **22**, 4 (December), 321–374.

1994. IEEE Storage Systems Standards Working Group. *Reference Model for Open Storage Systems Interconnection, Mass Storage System Reference Model Version 5.* IEEE Project 1244, September.

1995. Cole, J., and Jones, M. "The IEEE Storage System Standard Working Group Overview and Status," *Proc. 14th IEEE Symp. Mass Storage Systems.* Monterey, CA: IEEE Comp. Soc. Press.

1995. National Research Council. *Preserving Scientific Data on Our Physical Universe: A New Strategy for Archiving the Nation's Scientific Information Resources.* Washington, DC: National Academy Press.

1995. Rothenberg, J. "Ensuring the Longevity of Digital Documents," *Scientific American*, **272**, 1, 42–47.

1995. Watson, R., and Coyne, R. "The Parallel I/O Architecture of the High Performance Storage System (HPSS)," *Proc. 14th IEEE Symp. Mass Storage Systems.* Monterey, CA: IEEE Comp. Soc. Press.

J. L. Sloan

MATHEMATICAL PROGRAMMING

For articles on related subjects *see* DISCRETE MATHEMATICS; NUMERICAL ANALYSIS; and OPTIMIZATION METHODS.

This article provides an overview of *mathematical programming*—its scope, its methods, and the associated computer feasibility and efficacy of the methods. Mathematical programming as discussed here has nothing inherently to do with computer programming. Although mathematical programming is usually done by computer, this term refers to mathematical *optimization*, with or without constraints. A mathematical programming problem may be written without loss of generality as

Maximize: $c(x_1, \ldots, x_n)$,

Subject to: $a_i(x_1, \ldots, x_n) \leq 0 \quad (i = 1, \ldots, m) \quad (1)$

where $x_1, \ldots, x_n$ are real decision variables for which values are desired that will maximize the objective function $c(x_1, \ldots, x_n)$, subject to the m constraints

$a_i(x_1, \ldots, x_n) \leq 0$. There may be further restrictions requiring that the values of $x_j (j = 1, \ldots, n)$ are a proper subset of those values that satisfy the constraints. For example, all or some of the variables may be required to be integers.

With some imagination, one can see that almost any well-defined deterministic optimization problem (a problem in which all numbers in the functions of expression (1) are known constants) may be formulated as a mathematical programming problem. Many non-deterministic problems (those in which some numbers in the functions of expression (1) are probabilistic (i.e. are random variables)), can be formulated in this manner as well. Solving some types of mathematical programming problems is relatively straightforward and computationally inexpensive, while some others may be very difficult or expensive to solve.

Methods of mathematical programming may be divided into three groups: linear programming, integer linear programming, and nonlinear programming. Linear programming methods solve the problem for which the functions $c(x_1, \ldots, x_n)$ and $a_i(x_1, \ldots, x_n)$ are linear and the x_j may take on any values that satisfy the constraints. Linear programming problems are relatively easy to solve, and computers have great capability for solving such problems. Integer linear programming problems are those in which some or all variables must be integers. Nonlinear programming is literally everything else in mathematical programming. As might be expected, because of the availability of computer programs to solve large linear programming problems efficiently, there is a great incentive with nonlinear programming problems to reduce them somehow to linear programming problems or to find similar linear programming problems so that linear programming methods can be used to solve (or approximately solve) them. In addition, special methods have been developed to solve certain nonlinear programming problems that have special features.

This article discusses linear and nonlinear programming problems and methods for their solution. Also discussed are some necessary conditions for an optimal solution to a nonlinear programming problem that are also sufficient under restrictive circumstances. Finally, integer programming problems and methods are discussed, and some comments on computational feasibility are presented.

Linear Programming Problems

Linear programming is used to solve problems of resource allocation in which the employment of a resource has proportionately constant returns. This means that, for example, if four units of a resource can be employed to produce one unit of a product, then eight units of the resource can be used to produce two units of the product. It is also assumed that each unit of a product produced contributes the same amount to profits and to cover overhead.

The general linear programming problem may be written as follows:

Maximize: $c_1 x_1 + \cdots + c_n x_n$

Subject to: $a_{i1} x_1 + \cdots + a_{in} x_n \leq b_i, \quad i = 1, \ldots, m$

$$x_1, \ldots, x_n \geq 0 \qquad (2)$$

(Minimization problems may be handled by maximizing the negative of the objective function; variables unrestricted in sign may also be handled, as may $\geq$ constraints and equality constraints.) The a_{ij}, c_j, and b_i are constants. The above problem is solved by first converting the inequalities into equalities as follows: $a_{i1} x_1 + \cdots + a_{in} x_n + x_{n+1} = b_i$, $x_{n+1} \geq 0$, $i = 1, \ldots, m$ where the variables x_{n+1} are called *slack variables* (constraints of the $\geq$ type are converted to equalities by subtracting nonnegative variables called *surplus variables*). Adding slack variables to equation (2) yields an underdefined system of m equations in $(n + m)$ variables. A *basic solution* to this system is obtained by setting n variables to zero, and solving the resulting set of m equations for the remaining m variables. The variables set to zero are called *nonbasic* and the remaining variables are called *basic*. If a basic solution is *feasible* (i.e. if all solution values are nonnegative), it is called a *basic feasible solution*. If the problem has an optimal solution, then it can be shown that there is at least one basic feasible solution that is optimal. A naive way to solve linear programming problems would be to enumerate all basic feasible solutions and choose one that is optimal.

A practical way to solve linear programming problems is to begin with a basic feasible solution and then find a sequence of basic feasible solutions with monotonically increasing objective functions which terminates at an optimal solution. Each solution in this sequence is obtained from its predecessor solution by increasing the value of one nonbasic variable until a basic variable becomes zero. The nonbasic variable whose value is increased now becomes basic, and the basic variable that drops to zero becomes nonbasic in the new solution. In this procedure, a nonbasic variable is chosen if an increase in its value would lead to an increase in the problem's objective function value. This is the essence of the *simplex method* that has been widely used to solve linear programming problems.

APPLICATIONS

Linear programming has been used for a number of years by business, government, and industry to solve resource allocation problems. Some examples of applications are:

1. *Blending problems* in which a lowest-cost blend is desired to satisfy certain requirements subject to material availability, etc. The blending of animal feeds, peanut butter, and gasoline, and the specification of foods in hospital diets are examples of blending problems that have been solved using linear programming.

2. *Product-mix problems* in which the maximum profit mix of products is desired consistent with facility and material limitations, sales commitments to customers, and sales potential of products. Product-mix problems in the aluminum, manufacturing, oil, and steel industries (among others) have been solved by linear programming.

3. *Distribution problems* in which least-cost procedures are desired for distributing products from plants or warehouses to customers.

4. *Dynamic production planning* over a time projection.

EXAMPLE OF A LINEAR PROGRAMMING PROBLEM

We shall now develop an example of a linear programming problem that will also illustrate related concepts.

A small shop has two machines, A and B, used to make two products. Both machines are each operated 12 hours each day. Product 1 requires 2 hours on machine A and 1 hour on machine B, and produces a net profit (above the costs of materials) of $15. Product 2 requires 0.25 hour on machine A and 0.5 hour on machine B, and produces a profit of $10. The proprietor of the shop wants to maximize total profits. Assume that raw materials are abundantly available, and that all production will be salable. To formulate the problem, let x_1 and x_2 be the number of units of product 1 and product 2 produced on a given day, respectively.

We formulate the problem as a linear program as follows.

$$\text{Maximize:} \quad 15x_1 + 10x_2 \tag{3}$$

$$\text{Subject to:} \quad 2x_1 + 0.25x_2 \leq 12 \tag{4}$$

$$x_1 + 0.5x_2 \leq 12 \tag{5}$$

$$x_1, x_2 \geq 0 \tag{6}$$

The objective function gives the total profit from producing x_1 units of product 1 and x_2 units of product 2. Constraint (4) stipulates that the total amount of machine A time required should not exceed 12 hours, and constraint (5) stipulates a similar restriction with regard to machine B. Constraint (6) stipulates that the

number of units of a product to be produced must not be negative.

The problem may be solved graphically by plotting x_1 and x_2 as coordinates and graphing the constraints. A graph for this example is given in Fig. 1, in which the arrows on the four lines indicate the directions in which the four inequalities (4)–(6) are satisfied so that the shaded area represents the set of feasible solutions to the problem. The feasible region is bounded by line segments (*see* Fig. 1), and the points at which these segments intersect are called *corner points* (these are the basic feasible solutions). The corner points of the feasible set are indicated as C, D, E, and F in Fig. 1. The dashed lines of the form $15x_1 + 10x_2 = K$ are lines of constant profit K called *isoprofit lines*. We desire the line having the greatest value of K that intersects the shaded area. As can be seen, $K = 240$ is the maximum value of profits for which the associated isoprofit line intersects the feasible set. This line intersects the shaded area at point F; isoprofit lines having $K > 240$ do not intersect the feasible region. Accordingly, point F $(x_1 = 0, x_2 = 24)$ is the optimal solution. This analysis implies that the optimal solution to a linear programming problem always occurs on the boundary of the feasible region. The optimal solution is either a unique corner point, as in this example, or there may be multiple optimal solutions along the boundary.

Problems having more than two variables cannot be solved graphically. Such problems may be solved algebraically using the simplex method mentioned

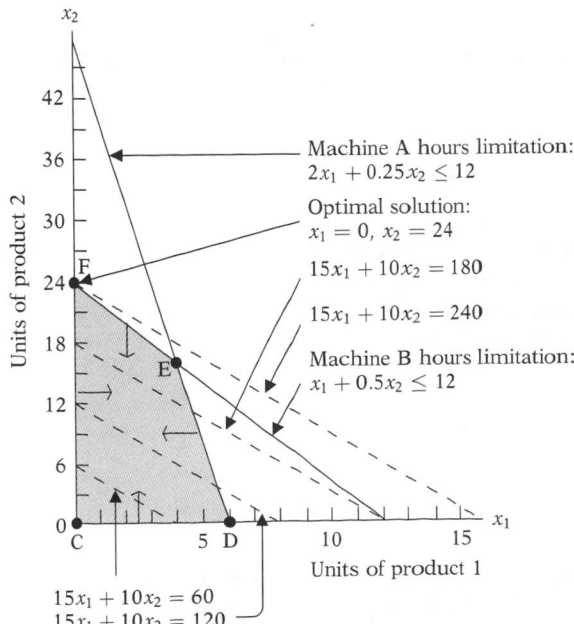

Figure 1. Graphical representation of example. The four short arrows indicate the directions in which the four inequalities (4), (5), and (6) hold.

earlier. For more information on the simplex method and its variants, see Sierksma (1996). Although the simplex method is an exponential time algorithm (*see* COMPUTATIONAL COMPLEXITY and NP-COMPLETE PROBLEMS) whose number of iterations grows as 2^n, it is nevertheless efficient for almost all practical values of n. Computer programs capable of solving problems with a very large number of variables and constraints are available.

DUALITY

Closely associated with the preceding problem is another linear programming problem called the *dual* problem. This is a pricing problem, as opposed to a resource allocation problem, and is of both practical and theoretical importance.

Example of a Dual Problem. Suppose the owner of the machine shop has been approached by an individual who would like to rent the facilities of the shop for one day. The assets of the shop consist of hours on machine A and hours on machine B. Designating the rental rate for each kind of hour as y_A and y_B, respectively, the owner will receive a daily rental of $12y_A + 12y_B$. However, if the *owner* were to use the shop to produce one unit each of products 1 and 2, a profit of \$15 and \$10, respectively, would be made. Hence, whatever rental price is decided on, the owner would not be willing to rent the machines unless

$$2y_A + y_B \geq 15 \tag{7}$$

$$0.25y_A + 0.5y_B \geq 10 \tag{8}$$

$$y_A, y_B \geq 0.$$

That is, the value that we place on the resources going into a unit of product must be at least as large as the profit that could be generated by making the product. For (7), recall that product 1 requires 2 hours on machine A and 1 hour on machine B; for (8), apply a similar argument for product 2. The *owner* wants to know the minimum rent he or she should accept, consistent with the alternatives of production. Thus, we want to solve the following linear programming problem:

$$\text{Minimize:} \quad 12y_A + 12y_B$$

$$\text{Subject to:} \quad 2y_A + y_B \geq 15 \tag{9}$$

$$0.25y_A + 0.5y_B \geq 10$$

$$y_A, y_B \geq 0.$$

The solution to (9), which may be found graphically, is $y_A = 0$, $y_B = 20$, with a total rental of \$240. It should not be surprising that the minimum acceptable rental is the same as the maximum level of profits that can be achieved. The owner should accept any offer of more

than \$240 rental per day, reject any offer of less than \$240 per day and be indifferent to an offer of \$240. (The reader may wonder why someone would be willing to pay a rental of more than \$240 per day. Such a person might have production options that the owner does not have available.)

Individual rental rates are of interest, too. Those rates (sometimes called *shadow prices* or *dual variables*) are the values of a unit of each resource. Recall that in the optimal solution to the owner's problem, only 6 machine A hours were used ($2(0) + 0.25(24) = 6$) and all 12 machine B hours were used ($1(0) + 0.5(24) = 12$). The dual variables, $y_A = 0$, $y_B = 20$ reflect the fact that the owner's profit will decrease by \$20 if 1 hour of machine B time is lost. Similarly, the owner's profit may increase as the amount of available resources increases. The dual variables will vary in general as a function of the number of units of resource lost or added. Dual variables give valuable measures by which to gauge the cost of resources. Fortunately, the solution of the dual problem is obtained as a by-product of solving the resource allocation problem.

The dual theorem of linear programming sums up the relationship between the two problems in a formal manner.

THE DUAL THEOREM OF LINEAR PROGRAMMING

Given the two linear programming problems:

$$\text{Maximize:} \quad c_1 x_1 + \cdots + c_n x_n$$

$$\text{Subject to:} \quad a_{11} x_1 + \cdots + a_{1n} x_n \leq b_1$$

$$\vdots$$

$$a_{m1} x_1 + \cdots + a_{mn} x_n \leq b_m$$

$$x_1, \ldots, x_n \geq 0$$

and

$$\text{Minimize:} \quad b_1 y_1 + \cdots + b_m y_m$$

$$\text{Subject to:} \quad a_{11} y_1 + \cdots + a_{m1} y_m \geq c_1$$

$$\vdots$$

$$a_{1n} y_1 + \cdots + a_{mn} y_m \geq c_n$$

$$y_1, \ldots, y_m \geq 0.$$

1. If one problem has an optimal solution, so does the other, and the objective function values of the solutions to the two problems are identical.

2. If one problem has an infinite optimal solution (i.e. the constraint set is not bounded and the optimal solution is infinite), then the other problem does not have any feasible solutions.

As a corollary to the dual theorem, there are the complementary slackness conditions, which we now state informally and give examples of from our problem. (The word "resource" is used in a general sense; every constraint is assumed to limit a resource. Similarly, the word "product" is used in a general sense; every variable is assumed to be a product.)

1. If the value of a resource (as measured by its dual variable) is positive, it should all be used ($y_B = 20$ implies that machine B has no idle hours: $x_1 + 0.5x_2 = 12$).

2. If a resource is not all used, its value is zero. (That machine A is not fully utilized (i.e. that $2x_1 + 0.25x_2 < 12$ in the optimal solution) implies that $y_A = 0$.)

3. If the value of resources required to produce a unit of product exceeds the profit of producing that product, the product will not be produced. (For product 1, $2y_A + y_B > 15$ implies that $x_1 = 0$.)

4. If a product is produced, the value of the resources used to produce the product exactly equals the profit associated with producing the product. (That product 2 is produced, or $x_2 > 0$, implies that $0.25y_A + 0.5y_B = 10$.)

KARMARKAR'S METHOD

Karmarkar (1984) developed a new approach for solving linear programming problems. The simplex method finds an optimal solution by examining a sequence of corner points (which are points on the boundary of the feasible region). By contrast, Karmarkar's method finds the optimal solution by examining the interior of the feasible region. In this method, an artificial variable is added to the problem and the problem is rescaled. The artificial variable is used to ensure that the point (say P_0) having all the decision variables $(x_1, \ldots, x_n)$ equal to 1 is feasible. By construction, such a point lies in the interior of the feasible region. Then, Karmarkar's method obtains a new point P_1 by moving from P_0 in a direction for which the objective function improves. The point P_1 is obtained using a linear transformation of the problem. Point P_1 therefore has the same properties as point P_0. This procedure is repeated from P_1 in an iterative manner until an optimal solution is found. A number of variants of Karkarkar's method have been developed in recent years (*see* Sierksma, 1996). Collectively these methods are known as *interior path methods*.

Karmarkar's method has been shown to be a polynomial time algorithm (*see* COMPUTATIONAL COMPLEXITY and NP-COMPLETE PROBLEMS) whose number of steps grows as $\sqrt{n}$. Thus, for sufficiently large n, Karmarkar's method will be faster than the simplex method. Practical experience has shown, however, that the simplex method is faster than Karmarkar's method for all but very large values of n.

Nonlinear Programming Problems

A mathematical programming problem of the form

$$\text{Maximize:} \quad c(x_1, x_2, \ldots, x_n)$$
$$\text{Subject to:} \quad X \equiv (x_1, x_2, \ldots, x_n) \text{ in } S \quad (10)$$

where S is a subset of Euclidean n-space, which is not a linear or integer programming problem, is classified as a nonlinear programming (NLP) problem.

If the function c in (10) is concave and the set S is closed, bounded, and convex, then an optimal solution occurs either at the global maximum of c or at a boundary point of S. A function c is concave if for all $X \equiv (x_1, x_2, \ldots, x_n)$ and $Y \equiv (y_1, y_2, \ldots, y_n)$ and $0 < \lambda < 1$,

$$c(\lambda(x_1, x_2, \ldots, x_n) + (1 - \lambda)(y_1, y_2, \ldots, y_n))$$
$$\geq \lambda c(x_1, x_2, \ldots, x_n) + (1 - \lambda)c(y_1, y_2, \ldots, y_n).$$

Intuitively, if the function is concave, then if a line is "stretched" between any two points on the function's surface, that line will be at or below the surface.

A set S is called convex if for any X and Y in S, the point $\lambda(x_1, x_2, \ldots, x_n) + (1 - \lambda)(y_1, y_2, \ldots, y_n)$ is also in S. If either c is not concave or S is not convex (or both), then an optimal solution could occur anywhere within S.

Methods for solving NLP problems exist, but many methods apply only to certain subsets of problems because they assume certain conditions about c or S (e.g. concavity or convexity). The problem of solving a general NLP problem can be compared to the problem faced by a person trying to walk to the highest point in the State of New York on a foggy day. From any point, the person can see only a short distance in any direction and hence never knows for sure if the "hill" on which he or she is standing is the highest hill.

Most algorithms used for solving general NLP problems involve some sort of neighborhood search method analogous to the method of the hiker in New York. There are four problems that such a method must overcome:

1. How can a local optimum be identified?

2. Which direction from a given point leads to an improvement in the function value?

3. If several directions improve the function, which is the "best" direction?

4. How far can the searcher move in the improving direction and still remain within S?

In the case of an NLP problem of form (1) in which the functions $c, a_1, a_2, \ldots, a_m$ are differentiable, an important theoretical result known as the Karush–Kuhn–Tucker conditions provides necessary conditions for a point to be a local optimum (*see* Sierksma, 1996).

Integer Linear Programming

Solving linear programming problems with the stipulation that some or all variables be integer-valued might seem to be a rather useless activity, particularly if we are concerned with determining the optimal number of four-door sedans General Motors should produce next year. It would appear that rounding a solution value such as 102,376.35 to a nearby integer value would make a negligible difference in the objective function value. On the other hand, if a variable represented the number of new bridges to be built across the Niagara River between the USA and Canada, and the optimal linear program solution value were 0.53, rounding to 0 or 1 would indeed make a great deal of difference in the objective function value.

Thus we may infer that, generally, large integer variables may be rounded arbitrarily, whereas small integer variables may not be. In addition, the requirement of integer values of variables may be made to insure that certain logical conditions are fulfilled (e.g. of two alternatives (x_1 and x_2), exactly one must be selected: $x_1 + x_2 = 1$, where $x_1, x_2 \geq 0$ and integer), or that certain peculiar nonlinear functions are involved that do not correspond to maximizing a concave function over a convex set.

Thus there are many applications for integer variables in addition to the obvious one that the number of units to be produced is to be integer. Integer programming methods have been successfully used to solve problems of airline crew scheduling, capital budgeting, and bank check clearing for large companies, as well as other problems.

In general, integer programming problems are difficult to solve, and no polynomial time algorithm exists for solving them. Usually, moderate-sized problems are solved to optimality using exponential time search procedures, and large problems are solved using heuristics (*q.v.*). Heuristics are used to obtain "good" and not necessarily optimal solutions. The performance of a heuristic is assessed using theoretical worst-case analyses and empirical investigations (*see* Parker and Rardin, 1988). We briefly describe the optimal integer programming methods in terms of four categories, as follows:

1. Cut methods.

2. Group theoretic methods.

3. Branch-and-bound methods.

4. Implicit enumeration methods.

Further, we will refer to the problem as an all-integer problem if all variables are required to be integer valued, and as mixed-integer if only some of the variables are required to be integer valued.

CUT METHODS

Cut methods, which were among the first methods developed, employ cut constraints derived from the original problem. Cut constraints have the desirable property that they exclude or cut off parts of the feasible solution space without cutting off any integer solution points. Some cut methods first require the solution of the linear programming problem before cut constraints are added; others do not. If the linear programming optimal solution should happen to have the required integer values, it is optimal. Otherwise, a cut constraint is added and a new optimal solution to the augmented problem is found. The procedure is continued until an integer solution is obtained. Other cut methods do not first solve the linear programming problem; instead they generate and use a cut constraint at every step of the solution process. There are cut methods for both all-integer and mixed-integer problems.

In recent years, an approach to the efficient solution of certain integer programming problems using cuts derived from polyhedral geometry has been developed. Cut constraints derived from polyhedral considerations are known as "valid inequalities" (*see* Parker and Rardin, 1988). Several specially structured large problems have been successfully solved to optimality by this approach.

GROUP THEORETIC METHODS

Group theoretic methods can be used only for problems in which all variables are required to be integers. The method begins by solving the linear programming problem. Assuming that the solution is not integer, the method then systematically constructs an integer solution to the problem by increasing to positive integer values certain variables that were set equal to zero in the optimal linear programming solution. Quite often, the constructed solution will be the optimal solution to the integer programming problem; where it is not, additional construction is required to generate the integer optimum. The method is based on mathematical group theory and works reasonably well on some problems. Although there is little available data on the efficiency of the methods, commercial computer codes using this technique are in use.

BRANCH-AND-BOUND METHODS

Branch-and bound methods are generally the most successful for solving integer programming problems—both for all integer and mixed integer. We outline one of a number of variations of the branch-and-bound procedure.

First solve the linear programming problem. If the solution does not satisfy the integer requirements, choose a variable in the solution that should be integer but is not. Suppose that the variable chosen has a solution value of 3.4. Then two new linear programs are solved, one stating that the variable must not exceed 3, and the other stating that the variable must be at least 4. Then the two problems and their solutions are stored in a list. The following procedure is then used.

Pick the best solution from the list; if it is integer, it is optimal. Otherwise, as above, choose a variable in that solution that is not integer but should be, and solve two linear programming problems, storing the resulting solutions in the list. Then the best solution on the list is chosen, a variable is branched upon, etc. The method is particularly successful because feasible integer solutions are usually found early in the solution process. Once such a solution has been found, the solution can be terminated at any time, as is often done in practice. A bound on how far the solution can be from optimal is known; it is the difference between the objective function value of the best-known integer solution and the objective function value of the best noninteger solution on the list.

IMPLICIT ENUMERATION METHODS

These are methods for solving all-integer problems. Most of the successfully implemented variations also require that all integer variables be either zero or one, but more general methods have been developed. The idea of the method is straightforward: if there are n variables, each of which must be 0 or 1, there are 2^n possible solutions to enumerate; explicit enumeration would require explicit consideration of each of them. By using tests that follow conceptually from using implied upper and lower bounds on variables, generally only a tiny fraction of all possibilities needs to be considered with the implicit treatment of all possibilities. Some auxiliary techniques used to accelerate implicit enumeration have been derived from linear programming.

Putting the Computational Considerations into Perspective

We conclude this article with a few comments about the current state of computational efficiency in mathe-

matical programming. Very large linear programming problems (having thousands of constraints) may be solved and have been solved, inexpensively, although it is certainly possible to dream up problems that are too large for solution. Fairly large nonlinear programming problems (including quadratic programming and separable programming) that employ methods based on linear programming methods may be solved at reasonable cost. Beyond that, linear constraints are much easier to handle than nonlinear constraints. In integer programming, although some fairly large problems have been and are being solved on a routine basis, there are still many relatively small problems that are computationally difficult to solve.

In perspective, mathematical programming gives a potentially very powerful means for formulating and solving optimization problems. Numerous methods have been developed and implemented in many computer systems, and are an effective means of solving many optimization problems.

Bibliography

1984. Karmarkar, N. "A New Polynomial Time Algorithm for Linear Programming," *Combinatorica*, **4**, 373–395.

1988. Parker, R. G., and Rardin, R. L. *Discrete Optimization.* New York: Academic Press.

1995. Bertsekas, D. P. *Nonlinear Programming.* Belmont, MA: Athena Scientific.

1996. Sierksma, G. *Linear and Integer Programming: Theory and Practice.* New York: Marcel Dekker.

Stanley Zionts and Ramaswamy Ramesh

MATHEMATICAL SOFTWARE

For articles on related subjects *see* ALGORITHM; APPROXIMATION THEORY; COMPUTER ALGEBRA; MATHEMATICAL PROGRAMMING; MATRIX COMPUTATIONS; NUMERICAL ANALYSIS; SOFTWARE LIBRARIES, NUMERICAL AND STATISTICAL; and SYMBOL MANIPULATION.

Mathematical software is software that implements algorithms that have a basis in mathematics. The scope of the term is generally accepted to include algorithms whose primary interest or motivation is mathematical and not merely the application of mathematics. Thus, a computer program to solve a system of first-order differential equations is considered to be mathematical software. A program to solve a chemical reaction problem is not mathematical software, even though the essence of the program might be an algorithm for solving differential equations. The scope of the term is much broader than a pure mathematician's view of mathematics; it includes some aspects of programming languages and computer systems. The scope is also much broader than traditional *numerical analysis*, for it includes such areas as statistics, symbolic mathematical analysis, and linear programming, which are clearly mathematical in nature.

The origins of mathematical software came with the advent of modern computers. A Mark I routine for $\sin(x)$ was published in 1944, and the first operational electronic computer (EDSAC) had a well thought out subroutine library in 1950. Activity and interest in the area grew steadily, and by 1970 mathematical software began to be recognized as a separate subdiscipline of the mathematics–computer science area.

Classification

Mathematical software can be classified from several points of view, and one of the most natural is according to complexity or mathematical level. At the bottom are algorithms for arithmetic; i.e. addition, subtraction, multiplication, and division. In many instances, these algorithms are more appropriately called *mathematical hardware*, since they are usually carried out by the hardware of central processing units (*q.v.*). The wide variety of algorithms here stems from the different representations and types of numbers used. Not only are there different radices (base 2, 10, and 16 are common), but there are also different lengths (6 to 15 equivalent decimal digits are common), plus multiple-precision, fixed- and floating-point (or integers and reals), and complex numbers. More specialized arithmetics include interval arithmetic (*q.v.*) and significance arithmetic. Each combination of these representations and types requires algorithms for the basic arithmetic operations.

The next higher mathematical level includes the evaluation of the functions of algebra, trigonometry, and analysis (e.g. roots and powers, sines and cosines, exponentials, logarithms, and a selection of "higher" functions). These are the *elementary functions* that are commonly included as the built-in mathematical routines of higher-level languages such as Ada, Algol, C, Fortran, and Pascal. These built-in routines allow one to write statements such as the following:

```
X = SIN(3.2) + ALOG(4.7)/5.1    (Fortran)

x := sin(3.2) + ln(4.7)/5.1     (Algol or Pascal)

x = sin(3.2) + log(4.7)/5.1;    (C)
```

The following algorithm illustrates how an efficient evaluation is made for the sine function $\sin(x)$.

> Set $Y = X \bmod (2\pi)$
> If $Y > \pi$ then set $Y = Y - \pi$, SIGN $= -1$
>   else set SIGN $= 1$
> If $Y > \pi/2$ then set $Y = \pi - Y$

> Set $Z = Y/3$
> Compute SIN(Z) using a cubic polynomial accurate to 10 decimal places
> Set $\text{SIN}(X) = \text{SIGN} * \text{SIN}(Z) * (3 - 4\,\text{SIN}^2(Z))$

One may obtain 20-decimal-digit accuracy by replacing the cubic polynomial by an appropriate sixth-degree polynomial. The state-of-the-art for this software is such that high-quality programs are tailored to exploit the specific characteristics of each computer's arithmetic-logic unit (*q.v.*).

The next level of mathematical software includes the algorithms of linear algebra (e.g. solving linear systems of equations) and the operations of calculus and advanced calculus (e.g. integration, differentiation, and solving nonlinear equations). These mathematical problems are an order of magnitude more difficult than those discussed above. This software is distinguished from the previous level by two other characteristics. First, it is well known that it is impossible to solve most of the underlying mathematical problems in complete generality. Thus, given any algorithm for integrating functions, one can construct a function for which the algorithm fails. This is true whether the integration algorithm is symbolic or numerical or a combination. Second, one should expect to discover new algorithms that are much superior to currently known ones.

The highest level of mathematical software is an integrated system for a particular branch of mathematics or all of mathematics up to a particular level. Several systems of this type, such as *Mathematica*, are described in the article COMPUTER ALGEBRA. Mathematica attempts to provide numerical, graphic, and symbolic capability up through calculus. One expects it to allow one to do mathematics at this level in ordinary mathematics terms, not using lower level, specialized algorithmic languages like Fortran, Pascal, Ada, or C. There are two primary goals of these mathematical systems. The first is to use standard mathematical notation; the system is to communicate with users in their own terms. Such systems allow statements like

$$A = \int_0^{1.8} \cos(x^2 + 1)\sqrt{x + 2}\; dx$$

$$\text{SOLVE } Bx^2 - 3.1e^{-x} = HBAR$$

$$F(T) = A'(T) + \int_0^{T+1} \sin(x)/(A(x) + 1)\, dx$$

The second goal is to incorporate high-quality, robust algorithms and software to carry out the mathematical procedures allowed in the language. These algorithms are integrated with one another and the overall system so that the results of one are automatically compatible with the others. The development of mathematical systems involves a broad range of mathematics and computer science. The computing areas involved most directly are symbolic manipulation, numerical methods, computational geometry (q.v.), and expert systems (q.v.), all supported by programming languages, operating systems, graphics, and powerful computers. These systems are examples of *problem-solving environments* (q.v.).

Mathematical algorithms can also be divided into two classes, according to whether the algorithm is "static" or "deterministic," or whether it is "dynamic" or "heuristic" (q.v.). This division is not precise, but it serves a useful intuitive purpose. An algorithm is said to be *static* if its operation is known fully in advance. Examples of static algorithms are those of arithmetic, symbolic differentiation, Simpson's rule for quadrature, and the evaluation of $\sin(x)$. The ambiguity of this classification arises from the word "known," and the division depends upon how much one knows. An algorithm is *dynamic* or *heuristic* or *adaptive* if its operation is somewhat unpredictable in advance.

Unpredictability normally comes from logical decisions that are made on the basis of quantities computed during the operation of the algorithm. An example of such software is a *polyalgorithm*, which is set of static algorithms plus a strategy for choosing and switching among them. Polyalgorithms were first introduced in the late 1960s with attempts to automate numerical analysis. Only a small portion of current mathematical software is dynamic, but this is an area with great potential significance and growth. As computing power increases and as knowledge about problem solving increases, these methods will gradually blur the distinction between algorithmic problem solving (q.v.—where the programmer is certain about all aspects of the method) and artificial intelligence (q.v.—where the system itself has helped to perfect aspects of the method).

Another common division of mathematical software is into *symbolic*, *numerical*, and *geometric* algorithms. This division is easily seen in simple cases. Integer addition and symbolic differentiation of polynomials are symbolic; the exact results are obtained after a finite number of symbolic operations. Newton's method for polynomial zeros and Simpson's rule for integration are numerical. Approximate results are obtained, but they can be made as accurate as one pleases with sufficient effort and precision in the arithmetic. The constructions of Euclidean geometry are graphical. Perhaps one could call them symbolic, but they are symbols very different from algebra. Geometric mathematical software is still in its infancy compared with symbolic and numerical software. The algorithms of arithmetic are symbolic, but—unfortunately and unavoidably—they

are incorrect due to the fixed precision of arithmetic. The algorithms of geometry are implemented using arithmetic, so they too are incorrect beyond a certain level of precision. This incorrectness introduces ambiguity in the distinction between symbolic, numerical, and geometric algorithms. For example, many of the algorithms of linear algebra are symbolic (e.g. Gaussian elimination for solving linear equations), but are considered to be part of numerical analysis. This is perhaps because one of the most important questions is the effect that incorrect arithmetic has upon these algorithms. On the other hand, polynomial manipulation is considered to be symbolic, and yet some programs for this take $(2X + 3) + (1/2) * (3X - 4)$ to be $3.5X + 1$, and thus are also subject to incorrectness due to the arithmetic. The depth and difficulty of understanding this distinction is much greater than one might conjecture. For example, there is a well-known formula to express the roots X_0 and X_1 of $ax^2 + bx + c = 0$ in terms of a, b, and c. However, given that a, b, c, X_0 and X_1 are representable in a particular computer, as yet there is no known program to produce X_0 and X_1 from a, b, and c which will always be correct (for this computer).

General Problems

Mathematical software contains three general problems and areas of great importance. One of these is the *dissemination of software*, and while it may be a somewhat mundane problem, it is also a very difficult one. The objective is simple: make the best and most effective software available to *everyone* in a natural, efficient, and automatic manner. Materials that fall into this area include *subroutine libraries*, *textbooks*, *published algorithms*, and *reference manuals*. All these materials are prone to weaknesses in documentation, effectiveness, efficiency, ease-of-use, and ease-of-access. The best solution to the dissemination problem is the creation of problem-solving environments for mathematics where the problem-solving know-how and abilities of the builders are incorporated into the system.

A second problem area of great theoretical and practical interest is the *evaluation of algorithms*. The problems here range from the foundations of mathematics to experimental investigations. Symbolic algorithms have been studied from the point of view of pure mathematics, and a variety of proof techniques of a very rigorous nature have been used. Complex and numerical algorithms are much less tractable for rigorous and mathematical proofs, and new techniques (both mathematical and experimental) are needed.

Finally, we come to the *resource allocation* aspect of mathematical software. A simple example of this is the trade-off between computation time and memory used. There are frequent instances in which significantly faster execution results by using significantly larger amounts of memory. The advent of sophisticated multi-programming systems and parallel computers with hierarchies of memories has introduced another dimension to the creation and evaluation of mathematical software.

Libraries

High-quality collections, libraries, and packages of mathematical software first appeared in the 1970s. These include two commercial libraries of algorithms and several systematized collections—the BLAS (Basic Linear Algebra Subroutines), EISPACK (56 routines for matrix eigensystems), FUNPACK (covers a number of the more difficult, higher transcendental functions), and LINPACK (linear systems of equations). All these collections are available for a modest handling fee. The Association for Computing Machinery *Transactions on Mathematical Software* and a few other journals regularly publish mathematical software; over 750 ACM algorithms have appeared, and those published since 1975 are available in machine-readable form from the ACM Algorithms Distribution Service or through *Netlib* (see below). Other packages appeared in the 1980s, covering a dozen or so subareas of mathematics (e.g. ordinary differential equations, partial differential equations (*q.v.*), numerical quadrature, homotopy maps).

There is now a substantial network infrastructure for locating and retrieving mathematical software. The *Guide to Available Mathematical Software* (GAMS) system provides an interactive online system to identify library routines for solving a broad range of problems. Its Web address is `http://math.nist.gov/gams/` and it covers major commercial and public domains libraries, about 10,000 routines in all. The *Netlib* system is a repository for public domain and freely usable mathematical libraries and packages. The source code of 10–15,000 routines can be obtained directly from `http://www.netlib.org` or by email; there have been almost 20 million requests to *Netlib* since it was established in the late 1970s.

Bibliography

1984. Cowell, W. R. *Sources and Development of Mathematical Software.* Upper Saddle River, NJ: Prentice Hall.
1987. Ford, B., and Chatelin, F. *Problem Solving Environments for Scientific Computing.* Amsterdam: North-Holland.
1991. Houstis, E., Rice, J., and Vichnevetsky, R. *Intelligent Scientific Software Systems.* Amsterdam: North-Holland.
1997. Boisvert, R. F. *Quality of Numerical Software: Assessment and Enhancement.* London: Chapman & Hall.

John R. Rice

MATHEMATICS, COMPUTERS IN

For articles on related subjects *see* BOOLEAN ALGEBRA; COMBINATORICS; COMPUTATIONAL GEOMETRY; COMPUTER ALGEBRA; COOPERATIVE COMPUTING; DISCRETE MATHEMATICS; FACTORING INTEGERS; FUZZY LOGIC; GRAPH THEORY; INTEGER SEQUENCES, ONLINE ENCYCLOPEDIA OF; NUMBER THEORETIC CALCULATIONS; SCIENTIFIC APPLICATIONS; and THEOREM PROVING.

Introduction

Many articles in this Encyclopedia are about the application of mathematics to computer science (and other subjects) through use of a computer. In this article we explore the converse, instances where a computer has been used to discover new mathematical knowledge.

Listed in order of increasing sophistication, a computer program can contribute to mathematics in one of five different ways:

1. by strengthening or refuting conjectures
2. by confirming the proofs of known theorems
3. by finding specific examples of structures known to exist by nonconstructive proofs
4. by completing partial proofs carried as far as possible by human mathematicians
5. by finding new conjectures and proving them when possible

Examples of each follow.

Strengthening and Refuting Conjectures

RIEMANN AND GOLDBACH

The empirical probabilities that two of the most famous outstanding conjectures in mathematics are true, the *Riemann hypothesis* (that all of the roots of the analytically continued Riemann zeta function have real part $1/2$) and the *Goldbach conjecture* (that all even numbers greater than 2 are the sum of two primes) have been greatly increased through the use of programs that have examined (literally) over a trillion cases without finding a counterexample to either. Such tests undoubtedly encourage mathematicians to continue to seek proofs for them.

MERSENNE NUMBERS

Numbers of the form $M_q = 2^q - 1$ where q is a prime number are called *Mersenne numbers* after Marin Mersenne (1588–1648), who was the first to study them extensively. When a number of the form $2^n - 1$ is prime, it can be proved that its corresponding n is also prime. Mersenne knew that the converse is not true ($M_{11} = 2047 = 23 \times 89$), but he thought that M_{67} and M_{257} were prime and they are not. Had he had access to even a very early computer, he would undoubtedly have found their factors (*see* COOPERATIVE COMPUTING).

SUMS OF POWERS

Euler thought that no integer raised to the nth power could be expressed as the sum of fewer than n other nth powers. In 1988, Noam Elkies used a computer search to find the first known counterexample for 4th powers, and Roger Frye did a more extensive supercomputer search to find the one involving the smallest numbers:

$$422481^4 = 95800^4 + 217519^4 + 414560^4.$$

Theorem Proving

Confirming the validity of proofs of known theorems has been a focus of theorem proving (*q.v.*) and computer algebra (*q.v.*), though not a principal one. Success here has been a striking example of artificial intelligence (*q.v.*) rather than of new mathematical discovery. (For an interesting example, *see* the description of Douglas Lenat's *Eurisko* program in HEURISTIC.) But sometimes the computer finds a *better* proof than had been known. The Newell–Simon–Shaw *Logic Theorist* found proofs for 38 of the 52 theorems from the Whitehead–Russell *Principia* including a much more straightforward proof of theorem 2.85 (a simple theorem in propositional logic) than had the authors. Lord Russell was impressed, and in 1956 wrote to Herbert Simon (*q.v.*):

> I am delighted to know that *Principia Mathematica* can now be done by machinery ... I am quite willing to believe that everything in deductive logic can be done by machinery.

The editor of the prestigious *Journal of Symbolic Logic*, however, was neither sufficiently impressed nor amused to accept an article allegedly co-authored by the *Logic Theorist* describing the shorter proof of theorem 2.85 (*see* MacKenzie, 1995).

Supplementing Nonconstructive Proofs

Sometimes a proof is known that some mathematical structure or relationship exists, but the proof is *nonconstructive*, that is, it does not in and of itself find a particular example. For example, the *fundamental theorem of algebra* states that an nth degree polynomial equation has n roots, some of which may be complex or multiple, but does not say how to find them. Algorithms for finding the roots to any desired degree of accuracy do exist, but using a computer to find them is just an extension of the longstanding use of calculators to do so, so the example is not particularly interesting. Similarly, there are tests that can prove that certain large integers are composite without specifying what their factors are. The search then degenerates into application of the best-known algorithms for factoring integers (*q.v.*). The author is indebted to Ian Stewart for citing these examples.

More interesting are cases where a heuristic (*q.v.*) rather than an algorithmic search has successfully found something long sought by mathematicians who knew, by nonconstructive proof, that what they sought must exist. Very recently, Divakar Viswanath did exactly that in his computer-assisted proof regarding probabilistic Fibonacci sequences, finding a new mathematical constant in the process.

In the classic Fibonacci sequence 0 1 1 2 3 5 8 13 ... each new term is the sum of the prior two. Then the nth term of the sequence is known to be the integer closest to $\varphi^n/\sqrt{5}$ where φ is the "golden ratio" $(1+\sqrt{5})/2 = 1.61803\ldots$. Now suppose we modify the usual rule for producing a Fibonacci sequence so that a coin toss (or any event that occurs with probability $1/2$) determines, at each step, whether a new term is formed as the sum of the prior two terms or their difference. Suppose we start with 0 1, flip a coin, and obtain HHHTHTTHT.... Then the sequence produced would be 0 1 1 2 3 −1 2 −3 5 2 3.... In his *American Scientist* column *Computing Science*, Brian Hayes (1999) calls such sequences "Vibonacci numbers" because their first few values "vibrate" between positive and negative values, but he presents graphical results that show that the sequence eventually rises exponentially.

In 1960, Hillel Furstenberg and Harry Kesten proved that for a general class of random-sequence generating processes that includes the random Fibonacci sequence, the absolute value of the nth member of the sequence will, with probability 1, approach a constant times the nth power of some fixed number. Now it is not obvious that the terms of the modified Fibonacci sequence just given are increasing in value, but according to the Furstenberg–Kesten theorem, the absolute value of the nth term must be proportional to some specific number raised to the nth power. But *what* number? Their proof was nonconstructive, and simple numerical experimentation is not fruitful because successive terms fluctuate chaotically in ways characteristic of fractals (*q.v.*). But Viswanath, using a combination of esoteric mathematics and carefully controlled multiple-precision arithmetic, found that the sought-after constant is $1.13198824\ldots$. Research continues to see if this number is related to one of the "Feigenvalues" (*see* SCIENTIFIC APPLICATIONS).

Proof Through Human–Computer Partnership

On rare occasions, a mathematician has been able to prove a theorem for all but a finite number of special cases, a number too large to cope with by hand, or to reduce the entire theorem to proof of a humanly intractable number of cases. By writing a computer program which confirms that the conjecture holds for each and every potentially troublesome case, the proof is completed (provided, of course, that the program is correct).

A CONVERGENCE THEOREM

The first instance of this method known to the author was the 1959 doctoral dissertation "On the Convergence of Infinite Exponentials" by Donald L. Shell (who is better known for his invention of *Shellsort*; *see* SORTING). Shell sought to prove that his conjecture held throughout a unit circle in the complex plane, but, unaided, was able to do so only up to a certain small distance from the circle's rim. But he was able to show that only a finite number of points needed testing within the troublesome annulus, and wrote a program to do so.

FOUR-COLOR THEOREM

A second example of this technique is much better known, the computer-assisted proof of the four-color theorem by Appel and Haken (1977). The Four-Color Problem dates back to 1852, when Francis Guthrie, while coloring a map of English counties, was surprised to note that he needed only four colors. He wondered whether it was true that *any* map can be colored using at most four colors in such a way that adjacent regions (i.e. those sharing a common boundary segment, not just a point) are colored differently. The conjecture was conveyed to Augustus DeMorgan, who found neither a proof nor a counterexample. The problem was first discussed in print by Arthur Cayley in 1878.

Even proving that there can be no map containing five regions each of which touches the other four is difficult, but that is not sufficient to prove the four-color theorem. Note from Fig. 1a on Color Page CP-11 that there can be four regions each of which touches the other three, but Fig. 1b on Color Page CP-11 shows a map that needs four colors even though it does not contain four mutually contiguous regions.

The four-color map problem can also be expressed as a vertex coloring of the map's equivalent graph (*see* GRAPH THEORY). What frustrated mathematicians was that they could prove that, for a map laid out on a torus, at most seven colors are needed (and some require seven), but for the seemingly simpler plane (or sphere), their best lower bound was five. Appel and Haken were able to show that if no more than four colors were needed for any of 1,936 basic cases, more than four would never be needed. (The number of basic cases was later reduced to 633.) When they

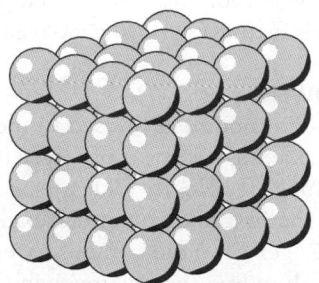

Figure 2. Oranges stacked inefficiently one over the other.

completed their proof through use of a computer program that eliminated these cases, other mathematicians were skeptical, but the proof has now been independently verified by Neil Robertson and his co-workers (1996) with a newer program that uses a slightly different technique.

SPHERE PACKING

Another centuries-old conjecture traceable to Johannes Kepler has been confirmed by this method very recently; the question as to how spheres of identical size, oranges or marbles perhaps, can be packed so as to waste the least possible space. More precisely, a maximally optimum packing density is sought for spheres packed into a bin so large that wall constraints can be ignored. The problem has more than recreational interest; it has application to the development of efficient error correcting and detecting codes (*q.v.*).

For a *lattice packing*—one in which the spheres have a regular geometric arrangement based on a unit cell that, when replicated, fills all of space—the packing density is defined as the ratio of the volume of the spheres in a unit cell to the total volume of the cell.

Figure 3. Thirty-five marbles stacked in a tetrahedral array.

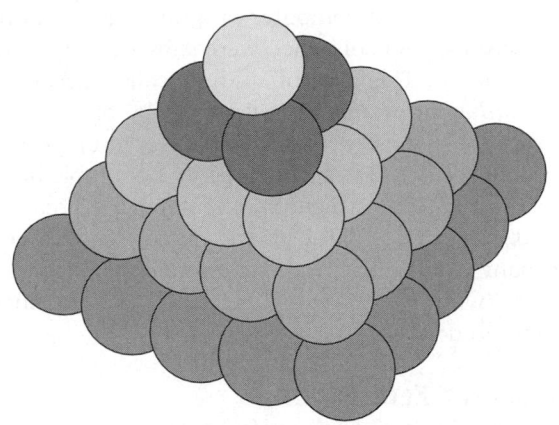

Figure 4. Fifty-five marbles stacked in a pyramidal array.

Stacking each rectangularly arranged layer of spheres directly over another layer as in Fig. 2 forms a cubic lattice whose unit cell has side $2r$ and volume $2r^3$, where r is the radius of every sphere. In that unit cell, there is $1/8$ of a sphere at each of the eight vertices (since each sphere is co-equally shared by 8 cells), which totals exactly one sphere. Thus the packing density is $\frac{4}{3}\pi r^3 / 8r^3 = \pi/6 = 0.5236\ldots$, which wastes 48% of available space.

Since Kepler first discussed the problem almost 400 years ago, it had remained a conjecture that letting each sphere fall into the depression formed by the group of four below it—the "grocer's" or "cannonball" arrangement—was optimum. Interestingly, the same allegedly best packing density is attained whether spheres are stacked in a tetrahedron (having a triangular base) as in Fig. 3 or in a pyramid (having a square or rectangular base) as in Fig. 4. In that figure, note that although the base layer is a rectangle, each of the four other faces (only two of which are visible) exhibits the same

"hexagonal-close-packed" pattern that is characteristic of any face of Fig. 3. For either a tetrahedral or pyramidal packing, the packing density is $\pi/\sqrt{18}$ which wastes only 26% of available space.

In 1832, Gauss proved that of all *lattice* packings, the grocer's arrangement attained the greatest density. But since it was still thought possible that some irregular packing might, when averaged over a large volume, achieve a still higher packing density, the conjecture that the grocer's arrangement was best of *all* packings remained outstanding. And to add to the frustration of the mathematical community, it was known that ellipsoids (or eggs!) could be packed much more densely than spheres.

A simple way to compute the packing density is to note that the centers of the spheres in the rectangular-based grocer's arrangement form what crystallographers call a *face-centered cubic* (fcc) structure. The 14 spheres that form such an arrangement are shown in Fig. 5a (where, for clarity, spheres are shrunk to much smaller ones that have the same centers). This fcc unit cell has, as was the case with the simple cubic cell, one eighth of a sphere at each of eight vertices and one-half of a sphere in the center of each of six faces, for a total of four spheres. These fractions are shown in Fig. 5c (and more esthetically in Fig. 6 on Color Page CP-11). Since the diagonal of any face is $4r$, its side is $\sqrt{8}r$ and the packing density is $\frac{16}{3}\pi r^3 / 8\sqrt{8}r^3 = \pi/\sqrt{18}$, the allegedly optimum density.

R. Buckminster Fuller thought he had proved the Kepler conjecture in 1975, as did Wu-Yi Hsiang about 10 years later, but their "proofs" did not withstand careful scrutiny. Finally, in a heralded breakthrough in 1998, Thomas Hales completed an elaborate 250 page proof that showed how to reduce the interstitial spaces

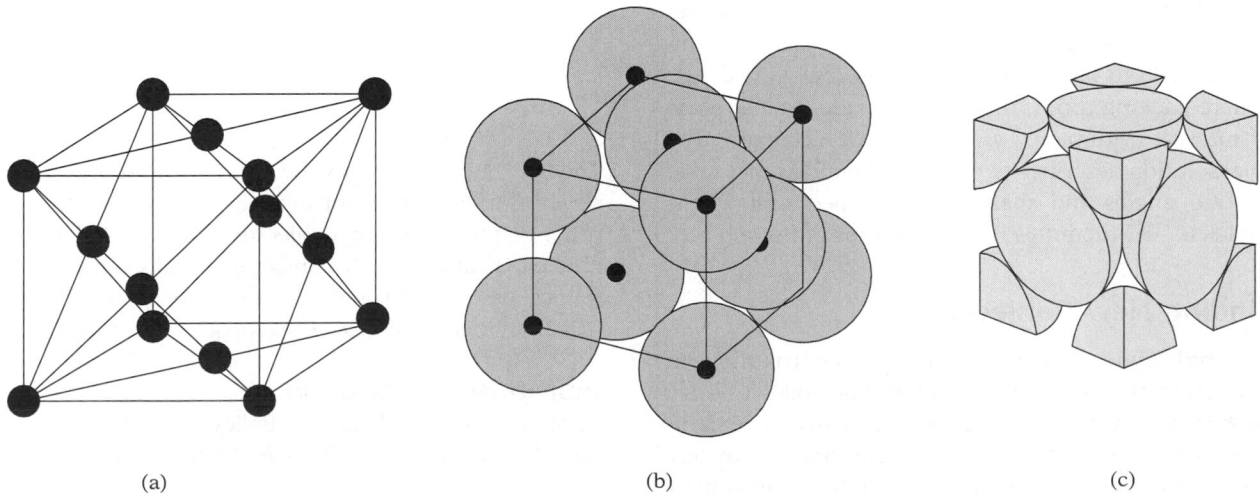

      (a)   (b)   (c)

Figure 5. (a) The centers of the 14 spheres that form an fcc lattice. (b) A view of the actual spheres in which only 10 of the 14 are visible. (c) Cutaway showing the fraction of each sphere that lies inside the fcc unit cell.

in any conceivable packing, lattice or not, to one of 5,094 "star" arrangements, each having a computable "score" relative to fcc packing. The lower the score, the greater the packing density. He then transformed each star into a problem in linear programming (*see* MATHEMATICAL PROGRAMMING) and wrote a program that found that none of the 5,094 stars had a score lower than the 8.0 score of the fcc packing. The program used interval arithmetic (*q.v.*) to make sure that no mistake was made due to round-off error (*q.v.*). Despite the length of the computer-assisted proof, mathematicians seem to have accepted its validity.

THE DOUBLE-BUBBLE THEOREM

For as long as soap bubbles have been studied, it has been recognized that the sphere has the minimum surface of all those that might be used to enclose a given volume. The proof of this 2,000 year old theorem is remarkably recent, however, dating back to Hermann Schwarz in 1882. But until 1995, the most efficient shape for enclosing *two* equal volumes remained uncertain. Mathematicians believed, but had not proved, that use of two coalesced spherical bubbles would be optimum, and even if that turned out to be true, the question would remain as to the size of the disk of separation relative to the radii of the spheres. Work by Michael Hutchings, Fred Almgren, Jean Taylor, and Brian White narrowed the problem down to two possible families of bubbles, the standard double bubble and the donut-shaped "torus" bubble, a donut with a dumbbell through the hole in the middle (*see* Fig. 7 on Color Page CP-11).

In 1995, Joel Hass and Roger Schlafly found a computer-assisted proof that a double-bubble separated by a flat disk, meeting along a circle at an angle of $2\pi/3$, is indeed optimum. The proof involves an exhaustive comparison of all possible minimizing surfaces, but only after narrowing the search of conceivable shapes to 200,260 particular calculations which their computer was able to run in about 20 minutes. As with the sphere packing proof, the authors made extensive use of interval arithmetic (*q.v.*) to ensure accuracy. The final solution describes two identical bubbles that meet at 120° angles and share a disk-shaped wall whose radius is $\frac{1}{2}\sqrt{3}$ (about 87%) of the radius of the spheres.

Finding New Conjectures

The fifth type of computer-related contribution to mathematics is the most profound. The ability to solve problems, however valuable, is not nearly as remarkable as the ability to pose them. Can anyone (or any thing) other than a human propose interesting conjectures? Could it prove those that it does find? We shall defer that last question for the moment and cite

examples where a computer program has found new conjectures, some of which were subsequently proved by a human. This area of study is called *experimental mathematics* and is now served by an electronic journal of precisely that name (*see* http://www.expmath.org). But the field has an honorable history that well antedates digital computers; the great Carl Friedrich Gauss (1777–1855) admitted that the source of many of his discoveries was numerical experimentation (with pencil and paper and his magnificent brain, no doubt).

RIEMANN'S ZETA FUNCTION

Consider the Riemann zeta function,

$$\zeta(n) = \sum_{k=1}^{\infty} k^{-n}$$

for integer values of $n > 1$. Euler, among others, knew that $\zeta(n)$ for even n was simply related to π^n; in particular $\zeta(2) = \pi^2/6$ and $\zeta(4) = \pi^4/90$. No one has yet found similar relations for odd n, but a program called *PSLQ* developed by H. R. P. Ferguson and David Bailey systematically searches for interesting relations among multiple values of $\zeta(n)$, including those of odd n. In 1993, Enrico Au-Yeung, then an undergraduate at the University of Waterloo, found experimentally that

$$\sum_{k=1}^{\infty} (1 + 1/2 + \cdots + 1/k)^2 k^{-2}$$

seemed to be equal to $\frac{17}{4}\zeta(4)$ and hence to $17\pi^4/360$. When asked to search for similar relationships called *Euler sums*, *PSLQ* then proceeded to propose, among others, the conjectures

$$s_h(2,2) = \tfrac{3}{2}\zeta(4) - \tfrac{1}{2}\zeta^2(2) = 11\pi^4/360$$
$$s_h(3,2) = \tfrac{15}{2}\zeta(5) + \zeta(2)\zeta(3)$$

where

$$s_h(m,n) = \sum_{k=1}^{\infty} (1 + 1/2 + \cdots + 1/k)^m (k+1)^{-n},$$

$$m \geq 1, n \geq 2.$$

The first of these has now been proved and, through a straightforward transformation, is equivalent to a proof of the Au-Yeung conjecture. It is probable that a proof of other *PSLQ* conjectures will eventually be found, perhaps through use of a computer algebra (*q.v.*) language such as *Maple* or *Mathematica*.

INDIVIDUAL DIGITS OF π

In another targeted search, Bailey *et al.* (1997) used the *PSLQ* program to discover the formula

$$\pi = \sum_{k=0}^{\infty} \frac{1}{16^k} \left(\frac{4}{8k+1} - \frac{2}{8k+4} - \frac{1}{8k+5} - \frac{1}{8k+6} \right)$$

which has now been proved. The formula is astonishing because, given the factor 16^{-k} as a clue, it allows the calculation of the nth digit of the hexadecimal representation of π without computing any of its prior digits! That algorithm is given at `http://www.mathsoft.com/asolve/plouffe/plouffe.html`. Using it and starting at the one hundred billionth (10^{11}) place, Fabrice Bellard obtained the hex digits 921C73C6838FB2. A group has formed that is using cooperative computing (*q.v.*) to obtain the one trillionth hex digit. Such sequences could have application as "one-time pads" in cryptography since, even if an "enemy" intercepted a message known to have used hex π as a key, he or she would not have the foggiest idea of the digit at which the sequence began. Guessing among, say, 10^{15} possibilities would be computationally intractable.

No similar formula is known for obtaining the nth decimal digit of π, but the decimal number system is no more fundamental, and arguably less so, than the hex (and hence binary) system. This should, but probably will not, end the continual *Guinness Book of Records*-like search for ever more decimal digits of π (*see* the Timeline in Appendix IX).

FINDING AND PROVING NEW CONJECTURES

To quote Douglas Hofstadter: "Clark Kimberling's work on theorem-discovery in geometry is about the most interesting use I have ever seen of computers for the purpose of exploration of mathematics. He first uses the computer to search for new theorems in Euclidean geometry (the geometry of the triangle, specifically), and then when it has found a conjecture (through numerical coincidences too unlikely to be just coincidences), he asks it to prove the theorem, and it often succeeds in doing so. So the computer acts the role of a full mathematician, in a sense, both making conjectures and proving them. It lacks, however, any sense of esthetics or interestingness, and hence it has to be guided or at least filtered by a human mathematician."

In the second part of this article, the creator of the Kimberling program describes some of its successes.

Bibliography

1959. Shell, D. L., "On the Convergence of Infinite Exponentials," *Ph.D. dissertation*, University of Cincinnati.
1977. Appel, K., and Haken, W. "The Four Color Theorem," *Scientific American*, **236**, 4 (October), 108–121.
1981. Davis, P. J., and Hersh, R. "Why Should I Believe a Computer?", in *The Mathematical Experience*, 380–387. Boston: Birkhäuser.
1995. MacKenzie, D. "The Automation of Proof: A Historical and Sociological Exploration," *IEEE Annals of the History of Computing*, **17**, 4 (Fall), 7–29.
1996. Hass, J., and Schlafly, R. "Bubbles and Double-bubbles," *American Scientist*, **84**, 5 (September–October), 462–467.
1996. Robertson, N., Sanders, D., Seymour, P., and Thomas, R. "A New Proof of the Four Color Theorem," *ERA Amer. Math. Soc.*, **2**, 17–25 (electronic). See also `http://www.math.gatech.edu/~thomas/FC/fourcolor.html`.
1997. Borwein, J. M., Borwein, P. B., Girgensohn, R., and Parnes, S. "Making Sense of Experimental Math," *Mathematical Intelligencer*, **18**, 4, 12–18.
1997. Bailey, D. H., Borwein, J. M., Borwein, P. B., and Plouffe, S. M. "The quest for Pi," *Mathematical Intelligencer*, **19**, 1, 50–57.
1998. Conway, J. H., and Sloane, N. J. A. *Sphere Packings, Lattices, and Groups*, 3rd Ed. New York: Springer-Verlag.
1998. Cipra, B. "Packing Challenge Mastered At Last," *Science*, **281**, *5381*, 1267.
1998. Sangalli, A. *The Importance of Being Fuzzy, and Other Insights from the Border between Math and Computers*. Princeton, NJ: Princeton University Press.
1999. Borwein, J. M., and Corless, R. M. "Emerging Tools for Experimental Mathematics," *American Mathematical Monthly*, **106**, 10 (December), 889–909.
1999. Hayes, B. "Computing Science: Vibonacci Numbers," *American Scientist*, **87**, 4 (July–August), 296–301.
1999. Wearne, D., and Aste, T. *The Pursuit of Perfect Packing*. Bristol, UK: IOP Publishing.
2000. Viswanath, D. "Random Fibonacci Sequences and the Number 1.13198824," *Mathematics of Computation* (to appear July).

Edwin D. Reilly

Computer-Based Theorem Discovery and Proof in Plane Geometry

Computer-based discovery of certain kinds of mathematical relationships has generated a resurgence of interest in the geometry of the triangle, and in some cases the method of discovery constitutes a proof. These developments proceed largely through two distinct but mutually reinforcing uses of the computer: (1) program-writing to detect certain "hits" (candidate conjectures) among many possibilities, and (2) visual output. These developments will be discussed under the separate headings of Methods and Software.

METHODS

Every point P in the plane of $\triangle ABC$ has homogeneous trilinear coordinates, or simply trilinears, written $x:y:z$, these being any numbers proportional to the directed distances from P to the sidelines BC, CA, AB, respectively. For example, the *incenter* of $\triangle ABC$ (where the angle bisectors meet), is $1:1:1$, since this point is equidistant from the three side lines. The vertices themselves are $A = 1:0:0$, $B = 0:1:0$, $C = 0:0:1$. Other points are defined in terms of the angles A, B, C or the side lengths a, b, c:

centroid (where the medians meet) $= 1/a:1/b:1/c$ $= \csc A:\csc B:\csc C$

circumcenter (where the perpendicular side-bisectors meet) $= \cos A:\cos B:\cos C$

orthocenter (where the altitudes meet) $=$ $\sec A:\sec B:\sec C$.

The incenter plus these three points are the ancient Greek centers, and the three just defined are collinear, defining an important line called the *Euler line*. Among many post-Renaissance centers are those defined by their trilinears as follows:

> *symmedian point* $= a : b : c$
>
> *Spieker center* $= a/(b + c) : b/(c + a) : c/(a + b)$.

There are also many 20th-century triangle centers, including

> *Schiffler point* $= 1/(\cos B - \cos C)$:
> $1/(\cos C - \cos A) : 1/(\cos A - \cos B)$
>
> *Hofstadter point* $= A/a : B/b : C/c$.

For constructions for these and a definition of "triangle center," see Weisstein (1999).

An important theorem is that three points $x_i : y_i : z_i$ are collinear if and only if $D = 0$ where D is the determinant of the matrix

$$\begin{bmatrix} x_1 & y_1 & z_1 \\ x_2 & y_2 & z_2 \\ x_3 & y_3 & z_3 \end{bmatrix}.$$

The rows represent the three vertices of a triangle, and when all three lie on the same line, the triangle is said to be *degenerate*. Algebraically, any row of the matrix representation of a degenerate triangle is a linear combination of the other two rows. According to a basic matrix theorem, this condition will ensure that $D = 0$. The converse is also true: if $D = 0$, then the rows are linearly dependent and the three points represented lie on the same line; there can be no false indication of collinearity.

Now consider a three-step program:

1. Memorize a list of n points $P_i = x_i : y_i : z_i$

2. For each selection P_i, P_j, P_k of three of the n points, compute D.

3. If $D = 0$, then print "Hit: $i, j, k =$"; i; j; k.

Such a program can be done symbolically, as by *Mathematica* or *Maple* (*see* COMPUTER ALGEBRA), or numerically. The latter is often preferable if the coordinates $x_i : y_i : z_i$ are laden with elaborate trigonometric functions.

For numerical work, double precision is necessary, and the criterion $D = 0$ must be programmed abs$(D) < \varepsilon$ for some appropriately small number ε. Each hit (i.e. possible new theorem) found for one choice of the side lengths a, b, c is then tested by a separate program in which D is evaluated for many values of a, b, c.

A list of 400 triangle centers appears in Kimberling (1998), and 360 of them are built into an available *Quick Basic* program named *Main*. Researchers can append new "trial points" to the program, which determines if the points are already in the list, and if not, which lines determined by the 360 triangle centers the trial points lie on.

The key to this method of theorem discovery and proof (whenever $D = 0$ symbolically, not just numerically) is that certain geometric properties are detectable by finding that a relevant matrix has a zero determinant. This simple key unlocks many kinds of new theorems, including collinearities of points and concurrences of lines, circles, conics, and other curves.

Another method depends on geometric inequalities, rather than equations. As an example representing hundreds of geometric inequalities found numerically and then tested for many values of the side lengths is the chain

$$d(G) \le d(S) \le d(I) \le d(K) \le d(H),$$

indicating that the orthocenter (H) is never closer to the centroid (G) than the symmedian point (K), which is never closer to (G) than the incenter (I), which is never closer than the Spieker center (S). The discovery of point-to-point and point-to-line distance relationships, typified by this one, is based on rather complicated formulas. It is largely the complexity of these formulas that accounts for the fact that many of these computer-discovered inequalities were found only recently and have yet to be proved.

Some researchers prefer to use barycentric coordinates instead of trilinears. The two systems are very closely related, and virtually everything (e.g. zero determinants) that works for trilinears works for barycentrics. For an elegant introduction to barycentric coordinates, see Coxeter (1969).

Among the most significant unsolved problems in triangle geometry is one sparked by the Schiffler point, Sc, and its relation to the incenter, I. A striking property of Sc is that the Euler lines of triangles BCI, CAI, ABI concur in Sc. The unsolved problem is to determine *all* triangle centers X for which the Euler lines of triangles BCX, CAX, ABX concur. (At least two solutions have been found by computer.) The significance of this unsolved problem is that it is meaningless unless "Euler line" is understood to be a function, not merely a line. That is, it is necessary to *evaluate* the Euler line at three different triangles. Similarly, centroid and incenter—indeed, all triangle centers and central lines (which by definition pass through two centers)—are functions of the variables *a, b, c*. The Schiffler problem was probably the earliest published in which geometric objects are necessarily regarded as functions. Others, with solutions found by computer methods, have been published subsequently.

SOFTWARE

There are two well-known software programs that enable virtually all plane Euclidean constructions. Descriptions of the programs, named *The Geometer's Sketchpad* and *Cabri*, are easily found on the Internet and in libraries. Here, we shall describe how *Sketchpad* has been used to discover new objects and properties.

Start with randomly chosen points *A, B, C* on the screen. Form their triangle and its incenter, *I*. Sketch the bisectors of angles *IBC* and *ICB* and their intersection with label $A_{\frac{1}{4}}$. Bisect angles *ICA* and *IAC* to obtain $B_{\frac{1}{4}}$, and angles *IAB* and *IBA* to obtain $C_{\frac{1}{4}}$. Sketch the lines $AA_{\frac{1}{4}}$, $BB_{\frac{1}{4}}$, $CC_{\frac{1}{4}}$ and discover that they meet in a point; label it $H_{\frac{1}{4}}$. Now vary point *A*, and watch the three moving lines: they always concur. The capacity of the program to show continuous change in this manner is called *dynamic geometry*.

To continue, bisect appropriate angles to obtain points $A_{\frac{1}{8}}$, $B_{\frac{1}{8}}$, $C_{\frac{1}{8}}$ for which the lines $AA_{\frac{1}{8}}$, $BB_{\frac{1}{8}}$, $CC_{\frac{1}{8}}$ concur in a point $H_{\frac{1}{8}}$. Repeat indefinitely to determine points $H_{\frac{1}{16}}, H_{\frac{1}{32}}, \ldots$ which approach a limit H_0. This remarkable limiting point was conceived using *Sketchpad* and is named the *Hofstadter point* after its discoverer, Douglas Hofstadter. Barycentric coordinates for H_0 are *A : B : C*. That is, H_0 is the point *X* inside $\triangle ABC$ for which the three areas *BCX, CAX, ABX* are proportional to the angles *A, B, C*.

A particularly powerful *Sketchpad* command is `locus`. As an example of its use to discover theorems, start with a sketch of a triangle *ABC*, its circumcircle Γ, incenter *I*, and incircle Γ' meeting sides *BC, CA, AB* at points *A', B', C'* respectively. Place *C''* anywhere on Γ' and determine points *A''* and *B''* on Γ' so that the angles *C''IC', B''IB', A''IA'* are equal. Sketch tangent lines to Γ' at *A'', B'',* and *C''*. Label the intersection of the last two tangent lines as A_t and label the other two points of intersection as B_t and C_t. Now, driving *C''* around Γ', watch the vertices of $\triangle A_t B_t C_t$ stay on the circumcircle, illustrating a famous theorem called *Poncelet's porism*. To discover theorems that may be new, construct a triangle center *X* of $\triangle A_t B_t C_t$, and use `locus`. If *X = K* (the symmedian point), *Sketchpad* suggests that the locus is an ellipse; if *X = S* (the Spieker center), the locus appears to be a circle; if *X = m* (midpoint of segment $B_t C_t$), the locus looks like a limaçon. These cases are shown in Fig 8. Rigorous proofs remain to be found.

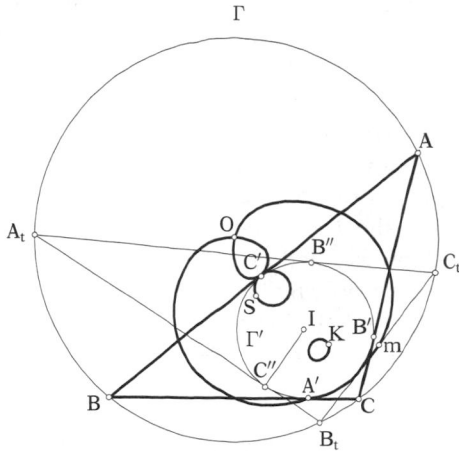

Figure 8. Triangle *ABC* with circumcenter Γ and incenter Γ'. As *C''* and the triangle $A_t B_t C_t$ that defines it (see narrative) are rotated around *I*, one known theorem is demonstrated (Poncelet's porism: points A_t, B_t, C_t stay on circumcircle Γ) and three conjectures are suggested, namely that the loci of triangle $A_t B_t C_t$'s symmedian point *K*, Spieker center *S*, and midpoint *m* of line segment $B_t C_t$ form, respectively, an ellipse, a circle and a limaçon.

Bibliography

1969. Coxeter, H. S. M. *Introduction to Geometry*, 2nd Ed. New York: John Wiley.
1995. David, P. J. "The Rise, Fall, and Possible Transfiguration of Triangle Geometry: A Mini-history," *American Mathematical Monthly*, **102**, 3, 204–214.
1998. Kimberling, C. *Triangle Centers and Central Triangles*, special volume of *Congressus Numerantium*, **129**, i–xxv, 1–295.
1999. Weisstein, E. W. *CRC Concise Encyclopedia of Mathematics*. Boca Raton, FL: CRC Press.

Clark Kimberling

MATRIX COMPUTATIONS

For articles on related subjects *see* ERROR ANALYSIS; LEAST-SQUARES APPROXIMATION; MATHEMATICAL SOFTWARE; NUMERICAL ANALYSIS; ROUNDOFF ERROR; and SCIENTIFIC APPLICATIONS.

A large proportion of the scientific calculations performed on computers involves *matrices*. Partly, this is because of the ubiquity of matrices in the mathematics of scientific problems, but it is also partly due to the fact that the use of matrices is ideally suited to the iterative type of calculation in which computers realize their full power.

Notation and Definitions

From the point of view of this article, a *matrix* is defined to be a rectangular array of elements, each of which will generally be a real or complex number. An $m \times n$ matrix will be denoted by a capital Roman letter, and the elements of such a matrix A will be denoted by a_{ij}, $i = 1, \ldots, m$, $j = 1, \ldots, n$. If $n = 1$, the matrix is called a *column vector* and a lower-case Roman letter will be used. The elements of a vector x of order m are denoted by x_i ($i = 1, \ldots, m$). The *transpose B* of an $m \times n$ matrix A is an $n \times m$ matrix defined by $b_{ij} = a_{ji}$. It is commonly denoted by A^T or A'. Similarly, the $1 \times m$ transpose of a column vector is denoted by x^T, and is called a *row vector*. The *Hermitian transpose B* of an $m \times n$ matrix A is defined by $b_{ij} = \bar{a}_{ji}$, where the bar over $\bar{a}$ denotes the complex conjugate, and is commonly denote by A^H or A^*; x^H is defined similarly.

If A and B are of the same dimension, their sum C is defined by $c_{ij} = a_{ij} + b_{ij}$. The product C of an $m \times k$ matrix A and a $k \times n$ matrix B is defined by

$$c_{ij} = \sum_{s=1}^{k} a_{is} b_{sj}.$$

Thus matrices A and B cannot be multiplied unless they *conform*: the number of columns of A must be equal to the number of rows of B.

The definition applies immediately to the product y of an $m \times n$ matrix A and an $n \times 1$ column vector x; we have

$$y_i = \sum_{s=1}^{n} a_{is} x_s.$$

In general, for square matrices A and B of the same size, $AB \neq BA$. In special cases where $AB = BA$, we say that A and B *commute*.

Finally, the product C of a matrix A by a scalar α is defined by

$$c_{ij} = \alpha a_{ij}.$$

A matrix or vector is said to be *null* if all its components are zero. Either "null" or "zero" will be denoted by the same symbol used for the zero scalar, the context providing adequate identification.

The *identity matrix* of order n is denoted by I_n, or by I if the order is obvious, and is defined by

$$i_{kk} = 1, \ i_{kl} = 0 \qquad (k \neq l).$$

The elements are usually denoted by δ_{kl} rather than by i_{kl}. From the definitions, $IA = A = AI$ whenever the dimensions are such that these exist.

It will be assumed that the reader is familiar with the concept of the scalar function of a square matrix A, known as its *determinant* and denoted by $\det(A)$. A square matrix A is said to be *singular* if $\det(A) = 0$;

otherwise, it is *nonsingular*. The matrix formed by the elements at the intersection of any collection of rows and columns is called a *submatrix*. The determinant of a square submatrix is called a *minor*; if the submatrix is formed from the intersection of the first r rows and columns, its determinant is called a *leading principal minor*. The *cofactor A_{ij}* of the element a_{ij} of an $n \times n$ square matrix A is defined by

$$A_{ij} = (-1)^{i+j} \det(\text{matrix formed by omitting} \\ \text{row } i \text{ and column } j).$$

The $n \times n$ matrix X with $x_{ij} = A_{ji}$ is called the *adjoint* of A, and it follows from the elementary properties of determinants that

$$AX = \det(A)I = XA.$$

Hence, if A is nonsingular, the matrix Y defined by $Y = X/\det(A)$ satisfies the relation $AY = YA = I$; Y is called the *inverse* of A and is denoted by A^{-1}.

The *rank r* of an $m \times n$ matrix A is defined to be the highest order of a nonzero minor. Clearly, $r \leq m, n$.

A set of matrices $A^{(1)}, \ldots, A^{(k)}$ is said to be *linearly dependent* if there exists a set of scalars α_i, not all zero, such that

$$\sum_{i=1}^{k} \alpha_i A^{(i)} = 0;$$

otherwise, they are said to be *linearly independent*. This concept is of particular interest when the $A^{(i)}$ are row or column vectors. If A is of rank r, then it has r independent rows and r independent columns; any k rows (or columns) with $k > r$ are linearly dependent.

The classes of square matrices defined below are of special interest in matrix computations.

Symmetric: $A = A^T$ (i.e. $a_{ij} = a_{ji}$).

Skew-symmetric (antisymmetric): $A = -A^T$
$$\text{(i.e. } a_{ij} = -a_{ji}).$$

Positive definite: A real, symmetric and $x^T A x > 0$
$$\text{for all real } x \neq 0.$$

Hermitian: $A = A^H$ (i.e. $a_{ij} = \bar{a}_{ji}$).

Unitary: $AA^H = A^H A = I$ (i.e. $A^H = A^{-1}$).

Orthogonal: A real and $AA^T = A^T A = I$.

Upper (lower) triangular: $a_{ij} = 0$, $i > j$ $\quad (i < j)$.

Tridiagonal: $a_{ij} = 0$, $|i - j| > 1$.

Upper-Hessenberg: $a_{ij} = 0$, $i > j + 1$.

The Solution of Simultaneous Linear Algebraic Equations

Perhaps the most fundamental of all computations is the solution of a system of m simultaneous linear equations in n unknowns:

$$\sum_{j=1}^{n} a_{ij}x_j = b_i \qquad (i=1,\ldots,m) \quad \text{or} \quad A\mathbf{x} = \mathbf{b},$$

where A is the $m \times n$ matrix (a_{ij}), and $\mathbf{x}$ and $\mathbf{b}$ are column vectors of order n and m, respectively. The mathematical theory is well known, the following being a brief summary.

Solutions exist if and only if rank $(A, \mathbf{b}) = \text{rank}(A)$. The general solution is based on the ability to solve any $r \times r$ system $C\mathbf{y} = \mathbf{d}$, where C is nonsingular. Such a system has the unique solution

$$\mathbf{y} = C^{-1}\mathbf{d},$$

the inverse C^{-1} existing since C is assumed to be nonsingular.

If $\text{rank}(A,\mathbf{b}) > \text{rank}(A)$, then there is no solution. If $\text{rank}(A,\mathbf{b}) = \text{rank}(A) = r$ (say), then the solutions are determined as follows: since A is of rank r, there is a nonsingular $r \times r$ submatrix of A; arrange the order of the equations and the order of the variables so that the leading principal $r \times r$ matrix is nonsingular. Then any solution of the first r equations is automatically a solution of the remainder. The first r equations may be written in the form

$$a_{i1}x_1 + \cdots + a_{ir}x_r = b_i - a_{i,r+1}x_{r+1} - \cdots - a_{in}x_n$$
$$= d_i \text{ (say)} \qquad (i=1,\ldots,r),$$

or
$$C\mathbf{x}^{(r)} = \mathbf{d}^{(r)},$$

where C is a nonsingular $r \times r$ matrix and $x^{(r)} = (x_1,\ldots,x_r)^T$. Hence, $x_{r+1},\ldots,x_n$ may be chosen arbitrarily, and for each such choice $x_1,\ldots,x_r$ are given uniquely as the solution of $C\mathbf{x}^{(r)} = \mathbf{d}^{(r)}$. If $r < n$, there is an $(n-r)$-fold infinity of solutions. If $r = n$, the solution is unique.

Of particular importance is the case $\mathbf{b} = 0$; the system is then called *homogeneous*. For such systems, rank $(A, \mathbf{b})$ certainly equals rank(A), and hence they are necessarily compatible, but if $r = n$, the only solution is $\mathbf{x} = 0$, the *null* solution. If $r < n$, there is an $(r-n)$-fold infinity of nonnull solutions.

The Practical Solution of a Nonsingular $n \times n$ System

The difficulties involved in solving a system of equations are almost entirely of a practical nature. It is essential that a method should be stable with respect to roundoff errors (*q.v.*) and be as economical as possible. Since the fundamental problem is the solution of a system with a square nonsingular matrix of coefficients, we now concentrate on this case. There are two main classes of methods. In *direct* methods the solution is obtained in a finite number of operations; without the intervention of rounding errors, it would be exact. In *iterative* methods a sequence $\mathbf{x}^{(k)}$ of solutions is obtained such that $\mathbf{x}^{(k)} \to \mathbf{x}$ is the true solution, as $k \to \infty$. In practice, iteration is terminated after a finite number of steps.

DIRECT METHODS

The best-known direct method is *Gaussian elimination*, which is merely a systematic version of the secondary school method of successive elimination of variables. We denote the original set of equations by

$$a_{i1}x_1 + a_{i2}x_2 + \cdots + a_{in}x_n = b_i \qquad (i=1,\ldots,n).$$

The variable x_1 is eliminated in each of equations $i = 2,\ldots,n$ by subtracting a multiple $m_{i1} = a_{i1}/a_{11}$ of the first equation from it. This gives the first derived set:

$$a_{11}x_1 + a_{12}x_2 + \cdots + a_{1n}x_n = b_1$$
$$a_{22}^{(1)}x_2 + \cdots + a_{2n}^{(1)}x_n = b_2^{(1)}$$
$$\cdots \qquad \cdots \qquad \cdots \qquad \cdots$$
$$a_{n2}^{(1)}x_2 + \cdots + a_{nn}^{(1)}x_n = b_n^{(1)}$$

The variable x_2 is now eliminated from each of the equations $i = 3,\ldots,n$ by subtracting a multiple $m_{i2} = a_{i2}^{(1)}/a_{22}^{(1)}$ of the second row from it. After $n-1$ such steps, we obtain an *equivalent* derived system of the following form:

$$a_{11}x_1 + a_{12}x_2 + a_{13}x_3 + \cdots + a_{1n}x_n = b_1$$
$$a_{22}^{(1)}x_2 + a_{23}^{(1)}x_3 + \cdots + a_{2n}^{(1)}x_n = b_2^{(1)}$$
$$a_{33}^{(2)}x_3 + \cdots + a_{3n}^{(2)}x_n = b_3^{(2)}$$
$$\cdots \qquad \cdots \qquad \cdots \qquad \cdots$$
$$a_{nn}^{(n-1)}x_n = b_n^{(n-1)}$$

or, in matrix form, $U\mathbf{x} = \mathbf{b}^{(n-1)}$, where U is *upper triangular*. This triangular set may now be solved by *back substitution*, computing x_n from the nth equation, x_{n-1} from the $(n-1)$th equation, $\ldots, x_1$ from the first.

The process breaks down if at any stage $a_{r+1,r+1}^{(r)} = 0$. This may be avoided by a simple modification. In the rth derived system, the last $n-r$ equations involve only the last $n-r$ variables. Any of these equations may be used to eliminate x_{r+1} from the remaining $n-r-1$. We may choose the equation that has the largest coefficient of x_{r+1}. It is convenient to think of terms of interchanging this equation with equation

$r + 1$. This modified process is known as Gaussian elimination with *partial pivoting*. Breakdown cannot now occur unless A is singular. (More accurately, unless A, modified by the rounding errors, is singular.) With this modification $|m_{ij}| \leq 1$. A more sophisticated form of pivoting is sometimes used. In the rth reduced set, the largest element $|a_{ij}^{(r)}|$ $(i, j \geq r + 1)$ is determined. If this is $a_{st}^{(r)}$, then equation s is used to eliminate x_t from the remaining $n - r - 1$ equations. This is best thought of in terms of interchanging the appropriate rows and columns. This process is *complete pivoting*. In general, Gaussian elimination with pivoting is remarkably stable with respect to rounding errors, but without pivoting it may be arbitrarily unstable.

If a matrix L is constructed from the multipliers m_{ij} by taking $l_{ij} = m_{ij}$ $(i > j)$, $l_{ii} = 1$, $l_{ij} = 0$ $(j > i)$, then the resulting unit lower triangular matrix (i.e. lower triangular with diagonal 1s) is such that $LU = A$. (In the case where partial pivoting has been used, the relation is $LU = \tilde{A}$, where $\tilde{A}$ is A with its rows suitably permuted; with complete pivoting, $LU = \tilde{A}$, where $\tilde{A}$ is A with both rows and columns suitably permuted.) The factorization $A = LU$ may be derived directly without producing the intermediate matrices $A^{(k)}$, and it is not difficult to combine this direct factorization with the equivalent of partial pivoting. The solution of $A\mathbf{x} = \mathbf{b}$ is then achieved by solving $L\mathbf{y} = \mathbf{b}$, $U\mathbf{x} = \mathbf{y}$. There is an analogous factorization in which U is unit upper triangular.

An important class of direct methods is based on the factorization of A into the product of an orthogonal matrix Q and an upper triangular matrix R. (The notation R is used rather than U for historical reasons.) If $A = QR$, then $Q^T A = R$, where Q^T is of course also orthogonal, and the factorization is commonly achieved in this way. Q^T is not derived directly, but as the product of a number of simple orthogonal matrices. Such factorizations are associated with the names of Givens and Householder. The QR factorizations have slightly more reliable numerical stability than the LU factorization with pivoting, but since they involve more work, the LU factorization is more commonly used for solving linear equations. However, the QR factorizations are of fundamental importance in connection with the eigenvalue problem and the least squares problem.

ITERATIVE METHODS

Basically, the simplest iterative methods for solving linear systems are those of Jacobi and Gauss–Seidel. The relations are most simply expressed if we write $A \equiv D - E - F$, where D is the set of diagonal elements, $-E$ is the set of subdiagonal elements, and $-F$ the set of superdiagonal elements. Jacobi's method may then be expressed in the form

$$D\mathbf{x}^{(k+1)} = b + E\mathbf{x}^{(k)} + F\mathbf{x}^{(k)}.$$

Clearly, the method can be applied only if the diagonal elements are nonzero. Writing $D^{-1}E = L$, $D^{-1}F = U$, this becomes

$$\mathbf{x}^{(k+1)} = D^{-1}\mathbf{b} + (L + U)\mathbf{x}^{(k)}.$$

If $\mathbf{x}$ is the true solution, then

$$\mathbf{x} = D^{-1}\mathbf{b} + (L + U)\mathbf{x}.$$

and writing $\mathbf{e}^{(k)} = \mathbf{x} - \mathbf{x}^{(k)}$, we have

$$\mathbf{e}^{(k+1)} = (L + U)\mathbf{e}^{(k)} = P\mathbf{e}^{(k)},$$

giving $\mathbf{e}^{(k+1)} = P^k \mathbf{e}^{(1)}$.

The process is therefore convergent if $P^k \to 0$ as $k \to \infty$ which is true if all the eigenvalues of P are less than unity in modulus (see later sections of this article). In the Gauss–Seidel method, the most up-to-date value of each component is used at this stage, the relevant relations being

$$D\mathbf{x}^{(k+1)} = \mathbf{b} + E\mathbf{x}^{(k+1)} + F\mathbf{x}^{(k)},$$

giving

$$(I - L)\mathbf{x}^{(k+1)} = D^{-1}\mathbf{b} + U\mathbf{x}^{(k)}.$$

The error matrix now satisfies the relations

$$(I - L)\mathbf{e}^{(k+1)} = U\mathbf{e}^{(k)}$$

or $\qquad \mathbf{e}^{(k+1)} = (I - L)^{-1} U\mathbf{e}^{(k)} = Q\mathbf{x}^{(k)},$

and the process is convergent if $Q^k \to 0$. When both methods are convergent, one might expect the Gauss–Seidel to converge faster, since it always uses the most recent information; this is true generally, but not always.

Research on iterative methods has mainly been concerned with *sufficient* conditions for convergence and methods for *accelerating* the rate of convergence. If A is real and symmetric with a positive diagonal, then a *necessary* and *sufficient* condition for Gauss–Seidel to converge is that it be positive definite. If L and U are nonnegative, then Gauss–Seidel and Jacobi are either both convergent or both divergent. In the former case, Gauss–Seidel converges the more rapidly.

A class of matrices that arises frequently in the study of partial differential equations (*q.v.*) is that for which the equations and variables can be reordered so that $L + U$ is of the form

$$\begin{bmatrix} 0 & P \\ Q & 0 \end{bmatrix}$$

where the null submatrices are square. These are said to have *Young's property* A. For matrices of this kind, when Gauss–Seidel converges, it does so twice as fast as Jacobi.

Acceleration of convergence of Gauss–Seidel can be achieved by making a change in each component that is ω times as great as that determined by Gauss–Seidel itself. The relevant relation is therefore

$$\mathbf{x}^{(k+1)} - \mathbf{x}^{(k)} = \omega[D^{-1}\mathbf{b} + L\mathbf{x}^{(k+1)} + U\mathbf{x}^{(k)} - \mathbf{x}^{(k)}],$$

$$(I - \omega L)\mathbf{x}^{(k+1)} = \mathbf{x}^{(k)} + \omega[D^{-1}\mathbf{b} - (I - U)\mathbf{x}^{(k)}],$$

giving

$$\mathbf{e}^{(k+1)} = (I - \omega L)^{-1}[(1 - \omega)I + \omega U]\mathbf{e}^{(k)}.$$

If $\omega > 1$ (<1), the method is known as *successive over-relaxation* (*under-relaxation*). The effectiveness of the method depends on a judicious choice of ω. Young has investigated fully the case when A has property A, and has shown that the optimum choice of ω is $2/(1 + (1 - \theta^2)^{1/2})$, where θ is the largest eigenvalue of $L + U$.

In iterative methods, one works throughout with the original matrix A, and for this reason it was at one time thought that such methods would be much more stable with respect to rounding errors than would direct methods. This advantage has proved to be less important than was thought. Much more important is the fact that if A has a high percentage of zero elements, then it is easy to take advantage of this and thereby reduce the storage requirements and the number of arithmetic operations. In direct methods, such as Gaussian elimination, the zero elements in the original matrix do not persist in the successive derived matrices.

The Algebraic Eigenvalue Problem

The practical importance of the algebraic eigenvalue problem springs mainly from its relation to the problem of solving a system of n simultaneous linear differential equations of first order with constant coefficients. In standard form such a system may be written as

$$\frac{d\mathbf{x}}{dt} = A\mathbf{x},$$

where A is an $n \times n$ matrix and $\mathbf{x}$ a vector. By substitution, $\mathbf{x} = \mathbf{u}^{\lambda t}$ is a solution if $\lambda\mathbf{u} = A\mathbf{u}$. Conversely, if λ and $\mathbf{u} \neq \mathbf{0}$ satisfy $\lambda\mathbf{u} = A\mathbf{u}$, then $\mathbf{x} = \mathbf{u}^{\lambda t}$ is a solution. The *algebraic eigenvalue problem* is the determination of such λ and $\mathbf{u}$. From the theory of linear algebraic equations, nonnull solutions exist if and only if $\det(\lambda I - A) = 0$. This is a polynomial equation of degree n, the coefficient of λ^n being unity. It is known as the *characteristic equation* of A. The roots of this equation are called the *eigenvalues*, *latent roots*, or *characteristic values* of A. Taking into account multiplicities, there are always precisely n eigenvalues. Corresponding to each eigenvalue there is at least one

nonnull solution to $\mathbf{u}$, and this is known as a corresponding *eigenvector*. The number of independent eigenvectors corresponding to a given eigenvalue λ may be less than its multiplicity; it is equal to $n - k$, where k is the rank of $A - \lambda I$.

Since the calculation of the eigenvalues is equivalent to finding the roots of the characteristic equation (an *apparently* simpler problem), early methods were based on the explicit determination of this equation. All such methods are inherently unstable, since very small errors in the coefficients of the equation may correspond to large changes in its roots even when the eigenvalues are not unduly sensitive to changes in the elements of A.

If the transformation $\mathbf{x} = P\mathbf{y}$ is made in the system of differential equations, it becomes $d\mathbf{y}/dt = (P^{-1}AP)\mathbf{y}$, assuming that P is nonsingular. The matrix $P^{-1}AP$ is said to be *similar* to A. Since $\det(P^{-1}AP - \lambda I) = \det(A - \lambda I)$, the eigenvalues of A are the same as those of any similar matrix. This is intuitively obvious from consideration of the differential equations. Many of the most effective methods for finding eigenvalues are based on determining a similarity transformation such that eigenvalues of $P^{-1}AP$ are readily available. The eigenvalues of a triangular matrix are its diagonal elements; hence, reduction to this form gives the eigenvalues immediately.

The theory of similarity transformations shows that, for any A, there exists a nonsingular P such that $P^{-1}AP$ is upper-triangular. In fact, such a transformation is always possible, even if P is restricted to the class of *unitary* matrices, i.e. matrices such that $PP^H = P^H P = I$. A real unitary matrix satisfies $PP^T = P^T P = I$ and is therefore orthogonal. Unitary similarity transformations are numerically very stable, and several of the best algorithms are based on their use. For such matrices, $P^{-1}AP = P^H AP$.

When A has distinct eigenvalues, there is always a P such that $P^{-1}AP = \text{diag}(\lambda_i)$, the diagonal matrix with λ_i on the diagonal. If A has any multiple eigenvalues, reduction to diagonal form is not generally possible, hence, *general* algorithms are not usually based on such a reduction.

REAL SYMMETRIC MATRICES

When A is symmetric, there is an advantage in taking P to be orthogonal, since $P^T AP$ is still symmetric. It is known that a real symmetric matrix is always reducible to diagonal form via an orthogonal P; Jacobi's method, one of the most effective algorithms, is based on such a reduction. P is not determined directly, but as a product of a sequence of elementary orthogonal matrices of the form R_{pq}, where

$$r_{pp} = r_{qq} = \cos\theta$$
$$r_{pq} = -r_{qp} = \sin\theta;$$
$$r_{ij} = \delta_{ij} \quad \text{(otherwise)}$$

This is known as a rotation in the p, q plane. Denoting the successive derived matrices by $A^{(k)}$, if $a_{p_k,q_k}^{(k)}$ is the off-diagonal element of largest modulus, then the next transformation is given by

$$A^{(k+1)} = R_{p_k,q_k}^T A^{(k)} R_{p_k,q_k}$$

with the angle θ being chosen so that

$$a_{p_k,q_k}^{(k+1)} = 0.$$

In general, an infinite number of transformations are needed to give the diagonal form, and iteration is terminated when the off-diagonal elements are all negligible. To reach this point, approximately $12n^3$ multiplications and additions are required.

A real symmetric matrix can be reduced to symmetric tridiagonal form by $(1/2) n(n-1)$ elementary orthogonal similarities of the above type, involving less than 10% of the computation in Jacobi's method. This algorithm is due to Givens; an alternative reduction involving orthogonal similarities and requiring half as much work is due to Householder.

The calculation of the eigenvalues of a symmetric tridiagonal matrix is a very economical process. Two methods are widely used. The first is due to Givens and is based on the fact that if T is tridiagonal, the leading principal minors p_r $(r = 0, \ldots, n)$ of $(T - \lambda I)$ can be computed from the relations

$$p_0(\lambda) = 1,$$
$$p_1(\lambda) = t_{11} - \lambda,$$
$$p_r(\lambda) = (t_{rr} - \lambda)p_{r-1}(\lambda) - (t_{r,r-1})^2 p_{r-2}(\lambda).$$

For any given value of λ, the number of agreements in sign between consecutive members of the sequence $p_0, p_1, \ldots, p_n$ equals the number of eigenvalues greater than λ. Any individual eigenvalue may be found by repeated bisection using this property, given only an initial upper and lower bound. The second method is described in the next section.

EIGENVALUES OF GENERAL MATRICES

The most efficient method for general matrices is based on the unitary similarity reduction to upper-triangular form. For real matrices, an analogous *real* reduction may be achieved, using only orthogonal similarities to give a triangular matrix apart from 2×2 diagonal blocks corresponding to complex conjugate pairs of eigenvalues. This reduction is much more economical

if the original matrix is first reduced to upper-Hessenberg form, which can be done by $(1/2) n(n-1)$ elementary orthogonal similarities, as in Givens' reduction of a symmetric matrix to tridiagonal form. Again, Householder has given an alternative requiring only half as much computation.

The Hessenberg matrix is then reduced to the quasi-triangular form by the Francis QR algorithm. In the basic QR algorithm, a sequence of similar matrices A is produced via the relations

$$A_s - k_s I = Q_s R_s, \qquad R_s Q_s + k_s I = A_{s+1},$$

where Q_s is orthogonal, R_s is upper-triangular, and the k_s are chosen so as to accelerate convergence. The matrix A_s tends to the quasi-triangular form, the speed of convergence being extraordinarily satisfactory. Upper-Hessenberg form is preserved by this algorithm, which greatly reduces the volume of computation.

The QR method is also extremely effective for finding the eigenvalues of a real symmetric tridiagonal matrix. The symmetric tridiagonal form is preserved, giving great economy in the volume of work. For finding all the eigenvalues, it is the most efficient of known methods.

Software

The most successful algorithms for computation with dense, stored matrices have been implemented in efficient, portable, standard Fortran software. LINPACK has subroutines for computing factorizations and solving simultaneously linear systems involving square general matrices, symmetric matrices, positive definite matrices, band matrices, and triangular matrices, as well as subroutines for computing orthogonal factorizations and solving least-squares problems for rectangular matrices. EISPACK has subroutines for solving various forms of the algebraic eigenvalue problem for several different types of matrices.

Software for iterative methods on large, sparse matrices, particularly those arising in finite difference and finite element methods for partial differential equations, is usually closely coupled to particular applications and so is not organized in general-purpose packages.

The Main Areas of Research

In the solution of linear systems, the main areas of research are devoted to the economical solution, by both direct and iterative methods, of large sparse systems. The work on direct methods concentrates on the development of efficient data structures (*q.v.*) for representing and manipulating sparse matrices, and on the development of pivoting strategies that reduce the number of new nonzero matrix elements created during factorization.

Much of the research work on iterative methods for linear systems is focused on refinements of the conjugate gradient method, particularly in connection with preconditioners that significantly accelerate the convergence.

In the eigenvalue field, there is active research on special matrix problems that occur in system theory, control theory, and signal processing. The singular value decomposition is a particularly effective tool in dealing with least squares data fitting problems and principal component analysis in the presence of noise and near-linear dependence.

Bibliography

1965. Wilkinson, J. H. *The Algebraic Eigenvalue Problem.* Oxford: Clarendon Press.

1971. Young, D. M. *Iterative Solution of Large Linear Systems.* New York: Academic Press.

1974. Smith, B. T., Boyle, J. M., Dongarra, J. J., Garbow, B. S., Ikebe, Y., Klema, V. C., and Moler, C. B. *Matrix Eigensystem Routines—EISPACK User's Guide,* 2nd Ed. Berlin: Springer-Verlag.

1977. Garbow, B. S., Boyle, J. M., Dongarra, J. J., and Moler, C. B. *Matrix Eigensystem Routines—EISPACK Guide Extension.* Berlin: Springer-Verlag.

1980. Parlett, B. N. *The Symmetric Eigenvalue Problem.* Upper Saddle River, NJ: Prentice Hall.

1981. Hageman, L. A., and Young, D. M. *Applied Iterative Methods.* New York: Academic Press.

1986. Duff, I. S., Erisman, A. M., and Reid, J. K. *Direct Methods for Sparse Matrices.* Oxford: Clarendon Press.

1989. Golub, G. H., and Van Loan, C. F. *Matrix Computations,* 2nd Ed. Baltimore: The Johns Hopkins University Press.

1997. Shi, T. K., and Steeb, W.-H. *Matrix Calculus and Kronecker Product with Applications and C++ Programs.* New York: World Scientific.

1998. Rao, C. R., and Rao, M. B. *Matrix Algebra and Its Applications to Statistics and Econometrics.* New York: World Scientific.

J. H. Wilkinson and Cleve B. Moler

MAUCHLY, JOHN W.

For articles on related subjects, *see* DIGITAL COMPUTERS, HISTORY OF: EARLY; ECKERT, J. PRESPER; ENIAC; and UNIVAC I.

John Mauchly, (b. Cincinnati, OH, 30 August 1907, d. Philadelphia, PA, 8 January 1980) was one of the major visionaries and pioneers of our current electronic digital computer era. The dedication of his brainchild, ENIAC, in 1946 totally changed the scientific and commercial information processing environment.

In 1925, Mauchly received a scholarship to attend the engineering school of the Johns Hopkins University. After two years, however, he decided that he didn't care for engineering and switched to physics. His Ph.D. was awarded in 1932 with a thesis on an analysis of the carbon monoxide molecule. He remained at Johns Hopkins the following year as a research assistant to Professor Joseph Eachus, where his work included calculating the energy levels of the formaldehyde spectrum. This research project, as well as his thesis work, involved a great deal of calculation, and Mauchly began to be interested in devising special techniques to cut down on the work involved.

He taught physics at Ursinus College from 1933 to 1941. During this period he developed an interest in the problem of weather prediction, and built an analog computer (*q.v.*) to do harmonic analysis of weather data. This work led to a paper (1940) on the quasi-periodicity of precipitation. He spent the summer of 1940 with H. Helm Clayton, who was interested in long-range weather forecasting, and he also presented a paper during this period to the Geophysical Union, using a statistical approach to the causes of sunspots.

In the summer of 1941, with war impending, he attended a defense training course in electronics at the Moore School of Electrical Engineering (University of Pennsylvania). He was subsequently invited to join the faculty of the Moore School as an instructor. The Moore School had long had a contract with the Army Ordnance to calculate ballistics tables, and Mauchly was assigned this work in addition to his regular teaching duties. All of his work of the prior decade seemed to come together in these ballistics calculations, and in 1942 he wrote a memorandum proposing that an electronic calculator be constructed to perform these vital

Figure 1. John William Mauchly.

computations. This original proposal was rejected, but it was revived a year later by Herman Goldstine, who had been assigned to Aberdeen Proving Ground to expedite the production of the firing data. Thirty months later, ENIAC, conceived by Mauchly and engineered by J. Presper Eckert, was publicly demonstrated (February 1946).

ENIAC, now retired to the Smithsonian Institution, operated successfully at Aberdeen Proving Ground for ten years. It well deserves its description as the first truly electronic general-purpose computer and the precursor of all that was to come.

Mauchly and Eckert left the Moore School in 1946 to found the Electronic Control Co., which became the Eckert-Mauchly Corporation in 1947. The company's first contract was to design a small binary computer for the Northrop Aircraft Corporation (BINAC, 1949). UNIVAC I followed, and the Bureau of the Census received the first completed model in 1951. In that same year, the Eckert-Mauchly Corporation became a division of the Remington-Rand Corporation, and Mauchly remained with it in various capacities until 1959 when he formed Mauchly Associates.

Mauchly was a founder of both ACM (*q.v.*) and SIAM. He served ACM as its first Vice-President and second President. He was a member of many other learned societies, including the American Physical Society, the Franklin Institute, and the National Academy of Engineering. He received numerous awards, including the Howard Potts Medal of the Franklin Institute (1949), the John Scott Award (1961), and (jointly with J. P. Eckert) the Philadelphia Man of the Year Award (1973). ACM's Eckert-Mauchly award is partially named in his honor. His scientific papers are housed in the Van Pelt Library of the University of Pennsylvania.

Bibliography

1942. Mauchly, J. W. "The Use of High Speed Vacuum Tube Devices for Calculating." Privately circulated memorandum, reprinted in *The Origins of Digital Computers*, 3rd Ed. (ed. B. Randell), 355–358. New York: Springer-Verlag, 1982.

1946. Kennedy, T. R. Jr. "Electronic Computer Flashes Answers, May Speed Engineering," *New York Times*, 15 February, 1, 16.

1947. Mauchly, J. W. "Preparation of Problems for EDVAC-type Machines," *Annals of the Computation Laboratory of Harvard University*, **16**, 203–207; reprinted in *The Origins of Digital Computers*, 3rd Ed. (ed. B. Randell), 393–397. New York: Springer-Verlag, 1982.

1969. Rosen, S. "Electronic Computers: A Historical Survey," *Computing Surveys*, **1**, *1* (March). Reprinted in "A Quarter Century View," *ACM*, 1971, 7–36.

1980. Stern, N. "John William Mauchly: 1907–1980," *Annals of the History of Computing*, **2**, *2*, 100–103.

1982. Mauchly, J. "Unpublished Remarks," *Annals of the History of Computing*, **4**, *3*, 245–256.

1995. Lee, J. A. N. "John William Mauchly," in *Computer Pioneers*, 453–460. Los Alamitos, CA: IEEE Press.

Henry S. Tropp

McDOWELL AWARD WINNERS

For an article on a related subject *see* TURING AWARD WINNERS.

The W. Wallace McDowell Award is made annually by the IEEE Computer Society for outstanding professional work in the computer field. The award currently includes a prize of $2,000. As might be expected of an electrical engineering society, the award is most often given for hardware and management achievements, but there is some intersection with the set of Turing award winners. The award is named in honor of William Wallace McDowell (1906–1985), who, in his 38-year IBM career, went from a designer in 1931 to Director of Engineering in 1950 and retired as a vice-president. His major computing contribution was to direct IBM's transition from electro-mechanical techniques to electronics and finally to solid state devices. Awards made since inception in 1966 have been:

1966   Fernando J. Corbató (1926–), for his leadership in time sharing (*q.v.*).

1967   John W. Backus (1924–), for Fortran (*q.v.*).

1968   Seymour R. Cray (1925–1996) (*q.v.*), for his series of supercomputers (*q.v.*).

1969   Herman Lukoff (1923–1979), for his contributions to early computers.

1970   Frederic P. Brooks, Jr (1931–), for his contributions to computer architecture (*q.v.*), programming, and education, and for skewering the myth of the man-month.

1971   Tom Kilburn (1921–) (*q.v.*), for his work on early powerful computers.

1972   Jean A. Hoerni (1924–1997), for inventing the planar process of semiconductor fabrication.

1973   David A. Huffman (1925–), for his solution of sequential circuit problems and his contributions to coding theory and for his teaching.

1974   Shmuel Winograd (1936–), for pioneering work in computational complexity (*q.v.*) and the efficiency of algorithms.

1975   C. Gordon Bell (1934–), for his work in technical design, education, and publication.

1976   Gene M. Amdahl (1922–), for his contributions to computer architecture and design and his business enterprise (*see* ENTREPRENEURS).

1977   Robert S. Barton (1925–), for stack (*q.v.*) processing, data stored with self-describing tags, and the direct execution of higher-level languages, as in the Burroughs B-5000 computer and its successors.

1978 Gordon E. Moore (1929–), for his development of semiconductor components and the microprocessor (*see* LAWS, COMPUTER and MICROPROCESSORS AND MICROCOMPUTERS).

1979 Grace Murray Hopper (1906–1992) (*q.v.*), for her single-minded drive for the acceptance of high-level programming languages.

1980 Donald E. Knuth (1938–), for his contributions to software engineering and education and for the scholarship and creativity of his classical texts that have made the essentials of computer science accessible to all.

1981 Maurice V. Wilkes (1913–) (*q.v.*), for his innovative contributions to software engineering (*q.v.*), structured programming (*q.v.*), distributed computing (*see* DISTRIBUTED SYSTEMS), database structures, time sharing (*q.v.*), storage hierarchies (*q.v.*), paging, and microprogramming (*q.v.*).

1982 Rex Rice (1918–), for the invention of the dual-in-line semiconductor component package and LSI semiconductor memories.

1983 Daniel L. Slotnick (1931–1985), for the centrally controlled parallel computer, ILLIAC IV.

1984 Thomas M. McWilliams (1952–) and Lawrence Curtis Widdoes, Jr. (1952–), for Structured Computer-Aided Logic (SCALD).

1985 William D. Strecker (1944–), for the VAX architecture and contributions to local area networks (*q.v.*), high-performance interconnects, cache memory (*q.v.*), and memory hierarchies.

1986 No award was made.

1987 Sidney Fernbach (1917–1991), for pushing for US supercomputers (*q.v.*).

1988 John W. Poduska, Sr. (1937–), for hardware and software developments and management expertise.

1989 Edward B. Eichelberger (1934–) and Thomas W. Williams (1943–), for the level-sensitive scan technique of testing logic circuits.

1990 Lawrence G. Roberts (1937–), for packet switching (*q.v.*) technology brought into practical use through the ARPA network (*see* INTERNET).

1991–1993 No awards were made.

1994 Federico Faggin (1941–), for the development of the silicon gate process, and the first commercial microprocessor.

1995 Ken Kennedy (1945–), for his contribution to the computer art through the theory and practice of compiler optimization (*see* COMPILER) and leadership in the development of software for parallel computation.

1996 Timothy Berners-Lee (1955–), for his innovative invention of the World Wide Web (*q.v.*), which extends hypertext (*q.v.*) to distributed information and has brought about a revolutionary transformation in the use of computers and networks (*see* ENTREPRENEURS).

1997 Marc Andreessen (1971–) and Eric J. Bina (1964–), for developing a multi-platform browsing tool for the World Wide Web (*see* ENTREPRENEURS).

1998 Tilak Agerwala (1950–), for outstanding contributions to the development of high-performance computers.

1999. Yale Patt (1939–), for impact on the high performance microprocessor industry via a combination of important contributions to both engineering and education.

Eric A. Weiss

MEDICAL APPLICATIONS

For articles on related subjects *see* BIOCOMPUTING; HOSPITAL INFORMATION SYSTEM; MEDICAL IMAGING; and TOMOGRAPHY, COMPUTERIZED.

Computers have made significant inroads in the healthcare industry so that computing systems are now commonplace in many medical settings. Products are available for individual clinicians, patients, and researchers, and for hospitals and other healthcare institutions as a whole. Applications can be found throughout clinical practice, clinical and basic science research, and education. The applications themselves are varied, spanning sophisticated instrumentation used for patient monitoring, information systems that coordinate communication and support clinical and financial management functions, analytical tools used by researchers, specialized programs designed to assist providers in clinical decision making, and instructional programs for healthcare workers and patients.

Clinical Applications

Computers have replaced manual methods for performing many repetitive and time-consuming clinical tasks. They have also been used to help clinicians access and interpret large amounts of complex data, such as patient information, bibliographic resources, clinical guidelines, and other institutional information.

MANAGEMENT OF PATIENT INFORMATION

Patient monitoring is a prime medical computing application. Computer-based patient monitors are commonly used to collect and display physiological parameters such as heart rate, respiratory rate, blood pressure, and blood oxygen content, and to sound alarms when intervention is required. Analysis of electrocardiograms (ECGs) is an application that has gained reasonable acceptance. Patient-monitoring devices are useful particularly in settings where frequent assessment of patient status is essential to effective therapy. Thus, patient monitors are standard equipment in intensive care units, operating rooms, and trauma centers.

Monitoring devices not only sample and convert biological signals to digital data, but also store the results, calculate derived variables that cannot be measured directly, format and print reports, flag abnormal values, and provide interpretations of data (Fig. 1).

Automated monitoring allows nearly continuous assessment of physiological parameters. The large amount of data collected, however, threatens to overload providers' capacity for interpretation. For this reason, some commercial vendors have designed data management systems that integrate, organize, and display data collected from multiple devices, as well as medication administration records and patient observations. To facilitate integration, researchers have defined standards for a medical information bus (MIB) that allows the interconnection of multiple devices. The MIB specifies requirements for physical connections, data communication protocols (*q.v.*), and data formats.

Closed-loop drug delivery systems are a direct application of computers in patient care. Functioning much like the thermostat of a heater, closed-loop control devices use a computer to sense and control a physiological variable by altering therapy directly.

Although monitoring devices are important, they deal only with certain types of patients, usually in a hospital setting. A great portion of healthcare delivery, however, is based on information from the medical record, which is the basis for healthcare in both in-hospital and out-of-hospital settings.

The electronic medical record has been a subject of intense research and development. The barriers to its full implementation in clinical practice include the user interfaces (*q.v.*), the lack of agreement about terminology, lack of perceived value-added for the clinician (or perception of an intolerable increase in documentation), and issues of patient privacy and confidentiality. Nevertheless, several hospitals have successfully implemented pharmacy, radiology, and laboratory order-entry and reporting systems. Applications that manage

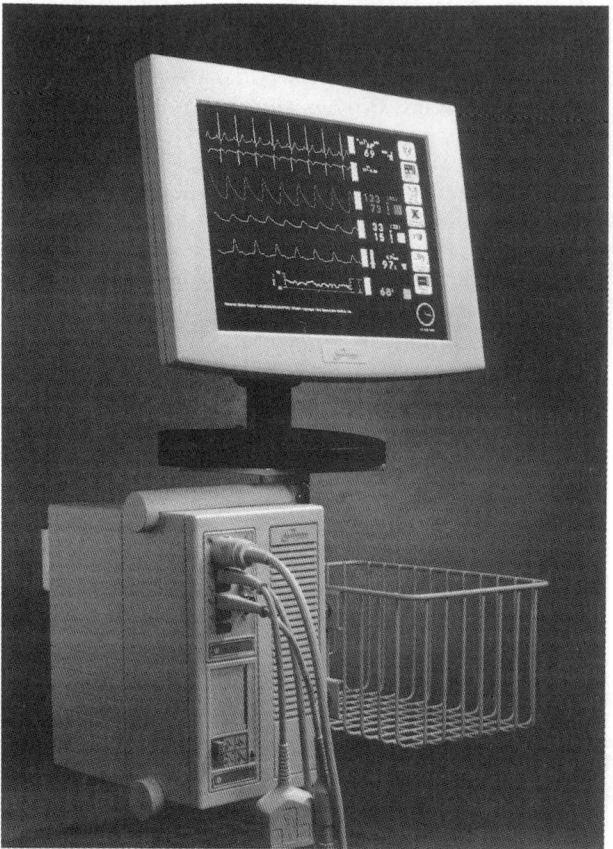

Figure 1. A computer-based patient monitor. These are common features of intensive care units (ICUs) and other critical care settings. Commercially available monitors collect, store, and evaluate physiological data, thus freeing nurses to perform other patient care functions. (Courtesy of SpaceLabs, Inc.)

text-based versions of medical and nursing records are also available.

PHARMACY

Computers are used in pharmacies to maintain accessible, legible, and up-to-date medication records, playing an important role in providing safe and effective drug therapy. Contemporary pharmacy systems also assist physicians and pharmacists directly by screening patients' computer-stored medication profiles, and by identifying drug allergies, potential drug interactions, and prior adverse reactions. With the development of integrated clinical databases, more sophisticated support is possible. The Brigham Integrated Computing System (BICS) developed at the Brigham and Women's Hospital in Boston, for example, allows clinicians to enter all laboratory orders and prescriptions online. These orders and prescriptions can be checked for accuracy and adequacy and alerts and reminders can be issued when necessary. The HELP system developed at LDS Hospital in Salt Lake City identifies abnormal chemistry levels, concurrent diseases, and other patient conditions that should be considered when particular drugs are prescribed. HELP has also been used to monitor the use of prophylactic antibiotics and to identify patients who could benefit from preventive drug therapy as well as patients who are receiving antibiotics unnecessarily.

A number of computer programs have been developed to assist physicians in individual dosing and timing drug administration. Most drugs may be safely prescribed in accordance with dosing guidelines developed for broad classes of patients. The effects of some drugs, however, are extremely sensitive to variability among patients, and dosing regimens must be individually tailored. These programs use mathematical models that relate measured drug concentration levels in the blood over time to drug-specific parameters (e.g. rate of drug elimination from the body) and patient-specific parameters (e.g. age, gender, ideal body weight, and concurrent disease factors). Physicians use these programs to forecast future drug levels and to choose the amount and timing of drug doses that will achieve target levels.

RADIOLOGY

Medical imaging (*q.v.*) is an active area for medical computing research. Many of the imaging modalities, such as ultrasound (US), computerized tomography (CT), and magnetic resonance imaging (MRI) are inherently digital. In CT and MRI, rather than depicting a directly measurable parameter (such as the attenuation of an X-ray beam as it travels through body tissues), the computer creates a functional image by performing complex calculations on measured data. Because of the enormous number of calculations to be performed, these modalities are only practical with powerful computers. Conventional X-ray images can also be captured directly or scanned and stored in digital memory, rather than on film.

Images stored in digital form provide opportunities for improved viewing and interpretation. For example, a variety of image processing (*q.v.*) techniques can be applied to enhance edges, to sharpen blurry images, and otherwise to improve the quality of images for human visualization. Image segmentation techniques can be used to identify relevant structures automatically. Digital images are also accessible for computer-assisted quantification of measurable parameters, such as the volume of a heart or the diameter of a fetus's head. Collection and storage of multiple, closely stacked image slices supports additional capabilities, such as displaying image slices on planes other than those originally collected, and displaying three-dimensional (3D) images. Three-dimensional imaging is particularly valuable for localization of lesions for radiation therapy, interventional radiological procedures, and surgery

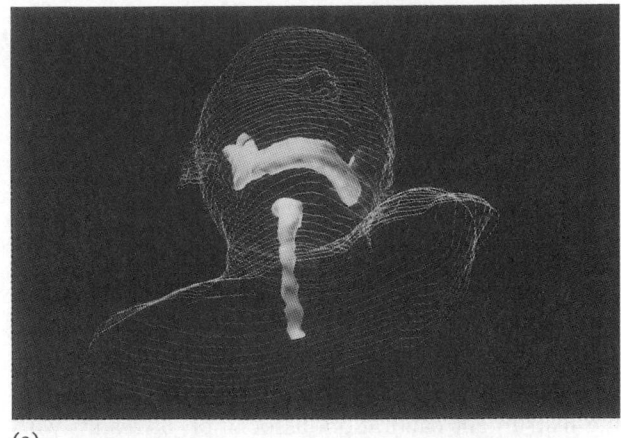

(a)

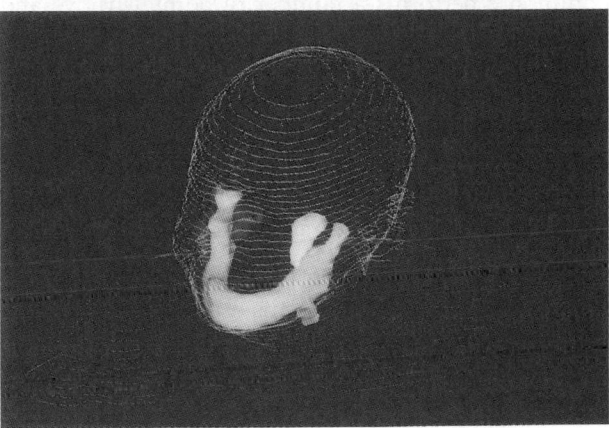

(b)

Figure 2. The FOCUS Treatment Planning System assists radiation oncologists in planning radiation therapy by evaluating competing plans to optimize parameters such as beam angle and radiation dose. Three-dimensional MRI and CT data can be displayed and rotated through different viewing planes, thus enhancing the radiation oncologist's ability to visualize the treatment beam in relation to the lesion and surrounding healthy tissues. (a) and (b) show two views of the same imaging data. (Courtesy of Computerized Medical Systems, Inc. and Hewlett-Packard Corporation.)

(Fig. 2). Reconstructions from 3D images have also been used to design and guide the creation of joint prostheses.

Picture archiving and communications systems (PACS) for image management and analysis are being used in some hospitals. Using specialized workstations (*q.v.*), radiologists can view multiple images for comparison, zoom in to examine subregions at greater magnification, alter image contrast, rotate images to alternative perspectives, and annotate images on screen.

LABORATORIES

One of the earliest areas of clinical application, clinical laboratories first used computers in the late 1950s to meet the growing demand for laboratory testing. Manual procedures were adequate when test volumes were low, but automated instruments became necessary to perform high volumes of repetitious tasks quickly and accurately, and the laboratory information system (LIS) was developed to manage the large amount of data generated. Several laboratory instruments perform panels of tests on a single specimen. These instruments contain preprocessors (*q.v.*) that convert raw data to digital form and transmit numerical results to the LIS for storage and report generation. Many instruments contain dedicated microprocessors that facilitate all phases of the testing process, including instrument calibration, association of results with individual specimens, and reporting of results. A LIS commonly performs a number of administrative and managerial functions, including specimen tracking, productivity analysis, and quality control. Many have optional subsystems to meet the unique needs of microbiology and anatomical pathology and to satisfy the stricter information management and reporting requirements of blood banks.

Computer-based tools have also been developed to support the professional functions of laboratory personnel. For example, programs are available to facilitate chromosome analysis and interpretation of some specialized laboratory tests, such as certain immunoassay tests.

CLINICAL DECISION SUPPORT

The past two decades have seen a proliferation of applications that support physicians in various aspects of medical practice. Medical record systems help to record and document a medical encounter. These systems usually produce textual narratives, and queries on specific items of the medical record are limited. Since the clinical findings are represented in narrative text, natural language processing (*q.v.*) tools are necessary to retrieve specific information. Other types of applications have been built to help clinicians interpret clinical situations and provide suggestions. Examples of these include programs to assist in management of hypertension and diabetes patients, interpretation of diagnostic exercise test results in coronary heart disease patients, health risk appraisal and evaluation of cardiac risk factors, interpretation of laboratory tests such as blood gases and blood counts, neurological assessment, and evaluation of physical impairment. Few of these systems have been integrated with the medical records or billing systems, so the need for redundant entry of information and the experimental nature of some of these systems have contributed to their limited success in clinical practice.

The development of computer-based tools to support clinical decision making has been an area of research since the 1960s. Multiple approaches have been pursued, including the application of simple algorithmic logic, symbolic processing techniques, and numerical approaches based on comparative analysis and probability theory.

Researchers have demonstrated a number of systems that assist physicians with clinical tasks such as diagnosis and therapy planning. For example, computer-based consultations regarding acid–base and electrolyte disorders are routinely available at Beth Israel Hospital in Boston, using an acid–base advisor developed by Bleich that is one of the best known examples of an algorithmic approach. During the early 1970s, Shortliffe at Stanford University developed the MYCIN system, one of the first rule-based systems. MYCIN was designed to assist physicians in selecting appropriate antibiotic therapy for patients with meningitis and bacterial infections of the blood. One of the first systems founded on the use of Bayesian probability theory, a program for diagnosis of abdominal pain, was developed by de Dombal at the University of Leeds. The system used sensitivity, specificity, and disease prevalence data for various signs, symptoms, and test results, to calculate the probabilities of seven possible explanations for acute abdominal pain.

Clinical decision support systems have been slow to achieve acceptance because of the complexity of medical domains, the potentially dire consequences of providing incorrect information, and resistance by the medical community. Decision-support tools are beginning to be used clinically, however, and a number of diagnostic support systems are commercially available. For example, the DXplain system, developed by Barnett and colleagues at Massachusetts General Hospital, is available on the World Wide Web. DXplain evaluates patients' signs, symptoms, and test results to suggest differential diagnoses and to indicate additional information that would help to narrow the diagnostic possibilities (Fig. 3).

Clinical practice guidelines have been a major emphasis in the era of managed healthcare. Healthcare managers believe that the standardization of care for certain types of patients results in better average outcomes at lower costs. Clinical practice guidelines have been developed in several institutions as an answer to this demand for standardization. Guidelines for prevention, diagnosis, and management of several conditions have been written and distributed to healthcare providers. Automation of these practice guidelines by computer systems that are able to suggest certain actions or make certain recommendations is being investigated by several researchers. This automation cannot occur without substantial integration of well-structured electronic medical records. The goal of sharing guidelines across

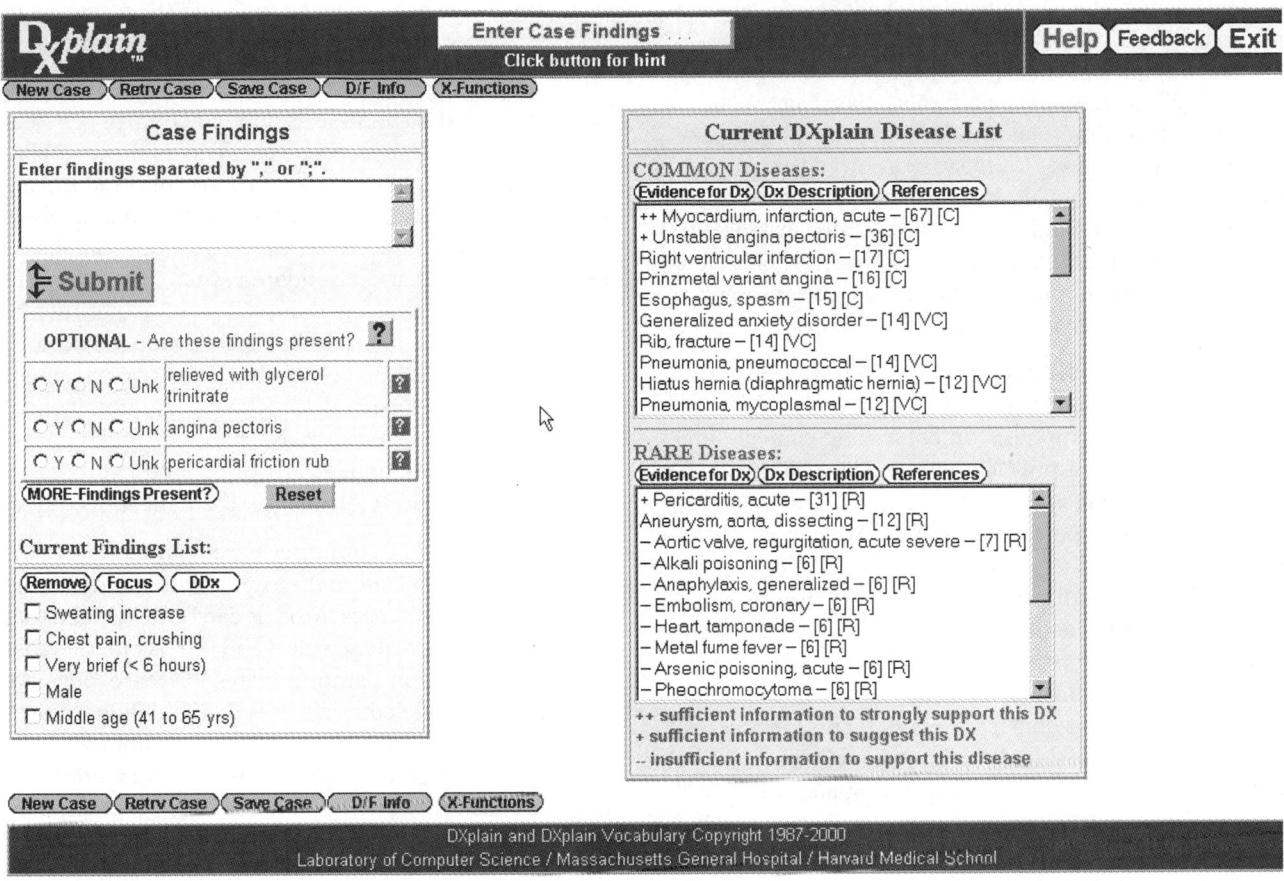

Figure 3. A physician using DXplain can enter one or more key findings to view a differential diagnosis of diseases that can account for those findings. (Courtesy of the Laboratory of Computer Science, Massachusetts General Hospital.)

different institutions has led investigators at Columbia, Harvard, and Stanford Universities to propose an interchange format for guideline representation.

BIBLIOGRAPHIC RESOURCES

More widespread than diagnostic aids are computer-based tools that assist health professionals with patient management by providing access to the biomedical literature and to detailed information in particular domains. Drug information bases are widely used, allowing physicians to retrieve comprehensive information on drug effects, interactions, contraindications, and dosing guidelines. Online bibliographic indexes are replacing conventional manual indexes, because complex online searches, infeasible when using printed indexes, can be performed rapidly and comprehensively. MEDLINE, the National Library of Medicine's major bibliographic database, contains references to the recent biomedical literature and additional backfiles to 1966. In addition, a variety of bibliographic databases is available for specific topic areas, such as psychology, toxicology, health planning, cancer research, and AIDS. Traditionally, these databases were accessed by spe-

cially trained librarians or search intermediaries. End-user searching has rapidly gained popularity, however, and many commercial products can assist users in formulating appropriate queries. A growing number of publishers and database distributors market biomedical information in CD-ROM format (*see* OPTICAL STORAGE) or via the World Wide Web (*q.v.*).

Hospital Management

Computers perform an array of activities in hospitals, processing and storing data to support patient management and patient care, as well as daily business operations and longer term strategic planning (*see* HOSPITAL INFORMATION SYSTEM). The most common applications of a hospital information system (HIS) are traditional financial functions such as payroll, billing, and accounts receivable management. Complementing the financial components of an HIS are modules designed to support healthcare delivery, including patient registration, order entry, results reporting, and management of ancillary areas such as the clinical laboratory, pharmacy, and radiology departments. In addition, specialty systems are available to support other hospital departments, assisting in inventory tracking and supplies purchasing, operating room management, staff scheduling, and diet planning. A large number of commercial vendors market a complete HIS or standalone specialty systems on hardware platforms, ranging from mainframes (*q.v.*) to networked microcomputers. Similar systems are also available to manage information in nonhospital settings, including outpatient clinics, nursing homes, physicians' group practices, and individual physicians' offices.

Until recently, an HIS performed mainly administrative and financially oriented functions. Currently, however, there is growing emphasis on enhancing clinical functions. The most sophisticated type of HIS provides integrated interfaces for ordering medications, procedures, and tests, performing contraindication checking, displaying online patient preparation instructions, and performing multilevel verification of orders. Nursing care modules assist in initial and ongoing patient assessment, development of nursing care plans based on patient problems, documentation of medication administration, and charting of nursing progress notes. Many health professionals believe that clinical systems can yield improvements in both the quality of patient care and the productivity of care providers and that significant benefits can be gained through the use of point-of-care-systems. The development of an integrated clinical database in an HIS represents one step toward the long-term goal of achieving a fully online medical record.

Clinical and Biomedical Research

A fundamental task of clinical research is the analysis of patient data that has been collected either retrospectively from medical records or prospectively during clinical trials. Computer-based clinical research systems provide investigators with tools for acquiring, maintaining, and analyzing such data sets to attain a better understanding of diseases and disease manifestations and of the relationships between medical interventions and clinical outcomes. Since the late 1950s, researchers have used the computer's superior computational power to perform statistical analyses. A number of general purpose statistical packages are available, including SAS, SPSS, S-Plus, and STATA.

Computers have been helpful in initial phases of clinical research. Exploratory data analysis that uses complex mathematical algorithms for clustering and data visualization was made possible with computers (*see* SCIENTIFIC VISUALIZATION). Machine learning methods are also being used for clinical *data mining* (*q.v.*). These algorithms, which include artificial neural networks (*q.v.*) and regression trees, among other statis-

tical methods such as linear and logistic regression, uncover important correlations among data and construct predictive models given new cases.

Confirmatory data analysis is done to confirm or reject hypotheses in clinical research. The highest quality clinical databases typically are those collected during prospective clinical trials. Manipulation and analysis of complex federations of heterogeneous databases uses mediators that consolidate results from different queries. The increasing complexity of experimental protocols in clinical trials has also produced a need for computer systems to support direct management of experiments. Systems for clinical studies include features such as audit trails, patient tracking and scheduling to minimize attrition, and automated randomization and treatment assignment tools.

The construction of computer-based simulation (*q.v.*) models provides an alternative method for studying the epidemiology of diseases. Models can be developed that represent various disease states and the risk factors that influence transitions among states. Disease development is then modeled as a series of state changes over time. Such compartmental modeling techniques have been used to study infectious disease and coronary heart disease in patient populations. By manipulating the parameters of computer-based simulation models, researchers are able to study interactions among variables and the effects of interventions on health outcomes, thus reducing the need for expensive and time-consuming real-world experiments. Simulations are useful for planning full-scale clinical trials and for focusing on the most promising programs when planning health services.

Computational biology is an important area of biomedical research that has received special attention because of the Human Genome Project sponsored by the National Institutes of Health. The primary goal of the project is to map the structure and function of human DNA. Computers are used to analyze the inheritance patterns of extended families in genetic linkage analyses designed to determine the chromosome locations of genes for inherited traits. Computers also support physical mapping experiments by executing algorithms (*q.v.*) used for genetic sequence comparison and for identifying possible overlaps in DNA fragments. The use of computers is not limited to storing and analyzing DNA; similar techniques have been used to predict the structure and function of proteins given sequences of amino acids.

Computer-Aided Education

Physicians can perform a large number of diagnostic procedures and choose from a wide array of alternative drugs. Many of these diagnostic and therapeutic choices have implications not only for patients' physical outcomes, but also for healthcare costs. To practice medicine effectively, physicians must have a firm foundation of knowledge and experience and continue to build and refine this base as medical science advances.

The use of computers in medical education offers one means for avoiding the shortcomings of traditional teaching methods. Advantages of computer-assisted instruction (CAI—*see* COMPUTER-ASSISTED LEARNING AND TEACHING) include the abilities to provide a medium for interactive learning, to offer immediate, student-specific feedback, to support individually tailored instruction, and to form a basis for objective testing. Computer-based simulations aimed at providers provide a forum for learning to manage both typical and unusual cases, and for experimentation without danger or inconvenience to real patients. Those applications designed to educate patients can be tailored to individual needs, such as language and educational background, and can save providers' time.

During the past two decades, CAI programs have proliferated. Virtually all medical schools and many nursing schools use computers to facilitate education. A number of publishing firms and specialty software companies are distributing educational programs on CD-ROMs or on the World Wide Web (*q.v.*). Programs are available to teach clinical skills such as neurological assessment and interpretation of laboratory test results and ECGs, and to address case management problems, such as the treatment of trauma and shock victims, advanced cardiac life support, and management of patients with diabetes. CAI programs have also been developed to educate patients regarding their diseases and treatments, such as the physiologic consequences of substance abuse and the pathology of several cancers.

Organizational Support for Research

The federal government has played a key role in funding medical computing research in the USA, mainly through the National Library of Medicine, the National Institutes of Health, and the Agency for Health Research and Policy. These agencies have promoted more general applications of computer technology in medicine, complementing the specific mission-oriented grants of organizations such as the National Cancer Institute. In Europe, much activity has been sponsored through national health maintenance organizations. Hospital computer systems have had specific governmental encouragement in Scandinavia, France, and Germany. As initial research approaches have proven feasible, commercial developers have moved to refine and market similar systems. In some areas, such as

medical imaging, hardware manufacturers have played an important role in technology development.

Sources of Information

For current information on specific applications, the journal *M.D. Computing* publishes annual surveys of commercially available medical computing systems and current vendors.

Journals devoted to medical informatics (the study of biomedical information and the applications of computers in medicine) include the *Journal of the American Medical Informatics Association*, *Computers and Biomedical Research*, *Methods of Information in Medicine*, *Computers in Biology and Medicine*, *M.D. Computing*, *International Journal of Bio-Medical Computing*, *Artificial Intelligence in Medicine*, and the *International Journal of Medical Informatics*. Selected articles are also published in medical journals, such as *JAMA* (the *Journal of the American Medical Association*), the *New England Journal of Medicine*, and the *Annals of Internal Medicine*, as well as the literatures of specific medical subspecialties.

In addition, a number of organizations provide a focal point for medical and healthcare computing, including the following:

◆ American Medical Informatics Association (AMIA), which sponsors the annual Spring and Fall AMIA meetings.

◆ Artificial Intelligence in Medicine (AIM), American Association for Artificial Intelligence.

◆ Engineering in Medicine and Biology Society, Institute of Electrical and Electronics Engineers.

◆ Healthcare Information and Management Systems Society (HIMSS), American Hospital Association.

◆ International Medical Informatics Association (IMIA), which sponsors the triennial international MEDINFO conference jointly with a special interest group of the International Federation for Information Processing (IFIP—*q.v.*).

◆ Special Interest Group on Biomedical Computing (SIGBIO), Association for Computing Machinery (*q.v.*).

Bibliography

1996. Clayton, P. D. and van Mulligen, E. "The Economic Motivations for Clinical Information Systems," *Journal of the American Medical Informatics Association*, **3** (Suppl.), 660–668.
1997. van Bemmel, J. H., and McCray, A. T. *Yearbook of Medical Informatics. Computing and Collaborative Care.* Stuttgart: Schattauer.
1997. Masys, D. R. (ed.) "The Emergence of 'Internetable' Health Care. Systems that Really Work," *Journal of the American Medical Informatics Association*, **4** (Suppl.).

Lucila Ohno-Machado and Leslie Perreault

MEDICAL IMAGING

For articles on related subjects *see* BIOCOMPUTING; IMAGE PROCESSING; MEDICAL APPLICATIONS; and TOMOGRAPHY, COMPUTERIZED.

Medical imaging is the study of human functions and anatomy through pictorial information. In order to generate this pictorial information, multidisciplinary knowledge, including biology, anatomy, physiology, chemistry, computer science, optical science, radiological science, electrical engineering, mathematics, and physics is required. Generally speaking, medical imaging studies the methods and procedures of:

1. Converting a conventional medical image, or synthesizing biological, anatomical or physiological information, to a digital image.

2. Analyzing the digital image according to a specific application or clinical need.

3. Extracting parameters and casting them into a format suitable for presentation, archiving, and decision making.

Some successful medical imaging applications in the early 1970s were the blood cell analyzer and the gamma camera in nuclear medicine (NM). The development of the computed tomography (CT or CAT for computer-assisted tomography) scanner resulted in the award of the Nobel Prize in Medicine to Allan M. Cormack and Godfrey N. Hounsfield in 1979. Major medical imaging developments in the 1980s and 1990s were electron microscopy (EM) and laser microscopy (LM), digital subtraction angiography (DSA), magnetic resonance imaging (MRI), positron emission tomography (PET), computed radiography (CR), direct digital radiography (DR), Doppler ultrasound, picture archiving and communication systems (PACS), and medical image informatics (MII). EM can reveal minute details in biological infrastructures as small as a few angstroms in size. LM yields thin serial images providing three-dimensional morphology of living cells. DSA allows real-time subtraction to enhance the vascularities in angiograms. Without the use of ionizing radiation, MRI reveals high-contrast images of three-dimensional anatomical structures of the body. MRI is the method of choice for neuroradiological, vascular, and musculoskeletal examinations.

PET provides chemical and physiological images of the human body that complement anatomical images obtained by using MRI and CT. The registration of MRI or CT with PET head images provides an insight into the specific function of various parts of the brain. CR and DR allow an X-ray image to be recorded directly as a digital image, opening new avenues for using digital image processing as an aid in medical diagnosis. An example is in direct digital mammography, which can reveal microcalcification in the breast of 50 microns in size.

PACS is a concept for medical image management and communication. When fully implemented, the system can revolutionize medical practice to improve health care delivery. PACS storage technology includes parallel transfer disks and optical disc/tape libraries. In the former, a conventional X-ray chest examination composed of posterior and lateral view images of 20 MB can be stored or retrieved from the parallel transfer disks within one second. In the latter, an optical disc/tape library that occupies a footprint of no more than 3×6 ft (1×2 m) allows the storage of five TB of information, equivalent to about five years' worth of all MR and CT examinations conducted in a large 600-bed teaching hospital.

In communication components, fiber optic systems with high-performance fiber optic transmitters and receivers like the ATM (asynchronous transfer mode— *q.v.*) and gigabit Ethernet technologies can transmit images at a rate of 1 gigabit per second. A conventional 10 MB X-ray image can be transmitted between two points in less than one second. For display, $2,000 \times 2,500$ pixel monitors are readily available that display digital X-ray images without loss of diagnostic quality. Three-dimensional display stations are used in various clinical applications.

PACS accumulates a very large volume of imaging data that leads to the concept of MII infrastructure (MIII). MIII allows for large-scale horizontal and longitudinal clinical studies, which opens up new horizons for large-scale imaging research.

Medical Image Detectors and Recorders

Medical image detection and recording methods can be categorized as being either photochemical or photoelectronic. An example of a photochemical method is the phosphorous screen and silver halide film combination system used for X-ray detection. The television camera and display monitor used in fluorography is a photoelectronic technique. The photochemical method has the advantage of combining image detection and image recording in a single step. The film in a screen/film system simultaneously detects and records the attenuated X-rays. A photoelectronic system, on the other hand, usually involves a two-step process; the image is detected first and then recorded in a subsequent step.

In the case of DSA, an image intensifier tube is used as the X-ray detector instead of a screen/film combination. The detected X-rays are converted first into light photons and then into electronic signals that are recorded by a video camera. The images from the video camera can be displayed on a TV monitor, and the video signal can be digitized to form a digital image. The photoelectronic system, while clearly more complicated, has one important advantage: the output information can be converted from light or electrons to digital format for image processing.

Fig. 1 shows an example of medical image detectors and recorders. In this case, an image of blood cells from a blood sample on a glass slide is to be recorded. The glass slide is first placed under the microscope. Three methods to record the image in digital form are shown in Fig. 1. One is to attach a 35 mm digital camera to the microscope to record the image of the blood cells digitally. Or a conventional 35 mm camera or a television or CCD (charge-coupled device) camera can be attached to the microscope, to record the blood cells on a film or as an electronic image on a TV monitor. In either case, the recorded image is in analog form. It can be converted to a digital image through an analog to digital (A/D) conversion process.

Digital Images

A digital image $P(x, y)$ is defined as an integer function of two variables x, y such that

$$0 \leq P(x, y) \leq N \quad \text{where} \quad 1 \leq x \leq m, 1 \leq y \leq n$$

and x, y, m, n, and N are positive integers. For simplicity of explanation, let $m = n$ (i.e. $P(x, y)$ is a square image). $P(x, y)$ is the gray-level value of a picture element, or *pixel*, at (x, y). The computer memory requirement for storing image $P(x, y)$ is $n \times n \times k$ bits, where $k = \lceil \log_2(N + 1) \rceil$. Thus, $n \times n \times k$ means that the image has n lines, each line has n pixels, and each pixel can have a discrete gray-level value that ranges from 0 to $2^k - 1$. A typical black and white microscopic digital image has 512×512 pixels and each pixel can have values from 0 to 255. A three-dimensional (3D) image $P(x, y, z)$ is an integer function of three variables in which the z-dimension can be time, or the third axis in the anatomy. For example, in DSA the third dimension is time, whereas in MRI the third dimension is the body axis. A picture element in 3D is called a *voxel*.

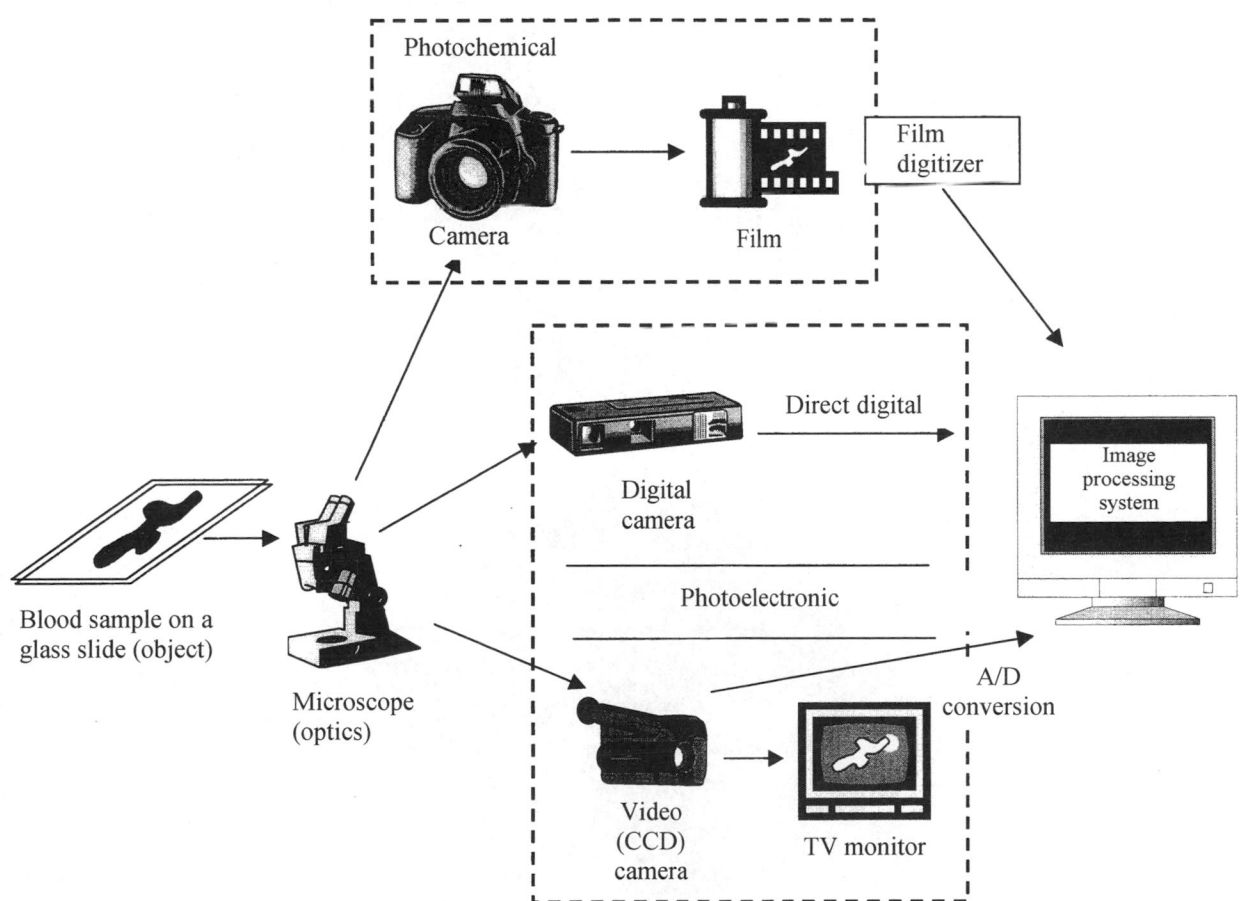

Figure 1. An example of biomedical image detectors and recorders. Three possible input methods: film digitizer, video signal A/D conversion, and direct digital camera.

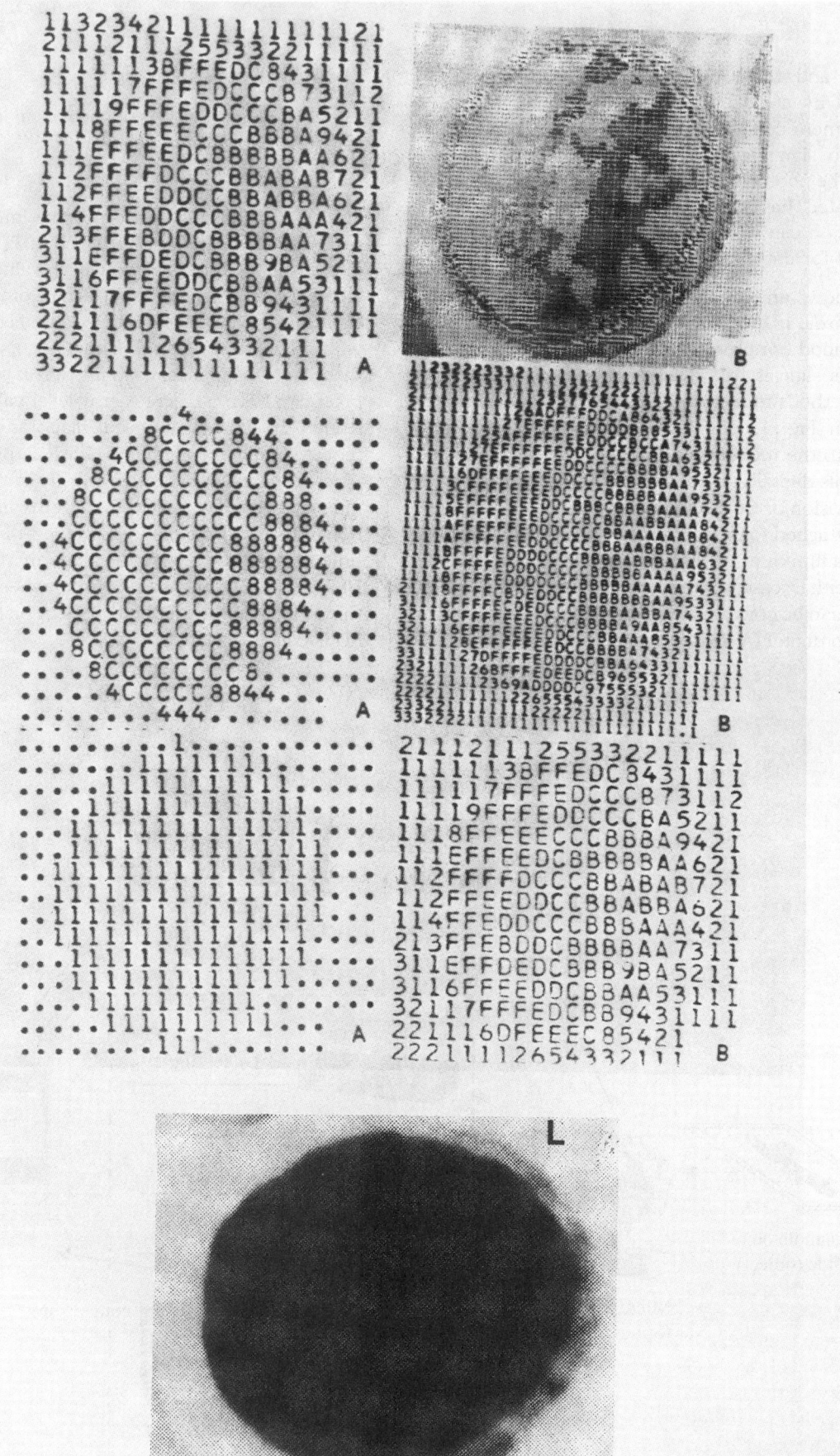

Figure 2. Illustration of spatial and density resolution, using a digitized lymphocyte image (L) as an example. (a) Fixed spatial resolution with variable density resolutions: 16, 4, and 2 gray levels. (b) Fixed density resolution (16 levels) with variable spatial resolutions. The 16 levels are represented by hexadecimal digits 0–F.

Spatial Density Resolution

The image quality of an object of interest is characterized by three parameters: spatial resolution, density resolution, and signal-to-noise ratio. Spatial resolution is a measure of the number of pixels used to represent the object, and density resolution is the total number of discrete gray-level values in the digital image. It is apparent that n and N are related to spatial resolution and density resolution, respectively. A high signal-to-noise ratio means that the image is very pleasing to the eye and hence has a better quality. Fig. 2 demonstrates the concept of spatial and density resolution of digital images of a lymphocyte. The left-hand column in Fig. 2 shows digitized images of the lymphocyte with a fixed spatial resolution (21×15) and variable density resolutions (from top to bottom: 16, 4, and 2 gray levels). The right-hand column depicts the digital representation of the same analog image with a fixed density resolution (16) and variable spatial resolutions (from top to bottom: high, medium, low). It is clear from this example that the upper right corner digital image has the best quality (highest spatial and density resolutions), whereas the lower left corner image has the lowest spatial and density resolutions. Depending on the application requirement, the spatial resolution, density resolution, and signal-to-noise ratio of the image should be adjusted during image acquisition. A high-resolution image requires a larger memory for storage and a longer time for image processing than a lower-resolution image.

Sources of Medical Images

By far the richest source of medical images is in radiology. Sometimes we call those images macroscopic to differentiate them from microscopic and infrastructural images. In radiology, about 70% of the examinations, including those that involve skull, chest, abdomen, and bone, produce images that are acquired and stored on X-ray film. These images have a spatial resolution of about 5 lp/mm. Line pairs per millimeter (lp/mm) is a measure of spatial resolution; one line pair represents two pixels. These films can be converted to digital format using a film digitizer. Among various types of digitizer, the laser scanning digitizer is considered the gold standard because it can best preserve the density and spatial resolutions of the original analog image. A laser film scanner can digitize a $14'' \times 17''$ X-ray film to 4000×5000 pixels (about 5 lp/mm), with 12 bits per pixel. At this spatial and density resolution, the quality of the original analog image and the digitized image is essentially equivalent. In clinical practice, however, we digitize an X-ray film to $2,000 \times 2,500$ pixels. Computed radiography (CR), which uses a laser stimulable luminescence phosphor imaging plate as a detector, is gradually replacing the screen/film as the

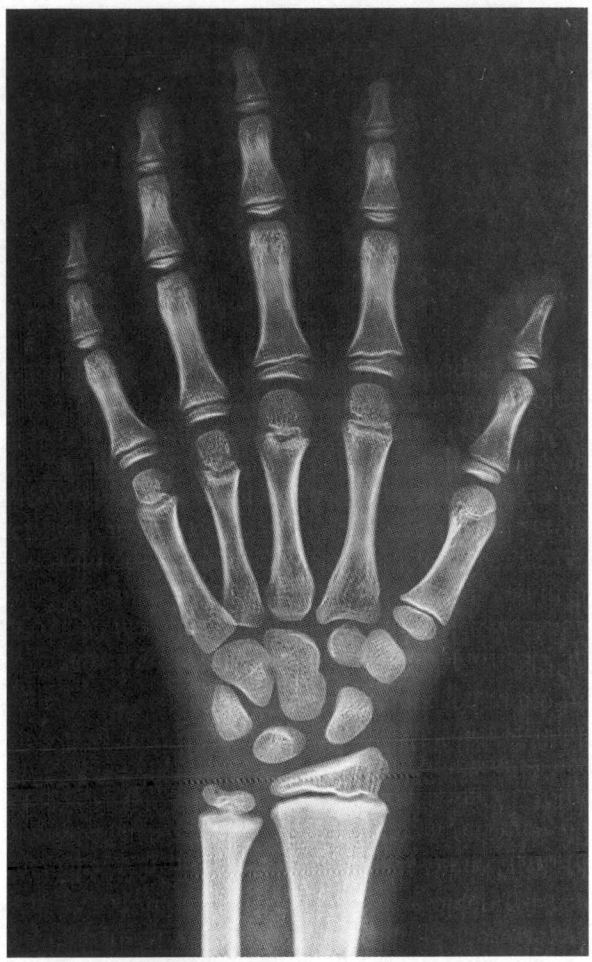

(a) Digitized radiograph of the hand and wrist. Both soft tissue and the detail of the bones are clearly delineated.

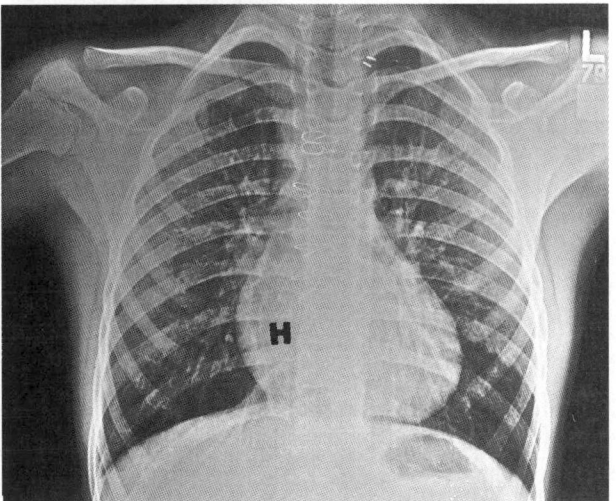

(b) CR (computed radiography) image of the chest: the image is $2,000 \times 2,500$ pixels and 10 bits/pixel. Excellent delineation of the blood vessels behind the heart (H).

Figure 3. Examples of medical images obtained from various energy sources.

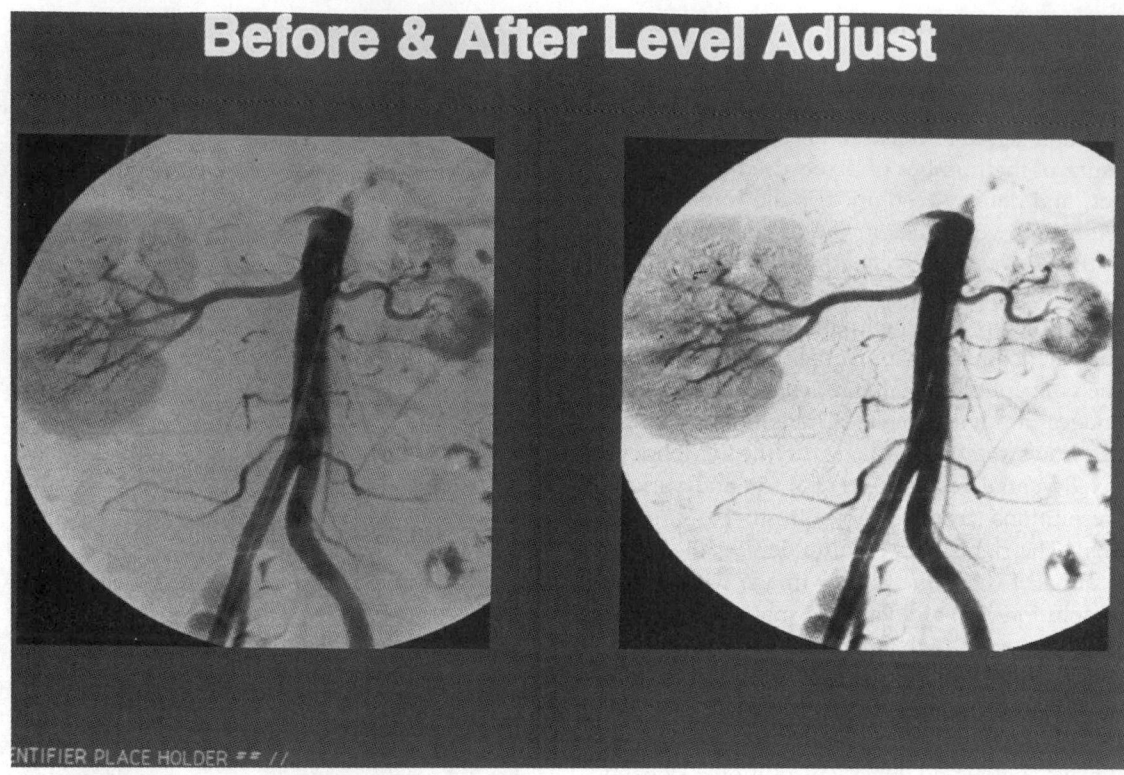

Figure 3(c). DSA (digital subtractlon angiography) of the kidneys showing contrast enhanced blood vessels. Left: before contrast injection; right: after contrast injection (black). (Courtesy of S. Balter.)

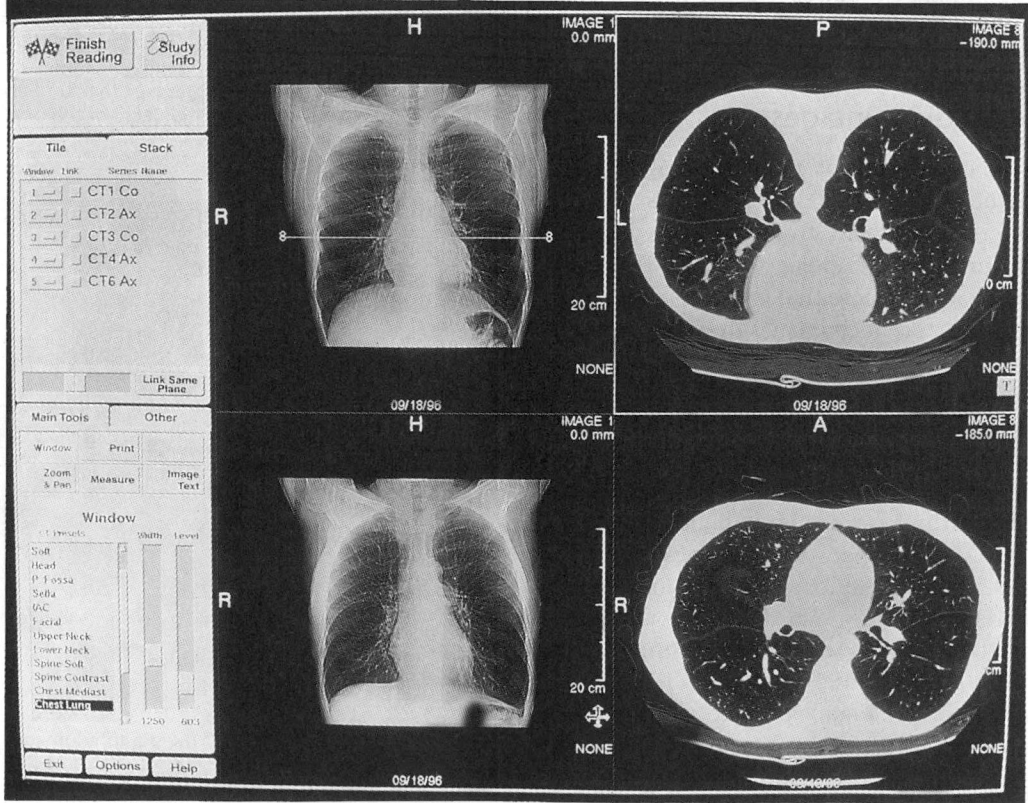

Figure 3(d). CT (computed tomography) image of the chest. Left: scout views, the horizontal line showing the scan level; right top: patient is in prone position; right bottom: patient in supine position.

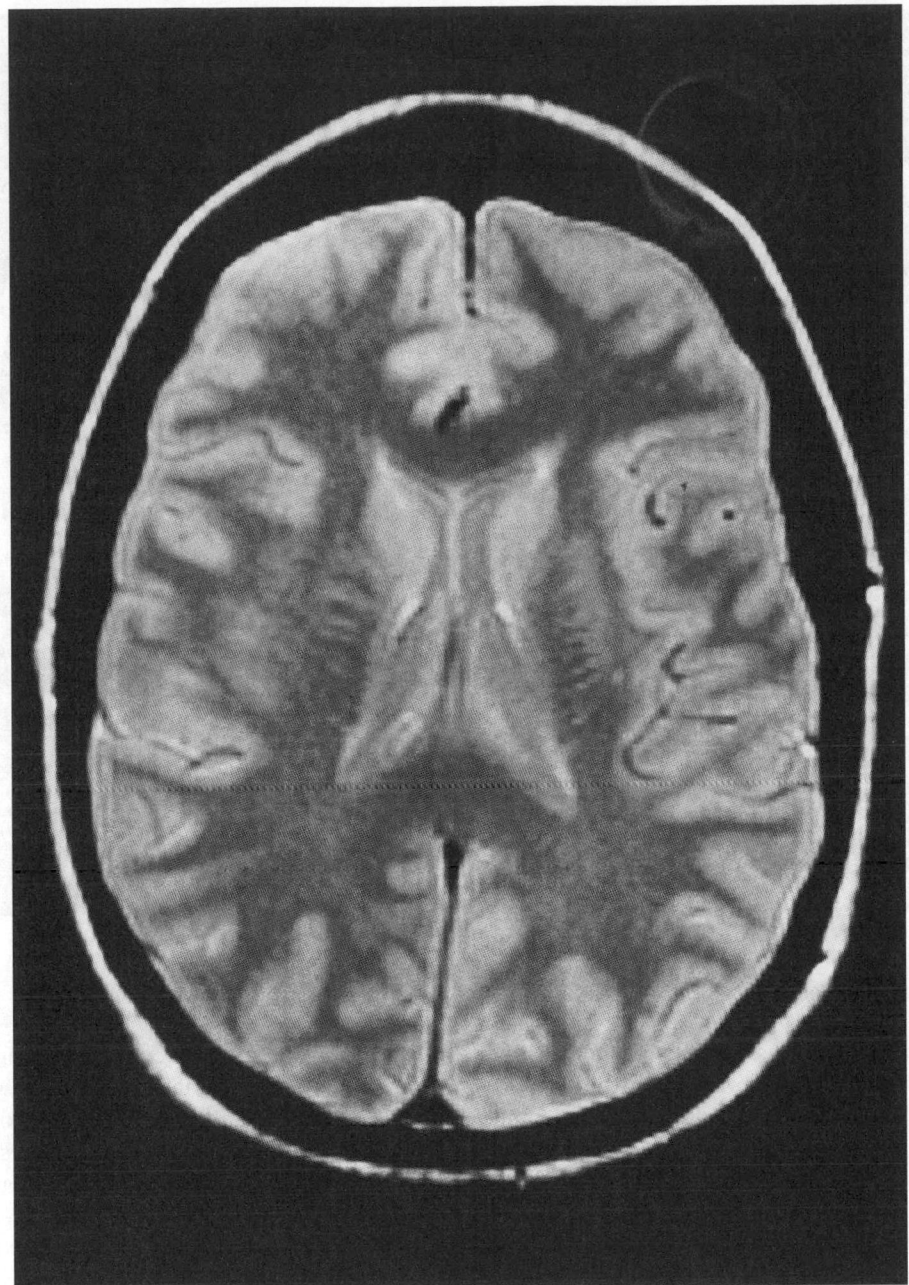

Figure 3(e)–(h). MR images of the head from the same patient in the transverse, sagittal, and coronal planes, and one view in the MR angiogram showing blood (white) supply to the Circle of Willis. Images from the three planes show fine structures of the brain. See next three pages for 3(f), (g) and (h).

image detector. In this case, a laser beam is used to scan the imaging plate that contains the latent X-ray image. The latent image is excited and emits light photons that are detected and converted to digitized electronic signals forming a digital X-ray image. Direct digital radiography (DR) does not require an intermediate step; after the detector system receives the attenuated X-rays, it converts the signal directly to a digital image. An example is direct digital mammography, which produces a $4,000 \times 5,000 \times 12$-bit digital image of the breast.

The other 30% of radiological examinations—those that involve computed tomography (CT), ultrasonography (US), magnetic resonance imaging (MRI), positron emission tomography (PET), and digital subtraction angiography (DSA)—produce images that are already in digital format. The image sizes are CT: $512 \times 512 \times 12$; US: $512 \times 512 \times 8$; MRI: $256 \times 256 \times 12$; PET: $128 \times 128 \times 12$; DSA: $512 \times 512 \times 8$. These techniques use different energy sources and detectors to generate images, and they complement each other in their clinical applications. CT uses X-rays as the energy

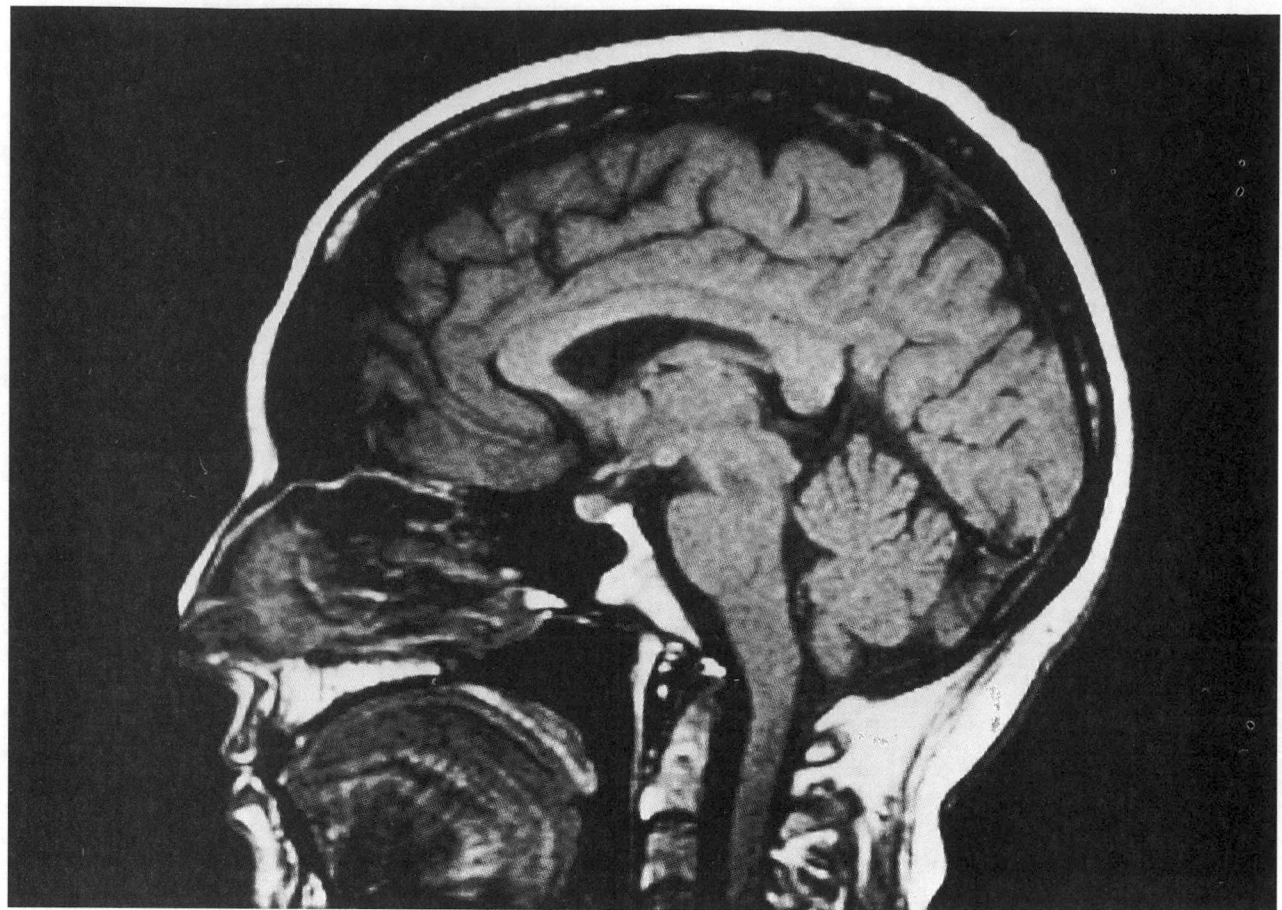

Figure 3(f).

source and gas or scintillating crystals as detectors. US uses an ultrasonic transducer as both the energy source and the detector. MR uses two energy sources, magnetic fields and radio-frequency electromagnetic waves, and a radio-frequency receiver as the detector. DSA uses X-rays as the energy source and an image intensifier tube as the detector. Conventional X-ray examinations and DSA produce a projection image, whereas CT, US, PET, and MRI give sectional images. Sectional images can be stacked to form a three-dimensional image set that represents the true three-dimensional object. All radiologic images are monochromatic except NM, PET, and Doppler US, in which pseudo-colors are used as an image enhancement tool. Thus, for example, a Doppler US will have an image size of $512 \times 512 \times 24$. Various color patterns are used to represent the direction of the blood flow toward or away from the transducer.

Other medical image sources used in anatomy, biology, and pathology are from light and electron microscopes. Images from these sources are collected with a video or a CCD camera and then digitized to a $512 \times 512 \times 8$ image (or 24 bits for true color) with a frame grabber (an areal A/D converter). Light microscopy produces true color images, using red, green, and blue filters for color separation. Thus, a color image after digitization yields three digital images, the combination of which produces a true-color digital image encoded at 24 bits/pixel. Figs. 3a–n show some examples of these medical images (for Figs. 3j and 3k, see Color Page CP-12). Table 1 describes the dimensions and storage requirements of some common medical images.

Image Processing Systems

After a medical image is formed, it is analyzed by an image processing system. The architecture of an image processing system (IP) consists of three major components: image processor(s), image memories, and video processor(s). They are connected by internal computer buses to form an integrated system. Fig. 4 shows the general block diagram of an integrated image processing system. For this particular system, only the IP controller is connected to the computer host bus. The image processor is a high-speed array processor. It is composed of arithmetic-logic units (*q.v.*), multipliers

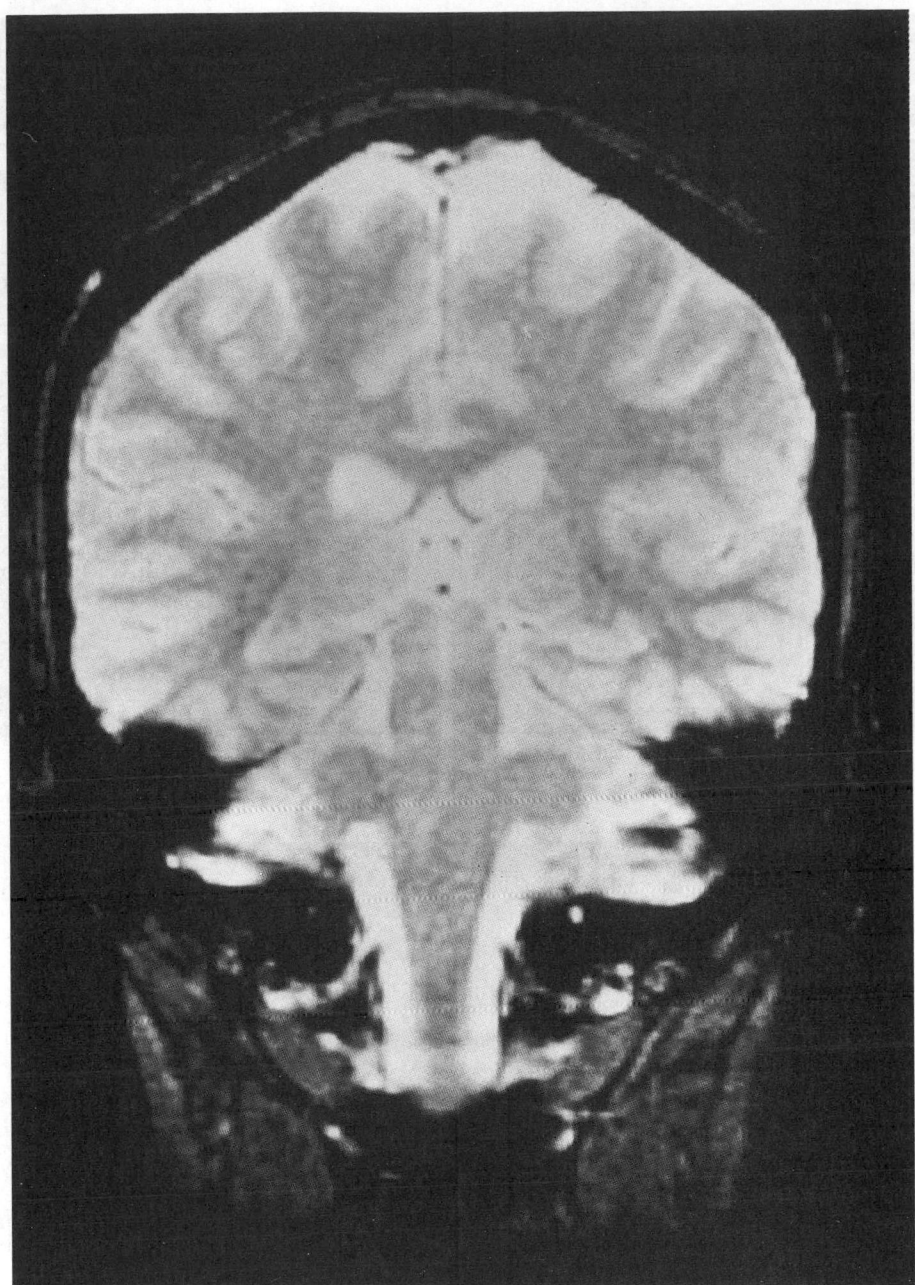

Figure 3(g).

and shifters, comparators, and look-up tables. The image memories can be partitioned into various sizes for efficient storage of image data. The video processor takes the images from the image memories and selectively displays them at high speed on video monitors.

An IP system requires extensive software support. The trend in IP software development is towards portability (*see* SOFTWARE PORTABILITY). Fig. 5 shows the general organization of IP software. Portability is preferred in the three higher levels of software so that they can be used again when the system hardware is up-

graded in the future. The two lower levels are machine dependent and have to be rewritten for each new hardware architecture. IP functions include pixel, local, global, and statistical operations. IP functions also consist of image database manipulation and image display. In the past, Fortran was used in most IP software development, but C (*q.v.*) running under the Unix (*q.v.*) or Windows NT operating systems is now standard.

In medical imaging applications, contour extraction of an object of interest is important because it leads to

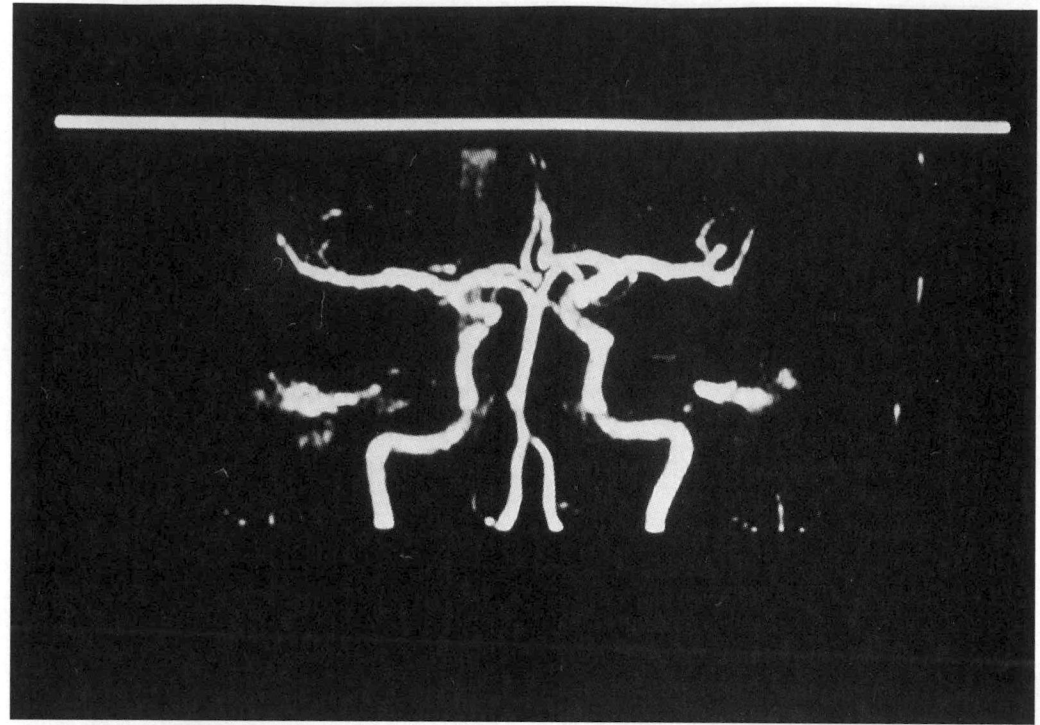

Figure 3(h).

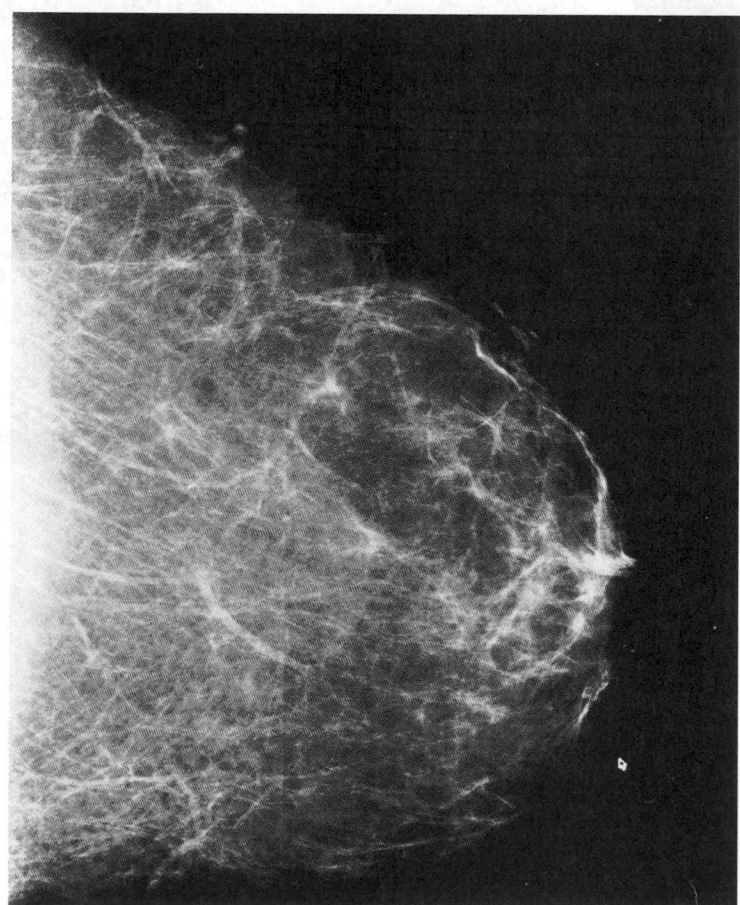

Figure 3(i). A direct digital mammogram. The image is 4,000 × 5,000 × 12 bits. (Courtesy of Drs. E. Sickles and A. Lou.)

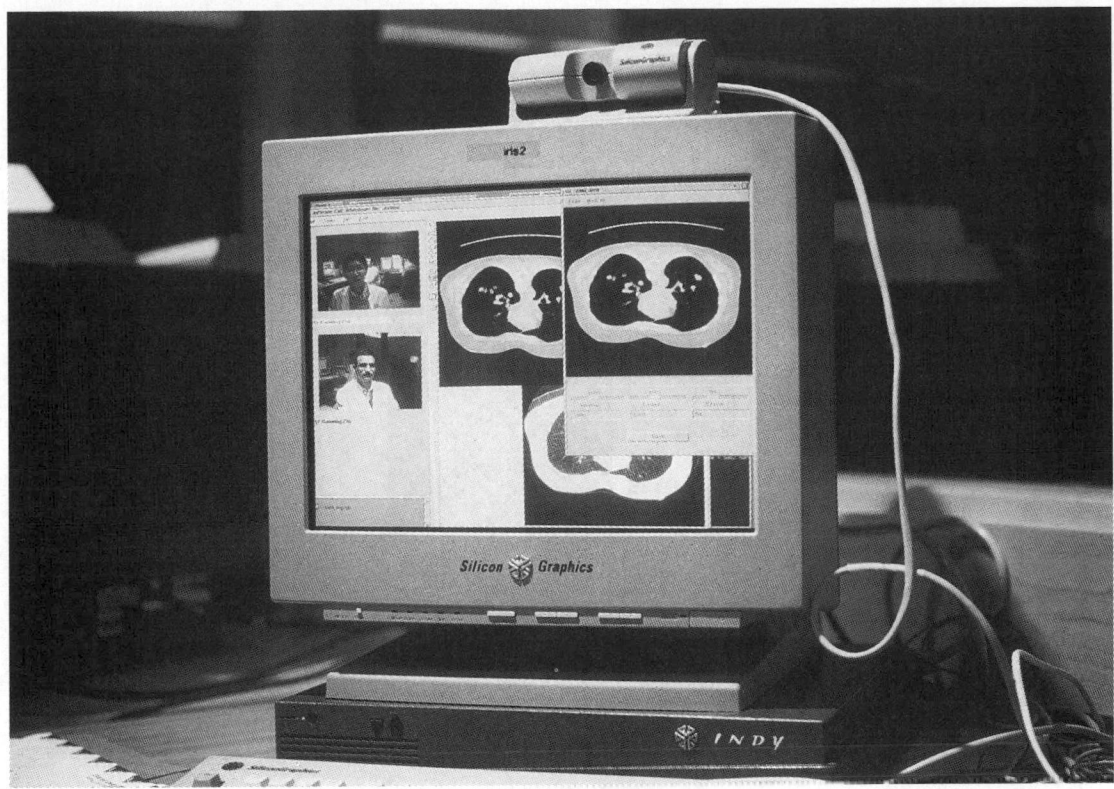

(l)

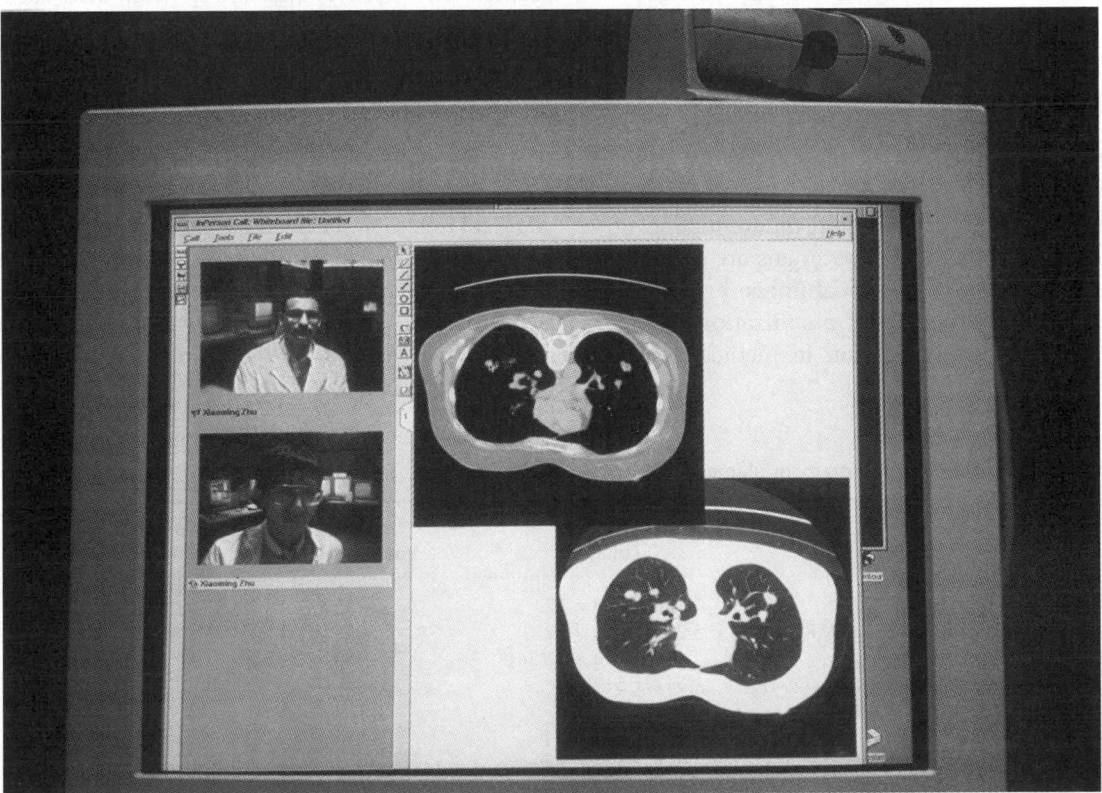

(m)

Figure 3(l, m). Two sites participating in a teleconferencing using CT images. Several windows are open at each site for the video and medical images presentation. Note that the two images in the video window at both sites are reversed.

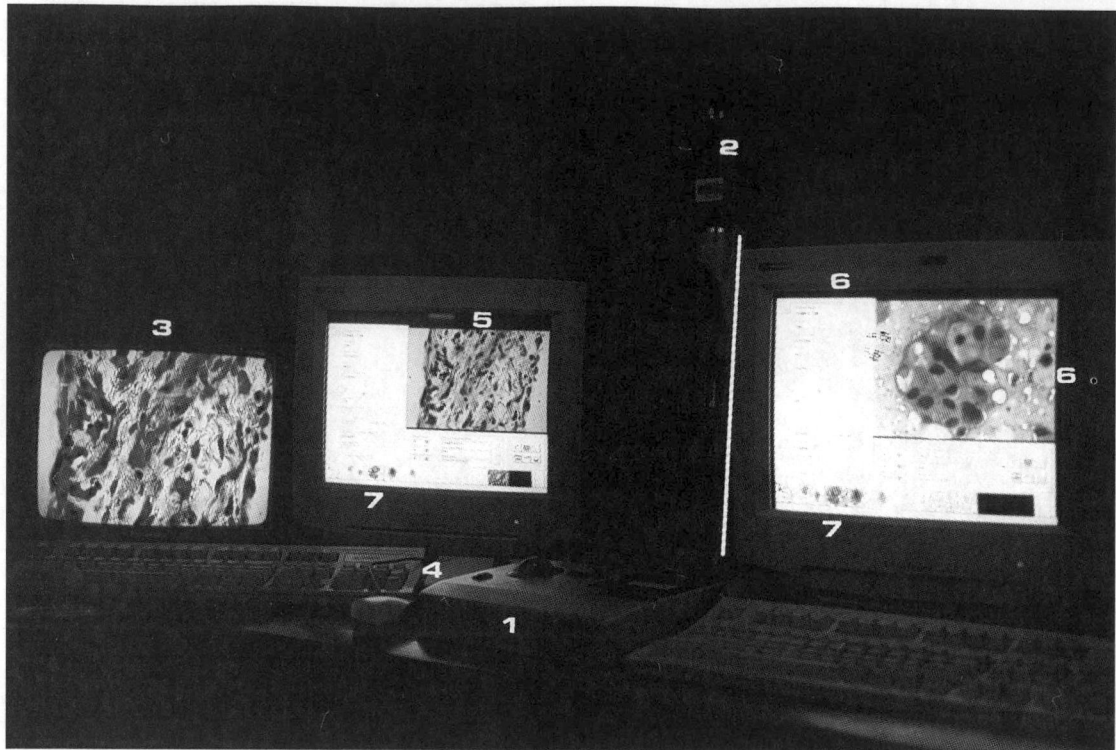

Figure 3(n). A digital tele-microscopic system. Left (from the white line): image acquisition workstation, automatic microscope (1); CCD camera (2); video monitor (3); computer with an A/D converter attached to the CCD, an image memory, a database to manage the patient image file (4); the video monitor (3) showing a life image from the microscope which is being digitized and shown on the workstation monitor (5). Right: remote diagnostic workstation (6) showing a previously transmitted image from the acquisition workstation. Thumbnail images in the bottom of both workstations are images which have been captured and sent to the diagnostic workstation from the acquisition workstation (7). Note that the last thumbnail image at the acquisition workstation has not been transmitted.

quantitative measurements. Despite many years of software research and development, soft tissue segmentation of radiologic images and differentiation of objects of interest in histology specimens are still very difficult tasks. Advances in medical image processing remain largely in the domain of quantization. Fig. 6 shows the levels of sophistication in medical image processing.

Tele-Imaging

Medical images have been an integrated component in medical practice since their inception. Recent health care reforms have prompted the use of telemedicine as a more efficient healthcare delivery system. For this reason, tele-imaging has drawn attention in recent years. In tele-imaging, teleconferencing (*see* COMPUTER

Table 1. Size of some common medical images.

	One image (bits)	No. of images/exam	One examination (MB)
Nuclear medicine (NM)	$128 \times 128 \times 12$	30–60	1–2
Magnetic resonance imaging (MRI)	$256 \times 256 \times 12$	60	8
Ultrasound (US)[1]	$512 \times 256 \times 8\ (24)$	20–230	5–60
Digital subtraction angiography (DSA)	$512 \times 512 \times 8$	15–40	4–10
Digitized electronic microscopy	$512 \times 512 \times 8$	1	0.26
Digitized color microscopy	$512 \times 512 \times 24$	1	0.79
Computed tomography (CT)	$512 \times 512 \times 12$	40	20
Computed radiography (CR)	$2048 \times 2048 \times 12$	2	16
Digitized X-rays	$2048 \times 2048 \times 12$	2	16
Digitized mammography	$4000 \times 5000 \times 12$	4	160

[1] Doppler US with 24 bit color images.

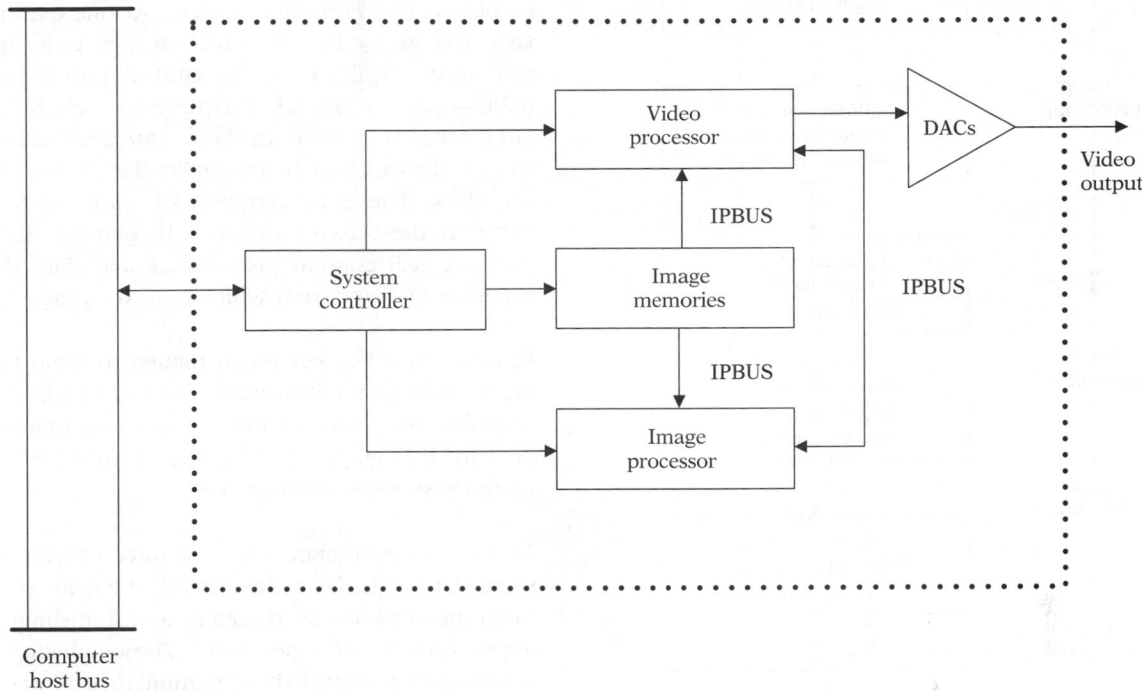

Figure 4. The general architecture of an integrated image processing system. Only the system controller is connected to the computer host bus.

CONFERENCING) and teleconsultation are two important clinical protocols both requiring the transmission of large medical image files (*see* Table 1) through some wide and local area networks (*q.v.*). When these image files are transmitted through a public network with limited bandwidth (*q.v.*), they will create a bottleneck. A major research effort in this area of research is to design the Next Generation Internet (NGI) in anticipation of the arrival of these medical images in the Internet. Figs. 3l and m show two sites participating in a teleconferencing using CT images, using a "store and forward" strategy in which medical images are prepared and stored at both sites before the teleconference. Fig. 3n shows a digital tele-microscopic

system with the remote image acquisition workstation (*q.v.*) on the left and the workstation at the expert site on the right.

Future Trends

The use of digital medical imaging in the radiological sciences is expected to increase about 40% in the next five years because of the introduction of CR and DR. New methods using different energy sources in producing medical images will not progress as fast, but image quality from existing imaging modalities will continue to improve. Traditionally, medical imaging is used only for diagnostic purposes, but there is a trend toward therapeutic applications as well. **PACS and MIII** will become vital image database management systems (*q.v.*). This will lead to the development of image knowledge databases requiring new IP hardware and software. The leading candidate in hardware design for medical image processing will be a modified parallel processing architecture that will shorten the time required for interprocessor communication. Mathematical advances may provide a new approach for image segmentation. Fractal (*q.v.*) analysis, wavelet transform, and mathematical morphology are promising methods for better image feature extraction and object definition. Neural networks (*q.v.*) may prove useful for medical pattern recognition, and other artificial intelligence (*q.v.*) techniques may bring medical imaging to the threshold of a mature science.

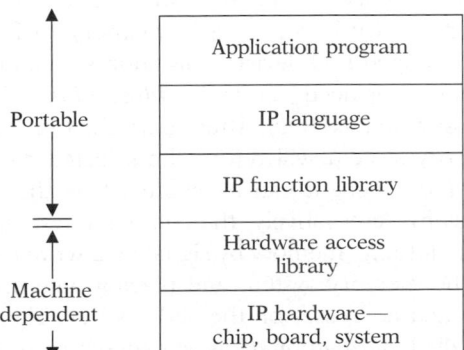

Figure 5. Organization of image processing software. The three higher levels of software should be portable for future hardware architecture.

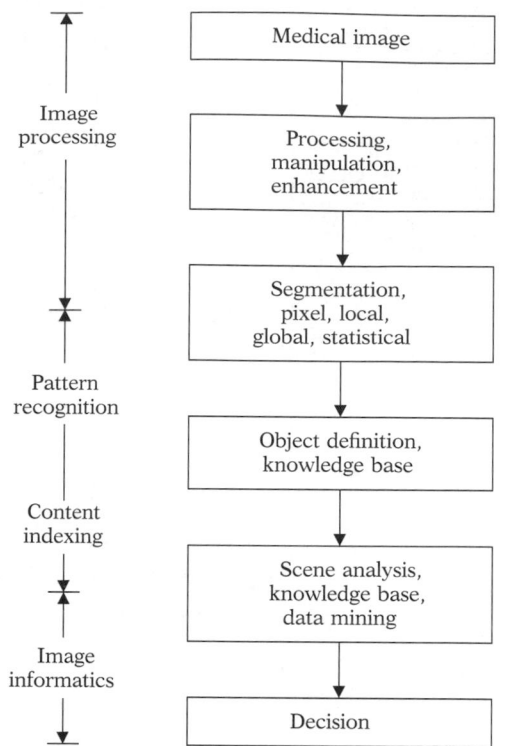

Figure 6. Levels of sophistication in medical image processing. Medical database, pattern recognition, content indexing, and image informatics are current major research topics.

Bibliography

1981. Huang, H. K. "Biomedical Image Processing," *CRC Critical Reviews in Bioengineering*, **4**, 185–271.

l990. Huang, H. K., Aberle, D. R., Lufkin, R., Grant, E. G., Hanafee, W. N., and Kangarloo, H. "Advances in Medical Imaging," *Ann. Int. Med.*, **112**, 203–220.

1996. Huang, H. K., Wong, A. W. K., Lou, S. L., Bazzill, T. M. *et al.* "Clinical Experience with a Second Generation PACS," *J. Digital Imag.*, **9**, *4*, 151–166.

1996. Huang, H. K. *Picture Archiving and Communication Systems in Biomedical Imaging*, 489. New York: VCH/John Wiley.

1997. Huang, H. K., Wong, S. T. C., and Pietka, E. "Medical Image Informatics Infrastructure Design and Applications," *Medical Informatics*, **22**, *4*, 279–289.

H. K. Huang

MEMORY

MAIN

For articles on related subjects *see* ACCESS TIME; ADDRESSING; ASSOCIATIVE MEMORY; CACHE MEMORY; DISKETTE; HARD DISK; INTEGRATED CIRCUITRY; LOCAL STORE; MASS STORAGE; MEMORY HIERARCHY; MEMORY MANAGEMENT; MEMORY-MAPPED I/O; MEMORY PROTECTION; OPTICAL STORAGE; PORT, MEMORY; READ-ONLY MEMORY; REGISTER; ULTRASONIC MEMORY; VIRTUAL MEMORY; and WILLIAMS TUBE MEMORY.

Different levels of memory (or *storage*) are usually employed in a computer system. At one extreme are very fast and relatively small storage units used as fast access *registers* by the central processing unit (CPU—*q.v.*). At the other extreme are relatively slow, large capacity units of *auxiliary storage*. The auxiliary storage devices may be magnetic disks, tapes, or optical discs. The characteristics of *main memory* lie between these two extremes. In general, the main memory will contain instructions and data that are accessed by a program while it is executing.

In this article the key terms related to main memory are described and illustrated. The logical components, organizations, and techniques of main memory are described. Finally, the technologies employed in main memory systems are described.

Memory performance and cost have evolved rapidly since the 1970s. Over this period, the price per bit of main memory has decreased at an astonishing rate of approximately 27% per year. These advances have come about primarily through miniaturization brought on by improvements in the integrated microelectronic technologies used to fabricate the storage devices (*see* INTEGRATED CIRCUITRY). The availability of fast, inexpensive memory has had enormous impact on computer technology.

Definitions and Terminology

Digital computers store data as a representation of binary digits. Each digit is called a *bit*, the minimum storage element. A bit may assume the value "1" or "0"; nothing else. Data may be both read from and written to any location in main memory. This type of memory is known as *random access memory*, or RAM. To access the data in main memory, some element of the computer system must first provide the memory system with an *address* which describes the location of the data in memory (*see* ADDRESSING). The address may come from the CPU, from a cache memory, or from a memory mapped I/O device. This address is a binary representation placed on the *address bus* of the memory system (*see* BUS). After an *access time* (*q.v.*), the memory system will return the selected data on its *data bus* where it can be captured by the computer system. Alternatively, the computer system can write data into the memory by signaling a write operation to the memory system and placing data on the data bus and addresses on the address bus. The data bus is called *bidirectional*, as it can serve to write data to and read data from the memory system. New data can be read from or written to the memory system every cycle time (*q.v.*). The access and cycle times are a function of both the technology and organization of the memory system.

Typically, each memory address refers to more than one bit of data in the memory system. The minimum uniquely addressable unit of data in main memory is typically eight bits, or a *byte*. However, the size of this addressable quantum, often called a *word*, depends upon the computer system, the memory unit, and the access mode. The choice of a *data path*, the number of bits simultaneously transferred per memory access, is governed by the trade-off between performance and cost. A wider data path will allow a greater rate of transfer of data in and out of the memory, but is accompanied by additional expense, power consumption, and system complexity.

An alternative technique for increasing the memory system data rate is the use of *interleaving* (*q.v.*). An interleaved memory system is physically implemented using a number M of independent memory subsystems, or banks, of similar size and performance. Adjacent memory addresses are assigned to different physical subsystems. Hence, if the processor accesses sequential memory locations, each memory subsystem can be activated concurrently. The peak memory system cycle time can be reduced by a factor M from the memory subsystem cycle time by using this technique. Implementation of an interleaved memory requires the use of a memory control function which analyzes the memory access address stream and determines the availability of the various memory subsystems to adjust the memory system timing. In the case of a nonsequential address access, the memory system cycle time must be lengthened. A portion of the memory address will be used to select the individual memory subsystem from which to read or write.

Even small computer systems now have relatively large memories. Since memory addresses are binary numbers, the memory size is typically related to a power of two and described in units of kilobytes (KB), megabytes (MB), gigabytes (GB), or (for mass storage—*q.v.*) terabytes (TB). A kilobyte is 2^{10} or 1,024 bytes (that is, approximately 10^3 bytes, which explains the use of the prefix "kilo"). A megabyte is 2^{20} or 1,048,576 bytes, a gigabyte is 2^{30} or 1.074×10^9 bytes, and a terabyte is 2^{40} or 1.10×10^{12} bytes. In 1999, main memory sizes ranged from 64 MB on an inexpensive personal computer to several GB on a mainframe (*q.v.*).

To translate the binary address provided by a computer system on the memory bus, the memory system makes use of *decoders*, which accept as input a binary address and as output activate one signal line chosen by the address. For example, a 6-bit address decoder would have 6 input bits and 2^6 or 64 output signals.

One of these 64 would be activated in response to each unique input address. Information inside the memory system is stored in *memory cells*. An individual memory cell can be uniquely selected by a signal from the decoder. However, in this simple realization a moderately sized memory would require an unrealistically large decoder circuit and associated signal wiring. To solve this problem, main memory addressing typically uses a hierarchical scheme. This is most easily understood in the case of a three-level hierarchy by visualizing the memory space as a three-dimensional cube with numbered lines containing integers starting with 0 on each axis of the cube. Separate memory cells are logically located at each Cartesian coordinate within the cube, thus forming a three-dimensional matrix of memory cells. The "address" of any cell is given by its Cartesian triplet (i.e. its *x*, *y*, *z* ordered triplet). The length of each axis is selected to be a power of two. In this way the entire address space may be represented by assigning specific bits from the address data word to a separate decoder for each axis that effectively chooses a specific position along that axis. In this three-level example, one portion of the address bits will choose a "plane" of cells, another portion of the address chooses a "row" of cells in the plane, and the final portion of the address bits choose a column within the row.

Use of a hierarchical address decoding scheme reduces the required number of decoded signals into the memory array. For example, a 1 MB memory system requires 20 bits to address. A one-level decoder would require 1,048,576 output signals. A two-level addressing scheme can be partitioned in a number of ways. A "square" representation would assign 10 address bits to one axis and the other 10 address bits to the other. This scheme would require two decoders, each with 1,024 output signals. A significant reduction in the number of decoded signal lines can result from this hierarchical addressing scheme. The choice of the number of levels in the addressing hierarchy and the number of unique addresses in each level depends on the desired cost, performance, power, and size of the memory system. The details of these trade-offs also depend upon the technology with which the memory cell and the decoders are realized. In a typical memory system using semiconductor memory, decoder cost and its associated signal wiring is much reduced when it can be integrated into the integrated circuit chip itself rather than being used to choose between chips or boards.

Memory Technologies

Memory cells for main memory may be realized by a number of technologies and designs that are distinguished by their unique characteristics of density,

TABLE 1. Relative characteristics of technologies used in main memories.

Technology	Density	Performance	Power	Cost per bit	Volatile
Semiconductor MOSFET DRAM	1	3	2	1	yes
Semiconductor MOSFET SRAM	2	2	3	2	yes
Semiconductor bipolar SRAM	3	1	4	3	yes
Magnetic core (obsolete)	4	4	1	4	no

1 (best) → 4 (worst).

performance (access and cycle time), power dissipation, and volatility. Density is important to the system through its impact on cost, size, and performance. A significant part of the delay in modern, high-speed computers comes from the delay along signal lines. Smaller, denser components allow the use of shorter signal lines and therefore improve performance. In integrated semiconductor technologies, the cost of the memory is strongly influenced by the density of the storage element. The smaller the memory cell, the cheaper the integrated memory chip and the cheaper the memory system. Power becomes a concern as it affects the overall system density or portability of the technology. When the number of storage elements in a main memory system is large and significant power is used by each individual memory cell, special cooling structures are required to remove the heat from the system. This increases the cost and reduces the density of the overall system.

Memory *volatility* refers to the inability of the memory to retain its data after power is removed from the system. Most main memories are volatile, that is, information is lost when power is removed. However, in some applications that require rapid restart after power failure or maintenance of data for intervals of power-off, nonvolatile memories are available at greater cost. In general, nonvolatile magnetic medium auxiliary storage devices are used to hold programs and data in the absence of system power. Table 1 describes the relative characteristics of popular main memory technologies. The "D" and "S" in "DRAM" and "SRAM" respectively stand for *dynamic* and *static*, properties defined in the next section.

Semiconductor Technologies

Main memory systems are most often realized using semiconductor technologies. To achieve high density and low cost, semiconductor memories use very large-scale integration (VLSI) to integrate many memory cells as well as decoder and detector circuits on the same semiconductor chips. Typically, each memory chip receives an address as input and outputs 1 to 32 bits corresponding to this address. Several memory chips will be activated at the same time to access an entire byte or memory word.

MOSFET DYNAMIC RAM

Metal Oxide Semiconductor Field Effect Transistor Dynamic Random Access Memory (MOSFET DRAM) is the dominant main memory technology. MOSFET DRAMs are chosen primarily for their characteristics of low cost, low power, and moderate performance that make them an ideal choice for large main memories. DRAMs achieve their low cost through use of a relatively simple semiconductor technology (CMOS) and a small memory cell consisting of a single transistor and a single capacitor. The CMOS technology provides both n-channel and p-channel field effect transistors (*see* INTEGRATED CIRCUITRY). The equivalent circuit of a DRAM memory cell, called the one device cell, is shown in Fig. 1. This one-device memory cell was invented by Robert Dennard in 1967. The value of the memory bit is represented by voltage stored on the cell's capacitor. This voltage is written into the storage capacitor by asserting the *word line* such that the transistor is turned "on." The desired data state is then imposed on the *bit line*. Since the transistor is on, this voltage will be transferred onto the capacitor. Next, the word line voltage is returned to a low voltage, which turns the transistor off, isolating the charge on the capacitor.

To read the information from the cell, the word line is again asserted after the bit line has been connected to the input of a sense amplifier circuit. The charge from the capacitor is then transferred to the amplifier, where it can be detected as a "1" or a "0." This readout procedure is destructive, since it disturbs the information in the storage capacitor. Hence, the read operation must be followed by a subsequent write operation.

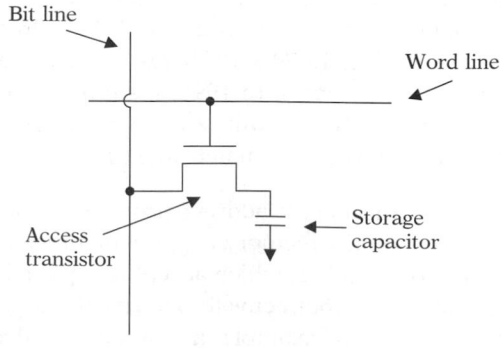

Figure 1. Equivalent circuit of a one-device DRAM memory cell.

Charge stored on the memory cell's capacitor does not remain on the capacitor indefinitely. Due to a variety of leakage paths, the charge can eventually leak off the capacitor, causing the memory cell to lose its information. To alleviate this problem, each memory cell in the memory must be periodically read, sensed, and rewritten to a full level. This *refresh* requirement distinguishes the "dynamic" RAM (DRAM) from a "static" RAM (SRAM). The implications of the refresh requirements on the operation of the memory system are described below.

Using modern integrated circuit technologies, a large number of one-device memory cells can be fabricated on a single integrated circuit chip (*see* MICROCOMPUTER CHIP). As of 1999, chips containing 64 megabits (Mb) are commonly available in large quantities. Chips containing a gigabit (Gb) have been demonstrated in the laboratory. DRAM density (bits per chip) has historically grown 60% per year for over 20 years. To provide the high packing density of the cells and to allow hierarchical addressing, the memory cells are physically configured in a square or rectangular array on the integrated circuit chip. A single bit line is shared by many memory cells. Also, a single word line is shared by many cells. By making the word and bit lines orthogonal, only one memory cell shares the combination of a given word and bit line, as shown in Fig. 2. This orthogonal configuration of control lines allows a two-level hierarchical addressing scheme. One level selects a single word line (often called a row). The second addressing level selects a single bit line (often called a column). Theoretically, a 4 Mb DRAM array could be constructed of 2K word lines and 2K bit lines. However, to improve array performance and signal margins, the 4 Mb chip will typically be segmented into a number of subarrays, with each subarray having fewer word and bit lines.

The important elements of a DRAM subarray are shown in Fig. 3. The *row decoder* accepts as input a

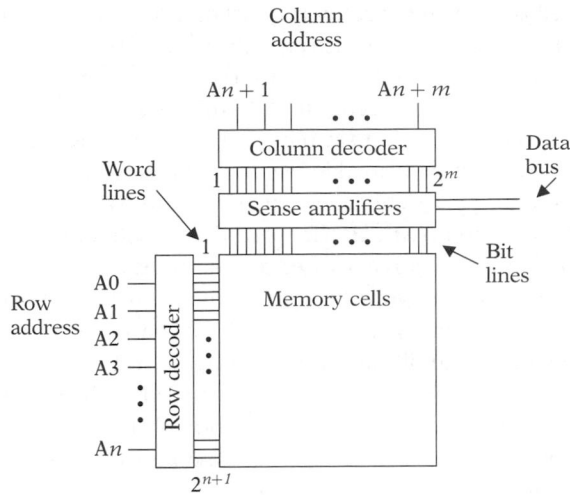

Figure 3. Important elements of a DRAM subarray.

portion of the data address presented to the chip. From this address, the row decoder activates one of the word lines. When this word line is activated, all of the memory cells located on this line are selected and the charge from their capacitors will be placed on the bit lines. Since this is a destructive read-out, each bit line must be equipped with *sensing write-back* circuitry. Once the signal on each of the bit lines is sensed and amplified, the *column decoder* uses as input a separate portion of the data address to select which sense amplifier output to connect to the *data bus*. Finally, if the array is segmented into a number of subarrays, the remainder of the address will be used to determine which segment data bus(es) to select as output from the chip. A single chip may output one or several bits. Typically, several memory chips will be activated at the same time to access an entire byte or memory word.

The sense amplifier and write-back circuitry are typically merged into one cross-coupled sense amplifier circuit, as shown in Fig. 4. Successful operation of this circuit requires the use of a *reference cell*, which is often implemented as an extra row of cells that store a voltage between a "1" and a "0." Whenever a memory

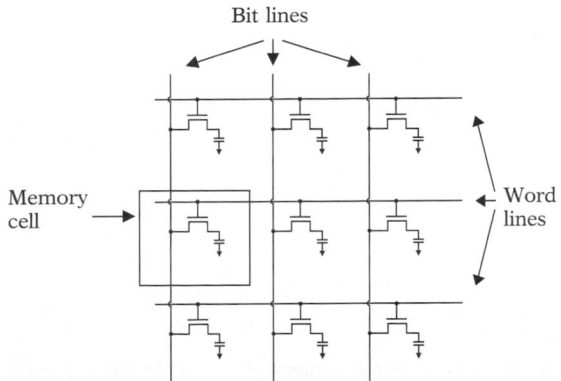

Figure 2. Schematic of a DRAM memory array.

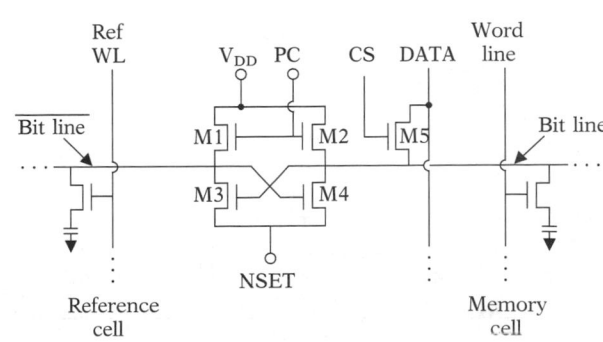

Figure 4. Cross-coupled sense amplifier circuit.

cell is accessed, a reference cell on a separate bit line is also selected. The sense amplifier compares the voltage on the reference bit line with the voltage on the memory cell bit line in order to determine the logical state of the memory cell. A simplified version of a DRAM sense amplifier is described in Fig. 5. Initially, the bit lines are precharged to a high level by transistors M1–M2 during time period t_1. Next, the word line selected by the row decoder circuit is activated at time t_2. At the same time, the reference word line is activated. The signal stored on the memory cell capacitor will be partially transferred to the bit lines during time period t_3. Since the bit line capacitance is large compared with the memory cell capacitance, only a fraction of the memory cell voltage is transferred. During time period t_4 the cross-coupled sense amplifier made up of transistors M3–M4 is activated by lowering the voltage on node NSET. This action will amplify the voltage difference present on the bit lines. This amplified level can now be transferred to the data bus during time period t_5 through transistor M5, which is selected by the column decoder circuitry. If it is desired to change the state of the cell, a voltage can be impressed on the data bus during time period t_6. This voltage is transferred to the selected bit lines through FET M5 and to the selected memory cell capacitor through the access transistor. Finally, during time period t_7 the word line is returned to ground and the signal is stored in the cell. In the case of unselected bit lines, the transistor M5 remains off and the information read from the cell is simply amplified and rewritten into the cell. This is the refresh operation. Hence, to refresh the array, one simply selects a word line, activates the sense amplifiers, and deselects the word lines. This must be repeated for all word lines in the chip at least once every refresh cycle time. A typical refresh cycle time is 64 ms. The chip refresh operation occupies only a small fraction of this 64 ms cycle time.

The sequencing of operations described above is controlled by circuitry on the DRAM chip. Several classes of DRAM chips exist. While they all share a common mode of operation in their core (as described above) their interfaces to the computer system differ. Three popular types of DRAMs include: Fast-Page-Mode DRAM (FP DRAM), Extended Data-Out DRAM (EDO DRAM) and Synchronous DRAM (SDRAM) as described below. The latter modes of operation have evolved in response to a need for ever-increasing data transfer rate from the main memory. FP DRAM and EDO DRAM have very similar characteristics. They operate "asynchronously," independent of the system clock. The typical signal sequences required to operate an FP or EDO DRAM chip are shown in Fig. 6a. The address pins are time multiplexed to serve as both the row and column addresses. When the $\overline{RAS}$ (row address strobe) signal falls, the chip accepts the signals present on the address lines as the row address. Next, when the $\overline{CAS}$ (column address strobe) signal falls, the chip accepts the signals present on the address lines as the column address. The $\overline{WE}$ (read–write enable) pin signals to the chip that the present operation is a read or a write. Data is transferred in and out of the chip via the data pin.

After a row access has occurred, data from the DRAM array is held in the sense amplifiers, waiting to be selected by a column operation. The sense amplifiers act similarly to a small cache accessible by a column address. The *fast page mode* operation of the DRAM accesses data already in the sense amplifiers, allowing a

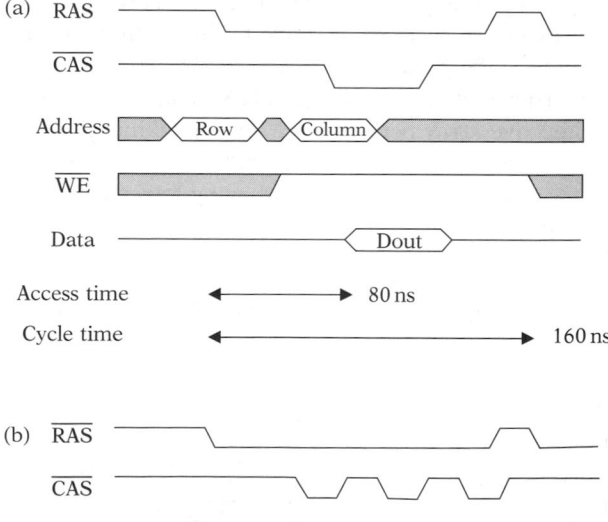

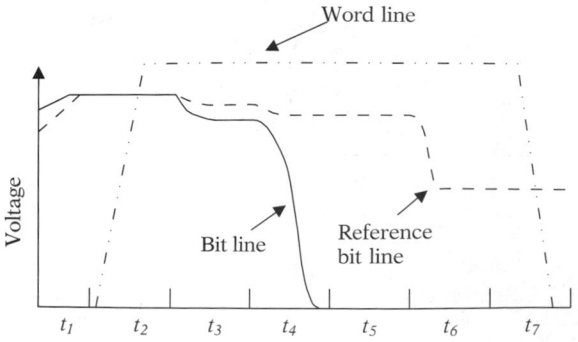

Figure 5.   Operation of the cross-coupled sense amplifier.

Figure 6.   Typical signal sequence for a DRAM chip. (a) Fast PAGE mode and EDO DRAM operating in page mode; (b) SDRAM operation.

reduced cycle time. In this mode, a single row address is latched in by a falling $\overline{RAS}$ signal, and then different column addresses can be presented accompanied by a falling $\overline{CAS}$ signal. Column addresses can be changed rapidly with new data resulting from each cycle. The EDO DRAM operates in a manner very similar to that of the FP DRAM, except that the data is maintained on the output pins for an extended time, even after the $\overline{CAS}$ signal returns high. This allows a reduction in column cycle time in the EDO part.

As the density of memory chips and the demands for higher data rates have increased, the SDRAM interface has appeared. The SDRAM differs from FP and EDO DRAMs in three important ways: (1) a clock signal is provided to the DRAM chip. All control and data signals to and from the chip are synchronized to this clock. The chip is controlled by the commands which are sent to it. The chip still accepts RAS, CAS, WE, and address signals; however, these are captured in the chip synchronously with the clock. (2) SDRAMs are laid out with multiple independent memory banks on the same chip. This allows for flexible interleaving to occur within a single memory chip. Furthermore, this increases the number of sense amplifiers which can hold data, allowing for greater opportunity for fast access. (3) The data stream is "burst" oriented. Rather than a single bit or word, the SDRAM can be commanded to send or receive a burst of 1 to 8 words, synchronized with the clock, from a given starting address. When operating at its highest transfer rate, the SDRAM can read or write new data on every clock cycle. SDRAM performance is often described by the maximum clock rate that it can support, that is, a 66 MHz SDRAM can operate with a 66 MHz clock. An SDRAM timing diagram is shown in Fig. 6b.

The technology employed in the fabrication of silicon MOSFET dynamic RAMs progressed at a rapid pace throughout the 1970s and 1980s. In 1991, 4 Mb DRAMs were commonly available from a number of manufacturers worldwide. The number of bits per DRAM chip has quadrupled every generation, with a new generation of DRAMs becoming available approximately every three years resulting in the aforementioned 64 Mb DRAMs in 1999. This density increase has been brought about through steady advances in three major elements: (1) manufacturing quality has improved, allowing fabrication of larger chips each generation; (2) fabrication tools have improved, allowing the individual elements of the DRAM cell to be smaller each generation; and (3) the invention of new memory cell structures in each generation has allowed the elements of a DRAM cell to be placed closer to each other, allowing a higher packing density. Each of these three elements contributes approximately an equal share to the increase in the number of bits per DRAM chip.

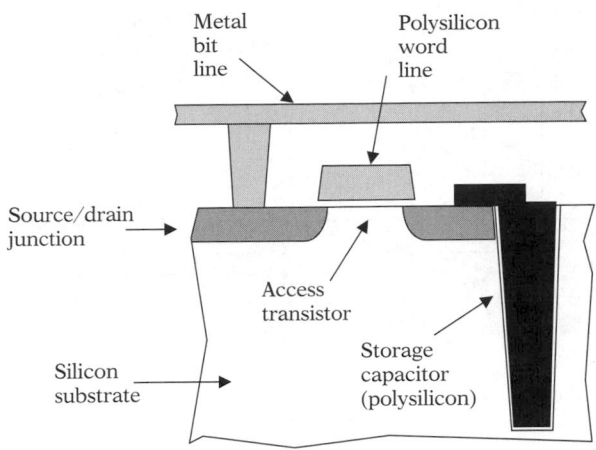

Figure 7. Cross-section of a typical trench capacitor DRAM cell.

The first dynamic RAMs made use of a planar storage capacitor. Here the memory cell capacitor is formed between the semiconductor substrate and an electrode called the *plate*. To ensure reliable operation of the memory cell, the capacitance of the memory cell's storage capacitor must be maintained above a minimum value of approximately 30 fF. In order to make the memory cell smaller while maintaining a large storage capacitor, modern dynamic RAM cells employ three-dimensional storage capacitor structures in the form of either *stacked* or *trench* capacitors. In a stacked capacitor cell, the memory capacitor is stacked above the access transistor of the cell, thus allowing sufficient area for the memory capacitor. In the trench capacitor DRAM cell, the storage capacitor is placed inside a trench that is etched into the silicon substrate. Use of a deep trench allows a large storage capacitor area. Fig. 7 shows the cross-section of a 4 Mb trench DRAM cell manufactured by IBM.

MOSFET STATIC RAM

To reduce the cycle time of the main memory, some computer designs choose to use static memory technologies. These circuits have the characteristics of not requiring a refresh operation and can be read out nondestructively. Since the memory cell need not be rewritten after every read, the memory cycle time can be reduced. The static RAM cell consists of cross-coupled inverter circuits (also known as *flip-flops*), as shown in Fig. 8, as well as two access transistors. The cross-coupled inverters possess two stable states. In one state, the right transistor (M2) is on and the left transistor (M1) is off. The second stable state has M1 on and M2 off. Each stable state represents a binary value. The memory cell's state is probed by raising the word line, turning on the access transistors. This transfers the state of the cross-coupled inverters onto the bit lines. The bit lines selected by the column decoders

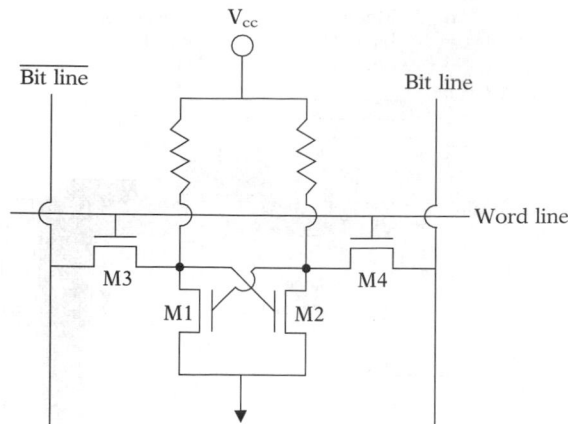

Figure 8. CMOS static RAM cell.

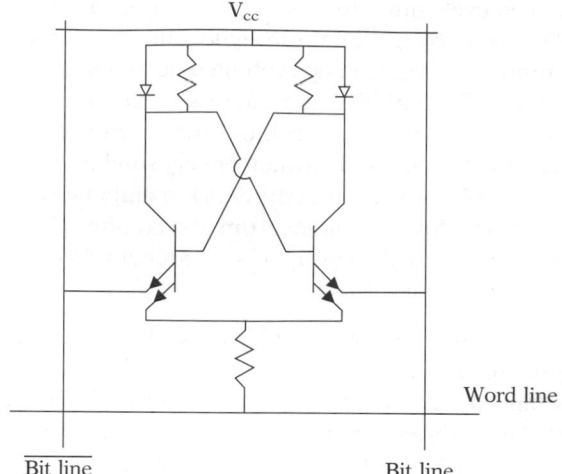

Figure 9. Bipolar SRAM cell.

can then be sensed and the data transferred onto the data bus and eventually off chip. Data is written into the cell by simply forcing a voltage onto the bit lines and turning on the access transistors. The memory cell's transistor characteristics are chosen so that the state of the bit lines can overcome the data state stored in the cross-coupled inverters to change the state of the cell.

Since each static memory cell requires either 4 FETs and 2 resistors or 6 FETs, the size of a static RAM cell is large compared to a dynamic RAM cell. For comparable technologies, SRAM chip densities tend to be approximately a factor of four less than that of DRAMs. This density is traded off for the improved performance of static RAMs.

Recently the performance of static RAMs has been enhanced by using a hybrid technology base called BiCMOS that integrates bipolar devices and CMOS devices on the same chip. BiCMOS static RAM chips use the CMOS technology to implement the memory cells. This is chosen as it results in a small memory cell with minimal power dissipation while the cell is storing its state. The bipolar devices are used to enhance the speed of the decoders, line drivers, and amplifiers on the chip.

BIPOLAR STATIC RAM

The first integrated semiconductor memory to be used in computer systems was the bipolar static RAM. Early IBM System 360 computers employed 64-bit bipolar static RAM chips. While this cell affords the fastest speed when compared to the previously discussed technologies, its high power dissipation makes it unusable for large main memory systems. The bipolar static RAM cell, shown in Fig. 9, is configured as cross-coupled inverter circuits. The load devices for the inverters include a resistor as well as a diode to improve speed. The cell access to the bit lines is provided

through one of the emitters of a split emitter transistor. In store mode, the voltage on the word line is low, and the current through the cross-coupled inverter flows through the emitter of the transistor into the word line. To access a cell, the word line voltage is raised above the bit line voltage of the selected cell. In this case, the cross-coupled inverter current flows onto one of the bit lines or the other, depending on the state of the cross-coupled inverter. This current flow in the bit lines is detected to read the status of the cell.

Ferrite Core Memory

Ferrite core memory was the first widely used technology for computer main memory. The idea of using magnetic loop toroids was first discussed by Jay Forrester in 1950. His concept of using Permaloy tape-wound cores was quickly extended to the use of mass-produced ferrite material. Fig. 10 shows a schematic representation of a single ferrite core memory cell. The ferrite core has the characteristic of hysteresis in its *remanence* shown in Fig. 10, which is used to represent the digital state of the cell. The remanence of the cell can be changed by passing a current through wires passing through the center of the toroid. The toroid's remanence exhibits a threshold behavior whereby if a current less than a critical value is passed through the toroid and then removed, no change in remanence results. If the current exceeds the threshold value, the remanence can be switched. Remanence can be returned to the original state by passing a current greater than the threshold value in the opposite direction. This threshold behavior can be used to provide a *cross-point* addressing scheme in a core memory. In this case an array of ferrite cores is constructed. Each row of cores has a common wire passing through the cores. This wire is selected by the row decoder. When

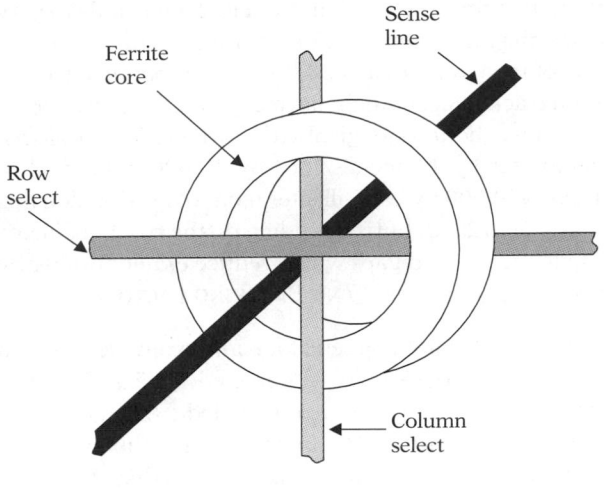

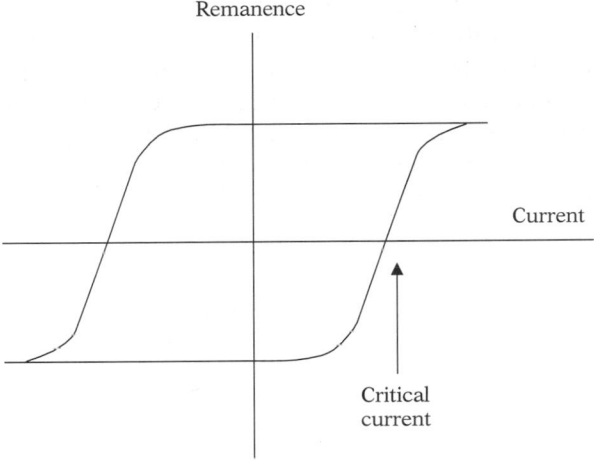

Figure 10. Ferrite core memory. (a) Schematic of a single memory cell; (b) remanence curve of a single ferrite core.

selected, a current greater than one-half the critical current but less than the critical current flows through the wire. Also, each column of cores has a common wire selected by the column decoder. One column wire will carry a current similar to the selected row wire. Only one core that has both the selected row and column wires passing through it will have a total current passing through the toroid greater than the critical value. Hence this selected cell is the only one that can switch remanence. The data state of this cell is detected by examining the current flow through the sense line. If the remanence of the core is switched by the select currents, a characteristic signal will be induced on the sense line. Since this read-out is destructive, the memory cell must be rewritten after sensing.

Bibliography

1964. Renwick, W. *Digital Storage Systems.* London: Spon.
1986. Chuang, K. *et al.* "A 1.0 ns 5-kbit ECL RAM," *IEEE Journal of Solid-State Circuits,* **SC-21** (October), 670–675.
1990. Itoh, K. "Trends in Megabit DRAM Circuit Design," *IEEE Journal of Solid-State Circuits,* **SC-25**, 778–789.
1991. Yoshinori, O. *et al.* "7 ns 4 Mb BiCMOS SRAM with Parallel Testing Circuit," *1991 International Solid-State Circuits Conference Digest*, 54.
1998. Various authors. "Special issue on the 1997 ISSCC: Digital, Memory and Signal Processing," *IEEE Journal of Solid-State Circuits,* **SC-32**, 1712–1765

Matthew R. Wordeman

AUXILIARY

> For articles on related subjects *see* ACCESS TIME; ASSOCIATIVE MEMORY; CACHE MEMORY; DISKETTE; HARD DISK; MASS STORAGE; MEMORY HIERARCHY; MEMORY MANAGEMENT; MEMORY-MAPPED I/O; MEMORY PROTECTION; OPTICAL STORAGE; PORT, MEMORY; READ-ONLY MEMORY; REDUNDANT ARRAY OF INEXPENSIVE DISKS; REGISTER; STORAGE ALLOCATION; ULTRASONIC MEMORY; VIRTUAL MEMORY; and WILLIAMS TUBE MEMORY.

Auxiliary memory is distinguished from main memory in that only from the latter are instructions taken for execution. In most computers, the central processing unit (CPU—*q.v.*) and main memory are a carefully designed pair of machine components, matched for speed and the width of the data path. Auxiliary memory comprises all other memories whose contents (whether instructions or data) must be fetched into main memory before processing by the CPU. It is used to store both current programs and data files and to provide backup storage as a safeguard against loss and for programs and data not in current use that will be needed again.

Most auxiliary memory is rewritable, i.e. it can be written, read, rewritten, etc. many times without deterioration. Certain types of optical auxiliary memory are read-only. Auxiliary memory generally uses electromagnetic or optical digital technology for storing data.

There are at least seven different types of auxiliary memory, and their variety and number continue to grow:

Magnetic tape

Cassette tape

Magnetic drum

Diskette (*q.v.*—once called "Floppy disk")

Fixed-head hard disks (*see* HARD DISK)

Moving-head hard disks (*see* HARD DISK)

Optical discs (*see* OPTICAL STORAGE)

Magnetic Tapes

The use of magnetic tape, once the dominant form of auxiliary memory, has diminished greatly as the availability of inexpensive random-access disks of large capacity has risen, although it is still a common form of backup storage. Four decades ago magnetic tapes were considered the epitome of data processing. Such action was what movies and TV always showed as being characteristic of a "modern" computer. Some computing centers had "tape jiggle" programs which would set every one of eight or so tapes spinning wildly, first one way and then the other, whenever high-ranking visitors came by to see how impressively "busy" the computer was.

Magnetic tapes are long narrow ribbons (typically 2,400 feet long and 0.5 inch wide) of plastic film coated with iron oxide and wound on hard plastic reels approximately 1 foot (30 cm) in diameter. Information is stored transversely on tape, once at 7 bits per *frame* (character of data recorded on tape), later at 9 bits per frame (one 8-bit byte plus a parity bit); *see* Fig. 1. Several frames are consecutively recorded as a *block* of data; blocks are separated by *inter-record gaps* (IRGs), and files of such blocks by *inter-file gaps* or "tape marks."

Longitudinally, data is typically stored at a density of 200, 556, 800, 1,600, 6,250, or 38,000 bits per inch (although the first two densities cited apply only to very early magnetic tapes). For example, a fully written reel of tape, recorded at 38,000 frames per inch (or, on each track, bits per inch, normally abbreviated as *bpi*), contains about one gigabyte computed as follows: 2,400 feet by 12 inches/foot by 38,000 bytes/inch = 1,094,400,000 bytes. Still later technology doubled this capacity to 2 GB, but, depending on the blocking factor used, inter-record gaps would reduce either number by about 1/3 (*see* BLOCK AND BLOCKING FACTOR).

Data is read from magnetic tape into main memory via a *tape drive* (or *transport*) depicted in Figs. 2 and 3. Referring to Fig. 3, the tape is pulled from the supply reel to the take-up reel by motors driving the two hubs. These motors operate independently, so that the length of tape between the two reels varies from instant to instant. This permits the take-up reel to accelerate quickly at the start of each read–write (R/W) operation without requiring synchronized acceleration of the supply reel. The inter-hub strand of tape droops into two vacuum columns in most tape drives, where it is held lightly taut by air-pressure differences. As the loop drops below a vacuum-sensing hold in the take-up

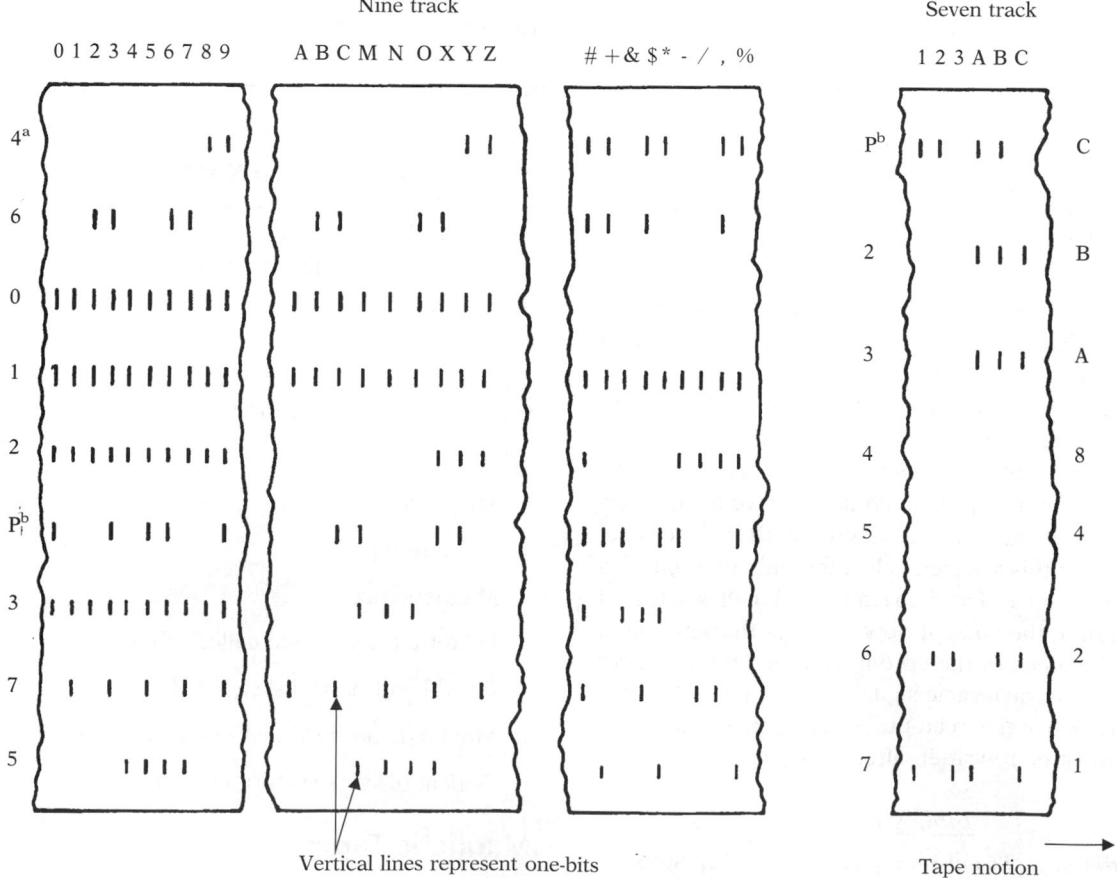

Figure 1. Nine- and seven-track tape data format. Notes: [a] Track numbering shows order in which bits are accumulated into bytes (characters); bit 0 is leftmost character and bit 1 is next, etc. Therefore, ignoring the parity bit, the EBCDIC character A has the bit representation 11000001 (hex C1) on a nine-track tape. [b] The parity bit.

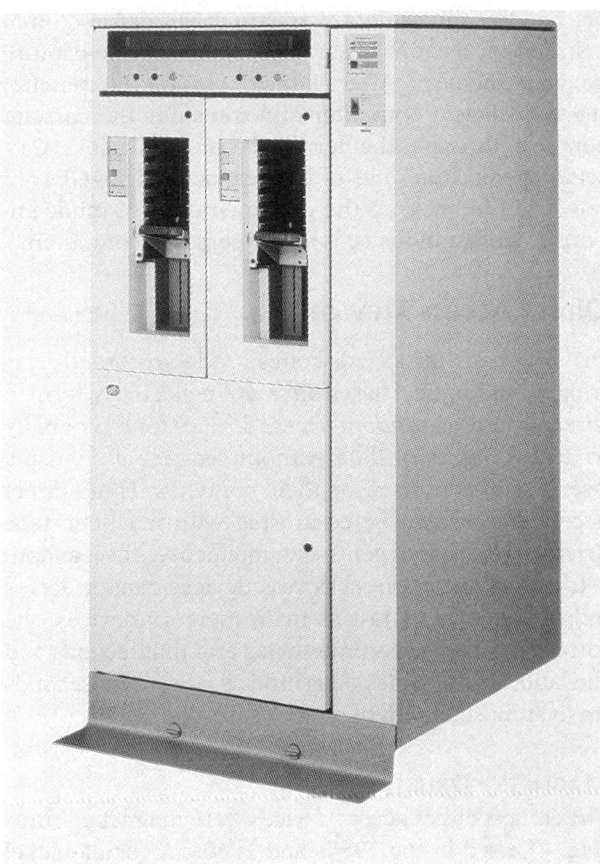

Figure 2. An IBM 3490 magnetic tape unit.

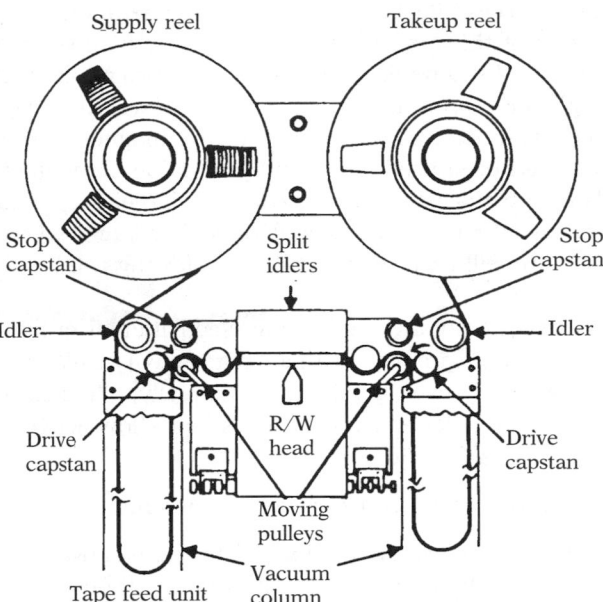

Figure 3. Tape-drive schematic.

column, an electric signal engages the take-up motor with the corresponding reel. The motor disengages as soon as the loop is pulled above a second vacuum-sensing hold. Analogous controls keep a varying-length loop suspended in the supply column.

Reading and writing are performed by a pair of read–write *heads* (seven or nine transformers) aligned transverse to the tape motion. During reading operations, the write head is inactive; the read head senses the flux produced by electromagnetic spots on the tape as it moves past the transformers. During writing operations, the write head furnishes strong electromagnetic signals at precisely timed instants. Whether the prior content of each frame is logical 0, 1, or "no value" (i.e. blank tape), the write signal creates a new frame of 0s and 1s (predetermined voltage levels). The read head checks newly written data a split second later by reading back the pattern of bits and comparing it to the pattern originally transmitted to the write head. These patterns should be identical; if not, a *write error* signal is sent by the tape drive to the computer. Error-retry operations follow, as described in the following paragraphs.

To detect (and, in some cases, to permit logical correction of) recording errors, two sets of check bits are written—*parity bits and longitudinal check bits*. One or two parity bits are furnished per frame on almost all tape drives, permitting detection of all single-bit errors (substitution of 0 for 1, or vice versa). At the end of each block of data, several frames of check bits are written, typically two (with their own parity bits, of course). The *tape subsystem* (one or more drives plus control unit) contains sophisticated checking logic that determines during each R/W operation whether all frames have been correctly transmitted to/from the tape. If a parity error is sensed during reading of one or more frames, the subsystem sets an internal latch; when the end of this block is reached, the subsystem sends status bits to the CPU (via an I/O *channel—q.v.*) so that rereading may be attempted.

Two different approaches to formatting and using magnetic tape data were prevalent, exemplified by tape drives furnished by IBM and DEC. IBM-compatible drives created variable-length blocks which could not be updated/overwritten in place; DECtape drives created fixed-length blocks which could be. In this respect, DECtape drives could be used like direct access devices (see next section), but were not nearly as fast.

TYPICAL USAGE

Until the early 1960s, magnetic tape was the prevalent auxiliary memory for scientific and commercial data processing; direct access devices were used only for executable programs and data (e.g. drums on the IBM 650 and Burroughs 205 computers), or for online real-time applications, such as inventory control and satellite monitoring. From 1963 to 1968, many sequentially stored files were transferred from magnetic tape to direct access devices. On the third-generation computers of this era, *scratch files* (intermediate storage required by compilers, sort and utility programs, and application programs) were typically allocated to disk and drum devices rather than to the magnetic tapes that had been used on second-generation computers. Although magnetic tapes have been largely replaced by cassette tapes, disks and optical storage, where they are still used, they fulfill the following roles:

1. Retention of low- and medium-activity master files. Common practice is that "high-activity" files are accessed over 300 times annually, "medium-activity" files at least 50 times, and "low-activity" files less than 50 times.

2. Backup of direct access device contents.

3. Initial capture of key-entered data and its subsequent presentation for computer processing (though diskettes have replaced magnetic tapes and cassette tapes for most such functions).

4. Interchange of data among computer installations by courier or mail service.

Magnetic tape is one of the cheapest ways to store machine-readable information over long periods of time, and it is far more compact than punched cards or paper records, traditionally used for data archives. Many medium-sized businesses have vaults containing a thousand or more tape reels; a large insurance company may store over 50,000 reels.

CASSETTE TAPES

The preceding section described magnetic tapes created and used primarily *within* large computing centers. Cassette tapes have been are increasingly used for data originating outside them, as follows:

Acquisition of data from laboratory instruments. Analog voltages are digitized and written onto a cassette. Paper tape punches had performed data acquisition for decades; cassettes and diskettes have generally displaced paper tape for these functions, though direct instrument–computer connections are now commonplace as well.

Cash register, gasoline, credit card, and other retailing applications. Some cassette-oriented devices are small and light enough to be hand-held. Typically, these cassette tapes are either 4 mm, 1/4-inch (~6 mm), or 8 mm wide and store several megabytes, in contrast to full-sized tapes, which are 1/2-inch wide and store up to a gigabyte. For minicomputers (*q.v.*) used in data acquisition environments, cassette tapes were sometimes used both to load programs into main mem-

ory and to capture data. Cassette drives are also often installed on terminals, serving as a local data-capture auxiliary memory. After all the data is on the cassette, the user dials a computer and transmits the cassette contents through the terminal–computer link. Cassette tape backup units of high capacity (5–10 GB) are now used to back up the disk memories of minicomputers, workstations (*q.v.*), and personal computers.

Direct Access Devices

Drums, hard disks, diskettes, video-recorded cartridges, and optical/laser discs are collectively termed *direct access* or *random access* devices for their ability to access blocks of data without sequentially passing over a major portion of their contents. Thus, direct access devices can be contrasted with magnetic tape drives, which are generally ineffective for random retrieval of data. Direct access devices cannot access individual bytes as fast as main memory devices, the former having access times of several milliseconds and the latter access times of as little as a few nanoseconds up to at most a tenth of a microsecond.

MAGNETIC DRUMS

The earliest direct access devices were magnetic drums (Fig. 4), used in the 1950s and 1960s. A cobalt–nickel substrate was coated with iron oxide, which was magnetized and sensed much as in magnetic tape operations. Drums were typically 8 to 20 inches (20 to 50 cm) in diameter, 2 to 4 feet (0.6 to 1.2 m) in length, and revolved at 1,800 to 3,600 rpm. Each character was stored on one or more tracks circumferentially, blocks of characters being separated by inter-record gaps of several thousandths of an inch. Densities of 4,000 bpi were commonplace, yielding R/W rates of 1 to 3 MB/sec.

As with magnetic tape, two types of formatting were possible: *fixed-length blocks* (often called "sectors") and *variable-length blocks*. With either format—and in contrast to conventional magnetic tape—it was possible to update blocks in place (i.e. without copying their contents to another part of the device). This facility was vital to the updating activities commonly performed during random retrievals from master files. In fact, all auxiliary memory except certain magnetic tapes and the photocopy/laser holography devices permit updating in place.

Drums hold considerably less data than do disks, magnetic tapes, etc. However, they can access blocks of data at random more quickly than other direct access devices, 5 to 8 ms on average because each track had its own read–write head. Since a drum is a narrow cylinder, its typical rotational speed of 3,600 rpm was considerably higher than that of disk drives of the same

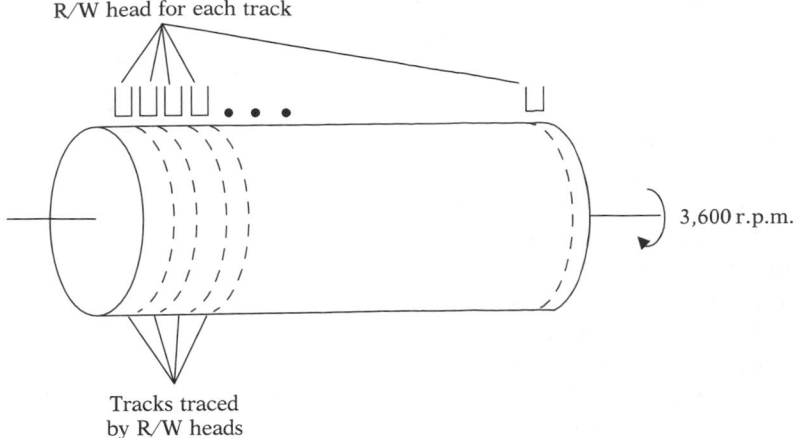

Figure 4. Magnetic drum.

era, typically 2,400 rpm. A speed of 3,600 rpm means an average rotational time of 16.7 ms. This compares to 12 to 80 ms for disk drives because of the time required to move the read–write head to the proper track. Therefore, drums were typically used for the following functions:

1. Prior to the development of magnetic core memories in the mid-1950s, drums were used as main memory (e.g. on the IBM 650 and Burroughs 205 computers).

2. Thereafter, frequently needed software (monitors, portions of the I/O error and program error supervisors, compilers, and sort programs, etc.) was often stored permanently on drums. Since drum storage is *nonvolatile*—electric power can be turned off and on without disturbing its contents—it is well suited for permanent storage of continually used software.

3. High-activity scratch files for the operating system, compilers, and other software was often allocated to drums.

4. Backing storage for virtual memory (*q.v.*) was a major role for drums dating from the Ferranti Atlas systems of the late 1950s. Thousand-word blocks of main memory contents could be shuttled to or from drums by the virtual memory control program.

5. In many airborne computers (and similar high-stress environments), drums were used for both main memory and auxiliary memory because of their high reliability, insensitivity to sudden force changes, and relatively light weight and small bulk.

Despite these advantages and applications, drums are now rarely used, their functions having been taken over by some form of disk storage or by semiconductor main memory.

DISKS

There are two major varieties of disk drives but the second discussed below is now the standard variety.

Fixed Head, Multiple Platter. Although their geometry is considerably different from that of drums, fixed head (FH) disks have comparable access times and transfer rates and greater storage capacity—up to a gigabyte.

Each FH drive contains several steel platters coated with iron oxide aligned vertically on a common spindle. R/W heads extend between the platters, facing up and down from the *comb* suspending the heads and containing signal cables. Since there is a head for each track, the only delay in accessing a data block is due to rotational *latency* (0 to 15 ms required for the block to revolve beneath the corresponding R/W head). Although track lengths vary linearly with distance from the spindle, R/W heads are calibrated in such a way that track capacities are all identical. Therefore, there is a universal transfer rate for data, whether read from inner or outer tracks. The average delay for reading a random block is half the maximum rotational latency, although *rotational position sensing* (RPS) considerably reduces inefficiencies caused by I/O, as follows.

The I/O supervisor keeps the queue of disk requests (i.e. R/W operations pending for one or more programs) ordered by angular displacement from an *index point*, a universal logical origin for the tracks. Index points for all platters are vertically aligned. As each R/W operation terminates, the I/O supervisor searches its queue for the nearest request in terms of angular position. This request may reference any track in the FH file, not necessarily that from which the preceding block was read. If *N* requests are queued with uniformly distributed angular displacements—a reasonable assumption for most computer environments—the average *interoperation latency* is only $(1/(N+1))$ times the maximum latency.

Moving Head. Since only two heads and associated electronics are required per platter, moving head (MH) drives are considerably cheaper to build than FH drives, although the former require sophisticated servomechanisms to move their read–write heads over the platters. Per-character cost for MH storage is typically 10 to 15% of the cost for FH storage. Some MH drives permit removal of their disk-and-spindle socket assemblies: a *disk cartridge* in the case of a single platter, a *disk pack* in the case of multiple platters. An installation can store an indefinite number of cartridges/packs offline to be mounted as required by various applications programs.

The *Winchester architecture* for disk packs superseded disk-and-spindle socket assemblies by the mid-1980s (*see* HARD DISK). Winchester drives (derived from IBM's pre-announcement product name) do not themselves contain R/W heads, the latter being manufactured together with the platters they access: Winchester modules. Small Winchester drives permitted shelf storage and mounting of the modules, although the latter were considerably more expensive than conventional disk packs. Winchester drives with high storage capacities (in 1999, 30 GB or more) do not have removable modules.

When removable disk packs were in common use, batch-processing installations with moving head drives would designate one subset as *resident* (also called *permanently mounted*, although this was a logical designation rather than a physical attribute), containing the operating system, scratch storage, and frequently referenced data files. Another subset of drives was designated *mountable*, where cartridges/packs were set up as required. Some current systems still use a term like *mount* for the operation of making a disk drive an active part of a file system, even though the disk is permanently installed in the system.

Moving-head drives may be either single platter or multiple platter.

- ◆ **Moving Head Single Platter (MHSP)** Typically, a *fork* (two-tined comb) that contains two R/W heads is used to enable reading from or writing to either surface; the fork is inserted/withdrawn radially according to the track address furnished with each I/O request.

- ◆ **Moving Head Multiple Platter (MHMP)** The MHMP (Fig. 5) drives generalize the MHSP type, with combs containing $2P-2$ heads, P being the

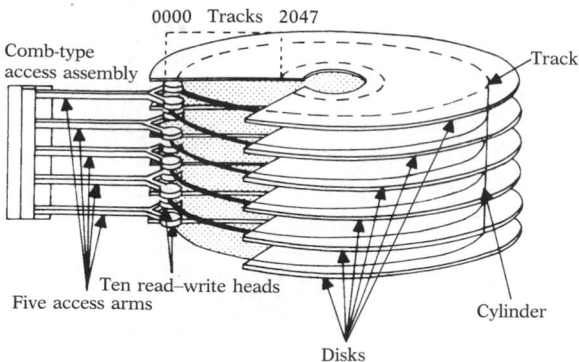

Figure 5. Moving head, multiple platter drive.

number of platters. (The top surface of the top platter and bottom surface of the bottom platter are not used on MHMP packs, since they are much more exposed to scratches and dust contamination than are interior surfaces.) Widely used drives have 3 to 12 platters, with capacities of approximately 1–35 GB. The range is due to variations in how densely the bits are packed on the surface; greater bit density requires more precise control of the drive mechanism. (The wide range of the latter figure is due to recent doublings of both radial and circumferential bit densities.)

After optical/laser discs, MHMP drives have the largest capacity of all hard-surface direct access devices. Diskettes, tapes, and video-recorded cartridges have flexible substrates and hence an inherently higher error rate—both *hard errors* (unrecoverable errors), where a small recording area becomes permanently defective, and *soft errors*, where rereading or rewriting successfully brushes off (or avoids) small oxide flecks. Hard-surface devices may operate for weeks or months without experiencing hard or soft errors—especially fixed head and Winchester drives, which have an air-sealed environment, in contrast to non-Winchester moving-head drives, in which cartridges or packs are exposed to dust during handling and offline storage.

A recent development is *network attached storage* (*NAS*). NAS systems are high-capacity systems of one or more disk drives with an intelligent disk drive controller (the hardware circuitry that communicates with the computer and manages disk access). These systems are connected directly to a local area network (*q.v.*) such as an Ethernet (*q.v.*) running the TCP/IP (*q.v.*) Internet protocol. Computer systems on the network can then mount and use the disk drives without any physical connection other than the network; the NAS plays the role of a file server (*q.v.*).

SOFT-SURFACE DIRECT ACCESS DEVICES

Diskettes ("floppy disks"), video-recorded cartridges, and similar devices compete against moving-head disk drives for selected application areas. Diskettes are structurally similar to MHSP hard-surface disk drives, except that their recording medium is a flexible plastic substrate—8, 5.25, or 3.5 inches in diameter—coated with iron oxide. The 3.5" size has now become the *de facto* standard, but is no longer called "floppy" since the recording medium is enclosed in a hard plastic case. Information is recorded and read back just as for an MHSP hard-surface drive. Unlike the latter, a diskette can be easily pocketed and even sent through the mail without extraordinary protective wrapping. They are very inexpensive, about 30 cents for a diskette pre-formatted to hold 1.44 megabytes. Very high capacity Iomega Corporation Zip drives are now available whose diskettes hold 250 megabytes and cost about $20 each, about eight cents per megabyte. A newer version, the Jaz drive, uses $100 diskettes that hold two gigabytes (5 cents per megabyte) and hence are attractive for backing up hard drives. In fact, Jaz peripherals are really hard drives, ones whose storage component is removable.

MASS STORAGE

During the 1970s, several manufacturers developed mass storage systems (*q.v.*): trillion-bit (tcrabit) storage devices based on reels, cartridges, or cassettes of videotape or wide magnetic tape. In late 1974, marketing of such devices to commercial users began with the IBM 3850 Mass Storage System, whose online capacity was 50 to 500 billion bytes, or *gigabytes* (0.4 to 4×10^{12} bits). A tape-based mass storage system typically had a large magazine of cartridges or cassettes from which a transport mechanism extracted requested units. Each cartridge or cassette contained approximately 50 megabytes, comparable to a fully packed reel of conventional magnetic tape. A full mass storage system of this type comprised 500 to 5,000 cartridges or cassettes, together with transports and read–write stations. Often, the transports and R/W stations were duplexed or triplexed to assure continuity of operation should one of these complex electromechanical devices malfunction. With modern disk technology, it has become easier to assemble terabyte mass storage systems with much better access time and transfer rate (*see* REDUNDANT ARRAY OF INEXPENSIVE DISKS (RAID) and MASS STORAGE). Dell, for example, markets a 2 terabyte (2 TB) disk system for $18,000—less than 1 cent per megabyte.

OPTICAL STORAGE

CD-ROM, DVD, and laserdisc memories are discussed in the article OPTICAL STORAGE. These are read-only auxiliary memories, prerecorded by the vendor. A variant called a CD-R (Compact Disc-Recordable) or WORM drive (Write Once, Read Many times) allows the user (once) rather than the vendor to do the recording. Yet other variants, generally called Erasable Optical (EO) or WMRM drives (Write Many, Read Many) devices are rewritable and hence are true auxiliary memory rather than just secondary storage. Among them are CD-RW (CD-ReWritable), Magneto-Optical

Table 1. Typical characteristics of various types of memory.

Memory	Access time	Transfer rate	Capacity	Device cost	Media capacity	Media cost	Cost/MB
Mainframes							
Main	20 ns	100 MB/sec	2 GB	$500 K	—	—	$250
Drum	5 ms	2 MB/sec	4 MB	$ 20 K	—	—	$5,000
FH Disk	10 ms	10 MB/sec	100 MB	$ 10 K	—	—	$100
MHMP disk	20 ms	1 MB/sec	—	$ 20 K	4 GB	$200	5¢
Magnetic tape	minutes	1 MB/sec	—	$ 10 K	2 GB	$26	1.3¢
Mass storage	50 ms	1 MB/sec	2 TB	$ 18 K	—	—	0.9¢
Personal Computers and Workstations							
Main	60 ns	40 MB/sec	128 MB	$320	—	—	250¢
Diskette	100 ms	0.2 MB/sec	—	$35	1.44 MB	25¢	17¢
Zip drive	29 ms	1 MB/sec	—	$200	250 MB	$ 20	8¢
Jaz drive	16 ms	7 MB/sec	—	$350	2 GB	$100	5¢
MO-RW	60 ms	4 MB/sec	—	$1,800	2.6 GB	$130	5¢
Hard disk	15 ms	5 MB/sec	30 GB	$900	—	—	3¢
CD-RW	80 ms	1 MB/sec	—	$500	650 MB	$ 7	1¢
CD-ROM (32X)	10 ms	4.8 MB/sec	—	$150	650 MB	$ 1	0.15¢
DVD-RAM	20 ms	1.3–2.4 MB/sec	—	$600	2.6 GB/side	$ 17	0.3¢
DVD (16X)	20 ms	2.4 MB/sec	—	$300	8.5 GB	$ 17	0.2¢
Cassette tape	minutes	1 MB/sec	—	$400	4 GB	$ 8	0.2¢

TB = Terabyte = 1,000 GB.
X = 150 KB/sec = 0.15 MB/sec, the transfer rate of first-generation CD-ROM drives.

(MO) drives of 5.25" CD-size that hold 500 MB, 3.5" floppy optical drives ("flopticals") that hold 20 MB, and DVD-RAM. No two of these use exactly the same technology, but some type of laser is fundamental to all four.

Summary

Table 1 provides comparative data for the various memory types, giving cost/benefit comparisons of using various types of memory for both mainframes and smaller computers. Not surprisingly, the general trend is that the greater the storage capacity, the lower the cost per megabyte and the slower the transfer rate.

Decade by decade, older forms of data storage obsolesce as ever-newer technology of greater capacity but lower cost per megabyte is developed. The only downside is the very worrisome problem of how important data recorded in earlier eras can be read and transferred to the newer devices. Is there a surviving drive, even if only in a museum, that can still read data from the old storage medium? Are the data bits still *there*, or have they crumbled to bits of another kind? For a fascinating discussion of this topic, see Rothenberg (1995).

Bibliography

1995. Rothenberg, J. "Ensuring the Longevity of Digital Documents," *Scientific American*, **272**, *1*, 42–47.
1998. Stone, M. D. "Removable Storage," *PC Magazine*, **17**, *8* (21 April), 153–179.
1998. White, R. *How Computers Work*, 4th Ed. Indianapolis, IN: QUE. Contains excellent color-illustrated descriptions of many of the devices discussed in this article.

David N. Freeman; revised by the editors

MEMORY ADDRESSING

See ADDRESSING.

MEMORY ALLOCATION

See STORAGE ALLOCATION.

MEMORY DUMP

See DUMP.

MEMORY HIERARCHY

For articles on related subjects *see* ADDRESSING; CACHE MEMORY; LOCAL STORE; MEMORY: AUXILIARY; REGISTER; and VIRTUAL MEMORY.

Introduction

Memory in a conventional digital computer is organized in a hierarchy as illustrated in Fig. 1. At the top of the hierarchy are *registers* (*q.v.*) that are matched in speed to the *central processing unit* (CPU—*q.v.*), but tend to use a large chip area and consume a significant amount of power. There are normally only a small number of registers in a processor, of the order of a few hundred or less. At the bottom of the hierarchy are secondary and offline storage memories, such as hard disks and magnetic tapes, in which the cost per stored bit is small in terms of money and power, but the access time is long when compared with registers. Between the registers and secondary/offline storage are a number of other forms of memory that bridge the gap between the two.

As the hierarchy level increases, greater performance is realized but at a greater cost. Table 1 shows some of the properties of the components of the memory hierarchy in the late 1990s. Typical Cost, computed by multiplying Cost/MB × Typical Amount Used, is approximately the same at each level of the hierarchy. But access times vary by approximately factors of 10 except for disks, which have access times 100,000 times slower than main memory. Additional properties not shown in the table include *persistence*: the ability of the memory to retain its contents when power is removed, and the amount of power required to operate the memory. Memory that is not persistent is said to be *volatile*.

Ordinary computation involves frequent accesses to the memory, and the computational power of the

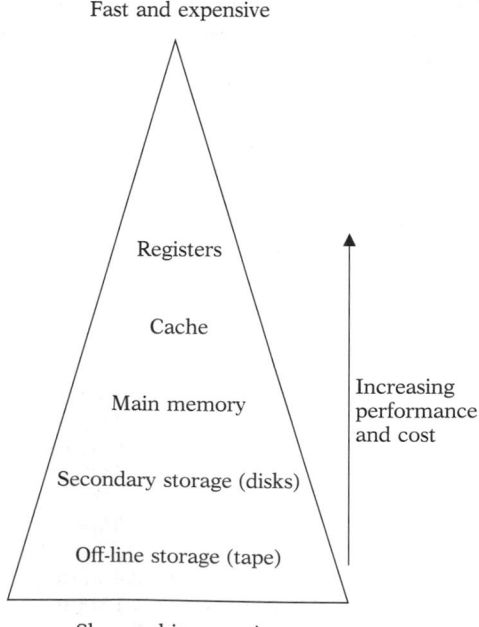

Figure 1. The memory hierarchy.

Table 1. Properties of the memory hierarchy.

Memory type	Access time	Cost/MB	Typical amount used	Typical cost
Registers	1 ns	High	1 KB	–
Cache	5–20 ns	$100	1 MB	$100
Main memory	60–80 ns	$1.10	64 MB	$70
Disk memory	10 ms	$0.05	4 GB	$200

computer will be wasted if the memory cannot keep pace with the CPU. The problem of matching the *bandwidth* (*q.v.*) of the CPU to that of the memory is difficult to solve with conventional technology for a number of reasons, the primary one being that in order to increase the speed of the memory, density (the number of bits stored per unit area) is sacrificed. Fortunately, the speed differences between the CPU and the different levels in the memory hierarchy can be bridged with architectural solutions.

Computer Memory

Computer memory consists of a collection of consecutively numbered locations, each of which stores exactly one binary value at any time, as shown in Fig. 2. Each of the numbered locations corresponds to a specific stored byte in this example. The unique number that identifies each byte is referred to as its *address* (*see* ADDRESSING). Since addresses are counted in sequence, beginning with 0, the highest address is one less than the size of the memory. The highest address for a 2^{32} byte memory is $2^{32} - 1$. The lowest address is 0.

The example memory architecture shown in Fig. 2 has a 32-bit *address space*, which means that a program can access a byte of memory anywhere in the range from 0 to $2^{32} - 1$. The address space for this example architecture is divided into distinct regions which are used for the operating system, input and output (I/O), user programs, and the system stack (*q.v.*), which comprise the *memory map*, as shown in the left side of

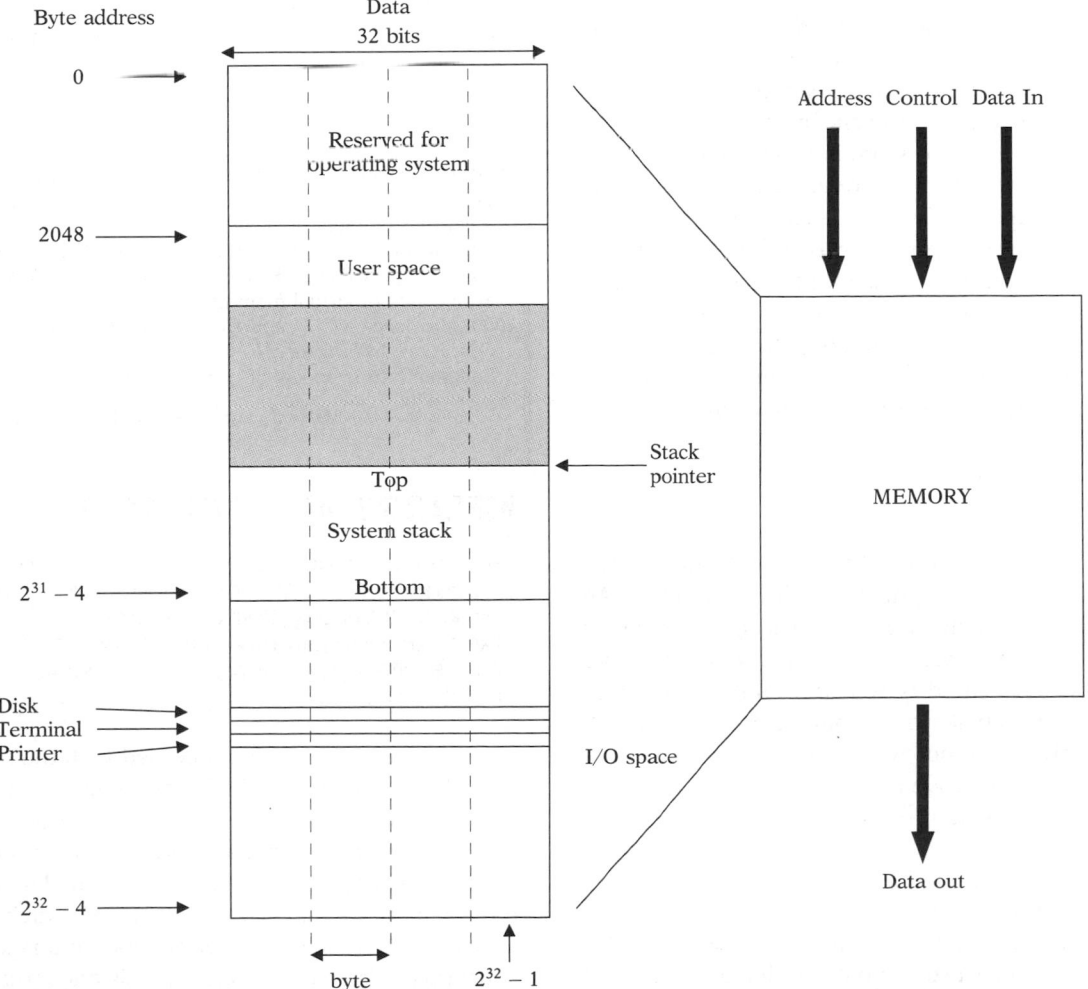

Figure 2. Example of a typical layout of computer memory. The memory map is shown on the left; the external architectural view is shown on the right.

Fig. 2. The memory map differs from one implementation to another. Notice that the portion of the address space between 2^{31} and $2^{32} - 1$ is reserved for I/O devices. The memory map is thus not entirely composed of real memory, and in fact there may be large gaps where neither real memory nor I/O devices exist. When I/O devices are treated like memory locations, this is referred to as *memory mapped I/O* (*q.v.*).

Locality

When an ordinary program executes on a conventional computer, most of the memory references are made to a small number of locations. Typically, 90% of the execution time of a program is spent in just 10% of the code. This property is known as the *locality principle* or more specifically as *locality of reference*.

Memory access is generally slow in comparison with the speed of the CPU, and so the memory poses a significant bottleneck in computer performance. Since most memory references come from a small set of locations, the locality principle can be exploited to improve performance. A small but fast *cache memory* (*q.v.*) in which the contents of the most commonly accessed memory locations are maintained, can be placed between the main memory and the CPU. When a program executes, the cache memory is searched first, and the referenced word is accessed in the cache if the word is present. If the referenced word is not in the cache, then a free location is created in the cache and the referenced word is brought into the cache from the main memory. The word is then accessed in the cache. Although this process takes longer than accessing main memory directly, the overall performance can be improved if a high proportion of memory accesses are satisfied by the cache.

Virtual Memory

OVERLAYS

One method of extending the apparent size of the main memory is to augment it with disk space. An early approach made use of *overlays*, in which an executing program overwrites its own code with other code as needed. In this scenario, the programmer has the responsibility of managing memory usage. Although this method works well in a variety of situations, an alternative method that can be managed by the operating system is *paging*.

PAGING

Paging is a form of automatic overlaying in which the address space is partitioned into equal sized blocks, called *pages*. Pages are normally an integral power of two in size, such as $2^{10} = 1024$ bytes. Paging makes the physical memory appear larger than it truly is by

mapping the physical memory address space onto some portion of the virtual memory address space, which is normally stored on a disk.

One problem introduced by paging is that every memory reference must be looked up in the page table before it is accessed. This means there must be two memory references to access a data item: one to look in the page table and another to access the data. Performance can be improved by keeping track of the most recent page table lookups inside the CPU, in what is known as a *translation lookaside buffer* (TLB). In the ideal case, the TLB contains the address of the data, and the cache itself contains the data.

SEGMENTATION

Paging is one-dimensional in the sense that addresses grow either up or down. *Segmentation* is a different form of virtual memory that allows several one-dimensional address spaces to exist simultaneously. This allows tables, stacks, and other data structures (*q.v.*) to be maintained as logical entities that grow independently. Segmentation allows for *protection*, so that a segment may be specified as "read only" to prevent changes, or "execute only" to prevent unauthorized copying.

Bibliography

1990. Hamacher, V. C., Vranesic, Z. G., and Zaky, S. G. *Computer Organization*, 3rd Ed. New York: McGraw-Hill. A classic treatment of cache memory.
1999. Tanenbaum, A. *Structured Computer Organization*, 4th Ed. Upper Saddle River, NJ: Prentice Hall. A readable explanation of virtual memory.
2000. Murdocca, M. J., and Heuring, V. P. *Principles of Computer Architecture*. Reading, MA: Addison-Wesley Longman. An overview of computer memory.

Miles J. Murdocca and Vincent P. Heuring

MEMORY MANAGEMENT

For articles on related subjects *see* CACHE MEMORY; DATA MODELS; DATA TYPE; DATABASE MANAGEMENT SYSTEM; DISTRIBUTED SYSTEMS; GARBAGE COLLECTION; LIST PROCESSING; MEMORY HIERARCHY; OPERATING SYSTEMS; POINTER; STACK; STORAGE ALLOCATION; VIRTUAL MEMORY; and WORKING SET.

Memory management is concerned with the organization of the storage in which data is placed in a computer and with the identification and enforcement of the rules for interpreting and assigning meaning to the bits in the storage. Thus, it is closely related to database management. While there is no agreed division, the principal differences are that database management is concerned with data of longer persistence (that is, the data exists for more than the execution time of one program), shared data, and data design in the context of planning large-scale systems, whereas memory management is primarily concerned with data used within a program for periods up to the duration of the program's execution.

Memory management supports three activities:

1. Allocation of space in which to hold data

2. Maintenance of *housekeeping data* describing the current use of the *allocatable memory*

3. Recycling memory when it is no longer needed so it can be used by new data

The term "memory management" is also used to cover address transformation and data movement between levels of the storage hierarchy, e.g. between main memory and processor caches and between disk and main memory using virtual memory. Modern memory management systems take account of the interaction between this kind of memory management and the three activities described above to improve performance significantly.

Disk Memory Management

Long-lived data is normally held on disk in files and databases. In this context, memory management, which is quite complex because of the properties of disk storage, is implemented in operating systems and database management systems respectively. Application programmers use databases and file systems as a matter of course and hence rely on automated memory management for disk storage and long-lived data.

Main Memory Management

AUTOMATED MEMORY MANAGEMENT

Programming practice for main memory management is undergoing a transition. Two regimes are available: *automated* memory management and *explicit* memory management. In the case of automated memory management, all of the required technology (see below) is built into the programming language; that is, all of the memory management activities occur implicitly. This regime has been available in research languages since Lisp (*q.v.*) appeared in the 1960s. Until recently, only a small proportion of commercial programming had used this regime, though it was available in many languages, such as Simula (*q.v.*), Smalltalk, Eiffel, Standard ML, and Modula 3.

EXPLICIT MEMORY MANAGEMENT

Many programmers, using languages such as C (*q.v.*) and C++ (*q.v.*), use an explicit regime and much legacy code (old programs still in use) depends on such regimes. That is, programs explicitly request or allocate space, explicitly return space, and maintain whatever information they need to decide when space can be returned for reuse. Operating systems provide an allocation system which can be used explicitly.

AUTOMATIC VERSUS EXPLICIT MEMORY MANAGEMENT

With an automatic regime, only the language implementers have to understand how to implement main memory management correctly and efficiently. With the explicit regime many more programmers have to tackle this challenging task. Not only does it prove laborious, it also proves error-prone. Three kinds of mistakes are typical:

1. Returning space that some other part of the program is still using (leaving a *dangling reference* and potential for later data corruption).

2. Failing to return space that has been allocated when it could be recycled (a *space leak*), which causes long-running programs to grow in size continuously.

3. Incorrect tracking of the boundaries of data items, so that operations on those items corrupt data in other items.

THE TREND TOWARDS AUTOMATIC MEMORY MANAGEMENT

Until recently, the relatively high computational cost of the automatic regime led many to think that the labor and unreliability costs of the explicit regime were worthwhile. This was reinforced by the use of languages such as C, which do not provide reliable information on which to base automatic memory management. In fact *conservative* policies were possible, which automated some aspects of space management, but the potential for errors remained. Faster processors, larger main memories, improved algorithms, larger application programs and rising programmer salaries have combined to tip the balance in favor of automated memory management. The advent and popularity of the Java language is both a consequence of these changes and a catalyst for the trend towards the increased use of improved automatic regimes. Java's definition ensures that an automatic memory management regime can be made reliable. Undoubtedly, any future languages which become popular will also have the same safety properties, for the economic reasons described above.

GARBAGE COLLECTION

In some computations it is relatively easy to determine when space is no longer needed. For example when *independent* processes or threads (of computation) terminate, their space may be returned. Similarly, return of space is straightforward when a window in a

GUI is closed. But in many computations, references to stored data are passed around and stored in multiple locations. In consequence, the application program cannot easily determine when it is safe to return space for fear of generating dangling references. Modern application programs are often built by large teams and frequently use substantial bodies of code that have been written by other organizations. This makes it progressively more and more impractical for application programmers to determine when space may be returned safely.

FRAGMENTATION

Memory can be viewed as a continuous range of allocatable cells, e.g. words or bytes. In an ideal system none would be wasted, that is, unused by the computation. However, it is hard to allocate space efficiently so that there are no gaps between useful cells. The occurrence of these unused gaps is called *fragmentation*. It can both increase the requirement for memory and slow down computation due to less efficient use of the storage hierarchy. Memory managers therefore invest some computation in reducing fragmentation.

Requirements for Storage Regimes

Programming languages have supported the automatic management of storage space by using one of two policies. *Static allocation* is a policy in which the provision of space is determined at compilation time. Fortran (*q.v.*) originally adopted this policy. *Dynamic allocation* is a policy in which the requirements for space are determined by the computation. Most modern languages use both policies, though dynamic allocation now predominates.

Dynamic storage regimes may be categorized by the demands made upon them, both by the objects stored and by the sequences of operations by which space is claimed and freed. The space required by an object to

be stored is called a *cell*. A cell is, therefore, a contiguous sequence of words or bytes in the computer memory. The cells may be of only one size, of a variety of sizes, or of varying size (i.e. an object once stored may change its size). The usage patterns that a memory management system may be expected to report can be classified into the following four groups.

1. The space may be claimed by successive demands and then all relinquished.

2. The space may be claimed by successive demands and be explicitly returned in reverse order.

3. The space may be claimed by a sequence of demands and returned in random order, interleaved with the demands.

4. The space may be claimed in sequence, and no space is explicitly returned.

A STACK REGIME FOR SPACE ALLOCATION

With a constant size or a variety of sizes, and with demand patterns 1 and 2 above, a space allocation strategy is straightforward. The total area of space available for allocation is viewed as a sequence of cells. A pointer records a position in this space indicating the start of the *next* place to allocate—the free cell. On making an allocation, the value of the pointer is returned as the address of the new cell, and the pointer is moved on, by the length of the space allocated, to the remaining cells. Such a scheme is shown in Fig. 1.

Such a regime is simple to implement and reasonably fast to operate. As space is relinquished in the reverse order from which it is claimed, the return of space is recorded by decreasing *next*. An allocated block may hold the previous value of *next*. When the block is returned, *next* is reset to that recorded value. This is the normal way of allocating *frames* holding local variables in block-structured languages (unless they implement higher-order functions) (*see* ACTIVATION RECORD).

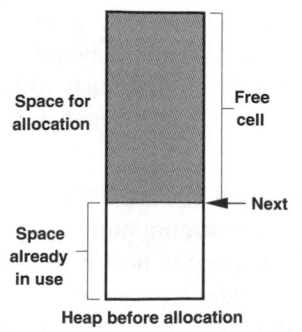

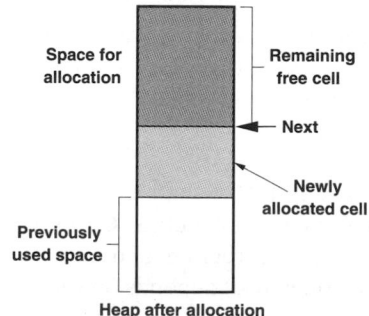

Figure 1. The operation of a stack regime.

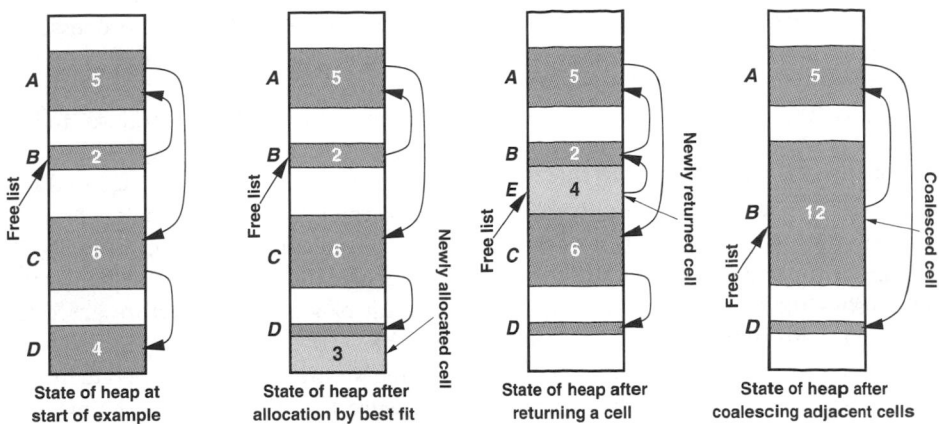

Figure 2. The operation of a best-fit strategy.

HANDLING RANDOM SEQUENCES OF REQUESTS AND DEALLOCATIONS

When demand is interspersed with return in some random sequence—case 3 above—then different strategies are appropriate depending on whether or not all the cells are of the same size. The range of memory from which cells are allocated and deallocated randomly is called a *heap*. A list (or a structure that is faster to search) is kept of all the cells available for issue. When a cell is returned, it is added to this list, which is called the *free list* or *list of available space*. If all cells are of the same size, when a cell is requested, the first one on the list is allocated.

CELL ALLOCATION STRATEGIES

When the cells vary in size, the first cell in the list may not be large enough, or will not be the optimum one to allocate. When choosing an algorithm to perform cell allocation, it is necessary to compromise between the computational cost of finding the cell and the optimality

of the cell found. The optimality depends on the rate of *fragmentation*; that is, on the proportion of small cells generated that are not contiguous and therefore cannot be coalesced and that are too small to be useful. Two extremes of this compromise are presented.

The Best Fit Strategy. The *best fit* algorithm requires a search of all cells available for allocation until one is found that is the correct size or is the smallest that is sufficiently large. In the example (Fig. 2), *A*, *B*, *C*, and *D* form the free list. If a cell of size 3 were requested, cell *D* would be allocated after a search of the entire free list. A structure such as several lists corresponding to defined ranges of cell size would accelerate the search for the optimum cell, but would also increase the cost of returning a cell.

Suppose that a cell is now returned consisting of the four words (memory locations) between *B* and *C*. Then the system could coalesce *B*, *E*, and *C*, as shown in Fig. 2, into a single cell.

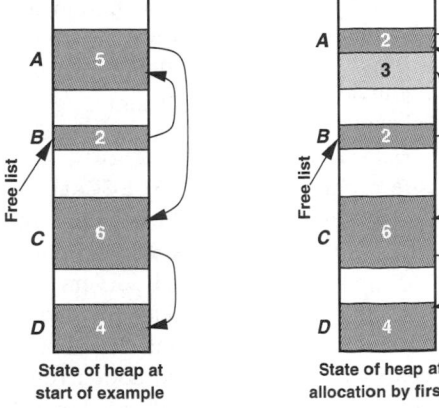

Figure 3. The operation of a first-fit strategy.

The First Fit Strategy. The *first fit* algorithm scans the list and allocates the first cell that is large enough, retaining the fragment left over. The operations involved in allocating a cell are shown in Fig. 3. Return of cells is similar to best fit.

RECYCLING SPACE BY GARBAGE COLLECTION

In case 4 above, a garbage collector is responsible for automatically determining which cells are still accessible to the executing computation; we call this the *live* data. It then replenishes the free list with the remainder of the heap. It may also move cells while insuring all references are suitably adjusted, either to form sufficiently large areas of contiguous space, to reduce fragmentation or to accelerate space allocation.

HOUSEKEEPING DATA

The memory management system has to maintain data to support all of its activities. This includes the current boundaries of the heap, the free lists, the sizes of cells, and whether they are currently in use. The data may be stored in the cells, e.g. as a cell header, or in separate data structures such as bitmaps. The garbage collector needs data which identifies all of the pointers into the heap and all of the pointers in each cell. To ensure safe management this housekeeping data needs to be protected from corruption. In operating systems it is placed in regions that are inaccessible to the application programs. Programming languages use a different approach. The compiler of a strongly-typed language, such as Java, is able to arrange the construction of all of the data needed and is also able to ensure that none of the generated code can corrupt it.

CONCURRENT COMPUTATION

Many applications require concurrent (multi-threaded) computation to handle asynchronous events and to exploit parallel processors. Therefore languages such as Ada (*q.v.*), Modula 3, and Java provide concurrency within an application program. As a result the memory management system must support arbitrarily interleaved streams of requests from each thread. The memory management algorithms therefore have to be made thread safe, that is, they must never corrupt their housekeeping data because of the coincidence of two requests. To avoid imposing excessive synchrony between threads making requests, a two-level allocation system may be used. This will issue a parcel of space at a time to a thread, and that thread will allocate from this until it needs another parcel.

Advances in Memory Management

A few examples of the recent advances in memory management are presented to illustrate its growing sophistication.

THE STORAGE HIERARCHY

It is now common for processors to have on-chip memory caches and other nearby caches that are between 100 and 1000 times faster to access than the large volume RAM. Modern memory management algorithms attempt to exploit this. It has been observed that most cells are allocated, used for a very short time and then are free for reallocation. If these short-lived cells are kept in the fast cache a significant acceleration is achieved. Therefore allocators and the current generation of garbage collectors are often tuned to try to achieve this. Once multi-threaded programs are running on multiprocessor architectures, it is necessary to ensure that these allocation spaces are in the appropriate processor.

Although RAM may now be very large, perhaps many gigabytes, it is invariably underpinned by a virtual memory mapping to disk. This again introduces a factor of 1000 in access time. To avoid incurring this penalty too often, it is necessary to insure that large heaps fit in the working set (*q.v.*), or that allocation and garbage collection minimize page faults (which bring portions of storage from the disk into main memory). For example, generational and incremental garbage collectors avoid complete scans that fault in every page.

DISTRIBUTED SYSTEMS

Many applications utilize distribution. In some it is possible to construct references from data in one processor to cells in other processors. This imposes additional complexity on the memory-management system. It now has to preserve the meaning of incoming references; i.e. it may not reallocate their referenced cells nor move cells so that the reference is lost. A protocol (*q.v.*) is therefore needed to ensure that processors inform others that their local memory manager has discovered it no longer needs a reference. However, this might retain data that is in fact no longer in use, because a cycle of references between data that extends across sites will never be collected by local collectors, even though no computation can reach any of these cells. This requires distributed algorithms, which are difficult to make safe, resilient to local failures and efficient.

LARGE-SCALE MEMORIES

The volume of RAM on computers has increased rapidly; 256 MB is not unusual on workstations (*q.v.*), and servers may have tens of gigabytes. The time taken to read or write this much memory is significant. This has led to the development of incremental and concurrent techniques for memory management that avoid over-long pauses for garbage collection and avoid scans and copies that yield little new free space.

The basic principle is to divide the space into separately administered partitions. Allocation and computation is then supported in the majority of these partitions, while housekeeping tasks such as garbage collection and archival dumping (saving data in long-term storage) are performed on the others. Interactions among partitions have to be monitored while this is going on to insure that the eventual result is consistent. As a result of introducing partitions, the recovery of trans-partition cycles of garbage (described above) becomes a problem. However, dealing with cycles in this context is easier than in a distributed system, since it is not necessary to deal with failures of some parts of the system.

PERSISTENT SYSTEMS

Long-lived data held on disk requires all of the techniques just introduced. Localizing space management on disk using a two-level system is essential to handle the typically concurrent load and to avoid disk-head movement for every allocation. Incremental algorithms are the only way to avoid inordinate delays and to offer a continuous service. It is common to introduce a localized indirect addressing mechanism to avoid the need to update data all over the disks when space has to be rearranged.

As type-safe programming languages (*see* TYPES, THEORY OF) become more prevalent, it is possible to integrate database technology and programming language technology into one consistent system that manages data on disk and in main memory. These systems then automate data movement between the long-term regime and the active program. Such automation often involves an object cache. The memory management then has several additional activities to perform:

1. Recognition of the objects now requiring persistence and their automatic promotion to long-term storage.

2. Detection that the computation now requires access to some long-lived object and its faulting into (being brought into) the object cache.

3. Detection that a faulted in object has been updated and then the preservation of its new state.

4. Space and identity management on disk, including garbage collection, archiving, and evolution facilities.

Typically, the transfers between disk and main memory also include translations. The object cache and the remainder of the main memory management interact. For example, they compete for space and space can be recovered either by garbage collection or cache eviction. Both of these have to handle references between transient and persistent space correctly.

Trends in Memory Management

Four forces combine to drive the trend towards dependence on automatic memory management.

1. Without it the large and sophisticated applications that are being developed are unreliable and uneconomic.

2. The sophistication of modern memory management algorithms is beyond the reach of application teams and is uneconomic to reprogram frequently.

3. The trend to faster processors and large multilevel memories with increasing speed discrepancies makes it imperative to use memory management tailored to the supporting hardware.

4. The requirement for the rapid introduction of "enterprise applications" that deliver continuous service for a business whose operations are supported by its computer network is driving substantial investment in memory management support.

While such safe and automatic memory management has been possible with research and academic languages for many years, it has just become significant in the commercial arena in the late 1990s. The use of type-safe languages will continue to grow, increasing the opportunities for automated memory management and the investment in its provision. Only a few specialized applications will need to use explicit memory management in the future.

This trend will undoubtedly have an impact on hardware. Support for memory management activities is appearing. Architectures will appear that reflect partitioned memory management. In these each memory component will support the local administration of its memory.

Bibliography

1983. Wiederhold, G. *Database Design*. New York: McGraw-Hill.

1984. Ungar, D. "Generation Scavenging: A Non-disruptive High Performance Storage Reclamation Algorithm," *ACM SIGPLAN Notices*, **19**, 5 (May), 157–167.

1995. Wilson, P. R., Johnstone, M. S., Neely, M., and Boles, D. "Dynamic Storage Allocation: A Survey and Critical Review," *Proceedings of the International Workshop on Memory Management*. New York: Springer-Verlag.

1996. Jones, R. E., and Lins, R. D. *Garbage Collection Algorithms for Automatic Dynamic Memory Management*. New York: John Wiley.

1997. Knuth, D. E. *The Art of Computer Programming, Vol. 1. Fundamental Algorithms*, 3rd Ed., Section 2.5. Reading, MA: Addison-Wesley.

1998. Jones, R. E. (ed.) *Proceedings of the First International Symposium on Memory Management*, Vancouver. New York: ACM Press.

1999. Atkinson, M. P., and Jordan, M. J. "Issues Raised by Three Years of Developing PJama: An Orthogonally Persistent Platform for Java," *Proceedings of the International Conference on Database Theory 99*, Jerusalem. New York: Springer-Verlag.

Malcolm P. Atkinson and Tony Printezis

MEMORY-MAPPED I/O

> For articles on related subjects *see* INPUT-OUTPUT OPERATIONS; MEMORY: MAIN; MICROPROCESSORS AND MICROCOMPUTERS; MONITOR, DISPLAY; PERSONAL COMPUTING; and PORT, MEMORY.

In some large computers equipped with a display monitor, a programmer must direct characters to the monitor in much the same way as output is directed to a tape, disk or other online I/O device; i.e. the program must execute an I/O statement that (typically) names the channel (*q.v.*) to which the display device is attached, the number of characters to be transmitted, the screen location where they are to be displayed, and the starting address in memory where the data to be transmitted may be found. Some mini- and microcomputers, however, now use a simpler and more flexible system known as *memory-mapped I/O*, whereby characters are transferred to the display monitor with the move or store instructions that are part of the processor instruction set (*q.v.*). In a computer with a small instruction set, this method of doing I/O has the merit of not requiring any additional instructions just for I/O.

There are two common sorts of memory-mapped I/O. In the first sort, typically used with character-based displays, several of the computer memory addresses are associated with data and control registers for the display rather than with conventional memory. Characters are displayed by examining status bits in the control register and copying a character into the data register when it is ready to receive one.

This I/O method is equally appropriate for other input and output devices such as keyboard, printers, or a mouse, and with some additional features, for high-speed devices like disk drives (*see* INPUT–OUTPUT OPERATIONS). A minicomputer may have a block of addresses set aside for the data and control registers of all the devices that are connected to it.

The other sort of memory-mapped I/O applies to graphics displays such as those on current personal computers or workstations. In this form, individual character positions on the screen are mapped one-to-one to bytes in the computer's main memory.

For example, suppose that a certain (hypothetical) 64×128 character display screen is mapped onto the 8,192-byte memory segment starting at hexadecimal address A000. This has a twofold advantage. First, to display, say, HELLO in the middle of the screen, one would merely store the five-byte ASCII (*see* CHARACTER CODES) equivalent of HELLO at hexadecimal memory locations A83E to A842, which correspond to the desired portion of the screen. Instantaneously and automatically, the desired message will appear without need for any further instructions. Second, unlike the programmer of a system without memory-mapped I/O, whose programs cannot detect what is currently on the screen, the programmer of a memory-mapped system need only check the current contents of the memory map area to ascertain what is being displayed. If a user at the console changes it through keyboard action, the storage map will change to conform.

When a display is in graphics mode, individual pixels are memory-mapped. This will, of course, take considerably more memory—a megabyte for a 1024×1024 array of pixels—but that is no longer a serious overhead storage penalty relative to the amount of main memory typically available on current computers.

A keyboard may also be memory-mapped in a similar way, with individual keys associated with memory addresses. This allows the software to use simple memory accesses to be able to sense at any given time which keys (or combination of keys) are being depressed and to take appropriate action.

The alternative to memory-mapped I/O is called *port-mapped* I/O (*see* http://hive.speedhost.com/code3.htm).

Edwin D. Reilly

MEMORY ORGANIZATION

See MEMORY HIERARCHY.

MEMORY PORT

See PORT, MEMORY.

MEMORY PROTECTION

> For articles on related subjects *see* ADDRESSING; MEMORY MANAGEMENT; MULTIPROGRAMMING; MULTITASKING; OPERATING SYSTEMS; STORAGE ALLOCATION; and VIRTUAL MEMORY.

Memory protection, as used in this article, is a hardware mechanism that limits or prevents access to specified areas in the central or main memory of a computer.

It first became important when systems became capable of permitting or requiring more than one program to be resident in memory at the same time. The possibility then existed that, while one of the programs was running, it might inadvertently (e.g. because of a bug) write in the area occupied by the other program and thus invalidate that program.

In *uniprogramming* operating systems (i.e. most first-generation systems), there were typically two programs resident in memory—an executive program and a user program. The earliest memory protection mechanism provided a switch register that could be set to a memory address that marked the upper limit of a protected area. The lower limit was zero. No program running outside the protected area could write into any location inside the protected area. The executive routine, presumably debugged, would reside *in* the protected area. The user program would run on the outside, and if it did anything improper, it could hurt only itself. The execution of a user program instruction that would result in a write into the protected area would abort the user program, and then, either automatically or through operator intervention, control would be returned to the executive, which could proceed to the next user program.

With the development of *multiprogramming* and *multitasking* (*q.v.*) systems, more elaborate memory protection mechanisms were needed. In such systems, supervisory programs and a number of user programs may reside in memory simultaneously. While a user program is running, it is important to be able to designate the areas that belong to that program and to limit its access to other areas. The supervisory programs must be able to designate and change the areas under protection, and the user programs must be denied this capability.

The first effective memory protection mechanism for a multiprogramming system used a *base register* (*q.v.*), now commonly called a *relocation register*, and a *limit register*. A program would reside in a contiguous area of memory; when that program was to run, the executive placed the program's origin (i.e. its lowest address) in the base register and its length in the limit register. Any attempt by a program to access a memory location outside its own area would cause control to switch to the executive routine.

Today it is common for a program to have several *segments*—one for the program code, one for its data, and perhaps one for its run-time stack (*see* ACTIVATION RECORD). Segments are disjoint regions of memory, and processors frequently have several relocation registers, one to hold the base address of each segment. The Intel Pentium II has six such "segment" registers for this purpose. Together with memory-management

(*q.v.*) hardware they provide rapid access to and protection for each segment (a code segment would be read-only; a data segment read–write). Since modern systems are multitasking, there can be many segments of memory (real or virtual), and an operating system will maintain segment tables to record the addresses of segments whose base values are not currently in the relocation registers. The combination of access-right protection for segments and protection against access outside a program's segments is now common in virtual memory systems. Errors give rise to messages such as "segmentation violation" for an attempt to use an address outside a segment or "general protection fault" for an attempt to write in a read-only segment.

Memory protection is an important feature of multiprogramming systems, but it does create problems in systems in which routines and data are to be shared among programs simultaneously present in memory. *Virtual memory* systems have been designed to permit and encourage such sharing.

Memory protection can also be important within a single program. One of the most frequent program bugs occurs when a program calculates a subscript that causes a value to be stored outside the array that is being referenced. Automatic checking of array bounds can be an extremely useful memory protection feature. This type of checking can be done by the run-time systems provided by many compilers, which generate code to check for references outside of the bounds that have been declared for arrays. Such checking slows a program, however, and thus it is sometimes employed during program development but then turned off in the final "production" version of a program. Programs that use pointers (*q.v.*) also risk data corruption if a pointer refers to an incorrect address. Some languages, such as Java (*q.v.*), do not provide pointers because of the difficulty of providing memory protection if they are used.

Saul Rosen

MEMORY, CACHE

See CACHE MEMORY.

MERGING

See SORTING.

METAFONT

For articles on related subjects *see* DESKTOP PUBLISHING; TEX; and TYPEFONT.

METAFONT is a computer-controlled system for specifying the shapes of letters and other symbols. It was designed by Donald E. Knuth at the same time as TeX, a computer-controlled typesetting system, and it shares the same goals of quality and portability. Like TeX, METAFONT was written in the **WEB** language and has been placed in the public domain.

Traditionally, a type designer has worked out the shape of each character by making many large-scale drawings. Then the scale is reduced to the desired size, and the type designer can see how the letters work together as blocks of text. Needless to say, it takes years of tedious work to develop a single new typeface with this method.

METAFONT allows the type designer to make changes in the shapes of letters almost instantly, and to see the letters in various sizes and combinations at will. The user can ask METAFONT to draw strokes with a specific kind of pen point—sharp, broad, round, rectangular or slanted. The pen point can be instructed to make an image either by following the center of a curve or by filling between the edges of a region that has been outlined. There are also erasers, which act like pens except that they remove parts of strokes.

METAFONT doesn't have any built-in information about the shapes of letters. It is just a robot draftsman, able to follow instructions about how to move pens and erasers. It is also a programming language

```
z1=(15u,16u); 1/2[z1,z2]=1/2[z3,z5]+(0,10u);
z3=(0,5u); z4=1/3[z3,z5]-(0,10u); z5=(50u,10u);

pickup pencircle xscaled 10u yscaled 3u
    rotated 30;
drawdot z1; drawdot z2;
draw z3..z4..z5;
```

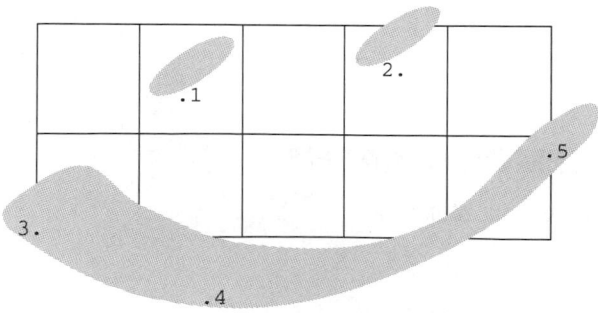

Figure 1. This METAFONT program defines five points $z_1, \ldots, z_5$, by specifying algebraic relations that they must satisfy. (The notation $1/2[z_1,z_2]$ used in the second equation stands for the point halfway between z_1 and z_2.) Then the computer is told to pick up a pen whose tip has an oval shape, holding it at an angle of $30°$ from the horizontal. The machine draws dots of this oval shape at points z_1 and z_2; then it uses the pen to draw a curved line from z_3 to z_4 to z_5.

(Fig. 1); the user writes a program for every letter, stating how that letter should be drawn.

Most statements in the METAFONT language are equations that express the designer's intentions about key parts of a shape to be drawn. For example, the designer may want a certain point to be one-third of the way between two other points. If the designer specifies a sequence of points, METAFONT will draw a smooth curve through them.

The design can be stated in terms of absolute physical dimensions, or it can be stated in terms of variable quantities or parameters that can be changed to produce a series of related fonts. For example, some parameters of a design could be the thickness of stem strokes and hairlines, the x-height of lower case letters and the heights of ascenders and descenders, the length of serifs, the width of an "em," the amount of oblique slant, etc. If a designer has written a METAFONT program in terms of such parameters, rather than in terms of absolute dimensions, other users can quickly and easily use the resulting design to generate a large family of fonts, simply by specifying different sets of numerical values for the parameters. Knuth has constructed an example of such a "meta-design," called the Computer Modern family of typefaces. Computer Modern fonts are based on traditional styles of type that had been used in his series of books, *The Art of Computer Programming*.

With an almost infinite set of possibilities, type designers must use their esthetic sense and professional experience to choose shapes that are beautiful and robust under a variety of parameter settings. Thus, the design of a complete typeface family is still a major undertaking, even though the amount of non-creative labor has been reduced.

Many uses of METAFONT are much simpler. Individual special characters and a wide variety of geometric symbols and decorations can be created quickly and used immediately within typeset documents.

The METAFONT language is of interest to designers of programming languages because it is a declarative language that combines a macro capability with structured types, much as SIMULA 67 combines procedures with structured types.

A similar language called METAPOST, which produces technical illustrations instead of fonts, has been developed by John Hobby. See

```
http://cm.bell-labs.com/who/hobby/
                          MetaPost.html
```

Information about METAFONT is regularly published in *TUGboat*, the journal of the TeX Users Group.

Hundreds of fonts in METAFONT format are available from the Comprehensive TEX Archive Network: `http://tug2.cs.umb.edu/ctan/`

Bibliography

1982. Knuth, D. E. "The Concept of a Meta-font," *Visible Language*, **16**, 3–27.
1985. Knuth, D. E. "Lessons Learned from METAFONT," *Visible Language*, **19**, 35–53.
1986. Knuth, D. E. *The METAFONT book*, Volume C of *Computers & Typesetting*. Reading, MA: Addison-Wesley.
1986. Knuth, D. E. *METAFONT: The Program*, Volume D of *Computers & Typesetting*, Reading, MA: Addison-Wesley.
1986. Knuth, D. E. *Computer Modern Typefaces*, Volume E of *Computers & Typesetting*, Reading, MA: Addison-Wesley.
1989. Billawala, N. *Metamarks: Preliminary Studies for a Pandora's Box of Shapes*. Stanford University Computer Science Report STAN-CS-89-1256, May.
1992. Hobby, J. D. "Introduction to METAPOST," *Proceedings of Euro TEX92* (Brno: Masaryk University), 21–36.

Donald E. and Jill C. Knuth

METALANGUAGE

For articles on related subjects *see* BACKUS–NAUR FORM; GRAMMARS; PROGRAMMING LINGUISTICS; and VIENNA DEFINITION LANGUAGE.

A *metalanguage* is a set of symbols and words used to describe another language in which these symbols do not appear. The most common application is in the definition of programming languages. The first and best known example was the definition of Algol 60, and a small section of this follows as an example.

The metalanguage used in this case, Backus–Naur Form, consists of the symbols $\langle$, $\rangle$, |, ::=, together with a number of metalinguistic variables that are used to define the elements of Algol. The brackets $\langle \rangle$ are used as delimiters for the metalinguistic variables, the vertical stroke | has the meaning "or," and the symbol ::= means "is defined as." The following extract from the report on Algol 60 gives the definition of an integer and illustrates the use of the symbols:

```
⟨digit⟩ ::= 0|1|2|3|4|5|6|7|8|9
⟨unsigned integer⟩ ::=
          ⟨digit⟩
          |⟨unsigned integer⟩⟨digit⟩
⟨integer⟩ ::= ⟨unsigned integer⟩
          | + ⟨unsigned integer⟩
          | - ⟨unsigned integer⟩
```

The complete definition of Algol 60 in this form, together with some semantic interpretation, takes about 26 pages.

Note that in order to define the symbols of the metalanguage, we had to make use of another language, namely, English. This causes no confusion in the present case, but might do so if we were to try to define English itself by a metalanguage.

In the example above we made use of three metalinguistic variables: ⟨digit⟩, ⟨unsigned integer⟩, and ⟨integer⟩. In defining the complete language, there will normally be one metalinguistic variable that is never used in the definition of any other variable; this is known as the *starting type*. In programming languages, this would normally be ⟨program⟩, and in natural languages it might be ⟨sentence⟩.

The digits 0, 1...9 and the signs + and – are *terminal symbols* of the language; i.e. they will appear in statements written in the language. For this reason they are sometimes printed in boldface to distinguish them from the *non-terminal symbols* (digit, integer etc.), sometimes called *defined types* or *metavariables*.

Bibliography

1969. Sammet, J. E. *Programming Languages*. Upper Saddle River, NJ: Prentice Hall.
1980. Hill, I. D., and Meek, B. L. (eds.) *Programming Language Standardization*. New York: John Wiley (Ellis Horwood).
1990. Schildt, H. *The Annotated ANSI C Standard American National Standard for Programming Languages-C:ANSI/ISO 1989–1990*. Berkeley, CA: Osborn/McGraw-Hill.
1993. Fisher, A. E., and Grodzinsky, F. S. *The Anatomy of Programming Languages*. Upper Saddle River, NJ: Prentice Hall.
1999. Sebesta, R. W. *Concepts of Programming Languages*, 4th Ed. Reading, MA: Addison-Wesley.

Kathleen H. V. Booth

METROPOLITAN AREA NETWORK (MAN)

For articles on related subjects *see* ASYNCHRONOUS TRANSFER MODE; DATA COMMUNICATIONS; GATEWAY; INTEGRATED SERVICES DIGITAL NETWORK; LOCAL AREA NETWORK; NETWORK PROTOCOLS; and NETWORKS, COMPUTER.

Data communications networks have traditionally been divided into local area networks and wide area networks. This division actually represents two ends of a range of a number of parameters for a network:

1. Geographical (local—up to several buildings, wide —up to worldwide)

2. Organizational (the larger, the more organizations involved)

3. Technological (the larger, the older)

4. Topological (redundancy of routes)

5. Performance (throughput, delay, errors).

A *metropolitan area network* (MAN) can be placed at the midpoint of each of these ranges:

1. 1–100 km in diameter

2. Building-wide to city-wide

3. Fiber optic cable plant, electronic switching

4. Commonly dual route—some redundancy

5. 100 Mbps or greater throughput, delay in the millisecond range, one bit in ten billion in error.

The motivation for the development of a clear standard way of implementing MANs came from the confluence of new ideas from digital telecommunications and telephony with old ideas from data communications. Digitized speech (and video) are best carried over a network in fixed-size packets called *cells*. These are small (53 bytes, made from 5 bytes of control information and 48 bytes payload/user data). The 5 bytes also contain the source and destination addresses of the cell. The fixed size means that the network can offer a predictable service time, which is vital so as not to confuse the human end user. These ideas are embodied in the Broadband ISDN Asynchronous Transfer Mode service (ATM). Such networks are also designed to carry data.

Local area networks use variable-sized packets ranging from 50 to 4,000 bytes. Wide area networks have offered recovery from outages and efficient use of the network bandwidth by using statistical multiplexing (*q.v.*) of variable-sized packets from many end users. The main algorithms used with a MAN are:

1. The Distributed Queue, Dual Bus (DQDB) architecture (defined by the IEEE 802.6 Committee), also known as Queued Packet Switched eXchange (QPSX), used at 150 Mbps.

2. Fiber Distributed Data Interface (FDDI) I and II.

ATM is also used for MANs with the appropriate adaptation layer for a data service.

3. B-ISDN using AAL-5 to provide variable length frames for data services. This is a specialization of ATM technology for a particular environment and is an example of its scaling properties from LAN all the way to WAN.

With method 1 (*see* Fig. 1), physical recovery from loss of a cable can be effected by bypassing it until it is repaired. The physical length of the bus is constrained so that cells are not delayed more than 1.5 ms. The head nodes generate empty cells and transmit them down each bus.

DQDB offers three types of service to the user:

1. Connection-oriented service—this is designed to carry a compressed video service, with buffering to match the synchronous video stream to ATM cells.

2. Connectionless data service (like the LLC service of a LAN)—here, just as on Ethernet or Token Ring, large packets are carried from one station to another on a best effort basis. The large packets are built from a collection of cells (*see* Fig. 2).

3. Isochronous, equal time segments, fixed bandwidth service. Digitized video or voice are often sampled in the way that fits this service. Once an isochronous channel is established, the end system nodes know which cells map into it from the cells' time slot positions.

Types 1 and 2 are arbitrated by a distributed queue algorithm. Type 3 is non-arbitrated and is allocated on a fixed basis by a "head-end" specially designated station.

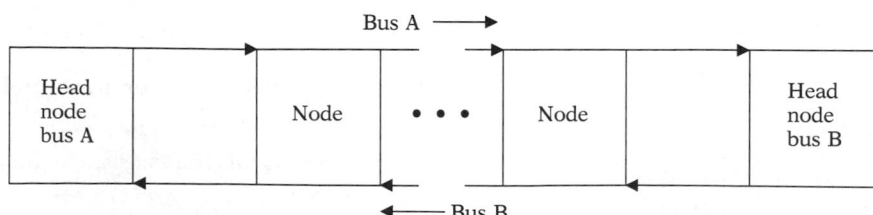

Figure 1. Distributed Queue, Dual Bus (DQDB) architecture.

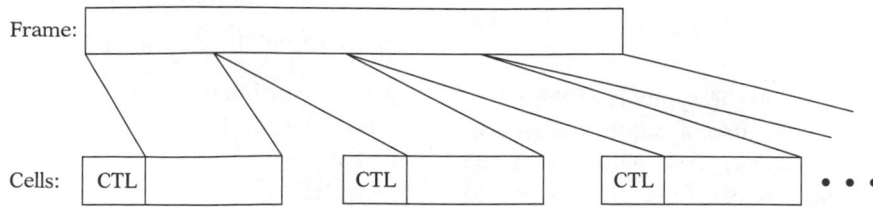

Figure 2. Mapping a large frame into cells by segmentation.

Operation of the Distributed Queue Algorithm

Access to each bus is requested by sending out requests on the other bus, which transmits in the reverse direction. Each node keeps a counter of requests seen for each bus. Whenever empty packets are seen (neither requests nor those that contain data), the counter is decremented. Empty cells must be for a "downstream" node, so they will have resulted from earlier requests. When a node has data ready to send and its counter is zero, it simply copies the data into the next empty slot that passes.

This algorithm ensures fairness of access to the MAN since, at worst, every other node has sent out a request just before a given one. Thus the given node will have access after all the others have had just one access. For an N node DQDB, it has to wait at most $N - 1$ cell service times.

FDDI—100 Mbps, Dual Fiber Optic Ring

FDDI is a token ring standard for MANs similar to the LAN 802.5 standard. It has been proposed to extend the services available to include connection-oriented services to carry compressed video, voice, and other services. This is a far less popular option than DQDB. FDDI runs over either a single fiber optic (*q.v.*) ring or a dual ring system.

ATM—Various Data Rates, Mesh of Switches

ATM is a mechanism for building cell-switched based networks. At the physical and transmission layer, typically SONET (or SDH in Europe) is used over copper for short haul, and fiber for longer distances. Above this the cell transfer service operates with ATM Adaptation Layer 5 as a mechanism to allow variable-length frames to be transmitted as a set of cells marked as belonging to the same data unit and reassembled at the receiver. A MAN can be built out of one or more switches, often operating with data rates ranging from 155 Mbps up to as much as 622 Mbps per port on the switch. Such a system is often used to connect together further switches, or else to connect routers at a set of sites within a metropolitan area. Redundancy can be provided by having a mesh of switches and links. There are no fixed standards in this area.

Bibliography

1989. IEEE 802.6, Draft Standard for Metropolitan Networks.
1989. *Data Communications Magazine*, Special Issue, December.
1997. Adams, J. *ATM for Service Providers*. London: Chapman & Hall.

Jon Crowcroft

MICROCOMPUTER CHIP

For articles on related subjects *see* INTEGRATED CIRCUITRY; MICROPROCESSORS AND MICROCOMPUTERS; MINICOMPUTER; and PERSONAL COMPUTING.

A *microcomputer chip*, often simply referred to as a *microchip* or just *chip*, is an integrated circuit component that is the building block of a computer system. Typically, microcomputer chips are very large-scale integrated circuit components (VLSI) containing millions to tens of millions of transistors. In 1999, the largest such components contained over one hundred million transistors. A computer will typically contain a large number and variety of such components or chips. A typical personal computer will contain about 40 chips of different varieties. Hand-held "personal digital assistants" have very few chips, to save battery power and to keep them small. The best known example of a microcomputer chip is the microprocessor, but "microcomputer chip" is a very broad term that refers to many different kinds of such components. Furthermore, the boundaries and distinctions between the particular forms are constantly changing.

Physical Description

Silicon wafers are typically 8 inches (20 cm) in diameter and thinner than cardboard. During semiconductor manufacturing, a single such wafer contains tens and possibly hundreds of individual microcomputer chips. The wafers are cut or diced into individual chips that are the size of a thumbnail (*see* Fig. 1). The surface of each chip is covered with transistors that are etched into the surface of the silicon through a complex sequence of superimposed photographically developed layers. The photographic layers provide a stencil for sequences of carefully controlled chemical procedures that create metal lines for signal flow, transistors, and the interconnections between various metal lines and transistors. The chips themselves are then typically placed into a package that provides a mechanically sound structure to keep them from being cracked.

Some packages have pins that allow them to be connected to a circuit board that subsequently allows interconnection to other components. The individual signal lines of the chip are connected to the package with gold wires that are finer than hair. Packages contain 50 to 500 pins (*see* Fig. 2). A more recent packaging technology allows tiny balls of solder to be deposited directly onto the silicon die; the die is then precisely positioned over a small fiberglass board with an array of metal squares imprinted on its surface, one square for every solder ball on the die. During manufacturing, the solder balls on the die are heated until the solder flows between the die and the fiberglass. For

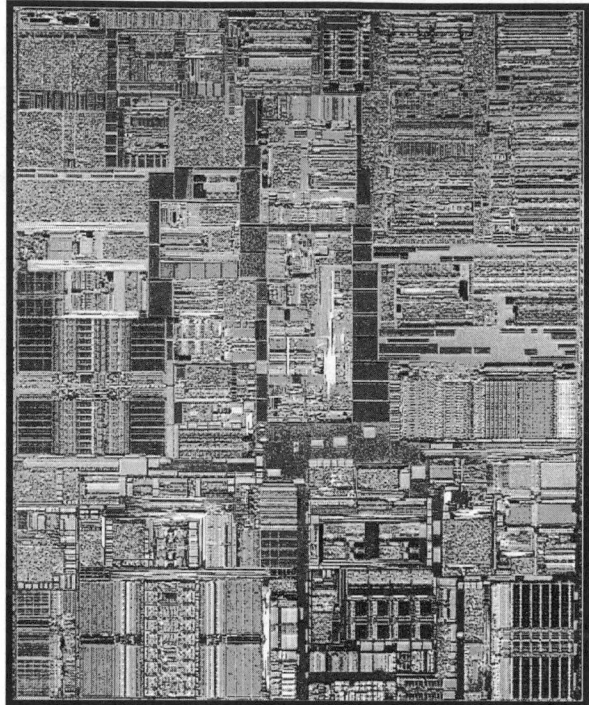

Figure 1. Die photo of Intel Pentium III microprocessor (courtesy of Intel Corporation).

(a)

(b)

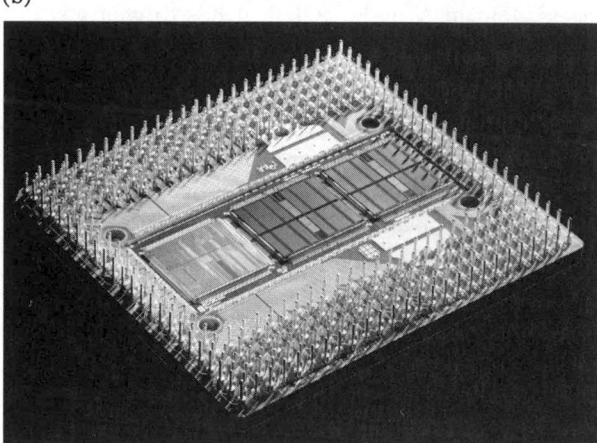

Figure 2. Packaged Pentium III chip (courtesy of Intel Corporation).

a considerably more detailed analysis of integrated circuits and their fabrication process, *see* INTEGRATED CIRCUITRY.

Over three decades, the number of transistors that can be fabricated as a single integrated circuit has more than doubled every two years (Fig. 3—*see* LAWS, COMPUTER). The largest microprocessor of 1990 had over one million transistors. Chips containing 50 to 100 million transistors will be in volume production in 2000, and many industry experts expect a production chip in 2010 to contain one billion transistors.

History

The precursor to the first microcomputer chip was the integrated circuit invented simultaneously by Jack Kilby of Texas Instruments and Robert Noyce (*q.v.*), then of Fairchild Semiconductor, in 1959. The microcomputer chip traces its origin to the microprocessor, invented in the early 1970s (*see* MICROPROCESSORS AND MICROCOMPUTERS). Prior to the microprocessor, integrated circuits were rather simple, performing a single function on an individual chip. The breakthrough of the microprocessor was the combination of several different computing elements or functional units of a computer into a single integrated circuit. The first such microprocessor was the Intel 4004 invented by Marcian (Ted) Hoff in 1972. In the case of the microprocessor,

the functions combined on a single chip were those that constitute most of a central processing unit (*q.v.*), the heart of a computer. These functions include items such as the arithmetic unit for addition and subtraction, register file, and memory address generation. The first significant variation following the microprocessor was the *microcontroller*, developed in the mid-1970s. The microcontroller combined memory with the microprocessor.

The memory typically contains the program or sequence of instructions that the microprocessor is to execute. In this way, the microcontroller can be embedded into a host system and perform a function repetitively, as needed, for extended periods of time. One example might be a traffic light controller whose memory is loaded with a program indicating what sequence of lights should be used for each conceivable configuration (*see* EMBEDDED SYSTEMS). Other common examples include the microcontrollers that govern modern automobile engines and antilock braking

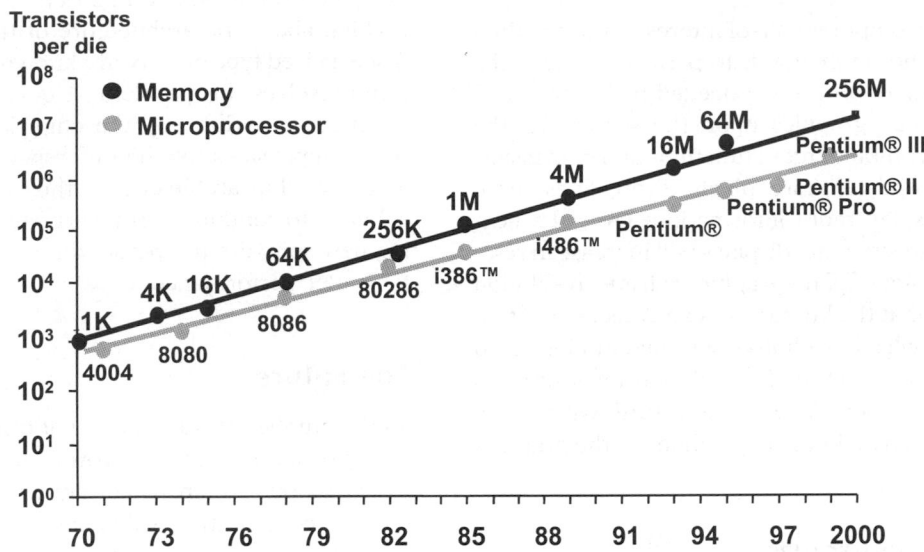

Figure 3. Chip size in number of transistors, 1970–2000, of one processor family and associated memory (courtesy of Intel Corporation).

systems. Embedded microcontrollers often include specialized input–output devices such as ports, analog-to-digital and digital-to-analog converters (*q.v.*), and timers, to keep overall system cost low and real-time performance high.

Integrating functions into a single chip has several significant advantages. First, the size of a system diminishes as functions are integrated. Thus systems built with microcomputer chips can provide much greater functionality in a smaller size. Second, signals travel smaller distances when combined into a single chip, so that the functions implemented on the chip operate at a higher speed, and waste less power. Single-chip solutions are more reliable than multiple chip designs, since there are fewer mechanical connections that could break, and they are much less expensive to make, since the silicon fabrication process is more highly concurrent than fiberglass board manufacturing. Finally, and most important, new techniques are possible when functions are integrated that are not possible when implemented discretely. For instance, when several functions are implemented as individual components, a designer is constrained to implementations that require a much smaller number of interconnections than would be possible on a single chip.

Types of Microchip

MICROPROCESSORS

Microprocessors combine all the capabilities of a central processing unit on a single chip and perform up to billions of instructions per second. The chip acts as the orchestra leader of the computer. Microprocessors have typically integrated new functions as required to remove bottlenecks that inhibit the performance of a

microcomputer system. Some examples are the integration of memory management (*q.v.*), cache memory (*q.v.*), floating-point operations, and recently, provisions for a single instruction to process multiple pieces of data simultaneously (*see* INSTRUCTION-LEVEL PARALLELISM and PARALLEL PROCESSING). Microprocessors can also be combined in systems known as multiprocessors (*see* MULTIPROCESSING and CLUSTER COMPUTING). Large database servers and engineering workstations (*q.v.*) are often configured in this way.

MICROCONTROLLERS

A single modern car may have as many as 25 microcontrollers that perform tasks ranging from audio systems to global positioning systems, ignition control, engine control, and suspension balancing. As microcontrollers have become very powerful (hundreds of millions of instructions per second) at very low costs (about US$20), they have begun to replace many special-purpose hard-wired chips. For example, a powerful microcontroller may perform a computer's disk control function. In addition to simply coordinating the disk accesses requested by the microprocessor, it also performs numerous other tasks. These tasks include searching for disk errors and correcting them and caching frequently used information, as well as compressing and encoding information stored on the disk to increase security and the amount of information that can be stored (*see* DATA COMPRESSION). Another example of a microcontroller is the *network controller* that can interpret higher-level communication protocols, perform network monitoring, and transfer information without any intervention from the microprocessor.

GRAPHICS

Another microcomputer chip of interest is the *graphics accelerator*, whose function is to perform some of the specialized display processing needed to put two- and three-dimensional graphics upon the screen. As the graphics chip combines more functions and runs faster, it is able to update more pixels, draw lines more quickly, or display more information. Over the next decade, it is expected that displays will increase in resolution to the point of photographic realism—resolution that exceeds what the human eye can detect—and that such displays will allow photographs and motion video to be played in real time. Three-dimensional displays will be more common. All of these features will require substantial increases in the capabilities of the graphics chip.

COMPUTER ARCHITECTURE

The chief characteristic that distinguishes microprocessors and microcontrollers from "hard-wired" devices is their programmability; software controls microprocessors and microcontrollers. Most software written for microprocessors is realized in a high-level language such as C (*q.v.*) or Java (*q.v.*). A program known as a compiler (*q.v.*) converts that high-level language program into the machine instructions of the target processor. Those machine instructions, along with certain other aspects of a processor, are collectively known as the processor's instruction set (*q.v.*) architecture.

There are many ways of implementing any given instruction set architecture. For example, the Intel Pentium III processor will correctly execute any program written for the much older Intel 486 processor, although the principles that underlie the Pentium III processor's design are quite different from those in the 486. Two different processor designs are compatible if and only if each instruction has exactly the same effect on program data from one processor generation to another, other than the actual speed with which the instruction executes. It is this property of processor families that allows a computer user to buy a new, much faster computer, yet continue to run older software already owned.

Microcontrollers also have instruction set architectures, but it is generally less important that they be strictly compatible, because they are programmed permanently and do not have to run older software.

Specialized microchips such as graphics controllers occupy a middle ground in terms of their required software compatibility. It is important for new chips to remain useful with older software, because computer users cannot afford to replace all their software just to use a new chip. But new chip designs would be seriously hobbled if they were strictly required to change nothing about the architecture of their predecessors. A specialized type of software known as a *device driver* (*q.v.*) resolves this problem. A device driver is a program (often written by the chip development team) that compensates for the differences between the old and new chip architectures, thus permitting the old software to continue to run correctly, while also allowing new software to operate differently where needed for better performance.

The Future

As the number of transistors that can be integrated on a single piece of silicon grows, the pervasiveness of microcomputer chips is certain to increase. Amazing levels of computation will be found in very small, inexpensive packages. A credit card-size personal phone book that recognizes spoken requests for addresses and names is just one possibility. Or better yet, a portable computing device that is always connected to the Internet (*see* MOBILE COMPUTING), and "knows" its exact physical location via global positioning satellites, would allow you to have instant access to all of your files, the Internet, your car, your home, and ready communication to everyone else similarly equipped.

The challenges for designers are growing, however. Eventually, performance will be limited by the laws of physics, some as early as 2002, which could potentially seriously constrain further improvements to silicon-based CPU design. For example, the process technology planned in 1999 uses layers of oxide that are only a few atoms thick; it is hard to see how to make them much thinner. Likewise, the amount of charge being stored in a memory chip has decreased to the point where stray cosmic rays can cause a loss of data. Fundamental thermodynamic limits have begun to impede our ability to make faster laptops and hand-held computers (*see* LIMITS OF COMPUTATION).

If there is one unmistakable message from the first 30 years of microchip development, it is this: every time the field has run into what was commonly assumed to be a showstopper, someone has found a way around it, and the field is off and running again.

Bibliography

1990. Hennessy, J., and Patterson, D. *Computer Architecture— A Quantitative Approach.* San Francisco: Morgan Kaufmann.
1991. Bell, T. "Incredible Shrinking Computers," *IEEE Spectrum*, **28**, 5 (May), 37–41.
1995. Malone, M. S. *The Microprocessor: A Biography.* New York: Springer-Verlag.
1998. Yu, A. *Creating The Digital Future.* New York: Free Press.

Patrick P. Gelsinger and Robert P. Colwell

MICROPROCESSORS AND MICROCOMPUTERS

For articles on related subjects *see* COMPUTER CIRCUITRY; EMBEDDED SYSTEM; INTEGRATED CIRCUITRY; INSTRUCTION-LEVEL PARALLELISM; MICROCOMPUTER CHIP; and REDUCED INSTRUCTION SET COMPUTER.

A *microprocessor* is a single-chip integrated circuit (IC) implementation of a general-purpose central processing unit (CPU—*q.v.*). It contains a controller to direct the execution of program instructions, registers to store control and data values temporarily, and an arithmetic logic unit (ALU—*q.v.*) to calculate results. A microprocessor chip is a (very) large-scale integrated (LSI or VLSI) circuit fabricated on a sliver of silicon less than 7 mm (about 1/4 in) square and 0.5 mm (1/50 in) thick, about the size of a baby's fingernail.

In thirty years, microprocessors have gone from being electronic curiosities capable of doing simple arithmetic to being the fastest single-CPU computers on earth. They are becoming brain cells in a planet-wide computing network linking all human knowledge and making it widely and rapidly available everywhere (*see* CYBERSPACE). Microprocessors are the enabling engines of the information revolution presently sweeping technological society.

There are many different kinds of microprocessors, designed for many different applications. In 1990, there were about 50 different microprocessor families, including 995 varieties of CPU chips; in 1999, there were 34,000 CPU and controller chip types sold by 200 vendors. Each CPU chip contains the equivalent of 4,000 to 20,000,000 transistors; and chip complexity increases roughly by a factor of 100 every decade. A transistor-equivalent is able to make one simple logic decision or to store one binary digit (a 0 or 1 bit). A popular CPU categorization is based on the width in bits of its internal data path, commonly 16-bit, 32-bit, or 64-bit.

Processor architecture, such as the DEC Alpha series and the Sun Sparc family, is sometimes distinguished from a particular implementation. Architectures specify programmer-visible functions. A flexible architecture takes advantage of technological progress that allows ever faster, more highly integrated microprocessors.

A *microcomputer* is a more complete system than a microprocessor, containing not only the CPU logic, but also memory for storing programs and data plus input–output (I/O) interfaces for exchanging data with peripheral devices. In 1990, most microcomputers combined a CPU chip with 1 to 200 support chips on a single circuit board no larger than a double book page. Most extra chips contained from 262,144 (2^{18}) to 4,194,304 (2^{22}) bits of memory. A 100-chip micro-

computer usually controlled a workstation (*q.v.*) with I/O interfaces for a graphics display, mouse (*q.v.*) input keyboard, storage disk, loudspeaker, and network communications; it executed from 64 to 300 different instructions at rates from 1 million to 80 million instructions per second (MIPS) and contained 9 to 36 million bytes (megabytes, or MB) of memory, including its display image. A memory byte is eight bits and can hold one alphabetic character, two decimal digits, eight display dots, one color value, or part of a large binary number.

By 1999, the circuitry for a personal computer had shrunk to a module the size of a deck of playing cards and containing about 10 chips: CPU, memory bus, memory controller, I/O bus, I/O controller, and 2 to 8 memory chips of 67,108,864 (2^{26}) to 1,073,741,824 (2^{30}) bits each, giving 64 MB to 1,024 MB of memory. Common execution rates were 100 to 1,000 MIPS.

The ever-increasing number of transistors that a single integrated circuit can hold has made possible *single-chip microcomputers* (Fig. 1), small systems with large application markets. They range in processing speeds from slow, tiny appliance controllers to near-super-computers (*q.v.*). A *digital signal processor* (DSP) is a microcomputer designed for high throughput (*q.v.*) numerical processing ("number crunching"). DSP

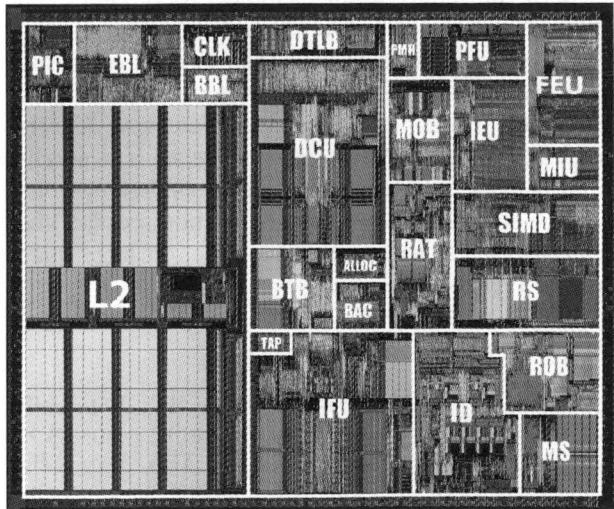

Figure 1. Photomicrograph of an Intel Pentium III processor introduced in 1999. It is a VLSI circuit with 28.1 million transistors. Among the major parts of the chip, marked with an overlay, are—left side: the cache memory (L2), and interface to the external bus (EBL); top center: data allocation units, including the data cache (DCU); bottom center: the instruction fetch unit and front-end of the instruction pipeline (IFU); top right: arithmetic execution units (IEU: integer execution), (FEU: floating-point execution), (SIMD: MMX technology instructions); bottom right: instruction decoder (ID) and associated logic for instruction scheduling. (Courtesy of Intel Corporation.)

chips are very useful for speech recognition and synthesis (*q.v.*). Their fast operations on arrays of numbers find many scientific applications. A *coprocessor* is an older, optional function unit on a separate chip that can rapidly execute complex floating-point arithmetic instructions (*see* COMPUTER ARITHMETIC). As of 1999, the millions of transistors on each fast CPU chip included all arithmetic units and logic for many DSP instructions.

A *bit-sliced microprocessor* is an obsolete type of fast CPU formed by combining several function blocks, each a separate chip. One chip family could be used to create prototypes of many different processors. The term *bit-slicing* (*q.v.*) describes the blocks for handling data within the CPU; they are 1 to 32 bits wide, but can be connected in parallel to form processors with any desired word width.

In the 1990s, a new technology became popular for making fast processor prototypes: *programmable gate arrays* (PGAs—*see* COMPUTER CIRCUITRY). Each chip holds regular arrays of hundreds of thousands of AND and OR gates with memory selectable interconnections. Some arrays, called *complex programmable logic devices* (CPLDs), also contain small fast RAMs for data and may have specialized DSP logic. Processor prototypes built with these logic devices execute programs hundreds of times faster than software simulators.

A *microcontroller* is a single-chip microcomputer built to control embedded systems, such as appliances and traffic lights. It typically has on-chip permanent program memory, a small amount of data memory for temporary values, and an assorted selection of interfaces and peripheral units such as serial and parallel ports, timers, and analog-to-digital converters (*q.v.*). Embedded applications usually do not require high performance, but need identical chips in huge quantities at very low prices.

Organization

A (micro) computer is organized into the three major von Neumann stored-program (*q.v.*) subsystems: processor, memory, and input–output. This design has stood the test of time surprisingly well, kept alive by improving implementation technology, even though it has an inherent speed limitation in exchanging data between the CPU and memory. Newer architectures, such as massively parallel machines that intersperse CPUs and input–output devices among memory modules, have the potential for high performance, but are of limited use, having yet to achieve standardization.

The *central processing unit* (CPU) contains the control units, execution units, and data registers that perform the instructions of a computer program. It can fetch instructions and data from the memory system, store results back into memory, and can exchange data with the input–output subsystem.

The *control unit* is in charge of decoding instructions and sequencing the actions of various functional units. It resolves conflicts between on-chip resources and responds to internal and external interrupts (*q.v.*). Control units are simple state machines (*see* SEQUENTIAL MACHINE), implemented directly in logic circuitry ("hard-wired") or by state table lookup ("microprogrammed"—*see* MICROPROGRAMMING). Hard-wired control is faster, but needs more IC space, is less flexible, and requires a simple internal architecture. A *pipelined* control unit can handle distinct parts of several simple instructions at once, greatly increasing execution rates. Processors with many complex instructions or legacy modes to emulate older CPUs are microprogrammed.

A *bus interface unit* controls instruction and data transfers to and from the CPU (*see* BUS). Architectures with separate instruction and data buses need two units—one for instruction fetch and one for data read and write. Sophisticated bus interfaces improve performance by prefetching instructions, buffering memory writes, and predicting branch instruction destinations.

There can be many *execution units*, commonly including an *arithmetic-logic unit* (ALU—*q.v.*), floating-point unit (FPU), and special-purpose units to execute graphics or vector instructions rapidly. The ALU executes most instructions on integer data, such as add, subtract, shift, rotate, and bitwise logical operations. If present, an FPU has specialized hardware to perform complicated floating-point arithmetic operations. FPUs often have distinct addition, multiplication, and division units, and dedicated registers. Many fast CPUs designed after 1997 have an on-chip graphics function unit.

A *register* (*q.v.*) is a storage location within an execution unit capable of holding one number. It is often part of a register set—a small on-chip data array that is explicitly or implicitly addressable by program instructions. Registers provide storage with the fastest possible access time and are included in all major microprocessors.

Registers are classified by function. *General-purpose registers* have no predefined functions; they can be used equivalently by programs to hold temporary data values during computations. Instructions access registers directly as operand (*q.v.*) sources or result destinations. Because reading a value from a register is much faster than reading from a memory location, keeping needed values in registers greatly improves execution speed. High-performance architectures all have dozens or hundreds of general-purpose registers. For fast execution, optimizing compilers (*q.v.*) must carefully allocate registers to values.

Dedicated registers play specific roles during execution of some instructions. For instance, the stack pointer in the Motorola 68000 is one of the general-purpose registers, but is implicitly modified by instructions that access the stack. Many architectures place the program counter and condition codes in dedicated registers. Some older CPUs used a single *accumulator* register to provide one operand for each arithmetic operation and to receive each result.

Floating-point registers are general-purpose registers accessible only by floating-point and data transfer instructions. They provide storage space for lengthy floating-point numbers, freeing the integer registers. Having them as separate registers simplifies control of instruction pipelines (*q.v.*). When the FPU is a coprocessor, putting floating-point registers on the coprocessor greatly speeds execution by not requiring slow off-chip data transfers. By 1999, high-end CPUs had all the floating-point and integer registers and logic on one chip.

To the CPU, the *memory* subsystem appears to be a large array of locations that can hold data values or program instructions. *Random access memory* (RAM) has become synonymous with "computer main memory." (*see* MEMORY). "Random access" means that any location can be referenced in the same time and manner. RAM can be dynamic (DRAM) or static (SRAM). DRAM is denser and needs much less power; SRAM is 10 times faster, but more costly. The densities achieved by DRAMs have made multi-megabyte primary memories affordable.

Read-only memory (ROM) is a simple type of memory with contents that cannot be changed, even by loss of electrical power. The contents are programmed during manufacture and are unalterable afterwards. ROMs are used for very high-volume control applications where simplicity and low per-unit cost, gained from mass producing the program within the memory chip, are critical.

PROMs, EPROMs, EEPROMs, and flash memory are erasable nonvolatile memories. A programmable read-only memory (PROM—*see* READ-ONLY MEMORY) can be written only once via an irreversible process. Data in Erasable PROM (EPROM) are reset by exposure to intense ultraviolet light. Both Electrically Erasable PROM (EEPROM) and flash memory are alterable by a high voltage input. Nonvolatile memories are very useful because they can survive power losses, but they can be rewritten only very slowly and for a limited number of times. Flash memory needs only 12 volts for

erasure and writes much faster than EEPROM; it can directly replace RAM for some applications. Recent research suggests that IC memories with minute magnetizable regions can be as fast to use and as easy to produce lithographically as DRAMs.

High-performance microprocessors need fast memory subsystems not costing much more than the cheapest memory arrays. The most important methods to improve price–performance are *cache memory* (*q.v.*) and paged *virtual memory* (*q.v.*). Caches greatly lower the average access time of system memory; virtual memory increases capacity. Both are part of a general memory hierarchy (*q.v.*) that encompasses all storage, from registers to magnetic tape.

Memory hierarchies rely on temporal and spatial locality of code and data references in running programs: after a memory location is accessed, it and nearby locations will often be needed many times. A large, cheap, slow memory can be combined with a small, expensive, fast memory to get both low cost and fast access. Currently needed regions are copied into fast memory and unneeded locations are returned to slow memory.

Cache memories are very fast SRAMs accessed directly by the processor and filled with copies of data from slower but cheaper DRAMs. Mappings between official DRAM addresses and actual SRAM locations are maintained by a cache controller. Average access times for memory with caching are one-fifth those for DRAMs alone. Paged *virtual memory* uses a similar, selective-copy scheme to make a slow disk appear to be a very large capacity RAM. Multitasking systems also use virtual memory to give each process its own separate memory, apparently starting at location zero. The virtual memory mappings of RAM to disk locations are maintained by the *memory management unit* (MMU) (*see* MEMORY MANAGEMENT). Cache memory started to be placed on CPU chips in the mid-1980s, and by 1999, most fast microprocessors had large caches on the CPU chip.

The *input–output* (I/O—*see* INPUT–OUTPUT OPERATIONS) subsystem includes all interfaces that connect the CPU to external peripherals, usually via device controllers that translate general commands from the CPU into specific details. A CPU may exchange I/O commands and data via direct I/O using special instructions, memory-mapped I/O (*q.v.*) by accessing controller registers as if they were memory locations, or direct memory access (DMA) by letting a sophisticated interface control the memory bus and transfer large blocks of data without CPU help. There are many types of device controllers, reflecting the many application areas for microprocessors. Most themselves contain an inexpensive microprocessor.

The most common I/O units are serial and parallel interfaces, or *ports* (*see* PORT, I/O). *Serial interfaces* accept data, such as 8-bit bytes, convert them into one-bit-at-a-time serial form, and send them over an optical fiber or a wire pair. The I/O interfaces must generate light or voltage signals corresponding to the data bits. *Parallel interfaces* are similar, but send or receive eight or more bits of data simultaneously on multistranded wire cables. *Network interfaces*, such as those for Ethernet (*q.v.*) and ATM (*q.v.*), allow computers to exchange data over communication links. They convert data to and from the special formats used in the network. All network devices have addresses. Propagation delays are longer than within a single computer system (*see* DATA COMMUNICATIONS).

Programmable *timers* interrupt the processor after a delay specified as a number of fundamental microcomputer clock cycles. They are very useful in real-time systems for providing a constant time delay between actions. *Analog to digital* (A/D) and *digital to analog* (D/A) converters (*q.v.*) are often provided on single-chip microcontrollers to transform analog input signals into digital form for processing, or vice versa.

Direct memory access (DMA) controllers can autonomously and rapidly transfer large blocks of data. They free the CPU to execute other tasks; they run transparently, without interfering with the CPU, by using the memory bus only when not needed by the CPU, in a process called cycle-stealing (*q.v.*). Fast disk controllers transfer data in DMA blocks.

Disk controllers are common peripheral interface units and one of the earliest produced in single-chip form. They convert I/O read and write requests into the right sequence of seeks, delays, and data transfer operations. Some disk interfaces—those following the small computer system interface (SCSI) standard, for example—assume that an intelligent controller in the disk drive accepts high-level commands to access stored data.

Video controllers put the electronics for a video display into one chip. Typically, they repeatedly read image data from memory, convert the data to pixels and colors, and send it to the screen. They calculate data addresses, look up colors, position pixels, and generate timing signals for the monitor. Some video controllers are general-purpose programmable microcomputers that also offer a number of different drawing primitives.

Special controller circuits for speech synthesis, speech recognition, and three-dimensional (3D) graphics imaging were added to I/O chips and some CPUs in the late 1990s. The Intel Pentium/MMX processor of 1997 and many later chips included special parallel floating-point instructions to speed calculations for 3D graphics images.

History

Microprocessors and microcomputers are products of a microelectronic revolution characterized by ever-shrinking costs and sizes for information processing devices. The history of microprocessors is tightly interwoven with the histories of integrated circuits and the semiconductor industry.

Microelectronics began at Bell Laboratories in 1947 with the development of small transistor amplifiers on the surface of semiconductor materials, such as pure germanium and silicon (sand and glass are mainly silicon dioxide). A transistor is hundreds of times smaller than a vacuum tube, which it replaced for building computers by the late 1950s. After learning how to use photographic masks to control diffusion of critical trace impurities into tiny regions of silicon, by the mid-1950s engineers could produce batches of hundreds of individual transistors from a single, thin wafer of silicon.

In late 1958, Texas Instruments created an integrated circuit of five connected transistors. In 1959, Fairchild produced a planar transistor, the first device using integrated circuit (IC) technology on silicon with layers of silicon dioxide for insulation and thin films of evaporated aluminum for connectors. In 1961, Fairchild marketed the first commercially available IC, a flip-flop (1-bit) memory circuit with four transistors and two resistors. Most other early ICs were single-logic gates. Hundreds of IC copies are photographically reproduced at once upon a silicon wafer; they are tested to eliminate defective copies, cut into individual circuits about 5–7 mm ($\frac{1}{5}$–$\frac{1}{4}$ in) square, and mounted in standard plastic or ceramic packages. The maximum number of elements per silicon IC has doubled every one to two years since 1959—an exponential phenomenon known as Moore's law (*see* LAWS, COMPUTER).

In 1967, ex-Fairchild executives formed Intel (*see* NOYCE, ROBERT). In 1969, Intel began developing a general-purpose chip set for handheld calculators. They abstracted the control mechanism into a programmable unit—the Intel 4004 chip. The idea of a controller on a chip originated with Gilbert Hyatt, who had the first microprocessor prototype running in 1968.

THE INTEL 80x86 FAMILY

The microcomputer revolution started in 1971, when Intel sold the first microprocessor chip, its 4004 controller. It contained 2,124 transistors, addressed 256

8-bit instructions, and operated on 4-bit data, each enough for a decimal digit (0–9). It was followed soon by the 4040 and several processors for 8-bit data: 8008 and 8080. The 8008 (1972) was designed to control video display terminals and keyboards. The 8080 and faster 8080A (1974) provided more registers, a stack (*q.v.*) for calling subroutines, and rudimentary 16-bit arithmetic. They executed 8-bit instructions, operated on 8-bit and 16-bit data, and had eight limited-use registers: a stack pointer (SP), three pairs of 8-bit registers (B, C, D, E, H, L), and an arithmetic accumulator (A). A register pair formed a simple index register addressing 2^{16} (65,536) memory bytes. The 8080 and 8080A were the first widely used microprocessors, used mainly in embedded control applications and in hobbyist systems that preceded personal computers (PCs). Their descendants are the 80x86 chips in many millions of PCs.

Improvements continued in 1978 with the 8086 and 8088, internally identical chips for 16-bit operations. The 8088 retained a narrow 8-bit external data bus for compatibility. Both used segmentation to extend the memory address range to 1 MB (2^{20} bytes). The 80186 (1981) was an 8086 with on-chip peripheral circuits for embedded applications. Subsequent improvements

to 8086 performance were made through the 80286 (1982), 80386 (1985), and the 80486 (1989) chips.

Starting with the 80386, the architecture was radically upgraded to form a 32-bit microprocessor supporting a nonsegmented 4 GB (2^{32} bytes) address space, virtual memory, and many new instructions. Compatibility with previous versions was provided by retaining the same register structure and supporting a virtual 8086 mode. The 80486 had the same instructions as the 80386, but added an on-chip memory cache, instruction pipelines, and a floating-point unit to improve performance greatly.

Although having few registers and maintaining 8086 compatibility hurt its performance, Intel retained the 80x86 architecture throughout the 1990s. The 80586 P5 Pentium (1993) had more on-chip cache and was superscalar: it could start two instructions per cycle to use both integer ALUs, or its single FPU plus one ALU (*see* INSTRUCTION-LEVEL PARALLELISM). The MMX CPU (1995) added "Matrix Math eXtension" instructions to perform two to eight, 32- to 8-bit vector integer operations at once in its 64-bit FPU, speeding calculations for 3D graphic images.

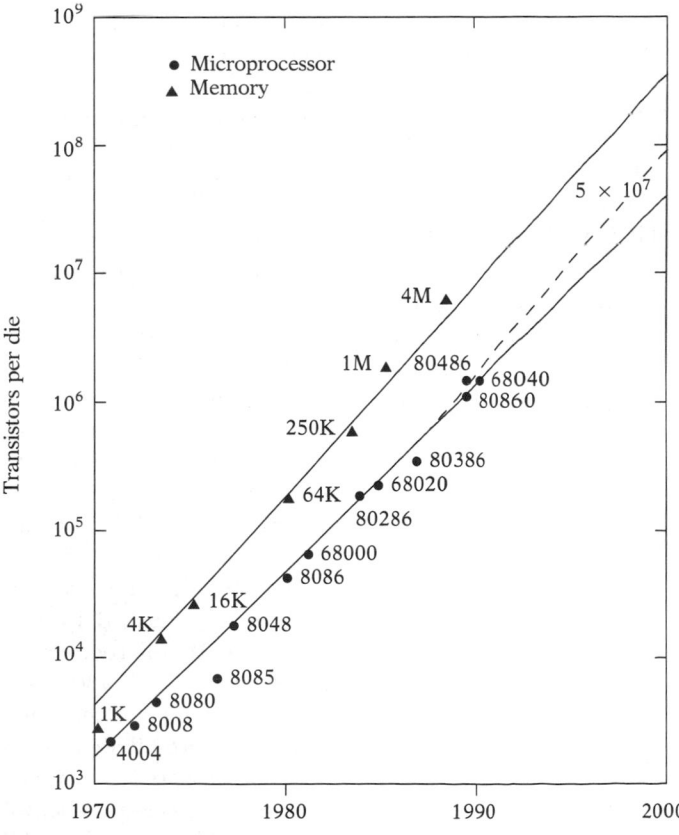

Figure 2. Almost annual doubling of transistors per chip for microprocessors and memories. The graph shows the densest memory chips and microprocessors from Intel (4044, 80xx, 80xxx) and Motorola (680xx). As microprocessors are built with more on-chip memory for fast access, the two lines will merge, as indicated by the dashed line (source: Intel Corporation).

The 80686 P6 Pentium Pro (1995) added level-2 (L2) cache on-chip and lessened pipeline delays after conditional branch instructions by speculative execution: guessing which instruction will follow a branch and starting to execute it immediately but not changing registers until the branch direction is known. The Pentium Pro did not execute its complex 80x86 family instructions directly; its decoding hardware translated them into simple instructions that pipelines could execute faster.

The Pentium II (1997) was a Pentium Pro with MMX instructions and an off-chip L2 cache, sold together on a heatsink module. Celeron (1998), a Pentium II with no L2, sold cheaply for under-$1000 PCs. It was too slow; a small on-chip L2 was added late in 1998. The Pentium III (1999) added a large on-chip L2 cache. The first 64-bit Intel processor (Itanium) was due for release in 2000.

Fig. 2 shows the growth in transistors/chip from 1970 to 2000.

OTHER EARLY MICROPROCESSOR FAMILIES

Eight-bit microprocessors were important because they were the first to address enough memory and to be powerful enough for general-purpose computing. Zilog was founded by designers of the Intel 8080A. The Z80 (1976) was upwardly compatible with the 8080A, but faster. It had more instructions, more addressing modes, and an alternate register set for fast interrupt responses. Its support chips were less expensive. It was used for most personal computers before IBM adopted the 8088 for the PC. The Z80 is still successful in embedded applications. Its descendants—(Z8, Z180, Z280 controllers; 16-bit Z8000 (1979); 32-bit Z80000— are well respected.

The Motorola 6800 (1974) was very different from the 8080. It had two accumulators, a stack pointer, and an index register (*q.v.*), but no data registers; it relied on powerful addressing modes to process data efficiently in main memory. Programs for the 6800 were more compact than for the 8080, saving expensive memory and execution time. The 6802 added a small, fast, on-chip RAM. The 6809 was the last 8-bit architecture from Motorola. It added two registers for base-page relative addressing and introduced a very sophisticated instruction set to improve code density and execution speed. The 6809 is a good example of instruction set design based on measured instruction usage patterns.

The Motorola MC68000 (1980) was significantly different. It used a 16-bit data bus to access 32-bit values and had eight data registers, eight index registers, two security levels, an orthogonal instruction set (with operand addressing modes chosen independently of the instruction), and a nonsegmented 16 MB (2^{24})

address space. It was much more elegant and powerful than the 8086 of the prior year. It was adopted for many personal computers and embedded applications. The 68010 (1982) restarted instructions after page fault interrupts to support virtual memory. The full 32-bit 68020 (1984) had a 4 GB address range, an on-chip memory cache, and many powerful new instructions and addressing modes. It became the standard CPU for high-performance Unix workstations. The 68030 (1989) added an on-chip MMU to map virtual addresses. The remarkably powerful 68040 (1990) used large on-chip caches, integrated floating-point, and aggressive pipelining to run four times faster than the 68030, but was the last of its family, which was buried by 80x86, PowerPC, and SPARC CPUs for PCs and workstations.

Although the 6800 and 8086 families prospered, 4-, 8-, and 16-bit CPUs vanished from new personal computers by 1990. Many found niches as low-cost microcontrollers.

MICROCONTROLLER FAMILIES

For microprocessors, the 1980s were a time of architectural innovation, improving performance, and market consolidation. By 1980, hundreds of types of CPU chips had flooded the market. Eight-bit microprocessors dominated, but some 16-bit minicomputer architectures had been put onto chipsets used to build single-board computers. In 1973, National Semiconductor sold the IMP-16C, the first *single-board* 16-bit microcontroller. It was followed by the Digital Equipment (DEC) LSI-11 (1975) single-board version of the popular PDP-11 minicomputer, the Data General MicroNova board (1976), and the Texas Instruments (TI) TM990 card (1979).

Single-chip microcomputers include on-chip, all CPU, memory, and I/O subsystems, permitting very small, flexible, and inexpensive control circuits for consumer products. There are many controller varieties, targeting different functionality/performance/price points. In 1974, TI introduced the first single-chip 4-bit microcomputer, the TMS1000, which at $2 was by far the most widely sold CPU in the world by 1980. The first Intel microcomputer chips were 8-bit: the 8048 (1977) with factory-masked ROM, 8748 with EPROM, and 8051 (1980). Microcomputer chips supplanted controller cards by 1980, but single-board computers reappeared in workstations in the late 1980s. Intel targeted the 16-bit 8096 (1984) and 32-bit 80960 (1987) microprocessors for fast embedded control, including automobile systems. The 80960 had on-chip floating-point, rapid context switching, instruction pipelines, superscalar execution, message passing, multiprocessing, and optional function units.

Microcontrollers based on existing microprocessors have inherently good software tools. The 68000 family includes the 68070 and 93C110 from Philips, plus the 68200 and 68300 from Motorola. Other designs focus on performance. The Harris RTX is a very fast, tiny 4,000-gate hardware implementation of Forth (*q.v.*), a popular real-time control language. Choices of on-chip support circuits and memory varieties determine suitability for many applications; many distinct controller chips coexist.

FAST REDUCED INSTRUCTION SET COMPUTER CHIPS

The late 1980s saw the rise of a new style of high performance CPUs, the single-chip RISC processors: the MIPS, Sparc, and PowerPC families. The key feature of these processors is efficient use of instruction pipelines made possible by easy-to-decode uniform code formats, large sets of registers for all arithmetic operands and results, and memory accesses limited to load and store operations. Other important features are that the entire CPU must fit on a single chip, since data exchanges are much faster on-chip than between chips; compilers must reorder instructions to keep pipelines busy; and alternative designs are evaluated by simulated execution of target programs.

The Control Data CDC 6600 supercomputer (1964) and IBM 801 chip prototype (1980) pioneered building fast computers using simplified instruction sets. The 6600 had many registers, a load–store architecture, simple three-address instructions executed in pipelines, multiple function units, and out-of-order instruction execution to avoid data conflicts. The 801 had 32 general-purpose registers, pipelined three-address single-cycle instructions, a delay slot to execute an instruction during each jump, and compiler instruction reordering. The 1981 Berkeley "Reduced Instruction Set Computer" (RISC) and 1982 Stanford "Microprocessor without Interlocked Pipe Stages" (MIPS) projects popularized simple instructions, pipelines, and code reordering. Limited to 100,000 transistors each in 1982, fast one-chip CPUs had circuit space for only the most useful instructions and hardware features. Early RISC chips had small, regular, hard-wired instruction sets, very different from the prevailing microcoded, complex instruction set computers (CISCs).

The RISC project succeeded. Hewlett-Packard began work in 1983 on a high-performance precision architecture (HPPA). Stanford engineers founded MIPS Computer Systems in 1984 and released the MIPS R2000 in 1986. In 1985, Sun Microsystems began designing its SPARC processor family based directly on the Berkeley RISC-II chip, and had CPUs by 1987. Many commercial RISC processors followed: Advanced Micro Devices (AMD) 29000 (1986), Motor-

ola 88000 (1988), Intel 80960 controller (1988), MIPS R3000 (1988), Intel 80860 graphics accelerator (1989), and the powerful "post-RISC" IBM Power-1 for the RS/6000 in 1989.

In the 1990s, RISC-style designs and shrinking IC device sizes greatly increased CPU performance: from 1.00 micron feature size (transistor length) in 1989 for the 25 MHz 32-bit CISC Intel 80486, to 0.18 microns in 1999 for the 480 MHz 64-bit RISC Sun/Texas Instruments UltraSPARC-3. IBM continued its 32-bit superscalar RS/6000 CPUs: Power-2 (1993) and Power-3 (1998), with eight function units allowing up to eight instruction completions per cycle. In 1992, IBM, Motorola, and Apple joined forces to redesign the Power-1 as a series of PowerPC CPUs to replace the 68040 and 80486 processors in Apple and IBM PCs: 601 (1993), 603 (1994), 604 (1995), and 750, marketed by Apple as G3, the third-generation PowerPC (1998).

In 1992, Digital Equipment (DEC) released its pioneering fast superscalar 64-bit RISC chip, the Alpha 21064 running at 150 MHz, then the 366 MHz 21164 (1995)—rated at 1,000 MIPS—and the 525 MHz 21264 (1998). In 1998, Compaq bought DEC in order to own Alpha. From the first, Alpha CPUs avoided the branch delay slots of MIPS and SPARC chips by speculative execution: guessing what instruction will follow a branch and starting to execute it immediately, but without changing register values until the branch direction is known. Delay slots work poorly for superscalar execution.

MIPS had a 64-bit R4000 chip in 1991, but its superscalar R10000 (1996) with on-chip FPUs was much faster. Sun Microsystems (design) and Texas Instruments (fabrication) released their 64-bit RISC Super-SPARC chip prematurely in 1992; it was slower even than Intel 80x86 CPUs. Their Russian-designed 64-bit UltraSPARC chip (1995) was much faster. It was superscalar (4 instructions issued per cycle) and had specialized instructions for moving I/O data blocks without disturbing the cache and for 3D graphics calculations.

FAST PROCESSORS AT THE END OF THE CENTURY

By 1999, the label RISC was a misnomer. Fast CPU chips held so many transistors—16 million in the Alpha 21264—that they could have the pipelines and general register sets characteristic of RISC chips as well as large CISC-like instruction sets and microcode to emulate older CPUs: PowerPC rapidly executes 68040 code (*see* EMULATION).

The PC and workstation processor market in 1999 was dominated by 32-bit 80x86 chips from Intel and three minor competitors: Advanced Micro Devices (AMD), Cyrix, and Integrated Device Technology (IDT). A few high-performance 64-bit alternatives remained: 525 MHz Compaq Alpha 21264 (1998), 480 MHz Ultra-SPARC-3 (1999), and IBM-proprietary 200 MHz Power3 (1998) processors. The 32-bit 400 MHz Motorola PowerPC G4 (1999) was used in one PC in 20. Its fast AltiVec instructions render images 10 times faster than a G3. It is poised to supplant MIPS CPUs in game controllers.

Fast CPUs were a small-volume, but high-revenue part of the microprocessor market. In 1998, four billion microcontroller chips sold for $13B (at an average price of $3) plus one billion fast CPUs for $19B—75% from Intel (at a $20 average price).

The exponential IC density curve has slowed slightly to two years per doubling, but every decade seems to show another 10 to 15 years of growth left. Near-future CPUs will use smaller devices, more parallel execution, and larger caches on-chip to execute 20 times faster. Cryogenic cooling may further increase CPU clock rates to 25,000 MHz (25 GHz) by 2010.

Applications

Microprocessors are most visible as the central processors of general-purpose computing systems. Almost all computers, even highly parallel and expensive supercomputers, use commercial microprocessor CPUs because of their unmatched performance to cost ratio. Only the very highest performance computers have architectures too complex or use implementation technologies too sparse to fit the CPU on one chip. In 1999, only a few supercomputers used fast gallium arsenide (GaAs) circuits to maintain a lead. In 1999 most techniques used to improve supercomputers for the previous 30 years were being implemented in high-end silicon-based CPU chips.

The great majority of microcomputers are dedicated to controlling everything from consumer appliances to cars to space probes. In embedded applications, microprocessors serve as cheap replacements for otherwise very complicated control circuitry and often offer functionality not feasible any other way.

Microprocessors are playing an increasingly important role in transportation industries, from automobiles to airplanes to traffic regulation. The automotive industry has found a number of uses for microprocessors: controlling fuel and air delivery to the engine for optimal performance, fuel efficiency, and exhaust emissions; monitoring brakes to prevent skidding (anti-lock braking systems—ABS); controlling shock absorbers to give more comfort under varying road conditions and better handling by leaning into turns; tracking road surface markings to warn when a car strays from its lane; and processing traffic information to recommend shortcuts that avoid traffic jams. Micro-

processors also regulate traffic by counting local vehicles and adjusting signal light timings accordingly. In aircraft, there is an even greater reliance on lightweight microprocessors. They monitor and operate many flight systems, like inertial navigation, and report status to flight computers that display summaries on video screens. New planes increasingly "fly-by-wire" under direct computer control.

Personal electronics is a ready match for microprocessors. Toddlers of today have cuddly toys that talk and show images. Their older siblings can build mechanical pets that roam around and come when called. Many household electrical appliances such as washers and dryers have replaced complex electromechanical systems with simpler and more reliable electronic ones. Digital keypads on microwave ovens allow programmed cooking sequences; an unattended video cassette recorder (VCR) can tape several programs at different times on different channels; a digital chess game can provide a challenging opponent; digital wristwatches can calculate and play music; and telephones can store frequently dialed numbers. There are exercise stations that report calorie losses and monitor heartbeat to help maintain optimal exercise rates. Devices such as compact disc players and cellular phones, autofocus cameras, hand-held calculators, television game machines, and personal computers have been made possible by inexpensive microprocessors. Computer-controlled active jewelry is imminent and peek-a-boo clothing will come eventually.

Industry has embraced microprocessor technology. On the factory floor, microcomputers store shapes to guide automated manufacturing machinery, control component placement, guide robot arms that insert components, and keep track of parts inventory (*see* ROBOTICS). In buildings, microprocessors control air conditioners, turn off lights in empty rooms, and maintain security by logging all door openings and limiting access.

In offices, they handle small business accounting and inventory, generate payrolls, and run word processors. In home offices, they control personal computers, facsimile (fax) machines, and modems (*q.v.*) that increasingly let people work in pleasant locations instead of commuting to centralized offices. On the salesroom floor, microprocessors scan product bar codes, update inventory databases from point-of-sale terminals, and enable just-in-time inventory methods to keep overheads low. In the field, microprocessors control instruments and log data to be relayed to larger computers. In medicine, microprocessor-controlled scanners generate three-dimensional images of the body. In outer space, microcomputers control satellites, telescopes, and interplanetary probes.

Future applications will be even more wide ranging. The most interesting and revolutionary will be ones related to information management and sharing among a mobile population. Microcomputers connected to the Internet can distribute information, make large central databases easily accessible, and allow a wide exchange of ideas. Radio-linked, notebook-sized computer displays and wall-sized flat screens may supersede printed media. Palm-sized personal assistants with cell-phone modems already let travelers stay linked to the Internet (*q.v.*) to find local maps, exchange email, and receive interesting news from electronic distribution services. Pocket-sized cell-phones are ubiquitous. Infrared emitting badges allow office computer systems to find any worker rapidly. Virtual reality (*q.v.*) displays and video cameras will soon be mounted in everyday eyeglasses. High-definition television and three-dimensional virtual-reality extensions will be heavily dependent on fast microprocessors for local reconstruction of compactly encoded complex images.

Microcomputers and microprocessors are leading an epochal revolution in manufacturing, communications, information management, and personal services. As microprocessors grow in importance, they are shrinking in size and becoming nearly invisible parts of tools, appliances, and homes. They are vanishing into the walls of modern buildings, much as the indispensable electrical power network begun in 1900 has become an invisible part of the cultural fabric. Microprocessors are profoundly affecting society.

Bibliography

1977. Toong, H. M. D. "Microprocessors," *Scientific American* (Special Issue on Microelectronics), *237*, *3*, 146–161.

1989. Gelsinger, P. P., Gargini, P. A., Parker, G. H., and Yin, A. Y. C. "Microprocessors Circa 2000," *IEEE Spectrum*, **26**, *10* (October), 43–47.

1989. Slater, M. *Microprocessor-Based Design: A Comprehensive Guide to Effective Hardware Design.* Upper Saddle River, NJ: Prentice Hall.

1996. Hennessy, J. L., and Patterson, D. A. *Computer Architecture: A Quantitative Approach*, 2nd Ed. San Francisco: Morgan Kaufmann.

Websites

Bayco, J. Great Microprocessors of the Past and Present. `http://www.cs.uregina.ca/~bayko/cpu.html`. Insightful vignettes on the distinguishing features of 40 great processors and their kin.

Burd, T. CPU Info Center. `http://bwrc.eecs.berkeley.edu/CIC/`. Archive site with Web links for all major microprocessors and latest Silicon Valley Industry news.

Gröner, J. Johannes' Computer Time Line. `http://home.t-online.de/home/Johannes.Groener/inhalt.htm`. Very complete list of computer names, dates, and makers worldwide, mainly in English.

Karbo, M. B. Click and Learn. `http://karbosguide.com`. An illustrated tutorial on the history and organization of Intel PCs. Easy reading.

Polsson, K. Chronology of Events in the History of Microcomputers. `http://www.islandnet.com/~kpolsson/comphist.htm`. A detailed list of computer industry events with no explanations.

Slater, M. *et al. MicroDesign Resources, Home for Microprocessor Report.* `http://www.mdronline.com`. Insider bible for Silicon Valley computer industry; older articles are free.

Larry D. Wittie

MICROPROGRAMMING

> For articles on related subjects *see* COMPUTER ARCHITECTURE; CYCLE TIME; EMULATION; FIRMWARE; HOST SYSTEM; INSTRUCTION SET; LOGICAL DESIGN; READ-ONLY MEMORY; REDUCED INSTRUCTION SET COMPUTER; and WILKES, MAURICE V.

Microprogramming is a technique used by designers to implement the control functions of a computer. Usually, it uses a read-only memory (ROM) to implement the instruction decoder. Microprogramming, as originally conceived by M. V. Wilkes in 1951, is a specific technique "to provide a systematic approach and an orderly approach to designing the control section of any computing system." In Wilkes' context, the term *control* is taken to mean the interpretation and execution of a machine instruction.

Microprogramming was widely used throughout the 1970s and 1980s as the preferred implementation of the instruction *decoder*. The IBM System/360/370 (*q.v.*) series and the DEC VAX systems are typical examples of microprogrammed control. The opcode of an instruction contained in the instruction register was used as an address (or part of an address) to a read-only control store. The contents of this address would define the first of a sequence of microinstructions or control words which specified the control values that implemented the required register-to-register data movements and ALU (*q.v.*) operations required for instruction execution. The regular implementation of the decoder through the use of storage provided a convenient way to change an instruction set by changing control store contents and also provided a debugging (*q.v.*) facility for designers. The availability of an extendible control memory also allowed for the execution of multiple separate instruction sets in a process called *emulation* of instruction sets. The IBM System/360/370 provided emulation of older instruction sets including the IBM 7090 and IBM 1401 (*q.v.*).

As the functions for microprogram control store increased, implementations changed so that the control store consisted of both a read-only portion and a read–write portion. This enabled certain microprogramming routines to overwrite a portion of the control store and facilitated functions such as microdiagnostics and fault location, as well as support for complex operating system functions and security checking.

There are a number of reasons why the microprogramming technique has fallen into disuse, but a major reason is speed. The access time required to retrieve data from a large control memory limits the cycle time (*q.v.*) of faster processors, and hence the attractiveness of the technique overall.

In early implementations, no speed problems developed because main memory was quite slow with a cycle time of the order of 10 μs, and the diode matrix had an access time of under 0.5 μs. The ratio of control access time to the main memory access time was an important one; namely, as long as there was a large number of internal cycles in each memory cycle, the microprogramming task was relatively simple and straightforward. One register-to-register transformation was performed per internal cycle, and performance was essentially limited by the main memory cycle. As the main memory access time decreased, however, microprogramming techniques became correspondingly more sophisticated. If only one or two internal machine cycles are available for each main memory cycle, it is necessary to have multiple data transfers in each machine cycle. That is, the microinstruction has to control simultaneously a number of resources internal to the system. This gave rise to a type of internal parallelism within the processor.

The second generation of microprogrammed systems was distinguished by its small number of internal machine cycles per main memory cycle. By the late 1960s, main memory access time (*q.v.*) had dropped below 1 μs, yet the technology for control store had not noticeably improved, and the best access for read-only store varied between 200 and 400 ns. In addition, the read-only storage technologies tended to be exotic. The technology was not common with any other part of the machine and not always reliable. However, by this time the arguments for using microprogramming went well beyond the reasons cited by Wilkes. In the beginning of 1964, with the announcement of the IBM System 360, an important application for microprogramming was added—emulation of multiple machines on a single host system. This was intended to make the customer's transition from an old to a new system much more palatable, in that the customer could, with one system, support old software as well as develop new applications with new programming languages and facilities (Husson, 1970).

The third generation of microprogramming dates from about 1970, with the advent of fast read–write control store. The development of bipolar monolithic technology created a storage medium with the same access time as combinational decisions, since they were made out of essentially the same material. The writable capability of control store represented an important transition, since the control store became a true member of the memory hierarchy. It was unnecessary for control store to contain dynamically all interpretations for each and every instruction for each and every machine that must be emulated. Rather, emulated routines could be overlaid, as required, into a common microstorage. Similarly, the same storage could be used to hold parameters and buffer data values. Where the flexibility of high-performance operation over a variety of machine languages was not required, the data buffering function could be split off into a separate memory, again with the same technology. Here, references to main memory are anticipated by transferring blocks of data into the buffer, giving rise to cache memory (*q.v.*).

After the mid-1980s, the technology had evolved so that the density of control store implementations became a problem for single-chip processors. The area occupied by a control store or microprogrammed implementation of a decoder exceeded that of a hardwired implementation. Additionally, the area budgets for processor implementations were tight. Still the Motorola 68000 family of processors used microprogrammed control in the late 1980s as logic density on chips improved. Motorola cited the importance of flexible extensions of the evolving instruction set as a major factor (Hilf and Nausch, 1989).

In the 1990s, the Intel Pentium processors had a vestigial form of microcode. Their instructions were composed of micro-operations, but typical instructions had three or four micro-operations that were generated directly by the instruction decoder. In the most complex cases, the micro-operations were fetched from a small microcode control store and were thus microprogrammed. In general, however, current processors use hardwired control circuits.

Bibliography

1970. Husson, S. *Microprogramming: Principles and Practices.* Upper Saddle River, NJ: Prentice Hall.
1988. Habib, S. *Microprogramming and Firmware Engineering Methods.* New York: Van Nostrand Reinhold.
1989. Hilf, W., and Nausch, A. *The M68000 Family*, Vol 1. Upper Saddle River, NJ: Prentice Hall.

Website

1999. Smotherman, M. *A Brief History of Microprogramming.* http://www.cs.clemson.edu/~mark/uprog.html.

Michael J. Flynn

MICROSOFT

For articles on related subjects *see* ENTREPRENEURS; and DIGITAL COMPUTERS, HISTORY OF: SINCE 1950.

Excepting only IBM, no company in the history of the computer industry has been so much written about as *Microsoft*, and few companies have been so completely identified with their founder. Microsoft's Bill Gates (born 1955) has been the subject of intense media interest, largely on account of his personal wealth (said to be about $50 billion of Microsoft stock in 1999), but also because of his reputation as a visionary and information-age pundit.

Microsoft was founded by Gates and his partner Paul Allen in 1975. The company initially developed an interpreter for the Basic (*q.v.*) programming language for the then nascent personal computer. For the first several years of its existence, Microsoft was a relatively obscure company specializing in the development of programming systems for personal computers, and by the start of the 1980s was still a small company with just 25 employees and a turnover of $2.5 million. In July 1980, however, in one of the most celebrated coups in the history of computing, Microsoft secured a contract with IBM to develop the operating system for the personal computer that IBM then had under development. Microsoft retained the right to market that system independently as MS-DOS. When the IBM PC was launched in summer 1981, it legitimized the personal computer for use in large-scale organizations, and quickly established an industry standard. IBM PC "clones" were produced by many other manufacturers and a copy of MS-DOS was supplied with most of them. Microsoft grew rapidly on the basis of its operating system sales and, when it made its initial public offering in 1986, it had over a thousand employees and its market value exceeded $600 million. The following year, Gates was lauded as America's youngest billionaire.

The revenues from the sales of MS-DOS enabled Microsoft to develop PC applications software, such as a word processor and a spreadsheet. Success usually eluded Microsoft on the first release of these new products, but the revenue stream from the sales of MS-DOS enabled the company to survive these initial failures, and success usually came with the second or third release. In November 1985, Microsoft released the first version of Windows, its graphical user interface and operating system for the IBM-compatible PC. Microsoft was one of a number of software companies attempting to produce a Macintosh-like interface for the PC in the mid-1980s, but none was successful at that time. Microsoft persisted with the venture, however, and achieved market success with the release of Windows version 3.1 in 1990. By this time Microsoft had become a major company with over 5000 employees and revenues of $1 billion. In 1993 Microsoft released Windows NT, a robust networked operating system, with the aim of competing with Unix (*q.v.*) and other products in the corporate operating system market.

During the first half of the 1990s, Microsoft achieved dominance of the two key markets for desktop software: operating systems and office applications, in both of which it was reported to have an 80–90% market share. Microsoft also began to diversify into recreational software (notably its *Encarta* CD-ROM encyclopedia), and into computer services through its online service, the Microsoft Network (MSN). In August 1995, Microsoft was perhaps at the peak of its powers with the launch of its new Windows 95 operating system, for which the publicity alone was said to have cost of the order of $200 million. By the end of the 1995–1996 financial year, Microsoft had over twenty thousand employees and revenues exceeding $8 billion, and its market valuation comfortably exceeded that of IBM.

Microsoft has been keenly studied by computer industry watchers, not only for its leadership of the PC software industry, but also for its novel software development processes and management techniques. Microsoft has eschewed many of the long-standing practices of the established software industry, such as rigid specifications, formal project management techniques, and elaborate quality assurance programs. By contrast, the company has developed a flexible, user-centered approach in place of rigid specification. It uses small programming teams and the discipline of the "daily build"—producing a complete working version of a product daily during its development—to achieve project convergence. The result has been to produce richly featured software that is sometimes late in delivery and sometimes underperforms in terms of speed and reliability. The market has thus far been willing to live with these shortcomings for the benefits of a high degree of functionality.

Microsoft's managerial practices have been much commented upon, particularly its lack of organizational hierarchy, and Gates's intimate personal control over all aspects of the business. Outside the information technology industry, Microsoft's elitist human resources policy of "hiring smarts" has been of particular interest. Microsoft—often Gates personally—has sought out the brightest and best for its employees: the company has attracted star players from the existing software industry for senior positions, and has recruited top graduates from American university campuses for its junior positions. Many Microsoft employees have become rich from stock options. This had made the company extremely attractive to young professionals; Microsoft is able to recruit only a small fraction of the tens of thousands of job seekers who make applications for employment each year. There have been some hostile press reports of exploitation and burn-out among Microsoft employees, but this has not been substantiated by the more analytical literature.

Microsoft's dominance of the PC software market has attracted antitrust concern since 1989. Underlying this concern is the new "information economics," which theorizes that because of the zero marginal cost of software products, natural monopolies tend to result and the rewards for the dominant producers are immense. Gates developed an early intuitive mastery of this phenomenon, for which he uses the term "positive feedback." In 1994 Microsoft entered a consent degree with the Department of Justice, by which it revised its charging policies for operating systems bundled with newly manufactured PCs. The following year it voluntarily withdrew its takeover bid for Intuit, manufacturer of the *Quicken* home finance software, amid speculation that such a strategic move might lead to Microsoft's eventual dominance of electronic commerce.

Microsoft's extraordinary success has inevitably attracted fear and loathing as much as admiration. The emergence of the Internet as a new computing paradigm around 1993, and the success of Netscape Communications Corporation in capturing the market for browser software, was seen as a long overdue counterbalance to Microsoft's hegemony of desktop software. However, Netscape's monopoly of the browser market did not last for long, and even Microsoft's most ardent critics have had to admire the speed and urgency with which the company came to terms with the Internet, first producing its own browser, Explorer, and then reshaping many of its software products to accommodate the new mode of computing.

In 1997 Microsoft "bundled" Explorer into all versions of its Windows operating system so that anyone who installed Windows automatically received an installed ready-to-use Explorer. The antitrust division of the US Department of Justice quickly filed suit against Microsoft claiming, among other things, that its purpose in combining Windows with Explorer was to undermine Netscape and attempt to put it out of business. In the subsequent trial, which began in 1998, the government's case, based in important measure on internal Microsoft email, was strenuously opposed by Microsoft. However, on 5 November 1999, Judge Thomas Penfield Jackson issued "findings of fact" which constituted a severe and wide-ranging denunciation of Microsoft's business practices. The eventual result is still unclear but an April 2000 ruling that Microsoft has violated anti-trust laws is likely to make it change its practices and a breakup of the company into several smaller ones is possible.

Bibliography

1992. Ichbiah, D., and Knepper, S. L. *The Making of Microsoft.* Rocklin, CA: Prima Publishing.
1995. Cusumano, M. A., and Selby, R. W. *Microsoft Secrets: How the World's Most Powerful Software Company Creates Technology, Shapes Markets, and Manages People.* New York: The Free Press.
1995. Gates, W. H., with Myhrvold, N., and Rinearson, P. *The Road Ahead.* New York: Viking Penguin.
1996. Stross, R. E. *The Microsoft Way: The Real Story of How the Company Outsmarts Its Competition.* Reading, MA: Addison-Wesley.
1998. Selby, R. W. *Microsoft Secrets: How the World's Most Powerful Software Company Creates Technology, Shapes Markets, and Manages People.* New York: Simon and Schuster.

Martin Campbell-Kelly

MILLENIUM BUG

See Y2K Problem.

MINICOMPUTER

For articles on related subjects *see* ADDRESSING; COMPUTER SYSTEM; DIGITAL COMPUTERS, HISTORY OF: SINCE 1950; INSTRUCTION SET; MICROPROCESSORS AND MICROCOMPUTERS; MICROPROGRAMMING; and PERSONAL COMPUTING.

While historically significant, the *minicomputer* has been largely replaced by the personal computer. It was developed at a time when expensive, large mainframes (*q.v.*) could be replaced by smaller digital computers whose price and functionality were sufficient to meet the needs of smaller applications (such as for data acquisition and control). However, the minicomputer's capability lies below that of today's workstation (*q.v.*) and is only marginally superior to a high-end personal computer.

Early workstations differed from minicomputers not in the processing engine (which was typically a microprocessor) but rather their graphical orientation and dependence on a network that supplied missing resources, such as hard disks and printers. At the other extreme, personal computers were first designed with 8- and 16-bit microprocessors that could address limited amounts of memory, store data on small capacity floppies, and display data in either a monochrome text mode or a limited graphics format (four colors and limited resolution).

The developmental history of minicomputer systems is paralleled by the later development of personal computers. Both types of computer eventually evolved to include high-resolution graphics display devices and fast network connections, along with increasingly larger main memories and hard disks. The minicomputer was different in that it was often relegated to the task of either providing time-sharing services to a large class of users, or was used as a standalone real-time processor. The personal computer has largely remained a single-user system. Also, with the advent of very large and fast hard disks, not available even on the later minicomputer systems, the personal computer has also taken on the role of an information or file server.

Minicomputers could be broadly classified as having 12-, 16-, 18-, 24-, or 32-bit word lengths with memory sizes of 128 MB to one gigabyte provided in modules of 256 KB or 1 MB. Nearly all minicomputers employed a parallel internal processor structure with a high-speed bus and a clock rate of 4–40 MHz. The basic configuration ranged in price from $4,000–$500,000, with the cost of peripheral devices usually far outstripping the cost of the machine. The use of low-cost LSI and VLSI logic removed many of the initial design constraints, such as:

1. Limited addressing capability

2. Lack of general-purpose registers and accumulators

3. Elementary I/O processing and devices

4. Limited interrupt schemes

Although it became increasingly difficult to distinguish differences in the range of applications found on minicomputers and larger-scale (mainframe) computers, there are some differences in usage which are worth mentioning.

1. For minicomputers with word lengths shorter than 32 bits, precision was limited without the use of multiple-precision software.

2. Although high-level languages were increasingly available, the use of assembly language for writing user application-specific programs was more common than on mainframes.

3. Although some minis ran in a closed-shop production environment, many were still run in an open-shop environment, with the user acting as operator, programmer, and application analyst. A typical installation is shown in Fig.1.

4. A substantial number of minis operated in a dedicated environment for which the system had been specifically configured. Today we call these embedded systems (*q.v.*), and they consist of microcontrollers such as those found in automobiles and missiles.

5. For other than standard applications, the mini user had to be more sophisticated and ingenious, since minicomputer operating systems did not necessarily provide the kind of environment (e.g. real-time) that a mini was often used for.

Figure 1. An HP 3000 minicomputer system (courtesy of Hewlett-Packard).

The trend of the minicomputer market shifted from an original equipment manufacturer (OEM) to an end-user market. As a result, more sophisticated software was developed, requiring additional hardware, such as memory management, user/supervisor modes, and multiple communication port boards. This allowed the user to buy a turnkey minicomputer system that had a complete operating system capable of supporting one or many users simultaneously. Indeed, when 32-bit machines were introduced, they looked increasingly like their mainframe counterparts.

The languages available on these machines usually included Fortran, Basic, APL, Cobol, PL/I, C, and Pascal, besides other proprietary dialects of these standards. As minicomputer systems evolved through new generations, the mini and large computer began to appear as one, at least from the point of view of the applications programmer.

Applications

The greatest use of minicomputers was in areas other than general-purpose computing. These areas included:

1. Industrial applications, such as control of power generation, petrochemical systems, data acquisition, and testing of equipment and devices.

2. Biomedical control for experiment monitoring.

3. As a part of larger computer systems which required communication and peripheral control, such as data concentrators, satellite peripherals, and intelligent terminals.

4. Intelligent graphics terminals and interactive graphics systems that were part of general-purpose, graphics-oriented computing.

5. Microprogrammable minicomputer systems that were capable of being tailored to specific applications and environments.

One important aspect of minicomputer design was the large-scale use of microprogramming (*q.v.*). The value of the microprogrammable machine could be found in its compatibility with other different machines by emulation (*q.v.*) of the same instruction set, in its ability to allow the user to tailor a machine at the most primitive level to accommodate particular requirements, or in its ability to allow the user the flexibility of experimenting with new ideas and designs.

Another distinction occurred between microprogrammable minis and minis with read-only memories (ROM—*q.v.*). Although ROMs are often used to hold microprograms, they could also be used to store programs for minicomputer applications that did not change and where the instructions could be locked into memory, providing decreased memory cycle time and greater integrity against accidental destruction. Many of these same features are found in today's microcomputers and microcontrollers.

Bibliography

1979. Eckhouse, R., and Morris, R. *Minicomputer Systems: Organization, Programming and Applications (PDP-11)*. Upper Saddle River, NJ: Prentice Hall.
1989. Levy, H. and Eckhouse, R. *Computer Programming and Architecture: the VAX*, 2nd Ed. Bedford, MA: Digital Press.
1999. Tanenbaum, A. *Structured Computer Organization*, 4th Ed. Upper Saddle River, NJ: Prentice Hall.

Richard H. Eckhouse

MINITEL

For articles on related subjects *see* BULLETIN BOARD; ELECTRONIC MAIL; VIDEOTEX; and WORLD WIDE WEB.

The *Minitel* terminal is the visible part of the Teletel service provided by the French telephone company, France Telecom. It consists of a small, low-cost terminal with a 9″ (23 cm) screen (320×240 graphic resolution) and a keyboard. The screen can display 25 lines of 40 videotex characters (alphanumeric and semi-graphic) or 80 ISO characters. It contains a modem (1200 cps originally but 9600 cps in more recent models) and can be directly plugged into a telephone outlet. A specialized but very small printer can be connected to print copies of the screen. Recent models include a memory card reader, which provides for secure money transactions, and can display photographs with 64 gray levels. A telephone with a Minitel screen is also available.

Using this terminal, present in almost every home in France and in many public places, people can browse the national phone book; order goods from telemarketing companies; consult train and plane timetables, order and pay for tickets to cinemas, theaters, trains or planes; manage their bank accounts and make money transfers; send telegrams or faxes, read news, register for exams or at universities; get their horoscopes or weather forecasts; have some text translated; obtain information about legal matters; send and read electronic mail; obtain the optimal road route from one place to another; participate in forums or chat rooms, and so on. The service book lists about 20,000 service providers.

The first experiments using Minitel were made in 1982. In 1983, France Telecom began creation of an "electronic phone book" which was extended to the whole of France by 1987. Minitels were provided to customers free of charge in place of the paper telephone book. This ensured a very large distribution of the terminals and of the concept. In 1984, the "kiosque" service was created by which a part of the phone bill is paid to the service provider, according to several cost rates, from $.05 per minute to about $1.50. This offered a very simple way to provide the various services mentioned above, completely avoiding the trouble of preliminary subscription. The first important uses, not anticipated by the developers, were mainly forums and chatlines, especially sex-oriented ones, but the current use is completely different.

In a country with 60 million inhabitants, 14.2 million are Minitel users, making 1.13 billion calls per year (which does not include use of the online phone book). The satisfaction rate is more than 90%. The phone book service provides access to a database of 24 million entries, with 40,000 updates every day and a natural language interface.

The success of the Minitel system stems from its initially free distribution, and from the simplicity of the kiosque service. Its main advantages, especially with regard to Web services, are that it is almost ubiquitous and extremely low-cost (the current monthly rental for the best model is about $3.50), requires no specific skills, and provides satisfactory performance and reliability. Its main drawbacks are its poor graphics capabilities, its incompatibility with other standards, and its limitation to the French market, although it is now possible to access foreign phone books. In the future, unless a link to the Internet (*q.v.*) is established, it will probably disappear.

Olivier Lecarme

MIS

See MANAGEMENT INFORMATION SYSTEMS.

MOBILE COMPUTING

For articles on related subjects *see* COMMUNICATIONS AND COMPUTERS; NETWORKS, COMPUTER; and PORTABLE COMPUTERS.

Mobile computing is computing using a device that can communicate through a wireless channel. The field of mobile computing is as broad as traditional computing. Consumers expect the same convenience and computing power in the mobile device as in the computer which sits on the desk. Furthermore, mobility opens up new venues for interesting and unique products and services. Freedom from geographic constraints can allow a more effective, convenient, and timely use of computing and communication. As people tend to think and work in places other than at their office desks, mobile computing lets the computer be used as a tool where it is needed, not where it is tied by a wire. Examples include the executive working on a laptop while traveling and the field engineer having remote electronic access to technical documentation and diagnostics, as well as emerging applications such as automated inventory or baggage checking with RFID (Radio Frequency Identification Devices), and location-dependent services such as local maps or weather reports.

The combination of the rapid reduction in computing device sizes, small portable displays and wireless networking capabilities has fostered the growing interest in *wearable computers*. Emerging experimental systems are small enough to be mounted on belts or helmets and often provide as much processing and networking power as their desktop counterparts. Besides the obvious capabilities for browsing the World Wide Web (*q.v.*) while performing mundane tasks, these "wearables" foster the creation of computer-mediated reality. Applications such as technicians having field manuals projected through glasses while they are working on a device, and computer-assisted facial recognition for instantly matching contact information with faces are just two examples of applications motivated by these devices. Similar applications have been proposed as computer resources for the disabled (*see* DISABLED, COMPUTERS AND THE). For example, there have been experiments with a wearable computer equipped with a camera and running a neural network (*q.v.*) program to recognize American Sign Language (ASL) and translate it into English for the benefit of the wearer who does not know ASL. Such wearable computers could also draw on the resources of more powerful ones through an Internet (*q.v.*) connection.

Several years ago mobile computing was defined in terms of the laptops used. However, this traditional view has changed significantly. Cellular phones already allow Web browsing and email reception, palmtop computers come with scaled-down versions of desktop operating systems and applications, and RFID devices provide intelligent communication and computing power with nearly any type of object. This myriad of new devices spans the technological and budgetary spectrums.

The explosion in mobile computing has been made possible through advances in certain key technological areas. Consider the relationships between mobility, portability, ergonomics, and cost. For example, in order to make a device portable it must be small and lightweight, which precludes the use of most standard hard drive and keyboard designs. Second, a fundamental requirement of today's computer is network connectivity. This generally calls for radio-frequency wireless communications for mobile devices. Although infrared mobile computer communications can also be used, interference from the Sun as well as the difficulty of non-line-of-sight communications make radio-frequency the preferred method for location-independent mobile communications. Third and most important are power considerations. Mobility requires a portable power source: a battery. Since battery power depends on size and weight, it is essential that all the parts of the mobile device are power-efficient. As battery capacities are not expected to increase by more than 30% in the near future (Powers, 1995), while computing capabilities and features have ever-increasing expectations, power efficiency has become a fundamental technology.

Mobility, Portability, and Utility

Mobile computing has benefited greatly from the advances in many areas of technology. High-density VLSI fabrication techniques, heat dissipation, and increased hard drive densities are examples of progress seen on the desktop which have also boosted the feasibility of mobile computing. The following are some of the more important areas of future device design (Harris *et al.*, 1995):

◆ *Display devices* Mobile devices which provide interaction with people require some sort of display device for feedback. In laptop computers, the design goal is usually to have displays which can provide the same resolution, refresh rate, and color capabilities as the desktop version in a screen which is less than an inch thick. Color liquid crystal is the most popular for this use but requires about 50% of the power of the entire mobile. Other mobile devices, such as Apple's Newton, are experimenting with different types of display designed specifically for their applications.

◆ *Integrated circuits* The most important part of the mobile computer, the CPU, is about the size of a thumbnail. Even with this high level of integration, advances are still being achieved in wireless transmitters, where items such as inductors are especially difficult to fabricate on a silicon die. Power also becomes a major issue, since the power required by the chip increases with the clock frequency.

◆ *Hard drive and other storage* As with integrated circuits, the density of hard drives has increased dramatically through the years. Typical methods to reduce the power consumed by these is to stop the rotation of the disk platter when it is not in use. Solid-state storage devices such as *flash memory* (a kind of reprogrammable ROM—*q.v.*) have also become very popular for mass storage as they require very low amounts of power and physical space.

◆ *Input devices* Input devices must also become smaller for the sake of mobility. Unlike traditional phones, where the minimum size is limited only by the ear-to-mouth distance, the input and output facilities of mobile computers still need to be large enough to be convenient to operate. One method of coping with this constraint is to combine the input and output facilities into a touch screen, such as the Apple Newton and AT&T's EO.

Mobile Networking

From the emergence of network-oriented languages such as Java (*q.v.*) to the legislatively encouraged convergence of communication technologies, communications has become an essential requirement of computing today. Mobile computing is no exception to this, with the additional challenge of utilizing the radio-frequency bandwidth (*q.v.*). When radio frequency signals are transmitted, they are reflected, refracted, and scattered by many objects on their way to the receiver. The resulting received signal is a combination of all of these paths, so that the phase and amplitude of the received signal can change drastically from even slight movements of the mobile or the surrounding objects. This time-varying random process, termed *multipath fading*, creates a potentially very high error rate on data being transferred to the mobile device, which can be significantly worse than that encountered in wired networks (Pahlavan and Levesque, 1995). There are a variety of methods used to combat these effects, including special error correcting and detecting codes (*q.v.*) added to each packet, spreading the packet's bits across multiple packets or frequencies, and enhanced modulation schemes.

There are three basic methods to connect a wireless computer to the rest of the world. All of these assume the existence of a wired base station infrastructure. Satellite communication may be possible as well, but it is typically extremely power-intensive. The first method is to use a modem (*q.v.*) over a voice-grade cellular phone. This is analogous to the way most people connect to the Internet (*q.v.*) from their homes by dialing to an Internet Service Provider (ISP) over a standard voice-grade line. Second, Mobitex and ARDIS are two examples of dedicated packet data networks which are emerging to meet the demand for higher efficiency and data rates than analog modems over radio can provide. Lastly, a hybrid of these two approaches uses the cellular networks designed for voice for transmitting packet data (*see* PACKET SWITCHING). CDPD (Cellular Digit Packet Data) is a system which uses idle voice channels on the analog AMPS voice cellular system to transmit data. Additionally, the newest digital cellular systems such as GSM (Global System for Mobile Communications) also include provisions for multiplexing packet data for transmission with digitized speech. Communication between mobile nodes without a base station as an intermediary is also possible and is termed *ad hoc* (improvised) networking. This method requires that some or all of the mobile nodes act as packet routers, and that the network protocols be robust enough to handle frequent, random topology changes as the nodes move (Corson and Macker, 1997).

In traditional desktop computing, the topology of the network is static. The physical location of the machine is encoded into its network address in protocols (*q.v.*) such as TCP/IP (*q.v.*). In the mobile network, the topology can be constantly changing as the devices move from cell to cell. The questions of how to change routing policies, update node addressing, and maintain mobile device location information are actively researched areas. An example of a protocol which does this while attempting to maintain compatibility with the existing Internet protocols is Mobile IP (Perkins, 1998).

The severely limited bandwidth is another fundamental challenge that mobile communications must consider. The part of the radio frequency spectrum usable for communications is limited and must be shared with television, radio, military, satellite communications, and many other services. Therefore, the frequency band available for mobile computer communication is extremely small when compared with that of a wire connected to a desktop computer. The challenge to mobile computing is to maintain high data rates in the presence of high errors while still maintaining fair access to a multitude of subscribers.

It is important that the wireless communication link not drastically deplete the mobile computer of its power.

Two areas are actively addressed: reducing the power used by the transceiver circuitry when it is on, or simply turning the transceiver off when it is not expected to be used. The latter method affects the mobile network in other ways, such as adding to the amount of delay experienced by a packet that is to be transmitted from the base station. Energy-conserving protocols (*q.v.*) such as those in Chlamtac *et al.* (1998) are designed to allow the mobile node to turn "off" the transceiver at deterministic times such that the base station can predict when the mobile is capable of receiving a packet. In the presence of a potentially very high node density and nonuniform traffic, the protocols allow a variable trade-off between the frequency of "on" time (and therefore consumed energy) and the amount of time before a packet can be transmitted from the base station. Similarly, the protocols in Imielinski *et al.* (1996) support energy-conservation in a mobile network where the base station periodically transmits large amounts of broadcast data such as news or stock quotes. These protocols intelligently organize the data with a directory so the mobile can reduce the amount of time that its receiver is "on" while watching the broadcast for the data of interest.

Conclusions

If success in the computing field is defined by market share and consumer interest, there is no question that mobile computing has already exceeded most expectations and is well on its way toward becoming one of the dominant forces of the entire information industry. From the array of palmtop computers available in budget superstores, to Intel's release of low-power mobile-oriented Pentium chips nearly immediately after the desktop version release, to the exorbitant sums of money paid by cellular operators for leasing radio towers and buying frequency space, there is little doubt about the potential of ubiquitous mobile computing. The challenges are complex, interrelated, and exacerbated by often hard, physical limitations (such as the limited RF bandwidth). However, if we try to gage the innovative potential of the computer industry by its past performance, it appears that that we have only begun to see the future of mobile computing.

Bibliography

1995. Harris, E. P., Depp, S. W., Pence, E., Kirkpatrick, S., Sri-Jayantha, M., and Troutman, R. R. "Technology Directions for Portable Computers," *Proceedings of the IEEE*, **83** (April), 636–658.

1995. Pahlavan, K., and Levesque, A. *Wireless Information Networks.* New York: John Wiley.

1995. Powers, R. A. "Batteries for Low Power Electronics," *Proceedings of the IEEE*, **83** (April), 687–693.

1996. Imielinski, T., Viswanathan, S., and Badrinath, B. R. "Data on Air: Organization and Access," *IEEE Transactions on Knowledge and Data Engineering*, **9** (May–June), 353–372.

1997. Corson, S., and Macker, J. *Mobile Ad-hoc Networking (MANET): Routing Protocol Performance Issues and Evaluation Considerations.* The Internet Engineering Task Force, Mobile Ad-hoc Networks Working Group, Internet Draft, draft-ietf-manet-issues-00.txt.

1997. Mann, S. "Wearable Computing: A First Step Toward Personal Imaging," *IEEE Computer*, **30**, *2* (February), 25–32.

1998. Chlamtac, I., Petrioli, C., and Redi, J. "Energy-conserving Access Protocols for Identification Networks," *IEEE Transactions on Networking*, **7**, *1* (Feb.), 51–59.

1998. Perkins, C. *Mobile IP: Design Principles and Practice.* Reading, MA: Addison-Wesley.

Imre Chlamtac and Jason Redi

MODEL CHECKING

For articles on related subjects *see* FORMAL METHODS FOR COMPUTER SYSTEMS; HARDWARE VERIFICATION; LOGICS OF PROGRAMS; and PROGRAM VERIFICATION.

Model checking is a technique of automatically verifying logical properties of the behavior of finite state systems. These properties are expressed in *temporal logic* (Burgess, 1984), a class of logics that is well suited to specifying the relationship of events in time. For example, in temporal logic, one can readily specify that condition p must eventually be followed by condition q, or that, after p, condition q must hold until the next occurrence of r, and so forth. A model checker determines whether a given finite state model satisfies a formula in the logic. In the negative case, it can supply a counterexample, that is, a behavioral trace that shows that the specified formula is false.

Model checking has been most successfully applied to the verification of computer hardware designs. This is because significant portions of a typical hardware design can be effectively modeled as a finite state transition system. As an example, model checkers have proved very effective at finding errors in the cache coherence (*q.v.*) protocols of multiprocessor systems. These errors tend to escape detection by simulation (*q.v.*), due to the infrequency of their occurrence.

Temporal Logic

In a propositional temporal logic, the usual operators of propositional logic (*see* BOOLEAN ALGEBRA and DISCRETE MATHEMATICS) are augmented by *tense operators*, which are used to form statements about how conditions change in time. For example, the formula Fq is true in the present if q is true at some moment in the future. The formula Gq is true in the present if q is true at *all* moments in the future. These operators can be combined to express more complex relationships. For example, the formula $G(p \Rightarrow Fq)$ can be read as "at all future times, if p holds, then q must hold at some later time." In the context of a hardware design, p might be the assertion of a signal that requests the use of a resource, such as a data bus, while q might be the assertion of the signal that grants access to the resource. Thus, $G(p \Rightarrow Fq)$ specifies that a request is always eventually answered by a grant of the resource. Temporal logics usually also include the "until" operator. The formula $p \, U \, q$ is true in the present if q holds at some moment in the future, and if p holds at all moments up to (but not necessarily including) that time. Thus, the formula $G(p \Rightarrow (p \, U \, q))$ could be interpreted to mean that "every request is eventually followed by a grant, and the request must remain asserted until the grant."

BRANCHING TIME

In a *linear* temporal logic (LTL), the model of time is a semi-infinite linearly ordered set of states. In a *branching* temporal logic (BTL), however, time is modeled as an infinite tree, where each infinite branch represents one possible evolution of the system. *Path quantifiers* can express the notions of possibility and inevitability in such a branching universe. That is, the formula Ep is true at the present moment if p holds for *some* branch containing the current state. Dually, Ap is true at the present moment if p holds *for all* branches containing the current state. For example, AFp can be read as "inevitably p", or "p holds in all possible futures," while EFp can be read as "possibly p", or "p holds in some possible future."

Branching time logic is of interest because of the ability to specify the possibility as well as the necessity of events. However, it is perhaps more important that the earliest model checking algorithm was given for the restricted branching temporal logic CTL. The practical significance of CTL is that it can express many useful properties, while offering a model-checking problem of lower complexity than that of LTL.

CTL model checking. The logic CTL (Computation Tree Logic) is a propositional branching temporal logic that allows tense operators only if they are immediately prefixed by path quantifiers. Thus, for example, $AG(p \Rightarrow EFq)$ is a CTL formula, whereas $A(Gp \Rightarrow Fq)$ is not. A model for CTL is a finite state graph where each state is labeled with the set of propositional letters true in that state. A formula of the logic is true in a given state of the model when it is true of the infinite tree obtained by unwinding the graph from the given state. Clarke and Emerson (1981) proposed this logic and later showed that the truth of a CTL formula could be determined in time proportional to sizes of the formula and the model (Clarke *et al.*, 1986). A model checking algorithm for a similar branching temporal logic, without "until," was independently proposed by Queille and Sifakis (1981).

CTL, though restricted in its syntax, can express many useful properties of systems, including, for example, the bus request/grant properties mentioned above. Using fairness constraints, it is also possible to specify, for example, that a protocol over a lossy channel always eventually makes progress, assuming the channel does not lose packets forever. Using the CTL model-checking algorithm, small but significantly complex finite state machines could be specified and verified, and some errors were found in the behavior of published state machine designs that were previously believed to be correct.

LINEAR TEMPORAL LOGIC MODEL CHECKING

For LTL, the model-checking problem is to determine whether all infinite paths in a finite state model, beginning with a given initial state, satisfy a given linear temporal formula. This problem can be solved by constructing an automaton that is equivalent to the LTL formula. Although the construction can be exponential in the size of the LTL formula, it is still linear in the model size. Thus, if the formulas to be checked are small, LTL model checking can be effective in practice, even for large models. This is of significant interest, since some properties expressible in LTL have no corresponding expression in CTL. LTL also has the advantage of simplicity, as it does not involve path quantifiers. In practice, both logics are used.

AUTOMATA-BASED SPECIFICATION AND VERIFICATION

While temporal logic model checking can be translated to operations on automata, there is also a school of thought in model checking, originated by Kurshan, which holds that specifications should be written directly as automata (Kurshan, 1994). That is, the exponential automaton construction involved in LTL model checking can be avoided by simply specifying the automaton directly. In fact, automata have a strictly greater expressiveness than linear temporal logic formulas (Wolper, 1983). For example, an automaton can characterize the sequences in which a condition p is true at all even times, but a temporal formula cannot. On the other had, LTL formulas have the advantage that they are easily complemented (i.e. negated) and that formulas can be nested within other formulas to build more complex properties.

In any event, LTL can be extended in various ways to provide the same expressiveness as automata. Second-order quantifiers can be added to the logic, although this leads to non-elementary complexity if the alternation depth of quantifiers is not bounded. Alternatively, hybrids that combine automata and logic can be made. However, a simple and adequate approach is to allow formulas to refer to auxiliary finite state machines. In this way, the advantages of both temporal logic and automata are obtained.

The State Explosion Problem

The primary practical issue in model checking is the *state explosion problem*. That is, finite state machines are seldom given as global finite state graphs. Rather, they are described as concurrent compositions of finite state machines, or machines that operate on finite data. The number of states in the model, while finite, grows exponentially with the number of finite state machines that are composed together, in the worst case. Thus, while model-checking algorithms are linear in the model size, it is more accurate to say that they are exponential in the model *description*. As it happens, the reachable state spaces of some highly complex systems and protocol models can nonetheless be small enough to construct in available computer memory, and thus to be verified by model checking. In general, however, state space explosion is the main practical limitation in the application of model checking. In response, a number of techniques have been explored' for exploiting some structural aspect of the state space of the model to mitigate the state space explosion problem. What follows is a representative, but far from complete, sample of such techniques.

SYMBOLIC MODEL CHECKING

Symbolic model checking is based on the idea that a set of states, or state pairs, can be characterized indirectly by a Boolean formula. Syntactically, this Boolean formula can be exponentially more compact than the set it represents. One representation of Boolean formulas that has proved particularly effective for this purpose is called an Ordered Binary Decision Diagram (OBDD) (Bryant, 1992) (*see* SWITCHING THEORY). This is a form of reduced decision graph in which Boolean decision variables occur in a fixed order. This representation is canonical, and has the advantage of providing polynomial time Boolean operations, such as logical "and," "or," and "not," and Boolean quantification.

Assuming that the transition relation of a finite state model is characterized implicitly by an OBDD, one can use Boolean operations on OBDDs to evaluate the predicate transformers whose fixed points characterize the CTL modalities (in essence, one can compute the image of a set with respect to a relation). Thus it is possible to verify CTL properties entirely using this indirect symbolic representation, and avoid actually constructing the state graph of the model. This technique was first used by McMillan in the SMV model checker (McMillan, 1983). Coudert, Madre, and Berthet independently developed a similar technique in the SIAM system for reachability analysis of finite state machines (Coudert *et al.*, 1989). In some cases, the technique made it possible to verify models whose state spaces are many orders of magnitude too large to construct directly. It was used by McMillan to verify an abstracted model of cache coherence protocols of a commercial multiprocessor (*q.v.*) design. Subtle protocol errors found in this experiment demonstrated that model checking could be used in a commercial environment to find errors that escaped extensive simulation.

Note that, in the worst case, information considerations dictate that any representation for Boolean functions is exponential in the number of Boolean variables. Thus, the symbolic model-checking technique does not improve the asymptotic complexity of the model-checking problem. However, because of its simplicity and generality, it is currently used in most commercial model-checking tools to extend the range of models that can be verified.

EXPLOITATION OF SYMMETRY

If symmetries in the state space of a model are known, they can be used to construct a reduced, but equivalent, model for the purposes of model checking. For example, suppose that the exchange of components c_1 and c_2 is a structural symmetry of a given system. Then intuitively, two states that differ only in the exchange of the states of processes c_1 and c_2 should be equivalent, at least with respect to any property that does not distinguish c_1 and c_2. Thus it should be sufficient to consider only one of these two states. Techniques based on this idea, though somewhat limited in their application, have been used to reduce significantly the state space size of protocols with many identical processes. An example of a model-checking tool using symmetry reductions is the Murphi system (Ip and Dill, 1996).

PARTIAL ORDER-BASED REDUCTIONS

One common source of the state explosion problem is the *interleaving* of concurrent actions. That is, if a set of local state transitions occurs asynchronously, the state graph will contain one execution path for each possible total order (i.e. interleaving) of these steps. This can result in a combinatorial explosion of states. Partial order methods treat this problem by grouping a set of executions that differ only in the order of concurrent events into an equivalence class called a *trace* and exploring only one representative execution from each trace. Various techniques are available for performing this simplification as the state graph is constructed, based on a static analysis of the interdependence of actions. These methods have proved effective, for example, in reducing the state space of protocol models using asynchronous message passing. An example of a linear temporal logic model checker using partial order reductions is the SPIN system (Holzmann, 1997).

Abstraction and Compositional Methods

Heuristic (*q.v.*) methods such as those described above can extend model checking techniques to somewhat larger problems. This, however, does not affect the fundamental asymptotic complexity of the model-checking problem. Thus we cannot expect model checkers to scale up to systems of arbitrary size. However, model checking can still be applied to the verification of large systems, provided the large verification problem can be reduced by some means to model-checking problems of tractable size. Such a reduction is, in general, not an automatic process, but rather requires some user understanding of the system under verification. Two important techniques that are used for this purpose are *abstraction* and *compositional methods*. These methods were pioneered in the automata theoretic framework by Kurshan (1994).

ABSTRACTION

The size of a verification problem can be reduced by replacing a detailed model by a simpler, more abstract one, from which information not relevant to the property being proved has been removed. This abstraction must preserve the property in question. That is, if the abstraction satisfies the property, we must be able to infer that the original model satisfies the property. This may be checked algorithmically, for example, by verifying a *homomorphism* (a property-preserving transformation) between the detailed and abstract models. Alternatively, the abstraction may be correct by construction. One example of the latter case is the method of *data independence* of Wolper (1986). This abstraction allows a data type with many values to be replaced by just a few representative values, given some constraints on the usage of data and the property being verified.

COMPOSITIONAL METHODS

Another approach to reducing the size of a verification problem is to prove some local properties of components of a system, and combine these properties into a proof of some global property of the system. This is known as *compositional* verification. Compositional methods based on temporal logic were originally described by Pnueli, in terms of an "assumption/guarantee" paradigm (Pnueli, 1984). Each component of a system is specified by those temporal properties which it assumes about its environment, and those temporal properties which it will guarantee, provided

the assumptions hold. For example, suppose a given process assumes *p* and guarantees *q*. Then, if we compose it with a process that guarantees *p* (under no assumptions), we can infer *q*. Other compositional approaches also allow for the mutual dependence of environment assumptions. This is important since, in practice, it is often difficult to find a local property that holds under no assumptions. Thus, there is often no point at which to begin an assumption/guarantee proof.

Compositional methods, though extensively studied, have yet to make a significant practical impact, largely because of the difficulty of specifying the environment of a small unit within a larger system. However, recent advances have shown some promise of overcoming this problem. For example, Eiriksson has reported the use of compositional methods to verify formally the low-level logic implementing the cache coherence protocol of a multiprocessor (Eiriksson, 1998). This work gives some indication that compositional methods can be applied in a scalable way to large designs.

Summary

Model-checking techniques are distinguished by the ability to verify properties of sequential, finite state systems automatically. These properties may be expressed either in a temporal logic or as the language of an automaton. Due to the state explosion problem, model checking is limited to relatively small models. Nonetheless, by means of abstraction and various heuristic methods for compactly representing or reducing large state spaces, it has proved possible to apply model checking to significantly complex systems, and thus to detect errors in real systems that escaped detection by other means.

Bibliography

1981. Clarke, E. M., and Emerson, E. A. "Synthesis of Synchronization Skeletons for Branching Time Temporal Logic," in *Logic of Programs: Workshop* (ed. D. Kozen). New York: Springer-Verlag.
1981. Queille, J. P., and Sifakis, J. "Specification and Verification of Concurrent Systems in CESAR," in *Proceedings of the Fifth International Symposium in Programming*, 337–371.
1983. Wolper, P. "Temporal Logic Can Be More Expressive," *Information and Control*, **56**, 72–99.
1984. Burgess, J. P. "Basic Tense Logic," in *Handbook of Philosophical Logic. Volume II: Extensions of Classical Logic* (eds. D. Gabbay and F. Guenthner), 89–134. Dordrecht: Reidel.
1984. Pnueli, A. "In Transition from Global to Modular Temporal Reasoning About Programs," in *Logics and Models of Concurrent Systems*, 123–144. New York: Springer-Verlag.
1986. Clarke, E. M., Emerson, E. A., and Sistla, A. P. "Automatic Verification of Finite State Systems Using Temporal Logic Specifications," *ACM Trans. Program. Lang. Syst.*, **8**, 2, 244–263.
1986. Wolper, P. "Expressing Interesting Properties of Programs in Propositional Temporal Logic," in *13th ACM POPL*, 184–193.

1989. Coudert, O., Berthet, C., and Madre, J. C. "Verification of Synchronous Sequential Machines Based on Symbolic Execution," in *Automatic Verification Methods for Finite State Systems, International Workshop, Grenoble, France* (ed. J. Sifakis). New York: Springer-Verlag.

1992. Bryant, R. E. "Symbolic Boolean Manipulation With Ordered Binary Decision Diagrams," *ACM Computing Surveys*, **24**, *3*, 293–318.

1993. McMillan, K. L. *Symbolic Model Checking*. New York: Kluwer.

1994. Kurshan, R. *Computer-Aided Verification of Coordinating Processes*. Princeton, NJ: Princeton University Press.

1996. Ip, C., and Dill, D. "Better Verification Through Symmetry," *Formal Methods in System Design*, **9**, *1–2*, 41–75.

1997. Holzmann, G. "The Model Checker SPIN," *IEEE Transactions on Software Engineering*, **23**, *5*, 279–295.

1998. Eiriksson, A. "Formal Design of 1M-gate ASICs," in *Formal Methods in Computer-Aided Design (FM-CAD '98)* (eds. G. Gopalakrishnan and P. Windley), 49–63. New York: Springer-Verlag.

K. L. McMillan

MODEM

> For articles on related subjects *see* BANDWIDTH; BAUD; COMMUNICATION CONTROL UNIT; CYCLIC REDUNDANCY CHECK; DSU/CSU; ERROR CORRECTING AND DETECTING CODE; NETWORKS, COMPUTER; and SYNCHRONOUS/ ASYNCHRONOUS OPERATION.

A *modem* is a device used to transmit data between computers, workstations, and other peripheral devices interconnected by means of conventional telephone communication lines supporting analog transmission. Modems transform (modulate) data from a digital device to analog form suitable for transmission over such lines. Since, in general, data flows in both directions, modems are also able to receive an analog signal from some remote device and restore (demodulate) it back to its original digital form, as shown in Fig. 1. The word "modem" stems from the *mo*dulation–*dem*odulation process performed. In addition to performing the basic transformation between digital and analog signals, modems also can perform a variety of control functions that coordinate data flow over the analog communication link. Terms usually used synonymously for modems include *data set* or *data phone*. A DSU/CSU (data service unit/channel service unit) performs the same function as a modem, but is used on communication lines supporting digital transmission conforming to AT&T publication 62310.

Modem Types

Many different types of modem are available, depending on their transmission speed, whether they are installed internally or connected externally to the computer with which they are used, and whether they are used for:

◆ Serial or parallel transmission;

◆ Synchronous or asynchronous transmission;

◆ Simplex, duplex, or full duplex operation;

◆ Long distance (long-haul) or limited distance (short-haul) operation;

◆ Operation over dedicated or dial-up lines; and

◆ Transmission of data only or faxes and data (fax modem).

Most modems transmit characters serially, bit by bit, but others are designed to transmit a character in one-bit time by receiving or transmitting its bits in parallel over several lines in order to increase the effective transmission rate. Some modems, called *acoustic couplers*, can be acoustically coupled to the telephone handset. Since parallel modems are not very common and since use of acoustic couplers is now rare, we shall only discuss serial modems that do not use acoustic coupling.

Internal modems are built into computing equipment such as personal computers. *External* modems have their own separate case with independent power supply and are connected to the computer by cable.

In synchronous transmission, the characters are transmitted at a fixed rate, usually at or in excess of 2,400 bits per second (bps). This mode of transmission was used primarily for high-speed communication between buffered systems. Synchronization between receiver

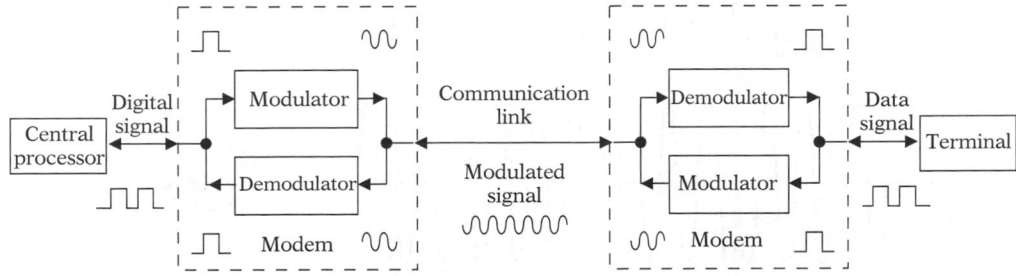

Figure 1. Computer-terminal communication with modems.

and transmitter is achieved by using special SYNCH characters at the beginning of each block or message. In asynchronous transmission, the characters are sent one at a time and the interval between them can vary arbitrarily. Synchronization is accomplished by adding *start* and *stop* bits to each character to allow delineation of adjacent characters. Synchronous transmission is more difficult to implement but is more efficient, since no start and stop bits are needed. Software for simultaneous support of many asynchronous devices, however, is generally much easier to implement than for a similar number of synchronous devices.

Most modern modems can operate in simplex, half duplex, and full duplex modes. *Simplex* refers to one-way transmission only and hence is rarely used. *Full duplex* refers to simultaneous transmission in both directions, while in *half duplex* systems the data may flow in both directions but not at the same time.

Today, most modems are long-haul: i.e. they function satisfactorily for unlimited distances over the public telephone network. One may also obtain limited-distance, or short-haul, modems which are specifically designed to work on short (usually 50 miles or less) point-to-point dedicated lines and, in general, offer higher transmission speeds than their similarly priced long-haul counterparts.

Modems that must operate over the public switched (telephone) network must have a dialing unit or auxiliary set to allow dialing from the originating device to establish a connection with the destination. The dialing unit may be manual, automatic (controlled by the computing device), or both. A conventional telephone suitably connected to a modem can perform this function.

Perhaps the most common modems today are the fax modems used with personal computers. They serve the dual purpose of sending or receiving faxes and supporting communication with distant computers over dial-up lines.

Modulation Techniques

Conventional telephone lines have a bandwidth of about 3,000 Hz (cycles per second). Data transmission over such lines is limited to 2,400 baud or line state changes per second. To modulate a digital signal over such a communication channel, a modem may use amplitude modulation (AM), frequency modulation

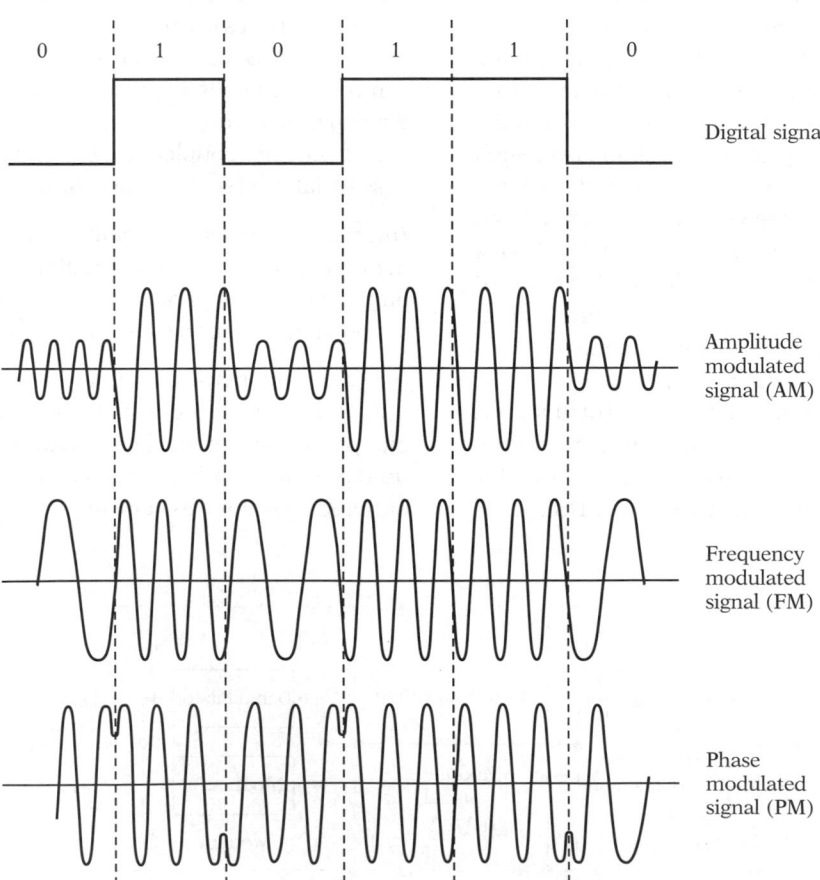

Figure 2. Types of modulation.

(FM), or phase modulation (PM), as shown in Fig. 2. The type of modulation used depends upon the transmission speed. FM, in the form of *frequency-shift keying* (FSK), is used almost exclusively for asynchronous communication up to 1,800 bps. A form of PM is used for synchronous communication at 2,000–2,400 bps. A combination of AM and PM, called *Quadrature Amplitude Modulation* (QAM), is used for speeds between 2,400 and 9,600 bps. At 9,600 bps, for example, 4 bits are encoded as one of 16 possible combinations of phase and amplitude, and 2,400 of these combinations are sent each second to achieve the desired 9,600 bps. Today, much more sophisticated modulation techniques, such as *Trellis Code Modulation* (TCM), are commonly used to achieve transmission rates of 33,600 bps but even 56,000 bps over conventional telephone lines.

Modem Design

Modems are continually becoming smaller, cheaper, faster, and smarter. Relatively inexpensive programmable modems operate at up to 56,000 bps and include features such as auto-dial, automatic speed detection, transmission error detection and correction (by means of cyclic redundancy checking), data compression, automatic fall back to a lower speed to reduce the number of transmission errors, automatic equalization to allow for the wide variation encountered on telephone lines, call-back security, and fax reception and transmission.

More sophisticated modems attempt to achieve the highest rate of error-free transmission for interactive and file transfer applications. Modems at both ends buffer the data and automatically append a cyclic redundancy check to transmitted blocks for error detection and correction through retransmission. Data compression hardware in the modem can provide an effective transfer rate up to 300% greater than conventional modems of the same speed. When the rate of retransmissions due to detected line errors exceeds a certain threshold, both the transmitting and receiving modems may automatically reduce the transmission speed to minimize the effect of adverse line conditions.

Call-back security provides a mechanism of protecting networks from unauthorized access. The modem can include a list of valid phone number–password combinations with routines for automatic password check and call back. Host sites can use this feature to call back remote sites immediately after being called by them. In addition to security, this feature can also redistribute and possibly reduce phone line costs through host site call origination.

Most modems in the USA use the EIA (Electronic Industries Association) Standard RS-232 specifica-

tions to define the interface between the modem and computing device. The international version of this interface is CCITT (Comité Consultatif Internationale de Télégraphie et Téléphonie) recommendation V.24. Other standards define frequency assignments for compatibility among modems and specifications for error control as well as data compression (*q.v.*) and decompression.

The newest modems use microprocessor technology, which allows them to provide some of the features discussed above at relatively low cost. All indications are that the number and sophistication of these features will continue to increase in the future. The goals are to simplify network management, improve its security and reliability, and maximize the effective (error-free) data transmission rate.

Bibliography

1988. McNamara, J. E. *Technical Aspects of Data Communication*, 3rd Ed. Bedford, MA: Digital Press.

John S. Sobolewski

MODULAR PROGRAMMING

For articles on related subjects *see* ABSTRACT DATA TYPE; ENCAPSULATION; INFORMATION HIDING; OBJECT-ORIENTED PROGRAMMING; PACKAGE; PROGRAM VERIFICATION; SOFTWARE ENGINEERING; and STRUCTURED PROGRAMMING.

A program or system *module* can be defined as a logically self-contained and discrete part of a larger program. A complete program can thus be considered to be a collection of modules. A properly constructed module accepts input that is well defined as to content and structure, carries out a well-defined set of processing actions, and produces output that is well defined as to content and structure.

In one view, associated with structured programming, a module packages a stage of processing. In this sense, a properly constructed module has only one entry point and only one exit point. If it is a subroutine, it always returns only to the statement following the one that invoked it. Breaking up a task into modules in this sense is a kind of functional decomposition, frequently called *procedural abstraction*. In many languages, a subroutine (procedure) can serve as a module, although some languages permit violations of the guidelines just stated, such as allowing multiple entry and exit points.

In another, now more common view, a module is a "responsibility center," which packages a set of operations on data that they share and to which only they have access. This is the notion of modularization that characterizes *object-oriented programming*, in which a module provides *data encapsulation* and *information hiding*. A module in this sense provides *data abstraction* as well as procedural abstraction.

The purpose of *modular programming* is to break a complex task into smaller and simpler subtasks which, among other things, facilitates writing correct programs. A program consisting of modules of properly designed scope (typically a page or two of coding at most) is much simpler to design, write, and test than the same program when it is not so modularized. Further, the interactions between parts of a program or system can be rigidly restricted to the interactions between modules, which greatly simplifies the understanding of how a program works.

In the development of large software systems by teams of programmers, good modularization is essential if the portions written by different programmers are to mesh effectively in a reasonable period of time. Finally, since all programs and systems that are used over a period of time have to be maintained and modified, good modularization also aids in doing these chores more quickly and accurately.

Good program design starts with the most general definition of the function of the program, and proceeds through a sequence of increasingly detailed specifications. This technique, called *top-down design*, is an aspect of structured programming and is greatly enhanced by modular programming.

Bibliography

1972. Parnas, D. L. "On the Criteria to be Used in Decomposing Systems into Modules," *Comm. of the ACM*, **15**, *12* (December),1053–1058.
1997. Meyer, B. *Object-Oriented Software Construction*, 2nd Ed. Upper Saddle River, NJ: Prentice Hall.

Daniel D. McCracken

MOLECULAR COMPUTING

For articles on related topics *see* BIOCOMPUTING; COMPUTATIONAL COMPLEXITY; NP-COMPLETE PROBLEMS; PARALLEL PROCESSING; and QUANTUM COMPUTING.

Molecular (or *DNA*) *computing* is founded on the idea that, given enough strands of DNA, and using certain biological operations, one can use DNA molecules to simulate some classic computations efficiently. The original insight is due to Leonard Adleman (1994) who showed how DNA can be used to solve the Directed Hamiltonian Path (DHP) graph problem (*see* GRAPH THEORY). Then Richard Lipton (1995) showed how to use DNA to solve more general problems, namely to find satisfying assignments for arbitrary Boolean formulas (*see* BOOLEAN ALGEBRA). Lipton's approach shows that DNA can be used to solve a large class of combinatorial search problems. Since then there have been many new ideas on DNA computation. In this article we review some of these proposals.

We begin with a brief explanation of some basic terms from molecular biology. A DNA strand is essentially a sequence (polymer) of four types of nucleotide distinguished by one of four bases they contain; the bases are denoted A, C, G, T (adenine, cytosine, guanine, and thymine). We will be dealing with short strands containing at most 10,000 nucleotides. Two strands of DNA are said to be Watson–Crick complements if their respective bases are complements—A matches T and C matches G. Under appropriate conditions two complementary DNA strands form a double strand that has the shape of the famous double helix. For our purposes we regard a single strand of DNA containing N nucleotides as a character string of length N over the alphabet $\{A, C, G, T\}$.

Molecular biology offers a variety of tools for manipulating DNA. DNA sequencing enables the biologist to "read" the sequence of nucleotides on a short DNA strand given a solution containing many copies of that strand. This is one way to read the output of a DNA computation. Biotin-avidin affinity purification is a technique for separating a solution of DNA strands into two solutions: those that contain a certain sequence and those that do not contain it. In some models this is the basic computational step of a DNA computer. The Polymerase Chain Reaction (PCR) is a technique for replicating all strands in a given solution of DNA. It provides an amplification technique crucial for reducing errors in a DNA computer.

At a high level one can think of a DNA computer as a massively parallel machine where each DNA strand serves as a separate processor. Assuming each strand contains fewer than 10,000 nucleotides, it is possible to dissolve 10^{18} strands in a liter of water. Unfortunately these processors are extremely slow, requiring several hours to complete the simplest Boolean operations. Still, a parallel computer that can perform 10^{18} Boolean operations every several hours seems promising.

Putting this computing power to work poses numerous difficulties. The first is the question of a useful application. Are there interesting problems that can be solved on an ultraparallel computer with very slow processors? The second is the issue of errors. Manipulating DNA strands is an error-prone process. Can the errors be controlled so that a meaningful result is produced? There is also the issue of scale. Do we have the physical means for handling the large volumes of DNA needed to solve large combinatorial problems? Other issues, such as automating the operation of a DNA computer, are also a concern. We address some of these issues at the end of this article.

Due to these problems and the fact that conventional silicon machines (i.e. transistor-based) are constantly getting faster, it is unclear today whether combinatorial search problems are the "correct" application for DNA computers. Recently several proposals, made by Leonard Adleman, Richard Lipton, Laura Landweber, and others, suggest that techniques of DNA computing be used to solve problems that are inherently embedded in DNA. Examples include molecular assembly, sequencing long DNA strands, DNA fingerprinting, and DNA mutation detection. For such applications there is no competition from conventional silicon machines, since they cannot directly manipulate DNA molecules. The next few years will tell whether DNA computing techniques can be used to tackle these classic problems.

Comparison of Several DNA Computing Results

Table 1 summarizes a few of the DNA computing models proposed thus far. The results listed there are compared according to two parameters. The first is the number of biological steps used by the algorithm. This roughly corresponds to the running time. The second is the number of DNA strands used. This corresponds to the volume of DNA needed to run the algorithm. Both parameters are equally important. If either one of them is too large, the algorithm cannot be implemented.

The six problems in Table 1 are described below:

1. This is Adleman's famous result (1994). A Hamiltonian path in a graph (*see* GRAPH THEORY) is a path that visits all nodes in the graph exactly once. Testing whether a graph has a Hamiltonian path is an NP-complete problem. Here n is the number of vertices in the graph.

   Adleman showed how to embed the graph in DNA such that the resulting DNA strands encode paths in the graph. He then described a procedure for filtering out all strands except the one representing a Hamiltonian path, if it exists. The actual Hamiltonian path in the graph can then be found by sequencing any of the remaining strands (i.e. reading the DNA sequence).

Table 1. DNA computing models.

Problem	Biological steps	Number of strands
1. Directed Hamiltonian path	$O(n)$	$n!$
2. Formula satisfiability	$O(s)$	2^n
3. Boolean circuit simulation	$O(s)$	2^n
4. 1-tape NTM	$O(t)$	2^N
5. Cellular Automata	1	$t \cdot S$
6. PSPACE	$O(S)$	2^{2S}

2. This is the result of Lipton (1995) that SAT (satisfiability for formulas in conjunctive normal form) and more generally contact network satisfiability (which includes general Boolean formula satisfiability) can be done in time linear in the size of the formula s. The number of strands needed is 2^n, where n is the number of variables in the formula. The importance of this result is that it shows that DNA computations can be used to solve general combinatorial problems.

   Lipton's idea includes a clever method of encoding all n-bit binary strings in DNA. In this encoding each DNA strand represents an n-bit binary string corresponding to an assignment of the variables. Lipton's encoding enable one to use biotin-avidin separation to filter out all strands that do not satisfy the given Boolean formula. Once the filtering is done only strands representing satisfying assignments remain. A satisfying assignment can then be obtained using DNA sequencing. To build the original library representing all 2^n binary strings, Lipton uses Adleman's technique of encoding paths in a graph in DNA.

   One can picture each strand as a processor in an ultraparallel computer. Initially each processor is given a random Boolean assignment of the variables. Each processor then checks whether its assignment satisfies the Boolean formula; if it doesn't, it shuts itself off (i.e. the strand is filtered out). Processors that remain on until the end represent satisfying assignments. Due to the large number of strands used, one can estimate that these techniques can be used to solve SAT problems with at most 60 variables (recall: at most 10^{18} DNA strands/liter, which is approximately 2^{60} strands/liter).

3. This simulation result, due to Boneh *et al.* (1996) shows how, given a function $F(x)$ taking n-bit binary inputs, one can construct a library of DNA strands representing all pairs $(x, F(x))$. In a sense, the entire lookup table for the function $F(x)$ is encoded in DNA. If the function F is computable by a Boolean circuit of size s, the construction requires $O(s)$ biological operations and produces a library of size 2^n. This result gives the first "real-world" application for DNA computers: breaking the Data Encryption Standard (DES) cipher (*see* CRYPTOGRAPHY, COMPUTERS IN). This application is discussed further in the next section.

4. Several research groups discovered how to simulate a Nondeterministic Turing Machine (NTM) using DNA (*see* Boneh *et al.*, 1996, for a survey). The N in Table 1 is the number of nondeterministic branches taken during a computation. This result is very important theoretically since it shows that DNA

computations are universal. From a practical standpoint these results are less significant since programming a Turing Machine (*q.v.*) is quite difficult.

5. This is a construction due to Erik Winfree that shows how complicated DNA patterns can be used to simulate cellular automata (*q.v.*). The number of nucleotides used by the DNA pattern is proportional to the product of the space used by the automata (S) and the number of generations for which it is run (t). The attractive feature of this model is that computations are done *in vitro*. Unlike other models, no intervention of a lab technician is required.

6. This result, independently discovered by Beaver, Reif, and Papadimitriou, shows how to simulate computations requiring polynomial space (PSPACE) with DNA operations; S denotes the space needed. These elegant ideas are mainly theoretical.

Applications

Applications for DNA computations fall into two categories: (1) solving combinatorial problems, and (2) solving problems that are inherently DNA based (as mentioned in the introduction). Here we discuss only the first type.

DNA computers have an immense amount of parallelism. The first "real-world" application is due to Boneh *et al.* (1996) showing how to break the Data Encryption Standard (DES)—a widely deployed symmetric cipher. The problem is this: given a plaintext M and a ciphertext C find a key K such that $C = DES(M,K)$. That is, find a key mapping the given plaintext to the given ciphertext. The number of possible keys is 2^{56}, which is well under 10^{18} (the number of DNA strands in a liter of water). The massive parallelism of a DNA computer is used to test all possible keys until the correct one is found. Testing a single key is a simple operation that can be performed by a single strand. It is currently estimated that a DNA computer will take several months to discover the key. Interestingly enough, after one spends the time to break one DES key using a DNA computer, subsequent DES keys can be broken in just a single day each. This can done by reusing the library of DNA strands produced in the initial break to crack many subsequent DES keys.

These ideas suggest that DNA may be used to solve interesting search problems. However, breaking DES is not a "killer application"; special-purpose hardware designed by Wiener in 1994 can also be used to break DES in roughly the same amount of time. However, Wiener's designs take advantage of the special structure of the DES circuit whereas the DNA simulation does not. In this sense, the DNA attack is more generic

and can be applied to any block cipher (so long as the key length is less than 60 bits).

Another possible application due to Eric Baum is to use a DNA computer as a large associative memory (*q.v.*). Each DNA strand encodes one word of information (e.g. 128 bits). This achieves 16×10^{18} bytes/liter, an attractive storage capacity. The disadvantage is that access is extremely slow. Furthermore, without additional techniques this cannot be used for long-term storage since DNA strands tend to disintegrate in solution.

It is fair to say that combinatorial search problems may not provide the "killer application" for DNA computers. Perhaps computations that are inherently done on DNA will.

Errors are a big concern in a DNA computer. The chemical manipulations involved are highly errorprone. The biggest problem is that the strand representing the desired solution might get lost (e.g. damaged, diluted, or incorrectly filtered out). To overcome these issues one must insure sufficient redundancy during the computation. Currently there are a number of proposals about how to make DNA computations errortolerant. Amplification via PCR plays a key role in this line of research.

Bibliography

1994. Adleman, L. "Molecular Computation of Solutions to Combinatorial Problems," *Science*, **266** (11 Nov.), 1021–1024.

1995. Lipton, R. "Using DNA to Solve NP-complete Problems," *Science*, **268** (28 April), 542–545.

1996. Boneh, D., Dunworth, C., Lipton, R., and Sgall, J. "On the Computational Power of DNA," *Discrete Applied Mathematics, Special issue on Computational Molecular Biology*, **71**, 79–94.

1997. Setubal, J. C., and Meidanis, J. *Introduction to Computational Molecular Biology*, Chapter 9. Boston, MA: PWS Publishing Company.

Dan Boneh

MONITOR, DISPLAY

For articles on related subjects *see* COMPUTER GRAPHICS; MULTIMEDIA; PERSONAL COMPUTING; TERMINALS; USER INTERFACE; and WINDOW ENVIRONMENTS.

Display monitors are the devices that produce realtime dynamic graphic images from computer output. They were originally used to monitor the state of the machine—hence the name. They are a "window" into the computer and, as the main way that the computer communicates data to the user, they have a critical role in the human–machine interface.

The monitor is the most common final device in the graphics subsystem in the computer. Although in the early days of computer graphics, displays were vector-based (that is they drew lines on the screen), virtually all displays are now *bitmapped* (*see* TYPEFONT).

The image on the screen is made up of individual dots known as pixels (short for *picture elements*). Each dot represents a location in the computer memory in an area known as the *frame buffer*. The frame buffer can be a designated part of main memory, or more often a separate type of memory designed specifically for the purpose. At each memory location a value is stored representing the color of the pixel. (The number of colors can vary, typically from 256 (8 bits per pixel) to 16.7 million (24 bits per pixel) depending on the size and arrangement of the buffer memory.) The number of pixels held in the frame buffer defines the *resolution*. The number of colors is known as the *color depth*.

Usually the practical frame buffer memory size is dictated by the availability and cost of chips as well as the width of the memory bus (*q.v.*) needed to address the buffer efficiently. Spare memory in the video buffer is often used to cache screen images and fonts during screen writing operations. Table 1 gives some typical resolutions, with the theoretical requirements and the typical loading of commercial products for two-dimensional applications.

The color value can either represent the direct color value (e.g. 8 bits for red, 8 bits for blue and 8 bits for green in a 24 bit system) or can represent an entry in a look-up table which stores the actual color values. The look-up table is known as the *color palette*. A palette is common for color depths below 15 or 16 bits, while those above 16 bits usually use direct color values.

The display is usually serially addressed, with pixels being sent to the display one at a time starting at the top left corner of the screen and scanning along each line sequentially until the bottom corner is reached. The vast majority of displays are analog, so the frame buffer color values are translated from binary data to a

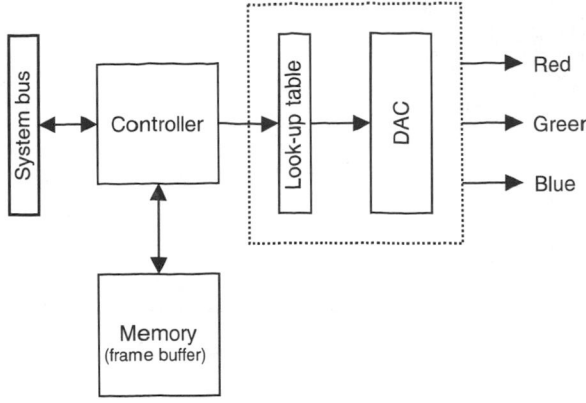

Figure 1. Block diagram of a graphics controller.

voltage for each color by a Digital to Analog Converter (DAC—*see* ANALOG-TO-DIGITAL AND DIGITAL-TO-ANALOG CONVERTERS) or by a Look-up Table DAC (LUTDAC) when a palette is used.

With the emergence of digital display technology there will be a shift from analog to digital displays, so over time the analog interface will be replaced by a digital one and the D/A stage is likely to disappear from the architecture. The use of digital interfaces eliminates the errors involved in digital–analog conversion, losses due to analog transmission and the conversion back to digital.

Look-up tables are still likely to be used as they allow the adjustment of the color values to compensate for the nonlinearities of different display technologies.

Because of the need to run the graphics output strictly in real time and the high data rates involved, most computers contain a special graphics processor chip that acts as a memory controller, but which is also likely to include special circuitry to accelerate both 2D and 3D graphics functions such as font rendering, block moves, and texture lighting and rendering. The processor is also likely to include special circuitry to process motion video for multimedia applications. Processes would typically include color space conversion from TV formats and scaling of image sizes. Fig. 1 shows a block diagram of a graphics controller.

Cathode Ray Tubes

The cathode ray tube (CRT) is the major display component used in computer monitors. The CRT, which was invented in 1897 by Karl Ferdinand Braun, is a type of thermionic tube and uses a beam of electrons from a heated cathode to excite materials called phosphors to emit light. An assembly called a *gun* focuses and shapes the beam of electrons (Fig. 2).

Table 1. Typical monitor resolutions and memory requirements.

Resolution	Colors	Minimum 2D memory	Typical board memory
640 × 480	16 (4 bit)	150 KB	256 KB
800 × 600	256 (8 bit)	469 KB	512 KB
1024 × 768	256 (8 bit)	768 KB	1 MB
1024 × 768	16.7 M (24 bit)	2.25 MB	4 MB
1152 × 864	256 (8 bit)	972 KB	1 MB
1280 × 1024	256 (8 bit)	1.25 MB	2 MB
1600 × 1200	256 (8 bit)	1.83 MB	2 MB
1600 × 1200	64 K (16 bit)	3.66 MB	4 MB
1600 × 1200	16.7 M (24 bit)	5.49 MB	8 MB

K = 1024; M = 1024 K

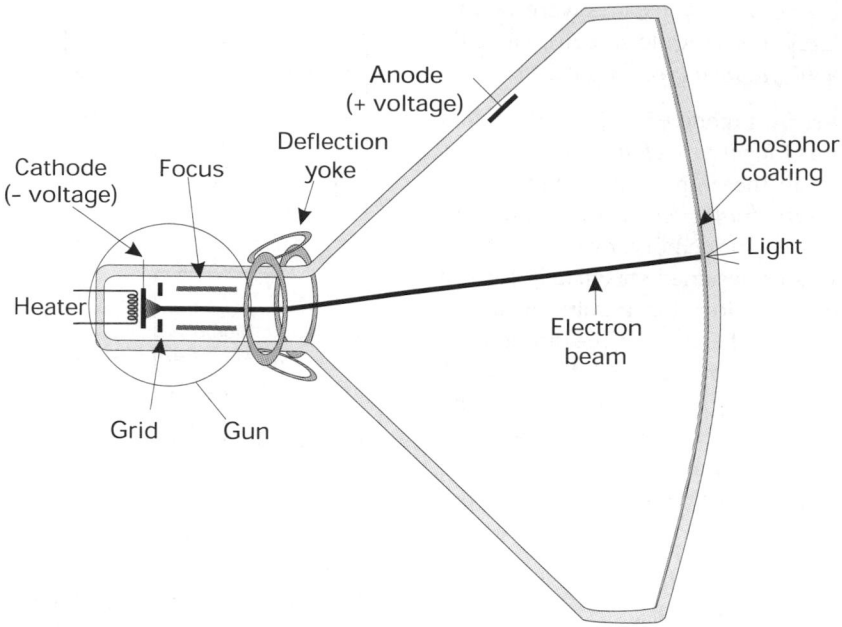

Figure 2. Cross-section view of a monochrome CRT.

The CRT uses horizontal and vertical magnetic deflection coils to bend and control the position of the beam and to scan the face of the CRT from side to side and from top to bottom to synchronize with the stream of pixels being sent from the graphics controller. Fig. 3 shows a block diagram.

The phosphor glow has persistence, so that the light emission is sustained after the beam has passed. By the careful choice of phosphors, the image on the CRT can be made to seem steady and flicker-free to the human eye when the full screen is scanned at 70–80 Hz or above (the *refresh rate*).

In a monochrome CRT, a single beam is used to create the image on the phosphor, with the display color controlled by the formulation of the phosphor. In a color CRT, three separate guns are used to excite three different kinds of phosphors that emit red, green, and blue (RGB) light. At the front of the CRT a masking

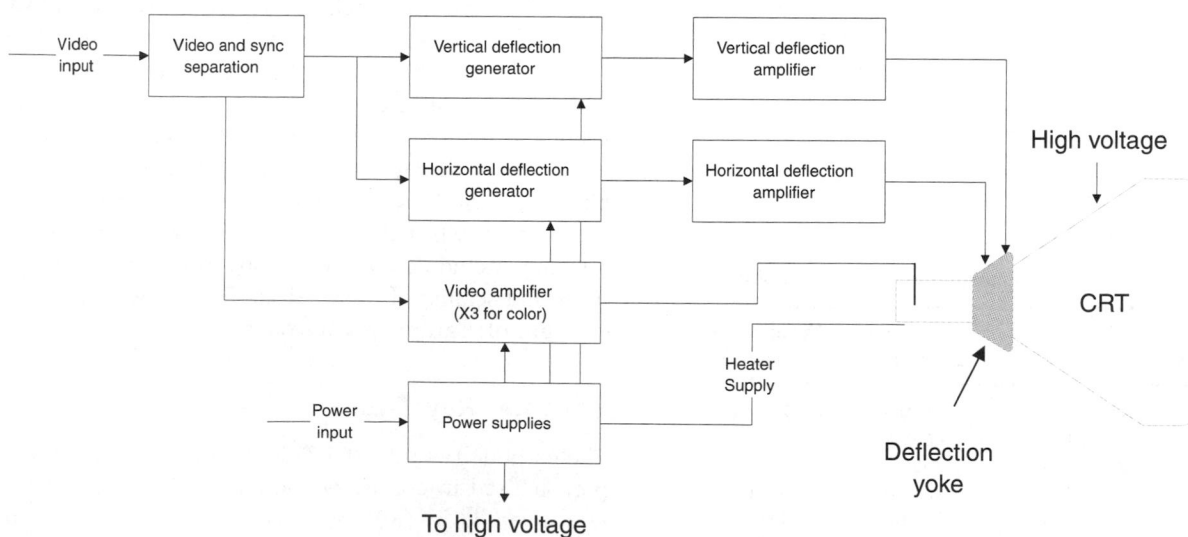

Figure 3. CRT monitor block diagram.

arrangement is used to ensure that the electrons from each gun land as nearly as possible on the right type of phosphor. The RGB phosphor dots are in groups of stripes or dots and the distance between the dots or stripes is known as the "dot pitch" or "stripe pitch" (*see* http://www.csf.org.uk). The dot pitch on most current CRT monitors is .28 mm. The lower the number, the better the resolution.

CRTs have a number of advantages. The scanning system means that CRTs are inherently very flexible and can run at a wide range of resolutions. The color quality and gamut is very good (although the gamut falls far short of the range of human color vision). The CRT phosphor is a Lambertian (relatively nondirectional) light source, so the picture looks the same from a wide range of angles. Above all, the CRT is cheap compared with other technologies.

However, CRTs also have a number of disadvantages, including bulk, weight, susceptibility to magnetic interference (including the Earth's magnetic field) and high power consumption. A display monitor will typically consist of an input amplifier, control circuitry, and deflection circuitry. Much of the skill in building a good monitor comes from the technology used to overcome some of the inherent weaknesses of the device.

LCDs

Although CRTs have many advantages, their power and bulk mean that they are unsuitable for portable devices. For portable applications the liquid crystal display (LCD) is the most common display device and is also being used in desktop monitors as prices come down and performance improves. Such "flat screen" monitors (Fig. 4) have a much smaller desk "footprint" than CRT monitors.

The LCD uses the special properties of a group of chemicals that are able to twist the polarization of light that is passed through them. In most types of LCD the degree of the twist is controllable by the application of an electric field along the length of the crystal.

In an LCD, light from a white source is passed through a polarizing filter. The light then passes through the liquid crystal (LC) material where the polarization is changed. On the top surface of the LCD is a second polarizer at right angles to the first. The LCD material twists the light through 90° (twisted nematic—TN—material) or 270° (super twist nematic—STN) allowing the light to pass through the second polarizer (Fig. 5).

When a field is applied across the crystal it "untwists" and less light passes out of the display allowing for different brightness levels (gray scales) for each pixel. In a color display, the front of the display is fitted with a color filter so that each pixel is red, green, or blue.

There are two broad categories of LCDs, defined by the way that each pixel is addressed. In a *passive matrix display*, the field for each pixel is applied serially. In order to avoid visible flicker, an LC formulation with a slow response time is needed. Unfortunately materials with a longer persistence are also relatively slow to turn on, so the monitor cannot respond to fast-changing screen items such as a rapidly moving cursor or motion video. This means that there is some smearing of the image on the screen where there is motion. The simple matrix connection system used to scan the display also tends to cause some crosstalk from bright or dark pixels to adjacent areas.

The solution to this problem is to put a switch under each pixel to maintain the field across the crystal for the whole of the frame period, allowing faster materials to be used. The array of switches is known as an *active matrix* (AM). In AM-LCDs, a transistor (usually a thin film transistor—TFT) is fabricated under each pixel to maintain the field. The performance improves significantly with no crosstalk and much reduced smearing, but with a penalty of cost. In order to make the matrix of transistors on the glass substrate, semiconductor processes must be used, making active LCDs cost about twice as much as passive LCDs.

A major disadvantage of the LCD is that the effect on the polarization of the light varies according to the angle of incidence of the light. Therefore, light traveling through the display at an angle can have a different brightness and color than light that passes through

Figure 4. A Mitsubishi LCD-80 flat screen monitor (courtesy of Mitsubishi Corp).

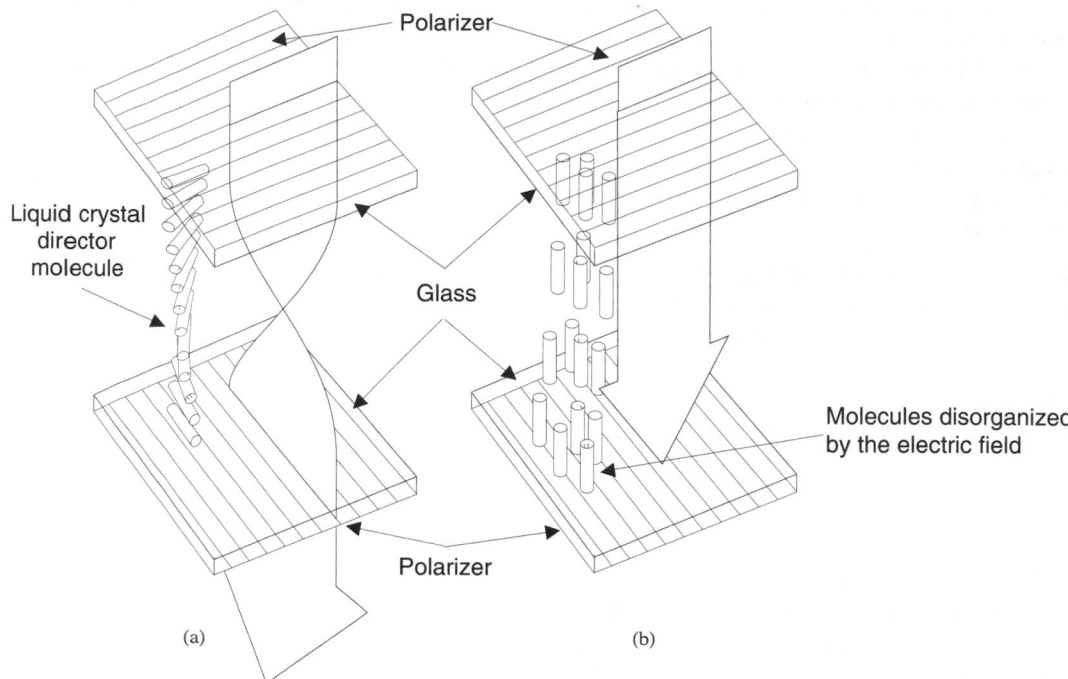

Figure 5. LCD structure. (a) The liquid crystal rotates the plane of polarization to transmit light; (b) without rotation, the second polarizer blocks the transmission.

at right angles. This means that the image performance and quality is consistent only over a limited range of angles. To compensate, a range of strategies are adopted including orienting the LC material differently (in-plane switching), subdividing the pixel area into sections with different crystal alignment (multidomain) and fitting special compensation films. All these approaches have some disadvantages of cost, complication, or power efficiency.

Although more power efficient than CRTs, 95% or more of LCD backlight can be lost in the process. Scientists continue to develop alternative technologies such as field emission displays (FEDs), plasma display panels (PDPs), organic LEDs (OLEDs) and light-emitting polymers (LEPs).

Projection

LCDs and CRTs are direct view displays, but some computers also use projection displays. In these displays a very bright image is created and is focused through a lens onto a screen from the front or from the rear. Projection displays can use special CRTs or LCDs as the source of the image. Projectors are often used as monitors on computers in control room and presentation systems.

A further device used in projection displays is the digital micromirror device, a chip-based technology that uses microscopic pivoting mirrors. When the mirror is in one position, light from a high intensity source is reflected into an absorber. When it is in the other position, the light is reflected out through the lens and onto a screen. Color projection devices can be built using one chip, illuminated by a light source modulated by a red, green, and blue color wheel, or up to three chips, where each chip is illuminated by a separate source.

Ergonomics

Because of the amount of time spent in front of display monitors by computer users, it is important to insure that the image is sharp in order to help reduce eye-strain and fatigue. It is also recommended that the display is positioned below eye level, as this minimizes the effort needed for close convergence and focus. The screen should be positioned at the very least 16″ (40 cm) from the user's eye but preferably at least 20″–24″ (50–60 cm) away. Care should be taken to ensure that the character size is not too small at longer viewing distances. Recommendations on detailed visual ergonomics are published in ANSI/HFS 100-1998 (USA) and EN29241/3 (Europe).

The number of times per second that the frame buffer is drawn on the screen should be at least 75 Hz for "black on white" images to avoid flicker with a CRT display. This is not an issue with LCDs, which use high-frequency fluorescent sources. The illumination of the workplace should also be considered, to avoid bright light falling onto the display surface or shining into the eyes of the operator.

Bibliography

1993. Peddie, J. *High-Resolution Graphic Display Systems.* New York: McGraw-Hill.

Website

The Computing Suppliers Federation. http://www.csf. org.uk.

Robert Raikes

MONITOR, SOFTWARE

See SOFTWARE MONITOR.

MONITOR, SYNCHRONIZATION

For articles on related subjects *see* ABSTRACT DATA TYPE; CLASS; CONCURRENT PROGRAMMING; and OPERATING SYSTEMS.

The term *monitor* in the context here denotes a control program that oversees the allocation of resources among a set of user programs. It was, along with *supervisor* and *executive*, an early synonym for *operating system.* An old example is the Fortran Monitor System (FMS), which appeared on the IBM 709 series beginning in the late 1950s to provide run-time support for Fortran programs. A more modern example is the Conversational Monitor System (CMS), a single-user interactive system that runs on a virtual machine (VM) implemented by the control program (CP) of the IBM VM/370 operating system.

In the early 1970s, the term *monitor* was applied to a formal program construct used to simplify operating systems by providing a separate scheduler for each class of resources. This kind of monitor has a syntactic form that generalizes the idea of an abstract data type or class; it defines a set of procedures for manipulating a set of objects concurrently. As with abstract data types, the monitor's procedures enable the caller to perform high-level operations on the monitor's resources; the details of resource status and structure are hidden inside the monitor (*see* INFORMATION HIDING). Unlike abstract data types, monitors have internal locks that permit only one process to execute monitor instructions at a time. Other processes must wait in a queue to enter the monitor. If a process in the monitor stops to wait for a resource to become available, the monitor must be unlocked so that another process (e.g. one that will release the desired resource) can gain access.

The following example of a *synchronization monitor* is adapted from Hoare (1974). Monitor RM handles the allocation of a set of resources whose indices $1, \ldots, N$ are initially in the set UNITS.

```
type RM = monitor:

    var nonbusy: condition;
    type unitnumber = 1..N;
    type UNITS = set of unitnumber;

    function entry acquire: unitnumber;
    var i: unitnumber;
    begin
        if UNITS = [] then nonbusy.wait;
                    ([] denotes empty set)
        i := "any member of UNITS";
        UNITS := UNITS - [i];
                    (Deletes i from UNITS)
        return i;
    end acquire;

    procedure entry release
                    (i: unitnumber);
    begin
        UNITS := UNITS + [i];
                    (Inserts i in UNITS)
        nonbusy.signal;
    end release;

begin
    UNITS := [1..N];
end RM;
```

The monitor condition "nonbusy" can be regarded as an (initially empty) queue of processes each awaiting a unit of resource. To acquire a unit of resource, a process executes the call:

```
i := RM.acquire;
```

As soon as this procedure returns, the caller has control over the ith unit of resource and the monitor is unlocked. If other processes come while there are no available units of resource, they will be enqueued when they perform the operation nonbusy.wait. To release unit i, the holder executes the call

```
RM.release(i);
```

The operation nonbusy.signal during this call permits one of the queued processes to proceed from its stopping point (at the statement nonbusy.wait). The monitor lock is held as long as any process is executing in the monitor; it is released either when a process exits from the monitor or gets queued for a condition.

Synchronization monitors in their modern sense have been used as tools for structuring operating systems and are provided by some languages for concurrent programming. They are used to implement synchronization in Java (*q.v.*).

Bibliography

1974. Hoare, C. A. R. "Monitors: An Operating System Structuring Concept," *Comm. of the ACM*, **17**, *10*, 549–557.

1977. Brinch Hansen, P. *The Architecture of Concurrent Programs.* Upper Saddle River, NJ: Prentice Hall.

1991. Andrews, G. R. *Concurrent Programming: Principles and Practice.* Reading, MA: Addison-Wesley.

Peter J. Denning and Walter F. Tichy

MONTE CARLO METHOD

For articles on related subjects *see* RANDOM NUMBER GENERATION; SCIENTIFIC APPLICATIONS; and SIMULATION.

In applied mathematics, the name *Monte Carlo* is given to the method of solving problems by means of experiments with random numbers. This name (after the casino at Monaco) was first applied around 1944 to the method of solving deterministic problems by reformulating them in terms of a problem with random elements which could then be solved by large-scale sampling. But, by extension, the term has come to mean any simulation that uses random numbers.

A classical example of what we would now call the Monte Carlo method is that of Buffon, who in 1733 pointed out that π could be determined experimentally by repeatedly throwing a needle onto a ruled surface and counting the number of times the needle crossed a line (*see* Fig. 1). The idea is more remarkable for its sophistication in geometric probability than for its practicality—a more accurate evaluation of π could be done with a piece of string, a ruler, and the plates and saucers in your kitchen. But the idea of Monte Carlo had been conceived, although the difficulty of using physical devices for sampling and the lack of suitable statistical theory made it little more than a curiosity until the advent of large-scale computers.

The development and proliferation of computers has led to the widespread use of Monte Carlo methods in virtually all branches of science, ranging from nuclear physics (where computer-aided Monte Carlo was first applied) to astrophysics, biology, engineering, medicine, operations research, and the social sciences.

The Monte Carlo Method of solving problems by using random numbers in a computer—either by direct simulation of physical or statistical problems or by reformulating deterministic problems in terms of ones incorporating randomness—has become one of the most important tools of applied mathematics. A significant proportion of articles in technical journals in such fields as physics, chemistry, and statistics contain articles reporting results of Monte Carlo simulations or suggestions on how they might be applied. Some journals are devoted almost entirely to Monte Carlo problems in their fields. Studies in the formation of the universe or of stars and their planetary systems use Monte Carlo techniques. Studies in genetics, the biochemistry of DNA, and the random configuration and knotting of biological molecules are studied by Monte Carlo methods. In number theory, Monte Carlo methods play an important role in determining primality or factoring of very large integers far beyond the range of deterministic methods (*see* FACTORING INTEGERS). Several important new statistical techniques such as "bootstrapping" and "jackknifing" are based on Monte Carlo methods.

The use of Monte Carlo method is so widespread that literature on it tends to be focused on particular fields. Interested readers will find Monte Carlo references spread throughout most technical journals. Calls such as "subject = monte carlo" or equivalent to the databases of most libraries will show numerous entries relating to such applications as artificial intelligence, hurricane wind speeds, polymer science, three-dimensional flow, microstructural lattices, statistical physics, economics, neutron transport, integrated circuits, and prediction of stock returns. Also listed will be a wide variety of proceedings of various conferences on Monte Carlo methods in special fields.

The references below list a few of the many books on Monte Carlo methods. Knuth's book describes and gives reference for Monte Carlo methods for factoring and determining primality. That book and those of DeVroye and Ripley give excellent discussions of methods for producing the random variables used in Monte Carlo simulations. The text of Hammersly and Handscomb was one of the first on Monte Carlo methods, and is still one of the best. Even by 1964, it listed several hundred references to Monte Carlo applications; by now a full list of references would number in the tens of thousands.

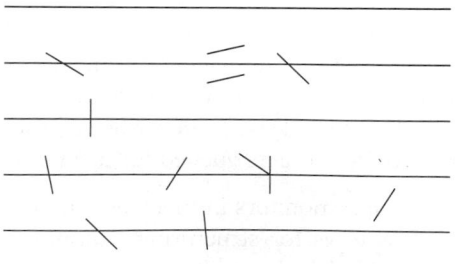

Figure 1. Buffon's needle problem. If a needle of length L (≤ 1) is dropped on a ruled surface of parallel lines spaced one unit apart, the probability that the needle will cross a line is $2L/\pi$. If the needle is dropped N times, the number of line crossings (say, X) should be about $2NL/\pi$, and hence $2NL/X$ is a Monte Carlo estimate of π.

Bibliography

1964. Hammersley, J. M., and Handscomb, D. C. *Monte Carlo Methods.* London: Methuen & Co.

1986. Kalos, Malvin H., and Whitlock, Paula A. *Monte Carlo Methods.* New York: John Wiley.

1997. Knuth, D. J. *The Art of Computer Programming: Volume 2/Seminumerical Algorithms,* 3rd Ed. Reading, MA: Addison-Wesley.

1998. Gentle, J. E. *Random Number Generation and Monte Carlo Methods.* New York: Springer-Verlag.

George Marsaglia

MOTHERBOARD

For articles on related subjects *see* BUS; INTEGRATED CIRCUITRY; and OPEN ARCHITECTURE.

The *motherboard* of a personal computer is its main logic board containing its central processing unit (CPU—*q.v.*) and memory chips. The term antedates personal computing since it was used by electronic hobbyists who often connected small ancillary "breadboard" circuits to a larger, principal circuit board that was dubbed "motherboard" to the smaller ones. On computers which employ an *open architecture*, the motherboard has attached *slots* into which specialized supplemental logic cards can be inserted to augment the primitive functions supported by the minimum configuration of the computer system.

Edwin D. Reilly

MOUSE

For articles on related subjects *see* INTERACTIVE INPUT DEVICES; and PERSONAL COMPUTING.

In computing, a *mouse* is a small hand-held interactive input device that, when rolled over a flat surface, controls placement of the cursor on a computer's terminal display screen. The palm-sized device has roughly an oval shape (or at least rounded corners) and is usually connected to the computer by a wire that is suggestive of a tail, hence the affectionate name "mouse." A mouse that deliberately exploits comparison to a live mouse is shown in Fig. 1.

The earliest mouse has been credited to Douglas Englebart and his colleagues at the Stanford Research Institute in 1965, but mouse technology has changed considerably since then. The Englebart mouse used a wooden housing with wheels placed at right angles to track cursor movement. The modern mouse senses movement either through use of a rolling ball or an optomechanical method that Logitech, the leading mouse manufacturer, considers optimal.

The mouse used with the Apple Macintosh is a one-button device. After positioning the cursor by moving the mouse, single or multiple clicks of its only button

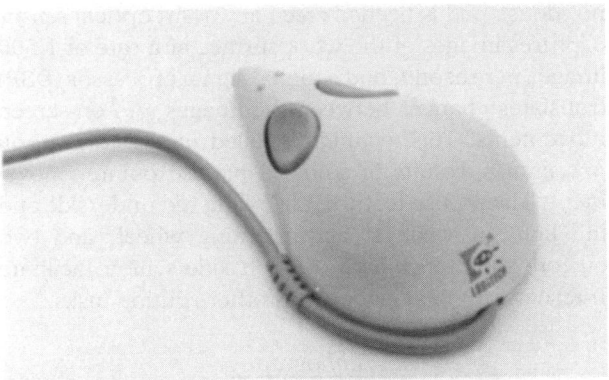

Figure 1. The Logitech Kidz Mouse (courtesy of Logitech).

select a course of action from a menu or, in word processing (*q.v.*), affect whether a word is to be highlighted for additional processing. Items such as screen *icons* (little pictures that stand for program applications) can be "dragged" across the screen by moving the cursor over them, holding the mouse button down, and moving the icon to a new position by moving the mouse and then releasing the button. The mouse used with the IBM and other PCs and with workstations (*q.v.*) is usually a two- or three-button device.

The most common mouse is electromechanical. As the mouse is moved over a flat surface, the rolling motion of a rubber-coated steel ball that protrudes from its bottom is detected by two orthogonal rollers that touch the surface of the ball. These rollers act as transducers that are able to convert the speed and direction of the the rolling ball to electrical signals that are fed to a software driver that moves a screen cursor accordingly (White, 1998). To provide good traction, an electromechanical mouse is generally used with a flat soft-cushioned *mouse pad.*

In late 1999, Microsoft introduced an electro-optical mouse, the *IntelliMouse Explorer*, that has no moving parts and may be used on any surface other than glass;

Figure 2. The Microsoft IntelliMouse Explorer (courtesy of Microsoft Corporation).

no mouse pad is needed (*see* Fig. 2). An optical sensor captures images of the work surface at a rate of 1,500 images per second, and a digital signal processor (DSP) translates changes between the images into on-screen movements. This technique, called *image correlation processing*, results in smooth, precise pointer movement. The mouse features a glowing red underside and tail light, a scrolling and zooming wheel, and two customizable buttons on its left side which facilitate Internet (*q.v.*) navigation and other routine tasks.

Bibliography

1992. Soberanis, P. "Of Mice and Trends," *CompuServe Magazine*, **11**, *2* (February), 29–30.
1998. White, R. "The Mechanical Mouse," in *How Computers Work*, 4th Ed., 160–161. Indianapolis, IN: Que/Macmillan

Edwin D. Reilly

MULTI-AGENT SYSTEMS

> For articles on related subjects *see* ARTIFICIAL INTELLIGENCE; DISTRIBUTED SYSTEMS; EXPERT SYSTEMS; and HEURISTIC.

Multi-agent systems are computational systems in which several artificial "agents", which are programs, interact or work together over a communications network to perform some set of tasks jointly or to satisfy some set of goals. These systems may consist of homogeneous or heterogeneous agents. Examples of agents would be ones for detecting and diagnosing network problems occurring on a segment of a local area network; for scheduling the activities of a group of machines in a workcell on a factory floor; or for locating agents that are selling a specific product and deciding on what price to pay. Agents may be characterized by whether they are benevolent (cooperative) or self-interested. Cooperative agents work toward achieving a set of shared goals, whereas self-interested agents have distinct goals but may still interact to further their own goals. For example, in a manufacturing setting, where agents are responsible for scheduling different aspects of the manufacturing process, agents in the same manufacturing company would behave in a cooperative way, while agents representing two separate companies, where one company was outsourcing part of its manufacturing process to the other company, would behave in a self-interested way. Agents often need to be semi-autonomous and highly adaptive due to their "open" operating environments, where the configuration and capabilities of other agents and network resources change dynamically. Agent autonomy relates to an agent's ability to make its own decisions about what activities to do, when to do them, and to whom information should be communicated. Scientific research and practice in this area, which is also called *Distributed Artificial Intelligence* (DAI), focuses on the development of computational principles and models for constructing, describing, and analyzing the patterns of interaction and coordination in both large and small agent societies.

Multi-agent systems provide a potential model for computing in the twenty-first century, in which networks of interacting, real-time, intelligent agents integrate the work of people and machines, and in which the effectiveness of computational agents in large distributed systems is improved by exploiting the efficiencies of organized behavior. Application domains in which multi-agent system technology is appropriate typically have a naturally spatial, functional, or temporal decomposition of knowledge and expertise among agents. By structuring such applications as a multi-agent system rather than as a single agent, the system will have some or all of the following advantages:

◆ Speed-up due to concurrent processing;

◆ Less communication required because processing is located nearer the source of information;

◆ More reliability because of the absence of a single point of failure;

◆ Real-time (*q.v.*) responsiveness due to processing, sensing, and effecting being collocated;

◆ Easier system development due to the modularity produced by dividing the program into agents.

Domains which have used a multi-agent approach include: distributed situation assessment (e.g. network diagnosis, information gathering, and monitoring on the Internet); distributed resource scheduling and planning (e.g. factory scheduling, network management); and distributed expert systems (e.g. concurrent engineering). A multi-agent approach is also useful in applications in which agents represent the interests of different organizational entities (for example, in electronic commerce (*q.v.*) where agents representing the interests of different buyers and sellers negotiate over an acceptable price for delivery of goods or services). Other emerging uses of multi-agent systems are in layered systems architectures, in which agents at different layers need to coordinate their decisions (e.g. to achieve appropriate configurations of resources and computational processing) and in the design of resilient systems in which agents dynamically reorganize to respond to changes in resource availability, software and hardware malfunction, and intrusions. In general, multi-agent systems provide a framework in which both the distribution of processing and information in an application and the complexities that come from issues of scale can be handled in a natural way.

Agents in such systems need to interact because they are solving subproblems that are interdependent, either through contention for resources or through relationships among the subproblems. This need for interaction may require them to cooperate extensively during problem-solving based on reasoning about subproblem interdependencies, the agents' current state of problem-solving, and the status of network resources. Such agent interactions are exemplified in a recently developed commercial multi-agent system for restoring service in an electricity transportation grid. This application has agents for fault detection, fault isolation and diagnosis, and network reconfiguration. Consider the example of two expert agents in this system performing different forms of fault diagnosis. Each of these agents, operating concurrently, uses very different algorithms to do its diagnosis and the information that they use is not identical. Both can make mistakes, but generally will not make the same mistake. They interact by exchanging partial results to focus their local diagnostic search processes towards promising areas of the grid where the fault probably originated, and away from unpromising ones. They also exchange final results to increase the confidence in the eventual diagnosis that they agree to. Thus, by working together, they not only produce a solution in which they have more confidence, but they also accomplish the task quicker.

Multi-agent systems must be designed to enable an agent to modify its problem-solving activity in response to the emerging state of the group problem-solving effort. Agents must be flexible, as they work with information of varying degrees of completeness and accuracy, and use resources of varying capabilities. For example, in the multi-agent system described above the agents doing the diagnosis should be able to work in a standalone manner, but also be able to take advantage of information from the other diagnostic agent if and when it arrives. In other words, hard-coded assumptions about information and resources are typically avoided. This flexibility requires agent autonomy and is in direct contrast to the less autonomous characteristics of agents in usual distributed processing applications.

The design, implementation, and assessment of multi-agent systems raises many specific issues. The major conceptual problem that researchers face in dealing with these issues is the possibility that the information an agent is using to make its decisions is incomplete, out-of-date or inconsistent with that of other agents. Obtaining all the appropriate non-local information is often not practical due to:

1. Limited communication bandwidth (*q.v.*) and computational capabilities which make it infeasible to

transfer, package, and assimilate pertinent information in a timely manner.

2. The heterogeneity of agents, which makes it difficult to share information and the possibility that competitive agents, out of self-interest, are not willing to share certain information.

3. The dynamic character of the environment due to changing problems, agents, and resources, and the inability to predict with certainty the outcome of agents' actions.

In order to deal with this uncertainty in problem-solving and coordination decisions, a number of formal and heuristic techniques have been developed. These techniques are oriented towards achieving effective, though not necessarily optimal, agent problem-solving and interaction, while limiting the computational and communication requirements. These include: group problem-solving strategies that can reach acceptable solutions even though an individual agent's local information may be incorrect or incomplete; coordination strategies that enable groups of agents to solve problems effectively through decisions about which agents should perform specific tasks and when, and to whom they should communicate the results of task execution; negotiation mechanisms that serve to bring a collection of agents to an acceptable state; and protocols (*q.v.*) by which agents may communicate and reason about interagent communications. Where formal techniques have been used, they have generally been based on game-theoretic ideas, market mechanisms, or logical formalisms, while heuristic approaches have their roots in knowledge-based AI search, planning and scheduling mechanisms. A recent trend is the use of machine learning (*q.v.*) to acquire the information necessary to implement these approaches.

The use of multi-agent systems technology is still in its infancy. There are only a handful of commercial applications to date. However, given the great interest in the field, the emerging multi-agent application development infrastructures, and the next generation of sophisticated network applications beginning to take shape, we may expect the impact of multi-agent systems on computer science to increase significantly during the next decade.

Bibliography

1988. Bond, A., and Gasser, L. (eds.) *Readings in Distributed Artificial Intelligence.* San Francisco: Morgan Kaufmann.

1994. Rosenschein, J. S., and Zlotkin, G. *Rules of Encounter: Designing Conventions for Automated Negotiation among Computers* (eds. M. Brady, D. Bobrow and R. Davis). Cambridge, MA: MIT Press.

1994. Jennings, N. R. *Cooperation in Industrial Multi-Agent Systems.* Singapore: World Scientific.

1995. *Proceedings of the First International Conference on Multi-agent Systems.* San Francisco: AAAI Press.

1995. O'Hare, G., and Jennings, N. R. (eds.) *Foundations of Distributed Artificial Intelligence.* New York: Wiley Inter-Science.

1996. *Proceedings of the Second International Conference on Multi-agent Systems.* Kyoto, Japan: AAAI Press.

Victor R. Lesser

MULTIMEDIA

> For articles on related topics *see* ASYNCHRONOUS TRANSFER MODE; COMPUTER-ASSISTED LEARNING AND TEACHING; COMPUTER CONFERENCING; COMPUTER GAMES; DATA COMMUNICATIONS; DATA COMPRESSION; ENTERTAINMENT INDUSTRY, COMPUTERS IN THE; HYPERTEXT; IMAGE COMPRESSION; SPEECH RECOGNITION AND SYNTHESIS; VIDEOGAMES; VIRTUAL REALITY; WORKSTATION; and WORLD WIDE WEB.

In the context of computing, *multimedia* has come to imply the integration of audio, video, and images with more traditional types of data such as text and numerics. It is an application-oriented technology that caters to the multisensory nature of humans and is based on the evolving ability of computers to store, transmit, and convey diverse types of information.

Multimedia computing is defined as the manipulation and presentation of such media in a computer system. There are applications of computing in many areas, including business, education, manufacturing, law, medicine, and entertainment, that were inconceivable prior to the introduction of this technology. Table 1 shows a few application domains and their media com-

Table 1. Multimedia and some applications.

Audio, video, images, text
Advertising
Consumer catalogs
Education/training
Electronic collaboration
Electronic mail
Sales agents
Tourist information

Images, text
Dictionaries
Legal information systems
Library
Newsprint publication

Images, text, numeric data
Geography
Weather
Office automation
Banking
Engineering, CAD/CAM

Telephony (with other media)
Command and control
Medical information systems

ponents. Increasingly, these capabilities are the norm as more and more computer applications become multimedia applications and multimedia computing is absorbed by mainstream computing.

The remainder of this article describes the essence of multimedia computing and the computer and networking components required to support multimedia applications.

Representative Applications

The following four areas exemplify multimedia applications.

ONLINE NEWS

Online news is the multimedia analog of the printed newspaper. Through a Web browser, a reader can browse through pages of a newspaper, read articles, and view pictures or audio/video presentations, as shown in Fig. 1. In addition, the user can perform index or relational database (*q.v.*) searches or queries to locate specific articles or advertisements. The user may also participate in chat groups and provide feedback to the editors. The presentation requires synchronization among media—the text, image, audio, and video elements. Other requirements of this application include the ability to format the data for display (e.g. fonts, panning, zooming, sequence control (stopping and starting of streaming video), and database navigation).

DISTANCE EDUCATION

Distance education enables students at remote locations to participate in live instruction via video conferencing; to collaborate on projects through shared "whiteboards"; or to replay instructional material that has been pre-recorded or pre-orchestrated. Fig. 2 illustrates an example of a multimedia distance learning application using the Web as a basis. In this example a student can browse through a database consisting of course material in various formats (images, audio and video recordings, and textual information). Alternatively, the student can issue queries to the database while reading text or viewing illustrations and audio/video presentations.

INTERACTIVE GAMING

Interactive games present perhaps the greatest demands on the multimedia delivery system due to the requirement for real-time, three-dimensional imaging coupled with interactions among multiple players. SwineOnline (Fig. 3) is an example of a Web-enabled game involving the raising of pigs by participants in a virtual state fair. Each participant is responsible for interacting with and nurturing the virtual pet as its weight increases. A characteristic of this application is the need for low-latency interactions and support for a large number of interacting players.

Figure 1. An example of an electronic news service from the Web (`http://www.boston.com/globe/`).

VIDEO-ON-DEMAND

Video-on-demand (VOD) refers to networked multimedia applications that use full-screen video. Examples include movies in the home delivered from a central video server. Although early attempts at VOD failed due to expensive system components, limited service offerings, and unsatisfactory revenue generation models, a resurgence in this technology is expected as residential broadband networks are installed, and the lessons learned from many successful Web-based applications are applied to video-rich content.

General Requirements for Multimedia Applications

The examples in the previous section belong to the class of distributed multimedia information system (DMIS) applications that together define multimedia technology. In a DMIS, there are many unique engineering challenges for both computer component designers and system integrators. Due to the large volume of multimedia data and inherent time dependencies, the components of such a system include high-speed networks, massive data servers, and specialized presentation devices which must be suitably selected and interconnected. A special case of a DMIS is the standalone workstation with multimedia capabilities including CD-ROM. Although not as rich in capabilities as a true distributed system (*q.v.*), workstations with multimedia capabilities are the norm for any new unit. However, the limited data universe of CD-ROMs does not match the universal appeal and reach of Web- and Internet-based data. In the rest of this section we elaborate on the requirements for the components that comprise a DMIS.

The major system-wide requirement for a DMIS is the ability to integrate real-time multimedia data retrieved

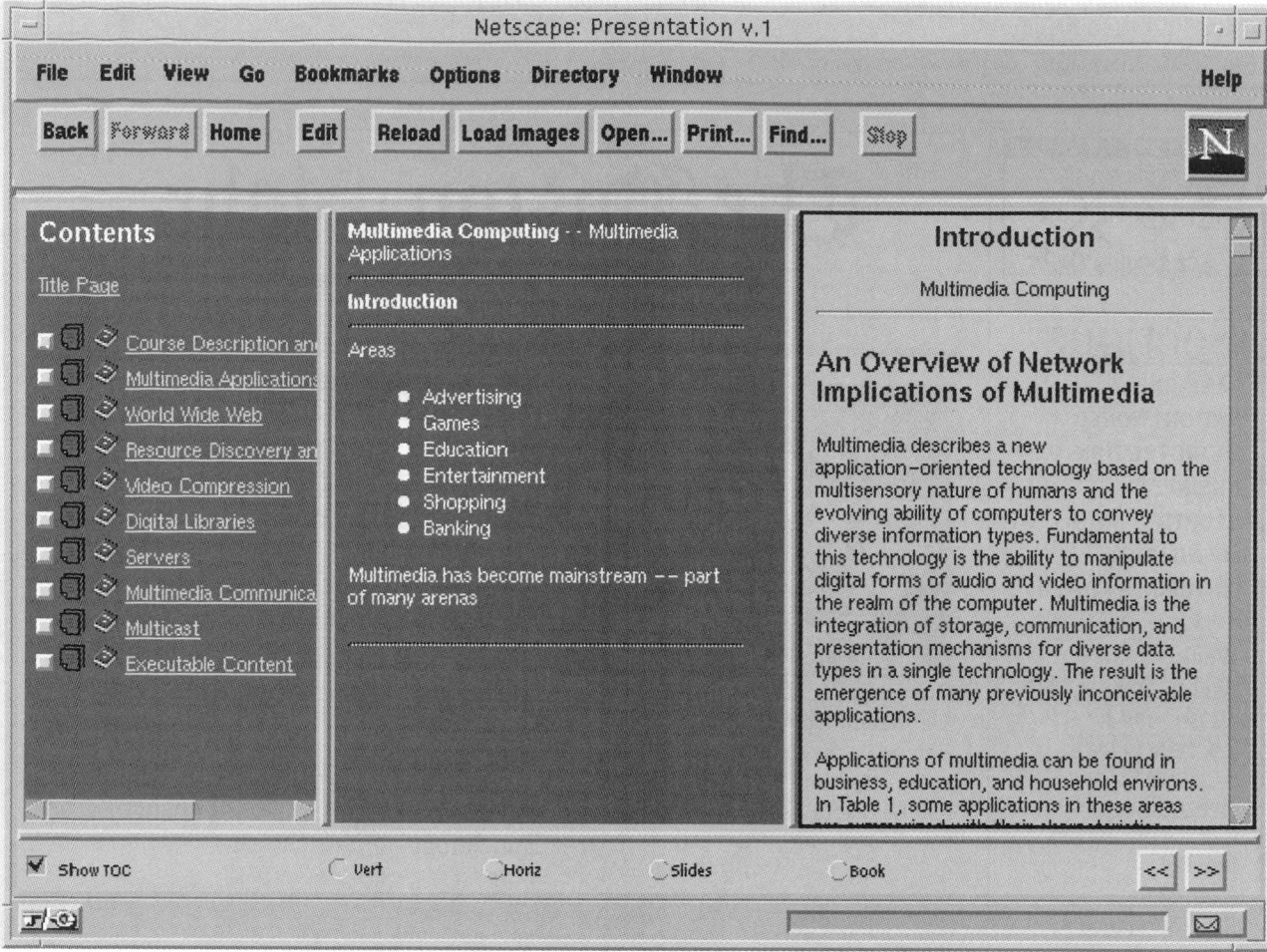

Figure 2. An electronic distance learning application of multimedia.

from distributed databases. This mode of integration differs drastically from the important problem of computer systems integration that is concerned with unifying heterogeneous operating systems, networks, instruction sets, and data formats. *Data integration, composition,* or *fusion* describes the assembly of multimedia data elements into presentation form depending on the temporal and spatial characteristics of the data. This requirement establishes the need for system components capable of performing real-time data retrieval, delivery, and presentation. Spatial integration requirements for multimedia data are unique to each medium and describe the assembly of objects in space (e.g. on a workstation—*q.v.*) at certain times.

For pictorial representations such as still images and graphics, integration operations include overlay (superimposing opaque or transparent images) and mosaic (juxtaposing images as tiles in the presentation window), and require processing such as scaling, cropping, color conversion, and position registration. For audio data, spatial integration is performed by

superposition, or mixing, of signals. Other "spatial" audio operations include gain, rate, and tone adjustment. For example, videoconferencing uses signal processing techniques to prioritize one speaker's voice among many, using volume or tone differences to signify "distance." Similarly, temporal integration describes the presentation of time-dependent data such as a sequence of video frames, which nominally occurs at a rate of 30 frames per second for NTSC (National Television Standards Committee) video, and requires specific video decoding hardware and scheduling for the retrieval and display of data elements.

These special characteristics of multimedia data require a detailed evaluation of the individual system components for their suitability for building a DMIS. The other technological requirements of a DMIS deal with the workstation technology, communication protocols, bandwidth (*q.v.*), internetworking, data storage, application interfaces and authoring tools, and information modeling and retrieval. We now briefly overview the requirements in these domains.

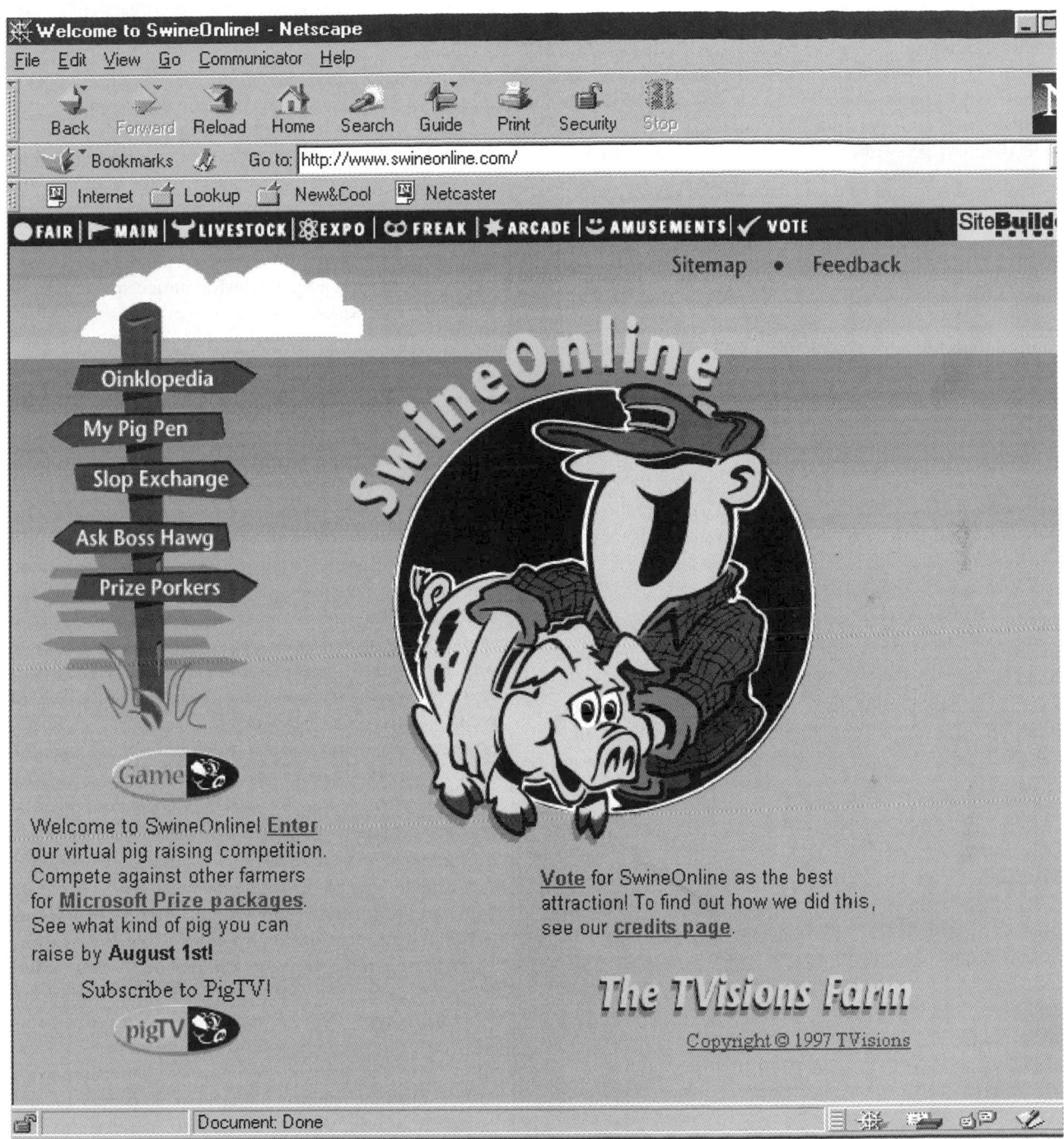

Figure 3. Interactive gaming with SwineOnline (http://www.swineonline.com).

WORKSTATION TECHNOLOGY

For multimedia applications we need appropriate multisensory input–output (I/O) devices. For presentation of data to a user, today's high-performance workstations with high-resolution monitors and audio output can be used as presentation devices. The output device must allow presentation of both the visual (text, graphics, video) and aural (voice, music) components of the application. For data capture, additional special-ized devices are required depending on the type of data. For example, still images can be captured using a scanner, voice can be captured with a microphone and digitizer, text can be input via a keyboard, and video can be handled with a camera and digitizer. Early multimedia systems showed that conventional devices for user interaction, such as the mouse (*q.v.*) and keyboard, are not suitable for many multimedia applications such as games because they provide poor control of the spatial manipulations required by the applications. Multiple axis joysticks, foot pedals, "data gloves" (gloves worn by the participant that translate finger and hand position to signals interpreted by the application), and eye motion tracking systems represent the next generation of multimedia I/O devices.

Other requirements of a workstation include the need to compress and decompress data for transmission and storage, and the need to handle the large data rates of live video. New video formats such as High-Definition Television (HDTV) will further tax the data handling capabilities of multimedia systems with their increased data rates. Evolving standards for image and video compression include JPEG (Joint Photographic Experts Group) for still image compression, and MPEG (Motion Picture Coding Experts Group) for motion picture image compression. Workstation add-on boards are available for real-time image compression with a compression ratio varying from 30 : 1 (VHS quality) to 500 : 1. Other add-on boards for multimedia workstations include TV tuners, and video encoders for producing recordings on tape.

Video and audio playout are now common functions of most workstations. Audio playout is supported by a hardware device, while video in various compression formats is handled by software decompression in conjunction with standard video display drivers. High-end solutions achieve video decompression with add-on boards that are becoming increasingly cheap.

COMMUNICATION PROTOCOLS

Interactive multimedia traffic places stringent real-time service demands on a communication system. Existing protocols, such as TCP/IP (q.v.) for data communication (q.v.), are not ideal for such traffic since they were not designed for time-critical delivery of data but for error-free service. Many multimedia application traffic types, such as some interactive voice and video applications, can tolerate errors in transmission due to corruption or packet loss without retransmission or correction since dropped packets do not seriously degrade the service. In fact, to meet real-time delivery requirements, late packets can be discarded to meet deadlines of others. The result of this characterization of the delivery requirements is that lightweight transmission protocols, which do not provide retransmission since this can introduce undesirable delay, can be employed.

Multimedia applications require high performance in terms of predictable end-to-end delays, a feature not provided by most of the existing protocols or operating systems. However, existing protocols can be used for multimedia applications, assuming the application can tolerate occasional long delays.

New protocols for real-time traffic, as required for multimedia applications, have been proposed at several levels of the OSI Reference Model to provide real-time delay-bounded service for continuous-media traffic. If a specific delay or throughput (q.v.) cannot be achieved under the currently existing conditions, then the connection is not allowed. In this manner, the traffic on the network is limited to provide guaranteed performance for all of the allowed connections. The transport mechanism can then prioritize traffic classes based on type, and achieve performance specifications for individual classes.

ATM (Asynchronous Transfer Mode) promises to provide a flexible communication mechanism for a variable Quality of Service (QoS) using variable-bandwidth channels in a form of packet switching (q.v.). This technique achieves a single network interface to communication channels for each media type, adaptability of the application's bandwidth requirements, flexibility for handling different data types, and a common signaling structure. However, implementations of ATM are expensive and it has yet to integrate both local (LAN—q.v.) and wide area (WAN) environments, or to support successfully multipoint applications. In contrast, conventional TCP/IP internetworks can be adapted for guaranteed service by the use of protocols such as RSVP (Resource reSerVation Protocol) or by overprovisioning with respect to the applications supported.

COMMUNICATION BANDWIDTH

Multimedia data, especially interactive data, requires enormous transmission rates. A summary of the data storage and communication requirements for various multimedia applications is shown in Table 2. As can be seen from this table, a single audio/video videoconference connection pair requires 150 Mb/s without compression. As mentioned, compression can reduce this bandwidth requirement, with acceptable signal degradation. For the enormous bandwidth necessary to support multiple sessions, high-speed networks are needed. Bandwidth (q.v.) availability is currently the most significant restriction on the ubiquitous deployment of multimedia applications and is the source of frequent complaints about the usability of the Web.

Table 2. Bandwidth requirements of high-end media delivery.

Medium	Nominal bandwidth
Text file	60 Kb/s
Image file	400 Kb/s
MPEG 1 compressed video/audio	1.5 Mb/s
MPEG 2 compressed video/audio	7 Mb/s
Internet streaming compressed video	28 Kb/s
Uncompressed video/audio	150 Mb/s

Bandwidth availability is the key to the viability of interactive TV or VOD consumption in the home. For residential networks, proposed solutions include Hybrid Fiber-Coaxial (HFC) (via the cable TV distribution system) and Asymmetric Digital Subscriber Line (ADSL) (via the telephone network) to provide the aggregate bandwidth for these applications.

INTERNETWORKING

In order to gain access to the thousands of public and private databases currently available, a DMIS must extend beyond the simple LAN environment. High-speed networks can link such geographically dispersed data stores and users requiring broadband services. Both LAN and Metropolitan Area Network (MAN—$q.v.$) technologies are being developed that are well-suited for such interconnections.

DATA STORAGE

Like communication bandwidth, the data storage requirement for multimedia data types is very large. For example, the storage of 10,000 full-screen color still images (3 colors/pixel × 8 bits/color × 1200 × 1200 pixels = 35 Mb) requires 350 Gb, or 43 GB of storage. Similarly, for digital video storage applications, a video archive of 500 movies of 120 minute duration each requires 531 Tb, or 66 TB of storage (3 colors/pixel × 8 bits/color × 512 × 400 pixels × 30/sec = 147 Mb/sec). With a compression of 20 : 1, this can be reduced to a "mere" 3.3 TB. This volume is particularly problematic when the multimedia applications require random access storage, for which streaming drives, such as magnetic tape, are not suitable. Furthermore, due to the limited data transfer rates of many storage devices, especially optical disc drives, these devices often have inadequate access bandwidth to satisfy a large number of user streams. For example, MPEG-2 compressed video requires a transfer rate of 6.2 Mb/sec. Although this rate is readily achievable from a typical magnetic disk drive or a large database server, it is not typical of a CD-ROM. The recent DVD (Digital Versatile Disk) standard addresses both the capacity and bandwidth limitations of CD-ROM; however, it is intended to support only a single video data stream (*see* OPTICAL STORAGE).

Applications Interfaces and Authoring Tools

Additional important problems faced by multimedia application developers are the design of user interfaces ($q.v.$) and the authoring of content for the applications. Tools for developing such interfaces include window systems and application programming interfaces (APIs) which permit the developer a full range of access to the utilities available in a DMIS. Substantial improvement in window-based interface models and toolkits has been achieved, particularly in the domain of the Web. These tools, which allow the rapid development of user interfaces for any application, often use an object-oriented ($q.v.$) approach, and are becoming *de facto* standards.

Multimedia content uses diverse data types. Construction of a multimedia application requires that there be instructions, or scripts, on how the content should be interpreted by the workstation. Authoring tools provide a means for technical and nontechnical content developers to produce multimedia works dealing with spatial layout and temporal presentation. Most of these tools produce proprietary data representations that are playable only with their own components. Increasingly, however, tools are being developed that yield standards-based output such as HyTime, SGML, or some other scripting language ($q.v.$) that is supported on a wider scale through open Web-based systems.

Executable content refers to scripting information that can be coupled directly with the content to be delivered. Most of the early Web-based content delivery approaches relied on both the workstation and server participating in interactions with the content. Executable content (e.g. programs written in Java—$q.v.$) allows for a tighter coupling of the content with the program that is required for its presentation. Thus, the content and the program can be transferred to a workstation from a server and subsequent interactions do not require participation by the server.

INFORMATION MODELING AND RETRIEVAL

New approaches to accessing information have also been developed that facilitate operation in novel ways. For example, high-end workstations can provide three-dimensional access to information via the use of large display devices and oscillating-aperture 3D glasses. For database applications, the trend is to move away from traditional relational query-type interfaces that require substantial knowledge of the content and structure of the stored information. Object-oriented and hypermedia models (nonsequential access by reference) are increasingly popular for managing very large multimedia data items such as *digital libraries* ($q.v.$). On the Web, the hypermedia or hypertext ($q.v.$) paradigm is fundamental, but is often coupled with conventional relational database components. In this paradigm, data or documents are interconnected as a network. This representation facilitates extensive cross-referencing of related items in a mode which allows a user to browse effectively through the data by following links connecting associated topics or keywords.

Summary and Future

Multimedia computing is here and is being absorbed into mainstream computing; however, for large-scale multimedia applications beyond the "desktop", there is still a need for significant advances in high-speed networking, storage servers, and low-cost presentation devices for delivery of multimedia applications to the consumer. The pace of development of multimedia technology is very rapid. Trends indicate that quite soon processing units will become faster, display devices will become cheaper, memory devices will become larger, and high-bandwidth network access will become ubiquitous. The end result will be a major impact of multimedia computer technology on society. It is becoming less of a novelty and more of a practical necessity.

Bibliography

1992. Blattner, M. M., and Dannenberg, R. B. *Multimedia Interface Design.* New York: ACM Press.

1994. Buford, J. F. (ed.) *Multimedia Systems.* New York: ACM Press.

1995. Gibbs, S., and Tsichritzis, D. C. *Multimedia Programming. Objects, Environments and Frameworks.* New York: ACM Press.

1995. Streinmetz, R., and Nahrstedt, K. *Multimedia: Computing, Communications and Applications.* Upper Saddle River, NJ: Prentice Hall.

1996. Furht, B. (ed.) *Multimedia Tools and Applications.* Norwood. MA: Kluwer Academic.

1997. *Communications of the ACM,* **40**, 2 (February).

Thomas Little

MULTIPLEXING

For articles on related subjects *see* BANDWIDTH; CHANNEL; COMMUNICATION CONTROL UNIT; CONTENTION; LOCAL AREA NETWORK; MODEM; NETWORKS, COMPUTER; PACKET SWITCHING; POLLING; TCP/IP; and TIME SHARING.

Multiplexing is a technique that allows a number of lower bandwidth communication channels to be combined and transmitted over a higher bandwidth channel. At the receiving end, *demultiplexing* recovers the original lower bandwidth channels. The main reason for multiplexing is to make efficient use of the full bandwidth of the communication channel and to achieve a lower cost per bit transmitted.

The three basic multiplexing methods in use are *space division multiplexing* (SDM), *frequency division multiplexing* (FDM), and *time division multiplexing* (TDM). The words *multiplexing* and *concentration* are sometimes used synonymously. Concentration, however, is a TDM technique in which traffic statistics and buffering play an important role. It usually involves a *concentrator*, a small computer programmed to perform the function of a time division multiplexer.

Space Division Multiplexing

Space division multiplexing refers to the physical grouping of many individual transmission channels

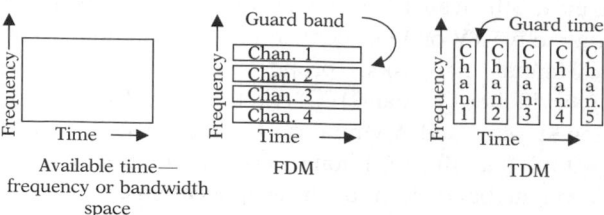

Figure 1. Relationship between frequency or bandwidth and time in FDM and TDM.

to form a channel with a much higher total aggregate bandwidth. Hundreds of twisted wire pairs, coaxial cables, and/or optical fibers can be grouped to form a larger diameter cable. Each wire pair, coaxial cable, or fiber in the main cable is an individual communication channel capable of being frequency or time division multiplexed. Such cables have enough total bandwidth to carry hundreds of thousands of two-way voice channels of 4,000 Hz each in a cable diameter of under 3 inches.

Frequency Division Multiplexing

As shown in Fig. 1, frequency division multiplexing (FDM) divides a higher bandwidth channel into many individual smaller bandwidth channels. Signals (data, voice, or video) on these channels are transmitted at the same time but at different carrier frequencies. *Guard bands* are needed between the channels to help reduce interchannel interference.

A familiar example of FDM is television broadcasting. Stations broadcast programs continuously, each at a different frequency, the atmosphere being the transmission medium. The tuning circuits in the television tuner select and separate one channel from the others.

Time Division Multiplexing

In time division multiplexing, the entire bandwidth of the channel is dedicated to one low-speed channel for a short period of time, and then to the other low-speed channels in round-robin fashion or some other predetermined sequence (see Fig. 2). In effect, the low bandwidth channels are accommodated on the high bandwidth channel by interleaving the former in the time domain. Guard times are used to separate time slices (*q.v.*), and the transmitting and receiving ends must be synchronized. A familiar example of TDM is the input–output bus (*q.v.*) of a computer servicing many peripherals, one at a time, for short periods of time.

The time slots may be allocated on a fixed, predetermined (*a priori*) basis or on a demand basis. TDM is, therefore, usually subdivided into the following categories:

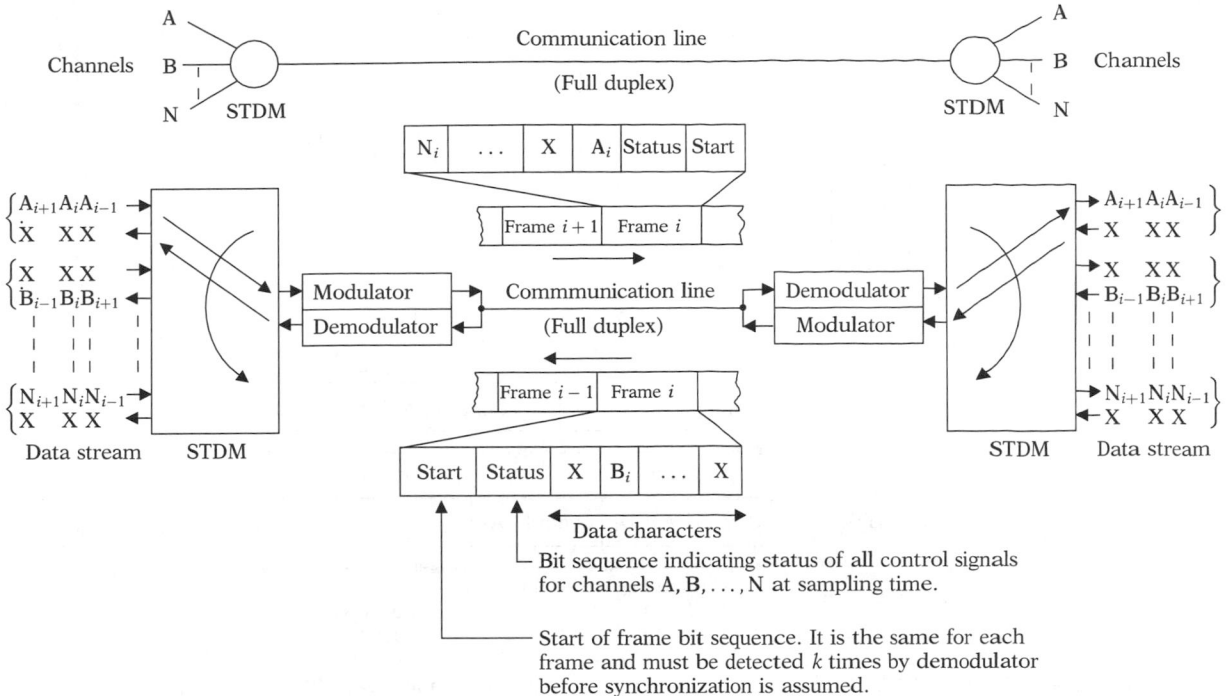

Figure 2. Typical character-interleaved STDM and associated frame format. After sending the start and status bit sequences, the STDM connects each channel in turn to the line for a very short time, forming the stream of data characters for each frame. A full duplex line is shown to enable simultaneous data transfer in both directions. The Xs represent an idle line condition.

1. Synchronous time division multiplexing (STDM)

2. Asynchronous time division multiplexing (ATDM)

3. Message switching multiplexing (MSM):

    (a) polling type

    (b) contention type

The time slots in STDM are allocated on a fixed basis, usually in a round-robin fashion, as shown in Fig. 2. The data stream may be bit or character interleaved, depending on whether each time slot within the frame is devoted to a bit or a character, respectively. Each channel is sampled one by one for 1 bit or character time, and the samples are assembled into a serial stream. At the receiving end, the stream is disassembled and the original streams are reconstructed.

A time slot in STDM is allocated for a channel even in the absence of data on that channel. ATDM (sometimes also called *statistical multiplexing*) overcomes this inefficiency by allocating time slots only for active channels. This requires a special control header in each frame to identify the active channels. Despite this header, the efficiency and effective throughput can be improved significantly, since some channels are idle much of the time. *See* Fig. 3.

STDM and ATDM may be interleaved by bit or character. The interleaving may also be on an entire

message, in which case it is sometimes called *message switching multiplexing* (MSM). Fig. 4 shows a leased communication line connecting a computer or master station to remote terminals or slave stations connected via modems designed for such lines. Each slave is assigned a unique address and the master performs the multiplexing function by *polling* or by *contention*. In a polled environment, each slave is addressed in turn to determine whether it has data to send or needs access to the master. If it does, the master authorizes the access for a finite period, and only one slave is permitted to receive or transmit data over the communication line at any one time. In a contention system, any slave device needing to communicate waits until there is no traffic on the line and then seizes the line to transmit its message. The line is then released to give another slave device the opportunity to seize the line. In such a system, the transmitted messages or data packets must be short to avoid unduly long wait times by the other devices on the line. Shared media Ethernet or FDDI networks work in a fashion similar to polling by contention, but the transmission tends to be peer-to-peer rather than on a master–slave basis.

Circuit and Packet Switching

A circuit switch refers to equipment that can transfer any one of m input lines to any one of n output lines or trunks ($m > n$), as shown in Fig. 5. Once established,

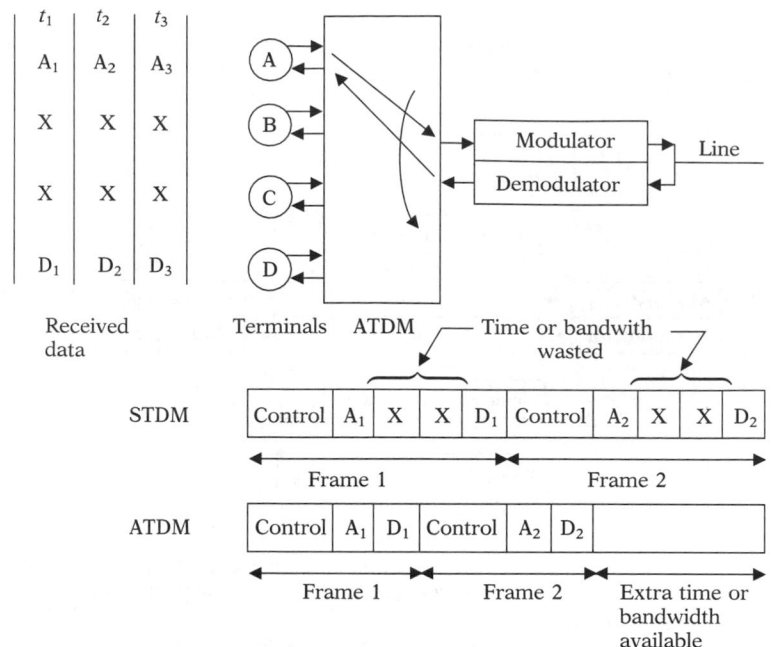

Figure 3. Comparison of STDM and ATDM. The sample shows reception of data on channels A and D, with B and C being idle, as indicated by the Xs. By assigning time slots only to the active terminals, ATDM results in less wasted bandwidth. The control signals in ATDM contain the addresses of the active terminals and the order in which they are sent.

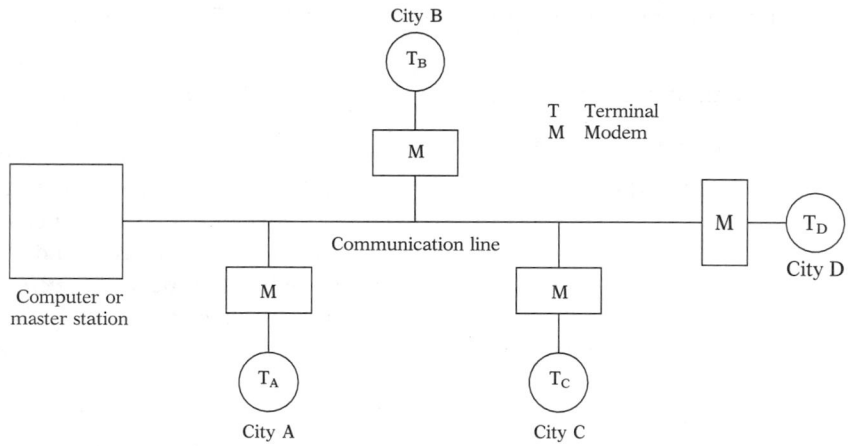

Figure 4. Multiplexing by polling or by contention.

the connection is typically held for the duration of the entire transmission of data, or voice call in the case of the telephone network. At the end of the transmission, the trunk is freed and is available for assignment to the next input line needing a trunk connection. An input can be connected to a trunk if at least one trunk is not being used. This technique is mainly used in telephone networks to establish an end-to-end circuit for the entire duration of a call and, although it has sometimes been called space division multiplexing, it is more appropriate to call it circuit or line switching. This should be contrasted with packet switching, in which the trunk is used only for the duration of the transmission of a packet rather than the entire duration of the call or transmission. By limiting the length

of packets, wait times for other users are limited. Packet switching is, therefore, very effective for transmitting data for interactive computing over a wide area network such as the Internet. Packet switching is a form of MSM and, therefore, TDM.

Multiplexer Hierarchies

As networks grow and get more complex, hierarchies of multiplexing are required in which low-bandwidth channels are multiplexed onto higher bandwidth channels, which in turn are multiplexed onto even higher bandwidth channels, etc. In the FDM hierarchy, multiplex levels correspond to increasingly higher frequency bands. In the TDM hierarchy, they correspond

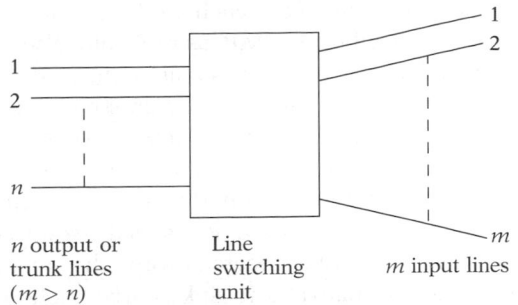

Figure 5. Line or circuit-switching unit connects any one of *m* input lines to any one of *n* trunk lines. This is widely used where the probability of all input lines being used at a given time is small, resulting in more efficient usage of the trunk lines.

to increasingly higher pulse rates. For example, 24 voice channels can be time division multiplexed on a T1 carrier operating at 1.54 Mbps (millions of bits per second), four T1 carriers can be multiplexed onto a T2 carrier operating at 6.312 Mbps, seven T2 carriers can be multiplexed onto a T3 carrier operating at 44.736 Mbps, while six T3 carriers can be multiplexed onto a T4 carrier operating at 274.176 Mbps using AT&T's multiplexing hierarchy.

Economics of Multiplexing

The basic reason for multiplexing is that the cost to transmit a fixed amount of data or voice traffic decreases as the total capacity of the communication channel increases, provided the amount of traffic justifies the higher capacity. Consequently, multiplexing is widely used for voice and data traffic, especially in wide area networks. It should be emphasized, however, that in modern data networks the multiplexing tends to be done primarily by using some variant of TDM (e.g. Ethernet, FDDI and Token Ring networks) rather than FDM, while for voice networks both TDM and FDM are widely used.

Bibliography

1985. Meadow, C. T., and Tedesco, A. S. *Telecommunications for Management*. New York: McGraw-Hill.
1996. Tanenbaum, A. S. *Computer Networks*, 3rd Ed. Upper Saddle River, NJ: Prentice Hall.
1997. Keshav S. *An Engineering Approach to Computer Networking: ATM Networks, the Internet and the Telephone Network*. Reading, MA: Addison-Wesley.

John S. Sobolewski

MULTIPROCESSING

For articles on related subjects *see* CACHE COHERENCY; CACHE MEMORY; CLUSTER COMPUTING; CONCURRENT PROGRAMMING; CONTENTION; MUTUAL EXCLUSION; MULTIPROGRAMMING; MULTITASKING; PARALLEL PROCESSING; and SUPERCOMPUTERS.

For the purpose of this article, *multiprocessing* is the simultaneous processing of two or more computational portions of the same program by two or more processing units. The simultaneous processing of different programs on a system with several CPUs (one program/CPU) sharing a common memory is considered here as an extension of multiprogramming rather than true multiprocessing.

With this definition, multiprocessing involves a departure from the classical von Neumann machine (*q.v.*) organization in which there is a single instruction stream (single program counter) and a single data stream (unique communication channel between CPU and memory). From an architectural viewpoint, extensions to this Single Instruction Single Data (SISD) organization will yield Single Instruction Multiple Data (SIMD) architectures and Multiple Instruction Multiple Data (MIMD) architectures. This classification is due to Flynn (1966). Here we restrict ourselves to MIMD systems.

MIMD architectures are differentiated according to whether they are shared-memory machines, i.e., communication occurs as the result of load–store instructions, or operate according to a message-passing paradigm. Although the tendency in recent systems is to try to support both programming models, we will consider only shared-memory multiprocessors. In shared-memory MIMD systems, further differentiation arises when one considers the switching structure between processors and memory modules. Typical switching structures in *tightly coupled* systems, where all processors operate under the control of a single operating system, are a common single shared bus, a multistage interconnection network, meshes or tori, or a crossbar (a switch that connects any processor to any memory module). Note, however, that one can stretch the definition of shared-memory multiprocessors by including networks of workstations (NOW) cooperating on solving the same problem. A fundamental difference between tightly coupled systems and NOW is the unit of communication, namely a few bytes (word or cache line) for the former and a few kilobytes (page) in the latter.

Single-Bus Systems

In the shared-bus architecture (which used to be called a *multi* (*see* Fig. 1) and now is often called *symmetric multiprocessors, SMP*), processors have access to a common *bus* (*q.v.*) via their off-chip caches. Global memory, common to all processors, is also attached to the bus. Since all processors access memory with the same latency, this architecture is of the *Uniform Memory Access* (UMA) type. Cache coherence is solved using snoopy protocols whereby each cache

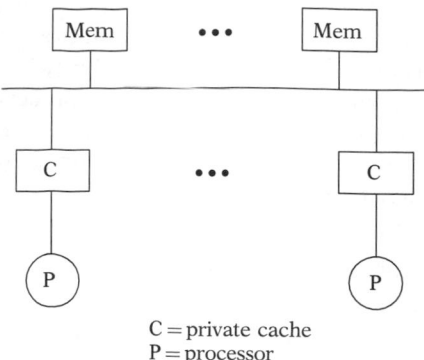

C = private cache
P = processor

Figure 1. Multi: multiprocessor with a shared bus.

controller listens to all bus transactions. The single bus is therefore a major source of contention, not only because it is on the unique access path to memory, but also because of the traffic generated by coherency operations. Early multis with (relatively) slow processors and (relatively) fast buses could consist of up to 30 processors (Sequent Balance and Symmetry, SGI Challenge). Recent offerings of SMPs are limited to four processors, since the processor speed is increasing much faster than the bus speed and width.

Non-Uniform Memory Access (NUMA) Systems

Larger multiprocessors (e.g. on the order of tens to a few hundred processing elements) require another switching structure. Multistage interconnection networks such as those in Fig. 2 ($O(\log n)$ stages for n processor and memory modules), as well as two- and three-dimensional meshes and tori, have been used to connect nodes—processors and associated memory modules. The number of switches, and stages, can be reduced by using 4×4 or 8×8 crossbars rather than

2×2 switches. Moreover, each node of the multiprocessor can itself be an SMP, as in Stanford's DASH experimental machine, or a small number (two to eight) of processors connected by a crossbar as in the SGI Origin and HP/Convex Exemplar. These more powerful nodes are often referred to as *clusters*. Cache coherence is maintained with the use of directories (maps showing where data is cached—*see* CACHE COHERENCY), generally located with the memory modules. An alternative is to link shared cache lines as in the SCI protocol.

In these larger systems, access to memory is nonuniform since the latency to reference memory within a node (home memory) is much smaller than access to the memory of a remote node; hence the name *distributed shared memory* for these systems. Care must be taken in designing applications for NUMA systems so that internode traffic is reduced as much as possible. In the case of clusters, adding a large cache shared by the processors of the cluster, as in the Sequent CC-NUMA, is very beneficial to performance.

Programming Shared Memory Systems

In multiprocessing systems, the increase in performance resides mainly in path parallelism, i.e. the concurrent execution of several different parts of the program, or of the same part with different data. In applications programming (*q.v.*), this requires an explicit indication of the parallelism either stated by the user or generated by the compiler, synchronization among the various paths, and scheduling of the processors.

The basic form of parallelism is via a FORK–JOIN pair where FORK indicates the creation of several paths that JOIN at a given point. A more modern and higher-level construct for FORK is the creation of concurrent threads that share common memory and have their own private stacks (*q.v.*). A *create* procedure with parameters for the number of threads, where they should start executing, and with what arguments, is a fairly common way to achieve this function. A *wait* construct implements the JOIN with an argument for the number of threads that must be ending before the flow of control can proceed with the statement following the wait. A special, and often present, case is the DO ALL statement which allows for the concurrent execution of independent loop instances. A *barrier* statement, a global synchronization primitive with an argument indicating the number of instances of the loop, is used to start (fork) and finish (join) the instances of the parallel loop.

In MIMD architectures, control and synchronization of the processors are sensitive areas. The most common type of control is a decentralized mode whereby each

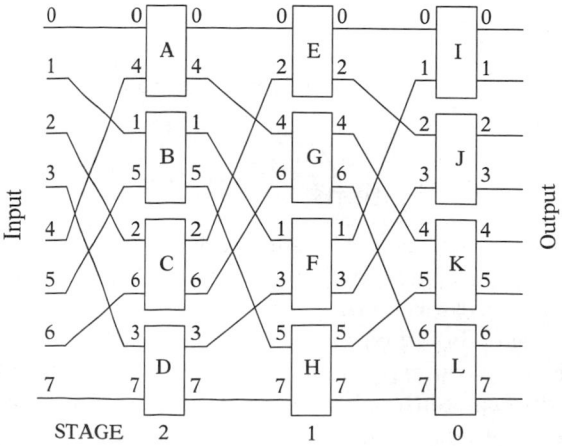

STAGE   2   1   0

Figure 2. Example of a multistage interconnection network: the Omega network.

processor can have access to the operating system (*q.v.*) and schedule itself. In this case, and more generally when a task is split into concurrent paths, it will happen that two concurrent processes will wish to access and modify the same data structures (*q.v.*), for example a work queue for self-scheduling or common modifiable data. Hence, there must be some means of preventing disorderly changes in the shared database. This has been referred to as the *mutual exclusion* problem. In any given path the portion of code that accesses the shared data is called the *critical section* of that path.

One way to provide the necessary protection is to associate a lock indicator with each shared data object. High-level constructs such as *acquire* and *release* of locks, implemented in an atomic fashion via the use of more primitive instructions, have been available in a variety of formats that are tuned to the shared-memory model seen by the programmer.

The presence of several processors adds a new dimension to the scheduling problem. In almost all cases, optimal schedules cannot be attained even with *a priori* knowledge of the exact time requirements of each task. Models have been devised, analytical solutions have been investigated, and a number of heuristic (*q.v.*) methods have been proposed to assess the performance of multiprocessing systems. This performance can be improved not only by an explicit expression of parallelism, but also by compiler-detected parallelism, and by designing new algorithms for parallel environments.

Bibliography

1966. Flynn, M. "Very High-speed Computing Systems," *Proceedings IEEE* (December).
1998. Hwang, K., and Xu, Z. *Scalable Parallel Computing.* New York: McGraw-Hill.
1999. Culler, D., Singh, J. P., and Gupta, A. *Parallel Computer Architecture. A Hardware/Software Approach.* San Francisco: Morgan Kaufmann.

Jean-Loup Baer

MULTIPROGRAMMING

For articles on related subjects *see* CONCURRENT PROGRAMMING; DATA SECURITY; INPUT–OUTPUT CONTROL SYSTEM; INTERLEAVING; MULTITASKING; OPERATING SYSTEMS; OVERHEAD; PARALLEL PROCESSING; PRIVILEGED INSTRUCTION; SCHEDULING ALGORITHMS; SWAPPING; TIME SHARING; and VIRTUAL MEMORY.

Today's computer systems typically provide far more resources than a single program requires. *Multiprogramming*—i.e. overlapping and interleaving the

executions of more than one program—can achieve several possible goals. It may achieve higher resource utilization by keeping the resources of the computer system working simultaneously as much as possible. It may permit two or more programs to operate in parallel, so their effects are observed simultaneously, rather than sequentially. Another objective is to complete what may be a lengthy, complex start-up phase of execution, leaving the program suspended in a state of readiness with relatively little time required for real-time reactivation. The concept of multiprogramming was conceived in 1962 at the University of Manchester and first implemented on an Atlas (*q.v.*) computer by a team led by Tom Kilburn (*q.v.*).

Early computer systems executed only one program (or *job*) at a time. Programs fell into two categories; certain programs were *input–output* (I/O) *bound*; i.e. their rate of progress was limited by the speed of input–output units. In mainframe (*q.v.*) computers, devices such as tape drives or card readers slowed execution; in desktop systems it is typically serial modems (*q.v.*) or printers that consume significant amounts of real-time. *Central processing unit* (CPU) *bound* programs performed mostly numerical calculations, with little input–output. Neither of these types of program can fully utilize the resources of the computer system. Clearly, if we could multiprogram, e.g. concurrently execute jobs from both of these classes, then better utilization of the available equipment could be realized.

Once a computer has begun to read data from a disk or modem, the processor can execute instructions while data is being transferred into an area of memory that is being used as a *buffer* (*q.v.*). Even if we have only a single CPU, it can perform work for many different programs by switching from one particular *task* to another. Each program requires allocated address space to hold the data and instructions being, or ready to be, executed. If sufficient memory and other resources exist and can be allocated to many programs in a manner such that each makes effective progress, then the computer can be multiprogrammed.

Fig. 1 is an example of how two programs can be interleaved and overlapped by multiprogramming. The first program (shown in Fig. 1a) is heavily input–output-bound, and uses the CPU only 10% of the time. The second program, shown in Fig. 1c, has the opposite nature, and would like to use the CPU 90% of the time. If these programs were executing alone, each would behave as shown in Figs. 1a and 1c, respectively, but Fig. 1b shows how often the demands of the first program and those of the second conflict because each wants to use the same resource. Notice that this happens about 20% of the time. We could have calculated

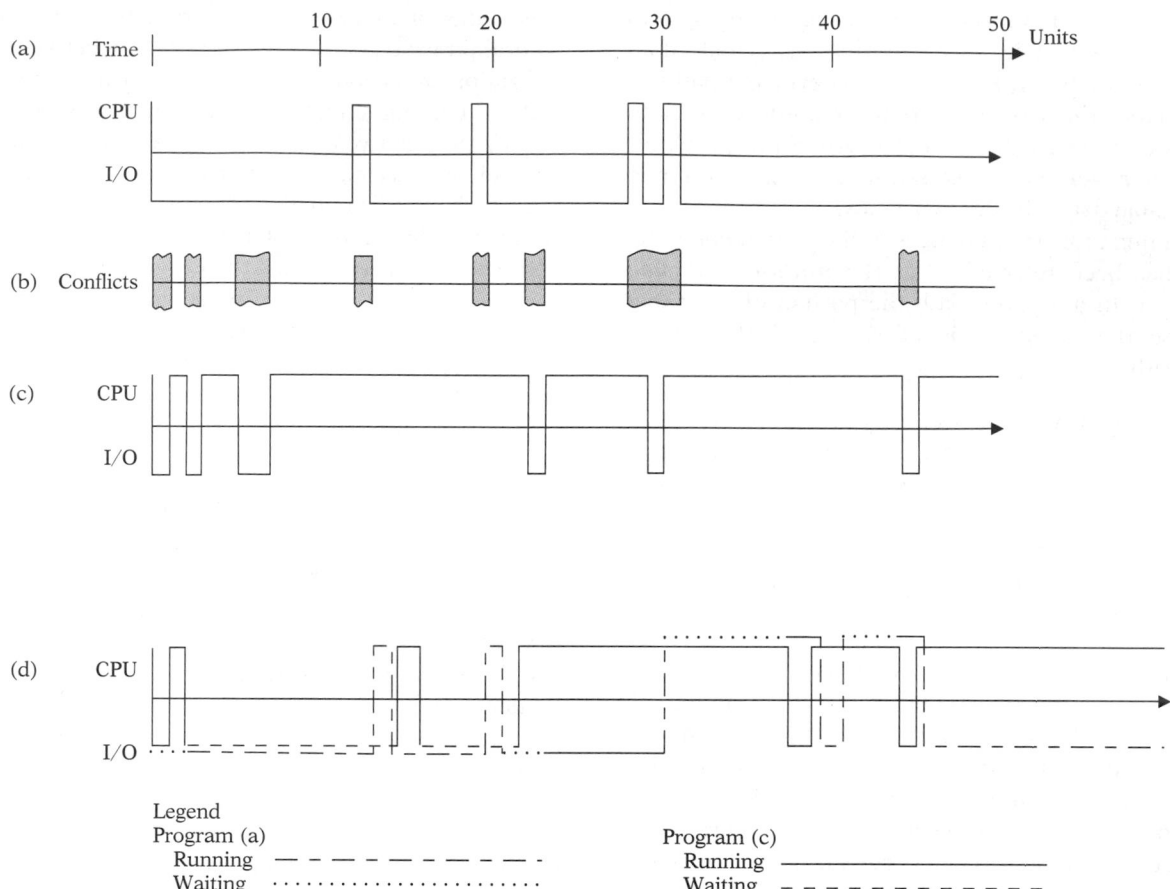

Figure 1. An example of the advantages of multiprogramming. The area of overlap between the I/O-bound program (a) and CPU-bound program (c) is shown in (b). In (d), one way of multiprogramming these two programs is shown.

this number by realizing that the program in Fig. 1a would like to use the CPU 10% of the time, but that the program in Fig. 1c probably wants to do the same. Conversely, the program in Fig. 1c wants to do some input–output about 10% of the time, when it is very likely that the program in Fig. 1a does also. Thus, we estimate that for 20% of the time there is a conflict for resources, while for 80% of the time the programs might be able to overlap by using different resources. Fig. 1d shows one way in which we can multiprogram these two programs. Assume that the following rule is used to determine which program will be active: whenever both programs request the use of the same resource, the CPU-bound program is allowed to proceed, and the I/O-bound program must wait, subject to the restriction that once an input–output operation is begun, it cannot be stopped and must be finished. (Such a decision rule is purely illustrative and is not necessarily the "best" rule to use for the types of jobs shown.) We see that, in the 50 units of time displayed, either the CPU or an I/O device is in use for 71 units. Since together we have resources for 100 units of work (50 from the CPU and 50 of I/O), we are achieving 71% *utilization* of the system. Sepa-

rately, the program in Fig. 1a or Fig. 1c would use only 50% of the available resources, so we have improved utilization of the system by about 40%. We could not expect utilization to go much beyond 90% (excepting some unusually favorable circumstances), since we calculated that for 80% of the time both resources could be in use, and that for 20% of the time only one resource is busy while one program waits for the other.

Multiprogramming does not require a large operating system in order to coordinate the demands of each program. On a small computer, such as is used for process control, it is common to provide a *background/foreground* system that permits two programs to execute. The foreground, or real-time, program may consist of a job to monitor periodically a number of instruments and perform some corrective adjustment. In between each measurement, the system may have sufficient resources to permit a background program to execute, doing compilations or calculations. These two programs might cooperate by mutual understanding; i.e. the programmers could insure that each would not interfere with the use of the system by the other.

While in very simple situations it may be feasible to multiprogram cooperatively, often we must be sure that, if one program somehow violates the rules of the system, it does not corrupt the whole environment. Thus, most multiprogramming systems require a *monitor* (also called an *executive* or *supervisor*).

It is the responsibility of the monitor to maintain the integrity of the system. In the case of the background/ foreground system used as an example, we would like the monitor to guarantee that the foreground real-time program will be able to take its measurements, even if the background program goes into a loop and never voluntarily relinquishes control. Thus, our computer system must have the capability to *preempt* a resource (such as the CPU) from a program and to ensure that the foreground program or the monitor gains control. The monitor must be *protected* from accidental or malicious destruction by a *user* program. User programs must also be protected from one another by intercepting, usually through hardware features, attempts to change or access memory that is "out of bounds" to a particular program. We also require some form of preemption to achieve acceptable levels of multiprogramming when an arbitrary collection of non-cooperating programs are executing, to prevent one of them from inadvertently monopolizing a resource.

In order to control resources effectively such as space for data or file storage, modern systems centralize all input–output operations in an *operating system* that performs services on behalf of the user programs. In this manner the users of the system cannot corrupt each other's data or invade the privacy of secure information.

To permit the construction of a system with these capabilities, computer systems generally possess *privileged instructions* that user programs cannot execute. For example, all input–output instructions (*q.v.*), or those instructions associated with the protection of one area of memory from a program executing in a different area, are reserved for the *kernel* (*q.v.*). When the computer is executing in kernel (or *master*) mode, these functions are permitted. The kernel has the responsibility of ensuring that when control is given to a user program, the system is switched to user (or *slave*) mode. In slave mode, any attempt to execute privileged instructions will give control back to the kernel.

In desktop systems, the decision to start or stop specific programs is totally under control of the user sitting at the keyboard. For larger shared computer systems this is not the case, and we require the operating system to implement a *scheduling algorithm*.

Scheduling in a multiprogrammed environment is often complex. The concept of multiprogramming entails the *global* optimization of the resources of the entire system. However, users are generally concerned with their own tasks, and attempt to optimize *locally*; i.e. they try to make their programs perform better or faster, without regard to the total environment.

Consequently, in a large data processing center it is common to find the ultimate scheduling performed external to the system itself, either by administrative decisions concerning the categories (or *classes*) of jobs that are permitted at certain times of day, or by the operator of the system. The operator may be able to start or suspend programs from an operator's console based on the performance of the system. Meanwhile, the scheduler program of the operating system performs the microscopic decisions, such as initiating input–output operations or deciding which program is to be given the resources of the central processor.

One common form of scheduling is provided by a *priority* assigned to each job or task within the system. The actual value of the priority may be based on external factors, such as the fact that the results are needed quickly (or the converse), or it may be based on the overall resource requirements of the job when submitted to the computer system. This priority may change dynamically as the program evolves, or it may increase as time progresses if the job is not making effective progress. Priority may also be changed by an operator from a console. The detailed nature of scheduling depends heavily on the nature of the service the system is expected to provide.

If too many jobs are begun at once, they can interfere with each other and waste resources. In fact, it is even possible to cause a *deadlock* to occur when a number of programs have begun but cannot continue until additional resources are available, and yet those resources are tied up by other jobs. The algorithm used for scheduling must have enough information to avoid such situations, or should possess the means to "untangle" them if they occur; otherwise, system performance degrades as it enters a very active but non-productive state called *thrashing* (*q.v.*).

Multiprogramming may also take place within a single job. For example, the system may be able to overlap the computational needs of a single program with its input–output needs. The capability of a program to spawn (or create) additional tasks (user processes) that are to be executed as if they were jobs, but which possess a filial relationship to the parent task, is referred to as *multitasking* or *multithreading*.

Multiprogramming is accepted as the standard means of using all but the smallest of today's computer systems. The advantages offered by multiprogramming are now present on some very small systems such as hand-held *personal information managers* (*see* PORTABLE COMPUTERS), and are omnipresent on dedicated, one-user desktop systems. Created initially to address the efficient utilization of expensive and unique central computer systems, multiprogramming is now critical to the desire of desktop users to switch rapidly between a variety of activities in a manner supporting apparent simultaneity.

Bibliography

1972. Lorin, H. *Parallelism in Hardware and Software: Real and Apparent Concurrency.* Upper Saddle River, NJ: Prentice Hall.

1997. Silberschatz, A., and Galvin, P. B. *Operating Systems Concepts*, 5th Ed. Reading, MA: Addison-Wesley.

Harry J. Saal

MULTITASKING

For articles on related subjects *see* CONCURRENT PROGRAMMING; MULTIPLEXING; MULTIPROCESSING; MULTIPROGRAMMING; OPERATING SYSTEMS; PARALLEL PROCESSING; REAL-TIME SYSTEMS; TIME SHARING; and TIME SLICE.

Multitasking refers to an operating system's ability to support multiple processes simultaneously. A *process* is a program in execution. Support for multiple processes is necessary in applications where several computations must proceed in parallel. On a PC, a user may edit a file while another file is being printed and electronic mail (*q.v.*) is received. These three activities are best supported by three processes running simultaneously. Multitasking is also needed on servers and time-sharing systems where multiple users share a single computer system and all processes created by them should, at least in principle, execute simultaneously. Real-time systems that control multiple devices also need to support multiple processes. For instance, an avionics computer on board an aircraft runs processes for monitoring the engines, updating the flight instruments, processing radar signals, and keeping the airplane on course. Batch operating systems depend on multitasking for overlapping computation with I/O operations: when a process performs I/O, the operating system runs another process to avoid idling the central processor for long periods of time.

Modern operating systems distinguish between two types of processes. *Lightweight processes* or *threads* are described by their *stateword* or *statevector*, i.e. the contents of the processor registers such as the program counter, stack pointer, general purpose registers, condition codes, etc. A *user process*, also called a *task*, is a significant extension. It includes at least one thread, a virtual memory (*q.v.*) containing a program (instructions and data), and context information such as descriptors for open files and communication channels

(Tanenbaum, 1997). Multitasking must be supported on both the thread and task levels.

Thread-Level Support for Multitasking

The simplest way to execute multiple threads simultaneously is to assign each thread to its own processor in a multiprocessor system. If the number of threads exceeds the number of processors, then processors must be multiplexed among the threads. *Processor multiplexing* implements quasi-parallelism: by switching a processor rapidly from one thread to the next, it appears to the observer as though all threads are making progress, even though the processor can execute instructions of only one process at a time.

Processor multiplexing works as follows. Time is divided into disjoint intervals called *time slices*, and the processor is assigned to at most one thread during each interval. At the end of a time slice, the operating system performs a *context switch*: it switches the running thread off its processor by first saving the processor registers into memory, and then loads the stateword of the next thread into the processor registers.

There are two major techniques for determining the end of a time slice. In simple batch operating systems, a time slice ends when the thread must wait for an event such as the completion of an I/O operation or a signal from another thread. While this approach insures high processor utilization, it allows a thread performing little or no I/O to monopolize the processor. In order to give all threads a fair share, most operating systems additionally implement a limit on the maximum period during which a thread may run continuously. When a thread begins its time slice, a timer in the processor is set to a standard value and decremented during every instruction cycle. When it reaches zero, the timer generates an interrupt (*q.v.*). The interrupt handler then performs a context switch.

The choice of thread to be loaded onto the processor by a context switch is determined by a *scheduling algorithm* (*q.v.*). Most scheduling algorithms simply select the thread with the highest priority. To ensure adequate response time in time-sharing systems, interactive threads are usually given higher priority than compute-intensive threads. This setting works well, since interactive threads spend most of their time waiting for input and do not need much compute time, but can regain the processor quickly when needed. In real-time systems, where threads must meet specified deadlines, priorities are not sufficient. Instead, a schedule for the entire set of available threads must be computed (Xu, 1990)

While processor multiplexing implements only quasi-parallelism, peripheral devices can provide true parallelism even if the computer system contains only a single central processor. Peripheral devices can be regarded as specialized processors that operate concurrently with the central processor. A device runs a single process specialized, for example, for printing a page or writing a disk block. The device receives commands from a device driver process which itself runs on the central processor. After a device driver has issued a command to a device, the driver waits for a completion signal (implemented by the interrupt system). During this wait, the main processor switches its attention from the device driver (*q.v.*) to other threads. With multiple processors (devices and CPUs), the potential for true parallel processing is increased.

Task-Level Support for Multitasking

At the task level, memory management (*q.v.*) is an important issue. A simple approach is *swapping* (*q.v.*): the operating system keeps only a single task's program in the main memory at a time; the programs of other tasks are stored in secondary storage (usually disk). As part of a context switch, the operating system must first unload its memory to disk and then reload it with the program of the next task. In order to reduce I/O traffic, a multiprogrammed operating system keeps programs or program segments of several tasks in main memory simultaneously. Multiprogramming reduces the number of reads and writes to secondary storage, provided main memory is large enough to hold the working sets (*q.v.*) of several tasks. Multiprogramming is facilitated by virtual memory (*q.v.*), a mechanism that simulates an address space much larger than the physical memory available to each task; it is discussed in detail elsewhere in this Encyclopedia.

If tasks contain several threads, then thread management becomes an issue as well. The threads of a task form a team and share memory and context information. To ensure rapid progress of tasks, the operating system must perform *co-scheduling*, i.e. schedule the threads of a task together. A task may also create and manage subtasks containing independent teams of threads and virtual memories.

Specifications of the operating system functions provided at the thread and task levels appear in the article OPERATING SYSTEMS.

Bibliography

1990. Xu, J., and Parnas, D. L. "Scheduling Processes with Release Times, Deadlines, Precedence and Exclusion Relations," *IEEE Transactions on Software Engineering*, **16**, *3* (March), 360–369.
1997. Tanenbaum, A. S. *Operating Systems—Design and Implementation*, 2nd Ed. Upper Saddle River, NJ: Prentice Hall.

Walter F. Tichy

MUSEUMS, COMPUTER

For articles on related subjects *see* COMPUTER ART; HUMANITIES APPLICATIONS; and WORLD WIDE WEB.

Computer museums are places, both real and virtual, that seek to preserve, celebrate, and explain humankind's most profound technical achievement of the mid- to late-20th century, the computer. Just as there exists enormous variety in the form, appearance, and performance of computers, so are there broad differences among computer museums in emphasis, funding, size, and intended audience.

Computer museums of any type share many of the same challenges and opportunities as do more traditional art, technology, or specialist museums. To some extent, all such institutions exist to place objects in a context which no longer exists outside museums and to foster the scholarly study and preservation of such objects as a means of reconstructing this context and the object's relationship to it. Museums also serve as a place to gain an esthetic understanding of individual objects, often eliciting a "sublime" response, and placing the computer architect or manufacturer in the role of "artist." Much as Goethe noted that "architecture is music frozen," so are the objects in a computer museum congealed embodiments of the technical constraints, economic possibilities, and expressive power of the human mind at particular instants. There is frequently an elegance in an object, one which appeals to museum visitors on a visceral level, and which is evocative of the virtuosity of its creators. This latter effect is one of the advantages that a "real" (physical object-based) museum has over a virtual one; it is akin to the difference between reading about Roman ruins and actually visiting the Colosseum. Conversely, while real computer museums are expensive to operate, frequently face funding challenges, and require large infrastructures, Web museums allow rapid dissemination of information and allow the historical net (to capture history) to be cast wider and audience size to be increased dramatically. It is clear as well that for the great majority of museum "visits," people will increasingly be using the Web rather than traveling to a physical location; hence even real museums now integrate their holdings, exhibits, education, and outreach programs into Web-based knowledge architectures.

Common Features

Given the variety and scope of computer museums and of the approaches and capabilities of the people who create them, both museum types nonetheless have certain features in common. Both embody, either explicitly or implicitly, meta-level guiding principles meant to facilitate execution of their institutional focus or curatorial mandate. Some of the more popular collections guidelines across all museums include:

1. *The first of something.* Also known as the "cult of champions," or the *Guinness Book of Records* approach. This comprises the "successes" of the industry, for example, representative instances of an IBM System/360 (*q.v.*) or the first Fortran (*q.v.*) compiler (*q.v.*). "Firsts," however, are frequently matters of controversy or interpretation and may change over time (e.g. the Atanasoff (*q.v.*)/Mauchly (*q.v.*) case) so care needs to be exercised with respect to both object selection and the knowledge claims made on behalf of such objects.

2. *Mass-produced.* Driven by market success, the object becomes collectible precisely because it is so common. The IBM PC (*q.v.*) is the classic example.

3. *Special provenance.* Something owned or used by an important inventor, for example, John von Neumann's (*q.v.*) slide-rule. While the scholarly value of such items is often unclear, these objects appeal to people's fascination with anything a famous person may have touched or used (*see* Fig. 1). In rare cases, these items may actually reveal something of significance given the proper forensic or analytical procedures.

4. *Failures.* Rule (1) is often problematic because it fosters an oversimplification of the invention process—obscuring, for example, the fact that concurrent invention happens frequently, given equivalent initial conditions. For this reason, many researchers find "failures" to be more instructive of invention than successes at the "environmental" or disciplinary level (*see* Fig. 2).

5. *Seminal inventors.* Certain people do seem to contribute a disproportionate amount of disciplinary knowledge (e.g. Seymour Cray (*q.v.*) or Donald Knuth) and, as such, objects they have created or supervised are of interest here.

Even with these simple guidelines, the variety of objects is overwhelming. To impose order on such objects, most museums construct a taxonomy by which to organize their current and future holdings. For more specialized museums, as is typical of Web-based ones, such taxonomies are often very straightforward, tending to focus on one type of machine product family or category (e.g. "Commodore Amigas," or "DEC (*q.v.*) minicomputers (*q.v.*)"). Larger institutions generally employ some form of hierarchical nomenclature, reminiscent of the Whittaker Five Kingdoms model used in biology. Although formal computer organizing systems by research and professional organizations have been devised, they tend to be overly formal, are inordinately comprehensive, and rapidly become out-of-date. For this reason, new taxonomies are frequently created by computer museums themselves to reflect their own unique collections practices and institutional focus. The PMS system (*see* HARDWARE DESCRIPTION LANGUAGES), devised by Bell and Newell, is one such

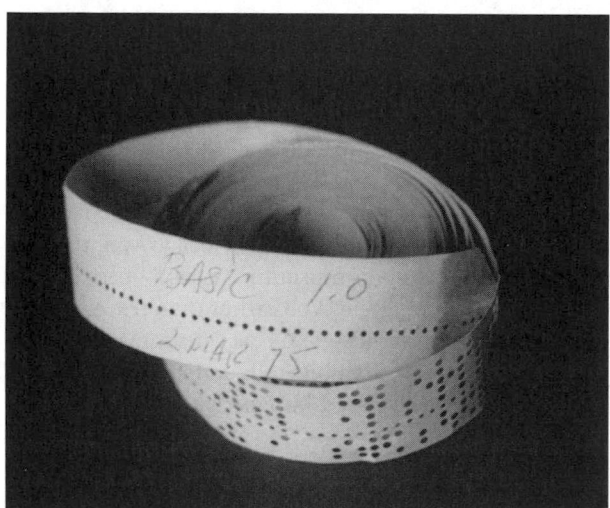

Figure 1. Bill Gates' Original BASIC Paper Tape. The Altair microcomputer inspired Bill Gates, then at Harvard University, to write a BASIC interpreter so that users could easily program the machine. This was the start of Microsoft, then known as "Micro Soft." From the collection of The Computer Museum History Center (X507.84).

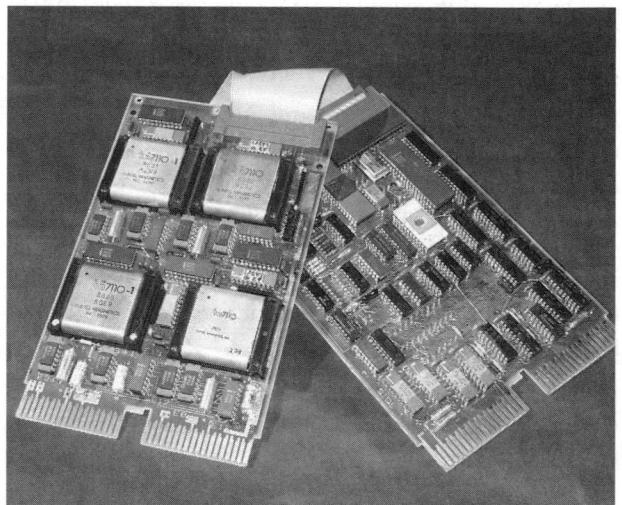

Figure 2. A 4 MB Intel bubble memory module. Magnetic bubble memory, a technology whose introduction seemed imminent for over a decade, was finally abandoned in the early 1980s as inexpensive DRAMs made it uneconomical. Although bubble memory had the advantage of being non-volatile, that advantage was also eclipsed by advances in semiconductor technology, specifically the EPROM and battery backed-up DRAM. From the collection of The Computer Museum History Center (X8.81 A-B).

system used by one of the larger museums—this is a hierarchical superstructure, derived from computer science, that classifies objects as Processors (P), Memory (M), or Switches (S). Regardless of a museum's taxonomy, formal schemas frequently omit significant developments that defy such classifications (e.g. "Totalisator" technology) so exceptions are occasionally made.

Types of Collected Objects

Parallel to these taxonomies are "object types" related to the central item being collected. What, for example, will a specific museum collect about an Altair microcomputer? Types of objects a computer museum might consider collecting fall into five broad categories: hardware, software, ephemera, documentation, and media. Let us briefly examine these five object types.

HARDWARE

Collecting and displaying hardware has been termed "the most expensive means of preserving computer history," yet it is also the means with the greatest visitor impact, something a physical museum must always consider. From a research perspective, having a physical object also establishes an epistemic datum one cannot obtain from books, Websites, or other simulacra of an object (*see* Fig. 3). This is particularly true in cases of a machine's device, manufacturing, and packaging technologies, and in a host of other physically based questions scholars may be seeking to answer by having real hardware in front of them for interrogation.

Figure 3. The Enigma enciphering machine used by Nazi forces in the Second World War, for secure communications. Breaking Enigma transmissions, undertaken in part by Alan Turing and others at Bletchley Park outside of London, UK had a dramatic impact on the outcome and conduct of the war. From the collection of The Computer Museum History Center (B197.81).

The issue of whether or not hardware needs to operate to be valid museologically is a matter of some debate and is something emulation (discussed below) often addresses satisfactorily. Generally, an inverse relationship exists between a machine's age and its likelihood of operating again. There are many factors in this equation but preeminent among them are: (1) the power and air-conditioning requirements, which are usually of the same order of magnitude as the power requirements of the (present-day) building in which they are displayed; (2) the difficulty in obtaining replacement parts; and (3) probably most important, the lack of subject matter experts who can understand the many tacit (unexpressed, unrecorded) means of getting a machine to run, i.e. loss of the "recipe" for testing, debugging, and booting. More specifically, museums which begin their hardware collections any time prior to the microcomputer era, roughly 1975, face special challenges by virtue of the significant size of computer hardware up to that time. If the focus is enlarged to comprise the entire span of electronic computing history, which begins in about 1945, the challenges become Herculean in scale. Such machines frequently occupied entire buildings or certainly entire floors within buildings, had power requirements in the hundreds of kilowatts, and were moved with cranes or forklifts. Aside from their now extreme rarity, such machines are rarely intact and often badly damaged by human or natural elements making any hope of operation a distant prospect. Nonetheless, a museum with hardware from this era—operating or not—is in a league of its own: there are probably fewer than five museums worldwide that contain significant amounts of hardware from this "prehistoric" epoch.

SOFTWARE

While hardware, being rooted in physical reality, tends to linger on, thus making collecting perhaps more obvious, software seems particularly evanescent as a museum object. Particularly in large institutions, this impermanence is exacerbated by the museological uncertainty concerning under whose professional jurisdiction its preservation should fall: curators (who generally collect physical objects) or archivists (who collect paper). As a result of this uncertainty, many museums have forestalled resolution of this debate with the regrettable outcome that software is not being preserved at all or is being collected only very haphazardly. This is another advantage of Web-based museums for whom such jurisdictional quagmires are usually moot and the subject of arid academic debates. Regardless of who is collecting them, many critical programs have apparently already been lost. The earliest versions of Unix (*q.v.*), for example, in either source or executable form, appear to have disappeared forever.

Reading old media to obtain the information in the first instance is also a serious issue. Like the hardware on which such reading frequently depends, the older the media, the more difficult will recovery be. Without the host hardware (or a backwards-compatible reading device), these objects remain as mute physical objects, not as information carriers. Related to this is the selection of preservation media. Most computer museums understand that device technologies continue to develop and improve and so have come to an understanding that archived digital information will likely have to be transferred to different media about once a decade. For example, while CD-ROMs, DVDs, and DLTs (Digital Linear Tapes) are currently a good choice for archival purposes, by 2010 new technologies will unquestionably change the economics and usability of these formats. Some have suggested using network file systems—essentially keeping the information circulating amongst file servers on the Internet—as the best long-term solution.

In terms of such preservation, what is it that a museum's core constituencies would find most useful about collected software? Source code, object code, something else? Will museum users be interested in understanding the intellectual underpinnings immanent in source code (i.e. its logical superstructure) or in just seeing the program running (i.e. the user experience)? Given the often mutually reinforcing nature of code and hardware (e.g. interdependent patches between both or certain copy-protection schemes) is such code valid without host hardware on which it can execute? Operating systems, applications, utilities— what of these should a museum collect? Is anything less than a bit-perfect record valid? Each museum must answer these questions as best it can based on available resources, mandate, and constituency. A good solution to, at least, the hardware-dependency issue is offered by emulators (*see* EMULATION).

Emulators mimic machine architectures to the functional level; simulators, being a subset of emulators, do so to the register-transfer, gate, or behavioral level. Both allow the running of historical software on present-day (i.e. non-native) hardware. In some cases, the fidelity of these emulators is remarkable—even unpublished machine features are emulated—resulting in extremely accurate portrayals of a machine's operation. Often these emulators include a graphical user interface (GUI) which directly implements the physical appearance of the original hardware as well, a further refinement towards verisimilitude. Researchers and enthusiasts have even devised emulator metalanguages (*q.v.*) and there exists a vibrant user community focused on emulating a very large fraction of machines built over the last 40 years. When one considers more distant time horizons (centuries hence), the difficulty of

maintaining operating hardware means that whatever approach a computer museum takes to collections, emulation is sure to form part of the preservation toolkit.

EPHEMERA

Ephemera refers to the cultural objects accreting around a physical item, including software. At once the most superficial and the most profound object type, items in this category include T-shirts, coffee mugs, lucite-encased mementos, marketing literature, buttons, posters, lab notebooks—in essence, any item directly or peripherally related to a machine or program that, while not required for such items to function, yield information about the intended purpose and function of such objects. Just as hardware and software embed the technical and corporate policy choices made by computer companies and designers, so does ephemera allow a cultural decoding of the time and context in which such products were introduced. In particular, marketing decisions (competitive environment, pricing strategies, target markets), which are difficult or impossible to infer without a cultural or economic context, are often readily discernible from such items.

In preservation terms, ephemera usually have a brief lifespan, introducing the paradox (well known to historians) that the most common objects of everyday life are precisely those that are not preserved and are the ones most likely to disappear. Ephemera are also very useful to any computer museum engaging in exhibit design and production. Recreating a "Programmer's Office of the 1960s," for example, might include such items as original furniture, an ashtray, a chocolate bar, issues of *Datamation*, and racks of software manuals—all of which help to explain how and why the central object was used.

DOCUMENTATION

This is certainly the most traditional category for researchers—who tend to be text-bound—to understand and use, although its granularity may be overwhelming to the casual visitor seeking something else. This category includes items such as technical manuals, quick reference cards, schematics, memoranda, and books. For either type of computer museum, there is great research utility in converting at least the more significant documentary holdings into electronic format. A popular method is to make these documents available in Portable Document Format (PDF), a format that maintains the original "look" of a document while permitting searching and indexing.

Documentation is particularly important in understanding software and hardware and, of course, is the bedrock upon which academic historians and many intellectual property specialists operate (*see* LEGAL ASPECTS OF COMPUTING).

MEDIA

Media refers to film, videotape, photographs, and their digital equivalents. Museums often maintain at least a minimal archive for exhibit support but such archives can also be a significant source of revenue. Like ephemera, the various media types can be useful in elucidating context for a particular machine. An inexpensive, simple, and historically-useful activity is to make video recordings of operating machines just prior to their decommissioning. The sights and sounds of such machines can be highly evocative and can provide insights that no amount of text, code, or mute hardware can provide. Recordings are also of crucial importance in capturing oral histories of computer pioneers, technicians, company executives, and machine user communities. While the usual caveats relating to oral and participant histories should be understood, such recordings can be an invaluable source of historical information, particularly when cross-checked and refined against other sources.

All five of the object types above are complementary in that they contribute more in combination than any could individually. This allows "thick" histories to be created—histories that tell us as much as possible about a technology and the environment in which it existed by preserving everything *about* an object as well as preserving the object itself.

Summary

Computer museums are a relatively new invention, like the very objects they seek to preserve, and have many constituencies, ranging from a small cadre of enthusiasts preserving a game machine from the 1970s on the Web, to casual visitors, scholars, legal analysts and schoolchildren. On the one hand, Web-based museums, with their almost nonexistent barriers to entry, can be both tremendous resources and propagators of inaccurate research or claims. While physical museums are not immune to these shortcomings, there are generally well-established methods of peer-review which tend to minimize them. On the other hand, physical museums have the problem of garnering funding, often from an industry which looks forward rather than backward, of physically handling very large objects, operating a physical plant, and of constructing specialized conservation environments. Like the types of objects they collect, however, both real and virtual museums are, in fact, highly complementary.

Finally, one vitally important constant between both types of museum is the importance of the volunteer community. Few museums would make much progress towards their institutional mandate (however modest) without individuals who believe the preservation and study of computers to be a worthy goal in itself. Certainly few could afford to hire people who possess the range of talent volunteers have obtained, often through decades of industry experience; and this applies equally to the dedication, enthusiasm, and work ethic of such people—which no amount of money can purchase. Such volunteers both gain and contribute to the very perspective that is the purpose of all museums—a perspective that goes beyond "how we got here from there" to one that presents the history of computing on its own terms as an organic and path-dependent interplay of technology, economics, culture and, most important, of people. Just like Goethe's "frozen music," such a perspective also reveals that the history of computing itself has an architecture and that it is the responsibility of computer museums to reveal the underlying blueprint.

Bibliography

Here are some useful Web links to computer museums and other institutions with significant computer history holdings.

Computer Museums
The Computer Museum History Center (USA). http://www.computerhistory.org.
The Heinz Nixdorf Museum Forum (Germany). http://www.hnf.de/index_en.html.
Charles Babbage Institute (USA). http://www.cbi.umn.edu.
The National Museum of Science and Industry (UK). http://www.nmsi.ac.uk.
The Smithsonian Institution (USA). http://www.si.edu.

Historic Machines Project
Computer Conservation Society (UK). http://www.cs.man.ac.uk/CCS/.

Links of Links (Museums and General Computer Historical Resources)
Enjoy the infinite regress of link surfing at http://www.vintage.org/vcf/vcflinks.htm.

Dag Spicer

MUSIC, COMPUTER

See COMPUTER MUSIC.

MUTUAL EXCLUSION

For articles on related subjects *see* CONCURRENT PROGRAMMING; CONTENTION; DATABASE CONCURRENCY CONTROL; MONITOR, SYNCHRONIZATION, MULTIPROCESSING; MULTIPROGRAMMING; and MULTITASKING.

When several processes are executing simultaneously, it may happen that two (or more) of these processes want to access and modify the same data. For example, in a multiprogramming system a WRITE process (producer) and a READ process (consumer) might share the same buffer area, so that the consumer has to be protected from having its data garbled by the producer before the READ is completed. As a second example, in a system with multiple CPUs two processors can be idle and request a new task at the same time. If no precaution is taken, both will access the table where the list of waiting tasks is stored, and both may initiate the same task. To circumvent this problem, means must be provided to protect the shared data from disorderly changes. Such means are usually called *mutual exclusion*, or *lockout*. The portion of code in a process that accesses a shared area is called a *critical section* of that process.

At the hardware level, the implementation of mutual exclusion is based on the atomic (indivisible) exchange of a value in a register with a value in memory. In older machines this was realized with a TEST-AND-SET instruction which tests a value, e.g., for 0, and sets it, e.g., to 1, if the answer is 0. However, TEST-AND-SET has the drawback of freezing the memory bus during its execution. An alternative is to use a pair of instructions such as LOAD LINKED and STORE CONDITIONAL (Hennessy and Patterson, 1996). The STORE CONDITIONAL will fail, e.g., return 0, if either the contents of the value loaded via LOAD LINKED has changed or if a context switch from one process to another has occurred. Otherwise, it will succeed and return 1.

Similar schemes have been proposed for high-level languages. In order to allow programs to be independent of specific implementations of mutual exclusion, Dijkstra (1968) defined a new type of variable, called a *semaphore*, which can assume only nonnegative integer values. Dijkstra's elegant solution is based on two primitive and indivisible operations on semaphores, namely:

$V(S)$ defined as: $S \leftarrow S + 1$.

$P(S)$ defined as:

if $S = 0$ **then** block process **else** $S \leftarrow S - 1$.

Basically, the philosophy behind the use of semaphores is as follows: (for purposes of clarity we restrict the semaphore S to take only the values 0 and 1). Initially, the semaphore is set to 1. Before entering a critical section, the process performs a P operation. If S is 1, the process decrements S and enters its critical section. Since S is now 0, no other process may enter its critical section. If S were 0, the process would be blocked and would remain so as long as another process was executing in a critical section. When a process terminates its critical section, it performs a V operation, setting S to 1 and thus allowing another process to enter its critical section.

The semaphore concept has become ubiquitous as an efficient means of protection between cooperating processes and has been implemented in various forms in most operating systems (*q.v.*). Because reasoning about semaphores might be tricky, some high-level language constructs such as *monitors* and associated *condition variables*, whose underlying structures rely on the semaphore concept, have been introduced to facilitate writing correct interprocess communication programs (*see*, for example, Tanenbaum and Woodhull, 1997).

Bibliography

1968. Dijkstra, E. W. "Cooperating Sequential Processes," In *Programming Languages* (ed. F Genuys). New York: Academic Press.
1996. Hennessy, J., and Patterson, D. *Computer Architecture: A Quantitative Approach*, 2nd Ed. San Francisco: Morgan Kaufmann.
1997. Tanenbaum, A., and Woodhull, A. *Operating Systems Design and Implementation*, 2nd Ed. Upper Saddle River, NJ: Prentice Hall.

Jean-Loup Baer

NAPIER, JOHN

For an article on a related subject *see* CALCULATING MACHINES.

John Napier (Fig. 1), the eighth Laird of Merchiston, was born in Merchiston, Scotland in 1550. He is best known for his invention of logarithms, but he also took an active part in the development of other forms of computational methods and instruments, was very active in the religious controversies arising out of the Scottish reformation, and invented a great many devices for agricultural and military use.

Logarithms are, undoubtedly, his most famous invention simply because they were the fundamental basis for all serious computation from the early 1600s until the invention of the electronic computer. Napier's original 1614 publication, *Mirifici Logarithmorum Canonis Descriptio*, contained 90 pages of logarithm tables and an introduction describing how they were to be used. The tables were not the common base 10 logarithms that are used today, but were actually logarithms of sines, whose base was a fractional quantity (different from what are known today as "Napierian logarithms") that arose naturally by reason of the method by which they were computed. Henry Briggs, a professor at Gresham College in London, suggested to Napier that the tables be changed to the common base 10 logarithms. Although Napier agreed to the change, his advanced years and ill health prevented his taking part in the production of the new tables. Henry Briggs published the first book of modern base 10 logarithms in 1624.

In 1617, three years after the publication of his first book on logarithms, Napier published a small volume entitled *Rabdologia*, which contained a description of three other devices that could be used to aid the process of multiplication and division. These were

Figure 1. John Napier. (Courtesy of the Mary Evans Picture Library.)

specifically designed for people who preferred to work with the natural numbers, rather than the logarithms of numbers.

The first and most famous of these devices is the one that Napier called rabdologia, but almost everyone else called *Napier's bones*. They obtained this nickname because the better quality sets were made from bone or ivory. In essence, they were simply vertical strips cut from a 10 by 10 multiplication table which could then be rearranged into the order required to produce a single-digit multiplication table for a multi-digit number.

The other two devices never gained any popularity, primarily because they were either too difficult to manufacture or involved concepts that were unintelligible to most. His second device, the *multiplicationis promptuarium*, was a more complex version of the bones. It consisted of two sets of strips, to be stacked on top of and at right angles to one another, to create a multiplication table for any two multi-digit numbers. The third was a form of a table abacus that was set on a chessboard, the rows and columns of which represented places within the binary number system.

Napier died in 1617 in Merchiston, the same town in which he was born 67 years earlier.

Bibliography

1914. Horsburgh, E. M. *Handbook of the Napier Tercentenary Celebration on Modern Instruments and Methods of Calculation.* Edinburgh: The Royal Society of Edinburgh (reprinted by The MIT Press and Tomash Publishers, 1982).

1983. Williams, M. R. "From Napier to Lucas, the Use of Napier's Bones in Calculating Machinery 1617–1900," *The Annals of the History of Computing,* **5**, *3*, 279–296.

1988. Hawkins, W. F., Tomash, E., and Williams, M. R. "The Promptuary Papers," *Annals of the History of Computing,* **10**, *1*, 35–67.

1991. Napier, J. *Rabdology.* (Reprint #15 of the CBI for the History of Computing.) Cambridge, MA: MIT Press.

Michael R. Williams

NATURAL LANGUAGE PROCESSING

For articles on related subjects *see* ARTIFICIAL INTELLIGENCE; DATABASE MANAGEMENT SYSTEM; GRAMMARS; HUMANITIES APPLICATIONS; KNOWLEDGE REPRESENTATION; LOGIC PROGRAMMING; MACHINE TRANSLATION; RELATIONAL DATABASE; and SPEECH RECOGNITION AND SYNTHESIS.

Natural language processing (NLP) refers to computer systems that analyze, attempt to understand, or produce one or more human languages, such as English, Japanese, Italian, or Russian. The input might be text, spoken language, or keyboard input. The task might be to translate to another language, to comprehend and represent the content of text, to build a database or generate summaries, or to maintain a dialogue with a user as part of an interface for database/information retrieval (*q.v.*). This article addresses issues in natural language comprehension and generation from text or keyboard input. Similar techniques can be used for spoken language by adding a system for speech recognition (*see* SPEECH RECOGNITION AND SYNTHESIS).

It is extremely difficult to define how we would ever know that a system actually "understands" language. All we can actually test is whether a system appears to understand language by successfully performing its task. The Turing test (*q.v.*), proposed by Turing (1950) (reprinted in *Computers and Thought* (1963)), has been the classical model. In this test, the system must be indistinguishable from a human when both answer arbitrary interrogation by a human over a terminal. This test has the unfortunate property that, while it sets the ultimate goal, it provides for no intermediate evaluation of work along the way. A growing concern in NLP is with developing more sensitive models of evaluation that can measure progress, given current performance levels. The usual approach is to develop evaluation tests within limited domains to test specific capabilities. For example, in the area of natural language interfaces for data query, statistical performance measures can be determined based on test sets of human-generated questions collected in protocols (*q.v.*) that use another human to simulate the system. It remains an area of active concern, however, as to how more complex systems that can handle extended dialogue can be evaluated.

The principal difficulty in processing natural language is the pervasive ambiguity found at all levels of the problem. For example, all natural languages involve:

◆ Simple lexical ambiguity (e.g. "duck" can be a noun [the animal] or a verb [to avoid something thrown]).

◆ Structural or syntactic ambiguity (e.g. in "I saw the man with a telescope," the telescope might be used for the viewing or might be held by the man being observed).

◆ Semantic ambiguity (e.g. "go" as a verb has well over 10 distinct meanings in any dictionary).

◆ Pragmatic ambiguity (e.g. "Can you lift that rock?" may be a yes/no question or a request to lift the rock).

◆ Referential ambiguity (e.g. in "Jack met Sam at the station. He was feeling ill . . . ," it is not clear who is ill, although the remainder of the sentence might suggest a preferred interpretation).

Of course, all these forms of ambiguity may interact, producing an extremely complex interpretation process. It is the prevalence of ambiguity that distinguishes natural languages from precisely defined artificial languages, such as logic and programming languages. It also makes most of the techniques developed in programming language grammars, parsing, and semantics ineffective for NLP unless significantly modified.

Natural Language Database Query Systems: Syntax and Semantics

The most successful NLP systems to date have been front ends to databases. These systems can understand isolated questions dealing with the content of the database; several systems that do so are commercially available. While they have not been precisely evaluated, these systems provide a wide coverage of English questions, including quite complex quantified database queries. The LUNAR system was the first system to develop this technology and serves as the prototype for many current-day commercial systems. The core of the LUNAR system was a syntactic grammar in a formalism called an Augmented Transition Network (ATN) Grammar (Woods, 1970). An ATN is a graphical notation that can be shown to be equivalent to context-free grammars. The exception is the augmentation: each arc in the grammar may have a procedurally defined augmentation that can enforce non-context-free restrictions that provide a representation of the sentence convenient for semantic interpretation. The principal contribution of the LUNAR system was to demonstrate that such augmented systems could retain the efficiency of pure context-free parsing algorithms, yet handle the context-sensitive aspects found in natural language. The architecture of a typical NLP database query system is shown in Fig. 1. Examples of natural language interfaces are TEAM (Grosz *et al.*, 1987) and IRUS (Bates *et al.*, 1986). An example of a natural language query to TEAM is *Which employees earn more than their manager's salary?*, which, after syntactic and semantic processing would result in a query, such as the following, to a relational database:

```
(IN $E EMPLOYEE) (IN $D DEPT) (EQ ($E DEPT)
($D NAME)) (IN $M EMPLOYEE) (EQ ($M NAME)
($D MANAGER)) (GT ($E SALARY) ($M SALARY))
(($E NAME)).
```

The other major development in the area of grammars and parsing for natural language was the development of definite clause grammars (DCGs) based on Prolog (*see* LOGIC PROGRAMMING: LANGUAGES). Prolog offers an efficient mechanism for parsing context-free grammars simply by writing each context-free rule as a Prolog clause. The additional power required to handle natural language is obtained by using variable bindings and unification to add additional restrictions and to build a convenient representation of the sentence for semantic interpretations. Prolog-based systems have the additional advantage that the semantic processing and the database itself, for that matter, can be represented within the same notation. Pereira and Warren (1980) describe this approach in some detail.

New grammatical formalisms that slightly extend context-free grammars are an active area of research in both computational and theoretical linguistics. These theories require finer distinctions than found in the traditional Chomsky Hierarchy (*q.v.*) to characterize their generative power. A good survey of such formalisms has been given by Perrault (1984).

As for semantic processing, the technology is at a considerably less developed stage, and most work is still being done within research prototypes of limited scope; there are very few commercial applications. Within limited-scope domains, such as database query applications, the semantic component is not much more than a translation program from the output of the parser into a database query language. In the more general research systems, the semantic interpretation phase produces a mapping from the parser output to a knowledge representation that supports inference and the later stages of pragmatic interpretation.

Semantic interpreters can be placed into two major classes: the *compositional* and the *noncompositional*. The noncompositional allows arbitrary transformations from the parser output to the final form. The compositional requires that interpretation rules are applied in accordance with the structure of the parser output. In its strongest form, compositional semantics requires a single semantic interpretation rule for each syntactic rule, and can support simultaneous syntactic and semantic processing while parsing. While

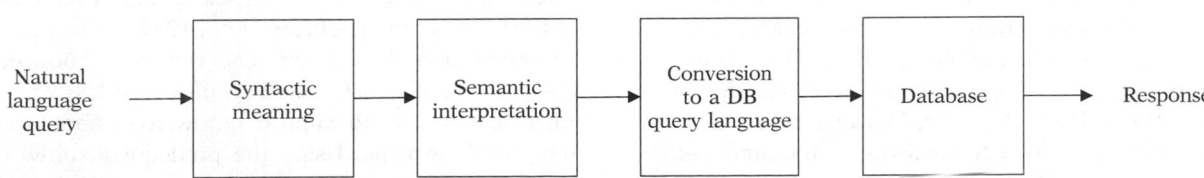

Figure 1. The architecture of an NL database query system.

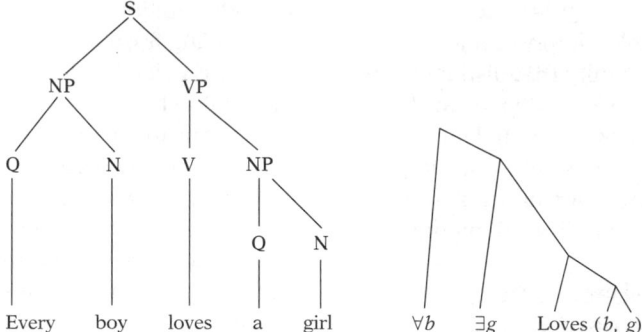

Figure 2. The structure of natural language compared with FOPC quantification. [S: Sentence; NP: Noun Phrase; VP: Verb Phrase; N: Noun; V: Verb; Q: Quantifier].

noncompositional schemes were common in early systems because of their greater power and flexibility, the compositional approaches are now more frequently used because they are significantly more modular and extendable. However, by working within the stricter constraints that a compositional approach imposes, difficult problems arise that require solutions when the syntactic structure of the sentence differs significantly from the structure of the final meaning representation. For example, consider the form of quantification in language versus quantification in a logic in Fig. 2. The structure of the English sentence *Every boy loves a girl* is quite different from the structure of the logic formula $\forall b \, \exists g \, Loves(b, g)$. English puts the quantifiers within the noun phrases, whereas in logic all the quantifiers are outside the scope of the proposition representing the sentence. In addition, there is no natural subpart of the logical formula that corresponds to the interpretation of the noun phrase *a girl*. Rather, the interpretation is spread between the quantifier outside the scope of the predicate and the variable within the scope of the predicate. Proposals for handling this problem within the compositional framework involve introducing an intermediate form of representation that can be built compositionally from the syntactic structure. This representation is then used as input for a second interpretation phase called *quantifier and operator scope determination* that produces the final meaning representation. This identifies yet another source of ambiguity in language: the scope of quantifiers and sentential operators.

Most current NPL systems use a knowledge representation expressively equivalent to or weaker than the first-order predicate calculus (FOPC). But significant aspects of language appear to remain outside the range of first-order logic, and considerable basic research into more expressive formalisms is required before systems will be able to represent the meaning of a significant subset of natural language.

Text Understanding: Pragmatics and World Knowledge

Understanding extended text, such as newspaper articles, paper abstracts, or books, requires significant additions to the capabilities required for question-answering systems discussed above. In particular, there is a strong pragmatic component as well—namely, the use of common everyday knowledge about the world in order to determine the relationships between the sentences in the text. There is a need for significant world knowledge even within single sentences. For example, the sentence *Jack couldn't drive to work because he lost his keys* requires knowledge about cars and keys (e.g. you need a key to start a car, driving to work requires starting the car, etc.). Without this basic knowledge, a system will not be able to determine why Jack couldn't drive to work. The need to use large amounts of common knowledge for natural language understanding was a major focus of the work by Roger Schank and his students. This work focused primarily on representing general knowledge about everyday actions and using this knowledge in interpreting language. These systems could understand simple stories about everyday activities, such as eating in a restaurant or taking public transit. To demonstrate this, they answered questions that required information necessary to understand the story, but not explicitly given in the story. A good description of the techniques is Schank and Riesbeck (1981).

The same motivations were used in the development of the GUS system (Bobrow *et al.*, 1977), which used a representation based on encapsulated knowledge about a specific task called *frames* (*see* KNOWLEDGE REPRESENTATION) to capture knowledge about planning airplane trips. Using the predefined knowledge that captured the structure of the information involved in planning trips, the system "understood" requests in this domain by instantiating the general knowledge to the specific knowledge described in the sentences. Such frame-based approaches still play an important role in current text-understanding systems. Typical application areas for current research systems include understanding messages regarding equipment failures, and extracting the key facts (i.e. those for which slots are defined in the frame) from newspaper articles about takeover attempts in the financial market. The following is an example of the analysis of an article by the SCISOR system, developed by GE Labs (Jacobs and Rau, 1990).

PILLSBURY SURGED 3 3-4 TO 62 IN BIG BOARD COMPOSITE TRADING OF 3.1 MILLION SHARES AFTER BRITAIN'S GRAND METROPOLITAN RAISED ITS HOSTILE TENDER OFFER BY $3 A SHARE TO $63. THE COMPANY PROMPTLY REJECTED THE SWEETENED BID, WHICH CAME AFTER THE TWO SIDES COULDN'T AGREE TO A HIGHER OFFER ON FRIENDLY TERMS OVER THE WEEKEND (Dow Jones News Service, 12 December 1988)

The system extracts the following information from the story:

```
Corporate-takeover-event:
        Target:        Name:  Pillsbury-Corporation
        Suitor:        Name:  Grand Metropolitan
                       Country:   United Kingdom
        Type:          Hostile
        State:         Rejected-offer
        Price:         $63/share
        Stock-exchange: NYSE
        Volume:        3.1 million
        Subevent:      Increased-offer:
                       Effect-on-stock
                       Increment:  3 3-4
                       Direction:  Up
                       Type:  Surge
                       Final-Value:  $62/share
        Previous-state: Negotiated-offer:
                       Type:  Friendly
```

It is realistic to expect 90% (combined recall and precision) accuracy for certain useful, carefully constructed tasks, but unrealistic to expect much higher. Many difficulties in reading texts appear when trying to achieve better results, but the most common limitation seems to be the degree of real inference required for understanding. In spite of its fairly sophisticated methods for combining linguistic and world knowledge, SCISOR has very little of the latter.

Dialogue Systems: Discourse and Communication

Systems that can engage in extended natural dialogue present particular challenges in addition to the issues described above. In order to account for dialogue phenomena, a model of conversational interaction needs to be developed. In addition, significant reasoning is required, both to recognize the other speaker's intentions and to produce reasonable responses. The most promising model so far has been based on the notion of speech acts—actions that are performed by speaking, such as requesting, informing, warning, etc. Computational speech act models have been developed by using models of actions and planning developed in work in knowledge representation (Cohen and Perrault, 1979). Plan recognition becomes an important technique for understanding the underlying motivations behind questions. These models can be used to generalize question-answering systems so that the answers generated are more useful and appropriate. These models, however, are not yet capable of explaining dialogues longer than a few sentences. In addition, structural models of discourse have been developed (Grosz and Sidner, 1986) that appear promising. There are currently no systems that come close to having human dialogue capabilities, which involves considerable clarification and correction subdialogues, topic change, and other complexities. It is reasonable to expect that prototype systems will be developed in the next few years that can handle dialogues within limited-topic application domains.

Machine Translation

Machine translation (language translation) was one of the first applications that led to AI work on natural language processing. Machine translation is a very active area of research, especially in Europe and Japan, and is now undergoing a resurgence in the USA. There are two primary approaches. The first is based on defining corresponding lexical, syntactic, and semantic correspondences between a pair of languages, and defining a transducer based on these rules. The second is based on a notion of a language-independent representation or *interlingua* (*cf.* INTERMEDIATE LANGUAGES). To translate, one would parse one language into the interlingua and then from that generate text in the second language. While the second is the more general approach, the most successful systems to date are based on the former techniques. It seems commonly accepted that, except in limited technical domains, high-quality machine translation of general text is either impossible or a very long way off in the future. What is feasible currently, however, is the development of machine translation tools to aid human translators, and the development of translation systems that then require post-editing by a human. While this might seem a failure, using such techniques can in practice significantly increase the productivity of each human translator. There are commercial systems available that offer these abilities, and we can expect considerable growth in the use and development of machine-translation "workstations" in the next decade.

A rudimentary system currently in place is part of the AltaVista search engine on the World Wide Web (*q.v.*). A user who obtains a "hit"—a short possibly relevant text passage received in a "foreign" language—can request automatic translation into the user's native language.

Generation

An issue that arises in dialogue systems, in text summarization applications, and in many machine translation systems is natural language generation (i.e. the production of sentences to describe a given body of knowledge). There are two primary problems in generation: deciding what content needs to be communicated and then deciding how to realize that content in language. The former problem is related to the reasoning abilities of the system, say those required for participating in a dialogue, whereas the latter is related to inverting the parsing and semantic interpretation processes. Typically, generation systems have been developed independently of the understanding component because each component faces a different set of issues. Present-day generation systems can generate paragraph-length text to describe a prespecified body of information in some knowledge representation. The issue of intelligently choosing what knowledge needs to be realized is just beginning to be addressed.

Speech

Another active area of research is aimed at developing natural language systems that use spoken, rather than written, language (*see* SPEECH RECOGNITION AND SYNTHESIS). But there is more to building a spoken language system than combining a speech recognizer with a natural language system. In particular, new uncertainty and ambiguity is introduced, since the parser does not know precisely what the input words are. On the other hand, other sources of information, such as intonation and prosody, are available to aid the interpretation. It is believed that such information will greatly aid discourse processing, as there appear to be strong intonational clues to discourse structure and communicative intent. To solve these problems and to take advantage of the additional information found in spoken language, new methods of integrating speech recognition and natural language systems must be developed. Systems currently in place include email processors that articulate their messages to the recipient, and systems that "listen" and react to a user's spoken commands.

Prospects

Natural language processing should make considerable strides early in this millennium. Large-scale grammars of natural languages are being written, and there is considerable effort in building large English lexicons using automatic techniques. We can expect to see the emergence of quite sophisticated question-answering systems if there is sufficient economic demand for such technology. In the area of text skimming and summarizing, substantial progress should be made in identifying and capturing a specific set of predetermined topics (e.g. a brief summary of the major financial transactions described in the *Wall Street Journal*). Such a system could automatically read the newspaper and build a database of the transactions described, which could then be searched and used to generate short paragraph summaries of the information extracted. We can also expect considerable progress in the area of dialog systems, although such systems in realistic-sized domains will likely remain as research prototypes.

Bibliography

1950. Turing, A. M. "Computing Machinery and Intelligence," *Mind*, **59** (October), 433–460.
1963. Feigenbaum, E. A., and Feldman, J. (eds.) *Computers and Thought*. New York: McGraw-Hill.
1970. Woods, W. A. "Transition Network Grammars for Natural Language Analysis," *Comm. of the ACM*, **13**, *10*, 591–606.
1977. Bobrow, D., Kaplan, R., Kay, M., Norman, D., Thompson, H., and Winograd, T. "GUS: A Frame Driven Dialog System," *Artificial Intelligence*, **8**, 155–173.
1979. Cohen, P., and Perrault, C. R. "Elements of a Plan-based Model of Speech Acts," *Cognitive Science*, **3**, *3*, 177–212.
1980. Pereira, F. C. N., and Warren, D. H. D. "Definite Clause Grammars for Language Analysis—A Survey of the Formalism and a Comparison with Augmented Transition Network Grammars," *Artificial Intelligence*, **13**, *3*, 231–278.
1981. Schank, R. C., and Riesbeck, C. K. *Inside Computer Understanding*. Hillsdale, NJ: Lawrence Erlbaum.
1984. Perrault, C. R. "On the Mathematical Properties of Linguistic Theories," *Computational Linguistics*, **10**, 165–176.
1986. Bates, M., Moser, M. G., and Stallard, D. "The IRUS Transportable Natural Language Database Interface," in *Expert Database Systems* (ed. L. Kershberg), 617–630. Menlo Park, CA: Benjamin/Cummings.
1986. Grosz, B., and Sidner, C. "Attention, Intentions, and the Structure of Discourse," *Computational Linguistics*, **12**, *3*, 175–204.
1986. Grosz, B., Sparck-Jones, K., and Webber, B. *Readings in Natural Language Processing*. San Francisco: Morgan Kaufmann.
1987. Grosz, B. J., Appelt, D., Martin, P., and Pereira, F. "TEAM: An Experiment in the Design of Transportable Natural-Language Interfaces," *Artificial Intelligence*, **32**, *2*, 173–244.
1990. Jacobs, P. S., and Rau, L. F. "SCISOR: A System for Extracting Information from On-line News," *Comm. of the ACM*, **33**, *11*, 88–97.
1992. Shieber, S. *Constraint-Based Grammar Formalisms*. Cambridge, MA: MIT Press.
1995. Allen, J. *Natural Language Understanding*, 2nd Ed. Reading, MA: Addison-Wesley.
1997. Suereth, R. *Developing Natural Language Interfaces: Processing Human Conversations*. New York: McGraw-Hill.

James F. Allen

NETWORK ARCHITECTURE

For articles on related topics *see* LOCAL AREA NETWORK; NETWORKS, COMPUTER; NETWORK PROTOCOLS; OPEN SYSTEMS INTERCONNECTION; and TCP/IP.

Modern computer networks may consist of thousands of computing devices of various kinds, often made by different vendors and interconnected by many types of transmission media, including standard telephone lines, satellites, digital microwave radio, optical fibers, or digital data lines. They may include local or wide area configurations. For such a group of heterogeneous devices to be linked, either the hardware and software need to be compatible or else complex interfaces need to be built to allow meaningful communication. *Network architecture* helps achieve this compatibility.

Objectives

A *network architecture* defines the message and data formats as well as the protocols (*q.v.*) and other standards to which hardware and software must conform to meet desired network objectives. Most network architectures are designed to achieve the following objectives:

1. *Connectivity* to permit diverse hardware and software built in conformance with the architecture to intercommunicate over the network.

2. *Flexibility* to permit easy modification as user needs change or available technologies improve. These modifications should be possible without the need for costly new interfaces or program modifications.

3. *Modularity* to permit mass production of hardware and software modules (building blocks) that can be used in a wide variety of devices.

4. *Reliability* to permit error-free communication by providing appropriate error detection and correction capabilities.

5. *Simplicity* to permit easy implementation, installation, and reconfiguration of the network and its services.

6. *Diversity* of network services that can be easily used and yet isolate users from the details of network structure or implementation.

Implementation

Although the above objectives may seem straightforward, designing a network architecture to achieve them is a difficult task given the many trade-offs that are possible. Furthermore, a modern network architecture must support a wide variety of functions. Consequently, the common set of rules for generating and interpreting messages sent and received by the communicating devices to implement these functions can be large and complex. For this reason, the entire set of rules is often partitioned into groups or layers of manageable size, with each layer containing only those rules needed to perform some specific subset of functions. By making the functions in each layer independent of those in other layers, new functions or enhancement of existing functions can be implemented with little or no disruption to other layers. This layered approach, therefore, helps reduce design complexity and offers the advantages of ease of modification and flexibility.

The Reference Model for Open Systems Interconnection (often referred to as the OSI model) is shown in Fig. 1 and is an example of a model for a layered network architecture. It has been widely adopted and its primary purpose is to provide the basis for coordinating standards for interconnection of systems using data communication facilities. The term "open" denotes the ability to transfer information between any two systems that conform to the model and its associated standards. The actual transfer of data occurs through the physical medium (telephone line, coaxial cable, or some other transmission medium) located just below layer 1 of the model. The seven layers collectively provide all the functions necessary for communication between two systems, with each layer providing a service to the layer above and enhancing the service provided by the layer below. With this approach, a process initiated at the highest

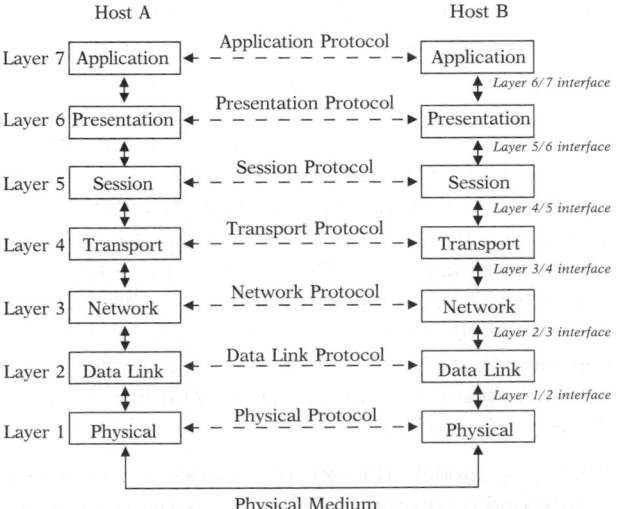

Figure 1.   Information exchange between two systems in the seven-layer OSI model, showing the peer-to-peer protocols and interfaces between the layers.

layer has the full set of services at its disposal. For a more extensive discussion, *see* OPEN SYSTEMS INTERCONNECTION.

Virtual and Physical Data Transmission in the OSI Model

For two machines to intercommunicate, the same set of layered functions must exist on each machine. Each layer, n, on one machine can be thought of as communicating with the corresponding layer on the other machine as a peer process using the appropriate layer n protocol. This is illustrated by the dotted horizontal lines in Fig. 1. An application on machine A requiring a file transfer from machine B, for example, will invoke a file transfer process on machine A that will communicate with its peer process on machine B, using a file transfer protocol (part of the application layer suite of protocols) designed to communicate the name of the file and other needed details of the request. If compression/decompression is used for data transmission, the application layer on machine B will pass the file to its presentation layer (via the level 6/7 interface) to perform the data compression, while the peer process on machine A will perform the corresponding decompression and pass the decompressed data through its application layer to the application that made the original request. Again, the compression/decompression can be thought of as being performed by communication between peer processes, using the appropriate presentation layer protocols.

The above example helps illustrate the relation between virtual and actual data transmission within the model. While the peer processes in layer n think of their communication as being horizontal using the layer n protocol, no data is directly transferred from layer n of one machine to layer n of another machine. Instead, during transmission each layer passes data and control information to the layer below until the lowest (physical) layer is reached. Below this layer is the physical medium through which the actual transmission occurs. Conversely, on the receiving end, each layer passes data and control information to the layers immediately above. In Fig. 1, the virtual communication between peer processes is shown by the horizontal dotted lines, while the actual or physical communication is shown by the solid vertical lines between layers and the solid horizontal line denoting the physical medium.

With this model, the set of functional layers and corresponding protocols defines the network architecture. Their specifications must contain enough information to allow design and implementation of the necessary hardware and software to insure that each

Table 1. OSI layers and the Internet protocols.

OSI layer	IP protocol stack
7. Application	Many, e.g. HTTP, FTP, Telnet, NFS
6. Presentation	Not specified
5. Session	Not specified—sockets/streams commonly used
4. Transport	TCP/UDP
3. Network	IP
2. Datalink	Many—network-dependent
1. Physical	Many—network-dependent

layer obeys the appropriate protocols. Neither the specification of the interfaces between the layers nor the implementation details are part of the architecture, to insure that the designer has full implementation flexibility. All that is needed is to insure that all machines can correctly use all the protocols.

The TCP/IP suite of protocols, used by the Internet, supports many different protocols at the application level. Using the HyperText Transfer Protocol (HTTP) for the World Wide Web as an example of an application level protocol, Table 1 shows the Internet protocol stack in relation to the OSI model. Sockets/streams are used to provide the session layer services while the network and transport layer services are provided by the Internet Protocol (IP) and the Transmission Control Protocol (TCP)/User Datagram Protocol (UDP) respectively. Since the Internet does not specify a physical or datalink layer standard, the IP can be layered over many types of networks, including Ethernet, Token Ring, FDDI, and ATM networks.

Bibliography

1989. Keiser, G. E. *Local Area Networks.* New York: McGraw-Hill.
1993. Spohn, D. *Data Network Design.* New York: McGraw-Hill.
1996. Tanenbaum, A. S. *Computer Networks*, 3rd Ed. Upper Saddle River, NJ: Prentice Hall.

John S. Sobolewski

NETWORK PROTOCOLS

For articles on related subjects, *see* COMMUNICATION CONTROL UNIT; HANDSHAKING; INTERNET; NETWORK ARCHITECTURE; NETWORKS, COMPUTER; OPEN SYSTEMS INTERCONNECTION; PROTOCOL; and TCP/IP.

A *protocol* is the set of formal operating rules, procedures, or conventions that govern a given process. A *communication* or *network protocol*, therefore, describes the rules that govern the transmission of data over communication networks. These rules are designed to help provide needed network services or to solve operating problems, including:

1. Formatting, or *framing*, which defines which group of bits or characters within a frame or a packet constitutes data, control, addressing, or other information.

2. *Error control*, which refers to the acceptance of correct messages, the detection of errors (usually by means of cyclic redundancy checks—*q.v.*), and the retransmission of messages in which errors were detected.

3. *Sequence control*, which defines the method of numbering (or sequencing) messages to detect loss or duplication of messages, and to identify correctly messages that are retransmitted by the error control mechanism.

4. *Flow control*, which defines the mechanisms used to ensure effective utilization of network resources without causing traffic congestion.

5. *Initiation and termination control*, which define how connections are established, maintained, and terminated across the network.

6. *Routing control*, which provides sufficient information to allow data to be routed from source to destination.

7. *Recovery control*, which defines mechanisms used for graceful recovery in case of abnormal conditions, such as loss of a message or an inquiry or cessation of information flow that may be caused by line, equipment, or software failures.

Types of Protocols

Protocols may be divided into three general categories, depending upon the technique used for message framing. They include:

1. *Bit-oriented protocols*, in which a unique flag character delimits individual message frames. An example is IBM's Synchronous Data Link Control (SDLC) protocol in which the beginning and ending characters of a frame must be 01111110. This is very similar to asynchronous transmission where start and stop bits bound a character rather than a frame consisting of a series of characters.

2. *Character-oriented protocols*, which use special characters to delineate the various fields within a message and to provide needed control functions. An example is IBM's Binary Synchronous Communications (BISYNC) protocol. It consists of two or more SYN characters (to synchronize the receiver and transmitter), followed by an SOH (start of header) to delineate the optional header, an STX (start of text) to delineate text, and an ETB or ETX

character to delineate the end of a block of data or end of text (no more text coming) and inform the receiver that the subsequent two characters are the cyclic redundancy check characters for error control.

3. *Byte count-oriented protocols*, which keep track of the number of bytes transmitted. An example is the Transmission Control Protocol/Internet Protocol (TCP/IP) used for communication on the Internet.

Byte count protocols have been implemented to help overcome problems encountered with the other two types of protocols in transmitting transparent data where special precautions must be taken when the data fields contain special characters, such as 01111110, SOH, STX, ETX, and others used to delineate and format messages.

TCP/IP

TCP/IP (Transmission Control Protocol/Internet Protocol) is a widely used set of byte count-oriented routing protocols that evolved from the implementation of the ARPA network (Arpanet), an early packet switching network. The Internet Protocol (IP) allows data packets to be sent and received across networks, while the Transmission Control Protocol (TCP) provides flow control and reliable transmission using cyclic redundancy checking. TCP/IP is supported by the Unix operating system (*q.v.*), as well as by personal computer operating systems, and is one of the more popular communication protocols in use today.

Fig. 1 illustrates the protocol stack and flow of frames or packets through a layered architecture such as the OSI model. Each protocol layer removes or adds header information depending on whether the frames are flowing up or down the stack. The header characters added by the data link layer include special information or characters to synchronize the transmitter and receiver and to add cyclic redundancy characters for error control. The physical layer then transmits the entire frame, which is routed over the network (perhaps through intermediate nodes) to its final destination.

Fig. 2 shows the header format added by the TCP (Transport Layer). The source and destination port addresses identify the applications associated with this message. The sequence number identifies the position of the sender's byte stream, and the acknowledgment number identifies the next byte expected by the receiver. The header length is needed because the TCP header can be of variable length, since it may include one or more optional fields. The six flag bits (URG, ACK, RST, etc.) determine the use of the

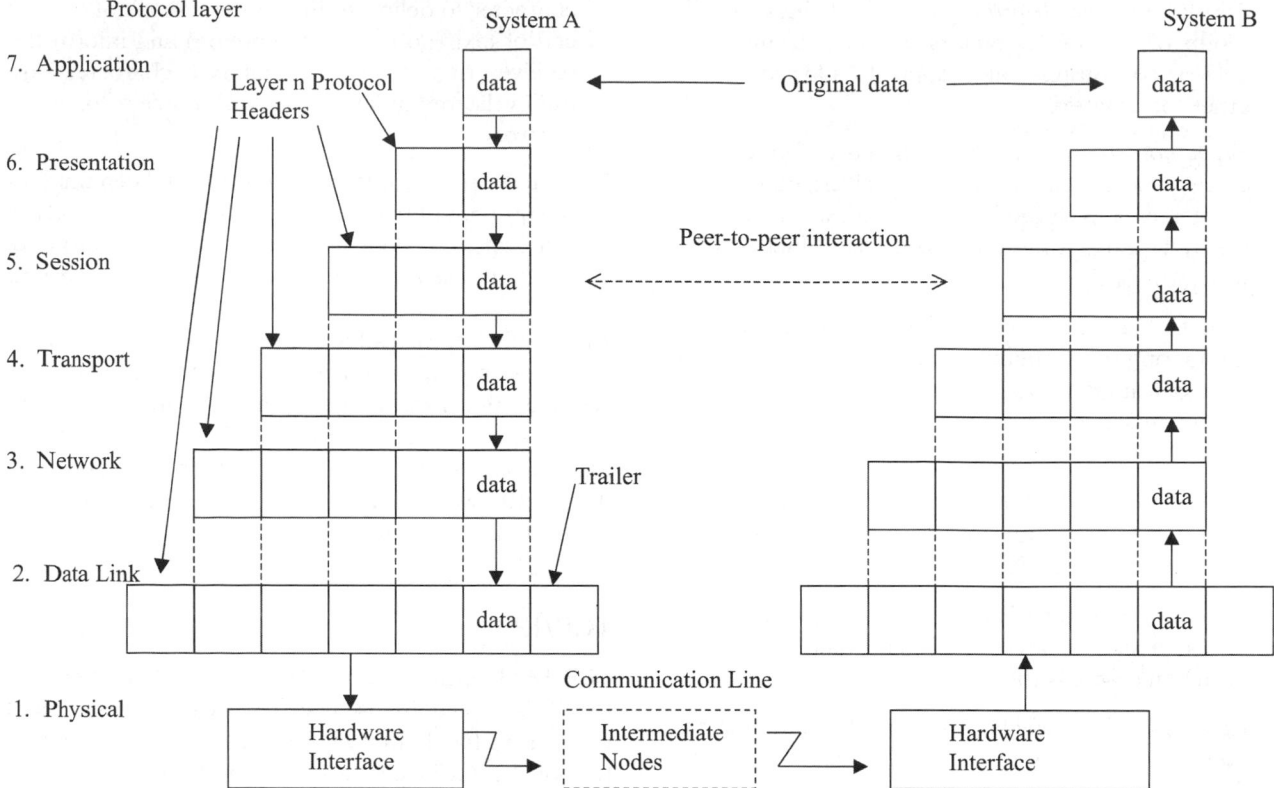

Figure 1. Protocol stack and flow of information through a typical layered architecture. The arrows show the flow when system A transmits data to system B. The messages plus the headers at each layer become the data field for the next lower layer on transmission and vice versa on reception.

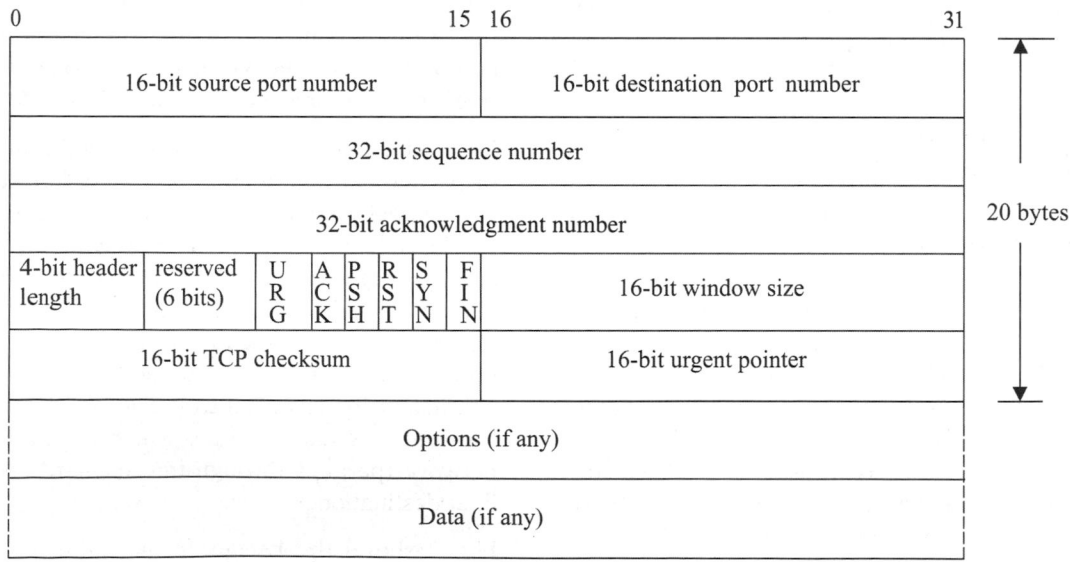

Figure 2. Transmission Control Protocol (TCP) header format.

segment—the RST bit, for example, resets the receiver during a TCP three-way handshake (Keshaw, 1997, section 12.4.4). The window size defines the amount of data the application is willing to accept, the TCP checksum (cyclic redundancy check) is for error control, the *urgent pointer* points to the last byte in the frame that has "urgent" data, and the option field is application-specific.

Protocol Implementation

Besides specifying the frame and message formats, network protocols specify the type of control messages needed for establishing and terminating connections, transmitting data, and recovering from various error conditions, as well as their sequence and allowable responses. This kind of "handshaking" between the transmitting and receiving stations over the network can be quite complex and is outside the scope of this article. The seven-layer model for network architecture helps reduce this complexity and simplifies protocol design at each layer of the model (*see* OPEN SYSTEMS INTERCONNECTION).

Bibliography

1988. McNamara, J. E. *Technical Aspects of Data Communication*, 3rd Ed. Maynard, MA: Digital Press.
1989. Keiser, G. E. *Local Area Networks*. New York: McGraw-Hill.
1997. Keshaw, S. *An Engineering Approach to Computer Networking: ATM Networks, the Internet, and the Telephone Network*. Reading, MA: Addison-Wesley.

John S. Sobolewski

NETWORK, LOCAL AREA

See LOCAL AREA NETWORK.

NETWORK, METROPOLITAN AREA

See METROPOLITAN AREA NETWORK.

NETWORK, WIDE AREA

See INTERNET; and NETWORKS, COMPUTER.

NETWORKS FOR LEARNING

For articles on related subjects *see* COMPUTER-ASSISTED LEARNING AND TEACHING; and COMPUTER CONFERENCING.

Networks that extended student access to computing played a major role in the development of instructional uses from the mid-1960s through the 1970s. Authors of instructional software found a larger audience for their programs and related materials, and obtained more feedback from users, since the applications were used on a network. Users benefited from access to the most current version of a program at the originating site or a central library. Because of their increasing capability and decreasing cost, during the 1980s personal computers replaced networks as a source of programs for instruction. During the 1990s the Internet (*q.v.*) and the World Wide Web (*q.v.*) again made networks a prime source of educational materials and provided many added benefits.

Research and development projects in the 1970s established computer-based conferencing and other electronic aids to educational communications as a major justification of remote access to computers as information systems for teaching and learning. Access to databases and other information services, now often via the Internet, along with communications among groups of learners, is now common at all levels of education.

Local area networks (LANs—*q.v.*) provide for group work within a school building or on a college campus. Collaborative writing and group research projects have become common applications. Students find others with whom to discuss their schoolwork as well as to organize special school projects and extracurricular activities. Databases related to local organizations and projects have become available to students, and members of the community are often encouraged to connect to the local network or Websites to participate in discussions. The Computer Supported Intentional Learning Environment from the Ontario Institute for Studies in Education evolved from classroom or school-based discussions and databases to make use of resources at science museums and other resource centers on the Internet.

National and international data networks link students in schools throughout the world. Kids Network was established by Technology Education Research Center (TERC) and *National Geographic* to explore science projects such as might be accomplished with data on acid rain from throughout the world. The Star Schools network set up by TERC was used to exchange data and ideas about mathematics, weather, alternative energy, and environmental concerns. The Interactive Communications Simulations project at the University of Michigan provided a variety of activities for students at schools throughout the world. After much success with role-playing (e.g. as a basis for study of international conflicts) and electronic publication (as in poetry stimulated and collected through international links among students), two of the staff members set off on an odyssey across Europe and North Africa, with students at participating schools posing questions for and collecting information from the two travelers. Schools have enjoyed many options for expanding learning opportunities and collaboration through network services, among them the AT&T Learning Network (for history, geography, social studies, science issues, and writing); Writers in Electronic Residence (writing, commentary, and discussion with well-known authors in Canada); SchoolNet (science and technology); NASA's Spacelink (astronomy and space sciences); MIT's MicroMuse Science Center (interactive exhibits in mathematics and science); and daily reports from travels and explorations (archaeology, geography, and oceanography).

The costs of network communications have at times required subsidies to schools to make them affordable. Network projects have extended communications among students in different parts of the world. Transfer speeds for large files result in some limitations, but clear benefits result from the collaboration within virtual communities which develops across national and cultural boundaries.

Uses of networks for learning have emerged as a major part of computers in education, providing students with electronic mail (*q.v.*), bulletin boards (*q.v.*), news services, computer-based conferences, access to databases, online tutoring, discussions with experts, and other resources that extend learning opportunities. Entire courses are offered via the Internet and some institutions offer certification and degree programs which minimize the constraints of distance and time. Rather than isolate students, such programs tend to encourage collaboration and the emergence of learning communities, and exploit the relevant tools of information processing.

Bibliography

1995. Berge, Z. L., and Collins, M. P. (eds.) *Computer-Mediated Communication and the Online Classroom.* Cresskill, NJ: Hampton Press.
1995. Harasim, L. M. *Learning Networks: A Field Guide to Teaching and Learning Online.* Cambridge, MA: MIT Press.
1996. Papert, S. *The Connected Family: Bridging the Digital Generation Gap.* Atlanta, GA: Longstreet Press.
1997. Schrum, L., and Berenfeld, B. *Teaching and Learning in the Information Age: A Guide to Educational Telecommunications.* Boston: Allyn and Bacon.

Karl L. Zinn

NETWORKS, COMPUTER

For articles on related topics *see* ASYNCHRONOUS TRANSFER MODE; COMMUNICATION CONTROL UNIT; DISTRIBUTED SYSTEMS; ETHERNET; INTERNET; LOCAL AREA NETWORK; METROPOLITAN AREA NETWORK; NETWORK ARCHITECTURE; NETWORK PROTOCOLS; OPEN SYSTEMS INTERCONNECTION; TCP/IP; TELEPROCESSING SYSTEMS; and WORLD WIDE WEB.

A *computer network* consists of a set of communication channels interconnecting a set of computing devices or nodes that can communicate with each other. The nodes may be computers, terminals, workstations (*q.v.*), or communication units of various kinds distributed over different locations. They communicate over communication channels that can be leased from common carriers (e.g. telephone companies) or are provided by the owners of the network. These channels may use a variety of transmission media, including optical fibers, coaxial cable, twisted copper pairs, satellite links, digital microwave radio, or one of the new emerging wireless technologies. The nodes may be distributed over a wide area (distances of hundreds or thousands of miles) or over a local area (distances of a hundred feet to several miles), in which case the networks are called wide area (WAN) or local area (LAN) networks, respectively. A metropolitan area network (MAN) is a network that spans distances between those of a LAN and a WAN.

In the past decade, modern computer networks have greatly increased in number and geographical area, in the number and variety of devices interconnected, and in the scope of applications supported. A modern network may consist of thousands of computing devices made by various manufacturers connected by a variety of transmission media spanning international and intercontinental boundaries. Design, operation, and management of such complex systems is a challenge. The sections that follow briefly describe network applications, design objectives, types of transmission media used, commonly used topologies, and standards, as well as some well-known networks that have been implemented.

Network Applications

The basic reasons for the explosive growth in computer networks include:

♦ *Resource access*—Networks can provide users with convenient access, at any time, to special computing resources, regardless of the physical location of the resources and the users. These resources may include specialized computers, software, or other devices that are expensive or unique and must be shared. An example is access to a corporate supercomputer (*q.v.*) from workstations at remote research laboratories.

♦ *Data access*—Networks can provide local and remote users with access to unique databases. Examples include remote access to stock exchange data, hotel or airline reservation systems, and the wealth of information on a virtually endless number of topics accessible via the Internet and the World Wide Web.

♦ *Communication and data exchange*—Networks allow users to exchange data, graphs, or documents and to communicate using electronic mail (*q.v.*), bulletin boards (*q.v.*) or by teleconference, irrespective of the time or their location.

In effect, networks can be considered as the information roads and highways over which data and information are transported to support the above applications as well as new applications that continue to evolve.

Network Objectives

The various types of network that have evolved share a common set of objectives. They include:

◆ *Connectivity* to permit various hardware and software products to be connected and communicate in a seamless way.

◆ *Simplicity* to permit easy installation and operation of all network components, including the software.

◆ *Modularity* to enable building of a wide variety of network devices from a relatively small set of mass-produced building blocks to help reduce the cost.

◆ *Scalability* to allow the network to grow in all dimensions when needed.

◆ *Reliability* to permit error-free transmission by providing appropriate error correcting and detecting (*q.v.*) capabilities. The network should be fully operational 24 hours/day, 7 days/week.

◆ *Flexibility* to permit the network to evolve as new needs arise or new technologies become available.

◆ *Diversity* of network services that can be easily used yet isolate users from the technical details of network structure and implementation.

◆ *Manageability* to detect and isolate problems, and to take appropriate corrective action.

Network Architecture

While the above objectives may appear to be simple, their implementation is very complex, since many trade-offs are involved. Moreover, linking a wide variety of computing devices made by different vendors requires hardware and software compatibility for seamless communication. A number of network architectures have evolved to help ensure this compatibility.

A *network architecture* defines the protocols, message formats, and other standards to which communication hardware and software must conform to achieve the network objectives. Computing devices complying to a given network architecture can intercommunicate. Communication between devices that conform to different network architectures is possible only through routers and complex gateways (*q.v.*) designed to translate the protocols between them.

Some popular early implementations of network architectures include the Xerox Network Systems (XNS) architecture, IBM's System Network Architecture (SNA), and DEC's Digital Network Architecture (DNA). Today, by far the most widely used network architecture is that of the Internet which is based on the suite of protocols (notably TCP/IP) developed by the Department of Defense for the Arpanet. In 1978, the International Organization for Standardization (ISO) recognized the importance of a standard for the exchange of information within and between networks and issued a recommendation for a standard network architecture. This recommendation has been widely accepted and is in the form of a seven-layer model known as the Open Systems Interconnection (OSI) Reference Model. The term "open" denotes the ability to transfer information between any two systems that conform to the reference model and its standards.

Network Topology

Two important network parameters are its topology and the transmission media used. The topology refers to the geometrical arrangement and connection of network nodes. The basic topologies are illustrated in Fig. 1 and include:

◆ *Point-to-point connection*. This has the advantage of simplifying routing decisions among nodes, but the reliability of the network depends on the reliability of the weakest links.

◆ *Linear bus* (*q.v.*), in which all network nodes have unique addresses and are connected to a common transmission medium. When a device transmits data onto the bus, it is received by all devices and is ignored, except by the one that is addressed. Local area networks based on the *Ethernet* use this topology.

◆ *Ring connection*, in which consecutive nodes are connected by point-to-point links arranged to form a closed path (ring). Information is passed from node to node around the ring until it arrives at the node that is addressed. *Token ring networks* use this topology.

◆ *Star connection*, in which all nodes are connected to a node called the *central node* or *hub*. The central node can be active or passive. If it is active, it is usually used to control the entire network and performs all the routing. This topology is used in applications where a central computer communicates with remote terminals or workstations.

◆ *Multiconnected networks*, in which nodes are connected by point-to-point links in an arbitrary fashion, with each node connected to at least two others. This improves reliability and reduces the likelihood of congestion, but makes routing much more complex, since many paths are possible between any two nodes.

Large and complex networks use various combinations of these basic topologies.

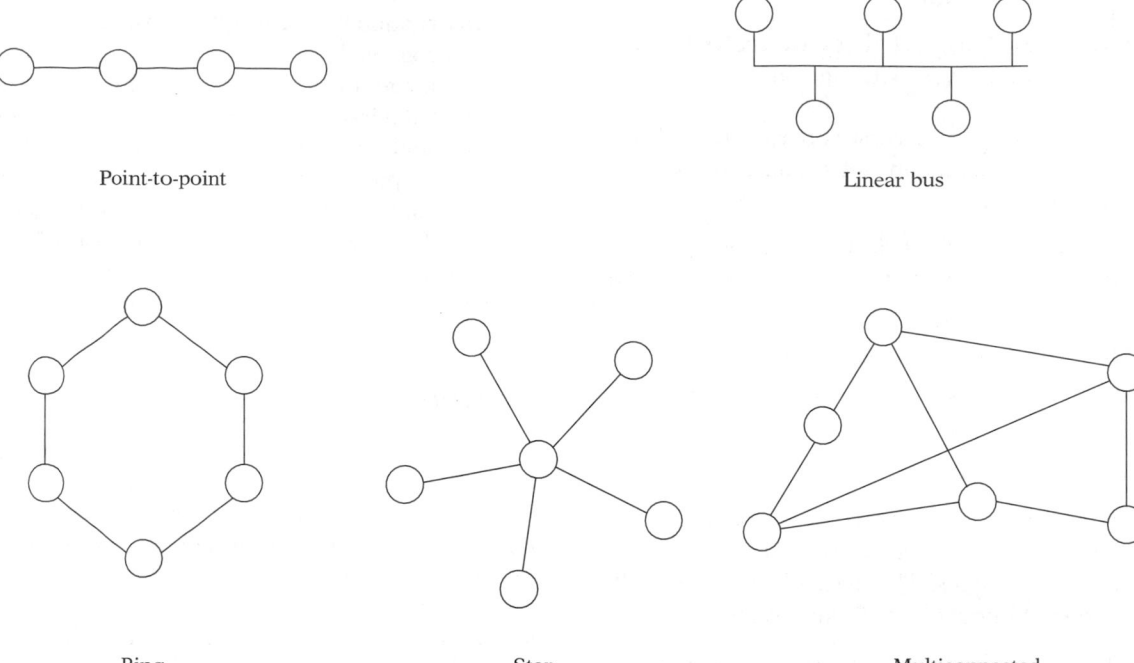

Figure 1. Basic methods of interconnecting nodes in a network. The circles represent computing devices or network nodes.

Transmission Media

Data transmission media provide the physical communication channel to interconnect nodes in a network over which the data is actually transmitted. Commonly used media for computer networks include:

♦ *Unshielded twisted wire pairs.* These are made of insulated copper wire, and are commonly used for connections within buildings. They are popular because they are relatively inexpensive, easy to install, and can operate at up to 155 Mbps over most typical distances encountered within buildings.

♦ *Shielded twisted pairs.* These have similar properties to unshielded twisted pairs, but include a metallic shield around both conductors to enhance reliability by reducing susceptibility to electromagnetic noise. However, with the newer generations of line drivers/receivers, unshielded twisted pairs have replaced shielded pairs except in the noisiest environments.

♦ *Coaxial cables.* They can be used over short (tens of feet) or long (hundreds of miles, with appropriate repeaters to help amplify the signal) distances at bandwidths (*q.v.*) of up to 500 MHz. They are easy to install and were once very popular, especially for local area networks. Such cables consist of an inner conductor completely surrounded by an outer conductor, with a layer of insulation in between. They are widely used for cable television but are being replaced by unshielded twisted pairs for short distances and by optical fibers for long distances.

♦ *Optical fibers.* These are thin, flexible glass or plastic fibers through which light is transmitted (*see* FIBER OPTICS). Although they are more difficult to work with than twisted pairs or coaxial cables, their use is increasing very rapidly since they can support transmission rates of tens of Gbps/fiber over short or long distances using currently available technologies.

♦ *Microwave radio.* This uses highly directional antennas for line-of-sight transmission between repeater stations. The antenna spacing may vary from several hundred feet (e.g. from building to building) to 20–30 miles, depending upon the geographical terrain and the transmitter power permitted by regulatory agencies. Microwave radio links can support very high transmission rates and compete with coaxial cables as a transmission medium. They are particularly effective in rough terrain or cities where laying coaxial cable can be very costly.

♦ *Satellite links.* These consist of line-of-sight propagation paths from a ground station to a communication satellite (up link) and back to a ground station (down link) that is the destination. The satellite is usually placed in a geosynchronous orbit about 22,300 miles above the Earth so that it appears stationary at any point from which it is visible. In effect, the satellite acts like a repeater in the sky. This medium is usually used for very high transmission rates over long distances, and its use for transmission of voice, data, and video signals is increasing very rapidly. While satellite links are used for computer communication, especially in very remote areas, their main disadvantage is the round trip delay time of the signal, which can be annoying for interactive computing but is quite acceptable for broadcasting.

◆ *Wireless radio.* Rapid improvements in high-frequency, low-power radio transmitter/receiver design are making wireless data communication possible over short (local or small metropolitan area) distances. Wireless communication, using technologies such as cellular or packet radio, provide a convenient mechanism for the rapid deployment of mobile computing (*q.v.*).

Networks usually use a combination of the above media. A corporate network, for example, may use twisted pairs within buildings, optical fibers between local buildings, microwave radio to access buildings within 20 miles, and satellites to access branches distributed across a nation. Special hardware interfaces are required to interconnect the different media. In general, the wiring within buildings and between buildings on a corporate campus is owned by the corporation, while the links to distant branches are leased from common carriers, such as telephone companies.

Computer Network Hardware

Communication adapters of various kinds provide the interface between the computer or workstation and the physical transmission medium over which data is actually transmitted. They vary in function from simple Ethernet cards that connect a personal computer to a local Ethernet to more complex adapters that support 620 Mbps data rates using Asynchronous Transfer Mode (ATM) networks to connect a super-computer to network-attached storage. Networks may also include a variety of of other devices, such as routers, switches and gateways, that are described elsewhere (*see* COMMUNICATION CONTROL UNIT and GATEWAY).

Types of Networks

As noted earlier, networks can be characterized as local area networks (LANs), metropolitan area networks (MANs), or wide area networks (WANs). As their names imply, the first two are usually limited to a geographical area that extends no more than a few miles between the extremities. Because of the smaller distances involved, LANs usually operate at relatively high speeds

of between 10 and 1,000 Mbps. The Ethernet, the token ring, FDDI (fiber distributed data interface) and ATM are examples of commonly used LAN technologies operating at speeds up to 10, 100, 155, and 622 Mbps respectively. WANs can cover distances of hundreds or thousands of miles and, in general, use a variety of transmission media leased from common carriers.

Instead of characterizing networks by geographical coverage (as done above), networks can also be characterized by the way they are funded. For example, we may have:

◆ *Private networks.* Such networks are usually owned by some corporation or other private entity that confines access and use of the network and its services to its employees and/or customers.

◆ *Public networks.* This usually refers to entities that offer networking or network services to any organization or individual that wishes to subscribe and pay for the goods or service provided. The telephone system is an example of a public network. Besides providing basic telephone services, telephone companies also sell or lease a variety of local and wide area communication services to their customers.

◆ *Cooperative networks.* This refers to networks that are supported and managed by their users. Bitnet was an example of a cooperative network used by educational institutions prior to the implementation of the Internet as we know it today.

Internets

Despite the growing acceptance of the OSI reference model for network architectures, the current abundance of incompatible network types will not go away very soon. The need arises, therefore, to interconnect two or more compatible or incompatible networks to form an *internet* or a network of networks. This is usually done by using communication control units called *routers* or *gateways* whose complexity depends mostly on the similarity of the networks connected in terms of frames, messages, protocols, and services supported.

Network Planning and Design

Planning, implementing, and operating a computer network can be a very complex task because of the number of often conflicting requirements that need to be satisfied and the variety of potential solutions that must be considered. The objective is to satisfy all, or at least most, of the requirements at the lowest cost. Factors to consider in planning include the:

◆ Type of applications for which the network will be used.

◆ Number and geographical distribution of the nodes.

◆ Amount and distribution of data to be transmitted.

◆ Access and response times required.

◆ Type of equipment that needs to be connected.

◆ Expected reliability and availability of network services.

◆ Need for future expansion.

◆ Needed compatibility with existing hardware and software.

◆ Simplicity of installation and ease of use.

◆ Security and management needs.

◆ Quality of service requirements. An example might be the reservation of some minimum bandwidth for computer teleconferencing (*see* COMPUTER CONFERENCING).

The design process includes the choice of the appropriate architectures, network topologies, transmission media, communication adapters, network electronics, and software so that all devices can intercommunicate seamlessly and transparently.

Examples of Networks

Tens of thousands of networks of various kinds are currently operating around the world. They differ in the services provided, the users served, the technologies used, and their administration. The sections that follow describe some well-known networks that have played, or will play, an important role in modern networking.

The Arpanet

In the late 1960s, the Advanced Research Projects Agency of the US Department of Defense (DoD) began funding research in computer networks. This research led to an experimental four-node network in late 1969, which expanded to include almost 1,000 computers by the early 1980s. Although the Arpanet, as it was called, spanned half the globe from Hawaii to Sweden, most of these systems were located at US universities and research laboratories that had DoD research contracts.

When the Arpanet technology had proven itself by years of reliable operation, Milnet (Military Network) was implemented, using the same technology, and extended to Europe. It was connected to Arpanet, but the traffic between the two was tightly controlled to ensure Milnet security. Since many user organizations connected their own local area networks to Arpanet and Milnet, the resulting ARPA internet included thousands of interconnected computing devices and a total of about 100,000 users by 1985. After 1985, ARPA continued to support Milnet, but began phasing out support of the Arpanet.

Much of our present knowledge about computer networking is a direct result of the Arpanet project. The major nodes or local area networks were interfaced to the network through communication processors known as IMPs (interface message processors, which were the forerunners of modern routers) and TIPs (terminal interface processors, which were the forerunners of today's terminal servers), connected mostly with 56 Kbps leased lines, with some operating at rates as high as 230.4 Kbps. The project led to the development of the TCP/IP (Transmission Control Protocol/Internet Protocol) family of protocols now used so widely to interconnect nodes using the Unix (*q.v.*) and other operating systems. The IP protocol was designed to handle the interconnection of the vast number of LANs comprising the Arpanet. Other important Arpanet protocols include the File Transfer (FTP) and Simple Mail Transfer protocols (SMTP), as well as Telnet, which supports login to a remote computer.

BITNET

BITNET (Because It's Time NETwork) was started in 1981 by the City University of New York and Yale University. The goal was to create an inexpensive mechanism for universities to communicate with each other by using electronic mail (*q.v.*) and exchange information using file transfer. It used an old IBM protocol and, at its peak, it connected about 3,000 mainframes (*q.v.*) at universities in the USA, Canada, Europe, South America, Asia, and Australia. By 1990, it had been largely replaced by NSFNET. Bitnet's popularity stemmed from the unusual financing mechanism used to support it. To join, a university had to pay for a leased line to some other (usually the nearest neighbor) university, and also to allow others to connect to it. As such, it was an early form of a cooperative network entirely funded by its user community.

NSFNET

In the early 1980s, the importance of the Arpanet for sharing resources and information among academic researchers had become obvious. But Arpanet was funded by the Department of Defense, and its use was therefore restricted to academic departments with DoD research contracts. As the DoD began phasing out its support for Arpanet after 1985, the National Science Foundation (NSF) began funding a number of network initiatives to ensure that university researchers could continue to communicate with each other and have convenient access to the national supercomputer centers (*q.v.*) established to help support NSF funded research.

The network that emerged from these initiatives in the late 1980s became known as NSFNET. It was based on the TCP/IP suite of protocols and consisted of a high-speed multiconnected backbone network designed to handle expected traffic patterns and provide reliability through redundant data paths. Initially, this backbone consisted of 56 Kbps leased lines, but these were upgraded to 1.54 Mbps (T1 lines) in 1990 and to 45 Mbps (T3 lines) three years later because of the exponential growth in data traffic. This growth was due a combination of factors, including connections to other national and international networks, deployment of ever improving network services (e.g. World Wide Web and network browsers), and the lifting of NSF restrictions on commercial and private use of the NSFNET, which was becoming known as the Internet.

As commercial and private use of the Internet kept growing, the Internet was increasingly becoming a commodity and NSF started phasing out the funding for university connections. By 1995, the US Internet traffic was carried exclusively by commercial Internet providers. By 1996, the number of Internet hosts reached a total of 12.8 million and the network was becoming more and more congested.

Advanced Networks

The current Internet delivers traffic on a "best effort" basis. While this may be adequate for applications such as electronic mail and Web browsing, it is inadequate for new generations of applications such as scientific visualization (*q.v.*), tele-immersion (i.e. virtual reality—*q.v.*) and advanced computer-based education systems that include audio and video clips. This new breed of applications requires guaranteed Quality of Service (e.g. bandwidth reservation for video and visualization applications) which cannot be provided by the current Internet. Consequently, there are a number of initiatives to build the next generations of networks to support new emerging applications. Some of these include:

◆ *The vBNS (very high Bandwidth Network Service* —This is an NSF initiative to support research requiring very high speed network connections that can guarantee Quality of Service for applications that need it. The current backbone operates at OC-12 (620 Mbps) speed with most connections to it operating between DS3 (45 Mbps) and OC-3 (155 Mbps) speeds.

◆ *Internet2*—This initiative was announced in 1996 by a consortium of research universities to build a new educational network with a mission to "facilitate and coordinate the development, deployment, operation. and technology transfer of advanced, network-based applications and network services to further US leadership in research and higher education and accelerate the availability of new services and applications on the Internet." In 1997, it was announced that the vBNS would be the forerunner of Internet2.

◆ *NGI (Next Generation Internet)*—Soon after the Internet2 announcement was made, the White House announced the Next Generation Internet Initiative. It will provide funding to a number of federal agencies, including NSF, for the support of research into advanced networks and network applications.

During the next few years, these initiatives are likely to result in new generations of commercial networks that support not only current applications, but also new applications that will further change the way we play, teach, learn, work, and communicate. Like the earlier networks, the new networks will create new opportunities for business and services we cannot fully anticipate today.

Bibliography

1990. Robertazzi, T. G. *Computer Networks and Systems.* New York: Springer-Verlag.
1996. Tanenbaum, A. S. *Computer Networks*, 3rd Ed. Upper Saddle River, NJ: Prentice Hall.

Websites

1999. MCI's vBNS site. http://www.vbns.net.
1999. http://www.cise.nsf.gov/anir/vbnsrep.html.
1999. Internet2 home page. http://www.internet2.edu.
1999. NGI Initiative home page. http://www.ngi.gov.

John S. Sobolewski

NEURAL NETWORKS

For articles on related subjects *see* ARTIFICIAL INTELLIGENCE; ARTIFICIAL LIFE; COMPUTER VISION; EXPERT SYSTEMS; GENETIC ALGORITHMS; PARALLEL PROCESSING; PATTERN RECOGNITION; PERCEPTRON; ROBOTICS; and SPEECH RECOGNITION AND SYNTHESIS.

Introduction

The human brain performs perceptual tasks such as visual pattern recognition, distinguishing acoustical harmonics, and speech understanding remarkably well. Such cognitive tasks remain difficult for digital computers to accomplish. The promise of neural computing relies on the rapid solution of such problems through massive parallelism, where information is not transferred between computing units, but is encoded through patterns of interconnectivity in a distributed fashion. The study of *neural networks* includes the notions of *connectionism, parallel distributed processing, self-adaptive systems*, and *self-organizing systems*.

Neural network architecture has been inspired by biological knowledge of the brain. Historically, neural systems have been studied by first creating simplified theories and then modeling those theories by simulation (*q.v.*) on conventional computers and VLSI implementation. By studying neural models, researchers hope to gain the insight needed to build machines with perceptual and cognitive capabilities that can understand what we say, read what we write, and recognize what we see. For example, neural networks provide speech recognition, capabilities that are now being embedded in computer applications to allow us to use machines more naturally. Additional cognitive capabilities will not only make computers more effective in handling real-world tasks, but could significantly change how we, as humans, interact with machines in the future.

In general, neural net or parallel distributed processing (PDP) models are specified by network topology, node characteristics, and training or learning rules. Networks are composed of a large number of simple processing units, each interacting with others via excitatory and inhibitory connections. Representations distributed over a massive number of units, together with local interconnections among processing units, provide fault tolerance (*see* FAULT-TOLERANT COMPUTING). Learning is achieved through a simple rule that adapts connection weights in response to input patterns. Alterations in the degree of interconnectedness (i.e. the weight associated with a connection) permit adaptability to new situations. Developments in net topologies and refinements in learning algorithms continue to drive the field of neural computing forward and inspire new applications for neural networks.

Historically, the study of artificial neural systems has been interdisciplinary, exciting the interest of scientists from the fields of neurobiology, psychology, computer science, biomedical engineering, and physics. The development of mathematical models for neural computing began more than 40 years ago with the work of McCulloch and Pitts (1943), Hebb (1949), Rosenblatt (1959), Widrow (1960), and others. While some researchers adhered closely to known biological mechanisms, others evolved new computational paradigms using simpler models. Such models have been successful in solving difficult optimization problems (Kirkpatrick, 1983) and in implementing associative memories (Kohonen, 1984). Researchers have also combined conventional symbolic and heuristic (*q.v.*) approaches of artificial intelligence (AI) with new parallel distributed approaches. Unlike traditional expert systems, where knowledge is made explicit in the form of rules, neural networks generate their own "rules" through learning encounters. However, hybrid models of neural computation are also possible where established techniques are used in conjunction with neural networks. For example, in the recognition of characters, one could use a Fast Fourier Transform (*q.v.*) to reduce an originally large input representation to a smaller set of vectors from which a neural network might be trained more efficiently.

Current estimates place the number of neurons in the human brain at 100 billion (10^{11}). In contrast to the accuracy and high speed of modern-day digital computers, the brain is relatively slow and imprecise. Even if we project into the future, however, and imagine electronic circuit switching times a million times faster than neurons, artificial neural models face severe size constraints. Conventional chips typically have an average fan-out between 10 and 100, while single cortical neurons can have from 1,000 to 100,000 synapses (connections) on their dendrites and can make from 1,000 to 100,000 synaptic connections on the dendrites of other neurons. Thus, while biologically motivated massive parallel solutions may offer important insights, their practical implementations may require reformulation to make them realizable with respect to existing and near future technology.

The remaining sections of this article provide an overview of a framework for neural computing and describe a neural network capable of arbitrary mapping.

Framework for Neural Computing

Rumelhart and McClelland (1986) identify eight major aspects of a parallel distributed model:

1. A set of *processing units*.

2. A state of *activation*.

3. An *output function* for each unit.

4. A pattern of *interconnectivity* among units.

5. A *propagation rule* for propagating patterns of activities through the network.

6. An *activation rule* for combining the inputs on a unit with its current state to produce a new level of activation.

7. A *learning rule* whereby patterns of connectivity are modified by experience.

8. An *environment* within which the system must operate.

A set of N processing *units* may represent distinct objects, such as features, letters, and concepts (*local representation*), or abstract elements over which meaningful patterns are defined (*distributed representations*). In the latter case, each entity is represented by a pattern of activity distributed over many units, and each unit may be involved in representing several entities. The architecture of neural networks distinguishes between three types of unit: *input, output,* and *hidden.* Input units receive information from the environment (outside world) in which the model is embedded. Output units transmit information out of the systems, either directly affecting control or driving other systems. Hidden units are those contained within the input and output layers of the network and are thus not "seen" outside the system.

Mathematically, the state of the system at time t may be defined by a vector of N real numbers representing a pattern of activation over a set of processing units. The activation of unit u_i at time t is $a_i(t)$ (*see* Fig. 1). It is the patterns of activation over a set of units that identifies what the system represents at some time t. *Activation values* may be continuous or discrete, bounded or unbounded. Indeed, assumptions concerning the domain and range of activation values account for most differences among neural models.

Each *unit* communicates with its neighbors via the strength of its output signals. For each unit u_i, output $o_i(t) = f_i(a_i(t))$. *Output functions f* may assume distinct characteristics depending on the nature of the problem domain (environment). For example, they may simply be the identity function, $f(x) = x$ (linear models), a threshold function (nonlinear models), or a stochastic function in which the output depends in a probabilistic fashion upon its activation values.

The *pattern of connectivity* among units implicitly specifies *what* the system represents and *how* it responds to arbitrary input. In a simple model, signals coming into a unit are multiplied by weights and summed to produce an output signal. Typically, positive weights represent excitatory types of input while negative weights represent inhibitory types of input. Thus, for a weight matrix W, each entry value w_{ij} represents the connection strength (magnitude) and type (sign) from unit i to unit j.

A *propagation rule* sends patterns of activities throughout a network. Signals may flow unidirectionally or may feed back to other units within a network. In a *feed-forward* model, activations are computed in sequence starting with the input layer and propagated towards the output layer. The structure of communication links is reflected by the connectivity matrix of each layer.

In general, a *propagation rule* combines an output vector $o(t)$ with its associated connectivity weight matrix to produce a resultant input to the next layer. Let net_j be the resultant input connections to unit j. Typically, the propagation rule is simply the weighted sum of the inputs (i.e. $net(t) = Wo(t)$).

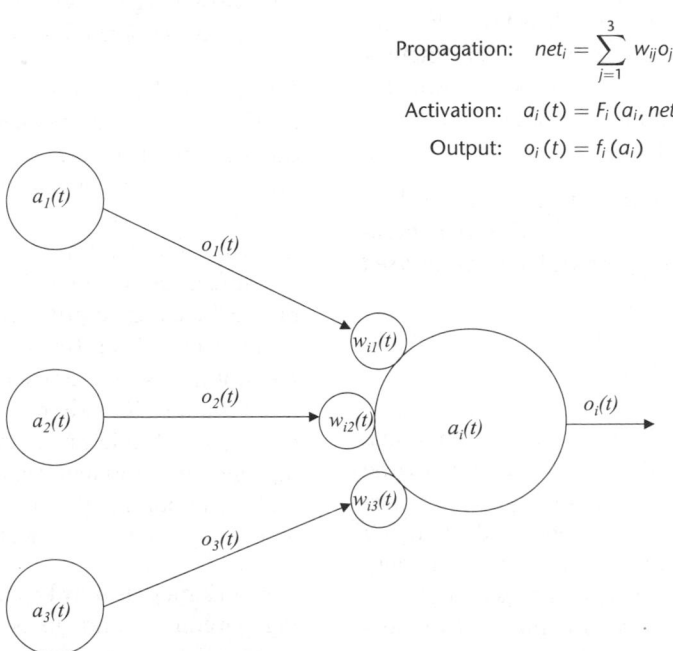

Propagation: $net_i = \sum_{j=1}^{3} w_{ij}o_j$

Activation: $a_i(t) = F_i(a_i, net_i)$

Output: $o_i(t) = f_i(a_i)$

Figure 1. The basic components of a neural computing system.

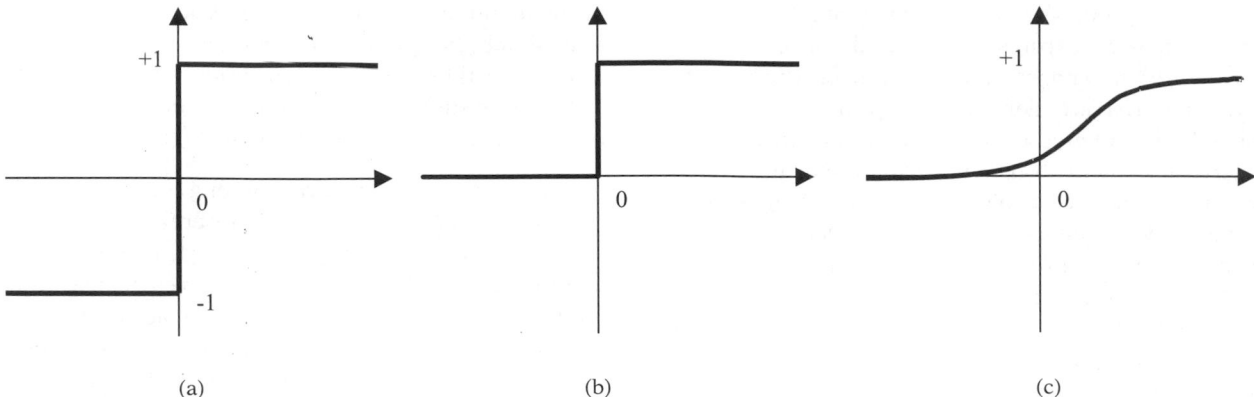

Figure 2. Three nonlinear activation functions: (a) hard limiter, (b) threshold logic, and (c) sigmoidal.

An *activation rule F* combines all net inputs of a unit with its current activation value to produce a new level of activation. The activation is formulated by an expression of the form

$$a_i(t+1) = F(net_i(t)) = F\left(\sum_j w_{ij}o_j(t)\right)$$

as shown in Fig. 1. For most neural models, each unit sums its weighted input and passes the result through some nonlinear process. Activation rules may be characterized by an internal threshold parameter and by the kind of nonlinearity. Fig. 2 shows three representative nonlinear activation functions: hard limiters, threshold logic, and sigmoidal functions. In the case of a hard limiter as shown in Fig. 2a, if the weighted sum of inputs is greater than or less than zero, the input pattern will be mapped onto the values $+1$ or -1, respectively. The earliest neurons (*McCulloch–Pitts neurons*) were such binary threshold devices. Timing of the activation rule may be driven synchronously or asynchronously. In models where updates are asynchronous and random, the network is more likely to avoid oscillations (Hopfield and Tank, 1986).

Learning strategies are the focus of much research in the field. In the next section we describe two paradigms by which networks may be trained: *supervised* and *unsupervised* learning.

Learning Paradigms

Changing the processing and/or knowledge stored in a network involves three kinds of modification to the patterns of interconnectivity: developing new connections, destroying existing connections, and changing the strengths of connections by attenuation or gain. The modification of interconnections is accomplished by adjusting the weights between connections whenever the neural net learns something in response to new inputs (created either by experience or changes

in the environment). In general, most learning rules increase or decrease synaptic weights in proportion to some *reinforcement signal*.

In *unsupervised learning*, no information concerning correct classification is provided to reinforce training patterns. The earliest example of unsupervised learning is the Hebbian learning rule: if cell A persistently participates in firing cell B, then A's efficiency in firing B is increased (Hebb, 1949). This rule may be approximated by $w_{ij}(t+1) = w_{ij}(t) + \eta a_i(t)o_j(t)$, where η is a gain parameter for the rate of learning. However, using this simple rule, networks can learn only orthogonal input patterns. A more sophisticated form of unsupervised learning is a variant of Hebb's rule called *competitive learning* $\Delta w_{ij} = \eta(u_j(t) - w_{ij}(t))a_i(t)$, where changes are balanced against previously established clusters. Kohonen's feature-map-forming sets (1984) and Grossberg's ART (Adaptive Resonance Theory, 1986) have evolved from competitive learning models.

Supervised learning paradigms require a "teacher," reinforcing correct associations between inputs and outputs by providing the correct or desired output during training periods. For example, consider the *Widrow–Hoff* rule, $\Delta w_{ij} = \eta(u_i(t) - a_i(t))o_j(t)$. In this rule, the reinforcement signal is proportional to the difference between the desired activation provided by the "teacher" input $u_i(t)$ and the current activation signal $a_i(t)$. Using this error-correcting rule (or *delta rule*), it is possible to train a network to recognize patterns that are linearly independent rather than strictly orthogonal. Models using methods of supervised learning, include Hopfield nets (1986), perceptrons (*q.v.*), and Boltzmann's Machine, and may be described as associative memories or classifiers (Fig. 3).

Network models may be classified based on their learning paradigms and goals. The goal of *pattern associators* is to map one set onto another. For example, *auto associators* can be used to recover a pattern from

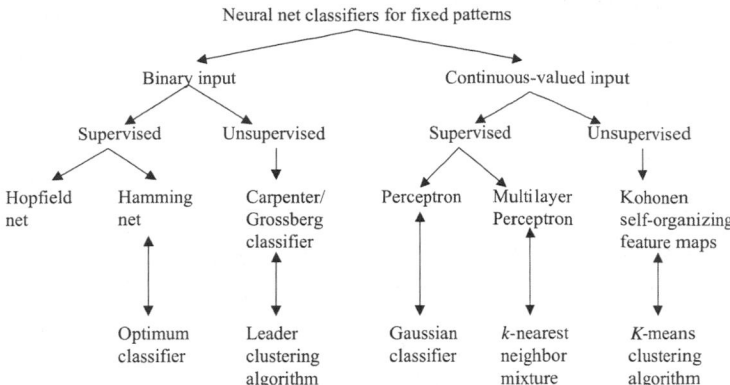

Figure 3. Neural net classifiers for fixed patterns. (From R. Lippman, "An Introduction to Computing with Neural Nets," *IEEE ASSP Magazine*, April 1987. © 1987 IEEE.)

a degraded version. *Regularity detectors* discover useful (invariant and efficient) features of an input population. *Reinforcement learning* provides feedback on input stimuli. However, Hebb's original idea remains a common thread in these paradigms. In the next sections, we describe how these goals of learning may be achieved in the context of linear and nonlinear models.

Linear Models

In linear models, activation values are unbounded real numbers and consist of two sets of units—input and output. There is no need for hidden units in linear systems because all multiple step computations may be accomplished in a single integral step. Units may be fully connected, and all connections are of the same type. For example, a linear model with a simple Hebbian learning rule is called a "linear associator." Applied as a pattern associator, the presentation of one pattern makes the network produce a previously learned pattern associated with some input. The new pattern may be associated with itself (auto association). In this case, when presented with a portion of the input, a trained network generates a completed version of that pattern. Thus, in terms of function, these networks can accomplish *mapping* and *pattern completion*.

The orthogonal constraint of linear systems may be overcome by using nonlinear units within multilayer systems. In the next section, we describe a nonlinear model, the perceptron, and discuss its significance with respect to the evolution of a learning rule for multilayered networks called the *generalized delta rule*.

Nonlinear Models

The simplest nonlinear system consists of linear threshold units. As shown in Fig. 2b, if the weighted sum of inputs is greater than some threshold, the activation value is 1, otherwise 0. A *perceptron* is a single-layer

network of linear threshold units without feedback. Rosenblatt (1959) first studied perceptrons, using a learning rule similar to the delta rule described earlier. The perceptron convergence theorem claims that such a system is guaranteed to find a set of weights that correctly classifies a set of input vectors *if such a set of weights exists*. Unfortunately, as Minsky and Papert pointed out in their 1969 book, *Perceptrons*, such a set of weights does not always exist. Perceptrons can solve only the class of functions that are *linearly separable*. Thus, if the input patterns are not linearly independent, they cannot be discriminated by a simple linear network. The simplest example of a function that cannot be computed by a single-layered perceptron is exclusive-or (XOR). However, a multilayered perceptron is capable of computing the XOR function.

The perceptron (nonlinear models) and delta rule (linear models) provided a simple guaranteed learning rule for all problems solvable without hidden units. The lack of such a learning rule for networks with hidden units delayed the development of neural networks for many years. A revitalization of neural computing was sparked by the development of learning algorithms for multilayered networks. Rumelhart and McClelland (1986), Werbos (1984), and Parker (1985) independently developed a generalized form of the delta rule for multilayered networks, capable of learning arbitrary mappings. Their work remains significant because it shows that the limitations of single-layer perceptrons do not apply to more complex networks. In the next section we describe a generalized delta rule applied to a feed-forward network having a differentiable activation function.

Learning by Back Error Propagation

The generalized form of the delta rule combines the benefits of nonlinear perceptron-like classification capability with a method of minimizing an error measure for learning called *gradient descent*. Widrow and Hoff (1960) first used gradient descent for learning in linear systems by the least mean square (LMS) method. The LMS procedure finds a set of connection weights that minimize the mean squared error between some desired output and actual output over a set of input patterns using gradient descent.

Similarly, learning by back error propagation exploits the method of gradient descent: Changes in weights are made in proportion to the negative of the derivative of an error term, as measured on some pattern with respect to existing weights. For example, given pattern p, the learning rule becomes

$$\Delta w_{ij} = -k \frac{\partial E_p}{\partial w_{ij}} \qquad (1)$$

where k is a proportionality constant. Computing the derivative in equation (1) shows that the generalized rule takes the same form as the original delta rule, $\Delta w_{ij} = \eta \delta_{pi} o_{pi}$. Thus, the delta rule *implements* gradient descent in E (Fig. 4). Each connection weight is changed by an amount proportional to the product of an error term called δ times the output signal of the unit sending activation along each connection.

The generalized delta rule requires *semilinear* activations. A semilinear activation function is a nondecreasing differentiable function of net output, such as the sigmoid logistic function shown in Fig. 2c.

$$o_{pj} = \frac{1}{1 - e^{-net_{pj}}},$$

where

$$net_{pj} = \sum_i w_{ji} o_{pi} + bias_j.$$

The parameter *bias* is similar in function to the threshold of the perceptron and is treated just like any other weight. The linear threshold function (Fig. 2b) on which the perceptron is based is discontinuous, and cannot be used since the new learning rule requires that the derivative of the activation function $f_i'(net_i)$ exist.

For purposes of back-propagation, the error signal δ is computed in two distinct ways. The error signal for output units is similar to the standard delta rule and is computed by

$$\delta_{pi} = (t_{pi} - o_{pj}) f_i'(net_{pi}), \qquad (2)$$

where f_i' is the derivative of the activation function. The error signal for hidden units for which there is no specific target is computed recursively in terms of the

where

$$F: R^n \to I^m$$
$$R = (-\infty, \infty), \ I = (0, 1)$$

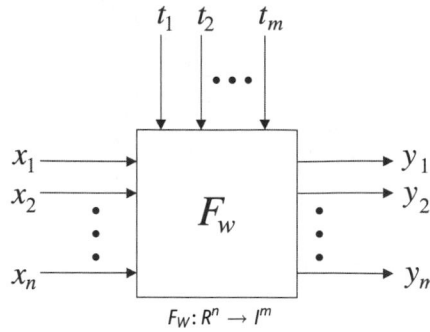

$F_W: R^n \to I^m$

$x \in R^n$: input signal $y \in I^m$: output signal

$t \in I^m$: teaching signal $w \in R^p$: connection weight

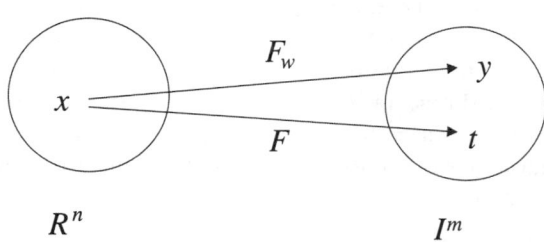

R^n I^m

Figure 4. A back-propagation net as a mapping device. Learning rule: Search for w such that $F = F_w$ by (1) Select training set $T \subseteq R^n$. (2) Minimize error function

$$E = \frac{1}{|T|} \sum_{x \in T} \| F(x) - F_w(x) \|$$

with

$$\Delta w = -\eta \frac{\partial E}{\partial w}$$

by method of gradient descent. (From T. Kimura, Department of Computer Science, Washington University, St Louis, MO. © 1989 Class notes. Reprinted with permission.)

δ values of units to which it directly connects and the weights of those connections. That is,

$$\delta_{pi} = f_i'(net_{pi}) \sum_k \delta_{pk} w_{kj}, \qquad (3)$$

Thus, learning by back-propagation requires that the generalized rule be applied in two phases. In the first phase, an input is presented and propagated forward through the network to compute an output value o_{pj} for each unit. Output unit values are then compared with a target pattern associated with an input, and a δ term is computed for each output unit using equation (2). In the second phase, a backward pass through the network allows the recursive computation of δ as shown in equation (3).

The network is trained by initially selecting small random weights and internal thresholds and presenting training input patterns repeatedly. Weights are adjusted after each pattern set until the weights converge and the cost function (E) is reduced to some acceptable value. Finding the global minimum is not guaranteed by this method alone (Hinton *et al.*, 1984). Convergence is sometimes faster and escape from local minima is possible if a momentum term is added, smoothing the weight changes.

Concluding Remarks

Artificial neural computing is beginning to appear in consumer products such as voice and character recognition applications. However, the full potential of this remarkable technology has yet to be reached. The back-propagation network described above is an example of a functional component that may be part of more complex systems in the future. Current research is focused on analyzing learning and self-organizing algorithms used in multilayered networks, on building complete systems for image understanding, computer vision (*q.v.*) for robots, and in advancing VLSI implementation strategies pioneered by Graf *et al.* (1986) and Mead and Ismail (1989). High-speed processing though massively parallel computing holds the promise of realizing practical real-time neural net systems.

For further reading see Schalkoff (1997), Gurney (1997), Landau and Taylor (1997), and Bose and Liang (1996).

Bibliography

1943. McCulloch, W. S. and Pitts, W. "A Logical Calculus of the Ideas Immanent in Nervous Activity," *Bulletin of Mathematical Biophysics*, **5**, 115–133.

1949. Hebb, D. O. *The Organization of Behavior.* New York: John Wiley.

1959. Rosenblatt, R. *Principles of Neurodynamics.* New York: Spartan Books.

1960. Widrow, B., and Hoff, M. E. "Adaptive Switching Circuits," *1960 IRE WESCON Conv. Record, Part 4*, 96–104, August.

1969. Minsky, M., and Papert, S. *Perceptrons: An Introduction to Computational Geometry.* Cambridge, MA: MIT Press.

1982. Hopfield, J. J. "Neural Networks and Physical Systems with Emergent Collective Computational Abilities," *Proc. Natl. Acad. Sci. USA*, **79** (April), 2554–2558.

1982. Feldman, J.A., and Ballard, D. H. "Connectionist Models and their Properties," *Cognitive Science*, **6**, 205–254.

1983. Kirkpatrick, S., Gellatt, C. D., Jr, and Vecchi, M. P. "Optimization by Simulated Annealing," *Science*, **220**, 671–680.

1984. Hinton, G. E., Sejnowski, T. J., and Ackley, D. H. "Boltzmann Machines: Constrained Satisfaction Networks that Learn," *CMU-CS-84-119*, Carnegie Mellon University (May).

1984. Kohonen, T. *Self-Organization and Associative Memory.* Berlin: Springer-Verlag.

1984. Werbos, P. *Beyond Regression: New Tools for Prediction and Analysis in Behavioral Sciences.* Ph.D. Dissertation, Harvard University.

1985. Parker, D. B. *Learning-logic* (TR-47). Center for Computational Research in Economics and Management Science, Cambridge, MA: MIT Press.

1986. Rumelhart, D. E., and McClelland, J. L. *Parallel Distributed Processing: Explorations in the Microstructure of Cognition.* Cambridge, MA: MIT Press.

1986. Grossberg, S. *The Adaptive Brain I: Cognition, Learning, Reinforcement,* and *Rhythm* and *The Adaptive Brain II: Vision, Speech, Language, and Motor Control.* Amsterdam: Elsevier/North-Holland.

1986. Hopfield, J. J., and Tank, D. W. "Computing with Neural Circuits: A Model," *Science*, **233** (August), 625–633.

1986. Graf, H. P., Jackel, L. D., Howard, R. E., Straughn, B., Denker, J. S., Hubbard, W., Tennant, D. M., and Schwarz, D. "VLSI Implementation of a Neural Network Memory with Several Hundreds of Neurons," in *AIP Conference Proceedings 151, Neural Networks for Computing* (ed. J. S. Denker). Snowbird, UT: AIP.

1988. *Science.* Special Issue: Frontiers in Neuroscience, **242**, 633–828 (November).

1989. Mead, C. A., and Ismail, M. (eds) *Analog VLSI Implementation of Neural Systems.* Boston: Kluwer Academic.

1996. Bose, N. K., and Liang, P. *Neural Network Fundamentals with Graphs, Algorithms, and Applications.* New York: McGraw-Hill.

1997. Landau, L. J., and Taylor, J. G. (eds) *Concepts for Neural Networks, A Survey.* New York: Springer-Verlag.

1997. Schalkoff, R. J., *Artificial Neural Networks.* New York: McGraw-Hill.

1997. Gurney, K. *An Introduction to Neural Networks.* London: UCL Press.

1999. Sarle, W. S. (ed.) *Neural Network FAQ.* Periodic posting to the Usenet newsgroup comp.ai.neural-nets. `ftp://ftp.sas.com/pub/neural/FAQ.html`.

Andrew Laine

NIXDORF, HEINZ

For articles on related subjects *see* COMPUTER INDUSTRY: EUROPE; and DIGITAL COMPUTERS, HISTORY OF: EARLY.

Heinz Nixdorf (1925–1986) (*see* Fig. 1), came to stand for successful, innovative entrepreneurship in the German computing industry. Under his leadership the company that he had founded in 1952, Nixdorf Computer AG, became the second biggest information technology company in Germany—second only to Siemens. He enjoyed such prestige as an entrepreneur and manager in the 1980s that *Fortune* voted him the most capable manager in Europe.

In 1951 Heinz Nixdorf, a physics student strapped for cash, took up a job at the Remington Rand electronics department in Frankfurt, where he got to know Walter Sprick, head of the electronics laboratory there, and assisted him in developing an electronic calculating machine. In 1952, when Remington Rand had discontinued these development activities, Nixdorf set up his own company—the Labor für Impulstechnik (LFI)—to develop electronic calculating machines on the basis of Sprick's patents.

Figure 1. Heinz Nixdorf, founder and head of the Nixdorf Computer AG, Paderborn, Germany.

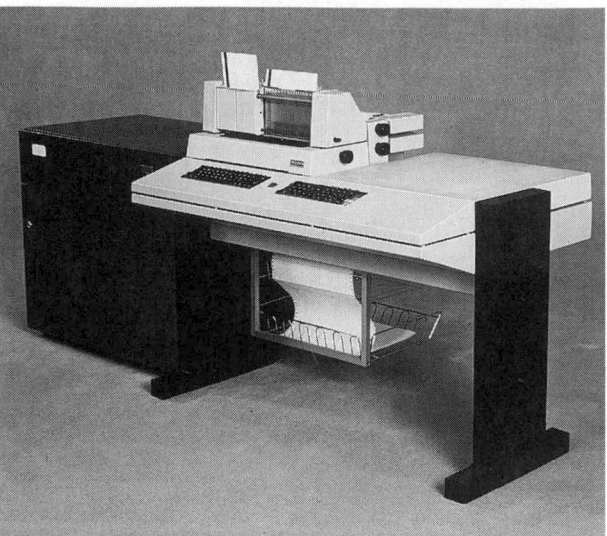

Figure 2. The Nixdorf 820 system, 1970.

Nixdorf's first customer was RWE, a power utility based in Essen. RWE ordered an electronic calculating machine from Nixdorf, and provided him with funds and a room to work in. This machine was to be connected to a Remington Rand tabulating machine in order to calculate electricity prices.

A crucial factor in the early stages of LFI was the company's contacts with Exacta (later known as Wanderer Werke), a Cologne-based maker of office machines, for which Nixdorf built electronic arithmetic-logic units (q.v.) to be incorporated in the Bull punched card equipment that Wanderer marketed. Starting in 1958, Nixdorf built electronic multiplication units for the Multitronic 6000, an electromechanical accounting machine that was produced by Wanderer, and, in 1964, one of the first electronic calculators with a printing unit (Conti)—again for Wanderer.

Nixdorf made his breakthrough as a computer manufacturer with the Logatronic, which was a programmable minicomputer (q.v.) for billing that was developed by Otto Müller in 1964. The huge commercial success of the Logatronic enabled Nixdorf to buy Wanderer in 1968, which until then had been almost his only customer. In the same year he renamed the company Nixdorf Computer AG (NCAG) and relocated it to his home town of Paderborn.

Wanderer's efficient sales network was expanded systematically over the following years, allowing Nixdorf to market his products successfully under his own name. The most successful products in the 1970s were the Nixdorf 820 (Fig. 2), a further development of the Logatronic, and its successor, the Nixdorf 8870. Equipped with special peripherals, the systems sold particularly well in the banking and retail sectors. In the Nixdorf 820, NCAG had created a minicomputer for commercial and administrative applications which was inexpensive and was thus also affordable by small businesses. The name Nixdorf was synonymous with office computers, or "Mittlere Datentechnik," as the technology was known in Germany at the time.

When Wanderer was taken over in 1968, NCAG had 1,800 employees and annual sales of DM105 million. By the mid-1980s, with sales growing by more than 20% a year, NCAG had become the fifth largest computer maker in Europe—after IBM, Siemens, Olivetti and DEC. By the time Heinz Nixdorf died in 1986 the company had manufacturing plants at seven locations—in Germany (Fig. 3), Ireland, Spain, USA, and Singapore—and was running subsidiaries in 44 countries. It had sales of DM5.4 billion, with 26,000 employees.

In 1988 the company ran into a crisis because of outdated products and general mismanagement. Heavy losses compelled NCAG to look for a partner. In 1990

Figure 3. Production plant in Paderborn, 1988.

Siemens acquired a majority stake in NCAG and merged the company with its own computer division to form Siemens Nixdorf Informationssysteme AG (SNI). Since 1992 SNI has been a fully owned subsidiary of Siemens.

Bibliography

1984. "Europe's Ablest Managers," *Fortune International*, 9 July, 16–27.
1985. Gee, J. "Over Here or Over There, Nixdorf Scraps with IBM," *Electronic Business*, 1 April, 51–60.

Margret Amedick and Ulf Hashagen

NO-OP

For articles on related subjects *see* ASSEMBLER; INSTRUCTION SET; and MACHINE AND ASSEMBLY LANGUAGE PROGRAMMING.

A *no-op* ("no operation") is a machine language instruction that can safely be placed in the flow of control of a program but that does nothing to advance the computation in progress. A true no-op does not change the status of any bit or register (*q.v.*) in the computer other than the program counter (*q.v.*), which, when control reaches the no-op, advances to the next meaningful instruction (or another no-op). The usual reasons for embedding a sequence of one or more no-ops in the flow of control are that the programmer wants to introduce a deliberate delay in processing for the sake of either time or address synchronization (to reach an even-numbered address, perhaps), or that space must be reserved in the object code that will be overwritten with a meaningful instruction at some point during execution of the program. (The latter practice is now discouraged because the resulting code would not constitute a reentrant program (*q.v.*).)

The instruction sets (*q.v.*) of a CISC (complex instruction set computer) often include one op-code (operation code) that is itself a no-op, but not all computers built in accord with the reduced instruction set (RISC–*q.v.*) philosophy can afford to devote one of their precious few op-codes to such a (non-) function (though Sparc, a RISC computer, does have one). But a no-op can be synthesized on virtually any computer by writing such instructions as adding zero to a register, shifting a register zero places left, or branching to the next instruction.

Edwin D. Reilly

NONMONOTONIC LOGIC

For articles on related subjects *see* ARTIFICIAL INTELLIGENCE; DEDUCTIVE DATABASE; DISCRETE MATHEMATICS; EXPERT SYSTEMS; FUZZY LOGIC; HEURISTIC; KNOWLEDGE REPRESENTATION; LOGIC PROGRAMMING; MULTI-AGENT SYSTEMS; and WELL-FORMED FORMULA.

A major goal of artificial intelligence is the development of automated agents that are capable of making decisions, responding to the actions of others, and determining the consequences of their own actions. In order to achieve this behavior, these agents must have access to information describing the objects in the environment and the relationships of the objects to each other and to the agent itself. Much of the pioneering work in artificial intelligence used the *predicate calculus* as a language for representing and analyzing domain information. Unfortunately, the predicate calculus does not have the flexibility to perform many types of inference required for common sense reasoning. A fundamental property of the predicate calculus is that the acquisition of new information preserves previous conclusions. Any system in which the set of conclusions grows with the addition of information is said to be *monotonic*.

Frequently, it is necessary to make decisions or take actions when only incomplete knowledge of the environment is available. In many such cases, generalizations and heuristics (*q.v.*) derived from experience are employed. Decision-making under these conditions uses *plausible reasoning* to make tentative conclusions and *belief revision* to retract these conclusions when the acquisition of additional information necessitates such a change. The ability to produce and then retract tentative conclusions produces *nonmonotonic* reasoning systems. Extensions or modifications to the predicate calculus that produce nonmonotonic reasoning are said to be nonlogical since they permit the generation of conclusions that cannot be obtained by strictly following the laws of logic.

Predicate Calculus as a Representation Language

We will give a brief introduction to a subset of the predicate calculus that is sufficiently rich to demonstrate the subtleties of plausible reasoning. A description of the complete predicate calculus and its role as a representation language for artificial intelligence can be found in Genesereth and Nilson (1987). The building blocks of a predicate calculus language $\mathcal{L}$ are the terms and predicate symbols of the language. The *terms* of $\mathcal{L}$ consist of constants $(A, B, C, \ldots)$ and variables $(x, y, z, \ldots)$. Predicate symbols are used to represent properties of objects. The *arity* of a predicate symbol designates the number of arguments of the predicate. An *atomic formula* is an expression of the form $T(t_1, \ldots, t_n)$ where T is an n-ary predicate symbol and $t_1, \ldots, t_n$ are terms. Atomic formulas obtained from unary (1-ary) and binary (2-ary) predicates have the form $P(t_1)$ and $Q(t_1, t_2)$, respectively. A *ground atomic formula* is an atomic formula that contains only constants as arguments.

The *well-formed formulas* or *wffs* of $\mathcal{L}$ are constructed recursively from the atomic formulas using the logical connectives $\wedge$ (and), $\vee$ (or), $\neg$ (not), $\rightarrow$ (implies) and the quantifiers $\forall$ (for all) and $\exists$ (there exists). The *scope* of the quantifier in a formula $\forall x(\phi)$ or $\exists x(\phi)$ is the wff ϕ which follows it. A *sentence* is a wff that contains no unquantified variables.

The wffs provide only the syntax of the language; there is no meaning associated with the constants or the predicate symbols. Semantics are obtained through an *interpretation* of the symbols of the language. An interpretation is a mapping from the constants and predicate symbols to a set of objects called the *universe* of the interpretation. The mapping associates an object in the universe with each constant and a set of n-tuples of objects with each n-ary predicate symbol. If an n-tuple of objects $(o_1, \ldots, o_n)$ is in the set associated with an n-ary predicate T, then the predicate T is true for objects $(o_1, \ldots, o_n)$ in the interpretation. The truth value of any sentence can be obtained from those assigned to the predicates by the interpretation.

A finite set of sentences of a language $\mathcal{L}$ is used to describe relationships among the constants and the predicates. In mathematics the sentences are called *axioms* while in database theory they are frequently referred to as the *assertions* or *facts* of the database. A *model* of an axiom set Δ is an interpretation of the symbols of $\mathcal{L}$ in which all the sentences in Δ are true. A sentence w is *logically entailed* by Δ, written $\Delta \models w$, if w is true in all models of Δ.

Predicate calculus is *monotonic* because $\Delta \models w$ implies that $\Delta \cup N \models w$ for any set of additional sentences N. The monotonicity of predicate calculus follows directly from the definition of logical entailment: if w is true in every model of Δ, then it is true in those models of Δ that also model the extended set of axioms $\Delta \cup N$.

Example

Representation using a predicate calculus language and limitations imposed by monotonic logic are demonstrated by the analysis of two simple axioms to describe the aviational capabilities of birds.

Constants: Tweety, Opus
Predicates: $BIRD(x)$, $FLIES(x)$, $PENGUIN(x)$

Δ: $BIRD$(Tweety), $BIRD$(Opus)
S1: $\forall x(BIRD(x) \rightarrow FLIES(x))$
S2: $\forall x(PENGUIN(x) \rightarrow \neg FLIES(x))$

A model of Δ that tries to capture the standard meanings of the predicate symbols may have the set of all animals as its universe. With this intended interpretation, the predicates *BIRD*, *PENGUIN*, and *FLIES* are true for all animals that are birds, are penguins, and that fly, respectively. Moreover, the sentences *BIRD*(Tweety) and *BIRD*(Opus) in Δ require that the constants Tweety and Opus denote animals that are birds.

The sentence S1 represents the general assertion that any object that satisfies the *BIRD* predicate also satisfies the *FLIES* predicate or, intuitively, that all birds fly. The axioms logically entail *FLIES*(Opus), since *FLIES*(Opus) is true in every interpretation in which S1 and *BIRD*(Opus) are true. If we later learn that Opus is a Penguin, adding *PENGUIN*(Opus) to Δ will produce an inconsistency since $\Delta \cup \{PENGUIN(\text{Opus})\}$ entails both *FLIES*(Opus) and $\neg FLIES$(Opus). Note that monotonicity is maintained with the addition of the fact *PENGUIN*(Opus) to the axioms. The new conclusion is simply added to the previous conclusions, since *FLIES*(Opus) is still logically entailed by *BIRD*(Opus) and S1.

The example illustrates a shortcoming of the predicate calculus as a representation language for plausible reasoning. Upon the acquisition of the information that Opus is a penguin, we would like to retract the original conclusion *FLIES*(Opus) and replace it with $\neg FLIES$(Opus). However, monotonicity ensures that the original conclusion remains in the set of logical consequences of the extended set of axioms. Thus, a monotonic inference system would produce an inconsistency since both *FLIES*(Opus) and $\neg FLIES$(Opus) are logically entailed by the axioms.

One potential solution is to be more careful with the selection of the axioms. Replacing S1 with

$\quad$ S1$'$: $\forall x((BIRD(x) \wedge \neg PENGUIN(x)) \rightarrow FLIES(x))$

would avoid producing an inconsistency upon learning that Opus is a penguin. However, penguins are not the only birds that do not fly. Ostriches, fried chickens, birds with no wings, wooden ducks, etc. share the inability to fly. Listing all conditions that may inhibit flight is probably impossible. Even if such an enumeration were possible, an axiom that includes each exception would be impractical; knowing that Tweety is a bird would provide no information about his ability to fly until it has been determined that Tweety does not belong to any of the exceptional cases.

A Nonmonotonic Logic— The Closed-World Assumption

The *closed-world assumption* (CWA) provides an example of a nonlogical assumption that facilitates drawing plausible inferences in database applications. The addition of the closed-world assumption produces a nonmonotonic logical system since inferences made based on this assumption may be retracted upon the acquisition of additional information.

We will demonstrate the motivation behind the closed-world assumption by considering two distinct interpretations of the predicate calculus language obtained from the following constants and predicates:

Constants: New York, Chicago, Detroit, Dayton, Columbus
Binary Relations: $DIRECT(x, y)$, $CONNECT(x, y)$

The binary predicates $DIRECT$ and $CONNECT$ are intended to represent the presence of commercial flights between the cities: $DIRECT(x, y)$ indicates that there is a direct flight from city x to city y, and $CONNECT(x, y)$ indicates that there is a way to get from x to y but it may require changing planes in intermediate cities. An axiom set Δ describes the available connections.

Δ: $DIRECT$(New York, Chicago),
   $DIRECT$(Chicago, Detroit),
   $DIRECT$(Columbus, Dayton)
S1: $\forall x \forall y (DIRECT(x, y) \rightarrow DIRECT(y, x))$
S2: $\forall x \forall y (DIRECT(x, y) \rightarrow CONNECT(x, y))$
S3: $\forall x \forall y \forall z ((CONNECT(x, y)$
   $\land CONNECT(y, z)) \rightarrow CONNECT(y, z))$

In a model of Δ, the satisfaction of sentence S1 indicates that if there is a direct flight from city x to y, then there is also one from city y to x. S1 illustrates an advantage of the expressibility obtained by including predicate calculus sentences in deductive databases: the inclusion of S1 in Δ eliminates the need to enter $DIRECT(y, x)$ into the database when $DIRECT(x, y)$ is in the database. S2 indicates that cities connected by a direct flight are connected while S3 expresses the transitivity of the predicate $CONNECT$.

The universe of Δ for both the model M_1 defined above and M_2 to be defined below consists of the cities designated by the constants. The interpretation of the predicates are described by specifying the truth values of $DIRECT$ and $CONNECT$ for each pair of cities in the universe. In model M_1, $DIRECT$ and $CONNECT$ are true for every pair of cities. It is easy to see that atomic formulas and sentences S1, S2, and S3 in Δ are satisfied by this model.

The model M_2 assigns false to the negation of ground atomic formulas that are not in Δ or entailed by Δ. The truth values of M_2 are given in the following table. Each pair of cities is written only once since $DIRECT$ and $CONNECT$ are symmetric in M_2.

M_2:

$DIRECT(x, y)$	$\neg DIRECT(x, y)$
New York, Chicago	New York, Dayton
Chicago, Detroit	Chicago, Dayton
Dayton, Columbus	Detroit, Dayton
	New York, Columbus
	Chicago, Columbus
	Detroit, Columbus
	New York, Detroit

$CONNECT(x, y)$	$\neg CONNECT(x, y)$
New York, Chicago	New York, Dayton
Chicago, Detroit	Chicago, Dayton
New York, Detroit	Detroit, Dayton
Dayton, Columbus	New York, Columbus
	Chicago, Columbus
	Detroit, Columbus

Neither $CONNECT$(New York, Dayton) nor $\neg CONNECT$(New York, Dayton) is logically entailed by Δ since the former is true in model M_1 and the latter in model M_2. Thus, based solely on a logical analysis of the axioms, no conclusion may be made concerning the existence of a connection between those two cities.

The assertions in M_2, however, coincide with an intuitive analysis of entries in the database: relations that are not entailed by the database are assumed not to hold. We would not expect an airline database to list pairs of cities that do not have direct flights. The absence of an entry $DIRECT(x, y)$ is taken to mean that no direct connection exists between x and y; in other words, that $\neg DIRECT(x, y)$ is true.

The closed-world assumption formalizes the intuitive notion of assuming that all and only the positive entries are given in a database. The original set of axioms Δ is augmented with an assumed set of axioms Δ_{asm}. The set of assumed axioms contains a ground atomic formula $\neg \phi$ whenever ϕ is not logically entailed by Δ. The closed-world assumption of Δ consists of all sentences that logically follow from $\Delta \cup \Delta_{asm}$.

It is important to note that Δ_{asm} does not contain the negation of every ground atomic formula that is not in Δ. The atomic formula $CONNECT$(New York, Detroit) is not in Δ but is entailed by Δ; consequently its negation is not added to Δ_{asm}.

A deductive variant of the closed-world assumption, *negation by failure*, is commonly employed in logic programming languages and deductive databases. If a sentence ϕ is not provable, then it is assumed that $\neg \phi$ is the case. This is clearly nonmonotonic, since the incorporation of additional axioms may provide a proof of ϕ.

Additional Nonmonotonic Logics

Default rules and *predicate circumscription* provide two additional nonlogical extensions of the predicate calculus used for constructing nonmonotonic logical systems. Default logic employs nonlogical inference rules, called *default rules*, to augment the set of axioms. Default rules are constructed to replace universal propositions such as *all birds fly* with rules that will not produce inconsistencies when nonflying birds are encountered. Rather than including the universal sentence *all birds fly* in the axiom set in the example, a default rule can be employed to capture the notion that "unless believing so produces an inconsistency, birds fly."

Predicate circumscription was developed to enforce the intuitive criterion that the only formulas that are true are those required to be so by the axioms. Adding the circumscription of the predicates *DIRECT* and *CONNECT* to the axioms of the airline routing example produces a theory in which the predicates are satisfied only by those pairs of cities required by the axioms. That is, M_2 is the only model of the extended set of axioms.

Further Reading

The practicality and ubiquity of plausible reasoning has provided the impetus for the development of nonmonotonic logical systems. Reiter's presentation of the closed-world assumption and default rules, and McCarthy's introduction of circumscription may be found in Ginsburg (1987), which is a compilation of the seminal papers on nonmonotonic systems. An introduction to other nonmonotonic systems, including the nonmonotonic modal logic of McDermott and Doyle, Moore's autoepistemic logic, and the related work on belief revision using Truth Maintenance Systems, can be found in this collection and in Antoniou (1997).

Probabilistic logic and fuzzy set theory (*see* FUZZY LOGIC) have also been used to represent the properties of normality. In Sombé (1990), a single example is presented to compare the representational capabilities and semantics of these systems with the approaches described above.

Bibliography

1983. Allen, J. "Maintaining Knowledge About Temporal Intervals," *Comm. of the ACM*, **26**, *11*, 832–843.
1987. Genesereth, M. R., and Nilsson, N. J. *Logical Foundations of Artificial Intelligence*. San Francisco: Morgan Kaufmann.
1987. Reiter, R. "Nonmonotonic Reasoning," in *Annual Review of Computer Science*, Vol. 2 (ed. J. Traub), 147–186. Palo Alto, CA: Annuals Reviews Inc.
1987. Ginsburg, M. (ed.) *Readings in Nonmonotonic Logic*. San Francisco: Morgan Kaufmann.
1990. Sombé, L. *Reasoning Under Incomplete Information in Artificial Intelligence*. New York: Wiley Professional Computing.
1997. Antoniou, G. *Nonmonotonic Logic*. Cambridge, MA: MIT Press.

Thomas Sudkamp

NONPROCEDURAL LANGUAGES

For articles on related subjects *see* DATAFLOW; FUNCTIONAL PROGRAMMING; LOGIC PROGRAMMING; PROBLEM-ORIENTED LANGUAGES; PROCEDURE-ORIENTED LANGUAGES; PROGRAMMING LANGUAGES; and SETL.

Basic Concepts

TERMINOLOGY

This article describes some of the basic characteristics of the class of programming languages commonly referred to as *nonprocedural* or *very high level* (*see* Leavenworth and Sammet, 1974). Some of the descriptive terms that have often been applied to the word "language" to convey essentially the same concept are the following:

Nonprocedural	Relational
Very high level	Problem statement
Less procedural	Problem definition
Goal-oriented	Problem description
Problem-oriented	Specification
Pattern-directed	Result specification
Declarative	Task description
Functional	

The most common term used has been *nonprocedural*, which denotes emphasis on the goals to be achieved (i.e. *what*), rather than the specific methods used to achieve them (i.e. *how*).

PROPERTIES OF PROGRAMS

No programming language is nonprocedural in any absolute sense because the term is a relative one that changes as the state of the art changes. We can, however, say that a language possesses certain nonprocedural features. In order to see why this is so, we review briefly some fundamental properties of programs and programming languages.

In general, a *program* is a prescription for solving a particular problem. A *procedure* is a series of steps followed in a regular, orderly, definite way. Procedural programming is based to a great extent on the necessity to conform to the inherent sequential organization of the conventional digital computer. Therefore, a possible definition of a nonprocedural program is that it is a prescription for solving a problem without regard to any arbitrary sequencing requirements. More generally, we will say that a nonprocedural program is a prescription for solving a problem without regard to the details of *how* it is solved. That is, the solution should be specified in terms of structures or abstractions that are relevant to the problem rather than those operations, data, and control structures (*q.v.*) that are based on some particular machine organization.

RELATIVE NATURE OF THE TERM "NONPROCEDURAL"

In many ways, the term *less procedural* is better than nonprocedural because it makes clear the relative nature of the concept. Fig. 1 should make this clearer. A comparison of Figs. 1a and 1a* shows the difference between assembly language and Fortran-like languages. Prior to the existence of Fortran (*q.v.*), the expression A = (B + C) * D + E * F could have been

considered nonprocedural because it could not be directly translated by any language processor. Similarly, Figs. 1b and 1b* indicate another level of relativity, since the Fortran program to do matrix multiplication can be handled by one statement in APL. The use of a subroutine in Fortran would not give additional nonprocedurality, since the procedurality is based on the language primitives. Finally, the illustration of Fig. 1c*, which is a program to CALCULATE THE SQUARE ROOT OF THE PRIME NUMBERS FROM 3 TO 95 AND PRINT THE NUMBERS AND THEIR SQUARE ROOTS IN TWO COLUMNS, cannot be handled by any translating system known today, but, if it could be, the language would be considered nonprocedural by the standards of 1999. (It is essential to realize that the two forms shown in Fig. 1c* are logically equivalent, and the desirability of one form over the other (i.e. formal notation versus English) is a matter of personal preference.) The ability of a system to "understand" English is not at issue here; phrases that look like English may really depend on specific programming techniques (e.g. pattern matching and macro (*q.v.*) expansion), rather than English grammar. It is entirely possible to design a formal language for doing mathematical problems in which the statement CALCULATE THE SQUARE ROOT OF THE PRIME NUMBERS FROM 3 TO 95 AND PRINT THE NUMBERS AND THEIR SQUARE ROOTS IN TWO COLUMNS is acceptable. At the other extreme, a natural and elegant looking phrase such as FIND X SUCH THAT X**2 = 5 is really equivalent to invoking a square root routine. Thus, nonprocedurality and English notation are completely independent issues.

We actually have two types of relativity: one involves the problem or application area as described above and one involves the actual hardware. With respect to the hardware, as the machine changes, so does the relativity. The reason that one must consider the hardware is that certain features or facilities that might be available on one machine are not on another. Thus, prior to the availability of floating-point instructions in essentially all hardware, the capability to perform floating-point arithmetic had to be included explicitly in the programming language, and thus would be considered higher level with respect to the machine. Once floating-point hardware became virtually universal on computers, it was removed from serious language consideration.

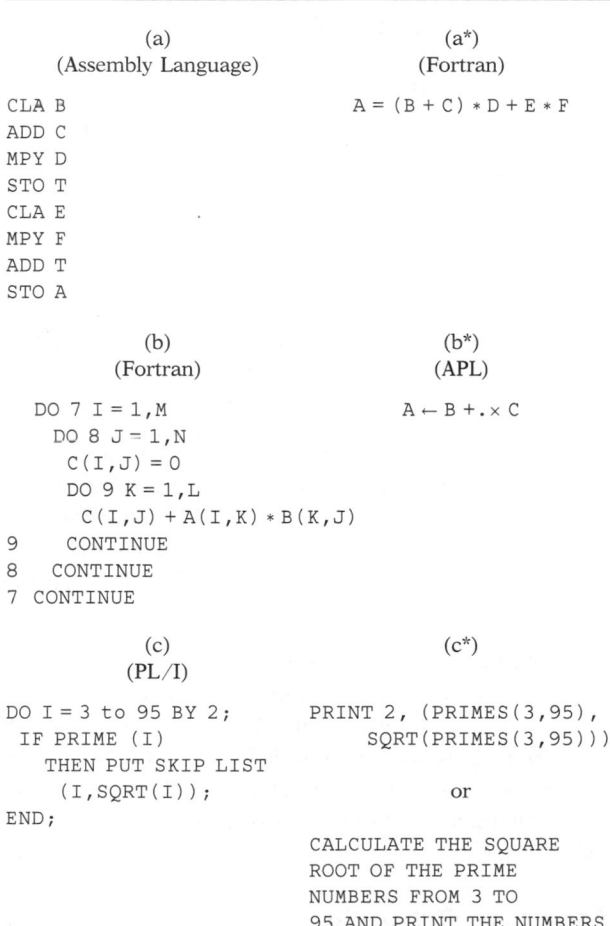

<table>
<tr><td>(a)
(Assembly Language)</td><td>(a*)
(Fortran)</td></tr>
</table>

```
CLA B                      A = (B + C) * D + E * F
ADD C
MPY D
STO T
CLA E
MPY F
ADD T
STO A
```

<table>
<tr><td>(b)
(Fortran)</td><td>(b*)
(APL)</td></tr>
</table>

```
  DO 7 I = 1,M             A ← B + . × C
    DO 8 J = 1,N
    C(I,J) = 0
      DO 9 K = 1,L
      C(I,J) + A(I,K) * B(K,J)
9   CONTINUE
8   CONTINUE
7 CONTINUE
```

<table>
<tr><td>(c)
(PL/I)</td><td>(c*)</td></tr>
</table>

```
DO I = 3 to 95 BY 2;       PRINT 2, (PRIMES(3,95),
  IF PRIME (I)                 SQRT(PRIMES(3,95)))
    THEN PUT SKIP LIST
      (I,SQRT(I));                    or
END;
                           CALCULATE THE SQUARE
                           ROOT OF THE PRIME
                           NUMBERS FROM 3 TO
                           95 AND PRINT THE NUMBERS
                           AND THEIR SQUARE ROOTS
                           IN 2 COLUMNS
```

Figure 1. Each example on the right is less procedural than the one on the left.

SEQUENCING

There is a difference between sequencing across statements and sequencing within one statement. The former requirement tends to be obvious in a problem. However, sequencing within a single statement may or may not be explicit, and this affects the nonprocedurality of the statement. Moreover, it is not always obvious from looking at a statement whether sequencing information is embedded in it. For example, sequencing is inherent in any mathematical expression that has precedence among its operators. Any data dependencies that are inherent in the problem statement may also affect the sequencing by requiring the data to be obtained in the correct order. A trivial illustration of this is obvious by merely noting that one cannot produce outputs until after one has performed calculations on the inputs.

As another illustration of the significance and relevance of sequencing, consider the problem statement shown in Fig. 1c*. This calculation could actually be performed in several ways. One way is to follow each number through the three "computations"; i.e. test for primality, and if the number is prime, then compute its square root and print it. However, depending on the particular hardware and software, it might be more efficient first to determine all the primes, then to calculate all the square roots of the identified primes, and then to do all the printing. This is a prototype of a calculation involving a sequence of tasks, each of which supplies data to the next, but where each input datum is independent of the others. The program given in Fig. 1c chooses only one of the alternatives; no discretion is left to the translator, whereas the statement in Fig. 1c* could—as indicated above—be translated in several significantly different ways that could have a major impact on efficiency. The explicit sequencing used in the program of Fig. 1c is not required for solution of the problem. One way of characterizing nonprocedurality is to say that the specification of sequencing of any information by the programmer (except that which is inherent to the logic of the problem) is irrelevant.

History

In the very early stages of programming (i.e. in the first half of the 1950s), the phrase *automatic programming* was used to mean the process of writing a program in some high-level language. In that context, "high-level" was by comparison with machine code. As time went on, it became clear that the coding was only a portion of the entire problem-solving task, and therefore the phrase *automatic coding* came into use as meaning the use of a language such as Fortran. Thus, even in the very early days, the proper distinction was made between coding (which is one aspect of the entire programming task) and the larger activity of specification and design. One of the first significant accomplishments was the work of the Codasyl Language Structure Group (1962) in the development of its Information Algebra. This was essentially a mathematically oriented way of describing a data processing application in terms of its input–output relationships;

these were actually defined by means of transformations on sets of entities called *areas* (analogous to files). As another example, we note that a string- and pattern-directed language such as Snobol or Icon (*see* STRING PROCESSING: LANGUAGES) is much less procedural for those features than a language such as Fortran or Cobol (*q.v.*).

Features of Nonprocedural Languages

We discuss three features that are considered of major importance for inclusion in a programming language that claims to be nonprocedural. Some examples of languages possessing some of these features are included.

ASSOCIATIVE REFERENCING
We will use the term *associative referencing* to denote the accessing of data according to some intrinsic property of the data (rather than by its location). Associative referencing is usually provided in those languages that contain sets as a data structure (*q.v.*). The operation of selecting elements from previously defined sets, and of defining new sets from old based on some property of the members, is sometimes called the *set former* (*see* SETL). An example of the power of SETL can be seen by the following expression, which specifies the prime numbers between 2 and 100.

$$\{P, 2 <= P <= 100 \uparrow (\forall 2 <= N < P \uparrow (P//N)NE. 0)\}$$

This can be read as "the set of 'P's between 2 and 100 such that for every N greater than or equal to 2 and less than P, the remainder of P/N is not equal to zero." (This specification is obviously not an efficient one; a practical algorithm would at the very least consider only the odd numbers from 3 to 100.)

The importance of associative referencing in nonprocedural languages is that the programmer does not have to specify access paths explicitly or program an algorithm to conduct a search for a specific data structure. Associative referencing is also used in database management languages.

Relational databases (*q.v.*) provide the traditional set operations of Cartesian product, union, and intersection. They also have relational operations: projection, join, division, and restriction (*see* Codd, 1972). These operators (*see* Aggregate Operators and Database Languages, below) effectively provide associative referencing.

AGGREGATE OPERATORS
It is possible to avoid writing loops in some programming languages that provide aggregate operators. The + operator in APL is the simplest example of an operator that applies equally to scalars and aggregates. For

example, the addition of two vectors x, y is obtained merely by writing x + y, whereas, in most programming languages, the elements of the result vector would have to be obtained one at a time under the control of a loop. Another example of an aggregate operator in APL is the use of the reduction operator to sum the elements of a vector x, as shown in the following expression: +/x.

There is a close relationship between associative referencing and aggregate operators It is clear that the algebraic operators defined by Codd (1972) on relations are aggregate operators. The elimination of explicit sequencing by this means is a nonprocedural feature.

ELIMINATION OF ARBITRARY SEQUENCING

We will define *arbitrary sequencing* as any sequencing that is not dictated by the data dependencies of the application.

A pure functional programming language is one that does not contain any assignment, iteration, or goto statements. "Functional" thus appears to be a synonym for "nonprocedural," since it means that a program specifies the outcome desired as a function of the inputs, rather than indicating a step-by-step sequence of program steps. A program in a functional language such as pure Lisp (*q.v.*) or Haskell avoids side effects (*q.v.*), which are a concomitant of procedural programming. A side effect may be caused in procedural languages during expression evaluation by the modification of memory by an assignment statement (e.g. during repeated iterations of a loop). Pure functional languages produce no side effects, since they have no assignment operation and cannot modify memory during expression evaluation.

Fig. 2 is a Haskell function that computes square roots of primes as specified in Fig. 1c*. It specifies solely the sequencing needed by the problem statement (e.g. get a prime before finding its square root), and we do not need to know if the Haskell system will produce all 23 primes first and then find the roots, or calculate and print each root as the prime is found. (In fact, since

```
map (\x -> output(x, sqrt(fromInt x)))
    (takeWhile (\x -> x < 95) odd_primes)
  where
  odd_primes = sieve [3,5..]
  sieve (prime:rest) =
    prime:sieve [r |r <- rest,
                    r 'rem' prime /= 0]
```

Figure 2. A Haskell function to do the computation of Fig. 1c*. It generates the set of odd primes (sieve) and selects those less than 95 (takeWhile). Map applies the output function to the resulting list, printing those values and their square roots (the definition of output is not shown). The notation \x -> ... is read: the function that takes x and returns . . . .

the function starts by computing the list of odd primes, it evidently does not generate them all before selecting the first 23, or it would never complete.)

Another example of functional programming would be APL "one-liners" (without assignments, or without function calls with side effects). The following APL one-line function will delete leading elements from a vector X up to but not including the first element of X which is not in Q, where Q represents a quoted character string or a numeric vector that contains examples to be deleted. Thus 'BAR' DELETE 'ABRACADABRA' returns 'CADABRA'.

```
∇R ← Q DELETE X
[1] R ← (~∧ \ X∈Q)/X
∇
```

The Prolog language (Clocksin and Mellish, 1994) is another example of a language that possesses some of the attributes we have been describing (*see* LOGIC PROGRAMMING: LANGUAGES). Prolog allows one to describe known facts and relationships about a problem, rather than prescribing a sequence of steps. Prolog uses pattern matching and "backtracking" to infer new facts from given facts. It therefore satisfies the associative referencing and lack of arbitrary sequencing criteria for nonprocedurality. For example, if the following relationship (rule) is declared:

X is mortal if X is human.

and the following simple fact is also declared:

Socrates is human.

then Prolog can "infer" that Socrates is mortal, even though this fact is not declared explicitly. Moreover, Prolog may be used to model a relational database from which retrievals may be made by pattern matching. For example, if the following facts are asserted:

```
s(s1,smith,20,london),
s(s2,jones,10,paris),
s(s3,blake,30,paris),
```

then the query to find s# and status for suppliers in Paris (*see* Database Languages below) could be written

```
?- s(S, _, Status, paris),
```

where lowercase names denote constants, uppercase names denote variables, and "_" represents a "don't care" value. The result of this query would be:

```
S = s2
Status = 10;
S = s3
Status = 30;
no                    (meaning no further solutions).
```

The ultimate expression of lack of arbitrary sequencing is a pure *dataflow* (*q.v.*) programming language. In this formalism, a program is composed of a set of modules that produce data or consume it, organized so that consumers wait for their data to be produced (*see* CONCURRENT PROGRAMMING). The sequencing is governed solely by these data dependencies (*see* Fig. 1c* and Fig. 2). An example of a well-known dataflow programming language is GPSS (General-Purpose Systems Simulator), in which sequencing of a simulation program is controlled by transactions (data) moving through the model.

Database Languages

Database languages have many of the characteristics we have been discussing. We will give one example from relational algebra (Date, 1999), which may be considered to be representative of a class of languages rather than a specific implementation. The relational algebra, which was developed originally by Codd (1972), consists of the operators SELECT, PROJECT, and JOIN, among others. Each operation of the relational algebra takes either one or two relations as its operand(s) and produces a new relation as a result. A relation has a precise mathematical definition, but can be considered to be a *table* for our purpose. An example of a relation (table) called S is shown below:

S	S#	SNAME	STATUS	CITY
	S1	Smith	20	London
	S2	Jones	10	Paris
	S3	Blake	30	Paris

The heading SNAME stands for supplier name, and the first row can be interpreted as the supplier Smith who has supplier number (S#) S1, has status 20, and is in London. The SELECT operator constructs a new relation by taking a horizontal subset of the argument table (i.e. all rows that satisfy some condition) and the PROJECT operator constructs a new relation by taking a vertical subset of the argument table. As an example, consider the query to find S# and STATUS for suppliers in Paris. This can be determined in two stages:

```
TEMP ← SELECT S WHERE CITY = 'PARIS'
```

This returns the table:

TEMP	S#	SNAME	STATUS	CITY
	S2	Jones	10	Paris
	S3	Blake	30	Paris

We then do a projection:

```
RESULT ← PROJECT TEMP OVER S#, STATUS
```

The result is the relation:

RESULT	S#	STATUS
	S2	10
	S3	30

Note that the SELECT operator uses associative referencing and is an aggregate operator. PROJECT is an aggregate operator, too.

It is not necessary to break up the retrievals into two distinct steps as indicated above. We could combine the query into one operation using the following syntax.

```
SELECT S#, STATUS
FROM S
WHERE CITY = 'PARIS'
```

Many of the newer database languages, such as SQL (Date, 1999), have extensive data manipulation capabilities in addition to their retrieval function.

Relation of Other Systems to Nonprocedural Languages

Spreadsheets are a form of nonprocedural language in the following sense. A spreadsheet (*q.v.*) is a two-dimensional grid of cells, where a cell may contain a datum (number or string) or a formula for computing a number based on values computed in other cells. There is no notion of sequencing other than dependencies that are implicit in the cell formulas, so that a spreadsheet is a form of dataflow language, with the user as the ultimate producer of data.

RPGs (report program generators) are often mentioned when discussing nonprocedural languages. It is certainly true that the output format of an RPG is specified by stating what is wanted rather than how it should be produced. It should be noted, however, that the Calculation section of an RPG program is decidedly low-level. This confirms our statement that no language is nonprocedural in any absolute sense.

Fourth-generation languages (4GLs) are rather poorly named and not clearly defined; most tend to have both procedural and nonprocedural components. It is only the latter that are of concern here. The major nonprocedural elements of a fourth-generation language are generally similar to database languages and report writers, and thus do *not* represent a new nonprocedural concept. Some of the fourth-generation language systems actually generate code for procedural languages such as Cobol, or link to them.

Summary

It is not possible to state that a given programming language is nonprocedural in any absolute sense because it is a relative term that changes as the state of the art changes. However, it can be said that a language possesses certain nonprocedural features relative to a specific time. The best examples of languages in 1999 that possess the "most" nonprocedural features are probably Prolog and constraint logic languages, Miranda (Turner, 1986), Haskell, and many of the database query languages. APL has high-level operators, but does not have the concept of associative referencing as a primitive notion. However, the elimination of arbitrary sequencing can be achieved in APL programs by exploiting the power of the aggregate operators.

Bibliography

1962. Codasyl Language Structure Group. "An Information Algebra Phase I Report," *Comm. of the ACM*, **5**, *4* (April).

1972. Codd, E. F. "Relational Completeness of Data Base Sublanguages," in *Data Base Systems* (ed. R. Rustin), 65–98. Upper Saddle River, NJ: Prentice Hall.

1974. Leavenworth, B. M., and Sammet, J. E. "An Overview of Nonprocedural Languages," *Proc. ACM SIGPLAN Symposium on Very High Level Languages, ACM SIGPLAN Notices*, **9**, *4* (April).

1986. Turner, D. A. "An Overview of Miranda," *ACM SIGPLAN Notices*, **21**, *12* (December).

1994. Clocksin, W. F., and Mellish, C. S. *Programming in Prolog*, 4th Ed. New York: Springer-Verlag.

1999. Date, C. J. *An Introduction to Database Systems*, 7th Ed. Reading, MA: Addison-Wesley.

Burton M. Leavenworth and Jean E. Sammet,
revised by David Hemmendinger

NORC

> For articles on related subjects *see* DIGITAL COMPUTERS, HISTORY OF: EARLY; and ECKERT, WALLACE J.

The NORC, the Naval Ordnance Research Calculator, (Fig. 1) was built by IBM for the US Navy Bureau of Ordnance under a non-profit research and development contract to build the most powerful and effective calculator that the state of the art would permit (as of 1951). It was designed for the rapid and convenient solution of the very largest computational problems of science, including partial differential equations (*q.v.*) in three space dimensions and time. It was the outgrowth of a research project under Byron L. Havens at IBM's Watson Scientific Computing Laboratory at Columbia University, where Dr. Wallace J. Eckert had assembled a group of electronic specialists in 1946 to further the development of electronic computers. Early in the project, Havens developed a fundamental circuit, the microsecond delay unit, which operated reliably at 1 MHz. The NORC was designed and built at the Laboratory. Assembly started in late 1953 and it was demonstrated and turned over to the Navy on 2 December 1954, at which time it calculated pi to over 3,000 places. It was installed at the Naval Proving

Figure 1. The NORC computer. (Courtesy of IBM.)

Ground, Dahlgren, VA, in the summer of 1955 and remained in highly productive use until replaced by an IBM Stretch (*q.v.*) computer in 1968.

NORC was based on the use of the Havens microsecond delay unit, diode switching, a 3,600 word cathode ray tube storage unit with 8 μs access, and high-speed four-channel magnetic tape units (which transferred 71,340 decimal digits per second). The calculator operated on decimal numbers of 13-digit precision and a range of 10^{-30} to 10^{30}.

Computing speed was 15,000 three-address instructions per second. Each instruction provided for modifying each address by any of three modifiers, fetching two operands from electronic storage, carrying out a floating-point, specified point, or fixed decimal point (i.e. integer) arithmetic operation, checking the result with an independent modulo-9 arithmetic unit, and storing the result. The arithmetic unit featured fast multiplication using serial digit-by-digit addition and serial generation of the nine multiples of the multiplicand. A pipeline (*q.v.*) of 12-decimal adders, each of which introduced a microsecond of delay while adding, combined a digit from each one-digit product and output one digit of the result every microsecond. The product of two 13-digit numbers required 31 μs.

Checking of the operation of the calculator was continuous. In addition to the modulo-9 arithmetic check, a check digit accompanied each word of instruction or data. This check digit was calculated when the data was read from punched cards, and verified each time it was read from tape or storage or refreshed in storage and after printing by echo pulses generated during printing. The cathode ray tube storage was further checked by an independent check on each bit column of storage. These two orthogonal checks pinpointed for correction any single bit in storage that was in error.

The instruction set (*q.v.*) took advantage of the three-address format to perform arithmetic (including multiple precision numbers), modification of the address modifiers, machine and operator interrupts, and three-way transfer of control with a single instruction wherever possible. Reading tape forward or backward, or writing tape with a variable length block of words, were done with a single instruction (*see* BLOCK AND BLOCKING FACTOR).

The microsecond delay unit that was used throughout the calculator for the registers, arithmetic units, and logical control functions acted as a storage unit with an output that regenerated a full pulse the microsecond following the receipt of an input pulse. It was highly reliable and facilitated offline maintenance of the pluggable units of which the machine was composed. Fifty percent of the total circuitry employed only six types of unit, and 80% employed only 18 types.

The peripheral equipment for the NORC was built by the IBM Poughkeepsie and Endicott laboratories. It included eight tape units operating at 70,000 characters per second reading or writing, two 150 line-per-minute printers with buffered input permitting calculation to proceed during printing, and a card-to-tape-to-card machine for card input and output.

One of the early uses of the NORC was computing the exact positions of the Moon, Earth, and planets in space at all times to the year 2000 for Project Vanguard. This was done by Dr. Paul Herget, Director of the Cincinnati Observatory in a 10 hour run on the NORC. Another was a simulation of neutron motion in a nuclear reactor. Mathematical models of various aspects of the Earth satellite programs, evaluation of various guided missile designs, and study of the re-entry of satellites into the earth's atmosphere were other early uses of the NORC. One of its last jobs was a large astronomical calculation for which the answers could be rigorously checked. The NORC run lasted 65 hours, performing over 75 billion operations without error.

Bibliography

1954. Anon. *IBM Business Machines*, **37**, *26*, 1, 4–11 (23 December).
1955. Eckert, W. J., and Jones, R. *Faster, Faster.* New York: McGraw-Hill.
1963. von Neumann, J. *Collected Works*, (ed. A. H. Taub), **5**, 238–247. New York: Oxford University Press.
1971. Brennan, J. F. *The IBM Watson Laboratory at Columbia University: A History.* Armonk, NY: IBM, **18**, 26–29.

John C. McPherson

NOTEBOOK COMPUTER

See PORTABLE COMPUTERS.

NOYCE, ROBERT NORTON

For articles on related subjects *see* INTEGRATED CIRCUITRY; MICROCOMPUTER CHIP; and MICROPROCESSORS AND MICROCOMPUTERS.

Robert Norton Noyce (12 December 1927–3 June 1990) was born in Burlington, IA, the son of the Rev. Ralph Noyce, Congregational Minister, and Harriet (Norton) Noyce. In 1937 Rev. Noyce was appointed assistant superintendent of the Iowa Conference of Congregational Churches, whose offices were located on the campus of Grinnell College. The family lived on campus, and three of the four Noyce boys would later attend the college.

Valedictorian of his class at Grinnell High School, Noyce entered Grinnell College in 1945. In 1948, his mentor, Prof. Grant Gale, learned by chance of the invention of the transistor at the Bell Telephone Laboratories and immediately contacted Oliver Buckley, director of research there and a Grinnell graduate, and John Bardeen, one of the inventors and a family friend, in order to obtain the new device. Noyce joined Gale in studying the device, a rare opportunity at the time. He graduated in 1949 with a Bachelor of Science degree in physics and mathematics. He enrolled in the graduate program at the Massachusetts Institute of Technology to study electronics, but was disappointed by the lack of opportunity to deepen his knowledge of transistor technology. In 1953, he completed a Ph.D. in physical electronics with a dissertation on the "Photo-electronic Study of Surface States on Insulators." Soon thereafter, he married Elizabeth Bottomley; they would have a boy and three girls.

Figure 1. Robert Norton Noyce. (Courtesy of the Intel Corporation.)

Noyce accepted a position with Philco, a relative newcomer to the transistor field, reasoning that he would be a "necessary cog in the machine." Philco's lack of commitment to transistor research disappointed him, and after a few years he contacted William Shockley, who had led the transistor research team at Bell Laboratories, received the Nobel Prize for Physics in 1956, and founded the Shockley Semiconductor Laboratory in Mountain View, California. In 1956, Shockley hired Noyce to join his research laboratory. The Shockley Lab provided Noyce with his first exhilarating taste of dedication to transistor research. By the summer of 1957, however, technical disagreements, clashes with Shockley's managerial style, and entrepreneurial opportunities in the nascent semiconductor industry led a group of seven researchers from the lab—Gordon E. Moore, Victor H. Grinich, Sheldon E. Roberts, Eugene Kleiner, Julius Blank, Jean Hoerni, and Jay Last—to break away and set up a new company, a move Noyce would later call an "in-house revolt." With the help of Arthur Rock at the investment firm of Hayden Stone, this group gained the financial backing of Fairchild Camera and Instrument Corporation. Noyce agreed to join this group, now dubbed the "Fairchild Eight," and became Director of Research of the new Fairchild Semiconductor Company. In 1959, he became Vice-President and General Manager. Fairchild Semiconductor became the seedbed for a generation of high-technology firms that defined the phenomenal growth of the region known after 1970 as "Silicon Valley." When Fairchild Camera exercised its option to buy out the shares of the eight founders in 1959, they all became wealthy men.

Noyce's greatest technical achievement at Fairchild was the integrated circuit, or IC. The IC that he devised in 1959 and patented in 1961 built upon Jean Hoerni's invention of the "planar transistor," which had greatly improved transistor reliability; the IC connected these transistors and other electrical circuit elements on silicon. A conductive aluminum layer replaced wires to link the components, a technique known as the "metal over oxide" process. Fairchild could thus manufacture completed circuits, rather than cutting up silicon wafers to make transistors and then shipping them to customers to assemble the circuits. The conceptual simplicity and resulting efficiency of this innovation led Noyce later to characterize it as arising out of his "own laziness." It reduced the complexity of circuit fabrication and set the stage for huge increases in the density of microcircuits. An independent version had been invented several months earlier by Jack Kilby at Texas Instruments, but Noyce's IC proved to be more easily manufactured. The IC, or "chip," established a foundation for the burgeoning semiconductor industry.

Despite rapid commercial and technological success at Fairchild, Noyce grew dissatisfied with its hierarchical, risk-averse management structure. Convinced that it was time to start a smaller company along different lines, Noyce, Moore, and Andrew Grove left Fairchild in 1968 to found Intel Corporation (originally N. M. Electronics) in Santa Clara, CA. Noyce became its first president and Chief Executive Officer. Intel's first major products were the 1103 Dynamic Random Access Memory, or DRAM, introduced in 1970, using the new metal oxide semiconductor (MOS) fabrication process, and the erasable, programmable read-only memory (EPROM), brought to market in 1971. With MOS fabrication and the EPROM, Intel established its identity as a company built to create and exploit technological advantages. Later in 1971, Intel announced the 4004 microprocessor, the first "computer on a chip." The microprocessor inaugurated what Intel advertising called "a new era of integrated electronics." Within a few years, the microprocessor led to the microcomputer, and Intel had honed its strategy of maintaining technological leads, which it vigorously defended through successive generations of microcomputer technology.

Under Noyce, Moore, and Grove, Intel established itself as one of the leading technology companies in Silicon Valley, but by the mid-1970s, Noyce's role changed. In 1975, he stepped down as president to become Chairman of the Board, a position he held until 1979. He devoted more attention to industry-wide issues, such as the competitiveness of the US semiconductor industry and technology policy. As an industry spokesman, particularly in the policy arena, he worked closely with the American Electronics Association and, in 1977, co-founded the Semiconductor Industry Association. He led the SIA in the founding of the Semiconductor Research Cooperative in 1981 and also served on advisory boards at MIT and Stanford. In 1982, he was appointed to the Board of Regents of the University of California, on which he served until 1988. His position as an industry leader during the technological competitiveness debate of the 1980s led to a seat on President Reagan's Commission on Competitiveness, a founding role in the California Legal Reform Project and the vice-chairmanship of the Association for California Tort Reform. In 1988, Noyce accepted the position of Chief Executive Officer of a new research consortium, SEMATECH (Semiconductor Manufacturing Technology), located in Austin, Texas, which he held until May of 1990. By then, the recovery of the US semiconductor industry was well under way, with Intel taking the lead as its most profitable company.

Noyce's career spanned the technological, industrial, and political development of American microelectronics from the early exploitation of the transistor through the integrated circuit, microprocessor, and personal computer. Awards recognizing Noyce's contributions were numerous and included election to the National Academy of Engineering in 1969, the National Medal of Science in 1979, the Faraday Medal of the IEEE in 1979, the National Medal of Technology in 1987, and the first Charles Stark Draper Award (with Jack Kilby) in 1990. Bob Noyce died suddenly of a heart attack on 3 June 1990 in Austin, TX.

Bibliography

1981. Noyce, R. N., and Hoff, M. E., Jr. "A History of Microprocessor Development at Intel," *IEEE Micro*, **1** (February), 8–21.
1990. SEMATECH. *Robert N. Noyce: 1927–1990.* Austin: SEMATECH.
1993. Wolfe, T. "The Tinkerings of Robert Noyce: How the Sun Rose on the Silicon Valley," *Esquire* (December), 346–373.

Websites

American Electronics Association. `http://www.aeanet.org`.
Intel. `http://www.intel.com`.
Sematech. `http://www.sematech.org`.
Semiconductor Industry Association.
  `http://www.semichips.org`.

Henry Lowood

NP-COMPLETE PROBLEMS

> For articles on related subjects *see* ALGORITHMS, ANALYSIS OF; ALGORITHMS, THEORY OF; COMBINATORICS; COMPUTATIONAL COMPLEXITY; DISCRETE MATHEMATICS; and MATHEMATICAL PROGRAMMING.

There are many practical computational problems for which no effective computer algorithms have been devised. Many of these seemingly intractable problems belong to a class of problems known as *NP-complete problems*. NP stands for *nondeterministic polynomial*, a concept discussed below. The only known algorithms for these problems require an amount of time that is an exponential function of the problem size (measured by some parameter, n, on which the problem depends). Such algorithms are called *exponential time algorithms*. Technically, problem size is measured by the number of bits in the problem description, but often the running time of an algorithm is more conveniently expressed in terms of some other (roughly equivalent) measure of the amount of input data. For problems of size n, exponential time algorithms may take time 2^n, $2^{n^{1/2}}$, 3^{n^2}, etc. In contrast, many problems can be solved by algorithms that require an amount of time that is a polynomial function of the problem size. These algorithms are called *polynomial time algorithms*. For problems of size n, they may take time

n, $n \log n$, n^2, n^3, etc. Because polynomials grow more slowly than exponentials, polynomial time algorithms (even with a large exponent) are efficient in comparison with exponential time algorithms. As a first cut at categorizing algorithm complexity, polynomial time algorithms are regarded as "efficient," and exponential time algorithms as "inefficient."

Computer scientists have proved that if one efficient (i.e. polynomial time) algorithm can be found for *any* of the NP-complete problems, then efficient algorithms can be devised for *all* of these problems. Conversely, if any of these problems requires exponential time, they all do. Most computer scientists are pessimistic about the possibility that non-exponential algorithms for these problems will ever be found, so proving a problem to be NP-complete is now regarded as strong evidence that the problem is intrinsically intractable. If, however, an efficient algorithm can be found for any one (and hence all) NP-complete problems, it would be a major intellectual breakthrough with immense practical implications.

We illustrate these concepts with three NP-complete problems—one from graph theory (*q.v.*), one involving summing numbers, and one involving sets.

Clique Problem

A *graph* is a set of nodes with edges connecting certain pairs of nodes (such as the graph in Fig. 1). A *clique* is a set of nodes from a graph where every pair of nodes in the set is connected by an edge. In the figure, $\{1, 3, 7\}$ is a clique set. Set $\{2, 4, 5, 6\}$ is not because nodes 5 and 6 in this set are not connected by an edge.

Problem. Given a graph and a "clique size" k, decide if the graph has a clique of that size. For the problem given in Fig. 1 and $k = 4$, the answer is "YES" because $\{1, 2, 4, 5\}$ is a clique of size 4. If, instead, the clique size in the problem were 5, the answer would be "NO."

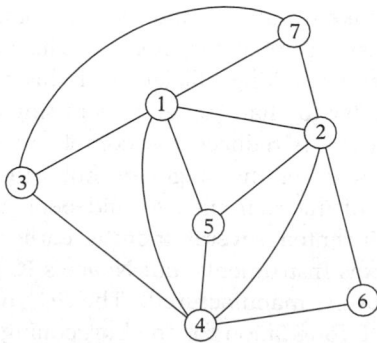

Figure 1. Example of a clique problem. Is there a clique of size 4?

List of numbers: 4 7 13 18 25 32 42 49
Knapsack size: 89

Figure 2. Example of a knapsack problem.

Knapsack Problem

Given a list of numbers and a "knapsack size," determine if some subset of the listed numbers adds up to the knapsack size. For the problem given in Fig. 2, the answer is "YES" because

$$4 + 18 + 25 + 42 = 89.$$

If, instead, the knapsack size were 90, the answer would be "NO."

Set Covering Problem

For a given set, a collection of subsets is said to cover the set if each member of the set belongs to at least one set in the collection.

Problem. Given a set to be covered, a list of available subsets, and a "cover size" k, determine whether k of the available subsets can be chosen so that the collection of chosen subsets covers the given set. For the problem given in Fig. 3, the answer is "YES" because the three subsets S_3, S_6, and S_7 can be chosen. If, instead, the cover size were 2, the answer would be "NO."

The three problems illustrated have the common property that, if the answer is "YES," there is a short, easily verified demonstration of this fact. For the clique problem, the demonstration is a list of nodes, equal in number to the clique size, that form a clique. For the knapsack problem, the demonstration is a subset of the listed numbers whose sum equals the knapsack size. For the set covering problem, the demonstration is a collection of the available subsets that contain every element of the set to be covered. This common property suggests a common approach to solving these problems; namely, enumerate the potential demonstrations and check each potential demonstration to see if it is an actual demonstration. For the knapsack problem, this means enumerating the subsets of the given numbers and adding the numbers in each subset to see if their sum is the knapsack value. Unfortunately, these enumerate-and-check algorithms require exponential time due to the number of things to be enumerated. In the knapsack case, with n numbers, there are 2^n subsets to be checked.

Set to be covered: $\{a, b, c, d, e, f, g, h\}$
Available subsets: $S_1 = \{d\}$, $S_2 = \{a\}$, $S_3 = \{a, b, c\}$,
$S_4 = \{f\}$, $S_5 = \{b, e, g\}$, $S_6 = \{c, d, e, h\}$, $S_7 = \{f, g, h\}$

Cover size: 3

Figure 3. Example of a set covering problem.

The preceding problems are called *recognition problems* because the answer for a given problem example is "YES" or "NO." A recognition problem is called *nondeterministic polynomial* (or NP) if, whenever the answer is "YES," there is a "polynomial" demonstration of this fact. A problem is considered to have polynomial demonstrations if there are constants c and k such that, for all n, a problem example of size n with answer "YES" has a potential demonstration that can be verified correct in at most cn^k steps. Thus, if the answer is "YES," a lucky person might guess a correct demonstration and verify his or her guess, all in polynomial time. However, the word *nondeterministic* is not meant to imply randomness or any use of probability. *Nondeterministic* signifies only that no rule is given for determining what the guess should be.

The key concept in relating problems to each other is *polynomial-time reducibility*. Problem A is said to be *reducible* to problem B if problem A can be solved using as a subroutine an algorithm that solves problem B. In particular, problem A is *polynomial-time reducible* to problem B if there is a polynomial bound on the number of steps taken by a main program to solve problem A, where the main program can call a subroutine for problem B. Note that the number of steps taken by the subroutine is not counted. If there is an efficient (i.e. polynomial-time) algorithm for solving problem B, then using that algorithm as the subroutine produces an efficient algorithm for problem A. Conversely, if problem A is intrinsically hard (i.e. cannot be solved in polynomial time), then no efficient subroutine for B can exist, and so problem B is also intrinsically hard.

To illustrate a polynomial-time reduction, Fig. 4 outlines a main program for reducing the clique problem

Main Program for Clique Problem
Step 1
Input graph G and clique size k
Step 2
Construct new graph $\overline{G}$ with:
   (a) The same nodes as G
   (b) An edge between two nodes if and only if there is no edge between these two nodes in G
   (c) A unique name for each edge in $\overline{G}$
Step 3
Let S = set of edges in graph $\overline{G}$
(S is set to be covered)
Step 4
For each node x in graph $\overline{G}$, let S_x = members of S with endpoint x (each S_x is an available subset)
Step 5
Let cover size = number of nodes − clique size
Step 6
Call subroutine for set covering problem, passing it the problem example constructed in steps 3, 4, and 5.
Step 7
If subroutine answers "YES," then ouput "YES"
If subroutine answers "NO," then output "NO"

Figure 4. Reduction of clique problem to set covering problem.

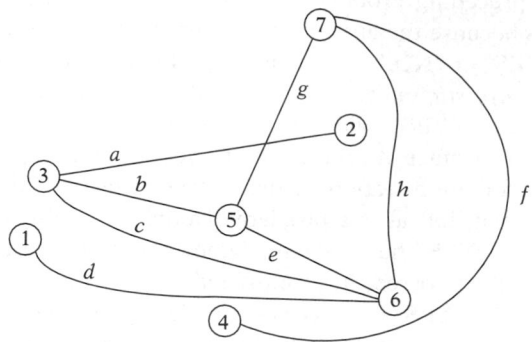

Figure 5. The graph $\overline{G}$ related to the graph G of Fig. 1.

to the set covering problem. If step 1 of the main program is given the clique problem example of Fig. 1 as input, the graph $\overline{G}$ constructed in step 2 is the graph of Fig. 5. For instance, the edge named b appears in $\overline{G}$ because G does not contain an edge between nodes 3 and 5, and $\overline{G}$ has no edge between 1 and 3 because G does have an edge between 1 and 3. Steps 3, 4, and 5 construct the set covering example of Fig. 3. Notice that set S_3 has members a, b, and c because a, b, and c are the edges of $\overline{G}$ having node 3 as an endpoint. The subroutine returns with answer "YES" (because of cover S_3, S_6, and S_7), and the main program outputs "YES."

The reason the program works is that for a graph with n nodes, there is a direct relationship between the nodes that form the clique of size k and the $n - k$ covering subsets that solve the constructed set covering problem. Specifically, the clique consists of the nodes corresponding to the available subsets that are not part of the cover. In the example, it is the available subsets S_1, S_2, S_4, and S_5 that are not in the cover S_3, S_6, S_7, and it is nodes $\{1, 2, 4, 5\}$ that form the clique.

A problem is said to be *NP-complete* if it is an NP-problem and every NP-problem is polynomial-time reducible to it. Thus, an algorithm for an NP-complete problem is universal in that it can be used as a subroutine for any NP-problem.

To show that a new problem is NP-complete, it suffices to show that it is an NP-problem, and that any one problem already known to be NP-complete is polynomial-time reducible to it.

As the number of problems already known to be NP-complete increases, there are more problems available for showing other problems NP-complete, and so the task of proving NP-completeness becomes easier and easier. In 1971, Cook formulated the concept of NP-completeness and showed that the problem of testing a logical formula for satisfiability is NP-complete. Shortly thereafter, Karp (1972) extended the set of known NP-problems to include about 20 other prob-

lems of practical interest. This gave momentum to the search for NP-complete problems and now thousands are known (*see*, for example, Garey and Johnson (1979)). It is now routine for a computer scientist confronting an apparently hard problem to investigate whether the problem is NP-complete.

The concept of NP-completeness is relevant not only to recognition (i.e. YES–NO) problems, but also to optimization problems. This is because optimization problems have closely related recognition problems. The clique problem is the recognition problem closely related to the optimization problem of finding the largest size clique in a graph. The knapsack problem is the problem closely related to the optimization problem of finding a subset of listed numbers that has the largest sum not exceeding the knapsack size. The set covering problem is the problem closely related to the optimization problem of finding the smallest collection of available subsets that cover a given set. In each case, the answer to the optimization problem also provides an answer to the recognition problem. For example, if the answer to the clique optimization problem is a clique of size n, the clique recognition problem has answer "YES" if $k \leq n$ and "NO" if $k > n$. Thus, optimization must be at least as hard as recognition. Some well-known optimization problems with closely related NP-complete recognition problems are the traveling salesman problem, integer programming, job-shop scheduling, and graph coloring.

For an optimization problem, one can sometimes develop an algorithm which always runs quickly, but produces an answer which is not necessarily optimal. Moreover, a worst-case time bound can sometimes be obtained on how much the answer produced may differ from the optimum, so that a reasonably close answer is assured. The degree to which problems can be approximated varies considerably from problem to problem. The three problems discussed earlier illustrate this variability.

Consider first the knapsack problem. There is a method of solving the YES/NO and optimization knapsack problems in time proportional to ℓk where ℓ is the length of the list of numbers and k is the knapsack size. This algorithm is exponential in the length of the input because k may be exponential in the length of the input (d digits produce a number of size 10^d). However, for many applications, the algorithm is quite practical because k is not too large. This algorithm is also the basis of a good approximation using a technique known as "rounding and scaling."

In rounding and scaling, the numbers on the list and the knapsack size are divided by some selected value. After division, each list number is rounded up to the nearest integer (thereby overestimating its size) and the knapsack size is rounded down (thereby underestimating its capacity). The optimum for the new problem is found using the ℓk algorithm and the result is translated back. For example, if we modify the problem of Fig. 2 with scaling value 5, the numbers become 1, 2, 3, 4, 5, 7, 9, 10 and the knapsack size becomes 17. One optimal solution to the modified problem is obtained by selecting the numbers 7 and 10. The numbers 7 and 10 were originally 32 and 49 so selecting 32 and 49 is the approximate solution to the original problem. Note that this choice is not optimal because $32 + 49$ is only 81 whereas the actual optimum sums to 89. The ratio of the approximation to the optimum is $81/89 = 0.91$. The closer this ratio is to one, the better.

The error in the approximation is due to the loss of accuracy caused by the rounding. The smaller the value selected for the scaling, the better the approximation, but the more time required to obtain the approximation due to the larger knapsack size after the scaling. Given any desired ratio less than one, there is a method of constructing a polynomial time algorithm that systematically selects a scaling value so as to guarantee the desired ratio.

The set cover optimization problem can be solved approximately by the following algorithm:

> Pick a subset which covers the most set elements. Then repeatedly pick a subset which covers the most not-yet-covered elements. Stop when all elements are covered.

In the example of Fig. 3, the first subset picked would be S_6 because it is the largest. Then subset S_5 might be picked which covers two of the remaining elements. (Two other subsets also cover two elements.) Finally, S_4 and S_2 might be picked, each covering one of the two remaining elements. Altogether, four subsets have been picked instead of the optimal three, for a ratio of $4/3 = 1.33$.

The closer the ratio is to 1 the better. (For maximization problems, the ratio cannot exceed 1 and for minimization problems the ratio cannot be below 1.) This algorithm uses what is known as the *greedy approach*. In general, an algorithm is called greedy if it makes a series of quick decisions in accord with a particular criterion, never revising a decision it has already made. (For the set covering algorithm, a decision consists of picking a subset to be included in the cover.) Each decision is based on the choice that makes the most progress toward the ultimate goal. (For the set covering algorithm, the ultimate goal is to cover all elements and progress is measured by how many additional elements are covered.)

It can be shown that the above greedy algorithm for the set covering problem guarantees a ratio of $\ln(n + 1)$,

where n is the maximum number of elements of any of the available subsets. Furthermore, it has been shown that, if there exists a polynomial time algorithm guaranteeing any better ratio such as $0.999 \ln n$, then $P = NP$ (which is considered unlikely).

For the clique problem, the best known approximation algorithm is very complicated and has a very poor performance ratio. A trivial approximation method for cliques is simply to find a clique of size one. (Every graph node is a clique of size one!) This method gives a worst case ratio of $1/n$ where n is the number of nodes. (The graph may have a clique of size n.) A small improvement on this terrible performance would be to find a polynomial time algorithm guaranteeing a ratio of $1/n^{0.999}$. However, it has been proven that, under an assumption similar to $P \neq NP$, no such approximation exists.

In the three examples above, the knapsack problem has excellent approximations, the set covering problem has a decent approximation, and the clique problem can only be approximated in a very unsatisfactory way.

Many NP-complete problems have special cases which are much easier to solve than the general case. For example, we have seen that the clique problem is NP-complete. However, for graphs in which every node has at most d edges (where d is some fixed constant such as 7) the problem can be solved in time proportional to n^d. Thus, if for some application, there is a d such that all graphs occurring in the application have at most d edges at each node, the problem can be solved in polynomial time.

To summarize, NP-completeness effectively eliminates the possibility of developing a completely satisfactory algorithm. However, the situation is not necessarily hopeless for the following reasons:

1. Even an exponential algorithm can be satisfactory for small cases.

2. There may be fast approximation algorithms with satisfactory accuracy.

3. The problems of most interest may be special cases for which a fast algorithm is available.

4. Although an algorithm may be bad "in the worst case," it may solve most cases in a satisfactory amount of time.

Bibliography

1971. Cook, S. A. "The Complexity of Theorem-Proving Procedures," *Proc. Third ACM Symposium on Theory of Computing*, 151–158.

1972. Karp, R. M. "Reducibility Among Combinatorial Problems," in *Complexity of Computer Computations* (eds. R. E. Miller, and J. W. Thatcher), 85–104. New York: Plenum Press.

1979. Garey, M. R., and Johnson, D. S. *Computers and Intractability: A Guide to the Theory of NP-Completeness.* San Francisco: W. H. Freeman and Co.

1989. Dewdney, A. K. *The Turing Omnibus*, Chapters 31, 38, 50. Rockville, MD: Computer Science Press.

1992. Harel, D. *Algorithmics: The Spirit of Computing*, 2nd Ed., Chapter 7. Reading, MA: Addison-Wesley.

Daniel J. Rosenkrantz and Richard E. Stearns

NUMBER THEORETIC CALCULATIONS

For articles on related subjects *see* COOPERATIVE COMPUTING; CRYPTOGRAPHY, COMPUTERS IN; FACTORING INTEGERS; MATHEMATICS, COMPUTERS IN; and NUMERICAL ANALYSIS.

The theory of numbers is primarily concerned with the properties of the *natural numbers* $1, 2, 3, \ldots$. The fundamental theorem of arithmetic states that each natural number greater than 1 can be expressed uniquely (up to order) as a product of *prime numbers*. A prime number is a natural number greater than 1 having no divisor other than 1 and itself. A natural number which is not prime is called *composite*. Much of the research in number theory, both theoretical and computational, has dealt with properties of the primes. This article will report some major advances in computational number theory made during the past ten years. It will be subdivided into these areas:

1. Prime testing.

2. The largest known primes.

3. Fermat's last theorem.

4. Waring's problem.

5. The Riemann zeta function.

Prime Testing

This is the problem of deciding whether a number n is prime or composite. Methods for factoring composite numbers are described in the article FACTORING INTEGERS. If n has only a few decimal digits, we can show that it is prime by trial division up to its square root. If n is composite, then it must have a prime divisor $\leq \sqrt{n}$.

A better procedure is needed for larger numbers. A simple test is based on *Fermat's little theorem*, which states that if n is prime and n does not divide a, then

$$a^{n-1} \equiv 1 \pmod{n} \qquad (1)$$

(That is, n divides the difference $a^{n-1} - 1$). Although the converse of this theorem is false, very few composite numbers n satisfy (1). Odd numbers n which

satisfy (1) for several randomly chosen values of a are called *industrial grade primes* because they are almost certainly prime, although this calculation does not prove it. One can raise a to the $n - 1$ power (modulo n) in roughly $\log_2 n$ steps by a simple procedure (*see* Lehmer (1969, 125) or Bach and Shallit (1996, 102–103).

More computation than (1) is needed to obtain a rigorous proof that n is prime, but (1) is often used to decide whether to attempt a rigorous prime proof or to try to factor n. If (1) holds and if one can factor either $n - 1$ or $n + 1$ completely, then there is a quick method for proving that n is prime via more calculations like that in (1). This method works well for large numbers n for which either $n - 1$ or $n + 1$ has only small prime factors. The largest known primes (see below) all have this special form. For general n, the method becomes impractical at about 50 digits because some numbers of that size take a while to factor and there are better methods for larger numbers.

In 1983, Adleman, Pomerance, and Rumely published an algorithm which uses algebraic number theory to decide whether n is prime in about $n^{\log\log\log n}$ steps. A practical version of it can test a 100-digit number for primality in a few seconds. *See* Bach and Shallit (1996, 285–293), for a description.

In the past few years, Goldwasser, Kilian, and Atkin have invented powerful prime tests which use elliptic curves. They work well for most primes, but may fail to work or be very slow for certain primes. Morain has turned these methods into a distributed algorithm for proving primality using elliptic curves. He ran this algorithm on 12 Sun workstations for 1.5 months to prove that the 1065-digit number $(2^{3539} + 1)/3$ is prime. The workstations independently tried to factor certain auxiliary numbers used in the proof. *See* Riesel (1994) for more details.

Adleman and Huang invented a polynomial time prime test which uses Abelian varieties, but this test seems useless in practice.

The Largest Known Primes

There is an especially simple prime test for *Mersenne numbers* $2^p - 1$ (*see* Riesel (1994, 119) or Bach and Shallit (1996, 273). For most of the past 400 years, the largest known primes have had this special form. There are 38 known Mersenne primes. The largest one, $2^{6972593} - 1$, which has 2 million digits, was discovered in 1999 by Nayan Hajratwala as part of the Great Internet Mersenne Prime Search (http://www.mersenne.org/prime.htm). *See* Ribenboim (1988), for more on Mersenne primes.

Fermat's Last Theorem

This statement, proved by Wiles in 1993 after being an unsolved problem for more than 350 years, asserts that if $n > 2$, then the equation $x^n + y^n = z^n$ has no solution in positive integers. Computers have been used to check the conjecture for particular n. In 1993, Buhler, Crandall, Ernvall, and Metsänkylä verified the conjecture for all n up to 4,000,000. Although Fermat's Last Theorem has been proved, the calculations which were used to check the conjecture remain interesting because they describe the structure of cyclotomic fields. *See* Ribenboim (1979) for a very readable exposition of these calculations.

Waring's Problem

Waring conjectured that for every integer $k > 1$ there is an integer r so that every natural number can be expressed as the sum of r exact kth powers. For example, every positive integer is the sum of four squares, nine cubes, etc. Hilbert proved this conjecture in 1909. Let $g(k)$ denote the smallest such r, so that $g(2) = 4$, $g(3) = 9$, etc. It has been proved that for $k \geq 6$ we have $g(k) = 2^k + q - 2$ provided $r + q \leq 2^k$, where q and r are the quotient and remainder when 3^k is divided by 2^k. (There is a different formula for $g(k)$ when this condition fails.) In 1989, Wunderlich and Kubina used a CRAY-2 to verify the condition for all $k < 470,000,000$.

The Riemann Zeta Function

Our final topic concerns the function

$$\zeta(s) = \sum_{k=1}^{\infty} k^{-s}$$

of the complex variable $s = \sigma + it$. The formula

$$\zeta(s) = \prod_p (1 - p^{-s})^{-1},$$

where the product is taken over all prime numbers, shows the connection between $\zeta(s)$ and prime number theory. From this relationship and the fact that $\zeta(1 + it)$ is never zero, one can prove the *prime number theorem*, which says that the number of primes $\leq x$ is asymptotic to $x/\log x$. The celebrated Riemann Hypothesis conjectures that all zeros of $\zeta(s)$ with $\sigma > 0$ satisfy $\sigma = 1/2$. Many important results in number theory would follow if this conjecture was proved. In 1986, van de Lune, te Riele, and Winter verified that the first 1,500,000,001 zeros of $\zeta(s)$ have real part $1/2$. See Ribenboim (1988) for more on this subject.

Bibliography

1969. Lehmer, D. H. "Computer Technology Applied to the Theory of Numbers," *Studies in Number Theory*, MAA Studies in Mathematics, Vol. 6. Upper Saddle River, NJ: Prentice Hall.
1979. Ribenboim, P. *13 Lectures on Fermat's Last Theorem.* Berlin: Springer-Verlag.
1988. Ribenboim, P. *The Book of Prime Number Records.* Berlin: Springer-Verlag.
1994. Riesel, H. *Prime Numbers and Computer Methods for Factorization*, 2nd Ed. Progress in Mathematics, Vol. 126. Boston: Birkhäuser.
1996. Bach, E., and Shallit, J. *Algorithmic Number Theory, Vol. I: Efficient Algorithms.* Cambridge, MA: MIT Press.
1997. Singh, S. *Fermat's Enigma: The Quest to Solve the World's Greatest Mathematical Problem.* New York: Walker.

S. S. Wagstaff, Jr.

NUMBERS AND NUMBER SYSTEMS

For articles on related systems *see* ARITHMETIC, COMPUTER; COMPLEMENT; INTERVAL ARITHMETIC; NUMERICAL ANALYSIS; PRECISION; and SIGNIFICANT DIGIT.

The representation in which we normally write decimal numbers, for example

$$276.1069 \tag{1}$$

is nothing more than shorthand symbolic representation for the precise mathematical equivalent

$$2 \times 100 + 7 \times 10 + 6 \times 1 + 1 \times 0.1$$
$$+ 0 \times 0.01 + 6 \times 0.001 + 9 \times 0.0001 \tag{2}$$

or

$$2 \times 10^2 + 7 \times 10^1 + 6 \times 10^0 + 1 \times 10^{-1}$$
$$+ 0 \times 10^{-2} + 6 \times 10^{-3} + 9 \times 10^{-4} \tag{3}$$

Equations (2) and (3) express clearly that the decimal system we use has a *base*, or *radix*, $R = 10$. By analogy, therefore, the *binary*, or *base 2* (i.e. $R = 2$), system so commonly used with computers can become immediately understandable, as presented below. The notation (1)—often called *positional notation* because the position of a digit specifies the power of 10 in (3) that is associated with it—effectively hides the real mathematical content of a number.

Radix Representation

The notation in (2) or (3) above is called the *radix representation* of a number. The general form of any decimal number may be written

$$\sum_{i=-m}^{n} d_i \cdot 10^i \qquad 0 \leq d_i \leq 9 \qquad (d_i \text{ an integer})$$

which in the case of (3) specializes to

$$m = 4, \qquad n = 2$$
$$d_{-4} = 9, \qquad d_{-3} = 6 \qquad d_{-2} = 0, \qquad d_{-1} = 1$$
$$d_0 = 6, \qquad d_1 = 7, \qquad d_2 = 2$$

Besides decimal, the two other number systems most important in computing are binary and *hexadecimal* ($R = 16$). In binary, numbers are represented as

$$\sum_{i=-m}^{n} b_i \cdot 2^i \qquad b_i = 0 \text{ or } 1. \tag{4}$$

In the hexadecimal, or base 16, system, numbers are represented by

$$\sum_{i=-m}^{n} h_i \cdot 16^i \qquad 0 \leq h_i \leq 15 \qquad (h_i \text{ an integer}).$$

An important task in any number system is to be able to *count*. The rule for counting in a number system of radix R, whose digits range from 0 to $R - 1$, is as follows:

1. When the rightmost digit of the number whose successor is desired is less than $R - 1$, increase that digit to its successor digit.

2. When the rightmost digit of the number whose successor is desired is equal to $R - 1$, replace $R - 1$ by 0, "carry" a 1 to the second radix position from the right, and repeat this two-step process until carries no longer need to be propagated to the left.

If $R = 10$, this algorithm will successfully generate the familiar sequence of decimal numbers. But when $R = 2$, we get the sequence of binary numbers, the first 18 of which are

0	1	10	11	100	101
110	111	1000	1001	1010	1011
1100	1101	1110	1111	10000	10001

BINARY

The addition and multiplication tables for binary numbers are particularly simple (Table 1) and, once learned, so is binary arithmetic using these tables. Fig. 1 gives examples of all four arithmetic operations in binary, with the corresponding decimal arithmetic also given. Finding the decimal integer equivalent to a given binary integer is very simple using Eq. (4). Thus, for example,

$$1011010 = 1 \times 2^6 + 0 \times 2^5 + 1 \times 2^4 + 1 \times 2^3$$
$$+ 0 \times 2^2 + 1 \times 2^1 + 0 \times 2^0$$
$$= 64 + 16 + 8 + 2$$
$$= 90.$$

Table 1. Binary addition and multiplication tables.

+	0	1		×	0	1
0	0	1		0	0	0
1	0	10		1	0	1

Addition

```
Carries   10011
          11001    25
         +10011   +19
         ------   ---
         101100    44
```

Subtraction

```
Borrows  10  1  1
          0  0 10 10 10
          1  1  0  0  0   24
         -0  1  1  0  1  -13
         ----------------  ---
             1  0  1  1   11
```

Multiplication

```
    1101      13
  ×1110     ×14
  ------     ---
  11010      52
  1101       13
  1101       ---
  ------     182
10110110
```

Division

```
           11        3 1/9
1001 |11100     9 |28
      1001
      ----
      1010
      1001
      ----
         1
```

Figure 1. Binary arithmetic.

Later in this article, we will consider the general problem of conversion from a number in one system to another.

HEXADECIMAL

This system became especially important with the advent of the IBM 360 system (*q.v.*), which, while binary internally, from the user's point of view used hexadecimal arithmetic for descriptive purposes and as the base of the exponent in floating-point numbers. Because hexadecimal requires 16 distinct characters, 6 characters in addition to $0, 1, \ldots, 9$ are needed to represent $10, 11, \ldots, 15$. These are usually taken to be A, B, C, D, E, F.

A binary number is easily converted to a hexadecimal number by dividing the bits of the binary number into groups of bits, starting from the binary point and working in both directions. Thus,

$$111|1010|0001|.0010|0001|110$$

becomes

$$7\,A\,1.2\,1\,C$$

in hexadecimal with the 7 corresponding to 111 with an implicit leading zero and the C corresponding to 1100 with the final 0 implicit.

At one time *octal* (base 8) representation was quite widely used in computing because binary numbers are easily converted to octal by using groups of 3 bits.

However, since the preponderance of computers in current use—mainframes and all popular personal computers—have word lengths that are divisible by four but not by three (16, 32, or 64 bits), octal is almost never used now.

Other Number Systems

BALANCED DIGIT SYSTEMS

In a balanced digit system the allowable digits in each position range in value from $-s$ to $+s$, with negative numbers usually denoted by an overbar. Thus, a balanced binary system would have digits $-1, 0, 1$ with -1 written as $\bar{1}$. In this system,

$$10\bar{1}\bar{1} = 2^3 - 2^1 - 2^0 = 5$$

and

$$\bar{1}101 = -2^3 + 2^2 + 2^0 = -3$$

One property of such a system, sometimes useful in the design of arithmetic units in computers, is the *redundancy* that occurs when a number has more than one possible representation. For example, in the system described above, 5 may, as in the usual binary system, also be represented by 101.

In any balanced digit system where s is less than the base, the leftmost digit gives the sign of the number so that no explicit sign is needed. In addition, given any number A, its negative may be found by changing all digits to their negatives (i.e. removing all overbars and inserting overbars where there were none). Thus, for example,

$$10\bar{1}10 = 2^4 - 2^2 + 2^1 = +14$$

and

$$\bar{1}01\bar{1}0 = -2^4 + 2^2 - 2^1 = -14$$

A particularly interesting balanced digit system, which does not yet appear to have been applied in computers, is *balanced ternary* (Knuth, 1969), which has radix 3 and where, as above, the digits, called *trits*, are 1, 0, and $\bar{1}$. This system is nonredundant and, in addition to the properties mentioned above, has the additional useful property that a number may be rounded to the nearest integer merely by deleting its fractional part. Thus,

$$10\bar{1}.\bar{1}\bar{1} = 3^2 - 3^0 - 3^{-1} - 3^{-2} = 7\tfrac{5}{9}$$

and

$$10\bar{1} = 8$$

RESIDUE SYSTEMS

A residue system is one in which (1) each digit position corresponds to a different radix; (2) all pairs of radices are relatively prime; i.e. the only common divisor of

any pair of radices is 1; and (3) the value of the digit d_i for integer A in position i corresponding to radix r_i is given by $d_i = A$ modulo r_i, i.e. the remainder when A is divided by r_i.

For example, if $r_2 = 5$, $r_i = 3$, $r_0 = 2$, then 13 is represented by 311 and 29 is represented by 421.

Because of property (2), the range of values that can be expressed is from 0 to 1 less than the product of the radices used.

Radix Conversion

To convert a number in a system with base p to a number in base q, we consider the integer and fractional parts of the number separately. Let $(I)p$ and $(F)p$, respectively, be the integer and fractional parts of the number in base p, which we wish to convert to base q; let $(q)_p$ be the expression of q in the p system (e.g. to convert from binary to decimal $(q)_p = (10)_2 = 1010$). Figs. 2a and 2b contain algorithms in pseudocode to perform the conversions of the integer and fractional parts, respectively. We illustrate these algorithms with two examples.

Example 1

Convert 6753.31 in decimal to binary. Here $p = 10$, $q = 2$, $(I)_p = 6753$, $(F)_p = 0.31$, and $(q)_p = 2$. From Fig. 2(a) we calculate the integral part and find it, reading up in the following table, to be 1101001100001.

(a) Integer part

```
quot ← I                          [I is initial integer part]
j ← 1
repeat
        quot, rem ← quot div q, quot mod q
                         [Divide quotient by new base to
                          get next quotient and remainder]
        result[j] ← (rem)q
                             [Express remainder in base q to
                              get jth digit to left of point]
        j ← j+1
until quot=0
```

(b) Fractional part

```
fract ← F                         [F is initial fractional part]
j ← 1
while j≤K and fract>0    [K is maximum digits desired]
        int ← intpart(fract * q)
                         [Obtain digit of fractional part]
        fract ← fract * q - int           [New fraction]
        result[j] ← (int)q
                             [Express integer in base q to
                              get jth digit after point]
        j ← j+1
endwhile
```

Figure 2. Radix conversion.

	Quotient	Remainder
6753/2	3376	1
3376/2	1688	0
1688/2	844	0
844/2	422	0
422/2	211	0
211/2	105	1
105/2	52	1
52/2	26	0
26/2	13	0
13/2	6	1
6/2	3	0
3/2	1	1
1/2	0	1

From Fig. 2b, with $K = 6$, we calculate the fractional part, and find it, reading down, to be 010011.

	Fractional part	Integral part
0.31×2	0.62	0
0.62×2	0.24	1
0.24×2	0.48	0
0.48×2	0.96	0
0.96×2	0.92	1
0.92×2	0.84	1

Thus, 6753.31 in decimal is equivalent to

$$1101001100001.010011\ldots$$

in binary. Note that the binary fraction is nonterminating (i.e. not expressible in a finite number of bits), even though the decimal fraction is finite.

Example 2

Convert 1001100.011 in binary to decimal. Here, $p = 2$, $q = 10$, $(I)_p = 1001100$, $(F)_p = 0.011$, and $(q)_p = 1010$, which is the binary representation of 10 in decimal. From Fig. 2a,

	Quotient	Remainder
1001100/1010	111	$110 \rightarrow 6$ in decimal
111/1010	0	$111 \rightarrow 7$ in decimal

Thus, the integral part of the decimal number is 76. From Fig. 2(b),

	Fractional part	Integral part
0.011×1010	0.110	$11 \rightarrow 3$ in decimal
0.110×1010	0.100	$111 \rightarrow 7$ in decimal
0.100×1010	0.000	$101 \rightarrow 5$ in decimal

Thus, the decimal equivalent of 1001100.011 is 76.375. In this instance a finite binary fraction became a finite decimal fraction. This is always the case because all the negative powers of 2 have finite fractional expansions in the decimal system.

Because of our natural facility with decimal arithmetic, an easier way to do Example 2 is to apply expression (4) directly:

$$1001100.011 = 1 \times 2^6 + 1 \times 2^3 + 1 \times 2^2$$
$$+ 1 \times 2^{-2} + 1 \times 2^{-3}$$
$$= 64 + 8 + 4 + 0.25 + 0.125$$
$$= 76.375$$

The conversions illustrated in Examples 1 and 2 are indeed precisely those performed when

1. A program written in a high-level language in decimal notation is compiled into the machine language of a binary computer.

2. The results computed in that binary computer are printed out as decimal numbers.

Bibliography

1969. Menninger, K. *Number Words and Number Symbols.* Cambridge, MA: MIT Press. (This book, subtitled "A Cultural History of Numbers," is a fascinating account of the history and uses of numbers in many natural languages.)

1994. Omondi, A. R. *Computer Arithmetic Systems: Algorithms, Architecture, and Implementation.* Upper Saddle River, NJ: Prentice Hall.

1997. Knuth, D. E. *The Art of Computer Programming*, Vol. 2, 3rd Ed. Reading, MA: Addison-Wesley.

Anthony Ralston

NUMERICAL ANALYSIS

For articles on related subjects see ALGORITHM; APPROXIMATION THEORY; DISCRETE MATHEMATICS; ERROR ANALYSIS; FAST FOURIER TRANSFORM; FINITE ELEMENT METHOD; INTERVAL ARITHMETIC; MATHEMATICAL PROGRAMMING; MATHEMATICAL SOFTWARE; MATRIX COMPUTATIONS; PARTIAL DIFFERENTIAL EQUATIONS; ROUNDOFF ERROR; SCIENTIFIC APPLICATIONS; and SPLINE.

Numerical analysis is concerned with the development, analysis, and use of algorithms that simulate physical and social processes. It is a practical science, involving as it does the production of numbers that approximate the solution of mathematical models of physical and social systems. It is a very old science. Many famous mathematicians from the seventeenth, eighteenth and nineteenth centuries—including Gauss, Newton, and Fourier—developed numerical algorithms that are still widely used. The advent of computers provided a tremendous impetus to the study and development of numerical analysis, and indeed led to so many new advances that it is now common to refer to the period from 1950 to the present as the era of "modern numerical analysis." High-speed computers have made it possible to solve ever more complex problems and, as a result, to gain much better insight into complex processes. Modern technological achievements in such areas as space and atomic energy would have been impossible without high-speed computers and advances in numerical analysis.

Computers have affected the direction of numerical analysis in several important ways. They have forced numerical analysts to search for algorithms that are computationally fast and efficient, and to search for a better understanding of error analysis. Algorithms that produce speed-up factors of the order of 100 or more have been discovered in such areas as harmonic analysis, the solution of large linear systems by iterative methods, and matrix eigenvalue problems. Computers have also generated new problems for numerical analysts. For example, because computers work with finite word lengths and because of the inexactness of conversion from one number base to another, roundoff errors are inevitably introduced. These errors in turn propagate in very complicated ways. Numerical analysts are concerned about the effect of the totality of such errors on the accuracy of the results. Statistical methods of error analysis hold some promise in this area, but the most effective approach to date is that of backward error analysis, due to Wilkinson (1960).

In backward error analysis, one shows that the *computed* results are the exact solutions of a perturbed problem and that the bounds for the perturbations can be obtained numerically. By comparing the perturbed problem and the given problem, one can then decide how much confidence to place in the computed results.

Another problem introduced by computers is that of numerical instability. Errors introduced into a computation, from whatever source, propagate in different ways. In some algorithmic processes, these errors tend to grow exponentially, with disastrous computational results. An algorithm that exhibits such exponential error growth is said to be numerically unstable. Numerical analysts therefore seek algorithms that are not only fast and efficient, but also stable.

The complexity of error analysis has also led to the development of automatic error analysis procedures. In such automatic error procedures, an attempt is made to have the computer monitor the error at each stage of the computation and to adjust parameters automatically so as to reduce the error in subsequent computations. The adaptive integration schemes for quadrature, which will be described in a later section, provide one example of such automatic error-monitor algorithms.

In recent years aspects of the implementation of algorithms have become of increasing importance. Teams of specialists have produced computer programs that implement the best available algorithms for important standard problems, such as the solution of linear equations, integration of differential equations, and evaluation of important functions of physics and chemistry. These programs, usually written in Fortran (*q.v.*), have gone a long way toward making high-quality standardized algorithms readily available. The most famous example is the LINPAK project, a collection of programs for matrix computation developed at the Argonne National Laboratory. See Dongarra *et al.* (1979).

An important new trend in numerical analysis is the construction of algorithms to take advantage of specialized computer hardware. Some new computers can perform simultaneous calculations, such as multiply and add. On several multiprocessing and parallel processing (*q.v.*) computers, it is possible to divide a computation into pieces, each of which will be done on a separate computing "node" with an overseer program synchronizing and combining the results. As computer networks improve, it will also be possible for the nodes to be widely separated. Developing efficient algorithms becomes much more difficult in these cases and is an active topic of current research.

In the early days of computers, the graphical representation of data was secondary to the calculation, which was thought of as a major task. Today this view has largely been replaced by the realization that the representation of results is often as important as what is calculated. By examining pictures, plots, and animated sequences, scientists can often analyze the output of computer runs much more effectively than by reading tables (*see* SCIENTIFIC VISUALIZATION). However, displaying graphical data presents its own demands on computer resources. The graphical output device must be able to translate commands and numbers into pictures. In addition, the numerical description of a picture often requires that a large amount of data be generated and moved rapidly from the computer to the graphics device, implying the need for "high bandwidth" communication paths. Nevertheless, a recent trend in numerical analysis is the use of sophisticated interactive graphics, in which the scientist views partial solutions to the posed problem and then advises the computer, graphically, on how to proceed. A related development has been the increasing use of "user-friendly" programs that assist scientists who have little or no programming knowledge.

Traditional numerical analysis usually deals with some aspects of the following topics.

1. Root-finding methods for a single equation or for systems of equations.

2. Interpolation.

3. Approximation.

4. Least-squares calculations.

5. Numerical differentiation.

6. Numerical integration.

7. Solution of linear equations.

8. Matrix eigenvalue problems.

9. Solution of ordinary differential equations.

10. Boundary value problems.

11. Solution of partial differential equations.

12. Generation of pseudo-random numbers.

13. Fourier analysis and the fast Fourier transform.

In an article of this length, one cannot provide more than a brief glimpse into some of these areas. There follows elementary discussions of root finding, interpolation, numerical differentiation, quadrature, and ordinary differential equations. More detailed treatments are given in Ortega and Rheinboldt (1970), Gautschi (1997), Golub and Van Loan (1983), Kahaner, Moler, and Nash (1989), and Shampine and Gordon (1975). Topics 4, 7, 8, 11, 12, and 13 above are discussed in separate articles in this Encyclopedia.

Roots of Equations

We consider first the problem of finding the roots of equations of one variable. Some examples of equations that arise in physics and engineering are:

1. $x^3 - x - 1 = 0$

2. $e^x - \cos x = 0$

3. $2x - \tan x = 0$

It is only rarely possible to find roots of such equations explicitly, and we must therefore rely on numerical methods that produce approximate solutions.

The simplest of all methods for finding a simple real zero of a continuous function $f(x)$ is the *bisection method*. The process begins by finding an interval (a_0, b_0) which contains the desired zero α. If the zero is simple, then $f(a_0)$ and $f(b_0)$ must be opposite in sign, the usual test for this being based on the inequality

$$f(a_0)f(b_0) < 0$$

The next step is to bisect the interval (a_0, b_0); i.e. compute $m = 1/2(a_0 + b_0)$. We then evaluate $f(m)$ and form the product $f(a_0)f(m)$. If this product is nega-

tive, then we know that the zero lies in the interval (a_0, m); otherwise, it must be in the interval (m, b_0). Of course, if $f(a_0)f(m) = 0$, then m is the desired zero. We now bisect the smaller interval, which is known to contain the zero α, and the entire process is repeated until the zero is obtained to the accuracy desired. The procedure is summarized in algorithmic form as follows:

Given a function $f(x)$ continuous on the interval (a_0, b_0) and such that $f(a_0)f(b_0) < 0$.

For $n = 0, 1, 2, \ldots$, until satisfied, do:

Set $m = (a_n + b_n)/2$.

If $f(a_n)f(m) \leq 0$, set $a_{n+1} = a_n, \quad b_{n+1} = m$;

otherwise, set $a_{n+1} = m, \ b_{n+1} = b_n$.

Then $f(x)$ has a root in the interval (a_{n+1}, b_{n+1}).

The phase "until satisfied" used in this algorithm must be made precise in a program and is usually based on one of the following criteria.

1. $|f(m)| < \varepsilon$;

2. $|b_{n+1} - a_{n+1}| < \delta$

where ε, δ are selected to achieve the desired accuracy.

As a simple example, consider the function $f(x) = x^3 - x - 1$. It is easy to verify that

$$f(1) = -1 < 0 < 5 = f(2).$$

Hence, there must be at least one zero of $f(x)$ on the interval $(1, 2)$. In fact, there is exactly one zero on $(1, 2)$. We call this zero α. The midpoint of the interval $(1, 2)$ is 1.5, and we know that $\alpha \approx 1.5$ with an absolute error of at most 0.5. Now $f(1.5) = 0.875$ and $f(1)f(1.5) < 0$; hence the zero lies in the interval $(1, 1.5)$. Therefore, $\alpha \approx 1.25$, with absolute error less than 0.25. After 20 steps of this algorithm we find that

$$1.3247175 = a_{20} \leq a \leq b_{20} = 1.3247184,$$

$$f(a_{20}) = (-1.857\ldots)10^{-6},$$

$$f(b_{20}) = (2.209\ldots)10^{-6}.$$

At this point we have six significant digits of accuracy. As this example shows, the bisection method always brackets the zero and provides an automatic bound on the accuracy of the approximation. Its simplicity makes it ideal for computer solution. On the other hand, it usually converges very slowly. If the function is complicated, this method is not very efficient and we are led to a search for methods that converge faster.

One such method is due to Newton. The algorithm for Newton's method is also quite simple:

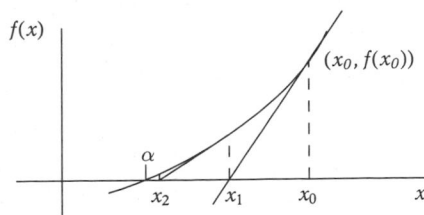

Figure 1. Newton's method.

Given $f(x)$ continuously differentiable and a starting approximation x_0. For $n = 0, 1, 2 \ldots$, until satisfied, calculate

$$x_{n+1} = x_n - \frac{f(x_n)}{f'(x_n)} \qquad (1)$$

Geometrically, Newton's method takes as a next approximation the intersection of the tangent to the curve $f(x)$ at the point x_n with the x-axis (*see* Fig. 1). We note that Newton's algorithm requires that the derivative $f'(x)$ be available.

For the example used above, $f(x) = x^3 - x - 1$, so that $f'(x) = 3x^2 - 1$, and Newton's algorithm leads to the iteration

$$x_{n+1} = x_n - \frac{x_n^3 - x_n - 1}{3x_n^2 - 1}$$

Starting with $x_0 - 1$, we obtain the values in Table 1. Since the iterates x_4, x_5 agree to seven significant digits, we take x_5 as an approximation to α, which is correct to at least that many digits.

The rapidity of convergence in this problem, even considering the fact that we do more work per step, shows that Newton's method is much more efficient than the bisection method. The tabular results also illustrate another important feature of this method. The number of correct digits, those underlined in Table 1, appears to double with each iteration. This observation is made more precise by the following theorem.

Theorem: Newton's Method. Let $f(x)$, $f'(x)$, $f''(x)$ be continuous and bounded on an interval containing the zero a. If x_0 is picked sufficiently close to α, then the

iteration of Eq. (1) converges; moreover, for n large enough,

$$(x_n + 1 - \alpha) \approx K(x_n - a)^2, \qquad (2)$$

where K is a constant that depends on the derivatives of $f(x)$ at the point α.

The last inequality shows that the error of the $(n + 1)$st iterate is proportional to the square of the error at the nth iterate, and demonstrates the eventual quadratic convergence of Newton's method. For this reason it is a very popular method. The most important disadvantage of Newton's method is that it will sometimes diverge or that it will converge to some zero other than the one desired. While the theorem guarantees convergence if x_0 is sufficiently close to α, it is difficult in practice to know what "sufficiently close" implies. A second disadvantage of Newton's method is that it requires that $f'(x)$ be computable. In many cases we may know $f(x)$ but not $f'(x)$.

A method that retains most of the advantages of Newton's method, but that does not require knowledge of $f'(x)$, is the secant method. It can be derived directly from Eq. (1) by replacing $f'(x_n)$ by a difference quotient:

$$f'(x_n) \approx \frac{f(x_n) - f(x_{n-1})}{x_n - x_{n-1}}. \qquad (3)$$

We know from calculus that this difference quotient is a reasonable approximation to $f'(x_n)$, provided x_{n-1} is sufficiently close to x_n. Substituting expression (3) into Eq. (1), we obtain the secant iteration:

$$x_{n+1} = x_n - f(x_n) \frac{x_n - x_{n-1}}{f(x_n) - f(x_{n-1})}. \qquad (4)$$

Here is the statement of the secant method in algorithmic form:

Given a function $f(x)$ and two points x_{-1}, x_0. For $n = 0, 1, 2, \ldots$ until satisfied do:

Calculate x_{n+1} using (4).

Geometrically, as shown in Fig. 2, the secant method takes x_{n+1} as the intersection with the x-axis of the secant passing through the points (x_n, f_n) and

Table 1. Newton's method applied to $f(x) = x^3 - x - 1$.

n	x_n
0	1.0
1	1.5
2	1.3478261
3	1.3252004
4	1.3247182
5	1.3247180

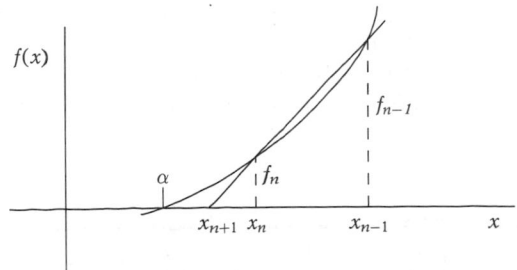

Figure 2. Secant method.

(x_{n-1}, f_{n-1}). This method converges much more rapidly than the bisection method, but less rapidly than Newton's method.

There are many other methods that could be considered, including fixed-point iteration, the modified regula falsi, Steffensen iteration, etc. Those mentioned above are, however, used most commonly in practice. Moreover, each of these methods can be generalized to apply to systems of nonlinear equations. As applied to systems, however, these methods frequently fail to converge, and in fact a great deal of research remains to be done to produce an effective computational method for finding zeros of nonlinear systems.

Interpolation

We now describe briefly the process of interpolation. In its simplest form, we are given the values of a function $f(x)$ at a selected set of points $\{x_i\}$ $(i = 0, 1, \ldots, n)$. The function $f(x)$ is usually not known explicitly, but its values at the selected points can be obtained either from a table of values or experimentally. The problem is to estimate the value of $f(x)$ at some non-tabular point $\bar{x}$. In Table 2, for example, we are given the values of an unspecified function $f(x)$ at the indicated points. We may now be required to estimate the value of $f(x)$ at, say, $\bar{x} = 2.1$, or at any non-tabular point. To do so, it is customary to select a simple class of functions, most commonly polynomials, that agree with the function $f(x)$ at the tabular points. We can then evaluate this polynomial at the point $x = \bar{x}$ to obtain the desired estimate. The simplest case is that of linear interpolation. Here we are given two points $\{x_0, x_1\}$ and the corresponding values $\{f(x_0), f(x_1)\}$. The equation of the linear polynomial (a straight line) that passes through the points $(x_0, f(x_0))$ and $(x_1, f(x_1))$ may be written in the following equivalent forms:

$$y = f_0 + \frac{f_1 - f_0}{x_1 - x_0}(x - x_0), \tag{5a}$$

$$y = f_0 \frac{x - x_1}{x_0 - x_1} + f_1 \frac{x - x_0}{x_1 - x_0}, \tag{5b}$$

where we have used the notation $f_0 = f(x_0)$, $f_1 = f(x_1)$. From either form it is easily verified that when $x = x_0$, $y = f_0$; and when $x = x_1$, $y = f_1$. Hence the line passes through the two tabular points (x_0, f_0) and (x_1, f_1). Linear interpolation is pictured geometrically in Fig. 3.

Table 2.

x	2.0	2.2	2.4	2.6
$f(x)$	0.30103	0.34242	0.38021	0.41497

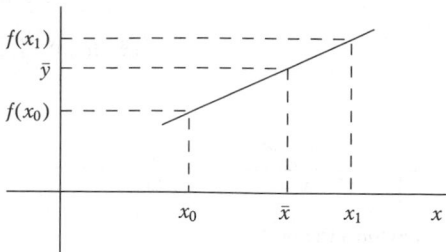

Figure 3. Linear interpolation.

To estimate $f(2.1)$ for the data in Table 2, using linear interpolation, substitute $x = 2.1$ into Eq. (5a) to obtain

$$y = 0.30103 + \frac{0.34242 - 0.30103}{2.2 - 2.0}(2.1 - 2.0)$$

$$= 0.30103 + 0.020695 = 0.321725.$$

This result "appears" to be reasonable, but we cannot say much about its accuracy. If the function varies greatly over the interval $[x_0, x_1]$, linear interpolation will generally give poor accuracy. It is reasonable to expect that, if the actual function $f(x)$ is smooth, interpolation based on a higher degree polynomial will give better results than that based on lower-degree polynomials.

If we are given $n + 1$ values of x and $f(x)$, say $\{x_i, f_i\}$ $(i = 0, 1, \ldots, n)$, then we can pass a polynomial of degree n through these points. It can be proved that if the points x_i are distinct, the interpolating polynomial of degree less than or equal to n is unique. However, it can be expressed in many different forms. One such form is the Lagrangian form defined by

$$P_n(x) = \sum_{k=0}^{n} f(x_k) l_k(x), \tag{6a}$$

where the $l_k(x)$, $k = 0, 1, \ldots, n$ are defined by

$$l_k(x) = \prod_{i=0, i \neq k}^{n} \frac{(x - x_i)}{(x_k - x_i)}.$$

Since each $l_k(x)$ is a polynomial of degree n, it is obvious that $p_n(x)$ is a polynomial of degree *at most* n and, furthermore, it is evident by direct substitution that $p_n(x_j) = f(x_j)$ $(j = 0, 1, \ldots, n)$. Another form of the interpolating polynomial that is more convenient than the Lagrangian form is the "Newton Divided Difference Polynomial." It is defined by

$$p_n(x) = a_0 + a_1(x - x_0) + a_2(x - x_0)(x - x_1) + \cdots$$

$$+ a_n(x - x_0) \cdots (x - x_{n-1}). \tag{6b}$$

In order for this polynomial to interpolate properly at the $n + 1$ distinct points $[x_k, f(x_k)]$, the coefficients a_k, $k = 0, 1, \ldots$ must be chosen properly. This can be done conveniently by use of a *divided difference table*; see for example Conte (1972). For the data of Table 2 the interpolating polynomial (Eq. 6b) now becomes

$$p_3(x) = 0.30103 + 0.20695(x - 2)$$
$$-0.04500(x - 2)(x - 2.2) \qquad (7)$$
$$0.011875(x - 2)(x - 2.2)(x - 2.4).$$

To find an estimate for $f(2.1)$, we set $x = 2.1$ in (7) to obtain

$$f(2.1) \approx p_3(2.1) = 0.30103 + 0.020695 + 0.00045$$
$$+ 0.000035625 = 0.3222106. \qquad (8)$$

This example illustrates two important features of Newton polynomial interpolation. First, we can increase the degree of the interpolating polynomial by simply adding on additional terms. No recalculation of coefficients once obtained is necessary. Second, the error of the interpolating polynomial of a given degree can be estimated by examining the next term. Thus, in Eq. (8) the error in linear interpolation is approximately 0.00045, while the error in second-degree interpolation is 0.000035625. Notice that each term decreases in magnitude. A thorough study of the error in the interpolating polynomial is beyond the scope of this article.

Although an interpolating polynomial is guaranteed to reproduce its input data (e.g. the points in Table 2), what happens for other values of x is much more difficult to predict. It is known that polynomial interpolants often "wiggle" or oscillate between the data points, and this is rarely desirable. One approach that often works better is to use a "piecewise" polynomial as an interpolating function. The idea is that in practice, it is usually better to use a low-degree polynomial over a

smaller range of the points than to use a high-degree polynomial over a large range. For example, if successive data points in Table 2 were connected by a straight line, the result would be a piecewise linear interpolant. Between each pair of points the interpolant is linear. This is simple, but the interpolant has "corners" (*see* Fig. 4). To make the interpolant smoother, one can use higher-degree polynomial "pieces." It is common to allow the interpolant to be a different cubic between each pair of points, and to force them to join together smoothly. If, at each joint the cubics on the right and left side have the same first derivative, the interpolant is called a Hermite cubic. If they have the same first and second derivatives at these points (continuous curvature), the interpolant is called a *cubic spline* (*see* SPLINE). Piecewise polynomials can be very successful in representing physical data and have become an indispensable part of most programs for computer-aided design (*q.v.*).

Numerical Differentiation

We turn next to a consideration of numerical differentiation. In the calculus, differentiation is a well-defined process if the function to be differentiated is given explicitly. Thus, if $f(x) = \sin x$, $f'(x) = \cos x$ and if $f(x) = x \sin x$, then $f'(x) = \sin x + x \cos x$. Often, however, the function is not known explicitly. $f(x)$ may, for example, be known only at a set of tabular points. How do we then obtain an estimate of the derivative at a point? One answer is to rely on finite difference approximations to the derivative. The simplest of these approximations is the "forward difference formula," given by

$$f'(x_0) \approx \frac{f(x_0 + h) - f(x_0)}{h} = \frac{\Delta f_0}{h}, \qquad (9)$$

where the forward difference operator Δf_0 is defined by (9) as $f(x_0 + h) - f(x_0)$. Since the limit on the right as $h \to 0$ is the definition of $f'(x_0)$, if it exists, then we can expect that for h small enough, the difference quotient will be close to $f'(x_0)$. Geometrically, as shown in Fig. 5, the difference quotient is the slope of the chord joining the points $(x_0, f(x_0))$ and $(x_0 + h, f(x_0 + h))$.

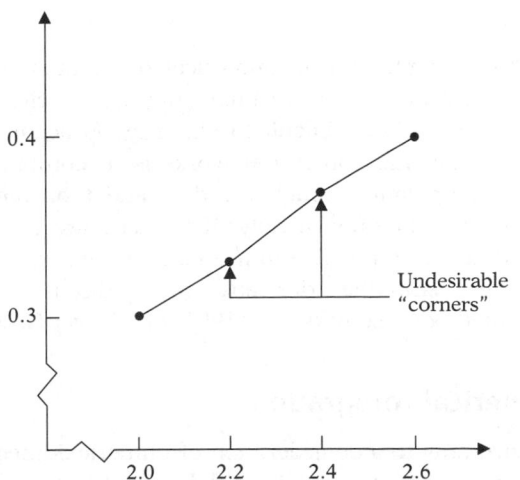

Figure 4. Piecewise linear interpolation.

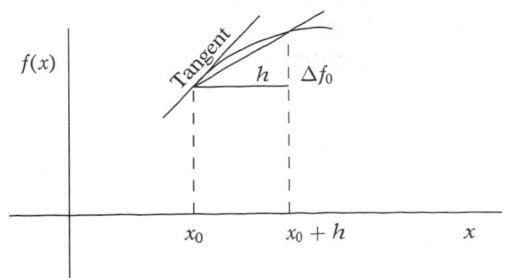

Figure 5. Numerical approximation to $f'(x_0)$.

It can be shown that the error in the forward difference formula is proportional to h. Hence, the approximation (9) is generally quite poor unless h is very small. If, however, h is taken very small, then there is a possibility of serious loss of accuracy due to the fact that we will be subtracting two quantities, $f(x_0 + h)$ and $f(x_0)$, which are nearly equal in magnitude. This type of error arises because computers have fixed word lengths. It is usually referred to as a "loss of significant digits (*q.v.*) due to subtraction." For example, if $f(x_0) = 0.76482122$ and $f(x_0 + h) = 0.76482333$, then $f(x_0 + h) - f(x_0) = 0.00000211$, which in floating-point arithmetic will then be written as 0.211×10^{-5}. Even if $f(x_0)$ and $f(x_0 + h)$ were correct to eight significant digits, the difference will be correct to only three significant digits. How, then, do we avoid this loss of significance? One way is to use a formula that has a smaller error term and hence will not require so small a value of h for a desired accuracy. One such formula is the "central difference formula":

$$D(f, h) = \frac{f(x_0 + h) - f(x_0 - h)}{2h}. \qquad (10)$$

The error term for this formula is of the order h^2 ($O(h^2)$); i.e.

$$f'(x_0) - D(f, h) = ch^2 \qquad (11)$$

for some constant c, while the error for the forward difference formula is only $O(h)$. An even more accurate formula is

$$D^2(f, h) = -\frac{1}{12h} \{ f(x_0 + 2h) - 8f(x_0 + h) \\ + 8f(x_0 - h) - f(x_0 - 2h) \}. \qquad (12)$$

The error of this formula is given by

$$f'(x_0) - D^2(f, h) = O(h^4). \qquad (13)$$

Of course, Eq. (13) requires more information about the function. Nevertheless, there is much less danger of loss of significance from subtraction, since we can use a considerably larger value of h.

To illustrate these formulas, consider the data in Table 3. Suppose that we wish to find an estimate of $f'(1)$, using this data. The function tabulated in Table 3 is $f(x) = e^x$, and since $f'(x) = e^x$, $f'(1) = e \approx 2.7183$. Using the forward difference formula (9) with $h = 0.1$, we get

$$f'(1) \approx \frac{f(1.1) - f(1.0)}{0.1} = \frac{3.0042 - 2.7183}{0.1} = 2.8590,$$

while for $h = 0.01$, we get

$$f'(1) \approx \frac{f(1.01) - f(1.0)}{0.01} = \frac{2.7456 - 2.7183}{0.01} = 2.7300.$$

Table 3.

x	$f(x)$
0.80	2.2255
0.90	2.4596
0.96	2.6117
0.98	2.6645
0.99	2.6912
1.00	2.7183
1.01	2.7456
1.02	2.7732
1.04	2.8292
1.10	3.0042
1.20	3.3201

Neither result is very good.

If we now use the central difference formula (10) with $h = 0.1$, we obtain

$$f'(x_0) \approx \frac{f(1.1) - f(0.9)}{0.2} = \frac{3.0042 - 2.4596}{0.2} = 2.7230,$$

while for $h = 0.04$ we obtain

$$f'(x_0) \approx \frac{f(1.04) - f(0.96)}{0.08} = 2.7188.$$

Finally, for $h = 0.01$ we find that

$$f'(x_0) \approx \frac{f(1.01) - f(0.99)}{0.02} = 2.7200.$$

These results are clearly better than those for the forward difference formula, but notice that the results for $h = 0.01$ are worse than those for $h = 0.04$. This is due to loss of significance. If we now use formula (12) with $h = 0.1$, we obtain

$$f'(x_0) \approx \frac{-1}{0.12} \{ f(1.2) - 8f(1.1) + 8f(0.9) - f(0.8) \}$$
$$= 2.7185,$$

a greatly improved result even with a rather coarse step h.

As this example shows, numerical differentiation is an unstable process. Even under the best of circumstances, it is often difficult to obtain good accuracy. A technique that sometimes works is to compute a spline interpolant through the data and then differentiate the spline analytically. If the data are equally spaced, it is also possible to use Fourier techniques to compute a smoothed derivative. For a discussion of these methods, see Atkinson (1993) or Weaver (1983).

Numerical Integration

We turn now to a consideration of numerical integration. In contrast to numerical differentiation, integration is usually a very stable process. The problem here

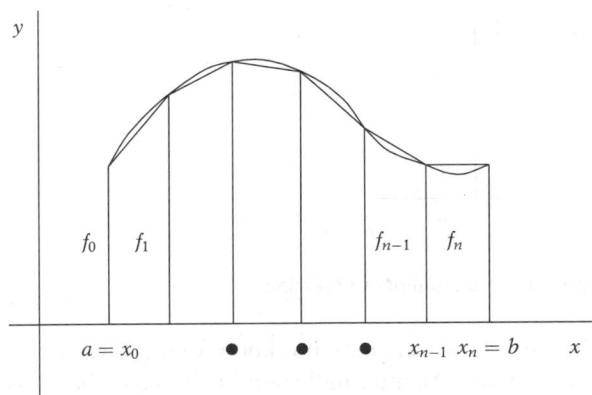

Figure 6. The trapezoidal rule.

in its simplest form is to compute an approximation to the definite integral

$$I = \int_a^b f(x)\,dx. \qquad (14)$$

Geometrically, we can interpret this problem as that of finding the area between the curve for $f(x)$ and the x-axis on the interval (a, b) (*see* Fig. 6).

The simplest usable formula based on equally spaced points for this purpose is the *trapezoidal rule*. This rule in its composite form consists of subdividing the interval (a, b) into N parts, each of length h, so that $Nh = b - a$. Also let $x_0 = a$, $x_1 = a + h, \ldots, x_N = b$, and $f(x_0) = f_0, f(x_1) = f_1$, etc. The area of a trapezoid over one panel (say, the first) is

$$T = \frac{h}{2}(f_0 + f_1).$$

Adding the areas over each panel leads to the composite trapezoidal formula

$$T_N = \frac{h}{2}(f_0 + 2f_1 + 2f_2 + \cdots + 2f_{N-1} + f_N).$$

How good is T_N as an approximation to the integral I? It is impossible to answer this question for all integrable functions $f(x)$. Sometimes the results are remarkably accurate, in some cases even exact. If we assume that the class of functions we are considering is sufficiently smooth, then we might try to answer the question by examining the error in the approximation T_N. It can be shown that the error is given by

$$E = I - T_N = \frac{h^2(b-a)}{12} f''(\eta), \qquad a < \eta < b.$$

The error here is called the *discretization error*. In general, we will not know $f''(\eta)$, but we see that the error in T_N is proportional to h^2, where $h = (b-a)/N$. We can achieve any desired accuracy, at least mathematically, by taking h sufficiently small. As we decrease h, however, the required number of function

evaluations will increase and the danger of roundoff error accumulation will also increase.

We have thus encountered a situation that arises frequently in numerical computation. The total error comes from two sources: a discretization error caused by using an approximate expression for the true mathematical operator, and a roundoff error. To achieve good accuracy in the mathematical sense (i.e. to reduce the discretization error), we need to take smaller divisions of h. Roundoff error, however, is inversely proportional to h. Hence, decreasing h increases roundoff error. The numerical analyst must therefore seek algorithms that in some sense minimize the totality of errors, those due to the sum of the absolute values of the discretization and roundoff errors.

Table 4 presents the results of applying the trapezoidal rule for various values of N to the integral

$$I = \int_0^1 e^{-x^2}\,dx$$

calculated using both single-precision (SP) and double-precision (DP) arithmetic.

The correct value of I to eight significant figures is 0.74682413. As N increases from 50 to 400, $T_N(\text{SP})$ approaches the correct result. However, for $N = 800$, the result is worse. The difference between the single precision result and the double precision result shows that the poorer results are due entirely to roundoff error. Thus, for this example, the optimum single precision result would be obtained for a value of N considerably less than $N = 800$. Even $N = 400$ requires considerable computational effort. This effort can be reduced by using a formula with a smaller discretization error.

One such formula is known as *Simpson's rule*. It begins by subdividing the interval (a, b) into $2N$ equally spaced panels, each of length h. Hence, $2Nh = b - a$. Again the subdivision points are labeled x_i $(i = 0, 1, \ldots, 2N)$ and the functional values $f(x_i) = f_i$ $(i = 0, 1, \ldots, 2N)$. Over each panel of width $2h$, one now assumes that the function $f(x)$ can be approximated by a polynomial of degree 2 passing through the points $(x_{2j}, f_{2j}), (x_{2j+1}, f_{2j+1}), (x_{2j+2}, f_{2j+2})$, $(j = 0, 1, \ldots, N-1)$. Integrating the polynomial over

Table 4. Trapezoidal rule results for $I = \int_0^1 e^{-x^2}\,dx$.

N	$T_N(\text{SP})$	$T_N(\text{DP})$
50	0.74679947	0.74679961
100	0.74681776	0.74681800
200	0.74682212	0.74682260
400	0.74682275	0.74682375
800	0.74682207	0.74682404

this panel then yields an approximation to the integral of $f(x)$ over this panel. Adding these approximations over all subpanels of width $2h$ leads to Simpson's quadrature formula S_{2N},

$$S_{2N} = \frac{h}{3}(f_0 + 4f_1 + 2f_2 + 4f_3 + \cdots + 4f_{2N-1} + f_{2N}).$$

$$(15)$$

The error of this formula is given by

$$E = I - S_{2N} = \frac{-h^4(b-a)}{180} f^{iv}(\xi), \qquad a < \xi < b.$$

Again, we do not in general know $f^{iv}(\xi)$, but the error is proportional to h^4. Thus, for functions that are sufficiently smooth, Simpson's formula should require fewer subdivisions, at least theoretically, to obtain a required accuracy compared with the trapezoidal rule. In fact, for the example considered above, Simpson's rule with $N = 50$ yields the result 0.74682400 in single precision and the result 0.74682413 (which is correct to eight significant figures) in double precision. Obviously, Simpson's rule is computationally much more efficient than the trapezoidal rule in this case, and this remains true in general for most functions $f(x)$.

Having selected a method and a step h in either Simpson's formula or the trapezoidal rule, we are faced with the question: "How good are the results produced?" The error term normally provides little help, since we usually cannot evaluate the derivatives involved. One way to build some confidence in the results is to solve the same problem several times with different values of h and then compare the results. Thus, if one uses Simpson's rule with a step h and then with a step $h/2$, one will have two approximations to the integral. If these two approximations agree to s significant figures, the assumption is then made that the results are correct to s significant figures. This method, while not conclusive mathematically, does provide some basis for confidence in the results. Each halving of the step size doubles the amount of work, however, and if the function $f(x)$ is not "smooth," the halving process may have to be repeated many times. We will not precisely define "smoothness" of a function here. However, a function that wiggles a great deal on part of an interval will be harder to integrate than one that does not, and some functions may even have singularities within the interval. In Fig. 7 we exhibit a function of this type.

A finer subdivision will be required over the interval (a, c) than over the interval (c, b). At the point c there is a discontinuity in the function. If this is known to the user, then it is reasonable to write

$$\int_a^b f(x)\,dx = \int_a^c f(x)\,dx + \int_c^b f(x)\,dx.$$

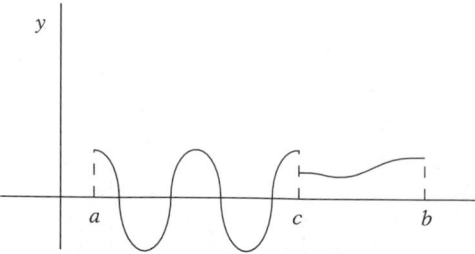

Figure 7. A discontinuous function.

The user, however, may not know that c is a point of discontinuity. An automatic approach, which has been used to handle such a situation in an efficient manner, is known as *adaptive integration*. It can be based on any basic integration formula, but we choose Simpson's rule for illustrative purposes. We are given an interval (a, b), the function $f(x)$, and an error ε, and a starting step size h.

The procedure for adaptive integration is as follows. Denote by $S(I)$ the result of applying Simpson's rule to the integrand on an interval I, and by ε the user-requested accuracy, such as 10^{-4}. Denote by $E(I)$ the magnitude of the difference between $S(I)$ and $S(I_1) + S(I_2)$, where I_1 and I_2 are the left and right halves of I.

The procedure for adaptive integration is as follows:

1. Initialize Q to $S([a, b])$ and E to $E([a, b])$.

2. If $E < \varepsilon$ stop. Report Q as the best estimate of the integral, and report E as the best estimate of the error in Q.

3. Otherwise, select the subinterval I with largest $E(I)$. (At the first step, there is only one interval $([a, b])$. Bisect I into I_1, I_2 and compute $S(I_i)$, $E(I_i)$, $i = 1, 2$.

4. Update,
$$E = E - E(I) + E(I_1) + E(I_2),$$
$$Q = Q - S(I) + S(I_1) + S(I_2).$$

5. Delete interval I and add I_1, I_2 to the collection of intervals.

6. Go to 2.

The advantage of adaptive schemes is that they do only as much work as necessary on each subinterval. Even discontinuities can be handled reasonably well by this approach.

Among other formulas based on equally spaced points are the *Newton–Cotes formulas* and *Romberg integration*. These quadrature formulas are capable of producing higher-order error terms and thus hold the promise of further reduction in computational error.

Somewhat different in nature are integration formulas of the Gaussian type. All the formulas considered above are based on equally spaced points. In Gaussian formulas, one attempts to select the integration points as well as the weights so as to produce a "best" integration formula. Such formulas have the form

$$I = \int_a^b f(x)\, dx \approx \sum_{i=0}^n w_i f(x_i),$$

where the points x_i as well as the weights w_i are to be determined. Such formulas, for a given number n of points, are capable of much higher accuracy. Gaussian methods can also be used to treat integrals with singularities

The points x_i and weights w_i of most Gaussian formulas are irrational numbers that can be obtained only after substantial calculation; programs incorporating these formulas use embedded tables. Also, there had been no practical way to estimate the error in Gaussian integration rules, a disadvantage if the program is to be automatic until, in 1968, the Russian computer scientist Kronrod developed a technique that pairs a Gaussian rule with a new rule using all the Gaussian points as well as others. For example, a common pair is the 7-point Gaussian rule, G_7, and the 15-point "Kronrod" rule, K_{15}. The difference between these is a good estimate of the error in G_7. Pairs such as these are at the heart of many automatic integration programs such as Quadpack. *See* Piessens *et al.* (1983). A more complete discussion of the integration formulas can be found in Davis and Rabinowitz (1984).

Differential Equations

Now we consider methods for solving ordinary differential equations. In this section, we restrict ourselves to a first-order initial value problem; i.e. we are given an equation involving a function $y(x)$ and its derivative

$$y' = f(x, y) \qquad (16a)$$

and an initial value such as

$$y'(x_0) = y_0. \qquad (16b)$$

We seek a continuous function $y(x)$ that satisfies Eq. (16a) subject to the initial value (16b). The theory of differential equations tells us that Eqs (16a) and (16b) have a unique solution provided certain conditions on $f(x, y)$ are satisfied. Closed-form solutions are sometimes, but not very often, possible. For example, the differential system

$$y' = y, \qquad y(x_0) = y_0$$

has the solution $y(x) = y_0(\exp(x - x_0))$. More often we must rely on numerical methods to obtain an approximation to the solution over a given interval.

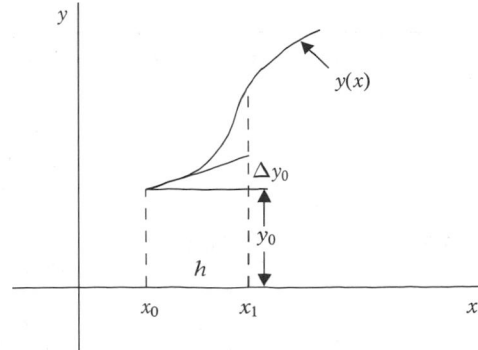

Figure 8. Euler's method.

Let a solution be required over an interval (x_0, b). We first subdivide the interval (x_0, b) into N equal parts of length h so that $Nh = b - x_0$, and we label the subdivision points $x_n = x_0 + nh$ $(n = 0, 1, \ldots, N)$ with $x_N = b$. We will consider several methods that yield approximations y_n to the true solution $y(x_n)$ at the subdivision points. The simplest of all methods is that of Euler, depicted in Fig. 8.

Geometrically, we find an approximate value of y at x_1 by extending the tangent to $y(x)$ at x_0 to the line $x = x_1$ and then adding to y_0 the increment $\Delta y_0 = hf(x_0, y_0)$. We thus obtain

$$y(x_1) \approx y_1 = y_0 + hf(x_0, y_0).$$

Note in Fig. 8 that the slope of the curve $y(x)$ is available immediately from the given equation $y' = f(x, y)$. Now that we have an estimate y_1 at $x = x_1$, we can calculate $y' = f(x_1, y_1)$, and thus we can step ahead to obtain

$$y(x_2) \approx y_2 = y_1 + hf(x_1, y_1).$$

The general formula, which yields y_{n+1} when we know x_n and y_n, is

$$y_{n+1} = y_n + hf(x_n, y_n), \quad n = 0, 1, \ldots, N - 1. \quad (17)$$

As an example, consider the equation

$$y' = -y^2 \qquad y(1) = 1 \qquad (18)$$

We choose $h = 0.1$ and apply formula (17) over the interval $(1, 2)$. The results are given in Table 5. The exact solution of Eq. (18) is $y = 1/x$. The results of Euler's method with a step $h = 0.1$ produces about one-digit accuracy.

An estimate of the error in Euler's method can be obtained by expanding $y(x_n + h)$ about x_n. Application of Taylor's theorem with remainder yields.

$$y(x_n + h) = y(x_n) + hy'(x_n) + \frac{h^2}{2} y''(\xi),$$

$$x_n < \xi < x_n + h.$$

Table 5.

n	x_n	y_n	$y(x_n) = 1/x_n$	$f(x_n, y_n) = -y_n^2$
0	1	1.	1.	-1
1	1.1	0.9	0.9090	-0.81
2	1.2	0.819	0.8333	-0.6708
3	1.3	0.7519	0.7692	-0.5654
4	1.4	0.6954	0.7143	-0.4836
5	1.5	0.6470	0.6667	-0.4186
6	1.6	0.6051	0.6250	-0.3661
7	1.7	0.5685	0.5882	-0.3232
8	1.8	0.5362	0.5555	-0.2875
9	1.9	0.5074	0.5263	-0.2575
10	2.0	0.4817	0.5000	-0.2320

Hence, the error in one step of Euler's method is

$$y(x_n + h) - \{y(x_n) + hf(x_n, y_n)\} = \frac{h^2}{2} y''(\xi_n).$$

This is called the *local error*, since it is based on the assumption that x_n and $y(x_n)$ are known exactly. Errors committed at each step will themselves propagate, and the global or total error at the end of N steps will be considerably larger. In fact, the global error of Euler's method can be shown to be of order h instead of h^2. To achieve any kind of accuracy for the problem presented above will clearly require a much smaller value of h. As we decrease h, however, the amount of work increases because we must evaluate $f(x, y)$ once for each step and, in addition, our roundoff error problems will increase. In practice, therefore, it is advisable to use formulas that are of higher order; i.e. we seek formulas for which the error is $0(h^p)$ with p greater than 1.

A direct use of Taylor's theorem carried to more terms would yield a formula of the form

$$y(x_n + h) = y(x_n) + hy'(x_n) + \frac{h^2}{2} y''(x_n) + \cdots$$
$$+ \frac{h^k}{k!} y^{(k)}(x_n) + \frac{h^{k+1}}{(k+1)!} y^{(k+1)}(\xi_n) \quad (19)$$

If we use the first $k + 1$ terms of this formula to predict $y(x_{n+1})$, then the error would be of order h^{k+1}. Taylor's theorem in this form is difficult to use because the higher derivatives of $y(x)$ are generally not easily computable. Runge first discovered formulas that achieve agreement with the Taylor expansion for different values of k, but that depend only upon the evaluation of $f(x, y)$. One such formula is

$$y_{n+1} = y_n + \frac{h}{6} (k_1 + 2k_2 + 2k_3 + k_4), \quad (20)$$

where:

$$k_1 = hf(x_n, y_n),$$
$$k_2 = hf\left(x_n + \frac{h}{2}, y_n + \frac{k_1}{2}\right),$$

$$k_3 = hf\left(x_n + \frac{h}{2}, y_n + \frac{k_2}{2}\right),$$
$$k_4 = hf(x_n + h, y_n + k_3).$$

The local error of this method is $0(h^5)$ and the global error is $0(h^4)$. It is called a *Runge–Kutta fourth-order method*; no derivatives of y other than $y' = f(x, y)$ are required. We note, however, that we must evaluate $f(x, y)$ at four different points for each step of the integration. By comparison with Euler's method, this Runge–Kutta method is far more efficient and, in addition, roundoff error is considerably less for the same accuracy. For the example presented in Eq. (18), again using $h = 0.1$, at $x = 1.1$ we obtain $y_1 = 0.090909$, which agrees with the exact result $1/1.1$ to all digits shown, indeed a remarkable improvement over the Euler result. The Runge–Kutta method and variations of it are very popular. It provides good accuracy, it is simple to program, it requires minimum storage, and it is stable. Its principal disadvantage, compared with methods based on finite differences, is that it requires four function evaluations per integration step.

Next we discuss the so-called multistep methods, which make it possible to achieve comparable accuracy with about half the amount of work. Runge–Kutta methods are called "one-step" methods because they use information at a single point to estimate y at the next point. Let us suppose that we have already estimated $y(x)$ at several successive subdivision points. For definiteness, assume that we know

$$(x_n, y_n, f_n), \quad (x_{n-1}, y_{n-1}, f_{n-1}),$$
$$(x_{n-2}, y_{n-2}, f_{n-2}), \quad (x_{n-3}, y_{n-3}, f_{n-3}),$$

where f_n represents $f(x_n, y_n)$, etc. How can this information be used to extrapolate a value for y at x_{n+1}. The theory of interpolation suggests one possible approach. If we integrate the equation $y' = f(x, y)$ from x_n to x_{n+1}, we obtain

$$y(x_{n+1}) - y(x_n) = \int_{x_n}^{x_{n+1}} f(x, y(x)) \, dx.$$

Since we know the value of f at the four successive points $x_n, x_{n-1}, x_{n-2}, x_{n-3}$, we can pass a polynomial of degree 3 through these points. Integrating the resulting polynomial and evaluating it between the limits x_n to x_{n+1} will then yield an approximate formula for $y(x_{n+1})$. One such formula is that of Adams, which after simplification, takes the form

$$y_{n+1} = y_n + \frac{h}{24} (55f_n - 59f_{n-1} + 37f_{n-2} - 9f_{n-3}).$$
$$(21)$$

The local error of this formula is $0(h^5)$ and the global error $0(h^4)$, just as for the Runge–Kutta method of order 4, discussed earlier. Notice that only one new function evaluation is required to compute y_{n+1}. It would thus appear that a formula of this type should be computationally more efficient than the Runge–Kutta method. It turns out that the accuracy of Adams' formula (21) is not quite as good as that of the Runge–Kutta method, even though both are of the same order, because the coefficient in the error term is somewhat larger. It is customary to consider the result of applying Eq. (21) as a predicted value and to correct it by using the formula

$$y_{n+1}^c = y_n + \frac{h}{24}\{9f(x_{n+1}, y_{n+1}^p) + 19f_n - 5f_{n-1} + f_{n-2}\},$$
(22)

where y_{n+1}^p is the value obtained from Eq. (21). The global error of Eq. (22) is also $0(h^4)$. The pair of formulas (21) and (22) is called a predictor–corrector pair. It yields results comparable in accuracy to the Runge–Kutta method with about half as much work. Multistep formulas such as (21) and (22) have the disadvantage of requiring special techniques for starting, since initially we have information at one point only. Some multistep methods also suffer from numerical instability, a phenomenon that can lead to disastrous results, and hence they should not be used indiscriminately.

Two important issues have propelled recent research in ordinary differential equations. The first is the need to develop reliable programs that can be used by non-specialists. The second is the need to solve "stiff" problems.

Programs for solving differential equations usually accept as input an error request ε and deliver a solution to the appropriate accuracy, much as for numerical integration. This implies the need to assess the accuracy of each integration step. If the estimated error is too large, the step is not accepted and a smaller one is tried instead. If the estimated error is sufficiently small, the step is accepted and an estimate is made to see if a larger step could be used from this point forward. A great deal of work has been done recently on estimating errors and developing variable step and variable order algorithms that are reliable and efficient. Nevertheless, the best programs, such as **LSODE** by Hindmarsh (1980) or **DEABM** by Shampine and Gordon (1975), still blend theory and experience. The reader is referred to Gear (1971), Shampine and Gordon (1975), or Shampine, Watts, and Davenport (1975) for a discussion of these methods.

When a differential equation is modeling two interrelated phenomena, with one changing rapidly and one changing slowly, difficulties can arise. An example might be a model of a beating drum where there are rapid vibrations corresponding to the tone of the drum, along with a slow decay in the volume of the sound. Many small integration steps would have to be used to model the rapid vibrations, leading to a great many calculations. However, a short time after the drum is struck, these rapid vibrations will be less important than the general decay, which can be approximated well by using only a few steps. Such a problem is called "stiff." The traditional numerical methods described in the early portion of this section have difficulty with stiff problems, since they slavishly follow the rapid motions even when they are less important than the general trend in the solution. Special algorithms have been devised for solving stiff problems; *see* Aiken (1985).

Boundary Value Problems

Differential equations of order higher than one are classified as *initial value problems* or as *boundary value problems*. In general, a differential equation of order n that can be expressed in the form

$$y^{(N)}(x) = f(x, y(x), y'(x), \ldots, y^{(N-1)}(x))$$

requires N conditions if it is to yield a unique solution. If these N conditions are all specified at one point, say $x = x_0$, then we have an *initial value problem*. If these conditions are specified at more than one point, than we have a *boundary value problem*. The methods previously considered for a single differential equation can be directly adapted to apply to initial value problems of any order. Boundary value problems are more complicated and require a different approach. Among the methods most commonly used for such problems are *finite difference methods*, the *finite element method*, *shooting methods*, and *collocation methods*. We shall restrict our discussion to a consideration of the finite difference method as applied to a second-order equation. We assume a second-order equation in the form

$$y''(x) + f(x)y'(x) + g(x)y(x) = q(x)$$
(23)

subject to the boundary conditions

$$y(a) = \alpha, \qquad y(b) = \beta,$$
(24)

where $f(x)$, $g(x)$, and $q(x)$ are given coefficient functions with sufficient continuity requirements. The problem is to find an approximate solution of Eq. (23) over an interval (a, b) that satisfies the boundary conditions (Eq. 24) at $x = a$ and $x = b$.

We first divide the interval (a, b) into N equal parts of width h so that $Nh = b - a$. We set $x_0 = a$, $x_N = b$ and we define the *mesh points* $x_n = x_0 + nh$ ($n = 0, 1, \ldots, N$). The corresponding values of y, f, g, and q are denoted by $y_n = y(x_0 + nh)$, etc. The next step is to replace each derivative appearing in Eq. (23) by an appropriate finite difference approximation. We use central difference approximations defined by

$$y'(x_n) \approx \frac{y(x_{n+1}) - y(x_{n-1})}{2h} = \frac{y_{n+1} - y_{n-1}}{2h},$$

$$y''(x_n) = \frac{y(x_{n+1}) - 2y(x_n) + y(x_{n-1})}{h^2}$$

$$= \frac{y_{n+1} - 2y_n + y_{n-1}}{h^2}$$

Substituting these into Eq. (23) leads to the finite difference equation

$$\frac{y_{n-1} - 2y_n + y_{n+1}}{h^2} = f_n \frac{(y_{n+1} - y_{n-1})}{2h} + g_n y_n = q_n.$$

Multiplying by h^2 and grouping terms we obtain

$$\left(1 - \frac{h}{2} f_n\right) y_{n-1} + (-2 + h^2 g_n) y_n$$

$$+ \left(1 + \frac{h}{2} f_n\right) y_{n+1} = h^2 q_n. \quad (25)$$

When Eq. (25) is written out for $n = 1, 2, \ldots, N - 1$, we will obtain a linear system of $N - 1$ equations for the $N - 1$ unknown values $y_1, y_2, \ldots, y_{N-1}$. Of course, y_0 and y_N are specified by the conditions of Eq. (24). More explicitly, we obtain the system

$$(-2 + h^2 g_1) y_1 + \left(1 + \frac{h}{2} f_1\right) y_2 = h^2 q_1 - \left(1 - \frac{h}{2} f_1\right) \alpha,$$

$$\left(1 - \frac{h}{2} f_2\right) y_1 + (-2 + h^2 g_2) y_2 + \left(1 + \frac{h}{2} f_2\right) y_3 = h^2 q_2;$$

$$\cdots$$

$$\left(1 - \frac{h}{2} f_{N-2}\right) y_{N-3} + (-2 + h^2 g_{N-2}) y_{N-2}$$

$$+ \left(1 + \frac{h}{2} f_{N-2}\right) y_{N-1} = h^2 q_{N-2},$$

$$\left(1 - \frac{h}{2} f_{N-1}\right) y_{N-2} + (-2 + h^2 g_{N-1}) y_{N-1}$$

$$= h^2 q_{N-1} - \left(1 + \frac{h}{2} f_{N-1}\right) \beta. \quad (26)$$

This linear system of equations can be readily solved by standard methods, some of which are described in the article on MATRIX COMPUTATIONS. Actually, because the matrix of coefficients of the system shown (Eq. 26) is *tri-diagonal*, a computer solution can be found very efficiently. The solution of this system will be the values $y_1, \ldots, y_{N-1}$ which approximates the solution function $y(x)$ at the mesh points. The accuracy of these approximations will depend upon how fine a mesh is chosen; i.e. on the value of h or N.

The method of finite differences works quite well on linear differential equations of any order. However, if the differential equation is nonlinear, this method becomes more complicated, and in such cases the shooting or collocation methods may be more appropriate.

Conclusion

In a short article on numerical analysis, one can hope to present to the reader only a synopsis of the work of the numerical analyst. We have discussed only a small number of algorithms. These algorithms work well on some classes of functions, but no algorithm is uniformly best for all classes of functions. The numerical analyst must be constantly alert to indications that an algorithm is not functioning properly. We have tried to stress those qualities of good algorithms that are important for computational purposes. These qualities are speed, efficiency, and automatic error analysis and control. There are many good books on numerical analysis at various levels for the reader interested in pursuing this subject, among which are Atkinson (1993), Gautschi (1997), Ralston and Rabinowitz (1978), and Hamming (1973).

The rapid movement of computers into homes, offices, and schools, as well as the much increased interest in communication via the Internet (*q.v.*) and the World Wide Web (*q.v.*), have led to new opportunities and issues for numerical analysis. The trend toward greater importance of data visualization and user-friendly programs is being amplified by new computer and communication technologies. With more computers and more users, the average level of understanding of computational techniques diminishes. As the 1990s drew to a close, fewer and fewer scientists were writing their own programs *ab initio*. The application of prewritten numerical analysis modules is growing, and there is even more rapid growth in the use of totally self-contained software systems which require no programming to solve specific end-user problems. Traditional numerical analysis is frequently being embedded into application disciplines, such as fluid flow, structural mechanics, electronic circuit design, scheduling optimization, etc. Further, when programming is required, new languages such as C, C++, HPF (High Performance Fortran), Matlab, Java, and others, are supplementing (and in many cases replacing) Fortran, which has been the standard for scientific computation.

Finally, the Internet is suggesting a variety of opportunities for collaborative and distributed computing. For example, recent experiments have shown that large collections of inexpensive PCs can be connected together to provide very effective problem solvers (*see* CLUSTER COMPUTING). As more people are using networks, the importance of data security increases.

Although traditional numerical analysis deals heavily with topics such as differentiation, integration, etc., a very interesting trend is the growth of numerical computation for discrete, combinatorial problems such as those associated with data encryption and decryption.

Bibliography

1960. Wilkinson, J. H. "Error Analysis of Floating Point Computations," *Num. Math.*, **2**, 319–340.

1970. Ortega, J. M., and Rheinboldt, W. C. *Iterative Solution of Nonlinear Equations in Several Variables.* New York: Academic Press.

1971. Gear, C. W. *Numerical Initial Value Problems in Ordinary Differential Equations.* Upper Saddle River, NJ: Prentice Hall.

1972. Conte, S. D., and deBoor, Carl J. *Elementary Numerical Analysis: An Algorithmic Approach.* New York: McGraw-Hill.

1973. Hamming, R. W. *Numerical Methods for Scientists and Engineers,* 2nd Ed. New York: McGraw-Hill.

1975. Shampine, L., and Gordon, M. *Computer Solution of Ordinary Differential Equations—The Initial Value Problem.* San Francisco: Freeman.

1975. Shampine, L., Watts, H., and Davenport, S. *Solving Non-Stiff Ordinary Differential Equations—The State of the Art,* SAND 75-01812. Albuquerque, NM: Sandia Corp.

1978. Ralston, A., and Rabinowitz, P. *A First Course in Numerical Analysis,* 2nd Ed. New York: McGraw-Hill.

1979. Dongarra, J. J., Moler, C. B., Bunch, J. R., and Stewart, G. W. *LINPACK Users' Guide.* Philadelphia: SIAM.

1980. Hindmarsh, H. "LSODE and LSODEI, Two Initial Value Ordinary Differential Equation Solvers," *ACM SIGNUM Newsletter,* **15**, 10–11.

1983. Golub, G. H., and Van Loan, C. F. *Matrix Computations.* Baltimore: The Johns Hopkins University Press.

1983. Piessens, R., de Doncker, E., Uberhuber, C., and Kahaner, D. *QUADPACK: A Subroutine Package for Automatic Integration.* Berlin: Springer-Verlag.

1983. Weaver, H. J. *Applications of Discrete and Continuous Fourier Analysis.* New York: John Wiley.

1984. Davis, P., and Rabinowitz, P. *Methods in Numerical Integration,* 2nd Ed. New York: Academic Press.

1985. Aiken, R. (Ed.) *Stiff Computation.* Oxford: Oxford University Press.

1989. Kahaner, D., Moler, C., and Nash, S. *Numerical Methods and Software.* Upper Saddle River, NJ: Prentice Hall.

1993. Atkinson, K. *Elementary Numerical Analysis.* New York: John Wiley.

1997. Gautschi, W. *Numerical Analysis: An Introduction.* New York: Springer-Verlag.

1998. Gerald, C. F., and Wheatley, P. O. *Applied Numerical Analysis.* Reading, MA: Addison-Wesley.

Sam D. Conte and David K. Kahaner

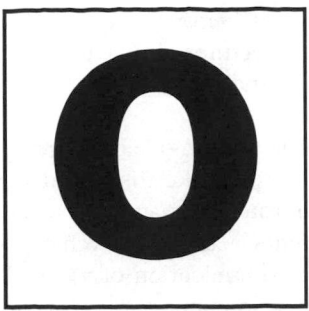

OBJECT-ORIENTED ANALYSIS AND DESIGN (OOAD)

For articles on related subjects *see* ABSTRACT DATA TYPE; CLASS; COMPONENT SOFTWARE; COMPUTER-AIDED SOFTWARE ENGINEERING; DATA MODELS; FORMAL METHODS FOR COMPUTER SYSTEMS; INFORMATION HIDING; OBJECT-ORIENTED PROGRAMMING; SOFTWARE DESIGN PATTERNS; and SOFTWARE ENGINEERING.

Introduction

Object-oriented analysis and design (OOAD) is a software engineering approach to constructing software systems by building object-oriented models that abstract key aspects of the target system and by using the models to guide the development process. The model concepts and the notation are intended to capture design decisions that have a large impact on the final system.

A complete object-oriented development approach has the following constituents:

◆ A set of fundamental modeling concepts for capturing semantic knowledge about a problem and its solution. The modeling concepts are independent of how they are visualized. They are the inputs for semantic tools, such as code generators, semantic checkers, and traceability tools. Typical modeling concepts include discrete entities, such as *class*, *operation*, *state*, and *value*, as well as relationships among the discrete entities, such as *association*, *generalization*, *dependency*, and *transition*.

◆ A set of *views* and *notations* for presenting the underlying modeling information to humans and allowing them to examine and modify it. Views may be pictorial, tabular, or textual. Pictures use a combination of geometric shapes, text, connectivity, and containment to represent semantic information. Pictures also use geometric arrangement and graphic markers (such as shape, line style, texture, and font) to highlight portions of the semantic information without changing its meaning. Usually each view shows only a part of the entire semantic model and different views can present the same semantic information in different forms.

◆ A development process for constructing models and implementations of them. A process operates at various levels of granularity. A process may include: a step-by-step description of what to do; rules to be applied whenever they are valid, not always during the same step; and general guidelines and procedures for building good models. The process describes which models to construct and how to construct them. It may also specify measures of goodness to evaluate proposed designs.

◆ An experience base that a designer can use in constructing a system. This includes reusable software (*see* SOFTWARE REUSE) components (classes, procedures, libraries), design patterns, application frameworks, and design rules. The concept of *patterns* is an attempt to describe expert experience in a uniform way. Patterns represent specific design solutions to recurring problems. These may apply at various levels of detail, from large-scale architectures down to low-level data structures (*q.v.*) and algorithms (*q.v.*).

The set of modeling elements together with their visual representation is called a *modeling language*; like a human language or a programming language it represents a universal vehicle for the representation and communication of ideas. A modeling language plus a development process is called a development *method*.

Models

The ultimate job of a development method is to capture knowledge about a system and build a solution of it. A *model* is a formal representation of a system at some level of abstraction. The goal of a model is to express precisely the essential features of a system and its solution in terms meaningful to a practitioner in the subject area. Each development method defines several different kinds of models that together provide a complete description of a system. Each kind of model has its own area of concern and notation. A developer constructs models to organize knowledge of the system and to verify that the knowledge is correct and consistent.

One kind of model found in all methods describes the classes (kinds of objects) in a system and their relationships to each other. This is usually called a *class model*. For example, a model of an order-processing system would be expressed in terms of classes such as *Order*, *Customer*, *Item*, *Payment*, and so on. Each class contains lists of attributes, operations, and (depending on the particular method) other things such as responsibilities (what a class knows and does) and rules. *Associations* (also called *relations* or *relationships*) show semantic connections between classes. Associations are abstractions of connections between objects. In the order-processing system class *Order* has associations to classes *Customer*, *Item*, and *Payment*.

Multiplicity is an important property of an association constraining how many instances of a class may be associated with an instance of another class. A multiplicity is a set of integers; for example, "1" means exactly one instance (a mandatory value), and "0..*" means zero through an unlimited number of instances (usually called "many"). Associations are often implemented using pointers, but an association is a logical relationship and a pointer is an implementation mechanism. *Generalization* (also called *inheritance*, *specialization*, *subclassing*, and *subtyping*) relates a general class to other more specific versions of it. In the order-processing system, *Customer* is specialized as *CorporateCustomer* and *PersonalCustomer*. The information common to both subclasses is placed in the superclass *Customer*; each subclass contains the additional information relevant to it alone. Fig. 1 shows part of the class model for the order-processing system using the Unified Modeling Language notation; other notations are similar. Rectangles represent classes, with their attributes and operations shown in separate compartments; lines represent associations with multiplicities shown on each end; and arrows with triangular arrowheads represent generalization from a child class (the more specific one) to the parent class (the more general one).

Models are useful for eliciting information from experts and verifying that the system has been correctly understood. Models may be used to answer questions about the system, such as: How many items may exist in one order? May an order have more than one customer? What transitions does an order undergo during its lifetime? Which class is responsible for handling orders that are canceled? The first two questions can be answered from the multiplicities in the class model; the others require other models. If important questions cannot be answered or yield the wrong answers, then the model must be modified until it is correct. The benefit of modeling is that it is easier to answer questions using a model instead of code,

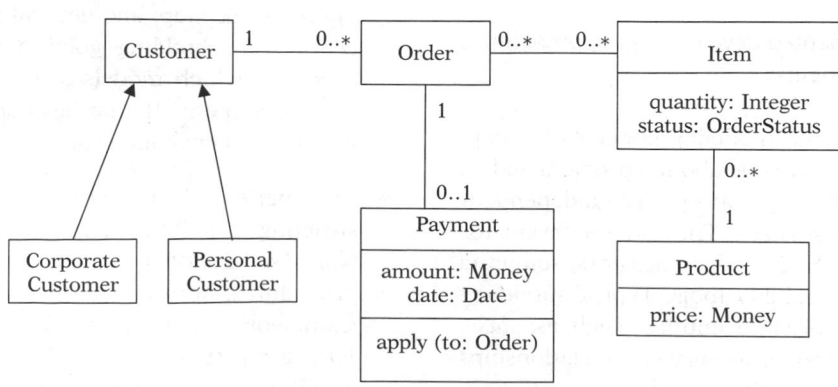

Figure 1. Class model for order-processing application.

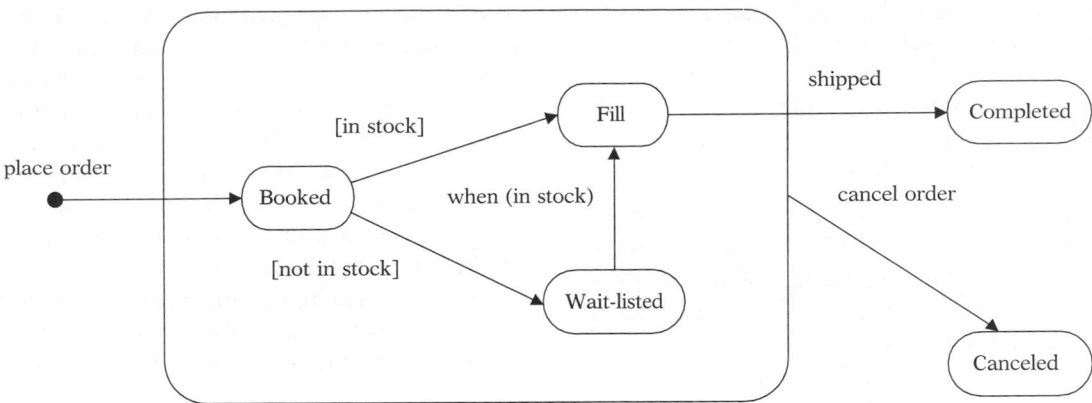

Figure 2. State model for Order class.

because a model contains less extraneous detail. It is also much easier to fix an incorrect model than to fix incorrect code.

Models can also be used to generate code for programming languages, databases, or special languages. A class model can be used to generate class declarations for most object-oriented programming languages with little difficulty. If the target language lacks one or more features, they can be mapped to other language features (which is what a compiler does for any language anyway). For example, if a target language lacks inheritance then it can be implemented in a different way.

Behavior Models

There is considerable variation among methods in modeling behavior. A *state model* shows the life history of an object or other entity in response to stimuli from other objects. The model contains a set of *states* that characterize periods during the life of the object during which it satisfies certain conditions. States are connected to other states by *transitions*, each of which indicates a change of state by an object in response to the occurrence of a certain trigger *event*. An event is a meaningful occurrence, such as an action by another object, the satisfaction of some condition, or the passage of a designated amount of time. A state model is a reductionist view of behavior; it shows the behavior of one object at a time in isolation. Fig. 2 shows a state model for the Order class in the order-processing system. The rounded rectangles represent states and the arrows represent transitions, with their trigger events shown as strings and their conditions shown as strings in brackets.

An *interaction model* shows a pattern of *messages* among a community of objects to implement a given higher-level operation or action. A message is a communication from one object to another that may include data arguments. A message may be synchro-

nous (a procedure call) or asynchronous (a one-way signal). An interaction model represents a holistic view of behavior; it shows the overall behavior of an entire community of objects. Message sequences can be shown in various ways, including sequential arrangement within a diagram or by using sequence numbers.

A *use case* is a complete transaction representing a chunk of functionality provided by a system that is meaningful to an outside agent, such as a person or another system. The entire set of use cases encompasses the functionality of a system. The set of use cases in a system together with the outside agents (called *actors*) with which they communicate are shown in a *use case model*. The details of a use case can be shown in an interaction model, as shown in Fig. 3. In this diagram, each object participating in the interaction is shown as a vertical line and time proceeds downward; an arrow represents a message sent from one object to another.

Other Kinds of Models

Organizational models organize the elements in a system into working units for purposes of understanding, configuration control, and concurrent work

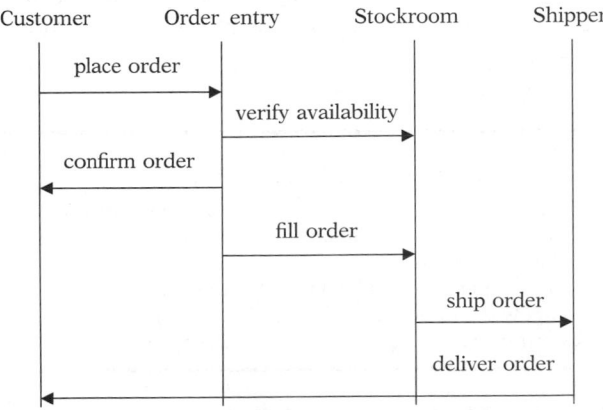

Figure 3. Interaction model of Customer–Order use case.

on different units. Usually these units may recursively contain other units of the same kind, so that the entire system is a tree (*q.v.*) or a partial order graph (*q.v.*) whose leaves are primitive elements. Such organizational units are called *packages* (*q.v.*), *subsystems*, and *models* in some approaches.

Various kinds of physical constructs from an implemented system may be modeled. Physical constructs include *containers* for organizing or distributing source, binary, or executable code; and computational resources in a run-time system environment, such as processors, memories, and devices. Such models also show the mapping of logical elements onto physical elements and the dependencies that result from such mappings.

CRC Cards

One simple modeling tool is the Class-Responsibility-Collaboration (CRC) card (Fig. 4). The information about each class is written on a paper index card. Each card contains the name of the class and two lists: one list contains the *responsibilities* of the class (the things it must do) and the other list contains its *collaborations* with other classes that enable it to satisfy responsibilities that it cannot perform by itself. A related technique is *role playing*, in which the members of a design team each play the part of one of the objects in a system, especially exploring the messages that the objects send each other to accomplish certain goals. These techniques help developers to understand the behavior of a design without getting bogged down in coding details.

Different methods use a variety of other models and notations, but the purpose in all cases is to capture key information about some aspect of a system.

The Development Process

A *development process* is the advice that a method provides about how to develop a model. Some methods have very detailed processes while others are much

Class: Order	
responsibility	*collaborates with*
Know which items it contains	Item
Maintain its status	
Know the customer and date	Customer
Compute total price	Pricelist, Item
Record payments	Payment

Figure 4. Class-Responsibility-Collaboration (CRC) card for class Order.

looser. The development process may be evolutionary or translational. In an evolutionary process an initial model is developed that is then evolved into a final model by a series of small changes. For example, a model of the real-world objects in a system may be augmented with internal objects that help to perform the computation. In a translational process an initial model is developed that is then translated (using rules specified as part of the process) into a final model, which may be expressed in the same form or a different form from the initial model. Most published methods contain a mixture of evolutionary and translational steps.

The typical development process may be summarized as follows:

◆ Build models of the problem domain and application that capture the key aspects of the system requirements. Use the models to validate the requirements and to expose errors, ambiguities, and omissions by examining them for consistency and consulting domain experts. The terms in this model should be meaningful to practitioners of the problem domain.

◆ Decide how to implement the target application and then produce design models to capture the essential features of the design. In an evolutionary process the design models may be produced by gradual modification of the requirements models. The design model may include computer science concepts in addition to application domain concepts.

◆ Finally generate some programming language code from the final design models and write the remaining code by hand.

If the problem and its formulation are highly constrained, it may be possible to state the requirements model fully, then produce design models or final code by evolution or translation using a *linear* one-pass approach (often called a *waterfall* approach). In a more complicated system, especially if the requirements are not well known in advance, an *iterative* approach may work better; this consists of building a requirements model of part of the system, driving it forward to obtain a design model and executable code for part of the system, then iterating the entire sequence several times to implement the complete functionality of the entire system. An iterative approach can more easily accommodate changes, but may involve some redundant effort. A linear approach, however, risks much greater wasted effort if it should fail to converge quickly.

Note that this generic description of development processes applies to many non-object-oriented approaches as well. The focus on object-oriented models makes a process object-oriented.

Object-Oriented Methods

Early object-oriented methods with class models and behavioral models include OMT (Rumbaugh *et al.*, 1991), Booch (1994), Fusion (Coleman *et al.*, 1994), Coad–Yourdon, Shlaer–Mellor, and Martin–Odell. These models are similar, although there are slight differences in semantics and major differences in notation. Other popular methods with more behavioral focus include Objectory (Jacobson, 1992), ROOM (Selic *et al.*, 1994), and RDD (Wirfs-Brock *et al.*, 1990). More recent work has focused particularly on the development process.

Unified Modeling Language

The Unified Modeling Language (UML) began in 1994 as an attempt to unify the Booch and OMT models but quickly developed into a broadly based effort to standardize object-oriented modeling concepts, terminology, and notation. Ultimately researchers from 17 companies submitted a proposal to the Object Management Group (OMG) that was unanimously adopted as a standard in 1997 after extensive feedback from the general public. The UML specification contains a metamodel (a model of legal models) of modeling constructs, constraints on well-formed models, definitions of semantics of the constructs, and notation for expressing models visually. UML does not standardize the development process; it is intended to support many current and future processes. UML has been widely accepted by the object-oriented community to replace the plethora of earlier notations. The Object Management Group has the responsibility for future evolution of the UML.

Support Tools

Large system development requires the assistance of automated editing tools to construct, verify, and maintain large models. Such tools are available from a number of vendors. A typical full-featured model editing tool permits the interactive drawing of models, the ability to browse the model both graphically and textually, code generation and reverse engineering of existing code, and facilities for organizing models into modules and for coordinating the work of multidveloper teams. Tools perform bookkeeping that would otherwise be tedious and error-prone; they also edit and display model diagrams interactively and present different views of a model on user request. Different tools support a variety of target implementation media, including various programming languages, object-oriented and relational databases (*q.v.*), fourth generation language (4GL) systems, and certain specialized environments. Models can also be constructed without producing any target application, for example, to understand the structure of a business organization.

Bibliography

1990. Wirfs-Brock, R., Wilkerson, B., and Wiener, L. *Designing Object-Oriented Software*. Upper Saddle River, NJ: Prentice Hall.
1991. Rumbaugh, J., Blaha, M., Premerlani, W., Eddy, F., and Lorensen, W. *Object-Oriented Modeling and Design*. Upper Saddle River, NJ: Prentice Hall.
1992. Jacobson, I. *Object-Oriented Software Engineering*. Reading, MA: Addison-Wesley.
1994. Booch, G. *Object-Oriented Analysis and Design with Applications*, 2nd Ed. Redwood City, CA: Benjamin/Cummings.
1994. Coleman, D., Arnold, P., Bodoff, S., Dollin, C., Gilchrist, H., Hayes, F., and Jeremaes, P. *Object-Oriented Development: The Fusion Method*. Upper Saddle River, NJ: Prentice Hall.
1994. Selic, B., Gullekson, G., and Ward, P. T. *Real-Time Object-Oriented Modeling*. New York: John Wiley.
1995. Firesmith, D., and Eykholt, E. *Dictionary of Object Technology*. New York: SIGS Books.
1995. Goldberg, A., and Rubin, K. *Succeeding with Objects*. Reading, MA: Addison-Wesley.
1999. Rumbaugh, J., Booch, G., and Jacobson, I. *The Unified Modeling Language Reference Manual*. Reading, MA: Addison-Wesley.

James Rumbaugh

OBJECT-ORIENTED PROGRAMMING (OOP)

For articles on related subjects *see* ABSTRACT DATA TYPE; C++; CLASS; ENCAPSULATION; INFORMATION HIDING; JAVA; OBJECT-ORIENTED ANALYSIS AND DESIGN; PACKAGE; SIMULA; SOFTWARE ENGINEERING; SOFTWARE DESIGN PATTERNS; and STRUCTURED PROGRAMMING.

Introduction

The essence of object-oriented programming is to model systems of real entities with the goal of separating their internal structure from their external, visible interactions. It emphasizes the hiding or *encapsulation* of the "inner" state of entities and the specification of interactive properties of entities by an interface of operations (the events in which they may participate). This separates the inner functioning of entities like banks, aircraft, or people from their external behavior in interacting with other entities. The separation is realized by partitioning the state of a system of entities into chunks associated with objects so that each chunk is responsible for its own protection against access by unauthorized operations. In a concurrent environment, objects protect themselves against asynchronous access, removing the synchronization burden from processes that access the object's data.

A programming language is said to be *object-based* if it supports objects as a language feature, and is said to be *object-oriented* if, additionally, objects are required to belong to *classes* that can be incrementally modified through *inheritance* (whereby a class may *inherit* the capabilities of a base class and also extend or modify these capabilities). Among the object-oriented languages are Simula, Smalltalk, C++, Eiffel, Ada (*q.v.*), and Java, but not Fortran, C, or Pascal. Originally Ada was object-based, supporting the functionality of objects, but was not object-oriented, since it did not support the management of objects through classes and inheritance. The current Ada 95 standard, however, provides a type-extension mechanism to implement inheritance, and may thus be considered object-oriented.

Early programmers thought of programs as instruction sequences. Procedure-oriented languages (*q.v.*) introduced procedural abstractions that encapsulate sequences of actions into procedures. Object-oriented languages encapsulate data as well as sequences of actions, providing a stronger encapsulation mechanism than procedures and, consequently, a more powerful modeling tool. Both procedures and objects are server modules that may be called by clients to determine a stimulus/response behavior in interacting with their environment (*see* CLIENT–SERVER COMPUTING. The role of procedures is to transform input data specified by parameters into values, while the role of objects is to serve as a repository of data (the current system state) and to respond in a manner determined by the current system state. For example, the response of a bank to a withdrawal request depends on the value of the current balance. Object-oriented programming is a modeling paradigm that models objects of the real world by collections of interacting objects of a programming system.

The procedure-oriented paradigm has strong organizing principles for managing actions and algorithms, but has weak organizing principles for managing shared data, while object-oriented systems organize data by restricting applicable operations to those associated with a specific object or class. Inheritance provides a second layer of structure by structuring classes into hierarchies. We can think of classes as a mechanism for classifying objects into categories with similar interface behavior, and inheritance as a mechanism for classifying classes by factoring out properties common to several subclasses into a superclass.

Functional, logic-based, and procedure-oriented paradigms execute algorithms whose semantics are described by computable functions, while objects provide persistent services to clients over time that cannot be entirely described by computable functions. Objects determine interactive "marriage contracts" with clients over the lifetime of the object that cannot be entirely described by algorithmic "sales contracts" (Wegner, 1997). Objects can better model embedded systems, graphical user interfaces, and distributed systems than

procedures and algorithms, supporting more powerful forms of problem solving, like distributed ATM banking systems and airline reservation systems.

Objects

Objects in programming languages are collections of operations that share a state. The operations determine the messages (calls) to which the object can respond, while the shared state is hidden from the outside world and is accessible only to the object's operations (*see* Fig. 1). Variables representing the internal state of an object are called *instance variables* and its operations are called *methods*. The collection of methods of an object determines its *interface* and its behavior:

```
name:object
  local instance variables (shared state)
  operations or methods (interface of
      message patterns to which the
      object may respond)
```

An object named `point` with instance variables x, y and methods for reading and changing them may be defined as follows:

```
point:object
    x:=0; y:=0;
    read-x: ↑x; -return value of x
    read-y: ↑y; -return value of y
    change-x(dx):x:=x + dx;
    change-y(dy):y:=y + dy;
```

The object `point` protects its instance variables x, y against arbitrary access, allowing access only through messages to `read` and `change` operations. The object's behavior is entirely determined by its responses to acceptable messages and is independent of the data representation of its instance variables. Moreover, the object's knowledge of its callers is entirely determined by its messages. Object-oriented message-passing facilitates two-way abstraction: senders have an abstract view of receivers and receivers have an abstract view of senders.

An object's interface of operations (methods) can be represented by a record:

```
untyped object interface: (op1,op2,..,opN)
```

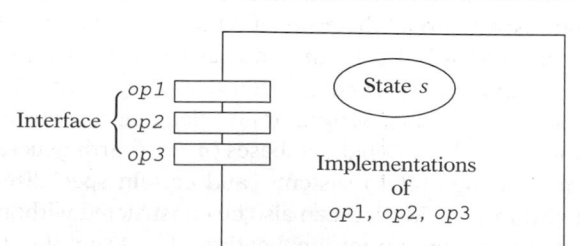

Figure 1. Object modules.

Objects whose operations `opi` have type `Ti` have an interface that is like a typed record, but differs from records in that fields of object records may be interdependent because of the shared state. Typed record interfaces are called *signatures*.

```
Typed Object Interface (Signature):
              (op1:T1,op2:T2,..,opN:TN)
```

The `point` object has the following signature:

```
point-interface =
    (read-x: Real,
     read-y: Real,
     change-x: Real → Real,
     change-y: Real → Real)
```

The parameterless operations `read-x` and `read-y` both return a **Real** number as their value, while `change-x` and `change-y` expect a **Real** number as their argument and return a **Real** result.

The operations of an object share its state so that state changes by one operation may be seen by subsequently executed operations. Operations access the state by references to the object's instance variables. For example, `read-x` and `change-x` share the instance variable x, which is nonlocal to these operations, although local to the object.

Nonlocal references in functions and procedures are generally considered harmful, but they are essential for operations within objects, since they are the only mechanism by which an object's operations can access its internal state. Sharing unprotected data within an object is combined with strong protection (encapsulation) against external access. The strong encapsulation at the object interface is realized at the expense of modularity (and reusability) of component operations. This captures the distinction within any organization or organism between closely integrated internal subsystems and contractually specified interfaces to the outside world.

Classes

We distinguish between object-based languages that support objects as a language primitive and object-oriented languages that additionally support the management of objects through classes (*q.v*) and inheritance. In object-oriented languages, the behavior of objects is specified by classes, which are like the types of traditional languages, but serve additionally to classify objects into hierarchies through the inheritance mechanism.

Classes serve as templates from which objects can be created. They are record-structured templates whose instantiation creates objects whose interfaces are record-structured. The class `point` has precisely the same instance variables and operations as the object

point, but their interpretation is different. Whereas the instance variables of a `point` object represent *actual* variables, class instance variables are *potential*, being instantiated only when an object is created:

```
point:class
  local instance variables
    (private copy for each object of the class)
  operations or methods (shared by all
    objects of the class)
```

Instances of a class can be created by a make-instance operation, which creates a copy of the class instance variables that may be acted on by the class operations:

```
p:= make-instance point; -- create a new
        instance of the class point, call it p
```

Instance variables in class definitions may be initialized as part of object creation:

```
p1:= make-instance point (0,0); -- create
        point initialized to (0,0), call it p1
p2:= make-instance point (1,1); -- create
        point initialized to (1,1), call it p2
```

The two points p1, p2 each have private copies of the class instance variables and share the operations specified in the class definition. When an object receives a message to execute a method, it looks for the method in its class definition. We may think of a class as specifying a behavior common to all objects of the class. The instance variables specify a data structure (*q.v.*) for realizing the behavior. The public operations of a class determine its behavior, while the private instance variables determine its structure.

Inheritance

Inheritance is a mechanism for sharing code and behavior. It allows reuse of the behavior of a class in the definition of new classes. Subclasses of a class inherit the operations of their parent class and may add new operations and new instance variables.

Fig. 2 describes mammals by an inheritance hierarchy of classes (representing behaviors). The class of mammals has persons and elephants as its subclasses. The class of persons has mammals as its superclass and students and females as its subclasses. The instances John, Joan, Bill, Mary, and Dumbo each have a unique base class. In *single inheritance*, illustrated here, membership of an instance in more than one base class, such as Joan being both a student and a female, cannot be expressed. We discuss *multiple inheritance* below.

Why does inheritance play such an important role in object-oriented programming? Inheritance can express relations among behaviors such as classification,

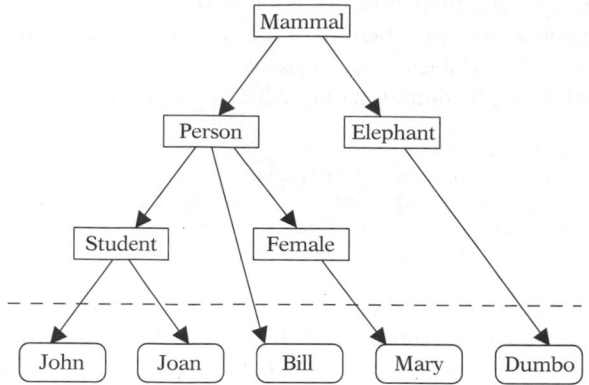

Figure 2. Example of an inheritance hierarchy.

specialization, generalization, approximation, and evolution. Thus, in Fig. 2 we classify mammals into persons and elephants. Elephants specialize the properties of mammals, and conversely mammals generalize the properties of elephants. The properties of mammals approximate those of elephants. Moreover, elephants evolved from early species of mammals.

Inheritance classifies classes in much the same way that classes classify values. The ability to classify classes provides greater classification power and conceptual modeling power. Classification of classes may be referred to as second-order classification. Inheritance provides second-order sharing, management, and manipulation of behavior that complements first-order management of objects by classes.

Inheritance can be expressed by record extension. If a class is specified by a record $\langle$op1:T1, op2:T2$\rangle$ then inheritance can extend this record by horizontal extension that adds one or more new operations and by vertical extension that modifies existing operations. The Oberon language, a successor to Pascal (*q.v.*) and Modula-2, uses record extension to implement inheritance, as does Modula-3. Languages like Self abandon inheritance at the class level in favor of *delegation*, which is a form of inheritance at the object level that is more flexible than inheritance in handling objects that may change their class, like students who become professors, or lawyers who become judges. In delegation, if an object of a subclass is called upon to execute an operation defined in a parent class, it delegates that operation to the parent class, e.g. by sending it a message. If an object changes its class, it can then delegate such an operation to the new parent.

Virtual classes are incomplete behavior specifications that require subclasses to complete their behavior specification before they can be instantiated. The class of mammals in Fig. 2 is a virtual class. It specifies behavioral attributes common to all mammals and must be supplemented by behavioral attributes of

specific mammals (persons or elephants) before instances like Joan and Dumbo can be created. Summarizing:

- *virtual class*: incomplete behavior specification, cannot be directly instantiated (mammals)

- *subclass*: completes virtual behavior specification (persons or elephants)

Incomplete behaviors are natural building blocks in constructing composite behavior specifications. Composition of incomplete behaviors during program development may be contrasted with modification of already complete behaviors during maintenance and enhancement.

Tree (*q.v.*) structure is a general mechanism for sharing of the properties of ancestors by descendants. Just as block structure facilitates the sharing of data declared in ancestor blocks by descendant blocks, inheritance hierarchies facilitate the sharing of code and behavior of superclasses by subclasses.

Multiple inheritance, which supports subclasses that share the behavior of several superclasses, gives rise to more complex structures, such as directed graphs (*see* GRAPH THEORY), since a subclass can inherit from several parents. It is natural in some contexts, but is conceptually complex in part because classes mix specification and implication in a single language construct. C++ and Eiffel have multiple inheritance; Simula and Smalltalk have single inheritance. Java separates the notion of interfaces as behavior specifications from the notion of classes as implementations, and permits multiple inheritance of interfaces to be specified in a cleaner way than is possible for multiple inheritance of classes.

Implementation of Class Inheritance

The following implementation of inheritance is simple, though not the most efficient. Consider a class *A* with instance *a* and a subclass *B* with instance *b*, as in Fig. 3. Both *A* and *B* define behavior by operations shared by their instances, and have instance variables that cause a private copy to be created for each instance of the class or subclass. The instance *a* of *A* has a copy of *A*'s instance variables and a pointer to its base class. The instance *b* of *B* has a copy of the instance variables of both *B* and its superclass *A* and a pointer to the base class of *B*. The class representation of *B* has a pointer to its superclass *A*, while *A* has no superclass pointer, since it is assumed to have no superclass.

When *b* receives a message to execute a method, it looks first in the methods of *B*. If found, the method is executed using the instance variables of *b* as data. Otherwise, the pointer to its superclass is followed. If

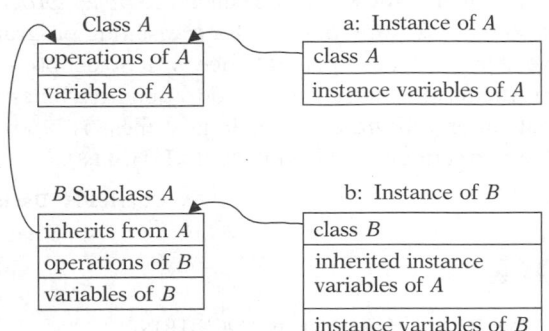

Figure 3. Implementation of inheritance.

it finds the method in *A*, it executes it on the data of *b*. Otherwise, it searches *A*'s superclass if there is one. If *A* has no superclass and the method has not been found, it reports failure. This search algorithm may be defined by the following procedure:

```
procedure search (name, class)
    if (name = localname) then
        do localaction
    else if (inherited-module = nil)
        then undefinedname
    else
        ocarch (name, inherited-module)
```

Actual implementations avoid the run-time search for the appropriate method. When a program is compiled, the compiler can determine in what class or superclass any method is declared, and can generate the code needed to invoke it at run time. There are two possible complications. If the language provides multiple inheritance, then any call of a multiply-inherited method must specify which version is meant, which may be done as in C++ by attaching the parent class name to the method name: `parent_class:: method_name`.

The other complication arises because it is possible for a method binding to change dynamically, as when a function in a virtual class is bound to a specific operation. A common technique is to maintain a *virtual methods table* (VMT) for each class. An object has a pointer to its VMT, and if a run-time assignment changes the binding (e.g. if an elephant becomes a circus-elephant), only the VMT pointer must change. The VMT requires an extra step to look up each function, but no run-time searching.

Evolution of Object-Oriented Programming

Simula 67 (Dahl *et al.*, 1968) was the first object-oriented language. Its language primitives included objects, classes, and inheritance, and it was used extensively for simulation and other applications, primarily in Europe. Smalltalk (Goldberg and Robson, 1983),

developed by the software concepts group at Xerox PARC in the 1970s and embodied in a stable implementation in Smalltalk 80, caught the public imagination because of its implementation on personal computers and its interactive graphical interface that permitted browsing and the display of objects in multiple windows. Smalltalk implementations were initially too slow to be commercially viable, but in the 1990s became increasingly competitive with traditional languages.

The US Department of Defense language Ada (*q.v.*) included the notion of packages, which are like objects, but did not have a notion of classes or inheritance in its 1983 version. Starting in the mid-1980s, object-oriented programming became a popular term, and object-oriented dialects of existing programming languages began to appear, like Object-Pascal, Objective C, and C++. C++ has proven to be a popular object-oriented language because it is upward compatible with C.

The preeminence of C++ as the dominant object-oriented programming language is being challenged by Java, which has a cleaner design, built-in threads that support concurrency (*see* CONCURRENT PROGRAMMING), an impressive collection of class libraries for graphical user interfaces and system software, and excellent documentation through textbooks written by the language designers. Java is increasingly being adopted as a language for first courses in computing and has a chance of displacing C++ as the dominant object-oriented language.

As object-oriented technology is being adopted by the software engineering community, attention is shifting from object-oriented languages to object-oriented design, epitomized by design methods like OMT, UML and OOAD (*see* OBJECT-ORIENTED ANALYSIS AND DESIGN), and component software (*q.v.*) systems like CORBA/OpenDoc, COM/OLE/ActiveX, and Java/JavaBeans. There is also much work on computer-aided software engineering (CASE—*q.v.*) tools for object-oriented programming. There is no doubt that object-oriented technology is a permanent part of the computer landscape. Object-oriented systems are not merely a more scalable technology for design; they are actually more expressive than procedure-oriented technology and allow systems that provide services over time to be designed in an integrated fashion that could not be designed in the procedure-oriented paradigm without introducing *ad hoc* shared data structures.

Is Object-Oriented Programming Fundamental?

The popularity of object-oriented programming in the late 1980s and 1990s rivals the fashionability of structured programming (*q.v.*) in the 1970s. It provides high-level structure in objects, classes, and class hierarchies, complementing structured programming techniques for microstructure at the level of statements and expressions. Object-oriented programming is more specific and comprehensive in its prescription for problem solving than structured programming is. The latter is concerned with "structure" in general, while object-oriented programming focuses on a specific form of structure: that associated with objects.

Modeling entities by their behavior (their response to messages) is a central principle of scientific method in many disciplines: behaviorism in psychology, operationalism in physics, and Platonic ideals in philosophy. Objects are a canonical form of description for any discipline or domain of discourse. Its universality as a representation, modeling, and abstraction technique supports the view that the object-oriented paradigm is conceptually and computationally fundamental.

Bibliography

1968. Dahl, O. J., Myrhaag, B., and Nygaard, K. *Simula 67 Common Base Language.* Norwegian Computing Center. Revised in 1970, 1972, and 1984.

1983. *Reference Manual for the Ada Programming Language.* US Dept of Defense.

1983. Goldberg, A., and Robson, D. *Smalltalk 80: The Language and its Implementation.* Reading, MA: Addison-Wesley.

1990. Wegner, P. "Concepts and Paradigms of Object-Oriented Programming," *OOPS Messenger*, **1**, *1* (August), 7–87.

1991. Rumbaugh, J., Blaha, M., Premerlani, W., Eddy, F., and Lorensen, W. *Object-Oriented Modeling and Design.* Upper Saddle River, NJ: Prentice Hall.

1997. Wegner P. "Why Interaction is More Powerful than Algorithms," *Comm. of the ACM*, **40**, *5* (May), 80–91.

1998. Arnold, K., and Gosling, J. *The Java Programming Language*, 2nd Ed. Reading, MA: Addison-Wesley.

Peter Wegner

OBJECT PROGRAM

For articles on related subjects *see* LANGUAGE PROCESSORS; LINKERS AND LOADERS; PROCEDURE-ORIENTED LANGUAGES; and SOURCE PROGRAM.

An *object program* is the output of a translating program, such as an assembler or a compiler, which converts a *source program* written in one language into another language, such as machine language, capable of being executed on a given computer.

This output may be in one of several forms: It may be in an intermediate language (*q.v.*), needing further translating; it may be *relocatable*, in which data and program references are still expressed relative to a base address; or it may be *absolute*, in which all linkages between program elements have been made and absolute address assignments established so that the program is ready to be loaded and executed. Usage varies

as to which of these may be called the *object program*. In some sense, any output of a translating program is the object of that step, and hence is an object program, but the term is most often used to denote a binary file that, after *linking* to other binary files, is ready for direct execution (*see* LINKERS AND LOADERS).

Charles H. Davidson

OCR

See OPTICAL CHARACTER RECOGNITION.

OFFICE AUTOMATION

See ELECTRONIC OFFICE.

ONLINE CONVERSATION

For articles on related subjects *see* BULLETIN BOARD; COMPUTER CONFERENCING; ELECTRONIC MAIL; GROUPWARE; INTERNET; and WORLD WIDE WEB.

Online conversation is communication between two or more participants in which there is little or no perceived delay between sending a message and it being received and read. Whereas electronic mail may be compared to sending or receiving a letter by post, online communications are very much like conversations carried out in person or on a telephone.

Two online conversation methods whose popularity and use grew explosively in the late 1990s are Instant Messaging (IM) and Chat. IM extends a service to the Internet that had been available on many time-shared computer systems for years. This service would typically allow a user to determine whether another user was logged in and, if so, to send a message directly to his or her terminal, or to open up a two-way "talk" session with split screens for the two sides of the conversation. IM services make this possible on the Internet via a "Buddy List" of the set of online users with whom a user may exchange instant messages. In order to use this service, an Internet user must run an IM program which displays the Buddy List. These programs connect to specialized servers which keep track of everyone currently running that IM program as well as which of these users have "buddied" with which other users. When a user on someone's list comes online (and runs a copy of the IM program), the first user's list will indicate that this user is online (and vice versa) and will allow instant messaging. When a message is sent it usually pops up in a window on the recipient's computer screen. If the recipient chooses to reply, a conversation is begun.

IM was first popularized by America Online and brought to the Internet largely by Mirabalis' ICQ (pronounced "I seek you") product (Mirabalis, an Israeli company, was subsequently purchased by AOL). Eventually other entrants to the IM market included Yahoo! with Yahoo! Messenger and Microsoft with Microsoft Messenger. As of mid-1999 these online communities were isolated from one another, and users in one could not send IMs to users in the others. However, standards organizations have done work to build bridges between the communities and it seems likely that at some point IM will become as universal to the Internet as the phone system is to the outside world.

IM is effectively an online version of email. Chat, on the other hand, may be thought of as an interactive version of the bulletin board communities that grew up in the early years of the Internet. Chat is an electronic conversation between several participants, usually centered in a virtual place (often called a "chat room"). The participants rendezvous at that virtual place and using specialized software send messages which are seen by all the users currently in that room. Chat, like IM, evolved from early time-shared programs which allowed users to communicate in real time. In the late 1970s MUDs, or Multi-User Dungeons, appeared. A MUD is a fantasy-based game in which multiple participants play (and chat) with one another. In 1988 Jarkko Oikarinen wrote a program called the Internet Relay Chat (IRC) which brought multiperson conversations to the Internet. It was designed to replace "talk" and became an institution on the net. MUDs were quickly adapted to use IRC and to open the games to users throughout the Internet. (These games proved very popular and a number of variations quickly sprung up, notably programmable versions in which the games could be easily expanded. MUSH's (Multi-User Shared Hallucinations) and MOO's (MUD, Object-Oriented) are two of the most common programmable MUDs. *See* http://www.lysator. liu.se/mud/faq/faq1.html and http://www. moo.mud.org/moo-faq/.) Meanwhile, America Online has offered chat services to its online community for years. In the late 1990s chat moved with the Internet into the mainstream and many new Internet chat services quickly sprung up. The most popular of such services, Yahoo! Chat, includes hundreds of chat rooms through which users may virtually stroll searching for a conversation that interests them. Also popular are "event chats," in which celebrities and others participate in chat conversations with fans, and private chat rooms in which, for example, only members of a family can communicate with each other.

Bibliography

1993. Oikarinen, J., and Reed, D. "Internet Relay Chat Protocol," *Request for Comments 1459* (May). http://www. ietf.org/rfc/rfc1459.txt.

1999. Day, M., and Rosenberg, J. "A Model for Presence and Instant Messaging," *Internet Draft, Internet Engineering Task Force* (June). http://www.ietf.org/ids.by.wg/ impp.html.

1999. Day, M., Mohr, G., Aggarwal, S., and Vincent, J. "Instant Messaging/Presence Protocol Requirements," *Internet Draft, Internet Engineering Task Force* (June). http://www. ietf.org/ids.by.wg/impp.html.

1999. http://www.apocalypse.org/pub/u/lpb/ muddex/. *The MUDdex* (History of MUDs).

1999. http://www.irchelp.org. IRC help site: includes FAQ, tutorial, etc.

Geoff Ralston

ONLINE INFORMATION SERVICES

For articles on related subjects *see* BULLETIN BOARD; DIGITAL LIBRARY; ELECTRONIC MAIL; INFORMATION RETRIEVAL; INTERNET; and WORLD WIDE WEB.

An *online information service* is a kind of current awareness system—a service for notifying an individual of newly published or newly created information in the area of the person's interest. While some current awareness services consist of predefined special interests, others allow the users of the service to define their own search criteria or areas of interest.

The daily newspaper, with its category sections on world news, local news, sports, weather, entertainment, etc. is a ubiquitous example of a current awareness service—in the broadest sense of the concept—that has successfully helped generations of people keep abreast of new information in their areas of interest. And for several hundred years, specialized journals, both scholarly and popular, have served the same function for specialized areas of research.

The explosion of knowledge and information dissemination after the Second World War created a need for more effective and more focused tools to keep scholars and researchers abreast of the latest developments in their areas of interest. Selective Dissemination of Information (SDI) was the first computer-based current awareness system. It was developed by researchers at IBM in the late 1950s, and quickly became the most common computer-based current awareness tool. It consisted of automatic searching of specialized computer-based bibliographic abstracts and indexes (A&I), using search arguments selected by users or by trained searchers familiar with users' interests. After an initial search, only updates to the A&I database would be searched to insure that the user of the service received only newly published information.

Many specialized libraries and commercial services developed SDI systems that provided researchers and scholars with both the results of the search—done either manually by librarians or other information professionals, or automatically by computer-generated searches—and, if the library or information service had the appropriate journal issue, with the actual text of the published work.

The development of commercial online database services in the 1970s formed the foundation of modern online information services. DIALOG, ORBIT and BRS began offering online access to hundreds of A&I databases via emerging telecommunications networks such as Telenet and Tymnet. By1980 all three systems offered an SDI service consisting of automatic searching of new additions to selected databases based on user defined profiles, and the mailing of the subsequent retrieved citations to users on an ongoing basis.

With the development of the Internet in the 1980s came programs that laid the groundwork for the Internet-based current awareness tools in use today. Communication services such as listservers and Usenet newsgroups were among the first Internet services to develop, and they provided means for researchers in specialized areas to communicate with each other. Many such lists and newsgroups now serve as information services for researchers and others. Electronic mail, another early Internet communication service, is now an integral component of many Internet-based information services.

The need for effective Internet searching tools led to the development of Gopher, a server-based menu-presentation protocol developed at the University of Minnesota. It enabled the creation of menus by which Internet users could locate information among many Internet sites and its use quickly spread throughout academic and research communities. Gopher was followed by the development of the Wide Area Information Server (WAIS) by Brewster Kahle, working at the then computer manufacturer Thinking Machines, Inc. WAIS was a bibliographic and full text client–server (*q.v.*) search and retrieval protocol that enabled Internet users to search simultaneously both bibliographic and full-text databases at multiple Internet sites. At about the sametime, Tim Berners-Lee developed the Hypertext Markup Language (HTML) (*see* MARKUP LANGUAGES) and the HyperText Transfer Protocol (HTTP) for retrieving and presenting text, graphic images, and audio over the Internet, and the Universal Resource Locator (URL), a file linking protocol that allowed users to access linked resources quickly on any host connected to the Internet. In the early 1990s Marc Andreessen of the National Center for Supercomputer Applications (NCSA) at the University of Illinois developed and freely distributed easy-to-use software based on HTML (*see* ENTREPRENEURS). The World Wide Web—or simply the Web, as it has come to be known—became the *de facto* Internet information presentation tool. Gopher use has all but vanished since the Web became ubiquitous.

By 1996 most Internet access was via Web clients—or browsers as they came to be called—accessing Web servers at host sites. The Internet itself had become the *de facto* networked computer environment of the modern era. This ubiquitous adoption of HTML provided a common computer environment for both electronic communication and publication and led to the rapid growth of the Internet, especially for commercial purposes. At the same time, search engines compatible with Web browsers and able to search multiple Internet sites—such as AltaVista, developed by the Digital Equipment Corporation—quickly supplanted the use of WAIS.

Based on these communication services and searching capabilities, many new types of current awareness services for Internet-based information have been developed recently. Many of these services are commercial and are sold to both individuals and institutions, while others are provided by information centers and academic libraries for their clientele. As Web search engines become increasingly sophisticated, many new current awareness services, based on these search engines and on rapidly developing HTML and XML standards, are being offered to the general public. Search engines are now frequently just one component of Web "portals" that provide general and customized information services on numerous topics. Some of these mass market services charge information seekers, while others rely on advertising revenue.

Among the newer types of current awareness tools spawned by the rise of the Internet are "webliographies," narrowcasting, and intelligent agents. A webliography, as the name implies, is the Internet equivalent of the bibliography. They are typically developed and maintained by librarians at higher education institutions, but because they describe Internet-based information, they are by nature dynamic and are frequently updated. Most webliographies have a current awareness service as part of the webliography, or they point to other available Internet-based current awareness services.

Narrowcasting, some forms of which have come to be known as "push technology," is an Internet "broadcast" service that can be individually tailored by each person who receives the service. Providing news tailored to individual interests is at present the most common use of this technology. An intelligent agent is client software that searches the Internet for information of interest to the user. These types of program are designed, through feedback, to become ever more adept at retrieving the information that best meets the user's requirements. Intelligent agents can run in the background while the computer is unattended or while the user is doing other things.

In addition to the development of these new services, traditional library catalogs are evolving into comprehensive information systems that feature SDI services coupled with the delivery of full text for journal articles available via the Internet. Many universities now give students and faculty the ability to fill out search profiles on the Web. These profiles are then used to search selected A&I databases, and the results of the search are sent to the searcher via email. After viewing the abstracts, users can often order the full text of the article via either online or offline delivery.

Internet search tools are becoming increasingly sophisticated. Together with the development of common Internet protocols for the transport and display of multimedia information, they are continuing to increase the percentage of the world's information output that is available on the Internet. And these trends in turn are giving rise to the development of ever more effective tools for keeping information seekers aware of current information in their areas of interest. With respect to Internet use, there is a clear trend toward the merger of current awareness systems with information retrieval in general—for scholars, for students, and for the general public.

Bibliography

1981. Harper, L. G. "A comparative review of BRS, DIALOG and ORBIT," *References Services Review*, **9**, *1* (January), 39–51.
1995. Hamilton, F. *Current Awareness, Current Techniques.* Aldershot, UK, Brookfield, VT: Ashgate Publishing.

Websites

Search engines general:
Alta Vista: www.altavista.com (Has a nice language translation feature)
AOL Net Find: www.aol.com/netfind (Widely used because of number of AOL users)
Ask Jeeves: www.ask.com (Allows full-sentence English queries)
Excite: www.excite.com
Fast Search: www.alltheweb.com
Go/Infoseek: www.go.com
Google: www.google.com
GoTo: www.goto.com
Hot Bot: www.hotbot.com
Lycos: www.lycos.com
Northern Light: www.northernlight.com (Indexes largest percentage of the Web)
Phoaks: www.phoaks.com (Searches Usenet sites and classifies information)
Snap: www.snap.com (Noted for relevant responses)
Yahoo!: www.yahoo.com (Highly organized categories)

Metasearch engines (that invoke several of the above, plus others, and combine the results):
Dogpile: www.dogpile.com
Infind: www.infind.com
Metacrawler: www.metacrawler.com
Metasearch: www.metasearch.com
ProFusion: www.profusion.com
Savvy Search: www.savvysearch.com

David Dorman

OPEN AND CLOSE A FILE

For articles on related subjects *see* BLOCK AND BLOCKING FACTOR; FILE; INPUT–OUTPUT CONTROL SYSTEM; and LOGICAL AND PHYSICAL NAMES.

A file is considered *open* when it may be accessed for reading, writing, or possibly both. It is considered *closed* when it cannot be so accessed. An *open* routine changes the state of a file from closed to open; a *close* routine does the opposite.

The open and close routines are the primary mechanisms by which various parameters in the logical device tables and physical device tables are initialized, or stored, and the associations between logical and physical device tables are maintained. The open and close routines also handle the initialization and update of tape and file labels. After the open routines have been executed, all data needed for further processing is available in the appropriate table. When a file has been closed, the file is in a state suitable for subsequent reopening.

When a program opens a data file, it often declares a number of attributes that the file will have. It is the responsibility of the open routines to initialize the proper table entries to reflect the declared attributes. For example, a file typically may be opened for reading only, writing only, or in some cases for both reading and writing (update). As another example, most systems allow a programmer to create a *scratch file* for temporary storage of data during program execution. In such cases, the temporary file is usually destroyed automatically at the end of the job or interactive session.

Upon receipt of a request to open an existing permanent file, the open routines must first find the file, which usually involves the accessing of the system directories. In MS-DOS, for example, the device name (A:, B:, C:, etc.) must often be supplied to resolve ambiguity. With indexed sequential files where the index is to be kept in main storage, the open routines will locate the index and read it into an internal buffer (*q.v.*).

The next task is one of label verification and initialization of logical and physical device tables with parameters that are carried in the file description block. These parameters will be copied to the proper fields in the logical and physical device tables.

The open routines will also set the read/write/update status so that subsequent requests can be checked for validity. If the file is to be written, then a fresh directory entry must be created, giving the date written, the edition number (multiple copies of files with the same name are updated by editions, much like newspapers), and other pertinent data.

File directory information is stored with the file and gives information concerning blocking factors, storage allocation, and storage organization. The storage organization information will often be complex. For example, the strategy to be used when storing new records that might not fit in a given storage area (*overflow policies*) would be part of the file control information for some files stored on a disk.

The routines to close a file have a number of tasks to perform before the file is ready for subsequent reopening. First, some of the data that has been logically "written" may still reside in a buffer because the buffer was not full and no physical "write" had yet been generated. The close routines will cause actual transfer of data to the recording medium. For this reason, closing a file that was open for writing—and doing so prior to the end of program execution—is much more important than closing a file that was merely opened for reading. If the file resides on tape, an end-of-file marker and perhaps also an end-of-file label will then be written. Alternatively, if the file is on a direct-access device, the close routine will restore indices and file directory information, updating such parameters as the size of the file in bytes. Closing a temporary file usually results in the release of the allotted file space.

Closing a file also results in the logical device table for the appropriate logical device being restored to a state that indicates that there is no file currently attached to this device. This allows subsequent requests on the logical device to be invalidated.

Robert W. Taylor

OPEN ARCHITECTURE

For articles on related subjects *see* BIOS; BUS; DIGITAL COMPUTERS, HISTORY OF; MOTHERBOARD; and PERSONAL COMPUTING.

The term "open architecture" is of recent vintage and pertains primarily to personal computers. An *open architecture* is one that allows insertion of additional logic cards to the interior of the computer chassis beyond those used with the most primitive configuration of the system. This is done by inserting the cards into *slots* in the computer's *motherboard* (*q.v.*), the main logic board that holds its central processing unit (CPU—*q.v.*) and memory chips. A computer vendor who adopts such a design knows full well that, since the electronic characteristics of the motherboard slots will be public knowledge, other vendors who wish to do so can design and market customized logic cards. The rationale is that the greater the variety of cards marketed, the greater will be sales of the host computer itself. The logic cards provide a host of services,

such as one form of hard disk (*q.v.*), greater degrees of color graphics resolution, supplemental memory, sound, and enhanced floating-point processing power through use of *coprocessor* boards.

Interestingly, a reversal of position with regard to the merits of an open architecture has played a significant role in the commercial history of Apple Computer (*q.v.*). Its initial, highly successful products, the Apple I and II (particularly the latter) used an open architecture, whereas its Macintosh line used a closed architecture. Just as significantly, about the time of introduction of the Macintosh, IBM brought out its PC, which was based on an open architecture. The combination of open architecture and a bus and BIOS system that were easy to reverse-engineer led to the marketing of a plethora of IBM-PC compatibles which, perhaps more than any other factor, led to the rapid growth of personal computing. The Macintosh, which was more difficult to clone, also enjoyed sales success, but not to the same degree as the aggregate of PC-compatible products.

Software can also be constructed to be compatible with other software through a choice of standard, public formats and interfaces. The term *open architecture* applies to such software as well as to hardware, and the interest in component software (*q.v.*) reflects a growing demand for open software architecture. As with hardware, software providers may choose to lock in customers through a closed architecture, or to increase demand for a product by designing it to be readily coupled with other software, including packages from other suppliers.

Edwin D. Reilly

OPEN SYSTEMS INTERCONNECTION (OSI)

For articles on related subjects *see* COMMUNICATIONS AND COMPUTERS; DATA COMMUNICATIONS: STANDARDS; GATEWAY; NETWORK PROTOCOLS; and PROTOCOL.

Two computer systems can communicate successfully only if they are prepared to use the same set of communication *protocols*. If machines from different manufacturers each use their own unique protocol, they will not generally be able to communicate. Each machine could, in principle, be provided with facilities for translating foreign protocols, but if the range of systems involved is large, this becomes a burdensome task.

The alternative is for all machines to use the same set of protocols so that no translation is needed. The objective of the *open systems interconnection* (OSI) is to create a single set of standard protocols, drawing on the best features of existing practice. Use of the OSI protocols thus opens the possibility of communication between any two computer systems, regardless of their origin.

The term "open" is used here in the sense of freedom from technical barriers to communication. The decision as to what information should be communicated and when communication should take place must be taken by the owner of each system, and the OSI standards include the facilities to provide the security mechanisms that may be necessary.

The OSI standards define only the protocols between systems. They do not constrain the internal structure of the systems that use them, because to do so would limit the freedom of the vendors to improve their designs. Thus, the same protocol may be used to convey information between systems with totally different internal structures and user interfaces. In testing that a system conforms to the published standard, only the data that flows between them is considered.

The work to create the set of OSI standards was begun by the International Organization for Standardization in 1978. The first step was the creation of the OSI Reference Model, the communication architecture that provides a framework for the various component standards making up the OSI family of protocols. This was followed by a series of standards for the individual members of the family, which were published one by one throughout the 1980s.

The OSI Reference Model divides the process of communication into a number of functional layers, splitting it up into pieces that are small enough to handle and specify separately. The layers build up progressively, starting from the underlying electrical signals transmitted to a much more abstract description of the user activity that exploits the communication.

Two types of standard are defined for each layer. The first is a *service definition*, which states what the layer does on behalf of the layers above, so that higher layers are shielded from lower layer detail. The second is the *protocol specification*, which sets out how the layer performs its function, and achieves the service by defining the messages actually exchanged using the services of the layer below and the actions taken in consequence.

The OSI Reference Model defines seven layers of protocol (Fig. 1). Starting from the most abstract, these provide the following functions:

Level 7 The *application layer* performs the functions that are the reason for the communication. They are determined or selected by the enterprise using the network. Only some of these can be standardized.

Level 6 The *presentation layer* manages the problems of format and encoding between the two systems, providing a typed data channel.

Level 5 The *session layer* provides tools for the structuring of the dialogue between the two application entities.

Level 4 The *transport layer* handles problems of end-to-end reliability and quality of service.

Level 3 The *network layer* allows networks to be used in combination and handles problems of routing and switching.

Level 2 The *data link layer* provides an orderly error-free path between adjacent systems.

Level 1 The *physical layer* is concerned with electrical compatibility (or its equivalent in optical or radio transmission systems).

Bibliography

1988. Henshall, J., and Shaw, S. *OSI Explained: End-to-End Computer Communication Standards.* New York: Ellis Horwood.
1993. Hebrawi, B. *Open Systems Interconnection: Upper Layer Standards and Practices.* New York: McGraw-Hill.

Peter F. Linington

OPERAND

For articles on related subjects *see* ADDRESSING; ARGUMENT; COMPUTERS, MULTIPLE ADDRESS; EXPRESSION; and POLISH NOTATION.

An *operand* is an entity on which operations are performed. In a typical computer, an instruction will specify an operation such as FETCH, ADD, MOVE, MULTIPLY, or EDIT. It will also usually specify one or more operands (*see* Fig. 1). The operands are the data items that will be fetched, added, moved, multiplied, edited, etc.

In some special cases the operand itself may be contained in the instruction, in which case it is usually

| Application |
| Presentation |
| Session |
| Transport |
| Network |
| Data link |
| Physical |
| Physical medium |

Figure 1. The seven OSI protocol layers.

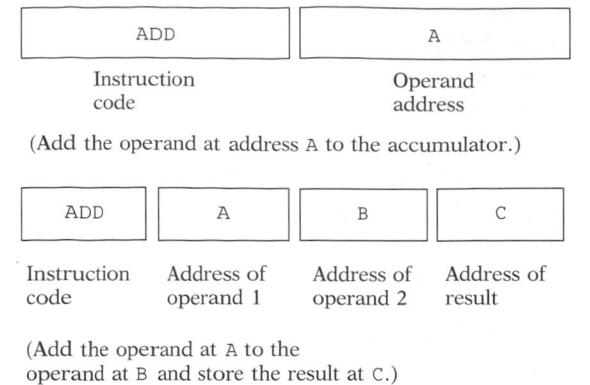

Figure 1. Typical single operand and multiple operand computer instructions.

called *immediate*. Usually, the instruction contains a memory address, or a number of fields from which a memory address can be calculated. That memory address is then a pointer (*q.v.*) that points to the operand and that permits the operand to be retrieved.

Many computers provide single-precision arithmetic operations in which the operands are numbers stored in single computer words. Some provide double-precision or multiple-precision operations in which operands may occupy two, three, or more words each.

In many non-arithmetic operations (and even in some arithmetic ones), the operands are strings of characters (or bytes). The operand address points to the beginning of the string. The extent of the string may be specified in the instruction, but in many cases it is determined by a count field or by a termination code in the operand itself.

Saul Rosen

OPERATING SYSTEMS

> For articles on related subjects *see* ACCOUNTING SYSTEM, COMPUTER; BOOTSTRAP; CACHE MEMORY; CLIENT–SERVER COMPUTING; CONCURRENT PROGRAMMING; DIRECTORY; DISTRIBUTED SYSTEMS; FILE SERVER; INTERRUPT; KERNEL; LOGIN FILE; MEMORY MANAGEMENT; MEMORY PROTECTION; MULTIPLEXING; MULTIPROCESSING; MULTIPROGRAMMING; MULTITASKING; PARALLEL PROCESSING; PRIVILEGED INSTRUCTION; QUEUEING THEORY; SCHEDULING ALGORITHMS; SHELL; SUPERVISOR CALL; SWAPPING; TCP/IP; THRASHING; THROUGHPUT; TIME SHARING; UNIX OPERATING SYSTEM; USER INTERFACE; VIRTUAL MEMORY; WINDOW ENVIRONMENTS; and WORKING SET.

GENERAL PRINCIPLES

Introduction

Early *operating systems* were control programs a few thousand bytes long that scheduled jobs, drove peripheral devices, and kept track of system usage for billing purposes. Modern operating systems are much larger, ranging from hundreds of thousands of bytes for personal computers (e.g. MS-DOS, Xenix) to tens of millions of bytes for mainframes (e.g. Honeywell's Multics, IBM's MVS, AT&T's Unix) and hundreds of millions of bytes for some servers (Microsoft's Windows NT). In addition to managing processors, memory, and dozens of input–output devices, modern operating systems also provide numerous services such as Internet communications, Web communications, interprocess communications, file and directory systems, data transfer over local networks, and command languages and graphical user interfaces for invoking and controlling programs. These high-level services hide the primitive facilities of the base computer, such as interrupts, status registers, and device interfaces, from the user. The operating system builds its high-level services by wrapping the low-level hardware facilities in layers of software, resulting in a powerful virtual machine that is much easier to use than the basic hardware. Thus an operating system provides two classes of functions: orderly allocation of computing resources among processes contending for them, and an extended machine that provides a powerful programming environment. These two classes are not independent; poor structure can make resource allocation a nightmare. The microkernel architecture to be discussed below is a good structure that enables efficient resource allocation and powerful programming environments.

Historical Development of Operating Systems

Most operating systems for mainframes and servers are descendants of third-generation systems, such as Honeywell Multics, IBM VMS, VM/370, and CDC Scope. These systems introduced important concepts such as time sharing, multiprogramming, virtual memory, sequential processes cooperating via semaphores, hierarchical file systems, and device-independent I/O (Denning, 1971, 1976). These concepts all helped to improve system throughput and utilization and insulate programming from the details of a particular machine.

During the 1960s, many projects were established to construct time-sharing systems and test many new operating system concepts. These included MIT's Compatible Time-Sharing System (CTSS), the University of Manchester Atlas, the University of Cambridge Multiple Access System, IBM TSS/360, and RCA Spectra/70. The most ambitious project of all was Multics (short for Multiplexed Information and Computing Service) for the General Electric 645 processor (later renamed the Honeywell 6180) (Organick, 1972). Multics embraced every important system concept of the day: processes, interprocess communication, segmented virtual memory, page replacement, linking new libraries to a computation on demand, automatic multiprogrammed load control, access control, protection rings, security kernel, hierarchical file system, device independence, I/O redirection, and a high-level language shell.

Perhaps the most influential current operating system is Unix. Originally developed at AT&T Bell Laboratories for DEC PDP computers, Unix distilled the most useful features of Multics into a kernel that fit into the small memory of a minicomputer (*q.v.*). Unix retained its predecessor's processes, hierarchical file system, device independence, I/O redirection, and a high-level language shell. Though the first version of Unix did not have virtual memory, most later versions did. It introduced an innovation, the *pipe*, which enables programs to be strung together by directing (piping) the output of one program for use as input of the next. Arbitrarily long pipelines can be constructed from simpler programs to solve complicated problems. Unix offered a large library of utility programs that were well integrated with the command language. The most important innovation introduced with Unix is the use of a high-level programming language (in this case C—*q.v.*) for the vast majority of kernel programming. This allowed Unix to be transported to a wide variety of processors, from mainframes to personal computers (Ritchie and Thompson, 1974; Kernighan and Pike, 1984).

In the 1980s, a new genre of operating systems was developed for personal computers, including MS-DOS, PC-DOS, Apple-DOS, CP/M, Coherent, and Xenix. All these systems were of limited function, being initially designed for 8- and 16-bit microprocessor chips with small memories. In many respects, the growth path of personal computer operating systems in the 1980s recapitulates that of mainframes in the early 1960s. For example, multiprogrammed operating systems for microcomputers appeared late in the 1980s in the forms of multiple background tasks. Multiprocessing operating systems soon followed, e.g. Windows NT and OS/2. This repetition parallels that of the hardware development. Mainframes were initially CPU-limited, then memory-limited, and finally I/O-limited. Microcomputers went through these same development stages. Processor speeds and memories of personal computers are now sufficient to support full-fledged operating systems.

With multiprocessors and computer networks in the early 1980s, operating systems began to manage the resources of multiple computers. An early example is StarOS, an operating system for the CM* (pronounced "CM star") machine, a multicomputer consisting of several dozen individual computers linked by a special network; StarOS supported the "task force," a group of processes cooperating in a distributed computation (Jones, 1979). Medusa, another operating system for CM*, was composed of several "utilities," each of which implemented a particular abstraction such as a file system; there was no central control (Ousterhout *et al.*, 1980).

Xerox's Grapevine, a distributed database and message delivery system, contained special name servers that located users, groups, and other services when given their symbolic names. Because Grapevine had no central control, it could survive failures of the name server machines (Birrell *et al.*, 1982).

Established, single-machine operating systems such as Unix and DEC's VMS evolved to accommodate networks of computers. Such operating systems typically support standards for accessing files on remote servers from any machine in a network. Locus (Popek *et al.*, 1981) and Apollo DomainOS are early examples of operating systems providing a directory (*q.v.*) hierarchy that spans an entire network. Sun's Network File System (NFS) was one of the first open, and hence widely available, Unix-based network file systems (Sandberg *et al.*, 1985). Carnegie Mellon's Andrew system provides a Unix-based network file system that spans thousands of computers around the campus; it allows users to access files without having to know their locations and it improves performance by caching whole files at individual nodes in the network (Howard *et al.*, 1988). The Mach operating system, also developed at Carnegie Mellon University, handles a variety of distributed system operations, including a uniform file name space, a virtual shared computational memory, and multiprocessing; it is compatible with Unix (Accetta *et al.*, 1986; Rashid *et al.*, 1988). Many of these systems rely on a remote procedure call facility within the operating system to support operations distributed among many machines.

The merging of mainframe (*q.v.*) functions into personal computer operating systems was complete by the end of the 1990s. The Mach kernel was incorporated in the NeXTStep operating system, which was acquired by Apple Computer in 1997 and will be offered in Apple's MacOS X. Linux, NetBDS, and FreeBSD, free software versions of Unix, are widely available for personal computers and network servers.

Many organizations have found that distributed systems can have unacceptably high costs for system administration—e.g. the separate installation of a new version of software into hundreds of workstations. For this reason, large networks of computers require simplified central management. Network management functions can be found in server operating systems such as Sun Microsystem's Solaris, Microsoft's NT, and the free Linux operating system.

Personal computers, workstations, and networks do not constitute the entire universe of machines needing operating systems. Demands for high-performance computing have led to massively parallel computers containing thousands and more processors. Operating systems for these machines must provide a single system view, meaning that thousands of processors or computing nodes in a cluster can be operated and programmed as a single resource (see CLUSTER COMPUTING). Operating systems must support extremely fast synchronization and communication. Each processor may have its own devices attached, and hence the operating system must control thousands of I/O channels (*q.v.*) at once. Virtual memory and time sharing must be extended to accommodate massive parallelism. In parallel computers with shared memory, programs run in a uniform address space without seeing processor/memory boundaries. In distributed memory computers, a programmer must distinguish local memory, which is accessed through normal instructions, and remote memory, which is accessed by sending messages—but some operating systems are seeking to hide even this within a virtual memory. Processes need not run on a fixed processor, but may migrate through a network. Perhaps the most important challenge is that the programming environment should permit parallel programs to be written with only modest effort beyond that required for sequential ones (Denning and Tichy, 1990). Current operating systems research addresses these problems.

A Model Operating System

OVERVIEW

Over the years, operating system designers have tended to use just two strategies for organizing the software: the monolith and the kernel architectures. The monolith results from a design strategy based on defining modules for operating system functions; any module can call any other provided it follows the interface specifications. All the modules must be linked to create the operating system executable file, and that file must be completely loaded into the computer's memory. Every module operates in supervisor mode so that it can have access to the hardware resources of the computer; application programs run in user mode, which has no such access. When an application program requires access to a resource, say a scanner, it must make a supervisor call to invoke a module to perform that access on its behalf. The supervisor call switches the computer from user mode to supervisor mode and forces entry to one of the operating system modules.

Monolithic operating systems can become extremely large and unwieldy. The monolith accumulates all the software that might ever be needed on all platforms, while the computer on which it is actually running needs only a fraction of it. The operating system becomes difficult to adapt to different hardware configurations, and difficult to extend and contract. Microsoft Windows 98, Windows NT, and Apple MacOS, all illustrate this trend. Both Windows and MacOs require 16–32 MB of RAM, and their disk files run upwards of 100 MB. Both systems are well known for numerous bugs and frequent crashes, problems that seem only to grow worse with each new (and larger) release.

The kernel architecture avoids these problems by careful design of the modules. The kernel is designed as a small set of modules that must run in supervisor mode; every other operating system function (and application) is designed as an extension that can be invoked as needed, does not have to be memory resident, and does not have to operate in supervisor mode. A typical kernel implements interrupts, low-level I/O, processes, semaphores, virtual memory, and interprocess communication. Everything else is treated as an extension—files, directories, network services, user interfaces. Since the number of sensitive kernel functions is small, these systems tend to be much more bug-free and stable than their monolithic counterparts. An error occurring in one of the extended functions may crash that function, but it is very unusual to crash the kernel. The term *microkernel* is now frequently used to call attention to compact kernels.

The principle of levels can be used to structure either a monolithic or kernelized system. Software is built up as a hierarchy of levels, each one constructed on the ones below it. The programs at a given level depend only on functions provided by lower levels. The bare hardware is the lowest layer, the application programs the highest. The microkernel itself, layered directly over the hardware, consists of several levels. The levels structure gives a systematic way of building the software, testing it, and proving it correct.

Each level adds new functions or operations and hides selected functions at lower levels. The functions visible at a given level form the instruction set (*q.v.*) of an abstract or virtual machine. Hence a program written at a given level can invoke visible operations at lower levels, but not operations on higher levels.

The first operating system constructed as a hierarchy of levels was Dijkstra's THE of 1968 (Dijkstra, 1968). The idea has been extended to generate families of operating systems for related machines (Haberman *et al.*, 1976) and to increase the portability of an operating system kernel (Cheriton, 1982). The Provably

Secure Operating System (PSOS) is the first complete level-structured system reported and formally proved correct in the open literature (Neumann *et al.*, 1980). XINU (*Unix* backwards) (Comer, 1984) demonstrates that the level-structure principle can lead to exceptionally compact microkernels that can fit into the small memory of a microchip. A distributed operating system design with 10 levels appears in Brown *et al.* (1984). Mach, Chorus, and Amoeba are three microkernel architectures that support multiprocessors; for a comparison see Tanenbaum (1995).

THE MICROKERNEL

Table 1 shows the minimal set of abstractions in a microkernel. The microkernel contains no file or directory system, offers no remote procedure call, and may even require some of the memory management to be performed in user mode. The functions in the microkernel are included there because they are difficult or inefficient to provide elsewhere.

Level 1 dispatches interrupts and manages access to peripheral devices. The interrupt dispatcher receives signals from condition detectors and responds by immediately transferring control of the CPU to a corresponding condition-handler routine. Condition handlers are defined at each level that must respond to conditions associated with that level; for example, the memory manager responds to missing-page faults and the IPC level to interrupts signaling the arrival of packets from the network. The entry points of condition handler procedures are stored in the interrupt vector, a list used by the interrupt dispatcher to locate them. Device driver programs manage operations such as positioning the head of a disk drive and transferring blocks of data. Software at a higher level determines the address of the data on the disk and places requests for it in the device's queue of pending work; the requesting process then waits at a semaphore until the transfer has been completed.

Level 2 implements threads. A *thread* is a single flow of control in some address space. It is an abstraction for the instruction trace of a CPU executing program code. Each thread operates in a context that includes a program stack (*q.v.*), the CPU register contents, interrupt masks, and any other flags or state information needed by the CPU to continue running the thread. This level provides a context switch operation, which transfers a processor's attention from one thread to another by saving the context of the first and loading the context of the second. A scheduler in this level selects the next thread to run from a "ready list" of available threads. The scheduler usually accommodates machines with more than one processor available. This level provides the clock interrupt handler, which forces the scheduler to switch threads at regular intervals. This level also provides semaphores, the special variables used to cause one thread to stop and wait until another thread has signaled the completion of a task. Threads are analogous to "system processes" in PSOS and "lightweight processes" in Locus.

Level 3 manages the computer's main memory, or RAM (random access memory). The memory manager does two jobs: (1) it enforces separation of address spaces, and (2) it moves blocks of data between RAM and secondary storage media. An address space is the set of addresses that a CPU can generate. The simplest form of address-space separation is a partition of the RAM into disjoint regions, each delineated by a base-and-bound register; an address generated by the CPU is taken to be relative to the base register and must not exceed the bound. A group of threads can be created in the same address space; they cannot be protected from one another, but they can communicate very easily through common variables. Virtual memory distinguishes between address space (CPU addresses) and memory space (RAM addresses). With each address space it associates a mapping table that converts a CPU address into a RAM address. Virtual memory permits a

Table 1. Microkernel layers.

Level	Name	Objects	Example operations
5	Processes	Process	Fork, suspend, resume, join, signal, exit, kill
4	Interprocess communication	Message, port	Send, receive, transmit
3	Memory management	Address, segment	Create, destroy, map
2	Threads	Thread, ready list, semaphore,	Fork, suspend, resume, wait, signal, kill
1	Low-level I/O	Device, device driver	read, write

CPU to access only the memory locations visible through the mapping table, thereby enforcing separation (partition) among address spaces. The mapping table stores access flags so that the CPU can be further restricted by denying read or write access to individual objects. Virtual memory can be configured to move blocks of data between RAM and disk automatically, thereby automating swapping of data between memory levels and relieving the programmer of any necessity to compile different versions of the program for different RAM sizes (Denning, 1970). Automation of swapping is achieved by adding a "presence bit" to the mapping table. When the CPU generates the address of an object marked as not present, the mapping hardware generates an address-snag interrupt that invokes the missing-object interrupt routine in Level 3. That routine locates the missing block in the secondary store, frees space for it in the RAM, and moves the missing block in.

Whether to use virtual memory or simple memory partition is a design trade-off between system complexity and protection. For applications that run a small number of mutually trusting threads and where the entire application can fit into a memory partition, virtual memory would be unnecessary. These include digital organizers and embedded applications. For applications whose memory demands are unpredictable or for which a high degree of protection is required, virtual memory would be the best approach. To facilitate the trade-off, some systems do not include all the virtual memory functions in their microkernel, placing them instead in a module outside the kernel. The kernel architecture of the Mach operating system is like this; it provides only an interface for reading and writing blocks of main memory and lets a user process determine which blocks to replace. The JavaOS, a small operating system for embedded systems (*q.v.*), goes further: it leaves memory management up to the run-time system of the language.

Level 4 implements interprocess communication (IPC). Threads that do not share the same address space and threads running on different computers in a network exchange messages through IPC. Messages are exchanged via ports which are buffers that retain messages in transit. A message contains the sender port number, the receiver port number, and a data field, enabling the receiver to identify the sender and send a reply.

Level 5 supplies the full-blown process, a program in execution on a virtual computer. A process consists of one or more threads, an address space, one or more input ports for incoming messages, and output ports for outgoing messages. The threads of a process share access to the address space and the ports. A process can create offspring (child) processes. This level tracks all processes in a tree (*q.v.*) of parent–child relationships and restricts certain actions accordingly; for example, a parent can force the termination of only its children and cannot terminate unless all its children have terminated.

USER-LEVEL SERVERS

The remaining levels of the operating system are structured according to the client–server (*q.v.*) model. In this model certain processes are designated as servers because they perform functions for other processes, called clients, on request. Clients and servers use IPC to exchange requests and responses. Fig. 1 shows how clients send messages through the kernel to servers on the same machine; Fig. 2 illustrates the distributed case.

When a server process is the only server on a machine, the machine itself is often called the server; a common example is a file server. Some servers, such as printer servers, directory servers, mail servers, authentication servers, and Web servers, can run alone on a machine or can be part of a group of services offered from a single machine. With this architecture it is possible to run several versions of a server at once—for example, a Unix file server and a Windows NT file server. Because all these servers sit on top of the same microkernel, any client can communicate with any server via the same IPC mechanism.

Although clients and servers communicate with messages, most systems allow programs to invoke services as procedure calls. This means that all services, local and remote, are called in the same way, and no

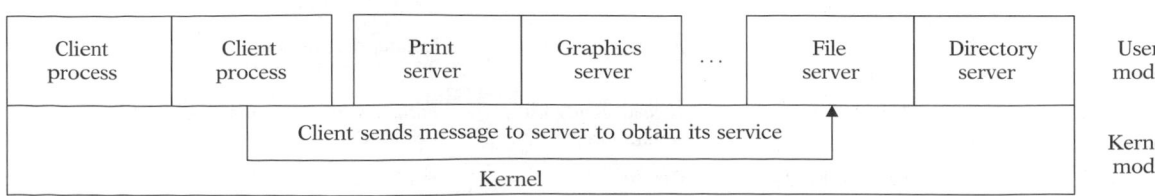

Figure 1. The client–server model on a single machine.

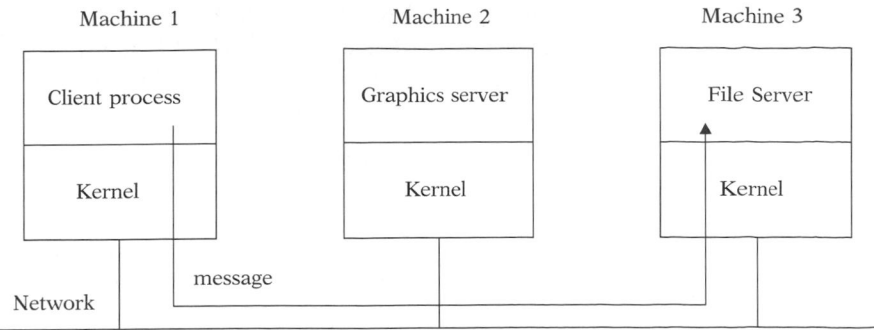

Figure 2. The client–server model in a distributed system.

programmer is required to know which is which. The mechanism for this, called remote procedure call (RPC), is implemented completely by compilers and does not have to be a component of the IPC level. When it encounters a procedure call P(parameters) in a program, the compiler substitutes a call on a "stub" of the form RPC(P,parameters). The stub either calls the procedure P locally, or it sends a message with a copy of the parameters to the remote server on which P resides; that server calls P(parameters) locally and returns the result to the calling stub, which then returns it to its caller.

Level 6 (*see* Table 2) implements a common interface to *information objects*. Info-objects produce, consume, store, or transmit streams (sequences) of bytes. There are three types of info-objects: devices, files, and pipes. Devices are external equipment that either produce or consume streams of bytes; a keyboard is an example of an input (stream-producing) device and a display is an example of an output (stream-consuming) device. A file stores a stream of bytes for an indefinite time. A pipe conveys a stream of bytes from a sender process to a receiver. The importance of treating devices, files, and pipes as info-objects is that they can all be accessed by the same interface: OPEN, CLOSE, READ, and WRITE. OPEN(object) establishes an efficient and fast communication pathway between a process and the object; CLOSE shuts it down. READ(open object) transfers bytes from the open object to the calling

process and WRITE(open object) transfers bytes from the calling process to the open object. The stream manager calls microkernel services as needed to implement the requested operation. It uses low-level I/O to perform the actual data transfers between address space and secondary storage or external devices. It uses the IPC level to transmit pipe-streams. This architecture makes the three kinds of object interchangeable. A programmer can say READ(open object) without knowing in advance whether the object is an open device, a file, or a pipe.

Level 7 manages a hierarchy of directories that catalogs the hardware and software objects to which access must be controlled throughout the network: files, devices, pipes, ports, processes, and other directories. A *directory* is a table that matches *external names* of objects to *internal names*. An *external name* is a string of characters chosen by a user; an internal name is a binary code chosen by the system. Internal names can be guaranteed to be unique for all time, which enables users to share objects without prior arrangements on what to name them. Internal names are generated for every sharable object—file, pipe, device, directory, process, or port. The directory allows the user to deal solely with recognizable, meaningful strings as object names without having to import system names into an address space (where they can be misused or damaged). Path names in directory hierarchies can be used to identify objects uniquely.

Table 2. Layers in the user services.

Level	Name	Objects	Example operations
9	Graphics server	Window, input event	Resize, move, draw, receive, send
8	Shell	Application program	Statements in shell language
7	Directories	Directory	Create, delete, enter, remove, search, get
6	Streams	File, device, pipe	Create, delete, open, close, read, write

The directory level is responsible only for recording the associations between the external and internal names; other levels manage the objects themselves. Thus, when a directory of devices is searched for the string "laser," the result returned is merely an internal name for the laser printer. The internal name must be passed to a program at level 6 (streams), which handles the actual transmission to that printer.

Level 8 provides command language interfaces called *shells*. The shell derives its name from a metaphor: it is the layer of software that separates the user from the rest of the machine. The user expresses a command to the shell which, in turn, invokes low-level and kernel services as appropriate to implement the command. The shell is in essence a parser that interprets commands in the syntax of the command language; it creates processes and pipes and connects them with files and devices as needed to carry out the command. A graphical user interface uses point-and-click facilities (windows, icons, mouse, menus) to accomplish the same objective.

At level 9, a graphics server provides user programs with the ability to present pictorial information to the user and coordinate that information with input from user devices such as a keyboard, a mouse (*q.v.*), or a joystick. The server enables several programs to share screen space without interfering with one another. Standard libraries have been developed to provide a large number of graphical user interface (GUI) elements such as buttons, sliders, menus, check-boxes, tree displays, dialog boxes, dials, meters, and table displays—all providing intuitive controls for applications. The distinction between the graphical server and the graphical user interface is that the server provides graphical control and display for applications while the interface provides standardized components for a uniform appearance and behavior of interface elements. These interface elements are displayed by the graphical server.

General Comments on Operating System Architecture

LEVEL STRUCTURE
The level structure is a hierarchy of functional specifications designed to impose a high degree of modularity and enable incremental software verification, installation, and testing.

In a functional hierarchy, a program at one level may directly call any visible operation of a lower level; input is communicated directly to the lower-level operation without any intermediate level's involvement; and output is returned directly to the caller. The level structure can be completely enforced by a compiler (*q.v.*), which inserts procedure calls or expands functions inline (Habermann *et al.*, 1976). A well-documented example of its use is XINU, a distributed operating system for microcomputers.

It is important to distinguish the level structure discussed here from the layer structure of the International Organization for Standardization (ISO) model of long-haul network protocols (*see* OPEN SYSTEMS INTERCONNECTION and Tanenbaum (1996)). In the ISO model, data input to a remote operation is passed down through all the layers on the sending machine and back up through all the layers on the receiving machine; return data follow the reverse path. Because each layer adds delay to a data transmission, whether or not that layer's function is required for the transaction, long-haul network protocols (*q.v.*) are likely to be inefficient in a local network (Popek *et al.*, 1981). A significant advantage of functional levels over information-transferring layers is efficiency: a program that does not use a given function will experience no overhead from that function's presence in the system.

NAMES
Naming of objects is a very important design problem in operating systems. The system of object names has two principal requirements: (1) It must allow individual users to choose local names as character strings that make sense to them, and (2) it must also allow any two users to share an object even though they have no prior agreement on the name that each will use for the object. These requirements can be met by allowing objects to have two names: the user-assigned (external) name and a system-assigned (internal) name. Although users can reuse external names at will, internal names must be unique in both space and time: in space because the object name may be passed to anyone anywhere; and in time because object names cannot be reused lest someone access the wrong object.

A two-level mapping scheme is used to convert an external name to an object location. The first level converts user-defined character strings into internal system names; the second level converts system names to object locations. In the architecture described below, the directories implement the first level and the individual object managers implement the second.

The simplest internal names are bit-strings, called *handles*, generated by the operating system when an object is created. Whenever a program requests the creation of an object such as a process, port, pipe, or file, the operating system returns an internal name for that object. The internal name is used to identify the object in subsequent operations. In its simplest form, a handle is a pointer (*q.v.*) to the object or an index into a table of objects managed by a particular level.

On a network comprising many machines, two extensions to handles are necessary. First, handles are extended by adding extra bits to hold the identifier of the creating machine; this makes handles unique throughout the network. Second, the mapping from handles to object locations must be augmented with search rules to help find objects that reside on other machines: object managers must poll other machines during searches for objects. To speed up multiple accesses to the same object, an object manager can maintain a cache which notes the locations of recently requested objects. Policies of moving or replicating objects to requesting machines and updating caches were explored in the Purdue Ibis (Ruan and Tichy, 1987) and Carnegie Mellon Andrew (Howard *et al.*, 1988) file systems, as well as in the Xerox Grapevine system (Birrell *et al.*, 1982).

These simple handles are good for object sharing but inadequate for access control. Nothing prevents anyone from passing a handle for an object to the wrong type manager, or from attempting to overwrite a read-only object. To overcome these limitations, some systems rely on *capabilities* rather than handles. A *capability* is a handle augmented with type and access codes (*see* CAPABILITY-BASED ADDRESSING). These codes can be checked by an object manager to make sure that it performs only the operations allowed by the access code only on its type of object. Fabry (1974) advocated capabilities as the most efficient solution to the two naming requirements stated earlier.

Capabilities were explored, among others, in the Carnegie Mellon Hydra system (Wulf *et al.*, 1981), the Cambridge CAP system (Wilkes and Needham, 1979), and the Intel iMax system (Organick, 1983). The Amoeba system (Tanenbaum, 1995) provides encrypted capabilities for both kernel and user-space objects. Amoeba capabilities can be passed safely across machine boundaries and stored in arbitrary data structures. Objects referred to by capabilities are located by broadcast, with the result cached for future use.

HETEROGENEOUS SYSTEMS

The systems discussed above deal with many computers on a network by running the same operating system on each machine, an approach often called *homogeneous distributed computing*. In such an environment, sharing information and moving objects among the machines is straightforward.

The open system philosophy, now practiced by many manufacturers of hardware and software, aims for networks whose components can be supplied by different vendors and which will work together anyway because those vendors follow basic standards. These are often called *heterogeneous distributed computing systems* because they may not have the same operating system or internal understanding of formats and structures. To make such an environment work, all machines will have to use a standard interprocess communication system (e.g. TCP/IP—*q.v.*). They may require translating filters to convert formats and structures as they are sent between machines with different operating systems.

A Closer Look

Let us now look a little more deeply into the operations and assumptions of the operating system levels outlined above.

LOW-LEVEL I/O: LEVEL 1

This level (Table 3) offers simple transfers of blocks of information between devices and the main store (RAM). It hides such details as device startup, parameter passing, device registers, device controller management, and interrupts.

Each device has a detailed specification that includes its hardware address, speed and bandwidth parameters, error codes, command codes, and driver (*q.v.*). A device driver is a program that interprets the command codes available to the system; for example, the disk driver instructs the disk controller to move the disk arm to a particular cylinder in response to

Table 3. Specification of low-level I/O (level 1).

Form of call	Effect
dev_handle := INSTALL_DEV(spec)	Adds the specification of a new device to the device table.
REMOVE_ DEV(dev_handle)	Frees the entry occupied by the given device in the device table.
READ_SEG(mem_addr, dev_handle, dev_ addr, size)	Copies size bytes from the device, starting at address dev_addr, to the segment of memory starting at base mem_addr.
WRITE_SEG(mem_addr, dev_handle, dev_ addr, size)	Copies size bytes from the segment of memory at base mem_addr to the device starting at address dev_ addr.

the disk command `seek(disk address)`. All device specifications are stored in a device table in a main-memory segment. The operations `INSTALL_DEV` and `REMOVE_DEV` are used to add and remove entries from this table.

A device-to-memory transfer is initiated by a `READ_SEG` operation. It copies a number of bytes given by a size parameter from the device to a segment of memory. Similarly, a `WRITE_SEG` operation carries out a memory-to-device transfer by copying a specified number of bytes from a memory segment to the device. Many systems support block devices where the basic unit of transfer is a block of data (typically between 512 and 4096 bytes) instead of a byte.

Once the system is booted, new devices can be added by copying their specifications from any storage medium for which there is a driver. During the boot sequence, an initial set of drivers must be loaded as part of the loading of the operating system executable file. This initial set may be determined by probing for known devices, then loading just the drivers corresponding to the devices that are available.

THREADS: LEVEL 2

A thread, or primitive process, is described by its *context*, i.e. its stack and the register state. The register state, known also as its *stateword*, holds the contents of *all* processor registers—including not only the general purpose registers holding program data and addresses, but also the program counter (*q.v.*), condition codes, interrupt masks, stack pointer, and any other registers that control or delimit the execution of a program. To run a process, its register state must be loaded into a processor's registers. The operation of saving one thread's state and loading another is called *context switch*. The thread level interface specification is shown in Table 4.

A thread is in one of four states: running, ready, waiting, or suspended. A running thread controls a processor: its register state has been loaded into a processor, and that process is executing instructions from its program. A ready thread is authorized to execute instructions on a processor as soon as one is available. A waiting thread is waiting for a semaphore signal and is ineligible for execution until the signal arrives. A suspended thread is waiting for a signal

Table 4. Specification of thread level interface (level 2).

Form of call	Effect
`thread_handle :=` 　　　`T_FORK(addr, priority)`	Creates a suspended thread at the given `priority` level by allocating a context for it. Sets its program counter to `addr` and returns a handle to the thread.
`T_KILL(thread_handle)`	Deletes the given thread (undoes `T_FORK`).
`T_SUSPEND(thread_handle)`	Transfers the given thread into the suspended state, removing it from its current state (running, ready, waiting). Remembers its prior state.(No effect if the thread is already suspended.)
`T_RESUME(thread_handle)`	Returns the thread to its prior state. A new thread is transferred to the ready state. (No effect if the thread is not suspended.)
`sem_handle := CREATE_SEM(val)`	Creates a semaphore with `val` as initial nonnegative integer counter value and an empty waiting list.
`DELETE_SEM(sem_handle)`	Removes the given semaphore (undoes `CREATE_SEM`).
`WAIT(sem_handle)`	Subtracts 1 from the counter of the given semaphore. If the counter is now negative, `WAIT` suspends the invoking thread, enqueues it on the semaphore's waiting list, and switches to the next ready thread. Otherwise, returns immediately to caller.
`SIGNAL(sem_handle)`	Adds 1 to the counter of the given semaphore; if the counter is now zero or still negative, transfers a thread from the semaphore's waiting list to the ready list. Returns immediately to caller.

from its parent. The ready and waiting states are represented by lists—all the threads waiting for a processor are linked to the *ready list* and all those waiting for a particular semaphore are linked to that semaphore's *waiting list*. The ready list is commonly organized as a set of queues for each priority level. When a thread is added to the ready list, it may preempt a lower-priority running thread, returning it to the ready list. Each thread has a private semaphore on which only it can wait. A thread is first created in its suspended state and will not become ready until its creator gives the signal.

Thread priorities are determined partly by the users and partly by the operating system. An example user-set priority is the high priority given to threads that must react quickly to time-critical events (such as completion of an operation on a high-speed I/O device). Examples of system-set priorities are assigning a background thread lower priority than a foreground thread, and the demotion of a thread that has been executing for a long time, in a system aiming to favor short jobs. The lowest priority of all is assigned to the *idle threads*. They consist of infinite loops of no-ops (*q.v.*) (empty instructions) and run only if there is no other ready thread; they are needed because otherwise a processor will crash if it has no instructions to execute.

Most operating systems allow many more threads to be created than there are processors. To prevent any one of them from monopolizing a processor, operating systems implement *time slicing*, a policy of limiting the maximum period that a thread can run continuously. At the start of a thread's interval of execution, a timer register in the processor is set to a standard value, called the "time quantum"; the timer triggers a clock interrupt when it reaches zero. The clock interrupt handler (part of the threads level) returns the running thread to the ready list, resets the timer to the time quantum, and switches to the next ready thread.

Requests for I/O are the most common events generated by threads. A thread requesting I/O places a request in the work queue of the device driver, signals the driver, and stops to wait on its private semaphore. The request includes the components

```
requesting thread id
request type (read or write)
memory address
device address
size
```

The device driver will cause the requested transfer to take place; when done, it signals the requesting thread via its private semaphore. The interrupt handler that receives the device's completion signal awakens the device driver from the point where it had paused to wait for the device's completion signal.

I/O is not the only example of thread coordination. Other common examples include: (1) several threads must stop and wait while another thread executes the instructions of an operation on a shared object; (2) a producer thread cannot add items to a full buffer and a consumer thread cannot remove items from an empty buffer; (3) threads borrow resource units from a pool and others must wait if the pool is temporarily empty. The semaphore is a single mechanism that provides simple solutions to these coordinations (and many others; *see* CONCURRENT PROGRAMMING).

A semaphore consists of a counter and a queue. The counter records the number of signals sent but not yet received; when it is negative, each thread waiting for a signal is listed in the queue. The operation WAIT implements the request to obtain a signal from the semaphore; SIGNAL provides a signal that can release a waiting thread (if any are waiting). The private semaphore is uniquely and permanently assigned to a thread; its implementation can be simplified because it only needs to record whether or not its owner is waiting on it.

In the first example of thread coordination cited above, threads must be allowed access to shared data one at a time. For example, if two teller machines attempt to add deposits to the same account simultaneously, one deposit will be lost; which is lost and which is recorded depends on the relative speeds of the two tellers. This problem can be prevented by defining a semaphore *mutex* (for "mutual exclusion") with an initial count of 1, and then bracketing the shared access with a WAIT/SIGNAL pair:

```
WAIT(mutex)
    access to shared data
SIGNAL(mutex)
```

Any section of code that must be constrained to be executed by only one thread at a time is called a *critical section*.

In the third example of thread coordination cited above, threads access a critical section that allocates resource units. The number of resources units is the initial value of a semaphore named *pool*:

```
WAIT(pool)
WAIT(mutex)
    get unit number from free list
    return (unit number)
SIGNAL(mutex)
```

A thread returns a unit to the pool:

```
WAIT(mutex)
    add unit number to free list
SIGNAL(mutex)
SIGNAL(pool)
```

One of the original motivations for semaphores was to avoid *busy waiting*—a form of waiting in which the processor loops while testing for a go-ahead condition. Busy waiting can waste a lot of processor time. The WAIT and SIGNAL operations avoid busy waiting.

MEMORY MANAGEMENT: LEVEL 3

The simplest responsibility of a memory manager is to partition the memory among address spaces so that parallel threads in different address spaces cannot interfere with one another. This can be accomplished through a method called *segmentation* (Table 5). A segment of memory is a region of L (for length) contiguous addresses starting at a base address B. The pair of values (B,L) is called a *descriptor* for the segment and is part of the register state of a processor. The addressing hardware of the processor checks that a process-generated address A does not exceed L and, if not, presents the address B+A to memory.

Memory managers are often asked to do more than simply partition the main memory among disjoint tasks. They are asked to swap segments automatically between a backing store (usually a disk) and the main memory. This kind of memory manager is called *virtual memory* (Table 6). By creating the illusion that the entire address space fits into main memory, virtual memory frees programmers from managing swaps.

Two mechanisms are needed to accomplish this. First, every address space must be represented as a table containing one entry for each segment of the address space. An entry tells whether the segment is present in main memory, and if so gives its descriptor. The processor's addressing hardware presents the segment number to the memory mapping unit (MMU), which looks up the descriptor in the table and computes the memory address as above. If the MMU finds the segment marked as "missing," it generates a missing-segment addressing fault signal. The fault signal invokes the segment-fault handler (part of this level). Second, the fault handler frees up space in main memory for the new segment by copying one or more segments back to disk (and marking them as missing), then swapping in the new segment (and marking it as present), and then allowing the interrupted thread to resume and retry the address. *See* VIRTUAL MEMORY.

INTERPROCESS COMMUNICATION: LEVEL 4

Interprocess communication (IPC) is used to exchange messages among threads in different address spaces on the same or different machines. IPC is the basis for client–server communication and remote procedure call (RPC).

Senders expect messages to be delivered even if the receiver is not able to accept messages exactly when

Table 5. Specification of physical memory (level 3).

Form of call	Effect
(B,L) := ALLOC(size)	Returns the base and length of a free segment of memory of the given size (L = size).
FREE((B,L))	Returns the segment (B,L) to the pool of free space in memory.

Table 6. Specification of virtual memory (level 3).

Form of call	Effect
vm_handle := CREATE_VM(size, dev_addr, dev_handle)	Creates a new virtual memory of given size, initialized to the contents of the file at the given address on the given secondary storage device.
DELETE_VM(vm_handle)	Deletes the given virtual memory and frees the space it occupied in the secondary storage system.
A := MAP(V, vm_handle)	Translates the virtual address V generated by a processor into an address A in the main store, using the mapping table of the given virtual memory. If the mapping table says that the block containing V is not present, generates a mapping fault (the fault handler will move the missing block into memory, update the table, and retry the MAP operation).

they are sent. To accomplish this, messages are not sent directly to processes or threads; they are sent to special buffers called *ports*. Each port has a network-wide, unique identification number. A random large number (96 to 128 bits) is good enough to ensure that two ports have distinct numbers.

Table 7 shows the main operations of IPC. A port is created with CREATE_PORT and deleted with DELETE_PORT. ATTACH_PORT opens a connection to an existing port, either for receiving messages from it or sending messages to it. To complete this operation, the IPC software must identify the machine on which the port is located. On a small local network, this can be done by broadcasting a message "who has port_id?". On a larger network this is done by consulting a *name server*. A name server is a database that records the associations between ports and machines; it provides an interface for registering ports and looking them up. In either case—broadcast or name server—the IPC software caches the result for fast future lookup.

The operation SEND delivers a message to a port and RECEIVE retrieves it. Both operations are synchronous, meaning that SEND blocks until the message has been copied into the port and that RECEIVE blocks until a message is available in the port. Some operating systems also provide asynchronous versions, in which both SEND and RECEIVE return immediately, providing a return code indicating that the operation is incomplete. In this case, the IPC interface needs additional operations that allow sender and receiver to find out whether previous operations have completed.

The operation TRANSMIT combines SEND and RECEIVE; it is useful for RPC. A client uses TRANSMIT to send a message to a server port and wait until a reply is returned. The port at which the reply is expected is sent along with the original message.

When messages are sent to a port on another machine in a network, a *network service* is used. A network service speaks several different protocols (*q.v.*) for exchanging messages with other computers. When sending a message, it breaks large messages into smaller packets, encapsulates them into the appropriate protocol wrappers, forwards the packets one by one to the receiver, and retransmits them if they are lost or corrupted. The receiving machine's network service reassembles the message from the fragments, even if they arrive out of order. A network service provides a host of additional functions. For example, it translates data types from one machine's representation to another's, authenticates other network services, acts as a gateway (*q.v.*) that bridges different networks, and performs simple name lookup. A network service can be run in kernel or user mode, similar to virtual memory management. For more details on the subject of this section *see* NETWORK PROTOCOLS, CLIENT–SERVER COMPUTING, and CONCURRENT PROGRAMMING.

PROCESSES: LEVEL 5

A *process* (Table 8) is a program in execution on a virtual (simulated) machine. It consists of one or more threads, an address space, and communication ports. The threads within the same process form a "team"

Table 7. Specification of IPC (level 4).

Form of call	Effect
port_id := CREATE_PORT()	Creates a new port with a randomly chosen identification number.
DELETE_PORT(port_id)	Deletes the port given by port_id
port_handle := ATTACH_PORT(port_id, rw)	Opens a connection to the port port_id; initializes it for sending or receiving, depending on the value of rw.
DETACH_PORT(port_id)	Drops the connection to the port port_id.
SEND(sport_id, sbase, ssize)	Sends message of length ssize beginning at sbase to port given by sport_id. Blocks until all data have been transferred to the port.
(rbase, rsize) := RECEIVE(rport_id)	Blocks until a message has arrived at port rport_id, then returns it in segment (rbase, rsize).
(rbase, rsize) := TRANSMIT (sport_id, sbase, ssize, rport_id)	Sends a message of length ssize beginning at sbase to sport_id and blocks until the reply message has been received from rport_id.

Table 8. Specification of process operations (level 5).

Form of call	Effect

`proc_handle :=`
` CREATE_PROC(file_handle,`
`              port_list)`
	Allocates a process control block that points to the thread, address space, and ports of the process. Creates a single suspended, thread and a virtual memory containing the executable file denoted by `file_handle`. Attaches to the ports given in `port_list`. Adds the new `proc_handle` to the list of children of its caller.

`KILL(proc_handle)`	Terminates the given process, but only if it is a child of the caller: deletes the threads and virtual memory and detaches from its ports; releases its process control block; and deletes it from the list of existing children of its parent.
`EXIT()`	Terminates the caller process and deducts 1 from the UNDONE variable of the parent process.
`JOIN(m)`	Sets caller's UNDONE variable to `m`, then waits until it reaches 0.
`SUSPEND(proc_handle)`	Puts the threads of the given process into the suspended state, but only if the process is a child of the caller.
`RESUME(proc_handle)`	Puts the threads of the given process back into the state they had at the time of the last SUSPEND operation on the process, but only if the given process is a child of the caller.

that must cooperate toward a common computational goal; they share the same address space and cannot be protected from one another. When it is created, a process has one thread; it can create and control additional threads with the facilities of the Threads Manager (Level 2). A process's creator also passes it a small set of ports for sending and receiving messages; they can be used later to exchange control information and port identifiers for additional communication channels.

The system keeps track of the creator of each process and restricts process control operations accordingly. The creator of a process is called a *parent* and the new process the *child*. A parent may suspend, resume, or kill any of its children but no others. These operations apply to all descendants of the affected child process— *suspend* and *resume* apply to all threads of a process; *kill* applies to the process and all its children. The JOIN operation allows a parent to stop and wait until all its children have completed their tasks; each child uses the EXIT operation to tell the parent it has done so.

The operating systems Unix and Mach separate process creation into two parts: FORK and EXEC. FORK creates a clone of the parent and EXEC performs a

context switch to a child program. This approach is quite powerful but can be expensive on multiprocessor systems without shared memory.

STREAM I/O: LEVEL 6

Stream I/O is the common interface to the information objects files, devices, and pipes. Each deals with streams of bytes. The common operations—OPEN, CLOSE, READ, and WRITE—are used to open and close data sources and sinks, to read blocks of data from a source, and to write blocks of data into a sink. The common interface supports *I/O independence*, the principle that READ and WRITE operations can be independent of the type of data source or sink. All READ and WRITE statements in a program refer to stream handles, which are attached to files, devices, and pipes when the program is executed.

This strategy can greatly increase the versatility of a program. A library program (such as the pattern-finding "grep" program in Unix) can take its input from a file or directly from a keyboard and can send its output to another file, to a window on a display, or to a printer. Without I/O independence, different versions of a program would have to be written for each possible combination of source and sink.

I/O independence works because files, devices, and pipes all rely on the same model of data: streams (sequences) of bytes. Corresponding to each of these objects is a pair of pointers, r for reading and w for writing; r counts the number of bytes read thus far and w those written thus far; r cannot exceed w. Each READ request begins at position r and advances r by the number of bytes read. Similarly, each WRITE request begins at position w and advances w by the number of bytes written.

The stream I/O interface uses "dynamic dispatch" to route a request to the appropriate file, device, or pipe manager. The dispatch vector points to the type managers for each type of info-object (three in this case). To see how this works, take the stream READ as an example. READ is provided with an open-object handle, which contains within it a type indicator of the info-object to which it points; using the dispatch vector, READ then passes control to the device manager, file manager, or pipe manager. A knowledgeable programmer can extend the same interface to deal with a new type of stream object by providing a type manager and adding a pointer to it to the dispatch vector.

The stream model is not used in every operating system. Multics used another approach (Organick, 1972). Multics had a segmented address space that subsumed the file system. Each segment was permanent, just like a file, and had a unique path name in a directory tree. The first time a process referred to a segment (via its directory path name), a "linkage" fault interrupted the process, calling in the linker, which loaded the missing segment; thereafter, the process could refer to the segment using ordinary virtual addressing. Certain segments of the address space were permanently bound to devices: read (writing) and one of them reads (writes) the associated device. Fabry offered arguments that explain why the shared-handle approach to naming info-objects leads to a simpler I/O system than Multics had (Fabry, 1974).

Files. A file server implements a long-term store for files. Files are named sequences of bytes of known (but

Table 9. Interface for files (level 6).

Form of call	Effect
file_handle := CREATE_FILE()	Creates an empty file and returns a handle for it. (If the caller is a process, it can store the handle in a directory entry and make the file available throughout the system.)
DELETE(file_handle)	Deletes the given file (undoes the corresponding CREATE_FILE).
ofile_handle := OPEN(file_handle, rw)	Opens the given file by allocating buffer storage and loading the file index table into main memory. The file is enabled for reading, writing, or both, depending on the value of rw. The read pointer r is set to zero, and the write pointer w to the file's length (fl). (Fails if the file is already open).
CLOSE(ofile_handle)	Undoes OPEN.
READ(ofile_handle, buf, n)	Sets m := min(fl − r, n). Copies m bytes from the given file, starting with position r, into segment buf. Updates fl to fl+m. (Fails if reading is not enabled.)
WRITE(ofile_handle, buf, n)	Copies the first n bytes of segment buf into the given file, starting with position w. Sets fl := max(fl, w+n) and w := fl. (Fails if writing is not enabled.)
SEEK(ofile_handle, pos, rw)	Stores the value of pos into the read pointer r, the write pointer w, or both, depending on the value of rw. (Fails if pos is larger than file length fl.)
ERASE(ofile_handle)	Sets file length, read and write pointers to zero; releases secondary storage blocks occupied by the file. (Fails if writing not enabled.)

arbitrary) length that persist until deleted and are accessible from all machines in the network. The file server offers a set of file operations (Table 9) that includes the four generic stream operations.

To establish a connection with a file, a process presents a file handle to the OPEN operation. OPEN contacts the file server via a known port. The file server locates the file in its secondary storage and allocates ports for transmissions between itself and the caller; it may even create and assign a dedicated thread to manage the file session. A READ operation copies the requested data from the file server to the client's buffers (*q.v.*) (assigned when the file was opened), then copies those data to the caller's address space, and finally updates the file's read pointer. A WRITE operation performs similarly in the reverse direction. The SEEK operation can change the read and write pointers to allow for random (non-sequential) file access. Examples of such remote file implementations are the Berkeley Cocanet System (Rowe and Birman, 1982) and the Network File System (NFS) (Sandberg *et al.*, 1985).

Caching is often used to improve performance of file READ and WRITE operations. When the file is opened, a copy is read into the client's buffers; READ operations do not require further transmissions from the file server. However, the cache must be copied back to the file server shortly after any WRITE operation. Examples are Purdue's Ibis (Ruan and Tichy, 1987) and CMU's Andrew (Howard, 1988).

Some file systems also provide improved synchronization and version control. *Synchronization control* means implementing a solution to the "multiple readers and writers" problem as part of READ and WRITE operations (Holt 1983; Tanenbaum, 1995). Version control means to retain previous versions of a file so that older versions can be retrieved even after the file is "overwritten" (*see* SOFTWARE CONFIGUREMENT MANAGEMENT).

Devices. The device level implements a common interface to a wide range of external I/O devices, including keyboards, scanners, displays, printers, plotters, and time-of-day clock. The interface attempts to hide differences in devices by making input devices appear as sources of data streams and output devices as sinks. Obviously, the differences cannot be completely hidden—for example, cursor-positioning commands must be embedded in the data stream sent to a graphic display—but a substantial degree of uniformity is possible.

Corresponding to each device is a *device driver program* at Level 1. The stream implementation of device access translates between the model of streams and the device access model assumed by the device driver. (Considerable effort is required to construct reliable, robust device drivers; the stream level does not attempt to duplicate that work, but only to interface with it.) Some devices are operated by dedicated servers—print servers are notable examples—and in these cases the

Table 10. Interface for devices (level 6).

Form of call	Effect
dev_handle := CREATE_DEV(type, address)	Creates a control block for the stream interface to a device driver or server. Returns a handle referring to this control block. (If the caller is a process, it can store the handle in a directory entry and make the device available throughout the system.)
DELETE(dev_handle)	Releases the given device control block (undoes the corresponding CREATE_DEV).
odev_handle := OPEN(dev_handle, rw)	Opens the given device by allocating buffer storage and performing setup operations. The device is enabled for reading, writing, or both, depending on the value of rw and on whether the device is an input or output device or both. (Fails if the device is already open)
CLOSE(odev_handle)	Undoes OPEN.
READ(odev_handle, buf, n)	Reads n bytes into segment base address buf, as for files. (No effect for output device.)
WRITE(odev_handle, buf, n)	Sends the n bytes of segment {base address buf to the device, as for pipe. (No effect for input device.)

translation is nothing more than a remote procedure call to the server.

The stream devices can add semantics appropriate for the device. For example, a READ operation applied to a keyboard may be programmed to return the next full line of input, regardless of its length.

Table 10 summarizes the interface for external devices. It is similar to the interface for files, without the SEEK and ERASE operations.

Pipes. Pipes (Table 11) move a continuous stream of data from a writer process to a reader process on the same or different machines. The most important property of a pipe is that a reader must stop and wait until a writer has put enough data into the pipe to fill the request. The main difference with IPC is that a pipe provides a continuous stream; IPC would treat a stream as a series of chunks, each transmitted separately.

When the reader and writer processes are on the same machine, a pipe between them can be stored in shared memory and the READ and WRITE operations are implemented in the same way as SEND and RECEIVE operations for message queues (Brinch Hansen, 1973). When the two processes are on different machines, IPC ports are used.

The semantics of READ and WRITE operations must be defined even if one end of the pipe is not connected. Should a writer be blocked from entering data until the reader opens its end? What happens if either the reader or writer breaks its connection? Such questions are answered by a *connection protocol*. The specifications in the table use the "rendezvous on open and close" connection protocol:

Table 11. Interface for pipes (level 6).

Form of call	Effect
pipe_handle := CREATE_PIPE()	Creates a new empty pipe and returns a handle for it. (If the caller is a process, it can store the handle in a directory entry and make the pipe available throughout the system.)
DELETE(pipe_handle)	Deletes the given pipe (undoes the corresponding CREATE_PIPE).
opipe_handle := OPEN(pipe_handle, rw)	Opens the given pipe by allocating buffer storage and performing setup operations. Initially, the pipe is empty. If rw = read the pipe is opened for reading (but only if the pipe is not already open for reading). If rw = write, it is opened for writing (but only if the pipe is not already open for writing). If both reader and writer are on the same machine, the pipe can be implemented in shared memory; otherwise it must be implemented using IPC ports.
CLOSE(opipe_handle)	If executed by the reader: closes down the pipe and sends an error message to a waiting writer. If executed by the writer: waits until reader empties the pipe, then closes it down.
READ(opipe_handle, buf, n)	Waits until there are at least n bytes in the open pipe, then moves them from the pipe into the caller's address space at base address buf. Awakens waiting writer if the read has freed up enough space in the pipe to accommodate the writer's request. (Fails if the open pipe does not permit reading.)
WRITE(opipe_handle, buf, n)	Copies n bytes from the caller's address space at base address buf into the given pipe. Waits if pipe cannot accommodate the requested bytes. May awaken waiting reader. (Fails if the open pipe does not permit writing.)

- The open-for-reading and the open-for-writing request may be called at different times; each returns immediately.

- The CLOSE operation, executed by the reader, shuts both ends of the pipe; when executed by the writer, the operation is deferred until the reader empties the pipe.

DIRECTORIES: LEVEL 7

Level 7 manages a hierarchy of directories containing handles for sharable objects. In our model, ports, pipes, files, devices, and directories are sharable; but handles for processes, threads, semaphores, virtual memories, and for open pipes, files, devices, are not sharable and cannot appear in directories. A hierarchy arises because a directory can contain handles for subordinate directories.

A directory is a table that matches an external name, stored as a string of characters, with a handle. (An access code for the object is contained in the handle.) The first ("self") entry of a directory contains a copy of the directory's own handle and the second entry is reserved for the handle of the parent directory. These two handles facilitate certain common operations such as copying an entry to the current directory or changing the current directory to the parent. In a tree of directories (Fig. 3), the concatenated sequence of external names from the root to a given object serves as a unique, system-wide external name (path name) for that object. Since directories are at a higher level than files, the file system can be used to store directories.

The principal directory operation is a search command that locates and returns the handle corresponding to a given external name. Thus, the directory level is merely a mechanism for mapping external names to internal ones. Information about attributes of objects, such as ownership, time of last use, or time of creation, is not kept in directories but rather in the object descriptor blocks within the various object-manager levels.

Portions of the directory hierarchy may be replicated across machines. The replication methods must guarantee consistency of the replicated portions; distributed database methods have been used for this purpose (Selinger, 1980), as have others (Ruan and Tichy, 1987; Howard *et al.*, 1988). To control the number of update messages in a large system, the full directory database may be kept on only a small number of machines. Other machines can cache the portions of the directory database accessed by their users. Operations that modify an entry in a directory must send updates to the directory database machines, which relay the updates to other machines.

The specifications for the directory level in the Table 12 are not complete; specific systems will provide other operations as needed.

The CREATE_DIR operation creates an empty, unattached directory. The access codes passed to this operation indicate which classes of processes have the right to search or modify the directory. The ATTACH operation is used to create a new entry in a target directory. When the new entry is a directory, this operation sets that new directory's parent pointer to the target directory. The DETACH operation only removes entries from directories but has no effect on the object to which a handle points; to delete an object, the DELETE operation of the appropriate level must be used. To minimize inadvertent deletions, the operation to delete a directory fails if applied to a directory containing anything else but the self and parent pointers.

The ATTACH and DETACH operations must notify other machines so that changes become effective throughout the system. By maintaining two conditions, this process is unlikely to yield inconsistencies: (1) an empty directory must first be attached to the global directory tree before entries are made in it, and (2) a directory must

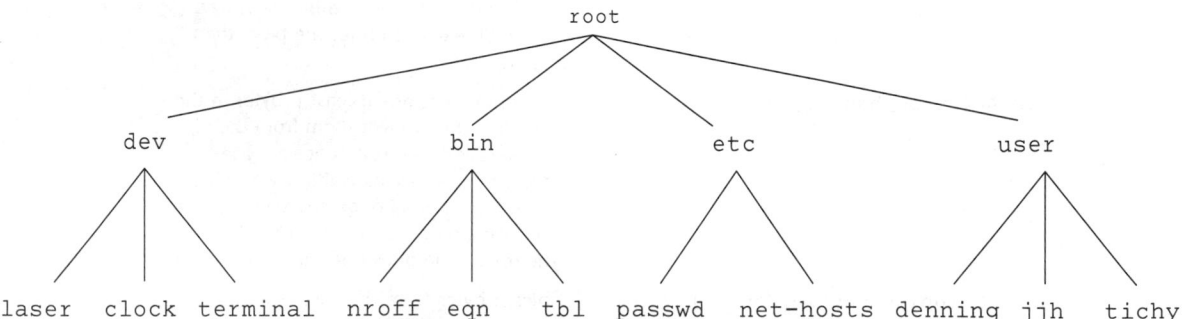

Figure 3. A directory tree. Some directories of the directory tree are permanently reserved for specific purposes. For example, the `dev` directory lists all the external devices of the system. The `lib` directory lists the library of all executable programs maintained by the system's administration. A `user` directory contains subdirectories for each authorized user; that subdirectory is the root of a subtree belonging to that user. In Unix, the unique external name of an object is formed by concatenating the external names along the path from the root, separated by / and omitting the root. Thus, the laser printer's external name is `/dev/laser`.

Table 12. Specification of a directory manager interface (level 7).

Form of call	Effect
`dir_handle := CREATE_DIR(access)`	Allocates an empty directory, sets its access codes to `access`, generates a handle for it, and places a copy of the handle in the first entry. Marks the new directory as unattached to the directory tree.)
`DELETE(dir_handle)`	Deletes the given directory. (Fails if any entry of the directory is nonempty, other than the self and parent entries, or if the directory is attached to the directory tree.)
`ATTACH(dir_handle,` `        name, obj_handle)`	Makes an entry (`name obj_handle`) in the given directory. If `obj_handle` denotes a directory, sets its parent entry to `dir_handle`. Notifies the directory databases of the change. (Fails if `name` already exists in the directory, if the directory `dir_handle` is not attached, if `obj_handle` denotes an already attached directory, of if `obj_handle` denotes a nonsharable object.)
`DETACH(dir_handle, name)`	Removes the named entry from the given directory. Notifies the directory databases of the change. (Fails if the given name does not exist in the given directory, or if it names a nonempty directory, or if the access codes of the directory prohibit changes.)
`obj_handle :=` `      SEARCH(dir_handle, name)`	Finds the entry of the given name in the given directory and returns a copy of the associated handle. (Fails if the name does not exist in the given directory, or if the access codes of the directory prohibit searching.)
`n := COUNT(dir_handle)`	Returns the number of entries in the given directory. (Fails if the the access codes of the directory prohibit searching.)
`(name, handle) :=` `      GET(dir_handle, i)`	Returns the ith entry of the directory. (Fails if there is no such entry or if the entry is blank.)
`RENAME(dir_handle, name, newname)`	Locates the named entry and replaces the name with the new name. (Fails if the directory access codes prohibit changes.)

be empty before being detached. A more complicated notification mechanism will be needed if a process can construct a directory subtree before attaching its root to the global directory tree. The COUNT and GET operations are used by a formatting program to prepare a summary of the objects listed in a directory.

SHELL: LEVEL 8

Most system users spend most of their time executing existing programs, not writing new ones. The shell is the program that listens to the user's console and interprets inputs as commands to invoke existing pro-

grams in specified combinations with specified inputs. When a user logs in, the operating system creates a process containing a copy of the shell program with its default input connected to the user's keyboard and its default output connected to the user's display.

The shell scans each complete command line of the input to pick out the names of programs to be invoked and the values of arguments to be passed to them. For each program called in this way, the shell creates a process. The processes are connected according to the data flow specified in the command line. Multics was one of the first systems to have a shell (Organick,

1972); Unix adapted the shell model (Ritchie and Thompson, 1974).

Operations of substantial complexity can be programmed in the command language of the Unix shell. For example, the operations that format and then print a file named `text` can be set in motion by the command line:

```
tbl < text | eqn | lptroff > output
```

The first program is `tbl`, which scans the data on its input stream and replaces descriptions of tables of information with the necessary formatting commands. The < symbol indicates that `tbl` is to take its input from the file `text`. The output of `tbl` is directed by a pipe (the | symbol) to the input of `eqn`, which replaces descriptions of equations with the necessary formatting commands. The output of `eqn` is then piped to `lptroff`, which generates the commands for the laser printer. Finally, > indicates that the output of `lptroff` is to be placed in the file `output`. If < `output` is replaced with | `laser`, the data are instead sent directly to the laser printer.

After the components of a command line are identified, the shell obtains handles for them by a series of commands:

```
h1 := SEARCH(CD, "tbl");
h2 := SEARCH(WD, "text");
h3 := CREATE_PIPE();
h4 := SEARCH(CD, "eqn");
h5 := CREATE_PIPE();
h6 := SEARCH(CD, "lptroff");
h7 := CREATE_FILE();
ATTACH(WD, "output", h7);
```

The variable `CD` holds a handle for a commands directory and `WD` holds a handle for the current working directory. Both `CD` and `WD` are part of the shell's context.

The shell then creates and resumes processes that execute the three components of the pipeline and awaits their completion:

```
RESUME(CREATE_SHPROC(h1, (OPEN(h2,r),
                          OPEN(h3,w))));
RESUME(CREATE_SHPROC(h4, (OPEN(h3,r),
                          OPEN(h5,w))));
RESUME(CREATE_SHPROC(h6, (OPEN(h5,r),
                          OPEN(h7,w))));
JOIN(3);
```

(`CREATE_SHPROC` works almost like `CREATE_PROC` of level 5. It first extracts the ports from the open stream descriptors in its second argument and passes these ports and the first argument, and executable file, to `CREATE_PROC`.) After the join completes, the shell can kill these processes, close all open objects, and acknowledge completion of the entire command to the user through a "prompt" symbol on the user's display.

If the specification < `text` is omitted, the shell connects `tbl` to the default input, which is the same as its own, namely the keyboard. In this case, the second search command is omitted and the first process creation is

```
CREATE_SHPROC(h1,(STD_IN, OPEN(h3,w)));
```

where `STD_IN` is the standard input for a process. Similarly, if > `output` is omitted, the shell connects `lptroff` to the default output, the shell's `STD_OUT`. If an elaborate command line is to be performed often, typing it can become tedious. Unix encourages users to store complicated commands in executable files called *shell scripts* that become simpler commands. A file named *format* might be created with the contents

```
tbl < $1 | eqn | lptroff > $2
```

where the names of the input and output files have been replaced by variables $1 and $2. When the command `format` is invoked, the variables $1 and $2 are replaced by the arguments following the command name. For example, typing

```
format text output
```

would substitute `text` for $1 and `output` for $2 and so would have exactly the same effect as the original command line.

GRAPHICS SERVER: LEVEL 9

The graphics server (Table 13) provides a standard way for programs to interact with the user pictorially. The basic abstractions are the *window* and the *event*. The window enables a program to display something for the user without interfering with the output of other programs. The event encapsulates information from input devices such as a keyboard, a mouse (*q.v.*), or a joystick, and messages sent between windows. The server maintains a policy (focus) for deciding to which window a given event belongs.

A user program can draw in a window regardless of whether it is visible or not. The server tries to maintain the contents of the window. If it loses the content, it can send a redraw event to the user program to request reconstruction of the context.

Each user program normally has an event loop to scan for and react to events. After initializing its windows, the program dedicates a thread to the event loop and to each of the actions linked to events. When an event arrives, the loop thread decides what action to take, invokes the corresponding action thread, then waits again. The event loop generally does not terminate until the user program does.

A special program called the *window manager* may be provided to assist the user. This program makes it easy for the user to manipulate windows on the screen (e.g.

Table 13. Graphics server (level 9).

Form of call	Effect
handle := CREATE(display)	Creates a new window on the given display.
DELETE(handle)	Removes the given window and its context from the display and releases its resources.
MOVE(handle, x, y)	Repositions the window at a new location.
RESIZE(handle, width, height)	Changes the size of the window.
MOVE(handle, x, y)	Repositions the window at a new location
SHOW(handle)	Makes the given window visible by placing it on the display.
HIDE(handle)	Removes the given window and its contents from the screen but maintain its state.
UP(handle)	Repositions the window over the window that most immediately overlaps it.
DOWN(handle)	Repositions the window under the window that it most immediately overlaps.
event := RECEIVE(handle)	Gets the next event that was sent to the window from its event queue.
SEND(handle, event)	Sends an event to the given window.

resize by dragging a corner, reposition by dragging the title bar), start and end programs, and even provide virtual screen space that is much larger than the actual screen. The user may even be able to choose what window manager to run. For example, the X Window server offers a wide variety of window managers to choose from (with acronyms including fvwm, twvm, mwm, kde, and gnome).

Window-system "class libraries" provide extensible building blocks for windows. With these libraries, a programmer can construct control windows that make it easier to present information to the user and get the user's feedback. Examples of control-window elements are icons, buttons, sliders, menus, checkboxes, tree displays, and table displays. The *Swing* library in Java (*q.v.*) is a good example. A windows manager and its class (*q.v.*) library offer the applications developer a powerful way of organizing user interactions with the application.

System Initialization

One small but essential piece of an operating system has not been discussed—the method of starting up the system. The startup procedure, called a *bootstrap* sequence, begins with a very short program copied into memory from a permanent read-only memory (ROM). This program loads a longer program from disk, which then takes control and loads the operating system itself. Finally, the operating system creates a special login process connected to each terminal of the system. When a user correctly types an identifier and a password (*q.v.*), the login process will create a shell process connected to the same terminal. When the user types a logout command, the shell process exits and the login process resumes.

Conclusion

We have used the levels model to describe the functions of multimachine operating systems and how it is possible to hide systematically the physical locations of all sharable objects while being able to locate them quickly when given a name in the directory hierarchy. The directory function is not simply a way of naming files; it is a way of naming any sharable object. No user machine needs to store locally a full copy of the entire directory structure; it need only save a copy of the view with which it is currently working. The full structure is maintained by a small group of machines implementing a reliable, dependable storage system.

The model can deal with heterogeneous systems consisting of general purpose user machines, such as workstations, and special purpose machines such as stable storage systems, database servers, file servers, and supercomputers (*q.v.*). Only the user machines need a full operating system; the special purpose machines require only a microkernel compatible with the microkernels on the workstations.

The model can also deal with the growing number of real-time systems (*q.v.*) such as bank customer inquiry systems, Web servers, airline reservation systems, transportation monitoring and control systems, manufacturing plant control systems, and hospital patient-monitoring systems. The common element in these systems is that each deals with a specified set of external events that trigger system responses, and the system responses must be completed within a specified deadline. The microkernel can be used to field the event signals and trigger the responses; the response programs can be established at the higher levels and use microkernel operations to coordinate their operations.

As computer systems proliferate we will rely more and more on networks of computers. The network will act as a "nervous system" connecting many sensors, actuators, motors, and service nodes. The networks will have to react to sensor input rapidly and effectively. The principles of operating systems, as outlined above, will be used to achieve these ends. Today's operating system principles, understood as software structuring principles, may well become principles for the design of chips and microcomputers—they are that fundamental.

Enterprise computing offers new challenges that can be accommodated within the levels mode. In organizations, the operating system is no longer limited to "managing the flow of work through the network of computers." It is concerned with helping people manage the flow of work in their organization. This form of operating system needs to incorporate a new level, a level that recognizes the distinctions of action in enterprises, a level higher in our hierarchy than the graphics server. The new, enterprise level is higher because it addresses ongoing never-ending coordinated, real-time actions among many people.

The levels mode is powerful because it is based on the same principle found in nature to organize many scales of space and time. At each level of abstraction are well-defined rules of interaction for the objects visible at that level; the rules can be understood without detailed knowledge of the smaller objects making up those objects. The many parts of an operating system cannot be fully understood without keeping this principle in mind.

Bibliography

1968. Dijkstra, E. W. "The Structure of the THE-Multiprogramming System," *Comm. of the ACM*, **11**, 5 (May), 341–346.

1970. Denning, P. J. "Virtual Memory," *Computing Surveys*, **2**, 3 (September), 154-216.

1971. Denning, P. J. "Third Generation Computer Systems," *Computing Surveys*, **3**, 4 (December), 175–212.

1972. Organick, E. I. *The Multics System: An Examination of its Structure.* Cambridge, MA: MIT Press.

1973. Brinch Hansen, P. *Operating System Principles.* Upper Saddle River, NJ: Prentice Hall.

1974. Fabry, R. S. "Capability-based Addressing," *Comm. of the ACM*, **17**, 7 (July), 403–412.

1974. Ritchie, D. M., and Thompson, K. L. "The UNIX Time-sharing System," *Comm. of the ACM*, **17**, 7 (July), 365–375.

1976. Denning, P. J. "Fault-tolerant Operating Systems," *Computing Surveys*, **8**, 4 (December), 359–389.

1976. Habermann, A. N., Flon, L., and Cooprider, L. W. "Modularization and Hierarchy in a Family of Operating Systems," *Comm. of the ACM*, **19**, 5 (May), 266–272.

1979. Jones, A. K., Chansler Jr., R. J., Durham, I., Schwans, K., and Vegdahl, S. R. "StarOS, a Multiprocessor Operating System for the Support of Task Forces," *Proceedings of the Seventh Symposium on Operating Systems Principles* (December), 117–127.

1979. Wilkes, M. V., and Needham, R. M. *The Cambridge CAP Computer and its Operating System.* Amsterdam: Elsevier/North-Holland Publishing Co.

1980. Neumann, P. G., Boyer, R. S., Feiertag, R. J., Levitt, K. N., and Robinson, L. "A Provably Secure Operating System, its Applications, and Proofs," *CSL-116*, 2nd Ed. Menlo Park, CA: SRI International.

1980. Ousterhout, J. K., Scelza, D. A., and Sindhu, P. S. "Medusa: An Experiment in Distributed Operating System structure," *Comm. of the ACM*, **23**, 2 (February), 92–105.

1980. Selinger, P. G. "Replicated Data," in *Distributed Data Bases* (ed. F. Poole), 223–231. Cambridge: Cambridge University Press.

1981. Popek, G. J., Walker, B. J., Chow, J. M., Edwards, D. A., Rudisin, G., and Thiel, G. "Locus: A Network Transparent, High Reliability Distributed System," *Proceedings of the Eighth Symposium on Operating Systems Principles* (December 1981), 169–177.

1981. Wulf, W. A., Levin, R. and Harbison, S. P. *HYDRA/C.mmp, An Experimental Computer System.* New York: McGraw-Hill.

1982. Birrell, A. D., Levin, R., Needham, R. M., and Schroeder, M. D. "Grapevine: An Exercise in Distributed Computing,"*Comm. of the ACM*, **25**, 4 (April), 260–274.

1982. Cheriton, D. R., *The Thoth System: Multi-process Structuring and Portability.* New York: Elsevier Science.

1982. Rowe, L. A., and Birman, K. P. "A Local Network Based on the UNIX Operating System," *IEEE Trans. Software Engineering*, **SE-8**, 2 (March), 137–146.

1983. Holt, R. C. *Concurrent Euclid, Unix, and the Tunis Operating System.* Reading, MA: Addison-Wesley.

1983. Organick, E. I. *A Programmer's View of the Intel 432 System.* New York: McGraw-Hill.

1984. Brown, R. L., Denning, P. J., and Tichy, W. F. "Advanced Operating Systems," *IEEE Computer.* **17**, 10 (Ocober), 173–190.

1984. Comer, D., *Operating System Design: The XINU Approach.* Upper Saddle River, NJ: Prentice Hall.

1984. Kernighan, B. W., and Pike, R. *The Unix Programming Environment.* Upper Saddle River, N.J: Prentice-Hall.

1985. Sandberg, R., Goldberg, D., Kleiman, S., Walsh, D., and Lyon, B. "Design and Implementation of the Sun Network Filesystem," *Proceedings of USENIX 1985 Summer Conference* (June), 119–130.

1985. Tichy, W. F. "RCS—A System for Version Control," *Software–Practice & Experience*, **15**, 7 (July), 637–654.

1986. Accetta, M., Baron, R., Bolosky, W., Golub, D., Rashid, R., Tevanian, A., and Young, M. "Mach: A New Kernel Fundation for Unix Development," *Proceedings of USENIX 1986 Summer Conference*, 93–113.

1987. Ruan, Z., and Tichy, W. "Performance Analysis of File Replication Schemes in Distributed Systems," *Performance Evaluation Review*, **15**, 1 (May), 205–215.

1988. Howard J. H., Kazar, M. L., Menees, S. G., Nichols, D. A., Satyanarayanan, M., Sidebotham, R. N., and West, M. J. "Scale and Performance in a Distributed File System," *ACM Transactions on Computer Systems*, **6**, 2 (February), 51–81.

1988. Rashid, R., Tevanian, A., Young, M., Young, D., Baron, R., Black, D., Bolosky, W., and Chew, J. "Machine-independent Virtual Memory Management for Paged Uniprocessor and Multiprocessor Architectures," *IEEE Transactions on Computers*, **37**, *8* (August), 896–908.

1990. Denning, P. J. and Tichy, W. F., "Highly Parallel Computation," *Science*, **250** (30 November), 1217–1222.

1995. Tanenbaum, A. S. *Distributed Operating Systems*. Upper Saddle River, NJ: Prentice Hall.

1996. Tanenbaum, A. S. *Computer Networks*, 3rd Ed. Upper Saddle River, NJ: Prentice Hall.

Peter J. Denning and Walter F. Tichy

CONTEMPORARY ISSUES

The Role of an Operating System

From a functional viewpoint, an operating system is a collection of programs that acts as an intermediary between the hardware and its users, providing a high-level interface to low-level hardware resources, such as the CPU, memory, and I/O devices. The operating system provides various facilities and services that make the use of the hardware convenient, efficient, and safe. Examples of these facilities and services are memory management (*q.v.*), process management, communication facilities, a command language interpreter (*see* SHELL), and a file system. The *sharing* of resources among users and programs is an essential goal of most operating systems.

From a structural viewpoint, an operating system offers services to clients. The fundamental task is to control interaction among users and also between users and system services. On the one hand, the operating system protects users and system services against corruption through others. On the other hand, it offers controlled communication channels. The combination of protection and system-controlled communication is the basis for achieving sufficient reliability and to establish security policies.

Wide variations are encountered both in the demands that are placed upon operating systems, and in the operating system structures that are adopted in response to those demands. Real-time systems (*q.v.*), personal computers, workstations (*q.v.*), time-sharing (*q.v.*) systems, and supercomputers (*q.v.*) may impose significantly different demands on their operating systems. Operating system structures range from highly monolithic to highly modularized and decentralized.

A Historical Perspective

The earliest computer systems were employed by a single user at a time to run a single program at a time. By operating toggles on the front panel of the system, the user would cause a machine language program to be loaded at a specific memory address from a simple device, such as a paper tape reader. Execution of the program would be commenced manually, again using toggles to specify an address to which control should be transferred. During execution, the program might read input or produce output; low-level machine instructions to operate I/O devices would be embedded in the program. Execution would terminate when the program branched to a "halt" instruction. When the lights stopped flashing, the job was finished.

Among the drawbacks to this style of operation were that every user had to know the computer system at a detailed level. Even for the single active program, the operation of the system was essentially sequential: read input, compute, read more input, compute, write output, etc. The sharing of the computer system was very inefficient; and facilities that we take entirely for granted today, such as large virtual memories and file systems, did not exist.

Some of the requirements for detailed knowledge of the computer system were ameliorated by the simple expedient of sharing partial programs: a single individual would write routines to control the I/O devices and would make these routines available (physically) to others. In some sense, these were the first operating system routines. The idea of a *resident monitor* was a further improvement: these routines would be permanently loaded in a region of memory (*see* Fig. 1), and user programs (loaded in the remainder of memory) would call them. The resident monitor often controlled an operator's console, providing a "soft substitute" for the physical toggles: the user could cause a program to be loaded and initiated by entering simple console commands. The existence of a resident monitor immediately raises the issue of protection. Without protection, an errant program could eradicate the resident

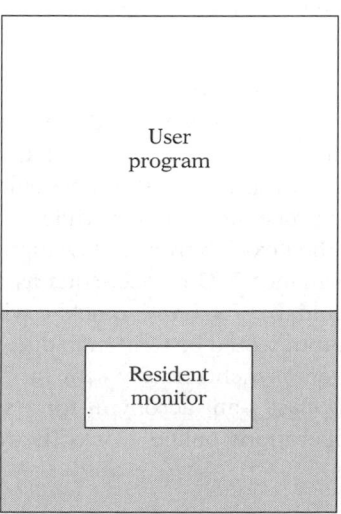

Figure 1. Resident monitor.

monitor, affecting not only the current user (who at least was presumably responsible for the accident) but future ones, and requiring the resident monitor to be reloaded.

The word *boot*, short for *bootstrapping*, is used to denote the initial loading of the operating system (*see* BOOTSTRAP)). In these days of large read-only memories, it is easy to forget the relevance of this term. Imagine, though, how the user program or the resident monitor was read into the memory of an early computer. Typically, the hardware of the CPU or of the I/O device was capable of independently reading some small amount of binary data—say, several words—into a fixed memory location. In a typical bootstrap procedure, this binary data would be a very small program that was capable of commanding the I/O device to read a somewhat larger amount of data, which would be a slightly larger program that was capable of commanding the I/O device to read more data, and so forth. Into the 1970s, computer systems were bootstrapped from card decks in which successive cards had greater amounts of binary data punched into them; "hauling yourself up by your own bootstraps" is indeed an apt analogy.

The inefficiencies that resulted from the sequential nature of system operation were ameliorated by overlapping I/O with computation within a single job. The program would initiate a physical input operation before the data was actually required; the I/O device would read the data into a buffer other than the one the program was currently accessing. Output also used multiple buffers. The obvious performance benefit was accompanied by a significant drawback: programs became more complex, particularly because concurrent activities now had to be managed. Indeed, nearly all operating systems are complex concurrent programs, but many of them suffer because of the historical precedent of handling this concurrency in an *ad hoc* manner.

I/O devices, such as paper tape readers and punches, card readers and punches, and line printers, are inherently slow. Even in a system that ran a single user program at a time, considerable efficiency could be gained by processing one job while simultaneously transferring the next job from a slow input device to a higher-performance I/O device, such as a disk, from which it could be retrieved quickly when needed. Similarly, output would be written to disk when generated, and then asynchronously sent to the punch or printer. SPOOLING—an acronym for "simultaneous peripheral operations online"—was the term used to describe this.

Time-sharing (multiuser interactive computing) was possible, even on computer systems that ran a single program at a time. MIT's Compatible Time-Sharing System (CTSS) was a very simple landmark time-sharing system. The memory of the computer system on which CTSS ran was only large enough to accommodate a single user. At the end of a time slice (*q.v.*), *swapping* (*q.v.*) was used to suspend temporarily the execution of one user program and allow another to execute. The former program's memory image was sent to disk, after which the latter's memory image was retrieved from disk. (Clearly, the swap image needed to contain more state information than simply the contents of memory to make it possible to resume the user program at the point where it had been suspended.)

Multiprogramming was a significant advance, for it allowed multiple users to share a computer system simultaneously, rather than sequentially. In early multiprogramming systems, the memory of the computer system was partitioned into a fixed set of regions of various sizes (*see* Fig. 2). The *long-term scheduling* algorithm determined which of the waiting jobs would be allocated the next available region of memory. The *short-term scheduling* algorithm determined which of the memory-resident jobs would be allocated the CPU. In a multiprogramming system, programs needed to be *relocatable*, since the address range of the program depended on the region to which it was assigned. (Hardware techniques such as *base registers* or *relocation registers* were typically employed—*see* MEMORY PROTECTION.) It also was mandatory that the operating system be responsible for I/O activity, since the simultaneous physical sharing of I/O devices by user programs was fraught with peril. Typically, users ceased to attempt to overlap their own CPU and I/O activity; the operating system achieved overall efficiency by overlapping the I/O of one user with the computation of another.

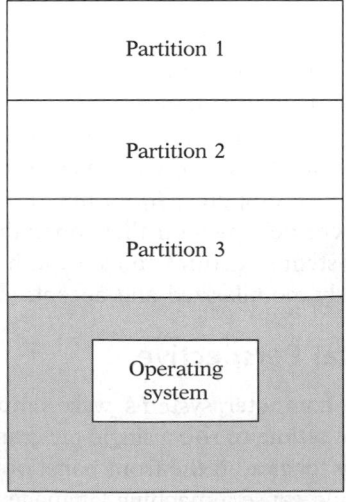

Figure 2. Multiprogramming with a fixed number of partitions.

More sophisticated multiprogramming systems divided memory into a variable number of regions of sizes tailored to the specific requirements of jobs. *Memory fragmentation* was a problem with either fixed-partition or variable-partition multiprogramming systems: *internal* fragmentation if a program was allocated a larger region than it required; *external* fragmentation if regions went unused because of a mismatch with the actual demands of the available jobs.

A drawback of all of the operating system designs discussed thus far is that each user program was required to be fully resident in a contiguous region of memory. *Paging* and *segmentation* are two approaches to removing the requirement for contiguity by using an indirection table. *Virtual memory* systems remove the requirement for full residency. A *page fault* occurs when a reference is made to a portion of a program's address space that is not memory-resident, and this page is fetched from secondary storage and the program resumed.

Concepts such as protection, asynchronous I/O, multiprogramming, virtual memory, and file systems are as important in single-user workstation systems as they are in multiuser time-sharing systems. A single user may wish to continue computing while the printer is active and to run multiple programs simultaneously (e.g. an editor and a compiler). These programs may not fit in the available physical memory, may be untrustworthy and need to be protected from one another; etc. One of the most interesting phenomena of the recent past has been to see operating systems for personal computers quickly recapitulate the 40-year history of development of operating systems for mainframes (*q.v.*).

Concurrency in Operating Systems

Concurrency is a prevalent theme in operating systems. There is physical concurrency: multiple I/O devices simultaneously active. There is logical concurrency: multiple users sharing the system, even though only one can actually be using the CPU at a particular instant (on a uniprocessor system).

In early operating systems, this concurrency was managed using *ad hoc* techniques. A user program would *trap* (*q.v.*) to the operating system, requesting some service. The program's state would be saved as part of the trap procedure. The operating system would initiate the requested activity, typically by sending a *start I/O* command to a device. The operating system would then *resume* some other program, restoring its previously saved state. When the I/O completed, the device would *interrupt* whatever program happened to be running at the time, saving the program's state and

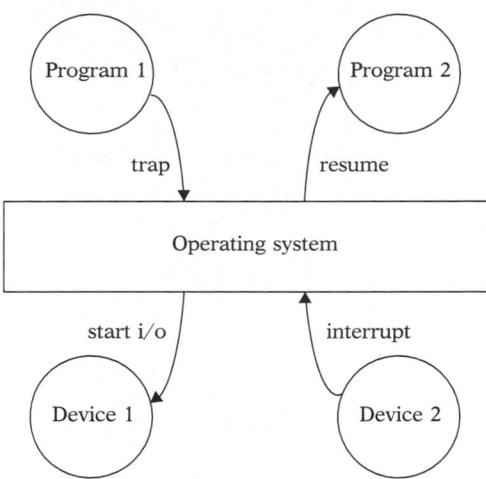

Figure 3. Communication with the operating system.

transferring control to an *interrupt handling routine* in the operating system. The operating system would resume the program that had been waiting for the I/O to complete (*see* Fig. 3). Errors were avoided by *disabling interrupts* when the operating system was active, thereby preventing the operating system from being interrupted at inopportune moments (such as when a critical shared data structure (*q.v.*) was in some intermediate state).

An operating system structured in this way is a bit like a juggler with lots of balls up in the air: as long as nothing out of the ordinary happens, things are fine, but the entire operation is somewhat fragile. There are a huge number of critical shared data structures, of which the corruption of any one could potentially wreak havoc on the system's operation. Techniques to cope with the complexities arising from concurrency were a major accomplishment of operating systems research in the 1960s.

Sequential Processes

The most important of these techniques was the idea, due to Dijkstra, of structuring the system as a collection of *cooperating sequential processes*. A *process* is the execution of a program by a (virtual) CPU. A *sequential* process does not deal with asynchronous events, although it does communicate with other processes through a well-defined synchronous interface. An individual process may be in one of three states: *running* (i.e. actively computing), *ready* (i.e. ready to run, but not currently allocated the CPU), or *blocked* (awaiting some event, such as a message or an interrupt) (*see* Fig. 4). These multiple processes, *cooperating* through the communication interface, can be used to implement an operating system.

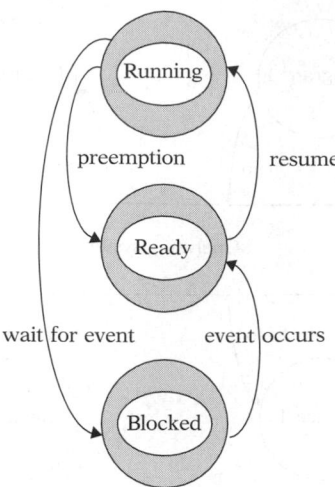

Figure 4. The states of a process.

Microkernels

A system design based upon the idea of cooperating sequential processes would involve a small kernel (*q.v.*), a *microkernel*, whose main responsibilities are to support processes and interprocess communication. Most operating system functions are then performed by processes. For example, separate processes are used to manage each I/O device, to implement spooling, to represent each user, to manage virtual memory, etc. These processes interact by means of mechanisms such as *monitors* (*see* MONITOR, SYNCHRONIZATION) or *message passing*. When a user program has an I/O request, the request is communicated by the user's process, through the kernel, to the manager process for the appropriate device. The user's process is then blocked. The device manager process, which was blocked waiting for a request message, is unblocked. In response to the message, it contacts the kernel to initiate the physical I/O and then blocks again. The effect of a device interrupt is to cause the kernel to ready the appropriate device manager process, which takes whatever actions may be necessary, and eventually signals the blocked user process that it can continue by communicating with it through the kernel. The role of the kernel is to translate asynchronous interrupts into synchronous signals that awaken device manager processes, and more broadly to implement interprocess communication and process scheduling. The kernel interface supports operations such as `Create` (create a new process), `Destroy` (kill a process), `Send` (send a message to a process and block, awaiting a response), and `Receive` (block, awaiting a message from some process). In addition, the kernel would makes resource allocation decisions among processes, at least at the level of allocating the CPU. Asynchrony is an issue when programming the kernel,

but not when programming the remainder of the operating system. Interrupts must be disabled only during the very brief periods of time when the kernel itself is active.

Version 3.0 of the Mach operating system and the Chorus kernel are some of the first commercial systems to be structured as microkernel operating systems. Various research systems (e.g. Solo, the V system, Amoeba) have been structured in this manner since the early 1980s.

Most early microkernels suffered from performance problems. In particular, the two key mechanisms, interprocess communication and process switching, were too expensive. Faster cache-based processor architectures made such mechanisms even more expensive relative to the ever-increasing processor speed. However, new research kernels, e.g. L4 and Exokernel, overcome that strategic performance problem. Communication and process switching is now typically one to two orders of magnitude faster than before and seems to scale well with increasing processor performance. Furthermore, second-generation microkernels offer an even higher flexibility than the first generation did. They are almost completely free of resource-management policies, which are instead provided by library routines that can be adapted for different uses. They can thus be used not only for conventional workstations and servers but also for real-time systems and pervasive devices such as wearable computers.

Monolithic Kernels

Although most contemporary operating systems support the notions of processes and structured interprocess communication, few go to the extreme of delegating all traditional operating system functionality to processes, despite the obvious advantages of this sort of microkernel structure. The first reason is inertia. The second is performance. A microkernel operating system places significant demands on the interprocess communication mechanism and will perform poorly if this mechanism is not efficient. Therefore most industrial operating systems have been built as *monolithic kernels* where all system services and the process system are integrated in one large kernel. Typical monolithic kernel sizes are 0.5 to 1 MB. Some research systems, e.g. Spin and Vino, try to achieve microkernel flexibility enabling them to extend monolithic kernels dynamically by user-defined modules.

Concurrent Programming Using Monitors

Monitors, attributed to Hoare, are one key approach to programming operating systems. As a first example, consider the *critical section problem*, which arises frequently in operating systems. A *critical section* is any piece of code that must be accessed by only one process at a time. For instance, suppose that several processes are counting occurrences of some type of event, such as I/O operations on various disks. When an I/O operation takes place at the disk being managed/observed by a particular process, this process loads the value of a shared counter, adds one, and stores back the result. The code to increment the counter is a critical section, for consider the following interleaving of operations:

Time	Observer A	Observer B
1	load	
2		load
3	add 1	
4		add 1
5	store	
6		store

Two events occur, but the value of the shared counter increases by only one.

To make the problem more interesting, we introduce a different type of process, one which periodically reports the number of events that have occurred in the reporting interval. It does this by reading the value of the counter, displaying it on a terminal, and zeroing the counter. (This example is due to Holt.) Consider the following interleaving of operations:

Time	Observer A	Reporter
1	load	
2		load
3	add 1	
4		display
5	store	
6		store 0

The event being tallied by Observer A is "lost."

Clearly, the observers and the reporter are interacting sequential processes: they loop, working largely independently but sharing the counter. However, some discipline must be imposed on accesses to the shared counter to turn the interaction into cooperation and avoid erroneous results. A *monitor* is one way to discipline this interaction.

A monitor includes data structures that are accessed by multiple processes (in this case, just the shared counter) and procedures that are used to access these data structures (in this case, a procedure Count, which is called by the observers, and a procedure Report, which is called by the reporter).

Thus far, monitors sound like abstract data types (*q.v.*) that encapsulate data structures. Each monitor, however, has the key property that at most one process may be executing its procedures at any time.

This is implemented by calls to the kernel at the start and end of each of the monitor's procedures. The kernel call at the start, Monitor_Enter, checks a flag to see if the monitor is occupied. If not, this flag is set and the process is allowed to continue. If so, then the process is blocked and placed on a kernel queue, waiting for the monitor to be free. The kernel call at the end, Monitor_Exit, checks the queue to see if any processes are waiting for the monitor. If not, the flag indicating that the monitor is occupied is unset. If so, then one of the waiting processes is made ready. In either case, the process exiting the procedure remains ready. The kernel calls themselves (Monitor_Enter and Monitor_Exit) must be done under hardware-level mutual exclusion (e.g. by disabling interrupts) to ensure the integrity of the kernel's queues and flags.

It is easy to see that this mechanism solves the problem just posed. To motivate the remaining properties of monitors, consider the more complex example of the *bounded buffer producer–consumer problem*, which again arises in many places in an operating system. The *producer* is a process that generates something, e.g. lines of output destined for a printer. The *consumer* is a process that disposes of what the producer generates, e.g. the device manager process for the printer. The producer and the consumer interact through a set of buffers (in this case, a fixed number of one-line buffers managed as a ring). The producer and the consumer run at irregular rates. The buffers increase overall throughput by allowing some "elasticity" between these two processes. However, discipline is necessary: if the consumer is operating slowly and all of the buffers are full, the producer must block; if the producer is operating slowly and all of the buffers are empty, the consumer must block.

In this case, the data within the monitor includes the ring of buffers, a counter indicating the number of buffers that are full, and pointers to the next buffer to be filled and the next buffer to be emptied. There are two access procedures: Deposit (called by the producer), and Remove (called by the consumer). Within the Deposit procedure, the producer checks to see if any empty buffers are available. If so, the producer deposits its data in the appropriate buffer, updates the counter and the pointer to the next buffer to be filled, and executes a Signal statement on a *condition variable* used to indicate that there is at least one full buffer. If not, the producer executes a Wait statement on a condition variable used to indicate that there is at least one empty buffer. This causes the producer to block, logically outside of the monitor, until the condition is signaled. Within the Remove procedure, the consumer checks to see if any full buffers are available. If so, the consumer removes the data from the appropriate buffer, updates the counter and the pointer to the next buffer to be emptied, and executes a `Signal` statement on a condition variable used to indicate that there is at least one empty buffer. If not, the consumer executes a `Wait` statement on a condition variable used to indicate that there is at least one full buffer. This causes the consumer to block, logically outside of the monitor, until the condition is signaled.

Monitors are an appropriate mechanism for concurrent programming within an operating system. A kernel supporting monitors would simply need to implement the procedures `Monitor_Enter`, `Monitor_Exit`, `Signal`, and `Wait`, plus the appropriate queues and flags. They are a better tool for structuring concurrent programs than is the lower-level semaphore construct described in the GENERAL PRINCIPLES section of this article, and monitors or variations on them are common.

Deadlock

Deadlock is a problem that can arise in concurrent systems when one process is waiting for a resource that is held by a second process, which in turn is waiting for a resource that is held by the first process. For example, suppose that the system's input spooler fills the disk with jobs waiting to run, with the result that there is no space in which to put the output of jobs that are trying to complete. (Things can, of course, be much more complicated than this.)

The deadlock problem was studied extensively in the early 1970s. A number of algorithms exist for preventing deadlock, offering various trade-offs between concurrency and overhead. One such algorithm is to have each process claim every resource it will need at the outset, aborting if this is not possible; this is clearly safe, but may dramatically restrict the set of jobs that can execute concurrently. A second algorithm is to number resources and require that resources always be acquired in ascending order; this algorithm is also safe (less obviously so) and is less restrictive. A third algorithm, called the *Banker's algorithm*, requires each process to state at the outset its maximum simultaneous requirement for each type of resource. Then, whenever a process requires a unit of a resource, the "banker" sees if this allocation would lead to deadlock if every process then requested its maximum claim. (Implicit in this is the fact that efficient algorithms for *detecting* deadlock also have been devised.) If not, the allocation is made; if so, the process is blocked.

An alternative to preventing deadlock is to allow it to occur (rarely, it is hoped), and then detect this occurrence and correct it, typically by terminating one of the offending processes. The cost/performance trade-

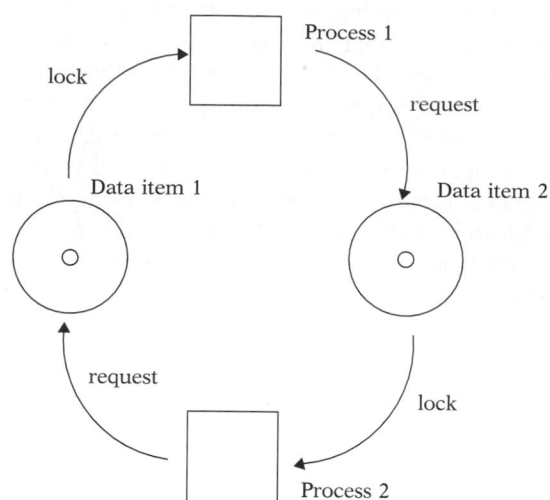

Figure 5. Two-process deadlock.

offs between prevention and detection/correction are highly system- and application-dependent.

Renewed interest in the deadlock problem has arisen from the advent of transaction processing (*q.v.*) systems in which data items are locked to avoid concurrency-related errors. If process A locks data item 1 and process B locks data item 2, and then process A attempts to lock data item 2 and process B attempts to lock data item 1, a deadlock results (*see* Fig. 5).

Virtual Address Spaces

In a traditional multiprogramming system and in many small personal computers, there is a single *address space* with a size equal to the size of physical memory. Different programs are allocated different parts of this address space, with protection typically achieved by hardware tags associated with fixed-size pieces of memory.

This organization is simple, but, as noted earlier, has several drawbacks. A program must be fully resident in a contiguous region of memory, with provision made for relocating the program once its region is determined.

Most computer systems today, even personal computers, employ some form of paged virtual memory. In a paged virtual memory system, each program has its own address space, which begins at address 0 and runs to some hardware-defined maximum. All address references in the program are within this address space. All address spaces are logically divided into *pages* of some fixed size. The physical memory is physically divided into *page frames* of the same fixed size. Any logical page can be stored in any physical page frame, which greatly simplifies memory allocation for the operating system, and eliminates external fragmentation. The mapping from program addresses (referred to as *virtual addresses*) to memory addresses (referred to as *physical addresses*) is accomplished by indirection using a *page table*—one per address space. A virtual address consists of two parts: a page number and an offset within that page. When the program issues an address, a *dynamic address translation* unit uses the page number as an index into the appropriate page table (determined from the ID of the address space that is active). The contents of the indexed page table entry are the physical memory address of the start of the *page frame* holding the correct page of data. The offset (from the virtual address) is added to this address to form the physical address, and the reference takes place. (*See* Fig. 6; note that there are other possible organizations for page tables.)

Most contemporary computer systems also support some rudimentary form of *segmentation*. In a fully flexible segmentation system, such as that employed by Multics, each program element is assigned to a variable-sized segment, and dynamic linking between segments is supported. More common is to have just a few segments in each address space, e.g. an operating system segment, a user code segment, and a user data or stack segment. (The VAX VMS operating system supported a scheme similar to this—*see* DIGITAL EQUIPMENT CORPORATION.)

Paging and segmentation ease a number of the problems of protection and sharing. A process or program can generate addresses only within its address space. The address space is defined by the page table. The page table is built by the operating system. As long as the operating system is correct, the potential for one user illicitly reading or destroying the data of another (or of the system, which has its own address space) is

eliminated. Sharing between two processes can be accomplished by having certain page table or segment table entries for these processes be the same.

DEMAND PAGING

A key point is that a page table entry may be marked as *invalid*, meaning that the correct page of data is not resident in memory. Should a reference to such a page occur, the dynamic address translation unit generates a *page fault* interrupt. The operating system gets control, brings the desired page from secondary storage to a page frame in primary memory (retiring the page that had occupied that frame, if any, to secondary storage), updates the page table entry, and then restarts the user program. This allows a program's physical memory allocation to be less than the size of its address space— sometimes by a very large factor.

Most systems rely on *demand paging*: they do not attempt to anticipate the pages that a program will need, but rather wait for a fault to occur and then fetch the page. (Obviously, some other program is run during the I/O activity.) An exception to this rule is that, when a program is temporarily suspended and swapped out, performance may be improved by writing all of its memory-resident pages to a contiguous swap area on disk, and then reading all of these pages back in prior to restarting the program.

A variety of *page replacement algorithms* is used to determine which page frame should be allocated to a page that has been faulted in. Some variation of *least recently used* (LRU) is common in practice. A thorough discussion of this topic is beyond the scope of this article.

Multiple-address-space Systems

Most operating systems provide process-specified address spaces. Each process (or group of tightly coupled processes) uses its own address spaces. The address spaces are independent of each other so that the computer memory is virtually replicated for each user. This method automatically protects users against each other: data and code accesses always work inside their own address space. Furthermore, it enables user-specific object/memory allocation and code generation: code can be generated and memory can be allocated independent from other users.

On the one hand, address conflicts between users are impossible; on the other hand, virtual addresses cannot be used for communication between multiple users or for identifying global objects. The latter restriction is not a real disadvantage on 32-bit systems since their address spaces are simply too small to include all system-global objects such as data on a disk in a single address space. Even many current laptops

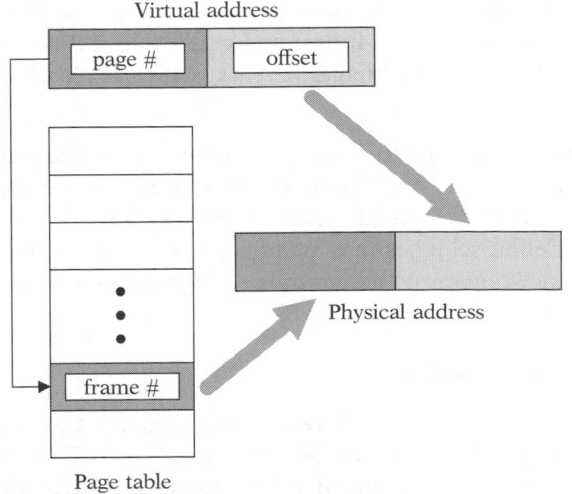

Figure 6. Address translation.

offer hard disks that cannot be mapped into a 4 GB virtual address space. Therefore, such systems always extend the address-space paradigm by a system-global *namespace*. Names are associated with global objects, e.g. files and processes, so that the objects can be referenced by their names. Very often, the *file system* acts as a name server that implements the namespace and offers system operations to identify the objects (`Open`) and to access them (`Read`, `Write`). Read–write operations typically require copying data between the system buffers and user address space. This makes according object access unnecessarily expensive and complicates the task of writing a program that accesses the object correctly and efficiently.

Newer systems therefore also offer a `Map` operation that maps the object/file dynamically into the user's address space. Then, a program can access the file like ordinary program variables. The implementation is straightforward: a page fault on a page that belongs to an address-space region that is backed by a mapped file is handled by the file system acting as a pager.

Single-address-space Systems

Forthcoming 64-bit processors enable a radically different paradigm, the *single-address-space operating system* (SASOS) where all processes share the same huge address space. Per-process *protection domains* control how each process can access that single address space. Here, a protection domain is the subset of the single address space that is visible to the corresponding process.

In contrast to conventional multi-address-space systems, virtual addresses are unique in the system and are valid throughout all processes whose protection domains include the corresponding address-space region. Consequently, objects can easily be shared or transferred between processes. For sharing an object between multiple processes, it is sufficient to include the object (its address-space region) in the protection domains of those processes. Transferring an object to another process is done by removing its region from the sender's protection domain and adding it to the receiver's one. The object's (virtual) address always remains the same.

Consequently, virtual addresses can be used as system-global identifiers. File names—although useful for humans—are no longer necessary for data that should be accessed by multiple processes or that should be persistent. Provided that the single address space is persistent (i.e. that it can survive a system shutdown or crash), file systems are no longer necessary to keep internal data and executable files. Executing a program is simply a procedure call to its virtual start address;

internal data like the registry, user preferences, etc. is accessed directly by load/store instructions in the same way as all other program variables. File read–write operations are not required.

Conventional multi-address-space systems typically require code relocation or *pointer swizzling* (mapping data references to address pointers) when an object is transferred to a different address space. (Reading or writing the object from or to a file can be regarded as such an operation.) Sharing objects between multiple address spaces generally relies on mapping the object identically in all address spaces, a method that soon leads to address conflicts.

Such problems disappear in a single-address-space system, since an object occupies the same address-space region throughout all processes and intra-object pointers are thus automatically valid in every process (provided the object is accessible in that protection domain).

A naive method for allocation and deletion of objects in a single-address-space system is based on the huge size of the address space: objects are allocated contiguously. Deleting an object releases its physical resources and makes its corresponding address-space region inaccessible (removes it from all protection domains). The regions of deleted objects are never recycled, i.e. they will never be reused for new objects. Advantages of the scheme are that object references are unique over time—you can never access the wrong object by using an outdated object reference—and that the allocation is very simple. On the other hand, the address space will be exhausted after some time.

Current processors offer 64-bit address spaces, approximately 1.8×10^{19} bytes. That might be sufficient for single workstations and medium-sized clusters: each minute, a 100 MB object can be created and deleted for over 5000 years. However, large servers and/or clusters might well create or delete at the rate of 100 GB per minute in the future and could thus exhaust the address space within five years, which is clearly not acceptable.

Since single-address-space systems are of particular interest for very large databases and other large distributed systems, more sophisticated allocation/deletion schemes may be required that reuse address space regions no longer in use. Practical experience is not yet available.

File Systems

Typical file-system operations are `Create`, `Destroy`, `Open`, `Close`, `Read`, `Write`, and `Seek`. Four key issues in the design of a file system are *allocation*, *organization*, *naming*, and *protection*.

Allocation concerns the way in which a file is mapped onto the physical disk. Among the desirable properties for an allocation strategy are ease of file creation and expansion, rapid direct access (access to a specific byte of the file), rapid sequential access (access to consecutive bytes of the file), and minimization of wasted disk space. Two extreme allocation strategies are *contiguous* and *linked*. Under contiguous allocation, the file is allocated in a contiguous area on disk. This makes access rapid, but makes creation and expansion difficult and may result in considerable wasted space. Under linked allocation, the file is allocated in fixed-size blocks that are linked together. This makes creation and expansion easy and reduces wasted space, but access is slow. A compromise is indexed allocation: the file is allocated in fixed-size blocks that are accessed through a set of index blocks, making random access efficient (although sequential access still requires many slow disk seeks). Some cleverness is required to insure that the index itself remains of manageable size. Unix (*q.v.*) uses an indexed allocation scheme in which each file is headed by an *i-node* containing (among other things) a small number of pointers (13 in one implementation), the first few of which point to 4 KB blocks of data, but the last three of which point, respectively, to a 4 KB block of pointers to 4 KB blocks of data, a 4 KB block of pointers to 4 KB blocks of pointers to 4 KB blocks of data, and a 4 KB block of pointers to 4 KB blocks of pointers to 4 KB block of pointers to 4 KB blocks of data (*see* Fig. 7). (Obviously, neither data blocks nor pointer blocks are allocated until the file expands to require them.) This scheme allows the efficient representation and access of files ranging from very small to very large. While Unix supports only this one allocation strategy, many production operating systems support several.

Organization concerns the "file model" available to the programmer. In Unix, all files adhere to a single model: files are sequential *streams* of bytes. This has the advantage of simplicity, and integrates well with other fundamental abstractions of Unix (e.g. pipes). Most operating systems support several file models (indexed, for example, in addition to sequential byte stream). The organization and the allocation strategy interact closely. Certain allocation strategies are most efficient for particular organizations.

Nearly all modern operating systems employ a hierarchical directory structure for naming. A directory (*q.v.*) maps names to files; files can be either data or other directories. A hierarchical directory structure allows the user to organize files in a structured and intelligent manner.

Protection is a significant issue that transcends the file system and cannot be treated fully in this article. *Access control lists* (lists associated with each file specifying who can access the file in what ways) and *capabilities* (unforgeable entities handed to users that indicate what files they can access in what ways) are two well-studied approaches to file protection.

The scheduling of disk operations is a topic that received much attention in the 1960s and 1970s. Four common algorithms are *first come, first served* (FCFS), *shortest seek time first* (SSTF), *scan*, and *sweep*. In the presence of a large queue of requests, FCFS offers a fairly uniform but fairly large response time. In SSTF, service is always given to the request whose seek distance is the shortest from the current head position; SSTF offers excellent average response time but a high variance, because requests located on the inner or outer cylinders may be "starved." In scan and sweep, the head moves from one edge of the disk to the other, handling all requests it encounters. (These algorithms differ only in their details.) Scan and sweep offer good compromise performance: mean response time almost as low as that of SSTF, and variability almost as low as that of FCFS. In truth, though, on most systems (particularly those with multiple disks), the length of the disk request queue is seldom long enough to benefit appreciably from clever scheduling.

Processor Scheduling

Processor scheduling (*see* SCHEDULING ALGORITHMS) is another aspect of process management that has been thoroughly studied and is well understood. The most important theoretical result is that *shortest remaining*

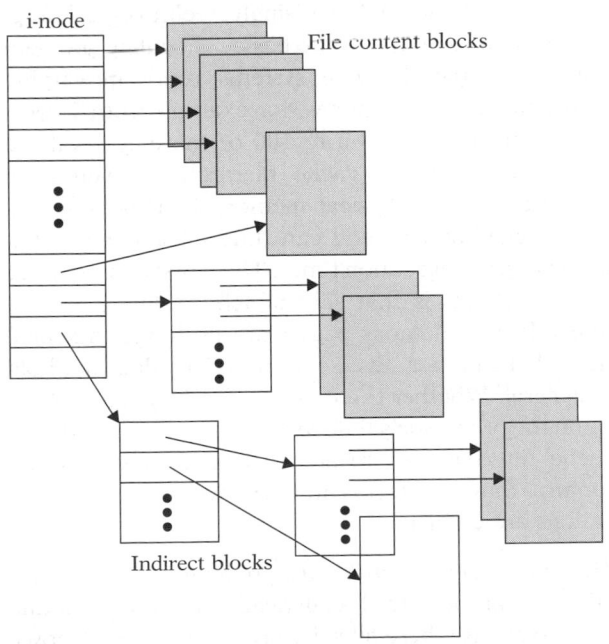

i-node

File content blocks

Indirect blocks

Figure 7. Unix file allocation.

processing time first (SRPT) is the optimal strategy to minimize response time when jobs' service times are deterministic and known at the instant the job arrives. Unfortunately, neither of these things is typically true in time-sharing systems, but most actual schedulers attempt in some way to mimic the behavior of SRPT.

Round-robin is a practical policy that preemptively rotates the CPU among the ready jobs, giving each job some *quantum* of service before moving on to the next. Its advantage over *first come, first served* is that a short job cannot get "stuck" behind a long job.

Feedback policies are an enhancement of round-robin in which a job, after receiving a certain amount of round-robin service, is "demoted" to a sequence of lower-priority queues. The relationship to SRPT is clear: service times aren't known in advance, but as jobs prove themselves to be long-running, they receive progressively worse service. Each newly arriving job is given the "benefit of the doubt" and begins its service in the highest priority queue. Most time-sharing systems use some variation of feedback scheduling.

Real-time tasks require different scheduling policies. The goal is then no longer to minimize the response time but to meet all *deadlines*. One of the first policies for scheduling periodic tasks was *rate-monotonic scheduling*. Rate monotonic is a static policy that gives the highest priority to the task with the shortest period. Dynamic policies, e.g. *earliest deadline first* (EDF) that dynamically associates the highest priority to that task whose deadline is closest to the current time, can schedule both periodic and aperiodic tasks.

Real-time Systems

There is a conceptual difference between non-real-time systems and real-time systems (*q.v.*): the first ones can be fast or slow. The latter ones cannot: either they meet their deadlines or they are incorrect. A *hard real-time* system must always, under every circumstance, meet its deadlines. A *soft real-time* system may sometimes (very seldom) miss a deadline. Soft real-time is, for example, sufficient for a video system that may sometimes, perhaps once per hour, deliver a frame too late. Clearly, that is unacceptable for an aircraft control system, which must meet real-time constraints. Real-time operating systems therefore focus on how to guarantee *predictability*, not on optimizing average behavior. Only predictable worst-case behavior matters.

Admission control is the basic method to insure that the system always behaves correctly, i.e. that each application meets its deadline. Before a new real-time activity starts, e.g. delivering a movie to a client, the admission control checks whether the new activity can be scheduled so that it meets its deadlines and that all currently active activities still behave correctly, i.e., meet their respective deadlines. If the admission control finds such a schedule, the new activity is accepted. Otherwise, the new activity is rejected. This guarantees that every started activity will continue to behave properly and always meet its deadlines (provided the activity's implementation is correct).

In an aircraft-control system, all such activities will typically start before turning on the engines. If the admission control does not accept all required activities, the aircraft is defective and will stay on the ground. If the admission control accepts all activities, the operating system guarantees that they will have sufficient resources for the entire flight.

A video server may handle requests more liberally. New requests for movies can show up any time. The admission control accepts or rejects them depending on the current load, so a customer has no guarantee that the system will accept a request, but once accepted, the system guarantees that the customer can watch the requested movie without disturbance.

The video-server example illustrates the principal difference from a time-sharing system. A real-time system accepts only up to n clients simultaneously. Due to its best-effort policy, a time-sharing *system* would, however, accept e.g. $2n$ clients but show the movies only with 6 frames per second, i.e., it would serve no client well at all.

Admission control has to take into consideration all relevant resources. Not only processor time but also memory, disk bandwidth, and network bandwidth have to be scheduled. Surprisingly, technological progress in hardware makes the basic scheduling problem harder. Multilevel cache systems result in varying instruction-execution times, for example from 1 cycle for an on-chip cache hit to 100 or more cycles if the access misses in all cache hierarchies. Even page allocation in the physical memory influences secondary cache conflicts and can thus substantially influence program execution times. The worst consequence of such effects is that schedulable *atoms*, e.g. time intervals and memory pages, are no longer independent of each other. Even commutativity does not hold in general. Whether three tasks are scheduled as $T_1 \, T_2 \, T_3$ on the processor's time axis or $T_2 \, T_1 \, T_3$ can—due to cache interference—result in substantially different timings. Similar effects can occur when memory allocations are changed.

The *interference problem*—predicting interference effects—can be solved analytically only for small and static systems where all software is completely known to the scheduler. In many cases, the systems are too large, or they include unpredictable components, e.g. randomly incoming packets from the network. Some systems will even run (unknown) time-sharing applications and real-time activities concurrently. Currently, only two strategies are known to solve the interference problem in those cases: (a) the operating system allocates memory in such a way that cache interference between predictable and unpredictable components is minimal. (b) The admission control uses a very pessimistic estimate for the worst-case costs of each activity. For hard real-time, the latter strategy usually has to estimate such high worst-case costs that the method is practically unusable. However, soft real-time enables better estimates. Since the estimated costs no longer have always to be correct but only in, for example, 99.99% of all cases, estimates can be derived from test runs instead of theoretical worst-case analysis.

Personal Workstations

The idea of dedicating the power of a traditional multi-user computer to a single user, of coupling this computing power to a high-resolution bitmap display, and of viewing these workstations (q.v.) as participants in a distributed system (q.v.) rather than as isolated computers, was pioneered by Xerox in the 1970s and was made commercially successful by a number of vendors in the 1980s.

The basic operating system requirements for a single-user workstation differ little from those for a more traditional multiuser computer. Unix, developed in the early 1970s as a time-sharing system, has become widely accepted as a workstation operating system, with the key addition of a *window system* to provide multiple logical displays on the single physical bitmap display. (Menu-oriented window environments (q.v.) are largely replacing more traditional command language interpreters as the user interface (q.v.) on a wide range of computer systems.)

In the 1980s, *personal computers* (PCs) became available, in particular through Apple and IBM. The first PCs can be regarded as low-level workstations that were cheap but offered only restricted services, low speed and small capacity compared to large workstations. Operating systems for personal computers have quickly recapitulated the developmental history of operating systems for mainframes. Early personal computers had simple resident monitor operating systems. A single application program ran at a time, fully resident in a contiguous region of physical memory. I/O was done through synchronous system service calls—the application was blocked while the I/O was in progress.

In the 1990s, the hardware capabilities of personal computers have evolved so rapidly that now PCs are effectively workstations. Accordingly, the differences between PC operating systems and workstation operating systems have largely disappeared.

The user interface aspects of personal computers and workstations have advanced faster than other aspects of their operating systems, with many personal computer operating systems supporting menu-oriented window systems on bitmap displays. Microsoft Windows and the Macintosh operating system are examples of such systems: they support highly refined user interfaces and a huge suite of user-friendly applications, but otherwise are relatively primitive. By supporting true multitasking—multiple address spaces and multiple processes—IBM's OS/2, introduced around 1990, and Windows NT closed the gap with the Unix family that had been dominant on classical workstations.

Clients and Servers

In the context of a distributed system, the terms *client* and *server* (see CLIENT–SERVER COMPUTING) are used to differentiate between types of host nodes. The same terms are, however, used to denote different processes (with per-process address spaces) in an operating system. In both cases, clients request services from servers, e.g. file access from a file server, printing from a print server, etc. The concept of client–server processes can be applied on a single machine as well as on a cluster of machines. Client process and server processes may reside on different machines or on the same machine. The communication principles are similar, although timing and security might be quite different.

Remote procedure call (RPC) has received wide acceptance as a program-level communication mechanism. RPC can be used for interprocess communication, across-address-space on the same machine as well as across-machine. The goal of remote procedure call is to provide syntax and semantics that resemble as closely as possible those of the familiar local (intra-process) procedure call: the synchronous transfer of control and parameters. In remote procedure call, the *client* and *server* programs are linked to *stubs* that are mechanically generated from a description of the *server interface*. To the client, its stub looks like the server. To the server, its stub looks like the client. The stubs insulate the client and the server from the details of communication (see Fig. 8).

Distributed Systems

Distributed systems involve multiple computer systems (*hosts*) connected by networks. The hosts are often high-performance single-user workstations or personal

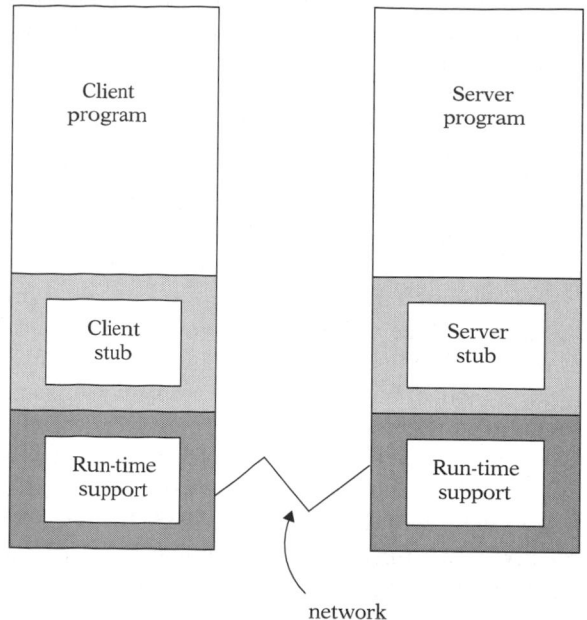

Figure 8. Remote procedure call structure.

computers. A number of key issues arise from distribution. Among these are *communication, file systems, authentication and security,* and *distributed programming support.*

File sharing in a distributed system can be achieved by a mechanism as crude as the explicit transfer of files (using, for example, the Internet's File Transfer Protocol (FTP) or the remote copy (`rcp`) command of Berkeley Unix). Much greater integration, though, is provided by file systems such as the Network File System (NFS) and the Andrew File System (AFS).

NFS can be viewed as a fairly straightforward extension of the Unix file system, in which remote directory subtrees can be *mounted* so that they appear to be (and behave as if) part of the local file system. As originally designed and implemented, NFS does not provide replication or nice semantics for files actively shared by users at multiple sites. AFS is also integrated into Unix, but pays considerable attention to scalability, security, file sharing semantics, and system management. These are critical issues in distributed file systems.

Authentication (*q.v.*) is more difficult in a distributed system than in a centralized system because one entity cannot necessarily trust another. In a centralized system, once the user is authenticated (say, by the entry of a password), all parts of the system accept the identity of the user. Not so in a distributed system. *Kerberos* is an example of an authentication service that offers considerable promise in the distributed environment. Kerberos is a scalable system that employs a secret key cryptographic protocol for initial authenti-

cation, and then grants "tickets" of finite lifetime, enabling the use of specific services.

Security is more difficult in a distributed system than in a centralized one because there are many opportunities for eavesdropping. Both public-key and private-key cryptographic systems have been used to provide secure communication (*see* CRYPTOGRAPHY, COMPUTERS IN).

The issue of distributed programming support is a complex one. A distributed application differs from a centralized application in more respects than merely communication. A distributed environment provides the potential for partial failure, which must be dealt with. At the same time, *replication* offers the potential for much higher overall reliability, availability, and performance than is possible with a centralized service. The critical question is which programming techniques make it easiest to realize this potential. The integration of *transactions* into distributed programming systems is one approach, as exemplified by the Argus and Camelot systems. *Group communication* with virtual synchrony, as seen in the Isis and Horus systems, is another research approach. Many commercial *middleware* systems help programmers to develop distributed applications. Most of them are based on the CORBA standard; COM/DCOM is a proprietary solution.

Multiprocessor Systems

Multiprocessor computer systems are becoming increasingly common because they offer the promise of significantly improved cost/performance for midrange systems, and significantly improved absolute performance for high-end systems. *Symmetric multiprocessing* (SMP) processors operate independently on a shared memory. The single shared memory inherently limits SMP scalability. Even with very large per-processor caches, more than four or eight processors cannot be served without the memory substantially degrading processor performance. *Nonuniform memory access* (NUMA) systems are much more scalable. Systems with tens of thousands of processors can be built. Typically, they consist of multiple SMP nodes with fast interconnect hardware. Memory access to local memory is then much faster than accessing memory that belongs to a different node. For simplicity, however, we restrict our attention to SMP processors.

It is possible, although not trivial, to take a uniprocessor operating system (e.g. Unix) and make it run on a multiprocessor. The difficulty arises because the way in which shared kernel data structures are protected from corruption in uniprocessor operating systems usually relies on the existence of only a single processor. In particular, when the kernel is active, hardware-level mutual exclusion is achieved by disabling interrupts. This does not work correctly on a multiprocessor because a second processor can execute in the kernel even in the absence of interrupts. Thus, the mechanism for achieving hardware-level mutual exclusion must be changed, for example to one involving *busy-waiting* (*spin-locks*) to make a processor idle while another is (briefly) executing in the kernel.

Once accomplished, such a change would yield a multiprocessor operating system that worked, but likely with mediocre performance. There are two separate issues that must be addressed to improve this performance: parallelism in applications and parallelism in the operating system.

Although multiprocessors can be used to execute a conventional workload, the more interesting application domain involves parallel programs—programs that bring multiple processors to bear on a single problem. An example is matrix multiplication (*see* PARALLEL PROCESSING: ALGORITHMS). In multiplying two $N \times N$ matrices A and B to yield an $N \times N$ result matrix C, each entry $[i, j]$ of C is computed as:

$$C[i, j] = \sum_{k=1}^{N} A[i, k] B[k, j]$$

It is clear that N^2 processors can easily be employed in computing the product of two matrices.

A key thing that a multiprocessor operating system must provide, then, is a facility for running parallel programs. The process mechanism, discussed earlier, is conceptually suitable, but such large overheads may be incurred for creating and synchronizing processes that only parallel computations with very coarse *granularity* (a word used to denote the relative size of a parallel unit of work) can be run with reasonable efficiency. (In the worst case, converting a sequential program into a parallel program may yield a slow-down rather than a speedup!) Much effort in the design of multiprocessor operating systems has been devoted to the design of *lightweight threads*—threads of control that can be created and synchronized more efficiently than traditional processes, and thus can be used in programming fine-grained applications.

It is also important to exploit parallelism in the operating system itself. Earlier, we showed how to achieve a correct operating system by changing the hardware-level mutual exclusion mechanism to ensure that only one processor at a time would execute in the kernel. Unfortunately, however, measurements show that computer systems often spend between 25% and 50% of the time executing operating system code as opposed to user code. If the bulk of this operating-system code is single-threaded, the overall speedup of the system will be dramatically limited. *Amdahl's law* (*see* LAWS, COMPUTER) states that the maximum attainable speedup for a program is $1/S$ if an S-fraction of the program executes inherently sequentially. Imagine that 25% of the uniprocessor execution time is spent executing inherently sequential operating system code. Then, the overall system speedup will be at most 4, even if all user programs have unlimited parallelism and there are an unlimited number of processors. Thus, in order to achieve good performance from a multiprocessor operating system, it must be structured to allow the maximum possible internal physical concurrency.

Current Issues

◆ *High-bandwidth, low-latency networks* For 15 years, local area network bandwidth remained at 10 Mb/sec. Then 100 Mb/sec became widely used and now relatively cheap Gigabit Networks have become available. This 100-fold increase in bandwidth presents a number of opportunities, particularly if accompanied by operating system structuring techniques that reduce the access latency.

◆ *Very large distributed systems* The Internet connects hundreds of millions of computer systems. How can file systems (organization, naming, and access), authentication, administration, etc., be designed to function effectively on a national or international scale?

◆ *Dynamically downloaded code* Programs, applets (code transferred over a network to run on a user's computer) as well as normal code, are increasingly downloaded to a personal workstation from the World Wide Web (*q.v.*). This mechanism offers major new opportunities but also makes workstations extremely vulnerable. Operating system technology has to ensure an applet's integrity and to enforce customer-defined and vendor-defined security policies.

◆ *Ubiquitous networks and mobile computing* Ever-decreasing computer size, weight, and power consumption, combined with improved batteries made mobile computing (*q.v.*) attractive. Upcoming ubiquitous networks based on cellular radio network technology add another dimension. From an operating system's perspective, there are challenging new problems in handling heterogeneous networks, temporarily being partitioned from the network, frequently switching to a different network, and unpredictable large variations of a network's quality of service, particularly for radio-based networks.

◆ *Pervasive systems* Hardware integration has improved such that very small but powerful computing devices become possible that are helpful in everyday life, wristwatches with a network browser, intelligent glasses that help driving a car, etc. Operating systems have to become highly configurable and customizable while nevertheless becoming much more robust than most current workstation/PC operating systems.

Controlling Complexity

The ever-increasing size and complexity of computer-based applications leads to an ever-increasing operating-system complexity (and size). Managing and controlling this complexity will be an extremely challenging problem in future operating system research. It may become even harder to find structures and methodologies that enable robust operating-system components that insure certain policies and functionalities independent of whether other system components or applications behave properly. Due to the huge number of software components that are used to build a system, system creators and administrators will typically have only incomplete, sometimes even wrong, knowledge of many components. Nonetheless, the structures mentioned and methods discussed here should be applicable and useful.

Bibliography

1983. Holt, R. C. *Concurrent Euclid, the UNIX System, and TUNIS.* Reading, MA: Addison-Wesley.

1984. Birrell, A. D. and Nelson, B. J. "Implementing Remote Procedure Calls," *ACM Transactions on Computer Systems*, **2**, 1, 39–59.

1984. Lazowska, E. D., Zahorjan, J., Graham, G. S., and Sevcik, K. C. *Quantitative System Performance: Computer System Analysis Using Queueing Network Models.* Upper Saddle River, NJ: Prentice Hall.

1984. Schroeder, M. D., Birrell, A. D., and Needham, R. M. "Experience with Grapevine: The Growth of a Distributed System," *ACM Transactions on Computer Systems*, **2**, 1, 3–23.

1988. Shaw, A. C. (ed.) Special Issue on Operating Systems. *Comm. of the ACM*, **31**, 3.

1989. Leffler, S. J., McKusick, M. K., Karels, M. J., and Quarterman, J. S. *The Design and Implementation of the 4.3BSD UNIX Operating System.* Reading, MA: Addison-Wesley.

1989. Satyanarayanan, M. "A Survey of Distributed File Systems," *Annual Review of Computer Science*, **4**, 73–104. Palo Alto, CA: Annual Reviews.

1993. Stankovic, J. A., and Ramamritham, K. (eds.) *Advances in Real-Time Systems.* Los Alamitos, CA: IEEE Computer Society Press.

1996. Liedtke, J. "Toward Real Microkernels," *Comm. of the ACM*, **39**, 9, 70–77.

1998. Stallings, W. *Operating Systems: Internals and Design Principles*, 3rd Ed. Upper Saddle River, NJ: Prentice Hall.

Edward D. Lazowska, revised by Jochen Liedtke

OPERATOR OVERLOADING

For articles on related subjects *see* EXTENSIBLE LANGUAGE; OBJECT-ORIENTED PROGRAMMING; PROCEDURE-ORIENTED LANGUAGES; and SUBPROGRAM.

Operators in programming languages are like arithmetic operators: they generally take two arguments, frequently but not always of the same type, and return a value of the type of one (or both) of the arguments. When binary, they are written in *infix* form, between the arguments, so that one can write x:= y + z, for example.

An operator symbol is *overloaded* when it is used to denote multiple operations on variables of different types. Most programming languages overload common arithmetic operators like + and *, which are operations both on integers and on real numbers (and perhaps also on strings or sets). The term *operator overloading* is commonly used to characterize programming languages that permit a programmer to assign new meanings to operator symbols, in addition to the predefined ones.

Operator overloading provides a convenient notation for user-defined functions when they represent mathematical operations that go by familiar names. If a program has vectors (one-dimensional arrays) or matrices (two-dimensional arrays), overloading lets us define vector or matrix addition or multiplication with the same notation that one would use in mathematics: for example, v1 + v2, or M * N, rather than the more cumbersome notation required by a programming language that requires that these operations be written as subprogram (*q.v.*) calls.

Extensible languages generally allow programmers to define new operators, but if their names cannot be overloaded, the programmer is forced to coin new names that may not indicate their meanings clearly. Good notation is important in programming as well as in mathematics. In object-oriented programming, where we define abstract data types (*q.v.*) that package together data and operations, it is desirable (less error-prone) if the vector type, the matrix type, and the complex number type can all use + as their addition operator, rather than arbitrarily assigning ++ to one, +++ to a second and ++++ to the third.

One commonly used overloaded operator in C++, for example, is <<, which is the output operator. Each C++ class (*q.v.*) that defines objects whose values can be printed can have its own definition of <<, and the user can simply write

```
cout << I << R << S
```

to print on output stream cout the integer I, real R, and string S, and three different output operations will be executed.

Subprogram names can also be overloaded when a language processor (*q.v.*) can use information about the number or types of the subprogram parameters to recognize which subprogram is being called. Ada (*q.v.*) allows such overloading, as does Prolog (*see* LOGIC PROGRAMMING).

Operator overloading is sometimes called *ad hoc polymorphism*, because the multiple meanings of a name are not necessarily related to one another. Some languages, like the functional languages (*q.v.*) ML and Haskell, have *parametric polymorphism*: a *single* list-processing (*q.v.*) function, for example, can operate on lists of any type of object. Such parametric polymorphism is a property of a single generic function, while overloading is a property of a single name, one used for many different functions.

Overloading should also be distinguished from *coercion* (*q.v.*). Many languages allow expressions like n + r where n is an integer and r a real number. This is not because there is an addition operator tailored to such a pair; rather, one argument is *coerced* to the type of the other, where coercion means that a new value of the required type is formed and that value is used in the operation.

Operator overloading is a valuable tool for expressing similar concepts in similar notation, and thus a means of achieving program clarity. It can also be misused to suggest such similarity where there is none, and it is the programmer's responsibility to take care to use it wisely.

Bibliography

1985. Cardelli, L., and Wegner, P. "On Understanding Types, Data Abstraction, and Polymorphism," *Computing Surveys*, **17**, 4 (December), 471–522.
1993. Louden, K. C. *Programming Languages: Principles and Practice*. Boston: PWS-Kent.

David Hemmendinger

OPERATOR PRECEDENCE

For articles on related subjects *see* COMPILER; EXPRESSION; GRAMMARS; LANGUAGE PROCESSORS; OPERATOR OVERLOADING; POLISH NOTATION; PROGRAMMING LINGUISTICS; and WELL-FORMED FORMULA.

Operator precedence refers to the hierarchy of precedence relations that determines the order in which operators are applied to their operands in a high-level language expression.

As an example of the need for such relationships, consider the expression A + B * C.

Is this to be interpreted as A + (B * C) or (A + B) * C? One way to solve this problem would be to enforce a strict left-to-right or (as in APL) a right-to-left order of evaluation. However, most programming languages resolve possible ambiguities by establishing precedence relations that determine the order in which operators are applied. A major purpose of such relations is to assure that as many expressions as possible have their "natural" interpretation (e.g. most people would regard A + (B * C) as the natural interpretation of A + B * C).

The operator hierarchy includes not only arithmetic operators but also relational operators ($<$, $>$, $\leq$, $\geq$, $=$, $\neq$), logical operators (**and**, **or**, **not**), concatenation, and other operators (such as those that apply to bit strings). Table 1 gives the arithmetic, relational, and logical operator hierarchy in Fortran, Pascal, and C. It is to be interpreted as follows: in an expression containing more than one operator, the operator to be applied first is the one that is highest in the hierarchy. Thus,

Expression	Interpretation
3 + 4 * 5 − 6	3 + (4*5) − 6 = 17
16 / 4 + 8	(16/4) + 8 = 12
3 < 4 + 5	3 < (4 + 5) = true

Note that the position of the relational operators relative to the arithmetic operators is forced if expressions containing a combination of these operators are to be meaningful. Thus, the Pascal or Ada expression 3 < 4 + 5 makes sense only if interpreted as 3 < (4 + 5).

When an expression contains two operators of equal precedence, the usual rule is to evaluate them from left to right (although successive exponentiations are often evaluated right to left). Thus, A/B * C is to be

Table 1. Operator hierarchy.

	Fortran	Pascal	C
High	**		
		not	!
	− (unary)		− (unary)
	*, /	*, /, **div**, **mod**, **and**	*, /, %
	+, −	+, −, **or**	+, −
	Relational ops.	Relational ops.	<, <=, >, >=
			==, !=
	.NOT.		
	.AND.		&&
	.OR.		||
	.EQV.		
Low	.NEQV.		

**
Exponentiation
div   Integer quotient of integer division
mod and %   Integer remainder of integer division
==   Equality

interpreted as (A/B)*C. In all languages, parentheses may always be used to override the precedence rules.

The operator precedence rules together with the rule just stated about parentheses are used to enable the compilation of a program written in a high-level language into machine executable code. This procedure is referred to as the *arithmetic scan*, in which the first step is a transformation that converts normal infix form (i.e. the form in which the operator is placed between its operands as in the examples above) to a Polish form, in which there exist no parentheses and the order of execution of the operators is specified by their positioning. Such a transformation is required because of the difficulty of associating operands with operators in infix notation. As an example, consider the expression

$$(A*X+B)/(C*X-D) \tag{1}$$

which, because of the precedence relations discussed above, is to be interpreted as

$$(((A*X)+B)/((C*X)-D)). \tag{2}$$

By use of a classical algorithm that scans across the string in expression (1) from left to right just once, this string can be converted to the Polish postfix string

$$AX*B+CX*D-/ \tag{3}$$

which, without a need for parentheses or precedence relations, has the unique interpretation of expression (2). With just one more scan across the string, it can be compiled into machine code.

The arithmetic scan described here is a special case of a general syntactic analyzer that uses precedence relationships (*see* COMPILER).

Anthony Ralston

OPTICAL CHARACTER RECOGNITION (OCR)

For articles on related subjects *see* IMAGE PROCESSING; PATTERN RECOGNITION; PERCEPTRON; and UNIVERSAL PRODUCT CODE.

Optical character recognition (OCR) is performed by optical character readers which are automated electronic systems. OCR may be defined as the process of converting images of machine printed or handwritten numerals, letters, and symbols into a computer-processable format. The long history of research in this area, commercial success, and the continuing need and ability to handle less restricted forms of text make OCR the most important application area in machine perception to date.

Two types of automated reading equipment, distinct from optical character readers, are optical mark readers (OMRs) and magnetic ink character readers (MICRs). OMRs characteristically read nontextual input such as bar codes. Examples of OMRs are grocery store bar code readers that read the Universal Product Code (UPC) and the United States Postal Service's wide-area bar code reader that reads ZIP codes encoded in the PostNet code. MICRs classify alphanumeric characters by sensing the pattern corresponding to the magnetic field generated by character ink. One common MICR is a bank check reader that reads account numbers on the bottom of checks.

Commercial OCR predominantly handles machine-printed text. Although neatly printed handwriting is accepted by OCR systems, the technology for handwriting recognition is generally distinct from OCR technology for machine-printed text. Handwriting recognition systems can be divided into two types: online and offline. Online systems allow recognition of characters and words as they are written on a surface. The interactive nature of these systems enables recognition algorithms to use information about how characters are written. Many online systems allow interactive correction of misrecognized characters. Examples of applications using online recognition include the Apple Newton, the 3Com PalmPilot and Cross's Crosspad. Offline systems recognize characters that have been previously written on a document. Therefore no information is available on the writing style or the implement path used to create the character strokes. Examples include address reading machines used by post offices and check amount reading machines.

The following discussion explores the structure, technological attributes, application areas and availability of commercial OCR.

OCR Systems

A typical OCR system (*see* Fig. 1) contains three logical components:

1. Image scanner

2. OCR software and hardware

3. Output interface

The image scanner optically captures text images to be recognized. Text images are processed with OCR software and hardware. The process involves three operations: document analysis (extracting individual character images), recognizing these images (based on shape), and contextual processing (either to correct misclassifications made by the recognition algorithm

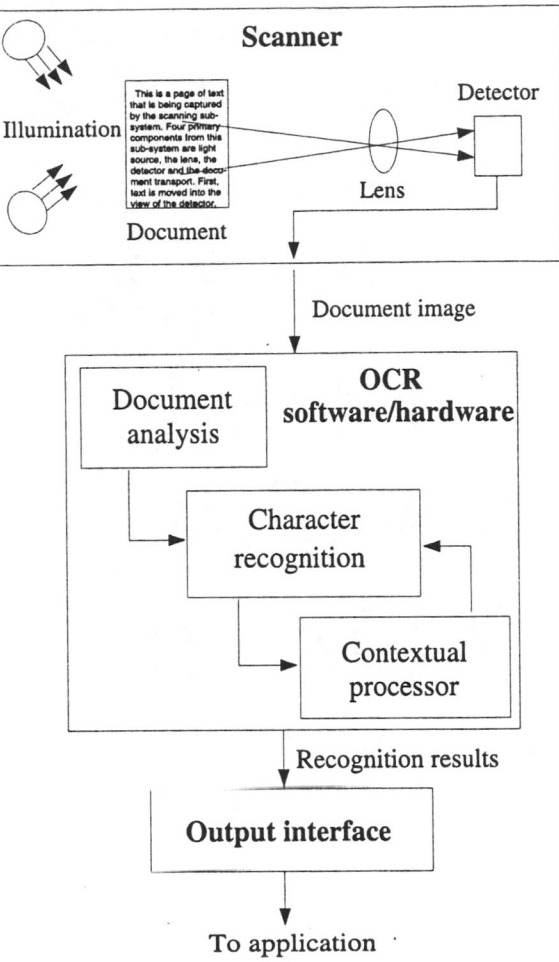

Figure 1. General structure of an OCR system.

or to limit recognition choices). The output interface is responsible for communication of OCR system results to the outside world.

IMAGE SCANNER

Four basic building blocks form functional image scanners: a detector (and associated electronics), an illumination source, a scan lens, and a document transport. The document transport places the document in the scanning field, the light source floods the object with illumination, and the lens forms the object's image on the detector. The detector consists of an array of elements each of which converts incident light into a charge, or analog signal. These analog signals are then converted into an image. Scanning is performed by the detector and the motion of the text object with respect to the detector. After an image is captured, the document transport removes the document from the scanning field.

Recent advances in scanner technology have made available resolution in the range of 600 pixels per inch (ppi) to 1200 ppi. Recognition methods that use features

(as opposed to template matching) use resolutions in the range of 200 ppi to 400 ppi, and careful consideration of gray scale. Lower resolutions and simple thresholding tend to break thin lines or fill gaps, thus invalidating features.

OCR SOFTWARE AND HARDWARE

Document analysis. Text is extracted from the document image in a process known as *document analysis*. Reliable character segmentation and recognition depend upon both original document quality and registered image quality. Processes that attempt to compensate for poor quality originals or poor quality scanning include image enhancement, underline removal, and noise removal. Image enhancement methods emphasize character versus non-character discrimination. Underline removal erases printed guidelines and other lines which may touch characters and interfere with character recognition, and noise removal erases portions of the image that are not part of the characters.

Prior to character recognition it is necessary to isolate individual characters from the text image. Many OCR systems use connected components for this process. For those connected components that represent multiple or partial characters, more sophisticated algorithms are used. In low-quality or nonuniform text images these sophisticated algorithms may not correctly extract characters, and thus recognition errors may occur. Recognition of unconstrained handwritten text can be very difficult because characters cannot be reliably isolated, especially when the text is cursive handwriting.

Character recognition. Two essential components in a character recognition algorithm are the *feature extractor* and the *classifier*. Feature analysis determines the descriptors, or feature set, used to describe all characters. Given a character image, the feature extractor derives the features that the character possesses. The derived features are then used as input to the character classifier.

Template matching, or *matrix matching*, is one of the most common classification methods. In template matching, individual image pixels are used as features. Classification is performed by comparing an input character image with a set of templates (or prototypes) from each character class. Each comparison results in a similarity measure between the input character and the template. One measure increases the amount of similarity when a pixel in the observed character is identical to the same pixel in the template image. If the pixels differ, the measure of similarity may be decreased. After all templates have been compared with the observed character image, the character's identity is assigned as the identity of the most similar template.

Template matching is a trainable process because template characters may be changed. In many commercial systems, PROMs (programmable read-only memory) store templates containing single fonts. To retrain the algorithm, the current PROMs are replaced with PROMs that contain images of a new font. Thus, if a suitable PROM exists for a font, template matching can be trained to recognize that font. The similarity measure of template matching may also be modified, but commercial OCR systems typically do not allow this.

Structural classification methods use structural features and decision rules to classify characters. Structural features may be defined in terms of character strokes, character holes, or other character attributes such as concavities. For instance, the letter "P" may be described as a vertical stroke with a loop attached to the upper right side. For a character image input, the structural features are extracted and a rule-based system is applied to classify the character. Structural methods are also trainable, but construction of a good feature set and a good rule-base can be time-consuming.

Many character recognizers are based on mathematical formalisms that minimize a measure of misclassification. These recognizers may use pixel-based features or structural features. Some examples are discriminant function classifiers, Bayesian classifiers, artificial neural networks (ANNs) (*see* NEURAL NETWORKS), and template matchers. Discriminant function classifiers use hypersurfaces to separate the featural description of characters from different semantic classes and in the process reduce the mean-squared error. Bayesian methods seek to minimize the loss function associated with misclassification through the use of probability theory. ANNs, which are closer to theories of human perception, employ mathematical minimization techniques. Both discriminant functions and ANNs are used in commercial OCR systems.

Character misclassifications stem from two main sources: poor-quality character images and poor discriminatory ability. Poor document quality, image scanning, and preprocessing can all degrade performance by yielding poor-quality characters. On the other hand, the character recognition method may not have been trained for a proper response on the character causing the error. This type of error source is difficult to overcome because the recognition method may have limitations and all possible character images cannot possibly be considered in training the classifier. Recognition rates for machine-printed characters can reach over 99%, but handwritten character recognition rates are typically lower because every person

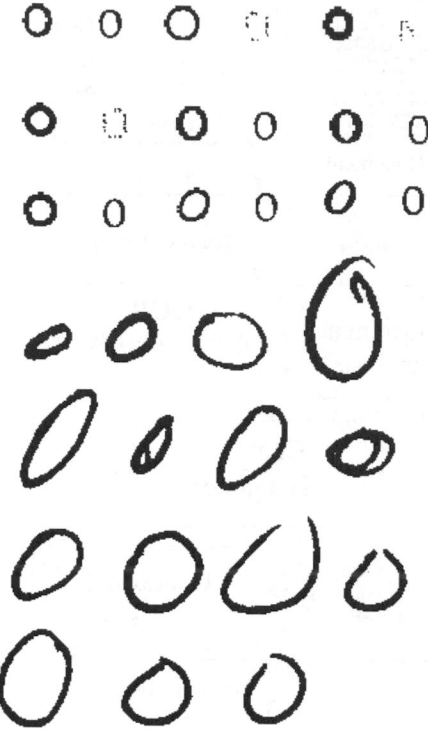

Figure 2. Machine-printed and handwritten capital "O"s.

writes differently. This random nature often results in misclassifications. Fig. 2 shows several examples of machine printed and handwritten capital "O"s. Each capital O can be easily confused with the numeral 0 and the number of different styles of capital "O"s demonstrates the difficulties recognizers must cope with.

ICR. *Intelligent character recognition* refers to the reading of handwritten characters. The term "ICR" was first coined by Kurzweil Computer Products, Inc. in the late 1970s to highlight its own "omni-font" OCR system, which was trainable and could learn new fonts. In the late 1980s this term was usurped to describe the systems developed to read handwritten characters. By its very nature, the variations in handwriting are limitless, so any algorithm which attempts to read handwritten characters will have to be more intelligent than, say, an OCR algorithm which reads only a limited set of fonts. Hence the term "ICR."

A typical ICR algorithm starts by slant-correcting the input image. Unlike machine-printed characters, handwriting is often written with a certain slant that can vary with factors such as the writing instrument, position of the writer, the surface, etc. Slant is corrected by calculating the average angle of slant of the major vertical strokes, and it is corrected by shearing the image.

The next step is size-normalizing the input image. Handwritten characters in general are much bigger than machine-printed characters, as can be seen in Fig. 2. In this step, the input image is reduced (or in the unlikely event that it is smaller than the target size, it is enlarged) to fit a target size, usually something on the order of 32×32 pixels. This entire process is called "preprocessing."

Once the input has been normalized in this fashion, some of the traditional pattern recognition techniques can be applied to recognize the resulting image. ANNs are a common choice for classification, but they suffer from the drawback that sometimes, when the input image is hopelessly complex (for example, when a writer tries to correct a mistake and writes over another character), the network may choose an incorrect classification with high confidence.

Human handwriting is not limited to isolated digits and characters. Quite often ICR algorithms have to cope with touching digits or characters. For example, it is common to write two 0s with a ligature joining them. Some ICR algorithms include modules to segment (separate) touching characters. When such intelligence is built into an ICR system, it is said to be able to read "natural handwriting."

The other extreme in ICR is cursive word recognition. Here, the input is a word (or a phrase) written cursively and naturally, along with a "lexicon" of possibilities. The aim is to find the closest match in the lexicon to the given word image.

There are some systems that claim to perform cursive word recognition. Most of these systems start by performing preprocessing operations like slant normalization. However, sometimes the base of the cursive writing is skewed and that has to be corrected using a skew-removal algorithm.

Some of these cursive word recognition systems work by looking for ligatures joining the individual characters and separating the individual characters that make up the word at these ligatures. The characters are then processed, and the closest match in the lexicon is found.

Other algorithms take a more "holistic" approach, based on the observation that when writing cursive words, people are sloppy and the individual characters cannot be isolated with great accuracy (as shown in Fig. 3). Due to this fact, they try to look for holistic features in the input image, like ascenders (tops of "b," "d," "l," etc.), descenders (bottoms of "g," "p," "q," etc.), loops (like those in "o," "a," etc.), and match the presence or absence and the location of these features with the input lexicon. The closest lexicon entry is the most likely choice.

Figure 3. Two cursive words.

Contextual Processing. Contextual information can be used in recognition. The number of word choices for a given field can be limited by knowing the content of another field, e.g. to recognize the street name in an address, first recognize the ZIP code, and then the street name choices can be limited to a lexicon. Alternatively, the result of recognition can be post-processed to correct the recognition errors. One method used to post-process character recognition results is to apply a spelling checker (*q.v.*) to verify word spelling. Similarly, other post-processing methods use lexicons to verify word results or recognition results may be verified interactively with the user. Additional methods to correct or prevent errors using contextual knowledge are state-of-the-art and should appear in commercial systems shortly.

Non-Roman character recognition. Recognition of scripts other than Roman has worldwide interest. There are some 26 different scripts in use today. Some of the scripts have had little work done on their recognition, e.g. Kannada, while a significant amount of work has been done on others, e.g. Japanese. In addition to letters and numerals, Japanese text uses Kanji characters (Chinese ideographs) and Kana (Japanese syllables). Therefore, it is more difficult to recognize Japanese text because of the size of the character set (more than 3,300 characters) and the complexity and similarity of the Kanji character structures (*see* Fig. 4). Low data quality is an additional problem in all OCR. A Japanese OCR system is usually composed of two individual classifiers (pre-classifier and secondary classifier) in a cascade structure. The pre-classifier first performs a fast coarse classification to reduce the character set to a short candidate list (usually containing no more than 100 candidates). The secondary classifier then uses more complex features to determine which candidate in the list has the closest match to the test pattern.

OUTPUT INTERFACE

The output interface allows character recognition results to be electronically transferred into the domain that uses the results. For example, many commercial systems allow recognition results to be placed directly

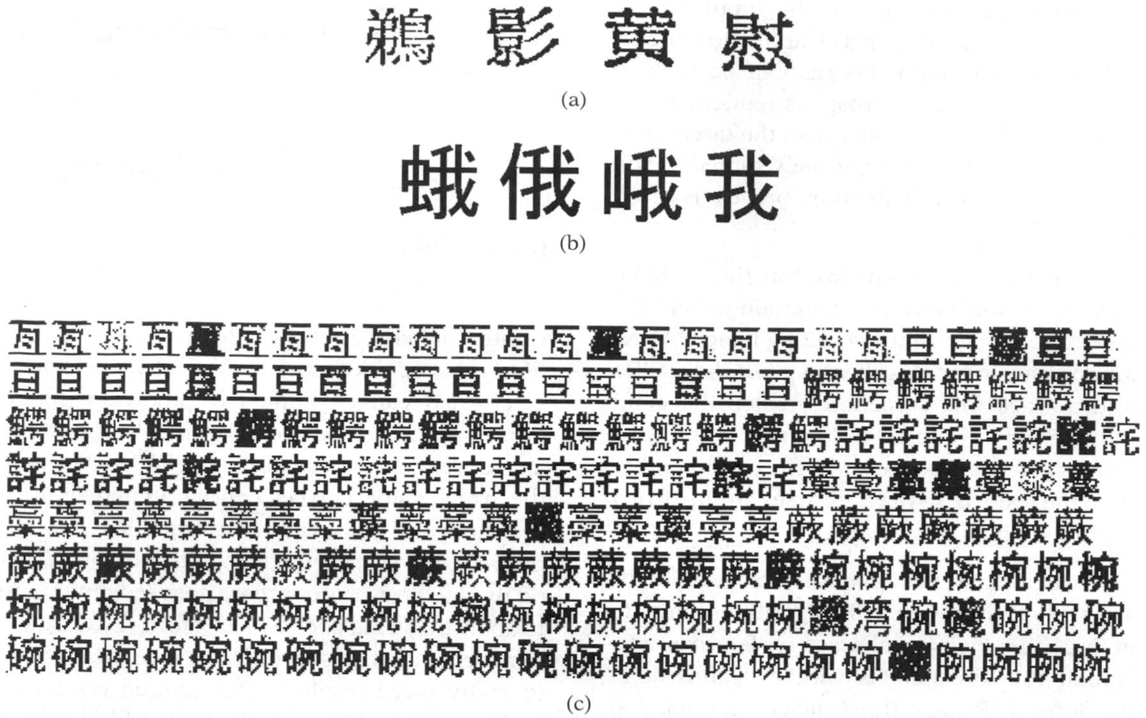

鶒　影　黄　慰

(a)

蛾俄峨我

(b)

(c)

Figure 4. Difficulties in Japanese character recognition: (a) presence of complex Kanji characters; (b) many characters share the same lexicographical element; and (c) diverse print qualities (each row repeats the same character).

into spreadsheets (*q.v.*), databases, and word processors. Other commercial systems use recognition results directly in further automated processing, and when the processing is complete, the recognition results are discarded. In any event, the output interface, while simple, is vital to the commercial success of OCR systems because it communicates results to the world outside of the OCR system.

Historical Perspective

An ideal model OCR system uses the human eye as the scanner and the human brain as the character recognizer. Accordingly, many of the early developments in OCR technology stemmed from attempts to help visually impaired people to read (*see* DISABLED, COMPUTERS AND THE). According to H. F. Schantz, the first steps towards OCR systems were made in 1809 when the first patents for reading devices to aid the blind were awarded. The first retinal scanner was developed by C. R. Carey in 1870 by using a mosaic of photocells to scan characters. In 1890, P. Nipkow developed a scanning disk that many consider a forerunner of modern television cameras, and in 1912, E. Goldberg converted scanned text into Morse code to be sent over a telegraph line.

Modern OCR technology was born in 1951 with David Shepard's invention, GISMO—A Robot Reader-Writer. In 1954, J. Rabinow developed a prototype machine that was able to read upper case typewritten

output at the "fantastic" speed of one character per minute. Several companies, including IBM, Recognition Equipment, Inc., Farrington, Control Data, and Optical Scanning Corporation, marketed OCR systems by 1967. During the late 1960s, the technology underwent many dramatic developments, but OCR systems were considered exotic and futuristic, being used only by government agencies or large corporations. Systems that cost one million dollars were not uncommon.

In the early years of OCR many standards (*q.v.*) were developed to help guide automatic document processing. These standards included:

◆ Character Set for Optical Character Recognition (OCR-A). ANSI X3.17-81.

◆ Character Set for Optical Character Recognition (OCR-B). ANSI X3.49-75.

◆ Paper Used in Optical Character Recognition Systems. ANSI X3.62-87.

◆ Optical Character Recognition (OCR) Inks. ANSI X3.86-80.

◆ Optical Character Recognition (OCR) Character Position. ANSI X3.93-81.

The two ANSI-standard machine-printed fonts, along with the ANSI-standard handwritten font, are pictured in Fig. 5.

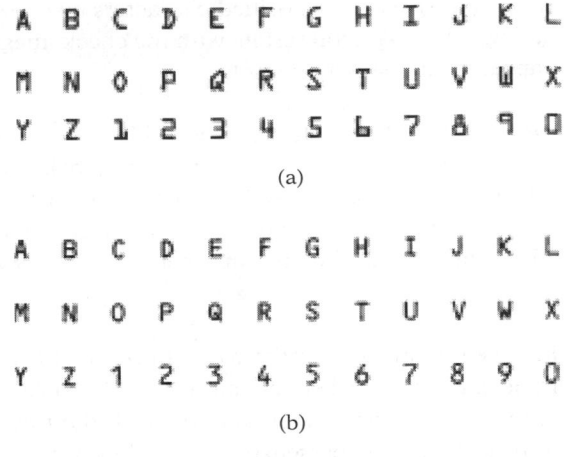

Figure 5. Standardized fonts: (a) OCR-A font; (b) OCR-B font; and (c) handwritten font.

Current OCR systems are cheaper, faster, and more reliable. It is not uncommon to find PC-based OCR packages for under $200 capable of recognizing several hundred characters per second. More fonts than ever can be recognized with today's OCR systems and some systems advertise themselves as omnifont—able to read any machine printed font. Less expensive electronic components and extensive research have paved the way for these new systems. With continued commercial demand for OCR systems, these trends will continue. Increased productivity by reducing human intervention and the ability to store text efficiently are two major selling points.

Current research areas in OCR include handwriting recognition and form "reading." Reliable recognition of handwritten cursive script is now under intense investigation. In addition, research is being conducted into "reading" forms, that is, using all available information to formulate an interpretation of the document. For instance, some United States Postal Service research focuses on assigning ZIP codes to letter images which may not contain any ZIP code. Such an assignment can be made by understanding the various address fields. The use of contextual information in both handwriting recognition and form reading is essential.

Commercial Applications

Hundreds of OCR systems have been developed since the 1950s and many are commercially available today.

Commercial OCR systems can largely be grouped into two categories: *task-specific readers* and *general-purpose page readers*. A task-specific reader handles only specific document types. Some of the most common task-specific readers read bank checks, letter mail, or credit card slips. These readers usually use custom-made image lift-hardware that captures only a few predefined document regions. For example, a bank check reader may just scan the courtesy amount field and a postal OCR system may just scan the address block on a mail piece. Such systems emphasize high throughput rates and low error rates. Applications such as letter mail reading have throughput (*q.v.*) rates of 12 letters per second with error rates less than 2%. The character recognizer in many task-specific readers is able to recognize both handwritten and machine-printed text.

General-purpose page readers are designed to handle a broader range of documents such as business letters, technical writings, and newspapers. These systems capture an image of a document page and separate the page into text regions and nontext regions. Nontext regions such as graphics and line drawings are often saved separately from the text and associated recognition results. Text regions are segmented into lines, words, and characters and the characters are passed to the recognizer. Recognition results are output in a format that can be postprocessed by application software. Most of these page readers can read machine-written text, but only a few can read hand-printed alphanumerics.

TASK-SPECIFIC READERS

Task-specific readers are used primarily for high-volume applications which require high system throughput. Since high throughput rates are desired, handling only the fields of interest helps to alleviate time constraints. Since similar documents possess similar size and layout structure, it is straightforward for the image scanner to focus on those fields where the desired information lies. This approach can considerably reduce the image processing and text recognition time. Some application areas to which task-specific readers have been applied include:

◆ Assigning ZIP codes to letter mail

◆ Reading data entered in forms, e.g. tax forms

◆ Automatic accounting procedures used in processing utility bills

◆ Verification of account numbers and courtesy amounts on bank checks

◆ Automatic accounting of airline passenger tickets

◆ Automatic validation of passports

Address readers. The address reader in a postal mail sorter locates the destination address block on a mail piece and reads the ZIP code in this address block. If additional fields in the address block are read with high confidence the system may generate a nine-digit ZIP code for the piece. The resulting ZIP code is used to generate a bar code which is sprayed on the envelope.

The *Multiline Optical Character Reader* (MLOCR) used by the United States Postal Service (USPS) locates the address block on a mail piece, reads the whole address, identifies the ZIP+4 code, generates 9- or 11-digit bar code, and sorts the mail to the correct stacker. The character classifier recognizes up to 400 fonts and the system can process up to 45,000 mail pieces per hour. The system is shown in Fig. 6.

Form readers. A form reading system needs to discriminate between preprinted form instructions and filled-in data. The system is first trained with a blank form. The system registers those areas on the form where the data should be printed. During the form recognition phase, the system uses the spatial information obtained from training to scan the regions that should be filled with data. Some readers read hand-printed data as well as various machine-written text. They can read data on a form without being confused by the form instructions. Some systems can process forms at a rate of many thousands of forms per hour.

Check readers. A check reader captures check images and recognizes courtesy amounts and account information on the checks. Some readers also recognize the legal amount on checks and use the information in both fields to cross-check the recognition results. An operator can correct misclassified characters by cross-validating the recognition results with the check image that appears on a system console.

Bill processing systems. In general, a bill processing system is used to read payment slips, utility bills and inventory documents. The system focuses on certain regions on a document where the expected information is located, e.g. account number and payment value.

Airline ticket readers. In order to claim revenue from a airline passenger ticket, an airline needs to have three records matched: reservation record, the travel agent record, and the passenger ticket. However, it is impossible to match all three records for every ticket sold. Current methods which use manual random sampling of tickets is far from accurate in claiming the maximal amount of revenue.

Several airlines are using a passenger revenue accounting system to account accurately for passenger revenues. The system reads the ticket number on a passenger ticket and matches it with the one in the airline reservation database. It scans up to 260,000 tickets per day and achieves a sorting rate of 17 tickets per second.

Passport readers. An automated passport reader is used to speed returning US passengers through custom inspections. The reader reads a traveler's name, date of birth, and passport number on the passport and checks these against the database records that contain information on fugitive felons and known smugglers.

GENERAL-PURPOSE PAGE READERS

There are two general categories of page readers: *high-end page readers* and *low-end page readers*. High-end page readers are more advanced in recognition capability and higher data throughput than the low-end page readers. High-end readers cost about $5,000 or more, and the more expensive ones are bundled into one hardware + software solution.

Low-end page readers usually do not come with a scanner and are compatible with many flat-bed scanners. They are mostly used in an office environment with desktop workstations (*q.v.*), which are less demanding on system throughput. Since they are designed to handle a broader range of documents, a sacrifice of recognition accuracy has to be made. Many scanners today come bundled with free low-end OCR software.

As the speeds of CPUs rise, the distinction between "high-end" and "low-end" machines tends to blur.

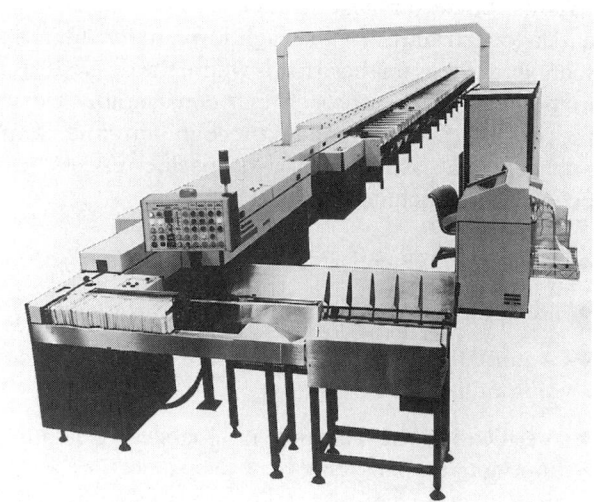

Figure 6. A Multiline Optical Character Reader used by the USPS.

Most OCR vendors offer a wide range of solutions to fit every need. In 1999, a Caere Corporation low-end system, the Omnipage Pro, cost about $99, and a high-end Forms/Free Text toolkit, about $5,000. Most of the other vendors, like Expervision, Mitek, NewSoft, and ScanSoft, offer a similar range of products.

Voting systems. A new trend today is to integrate OCR engines from diverse vendors, and perform recognition independently using each of them. The recognition results are then combined ("voted") to yield the final result. The advantage of this approach is that the multiple engines are able to compensate for each other's weaknesses, resulting in a significantly higher recognition rate. PrimeOCR is one such vendor whose main product is a voting OCR system.

Bibliography

1982. Schantz, H. *The History of OCR.* Manchester Center, VT: Recognition Technologies Users Association. (The history of OCR is related from its inauspicious beginnings up to its current commercial success.)

1985. Smith, J. W., and Merali, Z. *Optical Character Recognition: The Technology and its Application in Information Units and Libraries.* The British Library. (This report is intended for use by anyone who is considering OCR in an information or library context. Since minimal knowledge of OCR is assumed, general background material is abundant.)

1990. Adams, R. *Sourcebook of Automatic Identification and Data Collection.* New York: Van Nostrand Reinhold. (This book is a good general reference for OCR. It also considers a number of commercially available OCR systems. Names, addresses, and phone numbers of many OCR vendors are given.)

1999. Rice, S. V., Nagy, G., and Nartker, T. A. *Optical Character Recognition: An Illustrated Guide to the Frontier.* Boston: Kluwer.

Sargur N. Srihari, Ajay Shekhawat, and Stephen W. Lam

OPTICAL COMPUTING

For articles on related subjects *see* FIBER OPTICS; OPTICAL CHARACTER RECOGNITION; OPTICAL STORAGE; and UNIVERSAL PRODUCT CODE.

Digital computing with the use of optical components was considered at least as early as the 1940s by John von Neumann (*q.v.*), a pioneer in electronic computing. If lasers had been available at the time, the first digital computers might well have used optics. Historically, optical technology has found a few special purpose uses as an adjunct technology to electronics for analog and digital computing. Starting in the early 1960s, optical technology has been used for computing (fast) Fourier transforms (FFT—*q.v.*) of military images in matched filtering operations (McAulay, 1991). A simple lens setup realizes a Fourier transform, which maps a two-dimensional image from the space domain to the frequency domain. Aerial views of isolated objects are scanned by an optical/electronic setup that identifies features of interest in the frequency domain. Synthetic aperture radar (SAR) signal processing is an optical pattern recognition application that matches images in stored photographic form with input images at a very high rate. Spectrum analysis is another application that is performed with acousto-optic signal processing. These applications as well as others are performed optically when the need for high bandwidth (*q.v.*) exceeds electronic capability.

There was renewed interest in optical information processing in the late 1970s as advances were made in optical transmission and optically nonlinear materials. The limitations of electronic digital circuits grew increasingly severe as the need for communication bandwidth increased, and attention returned to digital optical computing.

The fastest transistors switch on the order of 5 picoseconds (ps), but the fastest computers have cycle times of the order of 1 nanosecond (ns), 1/200th as fast. This disparity arises from a number of problems related to conventional electronics which include:

◆ electromagnetic interference at high speed

◆ distorted edge transitions

◆ complexity of metal connections

◆ drive requirements for pins

◆ large peak power levels

◆ impedance matching effects

Electromagnetic interference arises because the inductances of two current-carrying wires are coupled. Sharp edge transitions must be maintained for proper switching, but higher frequencies are attenuated more than lower frequencies as an electrical pulse travels through a wire, resulting in sloppy edges at high speeds. The complexity of metal connections on chips, on circuit boards, and between system components affects connection topology and introduces complex fields and unequal path lengths. This translates to signal skews that are overcome by slowing system speeds so that signals overlap sufficiently in time. Large peak power levels are needed to overcome residual capacitances, and impedance matching effects at connections require high currents, which are generated by driver circuits that increase delays between integrated circuits (ICs).

A technology based on optics offers solutions to these problems if the advantages of optics are exploited without introducing new complexities or limitations that render their use ineffective. Advantages of optics include:

- ◆ high connectivity through imaging

- ◆ no physical contact for interconnects

- ◆ non-interference of signals

- ◆ high spatial and temporal bandwidth

- ◆ no inherent feedback to the power source

- ◆ Inherently low signal dispersion

High connectivity is achieved by imaging a large array of light beams onto an array of optical logic devices. There is no need for physical interconnects unless fiber optics or waveguides are used, so that connection complexity is simplified and drive requirements are reduced. Optical signals do not interact in free space, which means that beams can pass through each other without interference. This allows for a high density of signals in a small volume. High bandwidth is achieved in space because of the noninterference of optical signals, and high bandwidth is achieved in time because propagating wavefronts do not interact. There is no inherent feedback to the power source as there is in electronics, so that there are no data-dependent loads. Finally, inherently low signal dispersion means that the shape of a pulse as it leaves its source is virtually unchanged when it reaches its destination.

The success of digital optics depends heavily on advances in optical hardware, and a number of efforts have focused on the creation of optical logic gates, optical interconnection networks, optical power supplies, novel cooling methods, and problems related to the manufacture of optical systems. The development of suitable optical logic gates has historically been one of the most critical obstacles to achieving an all-optical digital computer and continues to pose a significant challenge. The properties expected of optical logic gates are that they support a fan-in and fan-out of at least two, comprise a logically complete set such as {AND, OR, NOT}, {NAND}, or {NOR}, support indefinite cascadability, operate at low switching powers, and switch at high rates with respect to electronics. For some configurations it is also necessary to have signal inputs and outputs oriented normal to the surfaces of the device substrates so that free space is used for interconnection. Devices that meet these goals are typically fabricated from semiconductor materials such as GaAs and GaAlAs, although promising devices are also made from other materials. Device research is a quickly moving area and is difficult to capture in its entirety, but the underlying idea is that light is used to switch light through an optically sensitive medium, such as GaAs at a wavelength of 850 nm.

There are a number of ways that optics can supplement or replace electronics in computing. Optical fibers typically transport information over long distances, of the order of several tens of kilometers, without a need for signal restoration. Fiber optics is a preferred medium for long-haul transmission because of low losses and high information-carrying capacity. Fibers are also used for distances on the order of a few tens of centimeters in connecting circuit boards. Both of these applications address transmission problems, but optics can be used for computation as well as transmission of information. Information in electronic digital computers is carried in binary values 0 and 1 (typically low and high voltages) and computing is done with configurations of transistors that use a weak signal to control a strong signal. Similarly, in optical digital computing, information is carried by beams of light and computing is done with the optical equivalent of a transistor.

The FET-SEED (D'Asaro *et al.*, 1993) is a more recent version of the SEED (Miller *et al.*, 1985) which has been used in optical processor testbeds at AT&T Bell Laboratories (now Lucent Technologies). The SEED is based on an electrically coupled optical modulator and detector pair. The basic device is made up of approximately 1200 alternating layers of GaAs and GaAlAs in an 8 μm thick quantum well structure placed inside a PIN photodiode detector, as shown in Fig. 1. When light is applied to the detector, a current is generated that reduces the potential across the quantum well. When a strong enough current is created, the positive feedback allows the device to retain its state after the light source is removed. One of the operating modes of the device is to pass light of low intensity and to absorb light of high intensity, implementing negating logic. The electrical properties of the device make it relatively easy to use in experimental setups, and since communication is handled optically, the system speed of a computer made up of these devices is limited only by the device speed. Operating rates for the FET-SEED are several hundred megahertz, and the devices can be monolithically integrated with digital electronics (Hinton *et al.*, 1994).

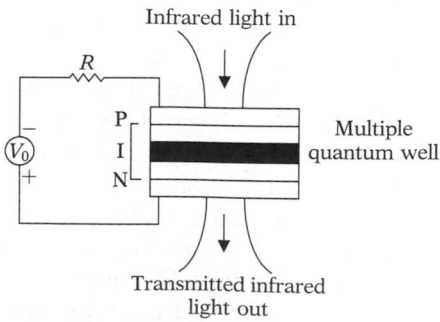

Figure 1. Schematic of the self-electro-optic effect bistable device (Miller *et al.*, 1985).

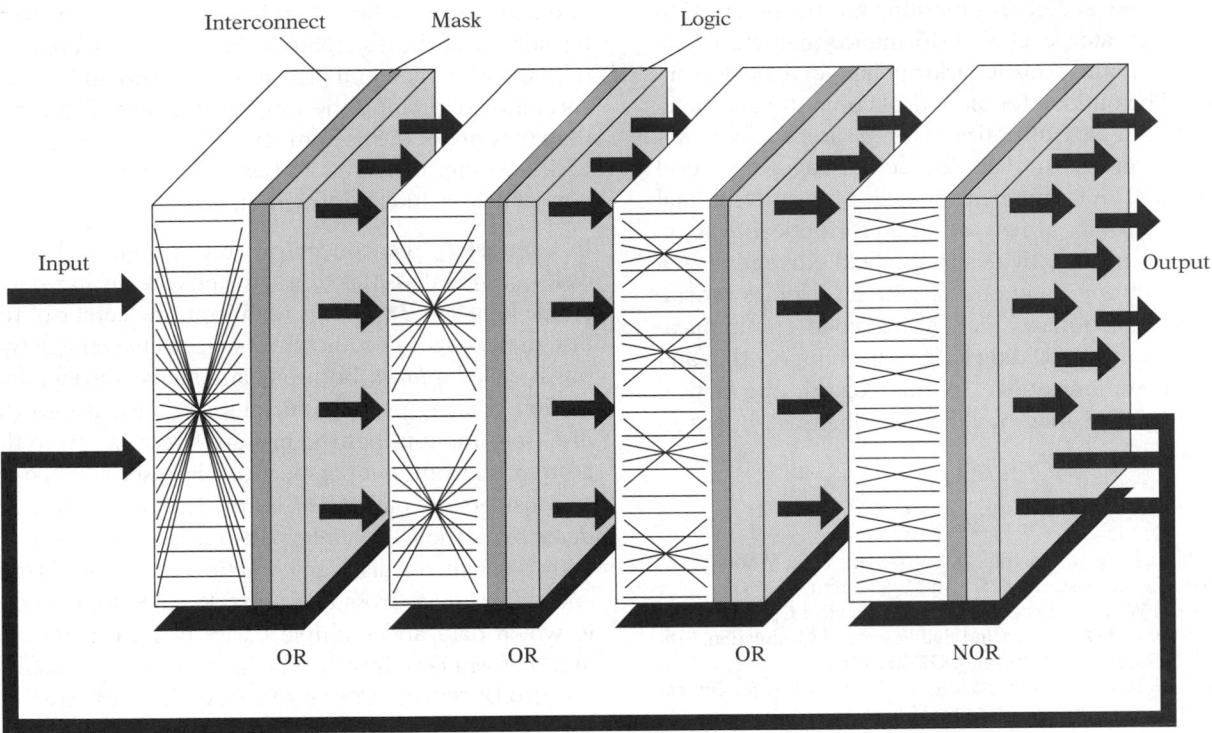

Figure 2. Arrays of optical logic gates are interconnected holographically or with passive components made of glass or metal such as beam-splitters, mirrors and lenses. Masks in the image planes customize the gate-level interconnects by blocking light at selected locations (Murdocca, 1990).

Interconnections among optical logic gates can be handled in a number of ways. Holography provides enormous flexibility by imaging light sources onto receivers in a wide range of configurations. Bulk optical components such as beam-splitters, prisms, mirrors, and lenses are generally easier to manufacture than holograms, but support more limited interconnection schemes, restricting connections to well-defined patterns. Guided wave (fiber) approaches can also be used, especially when connection density is not a major issue.

A conceptual layout of a digital optical circuit based on arrays of optical logic gates and free space optical interconnects (Murdocca, 1990) is shown in Fig. 2. Optical signals travel orthogonal to the device substrates, through alternating connection and logic stages. Masks in the image planes block light at selected locations, which allows the interconnects to be customized for specific functions such as binary addition and multiplication. The system is fed back onto itself and an input channel and an output channel are provided allowing for a conventional model of a digital circuit. Feedback is imaged with a single row vertical shift so that data spirals through the system, allowing a different section of each mask to be used on each pass. A four-stage implementation of this architecture using free space interconnects was constructed at AT&T Bell Laboratories (Prise *et al.*, 1990) as shown in Fig. 3. The system

is composed of four S-SEED arrays with an 8×4 matrix of NOR gates in each array. Fan-in of the logic gates is two and fan-out is two. The four modules occupy an area that is approximately $60 \, \text{cm} \times 60 \, \text{cm} \times 15 \, \text{cm}$, but several subsequent improvements in device technology and interconnection technology allow the size of this style of architecture to be dramatically reduced.

Figure 3. An optical implementation of the model shown in Fig. 2 is made up of four 4×8 arrays of S-SEED NOR gates and free-space interconnects. Size is approximately $60 \, \text{cm} \times 60 \, \text{cm} \times 15 \, \text{cm}$ deep. (Photograph provided by the courtesy of Nicholas Craft, AT&T Bell Laboratories.)

Although optical digital computing has the potential to achieve a greater level of performance than electronic digital computing, this superiority has yet to be demonstrated. The outlook for all-optical computing is one in which the impact of optics is far greater for communication bandwidth than for actual logic gate-level switching. The component densities for conventional digital electronics are greater than for optical technologies, and major activities in the field currently use a mix of electronics and optics, with electronics providing logic functionality and short-range communication, and optics providing long range (chip-to-chip and longer) communication. In this regard, the optical computing field may best be described as "optics in computing."

Bibliography

1985. Miller, D. A. B., Chemla, D. S., Damen, T. C., Wood, T. H., Burrus, C. A., Gossard, A. C., and Wiegmann, W. "The Quantum Well Self-electro-optic Effect Device: Optoelectronic Bistability and Oscillation and Self-linearized Modulation," *IEEE J. Quantum Electronics*, **QE-21**, 1462.

1990. Murdocca, M. J. *A Digital Design Methodology for Optical Computing.* Cambridge, MA: MIT Press.

1990. Prise, M. E., Craft, N. C., LaMarche, R. E., Downs, M. M., Walker, S. J., D'Asaro, L. A., and Chirovsky, L. M. F. "Module for Optical Logic Circuits Using Symmetric Self-electro-optic Effect Devices," *Applied Optics*, **29**, 2164.

1991. McAulay, A. D. *Optical Computer Architectures.* New York: John Wiley.

1993. D'Asaro, L. A., Chirovsky, L. M. F., Laskowski, E. J., Pei, S. S., Woodward, T. K., Lentine, A. L. Leibenguth, R. E., Focht, M. W., Fruend, J. M., Guth, G. D., and Smith, L. E. "Batch Fabrication and Operation of GaAs–Al$_x$Ga$_{1-x}$As Field-effect Transistor–Self-electrooptic Effect Device (FET–SEED) Smart Pixel Arrays," *IEEE J. Quantum Electronics*, **29**, *2*, 670–677.

1994. Hinton, H. S., Cloonan, T. J., McCormick, Jr, F. B., Lentine, A. L., and Tooley, F. A. P. "Free-space Digital Optical Systems," *Proc. IEEE*, **82**, *11*, 1632–1649.

Miles J. Murdocca

OPTICAL STORAGE

For articles on related subjects *see* MEMORY: AUXILIARY; and READ-ONLY MEMORY.

In contrast to memory that functions magnetically, an *optical storage* device uses a laser to etch and later detect microscopic pits in the surface of its recording medium. There are three principal kinds used as auxiliary computer memory, two of which had their origin as audio or audiovisual entertainment media.

CD-ROM

CD-ROM (compact disc read-only memory) is an optical storage medium used primarily with personal computers (*see* Fig. 1). Information is recorded on a 12 cm disc by using a laser to etch billions of tiny pits

into a thin metallic layer that is very much closer to the top surface of the disc than the bottom. Thus, contrary to popular opinion and practice, users should be more careful of scratching the top, printed side of the disc than they are of the bottom, even though it is the latter which so impressively and beautifully reflects a rainbow of colors due to diffraction.

In contrast to the concentric tracks used with hard disks (*q.v.*) or diskettes (*q.v.*), the pits are arranged in a 3-mile long spiral which is read from the center of the disc to the edge. The unetched space between any two pits is called a *land*. Both pits and lands convey information. During production, pits are burned into the disc from the top, but the pits are later read from the bottom, so from that perspective, the laser which does so considers the pits to be *bumps*. The laser, called the *detector*, is the CD counterpart of the read head used with a magnetic disk. Information on audio CDs is encoded using a Cross Interleave Reed–Solomon code in which data and multiple parity bits are combined into uniform-length code words. (*See* ERROR CORRECTING AND DETECTING CODES.) These code words are then super-encoded in accord with an algorithm called EFM (Eight to Fourteen Modulation) which produces 14-bit sequences, called "channel bits," all of which contain at least two consecutive 0-bits between any two 1-bits but never more than ten. To minimize "intersymbol interference," three zeros called "merge bits" are added to the end of each channel sequence, making 17 bits in all.

The depth of all pits is uniform, but their length varies from that needed to store three bits (0.833 μm) to that needed to store 11 bits (3.05 μm). A form of *run-length encoding* is used in which transitions between pits and lands indicate 1-bits, and the length of each

Figure 1. CD ROM.

pit and land is proportional to one plus the number of intervening 0s. Thus, in accord with the EFM restrictions on 1s and 0s, the shortest pits and lands represent the 3-bit sequence 100, the second shortest 1000, the third shortest 10000, etc., up to the longest pits which represent the 11-bit sequence 10000000000. Thus it always takes a combination of two or more pits and lands to represent a full 17-bit channel code.

When, during reading, a sufficient number of dispersed (interleaved) pits and lands are encountered which encode a *frame* of 24 data bytes and 8 parity bytes, those bytes are extracted from their channel codes, parity is checked in accord with R-S rules, errors are corrected when possible (bursts of hundreds of errors or more can be corrected), and the parity bytes are discarded, leaving just verified data.

Magnetic disks rotate at constant speed (constant angular velocity, or CAV), but CD rotational speed varies, decreasing toward the periphery, in order to provide constant linear (tangential) velocity (CLV). This allows use of the same pit density throughout the CD's single spiral track.

CD-ROM storage was adapted from audio CD, developed in the mid-1970s by Sony and Philips, and CD-ROM units have been available for personal computers since the mid-1980s. The capacity of a CD-ROM is 650 MB, enough to hold roughly 80 copies of this Encyclopedia, exclusive of space for digitized photographs and figures. At the time of its introduction, CD-ROM was distinguished as relatively slow, high-capacity removable-media, read-only storage. Today CD-ROM is distinguished by its low cost. The data transfer rate, which was initially limited to the 150 KB/sec needed for recorded music, has increased by 30 to 40 times, and drive cost has fallen from nearly $1,000 to under $100.

These performance improvements, coupled with proliferating applications, have led to CD-ROM drives becoming nearly standard equipment on personal computers. Infotech (www.infotechresearch.com), a market research firm specializing in optical media and multimedia applications, reported that 74.1 million CD-ROM drives were sold during 1997, and the installed base was 195 million units at the end of that year. They project sales increasing until the year 2000, when replacement by DVD-ROM drives will begin to slow shipment rates.

CD-ROM applications were pioneered by Gary Kildall and Bill Gates (*see* ENTREPRENEURS). Kildall, author of CP/M, an operating system that was widely used on early personal computers, worked with Grolier to publish the Academic American Encyclopedia in 1985. Gates, co-founder of Microsoft (*q.v.*), sponsored an annual CD-ROM conference in the early years of the

industry and spearheaded early PC and Macintosh standards efforts for the CD-ROM. Microsoft has also been an important publisher of CD-ROM titles.

CD-ROM applications include reference material, games, and software distribution. CD-ROM has revolutionized the encyclopedia industry, totally replacing some print encyclopedias (but not this one!). It has also been used widely in games for personal computers and specialized game machines. As the size of software packages has grown, CD-ROM has become a near-universal medium for program distribution. Hybrid titles, combining information on CD-ROM and the Internet (*q.v.*), are also growing in popularity. Infotech estimates there will be over 25,000 hybrid titles available by 2000. The rapid price decline of CD-RW drives (see below) has also led to their use in proprietary applications within organizations, for example, in internal information dissemination and backup for magnetic media.

There are now CD-R (Compact Disc Recordable) drives available that record information on a conventional blank CD, but only once, and hence are a type of WORM device (Write Once, Read Many). But even better, there are also CD-RW (Compact Disc ReWritable) drives available at somewhat higher cost that provide true auxiliary memory that can be recorded (up to about a million times) and read back and are thus a type of WMRM (Write Many, Read Many) drive.

One way to create a CD-R drive for a computer would be to equip the drive with a laser as powerful as the lasers used to burn pits into CDs at a commercial plant, but this has proved impractical because of size and cost considerations. So what is done instead is to use a less expensive laser which is able to create simulated pits which are really "stripes" of amorphous material on a metallic surface that was initially uniformly crystalline. Each stripe scatters light in the same pattern as a pit would have done. And once there were no virtually immutable pits that would be very difficult to fill in, the path was cleared for the development of the rewritable CD drive, a CD-RW. With such a drive, re-recording is done by first erasing old information through intense laser action that heats each amorphous stripe to that temperature just below its melting point where it recrystallizes. Then, after a few milliseconds of cooling to complete the process, a less intense laser action is used to record new information.

Laserdisc

Eventually, computer-based motion video will be digitally encoded on DVDs (see next section) but most of today's motion video applications involve the presentation of analog video under computer control. The *laserdisc*, originally called *videodisc*, is the most common source of *analog* video material for interactive applications because it allows random access, and the economies of scale derived from the extensive home and entertainment market have reduced player prices.

Laserdiscs are either 8 or 12 inches in diameter, with 12-inch discs being most common. As with CD-ROM, information is recorded by pressing a spiral of microscopic pits into a polished surface. There are about 14 billion pits on one side of a 12-inch disc. Information may be recorded at either constant linear velocity (CLV) or constant angular velocity (CAV). Each side of a 12-inch laserdisc holds a half-hour of video when recorded in CAV format, and an hour when recorded with CLV. The drive speed of a CLV disc varies from 600 to 1,800 rpm as a function of head position. The innermost "track" (rotation) of a 12-inch, CLV disc holds one frame, the outermost track holds three frames. With the CAV format, the disc rotates at a constant 1,800 rpm and there is always one frame per track. CAV discs are most commonly used in computer-based systems because they allow random access to any track, freeze frame, step frame, and multi-speed playback. The remainder of this section assumes CAV discs.

Audio information is recorded along with the video. There are two frequency-modulated (FM) channels with signal-to-noise ratios of 70 dB. The FM channels may be used as a single stereo soundtrack or two independent (typically bilingual) soundtracks. National Television System Committee (NTSC) discs have the capacity for an additional digital audio track with a signal-to-noise ratio of 96 dB; however, this track is not available with Phase Alternate Line (PAL) discs.

With an LD-ROM (laserdisc read-only memory), all or a portion of the digital audio may be replaced with digital information in the CD-ROM format. This allows up to 270 MB of program or data to be stored on the disc along with the video and FM audio.

Laserdisc players accept commands to seek a specified frame, play forward or reverse at normal or variable speed, freeze a frame, etc. It is common to speak of three levels of laserdisc, depending upon how these commands are issued. Level 1 refers to manual control with the user issuing commands using a remote control device or buttons on the player console. Level 2 players can display characters over the video image and store sequences of commands in an internal memory. Using the overlaid characters for multiple choice questions allows simple branching programs. The control information may be read from the disc or, more commonly, by using a barcode reader with printed material that accompanies the disc.

In Level 3, the player is connected to a computer through an RS-232 interface (*see* PORT, I/O), and con-

trol commands are issued by the computer. The video image may either be displayed on the computer display screen or an independent monitor or television set. Both approaches have advantages and disadvantages. Displaying the image on the computer screen focuses the user's attention on one monitor, reduces the system footprint, and saves the cost of a second monitor; however, it requires a special video adapter for the computer. Displaying the video image on an independent monitor gives additional viewing area and simplifies programming. If a television set is used, it may also play the audio; otherwise, a sound system must be provided. Playing an LD-ROM disc requires a special adapter, with a SCSI interface to the computer.

Level 3 laserdisc is used for applications, including industrial training, education, games, and retail sales support. The bulk of early applications were in industrial training, using IBM's InfoWindow system for the computer controller and development software. Development tools, and hence applications, have proliferated in recent years. In addition to authoring systems tailored to education and training, there have been laserdisc control extensions to HyperCard, HyperPad, ToolBook, and other general-purpose tools for creating interactive applications on personal computers (*see* HYPERTEXT). A developer may either produce a custom laserdisc or reuse a previously existing disc. Producing a custom disc requires video production equipment and skills, a one-time mastering charge, and disc reproduction charges. While producing a custom disc requires considerable expense and professional expertise, general users such as classroom teachers and industrial trainers can produce interactive material using pre-existing discs and the development tools mentioned earlier.

The pre-existing disc may be a movie, documentary, "how-to" disc produced for the home and entertainment market, or a disc produced specifically for use in interactive computer applications. The number of education and training video disc titles has grown from fewer than 200 in 1985 to over 12,000 in 1999.

DVD

A DVD (Digital Versatile Disc, formerly Digital Video Disc) has the same 12 cm ($4\frac{3}{4}$") size as a CD but is called "versatile" because it appears destined to replace not only the laserdisc and the audio CD for entertainment but also the CD-ROM for use as auxiliary computer memory (*see* Fig. 2). DVD technology uses a higher frequency (shorter wavelength) laser to etch pits than is used to make a CD, so the pits are much smaller. Furthermore, the DVD's spiral tracks are more dense than those of a CD, both circumferentially—0.4 μm rather than 0.83 μm—and radially—0.74 μm rather

Figure 2. The Hitachi GD-2500BX DVD ROM drive.

than 1.6 μm. These attributes and other compression techniques allow a DVD to contain up to 8.5 GB, thirteen times as much as a 650 MB CD (and twice again as much—17 GB—when recorded on both sides). And they are able to do this with greater fidelity than a CD through use of the Reed–Solomon Product Code (RS–PC), an error-correcting code that is ten times more robust than the Cross Interleave Reed–Solomon code used with CDs, and use of EFM PLUS, 8 bit to 16 bit modulation rather than 8 to 14. But, in keeping with the claim of versatility, a DVD drive can still read CDs.

Like CD-ROM and LD-ROM, an ordinary DVD is DVD-ROM, that is, its prerecorded pit-encoded information can be read but not rewritten. But DVD-RAM drives are now available which, through use of technology similar to that described earlier for use with CD-RW, are WMRM devices (*see* Fig. 3). These are likely to

Figure 3. The Hitachi GF-1000 DVD RAM drive.

become the optical storage medium of choice for use with personal computers (*see* MEMORY: AUXILIARY). Infotech predicts that by 2002, small computers and workstations will be routinely shipped with some kind of DVD rather than a CD-ROM.

Bibliography

1992. Pohlmann, K. C. *The Compact Disc Handbook*. Madison, WI: A-R Editions Inc.
1998. White, R. *How Computers Work*, 4th Ed. Indianapolis, IN: QUE.
1999. Goodwin, M. "Taking DVD for a Spin," *PC World*, **2**, 2 (February), 143–154.

Larry Press

OPTIMIZATION METHODS

For articles on related subjects *see* LEAST-SQUARES APPROXIMATION; MATHEMATICAL PROGRAMMING; NUMERICAL ANALYSIS; PARALLEL PROCESSING; QUEUEING THEORY; SIMULATION; and TOMOGRAPHY, COMPUTERIZED.

Mathematical optimization deals with the problem of finding (or approximating) a point that gives an *optimal* (minimal or maximal) *value* to some function (called the *objective function*), subject to some additional conditions (called *constraints*).

Many problems in various scientific and technological fields, such as physics, engineering, chemistry, economics, and operations research, as well as other fields of mathematics, can be cast as optimization problems and thereby benefit from and contribute to the reservoir of knowledge of mathematical optimization. In this area, numerical analysis, computational methods, and other branches of mathematics, as well as the study of practical applications, interact with and fertilize one another and promote our understanding and ability to solve concrete problems.

The two main branches of optimization are *dynamic optimization* and *static optimization*. The latter is more commonly called *mathematical programming*.

Dynamic optimization is particularly concerned with decision-making situations or economic growth models and mathematical formulations of problems involving moving objects in which the time variable enters naturally into the optimization problem and therefore also appears in its solution. The objective function here usually takes the form of an integral, while the constraints are described by a system of differential equations. The forerunner of this discipline was the *calculus of variations*, which, later on, upon the formulation of *Pontryagin's maximum principle*, developed into the modern theory of *optimal control* (*see* McShane, 1978). In between, the theory of *dynamic programming* appeared. This proved itself particularly efficient in handling multistage decision processes (*see* Bertsekas, 1995).

Static optimization is concerned with all forms of time-independent optimization. In the general formulation of the static optimization problem (*see* MATHEMATICAL PROGRAMMING), there is a function of n variables to be optimized (i.e. maximized or minimized), called the *objective function*, subject to m constraints on the variables. When the objective function and the constraints are all linear, this area is called *linear programming* and the best known method is called the *simplex method*. A modern treatment of this field can be found in Roos *et al.* (1997).

Obviously, the rest of mathematical programming is called *nonlinear programming*, of which one sub-branch is *convex programming*, in which the objective function is a convex function and the *feasible set* (i.e. those points in the Euclidean n-space R^n that satisfy the constraints) is a *convex set*. Part-way between linear and convex programming lies the theory and practice of *quadratic programming*, dealing with problems where the objective function is a positive definite quadratic function and the constraints are linear.

If the additional condition that some or all variables should take only integer values is imposed on the problem, *integer programming* is obtained.

Other specialized branches of mathematical programming are *stochastic programming*, *geometric programming*, *multiobjective programming*, and *large-scale programming*. Expository articles on these and other important topics in optimization appear in Nemhauser *et al.* (1989).

Real systems most often lead to large optimization problems which can be solved practically only by implementation of appropriate solution algorithms on a computer. Success or failure then depends strongly on computer programming talent, acquaintance with machine specifications, and the right methodology of implementation.

Some Optimization Methods

In this section, we shall sample briefly the huge number of methods of mathematical optimization.

SOLVING NONLINEAR EQUATIONS

The general problem is that of solving a system of equations $F\mathbf{x} = \mathbf{0}$, where F is an operator mapping some domain D of the Euclidean R^n space into R^n. This problem arises frequently in applications so that the importance of having at hand effective methods

of solution can hardly be exaggerated. One fruitful approach is to replace it by an equivalent optimization problem. With the aid of a real-valued function $f(\mathbf{x})$ on R^n, which has the property that its global minimum is uniquely attained at $\mathbf{x} = \mathbf{0}$, a new function g is defined by

$$g(\mathbf{x}) = f(F\mathbf{x}) \quad \text{for } \mathbf{x} \in D.$$

Then the optimization problem

$$\text{Minimize } g(\mathbf{x})$$
$$\text{such that } \mathbf{x} \in D$$

has to be solved to find $\mathbf{x}* \in D$, which gives g its global minimum on D.

If $F\mathbf{x} = \mathbf{0}$ has a solution, then this must be $\mathbf{x}*$. If $F\mathbf{x} = \mathbf{0}$ has no solution in D, then $\mathbf{x}*$ is called an *f-minimal solution* of $F\mathbf{x} = \mathbf{0}$ (*see* Ortega and Rheinboldt, 1970). The special choice $f(\mathbf{x}) = \mathbf{x}^T\mathbf{x}$ gives rise to an f-minimal solution, which is called a *least-squares solution* of $F\mathbf{x} = \mathbf{0}$ (*see* LEAST-SQUARES APPROXIMATION).

THE METHOD OF STEEPEST DESCENT

Also called the *gradient method*, this method for minimizing a real-valued, continuously differentiable function f, defined on R^n, consists of an iterative algorithm

$$\mathbf{x}^{k+1} = \mathbf{x}^k - \alpha_k \nabla f(\mathbf{x}^k)$$

in which $\mathbf{x}^{k+1}$ and $\mathbf{x}^k$ are the new and old iterates, respectively, $\nabla f(\mathbf{x}^k)$ is the gradient vector of f calculated at $\mathbf{x}^k$, and α_k is a nonnegative scalar minimizing $f(\mathbf{x}^k - \alpha \nabla f(\mathbf{x}^k))$. This means that from the point $\mathbf{x}^k$, a search is made along the direction of the negative gradient $-\nabla f(\mathbf{x}^k)$ to a minimum point on this line that is taken to be the next iterate.

NEWTON'S METHOD

Newton's method for solving a system of equations (for the case of a single equation, *see* NUMERICAL ANALYSIS) may be applied to the system.

$$\nabla f(\mathbf{x}) = \mathbf{0}$$

which describes the necessary condition for a minimum of the function f. To do this, f has to be twice continuously differentiable and its Hessian $\nabla^2 f(\mathbf{x})$ (the matrix of all second-order partial derivatives) must be invertible at every iteration point. The resulting Newton-type optimization method then takes the form:

$$\mathbf{x}^{k+1} = \mathbf{x} - [\nabla^2 f(\mathbf{x}^k)]^{-1} \nabla f(\mathbf{x}^k),$$

where the -1 denotes matrix inversion. Various modifications of this method have been suggested for these as well as a great variety of other optimization methods (*see* Nash and Sofer, 1996).

Applications of Optimization Methods

Examples of problems from various fields of application to which optimization methods are applied are abundant and can be found in the books cited in the references. *Optimal planning* in economics and *optimal allocation of resources* lead to optimization problems. So do many other applications in *mathematical economics*, *decision theory*, and *game theory*. Numerous real-world *engineering* problems in virtually every field are cast as optimization problems and are solved by optimization methods. In mathematics, one finds optimization problems in *approximation theory*, *numerical analysis*, and *functional analysis*. Specific models in physics, chemistry, biology, and other sciences lend themselves to treatment with optimization methods. Problems of *least-squares approximation* (*see* Björck, 1996) and *entropy optimization* occur in statistics and *data analysis*. The list of applications of optimization methods is extensive and, not surprisingly, also includes problems within computer science, such as *computer networks* (*see* NETWORKS, COMPUTER) and *image processing* (*q.v.*).

One such recent application of great importance is the problem of *image reconstruction* in which an image (a function of two variables) has to be recovered from experimentally available integrals of its grayness (i.e. its overall brightness) over thin strips. An important version of this problem in medicine, called *computerized tomography*, is concerned with the recovery of the density distribution within the human body from its measured X-ray projections.

In the *series expansion approach* to the image reconstruction problem (other approaches are available—*see* Herman, 1980), the mathematical formulation takes the form of a system of equations

$$\mathbf{p} = M\mathbf{x} + \mathbf{e}$$

where $\mathbf{p}$ is the m-dimensional vector of actual measurements, $\mathbf{x}$ is the n-dimensional unknown vector representing the grayness levels of the image to be reconstructed, and $\mathbf{e}$ is an (also unknown) m-dimensional vector of the errors that are due to the inaccuracy of the physical measurements and possibly also to the *discretization* of the original problem. The $m \times n$ matrix $\mathbf{M}$ is huge (of the order of magnitude $10^5 \times 10^5$) and sparse (i.e. has many zero elements), but lacks any structure in its sparsity.

By setting up various optimization criteria (i.e. objective functions), according to which a "solution" that agrees with the measurements is sought, the problem is transformed into an optimization problem. Quadratic optimization and entropy optimization have received considerable attention (*see* Censor and Herman, 1987, for a unified approach).

Parallel Optimization

Parallel computation techniques are becoming widespread and researchers in mathematical optimization are playing a leading role in demonstrating the effectiveness of parallelism in speeding up the solution of large-scale problems. In many areas of optimization theory, new algorithms are being developed which do not just use parallelism in the implementational phase but are also inherently parallel in their mathematical logic. For example *block-iterative projection* (BIP) methods allow the processing of "blocks" of constraints of the optimization problem. Parallelism can be realized within blocks or between blocks, depending on the problem at hand (*see* Censor and Zenios, 1997). Other sources on parallel optimization are Schnabel (1995) and Bertsekas and Tsitsiklis (1989).

Bibliography

1970. Ortega, J. M., and Rheinboldt, W. C. *Iterative Solution of Nonlinear Equations in Several Variables*. New York: Academic Press.

1978. McShane, E. J. "The Calculus of Variations from the Beginning Through Optimal Control Theory," in *Optimal Control and Differential Equations* (eds. A. B. Schwarzkopf, W. G. Kelly, and S. B. Eliason). New York: Academic Press.

1980. Herman, G. T. *Image Reconstruction From Projections: The Fundamentals of Computerized Tomography*. New York: Academic Press.

1987. Censor, Y., and Herman, G. T. "On Some Optimization Techniques in Image Reconstruction from Projections," *Applied Numerical Mathematics*, **3**, 365–391.

1989. Bertsekas, D. P., and Tsitsiklis, J. N. *Parallel and Distributed Computation: Numerical Methods*. Upper Saddle River, NJ: Prentice Hall.

1989. Nemhauser, G. L., Rinnooy Kan, A. H. G., and Todd, M. J. (eds.). *Optimization*. Handbooks in Operations Research and Management Science, Volume 1. Amsterdam: Elsevier Science Publishers.

1995. Bertsekas, D. P. *Dynamic Programming and Optimal Control*, Volumes I and II. Belmont, MA: Athena Scientific.

1995. Schnabel, R. B. "A View on the Limitations, Opportunities, and Challenges in Parallel Nonlinear Optimization," *Parallel Computing*, **21**, 875–905.

1996. Björck, A. *Numerical Methods for Least Squares Problems*. Philadelphia, PA: Society for Industrial and Applied Mathematics.

1996. Nash, S. G., and Sofer, A. *Linear and Nonlinear Programming*. New York: McGraw-Hill.

1997. Censor, Y., and Zenios, S. A. *Parallel Optimization: Theory, Algorithms and Applications*. New York: Oxford University Press.

1997. Roos, C., Terlaky, T., and Vial, J.-Ph. *Theory and Algorithms for Linear Optimization: An Interior Point Approach*. New York: John Wiley.

Yair Censor

OVERHEAD

For articles on related subjects *see* ACCOUNTING SYSTEM, COMPUTER; OPERATING SYSTEMS: GENERAL PRINCIPLES; and SCHEDULING ALGORITHMS.

Overhead in computer systems is like overhead in organizations—shared functions that benefit everyone but which cannot be allocated conveniently to any one activity. In organizations, rent, furnishings, electricity, telephones, utilities, supplies, auditing, accounting, general clerical support, and management are counted as overhead. In computer systems, allocation of resources, scheduling, conflict resolution, error correction, exceptional conditions, protection, security, performance monitoring, auditing, accounting, input–output control, caching, distributed functions, and network protocols (*q.v.*) are all counted as overhead. As in organizations, excessive overhead diminishes capacity and increases cost without increasing revenue or productivity. Overhead in computer systems shows up as slower processing, less memory, less network bandwidth (*q.v.*), or bigger latencies than would be expected from reading the system specifications.

Overhead is not always easy to measure. The time an operating system spends in supervisor state (*see* PRIVILEGED INSTRUCTION) is not pure overhead because many important operations requested by user tasks are implemented as system functions that run in supervisor state; examples are input–output, file operations, and message-passing. A measurement that an operating system spends 80% of its time in supervisor state does not mean that the system spends only 20% of its time doing useful work: we need to know what portion of the 80% is spent responding to requests from user tasks. Moreover, many operating systems use special coprocessors to perform important overhead tasks such as virtual memory control, external communications, or peripheral device management; these coprocessors do not diminish processor capacity, memory capacity, or bandwidth available to user tasks. A measurement that a processor spends 90% of the time running user tasks does not mean that overhead is low if there are eight or more coprocessors carrying out systems functions.

Listed below are the main functions that usually count as overhead. Each has a cost in processing time, memory space, network bandwidth, and latency (response time).

◆ *Allocation of resources* Many resources such as CPU cycles, disk sectors, main memory page frames, local network packet slots, and shared files can be used by only one task at a time. To prevent conflicts and deadlocks, operating systems implement schedulers for these resources. The time spent running a scheduler and the memory occupied by a scheduler's queues count as overhead.

◆ *Error correction* Data is stored and transmitted with redundant bits that permit detection and correction of errors (*see* ERROR CORRECTING AND DETECTING CODE). These bits consume some space and bandwidth.

◆ *Exceptional conditions* Most system functions have normal and error returns; the instructions that test for and respond to errors consume some space and processing time. Examples are arithmetic contingencies, data transmission failures, addressing snags, and illegal actions.

◆ *Protection and security* Monitors, firewalls, authenticators, backup systems, virus detectors, and other means of securing systems against unauthorized use, denial of service, and intruders are necessary but often expensive.

◆ *Performance monitoring, auditing and accounting* Recording key actions and events, logging each task's usage of resources, figuring costs and billings to users of the system, and generating statistics on resource usage and performance all have costs.

◆ *Input–output control* Many I/O operations are easy to specify at the user level—e.g. open or read a file. But the device spoolers and drivers can be quite complex because they must queue up requests from multiple tasks, translate each request into the low-level instruction sets of the devices, automatically work around known problems such as bad disk sectors, and handle interrupt conditions from their devices.

◆ *Caching* The speed of operations on secondary storage devices or remote servers can often be significantly improved by keeping a copy of the data in a local cache memory (*q.v.*). Microcomputer register-windows (multiple sets of registers), virtual memories, disk drivers, open-file managers, and network browsers are among the many prominent examples of caching. Caching consumes memory and processing time to locate and load copies of items into the cache and to maintain consistency with the originals.

◆ *Distributed functions* Modern operating systems distribute their functions transparently over a collection of servers and workstations connected by a high-speed local network. Examples are file servers, printing servers, compute servers, authentication servers, and workstations. Maintaining the appearance that files, printers, processors, and login-sites are location-independent significantly improves usability but is not cheap.

◆ *Network protocols* (*q.v.*) Protocols for opening connections, transferring data, obtaining encryption keys, routing, and authenticating access all cost processing time, memory, and bandwidth.

The cost of the overhead is borne by the users of the system. Where possible, these costs are allocated to the tasks that caused the overhead function to be performed (e.g. initiating a task, switching a processor to a task, moving information of a task among the levels of memory). Otherwise, these costs are distributed among all users according to some *pro rata* formula.

Overhead detracts from system performance only to the extent that the overhead functions do not add to the productivity of user tasks. Many services are provided by the system to relieve programmers from having to provide these functions themselves or to prevent expensive breakdowns. As long as the system can provide these functions more efficiently than its users, the resulting increases in overhead are offset by better service, improved performance, and lower overall costs.

Peter J. Denning

PACKAGE

For articles on related subjects *see* BLOCK STRUCTURE; ENCAPSULATION; GLOBAL AND LOCAL VARIABLES; INFORMATION HIDING; MODULAR PROGRAMMING; and OBJECT-ORIENTED PROGRAMMING.

A *package system* is that part of a programming language that supports multiple name spaces, a name space being the collection of names which have meaning within a particular package. Package systems were developed in part to prevent name space collisions. Name space collisions occur when different programmers accidentally use the same variable or function name with different meaning when working on different parts of a program within the same name space. Many early programming languages had only one name space.

Conceptually, a *package* is a data structure (*q.v.*) used by a package system to maintain a mapping between names and their values, the variables or functions denoted by those names. A package system requires programmers to be explicit about shared variables and functions. Variables and functions that are not explicitly shared are safely hidden in the package. Named values visible outside their package are said to be *exported*. Named values from outside a package that are visible inside a package are said to be *imported*. Every name belongs to some package. Packages help manage large software systems because the public interface to package services is usually much smaller and more comprehensible than the total number of names used within the package—users see only the operations and objects required to maintain the abstraction which the package presents. Many modern programming languages have a package mechanism; C++ (*q.v.*) calls them *namespaces*, Java (*q.v.*) and Common Lisp (*see* LISP) have *packages*.

In some programming environments packages are primarily a compile- and link-time mechanism, and name lookups are precalculated for speed. In other systems, packages are mutable and may be changed at run time. In such mutable package systems, name lookup may be done dynamically according to the currently active package. Some programming languages allow different areas within a single unit of source text to be associated with different packages, a practice which can be a source of confusion to the casual reader. In languages, such as Modula-2 and Ada (*q.v.*), where packages are directly identified with the unit of compilation, they are frequently called *modules*.

Kenneth A. Dickey

PACKAGES, SOFTWARE

See SOFTWARE LIBRARIES, NUMERICAL AND STATISTICAL; and MATHEMATICAL SOFTWARE.

PACKET SWITCHING

For articles on related subjects *see* ASYNCHRONOUS TRANSFER MODE; COMMUNICATIONS AND COMPUTERS; DATA COMMUNICATIONS; DISTRIBUTED SYSTEMS; NETWORK PROTOCOLS; NETWORKS, COMPUTER; INTERNET; INTEGRATED SERVICES DIGITAL NETWORKS; and TCP/IP.

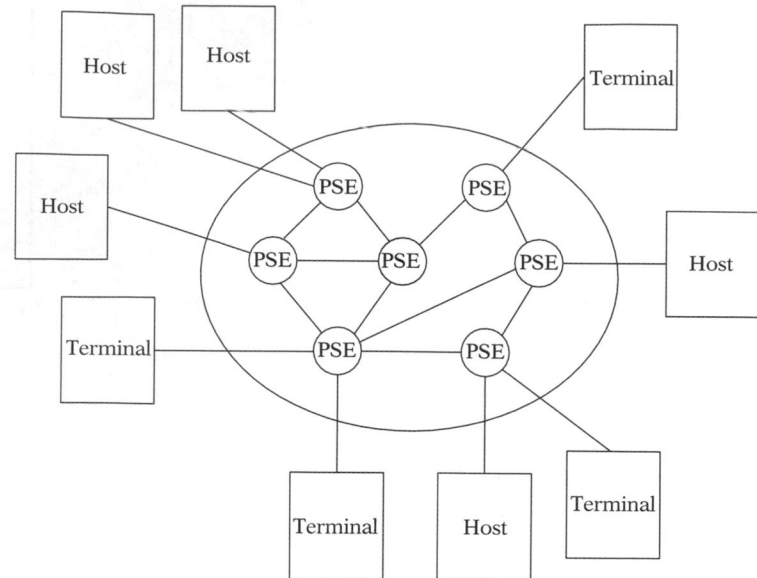

Figure. 1. Typical packet-switched network.

Packet switching is a term used to describe the internal operations of a particular type of data communications network that usually has a fixed topology and uses software to route information in a special format through the network from source to destination. A packet-switched data communication network is composed of a number of geographically separate nodes connected by dedicated high-speed data links. The nodes are (usually) stored program computers that have internal data link connections to the other nodes and external data links connected to local terminals and computers. Fig. 1 illustrates an example of a packet-switched data communications network.

The general theory of operation is that a unit of information, called a *packet* (usually 128 bytes or less), is routed from one *packet-switching exchange* (PSE) to another via transmission lines until the packet reaches its destination. The destination address for the information is contained in the header of the packet. Each packet may, therefore, go to a different destination; hence the term *packet switching*. A variant of packet

switching has evolved called *cell switching* where the packets are a fixed size of 48 bytes. Cell switching is the technology used in ATM and *broadband ISDN* services.

When a packet arrives at a PSE, the exchange determines whether it is a transit node or a destination node. If the former, it chooses a transmission line to send the packet toward its destination. This type of operation is called *store-and-forward* transmission, a term created in message-switching systems. In packet-switching systems, the store-and-forward operations generally occur in tens of milliseconds. End-to-end transmission delay (source to destination) is typically about 100 milliseconds for transcontinental packets on the Internet in the USA, though it can be a second or more on slower portions of the Internet.

Fig. 2 shows some of the history of packet switching. In 1976, the international standards body responsible for worldwide telecommunications standards (ITU-T) recommended the first interface protocol, called X.25, for attaching terminal equipment to a packet network.

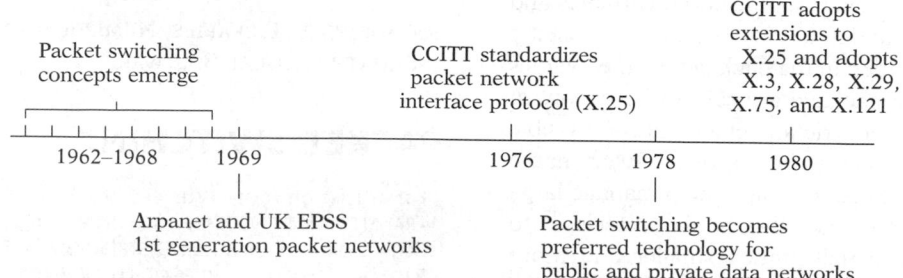

Figure 2. Evolution of packet switching. CCITT is now the International Telecommunications Union (ITU).

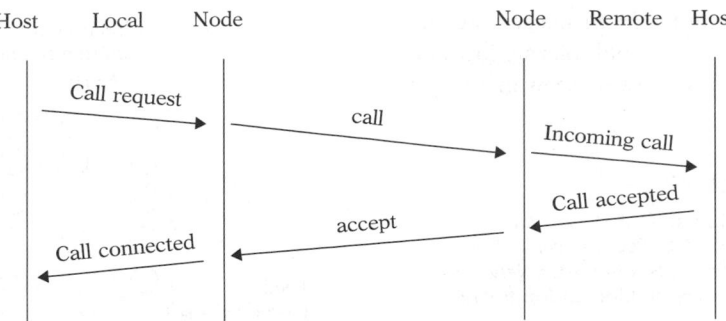

Figure 3. Virtual circuit setup.

Two alternative strategies have evolved in the implementation of packet-switching systems—*datagrams* and *virtual circuits*. In the datagram (also called *connectionless*) strategy, each packet of information is totally independent of all others. They are independently routed and have the properties that they can be lost or duplicated (this phenomenon is caused by transmission errors and retransmissions) with some probability, and transmission order between packets is not preserved. Proponents of the datagram approach argue that a simpler network interface can be achieved and that transmission of datagrams can easily be routed around failed links and nodes. The Internet uses datagrams and a protocol called IP (*see* TCP/IP) for controlling routing and transmission.

In the virtual circuit (VC) approach, a logical path is created by the network between the source and destination (*see* Fig. 3). The virtual circuit allows the network to maintain order, discard duplicates, and detect missing packets. The VC uses special packet types to establish and clear calls. VC proponents argue a simpler end-to-end protocol, better flow control by the network, and lower transmission and processing overhead

as the VC's chief assets. Public data networks that use the VC approach include X.25, frame relay, and ATM.

Packet-switching networks provide interfaces to terminals not supporting the packet mode of operation. These terminals are supported through PADs (packet assembler–disassemblers) which convert the native protocols (such as asynchronous communications used by most personal computers) into packet format for transmission through the network (*see* Fig. 4).

An important issue in the use of packet-switching is the *Quality of Service* (QoS) required by an application. The Internet IP protocol provides "best effort" service, which routes packets without any guarantee of minimum throughput (*q.v.*). This is appropriate for "traditional" Internet services like file transfer and email, but not for real-time audio or video, which will fail to be intelligible if the packet delivery rate falls too low. The appropriate *service models* for different sorts of packet-switching applications is a subject of current study. A service model for real-time packet-switched video, for example, would require that switching nodes guarantee it a certain minimum bandwidth, but might

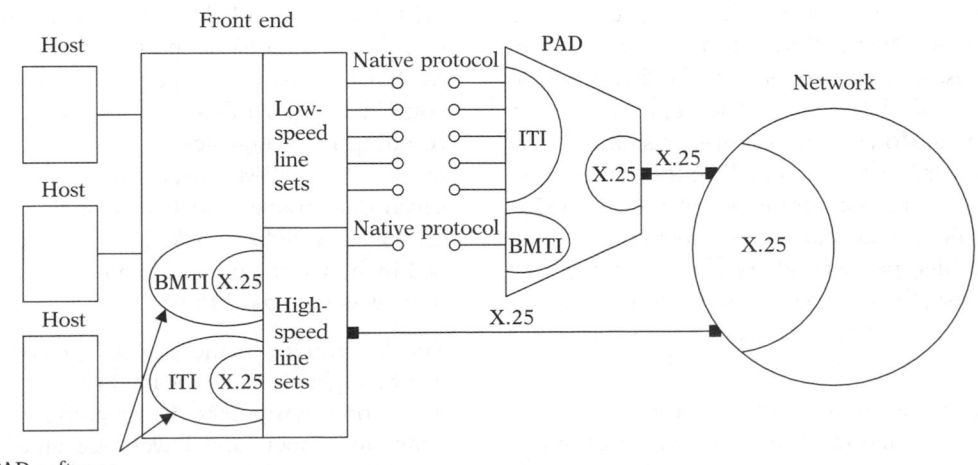

Figure 4. Typical interfaces to hosts. (X.25 above indicates hardware and software that implements the X.25 standard; BMTI is Block Mode Terminal Interface and ITI is Interactive Terminal Interface.)

not require complete immunity from occasional bit-errors. A file transfer, however, could tolerate low and variable transfer rates, but loss of even a few bits might render the file useless.

Bibliography

1996. Metcalfe, R., Salus, P. H., and Cerf, V. G. *Packet Communications.* Menlo Park, CA: Peer-to-Peer.
1996. Peterson, L. L., and Davie, B. S. *Computer Networks: A Systems Approach.* San Francisco: Morgan Kaufmann.

Barry D. Wessler

PAGED MEMORY

See VIRTUAL MEMORY.

PALMTOP COMPUTER

See PORTABLE COMPUTERS.

PAPER TAPE

For articles on related subjects *see* BAUDOT CODE; CHARACTER CODES; and CODES.

Punched *paper tape* is a storage medium used for the preparation, storage, and transmission of data in various applications. Slow-speed paper tape may be used as a control device for numerically controlled machine tool operations. At higher speeds, paper tape was once used for typesetting, telegraphic and data transmission, automated typewriting, for storing computer programs and data, and also for other data processing functions (e.g. to control the carriage movement in line printers), but few if any such applications are in current use.

The use of punched paper tape for data preparation, storage, and transmission is an old technique. It was introduced by Sir Charles Wheatstone in 1857 for telegraphic purposes, just 21 years after the first practical demonstration of the electric telegraph. One year later, in 1858, a Morse tape reader–transmitter operated at 100 words per minute. Five-track tape keyboard punches were in common use in 1908. In 1925, five-track readers were commonly operating at four letters, or 20 bits, per second. When multiplexed for transmission use, the line speed was 80 bits per second. Adoption of this technique for data processing saw a vast increase in applications of punched paper tape.

Speed requirements and therefore performance increased manyfold, and the available number of tracks increased from five to eight to accommodate the various alphabets required. Small sprocket holes appear along the length of the tape and were used to feed the

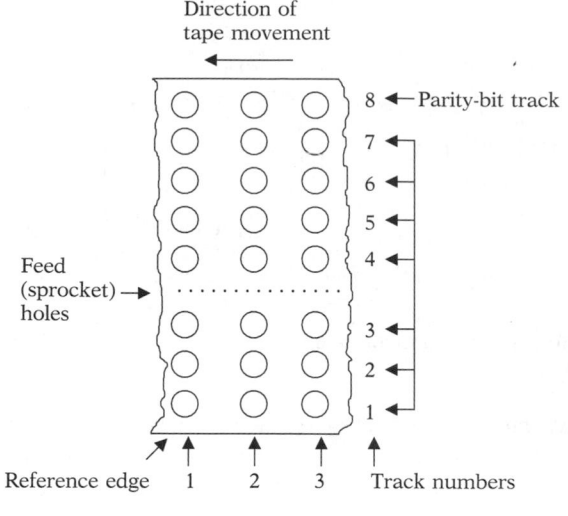

Figure 1. Punched paper tape terminology. Note: each data row represents one seven-bit character.

tape mechanically as they engage toothed wheels in slow-speed readers; in high-speed machines, these sprocket holes (or feed holes) act as a clock pulse when a tape is read by a photoelectric head (*see* Fig. 1). Data is recorded in the tape by punching holes in a row across its width. Each row represents one character, and the pattern of the holes punched indicates the particular character.

In the narrowest tape (with five tracks, and which was 11/16-inch wide), a hole can be punched in any track, so the number of unique hole combinations possible is 2^5, or 32. Thus, 32 characters can be represented by a five-hole code. More than 32 separate items can be identified if each code group is made to represent two or more characters, and a special character (e.g. letter or figure shift) precedes the punched data to indicate which interpretation is to be used.

With the advent of the second generation of computers, the limitations of the five-track tape led to introduction of a sixth track, giving the possibility of 64 code combinations. To this was also added a parity track, resulting in seven-track paper tape whose width was about 7/8 in. IBM's paper tape code, however, used seven data tracks and had a single character ("new line") in the eighth track. This resulted in a tape width of 1 inch, and the maximum number of code combinations was increased to 65.

The demand for further paper-tape code combinations was brought about by the larger character sets of third-generation computers. These computers had discrete codes for upper- and lower-case characters, a larger number of special symbols for both control and graphical characters, and transmission control codes. Seven-bit codes for information interchange were set up and internationally adopted, and standards such as ASCII were based on it. Eight-track paper tape was then used so that the first seven tracks accommodated the seven-bit code and the eighth track was used for parity.

Despite the inexpensiveness of paper tape and its usefulness as a by-product (e.g. from a cash register or ticket issuing machine), its disadvantages, such as the difficulty of correcting errors and the relatively slow speeds at which it can be read, have led to its disappearance as a computer input medium.

Jiri Necas

PARALLEL I/O

See INPUT–OUTPUT OPERATIONS; and PORT, I/O.

PARALLEL PROCESSING

For articles on related subjects *see* CLUSTER COMPUTING; COMPUTER ARCHITECTURE; CONCURRENT PROGRAMMING; DATAFLOW; MULTIPROCESSING; SUPERCOMPUTERS; and SYSTOLIC ARRAY.

PRINCIPLES

Parallel processing is the use of concurrency in the operation of a computer system to increase throughput (*q.v.*), increase fault-tolerance, or reduce the time needed to solve particular problems. Parallel processing is the only route to the highest levels of computer performance. Physical laws and manufacturing capabilities limit the switching times and integration densities of current semiconductor-based devices, putting a ceiling on the speed at which any single device can operate. For this reason all modern computers rely upon parallelism to some extent. The fastest computers exhibit parallelism at many levels.

We begin by describing *pipelining* (*see* PIPELINE) and *parallelism*, the two traditional methods used to increase concurrency in a computer system. We then survey low-level and high-level parallel processing mechanisms that appear in hardware followed by Flynn's taxonomy, the most popular way of classifying parallel architectures. The final section discusses parallelism in software.

Pipelining and Parallelism

To reduce the time needed for a mechanism to perform a task, we must either increase the speed of the mechanism or introduce concurrency. Two traditional methods have been used to increase concurrency: pipelining and parallelism. If an operation can be divided into a number of stages, *pipelining* allows different tasks to be in different stages of completion. An auto-mobile assembly line is an example of pipelining. *Parallelism* is the use of multiple resources to increase concurrency. A group of combines working together to harvest a wheat field is an example of parallelism.

To illustrate and contrast these two methods for increasing concurrency, we present the following pizza-baking example. Suppose a pizza requires 10 minutes to bake, and the baking time cannot be reduced without ruining the quality of the pizza. An oven that holds a single pizza can yield 6 baked pizzas an hour. To increase the number of pizzas baked per hour, a way must be found to have more than one pizza baking at a time.

One way to increase production is through use of parallelism. If 5 ovens are used, the ovens yield 5 pizzas every 10 minutes and 30 pizzas an hour. Note that the 5 ovens are used most efficiently if the number of pizzas needed is a multiple of 5. For example, the ovens require the same amount of time—20 minutes—to produce 6, 7, 8, 9, or 10 pizzas.

Another way to increase production is through the use of pipelining. Imagine a conveyer belt running through a long pizza oven. A pizza placed at one end of the conveyer belt spends 10 minutes in the oven before it reaches the other end. If the conveyer belt has room for 5 pizzas, a cook can place an unbaked pizza at one end of the belt every 2 minutes. Ten minutes after the first pizza has been put into one end of the oven, it appears as a baked pizza at the other end. From that time on another baked pizza will appear every 2 minutes, and the production of the oven will be 30 pizzas an hour. The pizza-baking speeds of the single-oven, parallel-oven, and pipelined-oven methods are compared in Table 1.

The speedup achieved is the ratio between the time needed for the single pizza oven to produce some number of pizzas and the time needed to produce the

Table 1. Contrasting the pizza-baking times of a single oven, five ovens, and a conveyor-belt oven.

Pizzas baked	Single oven	Five ovens	Conveyor oven
1	10 min.	10 min.	10 min.
2	20	10	12
3	30	10	14
4	40	10	16
5	50	10	18
6	60	20	20
7	70	20	22
8	80	20	24
9	90	20	26
10	100	20	28
11	110	30	30
12	120	30	32

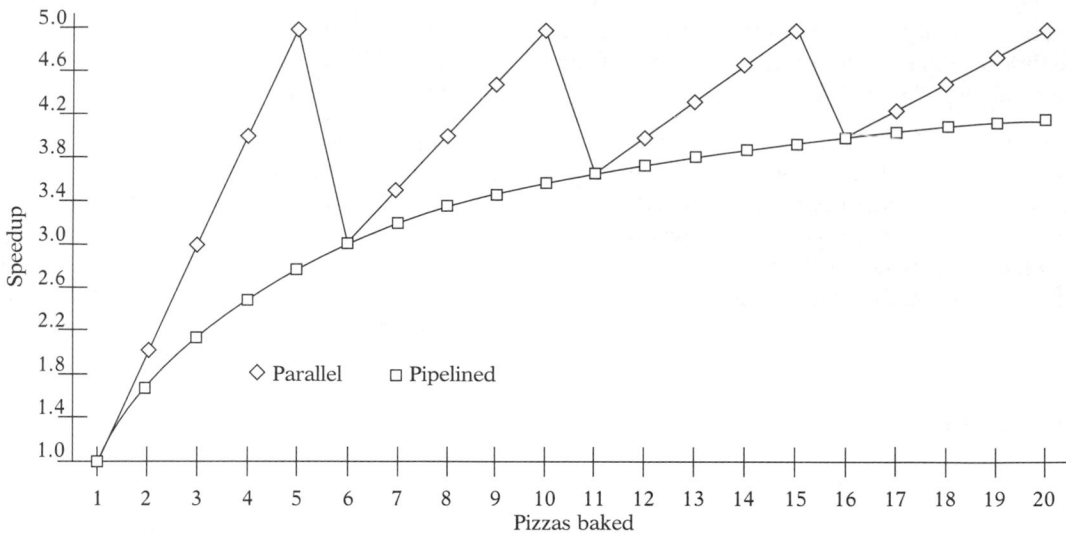

Figure 1. Contrasting the speedup achieved through pipelining and parallelism.

same number of pizzas using pipelining and/or parallelism. For example, producing 8 pizzas requires 80 minutes using a single pizza oven, 20 minutes using 5 pizza ovens, and 24 minutes using the conveyer belt oven. The speedup achieved using 5 pizza ovens to bake 8 pizzas is $80/20 = 4$; the speedup achieved using the conveyer belt oven to bake 8 pizzas is $80/24 = 3\frac{1}{3}$. Speedup can be plotted as a function of problem size. Fig. 1 illustrates the speedup achieved by the parallel and the pipelined pizza ovens as a function of the number of pizzas baked. Observe the jagged speedup plot of the parallel scheme; speedup is equal to 5, the number of ovens, only when the number of pizzas is a multiple of 5. The speedup curve of the pipelined machine is a monotonically increasing function approaching an asymptote of 5, the concurrency of the pipeline. Because of the time needed to fill and empty the pipeline, speedup never reaches 5. However, because this filling and emptying time is a constant, it becomes less and less significant as the problem size increases.

Parallelism in Hardware

Virtually all modern computer systems take advantage of at least some low-level hardware parallelism in order to improve performance. We summarize the most common sources of low-level parallelism. A *bit-parallel memory* allows all the bits in a word to be accessed in parallel. A *bit-parallel arithmetic unit* performs an arithmetic operation on all bits of a pair of operands in parallel. An *I/O processor*, or channel (*q.v.*), receives I/O instructions from the CPU but then works independently, freeing the CPU to resume arithmetic processing. An *interleaved memory* is a memory unit divided into a number of memory banks, which can be accessed concurrently (*see* INTERLEAVING). Computers

with *instruction lookahead*, or *instruction buffering*, prefetch instructions from memory, which reduces the amount of waiting done by the instruction unit. *Instruction pipelining* is the use of pipelining to allow more than one instruction to be in some stage of execution at the same time.

In the fastest contemporary computers, parallelism also appears at higher levels in the architecture, allowing large numbers of arithmetic-logic operations to be performed concurrently. Two important categories of high-speed computers are vector computers and multiple-CPU computers.

A *vector computer* is a computer with an instruction set that contains operations on vectors as well as scalars (Fig. 2). Processor arrays and pipelined vector processors are two examples of vector computers. A *processor array* is a set of identical synchronized processing elements, managed by a single control unit, that are capable of simultaneously performing the same operation on different data elements in parallel. By associating each processing element with a vector element, vector operations, such as element-wise vector addition (Fig. 2b), can be performed in a single step. A pipelined vector processor pipelines the flow of data from memory through pipelined functional units and back to memory, eliminating the overhead involved in fetching, manipulating, and storing the individual scalar elements of a vector.

A multiple-CPU computer contains multiple CPUs, each capable of independently executing its own instruction stream. A *multiprocessor* is a multiple-CPU computer with a single address space. Every processor can read from and write to every memory location. The globally accessible memory may be centralized, but

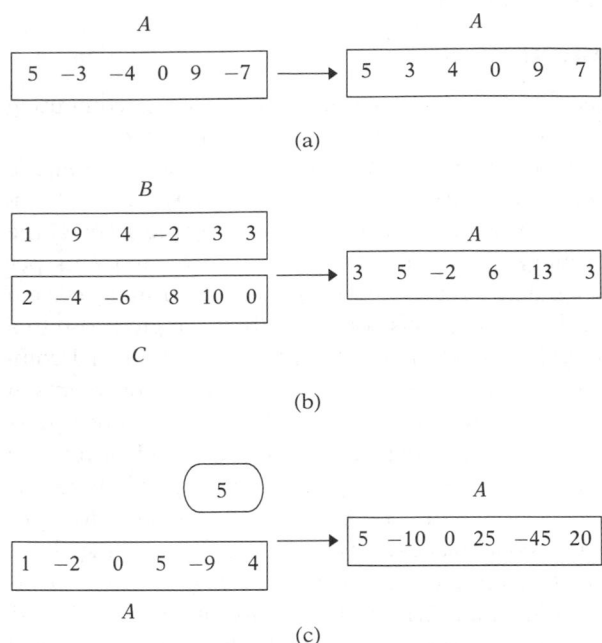

Figure 2. A vector is an ordered collection of values. Here are three examples of vector operations. (a) $A \leftarrow |A|$. (b) $A \leftarrow B + C$. (c) $A \leftarrow 5 \times A$.

more commonly it is distributed among the processors, so that a processor will have faster access to some memory locations than to other locations. A *multicomputer* is a multiple-CPU computer in which each CPU has its own local address space. Since a processor cannot directly access nonlocal memory locations, communication and synchronization between processors is accomplished solely through message passing.

Frequently, parallel computers are hybrid designs. For example, a collection of multiprocessors can be connected by a fast switching network to form a multicomputer (*see* CLUSTER COMPUTING).

Flynn's Taxonomy

The taxonomy proposed by Flynn (1966) is still the best-known classification scheme for parallel architectures. The taxonomy is based upon the amount of concurrency present in the instruction and data streams. The hardware may support only a single instruction stream, or it may have multiple program counters and other control hardware needed to support the simultaneous execution of multiple instruction streams. Likewise, the hardware may allow arithmetic operations to be performed on only a single pair of operands at a time, or it may support the simultaneous application of an operation to multiple data items. These combinations result in four classes of computer.

◆ *Single Instruction Stream, Single Data Stream (SISD)*: Uniprocessors fall into this category.

◆ *Single Instruction Stream, Multiple Data Stream (SIMD)*: Processor arrays fall into this category. A processor array executes a single stream of instructions, but contains a number of arithmetic processing units, each capable of fetching and manipulating its own data. Hence, in any time unit, a single operation is in the same state of execution on multiple processing units. SIMD computers are usually constructed out of custom-designed arithmetic processors.

◆ *Multiple Instruction Stream, Single Data Stream (MISD)*: No current architectures fit naturally into this category.

◆ *Multiple Instruction Stream, Multiple Data Stream (MIMD)*: Multiprocessors and multicomputers fall into this category. These systems contain multiple CPUs, each capable of executing its own instruction stream and performing operations on its own data stream. MIMD computers are typically constructed out of off-the-shelf microprocessors.

Many early parallel computers were SIMD architectures, but most contemporary parallel computers are MIMD systems. MIMD architectures have two important advantages over SIMD machines. First, because they have multiple CPUs, MIMD computers may accommodate more than one user at a time, making them more general purpose. Second, MIMD computers can take advantage of the price/performance advantages associated with off-the-shelf microprocessors. For example, in December 1996 the Department of Energy announced that a $55 million multicomputer manufactured by Intel out of more than 9,000 Pentium Pro microprocessors was the first general-purpose computer in the world to exceed one teraflops (one trillion floating-point operations per second) on a real application.

It is difficult to fit computers achieving concurrency through pipelining into Flynn's taxonomy. According to Flynn's definition, pipelined vector processors should be classified as SISD computers. However, from a programmer's point of view, pipelined vector processors are similar to SIMD processor arrays, because both architectures support vector instructions.

Parallelism in Software

In order to take advantage of parallel hardware to solve a particular problem more quickly, there must be some way to express parallelism in, or extract parallelism from, a user's program. In the case of a vector computer, which executes a single instruction stream containing vector as well as scalar operations, all that is needed is some mechanism to express or extract vector operations. In the case of a multiple-CPU computer that supports the concurrent execution of multiple instruction streams, there must be some way to express or extract the generation and cooperation of parallel processes. The remainder of this section discusses process control issues for multiple-CPU computers. This aspect of parallel processing has been heavily influenced by what has been learned about managing cooperating processes for multiprogrammed operating systems (*q.v.*).

Process generation may be explicit or implicit. Many different constructs have been proposed for explicitly generating processes in an imperative programming language: these include the *fork/join* construct of the Unix system, provided in its C (*q.v.*) language libraries, *cobegin/coend* style constructs in Algol 68 (*q.v.*) and Occam, and *process declarations* in the Distributed Processes and SR languages. If process generation is implicit, as in a program written in an ordinary sequential programming language, a functional programming (*q.v.*) language, or a logic programming (*q.v.*) language, then a greater burden rests upon the compiler.

In order for processes to cooperate, they must have the ability to communicate and synchronize. Communication is achieved either through shared variables or through message passing. The underlying architecture may dictate the communication mechanism. For example, because multicomputers do not have a shared memory, communication is possible only through message passing.

Synchronization has two uses: to constrain the order of events and to control process interference. For example, consider an algorithm in which at some point a global sum of a list of values must be computed. Every process sums a portion of the list, and then the subtotals are combined to form the global sum. The first kind of synchronization is needed to ensure that the global sum is initialized to zero before any process adds its subtotal. The second kind of synchronization is needed to ensure that only one process at a time adds its subtotal to the current value of the global sum.

Bibliography

1966. Flynn, M. J. "Very High-speed Computing Systems," *Proceedings of the IEEE*, **54**, *12* (December), 1901–1909.
1987. Perrott, R. H. *Parallel Programming*. Reading, MA: Addison-Wesley.
1988. Gehani, N., and McGettrick, A. D. (eds.) *Concurrent Programming*. Wokingham, UK: Addison-Wesley.
1994. Quinn, M. J. *Parallel Computing: Theory and Practice*, 2nd Ed. New York: McGraw-Hill.
1996. Patterson, D. A., and Hennessy, J. L. *Computer Architecture: A Quantitative Approach*, 2nd Ed. San Francisco: Morgan Kaufmann.
1998. Culler, D. E., Singh, J. P., and Gupta, A. *Parallel Computer Architecture: A Hardware/Software Approach*. San Francisco: Morgan Kaufmann.

Michael J. Quinn

ARCHITECTURES

Introduction

Serial computers have been the staple of computing since the development of stored-program computers, such as the Electronic Discrete Variable Automatic Computer (EDVAC—*q.v.*), in the early 1950s. Technological advances, such as increasing the speed of the circuitry, increasing the number of components per integrated circuit chip (IC), and performing certain low-level operations concurrently, have given rise to a roughly 10-fold increase in the speed of a serial computer every five years. In fact, rapid improvements in component technology led early component designers to believe that increases in speed could always be obtained by better component design. Unfortunately, the speed of light (3×10^8 m/sec, or about 1 foot per nanosecond) places a physical limitation on the speed at which electronic components of a given size can operate. (Seymour Cray designed his late 1970s CRAY-1 supercomputer in the shape of a horseshoe instead of a straight line to mitigate such physical limitations.) Since serial computers are now within two orders of magnitude of this limit, alternative solutions must be considered for problems that require orders of magnitude more computing power than today's fastest uniprocessor machines. Such problems include weather prediction, molecular modeling, and flow dynamics.

An alternative to the traditional single processor (serial) machine is the multiprocessor machine, often called a *parallel computer, multiprocessor,* or *multicomputer,* although there are minor distinctions among the terms. By the late 1990s, most supercomputers being manufactured contained multiple processors, many departmental computing engines contained multiple processors, and personal computers (PCs) containing multiple processors have become commonplace. Therefore, many claim the 1990s to be the "decade of parallel computing."

In 1952, John von Neumann (*q.v.*) designed (with paper and pencil) a machine, which he called a "cellular structure," that consisted of a two-dimensional array of simple processors. In the late 1950s, another parallel computer was designed by S. H. Unger, who proposed a two-dimensional array of processors targeted at problems in image processing (*q.v.*) and pattern recognition (*q.v.*). Unger also considered arrays of different dimensions and shapes.

Eventually, such theoretical designs led to the production of what was then called "the first highly parallel supercomputer," the 64-processor ILLIAC IV, which was designed in 1967 and became operational in 1975. The 64 processors were connected as an 8×8 two-dimensional grid. The ILLIAC IV, originally designed to

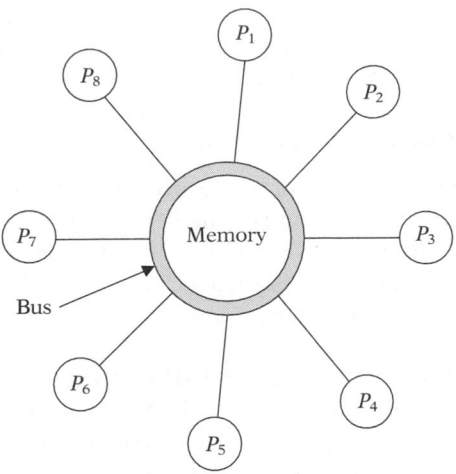

Figure 1. A shared memory system in which the processors (P_i) are connected to a common global memory via a bus.

have four 8×8 arrays of powerful processors, was targeted at applications involving matrices and partial differential equations (*q.v.*). It consisted of a control unit that broadcast one instruction at a time to all processors. Each processor executed the instruction on the contents of its own local memory. Unfortunately, due to technological limitations and inadequate software, many of the early parallel machines were destined to fail.

However, due to advances in computer chip (VLSI), compiler (*q.v.*), language, and operating system (*q.v.*) technology, as well as the realization that serial computers would not be able to provide sufficient computing power, commercially available parallel computers have become the computing systems of choice in computationally intensive settings and are currently being used to solve significant scientific and industrial problems (*see* SCIENTIFIC APPLICATIONS).

Terminology

The field of parallel computing is still changing, which means that not all terminology has become standardized. However, in this section we present some fundamental terms and concepts that are fairly well accepted.

SHARED MEMORY VS. DISTRIBUTED MEMORY

In a *shared memory* machine, there is a single global set of memory that is available to all processors, as shown in Fig 1. The processors in a shared memory system are connected to the common global memory by a bus or switch. Memory and bus contention in such a system is a primary concern when developing algorithms. For example, care must be taken when two processors try to write to the same memory location simultaneously.

Each processor in a *distributed memory* machine has access only to its own private (local) memory, as shown in Fig. 2. Distributed memory machines avoid the memory contention problem. Access to nonlocal data in a distributed memory system is provided by passing messages between the processors through the interconnection network (defined below). In a distributed memory system, contention (*q.v.*) for message-passing channels is a major concern.

GRANULARITY

When discussing parallel architectures, the term *granularity* is often used to refer to the relative number and complexity of the processors. A *fine-grained machine* typically consists of a relatively large number of small, simple processors (in terms of local memory and computational power), while a *coarse-grained machine* typically consists of a few large, powerful processors. With respect to late 1990s technology, fine-grained machines have of the order of 1,000,000 simple processors, while coarse-grained machines have on the order of 100 powerful processors. *Medium-grained* machines having the order of 1000 processors represent a compromise in performance and size between that of fine-grained and coarse-grained machines.

Fine-grained machines typically fall into the SIMD category, where all processors operate in lockstep fashion (i.e. synchronously) on the contents of their own small local memory. Coarse-grained machines

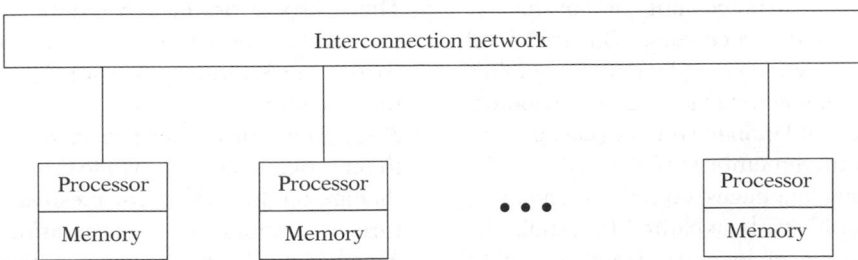

Figure 2. A distributed memory system. Every processing element consists of a processor and memory module.

typically fall into the shared-memory MIMD category, where processors operate asynchronously on the large shared memory. Medium-grained machines of the late 1990s typically fall into the distributed memory MIMD category, where the programming style is often that of *single program, multiple data (SPMD)*. In SPMD, all processors store an identical copy of the same program, which consists of computations on local data interspersed with communication steps for retrieving necessary data from nonlocal memory. Notice that due to data dependencies, at any given time different processors could be executing different sections of the code.

The field of parallel computing has matured and standards are beginning to emerge across commercially available machines. The wide variety of multi-processor machines that existed in the 1980s has been replaced by only a few architectures in the late 1990s. The vast majority of such machines fall into one of three categories, as follows.

1. Many manufacturers are creating coarse-grained departmental compute servers that appear as a shared-memory machine to the user. Typically, these machines fall into the *Non-Uniform Memory Access (NUMA)* model, where the time to fetch data from memory varies widely with the locality of the data, be it in local cache, in local memory, or in the memory of a distant processor-memory module.

2. The marriage of scientists demanding inexpensive cycles, the observation that enormous numbers of cycles on desktop workstations are not being used, and the deployment of packages of communication standards that can work efficiently in heterogeneous platforms, has led to the emergence of *Networks of Workstations* (*NOWs*), sometimes referred to as *Clusters of Workstations* (*COWs*) (*see* CLUSTER COMPUTING). This computational model provides a viable and affordable alternative to the more traditional parallel computers that come packaged with relatively large numbers of processors per box.

3. Finally, there are a few "massively parallel" machines being constructed out of commodity workstation/PC-based processors. On many of these machines, software is in place that will allow the user to treat the machine as either a distributed-memory machine (and manage the message passing explicitly) or a shared-memory machine (where the software, including languages, compilers, and operating system primitives, is exploited to handle the parallelism and data movement). Traditional massively parallel fine-grained SIMD machines no

longer have a significant presence in the market-place. It is quite reasonable to view such compute engines as special-purpose machines.

Interconnection Networks

Interconnection networks are used for processor-to-processor (in distributed memory machines) and processor-to-memory (in shared memory machines) communication. In this section, we briefly discuss a small subset of these interconnection networks.

PROCESSOR-TO-PROCESSOR INTERCONNECTIONS

In order to discuss some specific processor-to-processor interconnection networks, some terminology is needed. The *degree of a processor P* is defined to be the number of other processors that P is directly connected to via bidirectional communication links. The *degree of the network* is defined to be the maximum degree of any processor in the network. The *communication diameter* of the network is defined to be the maximum of the minimum distance between any two processors.

In the sections that follow, we will see that a set of n processors connected as a ring (*see* Fig. 3a) has a degree of 2 (each processor is directly connected to two other processors) and a communication diameter of $\lceil n/2 \rceil$. We will also see that if the processors are connected as a hypercube (*see* Fig. 3c), the degree of the network is $\log_2 n$ and the communication diameter is $\log_2 n$. Naturally, one of the goals in designing processor-to-processor interconnection networks is to minimize both the degree of the network and the communication diameter, subject to physical layout constraints. Unfortunately, reducing the communication diameter of a network often requires increasing the degree of the network, and vice versa.

RING

In a *ring* network, as shown in Fig. 3a, the n processors are connected in a circular fashion so that processor P_i is directly connected to processors P_{i-1} and P_{i+1}. While the degree of the network is only 2, the communication diameter is $\lceil n/2 \rceil$, which is quite high.

MESH

The n processors of a two-dimensional square mesh network, as shown in Fig. 3b, are typically configured so that an interior processor $P_{i,j}$ is connected to its four neighbors, processors $P_{i-1,j}$, $P_{i+1,j}$, $P_{i,j-1}$, and $P_{i,j+1}$. The four corner processors are each connected to their two neighbors, while the remaining processors that are on the edge of the mesh are each connected to three neighbors. So, by increasing the degree of the network to 4, the communication diameter of the network is reduced to $2(n^{1/2} - 1)$.

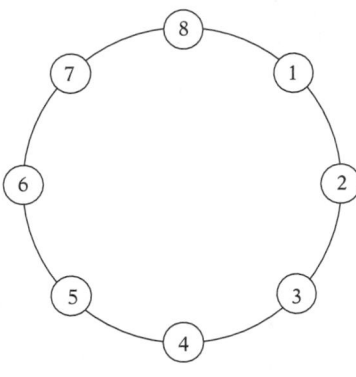

(a) A ring of size 8

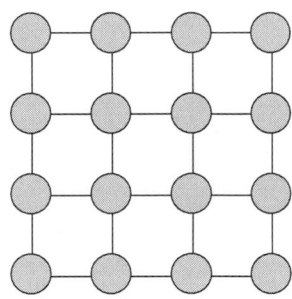

(b) A mesh of size 16

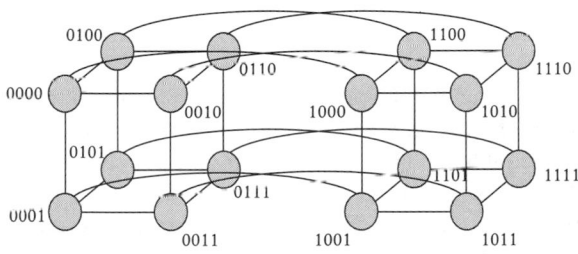

(c) A hypercube with 16 processors indexed by their binary representations

Figure 3. Processor-to-processor interconnection networks.

HYPERCUBE

A hypercube with n processors, where n is an integral power of 2, has the processors indexed by the integers $\{0, \ldots, n-1\}$. Viewing each integer in the index range as a $(\log_2 n)$-bit string, two processors are directly connected if and only if their indices differ by exactly one bit, as illustrated in Fig. 3c. A disadvantage of the hypercube is that, unlike the fixed degree ring and mesh networks, the number of links that are needed by each processor in a hypercube grows as $\log_2 n$. This makes it difficult to manufacture reasonably generic hypercube processors. The advantage of a hypercube is that the communication diameter is only $\log_2 n$. Notice that the hypercube in Fig. 3c has a degree and communication diameter of 4.

Processor-to-Memory Interconnections

In this section, some common processor-to-memory interconnections are discussed.

BUS

In a *single bus-based system*, the processors, memory modules, and I/O devices are connected by a single high-speed bus (*q.v.*). This is the least complicated interconnection network, but it has the disadvantage that only one processor can access the shared memory at a time. An alternative to using a single bus is to use *multiple buses*, where each of the processors and memory modules are connected to multiple buses. *See* Fig. 4, which also shows cache memory (*q.v.*) to keep frequently used data local to a processor.

CROSSBAR SWITCH

A *crossbar switch* provides every one of the n processors with a logical connection to each of the m memory modules. This allows every processor to communicate simultaneously with a distinct memory module without contention, but requires nm switches, as shown in Fig. 5.

MULTISTAGE INTERCONNECTION NETWORKS

A *multistage interconnection network* (*MIN*) connects processors and memory modules through a specialized switching network. Typical MINs include the Omega network, the Benes network, and the butterfly network. These networks typically have logarithmic depth (i.e. a message must go through a logarithmic number of switches to get from the processor to the memory module). An advantage of MINs is that they permit multiple paths between processors and memory modules and require fewer components than a crossbar switch, while still allowing good connectivity between the processors and memory.

Additional Models

In this section, we briefly describe some traditional parallel models that have not been touched on previously in this article.

DATAFLOW COMPUTERS

Dataflow (*q.v.*) computers are similar to conventional computers in some aspects. For example, dataflow computers execute stored programs, and machine-level programs consist of individual instructions that call for conventional operations to be performed. The difference is in the manner in which instructions are identified for execution. There is no program counter (*q.v.*) in a dataflow computer. Instead, an instruction is activated when it has received (as results from other instructions) the data it needs to operate.

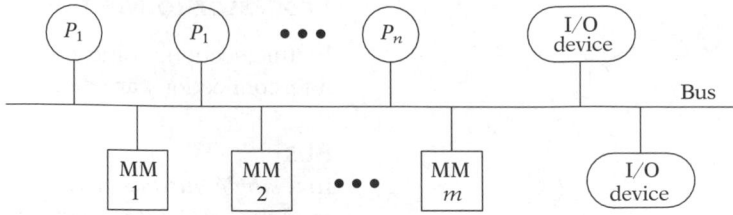

(a) A single bus-based system with n processors and m memory modules

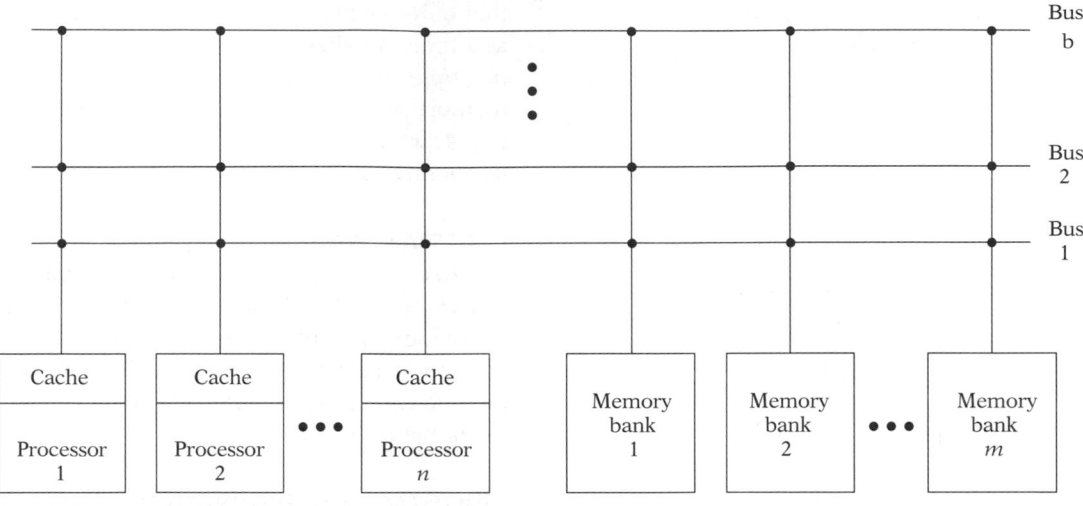

(b) A multiple-bus system with n processors and m memory modules.

Figure 4.   Bus-based systems.

A dataflow computer generally consists of many *processors*, a *packet routing network* that allows any processor to send information packets to any other, and *array memory units* for holding large databases of information required by many problems.

A dataflow processor typically consists of mechanisms for reorganizing when instructions are enabled, and mechanisms for carrying out their execution (*see* Fig. 6). The dataflow instructions assigned to a processor are held in the processor's *activity store*. A simple queue holds addresses of those instructions which are enabled. The *fetch unit* picks the address of some enabled instruction from the queue, fetches the instructions (with its operands) from the activity store, and delivers it to an *operation unit*. Execution of the instruction creates one or more result packets, which are sent on to the *update unit*. The update unit places the result value in the operand field of the target instruction, and decides whether the instruction has become enabled. If the instruction is enabled, its address is entered in the queue. If the target instruction of a result packet resides in some other processor of the machine, then the packet is sent off through the network. While experimental and prototype dataflow machines have been designed since the mid-1970s, the entry of such machines into the commercial market has been extremely limited.

SYSTOLIC ARRAYS

A *systolic system* consists of a set of interconnected processors, each capable of performing some simple operation. The processors in a systolic system are typically interconnected to form a *systolic array* (*q.v.*), where "systolic" is used to mean that pipelined

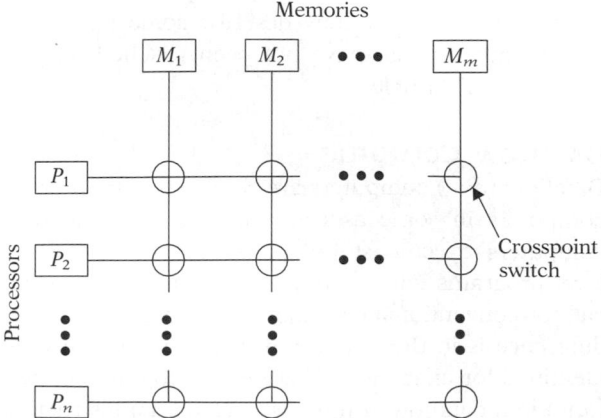

Figure 5.   A crossbar switch with n processors and m memory modules.

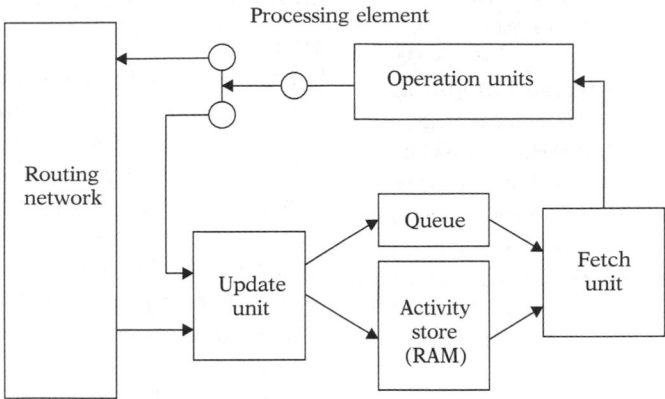

Figure 6. A dataflow processor.

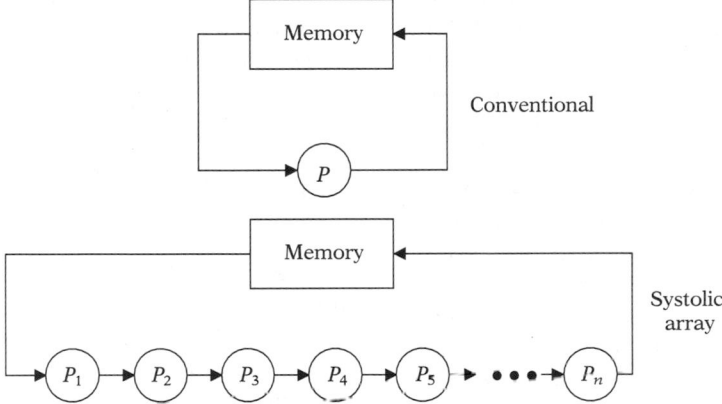

Figure 7. Comparison of a single processor machine with a systolic array. The systolic array has data brought out of memory and "pulsed" through an array of processors before returning to memory.

(assembly line) computations take place along all dimensions of the array. Communication with the environment occurs only at the boundary processors. The basic principle of a systolic architecture is that by replacing a single processor with an array of processors, a higher computation throughput can be achieved without increased memory bandwidth (*q.v.*). Data is typically viewed as being "pulsed" through the array of processors from the memory. Once a data item is brought out from memory, it can be used effectively at each processor it passes while being "pumped" from processor to processor along the array; *see* Fig. 7.

Bibliography

1984. Hwang, K., and Briggs, F. A. *Computer Architecture and Parallel Processing.* New York: McGraw-Hill.
1988. Babb, R. G. *Programming Parallel Processors.* New York: Addison-Wesley.
1989. Almasi, G. S., and Gottlieb, A. *Highly Parallel Computing.* New York: Benjamin/Cummings.
1992. Leighton, F. T. *Introduction to Parallel Algorithms and Architectures: Arrays, Trees, Hypercubes.* San Francisco: Morgan Kaufmann.
1994. Geist, A., Beguelin, A., Dongarra, J., Jiang, W., Manchek, B., and Sunderam, V. *PVM: Parallel Virtual Machine—A User's Guide and Tutorial for Network Parallel Computing.* Cambridge, MA: MIT Press.
1994. Quinn, M. J. *Designing Efficient Algorithms for Parallel Computers,* 2nd Ed. New York: McGraw-Hill.
1996. Miller, R., and Stout, Q. F. *Parallel Algorithms for Regular Architectures.* Cambridge, MA: MIT Press.
1998. Hwang, K., and Xu, Z. *Scalable Parallel Computing: Technology, Architecture, and Programming.* New York: McGraw-Hill.

Russ Miller

ALGORITHMS

Introduction

For computationally intensive problems such as processing data collected from satellites to predict the Earth's weather, it is estimated that information needs to be processed at a minimum of 10^{13} operations per second, where an operation may be defined as the addition or multiplication of two values. In fact, applications such as three-dimensional image reconstruction (*see* IMAGE PROCESSING), aircraft testing, and modeling fusion reactors require machines that can process 10^{15} operations per second. In 1997, as part of the US *Department of Energy's Accelerated Strategic Computing Initiative (DOE's ASCI program)*, an Intel Paragon constructed from 9000 Pentium 200 MHz processors became operational at Sandia National Laboratories. This machine delivered 1.8 Tflops (teraflops—trillion floating-point operations per second). Subsequent machines in the ASCI program are targeted at reaching 100 Tflops within a small number of years. By contrast, the fastest serial machines (e.g. the Cray T90 series) circa 1997 are only in the 2 Gflops range.

The *Architectures* section of this article describes a variety of ways in which such multiprocessor machines can be constructed. This section considers algorithms which exploit the potentially massive parallelism available from such machines. There are a number of basic approaches that can be used in developing efficient parallel algorithms. One approach is to port existing sequential algorithms to these new machines (either by hand or by using parallelizing tools). However, many algorithms that run well on serial computers are not easily ported to run efficiently on parallel computers. Another approach is to design a new solution to the problem with parallelism in mind. A third approach is to adapt an existing parallel algorithm, which was developed to solve a different problem, to solve the problem under consideration. Each approach has its place, and examples of the first two are discussed in this article.

Most of the large software packages that have been implemented on existing parallel machines rely on numerical algorithms to solve scientific problems. It is fortunate that many such algorithms can be implemented in a relatively straightforward fashion on existing parallel machines, since these operations are often critical in solving problems involving air-traffic control, the design of airplanes and automobiles, and the modeling of various physical situations, as well as problems in biology, chemistry, physics, geology, and astronomy. The thrust of most theoretical work, however, is on developing efficient parallel algorithms to solve problems in areas such as computational geometry (*q.v.*), intermediate-level image analysis, and graph theory (*q.v.*), areas that often require designing new algorithms and paradigms.

The purpose of this article is to give the reader a basic understanding of the field of parallel algorithms. We give examples for fundamental operations, matrix operations, and a fundamental problem in image analysis. In addition, general paradigms and fundamental operations are discussed that serve as building blocks for designing efficient parallel algorithms.

Examples and Discussion

SUM

Suppose that we need to sum n values, initially distributed one per processor on a fine-grained machine with n processors. Consider an algorithm for a square mesh ($n^{1/2} \times n^{1/2}$) of processors. First, sum the values in each row simultaneously and independently so that the leftmost processor in each row knows the sum of its row. Then, in the first column sum these partial sums to the topmost processor. Finally, the sum of these n values, which is stored in the top-left processor of the mesh, can be distributed to all processors by reversing the previous data movement, as follows. Send the solution from the top-left processor to all processors in the first column, and then in a similar fashion distribute the solution in parallel within each row. So, if processor $P_{i,j}$ starts with value $v_{i,j}$, then the following code shows how to compute the sum of these values.

```
for j := n^{1/2} downto 2 do
    v_{i,j-1} ← v_{i,j-1} + v_{i,j}
                (simultaneously for all rows i)
for i := n^{1/2} downto 2 do
    v_{i-1,1} ← v_{i-1,1} + v_{i,1}
```

Notice that while summing n values on a serial machine takes $O(n)$ time, this mesh algorithm only requires $O(n^{1/2})$ time (see Appendix II for a description of "Big O" notation). While this is asymptotically optimal for the mesh, since the communication diameter of the mesh is $O(n^{1/2})$, other architectures can compute the sum even faster. For example, a hypercube with n processors can compute the sum in $O(\log n)$ time.

MATRIX TRANSPOSE

Consider computing the transpose of a matrix on a mesh computer. Given an $n \times n$ matrix A, stored so that processor $P_{i,j}$ contains element $a_{i,j}$, it is possible to compute the transpose of A in $O(n)$ time, where the transpose of A, denoted A^T, is given by $a_{i,j}^T = a_{j,i}$. The algorithm consists of two complementary phases that are each completed in $O(n)$ time, as follows. Denote diagonal processors $P_{i,i}, 1 \leq i \leq n$, as *routers*. For all above-diagonal processors $P_{i,j}, i < j$, send the value of $a_{i,j}$ down to diagonal processor $P_{j,j}$ in lockstep fashion. Each value $a_{i,j}, i < j$, reaches diagonal processor $P_{j,j}$ in $k = j - i$ steps. As each router $P_{j,j}$ receives an $a_{i,j}$, it sends the data to the left where it will move for $k = j - i$ steps, until it reaches below-diagonal processor $P_{j,i}$. Next, in a similar fashion, all below-diagonal processors $P_{i,j}, i > j$, send their data to the right, where diagonal processor $P_{i,i}$ routes the data upwards. Finally, in $O(n)$ time every processor $P_{i,j}$ contains $a_{j,i}$. As with the previous example, due to the communication diameter of the mesh, it is easy to see that this algorithm is asymptotically optimal for the mesh. However, as before, other architectures can compute the transpose substantially faster.

MATRIX MULTIPLICATION

We now consider matrix multiplication, a more computationally intensive problem than the previous ones. Given two $n \times n$ matrices, A and B, the matrix product $C = AB$ is given by $c_{i,j} = \sum_{k=1}^{n} a_{i,k} b_{k,j}$. The algorithm we give shows how to compute $C = AB$ in $O(n)$ time on a mesh with $4n^2$ processors. Assume that matrix A is stored in the lower-left $n \times n$ quadrant, matrix B is stored in the upper-right $n \times n$ quadrant, and that the resultant matrix C is to be constructed in the lower-right $n \times n$ quadrant of the mesh, as shown in Fig. 1. At time 1, in lockstep fashion all processors containing an element of the first row of A send their values to the right and all processors containing an element of the first column of B send their values down. The processor responsible for $c_{1,1}$ can now begin to compute its running sum. At time 2, row 1 of A and column 1 of B continue to move in the same direction, and row 2 of A and column 2 of B start to move right and down, respectively. In general, at time i, the ith row of A and the ith column of B start to move right and down, respectively. Each processor that simultaneously receives a piece of data from a processor to its left and from a processor above computes the product of these two values and adds it to the running sum. At time $i + 1$, every processor sends the values received during time i to neighboring processors in the direction that they were moving. So, at time k, rows $1 \ldots k$ of A and columns $1 \ldots k$ of B

move right and down, respectively, where this is the first such movement for row k of A and column k of B. Therefore, row and column n of A and B start moving at time n, $c_{n,n}$ is the last value computed, and $c_{n,n}$ is fully computed at time $3n - 2$. Hence, the algorithm runs in $O(n)$ time on a mesh of size $4n^2$. Since each matrix element must be processed at least once, this is asymptotically optimal for a fine-grained machine constructed of $O(n^2)$ processors. Since the algorithm runs in $O(n)$ time with $O(n^2)$ processors, the total amount of work performed by the machine is $O(n^3)$, which is asymptotically optimal with respect to the number of operations required by the standard sequential matrix multiplication algorithm.

PARADIGMS AND DATA MOVEMENT

In developing efficient parallel algorithms, one often relies on general paradigms such as divide-and-conquer, which is particularly useful in a parallel setting since subproblems can be solved simultaneously (*see* ALGORITHMS, ANALYSIS OF and ALGORITHMS, DESIGN AND CLASSIFICATION OF). Data reduction techniques are often used to reduce an initial set of data to a smaller pertinent set of data that can be used to solve the problem efficiently. In addition to these techniques, it is becoming more common to design parallel algorithms in terms of a variety of fundamental operations. These operations include *sorting*, which is frequently used to route data on parallel machines (i.e. by sorting with respect to a destination address), *parallel search*, and *parallel prefix* (given a_i stored in processor P_i, and an associative binary operator $\otimes$, compute the initial prefix $a_1 \otimes a_2 \otimes \ldots \otimes a_i$ simultaneously for all P_i), which can be used to sum elements, detect a minimum value, broadcast values, and compress data. The next example will incorporate some of these techniques and operations

COMPONENT LABELING

The *component labeling problem* requires that all *figures* (i.e. maximally connected components) be uniquely labeled. We assume that an $n \times n$ digitized picture $A = \{a_{i,j}\}$ is stored one *pixel* (*picture element*) per processor on a machine with n^2 processors. The pixels are assumed to be in one of two states: black or white. It is helpful to think of this digitization as being a black picture on a white background. The picture is stored so that pixels that are adjacent in the picture are mapped to processors that are directly connected in the machine. Define a black pixel $a_{i,j}$ to be a *neighbor* of black pixels $a_{i+1,j}$, $a_{i-1,j}$, $a_{i,j+1}$, and $a_{i,j-1}$. (Notice that black pixels $a_{i,j}$ and $a_{i+1,j+1}$, for example, are not considered to be neighbors, though they may still be in the same figure if there is a path of neighboring black pixels between them.)

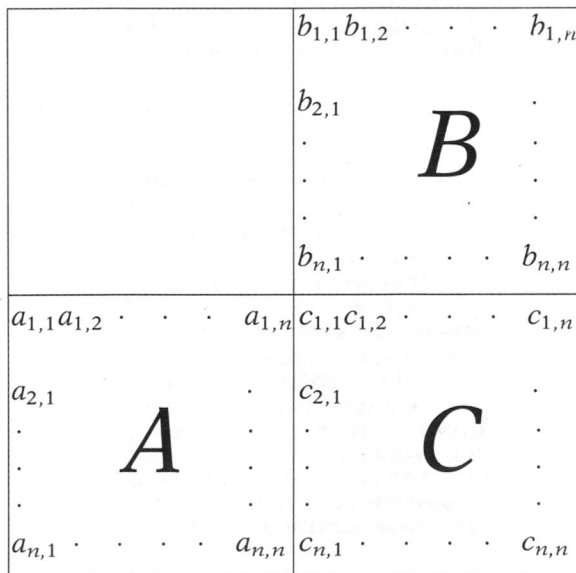

Figure 1. Multiplying two $n \times n$ matrices on a mesh with $4n^2$ processors.

Each processor that contains a black pixel uses its unique index as the label of the pixel that it contains. When a labeling algorithm terminates, each processor that contains a black pixel will store the label of the smallest labeled black pixel that its pixel is connected to. That is, each such processor will know the label of the figure that its pixel is a member of.

A simple parallel *propagation* algorithm can be used to label the figures, as follows. Each black processor (i.e. a processor containing a black pixel) initially assumes that the label of its pixel is the component label of the figure that its pixel is a member of. During each iteration of the algorithm, each black processor sends its current component label to its (at most) four black neighbors. Each black processor then compares its current label with the (at most) four labels just received, and keeps as its new label the minimum of these labels. It is easy to see that for each figure, the minimum label L is propagated from processor P_L (i.e. the processor with index L) to each black processor P_i in its figure in the minimum number of steps required to pass a message from P_L to P_i, under the restriction that data is passed only between neighboring black processors. Therefore this labeling algorithm terminates in $\Theta(D)$ time, where $\Theta(D)$ is the maximum amount of time that it takes any figure to propagate its minimum label to all processors in its figure. So, given "blob-like" figures as in Fig. 2, all processors can know the label of their figure in $O(n)$ time. However, it is easy to construct non-"blob-like" figures, such as spirals or snakes, as in Fig 3, for which this propagation algorithm would require $\Theta(n^2)$ time.

Next, we outline a general parallel algorithm that is much more efficient, in the worst-case, than the $O(n^2)$ time propagation algorithm for labeling all figures, regardless of the number, shape, or size of the figures.

The algorithm follows a recursive divide-and-conquer solution strategy that relies on efficient data reduction. The first step of the algorithm is to label recursively the four quadrants of the picture independently. After this step, the only figures that could have an incorrect global label are those figures that have a pixel on the border between the quadrants. For instance, assuming Fig. 4 represents the labels of figures after the independent and parallel recursive labeling of the quadrants, then figures A and H are labeled correctly in a global sense, while the other figures do not necessarily have the correct final labels since they have pixels along the border between quadrants. Two common methods for resolving conflicts are

1. To compress $O(n)$ pieces of information representing the border pixels into a subregion of the machine where interprocessor communication is minimized, resolve the conflicts, and inform all processors of their final label.

2. To create an adjacency matrix representing the connections between border pixels, compute the transitive closure of the matrix to resolve the conflicts, and inform all processors of their final label.

(a) A spiral is not a "blob-like" figure.

(b) A snake is not a "blob-like" figure.

Figure 3. Pictures consisting of non-"blob-like" figures.

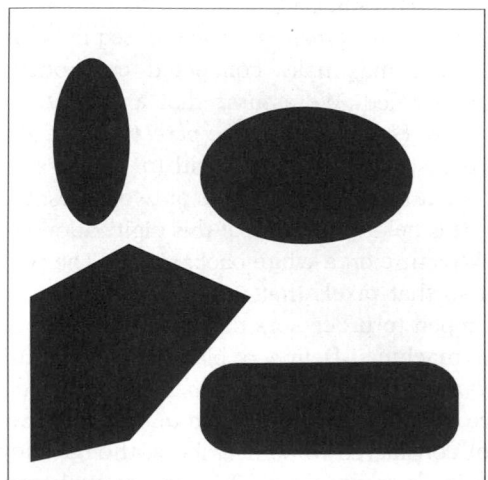

Figure 2. A picture containing "blob-like" figures.

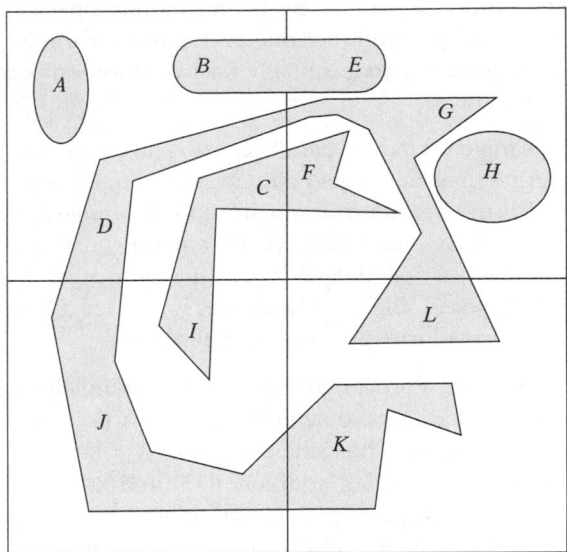

Figure 4. Sample labeling after recursively relabeling each quadrant.

Both resolution techniques exploit the fact that the pertinent data has been reduced from an amount proportional to the area of the image to an amount proportional to the perimeter of the image. The running time of component labeling on a serial machine is linear in the number of pixels. So, for an $n \times n$ image, the sequential running time is $O(n^2)$. On a mesh, the running time of the algorithm just described is $O(n)$, while on a hypercube the running time is $O(\log^3 n)$.

Final Comments

Research in parallel algorithms considers developing efficient paradigms, algorithms, and fundamental operations for a variety of real machines and theoretical models of computation. Efficient parallel algorithms for computing matrix operations, solving linear systems of equations, computing the eigenvalues of a system of equations, and solving partial differential equations have been implemented on a wide variety of commercially available and experimental machines to solve problems in areas such as biology, chemistry, engineering, vision, geology, and physics. Efficient parallel algorithms for solving fundamental problems, as well as for solving problems in computational geometry, image analysis, and graph theory, have been designed for a variety of theoretical models of computation.

The theoretical RAM (random access machine) model closely matches real serial machines in that the observed performance of an algorithm on a real serial machine can be expected to closely match the theoretical analysis provided by the RAM. Unfortunately, a corresponding situation does not exist for parallel machines. The parallel model that corresponds most closely to the RAM is the so-called *PRAM (parallel RAM)*, which consists of a set of processors all of which have unit-time access to a shared memory. Unfortunately, while ignoring communication costs allows one to concentrate on developing lower bounds for parallel algorithms, it does not have much effect on making decisions as to which algorithms to implement on real parallel machines, especially when these machines do not belong to the fine-grained SIMD family. Distributed memory models, such as the mesh and hypercube, are somewhat better at modeling real parallel machines, especially their fine-grained SIMD counterparts. However, even with the fine-grained distributed memory models, the constants that are masked in the asymptotic analysis of algorithms become critical when implementing algorithms on real machines since existing machines are not currently large enough to consume the overhead.

The number of multiprocessor vendors has been reduced significantly since the late 1980s. In addition, the number of distinct programming and architectural models has also been falling. Commercially available multiprocessor machines currently fall predominantly into two (not completely distinct) categories. The first category consists of machines that contain a relatively small number (e.g. tens or hundreds) of processors that present a shared-memory model to the user. However, these machines typically yield a *nonuniform memory access (NUMA)* paradigm in that the time to access memory is a function of locality. For example, it is faster for a given processor to access memory in its cache, slower to access its local memory, and slower yet to access memory that is physically located within some other processor-memory unit. While a number of theoretical models have been proposed to represent such machines, there has not been a convergence on a model and there has not been a body of literature that provides a wealth of critical theoretical algorithms which map efficiently to commercially available machines.

The other multiprocessor system that is gaining in popularity, particularly among scientists who require large numbers of inexpensive cycles, is that of *networks of workstations (NOWs)*. The advantage of such a system is that many departments, laboratories, and institutions have numerous workstations which sit idle for a large number of hours per day. Software has been, and continues to be, developed that allows users to exploit such, typically heterogeneous, systems. In fact, as standards such as PVM and MPI (*see* PARALLEL PROCESSING: LANGUAGES) begin to emerge, both the shared-memory machines and the NOWs have the potential to sustain a significant presence in the marketplace, which will be welcome to a software community that cannot continue to invest significant funds into porting software between incompatible platforms. This should have a profound effect on research and development in parallel algorithms.

Bibliography

1992. Leighton, F. T. *Introduction to Parallel Algorithms and Architectures: Arrays, Trees, Hypercubes.* San Francisco: Morgan Kaufmann.

1994. Geist, A., Beguelin, A., Dongarra, J., Jiang, W., Manchek, B., and Sunderam, V. *PVM: Parallel Virtual Machine—A User's Guide and Tutorial for Network Parallel Computing.* Cambridge, MA: MIT Press.

1994. Quinn, M. J. *Designing Efficient Algorithms for Parallel Computers.* New York: McGraw-Hill.

1996. Miller, R., and Stout, Q. F. *Parallel Algorithms for Regular Architectures.* Cambridge, MA: MIT Press.

1997. Akl, S. G. *Parallel Computation: Models and Methods.* Upper Saddle River, NJ: Prentice Hall.

Russ Miller

LANGUAGES

Parallel programming languages can be categorized according to whether the parallelism inherent in a program must be specified explicitly by the programmer or may be left implicit. Languages in which potential parallelism is implicit include common imperative programming languages such as Fortran (*q.v.*) and C (*q.v.*); functional programming (*q.v.*) languages such as Haskell and VAL; and logic programming (*q.v.*) languages such as Prolog. In order for a program written in such a language to take advantage of the power of parallel hardware, a *parallelizing compiler* must determine which operations may be executed in parallel.

Because of the huge investment in software written in conventional imperative programming languages, there has been a great deal of interest in the development of parallelizing compilers, particularly for Fortran. These compilers have been most successful in transforming Fortran DO loops into vector operations suitable for high-speed execution on pipelined vector processors. These compilers have been less successful transforming Fortran programs into code that executes efficiently on multicomputers; the absence of a shared memory and the resulting problem of distributing data among the local memories of many processors makes parallelization particularly difficult.

Research into parallelizing compilers for functional and logic programming languages has led to even less impressive results so far.

Languages with Explicit Parallelism

We will now consider languages in which the programmer indicates explicitly those operations that may be performed in parallel. By making parallel operations explicit, the programmer makes it easier for the compiler to generate code suitable for execution on parallel computers.

The simplest kind of parallelism to introduce into a programming language is *data parallelism*. Data parallelism is the simultaneous application of a single operation across an entire data set. Data parallel extensions to Fortran, C, Modula-2, and other languages have been proposed. Different languages introduce different mechanisms for expressing data parallelism.

For example, Fortran 90 supports data parallelism by allowing operations to be performed on arrays as well as scalar values. Thus, the statement A = B + C may express either scalar addition if B and C are real numbers or integers, or array addition if B and C are arrays. Fortran 90 programs are often shorter and easier to read than the corresponding older Fortran 77 programs because a single-line array operation can replace a multiple-line DO loop manipulating one element at a time.

Here is an example Fortran 90 program that performs numerical integration to compute an approximation to π. The area under the curve $4/(1 + x^2)$ between 0 and 1 is π. The interval $[0, 1]$ is divided into n subintervals of width $1/n$. For each subinterval the program computes the area of the rectangle whose height is such that the curve $1/(1 + x^2)$ intersects the top of the rectangle at its midpoint. The sum of the areas of the n rectangles approximates the area under the curve.

```
program main
      integer n
      double precision integrate, pi
      print *, 'Enter the number of
                              intervals: '
      read (*,*) n
      pi = integrate(n)
      print *, 'Estimate of pi is ', pi
      stop
      end

function integrate(n)
      double precision integrate, width,
                              x(n), y(n)
      integer n, id(n)
      width = 1.0d0 / n
      id = (/ (i, i = 1, n) /)
      x = (id - 0.5d0) * width
      y = 4.0d0 / (1.0d0 + x * x)
      integrate = sum(y) * width
      return
      end
```

The data-parallel array operations appear in function integrate. On the fifth line of the function a single assignment statement assigns the value i to id(i), for all i between 1 and n. On the sixth line every element of array x is assigned the value of width multiplied by the corresponding element of id less 0.5. On the following line is another array assignment statement. Every element of y is assigned the quotient of 4 divided by 1 plus the square of the corresponding element of x. Finally, on the eighth line of function integrate is the function sum, which computes in a single logical step the sum of all of the elements of y.

High Performance Fortran (HPF) is an extension of Fortran 90 that has received a great deal of attention, because a large group of parallel-computer vendors were involved in its specification. HPF extends Fortran 90 with additional parallel constructs and directives, which are designed to make it easier for compilers to translate HPF programs into code that executes efficiently on parallel computers.

For example, not every data-parallel assignment can be expressed using the array assignment statement of Fortran 90. HPF introduces the FORALL statement to allow more general data-parallel assignments. For example, the statement

```
FORALL (i = 1:n, j = 1:n, i < j) Y(i,j) = 0.0
```

sets to zero all elements in the upper right triangle of matrix Y.

Despite the advances being made in compiler technology for data-parallel languages such as Fortran 90 and High Performance Fortran, the best performance is still achieved by writing parallel programs using a low-level approach based on message passing. This approach is called SPMD (single program, multiple data). The programmer writes a single program in a language such as Fortran or C. A set of processes executes the program concurrently. Each process manipulates a subset of the data structures. The processes may be mapped to processors of a single parallel computer, or they may be distributed across a network. Processes coordinate their actions and communicate with each other through calls to a message-passing library.

Early developers of multicomputers all developed their own message-passing libraries, which made it difficult to move programs from one system to another. In 1993 a group of parallel computer vendors, researchers, and applications developers met to develop a standard portable message-passing library definition called MPI (Message-Passing Interface). The MPI specification describes a library of 129 functions which can be called from C and Fortran programs. These functions initiate and terminate MPI computations, allow processes to determine the total number of parallel processes and their unique identifier number, enable processes to send and receive messages, and support collective communication operations.

The Fortran/MPI program (Gropp *et al.*, 1999) in Fig. 1 implements the same numerical integration algorithm as the Fortran 90 program shown earlier. Remember that a group of processes executes this program in parallel. To insure that only a single process queries the user for *n* and prints the result, the input–output code must be surrounded by an if statement that ensures that only process 0 performs these steps.

Another communication-oriented system is based on the *Bulk Synchronous Parallel* (BSP) model, proposed by L. G. Valiant. Central to BSP programming is the idea of a superstep. A step is a basic operation performed by a process on its local data. A *superstep* is a sequence of steps followed by a *barrier synchronization* among the processes at which point nonlocal data accesses take effect. (When a process reaches a barrier it waits until all processes have also reached that point.) Because requests for nonlocal data may be made at any point during a superstep but are not guaranteed to be completed until the end of the superstep, the compiler and run-time system may perform various optimizations, such as combining communications or overlapping communications with computations.

Linda (Carriero and Gelernter, 1990) is the name given to a set of primitives allowing multiple sequential processes to communicate and synchronize through a global data area called *tuple space* (*see* COORDINATION LANGUAGES). Processes may insert tuples into tuple space, remove tuples from tuple space, and copy tuples from tuple space. A tuple may represent a piece of data or a function to be evaluated. Linda makes it easy to develop parallel applications based on the manager–worker model.

In a manager–worker program, one process (the manager) is responsible for dividing a job into tasks and collecting the results. The other processes (workers) go to the manager to get tasks. They complete the tasks independently and return the results to the manager. Workers continue to take tasks until the entire job has been completed. Implementing manager–worker programs in Linda is easy, because the shared tuple space is a convenient repository for tuples representing tasks and results.

Prognosis

Given the variety of parallel computers available, it is to a programmer's advantage to develop software in a language supported on many different platforms. At this time two environments widely supported among parallel-computer vendors are HPF and MPI. Both of these environments are based on explicit parallelism: the programmer must provide the compiler with information about operations that ought to be performed in parallel. At this time the lower-level

```
          program main
              include "mpif.h"

              double precision mypi, pi, h, sum, x
              integer n, myid, numprocs, i, ierr

c         Start up an MPI computation

              call MPI_INIT(ierr)

c         Each process learns its own id number

              call MPI_COMM_RANK(MPI_COMM_WORLD, myid, ierr)

c         Each process learns the total number of processes

              call MPI_COMM_SIZE(MPI_COMM_WORLD, numprocs, ierr)

c         Process 0 inputs n and broadcasts it to the other nodes

              if (myid .eq. 0) then
                 print *, 'Enter the number of intervals: '
                 read (*,*) n
              endif

c         Process 0 broadcasts the value of n to the other processes

              call MPI_BCAST (n, 1, MPI_INTEGER, 0, MPI_COMM_WORLD, ierr)

c         Each process finds the area of its share of the intervals

              h = 1.0d0/n
              sum = 0.0d0
              do 10 i = myid + 1, n, numprocs
                 x = h * (dble(i) - 0.5d0)
                 sum = sum + 4.0/(1.0d0 + x*x)
      10      continue
              mypi = h * sum

c         Add all the subtotals into a grand total

              call MPI_REDUCE (mypi, pi, 1, MPI_DOUBLE_PRECISION, MPI_SUM, 0,
         *       MPI_COMM_WORLD, ierr)

c         Process 0 prints the answer

              if (myid .eq. 0) then
                 print *, 'Estimate of pi is ', pi
              endif

              call MPI_FINALIZE(ierr)
              stop
              end
```

Figure 1. Parallel numerical integration using Fortran/MPI.

approach, exemplified by MPI, is much more likely to yield high performance parallel programs than the higher-level approach, exemplified by HPF. It remains to be seen to what extent improvements in compiler technology can narrow the performance gap. Other approaches, such as BSP and Linda, have numerous advocates. Still, the most common parallel programming methodology in the near future is likely to be SPMD programming based on message-passing, as exemplified by MPI.

Bibliography

1990. Carriero, N., and Gelernter, D. H. *How to Write Parallel Programs*. Cambridge, MA: MIT Press.
1990. Valiant, L. G. "A Bridging Model for Parallel Computation," *Comm. of the ACM*, **33**, *8* (August), 103–111.

1990. Metcalf, M., and Reid, J. *Fortran 90 Explained.* New York: Oxford University Press.

1994. Koelbel, C. H., Loveman, D. B., Schreiber, R. S., Steele, G. L., Jr, and Zosel, M. E. *The High Performance Fortran Handbook.* Cambridge, MA: MIT Press.

1996. Wolfe, M. J. *High Performance Compilers for Parallel Computing.* Reading, MA: Addison-Wesley.

1999. Gropp W., Lusk, E., and Skjellum, A. *Using MPI: Portable Parallel Programming with the Message-Passing Interface,* 2nd Ed. Cambridge, MA: MIT Press.

Michael J. Quinn

PARAMETER PASSING

For articles on related subjects *see* ARGUMENT; CALLING SEQUENCE; EXPRESSION; SIDE EFFECT; and SUBPROGRAM.

When a subprogram is called, information may be passed to it by means of a *parameter*, or *argument*. The placeholder within the subprogram for this information is called the *formal parameter*; the information that is actually passed on a given invocation is called the *actual parameter*. This article is concerned with the means by which the actual parameters supplied to a procedure or function are transferred to the formal parameters. There are three basic techniques:

1. Call by value

2. Call by reference

3. Call by name

Call by Value

In *call by value*, the actual parameter is evaluated at the time of the subprogram call and its value is copied into the formal parameter. There are two important points:

1. The actual parameter is evaluated whether or not the formal parameter is ever used inside the subprogram. For this reason call by value is sometimes called *eager evaluation*.

2. Since the formal parameter receives a copy of the actual parameter, modifications to the formal parameter have no effect on the actual parameter. In this manner the calling routine is insulated from the actions of the subprogram.

Call by value is illustrated using Pascal syntax in Fig. 1a.

Call by Reference

In *call by reference*, the calling routine does not provide the value of the actual parameter to the subprogram but instead provides the address of the memory location at which that value can be found.

(a) Call by value (Pascal). X holds the *value* of Y * Z and operations on X cannot affect Y or Z.

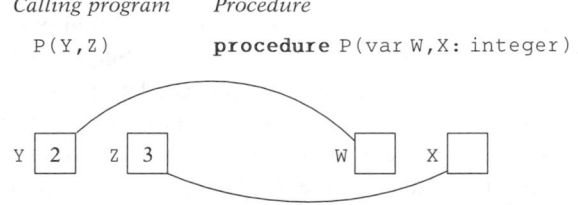

(b) Call by reference (Pascal). Since W and X hold the *locations* of Y and Z, whatever P does to the variables W and X is stored in Y and Z.

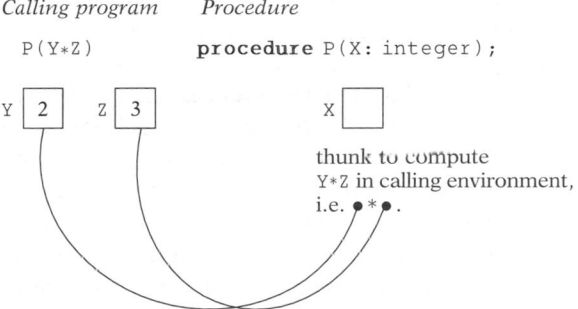

(c) Call by name (Algol). Within P, X will hold the value of Y * Z, which is evaluated whenever the value of X is needed.

Calling program   *Procedure*

   P(Y*Z)   **procedure** P(X: integer);

Y [2]   Z [3]   X [ ]

                                    thunk to compute
                                    Y*Z in calling environment,
                                    i.e. ● * ●.

Figure 1.   Passing arguments to procedures.

Thus the formal parameter shares memory with the actual parameter. It is the responsibility of the subprogram to access the data through this address; from the programmer's standpoint, the formal and actual parameters share memory directly. Call by reference is illustrated using Pascal syntax in Fig. 1b.

For an actual parameter that is an expression rather than a variable name, like Y*Z in Fig. 1a, there is no automatically corresponding address in the calling program. Therefore, if Y*Z were passed by reference, the calling routine would have to create a location for the value of Y*Z, evaluate Y*Z, put it in this location, and then transfer the address of this location to the subprogram, having essentially the same effect as passing by value. Some languages, such as Fortran (*q.v.*), do exactly this; most others, such as Pascal (*q.v.*), do not allow expressions to be passed by reference.

The difference between call by reference and call by value is important in two ways:

1. In call by value, modification of a formal parameter does not affect the value of the corresponding actual parameter. But in call by reference, the formal and

actual parameters share memory, so any modification of a formal parameter modifies the actual parameter as well. This means that in call by value information can be passed only into the subprogram, while in call by reference information can be passed both into the subprogram and back to the calling routine. For this reason value parameters are sometimes called *input parameters* and reference parameters are sometimes called *output parameters* or *input–output parameters.*

2. In call by value, a copy of the entire actual parameter is passed to the subprogram, while in call by reference a single address is passed. This means that when a large data structure is passed, significant space savings can be realized using call by reference instead of call by value. In C++ (*q.v.*), the economy of call by reference can be combined with the safety of call by value by declaring a by-reference input parameter with the keyword `const`, which prevents its being changed by the subprogram.

An alternative to call by reference is call by value/result, in which the value of the actual parameter is copied into the formal parameter as for call by value, but when the subprogram terminates the value of the formal is copied back into the actual one. This provides an input–output parameter without having the formal and actual parameters share memory as in call by reference. Call by reference and call by value/result are semantically equivalent if the subprogram does not make any nonlocal references to the actual parameter and if it completes normally rather than by raising an exception. Indeed, Ada (*q.v.*) provides an `IN OUT` parameter that provides information flow both from the actual to the formal and from the formal back to the actual, but does not specify whether it will be implemented as call by reference or call by value/result.

Call by Name

In *call by name*, the entire actual parameter expression is passed to the subprogram (so that it might better have been called *call by expression*). What is passed is not the symbolic string that defines the expression, but a machine language subprogram created by the compiler, sometimes called a *closure* or *thunk*. The use of this term is due to P. Z. Ingerman (1961) and refers to the fact that in such a closure, the environment in which an expression is to be evaluated has already been "thought out" by the compiler, hence "thunk." In addition to the code to be evaluated, the closure contains the referencing environment for variables in that code, since it may be different from the referencing environment (i.e. the association of names with objects) in the called subprogram. This is illustrated in Fig. 1c using Algol syntax. In the subprogram, each time the formal

parameter is referenced the closure is executed and the current value of the argument expression is determined and used as the value of the parameter. Such values may change during the execution of the subprogram as the result of side effects. When the actual parameter is a simple (i.e. unsubscripted) identifier the process of call by name is equivalent to call by reference, but interesting differences can arise when an expression or a subscript and an array variable that depends on that subscript are passed by name.

Call by name was used in Algol (*q.v.*), but has not been common. It is a form of *late binding* (*see* BINDING), which offers flexibility but can be difficult to use. Some functional programming (*q.v.*) languages use call *by need*, or *lazy evaluation* (note contrast to *eager evaluation*), a variation on call by name in which the expression that is passed is evaluated exactly once, the first time its value is demanded in the subprogram. In the absence of side effects that complicate call by name, call by need is semantically equivalent to call by name, but may be more efficient to implement as it eliminates the reevaluation of the actual parameter.

Parameter Passing in Common Languages

Call by value is the most widely used parameter-passing mechanism, but many languages offer alternatives. In Fortran, all parameters are passed by reference. In Pascal and C++, the programmer may choose between call by value and call by reference. In C, all parameters are passed by value, but the programmer can explicitly pass the address of any variable, so the effect of call by reference can be achieved as well. In Java, all parameters are passed by value, but when a reference variable is passed the reference is copied, not the object it refers to, so objects are effectively passed by reference. In Algol, all parameters are passed by name unless call by value is specified. Functional programming languages are divided into *lazy* or *nonstrict* languages, such as Haskell, which use call by need, and *strict* languages, such as Scheme [a dialect of Lisp (*q.v.*)], which use call by value.

Whatever the language used, the programmer must always be aware of how that language implements parameter passing. Otherwise, programs may not execute as planned.

Bibliography

1961. Ingerman, P. Z. "Thunks," *Comm. of the ACM*, **4**, *1.*

1964. Randell, B., and Russell, L. J. *Algol 60 Implementation.* New York: Academic Press.

1986. Peyton Jones, S. L. *The Implementation of Functional Programming Languages.* Upper Saddle River, NJ: Prentice Hall.

1989. Reilly, E. D., and Federighi, F. D. *Pascalgorithms.* Boston, MA: Houghton-Mifflin.

1996. Dybvig, R. K. *The Scheme Programming Language*, 2nd Ed. Upper Saddle River, NJ: Prentice Hall.

1996. Gosling, J., Joy, B., and Steele, Jr, G. L. *The Java Language Specification*. Reading, MA: Addison-Wesley.

1997. Stroustrup, B. The C++ Programming Language, 3rd Ed. Reading, MA: Addison-Wesley.

1998. Ghezzi, C., and Jazayeri, M. *Programming Language Concepts*, 3rd Ed. New York: John Wiley.

1999. Thompson, S. *Haskell: The Craft of Functional Programming*, 2nd Ed. Reading, MA: Addison-Wesley.

Adrienne Bloss and J. A. N. Lee

PARITY

> For articles on related subjects *see* CODES; CYCLIC REDUNDANCY CHECK; ERROR CORRECTING AND DETECTING CODE; and UNIVERSAL PRODUCT CODE.

In mathematics, two integers have the same *parity* if they are both even or both odd. A bit sequence has even parity if it contains an even number of 1 bits in it; otherwise it has odd parity. The parity of a set of bits, such as data recorded on a disk or transferred over a network, may be used for error detection, and this parity checking is an extensively used facility.

Suppose that we include one extra bit in the collection and set it to the value that will make the total number of 1 bits an even number. The bit collection including the parity bit then has even parity. When this bit collection is transferred to its destination, the receiver may calculate the parity of what is received. If that parity is odd, an error must have occurred. Such a check is normally performed by hardware.

A *parity bit* is thus a check bit whose binary value (0 or 1) depends upon whether the sum of bits with value 1 in the unit of data being checked is to be odd or even. Checking methods may use either even or odd parity. Each information system must use the same parity principle, even or odd, throughout. An error caused by incorrect parity detected as a result of a parity check is called a *parity error*.

The unit of data to which a parity check is applied may be a character, a byte, a word, etc., the character parity check being most common. Since two or any even number of errors in the unit of data cannot be detected by a single parity bit, the smaller the unit of data to which the check is applied, the higher the probability that multiple errors will not occur.

Jiri Necas

PARTIAL DIFFERENTIAL EQUATIONS

> For articles on related subjects *see* FINITE ELEMENT METHOD; MATRIX COMPUTATIONS; NUMERICAL ANALYSIS; SCIENTIFIC APPLICATIONS; and SOFTWARE LIBRARIES.

A major application of high-performance digital computers is to the numerical solution of problems involving *partial differential equations* (PDEs). These problems arise in scientific applications involving simulation and modeling in areas such as weather forecasting, fluid and supersonic flow, nuclear diffusion studies for reactor design, elasticity, and many others. These and other science and engineering problems are some of the primary uses of vector and parallel supercomputers (*q.v.*).

An important class of partial differential equations is *linear equations of second order* in two independent variables. The most general such equation is

$$L[u] = Au_{xx} + 2Bu_{xy} + Cu_{yy} + Du_x + Eu_y + Fu = G,$$

where $A, B, C, D, E, F,$ and G are functions depending on x and y. This equation is said to be *elliptic, hyperbolic,* or *parabolic* at a mesh point (x, y) according to whether the discriminant $B^2 - AC$ is negative, positive, or zero, respectively. Simple examples are the Laplace equation $u_{xx} + u_{yy} = 0$ (elliptic); the wave equation $u_{xx} - u_{yy} = 0$ (hyperbolic); and the heat or diffusion equation $u_{xx} - u_y = 0$ (parabolic).

Two important classes of problems involving partial differential equations are *initial-value problems* and *boundary-value problems*. For an initial-value problem in two variables, the desired function $u(x, y)$ is required to satisfy the differential equation in an unbounded region R and to satisfy certain auxiliary conditions on the boundary δR. Such conditions might involve prescribing the values of $u(x, y)$ on δR or (as in the Cauchy problem) u and the normal derivative $\partial u / \partial n$ might be prescribed on δR. For a boundary-value problem, the region R is bounded, and one prescribes either u, $\partial u / \partial n$, or a linear combination of u and $\partial u / \partial n$ on δR. For the Laplace equation, these conditions correspond to Dirichlet, Neumann, or mixed conditions, respectively.

Before attempting to solve a problem involving a partial differential equation, one should determine whether or not it is *well posed*. To be well posed, there should exist a unique solution that depends continuously on the boundary data. For linear equations of second order, boundary-value problems involving hyperbolic or parabolic equations are usually not well posed, nor are initial-value problems involving elliptic equations.

A basic tool in the solution of partial differential equations is the method of finite differences. Here one covers the region under consideration with a mesh (i.e. a grid), usually consisting of horizontal and vertical lines, and one seeks approximate values of the solution at the intersection points, or *nodes*. The partial derivatives appearing in the PDE are approximated by finite difference stencils. For example, we can use the standard central difference approximations

$$u_{xx} \approx \frac{1}{h^2} \left[u(x+h, y) + u(x-h, y) - 2u(x, y) \right],$$

$$u_{yy} \approx \frac{1}{h^2} \left[u(x, y+h) + u(x, y-h) - 2u(x, y) \right],$$

where h is the spacing between the adjacent lines in the grid. Substituting these finite difference approximations in the partial differential equation leads to a difference equation. For a boundary-value problem, one then obtains a system of linear algebraic equations, with the number of equations equal to the number of interior mesh points. It can usually be shown without difficulty that the linear system has a unique solution. To solve the linear system of equations either a direct method or an iterative method is used. For sparse linear systems, some direct methods are variations of Gaussian elimination and they are usually designed to take advantage of sparseness and to minimize the fill-in. Examples of iterative methods are the *successive overrelaxation* (SOR) method and procedures involving a basic iterative method combined with Chebyshev acceleration or conjugate gradient acceleration. Among other basic iterative methods that may be used are the Jacobi method, the symmetric SOR method, and methods based on approximate factorizations of the matrix of the system.

As an example, consider the problem of solving the Poisson partial differential equation

$$u_{xx} + u_{yy} = f(x, y),$$

in the L-shaped region shown in Fig. 1. The unknown function $u(x, y)$ is required to agree with a given continuous function $g(x, y)$ on the boundary of the region. For each interior mesh point, we have the difference equation

$$\frac{1}{h^2} \left[u(x+h, y) + u(x-h, y) - 2u(x, y) \right]$$

$$+ \frac{1}{h^2} \left[u(x, y+h) + u(x, y-h) - 2u(x, y) \right] = f(x, y).$$

This leads to a systems of equations each of which is of the form

$$4u_{ij} - u_{i+1,j} - u_{i-1,j} - u_{i,j+1} - u_{i,j-1} = -h^2 f_{ij},$$

where u_{ij} denotes a solution of the difference equation at the mesh point (ih, jh). Here $i, j = 0, 1, 2, \ldots, N+1$ and $h = 1/(N+1)$. Also, the known boundary values g_{ij} are stored in corresponding values of u_{ij}. Hence we obtain a linear system of equations and its solution gives approximate values at the mesh points to the solution of the Poisson equation. We can order the mesh points in a number of different ways—two common orderings are the *natural ordering* (left-to-right/

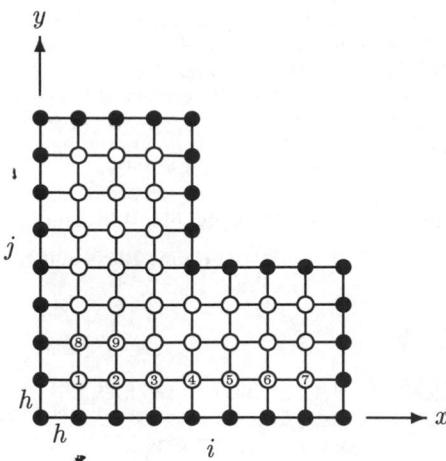

Figure 1.   Mesh points on an L-shaped region.

bottom-to-top) and the *red–black ordering* (checker board). We obtain the natural ordering by letting $x_k = u_{k1}$, for $k = 1, 2, \ldots, N$, be the unknowns on the first line of mesh points, by letting $x_k = u_{k-N,2}$ for $k = N+1, N+2, \ldots, 2N$, be the unknowns on the second line, and so on. We can write the system in the form

$$\mathbf{Ax} = \mathbf{b},$$

where

$$\mathbf{x} = (u_{11}, u_{21}, \ldots, u_{N1}, u_{12}, u_{22}, \ldots, u_{N2}, \ldots)^T.$$

The right-hand side **b** of the system consists of the quantities $-h^2 f_{ij}$ as well as the known boundary values. The coefficient matrix **A** can be written in a block form. (Different orderings lead to different patterns of the nonzeros within the coefficient matrix **A**.) This is an example of a diagonally sparse matrix and consists of at most five nonzero entries per row. We could apply the Jacobi method (*see* MATRIX COMPUTATIONS) in the form

$$u_{ij}^{(k+1)} = \frac{1}{4} \left[u_{i+1,j}^{(k)} + u_{i-1,j}^{(k)} + u_{i,j+1}^{(k)} + u_{i,j-1}^{(k)} - h^2 f_{ij} \right].$$

For Laplace's equation $f_{ij} = 0$, and the Jacobi method shows that the next iterate at the (i, j) mesh point is the average of the current iterate values at the neighboring mesh points (east, west, north, south).

An alternative procedure for solving boundary-value problems is the *finite element method*. Here, again, one eventually obtains a linear system. However, instead of using finite differences, one generates the linear equations based on functional approximation techniques, using certain subsets of the region (elements), and based on variational procedures, Galerkin procedures, or collocation procedures. With these techniques, the grid is seldom regular and adaptive grid schemes are used to refine the mesh points in critical areas within the region.

Multigrids are also often used to solve PDEs. With these methods, there are one or more coarse grids in additional to the basic (fine) grid. An approximate solution on the fine grid is projected or restricted up onto a coarse grid so that new approximate values may be obtained via some iterative or smoothing procedure. Then these newly computed values are interpolated back down onto the fine grid points. If a complete up and down sweep is performed, it is a V-cycle, and if repeated twice, a W-cycle. By working alternately on the fine grid and on the coarse grids, it is often possible to improve greatly the rate of convergence of the overall procedure.

One class of initial-value problems involves the partial differential equation $u_t = L[u]$, where $L[u]$ is an elliptic operator in one or two *space* variables. Frequently, one is given $u(\mathbf{x}, 0)$ for all $\mathbf{x}$ in the region and given $u(\mathbf{x}, t)$ for $\mathbf{x}$ on the boundary and for all $t > 0$. Here $\mathbf{x}$ represents x when there is one space variable and (x, y) when there are two. In the method of finite differences, one constructs a mesh in the space variables, as in the case of a boundary-value problem. In the *forward-difference method*, one replaces u_t by $[u(\mathbf{x}, t + \Delta t) - u(\mathbf{x}, t)]/\Delta t$ and sets it equal to $L_h[u](\mathbf{x}, t)$, where $L_h[u](\mathbf{x}, t)$ is a finite difference representation of $L[u](\mathbf{x}, t)$. The determination of $u(\mathbf{x}, \Delta t)$, $u(\mathbf{x}, 2\Delta t)$, etc. can be carried out explicitly. However, numerical stability considerations require that $\Delta t/h^2$ be bounded as $h \to 0$, where $h = \Delta x = \Delta y$. The work required is usually prohibitive since this requirement results in an excessively small value of Δt.

A widely used method is the *Crank–Nicolson method*, in which $L_h[u](\mathbf{x}, t)$ is replaced by $\frac{1}{2}\{L_h[u](\mathbf{x}, t) + L_h[u](\mathbf{x}, t + \Delta t)\}$ and the restriction on Δt is greatly relaxed. An implicit rather than an explicit procedure is thus developed. However, with one space dimension, the implicit calculation involves solving a linear system with a tridiagonal matrix. (This is relatively easy.) With two space dimensions, one must solve a boundary-value problem for each time step. However, certain iterative methods can be shown to converge much more rapidly than in the case of a pure boundary-value problem.

As an example, consider the diffusion equation

$$u_t = u_{xx} \quad \text{for} \quad 0 < x < 1, \quad t > 0,$$

subject to the boundary conditions $u(0, t) = g_1(t)$ and $u(1, t) = g_2(t)$, for $t > 0$, and the initial condition $u(x, 0) = f(x)$ (*see* Fig. 2). Here $g_1(t)$, $g_2(t)$, and $f(x)$ are given functions. The forward difference method is given by

$$\frac{1}{\Delta t}[u(x, t + \Delta t) - u(x, t)]$$

$$= \frac{1}{h^2}[u(x + h, t) + u(x - h, t) - 2u(x, t)].$$

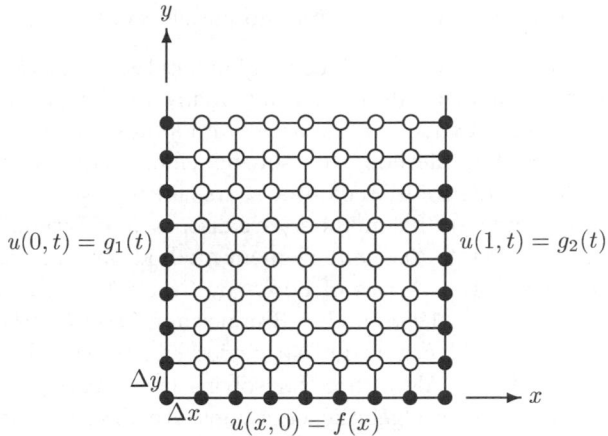

Figure 2. Mesh points on an open region.

From this, the values of $u(x, t + \Delta t)$ can be calculated explicitly in terms of values of $u(x, t)$. For the Crank–Nicolson method, the right-hand side is replaced by

$$\frac{1}{2}\left\{\frac{1}{h^2}[u(x + h, t) + u(x - h, t) - 2u(x, t)]\right.$$

$$+ \frac{1}{h^2}[u(x + h, t + \Delta t) + u(x - h, t + \Delta t)$$

$$\left. - 2u(x, t + \Delta t)]\right\}.$$

The approximate solution values are obtained by solving a system of equations. Hyperbolic equations of the form $u_{tt} = L[u]$ can often be treated in a manner similar to that described above. Other hyperbolic equations, or systems of equations, are treated by the *method of characteristics*.

Another approach is the *method of lines* in which the partial differential equation is approximated by an ordinary differential equation (ODE). Then ODE software is used to obtain numerical solutions on the grid lines.

Computer programs and packages have been developed for solving partial differential equations. One such software package is ELLPACK, which was developed at Purdue University and which is designed as a research tool for evaluating the performance of software for solving elliptic PDEs (Rice and Boisvert, 1985). ELLPACK has a large number of problem solving modules including mesh generation, discretization, equation solution, and many others. ELLPACK is being extended for use in parallel computing environments and for use in a Web-based network of computing systems. The ITPACK Project at The University of Texas at Austin has involved the development of computer programs for solving large sparse linear systems using iterative methods (Kincaid and Young, 1988). Some of the iterative algorithms developed as part of ITPACK have been used as equation solution modules within

ELLPACK. Some of the ITPACK programs have been adapted for use with vector and parallel computers.

Textbooks such as Lapidus and Pinder (1982) describe numerical methods for solving many of the partial differential equations that are common in science and engineering. Methods for solving elliptic equations, including the solution of large sparse linear systems by direct and iterative methods, are discussed by Birkhoff and Lynch (1984). Finite element methods are treated in a six-volume series of books by Carey, Oden, and Becker (1981–1986) and in Brenner and Scott (1994). Adaptive grid generation strategies can be found in Carey (1997). Algorithms for solving large sparse systems of linear algebraic equations are described in books such as Hageman and Young (1981), Axelsson (1994), and Saad (1996).

Information is available on the Internet on a large variety of mathematical software for solving PDEs. For example, *Netlib* is a repository for mathematical software, documents, and other useful information that can be accessed at `http://www.netlib.org`. Another repository is the Guide to Available Mathematical Software at `http://gams.nist.gov`. It is maintained by the National Institute of Standards and Technology and contains mathematical and statistical software for use in computational science and engineering. Keyword searches are available in both of these systems.

Bibliography

1981–1986. *Finite Elements: Vol. 1 A First Course* (Becker, E. B., Carey, G. F., and Oden, J. T., 1981); *Vol. 2 A Second Course* (Carey, G. F., and Oden, J. T., 1982); *Vol. 3 Computational Aspects* (Carey, G. F., and Oden, J. T., 1984); *Vol. 4 Mathematical Aspects* (Oden, J. T., and Carey, G. F., 1982); *Vol. 5 Solid Mechanics* (Oden, J. T., and Carey, G. F., 1983); *Vol. 6 Fluid Mechanics* (Carey, G. F., and Oden, J. T., 1986). Upper Saddle River, NJ: Prentice Hall.
1981. Hageman, L. A., and Young, D. M. *Applied Iterative Methods.* New York: Academic Press.
1982. Lapidus, L., and Pinder, G. F. *Numerical Solution of Partial Differential Equations in Science and Engineering.* New York: Wiley-Interscience.
1984. Birkhoff, G., and Lynch, R. E. *The Numerical Solution of Elliptic Problems.* Philadelphia: SIAM.
1985. Rice, J. R., and Boisvert, R. F. *Solving Elliptic Problems Using ELLPACK.* New York: Springer-Verlag.
1988. Kincaid, D. R., and Young, D. M. "A Brief Review of the ITPACK Project," *Journal of Computational and Applied Mathematics,* **24**, 121–127.
1994. Axelsson, O. *Iterative Solution Methods.* New York: Cambridge University Press.
1994. Brenner, S. C., and Scott, L. R. *The Mathematical Theory of Finite Element Methods.* New York: Springer-Verlag.
1996. Saad, Y. *Iterative Methods for Solving Linear Systems.* Boston: PWS.
1997. Carey, G. F. *Computational Grids: Generation, Adaptation, and Solution Strategies.* Washington, DC: Taylor & Francis.

David M. Young and David R. Kincaid

PARTIAL EVALUATION

For articles on related topics *see* AUTOMATIC PROGRAMMING; COMPILER; COORDINATION LANGUAGES; and LANGUAGE PROCESSORS.

Partial evaluation is an automated program transformation technique for specializing programs. Given a *source program* $P\langle x, y \rangle$ with the input parameters x and y, and a value s for x, a partial evaluator PE specializes P with respect to s, yielding the residual program $P_s\langle y \rangle$. To this end, PE precomputes all the parts of P that depend only upon the value of x, thus "partially evaluating" P, i.e., evaluating (executing) only the parts of P that do not depend on the value of y. The specialization process ensures the compatibility between source and residual programs: for any data item d in y's domain, running P_s on the remaining input $\langle d \rangle$ computes the same output as running P on the complete input $\langle s, d \rangle$.

The overall motivation for program specialization is that running P_s on d is often more efficient than running P on both s and d, since PE has already precomputed the portions of P that depend only on s. This *staging* of P using PE pays off if P is repeatedly used with the x parameter set to s. Since its value is fixed, x is called a *static* parameter, while y, which may vary, is called a *dynamic* parameter.

A simple example

Consider the following C (*q.v.*) function, which squares the sum of its two arguments.

```
int square_sum (int x, int y) {
    return (x*x + 2*x*y + y*y);
}
```

Specializing this function with x set to 3 yields the following residual function:

```
int square_sum_3_u (int y) {
    return (9 + 6*y + y*y);
}
```

This specialized function is obtained by retaining the unknown parameter y, propagating the constant 3 in the body of square_sum, and by evaluating the expressions $x*x$ and $2*x$ that do not depend on y.

Partial evaluators employ techniques found in optimizing compilers such as constant propagation and folding (evaluating expressions (*q.v.*) with constant parameters), loop unrolling (reducing the number of iterations by replicating a loop body). Since a partial evaluator is usually given more latitude than an ordinary compiler, it makes a more aggressive use of these techniques, propagating compound values (not merely scalars) across procedure boundaries, using nontrivial memorization (saving computed values for reuse) and caching techniques to share residual (partially evaluated) procedures, etc.

The two standard approaches to writing a partial evaluator are monolithic (*online*) and staged (*offline*). An online partial evaluator is essentially a symbolic interpreter, determining opportunistically which parts of the program to execute and which ones to retain. In contrast, an offline partial evaluator proceeds in two phases: (1) a *binding-time analysis* calculates dependency information in the source program and classifies each program construct as either (a) dependent upon the static parameters only, or (b) possibly dependent on the dynamic parameters as well; and (2) a *specialization phase* executes the static program constructs and generates code for the others, yielding the specialized program.

Partial evaluation is usually expressed as a *source-to-source* transformation, which facilitates portability and further transformation and optimization of specialized programs. Some static data, however, becomes available only at run time. But the naive idea of specializing at run time, compiling the residual program, and dynamically linking the resulting object code is much too costly. Therefore, modern partial evaluators perform *run-time code generation* instead. These *dynamic partial evaluators* produce programs that generate specialized object code at run time once the data becomes available.

Applications of partial evaluation occur throughout computer science to customize general-purpose programs or software libraries. Classical examples include multiplication of sparse matrices, pattern-matching compilation, and compilation of database queries. Two such applications, in particular, have been extensively explored: *programming language interpreters* and *partial evaluators* themselves:

◆ *Interpreters*: given a definitional interpreter INT and a program P in the defined language, one can specialize INT with respect to P to remove its interpretive overhead:

$$\begin{cases} \text{run PE}\langle\text{INT},\text{P}\rangle = \text{INT}_\text{P} \\ \text{run INT}\langle\text{P}, d\rangle = \text{run INT}_\text{P}\ \langle d\rangle \end{cases}$$

Thus, running INT_P on input d is equivalent to running the original INT on inputs P, d. This pattern of specialization is called a *Futamura projection*. It facilitates the use of interpreters for prototyping without performance penalty.

◆ *Self-application*: given a partial evaluator PE whose implementation language is a subset of its source language, and a program P, one can specialize PE

with respect to P in order to obtain a *generating extension*: a lightweight specializer dedicated to P:

$$\begin{cases} \text{run PE}\langle\text{PE},\text{P}\rangle = \text{PE}_\text{P} \\ \text{run PE}\langle\text{P}, d\rangle = \text{run PE}_\text{P}\ \langle d\rangle \end{cases}$$

For a very simple example, we give a generating extension corresponding to square_sum when its first parameter is fixed. This generating extension is a C function that outputs the C source code of a specialized function.

```c
void gen_square_sum_k_u (int x) {
  printf(
    "int square_sum_%d_u (int y){\n", x);
  printf(
    "return (%d + %d*y + y*y);\n",x*x, 2*x);
  printf("}\n");
}
```

A call gen_square_sum_k_u(3) produces as output the specialized function described earlier:

```c
int square_sum_3_u (int y) {
  return (9 + 6*y + y*y);
}
```

As specialized partial evaluators, generating extensions are often more efficient than a general-purpose partial evaluator. They are especially useful when the same program needs to be specialized repeatedly. In fact, some partial-evaluation systems produce generating extensions by default to carry out program specialization.

Contemporary applications of partial evaluation include implementing domain-specific languages (*see* PROBLEM-ORIENTED LANGUAGES) by interpreter specialization, removing layers of interpretation in coordination languages (*q.v.*), collapsing network protocol stacks for efficiency, optimizing graphics systems, dynamically specializing circuits on field-programmable gate arrays, and optimizing the verification of reactive systems (*see* REAL-TIME SYSTEMS).

Bibliography

1993. Jones, N. D., Gomard, C., and Sestoft, P. *Partial Evaluation and Automatic Program Generation*. Upper Saddle River, NJ: Prentice Hall. Available online at http://www.dina.kvl.dk/~sestoft/pebook/pebook.html.

1996. Danvy, O., Glück, R., and Thiemann, P. *Partial Evaluation* (Lecture Notes in Computer Science 1110). New York: Springer-Verlag.

Websites

1999. The TOPPS Group (University of Copenhagen). http://www.diku.dk/research-groups/topps/.

1999. The COMPOSE Group (IRISA/INRIA). http://www.irisa.fr/compose/.

Both sites keep pointers to current partial-evaluation research for all language paradigms: imperative, functional, logic, object-oriented, etc.

Olivier Danvy and John Hatcliff

PASCAL

For articles on related subjects *see* CONTROL STRUCTURE; DATA TYPES; PROCEDURE-ORIENTED LANGUAGES; PROGRAMMING LANGUAGES; and STRUCTURED PROGRAMMING.

Pascal was developed by Niklaus Wirth (1971) in the late 1960s and early 1970s following some earlier work by Wirth and Hoare (1966) to improve upon Algol (*q.v.*) in the area of data-structuring facilities (data types). While Pascal was designed in part to serve as a language for teaching computer programming as a systematic discipline, Wirth also showed that a reliable (error-free) and efficient (in size and speed) implementation of a large procedure-oriented language was possible on real computers then available, such as the one that his research group used, a Control Data (*q.v.*) 6000/Cyber mainframe. Pascal was the first widely adopted computer programming language to embody fully the principles of structured programming (Dahl *et al.*, 1972).

One of the distinguishing characteristics of Pascal is the small size of its definition, both syntactic (as specified in the Pascal Report—Jensen *et al.*, 1991) and semantic (as specified in the axiomatic definition—Wirth and Hoare, 1973). Wirth (1976) achieved this by carefully choosing a set of orthogonal control structures (statements) and data structures (declarations).

In fact, every structured type in Pascal has a corresponding control structure (in the sense that these control structures are used for typical ways of processing data of that type):

array;	`for-do`
record;	`if-then-else`
set;	`case-of`
file;	`while-do`
pointer;	(recursive procedures)

For example, sets are small collections of values of a discrete type, which may be processed with a `case` statement, and files, being of arbitrary size, may be processed with indefinite iteration using a `while` loop.

Pascal was designed to be compiled efficiently while requiring only a single pass through the source code (*see* COMPILER). This property made its compilers relatively small and fast, a practical advantage for their use in teaching. It also contributed to some aspects of the design of the language. For example, every procedure or function had to be declared before it was used, with the main program body at the end of the program, unlike, say, C, which can have the main program first

and the secondary routines later. Such declare-before-use also helps with error-checking.

Pascal supports both data and procedural abstraction, which allows the definition of data structures (*q.v.*) and program statements to model their corresponding physical entities closely. Pascal programmers benefit from Pascal's notion of "type," which rigorously defines the set of valid values and organizing structure that data may assume, as well as the valid set of operations upon that data. By holding the concept of "type" paramount, Pascal compilers are able to detect many errors at compile time by checking assignment statements and procedure parameter lists for mixed types and out-of-range operations. It is not unusual for Pascal programs, once syntactically correct, to execute error-free almost immediately, and if they do not, Pascal's type-checking allows the programmer to focus on possible logic errors. The sample Pascal program in Fig. 1 is adapted from Wirth (1973).

Besides the fact that Control Data computers were fortuitously used by many large universities in the USA, the spread of Pascal was greatly accelerated in the 1970s by Wirth's research group. They wrote and distributed a portable "Pascal-P" compiler which produced an intermediate ("P-code") language (*see* INTERMEDIATE LANGUAGES) for a hypothetical stack computer and could be used as a kit to bootstrap itself on a real computer with a modest programming effort.

By 1977 compilers existed for every available commercial computer from the Intel 8080 to the Cray-1 and their availability was coordinated by the Pascal Users Group (Mickel, 1996). In fact Pascal became the first serious programming language on the early microprocessor systems (which had limited memory) thanks to data-compression techniques applied to the P-code by a group led by Ken Bowles at the University of California at San Diego. "UCSD Pascal" became the basis for most personal computer implementations of Pascal for the next several years (including DEC, HP, Apple, and IBM). According to Wirth (1996, p. 111), UCSD Pascal played a major role in promoting widespread use of Pascal. For almost two decades, Pascal was the language of choice for most introductory computer science courses, a role now assumed by C++ (*q.v.*).

Pascal standards efforts began in Europe with the British Standards Institution, the first non-USA programming language standards initiative. The development of the resulting ISO Standard (1983) was aided by the Joint Pascal Committee of the IEEE and ANSI in 1978–1982.

Several languages can trace their origins to Pascal, including Concurrent Pascal, Modula-2, Object-Pascal,

```
program GeneratePrimes (Output);              {number of primes to compute}
   const n = 25;                              {scalar data type is subrange of Integer}
   type Index = 1 .. n;
   var x: integer;
       i, k, limit: Index;                    {variables i, k, limit are of type Index}
       Prime: boolean;                        {prime is either True or False}
       p: array[Index] of integer;            {p[i] is ith prime}
begin
   p[1] := 2;                                                        {first prime}
   writeln(2);                                         {output this prime on one line}
   x := 1; limit := 1;                                          {initialize method}
   for i := 2 to n do                              {compute next n - 1 prime numbers}
     begin
       repeat
         x := x + 2;                          {only odd numbers need to be considered}
         if sqr(p[limit]) <= x then limit := limit + 1;
                                        {to determine greatest prime needed as a divisor}
         k := 2; Prime := True;
         while Prime and (k < limit) do
             begin
             Prime := (x div p[k]) * p[k] <> x;
                                               {div results in integer part of quotient}
             k := k + 1
             end
       until Prime;                     {if Prime is True, no prime divisor of x exists}
       p[i] := x;
       writeln(x)                                                 {output the prime}
     end                                                            {of for loop}
end.                                                            {GeneratePrimes}
```

Figure 1. A Pascal program to print prime numbers.

Ada, and Oberon. Following an evolution from structured, to modular, to extensible programming, Wirth designed Modula-2 and Oberon as Pascal successors for machine-independent systems programming (*q.v.*). Modula-2 (late 1970s) extended Pascal to support the modularity concepts of information hiding (*q.v.*) and separate compilation while maintaining type consistency checks (*see* MODULAR PROGRAMMING). Oberon (late 1980s) is a small, powerful language which adds support for extensible data types and extensible procedures, popularly known as "object-oriented programming" (*q.v.*), to a minimal Pascal-like core.

Bibliography

1966. Wirth, N., and Hoare, C. A. R. "A Contribution to the Development of Algol," *Comm. of the ACM*, **9**, *6*, 413–431.

1971. Wirth, N. "The Programming Language Pascal," *Acta Informatica*, **1**, *1*, 35–63.

1972. Dahl, O. J., Dijkstra, E. W., and Hoare, C. A. R. *Structured Programming*. New York: Academic Press.

1973. Hoare, C. A. R., and Wirth, N. "An Axiomatic Definition of the Programming Language Pascal," *Acta Informatica*, **2**, *4* (December), 335–355.

1973. Wirth, N. *Systematic Programming: An Introduction*. Upper Saddle River, NJ: Prentice Hall.

1975. Wirth, N. "An Assessment of the Programming Language Pascal," *IEEE Transactions on Software Engineering*, **1**, *2* (June), 192–198. Reprinted in 1987, Horowitz, E. (ed.) *Programming Languages: A Grand Tour*, 3rd Ed., 117–122. Rockville, MD: Computer Science Press.

1976. Wirth, N. *Algorithms + Data Structures = Programs*. Upper Saddle River, NJ: Prentice Hall.

1977. Welsh, J., Sneeringer, W., and Hoare, C. A. R. "Ambiguities and Insecurities in Pascal," *Software—Practice and Experience*, **7**, *6* (November–December), 685–696.

Reprinted in 1987, Horowitz, E. (ed.) *Programming Languages: A Grand Tour*, 3rd Ed., 105–116. Rockville, MD: Computer Science Press.

1983. International Organization for Standardization. *Specification for Computer Programming Language Pascal*, ISO 7185-1983.

1991. Jensen, K., Wirth, N., Mickel, A., and Miner, J. *Pascal User Manual and Report*, 4th Ed. New York: Springer-Verlag.

1992. Reiser, M., and Wirth, N. *Programming in Oberon, Steps Beyond Pascal and Modula*. Reading, MA: Addison-Wesley.

1996. Wirth, N. "Recollections About the Development of Pascal" and Mickel, A. "Pascal Users Group and the Rise of Pascal," in *History of Programming Languages—II* (eds. T. J. Bergin, Jr, and R. G. Gibson, Jr). Reading, MA: Addison-Wesley.

Andrew B. Mickel

PASCAL, BLAISE

> For articles on related subjects *see* CALCULATING MACHINES; DIGITAL COMPUTERS, HISTORY OF: ORIGINS; and LEIBNIZ, GOTTFRIED WILHELM.

Blaise Pascal (b. Clermont, France, 1623; d. Paris, 1662) was educated by his father Etienne, and, after discovering a proof of Euclid's Proposition 32 at age 12, he became a participant in the mathematician Mersenne's Circle. Four years later he presented to them his well-known theorem in projective geometry.

In 1640, he started developing a calculating machine to help in his father's tax work in Rouen. He completed the first operating model in 1642 and built 50 more during the next ten years. The machine, called

Figure 1. Blaise Pascal (courtesy of the Mary Evans Picture Library).

Pascaline, was a small box with eight dials (resembling telephone dials), each geared to a drum that displayed the digits in a register window. Pascal's fundamental innovation was a ratchet linkage (*sautier*) between the rotating drums, which transferred rotating motion from one drum to the next higher-position drum only during carryover. This kept the digit of each drum aligned with its display window. The machine added and subtracted directly, and multiplied and divided by using repeated additions and subtractions, analogous to present-day pencil-and-paper algorithms. The machine was presented publicly in 1645.

In 1646, Pascal learned of Torricelli's experiment with the vacuum and successfully repeated it. Because of illness, he moved back to Paris in 1647, where he associated with Roberval, met Descartes, published treatises on the vacuum and on conics, and prepared the Puy-de-Dômes (barometer) experiment. Around 1651, he met the Duc de Roannez and the Chevalier de Mere and became reinvolved in research; in 1654, he produced two papers establishing the foundations of the integral calculus and of probability theory. In 1658, using the pseudonym Amos Dettonville, he challenged mathematicians to a mathematical contest and created a controversy by awarding himself the prize. No further significant research followed.

Pascal had been converted to Jansenism in 1645 and, in 1654, he had an ecstatic religious experience that drew him into the Port-Royal Jansenists' machinations with the Jesuits, resulting in his writing the *Provincial Letters*, the beginning of French classical literature. His general health, which had been poor, degenerated and he became more mystical in his interests. During his last months in 1662, he created the first public transportation system—an omnibus service in Paris.

Bibliography

1995. Adamson, D. *Blaise Pascal: Mathematician, Physicist, and Thinker About God.* New York: St Martin's Press.

Charles V. Jones

PASSWORD

For articles on related subjects *see* AUTHENTICATION; COMPUTER CRIME; CRYPTOGRAPHY, COMPUTERS IN; DATA SECURITY; HACKER; PRETTY GOOD PRIVACY; and PRIVACY, COMPUTERS AND.

Multiuser computer systems generally have an *account* for each user, which gives the user access to his or her files and to public files and programs. An account is protected by a *password*; as in ordinary usage, a password is a word or phrase that must be supplied in order to authenticate a user and permit access to a place or to information. Password-protected accounts typically reside on time-shared computers such as those run by an Internet Service Provider or by an employer, on workstations (*q.v.*) with a networked file server (*q.v.*), or even on a single-user computer that may be used by several people. Specific services such as email (*q.v.*) may also require password authentication to gain access to their data.

Since the purpose of requiring a password is to protect against unauthorized access, it would be most unwise to store actual passwords in the same memory as holds user files. In fact, the best practice is that passwords are not only encrypted, but that the encryption is done in such a way that even a system operator with access to all information in the computer cannot recover the original password. Commonly, the user's password is used as a key to encrypt a known common character string through a "one-way" algorithm similar to that of the Data Encryption Standard (DES—*see* CRYPTOGRAPHY, COMPUTERS IN). Once encrypted, the original password is discarded. When a user logs on and enters the password, the same encryption is performed and the result is compared to the stored string. Since the password itself cannot be recovered from the encrypted form with such a system, the user who forgets a password must endure the nuisance of having to ask for a new one, but the dividend is a much more secure system.

Of course, there are always malicious hackers ("crackers") who try to break into computing systems, and the more allegedly secure the system, the greater the challenge. While systematically trying all possible strings of characters is rarely feasible, they can try to guess the password that is associated with a user ID. (User IDs are frequently known because they are a part of email addresses.) And guessing the password of someone known to you is often easy because many people, concerned that they will not remember their password, choose something associated with them such as the name of a child, their spouse, their pet, or their car.

Some hackers automate password guessing, using their own local computer to test, one by one, words from a dictionary as possible passwords. To thwart this practice, most systems will terminate the connection and make you try again if, say, three attempts to log in fail. But this will not deter those who use their own account on a system to run a program to try to guess other users' passwords. Because of this, users are advised not to use short passwords, not to use names or phrases connected to them, and not to use a dictionary word, whether forward or reversed.

Suppose, for example, that an incautious user does choose a six-letter word from a dictionary. Then, since there are only about 10,000 valid six-letter English words, it does not take even a moderately fast computer very long to check them all. But now suppose that the user is willing to concoct not a six-*letter* password, but rather a six-*character* password, such as $2b+\sim 2B$. Since there are approximately 100 printable ASCII characters any one of which might occur at any of the six positions, there are now $100^6 = 10^{12}$ or one trillion possible passwords. That is likely to keep the cracker's program busy for so long that the intruder will lose interest. For those still worried, lengthening the password by just two more characters—making eight in all—raises the odds against the cracker to a virtually insurmountable 10^{16} to 1.

Many computer systems now require that a user choose a password not in the system's dictionary, and not derived from the user's name or ID. Some systems have password-generating programs that produce meaningless strings of characters. If these generate strings like "&Jkpzq@P2E", however, users may breach security by writing them down, since they are hard to remember. A better strategy is to generate strings of nonsense syllables that can be pronounced and hence more readily remembered. Another protection against break-ins is *password aging*, which requires that users change passwords regularly. This, too, may be counterproductive if too-frequent changes encourage users to write down passwords.

Another hazard is that early Internet programs for remote login, like ftp and telnet (*see* INTERNET), transmit passwords as clear text, since they were developed when the precursor of the Internet, the Arpanet, was used by a small community of researchers and security was not a central concern. It is possible to use a program that monitors all packets (*see* ETHERNET) transmitted over a local segment of the Internet and to search for strings that follow "Password:", which are user passwords. The best protection against such violations is to use more recently developed remote-login programs called *secure shells* that encrypt the text that they transmit. Of course, those who display their password on a Post-It note might be thought to deserve whatever happens to them.

Bibliography

1994. Cheswick, W. R., and Bellovin, S. M. *Firewalls and Internet Security: Repelling the Wily Hacker.* Reading, MA: Addison-Wesley.

1995. Cohen, F. B. *Protection and Security on the Information Superhighway.* New York: John Wiley.

1995. Kaufman, C., Perlman, R., and Speciner, M. *Network Security: Private Communication in a Public World.* Upper Saddle River, NJ: Prentice Hall.

1996. Schneier, B. *Applied Cryptography: Protocols, Algorithms, and Source Code in C,* 2nd Ed. New York: John Wiley.

Edwin D. Reilly

PATTERN RECOGNITION

For articles on related subjects *see* ARTIFICIAL INTELLIGENCE; COMPUTER VISION; DATA MINING; IMAGE PROCESSING; NEURAL NETWORKS; OPTICAL CHARACTER RECOGNITION; and PERCEPTRON.

Pattern recognition is concerned with the classification or description by computer of objects, events, or other meaningful regularities in noisy or complex environments. As an area of computer science and engineering, pattern recognition is the study of concepts, algorithms, and implementations that provide artificial systems with a perceptual capability to put abstract objects, or patterns, into categories in a simple and reliable way. As a human experience, pattern recognition refers to a perceptual process in which patterns in any sensory modality (vision, hearing, touch, taste, or smell) or patterns in conceptual or logical thought processes are analyzed and recognized (or classified) as being familiar either in the sense of having been previously experienced or of being similar to or associated with a previous experience.

Motivation for the study of pattern recognition is threefold. First, it is a part of the broader field of *artificial intelligence*, which is concerned with techniques that enable computers to do things that seem

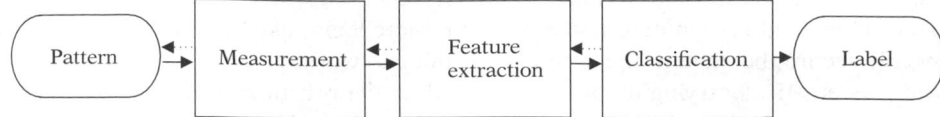

Figure 1. Stages in a pattern recognition system.

intelligent when done by people. Second, it is an important aspect of applying computers to solve problems that involve analysis and classification of measurements taken from physical processes. Third, pattern recognition techniques provide a unified framework for the study of a variety of techniques in mathematics and computer science that are individually useful. For example, pattern recognition algorithms are based on statistical, linguistic, geometrical, and graph-theoretic concepts, and data structures (*q.v.*) issues for pattern representation encompass a spectrum extending from the simple concept of a vector to knotty questions concerning knowledge representation (*q.v.*).

The major applications of pattern recognition fall into three categories: (1) patterns in images (spatial patterns); (2) patterns in time (temporal patterns); and (3) patterns in more abstract data environments. The most important image processing applications are optical character recognition (OCR) for systems ranging from bank check processing to reading machines for the blind, industrial robot vision, and unmanned planetary exploration systems; biomedical analyses, such as automated cytology and computerized tomography (*q.v.*); and remote sensing applied to earth resources, meteorology, and military applications. Signal processing applications include speech recognition (*q.v.*), radar and sonar signal analysis, seismological monitoring, and medical waveform analysis, as in electrocardiography (EKG) and electroencephalography (EEG).

Terminology

The process of a general pattern recognition system is shown in Fig. 1. In observing a pattern, *measurements* of an object are made that directly or indirectly reflect attributes of the object that distinguish it from other objects. *Features* are functions of the measurements intended to recover the defining attributes. The extracted features are used by a *classification procedure* to give a class assignment to the object. Since the overall process is one of reducing the pattern data in stages, pattern recognition may also be viewed as an information-reducing process.

As an example, let us consider the recognition of handprinted characters on a page. The measurement process consists of optically scanning a region of the paper where the character (i.e. pattern) is written so as to

represent the pattern as a two-dimensional array whose values represent shades of gray from white to black. A second stage of the measurement process is concerned with enhancing the data prior to analysis and includes operations such as smoothing to reduce noise (irrelevant variations), sharpening to enhance edges, segmentation of the image into separate characters, and transformations to allow for variations in size, position, and orientation of the characters to be recognized. The feature extraction stage searches for features in the input, *global* features such as the number of holes in the character, the number of concavities in its outer contour, or the relative protrusion of character extremities, or *local* features such as the relative positions of line-endings, line crossovers, and corners. The final classification stage identifies each input character by considering the detected features. In practice, it is difficult to choose a set of features that reliably distinguishes handwritten characters (see for example, Fig. 2, in which the letters H and A are represented almost identically). Thus, the later phases may need to reinvoke earlier phases to re-examine ancillary (often contextual) evidence to help in the development of a particular interpretation. The *top-down* flow of control information (as opposed to the *bottom-up* flow of pattern information), necessary to use *context*, is represented by dotted lines in the process organization diagram of Fig. 1.

Class Definitions

A *class* is a group or set of patterns that are similar or equivalent in some sense. Class definitions are based on the intuitive notion that members of a class share some common properties or attributes. To represent a class, either a prototype (an ideal form on which all member patterns are based, the class "essence") or a set of samples must be known. A philosophical distinction may be made between *canonical*, or natural, pattern classes, such as animal species and diseases, and *conventional*, or symbolic, pattern classes, such as letters

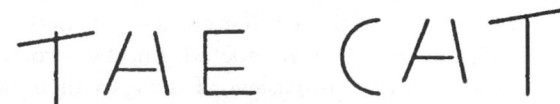

Figure 2. Identical patterns in different contexts have different meanings; most people read the same patterns as "H" in the first word and "A" in the second.

and musical notes. The feature selection process attempts to recover the pattern attributes characteristic of each class. For canonical classes, appropriate features may be inferred from an understanding of the natural phenomenon. For conventional classes, the features may be specified by the class definition, although, as in the case of hand-printed characters, they may not be explicit.

Depending on the nature of the data analysis problem, the various classes may or may not be distinguished *a priori*. In the first case, representative samples are available for each class and the problem is one of classification of subsequently observed patterns. In the second case, referred to as the *clustering problem*, the data consists of an unlabeled collection of samples and the analytic task is the detection and description of naturally occurring groups or clusters in the data. Additional samples may then be classified into the empirically established groups.

Approaches to Pattern Classification

Ultimately, the process of pattern recognition consists of assigning a pattern to a class. The assignment is made by a classification algorithm (or *classifier*), based on the features extracted and the relationships among the features. Since members of a class are equivalent or similar inasmuch as they share defining attributes, the measurement of similarity, either explicitly or implicitly, is central to any classifier. Depending on the features extracted—which, in turn, depend on the data environment, variability within classes, and defined attributes—classifiers are derived by using quite different approaches.

In the statistical approach, patterns are represented by points in a multidimensional *feature space*. Each component of the feature space is a measurement or feature value, which is a random variable reflecting the inherent variability within and between classes. A classifier partitions the feature space into regions associated with each class, labeling an observed pattern according to the class region into which it falls. The partition is based on the multivariate probability distribution of each class, as specified by a sample set of patterns (e.g. means, covariance matrices) or, identically, the joint probability density function of the random variable features. The classification algorithm commonly employs generalized distance measures in n-dimensional feature space.

Although many problems are successfully dealt with using the statistical approach, it is often more appropriate to represent patterns explicitly in terms of relationships among features other than statistical covariance. In such cases, the structure or arrangement of components or primitive elements is taken as the defining attribute of the pattern. The *structural* approach to pattern recognition represents patterns in terms of *primitives* and *relations* among primitives in order to describe pattern structure explicitly. Computer vision, where the primitives are simple objects and the relations are spatial, is an application that uses this approach. Most commonly, the concepts of formal languages (*q.v.*) are employed to represent pattern structure in terms of rules of syntax and classes in terms of grammars and their associated languages. An observed pattern is assigned to the class whose grammar allows a successful parsing.

Statistical Pattern Recognition

In the statistical approach to pattern recognition, a pattern that is represented by a set of m measurements is thought of as a point **p** in an m-dimensional measurement space. Feature extraction is expressed as a transformation that maps **p** into a point **x** in an n-dimensional feature space; it may be viewed pragmatically as a process that reduces pattern space dimensionally and consequently simplifies the classification task. The classifier then assigns **x** to a class by mans of a decision function $d(\mathbf{x})$, which, in effect, is a method of partitioning the feature space into territories corresponding to different classes. The performance of the classifier is measured by an objective function, which is usually the probability of error (misclassification).

An example of feature space partitioning used to classify a data set of 50 characters into five different classes $\{C, E, T, X, Y\}$ is illustrated in Fig. 3. The decision functions for each class are measures of distance from the classes (see geometric classifiers, below), and the dotted lines are equidistant from the classes they separate. The positions of some characters in the feature space show that two features are not enough to separate the characters with an acceptably low misclassification probability.

If we considered the entire alphabet (i.e. all 26 characters), samples of different character classes may not be clustered equally close about class centers and features may interact with each other, producing ellipsoidal rather than spherical distributions.

We will discuss a variety of mathematical techniques that have been developed to handle such problems. The techniques themselves are conveniently grouped into three categories: feature extraction methods, classification methods, and clustering methods.

FEATURE EXTRACTION

On a conceptual level, feature extraction is concerned with recovering the defining attributes obscured by imperfect measurements. Ideally, the feature extraction transformation would be derived according to a

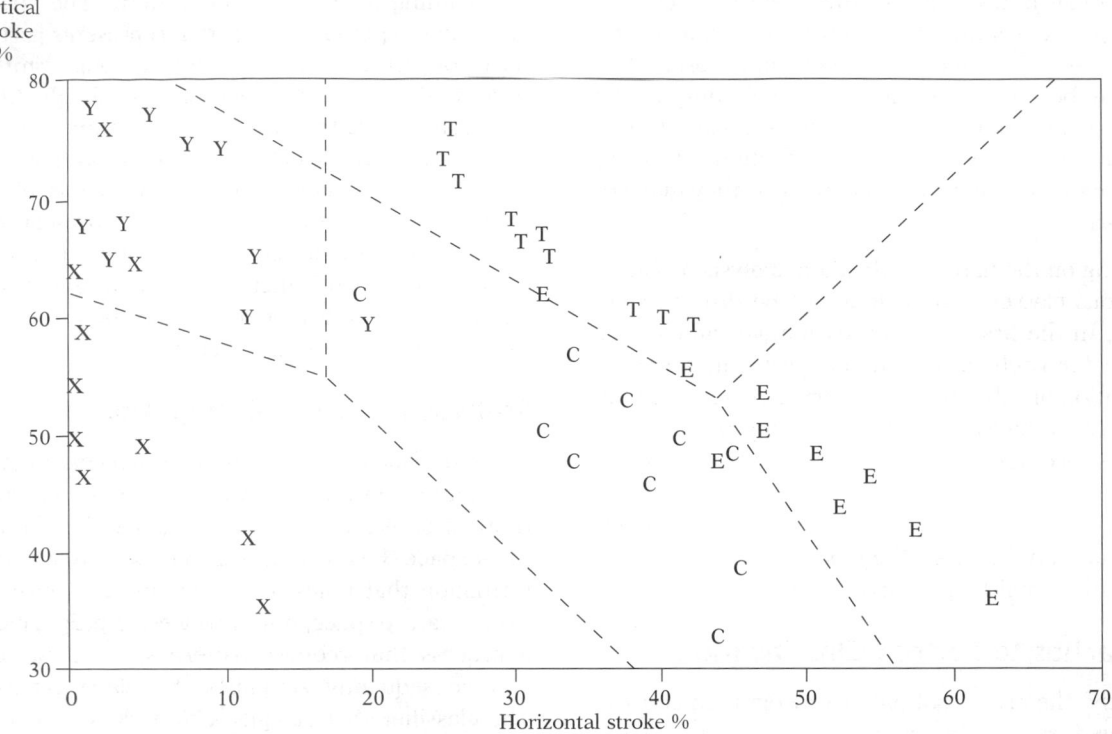

Figure 3. Classes are separated into categories by partitioning the feature space. The data set consists of 50 printed characters in different fonts from five different classes $\{C, E, T, X, Y\}$. The feature space represents the percentage of black pixels in the horizontal and vertical strokes.

minimum probability of error (or misclassification) criterion, but in most practical situations this approach is not possible. Consequently, feature extraction schemes generally attempt to choose features that minimize within-class variability; i.e. find a feature space in which the samples within each class are as close together as possible while insuring that the different class sets are well separated. Other feature selection criteria include measures of correlation between features (different features should be uncorrelated, to minimize redundancy in the representation object) and information theoretic measures relating features to classes. The mathematical transformation of the measurements obtained using such criteria generally results in features that are functions of the original measurements and that may or may not have physical interpretations. In general, if the system's performance in the resulting feature space is ultimately inadequate, additional measures and features must be sought.

CLASSIFICATION

On the basis of their implementations, statistical pattern classifiers may be distinguished as being *probabilistic*, *geometric*, *discriminant-based* or *conceptual*. Other elaborations also exist. The first of these uses *context* in making decisions. We shall discuss this

technique in greater detail in a subsequent section. A second elaboration is based on *sequential decision theory*, which applies to a situation in which successive features are measured only as necessary, to achieve a desired expected probability of error. Finally, the theory of *fuzzy sets* (*see* FUZZY LOGIC) has been applied in classification problems where a nonexclusive assignment of patterns to classes is desired. If the classes do not have precisely defined criteria of membership (e.g. tall people, beautiful women, numbers much greater than one), the concept of a membership function with value between 0 and 1 is a useful characteristic. Rather than probabilistically assigning a pattern to one class or another, but not both simultaneously, a fuzzy classifier would provide the degree of membership of a pattern to each of the classes. One can usually find mathematically equivalent algorithms by using each approach.

Probabilistic classifiers are based on the principle that a pattern should be assigned to the class that is most probable, given the observed features; i.e. a point $\mathbf{x}$ of feature space is assigned to the class that maximizes the *a posteriori* probability $P(C_i|\mathbf{x})$ over the set of classes $\{C_i\}$. From the Bayesian theory of conditional probabilities, this is mathematically equivalent to assigning $\mathbf{x}$ to the class C_i that maximizes $p(\mathbf{x}|C_i) * P(C_i)$, where $p(\mathbf{x}|C_i)$ is called the *class-conditional probability* *density function* (it gives the probability that the pattern has value **x**, given that it is in the class C_i) and $P(C_i)$ is the probability of class C_i before the pattern is observed (the *a priori* probability). Labeled samples representative of each class are generally used to determine the $p(\mathbf{x}|C_i)$ and $P(C_i)$ values necessary to implement such a classifier. In some cases, the functions $p(\mathbf{x}|C_i)$ may be assumed to have a particular form (normal, binomial, etc.) and samples are used to estimate their parameters (mean, covariance, etc.). More often, the forms of $p(\mathbf{x}|C_i)$ are unknown, in which case nonparametric estimation techniques are used that are usually based on computing the sample histogram. In either case, the estimates are used in the classifier with a result that is optimum to the extent to which the estimates are accurate.

Geometric classifiers are based on a kind of template matching in which the observed pattern is compared to *templates* (or *prototypes*) that represent each class and are classified according to the best match (or minimum mismatch). The distance between pattern **x** and the prototype of class C_i is computed by a *metric function* $d(\mathbf{x}, C_i)$ and **x** is assigned to the class that minimizes this function. $d(\mathbf{x}, C_i) = (\mathbf{x} - \mathbf{m}_i)^T S_i^{-1}(\mathbf{x} - \mathbf{m}_i)$, where $\mathbf{m}_i$ and S_i are the mean and covariance matrix of class C_i.

A metric that is useful for patterns having binary valued features is the *Hamming distance*—the number of features in which the observed pattern differs from the prototype of class C_i. A character recognition example using three prototypes and the Hamming distance measure is shown in Fig. 4.

Variations of the template matching scheme can be obtained by defining a similarity measure instead of a distance measure. For example, if n_{ij} is the number of pixels having values i and j in the template and pattern, then in a pattern of 0s and 1s, $n_{11}/(n_{11} + n_{01})$ is the ratio of the number of correct matches of 1s to the number of 1s in the unknown target pattern. Thus, the procedure ignores matches of 0s and does not penalize incorrect matches. Measures are often constructed by weighting individual matches and mismatches according to their statistical separability. A metric that is commonly used for patterns with continuous (or real) valued features is the Euclidean distance.

In addition to specifying the metric distance, it is necessary to choose a prototype pattern for each class carefully. Using the class means as a prototype results in a classifier that is well-suited for classes that are spherically distributed about the mean in the feature space. By using the member of C_i nearest to **x** as the prototype, the *nearest neighbor* rule tends to provide for more general (i.e. nonspherical) distributions.

Discriminant function classifiers associate a function $f_i(\mathbf{x})$ with class C_i and assign **x** to the class that has the maximum discriminant function value. In the case where the classes are *linearly separable* (i.e. there is a linear decision function that is greater than zero for all samples in one class and less than zero for all samples in the other class) in the chosen feature space, an iterative algorithm known as the *perceptron* (*q.v.*) finitely converges to discriminant functions that correctly classify all given samples. For linearly nonseparable classes, various criterion functions can be used

Templates

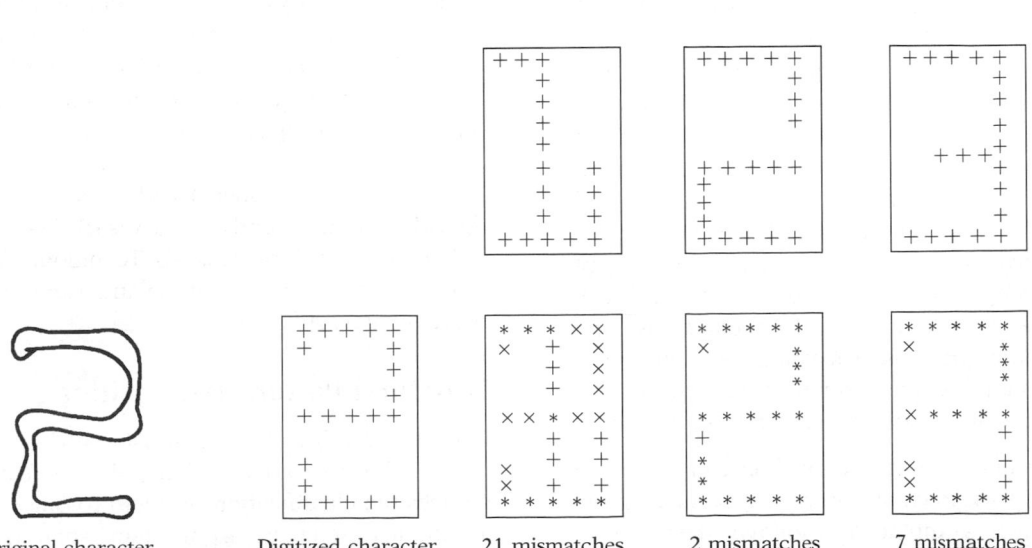

Original character   Digitized character   21 mismatches   2 mismatches   7 mismatches

Figure 4. Template matching using the Hamming distance. All points of the digitized character (i.e. features) are compared with corresponding points in each template. If the two are not the same (i.e. both 0 or both 1), a mismatch, or distance 1, is counted. Here, the second template is selected as a result of minimum mismatch ($\times$: mismatch; $*$: match).

in gradient descent procedures to obtain discriminant functions. As with geometric classifiers, some of the discriminant function classifiers are equivalent to probabilistic classifiers.

For instance, polynomial discriminant functions can be adopted to perform character recognition. Typically, a character is represented as a feature vetor $\mathbf{x}$. The binary character image is first mapped into an $n \times n$ binary array. The image is then represented by an $n^2 = N$-element column vector $\mathbf{v} = (v_1, v_2, \ldots, v_N)^t$. Using the components of $\mathbf{v}$ as linear terms and products of the components as polynomial terms, an M-element polynomial feature vector $\mathbf{x}$ is constructed by a predefined mapping $\mathbf{x} = p(\mathbf{v})$. Generally, the components of $\mathbf{x}$ are of degree two or less, which results in a quadratic feature vector of the form,

$$\mathbf{x} = (x_1, x_2, \ldots, x_M)^t$$
$$= (1, v_1, v_2, \ldots, v_N, v_1 v_2, \ldots, v_{N-1} v_N)^t.$$

Not all pixel pairs are typically used, and M tends to be far smaller than $(1 + N(N + 1)/2)$.

Given K classes to be discriminated, based on the polynomial feature vector $\mathbf{x}$, a K-dimensional discriminant vector $\mathbf{d} = (d_1, \ldots, d_K)$ is formed. Each of the K discriminant functions d_i is defined to be a linear expression in the components of $\mathbf{x}$,

$$d_i = a_{i1} x_1 + \cdots + a_{iM} x_M \qquad i = 1, \ldots, K$$

and thus a quadratic polynomial expression in the components of $\mathbf{v}$. The discriminant vector $\mathbf{d} = (d_1, \ldots, d_K)^t$ can therefore be written as $\mathbf{d} = A^t \mathbf{x}$, where A is an $M \times K$ matrix, whose ith column, $i = 1, \ldots, K$, consists of the elements $a_{i1}, \ldots, a_{iM}$.

Conceptual processing. With reference to character recognition, contextual processing techniques use knowledge at the word level to correct errors in character recognition. These methods use information about other characters that have been recognized in a word, as well as knowledge about the text in which the word occurs to carry out the task. Typically, the knowledge about the text takes the form of a dictionary (a list of words that occur in the text). For example, character recognition may not be able to distinguish reliably between a u and v in the second position of *qXote*. A contextual postprocessing technique would determine that u is correct, since it is very unlikely that *qvote* would be in the English language dictionary.

The problem of assigning a set of character images to a symbol string is known as compound decision theory. The problem is formulated as follows. The observed sequence of patterns (or vectors with feature elements) is $\mathbf{X} = (x_1, \ldots, x_m)$. Each pattern x_i is to be assigned to one symbol (character class) in the set $\mathbf{L} = \{L_1, L_2, \ldots, L_r\}$. Since there are r possible choices for each pattern, there are r^m possible assignments for $\mathbf{X}$. The goal is to choose that assignment $\mathbf{W}_j = (w_{j1}, \ldots, w_{jm})$, $w_{ji} \in \mathbf{L}$ that has the maximum probability over all possible assignments $j = 1, \ldots, r^m$.

Estimating all joint probabilities in order to perform the exact probability computation is impractical. One simplifying assumption is to assume that a character icon string arises from a Markov source. Assuming a first-order Markov source, the task of determining the joint probability of a given word reduces to a product involving first-order transitional probabilities between letters and the class-conditional (or confusion) probabilities associated with each pattern. The word with the highest probability is computed efficiently by a method known as the Viterbi algorithm; it involves $(m - 1)r^2$ computations instead of r^m computations.

CLUSTERING

Both feature extraction and classification depend critically on the nature of the *a priori* information about the classes with which the system is to deal. An important class of problems deals with unlabeled data sets in which class definitions must be determined empirically. Clustering algorithms are concerned with establishing any empirical classes—sets of samples that are more similar to each other than to patterns outside the set—that are present in the given set of unlabeled samples.

Simpler clustering algorithms establish clusters on the basis of the similarity of (distance between) individual samples, while more complex schemes employ formal criteria, such as measures of within and between cluster scatter (variability) in iterative optimization algorithms. In the first category are the hierarchical clustering algorithms, such as the *nearest neighbor algorithm*, in which clusters are merged (or split) in a hierarchical fashion according to the proximity of the nearest neighbors, and graph-theoretic algorithms that relate clusters with connected subgraphs, patterns with nodes, and similarities (distances) with edges. A well-known algorithm of the second category is ISODATA (Iterative Self-Organizing Data Analysis Technique Algorithm), which combines scatter criteria and user intuition in an effective interactive scheme.

Structural Pattern Recognition

Interpreting a list of characteristic attributes of a pattern as the coordinates of a point in feature space reduces the classification problem to one of partitioning the feature space. In problems such as computer vision, the patterns are quite complex and the number of features required is often very large. Thus, the idea of using the structural information that describes each

 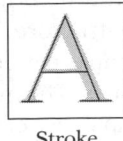   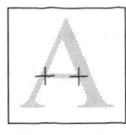 

| Image | Stroke | Concavity | Hole | Cross point | End point |

Figure 5. Structural features of stroke, concavity, hole, cross points, and end points can be used as the dimensions of a feature space to classify characters; the locations of these features for "A" are illustrated.

pattern to simplify its representation is attractive. The basic idea of the structural approach is to describe complex patterns in terms of a composition of simpler patterns. Another approach is to extract structural features and represent them as a feature vector and use statistically determined discriminant functions.

When asked to describe an alphanumeric character, people are most likely to use structural features (Fig. 5). For example, an upper case 'A' has two straight lines (strokes) meeting with a sharp point (end point) at the top, and a third line crossing the two at approximately their midpoint (cross points), creating a gap in the

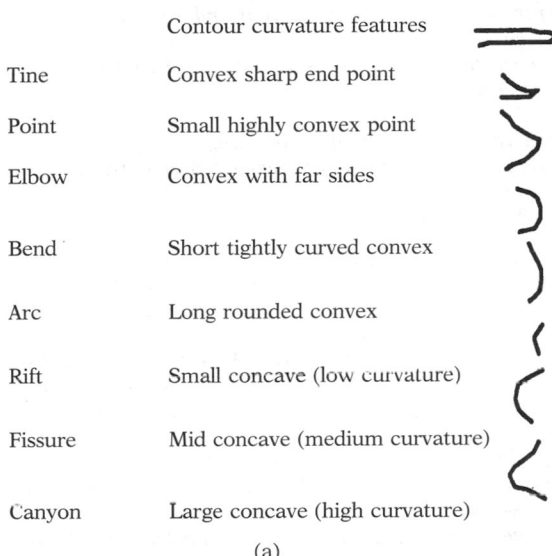

Contour curvature features

Tine	Convex sharp end point
Point	Small highly convex point
Elbow	Convex with far sides
Bend	Short tightly curved convex
Arc	Long rounded convex
Rift	Small concave (low curvature)
Fissure	Mid concave (medium curvature)
Canyon	Large concave (high curvature)

(a)

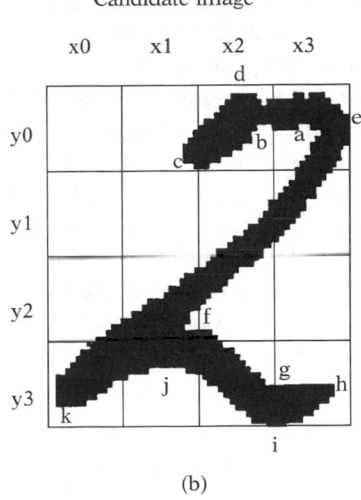

Candidate image

(b)

Features extracted

a = Canyon, West at (x3, y0)
b = Rift, South at (x2, y0)
c = Tine, West at (x1, y0)
d = Arc, North-West at (x2, y0)
e = Bend, North-East at (x3, y0)
f = Canyon, East at (x1, y2)
g = Rift, North at (x3, y3)
h = Tine, east at (x3, y3)
i = Arc, South at (x2, y3)
j = Fissure, South at (x1, y3)
k = Tine, South-West at (x0, y3)

(c)

Symbolic Description of a "2"

1: Canyon @ x1x2x3y0y1 @ SE | S | SW | W
2: Tine @ x0x1x2y0y1 @ S | SW | W | NW
3: Elbow | Bend | Arc @ x2x3y0y1 @ N | NE | E
4: Fissure | Canyon @ x0x1x2x3y2y3 @ N | NE | E | SE
5: Tine @ x0x1x2x3y2y3 @ N | NE | E | SE | S
6: Tine @ x0x1x2x3y2y3 @ SW | W | NW

(d)

Feature—rule correspondence

Feature	Rule
a	1
c	2
e	3
f	4
h	5
k	6

(e)

Figure 6. Contour feature analysis: (a) contour features, (b) digitized image, (c) extracted features, (d) rules in database that need to be satisfied for a digit 2, and (e) extracted features that match the size rules.

upper part (hole). The basis of any structural technique is the representation of the pattern with a set of feature primitives that are able to describe all encountered patterns and to discriminate between them.

An example of structural approaches to numeric patterns is illustrated in Fig. 6. It is based on the curvatures around the inner and outer contours of the pattern. The primitive feature set has eight features: five concave features (three simple arc-like structures of varying curvature and two end points) and three convex features of varying curvature (Fig. 6a). Associated with each feature is a direction quantized to eight compass points, and the location quantized to a 4 × 4 Cartesian grid with the origin at the upper left (Fig. 6b, c). The contour of the figure is first represented in the form of a chain-code; the chain code is an eight-direction code following the contour such that a change of one unit in the positive direction of the chain code represents a 45° turn in the positive direction and a negative change of one unit represents a 45° turn in the other direction. The chain code contour trace is converted to a curvature trace around the figure. The relative degree of curvature for each point along the original image is calculated. Local variations and noise are filtered by looking at the preceding and following points when calculating the curvature at the current point. Points along the image contour where the degree of curvature changes are the places where the features are defined.

A rule base is used to classify the extracted feature string. The rule base is designed as a decision tree, where each successive branch narrows down the possible candidates that can match the feature string. The rules are generalized to have a one-to-many relationship. Each class can be fully covered by just a few rules (Fig. 6d, e).

In the case where patterns consist of (one-dimensional) waveforms or (two-dimensional) images of flat objects, the structure of patterns can usually be described in a manner analogous to the syntax of languages. Patterns are specified as being hierarchically built up from subpatterns in various ways of composition by a grammar. In this approach, also called the *syntactic approach*, the important element is the pattern description language that provides the structural description of patterns in terms of a set of pattern primitives (or *morphs*) and their composition operations defined by the grammar.

In the syntactic approach, after each primitive within a pattern is identified in the feature extraction stage, classification is accomplished by analyzing syntax (or parsing) of the sentence describing the given pattern to determine whether or not it is syntactically correct with respect to the specified grammar. Syntax analysis produces a structural description of the given pattern in the form of a tree structure. The grammar itself may be inferred from sample patterns by using *grammatical inference* techniques. The most attractive aspect of this approach is its capability of using the recursive nature of a grammar to express in a very compact way some basic structural characteristics of infinite sentences. Again, for this approach to be practical, recognition of the simple pattern primitives and their relationships, as represented by the composition operations, is essential.

Bibliography

Journals that regularly contain research papers in pattern recognition include:

IEEE Transactions on Pattern Analysis and Machine Intelligence
IEEE Transactions on Acoustics, Speech and Signal Processing
Pattern Recognition
Artificial Intelligence
Computer Graphics and Image Processing
International Journal of Pattern Recognition and Artificial Intelligence
Machine Vision and Applications

1973. Duda, R. O., and Hart, P. E. *Pattern Classification and Scene Analysis.* New York: John Wiley. (A classic in the field. Discusses both statistical and structural approaches in depth up to its time of publication.)

1978. Gonzalez, R. C., and Thomson, M. G. *Syntactic Pattern Recognition.* Reading, MA: Addison-Wesley. (Describes the application of formal language and automata theory to the description of patterns.)

1980. Lea, W. A. (ed.) *Trends in Speech Recognition.* Upper Saddle River, NJ: Prentice Hall. (Overviews of approaches to speech recognition taken by different research groups.)

1981. Bezdek, J. C. *Pattern Recognition with Fuzzy Objective Function Algorithms.* New York: Plenum. (Models of feature selection, clustering, and classification based on fuzzy set theory are discussed.)

1982. Fu, K. S. *Syntactic Pattern Recognition and Applications.* Upper Saddle River, NJ: Prentice Hall. (Syntactic methods applied to the recognition of patterns in a variety of applications.)

1982. Devijver, P. A., and Kittler, J. *Pattern Recognition: A Statistical Approach.* Upper Saddle River, NJ: Prentice Hall. (A collection of papers on statistical methods.)

1984. Srihari, S. N. *Computer Text Recognition and Error Correction.* Silver Spring, MD: IEEE Computer Society Press. (A tutorial, including landmark papers, in contextual character recognition.)

1986. Devijver, P. A., and Kittler, J. *Pattern Recognition Theory and Applications.* Berlin: Springer-Verlag. (A collection of papers representing major areas of recognition.)

1988. Simon, J. C. *From Pixels to Features.* New York: North-Holland. (A collection of papers dealing with implementation of pattern recognition systems and underlying concepts.)

1993. Rabiner, L., and Juang, B.-H. *Fundamentals of Speech Recognition.* Upper Saddle River, NJ: Prentice Hall. (Describes principles and underlying theory of speech recognition.)

1996. Theodoridis, S., and Koutroumbas, K. *Pattern Recognition.* New York: Academic Press.

S. N. Srihari and V. Govindaraju

PDA

See PORTABLE COMPUTERS.

PERCEPTRON

For articles on related subjects *see* NEURAL NETWORKS; and PATTERN RECOGNITION.

In 1957 the psychologist Frank Rosenblatt proposed "The Perceptron: a perceiving and recognizing automaton" as a class of artificial nerve nets, embodying aspects of the brain and receptors of biological systems. Fig. 1 shows the network of the Mark 1 Perceptron. Later, Rosenblatt protested that the term *perceptron*, originally intended as a generic name for a variety of theoretical nerve nets, was actually associated with a very specific piece of hardware (Rosenblatt, 1962). The basic building block of a perceptron is an element that accepts a number of inputs x_i, $i = 1, \ldots, N$, and computes a weighted sum of these inputs where, for each input, its fixed weight ω can be only $+1$ or -1. The sum is then compared with a threshold θ, and an output y is produced that is either 0 or 1, depending on whether or not the sum exceeds the threshold. In other words,

$$y = \begin{cases} 1 & \text{if } (\sum_{i=1}^{N} \omega_i x_i) \geq \theta \\ 0 & \text{if } (\sum_{i=1}^{N} \omega_i x_i) < \theta \end{cases}$$

A perceptron is a signal transmission network consisting of sensory units (S units), association units (A units), and output or response units (R units). The receptor of the perceptron is analogous to the retina of the eye and is made of an array of sensory elements (photocells). Depending on whether or not an S-unit is excited, it produces a binary output. A randomly selected set of retinal cells is connected to the next level of the network, the A units. Each A unit behaves like the basic building block discussed above, where the $+1$, -1 weights for the inputs to each A unit are randomly assigned. The threshold for all A units is the same.

The binary output y_k of the kth A unit ($k = 1, \ldots, m$) is multiplied by a weight a_k, and a sum of all m weighted outputs is formed in a summation unit that is the same as the basic building blocks with all weights equal to $+1$. Each weight a_k is allowed to be positive, zero, or negative, and may change independently of other weights. The output of the perceptron is again binary, depending on a threshold that is normally set at 0. The binary values of the output are used to distinguish two classes of patterns that may be presented to the retina of a perceptron. The design of a perceptron to distinguish between two given sets of patterns involves adjusting the weights a_k, $k = 1, \ldots, m$, and the threshold θ.

Rosenblatt (1962) proposed a number of variations of the following procedure for "training" perceptrons. The set of given patterns of known classification are presented sequentially to the retina, with the complete set being repeated as often as needed.

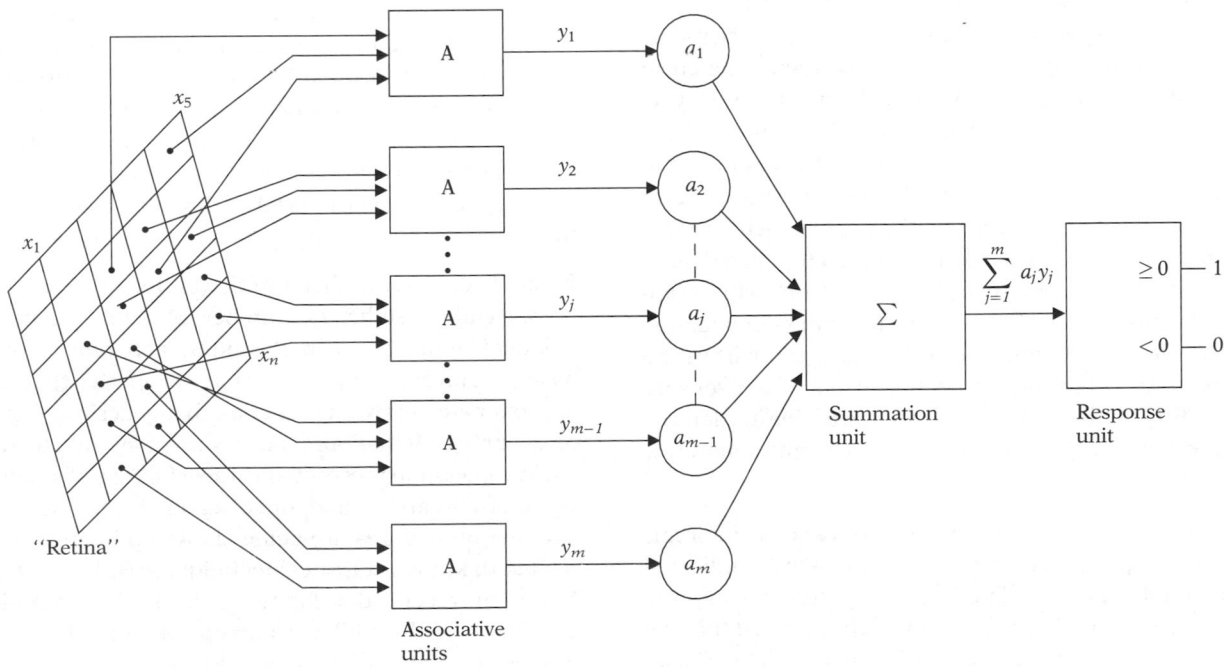

Figure 1. Mark 1 Perceptron structure.

The output of the perceptron is monitored to determine whether a pattern is correctly classified. If not, the weights are adjusted according to the following "error correction" procedure: if the nth pattern was misclassified, the new value $a_k(n+1)$ for the kth weight is calculated as

$$a_k(n+1) = a_k(n) + y_k(n) \times \delta(n),$$

where $\delta(n)$ is 1 if the nth pattern is from class 1 and $\delta(n)$ is -1 if the nth pattern is from class 2. No adjustment to the weight is made if a pattern is correctly classified.

If there exists a set of weights such that all patterns can be correctly classified, the pattern classes are said to be linearly separable. It was conjectured by Rosenblatt that, when the pattern classes are linearly separable, the error correction "learning" procedure will converge to a set of weights that correctly classifies all the patterns. Many proofs of this perceptron convergence theorem were subsequently derived, the shortest by A. J. Novikoff. Subsequent contributions related the simple perceptron to statistical linear discriminant functions and related the error-correction learning algorithm to gradient-descent procedures and to stochastic approximation methods that were originally developed for finding the zeros and extremes of unknown regression functions (see e.g. Kanal, 1962).

The simple perceptron described is a series-coupled perceptron with feed-forward connections only from S units to A units and A units to the single R unit. The weights a_k, the only adaptive elements in this network, are evaluated directly in terms of the output error. This is sometimes referred to as a *single-layer perceptron*. There is no layer of "hidden" elements—i.e. elements for which the adjustment is only indirectly related to the output error. A perceptron with one or more layers of hidden elements is termed a *multilayer perceptron*. Rosenblatt investigated *cross-coupled perceptrons* in which connections join units of the same type, and also investigated *multilayer back-coupled perceptrons*, which have feedback paths from units located near the output. For series-coupled perceptrons with multiple R units, Rosenblatt proposed a "back-propagating error correction" procedure that used error from the R units to propagate correction back to the sensory end. But neither he nor others were able to demonstrate a convergent procedure for training multilayer perceptrons.

Minsky and Papert (1969) proved various theorems about simple perceptrons, some of which indicated their limited pattern-classification and function approximating capabilities. For example, they proved that the single layer perceptron could not implement the Exclusive OR logical function (see BOOLEAN ALGEBRA) and

several other such predicates. Later, many who wrote on Artificial Neural Networks (ANN) would blame this book by Minsky and Papert for greatly dampening interest and leading to a demise of funding for research on ANNs. The section on "Alternate Realities" in Kanal (1992) details why the blame is misplaced. As noted there, by 1962 many researchers had moved on from perceptron-type learning machines to statistical and syntactic procedures for pattern recognition. The demise of funding for perceptron-type networks should be blamed on the inadequate technology and training algorithms available for multilayer perceptrons and the premature, overblown results promised the funding agencies.

Minsky and Papert's results did not apply to multilayer perceptrons. Research on ANNs, biologically motivated automata, and adaptive systems continued in the 1970s in Europe, Japan, the Soviet Union and the USA, but without the frenzied excitement of previous years. In a 1974 Harvard University dissertation, Paul Werbos presented a general convergence procedure for adaptively adjusting the weights of a differentiable nonlinear system so as to learn a functional relationship between the inputs and outputs of the system. The procedure calculates the derivatives of some function of the outputs, with respect to all inputs and weights or parameters of the system, working backwards from outputs to inputs. However, this work by Werbos went essentially unnoticed, until a few years after Rumelhart, Hinton, and Williams independently popularized a special case of the general method to adjust adaptively the weights of a multilayer, feedforward perceptron for pattern classification applications when learning samples are available. This algorithm, which adapts the weights using gradient descent, is known as error backpropagation or just *backpropagation*. It propagates derivatives from the output layer through each intermediate layer of the multilayer perceptron network. The resurgence of work on multilayer perceptrons and their applications in the 1980s is directly attributable to this convergent backpropagation algorithm.

It has been shown that multilayer feedforward networks with a sufficient number of intermediate or "hidden" units between the input and output units have a "universal approximation" property: they can approximate nearly any function to any desired degree of accuracy. It has also been shown by White that backpropagation is essentially a special case of stochastic approximation, and once again neural network learning procedures are being shown to be intimately related to known statistical techniques (Bishop, 1995). More on recent developments in backpropagation algorithms and multilayer perceptrons may be found in Werbos (1994), Chauvin and Rumelhart (1995), and Mehrotra *et al.* (1997).

Bibliography

1962. Rosenblatt, F. *Principles of Neurodynamics.* New York: Spartan Books.

1962. Kanal, L. "Evaluation of a Class of Pattern-Recognition Networks," in *Biological Prototypes and Synthetic Systems* (eds. E. E. Bernard and M. R. Kare), 261–269. New York: Plenum Press.

1969. Minsky, M., and Papert, S. *Perceptrons.* Cambridge, MA: MIT Press.

1992. Kanal, L. N. "On Pattern, Categories, and Alternate Realities," 1992 K.S. Fu award talk at IAPR, The Hague, in *Pattern Recognition Letters,* **14**, 241–255.

1994. Werbos, P. *The Roots of Backpropagation: From Ordered Derivatives to Neural Networks and Political Forecasting.* New York: John Wiley.

1995. Chauvin, Y., and Rumelhart, D. E. (eds.) *Backpropagation: Theory, Architectures, and Applications.* Mahwah, NJ: Lawrence Erlbaum Associates.

1995. Bishop, C. M. *Neural Networks and Pattern Recognition.* Oxford: Oxford University Press.

1997. Mehrotra, K., Mohan, C. K., and Ranka, S. *Elements of Artificial Neural Networks.* Cambridge, MA: MIT Press.

Laveen N. Kanal

PERFORMANCE MEASUREMENT AND EVALUATION

For articles on related subjects *see* ACCOUNTING SYSTEM, COMPUTER; BENCHMARKS; LAWS, COMPUTER; OPERATING SYSTEMS; OVERHEAD; QUEUEING THEORY; SCHEDULING ALGORITHMS; SIMULATION; SOFTWARE MONITOR; THROUGHPUT; and TIME SHARING.

The main purposes of the *measurement* and *evaluation* of computer systems are to:

1. Aid in the design of hardware and software.

2. Aid in the selection of a computer system.

3. Improve the performance of an existing system.

The first of these must use some type of model of the system being designed. The latter two may use actual measurements or models or some combination of the two.

Measurement and evaluation of computer system performance is difficult due to the complexity of the internal structure of computer systems and because of the difficulty of describing and predicting the workload. As shown in Fig. 1, a computer system is composed of subsystems, each of which can be viewed as a system with its own workload and performance. Total system performance is related to the performance of the subsystems, although the relationship can be complex.

Computer system and subsystem performance measures fall into three categories—*responsiveness*, *throughput*, and *cost*. The response time for interactive commands or the turnaround time for batch jobs are typical measures of responsiveness. Throughput is a measure of the computational work accomplished by the system per unit time. There is, however, no generally acceptable definition of a unit of computational work. Measures such as jobs per unit time or transactions per unit time become meaningful only when the resource requirements of these tasks are described; this is one aspect of the workload characterization problem. The cost of a computer system is the monetary amount required to buy or lease the system. Response and throughput characteristics have to be evaluated in terms of the cost of the system.

It is necessary to characterize the load on a system in order to make meaningful statements about its performance. One aspect of this problem is determining which characteristics of the load largely determine the performance measures of interest. Another is determining the values of the workload model parameters for a particular performance study and is particularly difficult if the system is not yet operational. But even with an operational system, the workload may vary with time, and the workload characteristics measured will depend on the measurement period chosen.

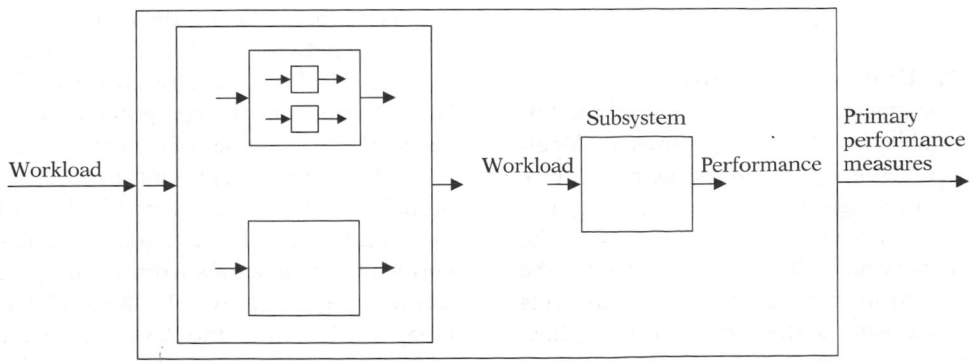

Figure 1. A computer system and its subsystems.

This article is concerned with the use of measurement data in computer system performance evaluation and not with the techniques for collecting the appropriate data. For some details on computer system monitoring methodologies, *see* SOFTWARE MONITOR.

Purposes of Performance Measurement and Evaluation

In this section, we provide some detail about the goals and constraints of the types of performance studies listed at the beginning of the article.

OPTIMIZATION

Computer systems offer a number of options in terms of hardware and software configuration that allow wide flexibility in tailoring a given installation to the workload and the desired performance characteristics. Some examples of the options are main memory size, number, type, and interconnection of channels (*q.v.*) and I/O devices; location of files on secondary storage; selection of nonresident portions of the operating system; and parameters for resource allocation algorithms. *System tuning* refers to the optimization of software-related options, and *reconfiguration* refers to the hardware aspects.

COMPUTER SYSTEM SELECTION

One of the considerations in the selection of a new system is the comparative cost/performance of the systems being considered. Judgments as to expected performance can be made informally based on the experience of others or the manufacturer's claims. More formal studies involve experimentation using benchmarks or system models. Prediction of the workload is an obvious problem if the system is being acquired for a new application. However, even upgrading of an existing system usually involves new functionality and features that have to be accounted for in the projected workload. Optimization is a part of the selection problem, since it is only reasonable to compare the cost/performance of systems that are tuned to the workload.

EVALUATION OF DESIGN ALTERNATIVES

The simulation or mathematical models used for this purpose require values for workload parameters. Measurements from currently operational systems can give some insight into the range of parameters that might be expected for the new system. Specific details of the workload can be very difficult to predict, since (1) the system may be used in many different environments and (2) the characteristics of the system can affect how it is used. However, general characteristics of program behavior have been isolated and found to be useful in system design. A good example is the characteristic of

locality of reference—the tendency of programs to execute in phases such that, in each phase, the program references only a restricted portion of its address space (a locality) or a subset of its pages. This is the basis for most memory management (*q.v.*) policies of paged memory systems (*see* VIRTUAL MEMORY).

Models of Computer System Performance

As a practical matter, when actual measurements cannot be made, we must use models. Two kinds of models need to be considered—system models and workload models.

SYSTEM MODELS

System models are simplifications of the real system that describe the relationship between workload measures and performance measures. The major types of system models are given below.

FUNCTIONAL MODELS

These describe the operation of the system. They may be written down (e.g. as a flowchart (*q.v.*) or as a Petri net—*q.v.*), but often they exist only in the mind of the performance analyst. This type of model is used informally to relate observed load and performance measures, or as a first step in developing a more formal model.

SIMULATION MODELS

Discrete event simulation is still the most commonly used technique in computer system modeling because of its flexibility in modeling details of the system. Its disadvantage is the cost of developing and then using a complex simulation (*see* SIMULATION).

STOCHASTIC MODELS

The range of applicability of queueing models has greatly expanded since the early 1970s, when queueing network models of computer systems began to be explored. A queueing network is a multiple resource model in which jobs "visit" the resources in a sequence that is probabilistically defined. A special case of a queueing network, called a *central server model*, is illustrated in Fig. 2. The resources in this example are labeled to indicate the computer system resources represented. The numbers P_i on the arcs from the CPU to the I/O devices represent, for each I/O device, the probability of that device being visited by a job after receiving CPU service. The goal is to obtain closed-form performance equations from which performance predictions may be easily calculated. However, there are many restrictions on the class of queueing networks for which closed-form performance equations are known. For example, priority scheduling and some other common scheduling disciplines are not permitted, and no

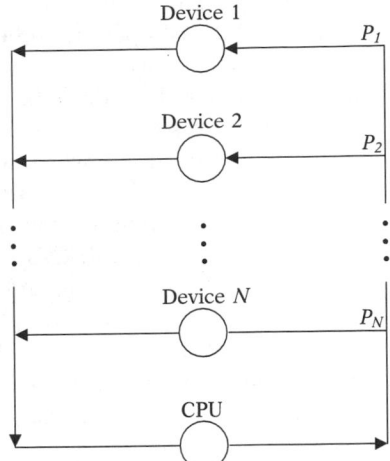

Figure 2. Central server queueing network model.

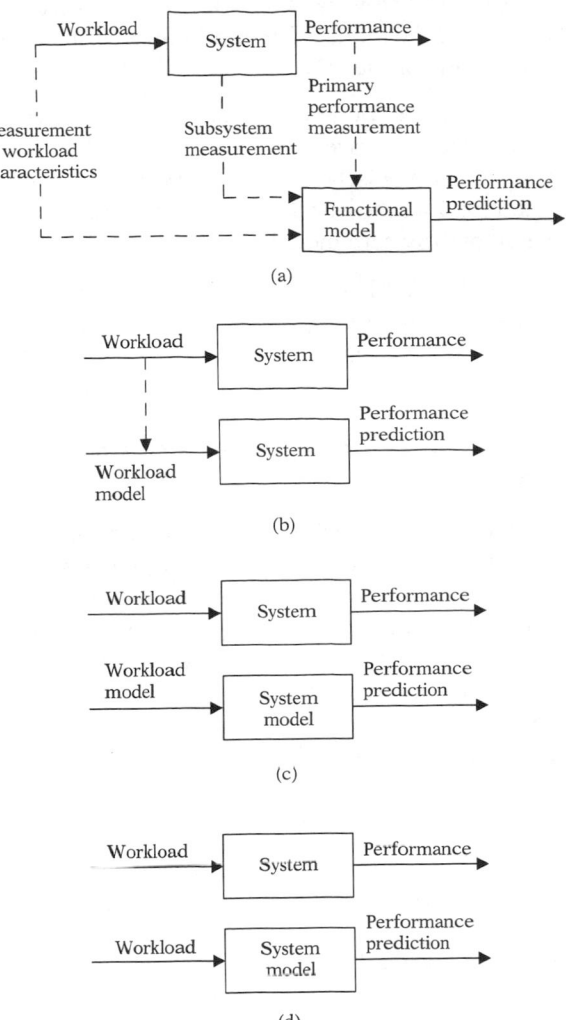

Figure 3. Uses of workload and system models.

limit can be set on the number of jobs at a resource or in a subset of the network (*see* QUEUEING THEORY).

Often analysis methods are combined. *Hierarchical decomposition* refers to a methodology in which subsystems are analyzed to obtain their performance characteristics, and these results are then used in a higher level analysis of the system. For example a stochastic model may be used for a subsystem and the results used in a simulation to represent the subsystem more efficiently.

WORKLOAD MODELS

An *executable* workload model is either a set of benchmark programs selected from the real workload or a set of synthetic programs that have been designed to exhibit certain resource utilization patterns expected in the real workload. These programs are directly executable on the system(s) being studied, and the performance of the system can be measured in actual operation. A *nonexecutable* workload model is a parameterization of the real workload that is to be used in conjunction with a simulation or stochastic system model. A nonexecutable workload model may be a sequence of events recorded from actual programs or a statistical model.

Use of Models

The various uses of workload models and system models are illustrated in Fig. 3. Fig. 3a indicates measurement of an operational system. A functional model is used to diagnose a performance problem and to hypothesize a remedy. Measurements taken after implementing the remedy are used to validate the hypothesis.

Fig. 3b illustrates the use of a workload model that is executable on the system under study. The workload model in this case consists of a set of programs or "scripts" of interactive user commands that are representative of the real workload (*see* BENCHMARK). This method is common in computer system selection in which the experiment is repeated for systems being considered and their performance compared.

In Fig. 3c, both a workload model and a system model are used. This is the case with simulation and analytic modeling. If a model is being developed for an operational system, measurement experiments are useful for calibrating the model. The workload parameters and performance are measured for a number of measurement periods. The model can be calibrated by driving it with the workload parameters from each measurement period and comparing the model performance predictions with the observed system performance in the corresponding period: the model is corrected or refined until the performance predictions are sufficiently close to the measured variables. Clearly, the calibration of a model gives some confidence in its ability to model the real situation. Confidence in the predictions of the model after alteration is a function of the magnitude of the alteration.

Fig. 3d illustrates the last possibility, which is using a real workload to drive a system model. This is not feasible to do precisely, but it can be approximated. For example, a real workload might be interpretively executed on a system model.

To illustrate how these techniques are actually used, we consider, first, the optimization of computer system performance, and then the prediction of system performance.

Optimization of Computer System Performance

Fig. 4 illustrates a model of major resources of a computer system and their interconnection. The resources explicitly shown are the CPU, the main memory (*q.v.*), channels (*q.v.*), and the secondary storage devices. The active set of tasks constitute those that have been allocated main memory and are competing for the CPU and I/O system resources. The box labeled "Task queues" represents tasks that are waiting for entry into the active set. This simple model can be used to describe the notion of a *system bottleneck*.

As a first-order approximation, assume that tasks submitted to the system require known mean amounts of service at each resource. For example, the mean CPU time required per task might be 20 seconds. (This is the total CPU time required, which is received in many "visits" to the CPU.) Then the throughput of the system cannot be greater than 1/20 tasks per second (or three tasks per minute), since the CPU, even if 100% busy,

cannot process tasks at a higher rate. This is the capacity of the CPU measured in tasks per unit time. Similar calculations can be made for the other resources. The throughput of the system is bounded above by the capacity of the individual resources. If one resource has a capacity that is significantly lower than that of any of the other resources, then the usual effect is that this resource has a relatively high utilization and a relatively long queue of tasks waiting for it. This resource is called a *bottleneck* or *limiting resource*, and is generally a major contributor to reduced throughput and poor responsiveness. The contrary situation, a balanced system, occurs when all resources have similar utilizations. Balanced resource utilization generally results in greater throughput, since there is greater concurrent utilization of resources (CPU and I/O).

Using the model of Fig. 4 and an appropriate workload model, *system profiles*, which are a set of measurements giving the utilization of the major system resources and the amount of overlap in CPU and I/O utilization, can be generated. These values might be simply given in table form, but are more easily interpretable if shown as a Gantt chart (Fig. 5). This data is useful in the exploratory phase of a performance optimization study to determine system bottlenecks, which then have to be studied in more detail. When considering the possible reasons for the observed resource utilizations, it is useful to consider the following factors:

1. System overhead.

2. The hardware characteristics of the resource.

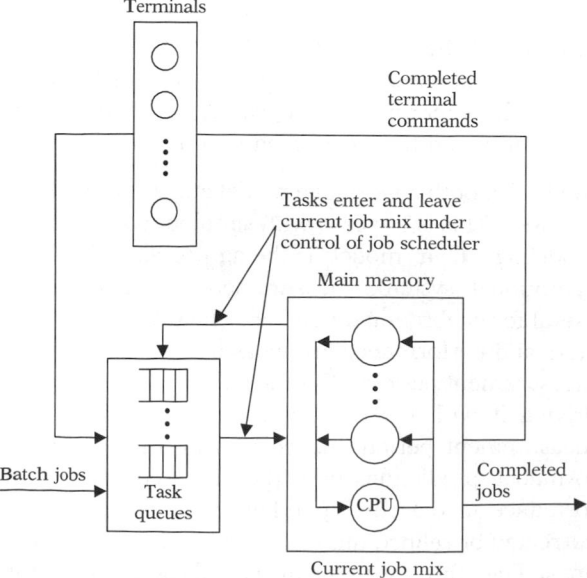

Figure 4. Simple computer system model.

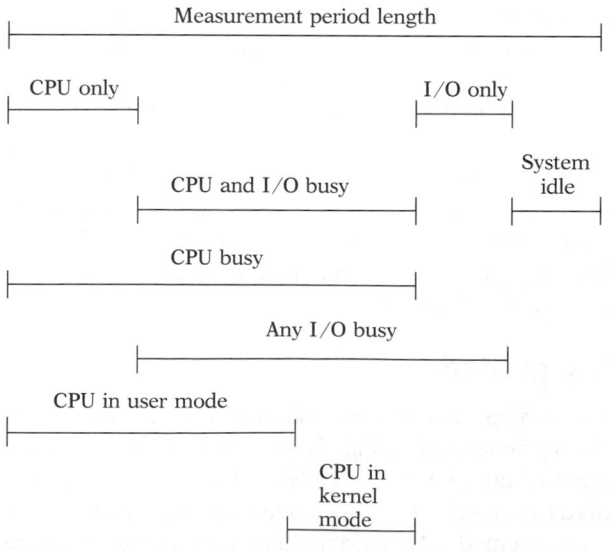

Figure 5. System profile shown as a Gantt chart. Each line represents a possible state of the system, and the length of each line corresponds to the total time the system was in that state during the measurement period.

3. Intrinsic resource requirements of the tasks.

4. The scheduling algorithm used to manage the resource.

5. Interactions among tasks; e.g. thrashing (*q.v.*) in main memory, contention (*q.v.*) on a disk.

6. Complex interactions between resources; e.g. the relationship between channel and disk utilization. Disk utilization can appear artificially high because of a bottleneck in the channel. A major portion of the disk utilization might then be due to waiting for the channel to become free.

Several examples of behavior that might be observed from a system profile and a partial list of possible explanations are given below.

Low utilization of CPU and I/O resources:
1. Insufficient workload.
2. Insufficient main memory to fit enough tasks in the active set to utilize resources.
3. Poor memory management policy that results in insufficient active set size.

High CPU utilization and low I/O device utilization:
1. Excessive CPU overhead.
2. Workload is CPU intensive.
3. Poor job mix scheduling algorithm.
4. Poor CPU scheduling algorithm; e.g. not giving priority to I/O-bound jobs.

Computer System Performance Prediction

The information gathered to aid in diagnosing a performance problem often suggests a remedy for the problem. Easy and inexpensive remedies are often implemented and the effects observed. Tuning of system parameters falls into this category. But if a large number of alternatives must be examined or the changes are costly to implement, some more formal method of predicting the effect of the changes is desirable. Simulation or stochastic modeling are alternatives, particularly when the cost of model development can be amortized over many applications; e.g. when the model is to be used for tuning or capacity planning for many installations. One approach called *operational analysis* is briefly discussed next.

In operational analysis, precise definitions of measured values and minimal assumptions about the system are used to derive invariant relationships among the measured data. These relationships can be considered to be consistency requirements for the values measured in any particular measurement experiment. The following formula for the average response time for an inter-

active system is an example of the type of result available from operational analysis.

$$R > N/X - T$$

where:

R = average response time

N = number of active terminals

X = number of terminal commands completed, divided by measurement period (rate of terminal command completion)

T = average think time at terminals (think time is the time elapsed from the instant the system finishes one command until the user gives the next command).

Under very general conditions, the above relationship can be shown to be *exact* for any measured period. This is an invariant relationship between measured values and not a formula for computing the average response time. However, it can also be useful for prediction of performance under changed conditions, although the problem of estimating or bounding new values for some of the variables is still present. For example, if the effect on the rate of terminal command completion X due to a proposed system change could be estimated, then the equation yields an estimate of the new value for R as a function of N and T. Bounding X also yields some information. For example, if it can be determined that $X < X_0$, then

$$R > N/X_0 \quad T.$$

A value for X_0 might be estimated by considering system bottlenecks as previously discussed.

Operational analysis has succeeded in developing relationships among performance and load measures that are analogous to many of the results available from queueing theoretic models but without the strong assumptions typically required in queueing theory. However, operational analysis has limitations and is not as powerful as queueing theoretic methods for analysis.

Bibliography

1978. Ferrari, D. *Computer Systems Performance Evaluation.* Upper Saddle River, NJ: Prentice Hall. (A comprehensive treatment of the issues discussed in this article.)

1983. Lavenberg, S. S. (ed.) *Computer Performance Modeling Handbook.* New York: Academic Press. (An in-depth treatment of queueing models and simulation as applied to computer systems modeling.)

1984. Lazowska, E. D., Zahorjan, J., Graham, G. S., and Sevcik, K. C. *Quantitative System Performance.* Upper Saddle River, NJ: Prentice Hall.

1989. Molloy, M. K. *Fundamentals of Performance Modeling.* New York: Macmillan. (An accessible account of queueing and simulation with case studies.)

1991. Jain, R. *Techniques for Experimental Design, Measurement, Simulation and Modeling; The Art of Computer Systems Performance Analysis.* New York: Wiley-Interscience. (An introduction to measurement techniques and tools, experiment design, simulation and queueing models.)

1991. Kant, K. *Introduction to Computer System Performance Evaluation.* New York: McGraw-Hill. (Contains a good discussion of queueing network models.)

Richard R. Muntz

PERIPHERAL

See HARD DISK; MEMORY: AUXILIARY; MONITOR, DISPLAY; MULTIMEDIA; OPTICAL CHARACTER RECOGNITION; OPTICAL STORAGE; and PRINTERS.

PERLIS, ALAN J.

For articles on related subjects *see* ALGOL; SOFTWARE HISTORY; and WHIRLWIND.

Alan J. Perlis was born in Pittsburgh on 1 April 1922 and died in New Haven, Connecticut, on 7 February 1990. He was renowned as a developer of programming systems and languages and as an educator—indeed, as a founding father of computer science as a separate discipline.

Perlis received a B.S. in chemistry in 1942 from the Carnegie Institute of Technology (now Carnegie Mellon University), and did graduate work at both the California and the Massachusetts Institutes of Technology in mathematics. He received a Ph.D. from the latter in 1950, and spent the next two years developing programs for the multi-machine computing laboratory of the Ballistic Research Laboratories at Aberdeen Proving Ground and for Whirlwind (*q.v.*) at MIT.

While an assistant professor at Purdue University from 1952 to 1956, he also served as head of a computing center that first had an IBM CPC (card programmed calculator) and then later a Datatron 205. Similarly, he served as associate professor of mathematics and head of its IBM 650-based computing center at Carnegie Tech from 1956 to 1960. Starting at Purdue and continuing at Carnegie Tech, he headed a group that defined the language IT (Internal Translator) and developed compilers for it. IT was quickly in wide use on 650s around the country, as were a succession of algebraic languages and assemblers that were also designed by the group that he led.

Perlis served as a professor at Carnegie Tech from 1960 to 1971. In 1965, he helped establish and became the first chairman of a graduate department of computer

Figure 1. Alan J. Perlis.

science. In 1971, he joined the new computer science department at Yale University as Eugene Higgins Professor of Computer Science, serving as chairman several times until his death. Many of the dozens of graduate students who received their degrees under his guidance at Carnegie Mellon and Yale are now well-known leaders in teaching and research in the USA and elsewhere.

In 1957, ACM president John W. Carr III appointed Perlis chairman of a programming language committee and head of a subcommittee that met in Zurich with a similar subcommittee of GAMM (Gesellschaft für angewandte Mathematik und Mechanik). This group of eight persons specified Algol 58, whose report by Perlis and Klaus Samelson became the basis of a formal specification of Algol 60. During the 1960s, he developed such extensions as Formula Algol and LCC, a form of Algol adapted to interactive, incremental programming.

Perlis was the first editor-in-chief of the *Communications of the ACM* (1958–1962), President of ACM (1962–1964), and, in 1966, the first recipient of ACM's Turing Award (*q.v.*). He received honorary degrees from Davis and Elkins College, Purdue, the University of Waterloo, and Sacred Heart University. He was invited to give numerous lectures abroad, in, among others, the Soviet Union, Denmark, Italy, China, Israel, Mexico, Peru, Venezuela, Scotland, and The Netherlands.

Throughout his career, Alan Perlis served on national and international committees and boards related to medical research, natural language processing (*q.v.*) and machine translation (*q.v.*), and software engineering within such organizations as the National Science Foundation, the Pennsylvania Council on Science and Technology, and the National Research Council Assembly on Engineering. He was elected to the American Academy of Arts and Sciences (1973), the National Academy of Engineering (1976), and he received the AFIPS Education Award in 1984.

Bibliography

1970. Galler, B., and Perlis, A. *A View of Programming Languages.* Reading, MA: Addison-Wesley.

1975. Perlis, A. J. *Introduction to Computer Science.* New York: Harper & Row.

1981. Perlis, A. J. "The American Side of the Development of ALGOL," in *History of Programming Languages* (ed. Richard L. Wexelblat), 75–91. New York: Academic Press.

1987. Perlis, A. J. "The Synthesis of Algorithmic Systems," and "Postscript 20 Years After" in Turing Award Lectures, 5–16. Reading, MA: Addison-Wesley.

Saul Gorn

PERSONAL COMPUTING

For articles on related subjects *see* APPLE COMPUTER, INC.; BULLETIN BOARD; CACHE MEMORY; DISKETTE; ELECTRONIC MAIL; ENTREPRENEURS; FREEWARE AND SHAREWARE; HARD DISK; IBM PC; INTERNET; MICROSOFT; MODEM; MONITOR, DISPLAY; MOTHERBOARD; MULTIMEDIA; OPTICAL STORAGE; PORTABLE COMPUTERS; POWER USER; PRINTERS; SOCIETY, COMPUTERS IN; SPELLING CHECKER; USER INTERFACE; WINDOW ENVIRONMENTS; WORD PROCESSING; WORKSTATION; and WORLD WIDE WEB.

Introduction

Personal computing, simply enough, is computing done on a personal computer. And a *personal computer* (PC) is, in turn, a digital computer (*q.v.*) sufficiently inexpensive that it can be purchased and used as a home appliance, or purchased in quantity by an employer and dedicated to the exclusive use of an individual worker.

Prior to the late 1970s, even the least expensive small computers, minicomputers (*q.v.*), cost at least a few tens of thousands of dollars, well beyond affordable levels to almost all individuals. The personal computer has been in existence only since 1974 and did not gain widespread popularity until the 1980s. Yet in this very short time span, it has radically changed the way

society does business, learns, plays, and gathers information. Bill Gates has said that when he and Paul Allen, both teenagers, founded Microsoft in the mid-1970s to write software for a computer whose sales were in the low hundreds, they set as a goal for their fledgling company to have a computer in every office and home in the country running Microsoft software. Less than 20 years later, their seemingly farfetched dream has come close to reality in the sense that virtually every office and a steadily increasing number of homes do indeed house a personal computer. And Microsoft, though far from the only supplier of PC software (*q.v.*), is the current dominant source.

Personal computing, the ability of average persons to perform computing tasks for themselves, has had a profound effect on society, an effect that has been possible only through a combination of technological advancement and the introduction of a new metaphor or vision of what is meant by computing. The personal computer has, in a very short time, made the typewriter, slide rule, accountant's pads, teletypes, and large reference libraries close to obsolete. It has changed the way virtually every industry, from printing and publishing to the law, to television and movies, and to military defense, does business. It has moved society dramatically toward a democratization of information, when all sizes of businesses and all classes of people have access to legal, financial, and scientific information. It has brought with it a raft of legal, ethical, and moral problems concerning the value of information, constitutional rights of electronic information publishers and bulletin board operators, access to computer training and use, government control over computer communications, health hazards related to long-term computer use, and threats to privacy made possible by computer technology.

History

In Albuquerque, New Mexico, in 1974, a small manufacturer named MITS developed a kit to build a microcomputer. Named the *Altair* by reviewer Leslie Solomon at the suggestion of his teenage daughter (after a fictitious planet on the *Star Trek* television series, not after the real star Altair), the system was built around an Intel 8080 microprocessor. When Solomon's story about the kit appeared as a cover feature in the January 1975 issue of *Popular Electronics* magazine, MITS was deluged with orders and the age of personal computing began.

Soon other companies began offering add-on parts or peripherals for the Altair, and Gates and Allen founded Microsoft to develop an *interpreter*, a program to allow programmers to use the Basic (*q.v.*) programming language on the Altair. Other firms began to develop commercial software for the computer, and competitive computer manufacturers began to appear. One of the earliest, Processor Technology, came quickly to market with a system, the Sol, designed by industry pioneer Lee Felsenstein and named after Leslie Solomon. Computer retail stores came into existence to market the new computers and in September 1975, *Byte* magazine became the first of the half dozen periodicals that would spring up within a year to address the new market. In short, the microcomputer was upon us (*see* MICROPROCESSORS and MICROCOMPUTERS).

Early personal computers, however, had little overall impact on society. The majority were built from kits and attracted only a group of hobbyists and electronics tinkerers across the country. These early computer users banded together into computer clubs where people could gather and exchange information about these novel new machines.

Shortly thereafter, two existing companies, Commodore and Radio Shack, entered the marketplace with their Pet and TRS-80 systems (*see* Fig. 1). These systems differed from those that had come before in that they were preassembled and were intended to attract not just hobbyists, but also end-users: people who saw the new device as a tool to do things, rather than as an end in itself.

While the Pet and TRS-80 made personal computers available to the nonhobbyist, it was the rise of Apple Computer and the development of a software product called VisiCalc that fostered the proliferation of personal computers throughout corporate America. Apple

Computer had its genesis at the California Homebrew Computer Club, where Steve Wozniak, a young Hewlett-Packard engineer, hung around and frequently brought in computers that he had designed. Another member, Steve Jobs, became convinced of the business opportunities attendant to this new technology and, after much effort, persuaded Wozniak to leave Hewlett-Packard (which had exhibited no interest in Wozniak's creations) and join with him in founding Apple Computer, Inc. Although the company began operations in Jobs's garage and living room, where the moderately successful Apple I was created and marketed, the firm grew rapidly when Jobs was able to entice retired millionaire A. C. "Mike" Markkula to join the firm as a partner. Markkula was able to bring establishment venture capital into the firm to provide the funding necessary for Apple's development. Apple's second venture, the Apple II, built around the Mostek 6502 processor and the floppy disk drive was extremely successful with computer enthusiasts and brought much technical praise to largely self-taught engineering genius Wozniak.

As the Apple II was gaining in popularity, a young graduate student at the Harvard School of Business, Daniel Bricklin, was groping with the case method system used in business school that required students to redo continually large financial workpapers or spreadsheets (*q.v.*) to show the effect of such normal business occurrences as interest rate changes, tax increases or decreases, inflation, etc. The process was extremely tedious and often required recalculating a large number of formulas and totals dependent in some way on

Figure 1. A Radio Shack TRS-80 Microcomputer system.

the changed variable. Bricklin, a former programmer at Digital Equipment Corporation (*q.v.*), reasoned that there must be something that could be done with these new inexpensive personal computers to reduce the effort involved. He and a friend, Bob Frankston, designed what became the first electronic spreadsheet, VisiCalc.

Since each of the existing computers of that time used a different microprocessor, it was necessary for Bricklin and Frankston to decide which of the existing microcomputers to choose as a host for VisiCalc. Because of its design and the availability of disk drives for the system, they chose the Apple II and completed the product for that system. Upon product completion, they took out a small ad in *Byte* magazine and began to sell the product through a software publisher, Personal Software.

As part of their marketing effort, Bricklin and Frankston were able to get a copy of VisiCalc into the hands of the editor of the prestigious *Morgan Stanley Electronics Letter* (MSEL), Benjamin M. Rosen. Rosen, extremely impressed with the potential of such a product and what he saw as its possible impact on Apple II sales, wrote in MSEL that VisiCalc might be the software tail that wags the hardware dog. Rosen's prediction became reality when people went into computer stores in droves asking for VisiCalc (at that time, $100) and something to run it on (which, at that time, could only be an Apple II, which cost anywhere from $3,000 to $9,000 depending on the type of printer, monitor, and disk drive attached to the computer). VisiCalc and the Apple II swept through corporate offices, often bucking the resistance of data processing managers unprepared for end-users having direct access to computer power.

With the success of VisiCalc and the Apple II in large corporations, it became only natural for people wishing to develop products for that marketplace to choose the Apple II as their platform. One, Mitchell Kapor, a graduate school student at Yale, produced a graphics and statistics program, Tiny Troll, which he sold from his house for the price of $100. Another, John Draper, who had previously served a prison sentence for phone-phreaking (using telephone systems for long distance calls without paying) developed a word processing program, EasyWriter, which allowed people to use the Apple II to write and revise material before final printing. A third, Dennis C. Hayes, developed a microprocessor, the Hayes Micromodem II, which allowed the Apple II to communicate over telephone lines and obtain information from the many large databases that were beginning to spring up, such as Dow Jones, CompuServe, the Source, and Dialog. Each of these products generated additional sales for the Apple II and caused new developers to come into the market.

As the number of products grew, it became clear that the lack of integration among them caused annoyance to users. A person using both VisiCalc and Tiny Troll to analyze data had to enter it twice through the keyboard, a practice that was both time-consuming and error-prone. To eliminate this problem, Personal Software, now renamed VisiCorp, contracted with Kapor, the developer of Tiny Troll, to produce a new product, VisiTrend + VisiPlot, with improved features and the ability to exchange data with VisiCalc, using a new standard file format, Data Interchange Format (DIF).

Computer industry giant IBM (*q.v.*) had remained on the sidelines for most of the early rapid development in personal computers. Its desktop offerings, the 5100 series, had been overly expensive for most and had fallen far short of the Apple II in user-friendliness. In an effort to develop a system that could properly compete in this marketplace, IBM set up a business component under the direction of Philip D. "Don" Estridge in Boca Raton, FL, and gave it the charter to do whatever was necessary to enter the market successfully.

Estridge and his staff embarked on a program unlike anything in IBM's history and formed alliances with strong players in the microcomputer field to develop versions of existing successful software products for the planned IBM personal computer. When the IBM-PC was introduced in August 1981, there were versions of VisiCalc, EasyWriter, the PeachTree Accounting System, and Microsoft Adventure ready to run on the brand new equipment. As its operating system (*q.v.*), IBM chose MS-DOS, a system adapted by Microsoft from a product developed by a small West Coast firm. They called their version PC-DOS.

From the moment of its introduction, the IBM-PC was dramatically successful. Data processing managers, weary of confrontations with accountants, analysts, engineers, portfolio managers, etc., who wanted to buy and use strange sounding computers named Apple and Pet, could now recommend a firm that they knew well and that had decades of experience in data processing (*q.v.*).

VisiCalc actually ran faster and used less memory on the Apple II than on the newer system. The Apple technical advantage was, however, short-lived. When VisiCorp asked Mitchell Kapor to create a version of VisiTrend for the IBM-PC, Kapor chose to sell his rights to the $265 product to VisiCorp for $1.5 million and go off on his own to develop a new product. Kapor took the proceeds (together with an additional $1.2 million amassed in royalties) to the recently started venture capital firm, Sevin-Rosen Management (Rosen being the same Ben Rosen who started the VisiCalc ball rolling with his MSEL article). Sevin-Rosen raised $4 million dollars and Kapor set up Lotus Development Corporation and, with co-developer Jonathan Sachs, developed Lotus 1-2-3, a spreadsheet program that, at that time, became the most successful computer program in history. When 1-2-3 was introduced at a press conference at New York City's World Trade Center, the advertising budget for the first year of the product was announced to be $6 million dollars—a far cry from a short time before when Bricklin took a small ad for VisiCalc in *Byte* and sent a copy of the program to Ben Rosen, hoping for publicity.

Lotus 1-2-3 became the VisiCalc of the IBM-PC, causing sales of the new system to skyrocket. The success of the system caused other manufacturers to come into the marketplace with compatible computers that ran like the IBM-PC. While the Apple II contained proprietary hardware that was illegal to copy, the IBM, based on *open architecture* (*q.v.*), did not, and firms of all sizes brought compatible machines to market. Initially the most successful of these, Compaq Computer Corporation, started with a transportable system, a 22 lb (10 kg) computer with a handle and built-in monitor and disk drives that could be rapidly moved from place to place. Computers made by firms that attempted, as Compaq did, to compete with IBM on the basis of power or features tended to be considered *compatibles*, while products whose prime attraction was low price were usually called *clones*. (Many clones were manufactured in Asia and imported to the USA and sold under innocuous American names such as Apricot.) Soon, the description of the machines that ran like the IBM-PC evolved from IBM-compatible to simply an MS-DOS machine (i.e. a system that ran under the Microsoft MS-DOS operating system). This slight change in nomenclature was in reality an indication that the industry's view was moving from one that saw IBM as the standard-maker to one that looked to Microsoft for that role.

While the majority of IBM's competitors in the personal computer market, such as Tandy, Zenith, Hewlett-Packard, Digital, Data General, Texas Instruments, and AT&T, eventually marketed MS-DOS systems, Apple Computer chose to go in its own direction and, building on technology originally pioneered by Xerox with its Star microcomputer, developed a system, the Lisa, which made use of an operating environment in which all programs worked in generally the same fashion and which used a pointing device called a mouse (*q.v.*) to perform routine activities. Although the Lisa failed commercially, both because of its pricing and the lack of a wide universe of software, its graphical user interface (GUI) became the basis of Apple's highly successful Macintosh computer and,

following that success, of Microsoft's Windows operating environment (*see* USER INTERFACE). The Commodore Amiga also used a GUI and earned a modest share of the personal computer market into the early 1990s, based on the offering of features similar to the Macintosh at a much lower price. Both the Macintosh and the Amiga used the Motorola 68000 processor.

The Macintosh's GUI, its ease of operation, and its what-you-see-is-what-you-get (WYSIWYG) approach to text processing gained popularity, in large part, because of the development of high-quality laser printers, the introduction of a page definition language (PDL) called PostScript (*q.v.*), and the publication of a program known as PageMaker. This combination of operational environment, hardware, and software products spawned a new industry called desktop publishing (*q.v.*). The new industry provided a path for the Macintosh into small and large businesses alike and revolutionized the production of newsletters, magazines, and advertising copy.

The increased penetration of the Macintosh into businesses and the expanded exposure of the graphical user interface gave impetus to Microsoft's Windows environment, which provided for MS-DOS machines many of the same features as the Macintosh. It also resulted in the development of GUIs for the Unix operating system (*q.v.*), a system that had been developed in a highly technical environment at Bell Laboratories and had not originally been considered an operating system for nontechnical users. Additionally, Microsoft and IBM cooperated on the development of a new operating system, OS/2, also based on a graphical user interface. In short, the user interfaces—the way that persons interact with the computer—were converging even though the underlying computers were quite different.

While the software and operating systems were developing, the equipment (i.e. the hardware itself) was growing rapidly in speed and capacity. The Intel 8088 processor on which the IBM PC and other compatible systems was based has had many compatible descendants: the 8086, the 80286, the 80386, the 80486, and several increasingly powerful versions of the 80586 (Pentium) with each chip having greater speed and the ability to address more memory than its predecessor (*see* MICROCOMPUTER CHIP). As of the end of 1999, Pentium-based machines were capable of over 700 MHz, about 300 times faster than the 8088. IBM PC compatibles that use an Intel or Intel-compatible 80x86 chip and the Microsoft Windows operating system are called "Wintel" machines. The principal competitor to Intel, Advanced Micro Devices, Inc., claims that its AMD K6 chip is 50% faster than the fastest Pentium. In addition to IBM, Wintel machines

Figure 2. The Compaq Deskpro system (courtesy of Compaq).

Figure 3. The Apple G4 computer (courtesy of the Apple Picture Library).

are marketed by Compaq, Dell, Gateway, Hewlett-Packard, Micron, and many other firms. An image of a PC made by Compaq is shown in Fig. 2.

Disk storage, once limited to 160,000 characters on a $5\frac{1}{4}$-inch floppy disk, is now available in units of 1.44 MB, 100 MB, or 250 MB on $3\frac{1}{2}$-inch diskettes and hard disks of capacity in the tens of gigabytes (1 billion characters). Display monitors now allow crisp color images and are available for desktop publishers in models that will display two full document pages at once. Inexpensive laser and color inkjet printers abound (*see* PRINTERS). The speed at which personal computers may pass information across telephone lines has increased over 100 times since the introduction of the Hayes Micromodem II in 1990, and fiber optic (*q.v.*) Internet connections are considerably faster yet. Personal computers with considerably more power than the original IBM PC are now available in laptop and even notebook or palmtop models (*see* PORTABLE COMPUTERS).

On the Macintosh and Amiga side, the original Motorola 68000 processor soon fostered the 68020, 68030, and 68040 processors. The Amiga is no longer marketed, but Apple Computer, Inc., after going through a period in which its loyal customers feared for its survival, has undergone a recent resurgence. See the INTERACTIVE INPUT DEVICES color section for a picture of the popular Apple iMac, Apple's least expensive computer. The top of Apple's line, the PowerPC, is now based on the G4 chip developed for Apple by IBM and Motorola (*see* Fig. 3). The G4 has a 128-bit data

path rather than the 16-bit (early) or 32-bit (most recently) data paths used with IBM PC compatibles, and is capable of a sustained speed of one gigaflop (one billion floating-point operations per second). This is supercomputer (*q.v.*) speed, which, according to an amusing Apple advertisement, makes the PowerPC G4 a "weapon" restricted for export under US law.

The phenomenal increase in processing power is not due solely to the rapid improvement of hardware and software. There has been tremendous progress in the ability to link computers for the purposes of gathering information, exchanging data, transmitting electronic mail (email), trading stock, bidding at auctions, buying products, and sharing resources. Computers are routinely connected in offices and classrooms through local area networks (LANs—*q.v.*). Information is gathered from huge remote databases maintained on America Online, Yahoo!, Dow Jones, Prodigy, Lexis, NewsNet, and many, many others. Email is sent through many of the same services as well as through MCI, Sprint, and AT&T, and the Internet. Society is close to the realization of ideas promulgated by industry pioneers Ted Nelson and Alan Kay in the 1970s who predicted the ability of users to obtain information without having to know either the location of the information or arcane computer commands to call for it.

Issues

The advent of mass computing and telecommunications has brought new ethical and legal problems to society. The problem of software piracy—the obtaining of copies of programs by people who have not paid for them—has brought lawsuits, financial settlements, and debates. The ability to copy electronic documents surreptitiously without destroying the original has raised questions concerning intellectual property (*see* LEGAL ASPECTS OF COMPUTING) and the value of information. The advent of electronic publishing—the distribution of material to online subscribers—raises legal questions, since electronic publishers do not receive the same protection as publishers of printed material. The filing of "look and feel" lawsuits (pertaining to ownership of the way programs appear on the computer screen) by Apple, Ashton-Tate, and Lotus raises questions of copyright law and industry practices. MP3 data compression (*q.v.*) now allows high-quality music to be downloaded from the Internet in reasonable times, a development that is wreaking havoc with longstanding copyright and licensing practices. The proven ability of computer hackers (*q.v.*) to gain unauthorized access to computer systems raises serious questions about security and ownership of information (global communications has even brought espionage by computer). Perhaps most important, the ability of credit, marketing, and government organizations to collect, massage, and disseminate an individual's financial, household, and employment information without the individual's prior approval has raised serious privacy issues.

These questions are complex and require careful and reasoned answers if we are to move forward technologically while retaining the freedoms and privacy to which we are accustomed. The concern for these issues is evidenced in the action of Harvard professor and constitutional law scholar Laurence H. Tribe, who, in 1991, suggested a constitutional amendment to specify the new electronic methods of communication and expression as protected rights.

The Future

The personal computer has become ubiquitous in many developed countries—an appliance that becomes a word processor, a communications device, a financial analysis tool, an artist's palette, and, coupled with access to the Internet, a shopper's paradise. It has the power and capability to be all of these. Both in terms of raw processing speed and memory storage capacity, a US$1,500 PC is many thousands of times more powerful, and hundreds of times smaller, than computers of the 1960s which *rented* for US$100,000 per month. Progress in accord with Moore's Law (*see* LAWS,

COMPUTER) continues unabated; every 18 months on average, a PC becomes available that is twice as capable as its predecessor—for the same price! Very few users routinely tap more than a fraction of their sheer computational power. But added speed and storage, coupled with advances in communications technology, allow PC users access to a continually growing font of knowledge on the Web, and to maintain contact with hundreds of other people—many in countries other than their own—more than was ever before possible.

Periodicals

Byte magazine is no longer in print, but does continue in electronic form (`http://www.byte.com`). Still the most technically informative, *Dr. Dobb's Journal* continues to flourish (`http://www.ddj.com`). The most widely read Wintel PC periodical is *PC Magazine* (`http://www.zdnet.com/pcmag/`), and the most popular magazines that relate to Apple products are *Macworld* (`http://www.macworld.com`) and *MacUser* (`http://www.macuser.co.uk`). For a much more extensive list, see the section entitled "Popular Computer Magazines" in Appendix III.

Computer Clubs

Among the best sources for information about personal computers are local computer clubs. They hold monthly meetings, publish newsletters, and distribute public domain software (programs that the authors are willing to give away) and shareware (programs that the authors are willing to have the user try and, if the program is useful, send a nominal payment). Information on local clubs may be obtained by browsing the Web. *See also* USER GROUPS.

Bibliography

1997. Grossman, W. M. (ed.) *Remembering the Future: Interviews from Personal Computer World.* New York: Springer-Verlag. Interviews with many of the founders of personal computing.

1998. Roman, S. (ed.) *Understanding Personal Computer Hardware: Everything You Need to Know to Be an Informed PC User, PC Buyer, PC Upgrader.* New York: Springer-Verlag.

1999. Collin, S. M. H. *Dictionary of Personal Computing and the Internet.* London: Peter Collin.

1999. Norman, D. A. *Invisible Computer: Why Good Products Can Fail, the Personal Computer Is So Complex and Information Appliances Are the Solution.* Cambridge, MA: MIT Press.

1999. *PC Complete.* San Francisco: Sybex. A guide to Wintel machines.

1999. Buchanan, W. *PC Interfacing, Communications, and Windows Programming.* Reading, MA: Addison-Wesley.

1999. O'Donnell, B. *Personal Computer Secrets.* New York: IDG Books Worldwide.

1999. Norton, P. and Goodman, J. M. *Peter Norton's Inside the PC.* Indianapolis, IN: Sams.

1999. Rittner, D., and Kawasaki, G. *The iMac Book*. Scottsdale, AZ: The Coriolis Group.
2000. Freiberger, P. and Swaine, M. *Fire in the Valley: The Making of the Personal Computer*, 2nd Ed. New York: McGraw-Hill.

**Barbara E. McMullen and John F. McMullen;
revised by Edwin D. Reilly**

PERSONAL DIGITAL ASSISTANT

See PORTABLE COMPUTERS.

PERSONAL FINANCE

For articles on related subjects *see* ADMINISTRATIVE APPLICATIONS; DATABASE MANAGEMENT SYSTEM; ELECTRONIC COMMERCE; ELECTRONIC FUNDS TRANSFER; PERSONAL COMPUTING; SPREADSHEET; and TRANSACTION PROCESSING.

Introduction

Personal finance applications are programs devised to facilitate the tasks of budgeting, banking, financial strategizing, investing, retirement planning, and tax planning and filing, primarily on personal computers. Starting with the advent of personal computing in the early 1980s, personal financial management software has rapidly developed into one of the most widely used PC computer applications with over 12 million users in the USA alone. Many personal finance applications include the ability to interact with the Internet (*q.v.*) and particular financial institutions. Financial management programs are intuitive easy-to-use tools that can shorten the time required for household or home business financial tasks.

The goal of personal financial management software is to help people create a financial profile, set goals, and save money to meet those goals. Accounts are developed that list the value of all the user's assets and liabilities. The software tracks expenses and income until it accumulates enough data to develop yearly cash flow statements. This allows individuals to structure budgets that are used to meet financial goals, such as increasing savings. Some financial management programs include "what if " scenarios that suggest ways to reduce taxes and other expenses or to increase income. The software then monitors expenditures to ensure that budgeting stays on track. Individuals may check their continually updated net worth statements periodically to see if they are on target.

Brief History

The first personal finance software appeared between 1980 and 1983. These programs began as electronic checkbook "add-ins" for spreadsheet programs but soon progressed to include sufficiently well-automated financial management functions to become standalone programs. When Intuit's *Quicken* was introduced in 1984, it faced 40 competitors. In that same year, Mecca launched *Manage Your Money*, a financial management program that included computerized financial planning advice from financial management expert Andrew Tobias. *Microsoft Money* debuted in 1992. By 1998, there were over 12 million users of personal finance software, with *Quicken* and *Money* dominating the market. Current personal finance packages are full-featured financial planners with audio and video help files. Personal financial management software is typically priced from $30 to $100 in the USA, depending upon the product's features. Trial evaluation versions and complete programs can be downloaded from the Internet, mail ordered, or purchased in stores. The leading programs require a computer with a minimum of 40 MB of RAM, 120 MB of hard disk (*q.v.*) space, and, of course, a modem (*q.v.*).

Basic Operations

The three leading personal finance software programs —*Managing Your Money*, M*icrosoft Money* (Fig. 1), and *Quicken*—are shipped with a Web browser and include automatic onscreen help, links to relevant Websites, online tutorials, and personalized financial advice based on user input. These personal finance software programs include predefined reports and support the ability of users to customize content and appearance, to import data from other sources, to create instant reports from transactions, and to view supporting data. Graphics include three-dimensional charts and graphs that can be personalized and displayed simultaneously in multiple windows.

Personal finance software typically includes the following functions:

◆ *Budgeting* Budgeting support includes the splitting of transactions among several categories, automatically setting up budget accounts based on the user's input from the prior year, and automatic preparation of a preliminary budget based on that prior year.

◆ *Checking and bill paying* Personal finance software can track from one to a dozen bank accounts, memorize recurring transactions, schedule future transactions, reconcile bank statements, and link to credit card statements and bill-reminder and bill-paying services offered by banks and "middleware" vendors such as Pay Online, Intuit CheckFree Financial Services, and similar companies.

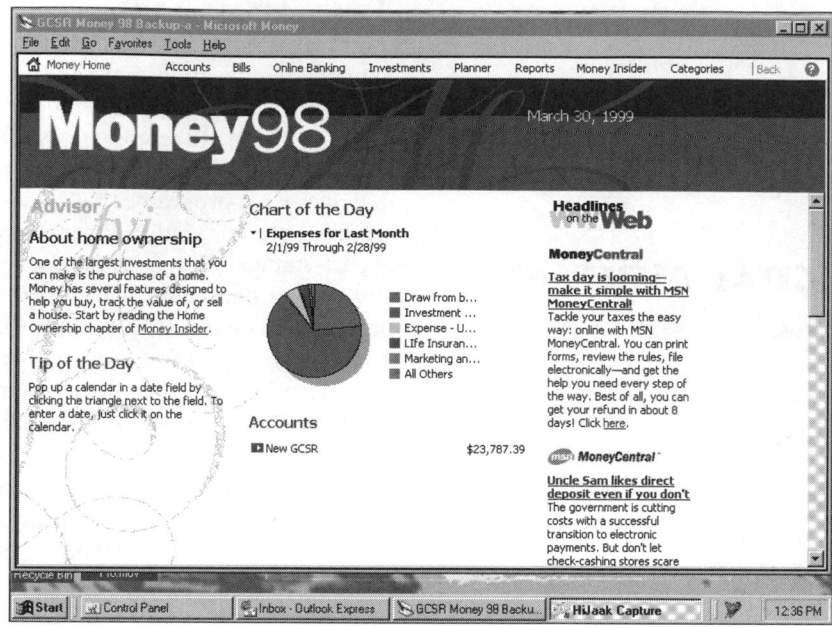

Figure 1. A screen from Microsoft Money, the Microsoft personal finance software program (courtesy of Microsoft).

◆ *Financial planning* Financial planning includes loan calculation and amortization tables; automatic crediting of loan payments transferred from checking accounts; accounting for the splitting of payments among principal, interest, and escrow; analyses of net worth, expenditure patterns, and cash flows; and "what if" scenarios to help users determine their life insurance needs and plans for debt reduction and retirement.

◆ *Investing and portfolio management* This function provides links to free online stock, bond, and mutual fund quotation services; online trading; portfolio optimization and analysis; tracking stocks, bonds, and real estate and other investments; and several user-customized views of multiple portfolios.

◆ *Mortgage information* This function helps users decide whether to rent or buy; records home purchases and calculates the cost savings for refinancing an existing mortgage loan; and indicates the cost savings of early mortgage repayment.

◆ *Small or home business advice* This function provides advice for making a business more successful; suggests ways to find specific information; compares a business to other similar businesses; guides the user to relevant industry news; and includes information on paycheck creation and tax withholding adjustments.

◆ *Tax planning* This function helps identify tax deductions; establishes tax liability; links categories to specific tax forms and schedules; exports data to major tax programs; and allows the viewing and printing of preliminary forms and schedules.

Home Banking

Home banking provides customers who have a computer, modem, and appropriate software with the ability to download their personal bank data; transfer funds from one account to another; monitor checking and savings accounts; and pay bills electronically by sending payment authorizations directly to financial institutions. Some online banking programs allow consumers to buy and sell securities. Bank data can include savings account, checking account, mortgage, loan, and credit card information.

There are three ways consumers can access their personal banking data: bank-owned software using a direct dial-up, Internet access, and personal finance software. The following explains each method.

PROPRIETARY BANK SOFTWARE
A few banks have developed their own software and others have purchased off-the-shelf programs. For example, in May 1995 NationsBank and Bank of America purchased Mecca's *Manage Your Money* for $35 million. At that time, the program accounted for about 5% of the total personal finance software market. After the purchase, NationsBank and Bank of America took Manage Your Money off the market so that it could be used as their proprietary online banking application. Bank customers receive the software free of charge, use bank dial-up instructions, and access their personal financial data.

INTERNET ACCESS

For Internet access, consumers use browsers that support securely encrypted transactions. They may access their personal bank data, transact business, and get real-time information about their account balances, payments and investment securities. Customers do not need to use special bank software or personal finance software. In the USA about 150 traditional banks including Wells Fargo use this method, but there are also Internet-based banks. Data is stored at the Internet host site and is not downloaded to local personal finance software. The first Web-based bank, Security First Network Bank, was launched in 1995. Such banks have account access via the Internet, but maintain no "bricks and mortar" branch offices.

PERSONAL FINANCE SOFTWARE

Over 125 banks use personal finance software such as Intuit's *Quicken* or Microsoft's *Money* for online banking. These personal finance software programs allow users to connect to the bank by dialing directly from the user's computer. Once connected, users can issue electronic payment instructions and download their personal financial data to local personal finance software or to a spreadsheet. Putting your accounts on Quicken or Money helps you organize, but electronic banking and bill paying offer the greater time savings. You begin by telling your bank which accounts should have electronic connections to Quicken or Money. When you first go online and type your PIN, either program will download the last 30 to 90 days of transactions to your local files. After that, you can stay current without having to call or visit your bank or wait for statements.

Middleware

The development of *middleware*—applications that link databases to a user interface—has extended the capabilities of personal finance software and made online banking popular. Home banking includes electronic bill payment requests that are sent to middleware companies. These firms pay bills, but account transfers and balance information requests are handled by the appropriate financial institution. Middleware companies started in 1981 when Peter Kight established CheckFree in order to collect monthly health club membership fees electronically. The company quickly realized the need for electronic bill presentment and payment services and proceeded to form the necessary bank partnerships and develop the needed software. Middleware companies proliferated to the point where, in March 1996, Microsoft launched Open Finance Exchange (OFX), a specification for middleware created in a joint effort with CheckFree and Intuit. This specification enables customers or small

Table 1. Personal finance software access to online banking.

Description	1995	1996	1997	1998
No. of banks providing access to personal finance management (PFM)	19	59	120	350
PFM online bank users	20,000	510,000	800,000	2,500,000
Online banking households		1,800,000	3,500,000	4,400,000

businesses to connect directly to their financial institutions in order to issue and download their own data. In September 1996, Intuit announced Open Exchange and three months later merged with OFX, though a bill presentment specification was not added until June 1997. All this resulted in a standard that developers use to create software that allows consumers to connect directly to their brokerages, banks, and other financial institutions. The specification also allows consumers to have their choice of computer platforms, processors, and personal finance or other software applications.

In July 1995, Microsoft Money and Intuit's Quicken personal software programs were upgraded to include the tools necessary for online banking and electronic bill paying. Table 1 shows the number of banks that provide online banking access by personal finance software, the number of consumers who subscribe to the service, and the total number of online banking households in the USA.

In 1995, only 19 banks provided consumers with the ability to download account information and pay bills electronically via their personal finance software, and only 20,000 bank customers subscribed to the service, but these numbers increased dramatically over the next four years. The increased use of the Internet, a large base of installed PCs, and ease of use of software have now brought a reasonable level of maturity to online banking. By 1998, about 2.5 million of 4.4 million online banking households subscribed to the services of 350 financial institutions. Despite the growth, these are actually small numbers considering that there are 12 million personal finance software users and over 100 million checking account holders in just the USA. But forecasts indicate that by 2003 there will be 25 million online banking households. In 1995, personal finance software sales totaled just $212 million, but sales are expected to reach $1.2 billion by 2003.

Personal Finance Programs As Value-Added Browsers

In 1993 the Internet lifted a ban against commercial transactions. By May 1995, *Quicken 96* included an

Internet connection in its personal finance software that allowed users to access the company's Website to read personal finance tips, read reviews of online banking services, and order Intuit software. Shortly thereafter, that Website began to offer free online stock quotes and other financial management data. Now both *Microsoft Money* and Intuit's *Quicken* include browsers that let users move seamlessly between the software and online resources.

Quick Web entry and one-step update functions also speed up access to Internet-based online accounts. This makes the latest personal finance software programs look and behave like *value-added browsers* rather than standalone software products. These new programs look like Web pages, even down to a portal to different sections of the software program such as online banking, investing, and tax planning. They offer direct connections to Web-based insurance quotes, car-buying guides, virtual travel agencies, and real estate listings. Features include online banking and bill payment through financial institutions that support *Money* and *Quicken*. Today's personal finance software programs allow users to access the Web to trade shares, transfer funds, and retrieve statements from credit card companies and brokerage houses, and then automatically post the updated information to the user's personal finance program files.

Other Products

In addition to *Quicken*, Intuit also markets a very popular program called *TurboTax* which, given relevant data, will prepare a user's US federal income tax return, right down to filling out forms, printing them out, and, at the user's request, electronically filing the return with the IRS. Supplements purchased separately will do the same for any state income tax return. Intuit also sells *QuickBooks* which, though simple to use, does all of the intricate bookkeeping and accounting necessary to run a small business. Peachtree Software offers a competitive package.

The Future of Personal Finance Applications

Future personal finance applications are all likely to be value-added browsers. Features that are now available will become faster and more sophisticated. It will be difficult for financial institutions to "brand" their products because consumers will have a hard time differentiating between the features of the personal finance software and those of the financial institutions they have selected. Relative to the rapidly increasing number of users of online personal financial services, those who choose not to use them are more likely to suffer

from the results of inaccurate bank information, improperly prepared tax returns, and losses due to the lack of investment monitoring.

Bibliography

1996. Goldstein, D., and Flory, J. *The Online Guide to Personal Finance Investing*. Chicago: Irwin Professional Publishing.
1997. Morris, K. M., and Siegel, A. M. *The Wall Street Journal Guide to Understanding Personal Finance*. New York: Lightbulb Press.
1998. Langer, M. *Quicken 99: The Official Guide*. New York: McGraw-Hill.
1998. Nelson, S. L. *Microsoft Money 99 at a Glance*. Redmond, WA: Microsoft Press.
1999. Franco, S. C., and Klein, T. M. *Online Financial Services Update, Fourth Quarter 1998*. Piper Jaffray Equity Research, Online Financial Services Update (http://www.piperjaffray.com).
1999. Gilbert, J. *Teach Yourself Turbotax Deluxe in 24 Hours*. New York: Macmillan.
1999. Sindell, K. *Investing Online for Dummies*, 2nd Ed. Indianapolis, IN: IDG Books.
1999. Sindell, K. *CheckFree: About the Corporation*. http://www.checkfree.com.

Kathleen Sindell

PERSONNEL IN THE COMPUTER FIELD

For articles on related subjects *see* COMPUTER SCIENCE—PH.D. STATISTICS; INFORMATION TECHNOLOGY; PROGRAMMER; SYSTEMS ANALYST; and WOMEN AND COMPUTING.

Introduction

During the last years of the 20th century, the increase in the number of computers in use in business and industry, corporations, government, and the home caused more jobs to be created than ever before. During the 1980s the personal computer and workstation (*q.v.*) became prevalent, but during the 1990s the computer became ubiquitous and connected to the world. The Internet (*q.v.*) became a major communications tool, with access becoming available in the workplace, libraries, hotel rooms, at home, and even at cyber-cafes. The information technology business, usually defined as computing combined with telecommunications and networking, is now the largest industry in the USA.

Every discipline has been affected by information technology. Librarians now work with computers every day, as do journalists, farmers, doctors, and artists. "Across careers, information technology opens up new niches" (Cyberjobs, 1995). Positions such as computer programmer, systems analyst, database administrator, systems administrator, etc. continue to exist, with new positions arising, such as Web developer, Internet coordinator, computer security officer, and help-desk worker. Other positions in network security, electronic commerce, and project management have increased recently. (Many positions related to the Year 2000 Problem (*see* Y2K PROBLEM) were created near the end of the millennium but most of these are not likely to endure.) As the commercial sector moved away from large mainframe-based systems to connected workstations, the demand was great for client–server (*q.v.*) network experience. Jobs continued to be highly specialized with respect to the area, such as software engineering (*q.v.*), as well as to the environment consisting of the operating system, the vendor brand of hardware, and the language tool. Companies advertised for computer programmers with specific skills, such as Visual Basic, C and C++, Powerbuilder, Microsoft Access, and Java.

Qualifications for the Work

Because many of the job skills in demand were for specific vendors' products, personnel took specialized training and took tests given by the manufacturers or training vendors to obtain certification of knowledge of the product, as a way to show employers they were qualified. The certification examinations of the Institute for Certification of Computer Professionals (ICCP— *q.v.*), created with the support of eight professional associations, offered an alternative to workers to show what they know. ICCP examinations are not vendor-specific, but cover the principles and concepts of the body of knowledge. Completion of certain of the examinations can lead to the Associate Computing Professional (ACP) credential, the Certified Computing Professional (CCP) credential, or the passing of a specialty proficiency examination. The Computing Technology Industry Association (CompTIA), an industry trade association of vendors, now offers several certification examinations, most of them with a non-vendor-specific emphasis. Their examinations include A+ for computer service technicians, a networking examination, and an examination for a certified document imaging architech.

Although software engineers employed in the high-technology industries usually have college or university degrees, many of the computer programmers employed do not. Those workers who started in the computing industry in its early years usually had degrees in mathematics, while those who started in the data processing business were usually from the accounting field. Most of those workers are now nearing retirement. They are being replaced by young people who are excited about the computing industry, enthusiastic about the work, and eager to show what they can do. Many of these young people, sometimes called "geeks" or "nerds," work long hours on the job, often sleeping and eating there for days at a time.

Corporations who wish to attract and keep these eager young people often provide them with additional benefits to make life easy for them. "In Silicon Valley, everyone wants to be a nerd" (Strauss, 1998, p. 50).

Students in the USA can now major in several different types of programs, some available in secondary schools or vocational technical schools, while others are found in colleges, universities, and community colleges. Degrees in Computer Applications, Computer Support Services, Computer Technology, Computer Science, Information Systems, Computer Engineering, Management Information Systems, and Information Technology are now available. Many students are lured into jobs before they complete their program of study, as the demand is great. Companies offer high salaries and many additional incentives to attempt to hire well-qualified workers. When colleges don't provide enough workers, corporations and colleges often form partnerships. When Intel Corporation could not get sufficient semiconductor manufacturing technicians, they invested $8.6 million to set up a program with local community colleges in New Mexico (Butler, 1997). When the US Government could not find Information Resources Managers, it established a program called "1000 by the year 2000" to develop these managers by using regional university programs. The US Congress also crafted legislation that created the National Skills Standards Board to facilitate voluntary, unified standards for use in education and the workplace. Computing skills standards are included in the industry cluster with telecommunications, arts and entertainment, and information (NSSB, 1998).

The work of the computer programmer, software engineer, database administrator, Web developer, systems administrator, systems analyst, systems designer, and network specialist is often highly detailed, with intricate complexity. The work is often urgently needed, behind schedule, with cost overruns, causing a high level of pressure on the job. Many computer personnel get "job burn-out" and have health problems after some time in that environment; others decide to leave the field for something more tolerable.

Job Supply and Demand

In most cities, and even in small towns, employment opportunities abound for the college student or graduate who has skills in information technology. Finding these personnel is a challenge, as colleges and universities have not been graduating them in sufficient numbers. In a 1997 poll of 402 large and medium-size US employers, 48.5% reported information technology workers in short supply. After a time of organizational downsizing during the 1980s that included the layoff of many computer personnel, fewer students chose computer-related courses, resulting in a decrease in the numbers of graduates. As the word of shortages spread in 1996 and 1997, more students began choosing computer-related programs, with resulting large increases in enrollments.

Several reports have recently been done on the issue of the shortage of information technology workers in the United States. The trade association, Information Technology Association of America (ITAA) sponsored a study stating a serious workforce gap existed in the information technology area, resulting in a national policy debate. Later studies were done by the Department of Commerce, ITAA, and the Computing Research Association (*q.v.*). The result of the last-named study is a fairly comprehensive examination of several aspects of the situation with the supply of information technology workers (CRA, 1999). These studies of both supply and demand seem consistent with the projections of the Bureau of Labor Statistics, US Department of Labor, which stated in the mid-1990s that the three fastest growing occupations before 2005 will be systems analysts, then computer scientists, then computer engineers. Computer programmers were also listed as a category for faster-than-average growth (http://www.bls.gov). But the number of graduates from bachelor's programs in computer science in the USA declined 42% between 1986 and 1994, from 41,889 to 24,200. However, the number of graduates from master's programs grew 29% from 1986 to 1994, from 8,070 to 10,416, while the number of Ph.D. graduates grew 135%, from 344 to 810 in that same period. Data from the last four years of the Computing Research Association Taulbee Survey indicate that doctoral graduates have shifted substantially towards placement in industry rather than academe, leaving a shortage there as well. In all these numbers, women and minorities are a significantly underrepresented percentage of the population earning degrees in computer science. Employment growth in the computer and data processing services industry is projected to grow 108% from 1996 to 2006, so that high demand for information technology workers is expected to continue for some time.

As would be expected from the shortages of personnel, salaries for computer information technology graduates have been rapidly increasing. In 1996, computer science baccalaureate graduates received about $35,000 per year on average, the most of any field. The median salary for a Director of Management Information Systems/Data Processing was $58,500 in 1996, but the highest paid in that group earned over $250,000 annually. Salaries continue to rise for the right combination of skills, with $75,000 quite common after only a few years' experience. These salaries have certainly risen considerably since 1996.

Bibliography

1995. "Cyberjobs: 1996 Career Guide," *U.S. News and World Report*, 30 October.

1996. Bureau of Labor Statistics (BLS). *Occupational Outlook Quarterly*, **37**, 3.

1997. Butler, P. "Computer Chip Makers Desperate for Techs," *The Albuquerque Journal*, 6 April.

1998. Strauss, R. "Geeks Rising," *Inquirer Magazine*, Philadelphia, 15 February, 50–54.

1998. National Skills Standards Board. *Annual Report*. Washington, DC. (http://www.nssb.org.)

1999. Freeman, P., and Aspray, W. *The Supply of Information Technology Workers in the United States*. Washington, DC: Computing Research Association.

Joyce Currie Little

PETRI NET

> For articles on related subjects *see* AUTOMATA THEORY; CHOMSKY HIERARCHY; CONCURRENT PROGRAMMING; DATAFLOW; FORMAL LANGUAGES; MULTIPROCESSING; and PARALLEL PROCESSING.

Petri nets are a popular and useful model for the representation of systems with concurrency or parallelism. They are named for Carl Adam Petri, who developed them in the early 1960s at the University of Bonn, Germany. A *Petri net* (*see* Fig. 1) is a graph with two types of nodes—*places* and *transitions*. Places are drawn as circles, while transitions are drawn as bars. Directed arcs (arrows) connect places to transitions and transitions to places. For each transition, the directed arcs define its *input* places (arc from place to transition) and its *output* places (arc from transition to place).

A Petri net is *executed* by defining a *marking* and then *firing* transitions. A marking is a distribution of *tokens* to the places of the Petri net. A token is represented on a Petri net graph by a small solid dot in a place. A transition is *enabled* whenever all of its input places have one or more tokens. A transition *fires* by removing one token from each of its input places and adding one token to each of its output places.

For example, in the marked Petri net of Fig. 1, two transitions are enabled. Transition b has one input (p_2), and that place has a token, so transition b is enabled. Similarly, transition e has tokens in both of its input places (p_4 and p_7), so it is also enabled. Transition d is not enabled, since there is no token in place p_5, one of its inputs. To fire transition b, we remove the token from p_2 and put a token in p_5 and a token in p_8 (its two outputs). This would enable transition d. Firing transition e will remove a token from both p_4 and p_7 and put a token in p_{10}.

If more than one transition is enabled, the firing of these transitions is generally asynchronous—they may fire simultaneously or at different times before or after

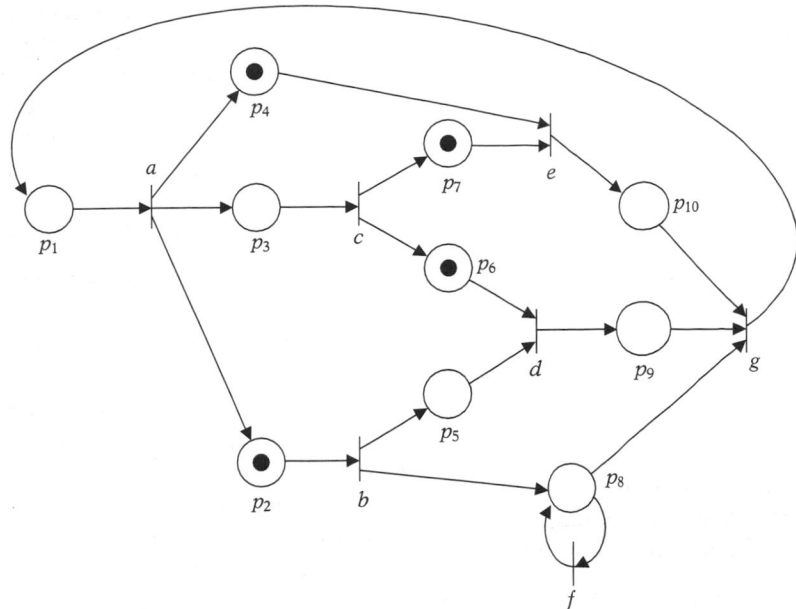

Figure 1. An example of a Petri net.

each other. For example, in Fig. 1, transitions b and e are enabled and may fire completely independently. If two transitions share input places, then they are in *conflict* and only one can fire. In Fig. 1, transitions f and g are in conflict when a token is in place p_8.

Petri nets are a simple, elegant model of information flow. This makes them useful for describing and explaining systems, especially systems with concurrency and synchronization. Petri nets have been used mainly to model computer hardware (e.g. asynchronous circuits, pipelined computers, and computers with multiple functional units, such as the CDC 6600 and IBM 360/91) and computer software (e.g. sets of cooperating processes, communication protocols, and operating systems). Transitions represent *events* in the modeled system, while places represent *resources* or *conditions*. For example, Fig. 2 is a Petri net model of a disk sched-

uling algorithm with two disk drives, a disk controller, and a channel (*q.v.*). The two available disk drives are represented by two tokens in the "disk drive available" place. Only one disk controller is available.

A Petri net can be associated with a nondeterministic automaton whose states correspond to the markings of the net. An execution of this automaton defines a *string* of events corresponding to a firing sequence of the Petri net. The set of all possible strings for a Petri net is its *language*. For example, if we associate the symbols (a, b, c, d, e) with the transitions as shown in Fig. 2, then one possible string is *abcdebcde*; another string is *aabcdeabcdebcde*. In general, for Fig. 2, any string is made up of the substrings a and *bcde* such that the number of bs never exceeds the number of as, from left to right. The as can otherwise be arbitrarily interleaved with the *bcde* substrings.

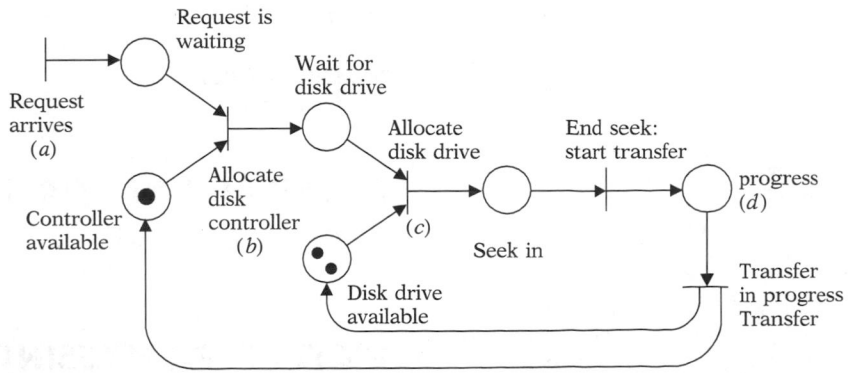

Figure 2. A Petri net model of an algorithm for allocating a disk controller and disk drives.

The class of Petri net languages has been used as a basis for comparing the Petri net model with other models of parallel systems: if the class of languages of a model A is strictly contained in the class of languages of a model B, then model A is strictly less powerful than model B; if the two classes are equal, then the models are considered equivalent. The results of such comparisons must be judged with caution, since the representation of an execution by a linear string does not distinguish between the resolution of conflict (where only one sequence is possible) and parallelism (where many arbitrary interleavings of events are possible, but only one happens to occur). With this reservation, it can be stated that the Turing machine (*q.v.*) model is strictly more powerful than the Petri net model, while Petri nets are strictly more powerful than finite state models. All regular languages are Petri net languages, and all Petri net languages are context-sensitive (*see* Fig. 3).

A Petri net can be *analyzed* to determine properties of the modeled system. Analysis techniques have been developed to decide if the number of tokens in a Petri net is bounded, if tokens are conserved, if deadlocks can occur, or if mutual exclusion is violated. These correspond to important problems for concurrent systems, but more general analysis techniques would be useful. Current techniques are based on either of two approaches: (1) a matrix representation of the Petri net, or (2) representation of its state as a tree (*q.v.*).

One typical analysis technique is the *reachability problem*: given a Petri net with an initial marking and a desired final marking, is it possible to fire transitions and change the initial marking to the desired final marking? Researchers have shown that the reachability problem is decidable, although expensive. In the worst case, the time and memory (computational complexity—*q.v.*) needed to analyze a Petri net grows exponentially with the size of the net.

Petri net execution does not include a concept of time, only the relative order of events. When performance metrics of systems are desired, the execution time of a transition must be defined. (A few models that associate time with places have been suggested, but they can be shown to be equivalent to times associated with transitions.) Two extended Petri net models are used for performance analysis: *Timed Petri nets* and *Stochastic Petri nets*. Both models have the concept of time (or a clock) associated with transition firings. For Timed Petri nets, the time value is constant; for Stochastic Petri nets, the time is a random variable (typically exponentially distributed).

The addition of a time for the firing transitions adds significant complexity to the model. In the case of Timed Petri nets, the reachability set may be a subset of the reachability set of the underlying Petri net. When the time is a constant value, even the boundedness question is undecidable. In the case of stochastic Petri nets, the reachability set does not change with the introduction of time (assuming that the probability density of the random variables is nonzero on the interval 0 to ∞).

Continued work on Petri nets and their use is resulting in the development of a new research area called *general net theory*. Within this general theory, *special net theory* corresponds to the Petri net model described here.

Bibliography

1977. Peterson, J. L. "Petri Nets," *Computing Surveys*, **9**, *3*, 223–252.
1979. Agerwala, T. "Putting Petri Nets to Work," *Computer*, **12**, *12*, 85–94.
1981. Peterson, J. L. *Petri Net Theory and the Modeling of Systems*. Upper Saddle River, NJ: Prentice Hall.
1985. Reisig, W. *Petri Nets*. Berlin: Springer-Verlag.
1989. Murata, T. "Petri Nets: Properties, Analysis, and Applications," *Proc. of the IEEE*, **77**, *4* (April), 541–580.
1992. Reisig, A. *A Primer in Petri Net Design*. New York: Springer-Verlag.
1997. Anisimov, N. A. *Compositional Methods for Communication Protocol Design: A Petri Net Approach*. Singapore: World Scientific.
The Petri Net WWW Pages. `http://www.daimi.au.dk/ ~petrinet/`.

Michael K. Molloy and James L. Peterson

PGP

See PRETTY GOOD PRIVACY.

PHYSICAL UNIT OR NAME

See LOGICAL AND PHYSICAL NAMES.

PICTURE PROCESSING

See IMAGE PROCESSING; and MEDICAL IMAGING.

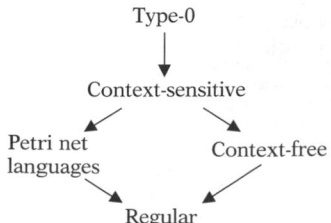

Figure 3. The place of Petri net languages in the Chomsky hierarchy (*q.v.*) of languages. An arrow indicates proper containment.

PIPELINE

For articles on related topics *see* CENTRAL PROCESSING UNIT; COMPUTER ARCHITECTURE; INSTRUCTION DECODING; INSTRUCTION-LEVEL PARALLELISM; PARALLEL PROCESSING; and SUPERCOMPUTER.

Pipelines have been used for many years by designers of high-performance computers in order to improve the performance of their machines. Similar to assembly lines in manufacturing, pipelines partition the processing of an instruction into a set of steps. The pipeline then allows multiple instructions to be at different stages of processing simultaneously. This parallelism leads to the performance improvement.

The performance of a computer is usually measured by the amount of work (or number of instructions) it completes in a fixed amount of time, or alternatively the amount of time it takes to complete a fixed amount of work. This can be described by the following equation:

Time to execute program =

Number of instructions in program

$\times$ Clock cycles needed per instruction (CPI)

$\times$ Time of one clock cycle.

If we assume the number of instructions is held constant, then improving performance will require a reduction in the second term (the CPI) and/or the third term (the cycle time).

Most computers employ an internal signal called a "clock" that alternates between a high state and a low state. This clock is used to synchronize operations within the computer and between the computer and external devices. The number of times this signal oscillates per second is referred to as the "clock frequency," and is measured in hertz (Hz). The amount of time between successive high (or low) points is called the "clock cycle time." Therefore, a clock with a frequency of 500 MHz oscillates 500 million times per second and the time for one oscillation is 2 nanoseconds. Since a higher clock speed corresponds to a decrease in the time per cycle, the third term in the equation above will be reduced and execution time will be shortened. Increasing the clock speed is primarily a function of technology and the size of the physical devices used. Higher clock speed has been a major driving force behind the tremendous increase in computer performance over several decades.

Another approach to improving processor performance is to overlap the execution of multiple instructions, reducing the average number of clock cycles needed per instruction. Increasing the clock rate and overlapping instruction execution are not mutually exclusive—it is entirely possible (and in fact quite common) for a designer to do both. In the realm of computer design, the latter technique is referred to as *instruction level parallelism* (having multiple instructions executing in parallel) and one of the oldest and best-understood techniques for achieving this is a technique called "pipelining."

A typical general-purpose processor must perform a sequence of well-defined steps in order to execute an instruction. First, the instruction must be fetched from its location in memory. Once it has been retrieved, the processor must "decode" the instruction to determine the operation that it specifies, and to identify its operands. Finally, the specified operation is performed (executed). This sequence of steps must be repeated for *every* instruction that is to be executed, and is commonly called the *Fetch–Decode–Execute* (FDE) cycle.

Performing all of these steps in a single clock cycle will reduce the CPI term to 1, but that requires that the cycle time term be big enough to allow all three steps to complete. The cycle time term can be reduced by making each step take one cycle, but doing this will mean that each instruction will take three cycles to complete (the CPI will go to 3).

Fortunately, as long the operations of each step] (also known as a stage) can be kept independent of the subsequent stages, it is possible to have instructions in each stage simultaneously. For example, while one instruction is being fetched from storage, another instruction can be in the decode stage and a third instruction can be in the process of being executed. This is "pipelining" and works as follows:

```
                Time
Inst  1    2    3    4    5    6    7
  1   IF   ID   EX
  2        IF   ID   EX
  3             IF   ID   EX
  4                  IF   ID   EX
  5                       IF   ID   EX

IF = Instruction Fetch
ID = Instruction Decode
EX = Instruction Execution
```

A processor pipeline works in much the same way as an actual pipeline. In an oil pipeline, for example, oil is pumped in one end and flows out the other. If the pipeline is empty, then it will take some time before the oil starts appearing at the output, but if the pipeline is full then the oil flows out as fast as it is put in. A given oil molecule will take a fixed amount of time to get from one end of the pipeline to the other, but rate of flow at the output end should be the same as at the input end. As seen above, the first instruction enters the pipeline at time 1, but does not leave until time 3. After this initial delay, the following instructions finish at a rate of one per cycle. So, while each instruction requires three clock cycles to be processed, on average instructions complete execution at a rate of one per cycle. Pipelining thus produces a factor of three speed-up over processing the instructions in a non-overlapped fashion.

This discussion suggests that further performance improvements can be achieved by subdividing the pipeline into more steps, providing more instruction overlap. In fact, most pipelined machines have more stages than those described above. Consider that an instruction operates on data items (operands—*q.v.*) and produces a result. The execute stage must perform three steps—fetch the operands, operate on them, and return the result to its destination. The execute stage can thus be divided into three stages: OF, EX and WB, one for each of these steps (respectively). In this way, the three-stage FDE pipeline is turned into a five-stage pipeline, and the previous diagram is modified to look as follows:

```
                          Time
Inst    1    2    3    4    5    6    7    8    9
 1     IF   ID   OF   EX   WB
 2          IF   ID   OF   EX   WB
 3               IF   ID   OF   EX   WB
 4                    IF   ID   OF   EX   WB
 5                         IF   ID   OF   EX   WB

IF = Instruction Fetch
ID = Instruction Decode
EX = Instruction Execution
OF = Operand Fetch
WB = Write (result) Back
```

Here there is a longer latency (five cycles) than in the simpler pipeline—however, once the pipeline is full, instructions still finish at a rate of one per cycle.

It might appear that it would be advantageous to continue to divide a pipeline into more and more stages indefinitely. For example, multiplication uses repeated addition, so multiplication is typically divided into several stages. The same is true for operations such as division and floating-point operations. In some implementations even the Fetch and Decode stages are subdivided into several stages each. Unfortunately, there are several practical reasons for limiting the number of pipeline stages (the "pipeline depth") that have to do with how the pipeline is implemented in hardware and the interactions among instructions in the pipeline.

The primary hardware limitations are an an imbalance between the timing of stages and an overhead term introduced per stage. This can be explained through another analogy: the processing of an instruction by a pipeline is very similar to the building of an automobile on an assembly line. Just as the processing of an instruction is broken down into steps, the assembly of an automobile is also broken down into a number of steps. As an automobile travels down an assembly line it must

pass through each phase of assembly in a particular order and can get through the assembly line no faster than the automobile in front of it. The speed of the assembly line is limited by the slowest phase on the line. In a similar way, the slowest stage in a pipeline determines the cycle time for all the stages in the pipeline. If the slowest stage takes twice as long as the fastest, it does no good to subdivide the fastest stage further. And there are certain tasks that are much more difficult to subdivide than others. This fact can lead to a limit on the amount of *useful* subdividing that can be performed.

The overhead term is related to the fact that pipelining requires a certain amount of extra logic (circuitry) between stages, logic that would not be there if the machine were not pipelined. This extra logic introduces a fixed time that cannot be subdivided further.

The interactions among instructions are arguably a more severe limitation on the practical depth of a pipeline and the performance improvements that can be achieved through pipelining. These problems are related to the dependencies that exist between instructions. In the descriptions above, instructions moved through the pipeline in order, but independent of one another. However, consider two instructions that perform the following operations:

```
i:      A = B + C
i+1:    D = A + E
```

Now consider how these instructions flow down a 5-stage pipeline.

```
                          Time
Inst    1    2    3    4    5    6    7    8    9
 i     IF   ID   OF   EX   WB
i+1         IF   ID   OF   EX   WB
```

Instruction i will produce its result, A, at time 5. However, instruction i+1 needs to read the operand A at time 4 (before it is produced). This *data* dependence between instructions is called a Read-after-Write (RAW) hazard, and requires special handling. Typically, circuitry is added to a pipeline to check for such a situation, and if it is detected, instruction i+1 is prevented (blocked or *stalled*) from proceeding down the pipeline until the value it requires is produced. This stalling of instruction i+1 causes a "bubble" to be formed in the pipeline. As shown below instruction i+1 is blocked in the ID stage and must wait until time 6 before it can read the operand it needs.

```
                          Time
Inst    1    2    3    4    5    6    7    8    9   10   11
 i     IF   ID   OF   EX   WB
i+1         IF   ID   st   st   OF   EX   WB
i+2              IF   st   st   ID   OF   EX   WB
i+3                        IF   ID   OF   EX   WB
i+4                             IF   ID   OF   EX   WB
```

This shows how stalls (st) due to the data dependencies between instructions reduce the rate at which instruction are processed. Comparing the diagram above with the original five-stage pipeline diagram reveals that two extra cycles are needed to process the five instructions. The rate at which instructions are processed will, therefore, depend on how many data dependencies exist between the instructions in a given program. It will also depend on the complexity of the pipeline—it is possible to add "bypass" logic, for example, that will allow the EX stage to deliver its result directly to the OF stage, bypassing the WB stage. Such logic can help eliminate some cycles lost to data dependencies, but can also substantially complicate the circuitry and introduce new problems. (It should be pointed out that other types of hazards also exist in more complex pipelines and must be handled properly as well.)

In addition to data dependencies, there are dependencies between instructions that are responsible for calculating the correct path to follow through the program. These types of dependencies are called "control" dependencies, and and are a function of the type of high-level language constructs used by the programmer. An example would be an if statement, implemented, as in this example, with a goto in the machine code:

```
i    D=1
i+1  if (A = B) goto i+3
i+2  D=0
i+3  print D
```

The value of D that will be printed will depend on whether or not A was equal to B. A is generally compared with B by using the subtraction logic in the execute stage. Here is the pipeline diagram of these instructions:

```
                   Time
Inst  1  2  3  4  5  6  7  8  9  10  11
 i    IF ID OF EX WB
i+1      IF ID OF EX WB
i+2         IF ID OF EX WB
i+3            IF ID OF EX WB
i+4               IF ID OF EX WB
```

The problem is clear—the value of the comparison won't be known until time 5, so what instruction should be fetched at time 3?

As was the case with the data dependencies, there are a number of increasingly complicated ways to deal with this problem. The simplest approach is to stop fetching when a branch is recognized and wait until the condition has been calculated. This introduces "bubbles" into the pipeline after every branch. A slightly more complicated way is to decide always to fetch the instructions after the branch (predict that the branch is not taken) which keeps the pipeline full of instructions. This is a *static prediction*, since no run-time information is used, and will not be very accurate in general.

It also requires a mechanism for invalidating those instructions that were not supposed to have been fetched (as do *all* techniques that involve predicting a branch choice).

In order to increase the accuracy of the prediction (and thereby keep the pipeline full of instructions that will be executed and not invalidated), a wide variety of approaches have been developed. More accurate static predictors attempt to exploit what is known about a program—for example, loop-terminating branches are usually taken (back to the beginning of the loop), and loop-exiting branches are usually not taken (branches that detect errors and exceptional conditions). However, without using any dynamic (run-time) information, the achievable accuracy of static branch prediction schemes is very limited.

Dynamic predictors are capable of much higher degrees of accuracy by storing information about the execution of previous branches and using that information to make new predictions. Dynamic predictors vary from simple models (a single bit that stores whether or not the branch was previously taken) to enormously large and complex multiple-level predictors which use different types of prediction mechanisms for different types of branches. As a rule, the more complex the predictor, the more accurate it becomes. Complex dynamic predictors can be designed with average accuracies over 90%. However, because of the nature of these control dependencies and the way that they are distributed throughout a program (what if the instruction at i+2 had been another branch, for example?), some predictors work better for a given program than others. Highly accurate branch predictors are crucial to reducing the problem of control dependencies.

This brief discussion merely highlights some of the issues involved in using pipelining to improve the performance of a processor. For example, the handling of interrupts (*q.v.*) in a pipelined machine has not been described. The proper handling of an interrupt is itself a major concern, but beyond the scope of this discussion. However, what has been presented here is the essence of why a processor is pipelined and the kinds of problems pipelining introduces. All of today's commonly used high-performance processors, such as the Intel Pentium III, the Sun Microsystems Sparc, the Compaq Alpha, and the Motorola/IBM PowerPC, use pipelining to some extent. The details of their pipeline structure vary, but the overall strategy outlined above is basically the same.

Bibliography

1996. Heuring, V. P., and Jordan, H. F. *Computer Systems Design and Architecture*. Reading, MA: Addison-Wesley.

1997. Hennessy, J. L., Patterson, D. A., and Peterson, D. A. *Computer Organization and Design: The Hardware/Software Interface*, 2nd Ed. San Francisco: Morgan Kaufmann.
1999. Omandi, A. *The Microarchitecture of Pipelined and Superscalar Architectures.* Norwell, MA: Kluwer Academic Publishers.

Matthew K. Farrens and Andrew R. Pleszkun

POINTER

For articles on related subjects *see* ADDRESSING; DATA STRUCTURES; LIST PROCESSING; and TREE.

A digital computer memory contains *cells*, which may be referred to by *addresses*. The address of a memory cell is sometimes referred to as a *pointer*, since it may be thought of as pointing to the memory cell to which it refers. A memory cell that contains the address of another cell is also called a pointer.

Pointers may occur at the level of machine language both as direct addresses and as indirect addresses.

LOAD 100   This assembly-language instruction specifies that the content of memory cell 100 is to be loaded into the accumulator. The address 100 is a pointer to the memory cell whose address is 100.

LOAD *100   This indirect-addressing assembly-language instruction (indicated by the *) specifies that location 100 contains the address of the quantity to be loaded into the accumulator. The address 100 is a pointer to a pointer.

In general, a pointer p_1 may point to a cell containing a pointer p_2, and the pointer p_2 may in turn contain a pointer to a cell containing a pointer p_3. A sequence of pointers $p_1, p_2, p_3, \ldots$ such that p_i points to a cell containing p_{i+1} for $i = 1, 2, \ldots$ is called a *pointer chain*.

Pointers also occur in high-level languages such as C (*q.v.*) and C++ (*q.v.*). In C and C++ the declaration

```
int *p
```

defines p to be of type "pointer to integer." If A is a variable of type integer, then the address of A can be assigned to p by writing

```
p = &A
```

Some languages, like standard Pascal (*q.v.*) and Ada (*q.v.*), do not have an "address-of" operator, but assign a value to a pointer variable by a call to an operation that allocates storage for a data structure and puts its address in the pointer variable. If p is a variable that can point to a structure of type *data*, then

```
p := new(data);
```

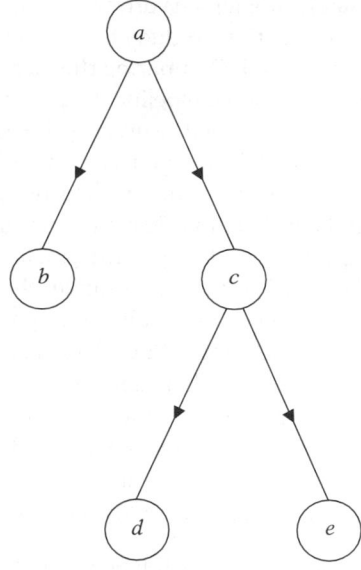

Figure 1.

would place the address of an anonymous variable of type *data* in p.

Dynamic data structures may be implemented as directed graphs in which vertices represent memory cells and directed edges represent pointers between memory cells. For example, the tree structure in Fig. 1 contains five memory cells *a*, *b*, *c*, *d*, *e*, with a pointer from *a* to *b* and pointer chains from *a* through *c* to *d* and *e*.

In general, pointers may be used to connect individual memory cells and also to point from one composite data structure to another. For example, in the diagram the pointer from *a* to *c* may be thought of not merely as a pointer from *a* to the cell *c*, but also as a pointer from *a* to the subtree having *c* as its root.

Pointers are essential in any composite data structure for linking components of the data structure. Nevertheless, they must be used with care because indiscriminate use of pointers leads to undesirable complexity in data structures in much the same way that indiscriminate use of gotos leads to control structure (*q.v.*) complexity.

Bibliography

1998. Liberty, J. "A Few Pointers," *C++ Report*, **10**, *10* (Nov.–Dec.), 57–62.

Peter Wegner

POINTING DEVICE

See INTERACTIVE INPUT DEVICES.

POLISH NOTATION

For articles on related subjects *see* COMPILER; EXPRESSION; LANGUAGE PROCESSORS; PROCEDURE-ORIENTED LANGUAGES; and STACK.

In the 1920s the Polish logician Jan Łukasiewicz devised a *parenthesis-free* notation for logic. This notation, extended for use in algebra and other operator–operand systems, has become known as *Polish notation*. Basically, by consistently placing operators before (or after) their operands, the need for parentheses is eliminated, provided each operator has a fixed number of operands.

Polish notation was originally developed in the *prefix* form, in which the operators precede the operands. The *postfix* or *suffix* form, also known as *reverse Polish notation* or *RPN*, which is logically equivalent to the prefix form, has been widely used in computing. Many compilers first transform an arithmetic expression from its ordinary or *infix* form into RPN, so that its evaluation can be done in a single left-to-right scan. RPN is also used as the basis of operation for some pocket calculators, such as those produced by Hewlett-Packard. However, many people find it difficult to shift their thinking from the infix notation that they have used for years to the concept of providing all of the operands before the operator, so RPN calculators have never had a major share of the market.

Parenthesis elimination is made possible by the fixed number of operands for each operator. Thus if $+$ denotes ordinary addition, we expect two operands. Hence $+ab$ (prefix) and $ab+$ (postfix) are as clearly understandable as $a + b$. The minus sign could cause a problem, since it may be associated with one operand (negative numbers) or two (subtraction). One way of handling this is to use $-$ for ordinary subtraction $(a - b)$ and to use another symbol (such as $\sim$) for unary negation as in $\sim a$ for $(-a)$. Łukasiewicz's original notation used upper-case letters for logical operators, for example, N for logical negation and C for *if-then*, so that $CNpq$ is equivalent to "if not p then q". Table 1 gives several examples of Polish notation.

If a prefix expression is evaluated from right to left, then whenever an operator is encountered, its operands are those that have most recently been evaluated.

Table 1. Polish notation.

Expression	Prefix	Postfix
$a + (-b)$	$+a - b$	$ab - +$
$(-a) + b$	$+ - ab$	$a - b +$
$a*(b + c)$	$*a + bc$	$abc + *$
$(a*b) + c$	$+*abc$	$ab*c +$
$(p \Rightarrow q) \equiv (\sim p \vee q)$	$\equiv \Rightarrow pq \vee \sim pq$	$pq \Rightarrow p \sim q \vee \equiv$

Hence the operator can be immediately processed. The same is true of a postfix expression evaluated from left to right. For example, the evaluation sequence for $*a+bc$ is (with parentheses inserted only to improve readability) $c, b, (+bc), a, *a(+bc)$ which is equivalent to the evaluation of the infix expression $a*(b + c)$ (where now the parentheses are necessary). Similarly, the expression $+*abc$ is evaluated in the order $c, b, a, (*ab), +(*ab)c$ and is equivalent to $(a*b) + c$. Thus, evaluated subexpressions placed on a stack are naturally "popped" from the stack in the order of their use. These two properties—ease of evaluation and unique representation of an expression without use of parentheses or other punctuation—justify Polish notation for use with computer languages and in language processors.

A variant of the prefix notation known as *Cambridge Polish notation* underlies the syntax of the programming language Lisp. Cambridge Polish notation allows operators to have a variable number of operands or *scope*, but requires that the operator and all of its operands be enclosed in a pair of parentheses. The operator ADD, for example, can then be used to add together any list of numbers:

(ADD 5 7) evaluates to 12

(ADD 3 7 −2 5 9) evaluates to 22

(ADD 11) evaluates to 11

Bibliography

1979. Copi, I. *Symbolic Logic*, 5th Ed. Upper Saddle River, NJ: Prentice Hall.

Robert R. Korfhage

POLITICAL APPLICATIONS

For articles on related subjects *see* SOCIAL SCIENCE APPLICATIONS; and SOCIETY, COMPUTERS IN.

The political process admits definitions ranging from the very narrow, restricting the term to the campaign process, to a very broad definition that includes much of the legislative and executive activities. In this brief review of computers and politics, we adopt a relatively restrictive view. Our description of the employment of computers will be discussed under three major applications: (1) the campaign process, (2) vote projection, and (3) political reapportionment.

Campaign Process

By far the major employment of computers in political campaigns takes advantage of the equipment to maintain mailing lists and generate computer-composed letters that are personalized to the extent that sentences or paragraphs reflect the previously indexed interests of the addressee. Frequently, that individual's name is embedded in the text of the letter to enhance personalization even further.

Mailing lists are maintained that specify for each person a set of personal characteristics, such as residence, degree of economic affluence, education, sex, race, ethnicity, religion, and political affiliation. In addition, the lists are indexed to reflect a history of prior campaign contributions and those political, social, and economic issues sufficiently interesting to the individual to have promoted a previous expression of opinion to a legislator or a candidate.

Although no hard statistics are available, it is estimated that 90–98% of computer applications in the campaign process relate to direct mail, whose intent is to influence opinion or to solicit contributions. The small remaining balance includes more sophisticated uses of computers in the management of a campaign. Among these applications are (1) the organization and maintenance of and coping with changes in the campaign activities and (2) the development and use of models for the allocation of funds or of the candidate's time and the simulation of a campaign in different jurisdictions, where the interplay of the emphasis of different issues will have varying effects upon the voting population. Such models require a large database of voter attitudes towards issues and knowledge of the extent to which the emphasis, either in support of or in opposition to a particular issue, will sway an already committed or politically leaning voter.

The existence of a database of this type allows a final application of computers to the campaign process, the tabulation and analysis of public opinion polls wherein voter opinions on issues are related to degrees of candidate support. The results of the analyses serve as aids to campaign strategy in determining issues and areas of strength and weakness that may be defined geographically or in terms of characteristics of segments of the voting population. A candidate's campaign strategist may be able to identify issues that may influence "undecided" or "leaning" voters, without alienating those who have already decided to support the candidate.

The near universal availability of increasingly powerful personal computers that have access to centralized databases has made the computer an essential tool used by political theorists and campaign strategists.

In 1996, both US presidential candidates maintained extensive Internet Websites. By 1998, virtually all elected officials also did so.

Unfortunately, the ubiquity of computers provides an environment in which there is great temptation to mis-

chief. In addition to the existence of the official Websites managed by candidates and elected officials, there are many unauthorized sites that are parodies of the official ones. And modern image and speech processing techniques make it quite easy for unscrupulous Webmasters to post pictures and sound bites of events that never happened.

Occasionally, computers can be enlisted to undo attempts to mislead. In 1998, the governor of New York reluctantly and belatedly kept a promise to provide records of campaign contributors by releasing them alphabetized by first name, making it difficult to locate an individual contributor's name. But all it takes to thwart this is a scanner and a short program that knows how to read and permute first and last names prior to sorting them by last name.

Vote Projection

The use of computers by the television networks to project early voting returns into estimates of the final result was the first introduction of the computer and its possibilities to large parts of the US population. The first broad-scale application of computers to vote projections began in the 1952 Eisenhower–Stevenson race, making use of a UNIVAC I (*q.v.*). By the time of the 1960 election, all networks were using some form of computer assistance, and the 1964 presidential election saw the first full, large-scale, three-network competition, each network making use of its own system and its own computer to project the election results. The mathematical models that form the basis of the projection procedures for the three networks differed markedly at the time. Since then, there has been a tendency to conform to a more uniform philosophy, although considerable differences in approach and in execution still exist among the four major US TV networks.

As an example, the technique used by one network makes use of an equation of the form

$$P = w_b P_b + w_p P_p + w_v P_v$$

where the ws are weights and the Ps are individual estimates of the vote for, say, the Democratic candidate obtained by considerations of the baseline (b), key precincts (p), and raw vote (v). P_b is an estimate based upon exit polls and a compilation of all available pre-election information, including polls and informed opinion. P_p is an estimate based upon the change in a select sample of key precincts over a prior compar-able election. The sample precincts are checked carefully to ensure that the characteristics of the voting population in each precinct have not varied significantly since the prior comparable election; e.g. that what had been a blue-collar working class precinct has not been replaced by a luxury high-rise development. The estimate provided by P_v is the actual raw vote as it is assembled at state or regional collection centers from counties and individual precincts and transmitted to the networks. The raw vote may be adjusted for reporting patterns if, for example, a larger proportion of the more Democratic urban vote is typically reported before the more Republican rural vote in a state.

All quantities in the equation are constantly changing. At any time, the sum of the weighting coefficients, the ws, must be unity. They reflect the relative importance of the factors associated with them in the equation. At the beginning of the evening, $w_b = 1$ and the other two coefficients are zero, reflecting the fact that the only component of the estimate is the pre-election baseline. As the evening continues, the dominant effect is generally assumed by the second term w_pP_p, with its magnitude being a function both of the number of key precincts whose returns have been entered into the model and the degree of consistency they have shown. As more raw vote is received, the first two coefficients tend to zero; w_v assumes dominance and ultimately becomes 1 when all precincts have reported. In those states where absentee ballots are counted in a special way after the votes cast on election day are counted, provision is made to incorporate the effect of the absentee ballots into the model.

Operations of the networks have evolved from intense competition in reporting the largest vote returns and earliest (accurate) projections to a pooled operation that, incidentally, saves each network several million dollars each quadrennial election cycle. Pooling has eliminated the differentiating characteristics of the networks, except for the subjective appeal of their on-air talent and the interpretation and analysis of the vote results.

The major networks and wire services combined to form the News Election Service (NES), which was responsible for collecting the actual vote at local precinct, county, and ward levels, aggregating this vote into higher-level political jurisdictions, and sending updated totals at rapid intervals to all subscribers simultaneously. The networks agreed that the NES vote would be the only vote displayed.

Beginning with the 1990 election, Cable News Network (CNN) and the other networks combined to support Voter Research and Surveys (VRS), whose nucleus was the CBS operation and its key staff. VRS was organized to provide the actual vote, exit poll data, and projections of individual races. VRS advocates claimed that, as a result, "there was no longer the fierce, and somewhat artificial, competition" that previously marked network election broadcasts. Unfortunately, however, the VRS operation failed to perform as promised in delivering results of exit polls and other data as promised to its subscribers, including several of the nation's leading newspapers. It was reported that VRS personnel were afraid a power surge would short out the computers at a critical stage of the operation, and VRS projections, absent the competition, were conservative and relatively slow. Even so, one projected race was "uncalled" for a long time before being reinstated as correct.

Political Reapportionment

The Supreme Court's "one person-one vote" decision in *Reynolds v. Sims* in 1964 led to an investigation of the use of computers to aid legislators in reapportioning their electoral jurisdictions to be acceptable to the Court's dictum. Most applications have been to state legislatures, but there have also been applications to Congressional redistricting within a state and in the drawing of district lines by municipal councils.

The various models that have been developed, most of which depend upon a computer for their practicality, differ in their approach to the specification of initial conditions for the legislative reapportionment and in the criteria used to find the best allocation.

The less politically sophisticated "nonpartisan" models attempt to lay a rectangular grid across a state, modifying the lines so as to obtain as nearly an equal proportion of the electorate in each of the districts as possible. Other models that reflect a greater degree of political sophistication commence with an initial allocation based upon the existing legislative boundaries and then perturbing them in such a way as to obtain population parity. To be practical, all models must recognize political boundaries, such as towns and counties, and major geographical barriers, such as bodies of water and mountain ranges.

Mathematical models and associated computer programs have been developed by various academic and commercial organizations. They differ in their degree of political sophistication, the extent to which online graphics are used, and in their ability to introduce degrees of partisanship, such as to give as great a representation as possible to one political party or one ethnic group.

Bibliography

1972. Chartrand, R. I. *Computers and Political Campaigning.* New York: Spartan Books.

1973. Moshman, J., and Kokiko, E. M. "A Redistricting Algorithm Applied to Geographic Reorganization of Circuit Courts," *Annals of the New York Academy of Sciences,* **219**, 236–245.

1990. Berke, R. L. "TV Networks Join in Voter Surveys," *New York Times,* **CXL**, 7 November, A1 and B6.

1996. Browning, G., and Weitzer, D. J. *Electronic Democracy: Using the Internet to Influence American Politics.* Wilton, CT: Pemberton Press.

1996. Sardar, Z., and Ravetz, J. R. *Cyberfutures: Culture and Politics on the Information Superhighway.* New York: NYU Press.

1997. Rash, W. *Politics on the Nets: Wiring the Political Process.* New York: W. H. Freeman.

1998. Hill, K. A., and Hughes, J. E. *Cyberpolitics: Citizen Activism in the Age of the Internet: People, Passions, and Power.* Lanham, MD: Rowman & Littlefield.

1998. Senlow, G. W. *Electronic Whistle-Stops: The Impact of the Internet on American Politics.* Westport, CT: Praeger Publications.

Jack Moshman, revised by Edwin D. Reilly

POLLING

For articles on related subjects *see* CONTENTION; LOCAL AREA NETWORK; MULTIPLEXING; and NETWORKS, COMPUTER.

In computing, a number of processes or devices often compete for shared resources. *Polling* or contention techniques are used to resolve such problems and enforce discipline.

In polling, the order of accessing the shared resource is managed so that competition is avoided and each process or device can use the shared resource for a limited time only. Polling can be centralized or distributed.

Centralized polling requires a master process or device to control access by devices subservient to the shared resource (*slaves*). The master simply addresses or polls each slave to provide access when it is needed. If access is not needed, the addressed slave sends a *negative acknowledgement*, which causes the master to poll the next slave. A polling system has the advantage that either all slaves can receive equal access, or else priority can be given by polling some slaves more often than others. Furthermore, a polling system can be arranged to function effectively over long distances since it can be adjusted to compensate for long propagation delays. For this reason, it can be used to connect a large number of widely separated slave stations to a master station or computer over a single communication line. The disadvantage is that there is a single point of failure. When the master goes down, so does the entire system. Centralized polling is often used by mainframes to check periodically the status of attached peripherals. The situation is similar to a chairperson who controls a meeting by choosing the order in which people are to speak.

Distributed polling is usually implemented by passing a *token* in a predetermined order amongst devices connected by a bus (*q.v.*) or a ring. The owner of the token, which is a special bit pattern, has the exclusive use of the bus or ring if it has data to transfer. If not, it passes the token to the next device. The *token bus* or *token ring* systems, as they are called, provide the fairness and distance insensitivity of the polling system. However, they rely on the reliability of the nodes, and provision must be made to recover gracefully from failures that cause the token to disappear. IBM's token ring network uses this technique to transfer data between a mainframe and devices attached to a network. Here, the situation is similar to a meeting where people have the opportunity to speak in some predetermined order, such as the alphabetic order of their names.

John S. Sobolewski

PORT, I/O

For articles on related subjects *see* BUS; DRIVER; ETHERNET; HARD DISK; MODEM; PRINTERS; SYNCHRONOUS/ASYNCHRONOUS OPERATION; and TERMINALS.

I/O ports are the interfaces through which computers communicate with external devices such as printers (*q.v.*), modems (*q.v.*), joysticks, and terminals. They are superficially distinguished by their connectors, which have different shapes and numbers of contact pins, and by the varieties of devices that may be connected to them. A more significant difference is the variety of protocols (*q.v.*) that are used with them—the protocols specify what control and data signals the port uses, and how they are to be interpreted.

This article will describe the common ports found on personal computers and workstations. Larger computers will typically have many of them as well, perhaps together with specialized ports for high-speed I/O (*see* INPUT–OUTPUT OPERATIONS).

Parallel Ports

A *parallel port* transmits the bits of a byte of data in parallel, so it has eight data lines as well as more for control of devices. It is a simple and widely used way to connect a printer to a computer. The original parallel port was designed by Centronics, and had 36 pins. IBM developed parallel ports with 25 pins; in both cases not all the pins needed to be used. Some carried control signals appropriate for high-speed line printers but not needed for small printers.

Because parallel ports transmit an entire byte at a time, they can operate at relatively high speeds and have been adapted for use with magnetic tape devices for computer backups and for transferring data between systems. Some of these uses require two-way communication, and there are now bidirectional parallel ports, defined by a standard, IEEE 1284.

Although parallel ports can use simple protocols, by virtue of transmitting data in parallel, their cables must be relatively large, with 18 to 25 or more wires. Interference among the multiple signals limits the cables to relatively short distances, roughly 10 feet (3 meters).

Serial Ports

Serial ports are designed for relatively low-speed communication, such as with a keyboard, character-oriented terminal, mouse (*q.v.*), or slow communication line. They transmit the bits of a byte one at a time. The serial port interface is a UART (Universal Asynchronous Receiver–Transmitter), containing a shift register that loads a byte in parallel from the computer and shifts its bits serially through the port (*see* SHIFTING). At the other end, the bits are reassembled into the byte. A serial-line cable can be simple, with as few as two signal lines (for transmitting and receiving) and ground.

A serial port transmits a simple stream of bits. The serial port protocol uses start- and stop-bits to delimit bytes. The two sides of the connection must agree on whether to use a bit for a parity (*q.v.*) check and on the rate for bit transmission (110 bits/sec for the early Teletypes, and up to 115,200 bits/sec for current PC ports. A failure to agree on these typically produces the gibberish familiar to those who configure modem connections.

Although serial communication can use as few as three wires, serial ports frequently use one or more additional ones to synchronize data transmission, and the RS-232C standard for serial lines defines 10. The original connectors had 25 pins, and the newer IBM "AT" connector has nine (a little-used chassis ground is omitted). Serial cables can be 25 feet (8 meters) or longer, though a long cable will limit the maximum possible bit-rate.

USB

The *Universal Serial Bus* port was introduced in 1996 to simplify the connection of serial devices. As with other buses, multiple devices may be connected to a USB port (through a simple *hub*). The USB protocol allows devices to identify themselves to the computer, and to exchange data with it at their own rates, not all the same. The USB port controller interrogates the devices to determine their characteristics and assigns each a 7-bit address (with one bit-pattern reserved, there can be up to 127 devices connected to a USB port). The devices all share in the total data bandwidth (*q.v.*) of the bus, 12 Mb/sec for shielded-wire cables; 1.5 Mb/sec for unshielded.

The USB cable has four wires, two for data and two for power to the devices. The cable is limited to 16 feet (5 meters) between hubs, which serve as *repeaters* to restore signal strength. The USB protocol achieves higher speeds than the RS-232C protocol does by using *differential signaling*. The signal is the difference between the voltages on two lines, rather than the value of the voltage on a single line. This technique is less interference-prone, since noise will affect the two lines similarly and will be largely canceled in subtracting the two values.

In addition to being used for devices with low data rates, USB ports can be used for external disk drives. 12 Mb/sec is a low transfer rate, but it suffices for disks used for backing up internal disks.

Firewire

Firewire is a new IEEE standard (1394) for a high-speed serial port. As of 1999, it could operate at speeds of 100 to 400 Mb/sec, fast enough to carry video signals between a video camera and computer with no loss of image quality or size. It is intended for high-bandwidth multimedia (*q.v.*) data, but is fast enough to be used as a disk-drive connection too. Multiple devices can be connected to a Firewire port, and they take turns transmitting packets of data.

The Firewire connection has six wires; four for data. Like USB, Firewire uses differential signaling for high bandwidth. Firewire uses two pairs of data lines to maintain synchronization at its high speeds, and the cables can be about 15 feet (4.5 meters) long.

Other Ports

Two other kinds of ports are SCSI ("scuzzy") (*see* HARD DISK) and Ethernet. The parallel SCSI port is used for internal and external disk drives on Apple computers and workstations, among others, and for other high-speed devices like tape and CD-ROM drives. Like USB it is a bus protocol, and multiple devices can be connected to a SCSI port in a serial "daisy-chained" fashion. It can currently operate at up to 40 MB/sec. An Ethernet port connects a controller in the computer to a local area network (LAN—*q.v.*) using the Ethernet bit-serial protocol. It may use a shielded, coaxial cable, but more commonly now it uses a "10base-T" or "100base-T" twisted-pair wire (the number designates the speed in Mb/sec). The latter cables have modular connectors similar to the common modular plug for telephones.

Bibliography

1999. Rosch, W. L. *The Winn L. Rosch Hardware Bible*, 5th Ed. Indianapolis, IN: Que Corp.

David Hemmendinger

PORT, MEMORY

For articles on related subjects *see* BUS; CHANNEL; INPUT–OUTPUT CONTROL SYSTEM; INPUT–OUTPUT INSTRUCTIONS; and MEMORY: AUXILIARY.

In some early computers the main memory had a single *port* (Fig. 1a) or logical connection through which to transfer data under CPU control. In current systems, a single memory port is connected to a *bus* (*q.v.*) through which several CPUs and I/O devices have memory access (Fig. 1b). On the more powerful systems, bus traffic can become so intense that, with only a single memory port, the speed of some important high-speed activity may be sacrificed. Thus, a second port may be added to the memory to serve the CPU separately from the bus (Fig. 1c).

Dual-port memory has several other uses. Some multi-processing (*q.v.*) systems of the NUMA (Non-Uniform Memory Access) variety use dual-port memory to give each processor rapid access directly to its own

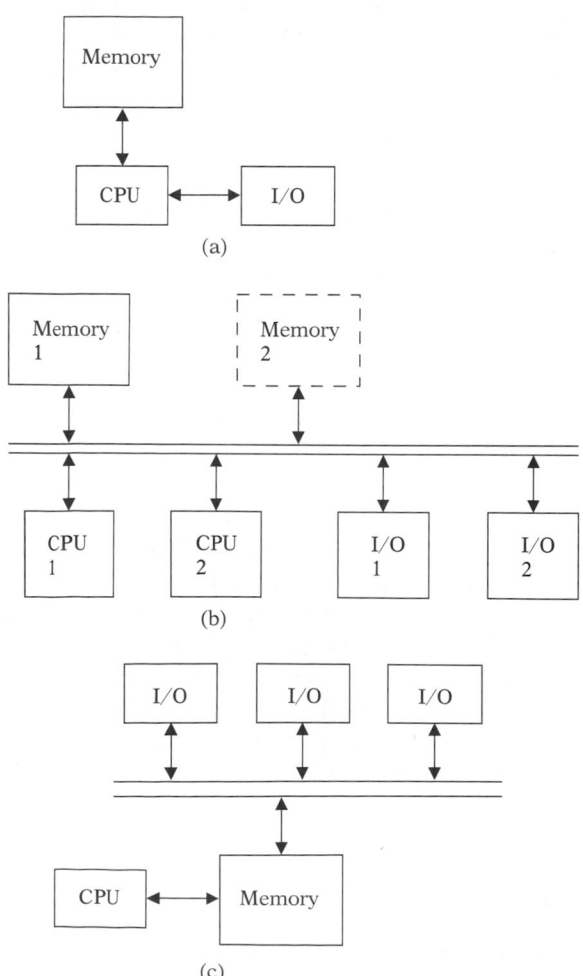

Figure 1. Memory port connections: (a) single port, simply connected; (b) single-port, bus-connected; (c) dual-port memory serving a CPU and a bus.

memory through one port, while connecting the system bus to the other port, thereby allowing any other processor slower access to that memory via the bus (*see* SUPERCOMPUTERS).

Dual-port memory can be used in digital signal processing (DSP), which uses the fast Fourier transform (*q.v.*), making repeated calculations of arithmetic expressions of related variables. Dual-port memory can speed up this intensive computation by allowing several calculations to be done at once. Another application of dual-port memory is in computer video memory, since the dual ports let the video controller display an image stored in memory while the processor is also updating it.

Within a multiport memory there must, of course, be some form of interlock (*q.v.*) mechanism to arbitrate conflict between port requests when both attempt to write the same memory cell (*see* MUTUAL EXCLUSION). The interlock may be a circuit that uses a "busy" signal to prevent one of the writes from taking place, or it may be an interrupt (*q.v.*) mechanism that can be used to implement turn-taking. Because of the complexity of arbitration, multiport memory generally has two ports; four ports are feasible, but not common. The 10-processor Univac 1100/94 had a 10-port memory, with arbitration done by the operating system.

Bibliography

1998. Baumann, M. *The Most Commonly Asked Questions about Dual-Ports.* AN-91. Santa Clara, CA: Integrated Device Technology, Inc. http://www.idt.com/docs/7130_AN_9477.pdf.

David Hemmendinger

PORTABILITY

See SOFTWARE PORTABILITY.

PORTABLE COMPUTERS

For articles on related subjects *see* MOBILE COMPUTING; and PERSONAL COMPUTING.

A *portable computer* is small, light enough to be carried, and can operate on an internal battery. Although many portables do not need a separate source of electrical power, they can use one when available. Running a portable on AC power can recharge the battery as well as power the computer. In terms of decreasing weight and the order in which they were developed, portable computers can be classified as:

◆ luggable

◆ laptop

◆ notebook

◆ palmtop (or hand-held, or PDA—*Personal Digital Assistants*)

Hand-held computers resemble pocket calculators but possess many of the capabilities of a personal or even a mainframe (*q.v.*) computer. *Laptops* and *notebook* computers offer complete personal computer functionality in a size convenient for holding on a person's lap. Luggable computers, no longer competitive because of weight, furnished fully functional machines in a small-suitcase-sized package.

The enabling technologies for the laptop computer, the most prevalent type of portable computer in 1999, include: flat-panel displays; electronic components and disk drives that use very little power; long-life, rechargeable batteries; and a compact keyboard that provides some special way to move the display cursor other than through an external mouse (which can be added as an option). A telecommunications capability can be added through use of a miniaturized modem having the form of a PCMCIA card or by an Ethernet connection.

Evolution of Portable Computers

The first portable computers weighed 28–33 pounds (12.5–15 kg) and were packaged in a ruggedized case very similar to the housings used for their desktop counterparts. This modified case provided a handle for carrying the machine, and frequently used a detachable keyboard that doubled as a cover for the display and front panel area. The Osborne 1 Portable, introduced in 1981, was the first such "luggable" computer. It used a standard cathode-ray tube (CRT) screen that measured a scant 5 diagonal inches— a screen very similar to that of an oscilloscope. This small screen, which displayed only 40 characters by 15 lines, was very difficult to read. The machine came with dual built-in floppy disk drives and a detachable keyboard. It required AC power, and used CP/M, the standard operating system of the day.

In that same year, Epson America introduced the first laptop computer. Its HX-20 used a 20 character by 4 line liquid crystal matrix flat-panel display (LCD). The computer ran on standard lead-acid batteries. It even sported a built-in printer very similar to a cash register tape printer. The built-in software and small display made the machine only marginally useful.

In 1983, Radio Shack proved the usefulness of the laptop computer concept with the introduction of the TRS-80 Model 100. This 4-pound (2 kg), battery-operated computer used a 40 character by 6 line LCD screen and provided useful built-in text editing and communications software. The machine soon became a favorite of newspaper and magazine journalists who found that its small size and easy-to-use text creation and transmission software made the computer an ideal writing tool to take on the road. A later version, the Model 200, provided a built-in disk drive, a larger screen, and a "clamshell" design (adopted by most subsequent laptops), in which the screen folded onto the keyboard when the computer was not in use.

The evolution of the laptop computer accelerated in response to the success of the Model 100. The IBM PC and its PC-DOS operating system rapidly became the standard for business personal computing after 1982, and laptops touting IBM PC compatibility sprang up from many sources. Through this period portable computers, such as the Compaq portable (introduced in 1982), acquired 9-inch CRT screens while dropping in weight to the 17–22 pound (8–10 kg) range. Portable computers started providing hard disk capacity in 1985, and laptops later added first floppy disk and then hard disk storage as well. In 1988, the NEC UltraLite machine heralded the arrival of the "notebook" computer, a laptop the size of a notebook that weighed under 5 pounds (2.5 kg), and provided all the functionality of an IBM PC-AT class computer. Gradually, vendors began calling their laptops "notebooks" even when by weight—8 to 10 pounds (3.5–4.5 kg)—they really do not qualify. In response, vendors of machines weighing 5 pounds (2.5 kg) or less began to call them "subnotebooks."

As of 1999, the state-of-the-art in notebook computers provide a fast Intel Pentium, Sparc, or PowerPC microprocessor; CD-ROM, diskette, and hard-disk storage; a high-resolution flat-panel color screen; built-in networking and telecommunications capability; and the ability to run almost all desktop computer applications consistent with its processor. Battery-powered, these machines can run for 4–8 hours between charges. These capabilities come packaged in a notebook-sized machine that costs about $2,000 and weighs less than 8 pounds (3.5 kg). One of the lightest and thinnest is the Toshiba Portégé 3010CT whose screen has a 10.4″ diagonal, is only $\frac{3}{4}''$ thick and weighs less than 3 pounds (1.5 kg) (*see* Fig. 1).

Enabling Technologies

One of the most important of the enabling technologies for laptop and notebook computers resulted from improvements in semiconductor fabrication. A fabrication technique called complementary metal-oxide semiconductor (CMOS) allowed the building of integrated circuit (IC) (*see* INTEGRATED CIRCUITRY) components that required very small amounts of electrical power and produced negligible amounts of heat.

Figure 1. The Toshiba Portégé 3010CT notebook computer.

CMOS-based microprocessors, memory chips, and other circuits along with design innovations like surface mounting of ICs let laptop manufacturers pack more computing power into a smaller space. Furthermore, CMOS components draw small enough quantities of electricity that they can be powered by a battery for extended periods of time.

Another key component of laptop computers—the flat panel display (*see* MONITOR, DISPLAY)—evolved rapidly in the 1980s due to heavy research and development by the Japanese. LCD (liquid crystal display) technology evolved from low-contrast, narrow-viewing angle twisted-nematic LCDs in 1984, through supertwist LCDs in the late 1980s, to the active matrix or thin-film-transistor (TFT) displays that became standard on the high-end laptops of the late 1990s. Each of these technologies increased the resolution and the readability of the machine's screens but also increased their cost and decreased the time that one battery charge would power a computer.

Battery technology improved to keep pace with the increased power demands of higher-resolution displays and the addition of floppy and hard disk drives. Some early laptops used flashlight batteries, but the later more sophisticated machines use rechargeable lithium ion or nickel hydride batteries. The nickel–cadmium battery was the standard for a good part of the 1990s because of its good weight-to-power ratio

and its nearly constant power output voltage, regardless of charge. But the increased power demands, typically 17 to 22 watts, of today's high-end machines have kept battery designers struggling to keep up with users' demands.

Laptop computers became the personal computer of choice for a substantial number of business people in the 1990s. As a result, the trend in displays is toward bigger, not smaller, screen sizes. While the 10.4-inch display was standard for some time, screen sizes up to 15″ are rapidly gaining favor. Larger screens require more power. Battery innovations under development include lithium polymer batteries which make use of a shapable plastic electrolyte, and zinc–air batteries which can power a laptop for up to 12 hours but at the cost of a housing almost as big as the computer itself.

Hand-held computers

More innovative technologies, such as stylus and pen-based input devices coupled with character-recognition software in a hand-held sized package, have created a whole new generation of very small computers variously called hand-held PCs (HPCs), pen computers, palmtops, or Personal Digital Assistants (PDAs). The typical palm computer with dimensions of about $5 \times 3 \times \frac{1}{2}$ in and weight less than a pound fits easily into the pocket. In lieu of a physical keyboard, input is entered by writing on a touchscreen display or by entering words letter-by-letter by touching a displayed keyboard. One of the first of these was the Apple Newton but this was not a commercial success because users claimed that it was not as good in recognizing handwritten screen notes as they had expected.

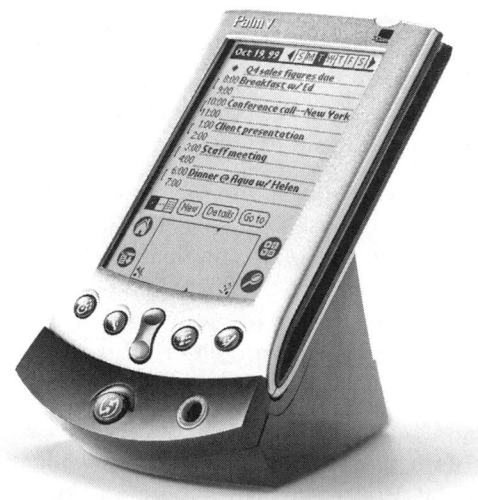

Figure 2. The 3Com PalmPilot V palmtop computer.

But the 3Com Corporation has sold several million of its popular PalmPilot PDAs. The 1999 PalmPilot V version costs about $450, has 2 MB of memory, and a proprietary operating system, Palm OS, that supports a wide variety of software (*see* Fig. 2.) The IBM WorkPad is very similar.

Not surprisingly, the Microsoft Corporation began to recognize the importance of the hand-held computer market as early as 1996 when it introduced a stripped-down version of its Windows operating system called Windows CE (which computer magazines call WinCE). Microsoft has never said what CE stands for, though a reasonable guess would be "Compact Environment." WinCE was soon adopted as the standard operating system (*q.v.*) by the makers of a number of hand-held computers (those with large enough memories to make use of it). This has led to a dichotomy which may not last, namely, that the hand-held computers that use WinCE are called HPCs and the smaller computers (both in size and memory) that do not are called palmtops.

Bibliography

1997. Sweeney, D. "Is Bigger Always Better?" *Mobile Computing and Communications*, **8**, *3*, 66–72.
1997. Bassak, G. "Running On Empty," *Mobile Computing and Communications*, **8**, *6*, 76–85.
1999. Bassak, G. *PC Novice Guide to Computing: Portables and Windows CE*, **6**, *11* (January). Lincoln, NE: Sandhills Publishing.

G. Michael Vose

POSTSCRIPT

> For articles on related subjects *see* DESKTOP PUBLISHING; MARKUP LANGUAGES; METAFONT; PROBLEM-ORIENTED LANGUAGES; PROGRAMMING LANGUAGES; T_EX; TYPEFONT; and WORD PROCESSING.

PostScript is a device-independent page description language. Page description languages are programming languages that are optimized to render document images on display devices. Display devices may be workstation (*q.v.*) screens, laser printers, film recorders, fax machines, or phototypesetters. PostScript programming is especially applicable to situations where a user has a mathematical description of an image and wants to know what it looks like.

The PostScript Language

The language specification for PostScript is in the public domain. It is derived from work that was done at Xerox PARC in the late 1970s and early 1980s. When Xerox declined to make this work the basis of a product, the Adobe Systems Corporation was formed and developed a PostScript implementation that has be-

come the *de facto* standard page description language. Adobe Systems licensed the technology to printer manufacturers, most notably to Apple Computer for the Apple LaserWriter product which was introduced in January 1985. Steve Jobs (*see* ENTREPRENEURS) saw PostScript and the Apple LaserWriter as the missing pieces required to create a larger market for the Apple Macintosh computer. Barely three years later, publishing products had to support PostScript output in order to be commercially viable. PostScript is as responsible as anything else for creating the demand for desktop publishing technology that is often credited to the program Aldus PageMaker. Most printer manufacturers now offer PostScript printers. Ghostscript is a freely available PostScript interpreter that runs on personal computers and workstations.

PostScript source code is characterized not only by device independence, but also by an all-ASCII representation and a postfix syntax (*see* POLISH NOTATION) that makes it easy to generate from programs. Like Forth (*q.v.*), its stack-oriented operations are interpreted and not compiled (*see* LANGUAGE PROCESSORS). Dynamic binding (*see* BINDING) and the postfix syntax make it possible to produce fast interpreters. PostScript supports a relatively small number of data types (*q.v.*) and a rich set of more than 200 primitives that allow specification of text, line drawings, images, and color. It supports system-defined operators, names, and dictionaries that are accessible and easily modified by expert-level programmers. PostScript programs may be executed by interpreters running on desktop computers or on microprocessors embedded within PostScript printers.

In PostScript, a page is represented as a bitmap, one bit per picture element (*pixel*). When an actual page is printed, each pixel corresponding to a 1-bit is printed in black and each pixel corresponding to a 0-bit is printed in white (actually, left blank). To preserve machine independence, however, one is not allowed to read from or write to the bitmap. Instead, programs include "painting" operators that set and clear bits within defined areas of the bitmap.

PostScript is designed to be portable. The all-ASCII representation allows PostScript files to be transmitted across electronic networks easily and reliably. The descriptions of objects and paths are separated from their imaging for any particular display technology or device. Objects can be stroked or filled. *Stroking* a path produces an image on the page consisting of a line of specified thickness. Filling a path paints areas inside the path with a specified gray level. Paths and outlines can be specified as sequences of lines, circular arcs, and Bezier cubic *splines* (*q.v.*). PostScript also supports embedded bitmap images.

```
%
% Define a procedure to print the words
% "Heather and Courtney" on the three sides
% of an imaginary box centered at the origin.
/hcprint
  {
    gsave
    90 rotate
    -45 90 moveto (Heather) show
    -90 rotate
    -21 90 moveto (and) show
    -90 rotate
    -54 90 moveto (Courtney) show
    grestore
  }
def

% Make the current font 30 point Times
% Roman
/Times-Roman findfont 30 scalefont setfont

% Move the coordinate system origin 3
% inches up and right
216 216 translate

% Draw a 240 degree circular arc centred
% near the origin
9 9 72 -30 210 arc stroke

% Print "Heather and Courtney" 20 times at
% 20 increasingly dark gray levels, each
% time moving the origin slightly up and
% to the right
.95 -.05 0 {setgray hcprint 1 1 translate}
for

% Print "Heather and Courtney" one more
% time in white.
1 setgray hcprint

% Produce the printed page.
showpage
```

Figure 1.　A short PostScript program.

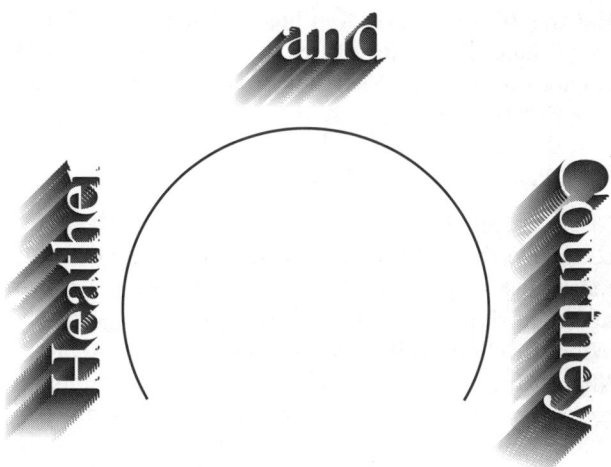

Figure 2.　Output of program in Fig. 1.

PostScript's generality, power, and flexibility is a two-edged sword. Coding and debugging complex images using native PostScript can be time-consuming and difficult. Unless special care is taken, name collisions can occur between system and user operations, and applications can suffer at the hands of redefined system operators.

A typical small PostScript program is shown in Fig. 1. Lines that begin with the percent sign (%) are comments. The printed output generated by the program is shown in Fig. 2.

Encapsulated PostScript

Since users often want to be able to reuse data and information, it is essential for one application to gener-

ate well-behaved PostScript code for use by another; that is, it should be easy to import and export Post-Script code among different applications. For example, graphics objects or spreadsheet (*q.v.*) results often need to be incorporated into documents produced, using different desktop publishing software products. *Encapsulated PostScript* provides software developers with rules and guidelines for producing PostScript code that can be easily exported. It defines a control block that contains specific information in a standard format, followed by a PostScript definition of an image and, optionally, by a hex-encoded bitmapped representation of the image for display on raster devices that do not support a PostScript interpreter (e.g. bitmapped screens on personal computers and workstations).

PostScript Fonts

PostScript has revolutionized the way people think about and use fonts. Characters in font families (e.g. Times Roman, Helvetica) and font style (e.g. normal, italic, bold) are largely treated as special cases of filling outlines. For this reason, characters can be scaled (e.g. 10 points, 18 points, 72 points (1 inch)), stretched, or rotated just like any other PostScript object. Outline fonts are compact, on the order of 150 KB, and contain specially encoded "hints" to the PostScript interpreter that improve their appearance at the relatively low 300 dots/inch resolution of early laser printers. By contrast, characters stored as rasters (i.e. bitmaps) do not scale well beyond about 15% of their design size and grow in storage requirements in proportion to the square of the resolution (e.g. doubling the resolution quadruples the storage requirement for a character at a particular point size). However, fonts available in raster format but not as outlines can be downloaded and processed using PostScript's support for bitmapped images.

Bibliography

1985. Adobe Systems, Inc. *PostScript Language Tutorial and Cookbook*. Reading, MA: Addison-Wesley.

1990. Smith, R. *Learning PostScript: A Visual Approach*. Reading, MA: Addison-Wesley.

1997. Weingartner, P. *A First Guide to PostScript*. http://www.cs.indiana.edu/docproject/programming/postscript/postscript.html.

1997. Adobe Systems, Inc. *PostScript Language Reference*, 3rd Ed. Reading, MA: Addison-Wesley.

1999. http://www.cs.wisc.edu/~ghost/. The source of Ghostscript and related programs and documentation.

David L. Rodgers

POWER USER

For articles on related subjects *see* GURU; and WIZARD.

A *power user* is a person who knows and uses a particular piece of software to its maximum extent. The term is always qualified by the name of the applicable software; we speak of a Unix power user, a WordPerfect power user, an Excel power user, etc. Such a person is not usually a programmer who can modify the system, but rather one who knows its reference manual inside out and who can apply not only that knowledge, but also additional "lore" that he or she constantly gleans from trade magazines, Internet surfing, bulletin boards (*q.v.*), conferences, user groups (*q.v.*), and email caucuses with others who share a similar desire to master use of a particular item of software.

Edwin D. Reilly

POWERS, JAMES

For articles on related subjects *see* HOLLERITH, HERMAN; HOLLERITH MACHINE; IBM CORPORATION; PUNCHED CARD; and PUNCHED CARD MACHINERY.

James Powers, born in Odessa, Russia, in 1871, was an inventor of punched card accounting machinery and founder of the Powers Accounting Machine Company. He graduated from the Technical School of Odessa and was for a time employed in a mechanical shop connected with the University of Odessa in making scientific instruments. He emigrated to the USA in 1889 and was employed by various engineering concerns, including Western Electric. He obtained several patents in his own name and did experimental work on office machines, including typewriters, adding machines, and cash registers, as well as early work on telephones and automatic machines of various types.

In 1907, the United States Bureau of the Census employed Powers as a mechanical expert to improve the punched card tabulating machinery developed by

Figure 1. James Powers.

Herman Hollerith for the 1890 and 1900 censuses. Hollerith himself had broken with the Bureau in 1905 following a dispute with the director of the census. Powers introduced several major improvements to the existing census machinery, including an electrically operated card punch and a printing tabulator. In 1911, Powers left the Bureau of the Census and incorporated the Powers Accounting Machinery Company to develop punched card machines for commercial applications. (In doing so, Powers followed the precedent of Herman Hollerith, who, in 1896, incorporated the Tabulating Machine Company, which later became IBM.) During 1912–13, Powers and his assistant, W. W. Lasker, developed a range of machines that included the "slide" and "visible" card punches, the "double-deck" horizontal sorter, and printing and non-printing tabulating machines. The machines were actively marketed beginning in 1913, and the first overseas operations were established shortly afterwards. Although the early Powers machines had several important advantages over those offered by Hollerith, the US Powers organization never prospered as well as its competitor. The overseas operations, however, developed largely independent of the parent company, and in their territories they competed with IBM on much more nearly equal terms. In 1927, the US Powers organization was acquired by Remington Rand, and Powers himself retired into obscurity and died in 1935.

Martin Campbell-Kelly

PRAGMATICS

See SYNTAX, SEMANTICS, AND PRAGMATICS.

PRECEDENCE

See OPERATOR PRECEDENCE.

PRECISION

For articles on related subjects *see* ARITHMETIC, COMPUTER; NUMBERS AND NUMBER SYSTEMS; and SIGNIFICANT DIGIT.

For a numeric representation that employs strings of symbols from a finite alphabet to represent numbers, the *precision attribute* of a symbol string denotes the *length* of the string, and possibly also positional information for determining a base point of the string. Those numbers representable by finite length symbol strings are termed the *finite precision numbers* of that numeric representation.

For the fixed-point radix representation $d_m d_{m-1} \cdots d_1 d_0 \cdot d_{-1} d_{-2} \cdots d_l$, $d_m \neq 0$, the precision attribute is the triple $(m - l + 1, -l, m + 1)$; e.g. 310.25 has precision $(5, 2, 3)$ and 0.0024 has precision $(2, 4, -2)$. If $l \leq 0 \leq m$, then $-l$ and $m + 1$ may be interpreted as the number of digits in the fractional and integer parts, respectively, of the $m - l + 1$ digit number. The precision triple $(m - l + 1, -l, m + 1)$ thus provides both the number of digits and base-point normalization information.

For a radix number system where computed radix representations are truncated to exhibit only significant digits, the precision attribute identifies the significant digits. In this restricted environment, precision is a measure of accuracy. For integer radix number systems such as the "8-digit decimal integers" or the "6-digit hexadecimal integers," the precision attribute provides simply a measure of the magnitude of the representable integers.

The precision attribute is used for numeric formats in input, output, and internal storage allocation in high-level programming languages. In PL/I, for example, precision rules are employed to compute the precision attribute of program variables at compile time to help optimize storage utilization.

Precision, as defined here, is intimately related to the displayed representation of a number, in contrast to *accuracy*, which is concerned with freedom from error. Thus, a highly precise number (i.e. one displayed with many digits) may be quite misleading regarding accuracy, since the accuracy would still be limited to the number of significant digits independent of the number of digits displayed.

Bibliography

1976. Matula, D. W. "Radix Arithmetic: Digital Algorithms for Computer Architecture," in *Applied Computation Theory: Analysis, Design and Modeling* (ed. R. Yeh). Upper Saddle River, NJ: Prentice Hall.

David W. Matula

PREPROCESSOR

For articles on related subjects *see* LANGUAGE PROCESSORS; MACRO; OBJECT PROGRAM; and SOURCE PROGRAM.

A *preprocessor* is a language processor that accepts, as input, statements written in one computer language and writes to an output file statements that are acceptable to a similar but less complete language. Suppose, for example, that we have available a standard Pascal compiler but that we would like to be able to write programs that are compatible with extended versions of Pascal that are richer in string manipulation constructs. As input file is prepared that contains source code for a particular program written in the extended language. The preprocessor must read each statement and parse it to see if its syntax pertains to string manipulation. If not, the preprocessor passes the statement along unchanged. If so, the preprocessor writes a sequence of standard Pascal statements that, when later compiled and executed as part of the artificially created (and longer) source file, produces the same effect as the desired string manipulation statement. The process is shown schematically in Fig. 1.

As the figure shows, preprocessing inevitably requires two translation passes rather than one, but on most

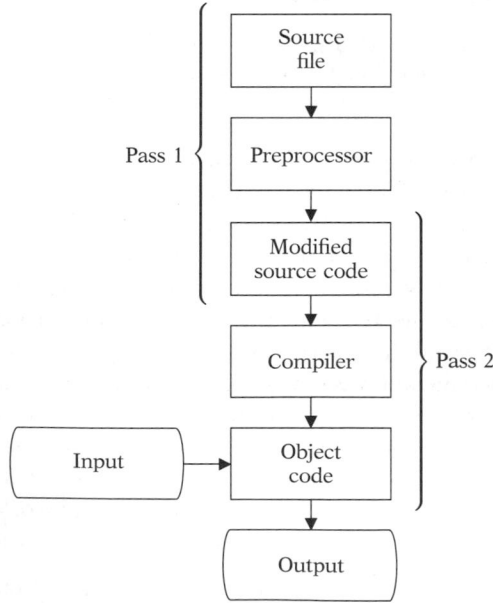

Figure 1. Preprocessing, shown as pass 1, precedes compilation and execution, shown as pass 2.

computers the user can be given the feel of one-pass translation through creation of a library of system commands which, when invoked, runs through the multiple operations in response to a short sequence of keystrokes or one click of a mouse.

A C language compiler includes a preprocessor that translates several commonly used directives. The line `#include <math.h>` is an example: it directs the preprocessor to include a *header* file that contains declarations of standard mathematical functions, so that they will be recognized by the compiler if they are used later. The directive `#define PI 3.14159` instructs the preprocessor to replace every occurrence of the string `"PI"` by the numerical value, so that the compiler itself never sees `"PI"`.

Preprocessor operation is very similar to macro expansion, but takes place at an early phase of language translation. Macro languages and assemblers that support a macro facility accept macro definitions as an integral part of language translation and then expand instances of the macro when encountered in the source code. To cope with a language that lacks a macro facility, we can write a preprocessor whose macro definitions are essentially embedded in its parsing logic. The definitions correspond to the syntactical constructs we wish we had in the host language but do not. The preprocessor then detects incoming statements that correspond to these constructs and expands them before the host language translator has a chance to reject them as being ungrammatical.

Edwin D. Reilly

PRETTY GOOD PRIVACY (PGP)

For articles on related subjects, *see* AUTHENTICATION; CRYPTOGRAPHY, COMPUTERS IN; DIGITAL SIGNATURE; ELECTRONIC MAIL; LEGAL ASPECTS OF COMPUTING; PASSWORD; and PRIVACY, COMPUTERS AND.

PGP (*Pretty Good Privacy*) is (1) a program that was popularized in the 1990s for encrypting electronic mail (*q.v.*); (2) a company that was founded by the program's author, Phil Zimmerman; and (3) a trademarked brand of encryption products offered by Network Associates, a US firm that markets computer security software and consulting services.

The PGP program is (partially) based on the RSA data encryption algorithm invented in 1977 by MIT professors Ronald Rivest, Adi Shamir, and Len Adleman. Unlike the symmetric encryption algorithms of the time, which used the same key for encryption and decryption, the RSA algorithm was asymmetric. That is, RSA used one key for encryption and a second key for decryption. For optimal security, both keys had to be based on prime numbers hundreds of digits long (*see* CRYPTOGRAPHY, COMPUTERS IN). The algorithm was published in MIT Laboratory for Computer Science Technical Memorandum #82 (April 1977), and popularized in the August 1977 issue of *Scientific American*. MIT filed for a patent in the fall of 1977 which was issued on 20 September 1983, but the algorithm did not find widespread use because computers of the 1970s were too slow to perform the mathematical operations necessary to implement it.

In 1980, Charlies Merritt, a programmer in Arkansas, discovered a technique for performing RSA encryption on low-cost microcomputers. Merritt's program, *DEDICATE/32*, could encrypt a small file in 20–30 seconds. Unable to find many businesses or consumers interested in the technology, Merritt telephoned computer manufacturers, hoping to find one that would be interested in bundling the product with their systems. He had no success until 1983, when he called Metamorphic Systems, a small computer vendor in Boulder, CO, and spoke with a programmer named Phil Zimmermann. Merritt was unable to convince Metamorphic to purchase the software—Metamorphic was having financial difficulties, and the company soon failed—but Zimmermann and Merritt became close friends. Over the next two years Merritt taught Zimmermann the techniques for performing mathematical operations with large numbers on small computers.

In 1986, Merritt and Zimmermann had their first face-to-face meeting. They were joined by Jim Bidzos, the president of RSA Data Security, a small company that had been created by Rivest, Shamir, and Adleman to commercialize the patented algorithm which they held jointly with MIT. Earlier that year Rivest had created for RSA an email encryption program called MailSafe that used the RSA algorithm. Bidzos demonstrated the program for Merritt and Zimmermann, and left a copy at Zimmermann's house.

After the meeting, Zimmermann decided to write his own email encryption program routine and started on the program in earnest in the spring of 1990. In April 1991 he wrote a letter to RSA asking for a "royalty-free license for your RSA algorithm." Zimmermann needed such a license because he wanted to place his program in the public domain so that it could be used by anyone who felt the need for electronic privacy—especially people who wanted privacy from their own government. RSA refused. Zimmermann nevertheless finished his program during the summer of 1991 and called it *Pretty Good Privacy*.

At about that the same time, the US Senate was considering an omnibus anti-crime bill. At the behest of the FBI, Senator Joseph R. Biden inserted language into the legislation that would have outlawed the use of encryption systems within the USA that did not "permit the government to obtain the plaintext contents of voice, data, and other communications when appropriately authorized by law." Fearing that use of his program would soon be illegal, Zimmermann gave copies of PGP 1.0 to a few of his friends. One of those friends uploaded the program to a few bulletin board (*q.v.*) systems in Colorado. The program was subsequently republished on the Internet (*q.v.*) and distributed around the world.

Subsequent cryptographic analysis of PGP 1.0 revealed that while Zimmermann's RSA implementation was secure, information encrypted with a second algorithm employed by the product (an algorithm that Zimmermann invented and called Bass-O-Matic) could be easily decrypted. Thus, while PGP 1.0 did provide "pretty good" privacy, it did not provide the military-strength encryption that Zimmermann felt the world needed.

Throughout the fall of 1991 and 1992, Zimmermann guided a team of programmers who had volunteered to rewrite the PGP program and make it a worldwide standard for strong email encryption. One important change was to replace the program's Bass-O-Matic algorithm with a new cipher called IDEA (International Data Encryption Algorithm) invented by Xuejia Lai and James Massey. A second change was to modify the program so that its user interface (*q.v.*) could be easily translated from one language to another, greatly increasing the program's portability (*q.v.*). This program, PGP 2.0, was released on the Internet in late 1992.

In February 1993 the US Customs Department launched a formal investigation of Zimmermann. Although the investigation was originally based on the exporting of a program that violated RSA's patent, the investigators quickly refocused on the exportation of a program that allegedly violated the US laws prohibiting the export of cryptographic software without a license. The investigation was dropped on 11 January 1996.

During the summer of 1993 Zimmermann licensed commercial rights to the PGP program to ViaCrypt, which could legally sell PGP since it already had a license to use the RSA algorithm. But Zimmermann still firmly believed that there should be both commercial and noncommercial, or free, versions of PGP available for all to use. The patent issues for the noncommercial version of PGP were resolved in the spring of 1994. On 14 May 1994, RSA Data Security released a cryptographic toolkit allowing noncommercial use of the RSA algorithm. On 26 May 1994, MIT released PGP Version 2.6, based on the RSA toolkit.

In March 1996 Zimmermann founded PGP, Inc., a new company that would develop and sell a variety of encryption-based products designed to promote privacy. On 1 July 1996, the company acquired ViaCrypt, and along with it both commercial rights to the PGP program and the coveted RSA license. PGP, Inc. went on to develop several new products including a telephone encryption system and a disk-drive encryption program called *PGPdisk*. But despite good technology, PGP, Inc. faltered, and, in February of 1998, was sold to Network Associates, a company formed just a year earlier through the merger of Network General and the McAfee company known for its virus protection software (*see* VIRUS, COMPUTER).

Bibliography

1994. Stallings, W. *Protect Your Privacy—A Guide for PGP Users.* Upper Saddle River, NJ: Prentice Hall.
1995. Garfinkel, S. *PGP: Pretty Good Privacy.* Sebastopol, CA: O'Reilly & Associates.
1995. Zimmermann, P. *The Official PGP User's Guide.* Cambridge, MA: MIT Press.
1995. Zimmermann, P. *PGP: Source Code and Internals.* Cambridge, MA: MIT Press.
1995. Bacard, A. *The Computer Privacy Handbook: A Practical Guide to E-mail Encryption, Data Protection, and PGP Privacy Sofware.* Berkeley, CA: Peachpit Press.
1996. Schneier, B. "Pretty Good Privacy (PGP)," section 24.12 of *Applied Cryptography*, 2nd Ed., 584–587. New York: John Wiley.

Simson Garfinkel

PRINTERS

For articles on related subjects *see* COMPUTER GRAPHICS; DESKTOP PUBLISHING; ELECTRONIC OFFICE; METAFONT; POSTSCRIPT; TEX; TEXT EDITING; TYPEFONT; and WORD PROCESSING.

Introduction

Early predictions that computerized data would lead to the "paperless office" have not been fulfilled. Not only are more printouts than ever before being created, but computer printing has turned into a fine art. The very essence of a whole new category of computing—desktop publishing—is the production of printed pages of ever higher quality.

In the age of the typewriter, there wasn't much you could put on paper except black letters and numbers—most often in an efficient but drab typeface called *Courier*, a "monospaced" font in which all letters have the same width. What forecasters did not foresee was that computer software and printing technology would make possible fast, easy, graphic, colorful hard copies of reports, newsletters, graphs, and, yes, company budgets and greeting cards better than even IBM's best *Selectric*—the state of the art in typewriters before they died—could ever come close to producing.

Speed and ease were the first improvements in computer printing. Where in the past a simple (type-written) error might just be whited out or hand-corrected with a pen, now—because of the speed of printers—it is easier just to correct a mistake on screen and print a fresh, flawless copy.

Graphics were the next big advance. The day of the all-text document ended with the first software that could print even the crudest line graph on a dot-matrix printer. Now anything that is visual, from line art to a halftone photograph, can be printed on a standard office printer. And since the image of a letter of the alphabet is an image like any other, even if a small one, there is no particular problem in using any one of a wide variety of typefaces, each available in roman, italic, or bold forms over a wide range of sizes (*see* TYPEFONT).

Dazzling color is the current frontier. The quality and speed of color printers is increasing as their cost is decreasing. Because they can double as black and white printers, color printers are more and more becoming the only kind used in home and office alike.

All computer printing is based on the *dot matrix*. This is a grid of dots that can vary from six across and eight down to as many as 2,400 dpi (dots per inch) in both directions. Whether it is a laser printer going through an intricate ballet of movement and time or an inkjet printer spitting dots of color on paper, the printer is limited to producing dots—thousands of dots on a single page—but still dots. This is a fundamental change in printing from all that went before it since Gutenberg. The freedom that Gutenberg's movable type afforded also created restrictions. Printing was done with fully formed characters, letters, and numbers. This was true with the first personal computer printers, which contained all the characters for a font on a *daisy wheel*, a circle of plastic that rotated swiftly to bring the correct characters into position to be struck by a plunger. There was no such thing as changing fonts or creating graphics on the fly. The dot matrix changed that. With it a printer could print anything that could be made up of many tiny dots, which is virtually anything.

Black and White Printers

DOT-MATRIX PRINTERS

The dot-matrix printer made its first appearance as the *impact dot-matrix printer*, an inexpensive and versatile device. It includes a *print head* that uses magnetic solenoids to pound various combinations of metal rods, arrayed in a matrix, against a ribbon coated with ink. The earliest dot-matrix printers used printheads containing 9 wires called *printing pins*, but later ones attained much better print quality by using 24 pins.

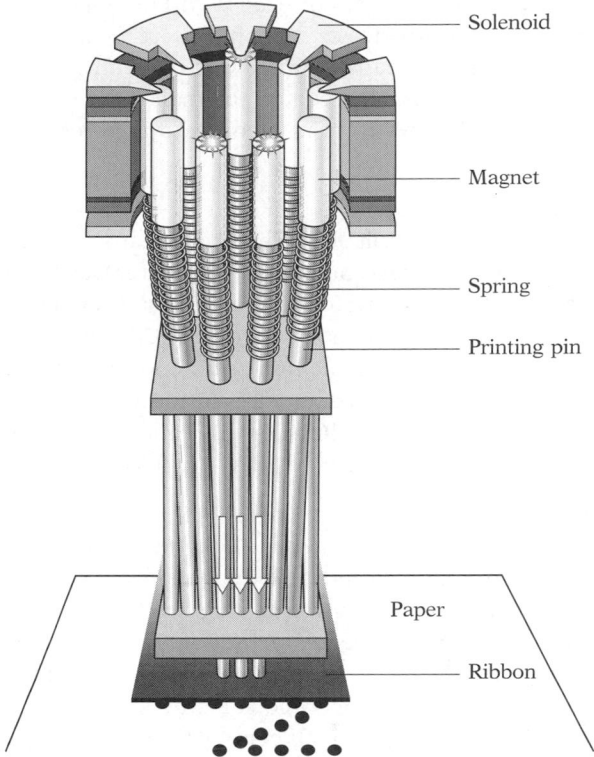

Figure 1. How a typical dot matrix printer works: 1. Electrical signals from a computer are fed to a selected number of solenoids that correspond to the printing pins in the print head. (The print head shown uses nine pins; dot matrix printers of higher resolution use 24.) Each solenoid (electromagnet) that is activated causes its pin to move toward the paper at high speed. 2. Each pin that moves strikes an inked ribbon and thus produces one individual dot on paper. When its solenoidal current is removed, a spring forces the pin back to its initial position. Then, in further response to signals from the computer, the print head continues firing different combinations of pins as it moves across the page in such a way that each character is formed as a linear sequence of vertically aligned dots.

For simplicity, Fig. 1 shows how a nine-pin dot-matrix printer works. By activating different solenoids as the printhead moves across the surface of a sheet of paper, the printer could produce any character in a crude but readable rendition.

Other printers make their dots without the miniature violence that an impact printer commits on a ribbon smeared with soot. But any printer, whether dot-matrix, inkjet, laser, dye sublimation, or solid ink, accomplishes essentially the same task: it creates a pattern of dots on a sheet of paper. The dots may be sized differently or composed of different inks that are transferred to the paper by different means, but all of the images for text and graphics are made up of dots. The smaller the dots, the more attractive the printout.

Because of their low speed and relatively poor print quality, dot-matrix printers are no longer widely used in office environments, nor even with PCs. Like background sports broadcasts, the characteristic sound of an operating dot matrix printer was once ubiquitous, but their use is now relegated to small quiet devices used in retail stores to print credit card invoices.

LASER PRINTERS

Laser printers—built by Hewlett-Packard, Canon, Epson, and other companies—have replaced the impact dot-matrix printer as the printer of choice in most businesses and many homes. Although it performs essentially the same task as an impact printer—placing dots of ink on paper—it is faster and produces smaller dots at 600–1400 dots per inch, providing the definition and sharpness of traditional typeset printing.

At the heart of the printer is the *print engine*—the mechanism that transfers black powder to the page—which is a device that owes its ancestry to the photocopier. To create the nearly typeset-quality output that is characteristic of a laser printer, the printer must control five different operations at the same time: it must (1) interpret the signals coming from a computer, (2) translate those signals into instructions that control the firing and movement of a laser beam, (3) control the movement of the paper, (4) sensitize the paper so that it will accept the black toner that makes up the image, and (5) fuse that image to the paper. It is a perfectly coordinated five-ring circus.

The laser printing process begins with the computer's operating system (*q.v.*) and software sending information to the laser printer's own microprocessor (*q.v.*) to determine where each dot of printing toner is to be placed on the paper. The instructions from the printer's processor rapidly turn on and off a beam of light from a laser (*see* Fig. 2). A spinning mirror deflects the laser beam so that the path of the beam is a horizontal line across the surface of a cylinder called the *organic photoconducting cartridge* (OPC), usually referred to as simply the *drum*. (Some laser printers replace the laser with a paper-wide row of *light-emitting diodes* (LEDs) that serve the same function.) The combination of the laser beam being turned on and off and the movement of the beam's path across the cylinder results in many tiny points of light hitting in a line across the surface of the drum. When the laser has finished flashing points of light across the entire width of the OPC, the drum rotates—usually 1/600th to 1/1200th of an inch in most laser printers—and the laser beam begins working on the next line of dots.

At the same time that the drum begins to rotate, a system of gears and rollers feeds a sheet of paper into the print engine along a path called the *paper train*. The paper is pulled along the paper train past an electrically

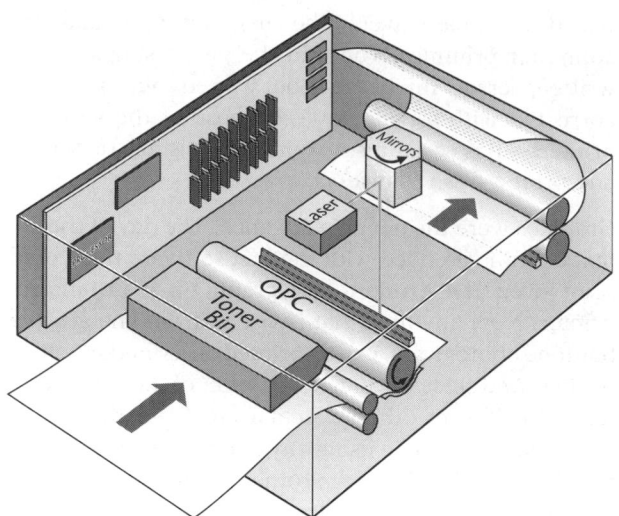

Figure 2. How a typical laser printer works: 1. The computer sends signals to the printer's own embedded processor to specify where printed dots are to be placed on paper. 2. Instructions from the printer's processor rapidly turn a beam of laser light on and off as needed. 3. A spinning mirror deflects light from the laser so that the path of the beam is a horizontal line across the surface of a cylinder called an *Organic Photoconducting Cartridge* (OPC), or more simply, a *drum*. The combination of the laser beam being turned on and off and the movement of the beam's path across the cylinder results in a line of many tiny points of light across the entire width of the drum. 4. The drum then rotates, perhaps 1/600 or 1/1200 of an inch depending on the resolution of the printer, and the laser beam begins work on the next line of dots. As the drum rotates, a system of gears and rollers feeds a sheet of paper along a path called the *paper train*. The paper is pulled past an electrically charged wire that places a static charge at designated points on the paper. 5. Each charge marks what eventually will become a black dot on white paper. 6. About halfway through its rotation the drum comes in contact with a bin that contains black powder called *toner* that will stick to the paper wherever it contains a static charge. 7. As the drum continues to turn, the paper moving with it gradually but rapidly accumulates the pattern of dots that comprise the text or image being printed.

charged wire that passes a static electrical charge to the paper. The charge may be either positive or negative, depending upon the design of the printer. For this example, we shall assume that the charge is positive. Where each point of light strikes the drum, it causes a negatively charged film—usually made of zinc oxide and other materials—on the surface of the drum to change its charge so that the dots have the same electrical charge as the sheet of paper. In this example, the light would change the charge from negative to positive. Each positive charge marks a dot that will eventually print black on paper. The areas of the drum that remain untouched by the laser beam retain their negative charge and result in white areas on the hard copy.

About halfway through the drum's rotation, the OPC comes into contact with a bin that contains a black powder called *toner*. The toner in this example has a negative electrical charge—the opposite of the charges created on the drum by the laser beam. Because particles with opposite static charges attract each other, toner sticks to the drum in a pattern of small dots wherever the laser beam created a charge. As the drum continues to turn, it presses against the sheet of paper being fed along the paper train. Although the electrical charge on the paper is the same as the charge of the drum created by the laser beam, the paper's charge is stronger and pulls the toner off the drum and onto the paper.

The rotation of the drum brings its surface next to a thin wire called the *corona wire*. It's called that because electricity passing through the wire creates a ring, or corona, around it that has a positive charge. The corona returns the entire surface of the drum to its original negative charge so that another page can be drawn on the drum's surface by the laser beam.

Another set of rollers pulls the paper through a part of the print engine called the *fusing system*. There pressure and heat bind the toner permanently to the paper by melting and pressing a wax that is part of the toner. The heat from the fusing system is what causes paper fresh from a laser printer to be warm. The paper train pushes the paper out of the printer, usually with the printed side down so that pages end up in the output tray in the correct order.

Color printing

There were two revolutions in computer printing in the last decade of the last century. One was the laser printer, which made typeset-quality printing of text and graphics readily available. The second was the development of inexpensive, fast, and high-quality color printing.

The complexity of color printing, of course, means trade-offs. At the low end is the color inkjet printer. It is in some ways a dot-matrix printer without the impact and with four times as many colors; that is, black plus three colors rather than just black. These may be combined in a way to be described to produce a wide spectrum of color. Since a color inkjet costs barely more than a black and white inkjet, the latter are no longer in wide use. The visual detail approaches that of laser printers, in some printers surpassing it. But inkjet technology is relatively slow. Color inkjets are the ideal printer for the home, where printing volume is small, the budget may be limited, and the flash of color in a school report or a greeting card is worth the extra wait.

All color printing uses *subtractive color* mixing, in which light is reflected—rather than emitted as in *additive color* mixing used by televisions and computer monitors. Four colored pigments are used; each color absorbs (subtracts) part of the spectrum that makes up white light. Color printing uses four pigments: Cyan (blue–green), Magenta (purple–red), Yellow, and blacK. This system is called CMYK, taken from the capitalized letters in the colors cited.

All color printers use tiny dots of those four inks to create various shades of color on the page. Lighter shades are created by leaving "dots" of unprinted white. Some printers control the size of the dots and produce *continuous-tone* images that rival photography, but less expensive printers create dots that are essentially the same size no matter how much of a particular color is needed. The earliest color printers created up to 300 dots of color per inch, for a total of up to about 8 million dots per page depending on the margins used. Current color printers typically use 600 or 720 dpi, and a few can create up to 2,400 dpi. Some use twice as many dots vertically as they do horizontally, densities (in dpi) of 1200×600 or 1400×720 being quite common. See Table 1 for typical characteristics of several different kinds of printers.

For all shades of color beyond the eight that are produced by overlaying the primaries, the printer generates a varied pattern of differently colored dots. For example, the printer uses a combination of one magenta dot to two of cyan to produce a deep purple. For most shades of color, the dots of ink are not printed on top of one another. Instead, they are offset slightly, a process called a *halftone* or *dithering*. The eye accommodatingly blends the dots to form the

Table 1. Characteristics of six types of printer as of late 1999.

Printer type	Resolution	Printing speed	Price range (US$)
Dot-matrix			
9-pin	90 dpi	100–400 cps	Obsolete
24-pin	240 dpi	100–300 cps	100–150
B/W laser	300–360 dpi	4–10 ppm	Obsolete
	600–720 dpi	8–17 ppm	400–750
	1200–1440 dpi	10–24 ppm	700–5,000
Color inkjet	300–360 dpi	6–12 ppm	Obsolete
	600–720 dpi	4–10 ppm	150–800
	1200–1440 dpi	4–10 ppm	250–1,300
Color laser	600–720 dpi	3–16 ppm	1,000–4,500
	1200–1440 dpi	2–12 ppm	2,000–7,500
Dye-sublimation	1200–2400 dpi	1–4 ppm	600–1,000
Multifunction	600–1440 dpi	4–10 ppm	400–700

Key to table: dpi = dots per inch; cps = characters per second; ppm = pages per minute.

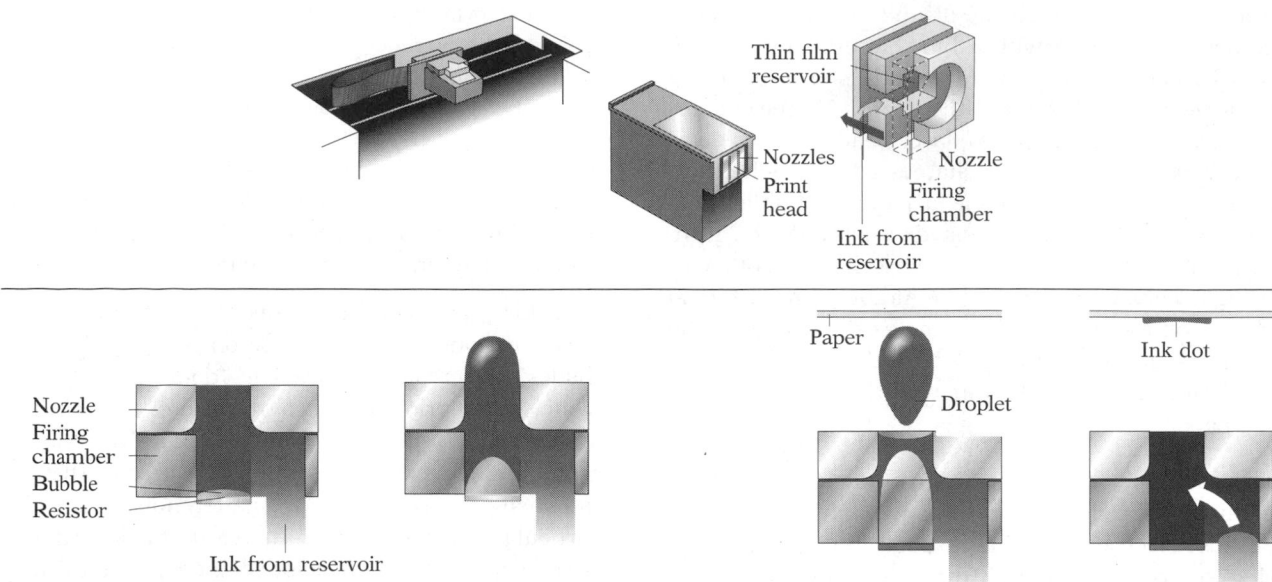

Figure 3. How a typical color inkjet printer works: 1. An ink-filled print cartridge, attached to the inkjet print head, moves across the width of a sheet of paper fed through the printer below to the print head. 2. The print head in the printer illustrated contains four ink cartridges—one for each magenta (red), cyan (blue), yellow, and black. Each cartridge contains about 50 ink-filled *firing chambers*, each attached to a nozzle smaller than a human hair. 3. An electrical pulse flows through thin resistors at the bottom of all the chambers of all colors that will be used to form a small section of a character or image on paper. 4. Each activated resistor heats a thin layer of ink at the bottom of a chamber to more than 900 degrees Fahrenheit for several microseconds. The ink boils and forms a vapor bubble. 5. As the bubble expands, it pushes ink through the nozzle to form a droplet at the tip of the nozzle. 6. The pressure of the bubble forces the droplet onto the paper. A typical character is formed by a 20 × 20 array of droplets. 7. As the resistor cools, the bubble collapses. The resulting suction pulls fresh ink from the attached reservoir into the firing chamber.

desired shade as it hides the jagged edges, or *jaggies*, produced by the dots. Use of this technique, a form of optical illusion called dithering, can produce nearly 17 million colors.

The type of paper used in color printing affects the quality of the hard copy. Uncoated paper, the type used with most black and white office machines, has a rough surface that tends to scatter the light, reducing the brightness, and it tends to absorb ink, which slightly blurs the image. Somewhat more expensive paper coated with a fine varnish or wax takes applications of ink more evenly so that it dries with a smooth surface that reflects more of the light hitting it. The coating also helps prevent the ink being absorbed by the paper, thus producing a sharper image.

INKJET PRINTERS

The biggest difference between an inkjet printer and its impact dot-matrix cousin is the inkjet's printhead. An inkjet printer spits little drops of ink onto paper (Fig. 3). The technology works much better than might be imagined, yielding both fine detail and vivid colors. An ink-filled *print cartridge* attached to the inkjet's print head moves sideways across the width of a sheet of paper that is fed through the printer below the print head. The print head is fed from a cartridge containing black, magenta, cyan, and yellow inks in separated

compartments. Because the black ink is typically consumed the fastest, many color inkjet printers separate the four colors into two separate cartridges, one containing only black ink and the other containing the other three (sometimes five) colors. Each color compartment is made up of some 50 ink-filled *firing chambers*, each attached to a nozzle smaller than a human hair. An electrical pulse flows through thin resistors at the bottom of all the chambers among all the colors that the printer will use to form a small section of a character or picture on paper. When an electrical current flows through a resistor, the resistor heats a thin layer of ink at the bottom of the chamber to more than 900 degrees Fahrenheit for several millionths of a second. The ink boils and forms a bubble of vapor. As the vapor bubble expands, it pushes ink through the nozzle to form a droplet at the tip of the nozzle. The droplet overcomes the surface tension of the ink, and the pressure of the vapor bubble forces the droplet onto the paper. The volume of the ejected ink is about one millionth that of a drop of water from an eyedropper, about 6 picoliters. A typical character is formed by an array of these drops 20 across and 20 high. As the resistor cools, the bubble collapses. The resulting suction pulls fresh ink from the attached reservoir into the firing chamber.

Instead of a heat-creating resistor, some inkjet printers use a *piezoelectric printer head*. The rear wall of the firing chamber is made of a piezoelectric crystal, a crystalline substance that flexes in proportion to the amount of current passing through it. As the wall moves back, it sucks ink in from the reservoir and back from the mouth of the nozzle. The farther the wall flexes, the more ink it pulls in, allowing the printer to change the amount of ink in a single dot.

MULTIFUNCTION PRINTERS

Several manufacturers now offer multifunction inkjet printers which, in addition to printing, can also function as a copier, scanner, and fax machine. The added features are restricted to use of single sheets of paper fed one at a time, so the device cannot be used to scan or copy pages of bound books or magazines. But the print quality is comparable to that of single-function inkjet printers, and despite the added features the multifunction machines sell for only about US$500.

HIGH-END COLOR PRINTING

Newer, more expensive color printers produce hard copy that rivals the resolution, brightness, and vividness of a photograph. A color laser printer works on the same principles as a black and white laser printer, but the color laser contains four bins of differently colored toner. It may use separate laser or LED rows for each color, producing a single page in one pass, or it may use only a single light source, requiring the paper to pass through the system four times for all the colors to be applied. The latter technique is used by a common office color-printing device called a *color thermal printer*. The process provides vivid colors because the inks it uses do not bleed into each other or soak into specially coated paper. But such a four-pass method is slow and wastes ink.

Two other color printing methods provide speed and photographic dazzle: *dye-sublimation*—also called *dye diffusion thermal transfer* (D2T2)—and *solid ink*. By controlling not only how many dots of color they put on the page but also the intensity of the dots, they produce *continuous-tone printing*. The result is virtually indistinguishable from a color photograph, even though its actual resolution may be no more than that of a laser printer.

Printer Characteristics

Typical printer characteristics as of late 1999 are given in Table 1. The price of a printer of any kind is roughly proportional to the dot density used and to its operating speed in pages per minute, which accounts for much of the wide variation in (US) prices quoted. And like most computer equipment, prices tend to fall over time, although prices of devices with mechanical components do not fall as fast as those that are predominantly electronic. Printing speed in pages per

minute covers a wide range both because of variation among products and because color printers can print black and white pages faster than those containing colors.

As mentioned earlier, most of the color inkjet printers (and the multifunction machines) use two cartridges, one containing black ink and one containing three to five other colors in separated compartments. Since color cartridges typically sell for US$25 and some for twice that, the owner of an inexpensive inkjet printer should expect that the cost of replacement cartridges throughout the printer's useful life will be several times the original cost of the printer. Toner cartridges for laser printers can cost US$100 or so for black toner and twice that for color toner, but the black cartridges last for many thousands of copies and the color ones for perhaps a thousand.

Bibliography

1996. Rosch, W. L. *Winn L. Rosch's Printer Bible*. New York: MIS Press/Holt.
1998. White, R. *How Computers Work*, 4th Ed. Indianapolis, IN: Que.

Ron White

PRIVACY, COMPUTERS AND

For articles on related subjects *see* COMPUTER CRIME; COMPUTER PROFESSIONALS FOR SOCIAL RESPONSIBILITY; ELECTRONIC MAIL; INFORMATION ACCESS; LEGAL ASPECTS OF COMPUTING; LEGAL ISSUES OF THE INTERNET; PRETTY GOOD PRIVACY; and SOCIETY, COMPUTERS IN.

The Right to Privacy

Privacy is a complex of social norms, laws, and regulation. It has proven particularly hard to codify privacy because it is both individual and circumstantial in nature, but it can generally be described as the desire for individual control over who obtains information about oneself and how that information is used.

There is a generally held feeling that all members of society have a right to privacy, but this right may not have constitutional support. In the USA, privacy is not mentioned in the constitution, although courts have at times interpreted the first, fourth and fifth amendments to include some rights pertaining to privacy. The 1948 Universal Declaration of Human Rights specifically mentions privacy in Article 12: "No one should be subjected to arbitrary interference with his privacy, family, home, or correspondence . . . ." Some more recent constitutions (e.g. Hong Kong, Malawi) include a similar right to privacy in relation to search or intrusion, but generally these are silent on the particular question of data privacy, which is one of the main issues in the concern about the impact of computers on privacy.

Computers and Privacy

Computer technology can affect privacy in a number of ways. First, computers allow the storage of masses of seemingly small bits of information about individuals over long periods of time. Techniques like *data mining* (*q.v.*) permit the analysis and use of this information in new and unanticipated ways. Second, previously separate databases of information gathered for unrelated purposes can be combined, creating a more revealing picture of individuals and their habits. Modern computing power permits the use of new technologies like biometrics, which use actual biological characteristics such as retinal scans, handprints and fingerprints. Biometric identification is designed to eliminate identity fraud but may also reduce the number of situations in which a person can act anonymously. These technologies and others can be used to trace an individual's physical location even without that person's knowledge, and thus increase the potential power of systems used for surveillance.

Data Privacy

Data privacy has been considered a basic human right for a number of decades. United Nations Resolution 45/95 of 14 December 1990, entitled "Guidelines for the Regulation of Computerized Personal Data Files," recommends that each nation develop regulations that require fairness, accuracy and transparency of data files, as well as a ban on using collected data for discriminatory purposes. Guidelines of the Organization for Economic Cooperation and Development (OECD) adopted at the 523rd meeting on 23 September 1980, on the "Protection of Privacy and Transborder Flows of Personal Data" advise that any personal data gathered should be relevant to the use of that data and should only be disclosed to others in relation to those purposes. These guidelines also include a right of individuals to obtain and challenge any personal data that is held by other parties.

Data privacy concerns have increased as computer technology has made it possible to gather, store and manipulate large amounts of data about persons. The early use of computers by US government agencies, as part of their enormous task of serving citizens, led to widespread concerns about a "Big Brother" state where one's every move would be watched and recorded. The US Privacy Act of 1974 places limits on the use of personal data by Federal agencies. Under the Act, individuals must be informed about what data is being gathered and how it will be used. They also have the right to examine this data and obtain corrections to erroneous entries. A key component of the Act prevents government agencies from sharing or exchanging data gathered for different purposes.

There is no related US legislation pertaining to the data-gathering activities of private entities, although states can enact their own laws in this area. At least 10 states have amended their constitutions to include the right of privacy, and others have passed legislation granting privacy rights in certain areas, including bank and telephone records.

Data privacy concerns increase with the development of electronic commerce (*q.v.*) because each transaction creates an audit trail. This information about consumers and their activities becomes a commodity in its own right and active markets exist for the purchase of information about consumers and their buying habits. The European Union's October 1998 Directive on Data Privacy (Directive 95/46/EC) requires each member nation of the EU to conform to privacy guidelines that protect the individual consumer, and prohibits data collection on the part of companies whose country's laws do not provide adequate privacy protection. The Directive specifically requires that:

◆ Individuals must be notified of data collection and must give their consent.

◆ Collecting agencies may collect only that data relevant to the transaction and may retain the data no longer than is necessary to fulfill its original use.

◆ Collecting agencies must take all reasonable steps to ensure that the data is accurate and complete.

◆ Individuals have recourse should they suspect that their data privacy rights are being violated.

Although general laws on consumer data privacy do not exist in the USA, consumer reaction to perceived threats to privacy have been effective in specific instances. In June of 1996 the Lexis-Nexis corporation, a large database provider, announced its P-TRAK database which provided access to the names, up to three addresses, maiden names, and Social Security numbers of over 300 million people. The company decided to abandon the product based on negative public reaction. The Social Security Administration had its Personal Earnings and Benefit Estimate Statement (PEBES) service on the Internet for less than a month before users demonstrated that they could retrieve the PEBES statements of others with little difficulty. The service was withdrawn and redesigned.

Privacy of Communications

The growth of the Internet (*q.v.*) from the late 1980s through the 1990s meant that tens or hundreds of millions of people were using computer technology as a communications system. In 1986 the USA enacted the Electronic Communications Privacy Act (ECPA) to update earlier laws that had specifically addressed wiretapping and telephone communications. ECPA protects digital communications from point-to-point across computer networks. Intrusions into computer systems, however, gave evidence that laws must be combined with strong computer security in order to have an effect. Mistrust of online communications was high and Internet users were advised to treat each email message "as a postcard, not a letter" in terms of expected privacy.

While ECPA protects the content of communications, transaction data and "clickstream" records are not protected. Owners of sites on the World Wide Web (*q.v.*) can gather information on who visits their sites, either by tracking requests for information or by placing small files called *cookies* on the user's computer. This information is linked to the computer that is requesting the information and does not necessarily reveal the identity of the person at the computer, but user distrust of such technology is often cited as a reason for not engaging in electronic commerce.

Encryption and Public Key Technology

Encryption has been offered as the solution to the communications privacy problem. The encrypting of messages has been a privacy technology since ancient times, with special application in the military and diplomatic arenas. The development of encryption techniques was greatly increased by the computational power of computers, and, by the late 1980s, a personal computer could securely encode messages in a way that would ensure privacy for most communications needs. The development of public key cryptography in the 1980s (*see* CRYPTOGRAPHY, COMPUTERS IN) promised to make cryptography available to all computer users.

Public key technology did not, however, enjoy widespread use because many countries, including the USA, have restrictions for national security reasons on the use of encryption technology. Phil Zimmerman, author of Pretty Good Privacy (PGP), an encryption program for personal computers, was under investigation by the US Justice Department for three years before he was cleared of charges that he violated US arms export laws by allowing his program to be transmitted beyond the US borders.

Computer Privacy and Law Enforcement

A long-standing concern has been the need to balance privacy with the information needs of an open, democratic society. There is also tension between the desire for privacy and the perceived needs of law enforcement. These tensions carry forward into the computer age.

Encryption arises frequently as a law enforcement concern. Law enforcement agencies maintain that encrypted communications could be used to hide crimes ranging from money laundering to terrorism. Many governments, including that of the USA, favor the requirement that anyone using encrypted messages be required to place a copy of each key in escrow with a trusted agency that would be authorized to reveal the key under specific circumstances. In 1994, the development of the Clipper Chip, a key-escrowed encryption technology for secure telephone communications that was considered a model for similar computer communications, drew a strong response from the Internet community and the technology never came into wide use. Key escrow schemes were also favored by European governments based on the same law enforcement concerns. Consumer acceptance of key escrow appears unlikely, especially since the cross-border nature of global communications systems would mean that consumer privacy would at times be in the hands of foreign governments.

Although electronic communications in the USA are protected by ECPA, law enforcement continues to have wiretap rights with a court order. Changes to telephone company technology from analog to digital switching, however, turned the once simple wiretap into a difficult technical problem. The USA passed the Communications Assistance for Law Enforcement Act of 1994 which mandated that communications companies retrofit their digital switches to facilitate law enforcement use of communications monitoring.

Privacy and the Workplace

In the USA it is primarily individual state tort law that governs privacy protection for employees. In general, employers may legally monitor electronic mail and Internet use by employees. A 1997 survey by the American Management Association showed that 63.4% of surveyed organizations practice one or more of the eight forms of electronic monitoring and surveillance, including keystroke counting, monitoring of computing files, and voice mail and electronic mail review. The Association strongly urged all employers to develop and distribute clear computer and Internet use policies to avoid any misunderstanding about the degree of privacy in the workplace.

Bibliography

1994. Branscomb, A. W. *Who Owns Information? From Privacy to Public Access.* NewYork: Basic Books.
1995. Alderman, E., and Kennedy, C. *The Right to Privacy.* New York: Knopf.

1996. Dichter, M. S., and Burkhardt, M. S. "Electronic Interaction in the Workplace: Monitoring, Retrieving and Storing Employee Communications in the Internet Age." Presented at the American Employment Law Council, Fourth Annual Conference, Asheville, NC, 2–5 October, (http://www.mlb.com/speech1.htm).

1997. Schneier, B., and Banisar, D. (eds.) *The Electronic Privacy Papers: Documents on the Battle for Privacy in the Age of Surveillance.* New York: John Wiley.

1998. Global Internet Liberty Campaign. "Privacy and Human Rights: An International Survey of Privacy Laws and Developments," October (http://www.gilc.org).

2000. Garfinkel, S. L. *Database Nation: The Death of Privacy in the 21st Century.* Sebastopol, CA: O'Reilly & Associates.

Karen Coyle

PRIVILEGED INSTRUCTION

For articles on related subjects *see* INPUT–OUTPUT OPERATIONS; INSTRUCTION SET; INTERRUPT; MULTIPROCESSING; OPERATING SYSTEMS; and SUPERVISOR CALL.

Improper use of certain instructions can easily affect system integrity in a multiprocessing environment, whether it is a single user multitasking (*q.v.*) or a multiuser environment. These particular instructions usually include storage protection setting, interrupt handling, timer control, I/O, and special processor status-setting instructions.

In order to prevent accidental or intentional misuse of these instructions, many computers have a special mode in which instructions of these types, called *privileged instructions*, are executed. In a processor that possesses such a mode, the instructions are divided into sets, with each set executed in its own mode. The privileged mode includes all instructions, whereas all lower-level modes exclude some of them. Historically, the number of modes used might be one (i.e. no special privileged mode), two (a user mode and a privileged mode), or more. The Digital Equipment Corporation PDP 11/45, for example, had three modes: user, supervisor, and kernel (*q.v.*). The attempted execution of a privileged instruction in a non-privileged state causes an interrupt (*q.v.*).

Current computers retain the concept, but because of the increased capacity of their instruction sets, due, for instance, to the complexity of the numeric floating-point standards, the number of modes is sometimes more difficult to enumerate. For example the IBM Power Architecture, originally the RS/6000, has a 64-bit Machine State Register in which the instruction set combination can be set by the Problem State bit—the old user/privileged bit—but also by two bits to control the behavior of the floating-point instructions, dividing them into sets that react differently in different modes, thus affecting the system behavior.

Another approach to the division of instructions into privileged and user subsets is to structure the computing system into two or more independent processors, each dedicated to one subset. Such division was originally made, for example, in the CDC 6000 and Cyber series of computers. In those machines, the central processor had no instructions that invoked any system functions unless explicitly directed to do so by another processor. (This was later changed by adding one additional instruction to the central processor.) This trend is mirrored today by the introduction of separate I/O processors and system processors into massive computational structures.

Bibliography

1994. May, C., and Warren, H. (eds.) *The Power PC Architecture,* 2nd Ed. San Francisco: Morgan Kaufmann.

1996. Kain, R. Y. *Advanced Computer Architecture.* New York: Simon & Schuster.

Gideon Frieder

PROBABILISTIC ALGORITHMS

For articles on related subjects *see* ALGORITHM; ALGORITHMS, ANALYSIS OF; ALGORITHMS, DESIGN AND CLASSIFICATION OF; ALGORITHMS, THEORY OF; COMPUTATIONAL COMPLEXITY; MONTE CARLO METHOD; NP-COMPLETE PROBLEMS; PROBABILISTIC AUTOMATA; RECURSION; and TURING MACHINE.

Let $Q(x, y)$ be the two-variable polynomial

$$Q(x, y) = (x + y)^7 - x^7 - y^7 - 7xy(x + y)(x^2 + xy + y^2)^2$$

and assume that we want to ascertain whether $Q(x, y)$ is identically equal to zero. A deterministic algorithm for this task would be to expand $Q(x, y)$ to individual terms, opening all parentheses, and then cancel out all equal terms with opposite signs. $Q(x, y)$ is identically zero if and only if all the terms cancel. A *probabilistic algorithm* for the same problem can be described as follows:

1. Choose at random integer values $\bar{x}$, $\bar{y}$ in the range $0 \leq \bar{x}, \bar{y} \leq 49$.

2. Evaluate $Q(\bar{x}, \bar{y})$ for the chosen $\bar{x}$ and $\bar{y}$.

3. Repeat steps 1 and 2 50 times.

If and only if $Q(\bar{x}, \bar{y}) = 0$ all through the execution of the algorithm, decide that $Q(x, y)$ is identically equal to zero. The probabilistic algorithm is based on the argument described below.

One can prove that, if $Q(x, y)$ is not identically equal to zero, then only a fraction $f < 1/2$ of all the 50^2 point vectors $(\bar{x}, \bar{y})$, $0 \leq \bar{x}, \bar{y} \leq 49$ can result in $Q(\bar{x}, \bar{y}) = 0$ (*see* Schwartz, 1980). We can therefore conclude that if $Q(\bar{x}, \bar{y})$ is not identically equal to zero, then the probability that $Q(\bar{x}, \bar{y}) = 0$ for 50 randomly and independently chosen point vectors $(\bar{x}, \bar{y})$ is less than 2^{-50}. Thus, an erroneous decision is extremely improbable.

The main features of the above and similar probabilistic decision algorithms can be summarized as follows:

1. The input belongs to a given discrete domain D (e.g. the domain of all multivariate polynomials, the domain of all integers, the domain of all graphs (*see* GRAPH THEORY)).

2. The algorithm must decide whether the input satisfies a given property (e.g. identically equal to zero for multivariate polynomials, primality for integers, connectedness for graphs).

3. It incorporates a randomizing step (step 1 in the above algorithm) that is repeated a certain pre-assigned number of times.

4. It terminates on every input.

5. The decision it provides may be erroneous, but the probability of error can be made as small as required by increasing the number of random choices invoked in its iterative step (step 3 in the example).

6. The adequacy of the algorithm is based on the following paradigm: If D is the domain, w the element of D at input, and P the property of w to be verified by the algorithm, then the repetitive and randomized step (step 1 in the example) of the algorithm consists of a binary test t, which is "easy" to perform. The test t is applied to w several times and its result is recorded. If at any time $t(w)$ is "no," then w does not satisfy the property P. If w does not satisfy the property P, then the probability of $t(w) = $ "yes" is less than some number $\varepsilon < 1$. If t has been executed n times and the result was always "yes," then the probability of this event, given that w does not satisfy the property P, is less than ε^n, which tends to zero with n. One may, of course, also have the symmetrical situation where the implications of the "yes" and the "no" results of the test are exchanged (i.e. w satisfies P when $t(w)$ is "no").

An additional example of a probabilistic algorithm of the above type is the algorithm of Rabin (1980—one of the first probabilistic algorithms in the literature) for deciding primality: the domain D is the domain of integers, the property P is primality, and the test t is described as follows.

Given an integer w, let b be a random number $1 \le b < w$. If either $b^{w-1} \not\equiv 1 \bmod w$ or there is an integer i such that $(w-1)/2^i = m$ is an integer and

$$1 < \gcd(b^m - 1, w) < w,$$

then $t(w) = $ "no". Otherwise $t(w) = $ "yes". It is easy to show that $t(w) = $ "no" implies that w is composite. It can be shown that if w is composite, then the probability that $t(w)$ is "yes" is less that one half.

The randomization concept inherent in the above algorithm had been exploited in Monte Carlo methods even before the invention of probabilistic algorithms. Based on this similarity, probabilistic algorithms as described above have been termed algorithms of Monte Carlo type. Another type of probabilistic algorithm can be illustrated by the Random Quicksort algorithm (*see* SORTING). This algorithm receives as input a list L of n numbers (or elements taken from an ordered domain) and outputs the same list in sorted order, using the following method.

1. An element of the list $s(L)$ is randomly chosen and called the *separator* (or *pivot*). (In the version of Quicksort listed in STRUCTURED PROGRAMMING, the first element of the list is used as pivot.)

2. A procedure is provided that constructs two lists L_1, containing all the elements in L smaller than $s(L)$, and L_2, containing all the elements in L larger than $s(L)$. The procedure runs in time that is proportional to the length of the list L.

3. The algorithm is applied recursively to the lists L_1 and L_2, resulting in the sorted lists S_1 and S_2 (*see* RECURSION).

4. Output S_1 concatenated to $s(L)$ concatenated to S_2.

The randomization introduced in step 1 has the effect that, most of the times when step 2 is applied, the lists L_1 and L_2 are almost equal in size. This implies that the number of iterations of step 2 is proportional to $\log_2 n$. As the algorithm proceeds, the number of lists to be processed at step 2 increases, but their total length is less than n (they are all disjoint sublists of the original list of n elements) and, since the time used by the procedure for any sublist is proportional to its length, the running time of each of the approximately $\log_2 n$ iterations on all the sublists produced up to that iteration is proportional to n. The running time of the algorithm is therefore proportional, on the average, to $n \log_2 n$, even though it might be proportional to n^2 in an extremely improbable worst case. As a matter of fact, the following properties of the Random Quicksort algorithm have been proved:

1. The average running time of the Random Quicksort algorithm is proportional to $n \log_2 n$.

2. For every ε, there is an n_0 such that for all $n \ge n_0$ the probability that the algorithm halts in less than $21 n \log_2 n$ steps is greater than $1 - \varepsilon$.

The main features of the Random Quicksort and similar algorithms, called algorithms of the Las Vegas type, are summarized below:

1. The input belongs to an infinite but discrete domain.

2. The algorithm incorporates a randomizing step (step 1 in the Quicksort example).

3. The algorithm terminates on every input.

4. The output *always* provides the correct answer.

5. The algorithm is "fast" on average and an "acceptable" bound $B(n)$ can be proved such that the running time of the algorithm is bounded by $B(n)$ with probability approaching 1 as n grows to infinity.

Notice also that the Random Quicksort algorithm is a computational algorithm, while the previously described algorithms are decision algorithms.

One should not confuse probabilistic algorithms with the probabilistic analysis of the running time of deterministic algorithms. In contradistinction to deterministic algorithms, probabilistic algorithms incorporate an inherent randomizing step. This randomizing step may subsequently induce probabilistic arguments in the analysis of the running time or the correctness of such algorithms.

In addition to the two types of probabilistic algorithm described above, there may be variations in several directions. For example, one may think of partial algorithms (algorithms that do not halt on every input) such that their probability of halting on any input is very high and such that, when they do halt, they either provide the correct answer or have a very small probability of being erroneous. One may also envision computational probabilistic algorithms that provide only an approximation to the required output and such that the approximation can be improved by increasing the running time of the algorithm.

Some Historical and Theoretical Comments

Randomization was first used in Monte Carlo computational methods. It was introduced in the 1960s and 1970s into theoretical models of computation (*see* PROBABILISTIC AUTOMATA and TURING MACHINES). In the 1970s and subsequently, many probabilistic algorithms were introduced for solving actual problems (primality, computational geometry, sorting, hashing, communication problems on networks, etc.—*see* Motwani and Raghavan (1995) for a treatise and survey). Particular emphasis has been on probabilistic algorithms whose running time is bounded by a polynomial in the length of the input (*see* COMPUTATIONAL

COMPLEXITY and ALGORITHMS, ANALYSIS OF). The class of those algorithms is denoted by RP (Random Polynomial). There are algorithms in RP such that there is no known deterministic polynomial algorithm that solves the same problems they solve. An example of such an algorithm is the foregoing primality algorithm. (No deterministic and polynomial algorithm for deciding whether a number is prime is known.) On the other hand, it has not been proved yet that the class P (deterministic and polynomial algorithms—*see* NP–COMPLETE PROBLEMS) is properly included in the class RP, which is an intriguing and important open problem in theoretical computer science. Another open and related problem is the question of whether the class RP is properly included in the class NP (*see* NP-COMPLETE PROBLEMS). A negative answer to either of the above two problems will solve the other, and the solution of either of those two problems will have a strong impact on the theory of computation.

Randomization and probabilistic algorithms played an important role in the development of the modern theory of cryptology (*see* CRYPTOGRAPHY, COMPUTERS IN). In particular, the concept of zero-knowledge proofs (roughly, convincing arguments that yield nothing but the validity of the assertion) depends heavily on a certain type of probabilistic algorithm.

Bibliography

1980. Rabin, M. O. "Probabilistic Algorithm for Testing Primality," *Journal of Number Theory*, **12**, 128–138.

1980. Schwartz, J. T. "Fast Probabilistic Algorithms for Verification of Polynomial Identities," *SIAM Journal on Computing*, *27*, *4*, 701–717.

1995. Motwani, R., and Raghavan, P. *Randomized Algorithms*. New York: Cambridge University Press.

Azaria Paz

PROBABILISTIC AUTOMATA

For articles on related subjects *see* AUTOMATA THEORY; FORMAL LANGUAGES; and SEQUENTIAL MACHINE.

A *probabilistic* or *stochastic automaton* (pa) is a device with a finite number of internal states that scans input words over a finite alphabet and responds by successively changing its state in a probabilistic way.

Let ρ be a vector with entries ρ_i representing the probability that the automaton was in its ith state to begin with; let $A(x)$ be a matrix with entries $a_{ij}(x)$ representing the probability that the automaton moved to state j from state i upon scanning the input symbol x. Let η be a column vector with some entries equal to one, the other entries being equal to zero. Then,

$$p(x_1 \cdots x_k) = \rho A(x_1) \cdots A(x_k)\eta$$

is a function representing the probability that the automaton entered a designated final state after scanning the input word $x_1 \cdots x_k$. The function p can be used as a sorting criterion to define the probabilistic language consisting of all input words $x_1 \cdots x_k$ with $p(x_1 \cdots x_k) > \lambda$, λ being a preassigned given threshold.

The study of pa's is concerned mainly with the study of probabilistic languages, their closure properties, and their relation to other types of formal languages.

Example
Consider a physical system (or animal) assumed to be in one of two possible states (healthy or ill), with probabilities 0.2 and 0.8 correspondingly. If a sequence of stimuli (medicines) is applied to the system (animal), it undergoes probabilistically successive changes of its states. Assume that the transition characteristics of the first stimulus are as depicted in Fig. 1, which is to be interpreted as meaning that with probabilities 0.7 and 0.3, the system will stay in its first state, or will go to the second state, respectively, if the stimulus has been applied while the system was in its first state, etc. The probabilities of being in one of the two states after the application of the first stimulus (after swallowing the medicine), will then be

$$(0.2 \quad 0.8)\begin{pmatrix} 0.7 & 0.3 \\ 0.9 & 0.1 \end{pmatrix} = (0.86 \quad 0.14)$$

and the process will continue in the same way.

Another and similar type of probabilistic finite state device studied in the literature is the probabilistic sequential machine (PSM). A PSM is an input–output device with finitely many internal states. It scans input words over a finite alphabet and responds by printing output words over (another) output alphabet, while changing its state in a probabilistic way.

Let ρ be a vector as in the previous definition and let $A(y \mid x)$ be a matrix with entries $a_{ij}(y \mid x)$ representing the probability that the machine printed the symbol y and moved to state j from state i, upon scanning the symbol x. Let η be a column vector with all its entries equal to one, then

$$p(y_1, \ldots, y_n \mid x_1, \ldots, x_n) = \rho A(y_1 \mid x_1) \cdots A(y_n \mid x_n)\eta$$

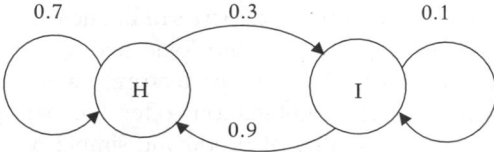

Figure 1. Transition characteristics.

is a function representing the probability that the machine printed the output $y_1, \ldots, y_n$ after scanning the input $x_1, \ldots, x_n$.

The study of PSMs is concerned with input–output relations induced by machines, minimization of states, and problems connected with input–output information systems with random behavior.

Example
A finite state communication channel (*see* e.g. Shannon, C. E., and Weaver, W., 1948, *The Mathematical Theory of Communication.* Urbana, IL: University of Illinois Press.), is specified by a conditional probability function $p_{ij}(y \mid x)$ interpreted as the probability of the output sent being y and the channel moving to state s_j given that the channel was in state s_i and received the input x.

Bibliography
1969. Carlyle, J. W. "Stochastic Finite-state System Theory," in *System Theory* (eds. L. A. Zadeh, and E. Polak), Ch. 10. New York: McGraw-Hill.
1971. Paz, A. *Introduction to Probabilistic Automata.* New York: Academic Press.

Azaria Paz

PROBLEM-ORIENTED LANGUAGES

For articles on related subjects *see* COMPUTER-AIDED ENGINEERING; EXPERT SYSTEMS; HARDWARE DESCRIPTION LANGUAGES; PROCEDURE-ORIENTED LANGUAGES; PROGRAMMING LANGUAGES; ROBOTICS; and SIMULATION.

The term *problem-oriented* languages, if taken literally, is too general to be useful in the taxonomy of programming languages. In its most general meaning, one would have to include any programming language that helps solve problems. Thus, Fortran (*q.v.*) is a problem-oriented language when one solves scientific or numeric problems. Cobol (COmmon Business-Oriented Language—*q.v.*) is problem oriented, even in its title, for business problems. However, accepted usage in computer science literature has imposed a narrower context for problem-oriented languages than one that could encompass Fortran and Cobol. From this more restricted point of view, synonyms for *problem-oriented* are *applications-oriented* or *special-purpose* or *specialized-application* or *domain-specific.*

This article discusses a number of applications-oriented and special-purpose programming languages. Some languages have been designed for very special applications, such as numerical control programming or electronic circuit analysis. Others are applications oriented, but at the same time are more general purpose. Examples of these would include simulation languages, statistical packages, and information retrieval systems. Discussion of the more general-purpose, problem-oriented languages is found in other sections of this Encyclopedia.

Numerous problem-oriented languages have been developed. Many of these languages have been described in Sammet (1969) and in her subsequent rosters of programming languages published in a number of journals, including the Association for Computing Machinery's *SIGPLAN Notices* (see Sammet, 1978). According to these rosters, the number of problem-oriented languages has consistently represented about half of all high-level languages used in the USA. The best source of technical information about a language is generally the reference manual provided by the developers or suppliers of the software.

Before looking at specific problem-oriented languages in current usage, we mention one of the earliest such languages and then review the characteristics of some commonly used languages in numerical control, civil engineering, electrical engineering, robotics, and expert systems. Finally, we will have a few things to say about trends in the future use and development of problem-oriented languages.

An Early Problem-Oriented Language—DYANA

Shortly after the successful introduction of Fortran as a programming language for scientific and engineering calculations, the General Motors Research Laboratories developed a specialized language for describing vibrational and other dynamic systems. DYANA (dynamic analyzer) was developed originally for the IBM 704 in 1958 and was an extension of Fortran (*see* Theodoroff, 1958).

DYANA provided for the definition of variables to specify the elements, excitation, and dependent and independent variables in a dynamic system. These variables have meaning in both Fortran and non-Fortran statements. The variables are constructed in such a way as to define the topology of the mechanical system.

Using a Problem-Oriented Language—APT

The essential goal of any problem-oriented language is to provide the user, who may or may not be a computer specialist, with a relatively simple and direct way of expressing a problem for computer solution. To be maximally effective, the language must be complete enough to express the functions, algorithms, and data

types that are normally used in the specific application. The value and effectiveness of a language is determined by how well this criterion is met.

To illustrate the process of using a problem-oriented language, we present as an example one of the most successful and widely implemented problem-oriented languages ever devised, namely, APT (IIT, 1967).

APT stands for *automatically programmed tools*. It was first developed at MIT in the early 1950s to assist in the production of punched tapes for numerically controlled machine tools. The early versions of APT were restricted to two-dimensional objects, using only straight lines and circles. Later developments, which were sponsored by the Aerospace Industries Association, resulted in a system called APT II. APT II used a specialized language to describe geometric surfaces. In the 1960s the APT Long-Range Program, sponsored by numerous industries and conducted by the Illinois Institute of Technology Research Institute, developed APT III, which eventually became the *de facto* standard for numerical control applications. Most of the currently used languages for numerical control programming are extensions, variations, or subsets of APT.

THE APT SYSTEM

The use of numerical control for machine tools is one of the most significant modern developments in manufacturing. Numerical control (N/C) has been applied to milling machines, drilling and boring machines, lathes, machine centers, automatic wiring machines, welding and flame-cutting machines, etc.

To use an N/C tool one must prepare a control tape that has recorded on it a description of all motions and machine functions required to fabricate the part on the tool. In the case of continuous path-control systems, literally thousands of computations must be performed to prepare a control tape.

The APT system includes a programming language, which provides a vocabulary for describing the geometry, motions, and machine functions necessary to produce a part using N/C, and a group of computer programs, called the *part program*, which translate APT language, perform the required calculations, and produce the control tape. The APT language provides a vocabulary to describe a large variety of two- and three-dimensional part geometry, to define tool shape, to specify tolerance, to command cutter motion, to indicate machining functions, to perform in-line computations, and to execute program logic and specify geometric transformations. These features, when used individually and in combination, offer the part programmer the possibility of producing simple or complex parts efficiently and economically.

THE APT LANGUAGE

We will illustrate the APT language by describing the process of writing a part program for a two-dimensional cam (Fig. 1). The APT language is used to:

1. Give names or symbols to the different geometrical elements of the part.

2. Describe the dimension and shape of the tool with which the part is to be cut.

3. Specify the computational tolerance. This tolerance is used by the computer to calculate the offset of the tool from the surfaces of the part and to determine successive cutter locations. By changing tolerances from run to run, machining can be varied from rough cuts to finer cuts.

4. Define the geometry of the part.

5. Describe the motion of the tool. Here, the part programmer acts as if sitting on the tool and driving it, like a car, around the part.

6. Specify auxiliary functions of the controller–machine tool combination.

With these elements, one obtains the part program shown in Fig. 1. The APT computer system calculates successive cutter positions to fabricate the part

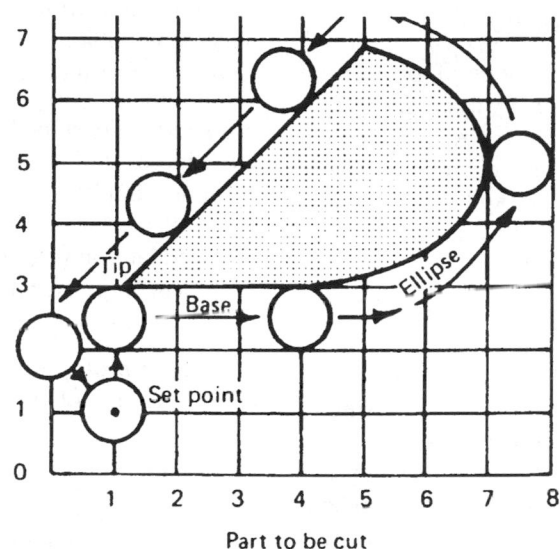

Part to be cut

Part program	Explanation
CUTTER/1	Use a 1 in diameter cutter
TOLER/.005	Tolerance of cut is 0.005 in
FEDRAT/80	Move tool at feed rate of 80 in/min
HEAD/1	Use head #1
SPINDL/2400	Turn on spindle. Set at 2,400 rpm
COOLNT/FLOOD	Turn on coolant. Use flood setting
PT1 = POINT/4,5	Define point PT1 as point with coordinates (4,5), used later to define ellipse
FROM/(SETPT = POINT/1,1)	Start tool from point called SETPT, defined as point with coordinates (1,1)
INDIRP/(TIP = POINT/1,3)	Aim tool in direction of point called TIP, defined as point with coordinates (1,3)
BASE = LINE/TIP, AT ANGL,0	Define line called BASE as line through point TIP, which makes angle of 0° with horizontal
GO/TO, BASE	Go to the line BASE
TL RGT, GO RGT/BASE	With tool on right of part with respect to direction of motion, go right along line BASE until tangency with next surface, the ellipse, is reached
GO FWD/(ELLIPS/CENTER, PT1,3,2,0)	Go forward along ellipse with center at PT1, semi-major axis = 3, semi-minor axis = 2, and major axis making angle of 0° with horizontal
GO LFT/(LINE/2,4,1,3,),PAST BASE	Go left along line joining points (2,4) and (1,3) past line BASE
GOTO/SETPT	Go to point SETPT in a straight line
COOLNT/OFF	Turn off coolant flow
SPINDLE/OFF	Turn off spindle
END	This is the end of machine control unit operation,
FINI	and the finish of part program

Figure 1. An APT program for the two-dimensional cam shown at top (from J. E. Sammet, *Progamming Languages: History and Fundamentals*, Prentice Hall, 1969).

specified, taking into account the defined tool shape, the tolerances, the part geometry, and the tool motions contained in the part program.

This application is typical of the procedures used in a problem-oriented language. The problem is defined in terms of variables and data types (points, lines, circles, ellipses, etc. in APT), certain declarations are invoked to establish the proper environment (cutter specifications, tool positions, coordinate transformations, tolerance, etc. in APT), and then statements are executed in a specific order to produce the desired result (tool motion, program logic, arithmetic operations, input–output control, etc. in APT). These same types of expressions, declarations, and statements are found in one form or another in all languages considered here.

Civil Engineering Applications

Some of the most active development of problem-oriented languages has been for civil engineering applications. The computer was recognized very early as an invaluable tool to the civil engineer in performing the numerous calculations and in handling the complex data that are involved in the design and construction of bridges, highways, harbors, etc.

The solution of civil engineering problems involves many disciplines. For example, in the design of a highway interchange, the engineer uses surveying, highway engineering, soil mechanics, structural engineering, hydraulic engineering, transportation engineering, etc. Computer aids to each of these fields have been developed over the past 40 years. Work was done to combine these separate applications into an integrated package of programs known as ICES (Integrated Civil Engineering System) which was initially developed in the mid-1960s. This section discusses some of the work that led up to the design and implementation of ICES, and then discusses ICES as an example of a unified system approach to problem-oriented languages.

Cogo

Cogo (*coordinate geometry*) is a programming language used to perform the geometric calculations required in surveying. It was developed originally by Professor C. Miller of the MIT Civil Engineering Department around 1960. It is now available on most computers and has also been implemented under several time-sharing systems.

Cogo provides the civil engineer with a large number of commands and associated programs to perform plane geometry computations. Some examples of Cogo commands are given below

`DIVIDE/LINE`	To divide a line into a specified number of segments
`LOCATE/AZIMUTH`	To define a point, given the distance and azimuth from a specified point.
`AREA`	To calculate the area of a triangle, given the three vertices.

STRESS

Structural Engineering Systems Solver (Stress) was developed (Fenves *et al.*, 1964) with the objective of facilitating the use of computers in analyzing structures. The principal objective of Stress was to provide a wide variety of structural analyses with a minimum of programming effort. It can be used to analyze two- and three-dimensional structures, with either pinned or rigid joints, with prismatic or non-prismatic members, and subjected to concentrated or distributed loads, support motions, or temperature effects.

Stress was developed in the early 1960s under the direction of Professor S. J. Fenves at MIT. Numerous computer implementations of this language have been accomplished since this early work. It was essentially replaced later in the 1960s by STRUDL. The following statements are examples of types found in Stress.

Size descriptors. Several statements are needed to define the size of the problem to be handled. These include:

```
NUMBER OF JOINTS
NUMBER OF SUPPORTS
NUMBER OF MEMBERS
NUMBER OF LOADINGS
```

Structural data descriptors. To describe completely a framed structure, it is necessary to provide information about its geometry, topology (interconnection of members and joints), mechanical properties (load–deflection relationships of the members), and the presence of local releases (such as hinges or rollers). Six types of statement are provided, and three are shown here:

1. Geometry is specified in terms of joint coordinates by the statement

   ```
   JOINT COORDINATES
   ```

   followed by the X, Y, Z coordinates of each joint (or X, Y for plane structures). These statements are also used to describe the status (i.e. free or support) of the joints.

2. The presence of hinges or rollers at support joints is given as

   ```
   JOINT RELEASES
   ```

followed by the joint numbers and the designation and orientation of the released (zero) force components.

3. The interconnection of the members is specified by the statement

    MEMBER INCIDENCES

followed by a list giving the starting and ending joint of each member. The meaning of this statement is best illustrated by the descriptive input form, which for a typical member may be MEMBER 17 GOES FROM JOINT 10 TO JOINT 7.

Loading data descriptors. The loading applied to the structure is specified in terms of loading condition descriptors, descriptors of individual loads, and descriptors of groups of loads, as follows.

The word

    LOADING

followed by any identifying information, delineates groups of loads (together comprising a loading condition) and serves as a loading condition header.

Individual loads are specified by statements such as

    JOINT LOADS

followed by the joint numbers and the components of applied load:

    JOINT DISPLACEMENTS
    MEMBER DISTORTIONS
    MEMBER LOADS

followed by a statement for each load, giving the member number, the orientation, magnitude, and type of the load.

ICES

The problem-oriented languages discussed to this point have provided the user with language capability to solve very special problems, such as producing tapes for numerically controlled machine tools, solving problems in plane geometry, and performing structural analysis. The *integrated civil engineering system* (ICES), on the other hand, was designed to function as a series of subsystems, each subsystem corresponding to an engineering discipline (Roos, 1981). Each subsystem in ICES uses its own data structure; nevertheless, it provides for common files of problem data. ICES also provides an engineering programming language, command-definition language, and data-definition language to create subsystems. Thus, ICES is a framework within which engineering programs can be embedded.

The engineering programming language is Icetran, which is an extension of Fortran designed to handle civil engineering programming. With Icetran, a programmer can develop problem-oriented subsystems that become part of the ICES package.

To provide for a common method of defining the language elements, the subsystem designer makes use of a command-definition language (CDL) to specify the commands needed for the necessary problem-solving capabilities, as well as the external data requirements and the internal data processing required for each command. This information is transmitted to the computer in the command-definition language. The command-definition language requests are processed by the command-definition system program (an ICES subsystem), which produces a command dictionary, a COMMON map, and command data blocks for the subsystem. The dictionary and the command data blocks are used by ICEX, the ICES executive program, which processes the engineer's problem-oriented language commands.

There are two types of command in ICES: system commands and subsystem commands. System commands are used by an engineer to specify the name of the ICES subsystem to be used. Examples of system commands are Cogo, STRUDL (structural design language), and Sepol (settlement problem-oriented language), etc. Subsystem commands refer to the engineering commands in each subsystem. The engineer specifies the appropriate system command, followed by the relevant subsystem commands. Assume, for example, that a structural engineer is working on a bridge design problem. First the BRIDGE system command will be given, followed by BRIDGE subsystem commands. Then, to design the bridge geometry, the Cogo system command will be issued, followed by the Cogo subsystem commands. After the bridge geometry has been calculated, the BRIDGE system command will be issued, which returns to the bridge subsystem.

Thus, the essence of ICES is the generation of appropriate subsystems for specific engineering applications, which are then used to solve a given class of problems. Once a new subsystem is generated, it becomes a part of the ICES package. The generation of a subsystem requires that a programmer:

1. Write a description of each subsystem command in CDL.

2. Write programs in Icetran to carry out the computations.

3. Design the load module structure.

4. Design the subsystem COMMON area.

Electrical Engineering Applications

Computers are essential aids to the electrical engineer in many applications. Circuit analysis is the "bread and butter" computation for most electrical engineering applications. The two most commonly used circuit analysis programs are ECAP (Electronic Circuit Analysis Program) and SCEPTRE (Jensen and Lieberman, 1968; Bowers and Sedore, 1971). ECAP allows the electrical engineer to perform dc, ac, and transient analysis. Under control of ECAP, network equations are formulated and solved after the appropriate topological information and element values of the network have been provided. SCEPTRE also performs dc and transient analysis, but was designed to provide several improvements over ECAP in transient analysis.

Robot Languages

One of the more recent specialized areas is the development of languages to program robots. While some of the languages bear a striking resemblance to the numerical control languages (e.g. APT), there are fundamental differences. Various authors represent robot programming on different levels, but the simplest way to consider the issue is to define only three conceptual levels: servo, manipulator, and task. At the servo level, a program consists of a series of endpoints, speeds, and input–output commands; the path between endpoints is generated by calculating a series of intermediate points between the endpoints. At the manipulator level, the program contains motion commands (e.g. move from Point A to Point B), some sensor capability (e.g. force specification), and branching and looping constructs (similar to what is in most programming languages). (Most robot programming languages are at this manipulator level.) At the highest (i.e. task) level, the program specifies tasks (e.g. put box A on box B) and decomposition will generate the motions necessary to perform the task; these generally will be at the manipulator level. (This is analogous to having a compiler translate a high-level language by generating an assembly language version of the source code.)

Unlike many of the other types of specialized languages —which tend to be "stand alone"—there are three major approaches to developing a robot language, and only one of them is pure standalone. Another approach is to add commands to numerical control languages, since many of the facilities (e.g. geometry, motion) are similar, while the third approach is to add facilities to existing general languages (e.g. Pascal—*q.v.*).

Expert Systems Languages

In the 1980s the concept of *knowledge-based systems* or *expert systems* (*q.v.*) became significant, with many practical applications developed. An expert system involves (1) a language, (2) an inference engine, and (3) specific rules and data for an individual application. Expert systems are specific software programs intended to operate at or close to the level of a human expert in a specific task domain (e.g. auto repair, computer configuration, medical diagnosis), although in a given case the system may be limited to a specific subset of the task domain (e.g. correcting poor auto performance, configuring minicomputers, controlling excessive bleeding). The purpose of the rules is to specify the information and choices to be used as the system is applied. The inference engine represents the methodology used to invoke the rules, and the language expresses the computations to be performed.

The program generally consists of a declaration section and an unordered set of rules written in a language that has well-defined syntax and semantics, and generally contains facilities for data types (both scalar and aggregate), and commands for comparison, arithmetic computations, branching, and input–output. The declaration section provides information about the data (*see* DECLARATION). The rules are often, but not always, expressed as IF...THEN statements. There are generally language facilities that allow the human expert to include in the data a "certainty" or "probability" factor with regard to the effect of the input on the conclusion. Included in the coding of a specific "expert program" are questions for the user that provide the program with the necessary information in a specific case.

The inference engine executes the program by using techniques of matching, data examination, nonsequential execution, and cycling as appropriate. Some expert systems are implemented by compilers, some are purely interpretive, and some are a combination of both.

An example of the user's view of an expert program for diagnosing an automobile problem in a language called OPS5 is shown in Fig. 2, taken from Sherman and Martin (1990). The program acts as a consultant to an auto repair business. It will ask the user pertinent questions about the condition of specific areas of the disabled auto (e.g. fuel system, electrical system, starter system, and temperature). The program will analyze the input data and make a diagnosis with recommended treatment. Fig. 2 shows what the user sees to provide input, and also what the user receives as output. The Certainty Factors (CF) indicate how sure the system is of its conclusions (0—very unsure, 1—certain).

Other Problem-Oriented Languages

Literally hundreds of problem-oriented languages have been developed over the past 35 years. We have looked

...CONSULTATiON PROGRAM VERSION TWO

...by asking questions about the functioning of specific areas of your automobile. Please type ... Any other input will produce erroneous results.

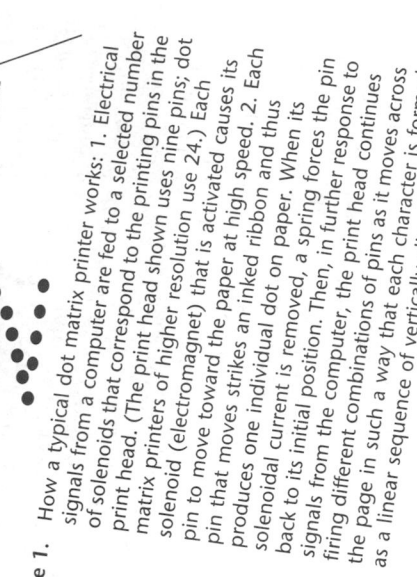

Figure 1. How a typical dot matrix printer works: 1. Electrical signals from a computer are fed to a selected number of solenoids that correspond to the printing pins in the print head. (The print head shown uses nine pins; dot matrix printers of higher resolution use 24.) Each solenoid (electromagnet) that is activated causes its pin to move toward the paper at high speed. 2. Each pin that moves strikes an inked ribbon and thus produces one individual dot on paper. When its solenoidal current is removed, a spring forces the pin back to its initial position. Then, in further response to the signals from the computer, the print head continues firing different combinations of pins as it moves across the page in such a way that each character is formed as a linear sequence of vertically aligned dots.

Speed and ease were the first improvements in computer printing. Where in the past a simple (type-written) error might just be whited out or hand-corrected with a pen, now—because of the speed of printers—it is easier just to correct a mistake on screen and print a fresh, flawless copy.

Graphics were the next big advance. The day of the all-text document ended with the first software that could print even the crudest line graph on a dot-matrix printer. Now anything that is visual, from line art to a halftone photograph, can be printed on a standard office printer. And since the image of a letter of the alphabet is an image like any other, even if a small one, there is no particular problem in using any one of a wide variety of typefaces, each available in roman, italic, or bold forms over a wide range of sizes (see TYPEFONT).

Dazzling color is the current frontier. The quality and speed of color printers is increasing as their cost is decreasing. Because they can double as black and white printers, color printers are becoming the only kind used in home and office alike.

All computer printing is based on the *dot matrix*. This is a grid of dots that can vary from six across and eight down to as many as 2,400 dpi (dots per inch) in both directions. Whether it is a laser printer going through an intricate ballet of movement and time or an inkjet printer spitting dots of color on paper, the printer is limited to producing dots—thousands of dots on a single page—but still dots. This is a fundamental change in printing from all that went before it since Gutenberg. The freedom that Gutenberg's movable type afforded also created restrictions. Printing was done with fully formed characters, letters, and numbers. This was true with the first personal computer printers, which contained all the characters for a font on a *daisy wheel*, a circle of plastic that rotated swiftly to bring the correct characters into position to be struck by a plunger. There was no such thing as changing fonts or creating graphics on the fly. The dot matrix changed that. With it a printer could print anything that could be made up of many tiny dots, which is virtually anything.

Black and White Printers

DOT-MATRIX PRINTERS

The dot-matrix printer made its first appearance as the *impact dot-matrix printer*, an inexpensive and versatile device. It includes a *print head* that uses magnetic solenoids to pound various combinations of metal rods, arrayed in a matrix, against a ribbon coated with ink. The earliest dot-matrix printers used printheads containing 9 wires called *printing pins*, but later ones attained much better print quality by using 24 pins.

For simplicity, Fig. 1 shows how a nine-pin dot-matrix printer works. By activating different solenoids as the printhead moves across the surface of a sheet of paper, the printer could produce any character in a crude but readable rendition.

Other printers make their dots without the miniature violence that an impact printer commits on a ribbon smeared with soot. But any printer, whether dot-matrix, inkjet, laser, dye sublimation, or solid ink, accomplishes essentially the same task: it creates a pattern of dots on a sheet of paper. The dots may be sized differently or composed of different inks that are transferred to the paper by different means, but all of the images for text and graphics are made up of dots. The smaller the dots, the more attractive the printout.

Because of their low speed and relatively poor print quality, dot-matrix printers are no longer widely used

years 1971–1977 sho...
sistently represented approximately 50% of...
level languages in use in the USA in a given year. There is reason to believe that this continues to be true, but no data has been collected since 1977 to confirm or reject that contention. However, these specialized application languages have generally been created by the users

Martin, J. C. *An OPSS Primer: Introduction to Rule-*

...guages rather than by computer scientists, ...ended to ignore this class of languages. ...omputer science research in programming ...uld affect the future developments in these ...pose languages. One area of research is the ...nt of techniques to permit users to define ...language requirements and have an auto-...cedure for generation of the specific syntax ...ntics, as well as a translator, for a language to ...e requirements. This goal has been stated for ...ars, but by the end of the 1990s had still not ...ieved. The closest we have ever come to that ...e in practical terms is the ICES system dis-...above, which is of course limited to civil engi-...applications.

...lvent of personal computers (*q.v.*) has both ...sed and decreased the need for those special-purpose languages. It has increased the need because of the additional millions of people using computers. Specialists in every discipline wish to communicate with the computer in languages that are comfortable for

Table 1. Illustrations of problem-oriented languages.

Application area	Program name
Statistics	SPSS: Statistical Package for the Social Sciences
	SAS Statistical Library
	OMNITAB
Computer-assisted instruction	TUTOR
	PLANIT
	COURSEWRITER
SImulation	GPSS: General-Purpose Systems Simulator
	SIMSCRIPT
	CSSL: Continuous System Simulation Language
Systems programming	AED: Automated Engineering Design
	BLISS: Basic Language for Implementing System Software
	C and C++
Computer design	CDL: Computer Design Language
	CSL: Computer Structure Language
	VHDL: VHSIC Hardware Description Language
Expert Systems	KRL: Knowledge Representation Language
	OPS5
Robotics	AML/2: A Manufacturing Language/2
	KAREL
	VAL: Versatile Assembly Language

them to use and that provide them with the greatest degree of expressiveness possible. However, this increase in the number of people using computers has been matched to some degree by the creation of an enormous number of program application *packages* that serve similar purposes but are not as general as a programming language covering the same area. Thus, while there could exist specific accounting languages, they are unlikely to be developed because of the existence of powerful spreadsheet (*q.v.*) programs.

As pointed out by Sammet (1969), the controversy over language structure will continue into the future. Some people advocate the use of English as a programming language. Others insist that many applications require a precision of expression that would be aided by a more formal and structured language than would be available when using natural language. Since this controversy is unlikely to subside in the near future, it seems reasonable to press for user-defined languages. In this way, the personal preference of the specific user could be satisfied. However, research in this field has been minimal.

Bibliography

1958. Theodoroff, T. J. "DYANA: Dynamics Analyzer-Programmer, Part I, Description and Application," *Proc. Eastern Joint Computer Conference*, 144–147.

1964. Fenves, S. J. *et al.* STRESS: *A User's Manual*. Cambridge, MA: MIT Press.

1967. IIT Research Institute. *APT Part Programming*. New York: McGraw-Hill.

1968. Jensen, R. W., and Lieberman, M. D. *IBM Electronic Circuit Analysis Program—Techniques and Applications*. Upper Saddle River, NJ: Prentice Hall.

1969. Sammet, J. E. *Programming Languages: History and Fundamentals*. Upper Saddle River, NJ: Prentice Hall.

1971. Bowers, J. C., and Sedore, S. R. *SCEPTRE: A Computer Program for Circuit and Systems Analysis*. Upper Saddle River, NJ: Prentice Hall.

1978. Sammet, J. E. "Roster of Programming Languages for 1976–77," *SIGPLAN Notices*, **13**, *11*, 56–85.

1981. Roos, D. (ed.) *ICES System: General Description*. Cranston, RI: ICES Users Group (July).

1983. Lozano-Perez, T. "Robot Programming," *Proc. IEEE*, **71**, 7 (July), 821–841.

1986. Blaha, J. R., Lamoureux, J. P., and McKee, K. E. *Higher Order Languages for Robots*. MTIAC-SOAR-86-01, Defense Logistics Agency, Dept of Defense.

1987. Cugini, J. V. *Programming Languages for Knowledge-Based Systems*. NBS Special Publication 500-145, Gaithersburg, MD: National Bureau of Standards, Institute for Computer Sciences and Technology.

1990. Sherman, P. D., and Martin, J. C. *An OPS5 Primer: Introduction to Rule-Based Expert Systems*. Upper Saddle River, NJ: Prentice Hall.

1991. Sammet, J. E. "Some Approaches to, and Illustrations of, Progamming Language History," *Annals of the History of Computing*, **13**, *1*, 33–50.

Benjamin Mittman and Jean E. Sammet

PROBLEM-SOLVING ENVIRONMENTS

For articles on related subjects *see* ALGORITHMIC PROBLEM SOLVING; COMPUTER ALGEBRA; MATHEMATICAL SOFTWARE; and SCIENTIFIC APPLICATIONS.

A *problem-solving environment* is a software system that provides all the computational facilities necessary to solve a target class of problems. These facilities include advanced solution methods, automatic and semi-automatic selection of solution methods, and ways to incorporate novel solution methods. Moreover, a problem-solving environment uses the natural language of the target class of problems so that users can try to solve them without specialized knowledge of the underlying hardware or software. By exploiting modern technologies such as interactive color graphics, powerful processors, and networks of specialized services, scientific problem-solving environments can track extended problem-solving tasks and allow users to review them easily. Ideally, they create a framework that is all things to all people; they solve

---

in office environments, nor even with PCs. Like background sports broadcasts, the characteristic sound of an operating dot matrix printer was once ubiquitous, but their use is now relegated to small quiet devices used in retail stores to print credit card invoices.

LASER PRINTERS—built by Hewlett-Packard, Canon, Epson, and other companies—have replaced the *Laser printers*—built by Hewlett-Packard, Canon, impact dot-matrix printer as the printer of choice in most businesses and many homes. Although it per-forms essentially the same task as an impact printer—placing dots of ink on paper—it is faster and produces smaller dots at 600–1400 dots per inch, providing the definition and sharpness of traditional typeset printing.

At the heart of the printer is the *print engine*—the mechanism that transfers black powder to the page—which is a device that owes its ancestry to the photocopier. To create the nearly typeset-quality output that is characteristic of a laser printer, the printer must control five different operations at the same time: it must (1) interpret the signals coming from a computer, (2) translate those signals into instructions that control the firing and movement of a laser beam, (3) control the movement of the paper, (4) sensitize the paper so that the black toner that makes up the black beam along a path called the *paper train*. It is a

Figure 2. How a typical laser printer works: 1. The computer sends signals to the printer's own embedded processor to specify where printed dots are to be placed on paper. 2. Instructions from the printer's processor rapidly turn a beam of laser light on and off as needed. 3. A spinning mirror deflects light from the laser so that the path of the beam is a horizontal line across the surface of a cylinder called an *Organic Photoconducting Cartridge* (OPC), or more simply, a *drum*. The combination of the laser beam being turned on and off and the movement of the beam's path across the cylinder results in a line of many tiny points of light across the entire width of the drum. 4. The drum then rotates, perhaps 1/600 or 1/1200 of an inch depending on the resolution of the printer, and the laser beam begins work on the next line of dots. As the drum rotates, a system of gears and rollers feeds a ... along a path called the *paper train*. The ... electrically charged wire that ...

simple or complex problems, support rapid prototyping or detailed analysis, and can be used in introductory education or at the frontiers of science.

While the concept of problem-solving environments has arisen in science, it encompasses much of computation. Thus Microsoft Word is a problem-solving environment for word processing (*q.v.*). Mathematica and Matlab are basic examples in scientific computing. The problem-solving environments Website `http://www.cs.purdue.edu/research/cse/pses.cgi` provides a lengthy list of examples and reference materials. The software architecture of a problem-solving environment is characterized by modularity using a software parts technology. An ideal one can make many decisions for the user by consulting its associated knowledge base. Thus a problem-solving environment is composed of four principal components: a user interface, a library of problem solvers, a knowledge base plus inference mechanism, and a software integration framework.

Bibliography

1994. Gallopoulos, E., Houstis, E. N., and Rice, J. R. "Computer as a Thinker/doer: Problem Solving Environments for Computational Science," *IEEE Computational Science & Engineering*, **1**, 2, 11–23.
1996. Rice, J. R., and Boisvert, R. F. "From Scientific Software Libraries to Problem Solving Environments," *IEEE Computational Science & Engineering*, **3**, 3, 44–53.

John R. Rice

PROCEDURE-ORIENTED LANGUAGES

SURVEY

For articles on related subjects *see* ABSTRACT DATA TYPE; ADA; ALGOL; ASSEMBLER; BLOCK STRUCTURE; C; C++; COMPILER; DATA STRUCTURES; DATA TYPE; EXPRESSION; FORTH; FUNCTIONAL PROGRAMMING; LIST PROCESSING: LANGUAGES; LOGO; MACHINE AND ASSEMBLY LANGUAGE PROGRAMMING; NONPROCEDURAL LANGUAGES; OBJECT-ORIENTED PROGRAMMING; PASCAL; POSTSCRIPT; PROGRAMMING LANGUAGES; RECURSION; SIDE EFFECT; STATEMENT; STRING PROCESSING; and TYPES, THEORY OF. *See also* articles on languages discussed in this article.

Procedure-oriented languages (POLs) are artificial languages used to define, in a form understandable to humans, the actions required by a computer to solve a problem. The higher-level form of a POL frees a programmer from the time-consuming and often tedious chore of expressing algorithms in lower-level languages such as assembly and machine language (*see* MACHINE AND ASSEMBLY LANGUAGE PROGRAMMING). Additionally,

in a POL actions are expressed in a machine-independent form that greatly eases the burden of moving a program from one computer to another (*see* PORTABILITY). This increases the lifetime and usefulness of the program.

The defining characteristic of a procedure-oriented language is the expression of a problem algorithm as a series of discrete statements or steps, each of which typically embodies far more logic than any one machine language instruction. Execution proceeds from one statement (*q.v.*) to the next in a sequential fashion, embodying a single flow or thread of control. This sequential stepwise processing of the program reflects the operation of most prevailing computer hardware (but *see also* PARALLEL PROCESSING).

The solution of a problem on a computer requires its expression in a form the machine can "understand." Usually, the solution begins as an algorithm expressed in a natural language. This identifies "what" needs to be done to derive a solution. It may be restated in a *specification language* (*see* PROGRAM SPECIFICATION) that states more precisely the requirements to be met by the solution. The informal or formal specification is then translated into a notation that contains the steps or machine instructions to be executed by the computer. The last form tells the computer "how" to get a solution. If the translation is directly from the specification into assembly language, most of the labor is done by the programmer. In most cases, however, a programmer expresses the "how" by writing in a procedure-oriented language that can be translated by a *compiler* program into machine language. The proportion of the translation process that can be done by the computer suggests the level of abstraction of the particular POL being used. Sophisticated compiler technology allows the programmer to use higher-level languages that approximate the original mathematical form of the algorithm.

Procedure-oriented languages belong to the higher-level category; yet they retain the "how to" flavor of machine language rather than the "what to do" flavor of mathematics or nonprocedural languages. A procedure-oriented language may be regarded as the language of a virtual computer that executes the steps of the POL as if they were single "machine" instructions. POLs vary in how powerful their steps are; that is, how much can be accomplished in a single statement of the language.

Procedure-oriented languages differ from machine and assembly languages in the level of data and expression abstraction available to the programmer. Data is stored in precise locations in the computer memory as sequences of bits. Assembly and machine language programmers use the data by specifying a memory address, and they have to manage all information such as the size and location of data themselves. The POL programmer accesses the data using variables that represent numbers and values with familiar types, such as real, integer, and character. Also, procedure-oriented language steps contain expressions (*q.v.*) with variables, constants, and operations on them. During execution, each expression will cause many machine-level actions to occur. The expressions and typed variables of the POL provide a higher level of abstraction that enables the programmer to develop algorithms in familiar terms.

As procedure-oriented languages have developed, they have increased the level of abstraction available to the programmer. A POL combines expressions into larger programming units called *procedures* or *subprograms* (*q.v.*). This *procedural abstraction* lets the programmer treat a complex sequence of operations as a single unit that can be reused. POLs also allow the grouping of data of homogeneous type into indexed aggregates called *arrays*. They provide *structures* or *records* (*q.v.*) to group complex heterogeneous data such as mixtures of numbers and character strings into single data objects. These structures can be combined, so that there can be arrays of records or records containing arrays or other records. Such data structures let a programmer model features of the problem being solved at a level more or less matching the problem statement.

Together with abstraction capabilities, POLs provide type checking, which prevents many run-time errors by detecting them during compilation. In addition to declaring complex data structures, in modern POLs, programmers define the *type* of each structure. A *phone_book*, for example, may be the name of a type defined as an array of records, each containing a string and a number). POLs generally require that the type of each variable be specified when the variable is first declared. The compiler then uses this type information to insure that the program uses its data structures correctly. A *strongly typed* language is one in which each entity has a precise type that cannot be changed in the program, and such languages provide considerable protection against programmer error.

One of the most important kinds of abstraction is to have program units that contain both data structures and the procedures that operate on them—that is, *abstract data types* (*q.v.*). These units may be compilation units called *modules*, or (in Ada) *packages*, or they may be *classes* (*q.v.*) that have multiple instances (*objects*). Such data abstractions separate a program into well-defined segments that permit access to the data structures only through their associated procedures. The segments can be reused in other programs,

or they can provide a basis for building new segments (*see* MODULAR PROGRAMMING and OBJECT-ORIENTED PROGRAMMING).

Most commercial and scientific application programs, existing or under development, use procedure-oriented languages, although there has been some growth in the use of functional languages (*q.v.*) that have less of the "how to" flavor that characterizes procedure-orientation. Despite the utility of procedure-oriented languages, some observers believe that the magnitude of the advances needed for future applications is not possible with these languages. One problem is to manage the complexity of very large programs. Today, that is often done with object-oriented languages and tools for organizing their multiple components (*see* SOFTWARE ENGINEERING and SOFTWARE CONFIGURATION MANAGEMENT).

The sequential stepwise execution requirements of a POL may also cause synchronization problems on multiprocessors. It remains to be seen whether current languages can be extended to support all forms of concurrency. A concern with multiprocessing POL extensions is the added complexity for the programmer. Nonprocedural languages can avoid the synchronization problems of stepwise execution and may be better choices for multiprocessors. In the late 1990s, however, most programming of multiprocessors was done with extensions of POLs, such as High Performance Fortran, which adds to Fortran constructs for specifying parallel execution. For the moment, some of the additional complexity of parallelism is being absorbed by sophisticated compilers, although programming parallel systems often uses POLs with relatively low levels of abstraction (e.g. in requiring the programmer to think about the location of storage for data).

Hundreds of procedure-oriented languages have been developed since the mid-1950s. This survey lists, in approximate historical order, general-purpose procedure-oriented languages that the authors regard as having been either popular or significant during that period. Many of these languages, marked by an asterisk in the following list, are discussed at greater length in articles devoted to them in this volume. The articles on list-processing, string-processing, and problem-oriented languages also include material on the procedural characteristics of these languages.

Fortran* Fortran is in some sense both the oldest and the newest language. Designed for numerical computations, the first versions of Fortran in the late 1950s proved that a higher-level language compiler could produce efficient machine code. Fortran has gone through numerous revisions, the most recent of which is Fortran 95.

Algol* Algol 60 was first defined by an international committee in the late 1950s. It introduced block structure (*q.v.*) and the explicit declaration of variable types (*strong typing*). It also introduced recursion (*q.v.*) to POLs. Though never commercially popular, at least in the USA, Algol is the ancestor of many important POLs—Pascal, Ada, and Modula-2, among others—the so-called "Algol family."

APL* APL was originally developed in the 1950s by Kenneth E. Iverson as a concise mathematical notation for expressing computer science concepts. It contains a rich set of operators on vectors and arrays that allow very compact statements. There are no control structures (*q.v.*), such as `while`, `if-then-else`, and `for`. These are replaced by recursion, array operations, and a single transfer-of-control operator, →, which means "go to".

Cobol* Cobol was developed in 1959 for business data processing applications, and became one of the most widely used languages. Cobol was the first language to place equal importance on data and procedures, providing separate specifications for each.

PL/I PL/I was specified by IBM and several of IBM's large computer user groups in 1964. It was an attempt to extend Fortran, primarily a scientific language, for use in commercial applications and *systems programming* (*q.v.*). The idea was to develop a single language that would be suitable for all programming efforts. A very large language, it was difficult to implement and was used mostly on IBM mainframes (*q.v.*). It is rarely used now.

Simula* Simula, introduced in 1967, was a general programming language intended specifically to be used for simulation (*q.v.*). It introduced the important concepts of *class* and *object*, and was thus the first object-oriented language.

Basic* Basic, developed in the late 1960s, was intended to be small, portable, and easy to learn. It was interpreted rather than compiled (*see* LANGUAGE PROCESSORS), which at that time gave it the advantage of rapid feedback on syntax and run-time errors. Its early versions lacked many of the resources needed for large programs, such as strong data typing and parameter-passing to subprograms. Later versions added more features including "visual" ones for Microsoft Windows applications.

Pascal* Pascal was developed in the early 1970s to refine the programming ideas of Algol into a small, compact, reliable, yet full-featured language suitable for teaching the principles of *software design* (*q.v.*). It became a major language for programming instruction, and provided user-defined data types, though not full data abstraction.

C* Developed in the early 1970s at Bell Laboratories as the implementation language for the Unix Operating System (*q.v.*), C and its successor C++ have become the primary languages of discourse in systems programming.

Modula-2 Modula-2, developed in the mid-1970s as a successor to Pascal, introduced data abstraction by means of an elegant module system. It was intended for systems programming as well as for software design, and provided support for coroutines (*q.v.*).

Ada* Ada, developed in the early 1980s, was the result of nearly 20 years of effort by the US Department of Defense to develop a single language for all applications – commercial, scientific, and particularly *embedded systems* (*q.v.*).

C++* C++ dates from the early 1980s. It was intended to preserve the efficiency of C but to add abstraction capabilities—stronger data typing and structuring features, and the object-oriented features of Simula. By the late 1990s, it had become one of the most popular languages for teaching, as well as for applications programming (*q.v.*) and systems programming (*q.v.*).

Eiffel was designed in the late 1980s as an object-oriented language with a carefully chosen set of features. Although less popular than C++, it is a useful language for teaching programming principles as well as for large-scale programming.

Java* Java, an object-oriented language of the early 1990s, uses much of the syntax of C++ but is intended to be free of the low-level features that C++ inherited from C. It avoids machine-specific operations like address manipulation, and is thus capable of being compiled on one system and run on another—such as in the *applets* that are part of the World Wide Web (*q.v.*).

Bibliography

1981. Wexelblat, R. L. (ed.) *History of Programming Languages*. New York: Academic Press.
1987. Horowitz, E. *Programming Languages: A Grand Tour*, 3rd Ed. Rockville, MD: Computer Science Press.
1996. Bergin, T. J., and Gibson, R. G. (eds.) *The History of Programming Languages II*. Reading, MA: Addison-Wesley.
1999. MacLennan, B. J. *Principles of Programming Languages*, 3rd Ed. Oxford: Oxford University Press.

Tony L. Cox, revised by David Hemmendinger

PROGRAMMING

For articles on related subjects *see* COMPILER; CONTROL STRUCTURE; DATA STRUCTURES; DEBUGGING; DECLARATION; DIAGNOSTIC; ERRORS; EXPRESSION; FUNCTIONAL PROGRAMMING; ITERATION; LANGUAGE PROCESSORS; MODULAR PROGRAMMING; OBJECT-ORIENTED PROGRAMMING; OBJECT PROGRAM; OPERATOR PRECEDENCE; PROGRAM; PROGRAMMING LANGUAGES; SOURCE PROGRAM; STATEMENT; STRUCTURED PROGRAMMING; SUBPROGRAM; and TYPES, THEORY OF.

In contrast with the tremendous advances in computer hardware, the level of machine and assembly languages (*q.v.*) has changed relatively little over the past five decades. Machine instructions are expressed as sequences of numerical codes. Moreover, the typical machine language instruction represents an activity that is trivial by human standards, offering no direct correspondence with our idea of a "step" in a problem solution.

Consequently, there is a gap between what the programmer wants to say and what the processor can recognize. High-level programming languages are designed to bridge this gap. This article addresses only procedure-oriented (also called *procedural* or *imperative*) languages; see articles on functional and logic programming for other types of languages (sometimes called *very high-level languages*). Object-oriented languages, a form of procedural language, are also discussed separately.

Each of the hundreds of procedure-oriented programming languages is designed to meet a particular set of objectives. Some are intended for use over a wide range of applications; others address a more limited spectrum of problem types characteristic of a specific discipline. All share a common property: the elemental vehicle for expressing the programmer's intention (i.e. the language statement) conveys a level of complexity consistent with the procedure being represented. Thus, the activity that can be described in a single "instruction" (a line of code) bears no direct resemblance to a single machine operation. Instead, many languages try to provide some similarity between a language *statement* and its counterpart in the notation appropriate to the application. For example, the following statement in the Fortran language,

```
H = 0.023*(C/D)*(D*V*R/U)
   **0.8*(U*P/C)**0.4,          (1)
```

is easily related to the same formula in conventional algebraic form:

$$H = 0.023 \frac{C}{D} \left(\frac{DVR}{U}\right)^{0.8} \left(\frac{UP}{C}\right)^{0.4}. \qquad (2)$$

This expression requires a considerable number of machine operations to produce the specified result (i.e. a value for H). Accordingly, the correspondence between the Fortran statement and the equivalent sequence of machine instructions produced by the language-translating program (the compiler) is not obvious at all.

This extensive insulation between machine and programmer has had a profound effect on the growth of computer use and the range of successful applications. Most programs are written in high-level languages, and most people who write programs are not computer specialists.

Despite the high-level character of procedural languages, their basic structure is relatively simple. They are sequences of statements (more properly called *commands*; hence the name *imperative* language). The most important statement is the *assignment* statement, which gives a value to a variable. There are *control* statements for decisions and repetition. As a program executes, variables are repeatedly assigned new values. A set of statements may be organized into a *procedure* or *function*, each of which is a subprogram. A procedure may then be executed by using its name as a program statement, and a function name may appear in expressions. Procedures and functions are used to identify operations that are used repeatedly, a process that simplifies the structure of a complex program. Languages generally provide some basic procedures and functions, particularly those that provide an interface with an operating system (*q.v.*), such as input and output operations.

Beyond these basic *executable* constructs, procedure-oriented (and other) languages have facilities (so-called *non-executable* statements) for describing and specifying program elements in terms appropriate to the problem being solved (*see* DECLARATION). These are at least as important for the organization of thought as the executable statement types just described. The following sections briefly describe the elements of procedure-oriented languages, specifically

- Specification capabilities: type systems
- Assignment and expressions: arithmetic and other forms
- Control structures: conditionals and repetition
- Subprograms: procedures and functions
- Program development facilities

Of the items in this list, it is the particular form and use of expressions, control structures, and subprograms that characterize procedure-oriented languages.

Specifications and Type Systems

A program in any language is eventually translated into elementary machine operations on strings of bits stored in memory. The distinction between low- and high-level languages is that in the former, the programmer must think in terms of storage and operations on what is stored, while in the latter, the programmer may think in terms of variable names. In assembly language, a programmer may introduce names, but only as labels attached to storage locations. In languages like Pascal, Ada, and Java, a programmer declares variables by name and the language translator associates the names with locations. The programmer is thus free to attend to the significance that the program variables have for the problem to be solved.

The association between a name and a location is part of the *binding* of the name (*see* BINDING). Depending on the language and the kind of variable (global to an entire program or local to one part of it, for example), the location may be determined by the translator at translation time, or it may not be fully determined until the program runs. Such issues must be resolved according to the language definition and its implementation.

In some early languages, like Fortran (*q.v.*), the first use of a variable name, such as H in Eqn. (1), would cause the compiler to allocate storage for it, and subsequent references to H would use that location. Reliance on such implicit *declarations* is poor programming practice, however, and if a programmer writes F where H was intended, the compiler will not warn of an error, but will simply provide storage for the spurious variable F.

Procedural languages now generally require every variable to be explicitly declared. A declaration specifies the *type* of the variable as well as its name. The type may be a primitive type of the language—real, integer, character—or it may be a programmer-defined type. The latter sort is particularly important in giving the programmer the ability to organize program data to correspond to the elements of the problem to be solved. A language that provides arrays of data but not heterogeneous records (*q.v.*), for example, would require that the programmer operate in parallel on an array of strings (names) and an array of integers (salaries), while a language with records, such as Pascal, C, or Ada, would let the programmer manipulate personnel records as units in the program, as they are in the problem domain. The following examples illustrate the forms of variable declarations in several languages.

```
Fortran   REAL X, Y, Z
C         double x, y, z, ar[100];
Pascal    var x, y, z : real;
          ar : array[1..100] of real
Ada       x, y, z : integer;
```

Each of these statements reserves storage for three variables x, y, and z to hold numerical values placed there later. Since nothing further is specified, internal language rules (*default conditions—q.v.*) will determine the amount of reserved storage and the form for the numerical values.

The declarations of the array ar in C and Pascal display a difference of level. In C, the array is declared as 100 real numbers; that is, the [100] directs the compiler to allocate an appropriate amount of storage. The Pascal declaration treats the ar as a distinct type, and specifies how it is to be indexed. (In C all array indexing starts from 0.)

Type declarations allow a compiler to check not only that a variable has been declared but that it is used correctly. Every type, both primitive and user-defined, has a set of operations that may be done on variables of that type. If a is an integer and s is a character string, a+s has a *type error*, since strings can't normally be added to integers, though a+a or s+s are legal, assuming that "+" for strings means concatenation, for example. A language is called *strongly typed* if the language implementation can detect any error due to the incorrect use of a type. In a *weakly typed* language not all such errors are detectable; that is, the language may permit operations to be done on variables inappropriately. If all type checking in a strongly typed language can be done at compile-time, the language is called *type-safe* or *statically typed*. In a type-safe language, a program that compiles correctly is guaranteed to have no type errors at run time. Ada is largely type-safe; the current ANSI C standard is more strongly typed than its predecessors, but less strongly typed than C++.

Object-oriented languages are procedure-oriented languages in which a type can be defined to be a data structure, together with a set of operations on it, in such a way that the data structure is accessible only through those operations. Such *abstract data types* (*q.v.*), called *classes* (*q.v.*), give the programmer still greater ability to define types that reflect the organization of the program's subject matter. A table such as a telephone book may be defined with operations to look up names, and to add and delete entries. The internal implementation of those operations in terms of lower-level types such as arrays or trees (*q.v.*) remains hidden, so that their details cannot affect the rest of the program (making it hard to write nonsense like adding 1 to a stored telephone number).

Assignment and Expressions

The statement in Eqn. (1) exemplifies a primary convenience a high-level language brings to its users—the ability to specify intricate steps with little loss in correspondence between the conventional description and its representation in a program. This intent is implemented by allowing a statement to be sufficiently large so as not to restrict the programmer's ability to maintain the integrity of a procedural step. Thus, it is usually the programmer, and not the computing system or the language, that determines the amount of activity to be specified in a single program "step" without serious regard to the number of actual machine steps these actions will eventually entail.

In procedure-oriented languages, the type of statement in which much of the actual computation is done is the *assignment statement*. An assignment statement has the form

$$variable \leftarrow expression \qquad (3)$$

The $\leftarrow$ in this construction symbolizes the operation of replacement, so that the general sense of the assignment may be stated as follows: "Evaluate the *expression* on the right-hand side of the $\leftarrow$ by performing the indicated operations; then let the result be the new value for *variable*, replacing its current value." The final step of placing the new value in *variable* may be a simple STORE machine instruction.

In many widely used high-level languages, such as Basic, C++ and Java, assignment is denoted (inaccurately) by the symbol "=". Algol, Pascal, and Ada use ":=" and APL uses an actual $\leftarrow$. Assignment must not be confused with mathematical equality. The C statement N = N+1 makes no sense as an equation, but is a simple increment operation as an assignment statement. (C, C++, and Java use "==" for equality, but Basic uses "=" for both assignment and equality, making the compiler—and programmer—rely on context to know which is meant.)

In (3), *variable*, the term to the left of $\leftarrow$, is a single variable name, because the effect of an assignment is to store a value at the address of the variable. In some languages it is restricted to be a simple data type such as an integer or real number; in others, it may be a compound data type such as a record.

An *expression* consists of a combination of *terms* and *operators* in which the rules of construction constitute a restricted version of those applicable in ordinary algebra. The two basic restrictions given below are imposed to accommodate the computer's functional limitations and to facilitate compilation by rules that avoid ambiguities.

◆ Each arithmetic operation must be indicated explicitly; it may never be implied. (For example, the expression $A(B + C)$, understandable in algebra, must be written as A*(B+C) in a program statement.)

◆ Expressions must be in linear form. For example, (A+B)/(C-D) is a more awkward, but unavoidable, substitute for the conventional algebraic equivalent:

$$\frac{A + B}{C - D}$$

The latter restriction reflects a physical limitation imposed by I/O media rather than any linguistic constraint.

As in algebra, a programming language expression like A+B/C*D would be ambiguous without *operator precedence* rules to specify the order in which to apply operators. Most procedural languages adopt precedence rules similar to algebraic ones, and give * and / higher precedence than + or -, and evaluate equal-precedence operators like * and / left-to-right. These languages, such as Pascal, C, and Java, would treat the expression above as equivalent to A + (B/C)*D. Some languages use a strict left-to-right or even right-to-left ordering, making the expression equivalent to ((A+B)/C)*D or A + (B/(C*D)), respectively. In all cases, however, the programmer may use parentheses to enforce a different precedence.

Expressions are not restricted to numbers in most procedural languages. At the very least, they also provide Boolean expressions, with the and, or, and not operators of Boolean algebra (*q.v.*), and generally also a small set of string expressions with operators such as concatenation. Some languages, including Pascal and Modula-2, have set expressions for set-theoretic operations such as union and intersection.

Correct use of an expression requires that the programmer guarantee that there is a value associated with each variable appearing in it, since compilers generally are designed to proceed on that assumption. Once the programmer makes sure that the variables have been defined (i.e. declared, so that storage has been made available for them, and values have been provided), the language presents no further obstacles with regard to the length or complexity of an expression.

To illustrate, we refer again to Eqn. (1), which uses the Fortran language. Assuming that values are available for each of the variables *D, V, R, U, P,* and *C*, the programmer has the prerogative of computing a value for *H* via a single statement, as in Eqn. (2), or using several statements to produce partial results that are stored in separate variables and used subsequently:

```
V1 = D*V*R/U
V2 = U*P/C
H = 0.023*(C/D)*(V1**0.8)*(V2**0.4).
```

The choice of form is governed predominantly by readability of the resulting program.

As in algebra, expressions combine with functions (see below) for still greater power. A function call returns a value, and thus may be a term in an expression, as in `X := Y + sqrt(Z)`. Although the preceding examples have used expressions as values to be assigned to variables, an expression may provide a value that is passed to a function, as in `C = sqrt(A*A + B*B)`, the equivalent of the algebraic $c = \sqrt{a^2 + b^2}$. In this case there is no program variable that is assigned `A*A + B*B`, but the compiler provides temporary storage for that value for the function to use.

Control Structures

Procedure-oriented languages have three basic control structures: sequences, conditionals and loops. A simple "straight-line" program is just a sequence of assignment statements, together with input and output operations. The power of digital computers, however, arises from their selecting alternative computations on the basis of the values of program variables (*conditional statements*) and their carrying out repetitive loops (*iterative statements*). In virtually all procedural languages today, *recursion (q.v.)* is another form of control in which a subprogram can solve a problem by calling itself repeatedly until the problem has been reduced to an elementary one.

Conditional and iteration statements both use Boolean (truth-value) expressions such as `(x < y)` or `(z > 0)`. They build on simple machine-level comparison instructions, together with branch instructions, which are machine-level *goto* statements. The latter are also available in high-level languages, but they can make a program difficult to understand and are rarely needed now.

CONDITIONALS

Early procedure-oriented languages like Fortran and Basic had `IF .. THEN ..` conditional statements. Later languages, including the current version of Fortran and Basic, all have the more convenient `if .. then .. else ..` conditional that lets the programmer write complex decision-structures without the use of `goto` (*see* STRUCTURED PROGRAMMING). It is described by the flowchart (*q.v.*) in Fig. 1, and its power can be summarized in three basic properties:

1. The formulation is simple and "natural," reflecting the flowchart given in Fig. 1: "Test the specified condition. If it is true, perform alternative action *A*, ignoring *B*. If it is false, perform *B*, ignoring *A*. Upon completion of the action, continue that part of the processing that is independent of the test condition."

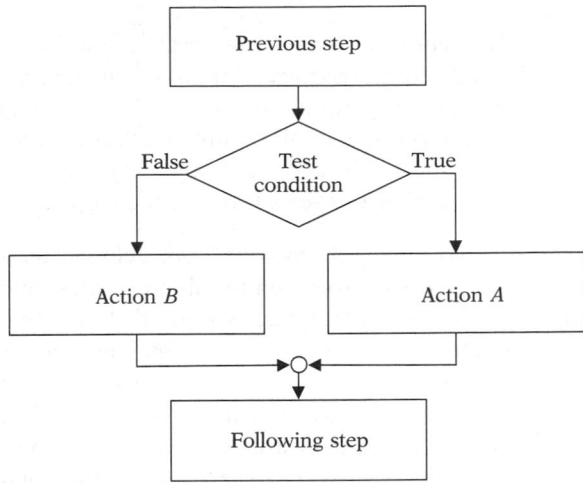

Figure 1. Flowchart for basic high-level language decision structure.

2. The test may be arbitrarily complex.

3. Either or both of the alternative actions may be arbitrarily complex, ranging from a very long sequence of program statements to no action at all.

There are minor syntactic variations among conditionals in current programming languages. C, C++ and Java, for example, omit "then", and Ada and some other languages have an `else if` construct that permits a series of alternatives to be expressed conveniently. The following compares C and Ada, and illustrates how each can specify a sequence of statements to be executed in the various alternative computations:

C:

```
if (x*y < z)
    { x = x + 7.8;
      y = 2*y;
    }
else if (x*y == z)
    z = z - 2.2;
else
    { x = x - 1.8;
      y = 0.85*y;
    }
t = x*y*z*(2.5*y + w);
```

Ada:

```
if x*y < z then
    x := x + 7.8;
    y := 2*y;
elsif x*y = z
    z := z - 2.2;
else
    x := x - 1.8;
    y := 0.85*y;
end if;
t := x*y*z*(2.5*y + w);
```

LOOPS

Procedure-oriented languages use iterative statements to specify and control repetitive operations. In general, these enable the programmer to identify the beginning and end of a *loop*, specify the number of repetitions, and define a mechanism for (automatically) keeping track of the number of cycles through the loop.

There are two principal kinds of loop: definite iteration, which repeats a specified number of times, and indefinite, which repeats as long as a specified condition is true (or until one becomes true). Definite iteration is appropriate for processing all elements of a fixed-size data structure like an array. Indefinite iteration is suited to processing all elements of a structure of unknown or varying size such as a file, or for processing parts of a fixed-size structure (e.g. searching an array for a given value).

As a simple example, we write a loop to place values $1, 2, \ldots, 14$ into a 14-element array A1, and to place the odd values $1, 3, \ldots, 27$ into array A2. The following are program fragments in Basic, Fortran, C, and Ada (recall that C arrays are indexed from 0).

Basic:

```
10  FOR I = 1 TO 14
20  LET A1(I) = I
25  LET A2(I) = 2*I - 1
30  NEXT I
```

Fortran:

```
DO 30 I = 1, 14
   A1(I) = I
   A2(I) = 2*I - 1
30 CONTINUE
```

C:

```
for (i = 0; i < 14; i++)
{
    a1[i] = i + 1;
    a2[i] = 2*i + 1;
}
```

Ada:

```
for i in 1..14 loop
   a1(i) := i;
   a2(i) := 2*i - 1;
end loop;
```

As with conditional statements the *body* of the loop—the portion executed repeatedly—may be complex, and may contain conditional statements or loops, permitting complex iterations to be programmed compactly.

Indefinite iteration is generally data-controlled. The following is a Pascal example of a loop that sums elements of a 14-element array *a*, stopping when the sum exceeds a specified value, or when the array is exhausted. We assume that the data are already in the array.

```
total := 0; i := 1;
while (total <= LIMIT) and (i <= 14) do
   begin
      total := total + a[i];
      i := i+1;
   end;
```

We note that the indefinite loop is the more general construct, since a for-loop can be implemented as a while-loop that explicitly increments the loop counter. In addition to the while-do loops shown here, languages frequently have a do-while loop (also called repeat-until) that executes the loop body before making the loop-termination test. It, too, can be implemented with a while-loop.

Subprograms

With the assignment statement, expressions, and the basic control structures, a programmer can write programs to solve complex programs. These programs will generally be long and difficult to follow. *Subprograms* help to simplify the task of writing a program and, equally important, the tasks of debugging and maintaining it. They are like small programs that can be passed inputs from a larger program, and that can provide it with results. Subprograms are either *procedures* or *functions*. They both take input arguments and produce results; a function does that by returning a value that can be used in an expression, while a procedure produces results by modifying some of its arguments, by giving values to variables through input statements, or by producing program output.

Subprograms make a program *modular* by partitioning it into units that perform distinct tasks. Each may be treated as a "black box" about which nothing is known but its input requirements and its outputs. These modules are *reusable*; subprograms may be used repeatedly in a single program, and may be used again in other programs. They are relatively small and self-contained, so that they isolate details that are not important in other parts of the program. Such modularity permits a programmer to think about a problem one piece at a time, and to define solutions that work independently of the solutions to other parts of that problem. This modularity is called *procedural abstraction*: once a computation has been made into a procedure, it can be used simply by writing the procedure name as a program statement (with the arguments that it needs). Procedural abstraction and the *data abstraction* provided by the type declarations discussed above are essential tools for large-scale programming.

In the history of programming languages, the importance of procedural abstraction was recognized first, for several reasons. Many early computer designers and programmers were mathematicians or engineers. Mathematicians were accustomed to defining functions in terms of simpler ones; engineers were accustomed to reusing well-tested solutions rather than developing each from scratch. Furthermore, programming in early machine language was arduous and error-prone, and the value of building collections of well-debugged subprograms was clear to programmers. As programming languages became more sophisticated, the problems tackled became larger, and the need for modularity and reusable components remained prominent.

Subprograms—procedures and functions—may be "built in" to a language, or they may be programmer-defined. Most languages have a square-root function, sqrt, for example. Some languages, like C and C++, have a large collection of *standard libraries* of subprograms that are specified by the language definition, including mathematical routines, input and output routines, string processing routines, and so on. Such libraries, together with other libraries that users may develop, extend the core of a programming language to make it more powerful.

In addition to subprograms in ready-to-use libraries, any program may be composed of subprograms specific to it. If a program needs to find the largest and smallest elements of arrays of reals, for example, it may have a procedure extremes that takes an array and finds these two values. In Ada, the procedure could be:

```
type vector is
  array(integer range <>) of real;
procedure extremes(
  A: in vector;
  small, big: out real) is
  begin
  small := A(1); big := A(1);
  for i in A'range loop
    if A(i) < small then small := A(i);
    if A(i) > big then big := A(i);
  end loop;
end extremes;
```

The first line of the procedure definition specifies that A represents any array of real numbers, and that small and big represent the variables in which the two results will be put. When the program *calls* the procedure, it must supply the *actual parameters* (*see* PARAMETER PASSING); for example it may call extremes (A1,s1,b1) if A1,s1,b1 are an array of reals and two real variables.

Procedural abstraction can be carried still further. Although extremes is too simple to require further abstraction, note that it is performing two similar actions to find the smallest and largest values. If there is a library function extreme that takes an array and a comparison *operation* as parameters, then extremes could be written in terms of it (in pseudo-Ada, since Ada does not allow subprograms to be parameters):

```
procedure extremes(
  A: in vector;
  small, big: out real) is
  begin
  small := extreme(A, "<");
  big := extreme(A,">");
end extremes;
```

Although passing subprograms or operators to another subprogram is a hallmark of functional languages, most procedural languages, including C, Pascal and object-oriented languages, also permit such procedure parameters, sometimes with constraints on how they may be used.

A recursive subprogram calls itself with successively simpler inputs until it reaches an elementary case whose solution is immediate. Recursive subprograms generally resemble the mathematical definition of the problem, making the step from specification to implementation smaller than in an iterative design. For example, the Euclidean algorithm for finding the greatest common divisor (gcd) of two non-negative integers, m, n says that if one integer is 0, the gcd is the other value. Otherwise, $gcd(m, n) = gcd(n, r)$, where r is the remainder when m is divided by n. The gcd function can be written in C (where % is the remainder operator) as a direct paraphrase of this statement:

```
int gcd(int m, int n)
  {
  if (n -- 0) return m;
  else return gcd(n, m % n);
  }
```

Program Development

Software is a product with negligible manufacturing but major development costs. The cost of programmer time to design and implement a program is often considerable. Equally significant are the maintenance costs to fix program errors and to modify a program to meet new requirements. The preceding sections have described how an appropriate level of expressive power in procedure-oriented languages can facilitate these tasks. Modular programming is central to reducing their complexity. In addition to organizing data and procedures into units of manageable size, modularity allows large problems to be partitioned into smaller ones on which several people may work concurrently.

Program development tools are not part of a programming language, but provide the environment in which programmers work. They fall into several categories, all of which, broadly speaking, are a part of software engineering (*q.v.*).

DESIGN TOOLS

Program design involves refining an initial statement of what a program is to do into a precise set of specifications, and from there to an outline of the program. There are specification languages (*see* PROGRAM SPECIFICATION) and modeling languages (*see* OBJECT-ORIENTED ANALYSIS AND DESIGN) to help with this task by making it more formal, or at least more systematic. Once program development is under way, version control tools help to ensure that a multiperson project will maintain consistency among its parts (*see* SOFTWARE CONFIGURATION MANAGEMENT).

COMPILATION AIDS

During the writing of a program, language-sensitive text editors can provide templates for sections of code (*see* TEXT EDITING); when a programmer writes "*if*", the editor can provide an *if-then-else* template, ready for statements to be inserted in each block. This helps to reduce minor typographical errors, such as missing punctuation. Compilers for procedure-oriented languages are sophisticated and can provide good diagnostics when a program contains syntax errors. Here are two examples from a C++ compiler:

◆ It is common to omit a symbol, such as the closing bracket in an array declaration. The declaration `int a[10;` produces the error message:

```
Error: line 3: expected a "]"
int a[10;
--------^
```

◆ If a variable is used without having been declared, either due to an omission or to a misspelling of a declared name, the compiler reports:

```
Error: line 4: identifier "b" is
  undefined
b = 1;
^
```

Not all compilers are as informative; for the first error, another C++ compiler reports only "`parse error before ';'`." All such compile-time diagnostics, however, become even more useful in a programming support environment (*q.v.*) in which, as each error message is selected, the corresponding portion of the program is highlighted in an editing window.

In many procedure-oriented languages there are also semantic errors that could be caught at compile-time but are not. A language definition may not require all such checking, perhaps to make compilation faster, though speed is rarely a problem now. For example, in Pascal one may declare a type as a subrange of another, but errors such as assigning a value outside a range may not be reported by the compiler:

```
type smallint = 1 .. 10;
var i : smallint;
...
i := 11;
```

Assigning `i` a value outside its range will usually be reported only at run time. In this case the compiler could easily detect the error, but of course, if `i` does not receive a value until run time, the compiler cannot detect the error.

RUN-TIME AIDS

Run-time errors include improper operations like division by 0, references to illegal memory addresses, or indexing outside an array range. There are also algorithmic errors, in which a program runs correctly but produces incorrect results because of design flaws. Whether the errors are *fatal*, terminating program execution, or not, diagnostic tools to show what happened include symbolic debuggers (*see* DEBUGGING) and trace (*q.v.*) packages. These tools allow a programmer to monitor program execution, to examine the values of variables whenever they change, or to stop a loop after a specified number of iterations. Good debugging tools are common now, though many programmers still debug by inserting output statements in a flawed program to observe its behavior.

There are also constructs in some procedural (and other) languages to help in error detection. Two mechanisms are *exceptions* (*q.v.*) and *assertions* (*see* LOOP INVARIANT). The former allow the programmer to specify in advance what actions should take place in the event of a run-time error, including printing an informative message. The latter let a programmer state what should be true of variable values at a certain point in a program. At run time, the assertion is tested, and if false, the program halts with an appropriate report.

Future Directions

High-level procedure-oriented languages evolved rapidly from the late 1950s to the early 1970s, and all of their basic features except for data abstraction capabilities were well established by the latter date. Since then, Ada, C++, Java, and less well-known languages like Eiffel have provided greater encapsulation (*q.v.*) and data abstraction capabilities. These are intended to make large-scale programming more readily managed, and they have had distinct successes. It is difficult to anticipate whether further gains will depend on more powerful software engineering tools for the specification, design, implementation, and testing of programs, or whether new kinds of high-level languages will also be required.

Program debugging tools work well with small program units, but less well with large programs because of the immense number of possible execution sequences. In addition to the modularity provided within programming languages, particularly in object-oriented languages, two recent approaches have been component software (*q.v.*), and automatic programming (*q.v.*). The former builds programs out of separately compiled components that satisfy a well-defined interface specification. The latter is an endeavor, still largely in research projects, to write programs that will take a programmer's specification of an algorithm and generate the program that implements it. If components can be shown to satisfy the specifications, and if the program generators can be shown to be correct, the burden of debugging large programs may be diminished, but if not, these tools may lead to programs that are still more difficult to debug. It is reasonable to suppose that the most appropriate languages and tools for large-scale programming are yet to be developed.

Bibliography

1972. Dahl, O.-J., Dijkstra, E. W., and Hoare, C. A. R. (eds.) *Structured Programming*. New York: Academic Press.
1976. Dijkstra, E. W. *A Discipline of Programming*. Upper Saddle River, NJ: Prentice Hall.
1987. Horowitz, E. (ed.) *Programming Languages: A Grand Tour*, 3rd Ed. Rockville, MD: Computer Science Press.
1996. Pratt, T. W., and Zelkowitz, M. V. *Programming Languages: Design and Implementation*. Upper Saddle River, NJ: Prentice Hall.
1999. MacLennan, B. J. *Principles of Programming Languages: Design, Evaluation, and Implementation*, 3rd Ed. New York: Oxford University Press.

David Hemmendinger

PROCEDURE

See SUBPROGRAM.

PROCESS

See JOB.

PRODUCT CODE

See UNIVERSAL PRODUCT CODE.

PRODUCTION

For articles on related subjects *see* BACKUS–NAUR FORM; CHOMSKY HIERARCHY; FORMAL LANGUAGES; GRAMMARS; PROGRAMMING LINGUISTICS; and WELL-FORMED FORMULA.

A *production* is a rule, often called a *rule of inference* or a *replacement rule*. Some expert systems (*q.v.*), called *rule-based*, represent their information as productions of the form IF ⟨condition⟩ THEN ⟨action⟩. In a grammar, a production describes how parts of a string (or word, or phrase, or construct) can be replaced by other strings. The set of productions of a grammar describes all the rules by which strings of the language can be generated by the grammar.

As an example, consider the grammar whose alphabet consists of the characters a and b and that is to generate any string consisting of any number (including zero) of bs followed by any number (including zero) of as.

A set of productions that generate this language is

$$S \rightarrow a$$
$$S \rightarrow b$$
$$S \rightarrow Sa$$
$$S \rightarrow bS$$

the first two of which read "a and b are constructs of the language" and the last two read, "If S is a construct of the language, then so is S followed by a or preceded by b." Sometimes this set of productions would be written as

$$S \rightarrow a \mid b \mid Sa \mid bS$$

where the vertical bar is to be read as "or."

Productions may be much more complex than those above. An example is the type of production found in *context-sensitive languages*,

$$S_1 SS_2 \rightarrow S_1 TS_2,$$

which states that, if the string S is found in the context (i.e. between) strings S_1 and S_2, then S may be replaced by the string T. Thus

$$abSba \rightarrow abaSaba$$

states that, if S is any string surrounded by ab and ba, it may be replaced by the same string preceded and succeeded by a.

Bibliography

1997. Sudkamp, T. A. *Languages and Machines*, 2nd Ed. Reading, MA: Addison-Wesley.

J. A. N. Lee and Anthony Ralston

PROGRAM

For articles on related subjects *see* ALGORITHM; ASSEMBLER; DOCUMENTATION; LITERATE PROGRAMMING; MACHINE AND ASSEMBLY LANGUAGE PROGRAMMING; MODULAR PROGRAMMING; OBJECT-ORIENTED PROGRAMMING; PROBLEM-ORIENTED LANGUAGES; PROCEDURE-ORIENTED LANGUAGES; PROGRAMMER; PROGRAMMING LANGUAGES; STORED PROGRAM CONCEPT; and STRUCTURED PROGRAMMING.

In order to solve a computational problem, its solution must be specified in terms of a sequence of computational steps, each of which may be effectively performed by a human agent or by a digital computer. Systematic notations for the specification of such sequences of computational steps are referred to as *programming languages*. A specification of the sequence of computational steps in a particular programming language is referred to as a *program*. The task of developing programs for the solution of computational problems is referred to as *programming*. A person engaging in the activity of programming is referred to as a *programmer*.

Programming is sometimes contrasted with *coding*. Coding generally refers to the writing and debugging of programs for given program specifications, while programming includes the task of choosing an applicable algorithm as well as that of writing the program. The text of a program is sometimes referred to as *code*, and lines of program text are referred to as lines of code, especially in the case of machine-language programs. The term *coder* is used, sometimes pejoratively, to describe a person engaged exclusively in implementing detailed program specifications prepared by others.

The programs for the earliest digital computers were written in a *machine language*. Pure machine-language programming required the programmer to write out the sequences of binary or decimal digits by which each instruction was represented in the computer memory. By the mid-1950s it was realized that programmers could specify instruction codes and memory locations by symbolic mnemonics, which could be translated into the internal machine language by a translation program called an *assembler*.

In the late 1950s and in the 1960s, *procedure-oriented languages* were developed to allow programmers to specify algorithms in a notation natural to the problem being solved. Programs specified in a procedure-oriented language were translated into the internal language of a particular computer by a translation program called a *compiler* (*q.v.*). The reader is referred to Sammet (1969) for brief descriptions of over a hundred programming languages developed in the 1950s and 1960s. (For languages of historical and current interest *see* Appendix VI: Key High-Level Languages.)

The flavor of programming in procedure-oriented languages can be experienced by following the logic in the Pascal function in Fig. 1, which finds the maximum of a list of n numbers.

A problem specification is generally given in terms of a desired relation between inputs and outputs that specifies *what* is to be computed. An algorithm or program for a given problem specifies *how* the given relation between inputs and outputs is to be achieved. It is the task of the programmer to convert "static" input–output specifications of *what* is to be computed into dynamic specifications that specify *how* the computation is to be performed.

A given input–output relation may be realized by a wide variety of different algorithms, and each algorithm may in turn be realized by a variety of different programming languages. There is thus considerable freedom in developing a program for the solution of any given problem. This freedom of choice in developing programs leads to the notion that programming is as much an art as it is a science.

There are also so-called "very high-level" languages (*see* FUNCTIONAL PROGRAMMING and LOGIC PROGRAMMING), where a program is closer to the static input–output specification. Such programs frequently use functions

```
function max(x: list; n: integer): real;              {Result is real}

{Given that main program has defined a type list as array [1..n] of real; for constant n
having a particular integer value, this function returns the largest number in the list.}

var i: integer; t: real;                              {Declare two local variables}

begin
  t:=x[1];                              {Initialize t to first number, the largest seen so far}
  for i:=2 to n do                                    {Test all remaining numbers}
    if x[i]>t then t:=x[i];                           {Update t if larger number found}
  max:=t                              {Bind the function's name to the desired result}
end {max}
```

Figure 1. A Pascal function. Comments are delineated by braces.

as inputs (data) to other function-building functions. For example, in the ML language, the max function could be simply

```
fun max(x::xs)=foldl Int.max x xs;
```

where `x::xs` is a list with first element `x` and remainder `xs`. `Int.max` is the function from the `Int` module that takes two integers and returns the larger, and `foldl` is the function-building function that applies `Int.max` successively to each list element in `xs` and the maximum from the preceding applications, starting with `x`. That is, it *encapsulates* the iteration pattern of the Pascal loop. Such encapsulation (*q.v.*), or abstraction, is vital to managing complexity in large programs.

Although the set of all programs for realizing a given problem specification is in general infinite, there are a number of criteria other than correctness that may be used to restrict the class of acceptable programs that realize a given problem specification. A good program should economize both on computation time and on the storage space required to represent the program and data structures (*q.v.*). It should have a modular structure in the sense that each well-defined subtask should be specified by a well-defined subprogram (*q.v.*). Modular design of a program is important because it makes the program easier to understand, facilitates debugging (*q.v.*), and allows modifications to be made easily. It is usually worth paying a price in computation time and memory space in order to achieve greater modularity. Modular construction is especially important in large programs, since the human mind is severely restricted in the complexity it can handle.

Programming was regarded as an art rather than a science in the 1950s and 1960s because it was felt that the choices among different styles of implementing a given problem were creative choices based on intangible criteria of style, just as in the case of literature. However, as more experience was gained in writing large programs, the freedom of the programmer to develop a personal style became increasingly restricted by programming conventions designed to mechanize programming style. For example, it has become accepted that `goto` statements should be avoided whenever possible, and that operators that preserve modularity, such as `while` statements, should be more heavily used (*see* STRUCTURED PROGRAMMING).

Another kind of modularity is achieving information hiding (*q.v.*) by constructing data abstractions (*see* ABSTRACT DATA TYPE) that package a data structure and operation on it, so that only the latter give access to the structure. Such abstraction is the basis of object-oriented programming (*q.v.*), and has become an important tool for writing large programs.

It has also been realized in recent years that maintenance of programs is more expensive than development, so reading of programs by humans is as important as writing them (*see* LITERATE PROGRAMMING). Documentation and other aids to readability are becoming increasingly important. The programs of a large system are increasingly viewed as one of several forms of system documentation and are stored in a database for manipulation by compilers (*q.v.*) and other system programming (*q.v.*) tools. Here, too, programs are data, or inputs to other programs.

Bibliography

1969. Sammet, J. *Programming Languages—History and Fundamentals.* Upper Saddle River, NJ: Prentice Hall.
1997, 1997, 1998. Knuth, D. E. *The Art of Computer Programming*, Vol. 1 (3rd Ed.), 2 (3rd Ed.), 3 (2nd Ed.). Reading, MA: Addison-Wesley.

Peter Wegner

PROGRAM CORRECTNESS

See PROGRAM VERIFICATION.

PROGRAM COUNTER

For articles on related subjects *see* INSTRUCTION SET; and MACHINE AND ASSEMBLY LANGUAGE PROGRAMMING.

Typically, a computer instruction is the specification of an operation to be performed, the address of operands on which the operation will be performed, the address for the location of the result, and a specification (an address) of the next instruction in the sequence. These specifications or addresses may be explicitly placed in the instruction or implicitly defined. By "implicit" is meant that the machine will assume that an operand will be in a certain place (e.g. the *accumulator*) rather than being specified in each instruction. In the case of the specification of the next instruction location, it is common for the machine to assume that the instructions lie in sequence. That is, the next instruction is contained in the address following the location of the current instruction. This address is kept in a register called the *program counter* (or, in some systems, the *program address register* or *instruction counter*). During the execution of an instruction, the program counter is advanced by one or more address units.

If the instruction lengths are not uniform (i.e. there are several different sizes), then the algorithm to increment the program counter must take this into account. For example, in the IBM System 360/370/390 (*q.v.*), instructions are of three different sizes: 2 bytes, 4 bytes, or 6 bytes. Since addresses always refer to bytes, the program counter must be incremented by either 2, 4 or

6, depending upon the type of instruction currently being executed.

In all systems that use program counters, there must be a mechanism for initializing its value and for changing values at certain points in the program. This latter mechanism is a special instruction, usually called a *branch* or *jump*. There are two basic kinds of branch instructions—*unconditional branch* and *conditional branch*. The unconditional branch causes a new value to be placed in the program counter and hence defines the start of the location of a new sequence of instructions. A particularly important type of unconditional branch is the subroutine call, which additionally saves the current value of the program counter for later restoration. The conditional branch has a similar action except that it is dependent upon the state of certain data items. Thus, whether the next instruction will be simply the next instruction in the current sequence or the beginning of a new sequence will depend upon the result (e.g. positive or negative) of a preceding instruction

Michael J. Flynn

PROGRAM LIBRARY

See MATHEMATICAL SOFTWARE; and SOFTWARE LIBRARIES, NUMERICAL AND STATISTICAL.

PROGRAM SPECIFICATION

For articles on related subjects *see* ABSTRACT DATA TYPE; AUTOMATIC PROGRAMMING; FORMAL METHODS FOR COMPUTER SYSTEMS; INFORMATION HIDING; PROGRAM VERIFICATION; SOFTWARE ENGINEERING; SOFTWARE PROJECT MANAGEMENT; SOFTWARE PROTOTYPING; and SOFTWARE TESTING.

The term *program specification* may refer to:

1. A statement of *requirements* for a program.

2. An expression of a *design* for a program.

3. A formal statement of conditions against which the program can be *verified*.

Properties of Specifications

Whatever the kind of specification, there are several concerns:

1. *Consistency*—Is the specification logically satisfiable?

2. *Implementability*—Is the specification practically realizable?

3. *Completeness*—Does the specification capture the *full* intent of the specifier?

4. *Nonambiguity*—Does the specification capture the *precise* intent of the specifier?

Uses of Specifications

Specifications can be used in all phases of program development. In the *requirement analysis* phase, a specification helps crystallize the customer's possibly vague ideas and reveals contradictions, ambiguities, and incompleteness in the requirements. In *program design*, a specification captures precisely the interfaces between the modules of a program. Each interface specification provides the module's client the information needed to use the module without knowledge of its implementation, and simultaneously provides the module's implementer the information needed to create the module without knowledge of its clients. In *program verification*, a specification is the statement against which a program is proved correct. Verification is the process of showing the consistency between a program and its specification. In *program validation*, a specification can be used to generate test cases for black-box testing. Together with the program, it can be used for path testing, unit testing, and integration testing. Finally, a specification serves as a kind of *program documentation*, since it is an alternative, usually more abstract, description of a program's behavior.

For a more detailed discussion of formal specifications, see Wing (1990).

EXAMPLE

Consider the specification of a data abstraction for a *bag* (in the sense of a sack that holds inserted items). This example is taken from Guttag *et al.* (1985). Using the Larch specification languages, we divide the specification into two parts. The first part, called a *trait*, specifies state-independent properties of data accessed by programs; the second part, called an *interface*, specifies state-dependent behavior (e.g. side effects (*q.v.*) and exceptional termination of program modules). In the Larch approach, there is an interface specification for each programming language. For example, a Larch/Pascal interface specification describes the behavior of a Pascal (*q.v.*) program; it would look different from a Larch/C interface specification.

Fig. 1 presents a trait that is useful for describing values of multisets and is written in the style of algebraic specifications. A multiset is an unordered collection of items that may contain duplicates. A trait defines a set of function symbols and a set of equations that define the meaning of the function symbols. The equations determine an equivalence relation on terms written using the function symbols. The `generated by` clause states that all multiset values can be represented by terms composed solely of the two function

```
MultiSet: trait
    introduces
        new: -> MSet
        insert: MSet,E -> MSet
        isEmpty: MSet -> Bool
        size: MSet -> Card
        count: MSet,E -> Card
        delete: MSet,E -> MSet
        numElements: MSet -> Card
    constrains MSet so that
        MSet generated by [new,insert]
        MSet partitioned by [count] for all [c: MSet, e, e1, e2:E]
            isEmpty(new) = true
            isEmpty(insert(c,e)) = false

            size(new) = 0
            size(insert(c,e)) = size(c) + 1

            count(new, e1) = 0
            count(insert(c,e1), e2) = count (c,e2) + (if e1 = e2 then 1 else 0)

            numElements(new) = 0
            numElements(insert(c,e)) = numElements(c) + (if count(c,e) > 0 then 0 else 1)

            delete(new, e1) = new
            delete(insert(c,e1), e2) = if e1 = e2 then c else insert (delete(c,e2),e1)
            implies converts [isEmpty,size,count,delete,numElements]
```

Figure 1. Specification of multiset values.

symbols, new and insert. This clause defines an inductive rule of inference and is useful for proving properties about all multiset values. The **partitioned by** clause adds more equivalences between terms. Intuitively, it states that two terms are equal if they cannot be distinguished by any of the functions listed in the clause. In the example, we could use this property to show that order of insertion of elements in a multiset does not matter (i.e. insertion is commutative). The **converts** clause is a way to state that this algebraic specification is sufficiently complete.

Fig. 2 gives a Larch/Pascal interface specification of a bag data abstraction. It introduces a type name, three procedures, and one function.

The body of each routine's specification places constraints on proper arguments for calls on the routine and defines the relevant aspects of the routine's behavior when it is properly called. It can be straightforwardly translated to a first-order predicate over two states by combining its three predicates into a single predicate of the form

> **requires** predicate ⇒
> (**modifies** predicate & **ensures** predicate).

An omitted **requires** is interpreted as **true**.

In the body of a Larch/Pascal specification, as in Pascal, the name of a function stands for the value returned by that function. Formal parameters may appear unqualified or qualified. An unqualified formal parameter stands for the value of that parameter when the routine is called. A formal parameter qualified by

prime ('), for example b', stands for the value of that formal parameter when the routine returns.

The values of variables on entry to and return from routines must be distinguished because Pascal is a language in which statements may alter memory. Since the function symbols in a Larch trait specification represent functions, this complication does not arise there, nor would it in an interface language for a functional programming (q.v.) language.

The **modifies** predicate is also related to the imperative nature of Pascal. The predicate **modifies at most** $[v_1, \ldots, v_n]$ asserts that the routine changes the value of no variable in the environment of the caller except possibly some subset of the variables denoted by the elements of $\{v_1, \ldots, v_n\}$. Notice that this predicate is really an assertion about all variables that do not appear in the list, not about those that do.

The **based on** clause associates the type *Bag* with the sort *MSet* that appears in trait *MultiSet*. This association means that Larch trait terms of algebraic sort *MSet* are used to represent Pascal values of type *Bag*. For example, the term "new" is used to represent the value that b is to have when *bagInit* returns. The **requires** clause of *bagAdd* states a precondition that is to be satisfied on each call. It reflects the specifier's concern with how this type can be implemented in Pascal. By putting a bound on the number of distinct elements in the *Bag*, the specification allows a fixed-size representation. It is quite natural for such considerations to surface in interface specifications, it would not be so natural for them to appear in traits.

```
type Bag exports bagInit,bagAdd,bagRemove,bagChoose
    based on sort MSet from MultiSet with [integer for E]
    procedure bagInit(var b: Bag)
          modifies at most [b]
          ensures b' = new

    procedure bagAdd (var b: Bag; e: integer)
          requires numElements(insert(b,e)) < = 100
          modifies at most [b]
          ensures b' = insert (b,e)

    procedure bagRemove (var b: Bag; e: integer)
          modifies at most [b]
          ensures b' = delete(b,e)

    function bagChoose (b: Bag; var e:integer): boolean
          modifies at most [e]
          ensures if ~isEmpty(b) then bagChoose & count(b,e') > 0
                      else ~bagChoose & modifies nothing
```

Figure 2. Interface specifications of a Larch/Pascal bag abstraction.

The most interesting routine is probably *bagChoose*. Its specification says that it must set *e* to some value in *b* (if *b* is not empty, where '~' denotes negation), but does not say which value. Moreover, it doesn't even require that different invocations of *bagChoose* with the same value produce the same result; in other words, the implementation may be *nondeterministic*. Our implementation is abstractly nondeterministic, even though it is a deterministic program (*see* Fig. 3). The value to which *e* is set depends on the order in which elements have been added to and removed from *b*, whereas this order does not affect *b*'s abstract value.

This interface specification has recorded a number of design decisions beyond those contained in the trait *MultiSet*. It says which routines must be implemented and, for each routine, it indicates both the condition that must hold at the point of call and the condition that must hold upon return. Thus, a contract that provides a *logical firewall* has been established between the implementers and the clients of type *Bag*. They can then proceed independently, relying only on the interface specification (*see* ABSTRACT DATA TYPE and INFORMATION HIDING).

The clients must establish the **requires** clause at each point of call. Having done that, they may presume the truth of the **ensures** clause on return, and that only variables in the **modifies at most** clause are changed. They need not be concerned with how this happens.

The implementers are entitled to presume the truth of the **requires** clause on entry. Given that, they must establish the **ensures** clause on return, while respecting the **modifies at most** clause.

Because the interface specification does not specify either the representation of the type or the algorithms in routines, yet another level of design is needed.

Because this level is hidden from clients of the data type, the design may be changed without affecting their correctness.

The specification of each routine in an interface can be understood without reference to the specifications of other routines—unlike traits, in which the specification constrains the operators by giving relations among them. Of course, to understand the type itself, to reason about it, or to design an efficient representation for it, the specifications of all its routines must be taken into account.

To illustrate the relation between an interface specification and an implementation, we give a Pascal implementation of type *Bag* in Fig. 3. Neither the data structure chosen for the representation nor the program itself is very interesting. Both the abstraction function and the representation invariant are presented informally. If we had included a formal specification of the type used in the representation, we could have presented them using a program annotation language. Then they could be mechanically combined with the interface specifications already given to derive a concrete specification for each routine, which could then be verified separately.

For example, to show that the implementation of *bagAdd* satisfies its specification, one assumes the precondition, which says that there cannot be more than 100 distinct elements contained in the bag if we were to insert *e*. The implementation of *bagAdd* then either finds an index *lastEmpty* at which to insert a new distinct element *e* in the *elems* array (and sets the corresponding count for *e* to 1) or finds the index *i* at which the *elems* array already stores *e* (and increments *e*'s count by 1). Notice that the implementation of *bagAdd* relies on the precondition since if we try to insert a new distinct element in a bag that already has 100 distinct elements then *lastEmpty* will be undefined

```
const MaxBagSize = 100;
type ElemVals = array [1..MaxBagSize] of integer;
   ElemCounts = array [1..MaxBagSize] of integer;
   Bag = record
              elems: ElemVals;
              counts: ElemCounts
              end;

{Abstraction function: the abstract bag is equivalent to the result of
inserting into the empty bag each integer in elems a number of times
equal to the corresponding number in counts.}

{Representation invariant: Each integer in counts is at least zero and
no integer appears in elems more than once associated with a positive
value in counts.}

procedure bagInit(var b: Bag);
   var i: 1..MaxBagSize;
   begin
      for i := 1 to MaxBagSize do b.counts[i] := 0
   end {bagInit};

procedure bagAdd(var b: Bag; e: integer);
   var i,lastEmpty: 1..MaxBagSize;
   begin
      i := 1;
      while (i < MaxBagSize) and (b.elems[i] <> e) do
         begin
            if b.counts[i] = 0 then lastEmpty := i;
            i := i + 1
         end;
      if b.elems[i] = e then b.counts[i] := b.counts[i] + 1 else
         begin
            if b.counts[i] = 0 then lastEmpty := i;
            b.elems[lastEmpty] := e;
            b.counts[lastEmpty] := 1
         end
   end {bagAdd};

procedure bagRemove (var b: Bag; e: integer);
   var i: 1..MaxBagSize;
   begin
      i := 1;
      while (not ((b.elems[i] = e) and (b.counts[i] > 0)) and (i < MaxBagSize)) do
         i := i + 1;
      if (b.elems[i] = e) and (b.counts[i] > 0) then
         b.counts [i] := b.counts [i] - 1
   end {bagRemove};

function bagChoose(b: Bag; var e: integer): boolean;
   var i: 1..MaxBagSize;
   begin
      i := 1;
      while (i < MaxBagSize) and (b.counts[i] = 0) do i := i + 1;
      if b.counts [i] = 0 then bagChoose := false else
         begin
            e := b.elems[i];
            bagChoose := true
         end
   end {bagChoose};
```

Figure 3. Pascal implementation of bag abstraction.

and an error presumably will occur in trying to access the *elems* array at an undefined index. Upon termination, *bagAdd* satisfies the postcondition of the specification, which says that the new bag value is the same as the old with the addition of the newly inserted ele-

ment. Furthermore, we can check that upon inserting an element in a bag, its final (multiset) value satisfies the desired properties as specified in the *MultiSet* trait: inserting a new distinct element into a multiset increases the number of distinct elements of the multiset by one; inserting an element already in the multiset does not; and regardless of whether the element is already in the multiset or not, the multiset's size increases by one.

Other specification languages for sequential programming are VDM (Vienna Development Method) and Z (pronounced "zed"). The latter is based on mathematical set theory and predicate logic, and has been used to specify industrial projects, particularly in Europe. There are also specification languages for concurrent programming (*q.v.*), which are less widely used, but have been applied to some safety-critical problems.

Bibliography

1985. Guttag, J. V., Horning, J. J., and Wing, J. M. "The Larch Family of Specification Languages," *IEEE Software*, **2**, *5* (September), 24–36.

1990. Wing, J. M. "A Specifier's Introduction to Formal Methods," *IEEE Computer* (September), 8–24.

1994. Morgan, C. C. *Programming from Specifications*, 2nd Ed. Upper Saddle River, NJ: Prentice Hall.

Jeannette M. Wing

PROGRAM VERIFICATION

For articles on related subjects *see* AUTOMATIC PROGRAMMING; FORMAL METHODS FOR COMPUTER SYSTEMS; LOGICS OF PROGRAMS; LOOP INVARIANT; MODEL CHECKING; PROGRAM SPECIFICATION; SOFTWARE TESTING; and STRUCTURED PROGRAMMING.

It is important to know that a computer program meets its specifications. Program errors might result in the loss of life or limb, the loss of information, or the loss of financial assets. With the massive penetration of computing technology into society, program errors can result in widespread inconvenience and risk (Neumann (1994) discusses and catalogs numerous failures of computing systems.) Various techniques can be used to determine whether a program satisfies its precise and rigorous specifications. Each technique provides varying amounts of assurance.

The most common technique is *testing* a program (*see* SOFTWARE TESTING). Sample data, presumed to be representative and to cover the necessary extreme cases, is given to the program and the results are compared against known or expected answers. The major problem is to know when to stop testing—how much more assurance of meeting specifications would be gained by additional cases. Or, as Dijkstra (1972) wrote, "Program testing can be used to show the presence of bugs, but never to show their absence!"

In contrast, but often as a supplement to testing rather than as a distinct alternative, is the technique of *program verification*. As that term is used in this article,

to *verify* a program means to demonstrate, via a mathematical proof, that the program is consistent with its specifications. It may be quite useful just to prove limited properties, such as that the program terminates (and without executing an operation whose result is undefined, such as division by 0) or that certain variables remain unchanged. The criterion of success requires a sufficiently believable proof, as do all mathematical proofs. Failure to complete the proof may be due to a problem with either the program or the specifications, as well as because of insufficient information about the problem domain or even actual inability to prove a true theorem.

Basic Technique and Example

The most common technique for verifying a program is known as the method of *assertions* (or *invariant assertions* or *inductive assertions*). The basic idea is to associate assertions with various points in the program. *Assertions* are propositions involving the variables of the program usually expressed in a system like the first-order predicate calculus (*see* DISCRETE MATHEMATICS). The intent is that each assertion be a true statement every time the execution of the program passes the point with which that assertion is associated. The proof requirement is to demonstrate that this intent is actually satisfied. Those assertions that appear at the end of a program are often called *postconditions*; assuming that the program terminates, these give the result of the program. Assertions that appear at the start of a program are called *preconditions*. Because programs do not accept arbitrary inputs, a precondition is intended to give a sufficient condition for the program to compute its result. For example, a program to compute the inverse of a matrix or the reciprocal of a number requires nonzero input and perhaps other conditions as well. The only other requirement on the association of assertions is that (the path formed by) every loop must have at least one point with an assertion. An assertion that is true for every execution of a loop is called a *loop invariant*. Such invariants can often be deduced from the program or, indeed, the loop can be constructed to preserve a previously given invariant. In either case, the loop invariant is an essential part of understanding why the program works as well as an essential ingredient of the verification.

The standard way to achieve the proof requirement is to focus on a particular assertion, say P_1, and to follow the program execution from P_1 along all possible paths, stopping on each path when another assertion, P_2, is reached (P_2 is often P_1 again if the path is a loop). One must show, for each such path, that P_1 and the effects of the statements between P_1 and P_2 imply that P_2 holds. Suppose we do this for all assertions, including the preconditions that may be assumed, and suppose that for each P_1 we can show that P_2 holds. In particular, the postconditions will be a P_2 for one or more P_1 preconditions. Thus, if the postconditions are actually reached (i.e. the program halts), they will be true. This argument by mathematical induction justifies the method and motivates some of its terminology.

As a simple example, consider the program whose aim is to count the nonnegative elements in the n-element array $A[1 \ . \ . \ n]$.

```
poscount := 0; i := 1;
while i ≤ n do
 begin
   if A[i] ≥ 0
   then poscount := poscount + 1;
   i := i + 1
 end
```

Fig. 1 is a flowchart (*q.v.*) of this program with assertions 1, 2, and 3 added. There the notation Positive (A, j, k) informally denotes the number of nonnegative elements of A in the range j to k inclusive. A formal recursive definition is

```
Positive(A,j,k) = if  j > k then 0
                  else if A(k) ≥ 0 then
                       1 + Positive(A,j,k-1)
                  else Positive(A,j,k-1)
```

For convenience, we assume n nonnegative. The postconditions 3 express the aim of the program. A very informal proof of this program might be simply that *poscount*, initially zero, is incremented for each nonnegative element encountered as A is inspected, element by element, by the **while** loop.

A more rigorous version of this informal proof uses the loop invariant 2 which appears just prior to the test to the **while** statement, thereby satisfying the requirement that each loop have at least one assertion point. There are four paths between assertions in this example: (a) 1 to 2, (b) 2 and $A[i] \geq 0$ back to 2, (c) 2 and not $A[i] \geq 0$ back to 2, and (d) 2 to 3. The four propositions to be proved follow:

(a) $n \geq 0$ **and** $poscount = 0$ **and** $i = 1 \Rightarrow$
$$1 \geq i \geq n + 1 \text{ and}$$
$$poscount = Positive(A, 1, i - 1)$$

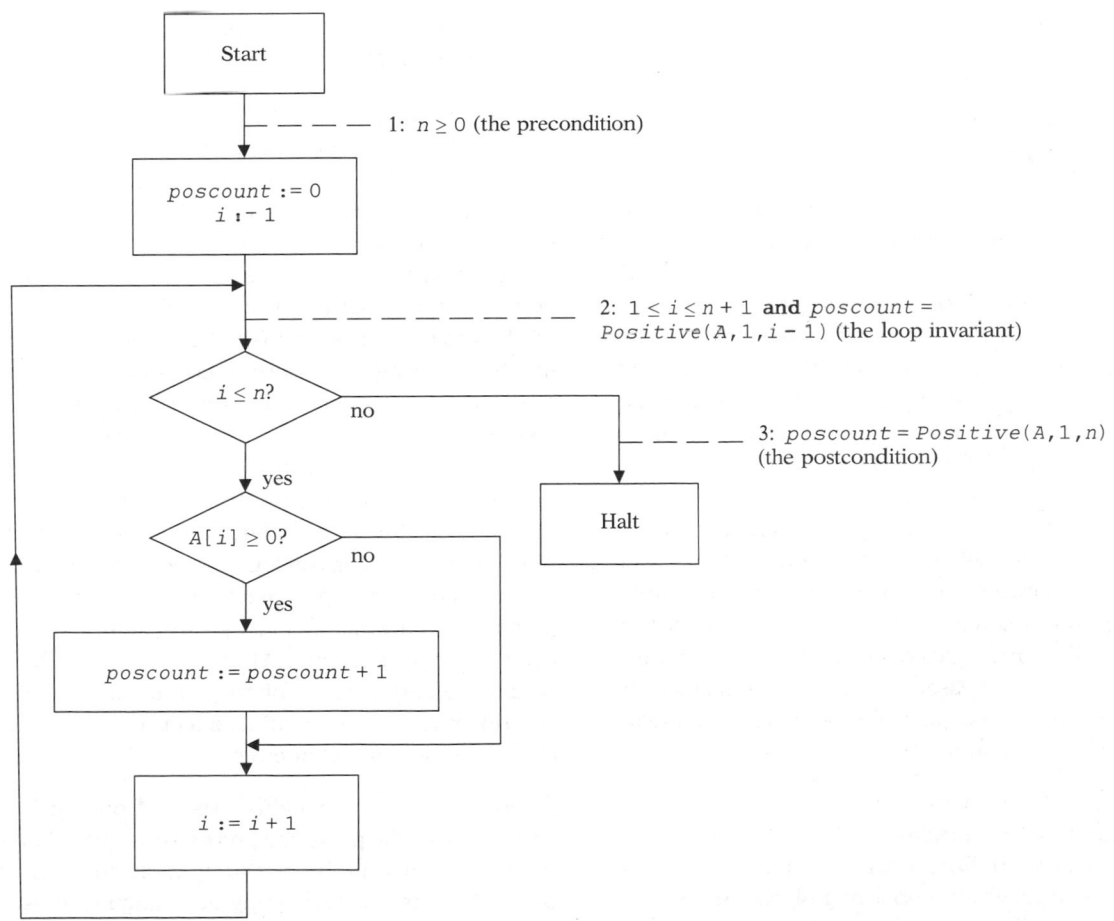

Figure 1. A flowchart, including assertions, of a program to count the nonnegative elements of array $A[1 \ . \ . \ n]$.

(b) $1 \le i \le n+1$ **and** $poscount =$
$\quad\quad$ `Positive(A,1 i -1)` **and** $i \le n$ **and**
$\quad\quad$ `A[i] >= 0` **and**
$\quad\quad\quad$ $poscount' = poscount + 1$
$\quad\quad$ **and** $i' = i + 1 \Rightarrow$
$\quad\quad$ $1 \le i' \le n+1$ **and**
$\quad\quad$ $poscount' =$ `Positive(A,1,i'-1)`

The prime (') has been introduced to denote the "new" value of a variable. The arrow denotes logical implication.

(c) As (b) except $poscount' = poscount$
$\quad\quad$ **and not** $(A[i] > 0)$.

(d) $1 \le i \le n+1$ **and** $poscount =$
$\quad\quad$ `Positive(A,1,i-1)`
$\quad\quad$ **and not** $(i \le n) \Rightarrow$
$\quad\quad$ $poscount =$ `Positive(A,1,n)`

Each of these propositions can be easily proved informally, using traditional and elementary mathematical reasoning, or formally, using the techniques of, say, the predicate calculus, which provides appropriate axioms and rules of inference for a deductive theory. Both kinds of proofs of (a), (b), and (c) use the three cases of `Positive`, respectively, plus substitution of equals for equals and simple inequality facts. For (d), it is necessary to obtain $i = n+1$ from $i \le n+1$ **and not** $(i \le n)$. With the completion of these four proofs, the example program is verified.

The main distinctions between formal and informal proofs are the required efforts to obtain each kind, the manner of presenting the proofs, and the likelihood of having a convincing proof. Informal proofs are easier to obtain (at least for the nonclerical part), are shorter, and must be read and judged by people. Formal proofs may have to be evaluated by people, but may also be constructed and/or checked by computer programs. The large number of formal details may swamp the human reader or human constructor. Thus we tend to have more faith in machine proofs than in human proofs, but we must always understand and question what axioms, lemmas, and other facts were simply assumed by the mechanical proof. Yet, going all the way back to first principles or giving too many details can easily obscure the essential elements of a proof. It should be noted that the example above is too simple to illustrate these distinctions.

Other methods for proving program correctness exist (e.g. Constable *et al.* (1986), Manna and Waldinger (1985), Gries (1981)). Furthermore, the various methods can apply to programs consisting of (recursive) subprograms, parallelism, nondeterminism, and abstract data types (*q.v.*).

Goals and Contributions of Verification

A major aim of program verification is to provide techniques for actually verifying programs in order to eliminate program errors and to know that this has been done in particular instances, thereby significantly decreasing the incidence of unreliable program behavior. The discipline of program verification also provides an important viewpoint that affects program construction, program specification, program decomposition, and language design. How would one actually verify a program being constructed? What are appropriate invariants? What are the specifications (preconditions and postconditions) of an auxiliary procedure? Only the publicly available specifications of a program component may be used in verifying uses of the component; hidden information or hidden assumptions may not be used. If the component is later modified without changing the public specifications, then only the component itself needs to be reverified, since the verifications of the uses of the component remain valid. One measure of the modifiability of a program is how much the proof changes in response to program changes. A modular program, when modified, will cause corresponding changes to the proof, but not changes otherwise. Verification concerns can also suggest appropriate decompositions of a programming task as well as appropriate abstractions to be used.

Verification concerns have also influenced the design of several programming languages; e.g. Euclid (Lampson *et al.*, 1977) and Eiffel (Meyer, 1997). In order that Euclid programs be semantically legal, it is necessary that conditions, known as *legality assertions* and made a part of the source language, be true at specific points in the program. For example, a pointer must not be the nil-pointer if it is to be dereferenced. Showing that each legality assertion holds falls to the verifier unless the compiler can show it itself. Also influenced was the procedure mechanism of Euclid, which was designed to satisfy a particular style of semantic definition. Global variables are allowed, but must be stated explicitly so that any changes are directly detectable. Another decision involving procedures was to insist that distinct formal parameters must always have distinct actual parameters in a call; i.e. no *aliases* such as the two array elements `A[i]` and `A[j]` with $i = j$, which are both names for the same variable. This restriction removes many subtle effects in procedure calls and makes it somewhat easier to specify procedures.

In addition to the benefits arising from performing proofs of specific programs, more substantial collateral benefits will accrue by providing tools and reasonably objective tests for developing and judging the success of new programming language designs, new language definition techniques, new programming strategies and methodologies, and new specification techniques. Since verification requires, for example, the definition of a programming language and the specifications of a programming task as integral parts of the verification effort, any inefficiencies, imprecisions, or inelegancies will soon surface. The concepts of verification have already had, and will continue to have, a deep impact on our thinking and understanding about programming and software technology.

Current Capabilities in Practice

While verification can be carried out by hand, one soon wishes to have computer assistance in this activity. Computer assistance increases the accuracy and credibility of the results and extends our abilities in achieving the requisite proofs. Various program verification systems have been implemented and have been applied to significant examples and applications. Capabilities exist to take annotated programs and produce the required propositions; to prove these propositions; to express mathematical concepts and prove consequences of those concepts; and to combine proofs of parts of programs or mathematical theories into proofs of programs or theories that use these parts. Additionally, these systems incorporate databases identifying the assumption basis, the progress of the development (including status of proofs), the dependencies of the parts, and reusable program components and mathematical theories.

The degree of automated support (especially with respect to automated deduction) varies from system to system. In no case can a user blindly submit a nontrivial annotated program with supporting mathematical theories and expect a quick proof with no interaction. Careful organization and decomposition of the entire programming task are required, just as these are required in programming itself. Automated deduction support varies from the level of proof checkers, which check that a presented proof satisfies the rules of a specific inference system, to highly automated provers, which might include decision procedures for various theories and heuristics (*q.v.*) for automatically generating induction hypotheses or simplifying propositions. Various verification systems are being used, though not widely, by industrial and governmental organizations. The focus of such uses is primarily that of critical systems.

Examples of successful verifications by these systems include computer science algorithms such as sorting (*q.v.*), searching (*q.v.*), pattern matching, implementations of abstract data types (*q.v.*), numerical calculations, and simple language compilers and interpreters. There is a slow but steady increase in the use of verification systems to analyze security- and safety-critical applications. Leading program verification systems include B (Abrial 1996) and EVES (Craigen *et al.*, 1993). Though a very coarse measurement, such systems have been successfully used to analyze programs with up to about 10,000 lines of code.

The survey by D. Craigen *et al.* (1993) and the compendium edited by M. G. Hinchey and J. P. Bowen (1995) discuss industrial applications of verification systems. The proceedings of the Formal Methods Europe symposia (e.g. Naftalin *et al.*, 1994) include articles describing new approaches for formally developing and reasoning about programs. The report by Clarke and Wing (1996) has an extensive bibliography of current work.

Bibliography

1972. Dijkstra, E. W. "Notes on Structured Programming," in *Structured Programming* (eds. O.-J. Dahl, E. W. Dijkstra, and C. A. R. Hoare), 1–82. New York: Academic Press.

1977. Lampson, B. W., Horning, J. J., London, R. L., Mitchell, J. G., and Popek, G. L. "Report on the Programming Language Euclid," *SIGPLAN Notices*, **12**, 2 (February).

1981. Gries, D. *The Science of Programming.* New York: Springer-Verlag.

1985. Manna, Z., and Waldinger, R. *The Logical Basis for Computer Programming.* Reading MA: Addison-Wesley.

1986. Constable, R. L. *et al. Implementing Mathematics with the NuPRL Development System.* Upper Saddle River, NJ: Prentice Hall.

1993. Craigen, D., Kromodimoeljo, S., Pase, B., Saaltink, M., and Meisels, I. "The EVES System," in *McMaster International Lecture Series on Functional Programming, Concurrency, Simulation and Automated Reasoning* (ed. P. Lauer), 349–373. New York: Springer-Verlag.

1993. Craigen, D., Gerhart, S., and Ralston, T. *International Survey of Industrial Applications of Formal Methods.* U.S. National Institute of Standards and Technology reports NIST GCR 93/626 (Volumes 1 and 2), March 1993. Also U.S. Naval Research Laboratories Formal Report 5546-93-9581/9582 (September 1993) and Atomic Energy Control Board of Canada reports INFO-0474-1 (Volume 1) and INFO-0474-2 (Volume 2), January 1995.

1994. Naftalin, M., Denvir, T., and Bertran, M. (eds.) *FME 94: Industrial Benefit of Formal Methods.* New York: Springer-Verlag.

1994. Neumann, P. G. *Computer-Related Risks.* Reading, MA: Addison-Wesley.

1995. Hinchey, M. G., and Bowen, J. P. *Applications of Formal Methods.* Upper Saddle River, NJ: Prentice Hall.

1996. Abrial, J.-R. *The B-Book: Assigning Programs to Meanings.* Cambridge: Cambridge University Press.

1996. Clarke, E. M., and Wing, J. M. (eds.) "Formal Methods: State of the Art and Future Directions," *ACM Computing Surveys*, **28**, 4 (December), 626–643.

1997. Meyer, B. *Object-Oriented Software Construction*, 2nd Ed. Upper Saddle River, NJ: Prentice Hall.

Website

Virtual Library Formal Method Page. `http://archive. comlab.ox.ac.uk/formal-methods.html`.

Ralph L. London and Daniel Craigen

PROGRAMMABLE CALCULATOR

See CALCULATORS, ELECTRONIC AND PROGRAMMABLE.

PROGRAMMER

For articles on related subjects *see* APPLICATIONS PROGRAMMING; CHIEF PROGRAMMER TEAM; DEBUGGING; DOCUMENTATION; HACKER; HUMAN FACTORS IN COMPUTING; OBJECT-ORIENTED ANALYSIS AND DESIGN; OBJECT-ORIENTED PROGRAMMING; PERSONNEL IN THE COMPUTER FIELD; PROGRAM; STRUCTURED PROGRAMMING; SYSTEMS ANALYST; SYSTEMS PROGRAMMING; and WIZARD.

The computer *programmer* is the link between a problem or process to be computerized and its successful realization on the computer. In the fullest meaning of the term, the programmer will participate in the definition and specification of the problem itself, as well as the algorithms to be used in its solution. He or she will then design the more detailed structure of the implementation, select the most suitable programming language, write and debug the necessary programs, and provide clear and complete documentation for both the user and other programmers who may need to modify the program.

The amount of this process that is done by any one individual is highly variable. A scientist who has a small problem may do all of the above tasks personally, while in a large airline reservation system, many hundreds of people may be involved in each phase of the process. However, even in this latter case, programmers should participate in the design and documentation of at least their own portions of the overall system. It is demoralizing for most programmers to be treated as *coders*, a pejorative term reserved for those in the programming profession whose work consists of almost a direct translation of detailed flowcharts (*q.v.*) into code. One of the major attractions of programming as opposed to coding as a career is its requirement for at least some creativity on a daily basis. It is a mistake for the manager of a programming group to overspecify the team's programming tasks and thereby stifle this creativity. On the other hand, the programmer must not let ego engender bad programming practices, such as the use of involved programming tricks that can only be easily understood by the programmer who used them. Good programmers write well-structured and clear programs that others can read and, if necessary, correct or modify. Documentation (*q.v.*) is therefore essential to good programming.

Both the amateur programmer (e.g. the scientist) and the professional programmer (e.g. a member of the airline reservation team) are examples of *applications programmers*. They most frequently use high-level languages (e.g. C++, Cobol, Fortran etc.) to write programs that serve particular applications. They approach the computer as a race car driver does a car—as a tool that enables a goal to be attained as efficiently as possible. As the race driver relies heavily on the mechanic, the applications programmer depends even more on the *systems programmer*, the elite member of the programming profession. The systems programmer is responsible for the compilers, assemblers, utility programs, operating systems, etc. that provide the environment for the applications programmer and is very close to the hardware. Usually, therefore, the systems programmer uses assembly language or, more frequently, the language C (*q.v.*), as this gives better access to the bits and bytes of the machine. It is hard to define what makes good systems programmers, but they are certainly a breed apart with a talent that is hard to teach. Although experience is of great importance, a good systems programmer can frequently be identified before education or experience have had a chance to have an effect. Almost any kind of background can be appropriate; once hooked, a systems programmer will find the mysteries of a full-blown operating system or windows environment (*q.v.*) a challenge for many years.

The distinction between applications and systems programmers is not clear cut. Applications programmers and system programmers frequently use the same language, and a large application such as the airline reservation system mentioned above is very much like an operating system and so would be written by many who consider themselves systems programmers.

One of the noteworthy aspects of programming is the great variation in programmer productivity, perhaps as great as a ratio of 10 : 1 from the best to the merely good. But for any programmer, applications or systems, there are some traits that are required if a programmer's full potential is to be realized. There is the need for creativity, of course, but it must be tempered with great patience and intense discipline if clever but unmanageable programs are to be avoided. Too many programs are written that may be a tribute to a programmer's ability to master complex logical structures but that have no place in a professional environment. The discipline of good programming practices is a severe one. *Egoless programming* is a technique that helps impose this discipline. Each member of a programming group will submit programs to the other members for criticism. The careful examination of another's program helps both the creator and the critic understand what makes a good, clearly written program. It is called "egoless" programming because, in order for it to be successful, all members must be able to submerge their own egos in the interest of their group. The importance of good programmers cannot be overstressed because of the great variation in programmer productivity. The application of good programming techniques can do much to decrease the 10 : 1 ratio mentioned above.

Bibliography

1976. Dijkstra, E. *A Discipline of Programming.* Upper Saddle River, NJ: Prentice Hall.

1992. Yourdon, E. *Decline and Fall of the American Programmer.* Upper Saddle River, NJ: Yourdon Press/ Prentice Hall.

1995. Brooks, F. P. *The Mythical Man Month*, Revised Ed. Reading, MA: Addison-Wesley.

1998. Weinberg, G. M. *The Psychology of Computer Programming*, Rev. Ed. New York: Dorset House.

Francis D. Federighi

PROGRAMMING LANGUAGE SEMANTICS

For articles on related subjects *see* ABSTRACT DATA TYPE; FUNCTIONAL PROGRAMMING; LAMBDA CALCULUS; LOGICS OF PROGRAMS; PETRI NET; PROCEDURE-ORIENTED LANGUAGES; PROGRAMMING LANGUAGES; PROGRAMMING LINGUISTICS; PROGRAM VERIFICATION; SYNTAX, SEMANTICS, AND PRAGMATICS; and VIENNA DEFINITION LANGUAGE.

Like English, French, and other "natural" languages, a programming language possesses both a syntax (grammatical laws that define the well-formed sentences) and a *semantics* (rules for giving meaning to well-formed sentences). Unlike natural languages, a programming language is a simple enough "artificial" language that precise definitions can be formulated for its syntax and semantics. The benefits of such precise definitions are: (1) the definitions standardize the programming language, so that implementors and users can agree on how the language behaves; (2) the definitions can be analyzed for correctness and efficiency properties; and (3) they can be used as input to automated prototyping tools like compiler generators.

Syntax is defined by a context-free grammar or a Backus–Naur form (BNF—*q.v.*) definition; here is an example BNF definition for a language of statements *S*, that contain expressions *E*, variable names *x*, statement sequences, and while-loops:

$$S ::= x := E \mid S_1; S_2 \mid \textbf{while } E \textbf{ do } S$$

where : : = is read as "is defined to be" and | is read as "or." Using this definition, one can verify that the program A:=2; while A>1 do A:=A-1 is grammatically correct. But just as important, one must state what the program *does* or *means*—this is the role of semantics.

There exist two main approaches to semantics definition: An *intensional* (*operational*) semantics describes the internal steps that a computer takes when it executes a program; an *extensional* semantics defines only program behavior that is observable to a user or external environment. The former is useful to implementors, who must build implementations that mimic the semantics, and the latter is useful to users, who must build programs whose behaviors satisfy system specifications. Indeed, a language can possess both an intensional and an extensional semantics, provided that the semantics are proved consistent with each other.

Perhaps the most popular presentation of a language's intensional semantics is an informal English description of "what the computer does" upon the language's sentence forms, but here we survey more precise formulations.

The classic intensional semantics is a *state-transition semantics*, where a program and the storage vector (representing program variables and their current values) are updated, step by step, in an *execution trace*. If *p* is a program and σ is a storage vector, we write $\sigma \vdash p$ to denote a *state* of the trace. For example, if the above program were executed then, with A set to 0 in the storage vector (denoted $A \mapsto 0$), the initial state appears as [A↦0]⊢A:=2; while A>1 do A:=A-1, and the trace proceeds as follows:

```
 [A↦0]⊢A:=2; while A>1 do A:=A-1
→[A↦2]⊢while A>1 do A:=A-1
→[A↦2]⊢A:=A-1; while A>1 do A:=A-1 (*)
→[A↦1]⊢while A>1 do A:=A-1
→[A↦1]
```

The trace shows the changes in the storage vector as the program executes; loop repetition is modeled by replicating the loop's body—see step (*). The above trace is generated from the following *state-transition rules*, which examine the first statement in a program and process it:

$$\sigma \vdash x := E; S' \to [x \mapsto v]\sigma \vdash S'$$
when the value of *E* with σ equals *v*
$$\sigma \vdash \textbf{while } E \textbf{ do } S; S' \to \sigma \vdash S'$$
when the value of *E* with σ equals *false*
$$\sigma \vdash \textbf{while } E \textbf{ do } S; S' \to \sigma \vdash S; \textbf{ while } E \textbf{ do } S; S'$$
when the value of *E* with σ equals *true*.

(Note: $[x \mapsto v]\sigma$ denotes σ with its *x* component updated to value *v*.) A modern and elegant way of presenting the state-transition rules is in *structural operational semantics* (*SOS*) style, where each statement form has its semantics stated as a logical *axiom* or *inference rule*. Here are the SOS rules for assignment and statement sequencing:

$$\sigma \vdash x := E \to [x \mapsto v]\sigma$$

$$\frac{\sigma \vdash S_1 \to \sigma'}{\sigma \vdash S_1; S_2 \to \sigma' \vdash S_2}$$

Notice that the axiom for assignment is separate from the inference rule for sequencing. The axiom and inference rule work together to generate an execution step, and the traces that result look the same as before, but properties are easier to prove with **SOS** rules.

The previous style of semantics is called *small-step*, because many small steps appear in the execution trace. There is also a "big-step" style of operational semantics (sometimes called "natural semantics"), where an entire execution trace is written as one computation step or derivation. In big-step semantics, one writes $\sigma \vdash p \Downarrow \sigma'$ to assert that state $\sigma \vdash p$ computes to final answer σ'. Here are sample big-step rules:

$$\sigma \vdash x := E \Downarrow [x \mapsto v]\sigma$$

$$\frac{\sigma \vdash S_1 \Downarrow \sigma_1 \quad \sigma_1 \vdash S_2 \Downarrow \sigma_2}{\sigma \vdash S_1 ; S_2 \Downarrow \sigma_2}$$

$$\sigma \vdash \texttt{while } E \texttt{ do } S \Downarrow \sigma$$
when the value of E with σ equals *false*

$$\frac{\sigma \vdash S \Downarrow \sigma_1 \quad \sigma_1 \vdash \texttt{while } E \texttt{ do } S \Downarrow \sigma_2}{\sigma \vdash \texttt{while } E \texttt{ do } S \Downarrow \sigma_2}$$
when the value of E with σ equals *true*

The big-step semantics of the example program is this assertion: $[A \mapsto 0] \vdash A := 2; \texttt{ while } A > 1 \texttt{ do } A := A - 1 \Downarrow [A \mapsto 1]$, which is derived by first noting $[A \mapsto 0] \vdash A := 2 \Downarrow [A \mapsto 2]$, which holds by the assignment rule, and then deriving

$$\frac{[A \mapsto 2] \vdash A := A - 1 \Downarrow [A \mapsto 1] \quad [A \mapsto 1] \vdash wh \Downarrow [A \mapsto 1]}{[A \mapsto 2] \vdash wh \Downarrow [A \mapsto 1]}$$

where *wh* stands for `while A>1 do A:=A-1`.

The primary advantage of big-step semantics is that one can reason about the entire execution trace as a single logical derivation. A disadvantage is that one cannot draw the trace of a divergent (endlessly looping) program.

In summary, operational semantics is best used to analyze executions of individual programs. It also proves useful as a standard for implementation building.

The other main approach to semantics, extensional semantics, defines properties of program behavior. There are two forms of extensional semantics that have survived the test of time—denotational and axiomatic semantics. A denotational semantics describes a program's input–output behavior: a program is a mathematical function that maps its input, the storage vector, to its output, the updated storage vector. (We call these the *input store* and *output store*, respectively.) Mathematical reasoning, especially equality laws and *function extensionality*, are used to prove properties about programs. (Function extensionality asserts that functions f and g are equal if $f(x) = g(x)$

for all legal arguments, x.) The function denoted by a statement, S, is written $\mathcal{S}[\![S]\!]$, where $\mathcal{S}$ is called the *valuation function*. Here is the valuation function for our example language:

$$\mathcal{S}[\![x := E]\!](\sigma) = [x \mapsto \mathcal{E}[\![E]\!](\sigma)]\sigma$$

$$\mathcal{S}[\![S_1; S_2]\!](\sigma) = \mathcal{S}[\![S_2]\!](\mathcal{S}[\![S_1]\!](\sigma))$$

$$\mathcal{S}[\![\texttt{while } E \texttt{ do } S]\!](\sigma) = \textit{if } \mathcal{E}[\![E]\!](\sigma)$$
$$\textit{then } \mathcal{S}[\![\texttt{while } E \texttt{ do } S]\!](\mathcal{S}[\![S]\!](\sigma)) \textit{ else } \sigma.$$

If σ is the input store, then $\mathcal{S}[\![S]\!](\sigma)$ is the value of the output store produced by S—internal computation steps are "hidden" inside the function. (Note: $\mathcal{E}[\![E]\!](\sigma)$ is the value of E with σ.)

With the input store, $[A \mapsto 0]$, we can calculate $\mathcal{S}[\![\texttt{A:=2; while A>1 do A:=A-1}]\!]([A \mapsto 0]) = [A \mapsto 1]$, because the valuation function tells us these equalities hold:

$$\mathcal{S}[\![\texttt{A:=2}]\!]([A \mapsto 0]) = [A \mapsto 2]$$

$$\mathcal{S}[\![\texttt{while A>1 do A:=A-1}]\!]([A \mapsto 2])$$
$$= \mathcal{S}[\![\texttt{while A>1 do A:=A-1}]\!](\mathcal{S}[\![\texttt{A:=A-1}]\!]([A \mapsto 2]))$$

$$\mathcal{S}[\![\texttt{A:=A-1}]\!]([A \mapsto 2]) = [A \mapsto 1]$$

$$\mathcal{S}[\![\texttt{while A>1 do A:=A-1}]\!]([A \mapsto 1]) = [A \mapsto 1]$$

Indeed, one can use function extensionality to prove a stronger result: $\mathcal{S}[\![\texttt{A:=2; while A>1 do A:=A-1}]\!] = \mathcal{S}[\![\texttt{A:=1}]\!]$; the two functions/programs are equal.

The valuation function for the `while` loop is problematic, because its definition is circular (recursive). The resolution, called *least fixed point semantics*, defines the recursion to mean $w_\infty = \cup_{i \geq 0} w_i$, where $\perp$ (read "bottom") denotes a program with no output:

$$w_0(\sigma) = \perp$$

$$w_{i+1}(\sigma) = \textit{if } \mathcal{E}[\![E]\!](\sigma) \textit{ then } w_i(\mathcal{S}[\![S]\!](\sigma)) \textit{ else } \sigma$$

The rationale goes as follows: to produce an output store, `while` E do S must terminate after finitely many iterations. Let w_i denote a loop that can iterate at most i times—if it must iterate more, the loop becomes exhausted and has no output. Define $\mathcal{S}[\![\texttt{while } E \texttt{ do } S]\!]$ as the union (more precisely, the *limit*), w_∞, of the w_i functions. We have this mathematical equality:

$$w_\infty(\sigma) = \textit{if } \mathcal{E}[\![E]\!](\sigma) \textit{ then } w_\infty(\mathcal{S}[\![S]\!](\sigma)) \textit{ else } \sigma$$

Hence w_∞ is a *fixed point* of the recursion; indeed, it is the *least* fixed point (*see* Schmidt, 1986).

The above reasoning comes from *domain theory*, a branch of discrete mathematics developed specifically for recursions in mathematical definitions. A notation called the *lambda calculus* is used to define valuation functions.

Because of its strong ties to mathematics, denotational semantics is best used for proofs of input–output correctness and program equivalence. It is also useful for comparing definitions of related languages and proving correctness of translations.

An *axiomatic semantics* abstracts program properties away from input–output behavior and into logical behavior: a standard example is *Hoare logic*, where program properties are formulas in propositional logic. For example, if program p computes the factorial of a nonnegative variable x and places the result in variable y, we might assert this as $\{x \geq 0\}p\{y = x!\}$. (Read $\{\phi\}p\{\psi\}$ as asserting that, if ϕ holds true prior to the execution of p, then ψ holds true when and if p terminates.)

An axiomatic semantics is defined by axioms and inference rules:

1. $\{[E/x]\phi\}\ x := E\ \{\phi\}$

2. $\dfrac{\{\phi_1\}S_1\{\phi_2\}\quad \{\phi_2\}S_2\{\phi_3\}}{\{\phi_1\}S_1 ; S_2\{\phi_3\}}$

3. $\dfrac{\{\phi \wedge E\}S\{\phi\}}{\{\phi\}\ \texttt{while}\ E\ \texttt{do}\ S\{\phi \wedge \neg E\}}$

(Read $[E/x]\phi$ as the substitution of E for all occurrences of x in ϕ.) Rule 3 is special: It states that if ϕ is preserved by a loop's body, then no matter how long the loop iterates, ϕ holds upon termination. ϕ is called a *loop invariant* (*q.v.*); loop invariants are the programming equivalent of induction hypotheses in mathematical induction proofs (*see* DISCRETE MATHEMATICS).

Let's prove that our example program always computes a positive value for variable A, that is, $\{true\}$ `A:=2; while A>1 do A:=A-1`$\{A>0\}$. We construct two subproofs: first, axiom 1 proves $\{[2/A]\ A=2\}$ `A:=2`$\{A=2\}$; that is, $\{2=2\}$`A:=2`$\{A=2\}$. Second, we note that A>0 is an appropriate loop invariant, so we attempt to prove $\{A>0\}$ `while A>1 do A:=A-1` $\{A>0 \wedge \neg(A>1)\}$ using Rule 3, and this requires the subproof $\{A>0 \wedge A>1\}$ `A:=A-1`$\{A>0\}$, which follows from Rule 1. Since A=2 implies A>0, Rule 2 assembles the two subproofs into one. (Note how elementary propositional logic laws are used throughout this proof.)

Varieties of axiomatic semantics are used to prove that programs satisfy specifications, to define type checkers, and to define static analysis algorithms for liveness and safety properties.

Historical Background

Operational semantics has a long history; the first comprehensive formalism was the Vienna Definition Language (VDL) of Lucas and Walk, which used state-transition rules to compute operations upon trees. Modern intensional semantics are primarily due to Plotkin (SOS) and Kahn (natural semantics); *see* Hennessy (1991) and Nielson and Nielson (1992) for good introductions. Denotational semantics was invented by Scott and Strachey; Stoy (1977) presents some history, and Schmidt (1986) gives standard applications. Domain theory is developed in depth by Gunter (1992). Axiomatic semantics evolved from the work of Dijkstra (1976), Hoare (1989), and others. Of the many textbooks on axiomatic semantics, one might start with Dromey (1989) and Gries (1981).

Recent Developments

In object-oriented programming (*q.v.*), objects can be parameters ("messages") to other objects' procedures ("methods"), and data-type casting laws based on *inheritance* allow controlled mismatches between actual and formal parameters. Carelessly defined castings cause unsound programs, so denotational and natural semantics have been used to formalize safe castings. Gunter and Mitchell (1994) survey a variety of approaches to inheritance, and the *object calculus* of Abadi and Cardelli (1996) gives a complete semantic model for object-oriented programming.

In concurrent programming (*q.v.*), multiple processes execute in parallel and synchronize through communication. Structural operational semantics has been adapted to this paradigm; a *Calculus for Communicating Systems* (*CCS*), developed by Milner (1989), is one such variant, and a related approach, *process algebra*, is described by Baeten and Weijland (1990). These two approaches are *interleaving semantics*, because they decode execution of multiple processes into a nondeterminism where only one process can execute an atomic step at any time instant. In contrast, *Petri nets* (*q.v.*) model truly parallel systems as graph structures, but proofs are more difficult with Petri nets than with interleaving semantics.

Finally, a longstanding research topic is the relationship between different semantic definitions of the same language—in what sense might a language's denotational and axiomatic semantics agree? In mathematical logic, one uses *soundness* and *completeness* to relate a logic's proof system to its interpretation, and in semantics there are similar notions of *soundness* and *adequacy* that relate one semantics to another. There is a stronger form of adequacy, called *full abstraction* (Gunter, 1992), which has proved difficult to achieve for realistic languages, although recent progress has been made.

Bibliography

1976. Dijkstra, E. *A Discipline of Programming.* Upper Saddle River, NJ: Prentice Hall.

1977. Stoy, J. *Denotational Semantics.* Cambridge, MA: MIT Press.

1981. Gries, D. *The Science of Programming.* New York: Springer-Verlag.

1986. Schmidt, D. *Denotational Semantics: A Methodology for Language Development.* Boston, MA: Allyn and Bacon.

1989. Dromey, G. *Program Derivation.* New York: Addison-Wesley.

1989. Hoare, C. "An Axiomatic Basis for Computer Programming," in *Essays in Computing Science* (eds. C. Hoare and C. Jones). Upper Saddle River, NJ: Prentice Hall.

1989. Milner, R. *Communication and Concurrency.* Upper Saddle River, NJ: Prentice Hall.

1990. Baeten, J., and Weijland, W. *Process Algebra.* Cambridge: Cambridge University Press.

1991. Hennesey, M. *The Semantics of Programming Languages: An Elementary Introduction Using Structured Operational Semantics.* New York: John Wiley.

1992. Gunter, C. *Semantics of Programming Languages.* Cambridge, MA: MIT Press.

1992. Nielson, H. R., and Nielson, F. *Semantics with Applications, a Formal Introduction.* New York: John Wiley.

1994. Gunter, C., and Mitchell, J. (eds.) *Theoretical Aspects of Object-Oriented Programming.* Cambridge, MA: MIT Press.

1996. Abadi, M., and Cardelli, L. *A Theory of Objects.* New York: Springer-Verlag.

David A. Schmidt

PROGRAMMING LANGUAGE STANDARDS

For articles on related subjects *see* COMPUTER GRAPHICS: STANDARDS; PROCEDURE-ORIENTED LANGUAGES; PROGRAMMING LANGUAGES; SOFTWARE PORTABILITY; STANDARDS; and VIENNA DEFINITION LANGUAGE.

One of the earliest formal standardization activities undertaken in the field of information technology was for programming languages. This reflects the importance to users of programming languages and the benefits of language standards. There are two primary benefits of standardization (over and above the benefits of the languages themselves). These benefits relate first to the people who use the language and second to the programs written in the language. First, common education can be provided for programmers who will use a standard language, and these programmers are able to write programs for multiple computing environments that support the language. Second, the standards permit the construction of programs that are portable across these multiple environments. In neither case is the portability likely to be perfect, since language standards typically have some specifications that are environment dependent, and language compilers usually contain additional capabilities or extensions beyond those specified in the standard.

While both of these benefits are important, the early impetus came as much from people portability as from program portability. In recent years, the interest in application portability has grown, resulting in greater emphasis on reducing environment dependencies in language standards in order to decrease the amount of conversion required to move a program from one environment to another. As the standard for a language is revised, it is normally expanded in function, reducing (but not eliminating) the need for implementers to provide language extensions in their products.

There was an early belief that there would be one standard language for each major application area, e.g. Cobol (*q.v.*) for business applications or Fortran (*q.v.*) for scientific applications. This belief was dispelled by several forces tugging in different directions. First, there has been a proliferation of languages designed with specific goals in mind, with many of them gathering an enthusiastic following. As each became more popular, its proponents desired to use it to program a wider variety of applications. Second, advocates of some languages have desired the prestige and increased implementations stemming from an official standard. Third, the borderline between differing types of applications has become increasingly blurred. The result has been a growing number of language standards, with each having greater functional capability over time.

Programming language standardization under the auspices of official standardization organizations began in the early 1960s. Standardization of Algol (*q.v.*) was initially undertaken internationally, while standardization of Fortran and Cobol began in the USA. Many others have followed (see Table 1).

The development of an initial standard tends to be long and difficult. This is true even when the standards committee starts with a very good base document, and there are several reasons for this. First, the rigor of the standard tends to be greater than the way base documents are normally written. Second, it is important to make absolutely clear what conformance to the standard means, both for implementations of the language and for programs written in the language; this requires a rigorous definition of all aspects of the language. Third, the language committee is usually composed of members with a variety of perspectives, depending on the applications and system environments to which they are accustomed, and these differences must be reconciled or compromised. Fourth, the committee may also differ as to the scope of what functionality should even be included in the standard. Fifth, they often differ as to what constitutes an improvement from the base document. Sixth, if there is experience from numerous implementations, the differences must be resolved, and, if there are few or no

Table 1. Language standards.

Language	ANSI ID	ANSI Dates	ISO/IEC ID	ISO/IEC Dates
Ada	MIL/STD-1815A (withdrawn)	1983	8652	1987
Ada	ISO/IEC 8652	1995	8652	1995
Ada (Generic Package of Elementary Functions)			11430	1994[1]
Ada (Generic Package of Primitive Functions)			11729	1994[1]
Ada (SQL Ada Module Description Language)			12227	1995[1]
Ada (Packages of Real & Complex Type Declarations and Basic Operations)			13813	1998
Ada (Generic Package of Complex Elementary Functions)			13814	1998
Ada (Semantic Interface Specification—ASIS)			15291	1999
Ada Conformity Assessment			18009	1999E
Algol 60			1538	1985 (withdrawn)
APL			8485	1989
APL, Extended			13751	2000E
APT[2]	X3.37	1974, 1977, 1980, 1987, 1995	3592	1978
			4342	1985
	NCITS 37	1999E	4343	1978, 1999E
Atlas	IEEE 416	1976[3], 1978, 1981, 1984		
C/Atlas	IEEE 716	1982, 1985, 1989, 1995		
Basic (Full)	X3.113	1987	10279	1991
Basic (Minimal)	X3.60	1978 (withdrawn)	6373	1979, 1984 (withdrawn)
BNF (Extended)			14977	1996
C	X3.159 (withdrawn)	1989	9899	1990, 1999E
	ISO/IEC 9899	1990, 1999E		
C (Integrity Amendment)	ISO/IEC 9899/AM1	1995	9899/AM1	1995
C++		1998	14882	1998
CHILL			9496[4]	1989, 1995, 1998
Cobol	X3.23	1968, 1974, 1985, 2001E	1989	1972, 1978, 1985, 2001E
Cobol (Intrinsic Function Module)	X3.23a	1989	1989/AM1	1991
Cobol (Corrections Amendment)	X3.23b	1993	1989/AM2	1994
DIBOL	X3.165	1988, 1992		
Forth	X3.215	1994	15145	1997
Fortran (Basic)	X3.10	1966 (withdrawn)	1539	1972
Fortran	X3.9	1966, 1978 (withdrawn)	1539	1980
Fortran[5]	X3.198	1992	1539-1	1991, 1997
	ISO/IEC 1539-1	1997		
Fortran (Variable Length Character String Module)			1539-2	1994
Fortran (Conditional Compilation)			1539-3	1999
Lisp (Common)	X3.226	1994		
Lisp (ISLISP)			13816	1997
Modula-2 (Base)			10514-1	1996
Modula-2 (Generics)			10514-2	1998
Modula-2 (Object-Oriented)			10514-3	1998
M [formerly MUMPS]	X11.1	1977, 1984, 1990, 1995	11756	1992, 1999
MUMPS (Open MUMPS Interconnect)	X11.2	1995	15851	1999
MUMPS (GKS Binding)	X11.3	1994		
MUMPS (X Window System Binding)	X11.4	1995		
M Windowing API			15852	1999
PANCM	X3.94	1985		
Pascal	IEEE770X3.97 (withdrawn)	1983	7185	1983
Pascal	ISO/IEC 7185	1990	7185	1990
Pascal (Extended)	IEEE770X3.160	1990	10206	1991

Continued

Table 1. *Continued.*

Language	ANSI ID	ANSI Dates	ISO/IEC ID	ISO/IEC Dates
Pilot	IEEE 1154	1991		
PL/B	X3.238	1994, 2001E		
PL/I	X3.53	1976	6160	1979
PL/I General Purpose Subset	X3.74	1981, 1987	6522	1985, 1992
Prolog (General Core)			13211-1	1995
Prolog (Modules)			13211-2	2000E
REXX	X3.274	1996		
Scheme	IEEE 1178	1991		
Smalltalk	NCITS 319	1998		
VDM-SL (Base)			13817-1	1996
VDM-SL (Modules)			13817-2	2001E
Z Notation			13568	2000E

[1] Will be withdrawn at the conclusion of the five-year review period.

[2] ISO 4342 covers the syntax and semantics of the APT language, ISO 3592 the structure of the resulting C1 file, and ISO 4343 the post processor language, all of which are included in ANSI X3.37-1995 and its revision, NCITS 37.

[3] The 1976 Atlas version was an IEEE standard but not an ANSI standard.

[4] Developed by ITU-T (formerly known as CCITT).

[5] X3.198 was called Fortran 90 in ANSI to distinguish it from X3.9, Fortran (78) which was retained until its withdrawal in 1997. ISO/IEC 1539-1:1997 is informally known as Fortran 95.

Notes:

1. Every standard in both ANSI and ISO/IEC is reviewed every five years to determine whether it should be affirmed, revised, or withdrawn.

2. Multiple dates indicate that the standard was revised in the subsequent year(s); revisions always supersede and make obsolete the previous edition.

3. An E next to a date indicates that it is a reasonable estimate of the future publication date of that standard.

4. For international standards, the older standards are ISO standards whereas most recent ones are combined ISO/IEC standards developed by ISO/IEC Joint Technical Committee 1 on Information Technology that was formed in 1987.

5. An ISO/IEC designation in the ANSI column means that ANSI has adopted the international standard rather than a separate ANSI standard. In several cases, the original ANSI standard was withdrawn in favor of the ISO/IEC standard.

6. A blank in either the ANSI or ISO/IEC columns means that no corresponding standard is being adopted in that arena.

implementations, there is generally large disagreement on what the standard should contain because of lack of experience.

Assuming there is agreement that a given functional capability should be part of a language standard, some believe it is helpful to have that functional capability "proven" by having been implemented and used prior to standardization. The experience of prior use can indicate those aspects that are well designed and those that should be improved, as well as indicating the general usefulness of the capability itself. On the other hand, if the standard "improves" the functional capability with desirable changes, it may cause program incompatibility problems for current users. If several vendors have implemented the functional capability differently, the experiences of these users may be helpful in discovering pitfalls, but may also cause difficulty in reaching agreement on a standard that does not place one or more group(s) of users at a significant disadvantage by making their current programs incompatible with the new standard. When actually updating an existing official standard, the problem of "improvement" versus "retaining compatibility" is one of the most difficult problems.

One issue that must be decided on early in the development of the standard is the method of documentation (*q.v.*) used. The basic question is whether to use natural language or a formal description technique for the language syntax and semantics. By now, all the syntactic definitions are formal. However, the decision on how formal the semantic definition should be may cause difficulty, since there may be disagreement as to who is the primary audience for the standard. An implementer may prefer a formal technique, since it reduces possible ambiguities. However, a formal definition of a programming language standard may be virtually unreadable to a user who may much prefer that the standard be written in a natural language such as English. This issue has been decided differently by different committees and, as a result, programming language standards vary considerably as to the documentation technique used. For example, the standards for Fortran and Cobol, while complex, are relatively easy to read and understand by a competent programmer. In contrast, the standard for PL/I is a fairly formal definition of the language and more difficult for even a professional to comprehend. One good result of the rigid PL/I definition, however, is that the PL/I committee has received only one request for interpretation or clarification since publication of the PL/I standard, whereas other language committees have typically received dozens.

In the USA most programming language standardization takes place in NCITS (National Committee for Information Technology Standardization), formerly known as X3. As of 1997, NCITS has active standards development committees for APT, C (*q.v.*), C++ (*q.v.*), Cobol, Forth, Fortran, Lisp (Common), Pascal (*q.v.*), PL/B, Prolog, REXX, Smalltalk, VDM-SL, and Z Notation. NCITS also has a committee on Java which is participating in the international group studying this subject in JTC1/SC22 (see below). Other US language standardization efforts are for Modula-2 in the IEEE Microprocessor Standards Committee, M[UMPS] in the M[UMPS] Development Committee (MDC), and Ada (*q.v.*) in the Department of Defense (DoD). The development and approval procedures differ significantly among NCITS (an Accredited Standards Committee), IEEE (an Accredited Standards Organization), and MDC or DoD (Organizations Accredited for Canvass), but all meet the basic requirements of the American National Standards Institute (ANSI) for due process and public review before adoption. For example, the canvass process requires a proposed standard to be circulated and reviewed by a canvass group that is representative of all affected industry interests, whereas standards developed by an Accredited Standards Committee (ASC) can be approved directly by the ASC, since the ASC is itself an open, balanced committee with representation from producer, consumer, and general interest segments of the industry.

In the 1960s and 1970s, programming language standards development tended to be concentrated in the USA. More recently, the development of many information technology related standards has shifted to international working groups and subcommittees. However, Subcommittee 22 (SC 22) of ISO/IEC Joint Technical Committee 1 (JTC 1), which is responsible for international standardization of languages for information technology, has in several cases undertaken standards development in ways that take advantage of the significant expertise in committees in the USA or other countries. In some cases, SC 22 has used "national body" development. In this mode, SC 22 assigns the development of the technical specifications for a standard to a national body (normally in the USA), with the request that working drafts be circulated for comment at appropriate times to members of the SC 22 working group from other countries and, when a stable draft document has been agreed upon, to send it to SC 22 to begin the usual international balloting process for adoption. International standards for Cobol, Fortran, and C have all been developed in this manner. In other cases, the SC 22 working group

retains development responsibility but works closely with the US committee, or in some instances the UK committee, perhaps even scheduling joint meetings of the international working group and the national committee. In the case of C++, joint meetings have been the normal mode of development.

As of 1999, JTC 1/SC 22 had working groups for the following programming languages: Ada, APL, C, C++, Cobol, Fortran, Lisp (ISLISP), Modula-2, and Prolog. SC 22 also has a study group on Java investigating alternatives for Java-related standardization. In the area of formal specification languages, SC 22 has a working group with responsibility for VDM/SL (Vienna Development Method/Specification Language), Z Notation, and Extended BNF (Backus–Naur Form). Also included within SC 22 are working groups for POSIX (Portable Operating System Interface for Computer Environments), PCTE (Portable Common Tool Environment), and Internationalization.

The topic of internationalization, also referred to as cultural adaptability, is representative of an important direction under way in information technology standardization. Historically, standards for computers in general, and for programming languages in particular, were written in English and were bound by interfaces provided to users in English-speaking cultures. It is now recognized that this is no longer sufficient. Significant efforts have been undertaken to address character-handling issues in order to allow use of natural languages with large character sets, and to consider other cross-cultural differences that cause difficulty for users, e.g. formatting of dates, representation of currency, meaning of icons, significance of colors, and use of "taboo" words. SC 22 is considering these issues in the development of future programming language standards and in revisions to current standards.

Programming language standards, no matter how comprehensive, cannot encompass all of the capability that modern users might wish. Many other standards have been adopted or are under development that must work in conjunction with programming language standards. Examples are standards for databases (e.g. SQL), graphics (e.g. GKS, PHIGS), and operating system interfaces (e.g. POSIX). The interface between these functional standards and programming language standards is called a *binding*. Standards for bindings are in place or under development for all of the examples just cited. In general, these bindings have been developed by the functional standards committee (e.g. graphics) rather than the programming language committee, since the bindings are usually expressed without adding new syntax to the programming language, e.g. by specifying parameters in a CALL interface. Where new syntax is desirable, the programming language committee undertakes the assignment, as was the case with the GKS binding to Basic (*q.v.*).

Programming language standardization continues to grow in importance as more languages are developed to meet user application needs, and existing languages are adapted to new user and application environments. Table 1 lists the programming language standards that have been approved (or are under way) as of mid-1999.

Robert H. Follett and Jean E. Sammet

PROGRAMMING LANGUAGES

For articles on related subjects *see* ADA; ALGOL; ALGOL 68; ASSEMBLER; BASIC; C; C++; COBOL; COMPILER; FORTH; FORTRAN; FUNCTIONAL PROGRAMMING; JAVA; LANGUAGE PROCESSORS; LISP; LIST PROCESSING: LANGUAGES; LOGIC PROGRAMMING: LANGUAGES; LOGO; MACHINE AND ASSEMBLY LANGUAGE PROGRAMMING; NONPROCEDURAL LANGUAGES; OBJECT-ORIENTED PROGRAMMING; PARALLEL PROCESSING: LANGUAGES; PASCAL; PROBLEM-ORIENTED LANGUAGES; PROCEDURE-ORIENTED LANGUAGES; PROGRAMMING LINGUISTICS; SETL; SIMULA; and STRING PROCESSING.

See also APPENDIX VI: KEY HIGH-LEVEL LANGUAGES.

The definition of the term *programming language* can vary with the context: these languages are both tools for directing the operation of a computer and tools for organizing and expressing solutions to problems. In order to lead up to the one proposed by this writer, we must consider various levels of languages used for dealing with the computer.

At the lowest level is pure binary code. This is so impractical to use that humans almost never use it, even though it is actually the only language that the machine "understands" and that does not need further translation. A step above this is what is generally referred to as *machine code* or *symbolic machine code*. In this case the user generally writes instructions using some type of alphabetic symbols (e.g. SUB for subtract, TRA for transfer control, etc.). Machine addresses are written in normal decimal form (e.g. 1723). At the next higher level is *symbolic assembly language* in which the names of variables are written in symbols (e.g. ALPHA, TEMP, X, Y, Z) so that the location can be referred to symbolically rather than numerically. Thus a user might write

```
CLA Z      (CLA = clear accumulator and add)
ADD ALPHA
STO TEMP   (STO = store)
```

meaning: "Add the values of variables stored in locations named Z and ALPHA and store the result in a location named TEMP." A program called an *assembler*

(*q.v.*) assigns absolute storage locations to the variables and fills in the numeric values for machine addresses in the instructions. The term *assembly language* is sometimes used for what was called above (symbolic) "machine code," and is sometimes used for what was called "symbolic assembly language."

The next level of complexity involves a *macroassembler* in which the user may define new "instructions" as sequences of assembly language statements and use them in a program, with their definitions being given elsewhere in the program; for example, INCR ALPHA might represent the use of a macro (*q.v.*) INCRement which adds 1 to its argument.

The previous levels bring us to what is frequently called *high-level language*, a term used here interchangeably with the term "programming language" (some would include assembly language in the scope of this term). The levels described so far require not only that a programmer use instructions that are close to machine code, but that the burden of storage management rests with the programmer. At the machine code level, the programmer must specify the physical address of each data item. At the symbolic assembly language level, the programmer can use names for data, but must still assign these names to storage locations. High level-languages provide more convenient instructions; they also take over most storage-management tasks. Both of these attributes abstract away machine-level details to permit fuller attention to the problem to be solved.

Definition of Programming Language[1]

A *programming language* is a set of characters, rules for combining them, and rules specifying their effects when executed by a computer, which have the following four characteristics:

1. It requires no knowledge of machine code on the part of the user. In other words, the user need only learn the particular programming language, and can use this quite independently of (perhaps nonexistent) knowledge of any particular machine code. This does not mean that the user can completely ignore the actual computer. For example, the user may need to know how floating-point numbers are represented, or may wish to take advantage of certain known machine resources which provide more efficient programs. In particular, the user obviously cannot use input–output equipment that does not exist on a particular computer configuration. However, the fundamental point is that a

---

[1] This section and the next three include material from Sammet (1969).

knowledge of the basic machine code for the given computer is not needed.

2. A programming language must have some significant amount of machine independence. This means that there must be some high potential of having a source program (a program written in a high-level language) run on two computers with different machine codes without major rewriting of the source program. (Although complete machine independence is an ideal that is often approximated rather than achieved, it is now increasingly common to move programs from one computer to another with little or no change.)

3. When a source program is translated into machine language, there is normally more than one machine instruction per executable unit created. For example, an executable unit in a programming language might be something of the form "A := B + C * D" or "OPEN FILE ALPHA." Normally, each of these executable units would be translated into more than one machine instruction.

4. A programming language employs a notation that is closer to that of the specific problem being solved than is machine code. Thus, for example, the example "A := B + C * D" might be translated into a sequence of machine instructions such as

```
CLA C
MPY D
ADD B
STO A
```

which is clearly less understandable than the programming language form.

Note that this definition of programming languages deliberately excludes menu-driven systems; they are extremely useful but they are *not* programming languages.

Benefits of Programming Languages

A major benefit provided by a programming language is that it is easier to learn than a lower-level machine or assembly language. Of course, an extremely powerful programming language might be harder to learn in its entirety than an assembly language on a computer which has only a dozen instructions. Given programming and assembly languages of approximately the same complexity in their relative classes, however, the programming language will be easier to learn. This actually has two facets. The programming language may itself be complex, but its ease of learning often comes because the notation is more closely related to the problem usage than is the machine code; furthermore, more attention can be paid to the language itself

rather than to the idiosyncrasies of the physical hardware, which is necessary when one deals in machine code.

A problem written in a programming language is generally easier to debug for two major reasons. First, the program is usually shorter than its assembly language equivalent because of the expansion factor indicated as the third characteristic of a programming language. Since the number of errors tends to be roughly proportional to the length of the program, there will normally be fewer errors. A second reason for the program being easier to debug is that the notation itself is more natural, and therefore more attention can be paid to the logic of the program with less attention paid to syntactic details.

Third, a program coded in a programming language is generally easier to understand and to transfer to someone other than the originator because of the notational advantages and relative conciseness already mentioned.

Fourth, the notation of a programming language automatically provides a part of the necessary documentation because the notation is easier to understand and the logic is easier to follow.

Fifth, a programming language that permits user-defined abstractions as well as those built into the language can be a powerful tool for organizing information in large programs. Such abstractions let a programmer represent data and operations on them at a level that fits the problem being solved, and to hide low-level details where appropriate. Virtually all programming languages today provide abstraction capabilities, though to varying degrees.

Finally, the above advantages tend to accumulate into two general advantages, which are that the total calendar time and the total cost required for the problem solution are generally reduced significantly.

Limitations of Programming Languages

Forty years ago, when programming languages were relatively novel, they were sometimes thought to have several disadvantages. Large programs could require a long time to compile, thus slowing the development of the program, possibly by more than was gained from easier debugging. Compilers might produce inefficient object code. Finally, there was concern that debugging could be even more difficult with a high-level language. (If the compiler did not provide good diagnostics and debugging tools, the user looking at a memory dump would have more trouble than in debugging an assembly language program, whose use of memory would be better understood.)

Today, these are generally not significant problems. Compilers are fast and produce efficient object code; indeed, with modern RISC (*q.v.*) processors they can often produce better assembly language code than human programmers. There are good symbolic debugging tools that map high-level language constructs to memory locations. Nonetheless, there can still be times when a user will be forced to think in detail about the correspondence between the high-level language and the machine details. This need is most common in systems programming (*q.v.*), but can arise on other occasions.

Classifications of Programming Languages

Programming languages can be classified in several ways. Two broad and overlapping ways are according to their internal structure, and according to their intended uses. In the first classification, languages are procedure-oriented or nonprocedural. In the second, languages are domain-specific or general (though "general-purpose" is really a misnomer). There are other categories as well; there are specification languages; and there are reference, publication, and hardware languages (the last three terms actually refer to forms in which a single language is presented). Note that several of the categories frequently referred to as "paradigms"—object-oriented, logic, and functional languages—are not singled out, as they are encompassed by the first classification scheme, although each offers specific important features.

PROCEDURAL AND NONPROCEDURAL
Procedure-oriented. A *procedure-oriented language* is one in which the user specifies a set of executable operations that are to be performed in sequence. These operations can be organized into *procedures* or subprograms (*q.v.*), and a program is constructed as a sequence of procedure calls and other statements. The key property here is that these constructs are definitely executable operations, and the sequencing is already specified by the user. Fortran, Cobol, and Ada are examples. (The relation of these to domains of application is discussed later.)

Object-oriented languages are procedural languages that allow data to be packaged with the procedures that operate on them and to hide implementation details of the data and of the operations. Such *data abstraction* (*see* ABSTRACT DATA TYPE and INFORMATION HIDING) is an important software engineering tool for the construction of large programs.

Nonprocedural. The term *nonprocedural language* (*q.v.*) does not have a precise definition. It is actually a relative term, characterizing the degree to which a

user can specify *what* is to be done rather than *how* to do it. The closer the user can come to stating a problem without specifying the sequential steps for solving it, the more nonprocedural is the language. Furthermore, there can be an ordered sequence of steps, each of which is "somewhat nonprocedural," or a set of executable operations whose sequence is not specified by the user. Both cases contribute to more "nonproceduralness." Thus, in languages like Fortran, the statement

$$Y = A + B * C - D/E$$

is nonprocedural because the order in which the operations are executed is not completely specified, although it may be one step in a procedural sequence of statements.

In 1999, the sentences CALCULATE THE SQUARE ROOT OF THE PRIME NUMBERS FROM 7 TO 91 AND PRINT IN THREE COLUMNS and PRINT ALL THE SALARY CHECKS cannot be translated into executable code by any compiler, but if they could be compiled, they would be nonprocedural because they do not give the specific steps required for their execution. They could, however, then be parts of procedural sequences.

Logic programming languages like Prolog and functional languages like Haskell and pure Lisp are among the best examples of nonprocedural languages today. In logic programming, in particular, a problem description can sometimes be a complete program. Other nonprocedural systems (not really languages) are report generators (RPG) and sort generators in which the individual specifies the input and the desired output without any description of the procedures needed to obtain the output.

The so-called "visual languages" are partly nonprocedural. They provide convenient ways of building programs by joining prepared elements like window menus and buttons. As such construction becomes more common (*see* COMPONENT SOFTWARE), programs may be built without explicit use of programming languages except for the "glue" that combines the parts. However, programming languages are still the means for writing these components themselves.

GENERAL- AND SPECIAL-PURPOSE LANGUAGES
General. Programming languages are designed for application to problem-domains of varying breadth. Fortran is designed to be primarily useful for numerical scientific problems, while Cobol is designed for business data processing. C originated as a systems programming language, and Simula as a language for simulation problems. Some languages, such as PL/I, Ada, and perhaps C++, are intended to be useful in multiple application areas. The term *general purpose*

is sometimes used for these languages, and even for Fortran and C, but there is *no* truly general-purpose language, in the sense of one that does all jobs equally well. Though any one of these *can* do any job, the "semantic gap"—the degree to which the language constructs fit the problem—may be larger than it would be with a different language.

We may still distinguish between languages for broad domains of problems and those that are narrower. Some of the former domains are scientific applications (Fortran), business data processing (Cobol), string processing (Snobol, Icon), real-time programming (Ada), and systems programming.

Domain-specific languages. Several related terms are in use. *Problem-oriented (q.v.)* has been used in many ways, but an appropriate use is to characterize languages that are well-adapted to a particular problem, and that are easier to use for that kind of problem than others are. If the term is construed broadly, of course, any language may be called problem-oriented, being intended to solve problems. Similarly, *application-oriented* is sometimes used to describe languages intended for particular purposes, but any language is application oriented, perhaps to a broad area like numerical computations.

Another term is *special-purpose* language: one that is designed to meet a single objective. The objective might involve the application area, the ease of use for a particular application, or pertain to efficiency of the compiler or the object code. A common and useful term today that covers all of these is *domain-specific* language, which indicates that the language has a limited rather than a broad domain. There are many such languages, for computer graphics, simulation, machine-tool control, robotics, expert systems, and architectural design, to name a few domains. There are languages intended specifically for implementing other programming languages; they are designed to be intermediate between high-level languages and machine languages (*see* INTERMEDIATE LANGUAGE).

SPECIFICATION AND DESCRIPTION LANGUAGES

A *problem-defining*, or *specification*, language is one that literally defines the problem and may specifically define the desired input and output, but it *does not* define the method of transformation. There are significant differences between a problem (and its definition), the method (or procedure) used to solve it, and the language in which this method is stated. These languages, such as Z (pronounced "zed") and UML (Unified Modeling Language—*see* OBJECT-ORIENTED ANALYSIS AND DESIGN) play an increasing role in software engineering.

A *reference* language is the definitive character set and form of a language. It usually has a unique character for each concept or character in the language, is one-dimensional, and need not be suitable as computer input. In some cases, the reference language contains English words considered as single characters; in other cases, a fixed set of symbols is provided. The concept of having a reference language, as distinguished from a publication or hardware representation language (discussed below), was introduced by the Algol committee in its first report. The reference language need not be particularly easy to read.

A *publication* language is some well-defined variation of the reference language that is suitable for publication of programs. It is designed to be suitable for printing or writing; therefore, it will have reasonable rules and characters for such things as subscripts, exponents, Greek letters, and other symbols. The publication language would normally be the means of communication between people (using printed media). There can be many publication languages and they can contain different characters, but there must be a well-defined mapping between the publication and reference languages. An illustration of this is the use of an "up" arrow to denote exponentiation in the Algol reference language, but the use of a raised symbol in the publication language, e.g. $A\uparrow 2$ becomes A^2.

A *hardware* language, sometimes called a *hardware representation*, is a mapping of the reference language into a form suitable for direct input to a computer. The number and types of characters used must be those accepted by the computer involved, and is often determined by those available on input devices. A hardware language must have a well-defined mapping between itself and the reference language; for example, ** might be a hardware representation of the $\uparrow$ in the reference language, and **begin** might be represented by 'BEGIN'.

PARALLEL-PROCESSING LANGUAGES

Languages for parallel processing *(q.v)* have some distinctive features, intended to handle the need to synchronize access to shared data and to provide communication between parallel activities. In most respects, however, they fall into the classifications already developed. Some, like High Performance Fortran, extend procedural constructs to cover multiple sequential activities, such as computations on many elements of a vector at once. Others are relatively non-procedural, specifying what is to be done in parallel rather than how to do it (*see* COORDINATION LANGUAGES). In certain respects, languages for parallel processing are at an early stage of development. As with assembly language programming, much programming for parallel systems requires that the programmer attend to low-level details of storage management like the placement of data in one part of memory or another, to minimize access time, or to reduce communication costs.

History and Statistics

A large number of high-level languages have been developed since the first ones in the early 1950s. By 1967, there were more than 115 implemented (Fig. 1) and in use at some time just in the USA. By 1999 there were well over 1,000 languages that had been used at one time or another, but many of them are no longer in use. Of these, roughly half were languages for specialized application areas (e.g. graphics, simulation, computer-assisted instruction, machine-tool control, equipment checkout, systems programming). The remainder are divided among the application areas cited earlier as being important and general. However, of this large number of languages developed in a 45-year time span, only a handful have been truly significant, and even fewer have been widely used.

Figure 1. The Tower of Babel, representing the large number of programming languages, is a concept that first appeared in the *Communications of the ACM*. The form shown above was used as the jacket design for *Programming Languages: History and Fundamentals* by J. E. Sammet, © 1969, Prentice-Hall, Inc., Upper Saddle River, NJ.

In approximate chronological order, the languages of major significance, and the approximate dates of their earliest public documentation and/or general availability, are shown below.[2] In some instances, notably IPL-V and Algol 60, earlier versions of the language contributed significantly to the ones listed here.

◆ APT (*A*utomatically *P*rogrammed *T*ools); 1957. The first language for a specialized application area.

◆ Fortran (*FOR*mula *TRAN*slation); 1956. The first high-level language to be widely used. It opened the door to practical usage of computers by large numbers of scientific and engineering personnel.

◆ Flow-Matic; 1958. The first language suitable for business data processing and the first to have heavy emphasis on an "English-like" syntax.

◆ IPL-V (*I*nformation *P*rocessing *L*anguage *V*); 1958. The first—and also a major—language for doing list processing.

◆ Comit; 1957. The first realistic string-handling and pattern-matching language; most of its features appear (although with different syntax) in any other language attempting to do string manipulation.

◆ Cobol (*CO*mmon *B*usiness-*O*riented *L*anguage); 1960. One of the most widely used languages on an absolute basis, and the most widely used for business applications. Technical attributes include real attempts at an English-like syntax and at machine independence.

◆ Algol 60 (*ALGO*rithmic *L*anguage); 1960. Developed for specifying algorithms, primarily numerical. Introduced many specific features in an elegant fashion and, combined with its formal syntactic definition, inspired most of the theoretical work in programming languages and much of the work on implementation techniques. More widely used in Europe than in the USA.

◆ Lisp (*LIS*t *P*rocessing); 1960. Introduced concepts of functional programming combined with a facility for doing list processing. Used by many of the people working in the field of artificial intelligence (AI—*q.v.*). Its Scheme dialect is used in teaching and research.

◆ Jovial (*J*ules *O*wn *V*ersion of *IAL*); 1960. The first language to include adequate capability for handling scientific computations, input–output, logical

---

[2] This list and subsequent text are based on material excerpted with some modifications and additions from "Programming languages: history and future," by J. E. Sammet, *Comm. of the ACM*, **15**, 7 (July, 1972), 603–604, used with permission.

manipulation of information, and data storage and handling. Most Jovial compilers were written in Jovial.

- ◆ GPSS (*General-Purpose Systems Simulator*); 1961. The first language to make simulation a practical tool for people.

- ◆ APL (*A Programming Language*); 1962. Provided many higher-level operators that permitted extremely short algorithms and fostered new ways of looking at some problems. An implementable version was not defined until 1967.

- ◆ Joss (*JOHNNIAC Open-Shop System*); 1964. The first interactive language; it spawned a number of dialects, which collectively helped to make time sharing practical for computational problems.

- ◆ Formac (*FORmula MAnipulation Compiler*); 1964. The first language to be used fairly widely on a practical basis for mathematical problems needing formal algebraic manipulation.

- ◆ Pascal; 1971. Introduced some new ideas about data typing and combined numerous known constructs in a neat and elegant manner in a fairly small language. Widely used for teaching purposes for many years.

- ◆ Prolog; 1971. Developed to provide facilities for logic programming. Has been significantly used in artificial intelligence applications.

- ◆ Smalltalk; 1971. This language has undergone numerous distinct versions since its earliest one, with the most widely used being that of 1980. Its most significant characteristic is the use of "objects" to permit object-oriented programming in a wide range of applications.

- ◆ C; 1974. Originally created to assist in developing the Unix operating system (*q.v.*), but subsequently became widely used and taught, primarily for systems programming, but also in other applications. C++, an object-oriented language, widely used in 1999, is an extension of C.

- ◆ Ada; 1979. A very large, powerful language developed initially for embedded computer systems under the auspices of the US Department of Defense. Has been used in multi-million line programs for nonmilitary government applications (e.g. FAA, NASA), as well as military applications. Has also been used in numerous commercial applications in the private sector and in diverse applications such as artificial intelligence and business data processing.

- ◆ Java; 1995. An object-oriented language developed for machine-independent programming and for programs that could be transferred over the World Wide Web for execution on the receiving computer. Resembles C++ in appearance, but without some of its low-level features for systems programming.

Some other languages have been more widely used or more comprehensive than those on the list, specifically Basic, PL/I, Simscript, Snobol, and Icon. In many cases they have almost completely replaced some of the languages on the list (e.g. Basic for Joss and its derivatives, Snobol and then Icon for Comit). The languages just cited are omitted from the list of languages of major significance for the following reasons: Basic, although simple and economical, added no new concepts, was not the first online language, and was not the first to be of major practical importance. PL/I has capabilities derived from Fortran, Cobol, and Algol, but has not succeeded in one of its implicit objectives, which was to replace these languages. It was preceded by Jovial in the attempt to combine capabilities for several application areas. Simscript built on the previous discrete simulation languages. Snobol was a good but fairly obvious improvement to the concepts introduced in Comit and then was largely superseded by Icon.

Appendix VI (Key High-Level Languages) contains a list of approximately 50 languages that are deemed to be the most significant ever developed.

Bibliography

1969. Sammet, J. E. *Programming Languages: History and Fundamentals*. Upper Saddle River, NJ: Prentice Hall.
1996. Pratt, T. W., and Zelkowitz, M. V. *Programming Languages: Design and Implementation*, 3rd Ed. Upper Saddle River, NJ: Prentice Hall.
1999. MacLennan, B. J. *Programming Languages: Design, Evaluation, and Implementation*, 3rd Ed. Oxford: Oxford University Press.

Website

Virtual Library, Computer Programming Languages. `http://src.doc.ic.ac.uk/bySubject/Computing/Languages.html`.

Jean E. Sammet, revised by David Hemmendinger

PROGRAMMING LINGUISTICS

For articles on related subjects *see* AUTOMATA THEORY; BACKUS–NAUR FORM; COMPILER; FORMAL LANGUAGES; GRAMMARS; LANGUAGE PROCESSORS; METALANGUAGE; PRODUCTION; PROGRAMMING LANGUAGE SEMANTICS; PROGRAMMING LANGUAGES; RECURSION; REGULAR EXPRESSION; STRING PROCESSING; SYNTAX, SEMANTICS, AND PRAGMATICS; VIENNA DEFINITION LANGUAGE; and WELL-FORMED FORMULA.

Languages for human communication have syntax (structure), semantics (meaning), and pragmatics (effects). Semantics and pragmatics are particularly complex subjects in human languages, and philosophers and linguists have studied them extensively. Computer languages are much simpler artificial languages, designed for the limited purpose of directing a computer to execute the operations needed to implement algorithms (*q.v.*). Their syntax and semantics are normally designed for ease of programmer use, translation, and implementation, all of which calls for simple rigid syntax and straightforward semantics.

This article is about methods for specifying the syntax and to a small extent, the semantics of programming languages—the latter is the subject of PROGRAMMING LANGUAGE SEMANTICS. For discussion of how such specifications are used *see* COMPILER and LANGUAGE PROCESSORS. We first describe the basic concepts of programming language specification, and then look at the implementation of these concepts.

Context-Free and Context-Sensitive Grammars

A *grammar* is a formal system of description of the relationships among the symbols that comprise a language over the operations of symbol substitution and concatenation. A grammar is composed of four parts:

1. An alphabet of the language (character set or symbol set).

2. A set of parts of speech (known as the *component names* or *metavariables*).

3. The initial language element, such as "sentence," from which all other sentences may be constructed.

4. A set of rules that directs the formation of instances of the language (called *productions*).

In the case of a language that may be described syntactically by rules of direct unconditional substitution and concatenation such that the substitution of a phrase for a component name is independent of the context of that component name, the language (and its grammar) is said to be *context free*. On the other hand, where such a substitution depends directly on the symbols or component names surrounding the component being replaced by substitution, the language is said to be *context sensitive*.

Language Descriptors

The terminology in which a language may be defined is a *metalanguage*, and must be uniquely distinguishable from the language being described. Thus,

attempts to define a language in terms of itself can lead to paradoxes due to the indistinguishability of the metalanguage and the language. For example, we may say in the metalanguage of English that a sentence has certain qualities, such as *it is grammatically correct* or *that sentence is true*. Consider, then, the sentence: *This statement is false*. If one is not given the information as to whether this sentence is written in the language or a metalanguage, one assumes that the word *this* refers to the statement itself; then the sentence is paradoxical. However, the same utterance on the part of a scholar pointing to some other statement is clearly valid. Thus, the metalanguage for the programming language Ada (*q.v.*), for instance, must be clearly distinguishable from Ada. By these requirements, the symbolism of a metalanguage must not include the symbols used in Ada. Hence there is a necessity to provide a distinct metalanguage that has applicability to the class of languages known as programming languages.

Symbolically, a grammar can be considered to be the definition of sets in terms of elements of other sets. For example, a member of the alphabet of Basic (*q.v.*) is a member of the set named (say) *character*; i.e.

$$character = \{A, B, C, D, E, \ldots$$
$$X, Y, Z, 0, 1, \ldots 8, 9, +, \star, /, -, \ldots\}$$

and, further, the class of objects named *variable* is composed of objects that are instances of the roman alphabet (*roman* $= \{A, B, C, \ldots X, Y, Z\}$) or the set of single instances of roman letters concatenated with single instances of the set of digits (in early versions of Basic); i.e.

$$variable = roman \cup (roman \times digit)$$

where $digit = \{0, 1, 2, \ldots 8, 9\}$ and the operation $\times$ signifies the cross-product of the two sets.

The rules for generation of sentences in a context-free language are composed of a set of productions in which each rule has the form

$$\alpha \rightarrow \beta_1\beta_2\beta_3 \ldots \beta_n \quad (n \geq 1),$$

where α is a member of the set of component names (called *metavariables*) and β_i is a member of the union of the set of component names and the alphabet of the language being defined. The string (or phrase) $\beta_1\beta_2\beta_3 \ldots \beta_n$ represents the concatenation of the individual elements β_i. The construct itself is taken to mean that the occurrence of α in any string may be replaced by the string $\beta_1\beta_2\beta_3 \ldots \beta_n$. The consistency of the set of production rules may be partially determined by ensuring that the following five conditions are met:

1. There shall exist only a single language component that is not derivable from other language elements.

This component is known as the *root component*, or *root symbol*, and generally is given the name of the object that the grammar describes, such as *program* or *sentence*.

2. All other components shall appear on the left-hand side of at least one construct rule, thereby assuring that there are no "dead ends" in the grammar.

3. For every component in the grammar, there must exist at least one sequence of substitutions using the production rules that will lead to a string composed totally of the characters in the alphabet of the language.

4. Starting at the root symbol, there must exist for each component in the language a sequence of substitutions based on the production rules that will result in a string in which the component occurs; i.e. there are no "useless" components.

5. For every string of characters in the language, there shall exist at the most one sequence of substitutions that permits the generation of that string; i.e. the language must be *unambiguous*.

In practice, there are (at least) three forms of syntactic specification in common use: BNF (Backus–Naur Form) and its variant, Extended BNF (EBNF); the Cobol (*q.v.*) language notation; and syntactic railroad charts. BNF was originally developed for the specification of the syntax of Algol 60 (*q.v.*). This method of specification has since been widely used in the literature of computer science and has become widely accepted as a result of its ease of use and its readability.

This notation is applicable to an alphabet that is composed of the union of the alphabet of the language being described and the set of component names (names of the "parts of speech") of the language. To distinguish between the character set (alphabet) of the language and the component names, the BNF system encloses component names in angle brackets, or corner braces (⟨and⟩), whereas the actual alphabet symbols are free of any enclosing marks.

While the original notation used for the Algol specifications was not subject to any constraints, such as those that need to be imposed to restrict, say, the number of characters in an identifier name, BNF has been extended to include notation from regular expressions so as to provide this needed control.

In the construction of the set of productions for a language, where there exists more than one possible substitution for any given component name α, two methods of description are possible: either there exist several production rules in which α occurs on the left-hand side, or the list of alternatives is specified on the right-hand side of a single production rule, separated by the alternation symbol |. Thus, the definition of a language composed of the set of binary digits (0 and 1) may take either of two forms:

```
⟨binary digit⟩ ::= 0
⟨binary digit⟩ ::= 1
```

or

```
⟨binary digit⟩ ::= 0|1
```

where ::= is to be read as "is defined to be."

As an example of a syntactic specification, consider the simple programming language (SPL) developed by Neuhold (1971) as the vehicle for the description of the Vienna Definition Language (*q.v.*). This language has two basic components, called *numbers* and *variables*:

```
⟨number⟩   ::= ⟨digit⟩|⟨digit⟩⟨number⟩
⟨digit⟩    ::= 0|1|2|3|4|5|6|7|8|9
⟨variable⟩ ::= ⟨letter⟩|⟨variable⟩⟨letter⟩
⟨letter⟩   ::= A|B|C|...|X|Y|Z
```

where two consecutive items, as with

```
⟨digit⟩⟨number⟩,
```

indicate that these items are to be concatenated.

In these two definitions, a recursive description system has been used which basically consists of two parts: a starter and an expander. That is, each definition contains an alternative which does not depend on the component type being formed, and an alternative which creates another instance of the component named on the left-hand side, given an instance of that component. Such recursive definitions permit the generation of unbounded strings of characters. Where an implementation restricts the length of a string (i.e. the number of characters that comprise the string), two alternative methods of description are available; either the set of permitted strings can be described individually, or a bounded repetition notation can be employed. The equivalence of these two descriptive methods is obvious. For example, let us assume that a particular implementation has restricted strings that represent *numbers* to three characters in length. Then the two representations could be

```
⟨number⟩ ::= ⟨digit⟩|⟨digit⟩⟨digit⟩
             |⟨digit⟩⟨digit⟩⟨digit⟩
```

or

```
⟨number⟩ ::= {⟨digit⟩}³₁
```

where the { } notation represents repeated concatenation of the object within the braces with itself, and the indices specify the upper and lower bounds of the number of repetitions.

SPL uses these elements to form programs that comprise statements that may be labeled optionally:

$\langle label \rangle$ ::= $\langle letter \rangle | \langle letter \rangle \langle label \rangle$
$\langle statement \rangle$ ::= $\{\langle label \rangle\}_0^1 \langle statement\ body \rangle$
$\langle program \rangle$ ::= $\langle statement \rangle | \langle program \rangle ;$
$\qquad\qquad\qquad\langle statement \rangle$

An SPL statement may take one of two forms: An arithmetic assignment statement (set statement) or a conditional branching statement (goto statement).

$\langle statement\ body \rangle$ ::= $\langle set\ statement \rangle |$
$\qquad\qquad\qquad \langle goto\ statement \rangle$
$\langle set\ statement \rangle$ ::= SET $\langle variable \rangle$ TO
$\qquad\qquad\qquad \langle expression \rangle$
$\langle goto\ statement \rangle$ ::= GOTO $\langle label \rangle$ IF
$\qquad\qquad\qquad \langle expression \rangle$

In the latter two descriptions (productions), the upper-case characters are elements of the language being described and therefore are without the angle brackets. Finally, the description of an *expression* is required:

$\langle expression \rangle$ ::= $\langle simple\ expression \rangle |$
$\qquad\qquad\qquad \langle simple\ expression \rangle$
$\qquad\qquad\qquad \langle operator \rangle \langle expression \rangle$
$\langle simple\ expression \rangle$ ::= $\langle number \rangle | \langle variable \rangle |$
$\qquad\qquad\qquad (\langle expression \rangle)$
$\langle operator \rangle$ ::= $+ | -$

This set of constructs completes the description of the syntax of the language and conforms to the five formation rules set forth previously.

As in the case of the specification of Algol 60, there existed a need in the development of Cobol for a means of syntactic specification. Whereas the Algol committee was composed of academicians and researchers, the Cobol committee was composed of a much more pragmatically-oriented group of people. Thus, the Cobol form of specification is much more oriented toward visual understanding than the (comparatively) mathematical form of BNF.

The latest version of this notation is presented in the specification of Standard Cobol (ANSI, 1985). This descriptive system uses lower-case strings to denote language components (called *generic terms* in the Cobol Standard) and upper-case strings to symbolize actual Cobol language characters. Further, upper-case strings that are underlined occur as key words in the language and must appear exactly as printed. On the other hand, upper-case characters that are not underlined are optional, and may or may not be present in the program. There are two sets of delimiters (*q.v.*): brackets, [ ], which denote users' options that may or may not appear in the program; and braces, { }, which denote alternatives, one of which must occur in the program. In this notation, the elements of the brackets or braces are listed vertically. There also exists a notation that means "and so on" that is represented by

the symbolism (...). According to the Cobol Standard (Chapter I, Section 5), the meaning of this becomes apparent in context.

Using this method of syntactic specification, the simple programming language (SPL) described earlier in BNF can be described as follows:

```
program: statement [; statement]...
statement: [label]
            {SET variable TO expression}
            {GOTO label IF expression  }
label: letter [...]
variable: letter [...]
number: digit [...]
expression:
        {number    }[{ + }          ]
        {variable  }[{   } expression]
        {(expression)}[{ - }         ]
        
letter:  {A}
         {B}
         {C}
         {...}
         
digit:   {0}
         {1}
         {2}
         {...}
```

The Cobol notation just used was adapted to produce EBNF, which simplifies BNF by specifying optional elements and repetition in a compact way. As in the Cobol notation, square brackets denote an optional item (i.e. 0 or one occurrence), and curly braces denote 0 or more repetitions. Thus, the SPL specifications has ENBF rules like:

$\langle number \rangle$ ::= $\langle digit \rangle \{\langle digit \rangle\}$
$\langle statement \rangle$ ::= $[\langle label \rangle] \langle statement\ body \rangle$

With the introduction of the programming language Pascal, the use of *syntax diagrams* or *railroad charts* for syntactic specification has become much more popular. Very similar in structure to the style of charts used in connection with finite state automata, these charts specify the alternative paths that may be taken in the construction of the allowable structures of a language.

Like both BNF and the Cobol notation, railroad charts can be constructed for each metavariable in the syntactic description of a language. Also like BNF, the railroad chart has been extended since its original conception to include a notation for the specification of the number of times a particular path in the chart can be traversed; this corresponds directly with the superscript and subscript notation that was added to BNF.

Using a BNF notation as a basic source of a syntactic rule, let us examine the procedures by which a railroad chart can be developed. For each BNF production, there exists a railroad chart which is named by the metavariable on the left-hand side of the BNF production.

Every occurrence of an actual language symbol (member of the language alphabet) is represented in the railroad chart by that symbol enclosed in a circle. Thus, the production

$$\langle A \rangle ::= x$$

would be represented by the chart:

Similarly, the occurrence of a metavariable on the right-hand side would be represented by a rectangle.

$$\langle A \rangle ::= \langle B \rangle$$

thus becomes

A BNF production having the form of a concatenated sequence of, say, metavariables would be represented by the sequential graph of their equivalent boxes. Thus

$$\langle A \rangle ::= \langle B \rangle \langle C \rangle \langle D \rangle \langle E \rangle$$

is represented by:

A: →[B]→[C]→[D]→[E]→

Alternatives in a production are handled very much the same as the two-dimensional scheme of the Cobol notation in which they are listed vertically with connecting arrows:

$$\langle A \rangle ::= \langle B \rangle | \langle C \rangle | \langle D \rangle | \langle E \rangle$$

becomes

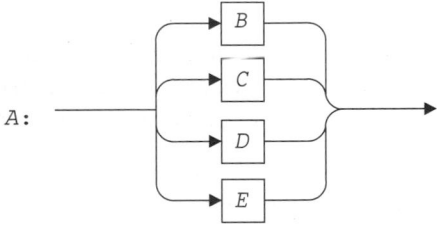

Repetition is represented by a graph that loops back on itself:

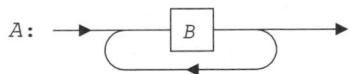

where the exit from the loop is clearly identified as the alternative route out.

For the case of repetition with the possibility of zero passes through the loop, the construction

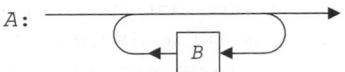

is the appropriate one (this is equivalent to the EBNF A ::= {⟨B⟩}).

Recursion is represented in BNF by $\langle A \rangle ::= \mathbf{a}\langle A \rangle \mathbf{b} | \langle B \rangle$ and thus by a graph that refers to itself:

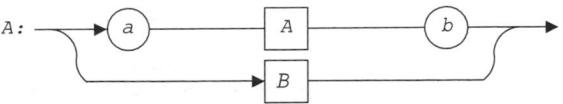

In Fig. 1 we present the railroad chart definition for the simple programming language we have used to illustrate the prior syntactic systems.

If the restriction had been placed on the construction of, say, variables that they should not contain more than five letters, then the notation used consists of a half circle in the connecting arrow containing the number of repetitions that are permitted. The minimum number of repetitions must be represented by an explicit number of occurrences of the object being repeated. Thus, if we were to add the additional constraint on variable names that they must contain at least two letters, the chart would be constructed as follows:

variable:

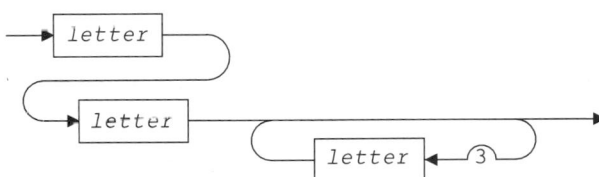

All these context-free descriptions are unable to specify context-sensitive constraints such as occur in programming languages in the rule that a variable be declared before it is used. Such a rule means that an assignment statement, say, is syntactically valid only if it has both the right form and if each variable has been declared to be of the appropriate type. Similarly, the description of a label that is a GOTO target in SPL requires that "the same label (mentioned in the GOTO statement) must appear exactly once as the prefix to some statement in the SPL program." It can be shown that context-free specifications cannot include such "long-range" dependencies among parts of a program. See the "Context Sensitivity" section, below, for ways of treating these dependencies.

Syntactic Ambiguity

As described in the preceding section, a grammar is considered to be ambiguous when there exists more than one sequence of substitutions that permit the generation of a single string of characters. In the English language, examples of syntactic ambiguities are common and appear most frequently in signs or titles. For example, consider the various ways in which the

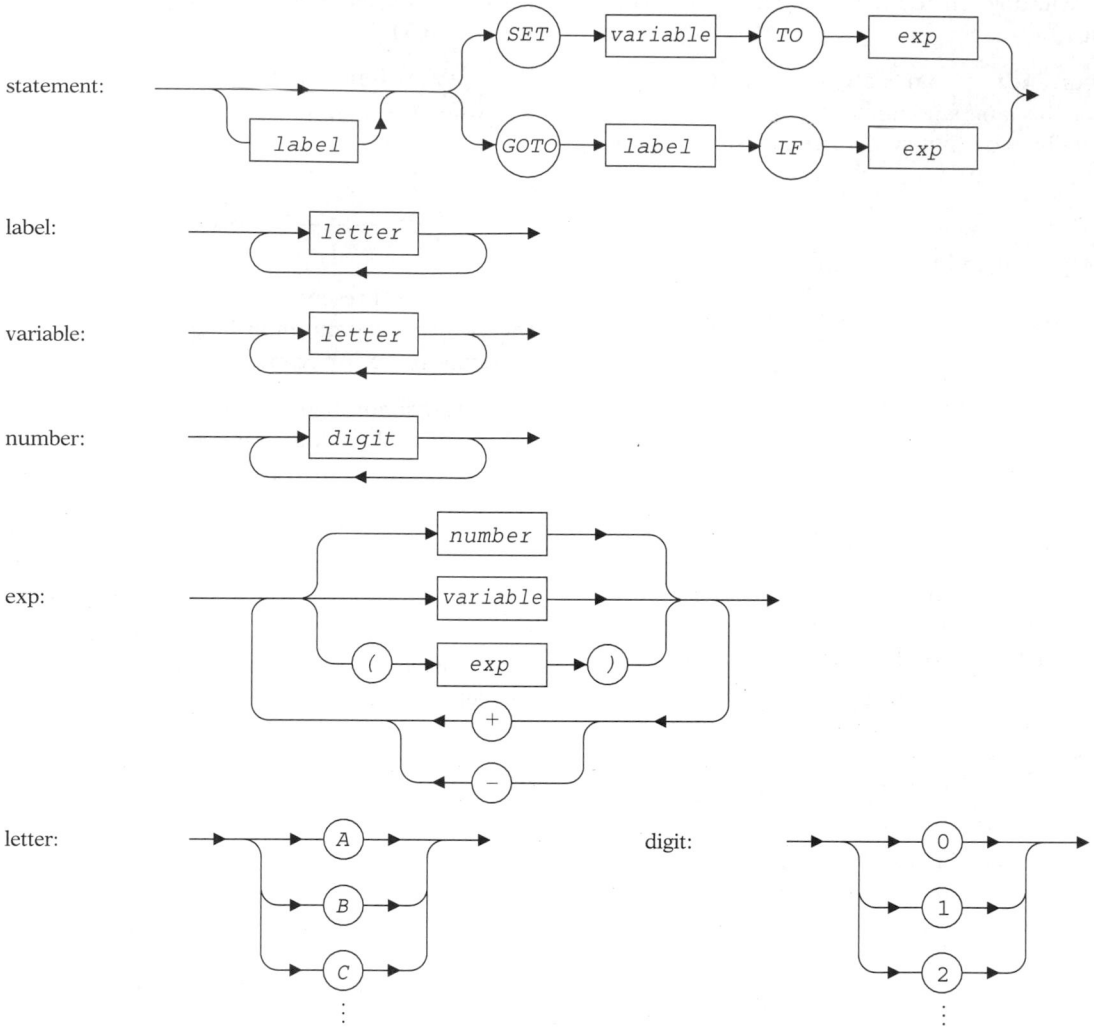

Figure 1. Railroad charts for the simple programming language (SPL).

following three phrases can be interpreted (or formally "parsed"):

> a half baked chicken
>
> hot tiled showers
>
> home made bake shop

Typically, an ambiguous grammar is one that contains a production rule which on its right-hand side references the same metavariable more than once, and does it in such a manner that it is impossible to discover the method of production of a string from its form. There is no known algorithmic technique to test for the existence of ambiguities in a grammar. However, examples of ambiguous grammars may help to indicate common sources of ambiguity. For example, consider the grammar

$\langle integer \rangle ::= \langle digit \rangle | \langle integer \rangle \langle integer \rangle$
$\langle digit \rangle \quad ::= 0 | 1 | 2 | 3 | 4 | 5 | 6 | 7 | 8 | 9$

Using this syntax, there are at least two possible generation sequences to generate any string composed of three or more digits. For example, consider the string 123:

Generation sequence (1)
$\langle integer \rangle \Rightarrow \langle integer \rangle \langle integer \rangle$
$\Rightarrow \langle integer \rangle \langle digit \rangle$
$\Rightarrow \langle integer \rangle \, 3 \Rightarrow \langle integer \rangle \langle integer \rangle \, 3$
$\Rightarrow \langle integer \rangle \langle digit \rangle \, 3 \Rightarrow \langle integer \rangle \, 23$
$\Rightarrow \langle digit \rangle \, 23 \Rightarrow 123$

Generation sequence (2)
$\langle integer \rangle \Rightarrow \langle integer \rangle \langle integer \rangle$
$\Rightarrow \langle digit \rangle \langle integer \rangle$
$\Rightarrow 1 \, \langle integer \rangle \Rightarrow 1 \, \langle integer \rangle \langle integer \rangle$
$\Rightarrow 1 \, \langle digit \rangle \langle integer \rangle \Rightarrow 12 \, \langle integer \rangle$
$\Rightarrow 12 \, \langle digit \rangle \Rightarrow 123$

The differences between these two generation sequences can best be seen by examination of the generation trees (syntactic trees) corresponding to these sequences. In these trees, the replacement of a component by the use of a production rule is represented by a single-level tree structure, with the component being replaced at the top and its replacement(s) below, and branch lines connecting the component and its replacement(s). Thus, sequence (1) is represented by the tree shown in Fig. 2, and sequence (2) is shown in Fig. 3. Obviously, these two trees are not equivalent, and thus we may state that this grammar appears to be ambiguous.

However, apparent ambiguity can result from a failure to be consistent in the order in which components in the partially expanded string are replaced. In fact, any rule that contains in its right-hand part more than one component is a potential source of apparent ambiguity. Thus, we insist that the order of replacement of components in a string be strictly left-to-right or right-to-left. That is, the leftmost (rightmost) component in a string is the candidate for replacement at each generation stage. Such a strict sequence of generations is known as *canonic* generation.

Returning to the definition of a digit string given above, it may be seen that a canonic generation would not alleviate the ambiguity of the grammar. However, a simple change in the grammar would solve this problem:

$\langle integer\rangle ::= \langle digit\rangle | \langle integer\rangle\langle digit\rangle$
$\langle digit\rangle \quad ::= 0 | 1 | 2 | 3 | 4 | 5 | 6 | 7 | 8 | 9$

From this grammar, it would appear that there are at least two distinct ways of generating the string 123, depending on the order of application of the production rules (i.e. left or right canonic generation).

Left canonic generation sequence (3):
$\langle integer\rangle \Rightarrow \langle integer\rangle\langle digit\rangle$
$\Rightarrow \langle integer\rangle\langle digit\rangle\langle digit\rangle$
$\Rightarrow \langle digit\rangle\langle digit\rangle\langle digit\rangle$
$\Rightarrow 1 \langle digit\rangle\langle digit\rangle \Rightarrow 12 \langle digit\rangle \Rightarrow 123$

Right canonic generation sequence (4):
$\langle integer\rangle \Rightarrow \langle integer\rangle\langle digit\rangle \Rightarrow \langle integer\rangle 3$
$\Rightarrow \langle integer\rangle\langle digit\rangle 3 \Rightarrow \langle integer\rangle 23$
$\Rightarrow \langle digit\rangle 23 \Rightarrow 123$

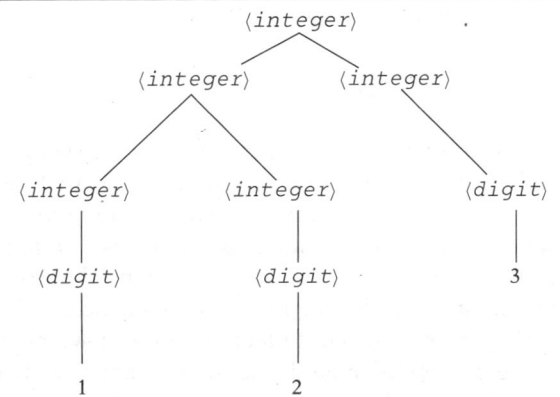

Figure 2. Generation sequence (1).

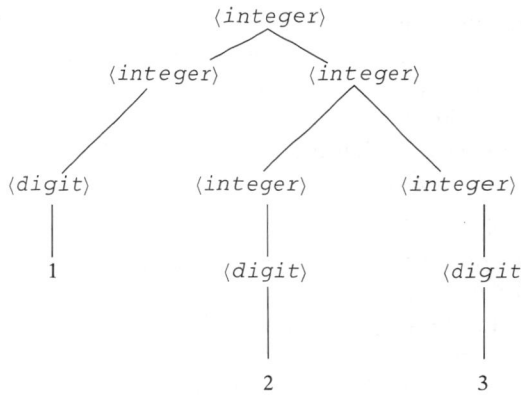

Figure 3. Generation sequence (2).

While it would appear that these two generation sequences are distinct, their generation trees are in fact identical, as is shown in Fig. 4.

In general, an ambiguous grammar will be formed when two grammars are combined to define languages that have at least one element in common. For example, consider the grammar

$\langle this\rangle ::= \{A\}_1^3$

which corresponds to the language with the sentences A, AA, and AAA. Then, if this were to be combined with the grammar

$\langle that\rangle ::= AA$

there would be two canonic generation sequences to develop the string AA. Thus, the grammar

$\langle this\text{-}or\text{-}that\rangle ::= \langle this\rangle | \langle that\rangle$

is ambiguous.

Although syntactic specification techniques are intended merely to provide a mechanism for describing the spatial relationships between the symbolic elements of the language, other structures inherent to the language are often introduced in order to provide guidance for compilers and other processors. The most common example is that of the arithmetic expression

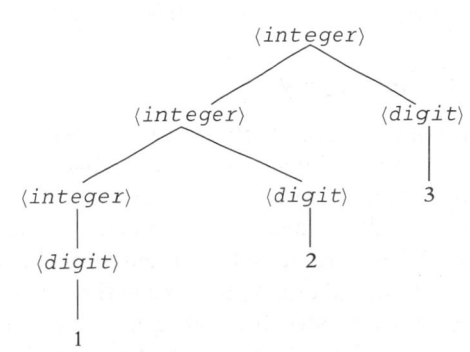

Figure 4. Canonic generation tree for sequences (3) and (4).

where the syntactic structure is organized in such a manner that it reflects the hierarchical execution (evaluation) structure of the expression. That is, if phrases within a syntactic tree are recognized in the same order in which the arithmetic factors are evaluated, then the two structures are synonymous.

Similarly, in connection with programming languages, it is important that languages be defined so that the desired meaning of a statement is unambiguous. As an example, it should be clear in defining an arithmetic expression that the implied meaning of an expression is unambiguous. Consider the simple expression

$$A - B - C$$

The interpretation (or parsing) of this string is usually considered to be equivalent to the string

$$(A - B) - C$$

and not

$$A - (B - C)$$

That is, $A - B$ is to be considered the first operand of the subtraction that contains C as its second operand. In terms of syntactic rules, this can be described by requiring that, in unparenthesized arithmetic expressions, the left (first) operand is always an `expression` and the right (second) operand is always a simple `element`, where a degenerate `expression` is an `element`. Thus, we might define

```
⟨expression⟩ ::= ⟨element⟩
              | ⟨expression⟩ - ⟨element⟩
```

If we now add a semantic interpretation scheme over the syntactic form, which specifies that only `expressions` can be evaluated and `elements` are number representations, we may see that

$$9 - 7 - 2$$

can be generated only by a sequence of productions such that $9 - 7$ is an `expression` (and hence can be evaluated) that is part of the larger `expression` $\overline{9 - 7} - 2$, where the overscore identifies the left-hand operand, which must have a value (i.e. be evaluated) in order to evaluate the second subtraction term.

Context Sensitivity

In the use of syntax productions, the progression from the root symbol to the actual string of characters may be visualized as the progressive substitution of components until all components have been replaced by elements of the character set of the language. This may be further visualized as the progression through certain branches of a tree structure wherein each branch is independent of all other branches. However, this tree-like structure with no interdependence of branches

exists only for *context-free* languages. If the left-hand side of a production contains more than one metavariable, then the production of the right-hand side is dependent on the occurrence of more than one metavariable, and the language is said to be *context-sensitive*. In such languages, productions of the type

$$⟨a⟩⟨b⟩⟨c⟩ ::= ⟨a⟩\pi⟨c⟩$$

indicate that in the context of ⟨a⟩ and ⟨c⟩ (either but not both of which may be empty strings), the component ⟨b⟩ is to be replaced by the string π, where π may be any combination of characters and components.

We noted that rules like declare-before-use, and type-checking rules in general, introduce context-sensitive elements into programming languages. It is possible to develop complete context-sensitive grammars to describe programming languages. They are not used, however, because they are complex and hard to work with, and because they are "overkill." Since most of the programming language syntax is context free, it is better to isolate the context-sensitive aspects and treat them by adding features to an underlying context-free notation.

There are several formalisms for this purpose, including *attribute grammars*, *two-level grammars* (W-grammars), *production systems*, and *affix grammars*. Pagan (1981) discusses the first two. Two-level grammars were used to specify Algol 68 (*q.v.*), but the notation is difficult, and attribute grammars are by far the most common, being frequently used to specify compiler designs. Attributes are introduced by annotations added to context-free rules, directing them to generate information or to use information generated by other rules. For example, a declaration (*q.v.*) would attach a "declared" attribute to a variable name, and later, the grammar rule for assignment statements could invoke a test to see if all variable names have that attribute. (Those production rules that don't use a particular attribute simply pass it along for later use.) Attribute grammars make production rules operate like procedures with parameters through which they inherit or generate attribute information.

Syntactic Analysis

The problem of associating a given string of symbols through a grammar to a language, such that an answer to the question "does this string belong to the language?" may be determined, is known as *syntactic analysis*. It is intended that, in determining the existence of the string in the language, the syntactic tree for that string can be created. In fact, in terms of syntactic trees, the process of analysis can be thought of as the determination of the syntactic tree that was used to generate the string.

Cheatham (1967) has likened the problem of tree generation to the game of dominoes, wherein the dominoes contain the left-hand side and the right-hand side of each syntactic production. The problem, then, is to fit the dominoes together in such a manner that there exists a complete tree between the root symbol and the string in question. Such a structure is shown in Fig. 5 and is discussed later in this section.

Another means for validating the existence of a string in a language is to generate all possible strings of that language and then to investigate the existence of the string in question in the generated set. Obviously, in some languages this is impossible, since the language is infinite. However, given a string of a prescribed length (i.e. number of distinct characters in the string), it is possible to generate all sequences of that length, provided the null element is rejected from the grammar. That is, if each and every production in a given grammar either maintains or increases the length of the generated string on application, then it is possible to discard many alternative generation sequences when the generated string is too long. In this sense, a string may consist of both characters in the language as well as components. Such strings are known as *sentential forms* of the language.

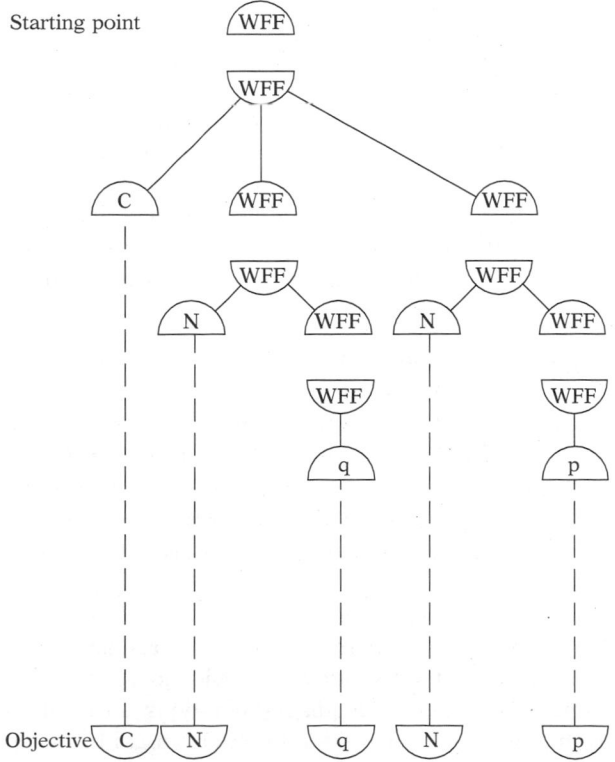

Figure 5. Syntactic tree as a dominoes game. Given a starting point and objective as semicircles, the game is finished when all semicircles match with another containing the same character or component name.

For example, given the grammar

(1) $\langle s \rangle ::= \langle e \rangle$
(2) $\langle e \rangle ::= \langle e \rangle + \langle t \rangle \mid \langle t \rangle$
(3) $\langle t \rangle ::= A\langle t \rangle \mid A$

we see that the initial symbol (root symbol) is $\langle s \rangle$ and that the character set of the language is $\{A, +\}$. The set of component names is $\{\langle s \rangle, \langle e \rangle, \langle t \rangle\}$. Given that $\langle s \rangle$ is the root symbol, then $\langle s \rangle$ is a sentential form of the language, and the replacement of any component in a sentential form by the use of one of the productions also develops a sentential form. Hence the sequence of sentential forms

$$\langle s \rangle \Rightarrow \langle e \rangle \Rightarrow \langle e \rangle + \langle t \rangle \Rightarrow \langle t \rangle + \langle t \rangle$$
$$\Rightarrow A\langle t \rangle + \langle t \rangle \Rightarrow AA + \langle t \rangle \Rightarrow AA + A$$

may be developed, showing that each form is *in* the language. However, we will usually be concerned with only those sentential forms that are composed totally of characters of the language; i.e. sentential forms that contain no components that are candidates for replacement through the use of any production. In the language defined by the grammar above, the *proof* that a string exists is the existence of a sequence of steps (using one production rule at each step) that leads from the root symbol to the desired string.

Such a definition of the proof of the existence of a string in a language is consistent with the definition of *proof* as related to formal systems (Mendelson, 1966):

A proof ... is a sequence $A_1, A_2, \ldots, A_n$ of well-formed formulas such that, for each i, either A_i is an axiom (of the system) or A_i is a direct consequence of some preceding well-formed formula by virtue of one of the rules of inference.

In terms of syntactic forms, the existence proof may be defined as follows:

An existence proof over a string of characters B_n in the language is a sequence $B_1, B_2, \ldots, B_n$ of sentential forms of the language such that, for each i, B_i is a sentential form that is the result of applying one of the production rules of the grammar to B_{i-1} and where B_1 is the root symbol of the language.

The means for determining this sequence is the task of a syntactic analyzer, and the sequence of productions that generates the sentential forms is known as the *parse* of the string. That is, for example, in the sequence of sentential forms that relate the root symbol $\langle s \rangle$ to the string $AA + A$ above, the parse is the sequence of rules applied. Thus, if the rules were numbered $i.j$ where i is the rule number and j the alternative used, then this sequence of sentential forms is equivalent to the parse

1.1, 2.1, 2.2, 3.1, 3.2, 3.2.

While we develop the parse of a string in the process of compilation, at least by implication, the most important derivative of a syntactic analysis of a string from the point of view of a compiler is the set of relationships between component names and the string. For example, it is comparatively easy to see in Fortran that the component name ⟨variable⟩ can be related to strings of characters in statements. Once this relationship has been established, then the generator of the compiler can (say) create addresses in target language instructions.

The task of analysis of a string must initially be to determine the existence of the string in the language. As noted above, one way to do this is by developing from the root component all strings of the same length as the string in question. Consider the grammar

$$\langle WFF \rangle ::= p \,|\, q \,|\, r \,|\, s \,|\, N \langle WFF \rangle \,|$$
$$\{ C \,|\, A \,|\, K \,|\, E \}^1_1 \langle WFF \rangle \langle WFF \rangle .$$

This simple grammar defines well-formed formulas of propositional logic in Polish notation (q.v.); the upper-case letters (N, C, A, K, E) represent the operators and the lower-case (p, q, r, s) the elementary operands. Fig. 5 shows Cheatham's domino game form of the generation tree of the string CNqNp. Now, obviously, since the definition of this language includes a recursive production, the language is an infinite language, and hence it will not be feasible to generate all possible strings in the language to test against any string that is believed to exist in the language. However, it is possible to generate all strings of a certain length and then to check the existence of some string in this generated set. For example, consider again the string CNqNp. This string is composed of five characters (symbols in the language); and, by an examination of the possible substitutions that can be made, it can be seen that there are approximately 2,500 five-character strings that may be generated from this grammar! Thus, even for strings with comparatively few (5 even) characters, the number of alternatives in the algorithm for analysis is extremely large. Therefore, we must search for an alternative approach.

Syntactic analyzers can broadly be classified into two types: (1) predictive methods, which, starting from the root symbol, attempt to predict the means by which the string was generated; and (2) reductive methods, which attempt to reduce the string to the root symbol. These methods are loosely termed *top-down* and *bottom-up* methods, respectively. The direction implied by these terms is related to the syntactic trees that may be generated wherein the root symbol is at the top of the page and the string at the bottom. It may then be seen that a predictive (top-down) method starts at the top of the (yet unconstructed) tree and builds down toward the string, whereas the bottom-up (*reductive*) method starts at the string and attempts to develop a tree that

converges to the root symbol. It can be seen, using Cheatham's domino game, that starting from the basic game board containing only the root symbol (at the top) and the string to be analyzed (at the bottom), the two stages of analysis are well exemplified by the order in which the players fit the pieces into the puzzle.

Semantic Descriptions

There are several ways to specify programming language semantics formally. They include

1. *Operational semantics*, which defines the meaning of programming language constructs in terms of how they are executed by an abstract machine that resembles a real von Neumann machine (*q.v.*). This is the original technique developed as the Vienna Definition Language and used (in a slightly informal form) in the ANSI (American National Standards Institute) standard PL/I definition.

   Operational semantics lends itself to language specifications for use in designing actual processors. An operational semantics is a kind of translation from the language being specified to the language of the abstract machine (which could resemble a real one closely). Attribute grammars have been used to express such translations (Farrow, 1984).

2. *Denotational semantics*, which is concerned with giving denotations (meanings) for the elements of a programming language in an abstract domain (possibly the domain of data items in the language) independent of either an actual or an abstract machine system. It has a rigorous mathematical foundation. Because of this foundation and its abstraction from any actual machine details, a denotational semantics specification can serve as a primary one for a programming language, from which others can be derived.

3. *Axiomatic semantics*, where programming language constructs are characterized by axioms of the form: if *P* is true before the execution of the language construct, then *Q* is true afterwards. Axiomatic semantics is useful in constructing proofs of program properties, either manually or with the aid of automated proof-tools (*see* PROGRAM VERIFICATION).

Although formal semantics specifications are more difficult to use than syntactic specifications, they play an increasing role in language definitions. In addition to the operational definition of PL/I, Pascal has been defined axiomatically, as have other languages. The functional language ML has been formally defined with a method that combines operational and denotational approaches (Milner *et al.*, 1997).

By analogy (but not necessarily in fact), these three descriptive methods correspond to the description of the interpreter for a programming language (operational semantics), the properties of the elements of the program (denotational) without regard for the end result, and the assertions that could be included in the program to show that it is correct (axiomatic definition).

Bibliography

1966. Mendelson, E. *Introduction to Mathematical Logic.* New York: Van Nostrand.

1967. Cheatham, T. E. *The Theory and Construction of Compilers*, 2nd Ed. Wakefield, MA: Computer Associates.

1971. Neuhold, E. J. "The Formal Description of Programming Languages," *IBM Systems Journal*, **10**, *2*, 86–112.

1976. ANSI. *American National Standard Programming Language PL/I, X3.53*. New York: American National Standards Institute.

1979. Gordon, M. J. C. *The Denotational Description of Programming Languages*. New York: Springer-Verlag.

1981. Pagan, F. *Formal Specification of Programming Languages: A Panoramic Primer*. Upper Saddle River, NJ: Prentice Hall.

1984. Farrow, R. "Generating a Production Compiler from an Attribute Grammar," *IEEE Software*, **1**, *4* (October), 77–93.

1985. ANSI. *American National Standard Cobol, X3.23-1985*. New York: American National Standards Institute.

1991. Jensen, K., Mickel, A., and Wirth, N. *Pascal User Manual and Report*, 4th Ed. New York: Springer-Verlag.

1997. Milner, R., Tufte, M., Harper, R., and MacQueen, D. *The Definition of Standard ML*, rev. ed. Cambridge, MA: MIT Press.

1997. Sudkamp, T. A. *Languages and Machines*, 2nd Ed. Reading, MA: Addison-Wesley.

1999. Sebesta, R. W. *Concepts of Programming Languages*, 4th Ed. Reading, MA: Addison-Wesley.

J. A. N. Lee, revised by David Hemmendinger

PROGRAMMING SUPPORT ENVIRONMENTS

For articles on related subjects *see* COMPUTER-AIDED SOFTWARE ENGINEERING; DEBUGGING; OBJECT-ORIENTED ANALYSIS AND DESIGN; SOFTWARE CONFIGURATION MANAGEMENT; SOFTWARE DESIGN PATTERNS; SOFTWARE MAINTENANCE; SOFTWARE REUSABILITY; and SOFTWARE TESTING.

Programming support environments are software tools that improve programmer productivity and enhance the usability of programming languages. All modern programming languages provide some programming support features, such as debugging tools. The Ada (*q.v.*) language project, in particular, has emphasized its programming support environment (APSE) from the start. Advanced environments can support programmers in designing, coding, debugging, testing, maintaining, browsing, documenting, project tracking, reverse engineering, and customizing software. In addition, online help and embedded instructions assist programmers learning to use programming environments. Some environments support groups of programmers who work collaboratively on large software development projects. CASE (computer-aided software engineering) tools automate aspects of the software development process and encourage the use of particular programming methodologies.

The need for improved programming support environments is growing, as the development and maintenance costs of large software systems continue to increase. In the remainder of this article, a sampling of some of the features and functionality provided in programming support environments will be presented.

Design

To improve the process of designing software, programming methodologies have been developed and integrated into some support environments. For instance, tools that support authoring and viewing entity-relationship database diagrams encourage the use of that methodology. Typically, CASE systems provide a user interface (*q.v.*) for authoring models of organizations and systems, specifying complex behaviors and processes, and laying out data structures (*q.v.*).

Coding

Libraries of subroutines and program templates allow the reuse and repurposing of software and therefore decrease the time and expense of writing new software (*see* SOFTWARE REUSABILITY). Online help systems and menu-based programming systems improve programmer productivity by decreasing the time programmers spend searching through manuals. More sophisticated coding support techniques include programming-by-example and automatic code generation from high-level graphic or symbolic specification languages.

Debugging

Programmers use a variety of support tools during the debugging process. A *stepper* allows programmers to monitor execution of code line by line. An *inspector* is used to examine and modify data structures in memory. A *stack backtrace* facility is used to examine the stack (*q.v.*) after an error is detected. A *breakpoint* and *watchpoint* facility is used to help track down side effects (*q.v.*). A *trace* facility is used to monitor function calls and argument values.

Testing

Test case libraries are used to insure that software meets design specifications. Tools that support developing, maintaining, and executing test cases are required. Bug tracking facilities are used to inform the development of test cases. An active area of research is concerned with automatic generation of test cases from software design specifications (*see* AUTOMATIC PROGRAMMING).

Maintenance

To perform software maintenance activities, programmers require tools that help them understand existing code that they may not have written. Tools exist to generate data flow, control flow, and calling hierarchy diagrams. If the source code is no longer available, techniques such as disassembly can be applied (*see* ASSEMBLER). Since the quality of documentation affects maintenance programmer productivity, an active area of research is concerned with techniques for better capturing the intentions of designers, the strategies of implementers, and the reasoning of maintainers.

Bibliography

1989. McClure, C. "The CASE Experience," *Byte*, 14 April, 235–236. Highstown, NJ: McGraw-Hill.
1989. Norman, R. J., and Nunamaker, J. F. "CASE Productivity Perceptions of Software Engineering Professionals," *Comm. of the ACM*, **32**, *9* (September), 1102–1108.
1995. Brooks, F. P. *The Mythical Man-Month: Essays on Software Engineering*, 2nd Ed. Reading, MA: Addison-Wesley.

James C. Spohrer

PROGRAMMING

See APPLICATIONS PROGRAMMING; AUTOMATIC PROGRAMMING; CONCURRENT PROGRAMMING; FUNCTIONAL PROGRAMMING; LIST PROCESSING; LITERATE PROGRAMMING; LOGIC PROGRAMMING; MACHINE AND ASSEMBLY LANGUAGE PROGRAMMING; MICROPROGRAMMING; MODULAR PROGRAMMING; OBJECT-ORIENTED PROGRAMMING; STRUCTURED PROGRAMMING; and SYSTEMS PROGRAMMING.

PROLOG

See LOGIC PROGRAMMING.

PROOF OF PROGRAM CORRECTNESS

See PROGRAM VERIFICATION.

PROPRIETARY PROGRAM

See LEGAL PROTECTION OF SOFTWARE.

PROTECTION, MEMORY

See MEMORY PROTECTION.

PROTOCOL

For articles on related subjects *see* BUS; COMMUNICATION CONTROL UNIT; GATEWAY; HANDSHAKING; INTERNET; NETWORK PROTOCOLS; SYNCHRONOUS/ASYNCHRONOUS OPERATION; and TCP/IP.

A *protocol* is an agreement or set of rules that two or more communicating entities use to structure their conversations. Protocols may be implemented in both hardware and software.

As an example of a hardware protocol, consider a computer system with several CPUs, memories, and I/O devices on a single bus. When a device wants to use the bus (e.g. to read a word from memory), it must request access to it. In most cases, a bus arbiter will examine the request and decide if it can be granted, depending on what else is using or requesting the bus. When permission is granted, the grantee can request a particular word by putting the address of that word on certain bus lines, and various control signals on other lines. In some systems, the memory is expected to respond within a fixed time (synchronous bus) or to give an explicit handshake signal when it is done (asynchronous bus). All of these rules—how the bus is requested, how it is granted, how reads and writes are requested, and how the responses are made—together form the bus protocol. Any device that obeys the bus protocol can be attached to the bus.

Software protocols are also important. Consider two machines communicating over a computer network. In order to be able to understand each other, they must agree on many things in advance—e.g. how long (in time) a bit is, how to recognize the start of data, and how to recover from errors, whether they are transmitting text in ASCII or an image in binary. These collective rules form the *network protocol*.

Because protocols are often highly complex, they are frequently structured in layers and implemented in both hardware and software. The lowest layer is typically concerned with the electrical aspects (e.g. how many volts) and mechanical aspects (e.g. how many pins on the connector). The middle layers deal with grouping the bits into well-defined units (frames, packets, messages) and reliably sending them from the originator to the destination, possibly hop-by-hop over several intermediate machines. The upper layers have to do with the meaning of the information sent, such as protocols for file transfer and electronic mail (*q.v.*).

Many protocols have become either *de facto* or *de jure* standards. Standardizing a protocol makes it possible for multiple vendors to produce products that can work together. An entire industry—the making of plug-in boards for the IBM PC (*q.v.*) and PC-compatibles—is possible only because IBM has defined and published the bus protocol for its PCs. Similarly, the Ethernet protocol makes it possible for workstations (*q.v.*) from multiple vendors to communicate, because they all use the agreed-upon rules for sending packets. The TCP/IP protocol makes it possible for millions of machines over the entire world to exchange electronic mail and other information over the Internet.

As networks and applications become more complicated, new protocols are needed. The International Organization for Standardization (ISO) has defined a complex set of protocols called the Open Systems Interconnection (OSI—*q.v.*) that are intended to cover the entire spectrum of networking applications, from the lowest layer to the highest.

Bibliography

1999. Tanenbaum, A. *Structural Computer Organization,* 4th Ed. Upper Saddle River, NJ: Prentice Hall.

Andrew S. Tanenbaum

PROTOTYPING

See SOFTWARE PROTOTYPING.

PUBLISHING

See DESKTOP PUBLISHING; and JOURNALISM, COMPUTERS IN.

PUNCHED CARD

For articles on related subjects *see* CHARACTER CODES; HOLLERITH, HERMAN; HOLLERITH MACHINE; POWERS, JAMES; and PUNCHED CARD MACHINERY.

Punched card data processing was invented by Herman Hollerith in connection with the 1890 US population census. In this first punched card application, a single $6\frac{5}{8} \times 3\frac{1}{4}$-inch card was punched for each citizen; the data recorded was essentially nonnumerical (e.g. gender, marital status, nationality). Following the success of the census, Hollerith incorporated the Tabulating Machine Company in 1896 to exploit his machines for statistical and accounting applications in commerce. These applications required data to be recorded in numerical form, and for this purpose the card was redesigned with a number of vertical columns, each of which could represent a single decimal digit; a numerical value was then represented by a *field* of several adjacent columns. Early forms of the punched card had 34 and 37 columns, but eventually Hollerith standardized on a $7\frac{3}{8} \times 3\frac{1}{4}$-inch 45-column card with round holes (Fig. 1). The 45 columns were arranged in 12 rows: the top row was known as the "12" or "Y" row; the second row was the "11" or "X" row; and the remaining rows were designated "0" through "9"; rows 0–9 were used to record the value of a digit, while the X and Y rows were used to indicate the sign of a number, or other control information. The 45-column format was also adopted by the rival Powers Accounting Machine Company, which was incorporated in 1911. (The Hollerith line subsequently became IBM, and Powers was acquired by Remington Rand in 1927.)

In 1928, IBM introduced the 80-column card using rectangular "slotted" holes. The new card enabled nearly twice as much information to be stored on the same size card. When IBM introduced alphanumeric equipment in 1932, the "Hollerith Code" was introduced (Fig. 2). In the 48-character Hollerith Code, the digits 0–9 were represented by a single "digit punch" using the same code as the 45- and 80-column numerical cards. To represent the letters of the alphabet, A–Z, a single-digit punch was supplemented with one of

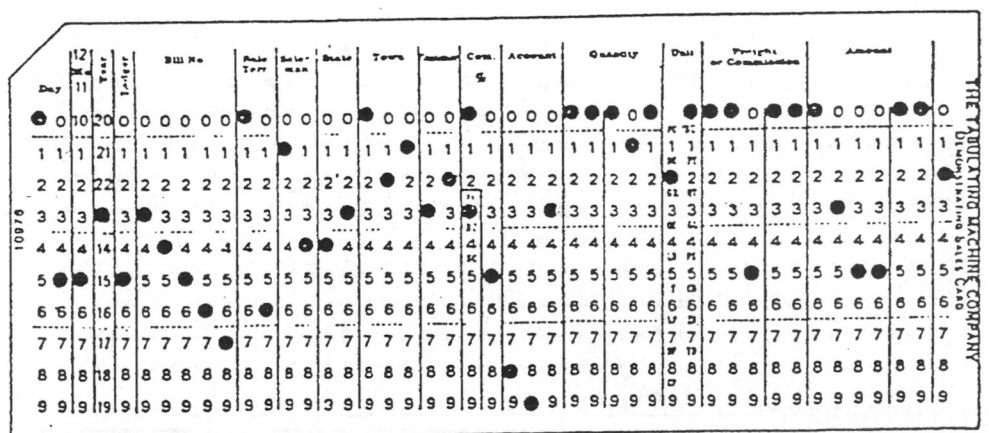

Figure 1. Example of a 45-column card, c.1913.

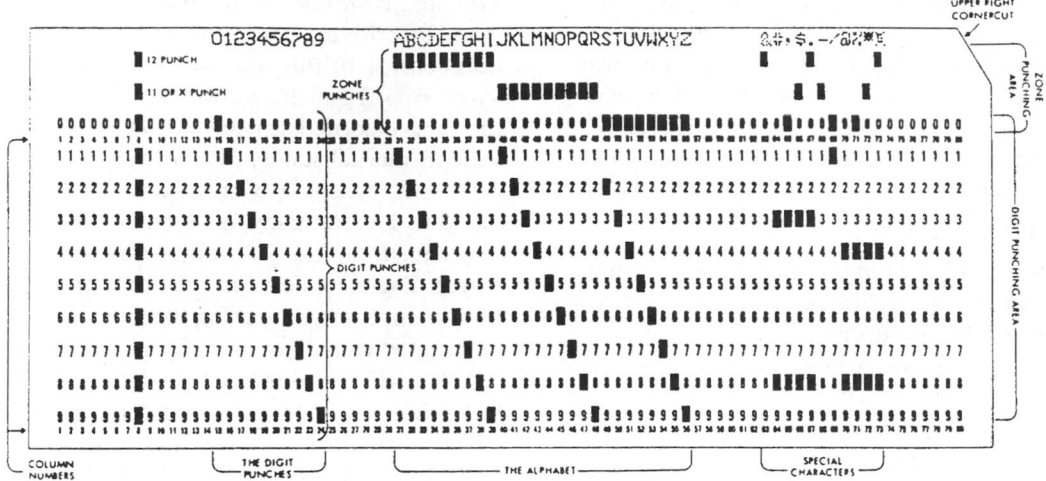

Figure 2. IBM 80-column card, introduced 1928.

three "zone punches." Special characters were generally coded by means of a zone punch and two-digit punches. The slotted-hole arrangement adopted by the Hollerith machines, which used electrical card-reading brushes, was not physically possible with the Powers machines since they used mechanical sensing pins that could not be spaced sufficiently closely. In order to increase the capacity of its card, therefore, Remington Rand introduced a 90-column card, which consisted of two 45-column tiers (Fig. 3). In the 90-column card, each character was represented by a 6-hole code. This code required a relatively complicated decoding mechanism and was not compatible with the 45-column card. Because of these disadvantages—and Remington Rand's smaller market presence—the 90-column card was always much less popular than the 80-column format. Although Remington Rand and its successor, Sperry Rand, clung doggedly to the 90-column card until well into the 1960s, Sperry Rand's Univac computers generally used the 80-column format.

In the 1950s and 1960s, 80-column punched cards became the dominant input medium for computers. During this period, the old Hollerith Code was superseded by more generous character sets. These included the 64-character set of the IBM 1400 series and other second-generation computers, the 128-character ASCII code, and the 256-character EBCDIC code, which was introduced with the IBM System/360 computers in 1964.

In 1969, IBM introduced a new, small card with the System/3 computer. The new card, which measured $3\frac{1}{4} \times 2\frac{11}{16}$ inches, held 96 characters arranged in three tiers of 32 characters. Each character was represented by a 6-bit code (Fig. 4). By this time, however, the use of punched cards was already in decline, and the 96-column card never achieved anything like the penetration of the 80-column card.

As an input medium to computers, punched cards long outlived the electromechanical machines for

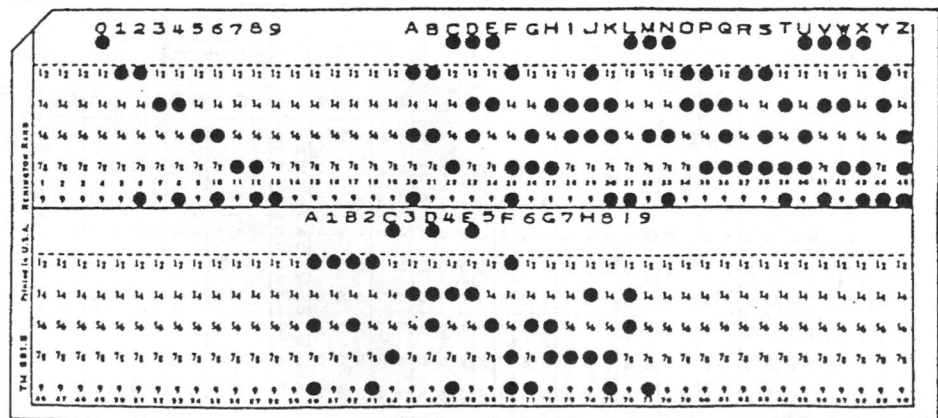

Figure 3. Remington Rand 90-column card, introduced 1930.

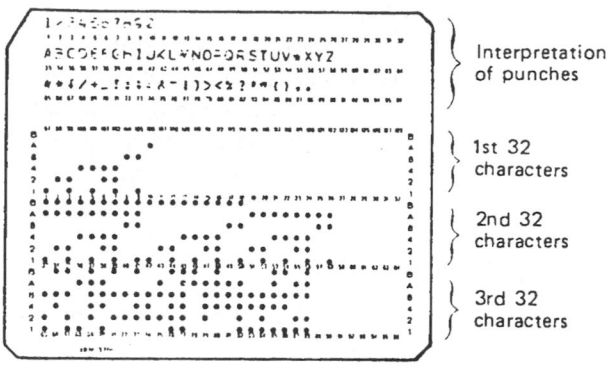

Figure 4.   IBM 96-column card, introduced 1969.

which they had been designed. But, from the beginning of the 1970s, the advent of key-edit equipment and interactive terminals caused a rapid falloff in punched card usage, which, for all practical purposes, ceased in the mid-1980s.

Martin Campbell-Kelly

PUNCHED CARD MACHINERY

For articles on related subjects *see* HOLLERITH, HERMAN; HOLLERITH MACHINE; IBM CORPORATION; IBM 1400 SERIES; POWERS, JAMES; PUNCHED CARD; and WATSON, THOMAS J., SR.

Until the advent of commercially available stored-program computers in the 1950s, punched card machines represented the most technologically advanced information processing capability that was routinely available. The leading punched card machine supplier was IBM which dominated the industry.

The origins of the punched card machine industry go back to Herman Hollerith, who developed his census machine for the 1890 US population census. The Hollerith system established the *unit-record* principle by which the data for a subject could be recorded on a single punched card. Once the card had been punched, the data on it could be repeatedly tabulated and sorted entirely by machine. The Hollerith tabulating system achieved a major improvement over existing manual data processing methods in terms of economy, speed, and accuracy.

In 1896, Hollerith incorporated a small business, the Tabulating Machine Company (TMC), to exploit his system for commercial applications. By the early 1900s, the company had focused its operations on the sale of cards and the rental of tabulating machines to the accounting departments of large-scale enterprises such as railroads, insurance companies, and engineering manufacturers. The early Hollerith equipment was based on three key machines that performed

the three key data processing tasks: the *recording*, *tabulating*, and *sorting* of data. (These machines are shown in Fig. 1, a photograph of an early punched card office.) The simplest machine, the *keypunch*—which was about the size of a small typewriter—was used to record original data onto a punched card. Introduced in 1901, the keypunch was to remain in use in essentially the same form for well over half a century and was a common sight in computer departments as late as the 1970s. The second machine was the *tabulator*. Introduced in 1906, the automatic tabulator was used to summarize and tabulate the data in a deck of cards at a speed of 150 cards per minute. The third machine, the *sorter*, was used to sequence a deck of cards according to some particular key field, and it operated at a speed of about 250 cards per minute. The early Hollerith sorter was known as the "vertical" model, an arrangement adopted to minimize the floor area taken up, but it soon became known as the "back breaker" because operators had to stoop to remove cards from the lower receiving pockets. It was replaced by a horizontal model in 1926.

Although Hollerith's Tabulating Machine Company was successful as a small-scale enterprise, it was not until the company was merged with two other businesses to form the Computing-Tabulating-Recording Company (C-T-R) in 1911, that it became a significant

Figure 1.   A typical Hollerith installation, c. 1920. The picture shows a vertical sorter (left of picture), an automatic tabulator (rear of picture), and two keypunches (on the table).

force in the booming office machinery industry. The same year, 1911, also saw the establishment of a rival punched card machine manufacturer, the Powers Accounting Machine Company, which introduced a highly competitive range of new machines. The Powers machines included an electrically operated card punch, a tabulator that printed its results, and a horizontal sorter. In 1924, the Powers company also introduced punched card machines for processing alphabetic data as well as numerical. From the time of the incorporation of the Powers company, rivalry between the Hollerith and Powers lines was intense, and it is a fair supposition that this competitive environment caused the machines to evolve more rapidly than otherwise would have been the case. Of the two companies, however, C-T-R—which changed its name to International Business Machines (IBM) in 1924—was much the more successful. In large part this was due to the charismatic leadership of its president, Thomas J. Watson, Sr. Although the Powers operation was fired with new vigor when it was acquired by Remington Rand in 1927, it never caught up with IBM.

Up to 1928, both Hollerith and Powers machines had used a common 45-column card format, but in that year IBM secured a major competitive advantage by introducing the greater capacity 80-column card. Remington Rand responded in 1930 by introducing a 90-column card, but it was less popular than the 80-column format (*see* PUNCHED CARD). This caused the Powers operation to be further eclipsed by IBM, which, according to contemporary accounts, sustained an 80–90% market share throughout the 1930s.

In 1931, IBM introduced the first of its 400 series accounting machines, and the following year the model 405 was announced, the first IBM tabulator to provide facilities for handling alphabetic data. The 400 series was a turning point for IBM: it marked the end of the transition from statistical machines to true accounting machines. The term "tabulator" was dropped at this time, and the machines were marketed as electric accounting machines (or EAMs). The IBM 400 series of punched card machines was to dominate the punched card scene for the next 30 years in much the same way that the IBM System/360 series was later to dominate the computer scene.

The 1930s was the heyday of the punched card machine. In the USA, IBM benefited greatly from the increase in government bureaucracy created by the new Social Security Act. In order to satisfy the burgeoning demand for punched card data processing in public administration and private enterprise, many new "auxiliary" machines were introduced to supplement the basic punched card setup. These new machines included the *multiplying punch*, the *inter-*

preter, and the *collator*. As well as new machines, there were evolutionary improvements in the specification, speed, and reliability of the existing machines. For example, the card punch was equipped with a full typewriter-style keyboard, the tabulator was equipped with an "automatic control" that enabled several levels of subtabulation to be achieved, and the speed of the sorter was progressively improved, eventually reaching 600 cards per minute.

During the Second World War there was a hiatus in punched card machine development so that in the immediate post-war period the punched card machine companies faced three technical challenges: first, to update their existing electromechanical products; second, to introduce electronic technology which had been brought to the fore during the war; and third, to respond to the invention of the stored-program computer. While the first challenge was swiftly addressed, the initial response of the punched card machine manufacturers to electronics and computers was evolutionary. For example, IBM's first electronic product was the 603 multiplier introduced in 1946. Operating at a rate of 100 cards per minute, the 603 multiplier was the functional equivalent of the 601 multiplier introduced in the 1930s, but the incorporation of an electronic arithmetic unit produced a tenfold improvement in its speed. The model 603 was followed by several other calculating punches, the best known of which was the model 604 introduced in 1948. The 604 calculator was to become the heart of the card-programmed calculator (CPC), a scientific calculating setup of which several thousand were sold during the early 1950s in the period before medium-priced stored-program computers became a commercial reality (Fig. 2).

The transition from punched card machines to computers, in fact, took longer and was more gradual than is often supposed. For example, throughout the 1950s, IBM continued to derive most of its revenues from its traditional punched card products; and as late as the early 1960s, Sperry Rand (the successor to Remington Rand) derived significant worldwide revenues from a transistorized calculating tabulator that was sold as the Univac 1004. It is now generally accepted that the key event that signaled the end of the punched card era and the dawn of the computer age was the launch of the IBM 1401 computer in 1959. As well as its low cost, a particular attraction of the new IBM computer was the model 1403 printer which operated at 600 lines per minute, enabling the system to absorb the workload of several traditional tabulators. The provision of magnetic tape and disk storage enabled the system to subsume the functions of the electromechanical sorters and collators. Finally, the central processor could take over the role of auxiliary machines, such as

Figure 2. An IBM card-programmed calculator (CPC), c. 1950. The CPC was a punched card-based computing system consisting of (left to right) a type 941 auxiliary memory unit, a type 402 electric accounting machine, and a type 604 calculating punch (two units—an arithmetic unit and a reader/punch). The CPC was a transitional product that provided a scientific computing capability until medium-priced stored-program computers became available.

multiplying and calculating punches. During the first half of the 1960s, some 14,000 IBM 1401 computers were sold, and sales of traditional tabulating equipment to first-time users faded away. Many existing punched card machine installations remained in operation throughout the 1960s, but by the 1970s, the great majority of data processing departments had switched to computers.

During this changeover period, the punched card remained the most common input medium for computers, and a new generation of card readers and card punches were marketed, both by IBM and the OEM (Original Equipment Manufacturer) suppliers to the computer industry. Card readers operated at speeds from 100 cards per minute up to 2,000 cards per minute for a high performance model, the latter corresponding to a data rate of 2,667 characters per second when all 80 columns of a card were punched. Card punches were slower, because of the relatively slow mechanical operation of the punching dies, and operated at a speed of 60 to 500 cards per minute.

The last major introduction of punched card-based equipment occurred with the launch of the IBM System/3 computer in 1969. System/3 introduced a new small 96-column card, and was equipped with optional offline electromechanical sorting equipment.

Active marketing of the 96-column equipment, however, was short-lived, as users turned increasingly away from card-oriented data processing methods to real-time transaction processing (*q.v.*). The use of both large and small punched cards declined steadily throughout the 1970s, and what use remains of punched cards is essentially vestigial. Surprisingly, however, there is an active market for new and refurbished punched card machines to process old data and even to record current information such as payrolls (*see* Dyson, 1999, and `http://www.cardamation.com`).

Bibliography

1985. Bashe, C. J., Johnson, L. R., Palmer, J. H., and Pugh, E. W. *IBM's Early Computers: A Technical History*. Cambridge, MA: MIT Press.
1990. Campbell-Kelly, M. *ICL: A Business and Technical History*. Oxford: Oxford University Press.
1990. Norberg, A. L. "High-technology Calculating in the Early 20th Century: Punched-card Machinery in Business and Government." *Technology and Culture*, **31** (October), 766–767.
1999. Dyson, G. "The Unread: A Technology That Won't Go Away," *Wired*, **7.03** (March), 141–145, 170–172.

Martin Campbell-Kelly

PUSHDOWN STACK

See STACK.

QUANTUM COMPUTING

For articles on related subjects *see* CRYPTOGRAPHY, COMPUTERS IN; FACTORING INTEGERS; FAST FOURIER TRANSFORM; LIMITS OF COMPUTATION; and LOGIC DESIGN.

In a conventional computer, information is represented by quantities that obey the laws of classical physics, such as the voltage levels in a logic circuit. But as the size of microelectronics shrinks, the underlying quantum physics will eventually become important. In the early 1980s this observation led Benioff and later Feynman to consider how to compute with information represented by quantum mechanical quantities. For example, an atomic electron has certain quantum states of motion with energies that are discrete or quantized. An electron in one of these states could be used to represent a binary 0 and when it is in a second, to represent a binary 1. A two-state quantum system that is used to store a single bit of information has come to be known as a *qubit*. (Other examples of qubits include: the two distinct polarizations of a photon or single particle of light; and the orientation of the intrinsic angular momentum or spin of an atomic nucleus, which can be either parallel or antiparallel to an applied magnetic field.)

With two or more qubits it becomes possible to consider quantum logical "gate" operations in which the state of one qubit changes in a way that is contingent upon the state of another. These gate operations are the building blocks of a *quantum computer* (QC). Quantum computation remained a largely abstract subject until 1994, when Shor showed that a QC could find the prime factors of composite integers much more efficiently than any conventional computer. Because integer factorization and related problems that are computationally intractable with conventional computers are the basis for the security of modern public key cryptosystems, Shor's result has turned quantum computation into a subject whose feasibility is now a very active research field. The practical realization of a QC is still in its infancy, but current experiments are producing encouraging results.

The logic gates in a QC are effected through quantum mechanical interactions between the qubits. Because the laws of nature are reversible in time, the logic operations themselves must also be reversible. Although many conventional logic operations are not reversible (e.g. neither a nor b can be recovered from the value of $a \vee b$), those required for quantum computation can be performed reversibly. For example, the input to a NOT gate can be recovered by feeding the output through a second NOT gate. Another fundamental reversible two-bit gate is the controlled-NOT or CNOT gate, in which a "control" bit and a "target" bit enter the gate and the target bit emerges XORed with the control bit, but the control bit emerges unchanged [and b can be recovered since $b = a \oplus (a \oplus b)$]. (With the NOT operation, the CNOT and a third reversible gate known as controlled-controlled-NOT [from which $c = (a \wedge b) \oplus ((a \wedge b) \oplus c)$], it is possible to perform any Boolean operation; *see* Fig. 1.) A computer based on these quantum operations would not necessarily be particularly powerful or fast. However, the real power

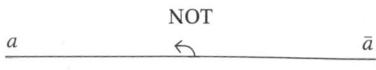

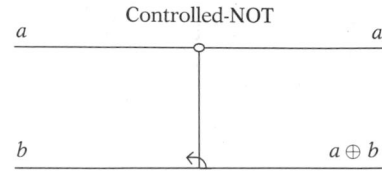

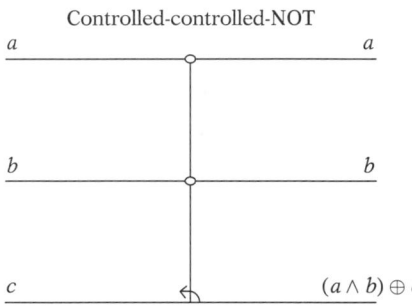

Figure 1. A set of three universal reversible Boolean logic gates, for which the input bit values (*a, b, c*) can be recovered from the output values by a second application of the same logic gate. All of the arithmetic functions for conventional computation can be constructed from this set of gates. The curved arrows represent the qubit in one of its two possible states.

of a QC would arise from the ability to perform much more general quantum gate operations that are not limited to the conventional Boolean operations of ordinary computers.

It is one of the most counterintuitive features of quantum physics that, at the atomic scale, material systems can behave with wavelike properties and exhibit the phenomenon of superposition, so that a qubit in a superposition state has aspects of *both* 0 and 1 simultaneously. Of course, once measured, a qubit in a superposition state will always be found to have a definite 0 or 1 value, with only the *probability* of each result being predictable by quantum mechanics, and determined by the amount of each component in the superposition. For example, quantum physics predicts that a horizontally propagating photon prepared with its polarization oriented at 45° to the vertical will pass through a vertically oriented polarizer with 50% probability and fail with 50% probability. (Superpositions are also the origin of the intrinsically probabilistic nature of quantum computation.) In 1986 Deutsch realized that a QC could exploit this distinctly nonclassical phenom-

enon of quantum superposition with a sort of continuously-valued (non-Boolean) logic to provide massive computational parallelism. In a QC a single-qubit operation can be used to prepare a superposition state. Similarly, with only *n* single-qubit operations, one for each qubit in the register, an *n*-qubit register could be prepared in a superposition of all possible 2^n values at once, providing a highly parallel memory.

The efficiency with which multi-qubit superpositions could be created in a QC also extends to the computation of functions. If we consider calculating a function that takes values on arguments from 0 to 2^{n-1}, we could create a single argument value in the *n*-qubit register and then create the function's value in a second register with appropriate quantum logic gates. But using instead a superposition of all 2^n values in the argument register, a *single* application of the same quantum logic gates would create *all* 2^n values of the function in superposition in the second register. (In contrast, on any conventional computer, even a parallel one, the values would have to be computed *individually*.) This "quantum parallelism" apparently allows an exponential amount of computational work in a single quantum operation, but if we are interested in the function values themselves, this feature of a QC is not directly useful because only a single value of the function is obtained on measurement. However, for *certain* problems where we are interested in some common property shared by all the values of the function, such as its period, the power of quantum parallelism can be harnessed using another nonclassical feature of quantum physics: quantum interference. Just as two waves can interfere constructively, when in-phase, to produce a stronger wave or destructively, when out of phase, to cancel each other out, the superposition states within a QC can be manipulated to produce constructive interference at correct answers and destructive interference at incorrect ones. The Fourier transformation is the natural mathematical device for such manipulations, and in 1994 Shor showed how non-Boolean operations could be used to perform a quantum Fourier transform (QFT) operation, with exponentially fewer operations than the classical fast Fourier transform. His QFT could be used to find the period of a function efficiently on a QC, and he related the problem of factoring an integer to a periodicity problem, showing that factoring could be solved efficiently on a quantum computer.

To put Shor's algorithm in perspective, during 1994 a 129-digit number known as RSA-129 was factored in 8 months, requiring 10^{17} instructions performed on over 1,000 networked computers (*see* COOPERATIVE COMPUTING). But a QC with a clock speed of 100 MHz could have factored this number in a few seconds, requiring a memory of about 2,000 qubits and 10^9 quantum logic gates. Furthermore, the number of quantum gates required to factor even larger numbers grows as only a polynomial function of the number of digits in the number being factored: a 250-digit number would only require about 10 times as many quantum logic gates. In contrast, conventional factoring algorithms have a much faster growth: a 250-digit number would require a factoring time of about 10^7 years by extrapolation from the RSA-129 result. The power of quantum parallelism becomes even clearer if we consider trying to simulate Shor's algorithm on a conventional computer: for factoring RSA-129 we would require $2^{2,000}$ memory bits.

At present there are only a few algorithms known in which quantum parallelism could provide an advantage over conventional computation. Shor has also invented a quantum algorithm to solve the discrete logarithm problem: given a prime number, p, and integer $g < p$ and another integer $y < p$, find the integer x, such that $g^x = y \bmod p$. Like factoring, this problem is computationally intractable on conventional computers and forms the basis for another class of public-key cryptosystems. The quantum factoring and discrete logarithm algorithms are particular instances of one class of quantum algorithms. Another class is based on Grover's quantum algorithm that finds a "marked" element in an unstructured database more efficiently than a classical computer. One of the most active areas of research in quantum computation is to understand the general nature of problems that are amenable to efficient solution on a QC.

A serious obstacle to practical quantum computation is the propensity for qubit superpositions of 0 and 1 to "decohere" into either 0 or 1. (This phenomenon of decoherence is invoked to explain why macroscopic objects are never observed in quantum superposition states.) However, over the past two years there have been breakthroughs in generalizing conventional error correction concepts to correct decoherence in a QC. A single logical bit would be encoded as the state of several qubits and quantum gate operations used to correct decoherence errors through a "majority vote." Moreover, these ideas have been shown to allow robust or fault-tolerant quantum computation with the encoded logical bits. It is now known that if a certain threshold precision per gate operation can be achieved, quantum error correction would allow a QC to compute indefinitely.

The requirements for practical quantum computing are simply stated but very demanding in practice. Firstly, a quantum register of multiple qubits must be prepared in an addressable form and isolated from environmental influences which cause the delicate quantum states to decohere. Secondly, although weakly coupled to the outside world, the qubits must nevertheless be strongly coupled together through an external drive in order to perform logic-gate operations. Thirdly, there must be a read-out method to determine the state of each qubit at the end of the computation. (In the quantum world measurement can be problematic.) At present, two hardware schemes have been used to demonstrate the basic operations of a QC with existing technology: the manipulation of nuclear spin qubits using nuclear magnetic resonance (NMR) methods; and photon polarization qubits manipulated with conventional linear optical elements. With these systems several logic operations with up to three qubits have been demonstrated, and even very simple instances of quantum algorithms, such as searching a four-element database using Grover's algorithm have been performed.

Although these systems will continue to be very useful for exploring the basics of quantum computation during the next few years, neither of them scales up easily to more than about 10 qubits. To go beyond this limit will require the use of other technologies now under development, such as laser manipulation of electronic energy levels in trapped ions and controlled quantum states of the electromagnetic field in microcavities. Single quantum logic operations have been demonstrated in both of these technologies. Estimates suggest that the trapped ion scheme should be particularly promising, with a computational potential of 30 or more qubits and many thousands of logic operations. Ion trap QCs should allow quantum computation to be developed into the realm where simulation of quantum computation on conventional computers is impossible. Even so, the computational capacity of an ion trap QC would allow the factoring of only small numbers. The long-term future of QC is therefore likely to involve solid-state schemes, although these are currently at a much earlier stage of development than the ion traps. A particularly promising silicon-based QC concept, which might allow large-scale quantum computation and industrial fabrication techniques, was proposed in 1998. This scheme is now under active development. However, the extrapolation to computationally significant problems is so great that it will be several years before the practical potential of quantum computation can be reliably assessed. Quantum computation is not only a new computational paradigm, but also opens up new perspectives on quantum physics. The future promises to be exciting for both fields.

Bibliography

1994. Shor, P. W. "Algorithms for Quantum Computation: Discrete Logarithm and Factoring," in *Proceedings of the 35th Annual Symposium on the Foundations of Computer Science* (ed. S. Goldwasser), 124. Los Alamitos, CA: IEEE.
1995. Lloyd, S. "Quantum Mechanical Computers," *Scientific American*, **273**, 4, (October), 140–145.

1996. Ekert, A. K., and Josza, R. "Quantum Computation and Shor's Factoring Algorithm," *Reviews of Modern Physics*, **68**, 733–753.

1996. Feynman, R. P. "The Feynman Lectures on Computation" (eds. A. J. G. Hey and R. W. Allen). Reading, MA: Addison-Wesley.

1996. Grover, L. K. "A Fast Quantum Mechanical Algorithm for Database Search," in *Proceedings of the 28th Annual ACM Symposium on the Theory of Computing*. New York: ACM.

1998. Gershenfeld, N., and Chuang, I. L. "Quantum Computing with Molecules," *Scientific American*, June, 66.

1999. Hey, A. J. G. (ed.) *Feynman and Computation*. Reading, MA: Perseus.

Richard J. Hughes

QUEUEING THEORY

For articles on related subjects *see* DISCRETE MATHEMATICS; PERFORMANCE MEASUREMENT AND EVALUATION; SCHEDULING ALGORITHMS; SIMULATION; and STATISTICAL APPLICATIONS.

A *queue* is a waiting line (like customers waiting at a supermarket checkout counter); *queueing theory* is the mathematical theory of waiting lines. More generally, queueing theory is concerned with the mathematical modeling and analysis of systems that provide service to random demands. A queueing model is an abstract description of such a system. Typically, a queueing model represents (1) the system's physical configuration, by specifying the number and arrangement of the *servers*, which provide service to the *customers*, and (2) the stochastic (that is, probabilistic or statistical) nature of the demands, by specifying the variability in the *arrival process* and in the *service process*.

For example, in the context of computer communications, a communications channel might be a server, and the messages the customers; the (random) times at which messages request the use of the channel would be the arrival process, and the (random) lengths of service time that the messages hold the channel while being transmitted would constitute the service process. Another example is a computer system where a programmer (customer) sitting at a terminal requests access to a CPU (server) for the processing of a transaction; both the arrival time of the request for access and the amount of processing time requested are random. Then, the mathematical analysis of the models would yield formulas that presumably relate the physical and stochastic parameters to certain performance measures, such as average waiting time, server utilization, throughput, probability of buffer overflow, etc. The art of applied queueing theory is to construct a model that is simple enough so that it yields to mathematical analysis, yet contains sufficient detail so that its performance measures reflect the behavior of the real system.

Queueing theory was born in the early 1900s with the work of A. K. Erlang of the Copenhagen Telephone Company, who derived several important formulas for teletraffic engineering that still bear his name today. The range of applications has grown to include not only telecommunications and computer science, but also manufacturing, air traffic control, military logistics, design of theme parks, and many other areas that involve service systems whose demands are random. Queueing theory is considered to be one of the standard methodologies (together with linear programming, simulation, etc.) of operations research and management science, and is standard fare in academic programs in industrial engineering, manufacturing engineering, etc., as well as in programs in telecommunications, computer engineering, and computer science. There are dozens of books and thousands of papers on queueing, and they continue to be published at an ever-increasing rate. But, despite its apparent simplicity (customers arrive, request service, and leave or wait until they get it), the subject is one of depth and subtlety. We will illustrate this by briefly visiting some of the most important models, and describing along the way some of the obvious features and some of the subtleties.

Queueing Models

The essence of queueing theory is that it takes into account the randomness of the arrival process and the randomness of the service process. The most common assumption about the arrival process is that the customer arrivals follow a *Poisson process*. One way to describe a Poisson arrival process is to imagine that time is divided into small intervals of length $\Delta\tau$. Assume that in each interval either an arrival occurs (with probability $\lambda \cdot \Delta\tau$, say, where the proportionality constant λ is the arrival rate) or it doesn't, independently of the occurrence or non-occurrence of arrivals in other intervals. Finally, imagine that $\Delta\tau \to 0$ (that is, take limits to pass from discrete time to continuous time). Then the arrivals are said to follow a Poisson process; and one of the properties of the Poisson process is that the times between arrivals (the *interarrival time*) are *exponentially distributed*. (A random variable X is said to be exponentially distributed if its distribution function $F_x(t)$ is given by $F_x(t) = 1 - e^{-\lambda t}$ for all $t \geq 0$, where $1/\lambda$ is the average value of X).

One of the most important queueing models is the *Erlang loss model*; it assumes that the arrivals follow a Poisson process, and that the blocked customers (those who find all servers busy) are *cleared* (that is, they are denied entry into the system, so the blocked customers are lost) (Fig. 1). The fraction of arriving customers who find all servers busy (the *probability of blocking*, or

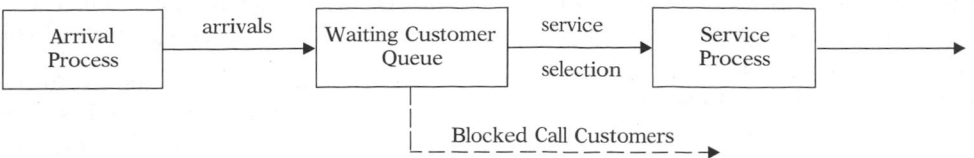

Figure 1. Elements of a queueing system.

loss probability) is given by the *Erlang loss* (or *Erlang B*) *formula*,

$$B(s, a) = \frac{a^s/s!}{\sum_{k=0}^{s} a^k/k!}, \qquad (1)$$

where s is the number of servers and $a = \lambda\tau$ is the *offered load* in *erlangs*, where in turn λ is the *arrival rate* and τ is the *average service time*. An important theorem is that formula (1) applies for *any* distribution of service times; this mathematically surprising and practically important result is an example of the phenomenon of *insensitivity*. Formula (1) is hard to calculate directly from its right-hand side when s and a are large, but is easy to calculate numerically using the following iterative scheme·

$$B(n, a) = \frac{aB(n-1, a)}{n + aB(n-1, a)}$$
$$(n = 1, 2, \ldots, s; \; B(0, a) = 1). \qquad (2)$$

For example, it is easy to write a program that implements (2), and to verify that $B(1, 0.8) = 0.4444$, $B(10, 8) = 0.1217$, $B(100, 80) = 0.003992$, and $B(1000, 800) = 10^{-12}$. (This means, for example, that when 8 erlangs of Poisson traffic are offered to 10 servers, then about 12% of the arrivals will be blocked.) Also, it can be shown that

$$B(s_1 + s_2, a_1 + a_2) < B(s_1, a_1) + B(s_2, a_2).$$

These examples illustrate the important fact that large systems are more efficient than small ones. The Erlang loss model is one of the fundamental models of teletraffic engineering (the "customers" are telephone calls and the "servers" are trunks, and the blocked calls are cleared from the system and thus are "lost" calls).

The *Erlang delay model* (also called M/M/s in queueing theory parlance[1]) is similar to the Erlang loss model, except that now it is assumed that the blocked customers will wait in a queue as long as necessary for a server became available. In this model, the probability of blocking (the fraction of customers

who will find all s servers busy and must wait in the queue) is given by the *Erlang delay* (or *Erlang C*) *formula*,

$$C(s, a) = \frac{a^s/[s!(1-\rho)]}{\sum_{k=0}^{s-1}(a^k/k!) + a^s/[s!(1-\rho)]}, \qquad (3)$$

where

$$\rho = \begin{cases} a/s & \text{if } a < s \\ 1 & \text{if } a \geq s. \end{cases} \qquad (4)$$

The quantity ρ defined by (4) equals the *server utilization* (the fraction of time, on average, that a server is busy), and $C(s, a) = 1$ when $\rho = 1$. The Erlang C formula (3) is easily evaluated by combining the iteration scheme (2) with the formula

$$C(s, a) = \frac{sB(s, a)}{s - a(1 - B(s, a))}. \qquad (5)$$

Using (5) and (2), it is easy to calculate $C(s, a)$ and to compare its values with the corresponding values of $B(s, a)$ computed earlier; the results are $C(1, 0.8) = 0.8$, $C(10, 8) = 0.4092$, $C(100, 80) = 0.01965$, and $C(1000, 800) = 5.6 \times 10^{-12}$. In each case the server utilization is $\rho = 80\%$, again showing that large systems are more efficient than small ones. Also, note that in each case, $C(s, a) > B(s, a)$. This can be explained by observing that in the Erlang B model the blocked customers are cleared from the system, whereas in the Erlang C model the blocked customers enter the system (and wait in the queue), thereby increasing the probability that future arrivals will find all the servers busy.

If the blocked customers are served in FIFO order (first in, first out), then the probability $P(t)$ that a customer will wait in the queue more than t before beginning service is

$$P(t) = C(s, a)\, e^{-(1-\rho)s\mu t}, \qquad (6)$$

where $\mu = 1/\tau$ is the *service rate*. For example, in a 10-server system operating at 80% utilization, the fraction of customers who will wait longer than one average service time is given by the right-hand side of (6) with $s = 10$, $\rho = 80\%$ (and therefore $a = 8$ and $C(s, a) = C(10, 8) = 0.4092$) and $t = \tau = 1/\mu$: $P(\tau) = 0.05538$.

---

[1] M/M/s denotes Memoryless (exponential) distribution of interarrival times/Memoryless distribution of service times/s servers.

Formula (3) (or (5)) predicts how many customers (more precisely, what fraction of arriving customers) will have to wait. Formulas (7) and (8) (below) predict how long the customers will have to wait; that is, if w denotes the average waiting time, then

$$w = C(s, a) \frac{1}{1 - \rho} \frac{\tau}{s}. \tag{7}$$

Significantly, although (6) is based on the assumption of FIFO service, (7) remains correct even when service is not FIFO, for example, LIFO (L=last) or SIRO (service in random order). This is true because interchanging statistically identical customers waiting in the queue does not change the number of customers or the amount of work waiting to be served, so average waiting time remains the same.

It is important to note that the Erlang delay model does *not* have the insensitivity property enjoyed by its Erlang loss counterpart; the Erlang C formula is derived under the assumption that the service times (like the interarrival times) are exponentially distributed. If the service times are not exponentially distributed, then results corresponding to (3), (6), and (7) are difficult to obtain, except in one very important case, the single-server ($s = 1$) queue. This fundamental model is often referred to as M/G/1 (the G denotes general distribution of service times). When $s = 1$ the analog of formula (7) is the *Pollaczek–Khintchine* formula,

$$w = \frac{\rho \tau}{2(1 - \rho)} \left(1 + \frac{\sigma^2}{\tau^2} \right), \tag{8}$$

where σ^2 is the variance (a measure of variability or "spread") of the service times. For example, when service times are exponential, then $\sigma^2 = \tau^2$ and (8) coincides with (7) (when $s = 1$). When service times are constant, then $\sigma^2 = 0$ and (8) shows that, all other things being equal, average waiting times are twice as long when service times are exponential as when they are constant. Remarkably, when $s = 1$ formula (3) remains valid for all service-time distributions.

These examples were chosen to illustrate the richness of queueing theory: simple models accurately describe real systems and often yield surprising insights. There is much more to this useful and mathematically interesting subject.

Bibliography

Heyman and Sobel (1982), Wolff (1989), and Ross (1993) provide good treatments of background material in probability and stochastic processes, together with material that relates directly to queueing theory. Cooper (1981) is a textbook on queueing theory, with some emphasis on models useful in teletraffic engineering; and Cooper (1990) is a survey with an updated list of references. Kleinrock (1976) is a classic textbook that emphasizes computer applications, and Bertsekas and Gallager (1992) has a similar focus but addresses more modern technology. Kulkarni (1995) is a recent textbook with many examples chosen from computer science and engineering, and Takagi (1991, 1993) is an encyclopedic compendium with a comprehensive bibliography.

1976. Kleinrock, L. *Queueing Systems, Vol. II, Computer Applications*. New York: John Wiley.
1981. Cooper, R. B. *Introduction to Queueing Theory*, 2nd Ed. New York: North Holland (Elsevier). Reprinted, with Solutions Manual, by University Microfilms International, Ann Arbor, MI.
1982. Heyman, D. P., and Sobel, M. J. *Stochastic Models in Operations Research, Vol. I, Stochastic Processes and Operating Characteristics*. New York: McGraw-Hill.
1989. Wolff, R. W. *Stochastic Modeling and the Theory of Queues*. Upper Saddle River, NJ: Prentice Hall.
1990. Cooper, R. B. "Queueing Theory," in *Stochastic Models* (eds. D. P. Heyman, and M. J. Sobel), 469–518. Amsterdam: North-Holland (Elsevier).
1991, 1993. Takagi, H. *Queueing Analysis*, Vol. 1 (1991), Vols. 2, 3 (1993). Amsterdam: North-Holland (Elsevier).
1992. Bertsekas, D., and Gallager, R. *Data Networks*, 2nd Ed. Upper Saddle River, NJ: Prentice Hall.
1993. Ross, S. M. *Introduction to Probability Models*, 5th Ed. San Diego: Academic Press.
1995. Kulkarni, V. G. *Modeling and Analysis of Stochastic Processes*. New York: Chapman & Hall.

Robert B. Cooper

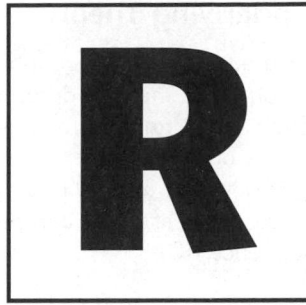

RAID

See REDUNDANT ARRAY OF INEXPENSIVE DISKS.

RANDOM-ACCESS MEMORY (RAM)

See MEMORY: MAIN.

RANDOM NUMBER GENERATION

For articles on related subjects *see* MONTE CARLO METHOD; SIMULATION; and STATISTICAL APPLICATIONS.

A *random number generator* is a computer procedure that scrambles the bits of a current number or set of numbers to produce a new number, in such a way that the result appears to be randomly distributed among the set of possible numbers and independent of the previously generated numbers. As experiments over the years have shown, this appears surprisingly easy to do. A wide variety of scrambling methods have been proposed. Random number generators are provided for most computer systems or software packages, and they work remarkably well—at least for limited use when only a few hundreds or thousands of numbers are required. But experience with very fast computers doing Monte Carlo problems requiring samples of hundreds of millions or billions of numbers has shown that the random number generator must be carefully chosen.

The most commonly used bit-scrambling method uses multiplication. Here is an example, using digits of the more familiar base 10, rather than the bits for base 2 that are used in computers; the current "random number" of, say, 10 digits is multiplied by a constant, then the last 10 digits of the product are taken as the new random number. For this example, start with an initial random number (the *seed*), say $x = 5323867883$, and multiply by a constant, say $a = 81734027$ to get an 18 digit product:

$$ax = 435141161293554841.$$

Then take the last 10 digits of that product as the new random number: $x = 1293554841$. For the next x, form the product $ax = 105727446300274707$, take the last 10 digits (reduce modulo 10^{10}) to get the new $x = 6300274707$, and so on. This is an example of a *congruential random number generator*. With proper choice of multiplier and modulus, a congruential generator produces a sequence of numbers that are difficult to distinguish from truly random numbers.

The first electronic computers of the late 1940s used random number generators much like the one above, and the intervening years have seen many arithmetic or algebraic schemes that seem to produce randomness, even though the results are completely deterministic. But modern computer speeds and exotic architectures make possible massive Monte Carlo simulations for which standard generators may not be suitable. A summary of some of the most common old, as well as promising new, random number generators is given below, after a description of the mathematical theory used to establish the nature and periods of the methods.

Underlying Theory

Virtually all random number generators are based on theory that may be described as follows: we have a finite set X and a function $f : X \to X$ that takes elements of X into other elements of X. Given an initial (seed) value, $x \in X$, (x might be a single computer word or an array of computer words), the generated sequence is

$$x, f(x), f^2(x), f^3(x), \ldots,$$

where $f^2(x)$ means $f(f(x))$, $f^3(x)$ means $f(f^2(x)) = f(f(f(x)))$ and so on. The three most common classes of random number generators are (1) congruential, (2) shift-register and (3) lagged-Fibonacci. An important property of any generator is its *period*, or how many numbers it produces before it enters a repeating pattern.

For *congruential generators*, the finite set X is the set of reduced residues of some modulus m and $f(x) = ax + b \bmod m$. Thus, with an initial element $x_0 \in X$, the generated sequence is

$$x_0, x_1, x_2, \ldots \qquad \text{with } x_{n+1} = ax_n + b \bmod m.$$

A wide variety of choices for a, b, and m have been described in the literature; see, particularly, Marsaglia (1972) or Knuth (1997) for methods for finding periods and establishing the structure of congruential sequences. With periods around 2^{32}, congruential generators have been used successfully in Monte Carlo simulations for the past 40 years. Most of the random number generators provided by computer systems or software packages are congruential generators. But random points in higher dimensions with coordinates produced by congruential generators show a crystalline regularity that makes them unsuitable for certain applications and that, taken with their relatively short periods, has led to the gradual adoption of longer-period generators for serious Monte Carlo studies.

For *shift-register generators*, the finite set X is the set of $1 \times k$ binary vectors $\mathbf{x} = (b_1, b_2, \ldots, b_k)$ and the function f is a linear transformation, $f(\mathbf{x}) = \mathbf{x}T$, with T a $k \times k$ binary matrix and all arithmetic modulo 2. With an initial binary vector $\mathbf{x}$ the sequence is

$$\mathbf{x}, \mathbf{x}T, \mathbf{x}T^2, \mathbf{x}T^3, \ldots$$

with the matrix T chosen so that the period is long and multiplication by T is reasonably fast in computer implementations. Shift-register generators are sometimes called *Tausworthe generators*.

The use of shift-register generators is declining. Those based on standard length computer words with $k = 32$, do not perform as well on tests of randomness as do congruential generators, and their periods are, like those of congruential generators, too short. Their main use is in forming part of a combination generator. The use of shift-register generators with extremely long binary vectors ($k = 607$, 1279, or even 9689 bits) still has some attraction, for the periods are extremely long ($2^k - 1$), and special hardware (called shift registers and hence the name of the general method) is easily constructed for their implementation. They are mainly used in special-purpose machines for Monte Carlo studies in physics.

For *lagged-Fibonacci generators*, the finite set X is the set of $1 \times r$ vectors $\mathbf{x} = (x_1, x_2, \ldots, x_r)$ with elements x_i in some finite set S on which there is a binary operation $\diamond$. The function f is defined by

$$f(x_1, x_2, \ldots, x_r) = (x_2, x_3, x_4, \ldots, x_r, x_1 \diamond x_{r+1-s})$$

where r and s ($1 \leq s < r$) are the two lag parameters.

Informally, a lagged-Fibonacci sequence is described by means of a set of r seed values followed by the rule for generating succeeding values:

$$x_1, x_2, \ldots, x_r, x_{r+1}, \ldots \qquad \text{with } x_n = x_{n-r} \diamond x_{n-s},$$

but to define and establish formally the period and structure of such sequences they must be viewed as iterates $\mathbf{x}, f(\mathbf{x}), f^2(\mathbf{x}), \ldots$ on the set X of $1 \times r$ vectors with elements in the set S on which the binary operation $\diamond$ is defined.

Various choices for S and $\diamond$ lead to interesting sequences—for example, when S is the set of reduced residues of some modulus m and $\diamond$ is addition or subtraction mod m; S is the set of reduced residues relatively prime to m and $\diamond$ is multiplication; S is the set of $1 \times k$ binary vectors and $\diamond$ is addition of binary vectors (exclusive-or); S is the set of floating-point computer numbers $0 \leq x < 1$ having 24-bit fractions and $x \diamond y = \{$if $x > y$ then $x - y$ else $x - y + 1\}$. Such generators are often designated $F(r, s, \diamond)$ generators.

Implementations of lagged-Fibonacci generators require a table of the previous r numbers, say $L(1)$, $L(2), \ldots, L(r)$ and two pointers I, J pointing to the last values used in the previous $x \diamond y$ operation. Then instructions equivalent to these are programmed:

```
K ← L[I] ◇ L[J]
L[I] ← K
I ← I − 1; if I = 0 then I ← r endif
J ← J − 1; if J = 0 then I ← r endif
return K
```

While examples of generators of each of the three standard methods described above are widely used and—for most purposes—work quite well, new methods are always being developed. All standard generators (with the exception of lagged-Fibonacci using multiplication) fail one or more stringent tests of randomness such as those described in Marsaglia (1985, 1995), and many of them have periods too short for the huge samples that current computer speeds make possible.

Combination Generators

Experience has shown, and there is theory to support it, that combining two different kinds of generators, by perhaps subtraction or multiplication, produces a *combination* generator that has much longer period and performs better, or no worse than, either component in tests of randomness. The McGill Random Number Generator Super-Duper, one of the most commonly used generators of the past 30 years, combines a congruential generator with a shift-register generator. Its period is about 2^{62}. An example of a simpler high-quality combination generator is given in Table 1.

Periods and Seed Values

An ideal generator should have period as great as the number of possible choices for seed values. Then, if the seed values are $x_1, x_2, \ldots, x_r$ and the sequence is strictly periodic, every possible r-tuple of x's will appear in the full sequence—a desirable uniformity property. Except for trivial cases of little interest, the lagged-Fibonacci generators—until recently the record holders for long periods—do not have this property. The lagged-Fibonacci generators $F(r, s, - \bmod 2^{32})$, $F(r, s, * \bmod 2^{32})$ or $F(r, s, - \bmod 1)$ have periods on the order of 2^{32+r}, 2^{30+r}, 2^{24+r}, far short of the ideals of 2^{32r}, 2^{30r} or 2^{24r} that are the number of possible choices of seed values. (Nonetheless, their periods are still far longer than those for $F(r, s, \oplus)$ generators using exclusive-or, for which the period is at most 2^r, whatever the word size.)

Of course, congruential generators satisfy that criterion: the period equals the number of choices for the seed value. But that period, of the order of 2^{32}, is far too short for modern needs. The full period can be quickly exhausted and it cannot provide the variety of possible k-tuples of numbers that probability theory says should be encountered in long streams.

There exist longer period generators for which the period equals the number of choices of seed values. One such class comes from extending the idea of a congruential generator for a prime modulus. For example, if p is the Mersenne prime $2^{31} - 1$ then the sequence produced by $x_n = 1999x_{n-1} + 4444x_{n-2} \bmod p$ has period $p^2 - 1$ for any initial seed values x_1,

Table 1. Examples of various kinds of random number generators.

Line	Seeds: number and type	Type and generating rule	Approximate period
		Congruential	
1	1 32-bit odd Integer	$x_n = 69069x_{n-1} \bmod 2^{32}$	2.1×10^9
2	1 32-bit integer	$x_n = 69069x_{n-1} + 1 \bmod 2^{32}$	4.3×10^9
3	1 31-bit integer $\neq 0$	$x_n = 16807x_{n-1} \bmod 2^{31} - 1$	2.1×10^9
		Extended congruential	
4	2 31-bit integers	$x_n = 1999x_{n-1} + 4444x_{n-2} \bmod 2^{31} - 1$	4.6×10^{18}
		Lagged Fibonacci	
5	17 32-bit integers	$x_n = x_{n-17} - x_{n-5} \bmod 2^{32}$	2.8×10^{14}
6	17 32-bit odd integers	$x_n = x_{n-17} * x_{n-5} \bmod 2^{32}$	7.0×10^{13}
7	17 32-bit integers	$x_n = x_{n-17} \oplus x_{n-5} \bmod 2^{32}$	1.3×10^5
8	55 32-bit integers	$x_n = x_{n-55} - x_{n-24} \bmod 2^{32}$	7.7×10^{25}
9	55 32-bit odd integers	$x_n = x_{n-55} * x_{n-24} \bmod 2^{32}$	1.9×10^{25}
10	97 reals	$x_n = x_{n-97} - x_{n-33} \bmod 1$	1.3×10^{36}
11	607 32-bit integers	$x_n = x_{n-607} - x_{n-273} \bmod 2^{32}$	10^{192}
		Subtract-with-borrow	
12	847 bits	$x_n = x_{n-240} - x_{n-847} - c \bmod 2$	9.4×10^{254}
13	1751 bits	$x_n = x_{n-472} - x_{n-1751} - c \bmod 2$	1.3×10^{527}
14	37 32-bit integers	$x_n = x_{n-24} - x_{n-37} - c \bmod 2^{32}$	4.1×10^{354}
15	30 64-bit integers	$x_n = x_{n-6} - x_{n-30} - c \bmod 2^{64}$	9.5×10^{577}
16	39 reals	$x_n = x_{n-25} - x_{n-39} - c \bmod 1$	8.6×10^{278}
		Combination	
17	2 32-bit x's, odd	$x_n = x_{n-1} * x_{n-2} \bmod 2^{32}$	
	3 y's $< 2^{30} - 35$	$y_n = y_{n-3} - y_{n-1} \bmod 2^{30} - 35$	
		$z_n = x_n - y_n \bmod 2^{32}$	2.3×10^{18}
		Multiply-with-carry	
18	32-bit x, 32-bit $c < a$	$x_n = ax_{n-1} + c \bmod 2^{32}$	4.6×10^{18}
19	16-bit x, 16-bit $c < a$	$x_n = ax_{n-1} + c \bmod 2^{16}$	2.6×10^9

x_2 not both zero, and there are $p^2 - 1$ possible choices. It is not easy, but one can find constants, c_1, c_2, c_3, so that $x_n = c_1 x_{n-1} + c_2 x_{n-2} + c_3 x_{n-3} \bmod p$ has period $p^3 - 1$ for any of the $p^3 - 1$ possible seeds x_1, x_2, x_3 not all zero, and so on: for any prime p, and any lag k, there are k constants such that the sequence $x_n = c_1 x_{n-1} + \cdots + c_k x_{n-k} \bmod p$ has period $p^k - 1$ for any choice of k seed values not all zero.

Unfortunately, implementations of these maximal-period generators require, for each new x, k multiplications and additions modulo the prime p. This makes them very slow unless k is small. A recently developed method that uses only two additions or subtractions and still produces nearly maximal periods is the subtract-with-borrow method described next.

Subtract-With-Borrow Generators

These new generators, developed by Marsaglia and Zaman, produce extremely long-period sequences. They are like lagged-Fibonacci generators using subtraction: each new x is obtained by subtracting, modulo some base b, two previous x's, except that a "carry" bit is also included:

$$x_n = x_{n-s} - x_{n-r} - c \bmod b.$$

Given r seed values $x_1, \ldots, x_r$ in $0 \le x < b$, not all zero, and an initial carry bit c, the rule for forming each new x_n and each new carry bit c is

Form $t = x_{n-s} - x_{n-r} - c \bmod b$.
If $t \ge 0$ then $x_n = t$ and $c = 0$,
Else $x_n = t + b$ and $c = 1$

As do lagged-Fibonacci generators, these generators require that the previous r values be kept in a table. This can be done with two pointers, as outlined above.

There are b^r choices for seed values, and certain choices of b, r, s, will attain virtually that maximal period. For example, with b near 2^{32} and r near 30, periods of the order of 2^{960} are obtained. Several examples are given in Table 1.

Multiply-With-Carry Generators

Experience has shown that multiplication is one of the best ways to scramble bits to produce new random numbers from old. If the CPU's built-in integer arithmetic is exploited to do this—in effect, using arithmetic modulo 2^{32}—for a congruential generator, the period is too short for modern requirements, and the trailing bits do not appear to be satisfactorily random. The period can be extended, and trailing bit behavior made satisfactory, if a prime modulus is used with a recursion such as $x_n = a_1 x_{n-1} + a_2 x_{n-2} \bmod p$. But arithmetic modulo a prime is awkward to implement. A new method, multiply-with-carry, has the advantage of exploiting the CPU's automatic integer arithmetic modulo 2^{16} or 2^{32} and yet provide longer periods as well as sequences that seem to pass all tests of randomness.

Similarly to subtract-with-borrow, a multiply-with-carry (MWC) generator keeps 32-bit current integers x and a current "carry," c. It has multiplier, a, chosen so that both $m = 2^{32}a - 1$ and $(m-1)/2$ are prime. (For 16-bit random integers $m = 2^{16}a - 1$.) Then the 64-bit expression $ax + c$ is formed. The lower 32 bits form the new x and the upper 32 bits, the new c. The successive values of x are the output of the generator. (For 16-bit integers, a 32-bit expression is formed with lower 16 bits the new x and upper 16 the new c.)

The period of such a MWC generator is $(m-3)/2$, typically about 2^{62} for 32-bit integers and 2^{30} for 16-bit integers. The theory behind these generators is in the PostScript (q.v.) file mwc1.ps in Marsaglia (1995). They are becoming the most common kind of random numbers in use today, because their apparently excellent randomness and ease of implementation in simple CPUs has made them widely used for slot machines and other gaming devices.

Unfortunately, most programming languages do not permit ready access to the double-length product of two single precision integers so machine language may be required to exploit fully the MWC method. But C++ or Fortran implementations can form random integers of double length by filling the upper and lower parts with two different MWC streams: 64-bit integers by two 32-bit streams or 32-bit integers by two 16-bit streams.

Here is an example in C++ programming: let w be an unsigned long word (i.e. 32 bits), with the current 16-bit integer x in the bottom half, the 16-bit carry in the top. The statement

```
w = 36969 * (w & 65535) + (w >> 16);
```

where & is bitwise AND and >> is the right shift operator, will create a new carry and a new 16-bit x in the top and bottom halves of w. Similarly, the bottom 16 bits after

```
z = 18000 * (z & 65535) + (z >> 16);
```

will create a separate stream of 16 bit random integers that can be concatenated with those of the w's to get a stream of about 2.9×10^{18} random 32-bit integers (the C routine would return $(z << 16) + (w \& 65535)$).

Tests of Random Number Generators

A random number generator is supposed to produce a sequence of independent uniform random variables

$U_1, U_2, \ldots$. Any function of the elements of such a sequence may be used to test that supposition; if the sampling distribution of the function is consistent with that called for by underlying theory, then the generator passes the test. Any number of tests are possible; many have been proposed. Probably the best test of a random number generator is to try it on a similar problem for which the answer—the probability distribution of the result—is known. A more or less standard set of tests is given in Knuth (1997), but most of those are tests the uniformity of the random numbers, not on their independence. More stringent tests of both uniformity and independence are given in Marsaglia (1985, 1995). Most of the standard generators, having periods of the order of $2^{32} \approx 4 \times 10^9$, fail one or more of the stringent tests if samples of millions or tens of millions of numbers are used. Such sample sizes are quite feasible for Monte Carlo simulations in current computers. Periods around 2^{32} are just too short to contain the variety of k-tuples of numbers that probability theory says should be encountered in large samples. However, newer generators, such as those in Table 1, having much longer periods, seem to pass stringent tests even with such large samples.

Some Examples

Table 1 lists examples of some of the most successful kinds of random number generators. Lines 1–3 are examples of three of the most frequently used congruential generators; line 4 is an example of an extended congruential generator with prime modulus p and period $p^2 - 1$. Lines 5–11 give examples of lagged-Fibonacci generators with increasingly long periods, except for line 7, which shows the drastic reduction of period arising from use of the exclusive-or operation rather than subtraction or multiplication.

The tremendously long periods of subtract-with-borrow generators are exemplified in lines 12–16, and line 17 gives an example of a very good generator that arises from combining two simple generators that individually are not very promising. Lines 18 and 19 indicate the general form of multiply-with-carry generators. For 32 bits, the multiplier a is chosen so that both $m = 2^{32}a - 1$ and $(m - 1)/2$ are prime. Then the period is $(m - 3)/2$. For 16 bits, use $m = 2^{16}a - 1$.

Bibliography

1972. Marsaglia, G. "The Structure of Linear Congruential Sequences," in *Applications of Number Theory to Numerical Analysis* (ed. Z. K. Zaremba), 248–285. New York: Academic Press.

1985. Marsaglia, G. "A Current View of Random Number Generators," Keynote Address, *Proceedings, Computer Science and Statistics: 16th Symposium on the Interface.* New York: Elsevier.

1987. Ripley, B. D. *Stochastic Simulation.* New York: John Wiley.

1995. Marsaglia, G. *The Marsaglia Random Number CDROM with the Diehard Battery of Tests of Randomness.* Produced by Dept. of Statistics, The Florida State University under an NSF Grant. Internet version available at `http://www.stat.fsu.edu/pub/diehard`.

1997. Knuth, D. E. *The Art of Computer Programming: Volume 2: Seminumerical Algorithms*, 3rd Ed. Reading, MA: Addison-Wesley.

George Marsaglia

READ-ONLY MEMORY (ROM)

For articles on related subjects *see* CYCLE TIME; EMULATION; FIRMWARE; MEMORY: MAIN; MICROPROGRAMMING; OPTICAL STORAGE; and PERSONAL COMPUTING.

Read-only memory (ROM) is based on a wide spectrum of storage techniques, many of which should be more accurately referred to as "slow write" storages. The basic idea behind read-only storage is that, for a number of applications, the contents of the storage are relatively fixed for a long period of time. In fact, for some applications, the contents of storage are not altered during the life of the machine. An example is the use of ROM in early microcomputers to hold an invariant copy of the processor for a high-level language such as Basic or Pascal. Another use of ROM is to hold the *bootstrap loader* (*see* BOOTSTRAP), a program that is run upon computer startup to start other programs and to transfer control to them.

Read-only memory can be factory programmed (and never altered) or field programmed [P(rogrammable) ROM]. In the latter case the user installs the storage contents and may subsequently change the contents. These programmable ROMs are erased by exposing the device to a special light source [E(rasable)PROM] or by using a special voltage line [E(lectrically)EPROM].

Michael J. Flynn

Figure 1. A 24,000-bit read-only storage chip, using field-effect transistor technology packaged in a 1-in square metallized ceramic substrate.

REAL-TIME CLOCK

See INTERVAL TIMER.

REAL-TIME SYSTEMS

For articles on related subjects *see* CONCURRENT PROGRAMMING; CONTROL APPLICATIONS; DATABASE CONCURRENCY CONTROL; DISTRIBUTED SYSTEMS; EMBEDDED SYSTEM; FAULT-TOLERANT COMPUTING; INTERRUPT; MULTIPROCESSING; MULTIPROGRAMMING; MULTITASKING; SCHEDULING ALGORITHMS; TIME SHARING; and TRANSACTION PROCESSING.

Real-time systems are those systems in which the correctness of the system depends not only on the logical result of computation, but also on the time at which the results are produced (Stankovic, 1988). Real-time systems span a broad spectrum of complexity from very simple microcontrollers (such as a microprocessor controlling an automobile engine) to highly sophisticated, complex and distributed systems (such as air traffic control for continental USA). Other examples of real-time systems include command and control systems, process control systems, flight control systems, flexible manufacturing applications, intensive care monitoring, intelligent highway systems, and multimedia and high-speed communication systems (Buttazzo, 1997; Kopetz, 1997; Stankovic and Ramamritham, 1988, 1994).

Typically, a real-time system consists of a *controlling system* and a *controlled system*. For example, in an automated factory, the controlled system is the factory floor with its robots, assembling stations, and the assembled parts, while the controlling system is the computers, sensors, actuators, and human interfaces that manage and coordinate the activities on the factory floor. The controlled system can be viewed as the *environment* with which the computer interacts.

The controlling system interacts with its environment based on the information available about the environment from various sensors. It is imperative that the state of the environment, as recorded by the controlling system, be consistent with the actual state of the environment. Otherwise, the effects of the controlling system's activities may be disastrous. Hence periodic monitoring of the environment as well as timely processing of the sensed information is necessary.

Timing correctness requirements in a real-time system arise because of the *physical impact* of the controlling system's activities upon its environment. For example, if the computer controlling a robot does not command it to stop or turn on time, the robot might collide with another object on the factory floor, possibly causing serious damage. In many real-time systems even more severe consequences will result if timing as well as logical correctness properties of the system are not satisfied; e.g. consider nuclear power plants or air traffic control systems failing.

In a real-time system, the characteristics of the various application tasks are usually known *a priori* and the tasks might be scheduled statically or dynamically. While static specification of schedules is typically the case for periodic tasks, the opposite is true for aperiodic tasks. When the periodic temperature monitor of a nuclear reactor senses a problem in the core, it can invoke another (aperiodic) task to activate the appropriate elements of the reactor to correct the problem, for example, to force more coolant into the reactor core. In this case, the deadline for the aperiodic task can be determined, in advance, from the physical characteristics of the reactions within the core. On the other hand, the deadline of a task that controls a robot on a factory floor must be determined dynamically from the speed and direction of the robot. The command to the robot forcing it to turn right, left, or stop should be generated before this deadline.

A large proportion of currently implemented real-time systems are static in nature, but by necessity, next generation systems will have to adopt solutions that are more dynamic and flexible. This is because such systems will be large and complex and will function in environments that are uncertain, and are also physically distributed. More important, they will have to be maintainable and extensible due to their evolving nature and projected long lifetimes. Because of these characteristics, real-time systems need to be *fast*, *predictable*, *reliable*, and *adaptive*.

Building a real-time system can vary from a simple task to an extremely complex task for which current techniques are not adequate. The difficulty depends on the characteristics of the real-time system, such as (1) how close or far away the deadlines are, (2) how important it is to meet the deadlines, (3) the level of reliability required, (4) the size of the system and degree of coordination among components of the system, and (5) the type of environment in which the system operates.

Aspects of Real-Time Systems

Achieving quantifiable real-time performance requires integrated solutions across many areas, including real-time kernels, real-time scheduling, real-time architectures, real-time databases, fault tolerance, programming languages, communication protocols, distributed systems, and design methodologies.

One focal point for developing real-time systems is the real-time operating system kernel (*q.v.*). The kernel must provide basic support for predictably satisfying real-time constraints, for fault tolerance and distribution, and for integrating time-constrained resource allocations and scheduling across a spectrum of resource types including sensor processing, communications, CPU, memory, and other forms of I/O.

There are extensive results about real-time scheduling. Theoretical results have identified worst case bounds for dynamic online algorithms, and complexity results have been produced for various types of assumed task set characteristics. Queueing theoretic analysis has been applied to real-time systems covering algorithms based on real-time variations of FCFS, earliest deadline, and least laxity (*see* QUEUEING THEORY). In FCFS, the queue of waiting tasks is ordered by first come, first served, while for earliest deadline it is ordered by the deadlines of the waiting tasks, and for least laxity by deadline minus computation time. Scheduling results have also been developed for imprecise computation (a situation where tasks obtain a greater value the longer they execute up to some maximum value). More applied scheduling results have also been produced with an extensive set of improvements to the rate monotonic (RM) algorithm. RM is a simple algorithm that assigns the highest priority to the most frequent periodic task, the second highest priority to the second most frequent periodic task, etc. RM has been extended to the *sporadic server algorithm* which integrates scheduling aperiodic tasks and periodic tasks. Additional results have been developed to address the problem of priority inversion (a situation where a low priority task may block a high priority task usually due to shared resources), and a set of algorithms that perform dynamic online planning.

A priori calculation of static schedules has been applied to provide what is called 100% guarantees for critical tasks. While these *a priori* analyses are very valuable, because these analyses are logical analyses, 100% guarantees do not mean that scheduling errors cannot occur in the actual running of the system. It is important to know that these 100% guarantees are based on many and sometimes unrealistic assumptions. If the assumptions are a poor match for what can be expected from the environment (more and more likely in a distributed environment), then even with 100% guarantees the system may miss deadlines. Hence two key issues are to choose an algorithm whose assumptions provide the greatest coverage of what *really* happens in the environment, and to have good error-handling capabilities. For all the scheduling results mentioned, the trend has been to deal with more and more complicated task sets and environment characteristics (e.g. multiprocessing, distributed computing, and tasks with precedence constraints). While many interesting scheduling results have been produced, the state of the art still provides

piecemeal solutions. Many realistic issues have not yet been addressed in an integrated and comprehensive manner.

Real-time systems are usually special purpose. The computer architectures (*q.v.*) used to support such applications also tend to be special purpose. However, the current trend is one in which more "off-the-shelf" components are being used to produce more generic architectures.

One aspect of architecture for real-time computing is the facility with which the worst-case execution time can be calculated. Worst-case execution times of programs are dependent on the system hardware, the operating system, the compiler used, and the programming language used. Many hardware features that have been introduced to speed up the average-case behavior of programs pose problems when information about worst-case behavior is sought. For instance, the ubiquitous caches, pipelining, dynamic RAMs, and virtual (secondary) memory, lead to highly nondeterministic hardware behavior. Similarly, compiler optimizations tailored to make better use of these architectural enhancements as well as techniques such as reorganization of loops contribute to poor predictability of code execution times. System interferences due to interrupt-handling, shared memory references, and preemptions are additional complications. Any approach to the determination of execution times of real-time programs has many complexities, but they must be solved for real-time computing.

Many real-time system architectures consist of multiprocessors, networks of uniprocessors, or networks of uni- and multiprocessors. Such architectures have potential for high fault tolerance, but are also much more difficult to manage in a way such that deadlines are predictably met. Fault tolerance must be designed in at the start, must encompass both hardware and software, and must be integrated with timing constraints.

A real-time database is a database system where (at least some) transactions have explicit timing constraints such as deadlines, and data may have validity intervals. For example, a data item representing pressure in a chemical process may only be valid for 100 milliseconds. In such a system, transaction processing must satisfy not only the database consistency constraints, but also the timing constraints of the transaction and data it uses. Real-time database systems can be found, for instance, in program trading in the stockmarket, radar tracking systems, battle management systems, and computer-integrated manufacturing systems. Some of these systems (such as program trading in the stock market) are *soft* real-time systems, so designated because missing a deadline is not catastrophic. Usually, research into algorithms and protocols (*q.v.*) for such systems explicitly addresses deadlines and makes a best effort at meeting them. In soft real-time systems there are no guarantees that specific tasks will make their deadlines. This is in contrast to *hard* real-time systems (such as controlling a nuclear power plant) where missing a deadline may result in catastrophic consequences. In hard real-time systems, *a priori* guarantees are required for critical tasks (or transactions).

Most current real-time database work deals with soft real-time systems. Here the need for an integrated approach that includes time-constrained protocols for concurrency control, conflict resolution, CPU and I/O scheduling, transaction restart and wakeup, deadlock resolution, buffer management, and commit processing has been identified. Many protocols based on time-cognizant locking, optimistic, and time-stamped concurrency control have been developed and evaluated in testbed or simulation (*q.v.*) environments. In most cases the optimistic approaches seem to work best. Most hard real-time database systems are main-memory databases of small size with predefined transactions, hand-crafted for efficient performance.

In summary, real-time systems are becoming more prevalent and important and their proliferation is being accelerated by high-speed networking, the Internet (*q.v.*), mobile computing (*q.v.*), and multimedia (*q.v.*), all of which have timing constraints that must be met.

Bibliography

1988. Stankovic, J. "Misconceptions About Real-time Computing: A Serious Problem for Next Generation Systems," *IEEE Computer*, **21**, *10*, 10–19.

1988. Stankovic, J., and Ramamritham, K. *Hard Real-Time Systems*, Tutorial Text. Washington, DC: IEEE Computer Society Press.

1994. Stankovic, J., and Ramamritham, K. *Advances in Real-Time Systems*, Tutorial Text, Washington, DC: IEEE Computer Society Press.

1997. Buttazzo, G. C. *Hard Real-Time Computing Systems*. Boston, MA: Kluwer Academic.

1997. Kopetz, H. *Real-Time Systems: Design Principles for Distributed Embedded Applications*. Boston, MA: Kluwer Academic.

John A. Stankovic

REBOOT

See BOOTSTRAP.

RECORD

For articles on related subjects *see* BLOCK AND BLOCKING FACTOR; DATA STRUCTURES; and FILE.

A *record* is an organized and identifiable aggregate of data transcribed on a computer storage medium. Each record comprises data values that have an underlying relationship to one another. For example, a personnel record usually contains data such as Social Security number, first name, middle initial, last name, date of birth, next of kin, and home address. All these data are *attributes* (descriptors, locators, identifiers, etc.) peculiar to this individual.

Data elements in a record may be of a similar or dissimilar type: bits, numbers, character strings, etc. The contents of punched cards and printer lines were often called *unit records*, since these document lengths were pre-defined for use with associated electromechanical devices. Magnetic tape and disk drives usually accommodate *variable-length records*, in which the amount of data per record varies according to activity, age, etc., of the individual. Records of the same type are usually grouped into larger aggregates, called *files* or *data sets* or *databases*. When written sequentially into a file, records are collected into intermediate aggregates called *blocks*, whose lengths are efficient for transcription to tape or disk devices. In theory, a file or database could comprise a single block containing all its records. In practice, a large file or database may contain hundreds or thousands of blocks, each containing one or more records. The number of records per block, called the *blocking factor*, is an important consideration in determining the efficiency of file processing.

High-level languages permit the creation of record types whose instances become the actual records to be stored in main memory or in external memory. The first widely used language to do so was Cobol. The corresponding C and C++ entities are called *structures*. Pascal record types are defined through use of the reserved word **record**. An example record type definition and corresponding variable declaration in Pascal follows:

```
type
    payrec=record
                name: array[1..28] of char;
                rate: real;
                hours: array[1..7] of real;
                union: boolean
            end;
var
    r:payrec; seq: array[1..100] of payrec;
    f: file of payrec
```

The variable *r* is now an individual instance of a *payrec*, the variable *seq* is an array of *payrec*s stored in main memory, and the variable *f* is a sequential file on an external storage medium to which *payrec* records may be written and later read with statements of the form *write(f,r)* and *read(f,r)*. On a computer whose real values occupy four bytes and booleans and characters occupy one byte, each `pay-rec` record transmitted would consist of a sequence of $488\ (= 28 \times 8 + 32 + 32 \times 7 + 1 \times 8)$ information bits plus any parity bits that may be added behind the scenes. Each binary record is copied as an aggregate without the programmer having to read or write record components one by one.

Record types in programming languages play an important role in allowing the programmer to reduce complexity by "chunking"—combining heterogeneous but related information into single units on which the program can operate. With some modification to permit information hiding (*q.v.*), they also provide a basis for objects in object-oriented programming (*q.v.*). Objects are like records that hold both private data and public routines that operate on the data. Finally, linked data structures such as lists (*q.v.*) and trees (*q.v.*) can be implemented by means of records that hold both data and links to the next part of the structure.

David N. Freeman and Edwin D. Reilly

RECURSION

For articles on related subjects *see* ACTIVATION RECORD; FUNCTIONAL PROGRAMMING; ITERATION; STACK; and TURING MACHINE.

Recursion refers to several related concepts in computer science and mathematics. One or more functions of an integer variable are defined by giving initial values and by giving the value for larger integers in terms of smaller ones. No single definition is generally accepted, so we will give examples of increasing complexity.

Recursion Relations

1. The Fibonacci sequence is given by the equations
$$f_0 = 1,$$
$$f_1 = 1,$$
$$f_{n+1} = f_n + f_{n-1} \qquad n \geq 1$$

2. When differential equations are to be solved numerically (*see* NUMERICAL ANALYSIS), *recursion relations* such as
$$f(x_0 + nh) = F(f(x_0 + (n-1)h), f(x_0 + (n-2)h),$$
$$\dots, f(x_0 + (n-k)h))$$
arise where f is, in general, a vector of real numbers.

3. When linear differential equations are solved by series, recursion relations for the coefficients of the powers of the independent variables arise.

Recursive Functions

The systematic study of recursion began in the 1920s when mathematical logic began to treat questions of definability, computability, and decidability. An important role is played by *primitive recursive functions*.

Primitive recursive functions are integer functions of integers built up from addition and multiplication of integers and previously defined primitive recursive functions by the primitive recursion scheme:
$$f(0, x_2, \dots, x_k) = g(x_2, \dots, x_k),$$
$$f(x_1 + 1, x_2, \dots, x_k) = h(f(x_1, \dots, x_k), x_1, \dots, x_k).$$

Here, g and h are primitive recursive functions of $k - 1$ and $k + 1$ arguments, respectively. As an example, we define $n!$, where n is a positive integer by $n! = f(n)$ where $f(0) = 1$ and $f(n+1) = (n+1) \cdot f(n)$. So, in this case, g is a function of 0 arguments, namely, the constant 1, and $h(u, v) = (v + 1) u$.

All the common functions of number theory are primitive recursive. Moreover, many important functions on countable domains other than the integers correspond to primitive recursive functions when we choose a specific enumeration for the domain.

Primitive recursive functions are included in general recursive functions. The definition of general recursive functions is like that given above for primitive recursive functions, except that the relations are replaced by an arbitrary finite collection of equations relating the values of f for different arguments, and the function is considered defined if and only if a unique value of $f(x_1, \dots, x_k)$ can be deduced from the equations for each k-tuplet $(x_1, \dots, x_k)$. Naturally, if someone gives you an arbitrary collection of such relations, you may not be able to determine whether $f(x_1, \dots, x_k)$ is uniquely determined, so you may not know whether you have a general recursive function. This difficulty is unavoidable. There is no way to give a definition scheme that is always guaranteed to give a function but which will give all computable functions. This fact is itself expressed in the terminology of recursive function theory by the statement that the set of computable functions is *recursively enumerable* but not recursive. The famous example of a general recursive function that is not primitive recursive is the *Ackermann function*, defined by the equations
$$A(0, n, p) = n + p, \qquad A(1, 0, p) = 0$$
$$A(m + 2, 0, p) = 1$$
and
$$A(m + 1, n + 1, p) = A(m, A(m + 1, n, p), p)$$

An important result for computer science is that the general recursive functions coincide with the functions defined by a Turing machine, which is a simple form of computer. They also coincide with the functions of integers defined by Pascal (*q.v.*) or C++ (*q.v.*) programs, assuming that the program can cope with whatever size integers arise.

Both programs and general recursion schemata, in general, give *partial functions* because the computation may terminate for some values of the arguments and not for others.

The study of computable functions is the domain of recursive function theory, an active branch of mathematics. The connection between current research in recursive function theory and computing practice, or even current research in computer science, is rather tenuous. This situation might change because of developments in either field.

Recursive Procedures

In programming, it is frequently convenient to have a procedure use itself as a subprocedure. If a procedure does this, it is called *recursive*. Recursive procedures are particularly natural in dealing with symbolic expressions because the structure of the programs often matches the structure of the data. As far as programming languages are concerned, recursive procedures are quite natural; it requires a special statement in the definition of the language to forbid them. However, implementing them requires that a special kind of object code be compiled, and early versions of programming languages like Fortran (*q.v.*) did not allow them. The problem is that variables in the program correspond to locations in the machine, and when the program is called by itself, it will use these same locations, overwriting their previous contents. Therefore, recursive programs use a data structure called a *stack* to store the contents of variables that must be saved. This storage can be done by the calling routine before it invokes the subroutine, or by the subroutine before it uses the program variables.

After the variables have been saved on the stack, the pointer into the stack is adjusted to account for the number and sizes of variables stored, so that subsequent saving on the stack will use fresh storage. When the subroutine exits, the contents of the saved variables are restored from the stack to their previous values, and the *stack pointer* is reduced by the amount it was previously increased. This is done by the caller or by the subroutine, according to whether the caller or subroutine did the original storing. An alternative technique is to use the stack for all temporary program variables. In this case, it is unnecessary to move data around, and it is only necessary to change the stack pointer when subroutines are entered and left.

This technique is now common (*see* ACTIVATION RECORD). Recursive programs can be written in any programming language by explicitly programming the saving and restoring.

The first languages to use recursive subroutines on a regular basis were the IPL languages of Newell, Shaw, and Simon. Lists were used for the stack and the saving and restoring was done explicitly by the programmer. The first language to provide an automatic mechanism for recursion was Lisp (*q.v.*). Algol 60 and all of its successors, such as Pascal, C++, and Ada, also allow recursion, as do virtually all other programming languages today, including Fortran 95.

Many computers have special instructions for handling stacks (e.g. the PUSH and POP instructions of the Digital Equipment VAX). Other machines, such as the Burroughs B5000 and its successors, had instructions that used a hardware stack directly. These special facilities give a modest increase in the efficiency of recursive programming.

Recursive Conditional Expressions

The recursive use of conditional expressions provides an economical and elegant way of specifying the functions that are computable in terms of a collection of base functions. This technique is the basis of the Lisp programming language and also of the theoretical system of Dana Scott for studying the properties of computer programs. A conditional expression has the form, in Algol-like notation, of

> **if** p **then** a **else** b.

It is evaluated by first evaluating the propositional expression p. If p is TRUE, the value of the conditional expression is that of a, and if the value of p is FALSE, the value of the conditional expression is that of b. It is important to note that only one of a or b is actually evaluated.

A simple example of the use of conditional expressions is to define the absolute value of a number by

> $|x| =$ **if** $x < 0$ **then** $-x$ **else** x.

Conditional expressions are used to define functions recursively by writing the definition in the form

$$f(x, \ldots, z) \leftarrow E\{x, \ldots, z, f, g, \ldots, h\}.$$

where E is an expression involving the variables $x, \ldots, z$, the function f being defined, and known or previously defined functions $g, \ldots, h$. An example of such a definition is

> $n! \leftarrow$ **if** $n = 0$ **then** 1 **else** $n \cdot (n-1)!$ (1)

The general method for evaluating recursive conditional expressions is illustrated by using the above definition to evaluate 3!. Namely, we have

```
3! = if 3 = 0 then 1 else 3 · (3 - 1)!
   = 3 · 2! = 3 · (if 2 = 0 then 1 else 2 · (2 - 1)!)
   = 3 · 2 · (if 1 = 0 then 1 else 1 · (1 - 1)!)
   = 3 · 2 · 1 · (if 0 = 0 then 1 else 0 · (0 - 1)!)
   = 3 · 2 · 1 · 1 = 6.
```

Note that the rule for evaluating conditional expressions ensures that the computer never attempts to evaluate $(-1)!$. This is necessary, since its evaluation would not terminate.

As a second example, the Ackermann function is written as a recursive conditional expression as follows:

```
A(m, n, p) ←
     if m = 0 then n + p
     else if n = 0 then (if m = 1 then 0 else 1)
     else A(m - 1, (A(m, n - 1), p), p).
```

Several remarks are worth making.

First, in a programming language that uses recursive conditional expressions, 3! would not be evaluated by the above symbolic manipulation. Either (1) would be compiled into a recursive subroutine (i.e. a subroutine of the type explained above that calls itself and uses a stack to save intermediate results and return addresses), or a recursive interpreter would interpret a list structure version of (1).

Second, (1) can easily be replaced by another expression for the factorial that can be compiled into a non-recursive program. Namely, we write

```
n! ← fact (n, 0, 1)
```

where

```
fact(n, m, p) ← if m = n then p          (2)
     else fact (n, m + 1, (m + 1) p).
```

Now (2) can be translated into a non-recursive program because the only occurrence of "fact" on the right-hand side of the definition appears at the outer level; i.e. fact $(n, m + 1, (m + 1)p)$ gives the value of fact (n, m, p), in contrast to the situation in (1) where $(n - 1)!$ must be multiplied by n to given $n!$. This allows the object program to contain an ordinary jump to itself rather than a subroutine call. When this is possible, the function definition is called *iterative* or *tail-recursive*. Thus, "fact" is iterative, while the definition (1) is not. Recursive definitions cannot in general be replaced by iterative definitions except by encoding the stack as a variable in the program, and, if this has to be done, there is no advantage in the replacement. However, modern optimizing compilers for functional and procedural languages can automatically implement tail-recursive subprograms as efficiently as explicit iteration.

Third, there may be several occurrences of the function being defined on the right-hand side of the recursive definition, and whether the evaluation terminates may depend on which occurrence is evaluated first. The following example due to Morris shows this:

```
f(x, y) ← if x = 0 then 0 else f(x - 1, f(y - 2, x)).
```

The reader should evaluate $f(2, 1)$ to see the problem.

It is also possible to use recursive conditional expressions to define functions that take functions as arguments or give functions as results. Before scope rules (*see* BLOCK STRUCTURE) for the binding of names to objects were well understood, it was difficult to ensure that such functions would always work correctly, but now such "higher-order" functions are standard tools in functional programming (*q.v.*) languages.

Source Material

McCarthy *et al.* (1962) has some discussion of the implementation of recursion in Lisp, and Randell and Russell (1964) discuss the implementation of recursion in Algol. Wirth (1976) discusses when to use recursion and when to use iteration. Peter (1967) has a thorough treatment of subclasses of general recursive functions. The standard reference on recursive function theory was written by Kleene (1952), who gave a more elementary treatment in a later book (1967).

Recursion is a technique for the specification and implementation of algorithms that is part of every computer scientist's "toolkit". It is a part of the mathematical theory of programming, which has as a major object the ability to prove assertions about programs and to check these assertions on a computer (*see* PROGRAM VERIFICATION). It also plays an important role in the theory of programming languages semantics (*q.v.*).

Bibliography

1952. Kleene, S. C. *Introduction to Metamathematics*. Princeton, NJ: Van Nostrand Reinhold.
1962. McCarthy, J., Abrahams, P. W., Edwards, D. J., Hart, T. J., and Levin, M. I. *Lisp 1.5 Programmer's Manual*. Cambridge, MA: The MIT Press.
1964. Randell, B., and Russell, L. J. *Algol 60 Implementation: Translation and Use of Algol 60 Programs by Computers*. New York: Academic Press.
1967. Kleene, S. C. *Mathematical Logic*. New York: John Wiley.
1967. Peter, R. *Recursive Functions*. New York: Academic Press.
1974. Manna, Z. *Mathematical Theory of Computation*. New York: McGraw-Hill.
1986. Roberts, E. S. *Thinking Recursively*. New York: John Wiley.
1990. Meyer, B. *Introduction to the Theory of Programming Languages*. Upper Saddle River, NJ: Prentice Hall.
1993. Dewdney, A. K. *The Turing Omnibus*, 2nd Ed. New York: W. H. Freeman.

John McCarthy

REDUCED INSTRUCTION SET COMPUTER (RISC)

For articles on related subjects *see* CACHE MEMORY; COMPUTER ARCHITECTURE; INSTRUCTION-LEVEL PARALLELISM; INSTRUCTION SET; MICROPROGRAMMING; and PIPELINE.

Until 1975, computer architecture and, consequently, computer design and implementation had grown more complicated with each successive generation. Instruction sets were large and individual instructions were complicated. Some of these complications were done to insure compatibility across a family, some were done to be better targets for compilers (*q.v.*) and some were done for performance enhancements. The result was often an architecture and implementation that had a lot of rarely used instructions and mechanisms because the nature of the compiler changed or because the compiler didn't change when it should have. Many other instructions were seldom used because they covered a very specific case or the implementation penalty was too large. Compilers and their run-time environments did not use some instructions because they did not fit in very well with generated code. Some complex instructions had such poor implementations that it was better to program an equivalent sequence than to use such instructions. Often, the implementation relied on a "micro-engine" to implement these numerous and complex instructions. The micro-engine, a small processor within the CPU, had a micro instruction set. Microprograms or microcode written in these microinstructions interpreted the complex instructions.

Prior to the mid-1970s, the only computer architect whose views differed significantly from the foregoing was Seymour Cray, who, while with the Control Data Corporation (*q.v*) in the early 1960s, designed the CDC 6600 supercomputer (*q.v.*) to have a small, simple instruction set.

At the beginning of 1975, a group was organized at IBM's T. J. Watson Research Center that had as its goal producing a "super mini" computer, one in which the compiler, the operating system, and the architecture and the implementation were done in concert while maintaining a very simple data format and addressing model and uniformity of instruction execution times. This machine would not have a micro-engine, but since the instructions were simple, all instructions would be directly implemented in hardware. Like many of the early computers the group chose a name for the project based on the building number in which it was done, in this case the 801 building. Hence the computer became the 801.

The original ideas for the 801 came from IBM Fellow John Cocke. His basic ideas were to make all instruc-tions simple and have a machine organization that could execute one instruction every machine cycle, where this cycle was very fast. The basic machine had an instruction fetch and decode stage and a register fetch and execute stage. These stages were organized into a two-deep pipeline; that is, the machine would be executing one instruction while fetching the next sequential instruction. The register write-back of a result was combined with the register fetch of the next instruction. There were two caches in front of main memory. One cache contained instructions and the other contained data. As long as the data or instruction needed was in the cache, there was a one cycle penalty on loads and a one cycle instruction fetch penalty if a branch was taken. The instruction cache was viewed as a replacement for the microcode memory; that is, the memory holding the microinstructions to be executed by the micro-engine. In other words, a general mechanism (instruction cache) was substituted for a special mechanism (microcode memory), thereby gaining significant improvements in the execution time of sequences of single-cycle instructions. In addition, the group contained several experts on optimizing compilers, people who knew both the techniques and theory and also had produced several compilers for various architectures. The definition of these simple instructions came from the compiler implementers' need for uniformity of instruction format and optimizable representations, along with the engineers' demand that the instruction execution fit into a regime of the single-cycle execution without negative impact on the machine cycle time.

A set of principles emerged from this work that has influenced the work of many others in this field:

1. A small instruction set consisting of simple, fixed length, fixed format instructions that execute in a single machine cycle (*see* INSTRUCTION DECODING)

2. A large number of registers with all instructions defined to have separate operands for register sources and register targets

3. Use of an optimizing compiler, where machine performance was directly dependent on the compiler's ability to manage many resources that had previously been managed by hardware, such as storage delays and branch penalties.

These ideas were picked up, enhanced, and promoted by David Patterson at the University of California at Berkeley and John Hennessy at Stanford University. It was Patterson who first used the term RISC (Reduced Instruction Set Computer) for this philosophy and contrasted it with CISC (Complex Instruction Set Computer). It was soon after this that the

RISC ideas took hold and many organizations began to participate.

Perhaps the best way to describe the RISC concepts is through examples.

Moving a data object from one location to another in a CISC may be done with one instruction, which specifies the source address, the target address and the length of the object (sometimes the length may be implied or even stored in the object). The implementation of this one instruction tests for all the cases: source and target alignment, overlap or not, destructive or not, out of bounds or not. This one instruction spends many cycles performing these tests and then more cycles doing the move. In a RISC, this move operation would be done with multiple instructions: first the tests for the various cases, then in a loop, a load from the source address, a store into the target address, source address increment, target address increment, test for end of move and a conditional branch to the loop. Obviously, the function in both CISC and RISC is the same. The contrast is between the ability of a CISC compiler to detect this situation and then generate this instruction and the ability of a RISC compiler to detect actual alignment, overlap, etc. and generate specific code for the actual situation. This specific code might be significantly better and should not be any worse than the underlying implementation of the CISC instruction. Furthermore, the code in a RISC, having exposed the many attributes of the move instructions, allows for the optimization of these instructions with other instructions around the move, whereas on a CISC little optimization is possible.

Another example is adding one to a counter in storage. In a CISC, one instruction might do this whole function: fetching from storage, adding one, and storing back. In a RISC, three instructions are needed. The difference is that in a CISC no register is used (CISCs usually have a small number of registers) and in a RISC a register is used to hold the counter value (RISCs have a large number of registers). Again, performance is no worse in the RISC and an optimizing compiler would look for the case when the counter value was already in a register and not reload it, but simply increment that register and store the counter. This emphasis on a large number of registers also allows a compiler to interlace instructions of different code sequences, thereby hiding the delays associated with memory access or branch delays. Consider updating a counter while fetching new data. In a RISC, a compiler could completely overlap the counter update and fetching of new data, covering memory access delays by rearranging (interlacing) new data fetching with updating.

Our last example is branching, particularly conditional branching. The problem with branching is knowing early enough that a branch is to be taken so that the instructions at the branch target can be fetched without delay. A CISC might solve this problem with significant hardware (a branch history table or multiple path fetches). A typical RISC, however, would define a new type of branch, often called a delayed branch, one in which one or more instructions after the branch are executed while the branch target is fetched. In this way, there is no lost time if the compiler can find instructions to be placed after the branch that are not part of the condition leading to the branch.

RISC architecture has led to many advances in machine organizations, especially in the areas of pipelining and instruction-level parallelism. It has brought a better understanding of machine organization along with metrics that could be used in evaluating alternative designs. It has given rise to new machine organizations, including superscalar and VLIW.

Over time many of the ideas of RISC architecture and implementation have come into CISC implementations, especially optimizing compilers and a machine organization that relies heavily on pipelines and caches. However, the underlying differences will remain: RISC is a simpler architecture and does not have all the baggage of the previous generations. Eventually it will acquire its own baggage and perhaps the architectural cycle between RISC and CISC will repeat itself.

Bibliography

1980. Patterson, D. A., and Ditzel, D. R. "The Case for the Reduced Instruction Set Computer," *Computer Architecture News*, **8**, *6*, 25–33. The pro side of the initial debate on the value of RISC.

1980. Clark, D., and Strecker, W. D. "Comments on the Case for the Reduced Instruction Set Computer," *Computer Architecture News*, **8**, *6*, 34–38. The con side of the initial debate on the value of RISC.

1982. Radin, G. "The 801 Minicomputer," *Proc. Symposium on Architectural Support for Programming Languages and Operating Systems*, Palo Alto, CA, 39–47. The original 801 paper.

1987. Hopkins, M. "A Perspective on the 801/Reduced Instruction Set Computer," *IBM Systems Journal*, **26**, *1*, 107–121. A broad discussion of the design decisions made in the 801.

1990. Cocke, J., and Markstein, V. "The Evolution of RISC Technology at IBM," *IBM J. of Research and Development*, **34**, *1*, 9–38. Shows the impact of RISC technology on subsequent machine organizations.

1991. Bhandarkar, D., and Clark, D. "Performance from Architecture: Comparing a RISC and a CISC with Similar Hardware Organization," *Proc. Symposium on Architectural Support for Programming Languages and Operating Systems*, Santa Clara, CA, 310–319. Shows the value of RISC over CISC at the architecture level.

1996. Hennessy, J. L., and Patterson, D. A. *Computer Architecture: A Quantitative Approach*, 2nd Ed. San Francisco: Morgan Kaufmann. Though RISC is not in its title, this is the definitive exposition of RISC philosophy.

Richard R. Oehler

REDUNDANCY

For articles on related subjects *see* ERROR CORRECTING AND DETECTING CODE; ERRORS; FAULT-TOLERANT COMPUTING; HARDWARE RELIABILITY; and REDUNDANT ARRAY OF INEXPENSIVE DISKS.

A system is said to be nonredundant or is said to have a *simplex structure* if it is designed such that only the absolute minimum amount of hardware is used to implement its function. If, even after using the finest components available, the desired system reliability is not achieved, or if failure tolerance is desired as a system capability, then *redundancy* is incorporated into the design; i.e. more system elements are used than are absolutely necessary to realize all the system's functions. The additional system elements, referred to as the redundant elements, need not all necessarily be hardware elements, but may also be additional software (*software redundancy*), additional time (*time redundancy*—e.g. performing a computation more than once and comparing the results), and additional information (*information redundancy*—e.g. the application of error-detection and correction codes).

Redundancies are often interrelated. Additional software requires additional memory and additional time is used to execute the added software. The term *protective redundancy* is often used to characterize redundancy that has an overall beneficial effect on the system attributes, since redundancy alone without proper application may well become a liability. Protective redundancy is used to realize *fault-tolerant digital systems* and *self-repairing systems* by such means as triple or *N*-tuple modular redundancy (TMR, NMR), quadded redundancy, standby-replacement redundancy, hybrid redundancy, software redundancy, and the application of error-detection and correction codes.

Redundancy as a procedure for designing more reliable systems than allowed by the intrinsic reliability of the constituent components is as old as the discipline of engineering itself. An example of the use of redundancy in ancient times is provided in structures where more than the absolute minimum required number of struts were provided to support a structure. Thus, early uses of redundancy were used as insurance against (1) the lack of accurate knowledge of underlying phenomena, and (2) the lack of confidence in the available data on the materials used. Redundancy as a procedure is even more basic. This is evidenced by the testimony of evolutionary processes of life, which make abundant use of it (e.g. in the human body there are two kidneys, two lungs, two cerebral hemispheres, etc.). Also, in societal systems, protective redundancy is advocated by the truism "two heads are better than one," and conversely, the improper use of redundancy

by "too many cooks spoil the broth." Among other societal systems exhibiting the principles of redundancy is the typical committee that has an odd number of members so that a tie in balloting cannot occur. This is analogous to the majority voting redundancy used in some computer systems. Other examples will readily occur to the reader.

For the computer age, redundancy has been used at all levels of technology, from very large-scale-integrated (VLSI) devices, circuit logic, subsystem computers, disk drives (RAID), and even to entire networks of digital systems.

Bibliography

1998. Siewiorek, D. P., and Swarz, R. S. *Reliable Computer Systems: Design and Evaluation*, 3rd Ed. Natick, MA: A. K. Peters.

Frank P. Mathur

REDUNDANT ARRAY OF INEXPENSIVE DISKS (RAID)

For articles on related subjects *see* ACCESS TIME; ERROR CORRECTING AND DETECTING CODE; HARD DISK; MASS STORAGE; and MEMORY: AUXILIARY.

Introduction

RAID (*Redundant Array of Inexpensive* [or *Independent*] *Disks*) is an architectural concept developed to turn relatively slow and inexpensive hard disks into fast, large-capacity, and more reliable storage systems. The RAID concept was introduced by a team of researchers from the University of California at Berkeley in 1987. RAID systems derive their speed from striping data across multiple disks (placing successive pieces of a file on different disks), thus allowing parallel data accesses. Reliability is generally achieved through replication ("mirroring") or by using error detection and correction schemes across the disk array. (Mirroring is a technique that predates RAID, being used, for example, in the IBM AS/400 minicomputer.) There are many levels of RAID, which differ in the way they provide for speed and/or reliability. The original Berkeley work has specified RAID levels 0–5. Slight modifications to these levels have recently resulted in the specification of levels 6 and 7.

Raid Levels

RAID-0

RAID-0 only stripes (splits) the data across the array disks, which achieves speed through parallelism. RAID-0, however, does not improve reliability. As indicated in Fig. 1, each data object is striped across all disks in the array.

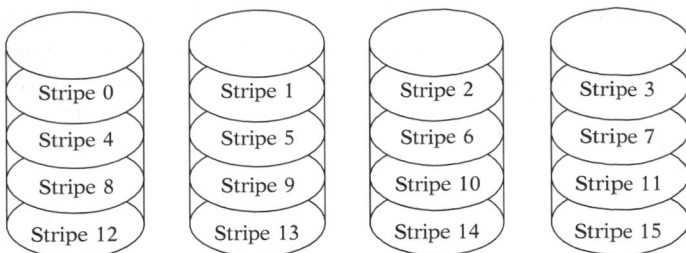

Figure 1. RAID Level 0 configuration showing the data striped across the disks of the array.

RAID-1

Unlike RAID-0, RAID-1 (Fig. 2b) focuses on reliability through redundancy, and does not offer speed. In this configuration two sets of disks are used, primary and secondary, where the secondary disks maintain an identical image of the primary disk data, which is striped across multiple disks as in RAID-0. Thus, if a disk in one set fails, one in the other set can replace it. This is clearly an expensive arrangement, as disk usage

drops to 50%. Furthermore, while reads can be faster since they can be done using the disk with the lower seek time, writes are slow, as there is always the need to write two copies.

RAID-2

In RAID-2, each block of data is striped across data disks by a stripe unit of either a bit or a byte to allow parallel accesses, as in RAID-0. In RAID-2, all the drive

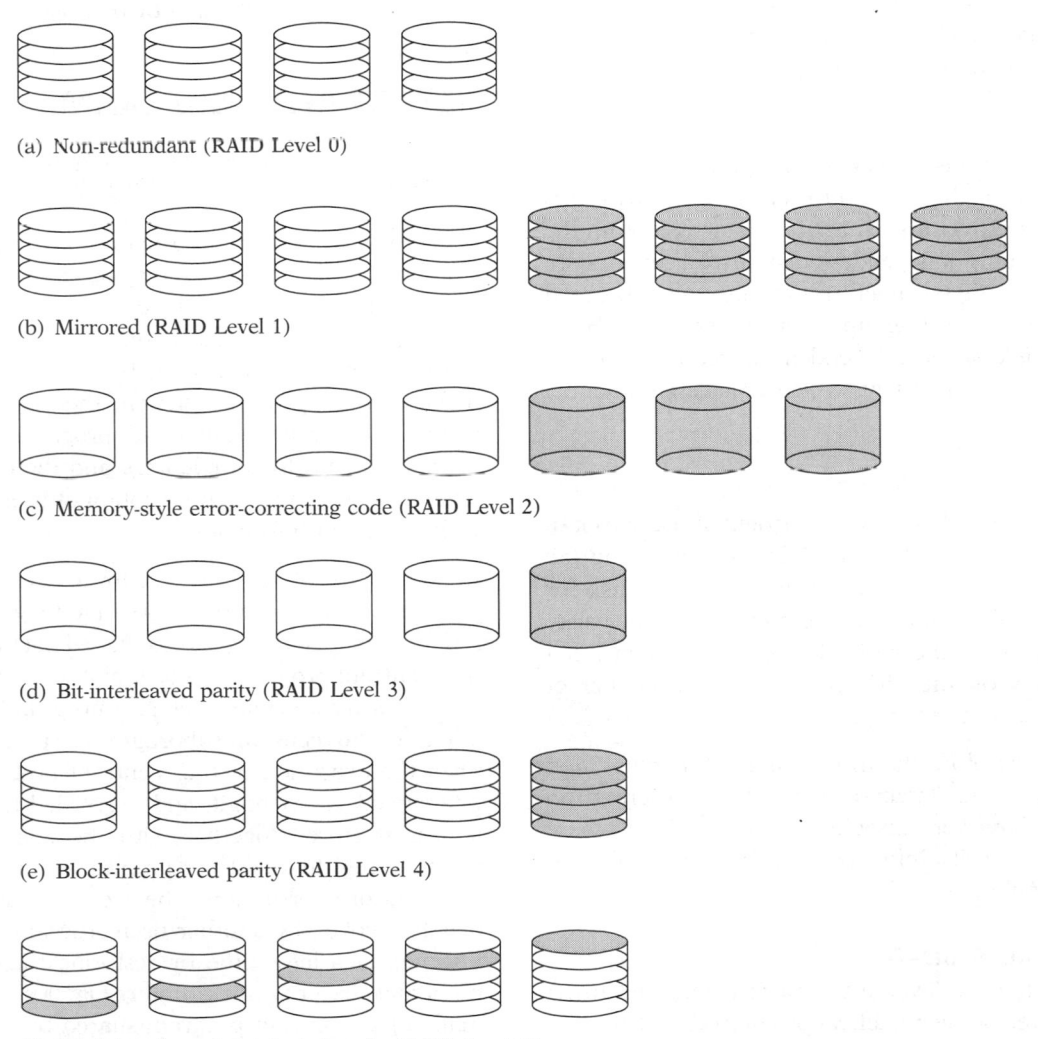

(a) Non-redundant (RAID Level 0)

(b) Mirrored (RAID Level 1)

(c) Memory-style error-correcting code (RAID Level 2)

(d) Bit-interleaved parity (RAID Level 3)

(e) Block-interleaved parity (RAID Level 4)

(f) Block-interleaved distributed parity (RAID Level 5)

Figure 2. Redundant array of inexpensive disks. Disks with multiple platters indicate block-level striping while disks without multiple platters indicate bit-level striping. The shaded platters represent redundant information (from Chen *et al.*, 1994, courtesy of ACM).

spindles have to be synchronized using a single actuator or multiple coupled actuators, as the data bits must be read in parallel. Error detection and correction is provided using additional disks, whose data is created using a Hamming error-correcting code, to allow recovery from a single disk failure (Fig. 2c shows four data disks and three for error correction). RAID-2 performs best for large transfers in which the seek time is rapidly amortized. It would deliver a performance close to that of a single disk for a short transaction, and would perform poorly, compared with independent disks, in doing a number of concurrent short transactions.

RAID-3

As seen in Fig. 2d, RAID 3 is similar to RAID-2, except that a single parity bit is used instead of the Hamming code, thus reducing the number of error detection/correction disks to one. If the parity bit indicates an error, disk controllers can then identify the faulty disk on their own without the need for an error-correcting code to locate the problem. The faulty disk can be then replaced and its data can be reconstructed using the remaining good disks and the parity disk.

RAID-4

RAID-4 (Fig. 2e) is similar in configuration to that of RAID-3, except that the unit used for data striping is the block (sector) rather than the bit or byte. With the large stripe unit, independent disk drive actuators are used and multiple small transactions can proceed concurrently, speeding up read transactions. However, multiple small independent writes must update the parity disk separately, which creates a sequential bottleneck.

RAID-5

RAID-5 (Fig. 2f) alleviates the sequential bottleneck of updating the parity disk in RAID-4 by spreading the parity information. Instead of using a single disk for parity, each of the data disks contains one of the parity blocks. Updating the parity blocks can thus proceed concurrently on the different disks by a number of small concurrent requests.

RAID-5 is therefore the most suitable for transaction processing, as in database applications. There is an overhead, however, associated with tracking where the relevant parity information is stored for a given data manipulation.

RAID-6 AND RAID-7

RAID-5 is the last level in the Berkeley-defined RAID architecture. Some modifications introduced by various implementations resulted in defining more levels. RAID-6 is an extension of level 5 in which disks are arranged in a two-dimensional array, and parity is determined in each dimension separately. RAID-7, in addition, uses dynamic mapping where each block of data does not always have to be stored in the same physical sector of a disk.

Conclusion

RAID-3 and RAID-5 are the two most popular levels of RAID. Which is better depends upon the application. RAID-5 is more suitable for database applications where small concurrent transactions can be supported efficiently. RAID-3, however, is most suited for large data accesses such as those found in scientific computing applications.

Bibliography

1994. Chen, P. M., Lee, E. K., Gibson, G. A. , Katz, R. H., and Patterson, D. A. "RAID: High-performance, Reliable Secondary Storage," *Computing Surveys*, **26**, *2*, 145–185.
1997. Raid Advisory Board. *The RAIDbook*, 6th Ed. http://www.raid-advisory.com.

Tarek El-Ghazawi and Gideon Frieder

REENTRANT PROGRAM

For articles on related subjects *see* COROUTINE; MULTIPROGRAMMING; and TIME SHARING.

In a time-sharing or multiprogramming environment, a number of user programs may be sharing a common pool of subprograms or processors. Therefore, it is necessary that the shared routines be written in such a form that each can be invoked by, say, user program 1 without running to completion, then be interrupted and invoked by some other user program (which may or may not run to completion), and then later be *reentered* at the point of interruption of user program 1 without loss of information.

In order to allow this reentrant capability, the programs must be written so that they contain no self-modifying features and so that all data required by the reentrant program can be maintained in regions of storage associated with each user program rather than as part of the reentrant subprogram or processor itself. Then the execution of the reentrant program can be interrupted at any point, and—provided that the data it uses is stored together with the contents of the machine registers and the program counter (*q.v.*) at the point of interruption—the program can be immediately invoked by another user program and can be resumed at a later time by restoring the data structures and the program counter. Fig. 1 shows a schematic of a reentrant program shared by *n* user processes. When UP*i* is interrupted, perhaps before it finishes using the reentrant program, and another user process (say, UP2) gets to use the reentrant program,

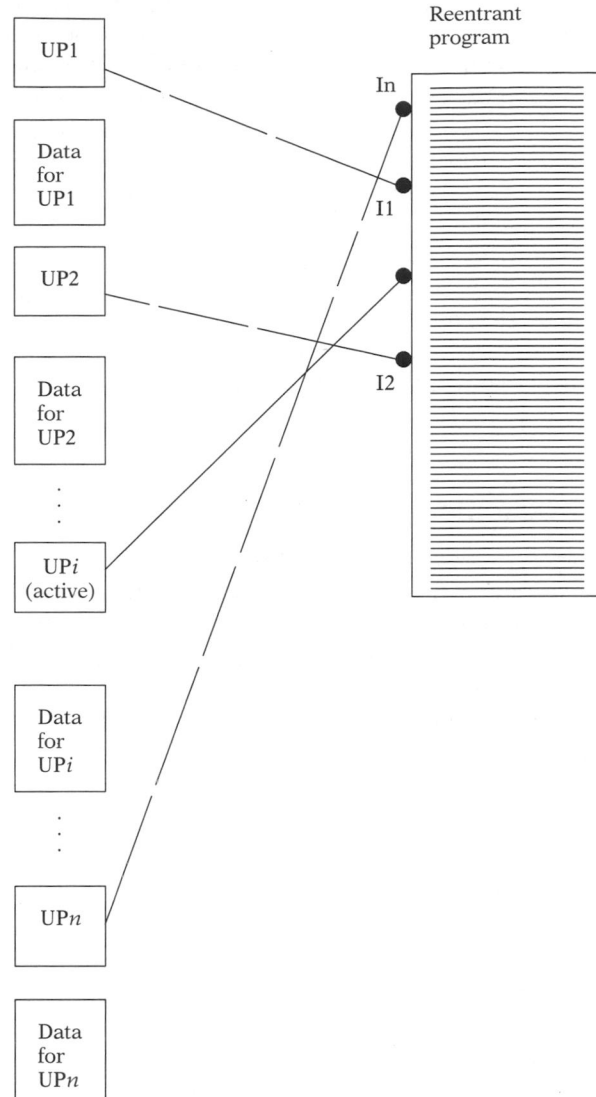

Figure 1. A reentrant program shared by *n* user processes; dotted lines indicate point in reentrant program at which user process was interrupted; solid line shows where reentrant program execution is taking place for the currently active user process.

the reentrant program must have communicated to it the location of the data for UP2 and the place I2 where previous execution was interrupted. Reentrant programs are sometimes called *pure procedures* or *sharable code*.

A subprogram is not reentrant if it maintains a single location where it stores the result of a computation, and provides the user program with the address of that location. If a second user program were to call the subprogram before a first had retrieved its data, the first user program would obtain the result of the second user's call. To make such a subprogram reentrant, each caller would have to pass a parameter to provide private storage for the subprogram result. Because the latter is more complicated, some versions

of the Unix operating system (*q.v.*), for example, have provided both non-reentrant and reentrant forms of certain of its functions, such as those concerned with network protocols (q.v.).

J. A. N. Lee

REGISTER

> For articles on related subjects *see* ARITHMETIC-LOGIC UNIT; CENTRAL PROCESSING UNIT; GENERAL REGISTER; INDEX REGISTER; PROGRAM COUNTER; and SHIFTING.

A *register* is a specialized storage element of the CPU consisting of digital storage elements that respond faster than those typically used to implement main memory storage locations.

The purpose of a register is to store a string of bits (often a word) representing related information: the digits of a number, the symbols of an alphanumeric word, the bits representing the status of various parts of a computer, the bits indicating the presence of interrupt requests, etc. The number of bits that can be stored in a register is its *length*. Registers of several different lengths may be found within the same system, but the most common length is the word length of the computer. The bits X_i that are stored in the n-bit register X are considered to be arranged in linear order and are identified by the indices i, usually chosen in the range $0 \leq i \leq n - 1$ (Fig. 1).

All registers within a computer or other digital device are uniquely identified by names or addresses. The names (e.g. X, ACC (Accumulator), PC (Program Counter), MSW (machine status word), index register, etc. often indicate the function of a register. The addresses are a set of N consecutive integers A ($0 \leq A \leq N - 1$) which identify registers within a storage array (often called *local memory*).

Registers are provided with the means to *load* new words or individual bits (writing) and to *sense* the register's contents (reading). If the reading and writing operations use all bits of a register simultaneously, the register is called *parallel*, but if one bit at a time is used, the register is called *serial*. The difference affects the reaction time of the register, but not the way a programmer uses it.

Registers may be provided with other functions in addition to reading and writing. A *shift register* is a

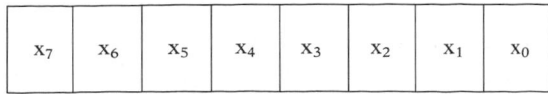

Figure 1. An eight-bit register X.

register in which all bits may be displaced by one or more positions to the left or to the right. A *counter* is a register in which the contents go through a specified sequence of states, normally those that represent consecutive binary integers. An *accumulator* is a register to which an adder circuit adds a specified number to its prior contents. Shifting, counting, and accumulation are performed upon receipt of appropriate machine-language commands.

Algirdas Avižienis

REGISTER ALLOCATION

For articles on related subjects *see* CALLING SEQUENCE; COMPILER; COMPUTER ARCHITECTURE; GENERAL REGISTER; INDEX REGISTER; INTERMEDIATE LANGUAGES; and REGISTER.

A *register* is one of a small number of high-speed memory locations in a computer's central processing unit (*q.v.*). Registers differ from ordinary memory locations in several respects:

◆ The set of registers is small, typically between 4 and 32; a register may be specified with just a few bits. Memory can be quite large; a memory location is usually specified indirectly, using an *addressing mode* that includes one more more register references.

◆ Registers are fast; typically, two registers can be read and a third written all in a single CPU cycle. Memory is slower with a single access requiring several cycles.

When a compiler translates a program to machine code, the high speed and limited size of the register set make it one of the critical resources in most computer architectures. An important part of compilation is management of the registers; that is, *register allocation*.

Classically, a compiler has three major phases: the front end, the optimizer, and the back end. The front end and optimizer are usually fairly machine-independent. The back end, or code generator, is necessarily machine-dependent and is responsible for instruction selection, instruction scheduling, and register allocation. Because the front end and optimizer are machine-independent, they are deliberately designed to have no knowledge of the target machine's register set. Instead, they work with abstract values, variables, and temporaries, assuming that the register allocator will correctly and efficiently bind all of these abstractions to concrete locations in the machine's registers and memory (*see* BINDING).

An Example

Imagine that we have a small routine written in some language and being compiled for some hypothetical target machine. The source code for our example is shown on the left-hand side of Fig. 1. An intermediate representation for this routine, as seen by the register allocator, might look something like the code shown on the right-hand side of Fig.1.

At this late stage of the compilation process, the intermediate form only remotely resembles the original source code due to the transformations that have been performed. On the other hand, it is quite close to final object code. The remaining task is register allocation. We must replace all references to *symbolic* registers (e.g. $r_a, r_b, \ldots$) with references to the machine's *physical* registers (e.g. $r_0, r_1, \ldots$). In cases where the code requires more registers than are actually available on the target machine, some values must be *spilled* to memory. Since spills can significantly slow the final code, the register allocator attempts to minimize the number and impact of required spills.

```
function dot(x,y,n)
    s ← 0
    do i ← 1 to n
        s ← s + x[i] × y[i]
    end
    return s
end dot
```

```
dot:  enter (r₀,r₁,r₂)        — parameters are passed in registers
      rₓ ← r₀                  — copy parameter registers
      r_y ← r₁
      r_n ← r₂
      r_s ← 0                  — initialize s
      r_a ← r_n × 4            — prepare loop limit (integers are 4 bytes)
      r_b ← r_a + rₓ
      if rₓ ≥ r_b goto exit    — branch around the loop
loop: r_c ← [rₓ]               — load value from x[i], where [rₓ]
                                    means "contents of the address in rₓ"
      r_d ← [r_y]              — load value from y[i]
      r_e ← r_c × r_d          — computes x[i] × y[i]
      r_s ← r_s + r_e          — update s
      rₓ ← rₓ + 4              — update pointer into x array
      r_y ← r_y + 4            — update pointer into y array
      if rₓ < r_b goto loop
exit: r₀ ← r_s                 — copy s into return register
      return r₀                — result is returned in r₀
```

Figure 1. Source and intermediate forms. Assume *x* and *y* are transferred by reference and *n* by value.

```
dot:  enter (r_0, r_1, r_2)          dot:  enter (r_0, r_1, r_2)
      r_3 ← 0                               r_3 ← 0
      r_2 ← r_2 × 4                         r_2 ← r_2 × 4
      r_2 ← r_2 + r_0                       r_2 ← r_2 + r_0
      if r_0 ≥ r_2 goto exit               if r_0 ≥ r_2 goto exit
                                            spill r_2 to b
loop: r_4 ← [r_0]                     loop: r_2 ← [r_0]
                                            spill r_3 to s
      r_5 ← [r_1]                           r_3 ← [r_1]
      r_4 ← r_4 × r_5                       r_2 ← r_2 × r_3
                                            reload r_3 from s
      r_3 ← r_3 + r_4                       r_3 ← r_3 + r_2
      r_0 ← r_0 + 4                         r_0 ← r_0 + 4
      r_1 ← r_1 + 4                         r_1 ← r_1 + 4
                                            reload r_2 from b
      if r_0 < r_2 goto loop               if r_0 < r_2 goto loop
exit: r_0 ← r_3                       exit: r_0 ← r_3
      return r_0                            return r_0
```

Figure 2. Two possible allocations.

If the target machine has an adequate number of registers, then no spill code will be required. One possible allocation using six registers is in the left-hand side of Fig. 2. Notice that the first three copy statements (e.g. $r_x ← r_0$) have been removed. This is a result of assigning the copy's source and destination to the same physical register. For instance, by assigning the symbolic register r_x to the physical register r_0, the copy statement $r_x ← r_0$ is rewritten as $r_0 ← r_0$, which is clearly useless and may be deleted. Thus we see that a clever choice of register assignments can result in fewer executable statements. This technique is sometimes referred to as *coalescing, subsumption,* or *copy propagation.*

Spill Code

If the target machine has insufficient registers, spill code will be required. Continuing our example, if we have a target machine with only four registers, the resulting code might look like the right-hand side of Fig. 2. Here we have had to spill two values to memory: the variable s and the loop limit which the compiler arbitrarily named b. Other spills were possible; this was simply one solution. Notice how much spilling has expanded the code—the loop has grown from seven to ten instructions. Worse yet, all of the spill instructions are memory references, each potentially requiring several cycles to complete; therefore, the execution time of the loop may have been increased by a factor of two or more due to spilling. A major goal of register allocation is to minimize the impact of spill code, especially inside loops.

Scope

The task of register allocation may be attacked at any one of several levels:

- ◆ The simplest form of register allocation works with one *expression* at a time. This technique is really a form of instruction scheduling, with the goal of ordering instructions so as minimize register requirements.

- ◆ More aggressive register allocators can manage registers over a complete *basic block* (a sequence of statements with no control flow) or over complete *loops.*

- ◆ *Global* register allocators work over an entire routine. The most common and effective techniques reduce the problem to that of coloring a graph (*see* GRAPH THEORY). The basic idea is to construct a graph where each vertex represents a symbolic register and the edges represent *interferences* between registers. To find a register allocation, we attempt to color the graph, using k colors, so that any two vertices connected by an edge get different colors. If k equals the number of physical registers available on the machine, then a k coloring gives a feasible allocation.

- ◆ *Interprocedural* register allocation works over a collection of routines, usually an entire program. Currently, most allocators of this form are research efforts.

Generally, the larger the scope, the more complex the allocation task and the better the results.

Optimality

Register allocation is quite difficult and an optimal solution is generally impossible to achieve. The basic difficulty is the compile-time unpredictability of branches. Even if we simplify the problem and assume some knowledge about which branches are executed most and how many time each loop will iterate, the general problem is at least NP-hard. If we further restrict the problem by disallowing the possibility of reordering instructions, then the problem is NP-complete (*see* NP-COMPLETE PROBLEMS). Therefore, compiler writers use *heuristic* (*q.v.*) approaches to avoid spending excessive compilation time, and accept that the resulting allocations are not generally optimal.

Other Considerations

The example above is rather idealized. One of the great difficulties inherent in writing a register allocator is handling the great variety of target-machine idiosyncrasies.

♦ Many machines have several types of register: floating-point registers, index registers, address registers, etc.

♦ In the example, the instructions were all *three-address* instructions, meaning that they specified two operand (*q.v.*) registers and a result register. While this is very flexible, some machines provide only less flexible two-address instructions, where the result of the instruction overwrites one of the operand registers.

♦ Many machines allow one of the operands of an instruction to be taken directly from memory, rather than requiring all operands to be in registers as is the case with Reduced Instruction Set (RISC—*q.v.*) computers. In some cases, they allow the result of an operation to be written directly to memory.

♦ Most machines have *calling conventions* that dictate the procedure-calling mechanism. Among other things, these conventions establish which registers must be preserved across procedure calls, which registers may have their values overwritten, and which registers are used for passing parameters and returning function values.

Each of these complications presents new challenges and opportunities and a good register allocation technique must be able to handle them all effectively. Finally, there are many interesting interactions between register allocation and other parts of the compiler, especially instruction scheduling and instruction selection. These interactions are a topic of current research.

Bibliography

1982. Chaitin, G. J. "Register Allocation and Spilling via Graph Coloring," *Proceedings of the SIGPLAN '82 Symposium on Compiler Construction*, *17*, 6 (June), 98–105.

1986. Aho, A. V., Sethi, R., and Ullman, J. D. *Compilers: Principles, Techniques, and Tools*. Reading, MA: Addison-Wesley.

1994. Briggs, P., Cooper, K. D., and Torczon, L. "Improvements to Graph Coloring Register Allocation," *ACM Transactions on Programming Languages and Systems*, *16*, 3 (May), 428–455.

Preston Briggs

REGULAR EXPRESSION

For articles on related subjects *see* AUTOMATA THEORY; FORMAL LANGUAGES; PRODUCTION; SEQUENTIAL MACHINE; and WELL-FORMED FORMULA.

The formal description of a language acceptable by a finite automaton or for the behavior of a sequential switching circuit is known as a *regular expression*. It tells how a language is built up from atomic languages, using regular operations. The atomic languages are the empty language ϕ and the singleton sets $\{a\}$, where a is a letter of some previously specified alphabet. The regular operations are *union, catenation*, and *catenation closure*. Union is the ordinary set theoretical union; the catenation (sometimes called *concatenation*) XY of two languages X and Y consists of all words xy with $x \in X$ and $y \in Y$; and the catenation closure X^* of a language X consists of the empty word and of all words of the form $x_1 \dots x_n$, where $n \geq 1$ and each $x_i \in X$. For example, $(ab \cup b)^*$ is a regular expression for the language X, obtained by catenating ab and b in an arbitrary fashion; i.e. X consists of the empty word and of all words over the alphabet $\{a, b\}$ ending with b and having no subwords aa. Regular expressions have turned out to be very useful in diverse areas, ranging from simple tasks of describing patterns of words to challenging problems of characterizing input and output formalisms in DNA computing (*see* MOLECULAR COMPUTING).

A formal definition of regular expressions is now given. Assume that V and $V_1 = \{\phi, \cup, *, (,)\}$ are disjoint alphabets. A word α over the alphabet $V \cup V_1$ is a regular expression over V if and only if (1) α is a letter of V or the letter ϕ, or (2) α is of one of the forms $(\beta \cup \gamma)$, $(\beta\gamma)$, or β^*, where β and γ are regular expressions over V. Each regular expression α over V denotes a language $|\alpha|$ over V according to the following conventions:

1. The language denoted by ϕ is the empty language.

2. The language denoted by $a \in V$ consists of the word a.

3. For regular expressions α and β over V,

$$|(\alpha \cup \beta)| = |\alpha| \cup |\beta|, \quad |(\alpha\beta)| = |\alpha| \, |\beta|, \quad |\alpha^*| = |\alpha|^*.$$

Very different looking regular expressions may denote the same language; e.g. each of the regular expressions

$$(a \cup ab \cup ba)^*, \quad (ba \cup a^*ab)^*a^*, \quad a^*(ab \cup ba^*a)^*$$

denote the same language.

The behavior of a finite automaton or a sequential switching circuit (see SEQUENTIAL MACHINE) is very often better understood after a simplification of the corresponding regular expression. Especially helpful is the reduction of the *star height*; i.e. the maximum number of nested stars in the regular expression. A finitary axiomatization can be given to all equations among regular expressions, although rules of inference stronger than substitution are necessary. Various algorithms are known for the transition from a regular expression to a finite automaton, and vice versa.

As a practical example of regular expressions, many operating systems (*q.v.*), screen editors, and word processing (*q.v.*) programs have generalized their string searching capability so that, in addition to being asked to find a particular string, they may be asked to find a string that matches a specified regular expression. Best known of these search tools is the Unix (*q.v.*) *grep* command, which stands for g/re/p, which can be paraphrased as: globally find regular expression and print.

Bibliography

1969. Salomaa, A. *Theory of Automata.* New York: Pergamon.
1991. Cohen, D. *Introduction to Computer Theory* (revised edition). New York: John Wiley.
1997. Paun, G., Rozenberg, G., and Salomaa, A. *DNA Computing: New Computing Paradigms.* New York: Springer-Verlag.

Arto K. Salomaa

RELATIONAL DATABASE

For articles on related subjects *see* DATABASE CONCURRENCY CONTROL; DATABASE MANAGEMENT SYSTEM; DATA MINING; DATA WAREHOUSING; and DEDUCTIVE DATABASE.

A *relational database* is one that is built and operated in accordance with the *Relational Model of Data* proposed by E. F. Codd (1970). This model has now gained wide acceptance and has engendered a great deal of additional study covering numerous aspects of database theory and practice. *The Third Manifesto*, by Hugh Darwen and C. J. Date (1995) is a modern reaffirmation and in certain respects a clarification of the Relational Model.

Primarily, the Relational Model provides a simple and intuitive method for defining a database, storing and updating data in it, and submitting queries of arbitrary complexity to it. More important, it provides a firm, sound, and consistent foundation for all the other topics that database management systems must commonly embrace, such as security and authorization, database integrity, transaction management, recoverability, and distribution of data.

The Relational Model is founded on the mathematics of *n*-ary relations, which is in turn founded on the disciplines of predicate calculus and set theory. Consider, for example, the proposition: "Brutus killed Caesar." In the context of a discussion about characters in Shakespeare's plays, we can say of this proposition whether it be *true* or *false*. If we were to construct a database of information about Shakespeare's plays, that database might well include a "record," such as (Brutus, Caesar), and that record might be one of a collection of similarly formed records, each asserting that some character killed some other character:

Brutus, Caesar

Hamlet, Laertes

Hamlet, Polonius

Laertes, Hamlet

Brutus, Brutus

Cassius, Caesar

⋮

Each of these records represents a proposition of the form "*x* killed *y*," where *x* and *y* are both names of Shakespearean characters. Such a record is not, *per se*, a proposition of that form, for the all-important word "killed" is omitted. In fact, "*x* killed *y*" is a *predicate* in two variables, and each record provides values for *x* and *y* to give one instantiation of that predicate.

The mathematical term *relation* occurs in the study of predicate logic but is most commonly used in connection with predicates of exactly two variables. See, for example, Lemmon (1978). In the Relational Model, a predicate of any nonnegative number, *n*, of variables is considered as an *n*-ary relation. If we want to say in which play each killing occurs, we might use the ternary (3-ary) relation "*x* killed *y* in *z*." If we want to record those characters who, like Cassius, were ambitious, we might use the unary relation "*x* was ambitious."

Here is how the binary (2-ary) relation "*x* killed *y*" might be represented according to the Relational Model:

KILLED	KILLER	VICTIM
	Brutus	Caesar
	Hamlet	Laertes
	Hamlet	Polonius
	Laertes	Hamlet
	Brutus	Brutus
	Cassius	Caesar

The verb of the predicate has become a *relation name*, KILLED, and the variables *x* and *y* have become *attribute names*, KILLER and VICTIM, defined in the *relation schema* of this relation. Associated with each attribute name, but not shown in the above representation, is an underlying *domain*, the set of permissible values for the attribute in question. In this case, both attributes would draw their values from the same domain, "names of Shakespearean characters."

A particular instantiation of a predicate in *n* variables is represented by an *n-tuple*. Thus, the 2-tuple (Brutus, Caesar), in combination with the relation schema of KILLED, represents the proposition "Brutus killed Caesar."

Arising from the visual representation of a relation are several informal terms in common use:

◆ *Table*, for *relation*.

◆ *Heading* for *relation schema*.

◆ *Column* (name) for *attribute* (name).

◆ *Row* for (*n-*)*tuple*.

◆ *Body* (or *extension*) for the set of tuples "in" the relation.

Four important principles are illustrated in the above example:

1. At each intersection of a row and column there is exactly one value. This is the principle of *first normal form*, fundamental in the relational model. While in natural language we might say "Hamlet killed Laertes and Polonius," the relational model does not allow us to put Laertes and Polonius in the same row and so requires us to say "Hamlet killed Laertes" and "Hamlet killed Polonius."

2. The order in which the rows are written is unimportant. The information conveyed—the single proposition formed by inserting the word "and" between the rows—is the same regardless of the order.

3. The order in which the columns are written is also unimportant. It is only important to know, for each value in a row, to which column that value pertains, and we achieve that by writing the value underneath the name of its column.

4. Writing the same row more than once is as redundant as would be writing the same proposition twice with the word "and" in between. Such redundancy can only confuse. For instance, if we had (Brutus, Caesar) twice, we would have to be very careful how we phrase the query that asks "How many people did Brutus kill?"—the Relational Model expressly prohibits duplicate rows.

A *relational database* is a collection of relations (more precisely, relation *variables*, to allow changes in the "contents" to reflect changes in the state of the enterprise, while the relation schemas do not change). A *relational database schema* is a collection of relation schemas, along with a collection of domain definitions, with the possible addition of integrity rules (usually known as *constraints*), access authorizations, and so on. A relational database management system (DBMS) must minimally provide for the definition of domains and relation schemas; the insertion, updating, and deletion of tuples; and a *relational query language* for defining new relations that may be derived from the "base relations" of the database. As of mid-1999, no well-known commercial product quite matches up to these stated requirements of a relational DBMS. Those based on the standard database language SQL (Structured Query Language) are commonly called relational DBMSs. However, SQL's concept of "tables," though similar to that of relations, turns out on close scrutiny to deviate in several important respects from the Relational Model. Further, SQL DBMSs have been particularly lacking in the area of domains. By this we do not mean failure to support the relational concept of domains, the concept now often referred to as data types (*q.v.*) or object classes (*see* CLASS), where a domain (or type or class) is a named set of values accompanied by a set of operators for operating on those values. Rather, we mean that SQL supports only a specific and very limited collection of domains, these being the data types (to use the SQL term) that it provides for representing and operating on numbers, character strings, dates, times and typically nothing else. Much work is currently under way to address this deficiency by providing comprehensive support for user-defined data types of arbitrary complexity. (Unfortunately, the current international standard for SQL does define a construct that goes by the name "domain," but this is not the concept referred to by that term in relational theory.)

A relational query language is one that embodies the fundamental principle that the operands *and* the result of any operator in the query language are relations. If query operations are thus closed over relations, then queries of arbitrary complexity can be expressed.

In practice, to achieve this end, relational query languages are founded on either or both of the *relational algebra* and the *relational calculus* proposed by Codd. Of these two, the algebra is considered, psychologically, to be the "lower-level" system (in the same sense in which programming languages are often described as "low-level" or "high-level"), but in fact the two systems have been shown to be equivalent—anything expressible in the algebra has an equivalent expression in the calculus, and vice versa.

The relational algebra draws on the notion that the body of a relation is a *set* (of tuples), and among its operators are specialized versions of the *union*, *difference*, and *intersection* operations of set theory. The algebra originally proposed by Codd included those three, two monadic operators—*project* and *restrict* (also known as *select*)—and the dyadic operator *Cartesian product*. Most authorities accept three further monadic operators—*attribute rename*, *extend*, and *summarize*. The non-primitive operators *natural join* and *divide* are so useful that they are normally presented as well.

Where the relational algebra draws on set theory, the *relational calculus* draws on the predicate calculus. It is characterized by its adoption of the universal and existential quantifiers ∀ ("for all") and ∃ ("there exists") of the predicate calculus.

While the calculus is in a sense "higher level" than the algebra and has more intuitive appeal to logicians and, potentially, to casual users of relational databases, it is the algebra that is more often used as a basis for theoretical discussion of many diverse aspects of database technology. Descriptions of the relational algebra and the relational calculus are given in Ullman (1982) and Date (1995).

To illustrate the completeness of the Relational Algebra and Calculus, we use our example relation, KILLED, and one other, DIED_BY, shown in the following table:

DIED_BY	VICTIM	METHOD
	Caesar	Daggers
	Hamlet	Sword
	Polonius	Sword
	Laertes	Sword
	Brutus	Sword

The predicate is "*y* died by *z*." VICTIM is the attribute name corresponding to y, and its domain is the same as that of VICTIM in KILLED. METHOD is the attribute name corresponding to z, and its domain is "methods of being killed." We assume that only one method of being killed is stated for each victim, choosing not to handle the possibility that one of Caesar's assassins used something other than a dagger.

Here, then, are some example queries against a database consisting of just those two relations. Each is expressed in (a) the relational algebra, (b) the tuple-oriented relational calculus and (c) SQL. The calculus solutions use the notation given in Date (1995), which

also describes a "domain-oriented" calculus as an alternative to the tuple calculus proposed by Codd. The result of each query is presented as a relation named ANSWER, and the attribute names are those that would arise from the algebraic solutions:

Who killed Caesar?

Algebra:

```
(KILLED WHERE VICTIM = 'Caesar') [KILLER]
```

The term WHERE signifies the relational operator known as *restriction*, the square brackets *projection*.

Calculus:

```
RANGE OF K IS KILLED
K.KILLER WHERE K.VICTIM = 'Caesar'
```

SQL:

```
SELECT DISTINCT K.KILLER FROM KILLED AS K
                 WHERE K.VICTIM = 'Caesar'
```

(which could in this case be abbreviated to

```
SELECT KILLER FROM KILLED WHERE VICTIM =
                                    'Caesar')
```

ANSWER	KILLER
	Brutus
	Cassius

Who was both a killer and a victim?

Algebra:

```
(KILLED[KILLER] RENAME KILLER AS
                     KILLER_VICTIM)
INTERSECT
(KILLED[VICTIM] RENAME VICTIM AS
                     KILLER_VICTIM)
```

We use *projection* and *rename* to make two unary relations, one of killers, the other of victims. The set operator *intersection* corresponds to the "both . . . and . . ." of the query.

Calculus:

```
RANGE OF K IS KILLED
RANGE OF V IS KILLED
K.KILLER WHERE EXISTS V (K.KILLER =
                              V.VICTIM)
```

SQL:

```
SELECT KILLER AS KILLER_VICTIM FROM KILLED
INTERSECT
SELECT VICTIM AS KILLER_VICTIM FROM KILLED
```

or

```
SELECT KILLER AS KILLER_VICTIM FROM KILLED
WHERE KILLER IN (SELECT VICTIM FROM KILLED)
```

(several other significantly different formulations are possible)

```
       ANSWER     KILLER_VICTIM
.........................................
              Brutus
              Hamlet
              Laertes
```

Which killers used daggers?

Algebra:

```
((KILLED JOIN DIED_BY) WHERE METHOD =
                    'Daggers') [KILLER]
```

The term JOIN signifies *natural join* of KILLED and DIED_BY "over" their common attribute, VICTIM.

Calculus:

```
RANGE OF K IS KILLED
RANGE OF D IS DIED_BY
K.KILLER WHERE EXISTS D (K.VICTIM =
     D.VICTIM AND D.METHOD = 'Daggers')
```

SQL:

```
SELECT DISTINCT K.KILLER FROM KILLED AS K,
                    DIED_BY AS D
WHERE K.VICTIM = D.VICTIM AND D.METHOD =
                    'Daggers'
```

```
       ANSWER     KILLER
..........................................
              Brutus
              Cassius
```

Show all cases where x killed y, and y killed z.

Algebra:

```
(KILLED RENAME KILLER AS KILLER1 RENAME
                    VICTIM AS KILLER2)
JOIN
(KILLED RENAME KILLER AS KILLER2)
```

Here we join the relation KILLED to itself, using *rename* to make VICTIM, on the one hand, and KILLER, on the other, the common attribute for the join.

Calculus:

```
RANGE OF K IS KILLED
RANGE OF V IS KILLED
K.KILLER, V.KILLER, V.VICTIM WHERE
                    K.VICTIM = V.KILLER
```

SQL:

```
SELECT K1.KILLER AS KILLER1, K1.VICTIM AS
                    KILLER2, K2.VICTIM
FROM KILLED AS K1, KILLED AS K2
WHERE
                    K1.VICTIM = K2.KILLER
```

ANSWER	KILLER1	KILLER2	VICTIM
	Laertes	Hamlet	Polonius
	Hamlet	Laertes	Hamlet
	Laertes	Hamlet	Laertes
	Brutus	Brutus	Brutus

Which killers always used the same method? Show the method as well as the killer.

Algebra:

```
DIED_BY DIVIDEBY KILLED
```

Relational *division* is a convenient non-primitive operator for use in queries that imply universal quantification, the "for all" of the calculus. Division can be expressed using several *projections*, *joins*, and *differences*, and that is best left as an exercise for the keen student.

(Yes, Cassius did, like Brutus, kill himself with a sword, but we forgot to record that, so we deserve what we get!)

Note that if we divided KILLED by DIED_BY, we would be asking for (KILLER, METHOD) pairs such that KILLER killed everybody who died by METHOD.

Calculus:

```
RANGE OF K IS KILLED
RANGE OF D IS DIED_BY
RANGE OF V IS KILLED
RANGE OF M IS DIED_BY
K.KILLER, D.METHOD WHERE FORALL M
     (IF K.KILLER = V.KILLER AND V.VICTIM =
     M.VICTIM THEN M.METHOD = D.METHOD)
```

SQL:

```
SELECT DISTINCT K1.KILLER FROM KILLED AS
                    K1, DIED_BY AS D1
WHERE K1.VICTIM = D1.VICTIM
AND NOT EXISTS (SELECT * FROM KILLED AS
                    K2, DIED_BY AS D2
          WHERE K1.KILLER = K2.KILLER
          AND K2.VICTIM = D2.VICTIM
          AND NOT (D1.METHOD =
                    D2.METHOD))
```

SQL's lack of an explicit universal quantifier means that it must be expressed with existential quantification and two negations.

```
ANSWER          KILLER          METHOD
..........................................................
                Hamlet          Sword
                Laertes         Sword
                Cassius         Daggers
```

How many people killed Caesar?

Algebra:

```
((SUMMARIZE KILLED GROUPBY VICTIM
ADD COUNT AS NUMBER_OF_KILLERS)
WHERE VICTIM = 'Caesar')
                         [NUMBER_OF_KILLERS]
```

Alternatively, the *restriction* can be done before the *summary*, in which case the grouping could be over no attributes at all, instead of over VICTIM.

Of course, the number would be bigger if we had remembered to record Casca and all the other assassins.

Calculus:

```
RANGE OF K IS KILLED
  COUNT (K.KILLER WHERE K.VICTIM = 'Caesar')
```

SQL:

```
SELECT COUNT(*) FROM KILLED WHERE VICTIM =
                                   'Caesar'
```

```
ANSWER     NUMBER OF KILLERS
...........................................
              2
```

In a database containing numerical information, the result of a query might be all sorts of calculated results, including complex statistical analyses.

Relational queries have many applications, not just the obvious one of delivering answers to interesting questions. They are used to define *views*, enabling individual users to work with customized database schemas instead of all having to use the same underlying schemas. They are used to define subsets of the database, to which access can be authorized discretely for different users or user groups. And they may be used in the definitions of integrity *constraints*.

Functional Dependence, Keys, and Normalization

The concept of *functional dependence* is completely orthogonal to the principles described above, but is usually included in any discussion of relational databases because of its importance in connection with database design, view updatability, query optimiza-

tion, and other topics. Indeed, the relational model itself makes certain recommendations arising from it. A *functional dependency* is a truth-valued expression, written as:

$$A \to B$$

and pronounced "A determines B" or "B depends on A." If A and B are both subsets of the attributes of some relation, R, then $A \to B$ is said to hold true in R if and only if any two tuples in R that agree in value for every attribute in A also agree in value for every attribute in B. For example, suppose that a relation, R, includes an attribute, z, whose values in R are constrained to be the sum of two other attributes in R, x, and y (perhaps z is thus computed, in some query). The following functional dependencies hold true in R:

$$\{x, y\} \to \{z\}$$
$$\{x, z\} \to \{y\}$$
$$\{y, z\} \to \{x\}$$

The left operand of a functional dependency is the *determinant*, and the members of the right operand are *dependants* of that determinant.

If K is a determinant in R such that:

◆ All the attributes of R are dependants of K;
◆ There is no proper subset of K, K′, such that all the attributes of R are dependants of K′; and
◆ This constraint holds true over time in a changing database;

then K is a *candidate key* of R. It follows from this definition that, if K is a candidate key of R, no two tuples in R can have the same combined value in the attributes of K.

The Relational Model requires at least one candidate key to be defined for every relation defined by a relation schema in the database schema. The functional dependency implied by such a candidate key is then treated as an integrity rule, prohibiting the insertion of a tuple, t, if there already exists some tuple agreeing in value with t for every attribute of that candidate key. When more than one candidate key is noted for the same relation, one candidate key is arbitrarily nominated as the *primary key*.

It is easy to prove that every relation has at least one candidate key, for if no proper subset of the heading is a candidate key, which is the case in our example, then the heading KILLED, is the only candidate key. The only candidate key of DIED_BY is {VICTIM}, because of our decision to state just one method for each victim.

The fundamental principle of *first normal form* of relations has already been noted. The study of database design involves further normal forms that are recommended to hold true for "base relations" (i.e. relations defined by relation schemas in the database schema) only. The most important of these is *Boyce–Codd normal form* (BCNF). BCNF is defined as holding true in a relation, *R*, if and only if every nontrivial determinant in *R* is a candidate key.

It can be shown that a base relation that is not in BCNF can involve redundancy (recording the same data more than once), giving rise to *update anomalies*, such as having to update the same data in the several different places where it occurs.

The reader is referred to Date (1995), Chapters 9–11, for a deeper discussion of functional dependence, keys, and normal form, where it will be found that even BCNF is not a thorough guarantee against update anomalies, and further normal forms sometimes need to be considered. One of these, called *fifth normal form*, is proved to complete the guarantee.

When a relation, *R*, includes some set of attributes, FK, such that every tuple in *R* is constrained to agree in value, for each attribute in FK, with its corresponding attribute in the primary key of a relation *S*, in some tuple of *S*, then FK is said to be a *foreign key* in *R*, *referencing S*. In our example database, VICTIM in the KILLED relation might be a foreign key "referencing" DIED_BY. We do not need to say which attributes of DIED_BY are involved in the reference, as the attributes of the primary key of the referenced relation are assumed. If we do declare this foreign key, we are prohibited from recording any killing without also recording its method.

Relational Databases and SQL

The database language SQL gained such wide acceptance during the 1980s, with a multiplicity of implementations and a diversity of dialects, that one authority was moved to characterize it as "intergalactic dataspeak." An international standard for SQL was first published in 1986, substantially extended in later editions (1989 and 1992) and augmented by the publication of additional parts in 1995 and 1996. The version currently in preparation stands at over 1500 pages in nine parts. The growth is partly due to the never-ending demands for extensions to the products, partly to the fact that not all aspects of the language were standardized in 1986, 1989, and 1992. Because SQL happens to be loosely based on relational theory, the term "relational" is now synonymous with "SQL" for many people. For that reason alone we are compelled to say a little more about it here, if only to dispel two popular misconceptions. The first misconception is, as we have already indicated, that "relational means SQL." SQL is merely one of many distinct attempts to implement the principles of the relational model of data. The second and more serious misconception is that SQL is relational or, to put it more kindly, that all the principles of the Relational Model of Data are embraced by SQL. In fact, authorities have noted several important deficiencies in SQL, such as:

◆ SQL does not properly support *domains*, though considerable attention is currently being paid to this matter, both in the leading products and in a new version, in preparation, of the international standard.

◆ In SQL, a table is permitted to contain *duplicate rows*.

◆ A table that is the result of a query can contain *unnamed columns*, and columns of the same name. In the original version of the language, no provision was made to allow column names to be given for results of scalar expressions; nor was any counterpart of relational algebra's *rename* operator available to avoid the duplicate column names that can arise when two or more tables are joined together. The most severe consequence of this error was that the query language was not truly closed over tables, thus limiting the complexity of expressions with resulting *incompleteness*. This was remedied in the 1992 version of the international standard. While many products have implemented column (re)naming, fewer have gone the extra step to relational completeness.

◆ SQL's treatment of "missing values," using *nulls*, has been shown to be unsound and inconsistent. The relational model of the early 1970s made no provision for the treatment of missing values. Furthermore, no subsequent extension of the model in this respect—Codd (1990) for example—has yet gained general acceptance among relational scholars.

Bibliography

1970. Codd, E. F. "A Relational Model of Data for Large Shared Data Banks," *Comm. of the ACM*, **13**, *6* (June), 377–387.

1978. Lemmon, E. J. *Beginning Logic.* Indianapolis, IN: Hackett Publishing Co.

1990. Codd, E. F. *The Relational Model for Database Management, Version 2.* Reading, MA: Addison-Wesley.

1995. Darwen, H. A. C., and Date, C. J. "The Third Manifesto," *SIGMOD Record*, **24**, *1* (March), 39–49.

1995. Date, C. J. *An Introduction to Database Systems: Volume I*, 6th Ed. "Part III: The Relational Model." Reading, MA: Addison-Wesley.

1997. Ullman, J. D., and Widom, J. *A First Course in Database Systems.* Upper Saddle River, NJ: Prentice Hall.

Hugh Darwen

RELIABILITY

See Hardware Reliability; and Software Reliability.

RESTART PROCEDURE

See Bootstrap.

REVERSE POLISH NOTATION

See Polish Notation.

RISC

See Reduced Instruction Set Computer.

ROBOTICS

For articles on related topics, *see* Artificial Intelligence; Automation; Computational Geometry; Computer Vision; Control Applications; Cybernetics; Pattern Recognition; Perceptron; and Telerobotics.

Introduction

Robotics is the study of reprogrammable, multifunctional manipulators designed to move materials, parts, tools, or specialized devices through programmed motions for the performance of a variety of tasks (Robot Institute of America, 1979). Taking a more general view, robots can be said to be programmable machines that either in performance or appearance imitate human activities. In contrast to purely algorithmic computing, which is concerned with the transformation of information from input to output, robotics is concerned with the transformation of the physical world from an input state to an output state. Robotics programs are real-time systems (*q.v.*); robotics programs must be able to service commands as close to instantaneously as possible.

As the range of capabilities of robots increase, so do their applications. Some unusual applications currently being studied or used include: dismantling of nuclear weapons (developed at the Sandia National Laboratory in New Mexico as part of START, the Strategic Arms Reduction Treaty); herding of sheep (developed at Silsoe Research Institute, UK); the Micro Electronic Fish Robot (Mefir), which searches the sea bed for dumped toxic waste (University of Central Florida); and robot insects that can fly, crawl, or swim, to be used for battlefield reconnaissance or to spy on terrorists holding hostages (Georgia Tech Research Institute). On the domestic front, an unusual

robot developed by the University of Western Australia is in use as a sheep shearer (*see* Fig. 1), and details of a robotic vacuum cleaner developed by Electrolux have recently been publicized in the UK. A similar device called Dustbot is discussed in Moravec (1998). It has omnidirectional wheels, stereoscopic eyes on all faces, and a BIPS (billion instructions per second) of processing power programmed to give it a three-dimensional sense of space.

History

For centuries, people have been fascinated with mechanisms that imitated parts of the human body. Priests in ancient Egypt sometimes attached mechanical arms to statues and then operated the arms in such a way as to claim to be acting under inspiration from their gods. To illustrate the science on which they were based, the Greeks built hydraulically operated statues which also found their way into temples.

During the 18th century, intricate mechanical puppets and automata were built in Europe. These included accurate models of people with arms, lips, and other body parts driven by linkages and cams controlled by rotating drum selectors. Some could write, some draw, and a famous one, a shepherd designed by Jacques de Vaucanson, could play a repertoire of 12 tunes on a flute. Since these automata did not respond to their environment in any way, they could not execute a different task unless they were completely rebuilt.

Until the middle of the 20th century, mechanically programmed automata were used solely for entertainment. Prior to this, however, considerable advances were made in "programmable" machines for specific industrial processes, starting with the Jacquard loom in 1801. Developments in technology, including the modern electronic computer, feedback control of actuators, and sensor technology, were required before programmable automata were sufficiently flexible to be of any practical use in manufacturing. The forerunners of programmable robots were mechanically fixed manipulators whose motions were set by mechanical cams or stops. These were custom-built to facilitate the manufacture of a specific product, a type of automation still used to make light bulbs.

Many people associate the word "robot" with something like R2D2 of *Star Wars*. Such a connection is appropriate because the word was actually coined on the stage, not in the factory. Robots first appeared in Prague in January 1921 in a play entitled R.U.R. (Rossum's Universal Robots), written by the Czechoslovakian dramatist Karel Čapek. Their first appearance on the New York stage occurred on 9 October 1922. The word *robot* is a derivative of the Czech word *robota*, which can be interpreted as "work," "forced

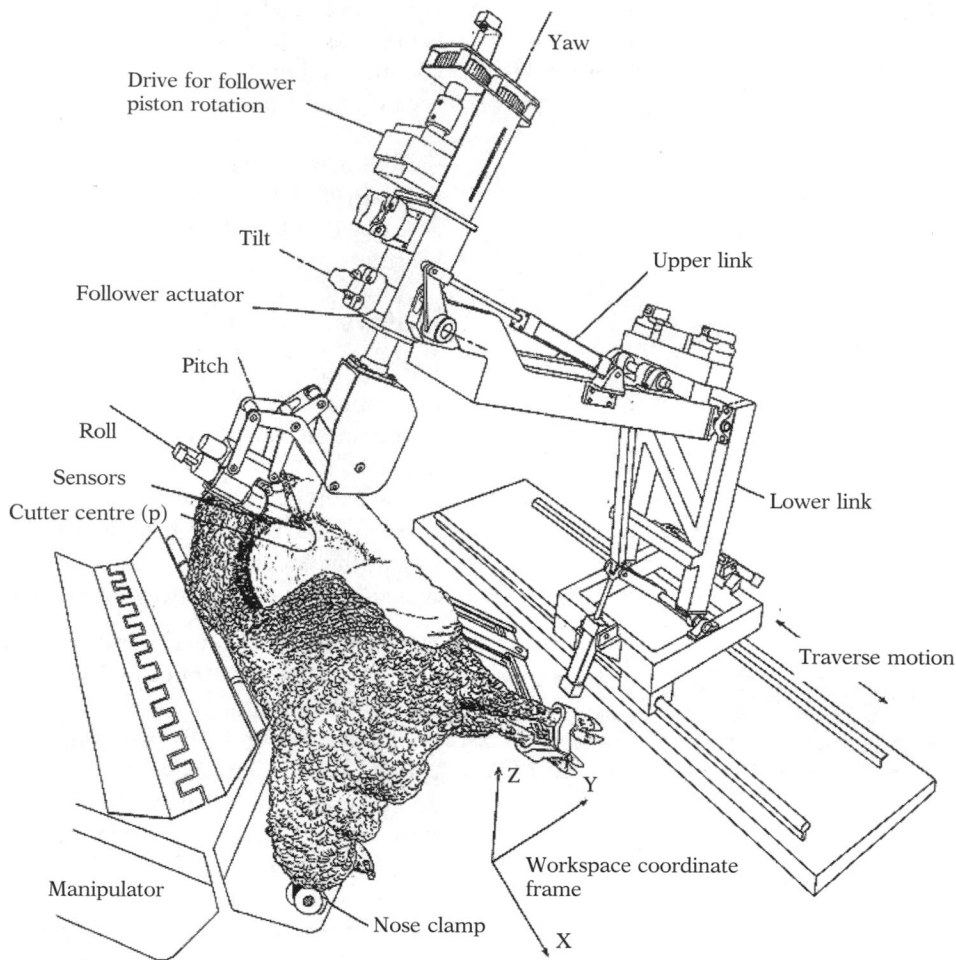

Figure 1. The University of Western Australia's robotic sheep shearer.

labor," "slave," or "serf." In 1926, the first movie involving robots, *Metropolis*, was released in Germany. The walking robot Electro and its dog Sparko were displayed at the New York World's Fair in 1939. Robot dogs are still popular; Fig. 2 on Color Page CP-12 depicts SONY's "AIBO" Entertainment Robot.

In 1956, more than 30 years after Čapek's play, but before *Star Wars*, a firm named Unimation was formed whose sole business was robotics. In 1972, 16 years and $12 million later, Unimation turned its first profit through sales of real industrial-grade robots. C. W. Kenward in Britain and George Devol in the USA developed the technology for this work in 1954. The initial device was called a *programmed articulated transfer device*. Joseph Engelberger, often called the father of the industrial robot, bought the rights to the Devol device and developed it further.

In parallel with the above developments, fundamental work was under way which led to the industrial robot as we know it now. In 1948, Ray Goertz built a bilateral mechanical master–slave manipulator at Argonne National Laboratory. In the same year, General Mills manufactured a unilateral manipulator based on electric motors with switch control. In 1954, Goertz built another electric master–slave manipulator incorporating servos and force reflection. In 1956, a General Mills manipulator was fitted for manned deep-sea operations. It was not until 1962 that General Motors installed its first Unimation robot. In 1968, R. S. Mosher at General Electric built a quadrupedal walking machine, referred to as the *walking truck*. It was 10 feet (3 m) long, weighed 3000 pounds (1360 kg), and was powered by a 90 hp (68 kW) gasoline engine. During the 1960s, work started on the design of prostheses to replace lost human limbs. The work on *teleoperators* (remote-controlled devices) and prostheses contributed significantly to the development of robots (*see* TELEROBOTICS).

The first robots that could be programmed to respond to external sensory information without direct human intervention were built in artificial intelligence laboratories to test theories in cognition and vision. H. A.

Ernst (1961) of the MIT Lincoln Laboratory equipped a robot arm with tactile sensors that were used to provide feedback to the control process. In 1962 L. G. Roberts demonstrated that a mathematical description of a three-dimensional scene could be recovered from a corresponding digital image. In 1969 a sophisticated mobile robot called *Shakey* (because of its shaky mechanical construction) was built at Stanford Research Institute to carry out experiments in using vision to control action. Shakey navigated highly structured indoor environments. In the late 1970s, another device, Hans Moravec's *Stanford Cart*, was the first robot to attempt an unstructured environment. Throughout the remainder of that decade, research and development focused on exploring the possibilities of sensor-based robot motion. Increasing applications followed increased technical developments in robotics. Industry further incorporated robots into manufacturing and non-engineering applications, and robot arms were employed in space, for example, in the Viking probes.

Perception

Measurement of the position and other parameters of a robot and the environment is fundamental to robotics applications. Most of today's industrial robots are restricted to some extent by their lack of sensing capabilities. Many of these robots can measure only joint position, plus a few interlocks and timing signals. These robots need to be taught the exact location of the manipulated work piece by manually moving the end effector (hand) to that location and recording the joint angles. If, during operation, the work piece is not in that exact location, the whole process can fail. Therefore, a robot that can "see" or "feel" the work piece and certain aspects of its surroundings has a considerable advantage over a robot that does not have artificial senses.

The sensing capability of a robot can have widely ranging degrees of sophistication in addition to a variety of sensing media. Sensing can be decomposed into a hierarchy with the sensor at the bottom or physical level of the hierarchy. Further up the hierarchy is the model level, where the sensed data is analyzed, reduced, and combined with other data to form a model of the world. The top level is the perception level, where the model is analyzed to infer the state of the world and the consequences of its actions.

In robotics, sensors are classified into two groups: internal and external. Internal sensors measure robot parameters relative to the reference frame of the robot such as joint angle, linkage deflection, and grip force. External sensors measure the environment and the position of the robot relative to the environment.

To model and control a robot, its position, motion, force and mass must be measured relative to coordinate reference frames attached to the robot. Kinematics modeling and control requires measurement of position and motion. Static modeling and control requires the measurement of force and of the mass of the work piece grasped by the end effector. Numerous sensors have been developed for internal sensing, including potentiometers, tachogenerators (d.c. motors used in reverse to measure angular velocity), variable differential transformers (a magnetic core which moves inside three cylindrical coils, used to measure linear and rotary displacements), linear velocity transducers, servo accelerometers (a closed-loop torque balance system), and piezo-resistive accelerometers (constructed by placing strain gauges on a cantilever beam).

External sensors are used to locate the robot with respect to the environment and to locate work pieces in the environment with respect to the robot. There are many kinds of external sensors, for "measurements" of touch, proximity, range, location, speech, sound, humidity, pressure and temperature. These measurements may be made in many ways; for example, proximity sensors may be optical or use electromagnetic induction. Range sensing may be done with time-of-flight measurements, radar, stereovision, or ultrasonic echolocation. Vision is probably the most important external sense. Computer vision in general is the capability to record, store, and reconstruct a graphic image that matches the original as closely as possible. The use of vision in robotics is more limited. Vision systems usually have a specific assignment, such as checking for proper part orientation, identifying parts, searching for specific defects, or checking alignment for assembly.

Tactile sensors serve two purposes, to determine the presence and characteristics of a work piece. Such sensors range from simple mechanically operated ones to those that attempt to simulate the human skin. The former types use a ferroelectric material, that is, material that is both piezo- and pyroelectric. Typically, they consist of a 16 by 16 array of force transducers at 1–2 mm spacing. The most sophisticated type of these is constructed from a VLSI wafer. This sensor includes local processing to decouple and amplify multiple sensor signals. The main disadvantage of this type of sensor is its inflexibility and susceptibility to damage. A more flexible tactile sensing array overcomes this problem. It is made with ferroelectric polymers consisting of a 100 μm thick layer of PVDF (polyvinylidene fluoride) to simulate the human dermis (inner layer of skin), and a 40 μm thick layer to simulate the epidermis (outer layer of skin), separated by an elastomer layer (Fig. 3). Since PVDF deforms only slightly under stress,

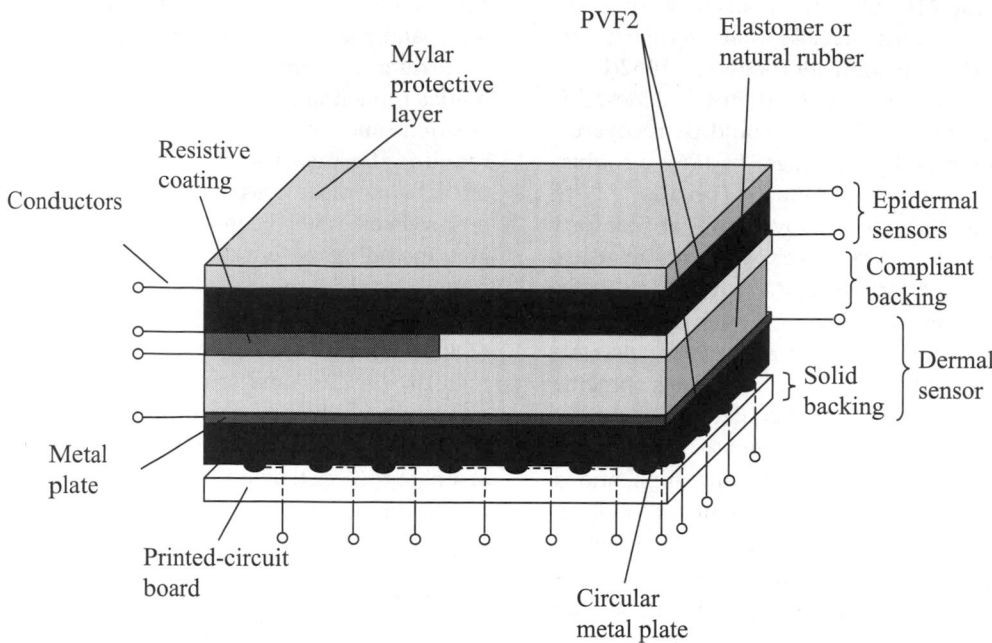

Figure 3. Construction of a polyvinylidene fluoride sensor.

and produces only a small charge when pressed, it is backed with a compliant elastomer layer. The result is an increase in the electric signal at the expense of spatial resolution due to extension of the polymer. Thus, the epidermal sensor is responsive to strain (extension), and the dermal sensor, which has a solid backing, is responsive to thickness changes. Thin metal electrodes are plated on the upper surface of the dermis, and the lower surface is bonded to a supporting printed circuit board, which has an array of circular metal pads etched on its surface. The dermis sandwich forms an array of capacitors. When a force is applied to the dermis, the resulting deformation generates a charge, which is capacitively coupled to the circular electrodes. Similarly, electrodes plated on the surface of the epidermal layer collect the charges generated there. A mylar layer protects the epidermal sensor, but reduces its sensitivity. A further development of this sensor enables it to obtain not only the shape and texture of a work piece but also its hardness and thermal qualities.

Actuation

The power sources used to drive robot joints and operate the end effector usually determine its performance characteristics and in turn, the feasibility of various applications. There are four principal power sources used—hydraulic, pneumatic, electric, and mechanical gear and cam. The source has to transmit power from an actuator to the work piece the robot is moving. Typical transmission devices are gears, tendons, and linkages. Recent developments have led to more advanced transmission devices that reduce or even eliminate problems experienced by traditional devices. These problems include difficulty in reversing, inaccuracies, and backlash (excessive play between mating parts). Such devices include harmonic drives (compact drives having inline parallel shafts, very high gear ratios, and near zero backlash). However, in recent years researchers have further improved the performance of robots by directly coupling a joint axis to the rotor of a rare earth magnet dc motor. These so-called direct drive systems have no backlash, low friction, low compliance, high reliability, and fast dynamic response. Experimental direct drive arms have been built at the MIT Artificial Intelligence Laboratory and the CMU Robotics Institute. The first commercially available arm using direct drive technology was the Adept One arm, manufactured by Adept Technology, Inc.

In robot motion we study the geometry of the robot arm with respect to a reference coordinate system, while the end effector moves along a prescribed path. This kinematics analysis involves two different kinds of problem; determining the coordinates of the end effector or end of arm for a given set of joints coordinates and determining the joints coordinates for a given location of the end effector or end of arm. Generally the location of the end effector can be defined in two ways: joint space and world space (also known as global space). In *joint space*, the joint parameters such as rotating or twisting joint angles and variable link lengths are used to represent the position of the end effector. In *world space*, rectilinear coordinates with reference to the basic Cartesian system are used to define the position of the end effector. The transformation of coordinates of the end effector point from the joint space to the world space is known as *forward kinematics transformation*. Similarly, the transformation of coordinates from world to joint space is known as *inverse kinematics transformation*.

To solve the kinematics equations of a robot with many joints, homogeneous transformations are applied. In robotics, the two common formulations of dynamics are derived from the Newton–Euler equations and Lagrange's equations, the fundamental equations governing three-dimensional motion of a rigid body. In forward dynamics, n second-order coupled non-linear differential equations describe the dynamics of an n-link robot.

Robots that can move about are starting to appear in industry, but their motion is still restricted. Before a general-purpose mobile robot can move freely in a factory, home, farm, or military environment, an "intelligent" connection between perception (sensing and understanding the environment) and action (control of robot motion within the environment) has to be achieved. This is a difficult problem in artificial intelligence, and has been the subject of extensive study for a number of years. It is the emphasis of most of the research into ALVs (Autonomous Land Vehicles) or mobile robots. Mobile robots can be based on either wheels or legs.

Wheeled robots are designed to maintain their wheels in contact with the floor at all times. Consequently, stability is designed into the robot and becomes a problem only when the robot is on a steep slope. The kinematics modeling of wheeled robots differs from the modeling of "fixed" robots because the contact of the wheels with the ground forms a multiple closed-link chain, whereas a "fixed" robot is a single open-link chain. The kinematics of wheeled robots can be decomposed into internal and external kinematics. *Internal kinematics* describes the relationship between the linkages within the robot. These relationships are important when steering the robot. *External kinematics* describes the relationships between the robot and the rest of the world, that is, the trajectory of the robot. A recent example of a wheeled robot application was the Pathfinder mission to Mars.

By contrast, legged robots lift their feet off the ground to walk. The motion of walking dynamically changes the stability of the robot. A robot is statically stable if the center of its gravity always lies within a triangle defined by the contact points between three feet and the ground. If the center of gravity lies outside this triangle, the robot is no longer stable and tends to fall over. For statically stable walking, a robot must have

four or more legs in order to have three feet in contact with the ground at all times. If fewer than three feet are on the ground, then the triangle reduces to a line on the ground or a point (one foot on the ground) and the robot tends to fall over. In these situations, the robot must be dynamically stable not to fall over. The repetitive pattern of foot placement when walking is called a *regular gait*. An irregular gait is mainly used to solve specific problems, e.g. a shuffle to get out of a tight corner. A statically stable gait always maintains at least three feet on the ground. A dynamic gait has fewer than three feet on the ground at some points and can have all feet off the ground for short periods. The latter situation arises in one-legged robots that travel by hopping from point to point.

There are legged robots with from one to eight legs; those with six or more tend to look like giant insects. In all of these robots, the problem of stability has had to be solved. Another problem is navigation. Any navigation scheme aims to reach a destination without getting lost or crashing into anything. Navigation involves three tasks: mapping, planning and driving. A higher-level process, called a *task planner*, specifies the destination and any constraints on the course, such as time.

A number of problems need to be overcome before wheeled or legged robots will match or even approach

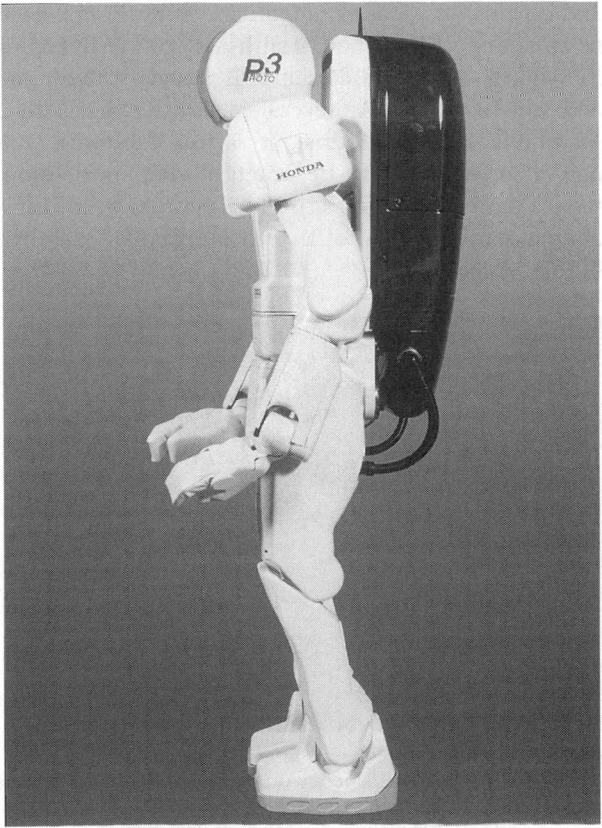

Figure 4. Honda (from Moravec (1998)).

Figure 5. The ALDURO wheeled robot (courtesy of Professor Hiller, Fachgebiet Mechatronik, Gerhard-Mercator-Universität-Duisburg, Germany).

the sophisticated navigation abilities of people. Such areas include planning in unknown environments, coordination between mobility and manipulability, computation environments for mobile robots, nonlinear control of mobile robots, and environmental modeling using advanced sensing technologies. A particularly interesting walking robot called Honda is shown in Fig. 4. Honda is a self-contained research robot developed over a decade by a group of 30 engineers at Honda Motors of Japan. Honda's backpack contains its computer and the battery power to run it. The robot has fully functional arms and camera eyes, and can find stairs and move objects. Its most advanced skill, so far, is walking on flat and sloped ground and up and down stairs. It is as human-like in its motion as in its appearance. If pushed, it shifts its posture or begins to walk to keep equilibrium. It stands 180 cm tall and weighs 210 kg. At several million dollars, with a 15-minute battery lifetime, it is too expensive and power-consumptive to be practical, but its development continues and it is surely a precursor of future universal robots. Two other mobile robots are shown in Figs. 5 and 6.

Figure 6. The Walking Gyroscope was the first dynamically stabilized walking toy on the market. It is shown here with the Tonka Hitchhiker robot which was based on the same idea. (Courtesy of its inventor, John Jameson, San Carlos, CA.)

Robot End Effectors

The end effector (also referred to as a hand or gripper) mounted on the wrist enables a robot to perform specified tasks. The selection of an end effector is a critical decision to be made by the automation engineer. This decision can be as important to the success of the application as the selection of the robot. End effectors come in a wide variety of configurations and are often designed by the customer to fit a particular application. In applications where a robot is required to manipulate a tool to perform an operation on a work piece, the end effector is used as a gripper that can grasp and handle a variety of tools and the robot has multitool handling function, similar to the automatic cutting-tool interchanging of machine tools. Services such as air and electric signals have to be turned off before the gripper is changed. However, in most robot applications, where only one tool is to be manipulated, the tool is directly mounted on the wrist and acts as an end effector. Spot welding tools, arc welding tools, spray-painting nozzles, and rotating spindles for drilling and grinding are typical examples of such setups.

All these end effectors have limitations. Though they can serve for many robot applications, a truly flexible robot will require end effectors with a flexibility and versatility approaching that of a human hand. Two important characteristics of human hands that need to be modeled are controlled impedance (where the hand in contact with the environment exerts pressure to sense it) and variable finger movement. A number of researchers have found ways to achieve these. Bell Laboratories has developed a controlled-impedance end effector, which has the fingers mounted on linear

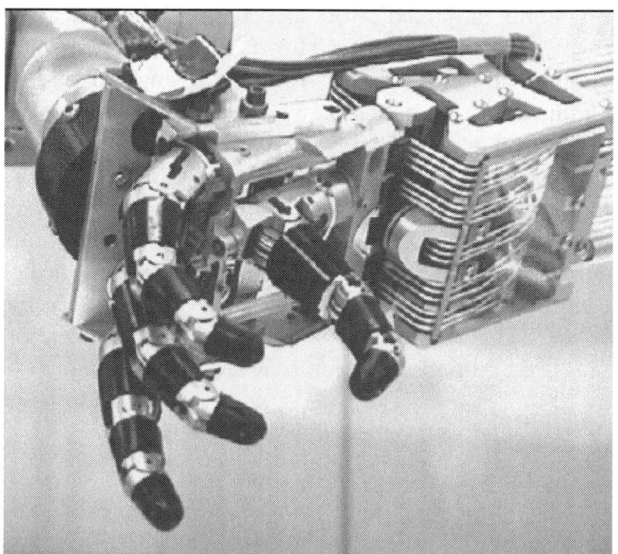

Figure 7. The MIT/Utah dexterous hand (courtesy of the University of Massachusetts Laboratory for Perceptual Robotics).

slides and driven independently by two dc servomotors through a rack and two pinions. Another development is the MIT/Utah dexterous hand (Fig. 7). However, human-like end effectors are likely to remain a subject of research for some time to come. The mechanical problems of packing all the actuator hardware in small enough space to fit a robot linkage, and the routing of tendons through wrists with three degrees of freedom, still have to be solved.

Programming

A key feature of robots is their capability to be reprogrammed for different tasks. Robot programming places special requirements on computer languages and systems. In addition to the data manipulation handled by normal programs, robot programs have to control motion, operate in parallel, communicate with programs which may be in other computers, synchronize with external events, respond to interrupts (q.v.) in real time, operate on sensor variables, and initialize and terminate in physically safe ways. Reprogramming was a feature missing from the manipulators seen before the advent of the industrial robot in the 1970s. The first robot programming language, WAVE, was developed for research purposes at Stanford Research Institute (SRI) in 1973, followed in 1974 by the AL language. Victor Scheinman and Bruce Simano subsequently combined the two languages into the commercial VAL language for Unimation.

Programming languages developed over the years were usually dialectical extensions of some popular general-purpose computer languages, such as Basic (q.v.). One such dialect is the ARMBASIC robot language, aptly named by Microbot, Inc., its creator and copyright owner. Another language based on Basic is AML, made popular by IBM's version of the SCARA robot.

Programming of robots is still to a large extent carried out either by using a *teach pendent* (a hand-held controller allowing an operator to move a robot through the desired motions by pressing buttons on the controller), use of a dummy robot, or *walkthrough* (referring to the manual dry-run mode employed for say, paint-spraying).

The potential offered by the flexibility of robots can be fully realized only when robots can be easily reprogrammed. The cost of programming a robot, even for simple tasks, can be very high. Consequently, reducing this cost will improve the economic viability of using robots in industry. This high cost can be overcome in a number of ways, such as improved sensing, parameterization of robot control procedures so that they are independent of physical assumptions, development of multifingered general-purpose end effectors coupled with a theory of grasping, development of

tools for task planning, and for converting task plans into robot programs.

To meet the goals of task-level planning, research has progressed from low-level machine code programming to higher levels of abstraction. A hierarchical decomposition similar to design of other computer programs is taking place in robot programming. This decomposition reflects the nature of robotic tasks and the nature of robots themselves.

Artificial Intelligence must have a central role in robotics if the connection of perception and action is to be intelligent. The application of AI to robotics involves practical problems in a real physical world as opposed to "traditional" applications that involve artificial problems in abstract domains. AI in robotics aims to tackle the problems of knowledge representation (q.v.) (particularly sensor data), how to perceive aspects of the world which affect the problems at hand, how to use knowledge in problem solving, and how to act on that knowledge in the robot's current situation. In robotics, researchers are working, and trying to copy, the human capabilities of mobility, dexterity, intelligence and sensory perception.

Prospects

Robotics is still in its infancy. In the laboratories, research into the science of robotics will contribute to maturing robotics technology. Research into sensors is focusing to a large extent on fusion (combining signals from several sensors to form a world model). Two areas are being examined. One is the design of a range of sensors with the same resolution, time base, field of view, and depth of field. But the perspective problem which arises from different locations of the sensors remains. The second area is the development of transforms that map each sensor into a similar field of view and then combine the images at specific moments. This is like overlaying several drawings on a drawing board.

The development of action-level and task-level languages hinges upon the ability to solve the problems of modeling the task while it is executing. This includes task description techniques, methods for modeling three-dimensional objects, and algorithms and heuristics (q.v.) for reasoning about relationships between objects in order to infer the results of actions on those objects. At a lower level, considerable work remains in the development of flexible robot-level languages and languages that are easily extendable to new applications. To improve the performance of robots, the problems of sensor integration, including the handling of sensor variables, and of interprocess communication, particularly between sensors and robot controllers, continue to be actively studied.

Models of the physical processes that robots are to execute, ranging from theoretical models of grasping to models of, say, machining processes need to be developed and refined. Other areas where considerable research is currently under way include the dynamics of motion and balance, the control of articulated fingers, perception of the environment from sensory information, hybrid control of robots and other objects in their environment, general solutions for inverse kinematics, control of robot dynamics, navigation in unstructured environments, three-dimensional vision, and the control of highly flexible robot links.

Moreover, the question of the social impact of robots has yet to be adequately addressed, but is likely to be significant.

Periodical Literature

Current developments in robotics are reported regularly in such periodicals as:

Autonomous Robots
The International Journal of Robotics Research
The International Journal of Robotics in Automation
Proceedings of the IEEE Conference on Robotics and Automation
Proceedings of the International Symposium on Industrial Robots
Robotica, the Journal of Robotics Systems

Additional journals are listed in the Appendix III category Automation, Cybernetics, and Robotics.

Bibliography

1994. Zheng, Y. F. *Recent Trends in Mobile Robots.* Singapore: World Scientific.
1996. Franklin, J. A., Mitchell, T. M., and Thrun, S. (eds.) *Recent Advances in Robot Learning.* Boston: Kluwer Academic Publishers.
1998. Fuller, J. L. *Robotics: Introduction, Programming, and Projects.* Upper Saddle River, NJ: Prentice Hall.
1998. Moravec, H. *ROBOT: Mere Machines to Transcendent Minds.* New York: Oxford University Press.
1999. Lee, T. H., Harris, C. J., and Shuzhi, S.G. *Adaptive Neural Network Control of Robotic Manipulators.* Singapore: World Scientific.
1999. Nof, S. Y. *Handbook of Industrial Robotics.* New York: John Wiley.

Websites

http://www.hompro.com/techkids/. Excellent for robotics for students and hobbyists and links to other related Websites.
http://www.fzi.de/ipt/WMC/preface/preface.html. A good pictorial reference for wheeled and legged robots.
http://www.cbc.umn.edu/~mwd/robot.html. Covers robotics, learning, chaos, complexity, systems theory, lots of links to other useful robotics related sites.
http://www.elet.polimi.it/section/compeng/air/robotics/mobile/. Covers a range of robotics research topics.

Raj Bhatti

ROM

See READ-ONLY MEMORY.

ROUNDOFF ERROR

For articles on related subjects *see* ERROR ANALYSIS; ERRORS; INTERVAL ARITHMETIC; and NUMERICAL ANALYSIS.

Computers typically deal with numbers of fixed length (i.e. with a fixed number of digits or bits) when performing arithmetic (although there are exceptions to this). For example, when multiplying two numbers each of which has n bits, the resulting $2n$-bit product is usually *rounded* (or, on some few computers, truncated) to n bits. The error that results from this is called *roundoff error*, or sometimes *rounding error*. With pencil and paper calculations, such roundoff is seldom significant, but with millions or even billions of arithmetic operations performed in computer calculations, the effects of roundoff can be considerable and sometimes disastrous. In addition, even a single roundoff error can be disastrous in large problems solved on a computer (see below for an example of this). Roundoff also occurs when the data for a calculation, which may be known exactly, must be rounded to n bits when read into and stored in a computer.

As examples of how large a single roundoff error can be, we consider two cases, both assuming the use of fixed-point arithmetic on a computer using 32-bit numbers with binary point at the left end, as shown in Fig. 1.

Case 1. Multiplication of two 31-bit numbers rounded to a 31-bit product. Rounding to a 31-bit product means that the thirty-second bit of the product is examined. If it is 0 (i.e. bits 32–62 represent less than $\frac{1}{2} \times 2^{-31}$), then nothing is done; if it is 1 (i.e. bits 32–62 represent greater than or equal to $\frac{1}{2} \times 2^{-31}$), then 1 is added into bit position 31 of the product. The magnitude of the error in the product is therefore no greater than

$$\tfrac{1}{2} \times 2^{-31} = 2^{-32}.$$

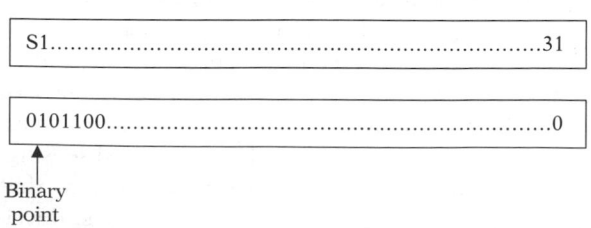

Figure 1. The 31-bit number shown with positive sign (0) has the value 0.1011 = 11/16.

Case 2. An exact datum is read into the computer and rounded to 31 bits. If the rounding is done as above, by looking at the thirty-second bit, then again the magnitude of the error is no greater than 2^{-32}.

The analysis of roundoff error in a long calculation is usually very difficult. Sometimes, by considering the worst possible error magnitude in each roundoff, a bound on the worst error in the result can be obtained, but this bound may be very conservative (i.e. much larger than the actual error). For example, suppose each of N numbers read into the computer, as in Case 2 above, are added. The quantity $N \times 2^{-32}$ is then a bound on the error in the sum, but this bound will occur only if all numbers have the maximum possible roundoff error *with the same sign*. Generally, individual roundoff errors will be less than the maximum possible and will have both positive and negative values so that there will be some cancellation of errors when they are added. Probabilistic analysis shows that, for this addition example, the *probable error*, defined as the value exceeded by the actual roundoff error one-half of the time, is given approximately by $0.2 \times N^{1/2} \times 2^{-32}$. The *square root rule* (i.e. replacing the number of operations N by $N^{1/2}$) is often used as a rule of thumb in making probable error estimates from maximum error bounds.

As an example of the disastrous effects that roundoff error can have, we consider the case of finding the zeros of the polynomial

$$(x-1)(x-2)(x-3)\cdots(x-20),$$

where the computer is given the coefficients A_0 to A_{19} in

$$x^{20} + A_{19}x^{19} + A_{18}x^{18} + \cdots + A_2 x^2 + A_1 x + A_0.$$

It is easily calculated that $A_{19} = -210$. Now suppose that the coefficients $A_0, A_1, \ldots, A_{18}$ are all stored exactly in the computer, but that, because of a roundoff error, A_{19} is stored as $-210 - 2^{-23}$, noting that 2^{-23} is approximately one ten-millionth. This one error changes the polynomial so that—even if the computer then calculated the zeros exactly (i.e. with no further roundoff errors)—instead of $1, 2, \ldots, 20$, it would obtain (correct to three decimal places)

1.000	6.000	$10.095 \pm 0.644i$
2.000	7.000	$11.794 \pm 1.652i$
3.000	8.007	$13.992 \pm 2.519i$
4.000	8.917	$16.731 \pm 2.813i$
5.000	20.847	$19.502 \pm 1.940i$

Not only have the larger zeros become quite inaccurate, but ten of them have also changed from real to complex conjugate pairs, all because of one error in the seventh decimal place. Problems in which a single, small roundoff error in the data or in subsequent calculation results in much larger errors in the answers, are called *ill-conditioned*. Recognition of ill-condition may be difficult, although some classes of problems— such as the calculation of the zeros of high-degree polynomials—are known to be generally ill-conditioned. Unless an ill-conditioned problem can be somehow transformed to a well-conditioned form, it is usually true that the only way to overcome ill-condition is by using multiple precision arithmetic in which the individual roundoff errors will be much smaller.

Bibliography

1963. Wilkinson, J. H. *Rounding Errors in Algebraic Processes.* Upper Saddle River, NJ: Prentice Hall. (Reprinted 1994, New York: Dover.)

Anthony Ralston

ROUTER

See GATEWAY.

RPN (REVERSE POLISH NOTATION)

See POLISH NOTATION.

RUN TIME

See COMPILE AND RUN TIME.

SCANNER, OPTICAL

See OPTICAL CHARACTER RECOGNITION, and UNIVERSAL PRODUCT CODE.

SCHEDULING ALGORITHMS

For articles on related subjects *see* INTERRUPT; MEMORY MANAGEMENT; MULTIPROGRAMMING; OPERATING SYSTEMS; QUEUEING THEORY; REAL-TIME SYSTEMS; SWAPPING; TIME SHARING; TIME SLICE; VIRTUAL MEMORY; and WORKING SET.

A computing system consists of a finite set of resources, such as processor cycles, memory locations, and input–output (I/O) devices which many programs or processes may need to use. The object of a *scheduling algorithm* is to allocate these resources to the programs that require them. At each decision point, a scheduling algorithm must decide which of several competing processes should next receive a given resource.

One crucial resource in any computer system is the processor itself, since every process residing in the system must have the processor allocated to it for some period of time in order for the process to complete execution and then leave the system. In this article, we will discuss processor scheduling algorithms for both single-processor and multiprocessor (*q.v.*) systems.

There are two main phases of processor scheduling activity. During the job management phase, several programs (or *jobs*) are selected for execution and are loaded into available memory. Then, during the dispatching phase, a processor is assigned to one after another of the memory resident programs. In general, the simpler dispatching algorithm is executed many times between any two executions of the more complex job management scheduling algorithm; the job management algorithm itself may be dynamically modified still more infrequently.

In describing the essential concepts of scheduling, we shall first assume a single-processor computer system. While our discussion will treat the dispatching and job management aspects of scheduling separately, these two functions are often integrated in existing systems. We first discuss the simpler dispatching function.

Dispatching involves the allocation of processor cycles to active programs, those programs that are currently in memory and competing for processor time. A given active program is in one of three states. It is either *executing*, *ready* to execute, or *blocked* waiting for the occurrence of some event, such as the completion of an I/O operation. It is the task of the short-term scheduling algorithm or *dispatcher* to decide which of the ready processes is to receive processor time and for how long (the *time slice*). The usual algorithm cycles *round-robin* through the set of ready programs, allocating the processor to each program in turn. The program executes until it blocks or terminates, or until its time quantum expires (*see* Fig. 1). This simple scheme is appropriate, since dispatching is done very frequently and the time involved in this type of scheduling (the *overhead*) must therefore be minimized.

The result of the dispatcher consecutively allocating processor cycles to several different memory resident processes is called *multiprogramming*. A single

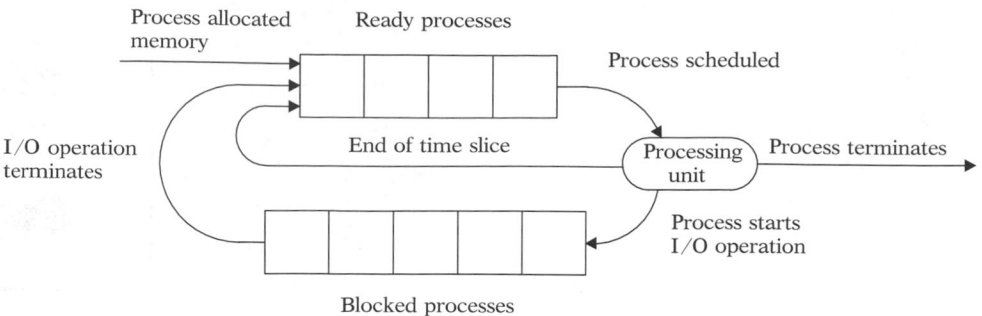

Figure 1. Dispatching.

processor appears to be executing multiple programs concurrently. Equivalently, we can say that a single processor is made to simulate the effects of several independent *virtual processors*. The task of the job management algorithm then becomes the assignment of one job to each virtual processor.

The object of the short-term scheduler or dispatcher is to maintain good utilization of the processor and I/O devices. The level of multiprogramming or, equivalently, the number of virtual processors is determined primarily by how many programs (or their *working sets* in a virtual memory system) fit comfortably in the memory, and this number may vary, depending on the job mix, or may be fixed.

The object of job management scheduling, in contrast, is to carry out management objectives with respect to total system utilization. The management policy may strive to satisfy a majority of casual users at the expense of a minority of users with very high resource demands. Alternatively, the management policy may favor production runs and allow casual use only when the system is otherwise underutilized. Regardless, it is primarily the task of the job management scheduling algorithm to achieve the stated management objectives.

Typically, to achieve this aim, a priority function is defined and each program in the system has a priority value that is updated at fixed decision points by the scheduling algorithm. The programs having the highest priority at each decision point are then assigned virtual processors. Between these job management decision points, the programs are managed by the simpler dispatching algorithm, which typically does not involve the overhead of priority calculations.

A great deal of work has gone into the development of different job management scheduling algorithms, and many different algorithms are used on current systems. We will discuss only some general approaches rather than giving the details of any particular system.

One important factor in this level of scheduling involves the choice of decision points. One could

choose to recalculate priorities only when a program enters an empty or underutilized system, or when a program terminates execution. It is more common, however, to define a preemptive scheduling algorithm where a fixed time interval is specified and the scheduling algorithm is executed at the end of each such interval. Depending upon the priority function chosen, use of this scheme can prevent a few long programs from monopolizing the processor. In general, more users are kept satisfied when shorter programs get preferential treatment.

The priority of each program may depend upon such static parameters as memory requirements, requirements for special I/O devices, or management-dictated preferential treatment; or upon such dynamic parameters as the amount of processor time already received, how long the program has been resident in the system, or recent frequency of I/O operations. The resulting set of priority values may uniquely order the waiting programs or merely group them. In the latter case, if several programs have the same highest priority, then the job management scheduling algorithm commonly cycles round-robin through these programs, giving each the opportunity to reside in memory for some time quantum.

Job management scheduling algorithms have also received much theoretical attention. The techniques of queueing theory have been used to model simple scheduling algorithms for statistically defined classes of programs, and to determine analytic system performance measures for them. While these models are necessarily somewhat simplistic, they do indicate the relative benefits of such different approaches as first in, first out (FIFO), shortest job first (SJF), shortest remaining time first (SRTF), and round-robin (RR).

As system load characteristics change over time, the management policy may be best implemented by also changing the job management algorithm. This can be done by either switching to a totally different algorithm or by modifying parameters in the existing algorithm. To implement this adaptive control of the scheduling algorithm, a set of system descriptors such as queue lengths must be identified and updated. As the values of these descriptors may vary significantly from desired norms, the job management scheduling algorithm is dynamically modified.

We now extend our discussion of single-processor scheduling to describe scheduling of time-shared, real-time, and multiprocessor systems.

In a time-shared system, the processor must be allocated to each terminal user in such a way that the computationally trivial interactive requests of the user are quickly responded to, and other requests requiring more resources have response times proportional to their resources demands. Typically, management objectives have shifted from efficient hardware usage towards satisfactory response time characteristics. In this environment, many user programs are in an inactive state waiting for the user to provide terminal input, and they need not be retained in memory. The active user programs are those that have a terminal request outstanding, and these programs must be brought into the physical memory for execution within some short time interval.

In such a time-sharing system, the scheduler may maintain two or more program queues in order to distinguish between active programs that have not received service and may therefore have just a trivial interactive request, and other active programs that have already received one or more full quanta of service, thus indicating a more substantive request. All new program requests in this multi-level treatment are serviced before the processor continues to execute any other unsatisfied requests, thus improving response characteristics. If all the active programs do not fit in memory, then response times may increase as active user programs are swapped in and out of memory to satisfy the requirement that all new active processes receive some service before others receive additional service.

Real-time systems, such as those used to control production machinery, are characterized as having certain programs whose execution must be completed within fixed time intervals. The key parameter of the job management scheduling algorithm is the length of time remaining until the program's deadline is reached. As the time leeway diminishes, the program's priority increases. Sophisticated special-purpose algorithms have been developed to predict accurately future resource requirements and availability; to manage explicitly processor, disk, and memory aggregates to achieve real-time goals; and to shut down selectively system functionality in such a way as to minimize external disruption.

We next consider scheduling for multiprocessors, which we characterize as consisting of several processors of similar power executing from a large common memory. The role of scheduling is the same as described before—to use the physical processors to simulate a possibly larger number of virtual processors; to allocate programs to these virtual processors; and to adapt the scheduling algorithm to changes in the workload. A key design decision for the multiprocessor concerns the choice of processor(s) to do the scheduling. The scheduling algorithms may always be executed by one processor, may float from processor to processor, or may be executed by each processor as it requires scheduling.

In a master–slave multiprocessor operating system, one processor is responsible for scheduling all work on the system. Whenever a slave processor requires service, it must request service and wait until the current program on the master processor is interrupted so that the scheduling algorithm can be executed. Although this control strategy is easy to implement, access to the scheduling processor may become a system bottleneck and any failure in the master processor stops the entire system.

In an operating system with a floating scheduler, any one processor at a time may perform the scheduling functions for the system, with either a software or hardware controller preventing two processors from scheduling simultaneously. While somewhat more difficult to implement, this form of control does have the potential for greater reliability than the master–slave organization.

In a multiprocessor operating system using distributed control, each processor is responsible for scheduling itself from a common table of scheduling information. System-wide conventions are used for processes entering into the scheduling queues and for assigning priorities; standard synchronization techniques are used to prevent two processors from accessing and changing the scheduling information at the same time. This organization, like that of the floating scheduler, has good reliability and is easily extensible to additional processors.

Over the past decades, decreasing hardware costs and increasing chip density have led to more and more powerful single-processor computers. Increasingly, these computers are networked to each other and to specialized filing, database, printing, and communications servers. System-wide scheduling has been simplified by allocating interactive tasks to single-user workstations (q.v.) and other time-critical tasks to dedicated network servers. There have been few attempts to schedule more effectively the total available computing resources in distributed computing environments.

Bibliography

1984. Comer, D. *Operating System Design—The XINU Approach.* Upper Saddle River, NJ: Prentice Hall.
1988. Finkel, R. A. *An Operating Systems Vade Mecum,* 2nd Ed. Upper Saddle River, NJ: Prentice Hall.
1995. Pinedo, M. *Scheduling: Theory, Algorithms, and Systems.* Upper Saddle River, NJ: Prentice Hall.

Leslie Jill Miller

SCIENTIFIC APPLICATIONS

For articles on related subjects *see* ARTIFICIAL LIFE; BIOCOMPUTING; COMPUTER GRAPHICS; FRACTALS; GENETIC ALGORITHMS; IMAGE PROCESSING; MATHEMATICS, COMPUTERS IN; MATRIX COMPUTATIONS; MEDICAL IMAGING; MOLECULAR COMPUTING; MONTE CARLO METHOD; NEURAL NETWORKS; NUMERICAL ANALYSIS; PARALLEL PROCESSING; PARTIAL DIFFERENTIAL EQUATIONS; PATTERN RECOGNITION; QUANTUM COMPUTING; SCIENTIFIC VISUALIZATION; SIMULATION; STATISTICAL APPLICATIONS; SUPERCOMPUTERS; SUPERCOMPUTING CENTERS; and TOMOGRAPHY, COMPUTERIZED.

Introduction

Computation has always played a central role in science. A new theory either gains acceptance or dies in direct proportion to its success in explaining known phenomena and predicting new ones, not just qualitatively but also quantitatively. Einstein's theory of relativity predicted not just that light should be deflected in passing by a massive object, such as the Sun, but also the precise amount by which it should be deflected. No computer is needed for such a prediction (indeed, the first such calculation antedated electronic computers by almost 50 years), but a certain minimum amount of arithmetic computation is nonetheless required.

Truly fundamental physical phenomena are governed by equations that describe what happens to small particles or energy bundles as they move through space and time. In the same way in which the physicist's quest to explore particle phenomena at ever higher ranges of energy leads to the construction of ever larger (and more costly) accelerators, the attempt to solve these equations in increasing detail has led to a continual need for computers of higher speed and greater memory capacity. The initial sections of this article attempt to explain why.

The Quest for High-Performance Computation

DIRECT CALCULATIONS

Monte Carlo. It is often of scientific interest to calculate the behavior of aggregates of particles over large regions of space or long time intervals. Scientists facing such a task usually have a choice of two basically different approaches. One can calculate the flight of an individual particle until it is scattered by a second particle, absorbed, or leaves the region of observation. The exact history of each particle depends on a sequence of random numbers chosen and used in such a way as to constrain the particle to experience one event or another in accord with its correct probability. Tracking and accumulating statistics on thousands of such particles then enable the calculation of quantities of physical interest. Such a technique is called the *Monte Carlo method* (*q.v.*), for obvious reasons, and finds application in such diverse situations as the behavior of neutrons in a reactor, light quanta in stellar atmospheres, and automobiles in heavy traffic. Monte Carlo calculations are inherently time-consuming, even on *supercomputers* (*q.v.*), because of the necessity to follow a sufficiently large number of particles to obtain results that are accurate within statistically acceptable limits of error.

Algebraic, integral and ordinary differential equations. The second principal line of computational attack occurs more often—namely when (1) the behavior of the quantity of interest is known to obey a linear or nonlinear algebraic equation, a differential equation, an integral equation, or an integro-differential equation over some region of space–time of given shape, and when (2) the desired quantity obeys specified boundary conditions in space (and initial conditions in time in time-dependent problems). Taking differential equations as an example, the simplest situations occur when the desired quantity (the dependent variable) is a function of only one independent variable, perhaps time or one space dimension. Such differential equations are called *ordinary*. In such cases, either an analytic solution is obtainable or the use of a simple difference equation approximation will allow the production of desired answers in a few seconds of computer time.

Partial differential equations. When the dependent variable is a function of two or more independent variables, the appropriate differential equation is called a *partial differential equation* (PDE) because it involves partial derivatives that indicate the change in the dependent variable as one or another of the independent variables change, while holding all other independent variables fixed. Except under special circumstances, the solution of such equations is computationally formidable. As an example, consider an electromagnetic wave impinging on a target of given shape and internal composition. In principle, Maxwell's system of differential equations and attendant boundary conditions completely specifies the behavior of the radiation scattered from the target. When the target is either a metallic (perfectly reflecting) sphere or a penetrable sphere of homogeneous and isotropic internal electrical properties, Maxwell's partial differential equations reduce to three ordinary differential equations, one each specifying the behavior of the scattered wave along the r, φ, and θ directions in spherical coordinates. This has been known at least as far back as 1908, and so-called Mie calculations (after their originator), while tedious, can be programmed and normally take only a few milliseconds of computer time.

Now imagine the target, while still spherical, to have internal electrical properties that are a function of radial position. Perhaps the core is dense and surrounded by a diffuse fringe. Then Maxwell's equations still separate into three ordinary differential equations, but the radial equation, which in the homogeneous case was known to have solutions familiar to scientists (Bessel functions), must now be solved from point to point by difference methods. A digital computer is now a virtual necessity.

Progressive relaxations of symmetry conditions will each greatly extend computer running time: nonspherical but still axially symmetric targets will require up to a second or two, and anisotropic targets will need several seconds to a minute or more (depending on spatial symmetry), and so on up to completely nonsymmetric anisotropic targets, which would take from several minutes to an hour, even on the fastest computers presently available.

Reactor design. The situation described above is typical of a number of physical situations. A scientist will often know that the subject of study is governed by equations whose full complexity places exact solutions beyond the capability of the computer available. A sufficient number of approximations is then made to bring a typical calculation down to an acceptable bound, usually an hour or less. When the host installation increases its capability by, say, a factor of four, the scientist will not necessarily be content to run four times as many cases in unit time, but will often remove a restriction or approximation, that will bring total running time back to what it had been for the simpler case. In reactor design, for example, it is known that neutron behavior is governed by a complex integro-differential equation known as Boltzmann's equation. This equation takes into account that, at any given spatial point, the rate of neutron flow depends on the speed and direction of individual neutrons and, to a certain extent, on their past history. The solution of such an equation everywhere throughout the reactor volume for all possible neutron velocities is a task beyond presently available computers.

What can be done, however, and usually is done, is to make approximations that replace the Boltzmann equation with a series of coupled partial differential equations, each of which calculates the neutron flux at a particular energy (speed) at a given space point. Each such equation, a so-called diffusion equation, is then calculated in either one, two, or three space dimensions, whichever the symmetry of the reactor (or expediency) demands. Any horizontal plane through a reactor core can be modeled in Cartesian (x, y) coordinates, but other geometric arrangements often dictate use of polar (r, θ) or cylindrical (r, z) coordinates. Any of these geometries reduces to this simple situation: given that p, a, c, d, and e are known functions of position (precalculated and stored in computer memory prior to the time-consuming calculation of neutron flux), we would like to know what values of neutron flux $(\varphi_P, \varphi_A, \varphi_C, \varphi_D, \varphi_E)$ balance the equation

$$p\varphi_P - a\varphi_A - c\varphi_C - d\varphi_D - e\varphi_E = 0$$

at every mesh-point P, where left, right, bottom, and top neighboring points are designated A, C, D, and E, respectively (B-back and F-front are conventionally reserved for 3D calculations). All questions of geometry, material composition, and boundary condition are buried in the calculation of the coefficients. Any one such equation has five unknowns, and hence cannot be solved uniquely, but since a similar equation must hold at every mesh point, a 100,000-point model (say) represents 100,000 equations in 100,000 unknowns. In principle, this can be solved by inverting a $100,000 \times 100,000$ matrix. Such an attempt would be not only foolish but unnecessary. Since most elements of such a matrix would be zero (the result of using only a nearest-neighbor numerical approximation to derivatives in the diffusion equation), the desired fluxes are best obtained iteratively. There are a variety of methods for doing this, but most process a line of points at a time, sweeping all lines a sufficient number of times to obtain the desired convergence. Here, "sweeping" means the consistent solution of just the 300 (say) points on a line by a systematic forward-elimination/backward-substitution method applicable to so-called three-term or *tridiagonal* linear systems (matrices whose only nonzero elements are on the diagonal or next to the diagonal).

Quantum chromodynamics. Although the preceding discussion assumed the use of a two-dimensional slice taken from a full three-dimensional reactor, the technique can be extended (at great expense in computer time) to all three space dimensions, or even to four dimensions: three spatial dimensions plus time. An example from another computationally intense field, elementary particle physics, is shown in Fig. 1 on Color Page CP-12 (Bitar and Heller, 1992). The three smaller spheres inside the larger one represent quarks that combine to form a single *hadron*, such as a neutron or a proton. The larger sphere represents a "bag" within which the quarks are forever confined, interacting in accord with the laws of quantum chromodynamics (QCD). To solve the time-dependent equations that describe these interactions, space–time is modeled by a four-dimensional grid, with force fields defined on the sites or links of the lattice. Coping with the nonlinear dynamics of the model has become one of the most demanding computational projects in physics. A typical QCD simulation on a $16^3 \times 32$ lattice (about 100,000 mesh points) requires 10^{16} floating-point operations. Fortunately, the fields at every node of the lattice are treated identically, so that such calculations are highly suitable for both vector supercomputers and massively parallel supercomputers.

Cosmology and astrophysics. At the opposite end of the size scale—the world of the very large rather than the very small—N-body calculations in cosmology and astrophysics are the most computationally intensive in all of science. The process by which galaxies form is among the most important unsolved problems in physics. Modern observations span the electromagnetic spectrum from radio frequency to gamma rays, but a firm theoretical understanding of photographic images of 40 years ago is still being sought. Even the question of why there are two families of galaxies, spiral and elliptical, is still a mystery.

The first step in understanding how galaxies and stars form is to understand the environment in which their formation occurs. Thus, scientists use computer simulation to study the shapes and dynamics of "dark matter" halos which are known to surround observed galaxies. The matter is called "dark" because it does not emit detectable radiation; its presence is inferred by its effect on galaxy rotation. In an astrophysical N-body simulation of dark matter, the phase space density distribution is represented by a large collection of "particles" which evolve in time according to Newtonian laws of motion and universal gravitation. Direct implementation of the system of equations that governs these particles is simply a double program loop. In the language of supercomputing, it vectorizes well and it parallelizes easily and efficiently (*see* PARALLEL PROCESSING: LANGUAGES). Unfortunately, in a simulation with N bodies, the time required to solve the equations exactly is proportional to N^2, which precludes their use for values of N larger than a few tens of thousands, even on the fastest parallel supercomputers. To compensate, researchers use an approximate method that employs an adaptive tree data structure (*q.v.*). The method reduces the time required to obtain an approximate answer to $O(N \log N)$, which allows for simulation of much larger systems. Speedups in excess of 400 over the single-processor

speed have been achieved on the Intel Delta Touchstone, a 512-node MIMD supercomputer.

In March 1992, researchers at Los Alamos, NM, ran a simulation with 8,783,848 bodies on 512 processors for 780 timesteps. The simulation was of a spherical region of space 10 megaparsecs on a side, a region large enough to contain several hundred typical galaxies. The simulation ran continuously for 16.7 hours, and carried out 3.24×10^{14} floating-point operations, for a sustained rate of 5.4 gigaflops. (A parsec is 3.26 light years. The abbreviation "*flops*" stands for "*fl*oating-point *o*perations *p*er *s*econd.") With a conventional $O(N^2)$ algorithm, it would have taken almost 3,000 times as long to obtain an equivalent answer. The speed of the Delta was sufficient to allow the simulated evolution of several hundred large galaxies simultaneously and provided statistics and information concerning environmental effects on evolution which cannot be obtained by simulating the formation of one galaxy at a time.

In June 1992, in response to the measurement of the microwave background anisotropy by the COBE satellite, the Los Alamos team ran two large simulations of the Cold Dark Matter model of the Universe. The COBE measurement constrained the last remaining free parameters left in the theory, and allowed the scientists to specify completely the statistical properties of the initial conditions. The simulations represented regions with diameters of 250 and 100 megaparsecs and had 17,158,608 and 17,154,598 bodies, respectively. With respect to the mass of the sun M_{Sun}, the individual particles each represented about $3.3 \times 10^{10} M_{\text{Sun}}$ and $2.0 \times 10^9 M_{\text{Sun}}$, respectively, so that galaxy-size halos are expected to form with tens to thousands of individual particles, enough to obtain reasonable statistics concerning the distributions and correlations of sizes. The spatial resolution was 20 kiloparsecs in both cases. The simulations ran for 597 and 667 timesteps, in 23.5 and 28.6 hours, respectively, and wrote 21 and 27 data files for a total of 11.53 and 13.72 GB. They respectively performed 4.33×10^{14} and 5.32×10^{14} floating-point operations, sustaining rates of 5.2 and 5.1 gigaflops, the largest N-body calculation done to that date. A graphical representation of the results of a typical cosmological N-body computation is shown in Fig. 2 on Color Page CP-12. The web-like clusters of galaxies are typical of what is actually observed.

Just three years later, Junichiro Makino and Makoto Taiji of the University of Tokyo reported an N-body calculation on a GRAPE-4 (GRAvity PipE) massively parallel computer of 1,692 pipelines that reached sustained speeds 100 times faster, 529 gigaflops, more than half a teraflop. The calculation simulated the behavior of two massive black holes in the core of a galaxy with 700,000 stars. By 1999, the NEC SX-5 and the Cray T3E were able to reach sustained rates eight times faster, about 4 teraflops.

Two-dimensional (2D) astrophysical calculations are far less demanding of computer time, but are nonetheless interesting. Since light from a distant point in the universe is bent by the gravitational fields of the stars which it passes, it is of interest to be able to compute the illumination pattern that will be produced by observing a particular configuration of stars. The relation to be solved is the Poisson equation $\nabla^2 \psi = -4\pi \rho(x, y)$ where the density ρ is 0 at most points x, y and nonzero at "sources" at particular x, y coordinates. The sources are "soft" lenses representing stars, "soft" implying a low index of refraction. Figs. 3a, b, c on Color Page CP-13 show, in order, a particular pattern of sources, the potential field that they induce, and, finally, the desired illumination field.

Chemical reactions. In some fields, the increasing speed and memory capacity of successive generations of digital computers have transformed the image that the computer conveys to the scientist from that of a tool—albeit a powerful one—to that of a new experimental device in its own right. Chemistry is a good example. The basic equation that governs the behavior of molecules, atoms, and (low-velocity) electrons has been known for over 70 years—the Schrödinger equation. Without a computer, only simple systems consisting of two or three particles can be studied in any detail. With the latest computers, however, ions of much larger atomic number can be followed kinetically as they interact with other ions to form molecules. If the chemist is able to watch the progression of such a reaction on a computer monitor, it is just as good or better (and less messy) than mixing the reagents in the laboratory. ("Better" because there are only limited means of varying the speed of an actual reaction, whereas the simulated reaction can proceed at "instant replay" slow motion on a display device through appropriate variation of the program parameters.)

INVERSE CALCULATIONS

All of the examples cited thus far are examples of *direct* calculational situations. We know the characteristics of a target and want to calculate its scattering properties. We know the reactor configuration and desire its lifetime behavior. We know the reagents and want to know their reactivity. As time-consuming as such calculations can be, they are routine in their demand for computer time compared with indirect or *inverse* calculations, where we have access to experimental data but no access at all to the source of the phenomena generating the data.

Interstellar dust. An example is the problem of interstellar dust particles. Astrophysicists and cosmologists would like to know the quantity, shape, and composition of these particles, since this knowledge has a bearing on theories of the origin and evolution of the universe. We cannot yet send spaceships to retrieve such matter, but we can observe quantities such as the polarization and absorption of light of various wavelengths passing through it. What kinds of particles produce the scattered light: Spherical? Elongated? Metallic? Anisotropic ferrite needles? Dirty ice? The question is far from settled, and the astrophysicist will need to experiment with many different models to achieve success without being at all sure that the answer is unique.

Planetary systems. A striking recent example of an inverse calculation was the deduction by astronomers that the star Upsilon Andromedae has a planetary system consisting of at least three large planets, each of a specific mass, orbital period, and eccentricity of orbit. Upsilon Andromedae is a bright star, visible to the naked eye, 44 light years away from Earth and roughly three billion years old, two-thirds the age of the Sun. This is the first multiple planet system ever found around a normal star, other than the nine planets in our Solar System.

The closest planet in the Upsilon Andromedae system was detected in 1996 by San Francisco State University astronomers Geoffrey Marcy and R. Paul Butler. Now, after years of observations at the Lick Observatory near San Jose, CA, the signals of two additional planets have emerged from extensive computer analyses of the data. Teams of astronomers from the Harvard-Smithsonian Center for Astrophysics (CfA) in Cambridge, MA, and the High Altitude Observatory (HAO) in Boulder, CO, independently found the two outer planets.

The method used by both teams was observation of the Doppler shift of the radial velocity of the star system. As a planet revolves around a star, the gravity from the planet pulls ever so slightly on that star. Astronomers use a spectrograph to study the light from a star suspected to have planets. Superimposed on the continuous spectrum obtained are many fine dark lines called absorption lines. Each of these lines represents a different element or compound in the atmosphere of the star. The positions of these lines are monitored over time to see if they move, an indication that a planet or some other astronomical companion is perturbing the motion of the star. If an object is moving towards or away from an observer, the positions of these lines shift back and forth as well, similar to the way the pitch of a train whistle changes as the train passes by. If the star is moving towards the observer, the spectrum is blueshifted; if moving away, it is redshifted (*see* Fig. 4 on

Color Page CP-13). By carefully monitoring a star's spectrum, the star's small wobble indicates what the mass of the planet is and its orbital period. When the data is sufficiently well reduced by intensive computer calculations, the presence of multiple planets of specific mass and orbital characteristics can be deduced.

The innermost of the three planets contains at least three-quarters of the mass of Jupiter and orbits only 0.06 AU from the star. (An Astronomical Unit (AU) is the distance from the Earth to the Sun.) It traverses a circular orbit every 4.6 days. The middle planet contains at least twice the mass of Jupiter and it takes 242 days to orbit the star. It resides approximately 0.83 AU from the star, similar to the orbital distance of Venus. The outermost planet has a mass of at least four Jupiters and completes one orbit every 3.5 to 4 years, placing it 2.5 AU from the star (*see* Fig. 5). Although the planetary masses are known, their densities and hence their sizes are not. The two outer planets have elliptical orbits, which is characteristic of the nine other known extrasolar planets in distant orbits around their stars. A computer simulation by Greg Laughlin of UC Berkeley showed that the three giant planets could coexist in stable orbits even if the star has additional but much less massive planets that could not be resolved by current methods.

A competitive method for the detection of planets, microlensing, is the inverse of the Poisson computation described in the prior section. Instead of computing the illumination pattern due to a known distribution of "microlenses," one must devise a computer program that processes an observed illumination pattern to deduce the pattern of lenses, possibly a planetary solar system, that produced it. The inverse calculation is far more demanding of computer resources than the direct calculation (DiStefano and Scalzo, 1999).

Crystallography. Crystallographic calculations are another example of inverse computations. It would be straightforward to calculate the pattern of X-rays diffracted from a known spatial distribution of known atoms, but we cannot get inside crystals or molecules the way Isaac Asimov's fictional scientists traveled through the circulatory system in the story and movie "Fantastic Voyage." We can observe the pattern of diffracted X-rays or neutrons impinging on a crystal of unknown structure, but in doing so, certain basic information (phase relations between atoms) is lost. Using what information is available, however, such as intensity data, suspected symmetries, and chemical formulas learned through destructive testing of portions of the same material, crystallographers are now able to use an organized trial-and-error method to deduce the structure of quite large molecules of up to 500 atoms or so, and the frontier is pushed ahead with each advance in computer technology. Figs. 6 and 7 on Color Page CP-13 show spectacular examples of how crystallographic structures can be rendered with modern computer graphics (*q.v.*).

As complex as they are, the structures of several proteins as well as the vitamin B-12 have been determined by computer techniques. Some programs are so sophisticated that they produce as a final result a stereo pair (Fig. 8) of similar views of the predicted molecular structure; viewing them through an appropriate optical device brings out the spatial arrangement and vibrational characteristics of a crystal's constituent atoms in stunning detail.

DNA sequencing. Traditionally, biologists have not used computers intensively, but that situation is changing rapidly (*see* BIOCOMPUTING). One of the more important types of inverse calculation is that needed to ascertain DNA sequences in molecular biology. Without high-speed computers, the Human Genome Project, whose goal is to deduce the gene sequences of all human chromosomes, would be impossible. For a discussion of the importance of computers in molecular biology, *see* Lander *et al.* (1991).

Geophysics. Just as the astrophysicist and the crystallographer are barred from entering the domain of the objects of their interest, so is the geophysicist unable

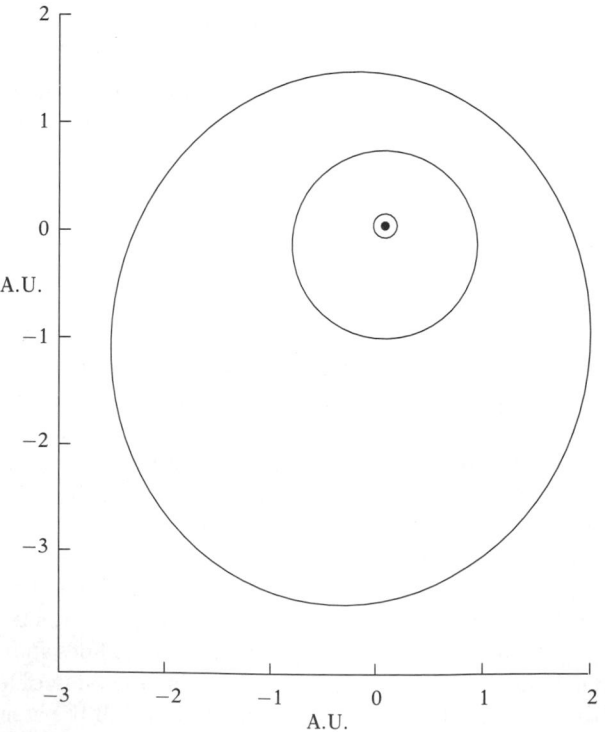

Figure 5. The orbits of the three massive planets of Upsilon Andromedae (the dot at [0, 0]).

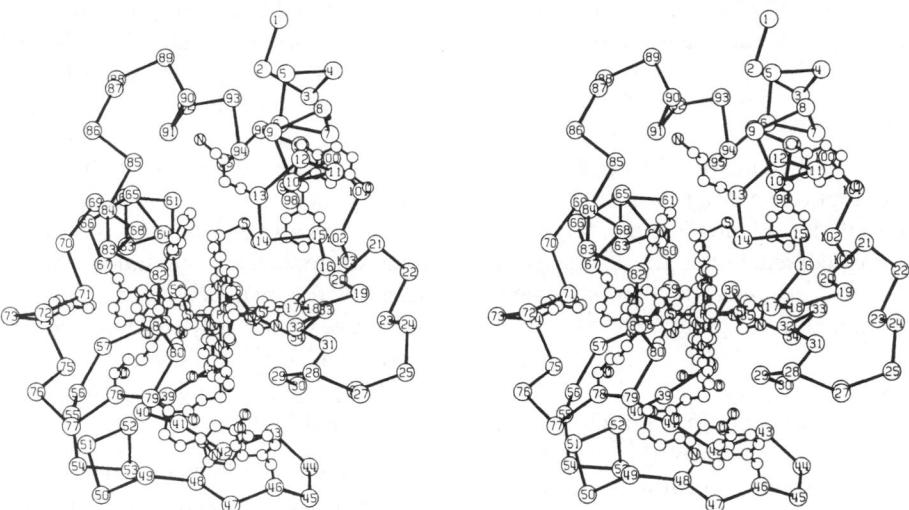

Figure 8. Stereoscopic pair of front view of reduced cytochrome *c* molecule from a tuna. (Source: R. E. Dickerson, California Institute of Technology.)

to examine more than a tiny fraction of the interior of the Earth. There is data, however, that gives extremely pointed clues as to the internal composition of the Earth—namely that provided through seismological records taken during periods of earthquake, volcanic eruption, and atomic testing. The Earth, like any (approximate) sphere of given internal composition, has certain characteristic modes of vibration, and allows elastic waves to propagate at certain speeds from point to point on its surface. By using digital computers to vary appropriate parameters in the equations that govern such phenomena, geophysicists have derived a profile of the Earth's interior with reasonable certitude, a confidence founded on agreement between the predicted characteristics of their model and observed properties. Based on such methods, they already predict a molten liquid core, and their detailed predictions of its shape and composition are being sharpened as they make increasingly detailed comparisons with experimental data of the effects that the liquid core might have on the Earth's rotational and magnetic properties. Similar methods are allowing geologists to map strain energies in the Earth in an attempt to understand earthquake phenomena.

Impact on Hardware Development

One obvious impact of the scientist's perceived need for ever higher performance computers to cope with the type of problems cited above is to create a market climate in which vendors are willing to design and develop supercomputers. Computers capable of 100 million floating-point operations per second (Mflops) are now rather commonplace and speeds in the teraflop (Tflop) range are attainable for certain problems running on massively parallel supercomputers.

Scientific users will have no difficulty absorbing the additional capacity that will be provided by ever-faster supercomputers. The four-dimensional QCD model described earlier used 100,000 mesh points, but only 16 along any one spatial dimension and 32 time-steps. Merely doubling the resolution in each dimension would require a computer 16 times faster in order to do a simulation in the same amount of running time. Simulation of supersonic flow over aircraft typically involves a million or more mesh points, so the scientific and engineering demand for ever larger main memories is also insatiable.

Similar points have been made with regard to modeling climate (Chervin, 1990). In the early 1970s, one hour of time on a CDC 6600 was needed to simulate one day of climate evolution using a very crude oceanic general circulation model. By the early 1980s, the same computation could be done in less than two minutes on a Cray 1A supercomputer. By the early 1990s, the Cray Y-MP8/832 reached a 1 gigaflop rate that reduced running time to a few seconds, but its doing so merely enticed the modelers to refine their model. The one they had been using had a resolution of only a half degree of latitude and longitude (about 35 miles at the equator) and 20 levels of altitude. Increasing the resolution will easily tax the added power of the latest teraflop supercomputers.

Fittingly enough, the advance of scientific research and the development of better computing devices are symbiotic. Faster speeds depend on faster switching devices, which, in turn, depend on such scientific advances as that of the Josephson junction, an outgrowth of research in solid state physics. Computers of the future that are able to use such junctions and certain other *superconducting devices* (*q.v.*) will lead to still further advances in solid state physics. The prospect of *quantum computing* (*q.v.*) is especially exciting.

Ancillary Roles

In addition to their obvious value for direct and inverse calculation, digital computers play a role in automating many other aspects of the scientist's personal workload. These will be discussed under the headings of instrumentation, information retrieval, computer algebra, and data reduction and presentation.

INSTRUMENTATION

Many of the instruments of modern research science have themselves become so complex that it is often expedient to control their operation automatically with a small computer directly connected to or embedded in the instrument. Nuclear reactors and particle accelerators are often controlled or at least monitored in this way, as are a wide range of other devices, such as radio and optical telescopes, nuclear magnetic resonance equipment, crystallographic apparatus, electron microscopes, and satellites controlled by telemetered signals emanating from computers on the ground below.

INFORMATION RETRIEVAL (*q.v.*)

The profusion of scientific papers being published makes it ever more difficult for working scientists to keep abreast of their fields, even in their own specialties. Some workers subscribe to computerized information retrieval services of one kind or another, or have access to libraries that do. Principal among these is the ability to file an interest profile with such a service center, and then be continually apprised of papers that match that profile as they are published. Another service makes a specific search over past literature according to certain keywords and key concepts. The development of the World Wide Web (*q.v.*) with its powerful search engines has now made it possible for ordinary researchers to keep abreast on their own. Many scientific journals now routinely post their articles on the Internet, and new specialized journals are being born at a rapid rate that exist only as electronic journals, or *e-journals*. The publishers of some journals—*Nature*, for example—email the current table of contents of their journal to all those who register for this cost-free service.

COMPUTER ALGEBRA

In an important sense, the digital "computer" has not been named to convey its most significant capability, namely, the ability to manipulate symbols. Babbage's assistant Augusta Ada Byron, the Countess of Lovelace (*q.v.*), forecast this very presciently in 1843 when she wrote "Many persons who are not conversant with mathematical studies imagine that because the business of the [Analytical] Engine (*q.v.*) is to give its results in numerical notation, the nature of its processes must consequently be arithmetical and numerical, rather than algebraical and analytical. This is an error. The Engine can arrange and combine its numerical quantities exactly as if they were letters or any other general symbols." More specifically, a digital computer can be programmed to automate the operations of applied mathematics, the very skill that the scientific theorist needs to cast predictions in calculable form (*see* COMPUTER ALGEBRA and SYMBOL MANIPULATION.) The most widely used commercial computer algebra programs are Derive, Macsyma, Mathematica, Maple, and Reduce.

Even when a mathematical derivation is tractable, it is reassuring to the scientist that a computer algebra program is able to verify the result. And there have been times when such a program has uncovered human error and countless others where a program has been able to carry analysis well beyond the point where the human brain can tolerate the strain. A specific example of the use of computer algebra in scientific analysis will be given in a later section.

DATA REDUCTION AND PRESENTATION

The data produced by an experimental instrument is seldom directly usable. It usually needs some kind of scaling, noise filtering, time integration, or other treatment that is ideally suited to computer processing. As a byproduct of this data reduction, a properly equipped computer can also display the reduced data, either in hard-copy form on a graph plotter or in a transient visual form on a display screen. Thus, a scientist may monitor an experiment in progress and perhaps even input feedback information that alters the later course of the research.

Pattern recognition. Some of the more interesting applications of data reduction occur in a pattern recognition (*q.v.*) context. The classic example is the widespread use of devices called *bubble chambers* in high-energy physics. Particles passing through such devices leave visible tracks composed of tiny bubbles that can be photographed and scanned for the occurrence of interesting branch-like structures that indicate the presence of a collision or reaction between particles. Although humans can do this quite well, a bubble chamber can snap a new picture every few seconds and easily reach an annual production of over a million frames. Such prodigious output can be coped with only by computerized pattern recognition techniques, and modern accelerators are serviced by large computers devoted almost exclusively to this task.

In a similar vein, pattern recognition by computer has been used by scientists in other fields. Biologists have successfully identified mutant chromosomes among normal ones through such techniques. Atmospheric scientists are experimenting with attempts to identify cyclone-like disturbances in cloud-cover satellite photos. Archeologists have successfully reconstructed murals from Egyptian temples by fitting together photographs of stone fragments as if they were pieces in a gigantic jigsaw puzzle solved by computer matching of similar patterns. In another application, but with far fewer pieces to worry about, earth scientists have tested theories of continental drift by doing a computerized comparison of how well the east coast of North and South America fits the west coast of Europe and Africa, and found the fit to be very plausible indeed.

Image processing. Pattern recognition, or at least computerized *image processing* (*q.v.*), also plays a vital role in planetary exploration. NASA space probes that flew by Mars (and Jupiter and Saturn) in recent years transmitted pictures back to Earth in digital form, specifically, as a series of 40,000 six-bit data points, each representing on a scale of 0 to 63 the shade of gray that was observed at the intersection of a 200×200 grid array superimposed on the visual scene. Once read into the memory of a high-speed computer, such a digitized picture was then easily "cleaned up" by removing spurious noise and enhancing its resolution for human viewing, thus producing the sharp and often breathtaking photos presented in news magazines at the time.

Scientific visualization. By *scientific visualization* (*q.v.*) is meant the ability to present data in simulated three-dimensional form on a high-resolution color graphics display device, rather than as a simple two-dimensional graph or, worse, the raw form that a printed sequence of numbers would provide. The object depicted may or may not be a "real" one that a human of suitable scale could ever see, or, even when it is, "false color" may be used to bring out interrelationships that would otherwise be difficult to ascertain. The pattern of Fig. 9 on Color Page CP-14 is fascinating because the object depicted does not exist as a pattern of matter that could ever be observed by the human eye or any optical instrument (Pickett *et al.*, 1992). The "image" is that of the calculated surfaces in momentum space (*Fermi surfaces*) for the charge carriers in the (relatively) high-temperature superconductor $YBa_2Cu_3O_7$. Such a beautiful "object" will never be seen directly and no artist would likely have rendered it from imagination. Nonetheless, even those who do not benefit from the scientific information it contains can nonetheless enjoy its esthetics through the medium of scientific visualization.

As was just observed, scientific visualization often results in illustrations of such remarkable beauty that

they qualify as computer art (*q.v.*). Another example is shown in Fig. 10 on Color Page CP-14 (Duncan, 1990). The "fountain" is really a theoretical representation of the mass and energy density distribution that would result from the collision of a star with a black hole.

Chaos and complexity. One of the prime applications of scientific visualization is to the study of chaotic behavior, or *chaos* (and its closely related area, the study of fractal (*q.v.*) geometry). The origin of the study of chaos as a distinct branch of scientific endeavor dates to the winter of 1961, when MIT atmospheric scientist Edward Lorenz created a simulated, or "toy," weather system on a primitive computer of that era. Given a particular set of initial conditions, his model weather program would grind away and print out changing patterns of rainfall and temperature that appeared to be very realistic. Ordinarily, the program would be started from scratch each time initial conditions were changed, but one day Lorenz decided to re-enter prior output data in order to repeat a sequence of results from an earlier run. To his surprise, however, the results obtained from the restarted run began to diverge from the original pattern after just a few time steps. After a few more, there was no resemblance whatsoever. Upon reflection, he realized that, though the program was carrying the equivalent of six decimal digits of precision throughout a run, he had re-entered data to only three digits of precision. The surprise was that two sets of initial conditions that differed on the average by only one part in a thousand would cause such vastly different output. The result has had a very sobering effect on those who were once optimistic that the evolution of ever faster computers would one day allow very precise long-range weather forecasts. The phenomenon described now carries the formal name "sensitive dependence on initial conditions," but is more affectionately known as the "butterfly effect." The latter term conjures the image that the flapping of a butterfly's wings in China might somehow affect the weather in New York a week or two later.

This "chaotic behavior," as characterized by the degree of difficulty of prediction based on numerical simulation, occurs not just in meteorology but also in many other physical systems whose dynamical equations are nonlinear. Their study has given rise to a whole new interdisciplinary branch of science called *complexity*, and the founding of the Santa Fe Institute in New Mexico to study it. For the fascinating story of its incorporation in 1984 by a group of Nobel Prize winners and the subsequent intellectual leadership of John Holland, *see* Waldrop (1992).

Although known to specialists for many years, the beauty of the chaotic images and widespread public acquaintance with chaos theory in general can be dated to the appearance of James Gleick's bestseller *Chaos: Making a New Science* (Gleick, 1987). Using text and pictures that were equally colorful, Gleick introduced the public to the Lorenz attractor and other *strange attractors*, diagrams that showed that certain chaotic systems exhibited a behavior that caused them to settle into, or oscillate around, particular loci in the diagram. The Lorenz attractor in meteorology is the solution of a set of differential equations in three-dimensional space. Other well-studied strange attractors are the Henon attractor in astrophysics, the Yorke attractor in chemistry, and the Logistic Map in ecology.

The Lorenz attractor has been reprinted so often (*see* FRACTALS) that we will not do so here, but an example of an even more beautiful strange attractor is shown in Fig. 11 on Color Page CP-14. The pattern shows the behavior of a pendulum whose bob is magnetized and allowed to swing freely from a chosen initial position above an array of magnets arranged on the plane below the pendulum. To produce the diagram, each magnet is imagined to carry a different color. The pendulum will move erratically ("chaotically"), tracing an irregular, aperiodic path among the magnets, but eventually settles down in the "basin of attractiveness" of a particular magnet. Each point of the figure is then colored to correspond to the color of the magnet that captures the bob released from that point. The attractors that can be readily identified are "strange" because they are sometimes able to capture bobs that are started much closer to competing magnets.

While doing numerical experiments with dynamical systems in 1975, Mitchell Feigenbaum discovered a family of new fundamental constants. While iterating the *logistic equation* $x_{i+1} = Rx_i(1 - x_i)$, he found that for values of R less than 1, x decayed to zero; for R between 1 and 3, x converged to the value $1 - 1/R$. For values of R from 3 to $R_\infty \approx 3.57$, there is a sequence of values $3 = R_0 < R_1 < R_2 < R_3 < \cdots$ such that for $R_{k-1} < R \leq R_k$, if the starting value x_0 is a sufficiently small positive number, the sequence $\{x_i\}$ converges to a *limit cycle* with 2^k values. That is, once convergence is attained, successive values of x_i alternate among 2^k values. Once R_∞ is reached, the successive values of x_i jump around in seemingly random ways; that is, the behavior becomes *chaotic*. The results are usually displayed as a *bifurcation diagram*, as shown in Fig. 12.

As can be read from the diagram, at $R = 1 + \sqrt{6} \cong 3.45$, the threshold for period doubling from 2 to 4, the system oscillates between (approximate) x values of 0.44 and 0.85. These values can be computed exactly by noting that if the system oscillates between two values x and y, they bear the relationship

$$x = Ry(1 - y); \qquad y = Rx(1 - x).$$

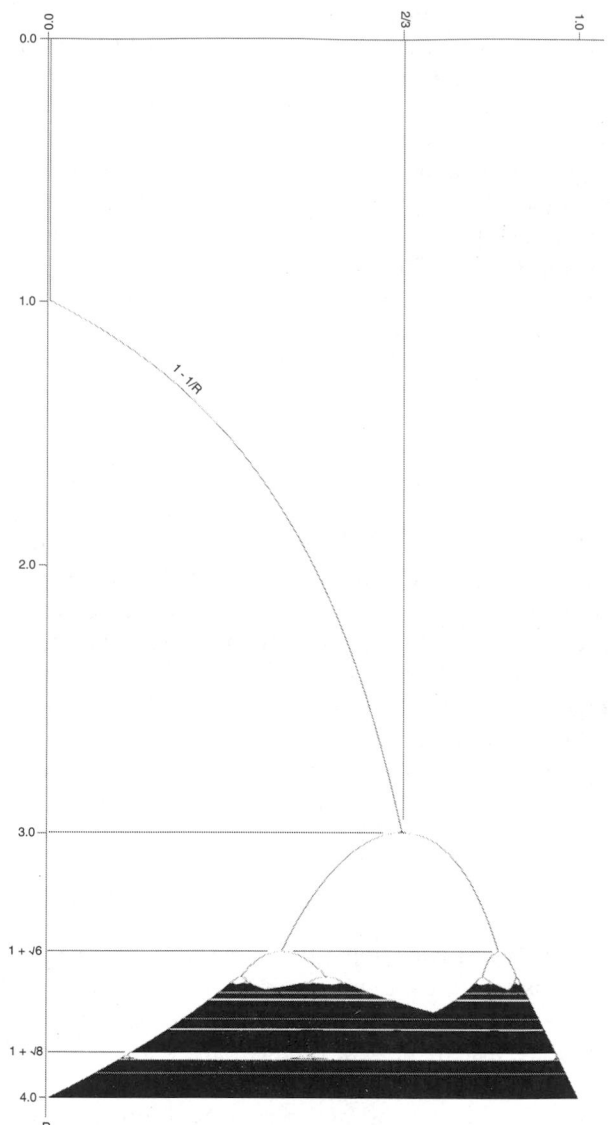

Figure 12. A bifurcation diagram showing a map of the stable and unstable regions for attempted solutions to the logistic equation $x_{i+1} = Rx_i(1 - x_i)$. The chaotic (unstable) regions form black bands separated by thin white bands of stable oscillation among a finite number of values of x.

Substituting the second equation into the first yields the cubic equation

$$R^3 x^3 - 2R^3 x^2 + (R^2 + R^3)x - (R^2 - 1) = 0$$

whose roots, according to the computer algebra program Derive, are

$$x_1 = 1 - 1/R; \qquad x_2 = (R + 1 - \sqrt{R - 3})\sqrt{R + 1})/2R;$$

$$x_3 = (R + 1 + \sqrt{R - 3})\sqrt{R + 1})/2R.$$

At $R = 1 + \sqrt{6}$, the second and third roots have values, to nine significant digits (*q.v.*), of 0.439960169 and 0.849937779. The first root indicates that the graph of $1 - 1/R$ in the bifurcation diagram could have been extended throughout the region of the 2-cycle, but the root is unstable. For $R = 1 + \sqrt{6}$, its value is 0.710102051..., an irrational number which cannot be exactly represented in the computer. When a value as close to this as is possible is used as a starting guess, the system will nonetheless, after a few hundred iterations at most, begin to gravitate toward oscillation between the *attractors*, roots x_2 and x_3; x_1 is effectively a *repeller*. For other examples of the use of computer algebra applied to dynamical equations, *see* Gutiérrez and Iglesias (1998).

It is interesting to consider the ratio of distances between consecutive doubling parameter values; i.e.

$$\delta_n = (R_{n+1} - R_n)/(R_{n+2} - R_{n+1}).$$

Then the limit as n goes to infinity is Feigenbaum's delta constant. To 25 decimal places, it has the value 4.6692016091029906718532038.... The interpretation of the delta constant is that, as chaos is approached, each periodic region is smaller than the previous by a factor of about 4.6692. Feigenbaum's constant is important because it is *universal*; it is the same for any function or system that approaches chaos by period doubling and has a quadratic (single hump) maximum. For example, the same constant arises through iteration of the equation $x_{x+1} = R \sin \pi x_i$. For cubic, quartic, etc. maxima, there are different Feigenbaum constants which, collectively with δ, are called *Feigenvalues* (Briggs *et al.*, 1991).

Among the many surprises in the seemingly rich detail of the bifurcation diagram is that in the midst of the chaotic region, there is a small band of R values starting at $1 + \sqrt{8}$ where the period is *three*. Anyone seeing the diagram for the first time without explanation would believe that its richness of detail represents a great deal of information, but note that it took only a few characters (and hence a few bits) to state the logistic equation and how to iterate it. Thus the result is fractal-like and indicates that even a turbulent phenomenon may have a great deal of underlying order. Feigenbaum arrived at his results by numerical experimentation, so that scientists at the time did not consider the result to be either mathematics *or* physics. But since a rigorous proof of universality was given by Oscar Lanford in 1979 and since logistic equations have been found to govern many real-world phenomena, Feigenbaum's discovery is now considered to be a fundamental contribution to the physics of dynamical systems.

Comparison of theory and experiment. Some physical situations are insufficiently well understood to be described according to fundamental principles and therefore must be treated phenomenologically. This implies that an equation devised to cover a phenomenon contains a number of adjustable parameters whose values are not known in advance, or known only within certain bounds. An example is the scattering of nuclear particles, such as protons and electrons, from atomic nuclei. In principle, the scattering properties are known (through solution of Schrödinger's equation) when the strength and shape of the force field (or *potential*) causing the scattering (i.e. the target nucleus) is known, but such characteristics of nuclei are extremely difficult to calculate quantitatively from first principles.

The solution is to characterize the potential as having a certain functional form containing several adjustable parameters, such as potential depth, nuclear radius, degree of surface diffuseness, and so on, up to as many as eight or nine such parameters. It then becomes a task worthy of a modern computer to vary these parameters to achieve that degree of agreement between theory and experiment that gives the best fit, in the *least squares approximation* (q.v.) sense. This is not a trivial task; it is something like trying to achieve the sharpest possible picture on a color TV set that has nine adjustable knobs and where adjusting one may make it necessary to readjust knobs already set by earlier trial and error. To achieve a reasonable fit, the computer must effectively search through an n-dimensional parameter space, recalculating the scattering at reasonably small steps in the parameters along the way. It is not unusual to consume hours of computer time in the process, but the scientist who does this considers the additional insights gained into nuclear structure well worth the effort.

Presentation of results. Historically, scientists have presented the results of their work in the specialized journals appropriate to their field. Special care is given to such things as the typography of equations and the choice of photographs, tables, and diagrams used. Until the last few years, any tools that facilitated typesetting were strictly the province of the publisher, and, similarly, any elaborate diagram or figure had to be drawn by a professional graphic artist. Now, many computer-based tools exist which allow scientists to display their equations using elaborate typefonts (q.v.) and to construct charts, graphs, and figures of professional quality (*see* COMPUTER GRAPHICS, TeX, TEXT EDITING, and WORD PROCESSING). Options for graphical output are now routinely provided in spreadsheets (q.v.), word processors, and computer algebra programs. And the scientist who wishes to take control of the whole process to produce "camera-ready" copy may use any of several powerful programs that automate *desktop publishing* (q.v.).

The World Wide Web (q.v.) has also prompted an increased emphasis on the quality of presentation of scientific information and results. Preparation of Web pages has now been facilitated through the availability of WYSIWYG page composition programs that obviate the need for the tedious HTML programming that was once required (*see* MARKUP LANGUAGES). HTML itself is being gradually replaced by the more general XML (eXtensible Markup Language), and a number of other markup languages customized to particular fields of science are in development: MathML that allows insertion of equations into Web pages with a few lines of simple text; CML (Chemical ML) that helps chemists sift through voluminous journal citations to find just those of immediate interest; BSML (BioSequence ML) to exchange and manipulate gene mapping and DNA sequencing; and AIML (Astronomical Instrument ML) to allow astronomers and space scientists to monitor and control telescopes and satellites through Internet browser software.

Simulation

Simulation (*q.v.*) of natural phenomena is a major scientific application of digital computers, and many of the examples already given involve simulation. Discussion of additional examples will be organized in accord with the three major purposes of simulation: for analysis, for design, and for education.

SIMULATION FOR ANALYSIS

A principal reason for simulating a complex physical system is analysis sufficiently detailed to enable prediction of its behavior. For example, the physical laws governing the motion of planetary bodies are intrinsically simple for two-body systems, but they are analytically intractable for the complex systems of Earth, Moon, multistage rockets of changing mass, satellites, etc., whose relative motions must be calculated with great precision in order to ensure the success of the most routine space mission. Of all the technological breakthroughs necessary to support the space programs of the USA, Europe, and Russia, none was more necessary than the development of reliable high-speed digital computers for analysis, prediction, design, and control.

A second and more extensive example of simulation for analysis was given earlier, the *N*-body calculations of cosmology and astrophysics, although in that case, waiting to verify predictions is clearly not feasible. But a third example of simulation (for both analysis and prediction) is the use of computers for weather forecasting. The equations governing the changes in temperature and pressure with time over even a small region of the Earth's surface require large amounts of computer time. With present speeds and memory capacities, it is difficult to forecast changes in weather patterns for a period of more than a few hours, but as machines improve, longer-range forecasts of reasonable reliability may be possible.

The Princeton Ocean Model (POM) is used to simulate the temperature, current, and salinity along coastal areas where topographical slopes are gradual, such as those in harbors, bays, and estuaries. It is also used to predict the environmental quality of coastal waters, model the effect of oil spills, and to predict ecocycles by modeling the movement of plankton and nutrients in tidal cycles and their effect on the viability of fisheries. Since the POM is used to predict currents, it is effective in modeling rescue efforts and in predicting oceanic weather effects such as storm surges (Piacsek *et al.*, 1998).

More common than heart attacks is a slower but equally dangerous disorder, a steady weakening of the heart muscle known as chronic heart failure. Computer simulations of the heart are helping clarify what causes the malfunction (*see* Service, 1999). Heart failure, which often sets in after a heart attack damages the muscle, occurs when the cardiac muscle cells contract less effectively. The result is that individual beats become longer and less forceful. The computer simulations, done by a team led by Eduardo Marbán, Raimond Winslow, and Brian O'Rourke of The Johns Hopkins University School of Medicine, suggest that the principal cause is altered production of two proteins that help control the concentrations of calcium ions in cells. Winslow and his colleagues constructed a computer model of a cardiac cell, incorporating everything known about the various proteins involved in ion movements and their interactions. Then, as they altered parameters representing concentrations of the various ionic components to match what is seen in heart failure, they tracked the effect on the cardiac cell's action potential and subsequent muscle contraction. An example of their program's graphic output is shown in Fig. 13 on Color Page CP-14. The simulations have important medical implications because they show how the biochemical changes might trigger fatal arrhythmias.

For other examples of simulation for analysis, see Gould and Tobochnik (1996).

SIMULATION FOR DESIGN

Once the analysis of a simulated physical model has advanced to the point where confidence can be placed in its predictions, the model can be used for the design of similar systems with variously different parameters. For example, the calculational problems associated with the behavior of neutrons in a reactor have been discussed previously, but the rationale for studying these problems was not considered. Initially, through the late 1940s and early 1950s, research data was reasonably fundamental, since the properties of neutron propagation in various materials under a variety of operating conditions were imperfectly understood.

As in other fields, however, the widespread use of digital computers accelerated the natural progression of a given type of activity, from research to applied science to engineering. The point has now been reached where most reactor calculations are part of a design engineering process whose aim is to simulate performance of tentative reactor designs *in lieu* of constructing an experimental prototype. By this technique, many hundreds of design variations can be tested in theory and only the most promising results need be tested in practice.

The preceding example is typical of many applications of simulation to design practice. In the same vein, other large scientific instruments can be engineered to desired specifications through preliminary simulation of a large number of alternative designs. It would now be extremely difficult for humans using pre-computer methods to design the large accelerators used in high-energy physics research or the large radio telescopes used in astronomy. Fig. 14 shows the design of the magnet used with the Relativistic Heavy Ion Collider at Brookhaven National Laboratory, an instrument that is exploring matter at temperatures and densities thought to be characteristic of the Big Bang. Because the magnet is located precisely at the intersection of two colliding 100 GeV beams, the strength of its field must vary by four orders of magnitude in only 6 mm. Using 3D software for the simulation of electromagnetic properties, Brookhaven scientists were able to evaluate a wide range of design alternatives that led to an optimal design (Tsoupas, 1998).

SIMULATION FOR EDUCATION

As the sophistication and availability of computer display devices increase, computers are being used more and more for educational purposes. Rather than running actual laboratory experiments to determine the behavioral characteristics of falling bodies, colliding spheres, pendulums, projectiles, etc., the event to be studied can be simulated at any desired rate on a display monitor. The student can then interact with the computer to study the effect of changing parameters, such as the mass of a pendulum bob, the angle of elevation of the initial launch of a rocket, or any one or more of the other factors that affect the experiment at hand.

Using such numerical simulation and display techniques, one can even examine phenomena that are closed to easy observation in the laboratory (e.g. the tunneling of a quantum mechanical particle through a potential barrier, the slow-motion fall of water droplets into a pool, or the crashing of water waves upon a beach). These simulations are instructive to watch, and are esthetically pleasing as well. Still photographs of such sequences are often examples of computer art, just as beautiful as other designs created deliberately.

Summary

Digital computers are now being used in every facet of scientific work, ranging from initial library research through the preparation of copy for final journal publication. Wherever there occurs an element of drudgery

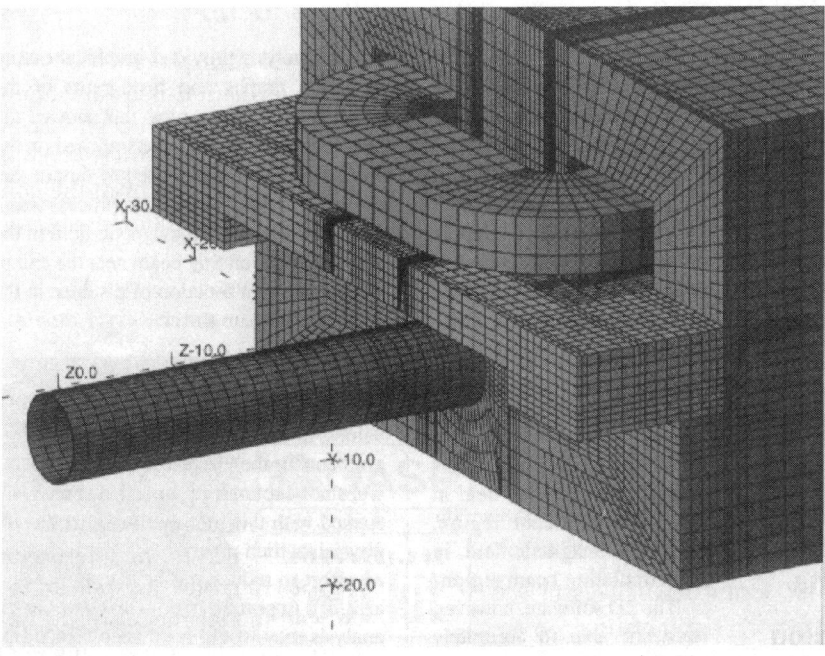

Figure 14. Computer generated design for the magnet, coil, and beam tube of the Relativistic Heavy Ion Collider at Brookhaven National Laboratory. (Courtesy: Nicholas Tsoupas, Brookhaven National Laboratory.)

in daily routine, there may be yet another computer application to lighten the load and leave the scientist free to concentrate on providing the human inspirational breakthroughs that cannot be automated. Although individual genius will create new systems in the future, as it has in the past, the average working scientist today cannot be competitive without access to a digital computer and reasonable proficiency in its use.

Bibliography

Journals

Computing in Science and Engineering. New York: IEEE and AIP. http://computer.org/cise/.
Journal of Computational Physics. New York: Academic Press. http://www.academicpress.com/jcp/.
Computers & Chemistry. New York: Elsevier. http://www.elsevier.nl/inca/publications/store/3/7/9/index.htt.
Computer Applications in the Biosciences. http://www.bio.net/bioarchives/BIO-JOURNALS/CABIOS/.
Computational Geosciences. Bussum, The Netherlands: Baltzer. http://www.baltzer.nl/comgeo/comgeo.asp.
Journal of Scientific Computing. New York: Kluwer Academic/Plenum Publishers. http://www.wkap.nl/journalhome.html/0885-7474/.
SIAM Journal on Scientific Computing. SIAM. http://www.siam.org/journals/sisc/sisc.htm.
Scientific Computing & Instrumentation. Morris Plains, NJ: Cahners. http://www.scimag.com.
Computing and Visualization in Science. New York: Springer-Verlag. http://link.springer-ny.com/link/service/journals/00791/index.htm.

Books and Articles

1987. Gleick, J. *Chaos: Making a New Science.* New York: Viking.
1990. Duncan, G. C. "Visualizing the Collision of a Star with a Black Hole," *Pixel*, **1**, *3* (July/August), 24–29.
1990. Chervin, R. M. "High Performance Computing and the Grand Challenge of Climate Modeling," *Computers in Physics*, **4**, *3* (May/June), 234–239.
1990. Nash, S. (ed.) *A History of Scientific Computing.* Reading, MA: ACM Press/Addison-Wesley.
1991. Lander, E. S., Langridge, R., and Saccocio, D. M. "Computing in Molecular Biology: Mapping and Interpreting Biological Information," *Computer*, **24**, *11* (November), 6–13.
1991. Burns, J. O., Norman, M. L., and Clarke, D. A. "Numerical Models of Extragalactic Radio Sources," *Science*, **253**, *5019* (2 August), 522–530.
1991. Briggs, K, Quispel, G.R.W., and Thompson, C., "Feigenvalues for Mandelsets," *J. Phys. A*, **24**, 3363–3368.
1992. Waldrop, M. M. *Complexity: The Emerging Science at the Edge of Order and Chaos.* New York: Simon & Schuster.
1992. Pickett, W. E., Krakauer, H., Cohen, R. E., and Singh, D. J. "Fermi Surfaces, Fermi Liquids, and High-temperature Superconductors," *Science*, **255**, *5040* (3 January), 46–53.
1992. Bitar, K. M., and Heller, U. M. "Lattice Field Simulations Press the Limits of Computational Physics," *Computers in Physics*, **6**, *1* (January/February), 33–40.
1994. Van De Velde, E. F. *Concurrent Scientific Computing.* New York: Springer-Verlag.
1995. Gobel, M., Muller, H., and Urban, B. *Visualization in Scientific Computing.* New York: Springer-Verlag.
1996. Gould, H., and Tobochnik, J. *An Introduction to Computer Simulation Methods.* Reading, MA: Addison-Wesley.

1996. Fosdick, L. D., Jessup, E. R., Donik, G., and Schauble, C. *An Introduction to High-Performance Scientific Computing.* Cambridge, MA: MIT Press.
1997. Arge, E., Bruaset, A. M., and Langtangen, H. P. (eds.) *Modern Software Tools for Scientific Computing.* New York: Birkhauser.
1997. Gander, W., Masaryk, J. H., and Hrebicek, J. *Solving Problems in Scientific Computing Using Maple and Matlab.* New York: Springer-Verlag.
1997. Heath, M. T. *Scientific Computing: An Introductory Survey.* New York: McGraw-Hill.
1998. Piacsek, S., Young, M., and Allard, R. "Porting the Princeton Ocean Model to High Performance Fortran Boosts Scalability," *Scientific Computing and Automation*, **15**, *10* (September), 26–28, 47.
1998. Tsoupas, N. "Computer Simulation Used to Design Magnet That Will Help Re-create the Big Bang," *Scientific Computing and Automation*, **15**, *6* (May), 37–40.
1998. Gutiérrez, J. M., and Iglesias, A., "Mathematica Package for Analysis and Control of Chaos in Nonlinear Systems," *Computers in Physics*, **12**, *6* (Nov.–Dec.), 608–619.
1999. Service, R. F. "Heart Failure Simulated," *Science*, **284**, *5411* (2 April) 33–34.
1999. DiStefano, R., and Scalzo, R. A., "Detection of Planetary Systems Through Microlensing," *Astrophysical Journal* (electronic), *512*, *564* and *579*.
1999. Thijssen, J. M. *Computational Physics.* New York: Cambridge University Press.

Edwin D. Reilly

SCIENTIFIC VISUALIZATION

For articles on related subjects *see* COMPUTER ANIMATION; COMPUTER GRAPHICS; DATA MINING; GEOGRAPHIC INFORMATION SYSTEM; IMAGE PROCESSING; MEDICAL IMAGING; SCIENTIFIC APPLICATIONS; TOMOGRAPHY, COMPUTERIZED; and VIRTUAL REALITY.

Introduction

Using visual display methods to examine scientific data and information is a time-honored technique (Tufte, 1983). Electronic or digital scientific visualization is a younger field, 10–20 years old. Scientific visualization applies techniques from the convergent fields of computer animation, computer graphics, image processing, computer vision (*q.v.*), computer-aided design and manufacturing (CAD/CAM—*q.v.*), signal processing, and user interface (*q.v.*) design studies (MacCormick *et al.*, 1987).

Scientific visualization transforms numerical or symbolic data and information into geometric computer-generated images. Data visualization tools allow scientists to observe and interpret their simulations (*q.v.*) and computations. Scientific visualization techniques can be applied to the interpretation of image data fed into a computer as well as to data generated from computational models. The final images can be displayed as static images, animated sequences or movies, or interactively in real time on a computer or workstation (*q.v.*).

Data visualization is closely related to the still-newer field of *data mining*. They differ in that the former processes data in accord with specific algorithms that exhibit relationships known to exist but which are not readily apparent when data is graphed conventionally, whereas data mining uses an admixture of algorithms and heuristics (*q.v.*) to uncover regularities and relationships not envisioned in advance, even by those who gathered the data being processed. For examples of the latter approach, see DATA MINING. For two examples of data (scientific) visualization, see Figs. 10 and 11 of SCIENTIFIC APPLICATIONS on Color Page CP-14.

There are three classes of scientific visualization tasks that are independent of data or technique. They include analysis and exploration, decision support, and presentation. Each of these tasks usually involves multidisciplinary and collaborative efforts between research scientists, artists, programmers, policy analysts, and other expert staff. We discuss each in turn.

ANALYSIS AND EXPLORATION

The task of analysis and exploration examines scientific data and information. These data-mining activities can encompass computer-aided design, medical imaging, remote sensing, and geographic information systems as well as large-scale computational output from super-computers (*q.v.*). Scientific visualization is also used as a diagnostic technique for calibrating the computational algorithms that are the components of large computer models. Here, interactive visualization tools are helpful for gaining insight into the impacts of modifying algorithms. Recently, scientific visualization methods have expanded to include comparisons and validation of data repositories located on the World Wide Web (*q.v.*).

DECISION SUPPORT

Scientific visualization techniques assist the decision-making process. For architectural site planning, interactive visualization systems help to understand the impact of specific construction activities. In environmental planning, research efforts use scientific visualization to examine the multidimensional impacts of air pollution, water quality, and subsurface contamination on ecosystem protection. In medicine, visualization is used to assist in medical diagnosis and to prepare surgeons for operations.

These activities frequently require customized visualization software to support specific decision-making functions. This software may incorporate trainable intelligent agents to assist in data mining and in constructing appropriate computer-generated visual displays across a heterogeneous network of workstations. These special interfaces free a user from having to attend to the complex details behind them. Here visualization techniques interact with human interface design and the networking infrastructure.

PRESENTATION

Scientific visualization and animation sequences can educate the public and inform high-level decision makers. These presentation visualizations often require the use of powerful animation tools and virtual reality display techniques. For animations, the final product is often a polished production with voiceover narration and background music sound tracks. New virtual reality techniques allow electronic virtual reality interactions to occur among small groups of people without their having to wear head-mounted displays.

Transforming Data to Three-Dimensional Pictures

The production of scientific visualizations involves transforming data into visual representations. The two most common approaches are conversion of mesh geometry and data directly into graphical primitives (e.g. points, lines, polygons), and data sampling (Gallagher, 1995).

CONVERTING TO GRAPHICS PRIMITIVES

Conversion of scientific data into computer graphics primitives is a three-stage process: filtering → mapping → rendering. *Filtering* takes modeled or collected data and "filters" it into another form which is more informative and less massive. Examples of filtering operations include computing derived quantities such as the gradient of an input scalar field, deriving a flow line from a velocity field, or extracting a portion of a solution.

The next step "maps" the filtered or newly derived data into geometric primitives such as points, lines, or polygons. Once a set of geometric primitives is chosen and calculated, the geometric data is "rendered" into pictures. At this stage, the user chooses coloring, placement, illumination, and surface properties for the visualized image.

DATA SAMPLING

Data sampling involves moving data into a structured grid of points using interpolation and extrapolation. The user specifies the resolution and position of the sampling grid and attempts to sample at a high enough frequency to capture the details of the solution. Once the data sample is placed on a regular grid, volume rendering techniques are used to create the visual display. *Volume rendering* is the process of creating a two-dimensional image directly from three-dimensional volumetric data. Conversion to graphics primitives is the most frequently used approach as it provides information that computer graphics hardware can process efficiently. This yields highly interactive scientific visualization systems. Data sampling, however, is ideal for volumetric representations and visualization techniques. An example of volumetric visualization would be reconstructing a sequence of two-dimensional slices obtained from magnetic resonance imaging (MRI) or computerized tomography (CT—*see* TOMOGRAPHY, COMPUTERIZED) into a volume model for medical visualization and diagnostic purposes (Kaufman, 1991).

Scientific Visualization Software

Over the last decade, a number of visualization systems have been developed. Some are defined as turnkey systems that are focused on specific types of visualization problems such as computational fluid dynamics, weather modeling, medical imaging, and so forth. There is also a group of software packages targeted more at the end user than at graphics programmers. These tools are called Modular Visualization Environments (MVEs—Cameron, 1995). With MVEs, software component *modules* are connected to create a visualization. MVEs allow the modules for filtering, mapping, and rendering to be combined into executable flow networks. To do this, the user selects modules from menus and places the icons representing the modules in a diagram. Each module appears as a box and connections between the modules are drawn as lines. Once the structure of the visualization application has been established, the MVEs execute the network and display the computer-generated image.

Each image that is produced is a visual representation of the scene defined by the modules. The user can interact with the image by moving or changing lights, by modifying surfaces, by rotating, shifting, or resizing objects, or by changing the point of view and angle of view.

Examples of Visualization Systems

We provide two examples of visualization systems: use of an MVE to explore geographic visualization, and a turnkey system to examine computational fluid dynamics.

GEOGRAPHIC VISUALIZATION

The process of visualizing ecological and earth sciences data often requires obtaining and merging multiple data sets stored in a Geographic Information System (GIS). Here we describe an MVE system that can access GIS data in real time and create interactive visualizations. The MVE is the Application Visualization System from AVS Inc. and the GIS is ARC-INFO for the Environmental Systems Research Institute

(ESRI). Using a specialized set of AVS-ARC modules, the AVS toolkit can directly access ARC-INFO data files and filter the geographic data into a format for registering and mapping into three dimensions. The AVS then renders and displays the three-dimensional image. The three-dimensional (3D) image shown as Fig. 1 on Color Page CP-14 is of the Great Smoky Mountains of Tennessee in the USA. Here a geographic map, obtained from the United States Geologic Survey, is mapped onto the three-dimensional terrain of the region. The coordinates of the map and the 3D terrain data were geographically registered in ARC-INFO and then moved into AVS using the AVS-ARC modules. The blue lines in this 3D image are various site selection criteria and represent an additional ARC-INFO data set. The user of this geographic visualization system can transfer multiple registered ARC-INFO data sets into the AVS environment. This visualization system allows an ecologist to obtain a precisely registered 3D view of merged data sets (such as land cover, vegetation, wildlife, and human population) for a particular geographic region (Rhyne and Fowler, 1997).

COMPUTATIONAL FLUID DYNAMICS

An example of a turnkey visualization system is the Flow Analysis Software Toolkit (FAST). FAST was specifically developed at the United States National Aeronautics and Space Administration (NASA) to assist computational fluid dynamics research. FAST is an integrated visualization tool for Unix (particularly Silicon Graphics) workstations. This visualization tool consists of a collection of programs that communicate with a central hub process which manages a pool of shared memory (Bancroft *et al.*, 1991). Data types or formats are first loaded or generated and stored in shared memory. Then a collection of programs (FAST modules) operate on the data and produce additional data (FAST objects) that is also put into shared memory. The objects are next rendered using the FAST viewing system. Data is analyzed by additional modules for visual inspection. Depending on the results of this analysis, the user changes input to any of the previous modules. Customized analysis modules can be developed under the FAST system. The 3D image shown as Fig. 2 on Color Page CP-14 depicts airflow around a building using a FAST module based on vector field topology. This topology module is unique to the FAST system (Globus *et al.*, 1992). The FAST system provides for real time visualization of computational fluid dynamics problems.

Future Directions

Further advances in computer graphics hardware and scientific visualization techniques will also allow the visual display of complex multiresolution data sets obtained from dispersed resources. This will increase the demand for the registration of multiple data, images, and signals. The integration of live analog video, volume rendering, and polygon-based graphics images will require expanding the traditional boundaries of scientific visualization.

Further research will need to examine the demands of interactive and collaborative visualization among users located at geographically remote sites. A comprehensive visualization research approach that includes new and improved computer graphics hardware, data compression (*q.v.*) algorithms, distributed and parallel computing, and complex network caching schemes will be necessary to achieve the goals of real-time interactive collaborative scientific visualization (IEEE-CS, 1996).

One of the more significant influences on future directions in scientific visualization is likely to be the continued evolution and refinement of the World Wide Web (*q.v.*). Tools to assist visualization of information and data accessible via the Web are under development. They call for exploring the application of visualization to multidimensional statistical data, video, images, hypertext (*q.v.*) documents, network topologies, and other less structured categorical data.

Bibliography

1983. Tufte, E. R. *The Visual Display of Quantitative Information.* Cheshire, CT: Graphics Press.
1987. MacCormick, B. H., DeFanti, T. A., and Brown, M. D. (eds.) "Visualization in Scientific Computing," *Computer Graphics,* **21**, 6.
1990. Nielson, G. M., Shriver, B., and Rosenblum, L M. (eds.) *Visualization in Scientific Computing.* Los Alamitos, CA: IEEE-CS Press.
1991. Kaufman, A. (ed.) *Volume Visualization.* Los Alamitos, CA: IEEE-CS Press.
1991. Bancroft, G., Merrit, F., Plessel, T., Kelaita, P., McCabe, K., and Globus, A. "FAST: A Multi-processed Environment for Visualization of Computational Fluid Dynamics," in *Proceedings of the IEEE Visualization 90 Conference,* October 1990. Los Alamitos, CA: IEEE-CS Press.
1992. Globus, A., Levit, C., and Lasinsk, T. "A Tool for Visualizing the Topology of Three-dimensional Vector Fields," *Proceedings of the IEEE Visualization 91 Conference,* October l991. Los Alamitos, CA: IEEE-CS Press.
1993. Watson, D., and Earnshaw, R. A. (eds.) *Animation and Scientific Visualization: Tools and Applications.* New York: Academic Press.
1995. Gallagher, R. S. (ed.) *Computer Visualization: Graphics Techniques for Scientific and Engineering Analysis.* Boca Raton, FL: CRC Press.
1995. Cameron, G. (ed.) "Modular Visualization Environments: Past, Present and Future," *Computer Graphics,* **29**, 2 (May).
1995, Rhyne, T.-M. "Scientific Visualization and Technology Transfer," *Computer,* **28**, 7 (July), 94–96.
1996. IEEE-CS. *Transactions on Computer Graphics,* **2**, 2 (June), Special Issue on Visualization.
1997. Rhyne, T.-M., and Fowler, T. "Examining Dynamically Linked Geographic Visualization," *Proceedings of the Computing in Environmental Resource Management Conference,* December 1996. Pittsburgh, PA: Air & Waste Management Association.
1997. Nielson, G. M., Hagen, H., and Müller, H. *Scientific Visualization: Overviews, Methodologies, and Techniques.* Los Alamitos, CA: IEEE-CS Press.

Theresa-Marie Rhyne

SCRIPTING LANGUAGES

For articles on related subjects *see* COMPONENT SOFTWARE; LANGUAGE PROCESSORS; OPERATING SYSTEMS; PROGRAMMING LANGUAGES; SHELL; UNIX OPERATING SYSTEM; and USER INTERFACE.

A *command language* (CL) is a language in which users of a computer can describe to the operating system the requirements of their jobs. Operating systems for mainframe (*q.v.*) computers provide a CL called *job control language* (JCL) in which the user can

1. Identify the job for accounting purposes

2. Specify the resources required by the job

3. Specify the input–output devices required, and define the way in which information is or should be organized or formatted on these devices

4. Specify the action to be taken in exceptional cases (e.g. compile-time error, missing or incorrect input data, device malfunctions etc.)

These languages are typically complex, difficult to learn, unnatural to use, and nonsystematic (Barron and Jackson, 1972).

Interactive Command Languages

With the advent of time-sharing (*q.v.*) systems, a new form of CL was developed. Since the user of a time-sharing system interacts directly with the computer in real time, typing in a single *command line* at a time and waiting for the system's response, interactive command languages are inherently simpler than batch languages. The user does not have to state in advance what the system should do under all possible conditions: these decisions can be made, one at a time, at the computer terminal.

The command-line interface is implemented by a command interpreter called a *shell*. (The name originates from the early days of the Unix operating system, reflecting the fact that an operating system is built up as a succession of layers, of which the shell is the outermost one.) Many command lines consist of just a command verb followed by one or more arguments to specify files to be operated on, or options to be set; however, the shell provides the user with a convenient syntax for redirecting input or output from the terminal to a file or files, and setting up *pipes* to link a sequence of commands so that the output from one command becomes the input for the next command in sequence, with the shell performing the necessary buffering.

The command-line syntax of the Unix shell, with input–output redirection and pipes, has been adopted by MS-DOS since Version 3. The only significant difference is that MS-DOS uses "/" to introduce options where the shell uses "–". However, the use of a command line interface in the PC world is decreasing as the graphical interfaces provided by Microsoft (*q.v.*) and Apple (*q.v.*) become almost universal.

Programmable Shells

Unix encourages the user to store complex commands or sequences of commands in an executable file called a *shell script*. The name of such a file can be typed as a command, causing the lines of the script to be processed as if they had been typed at the terminal. The "command" can be followed by up to nine arguments, which are referenced in the script as $1, $2, . . . , $9. (MS-DOS provides a similar facility in the form of *batch files*.)

Almost from the beginning, the Unix shell had a degree of programmability with gotos and labels: a powerful if command allowed a variety of conditions to be tested, and the shift command, which discarded the first argument and renumbered the remaining arguments, provided a convenient way of iterating over multiple arguments

The Bourne shell (Bourne, 1982) introduced in Unix version 7 added fully programmable capabilities, including conditional branches and looping. This makes shell scripts much more powerful, to the extent that they can be used instead of C (*q.v.*) to define complex new commands and to develop tools for system administration. However, the programmable shell has a very restrictive and inconvenient syntax, because it does not perform any syntax analysis but processes its input string left to right without any backtracking. The programmability is provided by adding internal commands: for example, the if, then and fi (end-if) of a simple conditional statement must each appear at the start of a line, since they are not syntactic keywords but names of internal shell commands.

Scripting Languages

The limitations of shell scripts, in particular the inconvenient syntax and the lack of string-processing capabilities, led to the development of a number of disparate languages that are commonly called *script-ing languages*. (The name is also applied to special-purpose languages for control of programmable devices like modems—*q.v.*)

Scripting languages can be broadly categorized as follows.

◆ *Interpreted, not compiled.* Scripting languages are interpreted (or compiled to an intermediate form which is then interpreted) because scripting is usually an interactive experimental activity that does not fit well with the edit–compile–link–run cycle of conventional programming.

◆ *Low overhead and ease of use.* Scripting languages have a minimum of "clutter"—typically no declarations; automatic initialization of variables; no types—variables hold numbers or strings, with automatic conversion as required; no machine architecture-determined limit on the size of numbers; no size or shape limits on arrays; and no concept of nested blocks and scopes.

◆ *Enhanced functionality.* Scripting languages usually have enhanced functionality in some areas: powerful string manipulation that exploits the power of regular expressions (*q.v.*) is common, as are associative arrays (arrays indexed by strings or other complex values). In some languages the enhanced functionality includes easy access to low-level system facilities.

◆ *Efficiency not an issue.* Ease of use is achieved at the expense of efficiency: many scripts will be used only once, other scripts will be used on a regular basis but do not call for high performance. Rapid development is more important, together with the ability to make speedy changes to meet new or unanticipated requirements.

We describe here three scripting languages in widespread use. All originated in the Unix world, but have been ported to many other platforms, particularly Intel-based PCs.

AWK

AWK was developed to meet the limitations of shell scripts in applications which call for data manipulation and reduction, which are common requirements in system administration. AWK (Aho, Kernighan, and Weinberger 1988—named after its authors) was originally conceived as a tool for editing and manipulating text files which were structured as *records* (lines) divided into fields separated by whitespace. It is based on an interesting paradigm. An AWK script consists of a list of *patterns* and associated *actions*: the target file is read sequentially, and as each record is loaded in turn into the processing buffer, all patterns are checked against the record, and any pattern that is satisfied (true) triggers its corresponding action. The power of AWK derives from the facts that the "pattern" can be specified as matching a regular expression, or as a relationship between values in fields, while the action can be a simple imperative operation like "print," or an arbitrary piece of code in a C-like language, in which the fields in the record can be treated as variables. Fig. 1 is a simple AWK script that removes blank lines from a file and prints the number removed at the end.

The use of AWK rapidly extended beyond its original purpose: being an interpreted language with a simplified syntax, it became a useful tool for writing "throwaway" programs, prototyping larger applications, and providing an acceptable substitute for C for much general-purpose programming. However, it has now been largely superseded by Perl.

PERL

Perl (*Practical Extraction and Report Language*) (Wall *et al.*, 1996) originated in the late 1980s when its author, Larry Wall, was the system administrator for a project developing secure wide-area networks. The project required a variety of reports to be generated on a semi-automatic basis, and the job stretched the combination of shell and AWK to their limits. Perl rapidly developed from being a fairly simple text-processing language to a fully-featured systems programming (*q.v.*) language, providing system-independent abstractions of files, processes, sockets, etc. The 1999 version (Version 5) also provides a full range of object-oriented capabilities. Perl provides "one-stop shopping" for system administrators: it is often called "the Swiss Army chain saw of languages," partly because its versatility resembles that of the Swiss Army knife, and partly because it is able to cut through difficulties with ease. (It is also affectionately known in some circles as the "Pathologically Eclectic Rubbish Lister.")

Although the underlying ideas are simple, Perl is an immensely rich language. It has unashamedly borrowed the best ideas from many sources, particularly

sed (Unix stream editor), awk, shell programming, and C, in pursuit of its aim of keeping easy things easy while making difficult things possible. Unlike most languages, which make a virtue out of forcing the programmer to do things in a particular way, Perl espouses the principle that "there's more than one way to do it." Consciously modeled on English usage, it allows different ways of expressing the same concept (e.g. unless/until as alternatives to if/while, and the ability to place "if/unless" and "while/until" conditions *after* a statement if so desired), it makes sensible assumptions in the face of apparently incomplete information, and it takes a relaxed view of syntactic conformity, e.g. brackets are required around the arguments of built-in functions only if they are needed to resolve ambiguity: if the meaning is unambiguously clear without the brackets, they can be omitted. Throughout the language there is a policy of "no surprises": Perl always seems to do what is obviously sensible in the circumstances. Fig. 2 is a Perl version of a program to remove blank lines.

In less than ten years, Perl has become one of the world's most popular programming languages. Larry Wall has observed that the explosive growth of Perl outside the Unix environment has been driven by former Unix programmers whose jobs have taken them into other less congenial environments; as a result of its origins in the Unix world, Perl is "a portable distillation of Unix culture" that such refugees can take with them. Another reason for the explosive growth can be found in the all enveloping World Wide Web (*q.v.*), where Perl was rapidly adopted as the language of choice for server-side (Common Gateway Interface—CGI) scripting.

TCL/TK

Tool Command Language/Toolkit (Tcl/Tk) (Ousterhout, 1994) is based on the philosophy that application development is best accomplished using a combination of two languages: "... one, such as C or C++ (*q.v.*), for manipulating the complex internal data structures where performance is key, and another, such as Tcl, for writing small-ish scripts that tie together the C pieces and are used for extensions." Thus Tcl (as seen by its inventor) is not so much a language—it has little

```
BEGIN { n = 0 }
/ ^ [ \t]*$/    { n++ }
/[ ^ \t]/       { print }
END { print n, "empty lines removed" }
```

Figure 1. An AWK script to remove blank lines from a file and report the number removed. The second line has a pattern that matches any line that contains only zero or more space or tab characters ([\t]*) between the start ("^") and end ($) of the line, and the action is to increment a counter. The next line matches any line that contains anything other than a space or tab (the "^" within brackets means "not").

```
while ((STDIN)) {
       / ^ \s*$/ ? $n++ : print
       }
print "$n empty lines removed\n";
```

Figure 2. A Perl script to remove blank lines. The loop condition is "while there are lines in the input." The "\s*" pattern matches 0 or more "whitespace" characters, and the "? .. : .." is a conditional: "if there is only whitespace between the start and end of the line, then add 1 to the counter; else print the line."

syntax and no inherent semantics—as an interpreter which can be embedded in an application to provide a simple command-line interface, making it a universal command language. A measure of the success of a language design is the extent to which it is used for purposes not intended, or even envisaged, by its designer, and on this measure Tcl is an enormous success: many large applications are written entirely in Tcl, with no C code at all.

Internally, everything in Tcl (even an array) is a string. Tcl itself is a pure string-substitution language: the syntax of a normal language is replaced by a collection of string-substitution rules which define the way in which a statement is decomposed into "words." The first word of a statement can denote a built-in function (e.g. if, while), another Tcl script (subroutine) or a function written in C: the interpreter then executes this with the remaining words passed as arguments. This typically involves recursive calls to the interpreter, which can also be explicitly invoked within a script by the "eval" function (a capability first used in Lisp—q.v.). This recursive interpretation, together with the overhead (q.v.) of handling all data items as strings, leads to poor performance. (Typically, Perl runs ten times slower than C for a given task, and Tcl runs ten times slower than Perl.) Despite this, Tcl has been used for a number of very substantial programming projects.

Tcl is probably at its best in the role originally envisaged for it: implementing a specialized language for an application where the hard work will be coded in some more appropriate language. The Tk toolkit, a major application of Tcl, illustrates the power of this approach to application development. Tk implements a graphical user interface (GUI) by providing a front end to a collection of C functions which realize a collection of useful visual objects (*widgets*) under the X Window system (*see* WINDOW ENVIRONMENTS): besides providing these building bricks (windows, menus, dialog boxes, etc.) it provides a harness for an event-driven system in which Tcl scripts are associated with the events (mouse clicks, key presses, etc.) recognized by the underlying operating system.

Object-based Scripting

In recent years the term "scripting" has acquired an entirely new meaning, being applied to the use of specialized languages to manipulate "scriptable objects"—*visual scripting*—and to compose "component-objects" into applications—*component-ware*.

Visual scripting first came to public attention in Visual Basic, a tool designed to facilitate the development of Windows applications. The user of Visual Basic is presented with a palette of visual "controls" which can be positioned on the screen to suit the application: each control has a number of "properties" that can be set initially by the designer with a screen dialogue, but can subsequently be changed at run time by code written in a scripting language also called (confusingly) Visual Basic. Chunks of code can be associated with *events* (mouse and keyboard operations) for each control. Thus a control can be viewed as an object with attributes (properties) and methods, the methods being invoked by external events. This model has extended into Web client software, where the browser exposes objects (e.g. the current window, the current URL, the history list) that can be controlled by *scripts* attached to events such as page load, mouse entering/leaving a region, mouse click on a link, etc. Microsoft and Netscape browsers implement an almost common object model so that the objects can be controlled (scripted) by various languages, including JavaScript, Jscript and VBScript. In addition, in Internet Explorer VBScript and Jscript can be used to control Visual Basic-like visual objects, known in this context as ActiveX Controls.

The idea of building applications from "off-the-shelf" components is not new—OpenDoc (Feiler and Meadow, 1996) was a brave attempt to establish this approach. However, whereas OpenDoc presupposed a C++ infrastructure, the idea of scriptable component-objects is that they are written so that they can be manipulated by any language that conforms to the chosen "scripting architecture." In a related development, the applications in the Microsoft Office suite are constructed so that they expose data and functionality at run time as a collection of objects with properties and methods that can be accessed from a scripting language. At present, this has to be Visual Basic for Applications (VBA; Chappell, 1996). VBA is licensed to other software companies, so in principle this need not be a Microsoft proprietary approach to system development.

Bibliography

1972. Barron, D. W., and Jackson, I. R. "The Evolution of Job Control Languages," *Software: Practice and Experience*, **2**, 2, 143–164.
1982. Bourne, S. R. *The Unix System*. Reading, MA: Addison-Wesley.
1988. Aho, A. V., Kernighan, B. W., and Weinberger, P. J. *The AWK Programming Language*. Reading, MA: Addison-Wesley.
1994. Ousterhout, J. *Tcl and the Tk Toolkit*. Reading, MA: Addison-Wesley.
1996. Chappell, D. *Understanding ActiveX and OLE*. Redmond, WA: Microsoft Press.
1996. Feiler, J., and Meadow, A. *Essential OpenDoc*. Reading, MA: Addison-Wesley.
1996. Wall, L., Christiansen, T., and Schwartz, R. L. *Programming Perl*, 2nd Ed. Sebastopol, CA: O'Reilly and Associates Inc.

Websites

Perl. http://www.perl.com.
Scriptics Tcl/Tk page 1. http://www.scriptics.com/products/tcltk/.
Microsoft Visual Basic: http://msdn.microsoft.com/vbasic/.
Microsoft Visual Basic for Applications. http://msdn.microsoft.com/vba/.

David W. Barron

SCSI

See HARD DISK; and PORT, I/O.

SEAC

For articles on related subjects *see* DIGITAL COMPUTERS, HISTORY OF: EARLY; EDVAC; and SWAC.

In 1947, with the encouragement of the US Navy, the National Bureau of Standards (NBS) established the National Applied Mathematical Laboratories under the leadership of John Curtiss. The purpose was to create a centralized national computation facility equipped with high-speed automatic computers which would provide a computing service for other governmental agencies and play an active part in the further development of computing machinery.

The Census Bureau, the US Air Force, and the US Navy all supported the Laboratories, and negotiations for the acquisition of computers from Eckert and Mauchly (later acquired by Sperry Rand), from Engineering Research Associates (a supplier to the security agencies), and from Raytheon Corporation (RAYDAC), were under way in 1948. Impatient with the slow development of computers, and feeling the need for more "hands-on" expertise, the NBS decided at a meeting in May 1948 to build its own computer; later in the same year the decision was made to build a second computer at the Institute for Numerical Analysis, an NBS field station located at the University of California at Los Angeles. These two Bureau computers became known as the SEAC and SWAC (Standards Eastern and Standards Western Automatic Computers).

The SEAC, built under the direction of Samuel Alexander, used mercury delay lines for storage (*see* ULTRASONIC MEMORY). Its design was based on the EDVAC (*q.v.*) at the University of Pennsylvania. The original memory used the same type of mercury delay lines, consisting of 64 eight-word lines operating at a clock rate of 1 MHz. Initial input and output was by punched paper tape (*q.v.*). Later, magnetic wire and magnetic tape replaced the paper tape, and a Williams tube memory (*q.v.*) was added to the system.

Addition time (including storage access) ranged from 192 to 1,540 ms, and multiply time from 2,300 to

Figure 1. The SEAC (courtesy of the National Institute of Standards and Technology, Gaithersburg, Maryland).

3,600 ms. The SEAC was the first stored-program computer (*see* STORED PROGRAM CONCEPT) to run in the USA. It was dedicated in May 1950 and was in operation until October 1964.

Bibliography

1951. Alexander, S. N. "The National Bureau of Standards Eastern Automatic Computer (SEAC)," *IRE Eastern Joint Computer Conference*, 84–89.
1953. Shupe, P. D. Jr, and Kirsch, R. A. "SEAC—A Review of Three Years of Operation," *IRE Eastern Joint Computer Conference*, 83–90.

Harry D. Huskey

SEARCH ENGINE

See WORLD WIDE WEB.

SEARCHING

For articles on related subjects *see* ALGORITHMS, ANALYSIS OF; DATA STRUCTURES; LIST PROCESSING; SORTING; and TREE.

Introduction

For a given searching problem, the particular choice of an algorithm and data structure depends on the nature of the storage medium (internal memory, disk other), on the nature of the data being organized change through insertions or deletions, is it a or numeric, are some elements more likely to occur as search objects than others, and so on), and on the requirements of the search (must it be fast on average or in the worst case, how much information is available, and the like). We describe here some of the most important algorithms and data structures.

We will assume that we are searching a *table* of n *elements*, in which each element has a collection of *fields* associated with it, one field for each of a number of *attributes*. One of these attributes will be the *key* that is used to refer to the element and on which the searching is based.

Lists

In organizing a table as a list, we can vary only two things: the order of the elements in the list and the implementation as either an array or a linked list. The elements may be in no particular order, in an order based on their frequencies as search objects, or in their natural order (alphabetic or numeric).

There is a trade-off between arrays and linked lists: the ease with which we can randomly access any element in an array makes it ideal under certain conditions, while under other conditions, the ease of insertion and deletion makes a linked list more appropriate. Situations also occur in which both efficient access and ease of modification are needed simultaneously, but neither arrays nor linked lists are then appropriate; instead, dynamic trees (discussed later) should be considered.

LINEAR SEARCH

Linear search examines each element in turn to see if it is the one sought, continuing until either the element is found or all the elements in the list have been examined. The order of the elements in the list does not affect the correctness of this algorithm, only the amount of time it requires.

The performance of linear search is based on the number of *probes* into the list: a probe is a comparison between the search object and the key of an element in the table. We evaluate all search strategies by the number of probes required to find an object, both in the worst case and on average. The amount of work in searching for an element is not entirely in the probes, but the total work done is usually proportional to the number of probes, since only a constant number of operations are done per probe. The behavior of linear search is summarized as

	Worst case	Best case	Average case
Successful search	n probes	1 probe	$\sum_{i=1}^{n} ip_i$ probes
Unsuccessful search	n probes	n probes	n probes

where p_i is the probability that the ith item on the list is sought. If all the probabilities $p_i = 1/n$, a successful search will use an average of $\sum_{i=1}^{n} ip_i = \sum_{i=1}^{n} i/n = (n+1)/2$ probes; that is, we expect to search half the list.

When the probabilities are not all equal, we can improve linear search by arranging the list so that the value $\sum_{i=1}^{n} ip_i$ is minimized. The minimum value occurs when the items are in decreasing order by frequency, that is, when $p_1 \geq p_2 \geq \cdots \geq p_n$, but it is seldom possible to determine the access probabilities *a priori*. Even empirical observation may not give an accurate picture of the probabilities if they fluctuate in time. We can still take advantage of nonuniform access probabilities, however, by allowing the order of the elements in the table to change dynamically so that those frequently accessed move to the front of the table. Such a list is called *self-organizing*.

The idea is that when an element is accessed, it is moved to a position closer to the beginning of the table. The amount of work to do this movement must be reasonable, so the possibilities are limited. If the table is an array, we can use the *move-ahead-one strategy* or the *interchange-to-the-front strategy*. If the table is a linked list we can, in addition, use the *move-to-the-front strategy*.

The move-ahead-one strategy, applicable to either linked lists or arrays, works well to keep the table well arranged if the table order is not too far from the desired order. However, it will take quite a while for the popular elements to propagate to the beginning of the list, since they move so slowly. On the other hand, the move-to-the-front strategy, applicable only to linked lists, works well to order the elements quickly when they are far out of order, but it causes erratic behavior in a table that is nearly in order; the interchange-to-the-front strategy is even worse in this regard. Thus it is most reasonable to apply the move-to-front strategy initially until the table order settles down, and continue thereafter with the move-ahead-one strategy.

ORDERED LISTS

If it is possible to maintain the list in some natural order (such as numeric or alphabetic), it is almost always advantageous to do so. Linear search can then be speeded up somewhat for unsuccessful searches, because in an ordered table the search can stop when it discovers the first element beyond what it is seeking, rather than go all the way to the end of the list.

The improvement for unsuccessful search times in tables in the natural order is minor in contrast to the fact that a single probe into the table can now get a good deal more information than when the table is in

```
procedure BinarySearch(
    var x: ArrayType;                          {array to be searched}
        l: integer;                   {the low end of the subrange to be searched}
        h: integer;                   {the high end of the subrange to be searched}
        z: ElementType;                        {the object of the search}
    var loc: integer);                    {the location of z in x, if it was found;
                                           loc= -∞ if it was not found. }

    var m: integer;
    begin { BinarySearch }
      loc := -∞;                                 {assume it won't be found}
      if l ≤ h then
        begin
          m := (l + h) div 2;
          if z < x[m] then                       {search left half recursively}
              BinarySearch(x,l,m-1,z,loc)
          else if z > x[m] then                  {search right half recursively}
              BinarySearch(x,m+1,h,z,loc)
          else                                              {found it}
              loc := m
        end
    end; { BinarySearch }
```

Figure 1. The binary search procedure.

some other order: by comparing the item sought with the key of the middle element of the table, we can determine which half of the table is of further interest. Continuing this idea recursively yields *binary search* (*see* Fig. 1) whose behavior is summarized by

	Worst case	Best case	Average case
Successful search	$\lceil \lg(n+1) \rceil$ probes	1 probe	$\left(1 + \frac{1}{n}\right)\lg(n+1)$ $+ o(1)$ probes
Unsuccessful search	$\lceil \lg(n+1) \rceil$ probes	$\lfloor \lg(n+1) \rfloor$ probes	$\lg(n+1) + o(1)$ probes

The function "lg" is the base-two logarithm, that is, $\log_2$. The symbol $\lfloor x \rfloor$ is the largest integer not larger than x; similarly, $\lceil x \rceil$ is the smallest integer not smaller than x.

The values given for the number of probes in the average successful and unsuccessful searches are based on the assumption that for successful searches each of the n elements is equally probable as the place for the search to end. This assumption is rarely justified in practice, but is the only reasonable one to make in the absence of any information. When the access probabilities are known, it is possible to use the optimal search trees discussed later.

There may be useful statistical properties of the table that can aid the search. For example, in looking up the name "Smith" in a phone book we would be unlikely to probe first at the midpoint and then at the three-quarters point, and so on, as in binary search. Instead, we would assume that under normal conditions the name "Smith" would be found near the end of the list-

ings, and we would begin our search nearer to the expected location of the search object. This idea leads to *interpolation search*.

For simplicity, assume we are dealing with numeric values $x_1 < x_2 < \cdots < x_n$ uniformly distributed in the range (x_0, x_{n+1}). If we are searching such a table for z, $x_0 < z < x_{n+1}$, the uniform distribution suggests that we interpolate linearly to determine the expected location of z. That expected location is $n(z - x_0)/(x_{n+1} - x_0)$, and this is where we should probe first. In general, if we know that $x_l < z < x_h$, then we should probe at location

$$l + \frac{z - x_l}{x_h - x_l}(h - l - 1).$$

The number of probes used in interpolation search is

	Worst case	Best case	Average case
Successful search	n probes	1 probe	$\lg \lg n$ probes
Unsuccessful search	n probes	2 probes	$\lg \lg n$ probes

The average behavior of interpolation search is a much different "average" from that considered for either linear search or binary search. In those cases the table of elements was fixed and the average was over the occurrences of the various elements as search objects; in this case the average is over search objects *and* tables whose elements follow a certain statistical pattern. If a particular table does not follow that pattern, the average search in that table will be poorer than expected. Furthermore, the greatly increased cost per probe in interpolation search means that interpolation search is inferior to binary search unless the tables are much larger than most tables occurring in practice.

Binary Search Trees

A *binary search tree* is a binary tree of the table elements in which every element x has the lexicographic property that the elements in the left subtree of x are before the key of x in the natural order and the elements in the right subtree of x are after the key of x in the natural order. This property of the tree makes it easy to search for an element z: compare z with the key of the root element; if the keys are equal, the search ends successfully, and if they are not, search the left or right subtree according to whether z is less than or greater than the key of the root element, respectively. Fig 2 shows a binary search tree of 16 common English words.

STATIC TREES

The application of binary search trees to static tables is concerned entirely with choosing the tree that minimizes search time; we assume that the table is constructed once and that its contents never change, or change so infrequently that the entire table will be reconstructed to make the change. If we want to minimize the worst-case search time, we simply use the tree corresponding to binary search, and we do not need an explicit tree at all. The more difficult problem is to minimize the average search time, given some frequency distribution of how the search will end. If the table consists of elements $x_1 < x_2 < \cdots < x_n$, then the search can end successfully at any of the x_i (internal nodes) and unsuccessfully in any of the $n + 1$ intervals (leaves) specified by the x_i and the endpoints. If we are given the relative frequencies with which the search ends in these $2n + 1$ ways, we can use dynamic programming to determine the optimal shape of the tree that minimizes the average search time.

The dynamic programming algorithm can be implemented in quadratic time, but it may not be worth spending so much time to construct the optimal tree if we have only inaccurate values for the relative frequencies. Instead, we should use a heuristic (*q.v.*) to construct a "near-optimal tree" rapidly.

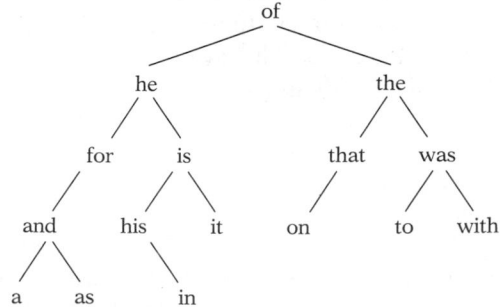

Figure 2. A binary search tree of 16 common English words.

The *balancing heuristic* chooses the root so as to equalize (as much as possible) the frequencies with which a search will end in the left and right subtrees. The cost of the resulting tree is always extremely close to the cost of the optimal tree. That the balancing rule does so well is even more remarkable since it can be implemented in time linear in the number of elements in the table.

DYNAMIC TREES

Binary search trees can be used for dynamic tables—tables whose contents change because of insertions and deletions. There is a conflict between efficient search algorithms and efficient modification: fast search requires a rigid structure, while fast modification needs a flexible structure; *balanced trees* provide a compromise between the two requirements.

Logarithmic search times can be achieved by keeping the tree nearly perfectly balanced at all times (as is implicit in binary search). Unfortunately, when the tree is thus constrained, it is quite costly to insert or delete an element. Instead, we allow a limited flexibility in the shape of the tree so that insertions and deletions will not be so expensive, yet search times will remain logarithmic. Such techniques keep the trees "balanced" so that they cannot become too skewed (and hence degenerate to linear search times). The height of such trees of n elements will be $O(\log n)$ so that search times are logarithmic. Insertions and deletions will require only local changes along a single path from the root to a leaf, thus requiring only time proportional to the height of the tree, which is logarithmic.

There are several strategies for keeping binary trees balanced as they undergo insertions and deletions. A binary tree is *height-balanced* if at any node in the tree the two subtrees of that node differ in height by at most one. A height-balanced binary tree of n elements will have height at most about $1.44 \lg(n + 1)$, so if a search tree is kept height-balanced, the worst-case search time will be logarithmic. A two-bit *condition code* is stored at each node; the condition code specifies whether the two subtrees have equal height, the left subtree is taller by one, or the right subtree is taller by one.

A binary tree is *weight-balanced* if, at any node in the tree, neither of the two subtrees contains more than a specified fraction f, $0 < f < 1/2$, of the nodes. A weight-balanced binary tree of n elements will have height at most about

$$\frac{\lg(n + 1)}{-\lg(1 - f)}$$

so if a search tree is kept weight-balanced, the worst-case search time will be logarithmic. The choice of f

allows an explicit trade-off to be made between search times and rebalancing times. If

$$\frac{2}{11} \le f \le 1 - \frac{\sqrt{2}}{2},$$

insertions and deletions can be accommodated so that a weight-balanced tree remains weight-balanced afterward. The size of the subtree is stored at each node.

Binary trees can also be kept balanced by a simple scheme in which the edges connecting nodes of the tree are colored either red or black. The balancing rule is that all paths from the root of the tree to a leaf contain the same number of black edges and that there are never two red edges in a row along such a path; the height of such a tree with n elements will be at most $2 \lg(n + 1)$. The trees are implemented by using a single bit at each node specifying the color of the incoming edge.

In the balanced trees discussed above, some explicit balance information is maintained in each node and the trees are rebalanced on the basis of that information. Instead of maintaining such information, *splay trees* adjust the tree at each access, as well as upon an insertion or deletion. The adjustment is made along the access path, and its effect is to bring the accessed item to the root of the tree; this is similar to the move-to-the-front strategy in self-organizing lists. The resulting trees are not guaranteed to have logarithmic height, so some accesses, insertions, and deletions will be relatively costly, but the *amortized behavior* of these trees is logarithmic: the total time required by any sequence of m tree operations starting with an initially empty tree is $O(m \log n)$, where n is the number of insertion operations. Even more remarkably, splay trees are, to within a constant factor, as efficient in the amortized sense as optimal binary search trees (above).

Digital Search Trees

We can use trees to organize tables based on the representation of the elements, rather than on the ordering of the elements as in the previous section. If the alphabet contains c characters, each node in the tree would be a c-way branch—one branch for each possible character. The structure thus obtained is called a *digital search tree* or *trie* (taken from the middle letters of the word "retrieval," but pronounced "try"). This concept is illustrated in Fig. 3 which shows eight mathematical constants.

To explain Fig. 3, we describe how to search it. Suppose we are given the number 1.414 as the object of the search. We consider each of the digits 1, 4, 1, and 4 in turn, starting at the root of the tree and proceeding as follows. Follow the branch labeled 1 out of

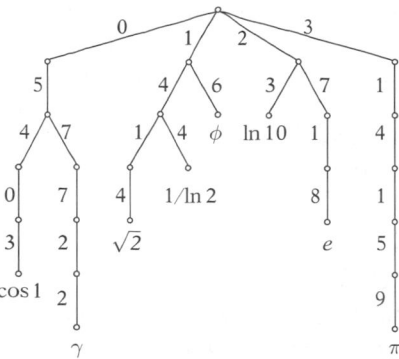

Figure 3. A trie of eight mathematical constants. The implicit decimal point is between the first and second edges of each path.

the root; at the next node follow the branch labeled 4, then the branch labeled 1, and finally the branch labeled 4. At that point we are at the bottom of the tree and the letters of the search object are exhausted, so we have successfully found 1.414 in the tree. If the search object had been 1.413, we would have followed down branches in the tree corresponding to 1, 4, and 1, but then there would be no branch labeled 3, indicating that 1.413 is not in the tree.

The advantage of a digital search tree is that in many circumstances the multiway branch required at every node of the tree will require little or no more time than a binary decision.

Hashing

In *hashing* an element is stored in a location computed directly from the key of the element. Suppose that we have an array of m table locations $T[0 \ldots m - 1]$ and are given an element z to be inserted; we transform z to a location $h(z)$, $0 \le h(z) < m$, where h is called a *hash function* and $h(z)$ is called the *hash address*. We then examine $T[h(z)]$ to see whether it is empty. If it is empty, we store z there, and we are done. If $T[h(z)]$ is not empty, a *collision* has occurred, and we must resolve it somehow. Taken together, the hash function and the collision resolution method are referred to as *hashing* or *scatter storage* schemes.

Under the proper conditions, hashing is unsurpassed in its efficiency as a table organization, since the average times for a search or an insertion are generally *independent of the size of the table*. Some important caveats are in order, however. First, in the worst case collisions occur every time and hashing degenerates into linear search. Second, while it is easy to make insertions into a hash table, the full size of the table must be specified *a priori*, because it is usually closely connected to the hash function used; this makes it extremely expensive to change dynamically. Third, deletions from the table are not easily accommodated in most schemes. Finally, the order of the elements in the table is unrelated to any natural order among the elements, and so an unsuccessful search tells us only that the element sought is not in the table; we obtain no information about how it relates to the elements that are in the table.

HASH FUNCTIONS

The hash function takes an element to be stored in a table and transforms it into a location in the table. If this transformation makes certain table locations more likely to occur than others, it is said to exhibit *primary clustering*. This increases the chance of collisions and decreases the efficiency of searches and insertions. The ideal hash function spreads the elements uniformly throughout the table without primary clustering.

There are four basic techniques used for constructing hash functions; while there are no absolute rules, there are several important principles. A hash function should be a function of *all* the bits of the element, not just some of them. A hash function should break up naturally occurring clusters of elements. A hash function should be quick and easy to compute. The properties of any particular hash function are hard to determine because they depend so heavily on the set of elements that will be encountered in practice.

The simplest hash functions merely extract a few scattered bits from an element, putting those bits together to form an address. Such *extraction hash functions* are generally a poor way to do hashing except in *ad hoc* situations where the table contents are completely known in advance and the bits to be extracted can be carefully chosen to prevent primary clustering. The weakness of extraction is that the resulting location depends only on a small subset of the bits of an element.

A simple way to get a location from an element in such a way that every bit of the element participates is to compress the bits of the element into the number required for an address. For example, one could break a bit string to be hashed into fixed-length segments and then add them as binary numbers or take their exclusive-or. One weakness of such a method of compression is that the operations of addition and exclusive-or are commutative, so that permutations of the segments yield the same hash value. It is better to shift different segments circularly by different amounts. *Compression hash functions* are most useful for converting multi-word elements into a single word, making it easy to apply either the division- or multiplication-based hash functions that we now describe.

Given a table $T[0 \ldots m-1]$, we can take $h(z) = z \bmod m$; that is, $h(z)$ is the remainder when z is divided by m. In using such a *division hash function* one must choose the value of m carefully to ensure that the hash location depends on all the bits of the element and that naturally occurring clusters are broken up. It generally works out best if m is prime. Furthermore, it is undesirable for $r^k \equiv \pm a \pmod m$, for "small" values of a and k, where r is the radix of the objects being hashed (bytes, digits, characters, or whatever).

Given a real number θ, $0 < \theta < 1$, we can construct a hash function $h(z) = \lfloor m \times (z\theta \bmod 1) \rfloor$; that is, compute the fractional part of the product $z\theta$, multiply it by m, and take the greatest integer in the product. Unlike division hash functions, with *multiplication hash functions* we need not be concerned with the table size m, but we do need some guidelines in choosing θ. The value of θ should not be too close to 0 or 1, nor should $r^k\theta \bmod 1$ be close to 1 for small values of k, where r is the radix of the objects being hashed. Values of θ approximately $i/(r^k - 1)$ are also problematic in terms of clustering.

COLLISION RESOLUTION

A *collision* occurs when the location $T[h(z)]$ is already filled at the time we try to insert z. A *collision-resolution scheme* specifies a list of table locations then to be considered for z; these locations are inspected (in order) until an empty one is found. There are two choices: store pointers describing the sequence explicitly (chaining), or specify the sequence implicitly by a fixed relationship with z (linear probing).

In *chaining*, a sequence of pointers is built from the hash location $h(z)$ to the location in which z is ultimately stored. In *separate chaining*, each table location $T[i]$ points to a linked list of those elements z with $h(z) = i$. These lists can be kept in order or not, as appropriate. Separate chaining is most efficient in cases where dynamic allocation can be used. If dynamic allocation is unavailable or undesirable, we can use *coalesced chaining* in which the record for each table location $T[i]$ contains a field NEXT. When $T[h(z)]$ is found to contain another element on an attempted insertion of z, we follow the NEXT fields until we reach one that is null; then we take an arbitrary empty table location, set that last null NEXT field to point to it, and store z there.

Assuming that we use a hash function devoid of primary clustering and that collisions are resolved by coalesced chaining, the average number of probes in a successful search in a table of m locations containing n elements is

$$S(\lambda) \approx 1 + \frac{1}{8\lambda}\left(e^{2\lambda} - 1 - 2\lambda\right) + \frac{1}{4}\lambda,$$

where $\lambda = n/m$ is called the *load factor* of the table. The behavior of a collision-resolution scheme is expressed in terms of λ because the behavior of the algorithms is governed by the fullness of the table in relative, rather than absolute terms. In an unsuccessful search the average number of probes is

$$U(\lambda) \approx 1 + \frac{1}{4}(e^{2\lambda} - 1 - 2\lambda).$$

For separate chaining the corresponding formulas are

$$S(\lambda) \approx 1 + \frac{1}{2}\lambda$$

and

$$U(\lambda) \approx e^{-\lambda} + \lambda$$

for unordered lists, and

$$U(\lambda) \approx 1 + \frac{1}{2}\lambda - \frac{1}{\lambda}(1 - e^{-\lambda}) + e^{-\lambda}$$

for ordered lists.

The simplest alternative to chaining that does not require the storage of NEXT fields is to resolve collisions by probing sequentially, one location at a time, starting from the hash address, until an empty location is found. This is called *open addressing with linear probing*, or simply *linear probing*. Again assuming we use a hash function devoid of primary clustering, when collisions are resolved by linear probing the average number of probes in a successful search in a table of m locations containing n elements is

$$S(\lambda) \approx \frac{1}{2}\left(1 + \frac{1}{1 - \lambda}\right)$$

and in an unsuccessful search

$$U(\lambda) \approx \frac{1}{2}\left[1 + \frac{1}{(1 - \lambda)^2}\right].$$

Linear probing exhibits *secondary clustering*: the tendency of two elements that have collided to follow the same sequence of locations in the resolution of the collision. Such a tendency will aggravate the unavoidable fact that long lists are more likely to grow than short lists. To avoid secondary clustering we want the sequence of locations followed in resolving a collision of z to be a function of z. This can be accomplished by only a minor change to linear probing—instead of probing sequentially for an empty location, increment by an amount that is a function of z. To ensure that every location in the table will be probed on a collision, the increment and m must be relatively prime. If m is a prime, we can use another hash function $\delta(z)$, $1 \le \delta(z) < m$ as the increment. This method is called *double hashing*.

Assume that we use a hash function devoid of primary clustering and further that our increment function $\delta(z)$ is ideal in the sense that all $m!$ probe sequences are equally likely in resolving the collision. Then, when collisions are resolved by double hashing, the average number of probes in a successful search in a table of m locations containing n elements is

$$S(\lambda) \approx \frac{1}{\lambda}\ln\frac{1}{1 - \lambda}$$

and in an unsuccessful search

$$U(\lambda) \approx \frac{1}{1 - \lambda}.$$

There may be a natural order of the elements that can be used to speed up unsuccessful searches in hash tables. Such an order is utilized by having an element being inserted "bump" a smaller element already in the table from its place during an insertion; the insertion then continues with the bumped element being inserted. The bumping makes the table appear as though its contents were inserted in decreasing order and this has the effect of reducing unsuccessful times, just as in the case of linear search. For double hashing the average cost of an unsuccessful search is reduced to

$$U(\lambda) \approx \frac{1}{\lambda}\ln\frac{1}{1 - \lambda}.$$

DELETION AND REHASHING

Except in separate chaining, deletion of an element from a hash table poses special problems. We cannot simply remove an element from the table, because such a removal will disrupt the probe sequence for elements that collided with the one to be deleted. We can mark the table location as containing an element that has been deleted. Such a location acts like an empty location with respect to insertions, but like a full location with respect to searches. This means that search times will not change for the better after a deletion; for example, if we fill a table to 90% of its capacity and then delete half the elements, the table still behaves like a table 90% full as far as searching is concerned.

The only solution to the problem of degraded search times is the ultimate reconstruction of the table by a process called *rehashing* in which each table location is scanned in turn and its contents, if any, are relocated as necessary. Such a rehashing process is expensive, since it requires time proportional to the table size.

TABLE LOOK-UP

Suppose that all the items z to be stored in Table $T[0 \ldots m - 1]$ have associated with them a unique key k such that $0 \le k < m$. Then the simplest conceivable hash function h is $h(k) - k$, i.e. k itself is usable as a naturally occurring index into the table. In such a case, hashing is collision-free and degenerates to simple table look up. If, for example, each of the 51 geographic units that comprise the USA is numbered 0 to 50 and their respective populations are stored in $T[0\ldots50]$, then we can "look up" the population of the kth state by accessing $T[k]$.

Tables in External Storage

The methods of table organization that have been presented so far are geared to internal memory—memory that can be accessed randomly at speeds matching the speed of the computer itself. For small or medium-sized temporary tables internal memory is fine, but for large or long-term tables we must rely on relatively slow external memory devices, such as magnetic tapes and disks.

MAGNETIC TAPES

Magnetic tape is a sequential storage medium, so that to examine the ith record on the tape it is necessary to have examined or moved past the first $i-1$ records. Essentially, then, organizing a table on magnetic tape is the same as using a linked list. Such a table must be searched in a linear fashion, and the only possible refinement is to order the records on the tape so as to minimize search time. The two relevant orders are (1) the natural order of the records (alphabetical or numerical) or (2) so that $p_1/L_1 \leq p_2/L_2 \leq \cdots \leq p_n/L_n$, where p_i is the probability that the ith record is the search object and L_i is its length—the cost of reading it into memory. In general, magnetic tapes are a poor choice for storing frequently accessed information unless that information will always be scanned in a linear fashion.

DISKS

Disks allow random access to all records stored, but the time required for such an access is great compared with internal memory speeds. There is a high overhead in time to initiate an *access*—that is, a transfer of records from the disk to internal memory. Efficient organization of tables on disks thus requires minimizing the number of times such an access is initiated and transferring large numbers of records on each access.

Since accesses are costly compared to probes, it is preferable to make many probes for each disk access. Thus to adapt search trees to disks we use m-way branches instead of two-way (binary) branches. Typically, m will be several hundred; the best choice for m depends on the precise physical characteristics of the storage device (access and transfer times), the size of the elements in the table, and the amount of internal memory available to store elements. As with binary search trees, it is quite time-consuming to keep the tree perfectly balanced while inserting and deleting: We only insist that all paths from the root to a leaf node are of equal length and that each node except the root has at least $\lceil m/2 \rceil$ subtrees. Such a tree is called a *balanced multiway tree* or *B-tree*. Search times remain logarithmic and insertions and deletions can be accommodated. In the worst case, B-trees waste about 50% of their space, but on average the storage utilization will be about 69%.

We can adapt hashing schemes to disks by having the address computed by the hash function be a disk address. To minimize the number of disk accesses needed on a search we should enlarge the basic table component from a single element to a group of b elements called a *bucket*; a hash address would specify the disk address of a bucket and a disk access would retrieve all the elements of the bucket. The elements in a bucket would then be searched. We should also spend much more time in computing the hash function so as to minimize collisions. Because we are hashing to buckets rather than individual table locations, we expect collisions to be no problem and we can use a relatively simple-minded scheme to resolve them.

Some schemes for hashing allow the table size to be extended dynamically. These schemes, which impose a tree-like structure on the hash table, are suitable for large hash tables on disks.

Bibliography

1974. Amble, O., and Knuth, D. E., "Ordered Hash Tables," *Computer J.*, **17**, 135–142.
1975. Knott, G. D. "Hashing Functions," *Computer J.*, **18**, 265–278.
1978. Guibas, L. J., and Szemeredi, E. "The Analysis of Double Hashing," *J. Comput. Syst. Sci.*, **16**, 226–274.
1979. Fagin, R., Nievergelt, J., Pippenger, N., and Strong, H. R. "Extendible Hashing—A Fast Access Method for Dynamic Files," *ACM Trans. Database Sys.*, **4**, 315–344.
1980. Gonnet, G. H., Rogers, L. D., and George, J. A. "An Algorithmic and Complexity Analysis of Interpolation Search," *Acta Informatica*, **13**, 39–52.
1984. Gonnet, G. H. *Handbook of Algorithms and Data Structures.* Reading, MA: Addison-Wesley.
1985. Sleator, D. D., and Tarjan, R. E. "Self-adjusting Binary Search Trees," *J. ACM*, **32**, 652–686.
1986. Reingold, E. M., and Hansen, W. J. *Data Structures in Pascal.* Boston, MA: Little, Brown and Company.
1997. Knuth, D. E. *The Art of Computer Programming, Vol. III: Sorting and Searching*, 2nd Ed. Reading, MA: Addison-Wesley.
1999. Sedgewick, R. *Algorithms in C++*, 3rd Ed. Reading, MA: Addison-Wesley.

Edward M. Reingold

SEMANTICS

See PROGRAMMING LANGUAGE SEMANTICS; and SYNTAX, SEMANTICS, AND PRAGMATICS.

SEQUENTIAL MACHINE

For articles on related subjects *see* AUTOMATA THEORY; BOOLEAN ALGEBRA; FORMAL LANGUAGES; PROBABILISTIC AUTOMATA; REGULAR EXPRESSION; and SWITCHING THEORY.

Basic Concepts

A *sequential machine* is a mathematical model of a certain type of simple computational structure. If a sequential machine has a finite number of states, it is frequently called a *finite-state machine*, or FSM. Sequential machines have numerous applications, for example, in asynchronous circuits, coding theory, concurrent systems, digital circuit design, formal language theory, hardware testing, protocol design, and software and hardware verification.

There are several varieties of sequential machine, of which the most common is the finite-state, synchronous sequential machine. It has an input σ, which can take on any value from a finite set Σ, called the *input alphabet*, and an output δ, from a finite *output alphabet* Δ, as shown in Fig. 1. The input and output values are of interest only at certain instants of time, which are usually identified with the integers $1, 2, 3, \ldots$. At any time t, the output $\delta(t)$ depends not only on the present input $\sigma(t)$ (as is the case in combinational circuits), but also on the past input *sequence* $\ldots, \sigma(t-k)$, $\sigma(t-k+1), \ldots, \sigma(t-1)$; hence the name *sequential machine*. In this section we shall, for simplicity, assume that $k = 0$.

The dependence of the output on past inputs implies that a sequential machine has memory. Usually, this memory is finite and corresponds to a finite set Q, called the set of *internal states*. At time t machine M is in some (present) internal state $q(t)$. It receives an input value $\sigma(t)$, and this present input and present internal state determine the next internal state $q(t + 1)$.

An example of a sequential machine is shown in Fig. 2. The machine is represented by a directed graph, its *state graph*, where the nodes correspond to internal states and the labeled edges to transitions among internal states. The labels are of the form σ/δ, where σ is the input value causing the transition and δ is the corresponding output value. For example, if M_1 of Fig. 2 is in state q_1 at time t, and if $\sigma(t) = 1$, then the transition labeled $1/0$ is relevant; the output produced during the transition is $\delta(t) = 0$, and the next state of M_1 is $q(t + 1) = q_2$. In general, if we are given an initial state $q(1)$ (i.e. the value of q at $t = 1$), and

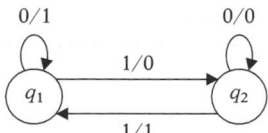

Figure 2. Machine M_1.

an input sequence $\sigma(1), \ldots, \sigma(t)$, we can determine from the state graph the resulting state sequence $q(2)$, $\ldots, q(t+1)$ and the corresponding output sequence $\delta(1), \ldots, \delta(t)$. A typical computation is shown in Table 1, where it is assumed that $q(1) = q_1$. The reader will verify that, if M_1 is started in state q_1, it will produce an output of 1 at time t if and only if the number of 1s in the sequence $\sigma(1), \ldots, \sigma(t)$ is even.

With each sequential machine we associate two functions: the *transition function* f, which determines the next state from the present state and the present input, and an *output function* g. In machine M_1, the present output depends on both the present state and the present input. Such a model, in which $\delta(t) = g(q(t), \sigma(t))$, is called the *Mealy model*. In another useful model, the *Moore model*, the present output is uniquely determined by the present state, i.e. $\delta(t) = g(q(t))$.

An example of a Moore machine is shown in Fig. 3. The input and output alphabets are $\Sigma = \{a, b\}$ and $\Delta = \{0, 1, 2\}$, respectively. Given an initial state and an input sequence, we can determine the state sequence, as in the Mealy model. Since the output is determined solely by the state, we associate it with the nodes of the state graph rather than with the edges. A typical computation for M_2 is shown in Table 2, assuming $q(1) = q_1$. The behavior of M_2 can be described as follows: the input value a is "ignored" by M_2, in the sense that no change of state results when $\sigma(t) = a$. The input b advances the state of M_2 cyclically. If the machine is started in q_1, the output $\delta(t + 1)$ is congruent modulo 3 to the number of bs in the input sequence $\sigma(1), \ldots, \sigma(t)$.

Table 1. Sequences for M_1.

Time:	1	2	3	4	5	6	7
Input:	0	1	0	0	1	1	
State:	q_1	q_1	q_2	q_2	q_2	q_1	q_2
Output:	1	0	0	0	1	0	

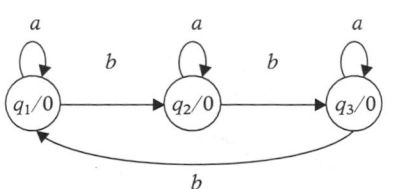

Figure 3. Machine M_2.

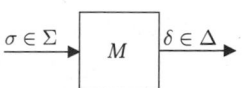

Figure 1. Sequential machine block diagram.

Table 2. Sequences for M$_2$.

Time:	1	2	3	4	5	6	7
Input:	b	a	b	a	b	b	
State:	q_1	q_2	q_2	q_3	q_3	q_1	q_2
Output:	0	1	1	2	2	0	1

The differences between Moore and Mealy models are only technical. From a general point of view, these models are equivalent as far as computational power is concerned. Another related model is the *finite automaton*. This is a special case of the Moore machine, where $\Delta = \{0, 1\}$. If the output corresponding to an internal state is 1, that state is called *accepting*, or *final*; if the output is 0, the state is called *rejecting*. A single initial state q_0 is usually specified in a finite automaton A, which can then can be viewed as an *acceptor* of input sequences. For the input sequence $\sigma(1), \ldots, \sigma(t)$, let $q(t + 1)$ be the state reached by A, when it is started in q_0. If $q(t + 1)$ is a final state, the sequence is accepted; otherwise, it is rejected.

An alternative point of view considers a sequential machine as a *sequence transducer*—a machine that transforms an input sequence into an output sequence, as in Tables 1 and 2.

Realization of Sequential Machines

The behavior of a sequential machine can be realized by a sequential switching circuit. We now describe an idealized model of such a circuit. The *sequential network* model reflects the logical properties of the switching circuit, but not its electronic properties. Thus it has the advantage of being independent of the actual technological implementation, while retaining many of the basic structural properties.

A block diagram of a sequential network is shown in Fig. 4. As is usually the case, we assume that all signals in a sequential network are binary, with 0 and 1 as the two possible values. The network has a finite number of binary inputs $x_1, \ldots, x_n$ and binary outputs $z_1, \ldots, z_m$. If the output values $z_i(t)$ at time t are uniquely determined by the input values $x_j(t)$, then it has no memory. In that case, it is called a *combinational network*, and its behavior can be described by m Boolean functions, one for each output z_i. A combinational network can be implemented by a network of logic gates *without* any feedback loops.

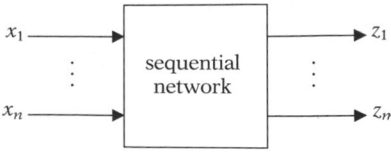

Figure 4. Sequential network.

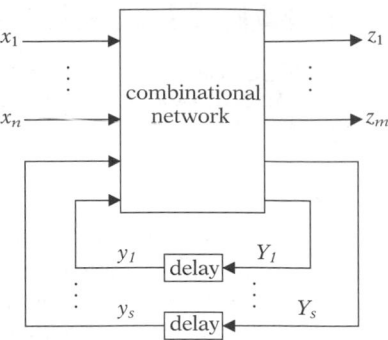

Figure 5. Sequential network with unit delays.

A switching network with memory is called *sequential*. The function of memory can be performed by gate networks *with* feedback. In general, such networks have no special timing signals and are called *asynchronous*. If a special periodic input, called *clock*, is provided to control the action of the network, the network is *synchronous*. In that case, the response of the network is of interest only at certain times, once during each clock period. These times correspond to the instants $1, 2, \ldots$ mentioned earlier.

A synchronous sequential network can be divided into a combinational part and a memory part. The units corresponding to memory are asynchronous networks called *flip-flops*. For theoretical considerations, the simplest memory module is the *unit delay*, whose output y is equal to the input x delayed by one unit of time; i.e., $y(t) = x(t - 1)$. The general form of a synchronous sequential network with unit delays as memory elements is shown in Fig. 5. The network can be described by two sets of equations.

1. Next-state equations: for $i = 1, \ldots, s$,

$$y_i(t + 1) = Y_i(t)$$
$$= f_i(x_1(t), \ldots, x_n(t), y_1(t), \ldots, y_s(t)).$$

2. Output equations: for $j = 1, \ldots, m$,

$$z_j(t) = g_j(x_1(t), \ldots, x_n(t), y_1(t), \ldots, y_s(t)).$$

The f_i in (1) and the g_j in (2) are Boolean functions.

The reader will easily verify that the sequential network model of Fig. 5 is a special case of the Mealy model, where Σ is the set of all binary n-tuples (binary words of length n), Δ is the set of all binary m-tuples, and Q is the set of all binary s-tuples.

Any abstract sequential machine can be realized by a sequential network of the type shown in Fig. 5. This can be done by representing each element of Σ by a suitable n-tuple $x_1, \ldots, x_n$, and Δ and Q must be coded similarly.

Table 3. State tables for flip-flops: (a) *D* flip-flop, (b) *T* flip-flop, (c) *SR* flip-flop, (d) *JK* flip-flop. Each table shows the value of $q(t+1)$.

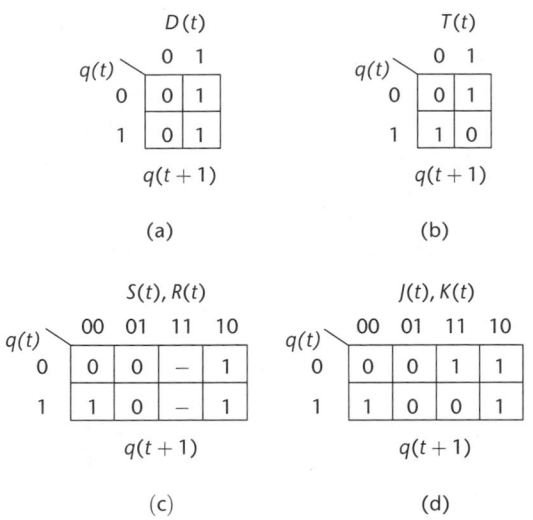

(a)

(b)

(c)

(d)

The unit delay is sometimes called the *D flip-flop*. Other types of flip-flops are the *T* (*toggle* or *trigger*) type, the *SR* (*set–reset*) type, and the *JK* type. In Table 3 we define the four types of flip-flops by their *state tables*, which constitute a common way (equivalent to the state-graph) of representing sequential networks. The rows of the state table correspond to the internal states, and the columns to input combinations. The entries represent the next state. The most general type of flip-flop is the *JK*. The condition $J=0, K=0$ is the *remember* condition, where no change takes place; $J=0, K=1$ corresponds to the *reset* condition (the flip-flop is reset to 0); $J=1, K=0$ is the *set* condition; and $J=1, K=1$ is the *toggle* condition (the state changes, or *toggles*). The combination 11 is not used in an *SR* flip-flop. Any sequential machine can be realized using logic gates and flip-flops of any one of the four types.

Behavioral Properties

Two states q and q' of a sequential machine M are *indistinguishable* if the input–output (I/O) behavior of M started in q cannot be distinguished by any external experiment from that of M started in q'. In other words, any input sequence applied to M started in q, produces the same output sequence as in the case when M is started in q'. Otherwise, q and q' are *distinguishable*. A sequential machine in which any two states are distinguishable is called *reduced*.

Two sequential machines M and M' are indistinguishable if for every state q of M there exists a state q' of M' such that the I/O behavior of M started in q is the same as that of M' started in q', and vice versa. For every sequential machine M, there exists a unique (up

to isomorphism) reduced sequential machine M_0 indistinguishable from M. Machine M_0 is the *minimal-state version* of M.

A set of sequences over a finite alphabet is called a *language*. It is useful to associate certain languages with sequential machines. For example, in the case of a finite automaton A, we define the *language* $L(A)$ of A to be the set of all accepted sequences. Similarly, the set L_{ij} of all sequences taking a sequential machine from state q_i to state q_j, or the set L_δ, of all sequences resulting in a particular output value δ, represent useful languages. All such languages of the form $L(A)$, L_{ij}, or L_δ are *regular languages*. It can be shown that any language defined by a sequential machine in the sense given above is regular, and, conversely, for every regular language there exists a sequential machine "recognizing" that language.

One basic function of sequential machines is counting. When the number of states is finite, a sequential machine can only count "up to a threshold" (see below) and then modulo an integer.

Another unique characterization of sequential machines is provided by the *syntactic semigroup* of the machine, defined as follows: for each input σ, the set Q of states of a reduced machine is transformed according to the transition function. The set of all transformations of states performed by all input sequences constitutes the syntactic semigroup. This representation is useful for certain structural properties.

Structural Properties

In a general network, as shown in Fig. 5, there may be *feedback loops*. For example, Y_1 may be a function of y_2, and Y_2 may be a function of y_1. In the special case where no such loops exist, the network is called *definite*. An example of a simple definite network is shown in Fig. 6, where the rectangles represent unit delays. The languages recognized by definite networks are particularly simple, since the behavior of such networks depends only on the last k symbols of the input sequence, for some k. In general, feedback is required to realize the behavior of an arbitrary sequential machine. It can be shown, however, that every sequential machine can be realized by a sequential network having a single feedback loop.

When *SR* flip-flops (instead of unit delays) are used as memory elements, the class of machines realizable without feedback is considerably larger than the class of definite machines. The languages recognized by

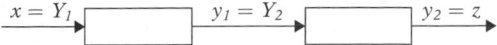

Figure 6. A definite machine.

machines in this class are the so-called *noncounting* regular languages. Such machines can only count to a threshold in the following sense: if the threshold is the integer $k \geq 0$, then the machine may be able to determine whether a certain sequence of symbols occurs in the input sequence $0, 1, \ldots$, or $k - 1$ times. After this, it cannot distinguish k occurrences from $k + 1$ occurrences, but can only conclude that the number of occurrences is at least k. Therefore, such machines cannot count modulo any integer greater than one, and are called *counter-free*. The languages corresponding to counter-free machines constitute a natural subclass of regular languages. They can be defined by regular expressions that use only Boolean operations and concatenation. Such expressions are called *star-free*. The syntactic semigroups corresponding to this class of machines and languages are *group-free* (i.e. contain only subgroups of order 1).

Sequential machines that can be realized by networks of unit delays and exclusive-OR gates are *linear* and constitute a proper subclass of sequential machines. Linear machines have important applications in coding theory, and also in circuit testing.

The problem of decomposing a sequential machine into a *cascade connection* of smaller sequential machines has received much attention. The cascade connection of two machines is shown in Fig. 7. This connection is also known as the *series connection*. The *parallel connection* of two machines is a special case of the cascade connection, where neither machine influences the other. We have already indicated that definite machines correspond to cascade connections of unit delays (*see* Fig. 6), and counter-free machines correspond to cascade connections of *SR* flip-flops. The Krohn–Rhodes theory shows that, in general, arbitrary sequential machines correspond to cascade connections of machines whose syntactic semigroups are simple groups, and *SR* flip-flops. Such results are of theoretical interest. For practical applications, an often-used connection is a *shift register*, which is a very simple cascade connection of flip-flops, used, for example in a computer connection to a serial communication line. Shift registers and counters constitute basic modules in the design of sequential networks.

Related Models

In practical applications, certain state-input combinations of a sequential machine may never occur. In this case, the next state and output may be irrelevant and need not be specified. The *incompletely specified* sequential machine model handles such cases.

The situation where the next state and output of a machine are not precisely predictable is modeled by *stochastic* or *probabilistic* sequential machines. The case where the transition and output functions vary with time is modeled by *time-varying* sequential machines. Stochastic and time-varying machines are both more powerful than ordinary machines in the sense that they can recognize some languages that are not regular.

A theoretically convenient model is the *nondeterministic* sequential machine. Here, for a given present state and input, the next state can be chosen from a set of states; i.e. it is not necessarily unique. As acceptors of languages, nondeterministic machines are no more powerful than deterministic machines; both types can recognize only regular languages. A nondeterministic machine can have fewer states than the corresponding reduced deterministic machine accepting the same language.

The concept of a *generalized sequential machine* (GSM) has applications in the theory of formal languages. In this model, for a given present state and input symbol, the machine can produce a sequence of output symbols, whereas the standard model permits only one output symbol. The GSM is also a more powerful model than the standard one.

In the discussion above, we have assumed that the term *sequential machine* implies that the number of states is finite. *Infinite-state* sequential machines have also been studied. They are obviously much more powerful than finite-state machines, and most of the results discussed above do not apply directly to the infinite-state case. Infinite-state linear sequential machines provide an example, in which a number of results from the finite-state case have their generalized counterparts in the infinite case. Finite-state machines can also operate on infinite strings. Such machines have applications to mathematical logic and to processes, such as operating systems, where nonterminating computations are used.

Sequential machines are widely used to verify hardware designs and computer programs which use only a finite amount of memory. Symbolic *model checking* (*q.v.*) is a method in which sets of states, rather than individual states, are analyzed. This leads to efficient algorithms that overcome the "state explosion" problem (the number of states is exponential in the number of system variables).

Sequential machines are also very useful in the design and verification of computer protocols (*q.v.*). In

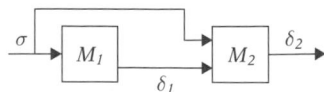

Figure 7. Cascade connection.

particular, concurrent processes can be represented as *communicating* finite-state machines. *Extended* finite-state machines are more versatile, since they permit variables, which can be used to control state transitions. Special models such as *Petri nets* (*q.v.*) and *FIFO nets* are also used in this area.

Bibliography

1968. Hennie, F. C. *Finite-State Models for Logical Machines.* New York: John Wiley.

1976. Eilenberg, S. *Automata, Languages, and Machines,* Vols. A and B. New York: Academic Press.

1978. Kohavi, Z. *Switching and Finite Automata Theory,* 2nd Ed. (especially Part 3). New York: McGraw-Hill.

1979. Hopcroft, J. E., and Ullman, J. D. *Introduction to Automata Theory, Languages, and Computation* (especially Chapter 11). Reading, MA: Addison-Wesley.

1985. Berstel, J., and Perrin, D. *Theory of Codes* (especially Chapter 4). Orlando, FL: Academic Press.

1989. Dewdney, A. K. *The Turing Omnibus* (Chapter 35). Rockville, MD: Computer Science Press.

1990. Perrin, D. "Finite Automata," in *Handbook of Theoretical Computer Science, vol. B, Formal Models and Semantics* (ed. J. Van Leeuwen), 1–57. Amsterdam: Elsevier.

1990. Thomas, W. "Automata on Infinite Objects," in *Handbook of Theoretical Computer Science, vol. B, Formal Models and Semantics* (ed. J. Van Leeuwen), 133–191. Amsterdam: Elsevier.

1991. Holzmann, G. J. *Design and Validation of Computer Protocols* (especially Chapter 8). Upper Saddle River, NJ: Prentice Hall.

1995. Brzozowski, J. A., and Seger, C-J. *Asynchronous Circuits* (especially Chapters 10–15). New York: Springer Verlag.

1996. Clarke, E. M., and Kurshan, R. "Computer-aided Verification," *IEEE Spectrum,* **33**, 6, 61–67.

1996. Hachtel, G. D., and Somenzi, F. *Logic Synthesis and Verification Algorithms* (especially Chapters 7 and 8). Boston: Kluwer Academic Publishers.

Janusz A. Brzozowski

SERIAL I/O

See INPUT–OUTPUT OPERATIONS; and PORT, I/O.

SERVER

See CLIENT–SERVER COMPUTING; and FILE SERVER.

SETL

> For articles on related subjects *see* CONTROL STRUCTURE; PROGRAMMING LANGUAGES; and NONPROCEDURAL LANGUAGES.

Very high-level languages are programming languages, such as functional and logic languages, in which algorithms can be expressed without getting into details of control and data structuring. SETL (*SET L*anguage) is a very high-level language designed for programming algorithms that involve sets and related structures.

SETL provides conventional control structures (`if-then-else`, `while`, `case`, etc.) as well as some specifically set-oriented ones (e.g. `forall` (the members of a set)), but its data structures are very general and include arbitrary finite sets nested to any length and nested tuples with arbitrary components as objects. More specifically, SETL admits the following structures:

Tuples are arbitrary length ordered sequences of component values, which may be primitive or may themselves be tuples. Tuples correspond closely to one-dimensional vectors in familiar languages except that they have no fixed length and can be extended dynamically simply by assigning a value to a previously nonexistent element. In SETL, tuples are used to represent both ordered sequences and unordered "bags" where equal elements may occur. In the latter case, the order of the elements in the tuple is not important.

Examples of SETL tuples, which are delimited by brackets, and of the results of operations on them are as follows:

$$t_1 := [0, 1.3, \text{'hello'}]; \ t_2 := [0, 0, [\text{'a'}, \text{'b'}]];$$
$$t_1(2) = 1.3, \ t_2(3) = [\text{'a'}, \text{'b'}],$$
$$t_2(2..3) = [0, [\text{'a'}, \text{'b'}]],$$
$$t_1 + t_2 = [0, 1.3, \text{'hello'}, 0, 0, [\text{'a'}, \text{'b'}]\}.$$

where + represents concatenation.

Sets are unordered collections of objects with the constraint that a given element cannot appear more than once. SETL provides the usual set-theoretic operations (union, intersection, etc.) and also the `arb` operator, which selects (nondeterministically) an arbitrary element from a set. Examples of sets and of the results of operations on them are the following:

$$s_1 := \{0, 1.3, \text{'hello'}\}; \ s_2 := \{0, [\text{'a'}, \text{'b'}]\};$$
$$s_1 * s_2 = \{0\}; \ s_1 - s_2 = \{1.3, \text{'hello'}\};$$
$$s_1 + s_2 = \{0, 1.3, \text{'hello'}, [\text{'a'}, \text{'b'}]\};$$

where * represents intersection; +, union; and −, set difference.

Maps in SETL are not a separate basic type, but are simply sets of tuples of length 2 (called pairs) whose first component is a domain value and whose second component is the corresponding range value. The set of tuples in a map, therefore, defines a function. Maps may be single or multiple valued, and SETL provides functional-style constructions for evaluating maps for a given argument value, assigning new map values, etc. Since maps are sets, all set valued operators can be used with maps. An example of a map and of operations involving it are:

```
numbvowels := {['hello',2], ['goodbye',3]};
numbvowels('hello') = 2;
numbvowels('zebra') = Ω/*undefined*/.
```

The following succinct "topological sort" program illustrates the use of SETL. We read a directed graph g, which is assumed to be a set of ordered pairs $\{[a, b], [c, d], ...\}$, each such pair representing an edge, and then attempt to arrange the nodes of g in a tuple in such a way that each directed edge goes from a lower to a higher numbered node (i.e. from an element of the tuple to one which follows it).

```
read(g);
  /*read in the graph, which is set of pairs */
set_of_nodes := {n(1):n∈g} + {n(2):n∈g};
                         /*all nodes of g*/
ordered_tuple := [ ];
   /*tuple to be built up is initially empty*/
(while exists n∈set_of_nodes suchthat
     (forall m∈set_of_nodes | [m,n]∉g)
            /*if no [m,n] is in g, add n to end
               of ordered tuple and remove
                  it from set_of_nodes */
        ordered_tuple := ordered_tuple + [n];
        set_of_nodes := set_of_nodes - {n};
end while
if set_of_nodes = { } then
        /* remaining set of nodes is not null*/
        print('topological ordering
                        is impossible');
end if;
        /*otherwise ordered_tuple includes
                             all nodes*/
```

SETL, first implemented at New York University, is available for many systems, including the IBM 370 and many Unix (*q.v.*) systems. It has been successfully used in large research projects, one of which was the first validated Ada (*q.v.*) compiler.

ISETL (*I*nteractive SETL) is a variant of SETL developed by Gary Levin while at Clarkson University. It was designed specifically for teaching and learning mathematical concepts.

SETL2, also from New York University, is intended for prototyping or building large applications. It extends SETL by including a package and library system similar to Ada's, and supports object-oriented programming (*q.v.*).

Both ISETL and SETL2 are available for common personal computers and for Unix systems.

Bibliography

1975. Schwartz, J., and Kennedy, K. "An Introduction to the Set Theoretical Language SETL," in *Computers and Mathematics with Applications*, **1**, 97–110. New York: Pergamon Press.

1986. Schwartz, J. T., Dewar, R. B. K., Dubinsky, E., and Schonberg, E. *Programming with Sets: An Introduction to SETL*. New York: Springer-Verlag.

1989. Baxter, N., Dubinsky, E., and Levin, G. *Learning Discrete Mathematics with ISETL*. New York: Springer-Verlag.

1989. Snyder, K. W. "The SETL2 Programming Language," Report 490. Courant Institute of Mathematical Sciences, New York University.

1996. Fenton, W. E., Dubinsky, E., and Fenton, W. N. *Introduction to Discrete Mathematics with ISETL*. New York: Springer-Verlag.

Jacob T. Schwartz and Kirk W. Snyder

SGML

See MARKUP LANGUAGES.

SHANNON, CLAUDE E.

For articles on related subjects *see* BUSH, VANNEVAR; CODES; DIFFERENTIAL ANALYZER; ERROR CORRECTING AND DETECTING CODE; INFORMATION THEORY; LIMITS OF COMPUTATION; and SWITCHING THEORY.

Claude Elwood Shannon, a native of Gaylord, Michigan, was born on 30 April 1916. He received bachelor of science degrees in electrical engineering and in mathematics from the University of Michigan in 1936, a master's degree in electrical engineering at MIT in 1940, and a Ph.D. in mathematics at MIT in 1940.

At MIT for these four years, he was in charge of the Differential Analyzer, a machine developed by Vannevar Bush for solving differential equations. In his master's thesis, Shannon showed how Boolean algebra (*q.v.*) can be used in the analysis and synthesis of switching (or computer) logical networks, a technique of enduring value. His doctoral thesis showed the application of algebraic theory to genetics. These early

Figure 1. Claude Shannon (courtesy of Lucent Technologies, Bell Labs).

works presaged Shannon's many later applications of mathematics to science and engineering.

Subsequent to receiving his Ph.D., Shannon was a National Research Fellow at the Institute for Advanced Study at Princeton. He joined Bell Laboratories in 1941. During the Second World War, he worked on the design of anti-aircraft gun directors and also on cryptographic problems. His publication "A Mathematical Theory of Cryptography" (published after the war) led to a deep interest in problems of communication.

In 1948, he published "A Mathematical Theory of Communication" in the *Bell System Technical Journal*. This founded what is now called *information theory*. The impact of information theory ranges from the efficient transmission systems for communication from Galileo and later spacecraft, the efficient encoding of television and speech, the analysis of radar systems, and the error-correcting encoding endemic in computers and compact discs, and on to new insights in cryptography and to many rather general applications in a host of fields.

In 1949, Shannon showed how a computer could be programmed to play chess, a goal realized years later (*see* COMPUTER CHESS). In 1952, he demonstrated a maze-solving mouse controlled by interconnected switching relays.

In 1958, Shannon became Donner Professor of Science at MIT, where he advised a number of brilliant graduate students. His later work includes various theorems on juggling.

Shannon is a member of the National Academy of Sciences, the National Academy of Engineering, the American Philosophical Society, and the American Academy of Arts and Sciences, as well as the Leopoldina Academy, the Royal Netherlands Academy of Arts and Sciences, and the Royal Irish Academy. He has received a dozen honorary degrees, and many prestigious awards, including the National Medal of Science (1966), the IEEE Medal of Honor (1966), and the Kyoto Prize in Basic Science (1985).

Shannon is best known for his invention and exploitation of information theory. His collected papers (1993) show a wide range of other important work. [Ed. note: Claude Shannon died on 24 February, 2001.]

Bibliography

1993. Sloane, N. J. A., and Wyner, A. D. (eds.) *Claude Elwood Shannon: Collected Papers*. New York: IEEE Press.

John R. Pierce

SHAREWARE

See FREEWARE AND SHAREWARE.

SHELL

For articles on related subjects *see* KERNEL; OPERATING SYSTEMS; REGULAR EXPRESSION; SCRIPTING LANGUAGES; and UNIX OPERATING SYSTEM.

A *shell* is a command interpreter through which the user gives commands to an operating system. The term reflects the principle that an operating system is constructed from a succession of layers, of which the shell is the outermost one. The shell separates the users from the rest of the operating system and provides a *virtual machine* that serves as a high-level programming environment.

Most system users spend a great deal of time executing programs, not writing new ones. When a user logs in, the operating system creates a process running a copy of the shell program. The shell "listens" to the user's terminal and interprets the inputs as commands to invoke existing programs in specified combinations and with specified inputs. The shell scans each command line of the input to pick out the names of programs to be invoked and the values of arguments to be passed to them. Each program called in this way is invoked as a subprogram (*q.v.*) or subprocess. The programs are connected according to the data and control flow specified in the command.

The Unix operating system has shells in which operations of substantial complexity can be programmed. As a simple example, the following sequence of commands prepares a five-column list of filenames in a directory, saves it as a file, and prints it.

```
ls | pr -5 > filenames
lpr filenames
```

The command `ls` lists the file names in the current directory. The pipe symbol "|" connects the output of one command to the input of the next, and `pr -5` produces a five-column format of the filenames. The symbol ">" redirects the output to the file named `filenames`, and the printer spooler `lpr` then sends the result to the printer.

If a command line is to be performed often, typing it can become tedious. Unix encourages users to store complicated commands in executable files called *shell scripts*, which become simpler commands. A Unix shell program is not necessarily a single line. Shell programs can be arbitrarily long and may include assignments to variables, control constructs for alternation and iteration, subroutine calls to commands in other files, and even interrupt (*q.v.*) handling. The Unix shell is a full-fledged, high-level programming language.

The shell language need not be different from a standard, interpreted programming language. Shell languages have been one of the inspirations for the development of more powerful scripting languages. In Lisp (*q.v.*) programming environments, the shell is typically a Lisp interpreter that allows operating system commands to be invoked as if they were normal Lisp functions (Teitelman and Masinter, 1981). The shell language is used interactively and hence must be interpreted rather than compiled.

Unix now has several shells, and each user may choose among them for the user's default environment. Some have several features in the shell interpreter that simplify interactive use. One of them is an input completion facility, with which the shell completes the names of commands and files once the user has typed a unique prefix. A spelling checker (*q.v.*) can help correct typing mistakes. A dialogue history supports the reissuing of elaborate commands. The dialogue history records all commands typed in by the user, who can then select any past command on this list by pointing to it or by identifying it by typing a unique prefix. The selected command can be reissued, or first modified and then reissued.

Not all operating systems have shells, or make them as visible and important as Unix does. Window environments (*q.v.*), with their graphical user interfaces (GUIs), allow users to execute commands without directly giving them to a command interpreter. Some, such as Apple's MacOS, do not have a shell, while others, such as Microsoft's Windows, have a shell that operates beneath the GUI, but it is intended for the Windows programmer, not for the ordinary user. In the X Window system for Unix, all of the traditional shells are still available within a user's command-window.

Bibliography

1979. Kernighan, B. W., and Mashey, J. R. "The Unix Programming Environment," *Software: Practice and Experience*, **9**, *1* (January), 1–15.
1981. Teitelman, W., and Masinter, L. "The Interlisp Programming Environment," *IEEE Computer*, **14**, *4* (April), 25–33.
1990. Kochan, S. G., and Wood, P. H. *Unix Shell Programming*. Indianapolis, IN: Hayden Books.

Walter F. Tichy

SHIFTING

For articles on related subjects *see* ARITHMETIC-LOGIC UNIT; COMPLEMENT; INSTRUCTION SET; MACHINE AND ASSEMBLY LANGUAGE PROGRAMMING; MASKING; and REGISTER.

Shifting is the process of moving data in a storage device relative to the boundaries of the device (as opposed to moving it in and out of the device). The device in which the shift is performed is called a *shift register*. In order to discuss the various modes of the shift operation, we assume that the register in which

the shift is to be performed is n bits wide, and number the bits from left to right, $1 \ldots n$.

A *left shift* is the operation in which the ith bit is replaced by the $(i + 1)$st one. This operation can be repeated an arbitrary number of times so that one can shift by any number of positions. The question of what replaces the nth (last) bit will be dealt with later, as will the question of what happens to bit 1.

A *right shift* is the operation in which the ith bit is replaced by the $(i - 1)$st bit. Again, this is easily generalized to a right shift by any number of positions.

There are three types of shift: logical, circular, and arithmetic (*see* Fig. 1). They differ in the treatment of the first and last bits, both in the left and right shift.

In *logical shifts* the bit shifted out is lost, and the bit shifted in is zero. Note in the left shift that the bit shifted out is bit 1, and the bit shifted in occupies position n, whereas in the right shift, the bit shifted out is the nth one and the bit shifted in occupies position 1.

In *circular shifts* the bit shifted out of one end is shifted into the other end. There is, therefore, no loss of information in the circular shift.

The *arithmetic shift* is designed to take advantage of the fact that shifting a bit string left multiplies the binary number it represents by 2, whereas shifting it right divides it by 2. Multiplication and division of a positive number by 2 can therefore be accomplished by logical shifts. However, when negative numbers are present, special care must be exercised in dealing with the sign bit.

In the sign-magnitude representation of negative numbers, the sign bit should be left intact. In the 2s complement representation, it should be kept intact upon left shift and should be replicated upon right shift; i.e. in the right shift, bit 2 should be replaced by bit 1 (the sign bit) and bit 1 should be left with its previous value. In the 1s complement representation, the equivalent operation is done by circular shifts. In either of these, there are cases in which *overflow* can be generated.

The precise definition of an arithmetic shift depends, therefore, on the way negative numbers are represented in the computer. For 2s complement representation (Fig. 1), the definition is as follows:

In a right arithmetic shift, the nth bit is shifted out and the first bit is preserved. In a left arithmetic shift, the nth bit is filled with zero and the sign bit is replaced with former bit 2. This will usually leave the sign intact because all but quite large negative numbers start with two or more 1-bits. Shifting a number that begins with 10 left one place changes a formerly

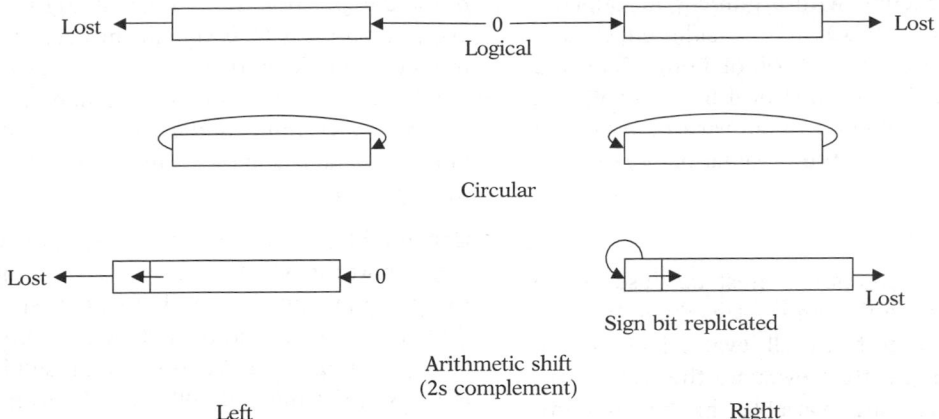

Figure 1. Various one-bit shift operations.

Table 1. 2s complement shift operations on a 5-bit word computer.

Bit string	Operation	Result	Comments
01011	Left logical	10110	
01011	Right logical	00101	Last bit lost
01011	Right circular	10101	
01011	Left circular	10110	
01011	Right arithmetic	00101	
01011	Left arithmetic	10110	Result incorrect (overflow)
11001	Left arithmetic	10010	
11001	Right arithmetic	11100	Last bit lost
11001	Left logical	10010	
11001	Left logical 2	00100	2-place shift

negative number to a positive one and indicates overflow. The converse would be true for a number starting with 01. Most computers will set condition codes to indicate such overflows.

Some examples of the effect of various shift operations on five-bit strings are presented in Table 1.

Shift operations are usually used in field alignments, packing and unpacking of data items into storage units, and high-speed multiplication and division, especially by constants. Among the more exotic uses is that for the creation of control patterns. For example, the pattern 10110111 can be used for a switch that will do an operation once, then skip (0), then do it twice, skip again, and finally do it three times with a left shift after each operation.

Many computers allow double-precision shift operations. In these shifts, two n-bit storage devices are used as one $2n$-bit device. Also, in certain computers the shift register is extended, usually by a carry indicator, so that the bit shifted out is not lost, but rather is shifted into an extra storage bit where it can be tested.

Gideon Frieder

SIDE EFFECT

For articles on related subjects *see* ARGUMENT; GLOBAL AND LOCAL VARIABLES; PARAMETER PASSING; PROCEDURE-ORIENTED LANGUAGES: PROGRAMMING; STRUCTURED PROGRAMMING; and SUBPROGRAM.

A *side effect* occurs when a procedure or function changes the value of a global variable. This is one reason why the use of global variables is deplored in programming; they allow the possibility of side effects, which are usually unplanned and, therefore, undesirable. But this is not always so; sometimes, as in database systems, the database itself is global to all procedures, and modifying it is just what many of the procedures in the system are supposed to do. Another example would be a procedure to generate random numbers where the ith random number, X_i, is generated as $f(X_{i-1})$ for some function f. A global variable X would contain the value of X_{i-1} and a side effect would replace this with X_i. A third example of benign side effects is in functions, such as input and output functions, that both produce results and return a value giving information about them. For example, the scanf function in the C I/O library reads values into its arguments (a side effect) and returns a count of the number of items read.

Procedures or functions that cause side effects can result in nasty problems whose solution may require the programmer to know more than should be necessary about how a program is processed (e.g. compiled) by a language processor. For example, consider the expression

    A + B * C

It should not matter to the programmer whether this expression is evaluated by first multiplying B times C and then adding A or by first fetching A, storing it away temporarily, multiplying B * C and then adding A although the former will usually be more efficient. But what if the expression is instead

    FCN(A) + B * C

where FCN is a function with argument A? Suppose the evaluation of FCN(A) has a side effect that modifies the value of B or C or of both. Then the value of the expression is different if B * C is evaluated before FCN(A) is evaluated or afterward. A related problem can occur in the evaluation of logical expressions such as

    I<20 and FCN(A)=5.

If $I \geq 20$, then the expression must be false. Some systems will recognize this and not evaluate FCN(A) at all. Others will perform all evaluations of the arguments of **and** and then evaluate the expression. If FCN(A) modifies other variables in the program, then it is vital to know how expressions are evaluated. The same problem arises in evaluating a function call like g(FCN(A), B) where the result may depend on which argument of g is evaluated first.

To avoid problems such as these, many languages specify left-to-right evaluation of logical expressions and a few specify how arithmetic expressions are to be evaluated. The best rule is that, whether or not these matters are specified, the programmer should be careful to avoid the possibility of the kinds of side effects described above.

Bibliography

1980. Wagener, J. *Fortran 77: Principles of Programming.* New York: John Wiley.
1989. Reilly, E. D., and Federighi, F. D., *Pascalgorithms.* Boston, MA: Houghton-Mifflin.

Anthony Ralston

SIGNIFICANT DIGIT

For articles on related subjects *see* ARITHMETIC, COMPUTER; INTERVAL ARITHMETIC; NUMBERS AND NUMBER SYSTEMS; PRECISION; and ROUNDOFF ERROR.

Let the positional digit sequence $d_m d_{m-1} \ldots d_0 . d_{-1} d_{-2} d_{-3} \ldots$, with $d_m \neq 0$ be an exact radix representation for a real number $x \geq 1$. (Note that a decimal point, or, in general, a *radix point*, is present between d_0 and d_{-1}.) Each digit d_i for $i \leq m$ is termed a *significant digit of the exact representation* of x, and the leading nonzero digit d_m is the *most significant digit* of x. For example, if $x = 700.3056$, all the digits are significant, and the 7 is the most significant.

When $x < 1$, its radix representation is conventionally written with a single 0 to the left of the radix point, $0 . d_{-1} d_{-2} d_{-3} \ldots$, and the most significant digit is the leftmost nonzero one. For $x = 0.030200$, $d_{-2} = 3$ is the most significant digit. Note that the leading zero digits $d_0 = 0$ and $d_{-1} = 0$ are not considered significant digits of x, even though the representation uses

$d_{-1} = 0$ to position the significant digits properly; d_{-3}, even though it is 0, *is* significant because it falls after the most significant digit, as is $d_{-4} = 2$. In the absence of additional information, any number of trailing zeros that follow a significant digit that comes after the radix point, d_{-5} and d_{-6} in the example under discussion, are *not* significant.

Conceivably, however, some experimentalist might well report that she has measured something accurate to five significant figures, that is, that she is confident that d_{-6} is an accurate and hence significant digit. (If so, she might have reported her result in some such form as 0.0302004 ± 0.0000002.) Conversely, she may sometimes admit that a result has fewer significant digits than appears to be the case. The statement that a measured value such as 23.185 has only three significant digits merely indicates that the digit value d_{-2} is not known with certitude, although $d_{-2} = 8$ might be possible (and perhaps represents a "best guess").

In any calculation, the number of significant digits present in input data is not necessarily preserved throughout extensive computation. Subtractive cancellation can result in a severe decrease in the number of significant digits, with the possibility that none at all are present in the output. *Roundoff error* (*q.v.*) can be equally insidious. Charles Babbage (*q.v.*) so worried about this that the design for his Analytical Engine (*q.v.*) called for use of a word length of 50 decimal digits. To the great relief of all those engaged in large-scale digital computation, his fear has proved unfounded. The typical single-precision IEEE-standard floating-point number of 7 decimal digit equivalence works quite well in most applications, and the corresponding double-precision number of 15 decimal digit equivalence is adequate for virtually all applications (*see* ARITHMETIC, COMPUTER).

Bibliography

1976. Matula, D. W. "Radix Arithmetic: Digital Algorithms for Computer Architecture," in *Applied Computation Theory* (ed. R. Yeh), Ch. 9. Upper Saddle River, NJ: Prentice Hall.

David W. Matula

SIMON, HERBERT A.

For articles on related subjects *see* ARTIFICIAL INTELLIGENCE; and LIST PROCESSING.

Herbert Alexander Simon (b. Milwaukee, WI, 1916) (Fig. 1) is best known in computer science for his work in artificial intelligence and cognitive psychology. As his receipt of the Nobel Prize in Economics for 1978 indicates, his intellectual range is far wider. Trained as a political scientist at the University of Chicago (Ph.D.

Figure 1. Herbert A. Simon (courtesy Carnegie Mellon University).

1943), he has made substantial and often major contributions not only to political science, but also to the study of organizations, public administration, econometrics, management science and operations research, the philosophical foundations of causality and Newtonian mechanics, and the nature of scientific discovery, as well as to psychology and computer science.

It is possible to emphasize the diversity in such a scientific career; e.g. a highly successful text on public administration (Simon *et al.*, 1954), an influential research monograph on the servomechanism analysis of factory production control (Holt *et al.*, 1960), etc. It is preferable, and equally valid, to emphasize the common theme that runs through all his work: to understand the nature of rational behavior in humans. Simon's first book in 1947 was an analysis of how the administrative human operates in formal organizations—a creature of institutional, informational, and computational limits who works within a frame of *bounded rationality*. This book, a core citation in the Nobel award, was central to establishing a model of economic decision making that has stood in contradistinction to the dominant model of the *homo economici*, global optimizers who know their preferences over all conceivable commodity bundles. This concern with bounded rationality—with behavior that *satisfices* rather than optimizes—also lies at the heart of his work in understanding in detail how computers and humans can behave intelligently.

Counterposed to the diversity of his intellectual career is the simplicity of his academic career. After relatively short stays at UC Berkeley and the Illinois Institute of Technology, he joined Carnegie Mellon University (then Carnegie Institute of Technology) in 1949 as a founding member of the Graduate School of Industrial Administration, which launched a revolution in graduate education in business, building it on scientific knowledge in economics, psychology, and operations research. He has been at Carnegie Mellon University ever since, the last 20 years most closely associated with its Psychology Department (as Richard King Mellon Professor of Psychology and Computer Science).

Simon's primary contribution in computer science was his collaboration with John C. (Cliff) Shaw and Allen Newell in the development of the first heuristic (*q.v.*) programs (the *Logic Theorist*, 1956; the *General Problem Solver*, 1958) and the first list processing languages (the IPLs, 1957). This team of three, along with John McCarthy, Marvin Minsky, and Oliver Selfridge, are generally credited with having founded the area of *artificial intelligence* (McCorduck, 1979). The early programs were also taken to be models of how human thinking occurs (then usually called simulation of thought processes). Simon has continued to produce a stream of programs and analyses that explore how intelligent action occurs—in problem solving, memorizing, inducting, behaving in semantically rich domains, and learning. Throughout, the connection with human thinking has been explicit and often dominant. A major work on human problem solving was published in 1972 (Newell and Simon, 1972) and the range of his work can be found in Simon (1979, 1989, 1996). In 1975, Simon (jointly with Newell) was given the ACM Turing Award (*q.v.*) for his entire line of work. Simon had earlier (1969) received the Award for Distinguished Scientific Contribution of the American Psychological Association for the psychological side of his work. As recently as 1995, he received the Research Excellence Award of the International Joint Conference on Artificial Intelligence.

Simon has received many other awards and honorary degrees, and is a member of the US National Academy of Sciences. He has been active in many professional societies, and in giving advice and counsel to government at all levels. His total scientific output is prodigious, even by the standards of his peers (15 books and some 600 papers). [Ed. note: Herb Simon died on 9 February, 2001.]

Bibliography

1954. Simon, H. A., Smithburg, D. W., and Thompson, V. A. *Public Administration.* New York: Knopf.
1960. Holt, C., Modigliani, F., Muth, J. F., and Simon, H. A. *Planning Production, Inventories, and Work Force.* Upper Saddle River, NJ: Prentice Hall.

1972. Newell, A., and Simon, H. A. *Human Problem Solving*. Upper Saddle River, NJ: Prentice Hall.

1979. McCorduck, P. *Machines Who Think*. San Francisco: Freeman.

1979. Simon, H. A. *Models of Thought*. New Haven, CT: Yale University Press.

1989. Simon, H. A. *Models of Thought*, Vol. II. New Haven, CT: Yale University Press.

1996. Simon, H. A. *Models of My Life* (reprint). Cambridge, MA: MIT Press.

1996. Simon, H. A. *The Sciences of the Artificial*, 3rd Ed. Cambridge, MA: MIT Press.

1997. Simon, H. A. *Administrative Behavior*, 4th Ed. New York: Free Press.

1997. Simon, H. A. *Models of Bounded Rationality: Empirically Grounded Economic Reason*, Vol. 3. Cambridge, MA: MIT Press.

Allen Newell, revised by the Editors

SIMULA

For articles on related subjects *see* ABSTRACT DATA TYPE; ALGOL; C++; CLASS; OBJECT-ORIENTED PROGRAMMING; and SIMULATION.

Simula 1 (1962–1964) and *Simula 67* (1967) were the first two object-oriented (OO) languages. Simula 67 introduced most of the key concepts of object-oriented programming: *objects*, *classes*, *subclasses* (usually referred to as *inheritance*), and *virtual procedures*, combined with safe referencing mechanisms for making the contents of separately compiled classes available to programs.

The Simula languages were developed at the Norwegian Computing Center, Oslo, Norway by the authors. Nygaard's work in operations research in the 1950s and early 1960s showed the need for precise tools for the *description* and *simulation* of complex human–machine systems. In 1961 the idea emerged for developing a language for both purposes, usable for human communication as well as for instructing a computer. Such a language had to contain a general algorithmic one, and thus Dahl's previous experience in language design and implementation became important.

The Simula 1 compiler was partly financed by Univac (*q.v.*) and was ready in January 1965. Simula 1 quickly got a reputation as a simulation language, but turned out to possess properties useful for other purposes as well. When the inheritance mechanism was invented in 1967, Simula 67 could be regarded as a general-purpose programming language that could also be specialized for many domains, including system simulation. Simula 67 compilers started to appear for UNIVAC, Control Data (*q.v.*), IBM (*q.v.*), Burroughs, DEC (*q.v.*), and other computers in the early 1970s.

Simula 1

Technically Simula 1 was an *ad hoc* extension of the Algol 60 programming language. One of the reasons for basing the new language on Algol was Algol's concept of *block*. Algol blocks combine data and operations by containing local variable and procedure declarations, as well as an action sequence pattern. Through the procedure call mechanism, many invocations of a block may coexist in an Algol program execution in the sense of being dynamically nested, each with its own local variables and declared procedures.

For the purpose of system modeling, it was useful to break away from the rigid dynamic nesting regime of Algol, introducing the concept of *quasi-parallel processes*, each an activation of (the body of) a so-called *activity* declaration, structurally similar to a procedure declaration. Quasi-parallel processing is a way of simulating concurrent action sequences within a single sequential computation (*see* COROUTINE). Control will jump from one process to another as the result of certain special sequencing statements, leaving behind a "reactivation point" indicating where in the process operations are to be resumed when control returns. At the same time a concept of *simulated time* was introduced. Each process was given a local time variable indicating the system time scheduled for its next active period, and a list was kept of processes ordered according to time values. A system invariant was established so that the process at the front of the time list would be the currently active one. Its local time value would define the current simulated time. Thus, a statement such as `hold(t)`, representing the passage of *t* units of simulated time, could be implemented by detaching the active process from the time list, increasing its local time value by *t*, and reinserting it into the time list according to its new time value. The process now at the end of the time list would be resumed at its reactivation point.

Explicit pointer values were introduced for the purpose of process identification (it follows that the language had list processing (*q.v.*) capabilities). Processes could interact through nonlocal variables and by accessing each other's "attributes," i.e. local variables and procedures, declared at the outermost block.

Algol 60 had introduced an important principle of high-level programming: that the behavior of any program accepted by the compiler should be explainable by reasoning completely in terms of the language semantics, independently of implementation details. In particular, there must be data access security in the sense that accessible data actually exist and are interpreted according to their declaration. In order to retain such security a special mechanism for the "remote" accessing of process attributes, called an *inspection block*, had to be invented, so that the "kind" of a referenced process could be ascertained by an explicit test before its attributes were accessed. In each inspection block the attributes of a process of the corresponding kind are directly accessible.

In Algol the storage for each block activation can be recycled upon exit, leading to a very simple and efficient storage management using a last in, first out stack (*q.v.*) regime. In Simula, Algol-like blocks can be treated similarly, but each process needs an independent stack, which necessitates a much more complicated dynamic store management. For the purpose of data access security, processes must not dispose of their storage, but have to remain in memory as long as there are accessible pointers to them. Thus, a garbage collection (*q.v.*) mechanism was required in order to achieve efficient memory usage.

Experience has shown that Simula 1 was a successful instrument for simulation purposes, as well as for system description. The fact that the whole of Algol was included in the language implied that it was easy to add facilities for special purposes such as pseudo-random number generation (*q.v.*) and data accumulation. Processes would typically range from full-fledged Algol-like programs to passive data structures with associated operators.

Simula 67

It became clear that features introduced in Simula 1 were of interest from points of view other than simulation modeling, especially the data structuring possibilities inherent in the process concept and the associated list-processing facilities. Also, coroutine-like sequencing could be useful without the use of a system time concept. In order to clean up the language, a *class* declaration was introduced, giving rise to block-like *objects* (with mechanisms for coroutine sequencing added), as well as direct typed object pointers in the manner of record handling as proposed by C. A. R. Hoare and implemented in the Pascal language (*q.v.*). Thus, if C is a class declaring an attribute A, and X is a `ref`(C) pointer, then $X.A$ is a secure access to the attribute A belonging to the referenced object.

The most important innovation in Simula 67 was a mechanism for declaring subclasses with inheritance. Let C be a class. Then

```
C class D; begin ⟨class body⟩ end
```

is a subclass of C, and D objects inherit all C attributes. C may express properties common to a number of subclasses in the same program, or, if separately compiled, it may serve as a reusable plug-in unit. The subclass mechanism also makes it possible to formulate "application languages" for special problem areas by collecting relevant concepts in a class. In particular, the special purpose simulation facilities of Simula 1 could be introduced using a built-in class declaration.

What are the reasons for the success of the class and subclass concepts? The following properties are probably important: the capacity for concept modeling and for providing reusable program components. Sometimes it is important that aspects of the real world can be directly mapped to program structures.

One final notion deserves to be mentioned: *virtual procedures*. It is sometimes useful to redeclare inherited attributes. The standard binding rule of attribute identifiers is that they refer to the last declaration "statically visible" at the subclass level of the accessing identifier occurrence. However, if a procedure attribute is declared "virtual," access is to the declaration occurring deepest down in the actual object, regardless of the subclass level of the accessing occurrence. This implies that a virtual procedure becomes more like a "replaceable part" or formal parameter. In some later OO languages virtual binding of procedure attributes is the only option.

At the time of writing (late 1990s) Simula 67 is still being used in many places around the world, but its main impact has been through introducing one of the major categories of programming, *object-oriented programming*.

In the 1980s tremendous resources were put behind the Ada language (*q.v.*) and the logic programming (*q.v.*) language Prolog, and many believed that these two languages would come to dominate practical programming in the next decade. Instead, object-oriented programming has become a dominant style of developing complex programs with large numbers of interacting components. Among the multitude of OO languages are *Eiffel*, *Clos*, *Self*, C++ (*q.v.*) and *Java* (*q.v.*). *Beta* is a very general object-oriented language in the Simula tradition.

Simula has influenced other important developments. The idea of data structures (*q.v.*) with associated operators has led to a notion of "abstract" data types (*q.v.*) (Dahl and Hoare, 1972). A modified version of the language was used in the design of VLSI circuitry (Intel, Caltech, Stanford). Alan Kay's group at Xerox PARC used Simula as a platform for their development of the Smalltalk language in the 1970s, extending object orientation significantly by the integration of graphical user interfaces (GUIs) and interactive execution. Finally, Bjarne Stroustrup started his development of C++ in the 1980s by bringing key concepts of Simula into the C programming language.

Bibliography

1966. Dahl, O.-J., and Nygaard, K. "Simula—an Algol-based Simulation Language," *CACM*, **9**, 9, 671–678.
1968. Dahl, O.-J., and Nygaard, K. "Class and Subclass Declarations," in *Simulation Programming Languages* (ed. J. N. Buxton), 158–174. Amsterdam: North Holland.

1972. Dahl, O.-J., and Hoare, C. A. R. "Hierarchical Program Structures," in *Structured Programming* (eds. O.-J. Dahl, E. W. Dijkstra and C. A. R. Hoare), 175–220. New York: Academic Press.

1975. Birtwistle, G. M., Dahl, O.-J., Myhrhaug, B., and Nygaard, K. *SIMULA*. New York: Petrocelli/Charter.

1981. Nygaard, K., and Dahl, O.-J. "The Development of the Simula Languages," in *The History of Programming Languages* (ed. R. L. Wexelblat), Ch. 9, 439–493. New York: Academic Press.

1994. Holmevik, J. R. "Compiling Simula: A Historical Study of Technological Genesis," *IEEE Annals of the History of Computing*, **16**, *4*, 25–37. Also at `http://lingua.utdallas.edu/jan/simula.html`.

Ole-Johan Dahl and Kristen Nygaard

SIMULATION

For articles on related subjects *see* ANALOG COMPUTER; ARTIFICIAL LIFE; COMPUTER GAMES; MONTE CARLO METHOD; QUEUEING THEORY; RANDOM NUMBER GENERATION; SCIENTIFIC APPLICATIONS; SIMULA; and VIRTUAL REALITY.

Introduction

DEFINITION

Simulation is the process of designing a model of a real or imagined system and conducting experiments with this model to understand the behavior of the system or to evaluate strategies for its operation. Assumptions are made about this system and mathematical algorithms (*q.v.*) and relationships are derived to describe these assumptions—this constitutes a "model" that can reveal how the system works. If the system is simple, the model may be represented and solved analytically. A single equation such as DISTANCE = (RATE ∗ TIME) may be an analytical solution representing the distance traveled by an object at constant rate for a given period of time.

However, problems of interest in the real world are usually much more complex than this. In fact, they may be so complex that a closed analytical model cannot be constructed to represent them. In this case, the behavior of the system must be estimated through a simulation. Exact representation is seldom possible in a model, constraining us to approximations to a degree of fidelity that is acceptable for the purposes of the study. Models have been constructed for almost every system imaginable, including factories, communications and computer networks, integrated circuits, highway systems, flight dynamics, national economies, social interactions, and imaginary worlds. In each of these environments, experimenting with a model of the system has proved to be more cost-effective, less dangerous, faster, or otherwise more practical than experimenting with a real system.

For example, a business may be interested in building a new factory to replace an old one, but is unsure whether the increased productivity will justify the investment. In this case, simulation could be used to evaluate a model of the new factory. The model could describe the floor space required, number of machines, number of employees, placement of equipment, the production capacity of each machine, and the waiting time between machines. Simulation runs would then evaluate the system and provide an estimate of the production capacity and the costs of a new factory. This type of information is invaluable in making decisions without having to build an actual factory to arrive at an answer.

HISTORY

One of the pioneers of simulation was John von Neumann (*q.v.*). In the late mid-1940s, together with physicist Enrico Fermi and mathematician Stanislaw Ulam, he conceived of the idea of running multiple repetitions of a model, gathering statistical data, and deriving behaviors of the real system based on these models. This came to be known as the Monte Carlo method because of the use of randomly generated variates to represent behaviors that could not be modeled exactly, but could be characterized statistically. Von Neumann used this method to study the random actions of neutrons and aircraft bombing effectiveness. Early civilian applications of this method were found in representations of factories attempting to determine maximum potential productivity.

Simulations derive much of their technique from models of the world found in other disciplines. Wind tunnels are models that replicate flight by moving the air rather than the aircraft; chess has been used to stimulate strategic thinking about warfare; and computer games are intended to generate believable worlds requiring mastery of a specified set of behaviors.

PURPOSE

Simulation allows the analysis of a system's capabilities, capacities, and behaviors without requiring the construction of or experimentation with the real system. Since it is extremely expensive to experiment with an entire factory to determine its best configuration, a simulation of the system can be extremely valuable. There are also systems, like nuclear reactions and war, which are too dangerous to activate for the sake of analysis, but which can be usefully analyzed through simulation.

LIMITATIONS

When conducting a simulation or contriving a model, certain limitations must be acknowledged. Primary among these is the ability to create a model that accurately represents the system to be simulated. Real systems are extremely complex and a determination must be made about the details that will be captured in the model. Some details must be omitted and the effects of these lost or aggregated into other variables which are included in the model. In both cases, an inaccuracy has been introduced and the ramifications of this must be known and accepted by the model developers. Another limitation usually results from the availability of data. It is possible, even common, for the model to require input data that is scarce or unavailable. This availability of data is best addressed prior to the design of the model to minimize its impact once it is completed.

Both of the limitations above lead to a simulation that provides approximate results or describes system behavior statistically. For this reason, simulation usually provides measurements of general trends, rather than exact data for specific situations or individuals. A simulation would be hard pressed to determine which piece of material will be ruined by a milling machine. It would be an excellent tool for determining the impacts of machine failure on factory productivity, using known statistical distributions for the failures of many machines.

Uses of Simulation

Simulation is used in some form in nearly all engineering, analysis, and technology disciplines. Many problems in these areas are too complex to solve analytically, but the reward for solving them is so great that a solution must be found—often via simulation. In each case, the expense of constructing a simulation may be significant in itself, but is minuscule compared with the cost of experimenting with an actual or a prototype system. There are several general categories of simulation uses.

DESIGN

Designers turn to simulation to allow them to characterize or visualize a system that does not yet exist and for which they wish to achieve the optimum solution. Manufacturing models may describe the capacities of individual machines, the time to prepare material for operation, time to transfer materials from one machine to another, the effects of human operators, and the capacities of waiting queues and storage bins. Simulations of new pieces of equipment may evaluate their performance, stress points, transportability, human interfaces, and potential hazards in the environment. Business process models may evaluate the flow of paperwork through a company to determine where redundancies or unnecessary operations are located, allowing them to redesign operations such that the same work can be performed with a fraction of the labor and time that has evolved into the process. Major

airlines use simulations to study complex routing patterns for large numbers of aircraft traveling around the world, to identify routes that serve the most passengers and use assets most efficiently. Factors such as aircraft capacity, ground time, flight time, scheduled maintenance, crew availability, weather effects, and unscheduled downtime are all considered in such models.

ANALYSIS

Analysis refers to the process of determining the behavior or capability of a system that is currently in operation. Unlike design, analysis may be supported by the collection of data from the actual system to establish model behaviors. The model can then be modified to determine the optimum configuration or implementation of the real system. A computer network can be described by the volume of traffic carried, capacity of the lines and switches, performance of a router, and the path taken from sender to receiver. Based on measured message patterns, the network can be configured to deliver the most information using the shortest or most reliable paths available. In the healthcare industry, it is important to schedule patient treatment to serve the most patients as quickly as possible with a limited set of practitioners, equipment, and facilities. Social trends can be simulated to determine what services or goods will be needed at a given time by a specific sector of society. The impacts of aging, health, family composition, and a host of other factors can be predicted from an appropriate social model.

TRAINING

Training simulations recreate situations that people will face on the job and stimulate the subject to react to the situation until the correct responses are learned. These devices prepare personnel without the expense of their making mistakes on the job. Perhaps the best known of these are flight simulators (Fig. 1 on Color Page CP-15), which model dangerous environments where life-threatening situations can be mitigated through learning in nonlethal environments. Military simulators may replicate the performance characteristics of the aircraft, instruments in the cockpit, effects of weapons, support from other combat systems, communications with other pilots, and terrain over which the events occur. Similar systems are used to train the captains of large ocean-going ships to dock without the danger of destroying both a real ship and a real dock. Entire mock-ups are made of nuclear power control centers to teach operators how to respond to emergency situations and to identify potential hazards before an emergency occurs. Modern medical equipment is so expensive and scarce that simulations have been constructed to allow interns and nurses to practice, develop, and have their skills certified without having to schedule time on the real equipment in competition with real patients. Fig. 2 on Color Page CP-15 shows a military training simulation.

ENTERTAINMENT

The entertainment industry makes wide use of simulation to create games that are enjoyable and exciting to play. These contain many, but usually not all, of the components of simulation described in this article. Arcade games, computer games, board wargames, and role-playing games all require the creation of a consistent model of an imaginary world and devices for interacting with that world. These simulations often appear very similar to training simulations, but differ in that their purpose is entertainment rather than practice for real-world events. This fact allows game simulation developers the freedom to modify the laws of physics and behaviors included in the simulation, rather than accurately replicating real-world equivalents. Advances in these simulations, together with the prevalence of the Internet, are allowing the creation of multiplayer online games that pit players against multiple opponents distributed around the world. Though the purpose of these simulations is entertainment, the technical challenges faced are often just as daunting as those in the other categories.

The Simulation Process

The creation and operation of a simulation was once a black art in which only experienced practitioners could claim competence and understanding. However, over the last several decades a definite process has evolved for developing, validating, operating, and analyzing the results of simulations. In this section we will describe the process, illustrated in Fig. 3.

DEFINE PROBLEM SPACE

The first step in developing a simulation is to define explicitly the problem that must be addressed by the model. The objectives and requirements of the project must be stated along with the required accuracy of the results. Boundaries must be defined between the problem of interest and the surrounding environment. Interfaces must be defined for crossing these boundaries to achieve interoperability with external systems. A model cannot be built based on vague definitions of hoped for results.

DEFINE CONCEPTUAL MODEL

Once the problem has been defined, one or more appropriate conceptual models can be built. These include the algorithms to be used to describe the system, input required, and outputs generated. Assumptions made about the system are documented in this phase, along

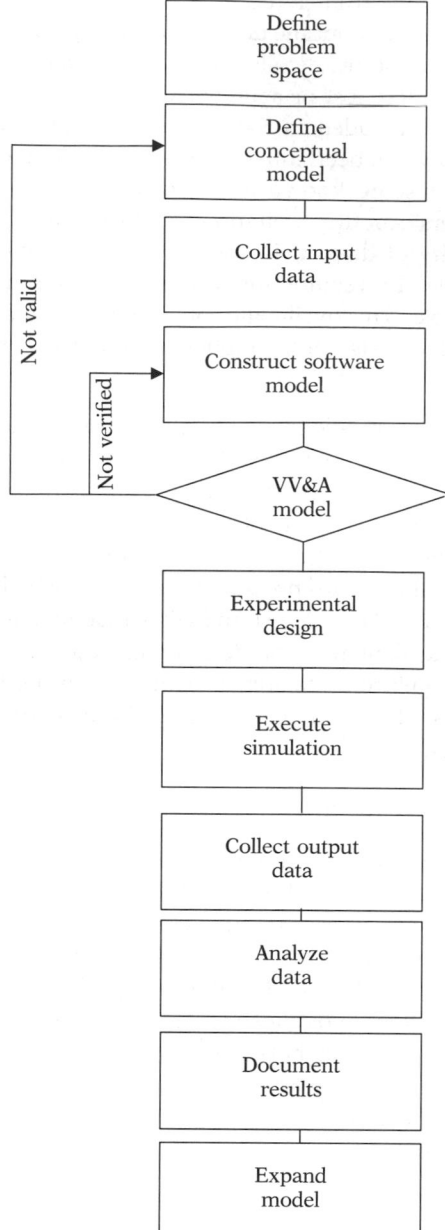

Figure 3. The simulation modeling process.

with the potential effects of these assumptions on the results or accuracy of the simulation. Limitations based on the model, data, and assumptions, are clearly defined so that appropriate uses of the simulation can be determined.

The conceptual model includes a description of the amount of time, number of personnel, and equipment assets that will be required to produce and operate the model. All potential models are compared and trade-offs made until there is a single solution that meets the objectives and requirements of the problem and for which algorithms can be constructed and input data acquired.

COLLECT DATA

Once the solution space has been determined, the data required to operate and define the model must be collected. This includes information that will serve as input parameters, aid in the development of algorithms, and be used to evaluate the performance of the simulation runs. This data includes known behaviors of working systems and information on the statistical distributions of the random variates to be used. Collecting accurate input data is one of the most difficult phases in the simulation process, and the most prone to error and misapplication.

CONSTRUCT SOFTWARE MODEL

The simulation model is constructed based on the solution defined and data collected. Mathematical and logical descriptions of the real system are encoded in a form that can be executed by a computer. The creation of a computer simulation, as with any other software product, should be governed by the principles of software engineering (*q.v.*).

VERIFY, VALIDATE, AND ACCREDIT THE MODEL

Verification, validation, and accreditation (VV&A), is an essential phase in ensuring that the model algorithms, input data, and design assumptions are correct and solve the problem identified at the beginning of the process. Since a simulation model and its data are the encoding of concepts that are difficult to define completely, it is easy to create a model that is either inaccurate or that solves a problem other than the one specified. The VV&A process is designed to identify these problems before the model is put into operation.

For the purposes of VV&A the simulation development process is divided into the problem space, conceptual model, and software model with definite transitions and quality evaluations between these stages as shown in Fig. 4. Validation is the process of determining that the conceptual model reflects the aspects of the problem space that need to be addressed and does so such that the requirements of the study can be met.

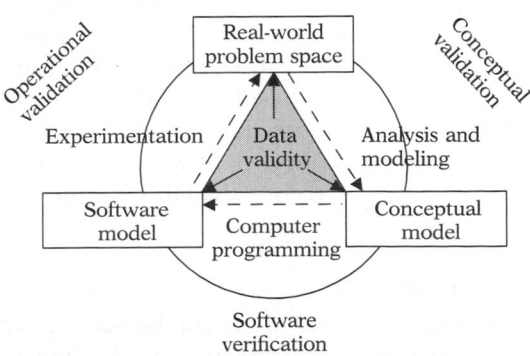

Figure 4. Verification, Validation, and Accreditation (VV&A).

Validation is also used to determine whether the operations of the final software model are consistent with the real world, usually through experimentation and comparison with a known data set. Verification is the process of determining that the software model accurately reflects the conceptual model. Accreditation is the official acceptance of the software model for a specified purpose, and software models accredited for one purpose may not be acceptable for another.

DESIGN EXPERIMENTS

This phase identifies the most productive and accurate methods for running the simulation to generate the desired answers. Statistical techniques can be used to design experiments that yield the most accurate data with the fewest number of simulation runs. When simulation runs are expensive and difficult to schedule, experimental design can ensure answers at the lowest cost and on the shortest schedules.

EXECUTE SIMULATION

This is the actual execution of the designed, constructed, and validated model according to the experimental design. The simulation runs generate the output data required to answer the problem initially proposed. In the case of Monte Carlo models, many hundreds or thousands of replications may be required to arrive at statistically reliable results.

COLLECT OUTPUT DATA

Concurrent with the execution of the model, output data is collected, organized, and stored. This is sometimes viewed as an integral part of the model, but should be distinctly separated since it is possible to change the data collected without changing the model algorithms or design.

ANALYZE DATA

Data collected during the execution of a simulation can be voluminous and distributed through time. Detailed analyses must be performed to extract long-term trends and to quantify answers to the driving questions that motivated the construction of the simulation. Analysis may produce information in tabular, graphic, map, animation, and textual summary forms. Modern user interfaces (*q.v.*) have greatly enhanced this phase by displaying data in forms that can be easily understood by diverse audiences.

DOCUMENT RESULTS

The results of the simulation study or training session must be documented and disseminated to interested parties. These parties identify the degree to which the simulation has answered specific questions and areas for future improvements.

EXPAND MODEL

Simulation models are expensive and difficult to build. As a result, once a model is built, it will often be modified for use on many related projects. New requirements will be levied, new users will adopt it, and the entire development process will be conducted many times over.

Modeling Essentials

Though simulations vary widely in their design and implementation, most share a few common features.

EVENT MANAGEMENT

A simulation is made up of states, events, and entities. *States* are groups of variables that describe the system at a specific time. *Events* are activities that change the state of the system. *Entities* are the objects represented in the simulation, the things described by the state variables and to which events occur. Events are the key items that make transformations in the model and drive it through its operations. These may include the arrival of a piece of material at a milling machine, the departure of an aircraft from an airport, the delivery of a message in a network, or an engagement between a missile and a fighter aircraft. These are typically managed through the use of multiple lists or *queues* in the model. The queues identify which events are ready to be processed, which are waiting until a specified time, and which must be triggered by specific conditions.

Queues manage events by ordering and releasing them according to various criteria. The most common types of queues are the first in, first out (FIFO), last in, first out (LIFO), ordered, and random. Each of these releases events into the simulation in a different order and each is useful for representing specific situations. The FIFO queue may contain a plan in the form of events to be executed, where each occurs after all previously added events have occurred. The LIFO queue may handle object reactions that interrupt and supersede planned events. In an ordered or *priority* queue, widely used in training simulations, the time that an event is to occur determines its insertion into the simulation. A random queue assigns no order to the events in the queue, processing any one without regard for its priority or arrival order.

TIME MANAGEMENT

In a simulation, time is represented by a variable that can be controlled like any other and is not tied to real time. Typically, simulations move forward through the use of event-based time (event-stepped) or incremental time advancement (time-stepped). An event-stepped simulation recognizes that in the model of the system, changes occur only at the points at which events occur.

Therefore, the model jumps from one scheduled event to the next, omitting the representation of intermediate times and speeding up the execution of the simulation by eliminating operations that do not affect the simulation state. Time-stepped simulations, on the other hand, are used when there are a large number of interactions among entities that share events. Training simulations use this method because of the need to present a consistent flow of time and events to a person who is interacting with the simulation.

Such simulations are called *discrete event* simulations because state variables change at distinct points in time. There are also *continuous* simulations, in which variables change continuously as a function of time. In practice, most simulations make use of both discrete and continuous state variables, but one type is predominant and determines the classification of the entire simulation.

RANDOM NUMBER GENERATION

Many models require the use of random numbers to introduce the variability caused by statistical rather than deterministic representations of events. Computer random number generators use algorithms that are actually deterministic and merely provide the impression of randomness. The algorithms are typically required to be repeatable, fast, use little storage space, and usually generate uniformly distributed numbers in the range (0,1). Other distributions, such as exponential or Poisson, can be produced by using the uniform distribution as the input to a second algorithm.

PHYSICAL MODELING

Traditionally, models have represented the capabilities of machinery and systems based on their physical characteristics and the basic laws of physics. The focus has been on understanding and representing the physical environment—distance, rate, weight, density, etc. In manufacturing systems, models represent entities entering a system in which events are generated by statistical distributions buffered by waiting queues. In analytical physics simulation, the models represent the specific behaviors of particles or chemicals under specified conditions. In training simulations, the models reproduce the physical world, allowing people to interact with terrain, buildings, and other entities. The impact of human decision making and process variability is handled through the use of statistical distributions that represent variation with the aid of random number inputs.

BEHAVIORAL MODELING

Some simulations need to model human behavior accurately. To accommodate this need, simulation developers have turned to artificial intelligence (*q.v.*)

for assistance. Behavioral modeling has been particularly useful in training applications where computer controlled adversaries with challenging and realistic behaviors are required.

MODEL MANAGEMENT

A computer simulation is a system of software and hardware that must be developed and managed in accordance with the same principles of systems and software engineering that govern other applications. Issues that are not germane to the *science* of simulation are very important to the *business* of simulation. An attractive and friendly user interface is important. Systems that have provided only textual input–output are giving way to those with graphical user interfaces and multidimensional representations of the simulated world. Configuration management of the models provides stability to a simulation program, ensuring that it can control its own evolution. Documentation (*q.v.*) provides stability by formally recording model assumptions, algorithms, data collection, and validation results. This establishes a foundation that can extend the useful life of a model beyond the tenure of its original developers.

Computer Technologies

Simulations depend on technologies from other areas of science. The need for a very complex simulation model and the information required to create it has often preceded the ability of computer hardware and software to represent it. However, simulation applications are growing larger and more useful as a result of developments in the computer field that provide tools powerful enough to represent the problems. A few of the most useful technologies are described here.

NETWORKS

Distributing a simulation across a network of computers makes it possible to have more detailed and complex models. Standard tools for distributed programming allow a single problem to be addressed with a large number of traditional computers on a network. When the network includes control systems, it is possible for a simulation to exchange data with these systems in real time, and, in effect, become part of that control system. This has blurred the boundary where real and simulated worlds meet.

The expansion of the Internet (*q.v.*) and the World Wide Web (*q.v.*) has led to experiments with simulations that are either distributed through the Internet or accessible from it. These simulations make use of standard protocols (*q.v.*) and allow the distribution of a simulation across multiple computers that are not directly controlled on a dedicated network.

PARALLEL COMPUTING

Parallel processing (*q.v.*) provides many of the advantages of distributed networked simulations, together with rapid and efficient communication. Some problems can be divided into many thousands of separate processes, but the interactions among these are so frequent that a general purpose network for delivering messages introduces delays that greatly extend the execution time of the simulation. In these cases, parallel computers can provide the close coupling between processors and memory that allows the simulation to execute more efficiently and thus handle larger models.

As simulations have grown to operate across networks of computers or on parallel computers, the models have been separated into pieces that represent portions of the problem, and that are programs that reside on multiple machines. It is necessary to maintain consistency among these programs, which cannot be done effectively with the simple queuing lists used within a single program. Parallel and distributed time management was initially achieved through the use of a shared clock to which all programs would refer. However, research has led to the use of algorithms which can ensure time synchronization without the use of a central shared clock.

Parallel and distributed time management can be accomplished through conservative or optimistic synchronization. Both methods use a mechanism to represent the time of each of the processes. Conservative synchronization then chooses to maintain consistency among all processes as the simulation executes. Optimistic synchronization, on the other hand, allows each process to move ahead as fast as computationally possible, putting each process at a different point in time. When an event is received from another process that affects past events in the local process, the simulation reverses its operations and "rolls back" in time to include the new event interaction. The conservative method assumes that interactions between processes are common enough that constant synchronization is the most efficient method of proceeding into the future. The optimistic method assumes that interactions are scarce and the problem can be solved more efficiently by working as fast as possible, rolling back only occasionally to take account of past events when information about them arrives.

ARTIFICIAL INTELLIGENCE

As mentioned earlier, the representation of human and group behavior has become essential in some parts of the simulation community. The use of techniques developed under the umbrella of artificial intelligence and cognitive modeling can solve some of these problems. Simulations are including expert systems (*q.v.*), neural networks (*q.v.*), case-based reasoning (*q.v.*), and genetic algorithms (*q.v.*) in an attempt to represent these behaviors with more fidelity and realism.

COMPUTER GRAPHICS (*q.v.*)

Simulation data lends itself very well to graphic displays. Factories and battlefields can be represented in full 3D animation using virtual reality techniques and special graphics hardware. Graphical user interfaces (GUIs) can provide easy model construction, operation, data analysis, and data presentation. These tools place a new and more attractive face on simulations that previously relied on the mind's eye for pictorial representation. This often leads to greater acceptance of the models and their results by the engineering and business communities.

DATABASES

Simulations can generate a large amount of data to be analyzed and may require as much input data to drive the models. The availability of relational and object-oriented databases has made the task of organizing and using this information much more efficient and accessible. Previously, model developers were required to build their own storage constructs and query languages, a distraction from the real focus of the simulation study.

SYSTEMS ARCHITECTURE

Like many kinds of software, simulations fall into families, or domains, that can use the same program architectures to represent entire classes of problems. These architectures are made up of components with capabilities and interfaces that allow their reuse in a variety of problems. The identification of common elements has led to the creation of a host of simulation products that encapsulate functionality used to model everything from factory operations to aircraft routing schedules.

Simulation Languages and Packages

A number of simulation languages and packages have been developed specifically to assist developers in constructing models of their systems. These languages are intended to serve a specific problem domain, rather than support general-purpose programming as do Fortran, C, Pascal, and Ada. However, general-purpose languages are still widely used to construct simulations in domains for which simulation-specific languages or packages do not yet exist or where the problem is so unusual that simulation tools cannot be created economically.

Some of the more popular languages and packages are described below and a sample comparison of three provided in Table 1.

DISCRETE EVENT SIMULATION

Discrete event simulation includes a wide array of both problems and commercial tools for solving them. The descriptions below are separated into those that use an actual programming language and those that are simulation applications or toolkits.

LANGUAGES

Simula (*q.v.*) from the Norwegian Computer Center was developed by O. J. Dahl and K. Nygaard in 1967. The language is actually a general-purpose programming language with specific extensions to support simulation. The first object-oriented language, many of its features, such as classes (*q.v.*), inheritance, encapsulation (*q.v.*), and multi-threading were motivated by its intended use for simulation.

GPSS/H from Wolverine Software is a block programming language improved from the original GPSS developed at IBM in 1969. This language provides an interactive debugging environment, a clock, and built-in mathematical, trigonometric, and statistical functions.

Table 1. Simulation language comparison.

GPSS/H	SIMAN	SLAM II
``` SIMULATE GENERATE RVEXPO(1,1,0) QUEUE SERVERQ SEIZE SERVER LVEQ DEPART SERVERQ TEST LN$LVEQ,1000,STOP ADVANCE RVEXPO(2,0.5) STOP RELEASE SERVER TERMINATE 1 START 1000 END ```	``` BEGIN; CREATE,,EX(1,1):EX(1,1) :MARK(1); QUEUE,1; SEIZE :SERVER; TALLY :1,INT(1); COUNT :1,1; DELAY :EX(2,2); RELEASE :SERVER :DISPOSE; END; ```	``` GEN,1,,,,,,72; LIM,1,1,100; NETWORK; RESOURCE/SERVER(1),1; CREATE,EXPON(1.0,1),1,1; AWAIT(1),SERVER; COLCT,INT(1),DELAY IN QUEUE,,2; ACTIVITY,EXPON(0.5,2),,DONE; ACTIVITY,,,CNTTR; DONE FREE,SERVER; TERM; CNTR TERM,1000; END; INIT; FIN; ```

It automatically collects basic simulation output data and supports the extension of this collection by the programmer.

SIMSCRIPT II.5 from CACI Products is an event-oriented and process-oriented language that evolved from the original SIMSCRIPT developed at the Rand Corporation in 1962. The language is actually a complete general programming language that can be used to build discrete-event, continuous, and combination simulations. It is supplemented by SIMGRAPHICS, which allows the user to develop input forms, output displays, and interactive controls for the simulation.

SIMAN/Cinema from Systems Modeling is a combined simulation language and animation system. SIMAN models are constructed graphically using the Cinema package and automatically converted into code. The language includes built-in functions for manufacturing and material handling systems, an interactive debugger, and analyzers for input and output data.

SLAM II from Pritsker Associates is predominantly used for process-oriented simulation, with extensions that support event-oriented simulation and combinations of the two. The language represents models in a network-like structure that includes nodes and branches. Support packages allow the developer to draw a network, which is then converted into the simulation code.

MODSIM from CACI is an object-oriented programming language with graphic extensions to support data input, execution monitoring and control, and output analysis. The language includes built-in routines for statistical distributions and simulation management operations. Interaction with the language is through

a development environment that includes a compiler (*q.v.*), object manager, and debugger.

LANGUAGE COMPARISON

To illustrate the syntax of some of the more common simulation languages, Table 1 provides the code for the same problem in GPSS/H, SIMAN, and SLAM II. This code represents a simple single-server queue with exponential interarrival and service times, such as a barber shop with one barber and a waiting queue. Though these languages are designed to serve efficiently the needs of model builders, their syntax is often equal to or more complex than general purpose programming languages. This fact has motivated the creation of the simpler graphic packages and toolkits described in the next section.

PACKAGES

Extend from Imagine That is a visual, interactive simulation package for discrete event and continuous modeling that allows users to build models and user interfaces graphically (Fig. 5). Model execution is carried out interactively on the graphic model representation. The package can accept data input through the inter-faces or from separate files. Extend provides built-in mathematical and statistical functions and can be customized through the addition of C and Fortran routines.

Workbench from SES is a visual simulation environment that allows models of complex systems to be built and executed graphically for performance analysis and functional verification. A model is specified graphically as a hierarchy of directed graphs; declaratively by filling in forms attached to each node in a

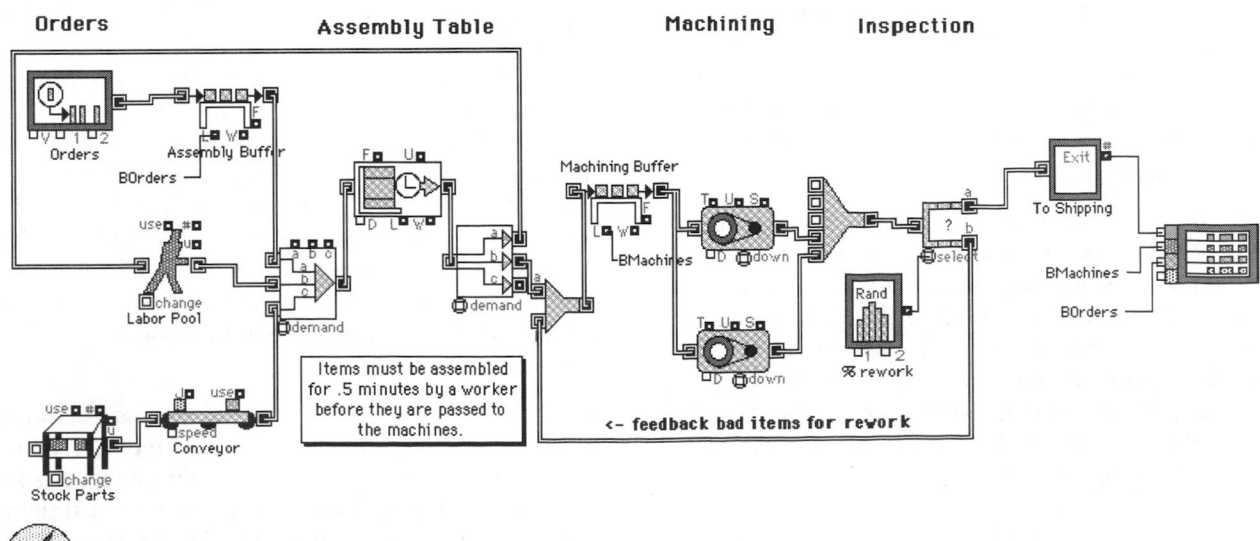

Figure 5. Simulation of a manufacturing production line. (Courtesy of Imagine That, Inc.)

graph; and procedurally by specifying procedural methods attached to the nodes where desired in an internal language that is a superset of C.

TAYLOR II from F&H Simulations is a graphic model building package based on four fundamental entities—elements, jobs, routings, and products. These are manufacturing-oriented, where elements can represent machines, buffers, conveyors, transport, paths, warehouses, and reservoirs. The three basic operations supported are processing, transport, and storage. During simulation execution, graphic interfaces provide 2D and 3D views of factory activities.

COMNET III from CACI Products is designed to simulate communications networks. It provides a graphic interface for model building, execution, and data analysis. It specifically provides statistical distributions and control data for communications and computer networks as used by telephone companies, cable television broadcasters, and computer networks.

BONeS Designer from the Alta Group models the protocol and messaging layers of computer architectures and communications systems. The tool provides graphical user interfaces for defining data structures, analyzing results, generating finite state machines, and directing interactive simulation runs.

CSIM18 from Mesquite Software is a library of classes, functions, procedures, and header files that describe the activities and statistical distributions of communications, transportation, microprocessors, and manufacturing systems. Library components can be combined with developed software in C and C++ to create a simulation model that has fast execution.

SimPack from the University of Florida is a toolkit written in C and C++ to support the development of simulation programs by the user. It contains routines to support basic simulation operations and management of declarative, functional constraint, and combination models. The software is intended to be combined with code written by the user.

CPSim from BoyanTech provides an execution kernel that manages synchronization, scheduling, deadlock prevention, and message passing, as well as a library of C functions that can be used to build an application. CPSim represents the system being modeled as a directed graph of communicating objects that are categorized as sources, nodes, and sinks. The tool supports portable models across single and multi-processor computers.

CONTINUOUS SIMULATION

The Advanced Continuous Simulation Language (ACSL) from MGA Software was developed specifically for modeling time-dependent, nonlinear differential equations and transfer functions. The language allows the user to develop code from block diagrams, mathematical equations, and Fortran statements. There are two distinct groups of user interactions: the first define the model and the structure of the system being represented; the second exercise the model allowing input variation and output analysis.

The Continuous System Modeling Program (CSMP) is constructed from three general types of statements—structural, which define the model; data, which assign numerical values to parameters; and control, which manage the execution of the model.

INTERACTIVE SIMULATION

In the interactive training arena a number of simulation products have emerged, particularly with military domain applications.

VRLink from MAK Technologies supports network protocols and simulation management for distributed military simulations. This package provides routines that format messages according to defined standards and manage the delivery and receipt of these messages across a number of computer platforms.

ITEMS from CAE Electronics provides a graphic environment for constructing simulated virtual worlds and the entities that populate them. The tool allows the creation of vehicles, aircraft, and humans and the specification of the physical characteristics and behavioral patterns. Terrain and weather data can be imported from standard formats or generated internally to create an operational environment. It provides a graphical user interface for executing and managing simulation runs.

FLAMES from Ternion is a simulation development and execution environment for military training and analysis. The system provides a simulation kernel to manage data distribution among multiple computers, time advancement, and simulation control. This supports models of equipment and organizations that actually replicate military events. The system includes tools for scenario generation, data analysis, simulation control, and two- and three-dimensional battlefield viewers.

MultiGenII from Multigen is a three-dimensional modeling tool for generating the visual representations of simulated objects, terrain, and cultural features for a complete synthetic environment to support training simulations. The tool simplifies the creation of the visual objects, allowing simulation developers to focus on more specific physical and behavioral models within the simulation.

Conclusion

THE GROWTH OF SIMULATION

Like all computer applications, the use of simulation is expanding as a result of improvements in computer hardware and software technologies. At one time simulation was performed entirely by specialists using expensive, dedicated computer systems. We have now reached a point where significant simulations can be performed on personal computers and workstations (*q.v.*). Simulation software tools allow experts in various fields to model their systems without a staff of simulation specialists. Modern languages, tools, and architectures encapsulate much of the difficult work of building a model. Knowledge of the system being studied is now sufficient for creating a model of the system.

Research in simulation itself is leading to an array of new technologies and methods for constructing and using models. Innovations include formalisms for defining models, interoperability of a diverse set of interactive simulations, metamodeling, human behavior modeling, and concurrent simulation.

FUTURE

The manufacturing, research, planning, and training communities, to name a few, have discovered that answers to their questions and insights into their problems can be obtained economically and quickly from simulation models. As the world evolves into the information age, more and more business, recreation, and government activities will operate through digital data and this information can be analyzed, organized, and predicted using simulation. For these reasons, the application of simulation will expand as the digitization of the world expands.

Bibliography

1991. Law, A., and Kelton W. *Simulation Modeling and Analysis.* New York: McGraw-Hill.
1991. Schriber, T. *An Introduction to Simulation Using GPSS/H.* New York: John Wiley.
1993. Cassandras, C. *Discrete Event Systems.* Boston: Aksen Associates.
1993. Knepell, P., and Arangno, D. *Simulation Validation: A Confidence Assessment Methodology.* Los Alamitos, CA: IEEE Press.
1995. Fishwick, P. *Simulation Model Design and Execution.* Upper Saddle River, NJ: Prentice Hall.
1996. Nance, R. "A History of Discrete Event Simulation Programming Languages," in *The History of Programming Languages—II* (eds T. J. Bergin and R. G. Gibson, Jr). Reading, MA: Addison-Wesley.

Websites

Discrete Event Simulation Server. http://masg1.epfl.ch/roso.mosaic/nino/devs.html.
Electronic Simulation Conference. http://www.scs.org/confernc/elecsim/elecsim.html.
On-line Executable Simulations. http://www.cis.ufl.edu/~fishwick/websim.html and http://ms.ie.org/websim/survey/survey.html.
Simulation Interoperability Workshop. http://siso.sc.ist.ucf.edu.
Society for Computer Simulation. http://www.scs.org.
Winter Simulation Conference. http://www.wintersim.org.

Roger D. Smith

SMALLTALK

See OBJECT-ORIENTED PROGRAMMING.

SNOBOL

See STRING PROCESSING LANGUAGES.

SOCIAL SCIENCE APPLICATIONS

For articles on related subjects *see* SOCIETY, COMPUTERS IN; DATABASE MANAGEMENT SYSTEM; GEOGRAPHIC INFORMATION SYSTEM; LEGAL APPLICATIONS ; POLITICAL APPLICATIONS; SIMULATION; and STATISTICAL APPLICATIONS.

Social science research requirements have challenged the limits of computation for over a century. Several major milestones in the early history of computing were sparked by attempts to advance the social sciences. It was the US census of 1890 that inspired Herman Hollerith (*q.v.*), a social researcher, to design the first automated data processing machinery. Hollerith's punched card (*q.v.*) system, while not a true computer, provided the foundation for contemporary computer-based data management.

In the late 1940s, anticipating the massive tabulations needed in the 1950 census, the US Bureau of the Census contracted for the building of Univac I (*q.v.*), the first commercially produced electronic computer. The need to count, sort, and analyze the 1950 census data on this milestone computer led to the development of the first high-speed magnetic tape storage system, the first sort–merge software package, and the first statistical package, a set of matrix algebra routines.

All of the social sciences plunged into computing during the 1960s. During this period, the first book of statistical computer programs was published (Cooley and Lohnes, 1962), and that same year the first book devoted entirely to social science applications was edited by Borko (1962). Not only were social scientists writing about how to apply computers, but they were designing and developing new software. One of the most popular statistical software packages, SPSS (Nie, Bent, and Hull, 1975), was designed and developed by social science graduate students at Stanford University.

In the three decades following what was done by these early pioneers, social science computing evolved rapidly. Computer applications were designed to augment or support every research task, even the more subjective ones like notetaking, interviewing, and content analysis. By the early 1990s, the processing power of desktop computers and workstations (*q.v.*) had become so compelling to social researchers that in most countries it is hard to find a social science researcher's office without one.

During the 1980s and 1990s, the volume of scholarly publications in social science computing expanded enormously. The primary source of articles on social science applications is the *Social Science Computer Review*, a quarterly publication of Sage Publications, Inc. (`http://hcl.chass.ncsu.edu/sscore/sscore.htm`). This journal also publishes reviews of social science software, social databases, and computer-related books. Another source of contemporary advances in social science computing is the anthology series *Computers and the Social Sciences*, from JAI Press.

Another major development during the last two decades was the emergence and institutionalization of computing as a subfield within the social science professional associations. In 1990 the American Sociological Association (ASA) formed a Section called "Sociology and Computers," and similar subgroups were established in the American Political Science Association, the American Psychological Association, and the American Anthropological Association. Perhaps most significant for the emerging discipline of social science computing was its first annual conference, Computing for the Social Sciences, held in 1990 at Williamsburg, VA. This conference continues annually under the auspices of the Social Science Computing Association. The best papers from the conference are published annually as a special issue of the *Social Science Computer Review*.

This review of applications begins by summarizing two important categories: quantitative and qualitative computing. Applications that straddle this dichotomy, such as data management and computer-assisted data collection, are discussed later.

Quantitative Computing

A large share of ongoing social research, like analysis of massive census files, would never get done without computer technology. For example, one use of LISREL, a computer procedure which analyzes linear structural relationships by the method of *maximum likelihood*, would consume weeks or months without a computer. The use of computing-intensive applications by social scientists are on the rise (Cirincione and Gurrieri, 1997). Some of the more common methods are *randomization* (Edgington, 1995) and *resampling* and *bootstrapping* (Mooney and Duval, 1993).

Not only does statistical computing save time but it offers unique views of the patterns in one's data. Without the ability to reorganize data quickly and display it in a variety of forms, social researchers could neglect important patterns and subtle relationships within complex data. Some patterns cannot be observed without special software tools. For example, Heise's (1988) computer program called Ethno gives the researcher a framework for conceptualizing, examining, and analyzing data containing event sequences. In addition, computer models by Cleveland (1993) and others for visualizing and analyzing data graphically give new ways that social researchers can deal with vast data resources.

Finding a statistical program tailored to a particular problem or technique is often challenging as the potential user community may be quite small. However, abstracts and reviews of such software appear in the *Social Science Computer Review*, *Educational and Psychological Measurement*, the *Journal of Marketing Research*, *The American Statistician*, and the annual *Sociological Methodology* (`http://depts.washington.edu/socmeth2/software.html`).

Qualitative Computing

Qualitative computing as it is practiced today consists of the manipulation of textual and other types of nonnumeric data for purposes of deciphering the embedded content and structure. Historically, quantitative computing has eclipsed qualitative computing within the social sciences, but there are signs of change. Qualitative computing in the social sciences began with computer-based "content analysis" (Stone, 1966), which emphasizes word classification and word counts. Refinement of computational methods for content analysis continues (*cf.* McTavish, 1997). Most qualitative analysis is not oriented toward word counts, but toward the classification and re-classification of text segments. Several general-purpose programs for qualitative analysis have been widely distributed (Tesch, 1989; Kelle, 1995). These tools make the analysis of large amounts of text more accurate and efficient, and potentially direct the focus of attention to analytic procedures. The general tasks of text entry, code assignment, counting, and data organization have been extended to include special routines for improving the quality of coding and code management. Hesse-Biber, Dupuis, and Kinder (1997) extended these methods to include the management and analysis of audio and video segments as well as text.

Data Management

One major development in social data management is interactive access to data via the Web (*see* WORLD WIDE WEB). A variety of strategies are used for access to both pre-formatted text files and pre-coded data files via the Web. Among the systems available are GSSDIRS from ICPSR at the University of Michigan (`http://www.icpsr.umich.edu/gss/`), IPUMS at the University of Minnesota (`http://www.ipums.umn.edu`), QSERVE from Queens College-CUNY (`http://www.soc.qc.edu/qserve/`), and SDA Archive from the University of California at Berkeley (`http://csa.berkeley.edu:7502/archive.htm`). Other major social science data archives on the Web are the Council of European Social Sciences Data Archives (CESSDA) (`http://www.nsd.uib.no/cessda/europe.html`) and Social Indicators of Development (`http://www.ciesin.org/IC/wbank/sid-home.html`), which contains the World Bank's data on the social effects of economic development. Here are some Websites that contain access points to other social science data:

- Demography and Population Studies WWW Virtual Library
  `http://coombs.anu.edu.au/ResFacilities/DemographyPage.html`

- WWW Virtual Library: Sociology—SOCNET—Courses, Resources
  `http://www.mcmaster.ca/socscidocs/w3virtsoclib/socnet.htm`

- SOCIOWEB A Sociology Resource Center
  `http://www.socioweb.com/~markbl/socioweb/`

- Research resources for the social sciences
  `http://www.socsciresearch.com`

- WeacTies (for Sociology of the Internet)
  `http://www.princeton.edu/~soccomp/weacties/`

Geographic data is particularly challenging for social science research. Geographic information systems (*q.v.*) are designed for the purpose of handling data with geographic coordinates. Not only do geographers depend upon such systems, but social and political scientists use them for redistricting and political campaigns (Novotny and Jacobs, 1997; Eagles, Katz, and Mark, 1999).

Simulation and Modeling

Early in the history of social science computing, Coleman (1962) designed computer simulation models and showed how they could be used to identify elusive implications of different theoretical assumptions. Others followed in his footsteps but the excitement of the pioneers was lost and few simulations and formal computer models were developed in the 1970s. During the past two decades, with the emergence of artificial intelligence (*q.v.*) techniques and other computing methodologies, many more social researchers have published simulation models of social processes (*cf.* Feinberg and Johnson, 1995; Hanneman, 1988; Markovsky, Lovaglia, and Thye, 1997). New computer simulations for social policy analysis have also emerged (Anderson, 1993).

Neural networks (*q.v.*) combined with other techniques of artificial intelligence and expert systems (*q.v.*) have excited a number of social scientists (Garson, 1990). Neural nets organize computer memory in ways that model the human brain and its ability to process many things in parallel. The possibilities of combining expert systems and neural net technology have generated substantial interest (Brent, 1999).

Computer-Assisted Data Collection

Most social science research centers now use computer-assisted telephone interviewing (CATI), which consists of online questionnaires or entry screens for telephone interviewers. These systems generally, but not always, have the following characteristics: centralized facilities for monitoring individual interviewer stations, instantaneous edit checks with feedback for invalid responses, and automatic branching to different questions depending upon the respondent's answers. CATI systems run on free-standing PCs, networked PCs, or large mainframe computers. Major variations on this mode of data collection include (1) computer-assisted personal interviewing (CAPI), face-to-face interviewing assisted with a laptop or handheld computing device (*see* PORTABLE COMPUTERS); (2) computerized self-administered questionnaires (CSAQ), online programs designed for direct input from respondents; and (3) data entry programs to facilitate the entry of data collected manually at a prior time. Rodman and Williams (1996) describe typical systems for these types of surveys.

The Social Sciences and the Web

As electronic mail (*q.v.*) systems continue to expand, they offer social researchers new opportunities for conducting studies using electronic networks. For instance, Gaiser (1997) explored issues of running online focus groups. Online surveys have become quite common in various forms: email texts, email attachments, entry forms on the Web, and as programs in external storage devices like diskettes and CD-ROMs (*see* OPTICAL STORAGE). Sampling problems and low completion rates pose the greatest challenges. Ongoing methodological investigations will be necessary to determine the potential and impact of this new mode of research.

Multimedia (*q.v.*) databases accessible over the Web may shape the future of the social sciences more than new data collection opportunities. Current technology allows for a limited range of analysis of quantitative data at remote sites. If these analytical capabilities expand and make it possible to manipulate and analyze large volumes of text, audio, and video data remotely, there will be an observable shift in the nature of social science research.

Conclusion

The application of computing to social research is not without problems. Errors in data and software abound. Data and software tend to be costly, and many impediments inhibit sharing of these critical resources. Research grants for the development of software methodologies are scarce. Meanwhile, new breakthroughs in computer technology continue, and major new opportunities may emerge. Many of the advances in social science computing during the next few years will undoubtedly follow the lines of progress already described: computing-intensive methods; hypertext (*q.v.*) networks; integrated, high-performance, graphic data analysis stations; qualitative methods; expert systems; neural networks and other complex models of social systems; and a variety of Web applications. The challenge for the future is to build upon and assemble these innovations, especially toward modeling and analyzing vast amounts of social data.

Bibliography

1962. Borko, H. (ed.) *Computer Applications in the Behavioral Sciences.* Santa Monica, CA: System Development Corporation.

1962. Cooley, W., and Lohnes, P. *Multivariate Procedures for the Behavioral Sciences.* New York: John Wiley.

1962. Coleman, J. S. "Analysis of Social Structures and Simulation of Social Processes with Electronic Computers," in *Simulation in Social Science: Readings* (ed. Harold Guetzkow). Upper Saddle River, NJ: Prentice Hall.

1966. Stone, P. J., Dunphy, D. C., Smith, M. S., and Ogilvie, D. M. *The General Inquirer.* Cambridge, MA: MIT Press.

1975. Nie, N., Bent, D., and Hull, H. *Statistical Package for the Social Sciences.* New York: McGraw-Hill.

1987. Brent, E., Scott, J., and Spencer, J. "The Use of Computers by Qualitative Researchers," *Qualitative Sociology*, 10, *3*, 309–313.

1988. Hanneman, R. A. *Computer-Assisted Theory Building.* Newbury Park, CA: Sage Publications.

1988. Heise, D. "Computer Analysis of Cultural Structures," *Social Science Computer Review*, 6, 183–196.

1989. Blank, G., McCartney, J. L., and Brent, E. (eds.) *New Technology in Sociology: Practical Applications in Research and Work.* New Brunswick, NJ: Transaction.

1989. Lyman, P. "The Future of Sociological Literature in an Age of Computerized Texts," in *New Technology in Sociology: Practical Applications in Research and Work* (eds. G. Blank, J. L. McCartney, and E. Brent). New Brunswick, NJ: Transaction.

1989. Tesch, R. "Computer Software and Qualitative Analysis: A Reassessment," in *New Technology in Sociology: Practical Applications in Research and Work* (eds. G. Blank, J. L. McCartney, and E. Brent). New Brunswick, NJ: Transaction.

1990. Brent, E., and Anderson, R. E. *Computer Applications in the Social Sciences.* New York: McGraw-Hill.

1990. Garson, G. D. "Expert Systems: An Overview for Social Scientists," *Social Science Computer Review*, 8, *3* (Fall), 387–410.

1993. Anderson, R. E. "Development of a Structured Sentencing Simulation," *Social Science Computer Review*, 11, *2*, 166–178.

1993. Cleveland, W. S. *Visualizing Data.* Summit, NJ: Hobart Press.

1993 Mooney, C. Z., and Duval, R. D. *Bootstrapping: A Nonparametric Approach to Statistical Inference.* Newbury Park, CA: Sage.

1995. Edgington, E. *Randomization Tests.* New York: Marcel Dekker.

1995. Feinberg, W. E., and Johnson, N. R. "FIRESCAP: A Computer Simulation Model of Reaction to a Fire Alarm," *Journal of Mathematical Sociology*, 29, *2–3*, 257–269.

1995. Kelle, U. *Computer-Aided Qualitative Data Analysis.* Newbury Park, CA: Sage Publications.

1996. Rodman, R. D., and Williams, J. O. "Hardware and Software for Telephoning Voters En Masse," *Social Science Computer Review*, 14, *2* (Summer), 190–196.

1996. Wellman, B., Salaff, J., Dimitrova, D., Garton, L., Guila, M., and Haythornwaite, C. "Computer Networks as Social Networks: Collaborative Work, Telework, and Virtual Community," *Annual Review of Sociology*, 22, 213–238.

1997. Anderson, R. E. "A Research Agenda for Computing and the Social Sciences," *Social Science Computer Review*, 15, *2* (Summer), 123–134.

1997. Cirincione, C., and Gurrieri, G. "Computer-intensive Methods in the Social Sciences," *Social Science Computer Review*, 15, *1* (Spring), 83–97.

1997. Gaiser, T. J. "Conducting On-line Focus Groups," *Social Science Computer Review*, 15, *2* (Summer), 135–144.

1997. Hesse-Biber, S., Dupuis, P., and Kinder, S. "Anthropology: New Developments in Video Ethnography and Visual Sociology—Analyzing Multimedia Data Qualitatively," *Social Science Computer Review*, 15, *1* (Spring), 5–12.

1997. Markovsky, B., Lovaglia, M., and Thye, S. "Sociology: Computer-aided Research at the Iowa Center for the Study of Group Processes," *Social Science Computer Review*, 15, *1* (Spring), 48–64.

1997. McTavish, D. E. "Scale Validity: A Computer Content Analysis Approach," *Social Science Computer Review*, 15, *4* (Winter), 379–393.

1997. Novotny, P., and Jacobs, R. H. "Geographical Information Systems and the New Landscape of Political Technologies," *Social Science Computer Review*, 15, *3* (Fall), 264–285.

1999. Brent, E., and Tompson, G. A. "Sociology: Modeling Social Action with Autonomous Agents," *Social Science Computer Review*, 17, *3* (Fall), 313–322.

1999. Schweik, C. M., and Green, G. M. "The Use of Spectral Mixture Analysis to Study Human Incentives, Actions, and Environmental Outcomes," *Social Science Computer Review*, 17, *1* (Spring), 40–63.

1999. Eagles, M., Katz, R. S., and Mark, D. "GIS and Redistricting: Emergent Technologies, Social Geography and Political Sensibilities," *Social Science Computer Review*, 17, *1* (Spring), 5–9.

Ronald E. Anderson

SOCIETIES, COMPUTER

See COMPUTER SOCIETIES.

SOCIETY, COMPUTERS IN

For articles on related subjects *see* BULLETIN BOARD; COMPUTER CRIME; COMPUTER ETHICS; COMPUTER LITERACY; DATA SECURITY; DISABLED, COMPUTERS AND THE; ELECTRONIC FUNDS TRANSFER; ELECTRONIC MAIL; ELECTRONIC OFFICE; FREEWARE AND SHAREWARE; HACKER; HUMAN FACTORS IN COMPUTING; INFORMATION ACCESS; INTERNET; LEGAL ASPECTS OF COMPUTING; LEGAL PROTECTION OF SOFTWARE; PERSONAL COMPUTING; POLITICAL APPLICATIONS; PRIVACY, COMPUTERS AND; SOCIAL SCIENCE APPLICATIONS; VIRUS, COMPUTER; WORLD WIDE WEB; and Y2K PROBLEM.

Introduction

Ever since the introduction of microcomputers in the late 1970s, computers have become more and more a part of everyday life. Computers are integral to communications, government, the military, medicine, and most businesses. When you visit the bank, you are likely to use an automatic teller machine. If your job once required a typewriter, the odds are good that you now use a word processor (*q.v.*). When you make an airline reservation, request a telephone number from directory assistance, or even order a meal in a fast-food restaurant, a computer system is likely to be centrally involved, even if consumers are not always conscious of that fact.

As computers have become cheaper and more powerful, society has become increasingly dependent on this technology. With increasing dependence comes increasing risks. For many years, any such risk was assumed to be insignificant in comparison to the enormous and largely self-evident promise of computing technology. However, as various incidents within the last two decades have demonstrated, such risks are real, and interest in understanding them and in assessing the long-term social effect of computing technology has begun to grow. Many computer science programs in colleges and universities now require courses in "computers and society" or "computers and ethics," and several academic journals now explore these issues. Several new organizations, including Computer Professionals for Social Responsibility (*q.v.*) or the Association for Computing Machinery's (*q.v.*) Special Interest Group on Computers and Society (SIGCAS), now exist to promote the responsible use of computing technology within society.

The risks associated with computers take two principal forms. First, there is a risk of *failure*. Designing a computer-based system, particularly when it requires extensive software development, tends to be so complex that it is difficult even to understand its failures, much less to predict or prevent them. The likelihood of such failures, coupled with our growing dependence on the underlying technology, represents an important social problem. Second, there is also a risk of *success*. As computers become essential to an ever-widening range of human activity, the nature of those activities and the social relations surrounding them will also change, sometimes in negative ways.

This article looks first at the phenomenon of our growing dependence on computers and the ways in which this dependence has been shaped by technological progress. It then examines the risks of both failure and success, considering first the question of computer reliability and the social implications of computer failures and then the effects of the growing use of computers on the individual and on society as a whole.

The Growing Dependence on Computers

On a historical scale, computers are a recent technological phenomenon. Sixty years ago, no digital computer yet existed. By 1997, there were an estimated 400 million computers worldwide, a number that continues to grow rapidly. Moreover, since the appearance of the first computer systems, there has been a consistent trend toward vast increases in computing power at ever-decreasing cost. The observation that computing power increases exponentially with time is commonly referred to as Moore's Law (*see* LAWS, COMPUTER), after computing pioneer Gordon Moore, who wrote in 1965 that transistor density on microchips tends to double every two years. This trend has in fact continued and, in many aspects of computing, has even accelerated. Since 1980 the power of a typical computer has doubled approximately every 18 months.

THE PERSONAL COMPUTER REVOLUTION

The continued improvement in price–performance ratio has had some profound effects, most notably the development and explosive growth of the personal computer industry. The first personal computer appeared in 1975; by 1999, there were over 400 million personal computers worldwide. The enormous growth of the personal computer industry, particularly since the introduction of the World Wide Web in the early 1990s, has meant that many more people have access to computing than they did a decade ago. According to the US Census Bureau, more than 36 percent of American households had personal computers in 1997—more than double the percentage at the beginning of the decade.

The power of the personal computer has increased as dramatically as its availability. Hardware has advanced in numerous ways: processors are faster, memory capacity has increased by three orders of magnitude, peripheral devices (including laser printers, telecommunications devices such as modems (*q.v.*), and input devices such as the hand-held mouse) have made revolutionary progress, size has been reduced to the point that truly portable computers (*q.v.*) are commonplace, and the price of all of these features has dropped sharply. Concurrently, software for personal computers has also been radically transformed in recent years, both in terms of the expected styles of interaction and in the way in which software is developed for popular consumption.

Based on the philosophy that computers should be sufficiently easy to understand that they can be used by nontechnical persons, the early 1980s witnessed a considerable shift in the style of computer–human interaction. Using technology pioneered at the Xerox Palo Alto Research Center in the late 1970s, Apple Computer's (*q.v.*) introduction of the Macintosh led the way to widespread acceptance of a new user interface (*q.v.*) paradigm emphasizing extensive graphics, mouse-oriented interaction, and ease of use. As this style of interaction has been adopted by the designers of other systems (as in the Microsoft Windows product for the IBM PC (*q.v.*) and other Wintel machines, computers have become accessible to the average citizen.

Strategies for software development have also been affected by the growth of personal computing. As the importance of personal computer systems expands, there is an ever greater premium on compatibility and integration. A software application that doesn't integrate well with the existing base of tools available on a particular platform is less likely to survive in the competitive marketplace. This emphasis on integration and compatibility has led to *de facto* standardization of certain operating systems and user interface paradigms, at the expense of others. Some industry observers have expressed the concern that this standardization threatens future innovation, but it has also certainly improved the quality and usability of the systems that emerge at the top of the heap.

The widespread availability of computers to individual programmers has also led to the development of a sizable cottage industry in computer software. Private system designers have in some cases had significant success developing and marketing computer applications. The fact that such individual entrepreneurs lack access to the large-scale distribution mechanisms of large companies has led to the development of *shareware*, software distributed freely over computer networks, with users encouraged to send in voluntary contributions if they are satisfied with the products (*see* FREEWARE AND SHAREWARE).

THE INTERNET AND THE WEB

Another aspect of the enormous changes in computing over the last two decades—and one that has significant social impact—is the growth of communications technology in general and computer networking in particular. In 1968, Bolt Beranek and Newman Inc. of Cambridge, MA, won a contract from the Defense Advanced Research Projects Agency to build a network that would connect computer systems at various universities, corporate research centers, and government agencies. In late 1969, the first four nodes of this system were in operation, and by 1977 the Arpanet system had grown to include 111 host computers. Since that time, network growth in both the public and private sector has been enormous. The Arpanet became the Internet, and its structure became much more sophisticated through the creation of domains and subdomains. As of 1999, almost 40 million computers in over 200 countries were connected to the Internet.

The importance of the Internet increased dramatically in the 1990s, in part because of the emergence of the World Wide Web, an internationally distributed collection of online documents connected by interactive links. The number of systems that serve as World Wide Web repositories has grown extremely rapidly, rising from approximately 500 in 1993 to over 4,000,000 in 1999.

THE INTEGRATION OF COMPUTERS INTO OTHER PRODUCTS

As microchip processors became smaller, cheaper, and more powerful, they have been incorporated into a wide variety of products, from microwave ovens to automobiles, from children's toys to high-tech military weapons. The addition of computing technology to such systems means that they can perform a more sophisticated set of functions and be more flexible in their operation. It also means that the systems increase in complexity, in the sense that their detailed operation is much less easily understood.

Reliability and Risk

Increasing reliance on sophisticated computer technology, particularly when such technology is employed in life-critical applications, carries with it the significant social risk that such technology will fail, in potentially catastrophic ways. In much of society, the idea that computers always give the correct answer is strongly embedded in cultural mythology. Given recent advances in computer engineering, this perception is now substantially correct for the hardware itself. Machines rarely give incorrect results through any sort of physical failure, and the reliability of computing hardware has been increasing steadily. Nonetheless, hardware failures do occur, and the results can be particularly frightening. In June 1980, the failure of a multiplexer chip at NORAD led to two false nuclear alerts in four days.

Computer systems, however, are much more complex than the hardware alone. In order to perform any useful tasks, computers must be programmed; they need software to control the hardware. While engineering advances have led to dramatic improvements in hardware reliability, the problems involved in the development of reliable software have proven much more difficult to solve. Software systems are complex, and there are myriad opportunities for error. These errors may be simple oversights or typographical mistakes, or they may represent more serious failures in the conceptual design. Often, software errors are manifest only when the system encounters some unexpected or unlikely situation, or when several individually innocuous events occur in concert. In such cases, it is common for the errors to remain undetected despite years of use.

EXAMPLES OF SOFTWARE FAILURE

In 1962, a single-character error in the controlling software for the Mariner 1 Venus probe sent the booster off course and forced mission controllers to destroy the launch vehicle, at a cost of $18.5 million. On 15 January 1990, the AT&T long-distance system suffered a catastrophic failure in which much of the national telephone network in the USA was out of service for nine hours. The problem was eventually traced to a problem in the routing software. In each of these instances, moreover, the error occurred in a part of the program responsible for failure recovery. These systems worked under "normal" operating conditions and had therefore passed most tests successfully. It was only when a special condition occurred, and the system needed to respond to that condition, that the software failure was triggered.

Two computer system flaws received a great deal of press coverage in the 1990s. In 1994, a bug was discovered in Intel's Pentium chip that caused floating-point division to return incorrect results when applied to certain data values. Initially, Intel argued that the flaw was extremely unlikely to occur, since the conditions required for failure would arise only once in every 40 billion operations on randomly chosen data. Critics argued that the flaw was much more serious given that certain faulty dividend–divisor pairs would arise much more frequently. Intel was eventually pressured into offering replacement chips to customers who requested them.

More recently, considerable attention has been focused on the "Year 2000" problem, which is often referred to as the Y2K problem or the Millennium Bug. The problem here is simply that many computer systems stored dates using only two digits for the year. This design decision seemed harmless in the early days of computing, when the turn of the century was decades away. As the year 2000 approached, there was considerable concern that the change from the year 99 to 00 would cause many systems to fail, as time appeared to run backwards. Commercial software systems, for example, might decide that credit cards with expiration dates in 00 had already expired or that a person's age had suddenly become negative. The Gartner Group consulting firm claimed that this problem would cost as much as $600 billion to fix worldwide, but most assessments suggested a considerably smaller figure. Several analysts have asserted that the costs of fixing the bug, although certainly substantial, would be less than the savings that were achieved in storage costs over the years by not having to store the full four-digit year.

Many "computer problems" are not necessarily the fault of the computer itself. Computers are most often used as parts of larger systems that involve both people and technology. In such systems, a common source of risk is the human–computer interface. If a computer system is designed in such a way that it is difficult to use or so that people are likely to make mistakes when using it, this is in itself a risk. One instance is the failure of the first test of the accuracy of ground-based laser stations as a candidate architecture for the Strategic Defense System. An operator entered the height of the ground station in feet, but the programmer had intended that this value be entered in nautical miles. Comically, when the Space Shuttle received this value, it turned upside down so that its mirror pointed out into space toward the top of a hypothetical mountain more than 10,000 miles high—well above the shuttle's orbit. A similar error occurred in 1999 when the $125 million Mars Orbiter was lost because of a failure to convert English units to metric.

Software failures have had more tragic consequences as well. In 1985 and 1986, poorly designed software in the Therac 25 X-ray machine caused it to deliver massive doses of radiation that killed three patients. Later analysis by Nancy Leveson and Clark Turner identified three causes of these failures. First, the software allowed users to edit commands in such a way that the system would execute those commands before the level of radiation had switched to a safe level. Second, the code contained an overflow bug involving a 6-bit counter, which caused safety checks to be bypassed once out of every 64 times. Third, the designers of the system had removed hardware interlocks present in earlier models on the grounds that they would not be needed with the new software.

A similar failure occurred in the design of the Patriot missile system that was deployed in the Persian Gulf War. On 25 February 1991, an Iraqi SCUD missile evaded detection by the Patriot's radar system and detonated inside a US military base near Dhahran in Saudi Arabia, killing 28 American soldiers and wounding 97. The error was traced to the fact that the software represented time values in both 24-bit and 48-bit forms. The mathematical difference between these representations caused small errors to accumulate over time, eventually reaching a point at which the system was unable to recognize radar tracks as incoming missiles.

Finally, many failures are caused by unanticipated interactions between the computer system and its environment. In 1980, a hospital patient was receiving treatment on a microwave-based arthritis therapy machine that had previously been used successfully on many patients. In this case, however, the patient died when the therapy machine inadvertently reprogrammed his pacemaker. And since 1982, there have been five crashes of the US Air Force Blackhawk helicopter, resulting in 22 deaths. Each of these crashes has been traced to radio interference affecting the helicopter's computerized control system.

These examples are not isolated instances or occasional flukes. Computer systems have been implicated, for example, in the near-meltdown of the Three Mile Island nuclear power plant, the stock market crash of October 1987, the downing of a civilian Iranian airliner by the USS *Vincennes* in 1988, and at least two crashes of the Airbus A320 fly-by-wire aircraft. These and thousands of other software failures have been documented over the years by Peter Neumann in his RISKS Forum digest, which has been published as an Internet newsgroup since 1985.

THE INEVITABILITY OF SOFTWARE RISK
It is interesting to speculate as to why the discipline of software engineering (*q.v.*) has not advanced to the point at which software designers can avoid software errors and their attendant risk. For the foreseeable future, such a goal is unlikely to be reached. Most experts in software engineering believe that software errors are inevitable in any large system. When the US Department of Defense convened the Eastport panel in 1985 to study the feasibility of the software required for a ballistic missile defense system, they concluded, "Simply because of its large size, the software capable of performing the battle management task for strategic defense will contain errors. All systems of useful complexity contain errors." In effect, errors are a

consequence of the complexity of the problems that computers are directed to solve.

In one important respect, software engineering differs from other engineering disciplines in which technological advances and the development of appropriate standards have made it possible to eliminate the major causes of catastrophic failures. Computers are discrete systems, whereas most engineering is concerned with continuous ones. A continuous system usually degrades in a predictable way: small changes have small effects. This property is not at all true of a computational system. A single character change in a program or its data may be completely innocuous, but on the other hand, it led to the loss of the Mariner 1 spacecraft. Small changes can, and do, have catastrophic effects.

A related problem is that most technologies permit the designer to *overengineer* a system in case of uncertainty. If a bridge designer is unsure whether a particular number of reinforcing supports will be sufficient to withstand an earthquake, it is usually reasonable, for example, to double the predicted number of supports "just for good measure." The same strategy is not available to the software designer. If that designer is unsure whether errors are lurking in a 10,000 line program, doubling the number of lines will decrease rather than increase confidence in the product. As we use computers to solve problems of increasing complexity, we need to accept a corresponding increase in risk. This observation has led some well-informed critics, including David Parnas, Charles Perrow, and Joseph Weizenbaum, to conclude that there must be limits on the level of risk that we, as a society, can accept. Moreover, limiting these risks imposes a parallel limitation on the complexity of systems that we should be willing to deploy in life-critical applications.

SOFTWARE LIABILITY
That computer systems are prone to failure has not been lost on software developers. Throughout much of its history, software development has not been subjected to the same standards of strict liability as have other engineering disciplines, and software vendors have gone to considerable pains to avoid liability for products that cause damage through software error. Almost every piece of software sold includes a standard disclaimer indicating that the product is sold "as is," with no responsibility whatever accruing to the vendor should the product fail to operate as advertised. The legal status of such blanket disclaimers is open to question, and the entire issue of liability for software errors is likely to become a central legal concern in the new millennium.

THE RISK OF MALICIOUS ATTACK

The enormous proliferation of computing technology and the degree to which computers interact, either through networks or the sharing of software, has led to a new concern. The hazards described in the previous section are caused by errors, oversights, or a failure to understand the complexities of a problem. In each of these cases, the results were unintended, even if they could have been foreseen. They are not deliberate assaults.

Beginning in the 1980s, however, several serious incidents have occurred in which the perpetrator was intentionally negligent, or at least reckless. Computer networks have been prime targets. In the summer of 1986, an astronomer-turned-computer-operator named Clifford Stoll discovered that someone was breaking into the computers at Lawrence Berkeley Laboratory and acquiring special privileges on that system. After more than a year of investigation, described in Stoll's book, *The Cuckoo's Egg*, the intrusion was traced through an astonishingly complex array of networks and computers to Germany, where a group of computer "hackers" was selling US military computing secrets to the Soviet KGB. In November 1988, Robert Morris, a graduate student at Cornell, unleashed a *worm* that exploited three different holes in the Unix operating system to replicate itself across the Internet, eventually affecting more than 6,000 machines. The worm's author evidently did not intend his program to cause real damage, but a software error in the program caused it to replicate itself much more rapidly than intended, overwhelming many of the machines it reached.

In the personal computer world, the dominant problem has been the *computer virus*. A virus is a program that can copy itself into other programs, which then will create further copies of the virus, etc. They may or may not have malicious consequences. Viruses are usually spread from one personal computer to another when a piece of software is copied. If the source machine is infected, it is likely to infect the diskette (*q.v.*) used to make the copy, and then to go on to spread the virus to the new machine. Since the appearance in 1986 of the first virus to be transmitted outside of the laboratory (the so-called "Brain" or "Pakistani" virus), the problem quickly became increasingly severe, so that by 1999 over 500 identifiable viruses and virus variants had been detected.

The proliferation of viruses and worms, and the threat of additional attacks by computer *hackers* have led to an increase in emphasis on system security. Some response to this threat is indeed necessary, but there is also concern that defending against such attacks may adversely affect research. The existence of relatively open computer networks and the widespread availability of software have both contributed to the successes of the computer age by making it far easier than it has ever been to build upon the work of others. If these channels are restricted, some fear that the advantages of an open environment will also be lost, to the ultimate detriment of the field.

COMPUTER CRIME

While computer hackers have captured most of the headlines in recent years, most observers believe that the real threat of malicious attack lies elsewhere. The danger represented by unauthorized users is probably small in comparison to the danger posed by authorized users who exploit their authorization with criminal intent. White-collar crimes, such as embezzlement and fraud, are familiar problems in business. In the computer age, however, these age-old problems can expand in magnitude because reliance on computers creates new opportunities for economic crime.

It is difficult to assess the actual impact of computer crime within the US or world economies. Possibly out of fear that disclosure of losses might weaken the confidence of consumers or investors, few companies are willing to prosecute computer crimes, preferring instead to handle such cases internally. In any case, losses are certainly high. A 1984 report by the American Bar Association (ABA) surveyed 278 companies and public agencies, concluding that "if the annual losses attributable to computer crime sustained by this relatively small survey are, conservatively estimated, in the range of half a billion dollars, then it takes little imagination to realize the magnitude of the annual losses sustained on a nationwide basis."

A few cases of computer fraud have drawn widespread attention. In 1979, a computer consultant to the Security Pacific Bank, who had acquired the access codes to the electronic funds transfer (EFT) system, was able to shift more than $10 million to his account in Switzerland. One of the largest computer fraud cases known is the Equity Funding scandal, uncovered in 1972. In this case, computers at Equity Funding were used to generate fraudulent insurance policies that were then resold to other insurance carriers, resulting in losses to investors and legitimate insurance companies that may have been as high as $2 billion. In 1987, the German Volkswagen corporation revealed that it had lost about $260 million through a computer-based foreign exchange contract scheme.

SOFTWARE PIRACY

The examples of computer crime cited in the previous section are those in which computers are the *instruments* of crime. Computers and their software are also the *objects* of crime. Theft of computer hardware has grown in importance as the size of the computers themselves (and the concomitant difficulty of moving them) has diminished. Even so, the economic impact of hardware theft is certainly dwarfed by that of what is often referred to as *software piracy*—the act of copying proprietary software without payment of any licensing fees. Particularly after the development of the personal computer opened up the home computing market, such copying of software has become enormously widespread, to the point that software vendors estimate that two to three copies are made for every program that is sold.

Once again, the actual extent of such copying, or the attendant economic costs, are difficult to assess. Ironically, one of the best indicators of the scope of the problem is the proliferation of computer viruses (as discussed above), because such viruses are most often spread through software copying. The extent of the problem was vividly illustrated by the "Peace Virus," which was designed so that on 2 March 1988, it would display a message promoting peace. According to Richard Brandow, publisher of the Canadian *MacMag* magazine and one of the creators of the virus, the virus was transmitted to 350,000 Macintosh computers within two months.

There is considerable debate as to the ethics of such unauthorized copying. Many computer users simply do not regard such copying as theft, pointing out that classical theft denies the original owner possession of an object of value, whereas software copying does not. An organization of programmers called the League for Programming Freedom, founded by Richard Stallman, opposes software patents and copyrights. Others counter that some form of protection analogous to copyright is essential in order to protect the intellectual property rights of inventors. In recent years, particularly with the introduction of lawsuits asserting protection for the "look and feel" of a particular product, this debate has quickly grown in importance so that it is now the foremost legal question facing the computing community.

THE SECURITY OF ELECTRONIC VOTE TABULATION

While most of the concern about the threat of fraud or data tampering is focused on economic crime, there are other concerns as well. For example, computer experts have expressed increasing concern that the proliferation of electronic vote-counting systems in the USA could threaten democratic rights. A small number of vendors supply the vast majority of voting systems for the country at every electoral level. There are many opportunities, both inside and outside those companies, to sabotage the vote tabulation software, and there are few safeguards to prohibit such tampering or even to detect it if it occurs. In most cases, election officials are

not even able to review the vendor-supplied voting software, since the companies providing that software regard it as a proprietary trade secret.

Although the possibility of fraud exists, most of the known problems in electronic vote counting have to do with computer failures and undetected software errors, and not with actual fraud. In the 1985 mayoral race in Dallas, for example, there was a momentary power outage during the tabulation process. When power was restored, the candidate who had been leading up to that time quickly fell behind, which aroused enough suspicion that the problem was investigated. That investigation determined that the software supplied for the election system was incorrectly reporting vote totals for the so-called "split precincts" lying partly inside and partly outside of the city limits. Still other problems were detected during further investigation. This fiasco eventually led the Texas legislature to amend the state election law and forced Dallas County to replace its entire vote-counting system.

Computers and the Changing Social Order

The preceding section focused on how computers affect society when they are either misused or fail to function as intended. This, however, is only one aspect of the social impact of computers. It is at least as interesting to consider how computers affect individuals and society when they operate as advertised.

COMPUTERS AND THE WORKPLACE

For many people in modern society, the greatest impact of computing technology has been in the workplace. As technological innovation produces computing equipment that is faster, more powerful, and less expensive than its predecessors, there is an increasing impetus toward using computer systems in an enormously wide variety of work environments. In the office, typewriters have been almost entirely replaced by word processing systems or workstations (*q.v.*). On the shop floor, technology has led to the development of significantly more sophisticated tools, such as computer-aided design and computer-aided manufacturing systems (CAD/CAM—*q.v.*). Computers have made their mark even in the fast-food industry, with systems that allow workers to ring up orders by pushing buttons with pictures of hamburgers, French fries, and the like.

In each of these environments, the introduction of computers has profoundly transformed the nature of the work process. One of the principal effects of computerization on the labor force itself has been to increase the polarization of job categories with respect to skill levels. Some jobs require increased skill levels on the part of employees, so that they can handle the new, more sophisticated tools; office jobs that require the use of word processors are one example. Many other jobs, such as that of the fast-food clerk pushing picture buttons, require less skill as a result of computerization. Some jobs can be eliminated entirely through the introduction of computing technology, although the extent to which this has occurred has been less than either its proponents or critics predicted. Thus, while there are more jobs requiring highly skilled workers and more requiring essentially no special skills, there are fewer jobs for workers with intermediate skill levels who nonetheless seek rewarding work that validates their talent and intelligence.

It is also difficult to assess precisely the economic impact of the massive introduction of computers into the workplace. Several studies have found that the introduction of computing—despite the significant investment in capital it represents—has had relatively little effect on the productivity of the workforce. This finding is often referred to as the *productivity paradox*. As of the late 1990s, there are some indications that productivity is in fact increasing and that earlier studies may have been distorted by failures of traditional measurement techniques to assess value in computer-related work.

Initially, one of the goals of management was to reduce the size of the required labor force through the introduction of new technology. While employment has decreased in some job categories, it has increased in others, and the overall effect on employment is unclear. Moreover, many computer systems have proven to be far less effective than was originally anticipated. In some cases, the failure of computer systems to meet the needs of the work environment into which they were introduced has been traced to a failure on the part of their designers to understand the precise requirements of the job. Understanding this source of failure has led to a new philosophy of software development, *participatory design*, which encourages greater participation by employees in the design of the systems they will eventually use.

One of the work environments in which the impact of computers has been most heavily studied is the electronic office. According to a 1987 report prepared by the Office of Technology Assessment of the US Congress, 20 million office workers in the USA use a computer as part of their job and that number is surely much greater now. Of these, somewhere between four and six million are evaluated on the basis of monitoring data collected by the computer system they use. This practice has raised new concerns. Electronic monitoring—the process of collecting performance statistics automatically as part of the standard operation of the computer system—is quite widespread. Although such performance statistics can be a useful tool for management in evaluating employee productivity and can help workers improve their own performance, several studies have shown that monitored workers often experience substantially increased levels of job stress. Moreover, electronic monitoring emphasizes those aspects of a job that are easily quantifiable, often at the expense of more subjective measures of the quality of job performance. Electronic monitoring has become a central question of labor policy at all levels of government, and is likely to become more important as this practice becomes more widespread.

In recent years, new concerns have been raised about the possible health and safety consequences of the growing use of computers on the job. The most significant problem for the computerized workforce has been the development of an astonishing number of cases of repetitive strain injuries, a debilitating condition that usually affects the hands and wrists ("carpal tunnel syndrome"), caused by repeated keyboard motions over extended periods of time. Such conditions now account for almost half of the total occupational safety and health claims in the state of California, which led the city of San Francisco in 1990 to pass new legislation mandating special health precautions for computer workers within the city limits. In addition to these problems, workers who use computers extensively also appear to have serious problems with eyestrain, headaches, and back pain. Two studies have also found evidence linking heavy use of video display terminals (VDTs) with increased miscarriage rates. As yet, the data on these health problems remains somewhat inconclusive, but there is certainly cause for concern and need for additional study.

PRIVACY IN THE INFORMATION AGE

Historically, one of the principal applications for computer systems has been record keeping. Computers provide an ideal mechanism for storing large quantities of data in a way that makes that data easy to retrieve or to manipulate. And because it is so convenient to maintain computer databases, the amount of information stored in computers has grown enormously over the last few decades. In his 1983 book, *The Rise of the Computer State*, David Burnham reports that the USA maintains four billion records about its citizens in the form of IRS tax data, Social Security and Medicare records, criminal justice data, and so forth. By now the number of such records has certainly increased. Private companies also record data about individuals, most commonly in the form of credit records. Credit-reporting companies, such as TRW and Equifax, maintain records on the majority of US citizens.

The existence of this vast amount of data raises important questions of privacy. Since the 1880s, the Supreme Court has recognized some constitutional protection for the right of privacy, and there is considerable concern that these rights are being eroded by the enormous growth in electronic databases. An ironic example of the danger was provided during the 1987 confirmation hearings for Supreme Court nominee Robert Bork, who disagreed with the idea of a constitutionally based right to privacy. An enterprising reporter managed to obtain and publish the list of videotapes Bork had rented, which were maintained in the computer system of the video rental store. In response, Congress passed a Video Privacy Protection Act, but has yet to deal with many more substantial questions that arise.

The question of privacy is compounded by the fact that it is easy to use electronically stored data for purposes other than that for which it was collected. A particularly dramatic example occurred when a restaurant chain offered free ice cream cones to children on their birthdays, keeping records on those customers, presumably to insure that only one birthday was recorded for each child per year. Allegedly, this data eventually made its way into the Selective Service system, which used the information to determine when those children had reached draft age. A more common example concerns the sale of mailing lists among companies or organizations. Ordering a magazine, for example, may result in an avalanche of unsolicited mail if that magazine sells its list of subscribers to other companies. In 1990, this problem caused a new level of concern when the Lotus Corporation announced that it would offer to sell companies a product called Household Marketplace containing information—including home addresses, buying habits, estimated income, "lifestyle" classification, and other information obtained from credit histories—on over 120 million Americans. Public pressure based on privacy concerns forced Lotus to cancel the product.

DATA ACCURACY
Civil libertarians are not only concerned that the collection of personal data may threaten individual privacy, but also that inaccuracies or errors in the data may harm the affected person. As more and more data is collected and stored in computerized form, it has become increasingly difficult to ensure that the stored information is correct and up to date. In 1982, the Office of Technology Assessment (OTA) undertook a study of the files maintained in the National Crime Information Center (NCIC) maintained by the FBI. Of the records in the wanted person file, the OTA study found that 11.2% of the warrants were no longer valid, 6.6% were inaccurate, and 15.1% were more than five years old. The FBI undertook its own study in 1984, and found error rates of 6.0%. An internal review of agency operations improved the data quality somewhat, but a second study undertaken in 1988 continued to show an error rate of 3.6%. While this error rate may seem small, the impact of those errors on innocent citizens can be high. A certain Terry Dean Rogan of Michigan was arrested for crimes committed by another man using that name, and because the NCIC records indicated that the suspect was armed and dangerous, the arrest was made at gunpoint. Even after the error was discovered, it proved to be difficult to correct the erroneous entries, and Rogan was arrested four more times in the next two years.

Computers and the Security State
For some critics of privacy policy, the increasing use of computing technology by law enforcement agencies raises the danger of a police state. Courts have ruled that electronic information is not subject to the same protection against wiretaps that have traditionally safeguarded telephone communication, for example. This raises fears among some people that the government may undertake extensive surveillance of electronic communication, leading to considerable interest in encryption on the part of many computer users. A request submitted by Computer Professionals for Social Responsibility under the Freedom of Information Act revealed that the Secret Service has monitored electronic transmission over computer networks, and that the agency has even set up special bulletin boards that they hope will entrap hackers who openly boast of their illegal activities.

COMPUTERS AND SOCIAL POWER
Finally, there is some concern that the proliferation of computers will affect the distribution of power in society, although opinions are divided as to whether the eventual result will be greater democratic participation or the reinforcement of existing imbalances between social classes. Those who see the computer as a democratizing force point out that personal computers have brought considerable computational power into the economic reach of common citizens. With a relatively small investment, for example, any individual or organization can use desktop publishing (*q.v.*) software to produce a high-quality newsletter or magazine. Others counter that computers are essentially a tool, and power will accrue disproportionately to those who have the economic resources to buy the biggest and best tools.

There is little quantitative data available to indicate which of these perspectives is more likely to be correct in the long run, but there are some disturbing trends. Access to computers in the educational system, out of which will certainly come the future programmers and software engineers, is clearly related to economic class. Students in private schools or those in well-funded public systems have much greater access to computers than do students in poorer districts, an imbalance of access that reinforces existing inequalities based on social class.

Conclusions

Although computers still qualify as a new technology in a historical sense, they are no longer the novelty they were in the 1970s. In the intervening years, computers have become integral to the functioning of society as they demonstrate their enormous promise. At the same time, we have become more aware as a culture that the use of computers, and particularly reliance on them, also involves significant risk. That risk is in part due to the fact that computer systems are susceptible to failure, usually as a result of software or design errors. Moreover, the very complexity of the tasks that these computer systems are used to solve makes it unlikely that we can eliminate such risks. But computers also have a profound, and possibly negative, effect on our lives, even when they operate as advertised.

Bibliography

1976. Weizenbaum, J. *Computer Power and Human Reason: From Judgment to Calculation.* San Francisco: W. H. Freeman and Company.

1983. Burnham, D. *The Rise of the Computer State.* New York: Random House.

1983. Pool, I. de S. *Technologies of Freedom.* London: Belknap Press.

1984. Perrow, C. *Normal Accidents: Living with High-Risk Technologies.* New York: Basic Books.

1985. Howard, R. *Brave New Workplace.* New York: Elizabeth Sifton Books/Viking Press.

1987. Bellin, D., and Chapman, G. *Computers in Battle.* New York: Harcourt Brace Jovanovich.

1989. Stoll, C. *The Cuckoo's Egg: Tracking a Spy through the Maze of Computer Espionage.* New York: Doubleday.

1990. Denning, P. J. (ed.) *Computers Under Attack: Intruders, Worms, Viruses.* Reading, MA: Addison-Wesley.

1991. Dunlop, C., and Kling, R. *Computerization and Controversy.* Boston, MA: Academic Press.

1993. Leveson, N., and Turner, C. "An Investigation of the Therac-25 Accidents," *IEEE Computer,* **26**, 7 (July), 18–41.

1994. Johnson, D. *Computer Ethics.* Upper Saddle River: Prentice Hall.

1995. Huff, C., and Martin, C. D. "Consequences of Computing: A Framework for Teaching Ethical Computing," *Comm. of the ACM,* **42**, 10, 75–84.

1995. Neumann, P. *Computer Related Risks.* Reading, MA: Addison-Wesley.

1995. Stoll, C. *Silicon Snake Oil: Second Thoughts on the Information Highway.* New York: Doubleday.

1996. Miller, S. *Civilizing Cyberspace: Policy, Power and the Information Superhighway.* New York: ACM Press.

1997. Baase, S. *A Gift of Fire: Social, Legal, and Ethical Issues in Computing.* Upper Saddle River, NJ: Prentice Hall.

Eric Roberts

SOFTWARE

For articles on related subjects *see* COMPONENT SOFTWARE; MATHEMATICAL SOFTWARE; OBJECT-ORIENTED PROGRAMMING; OPERATING SYSTEMS; PROGRAMMING LANGUAGES; all following articles that begin with SOFTWARE; SYSTEMS PROGRAMMING and USER INTERFACE.

Very early in the development of computers, people referred to the actual physical components—the tubes and relays, the resistors and wires, and chassis—as computer *hardware.* The word *software* was then coined to describe the non-hardware components of the computer, in particular the programs that were needed to make the computers perform their intended tasks. The word caught on rapidly, and was in quite general use by 1960. One speaks of software shops (i.e. organizations that produce software), software maintenance, and, more recently, software engineering. Actually, software is a very general term that includes many areas discussed elsewhere in this Encyclopedia. The most significant are operating systems, programming languages, and graphical user interfaces (GUIs).

Although the word *software* can be used in connection with all kinds of programs, it is usually used to denote programs whose use is not limited to one particular job or application. Thus, one speaks of systems software, of software systems, of mathematical software, of software for business applications, etc.

Early computers could run with relatively simple software systems. A loader (*see* LINKERS AND LOADERS) and a library of subroutines was considered sufficient for most first-generation computers. There were some very significant and sophisticated software developments associated with UNIVAC I (*q.v.*). Grace Hopper (*q.v.*) and her colleagues designed the first, very general, sorting systems, and developed the first high-level languages for business applications. Anatol Holt and William Turanski introduced many software system concepts in their GP (Generalized Programming) system, such as the *extended machine*, which refers to the *combination* of hardware and software that the user sees as the machine for which programs are written. An extended machine is now called a *platform*.

Still in the first generation, John Backus and his colleagues from IBM and from several IBM user installations developed the Fortran (*q.v.*) compiler for the IBM 704, perhaps the most significant piece of software ever written. Fortran (*q.v.*) became the language of discourse for scientific programmers throughout the world and throughout the computer industry, and once and for all established the importance and usefulness of high-level languages.

The separation of hardware and software, the idea that software was superimposed on hardware in order to enhance its capabilities, persisted throughout the first- and most of the second-generation computers (*see* GENERATIONS, COMPUTER). Even though this was already true in some earlier computers, especially those built by Univac, it is perhaps the distinguishing characteristic of third-generation and subsequent systems that the hardware system is designed to operate under control of a rather sophisticated software system. Especially in a multiprogramming (*q.v.*) multiprocessor system, it is essential that there be an operating system that maintains control of the allocation of system resources and that avoids problems of conflict, blocking, and interference among simultaneous users of the system. In particular, the input–output functions and the management of central and peripheral storage are software system functions that must be centralized and carefully controlled if chaos is to be avoided. These topics are discussed in detail in the article on operating systems.

The operating system provides a set of interfaces and conventions for using them that are reflected in all other major software products. A complete software system will contain, in addition to the operating system, a set of compilers (*q.v.*) for various languages, one or more system loaders, one or more database management systems (*q.v.*), sets of utility routines, special- and general-purpose debugging (*q.v.*) systems, and generalized subsystems for applications such as sorting (*q.v.*) and merging, mathematical programming (*q.v.*), engineering design, report generation, simulation (*q.v.*), graphics, etc. All of these must interface with the operating system and its input–output system, and in this sense they all form part of a single software system.

Up until about 1969, it was generally assumed that the purchase or rental of a computer hardware system entitled the customer to all general-purpose software produced by the manufacturer for that computer at no extra cost. The independent software industry, to the extent that it existed, was limited mostly to work on special-purpose systems and to applications programming. Software companies could attempt to produce software systems for sale that were better in some significant ways than those produced by the hardware manufacturers, but this could rarely be done on a profitable basis. The software companies argued that the manufacturers were actually selling software to their customers and including its cost in the price of the hardware. The hardware customer had to buy a bundle consisting of the hardware plus all available software. They urged the *unbundling* of software. This would presumably benefit the buyer, who would have to pay only for as much software as needed. It would also permit competitive marketing of software products.

In June 1969, IBM announced that it was introducing a new policy to implement the unbundling of computer software. With the exception of essential operating system software, all new software products would henceforth be priced separately. The decision to unbundle software was made under pressure as a response to charges of unfair competition, but it was probably not made reluctantly. It must have been clear to IBM that software sales could become a major source of revenue to computer manufacturers. Almost all other hardware manufacturers followed the lead of IBM and unbundled their software products.

Software Engineering

Techniques of software development advanced on an *ad hoc* basis along with the earliest computers. Application of these techniques to the production of very large software systems resulted in unexpectedly large expenditures for the relatively inefficient programs that were produced.

There has been a great deal of thought devoted to the technology of software production. In the third generation of computers the cost of producing software seemed to be excessive, and the methods used often showed little or no advance over those used on some of the earliest systems.

Attempts have been made, with varying degrees of success, to apply the engineering principles that have been reasonably successful in other disciplines to the problems of software production. The most usual proposal is to develop sets of modules that can be used as "off the shelf" components in the development of software products (*see* COMPONENT SOFTWARE). One of the factors that has limited the success of such ventures has been the continuing high rate of technological development of computer hardware. As memory becomes larger and cheaper, and processors more powerful, following the pattern of Moore's Law (*see* LAWS, COMPUTER), software capabilities and technology continue to change rapidly.

A more theoretical approach to the problems of program development arose from the work of Perlis (*q.v.*), McCarthy, Dijkstra, Wirth, Naur, Floyd, and others. This approach is based on *structured programming* (*q.v.*) and on the use of mathematical verification and proof techniques in connection with the production of programs (*see* PROGRAM VERIFICATION). The aim is to produce programs that have been proved to be correct before they are tested on a computer, and thereby to eliminate much of the program-testing activity. Although verification of large programs is still a goal rather than a routine practice, even partial steps toward it pay off in increased precision of software specifications and in early discovery of program design errors.

Since the 1980s *object-oriented programming* (*q.v.*) has become a prevailing form of software design. Like structured programming, it is intended to manage complexity, which it does by packaging data and operations into *objects* that have simple interfaces through which they interact (*see* ABSTRACT DATA TYPE, CLASS, ENCAPSULATION and INFORMATION HIDING). It is intended to facilitate software reuse by clearly separating the interfaces from the implementation details.

During the same period, distributed software has also become important. Since distributed systems (*q.v.*) are typically heterogeneous, platform-independent software standards have become essential, both for networking (*see* TCP/IP) and for the construction of component software that can be used in distributed environments.

Bibliography

Note: There are many books and journals devoted to the software field. Among the most important software journals are the ACM *Transactions on Programming Languages and Systems*, the IEEE *Transactions on Software Engineering*, and *Software: Practice and Experience*.

1967. Rosen, S. (ed.) *Programming Systems and Languages*. New York: McGraw Hill. (A survey of software up to the mid-1960s.)

1987. Freeman, P. *Software Perspectives: The System is the Message*. Reading, MA: Addison-Wesley.

1987. Levy, L. S. *Software Engineering and Software Economics*. New York: Springer-Verlag.

1991. Gelernter, D. H. *Mirror Worlds, Or: The Day Software Puts the Universe in a Shoebox*. New York: Oxford University Press.

1998. Szyperski, C. *Component Software: Beyond Object-Oriented Programming*. Reading, MA: Addison-Wesley.

Saul Rosen, revised by the Editors

SOFTWARE CONFIGURATION MANAGEMENT

For articles on related subjects *see* SOFTWARE ENGINEERING; SOFTWARE MAINTENANCE; and SOFTWARE PROJECT MANAGEMENT.

Configuration management (CM) is the discipline of controlling changes in large and complex systems. Its goal is to prevent the chaos caused by the numerous corrections, extensions, and adaptations that are applied to any large system over its lifetime. The goal of CM is to ensure a systematic and traceable development process, so that a system is in a well-defined state with accurate specifications and verified quality attributes at all times.

CM was first developed in the aerospace industry in the 1950s, when production of spacecraft experienced difficulties caused by inadequately documented engineering changes. *Software Configuration Management* (SCM) is CM tailored to systems, or portions of systems, that consist predominantly of software (Bersoff *et al.*, 1980). A major difference between SCM and traditional CM is that software changes faster than hardware, and therefore needs automatic support. Fortunately, software is online and hence can easily be placed under automatic programmed control.

Basic Definitions

The primary objects of interest in SCM are software configuration items, configurations, baselines, and derived items. A *software configuration item*, or simply *item*, is any separately identifiable, machine-readable information unit produced during the course of a software project. It consists purely of information. Examples include requirements documents, design documents, class diagrams, specifications, interface descriptions, source program modules, machine code modules, database files, test programs, test data, test output, user profiles, user manuals, VLSI designs, icons, images, digitized drawings, and sound recordings. A configuration item is the smallest unit of individual change: there are no practicable, smaller units contained in the item that vary independently.

By contrast, a *configuration* is an aggregate of several components, where the components are configuration items or other configurations. A configuration is changed by replacing, adding, or deleting components. An example is the configuration of hardware, software, and documentation making up an entire computer system. Each of the three main components is again a large configuration, ultimately composed of individual integrated circuits, code modules, or manual sections, for example.

A *baseline* is the description of a configuration. A baseline is a hierarchically structured parts list, stating precisely and unambiguously which components make up a given configuration. Since baselines are information units and may change, they are configuration items in their own right. Baselines serve as important reference points in the development of a system: once a baseline is established, subsequent changes are described relative to it, until the next baseline is recorded.

A *derived item* is generated fully automatically from other items. Examples include compiled code, linked systems, formatted text, and test output. Derived items are special in that they can be deleted, since they can be regenerated when needed (provided the inputs are available and the generator is operational). The space/time trade-off between storage and regeneration is handled by the system-building function of SCM (see below).

SCM Functions

The main functions of SCM that have been automated are identification, version control, configuration selection, configuration building, and change management. Additionally, process support tools help teams carry out updating steps involving many items. In software development organizations that are spread over multiple sites, all these functions must be capable of operating in a distributed environment.

IDENTIFICATION

Identification assigns a unique identifier to every configuration item. Reliable identification is crucial for effective CM. A great deal of confusion results if the same identifier is assigned to two different items, for example two different versions of a file. To avoid misidentification, a new and unique identifier is issued whenever an item is changed. A unique identifier typically consists of a descriptive name and several fields with version designators, serial numbers, or dates.

VERSION CONTROL

Issuing a new identifier for every change may obscure relations between items. One may want to record, for instance, that a given configuration item is a revision of another, correcting certain errors. The version control function of SCM records this information. It collects related configuration items into sets called *version groups* and manages the evolution of these sets. The items in a version group are linked by a number of relations. For instance, the relation *revision-of* records historical development lines; the relation *variant-of* connects items that differ in some aspect of function, design, or implementation, but are interchangeable in other respects. Fig. 1 illustrates a version group with two diverging lines of development; one is a corrective branch and the other, a parallel branch. The corrective branch is applied to an old version and merged into the main line at a later point.

For practical reasons, version control also incorporates the identification function by simply incrementing a version number for every new item added to the group. Team members update version groups by following the *checkin/checkout protocol*. Before commencing work on a configuration item, a developer performs a checkout. The checkout operation copies a selected version from its version group into the developer's workspace, as illustrated in Fig. 1. In a workspace, a developer can carry out modifications undisturbed from the activities of other workers. The checkout also places a reservation into the version group. This reservation gives the developer the right to deposit a new version of the item and attach it to the one that was checked out, in a straight line of descent. Other users wishing to modify the same original version can only create branches stemming from this version. Thus the reservation grants the right to extend the development history in a straight line of descent and prevents additional developers from depositing other changes "in between" the original and the new version. Once the holder of the reservation performs a check-in, the current version is copied from the workspace into the version group and linked into the history. Old versions are typically not deleted until it is certain that they are not used anywhere. Version groups with a hundred or more elements are not uncommon.

Version control also maintains a logbook recording the reasons for changes. The log entries typically record time of change and the identity of the developer, plus a short commentary describing the nature of the change. The log is convenient for surveying the changes that a system underwent over time. Version control also compresses the space occupied by a version group using *delta storage*. This technique saves only the differences between versions rather than complete copies. With modern delta generators, space consumption is reduced to from 2–10% of full storage (Hunt *et al.*, 1998). Whenever a version is needed, a decoder program first

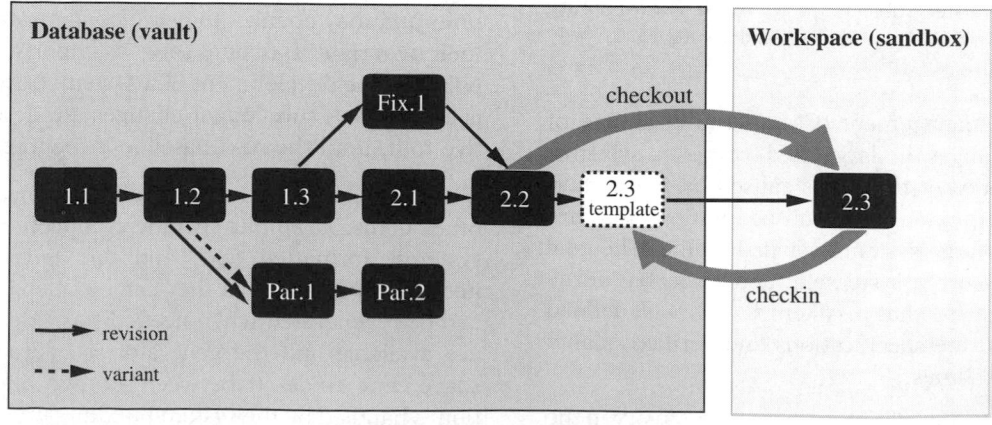

Figure 1. A version group and a workspace.

reconstructs the data from the differences. SCCS and RCS (Rochkind, 1975; Tichy, 1985) are early version control systems implemented with delta mechanisms.

CONFIGURATION SELECTION AND BUILDING

Configuration selection deals with the problem of which changes to include in a new configuration. For instance, developers would typically select their own changes plus those of others that have been tested, relative to the latest baseline. Another selection criterion is to choose all changes current and tested at a given point in the development history. Still another approach is automatic selection, where a configuration program is given a few key software modules, say the main program and a few others, and then searches the version groups for missing modules, using interface information to select the right ones.

Once selection is complete, the configuration is handed over to *configuration building* or system building. This function produces the desired set of derived items. It performs such tasks as compiling, linking, loading, pre- and post-processing, document formatting, etc. Efficiency is important, so building should avoid redundant processing steps. For example, a program module should not be compiled more than once. The Unix (*q.v.*) *make* system (Feldman, 1979) is a classic system-building tool. It is driven by a description of the desired configuration (albeit without version numbers), runs specified building processes automatically, and can even trigger tests. ClearCase (Leblang, 1994) offers flexible selection rules based on various version attributes, such as version numbers, branch names, development state, and ownership, and then runs building steps. Important for building tools is the ability to repeat the selection and the building steps reliably and exactly at any time, so older configurations can be reconstructed for maintenance.

An important step after configuration building is *regression testing*. It consists of re-running test suites after changes, and comparing the results with expected outputs. (The term derives from the fact that one wants to prevent a system from *regressing* to a worse state.) Once a test suite is defined, it is run against all future releases of a software system to avoid having old problems reappear. Regression testing is a mechanical task and can be triggered automatically.

Change Management

Change management is built on top of version control and configuration handling. It requires that every modification start with a formal change request; the individual developer can no longer carry out changes without an approved change request. A change request has a unique identifier and a short description of the change order. Change requests are stored in a database. The database tracks them through a series of states. After initial submission, a change request enters one of the states "approved," "rejected," or "delayed." If approved, it is assigned to a developer or team, and then passes through states such as "in progress," "tested," "accepted," and "released." Change requests are also linked to both the faulty configuration items and the corrected versions. This information can then be used by configuration selection for composing a system that implements a certain set of changes.

The change request database is an important management tool, because it can answer the following questions:

> "Which changes are complete, which in progress?"

> "Which change requests have been or will be implemented in a given release?"

> "Which changes are delayed, and which subsystems caused the delays?"

Without change management, progress tracking and planning remains informal and imprecise, because it requires asking individual workers to determine the change status of a system.

PROCESS SUPPORT

Once change management is in place, large teams may need process support. Process support for SCM helps manage the SCM database with its numerous versions, branches, and change requests. Process support is needed partly because of the sheer number of items that need to be handled, and partly because large teams work in parallel and the branching in the version groups can become unwieldy. Process support organizes branching and merging, tracks change sets (the items that were modified for a given change request), helps with updating workspaces with released changes by others, and organizes merging of the work of multiple teams.

A simple model for process support is the following. Each team automatically works on its own development branch in each version group it touches. Versions are moved from these branches to a designated release branch only after all conflicting changes have been resolved and tested. Teams work on their branches and in their workspaces in relative isolation. Periodically, say once a week, they synchronize their work with others. During the synchronization, process support delivers the appropriate configuration items from the release branch to the synchronizing workspace and helps resolve conflicts by staging merge runs. When completed, an integrator picks up the changes from a team's branches, tests one more time for conflicts, runs regression tests, and then places the changes onto the release branch. Process support thus simplifies dealing with large numbers of items, branches, and conflicting changes.

DISTRIBUTED SCM

Distributed SCM coordinates the work of geographically distributed teams. Distribution requires that the main SCM functions introduced above are all network enabled. In local area networks (*q.v.*), client–server (*q.v.*) implementations of these functions will do, but in wide-area networks the bandwidth (*q.v.*) between sites may not be sufficient. In this case, each site needs to replicate the relevant parts of the database and a periodic update process must synchronize them. Updates that travel over public networks should be encrypted to foil industrial espionage.

Distributed development places a strong emphasis on process support. If team members rarely meet, telephone calls may be difficult because of time-zone differences, and email round-trips may take a day, and informal arrangements on who works on what for how long may break down. In this situation, much more emphasis must be placed on automated support for scheduling, tracking work, and preventing information loss.

Summary

Software configuration management helps control evolving software systems and coordinate teams. It is an established subfield of software engineering, and one that provides recognized benefits for software developers and managers. As the demand for quality software increases, SCM will be crucial for developing and maintaining large, long-lived systems on time and within budget.

Bibliography

1975. Rochkind, M. J. "The Source Code Control System," *IEEE Transactions on Software Engineering*, **SE-1**, 4, 364–370.
1979. Feldman, S. I. "Make—A Program for Maintaining Computer Programs," *Software—Practice and Experience*, **9**, 3, 255–265.
1980. Bersoff, E. H., Henderson, V. D., and Siegel, S. G. *Software Configuration Management.* Upper Saddle River, NJ: Prentice Hall.
1985. Tichy, W. F. "RCS—A System for Version Control," *Software—Practice and Experience*, **15**, 7, 637–654.
1994. Leblang, D. B. "The CM Challenge: Configuration Management that Works," in *Configuration Management* (ed. W. F. Tichy), 1–37. Chichester, UK: John Wiley.
1998. Hunt, J. J., Vo, K.-P., and Tichy, W. F. "Delta Algorithms: an Empirical Analysis," *Transactions on Software Engineering and Methodology*, **7**, 2, 192–214.

Walter F. Tichy

SOFTWARE DESIGN PATTERNS

For articles on related subjects *see* OBJECT-ORIENTED ANALYSIS AND DESIGN; OBJECT-ORIENTED PROGRAMMING; and SOFTWARE ENGINEERING.

Patterns are proven solutions to recurring design problems. The term has a special sense in contemporary software design, most notably in the object-oriented programming community, one that is unrelated to pattern-matching languages or regular expressions. A broad collection of values and conventions guide the creation and use of software patterns. Patterns support, rather than supplant, existing design methods and practices. For example, the *Design Patterns* book (Gamma *et al.*, 1995), the most widely applied collection of software patterns, complements object-oriented design techniques.

The software community adapted patterns from urban design and the architecture of the built world, particularly from works of Christopher Alexander (Alexander *et al.*, 1977). Software practitioners use the pattern form—a stylized presentation of a context, problem, and solution—to describe important, recurring software design structures.

Patterns most often describe subtle structures that tie together modules produced by common design methods. Patterns also help capture domain knowledge for software development areas as diverse as human interface design, development organization and process, and teaching techniques.

What is a Pattern?

A pattern is a description of a mature solution for a particular design problem in a given context. The term "pattern" is used both for the description and any particular applied use of it. It relates a system of trade-offs, called "forces," recurring within a context, to a proven solution that resolves them.

Patterns are written in one of several *pattern forms* (see below). Pattern form helps the reader appreciate the severity of the problem, the subtleties of design trade-offs, and the effectiveness of the solution. There are several pattern forms, but most of them have these components:

Name: Pattern names, usually nouns or noun phrases, become an integral part of the domain design vocabulary.

Problem: A statement of the problem to be solved, usually in the form of a question.

Context: The context in which the problem arises; this often describes assumptions about patterns that have already been applied.

Forces: A description of the trade-offs that make this a hard problem. Forces help the reader understand why "obvious" solutions might not work.

Solution: The solution tells the reader how to solve the problem, in terms of steps that the reader can take using resources at hand.

Sketch: Many good patterns have strong visual analogies, and have a rough sketch depicting major relationships.

Some pattern forms include sections for *resulting context* that discusses advantages and disadvantages of the pattern, so the reader doesn't apply the pattern blindly; *related patterns*; *rationale*; *participants* (a description of the structural elements that participate in the pattern); and *known uses*.

Typical patterns capture mature design solutions to specific problems that elude general-purpose methods. Patterns often incorporate nontechnical esthetic issues.

An Example Software Pattern

This pattern from Gerard Meszaros appears in Coplien and Schmidt (1995):

Name: Half-object + Protocol (HOPP)

Problem: Sometimes objects must appear to be in more than one computing context (address space). How can we make the difference between single and multiple address spaces (e.g. between centralized and distributed processing) transparent?

Forces: The forces affecting the placement of objects into address spaces include complexity, distribution, information availability, cost, and performance.

Many computer systems must be implemented across multiple address spaces for reasons of cost, size, physical distribution, disparity of programming environments, regulatory reasons, and so on (*see*

DISTRIBUTED COMPUTING). Sometimes these systems can be easily decomposed into objects that each live in exactly one address space. Some objects are constrained to exist in certain address spaces by coupling to hardware (such as disk drives or sensors). Sometimes such coupling requires that an object exist in two distinct address spaces at the same time.

Solution: Divide the object into two interdependent half-objects, one in each address space, with a protocol between them (*see* Fig. 1). In each address space, implement whatever functionality is required to interact efficiently with the other objects in that address space. (This may result in duplicated functionality, i.e. functions implemented in both address spaces). Define the protocol (*q.v.*) between the two half-objects such that it coordinates the activities of the two half-objects and carries the essential information that needs to be passed between the address spaces.

HOPP also includes sections for *Related Patterns* and *Examples*.

Pattern Languages

Patterns can contain smaller patterns that balance additional forces, solve further problems, and improve the quality of the design. A group of patterns designed to work together this way is called a *pattern language*. This is an analogy to natural language, where individual patterns are like words and parts of speech, and the language describes how they go together to create meaning.

Pattern languages are *generative*: a pattern language generates a system as an emergent phenomenon. It combines individual patterns to address system issues and issues of wholeness that are more than the combination of the individual cause-and-effect solutions of individual patterns.

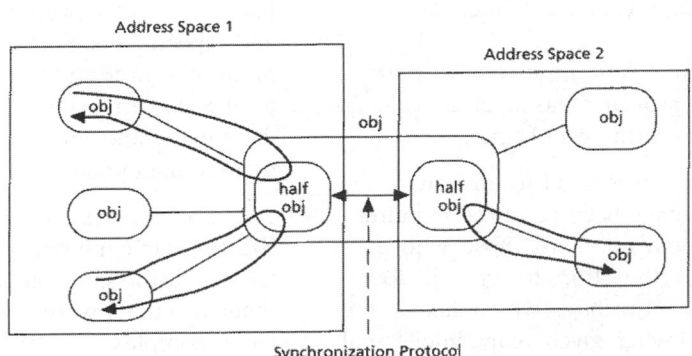

Figure 1. Two half-objects with a synchronization protocol.

History

Software patterns draw on the work of Christopher Alexander, who published a series of books on urban planning and architecture for the built world. His notion of patterns sought to capture timeless structures and practices that served human comfort, putting aside art for its own sake. His claim that beauty is objective is controversial in contemporary architecture.

The software pattern discipline gained critical mass in an "Architecture Handbook" workshop at the ACM Conference on Object-Oriented Programs, Systems, Languages and Applications (OOPSLA) in 1991. People from this workshop seeded a three-day meeting in the autumn of 1993 that crystallized the link between software and Alexander's patterns. That group grew into the Hillside Group, which went on to sponsor the early Pattern Languages of Programming (PLoP) conferences and to publish early software pattern literature.

At about the same time, several software practitioners started to capture important object-oriented "micro-architectures" in pattern form. The most noteworthy work whose foundations date to this time is the *Design Patterns* book (Gamma *et al.*, 1995).

The first PLoP conference took place in the fall of 1994 in Allerton Park, Illinois. The first European PLoP, EuroPLoP, took place in July of 1996. A body of literature precipitated from these conferences (Coplien and Schmidt, 1995; Vlissides *et al.*, 1996).

The Pattern Community and Culture

A pattern community and culture has grown around the workshop-style PLoP conferences. The culture is characterized by writers' workshops used to refine the pattern literature, by games designed to encourage creative thinking, and by architecturally-interesting meeting venues.

The culture is also characterized by a system of values designed to protect the quality of the literature produced and the interests of those who write, review, and use patterns. Major tenets include:

◆ *Aggressive disregard for originality*: The pattern community values proven ideas over new ideas which have not passed the test of time.

◆ *Intellectual currency*: It is good to give away key technical ideas that have been captured in pattern form, but always with credit to those who contributed expertise or the effort to write it down. Unlike conventional currency, which leaves the holder impoverished when given away, intellectual currency accrues to the originator the more it is given away.

◆ *Valuing expertise*: Pattern writers and "pattern miners" are admonished to gather patterns from authoritative sources. Pattern users are reminded that there is no adequate substitute for first-hand experience.

Today, the software pattern community has several workshop-style conferences and has a strong presence in many software conferences including OOPSLA and those of the ACM Special Interest Group on Computer–Human Interaction (CHI).

Bibliography

1964. Alexander, C. *Notes on Synthesis of Form*. Cambridge, MA: Harvard University Press.
1977. Alexander, C. *et al. A Pattern Language*. Oxford; Oxford University Press.
1995. Coplien, J. O., and Schmidt, D. (eds.) *Pattern Languages of Program Design*. Reading, MA: Addison-Wesley.
1995. Gamma, E., Helm, R., Johnson, R., and Vlissides, J. *Design Patterns: Elements of Reusable Object-Oriented Software*. Reading, MA: Addison-Wesley.
1996. Buschman, F., Meunier, R., Rohnert, H., Sommerlad, P., and Stal, M. *Pattern-Oriented Software Architecture: A System of Patterns*. New York: John Wiley.
1996. Gabriel, R. P. *Patterns of Software: Tales from the Software Community*. New York: Oxford University Press.
1996. Vlissides, J., Kerth, N., and Coplien, J. (eds.) *Pattern Languages of Program Design—2*. Reading, MA: Addison-Wesley.

James O. Coplien

SOFTWARE ENGINEERING

For articles on related topics *see* DEBUGGING; OBJECT-ORIENTED ANALYSIS AND DESIGN; PROGRAM VERIFICATION; SOFTWARE CONFIGURATION MANAGEMENT; SOFTWARE DESIGN PATTERNS; SOFTWARE ENGINEERING INSTITUTE; SOFTWARE MAINTENANCE; SOFTWARE METRICS; SOFTWARE PROJECT MANAGEMENT; SOFTWARE PROTOTYPING; and SOFTWARE TESTING.

Software engineering is the disciplined application of theories and techniques from computer science to define, develop, deliver, and maintain, on time and within budget, software products that meet customers' needs and expectations. Software products include the actual program source code and data structures (*q.v.*), as well as the documents necessary to produce these, and documents and interface programs necessary to use them in the intended environment.

The term *software engineering* was first used in the late 1960s in conjunction with a NATO-sponsored conference by the same name (Naur *et al.*, 1969). This and other meetings were held to discuss the problems of large, complex software development projects and to propose strategies to overcome the emerging "software crisis" of cost overruns and reduced functionality in delivered software. Though some have questioned the appropriateness of the term software *engineering* (Shaw and Garlan, 1996), it has nonetheless become common usage for this subfield of computer science. A brief description is given here of the fundamental activities of software engineering and the nature of the processes followed to complete them. Software engineering management is an important part of these processes, as is the pursuit of certain quality characteristics; these will be discussed in turn. Finally some remarks on the evolving nature of the field are included.

Software Development Activities

No matter what overall development approach is taken, there are some fundamental activities that must take place to produce the software: requirements specification, design, implementation, and verification/validation. These activities are not necessarily disjoint in concern nor in time of occurrence.

Specification of requirements involves modeling the system at an abstract level. It may consider just the software system, or may include models of the larger computer-based system of which the software is to be a part. The requirements document *what* the software will do.

The *design* activity defines the structure needed to implement the specified requirements. The design documentation tells *how* the envisioned solution will be implemented by programmers. It includes the software architecture (data and program structures) and the detailed processing algorithms (*q.v.*). The design models the software system again, in more detail than the requirements models. Some classes of software, such as real-time programs and graphical user interfaces, may use special design methods.

Implementation is the translation of the design to source code. The activity is driven by the needs of the particular language chosen for implementation and the tools available for code generation.

Verification and validation (V&V) involves the exercise of the code to ensure it meets the design and requirements specifications. It includes testing of the individual program units, the integrated units, and the software system as a whole. The assessment can be dynamic and static. In dynamic analysis the program or program segment is executed with representative inputs, and the output is compared with the expected results. Static analysis is performed without actually running the program; examples include symbolic execution, "cleanroom" approaches, and formal program verification. In the latter case, mathematics is used to prove that the program corresponds to the specifica-

tion. Testing may consider the code structure within a unit, referred to as *whitebox* testing, or it may disregard internal structure, in which case it is called *blackbox* testing. Generally, individual unit tests are whitebox, while system and integration tests are blackbox. The testing effort involves both objective and subjective means to assess the software under development. Whenever testing finds a discrepancy between the expected and actual results, debugging is used to find and remove the source of the error.

Two other activities are common to most software engineering efforts: maintenance and prototyping. Maintenance refers to any development or modification that takes place after the software is delivered to the customer. (Note that the customer and the developer may be one and the same.) It includes corrections for errors discovered after delivery, adaptations necessary due to environmental changes, and enhancements desired by the customer. If the changes are significant, the maintenance activity should embody the entire development process, though usually on a smaller scale.

Prototyping is a technique used within almost every development of large software systems. It has become even more prevalent in the wake of the recent emphases on graphical user interfaces (GUIs), and is essential for certain application areas such as real-time systems (*q.v.*). Prototyping is sometimes confused with simulation, and in some special cases may be a type of simulation (*q.v.*). Often a prototype has only the look and feel of what the software product will be like and little or none of the functionality, except perhaps the interface functions. A simulation is not required to look or feel like the product, but rather to match exactly the dynamic behavior of the actual system or some part of it. Though prototyping may be used throughout the development process, it is typically a part of the specification and design activities.

The Software Development Process

Every software engineering effort follows some process or ordered set of procedures and activities. Some processes are carefully planned out; others are more *ad hoc*. In the latter case, prediction of results is difficult at best, and often the process being followed is obscure until the retrospective look at the project's conclusion. There are nearly as many distinct software processes as there are development efforts; five of the general software development paradigms are: iterative, transformational, spiral, waterfall, and fourth generation.

The *iterative*, sometimes called *evolutionary*, process paradigm is a flexible scheme consisting of short development "steps" that each results in a software product (Boehm, 1988). The incremental product is developed through specification, design, implementation, and verification. Each of these products is refined until ultimately the final product is achieved through these iterative steps. Often the incremental products are delivered to the customer, whose feedback is used to guide the refinement in succeeding steps.

The *transformational* process model requires a formal specification of the requirements for the software system under development. A series of transformation steps are then applied to the formal representation to achieve the implementation. These transformations can be reapplied to derive an updated implementation if the specification changes (Balzer, 1981). The need for formal representations keeps this process paradigm from being widely used outside of research environments.

The *spiral* paradigm divides the *software life cycle* activities into four repeated stages: planning, risk analysis, development, and evaluation. Progress is made along an outward spiral through these stages (*see* Fig. 1), with the planning stage beginning each spiral loop. The evaluation and risk analysis phases end with a decision to proceed or not with the planned project (Boehm, 1988). The width of the spiral (number of loops) indicates the resources already consumed for the effort. The requirements specification activity takes place during planning, risk analysis, and development. Design and implementation activities are generally in the development stage. V&V activities occur in development and evaluation. Prototyping is often used in early spiral loops to guide decisions for the final implementation.

The traditional *waterfall* life cycle paradigm is the basis for most current practice and has many variations. Its name comes from the progression of activities based on the output of one phase "falling" as input to the following phase (*see* Fig. 2.) It is driven by the need to schedule project milestones which are provided by the completion of documents at each level or phase. A strict adherence to this model has the drawback that no product will be available to show to customers until after the implementation phase. It is also very costly to make changes to the requirements because they are set very early in the process. Some variations include feedback paths from one phase to the previous one to accommodate changes during development, and systems or feasibility analysis as an additional first phase.

Fourth-generation processes are designed around special languages and tools that automatically generate code from a high-level description. Software development techniques are often viewed historically as belonging to "generations." The first generation saw customized solutions by single developers using low-level programming languages. In the second generation, software was developed for multiple users using procedural languages. The third generation is characterized by high-level, general-purpose languages that were used to develop software for a multitude of industrial applications. The high-level, nonprocedural languages that followed are hence usually termed *fourth generation*. These techniques are not broadly applicable, but rather have been established for certain application domains and usually employ a database system to keep track of all development information. The nature of such specialized languages and tools restricts options during development; the intent is to lessen the amount of design and implementation effort necessary to complete the software product.

An important technique common to all these process models is *abstraction*; it is essential for the development of large systems. Abstraction allows engineers to focus on important aspects of the system under development without becoming overwhelmed by details that will be dealt with later. Sometimes the abstraction

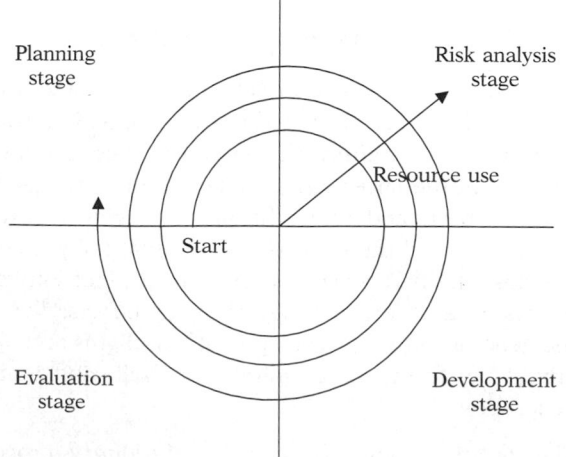

Figure 1.   Spiral model.

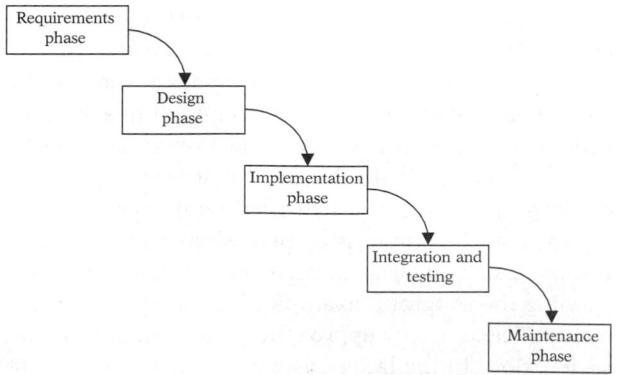

Figure 2.   Waterfall model.

is from a particular viewpoint. For example, the customer's view may only incorporate system level functionality; the software designers focus on the software component modules; a unit tester's concerns are with the strings of bits that implement a particular loop.

One type of abstraction for data definition is the abstract data type (ADT—*q.v.*). Here the type of the data and all the operations allowed on that type are encapsulated within one separate compilation unit (*see* ENCAPSULATION). The access to this information by other parts of the program is restricted, as only the names of types and operations are visible across the unit interfaces. This helps considerably when changes are needed, as all the information and operations are located together, and their integrity is assured. The use of abstraction through ADTs is an important part of contemporary software development techniques such as object-oriented and reuse approaches.

Software development processes generally follow a particular approach or orientation for the system definition and solution. The specification and design may be formal, i.e. written in a mathematical notation with a precise syntax and semantics. Some processes are organized around functions that the system is to provide, or by the flow of information through the system. The structure of input and output data may drive the process, or the focus may be on objects that the system is to include. The orientation of the process determines the particular levels of abstraction used to create the solution.

The focus of effort in early years was on getting a product delivered. Only resulting *products* were measured and considered as marks of progress for the field. In recent years the focus has shifted to the *process* of development. Osterweil suggested using programming languages to describe formally and study (program) the process followed for development (Osterweil, 1987). Curtis and others have described process modeling and approaches to finding the appropriate process for the project and developers (Curtis *et al.*, 1992).

Software Engineering Management

Management of a software engineering project is a challenging task, for the customer expectations are usually high and a new project is seldom like the last one. Management responsibilities include plans and organization, leadership and control, and assessment.

The *software project manager* is responsible for scheduling the development process activities. Before activities can be scheduled, the project manager predicts and plans for adequate resources throughout development, including time, personnel, and financial and physical resources. Without good planning, the "on schedule and within budget" goals of software engineering cannot be achieved. An estimation of financial and physical risk of the project must be made and used to make decisions about the obligations and commitments of the organization. The organizing function of management is concerned with assignments of personnel and tasks to teams, individual team structures, and coordination among all teams. Team structures may have central control, e.g. a chief programmer team (*q.v.*), or may have a democratic decentralized control, or some combination of the two (Mantei, 1991). The nature of the problem to be solved, the strictness of the schedule, and the experience and capabilities of the team members largely determine the team structure.

Software development managers provide the leadership to keep the organization focused and directed. They control the dynamic software process and make adjustments to staffing, schedule, and work environments as needed. A critical means of controlling the process is *configuration management*. Once a unit, such as a document or module, has been approved or *baselined*, any changes must be made through detailed procedures. Software configuration management (*q.v.*) keeps track of what changes have been approved and what the current versions of each program and document unit are. This is imperative during development and continues throughout maintenance of the products.

Timely information about the project status is a prerequisite to making trade-off decisions that will lead the project to successful completion. In addition to verification and validation activities for the software units, software metrics (*q.v.*) are used to measure both the software product, including documentation, and the software process for various attributes. Cost estimation metrics, with size and function measurements, are used to predict and schedule resources, including human resources, for the life cycle of the project. Progress towards the organizational and project goals is assessed by management using systematic measurement. These metrics are used as feedback to monitor and manage throughout development. Most of them relate to complexity of code units and defect appraisal. For example, work products may be subjected to formal reviews or inspections to find defects before testing.

A widely used strategy, due to Fagan (1986), consists of software inspections performed by small teams with specific roles for each participant in the inspection, e.g. author, moderator, recorder, reader, tester. These teams have from 3 to 5 members, and none of the members represents management. The work product being inspected (design, code, etc.) is available ahead of time for each person on the inspection team. The purpose of the inspections is to find errors by reviewing the work product, not to count employee mistakes.

Software Quality Characteristics

Quality is built into the software; it does not just happen to be there because the developers did a good job. Like management activities, quality assurance practices are concurrent with all process activities. Quality is defined as "the degree of excellence of something" (Glass, 1992). This implies a subjective factor; any project can be found lacking if measured against a vague notion of what high quality is. Glass goes on to say that software quality is measured via a set of attributes that are characteristic of high-quality software. Then we build into the requirements the attributes that are desired in the final product. These non-functional requirements are not the same as other functionality or behavior that is required; nonetheless they are part of the specification. The desired quality attributes are part of the standard for measurement on the project. It is not always possible to measure each attribute directly, but some form of relative measurement must be made. Common among the characteristics are: completeness, correctness, dependability, efficiency, maintainability, portability, robustness (the ability to minimize the impact of external factors, such as user errors or adverse environmental conditions), testability, and usability, but the list is not limited to these.

The key to insuring quality is interaction with the customer. No single project can achieve every quality characteristic. Time and financial resources are finite, and some characteristics will be in conflict with others. For example, it is not possible to have a system that is completely portable and still have maximum efficiency for a particular environment. Trade-offs are usually required for the desired quality attributes. The selection of which ones to require in the final product must be based on the value they add for the customer. This calls for continuing interaction with the customer, particularly in early phases, but in later phases also if at all possible. One means to facilitate such interaction is prototyping, mentioned above.

All the software engineering activities described here have quality assurance as an objective. Management selects the process that will put highest emphasis on the quality characteristics desired; software metrics are selected to measure certain quality attributes; life cycle activities aim to ensure the required characteristics.

Software Engineering Evolution

During its short life, the field of software engineering has been consumed with the search for the best method to develop software—all software. If these past 40 years have taught us anything it is that there is "no silver bullet" that will work for all organizations and for all projects (Brooks, 1995). Rather, the target is continually moving and therefore requires flexible, yet disciplined approaches that include feedback and proper adjustment of the development process throughout the product life cycle.

Industry and government have collaborated to research and develop methods and tools for implementing large, high-quality, software-intensive systems. Among these efforts are the Software Productivity Consortium (SPC) in Herndon, VA, Microelectronics and Computer Technology Corporation (MCC) in Austin, TX, and the Software Engineering Institute (SEI—*q.v.*) in Pittsburgh, PA. Though MCC curtailed software research in the early 1990s, the contributions of these and other collaborations have led to many new approaches and have had the intention of hastening the transfer of technology from the drawing board into actual industry practice (Gibson *et al.*, 1994).

In the early 1990s the SEI established a method for assessing the capability of an organization to develop software. This Capability Maturity Model (CMM) provides a framework for organizations to improve their development process. The five levels of maturity are shown in Fig. 3. The CMM defines key processes associated with the five levels which suggest areas for improvement to advance to that maturity level. Qualification for any level implies that the process embodies all the key processes of the lower numbered levels. Organizations are assessed by outside professionals to determine the level of the process they use. They are encouraged to improve their process, even if they have been assessed at level 5 (optimizing), where continuous improvement is a way of doing business. Note that the capability is evaluated, not the results. Even processes at the initial level may sometimes produce fine software, but this fortunate result is difficult to predict (Paulk *et al.*, 1993).

The CMM work has spawned a number of improvement initiatives. Representatives from industry *software engineering process groups* hold regional and

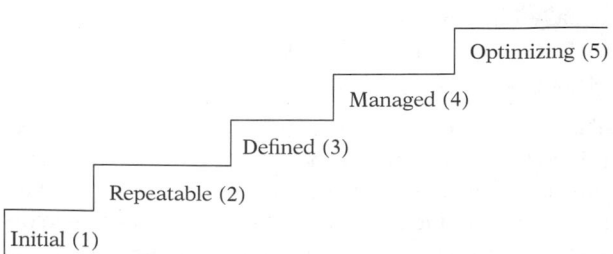

Figure 3. Capability maturity levels.

national meetings to discuss experiences with CMM and process improvement. The Personal Software Process extends the CMM concepts to the practices of individual engineers. The personal process that each engineer uses for development tasks can be assessed and improved through this evolutionary approach (Humphrey, 1996).

Practice in some companies includes company-wide standards for documents and processes. Though the profession as a whole lacks much in the way of standard practices, there are published standards for the professional community that include terminology, procedures for documenting requirements, and certain language syntax, for example those in IEEE (1994).

Probably the best evidence for the evolution of software engineering practice is the availability of Computer-Aided Software Engineering (CASE—*q.v.*) tools to support process activities. Some tools are for general use, while others support a particular technique or methodology. In fact, some methods would not be practical were it not for tool support (for example fourth-generation techniques). There are tools for management activities, such as configuration management, cost estimation, and scheduling; documentation tools, such as editors; design tools, such as rapid prototyping and modeling and simulation tools; programming aids, such as debuggers and code generators; testing tools; and maintenance tools. Some CASE environments have integrated tools for the whole development effort. These tool suites work in the same machine environment and accept the same data formats. They usually include configuration management tools to track intermediate products throughout development.

As the software engineering field evolves, different problems influence the focus of research and development. Over time, the dependability characteristic has expanded to include not only reliability but also issues of the safe operation of software-intensive systems. Software reusability (*q.v.*) has become an important quality characteristic, as more projects hope to have off-the-shelf components that can be reused for many software systems. Reverse engineering techniques are being developed to facilitate the maintenance of older systems for which development documentation does not exist or does not match the current evolved system.

Much progress has been made from the early days of programming; however, the discipline of software engineering still fails to influence sufficiently many actual practices. Despite collaborative endeavors, the transfer of new technologies from the research environment to industrial practice remains slow. As with any young field, more challenges remain. Formal analysis techniques, measurement techniques for process and quality characteristics, and tools for analysis and measurement are needed. Integration of software systems with other engineered systems is a difficult problem for the software engineering field, as is coping with the dynamic changes in customer needs. Solutions to these and other challenges will be found as software engineering evolution continues.

Bibliography

1969. Naur, P., and Randell, B. (eds.) *Software Engineering: A Report on a Conference Sponsored by the NATO Science Committee.* Brussels: Scientific Affairs Division, NATO.
1981. Balzer, R. "Transformational Implementation: An Example," *IEEE Transactions on Software Engineering,* **SE-7**, *1*, 3–14.
1986. Fagan, M. "Advances in Software Inspections," *IEEE Transactions on Software Engineering,* **SE-12**, 7, 744–751.
1987. Osterweil, L. "Software Processes are Software Too," *Proceedings of the 9th International Conference on Software Engineering,* Monterey, CA, 2–13.
1988. Boehm, B. "A Spiral Model of Software Development and Enhancement," *IEEE Computer,* **21**, 5, 61–72.
1991. Mantei, M. "The Effect of Programming Team Structures on Programming Tasks," *Comm. of the ACM,* **24**, 3, 106–113.
1992. Curtis, B., Kellner, M. I., and Over, J. "Process Modeling," *Comm. of the ACM,* **35**, 9, 75–90.
1992. Glass, R. *Building Quality Software.* Upper Saddle River, NJ: Prentice Hall.
1993. Paulk, M., Curtis, B., Chrissis, M., and Weber, C. *Capability Maturity Model for Software,* CMU/SEI-93-TR-24. Pittsburgh, PA: Software Engineering Institute.
1994. Gibson, D. V., Kehoe, C. A., and Lee, S. Y. K. "Collaborative Research as a Function of Proximity, Industry, and Company: A Case Study of an R&D Consortium," *IEEE Transactions on Engineering Management,* 41, 3, 255–263.
1994. IEEE. *Software Engineering Standards Collection.* Los Alamitos, CA: IEEE Press.
1995. Brooks, F. *The Mythical Man Month: Essays on Software Engineering.* Reading, MA: Addison-Wesley.
1996. Humphrey, W. "Using a Defined and Measured Personal Software Process," *IEEE Software,* **13**, 3, 77–88.
1996. Shaw, M., and Garlan, D. *Software Architecture: Perspectives on an Emerging Discipline.* Upper Saddle River, NJ: Prentice Hall.

Bonnie Melhart

SOFTWARE ENGINEERING INSTITUTE (SEI)

For articles on related subjects *see* SOFTWARE ENGINEERING; and SOFTWARE PROJECT MANAGEMENT.

The *Software Engineering Institute* (SEI) is a federally funded research and development center operated by Carnegie Mellon University in Pittsburgh, Pennsylvania. The institute was competitively awarded to Carnegie Mellon in December 1984 by the US Department of Defense (DoD) to improve the state of the practice of software engineering. It was established because the DoD recognized the need for advances in software practice in order to develop higher quality systems more economically.

The SEI works to transform software engineering from an *ad hoc*, labor-intensive activity to a managed, technology-supported engineering discipline. The SEI mission, as stated in its charter, is to

◆ Provide the means and leadership to bring the ablest professional minds and the most effective technology to bear on rapid improvement of the quality of operational software in software-intensive systems.

◆ Accelerate the reduction to practice of modern software engineering technologies.

◆ Promulgate the use of this technology throughout the software community.

◆ Foster standards of excellence for improving software engineering practice.

The strategy of the SEI in carrying out its mission is to address pervasive and important issues that impede the ability of organizations to acquire, build, and evolve software systems on time, within cost, and working as planned.

The Institute explores promising solutions to potentially significant problems, selects the best candidates, and works on them to determine their value. In some cases, the SEI works to overcome the limitations that prevent a solution from being of general use in the software community. Finally, the SEI moves mature solutions of proven value into widespread use; examples include the Capability Maturity Model (CMM), described below, and a model curriculum for a master's degree program in software engineering, the latter of which has been adopted by universities across the country.

SEI activities are grouped into two principal areas: software engineering management practices and software engineering technical practices.

Software Engineering Management Practices

Software engineering management practices activities focus on the software process—the ability of organizations to predict and control quality, schedule, cost, and productivity.

The most widely known aspect of this work is Capability Maturity Modeling. Capability maturity models provide structured, integrated collections of good practices that organizations in the software community can use to improve their performance. The SEI has also developed a Personal Software Process and Team Software Process, which enable individual software engineers and development teams, respectively, to improve dramatically their ability to manage and improve their own work processes.

Software Engineering Technical Practices

Software engineering technical practices concern the ability of software engineers to analyze, predict, and control selected properties of software systems. Work in this area involves the key choices and trade-offs that must be made when acquiring, building, or enhancing software systems.

One initiative concentrates on "survivable systems"—ensuring that appropriate technology and practices are used to prevent successful attacks on networked systems and to limit the damage caused by successful attacks. This work builds on SEI experience with the CERT® Coordination Center (formerly the Computer-Emergency Response Team), which counters intrusions into systems connected to the Internet, identifies security flaws that permit intrusions, and works to eliminate those flaws.

Another SEI initiative focuses on techniques for predicting the impact of software architecture decisions on a set of desirable system properties. Still others address a variety of technical issues: identifying and exploiting commonalities that exist across software systems in particular domains; evaluating and integrating commercial off-the-shelf (COTS) components (*see* COMPONENT SOFTWARE) into mission-critical systems while preserving key qualities; and performing incremental and online system upgrades even in the presence of faults caused by the upgrade.

The SEI believes that software organizations will continue to be expected to do more with less. The SEI program will continue to concentrate on key software engineering problems and on facilitating the widespread adoption of improvements that bring engineering insight and management discipline to the practice of software engineering.

Acknowledgment

Personal Software Process, and Team Software Process are service marks of Carnegie Mellon University. Capability Maturity Modeling, CMM, CERT, and CERT Coordination Center are registered in the U.S. Patent & Trademark Office.

Bibliography

SEI documents are available on line at: http://www.sei.cmu.edu/publications/publications.html, or from Customer Relations, Software Engineering Institute, Carnegie Mellon University, Pittsburgh, PA 15213-3890 (Phone: +1-412-268-5800).

1993. Paulk, M. "The Capability Maturity Model^{SM} for Software, Version 1.1," *SEI Technical Report CMU/SEI-93-TR-024*. Pittsburgh, PA: Carnegie Mellon University.

1995. Curtis, B., Hefley, W. E., and Miller, S. "Overview of the People Capability Maturity Model^{SM}," *SEI Report CMU/SEI-95-MM-01*. Pittsburgh, PA: Carnegie Mellon University.

1995. Systems Engineering Capability Maturity Model Project. "A Systems Engineering Capability Maturity Model^{SM}, Version 1.1," *SEI Report CMU/SEI-95-MM-003*. Pittsburgh, PA: Carnegie Mellon University.

1996. CERT® Coordination Center. *CERT/CC Annual Report*. Pittsburgh, PA: Carnegie Mellon University.

1996. Clements, P., and Northrop, L. "Software Architecture: An Executive Overview," *SEI Technical Report CMU/SEI-96-TR-003*. Pittsburgh, PA: Carnegie Mellon University.

1996. Ferguson, J., Cooper, J., Falat, M., Fisher, M., Guido, A., Marciniak, J., and Webster, R. *Software Acquisition Capability Maturity Model^{SM}, Version 1.01*. Pittsburgh, PA: Carnegie Mellon University.

1996. McFeeley, R. "IDEAL^{SM}: A User's Guide for Software Process Improvement," *SEI Handbook CMU/SEI-96-HB-001*. Pittsburgh, PA: Carnegie Mellon University.

1996. Mead, N., Tobin, L., and Couturiaux, S. "Best Training Practices Within the Software Engineering Industry," *SEI Technical Report CMU/SEI-96-TR-034*. Pittsburgh, PA: Carnegie Mellon University.

1996. Software Engineering Institute. "SEI Strategic Plan: 1997–2001," *Special Report CMU/SEI-96-SR-006*. Pittsburgh, PA: Carnegie Mellon University.

1997. Florac, W. A., Park, R. E., and Carleton, A. D. "Practical Software Measurement: Measuring for Process Management and Improvement," *SEI Technical Report CMU/SEI-97-HB-003*. Pittsburgh, PA: Carnegie Mellon University.

1997. Weinstock, C., and Gluch, D. "A Perspective on the State of Research in Fault-Tolerant Systems," *SEI Technical Report CMU/SEI 97-SR-008*. Pittsburgh, PA: Carnegie Mellon University.

Websites

SEI home page. http://www.sei.cmu.edu.
CERT home page. http://www.cert.org.

Linda Hutz Pesante

SOFTWARE HISTORY

For articles on related subjects *see* DATABASE MANAGEMENT SYSTEM; DIGITAL COMPUTERS, HISTORY OF; OPERATING SYSTEMS; PROGRAMMING LANGUAGES; and SOFTWARE ENGINEERING.

From the outset, the development of software has been directed toward the apparently contradictory, but in fact complementary goals of bringing the computer closer to the user while keeping the user at a distance. The first goal has involved the creation of programming languages and systems to facilitate the development of the applications that make the computer useful. The second has included the operating systems that oversee these applications and manage the hardware and software resources on which they draw. Looking back from the 1990s, one may divide the history of software into two major periods: an industrial period, during which the main areas of software—programming languages; operating systems; data handling; and

software tools, techniques, and methodologies—were established; and a consumer period, during which those products were adapted to the personal computer and to the needs and interests of nonexpert users. The second stage in particular has focused on making computers "user-friendly" by interposing layers of transparent software between the user and the machine (*see* TRANSPARENCY).

The term *programming language* refers to the specific form in which the user actually writes a program for input to the computer. The term *operating system* encompasses the general set of tools and techniques that enables both individuals and computer installations to accommodate effectively many jobs with minimum human intervention, allowing for parallel, sequential, interactive, and distributed modes. Real-time systems (*q.v.*) are also included within the framework of operating systems, although most real-time application programs are outside the operating system. The term *data handling* represents general capabilities, ranging from the early sort–merge generators to the current database management systems. *Software tools*, *techniques*, and *methodologies* run the gamut from subroutines to debugging (*q.v.*) tools (such as program tracers) from programming library support systems to computer-assisted software development environments. The category also includes application packages. Although the software facilities described in this section started on mainframe (*q.v.*) computers, they all became crucial in the practical use of the personal computer, starting in the early 1980s.

Programming Languages

The term *programming language* as used here is equivalent to *high-level language*. The development of assembly language and macroassemblers is not discussed.

Language development started as far back as 1945 with the unimplemented "Plankalkül" by Konrad Zuse (*q.v.*) in Germany. Various attempts at developing a language that was closer to the problem expression than was assembly language were made by numerous people and organizations, as described by Knuth and Trabb Pardo (1980) and Sammet (1969). The earliest *operational* compiler (*q.v.*) for a high-level language seems to have been that developed by Laning and Zierler for mathematical computations, which was running on the MIT Whirlwind (*q.v.*) in 1954. It provided the capability for writing mathematical expressions (with subscripts *and* superscripts), assignment, branching, input–output, subroutines, and some handling of differential equations. However, the first high-level language that received wide usage was Fortran (*q.v.*), developed by John Backus and others at IBM in the mid-1950s.

Originally intended for scientific and engineering computational problems, it has also been used for everything from payroll calculations to compiler writing. It proved the feasibility of high-level languages and thus provided a foundation for future work on languages.

In 1958, a group of Americans (representing ACM) and Europeans (representing GAMM) collaborated on a language for algorithmic processes known as IAL (*International Algebraic Language*); this language was eventually modified to become Algol 60 (*q.v.*) (Naur, 1960) and the earlier version was renamed Algol 58. Both Algol 58 and Algol 60 led to a major emphasis on and work in the area of programming languages by universities and industry. Several languages based on Algol 58 were developed (e.g. Jovial, Mad, Neliac), and compiler techniques were developed. Algol spurred the theoretical and research effort in programming languages, whereas Fortran had far more effect on the practical side.

In parallel with these developments in scientific languages were the efforts for business data processing; the first of these was Flow-Matic, developed by Grace Hopper (*q.v.*) and her colleagues at Remington Rand UNIVAC in the mid-1950s. As the first programming language oriented toward English, Flow-Matic was one of the major inputs to Cobol (Common Business-Oriented Language—*q.v.*), which was developed by a group of computer manufacturers' representatives and users organized in 1959 under Department of Defense sponsorship. Cobol had an effect on the programming of business data processing problems as large as or larger than Fortran had for scientific and engineering problems.

The two years 1958 and 1959 were probably the two most productive years in the history of programming languages. Joining Algol 58 for scientific computation and Cobol for business data processing were Comit and Lisp (*q.v.*), both developed at MIT. Comit was a string processing (*q.v.*) language designed primarily by Victor Yngve for use in translating natural languages. Lisp was a list processing language developed for artificial intelligence applications by John McCarthy and a number of others (primarily graduate students). While Lisp continues to be heavily used by the AI community, Comit was largely supplanted by varying versions of Snobol, which was developed initially by David Farber, Ralph Griswold, and Ivan Polonsky at the Bell Telephone Laboratories in the mid-1960s. Snobol has been widely used in general text manipulation applications, but has been superseded by Icon.

Because the early languages maintained the same dichotomy between scientific and data processing computations that the early computers did, it is not

surprising that eventually languages began to be developed that were meant to be more general. One of the earliest of those was Jovial (an outgrowth of Algol 58), developed by Jules Schwartz and others at the System Development Corporation in 1959–1960. The first language really *intended* for both scientific calculations and business data processing, as well as systems programming (Multics), was PL/I, developed as a joint project between IBM and SHARE (an early IBM users group—*q.v.*) in 1963–1964. The next large language developed was Algol 68 (*q.v.*), which was really a new development and *not* an upward extension of Algol 60. One of its major characteristics was orthogonality, meaning that it defined a small number of basic characteristics and systematic rules for combining them so as to eliminate many arbitrary restrictions. There was also a facility to allow the programmer to define new data types (*q.v.*) and operators on them. Algol 68 was defined with a new (and difficult) definitional technique and this seemed to have discouraged a number of people from seriously studying and using the language.

Beginning in 1975, the Department of Defense undertook to develop a single language suitable for embedded computer systems. (*Embedded systems* (*q.v.*) are those in which the computer is part of a system involving other equipment; e.g. air traffic control, process control, or weapons systems.) The preliminary specifications for this language, called Ada (*q.v.*), were issued in 1979, and the language specifications labeled "final" were issued in July 1980. This was the baseline for a potential standard, future development, and major implementations. Although originally intended for use on embedded computer systems, Ada has been used effectively in almost all types of application, including artificial intelligence and business data processing.

With the advent of interactive computing systems that permitted an individual to access a computer system from a remote terminal (see below), languages were developed for effective use in an interactive environment. The earliest was Joss, developed by J. Cliff Shaw at the Rand Corporation in 1963. The most popular, Basic (*q.v.*), originated as part of the Dartmouth (College) Time-Sharing System, developed under the leadership of John Kemeny and Thomas Kurtz and aimed at making the computer generally accessible to students. The language soon took on a life of its own, as it was implemented in a variety of dialects, first on minicomputers (*q.v.*) and then, most famously, on personal computers, and it remains in widespread use today.

A number of languages have been developed to do nonnumeric mathematics (i.e. formal algebraic manipulation—*see* COMPUTER ALGEBRA) on a computer. The first to receive wide usage was Formac, developed by Jean Sammet and her colleagues at IBM in 1962–1964. It was succeeded by Macsyma, initially developed in the early 1970s at MIT by Joel Moses and others, which gave way in turn by the early 1990s to the powerful Mathematica system developed by Stephen Wolfram and available on a wide range of computers.

Although the languages cited above are intended for relatively broad classes of applications, there has been a parallel development that has gone largely unnoticed or ignored by most computer scientists, namely, the development of languages for specialized application areas (*see* PROBLEM-ORIENTED LANGUAGES). The earliest of these was APT, for machine tool control, developed at MIT by Douglas Ross and others starting in 1956. Other popular specialized languages include Cogo (civil engineering), Coursewriter (computer-assisted instruction), and Atlas (equipment checkout).

From 1967 to 1977, Jean Sammet maintained a roster of high-level languages developed and used in the USA. The number in use in any given year was around 170, with roughly 25 to 30 simultaneously being added and deleted each time the annual or biannual count was made. An astounding phenomenon is that, since the tracking began, the languages for specialized application areas consistently have been about half of the total languages listed (*see*, for example, Sammet, 1978). However, the actual *usage* of these languages is much less than 50%.

As an indication of a value judgment on important languages, the ACM Special Interest Group on Programming Languages (SIGPLAN) sponsored a History of Programming Languages (HOPL) Conference in 1978. The program committee for that conference chose to discuss languages that met the following criteria: (1) they were created and in use by 1967; (2) they remained in use in 1977; and (3) they had considerable influence on the field of computing. The languages chosen were the following: Algol, APL, APT, Basic, Cobol, Fortran, GPSS, Joss, Jovial, Lisp, PL/I, Simula (*q.v.*), and Snobol. Languages that did not meet the "ten year usage and considerable influence" criteria at that time, but did by 1990, are Ada, C (*q.v.*), Pascal (*q.v.*), Prolog (*see* LOGIC PROGRAMMING), and Smalltalk (*see* OBJECT-ORIENTED PROGRAMMING). Papers on those languages were invited for the second ACM SIGPLAN History of Programming Languages in 1993. By the early 1980s, Pascal had become a practical base and spiritual catalyst of language development, just as Algol had been for the 1960s. Initially developed as a systems programming language for Unix (*q.v.*), C's popularity grew with the spread of personal computers, especially in its object-oriented version C++ (*q.v.*) (Stroustrup, 1994). Over the course of the 1990s, functional programming (*q.v.*) languages such as ML have gradually moved to the forefront of development.

In conjunction with the actual development of individual languages, of course, has come the development of concepts that appear in, or relate to, languages. Among the important enduring language concepts are block structure (*q.v.*) (Algol); data typing (*see* DATA TYPES), record (*q.v.*) structure, and separation in a program of the data and procedural aspects (Cobol); the class (*q.v.*) concept (Simula), which has led to modern concepts of data abstraction and object-oriented programming; and the strong data typing mechanisms (Pascal). In addition, the primary concept of a formal technique for defining language syntax came from Backus in 1959 and is known as BNF (for Backus Normal Form or Backus–Naur Form—*q.v.*); aside from the Backus paper proposing the concept, it was first used in the major publication of the Algol 60 report (Naur, 1960). The metalanguage (*q.v.*) of Cobol was developed independently and has been widely used. Research begun in the mid-1960s into the formal definition of programming language semantics based on the use of Church's lambda calculus (*q.v.*) as a metalanguage has since given rise to a family of functional programming languages, among them Standard ML (Milner *et al.*, 1991). Along with the development of these languages have come a myriad of compiler techniques, including optimization. Most recently, Java (*q.v.*) has achieved the longstanding goal of conceptual autonomy by including in its design the specifications for the virtual machine on which it runs.

Much of the early history of specific programming languages can be found in Sammet (1969); for the languages covered by the two HOPL Conferences, see Wexelblat (1981) and Bergin and Gibson (1996). A discussion of various approaches to the history of programming languages is in Sammet (1990). See also Appendix VI for a list of key high-level languages.

Operating Systems

The history of operating systems has so far received much less attention than that of programming languages, perhaps because it has taken longer for thematic issues to emerge from a variety of systems initially developed for a single computer or family of computers and only later, with Unix (*q.v.*) and the various microcomputer systems, designed for portability across platforms.

In the earliest days of computing, each programmer tended to operate the computer alone. Before long, it became clear that it was not an efficient use of a programmer's time to mount tapes, put cards in a reader, etc.; as a result, the separate function of computer operator came into being. However, it was *still* necessary for a *person* to put cards into a card reader and/or mount tapes separately for each job that was to be run.

As computers became faster, the amount of computer time that was lost between programs became significant, so various techniques and concepts were developed to allow efficient use of the physical computer time, which was scarce and expensive in the early days. Although computers had far greater speed and lower costs in the early 1980s than at any preceding time, the uses of computers had also grown enormously and the larger capacity was needed. Hence, operating systems continued to be needed, particularly because the vast speed precluded wasting time with human intervention. Even the desktop personal computers used by a single person, which started to become significant in the early 1980s, required operating systems to enable the user to be effective and comfortable in running programs, managing files, and accessing peripherals.

Around 1956, a simple operating system was developed jointly by General Motors and North American Aviation for the IBM 704. By the time Fortran became generally available, operating systems had been developed that provided facilities such as sequencing from one job to another, input–output control systems (*q.v.*), calling in components (e.g. assembler, compiler), and loading object programs along with library routines. By the early 1960s, batch operating systems such as IBSYS on the IBM 7090 could manage programs requiring differing services (e.g. separate compilers, assemblers) and provide printed results within hours (or days if there were many users). The programmer specified what functions the operating system was to perform via some special cards known as *job control cards*.

Around 1963, Burroughs released its Master Control Program (MCP) written in a high-level language and with facilities for multiprocessing (*q.v.*) and multiprogramming (*q.v.*). OS/360, developed in the middle 1960s for the IBM System/360 (*q.v.*), typified the very large and powerful batch system, although it was actually designed for a broad range of uses (including real time). It provided facilities for handling devices and data, job management, debugging (*q.v.*), and multiprogramming, often with printed results within minutes. It also provided growth, without recoding, across a family of machines by defining a common architecture and instruction set (*q.v.*), to which each machine was made compatible by microprogramming (*q.v.*).

The development of SAGE in the late 1950s demonstrated the feasibility of real-time systems (*q.v.*), in which the computer responds very rapidly (and sometimes seemingly instantaneously) to continuing input. The IBM–American Airlines SABRE system of 1963 (for airline reservations) seems to have been the earliest major system for transaction processing (*see* IBM CORPORATION and TRANSACTION PROCESSING) and was the forerunner of later facilities of that kind, as well as influencing OS/360.

The extension of real-time computing to interactive programming got under way with the development of the Compatible Time-Sharing System (CTSS) at MIT on the IBM 709/7090 under the direction of Fernando Corbató, starting in 1961 and becoming of significant use by 1963 (*see* TIME SHARING). This was the first significant general system with the following characteristics: (1) numerous typewriter-like terminals were connected to one computer and could be used at the same time; (2) each terminal user seemed to have available the full power and facilities of the computer hardware and software; and (3) users' tasks were carried out in small slices of time in rotation at a speed that gave them the feeling of having the entire machine devoted to their service. CTSS provided various language compilers, file manipulation facilities, and user-developed systems. It was used heavily at MIT and proved the practicality of general interactive systems. This capability contrasts with that in a system supporting Joss and Basic, which provided (only) a single language that could be used simultaneously by many people. By the 1970s, the most powerful and flexible of the general interactive systems was Multics, developed in the mid-1960s for the GE (later Honeywell) 645 as a joint effort of General Electric, MIT, and Bell Laboratories; it was heavily influenced by the MIT experience with CTSS.

Toward the late 1960s, the three operating system concepts of interactive, batch, and real time began to merge (although the similarity had been recognized earlier by some people). It became clear that the design requirement for all three concepts was resource management, and that the same basic design involving dynamic allocation of resources to independent processes could satisfy each of the "separate" problems. Included were various facilities to protect (1) the operating system against ruination from accidental or deliberate tampering by users, and (2) one user's files and programs from another user's access or tampering. Among the resources to be managed was virtual memory (*q.v.*), i.e. the facility whereby the user can write a program assuming the memory size is effectively unlimited, seems to have started in the late 1950s on the Atlas (*q.v.*) computer at Manchester University in the UK (*see* MANCHESTER UNIVERSITY COMPUTERS). A virtual memory facility was eventually put into the major operating systems of most of the computer manufacturers.

Since the early 1970s, Unix has become widely accepted as a model of a small but powerful interactive operating system designed to facilitate the work of the programmer. Reflecting the experience of Multics and

Genie, the initial version was developed by Ken Thompson and Dennis Ritchie of Bell Laboratories in 1969–1970 to run on the DEC PDP-7 and PDP-9 computers and proved readily portable to other machines. Blocked by a consent decree from commercializing Unix, Bell Labs made it and its source code freely available to universities, where it quickly became the system of choice. Written almost entirely in C, Unix invited tinkering and adaptation to local needs and thus spawned a variety of versions, perhaps most famous among them the Berkeley Software Distribution. During the 1980s it was ported in various flavors to microcomputers. Unix and related developments, in particular the notion of "software tools" (see below), are described in BSTJ (1978) and in Salus (1994).

At just about the same time, the first microcomputer operating systems, in particular CP/M and various versions of DOS, took shape on the model of then current mainframe (*q.v.*) and minicomputer systems, adopting in particular the hierarchical file structure, file redirection, and pipes of Unix. With those earlier models came also the notion of a layered system in which applications run on a virtual machine that communicates with the real machine through a kernel (*q.v.*). The rapid expansion of memory and processing speed dedicated to single, standalone use soon led to the commercial introduction by Apple (*q.v.*) of the graphical user interface (GUI or WIMP, for Windows–Icons–Menus–Pointers) pioneered at Xerox PARC (Palo Alto Research Center) in the mid–1970s and ultimately stemming from the work of Douglas Engelbart in the 1960s (Goldberg, 1988). While some GUI systems have preserved the user's access to the system through a command shell, others have effectively placed the system beyond the normal user's control, demanding of all applications that they be presented to the user through a standard WIMP interface while at the same time they address the computer through the virtual machine.

GUIs have separated the user from the computer in another, perhaps culturally more significant sense. In creating the image of a "desktop," or more recently, of a browser as a working environment, they have removed the computer itself from the user's view, transforming programming into a set of mediated actions that bear little resemblance to it. In so doing, they have moved beyond high-level programming languages to a point at which programming "languages" are no longer languages.

Details on some of the earlier systems mentioned above, as well as on some of the programming languages, are in Rosen (1967). A brief general history of operating systems is in Weizer (1981). For the early microcomputer systems, see Ceruzzi (1998).

Data Handling

The broad category of data handling refers to the tools and techniques used to manipulate large amounts of data. One of the earliest significant achievements in data handling was the 1951–1952 Sort–Merge Generator developed by Betty Holberton for the Remington Rand UNIVAC I (*q.v.*). Not only did this introduce the concept of a program that would be automatically tailored for a particular set of parameters, but also it helped initiate the development and widespread use of many data processing tools.

One concept that has pervaded work in the data handling area is the need for *data definition* facilities. This concept involves the tools and techniques for describing both full files and individual records (down to each field) as they are represented logically, and also physically. The earliest attempt at such a facility seems to have been the COMPOOL developed at the MIT Lincoln Laboratory for the SAGE Air Defense System in the early 1950s. The COMPOOL provided a way of defining the characteristics of the very large SAGE database, which was used by hundreds of programs. The COMPOOL concept was later carried over to the programming language Jovial. The early work on Flow-Matic provided this data definition facility initially in the programming language, and the first major culmination of that approach was reached in the Cobol Data Division.

Based on concepts from IDS (mentioned later), the Codasyl Cobol committee in 1969 developed their first schema Data Definition Language for defining a total database, and a Sub-Schema Data Manipulation Language (DML) for defining various aspects of the database associated with individual languages (e.g. Fortran). This work has subsequently been updated.

By the mid- and late 1950s, various systems were available for handling large collections of files and producing reports. Report writers started as early as 1956 with the development at the General Electric (Hanford, WA) operation of MARK I for the IBM 702. One of the first widely used report generators was the Report Program Generator (RPG) developed for the IBM 1401 in 1961. In 1962, a Report Writer module and Sort module were added in Cobol 61 Extended, thus freeing the user from the need to have separate programs to achieve those functions. However, many users still use independent RPGs.

File handling facilities also started at GE Hanford, and the two capabilities from there were the forerunner of 9PAC, developed on the IBM 709 around 1959 by users under the auspices of the SHARE users group.

With the advent of the first Cobol specifications in 1960, the need for file manipulation facilities separate from the actual programs could be eliminated because file manipulation facilities were embedded in the support provided by Cobol. But in most data processing environments, installations would create separate files for each set of applications; for example, an employee file was used for payroll purposes and a separate employee file was used for department assignment and transfer purposes. Eventually, it became clear that all of these separate files should be combined into a common framework, and this led to the concept now known as a *database management system* (DBMS—*q.v.*).

There have been three major technical approaches to database management systems. One is based on the Integrated Data Store (IDS), first proposed by Charles Bachman of General Electric in 1964. He proposed a network approach to storing data, and this was used as the basis for the work of the Codasyl Data Base Task Group. A second approach is the hierarchical system in which data is represented as a tree (*q.v.*) structure. The earliest manifestation of this approach seems to have been the work at North American Aviation Space Division and IBM in 1965; it is exemplified by IBM's Information Management System issued around 1969. A third approach is the relational database (*q.v.*) of E. F. Codd of IBM, first introduced around 1970. It involves the concept of linked tables of data where information is not repeated, as it must be in the hierarchical systems.

Each approach has been implemented in one or more commercial systems, has strong proponents and opponents, and tends to be useful in differing application environments, based to a large extent on the preferences of the individuals making the selections. A good technical description of these alternative approaches is given by Date (1981) and in ACM (1976). The article by Fry and Sibley (1976) provides a detailed history of early developments from which much of this section was derived.

By the late 1970s, database management systems were very important as an area of research viewpoint and as a major practical facility for large organizations. With the rapidly growing power of personal computers and their resulting spread into the business office, systems initially developed for mainframes became available in packages that provide tools for establishing, maintaining, and displaying databases, increasingly by means of a graphical user interface.

Software Tools, Techniques, and Methodologies

Many of the useful software tools and techniques for assisting programmers became so ingrained in the 1960s that it is hard to realize that these ideas did not exist in the early days and had to be developed. As one example of an early technique, the crucial concepts of subroutine and subroutine libraries (*see* SUBPROGRAM) were promulgated in a 1951 book by Wilkes (*q.v.*), Wheeler, and Gill. As another illustration, the symbolic assembly program, which freed the programmer from worrying about absolute machine addresses, was developed by Nathaniel Rochester of IBM by 1953; it replaced the concept of regional or floating addresses implemented on the MIT Whirlwind Comprehensive System (*see* MACHINE AND ASSEMBLY LANGUAGE PROGRAMMING).

Among the many other major software tools and techniques, only a few of the most important concepts can be mentioned. Specific early system names and dates are very difficult to identify.

Compilers are obviously a major class of tools, and initially the emphasis lay on developing techniques that provide rapid compilation and object code that is efficient both in speed of execution and in minimal use of memory. The earliest significant compiler was that for Fortran, as described by John Backus in Wexelblat (1981). The concept of a syntax-directed compiler was introduced by E. T. Irons in 1961; in addition to inspiring a great deal of research, it led first to diagnostic compilers that could catch syntactical errors and mismatches of type as they arose during compilation and then to syntax-driven editors which guided programming as it progressed.

The concept of a *list* seems to have been introduced by Allen Newell, Herbert Simon, and J. C. Shaw in the mid-1950s as a useful technique in their work on developing programs that would prove theorems in the propositional calculus. Although a sequence of list processing languages (*q.v.*) was also developed (named IPL-I, . . . IPL-V) to do list processing, only the last became significantly used and even it eventually faded from use, while the list *concept* remains as a cornerstone of software techniques.

Debugging (*q.v.*) tools and concepts were created as part of the early development of programming. The tools ranged from very simple to quite sophisticated, and have included static and dynamic traces and cross-references, simulators, measurements, and diagnostic features associated with compilers. In this connection, it is worth noting that, although testing is related to debugging, it was not until a conference in 1972 that software testing (*q.v.*) really began to be considered seriously as a distinct subdiscipline.

With interactive time-sharing systems came the development of online tools for file management, editing, and rapid prototyping by means of an interpreter, or shell language, operating interactively at the level of the file system and replacing the earlier job-control languages at the user interface (*q.v.*). The concept received full expression in Unix, where the notion of the *software toolbox* emphasized the utility of "little languages" such as *awk* and *eqn* used as successive filters in the transformation and editing of files. Such languages, which feature powerful pattern-matching engines and associative arrays, are now fundamental to Internet browsers in the form of tools like Perl (a successor to *awk*) and Javascript. As in the case of applications, so too programming itself has been adapted to the WIMP environment in the form of tools for visual programming, where syntax-directed editors, compilers, and debuggers work interactively and files, libraries, and other resources are available for selection from menus.

Attempts on a larger scale to make software development less of an art and more of a science or engineering discipline have been under way since at least 1968, when NATO sponsored a conference on "Software Engineering" (*q.v.*). There is still debate on the meaning of this term even in the late 1990s, but it is reasonably clear that it encompasses issues of management as well as of programming methodology, and extends over the full *life cycle* of software development. Research since the 1970s has focused in particular on formal methods of requirements analysis, specification, and design and on the implementation of these methods in computer-aided software engineering (CASE—*q.v.*). Efforts to make the programming process more manageable by constraining the way in which programmers write their code led to the structured programming (*q.v.*) concepts proposed by Edsger Dijkstra in the late 1960s and early 1970s (Dahl, Dijkstra, and Hoare, 1972). By the late 1980s, educational curricula for software engineering—separate from computer science—had been developed at both the graduate and undergraduate level.

A contribution to the developing discipline of programming has been the creation of ANSI standards. The main software standards have been the programming languages that started with the first Fortran standard in 1966. Other languages that have had one or more standards, either internationally or in the USA, are Ada, Algol 60, APL, APT, ATLAS, Basic, C, C++, Chill, Cobol, DIBOL, Forth, Mumps, PANCM, Pascal, Extended Pascal, Pilot, PL/I, and Scheme. Standardization has been under way for various other languages (*see* PROGRAMMING LANGUAGE STANDARDS for a fuller discussion of this subject).

The relatively easy availability of interactive systems caused a large interest in text editing systems (*q.v.*) that could be used by programmers for correcting and documenting their programs. Online editing systems then became widespread for use with ordinary text, not just programs. Major differences among the systems included the types of editing commands they used, and whether the basic unit of reference was a single line or some unit of text controlled by a delimiter (*q.v.*). One of the earliest text editors was the system running under the MIT Compatible Time-Sharing System (CTSS) in 1963. A small system oriented toward text-handling was the IBM Administrative Terminal System (ATS) available in the mid-1960s on the IBM 1401 (*q.v.*). More powerful systems developed in the late 1960s include WYLBUR (Stanford University on the IBM 360/67) and TECO (MIT on the DEC PDP computers). The SCRIPT system developed by IBM on the System 360/370 has evolved from earlier internal versions created in the late 1960s. On the Unix system, Runoff (later, troff), another product of MIT, served as the engine for an extensive set of formatting packages for texts ranging from typed memoranda to camera-ready copy for books, including equations, tables, graphs, and illustrations. The availability of more sophisticated terminals (*q.v.*) and display devices, especially on workstations (*q.v.*) and personal computers, subsequently led to the union of editing and formatting in the form of word processing (*q.v.*), which rapidly became one of the main uses of the personal computer.

Under the broad heading of this section are included application packages as well as the tools for easily developing them. Although some of these existed prior to the PC, it was the advent of the latter that spurred major developments. One of the earliest major systems was VisiCalc for spreadsheets (*q.v.*), which was eventually replaced by programs such as Lotus 1-2-3, Excel, Quattro Pro, and Supercalc. For some of the people involved in the development of these programs, see Lammers (1986). Within the last decade applications such as word processing, spreadsheets, databases, and Web browsers have been integrated with one another to form a single computing environment, in which the users supply input and select tasks to be carried out by the underlying software, often by simply moving one screen object onto another. Whether the users' actions constitute a form of programming is a matter of debate, but it is certain that it requires a lot of sophisticated software, none of which existed less than 50 years ago.

Bibliography

1951. Wilkes, M. V., Wheeler, D. J., and Gill, S. *The Preparation of Programs for an Electronic Digital Computer.* Reading, MA: Addison-Wesley.

1960. Naur, P. (ed.) "Report on the Algorithmic Language ALGOL 60," *Comm. of the ACM*, **3**, *5*, 299–314.

1967. Rosen, S. (ed.) *Programming Systems and Languages.* New York: McGraw-Hill.

1969. Sammet, J. E. *Programming Languages: History and Fundamentals.* Upper Saddle River, NJ: Prentice Hall.

1972. Dahl, O.-J., Dijkstra, E. W., and Hoare, C. A. R. *Structured Programming.* New York: Academic Press.

1976. *ACM Computing Surveys (Special Issue: Data-Base Management Systems),* **8,** *1* (March).

1976. Fry, J. P., and Sibley, E. H. "Evolution of Data-base Management Systems," *Computing Surveys,* **8,** *1,* 7–42.

1978. *Bell System Technical Journal (UNIX Time-Sharing System),* **57,** *6,* Part 2 (July–August).

1978. Sammet, J. E. "Roster of Programming Languages for 1976–77," *ACM SIGPLAN Notices,* **13,** *11,* 56–85.

1980. Knuth, D. E. and Trabb Pardo, L. "The Early Development of Programming Languages," in *A History of Computing in the Twentieth Century* (eds. N. Metropolis, J. Howlett, and G.-C. Rota), 197–273. New York: Academic Press.

1981. Weizer, N. "A History of Operating Systems," *Datamation,* **27,** *1,* 119–126.

1981. Wexelblat, R. (ed.) *History of Programming Languages.* ACM Monograph Series. New York: Academic Press.

1981. Date, C. J. *An Introduction to Database Systems,* 5th Ed. Reading, MA: Addison-Wesley.

1986. Lammers, S. *Programmers at Work: Interviews.* Redmond, WA: Microsoft Press.

1988. Goldberg, A. (ed.) *A History of Personal Workstations.* Reading, MA: Addison-Wesley.

1990. Sammet, J. E. "Some Approaches to, and Illustrations of, Programming Language History," *Annals of the History of Computing,* **13,** *1,* 33–50.

1991. Milner, R., Tofte, M., and Harper, R. *The Definition of Standard ML.* Cambridge, MA: MIT Press.

1994. Salus, P. H. *A Quarter Century of Unix.* Reading, MA: Addison-Wesley.

1994. Stroustrup, B. *The Design and Evolution of C++.* Reading, MA: Addison-Wesley.

1996. Bergin, T. M., and Gibson, R. G. (eds.) *History of Programming Languages II.* New York: ACM Press; Reading, MA: Addison-Wesley.

1998. Ceruzzi, P. E. *A History of Modern Computing.* Cambridge, MA: MIT Press.

Jean E. Sammet, revised by Michael S. Mahoney

SOFTWARE LIBRARIES, NUMERICAL AND STATISTICAL

For articles on related subjects *see* COMPATIBILITY; COMPUTER ALGEBRA; DOCUMENTATION; MATHEMATICAL SOFTWARE; SOFTWARE PORTABILITY; and SUBPROGRAM.

A *program library* is a collection of computer programs for a particular application. To be characterized as a library, such a collection should contain a substantial number of computer program modules designed to solve a wide range of problems in the given area. In addition, the programs in a library should be coherent, both in their external appearance and their internal design. In particular, they should

♦ present a similar user interface (*q.v.*),

♦ have a fixed documentation format,

♦ be designed to be used easily in combination,

♦ be built upon a common set of low-level utilities,

♦ share coding and portability standards.

This article describes program libraries for general-purpose numerical computation and statistical analysis. This includes, for example, the evaluation of the special functions of applied mathematics, the numerical solution of differential equations, regression, and analysis of variance. Most scientific computing facilities make libraries of this type available to their users.

Program Library Development

The first program libraries for numerical computation were written in machine or assembly language for a particular computer at a given site. Probably the earliest of these was a library written for the EDSAC (*q.v.*) computer in England by Wilkes (*q.v.*), Wheeler, and Gill in 1951. By the early 1960s computer manufacturers were working on program libraries to help customers and stimulate sales, and in 1961 IBM released the SSP (Scientific Subroutine Package) library, providing it free with a computer rental or sale.

At the same time, many groups in universities, government laboratories, and private industry began to feel the need to consolidate programming effort into useful libraries. For example, statisticians in the biomedical group at the University of California put together a group of statistical routines known as the BMDP library, the first edition appearing in 1961. Other statistical libraries originating in the early 1960s were SPSS (Statistical Package for the Social Sciences), originally written at Stanford University and further developed by the National Opinion Research Center at the University of Chicago, and SAS (Statistical Analysis System), developed at North Carolina State. Each of these is now supported commercially. By the late 1960s software library development was also occurring in the private sector, e.g. at Boeing and Monsanto, although the resulting libraries were primarily for internal use.

Libraries for numerical computation were also being built in England during this period. One was developed in 1963 for the IBM Stretch (*q.v.*) computer at the Harwell Atomic Energy Research Establishment; in 1967 the library was converted to the IBM 360; its successor remains available today. In 1970, six British computing centers began an effort to develop a library for their ICL 1906A/S computers, and in 1971 Mark 1 of the NAG (Nottingham Algorithms Group) library was released. Implementation for other computer systems followed, and, by 1976, a non-profit company, Numerical Algorithms Group Ltd, had been formed to continue development and distribution. The NAG effort continues to be characterized by close collaboration between a full-time coordination staff and a large number of specialists in numerical and statistical analysis in university and government research institutions worldwide. NAG now markets general-purpose numerical libraries in Fortran (*q.v.*), C (*q.v.*), and Ada (*q.v.*), as well as specialized libraries for parallel computing and other mathematical topics.

Probably the first commercial venture formed exclusively to market a general-purpose mathematical subroutine library was IMSL (International Mathematical and Statistical Libraries), which was incorporated in 1970. The next year IMSL released a library for the IBM 360/370 class of computers and sold seven copies. By 1976, when the company showed its first profit, it had 430 customers using its library on seven different computer systems. Today the IMSL Libraries are developed and marketed by Visual Numerics, Inc., which offers Fortran and C implementations for some 35 computer platforms, as well as specialized libraries for graphics and parallel and distributed computing.

In the early 1970s, the NATS (National Activity to Test Software) group was established at Argonne Laboratory under government and university sponsorship to produce quality software for specific areas of numerical computation. Two packages were produced by this project, EISPACK for eigenvalue–eigenvector computation (1972) and FUNPACK for special function evaluation (1975). The software produced by the NATS effort was very well received, its high standards for performance, transportability, testing, certification, documentation, and dissemination establishing a paradigm for subsequent numerical software development efforts; see Table 1 for a partial list.

Table 1. Some PACKs for Numerical Computation[1]

Name	Year[2]	Size[3]	Purpose
EISPACK	1972	70	Matrix eigenvalue problems
FISHPAK	1975	19	Separable elliptic partial differential equations
ELLPACK	1977	49	Elliptic partial differential equations
BLAS	1979	42	Elementary vector operations
LINPACK	1979	164	Matrix factorizations, linear systems, determinants, inverses
FNLIB	1979	204	Elementary and special functions
MINPACK	1980	10	Nonlinear systems and nonlinear least squares problems
FFTPACK	1982	18	Fast Fourier and related transforms
QUADPACK	1983	68	Numerical evaluation of one-dimensional integrals
ODEPACK	1983	6	Systems of ordinary differential equations
BLAS 2	1988	27	Elementary matrix–vector operations
BLAS 3	1990	48	Elementary matrix–matrix operations
LAPACK	1992	598	Numerical linear algebra
SCALAPACK	1995	26	Distributed numerical linear algebra

[1] Most of these packages are available from *netlib* at http://www.netlib.org.
[2] Date of first release.
[3] Number of user-callable subprograms in 1999.

Excellent public domain packages such as these have greatly influenced program library development, and many of them have been incorporated into larger, more widely distributed libraries, both public domain and commercial. Their availability, in fact, was one of the prime motivations for the development of the SLATEC (Sandia National Laboratory Albuquerque–Los Alamos National Laboratory–Air Force Weapons Laboratory Technical Exchange Committee) library. (Sandia National Laboratory Livermore, Lawrence Livermore National Laboratory, the National Institute of Standards and Technology, and Oak Ridge National Laboratory were also partners in the project.) These groups wished to integrate this software into a new highly portable common mathematical library which would be (a) free of licensing restrictions for use within the laboratories, (b) supported jointly, thus reducing local library maintenance costs, (c) immediately available on newly acquired supercomputer systems, and (d) an aid to the interchange of application software among the labs. The committee, which was active from 1977 to 1993, solicited software for inclusion, and developed and enforced standards for portability, documentation, and testing. The library was highly successful, and is still widely used today.

Traditionally, the interface to mathematical and statistical libraries has been the procedure call, typically in Fortran. This requires that users write a calling program (usually) in the same language in which the library is coded. This is ideal when libraries are to be used within large complex applications. However, this method of interfacing with library routines is inconvenient for more casual users who are not necessarily expert in computer programming. This problem was recognized quite early. In the early 1960s the National Bureau of Standards developed a general purpose, interpretive, and portable program called OMNITAB which allowed high-level access to a varied collection of library procedures for statistical and numerical data analyses. A modern version of this program is still in use, and was the basis for the MINITAB system, now available commercially. The development of such high-level user interfaces continued to be important to the statistics community, and all of the original statistical libraries such as BMDP, SPSS, and SAS developed sophisticated user interfaces, including graphics and windows.

The move toward high-level user interfaces for *mathematical* libraries came somewhat later. The ELLPACK system for elliptic boundary value problems, developed in the late 1970s, provided a high-level problem-statement language to describe problems and invoke and compose procedures for solving them. During the same period, Cleve Moler of the University of New Mexico developed an interactive system called

MATLAB to ease use of the LINPACK and EISPACK libraries for students. A much enhanced commercial version is now marketed by The MathWorks. In 1988 Wolfram Research released Mathematica, a system which combined numerical, symbolic and graphical tools in a single product, appealing to sophisticated and neophyte users alike. These events set the stage for the large number of general-purpose mathematical computing systems providing high-level interfaces to rich underlying mathematical and statistical software libraries which are now available.

Issues

We next describe some of the issues which must be addressed in the development and maintenance of large numerical program libraries.

PORTABILITY

The costliness of the effort to adapt libraries to ever-changing computer systems has led to a concern for portability. Although most of the libraries described here are written in common programming languages like Fortran and C, not all can be moved easily from one computer to another; instead, libraries are often provided in a different implementation for each type of computer system. Several things stand in the way of portability: first, the dialect of the programming language in use and, second, the arithmetic differences among computers, both in static hardware and dynamic behavior resulting from differences in compiler-generated code.

Considerable progress has been made in overcoming these problems. Libraries are now usually programmed in standard Fortran or C, and their adherence to the standard can be mechanically verified. To cope with arithmetic differences among computers, machine-dependent code fragments are often flagged to be set by a preprocessor (*q.v.*) before compilation. An alternative technique is to have only one source code, with machine-dependent quantities obtained at run time using standardized function calls. The PORT library, developed by AT&T Bell Laboratories in 1974, pioneered this technique. In PORT, machine-dependent constants are obtained from three Fortran functions, R1MACH, D1MACH, and I1MACH. These routines are freely available (from *netlib*, for example; see below) and have become the basis of portability for a number of other libraries such as SLATEC.

For systems that provide high-level user interfaces to library routines there is also the added complication of interaction with services provided by the operating system, as well as windowing and graphics systems. These are not addressed here.

PERFORMANCE PORTABILITY

Modern computer architectures are complex and varied. Architectural details such as number of processors, their type (e.g. vector), type and size of cache (*q.v.*), page sizes (*see* VIRTUAL MEMORY), etc. can have profound effects on the efficiency of numerical algorithms. As a result, library developers have also become concerned not only with a library routine's ability to perform correctly, but with its *efficiency*, measured in terms of elapsed time and memory usage, as one moves the routine from one platform to another.

One promising approach to achieving what has come to be known as *performance portability* has been to encapsulate low-level, but compute-intensive, operations into standardized utilities which have good generic implementations, but which can be optimized for each platform. This was pioneered by the Basic Linear Algebra Subprograms (BLAS), released in 1979, which formed the basis for LINPACK. These low-level vector functions provided a degree of performance portability between scalar systems and early vector processors like the CRAY I and the Cyber 205. Modern symmetric multiprocessor systems and cache-based processors require the encapsulation of higher-level operations to achieve effective performance portability. This has led to the development of the Level 2 and Level 3 BLAS, which provide matrix–vector and matrix–matrix operations; these form the basis for LAPACK. Many computer manufacturers have provided optimized BLAS for their systems, and these are used in many libraries.

ERROR HANDLING

In order to protect users from program failure and from their own programming errors, the best quality program libraries do careful error checking. Both the legality of the input parameters to a subprogram and the validity of the computation process must be scrutinized. Some errors must be signaled as *fatal* whereas others can be designated as less serious. Unfortunately, no standard has been adopted for error handling, and procedures vary from one library to another. Within a given library, however, errors are most often reported through a fixed error handler. Users can often control the behavior of the handler as a function of the error severity. In some cases it is reasonable to print a notification of a fatal error and abort the program, while in other cases users need the flexibility to regain control of execution with an error flag set so that they can take appropriate action. Good error handlers provide both of these mechanisms.

DOCUMENTATION

A program library is of no use unless it is supported by documentation explaining how to use each program.

The purpose of the program, its input and output parameters, and possible error situations must be clearly described. Most libraries have detailed manuals which provide this information, as well as extensive background on the problems addressed.

Increasingly, library documentation is being kept on-line, permitting users to access the information interactively. In some cases, as with the SLATEC library, documentation is provided only in machine-readable form (*q.v.*). Because of this, SLATEC established rigid documentation standards for subprograms accepted into their library. The *SLATEC Prologue*, which is included in each subprogram, includes sections on purpose, problem classification, precision, keywords, authors, description, related routines, references, routines called, and revision history. Such standards greatly ease the integration of online documentation into local systems.

Many libraries now provide separate interactive online documentation systems employing keyword search, problem classifications, and decision trees to help users locate appropriate software. The National Institute of Standards and Technology Guide to Available Mathematical Software (GAMS) problem classification system is in widespread use for this purpose. This system is the basis for an online software advisory system which integrates information about software in more than 100 libraries and packages; it is available at `http://math.nist.gov/gams/`.

THE FUTURE

Many challenges remain in the development of numerical and statistical program libraries. Among these are massively parallel computers, new computer languages, and network-based computing.

Library developers have begun to address the problem of revising algorithms and interfaces to achieve improved performance on distributed memory multiprocessors. Providing high levels of performance as well as high levels of portability for such environments is especially difficult. The SCALAPACK library represents a first effort to do this for the solution of linear systems; it has formed the basis for several recent commercially supported libraries. The need to integrate mathematical problem solving into applications with very high computational demands is also straining the traditional black-box approach to the delivery of libraries. Such applications cannot afford to map their data into forms best suited to the numerical algorithm, and may need to exercise more control over the process. This is leading to the exploration of new techniques for the delivery of the expertise of numerical analysts to customers. Some facets of object-oriented computing (*q.v.*) may play an important role here.

Library users are increasingly moving to new languages like Fortran 90, C++, and Java to do their work. This is providing new demand for redesigning numerical and statistical libraries to adapt to the new computing paradigms underlying these languages. The pervasiveness of computer networks also opens the possibility of network-based libraries which provide remote access to problem solution services rather than source code for a local machine.

Finally, expansion of libraries into new mathematical and statistical problem domains as well as the incorporation of improved algorithms will continue indefinitely.

Program Library Availability

Table 2 provides current information on the accessibility of the large program libraries mentioned in this article.

Libraries classified as mathematical generally include evaluation of special functions, linear algebra, interpolation and approximation, solution of nonlinear algebraic equations, optimization, quadrature, solution of differential equations, integral transforms, and sorting (*q.v.*). Libraries classified as primarily statistical generally include data summarization, data manipulation, elementary data analysis, statistical function evaluation, random number generation (*q.v.*), analysis of variance, regression, categorical data analysis, time series analysis, and cluster analysis.

Of course, there are many libraries and sources of programs not represented here. This has become especially true in recent years as commercial ventures seek to exploit the booming market in personal computers and workstations (*q.v.*).

Journals in several scientific fields regularly publish algorithms and programs which form the basis for new library routines. For example, the Association for Computing Machinery began publishing refereed algorithms in their *Communications* in 1960, and the *Collected Algorithms of the ACM* contains algorithms published since that time. In 1975, publication of algorithms was transferred to the *ACM Transactions on Mathematical Software (TOMS)*. Similar libraries have appeared in related fields. In 1969 a library of codes whose descriptions were published in the journal *Computer Physics Communications* was established at the Queen's University of Belfast. Although primarily a library of software for physics, many refereed general-purpose mathematical and statistical codes have appeared there. Such numerical and statistical packages developed by the research community are readily available for downloading from the Internet (*q.v.*). Most of the packages listed in Table 1, for example, as well as much additional freely available software, can be

Table 2. Some libraries for numerical and statistical computation.

Name	Version	Size[1]	Area	Distributor
ACM CALGO	1997	775	Math, statistics	ACM, 1515 Broadway, 17th Floor, New York, NY 10036-5701. `http://www.acm.org/calgo/`
BMDP	Classic	40	Statistics	SPSS Inc., 444 N. Michigan Avenue, Chicago, IL 60611. `http://www.spss.com`
CPC	1997	1500	Math, statistics	CPC International Program Library, School of Maths and Physics, The Queen's University of Belfast, Belfast BT7 1NN, Northern Ireland, UK. `http://www.cpc.cs.qub.ac.uk/cpc/`
HARWELL	12	640	Math	AEA Technology plc, Culham Science Centre, Abingdon, Oxfordshire, OX14 3ED, UK. `http://www.cse.clrc.ac.uk/Activity/HSL/`
IMSL	3.0	960	Math, statistics	Visual Numerics, Inc., 9990 Richmond Ave., Houston, TX 77042. `http://www.vni.com`
Mathematica	3.0	N/A	Math, statistics	Wolfram Research, 100 Trade Center Drive, Champaign, IL 61820-7237. `http://www.wri.com`
MATLAB	5	N/A	Math, statistics	The MathWorks, Inc., 24 Prime Park Way, Natick, MA 01760-1500. `http://www.mathworks.com`
MINITAB	11	N/A	Statistics	Minitab Inc., State College, PA 16801. `http://www.minitab.com`
NAG	Mark 17	1295	Math, statistics	Numerical Algorithms Group Ltd., Wilkinson House, Jordan Road, Oxford OX2 8DR, UK. `http://www.nag.co.uk`
OMNITAB	7.0	N/A	Statistics	NTIS, US Dept. of Commerce, 5285 Port Royal Rd., Springfield, VA 22161. `http://www.ntis.gov/fcpc/cpn5314.htm`
PORT	3	373	Math	Lucent Technologies, Software Solutions Group, 150 Allen Road, Suite 2000, Liberty Corner, NJ 07938-1995. `http://www.netlib.org/port/`
SAS	5.18	N/A	Statistics	SAS Institute Inc., Box 8000, Cary, NC 27511-8000. `http://www.sas.com`
SLATEC	4.1	741	Math	*netlib.* `http://www.netlib.org/slatec/`
SPSS	2.1	N/A	Statistics	SPSS Inc., 444 N. Michigan Avenue, Chicago, IL 60611. `http://www.spss.com`

[1] Approximate number of user-callable program modules.

obtained from the *netlib* service of the University of Tennessee at Knoxville and Bell Laboratories (`http://www.netlib.org`). A similar collection of statistical software is maintained at Carnegie Mellon University (`http://lib.stat.cmu.edu`).

Acknowledgment

This article is a contribution of the National Institute of Standards and Technology (NIST) and is not subject to copyright. Certain commercial products are identified in the article in order to describe the history of program library development. Such identification does not imply recommendation or endorsement by NIST, nor does it imply that they are the best available for the purpose.

Bibliography

1951. Wilkes, M. V., Wheeler, D. J., and Gill, S. *The Preparation of Programs for an Electronic Digital Computer.* Reading, MA: Addison-Wesley.
1971. Rice, J. R. (ed.) *Mathematical Software.* New York: Academic Press.
1978. Fox, P. A., Hall, A. D., and Schryer, N. L. "Framework for a Portable Library," *ACM Transactions on Mathematical Software*, **4**, 177–188.
1984. Cowell, W. R. (ed.) *Sources and Development of Mathematical Software.* Upper Saddle River, NJ: Prentice Hall.
1985. Boisvert, R. F., Howe, S. E., and Kahaner, D. K. "A Framework for the Management of Scientific Software," *ACM Transactions on Mathematical Software*, **11**, 313–355.
1990. Dongarra, J. J., Du Croz, J., Hammarling, S., and Duff, I. "A Set of Level 3 Basic Linear Algebra Subprograms," *ACM Transactions on Mathematical Software*, **16**, 1–17.

R. F. Boisvert

SOFTWARE MAINTENANCE

For articles on related subjects *see* COMPATIBILITY; DEBUGGING; ERRORS; OBJECT-ORIENTED PROGRAMMING; SOFTWARE CONFIGURATION MANAGEMENT; SOFTWARE ENGINEERING; and SOFTWARE PROJECT MANAGEMENT.

Introduction

The objective of *software maintenance* is to make required changes in software including changes to documentation (e.g. specification, design, listing, test plan) in such a way that its value to users is increased. Required changes can result from the need either to correct errors or to increase the capabilities of the software. Maintenance is not limited to making post-delivery changes. Rather, it starts with user requirements and continues for the life of the software

(Pigoski, 1996). Even the installation of and changes to a replacement system can be considered part of the maintenance process. Maintenance is a process of change management.

We present a brief overview of the various characteristics of maintenance, relate maintenance as a process to the reliability of the product it produces, and show how product measurements can be used to assess process stability.

Purpose of Maintenance

Maintenance activities can be broken down according to the purpose of the maintenance into the following three major categories: *perfective* (performed to enhance performance, improve maintainability, or improve executing efficiency), *adaptive* (performed to adapt software to changes in the data requirements or processing environments), and *corrective* (performed to identify and correct software failures, performance failures, and implementation failures) (Lientz and Swanson, 1980).

Perfective maintenance restructures code in accordance with structured programming (*q.v.*) principles (i.e. using constructs such as `if-then-else` and a single entry to a procedure and single exit from a procedure). Much early software was programmed before the benefits of structured methods were appreciated. Thus unstructured software ("spaghetti" code) is difficult to maintain because the consequences of making a change are not apparent (e.g. causing an error in another part of the code when attempting to correct an error in a given part). Therefore, restructured code will be easier to maintain.

Adaptive maintenance changes the format and method of handling data to be compatible with the way data is processed in an application package. This need could arise, for example, when a user decides to process data in a spreadsheet (*q.v.*) rather than continue to use the operating system's calculator to make computations on data elements in a text file. The data is now transformed to a column, row, and cell format, whereas before it had little or no structure.

Corrective maintenance changes the code in order to correct a fault or make a correction in a design document.

It should be noted that for the three types of maintenance to be done correctly, both the documentation (e.g. requirements specifications, design specifications, test plans) and the code must be changed so that the code and documentation (*q.v.*) remain consistent with one another.

High Cost of Maintenance

In the early days of information system development, most of the software that was written was new. Programmers had to write programs that made efficient use of the hardware because the latter was the most expensive element in an information system. Programmer salaries were an almost insignificant percentage of the information system budget. Now many years later, when hardware is inexpensive and programmer salaries are high, many programmers are required to maintain these efficient but hard to maintain programs, at considerable expense to their organizations. Unfortunately, these *legacy* programs cannot be discarded because so much of this software deals with the business needs of the organization. This software can be reengineered to improve its maintainability or reverse engineered (i.e. extracting its specifications from its behavior) in an attempt to discover its design rules, but it cannot be entirely discarded. Even if the code is rewritten, the design artifacts, to the extent that they exist, can be valuable to an organization as it integrates new business rules with the existing rules embedded in early designs.

Many vendors produce products that are not domain-specific (e.g. network servers) and have limited functionality (e.g. mobile phones). We call this software Commercial off the Shelf Components (COTS) (*see* COMPONENT SOFTWARE). With the emergence of COTS, much of an organization's software may be supplied from the outside (Schneidewind, 1998b). Yet this alien software must also be maintained along with the software developed in-house. The decision to employ COTS should not be based on development cost alone. Rather, costs should be evaluated on a total life cycle basis and product attributes like maintainability should be evaluated in a system context (i.e. COTS components embedded in a larger system).

Evolutionary Model of Software

Lehman suggests that change is intrinsic in software, and must be accepted as a fact of life, and since software undergoes change throughout its life, there is no reason to distinguish maintenance from initial development. Evolutionary development is inevitable (Lehman, 1980). Furthermore, the very act of installing software changes the environment; pressures operate to modify the environment, the problem, and technological solutions. Changes generated by users and the environment and the consequent need for adapting the software to the changes is unpredictable and cannot be accommodated without iteration. Programs must be more alterable and the resultant change process must be planned and controlled. According to Lehman, large programs are never completed, they just continue to evolve. In other words, with software, we are dealing with a moving target and, in effect, "maintenance" is performed continuously. Lehman suggests that the word "maintenance" not be used and that the term "program evolution" be used instead. This model of the software process suggests that change activity and change management should be an integral part of development and all other phases of the life of software. In this view, a change would be no more associated with "maintenance" than with development.

Relationship between Product and Process Evolution

We can apply this model of maintenance to obtain common measures of product and process evolution. They are desirable because the relationship between product quality and development, and maintenance process capability and maturity has been recognized as a major issue in software engineering, on the premise that improvements in process will lead to higher quality products. To illustrate this relationship, we use product reliability and process stability as defined and evaluated by trend, change, and shape metrics, across releases and within a release of the software. A shape metric specifies the direction and magnitude of the slope of a metric function (e.g. failure rate decreases asymptotically with total test time—Schneidewind, 1998a). Integrating product reliability and maintenance process measurement and evaluation serves the dual purpose of using metrics to assess and predict the reliability and risk of deployment and concurrently using these metrics for process stability evaluation.

Process Stability

To understand the effect of the maintenance process on product metrics like reliability, one would analyze trends in these metrics (Schneidewind, 1998a), looking at two types of trend: across releases and within a release. Either an increasing or a decreasing trend might be favorable. For example, an *increasing* trend in Time to Next Failure and a *decreasing* trend in Failures per KLOC (thousand [K] Lines Of Code) would be favorable. A favorable trend indicates maintenance stability. When the trend in a metric over time is favorable (e.g. increasing reliability), one may conclude that the maintenance process is *stable* with respect to that software metric (reliability). Conversely, when the trends are unfavorable (e.g. decreasing reliability), one may conclude that that process is *unstable*.

The Change Metric

Although looking for a trend on a graph is useful, it is not a precise way of measuring stability, particularly if the graph has peaks and valleys and the measurements

are made at discrete points in time. Therefore, a Change Metric (CM) was developed which is computed as follows (Schneidewind, 1998a):

1. Note the change in a metric from one release to the next (i.e. release j to release $j + 1$).

2. (a) If the change is in the favorable direction (e.g. Failures/KLOC decrease), treat this change as positive.

   (b) If the change is in the unfavorable direction (e.g. Failures/KLOC increase), treat it as negative.

3. (a) If the change under consideration is positive, divide it by the value of the metric in release $j + 1$.

   (b) If the change is negative, divide it by the value of the metric in release j.

4. Compute the average of the values obtained in repeating step 3 for a number of releases, taking signs into account. This is the change metric (CM). The CM is a quantity between -1 and 1. A positive value indicates stability; a negative value indicates instability. The magnitude of CM indicates the degree of stability or instability. Note that CM pertains only to stability or instability *with respect to the particular metric that has been evaluated* (e.g. Failures/KLOC). The evaluation of stability should be made with respect to a set of metrics and not a single metric.

Application of a Change Metric

An example of CM computations for NASA Shuttle flight software (Billings *et al.*, 1994) is shown in Table 1 for the metrics Mean Time to Failure (MTTF) and Failures per KLOC. The CM value for MTTF is -0.060, indicating a slight degree of instability with respect to MTTF and 0.087 for Failures per KLOC, indicating only a slight degree of stability with respect to normalized Total Failures (since large positive values are desirable). The corresponding standard deviations are 0.541

Table 1. Example computations of change metric (CM).

Software release	MTTF (days)	Relative change	Failures per KLOC	Relative change
A	179.7	—	0.750	—
B	409.6	0.562	0.877	−0.145
C	406.0	−0.007	1.695	−0.483
D	192.3	−0.527	0.984	0.419
E	374.6	0.487	0.568	0.423
F	73.6	−0.805	0.238	0.581
G	68.8	−0.068	0.330	−0.272
	CM	**−0.060**	CM	**0.087**
	STD DEV	**0.541**	STD DEV	**0.442**

and 0.442. The large variability in CM in this application is due to the large variability in functionality across releases. The CM is used to assess the long-term stability of the maintenance process, of which this example is only a small part.

Summary

Maintenance is performed continuously and the stability of the maintenance process has an effect on product reliability. Therefore, in analyzing the stability of the software maintenance process, we observe the reliability of the software that the process produces in order to evaluate that process. By integrating multiple factors into a unified approach, we can gauge the influence of various maintenance actions on the reliability of the software.

Bibliography

1980. Bennet, P. L., and Swanson, E. B. *Software Maintenance Management.* Reading, MA: Addison-Wesley.

1980. Lehman, M. M. "Programs, Life Cycles, and Laws of Software Evolution," *Proceedings of the IEEE*, **68**, *9* (September), 1060–1076.

1980. Lientz, B. P., and Swanson, E. B. *Software Maintenance Management.* Reading, MA: Addison-Wesley.

1994. Billings, C., Clifton, J., Kolkhorst, B., Lee, E., and Wingert, W. B. "Journey to a Mature Software Process," *IBM Systems Journal*, **33**, *1*, 46–61.

1996. Pigoski, T. M. *Practical Software Maintenance.* New York: John Wiley.

1998a. Schneidewind, N. F. "How to Evaluate Legacy System Maintenance," *IEEE Software*, **15**, *4* (July/August), 34–42.

1998b. Schneidewind, N. F. "Methods for Assessing COTS Reliability, Maintainability, and Availability," in *Proceedings of the International Conference on Software Maintenance*, Bethesda, Maryland (16–20 November), 224–225.

Norman F. Schneidewind

SOFTWARE MANAGEMENT

See SOFTWARE PROJECT MANAGEMENT.

SOFTWARE METRICS

For articles on related subjects *see* SOFTWARE ENGINEERING; and SOFTWARE PROJECT MANAGEMENT.

Definition

Software metrics are units of measurement of software. Software includes both the product (programs, documentation, reports) and the process by which the product is developed (the software *life cycle* phases of specification, design, implementation, testing, and maintenance). Software metrics make it possible for software to be compared, evaluated, and analyzed quantitatively. Example software metrics and related measures are program size (source lines of code), efficiency (execution time), reliability (mean time to failure), and programmer experience (years of programming in a particular language). Metrics and measures form the basis for numerous models of the software development process.

Background

Recognition of the software crisis in the 1960s brought an awareness of the need for better management capabilities in the production of software. Metrics and models provide the ability to quantify more precisely factors in the software development process so that improvements may be made, more control exercised, productivity increased, and better quality guaranteed. This led to considerable research activity in software metrics in the 1970s, 1980s, and 1990s. This research may be categorized into the areas of process metrics, product metrics, experimental studies, data collection, and studies of large system evolution. Publications in software metrics have been dated back to the late 1960s with an article by Rubey and Hartwick (1968).

Early process models in the 1970s included Wolverton's empirical model for cost projection and Walston and Felix's statistical model for projecting development effort. Boehm's Constructive Cost Model (COCOMO) (1981) was a process model for cost estimation and was the result of experience, empirical studies, and intuition. Development of product metrics has concentrated primarily on code metrics and is represented by the work of Halstead (1977) on software science and the control structure complexity of McCabe (1976). In the 1980s Henry and Kafura, and Albrecht and Gaffney developed models and metrics of modularity at the design and code levels. Chidamber and Kemerer (1994) have proposed a suite of metrics for object-oriented design. Long-term data collection over a period of 10 years by Belady and Lehman led in 1976 to the formulation of laws of software systems evolution and models of software change. Models of software errors and defects have been the basis of reliability studies by Musa *et al.* (1987). The work of Basili in conjunction with the Software Engineering Laboratory (*see* Basili and Green, 1994) is representative of many research groups that rely on the collaborative efforts between researchers and practitioners to define, collect and use software measures in actual software development situations. Fenton, Kitchenham, and Pfleeger (see Fenton and Pfleeger, 1997) have written extensively on the theoretical and practical aspects of software metrics.

Applications

The need for software metrics has been compared to the need for dials and gauges in a nuclear plant to monitor and control the underlying process. Without metrics and measures, it would be difficult, if not impossible, to understand and improve the complex process of software development and meet the goals of software engineering. In practice, software metrics are used: (1) to make projections about management concerns in the software process, such as costs, staffing levels, resource allocation, and completion estimates, (2) to provide feedback during the development process and to signal when standards and practices have been violated and when faulty products need to be corrected, (3) to evaluate the acceptability and quality of products, determining whether specifications have been met and user needs satisfied, (4) to monitor the software process, keeping track of time, staff, costs, and quality of products during the life cycle, (5) to measure the productivity of personnel and (6) to make comparisons and decisions about trade-offs.

Criticisms

Software metrics have been received with a great deal of skepticism by some software practitioners. This has been due largely to poor methodology, faulty data, and a sense that much of the research is *ad hoc*. Many models and metrics proposed by individuals for specific situations and tested in limited contexts cannot be readily generalized to other situations and contexts. Even where metrics appear to have generality, such as size, measures cannot be readily transformed across environments, applications, and languages. Investigators rely largely on intuition and experience rather than more traditional disciplined approaches when formulating new metrics and models. Experimental studies have been criticized for using faulty designs and improper statistical techniques. Much of the criticism is well-deserved, but efforts are under way to improve the situation.

Part of the problem can be attributed to the fact that there is no sound theoretical basis upon which to develop metrics. Software does not have a concrete realization except as documents or bit strings that do not convey the true nature of software (i.e. the dynamic aspects, the interaction with hardware and humans). Software does not wear out or break; its function is frequently changed from what it was originally designed to do. Thus the very ephemeral nature of software hampers research efforts. Fairley (1985) has compared software design to architectural design in the absence of gravity. At this time it is not clear whether the necessary scientific foundation for software is analogous to that of the natural sciences or to that of large, complex forecasting systems. In the former case, there should be identification of a set of laws, invariants, or common properties to serve as the foundation of metrics and models. In the latter case, it may not be possible to describe software completely with invariant principles, but rather to describe aspects of the process and product that can be combined into a general

theory analogous to weather forecasting or economic systems.

Apart from the lack of a science of software, there are also inherent difficulties for research due to the fact that software production involves large, complex systems. This makes it impossible to repeat experiments or try different approaches in order to make comparisons of various methodologies and techniques. Another major obstacle to research and experimentation has been the lack of common sources of data, both in actually developed sample software systems and in records of how the systems were produced and developed. Part of the problem has been due to the proprietary nature of the data; companies do not want to reveal details of internal practices, since it may cause embarrassment in the presence of poor practices, or it may give competitors an edge. It has been only recently that the need for such data has been recognized by industry, with attempts made to develop collection methods that are not intrusive and do not violate confidentiality. Large databases of collected data are also being built and made accessible to all interested researchers on a national basis. At the same time, experimental techniques are being refined so that validation studies have more applicability and reliability.

Example Measures

The following are among the more widely known and used software product measures. The first three are source code measures that are applied to program text during the implementation phase. The fourth measure is an example of a measure that can be applied earlier in the development cycle. The sample measures are used in a variety of metrics (e.g. size, complexity, productivity, reliability, testability, maintainability). Some have been used in specifications to control program quality (e.g. code modules should not exceed 50 lines or a McCabe measure of 10).

The following Pascal program segment implementing a selection sort will be used in the discussion of the measures given below:

```
type
    LISTTYPE = array [1..1000] of INTEGER;
procedure SORT (var L : LISTTYPE; N : INTEGER);
var
    I, J, TEMP, MINLOC : INTEGER;
begin
    for I := 1 to N - 1 do
        begin
            MINLOC := I;
            for J := (I + 1) to N do
                if L[J] < L[MINLOC] then MINLOC : = J;
            TEMP := L[MINLOC];
            L[MINLOC] := L[I];
            L[I] := TEMP
        end
end;
```

LINES OF CODE MEASURE (LOC)

Historically, this is one of the earliest program code measures. It is a simple intuitive measure in which the source lines of code in a program are counted. There are a variety of methods of taking the measure; the most common one counts all lines of program text except blank lines and those that contain only comments. The measure originated in the days when programs were punched on cards and a source line corresponded to a card. In current usage, a source line of code is understood to be a line printed in a listing. Even for such a simple measure, there are difficulties when applying it to different programming languages. Lines of code has been criticized as a measure because it does not take into account the content of the code being measured (e.g. a complex logical statement is counted the same as a simple assignment statement).

HALSTEAD'S SOFTWARE SCIENCE

Halstead (1977) proposed the notion that algorithms display characteristics similar to those of the natural sciences, and attempted to define a *software science*. His system models software in terms of counts of *tokens* in the program text, and, from these counts, measures of length, volume, effort, and development time are derived. Tokens are all symbols occurring in a program including punctuation and keywords. Tokens are split into two groups: operands and operators. Halstead's rules for counting tokens are language dependent and can be subject to the preferences of individuals implementing the counts. (Note again nonstandard measurement across programming languages.) For Halstead measures, the following are defined:

n_1 = number of unique operators

n_2 = number of unique operands

N_1 = total occurrences of operators

N_2 = total occurrences of operands

These are used in the following formulas:

Program vocabulary:

$n = n_1 + n_2$

Program length:

$N = N_1 + N_2$

Program volume:

$V = N \log_2 n$

Program level:

$L = V^*/V$

(V^* is the size of the minimal program implementing the algorithm)

Program effort:

$E = V/L \text{ or } E = V^2/V^*$

Program development time:

$T = E/S$

(S = number of mental discriminations per second or *Stroud number*, usually = 18)

Halstead hypothesized that these quantities could be estimated using only n_1 and n_2 to obtain an estimate of the length, namely

$$\widehat{N} = n_1 \log_2 n_1 + n_2 \log_2 n_2.$$

Tests using this length estimate ranging over a large number of samples show that it is fairly accurate for most reasonable programs (it is possible to construct pathological samples as counter-examples). Thus, simply by observing token counts and frequencies, level, volume, effort, and development time can be calculated and used to predict coding time, program complexity, size of programs, etc. Experimental results show that in some cases Halstead measures are reasonably good predictors. However, there has been no acceptance of the Halstead notion of a software science, due primarily to a lack of convincing proof. The individual Halstead measures are included in many commercial metrics packages and are available for a variety of languages. For the SORT example, the Halstead measurements are:

$$n_1 = 20$$
$$n_2 = 9$$
$$N_1 = 52$$
$$N_2 = 36$$
$$N = 88$$
$$\widehat{N} = 115$$
$$V = 296$$
$$L = 0.025$$
$$E = 11853$$
$$T = 658$$

MCCABE'S CYCLOMATIC COMPLEXITY MEASURE

The McCabe cyclomatic complexity measure is a measure of the control structure complexity of a program that is obtained by counting the number of linearly independent paths through program code. The measure is based upon graph theory (q.v.) and the cyclomatic number of a directed graph. A flowgraph (similar to a flowchart—q.v.) is created from the program text of the target program, and a count is taken of the number of nodes (n) and the edges (e) from the nodes. The McCabe complexity $v(G)$ is given as $e - n + 2$. For structured programs (no `gotos` or backward branches), $v(G)$ is obtained by counting the number of predicates and adding 1.

The quantity $v(G)$ is used in measuring program complexity (more paths imply more complex code), and is commonly used as a basis for comparison in program complexity experiments. Like the Halstead measures, McCabe's cyclomatic complexity has shown good correlation as a predictor in certain specific cases. The McCabe measure reflects more information about a program than the source lines of code measure. However, it omits nesting of control structures (q.v.) and data from its consideration. The McCabe measure for the SORT procedure is 4 (count 1 each for the two `for` statements, one for the single `if` statement, and add 1).

The software complexity measures mentioned above are useful to detect problematic code for the testing and maintenance stages in the software development cycle. But this is generally too late and too costly in the development process, and measures taken earlier in the design and specification phases are needed to anticipate problems. Efforts are currently under way to look for such measures. One such measure, commonly used in data processing environments, is the *function point* measure.

FUNCTION POINTS

Functions points are a measure of the interfaces between modules or subsystems in programs and large systems. The function point measure (FP) is a count of the number of external user inputs, inquiries, outputs, and master files in a subprogram (q.v.) or subsystem. These are then weighted by 4, 4, 5, and 10, respectively. The results are then summed to arrive at a value of FP. For the above SORT procedure, the FP measure is 13 (2 inputs: *list* and *num*; 1 output: *list*). Note that FP can be calculated without having any actual code. The weights can also be further adjusted to compensate for other factors, such as application, experience, and environment. The measure is frequently used in the development of business software and is found in metrics packages that measure commercial software. It has appeal because it anticipates problems in software development before the coding stage is reached. Intuitively, one can expect that modules with high function point measures in the specification and design phases will be more difficult to implement and require more resources. FP has not been used extensively in formal metrics research.

PROCESS METRICS

A software process is a series of activities related to the production of software. A process has some duration in time and process activities are usually ordered by time. The entire development cycle may be considered globally as a single software process or a process may be an activity within the development cycle, such as requirements analysis, configuration management, testing, or coding. *Process metrics* include measures of duration (time), effort, errors detected and changes made. Additional process measures can be derived from these measures and include quality, cost-effectiveness, and productivity. An example of a metric defined for the entire software development process is the Software Engineering Institute's (q.v.) Capability Maturity Model (Paulk *et al.*, 1994) with five defined levels of process maturity. Testing effectiveness and requirements stability are example measures for the subprocesses of requirements analysis and testing.

Among the more common process models are the predictive models that attempt to guide decision-making and provide estimates for future processes. Of these, perhaps the most widely known is Boehm's (1981) COCOMO model, used for estimating the development time, staffing levels, and costs of a software project. The COCOMO model for effort is:

$$E = aKDSIb$$

where E is effort in person months and *KDSI* is predicted size given in thousands of delivered lines of source instructions. The values of a and b depend on the type of software that is being developed and are derived from a set of empirical data Boehm collected in the 1970s at TRW. This effort model is applicable to early, intermediate and advanced stages of the development process with adjustment factors for each stage. Duration and cost models are based on the effort model. Boehm has revised the original model to COCOMO 2.0 (Boehm *et al.*, 1995) to incorporate advances in software engineering technology.

Current Trends

While few metrics are widely accepted, there is a growing awareness that metrics, even in limited cases, can be of value in understanding and controlling software products and the software development process. Increasingly, off-the-shelf metrics packages are becoming available and measures are tailored to suit each individual company's standards and practices. Management is beginning to install integrated metrics programs on a corporate basis that not only apply metrics to individual products and phases of development, but also collect, store, and analyze data taken during the entire development process. Studies are under way to determine the kinds of data, storage techniques, analysis techniques, and collection schemes that can be useful in these systematic programs. The long-range effects of these programs and the data collected should help to identify more relevant metrics and improve models of the software process.

Bibliography

1968. Rubey, R. J., and Hartwick, R. D. "Quantitative Measurement of Program Quality," *Proc. ACM National Conference*, 671—677.

1976. McCabe, T. J. "A Complexity Measure," *IEEE TSE*, **SE-2**, *4* (December), 308–320.

1977. Halstead, M. *Elements of Software Science*. New York: Elsevier North Holland.

1977. Walston, C. E., and Felix, C. P. "A Method of Programming Measurement and Estimation," *IBM Systems Journal*, *16*, *1*, 54–73.

1981. Boehm, B. W. *Software Engineering Economics*. Upper Saddle River, NJ: Prentice Hall.

1985. Fairley, R. E. S*oftware Engineering Concepts*. New York: McGraw-Hill.

1985. Kolence, K. W. *An Introduction to Software Physics*. New York: McGraw-Hill.

1986. Conte, S. D., Dunsmore, H. E., and Shen, V. Y. *Software Engineering Metrics and Models*. Menlo Park, CA: Benjamin Cummings.

1986. Jones, T. C. *Programming Productivity*. New York: McGraw-Hill.

1987. Musa, J. D., Iannino, A., and Okumuto, K. *Software Reliability: Measurement, Prediction, Application*. New York: McGraw-Hill.

1992. Grady, R. B. *Practical Software Metrics for Software Management and Process Improvement*. Upper Saddle River, NJ: Prentice Hall.

1994. Paulk, M. C., Weber, C. V., and Curtis, B. *The Capability Maturity Model for Software: Guidelines for Improving the Software Process*. Reading, MA: Addison-Wesley.

1994. Chidamber, S. R., and Kemerer, C. F. "A Metrics Suite for Object Oriented Design," *IEEE TSE*, **SE-20**, *6*, 476–493.

1994. Basili, V. R., and Green, S. "Software Process Evolution at the SEL," *IEEE Software*, *11*, *4*, 58–66.

1995. Boehm, B. W., Clark B., Horowitz, E., and Westlan, C. "Cost Models for Future Life Cycle Processes: COCOMO 2.0," *Annals of Software Engineering*, *1*, *1*, 1–14.

1997. Fenton, N., and Pfleeger, S. L. *Software Metrics— A Rigorous and Practical Approach*, 2nd Ed. New York: PWS Publishing Company.

1997. *IEEE Software*, *14*, *2*.

Patricia B. Van Verth

SOFTWARE MONITOR

For articles on related subjects *see* BENCHMARKS; PERFORMANCE MEASUREMENT AND EVALUATION; and STRUCTURED PROGRAMMING.

Types and Functions

A *software monitor* is, according to its most general definition, a piece of software used for performance measurement purposes. Like other types of instruments (e.g. hardware monitors), a software monitor is capable of measuring the performance of two kinds of objects—computer systems and computer programs. A *system-oriented* monitor usually measures system performance indices (e.g. response or turnaround times, throughput (*q.v.*) rates, component utilizations), as well as system and workload variables (e.g. CPU time demands, memory space demands, paging rates, degrees of multiprogramming—*q.v.*). A *program-oriented* monitor is usually capable of measuring such program performance indices as execution times, instruction execution counts and frequencies, total CPU times, uninterrupted CPU interval durations, numbers and types of I/O operations performed, and so on.

The main functions of any monitor are event detection, data collection, data reduction, and presentation of results (*see* Fig. 1). A software monitor is either *event-driven* or *sampling*. The basic type of event for an event-driven software monitor is the execution of a certain instruction within a program. This event can be detected by inserting into the program at that location a *checkpoint* (*q.v.*) or *software probe*; that is, an instruction that is executed whenever the monitored instruction is executed and that has the effect of recording the execution (e.g. by incrementing a counter). A wide variety of event types can be indirectly detected by this mechanism; for instance, the use of a variable, the coincidence of the value of a variable with a given value, the updating of a register, the execution of a given arithmetic operation, and so on. System events can be expressed in terms of these program event types when the program involved is the operating system.

With a sampling software monitor, event detection is performed by an interval timer (*q.v.*) that interrupts the CPU and causes the monitor to seize control. The main advantages of a sampling monitor over an event-driven one are its much easier addition to an existing system or program and the potentially lower interference with the object being measured. The main disadvantages are its lesser accuracy when measuring certain types of indices and, in some cases, its inability to collect protected system information.

With all types of software monitor, the detection of an appropriate event causes a certain amount of data

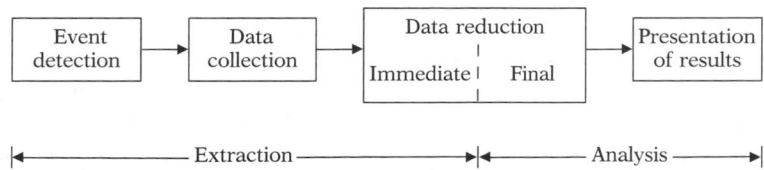

Figure 1. Principal functions of a software monitor.

accessible to the instrument to be collected and possibly processed for reduction purposes. The types of events to be detected, the amount of collected data, and the extent of their intermediate reduction vary with the instrument and may often be influenced by its user. When this is not possible, the monitor is said to be *fixed*. Examples of fixed software monitors are the *meters* (checkpoints that increment a software counter whenever they are executed) and all non-modifiable checkpoints inserted into a program (e.g. those that, within an operating system, measure resource consumptions for accounting and charging purposes). The extent to which monitors reduce data at collection time varies between the extremes of *counting* (maximum immediate reduction, minimum storage requirements, maximum loss of information) and *tracing* (no immediate reduction, maximum storage requirements, minimum or no loss of information).

Depending on the time that elapses between detection/collection and reduction/presentation, a monitor can be classified as *offline* or *online*. In an offline monitor, the completion of data reduction and the presentation of results are deferred until a later time. In the terminology of Fig. 1, the analysis follows the extraction at a relatively long temporal distance, so that, in an offline software monitor, there is no appreciable interference between the two operations. Online monitors are those that reduce data and present results at their full speed, which, for software monitors, is the speed of the system on which data is collected. In other words, in these monitors, analysis is performed on line with respect to extraction.

From the viewpoint of the duration of their operation, monitors can be classified as *permanent* or *temporary*. Permanent instruments are used in continuous monitoring (a fundamental aspect of performance management) and in resource usage accounting (*see* ACCOUNTING SYSTEM, COMPUTER). Since they are permanently incorporated into the object being monitored, their interference (i.e. their effects on the measured quantities) is always present and can therefore be generally ignored, though their impact on system overhead cannot be ignored. Temporary monitors find their main applications in the measurement studies needed for system or program tuning, capacity planning, and benchmark design for procurement projects. Temporary event-driven software monitors consist of removable checkpoints and of appropriate measurement routines called by the checkpoints. The insertion and the removal of checkpoints can be partially automated by an interactive approach. Sampling monitors may be system or user programs that can be started and stopped by their users. Online instruments are mostly used for fast short-term tuning, real-time detection and removal of sudden performance problems (infinite loops, deadlocks), and continuous monitoring. Any temporary instrument may be used for continuous monitoring by leaving it on without interruptions, or, more conveniently, turning it on periodically according to a performance management plan. However, in the former case, a fixed *ad hoc* monitor normally consumes fewer resources than a more general type of monitor; also, in the latter case as well as in all temporary uses of a system-oriented software monitor, its interference with the measured system cannot in principle be ignored.

The amount of interference caused by a software monitor depends on the data collection rate, on the access times of the data to be collected, on the degree of immediate data reduction, on the strategies adopted for storing the data, and on the efficiency of the monitor's code.

The events a software monitor can detect and the data it can collect belong to the class of those that are accessible at the software level. Voltage pulses, control states, microinstruction delays, or contents of microregisters, cannot be observed. On the other hand, variables such as the name of the jobs or transactions that have caused certain events, queue lengths, the names of the most frequently accessed files can only, or much more easily, be measured by a software monitor than by a hardware monitor. All types of software monitor are to some extent dependent on the hardware–software system on which they run. Thus, they are much less portable than hardware monitors.

Most existing event-driven software monitors have been constructed by operating system manufacturers. It is clearly much easier for the designers of a system than for outsiders to instrument it with suitable checkpoints. These monitors, like fixed instruments also based on the checkpoint technique, were originally implemented for the exclusive use of the manufacturer, but later have been distributed to the customers for their own performance monitoring or measurement projects. In some cases, the user is allowed to specify or select both the data collection operations that are to take place upon detection of the system events corresponding to the fixed checkpoints, and the subsequent data reductions. In the case of fixed monitors, such as those that collect accounting data, the user can specify the desired reduction operations; commercial software packages exist that exploit either possibility. Most of the commercial software monitors, however, and some of those offered by system manufacturers, are of the sampling type. The first system-oriented sampling monitor appeared on the market in 1968, and was immediately followed by the first program-oriented sampling monitor. Several years later, the first online system-oriented software monitor, of the sampling type, was announced.

Examples

Three simple examples of applications of software monitors are given below.

Measurement of device utilization during a time interval of duration T. It is assumed that the operating system keeps the information about the state (busy or idle) of the device in a memory bit S.

An event-driven monitor to solve the problem consists of two checkpoints, C_1 and C_2, and two program variables, A and B. The two checkpoints are inserted into the operating system code immediately after the instructions that update the contents of S.

$$\vdots$$
$$S \leftarrow \text{busy}$$
$$C_1: \quad B \leftarrow \text{clock}$$
$$\vdots$$
$$S \leftarrow \text{idle}$$
$$C_2: \quad A \leftarrow A + \text{clock} - B$$
$$\vdots$$

Initialization: $A \leftarrow 0$. Computation of the utilization (at the end of time interval T): $u = A/T$.

A sampling monitor samples the contents of S periodically (or at random times) N times during the interval: if $N_1 \leq N$ is the number of times S was found to contain "busy," then $u \cong N_1/N$.

Measurement of the mean length of a queue. It is assumed that the operating system keeps the instantaneous length of the queue in variable Q.

An event-driven monitor uses one checkpoint C consisting of two statements and two dedicated memory locations A and B. C is inserted into the operating system code just before the point at which an item is added to or deleted from the queue:

$$\vdots$$
$$C: \quad A \leftarrow A + Q * (\text{clock} - B)$$
$$B \leftarrow \text{clock}$$
$$Q \leftarrow Q + 1 \text{ or } Q \leftarrow Q - 1$$
$$\vdots$$

Initialization: $A \leftarrow 0$, $B \leftarrow \text{clock}$. Computation of the mean queue length (at the end of a time interval T): $mQl = A/T$.

A sampling monitor samples the contents of Q periodically (or at random times) N times during the interval and accumulates into location A the sum of the sampled queue lengths: if the initial contents of A

were 0 and a is the value of A at the end of the interval, then $mQl \cong A/N$.

Measurement of the profile of a program by a sampling monitor. The monitor samples the contents of the program counter periodically and is able to determine when the program to be measured is running. (In practice, the monitor gets its data from the program status word of the process that has just been interrupted.) A code utilization map is constructed by dividing the instruction space of the program into contiguous regions of 2^n words each, mapping each region onto one word in the map, and incrementing by 1 the contents of a map word whenever the program counter is found to point to an instruction in the corresponding region. If the map initially contains all zeros, at the end of the measurement interval it will show the utilization profile of the program during that interval with a resolution inversely related to the value of n.

Bibliography

1975. Hellerman, H., and Conroy, T. E. *Computer Systems Performance.* New York: McGraw-Hill.
1976. Svobodova, L. *Computer Performance Measurement and Evaluation Methods: Analysis and Applications.* New York: Elsevier.
1978. Ferrari, D. *Computer Systems Performance Evaluation.* Upper Saddle River, NJ: Prentice Hall.
1983. Ferrari, D., Serazzi, G., and Zeigner, A. *Measurement and Tuning of Computer Systems.* Upper Saddle River, NJ: Prentice Hall.
1988. McKerrow, P. *Performance Measurement of Computer Systems.* Reading, MA: Addison-Wesley.

Domenico Ferrari

SOFTWARE PIRACY

See LEGAL PROTECTION OF SOFTWARE.

SOFTWARE PORTABILITY

For articles on related subjects *see* COMPATIBILITY; CROSS ASSEMBLERS AND COMPILERS; SOFTWARE; SOFTWARE ENGINEERING; and TRANSPARENCY.

Software is said to be *portable* if it can, with reasonable effort, be made to run on computers other than the one for which it was originally written. Portable software proves its worth when computers are replaced or when the same software is run on many different computers, whether widely dispersed or at a single site.

The simplest aid to portability is the use of standard high-level languages such as C++, Fortran or Cobol. Such standard languages do, however, have the following deficiencies: (1) standards change over time;

(2) compilers often support non-standard language extensions; (3) standards are rarely completely precise; (4) programs sometimes require non-standard parts to interface with the local operating environment. Therefore, extra work is needed to make software properly portable. Useful methods include the use of language subsets, common to all compilers, and the use of verifier programs to ensure adherence to subsets; the use of *preprocessors* (*q.v.*) to map a source program into several alternative forms, thus catering to variations among compilers; and separating out machine-dependent aspects of software.

Portability of a language is enhanced if it has a compiler (or interpreter) that is itself written in a portable way. This makes it easy to implement the compiler on any desired platform, and thus to run programs written in the language that the compiler supports. Moreover, if the same portable compiler is used in all cases, this helps ensure that all the implementations are compatible with each other.

Java has been designed to be portable over networks. Java programs are converted into a simple and concise intermediate form, called *byte-code*, which is machine-independent. This intermediate form can be downloaded and interpreted by any computer on the network.

It costs planning and effort to produce software that is portable. Moreover, on any one computer, a portable program may be less efficient than a specially hand-tailored one. Nevertheless, given the huge cost of rewriting non-portable software, an investment in portability is normally one that will repay handsomely.

Bibliography

1996. Sommerville, I. *Software Engineering*, 5th Ed. Wokingham: Addison-Wesley. (Contains useful material on portability within the overall context of software engineering.)

Peter J. Brown

SOFTWARE PROJECT MANAGEMENT

For articles on related subjects *see* CHIEF PROGRAMMER TEAM; SOFTWARE CONFIGURATION MANAGEMENT; SOFTWARE ENGINEERING; SOFTWARE MAINTENANCE; and SOFTWARE SAFETY.

Software project management is concerned with managing the resources and work activities needed to develop and modify software-intensive systems. The primary success criteria for software managers are delivery of systems that satisfy stated needs and requirements, on time and within budget. Goals for software project managers include better quality, increased productivity, and improved predictability of software development efforts.

A large amount of software effort is concerned with modifying existing systems to provide additional functionality, to improve performance, to adapt the software to changing hardware environments, and to fix problems in the software. For the purposes of this article, we use the term *software development* to mean initial development of a system or significant modification of an existing system.

The major activities of software project management include planning and estimating, measuring and controlling, managing risk factors, leading and directing, and representing projects to project stakeholders and other interested parties. Effective planning requires detailed understanding of the needs, requirements, and design constraints for the system. Because requirements and plans tend to evolve together, they should be developed in an iterative manner.

Planning and Estimating

Factors to be considered in planning for software development include the work products to be delivered, the resources available, and the time allocated to system development. Other essential factors include organization of the development effort, the managerial processes to be used, and the technical processes to be employed.

Organizational factors include the process model to be used, the organizational structure, organizational boundaries and interfaces, and delegation of development responsibilities. A process model specifies the procedures, methods, and interactions among work activities for a software development effort. Current process models include the waterfall model, the incremental development model, the evolutionary model, and the spiral model (Pfleeger, 1998) (*see also* SOFTWARE ENGINEERING).

There are two types of issues concerning organizational structure for software development: the structure of the development organization and the structure of the development team. Organizational structures for software development include the project format, the functional format, and the matrix structure. Techniques for organizing the software development team include the democratic structure, the hierarchical structure, and the chief programmer team structure (Thayer, 1997).

Managerial process considerations include management objectives and priorities for the development effort, management dependencies and constraints, identification and analysis of development risks, the measuring and controlling mechanisms to be used, and the staffing and training needs of the development effort.

Technical processes to be planned include the methods, tools, and techniques to be used, the documentation requirements, and the supporting functions, such as quality assurance, configuration management, and validation and verification (*see* SOFTWARE ENGINEERING).

These planning considerations should be documented in a software development plan that includes detailed specification of the work activities, time dependencies among the activities, the resource requirements over time, allocation of the budget and resources to the work activities, and an overall schedule for the development effort. Planning is an ongoing activity for software development. Status reviews and replanning should continue throughout the lifetime of the development process.

IEEE Standard 1058 provides a structured format for a software development plan and the IEEE Tutorial on Software Engineering Project Management contains several articles on the planning process for software development (IEEE, 1998; Thayer, 1997).

Planning requires estimation. An estimate is a projection from past projects to a future project, suitably adjusted to account for differences between past projects and the future one. Adjustment factors must be applied to the projection because the future software project is always different from past ones. *See* Boehm (1981) for a discussion of adjustment factors for software projects. Three fundamental factors to be balanced in making an estimate are the requirements to be satisfied by the software to be developed, the time needed to conduct the project, and the numbers and types of required resources. Estimation techniques include analogy, rule of thumb, expert judgment, work breakdown structures and activity networks, and algorithmic models based on historical data.

Measuring and Controlling

Factors to be measured and controlled during software development include quality, productivity, schedule, budget, risk indicators, and progress. Quality factors include functional characteristics, such as response time, throughput (*q.v.*), memory utilization, and mean time between failure, plus nonfunctional characteristics, such as safety, security, ease of use, maintainability, and quality of the user instructions. Productivity is the amount of product produced per unit of resource expended. Typical measures of productivity include lines of code per programmer-month, function points

per programmer-day, and test cases run per programmer-hour. In software engineering, productivity includes both the quantity and quality of output produced.

Schedule and budget are often tracked using the earned-value technique, which compares the budgeted cost of work performed to the actual cost of work performed and the budgeted cost of work scheduled. If the actual cost of the work performed is greater than its budgeted cost, the project is over budget. If the amount of work scheduled, as measured by its budgeted cost, is greater than the amount performed, the project is behind schedule.

Progress is typically measured in terms of requirements designed/implemented/tested to date. Progress is not necessarily synonymous with productivity; it is possible to be extremely productive at doing the wrong thing.

Several articles on monitoring and controlling software projects are contained in the IEEE Tutorial on Software Engineering Project Management (Thayer, 1997). In addition, the text by Boehm (1981) provides detailed information on planning, monitoring, and controlling software development efforts.

Managing Risk Factors

A risk is a potential problem. Two fundamental attributes of risk are the probability that a potential problem might happen, and the resulting impact if it does. Risk areas for software projects include technology, schedule, resources, cost, and quality. A risk becomes a problem when an objective measure crosses a predetermined threshold; for example, failure to achieve a schedule milestone within an allowable slippage factor, an unacceptable number of defects found during design inspections, a shortfall in performance, or an excessive overrun of budgeted memory. Managing risk involves identifying the risk factors for a particular project, prioritizing the risk factors, deciding on a risk management strategy for the most serious risks, and implementing action plans and contingency plans for risks that are not avoided by changing the situation to eliminate them. Action plans are invoked to prevent future problems; contingency plans are invoked when a potential problem (a risk) becomes a real problem; i.e. when an objective measure crosses a predetermined threshold. Important attributes of a contingency plan are the criteria for determining that the problem has been solved and the allowed duration of the plan. A project enters crisis mode if the problem is not fixed within the specified duration of the contingency plan. The IEEE Tutorial on Risk Management (Boehm, 1989) contains numerous articles on risk management for software projects.

Leading and Directing

Because software development is a labor-intensive (intellect-intensive) activity conducted by teams of individuals, issues of leadership, motivation, and team building are of paramount importance to successful software project management. Leadership and management are related but distinct concepts. Management involves presiding over institutional processes, allocating resources and assigning responsibilities, and checking up on work assignments. Leadership, on the other hand, is concerned with issues such as organizational politics, vision, communication and coordination, values, motivation, and improving the work processes and work structures.

A particularly difficult issue for many software managers is delegation of technical decisions to those best qualified to make them. Every software development project should have a chief architect (i.e. lead engineer, senior designer). On small projects (three to five people), it may be possible (and desirable) for the manager to also play the role of chief architect. On larger projects, the manager and chief architect should be different persons because of the amount of work to be done and the different skills needed for managerial leadership and technical leadership.

Motivation is the drive to satisfy one's psychological needs. Studies of motivational factors for software developers have shown that the major motivators are autonomy, professional growth, and confidence in the technical leadership. Autonomy refers to the freedom to make decisions concerning the best way to do one's job. Professional growth is the opportunity to learn and apply new skills. Confidence in technical leadership refers to the confidence that one's technical skills and energy are being used to best effect. It is the leader's responsibility to create a work environment in which software developers can fulfill their psychological work needs and thus obtain a sense of job satisfaction.

Software systems are, for the most part, developed by teams rather than by individuals. It is therefore essential that the leader/manager knows how to build an effective team so that software developers can work in a cooperative manner toward shared common goals.

The tasks of a leader/manager are thus to communicate values, vision, and day-to-day information; to delegate technical decisions to those best qualified to make them; to provide a work environment in which individuals can satisfy their psychological needs; and to develop effective work teams. These tasks are particularly difficult for software managers who are promoted into management as a reward for their technical skills, rather than their "people" skills, and who may have received no training in leadership or team building. The text *Peopleware* (DeMarco, 1989) provides insightful details concerning the leading and directing of software engineers.

Representing the Project

The project manager is the project representative and spokesperson. Different stakeholders and constituencies have different needs for information concerning and involvement in a project. Stakeholders and constituencies for a software project include (perhaps) higher-level managers, supporting departments such as configuration management and quality assurance, subcontractors, affiliated projects (both hardware and software), affiliated contractors, customers, various types of users, and the system acquirer.

Bibliography

1971. Weinberg, G. *The Psychology of Computer Programming.* New York: Van Nostrand Reinhold.
1981. Boehm, B. *Software Engineering Economics.* Upper Saddle River, NJ: Prentice Hall.
1982. DeMarco, T. *Controlling Software Projects.* New York: Yourdon Press.
1985. Fairley, R. *Software Engineering Concepts.* New York: McGraw-Hill.
1989. Boehm, B. W. *IEEE Tutorial on Software Risk Management.* Los Alamitos, CA: IEEE Computer Society Press.
1989. DeMarco, T. *Peopleware.* New York: Yourdon Press.
1995. Brooks, F. *The Mythical Man-Month*, Rev. Ed. Reading, MA: Addison-Wesley
1997. Thayer, R. (ed.) *IEEE Tutorial on Software Engineering Project Management.* Los Alamitos, CA: IEEE Computer Society Press.
1998. Pfleeger, S. *Software Engineering Theory and Practice.* Upper Saddle River, NJ: Prentice Hall.
1998. *IEEE Std 1058, 1998 Edition; Standard for Software Project Management Plans.* Piscataway, NJ: The Institute of Electrical and Electronics Engineers, Inc.

Richard E. Fairley

SOFTWARE PROTOTYPING

For articles on related subjects *see* SOFTWARE ENGINEERING; SOFTWARE PROJECT MANAGEMENT; SOFTWARE REUSABILITY; and SOFTWARE TESTING.

A *software prototype* is an executable model of a proposed software system that accurately reflects chosen aspects of the system, such as display formats, the values computed, or response times. Software prototyping is an approach to software development that uses prototypes to help both the developers and their customers visualize the proposed system and predict its properties in an iterative process as shown in Fig. 1.

Prototypes are used extensively by designers and engineers working in other disciplines. For example, architects build scale models of buildings to aid visualization

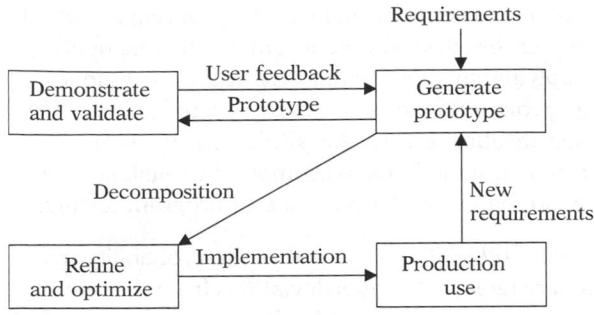

Figure 1. The software prototyping process.

of three-dimensional relationships, aeronautical engineers build scale models of airplanes to measure lift and drag in wind tunnel tests, and electrical engineers build breadboard circuits to check the validity of designs based on simplified ideal models of physical components. The common purpose of these prototypes is to reduce the uncertainty about the properties of a proposed design before it is implemented.

The main incentive for using prototypes is economic: scale models and prototype versions of most systems are much less expensive to build than the final versions. Prototypes should therefore be used to evaluate proposed systems if acceptance by the customer is in doubt. The motivation for software prototyping is essentially the same, and has become more urgent as systems being developed have grown more complex, and hence more expensive and more likely to have requirements errors (errors in specifying the system).

Software prototypes may not satisfy all of the constraints on the final version of the system. For example, a prototype may provide only a subset of all the required functions, it may be expressed in a more powerful or more flexible language than the final version, it may run on a machine with more resources than the proposed target architecture, it may be less efficient in both time and space than the final version, it may have limited capacity (databases may be implemented in main memory), it may not include facilities for error checking and fault tolerance, and it may not have the same degree of concurrency as the final version.

It is generally not possible to put a prototype into production use. The conceptual models and designs contained in a prototype, however, can usually be used in the final version. Precise specifications for the components of a prototype and clear documentation of its design are therefore critical for effective software prototyping.

Software prototyping has gained importance in recent years because new technologies have made computer-aided prototyping feasible. These technologies have

reduced the time and cost involved in producing a prototype, thus widening the gap between a software prototype and the cost of the final software system, and increasing the potential leverage of prototyping.

The new technologies are based on reusable code, computer-aided design, and automatic generation of programs. The most powerful systems are designed for specific problem domains. Some problem domains for which computer-aided prototyping tools have been developed include business information processing (*see* ADMINISTRATIVE APPLICATIONS), user interfaces (*q.v.*), programming languages (*q.v.*), and real-time systems (*q.v.*).

Generators for business information systems provide graphical interfaces to databases to define database schemas, queries, and reports by graphically defining table layouts (*see* RELATIONAL DATABASES). There are many commercially available tools in this category.

Interface generation systems (Linton *et al.*, 1989) generate graphical user interfaces based on a set of predefined components such as windows, menus, scroll bars, and buttons. These components are placed and adapted interactively via a mouse and menu interface (*see* WINDOW ENVIRONMENTS).

Generators for language processors are mostly based on attribute grammars. These systems can generate various tools for computer languages based on a context-free grammar for the language, augmented with equations defining computed attributes for the nodes of the parse tree (*see* FORMAL LANGUAGES). This technology can be used to prototype tools for computer languages, including translators, interpreters, pretty-printers, type checkers, dataflow analyzers, and so forth. Applications span programming languages, specification languages, data definition languages for databases, hardware description languages (*q.v.*), and command languages for applications programs (*see* SCRIPTING LANGUAGES). Attribute grammar processors have been coupled to generators for syntax-directed editors (Reps and Teitelbaum, 1988) and program transformation systems (Abraido-Fandino, 1987).

Computer-aided prototyping of real-time systems (*q.v.*) is supported by the prototyping language PSDL (Luqi *et al.*, 1988) and the associated prototyping system CAPS. CAPS uses a software base of reusable components, a program generator, a static scheduler, and a dynamic scheduler to realize systems containing both functions with hard real-time constraints and non-time-critical functions. PSDL provides a simple representation of system decompositions using dataflow (*q.v.*) diagrams augmented with non-procedural control constraints and timing constraints (maximum response times, maximum execution times, minimum inter-stimulus periods, periods, and deadlines). The language models both periodic and data-driven tasks, and both discrete (transaction-oriented) and continuous (sampled) data streams. The CAPS system provides automated tools for generating static schedules to guarantee hard real-time constraints as well as an execution support system that generates code for adapting, interconnecting, and controlling the execution of reusable software components.

In the future, prototyping will be integrated with final implementation. Progress in prototyping methods will hinge on automatic procedures for optimizing implementations. Prototypes will support refinement of the prototype into the final version by supplying additional information, and automatically transforming frequently used components to improve efficiency. Initially this will be done via optional implementation advice supplied by software engineers, in analogy to the *pragmas* in the programming language Ada (*q.v.*). In the longer term, prototyping systems will have reasoning capabilities and extensive knowledge bases which may include generic models of the problem domain, common goals of customers, common system structures, and generators producing specifications and code for classes of software components. Facilities for supporting formal verification of prototype decompositions are desirable to ensure that they are viable, especially if the subcomponents are to be built by different contractors.

Bibliography

1987. Abraido-Fandino, L. "An overview of REFINE 2.0," *Proceedings of the Second International Symposium on Knowledge Engineering*, Madrid, 8–10 April.

1988. Herndon, R., and Berzins, V. "The realizable benefits of a language prototyping language," *IEEE Trans. on Software Eng.*, **SE-14**, 6 (June), 803–809.

1988. Luqi, Berzins, V., and Yeh, R. "A prototyping language for real-time software," *IEEE Trans. on Software Eng.*, **14**, 10 (October), 1409–1423.

1988. Reps, T., and Teitelbaum, T. *The Synthesizer Generator: A System for Constructing Language-Based Editors*. New York: Springer-Verlag.

1989. Linton, M., Vlissides, J., and Calder, P. "Composing user interfaces with interviews," *IEEE Computer*, **22**, 2 (February), 8–22.

1996. "Special issue on computer-aided prototyping," *Journal of Systems Integration*, **6**, 1–2.

Valdis Berzins

SOFTWARE RELIABILITY

For articles on related subjects *see* DEBUGGING; PROGRAM SPECIFICATION; PROGRAM VERIFICATION; SOFTWARE MAINTENANCE; SOFTWARE METRICS; SOFTWARE MONITOR; SOFTWARE SAFETY; and SOFTWARE TESTING.

It is imperative to access the correctness of software for critical applications prior to actual use. Ideally we would like to verify formally that a program is correct. However, besides the practical difficulties encountered in applying current formal verification techniques to large programs, they cannot cope with the possibility of specification errors. An alternative approach is to use statistical methods to estimate the reliability of the software based on the outcome of program testing.

Software reliability is defined as the probability that a software fault that causes deviations from the required output by more than a specified tolerance, in a specified environment, does not occur during a specified exposure period. There are three distinct methods of estimating software reliability, namely, on the basis of its failure history, its behavior for a random sample of points taken from its input domain, or the number of seeded and actual faults detected by the test team where seeded faults are those that are deliberately inserted into the program at the start of the debugging phase.

Software Reliability Growth Models

Software reliability growth models attempt to predict the reliability of a program on the basis of its failure history. Failure history is defined to be the realization of a sequence of random variables $T_1, T_2, \ldots, T_n$, where T_i denotes the CPU time spent in testing the program after the faults causing the $(i-1)$th failure have been identified and removed until the ith failure is detected. These models can be further classified into fault-counting and nonfault-counting models depending on whether they express the reliability in terms of the number of faults remaining in the program or not.

Fault-counting models assume that the failure rates of the faults remaining in the program are independently identically distributed random variables and that the program failure rate is the sum of the individual failure rates. As an illustration, consider the General Poisson Model (GPM) which assumes that the failure rate, $r_j(t)$, after the faults causing the $(j-1)$th failure have been removed, is proportional to the number of faults remaining in the program and a power of the elapsed CPU time, i.e.

$$r_j(t) = \phi(N - M_j)\alpha t^{\alpha - 1}$$

where α and ϕ are constants, N is the number of faults originally present in the program, and $M_j = \sum_{i=1}^{j} m_i$ where m_i is the number of faults removed following the ith failure. Hence, the reliability of the program after the jth failure is given by

$$R_j(t) = e^{-\phi(N - M_j)t^{\alpha}}.$$

Given $m_1, m_2, \ldots, m_n$ and $t_1, t_2, \ldots, t_n$, where t_j is the CPU time required to detect the jth failure after the faults causing the $(j-1)$th failure have been removed, the maximum likelihood estimates (MLE) of the parameters (those with hats (^) below) of the model can be obtained by solving the following equations:

$$\sum_{j=1}^{n} \frac{1}{\hat{N} - M_{j-1}} - \sum_{j=1}^{n} \hat{\phi} t_j^{\hat{\alpha}} = 0;$$

$$\frac{n}{\hat{\alpha}} + \sum_{j=1}^{n} \log t_j - \sum_{j=1}^{n} \hat{\phi}(\hat{N} - M_{j-1}) t_j^{\hat{\alpha}} \log t_j = 0;$$

$$\frac{n}{\hat{\phi}} - \sum_{j=1}^{n} (\hat{N} - M_{j-1}) t_j^{\hat{\alpha}} = 0.$$

Nonfault-counting models consider the effect of a debugging action on the failure rate without concern as to the number of failures detected at a time. An example of a model in this category is the Musa–Okumoto logarithmic model. The inputs to the model are $t_1, t_2, \ldots, t_n$ where t_j is the CPU *time* (not interval as in the GPM model) at which the jth failure was observed. The failure rate is given by

$$r(t) = \frac{\lambda_0}{\lambda_0 \theta t + 1},$$

where λ_0 is the initial failure rate and θ is a failure rate decay constant. Thus, the model assumes that the failure rate decreases continuously over the testing and debugging phase, rather than at discrete points corresponding to failure detection and removal times. Further, the rate of decrease in $r(t)$ itself decreases with time, thus modeling the decrease in the size of errors detected as debugging proceeds. The reliability during the jth interval is given by

$$R_j(t) = \left\{ \frac{\lambda_0 \theta t_j + 1}{\lambda_0 \theta(t_j + t) + 1} \right\}^{1/\theta}.$$

The MLE of λ_0 and θ can be obtained by solving the following equations:

$$\frac{n}{\hat{\lambda}_0} - \hat{\theta} \sum_{j=1}^{n} \frac{t_j}{\hat{\lambda}_0 \hat{\theta} t_j + 1} - \frac{t_n}{\hat{\lambda}_0 \hat{\theta} t_n + 1} = 0;$$

$$-\hat{\lambda}_0 \sum_{j=1}^{n} \frac{t_j}{\hat{\lambda}_0 \hat{\theta} t_j + 1} + \frac{1}{\hat{\theta}^2} \log(\hat{\lambda}_0 \hat{\theta} t_n + 1)$$

$$-\frac{\hat{\lambda}_0 t_n}{\hat{\theta}(\hat{\lambda}_0 \hat{\theta} t_n + 1)} = 0.$$

Other approaches for estimating the reliability of a program from its failure history include Bayesian models (e.g. the Littlewood–Verrall model) and the use of artificial neutral networks (*q.v.*) to extrapolate patterns in the sequence of failures encountered during the testing and debugging phase to predict the reliability during the operational phase.

Sampling Models

The basic principle underlying these models is similar to the sampling technique used to determine the reliability of hardware components except that instead of selecting a random sample of components and subjecting them to operational use, the program is tested with a random sample of points from its input domain. Faults discovered in this process are not removed. If we observe n_f failures out of n runs, then the estimate of the reliability of the program for a single run is

$$\hat{R} = 1 - \frac{n_f}{n}.$$

Assuming that inputs are selected independently according to the same probability distribution used to choose the random sample, the reliability of the program over i runs is given by

$$\hat{R}(i) = (\hat{R})^i.$$

This method of estimating software reliability is the basis of the Nelson model.

While the theoretical foundations of the Nelson model are sound, it suffers from a practical drawback, namely the need to select a very large number of random test cases in order to have a high confidence in the reliability estimate. The Ramamoorthy–Bastani input domain based model overcomes this objection to the Nelson model. It was developed for assessing the reliability of critical real-time process control programs for which no failures should be detected during the reliability estimation phase, so that the reliability estimate is one. Hence, the important metric of concern is the confidence in the reliability estimate. This model provides an estimate of the conditional probability that the program is correct for all possible inputs given that it is correct for a given set of inputs. The basic assumption is that the outcome of each test case provides at least some stochastic information about the behavior of the program for points that are close to the test point. The main result of the model is a probability, P:

$P\{$program is correct for all points in $[a, a + V]$ given that it is correct for all test cases having successive distances x_j, $j = 1, \ldots, n - 1\}$

$$= e^{-\lambda V} \prod_{j=1}^{n-1} \left(\frac{2}{1 + e^{-\lambda x_j}} \right),$$

where λ is a parameter that is deduced from some measure of the complexity of the source code.

The above question is derived under the assumption that the correctness of an input, given that the program works for all its neighbors, depends only on its nearest neighbor. More general assumptions, such as the influence of boundary value test cases, result in mathematically intractable derivations.

One advantage of sampling models is the possibility of combining testing with formal verification. A simple approach is to divide the input space into partitions and verify high-usage partitions while testing low-usage partitions. Verifying high-usage partitions significantly reduces the number of samples needed for achieving a desired confidence in the reliability estimate. A more general approach is to use partial program proofs, such as the verification of lower level abstract data types (q.v.) and library functions and the proof of general correctness properties (e.g. proving that the program is deadlock free), to amplify the effect of test cases. That is, partial proofs are selectively applied so that testing the partially verified program with one test case is equivalent to testing the unverified program with a large number of test cases. The main effect of this type of test data amplification is to reduce the sensitivity of the reliability estimate to errors in the estimates of the operational profile.

Fault Seeding

This is an experimental approach for predicting the number of faults in a program. It was proposed and used by Mills and Basin. Artificial faults are inserted into the program without the knowledge of the test team. Assuming that the seeded faults have the same distribution as the original faults in the program, an approximate estimate of the number of faults remaining in the program given that m_a actual faults and m_s seeded faults have been have been detected is

$$\frac{m_a(M_s - m_s)}{m_s},$$

where M_s is the total number of faults artificially injected into the program.

The problem with the fault seeding approach is that there is no way to ensure that the seeded faults have the same distribution as the original faults. Simple changes to the source code, such as deleting some statements or modifying some expressions, do not adequately reflect subtle design and requirements specification problems. An alternative approach is to use two test teams and compare the set of faults detected by each team. Suppose that the first team finds m_{a1} faults while the second team finds m_{a2} faults, of which m_{a12} faults are the same as those found by the first team. Then, an estimate for M_a the total number of faults in the original program, is $m_{a1}m_{a2}/m_{a12}$. The number of faults remaining in the program is $M_a - m_{a1} - m_{a2} + m_{a12}$. The approach does not have to deal with the issue of selecting artificial faults. However, a problem here is that the faults detected by the two teams are likely to be correlated since faults with a high failure rate have a high probability of occurring in both the sets. Finally, there is no way to make reliability statements about a

program given just the number of faults remaining in it. This number, however, is useful in estimating the resources needed for future maintenance of the program.

System Reliability

Assuming that only one component is active at a given time, then an approach proposed independently by Cheung and Littlewood can be used to assess the reliability of a software system given the reliabilities of the models constituting the software. The system is assumed to consist of j components among which control is switched randomly according to a semi-Markov process. Assuming that the failure process of each component is a Poisson process with the ith component having parameter λ_i and that no failures occur during the transition from one module to another, the overall system failure process can be approximated as a Poisson process with failure rate

$$\lambda = \frac{\sum_{i=1}^{k} \sum_{j=1}^{k} \pi_i p_{ij} \mu_{ij} \lambda_i}{\sum_{i=1}^{k} \sum_{j=1}^{k} \pi_i p_{ij} \mu_{ij}}$$

where π_i is the steady state probability that component i is active and is given by $\sum_{j=1}^{k} \pi_j p_{ji}$ subject to $\sum_{j=1}^{k} \pi_j = 1$, where p_{ij} is the transition probability from component i to component j, and μ_{ij} is the mean CPU time spent in component i before switching to component j (the *sojourn* time).

Discussion

During the first decade of software reliability research the major emphasis was on developing models based on various assumptions. This resulted in a proliferation of models, most of which were neither used nor validated. Currently the consensus appears to be that perhaps there is no single model that can be applied to all types of projects. Hence, one area of active research is to investigate whether a set of models can be combined so as to achieve more accurate reliability estimates for various situations. A variety of automated tools have been used to experiment with several different models and with the selection of a model that is most appropriate for given failure data. Another trend is the investigation of possible relationships between parameters of software reliability models and software metrics (size, defect density, etc.) to predict the reliability of a program very early in its life cycle. These studies are also useful for identifying fault-prone components for optimal allocation of testing resources. Other research topics include developing methods of analyzing the confidence in the predictions of a model and using software reliability theory to assist with the management of a project throughout the software life cycle.

Bibliography

1982. Ramamoorthy, C. V., and Bastani, F. B. "Software reliability – status and perspectives," *IEEE Trans. Softw. Eng.*, **SE-8**, *4* (July), 354–371.

1985. Goel, A. L. "Software reliability models: assumptions, limitations, and applicability," *IEEE Trans. Softw. Eng.*, **SE-11**, *12* (December), 1411–1423.

1987. Musa, J., Iannino, A., and Okumoto, K. *Software Reliability: Measurement, Prediction, Application.* New York: McGraw-Hill.

1996. Lyu, M. R. (ed.) *Handbook of Software Reliability Engineering.* New York: McGraw-Hill.

Farokh B. Bastani and C. V. Ramamoorthy

SOFTWARE REUSABILITY

For articles on related subjects *see* ABSTRACT DATA TYPE; CLASS COMPONENT SOFTWARE; ENCAPSULATION; INFORMATION HIDING; MACRO; MODULAR PROGRAMMING; OBJECT-ORIENTED PROGRAMMING; PORTABILITY; and SUBPROGRAM.

Software reusability is an attribute of software that facilitates its incorporation into new application programs. Reusable software shares many attributes in common with "good" software (e.g. transportability, maintainability, flexibility, understandability, usability, and reliability).

Software reuse, as a means of saving time and resources, was initially proposed by Charles Babbage (*q.v.*) as part of the Analytical Engine (*q.v.*) through a mechanism analogous to a subroutine call. The first practical implementation of software reuse, a sub-routine library, was realized by Maurice Wilkes (*q.v.*) as part of the first stored-program computer, the EDSAC (*q.v.*), at the University of Cambridge in 1951. During the early days of computer programming, the most successful examples of software reuse were sub-routine libraries or system macros. The modern roots of software reuse can be traced to Doug McIlroy's 1969 paper "Mass Produced Software Components" at the NATO Conference on Software Engineering. McIlroy speculated on the viability of a Commercial-Off-The-Shelf (COTS) software parts industry furnishing the programming community with the building blocks necessary to create new software applications. Current interest in software reusability has been stimulated by advances in programming languages, such as Java, Ada, and C++, that support the adaptation of a more disciplined engineering approach to software development called object-oriented programming and design.

It is interesting to note that "reusability" is not usually a distinguishing attribute of artifacts in other engineering disciplines. That is, in areas other than programming there is little or no differentiation between "use" and "reuse" because reuse is taken for granted. That reusability is an issue in programming is indicative of the relative immaturity of the profession as well as a common lack of discipline in the programming process.

The reusability of software is contingent upon the identification of useful software abstractions that are common to a wide number of applications within a particular application domain (vertical domain analysis) or across several application domains (horizontal domain analysis). The degree of reusability of a software module or component can be increased by providing

```
generic
      type ELEMENT is private;
package STACK is
      type STACK is limited private;
      procedure INTIALIZE (THE_STACK : in out STACK);
      procedure PUSH(THE_ELEMENT : in ELEMENT;
                     ONTO_THE_STACK: in out STACK);
      procedure POP(THE_STACK : in out STACK);
      function TOP_OF(THE_STACK : in STACK)
            return ELEMENT;
      function IS_EQUAL(LEFT, RIGHT : in STACK)
            return BOOLEAN;
      function IS_EMPTY(THE_STACK : in STACK)
            return BOOLEAN;
      function LENGTH OF(THE_STACK : in STACK)
            return POSITIVE;

      OVERFLOW : exception;
      UNDERFLOW: exception;

      private
            type DATA_STRUCTURE;
            type STACK is access DATA_STRUCTURE;
end STACK;
```

Figure 1. A reusable Ada package.

parameters that generalize its use or by building the module so that its implementation dependencies (hardware, operating system, or database) are reduced, eliminated, or encapsulated through the use of a virtual or abstract machine interface.

There are several implementation techniques and programming technologies that enhance the reusability of software. These include:

1. Data encapsulation

2. Information hiding

3. Polymorphism (*see* OPERATOR OVERLOADING)

4. Abstract data types, classes, or methods

5. Pipes and filters (such as are used with Unix—*q.v.* and MS-DOS)

6. Inheritance (object-oriented programming)

7. Parameterization and genericity (macros and preprocessors—*q.v.*)

8. Application generators and fourth-generation languages (4GLs)

9. Virtual or abstract machine interfaces

The Ada package (*q.v.*) in Fig. 1 exports an abstract data type called STACK as an example of a parameterized abstract data type whose implementation exhibits data encapsulation and information hiding. This software component is reusable because it can be easily adapted to hold any type of data (i.e. it has a broad domain of applicability). Furthermore, because the data structure is completely encapsulated, the user can manipulate the contents of the stack only through the operations exported in the interface. Thus, the abstraction (stack) is prevented from being corrupted. Finally, the user has no indication of whether a linked list or an array was used to implement the data structure. (This information is hidden in the Ada package body, which is not shown in this example.) Conceivably, several implementations might exist that satisfy the same functionality, in which case the Ada specification serves as a virtual machine interface to a family of implementations that exhibit different time and resource attributes.

While parameterized types in Ada (*q.v.*) can be reused through instantiation with generic parameter values and abstract classes in Java (*q.v.*) can be specialized through inheritance and overriding the abstract methods, any reusable component needs to be adequately documented before it can be reused. Furthermore, the documentation associated with the component must be kept consistent with the current implementation, or else the software developer is faced with the undesirable task of looking at the code in order to understand how it can reused. Java has introduced a tool, Javadoc, to enhance the reusability of a component by supporting the automatic generation of hypertext documentation (i.e. HTML Web pages) from stylized comments embedded in the source code. As shown in Fig. 2, special tags (e.g. @param) inside Javadoc comments (i.e. /**) are used to generate standard format Web pages, which also may include HTML text formatting tags. The classes, packages, interfaces, and exceptions found in the Java Library API Package are

```
/**
 * An example to echo the run-time
 * parameters. <br>
 * <b>For example, if the user invokes this
 *                   application by typing:</b><pre>
 * ALittleMoreReusableExample This is good!
 * </pre><b>then the application prints out</b><pre>
 * This is good!</pre>
 * @version  2
 * @author   Will Tracz
 * @author   Lockheed Martin FS
 **/
public class ALittleMoreReusableExample {
This is an application not an applet<br>
/**
 * @param args An array of string variables
 *             to be printed out.
 **/
public static void main ( String [ ] args ) {
     for ( int i=0; i<args.length; i++ )
       System.out.print ( args [ i ] + " " );
     System.out.println (); // flush buffer
 } // end of "main" method
} // end of ALittleMoreReusableExample
//use javadoc >-author -version
```

Figure 2. A reusable Java class documented with Javadoc tags.

documented with JavaDoc, making them more readily learned, used, modified, and extended. They not only provide programmers with a rich set of application building blocks, but also provide examples of well-documented components.

If enough well-tested, well-documented, flexible, and reusable components are developed according to these principles and placed in inventory, programmers could easily construct new applications or *applets* simply by assembling and extending selected components. This paradigm shift to "component-based" programming is promoted by the COM (Component Object Model) in Java and Visual Basic and has resulted in the development of a reusable component industry.

Bibliography

1987. Booch, G. *Software Components with Ada*. Menlo Park, CA: Benjamin/Cummings.
1989. Biggerstaff, T. J., and Perlis, A. J. *Software Reusability: Volume I Concepts and Models, Volume II Applications and Experience*. New York: ACM Press.
1996. Brockschmidt, K. "How OLE and COM solve the problems of component software design," in *Microsoft Systems Journal*, **11**, *5*, 19–30.
1996. Tracz, W. *Confessions of a Used Program Salesman: Institutionalizing Software Reuse*. New York: Addison Wesley Longman.
1997. Chan P., and Lee, R. *Java^TM Class Libraries: An Annotated Reference*. New York: Addison Wesley Longman.

Will Tracz

SOFTWARE SAFETY

For articles on related subjects *see* EMBEDDED SYSTEM; SOFTWARE ENGINEERING; SOFTWARE PROJECT MANAGEMENT; and SOFTWARE TESTING.

Although software is not intrinsically dangerous in any physical sense, when it is used to control the behavior of physical processes it can be dangerous in the sense that the system it controls can become a safety risk.

There are many factors that make software dangerous; however, it is essential to observe that the safety of software is just one aspect of system safety and must, therefore, be considered in the system context. Combinations of electronic and software components must work in harmony with each other as well as with humans to provide for the safe operation and support of the total system according to stated requirements and further requirements that follow from them. Defining safe software is complicated due to the diversity of requirements placed upon such systems as well as the variety of solutions that can be and are being used.

Moreover, issues related to *software safety* must be treated from the engineering point of view as well as in relation to the technical and nontechnical processes employed during the life cycle of a product containing safety-critical software.

Fig. 1 is a diagram of the elements that enter the treatment of software safety issues. This model is a slightly modified version of a model developed by Pyle (1991). It contains human and material "actors" of various kinds; namely:

♦ *Physical system (PS)*—The system to be controlled, such as an oil refinery.

♦ *Embedded control system (ECS)*—Hardware system and software.

♦ *Operator(s)*—People who act in symbiosis with the system.

♦ *Potential victim(s) (PVs)*—The people or property susceptible to danger.

♦ *Environment*—The environment in which all actors operate.

The software part of the model is subdivided into infrastructure software, including a real-time operating system (*see* REAL-TIME SYSTEMS), and application software.

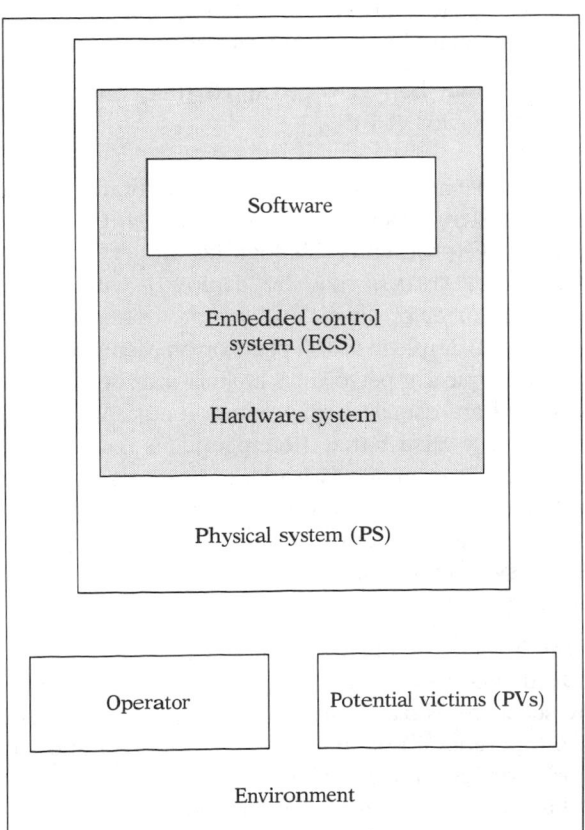

Figure 1. Model of a safety-critical system.

The ECS is connected to the other actors as follows:

◆ The ECS has sensor and actuator connections to the PS that are used in controlling the PS, and may also have connections to the operator.

◆ The ECS may also incorporate sensors which provide information from the environment and information concerning potential victims that can be relevant to the correct operation of the PS and in avoiding harm to the PVs.

Based upon the utilization of these connections, the ECS, when executed, is responsible for achieving proper interactions between the actors. More explicitly, the following properties can be observed:

◆ The software and hardware of the ECS define its behavior.

◆ The ECS senses and controls activities in the PS.

◆ The operator behavior can influence ECS behavior and vice versa.

◆ The PS has the possibility (to be avoided) of acting dangerously.

◆ The PS and the PVs together act within the environment.

◆ The PS may be able to sense the states of PVs and the environment but it cannot directly control them.

◆ There may be a part of the PS that can influence the behavior of PVs.

The complexity of the ECS for a particular safety-critical system product varies quite widely. On the low end, a PLC (programmable logic controller—*see* CONTROL APPLICATIONS) may be deployed with only a limited number of sensor and actuator signal connections; for example in a drill press or an escalator. Such systems typically perform a limited number of functions and are usually highly autonomous. At the high end, highly distributed heterogeneous control systems may be employed with large numbers of sensors and actuator connections where multiple interrelated or independent functions are provided (multiplexed) in the system; for example, a chemical plant or an airplane.

From a safety point of view, it is essential to identify hazards and risks in all parts of the system, including the software. Hazards are conditions in system execution (operational) or in system development and support (nonoperational) which can lead to a mishap. A hazard can be related to the nonavailability of a critical function, improper operation, or untimely operation. The very nature of software design, develop-

ment, and deployment introduces the potential hazard sources: for example, misinterpreted or incomplete requirements or specifications, design or coding errors, and inadequate test coverage and verification.

A significant portion of the engineering effort going into safety-critical products concerns hazard identification, the elimination of hazards through proper design and implementation, and the control of hazards that cannot be completely eliminated.

Typically, hazards are categorized according to their severity and probability. The probability of a hazard occurring may be classified as follows:

◆ Frequent   Likely to occur often

◆ Probable   Likely to occur several times in the unit life of the unit

◆ Occasional   Likely to occur some time in the life of the unit

◆ Remote   Unlikely to occur in the life of the unit, but possible

◆ Improbable   Extremely unlikely to occur

◆ Impossible   The probability of occurrence is zero

The severity of hazards is typically identified as belonging to the following categories: Catastrophic, Critical, Marginal, or Negligible.

The probabilities and severity form a matrix in which appropriate actions are indicated as to the treatment (that is, need to eliminate or control each hazard). The potential operational and nonoperational hazards associated with each hardware, software and human component of the safety-critical system must be identified at various stages of the life cycle of a product. A preliminary hazard analysis needs to be performed as well as analysis of hazards after design and implementation, and with respect to continued support and maintenance.

The identification of hazards is typically supported by one or more of the known techniques for hazard analysis. Some of the following techniques can and have been employed in analyzing software hazards.

◆ *FTA (Fault Tree Analysis)*—Employs Boolean logic to describe the combination of individual faults that can constitute hazardous events. The analysis starts from a top event (hazardous situation) and then proceeds (in a top-down manner) to identify the combination of faults that can lead to the hazardous situation. Developed originally at Bell Labs, FTA is widely used in the aerospace, electronics, and nuclear industries.

◆ *FMEA (Failure Modes and Effects Analysis)*—Starts by identifying all components and their failure modes. For each failure mode, the effects on all other system components are determined along with the effect on the overall system. The probabilities and the seriousness of each failure mode can be calculated from experience with component failure rates. This method originated in the field of reliability engineering for predicting equipment reliability.

◆ *HAZOP (Hazards and Operability)*—A quantitative technique intended to identify all possible deviations from the system design and expected operation, and all hazards associated with the deviations. Analysis is performed by a team of experts with an independent team leader. This method originated in the chemical industry in the UK.

Using the probabilities, products may be categorized according to SIL (Safety Integrity Levels). These levels are then used to determine the intensity of effort to be expended in identifying, analyzing, and treating hazards as well as the placement of requirements for the use of particular technical hardware or software solutions.

Risks are related to the possibility and impact of an operational or nonoperational hazard leading to an accident. Taking risks has varying consequences in relationship to the hazard. It is vital to assess the risks of hazards leading to accidents in order to determine a suitable level of risk assumption.

There are a number of architectural design decisions which may have a radical effect upon the ECS hazards and risks, including the following:

◆ employment of synchronous or asynchronous processing

◆ online and offline scheduling

◆ resource utilization

◆ scheduling strategy

◆ treatment of external interrupts

◆ fault handling (identification, isolation, recovery)

◆ specific safety features (guards, lock-in, lock-out, interlocks—*q.v.*)

◆ centralized or decentralized environment

◆ isolation of safety-critical from non-safety-critical functions

The treatment of these aspects dominates the ability to engineer safety-critical functions, to be able to test

and verify the product thoroughly, to provide reproducibility of execution, to operate in difficult physical environments, and to provide protection mechanisms for undesired control actuations.

The life cycle processes employed for dealing with technical and nontechnical (including managerial) aspects must also be scrutinized. For safety-critical products incorporating software, this includes all aspects of acquisition, supply, development, operation, and maintenance. Well-defined processes must exist for critical support, such as software configuration management (*q.v.*), documentation, verification, validation, joint reviews, problem resolution, and auditing. The practice of requiring a "safety case," that is, justification that all reasonable steps have been taken to ensure safety, is becoming a requirement in many application areas.

Bibliography

1991. Pyle, I. C. *Developing Safety Systems: A Guide Using Ada.* Upper Saddle River, NJ: Prentice Hall.
1995. Leveson, N. G. *Safeware.* Reading, MA: Addison-Wesley.

Harold W. Lawson

SOFTWARE TESTING

For articles on related subjects *see* DEBUGGING; PROGRAM VERIFICATION; SOFTWARE ENGINEERING; SOFTWARE MAINTENANCE; SOFTWARE MONITOR; and SOFTWARE RELIABILITY.

Overview

The term *software testing* can refer to any planned, risk-reducing activity that takes place during software development, operation, or maintenance. Examples of such activities include: (1) analyzing system requirements, (2) experimentation with prototypes, (3) static reviews of designs and other intermediate engineering products, (4) static and dynamic analysis of software products, and (5) retesting software products during maintenance. As these example show, software testing occurs at many stages of software development and operation. The article being analyzed during a test may be the actual software product, an early specification of its design, or a model of its intended use.

Two kinds of risks are addressed during a software test. The first risk is that the ultimate software product will fail to meet the needs and expectations of the end user. These expectations comprise the system *requirements*; the process of determining the likely extent to which the eventual software product will satisfy its requirements is called *validation*. As a complex software product evolves from a set of requirements in the minds of users to a working system, intermediate engineering products are produced. These may range from high-level system designs and partially functional prototypes to nonfunctional specifications of performance and reliability, and, ultimately, to working software. The second kind of risk is that developers may introduce technical incompatibilities or inconsistencies into these engineering products. The process of comparing these products with each other to insure that they are mutually consistent is called *verification*.

The critical elements of a software test are: (1) specifications of validation or verification products to be tested, (2) goals and thresholds for the test, (3) specifications of test activities and data, and (4) evaluations. A *validation and verification product* (or V&V product) is any engineering product analyzed during the test. An example of an early V&V product is a prototype graphical interface for validating ease-of-use by end users. An intermediate V&V product is a detailed design specification that is used to verify that elaboration of high-level design has been carried out correctly. A very late V&V product is a partially integrated software system. A *goal* or *threshold* for the test is a specification of what it means to pass or fail the test. Ideally, these are quantitative specifications that correspond to direct measurements of a V&V product. Examples of such specifications include observed failure rates, coverage criteria for correctness tests, and independent estimates of test data quality. A typical threshold requirement is that the input–output behavior of a given program unit must conform to its detailed design specifications on at last k test points chosen randomly from a specified probability distribution. The *specifications of test activities and data* refer to the procedures and conditions under which the test will be carried out. The *evaluations* comprise the important results of the test. The principal question answered by the evaluation is: does this test demonstrate that the specified goal or threshold has been achieved? These elements are frequently formalized in a series of *test plans*. The design, management, and use of an effective test plan is sometimes an engineering process as complex and costly as the software product development itself. National and international standards organizations have developed and distributed standards for test plans and test documentation.

Frequently the term "testing" is reserved for dynamic analysis (i.e. for those activities that involve running programs and observing outputs). Even in this restricted usage, however, intermediate V&V products may be involved and used for either validation or verification.

Theory of Software Tests for Correctness

The aspect of software testing that has received the most attention from researchers is *testing for correctness*

(i.e. the dynamic verification that a program is consistent with a detailed specification of its behavior) (*see* PROGRAM VERIFICATION). There is an extensive mathematical theory of correctness testing that revolves around test data quality; that is, the extent to which a given test demonstrates (or fails to demonstrate) consistency of a program and its specified behavior.

Given a program P and its specification F, a test data set D is said to be *reliable* if correctness on D implies correctness on all inputs. More precisely, let $P(x)$ represent the result of running program P on input x. Let $F(x)$ represent the specified behavior for input x. Then D is reliable relative to P and F if and only if:

$$P(x) = F(x), \text{ for all } x \in D$$

implies

$$P(x) = F(x), \text{ for all } x.$$

Equivalently, if P is not correct (i.e. if $P(x) \neq F(x)$ for some input x), then P will fail to match F on some input in a reliable test for P and F. Thus, the existence of a reliable test set guarantees that "bugs" (*q.v.*) in incorrect programs will be uncovered by the test. A related concept is test data *adequacy*; a test set is adequate if it distinguishes the program being tested from all nonequivalent ones. In mathematical terms, D is adequate for P if and only if for all programs Q:

$$P(x) = Q(x), \text{ for all } x \in D$$

implies

$$P(x) = Q(x), \text{ for all } x$$

Equivalently, if $P(x) \neq Q(x)$ for some input x, then some input in D distinguishes P and Q. Thus, the existence of an adequate test set can be used as "evidence" that P is correct: if P is correct, then it is not equivalent to any incorrect program and thus D distinguishes P from all incorrect programs.

Adequate and reliable tests are mathematical ideals. A method that is guaranteed to produce a reliable test set if the program is incorrect and an adequate test set if the program is correct would, in principle, solve the correctness testing problem. Such ideal methods are, in general, impractical (and, in some cases, impossible). In practice, a variety of other test set criteria are used to evaluate test data quality. The goal in selecting these criteria is to choose those that are most likely to result in reliable or adequate tests sets in a given test environment.

BLACK BOX CRITERIA
These criteria set requirements for a test set based upon external characteristics. A typical black box criterion is correct performance on a specified number of randomly chosen data points.

WHITE BOX CRITERIA

These criteria set requirements for a test based upon *coverage* of internal components or elements associated with the software. The most common white box criteria are *structural coverage* and *fault coverage*. A structural coverage criterion specifies the extent to which a given test exercises or "covers" structural components of the software (e.g. statements, branches, or dataflow chains). A fault coverage criterion specifies errors, faults, or classes of faults that are ruled out or "covered" if the given test is passed.

Major Software Testing Methodologies

Principal techniques for static analysis include reviews and inspections, measurement, reliability modeling, and other methods that have developed into subdisciplines in their own right. The following includes the major dynamic testing methodologies. There are no clear lines of demarcation between these methods, and a given set of test procedures may contain techniques drawn from several types of methods. In many cases, commercial or experimental tools have been developed to support the methodologies.

FUNCTIONAL TESTING

This is a family of black box testing criteria that generate tests based on specified properties (e.g. functional properties) of the software being tested. An example of a functional testing criterion is a "special values" test that generates data points at which correctly functioning software exhibits some special behavior.

RANDOM TESTING

Random tests are black box tests based upon known or assumed probability distributions of inputs. Random inputs may be chosen from operational profiles, simulations, or by purely statistical means. Random testing is sometimes associated with development methodologies and can be used to predict statistical parameters of operational software systems.

PROGRAM INSTRUMENTATION

These white box methods are used simply to gather measurements during tests. Software monitors or *probes* are incorporated into the program text or object code as a kind of instrumentation. These probes record or display dynamic characteristics. An important variation on instrumentation is the *executable assertion* (i.e. an embedded predicate that is evaluated during program execution). Modern programming languages like C++ (*q.v.*) and Eiffel include *assert* statements to encourage programmers to use executable assertions.

STRUCTURAL TESTING

The simplest family of white box methods, structural testing criteria, sets coverage thresholds for program components, such as statements, decision-to-decision branches, control flow paths, and dataflow chains (i.e. program segments between successive definitions and uses of specified variables). One hundred per cent statement coverage is frequently considered to be the lowest acceptable threshold criterion for an effective software test.

PARTITION TESTING

White box analysis of a program frequently leads to *partitions* of the input space to a program. For example, a typical partitioning scheme may identify all those input values that cause the program to execute the same control path. A partition testing method is used to select test data from the partitions. In one such method (domain analysis), a geometric model of the partitions is used as a guide to test data selection.

MUTATION TESTING

Mutation testing refers to a family of white box methods based upon fault coverage. The goal is to create tests that distinguish the program being tested from "mutant" programs that contain faults or bugs. A successful mutation test creates either a reliable test set if the program is incorrect or an adequate test set if the program is correct. Variations have been developed to study fault propagation (e.g. *relay* testing), early fault detection (e.g. weak mutation testing), and test case generation (error-sensitive test case analysis).

An important static analysis technique that is used in many of these dynamic methods is *symbolic execution*. With each possible control flow path in the program is associated a symbolic expression that represents the results of executing the statements along that path on symbolic inputs. Logical tools can be used to manipulate these symbolic expressions

Organizing Tests

Industry data indicates that the cost of finding and removing faults in a software product can increase by a factor of 100 or more as the design, development, and operation process proceeds. Consequently, much of the effort in test technologies is oriented toward "front-end" activities. As the V&V products increase in size and complexity, the cost of testing increases at a disproportionate rate. Balancing the costs and benefits of testing has resulted in an identification of distinct *phases* of testing. Each phase addresses a specific type of V&V product and is used to achieve a specific set of goals. All software tests are organized around the following sequence of testing phases. In simple software systems, only programmer and regression testing may actually be used. In large and complex system development efforts, however, all of these phases are present.

REQUIREMENTS ANALYSIS

This may include the static analysis of software requirements (e.g. to determine their "testability") or the dynamic analysis of prototypes for requirements validation.

DEVELOPMENT TESTING

Development testing includes all testing associated with system design and engineering. In early development testing, models of designs may be subjected to dynamic and static analysis. In late development testing software product components are tested for correctness.

PROGRAMMER TESTING

The least formal aspect of testing, programmer testing, consists of the testing of software components (e.g. units and modules), usually in isolation from other components. This is the testing phase in which a testing–fault isolation–fault removal cycle is the most apparent.

INTEGRATION TESTING

All testing activities associated with the assembling of a completed software product (software system integration), replacing software drivers (*q.v.*) constructed for development or programmer testing, removing instrumentation, or integrating a completed software product with its target environment are referred to as *integration testing*.

SYSTEM OR FUNCTION TESTING

Since it requires a completed system, function or system testing occurs very late in the development process. This kind of testing is usually oriented toward requirements validation and may also be associated with certification or other quality activities.

OPERATIONAL TESTING

When it is conducted formally (e.g. for large systems developed under government contracts), operational testing involves the black box testing of the system in a realistic environment using typical operator personnel. Testing carried out by the software developer is known as *alpha testing*. *Beta testing* is the informal operational testing of commercial products that may be carried out by selected, willing customers or other typical users through a program of "early" releases.

IN-LINE TESTING

As opposed to operational testing, in which the test environment is a realistic model of the operational environment, an in-line test is carried out on the end product in its operational environment using real users. In-line testing for software is less common than for hardware, but it is an essential component of all fault-tolerant systems (*q.v.*). Many other application domains (e.g. safety-critical applications, secure applications) use in-line probes and instrumentation and thus implement rudimentary forms of in-line testing.

REGRESSION TESTING

Regression tests are retests of systems after modifications have been made to enhance functionality or remove faults. A regression test can be conducted as either a black box or white box test; the critical factor in regression tests is the cost of the test so that regression tests are typically organized to minimize the amount of retesting.

Dividing the testing effort into these phases frequently facilitates hierarchical organization of the total testing process. During the earliest test phases, relatively little detailed information is available about the ultimate software product. A tester may have detailed information, for example, about overall architecture and user interface (*q.v.*) design, but may have to use "dummy" software or software stubs in place of actual system functions. A test that is organized in this way is called a *top-down* test. During later test phases—and particularly during integration testing—the situation is reversed. The tester has detailed tests results about relatively low-level system structures and uses a *bottom-up* strategy to combine them systematically into a composite test of the entire system. Regression tests frequently cannot rely upon hierarchical strategies at all and therefore require more extensive tooling for analyzing global software structures.

Economics and Management of Testing

Testing frequently dominates development costs. In a large, carefully managed system development, the cost of development testing is often 45% of the total development budget. During maintenance, regression testing costs can represent 70% or more of the total maintenance effort. Integration, system, and operational tests are frequently capital-intensive, requiring special hardware platforms, simulators, and test facilities.

The goal of managing a large and complex test is to balance the cost of a test and its effectiveness. Since the costs associated with late discovery of faults are often very high, managers of successful system developments are usually willing to invest a considerable portion of their resources in early test programs.

The high costs of testing also make managing the relationship between software testing and quality programs more important. Control of these activities may be given to independent oranizations who have overall responsibility for all quality aspects of the system.

Bibliography

1987. Howden, W. E. *Functional Program Testing and Analysis.* New York: McGraw-Hill.

1987. DeMillo, R. A., Martin, R. J., McCrackena, W., and Passafiume, J. *Software Testing and Evaluation.* Redwood City, CA: Benjamin/Cummings.

1995. Marick, B. *The Craft of Software Testing.* Upper Saddle River, NJ: Prentice Hall.

1999. Dustin, E., Rashka, J., and Paul, J. *Automated Software Testing: Introduction, Management and Performance.* Reading, MA: Addison-Wesley.

Richard A. DeMillo

SORTING

> For articles on related subjects *see* ALGORITHMS, ANALYSIS OF; SEARCHING; and TREE.

Internal Sorting

In computing, *sorting* is the process of rearranging an initially unordered sequence of records until they are ordered with respect to all of or that part of each record designated as its *key*. Usually, the desired result is that the records be placed in ascending order (smallest key first), but any sorting algorithm capable of placing records in ascending order can be easily modified to produce a sequence of records in descending order.

As used here, a *record* (*q.v.*) may be as small as a single bit, character, integer, or real (floating-point) number—in which case the entire record serves as a key—or it may be an arbitrarily large aggregate of data values of possibly mixed data types, in which case one or more constituent elements are designated as primary key, secondary key, tertiary key, etc. Multiple keys imply multiple sorting phases in which, for example, the goal might be to sort persons' names so that they are ordered primarily by last name and secondarily—within groups of the same last name—by first name.

The most common rationale for sorting a sequence of records is that the time to do so (once) will prove to be insignificant compared to the many times that the sequence will be searched in order to locate a particular record. When such a search is performed on an unordered sequence of n records, then, on average, $(n+1)/2$ records need to be examined during a successful search (and all n for an unsuccessful search).

But an ordered sequence of n records of uniform length can be searched by examining at most $\log_2 n$ records, which, for $n = 1,024$, is 51 times faster than the average successful sequential search. Thus, the incentive to maintain sorted (ordered) record sequences is quite clear (*see* SEARCHING).

There are many algorithms for sorting unordered data. In choosing or designing one, the foremost consideration is whether all data records reside in main memory (*q.v.*), or whether some or all are stored on an auxiliary mass storage (*q.v.*) device, such as magnetic tape or (more commonly now) magnetic disk. In the former case, one of a class of *internal sorting algorithms* may be used in which, because of the random access property of main memory, records may be freely accessed regardless of their position in what is then essentially an indexable array of records. But when records are stored in an auxiliary mass storage memory whose latency and additional access time (*q.v.*) imposes a severe penalty on retrieval of single records, one of a class of specialized *external sorting algorithms* must be used that processes as many records as possible for each probe into auxiliary mass storage memory. Because the average size of main memory has been increasing so rapidly, this article will emphasize internal sorting algorithms, but it does conclude with a brief discussion of external sorting methods.

For both internal and external sorting algorithms, an important consideration is stability. A sorting algorithm is *stable* if, during movement and possible rearrangement of records, no two records having identical keys ever have their original order reversed. For records that are "all key" or records that are to be sorted only on a primary key, stability is not a concern, but when a record sequence is to be sorted first on a secondary key and then a primary key (the logically necessary order of use of multiple keys), the desired result cannot be attained if the final sort on primary key permutes the order of records whose secondary keys differ, but whose primary keys are the same.

At least five considerations may influence the choice of an internal sorting algorithm:

1. *Running time*—How long does it take to sort n records, and by what factor does this time increase in order to sort $2n$ records?

2. *Memory space*—Do main memory limitations force choice of an algorithm that sorts "in place" (only one or two record spaces are needed beyond the space needed to hold n records), or are there an additional n record spaces available beyond the space needed to hold the data to be sorted?

3. *Initial order*—Are the records known to be already ordered with just a few exceptions? This is not the usual situation, but when it does occur, the most suitable algorithm may well be one that is not at all efficient when the initial order of the records is essentially random.

4. *Key range*—Do record keys span a very large range or possibly only a very restricted range (such as integers 0 to 999)? Certain algorithms applicable to keys of narrow range are not feasible for keys that span a large range.

5. *Programming language*—For reasons of local policy or availability, must a particular programming language be used, and if so, does that language support recursion (*q.v.*)? Many of the most efficient internal sorting algorithms are most naturally expressed recursively and hence would be awkward to encode in languages that do not support recursion.

Unless the number of records to be sorted is very small—perhaps 100 or fewer—by far the most important of these five considerations is running time.

Sorting algorithms may be classified as being either *comparative* or *distributive*. A comparative algorithm rearranges record order by comparing record keys. A distributive algorithm moves records to or close to their final correct position based on intrinsic key characteristics.

Comparative Sorting Algorithms

There is an easily derived theoretical upper limit to the rate at which records may be sorted by key comparison. There are $n!$ different sequences of n records, only one of which (ignoring records of equal key) is the correct ascendingly (or descendingly) ordered sequence. Imagine that these $n!$ permutations form the leaves of a *binary decision tree* (a binary tree in which each node has 0 or 2 children) each of whose nodes represents a comparison of two record keys. Then the shortest path from the root of the tree (where the first comparison decision is made) to the particular leaf that represents the desired final ordering requires a number of decisions equal to the height of the tree (*see* TREE). But a binary decision tree of m leaves has a height of at least $\lceil \log_2 m \rceil$ (i.e. the smallest integer greater than or equal to $\log_2 m$). Now let $m = n!$ and note that for large n the Stirling approximation to $n!$ is proportional to $(n/e)^{n+1/2}$. Then $\log_2 n! = 1.4 \ln n! = 1.4 (n + 1/2)(\ln n - 1)$ which is $O(n \ln n)$ (i.e. approaches a constant times $n \ln n$ as $n \to \infty$; *see* ALGORITHMS, ANALYSIS OF) and hence is also $O(n \log_2 n)$. Thus no sorting algorithm *based on key comparisons* can have

running time superior to $O(n \log n)$. Since the proof is not constructive, however, algorithms that attain this performance have to be discovered empirically. We will discuss four such sorting algorithms, but only after first examining why the four primitive algorithms of most straightforward logic fail to achieve $O(n \log n)$ performance.

SELECTION SORT

The first sorting algorithm likely to occur to anyone is called *selection sort*: look through all n records to find the one with smallest key, then through the remaining $n - 1$ records to find the one of next smallest key, etc. By exchanging each record of successively smaller key with the appropriate record at the top of the unsorted sequence of records, the records can be sorted in place, the length of the sorted sequence at the top growing gradually longer as the length of the unsorted sequence at the bottom shrinks to zero. Selection sort shares with the three other primitive algorithms to be discussed the undesirable property that when the number of records to be sorted is doubled, the time to do so quadruples, another way of saying that its running time is $O(n^2)$. The only desirable property of selection sort is that records of successively larger key are identified one by one, so that output of the sorted list can proceed virtually in parallel with the sort itself.

BUBBLESORT

A second reasonably obvious idea is based on the simplistic notion that if two adjacent records are out of order they should be exchanged. If this is done to successive (overlapped) record pairs, from the first through the record pair that starts at the $(n - 1)$st position, the original list will not necessarily yet be sorted, but one can be sure that the record of largest key (assuming an ascending order sort) will have reached the end of the list. Then, by repeating the process $n - 2$ more times, the entire list is certain to be sorted. Successive phases of the sort are called *passes* (since each requires that we reexamine (i.e. *pass through*), all remaining unsorted data). The name *bubblesort* stems from the fact that from pass to pass the records of "lighter" (smaller) key gradually rise ("bubble up") to their proper ultimate position. Because of the large number of record exchanges required, bubblesort is also known as *exchange sort*.

We will show shortly that both selection sort and bubble sort have $O(n^2)$ average and worst-case running times, but because, on average, each pass of bubblesort needs more exchanges to isolate a new largest key than selection sort needs to identify a new smallest key, bubblesort runs more slowly. In fact, bubblesort runs so slowly relative to most other sorting algorithms that its popularity with hobbyists can only be attributed to the ease with which its logic can be remembered.

The only exceptional feature of bubblesort—not enough to be a redeeming one—is that if, at the end of any pass including the first, it is noted that no exchanges were necessary, the process can be terminated and the record sequence declared to be sorted. Thus, in the best case of attempting to sort an already ordered list—a case that seldom occurs—bubblesort has $O(n)$ running time.

INSERTION SORT

The *insertion sort* algorithm is likely to occur to anyone who has sorted cancelled checks or playing cards by simply holding them in the hand and inserting them one by one into the proper position in the stack or hand of already sorted items. The computer version, of course, has more difficulty making room for new insertions. Sometimes room must be made for insertion of a record at the top of the list, necessitating movement of all records in the partially ordered list down by one position. But whenever a record is encountered whose key is larger than that of the last one in the partially ordered list, it merely needs to be appended to the list. This implies that in the best case of an already sorted list, or even one that is almost ordered to the point where few insertions need to be made near the beginning of the list, insertion sort is $O(n)$. For the average and worst cases, however, insertion sort is $O(n^2)$.

The gradually lengthening partially ordered list need not be stored in a separate storage area from the unsorted list; since the combined number of already sorted and remaining unsorted records remains n throughout the sort, insertion sorting can be done in place by letting the partially sorted list at the top of the combined sequences gradually displace the diminishing list of unsorted records stored directly underneath. A Pascal insertion sort procedure is given in Fig. 1. By making sure that the first element of the array to be sorted is smallest (by an $O(n)$ preamble), the procedure is made slightly faster. Doing so allows the inner loop to be controlled by exactly one test, **while** $A[k] > t$, there being no danger that the loop can run away at the top in a vain search for a number smaller than or equal to the key being inserted. The same effect could have been attained by storing the smallest negative integer in the 0th index position of the array to be sorted, but that would have required cooperation between the calling program and the insertion sort procedure so as to dimension the array of unsorted values $0..limit$ rather than $1..limit$ (while still placing the first meaningful unsorted data value in $A[1]$).

ENUMERATION SORT

Selection sort, bubblesort, and insertion sort all involve movement of data records as an integral part of each pass of the sort. An alternative is to leave actual data movement to a last pass and concentrate first on key comparisons. By comparing each key to all others, we can count how many keys are smaller than any given key. If, for example, the counting phase shows that there are 17 records whose keys are smaller than the key of the first record of the unsorted list, then that record can be moved into the 18th position of the ordered list being developed. The space needed is n locations of integer length to hold counts and n locations of record length to hold the records. A Pascal implementation of enumeration sort is given in Fig. 2.

Provided that the comparisons involved are programmed carefully, all four of the primitive sorting

```
procedure InsertionSort(var A: list; n : integer);
{
    Sorts the first n numbers of A, where type list =
    array [1..limit]
}
var
  i, j, k, t : integer,
begin            {Make sure first number of A is the smallest:}
  for i:=2 to n do if A[i] < A[1] then {exchange them:}
    begin t:=A[i]; A[i] :=A[1]; A[1] :=t end;
  for j:=1 to n-1 do
    begin
      t:=A[j+1];           {Save a copy of the next unsorted}
                           {item to be inserted}
      k:=j;
      while A[k] > t do      {Move down to make room}
                            {for the new item}
        begin
          A[k+1] := A[k];
          k:=k-1
        end;
      A[k+1] :=t              {Make the insertion}
    end
end {Insertion Sort};
```

Figure 1. A Pascal implementation of insertion sort.

```
procedure enumsort (var A : list; n : integer);
{
    Sorts the first n elements of A[1..lim], n <= lim
}
var
  i, j, k, t : integer ; B, count : list;
begin
  for i:=1 to n do count[i] := 0;       {Initialize counts}

  for j:=1 to n-1 do
    for k:=1 to n-j do
    if A[j] > A[k+j] then count[j] := count[j] +1
                else count[k+j] := count[k+j] +1;
    for i:=1 to n do B[count[i]+1]:=A[i];
          {Move keys to B array and then back to A}
    A:=B
  end {enumsort};
```

Figure 2. A Pascal implementation of enumeration sort.

algorithms are stable. From Figs. 3a–d, the $O(n^2)$ worst case running times of these four algorithms can easily be deduced from the principal portion of their highly similar structured flowcharts (Nassi–Shneiderman diagrams). Each has an inner loop that is executed an average of $n/2$ times ($n/4$ for insertion sort) for each outer loop index that ranges from 1 to $n - 1$, so that overall running time is $O(n^2)$.

Although none of the four primitive comparison sort algorithms realizes the theoretically possible $O(n \log n)$

behavior, three of the four have modifications that do. We will examine them in the same order: a modified selection sort called *heapsort*, modified exchange sorts called *quicksort* and *radix exchange sort*, and modified insertion sorts called *Shellsort*, *treesort*, and *mergesort*. We will then comment on the search for a modified enumeration sort.

HEAPSORT—A BETTER SELECTION SORT
In 1964, John Williams realized that the principal defect of selection sort was that important information

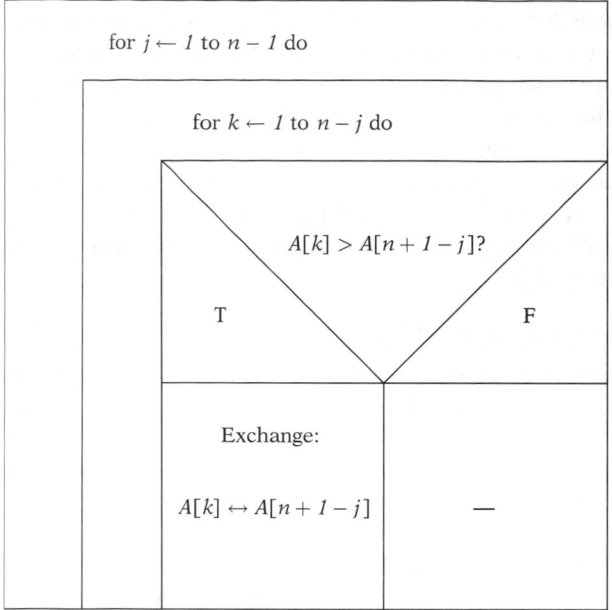

(a) Selection sort

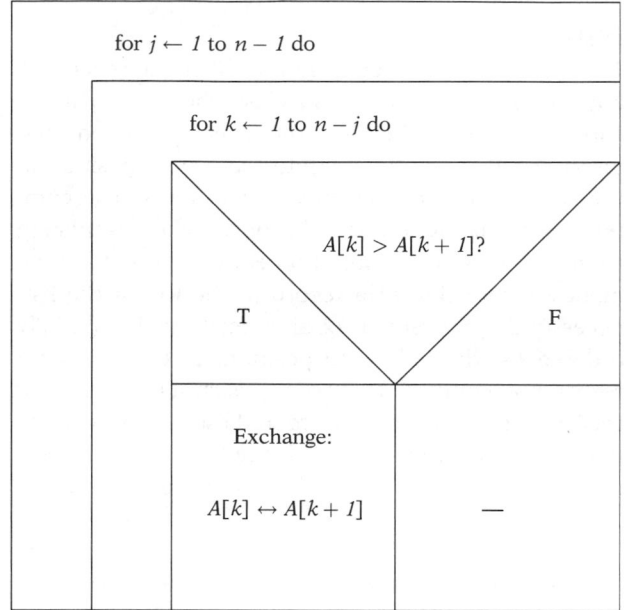

(b) Bubble sort

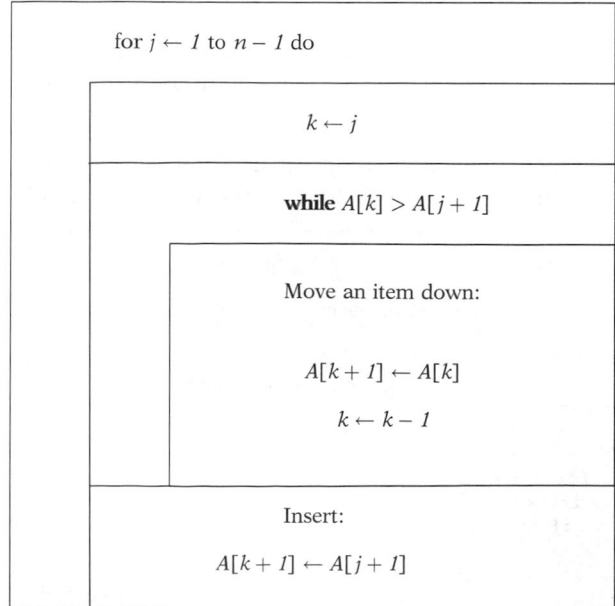

(c) Insertion sort

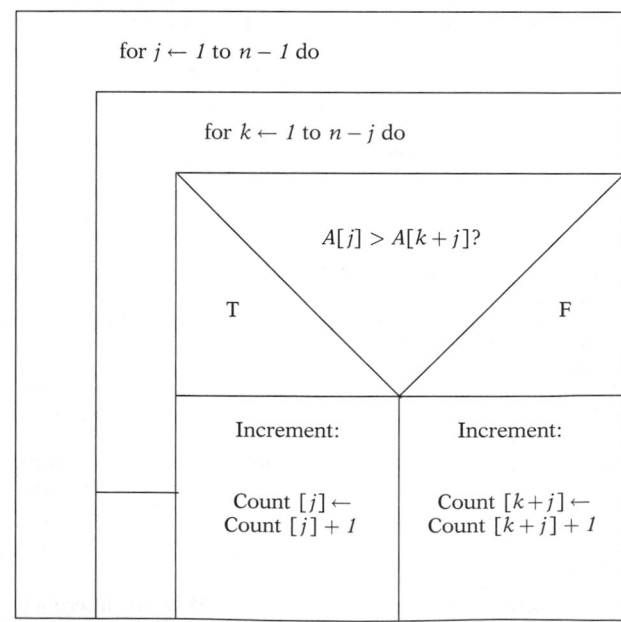

(d) Enumeration sort

Figure 3. Nested-loop structure of the four primitive $O(n^2)$ sorts.

was being developed but then discarded and lost during each pass that isolates the smallest key of the records remaining to be sorted: the value of the next smaller key. That key—almost the "winner" in the search for the smallest key—was being overwritten, perhaps at the last instant, with the smallest key. How could knowledge of that next smallest key—and the third smallest, perhaps, etc.—be preserved as the sort progresses? Williams invented an algorithm called *heapsort* based on two observations: (1) information about the relative sizes of keys could be stored in a special kind of binary tree called a *heap*, and (2) the nodes of a heap can be mapped one to one to successive cells of an *array*.

A *heap* (more particularly, a minheap) is a complete binary tree in which the value of every node is less than or equal to the value of either child node. (A maxheap is formed in a similar way, except that the value of every node is greater than or equal to either child node.) By "complete" is meant that there are no missing nodes except, perhaps, for one or more leaves at the right of the bottom level. Once the unsorted records are "heapified," the record at the root can be removed and made the first record of the sorted list (and issued as output, if desired, in parallel with the remainder of the sort). When the 2-tree forest that remains is reheapified, the new root will be the next record to be appended to the sorted list (or issued as output), and the process continues until the entire array of records is sorted.

The mapping of a complete binary tree of 7 nodes to successive elements of an array is shown in Fig. 4. A Pascal procedure that implements heapsort is shown in Fig. 5. For reasons of coding efficiency, the procedure forms maxheaps rather than minheaps, storing successive smaller new maximum values backward from the end of a subsidiary array. Since, unlike most $O(n \log n)$ algorithms, heapsort is iterative, the code given can easily be transliterated into Basic, Cobol, or Fortran. However complicated the record movement involved in the heapify procedure may sound, all that happens throughout is movement of a record from one indexed position in an array to another, so that heapsort might just as well have been called *array sort*. And, while the proof is omitted here, heapsort running time is $O(n \log n)$, even in the worst case, and the algorithm is stable.

QUICKSORT—A BETTER EXCHANGE SORT

In 1962, C. A. R. Hoare reasoned that the principal defect of exchange sort (bubblesort) was that the records that were exchanged never moved very far; each exchange moved the records only one record position closer to their ultimate location, a snail's pace. What if, he pondered, records were partitioned

```
procedure Heapsort(var a : data; n : integer);
var
    i : integer

    procedure exchange(var a, b : integer);
    var
     t : integer
    begin
     t:=a; a:=b; b:=t
    end {exchange};

    procedure rebuild(j,m : integer);
    var
        k : integer;
        sinking : Boolean;
    begin
        sinking:=true;
        k:=2*j;
        while (k<=m) and sinking do
          begin
            if k<m then if a[k]<a[k+1] then k:=k+1;
                                   {Find the larger child}
            if a[j]<a[k] then      {Exchange a[j] with the
                                       larger of its children}
              begin
                exchange(a[j],a[k]);
                j:=k;            {Advance j to point to latest point
                                            of insertion}
                k:=2*k          {Advance k to point to first child
                                            of old k}
              end
            else sinking:=false     {Change sentinel to force
                                            termination}
          end
    end {rebuild};

    procedure buildheap;
    var
      i:=integer;
    begin
      for i:=n div 2 downto 1 do rebuild(i,n)
    end {buildheap};

begin {Heapsort}
  buildheap;
  for i:=n downto 2 do
    begin
      exchange(a[1],a[i]);          {Exchange top of heap
                                     and current last element}
      rebuild(1, i-1)               {Restore heap}
    end
end {Heapsort};
```

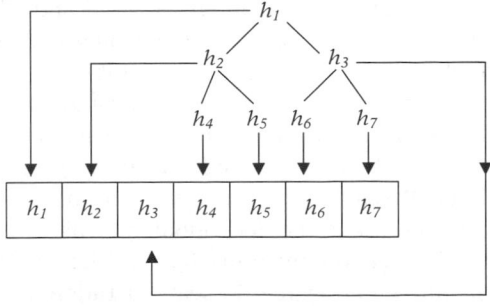

Figure 4. Mapping a binary tree to a one-dimensional array.

Figure 5. A Pascal implementation of heapsort.

with respect to a chosen *pivot*, a particular key taken from one of the records in the data set being partitioned. All records having a key less than or equal to the pivot would be placed in a left partition; all other records would be placed in a right partition and the pivot record would lie between them. Neither the left nor right partition would then necessarily be sorted, but the pivot record would be in its final location, never having to be moved again. Next, the left and right partitions are partitioned in the same way, etc. (recursively, in the easiest implementation to program). When all partitions have reached size 1, the sort is complete. Hoare called his algorithm *quicksort*, the name most commonly used, but it is sometimes called *partition exchange sort*.

A Pascal quicksort procedure is given in the article STRUCTURED PROGRAMMING. On average—i.e. for initial sequences of records whose keys are randomly distributed—quicksort has running time $O(n \log n)$. Running time is sensitive to the choice of pivot, however, and using the first record's key as pivot as that procedure does will yield $O(n^2)$ running time for sequences that are already in order, or are in reverse order.

For average data, experience has shown that quicksort is the fastest of all known comparison sorts. However, the conventional implementation of quicksort is unstable.

RADIX EXCHANGE SORT

Another improved version of exchange sort is the *radix exchange sort* invented in 1959 (before quicksort) by Paul Hildebrandt, Harold Isbitz, Hawley Rising, and Jules Schwartz. The basic idea is to look at the binary representation of the keys to be sorted bit by bit, a column (radix position) at a time, starting at the leftmost column that has at least one 1-bit. Then, analogously to a quicksort partition that progresses by moving a pair of pointers from the left and right sides of an array of records until they meet, pointers (*q.v.*) are moved down from the top and up from the bottom until they meet. During pointer motion, bitwise comparisons are made and, whenever a pair of keys is found such that the key having a 1-bit in the column under review lies above a key having a 0-bit in that position, the records are exchanged. When a pass is finished (complete processing of the bits in a given column), the data will have been organized into two groups—one with 0-bits in that column and (below it) one with 1-bits in that column. On the next pass, each group is examined separately with respect to bit comparisons on the next column to the right.

Suppose, for example, that there are a certain six numbers to be sorted. Begin by listing their binary representations and using variable j to label bit positions right to left:

Key	$j=4$	3	2	1	0
25	1	1	0	0	1
4	0	0	1	0	0
23	1	0	1	1	1
15	0	1	1	1	1
1	0	0	0	0	1
17	1	0	0	0	1

If these numbers were sorted, the "heavier" keys would be under the "lighter" keys; i.e. no number having a 1 at bit position 4 would be above a number having a 0 at that position. To proceed toward that status, we move index pointers i and k down from the top and up from the bottom, respectively, until i points to a 1 and k points to a 0; then we exchange all bits of the two numbers pointed at. If we continue moving i and k until they cross, we obtain

Key	$j=4$	3	2	1	0
1	0	0	0	0	1
4	0	0	1	0	0
15	0	1	1	1	1
23	1	0	1	1	1
25	1	1	0	0	1
17	1	0	0	0	1

The keys are still not in order, so the process is repeated for the group of numbers above the line at bit position $j = 3$, and the same is done separately for the group of keys below the line. Nothing happens to the top group (because they happen to be in order), though this is far less likely to be the case if there had been, say, 1,006 numbers to sort rather than just 6. But processing the bottom group at $j = 3$ will yield

Key	$j=4$	3	2	1	0
23	1	0	1	1	1
17	1	0	0	0	1
25	1	1	0	0	1

The next pass, at $j = 2$, will interchange 23 and 17 and complete the sort. Since the bookkeeping needed to keep track of the rapidly growing number of groups that need further processing is formidable, the algorithm is best implemented recursively. Also, the algorithm must be programmed in a language (such as C or Turbo Pascal) that gives the programmer some means of accessing the individual bits of a stored number. The version given in Fig. 6 exploits a Turbo Pascal feature whereby the Boolean operation and can be applied bitwise to a pair of integer operands.

```
procedure RadixExchangeSort (var a : data;
                                j, lo, hi : integer);
var
    i,k,mask : integer;

    procedure exchange(var a,b : integer);
    var t : integer;
    begin t:=a; a:=b; b:=t end

begin
    if (j>=0) and (lo<hi) then
    begin
      mask:=bitmask[j];
      i:=lo-1; k:=hi+1;
      repeat
        repeat i:=i+1 until ((a[i] and mask)>0) or
                                (i=k);
        repeat k:=k-1 until ((a[k] and mask)=0) or
                                (k=i);
        if i<k then exchange(a[i], a[k])
      until i>=k;
      RadixExchangeSort(a, j-1,lo,i-1);
      RadixExchangeSort(a, j-1,i,hi)
    end
end {RadixExchangeSort};
```

Figure 6. A Turbo Pascal implementation of the radix exchange sort.

The similarity of radix exchange sort to quicksort is striking. The effect is to partition numbers according to a phantom pivot of value 2^j that is not necessarily a member of the set of record keys being examined.

Since radix exchange sort indirectly involves key comparisons, albeit bit by bit, it is subject to the proof given earlier that a comparison sort runs, at best, in $O(n \log n)$. Knuth (1973) gives an extensive analysis that this is so, but the $O(n \log n)$ behavior does not set in until very high values of n; for up to at least 16,000 items sorted, the dominant behavior appears to be that radix exchange runs in $O(pn)$, where p (for precision) is the number of bit positions to be examined. But if we think of the keys as numbers, then the more data to be sorted, the more likely it will be that keys span an ever greater range. As the range increases (ever higher large values), the more bits there are in the binary representation of these large keys. Thus, there is a propensity that $p = \log n$, so that $O(pn)$ reduces to $O(n \log n)$ after all.

SHELLSORT—AN IMPROVED INSERTION SORT

An interesting algorithm that improves the performance of sorting by insertion was published by Donald L. Shell in 1959. In the best case—a list already in order—insertion sort is $O(n)$ because each newly stored item can just be appended to the end of the growing output list. If the data is almost but not quite in order, performance should still be close to $O(n)$ because so few items need to be inserted far up into the output list. So, if only we could do some work taking less than $O(n^2)$, to get the list "almost" sorted prior to a final $O(n)$ insertion pass, we might be able to

obtain an overall performance that is less than $O(n^2)$. What Shell proposed was that a certain number of preliminary passes be performed that are also insertion sorts, but of a special kind. Rather than processing all n numbers spaced one storage unit apart (as will be done on the last pass), each earlier pass divides the numbers into groups that are, say, eight index positions apart on the first pass, four apart on the second pass, two apart on the third, and then—finally—one apart on the fourth and last pass. Because of this strategy, Shellsort is also known as a *diminishing increment sort*. For a given increment i, each pass does i insertion sorts, each on a group of (approximately) n/i numbers spaced i apart. Here is how the algorithm would work for $n = 13$ and successive increments of 4, 2, and 1 (where the group of insertion sorts with a given increment i is called an *i-sort*):

original data	17	3	65	81	9	12	6	5	27	4	87	1	18
after the 4-sort	9	3	6	1	17	4	65	5	18	12	87	81	27
after the 2-sort	6	1	9	3	17	4	18	5	27	12	65	81	87
after the 1-sort	1	3	4	5	6	9	12	17	18	27	65	81	87

```
procedure Shellsort(var a : data; n : integer);
{type data=array[-29524..max] of integer;}
const m=10;
var
    i : array[1..m] of integer;       {Array of diminishing
                                              increments}
    j : 1..m; k,p,s,t,inc : integer;
begin
    i[m]:=-1;
    for j:=m-1 downto 1 do i[j]:=3*i[j+1]+1;
                                    {Calculate increments}
    for j:=1 to m do              {j controls # of sort passes}
      begin
        inc:=i[j];
        for k:=1 to inc do        {k controls # groups to be
                                      i[j]-sorted per pass}
          begin
            s:=inc+k;             {s marks current last item to be
                                              inserted}
            while s<=n do
              begin
                p:=s;
                t:=a[p];          {Save copy of item to be inserted}
                a[1-inc]:=t;      {Set sentinel to bound
                                      search for insertion point}
                while t<a[p-inc] do
                  begin
                    a[p]:=a[p-inc];  {Move item down
                                              one increment}
                    p:=p-inc         {Decrement position
                                          counter one inc}
                  end;
                a[p]:=t;          {Insert new item}
                s:=s+inc          {Prepare to get next item
                                      to be inserted}
              end
          end
      end
end{Shellsort};
```

Figure 7. A Pascal version of Shellsort.

Though we used increments of 4, 2, and 1 for the sake of illustration, it has been shown that if an *i-sort* is done followed by a *j-sort*, the array is still *i-sorted*. Therefore, interaction among the groups as the sequence of sorts progresses will cause the array to become more nearly sorted sooner if the increments are *not* multiples of one another. The Pascal procedure of Fig. 7 uses the ten increments 29,524, 9,841, 3,280, 1,093, 364, 121, 40, 13, 4, 1, where each increment is one more than three times the increment to the right.

The program of Fig. 7 sorts half a million numbers 1,200 times faster than does one insertion pass ($m = 1$; $i[1] = 1$). Though much faster than an $O(n^2)$ sort, the behavior of Shellsort still does not attain the theoretical $O(n \log n)$ performance that we hope to attain for a comparison sort. Empirical evidence is that Shellsort runs as $O(n^{1.2})$, or perhaps $O(n \log^2 n)$. Those two functions grow at a similar rate for values of n up to a million and theory has not yet provided a guide as to which, if either, function characterizes Shellsort behavior for very large values of n.

Shellsort endures in the face of better algorithms because it is quite fast for sorting up to several thousand items and because it is iterative rather than recursive. However, it is unstable.

SHORTSORT—AN ENIGMATIC SORT

Another diminishing increment sort was invented by John Piccard and communicated to this author in 1987. A Pascal implementation is given in Fig. 8. The code is so remarkably short that one might wonder how it can possibly accomplish its objective. Its outer loop is executed for a sequence of diminishing increments, the number of such increments being controlled by a real parameter f. Unlike Shellsort, whose nested inner loops represent a complete insertion sort (or, in a variant, a complete exchange sort) performed on the set of keys an increment apart, Shortsort uses a single inner loop that merely exchanges out-of-order keys spaced an increment apart.

The performance of Shortsort is very sensitive to the parameter f. The number of comparisons made can be shown to be

$$n\left(\frac{\log n}{-\log f} - \frac{f}{1-f} \right)$$

Accordingly, for $n = 512\text{K}$ (2^{19}), Shortsort runs about four times faster for $f = 0.4$ then it does for $f = 0.8$. But f needs to be at least 0.5 in order for Shortsort to perform the minimum $n(\log n - 1)$ comparisons. Unfortunately, however, with $f = 0.5$, Shortsort will not produce a sorted array for virtually any value of n. Experimentation with random integer keys and values of n up to 512K show that the critical value of f lies

```
procedure Shortsort(var ary : data;
                         arlength : integer);
const f=0.8;
var
   realgap : real;
   intgap,j,k,temp : integer;

begin {Shortsort}
   realgap:=f*arlength;
   repeat
      intgap:=trunc(realgap);
      for j:=1 to arlength-intgap do
        begin
          k:=j+intgap;
          if ary[j]>ary[k] then
            begin
              temp:=ary[j];
              ary[j]:=ary[k];
              ary[k]:=temp
            end
        end;
      realgap:=f*realgap
   until realgap<1
end {Shortsort};
```

Figure 8. A Pascal implementation of Shortsort.

between 0.775 (which yields missorted arrays) and 0.780 (which does not). At $f = 0.8$, Shortsort is reliable and runs in time virtually identical to that of Shellsort.

Shortsort is intriguing because of its speed and its short, nonrecursive code. But it will remain an enigma until some theorist can prove that for some critical, possibly n-dependent value of f, it can be guaranteed to sort without error.

TREESORT—ANOTHER IMPROVED INSERTION SORT

The principal defect of insertion sort is that records occasionally need to be placed high in the list of tentatively sorted records, necessitating downward movement of a large number of records stored as a sequential list in an array. What is needed is an alternative data structure into which new records can be inserted at much less operational cost. A more suitable structure for use with a type of insertion sort is a *binary search tree*, such as is described in the article TREE. Suppose that the data to be sorted is the initial sequence of integers 9 2 7 1 4 8 7 6 10. Their corresponding search tree is shown in Fig. 9.

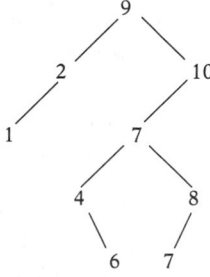

Figure 9.

The first unsorted integer becomes the root of the tree. Each successive integer is then inserted recursively into the left subtree if it is strictly less than the root, and into the right subtree if it is equal to (for stability) or greater than the root. If insertions are made according to this rule, then an inorder traversal of the search tree will produce the desired sorted sequence, in this case, 1 2 4 6 7 7 8 9 10. This algorithm, known as *treesort*, was first described by David J. Wheeler in 1957 and Conway M. Berners-Lee in 1958.

With the average case of randomly distributed keys, the search tree formed will be reasonably well-balanced and treesort will perform as $O(n \log n)$. But in the worst case of already ordered (or reverse ordered) keys, the search tree will consist of one long linear right (or left) subtree and treesort will degenerate to $O(n^2)$ performance.

MERGESORT

An improved insertion sort algorithm based on repetitive merging was discussed as early as 1945 by John von Neumann (*q.v.*). Merging, an information processing technique similar to that of sorting, makes no sense except when applied to two (or more) lists that are already separately in order. To *merge* such lists then means to intersperse their elements to form one overall output list that is entirely in order.

Fig. 10 shows an output list C in the process of being formed through the merging of ordered sublists A and B. Four ordered numbers have already been delivered to output list C; we have no way of knowing which of lists A and B they came from. The current heads of lists A and B are 40 and 48 respectively, so the lower one, 40, gets to go next. Unlike automobiles merging from two lanes to one, where courtesy would indicate that it's now the turn of the car in lane B to go next, numbers are selected strictly by their relative size. Thus, 43, which moved up one spot when 40 left, goes ahead of 48, then 48 moves out because it is lower than 52, etc., until all numbers have been processed. When there is a tie at the heads of the lists, then, ignoring stability, it is immaterial which number goes next. There is no requirement that the lists being merged have the same length.

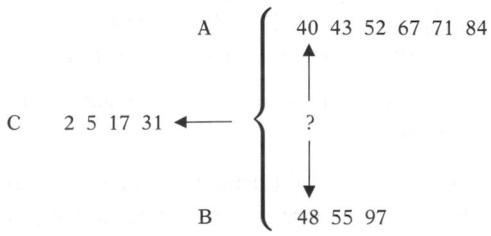

Figure 10. A merge in progress.

The merging algorithm can be stated in pseudocode as:

while { still more unmerged items in either list } **do**
  begin
    if *A is empty, take the next item from B,* **else**
    if *B is empty, take the next item from A,* **else**
    take the smaller of the two items at the heads
    of lists A and B
  end

In the course of being merged, each number in each list is processed only once. This means that the running time needed to merge two lists of size m and n will be proportional to $m + n$: processing time increases only linearly with increasing list sizes. Thus, merging is a far more efficient process than sorting, which, using poor algorithms such as bubblesort, takes running time proportional to the square of the number of elements to be sorted.

As von Neumann observed, repetitive merging can be made the basis of a very efficient sort strategy. Once we are able to form some initially sorted sublists no matter how short—and that is not difficult if the sublists need only be, say, two numbers long—we can merge two lists of length two to make one of length four, two fours to make eight, etc., until we have formed one ordered list. Recursion is used in order to make the machine's memory (the stack (*q.v.*) behind the scenes) remember all currently unprocessed lists. Fig. 11 is a diagram that shows how to apply repetitive merging to effectuate sorting:

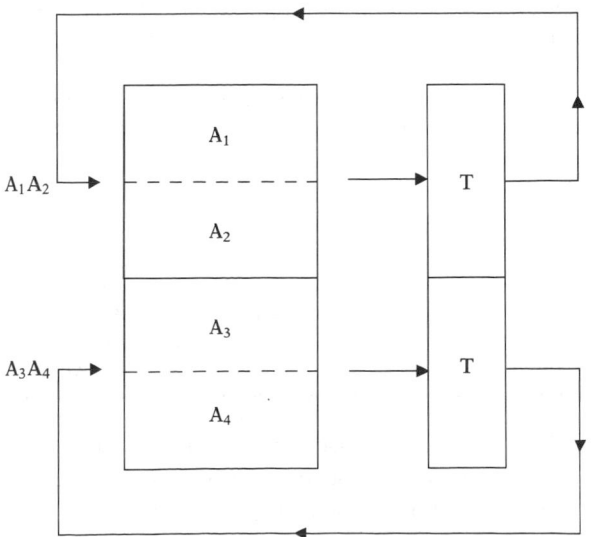

Figure 11. Sorting by repetitive merging. Given that data segments A, A_2, A_3, and A_4 are ordered already, A_1 and A_2 can be merged into T and then stored back to $A_1 A_2$, and the same can be done with A_3 and A_4. Finally, a merge of $A_1 A_2$ and $A_3 A_4$ completes the sort.

Strategy: Sort the bottom half. Sort the top half. Merge the halves.

Tactics: 1. Let the "sort" itself be a mergesort, i.e. use recursion with the termination condition being: if size < 2 do nothing. If size = 2, exchange the two items if necessary to produce the mini-sequences needed for later merging.

2. The merge procedure needed for mergesort must be slightly different than the earlier one so that merged sequences are stored back where they need to be to continue the repetitive process.

First version: Merge A & B → C
Needed now:
(a) Merge two halves of A → T
(b) A ← T

The temporary array T is needed because we can't place a partially completed merged list back on top of the original lists without destroying unprocessed parts of those original lists.

A Pascal *mergesort* procedure based on a slightly different strategy is given in ALGORITHMS, DESIGN AND CLASSIFICATION OF. Actual time measurements on one particular computer showed that mergesort was able to sort half a million numbers 500 times faster than bubblesort. To see why, let's make a crude analysis of how much work is involved in sorting some more manageable number of numbers, say 64, under the simplifying assumption that pairs of lists being sorted are of equal size.

# merges		# numbers/ merge		# numbers processed	
32	×	2	=	64	
16	×	4	=	64	
8	×	8	=	64	
4	×	16	=	64	6
2	×	32	=	64	
1	×	64	=	64	
Total operations			=	64 × 6	
or, in general				$n \times \log_2 n$	

The $O(n \log n)$ behavior of mergesort holds even in the worst case, and mergesort has the added advantage of being stable when properly programmed.

FASTCOUNT—A BETTER ENUMERATION SORT

Since three of the four primitive $O(n^2)$ algorithms—selection sort, bubblesort, and insertion sort—have one or more modified versions that run as $O(n \log n)$, one might expect that there should be a way to modify the fourth one—enumeration sort—to run as $O(n \log n)$, but the hypothetical *fastcount* has not yet been invented. A very efficient $O(n)$ sorting algorithm based on counting will be discussed in the next section, but it is distributive rather than comparative.

Distributive Sorting Algorithms

Instead of comparing keys, a distributive sorting algorithm moves each record to or close to its final destination based on some intrinsic property of the key itself. The first such sort we will examine is the oldest, one used as the basis for the special-purpose sorting machines that were first developed in the late 1800s by Herman Hollerith (*q.v.*) for processing census data.

RADIX SORT

For reasons that will soon become apparent, the algorithm used for sorting on physical card sorting machines is seldom used on a computer. That algorithm is called *radix sort* because it depends on multiple sort passes, one for each digit (radix) position of the maximum value number to be sorted. (On a card-sorting machine, the radix is invariably 10—the digits are decimal digits—but any radix may be used from two upward.) The earliest published description of radix sort cited by Knuth (1973) is by Leslie J. Comrie (*q.v.*) in 1929.

As cards flow through the machine on any given pass, they drop into the appropriate one of ten pockets numbered 0 to 9, corresponding to the digit in the position being used as a key. Suppose we are sorting three-digit numbers 000 to 999. Though it is not the procedure followed, we can easily envision the success of a three-pass procedure that proceeds left to right, sorting cards first into piles where, say, all of the 300s drop into one pocket and all of the 700s drop into another. Separately sorting each pile on their tens digits and, later, subpiles on their units digits will complete the sort. But such a procedure involves much more card handling than is necessary. Though not obvious, passes may be made in the opposite order, right to left from units digit to hundreds digit, provided the cards are collected and stacked properly after each pass. The entire deck participates in each pass. After all but the last pass, cards are collected by placing the 9-pocket stack on top of the 8-pocket stack, etc., picking up the 0-pocket stack last. After the last pass, collect cards in normal order, 0-pocket through the 9th.

There are two problems in adapting this algorithm for use on a computer:

1. Numbers are stored internally in binary, not decimal. One might program a binary radix sort, but it is more effective to treat binary keys as if they were octal by accessing successive groups of three bits

from right to left, or hexadecimal by accessing successive groups of four bits from right to left. (If all bits are accessed—the whole key—radix sort reduces to the hashsort algorithm to be described momentarily.)

2. On a physical card sorter, pockets are very deep relative to the size of the typical card deck being sorted. If pockets are simulated as arrays in a computer, each array has to be prepared to hold all n numbers being sorted (just in case they all have, say, a 7 in the same radix position). If the radix is 16 (hexadecimal), then $16n$ record locations are needed, a storage requirement that is just not competitive with the many algorithms that sort in place, or that use at most an extra n record locations. Linked lists could be used for pockets, but the resulting program is unwieldy.

Since, for a given radix r and bit precision p, the radix sort makes $\log_2 r$ passes, its running time is expected to be $O([p/\log r]n)$ in the best, average, and worst cases. Thus, for 16-bit integers and radix 16 (hexadecimal), the radix sort should run about four times more slowly than hashsort (see below).

SORTING BY ADDRESS CALCULATION (PERFECT HASHING)

An $O(n)$ distributive algorithm applicable to data of restricted range was described by Earl Isaac and Richard Singleton in 1956. Suppose that the data to be sorted are integers in the range 1 to *limit* with no duplicates. Then, if there is sufficient memory space to declare an array T of size *limit*, that array is initialized to zero (or any value outside the range 1..*limit*) and unsorted data values are directed, one by one, into the

unique space reserved for each: $T[7] \leftarrow 7$; $T[19] \leftarrow 19$, etc. (*see* Fig. 12). After distribution to the temporary array T, the nonzero values from $T[1]$ through $T[limit]$ can be output as the sorted list, or (as in the procedure of Fig. 13) nonzero values can be moved back on top of the original array of unsorted data. When either of these operations is done properly, it takes only $O(limit)$ time, or $O(n)$ time if n is close to *limit*. Since it takes only $O(n)$ time to store the numbers and $O(n)$ time to pack them, the overall performance of the algorithm is $O(n)$. This method was called sorting by *address calculation* in the days of machine language programming—each data value being directed to an address equal to itself—but could now be called sorting by *index calculation* when implemented in a high-level language. It is also called sorting by *perfect hashing* (*see* SEARCHING) because, since it was postulated that the data set contained no duplicates, each value can be "hashed" to a particular destination address without danger of "collisions."

Although the procedure given for the address calculation sort applies to records that are "all key" integers, it can easily be extended to apply to records of any uniform size (memory permitting) whose keys obey the restriction cited: integers in the range 1..*limit* with no duplicates.

HASHSORT

The condition that a sequence of record keys span the range 1..*limit*, as was required for sorting by address calculation, occurs fairly often, but the restriction that there can be no duplicates is unrealistic. What can be done to salvage sorting by hashing under threat of collisions (two or more records hashed to the same index position)? One way is to build a linked list of

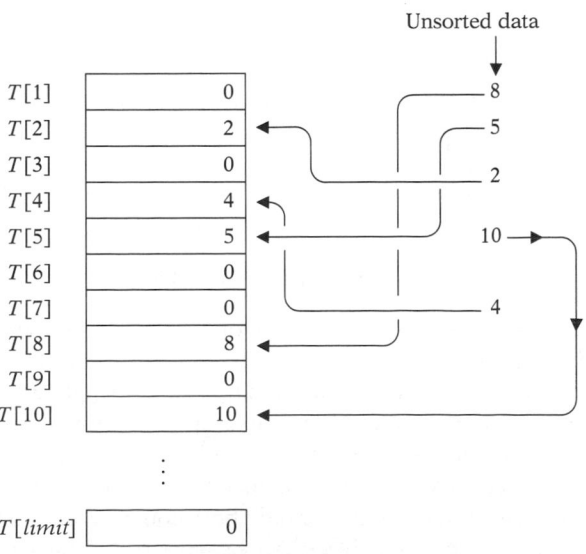

		Unsorted data
$T[1]$	0	8
$T[2]$	2	5
$T[3]$	0	2
$T[4]$	4	
$T[5]$	5	10
$T[6]$	0	
$T[7]$	0	4
$T[8]$	8	
$T[9]$	0	
$T[10]$	10	

$T[limit]$ | 0 |

Figure 12. Sorting data by address calculation.

```
procedure adcalcsort(var A : list; n : integer);
{
    Sorts the first n numbers of list A by address calculation,
    where type list = array[1..limit] of integer. Assumes
    that all numbers to be sorted are in [1..limit] and that there
    are no duplicates.
}
var
    i,j : integer; T : list;
begin
    for i:=1 to limit do T[i]:=0;              {Initialize T}
    for i:=1 to n do T[A[i]]:=A[i];
                              {Put each A[i] in its reserved slot}

{Now move nonzero elements of T back into A}

    j:=1;
    for i:=1 to limit do if T[i]<>0 then
      begin
        A[j]:=T[i];
        j:=j+1
      end {for}
end{adcalcsort};
```

Figure 13. A Pascal procedure for sorting by address calculation.

collided items at each target destination (*see* LIST PRO-CESSING). A Pascal procedure called *hashsort* based on this idea is given in Fig. 14. (Hashsort is also called *bucket sort* because every record is directed into a particular receptacle, or "bucket.") All elements of a target array are initialized to nil pointers, and then all keys that hash to a given index position are entered into a linked list, even if that list never contains more than one item.

But what kind of hash function is appropriate? If no key were larger than the length of the pointer table, then no hashing would be necessary, since all keys would land inside the table and only identical keys

would cause collisions. But if keys might be larger than the size of the pointer array, they must be cut down to size even though doing so will increase the frequency of collisions. If keys might be as large as, say, 9,999, and the table size is just 1,000 we could simply divide each key by 10. Then, 7,136 and 7,139 would both be mapped to index 713, but as long as the overflow list corresponding to index 713 is kept in order and its complete 4-digit components are later recovered in order, the collision will ultimately be resolved. Instead of always using 10 as a divisor, the procedure of Fig. 14 computes an optimum divisor based on the relative sizes of the maximum key and the pointer table used.

When hashsort encounters no collisions, it is clearly an $O(n)$ algorithm. At the other extreme, when the data to be sorted is so skewed that all n items hash to the same index, the sort would be only as good as the $O(n^2)$ running time needed to maintain an ordered singly linked list. But for randomly distributed keys and reasonable pointer table size, we expect collisions to be sufficiently rare that it would be hard to detect any degradation from the $O(n)$ performance obtainable with perfect hashing. This is in fact the empirical result of experimentation with hashsort. Its high speed is attained at the cost of high storage overhead—for "all key" integer records, the table of linked lists occupies space at least three times that of the array of unsorted items.

```
procedure Hashsort (var a: data; n: integer);
const m = 99999;                  {Upper limit of hash table}
typ ptr = ^node;
    node = record;
             val : integer;
             link : ptr
           end;

var
    h : array [0..m] of ptr;
    i, j, mpl : integer ;
    t : ptr;
    d : integer;    {Divisor to be used in the hash function}

    procedure insert (item : integer; var list : ptr);
    var p : ptr;
    begin
      if list = nil then begin
        new(p);
        p^.val := item;
        p^.link := nil;
           list := p
      end
      else if item <= list^.val then begin
             new(p);
             p^.val := item;
             p^.link := list;
                list := p
           end
      else insert (item, list^.link)
    end {insert};

begin                             {Logic of Hashsort itself}
  mpl := m + 1;
  d := 1 + trunc(maxnum / mpl);
  for i := 0 to m do h[i] := nil;    {Empty the hash table}
  for j := 1 to n do insert (a[j], h[a[j] div d]);
                                  {Insert all data}

  j := 1;        {Recover hashed items and store them back at
                                                       array a}
  for i := 0 to m do
    begin
      t := h[i];
        while t <> nil do
          begin
            a[j] := t^.val;
            j := j + 1;
            t := t^.link
          end
      end
  end {Hashsort};
```

Figure 14. A Pascal hashsort procedure.

ULTRASORT

When conditions permit, an extremely fast sorting algorithm with a worst-case performance of $O(n)$ can be based on *frequency counting*. Suppose that we want to sort an arbitrarily long sequence of single-digit integers. If we just count the integers, which we can do in $O(n)$ time, the counts of their relative occurrences might conceivably be

$$c[0] = 147 \quad \text{there are 147 0s}$$
$$c[1] = 89 \quad \text{there are }89\text{ 1s}$$
$$c[2] = 463 \quad \text{there are 463 2s}$$
$$\vdots$$
$$c[9] = 216 \quad \text{there are 216 9s}$$

Next, we overwrite the array of unsorted numbers with consecutively, 147 zeros, 89 ones, 463 twos, etc., up through 216 nines—all in $O(n)$ time. Single-digit numbers were used only as an example; the maximum size of the integers that can be handled with this often overlooked algorithm is limited only by how large a table can be allocated to hold the frequency counts. The algorithm, first described by Harold Seward in 1954, has no standard name. It was called *mathsort* by

```
procedure Ultrasort (var a:data; n:integer);
var
    c : array[0..maxnum] of integer;
    i,j,k : integer;
begin
    for j:=0 to maxnum do c[j]:=0;        {Initialize the
                                              counts}
    for i:=1 to n do c[a[i]]:=c[a[i]]+1;   {Increment
                              the bin having the same number}
    k:=1;
    for j:=0 to maxnum do        {Make c[j] copies of each
                                              count:}
        for i:=1 to c[j] do
          begin
             a[k] :=j;
             k:=k+1
          end
end {Ultrasort};
```

Figure 15. A Pascal ultrasort procedure.

Wallace Feurzig in 1960 and *ultrasort*, the name used here, by Reilly and Federighi (1989). A Pascal version is given in Fig. 15.

Sorting Large Records

The Pascal procedures given for the internal sorting algorithms described assumed that the records being sorted were "all key" integers. In most actual situations, the key that determines the collating order is just one part—a small one, perhaps—of some larger record. An example would be a nine-digit social security number that constitutes one field of a record of, say, 900 characters. The work of most sorting algorithms consists of making comparisons and moving data. When only small keys are involved, comparisons tend to dominate, but if large records are moved about, moves become very significant and can greatly distort the relative performances otherwise attainable from the various algorithms discussed herein. But large records should not be moved during sorting; only their keys and their original index positions should be shifted. Suppose, for example, that we wish to sort the array of records shown in Fig. 16, where the non-key portion of each record is quite large.

The sequence of scrambled indices represented by the $p[i]$ is in an important sense more valuable than the sorted $R[i]$ would be (which is why the APL (*q.v.*) language "grade up" function returns such indices rather than actually sorting its operand vector). Those indices (subscripts), applied in the order derived, can be used to output or move all or any part of the $R[i]$ to whatever destination is desired in precisely the order indicated by their keys.

Alternatively, we could maintain an array of pointers to the large records and, when comparison of record keys indicates an interchange, swap pointers rather than the records themselves. A pointer is a small item (a machine address); the record might be many hundreds of bytes long.

Comparative Performance of Internal Sorting Algorithms

The best, average, and worst-case performance of 14 internal sorting algorithms is given in Table 1. The running times (Table 2) for sorting 32K (K = 1024) six-digit random numbers up through 512K numbers in steps a factor of two apart were obtained on a 166 MHz Pentium machine for routines written in the version of

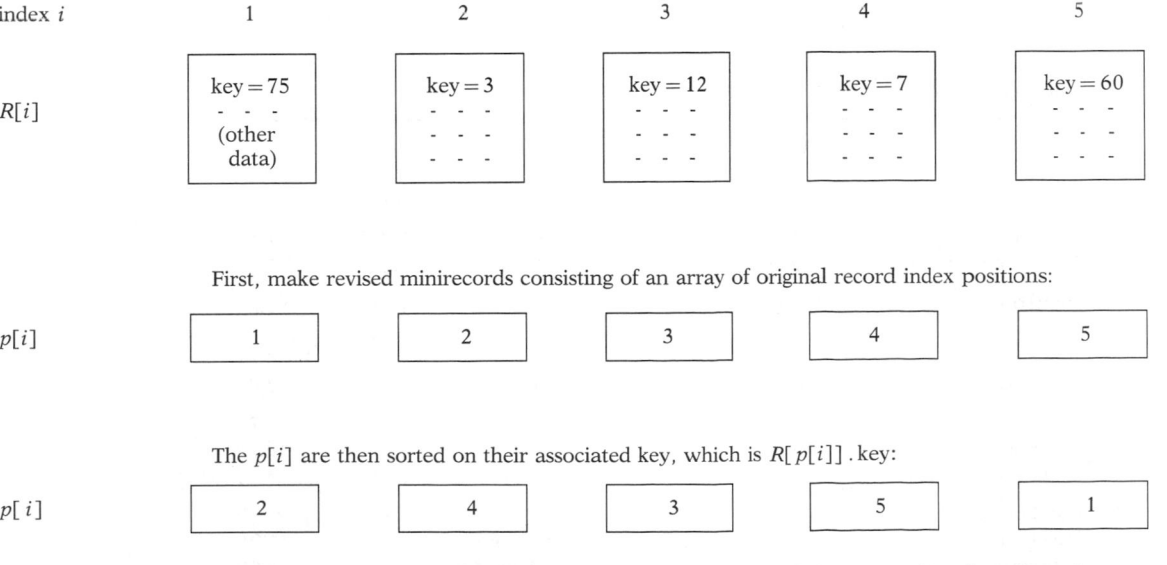

Figure 16. Sorting large records with minimum record movement.

Table 1. Expected performance of internal sorting algorithms.

Algorithm	Best-case performance	Average-case performance	Worst-case performance	Stability
Linear:				
Ultrasort	$O(n)$	$O(n)$	$O(n)$	NA
Hashsort	$O(n)$	$O(n)$	$O(n^2)$	Stable
Radix sort	$O([p/\log r]n)$	$O([p/\log r]n)$	$O([p/\log r]n)$	Stable
Radix exchange sort	$O(pn)$	$O(pn)$	$O(pn)$	Unstable
Logarithmic:				
Quicksort	$O(n\log n)$	$O(n\log n)$	$O(n^2)$	Unstable
Shortsort	$O(n\log n)$	$O(n\log n)$	$O(n\log n)$	Unstable
Heapsort	$O(n\log n)$	$O(n\log n)$	$O(n\log n)$	Stable
Mergesort	$O(n\log n)$	$O(n\log n)$	$O(n\log n)$	Stable
Treesort	$O(n\log n)$	$O(n\log n)$	$O(n^2)$	Stable
Polynomial:				
Shellsort	$O(n)$	$O(n^{1.2})$	$O(n^2)$	Unstable
Insertion sort	$O(n)$	$O(n^2)$	$O(n^2)$	Stable
Selection sort	$O(n^2)$	$O(n^2)$	$O(n^2)$	Stable
Enumeration sort	$O(n^2)$	$O(n^2)$	$O(n^2)$	Stable
Bubblesort	$O(n)^*$	$O(n^2)$	$O(n^2)$	Stable

$p =$ precision in bits
$* \Rightarrow$ use of flag to abort when no exchanges made during prior pass
$r =$ radix

Turbo Pascal included with the Borland Delphi development system. Since running time is data dependent, times reported are averages over several samples.

The $O(n^2)$ running time of the four basic polynomial time algorithms is readily apparent; ultrasort sorts a half million integers 80,000 times faster than enumeration sort. That bubblesort ran faster than enumeration sort was a surprise since, in accord with Knuth's prediction, bubblesort should be about 20% slower, the result obtained with the much slower computer used for this article in the third edition of this encyclopedia.

But as can be seen from Fig. 3, both routines make the same number of comparisons, and experiments show that, for random data, bubblesort has to exchange a pair of keys for about half of all comparisons made. Enumeration sort, on the other hand, has to increment a counter *every* time through its inner loop. Thus, the relative speed of the two routines must depend on whether, on a given machine, an addition (the incrementation) is slower or faster than half the time needed to exchange two numbers (three memory accesses). At least with regard to PCs, there appears to have been an inversion since 1992; acceleration of arithmetic has

Table 2. Relative running times of 14 internal sorting algorithms.

Algorithm	$n = 32K$	$n = 64K$	$n = 128K$	$n = 256K$	$n = 512K$
Ultrasort	12 ms	25 ms	50 ms	0.1 s	0.2 s
Quicksort	0.2 s	0.3 s	0.6 s	0.8 s	1.1 s
Radix exchange sort	0.4 s	0.6 s	0.9 s	1.2 s	1.7 s
Shortsort	0.4 s	0.7 s	1.1 s	1.5 s	3.2 s
Shellsort	0.4 s	0.7 s	1.1 s	1.5 s	3.2 s
Hashsort	0.4 s	0.7 s	1.1 s	1.7 s	3.7 s
Heapsort	0.6 s	0.8 s	1.3 s	1.9 s	3.8 s
Treesort	0.6 s	1.1 s	1.5 s	3.3 s	6.7 s
Mergesort	0.7 s	1.4 s	3.2 s	8.0 s	17.9 s
Radix sort ($r = 16$)	0.7 s	1.6 s	3.7 s	10.1 s	24.5 s
Insertion sort	15 s	1.0 min	4.1 min	0.3 h	1.1 h
Selection sort	31 s	2.2 min	8.8 min	0.5 h	1.9 h
Bubblesort	32 s	2.3 min	9.4 min	0.6 h	2.5 h
Enumeration sort	56 s	4.2 min	16.8 min	1.1 h	4.4 h

n is the number of integers sorted.

not quite kept pace with the increased speed of memory access afforded through sophisticated caching.

The running times of the supposedly faster linear and $n \log n$ routines appear to be sublinear, but this behavior certainly cannot continue much beyond sorting half a million numbers. The reason must be that a certain amount of overhead is "contaminating" predicted $O(f(n))$ performance. For example, a routine rated $O(n)$ for sample size n must really have running time t that obeys $t = a + bn$ where a and b are constant factors. Until n reaches sufficient size, the ultimate dominant term bn will not be apparent. Similarly, a routine rated $O(n \log n)$ would really have running time $t = a + bn + c(n \log n)$.

External Sorting

With the ever increasing size of main memory, the need for external sorting algorithms diminishes. Suppose, for example, that a file stored on a mass storage device consists of 200,000 100-character records. Such a file occupies 20 megabytes, which does not exceed the scratch main memory storage of many current PCs. To sort such a file, it is feasible to read the entire file into main memory, use an appropriate internal sorting algorithm (quicksort, perhaps, which sorts in place), and then rewrite the sorted file back onto mass storage. But what can be done when the size of the external file does not fit in main memory?

TAPE SORTS
The earliest widely used external storage medium was magnetic tape, so it is not surprising that so many external sorting algorithms were devised for sorting files stored on tape. Knuth (1998) devotes most of his discussion of external sorting to such algorithms. Three important tape sorts described by Flores (1969) both in his book and in SORTING in the third edition of this Encyclopedia are called *multiway merge, cascade merge*, and *polyphase merge*.

Since tape sorting algorithms are now mainly of historic interest, we will discuss only the first of these because it applies equally well to disk sorting.

Multiway merge. We have described merging where two lists were merged into a single list or distributed into two output lists. The number of lists that can be merged at one time is limited only by the complexity of the merge program and by the amount of main memory available in the machine. Fig. 17 shows a four-way merge, where L, M, N, and Q are input lists of ordered sublists and distribution takes place to U, V, W, and X. One sublist each from L, M, N, and Q is merged into a single sublist and distributed to the proper output list.

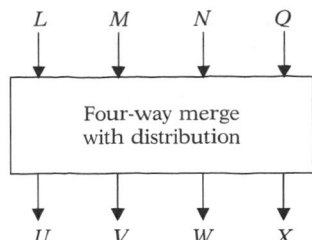

Figure 17. Multiway merge.

This method is described in detail in Flores (1969, p. 109).

The advantage of the multiway merge is that it gets the job done much more quickly. The disadvantage is that it uses many I/O devices—the four-way merge uses eight devices, although this is not a serious objection if disks rather than tapes are used.

DISK SORTS
Modern disk sorts use an efficient internal sort coupled with a balanced multiway merge. The *balanced merge* uses an equal number of input and output lists. For sorting with magnetic tape units, each list for merging, whether input or output, requires its own device. For the disk we have direct access; this means that it is easy to switch access from one list on a volume to another on the same volume, in contrast to serial access devices such as a tape unit.

The disk sort designer, therefore, does not face any inherent limitation arising from the number of lists to be used. Instead, the problem is to use an optimum number of lists and space these lists in an optimum way. The crucial factor in reducing sort time is the number of seeks required by the disk mechanism. Therefore, one tries to optimize the list selection and layout with respect to minimizing the total number and length of seeks involved over the entire sort.

Bibliography

1969. Flores, I. *Computer Sorting.* Upper Saddle River, NJ: Prentice Hall.

1971. Martin, W. A. "Sorting," *ACM Computing Surveys,* **3,** *4,* 147–174.

1972. Rivest, R. L., and Knuth, D. E. "Bibliography 26, Computer Sorting," *Computing Reviews,* **13,** *6,* 283–289.

1975. Lorin, H. *Sorting and Sort Systems.* Reading, MA: Addison-Wesley.

1977. Rich, R. P. *Internal Sorting Methods Illustrated with PL/1 Programs.* Upper Saddle River, NJ: Prentice Hall.

1980. Pratt, V. R. *Shellsort and Sorting Networks.* New York: Garland Publications.

1984. Bentley, J. "Programming Pearls: How to Sort," *Comm. of the ACM,* **27,** *4,* 287–291.

1985. Akl, S. *Parallel Sorting Algorithms.* New York: Academic Press.

1989. Reilly, E. D., and Federighi, F. D. *Pascalgorithms*. Boston: Houghton-Mifflin. (Figs. 4, 11, and 12 and portions of the text of this article are reprinted with permission.)

1995. Wilt, N. *Classical Algorithms in C++: With New Approaches to Sorting, Searching, and Selection*. New York: John Wiley.

1998. Knuth, D. E. "Sorting and Searching," in *The Art of Computer Programming*, Vol. 3, 2nd Ed. Reading, MA: Addison-Wesley.

Edwin D. Reilly

SOURCE PROGRAM

For articles on related subjects *see* COMPILER; LANGUAGE PROCESSORS; OBJECT PROGRAM; and PROCEDURE-ORIENTED LANGUAGES.

A *source program* is a computer program written in a language one or more steps removed from the *machine language* of a given computer. Machine language consists of the very explicit set of instructions and operation codes capable of direct execution by the hardware of the computer. It is, however, extremely tedious and error-prone, for it requires that instructions be spelled out in almost microscopic detail, specifying all data and program references in terms of actual addresses within the computer memory. Accordingly, other languages have been developed to make it easier for programmers' desires to be expressed. A program written in such a language is called a source program, and must be translated by one means or another into the language of the machine before it can be executed. Fortunately, other programs can carry out this translation on the computer itself.

If the source program is in assembly (i.e. symbolic) language, the process of translating it is called *assembling* and the result is an *object program* in machine language, ready to be executed. If the source program is in a high-level language like Pascal or C++, the translating process is called *compiling*, and may involve one or more stages (e.g. a Pascal program may be first compiled into assembly language or some other *intermediate language* (*q.v.*), and then that program is translated into machine language).

Source programs in high-level languages have great advantages in portability, for with only minor changes, if any, they can often be compiled to run on various machines.

Charles H. Davidson

SPECIFICATION

See HARDWARE DESCRIPTION LANGUAGE; and PROGRAM SPECIFICATION.

SPEECH RECOGNITION AND SYNTHESIS

For articles on related subjects *see* ARTIFICIAL INTELLIGENCE; COMPUTER VISION; DISABLED, COMPUTERS AND THE; IMAGE PROCESSING; NEURAL NETWORKS; PATTERN RECOGNITION; and PERCEPTRON.

The use of computers could be greatly expanded if human speech could be reliably used as an input–output medium. Such capability would allow humans to listen to synthetic speech output from a computer rather than read a display. Indeed, commercially acceptable synthetic speech can now be produced as output from a computer, even for unrestricted vocabulary and syntax. The ability of computers to recognize human speech would permit input to the computer without the use of a keyboard. Although commercial units of limited capability are available, *speech recognition* is a far more difficult problem than *speech synthesis*.

Speech Recognition

In order to understand the process of speech recognition, it is useful to assume first that all of the necessary information for recognizing spoken words is available in the speech signal itself. Indeed much research and system implementation is based on this assumption. The first task is thus to represent the speech signal in a form that contains fewer bits of information, but retains those facets that are thought to be useful for recognition. Most systems base this representation on derived attributes of a model for speech production called the *source-filter* model. The human vocal apparatus is modeled as one or two sources exciting a set of coupled resonators that intensify the sound in the neighborhood of the resonant frequencies. One source is the sequence of puffs of air that can be produced by the vibrating vocal cords, as in "voiced" sounds, such as those in the word "zen" (fricative "z," vowel "e," and nasal "n"). In addition, the vocal tract can produce turbulent airflow at any of a large number of constrictions, leading to noise-like sounds, such as the "s" in "son." Both forms of excitation can be combined, as in "z". Whatever the form of excitation, it can be considered to excite a set of resonances (called *formants*) that vary with the shape of the vocal tract. The resulting speech spectrum is thus the result of multiplying the source spectrum by the vocal tract filter spectrum. (An example is shown in Fig. 1.) Most speech recognition systems use some form of spectral representation as input to classification algorithms, since the relatively slow motion of the articulators is displayed in the formant trajectories, allowing for an insightful reduction of the input information rate. Precisely what frequency–time–amplitude features are computed is

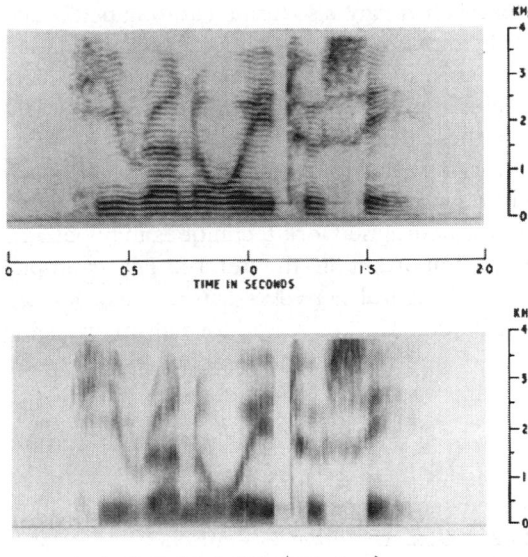

KHz
- 4
- 3
- 2
- 1
- 0

TIME IN SECONDS
0   0.5   1.0   1.5   2.0

KHz
- 4
- 3
- 2
- 1
- 0

h ɪ r æ n ə w eɪ t u s i

Figure 1. Spectrogram of the sentence "He ran away to sea." The upper record is a narrow-band analysis made with a 30 Hz bandwidth filter. The fine horizontal lines are due to individual harmonics in the buzzing sound produced at the larynx. The lower record is a wideband analysis made with a 240 Hz bandwidth filter. The fine vertical lines are due to the sound of individual pulses of air emitted by the larynx. The dark bands, or formants, are due to resonance peaks in the acoustic response of the vocal tract. Below the bottom figure the spoken phrase is written in phonetic symbols of the International Phonetic Association. Each "letter" represents a single sound.

an important attribute of any speech recognition system. In many contemporary systems, all input spectra are sorted into a group of spectral equivalence classes, usually about 200 in number. This process is referred to as *vector quantization*, and allows each spectrum (usually computed at centisecond intervals) to be labeled with the name of one of the equivalence classes in the vector quantization codebook, or *library*. All further processing uses only the class label designation, and no further reference is made to specific attributes of input spectra. On the other hand, some systems attempt to extract *features* from the input spectra, and use the set of such feature designations distributed over the input utterance as the reduced input representation. This approach seeks to represent directly those phonetic attributes thought to be significant to human speech perception or machine speech recognition, but such early feature detection must be marked as tentative, since it is impossible to recognize these features reliably.

Following parametric (either spectral- or feature-based) representation of the speech, end points of the utterance are detected, and normalization may be performed to compensate for spectral warping due to variation in vocal tract length. Matching against stored

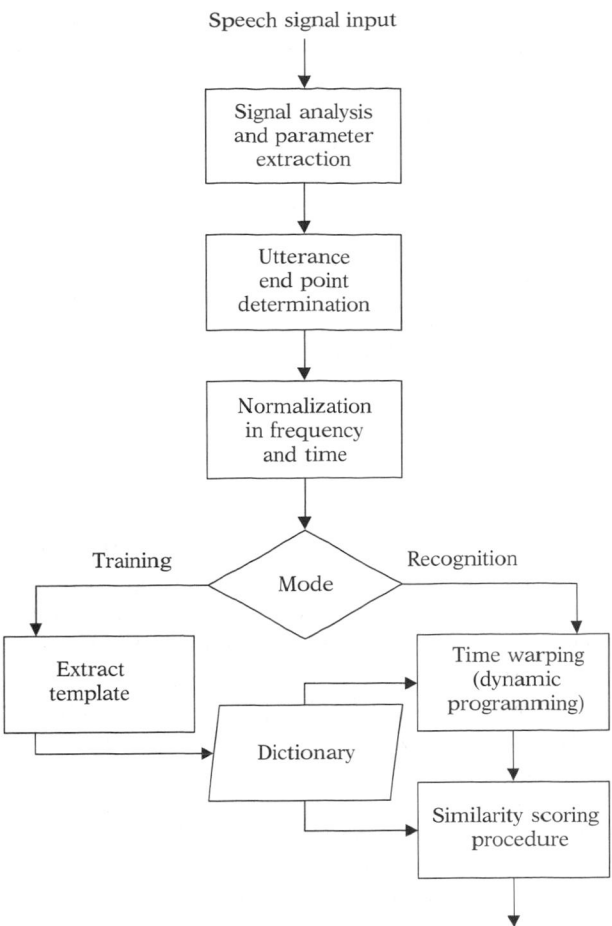

Speech signal input

Signal analysis and parameter extraction

Utterance end point determination

Normalization in frequency and time

Training — Mode — Recognition

Extract template

Dictionary

Time warping (dynamic programming)

Similarity scoring procedure

Figure 2. Pattern-matching speech recognizer. The pattern produced from the speech signal is normalized and compared with a set of patterns derived from words of known identity. The input word is assumed to be the same as that word whose stored pattern has the highest similarity score.

templates is then performed, often using abstract mathematical formalisms and sophisticated search procedures to obtain the best match. Many systems use a procedure called *dynamic programming* to warp the time dimension of the input to secure the best match, as computed by a variety of scoring methods. Some investigators feel that the use of optimal time warping is more important than the choice of spectral representation. Fig. 2 shows how these techniques are combined to perform the speech recognition task. Several commercial systems are available that provide speech recognition based on these procedures. These pattern matching approaches are based on the assumption that only the information in the speech wave form is necessary for correct recognition. It is always desirable to use the best possible acoustic–phonetic analysis of the speech signal, but other constraints of the language being spoken are also useful in recognition of the utterance. These constraints cover the allowable consonant clusters, syllable structure, morpheme sequences, phase- and clause-level syntax, semantics, and discourse structure derivable from the nature of the specific task being performed. The representation of these *knowledge sources*, their access, and means to combine their constraining effects on the output decision are reflected in a control structure that guides the searching and decision binding tasks.

During the 1980s, great emphasis was placed on the use of hidden Markov models for speech recognition. These models provide a way of representing the constraints on spectral template sequences presented by phonemes and their distribution in syllables, as well as the constraints of the word sequence represented by syntax, but summarized in statistical form. In this way, the pronunciation of individual words can be represented as a network of arcs connecting states. Using the hidden Markov model formalism, it is possible to train these networks so that the probability of traversing a given arc from one state to another can be automatically derived from many training utterances, and thus characterize a statistical picture of the sequence of states in the model corresponding to a particular speaker's (or a group of speakers') vocal articulations. Syntactic constraints are usually represented by "*N*-gram" statistics, which provide crude indications of syntagmatic word order constraints. Three-grams are often used, and it is remarkable how much improvement in performance is provided by their use. These "language models" are also trained automatically, so that word sequence constraints become a part of the overall hidden Markov model representation. It can also be shown that dynamic time warping techniques, which had previously been shown to provide substantial increases in performance, can be formally subsumed by the hidden Markov model mechanism. During the 1980s, a great deal of research was devoted toward refinements in the use of such models, leading to word error rates of a few per cent over large (20,000 word) vocabularies trained for a single speaker. Research continues to develop techniques for automatic multispeaker recognition of large vocabularies, as well as low error rates of 2–3 per cent in medium vocabularies of one or two thousand words. Hidden Markov modeling techniques have also been used for very small vocabularies, including the alphabet and numerals, leading to very compact and inexpensive systems of commercially acceptable performance. While hidden Markov models have been devised that can represent timing variations in speech, the representation within this framework of pitch contours is still under study. In addition, ways in which phonetic features can be incorporated within this abstract formalism are being used in experimental systems.

Neural network classifiers have also been proposed for use in speech recognition. These techniques, based on massive parallelism, are also trained automatically and can provide impressive performance in discrimination between classes, such as vowels. Such static classifiers can be useful in many applications, but it is more difficult to use these techniques for sequential constraints and time-varying behavior. Nevertheless, this approach has received far less study than hidden Markov modeling, and new neural network techniques may become increasingly important in the future. For example, ways in which neural networks can be incorporated within the hidden Markov model formalism are being explored in order to exploit the complementary virtues of the two approaches.

Despite requiring several hundred MIPS of computing power to provide real-time performance, speech recognition systems became viable commercial products in the late 1990s. Dictation systems accepting large vocabularies are available from several firms, notably Dragon Systems, Inc., IBM and the Kurzweil Educational Systems Division of Lernout and Hauspie. They are able to convert speech to text on screens with reasonable accuracy. Such systems will undoubtedly improve their performance rapidly in the first decade of the 21st century. Special purpose systems in which voice commands from a small vocabulary activate equipment, such as IN CUBE from Command Corporation, already give high quality performance. While the goal of building a comprehensive system that can, without training, recognize speech from multiple speakers using an unrestricted vocabulary and syntax is still elusive, substantial progress has been made in recent years and can be expected to continue in years to come.

Speech Synthesis

The inverse of speech recognition is speech generation (synthesis). Toys and robots that "speak" have been familiar objects for some time. There is also an increasing interest in interactive human–computer dialogue. In these applications, the human speaks to the computer, but the computer must respond using some form of synthetic speech. When the vocabulary is small, recorded or coded speech can readily provide the required voice.

Frequently, however, large vocabularies and unrestricted syntax is needed, or the vocabulary, while possibly small, is changing rapidly enough that recording is impractical. *Text-to-speech* capability has been developed for these needs and is available commercially. The quality of this speech is intelligible, but somewhat unnatural. Among the applications of text-to-speech synthesis are readers for the blind in which a scanner and a personal computer combine to provide voice output of books and documents (see also DISABLED,

COMPUTERS AND THE). Such systems are available from various sources, among them Elan Informatique and the Kurzweil Educational Systems Division of Lernout and Hauspie. Systems are also available which convert the contents of a computer screen to speech. As the cost of such systems decreases while the quality of their speech continues to improve, many new applications will be found for speech synthesizers.

Speech synthesis and speech recognition share common concerns, but there are also distinctive differences. Recognition implies the use of a sophisticated search strategy, techniques for representation of partial knowledge, and means for considering alternative pronunciations, whereas speech synthesis requires a rich lexicon, complex and interactive rule systems, and processes for contextual smoothing and realistic articulation. Research in each of these fields is mutually constructive. Speech synthesis, while commercially useful, still faces many difficult research questions similar to those pursued in speech recognition. Thus, the multiple ways in which speech sounds are produced in synthesis is of direct utility to speech recognition, and the extensive characterization of pronunciation patterns for use in speech recognition is of equal importance to speech synthesis. Consequently, there is an important need to view these two applications in one unifying context, such as discourse modeling. The benefits of such a view can be expected to improve both synthesis and recognition in future language-based systems.

Bibliography

1991. Furui, S., and Sondhi, M. (eds.) *Recent Progress in Speech Signal Processing*. New York: Marcel Dekker.

1993. Rabiner, L. R., and Juang, B-H. *Fundamentals of Speech Recognition*. Upper Saddle River, NJ: Prentice Hall.

1994. Roe, D. B., and Wilpon, J. G. (eds.) *Voice Communication between Humans and Machines*. Washington: National Academy Press.

1996. Van Santen, J. P. H., Sproat, R. W., Olive, J. P., and Hirschberg, J. (eds.) *Progress in Speech Synthesis*. New York: Springer-Verlag.

1998. Jelinek, F. *Statistical Methods for Speech Recognition*. Cambridge, MA: MIT Press.

Jonathan Allen

SPELLING CHECKER

For articles on related subjects *see* NATURAL LANGUAGE PROCESSING; ONLINE INFORMATION SYSTEMS; and WORD PROCESSING.

Computers are very useful for word processing. They are used to input, store, edit, format, and print text files ranging in size from short notes to multi-volume books. In addition to these conventional forms of word processing, computer programs can provide more advanced word processing assistance, such as *spelling checking*, *spelling correction*, and *grammar checking*.

The general operation of a spelling checker is simple: it checks each word in a document or file for correct spelling. Allegedly incorrect spellings are reported to the human user, who can then correct the errors. A spelling corrector checks each word (just like a spelling checker) and, in addition, will try to suggest the correct spelling for each misspelled word that is found.

Spelling checkers guarantee only that each word is *some* correctly spelled word, not necessarily the one you meant. If "or" is mistyped as "of" or if "affect" is misused for "effect," a spelling checker will not report an error. Detecting these kinds of errors would require a much more complicated program called a *grammar checker*.

An *interactive* spelling checker reads a document and presents each spelling error to the user as it is found. The user can see each alleged error in context and either change it immediately or leave it alone. A word processor (or email formatter or web page compositor) may incorporate spelling checking (or correction) directly into its processing, either in response to a menu option or continually as text is entered.

How does a spelling checker know if a word is correctly spelled? Most checkers use a *word list* to define the set of correctly spelled words. The word list may be the list of all words in a dictionary (without the definitions) or may be accumulated from existing documents. Despite having no definitions, most spelling programs call their word lists "dictionaries." The list of words is generally stored in a file. A word is considered to be correctly spelled if and only if it is found in the speller's word list. The main technical problem, particularly for an interactive program, is to search the list as quickly as possible.

Differing search and data structure (*q.v.*) techniques are used for differing environments. A batch checker, for example, may form an alphabetically sorted list of all words in an input document and then make one pass over a similarly sorted word list to check for misspelled words. A speller with large amounts of main memory can keep the entire word list in that fast memory in the form of a hash table and use standard hash table search algorithms (*see* SEARCHING). A system with a fast disk might keep its word lists on disk with an in-core index and a cache of the most frequently referenced disk blocks.

The correctness of a spelling checker is determined by its word list. As long as its word list has no incorrectly spelled words, a checker will never "miss" an incorrectly spelled word that is not, coincidentally, some other legal word. On the other hand, spellers often report correctly spelled words as possible spelling errors. These may be proper names, technical terms, or uncommon words that are not in the system word list. Most systems allow a user to augment its main word list with local auxiliary word lists for special subjects, authors, or documents. Doctors and lawyers, for example, generally use extensive auxiliary word lists designed for the specialized vocabularies of their fields.

Some systems, upon flagging a suspect word, allow the user several options, including: (1) correct the word, (2) add the word to the main word list, (3) add the word to an auxiliary word list, or (4) add the word to a transient word list that endures only for the duration of the document being checked.

A very large word list might seem desirable to avoid having a spelling checker incorrectly report correctly spelled words as possible errors. However, a very large word list tends to include unusual and infrequently used words. This increases the chance that a word will be misspelled as some other word and not be caught by the checker. The appearance of "dhow" in text might indicate that the author is writing about an Arab boat, but more likely signals a typographical error for "show." In general, word lists should be kept reasonably small, in the range of 50,000 to 100,000 words, even though there are over half a million English words (counting inflections).

One approach to keeping the word list short is to notice that many words are derived from a base word by the addition of common suffixes and prefixes. Some checkers keep only the base words in their word lists. If a suspect word is not in the word list, an attempt is made to remove suffixes and prefixes to find the base word. If the base word is in the word list, the suspect word is accepted as correctly spelled. Note that this approach may allow incorrect spellings to escape detection, such as if "designing" is misspelled "desinging" (which can be processed as "*de* + *sing* + *ing*").

A spelling corrector is invoked when an incorrectly spelled word is found. Its problem is to produce a list of possible correct spellings for the error. For correction, the set of correctly spelled words is thought of as a set of points in a multidimensional space. The corrector tries to find the nearest neighbor or neighbors of the spelling error in that space. If an error produces one candidate correction that is much closer to the error than other possible corrections, the speller may suggest an automatic correction.

The success of a spelling corrector depends largely upon the source of the spelling errors and the methods used to find nearest neighbors. For example, many systems assume that spelling errors occur because of one of the following four types of errors:

1. One extra letter in the word ("*feeel*").

2. One missing letter in the word ("*fel*").

3. One wrong letter in the word ("*feal*").

4. Two adjacent letters are transposed ("*fele*").

These types of errors may account for 80% to 90% of the typing errors in a document.

Another source of spelling errors is the difference between spelling and pronunciation—a word like "tough" may be spelled "tuff." The most common approach for correcting these types of errors is to map the error onto a sound-based encoding. Each word in the word list is also mapped, and candidate corrections with the same sound as the error are generated. The proper use of appropriate data structures and search algorithms to provide adequate performance is particularly important in this case.

Another common typing error is to repeat an entire word, commonly at the end of one line and the beginning of the next line, creating such obvious errors as "a a" and "the the." Some checkers check for duplicate adjacent words, but would then report spurious errors in those sentences with repeated words, such as "I knew that that boy had had the measles."

In addition to spelling and typing errors, there are errors of grammar. Grammatical errors are defined by incorrect groups of words, not individual words. Grammar checkers try to find errors in sentences or phrases rather than separate words. While it is possible to look for certain simple errors (such as two identical words in a row, incorrect use of "a" or "an", capitalization errors, or use of certain incorrect word combinations), the general problem of detecting true errors of grammar is still a research problem. We do not yet have computer programs that "understand" the structure of sentences. Understanding the structure of sentences would allow the detection of errors, such as a sentence with no verb or a plural subject with a singular verb ("they is").

Bibliography

1980. Peterson, James L. "Computer Programs for Detecting and Correcting Spelling Errors," *Comm. of the ACM*, **23**, *12*, 676–687.

James L. Peterson

SPLINE

For articles on related subjects *see* APPROXIMATION THEORY; CHEBYSHEV APPROXIMATION; LEAST-SQUARES APPROXIMATION; and NUMERICAL ANALYSIS.

Polynomials are the approximating functions of choice when a smooth function is to be approximated locally. For example, the truncated Taylor series $\sum_{j=0}^{n} D^{j} f(a)(x-a)^{j}/j!$ provides a satisfactory approximation for $f(x)$ if f is sufficiently smooth and x is sufficiently close to a. But if a function is to be approximated on a larger interval, the degree of the approximating polynomial may have to be chosen unacceptably large. The alternative is to subdivide the interval $[a, b]$ of approximation into sufficiently small intervals $[\xi_{j}, \xi_{j+1}]$ (with $a = \xi_{1} < \cdots < \xi_{l+1} = b$) so that, on each interval, a polynomial p_{j} of "low" degree can provide a good approximation to f. This can even be done in such a way that the polynomial pieces blend smoothly, i.e. so that the resulting patched function $s(x) := p_{j}(x)$ for $\xi_{j} \le x \le \xi_{j+1}$, all j, has several continuous derivatives. Any such smooth pp (piecewise polynomial) function is called a *spline*, the name given by I. J. Schoenberg, since a twice continuously differentiable cubic spline (with sufficiently small first derivative) approximates the shape of a drafter's spline.

While the *pp-form* of a spline (i.e. the description of a spline in terms of its *breakpoints* $\xi_{1}, \ldots, \xi_{l+1}$ and the *local polynomial coefficients* c_{ij} of its pieces $p_{j}(x) = \sum_{i=0}^{k} c_{ij} (x-\xi_{j})^{j}/j!$, is convenient for the evaluation and other uses of a spline, the *B-form* has become the standard way to represent a spline during its construction, since the B-form makes it easy to enforce matching of derivatives across breakpoints. The B-form describes a spline as a linear combination $\sum_{j=0}^{n} a_{j} B_{j,k}$ of B-splines, with $B_{j,k} = B(t_{j}, \ldots, t_{j+k})$ the jth *B-spline* of *order* k for the *knot sequence* $t_{1} \le t_{2} \le \cdots \le t_{n+k}$. In particular, $B_{j,k}$ is pp of degree $< k$, with breakpoints $t_{j}, \ldots, t_{j+k}$, is nonnegative, is zero outside the interval (t_{j}, t_{j+k}), and is so normalized that $\sum_{j} B_{j,k}(x) = 1$. The *multiplicity* of the knots governs the smoothness: if the number z occurs exactly r times in the sequence $t_{j}, \ldots, t_{j+k}$, then the $B_{j,k}$ and its first $k - r - 1$ derivatives are continuous across the breakpoint z, while the $(k - r)$th derivative has a jump at z. Since each B-spline has only small support, the linear system for the B-spline coefficients of the spline to be determined, by interpolation or best approximation or as the approximate solution of some differential equation, is *banded*, hence easily solvable. Also, many theoretical facts concerning splines are most easily stated and/or proved in terms of B-splines; e.g. it is possible to match arbitrary data at points $x_{1} < \cdots < x_{n}$ uniquely by a spline of order k with knot sequence $t_{1}, \ldots, t_{n+k}$ if and only if $B_{j,k}(x_{j}) \ne 0$ for all j (Schoenberg–Whitney Theorem). Computations with B-splines are facilitated by stable *recurrence relations*.

$$B_{j,k}(x) = \frac{x - t_{j}}{t_{j+k-1} - t_{j}} B_{j,k-1}(x) + \frac{t_{j+k} - x}{t_{j+k} - t_{j+1}} B_{j+1,k-1}(x)$$

(with $B_{j,k}(x) = 1$ for $t_{j} \le x < t_{j+1}$ and 0 otherwise), which are also of help in the conversion from B-form to pp-form. The *dual functional*

$$a_{j}(s) = \sum_{i<k} (-D)^{k-i-1} \psi_{j}(\tau) D^{i} s(\tau)$$

provides a useful expression for the jth B-spline coefficient of the spline s in terms of its value and derivatives at an arbitrary point $\tau \in (t_{j}, t_{j+k})$ (and with $\psi_{j}(t) = (t_{j+1} - t) \cdots (t_{j+k-1} - t)/(k-1)!$). This can be used to show that $a_{j}(s)$ is closely related to s on the interval $[t_{j}, t_{j+k}]$.

If the coefficients a_{j}, in the B-form $\sum_{j} a_{j} B_{j,k}$, are points in 2-space or 3-space instead of scalars, a spline *curve* results. More flexible parametric pp curves are available that are smooth (as curves) even though their parameterization is not. The simplest *bivariate* spline is obtained as the *tensor product* $\sum_{i,j} a_{i,j} B_{i,h}(x) B_{j,k}(y)$ of (univariate) splines. More general bi- or multi-variable pp functions usually have to be dealt with polynomial piece by polynomial piece, since multivariate B-splines (such as *box splines*) are available only for very special partitions.

The above *constructive* approach is not the only avenue to splines. In the *variational* approach, a spline is obtained as a "best interpolant" (e.g. as the function with smallest kth derivative among all those matching prescribed function values at certain points). Among the many such splines available, only those that are piecewise polynomial (or, perhaps, piecewise exponential) functions have found much use. Of particular practical interest is the *cubic smoothing spline* $s = s_{\lambda}$, which, for given data (x_{i}, y_{i}) with $x_{i} \in [a, b]$, for all i, and given corresponding positive weights w_{i}, and for given *smoothing parameter* λ minimizes

$$\sum_{i} w_{i}(y_{i} - f(x_{i}))^{2} + \lambda \int_{a}^{b} (f''(t))^{2} \, dt$$

over all functions f with two derivatives. The smoothing spline s is a cubic spline with a breakpoint at every data point. The art of using the smoothing spline consists in choosing λ so that s contains as much of the information and as little of the supposed noise in the data as possible.

Bibliography

1978. Boor, C. de. *A Practical Guide to Splines*. New York: Springer-Verlag.

1988. Chiyokura, H. *Solid Modeling*. Reading, MA: Addison-Wesley.

1993. Schumaker, L. L. *Spline Functions: Basic Theory*. Melbourne, FL: Krieger Publishing Co.

1995. Shikin, E. V., and Plis, A. I. *Handbook on Splines for the User*. Boca Raton, FL: CRC Press.

Carl de Boor

SPREADSHEET

For articles on related subjects *see* ADMINISTRATIVE APPLICATIONS; DATABASE MANAGEMENT SYSTEM; NONPROCEDURAL LANGUAGES; and STATISTICAL APPLICATIONS.

Introduction

An electronic *spreadsheet* is a matrix of data and formulas originally devised to facilitate financial and business modeling, primarily on microcomputers. First constructed in 1979, spreadsheets rapidly developed into one of the most widely used software products during the 1980s and 1990s. Their design, in the form of an accountant's spreadsheet of rows and columns, provides a programming environment that has proved to be accessible to managers, accountants, and a vast variety of other end users, as well as to other computer professionals. Even people with no programming experience generally have found spreadsheets to be intuitive, natural, and usable tools for business and mathematical modeling, decision making, simulation (*q.v.*), and problem solving. Originally regarded simply as applications programs, spreadsheets are in fact effective instruments for nonprocedural programming in general.

When first introduced, spreadsheets were used primarily with small models for low-level decision making, often by single individuals. Within a decade, however, spreadsheets had become a primary management tool, and are now used extensively as a medium for implementing increasingly larger models and for doing decision analysis in significant, high-level business decisions.

Spreadsheets are one of the three most widely utilized computer applications, along with word processors and games, and have contributed to the popularity of personal computers. The rapid growth of the use of spreadsheets helped drive many of the microcomputer hardware developments during the 1980s and 1990s. As larger and more sophisticated models were designed for spreadsheet implementation, the need for increased memory capacity and more sophisticated spreadsheet capabilities created a corresponding need for advances in the development of computer hardware.

Over the years, spreadsheets have found extensive use in a diverse range of disciplines as well as throughout the general population. Professionals in mathematics, engineering, science, medicine, the arts, social science, and education find the spreadsheet to be a natural tool for modeling, implementing and analyzing algorithms (*q.v.*), constructing laboratory reports, carrying out statistical analyses, and producing graphical displays.

Brief History

Bob Frankston and Dan Bricklin developed the first spreadsheet program, VisiCalc, in 1979. The program's idea emanated from creating an effective way to use computers to solve business school problems, with the spreadsheet concept patterned after a traditional blackboard production planning layout. Originally written in assembly language for a 32 KB Apple II, VisiCalc was a small spreadsheet with a terse single-line menu. However, its popularity and usefulness led to the rapid development of numerous other spreadsheets.

In 1981, SuperCalc was developed for the Osborne computer, and became the primary spreadsheet for 8-bit CP/M computers. In 1983 Lotus 1-2-3 was created for 16-bit MS-DOS computers. It contained many innovations and advanced features, including online help, sophisticated menus, graphic and database management capabilities, and macros (*q.v.*). It immediately became a best-selling software product, and set standards for competitive spreadsheet products that followed. As the number of spreadsheet users increased, the desire for additional features escalated. This led to the development of add-on features that now have been incorporated into spreadsheets. Recent years have seen the development of more powerful spreadsheets with advanced features and presentation-quality graphics. Originally created as small standalone programs, spreadsheets now typically are designed as fundamental components of large integrated programs that run under Windows. Current versions occupy hundreds of megabytes on a computer's hard drive and require at least 32 MB of RAM to operate effectively. The list of current leading spreadsheets includes Microsoft Excel, Lotus 1-2-3, and Quattro Pro. These programs are written in combinations of assembler and high-level languages.

Basic Operation

The spreadsheet format consists of a large rectangular array, a portion of which is shown on the screen. Spreadsheet columns are identified by letters, and rows by positive integers. Individual locations, or cells, are referenced by column and row. For example, E5 refers to the cell in column E of row 5. Fig. 1 contains a typical Excel screen display which shows a model for computing compound interest.

One cell is highlighted on the screen by a cursor. The cursor can be moved to other cells by using either arrow keys or a mouse (*q.v.*). After positioning the cursor on a cell, a user can enter into that location a label (or string), a number, or a formula that references other spreadsheet cells. The program calculates the value of a formula in a cell by using the values of

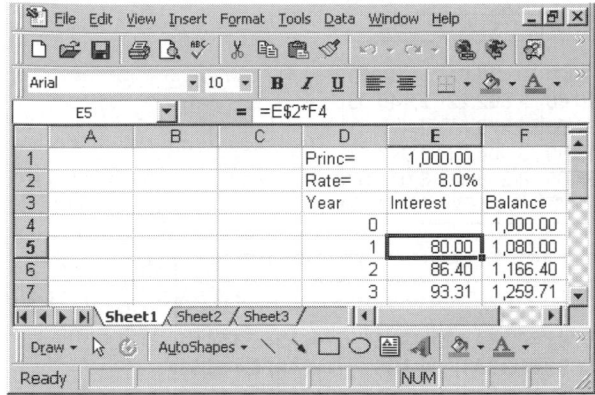

Figure 1. The Excel spreadsheet screen display.

	A	B
1	Tax Break	20,000
2	Low Rate	10.0%
3	High Rate	20.0%
4		
5	Income 1	23,000
6	Income 2	10,000
7	Income 3	12,000
8		
9	Income	45,000
10	Tax	7,000
11	Net	38,000

	A	B
1	Tax Break	20000
2	Low Rate	0.1
3	High Rate	0.2
4		
5	Income 1	23000
6	Income 2	10000
7	Income 3	12000
8		
9	Income	=SUM(B5:B7)
10	Tax	{below}
11	Net	=B9-B10

Note: B10: =IF(B9<B1,B2*B9,B2*B1+B3*(B9-B1))

Figure 2. Taxation spreadsheet model.

the cells that it references and displays the results on the screen. Generally, the calculation of a spreadsheet is performed in an order that first evaluates any of the cells referenced in another cell, although other options are available. In Fig. 1 the formula in cell E5, =E\$2*F4, computes interest as the product of the previous balance (F4) and the interest rate (E2). The initial = sign indicates that the expression is a formula. (The use of the \$ sign is discussed later.) Although such a formula may be entered by typing in the symbols directly, a conceptually superior approach is to enter the formula's cell locations by "pointing to them", i.e. by clicking on the referenced cells while entering the formula.

One of the popular attributes of a spreadsheet is its "What if...?" capability. If the value of any cell is changed, a spreadsheet's formulas are recalculated and the display is updated. This allows a user to interrogate a model by changing its parameters or data and observing the resulting effects. Thus, in financial models it is possible to examine the compound effects of changes of such interrelated components as projected sales, prices, production costs, interest rates, and profit.

Fig. 2 gives the output and formulas of a simple tax model, in which income is taxed at a rate of 10% on the first \$20,000 and 20% on amounts in excess of \$20,000. The parameters and data of the model are entered into cells B1 through B7. In cell B9 a library function, =SUM, computes the sum of the incomes in cells B5 through B7. The library function =IF used in cell B10 reads "IF income (B9) is less than the breakpoint (B1), THEN multiply income (B9) by the low rate (B2), ELSE add the tax on the amount below the break (B2*B1) to the tax on the amount above the break (B3*(B9-B1))". Cell B11 finds the net difference between Income and Tax.

Once constructed, a model like Fig. 2 can be used repeatedly simply by changing the parameters (breakpoint, tax rates) or the data. Such a model, called a *template*, is often created for multiple users. In a tem-

plate, data and parameter cells are initially blank, to be changed by the user, while cells containing the model's formulas can be protected by a command that prevents changes to those cells.

Spreadsheet Commands

Spreadsheet commands provide additional ways for a user to interact with a model. These commands may be selected by using a mouse to choose from a series of pull-down menus or through the use of keystrokes. Among options available are commands to load, save and print files, format output, create graphic displays, access objects, import or export data, and perform database operations. Other commands allow a model to be modified by inserting or deleting rows and columns, or by moving and copying blocks of cells, with the program automatically adjusting all formula references throughout the spreadsheet.

The copy and fill commands are particularly useful in creating models that repeatedly perform the same computations, eliminating the need to enter many formulas individually. Fig. 3's model projects the future values of a group of investments. Current investment values are entered in Column C, with annual interest rates in Column A. The model assumes that a flat management fee (cell C1) is deducted from each investment at the end of a year.

A principal p at an annual rate r increases in one year to a value of $p + rp = (1 + r)p$, less the annual fee. The formula =(1+\$A3)*C3-\$C\$1 is entered into cell D3 and then is copied into all of the cells of rows 3–5 of columns E,F,G,... The \$ symbol determines how a location identifier is interpreted by a copy command. An identifier without the \$ is treated as a relative location. Thus, in copying the formula in cell D3, the previous year's value, C3, is copied as a relative location, or as "the cell to the left." Identifiers preceded by a \$ are treated as constants. Thus, the fee \$C\$1 is unchanged in copying, while the interest rate \$A3 varies

	A	B	C	D	E	F
1	Ann fee:		100.00			
2	Rate	Stock	1999	2000	2001	2002
3	13.20%	ABC Inc	2,400.00	2,616.80	2,862.22	3,140.03
4	11.60%	Beta Co	2,000.00	2,132.00	2,279.31	2,443.71
5	12.30%	CST Ltd	2,600.00	2,819.80	3,066.64	3,343.83
6		Total	7,000.00	7,568.60	8,208.17	8,927.57
7	Ann rate:			8.12%	8.45%	8.76%

	A	B	C	D	E	F
1	Ann fee:		100			
2	Rate	Stock	1999	=1+C2	=1+D2	=1+E2
3	0.132	ABC Inc	2400	=(1+$A3)*C3-$C$1	=(1+$A3)*D3-$C$1	=(1+$A3)*E3-$C$1
4	0.116	Beta Co	2000	=(1+$A4)*C4-$C$1	=(1+$A4)*D4-$C$1	=(1+$A4)*E4-$C$1
5	0.123	CST Ltd	2600	=(1+$A5)*C5-$C$1	=(1+$A5)*D5-$C$1	=(1+$A5)*E5-$C$1
6		Total	=SUM(C3:C5)	=SUM(D3:D5)	=SUM(E3:E5)	=SUM(F3:F5)
7	Ann rate:			=D6/C6-1	=E6/D6-1	=F6/E6-1

Figure 3. Use of the copy command.

from row to row, but always comes from column A. The formulas in cells D2, C6, and D7 can be copied across their rows as well, with all locations relative.

Graphics commands allow the creation of a vast variety of graphs to display aspects of a model visually. Graphs and output can be displayed simultaneously so that the effects of changes in a spreadsheet model can be observed visually. Fig. 4 is a graph (or chart) created from the previous example produced using Excel. Some spreadsheets allow users to interrogate a model by varying graphic elements directly to generate changes in the model's parameters.

While spreadsheet notation is relatively easy to learn and use, the logic of a spreadsheet model, with its many interrelated cells, can be arduous to follow, making it difficult to modify and debug a complex model. More structured models can result from the adoption of standardized layouts in which data, parameters, and formulas are located in separate areas, and from the use of range names, macros, and multiple files or sheets. The name command allows ranges of cells to be named, making formulas more meaningful. For example, in Fig. 3 cells A3, A4, A5 can be named as Ratea, Rateb, Ratec, with cell C1 as Fee, and the range C3:C5 as Initial. The formulas in cells D3 and C6 are then =(1+Ratea)*C3-Fee and =SUM(Initial).

A macro (q.v.) is a program written within the spreadsheet. Macros can be used to simplify the process of carrying out a complex or often-repeated series of commands. Macros can also be used as programming tools and to implement procedures that are not easily performed in a spreadsheet. They can include the use of logic statements, loops, branching, and subroutines. One way to create a macro is to set the program to record a series of keystrokes and mouse operations while carrying out a given task. The spreadsheet then stores these commands as a program, often written in Visual Basic (q.v.). The macro can be invoked later to carry out this series of operations. Alternatively, a user skilled in programming can write the code for a macro directly. Frequently a macro will be attached to a button or other user-created device. This allows users to automate further the process that they have designed.

Fig. 5 illustrates the use of a sort command to sort a list of nations by their area (in 1000 km²) in descending order. Starting from the listing at the left and using Excel, a user issues the commands to turn on the

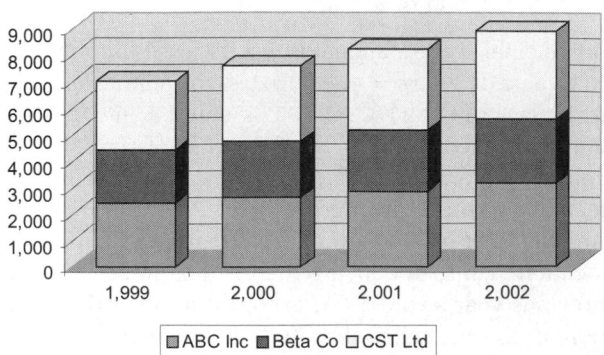

Figure 4. Sample graphical output from Excel.

	A	B
1	Nation	Area
2	Canada	9976
3	Cuba	114
4	Mexico	1973
5	USA	9385

	A	B
1	Nation	Area
2	Canada	9976
3	USA	9385
4	Mexico	1973
5	Cuba	114

Figure 5. Recording a macro for sorting.

macro recorder (Tools, Macro, Record New Macro, OK), uses the mouse to select the block A2:B5, selects the appropriate sort commands (Data, Sort, Area, Descending, OK), and finally turns the macro recorder off (Tools, Macro, Stop Recording). The display at the right is produced. For future use, rather than go through these steps again, a user simply refers to the macro, which is typically named as part of the process described above.

In the earliest spreadsheet programs, each model was created in a separate file. Current spreadsheets allow for multiple-page spreadsheet files or for several spreadsheet files to be linked by formulas that reference the other files. These permit the construction of modular and multidimensional models.

Spreadsheets contain many additional features. The screen display can be split into windows to show different sections of a spreadsheet or other files. Spreadsheets include numerical, string, table, and logic library functions from mathematics, finance, engineering, statistics, and computing. Some contain functions and commands for more advanced mathematics, including linear and multiple regression, matrix operations, random number generation, and linear programming. A variety of interactive buttons, scroll bars, and similar objects can be created by a user to help in designing more effective interfaces for interacting with models. For example, connecting a scroll bar to the cell containing one of a graph's parameters can produce animation effects in the graph.

Solver commands cause spreadsheets to vary one or more parameters of a model automatically to find the values that will produce desired target goals. A particular spreadsheet program can generally read from, and write to, files created by other spreadsheet programs, or from database, word processing, Web, and other files. Also, interactive, dynamic links can be established between spreadsheets, databases, and word processors. In particular, one can copy both numerical output and graphs from a spreadsheet into a word processing document. Spreadsheets also contain database structures and support a number of database operations. Like many other user packages, spreadsheets have built-in help libraries that can be used as

online manuals or invoked while entering a command to supply help on the specific command.

Because spreadsheets are used increasingly for the analysis of significant and critical financial decisions, it has become crucial to ensure the correctness of the spreadsheet models. To aid in this, most spreadsheets have auditing features that can be used to locate errors. Auditing commands display interconnections between cells, provide lists of ranges and functions, display cells of a certain data type, and step through macros. They also find, highlight, and display sources of possible errors, such as formulas that reference empty or text cells, cells not referenced, and circular references. Fig. 6 contains the layout for an interest computation in a savings account model. After clicking on Cell E5 the auditing toolbar can be used to indicate the precedence relations in the computation of interest as the product of the rate (E2) and the prior balance (F4). Colors are frequently employed by editors as another way to illustrate connections between formulas and the cells to which they refer.

Additional Applications

Mathematical algorithms that are iterative or recursive can usually be implemented on a spreadsheet through the use of recurrence relations. The model in Fig. 7 finds binomial probabilities. If an experiment (e.g. flip a coin) has only two outcomes, succeed and fail, and the probability, p, of a success does not change when the experiment is repeated, then the probability $P(n, k)$ of obtaining exactly k successes in n repetitions can be found by the recurrence relation

$$P(0,0) = 1, \quad P(n,0) = (1-p)^n, \quad P(n,n) = p^n$$
$$P(n,k) = pP(n-1, k-1)$$
$$+ (1-p)P(n-1, k)$$
$$\text{for } n > 0,\ 1 \le k \le n-1.$$

	A	B	C	D	E	F
1	p =	0.6	q =		0.4	
2						
3	n/k		0	1	2	3
4	0		1.000			
5	1		0.400	0.600	0.000	0.000
6	2		0.160	0.480	0.360	0.000
7	3		0.064	0.288	0.432	0.216

	A	B	C	D
1	p =	0.6	q =	=1-B1
2				
3	n/k		0	=1+C3
4	0		1	
5	=1+A4		=$B$1*B4+$D$1*C4	=$B$1*C4+$D$1*D4
6	=1+A5		=$B$1*B5+$D$1*C5	=$B$1*C5+$D$1*D5
7	=1+A6		=$B$1*B6+$D$1*C6	=$B$1*C6+$D$1*D6

Figure 7. Binomial probability model. Columns E and F are not shown in the lower part of the figure but would be analogs of column D.

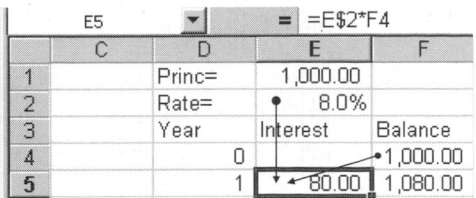

Figure 6. Showing formula precedences.

This formula is based on the fact that, to have k successes after n repetitions, after $n-1$ repetitions either there were (a) $k-1$ successes followed by a success (probability $pP(n-1, k-1)$) or (b) k successes followed by a failure (probability $(1-p)P(n-1, k)$). As spreadsheets treat references to blank cells as 0, a single formula (e.g. cell C5) can be copied throughout the table. In the example, $p = 0.6$. While this model is designed to illustrate the use of a recurrence relation, binomial probabilities can also be computed by using library functions.

Bibliography

1997. Boctor, D. *Office 97 Visual Basic: Step by Step*. Redmond, WA: Microsoft Press.

1997. Dodge, M., Kinata, C., and Stinson, C. *Running Microsoft Excel 97*. Redmond, WA: Microsoft Press.

1997. Moseley, L., and Boodey, D. *Mastering Microsoft Excel 97, Professional Edition*. San Francisco: Sybex.

1998. Neibauer, A., and Cowpland, M. *Corel WordPerfect Suite 8 Professional: The Official Guide*. Berkeley, CA: Osborne/McGraw-Hill.

1997. Sandberg, E. *Mastering Lotus SmartSuite 97*. San Francisco: Sybex.

Website

http://sunsite.univie.ac.at/spreadsite/ contains not only a wealth of mathematical and educational applications of spreadsheets, but also links to numerous general spreadsheet sites.

Deane Arganbright

SQL

See DATABASE MANAGEMENT SYSTEM; and RELATIONAL DATABASE.

STACK

> For articles on related subjects *see* ACTIVATION RECORD; DATA STRUCTURES; LIST PROCESSING; POLISH NOTATION; RECURSION; SUBPROGRAM; and TREE.

A *stack* is a structure that behaves like a linear list for which all insertions and deletions are made at one end of the list. The properties of a simple stack may be illustrated by a railroad switching network having a track into which railroad cars may be inserted and removed from only one end, as in Fig. 1. At any given time, only the most recently entered railroad car may be removed from the track. Railroad cars are said to enter and leave the track in a last in, first out (LIFO) order.

A stack may thus be defined as a structure whose elements may be inserted and deleted only in a last in, first out order. The rules or axioms (*see* ABSTRACT DATA TYPE and PROGRAM SPECIFICATION) that specify what a

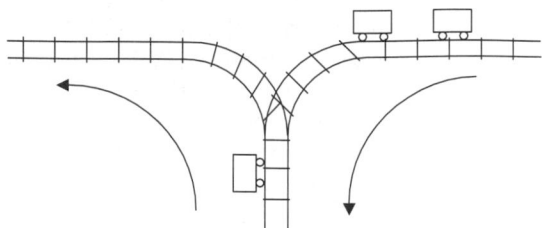

Figure 1. Railroad switching network.

stack is can be stated in terms of three operations, commonly called *push*, *pop* and *top*. *Push* adds an item to a stack, *pop* deletes the most recently added item, and *top* returns that item, leaving the stack unchanged. We can characterize a stack by means of axioms stating how these operations are related (a complete specification would also have axioms concerning empty stacks). Here *push* and *pop* are functions that return the stack after modification. The first axiom states that the most recently pushed item is at the top of the stack, and the second that pop removes that item.

$$top(push(item, stack)) = item$$
$$pop(push(item, stack)) = stack$$

Stacks arise in computational processes that deal with structures whose components are nested, as in the following example of arithmetic expression evaluation. The expression $(3 + (4*5))$ has a subexpression $(4*5)$, which is nested within the complete expression. It is conveniently evaluated by first converting it to the parenthesis-free postfix notation (*see* POLISH NOTATION) 345*+ (in which the operator $*$ immediately follows its operands 4, 5 and the operator $+$ immediately follows its operands 3 and (45*), and then using an operand stack for evaluation. The evaluation of the expression 345*+, using a stack, is illustrated in Fig. 2; it follows the rule:

Evaluation Rule for Postfix Expressions Scan the constituents (operators and operands) of the expression from left to right. If the constituent is an operand, push it onto the operand stack. If the constituent is an operator, apply it to the two top elements of the operand stack and replace these two elements by the result of that operation.

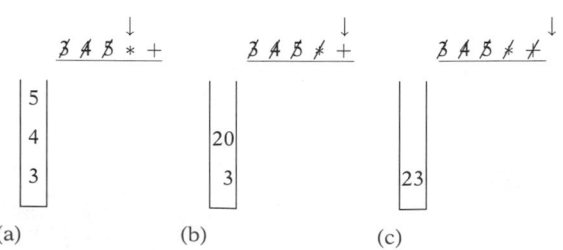

Figure 2. Evaluation of 3 4 5 $*$ +.

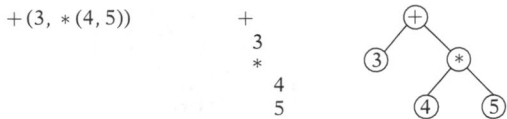

Figure 3. Three representations of a nested structure.

The elements 3, 4, 5 in Fig. 2a have been placed in the operand stack and the operator "*" is about to be scanned. According to the evaluation rules, * is applied to the two top elements (5 and 4) of the operand stack, which causes the elements 5 and 4 to be replaced by the value 20. The operator + is now applied to the two top elements (20 and 3) of the operand stack (Fig. 2b), which causes these elements to be replaced by the value 23 (Fig. 2c).Such arithmetic expression evaluation is conveniently implemented with a stack because expressions (*q.v.*) may contain subexpressions nested inside them to an arbitrary level.

Another example of nested program structure arises in the case of subroutines (procedures—*see* SUBPROGRAM). Subroutine calls have the property that a called subroutine must be completely executed before returning to the higher-level subroutine that called it. Thus, subroutines are executed in a last in, first out order (relative to the order in which they are called), and are conveniently implemented by a stack mechanism that creates and deletes information about subroutine parameters and the return address in a last in, first out order.

Nested structures may be represented by parentheses, indented outlines, or tree (*q.v.*) structures, as illustrated in Fig. 3.

There are many applications in which the elements of a nested structure (tree structure) must be "visited" in an order that requires the path by which the element was reached to be remembered. For example, if a tree is traversed by first visiting the root and then traversing the subtrees in a left-to-right order, then it is convenient to remember the path from the root to the current vertex on a stack, since successor subtrees of vertices along the path from the root to the current vertex must be examined in a last in, first out order if the traversal of all vertices of the tree is to be completed.

Bibliography

1997. Knuth, D. E. *The Art of Computer Programming*, Vol 1, 3rd Ed. Reading, MA: Addison-Wesley.

Peter Wegner, revised by David Hemmendinger

STAMPS, COMPUTING ON

For articles on related subjects *see* CALCULATING MACHINES; and DIGITAL COMPUTERS, HISTORY OF.

There are a large number of postage stamps featuring computers and related topics. Many of these stamps relate to the history of calculation and computation; others are more concerned with the present-day uses of computers in society. In this article we present a small selection of stamps, chosen to be as representative as possible.

From earliest times, men and women have needed to carry out computations of various kinds. Early methods of counting and calculating included *counting on the fingers* (Iran, 1966), the use in Peru of the *quipu*, a knotted cord employed for accounting and census purposes (Peru, 1972), and various forms of the *abacus* (Colombia, 1977[1]).

A major advance occurred in the seventeenth century with the invention of logarithms by John Napier and Henry Briggs. This simplified calculations enormously, and quickly led to such practical calculating devices as the *slide rule* (Romania, 1957). Around the same time, the first mechanical calculating machine was described by *Wilhelm Schickard* (West Germany, 1973[1]). Other early calculating machines, several of which still exist today, were constructed by *Blaise Pascal* (Monaco, 1973) and *Gottfried Wilhelm Leibniz* (*q.v.*) (West Germany, 1980).

The central figures of the nineteenth century were Charles Babbage (*q.v.*) (Great Britain, 1991[1]) and Ada Lovelace (*q.v.*). Babbage may be said to have pioneered the modern computer age with his Difference Engine (*q.v.*) and Analytical Engine (*q.v.*), even though the technology of the time was insufficiently advanced for efficient working versions to be constructed.

The modern computer age started in the 1940s. The machines of the 1940s were large and cumbersome, and for several years were run using *punched cards* (*q.v.*) (Norway, 1969[1]), *punched tape* (Switzerland, 1970[1]; Poland, 1971[1]), or *magnetic tape* (Canada, 1971[1]). Advances in electronic technology quickly led to the development of the *integrated circuit* (Japan, 1980[1]), and the *microchip* (Great Britain, 1989[1]).

Computers themselves came to be used for a wide variety of purposes, ranging from large-scale machines (Ivory Coast, 1972[1]; East Germany, 1966[1]) to conventional small-scale office equipment (Denmark, 1965). Recent technological developments have enabled computers to become increasingly compact, and desk computers in homes and offices are now commonplace (India, 1985; Austria, 1987).

Finally, computers have been used increasingly in the design of stamps. An interesting example is the set of five computer-designed stamps produced on the Eindhoven computer (Netherlands, 1970).

[1] See Color Page CP-15 for these stamps.

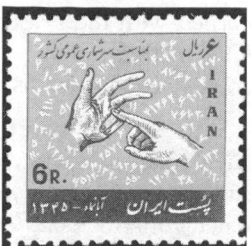

Iran

Peru

Romania

Monaco

West Germany

Denmark

India

Austria

Netherlands

Netherlands

Netherlands

Netherlands

Netherlands

Bibliography

For several years, the quarterly Springer-Verlag publication *Mathematical Intelligencer* has featured a "Stamp Corner" written by the author of this article. The stamps depicted feature mathematicians and mathematical topics, many of which relate to the history of computation.

Philamath, a journal of mathematical philately, is published by the Mathematical Study Unit of the American Topical Association. For information, contact the Secretary-Treasurer Estelle A. Buccino, 5615 Glenwood Road, Bethesda, MD 20817, USA.

1998. Dodson, L. *Computers on Stamps and Stationery.* Tucson, AZ: American Topical Association.

Robin J. Wilson

STANDARDS

For articles on related subjects *see* COMPUTER GRAPHICS: STANDARDS; DATA COMMUNICATIONS: STANDARDS; and PROGRAMMING LANGUAGE STANDARDS.

Overview

Standardization is one of the hallmarks of an industrial society. As a society becomes increasingly complex and its industrial base begins to emerge, it becomes necessary for the products, processes, and procedures of the society to fit together and to interoperate. This interoperation provides the basis for greater integration of the elements of the society, which in turn causes increased social interdependency and complexity. This trend has recently been accelerated by the so-called "global economy," and further spurred by the creation of seamless methods of transnational transfer of information and knowledge via the the Internet (*q.v.*) and the World Wide Web (*q.v.*). Both the Internet and the Web are currently based entirely upon voluntary standardization. Their result is increased information interdependence, which in turn will feed the need for increased application standardization. However, the standardization that will result from the application of these technologies will include social and economic standardization, a phenomenon whose depth and implications are just now beginning to be appreciated.

There are three possible types of standardization: *de jure*, *de facto*, and the development of publicly available specifications. A brief description of each follows, as well as comments about their relevance to the Information Technology (IT—*q.v.*) industry. It is necessary to remember that in all cases, standards are motivated by economic forces, and not by technological activity. A standard is effective (and hence, successful) only if it is incorporated into a product or service and deployed by multiple providers; organizations that create and sell products are usually "for profit" companies.

According to the International Organization for Standardization (ISO) and the International Electrotechnical Commission (IEC), a *standard* is formally defined as being a "document, established by consensus and approved by a recognized body, that provides for common and repeated use, rules, guidelines, or characteristics for activities or their results aimed at an achievement of the optimum degree of order in a given context. [Standards] should be based upon the consolidated results of science, technology, and experience and aimed at the promotion of optimum community benefits." (ISO/IEC Guide 2.) These are *de jure standards*, which are created only by recognized bodies, normally called Standards Developing Organizations (SDOs). By being open to all and having rules protecting everyone, an SDO can gain a limited immunity from claims of anticompetitive activities and collusion. The SDO operates under a set of rules that encourages open participation and consensus in creation of standards for a product, process, service, or technology. The reality is that the participants generally represent not only themselves, but also their organizations (usually a commercial entity), and their National Body, which represents the nation of the participant. The IT sector is usually well represented in the national SDOs of the developed countries.

De facto standards are those products and services that have gained market acceptance and are recognized as those against which others will be compared. There is usually no one reason why something becomes a *de facto* standard—usually, it is a combination of having the right product and right window of opportunity and the right marketing for product acceptance. Although creating *de facto* standards is the aim of many providers, this is usually not an ideal solution from a user's point of view, since a *de facto* standard can limit innovation or confer a monopoly position on the supplier. The continued survival of a *de facto* standard is usually in direct proportion to the amount of marketing and legal resources that the provider wishes to spend. (An example is the status of Microsoft Windows and the US government antitrust suit against Microsoft—*q.v.*)

Publicly Available Specifications (PASs) are those specifications which the market has accepted (or the providers wish that the market would accept) but which have not yet been through the formal (SDO) standardization process. PASs are normally created by consortia, which are groups of companies formed to unify their industry around a single specific technical specification. They usually operate in areas of fast-moving or contentious technologies, where formal SDOs have been judged too slow or too cumbersome to meet the needs of the industry for standardization. Consortia tend to be very focused on the creation of a single specification (or set of specifications) that respond to a singular industry problem (chip standardization, language standardization, automotive supply standardization, or any other problem that has natural constraints that make it a candidate for standardization) which a limited number of participants can solve. Consortia are "pay to play" organizations that are seeking solutions that are acceptable to the majority of players in the industry which supports them; they do not care, usually, about the "disaffected academic" or "concerned citizen" in the creation of their PASs. By and large, they are there to create a working solution to an industry problem. Consortia in the USA are often registered under the antitrust shelter provided by the National Cooperative Research and Production Act (NCRPA) of 1993 (which protects registered organizations from the risk of normal antitrust treble damages and liability for a plaintiff's attorneys' fees). Their historical success rate has been poor, but they do raise the awareness of standardization among the general public. The importance of standardization to the world economy is significant since standards can form the basis of much national, regional, and international trade. The Uruguay GATT (General Agreement on Tariffs and Trade, 1986–94) recognized the importance of standards as potential nontariff trade barriers and has worked to limit their use in this way. The Agreement on Technical Barriers to Trade recognizes that standardization can be a significant factor in reducing trade barriers, and the Agreement on Government Procurement states that internationally accepted standards are the preferred basis of procurement for governments. Additionally, the European Commission has created its own standardization bodies to deal with European regional standardization as a unifying tactic, acknowledging the power and influence of standardization in trade. Given this level of importance, it is surprising that standardization has been so overlooked by academic institutions. In the USA there are fewer than 15 institutions of higher learning offering any coursework on the subject.

The cost of the creation and implementation of standards by industrial users in the USA has been estimated at between $17 billion and $30 billion each year, but there is little or no definitive research on the issue. It is a significant activity in industrial policy (foreign and national), yet the level of formal understanding of the discipline is surprisingly poor. On the positive side, however, many business and governmental organizations do understand the nature and importance of standardization, and are learning and adapting to the standardization system or are forcing the system to adapt to their market needs.

Information Technology Standardization

Information technology standardization is probably the most dynamic standardization arena in the world. The changes that are taking place in the IT industry are mirrored in the rapid changes in the industry's standardization arena. This, of course, has created some severe stresses within the IT industry, because the traditional approaches to standardization (SDOs) are more suited to a "smokestack" industry, where product life cycles are lengthy. Additionally, because of the extraordinary requirements for openness, and the complexity of the review and agreement process, the formal standardization process rarely—if ever—produces a standard to a schedule. The lack of accountability and lack of real deadlines are probably the major impediments to the formal standardization process being taken seriously by the producers in the IT industry.

There were several responses that the IT industry—as a whole—had towards the perceived "time and relevance" problems of formal standardization. (The average time for a standard to be completed within the ISO framework, from initiation to completion, is between 36 and 42 months, which makes it late and, usually, irrelevant to IT product life cycles.) The first response involved the concept of anticipatory standardization by SDOs, the second was the creation of consortia, and the third involved changes to the discipline and practice of standardization.

The creation of *anticipatory standards* (i.e. standards developed in advance of the general implementation of technology in products) was initially perceived to be a viable idea. Anticipatory standards appeared to allow the recapture of some of the introduction and growth stages of the product life cycle by permitting public comment and review of basic specifications as these specifications (or standards) were created. They were also viewed as potential "change agents," driving the direction of the industry by their existence. It was hoped that SDOs would be forums where demonstrated and viable technology was standardized, allowing widespread adoption and multiple implementations. Reality soon overtook this concept, especially in the areas of POSIX and Open Systems Interconnection (OSI—*q.v.*). Both of these were massive standardization efforts that were anticipatory in nature—and both succumbed to provider pressures and market indifference. POSIX (Portable Operating System Interface for Unix) grew and grew—and generally was ignored by the commercial market. OSI, supported by major vendors, never caught on with the buyers because it could not guarantee product interoperability, one of the primary functions that users believed that a standard should supply. The failure of anticipatory standardization has hurt the relevance of the SDOs, who were the most dominant users of this concept in standardization. Also, due partially to arcane rules and procedures (often used to slow or stop a standardization effort) and partially due to the perceived lack of response to market needs, formal SDO standardization is less relevant to the IT industry in 1999 than at any time over the past five years.

The next option, the use of consortia, was based upon the belief that a consortium, because it was a collection of like minded companies who had invested in a common belief, would be a more efficient and effective way of standardizing. The consortia gained acceptance because they did succeed in creating publicly available specifications which, in many cases, did lead or stabilize the market. To complement their technical capabilities, many consortia had a budget for advertising their progress and their accomplishments, something that SDOs did not. However, as they struggled to gain consensus among their members, they often did not create or issue specifications with any more relevance or speed than did SDOs.

However, the consortia could change both their focus and rules (as well as come into existence or disappear) with greater facility than could SDOs—and it is this feature that is both the strength and weakness of consortia. Many consortia have modified their rules to begin to accept for standardization what the industry (as represented by their members) is currently practicing. These specifications are then distributed and—in many cases—implemented by the members of the consortium, which stabilizes the market for the specification and products that are based on the specification. The change from "anticipatory" standardization to "open industry practice" (where specific vendor implementation requirements are removed) responds to the market need for speed as well as satisfying the need for consensus, since consensus is obvious by market acceptance of the underlying practice. The best-known practitioner of this form of "open industry practice" standardization is the Internet Engineering Task Force (IETF), concerned with maintaining the Internet. One of the major claims opposing consortia specifications is that consortia are "not open." The people or groups who are not part of the consortium (for any of a number of reasons, but usually because they cannot afford the dues or because they oppose the underlying technology) claim that there is discrimination by the members of the consortium, who do not represent the "market." The point is that consortia were never meant to be a replacement for the SDOs; consortia are focused on achieving a solution to a market need in a reasonable time, and need not accept all opinions on the technology under consideration; they are meant to take into account only the opinions of their members. However, if the majority of the product-producing industry is represented in a consortium producing a specification, the only difference between the SDO and the consortium is in the naming of the final product (standard versus publicly available specification). In this case, the distinction between the two organizations tends to be somewhat artificial.

Finally, changes to the discipline and practice of standardization have begun to occur. ISO/IEC JTC 1 (see below) created a procedure for accepting the work of consortia as what we called earlier Publicly Available Specifications (PASs). This procedure—initiated in 1995—failed to garner much interest until Sun Microsystems, Inc. applied for permission to act as a submitting organization for the Java (*q.v.*) specification. The request was accepted by the National Body members of ISO/IEC JTC1 after much debate. During the debate, however, the use of the Web as a substitute for the traditional standards methodology surfaced. This concept—the ability to use the unlimited audience of the Web as a review body for technology—seems to be the panacea for the "lack of user participation" aspect of the current practice. The question is whether or not JTC1—and possibly all of ISO—can fold the technology being standardized into the process to make the process more responsive. It is probably upon this question that the entire process will either prosper or wither, and whether or not the formal process is seen as a viable complement to the other standardization options available to the market.

Standards Development

Standards development has a five-stage life cycle:

Stage 1: External to the formal process:
Preconceptualization (or market verification of need and selection of the general forum for standardization)

Stages 2, 3, and 4: Within the actual standardization process:
Conceptualization (where technical requirements are defined and a standardizing organization chosen or created)
Discussion (where the committee achieves understanding of its mission and defines the task at hand, as well as a methodology for succeeding)
Writing (in which complex mathematical algorithms are turned into unambiguous native language statements)

Stage 5: External to the formal process, but sometimes included within the remit of a consortium:
Marketing and *implementation* (where the standard or specification is actually put into practice)

Each of the stages of the life cycle has a great deal more complexity than indicated in the preceding list. The first and last stages are poorly understood, and in these areas lie most of the current opportunities for growth and increased utility of the process.

Standardization Organizations

There are various types and kinds of standardization organizations, from international SDOs to consortia to alliances, each having a role and place in the standards development hierarchy. This examination will look at SDOs (from an international, national, and governmental point of view), and then examine consortia and similar organizations, and will conclude with a look at the emerging "alliance–consortium" organizations.

INTERNATIONAL ORGANIZATIONS

The premier standards organization is the International Organization for Standardization, located in Geneva, Switzerland. ISO, which covers nearly every aspect of standardization (from machine screws to ornamental garden rocks), was born in the post-Second World War era of common international cooperative efforts. It was intended to unify standardization activities throughout the world, both to improve cooperation and to lessen national trade barriers. It is recognized today as being the international body for standards in most major areas, with electrotechnical devices (International Electrotechnical Commission (IEC)) and telecommunications/telegraphy (International Telecommunication Union (ITU)) being excepted from the ISO's purview. Voting in all of these organizations is by nation (i.e. the USA has one vote, as do Ghana, Switzerland, and Japan). The voting member of the ISO and the IEC for the USA is the American National Standards Institute (ANSI), which is recognized by the ISO as being the most representative standards body in the USA.

Until the late 1980s, both the IEC and ISO had committees devoted to looking at information technology standardization. However, with the growth of systems standards in the 1980s, the various IT-focused standardization committees of these two organizations began to expand their various scopes, leading to "turf wars" within the standards community. After several years of negotiations, the first joint ISO/IEC committee was created to deal with matters of information technology. This is ISO/IEC Joint Technical Committee 1 (JTC1), the only joint ISO/IEC committee and, until 1997, the only internationally recognized committee that dealt exclusively with IT standards and standardization. In the mid-1990s, however, the IEC once again formed its own committee to deal with areas of IT standardization. This committee (IEC Technical Committee Number 100: Audio, Video, and Multimedia Systems and Equipment) was a response by the IEC to what it perceived was the lack of activity by JTC1 to cover necessary topics in this arena. The conflict between the two organizations has not, as of 1999, become pronounced, although there is an increasing

Table 1. Subcommittees of JCT1.

SC 02	Coded Character Sets
SC 06	Telecommunications and Information Exchange Between Systems
SC 07	Software Engineering
SC 11	Flexible Magnetic Media for Digital Data Interchange
SC 17	Identification Cards and Related Devices
SC 22	Programming Languages, Their Environments and Systems Software Interfaces
SC 22/WG 20	Internationalization
SC 23	Optical Disk Cartridges for Information Interchange
SC 24	Computer Graphics and Image Processing
SC 25	Interconnection of Information Technology Equipment
SC 26	Microprocessor Systems
SC 27	IT Security Techniques
SC 28	Office Equipment
SC 29	Coding of Audio, Picture, and Multimedia and Hypermedia Information
SC 31	Automatic Identification and Data Capture Techniques
SC 32	Data Management and Interchange
SC 34	Document Description and Processing Languages
SC 35	User Interfaces

tension between the organizations. Additionally, JTC1 is in the process of restructuring itself, and the current committee structure is in the process of being realigned with the Information Technology industry. Table 1 lists the subcommittees of JCT1.

NATIONAL STANDARDS BODIES

Most nations have a single SDO that oversees creation of national standards. In Germany, the organization is the Deutsches Institut für Normung e.V. (DIN); in Canada, the Canadian Standards Association; and so on. However, in the US, there is only an umbrella organization, the American National Standards Institute (ANSI). It creates the rules by which standards are written and accredits organizations that write standards by the rules that ANSI publishes. The rules have a twofold aim: allowing free and open participation to any concerned party, and the achievement of consensus in the creation of a standard. Consensus can best be defined as a state achieved when all parties reach substantial agreement. This definition indicates more than majority approval, but does not imply unanimity. Rather, it indicates that all arguments have been heard, addressed, and dealt with in a constructive fashion.

ANSI usually accredits any organization to write standards that will agree to follow its rules. This has led to several hundred standards-making bodies being accredited in the USA. The federalist model of governance works well in a static organization; the commercial importance of standardization, however, has made the US standards scene very dynamic. As a result, the hegemony that ANSI managed to build based on the coveted designation of *American National Standard* (ANS) has been eroded over the last several years, and the tacit acceptance of consortia (outside of the ANSI framework) by the creation of the PAS process has further eroded the power of ANSI as the actual coordinator of US standardization. The decline in the importance of the ANS designation, however, is somewhat countered by the rise in importance of international standards since ANSI is the source of the US positions in the formal international standardization community. This role is one of increasing importance to ANSI, and may permit ANSI to regain its position as the leader in the US standardization arena.

Within formal standardization in the US, there are three types of standardization paths to pursue, depending upon the nature of the group that is doing the standardization.

The first type of group is the *Accredited Canvass Organization* (ACO), which is almost always a single-issue and single-effort organization. The canvass method of standardization begins with a completed specification, which is then exposed for public review. Comments from the concerned public on the specification are reviewed and included (where necessary) and, eventually, an American National Standard emerges. The process works well for noncontentious and stable specifications (usually of current practice) or where the potential audience for the specification is small and well known. Since the Canvass committee is a "committee of the whole," it is usually inefficient for contentious or specification-creating activities.

The *Accredited Organization* (AO) is usually an organization that is extant and which does standardization as a sideline. The IEEE is such an organization, since standards creation is only a minor part of the functions that the IEEE offers its members. The usual rationale for an AO is that the membership has a set of competencies which should or could be turned to standardization creation for "the good of the membership and the industry" from which the membership is drawn. Membership in the committee is usually, but not always, drawn from the membership of the organization. The AO has a more widespread competence than the ACO, but it, too, is usually limited by the competencies of the members of its parent organization.

Finally, there is the *Accredited Standards Organization* (ASC), which exists only to create standards. The ASC is open to all participants, is focused on standards creation, and tends to live a precarious existence because its fortunes ebb and flow with the status of standardization in the industry. The ASC will usually undertake standardization in any arena of interest to its

diverse membership, which, in turn, reflects the skill of the ASC in recruiting members. The most significant ASC in the USA in the IT arena is the National Center for Information Technology Standardization (NCITS), previously known as X3. Table 2 lists the technical committees of NCITS.

As noted above, ANSI holds the US vote at ISO, IEC, and other voluntary formal standardization organizations. However, because ANSI itself has no specific competence in the technical areas of standardization, it relies upon "Technical Advisory Groups" (TAGs) to provide it with the necessary position and vote. The TAGs are appointed by ANSI, and usually are based upon domestic standardization groups who have an interest in the area being standardized. For the IT industry, the TAG is composed of the members of the NCITS, the IEEE, and several other AOs/ASCs. This committee (the US JTC1 TAG) looks at the JTC1 issues

Table 2. NCITS technical committees.

A1	Optical Character Recognition (OCR)
B5	Flexible Magnetic Media and Formats
B9	Paper Forms/Layout
B10	Identification Cards and Related Devices
B11	Optical Digital Data Disks
H2	Database
H3	Computer Graphics & Image Processing
J1	Programming Language PL/I
J3	Programming Language Fortran
J4	Programming Language COBOL
J7	Programming Language APT
J9	Programming Language Pascal
J11	Programming Language C
J13	Programming Language LISP
J14	Programming Language FORTH
J15	Programming Language PL/B
J16	Programming Language C++
J17	Programming Language Prolog
J18	Programming Language Rexx
J20	Programming Language Smalltalk
J22	U.S. TAG to ISO/IEC JTC1 SC 22 Java Study Group
K5	Vocabulary for Information Processing Systems
L1	Geographic Information Systems (GIS)
L2	Codes and Character Sets
L3	Coding of Audio, Picture, Multimedia, and Hypermedia Information
L8	Data Representation
R1	Real-Time Computing Systems
T2	Information Interchange and Interpretation
T3	Open Distributed Processing (ODP)
T4	Security Techniques
T6	Radio Frequency Identification (RFID) Technology
T8	Fault Isolation
T10	I/O Interface—Lower Level
T11	I/O Interface—Device Level
T12	I/O Interface—Distributed Data
T13	I/O Interface—AT Attachment
V1	Text Processing: Office and Publishing Systems Interface
W1	Office Machines

from a US point of view, and then advises ANSI how to cast the ballot that represents the opinion of the US standardization experts in this arena.

CONSORTIA

Consortia have become the current drivers of standardization in many areas of IT standardization where there is a premium on rapid change and applications of new technology. Many of the interesting areas of IT, such as the Internet, the World Wide Web, programming languages, applications, and security are undergoing standardization in consortia. This phenomenon is growing, with consortia being created at a rate of about one per week in 1999.

Consortia are "pay to play" groups, and their attraction is that they can focus on the creation of a marketable specification, to which vendors build products and which users can specify and deploy. The key to a consortium's success is the ability to respond quickly to an immediate and pressing need of the market—and to focus only upon that need. Unlike an SDO, which must take a project/program in the general area of its charter, a consortium is under no such constraints. Consortia can look for high return or interest activities upon which to focus. Additionally, consortia, operating under their own rules and policies, have the ability to commit to and meet schedules, something that an SDO cannot do. Finally, a consortium can declare itself multinational and not have to deal with the problems of "national bodies."

The following list of consortia gives a sample of the nature and diversity of the species. It is not meant to be inclusive, but is rather a sampling of organizations to show the diversity.

◆ The Internet Engineering Task Force (IETF), is responsible for the creation, growth, and maintenance of the Internet. The membership is individuals. IETF is probably the most egalitarian and open standardization group in existence.

◆ The World Wide Web Consortium (W3C) is responsible for the technology and growth of the World Wide Web. Membership is by organization. This is an academic/commercial cooperative venture to ensure that their Web growth has some coherence.

◆ ECMA (European Computer Manufacturing Association) is an international Europe-based Information Technology standardization association with a close liaison with ISO JTC1. ECMA's expertise is in the standardization of "current practice" technology and accepted *de facto* standards. Membership is by organization.

◆ The Object Management Group (OMG) is responsible for most object-oriented programming (*q.v.*)

standardization. With over 800 organizational members, the group is one of the largest consortia. It has PAS status.

◆ The Open Group, responsible for "The IT Dialtone." This is an amalgamation of the Open Software Foundation and X/Open. The Open Group is redefining its role. It is best known for its testing and branding abilities. It has PAS status.

◆ The Open GIS Consortium focuses on Geospatial Information Systems (GIS), and works in conjunction with ISO's GIS Technical Committees. Membership is by organization.

◆ The Desktop Management Task Force (DMTF) is an organization that focuses on setting System Administration standards for desktop computers. It has PAS status.

◆ The Virtual Reality Modeling Language (VRML) Consortium exists to create the specification for VRML and forward it to ISO, and then to begin work on the next iteration.

◆ The Digital Imaging Group (DIG) is establishing a format for digital imaging to be sent and displayed over the Internet and for desktop applications of digital imaging.

REGIONAL GOVERNMENTAL AGENCIES

Comité Européen de Normalisation (CEN), Comité Européen de Normalisation, Electrotechnique (CEN-ELEC), and the European Telecommunications Standards Institute (ETSI) are three organizations created by the European Commission that are supposed to help unify the standards for commercial activities in the countries that make up the EU. The three organizations roughly parallel the activities of ISO, the IEC, and the ITU, but are focused on European regional activities. The activities of these groups have not been as successful as was hoped in the IT arena, but they have been very successful in standardization of non-IT arenas, such as the environment and quality management. With the growing access to the Web, and the conversion of the Web from a technical to a social phenomenon, the possibility that these organizations may become involved in the IT arena through social legislation (such as security and privacy issues) is growing.

THE NATIONAL INSTITUTE FOR STANDARDS AND TECHNOLOGY

The US National Institute for Standards and Technology (NIST) replaced the old National Bureau of Standards (NBS) in 1989. The Computer Systems Laboratory (CSL) is the federal government's primary player in the standardization arena. Although a formally chartered SDO in its own right, NIST rarely creates standards, preferring to rely upon the private process. The use of private sector standardization—which is becoming an increasingly popular governmental response to procurement—is increasing the trend to withdraw NIST from active standardization involvement.

Bibliography

1984. Cerni, D. M. *Standards in Process: Foundations and Profiles of ISDN and OSI Studies.* Washington, DC: NTIA Report 84-170.

1992. Weiss, M., and Cargill, C. "Consortia in the Standards Development Process," *Journal of the American Society for Information Science,* **43**, 8, 559–565.

1993. *Standard View, ACM Perspectives on Standardization.* New York: ACM.

1994. Wagner, C. S., Cargill, C. F., and Slomovic, A. *Standards and the National Information Infrastructure: Implications for Open Systems Standards in Manufacturing.* Santa Monica, CA: RAND.

1995. Kahin, B., and Abbate, J. (eds.) *Standards Policy for Information Infrastructure.* Cambridge, MA: MIT Press.

1995. Libicki, M. *Standards: The Rough Road to the Common Byte.* Washington, DC: National Defense University.

1997. Cargill, C. F. *Open Systems Standardization: A Business Approach.* Upper Saddle River, NJ: Prentice Hall.

Carl F. Cargill

STATEMENT

For articles on related subjects *see* CONCURRENT PROGRAMMING; CONTROL STRUCTURE; DECLARATION; DEFAULT CONDITION; DELIMITER; EXECUTABLE STATEMENT; EXPRESSION; PROCEDURE-ORIENTED LANGUAGES; PROGRAMMING LANGUAGES; and STRUCTURED PROGRAMMING.

In much the same way that a sentence is the structural unit of expression in a stream of natural language discourse, the *statement* may be viewed as the elemental organizational component of a procedural high-level language. As such, it embodies a unit of activity in terms of the algorithm being implemented. This is quite different from, and bears no direct correspondence with, processor activity. Although many types of statements are *executable* in that they instigate the compiler to produce operationally equivalent sequences of machine-language instructions, this relationship is arbitrary: a given type of statement may be expanded or contracted to designate a wide range of activities, all within the syntax of that statement. For example, the following two statements:

```
A = 7.82
B = (22.4 + (X/Y)**3) * (X * Y - Z)
```

are both syntactically legitimate assignment statements in the Fortran language, but there is clearly a considerable difference in the amount of computation

that each one specifies. This is completely consistent with the underlying idea that the user, rather than the processor, be the determining factor with regard to the amount of processing expressed in a high-level language statement.

Not all high-level language statements can be related to instructions in the machine language program ultimately produced. Many languages include statement types whose primary purpose is not to convey the intent of an algorithm, but rather to provide supportive information for compilation and other processes auxiliary to the actual execution of the program. These statements, which pertain to matters such as the allocation of storage and description of variables, correspond to a range of activities that do not generally show up as equivalent sequences of machine instructions. Accordingly, they are *nonexecutable*, and usually are treated as a distinct syntactic set of statements called *declarations*.

It is not always possible to provide the programmer with unlimited scope for expression in a single statement. Yet such capability is needed if the linkage between the statement and a meaningful activity is to be preserved. There are innumerable occasions in which a sequence of associated events, while clearly identifiable as a single procedural activity, contains arbitrarily diverse machine processes whose specification in a single statement would be linguistically impractical. Most high-level languages accommodate this necessity by allowing some type of compound construction. In some cases the construction is formed as a single statement with multiple clauses; in others, the idea of the *compound* statement is implemented as a group of single statements enclosed in special organizational statements or special words that serve as *delimiters* (*q.v.—see also* STRUCTURED PROGRAMMING). Such a compound statement may also be the executable body of a *subprogram* (*q.v.*).

Executable Statements

Since these statement types are characterized by their ultimate relationship to explicit processing action in the object program, their general form tends to resemble the imperative sentence in many natural languages. Accordingly, it is often true that the language elements used for specifying activities are verbs. For example, an input activity in Pascal is expressed in the form

```
read(filename, list)
```

where *filename* and *list* specify the source and destination of the input, respectively. The same construction prevails when data is to be transmitted from the central processor to the outside world, with the verb `write` indicating the direction. When similarity to natural language is a primary design objective, the correspondence may be more pronounced, as in the following Cobol statement:

```
ADD a TO b GIVING c.
```

The narrative construction persists in an alternative, more formulaic form:

```
COMPUTE c = a + b.
```

The Basic language designates the same operations in a similar manner ("LET" is now optional):

```
LET c = a + b.
```

The words COMPUTE and LET are included in the fixed vocabularies of their respective languages specifically to enhance the parallels with "real" sentences; the language translators clearly can operate properly without them, as they do in such languages as Fortran (*q.v.*), Pascal (*q.v.*), and C (*q.v.*). It should be noted, however, that the absence of such verbs does not change the inherently imperative syntax: though now more implicit, it still remains. Thus, the Pascal statement equivalent to the previous examples, namely,

```
c := a + b
```

can be read as a highly implicit form of this sentence: "The value in c is to be replaced by the result of the indicated operation on a and b."

The same construction generally carries over to compound statements. Though high-level languages vary in the type and extent of compounding their syntaxes allow, there is one category of compound activity sufficiently basic to all computing work to compel its representation across the entire spectrum of high-level languages. This is the fundamental decision mechanism in which a comparison is specified in conjunction with procedural alternatives based on the outcome of that comparison. In programmers' argot, this is termed the IF-THEN-ELSE construct. A "natural" way to articulate such a construction would be with some form of conditional sentence: "If a particular condition exists, take the action specified here; if it does not exist, ignore that action and perform this alternative action." This construction is followed closely in many languages.

To illustrate this, consider the situation in which two variables, X and Y, are to be compared. If X is less than Y, the X value is to be doubled; otherwise, X is to be decreased by 8.2. In either case, a variable Z is to be computed as the product XY. The appropriate compound statements for several languages are:

```
(Cobol)      IF X IS LESS THAN Y
                 MULTIPLY X BY 2
             ELSE
                 SUBTRACT 8.2 FROM X.
             COMPUTE Z = X * Y.
```

```
(Fortran 90)  IF (X .LT. Y) THEN
                  X = 2.0 * X
              ELSE
                  X = X - 8.2
              END IF
                  Z = X * Y
```

```
(Pascal)      if X < Y then
                  X := 2 * X
              else
                  X := X - 8.2;
              Z := X * Y;
```

These languages provide a variety of structural features that enable such decision mechanisms to be extended. One such extension, for example, allows either or both alternative actions at the ends of an if statement to be if statements themselves.

The ability to treat arbitrarily long sequences as single procedural activities receives formal emphasis in languages such as Pascal, whose vocabulary includes special organizational statements to indicate the bounds of such sequences. This is intended to encourage a modular approach to program design wherein the implementation of an algorithm is treated as a synthesis of related but logically (and structurally) distinct activities. Languages so oriented are often termed *block structured* (*q.v.*) languages. In Pascal, for example, decision alternatives may be extended arbitrarily by bracketing them with **begin** and **end** *delimiters*. C and C++ use { and } for this purpose.

On a somewhat larger scale, this method is used to enclose subprograms (*q.v.*) and other major program components (e.g. SUBROUTINE and END delimiters in Fortran, and **repeat** and **until** in Pascal).

Nonexecutable Statements

Completion of a high-level language program usually requires the inclusion of declarative statements (*declarations*) that do not correspond directly to steps in the algorithm being implemented. Rather, they provide the compiler with essential information from which it may determine the allocation of storage and other organizational characteristics of the final program. The command structure in these nonexecutable statements bears a less consistent resemblance to the imperative sentence than is found in other statement types.

A primary type of information transmitted by such statements concerns the definition and description of variables to be used in a program. For example, each of the following statements:

```
(Fortran 90)  REAL X, Y
              INTEGER Z
```

(Pascal)   **var** x, y : real;
              z : integer

associates the names *x* and *y* with certain amounts of storage, indicating further that the contents of these locations are to be treated as numerical values in floating-point form. In addition, the name *z* is associated with storage whose contents represent an integer value. Note that the expandability inherent in other statement types is available here, too, since it is possible to combine an arbitrary number of different declarations in a single statement.

Definition of entire arrays is no more complicated, since the same basic descriptive structure is used, augmented by information about the array's extent and organization. For instance, the following declarations:

(Fortran 90)   REAL X, Y
               INTEGER Z(18)
(Pascal)   **var** x, y : real;
               z: **array**[1..18] **of** integer

define variables *x*, *y*, and *z* as they did above, except that *z* is now an array of 18 elements, each of whose contents accommodates (and expects) an integer value.

Bibliography

1999. MacLennan, B. *Principles of Programming Languages: Design, Evaluation, and Implementation.* Oxford: Oxford University Press.

Seymour V. Pollack and Ron K. Cytron

STATISTICAL APPLICATIONS

For articles on related subjects *see* LEAST-SQUARES APPROXIMATION; MATHEMATICAL PROGRAMMING; MATHEMATICAL SOFTWARE; MATRIX COMPUTATIONS; NUMERICAL ANALYSIS; and SCIENTIFIC APPLICATIONS.

At the beginning of the 1980s, there were fewer than 20 commercial statistical software "packages." At the end of the 1990s, there were over 1,000 packages, and the annual revenue to the producers of those packages surpasses a billion dollars. This explosion in the availability of software to perform statistical calculations has caused a corresponding increase in both the available methodology and in the diversity of applications.

There is an extensive literature on computational techniques for the application of statistical methods. Standard graduate-level textbooks include Kennedy and Gentle (1980), Maindonald (1984), and Thisted (1988). There are a number of journals publishing current research in the area. Among these are *The Journal of Statistical Computations and Simulation, The Journal of Computational and Graphical Statistics,*

Statistics and Computing, and *Computational Statistics and Data Analysis.*

Not every package includes every statistical method, but several standard methods are included in most general-purpose packages and there are many special-purpose packages that include one or more of the less common statistical methods. The most widely used package on PCs and workstations is Statistica, also available in a "lite" version called Quick Statistica.

Methods

The standard methods include regression analysis, analysis of variance, discrete data analysis, cluster analysis, and time series analysis.

Regression analysis is used for exploring relationships between continuous variables. In it simplest form, a response variable is assumed to be a linear function of various predictor variables, and the coefficients of the predictor variables are estimated by the method of least squares. More complex forms of this method involve nonlinear relationships between the response and the predictors, multivariate responses, and robust methods for estimating the coefficients. An introduction to the method can be found in Weisberg (1985).

Analysis of variance is used for exploring relationships between a continuous response variable and categorical predictor variables. Such data often arises from designed experiments. In its simplest form, the response variable is assumed to be a linear function of the predictor variables, and the analysis assigns a portion of the squared variation in the response to each of the predictors. More complex forms of this method involve intentionally complex patterns in the predictor variables (fractional designs), continuous predictor variables (covariates), nonlinear relationships (response surface methods), and multivariate responses. An introduction to the method can be found in Box, Hunter, and Hunter (1978).

Discrete data analysis is used for exploring relationships between a categorical response variable and categorical predictor variables. In its simplest form the natural logarithm of the number of responses in a category is assumed to be a linear function of the predictor variables. This method is also called the method of *loglinear models.* More complex forms of this method involve hierarchical and other relationships among the predictor variables, continuous predictor variables, nonlinear relationships, and multivariate responses. An introduction to this method can be found in Santner and Duffy (1989).

Time series analysis is used for exploring the relationships between a continuous response variable and time (or some other single-ordered variable such as distance). The methods of analysis fall naturally into two categories: time-domain methods and frequency-domain methods. The time-domain methods are similar in many respects to regression analysis, with previous values of the single response variable serving as predictor variables. The frequency-domain methods are also similar in many respects to regression analysis; in this case, phase-shifted cosine functions of various frequencies serve as the predictor variables. An introduction to the method can be found in Kendall and Ord (1990).

Cluster analysis, sometimes called *numerical taxonomy*, is used for grouping similar objects. When the number and identification of the groups is assumed known, the method is often called *classification*. Cluster analysis is distinguished from other statistical methods by the fact that each cluster analytic method is specified by the algorithm used to calculate the results rather than by the model used to describe the data. An introduction to the method can be found in Hartigan (1976).

Applications

The applications listed below give some indication of the breadth of application of statistical methods:

Epidemiology—A major risk to public health in the USA appeared during the 1980s and reached epidemic proportions by 1990: Acquired Immune Deficiency Syndrome (AIDS) and its etiologic agent, the human immunodeficiency virus (HIV). The first cases of AIDS were reported in 1981. By 1990, the cumulative number of cases exceeded 150,000. Statistical methods were used in the earliest studies of the etiology of AIDS. Evidence for sexual transmission of the disease first came from controlled clinical trials among gay men. Unusual clusters of cases were found among sex partners and between blood transfusion recipients and donors.

Space—On 27 January 1986, the space shuttle *Challenger* exploded shortly after liftoff. The Presidential Commission on the Space Ship Challenger Accident (the Rogers Commission) subsequently determined that the cause of the explosion was a combustion gas leak through a joint in one of the two booster rockets, which was sealed by an O-ring. A subsequent statistical analysis of O-ring data from 23 of the 24 pre-*Challenger* flights by the Shuttle Criticality Review Hazard Analysis Audit Committee of the National Research Council (a review recommended by the Rogers Commission) strongly sup-

ports the conclusion that O-rings do not seal properly at low temperature. Furthermore, that analysis showed that the probability of catastrophic O-ring failure at a temperature of 31° Fahrenheit (the actual temperature at liftoff) was 16%.

Physics—In 1986, the Committee on Data for Science and Technology (CODATA) of the International Council of Scientific Unions released new estimates of the fundamental physical constants. These constants include the speed of light, the gravitational constant, the mass of the proton, the Avogadro, Plank, Bohr, Rydberg, and Compton constants, and other, more esoteric constants. The constants are of fundamental importance in the analysis and interpretation of large numbers of experiments in many scientific disciplines. The method by which the constants are estimated is entirely statistical using experimental data. In fact, the estimates are reported together with a relative uncertainty of one standard deviation. The full CODATA report gives the covariance matrix of the estimates, recognizing that not only are the estimates uncertain, but they are dependent on each other.

Forensics—DNA fingerprinting is a biochemical technique for transforming DNA (the genetic material of living cells) into a visible pattern of bands similar to the UPC bar codes that appear on grocery and other items (*see* UNIVERSAL PRODUCT CODE). It is believed that, except for random variation, these DNA fingerprints are unique to each individual; identical twins have identical DNA, although the prints of their fingertips are not identical. Unfortunately, there is considerable random variation in the process, both in the chemical process used to produce the bands and in the assignment of the bands to various categories. It is essential, therefore, to use statistical methods in the determination of whether two DNA fingerprints match or not.

Testing—The General Aptitude Test Battery (GATB) is a series of 12 tests, taking about 2.5 hours to complete, that measure a range of aptitudes. It was originally developed as a distillation of some 100 occupation-specific tests used by government employment services. Beginning in 1981, the United States Employment Service (USES) adopted a plan by which all applicants would be encouraged to take the GATB and all employers would be encouraged to require the GATB. Statistical methods were the basis of the original combination of tests, and statistical methods were behind the 1981 decision. On the basis of unadjusted test scores, relatively few minorities would be referred to jobs. Consequently, the USES adjusts the test scores by a statistical method. This practice has been called into question as reverse discrimination.

Demography—The US Decennial Census consists of an Enumeration Phase (EP), in which forms are mailed to every housing unit in the USA. Those housing units whose occupants do not return completed forms are visited by a census enumerator. After the EP, there is a Post Enumeration Survey (PES) of 150,000 households across the nation; the purpose of the PES is to assess the validity of the data collected in the EP. Most statisticians believe that more accurate estimates of the true population could be made by adjusting the EP numbers based on the PES and other data. Their rationale is that, despite extensive efforts to enumerate everyone, there is a significant undercount and that undercount is allegedly larger for the poor and for minorities. Federal Judge Joseph M. McLaughlin has held that the US Constitution "is not a bar to statistical adjustment" and that the "concept of statistical adjustment is wholly valid and may very well be long overdue." The Clinton Administration proposed use of statistical adjustment of the year 2000 census, but the initiative was fiercely opposed by the House Republican leadership. In 1999 the US Supreme Court ruled that statistical adjustments could not be used to apportion the House of Representatives but could be used for other purposes.

Bibliography

1976. Hartigan, J. A. *Clustering Algorithms.* New York: John Wiley.

1978. Box, G. E. P., Hunter, W. G., and Hunter, J. S. *Statistics for Experimenters.* New York: John Wiley.

1980. Kennedy, W. J., and Gentle, J. E. *Statistical Computing.* New York: Marcel Dekker.

1984. Maindonald, J. H. *Statistical Computation.* New York: John Wiley.

1985. Weisberg, S. *Applied Linear Regression*, 2nd Ed. New York: John Wiley.

1988. Thisted, R. A. *Elements of Statistical Computing.* New York: Chapman & Hall.

1989. Santner, T. J., and Duffy, D. *The Statistical Analysis of Discrete Data.* New York: Springer-Verlag.

1990. Kendall, M., and Ord, J. K. *Time Series*, 3rd Ed. New York: Oxford University Press.

1994. *Quick Statistica for Windows, Vols I & II: Statistics and Graphics.* Tulsa, OK: Statsoft, Inc. http://www.statsoft.com.

William Eddy

STIBITZ, GEORGE ROBERT

For an article on a related subject *see* BELL LABS RELAY COMPUTERS.

George Robert Stibitz was born in York, Pennsylvania, on 30 April 1904. He grew up in Dayton, Ohio, where his father taught ancient languages at a theological seminary of the German Reformed Church. In the seventh grade, he entered the Moraine Park School, an experimental school newly founded by Charles Kettering and Col. Edward Deeds. Its flexible curriculum and small classes provided an excellent environment for intellectual investigation and exploration.

Stibitz developed an interest in mathematics and physics while in high school, and after graduating in 1922 he received a scholarship to Denison University. Upon graduation from Denison in 1926 with a major in mathematics, Stibitz enrolled in the graduate program at Union College, where he received his M.S. degree in physics in 1927. He then took a year off and went to work for the General Electric Company in Schenectady, NY. In 1928, Stibitz enrolled in the Ph.D. program at Cornell University. Under the tutelage of his mathematics professor, Wallie Hurwitz, he generalized his interest in the vibrations of the telephone diaphragm into his Ph.D. study of the differential geometry of a non-planar membrane.

In the summer of 1929, he met his future wife, Dorothea Lamson, and they were married in September 1930 after he had completed his Ph.D. and had accepted a position as a "mathematical engineer" with Bell Laboratories, then located on West Street in New York City.

One weekend at home in 1937, observing the similarity between the two-state positions of telephone relays

Figure 1. George Stibitz.

and the binary notation for integers, Stibitz decided to experiment. He fastened two relays from the Bell Labs scrap pile to a piece of plywood, cut strips from a tobacco can, bought two dry cell batteries and some flashlight bulbs, and, with some electrical wire, constructed a one-digit binary adder. His colleagues were amused when he showed it to them in the lab the next day. This simple exercise might have ended there except for Stibitz's penchant for generalizing. Further evenings at home were spent sketching circuits for the arithmetic operations. When he presented his ideas to Thornton Fry, the head of the mathematical section at the Laboratory, Fry indicated a curiosity as to whether these little relay calculators could do complex arithmetic, which then involved a fair number of human computers in the Lab. With this target, Stibitz began to draw up relay circuits for the calculation of complex numbers. In February 1938 the circuits were completed, and Stibitz began to work in earnest with Sam Williams, a switching engineer. In 1939, the Complex Calculator was completed and put into use at the Laboratories. The machine was capable of performing all four arithmetic operations. The calculator was operated by remote access from either of three teletype machines located in different parts of the Laboratory. The first public demonstration of the Complex Calculator (and perhaps first remote control of a computer) occurred at a meeting of the American Mathematical Society at Dartmouth College in September 1940. Stibitz presented a paper describing the machine, followed by Dr. Fry showing how a problem could be introduced on a teletypewriter, transmitted to new York, and the answer then received on the teletypewriter. Attendees, among them Norbert Wiener (*q.v.*) and John Mauchly (*q.v.*), were then able to participate in using the Complex Calculator.

In 1940, Stibitz proposed that the Laboratory construct a general-purpose automatic computational device. He had developed circuit drawings to provide for interchangeable taped programs, and an assembly language, an error-deletion code, and a design for floating-point arithmetic. At this time the lab management showed no interest in the development of a general-purpose computational device. The onset of the Second World War provided the necessity for the design and construction of automatic computing machines. The first of a series of relay devices, the Relay Interpolator, was installed at West Street in September 1943. Late in the war it was moved to the Naval Research Laboratory, where it remained until 1961. The Relay Ballistic Computer (two copies, 1943–44) was a general-purpose device, as was its successor, the Error Detector Mark 22. This sequence of relay calculators was later renamed Models 1, 2, 3, and 4. Models 5 (two copies) and 6, the most ambi-

tious of the relay devices, were completed in 1946, 1947, and 1950, respectively. Model 3 (and its successors) contained error detection, halting trouble diagnosis, and an assembly language. Model 5 was the first to implement floating-point arithmetic. Each copy of the Model 5 incorporated a system of two arithmetic units and four problem positions. Problems were loaded into any positions that were idle, and upon the completion of one problem, the computer automatically picked up another. When the models were redesignated, Mrs. Stibitz suggested that the original one-digit binary adder be called Model K for the kitchen table on which it was constructed.

During the Second World War, Stibitz took a leave of absence from Bell Labs and joined Division 7 (Fire Control) of the NDRC (later OSRD), as a Technical Aide. The Dynamic Tester, a device developed by Division 7 to test and guide the design of newly developed anti-aircraft gun control directors, made great demands on the computers. Model 2 reduced the number of fundamental calculations for the early Dynamic Testers by a factor of about 10, and later models of the relay series further increased the speed and reliability of the calculations, thereby making enormous savings in human labor possible.

Stibitz did not return to the Labs at the end of the war. Instead, he established himself as a private consultant to government and business (1945–1964). One of his projects during this period grew out of his wartime association with Duncan Stewart, later President of the Barber Colman Company. Beginning in 1946, Stibitz began the design of a desk size electronic digital computer for use in the business world. Two working prototypes of the Barber Colman computer were completed, but in 1954 the project was abandoned for financial reasons.

In 1964, Stibitz was invited to join Dartmouth Medical School's Department of Physiology as a Research Associate. In this newest career, he did significant pioneering work in a field that is now referred to as biomedicine. Over the ensuing quarter century, he worked on a variety of biophysical problems, including the modeling of renal exchange processes, the computer display of brain cell anatomy, and a mathematical model of capillary transport phenomena. Although he retired as Professor Emeritus in 1974, Stibitz remained an active consultant to the Medical School for more than a decade.

George Stibitz's honors include the AFIPS Harry Goode Award (1965), IEEE's Emanuel Piore Award (1977), IEEE's Computer Pioneer Award (1982), election to the National Academy of Engineering (1981), and election to the National Inventors Hall of Fame (1985). He has also received honorary degrees from

Denison University (1976), Keene State College (1978), and Dartmouth College (1986). The George R. Stibitz Distinguished Professorship in Mathematics was endowed at Denison University in 1994.

George Stibitz died at his home on Tuesday 31 January 1995. On Sunday 30 April 1995, "A Gathering to Remember George Robert Stibitz" was held in the Kellogg Auditorium of the Dartmouth Medical School.

Bibliography

1967. Stibitz, G. R. "The Relay Computers at Bell Labs," *Datamation* (April) 35–44, (May) 45–49.

1973. Dartmouth College Library. *An Inventory of the Papers of George Robert Stibitz concerning the Invention and Development of the Digital Computer.* Hanover, NH. (Reprinted 1989.)

1993. Stibitz, G. R. *The Zeroth Generation: A Scientist's Recollections (1937–1955). From the early Binary Relay Digital Computers at Bell Telephone Laboratory and OSRD to a Fledgling Minicomputer at the Barber Colman Company.* Includes a Foreword by Jerome A. G. Russell and a Biography by Henry S. Tropp. Illustrations. Privately printed.

Henry S. Tropp

STORAGE ALLOCATION

For articles on related subjects *see* ADDRESSING; ASSOCIATIVE MEMORY; CACHE MEMORY; COMPUTER ARCHITECTURE; GARBAGE COLLECTION; MEMORY HIERARCHY; MEMORY: MAIN; MEMORY MANAGEMENT; SWAPPING; TIME SHARING; and VIRTUAL MEMORY.

Storage in a digital computer system must be *allocated* to programs and data that are being executed, just as for any other resource in the system. While the cost of hardware used for storage continues to decrease, the demands for storage generated by increasingly sophisticated software systems and application programs dilute the benefits from the availability of cheaper, larger storage.

A computer system will normally have several levels of storage, usually referred to as "main" (or primary) storage, "secondary" (or auxiliary) storage, etc. Main storage is implemented using fast but relatively expensive components. Secondary storage is slower and less expensive. A typical system will have more of secondary than of main storage. The lower levels of storage are intended for storing large amounts of information for relatively long periods of time. When some part of the information is to be referenced during a computation, it is usually transferred to main storage first; i.e. it is *loaded* into main storage.

Sound resource management dictates that programs and data should be allocated only the minimum amount of main storage that is necessary, but additional amounts are often acquired and released dynamically.

Thus, a program may be allocated an initial amount of *static* main storage when it is loaded from secondary storage, which it will use until its execution is completed. During the computation, there may be requests to an operating system (*q.v.*) for additional dynamically allocated main storage which will receive temporary values for subsequent computation or communication to other *processes*, and which may then be released back to the supervisory system when it is no longer required.

Another use for dynamically acquired storage (as well as the initially acquired storage) is for the introduction of additional segments of programs or data, while parts of the program or data that were used and are no longer needed are released or overwritten. This process is called an *overlay*. A considerable amount of program and data management is involved in an explicit overlay process. At one time, as much as 50% of a program development effort might have been concerned with the design and implementation of overlay procedures. For this reason, various software and hardware systems now include features that help to alleviate the overlay burden.

One concept introduced at least partly because of the overlay problem is *virtual memory* (*q.v.*). Here, program and data are assigned addresses independent of the amount of physical storage actually available and independent of the location from which the program will actually be executed. Thus, one might use 32 bits to represent an address (thus addressing about four billion items), while the available physical (main) storage might accommodate only about a quarter-million items (needing only 18 bits for the representation of a particular address). This large ratio of total virtual storage to total physical storage implies a potentially massive overlay problem, although only occasionally will a program or its data be expected to occupy a very large fraction of the virtual storage.

The program and data are thus allocated enough addresses in virtual storage to enable them to be accommodated without any worry about overlay, but given that the physical storage is smaller than the virtual storage, and will be shared with other programs and data in a typical time-sharing or multiprogramming (*q.v.*) system, it is necessary for the system to invoke an automatic overlay procedure. This is accomplished in a virtual storage system by bringing into physical storage from secondary storage only those parts of virtual storage that have been referenced (or can reasonably be expected to be referenced shortly). By recording in a table the mapping (i.e. the correspondence between parts of virtual storage and physical storage established when pieces of virtual storage are

Register 3 (containing base address of segment)

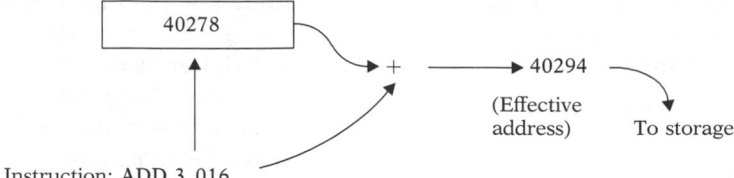

Instruction: ADD 3,016

Figure 1. Relocation within virtual storage.

brought into main memory), addresses may be translated dynamically. Those references to virtual addresses that are not already mapped into physical storage can be intercepted by special hardware, and that part of virtual storage now needed, called a *page*, can then be brought into main memory. Pages are usually of a fixed size and therefore may be deposited into physical storage wherever a space of that size can be found.

Because the current location is entered into a mapping table whenever a page is introduced into physical storage, *dynamic address translation* can provide up-to-date interpretation of addresses (see below). This allows the effect of dynamic relocation without the overhead of actually modifying the addresses within instructions. The determination of which pages are to be removed from physical storage to make room for the needed incoming pages has itself been the object of research (*see* WORKING SET).

Although it is possible to implement in software the mapping described above, the overhead is considerable, and computers that incorporate virtual storage concepts generally provide a hardware implementation for dynamic address translation. In addition, several computers have introduced an additional concept, *segmentation*. Here, one views virtual storage as having identifiable regions, called *segments*, each containing enough addresses so that programs or data stored in them will not try to assign the same addresses more than once, even if they expand during execution by means of dynamic allocation of additional virtual storage. Segments are thus different from pages in that page boundaries assume a predetermined relationship to blocks of physical storage, whereas segments are viewed as functional subdivisions of virtual storage (and usually contain a number of virtual pages).

An important motivation behind the use of segments is the facility for sharing programs and data. In physical storage systems, one often finds programs written so that all addresses are given as displacements from a *base address*, and this is implemented by maintaining the base address in a hardware register. In this way, different copies of the program (or data) can be placed into storage in different locations while executing. Simi-

larly, by establishing a convention that programs and data be *address-free* (i.e. that all addresses be represented as displacements from the expected contents of a base register) and by arranging for base addresses of segments to be maintained in registers during execution, relocation within virtual storage can be accomplished. This is illustrated in Fig. 1. Now the system may load individual users' programs or data into different areas of virtual storage (i.e. into different segments), but can arrange to share a copy that is actually loaded into physical storage through the paging mechanism. Fig. 2 illustrates this sharing.

Various hardware devices are included in systems to facilitate the implementation of paging, and—to a lesser extent—segmentation. One example of a hardware implementation of the dynamic address translation described above is given in Fig. 3. The virtual address is separated into three parts. The first, called the *segment number*, can be viewed (with an appropriate number of trailing zeros) as the base address of a segment of virtual storage. In the implementation as shown in Fig. 3, however, it is used as an index into a segment table maintained for that user to retrieve the appropriate page table; i.e. a table showing the virtual-to-physical mapping for those pages of the referenced segment for which the mapping exists. Once the page-table base address as been retrieved from the segment table, the page number obtained as the second part of the original virtual address is used as an index into the page table to retrieve the physical address corresponding to the base of that page in virtual storage. The third

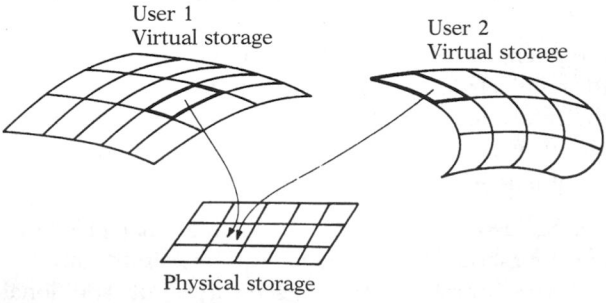

Figure 2. Sharing in physical storage.

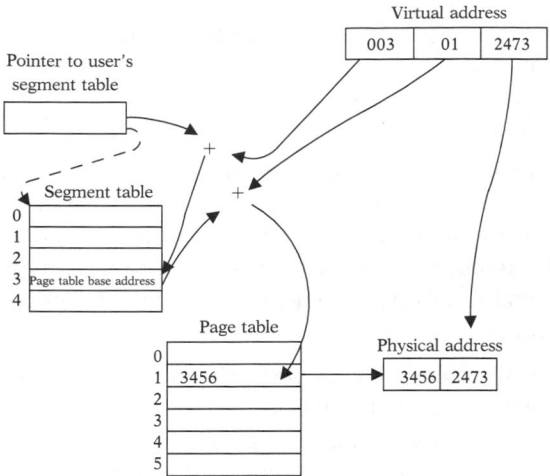

Figure 3. Mapping from virtual address to physical address.

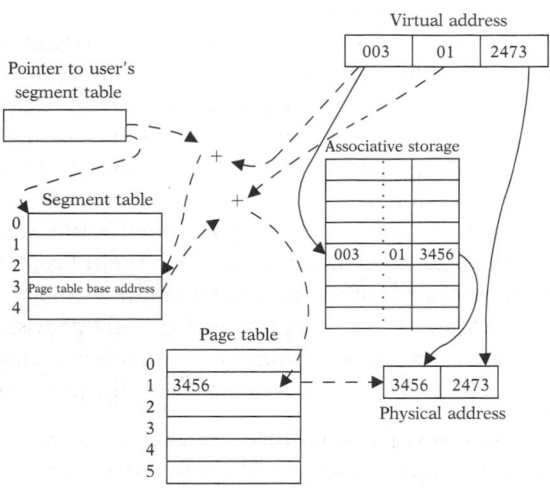

Figure 4. Mapping from virtual address to physical address, showing the use of associative storage.

part of the original virtual address is then added (in fact, appended, since trailing zeros are not included in the page table), and the result—generated in this manner by the hardware—is the desired physical address.

If the virtual page containing the reference address is not present in physical storage—and only a few will be, depending on the number of other users of the system and the amount of physical storage available—an *interrupt* (*q.v.*) will be generated, causing a delay in the execution of that program while the desired page is found and loaded into physical storage. (This system service is the substitute for the cumbersome overlay process described earlier.) Of course, all tables mentioned above must be protected by the operating system from access by programs that are not authorized to do so.

Accessing segment and page tables, as in Fig. 3, does imply additional storage references, thus potentially implying a large overhead. Several hardware systems include provisions for some *associative memory*, which retains several of the most recent mapping results. Thus, from a dozen to several hundred entries will be maintained, each consisting of a segment and page number pair, together with the corresponding physical-page/base-address. A subsequent search with the same segment-page pair will quickly produce the physical-page/base-address without the need for accessing the segment and page tables. This is illustrated in Fig. 4, where the segment table and page table would not be accessed once a match is found in associative storage.

Another interesting application of virtual storage is the implementation of the *virtual machine*. Here a program is written as if it has a segment of virtual storage as its physical storage, and most (nonprivileged) instructions are executed on the hardware at full speed. When interrupts are thus generated because of missing virtual pages (*page faults*) or the execution of privileged instructions, the intended system services are provided by means more conducive to an environment in which several users are actually sharing the hardware. In addition, because paging services are provided for the bulk of virtual storage, large storage can be simulated for each virtual storage machine at a fraction of the overhead incurred in the planning and implementation of overlay processing. To the users of such a system, it appears as if each one has a different physical (or software) system on which to run a program.

Bibliography

1997. Tanenbaum, A. S. *Operating Systems: Design and Implementation*, 2nd Ed. Upper Saddle River, NJ: Prentice Hall.
1998. Silberschatz, A., and Galvin, P. B. *Operating System Concepts*, 5th Ed. Reading, MA: Addison-Wesley.

Bernard A. Galler

STORAGE

See articles under MEMORY.

STORED PROGRAM CONCEPT

For articles on related subjects *see* ADDRESSING; ANALYTICAL ENGINE; ASSEMBLER; BABBAGE, CHARLES; DIGITAL COMPUTER; MACHINE AND ASSEMBLY LANGUAGE PROGRAMMING; MARK I, HARVARD; PROGRAM COUNTER; VON NEUMANN, JOHN; and VON NEUMANN MACHINE.

The key design feature of modern computers, which allows the instructions to be held in the internal store while they are awaiting execution, is known as the *stored program concept*. Many computers, beginning with the Analytical Engine of Charles Babbage, and including the Automatic Sequence Controlled Calculator (Harvard Mark I), were designed to perform discrete operations, each specified by a concisely coded instruction. Prior to the use of electronics, however, these instructions were taken by the control unit from a special input device that read a tape or belt. Program loops required a loop of tape to be mounted (and the Harvard Mark I had three readers) with provision for control to be passed from one to another to allow some flexibility in the logical structure of the program.

Electronics forced a departure from this arrangement because no tape reader could scan instructions fast enough to keep up with the internal speed of the computer. The first electronic computer, ENIAC (*q.v.*), went back to plugboard programming (as used on punched card machines), but this proved extremely clumsy. The stored program concept emerged as an alternative solution from discussions that took place at the Moore School of Electrical Engineering, where ENIAC was under construction in 1944. Participants in these discussions included J. Presper Eckert (*q.v.*), J. W. Mauchly (*q.v.*), John von Neumann, and H. H. Goldstine, and the concept was first documented in a Moore School report drafted by von Neumann (1945).

Besides solving the speed problem, the concept had two important long-term effects. First, program jumps could be used liberally without incurring the time penalty required to hunt along the program tape. (Some early machines, especially those based on drum stores, had some residual timing penalties affecting the arrangement of jumps, but these were comparatively unimportant.) Therefore, much more complex program structures could be contemplated. Secondly, and more significantly, the instructions held in the internal store were accessible to be operated upon the same way as the data during the execution of the program. Both these possibilities were quickly explored when the first stored-program computers, EDSAC (*q.v.*) and BINAC, came into service in 1949. Alteration of the programs during execution enormously increased the scope of automatic computing, and was heavily used in the early days. Since then, its use has diminished considerably, for several reasons, the main ones being the introduction of *index registers* (these achieved more economically the effect of address modification, which had been the commonest purpose of program alteration) and the trend toward time-sharing (*q.v.*) systems and run-time diagnostic systems. This required programs to be *pure procedures* or *reentrant* (*q.v.*) which means that code is not self-modifying and that all data storage is kept separate from program storage.

Another development that demanded the abandonment of program alteration during execution was the use of read-only memories (*q.v.*) for programs needed very frequently. This approach was once widely used in microcomputers.

The potentialities of program processing were much more fully exploited later in the preprocessing of programs by assemblers and compilers before execution, and, although the stored program concept was not essential to this development, it certainly encouraged it strongly.

From the beginning it was inherent in the stored program concept that the instructions be made to fit (perhaps in groups) into the same word length as the data so that the same store could be used interchangeably for both with reasonable efficiency. Indeed, the ability of the machine to modify its program depended on having the program accessible in the same way as the data. However, the Harvard Mark IV was remarkable in having separate stores for the instructions and the data.

A. M. Turing (*q.v.*) had touched on the stored program concept in a paper on mathematical logic in 1936 (which led to the term *Turing machine—q.v.*), though not in a form that showed its potential practicality. The first electronic stored program machine to obey instructions was that built by Williams and Kilburn in Manchester, England, and the first to carry out practical calculations was the EDSAC, built by Wilkes (*q.v.*) at Cambridge, England, which was operating in May 1949. Both EDSAC and EDVAC (*q.v.*), designed at the Moore School by Eckert and Mauchly, embodied many of the ideas incorporated in von Neumann's report (1945), but EDVAC did not become operational until 1951.

In the years that have followed these early implementations, the stored program concept has been elaborated in many ways. Programming techniques and languages of many kinds have been developed, as well as operating systems (*q.v.*) and all the various components of modern software. Perhaps the most fundamental variation from the original idea has been the introduction of program interrupts (*q.v.*), which means that the sequence of execution of the instructions is no longer uniquely determined by the program and its data, but can be affected by external events occurring during the execution.

These, however, are all auxiliary to the stored program concept itself, an essentially simple but profoundly important concept that has characterized the main stream of digital computer development since 1945. This concept, together with the practical development of electronics, has made possible the computer revolution as we now know it.

Bibliography

1945. von Neumann, J. "First Draft of a Report on the EDVAC," Contract No. W-670-ORD-4926. US Army Ordnance Department and University of Pennsylvania, Moore School of Electrical Engineering, University of Pennsylvania, Philadelphia, PA. (30 June). Reprinted in 1981. Stern, N. *From ENIAC to UNIVAC*. Bedford, MA: Digital Press.

Stanley Gill

STRACHEY, CHRISTOPHER

For articles on related subjects *see* MANCHESTER UNIVERSITY COMPUTERS; PROGRAMMING LANGUAGE SEMANTICS; and TIME SHARING.

Christopher Strachey (1916–1975) was Professor of Computer Science at Oxford University from 1971 until his death. He was born into the well-known Strachey family, associated with the English artistic circle, the "Bloomsbury Group." He showed a scientific bent, however, and graduated in physics from Cambridge University in 1939. During the Second World War he served in an electronics development laboratory at Standard Telephones and Cables where he gained some computing experience using a differential analyzer (*q.v.*). Strachey was a gifted teacher, and in 1944 he became a schoolmaster. While teaching at Harrow School in 1951, he began in his spare time

Figure 1. Christopher Strachey.

to program the Pilot ACE computer at the National Physical Laboratory and the Mark I computer at Manchester University. As a result of this early involvement with computers, in 1952 he became a technical officer with the National Research Development Corporation (NRDC)—a quasi-governmental organization created for the commercial exploitation of British technological innovations. While with the NRDC, he played a leading part in the calculations for the St Lawrence Seaway in Canada, and undertook the logical design of the Ferranti Pegasus computer. Each achievement was considered a *tour de force* in the late 1950s. Strachey was one of the first proselytizers of time sharing (*q.v.*). From 1959–65, he was a private consultant, and in 1962 he joined the University Mathematical Laboratory, Cambridge, on a half-time basis. At Cambridge he led the development of the CPL programming language. Although CPL was never satisfactorily implemented, the design of the language and the people associated with the project subsequently made their mark on programming language development. During this period, he also developed the General Purpose Macrogenerator. In 1965, Strachey wound up his consultancy in favor of the academic life—first spending a year at MIT, and in 1966 founding the Programming Research Group at Oxford University. He was appointed to a personal chair in 1971. During his last years, Strachey collaborated with the American logician Dana Scott, with whom he laid the foundations of denotational semantics. Although Strachey had a notorious reluctance to publish throughout his life, the few papers he did produce show the literary elegance and wit characteristic of his family.

Bibliography

1985. Campbell-Kelly, M. "Christopher Strachey, 1916–1975: A Biographical Note," *Annals of the History of Computing*, **7**, 19–42.

Martin Campbell-Kelly

STRETCH

For articles on related subjects *see* DIGITAL COMPUTERS, HISTORY OF: EARLY; LARC; and SUPERCOMPUTERS.

The *Stretch* computer (formally the IBM 7030) was the outcome of a research and development project started in 1955 and aimed at an advance in performance of about two orders of magnitude over the then existing computer technology and organization. It was a joint project between the IBM Corporation and the Los Alamos Scientific Laboratory of the US Atomic Energy Commission.

The first computer (Fig. 1) was delivered to Los Alamos in 1961. Although the machine did not "stretch"

Figure 1. The first Stretch computer being tested just prior to its installation at the Los Alamos Scientific Laboratory.

quite as far as the ambitious performance goal originally set, at that time it was still the most powerful computer in existence. After 10 years of service, the Los Alamos machine was dismantled in 1971. Seven other Stretch machines were built.

Stretch was the first major solid state computer developed by IBM, and its transistor, core, and disk storage technologies were applied extensively to other computers of the 7000 series. Its sophisticated internal organization (Buchholz, 1962) departed substantially from that of previous computers. An instruction look-ahead unit, for example, permitted up to six instructions at one time to be in various stages of execution; thus, Stretch became the first pipelined (*q.v.*) computer. While the sophistication contributed to the high speed of Stretch, the resulting complexity of implementation, in retrospect, also kept the speed somewhat short of the objective.

Other than speed, perhaps the most significant feature was the provision in one computer system of both the parallel floating-point arithmetic then associated with "scientific" computers, and the serial, variable-length, fixed-point arithmetic and character processing functions then found only in "commercial" computers.

The computer had been planned as the largest of a single line of general-purpose compatible machines. However, this concept did not materialize until the later IBM 360/370/390 (*q.v.*), which also adopted several other basic concepts of Stretch. Some of the terminology from the Stretch project (computer architecture, byte) has since entered general use.

A major non-arithmetical extension to Stretch, referred to as *Harvest*, provided very powerful data streaming and table look-up operations on a byte-by-byte basis

(Buchholz, 1962, Ch. 17). Only one Harvest machine was ever built and was installed at the National Security Agency.

Bibliography

1962. Buchholz, W. (ed.) *Planning a Computer System (Project Stretch)*. New York: McGraw-Hill.
1997. Blaauw, G. A., and Brooks, F. P. Jr. *Computer Architecture: Concepts and Evolution*, Sec. 13.3. Reading, MA: Addison-Wesley.
1999. Smotherman, M. *IBM Stretch (7030)—Aggressive Uniprocessor Parallelism*. http://www.cs.clemson.edu/~mark/stretch.html.

Werner Buchholz

STRING PROCESSING

For articles on related subjects *see* LIST PROCESSING; PROGRAMMING LANGUAGES; PROGRAMMING LINGUISTICS; and SCRIPTING LANGUAGES.

PRINCIPLES

In programming contexts, the term *string* usually refers to a sequence of characters. For example, ABC is a string of three characters. Strings are more prevalent in computing than is generally realized. In most cases, computer input is in the form of strings (e.g. commands entered at a terminal). Similarly, computer output is in the form of strings since printed lines are simply strings of characters.

Strings and String Processing

The facilities of the most widely used programming languages are concentrated on numerical and business data processing. However, a substantial amount of string processing is performed. For example, compilers accept strings as input, analyze them, and produce either bit or character strings as output. Command interpreters analyze command strings and perform appropriate actions. These kinds of programs are used heavily, so they must be extremely efficient. For this reason, they are often written in systems-programming languages such as C++ (*q.v.*) rather than in higher-level string processing languages. Nevertheless, higher-level string-processing languages offer many advantages for solving complex problems. Examples of such problems are machine translation (*q.v.*), computational linguistics, computer algebra (*q.v.*), text editing (*q.v.*), and document formatting (*see* DESKTOP PUBLISHING).

While mathematical notation for numerical computation has developed over centuries, string processing is a new area. There is no general agreement on what operations should be performed in string processing, nor is there a standard notation. The developers of string-processing languages started largely without conventions. As a result, notation, program structure, and approach to problem formulation are often radically different from those of more conventional programming languages.

Operations on Strings

Four string processing operations have achieved reasonably general acceptance: concatenation, identification of substrings, pattern matching, and transformation of strings to replace identified substrings by other strings.

Concatenation (sometimes called "catenation") is the process of appending one string to another to produce a longer string. Thus, the result of concatenating the strings AB and CDE is the string ABCDE. This operation is a natural extension of the concept of a string as a sequence of characters. A *substring* is a string wholly contained within another string. For example, BC and CDE are substrings of ABCDE.

The most important string operation is *pattern matching*, examining a string to locate substrings or to determine if it has certain properties. Examples are the presence of a specific substring, substrings in certain positions, and substrings in a specified relationship to each other. *Transformation* of strings is typically accomplished in conjunction with pattern matching, using the results of pattern matching to effect a replacement of substrings.

The language descriptions below emphasize approaches to string processing and the major facilities that deal with strings. No attempt has been made to describe these languages completely; details can be found in the references.

LANGUAGES

Comit

Comit (Yngve, 1963), designed in 1957–1958, was the first string-processing language. It was motivated by the need for a tool for mechanical language translation. Comit strongly reflects these origins and is oriented toward the representation of natural languages.

BASIC CONCEPTS

In Comit, unlike most other string processing languages, a string is composed of *constituents* which may consist of more than one character. Thus, a word composed of many characters may be a single constituent in a string. A string is written as a series of constituents separated by + signs—e.g.

```
FOURSCORE + AND + SEVEN + YEARS + AGO
```

The character – represents a space (blank). Thus, to include spaces between words, the string above becomes

```
FOURSCORE + – + AND – + SEVEN + – YEARS + – AGO
```

All characters other than letters have syntactic meaning. A star (asterisk) in front of a character other than a letter indicates that the character is to be taken literally rather than for its syntactic meaning. For example,

```
33 ARE IN THE TOP 1/2.
```

is written

```
*3*3 + – + ARE + – + IN + – + THE + – + TOP
                              + – + *1*/*2*.
```

Attention focuses on a *workspace*, which contains the string currently being processed. There are 128 *shelves*, any of which may be exchanged with the workspace to change the focus of attention. Thus, there may be at most 129 distinct strings in a program at any one time.

Comit programs are a sequence of rules, each of which has five parts:

```
name left-half = right-half / / routing goto
```

The `name` identifies the rule. The `left-half` is a pattern applied to the workspace, and the `right-half` specifies processing to be performed on the portion of the workspace matched by the `left-half`. The `routing` performs operations other than pattern matching. If a rule has no routing field, the slashes are not required. The `goto` controls program flow.

PATTERN MATCHING

The left-half may specify full constituents as written in a string, a specific number of constituents of unspecified value, an indefinite number of constituents, an earlier constituent referenced by its position in the left-half, etc. A full constituent is written as it is in a string. Other left-half constituents are represented by special notations. For example: $n matches n consecutive constituents, regardless of their value; $ matches any number of constituents. The integer n matches the same string that the nth constituent of the left-half matched. For example, the left-half

```
THE + $1 + $ + 2
```

has four constituents: the characters THE, followed by any single constituent, followed by any number of constituents until one is encountered that is the same as the one matched by the second constituent, namely, $1. Pattern matching is left to right. Left-half constituents must match consecutive constituents in the workspace.

If the workspace contains

```
THE  +  FIRST
└─┬─┘   └──┬─┘
  1        2

+ PERSON + IN + LINE + IS + SERVED + FIRST
└──────────────┬──────────────────┘ └──┬─┘
               3                        4
```

the match for each of the constituents is as shown. Note that the fourth constituent of the left-half matches the same constituents as the second constituent of the left-half. The third constituent of the left-half consequently matches the intervening five constituents. When a match occurs, workspace constituents are associated with the left-half constituents they matched and are subsequently referenced by the number of the corresponding left-half constituent.

The right-half may contain full constituents and integers that correspond to the constituents of the left-half. The matched portion of the workspace is replaced by constituents specified in the right-half. Continuing the example above, the rule

```
THE + $1 + $ + 2 = 1 + SECOND + 3 + 4
```

transforms the workspace into

```
THE + SECOND + PERSON + IN + LINE +
                         IS + SERVED + FIRST
```

SNOBOL

The first SNOBOL (string-oriented symbolic language) language was designed and implemented in 1962–1963. Its major motivation was the need for a general-purpose language for string processing. Manipulation of symbolic mathematical expressions was also an important consideration.

BASIC CONCEPTS

In SNOBOL, unlike Comit, a string is simply a sequence of characters. Enclosing quotation marks delimit the string, but are not part of the string. An example is

```
'FOURSCORE AND SEVEN YEARS AGO'
```

Such a string is said to be specified *literally*. Strings may be assigned to names for subsequent reference, e.g.,

```
FIRST = 'MORGAN'
```

assigns the string MORGAN to the name FIRST. There is no limit to the number of distinct strings. Storage management is automatic; there are no declarations. Concatenation is denoted by the juxtaposition of strings. Such strings can be given literally or as the value of names, e.g.

```
FULLNAME = FIRST 'ⴑ SMITH'
```

assigns the string MORGANⴑSMITH to the name FULL-NAME. The blank, shown here as ⴑ for clarity, is simply a character like any other.

A SNOBOL program consists of a sequence of statements. There are three kinds of statements: assignment, pattern-matching, and replacement. The respective forms are

```
label      subject = object          goto
label      subject pattern           goto
label      subject pattern = object  goto
```

An optional *label* identifies the statement. The *subject* provides the focus for the statement and is the name on which operations are performed. The *goto* controls program flow and is optional. An assignment statement assigns a value to a name. A pattern-matching statement examines the value of a name for a *pattern*, and a replacement statement modifies that part of the subject matched by the pattern.

PATTERN MATCHING

Patterns in SNOBOL consist of a sequence of components. There are two types of component: specific strings and *string variables*. A specific string may be given literally or referred to by name. A string variable is indicated by delimiting asterisks that bracket a name. There are several types of string variables. An *arbitrary string variable* can match any string. It is similar to the Comit $ notation, except that whatever the string variable matches is assigned to the name between the asterisks. Pattern matching is left to right, and components of the pattern must match consecutive substrings of the subject. For example, in

```
Z 'T' *FILL* 'N'
```

the value of Z is matched for any string that begins with a T and ends with an N. The substring between the T and N is assigned to the name FILL. If the value of Z is TEEN, the value assigned to FILL is EE.

A *balanced string variable* matches a string that is properly balanced with respect to parentheses like an ordinary mathematical expression. A *fixed-length string variable* matches any string of a specific length and is indicated by a / and a quoted number following the name. For example,

```
TEXT ',' *C/" 1/*
```

examines the value of TEXT for a comma and assigns the character following the comma to C.

Replacement is a combination of pattern matching and assignment in which the matched substring is replaced by the object. The statement

```
FULLNAME 'SMITH' = 'JONES'
```

replaces the substring SMITH by JONES and consequently changes the value of FULLNAME to MORGANⴑJONES.

INDIRECT REFERENCING

A string may be computed and then used as a name. A $ placed in front of a string uses the value of that string as a name. For example, the statements

```
X = 'NUM'
N = '3'
HOLIDAY = X N
$HOLIDAY = 'EASTER'
```

first assign the value NUM3 to HOLIDAY and then assign the value EASTER to NUM3. The indirect referencing operator, similar in concept to indirect addressing in assembly language, provides a way of constructing data names during execution.

OTHER FACILITIES

Input and output take place using specially designated names as subjects. Arithmetic facilities are rudimentary (e.g. integer arithmetic on strings of digits).

The goto part of a statement controls program flow. Gotos can be unconditional to a labeled statement, or conditional on the success or failure of pattern matching. Loops are programmed using the conditional nature of pattern matching.

SNOBOL4

SNOBOL4 (Griswold *et al.*, 1971) is a natural descendant of SNOBOL and is based on many of the same ideas and approaches to string processing. SNOBOL4, however, introduced a number of new concepts. The most important are those dealing with pattern matching.

PATTERNS

In Comit and the earlier SNOBOL languages, different types of patterns are indicated by specific notations. In SNOBOL4, patterns are data objects that are constructed by functions and operations. Consequently, quite complicated patterns can be built piecemeal.

There are two basic pattern-construction operations: alternation and concatenation. The alternation of two patterns is a pattern that will match anything that either of its two components will match. The concatenation of two patterns is a pattern that will match anything that its two components will match consecutively. Alternation is represented by a vertical bar and concatenation by a blank; e.g.

```
PET = 'CAT' | 'DOG'
PETKIND = PET '-LIKE'
```

The pattern PET matches either of the strings CAT or DOG, and PETKIND matches anything PET matches followed by the string -LIKE (i.e. CAT-LIKE or DOG-LIKE).

Pattern-valued functions generalize the concept of patterns and avoid special notations for each type. For example, the value returned by LEN(*n*) is a pattern that matches *n* characters, and the pattern returned by TAB(*n*) matches a substring through the *n*th character of the subject string. For example,

```
OPER = TAB(6) 'X'
```

creates a pattern that will match any string containing an X as its seventh character. Other pattern-valued functions create patterns that match any one of a number of specific characters, search for specific characters, etc. Examples are SPAN('0123456789'), which matches a substring consisting only of digits, and BREAK(';,'), which matches the substring beginning at the current position up to the next comma or semicolon.

As in SNOBOL, pattern matching is left to right, and components must match consecutive substrings of the subject string. When a component fails to match, alternative matches are attempted. If no alternative is specified, the pattern-matching process backs up to earlier, successfully matched, components, seeking other ways in which the entire pattern match can succeed. Conceptually, the pattern matching process manipulates a *cursor*, which is an imaginary marker in the subject string indicating the current position of the match. Movement of the cursor is implicit, not under direct control of the programmer, although in some patterns there is a direct correlation. Thus, LEN(3) moves the cursor to the right three characters. The cursor cannot be moved to the left by a successful match.

Names may be attached to components of patterns so that when the component matches a substring, that substring is assigned to the name. Attachment is indicated by the binary $ operator, e.g.

```
HEAD = LEN(7) $ LABEL
```

constructs a pattern that matches seven characters. The seven characters, when matched, are assigned to LABEL, so

```
CARD HEAD
```

assigns to LABEL the first seven characters of the string that is the value of CARD. If the match fails (as it would if that string had fewer than seven characters), no assignment is made to LABEL.

Another aspect of pattern matching is the ability to modify the pattern during matching depending on substrings matched by earlier components. Evaluation of an expression in a pattern may be deferred by prefacing the expression with *. The expression is then left unevaluated until it is encountered in pattern matching. An example of the power of this facility is given by

```
LIT = ('"' | '"') $ C BREAK(*C) . STRING LEN(1)
```

When LIT is used in pattern matching, the argument of BREAK is not evaluated until after the first part of the pattern has matched. The pattern matches a single or double quote and assigns it to C. The remainder of the pattern matches everything up to the next occurrence of character just assigned to C, assigns that substring to STRING, and then LEN(1) matches the second quote. Thus, LIT matches literal string constants as used in many programming languages.

OTHER FACILITIES

Other string-processing facilities include alphabetical comparison of strings, mappings from one set of characters to another, and deletion of trailing blanks. Earlier SNOBOL languages were purely string processing languages; SNOBOL4 includes many types of data. In addition to types such as integer and real, SNOBOL4 includes arrays as data objects, tables that provide associative look-up features, and a facility for defining record types during execution. In many cases it is possible to perform data type (*q.v.*) conversions between various types of data. It is possible to convert a string into program statements during program execution, and hence to modify or extend the program while it is running. SNOBOL4 is actually a general-purpose language that strongly emphasizes string processing and contains a number of exotic features.

STATUS

SNOBOL4, despite its age, is still used, and implementations are available for personal computers and several workstations.

Icon

The major emphasis in pattern matching in the SNOBOL languages, as in other string-processing languages, is on the *specification* of patterns that analyze strings. There is little facility for indicating *how* the matching is accomplished or for describing the synthesis of new strings from the results of pattern-matching.

In many cases, this bias toward pattern specification is useful; it frees the programmer from the necessity of spelling out too much detail concerning the actual matching. This is especially the case in SNOBOL4, in which the process of matching embodies a powerful search and backtrack algorithm that is particularly complex and obscure.

In other cases, however, programming tasks may fall outside the capabilities of the pattern-matching facility. Faced with this dilemma, programmers resort to inefficient or obscure techniques that are typically unrepresentative of the capabilities of the language as a whole. This situation is due largely to the inextensibility

of the pattern-matching facility. In SNOBOL4, for example, the pattern matching facility is not as extensible as is the rest of the language. While there is a facility for programmer-defined functions and data types, there is no facility for programmer-defined *matching* procedures (i.e. procedures, which are invoked during matching, that describe how a particular pattern is to be matched). This deficiency can be better understood by considering the pattern assigned to HEAD above:

    HEAD = LEN(7) $ LABEL

LEN(7) constructs and returns a pattern that, when applied, attempts to advance the cursor by seven characters. LEN itself plays no role in the matching—it merely constructs a data object that contains an indication of the action to be taken during pattern-matching. It is this latter component of the pattern that corresponds to the matching procedure and that cannot be defined by the programmer.

SNOBOL4 and its variants suffer a common problem: they are each, in reality, composed of two languages—a basic language and a pattern-matching language (Griswold and Hanson, 1980). In each language, the programmer is burdened with the construction of pattern-matching "programs." This corresponds to construction of a pattern, which is subsequently applied, or to the construction of the set of procedures, which eventually cooperate during pattern matching. This two-step process—pattern construction and pattern application—is due largely to the central role of patterns as distinguished objects in string processing languages. It is the elimination of patterns, but not of pattern-matching, that differentiates the newest string processing language, Icon, from its predecessors.

Icon (Griswold and Griswold, 1996), developed in the late 1970s, has a number of relatively low-level lexical primitives, some of which are related to patterns in SNOBOL4. Icon also has control structures and a goal-directed evaluation mechanism that make pattern matching—called *string scanning* in Icon—an integral part of the language. The central feature of Icon is this evaluation mechanism, which embodies a search and backtrack algorithm similar to, but simpler than, that used in SNOBOL4 pattern matching. An important aspect of this mechanism is that it pervades the entire language, instead of being restricted to a component of the language. The combination of the lexical primitives and the evaluation mechanism yields string-scanning capabilities comparable to those of SNOBOL4.

String scanning in Icon is accomplished in a manner that appears similar to SNOBOL4 but does not involve anything like pattern construction. The expression *s? e* establishes *s* as the subject to which string processing operations in *e* apply. The expression *e* typically includes string analysis operations, but may include *any* Icon operation. A *scanning environment* is characterized by a pair of implicit variables {subject,pos}; subject is the string to which scanning operations apply, and pos is a location with the subject and usually changes as the subject is analyzed. The expression *s?e* establishes a new scanning environment {*s*,1}, and then evaluates *e*. After evaluating *e*, the previous scanning environment is restored.

Some of the scanning operations in Icon operate on the position in the absence of other specifications. An example is move(*n*), which attempts to advance the position by *n* characters. If the advancement is successful, move returns the *n*-character substring between the initial and final positions. For example,

```
line ? write("[", move(7), "]")
```

writes the first seven characters of line enclosed in brackets to the output.

This simple example illustrates an important aspect of string scanning in Icon: move does not construct a pattern, but simply carries out the analysis in the current scanning environment. The SNOBOL4 equivalent involves construction of a pattern, followed by its application, and finally the output of the desired result.

Another important advantage resulting from the integration of string processing with the rest of Icon is that any language operation can be performed during string scanning. An example is

```
line ? while t := t || move(1) || "."
```

which produces a string t containing the characters of line separated by periods. The || operator denotes string concatenation, and while repeatedly evaluates

```
t := t || move(1) || "."
```

until it fails, which occurs when move(1) is invoked at the end of the subject string. Note the use of a standard control structure, while, within the ? expression.

String *synthesis* often accompanies string scanning. In the example above, t is synthesized during scanning, and it is t that is the result of interest. In some cases, the result of interest can be returned as the value of the scanning expression. The result of *s* ? *e* is the result of *e*, so both of the expressions

```
line ? write("[", move(7), "]")
write("[", line ? move(7), "]")
```

produce the same output.

The function move(*n*) is called a *matching function* because it returns the substring of the subject that is "matched" as a result of changing the position. Another matching function is tab(*i*), which moves

to position *i* in the subject and returns the substring between the old and new positions. For both move and tab, the new position can be to the left of the old position.

Lexical functions return positions in the subject instead of substrings in the subject. For example, find(*s*) returns the position of the string *s* in the subject following the current position, so the output of

```
"Icon is a programming language" ?
   write(find("program"))
```

is 11, the position of the "p" in "programming." Likewise, upto(*s*) returns the first position of any of the characters in string *s* in the subject string, and many(*s*) returns the position following the longest possible substring containing only characters in *s* starting at the current position in the subject string.

It is important to note that functions like many return positions, but the specific values of those positions are rarely important. Positions are used most often as arguments to matching functions like tab. For example,

```
line ? while tab(upto(&letters)) do
   write(tab(many(&letters)))
```

writes the "words" in line. The value of the keyword &letters is a string containing all of the upper- and lower-case letters. The expression tab(upto(&letters)) advances the position up to the next letter, and tab(many(&letters)) matches and returns the word, which is passed to write. The while loop terminates when tab(upto(&letters)) fails because there are no more words in line.

Icon has an alternation expression that resembles alternation in SNOBOL4: $e_1 \mid e_2$. The important difference is that, while the SNOBOL4 alternation operator constructs a pattern, alternation in Icon simply carries out the operation directly. The operation is similar to that performed during pattern matching in SNOBOL4 when the pattern constructed by P1 | P2 is applied.

In the Icon expression, $e_1 \mid e_2$, e_1 is evaluated first and, if that evaluation succeeds, the value of e_1 is the result of the entire expression. If, however, evaluation of e_1 fails, the result is the result of evaluating e_2. Another way in which e_2 can be evaluated is if the entire expression is used in a context where the value of e_1 is unacceptable. An example is

```
move(10 | 5)
```

The expression 10 | 5 has two literal subexpressions, and the first, 10, succeeds. Suppose, however, that the subject is only six characters long. In this case, move(10) fails. This causes the re-evaluation of

10 | 5, which yields the value 5. This time, `move(5)` succeeds. Note that

```
move(10 | 5)
```

is equivalent to

```
move(10) | move(5)
```

In Icon, operations that have the capacity for producing alternative values that are required by the context in which they appear are called *generators*. In addition to alternation, many of the low-level lexical primitives are generators whose behavior when used in string scanning is designed to facilitate string processing. For example, `find(s)` is capable of generating all of the positions at which *s* appears in the subject. If only one value is needed, only one is generated, so the output of

```
"a fish is a fish is a fish" ?
    write(find("fish"))
```

is 3. Additional values are generated as demanded by the context in which `find` is used; for example, in

```
"a fish is a fish is a fish" ?
    write(find("fish") > 20)
```

the first value produced by `find` is 3, which is less than 20. The comparison (>) fails, which causes `find` to be resumed. It produces 13 and the comparison again fails. Finally, `find` produces 23 and the comparison succeeds. A successful comparison returns its right operand, so the output is 20.

Icon's procedure mechanism allows the construction of programmer-defined generators. This capability corresponds to the definition of programmer-defined matching procedures in SNOBOL4. Generators are not limited to the string processing aspects of Icon, but are meaningful for many operations. Generators allow a more natural expression of some constructions than is possible in most other programming languages. It is often possible to express constructions more concisely and closer to the way that programmers think in mathematical and natural languages. For further information about this aspect of Icon, see Griswold *et al.* (1981).

STATUS

Icon has been implemented for many computers ranging from PCs to mainframes. It is the most widely used and generally available high-level string-processing language.

Other String-Processing Languages

Ambit (Wolfberg, 1972), developed in 1964, is a string-processing language oriented toward algebraic manipulation. Ambit is similar in many respects to Comit and the SNOBOL languages. However, its strings are parenthesized expressions that correspond to tree structures, and they are implemented as fully linked trees. In Ambit, unlike most other string-processing languages, two strings having the same sequence of non-blank characters are considered equivalent even if they differ in the position and number of blanks they contain. A *basic replacement* rule consists of a *citation*, specifying a pattern, and a *replacement*, which effects a transformation on the string under consideration. The citation may match only one way; the replacement rule must be unambiguous. An important aspect of Ambit pattern-matching is the explicit reference to pointers, which identify specific positions in strings.

Convert (Guzman and McIntosh, 1966) is an extension of Lisp (*q.v.*) incorporating pattern-matching and transformation operations. There are a number of fundamental patterns and facilities for constructing more complicated ones. The function RESEMBLE applies patterns to strings, and REPLACE performs transformations using skeletons that specify the structure of the replacement. A rule consists of a pattern and a skeleton. Convert applies the pattern to a string. If a "resemblance" is found, values of relevant parts are identified and substituted into the skeleton to effect the conversion.

Axle (Cohen and Wegstein, 1965), like Comit, has a workspace that is the focus of attention for pattern matching and replacement. Axle has *assertion tables*, which specify patterns. These specifications may be recursive. *Imperative tables* specify patterns to be matched and corresponding replacements. A pattern-matching procedure determines which imperative is applicable. Axle has *markers*, which may be positioned in the workspace. These markers may be used to avoid reprocessing previously transformed parts of the workspace.

Panon (Forino, 1968) is based on generalized Markov algorithms and includes a number of pattern-matching facilities and rules for transforming strings. A Panon program is itself a string, and hence susceptible to self-modification.

Bibliography

1963. Yngve, V. H. *Computer Programming with COMIT II.* Cambridge, MA: MIT Press.

1965. Cohen, K., and Wegstein, J. H. "AXLE: An Axiomatic Language for String Transformations," *Comm. of the ACM*, **8**, *11*, 657–661.

1966. Guzman, A., and McIntosh, H. V. "Convert," *Comm. of the ACM*, **9**, *8*, 604–615.

1968. Forino, A. C. "String Processing Languages and Generalized Markov Algorithms," in *Proceedings of the IFIP Working Conference on Symbol Manipulation Languages*, 141–206. Amsterdam: North-Holland.

1971. Griswold, R. E., Poage, J. F., and Polonsky, I. P. *The SNOBOL4 Programming Language*, 2nd Ed. Upper Saddle River, NJ: Prentice Hall.

1972. Wolfberg, M. S. "Fundamentals of the Ambit/L list-processing language," *SIGPLAN Notices*, **7**, *10*, 66–75.

1980. Griswold, R. E., and Hanson, D. R. "An alternative to the use of patterns in string processing," *ACM Transactions on Programming Languages and Systems*, **2**, *2*, 153–172.

1981. Griswold, R. E., Hanson, D. R., and Korb, J. T. "Generators in Icon," *ACM Transactions on Programming Languages and Systems*, **3**, *2*, 144–161.

1996. Griswold, R. E., and Griswold, M. T. *The Icon Programming Language*, 3rd Ed. San Jose, CA: Peer-to-Peer Communications.

Ralph E. Griswold and David R. Hanson

STRUCTURED PROGRAMMING

For articles on related subjects *see* ADA; C; CONTROL STRUCTURE; ITERATION; LITERATE PROGRAMMING; LOOP INVARIANT; MODULAR PROGRAMMING; OBJECT-ORIENTED PROGRAMMING; PROCEDURE-ORIENTED LANGUAGES: PROGRAMMING; PROGRAM; and PROGRAM VERIFICATION.

Structured programming (SP) may be defined as a methodological style whereby a computer program is constructed by concatenating or coherently nesting logical subunits that either are themselves structured programs or else are of the form of one or another of a small number of particularly well-understood *control structures*. Such a definition is inherently and deliberately recursive. Though the idea is of uncertain and undoubtedly multiple parentage, intense interest in the concept followed the publication of a letter to the editor in *Communications of the ACM* in March 1968 by Edsger Dijkstra. In this letter, entitled by the editor of CACM "Go To Statement Considered Harmful," Dijkstra reported his observation that the ease of reading and understanding program listings was inversely proportional to the number of unconditional transfers of control ("goto"s) that they contained. This rule of thumb is quite plausible since, when a programmer suddenly writes goto, what he or she is essentially saying to the reader is "However hard you were concentrating on the logical flow of my program, stop and find the continuation of this logic at another (possibly remote) physical point." That new point is presumably marked by a label of some sort (numeric in Fortran or Pascal, or alphanumeric in Algol or APL, etc.), which may not even be on the same page that contained the goto. The front page of any daily newspaper is full of gotos (e.g. "cont'd on p. 6") for the obvious reason that the editors want to draw attention to a large number of unrelated stories of approximately co-equal importance. At least some magazines are more considerate, however, and always finish one thought (article) before beginning another. Why can't programmers? Their ability to do so is at the heart of structured programming.

Control Structures for Structured Programming

One possible barrier to writing structured programs is lack of a sufficiently flexible grammar. Consider the Fortran IV segment:

```
IF (A .GT. B) K = K + 1
J = 3 * K
L = 7
```

Such a segment scans well because the possible detour consists of the single statement K = K + 1. But, when either branch requires two or more statements, the programmer is forced to write something like the following:

```
    IF (A .GT. B) GOTO 30
20      K = K + 1
        M = 2
30 J = 3 * K
    L = 7
```

Following the flow of control in even this simple example is not trivial; if the sequence of two statements that begins at label 20 had consisted of 30 or 50 or more statements, readability would suffer. At least as early as the development of Algol in the late 1950s, it was noted that use of a compound statement, two or more statements, each pair separated by a special character (say "; ") and delimited by others, typically "**begin**" and "**end**", could have a very beneficial effect. In Algol or Pascal, the last example can be rendered:

```
if A > B then begin K := K + 1; M := 2 end;
J := 3 * K; L := 7;...
```

In this example, the sequence starting with J := 3 * K is to be executed regardless of whether the consequent of the **then** is executed or not. When different and mutually exclusive actions are desired, the Algol or Pascal programmer can write:

```
if A > B then begin K := K + 1; M := 2 end
         else begin K := K - 1; M := 7 end
```

This **if-then-else** structure, which allows the selection of compound statement alternatives, turns out to be one of the essential control structures for structured programming. Interestingly enough, Cobol, which is seldom thought of as a structured language, has such a decision construct, whereas the more "scientific" language Fortran (in dialects up though IV) did not.

What else is needed? The answer was given in 1964 in a seminal paper by Böhm and Jacopini, who proved that every "flowchart" (program) however complicated, could be rewritten in an equivalent way using only repeated or nested subunits of no more than three

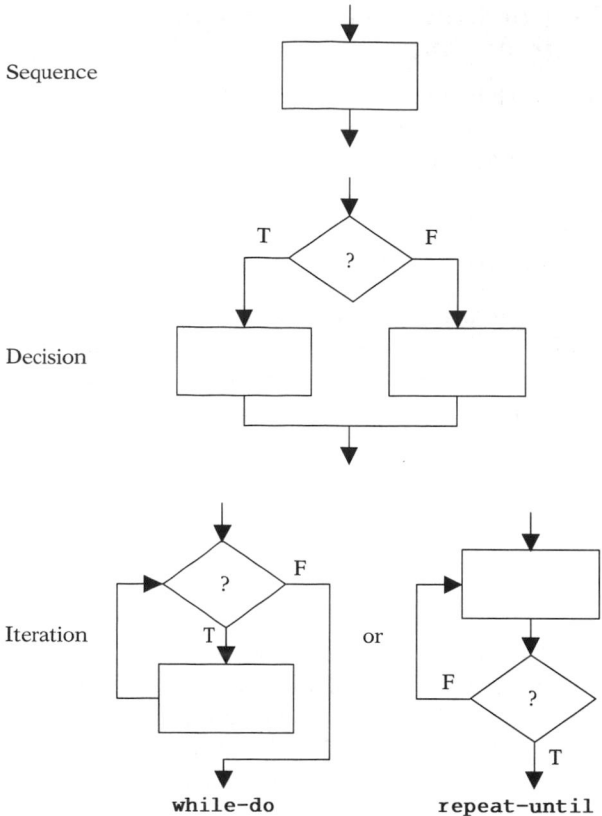

Sequence

Decision

Iteration   or

while-do   **repeat-until**

Figure 1. SP canonical forms.

different kinds—a *sequence* of executable statements, a *decision* clause of the `if-then-else` type described above, and an *iteration* construct, which repeats a sequence of statements `while` (or `until`) some condition is satisfied. Using conventional flowchart notation, these so-called *canonical forms* are typically rendered as in Fig. 1. Note that each of these control structures has a single entry point and a single exit, a key to their intelligible interconnectibility.

The two forms of iteration differ in this regard: the `repeat-until` variation of iteration does something first and asks a question later (as to whether a termination condition has yet become true), whereas the `while-do` variation of iteration cautiously asks a question first, since, if the condition tested is false, the loop under consideration is not executed at all. The Fortran `DO` statement is essentially a weak form of `repeat-until`; e.g. the Fortran segment:

```
    DO 17 I = 1,L
        ⋮
17  CONTINUE
```

will iterate until I > L becomes true.

Using most compilers for Fortran dialects up through IV, the loop will run once even if L < 1 (and hence

I > L) to start with. This can be avoided in Algol through use of the construction:

```
I := 0;
for I := I + 1 while I < L do
(a single, possibly compound, statement);
```

which does not iterate at all if L < 1.

Do we need both iteration variants? The Böhm–Jacopini theorem says "no," but that theorem addresses only constructibility and not convenience. For this reason, programmers like to have both variants, as they do in Pascal. For similar reasons of convenience, three other constructs—`case`, `exit`, and `return`—have proved to be desirable adjuncts to the canonical forms since each eliminates the need for an unconditional branch to a label under some circumstances. The utility of `case` is discussed in the article CONTROL STRUCTURE; `exit` (from a loop) and `return` (from a procedure) are closely related in that it is often contingently desirable to terminate a logic segment abruptly. Consider the following fragment of code in the language C or C++ (which uses `break` for `exit`):

```
true = 1; false = 0;
found = false;
for (i = 1; i <= 100; i++)
  if (a[i] == gold) {found = true; break;}
/* if executed, break sends control here */
```

where i++ is the same as i = i + 1 and == means "is identically equal to." Such a loop runs at most 100 times, but terminates sooner if the search is successful.

Without using `break`, a `goto` in disguise, the same logic can be expressed in C or C++ as

```
for (i = 1; !found && i <= 100; i++)
    found = (a[i] == gold);
```

where && and ! are, respectively, the Boolean operators **and** and **not**. Not all languages are as flexible, however, so even staunch SP advocates would consider the price too high and say, "If your language doesn't support `exit` or `break` then, by all means, use a `goto` or a Boolean flag to break a loop when necessary."

The occasional need for an explicit `return` for early exit from a procedure or function is quite similar. The foregoing logic embodied in a C or C++ function called "found" would be:

```
int found (int a[], int gold)
{int i;
  for (i = 1; i <= 100; i + +)
    if (a[i] == gold) return (true);
  return(false);
}/* end definition of found */
```

Input/Output Aspects of Structured Programming

None of the canonical control structures was specifically designed to handle input–output; yet the way such statements are treated can have a significant impact on program structure and intelligibility. As a minimum, embedded program comments should describe the significance and expected range of each quantity to be read or written. When valid data or results are available for transmission, read and write statements are merely particular examples of *sequence*. The principal problem that affects program structure arises when an abnormal or other special case occurs, such as the perennial problem of how best to handle the end-of-file condition. From the SP standpoint, one of the poorer ways is the PL/I (and typical microcomputer Basic) method of allowing the programmer to place a statement such as "On endfile do something" or "ON ERROR GOTO 5000" anywhere in the program— possibly far removed from the I/O statement it may affect. To the unwary reader of such a program, the logic being followed is subject to a "disembodied goto," i.e. something could occur during execution that could snatch control away from a presumably imperative statement that is actually a conditional one.

Even Fortran IV provides a better answer by means of such a statement as

```
READ (5, 12, END = 100) A,B,C
```

The Fortran-knowledgeable reader is now able to see the conditional nature of the READ statement explicitly; it is saying, "If possible, read three numbers from input unit 5 according to the FORMAT specified at statement 12. But if an end-of-file condition is detected prior to receipt of three valid numbers, go to statement 100." Though the implied goto (and associated label) is annoying, the meaning is quite clear.

Somewhat better is the Pascal solution:

```
while not eof do
   begin
      read (a,b,c);
      {process this data set}
   end;
```

Finally, the preferred solution would be the ability to write:

```
while reading(a,b,c) do
      {process data set}.
```

where "reading" is what Federighi calls a *gerund function*, one that returns a Boolean value **true** (when valid input is available) and **false** (upon encountering end-of-file) and whose *side effect* (something usually undesirable, but not so here) is the principal action desired, namely, the reading of data. An end-of-file, of course, terminates the **while** loop in

a way analogous to the **exit** construct discussed earlier. This is the only solution that both preserves structure and directly associates the end-of-file with its proximate cause.

Structured Programs

While a fully structured program has no **goto**s (and hence needs no labels), rewriting a program merely to eliminate **goto**s does not necessarily result in a structured program; more is needed.

Most experts agree that the term SP connotes certain basic principles:

1. *Control structures* Use of only those canonical control structures of Fig. 1 supported by the host language being used unless deviation therefrom removes a gross inefficiency or (most unlikely) enhances readability.

2. *Modular composition* Subdivision of a program into modules, where a *module* is a program segment that embodies a complete logical thought in about one page of code. Depending on their relative sizes, a module may be larger or smaller than a procedure, but the two should be kept commensurate; i.e. either one module consists of one or more small procedures, or else a large procedure is divided into several page-size modules. A program is divided into procedures both for the sake of processing efficiency and for ease of construction. It is divided into modules partially for ease of construction, but mostly for the sake of the human reader. Significant computer programs usually have only one or, at most, a few authors, but they may have many readers.

3. *Program format* Careful organization of each such page into clearly recognizable paragraphs based on appropriate indentation of iteration, decision, and nested structures.

4. *Comments* Judicious use of embedded comments that describe the function of each variable and the purpose of each module and procedure. A program whose every statement is annotated is often harder to read and understand than one that is devoid of comment; the right density is about one comment for every few lines of code that express a coherent logical action.

5. *Readability versus efficiency* A preference for straightforward, easily readable code over slightly more efficient but obtuse code.

6. *Stepwise refinement* Creation of the final program through an evolutionary process of *stepwise*

refinement (top-down design) whereby the overall logic is first sketched in using a generous admixture of English, which is then gradually replaced in subsequent versions by more detailed logic syntactically acceptable to the intended compiler (*q.v.*) or interpreter.

7. *Program verification* The ability to make assertions about key segments of a structured program to facilitate reasoning about program correctness (*see* PROGRAM VERIFICATION).

Before discussing further the prospective benefits of adhering to these rules, we make two observations. First, note that nothing in all of the foregoing referred to the concepts of *algorithm* or *data structure*. The selection of an appropriate algorithm and associated data structure is a strategic concept; the application of SP techniques is a tactical methodology. Neither a structured program that implements an inferior algorithm nor an unstructured program that implements an excellent one is as desirable as the constructive use of good strategy *and* good tactics. To paraphrase the title of Niklaus Wirth's classic book: "Algorithms + Data Structures = (possibly unstructured) Programs," but "(Good) Algorithms + (associated) Data Structures + SP Techniques = An Efficient Structured Program."

Second, a purported structured program can be examined by a reader who can form value judgments as to whether characteristics one through five have been met, but unless the author chooses to display intermediate versions, it is impossible to tell (nor need we care) whether the final result was attained using stepwise refinement. This is not to denigrate rule 6; there is now sufficient professional experience to support its continued advocacy.

Benefits of SP

Advocates claim at least the following benefits for SP:

1. Structured programs are more readable and hence more intelligible than unstructured ones.

2. This greater readability makes it easier to maintain and modify structured programs, especially by programmers other than the original author.

3. Structured programs are more likely to be correct in the first instance and are more easily shown correct by systematic program verification.

4. The greater likelihood of correctness cited above lessens elapsed time to create a new program because there are fewer bugs (*q.v.*) to find and fix. Instead of the routine expectation that a program

will not run properly the first time, the goal of the structured programmer is "zero defects"; reasonably complex structured programs have indeed been known to run perfectly on the first attempt.

Though the foregoing claims are difficult to substantiate quantitatively, there is no doubt that the majority of professionals who teach programming and language design have moved heavily toward the SP philosophy. This movement is reflected in at least four identifiable developments: (1) the widespread use of structured languages for teaching introductory computer science courses in universities; (2) the US government's decision to choose a structured format for its command and control language Ada; (3) the concession of the Fortran community that it was time to introduce some structure through the medium of Fortran 77 (and later, Fortran 90); and (4) the fact that all recently developed versions of Basic are structured.

Structured Flowcharts

Since SP has caused a significant change in programming, or at least in the way we think about programming, it should not be surprising that other related tools that once served us well need reformulation. One of these is the time-honored *flowchart* (*q.v.*), which so often contains a spaghetti-like maze of transfers from box to box, just the antithesis of SP. An interesting and useful remedy has been proposed by Nassi and Shneiderman, who recommend use of certain new diagrams for each principal SP control structure. Among these are a rectangular box for a declarative sequence (or process), "L" or inverted "L" structures for iteration, and other distinctive diagrams for binary (if-then-else) or multiple (case) decisions (Fig. 2). Since each diagram's outer outline is a rectangle and since the subdivision of any structure always leaves rectangles that may be further subdivided, a set of such diagrams can always be sequenced or nested within an outermost rectangle in a manner that models faithfully the recursive definition of a structured program given in the first sentence of this article. Examples of diagram intercombination are given in Figs. 3 and 4, which represent, respectively, procedures for calculating the factorial of N and the product of two $N \times N$ matrices. Such *structured flowcharts* are also called *iteration diagrams* or, after their inventors, *Nassi–Shneiderman diagrams*.

A significant feature of iteration diagrams is that the clarity with which nested logic is displayed often facilitates algorithm analysis; note in particular the three nested loops in Fig. 4, which so vividly emphasize that conventional matrix multiplication of $N \times N$ matrices takes running time proportional to N^3.

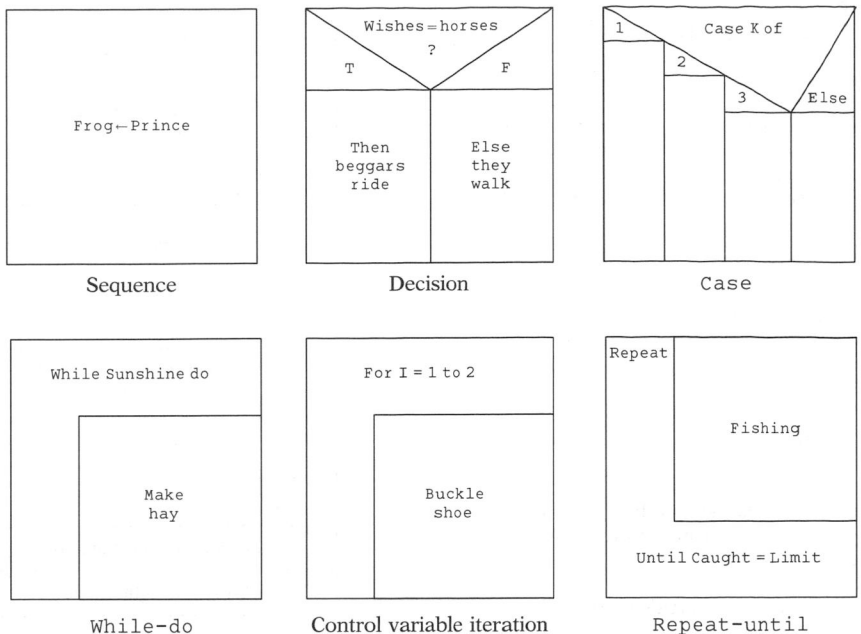

Figure 2. Structured flowchart building blocks.

An Example

As an example of SP, consider the classic *Quicksort* algorithm for sorting an initially unordered one-dimensional array of (say) integers. One step of this algorithm will partition the array into three parts—a single interior element called the *pivot*, which is guaranteed to have gravitated to its correct final position; a left partition, all of whose elements are less than or equal to the pivot; and a right partition, all of whose elements are greater than the pivot. Repetitive (i.e. recursive) application of this process to the left and right partitions and to their subpartitions (until all such subpartitions are reduced to size one) will complete the sort.

The program logic is illustrated progressively in four forms, stepwise-refined stages in Figs. 5 and 6, a structured flowchart in Fig. 7, and, finally, in Fig. 8, the completed structured program and an example of its operation on a specific data set.

Not only does the program shown work correctly for the data set shown, we can prove that the basic partitioning algorithm works for *any* data set if, according to the precepts of program verification, we can identify two relations say p and c, such that the combined truth of p and $\neg c$ (not c) guarantees a correct partitioning. The relation c is the loop control relation I<=J; i.e. an inspection of the program shows that the principal loop runs until $\neg c$ (I>J) is true. A more

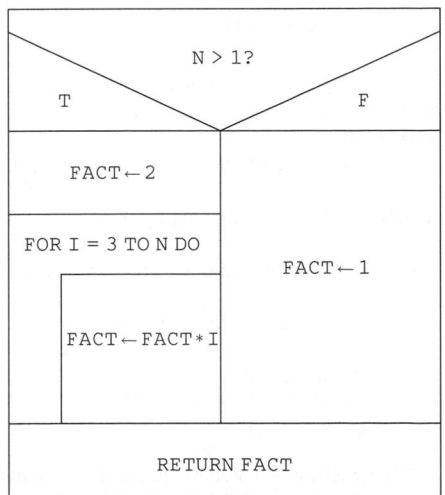

Figure 3. Factorial.

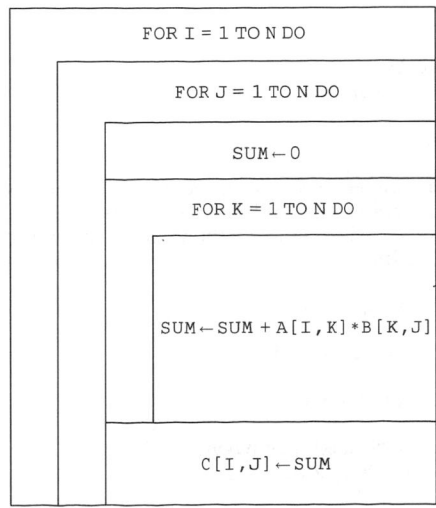

Figure 4. Matrix multiplication.

Procedure Quicksort (L, R : integer);
{sorts global array A[L..R] where A[R + 1] > any A[L..R]}

Choose pivot arbitrarily to be element at left end of array A.

[Set pointers to mark positions such that all elements to left of left pointer I are less than or equal to the pivot and all elements to right of right pointer J are greater than the pivot, leaving J − I + 1 elements between I and J (inclusive) to be examined.]

{The initial choices of I and J that satisfy the above are I = L + 1 and J = R.}

Move left pointer to right and right pointer to left until either

(a) the bracketed condition above is temporarily violated, in which case we exchange elements addressed by the pointers in order to restore that condition, and then continue moving the pointers, or
(b) the pointers cross.

Replace the first element with the element addressed by right pointer and then replace that right element with the pivot in order to achieve the desired partition.

Now operate similarly on left and right partitions until all subpartitions are of size one.

Figure 5. First version of Quicksort written primarily in English.

---

procedure Quicksort (L, R : integer);
{sorts global array A[L..R] where the main program has set A[R + 1] to "infinity"; i.e., a number guaranteed to be larger than any A[L..R]}

if L < R **then**
begin
by initializing a left pointer I := L + 1, which
    shall move to the right, and a right pointer J := R, which shall
    move to the left.

    As an arbitrary pivot element, select PIV := A[L], the first
    element. Now

repeat
    -edly move pointers toward each other in such a way that

while A[I] <= PIV we increment the left pointer, and then
while A[J] > PIV we decrement the right pointer.

    After this movement, if I still < J, then pointers haven't
    crossed so

    Exchange A[I] and A[J].
    After this exchange, keep moving pointers

until I > J.

    Now that pointers have crossed, copy A[J] to first position,
    A[L], and replace A[J] with the pivot element. This completes
    a partition. Finally, complete the work by recursively sorting
    the left partition via:

    Quicksort (L, J − 1)

and the right partition via:

    Quicksort (J + 1, R)

End logic performed only when L < R.
end procedure Quicksort.

Figure 6. Second version of Quicksort using English embedded in Pascal-like control structures.

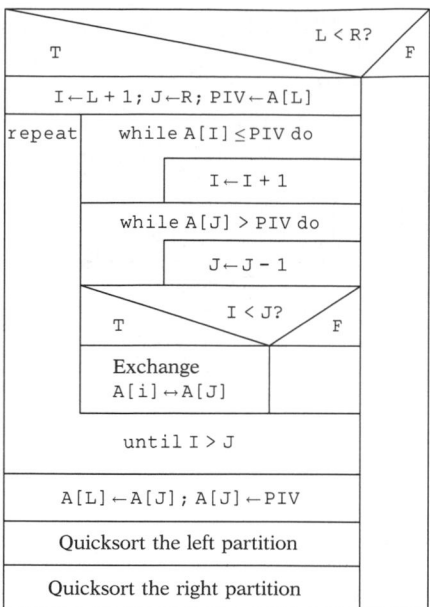

Figure 7. Procedure Quicksort (L, R).

careful inspection of the program reveals that *c* switches from true to false in such a way that ¬*c* is equivalent to the truth of J=I−1. The other relation, *p*, is the so-called *invariant relation* of the loop, one that was true before the loop began and whose truth is

---

```
program QuickDriver (input, output);
const max = 10001;
var
  A: array [1..max] of integer;
  i: integer;                        {Control variable}
  n: integer;          {number of integers to be sorted}

procedure Quicksort (L, R : integer);
{sorts global array A[L..R] where A[R+1] > any A[L..R]}
var I, J, PIV, T : integer
begin
  if L < R then
    begin
    I := L + 1; J := R; PIV := A[L];
    repeat
      {move pointers I and J inwards as far as possible}
        while A[I] <= PIV do I := I + 1;
        while A[J] > PIV do J := J − 1;
        if I {still} < J then {exchange items pointed to
                                              by I and J}
        begin T := A[I]; A[I] := A[J]; A[J] := T end
    until I > J;
    {now two final replacements finish a partition}
    A[L] := A[J]; A[J] := PIV;
    {finish by recursively sorting the left and
                                      right partitions}
    Quicksort (L, J − 1); Quicksort (J+1, R)
  end {logic performed only when L < R}
end {procedure Quicksort};
```

Figure 8. Final structured version of Quicksort implemented as a Pascal procedure and embedded in a sample driver together with an example of how a particular data set would appear after a single partitioning.

```
begin
  write ('Enter number of integers to be sorted: ');
  readln (n);
  for i := 1 to n do read (A[i]);        {Read integer data}
  A[n + 1] := maxint;          {Set "infinite" right guard}
  Quicksort (1,n);
  for i := 1 to n do write (A[i]:5); {Write sorted numbers}
  writeln;
end {qs driver}.
```

Example

```
I J
2 8 | 8  6 12 20  2  5 47 14   Initial array;
3 6 | 8  6  5 20  2 12 47 14   pivot = 8
4 5 | 8  6  5  2 20 12 47 14
5 4 | 2  6  5 [8] 20 12 47 14  Final result
                                of one partitioning
      Left partition    Right partition
```

To be further processed recursively (by 3rd-last line of the procedure) until partitions of size one result in completely ordered (sorted) data.

Figure 8. *Continued.*

preserved throughout the running of the loop (*see* LOOP INVARIANT). There may be many candidate relations for *p*, most of them irrelevant—we seek the particular one such that *p* and ¬*c* proves the desired "theorem." That particular *p* has been right before us all along; it is precisely the statement in square brackets in Fig. 5. When that invariant relation is written with the substitution J=I-1, we obtain:

> Set pointers to mark positions such that all elements to the left of the pointer I are less than or equal to the pivot and all elements to the right of the right pointer J are greater than the pivot, leaving 0 elements between I and J to be examined,

which "proves" our theorem to the degree of conviction we achieve that our chosen "invariant" relation really is an invariant; i.e. no program step destroys the validity it had prior to execution of the primary loop to which it pertains.

Structured Programming Languages

We shall adopt the criterion that a structured language must have, as a minimum, an **if-then-else** compound statement-oriented decision statement, and at least one form of iteration based on a Boolean decision; i.e. either **while-do** or **repeat-until**. The statements **case**, **exit**, and **return** are luxuries. Note that, although classical iteration based on a control variable is not cited as being necessary despite its obvious utility, most SP languages retain such a form in addition to **while-do** and/or **repeat-until**.

Table 1 summarizes the SP features of seven particular high-level languages. *Sequence* has not been tabulated because all of them have such a construct. Recursion, on the other hand, has been included because many procedures are much more intelligible (though, of course, not more efficient) when written in recursive form (as in our Quicksort example) than they are when written out nonrecursively. Also, since embedded comments play an important role in readability, a language is characterized in this regard as being *poor* if comments must be confined to separate lines, *fair* if they may be placed at certain restricted points internal to a statement, *good* if they may be placed within or at least to the right of statements, and *excellent* (exc.) if such comments are delimited by single characters (such as { .. } in Pascal) rather than the jarring double-character delimiters /* and */ that PL/I and C use.

The influence of the SP philosophy has now become quite pervasive, and deservedly so, even in environments where, for one reason or another, programs are still written in a traditional unstructured language. This is manifesting itself in several ways: (1) the creation of compilers for structured versions of languages

Table 1. Language features that facilitate SP.

	Algol 60	Pascal	Ada	PL/I	C	Fortran 90	Java
if-then-else decision	✓	✓	✓	✓	✓	✓	✓
Control variable iteration	✓	✓	✓	✓	✓	✓	✓
while	✓	✓	✓	✓	✓	a	✓
repeat-until	–	✓	–	–	✓	–	✓
case	–	✓	✓	✓	b	✓	b
exit (break)	–	–	✓	–	✓	✓	✓
return	–	–	✓	✓	✓	✓	✓
Recursion	✓	✓	✓	✓	✓	c	✓
Flexibility of comments	Good	Exc.	Good	Good	Good	Fair	Good

[a] *Not* in the standard but present in many actual implementations.
[b] The structure in C and Java does not have a common single exit and hence is more properly classified as a form of Fortran-like computed goto.
[c] Possible if a routine is explicitly declared to be recursive.

such as Basic, Lisp, and Snobol (i.e. versions in which, typically, options for `if-then-else` and `while-do` control structures are superimposed on the original language); (2) the creation of preprocessors (software translators), which change structured syntax into conventional statements acceptable to existing compilers; and, as a last resort, (3) hand translation of structured flowcharts or hypothetical structured code into transliterated conventional equivalents.

The major contributions of the SP approach have been twofold—the elevation of programming technique to something less of an art and more of a science, and also the demonstration that carefully structured programs can be creative works of sufficient literary merit to deserve being read by humans and not just by computers.

Bibliography

1964. Böhm, C., and Jacopini, G. "Flow Diagrams, Turing Machines, and Languages with Only Two Formation Rules," *Comm. ACM*, **9**, 5.
1968. Dijkstra, E. "Go To Statement Considered Harmful," *Comm. ACM*, **11**, 3.
1972. Dahl, O. J., Dijkstra, E., and Hoare, C. A. R. *Structured Programming*. New York: Academic Press.
1994. Nicol, D. *Structured Programming Design: A Designer's Handbook*. Boston: MA: Butterworth-Heinemann.
1995. Fowler, E. C. *Cobol: Structured Programming Techniques for Solving Problems*, 2nd Ed. Boston: Boyd & Fraser.
1996. Staugaard, A. C. *Structured and Object-oriented Techniques: an Introduction Using C++*. Upper Saddle River, NJ: Prentice Hall.
1997. Forouzan, B., and Gilberg, R. F. *Computer Science: A Structured Programming Approach Using C++*. Minneapolis, MN: West Publishing Group.

Edwin D. Reilly

SUBPROGRAM

> For articles on related subjects *see* ACTIVATION RECORD; ARGUMENT; BLOCK STRUCTURE; CALLING SEQUENCE; COROUTINE; GLOBAL AND LOCAL VARIABLES; PARAMETER PASSING; PROCEDURE-ORIENTED LANGUAGES; RECURSION; and SIDE EFFECT.

A *subprogram* is a portion of a high-level language program that performs a specific task necessary for that program. This term is often used interchangeably with the term *subroutine* when referring to high-level languages, although *subroutine* is more usual in the context of machine language programs.

Early in the development of programming languages, it was recognized that programs would be written in which the same process was to be executed at several different locations within the program. One example of such a process is the evaluation of mathematical functions such as logarithms, exponentials, and trig-

onometric functions such as sine or cosine. Another example is the printing of output in a particular format, or the updating of a central table with newly computed information. To accomplish these tasks conveniently, a facility was needed to permit the programmer to write the appropriate code once, and then call that code whenever it was needed. On each call it would be given the values on which it was to operate (its *arguments*, or *parameters*).

There are two basic kinds of subprograms: procedures and functions. A *procedure* is a sequence of code that performs an action but returns no value (except indirectly, perhaps by changing the value of a parameter). For example, a procedure might print a value or update a data structure (*q.v.*). A procedure call is therefore a statement, as statements perform actions. A *function* is a sequence of code that returns a single value, as do mathematical functions. A pure function does not perform an action that affects memory of concern to its calling program; a function that does perform such an action in addition to returning a value is said to have a *side effect*. Since it returns a value, a function call is an expression (*q.v.*) or part of one. Both functions and procedures are widely used in most general-purpose high-level programming languages, such as Pascal (*q.v.*), Ada (*q.v.*), and C++ (*q.v.*). Because procedure calls are statements, and the fundamental element of these languages is the statement, these languages are sometimes said to be *procedural* or *procedure-oriented*. Languages that rely solely on function calls, and in which the fundamental element is the expression, are said to be *functional* (*see* FUNCTIONAL PROGRAMMING).

Subprograms in high-level languages may be *intrinsic* (or *built-in* or *library*) or programmer-written. Intrinsic subprograms are those provided with the language so that the programmer need only cite them in a program to have them automatically invoked. This invocation requires only that the programmer give the name of the subprogram and its arguments. Pascal, for example, has numerous built-in functions, a short list of which is given in Table 1. If, for example, a programmer wishes to assign to variable A the absolute value of the sum of the cosine and sine of the argument, he or she may write:

```
A := abs(cos(X) + sin(X))
```

Table 1. Pascal functions.

Name of function	Mathematical definition	Pascal name
Sine	$\sin x$	`sin`
Cosine	$\cos x$	`cos`
Natural logarithm	$\ln x$	`ln`
Absolute value	$|x|$	`abs`
Square root	$\sqrt{x}$	`sqrt`

```
program test(input, output);
type array100 = array[1..100] of real;
var A, B, C, D: real;
  Q1, Q2, F, G: array100;

function prod(X,Y: array100):real;
var I: integer;
  sum: real;
begin {prod}
    sum := 0;
    for I := 1 to 100 do
            sum := sum + X[I] * Y[I];
    prod := sum
end; {prod}

begin {test}
    . . .
    C := A + (B*D)/prod(F,G);
    . . .
    A := B * prod(Q1,Q2);
    . . .
end. {test}
```

Figure 1. A Pascal function.

In addition to built-in functions, Pascal offers the built-in procedures read and write. Thus, the following Pascal code would read in a value, store it in X, add 1 to X, and print out the result:

```
read(X);
X := X + 1;
write(X)
```

Different high-level languages provide different sets of procedures and functions. For example, C provides a large library of subprograms as part of its standard environment, although they are not strictly part of the language itself. These include subprograms for input

and output, mathematical calculations, string manipulation, date and time representation, and so on. C does not distinguish between procedures and functions by name, but treats all subprograms as functions. However, a C function may have return type void, in which case it returns no value, and is thus a procedure. Furthermore, in C, any function may be called as a statement, in which case its return value is discarded. Thus, C functions that deliberately exploit side-effects can double as procedures.

The availability of intrinsic subprograms clearly suggests the need for a parallel facility to permit programmers to define their own subprograms that can be referenced in the same manner as intrinsic subprograms. Almost every general-purpose high-level language has such a *library* facility, although the details of how it can be used and how it is implemented vary considerably.

Fig. 1 provides an example of a programmer-written Pascal function to calculate the sum of the products of the corresponding elements of two 100-element arrays. Also shown are two main program statements calling this function. Note that in Pascal the value returned by a function is the value assigned to its name, and that the type of the return value is specified after the types of the parameters. Also note that the function is a *declaration* (q.v.) at the beginning of the *block* that is the Pascal program.

Pascal procedures are defined in a manner similar to Pascal functions. A procedure, however, returns no value and is expected to perform an action to modify something in its environment, something passed as a

```
program test2(input, output);
type matrix = array[1..50, 1..50] of real;
var A,B: matrix;

procedure trans(var A: matrix; N: integer);
var I,J: integer;
  temp: real;
begin {trans}
    for I := 2 to N do
        for J := 1 to I-1 do
            begin
                temp := A[I,J];
                A[I,J] := A[J,I];
                A[J,I] := temp
            end
end; {trans}

begin {test2}
    . . .
    trans(A,50); {Transpose the full 50x50 matrix A.}
    . . .
    trans(B,10); {Transpose the 10x10 matrix in upper left corner of B.}
    . . .
end. {test2}
```

Figure 2. A Pascal procedure.

parameter, or the input or output stream. Fig. 2 shows a Pascal procedure that transposes the elements of a two-dimensional square array (i.e. interchanges the (i, j) and (j, i) elements). Note that the action performed by this procedure is to modify the matrix whose name is passed as a parameter. The parameter is specified as a **var** (*variable*) parameter to allow the actual parameter to be modified when the formal parameter is (*see* PARAMETER PASSING).

In some languages, including Fortran (*q.v.*) and C++, subprograms are defined separately from the main program as opposed to being embedded in it as in block-structured languages such as Pascal. This facilitates separate compilation of the main program and subprograms, and may be convenient during debugging (*q.v.*). Some block-structured languages, such as Modula-2, Ada, and some dialects of Pascal, allow creation of modules that allow separate compilation of subprograms.

Bibliography

1999. Sebesta, R. W. *Concepts of Programming Languages*, 4th Ed. Reading, MA: Addison-Wesley.

Adrienne Bloss and J. A. N. Lee

SUBPROGRAM, CALLING A

See CALLING SEQUENCE; and PARAMETER PASSING.

SUPERCOMPUTERS

> For articles on related subjects *see* BIOCOMPUTING; CACHE COHERENCY; CLUSTER COMPUTING; COMPUTER-AIDED ENGINEERING; CONTROL DATA CORPORATION; CRAY, SEYMOUR; DATAFLOW; INSTRUCTION-LEVEL PARALLELISM; MULTIPROCESSING; PARALLEL PROCESSING; PIPELINE; SCIENTIFIC APPLICATIONS; SIMULATION; SUPERCOMPUTING CENTERS; and SYSTOLIC ARRAY.

The most powerful computers of any time have been called high-speed computers, supercomputers, high-performance computers and, most recently, high-end computers. The term *supercomputer* is used in this article to encompass all these terms.

Supercomputers are important tools for modern science. They are routinely used to simulate physical phenomena in an accurate and timely manner. Computer simulation (*q.v.*) is accepted today as a third mode of scientific research that complements experimentation and theoretical analysis. It enables the exploration of phenomena that otherwise cannot be observed or analyzed, and provides intuition to guide experimental and theoretical work. Supercomputers are also of great importance in engineering because computer simulations can give designers useful feedback on the quality and feasibility of new designs. Because of the large number of operations involved in simulations for science and engineering, supercomputers are an enabling technology, making possible advances that cannot be achieved by any other means.

Some examples of supercomputer applications in science and engineering, mentioned in the 1998 report of the US President's Information Technology Advisory Committee, are:

- designing new cancer-fighting and anti-viral drugs;

- understanding the causes and sources of air, water, and ground pollution, and devising solutions to these problems;

- forecasting local weather and predicting long-range climate changes;

- designing safer, more fuel-efficient vehicles;

- ensuring the safety and effectiveness of the nuclear stockpile;

- designing new aircraft, such as the Boeing 777.

Supercomputers have also been used for nonnumerical and seminumerical problems, although much less frequently than for the numerically intensive problems typical of science and engineering simulations. For example, supercomputers are used to compare normal and pathological genetic sequences to help researchers understand the molecular basis of disease. The 1997 victory of IBM's Deep Blue, a supercomputer designed to evaluate chess moves at very high speeds, over world chess champion Garry Kasparov is arguably one of the most important events in the history of computing (*see* COMPUTER CHESS). Supercomputers also have been used to decompose large numbers into prime factors, a seminumerical problem with applications for code breaking (*see* FACTORING INTEGERS; NUMBER THEORETIC CALCULATIONS; and CRYPTOGRAPHY, COMPUTERS IN).

Machine Organization

In the past, a high clock rate was one of the characteristics that distinguished supercomputers from ordinary machines. For instance, the high clock rate of Cray processors made them the fastest available during the 1980s, even if their arithmetic pipelines (see below) were not used. However, microprocessor clock rates have now matched, and in some cases surpassed, the clock rates of supercomputers. What distinguishes the supercomputers of today from ordinary computers is their high degree of parallelism; that is, their ability to perform a large number of operations simultaneously.

All modern supercomputers contain several processors (hence the term "multiprocessors") which can cooperate in the execution of a single program. Each processor can execute instructions following a program path independently of the others. Parallelism is achieved by decomposing programs into components, known as *tasks* or *threads*, that can be executed simultaneously on separate processors.

Multiprocessor parallelism is usually combined with internal parallelism of each processor. The maximum number of operations that a supercomputer can execute is the product of the number of processors by the maximum number of operations that each processor can execute simultaneously. Some modern supercomputers use conventional microprocessors capable of executing a few operations (<10) simultaneously. Other supercomputers are built around *custom-designed processors*, capable of executing large numbers of operations (>100) simultaneously. Although it is widely believed that all supercomputers of the future will be built using off-the-shelf microprocessors, several new supercomputers based on custom-designed processors were introduced as late as 1998.

The parallel execution of a program in a multiprocessor requires that the processors interact by coordinating their work and exchanging data. Multiprocessors may or may not have a global address space. In machines without a global address space, also known as *NORMA* machines (Fig. 1) (for NO Remote Memory Access), processors exchange information and coordinate their work by sending messages to each other. In a NORMA machine, each processor has access to a private memory. The only way a processor can get information stored in the private memory of another processor is by one processor executing a *send* operation while another processor executes a matching *receive* operation. Messages are also used to coordinate work between processors in NORMA machines, although hardware devices have sometimes been used to implement a popular coordination mechanism known as a *barrier*, which forces a collection of processors to rendezvous before allowing execution to continue in any of them.

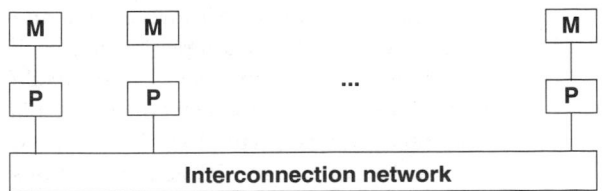

P: Processor
M: Private memory

Figure 1.   Schematic of a NORMA multiprocessor.

In multiprocessors with a *global address space* or *shared memory*, there is a region of memory that can be read and written by all processors (*see* MULTIPROCESSING). In these machines, processors may exchange data by fetching and storing in memory. Coordination is achieved by using software *locks* and barriers. Locks are typically used to enforce ordering between instructions executed by different processors and to guarantee that a section of code is executed by only one processor at a time. Locks and barriers can be implemented using special synchronization instructions which have the ability to read and modify a memory location in a single indivisible step (*see* MUTUAL EXCLUSION).

Machines with a global address space have existed since the early 1960s, when the first Burroughs B5000 and D-825 were delivered. However, in those days, multiprocessing was used most often to increase the reliability of the system and to overlap I/O with computation. Since the introduction of the Cray X-MP in 1984, there has been a growing interest in the use of multiprocessing to increase computation speed. Today, shared-memory machines are widely available with the largest systems containing hundreds of processors. The presence of a global address space facilitates programming, but shared-memory multiprocessors can be more costly to design and build than NORMA machines.

Shared-memory supercomputers may be classified according to the way processors and memories are interconnected and by the region of memory that can be buffered in their *cache memories* (*q.v.*). Cache memories, or simply caches, are an important component of practically all computer systems today, including conventional machines and multiprocessors. Copies of data and instructions originally found in main memory are kept in caches which can be accessed much faster than main memory to accelerate program execution. When the data and instructions accessed by the processor are often found in the cache, it is said that the cache hides the memory access delay (or *memory latency*) from the processor.

A popular classification of shared-memory multiprocessors is as follows:

1. *Uniform Memory Access (UMA)* This class of machines, depicted in Fig. 2, has a globally shared memory located remotely from all processors and connected to them by an interconnection network such that all data accesses to the global address space take approximately the same time to complete. Typically, UMA systems contain special hardware to keep the caches *coherent* across the machine as data is read and written by the different processors. That is, if several caches have copies of

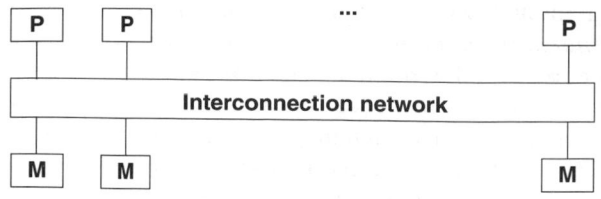

P: Processor
M: Memory module

Figure 2. Schematic of a UMA multiprocessor.

the same main memory location, the hardware will take the necessary actions to guarantee that the copies will have the same value in all caches. Perhaps the main advantage of UMA multiprocessors is that their simple memory model facilitates parallel program development. Today's UMA machines typically contain fewer than 64 processors.

2. *Non-uniform Memory Access (NUMA)* Although the typical number of processors in UMA machines may increase significantly in the near future, the machines with the largest numbers of processors will most likely be NUMA machines, due to cost and performance advantages. The defining characteristic of NUMA machines (Fig. 3) is the clustering of processors and memories. Instead of a single memory space placed equidistantly from all the processors, in NUMA machines processors and memories are clustered and a processor can access the memory in its cluster faster than the memory in other clusters. Thus, NUMA machines take advantage of physical proximity to accelerate some references to memory.

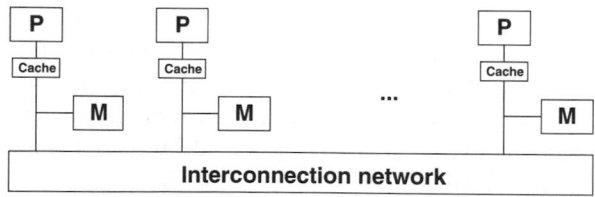

P: Processor
M: Local memory

(a) CC-NUMA

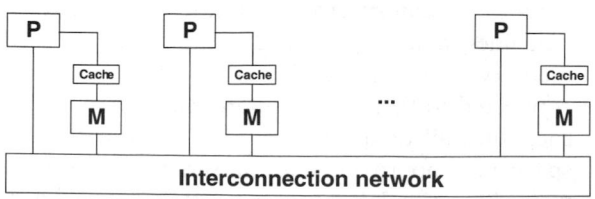

P: Processor
M: Local memory

(b) NC-NUMA

Figure 3. Schematic of NUMA multiprocessors.

NUMA machines can be further classified by section of memory buffered by the caches.

(a) *Cache-Coherent Non-uniform Memory Access (CC-NUMA)* These machines are similar to UMA machines in that there is a global address space, all of which is buffered by the caches. Coherency is usually guaranteed by the hardware.

(b) *Non-Cache-Coherent Non-uniform Memory Access (NC-NUMA)* These machines have a local memory and a data cache for each processor. They make no attempt to cache data that is not in the local memory, but still provide a global address space. Typically, remote data is copied to a temporary location in local memory before it is used. Once the remote data is used from local memory, it is cached along with the other local data accesses. It is the responsibility of the programmer (or the compiler) to guarantee that processors always use the correct value of remote data.

It can be argued that CC-NUMA machines are easier to program than NORMA and NC-NUMA machines because of cache coherency. On the other hand, effective programming of CC-NUMA machines may require more effort than programming UMA machines because the varying memory access time has to be considered.

Processor Organization

The total parallelism of a modern supercomputer is the combination of intraprocessor parallelism and multiprocessing. The processors of today's supercomputers contain two forms of parallelism: multiple functional units and pipelining. These two forms are discussed next, followed by a discussion of array processors, which is a third form of processor parallelism found in only a few machines today.

PROCESSORS WITH MULTIPLE FUNCTIONAL UNITS

A processor may contain two or more functional units to perform arithmetic and logic operations. The functional units can execute in parallel. Usually, the functional units are specialized to perform a subset of the operations that a conventional arithmetic-logic unit (ALU—*q.v.*) can execute. For example, in a certain processor, a functional unit could be devoted exclusively to floating-point multiplication and division while a second functional unit is devoted to floating-point addition and a third to integer and Boolean operations.

There are three strategies to control multifunction parallelism. In the first approach, parallelism is exploited at run time by a control unit that, under certain circumstances, can issue an instruction before preceding ones have completed. An instruction will not be issued if the functional unit it needs is busy or if it collides with an executing instruction. Two instructions are said to *collide* if both access the same location (memory or register) and at least one of these accesses is a write. In this approach, some of the parallelism present in sequential programs (or sequential components of parallel programs) can be exploited automatically by the hardware without the need for human intervention or compiler transformations. However, code reorganization, done manually or by the compiler, can increase program performance. The Bull Gamma 60, designed in the 1950s, is one of the earliest examples of a run-time-controlled multifunction processor. However, it was the introduction of the CDC 6600 and the IBM 360/91 in the early 1960s that made this a popular approach. Today, most processors have multifunctional parallelism supported by run-time control.

In the second strategy, the instructions contain several operations, each of which corresponds to a particular functional unit. Processors with this type of instruction are, for obvious reasons, known as *very-long-instruction-word* (VLIW) processors. To exploit the parallelism in VLIW machines, it is necessary to determine which operations can execute in parallel and then schedule their execution by grouping operations into instructions. This is difficult to do manually and, therefore, is usually left to the compiler. Although no pure VLIW machines exist today, some designs come close. For example, the Texas Instruments Digital Signal Processor TMS320C6701 uses sequences of instructions, called *fetch packets*, to express instruction-level parallelism explicitly. A bit associated with each instruction is used to specify whether or not the instruction is in the same fetch packet with the next instruction. Also, the IA-64 processor, designed by Intel and Hewlett-Packard, follows a similar strategy, known as *Explicitly Parallel Instruction Computing* (EPIC). The IA-64 is likely to become quite popular for everyday computing and, as a result, to become the processor of choice for many future supercomputers.

In the third strategy, known as *multithreading*, several program threads may share the functional units of the processor at the same time. With multiple threads, there are more opportunities to use the functional units which tend to improve efficiency. Furthermore, threading can be used to hide memory latency. A thread can be placed on hold while memory is being accessed; but, if enough threads are being run, the functional units can be kept busy, and therefore efficiency would remain as high as if there were no memory access delay. A current example of this type of processor in a supercomputer is the Tera MTA. This machine is unique in that it contains no caches. Instead of masking memory latency by caching data

values, it tolerates the latency of a memory access by quickly switching to a new thread of control after an access is issued. Each processor of the Tera machine can support up to 128 threads and can switch from one to the next in one clock cycle (3 ns). Lightweight synchronization is achieved by using a set of synchronization state bits stored with each memory location.

PIPELINING

In this approach, an operation is divided into stages, each accomplishing a fraction of the work required by the operation (*see* PIPELINE). For example, a floating-point multiplication can be divided into four stages: addition of the exponents, multiplication of the mantissas, rounding, and normalization of the result. The stages are connected in a linear sequence or *pipe*. An operation enters at one end of the pipe and proceeds from one stage to the next until, finally, the result exits at the other end of the pipe. Parallelism is achieved by operating the pipe like an assembly line (i.e. in such a way that several operations, each at a different stage, could be under way at any given time). Usually, pipes are synchronous and, at periodic intervals, the operations on all the stages move simultaneously to the next, and the first stage accepts a new operation. The length of time between such moves is called the *cycle time* of the processor. To see how much speed improvement can be derived from the pipelined approach, consider a pipe with s stages that is to perform a sequence of m operations. The pipe will take s cycles to be filled and, after that, one result will come out of the pipe at the end of every cycle. If the cycle time is T, the total time to complete the m operations will be $(s + m)T$. On the other hand, if pipelining were not used, the total time required to complete the m operations using the same s stages would be smT. For m much larger than s, pipelining is then approximately s times faster than the nonpipelined version. The maximum performance of a pipelined unit is $1/T$ operations per second if it includes only one pipe. In some machines, several identical pipes are used, which allows several operations to be processed simultaneously at each stage. A functional unit with n identical pipes has a maximum performance of n/T operations per second.

The major limitation of pipelining is that most functions can be broken into only a relatively small number of stages. In fact, pipes typically have from 2 to 15 stages. This small number of stages limits the amount of parallelism that can be exploited, and therefore also limits the potential of pipelining to achieve high computing speeds independently.

ARRAY PROCESSORS

An array processor consists of a number of identical arithmetic-logic units usually called processing

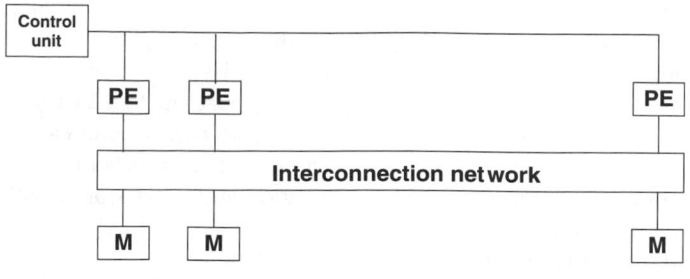

PE: Processing element
M: Memory module

Figure 4. Schematic of an array processor.

elements (PEs). The processor control unit broadcasts the commands corresponding to each instruction to all the PEs (Fig. 4). In this way, vector instructions could be executed by applying the same operation simultaneously to different (pairs of) array elements. ILLIAC IV, a machine designed at the University of Illinois by Daniel Slotnik in the late 1960s, is an early example of an array processor.

Vector supercomputers dominated in the late 1980s, but lost much popularity in the early 1990s due to the introduction of microprocessor-based multiprocessors. However, as late as 1998, new vector machines were still being introduced.

Commercially Available Machines

During the decade of the 1980s, there was an unprecedented proliferation of supercomputers, as well as a corresponding increase in the number of supercomputer manufacturers. Japan emerged during this decade as an important center of supercomputer design and manufacture (*see* COMPUTER, INDUSTRY: JAPAN). The decade of the 1990s, on the other hand, has seen the opposite trend. Many supercomputer companies have gone out of business, some before even producing a machine. Others, notably Cray Research and Convex, have been purchased by other computer manufacturers (Silicon Graphics and Hewlett-Packard, respectively). Nevertheless, despite these commercial setbacks, supercomputers are without question of great commercial importance, and several major manufacturers, such as IBM, SGI, and Sun Microsystems in the USA, and Fujitsu, Hitachi, and NEC in Japan, continue marketing and designing new supercomputers. However, due to the high cost and low demand for the very top-of-the-line systems, it is possible that custom-built supercomputers will grow in importance. A 1998 project that relies on custom-built supercomputers is the *Accelerated Strategic Computing Initiative* (ASCI)

whose main objective is to simulate nuclear weapons accurately in order to verify the safety, reliability, and performance of the USA's nuclear stockpile. Some of the most powerful supercomputers of today were custom-built for this project by Intel, IBM, and SGI.

Some important characteristics of several supercomputers are presented in Tables 1 and 2. Table 1 describes vector processor supercomputers that continue the line started in the 1970s with the Cray 1. Table 2 presents information on microprocessor-based supercomputers that have come of age in the 1990s. One of the values presented in these tables is the *theoretical peak performance*, which is the maximum number of floating-point operations that a machine can execute per second, assuming that all the floating-point units are continuously busy. This peak performance is never achieved in the execution of real-life programs, which are usually unable to fully utilize all the computational resources available in the machine. However, the theoretical peak performance can give some idea of the computational resources in the machine. The units used to measure the theoretical peak performance are *Megaflops* (millions of floating-point operations per second), *Gigaflops* (billions of floating-point operations per second), and *Teraflops* (trillions of floating-point operations per second).

Although parallelism inside the processor in the form of pipelined arithmetic units and multiple functional units is of crucial importance for all the machines in Table 1, the dramatic increase in theoretical peak performance for the machines delivered since 1995 is due to an increase in the number of processors rather than an increase in performance of individual processors. In fact, the use of the more cost-effective CMOS technology (*see* COMPUTER CIRCUITRY) since 1995 has meant longer cycle times and slower processors as a result. However, processor performance remains critical. To illustrate the importance of parallelism inside the processor, consider the NEC SX-5. Although its cycle time is 4 ns (250 MHz), each processor of the

Table 1. Characteristics of some vector processor supercomputers.

System	Year	Machine organization	Maximum no. of processors	Cycle time (ns)	Theoretical peak performance (Gigaflops)	Maximum memory size (Gigabytes)
Cray-1	1976	Uniprocessor	1	12.5	0.16	0.03125
Cyber 205	1981	Uniprocessor	1	20	0.4	N/A
Cray 2	1985	UMA	4	4.1	1.952	N/A
Fujitsu VP-400	1986	Uniprocessor	1	7.5	1.142	N/A
NEC SX-2	1986	Uniprocessor	1	6	1.3	N/A
Cray X-MP	1986	UMA	4	8.5	0.84	N/A
Cray Y-MP	1988	UMA	8	6	2.667	N/A
Hitachi S-820/80	1988	Uniprocessor	1	4	3	N/A
NEC SX-3	1991	UMA	4	2.9	22	2
Cray Research C-90	1992	UMA	16	4	16	4
Fujitsu VP2400/40	1992	UMA	4	3.2	5	2
Cray T90	1995	UMA	32	2.2	56	16
NEC SX-4	1995	UMA/NORMA	512	8	1,024	128
Fujitsu VP700	1996	NORMA	512	6.5	1,126	1,024
NEC SX-5	1998	UMA/NORMA	512	4	4,096	4,096
Cray SV1	1998	UMA/NORMA	1,024	4	1,024	1,024

N/A—Not Available.

SX-5 has a peak vector performance of 8 Gigaflops due to the 16 sets of pipelined units it contains (Fig. 5).

To accommodate the dramatic increase in the number of processors over the last few years, many recent machines in Tables 1 and 2 have been organized as clusters of UMA nodes. Memory is shared among the processors of a node, but communication between nodes is typically done using message passing. This type of organization is named UMA/NORMA in the tables. The SX-5 illustrates this mixed organization. Each UMA node of the SX-5 can contain 16 processors, and the machine can contain up to 31 nodes, illustrated in Fig. 6. Other examples of this organization are the two ASCI machines in Table 2. However, the number of processors in the UMA nodes of

Table 2. Characteristics of some microprocessor-based supercomputers.

System	Year	Machine organization	Interconnection network	CPU	Maximum no. of processors	Theoretical peak performance (Gigaflops)	Maximum memory size (MB)	Interprocessor channel bandwidth (MB/sec)
Ncube 2	1993	NORMA	N-D cube	Custom	8,192	27	32	2.22
IPSC/860	1989	NORMA	N-D cube	Intel i860	128	7.6	2	2.8
Fujitsu AP1000	1991	NORMA	2-D mesh	SPARC	1,024	12.8	16	25
Paragon XP/S	1992	NORMA	2-D mesh	Intel i860XP	2,048 (3-cpu nodes)	300	64	200
KSR-1	1992	CC-NUMA	Hierarchical ring	Custom	1,088	400	34	34
Cray T3D	1994	NC-NUMA	3D torus	DEC Alpha	2,048	307	128	300
SGI Power Challenge	1994	UMA	Bus	R10,000	36	13.68	4	N/A
HP/Convex Exemplar SPP2000X	1996	CC-NUMA	Crossbar + ring	PA-RISC	64	46.8	128	N/A
Fujitsu AP3000	1996	NORMA	2D torus	UltraSPARC	1,024	614	2,048	200
Hitachi SR2201	1996	NORMA	3D crossbar	Custom	2,048	614	2,048	300
SGI Origin 2000	1996	CC-NUMA	3D torus	R10,000	128	49.9	256	800
Intel ASCI Red	1997	UMA/NORMA	Split 2D mesh (2 x–y planes)	Pentium Pro	9,216	1,800	584	800
Cray T3E	1997	NC-NUMA	3D torus	DEC Alpha	2,048	2,400	4,096	300
IBM ASCI Blue-Pacific	1997	UMA/NORMA	Multistage network	Power PC	5,856	3,888	2,600	150
Sun Enterprise	1998	UMA	Crossbar	UltraSPARC II	64	51.2	64	N/A
Hitachi SR8000	1998	UMA/NORMA	3D crossbar	Custom	1,204	1,024	1,024	1,024

N/A—Not Available.

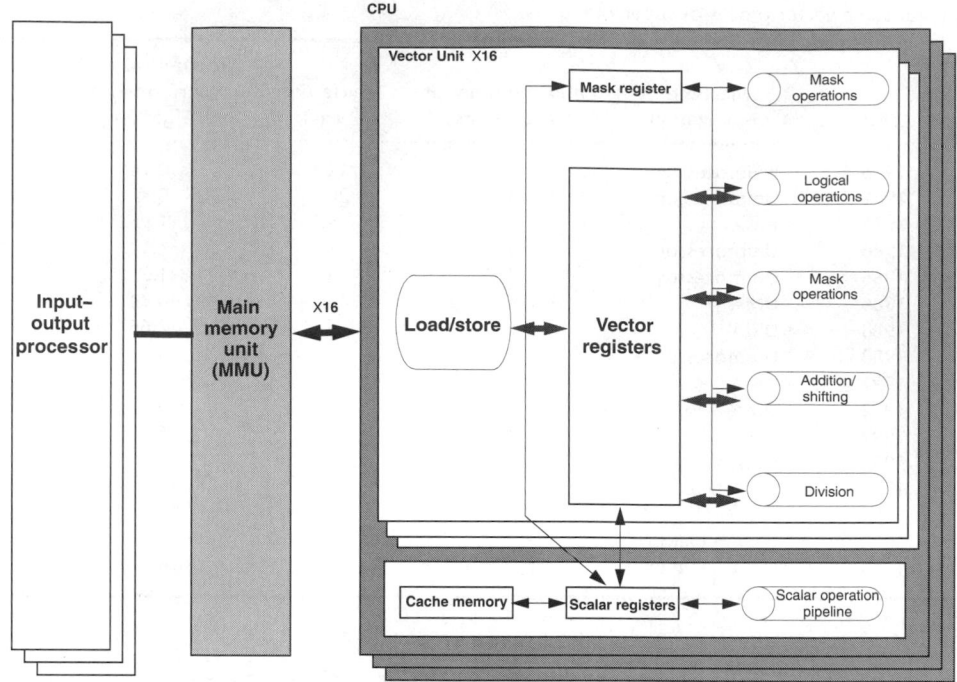

Figure 5. Internal organization of a NEC SX-5 processor.

these machines (two for the ASCI Red from Intel, and four for the ASCI Blue Pacific from IBM) are much smaller.

Programming Languages and Compilers

Supercomputers are usually programmed using conventional languages extended with parallel constructs, directives, or library routines. Parallel programming is typically done today using Fortran 90 vector extensions, OpenMP shared-memory parallelism directives, and Message Passing Interface (MPI) routines. These approaches are briefly discussed next.

Parallelism for vector processors has to be expressed in the form of vector operations. Until recently, this type of parallelism was usually expressed in Fortran 77 (*see* FORTRAN) to insure portability (*q.v.*) and to present a familiar programming environment. This forced programmers to represent vector operations as loops and to rely on *vectorizing compilers*, sometimes supported by annotations, to identify vector operations implicit in program loops. However, with the advent of Fortran 90, it became possible to express vector operations in a standard language. Fortran 90 includes vector expressions and a large number of powerful intrinsic functions for vector manipulation. The vector

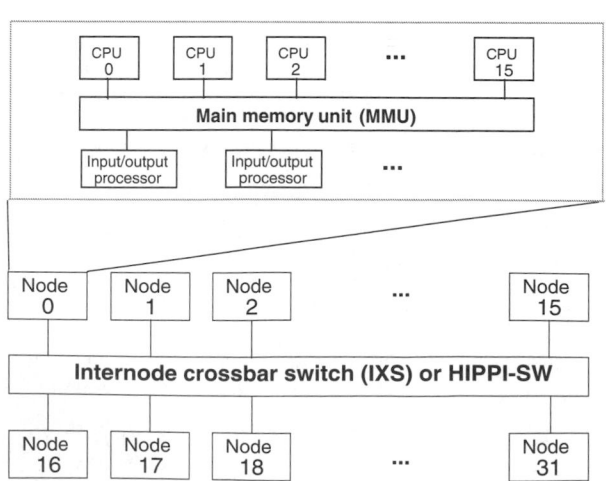

Figure 6. Overall organization of the NEC SX-5.

Figure 7. The Cray Research T3E Supercomputer.

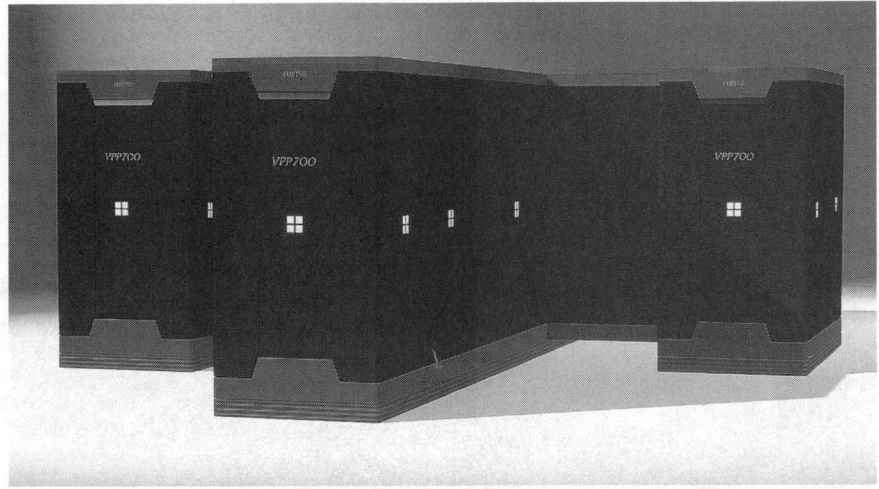

Figure 8. The Fujitsu VPP700 supercomputer with multiple processing elements.

capabilities of Fortran 90 and its successor, Fortran 95, are the culmination of a long line of vector languages that started in the 1970s when the first vector Fortran extensions were developed for the ILLIAC IV and the Texas Instruments-ASC. Another vector Fortran extension of the 1970s was VECTRAN, developed by researchers from IBM and heavily influenced by APL (*q.v.*), a vector language developed in the early 1960s by Kenneth Iverson. VECTRAN, in turn, had an important influence on Fortran 90. Today, there are Fortran 90 compilers for most vector supercomputers, including those from Cray, Hitachi, Fujitsu, and NEC.

Program parallelism for shared-memory multiprocessors is usually expressed in the form of parallel loops and threads. Although most shared-memory multiprocessor vendors have developed *parallelizing compilers* capable of automatically identifying and exploiting loop parallelism, today's parallelizing compilers are not as popular as vectorizing compilers were in the past. Most programmers now use directives to express shared-memory parallelism explicitly. Only vendor-specific directives, which precluded portability of parallel programs, were available in the past. However, in 1997, several supercomputer vendors and software houses (including SGI, IBM, Intel, and Kuck and Associates, Inc.) agreed to develop Fortran and C (*q.v.*) compilers that support a common set of parallelism directives known as OpenMP. Both loop and thread parallelism can be represented in OpenMP.

Although unstructured use of message passing in a parallel program may lead to code that is difficult to read and maintain, message-passing parallel programming is now the dominant paradigm. The most widely used message-passing libraries follow the MPI specification. The MPI standardization effort involved most current supercomputer vendors. Parallel programs written using MPI can be ported to all multiprocessor

systems regardless of whether the underlying hardware supports shared-memory or requires messages for communication. Furthermore, at least for numerical programs, it is possible to restrict the use of messages in such a way that the program is readable. Nevertheless, most would agree that the message-passing paradigm is not a very good programming model. For that reason, a Fortran extension, known as *High Performance Fortran* (HPF), was developed to facilitate the generation of message-passing code. An HPF program looks very much like a conventional Fortran 90 program except that it includes a few directives to control array alignment and distribution. These directives specify how an array that is to be processed

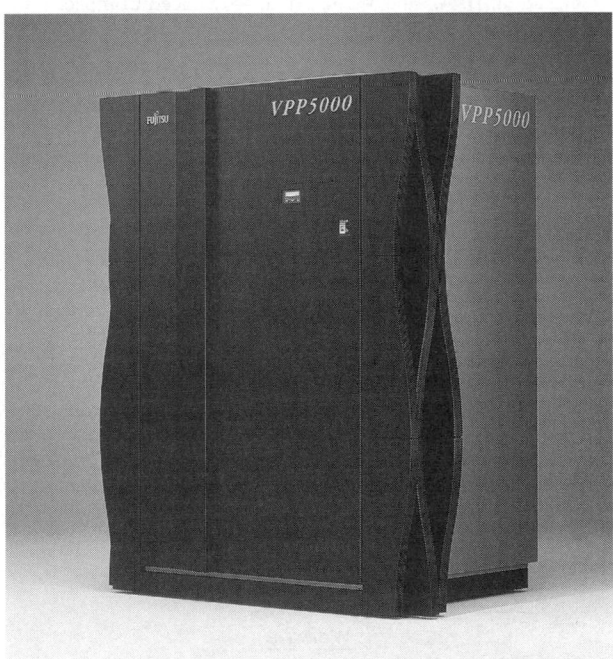

Figure 9. A single processing element Fujitsu VPP5000 supercomputer.

Figure 10. The NEC SX-5 series supercomputer.

in parallel should be broken into private arrays. Following these directives, HPF compilers generate parallel code and the necessary message operations. Although High Performance Fortran is promising, it has yet to become a mainstream language.

Bibliography

1986. Padua, D. A., and Wolfe, M. J. "Advanced Compiler Optimizations for Supercomputers." *Comm. of the ACM*, **29**, *12*, 1184–1201.

1993. Koelbel, C. H., Loveman, D. B., Schreiber, R. S., Steele Jr, G. L., and Zosel, M. E. *The High Performance Fortran Handbook*. Cambridge, MA: MIT Press.

1994. Almasi, G. S., and Gottlieb, A. *Highly Parallel Computing*. Redwood City, CA: Benjamin/Cummings.

1995. Flynn, M. J. *Computer Architecture. Pipelined and Parallel Processor Design*. Boston: Jones and Bartlett.

1995. Foster, I. T. *Designing and Building Parallel Programs. Concepts and Tools for Parallel Software Engineering*. Reading, MA: Addison-Wesley.

1996. Gropp, W., Lusk, E., and Skjellum, A. *Using MPI. Portable Parallel Progamming with the Message-Passing Interface*. Cambridge, MA: MIT Press.

1996. Kuck, D. *High Performance Computing. Challenges for Future Systems*. New York: Oxford University Press.

1997. Murray, C. J. *The Supermen: The Story of Seymour Cray and the Technical Wizards Behind the Supercomputer*. New York: John Wiley.

1998. Pfister, G. F. *In Search of Clusters*. Upper Saddle River, NJ: Prentice Hall.

Website

http://www.computer.org/paraphrase/.

David A. Padua and Jay P. Hoeflinger

SUPERCOMPUTING CENTERS

For articles on related subjects see CLUSTER COMPUTING; MULTIPROCESSING; PARALLEL PROCESSING: ARCHITECTURES; SCIENTIFIC APPLICATIONS; SCIENTIFIC VISUALIZATION; and SUPERCOMPUTERS.

In the early 1980s, the Lax Report, written by a panel convened by the US National Science Board and chaired by Peter Lax, indicated that the academic community lacked much needed high-performance computing resources. This report and other studies predicted that, unless support was given to computational science and engineering and the researchers who used such resources, science and the USA's economic competitiveness would suffer.

In 1985, therefore, Congress authorized the National Science Foundation (NSF) to establish a group of supercomputing centers, partnerships between academia, industry, and government to further research in computational science. The goal of the NSF centers was to allow researchers access to supercomputers to simulate phenomena that cannot be investigated in a laboratory. From 1985 to 1999, the four NSF supercomputing centers were joined by several dozen state- and university-sponsored supercomputing centers (see Table 1).

In response to the changing technological landscape, the NSF initiated the Partnerships for Advanced Computational Infrastructure (PACI) program in October 1997. Two of the NSF centers became the computational hubs of the new partnerships, while NSF funding for the other two was phased out over 18 months. The supercomputing centers had seen the explosive growth of the Internet, the birth of the World Wide Web, and tremendous increases in computing power. With the new PACI mission, the NSF shifted its focus from centralized facilities to nationwide partnerships, reflecting the growing importance to computational science of high-speed networking, distributed computing, and remote collaboration.

Under PACI, the National Computational Science Alliance led by the University of Illinois at Urbana-Champaign (UIUC) and the National Partnership for Advanced Computational Infrastructure led by the University of California, San Diego (UCSD), have joined dozens of research organizations across the USA in large-scale efforts to improve the technological environment available to computational scientists.

The NSF Supercomputing Centers

The NSF Supercomputing Centers program included four centers across the USA: the Cornell Theory Center at Cornell University; the National Center for Supercomputing Applications at the University of Illinois, Urbana-Champaign; the Pittsburgh Supercomputing Center at Carnegie Mellon University; and the San Diego Supercomputer Center at the University of California at San Diego. In addition to high-speed Internet links, the centers were four of the first five sites on the NSF-sponsored very-high-speed Backbone Network Service (vBNS)—the fifth site being the National Center for Atmospheric Research in Boulder, CO. The vBNS provides researchers with access to a research-only network at speeds many times faster than the typical Internet backbone—it is the initial interconnection network for Internet 2.

During 12 years of operation, tens of thousands of researchers from universities, research institutions, and industry have taken advantage of the high-performance computing resources available at the four centers. In addition to supporting the national community of computational scientists, the centers participate in various research efforts to advance enabling technologies and application tools.

Cornell Theory Center

Interdisciplinary research collaborations at the Cornell Theory Center (CTC) among academia, industry, and government have been funded by New York State, the Defense Advanced Research Projects Agency (DARPA), the National Center for Research Resources at the National Institutes of Health, IBM (*q.v.*), and other corporate partners, as well as the NSF.

CTC also participated in various research projects in addition to the center's NSF mission. The Advanced

Computing Research Institute, a joint effort with Cornell University's Computer Science Department, studied advanced architectures for scientific computation. The Computational Science and Engineering Research Group engaged in research on a variety of problems in computational science and developed new theoretical and computational methods for high-performance computing.

Following the phase-out of NSF funding, CTC continued to provide high-performance computing resources to Cornell University and New York State researchers and served the national computational biomedical community through its Parallel Processing Resource for Biomedical Scientists.

National Center for Supercomputing Applications

In addition to providing high-performance computing resources, the National Center for Supercomputing Applications (NCSA) at UIUC developed software to help users take advantage of computing resources. In 1992 the release of the network browser NCSA Mosaic provided the basis of a technology that generated the World Wide Web "gold rush" on the Internet. NCSA also created a powerful desktop-based collaborative software environment to help eliminate distance barriers for virtual teams (*see* COOPERATIVE COMPUTING).

NCSA's Virtual Environment Laboratory is one of the world's most advanced virtual reality (VR—*q.v.*) research laboratories available to academic and industrial researchers. The lab consists primarily of three projection-based modes of VR—the Computer Automatic Virtual Environment (CAVE), and the Immersa-Desk developed by the Electronic Visualization Laboratory (EVL) at the University of Illinois at Chicago, and the Infinity Wall developed by EVL in collaboration with NCSA and the University of Minnesota.

In addition to NSF funds, NCSA received support from DARPA, NASA, the DoD Modernization Program, corporate partners, the State of Illinois, and the University of Illinois. Under the PACI program, NCSA became the leading-edge site for the National Computational Science Alliance led by UIUC.

Pittsburgh Supercomputing Center

The Pittsburgh Supercomputing Center (PSC) was established in 1986 as a joint effort of Carnegie Mellon University, the University of Pittsburgh, and Westinghouse Electric Corporation, with additional funding from the National Institutes of Health and the Commonwealth of Pennsylvania.

The PSC has been a leader in developing and advancing heterogeneous computing and distributed file systems.

Table 1. Supercomputing centers: major equipment and projects (compiled by Susan Fratkin).

Center	Location	Major projects	Computing resources
Alabama Supercomputer Authority	Huntsville, AL	Computational Chemistry, Materials Science, Computational Fluid Dynamics, Structural Mechanics and Dynamics, Statewide Research and Education Network	SGI/Cray SV1, StorageTek Mass Storage, SGI Visualization Labs
Arctic Region Supercomputing Center	Fairbanks, AK	Explorations of Oceanic, Crustal, Atmospheric, & Ionospheric Phenomena, Arctic Biology and Arctic Engineering	Cray T3E900, Cray J932se, 4 VisLabs including Pyramid Systems ImmersaDesk
Arizona State University	Tempe, AZ	Support for ASU's research and computing needs	IBM RS 6000 Cluster, SGI Power Challenge, Beowulf Computing Cluster
Center for Advanced Computing Research— California Institute of Technology	Pasadena, CA	Numeric & Data Intensive Science & Engineering Applications; High Performance Networking; System Software Infrastructure	HP X2000, SGI Origin/2000, IBM SP, Beowulf Cluster, HPSS Archive
Center for Computational Sciences	Lexington, KY	Models for Engineering; Astronomical, Chemical, Physical, & Biological Systems	HP/Convex Exemplar
ORNL Center for Computational Sciences	Oak Ridge, TN	Materials Science, Analysis of Human Genome, Quantum Chromodynamics, Global Climate Modeling & Groundwater Modeling	Intel Paragon XP/S 150, XP/S 35, XP/S HPSS Archive, VisLab
Indiana University	Bloomington, IN	HPC Component & Distributed Computing Technology, Astronomy, Chemistry, QCD, VR, Bioinformatics. Support and services for HPC in a broad variety of disciplines	IBM RS/6000 SP, SGI Origin2000s, PC cluster (Linux and NT), HPSS mass storage system
Center for Research on Parallel Computation	Houston, TX	Fortran Parallel Programming Systems, Parallel Paradigm Integration, Linear Algebra, Optimization & Automatic Differentiation, Parallel Algorithms for Physical Simulations	Cray T3D, IBM SP1, Intel Paragon, Intel Touchstone Delta, SGI
Cornell Theory Center	Ithaca, NY	Biomedical Applications, Material Science, Structural Mechanics, Parallel Computing & Algorithms, Applied Mathematics	IBM SP
High Performance Computing Education and Research	Albuquerque, NM and Maui, HI	Image Processing, Remote Sensing, Modeling & Simulation, Database Applications, Benchmarking, Education, Visualization, Computational Chemistry, Computational Physics, Computational Mechanics, Cluster Computing	IBM SP2, SGI, HPSS, Linux Supercluster
Information Sciences Institute—University of Southern California	Los Angeles, CA	Distributed Computing, High-Performance Communications, Middleware, Computer Security, Parallel Tools, Data-Intensive Architecture, Visualization, Hardware Technology	IBM SP2, SGI Origin 2000, SGI Onyx 2, HP/Convex SPP-2000, SGI Visualization Lab
National Center for Atmospheric Research	Boulder, CO	Climate, Weather, Environmental & Social Impacts of Climate & Weather, Solar–Terrestrial Interactions, Atmospheric Chemistry	IBM SP/Nighthawk, SGI Origin 2000, Cray J90se, Compaq Regatta/ES40
National Center for Supercomputing Applications at UIUC	Champaign, IL	Virtual Environment Laboratory; CAVE, ImmersaDesk, & Infinity Wall, Industrial Partner & Outreach Initiatives Programs	HP/Convex Exemplar SPP-1200 & SPP-2000, SGI/Cray Origin 2000, SGI Power Challenge
National Energy Research Supercomputing Center	Berkeley, CA	Magnetic Fusion, High Energy/Nuclear Physics, Basic Energy Sciences, Health & Environmental Research	Cray T3E, Cray J90s, Cray C90
NSF Engineering Research Center for Computational Field Simulation	Starkville, MS	Computational Fluid Dynamics, Scalable Distributed Standards-Based Parallel Computing Environments, Geometry/Grid Generation, Collaborative Visualization, Integrated Simulation Environments, Data Acquisition and Microsystems, Remote Sensing	Sun Ultra HPC 10000 (64 proc.), SGI Power Challenge 10000 XL

Table 1. (*Continued*).

Center	Location	Major projects	Computing resources
National Supercomputer Center for Energy and the Environment	Las Vegas, NV	Energy Production, Impact of Human Engineered Energy Systems on Environment	Cray Y-MP, Convex, SGI Origin 2000, STK Mass Storage
North Carolina Supercomputing Center	Research Triangle Park, NC	Chemistry, Engineering, Physics, Biomedical Applications, Air Quality	Cray T916/4256, Cray 590, MCA 32-8, Cray T3 E, IBM SP2, IBM 3494 Tape Robot
Ohio Supercomputer Center	Columbus, OH	Lake Erie Weather Forecasting, Genetic Sequencing, Liquid Crystals, Medical Imaging, Coal Combustion, Aircraft Engine Performance	CRAY T94, CRAY T3E, 2 Origin 2000, Intel Cluster (133), IBM MagStar, 2 SGI ONYX-2, ImmersaDesk, SGI 540 Systems
Pittsburgh Supercomputing Center	Pittsburgh, PA	High End Computational Capability, Supporting Complex Projects in Biomedical, Materials, Environment	Cray T3E, 2 J90, DEC Turbolaser, SGI Power Challenge
Purdue University	West Lafayette, IN	Computational Geometry, Computer Graphics, Data Visualization, Multimedia, Image Analysis	IBM SP2, Intel Paragon XP/S, IBM RISC System 6000 Systems
San Diego Supercomputer Center	San Diego, CA	Molecular, Neuro-, and Earth System Sciences; Data-Intensive Computing and Metacomputing	Cray T3E, Cray T90, IBM SP2, Tera MTA, VisLab, HPSS Archive
SUNY – Buffalo Center for Computational Research	Buffalo, NY	Computational Crystallography, Computational Chemistry, Advanced Design, Computational Fluid Dynamics, Combustion, Bioinformatics	SGI Origin 2000, IBM SP, Sun Ultra5 Linux Cluster, ImmersaDesk
Supercomputer Computations Research Institute	Tallahassee, FL	Chemistry, Fluid Dynamics, Condensed Matter and High Energy Physics, Materials Sciences, Mathematical Sciences, Software Development, Structural Biology	Connection CM-2, IBM SP2, IBM RS/6000
Texas A&M University Supercomputer Center	College Station, TX	Computational Fluid Dynamics, Transition Metal Complexes and Catalysis, Structural Analysis, Climate Modeling, Visualization Sciences, Material Science, Solid State Physics, Hazardous Wastes Characterization	SGI Power Challenge 10000 XL, Cray J90, SGI Power Challenge, EMASS AML/J, SGI Origin 2000 (32 processors)
The Pennsylvania State University	University Park, PA	Computational Fluid Dynamics, Solid Modeling, Molecular Dynamics, Virtual Surgery, Climate Modeling, Combustion/ Propulsion, Materials Science, Network & Computer Resources Management	IBM SP, SGI Power Challenge, Cray J932/16, J90, IBM 3494 Tape Library, Dell Linux Clusters
University of Florida, Northeast Regional Data Center	Gainesville, FL	Quantum Physics, Imaging Science, Astronomy, Magnetic Resonance, Molecular Structure, & Brain Research	IBM 9672-R45, IBM 9672-R22, 3 IBM RS6000/SP
University of Maryland	College Park, MD	Data Intensive Computing; Earth System Science, Computational Astrophysics, Space & Plasma Physics, Fluid Dynamics	IBM SP2, DEC ALPHA Cluster, CM-5
The University of Texas Advanced Computing Center	Austin, TX	UT Center for Space Research (TOPEX/ POSEIDON/GRACE missions), Chemistry, Physics, Computational Fluid Dynamics, Subsurface Modeling, Mid-range resource center for the NSF NPACI Partnership	Cray T3E/88, Cray SV1/16, IBM SP, Origin 2000, STK/CRAY DMF Data Archive
University of Utah Center for High Performance Computing	Salt Lake City, UT	Calculating Large-Scale, Two- & Three-Dimensional Problems; Comp. Chemistry; Combustion Astrophysics; Earth Sciences; Medical & Scientific Visualization; C-SAFE (ASCI Center for the Simulation of Accidental Fires and Explosives)	72-processor IBM SP, 96-processor SGI 2000 with 8 Infinite Reality Engines, 16 Processor SUN E10000, Pentium/Linux cluster of 64 processors

A major portion of the center's resources is used for "capability" computing, that is, computationally massive, resource-intensive, and interdisciplinary projects. Many of these enabled significant scientific accomplishments in weather modeling, biomedical applications, and materials research.

PSC participated in a number of research projects related to high-performance computing. The Automated Interactive Microscope Project, a collaboration with the Center for Light Microscope Imaging and Biotechnology and the School of Computer Science at Carnegie Mellon University, extends the power of the light microscope to a dramatically new level by coupling the latest techniques for fluorescence-based light microscopy to advanced image processing (*q.v.*) and pattern recognition (*q.v.*) software running on a supercomputer. In the Grand Challenge Cosmology Consortium, a multi-institution project funded by the NSF, PSC worked to bring Grand Challenge-scale computing power to bear on fundamental questions in cosmology and make the resulting knowledge and computational methods as widely available as possible.

SAN DIEGO SUPERCOMPUTER CENTER

The San Diego Supercomputer Center (SDSC) began in 1985 on the UCSD campus, with a consortium of academic and research institutions to provide guidance to the center. Like the other centers, SDSC participated in a wide range of interdisciplinary projects. Under the PACI program, SDSC became the leading-edge site for the National Partnership for Advanced Computational Infrastructure led by UCSD.

SDSC research projects have spanned many disciplines. The Computational Center for Macromolecular Structure, a collaboration started in 1990 between SDSC, UCSD, and The Scripps Research Institute, distributed software to analyze macromolecular structures. The National Biomedical Computation Resource, an NIH-funded collaboration, developed tools for applying high-performance parallel computers to biomedical problems.

The Collaboratory for Microscopic Digital Anatomy, with the National Center for Microscopy and Imaging Research at UCSD and the Cornell Program of Computer Graphics developed a collaborative environment to increase access to specialized research equipment and sophisticated image processing, and the San Diego Bay Project assisted more than 30 federal, state, and local government agencies by developing visual, analytical, and predictive models of the bay.

The PACI Partnerships

The Partnerships for Advanced Computational Infrastructure program builds on the NSF Supercomputing Centers program and focuses on taking advantage of emerging opportunities in high-performance computing and communications. In shifting from centralized facilities to partnerships, the program will provide flexibility to adapt to evolving circumstances and to meet the need for high-end computation. PACI will continue to provide access to high-performance computing systems for the thousands of users of the supercomputing centers.

Under the PACI program, which began on 1 October 1997, two of the supercomputing centers became the leading-edge sites for two partnerships that encompass many of the leading research institutions in the country.

NATIONAL COMPUTATIONAL SCIENCE ALLIANCE

To realize the PACI mission, the University of Illinois and NCSA joined a broad range of individuals and institutions to create the National Computational Science Alliance, whose purpose is to prototype a National Technology Grid. The Grid built by the Alliance will serve as an early model for a full-scale Advanced Computational Infrastructure, which will be built by the computer, communications, and software vendors to support the USA's computational scientists and engineers in academia, industry, and government. (*See* Foster and Kesselman, 1988 and Glanz, 1998.)

To create the Grid, the Alliance will create a distributed set of computational facilities, eventually providing 10 teraflops in scalable, shared-memory computing power (*see* MULTIPROCESSING) with a consistent software environment. It will provide access to the USA's teraflop scalable supercomputer, using Intel processors and running Windows NT; build the world's first "visual supercomputer" infrastructure that couples an advanced graphical display system with parallel processing on the shared memory network of the supercomputers. It will deploy a distributed computing environment to create an integrated service consisting of distributed storage, computation, and virtual environment displays; and integrate the information management capabilities of major computing centers, providing an object–relational database user interface for building advanced environments that can support data sets in the petabyte range.

NATIONAL PARTNERSHIP FOR ADVANCED COMPUTATIONAL INFRASTRUCTURE

The National Partnership for Advanced Computational Infrastructure (NPACI) led by UCSD and SDSC teams 37 of the nation's leading academic and research institutions to revolutionize the computational infrastructure available to the nation's scientists and engineers. NPACI is developing the software infrastructure to link computers, data servers, and archival storage systems to harness the aggregate computing power. Further, NPACI has teamed applications scientists and computer scientists to support the development and application of new software and hardware techniques for improving the functionality and performance of supercomputers.

The planned NPACI infrastructure will be used to tackle currently intractable scientific and engineering problems, such as designing complex drugs to activate or deactivate a particular biochemical process. NPACI will also develop electronic environments for long-distance collaboration and more efficient delivery of electronic information.

NPACI partners will participate in deploying computing resources, developing technology and applications, and education and outreach activities. Focus areas will motivate, guide, and validate the evolution of the infrastructure. NPACI will focus initially on Molecular Science, Neuroscience, Earth Systems Science, and Engineering. Three technology areas will be pursued that are central to creating the planned computing environment: Metacomputing—forming a "virtual computer" out of a network of high-performance systems; Data-intensive Computing like weather modeling; and Interaction Environments that let researchers manipulate complex data, such as three-dimensional molecular models, in real time.

Bibliography

1998. Foster, I., and Kesselman, C. (eds.) *The Grid: Blueprint for a New Computing Infrastructure.* San Francisco: Morgan Kaufmann.
1998. Glanz, J. "Beyond 'Big Iron' in Supercomputing," *Science,* **279** (27 March), 2030–2032.

Website

http://www.computer.org/paraphrase/.

David L. Hart

SUPERCONDUCTING DEVICES

For articles on related subjects *see* COMPUTER CIRCUITRY; INTEGRATED CIRCUITRY; LIMITS OF COMPUTATION; and MICROCOMPUTER CHIP.

The Josephson tunnel junction, whose effect was predicted by Brian Josephson in 1962, typically consists of a thin insulating layer ($\sim 30\text{Å} = 3 \times 10^{-9}$ m, or about 10 atomic layers thick) sandwiched between two superconducting (zero resistance) films. When placed in suitable cryogenic environment (such as liquid helium at $4.2\,\text{K} \approx -269°\text{C}$), these junctions form the basis of ultrafast switching circuits with transitions times of picoseconds (ps) and power dissipations of less than a couple of microwatts. Such high speed and low power dissipation make the technology of Josephson junction devices a strong contender for use in the high performance systems.

The Josephson tunnel junction is characterized by two states, one of zero resistance and the other of non-zero resistance. When the junction is in the zero resistance state, an externally applied current is transported through the insulating layer, or tunnel barrier, by superconducting electrons (paired electrons) which, via a quantum mechanical tunneling mechanism, cross the barrier without resistance. If the junction is in the non-zero-resistance state, an externally applied current passes through the barrier as a normal electron tunneling current with an associated voltage drop. A current-biased (~ 1 mA) junction in the zero-resistance state can be switched to a non-zero voltage (~ 3 mV) by increasing the bias current above a particular value (the critical current) or by applying a magnetic field generated by a current in an overlying control line. The magnitudes of the current and the voltage lead to power dissipation measured in microwatts. The switching speed of ~ 1 ps is set primarily by the time required to charge the junction capacitance (measured in picofarads for devices with LSI dimensions). Josephson switching devices frequently consist of two or more junctions incorporated in a superconducting loop to form a Superconducting Quantum Interference Device (SQUID—*see* Fig. 1). In logic applications, current diverted from one SQUID as it makes a transition to a non-zero voltage state can be used to induce switching in another SQUID. Complete SQUID logic families have been successfully designed and tested.

Memory cells have also been constructed with Josephson devices. The cells rely on the phenomenon of "magnetic flux trapping," whereby a persistent circulating current can flow in a SQUID loop indefinitely with no loss of energy. Such a current can be initiated or terminated and its presence or absence can be detected by the use of Josephson junctions and SQUIDS. Again, the advantages of high speed and low power dissipation are significant.

The fabrication process for Josephson junction devices and circuits is similar in complexity to that of LSI semiconducting devices. Josephson structures are formed by multiple vacuum depositions on a silicon substrate rather than by diffusion and induced crystal growth (epitaxy), as is common with semiconductor devices. The vertical structure typically consists of a niobium groundplane followed by approximately ten layers of various metals (primarily niobium superconductors) interleaved with insulating layers (primarily silicon oxide). The most sensitive step in the fabrication process is tunnel barrier formation. A decrease of 1 Å in thickness of the barrier (nominally ~ 20 Å) leads to a typical critical current increase on the order

(a)

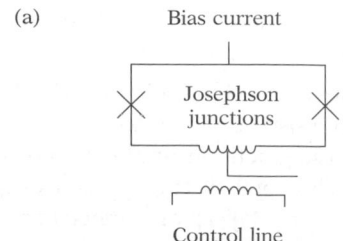

Bias current

Josephson junctions

Control line

(b)

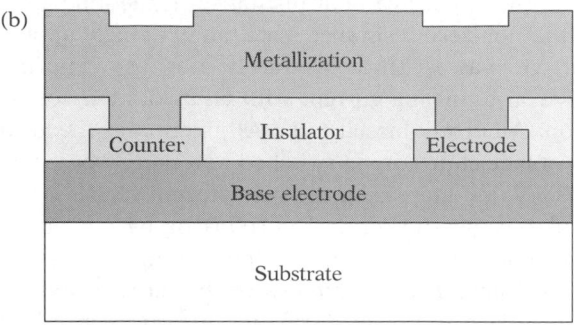

Metallization

Insulator

Counter

Electrode

Base electrode

Substrate

(c)

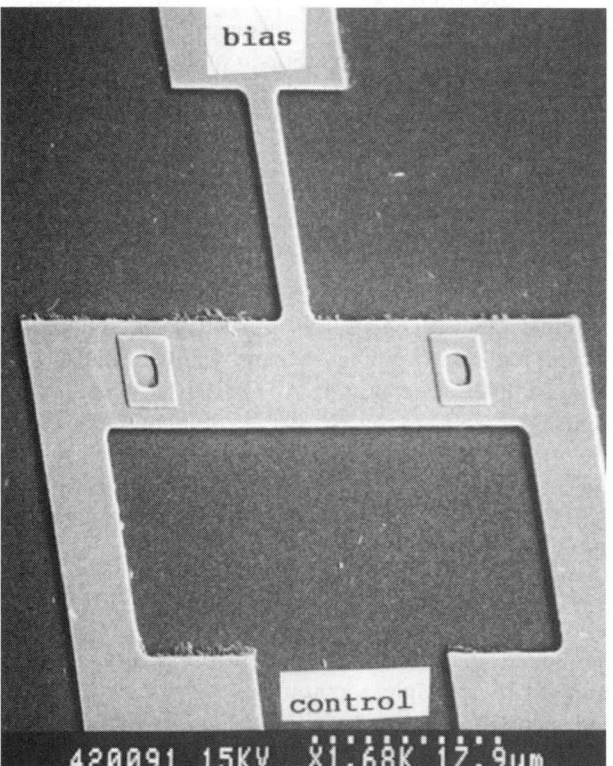

bias

control

420091 15KV X1.68K 17.9um

Figure 1. (a) Circuit diagram, (b) schematic cross-section, and (c) layout diagram of a two-junction Superconducting Quantum Interference Device (SQUID). The SQUID is normally biased in the zero-resistance state with bias current less than the critical current of the SQUID. When a current passes through the control line, it generates a magnetic field that interacts with the device and causes the SQUID to switch to a non-zero voltage. (Courtesy of HYPRES, Inc., Elmsford, NY.)

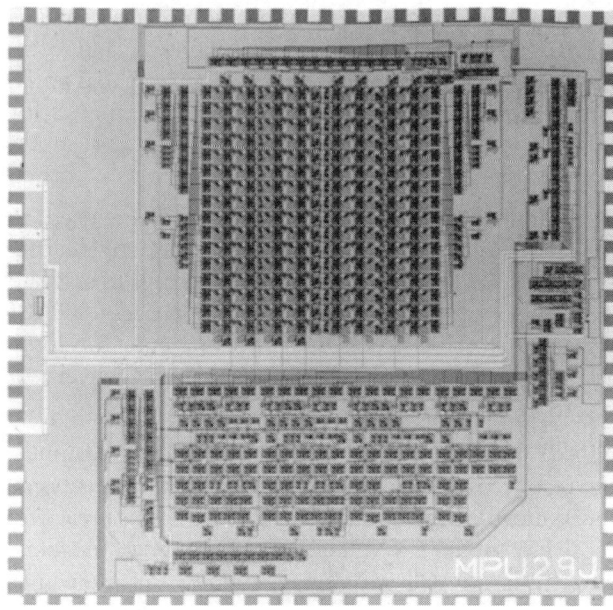

Figure 2. Photograph of a fabricated and tested digital signal processor. The die includes more than 23,000 Josephson junctions using 1.5 μm all-niobium technology. The chip has an architecture similar to a silicon-based processor and contains ALU, Multiplier, RAM, ROM, and Registers. (Courtesy of Fujitsu Limited, Atsugi, Japan.)

of 300%. The niobium used for junction electrodes is also used to make lossless transmission lines. Such lines with matched resistive terminations both serve to transport signals without loss or degradation on circuit chips and within the package in which the circuit chips are imbedded. Such chips have been fabricated and integrated into commercial systems as sampling oscilloscopes.

The primary advantages of Josephson technology arise from extremely fast switching speeds and low power dissipation. For example, the energy dissipation for the recently introduced Rapid Single Flux Quantum (RSFQ) logic family is less than 10^{-18} joules per bit. Chips cooled by natural convection in liquid helium can be packed tightly together in a three-dimensional package with lossless superconducting transmission lines for communication. A Josephson junction-based 8-bit digital signal processor has been designed and tested (Fig. 2). It performs 10^9 operations per second with only 12 mW of power dissipation at 4.2 K. For a large-scale computer based on Josephson technology, the cost of providing and maintaining the cryogenic environment will amount to a small fraction of the total cost of the machine.

For ultrahigh-performance machines, it appears that the cost of manufacturing and maintaining a Josephson computer will be similar to that for a semiconductor computer of comparable complexity. One of the major factors in determining the future of Josephson technology is the memory technology. Even though significant progress has been made in recent years in this area, improvements in the design as well as the fabrication process are necessary. The state of the art in memory technology in 1999 was a one Kb ROM with an access time of better than 400 ps and at 1.6 mW. Although much work remains to be done in these areas, the future for Josephson technology looks promising.

Bibliography

1988. Whiteley, S. R. *et al.* "Technologies for a Superconducting Sampling Oscilloscope/Time Domain Reflectometer," *Proceedings of SPIE Symposium on Advances in Semiconducting and Superconductors: Physics and Device Applications (Interconnection of High Speed and High Frequency Devices and Systems).* Newport Beach, CA, March.

1990. Aoyagi, M. *et al.* "A Josephson 10-bit Instruction 128-word ROM Unit," *IEEE Journal of Solid-State Circuits,* **25**, 971.

1990. Kotani, S. *et al.* "A 1 GOPS 8-bit Josephson Digital Signal Processor," *Proceedings of IEEE International Solid-State Circuits Conference,* February.

1995. Radparvar, M. "Superconducting Niobium and Niobium Nitride Processes for Medium Scale Applications," *Cryogenics,* **35**, 535.

1997. Likharev, K. "Superconductors Speed Up Computation," *Physics World,* **10**, 5 (7 May).

Masoud Radparvar

SUPERVISOR CALL

For articles on related subjects *see* INTERRUPT; MULTIPROGRAMMING; OPERATING SYSTEMS; and PRIVILEGED INSTRUCTION.

A typical operating system has a set of system programs, collectively known as the *supervisor*, whose function is to provide services for and to supervise the running of a number of user programs. Control goes to the supervisor every time the normal flow of processing is interrupted by a change of state in the system.

The purpose of a *supervisor call* is to provide a mechanism whereby a program can interrupt the normal flow of processing and ask the supervisor to perform a function for the program that the program either cannot or is not permitted to perform for itself.

The most typical supervisor calls have to do with input and output. In a multiprogramming system, it is essential to have system control of I/O devices, especially those devices shared by a number of programs.

Most computers that were designed for multiprogramming systems have a supervisory mode of operation and hardware *interlocks* (*q.v.*) that prevent certain supervisory operations from taking place except when the computer is operating in supervisory mode. This may be handled by means of special *privileged instructions* that can be executed only in supervisory mode, or only in some other way.

In the IBM 360/370/390 systems (*q.v.*), for example, a supervisor call is made through the execution of an instruction whose effect is to create an *interrupt* (*q.v.*). The instruction is two bytes long. The first byte is the supervisor-call instruction code, and the second byte describes the nature of the supervisor call. This second byte goes into a special register that is used in connection with all interrupts to transmit information to the system as to the status of that particular interrupt.

The interrupt now proceeds like any other interrupt. It stores the status of the computer (the old program status word) and loads a new status that gives control to a resident supervisor routine that operates in supervisor mode and whose function is the handling of supervisor calls. This routine then analyzes the second byte of the supervisor-call instruction and determines the nature of the call.

It is, of course, possible—and usually essential—that additional information is passed to the supervisory routine as a result of the supervisor call. This information may be in a *general register* (*q.v.*) or in an area of memory pointed to by a special register.

The supervisor may have resident routines for handling certain classes of supervisor calls, and may have available areas of central memory (transient areas) into which overlays can be loaded for the handling of less frequent supervisor calls. Fast response to supervisor calls is usually an important factor in system performance, and systems that have large amounts of central memory can often improve their responsiveness by increasing the number of resident supervisor-call routines.

Saul Rosen

SWAC

For articles on related subjects *see* DIGITAL COMPUTERS, HISTORY OF: EARLY; SEAC; and WILLIAMS TUBE MEMORY.

SWAC ([National Bureau of] Standards Western Automatic Computer) was dedicated in August 1950, and at that time was the fastest computer in existence. It was begun in January 1949 at the National Bureau of Standards' field station, the Institute for Numerical Analysis at the University of California at Los Angeles, and was designed and constructed under the direction of the author. Originally named the ZEPHYR, it was later renamed the SWAC to emphasize its relation to SEAC.

The SWAC was a parallel computer using a Williams tube memory (*q.v.*). The memory cycle was 16 ms consisting of an 8 ms action cycle and an 8 ms restore cycle (where some other memory location was restored). An

Figure 1. The SWAC.

addition of two 37-bit operands occurred in 64 ms, and multiplication occurred in 384 ms. Due to technical difficulties with Williams tube storage, the memory was never increased beyond 256 words. A 4,096-word magnetic drum was added to the system with coordinated addressing so that block transfers of 32 words between the two memories occurred with no latency.

Initial input and output was by typewriter and punched paper tape (*q.v.*). These were soon replaced by a card reader (240 cards per minute) and a card punch (80 cards per minute). The SWAC used a four-address command structure. A floating-point interpretive system named SWACPEC was developed, which made it much easier for users to write programs.

In 1953, the SWAC was producing about 53 hours of useful computing time per week. SWAC was used in a research computing environment, and therefore many of the problems tended to be quite large. Solution times from 177 to 453 hours are reported by Huskey *et al.* (1953). Some of the early problems included the search for Mersenne primes, the Fourier synthesis of X-ray diffraction patterns of crystals, the solution of systems of linear equations, and problems in differential equations.

When the National Bureau of Standards ceased to support the Institute for Numerical Analysis, the SWAC was transferred to the University and moved to the Engineering Building at UCLA. There it continued in useful operation until December 1967. Parts of the SWAC are now on exhibit in the Museum of Science and Industry in Los Angeles.

Bibliography

1951. Huskey, H. D. "Semiautomatic Instruction on the Zephyr," *Proceedings of a Second Symposium on Large-Scale Digital Computing Machinery*, 83–90. Cambridge, MA: Harvard University Press.

1953. Huskey, H. D., Thorensen, R., Ambrosio, B. F., and Yowell, E. C. "The SWAC—Design Features and Operating Experience," *Proceedings of the I.R.E.*, **41**, *10*, 1294–1299.

1978. National Computer Conference Pioneer Day. (Edited transcript available from the Charles Babbage Institute, Madison, WI. Also at `http://www.cbi.umn.edu/`.)

1980. Huskey, Harry D. "The National Bureau of Standards Western Automatic Computer (SWAC)," *Annals of the History of Computing*, **2**, *2*, 111–121.

Harry D. Huskey

SWAPPING

For articles on related subjects *see* MEMORY: AUXILIARY; SCHEDULING ALGORITHMS; TIME SHARING; TIME SLICE; VIRTUAL MEMORY; and WORKING SET.

Swapping is the transfer of programs or segments between main and secondary memory of a computer system. The term originated in the time-sharing systems of the early 1960s. Because there was no memory protection (*q.v.*) hardware to isolate multiple programs, these early systems permitted only one user program at a time to reside in the main memory. When a program reached the end of a time slice or stopped for I/O, the operating system exchanged it for another waiting program.

Modern operating systems use multiprogrammed virtual memory. In these systems, there are two kinds of information transfer between main and secondary memory:

1. Loading a program at the start of an execution period, and unloading it at the end of that period (called a *warm start*).

2. Fetching new pages or segments on demand during the execution period.

Swapping is often used to name the first type of information transfer, and *demand paging* the second type. The term *roll-in* is sometimes also used for loading a program, and *roll-out* for unloading.

The two types of transfer may not be used at the same time. Operating systems for personal computers, such as Windows 98 or MacOS, can be run with the virtual memory off; they then use swapping but not demand paging. Paged virtual memory systems, such as the OS/2 operating system, can start a program with an initially empty partition (called *cold start*); demand paging loads the program after the start of execution. This is not an effective use of demand paging. It is much more efficient to load and unload full working sets (*q.v.*) at the start and end of execution periods; demand paging should be used to add pages to the working set during the execution period.

Early time-sharing systems had to control the overhead of swapping. In CTSS, for example, the CPU would be idle during a swap because only one user program at a time could occupy memory. The CTSS multilevel scheduler started programs at priority levels whose quanta were at least as long as the swap time, thereby limiting to 50% CPU idle time due to swapping (Corbató *et al.*, 1962). Schedulers in modern multiprogramming systems do not give much weight to program loading because the swapping of one program occurs in parallel with the execution of another.

Bibliography

1962. Corbató, F. J., Merwin-Daggett, M., and Daley, R. C. "An Experimental Time Sharing System." *Proceedings of the Spring Joint Computer Conference 21*. In *Programming Languages and Systems* (ed. S. Rosen), 335–344. New York: McGraw-Hill (1967).
1992. Tanenbaum, A. *Modern Operating Systems*. Upper Saddle River, NJ: Prentice Hall.

Peter J. Denning

SWITCHING THEORY

For articles on related subjects *see* ARITHMETIC-LOGIC UNIT; BOOLEAN ALGEBRA; CODES; COMPUTER ARCHITECTURE; COMPUTER CIRCUITRY; DIGITAL DESIGN AUTOMATION; INTEGRATED CIRCUITRY; LOGIC DESIGN; and SEQUENTIAL MACHINE.

Switching theory is the abstract mathematical formalization used in the logic design of digital networks. It is so called because, when it was first developed by Claude Shannon (*q.v.*) in 1938, most logic networks were implemented using switches and electromechanical devices such as relays. Modern logic networks are usually constructed using electronic integrated circuits comprising networks of logical elements such as inverters, AND gates, and OR gates. These elements operate on binary signals; they are constrained to take on only two different voltage values (such as 0 or 5 volts). Switching theory uses a two-valued Boolean algebra (sometimes called *switching algebra*) as a notation to represent the operation of such logic networks. The two algebraic values are most often represented as "0" and "1," although "T" and "F" are sometimes used to emphasize the relation to propositional logic. The correspondence between the algebraic symbol used to represent a signal and the voltage present is arbitrary, although the *positive logic convention* in which the algebraic 1 represents the more positive voltage signal is now most common. Each input or output

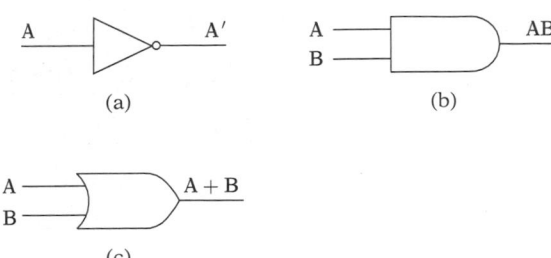

Figure 1. Elementary gate symbols: (a) inverter; (b) AND gate; (c) OR gate.

signal of a logic network is represented by a Boolean variable. Boolean algebra has three basic operations: inversion, logical addition, and logical multiplication; these operations are implemented directly by logic gates called inverters, OR gates, and AND gates. The symbols most often used to represent these gates are shown in Fig. 1. The output of an inverter always takes on the value opposite to the value of its input., The output of an OR gate is always equal to 1 unless all of its inputs are equal to 0, in which case the output is 0. The output of an AND gate is always equal to 0 unless all of its inputs are equal to 1, in which case the output is 1.

There are two classes of logic networks: *combinational networks* for which the output at any time depends only on the inputs present at the same time, and *sequential networks*, for which the output depends on past as well as present inputs.

Combinational Networks

A combinational network implements a Boolean function. Such a function can be represented by a Table of Combinations (or *truth table*) that lists all possible combinations of input values and the corresponding output values, as in Table 1(a), or by an algebraic

Table 1. An example of a Boolean function—the 2-bit multiplexer function (a) Table of Combinations (b) algebraic expressions

(a)			
x	*y*	*z*	*f(x, y, z)*
0	0	0	0
0	0	1	1
0	1	0	0
0	1	1	0
1	0	0	0
1	0	1	1
1	1	0	1
1	1	1	1

(b)

$$f(x, y, z) = xy + y'z = (x + y')(y + z)$$

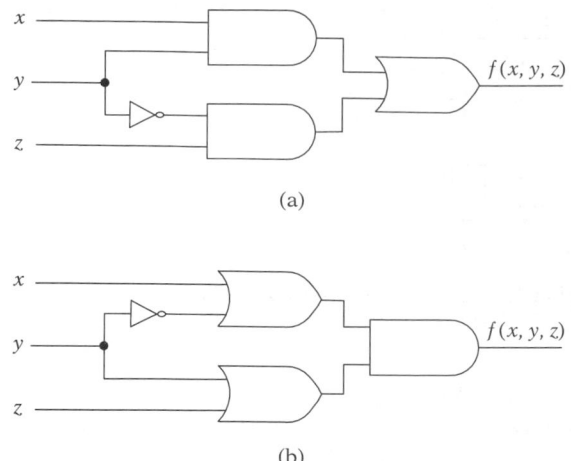

(a)

(b)

Figure 2. Logic networks that implement the function of Table 1. (a) $f(x, y, z) = xy + y'z$. (b) $f(x, y, z) = (x + y')(y + z)$.

expression, as in Table 1(b). This function is called the *2-bit multiplexer function*. Two logic networks that each implement this function are shown in Fig. 2.

ANALYSIS

Switching theory was developed to solve the two major issues of analysis and synthesis. In analysis, the Boolean function realized by a network is determined and compared with the specified function. Like many of the issues that arise in switching theory, this problem is very simple conceptually. It can be easily solved for functions of a small number of variables (up to 10) by comparing the Tables of Combinations for the network and the specification. The difficulty is that many important combinational designs have far more than 10 inputs and the time required to compare a design and its specification grows exponentially with the number of inputs. All that can be done is to invent techniques that require less computation for some of the possible Boolean functions.

Since the size of the Table of Combinations doubles for each additional input variable, other representations are needed. The most promising approach uses a binary tree called a *binary decision diagram* (BDD). In this diagram each level corresponds to one of the variables and the leaf nodes correspond to function values (0 or 1). Paths in the diagram correspond to assignments of values to the independent variables. A binary decision diagram for the 2-bit multiplexer is shown in Fig. 3.

SYNTHESIS

In synthesis, the problem is to find a network (preferably an optimum one) that realizes a given specification. There is no challenge to find a network. An algebraic expression, called the *canonical sum* or *disjunctive normal form*, is easily found for any function:

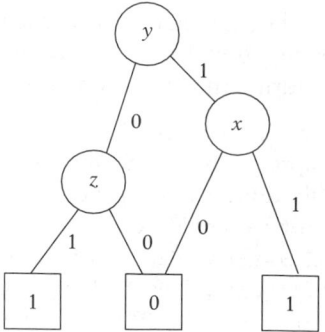

Figure 3. Binary decision diagram for the 2-bit multiplexer function.

this expression is a sum-of-products in which each product term (called a *fundamental product* or *minterm*) corresponds to a row of the Table of Combinations for which the function is equal to 1. The canonical sum for the 2-bit multiplexer function of Table 1 is: $f(x, y, z) = x'y'z + xy'z + xyz' + xyz$. The first product, $x'y'z$, corresponds to the second row of the Table of Combinations. The variables x and y are primed because the entries in this row for x and y are 0; z is unprimed since it corresponds to a 1 entry. When the input variables have the values given in the second row of the table, the first product will equal 1 and all other products will be 0. A network is easily drawn from the canonical sum: each product term is represented by an AND gate whose output is connected to an OR gate; the OR gate output is the network output (Fig. 4). Networks such as that in Fig. 4 in which there are (at most) two gates between an input signal and the output are called *two-stage networks*. Each network input is a signal representing either an input variable (such as x) or the complement of an input variable (such as x').

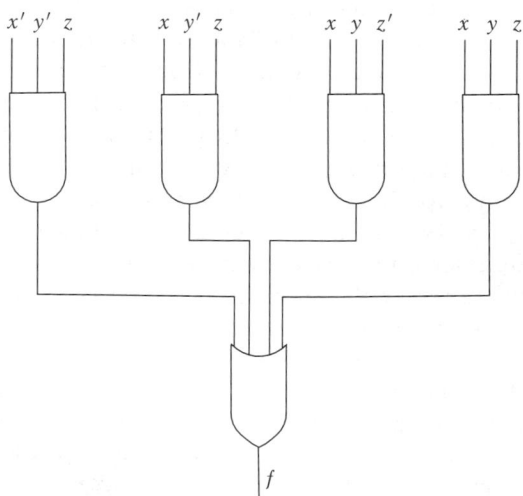

Figure 4. Network for the 2-bit multiplexer function derived from its canonical sum.

Although the canonical sum network is easily designed, it is often a very inefficient implementation—compare the networks of Figs. 2 and 4. The historical objective of switching theory is to develop techniques for synthesizing optimum networks. The first issue that arises is deciding which network characteristics to optimize. Cost usually comes first, although performance and testability are also very important. Silicon area is typically the major cost factor; it depends on which gates are required and how difficult it is to implement the required interconnections. A precise cost cannot be determined from an algebraic expression or logic network, but the total number of required gate inputs is usually a good approximation to relative cost. Most synthesis techniques attempt to minimize the gate-input count. This is done by finding an expression having the fewest possible literals (variables or complemented variables) present. Performance can be taken into account by limiting the maximum number of gates in any path from an input to an output. Testability is a more complex issue. Combinational synthesis tries to enhance testability by ensuring that there are no untestable (redundant) elements in the synthesized networks.

A canonical sum can be transformed into another expression by using the Boolean algebra theorems: $W + W = W$ and $WU + WU' = W$, in which W and U stand for arbitrary Boolean expressions. For example, in the canonical sum for the 2-bit multiplexer function

$$f(x, y, z) = x'y'z + xy'z + xyz' + xyz$$

the last two terms differ only in z, so they can be combined: $xyz' + xyz = xy$. A similar operation on the first two terms allows them to be replaced with the single product $y'z$. These operations result in a simpler expression for the 2-bit multiplexer function:

$$f(x, y, z) = y'z + xy.$$

This expression corresponds to the Fig. 2(a) network. Of all the possible sum-of-products expressions for this function, it is the one having the fewest literals. Such an expression is called a *minimal sum*. In the example just given, the theorem $W + W = W$ was not used; but for most functions this theorem is needed to find a minimal sum.

The minimal sum is a very important expression for synthesis: it corresponds directly to an efficient design for a PLA (programmable logic array) and is the starting point for many of the methods used to synthesize multistage gate networks. A minimal sum has two basic properties:

1. None of the product terms is redundant in the sense that it could be removed from the expression without changing the function represented, and

2. None of the product terms can have a literal removed without changing the function represented.

Product terms with property 2 are called *prime implicants*.

The Quine–McCluskey algorithm is a well-known procedure for finding a minimal sum for any arbitrary Boolean function. There are two parts to this algorithm: first, the two theorems just mentioned are used to find all possible prime implicants. Then, some of the prime implicants are chosen for use in forming the minimal sum. While this algorithm is straightforward, it is impractical for functions with many input variables. There are storage problems, since there can be as many as $3^n/n$ prime implicants for an n-variable function. This means that if $n = 15$, the number of prime implicants can be almost 1 million, and for $n = 20$, almost 175 million. The second step of choosing those prime implicants with which to form the minimal sum requires solving a minimum covering problem. This problem is NP-complete (*q.v.*); no algorithm is known for solving such problems faster than a running time that grows exponentially in the number of variables. This means that, for functions with more than 15 variables, it is not possible to guarantee finding a minimal sum in a reasonable time. Two approaches have been taken to handle such functions: one is to develop a procedure that will produce either a minimal sum or will not get any output in a reasonable time; and the other is to use a procedure that will always produce an output even though that output is not always a true minimal sum.

For very simple functions such as the 2-bit multiplexer function and for PLA implementations, the minimal sum produces the best design. For other technologies, such as gate networks or more complex functions, *multilevel networks*—those with more than two gates between input and output—are often more efficient. The Carry Function, $f(a, b, c) = ab + ac + bc$, is a very simple example of this situation. This sum-of-products expression corresponds to a two-stage network with nine gate inputs (Fig. 5a). This expression can be factored using the Boolean algebra theorem, $WU + WV = W(U + V)$, to form the factored expression $a(b + c) + bc$. The multistage network of Fig. 5b, with eight-gate inputs, results from this expression.

Another approach to finding efficient networks seeks to decompose the network into interconnections of subnetworks. The simple disjoint decomposition, illustrated in Fig. 6, is the most important such decomposition. Subnetwork N_1 implements the subfunction $G(x_1, x_2, \ldots, x_s)$, and subnetwork N_2 implements the subfunction $F(G, x_{s+1}, \ldots, x_n)$, which is equal to $f(x_1, x_2, \ldots, x_n)$. Not all functions can be decomposed

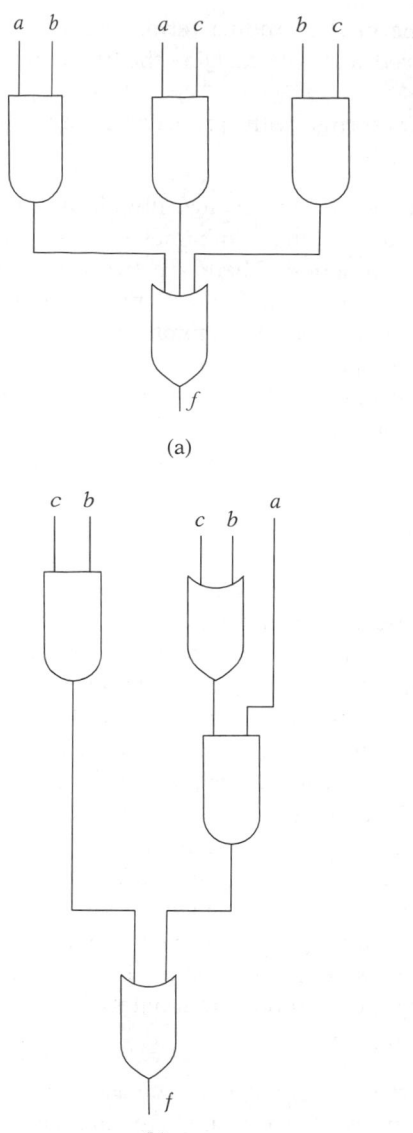

(a)

(b)

Figure 5. Two networks for the carry function. (a) Two-stage, (b) multistage.

in this fashion. Tests have been developed to check whether a given function can be realized by a network of this structure. It has been proved that most Boolean functions cannot be realized this way, but the functions used in computers are not typical and many of these functions can be decomposed effectively.

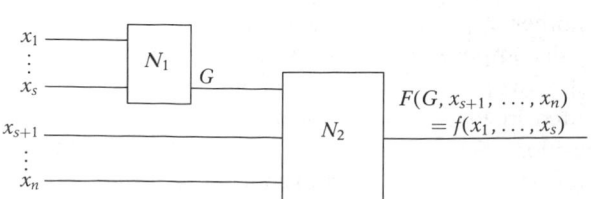

Figure 6. Simple disjoint decomposition.

Sequential Networks

The output of a sequential network depends on past as well as present inputs. Thus the network must have some internal memory, which is typically implemented with *latches* (flip-flops). These elements contain feedback loops that store signals. The stored signals constitute the *state* of the network. The most common form of sequential network is the *finite state machine*, which has one input (usually called the clock), on which pulse signals occur, while the remaining inputs have level signals. When a clock pulse occurs, the state of the machine may change to another state that is determined by the present state and the values of the remaining inputs. The network output is based on the state and the inputs.

The simplest finite state machine is the D flip-flop, which has two inputs: CK is the clock input and D is the level input (Fig. 7a). When a clock pulse occurs, the output Q becomes equal to the value at D and remains equal to this value until the next clock pulse. Clearly, there must be two states to "remember" the last D value between successive clock pulses. The operation of a finite state machine is usually described by means of a *state diagram*, a graph that has one node for each state and an edge for each transition between states. The state diagram for the D flip-flop is shown in Fig. 7b.

Synthesis of a finite state machine starts with a state diagram specification of the desired behavior. There are algorithms for checking to determine whether fewer states can be used (state minimization). After a minimum-state diagram is found, a binary encoding of the states must be chosen. The complexity of the final design depends on this encoding, but there are only heuristic (*q.v.*) procedures to choose a good encoding. Once the state encoding is fixed, the remaining steps

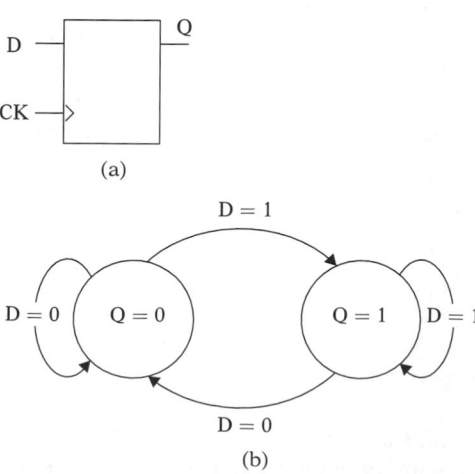

Figure 7. D flip-flop. (a) Symbol, (b) state diagram.

to complete the design are mainly combinational design problems.

With the increased power of modern design workstations, it is now possible to use switching theory synthesis techniques to carry out a major portion of the design of new computer systems.

Bibliography

1970. Kohavi, S. *Switching and Finite Automata Theory.* New York: McGraw-Hill.
1984. Brayton, R. K., Hachtel, G., McMullen, C., and Sangiovanni-Vincentelli, A. *Logic Minimization Algorithms for VLSI Synthesis.* Norwell, MA: Kluwer Academic.
1986. McCluskey, E. J. *Logic Design Principles.* Upper Saddle River, NJ: Prentice Hall.
1994. DeMicheli, G. *Synthesis and Optimization of Digital Circuits.* New York: McGraw-Hill.

Edward J. McCluskey

SYMBOL MANIPULATION

For articles on related subjects *see* AUTOMATA THEORY; COMPUTER ALGEBRA; LIST PROCESSING; STORED PROGRAM CONCEPT; and STRING PROCESSING.

The power of a modern computer derives from its being more than an arithmetic calculator. It is, in fact, a *general-purpose symbol-manipulating system.* A symbol *token* is a pattern that can be compared by an information processing system with some other symbol token and judged equal with it or different from it. The basic test for equality of tokens incorporated in an information processing system determines the fundamental alphabet of symbols it is prepared to recognize and distinguish. A symbol, then, is a class of equal tokens with respect to this basic test.

The key characteristic of symbols for an information processing system is its ability to *designate*, i.e., to have referents. This means that an information process can take a symbol token as input and use it to gain access to a referenced object in order to affect it or be affected by it in some way: to read it, modify it, build a new structure with it, and so on. Hence, four concepts are central to understanding symbol manipulation: the information processing system itself and its symbol structure, designation and representation.

Information Processing Systems

An information processing system (IPS) is a system (Fig. 1) consisting of a memory containing symbol structures, a processor, effectors, and receptors. Leaving out of account the effectors and receptors, we can summarize the characteristics of an IPS in this way:

1. There is a set of elements, called *symbols*.

2. Symbols may be formed into symbol structures by means of a set of *relations*.

3. There is a *memory*, capable of storing and retaining symbol structures.

4. There is a set of *information processes* that take symbol structures as inputs and produce symbol structure outputs.

5. The IPS has a component, the *processor*, that consists of (a) an ability to execute a set of *elementary information processes* (EIPs); (b) *short-term memory* (STM) that holds the input and output symbol structures of the EIPs; and (c) an *interpreter* that determines the sequence of EIPs to be executed by the IPS as a function of the symbol structures in STM.

SYMBOL STRUCTURES

We say that a symbol structure *designates* (or *references*, or *points to*) an object if there exist information processes that admit the symbol structure as input, and either: (1) affect the object; or (2) produce, as output, symbol structures that are affected by the object.

A symbol structure serves as a *program (q.v.)* if the object it designates is an information process, and the

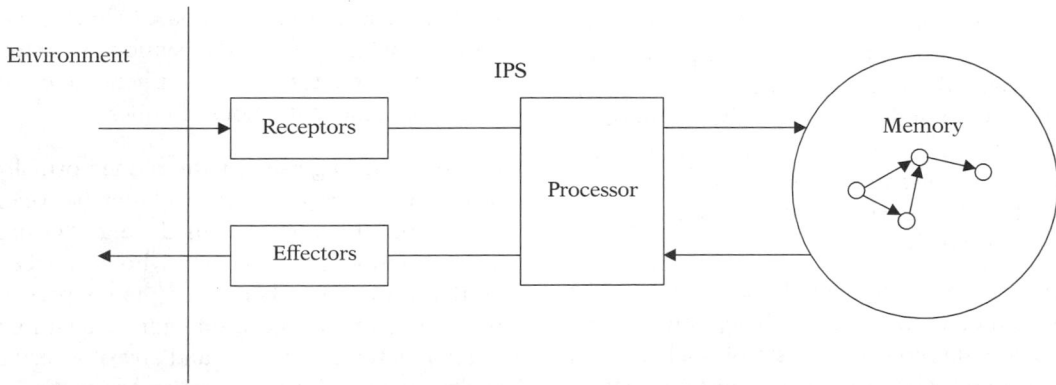

Figure 1. General structure of an information processing system. (From Newell and Simon, 1972.)

interpreter, if given the program, can execute the designated process.

A symbol is *primitive* if its designation is fixed by the elementary information processes or by the external environment of the IPS.

The "objects" that symbols designate may include symbol structures stored in the IPS memories (data structures (*q.v.*) and programs), processes that the IPS is capable of executing, or objects in an external environment of sensible (readable) stimuli. To *read* is to create in memory internal symbol structures (representations) that designate external stimuli; to write is to create responses in the external environment that are designated by internal symbol structures.

The relation between a designated symbol and its object may have any degree of directness or indirectness. A structure can point to a structure that points to a structure that points to . . . .

Example
The meaning of these concepts can be illustrated by an example. An IPS for receiving Morse Code will have to be able to perceive the basic external stimuli: dots, dashes, letter spaces, and word spaces. These stimuli could be represented internally by two different primitive symbol types, say "·" and "−", together with conventions for representing letters as lists of primitive symbols, and words as lists of letters. Sequences of stimuli could be represented by ordered sets (*lists*) of primitive tokens. Thus, if the external stimulus were a sequence of three dashes followed by a letter space, the read process might store the symbol structure $(-,-,-)$, the ")" representing the letter space.

In turn, each of these simple symbol structures would be assigned a *name*—i.e. a designating symbol. The structure $(-,-,-)$, for example, might be designated by S. Then, larger structures could be built up as lists of such naming symbols (e.g. (W, A, S), and so on indefinitely.

There would exist an elementary information process to find the member of a list next to a given member. Thus, given the token A and the list (W, A, S), this process would find the symbol token S. Another elementary process would test pairs of symbols for identity, to determine the equality, for example, of the second symbols of the lists (W, A, S) and (H, A, S), respectively.

The elementary processes would also have symbolic names, which could then be combined into composite processes, designated by lists of such names, thus allowing an arbitrary complex subroutine structure. For example, the process for testing symbol

identity could be combined with the process for finding the next symbol on a list to test whether two lists are identical.

To execute composite processes, the IPS could use an interpretive process. A symbol structure (the program) would designate the sequence of elementary processes to be executed. The interpreter would keep track of the current elementary process being executed, and after execution would find the next process to be executed.

Finally, additional information could be associated with the symbol structures. With the list (W, A, S) might be associated the descriptors—part of speech (verb) and tense (past)—the two pairs con-stituting a description of the list. There would then be additional elementary processes to obtain the descriptions, given the list.

These postulates for an IPS are entirely abstract, making no assertions about how the structures and processes are realized, whether physically or biologically. Digital computers are physical systems that fit this abstraction; some psychologists, though not all, believe that the human cognitive system is also an information processing system in the sense of these postulates. There are also differences in points of view about the degree of seriality or parallelism of the processing in the human system. These questions cannot be settled conclusively on the basis of the evidence now available, although there has been steady progress in modeling human thinking, particularly with serial symbolic systems, over a continually broadening range of cognitive tasks, including, for example, chess playing, scientific discovery and abstract and representational drawing and painting.

DESIGNATION

It would be more correct to say that symbol *structures* designate than to say that *symbols* designate. For example, if an information process takes as input the symbol structure (color, houseA) and produces the symbol "white," then the symbol structure (color, houseA) designates *white*, and hence indirectly designates the color of the house in question.

In discussing linguistic matters, one normally takes as prototypic of designation the relation between a proper name and the object named—e.g. "George Washington" and a particular man who was once President of the USA. One then attempts to pass from that relation to others more difficult to envision: e.g. the relation between "house" and any of a certain class of sheltering structures, and so on to "truth," "beauty," and "justice."

Any discussion of the basic characteristics of symbols and symbol structures always assumes the existence of information processes for acting on those symbols and structures. Each of the components, as is typical in abstract systems, remains essentially undefined, except when taken in conjunction with the other parts. Thus, the concept of *list* is inextricably mingled with the concept of a process for finding the *next* item on a list—i.e. for responding to the ordering relation that defines the list.

Some symbols have their meaning fixed by the existence of elementary information processes that treat them in fixed ways. The most important examples are:

1. Symbols that designate specific external events or structures (e.g. internal representations of real characters).

2. Symbols that designate elementary information processes, so that these EIPs can be executed when these symbols call for the execution.

The collection of symbols that is primitive for a specific IPS varies with the particular application. For example, for purposes of visual pattern recognition, the primitive symbols might be set up to correspond, more or less approximately, to the elementary discriminations of which the retina is capable, and it is usual in such applications to describe the sensory input as a two-dimensional array of intensities. Similarly, an information processing theory of speech recognition might take as primitive symbols the elementary features that are postulated to define phonemes. In applications where sensory discrimination is not the central concern, it may be more convenient to omit pattern recognition at this elementary level and to take encodings of familiar configurations of sensory objects as the alphabet of primitive symbols. Thus, for particular applications, letters of the alphabet, or even whole words, might be taken as primitive symbols. An important consequence of taking letters as primitive symbols is that we cannot then speak of one pair of letters as more closely resembling each other than another pair. There is no notion of degree of difference or similarity among them.

REPRESENTATION

A simple example has already shown how primitive symbols can be combined into lists and descriptions. A couple of additional examples will illustrate the wide range of representations that can be accommodated by these means. In storing chess information, the pieces can be designated by symbols that have descriptions—defining each piece's type (King, Queen, Rook, etc.), color, and position on the board. Squares can also be represented as described symbols whose descriptions include information about the geometry of the board, i.e. which squares adjoin them. A position, in this representation, is a symbol structure that associates with each square the symbol of the piece occupying that square, if any, and which identifies the adjacent squares in various directions.

A somewhat different representation might be suitable for expressions from symbolic logic; e.g. $(P \vee Q) \cdot (Q \supset R)$. This expression can be represented by just this list of symbols, including parentheses. The expression can also be represented by a list structure, whose main list is $(\cdot, A, B)$, where A is the symbol that designates the list $(\vee, P, Q)$, and B the symbol that designates the list $(\supset, Q, R)$. Alternatively, making use of the relations of left (for left subexpression) and right (for right subexpression), the same logic expression could be represented as a tree structure (Fig. 2). Yet another representation of the expression uses descriptions. Take as attributes *term, connective, left,* and *right,* and as symbols a number of nodes, $x1, x2, \ldots$ Then the

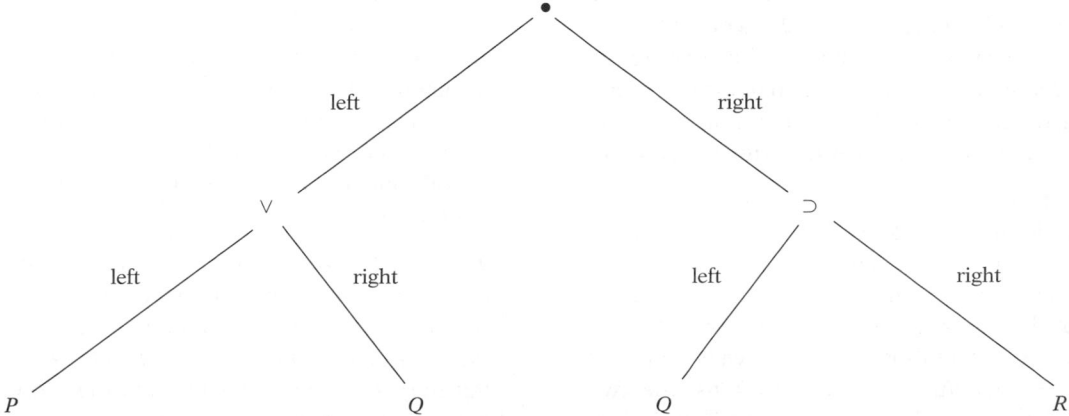

Figure 2. Tree structure for $(P \vee Q) \cdot (Q \supset R)$. (From Newell and Simon, 1972.)

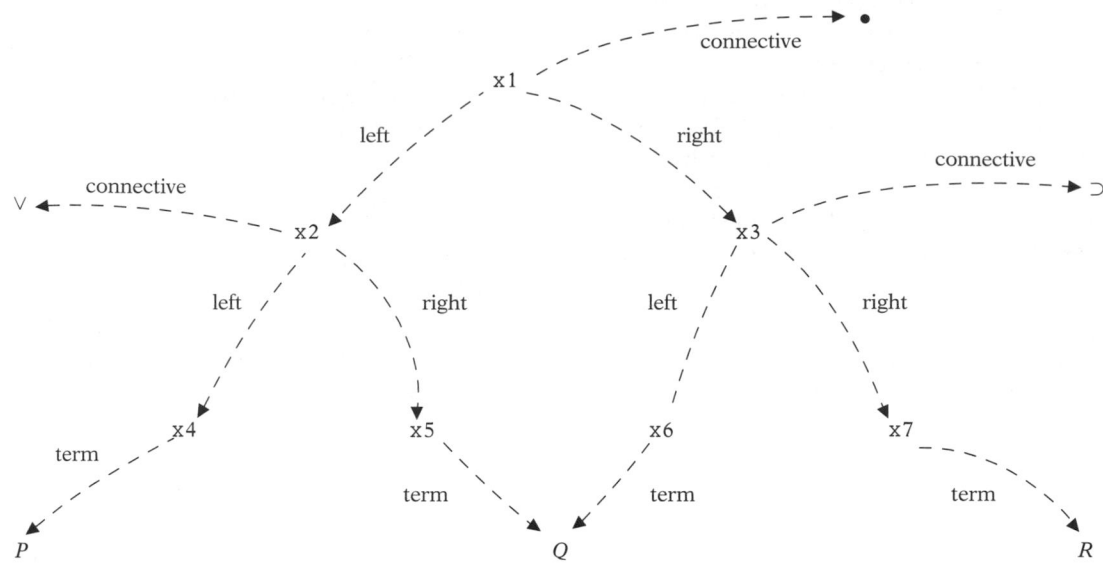

Figure 3. Association structure for $(P \lor Q) \cdot (Q \supset R)$. (From Newell and Simon, 1972.)

logic expression could be represented as the following set of descriptions:

connective($x1$) = ·	left($x1$) = $x2$	right($x1$) = $x3$
connective($x2$) = $\lor$	left($x2$) = $x4$	right($x2$) = $x5$
connective($x3$) = $\supset$	left($x3$) = $x6$	right($x3$) = $x7$
term($x4$) = P		
term($x5$) = Q		
term($x6$) = Q		
term($x7$) = R		

These associations can be represented pictorially, as in Fig. 3. All of these representations are very closely related. That there are many ways of representing something should not be surprising. We could give still others, e.g. Polish prefix notation (*see* POLISH NOTATION). All that is needed for a representation is some scheme of associations (relations) together with a set of information processes that can extract the appropriate information about connections. It is not usually possible to tell from its output exactly what internal representation is being used by an IPS, especially when alternate representations are as isomorphic as those presented here. However, in other cases, particularly in representing problems, the choice of representation can have striking observable consequences for external behavior.

If too limited a repertory of symbol structures and designations is provided by an IPS, the encoding of complex information can become an exercise in virtuosity that yields little benefit of any other kind. It appears that the structures essential to provide appropriate direct representation of a very wide range of stimuli are list structures and descriptions, the two types of structures we have used extensively in our examples. Other types of structure may be needed

occasionally, but these two types are the core of the representational capability used in most information processing systems.

Elementary Information Processes

There must be a sufficiently general and powerful collection of elementary information processes to extract from them all the macroscopic performances of the IPS. Furthermore, it is essential that these elementary processes be well defined so that they are realizable by known mechanisms. It is one of the major foundation stones of computer science that a relatively small set of elementary processes suffices to produce the full generality of information processing. On the other hand, there is no *unique* basis. However, all alternative schemes do incorporate certain fundamental types of EIPs that constitute a sufficient basic set. (Proof of their sufficiency is somewhat more involved.) Among these types are the following:

1. *Discrimination.* It must be possible for the system to behave in alternative ways, depending on what symbol structures are in its STM. Furthermore, the behavior needs to be *arbitrarily* alterable; i.e. transfer of control to an independent program must be possible.

2. *Tests and comparisons.* It must be possible to determine that two symbol tokens do or do not belong to the same symbol type. Comparisons are often directly coupled with conditional behavior, but they may equally well lead to the production of a conventional symbol (e.g. *true* or *false*) that can later be discriminated.

3. *Symbol creation.* It must be possible to create new symbols and set them to designate specified symbol structures. Again, this process must be performable arbitrarily; i.e. whenever a new symbol is desired, it can be created, but it should carry no meaning other than its designation of the specified symbol structure. Whether the system must also be able to destroy symbols depends primarily on whether memory capacity is limited.

4. *Writing symbol structures.* It must be possible to create a new symbol structure, copy an existing symbol structure, and modify an existing symbol structure, either by changing or deleting symbol tokens belonging to the structure or by appending new tokens with specified relations to the structure.

5. *Reading and writing externally.* It must be possible to designate stimuli received from the external environment by means of internal symbols or symbol structures, and to produce external responses as a function of internal symbol structures that designate these responses.

6. *Designating symbol structures.* It must be possible to designate various parts of any given symbol structure, and to obtain designations of other parts, as a function of given parts and relations. Again, this may be achieved in many ways, but there must not be any parts of symbol structures that are in principle inaccessible.

7. *Storing symbol structures.* It must be possible to remember a symbol structure for later use, by storing it in the memory and retrieving it at any arbitrary time via a symbol structure that designates it. How much memory is available, of course, conditions strongly how complex the totality of stored structures may be. The memory must be highly reliable over time.

Even the earliest stored-program computers essentially met these requirements for an information processing system. The abstract characterization of a system such as that outlined here was developed in close relation with the invention and application of list processing and string manipulation languages, particularly in the domains of artificial intelligence (*q.v.*), computer algebra, computer simulation (*q.v.*) of human cognitive processes, machine translation (*q.v.*) of language, and the design and construction of compilers. These applications make little use of the computer as a rapid arithmetic calculator, and depend basically upon its generality as a system for manipulating symbols.

Interaction with Environment

Progress in scene recognition and language recognition through visual and auditory sense organs has led to a rapid development of robotic (*q.v.*) symbol systems having substantial capabilities for interpretation of sensory information and its coordination with motor capabilities: including steering motor vehicles on highways at high speed, harvesting alfalfa, and playing robot soccer.

Source Information

This article is drawn in large part from pages 20–30 of Newell and Simon (1972). For a formal approach to symbol manipulation see Chapter 2 of Knuth (1997). Descriptions of two widely used list-processing languages illustrating many of the concepts discussed in this article can be found in Cooper and Wogrin (1988) and Jones, Maynard and Stewart (1989).

Bibliography

1972. Newell, A., and Simon, H. A. *Human Problem Solving.* Upper Saddle River, NJ: Prentice Hall.
1988. Cooper, T., and Wogrin, N. *Rule-based Programming with OPS5.* San Francisco: Morgan Kaufmann.
1989. Jones, R., Maynard, C., and Stewart, I. *The Art of Lisp Programming.* New York: Springer-Verlag.
1997. Knuth, D. E. *The Art of Computer Programming*, Vol. 1, 3rd Ed. Reading, MA: Addison-Wesley.

Allen Newell and Herbert A. Simon

SYMBOLIC MATHEMATICS

See COMPUTER ALGEBRA.

SYNCHRONOUS/ASYNCHRONOUS OPERATION

For articles on related subjects *see* CONCURRENT PROGRAMMING; CYCLE STEALING; CYCLE TIME; HANDSHAKING; INPUT/OUTPUT OPERATIONS; MULTIPLEXING; PETRI NET; and PROTOCOL.

The flow of information within a digital network may be said to be either *synchronous* or *asynchronous*. In the case of synchronous operation, a transfer of data from one point to another is assumed to occur within a fixed time interval known to both the sending and receiving devices. The sender and receiver are synchronized by a signal called the *clock*, which may be supplied externally to both, or generated by the sender with the data, and occasionally incorporated within it, but often sent on a separate signal line. In the case of asynchronous operation, the sending device or circuit need have no knowledge of the time-scale on which the receiver (and intervening connection) operates, but rather transmits its data with a "data ready" signal and then awaits a reply to the signal sent. Upon receipt of the reply by the sender, it removes its original data and status signal from the line, often (but not necessarily) waiting for the removal of the reply by the sender before proceeding with a second transfer.

The distinction between synchronous and asynchronous operation extends over an extremely broad range of digital design. It can apply to the logic gate and flip-flop level, to the logic unit interconnect level, to the bus transfer level, to the I/O device transfer level, and even to the level of communication with remote systems.

At the logic design level, the synchronous design technique is most straightforward and, accordingly, the most common. It is characterized by a cascade of alternating levels of combinational logic gates and synchronizing flip-flops driven by a common system clock. The system remains synchronized provided that the total worst-case propagation delay through the combinational logic, from one flip-flop level to the next, is less than the interval between consecutive clock events. Accordingly, in synchronous logic designs, it is usual practice to "capture" the state of the external environment by incorporating clocked flip-flops at the inputs, where, by means of the clock, a snapshot of the input is taken for processing. While the input sampling rate and internal clock rate are the same, the resulting process is essentially the one called *pipelining* in the context of large systems designs. In smaller-scale applications, the input sampling rate is usually at a small fraction of the clock rate of the internal logic, since the limited amount of hardware must be used in a succession of tasks between each input sample.

It is usual that the external inputs to a logic device are not inherently synchronized and thus may be said (causally) to be asynchronous. For example, the time at which an operator presses a button to signal a modified operation is quite random. As indicated previously, one approach is to synchronize such inputs by sampling them under control of the logic clock. However, it is possible to deal with them directly using logic operating in an asynchronous mode.

In asynchronous operation, the flip-flops used are of the simple unclocked reset–set (RS) kind, which wait in readiness for a gating event. Often, the event is directly applied. For example, the RS flip-flop used with mechanical single pole, single throw (SPST) input pushbuttons and switches to *debounce* them (i.e. to mask the intermittent connection provided by switch contact for a short time after its operation) is operating asynchronously; there is no clock; the flip-flop simply changes state upon the first transient contact of the bouncing switch element with its ultimate resting place.

Generally, in asynchronous logic design, a large network of race-free combinational logic, in which the

possibility of a transiently incorrect output (*glitch*) has been eliminated through care in the design of signal paths, may precede each RS storage element. A signal change at the input of this network is propagated to the flip-flop as fast as is possible at the actual speed of propagation of the intervening gates. While, for this part of the operation, no detailed knowledge is needed of the actual timing characteristics of the gates, it is quite difficult to know that gating is complete. Clearly, an estimate can be made from the specified worst-case propagation delays of all intervening gates.

On the larger systems level, synchronous and asynchronous operation are well illustrated by the signaling protocols that characterize both internal and external bus (*q.v.*) communications. Interestingly, one finds a synchronous protocol for links that are either very, very short or very, very long. The former choice is made when the environment is well controlled and the maximum delay assumptions underlying synchronism can be made. The latter choice applies when the cost of waiting in an asynchronous exchange is thought to be too great.

Fig. 1 illustrates the synchronous exchange of data between two devices, the sender acting as master (M) and the receiver acting as slave (S). (The letters M and S at the right edge of the waveforms in Figs. 1 and 2 indicate the association device to be either master or slave.) The bus clock is common to both. At t_1, the master transmits the address of the slave, I/O mode information for control of the slave, and data (if any). The clock falling at t_2 signals the slave(s) to look at the bus and accept data (if sent) or send data (if required). The interval t_1 to t_2 allows for the time of signal propagation in the drivers (*q.v.*), the line, and the receivers, as well as its variability (*skew*). At t_3, data, if requested by the master and sent by the slave, is gated into the master. The interval from t_2 to the following t_1 insures settling of the bus prior to the next cycle.

When a bus is very long and serves many devices of different characteristics, the time required to handle a

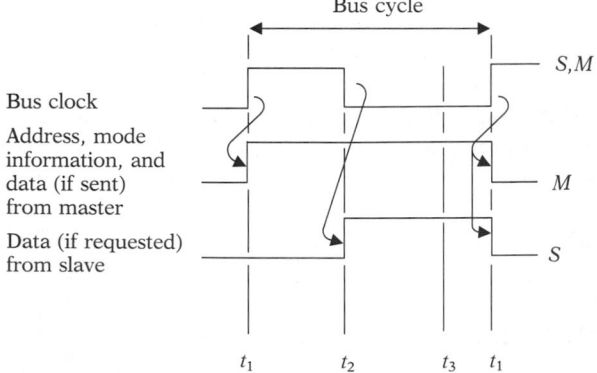

Figure 1. Timing of data exchange between master and slave on a synchronous bus under common clock control.

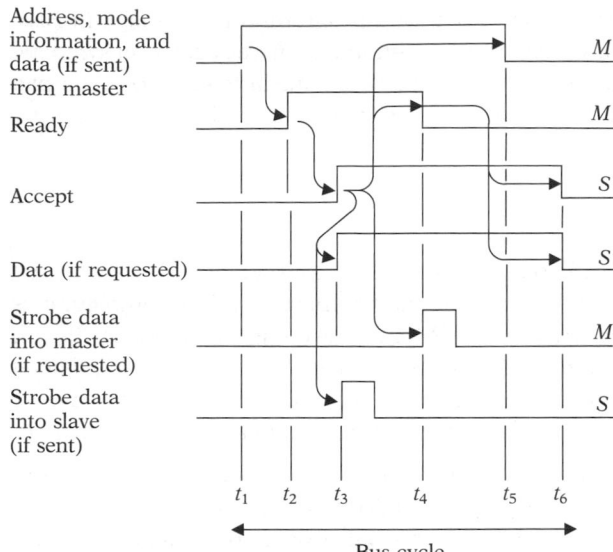

Address, mode
information, and
data (if sent)
from master

Ready

Accept

Data (if requested)

Strobe data
into master
(if requested)

Strobe data
into slave
(if sent)

t_1 t_2 t_3 t_4 t_5 t_6

Bus cycle

Figure 2. Timing of data exchange between master and slave on an asynchronous bus with handshake control.

given device may be highly variable. However, if the synchronous protocol is used, all must go as slow as the slowest. This problem is avoided with asynchronous operation, as indicated in Fig. 2. Here, one device, the master (M) initiates the process at t_1 (having checked that the bus is not busy by noting that Ready and Accept lines are low), sending address, mode and data (if any) to the slave (S). Later, to allow for bus skew (the propagation time difference between signals on two lines), the master raises Ready at t_2, which signal propagates to all slaves. One, recognizing its address (indicated to be valid by Ready) at t_3, takes in (*strobes*) the data (if sent) or sends data (if requested) and raises the signal Accept. Subsequently, at t_4, having noted Accept and allowed for bus skew, the master strobes data from the slave (if requested) and lowers Ready. However, to insure correct operation of the slave while Ready is high in the presence of bus skew, the Master waits until t_5 to remove the Address and Control information. Meanwhile, the slave, having sensed the fall of Ready, removes Accept and Data (if any) at t_6, preparing the bus for a new cycle. In systems in which the role of master is not fixed, another control line, called Busy, is used to prevent the use of the bus by another (third) device connected to it. In simple systems, such conflict cannot occur, since slave devices do not "speak unless spoken to."

For links of greater length, particularly between major components of a machine (such as CPU and memory, or CPU and disk) or between two machines (CPU and CPU), asynchronous operation tends to dominate, since the Ready–Accept exchange can compensate for both transmission uncertainties as well as for busy

states, etc., of one of the participating machines. However, as links lengthen, transmission time looms larger. Accordingly, for transmission at a distance, the message enlarges from a byte or two to a great many bytes. Within the message, the operation is synchronous, although the initiation and completion of the message as a whole remains asynchronous in nature. In the limit, for large distances, the asynchronous element virtually disappears. The situation may be likened to that of sending a telex. A message is sent with the assumption of availability of the recipient. If the receiver gets a garbled message, a repeat is requested. If no response at all is received by the sender, the message is sent again. These messages, while illustrating synchronism within themselves (i.e. locally), are embedded in a system that is asynchronous overall (i.e. globally).

Another important example of a combination of synchronous and asynchronous techniques occurs in the start–stop codes used in serial communications protocols such as the IEEE RS-232 protocol for computer serial ports. Transmission commences with one bit to signal the start bit, followed by the 0 and 1 bits of a serial code. When the bit string is complete (at the end of eight data bits for seven-bit ASCII), one or two "1" bits are sent, the *stop bits*, which signal to the receiver that a complete character has been sent, while preparing the line for the next transmission.

Bibliography

1996. Hamacher, V. C., Vranesic, Z. G., and Zaky, S. G. *Computer Organization*, 4th Ed. New York: McGraw-Hill.

Kenneth C. Smith

SYNTAX, SEMANTICS, AND PRAGMATICS

> For articles on related subjects *see* BACKUS–NAUR FORM; FORMAL LANGUAGES; GRAMMARS; LANGUAGE PROCESSORS; PROGRAMMING LANGUAGES; PROGRAMMING LANGUAGE SEMANTICS; and PROGRAMMING LINGUISTICS.

Every language is characterized by having both form (*syntax*) and meaning (*semantics* and *pragmatics*). The syntax of a natural language (one used for human communication) is generally referred to as its *grammar*, and this terminology has been extended to the specification of the syntax of programming languages as well.

The syntax of a language is a set of rules specifying which of its expressions are grammatically acceptable. For example, if a simple English sentence is specified to have the grammar

noun phrase   verb phrase

and a *noun phrase* is composed of an *article* followed by a *noun*, while a verb phrase is defined to be a *verb* followed by a *noun phrase*, we may see that the sentence

"The cat drank the milk."

is a syntactically correct English sentence, since the word "the" is in the class of *articles*, "cat" and "milk" are *nouns*, and "drank" is a *verb*.

Natural languages can have syntactic ambiguity. A prepositional phrase may modify either a noun or a verb, allowing two ways to read

"Mary saw John with a telescope."

(who had the telescope?). Ambiguous sentences have multiple semantic meanings (what the sentence is about). It is also possible for a syntactically correct sentence to have no (literal) meaning. The sentence

"The milk drank the cat."

is syntactically correct but literally meaningless, since cats are not liquid and milk is not capable of drinking, though it may have metaphorical meaning (the cat fell into a vat of milk).

In addition to being about some state of affairs (the semantic meaning), a sentence may have *pragmatic* meaning, sometimes called the *speaker's meaning*. The pragmatic meaning of a spoken or written sentence is what it is intended to convey or accomplish. If I exclaim "Your house is on fire!", and my neighbor replies "Hot, isn't it!", I would judge that the semantic meaning of the sentence was grasped, but not its pragmatic meaning.

Much humor depends on syntactic or semantic ambiguity, or on disparities between semantic and pragmatic meaning; these are part of what makes a natural language a rich symbolic system. The sentence

The box is in the pen

could be about a shelter in an animal's pen, or about the spy's fountain pen within which a tiny box is hidden. The sentence, "The door is on your left" could be factual, or could also be a request to get out. Philosophers and linguists have studied the complex relationships between semantics and pragmatics; *see* Grice (1991) for a recent discussion.

Programming languages, however, are not languages for two-way communication between human and machine, but only for encoding program instructions. They are not intended to convey multiple meanings or to permit metaphor. They do, however, still have syntax, semantics, and pragmatics, in part because as well as embodying instructions for computers, they have a secondary role as a human communication medium.

The specification of a programming language in BNF or other formal notation eliminates nearly all syntactic ambiguities. One that remains in Pascal, for example, is the *dangling* `else`. In

```
if C1 then
    if C2 then
        S1
    else S2
```

the Pascal grammar does not specify with which "`if`" the "`else`" should be matched. This ambiguity is resolved by a rule for Pascal compilers: associate it with the most recent `if` not matched by an `else`. All such syntactic ambiguities are resolved either by a rule or *ad hoc* when a programming language is implemented.

Programming language semantics also has little room for ambiguity. Put informally, the semantics of a language construct is what it does to the state of a program when it executes; an assignment statement, for example, changes a value in a storage cell. Language specifications frequently leave certain details explicitly unspecified, however, to allow implementations to be done efficiently on different architectures. For example, in evaluating a function expression like `f(x,y)`, the order in which x and y are evaluated is often unspecified. If the evaluation of x has a side effect (*q.v.*) that changes y, then the expression may have different semantics on different systems—one of several reasons for avoiding such side effects.

By analogy with natural language, pragmatic meaning is what a statement in a programming language is meant to accomplish in a program. For example, the C++ statement

```
mySalary = 2 * mySalary;
```

has the semantics of any assignment statement, but assuming that the variable name is appropriately chosen, the effect of the statement is to double the representation of my salary in that program, and if the program has print statements in it, perhaps to give me a larger paycheck. Pragmatic meaning is conveyed clearly in a program when it is well documented—when the names of program objects reflect their functions and when the documentation (*q.v.*) explains the purpose of each part. In such cases, the semantics of the program will reflect its pragmatics.

Bibliography

1991. Grice, H. P. *Studies in the Ways of Words*. Cambridge, MA: Harvard University Press.

David Hemmendinger

SYSTEMS ANALYST

For articles on related subjects *see* ADMINISTRATIVE APPLICATIONS; PERSONNEL IN THE COMPUTER FIELD; and PROGRAMMER.

The title *systems analyst* is most often applied to those who investigate, analyze, design, install, and evaluate information systems. Systems analysts first appeared in significant numbers in the 1940s, when the organization now called the Association for Systems Management (ASM) was formed.

Currently, systems analysts are usually located in or near the computer function in an organization. It is most common to find them in a project development department that reports to the Director of Information Systems. Less commonly, systems analysis and design is decentralized into the functional areas (e.g. marketing or finance) that process information.

The systems analyst needs to be competent as a communicator, a technician, and a business generalist. Communication skills needed are oral, written, and interpersonal. These include persuasive skills, the ability to be effective in leading and attending meetings, and supervisory skills. Technical skills include fact gathering, identification of information needs, feasibility analysis, equipment evaluation, and systems design. As a business generalist, the analyst needs to know the several business functional areas, the company, and the industry. Since systems analysts usually work in teams, the skill deficiencies of one team member may be compensated for by others.

The tasks performed by systems analysts and programmers are similar in that analysts program and programmers analyze. The main difference is in the frequency with which the tasks are performed. The tasks that differentiate the two occupations are shown below.

Tasks frequently done by a programmer/infrequently by a systems analyst

◆ Translate detailed flowcharts into programs

◆ Maintain program

◆ Debug or test

◆ Prepare test data

◆ Prepare operational instructions

Tasks frequently done by a systems analyst/infrequently by a programmer

◆ Define requirements

◆ Prepare functional specifications

◆ Prepare system specifications

◆ Prepare systems flowcharts

◆ Design forms and reports

◆ Design data items

◆ Define data organization

◆ Define systems calculations

Systems analysis is a rapidly growing occupation. A degree in business with an information systems emphasis is the preferred education. Some firms hire systems analysts, while others promote from programming or user areas. A growing number of organizations are now requiring masters' level education.

Some organizations choose to combine the jobs of systems analyst and programmer and use the title *programmer-analyst*. Others split the systems analyst job into administrative systems analyst and computer systems analyst. These differences, plus the use of the same or a similar job title for engineers and economists, make it difficult to infer competencies from the job title alone.

Bibliography

1975. Willoughby, T. C., and Senn, J. *Business Systems.* Cleveland: Association for Systems Management.

1997. Whitten, J. L., Bentley, L. D., and Dittman, K. C. *Systems Analysis and Design Methods.* Homewood, IL: Richard D. Irwin.

1998. Lejk, M., and Deeks, D. *Introduction to Systems Analysis Techniques.* Upper Saddle River, NJ: Prentice Hall.

Theodore C. Willoughby

SYSTEMS PROGRAMMING

For articles on related subjects *see* ASSEMBLER; COMPILER; CROSS ASSEMBLERS AND COMPILERS; DEBUGGING; DISTRIBUTED SYSTEMS; LINKERS AND LOADERS; MACHINE AND ASSEMBLY LANGUAGE PROGRAMMING; OBJECT PROGRAM; and OPERATING SYSTEMS.

Systems programming is concerned with the operating systems, utility programs, and library software needed to keep computer systems running smoothly. Unlike traditional areas of computer science, such as compilers, algorithms (*q.v.*), or data structures (*q.v.*), the topics included in systems programming are less focused and more diverse. In short, systems programming can be described as the glue that ties together a machine's hardware, its operating system, support utilities such as compilers, editors, and debuggers, and other aspects of proper day-to-day computer operation.

Using its most general definition, systems programming is practiced by all those who write or maintain systems software, in contradistinction to those who practice applications programming (*q.v.*). Thus most systems programmers work for large software development companies such as Adobe, Symantec, or Microsoft (*q.v.*). But this article focuses on the individual (or small group of) systems programmers who keep the computers at user application sites running.

In traditional large computing centers, systems programming involves three job categories. *System operators* (Sys Ops) are concerned with the nuts-and-bolts issues of keeping machines running, rebooting machines that crash, performing file system backups, running special jobs, mounting tapes, and so forth. *Systems programmers* focus on such software aspects as installing new releases of application and operating systems software or porting software to a new machine, while *systems analysts* (*q.v.*) focus on planning and managing growth, finding and eliminating performance bottlenecks, and improving overall throughput (*q.v.*) and response time. With the increasing prevalence of smaller systems or networked personal computers and workstations (*q.v.*), the three tasks may fall on a single systems programmer, which we assume to be the case in the following discussion.

A *systems programmer* is thus a handyperson whose overall responsibility is to keep machines and software running properly so that other computer users can get their work done. Those users, whether using or writing applications software, expect their computers to function properly. Most users operate at a high level, not knowing or caring to know low-level details of the systems they use. They work on specific application development projects, or use a small set of software utilities, such as spreadsheets (*q.v.*) or word processors (*q.v.*), on a regular basis.

In practice, keeping a computer system operating smoothly requires constant attention. New releases of software utilities and operating systems must be installed; hardware devices fail and require servicing; machines crash; errant programs consume excessive amounts of system resources, such as disk space, memory, or processing time, etc. It is the system programmer's task to insure that the software and hardware of a computer system function properly for its users and that systems resources are allocated fairly among them.

Historically, systems programmers tended to know one system particularly well, reflecting a time when computers were expensive and a site was likely to have only one or two machines. Today, most sites support a range of computers, from personal computers and workstations (*q.v.*) to mainframes (*q.v.*) and supercomputers (*q.v.*). The principal systems programmer's responsibility is that all machines function properly, and that they can communicate with one another across networks. For example, to reduce costs through sharing, printers and disks may be concentrated on a subset of the available machines, with individual machines accessing the resources across a network (*see* CLIENT–SERVER COMPUTING and FILE SERVER).

Systems programming begins with a basic understanding of the architecture of the machines in use because some software problems can be resolved only with an understanding of the underlying hardware. From a programmer's perspective, software that works correctly on one machine may crash on another. Although compilers can reduce the likelihood of such errors and debuggers can help pinpoint them, the recognition of such errors requires familiarity with the hardware.

Systems programming also requires basic knowledge of operating system principles, as well as specific information about the local operating system in use. The operating system *kernel* (*q.v.*) controls access to all hardware resources and defines the protection mechanism used to prevent processes created by one user from interfering with another. In addition, the operating system provides access to the file system, defining how files can be created, accessed, and destroyed; how the files of one user are protected from unauthorized access by another; or how a subset of users can share files protected from access by general users. Finally, the operating system supports and controls access to many services, such as accessing network devices, accessing tape drives, and using special printers and plotters.

With the increased variety of machine configurations, many sites need to tailor the operating system kernel to match their local configuration of peripheral devices. For example, some sites have more disk drives than others, or may use those supplied by different manufacturers. In addition, the actual job may influence kernel parameters. If a system runs programs that require a large virtual memory (*q.v.*), additional swapping (*q.v.*) space may need to be added to the system, or existing space may need to be distributed among multiple devices to reduce contention for backing store, thereby reducing latencies (access times—*q.v.*).

In addition to the operating system kernel itself, computer systems include a set of software libraries and utility programs. Some utilities help support proper system administration, such as programs that perform file system backups, read and write tapes, repair corrupted file systems, display system activity, and create or delete user accounts. Other utilities, such as editors, compilers, mail processing software, and word processors, are oriented towards end users. In either case, systems programmers use them during the course of their work, and must be able to locate, verify, and possibly fix problems related to their use.

When a user has problems with a particular utility or application, the systems programmer is often consulted for advice. The first step in locating the cause of the problem is to identify the system component causing the problem. The problem could be with the utility itself, with one of the system-supplied library routines, with the operating system, or with obtaining necessary resources (e.g. memory) to run the program. The systems programmer must be sufficiently familiar with each of these areas in order to isolate the problem. If the problem is with the program itself, a debugger would be used to obtain more information. In the early days of computing, debugging programs was an especially difficult task. Often, a dump (*q.v.*) of the program's memory contents was all that was available. More recently, interactive debuggers allow a user to set *breakpoints* at arbitrary statements in their program. When the program reaches a breakpoint, the debugger suspends the program and allows the user to display the contents of active variables by their symbolic names. Likewise, when a program error terminates the program, the debugger allows interactive inspection of its data structures, from which the high-level cause of the problem can be ascertained.

Compilers translate high-level programs into assembler language or directly into machine language. *Assemblers*, in turn, translate assembly language programs into object files, and a *linker* combines object files into a single executable load module. Because of their dependence on the underlying hardware and operating system, the creation and maintenance of assemblers, linkers, and loaders belongs to the realm of systems programming.

The availability of low-cost workstations and personal computers has led to the development of *distributed computing*. One of the most common applications of distributed computing—electronic mail (*q.v.*)—allows a user on one machine to send mail ("email") to someone having an account on another. One challenging aspect of systems programming is the configuration and maintenance of networked systems. Adding a new machine to the network requires configuring it into the local system, including the assignment of a low-level network address and a user-friendly name by which email users can refer to it. In addition, support software, such as name servers and file servers, may need to have the new machine registered with them so that existing machines can determine how to communicate with the new one.

A basic understanding of computer networks (*q.v.*) helps in the maintenance of systems in a distributed environment. The machines of various vendors may be unable to interoperate properly because one or the other (or both) fails to adhere to the appropriate protocol (*q.v.*) specification precisely. If each vendor blames the other, the systems programmer may be forced to locate the offender, perhaps with the aid of a network monitor and a description of the protocol specification.

In addition to networked systems, the availability and proliferation of low-cost computers has produced several interesting challenges for systems programmers.

First, because users prefer consistent environments, it is often necessary to install the same version of a software program on multiple machines. With the plethora of machine architectures and operating systems, porting an application from one system to another may pose difficulties (*see* SOFTWARE PORTABILITY). Applications may use a subtle operating system feature, or a compiler for one architecture may accept a slightly different language dialect than the compiler for another. Moreover, existing compilers are often modified to generate code for a new architecture, and some of its more advanced features, such as a code optimizer, may not generate correct code in all cases. The systems programmer must be prepared to recognize these potential pitfalls and take corresponding action.

Distributed and parallel processing (*q.v.*) systems pose special problems for systems programmers. Maintaining a system frequently requires that the programmer be able to monitor its state. The state of a distributed or parallel system, which has many activities going on at once, is difficult to observe, and sometimes difficult even to define precisely. Utilities and management tools for operating such systems are only beginning to become available, and to date they do not make the task easy.

Although most users make use of compilers, editors, and other tools, a systems programmer generally needs to have a more detailed understanding of such tools. The more information systems programmers have about a system, the better they are able to improve its performance.

Bibliography

1990. Beck, L. L. *Systems Software: An Introduction to Systems Programming.* Reading, MA: Addison-Wesley.
1996. Oney, W. *Systems Programming for Windows 95.* Redmond, WA: Microsoft Press.
1997. Clarke, D. L., and Merusi, D. E. *System Software Programming: The Way Things Work.* Upper Saddle River: Prentice Hall.

Thomas Narten

SYSTOLIC ARRAY

For articles on related subjects *see* PARALLEL PROCESSING; PIPELINE; and SUPERCOMPUTERS.

Systolic arrays are a family of parallel computer architectures capable of using a very large number of processors simultaneously for important computations in applications such as scientific computing and signal processing. This article gives a general description of systolic arrays, illustrates the idea by two simple examples, lists some applicable computations, and describes fine-grain interprocessor communication in systolic arrays.

General Description

Systolic arrays are suited for processing repetitive computations. Although this kind of computation usually requires a great deal of computing power, such computations are highly regular and parallelizable. The systolic array architecture exploits this regularity and parallelism to deliver the required computational speed.

In a systolic array, all processing elements, called *systolic cells*, perform computations simultaneously, while data, such as initial inputs, partial results, and final outputs, is being passed from cell to cell. When partial results are moved between cells, they are computed over these cells in a pipeline fashion. In this case, the computation of each single output is partitioned over these cells. This contrasts to other parallel architectures based on data partitioning, for which the computation of each output is computed solely on one single processor.

When a systolic array is in operation, computing at cells, communication between cells and input from and output to the outside world all take place at the same time to achieve high performance. This is analogous to the circulatory system; data is "pulsed" through all cells where it is processed.

Being able to perform many operations simultaneously is just one of the many advantages of systolic arrays. Other advantages include modular expandability of the cell array, simple and regular data and control flows, simple and uniform cells, efficient fault-tolerant schemes, and nearest-neighbor data communications. These properties are highly desirable for VLSI (Very Large-Scale Integration) implementations. Indeed, the advances in VLSI technology have been a major motivation for much interest in systolic arrays.

Two Systolic Array Examples

For illustration, consider first a simple systolic array for implementing a finite impulse response (FIR) filter. Given inputs x_i and weights w_j, the filtering problem is to compute outputs y_i, defined by $y_i = w_1 x_i + w_2 x_{i+1} + \cdots + w_k x_{i+k-1}$. Fig. 1 depicts a one-dimensional systolic array for a FIR filter with $k = 3$ weights, each of which is preloaded into a cell.

During computation, both partial results for y_i and inputs x_i flow from left to right, where the former

move twice as fast as the latter. More precisely, each x_i stays inside every cell it passes for one additional cycle, and thus each x_i takes twice as long to march through the array as does a y_i. One can check that each y_i, initialized to zero before entering the leftmost cell, is able to accumulate all its terms while marching to the right. For example, y_1 accumulates $w_3 x_3$, $w_2 x_2$, and $w_1 x_1$ in three consecutive cycles at the leftmost, middle, and rightmost cells, respectively.

Note that, although each output y is computed using several inputs x and several weights w, and each input and each weight is used in computing several outputs, the systolic array described here uses no "global" communication. More precisely, data communication at each cycle is always between adjacent cells.

Fig. 2 illustrates another systolic array. This is a two-dimensional array capable of performing matrix multiplication, $C = A \times B$ for 3×3 matrices $A = (a_{ij})$, $B = (b_{ij})$ and $C = (c_{ij})$. As indicated, entries in A and B are shifted into the array from left and top, respectively. It is easy to see that the c_{ij} at each cell can accumulate all its terms $a_{i1} b_{1j}$, $a_{i2} b_{2j}$, and $a_{i3} b_{3j}$ while A and B march across the systolic array.

Scope of Applicable Computations

A large number of systolic array designs have been developed and used to perform a broad range of computations. In fact, recent advances in theory and software have allowed some of these systolic arrays to be derived automatically. The following is a representative list of computations for which systolic designs exist:

◆ *Signal and image processing*—Digital filters, convolution and correlation, discrete Fourier transform, fast Fourier transform (FFT—*q.v.*), encoding/decoding for compression (*see* DATA COMPRESSION)

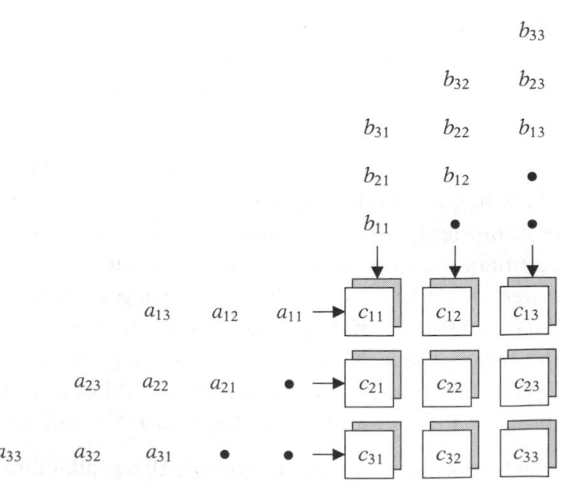

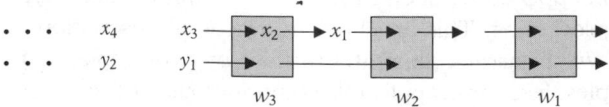

Figure 1. One-dimensional systolic array for implementing FIR filter.

Figure 2. Two-dimensional systolic array for matrix multiplication.

and error-correction (*see* ERROR CORRECTING AND DETECTING CODE), etc.

◆ *Matrix arithmetic*—Matrix multiplication, solution of linear systems of equations, solution of Toeplitz linear systems, QR-decomposition, least-squares computation, singular value decomposition, eigenvalue computation, etc. (*see* NUMERICAL ANALYSIS).

◆ *Polynomial and multiple precision integer arithmetic*—Multiplication, division, greatest common divisor, etc.

◆ *Nonnumeric applications*—Searching (*q.v.*), sorting (*q.v.*), pattern matching, regular language recognition, dynamic programming, relational database (*q.v.*) operations such as join and intersection, data structures (*q.v.*) such as priority queues, and graph and geometric algorithms such as minimum spanning trees, convex hull calculations, etc.

Fine-Grain Communication in Systolic Arrays

In a systolic array, each cell processes a data word immediately after it arrives, and sends out a data word immediately after it is processed. Therefore, the unit of communication is a single word. This contrasts to the classic message-passing communication, where the unit of communication is an entire message, which typically consists of a large number of words. Thus, supporting this fine-grain communication, also called *systolic communication*, is a unique architectural feature of a systolic array computer.

To support systolic communication, each cell in a systolic array allows its CPU to access the input and output ports directly, in addition to the local memory. This differs from message-passing machines for which each processor can access only its local memory. Fig. 3 illustrates the difference.

Summary

Systolic arrays are an effective parallel architecture for a wide range of computations that are repetitive in nature. By using fine-grain communication, the architecture can use a large number of processors simultaneously. Moreover, systolic arrays have a simple and regular design, so their implementations are relatively easy. As software and hardware technologies continue to advance to allow efficient systolic designs or programs to be derived automatically and routinely, and to allow very large systolic arrays to be implemented inexpensively, widespread use of systolic arrays can be expected in solving many computationally demanding problems.

Systolic array:

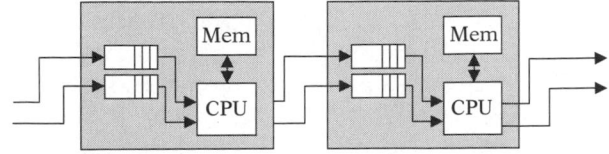

Message-passing machine:

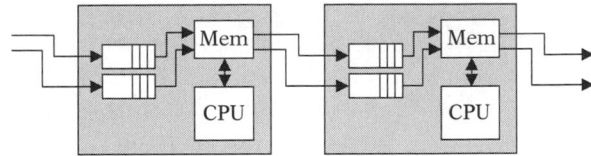

Figure 3. Comparing a systolic array with a message-passing machine.

Bibliography

1990. Lang, T., and Moreno, J. H. "Matrix Computations on Systolic-type Meshes," *Computer*, **23**, *4* (April), 32–51. Begins with an excellent tutorial on systolic parallel processing.

1990. Dostie, A. J., Seidman, S. B., and Clessas, A. C. "Systolic Computing on Transputer Networks," *Proceedings of North American Transputer Users Group*, Durham, SC, October 1989, 123–137. Amsterdams: IOS.

1991. Quinton, P., Robert, Y., and Craig, I. *Systolic Algorithms & Architectures*. Upper Saddle River, NJ; Prentice Hall.

1991. Evans, D. J. (ed.) *Systolic Algorithms*. London: Gordon & Breach.

1992. Gruska, J. *Systolic Computation*. New York: Springer-Verlag.

1992. Megson, G. M. *An Introduction to Systolic Algorithm Design*. Oxford: Oxford Science Publications.

1992. Moreno, J. H., and Lang, T. *Matrix Computations on Systolic-Type Arrays*. New York: Kluwer-Academic Press.

1993. Petkov, N. *Systolic Parallel Processing*. Amsterdam: North-Holland.

H. T. Kung

TASK

See JOB; and MULTITASKING.

TCP/IP

> For articles on related subjects *see* ETHERNET; GATEWAY; INTERNET; NETWORK PROTOCOLS; OPEN SYSTEMS INTERCONNECTION; PACKET SWITCHING; and SYNCHRONOUS/ ASYNCHRONOUS OPERATION.

TCP/IP is an abbreviation for two protocols within the Internet Protocol Suite (IPS). The abbreviations stand for "Transmission Control Protocol" (historically, the "P" stood for "Program") and "Internet Protocol." These are the protocols which allow transport of information from one "host" (*q.v.*) to another (i.e. from one end to the other of a connection) and were developed in the mid-1970s in order to provide connection between Arpanet and other networks being developed (e.g. SATNET) since the original Arpanet protocols were only relevant to a single network. IPS is the name of the suite of protocols used on the Internet. In functionality, the IPS protocols are similar to the Open Systems Interconnection (OSI) protocols (ISO/IEC 7498) and, indeed, it is feasible to run the higher level OSI protocols over the lower level IPS protocols (TCP/IP) by means of a simple interface described in Internet RFC (Request for Comments) 1006. TCP/IP was provided as the main communications protocol for computers using the Unix (*q.v.*) operating system (and variations) but is now available on a wide range of computers, especially personal computers (PCs). The various pro-

tocols are defined in Internet RFCs; those which are recognized as IAB (Internet Architecture Board) official standards are defined as such and are published in an RFC which is regularly updated (as of September 1999 the version is RFC 2500, June 1999). This document includes other relevant information.

This article covers the entire Internet Protocol Suite with particular emphasis on TCP/IP. The main protocols which comprise IPS are file transfer (FTP), electronic mail (SMTP, including multimedia extensions, MIME), virtual terminal and remote login (TELNET and rlogin), name lookup (DNS), routing (RIP, OSPF, etc.), network management (SNMP), and the Network File System (NFS).

Transmission Control Protocol (RFC 793)

TCP provides a reliable end-to-end connection across one or more computer networks and runs over the Internet Protocol. It provides a full-duplex (simultaneous two-way) link between a *socket* on the source computer system and a socket on the destination one (a socket appears to applications in the host computer in a very similar way to other input–output devices). A socket has a globally unique identifier consisting of the IP address (see below) of the computer plus a "port" number, assigned by the host computer. In order to overcome the requirement for all port numbers to be published (especially since they may be assigned dynamically), a set of port numbers is reserved, each for a different protocol. A connection is made to the "well-known socket" for each required service.

In order to provide a reliable service, TCP must implement services such as flow control, sequencing, error checking, acknowledgments and retransmission. It also provides facilities such as multiplexing (*q.v.*).

In many cases, there is no requirement for a connection-oriented protocol with the attendant overheads of setting up and clearing down a connection so a simpler, connectionless, protocol has been developed.

User Datagram Protocol (RFC 768)

This operates at the same level as TCP but is connectionless. It is used by other protocols such as the Domain Name Server (DNS) and the Simple Network Management Protocol (SNMP) where the reliability of TCP is not required.

Internet Protocol (RFC 791)

As mentioned, IP is intended to provide communications over a number of interconnected networks which are likely to implement different technologies; it corresponds to the OSI Network Protocol (ISO/IEC 8473: 1994).

It is a *connectionless packet-switched protocol*, which means that its data is broken up into blocks of data (called "packets"), each of which contains the source and destination addresses. IP does not itself provide facilities for error recovery or sequencing, so it is the responsibility of the destination to provide such facilities. IP packets may be duplicated or discarded (although the various errors are less likely on modern, relatively error-free networks than on early networks).

Each system which uses the Internet Protocol has an address (the IP address) and a name (the domain name). The IP address is a central feature of these protocols. It is a globally unique number and, as a result, is causing serious difficulties at the present time because of a shortage of numbers. In the original Arpanet (which was only intended to interconnect about 20 computers), the address space was eight bits, six of which defined the IMP (Interface Message Processor) and two of which the host connected to that IMP. This permitted a maximum of 64 IMPs with four hosts per IMP, leading to a maximum of 256 hosts. As the network grew, this became insufficient and the address space was increased to 16 bits, thus allowing a maximum of 65,536 hosts.

The Internet (IP) addressing scheme used 32 bits permitting, in theory, about four thousand million addresses. However, Internet addresses were structured into three classes—A, B and C—thus restricting the address space. The structure of the three classes was as follows:

Class A

0	network (7 bits)	local address (24 bits)

Class B

10	network (14 bits)	local address (16 bits)

Class C

110	network (21 bits)	local address (8 bits)

In the mid-1990s, with the explosive growth of the Internet (doubling in size every few months), it was clear that this address space would soon be used up and a new protocol was sought (originally called *IPng*, with *ng* for "next generation"). After consideration of a number of options, including the OSI 160-bit address mechanism (which was required to accommodate a large number of address formats), a new protocol was agreed, known as *IP version 6* (*IPv6*) (RFC 1833). This protocol uses 128-bit addresses and is "upward compatible" from the current IP (v4) so that it will be fairly straightforward to change to the new protocol over a period of time.

In order to permit IP packets to be transmitted over a wide variety of networks, the packet is "encapsulated" by each network (so that, for example, in an X.25 network, the data being transmitted appears to be an X.25 (High-Level Data Link Control—HDLC) frame but, within that frame, there is the IP packet). At the *gateways* (*q.v.*) between networks (also known as *routers*), the IP packet is taken out of its capsule, so the only devices on the various networks which require knowledge of IP are the routers.

IP addresses are currently 32 bits long and, for simplicity, are normally written as four decimal integers (one per eight bits) separated by "." (e.g. "204. 101.80.3"). Such an address is not "user friendly," so each system also has a "domain name" consisting of a set of text strings, separated by "." (e.g. "www.acm. org"). The domain name is mapped into the IP address using the *Domain Name Server* (DNS) protocol.

Internet Control Message Protocol (RFCs 792, 950)

Although this is formally a separate protocol (and, indeed, uses the facilities of IP), it is an integral part of IP and must be implemented alongside IP. It is used to transfer control (mainly error) information such as when a datagram cannot reach its destination.

File Transfer Protocol (FTP; RFC 959)

FTP is a higher-level ("application") protocol, using TCP (and thence IP) to transfer complete files from one host system to another. It uses two separate (duplex) TCP connections, one for the actual data and one for controlling the transfer. It does not permit parts of files to be accessed and transferred, whereas the corresponding OSI standard (ISO/IEC 8571—File Transfer, Access and Management) does.

Network File Service (RFCs 1813, 1094)

This is another high-level protocol which provides a virtual file store service whereby a host computer can make its file system available to a remote computer as if it were part of the latter's file system. This is often used in local area networks (*q.v.*), permitting PCs to access storage on a *network server*.

Simple Mail Transfer Protocol (SMTP; RFC 821) and Multimedia Extensions (MIME; RFC 1341)

SMTP is one of the most heavily used application level protocols. It permits the exchange of unstructured text messages between users ("electronic mail"—*q.v.*). A major disadvantage of SMTP is that it permits the transfer of only 7-bit characters and so binary (8-bit) files must be encoded by the sender and decoded by the receiver. Various encoding algorithms are used; an early one was UUE (Unix–Unix Encoding). More recently, MIME (Multipurpose Internet Mail Extensions) encoding standards have been developed for a variety of file formats such as video and audio; they provide similar features to the international X.400 standard, including some security services.

Hyptertext Transfer Protocol (HTTP; RFC 2068)

This protocol, which has probably done more to popularize the Internet than any other, was developed at the European nuclear establishment, CERN. It provides a distributed hypertext (*q.v.*) facility where the various documents (or parts thereof) are identified by a "Uniform Resource Locator" (URL), usually of the form "`http://www.acm.org`" where "`http:`" specifies the protocol and "`www`" is an abbreviation for "World Wide Web," essentially the set of Internet hosts which implement HTTP and which overlays the Internet. One of the earliest "Web browsers" (i.e. an HTTP client) was Mosaic; currently the most popular ones are Netscape Navigator and Internet Explorer.

Bibliography

1994–1997. Comer, D. *Internetworking with TCP/IP.* Vol. 1 Principles, Protocols and Architecture; Vol. 2 Design, Implementation and Internals; Vol. 3 Client/Server Programming and Applications for the Windows Sockets Version (versions of Vol. 3 for other operating systems are available). Upper Saddle River, NJ: Prentice Hall.

Internet Protocols and OSI Standards

RFC 768	*User Datagram Protocol*
RFC 791	*Internet Protocol*
RFC 792	*Internet Control Message Protocol*
RFC 793	*Transmission Control Protocol*
RFC 821	*Simple Mail Transfer Protocol*
RFC 950	*Internet Standard Subnetting Procedure*
RFC 959	*File Transfer Protocol*
RFC 1006	*ISO transport services on top of the TCP: Version 3*
RFC 1341	*MIME (Multipurpose Internet Mail Extensions): Mechanisms for Specifying and Describing the Format of Internet Message Bodies*
RFC 1833	*Binding Protocols for ONC RPC Version 2*
RFC 2068	*Hypertext Transfer Protocol—HTTP/1.1*
RFC 2228	*FTP Security Extensions*
RFC 2400	*Internet Official Protocol Standards*
ISO/IEC 7498:1994	*Information technology—Open Systems Interconnection—Basic Reference Model*
ISO/IEC 8473:1994	*Information technology—Protocol for providing the connectionless-mode Network Service*
ISO/IEC 8571:1988	*File Transfer, Access and Management*

Adrian Stokes

TELECOMMUNICATIONS

See COMMUNICATIONS AND COMPUTERS; DATA COMMUNICATIONS; and TELEPROCESSING SYSTEMS.

TELECONFERENCING

See COMPUTER CONFERENCING.

TELEPROCESSING SYSTEMS

For articles on related subjects *see* CLIENT–SERVER COMPUTING; COMMUNICATION CONTROL UNIT; DATA MINING; DATA WAREHOUSING; DISTRIBUTED SYSTEMS; INTERACTIVE SYSTEM; TIME SHARING; TRANSACTION PROCESSING; and WORLD WIDE WEB.

Teleprocessing refers to a form of online processing in which users at remote workstations are able to access a central computer to store, retrieve, or process data. *Teleprocessing systems* can provide a variety of services to many simultaneous users at many different locations without the necessity of having a computer and/or unique data at each such location. The basic types include:

1. *Inquiry and response systems* In these systems, the computer is used as a mass storage facility that can be accessed by a large number of users over a communication network. The best examples of such systems include document retrieval and airline and hotel reservation systems. The user enters a query at a workstation, causing the computer to search its files and send the retrieved information to the user.

2. *Data collection systems* In such systems, sometimes also called *data acquisition* or *data entry systems*, information from workstations (*q.v.*) or other input devices (e.g. cash registers in a store) is entered and stored. This data may be processed immediately or it may be used to update records that will be used for inquiry and response or in some other way. Examples of such systems include weather recording, bank transactions, and keeping track of store inventory.

3. *Data distribution systems* These systems are the converse of pure data collection systems in that the main flow of data is in the opposite direction (i.e. from computer to the workstation). Distribution of stock quotations or airline arrival and departure times are examples of such systems.

4. *Conversational systems* These systems are designed to permit many concurrent dialogues between a central computer and local or remote users. In this mode, each statement or command entered by a user is executed immediately, and a response or a prompt is sent back before the next command can be entered. Such systems are also called *time-sharing* or interactive systems, and usually allow access to a wide range of services, including compilers (*q.v.*) and application packages.

5. *Batch entry systems* Such systems are often called *remote job entry* (RJE) systems and permit submission of jobs from remote workstations. When received, these jobs are placed in the batch queue along with other jobs in the system. After execution, the output is usually sent back to the originating workstation. This may take several seconds or minutes, depending on the size of the job. Contrast this with conversational systems, where a virtually instantaneous response is expected.

6. *Message switching systems* These systems may be considered as special cases of data collection and data distribution systems. Information is collected from certain devices, stored, and then forwarded to other devices. Consequently, they are often called *store and forward systems*, and are used extensively for information transfer and electronic mail (*q.v.*) over a large network with distributed computers.

7. *Web serving systems* These systems can be thought of as a modern variation of inquiry response and data collection. Internet (*q.v.*) users can seek information provided on the World Wide Web or submit the information requested (for data collection) by Web servers.

8. *Data warehousing and data mining systems* A data warehouse usually stores some relevant subset of enterprise (e.g. a bank) data that can be queried without interfering with production systems. Data mining is the process of querying and analyzing warehouse data to discover new and relevant information and, in the case of businesses, to use that information to gain a competitive edge.

9. *Other systems* The systems described above serve only to summarize the general characteristics of teleprocessing systems. In practice, many variations and combination are possible, making the distinction between them difficult. *Monitoring systems*, for example, are similar to data collection systems, but the input is usually from some source other than a workstation (e.g. a transducer monitoring the temperature of a chemical process). *Process control systems* may be thought of as closed-loop monitoring systems that regulate a process (e.g. keep the temperature of a chemical process constant). Other examples include electronic funds transfer (*q.v.*), transaction-based applications, and video servers that digitally distribute video on demand over cable TV networks.

Characteristics of Teleprocessing Systems

Since teleprocessing systems may be required to serve hundreds or even thousands of local and remote users, the hardware and software must be designed for high reliability and availability, high transaction volumes, efficient and flexible file management capabilities, and an efficient communication access method to communicate with large numbers of local and remote terminals.

John S. Sobolewski

TELEROBOTICS

For articles on related subjects *see* AUTOMATION; COMPUTER ANIMATION; ROBOTICS; and VIRTUAL REALITY.

Introduction

Telerobotics denotes the technology of robotics controlled at a distance by human beings. When a task involving physical exploration, manipulation, and sampling is too dangerous or impractical to be performed directly by a human, it may be suited to a telerobot. In such a system, the human operator is physically removed from the task, sends commands to the robot over a telecommunication system, and receives information about the status of the task and its environment. Teleoperation therefore involves augmenting, supervising, or substituting artificial intelligence (*q.v.*) and control functions of the robot with the intelligence and pattern recognition abilities of the human operator.

This article describes some of the applications, challenges, and technologies of modern telerobotic systems while concentrating primarily on remote manipulation. Most of the ideas in this article will be applicable to other major segments of telerobotics, namely remote control of vehicles or mobile robots, and micromanipulation systems.

The first telerobots, called *teleoperators*, were developed in response to the needs of the Manhattan Project to handle highly radioactive material during the Second World War, and they thus predate the use of electronic computing in robotics. These early electro-mechanical, "master–slave," devices, pioneered by Ray Goertz at the US Argonne National Laboratory, nevertheless broke significant ground for robotics through their highly dexterous and precise mechanical design. Subsequent applications implemented from the 1940s through the present are dispersed throughout the world (and even the solar system). Undersea applications include oil rig servicing, exploration and oceanography, underwater construction, and military missions such as ordnance retrieval. Outer space applications include the well-known Space Shuttle remote manipulator system (RMS) and the Sojourner Mars rover vehicle. Experimentation in space has increased, as represented by such efforts as the German Robotic Technology Experiment (ROTEX) (April 1993) and the Japanese Space Agency's (NASDA) Manipulator Flight Demonstration (MFD) experiment (August 1997). Fig. 1 shows the JPL Rocky 7 long-range science rover.

The Mars Pathfinder rover, dubbed Sojourner (Matijevic *et al.*, 1997), was the first telerobot to gain the world's attention, as it was guided around the surface of Mars by operators at NASA's Jet Propulsion Laboratory in July of 1997. This 12 kg robot vehicle was

Figure 1. The Rocky 7 Mars Rover prototype with its sampling arm deployed. (Courtesy of the Jet Propulsion Laboratory, California Institute of Technology, Pasadena, CA. © 1999, California Institute of Technology. All rights reserved. US Government sponsorship acknowledged under NAS7-1407.)

truly a telerobot in that it had on-board laser sensors for obstacle avoidance and the capability to navigate the unknown terrain autonomously (using a surprisingly simple microprocessor capable of only 0.1 million instructions per second). Navigation objectives were sent from earth by radio requiring a round-trip time delay of about 20 minutes. Scientific users were surprised at the value added by the telerobot in opportunistically exploring the terrain.

Engineers are currently developing many new applications of telerobotics. These include remote surgery (*telemedicine*), cleanup of hazardous waste, micro-assembly, and interactive entertainment.

Technologies

Modern telerobots are made feasible by advances in computing price/performance ratio, lower cost for telecommunication bandwidth (*q.v.*), the Internet (*q.v.*), and improvements in mechanical design.

Early systems could function only with the master and slave devices being nearly identical copies of each other. With low-cost computing power, designers are free to modify the basic teleoperator architecture to create more powerful and friendly user interfaces (*q.v.*). This is because computation of the coordinate transformations required to adapt signals between differing master and slave devices was prohibitive until the late 1980s. Now designers can separately optimize the master side mechanism for effective human interaction and the slave side for the particular class of tasks.

In such a system, the computer must convert the operator's motion (which is measured by sensors in the joints of the master device) into Cartesian motion commands for the slave (the forward kinematic transformation), and also convert the Cartesian motion commands to commands for the joints of the slave device (inverse kinematic transformation). Control signals must be computed for the slave device through the use of sensor feedback signals, the joint motion commands, and a well-designed control law which may involve the dynamic equations of the master and slave devices. Finally, feedback information such as contact force between the slave and the task may be sent back to the operator through a related set of kinematic transformations.

CONTROL

Telerobotics represents a significant challenge to control engineering. The dynamics of robot manipulators are nonlinear because they depend strongly on the configuration, or "pose," of the robotic device. Furthermore, robots are frequently called upon to interact with an unmodeled environment and perform unforeseen tasks. As a robot manipulator picks up an object or pushes on something, its dynamic response completely changes. Human operators are also a source of significant model uncertainty. Precise mathematical modeling of the robot and human operator is impossible, so control laws must be robust to substantial variations. Instability of the controller must be avoided because of the obvious danger of uncontrolled motion of robots and user interaction devices.

COMMUNICATION

Improvements in telecommunication technology are also having a major impact on teleoperation. Telerobotics tends to use bandwidth asymmetrically because the "uplink," relaying commands from the human operator to the robot, requires a much lower data rate (less than 10 KB per second) than the returning sensor information (typically dominated by one or more video channels requiring on the order of megabits per second before compression).

For many applications, it is possible to teleoperate robots via the Internet (*q.v.*)—*see* Fig. 2. Goldberg (1995) pioneered such a demonstration in 1994. Rapid progress in the technology for video data compression is now beginning to have a major impact on telerobot designs. Through the use of emerging video data compression technology such as H.263 (*see* IMAGE

COMPRESSION), higher quality feedback in the form of improved television pictures will be available to the operator.

Advanced Challenges

HAPTICS (FORCE FEEDBACK)

When the task involves manipulation and contact with an unstructured remote environment, it was recognized in the 1940s that it was desirable to transmit contact force information from the slave manipulator to the human operator. For example, in an experimental system created by the Jet Propulsion Laboratory in the 1980s (Kim *et al.*, 1992), when the remote robot contacts an object of interest (or makes unintended contact), the contact forces and torques are measured at the robot's wrist, coordinate-transformed by the control computers, and applied to the user's hand through motors in the master device.

Such a system of "kinesthetic force feedback" creates a loop of information flow between the master and slave sides and thus introduces additional challenges for stable high performance control. This approach has been successfully implemented in several laboratories but is still rare in systems in the field. When round trip

Figure 2. This telerobotic installation developed at the University of Southern California allows WWW users to view and interact with a remote garden filled with living plants. Members can plant, water, and monitor the progress of seedlings via the intricate movements of an industrial robot arm.

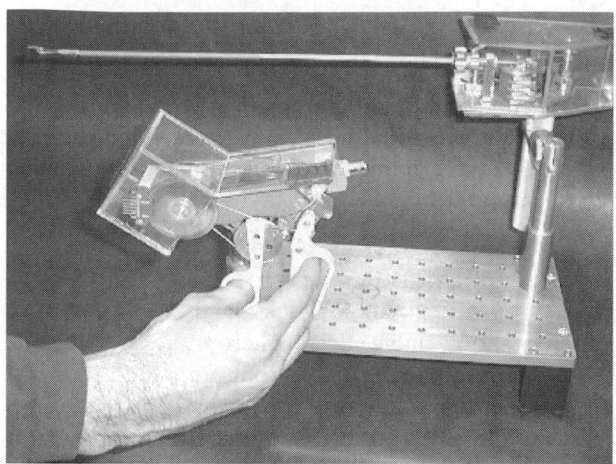

Figure 3. The Force Reflective Endoscopic Grasper (FREG) – Force Feedback Teleoperation Mode, for endoscopic surgery. (Courtesy of the University of Washington Biorobotics Laboratory.)

time delay of the communication link exceeds about 200 ms, no control approach has yet been developed which achieves a satisfactory balance between stable (safe) operation and force feedback performance. So far, force feedback systems have been limited to those involving only local communication; for example, in the surgical telerobot in Figure 3.

SUPERVISORY CONTROL

When intelligent functions are available in the computer of the remote robot, the system is usually configured for what Sheridan (1992) calls "supervisory control." In this mode, the operator acts as a supervisor of the robot's autonomous functions, helping it to plan high level strategies, detect task progress or failure, and assisting the robot to recover from errors. Low-level functions such as executing a move from one point to another, grasping an object already located within its jaws, or detecting simple visual features, are then performed by the remote robot on its own. As an example, the University of Washington's remote protein crystal mounting cell (Hannaford *et al.*, 1997) receives commands over the Internet which encode only the endpoint of manipulator motion and the duration of the motion. The local computer (known as the "server") generates the trajectory and performs servo control. The user verifies correct operation through numerical displays of slave position and moving images transmitted by three video cameras.

SHARED VS. TRADED CONTROL

Supervisory control can take two common forms: "shared control" and "traded control." In shared control, human operator and remote agent control different aspects of the system at the same time. For example, the human operator may control the posi-

tion of a robot end-effector (e.g. a grasping arm) while the robot autonomously controls the orientation. In another example, an operator may drive a remote vehicle while the vehicle's control system monitors its sensors for imminent collisions.

Traded control involves sequentially exchanging control between the operator and the robot's autonomous functions. A key challenge here is tracking the user's inputs and intent so that the autonomous control functions can keep track of the changes in state made by the inputs.

With a large set of possibilities for the control mode, it can be difficult for the user to track the state of the system and to make appropriate commands. For example, in the JPL system, each of the six degrees of freedom could be set in one of 10 possible modes. This generates one million possible control mode combinations. An effective user interface must allow users to manage this complexity in accordance with their level of training and experience.

Besides bandwidth, a major requirement of the communication link is that it minimize the latency or delay of transmission. This latency is rarely due to the fundamental speed of light limit, time $\geq$ distance/c, since c, the speed of light, is 300 000 km/sec. More commonly, the latency comes from computing delays as data is routed through multiple network hubs. When round trip delay exceeds about 250 milliseconds (ms), it becomes noticeable to the human operator. When it exceeds about 500 ms, it causes a noticeable impact on performance. As delay increases, the operator shifts to a "move and wait" strategy (Sheridan and Ferrell, 1963) in which he or she pauses at intervals to wait for the returning feedback to assess results. Real-time computer graphics (*q.v.*) animation has been used to provide a preview of the effects of the operator's commands without waiting for time-delayed information.

HUMAN–COMPUTER INTERACTION (HCI)

Because the telerobotic system relies so heavily on the intelligence of the human operator, its performance will depend strongly on the quality of the human–computer interface (*see* HUMAN FACTORS IN COMPUTING). Although humans are remarkable in their ability to adapt to human interfaces of varying quality, extensive training time, fatigue, and errors can be avoided with attention to HCI. Some requirements of telerobotic tasks may require advanced modes of human computer interaction such as stereoscopic vision systems and displays, computer simulation and animation (as with time-delayed teleoperation), and force feedback (haptic displays) for better control of contact forces and manipulation at the remote site.

Bibliography

1963. Sheridan,T. B., and Ferrell, W. R. "Remote Manipulative Control with Transmission Delay," *IEEE Transactions on Human Factors in Electronics*, **HFE-4**, 25–29.

1987. Bejczy, A.K., and Szakaly, Z. "Universal Computer Control System for Space Telerobotics," *Proceedings of the IEEE Conference on Robotics and Automation*, **1**, 318–324.

1992. Kim, W. S., Hannaford, B., and Bejczy, A. K. "Force-reflection and Shared Compliant Control in Operating Telemanipulators with Time Delay," *IEEE Transactions on Robotics & Automation*, **8**, 2, 176–185.

1992. Sheridan, T. B. *Telerobotics, Automation, and Human Supervisory Control.* Cambridge, MA: MIT Press.

1995. Goldberg, K., Mascha, M., Gentner, S., Rothenberg, N., Sutter, C., and Wiegley, J. "Desktop Teleoperation via the World Wide Web," in *Proc. 1995 IEEE Intl. Conf. on Robotics and Automation*, **1**, 654–659.

1997. Hannaford, B., Hewitt, J., Maneewarn, T., Venema, S., Appleby, M., and Ehresman, R. "Robotic System for Protein Crystal Handling," in *IEEE International Conference on Robotics and Automation*, Albuquerque, NM, April, 1997.

1997. Matijevic, J. R. *et al.* "Characterization of the Martian Surface Deposits by the Mars Pathfinder Rover, Sojourner," *Science*, **278**, *5344* (5 December), 1765.

Websites

JPL: `http://robotics.jpl.nasa.gov/groups/tra/homepage.html`.
NASDA MFD experiment: `http://jem.tksc.nasda.go.jp/JEM/Jem-j/mfd/index_e.html`.
ROTEX: `http://www.robotic.dlr.de/TELEROBOTICS/rotex.html`.
TELEGARDEN: `http://telegarden.aec.at`.
University of Washington: `http//rcs.ee.washington.edu/brl/`.

Blake Hannaford

TELNET

See INTERNET; and TCP/IP.

TERMINALS

For articles on related subjects *see* COMMUNICATIONS AND COMPUTERS; DATA COMMUNICATIONS; DISTRIBUTED SYSTEMS; DSU/CSU; INTERACTIVE INPUT DEVICES; INTERACTIVE SYSTEM; INTERNET; MODEM; MONITOR, DISPLAY; NETWORKS, COMPUTER; PERSONAL COMPUTING; TELEPROCESSING SYSTEMS; WORKSTATION; and WORLD WIDE WEB.

Introduction

A *terminal* is a device through which information from a remote computer is made available to an end user. This article addresses two categories of terminals: general-purpose and job-oriented. The personal computer is the embodiment of a general purpose terminal. Job-oriented terminals comprise all others which are designed to do specific tasks. Implicit in the notion of a terminal is that it is in communication with another device, usually one of greater capability.

The Personal Computer as a Terminal

General-purpose terminals commonly use as hardware a personal computer loaded with appropriate communications software. The distinguishing features that make it a terminal are a communications adapter and terminal software.

A personal computer is a stored program system consisting of at least a microprocessor, memory, and input–output devices. A block diagram of a typical system is shown in Fig. 1. The microprocessor executes the programmed instructions that are stored in memory, as are the data resulting from the operation. Human interaction occurs most frequently through use of a keyboard and mouse (*q.v.*) for input and a display monitor for output, although a wide range of other devices can be attached, such as printers, compact discs, scanners, voice recognition equipment, and speakers. In terminal applications, the stored programs can be sent from a host computer and loaded into the personal computer memory, or loaded from the PC's disk.

Personal computers are readily available off the shelf for most general-purpose terminal applications. Also readily available are items such as communication

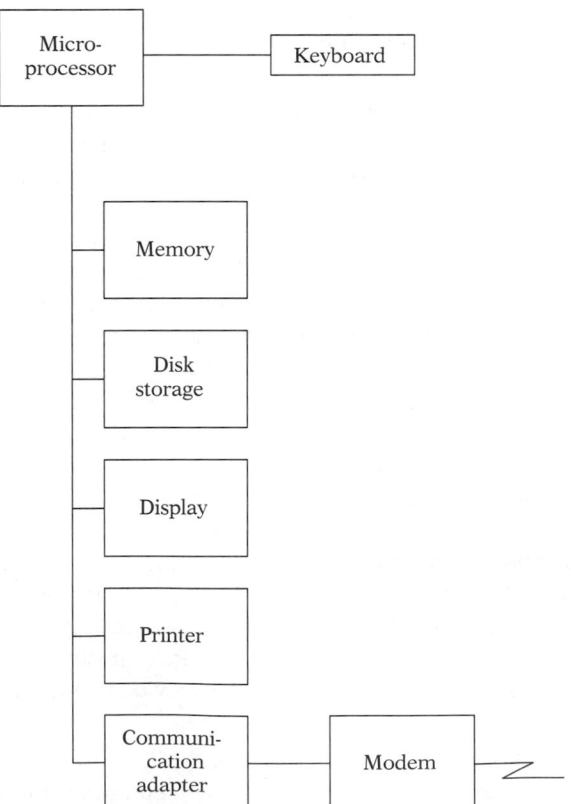

Figure 1. Block diagram of a typical personal computer system. The communication adapter is essential for a PC to become a terminal. If the communication line is analog, then a modem is also required.

adapters, modems, local area network adapters, terminal programs, and network programs.

Communication Facilities

A communication line of some sort must be connected to the user's device for it to be called a terminal. Frequently this is a telephone line, which most often is analog and which requires a modem. In business environments the terminal might be connected to a local area network (LAN—*q.v.*), which in turn interfaces to external communication facilities which are likely to be digital, and thus provide higher speed data transfers than traditional home telephone lines.

Terminal software consists of a program that can interpret the data in a standard form. For example, when receiving a data stream, the program knows which bytes are for the addressee, which bytes are the sender's address, which bytes convey data, which bytes are error correction codes, and which bytes tell where to direct the data. Fig. 2 shows a screen from the terminal software associated with Microsoft Windows applications. The operator is using the dialog boxes to convey some of the characteristics of the terminal being used so that a return message can be received.

If many terminals are communicating to one or several hosts or peers, a networking program will also be needed to establish such things as which terminal is allowed to send at a particular instant, which has priority, what facilities should be used, and what are the security levels.

Typical General-Purpose Applications

To provide a feeling for the range of jobs that can be done with a personal computer terminal, just a few of the general purpose applications will be discussed.

Internet

One of the most pervasive terminal applications is the Internet connection; a personal computer is all that is needed. It usually comes with a modem and browser software installed so that it can be connected to a telephone jack for access to all the information on the Internet. The personal computer terminal can display text and images, or produce audio.

Fig. 3 shows a Website which can access the storehouse of information at that site via further menu selections. Much research is done this way, with the Internet providing access to host databases at universities, government agencies, newspapers, and institutions. Another common use is to obtain product information from companies. The Internet is also the usual medium for sending and receiving electronic mail (*q.v.*).

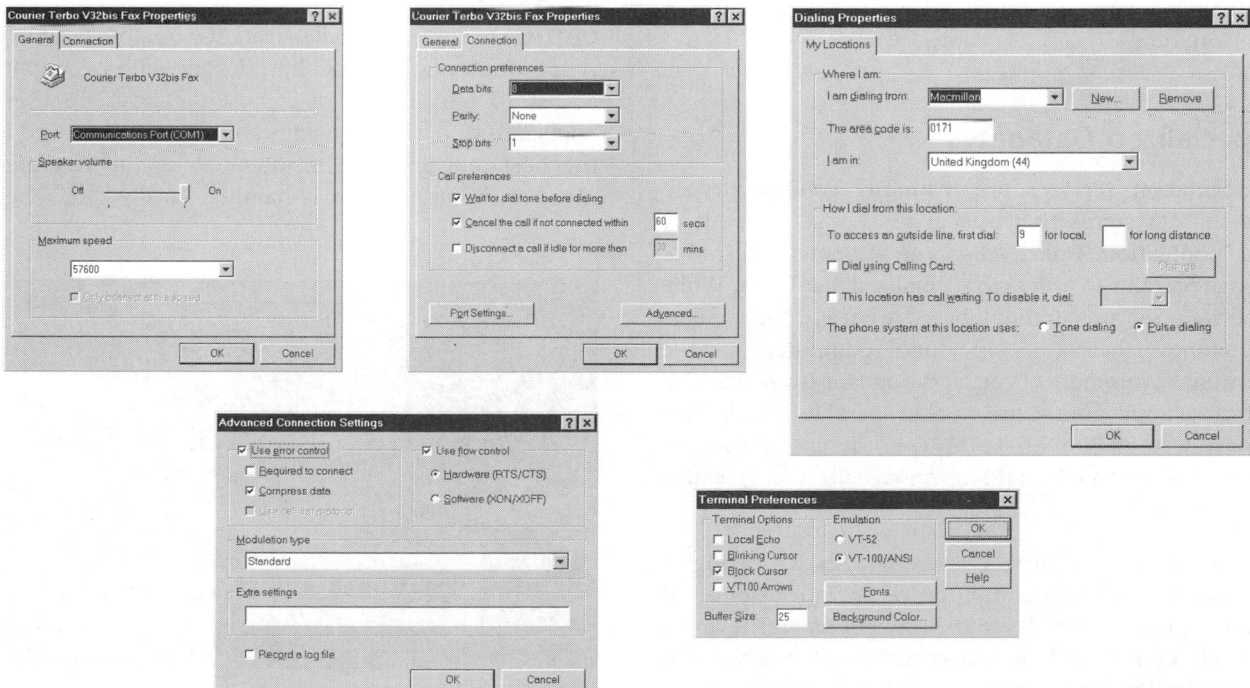

Figure 2. Microsoft Windows dialog boxes showing some of the choices to be made when setting up a terminal for communication.

Figure 3. An Internet screen. Other typical screens would display sales advertisements, stock quotes, news, reference articles, messages, and additional menus for navigating the Web.

Information Services

Information service companies such as America Online provide a range of general-purpose information to terminals that goes beyond what is available elsewhere on the Internet. These provide, in addition to an Internet connection, some host services such as mail retention, personal financial status, or customized information.

Specialized Databases

Information services are primarily general-purpose database systems that appeal to a large segment of the population. But a very large segment of terminal usage pertains to access to specialized databases. While special programs and databases are used, the applications nevertheless use personal computers as the terminal equipment. Typical, though far from inclusive of these applications, are stockbrokers' terminals, real estate terminals, CAD/CAM (*q.v.*) design and manufacturing terminals, and terminals used in business accounting and publishing.

For example, the broker's terminal shown in Fig. 4 would access a host computer for the latest stock and bond quotes, provide search functions, retrieve research reports, and make transactions. The terminal is a standard personal computer; what makes it a terminal is its connection to a network and the installation of terminal and network software.

Real estate terminals, as shown in Fig. 5, are also PC-based and use both a local as well as a remote database. What is unique in this application, beyond the usual searching and recalling of data, is the potential to store and display a photograph of the house or building that is for sale. Image information requires that a large storage capability be a part of the PC system.

CAD/CAM applications illustrate the combination of a significant amount of local processing with occasional access to information at a host database. In these applications, design drawings and data are archived at the host and accessed or updated by the terminal. Most of the interaction is handled locally, but when

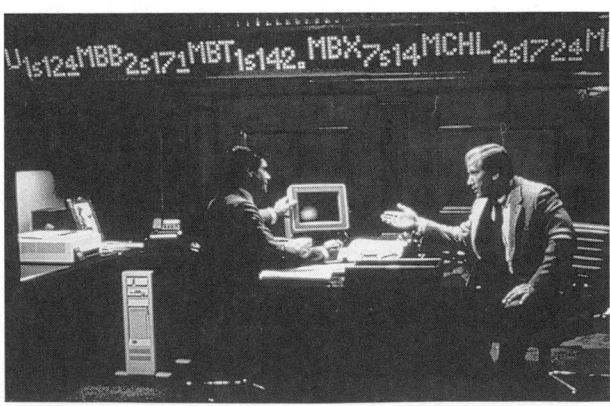

Figure 4. A broker's terminal, which is a PC that has been customized to perform the functions required at a stockbroker's desk. (Courtesy of IBM Corp.)

Figure 5. A PC in a real estate office that has been customized to perform the functions required at a real estate agent's desk. (Courtesy of IBM Corp.)

a request to the host is made, it generally involves a large file transfer. In these kinds of applications, it is important to have high-speed lines that can download a large file in a reasonable time.

Another variety of terminal configuration is typified by a publishing terminal, where news reports are received over communication lines and edited locally into a stylized publication that in turn may be sent over other communication lines to an off-site printer (*see* JOURNALISM, COMPUTERS IN).

Job-Oriented Terminals

With job-oriented terminals, the applicable job is so unique that something more or less than a personal computer is required. Typical applications include airline reservation terminals, automatic teller machines, credit card verification terminals, grocery store checkout terminals, fast food terminals, or terminals for hospital patient monitoring. In this class, the hardware and software are customized to fit the application.

Airline terminals provide a simple example where the customization is a stripped-down PC. Here the agent interacts with the host database to find routings, seat availability, and lowest cost fares, as well as to make reservations. The database is maintained at a central location and handles thousands of terminals on a time-shared basis with minimal delay times. In this application, fast response times, frequent interactions, and short message lengths are characteristic.

The hardware of an automatic teller machine (ATM) contains a magnetic stripe reader, a numeric keyboard, a display, an electromechanical device for cash issuing and deposits, and a receipt printer. All of these must be weather-resistant, vandal proof, and operable

Figure 6. An automatic teller machine (ATM), which has a cash issuing slot, a deposit receiving slot, a credit card slot, a keyboard, and a display. (Courtesy of First National Bank, Rhinebeck, NY.)

from a car window. Fig. 6 illustrates a typical walk-up terminal mounted on the outside wall of a bank building. These terminals connect to a local controller that continually monitors and activates the functions of the terminal. It is connected to another local business computer for account information, authorization for disbursement, and debiting the user's account. This local account computer is in turn connected to a larger network for credit and transaction processing when the user's account resides in some other bank or financial institution. These networks are so broad that users can access their accounts from most places in their own country as well as from many foreign countries. The terminal itself is a combination of technologies to do a specific job. The display usually is a cathode ray tube that has increased brightness so as to be visible in bright sunlight, and anti-glare treatment to reduce reflections, and displays large characters. The cash-issuing device consists of a stack of bills and a picker to disburse a precise number of them into a receiving tray. These devices can be adjusted to handle new bills or used ones. The plastic card readers use standard magnetic stripe technology. In some installations, it is merely a slot reader through which the user slides a credit or debit card, but in others such as shown in the photograph, the card slot must be designed to take the card within the machine to read it. This is done so that if credit is overdrawn or there is suspicion of a stolen card, it will not be returned to the customer. A greatly scaled-down version of the ATM is the credit verification terminal, where just the card reader is implemented and credit authorization is received from the user's credit card institution.

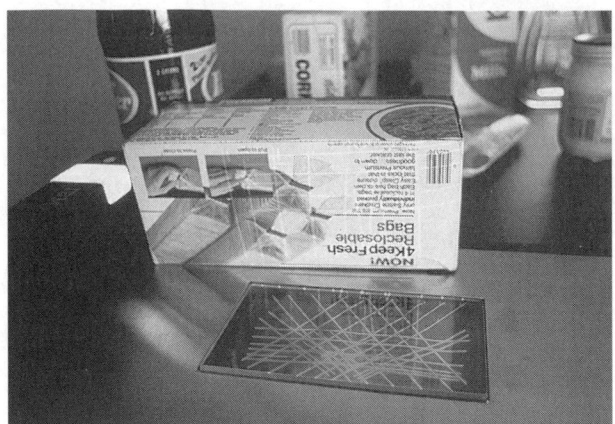

Figure 7. A supermarket scanner terminal showing a view of the pattern that the laser beam traverses to insure that it scans the bar code no matter where it occurs on the product. (Courtesy of IBM Corp.)

Figure 8. Education terminals in a library. Students can be viewing applications of their choice accessed from a central database. (Courtesy of IBM Corp.)

Another pervasive example is the supermarket checkout terminal, where the most unusual device is the laser bar code scanner as shown in Fig. 7. The terminal reads the universal product code (*q.v.*), opens the cash drawer, allows for key entry of some items, and prints the receipt. These checkout terminals are usually connected via a LAN to an in-store computer which may in turn communicate with a corporate host for inventory, reordering, and business performance processing. The in-store computer is updated on a daily basis with the latest prices. The bar code scanner consists of a laser beam that scans across the bar code (*see* UNIVERSAL PRODUCT CODE), and from this sequence of variable width bars the in-store computer can translate to a product item and its price. The laser beam sweeps across the bar code at a variety of angles and is able to read the code even when the code is not directly over the aperture. This technology is also adapted to other terminal applications, such as retail sales, manufacturing operations, or inventory data collection.

In applications such as fast food, the job-oriented terminal is designed for simplicity and ease of use by untrained operators. In patient monitoring, the terminal is equipped with sensors. The list of these special applications is too long to enumerate further.

Future Trends

The upward trend in terminal use will continue, not only because unique job-oriented applications are continually being developed but also because personal computers are becoming ubiquitous. The driving force is economics; computer applications can either reduce the cost of doing a function or the level of service can be increased, or both.

Fig. 8 shows PC-based education terminals. By far the dominant application is use of the Internet to access

information. As communication bandwidths become grater more dynamic video and audio will be available. There is a converging trend to combine TV with the presently available personal computer and Internet.

TV technology is now moving to greater use of digital circuitry in conventional sets to implement more stable circuits and to provide more function. High Definition TV (HDTV) will also depend on digital signal processing, data compression (*q.v.*), and bit-mapped buffers to obtain higher resolution with minimum use of the available broadcast spectrum.

Network Computers (NCs) are now being marketed in the sub-$1000 price range and have only the capability needed for this device to interact with a host or server. NCs are stripped down PCs usually without disk storage, CDs or other peripherals. NCs are used solely as a terminal and depend on the Internet and hosts to provide most of their function.

Bibliography

1997. Comerford, R. "The Battle for the Desktop," *IEEE Spectrum*, **34**, *5* (May), 20–28.
1998. Lange, L. "The Internet," *IEEE Spectrum*, **35**, *1* (January), 37–42.

David R. Baldauf

TESTING

See DEBUGGING; and SOFTWARE TESTING.

T_EX

For articles on related subjects *see* DESKTOP PUBLISHING; LITERATE PROGRAMMING; METAFONT; and TYPEFONT.

T_EX is a computer-controlled typesetting system designed by Donald E. Knuth. The name, which should be pronounced "tech" to rhyme with "blech," is the Greek root for English words such as "technique" and "technology."

In 1977, Knuth saw phototypeset proofs for a new edition of a book in his series, *The Art of Computer Programming*. The quality of the typesetting had deteriorated seriously from the previous editions, which had been set with lead type. Knuth had just learned about "digital" devices for typesetting, in which each image on each page is made up of tiny black dots arranged on a grid. He realized that such equipment gave him the power to make his books look good again; all he had to do was write a computer program to put tiny bits of ink in the right places. So he began the T_EX project, which turned out to be a 9-year long program of research in digital typography.

From the beginning, Knuth wanted to produce a system capable of high-quality typesetting, one that would incorporate the finest traditions of the printing industry. This meant that T_EX users would specify a bit more than was customary with ordinary typewriters. For example, the numeral "1" needs to be distinguished from the letter "l" (lowercase L); opening quotation marks are distinguished from closing quotes. Several kinds of hyphen and dashes can be used, just as in fine printing. T_EX is especially adept at mathematical typesetting (*see* Fig. 1), which involves embedded formulas, subscripts, superscripts, a multitude of symbols, and arrangements of tabular matter in rows and columns.

Portability and stability were also important goals. The system is designed to be device-independent; T_EX now runs on hundreds of different computers, from PCs to mainframes (*q.v.*) and high-performance workstations (*q.v.*), producing identical results on each. The finished output can be directed to many devices, including video screens, impact printers, laser printers, and phototypesetters. T_EX file prepared today should be able to produce the same output 20 or more years from now, on the machines of the future.

Knuth felt strongly that T_EX should be in the public domain, available to everyone without payment of royalties, and that the algorithms of T_EX should be published as a contribution to computer science. These algorithms may be freely incorporated into other systems. But Knuth requires that the name T_EX be restricted to systems that are fully compatible with the program he wrote, so that anybody using a system of that name can be sure that the system conforms to a definite standard.

The metaphor of boxes and glue (*see* Fig. 2) is used to illustrate the way T_EX assembles elements on a page. Each letter or character can be thought of as a small box containing an image. These boxes are glued together; a horizontal string of characters forms a bigger box to make up a word. Words, in turn, make sentences, which combine to make paragraphs, etc. Boxes can be glued together vertically as well as horizontally.

The glue used to assemble groups of boxes has the ability to stretch or shrink. Boxes can be set right next to each other with no glue at all, or they can be spaced far apart with thick glue. The capacity to control the stretching and shrinking of the glue is an important feature of T_EX that allows an almost infinite variety of formats to be defined in terms of a small number of basic operations.

Another unique feature of T_EX is the way it decides to break the text of a paragraph into individual lines (*see* Fig. 3). T_EX looks at the paragraph as a whole, instead of examining one line at a time. Penalties of varying severity are imposed upon bad line breaks, which are charged with a number of demerits. T_EX finds the combination of line breaks that adds up to the fewest demerits overall. Therefore, what comes later in a paragraph can influence the final appearance of lines in the earlier part. This aspect of T_EX was developed with the help of Michael Plass.

The procedure by which T_EX hyphenates words, developed by Frank Liang, is constructed in such a way that it can easily be adapted to different languages and to different conventions within a single language. Patterns that appear in a word are used to decide where hyphens are permissible and where they should be forbidden. For example, an English word containing the sequence "onc" normally permits a hyphen after the "n"; consider "bron-chitis," "discon-certing," "incon-clusive," "non-chalant," "recon-ciled," violoncello."

Input to T_EX:

> The names of variables in math formulas
> such as $e^{x_1^2+\cdots+x_n^2}$ are
> usually set in {\it italic type}.

Output from T_EX:

> The names of variables in math
> formulas such as $e^{x_1^2+\cdots+x_n^2}$ are
> usually set in *italic type*.

Figure 1. T_EX automatically chooses sizes and styles of type for mathematical material that the user has enclosed in dollar signs.

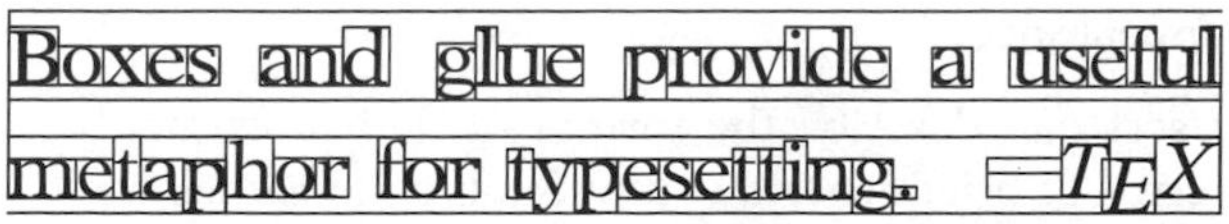

Figure 2. T_EX typesets pages by constructing boxes inside of boxes inside of boxes, with flexible glue to hold them in place.

Better spacing is often possible when the entire text of a paragraph is considered before it is broken into lines.

Better spacing is often possible when the entire text of a paragraph is considered before it is broken into lines.

Better spacing is often possible when the entire text of a paragraph is considered before it is broken into lines.

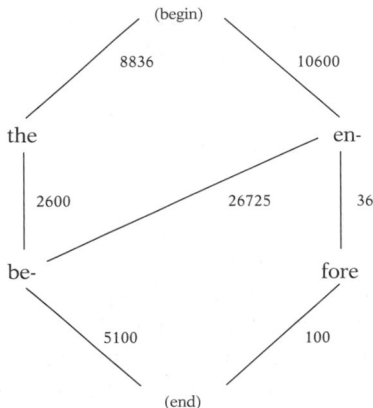

Figure 3.   Three ways to break a sample paragraph into lines. If the word "entire" is not hyphenated on the first line, the word "before" must be hyphenated on the second line. T_EX assigns demerits of $8836 + 2600 + 5100$, $10600 + 26725 + 5100$, and $10600 + 361 + 100$ to the respective paragraphs shown here, and chooses the third alternative because it has minimum total demerits. Optimum line breaks can be discovered by finding the least-cost path in a "demerit network," like the one shown here.

Version 3.0 of T_EX, released in 1990, introduced new capabilities for typesetting mixed-language texts with different hyphenation rules for each language. As a result, the use of T_EX has spread to almost every country in the world, and many facilities have been developed to adapt T_EX to the special needs of local users.

When users of T_EX find that they are repeating certain groups of instructions over and over, they can create macros (*q.v.*) to remember those sequences. Collections of macros help to define the appearance of specific kinds of documents (memos, business letters, newsletters, music programs, price lists, poetry verses, computer listings, chess games, etc.). This is particularly useful when many people are typing the same sort of document and each example should have the same appearance.

Users can describe the format of their documents in terms of brief generic codes. Such code names can be invented for personal use or borrowed from other systems. Once macros have been written that convert each brief code into a series of T_EX instructions, the

user needs only to type the codes; low-level typesetting commands rarely need to be specified directly.

Several children of T_EX have been born, each using its own set of macros. The most prominent of these is L^AT_EX, by Leslie Lamport, which encourages its users to create documents with nested structure; chapters, sections, subsections, illustrations, equations, etc. L^AT_EX has automatic facilities for assigning numbers to itemized lists, and for generating indexes and tables of contents. $\mathcal{A}_{\mathcal{M}}\mathcal{S}$-T_EX, by Michael Spivak, is designed for technical material that contains advanced mathematics. $\mathcal{LA}_{\mathcal{M}}\mathcal{S}$-T_EX is a collection of macros that extends L^AT_EX by providing the mathematical facilities of $\mathcal{A}_{\mathcal{M}}\mathcal{S}$-T_EX. The American Mathematical Society uses these systems to typeset most of its journals and books. Indeed, current estimates indicate that more than 90% of all publications worldwide in mathematics and physics since 1990 have been typeset with T_EX. Several hundred sets of macros for non-mathematical publications (such as legal texts, graphics, music, games) have also been developed to work with the standard L^AT_EX package.

An auxiliary program called B_{IB}T_EX, by Oren Patashnik, is a bibliography handler for T_EX and its offspring. B_{IB}T_EX removes much of the tedium in producing a bibliography, ensures consistency within the bibliography, and allows users to choose among many different bibliographic styles. Given a database with bibliographic information and a T_EX document containing citations, B_{IB}T_EX will automatically generate a bibliography that is formatted according to a chosen style. For example, if the database contains the entry

```
author = "Johannes Diderick van der Waals"
```

a B_{IB}T_EX style can render the name as "Johannes Diderick van der Waals," or "Waals, Johannes Diderick van der" or "van der Waals, J. D.".

At the simplest level, a T_EX user who relies on macros created by other people needs only to observe a few typing conventions related to quotes, hyphens, and dashes, and to insert brief codes when a change in typeface or spacing is desired. At the other end of the spectrum, an expert T_EXnician may fill computer files with T_EX instructions to create extremely complex formulas and charts.

As Knuth was writing T_EX, he also developed the WEB system of structured documentation. WEB encourages *literate programming*, in which a computer program is thought of as an essay to be read by human beings rather than a set of instructions to be read by computers. The program is broken into small parts and presented as a combination of informal text and formal computer language. These small parts are knit into a "web" that can be used in two distinct ways; it can either be processed by a compiler (*q.v.*) and executed by a computer, or it can be processed by TEX and printed as a document with automatic cross-indexing. The WEB system also includes macros and substitution facilities that greatly simplify the transportation of programs from one type of computer to another.

WEB predated the World Wide Web (*q.v.*), and has no relation to it. But TEX has many connections with the Internet (*q.v.*); indeed, one of the original motivations for WWW was the desire of physicists at CERN and elsewhere to share their TEX documents in a convenient way. Several systems are now available to convert TEX material into hypertext (*q.v.*) documents in HTML, PDF, or HDVI format. A Comprehensive TEX Archive Network (CTAN) containing several gigabytes of public domain files for the worldwide TEX community was established on the Internet in 1994; CTAN is a set of file servers in different countries which mirror each other's contents and make the files available to all Internet users.

The TEX Users Group (TUG), formed in 1979 and numbering about 1,500 members in 1997, publishes a quarterly journal called *TUGboat*. TUG holds annual meetings, provides publications, organizes short courses, and hosts a Website at `http://www.tug.org`. From this Website one can connect to other groups of TEX users that coordinate language-dependent activities: CSTUG for Czech and Slovak, CyrTUG for Russian, DANTE for German, GUST for Polish, GUTenberg for French, NTG for Dutch, and UKTUG for the United Kingdom. These groups also hold conferences and publish journals about current developments.

Bibliography

1979. Knuth, D. E. "Mathematical Typography," *Bulletin of the American Mathematical Society* (new series), **1**, 337–372.
1984. Knuth, D. E. "Literate Programming," *The Computer Journal*, **27**, 97–111.
1984. Knuth, D. E. *The TEXbook*, Volume A of *Computers & Typesetting*. Reading, MA: Addison-Wesley.
1986. Knuth, D. E. *TEX: The Program*, Volume B of *Computers & Typesetting*. Reading, MA: Addison-Wesley.
1990. Spivak, M. D. *The Joy of TEX*, 2nd Ed. Providence, RI: American Mathematical Society.
1992. Knuth, D. E. "The Errors of TEX," in *Literate Programming*, Chapters 10 and 11. Cambridge: Cambridge University Press.
1994. Goossens, M., Mittelbach, F., and Samarin, A. *The LATEX Companion*. Reading, MA: Addison-Wesley.
1994. Lamport, L. *LATEX: A Document Preparation System*, 2nd Ed. Reading, MA: Addison-Wesley.
1994. Walsh, N. *Making TEX Work*. Sebastopol, CA: O'Reilly & Associates.
1997. Goossens, M., Rahtz, S. P. Q., and Mittelbach, F. *The LATEX Graphics Companion*. Reading, MA: Addison-Wesley.
1999. Knuth, D. E. *Digital Typography* (CSLI Lecture Notes, No. 78). Stanford, CA: Center for the Study of Language and Information.

Donald E. and Jill C. Knuth

TEXT EDITING SYSTEMS

For articles on related subjects *see* DESKTOP PUBLISHING; HYPERTEXT; INTERACTIVE INPUT DEVICES; METAFONT; MOUSE; POSTSCRIPT; SPELLING CHECKER; TEX; TYPEFONT; USER INTERFACE; WINDOW ENVIRONMENTS; and WORD PROCESSING.

Introduction

Text editing is the use of a computer to generate and modify written words, usually in order to print out the text. It is one of the most common uses of computers today. Text editing systems enable the computer and its printer to act as a kind of super typewriter. This use has, as much as any of its many other capabilities, been responsible for the quick and indeed virtually universal acceptance of computing in every kind of office. In addition, it is one of the principal uses of home computer systems and the one with which users who are not computer professionals are the most familiar. Once primarily a tool for programmers to compose and edit work in programming languages, it has broadened in application so that all kinds of written text, from email (*q.v.*) that traverses the globe to novels, term papers, and letters to family members, are composed using a computer

Text editing systems that not only enable writers and editors to generate the text to be printed directly from their desks, but that also enable setup of the page layouts of newspapers, magazines, and books, are used routinely by newspapers and publishing firms. In practice, this has meant that typesetters have often been replaced by editors who organize and format computer-based textual information. Their computer-generated texts are sent directly to a printer who produces the final pages, rather than, as was done previously, retyping the text into machines that produced metal images of the text, to be inked and pressed onto the page. It is rare now to see a publication office that does not have a computer on each desk.

NATURAL LANGUAGE APPLICATIONS

Word Processing. *Word processing* is the name given to using the computer to write and edit general-purpose text with any of the many commercial products designed for this. The term *word processor* is used to designate both a software program enabling word processing and a computer designed solely for such manipulation of text and which looks like a typewriter with a computer screen. Currently, however, multipurpose computers are more often used than stand-alone word processors, because of the limited capacities of the latter. Very often, for example, the user will also want to store large amounts of previous text for reference or reuse or to send the text electronically to an intended recipient (in the case of letters, memos, or email) rather than just print it out, tasks for which a general-purpose computer is necessary.

Page Layout Systems. Editors of publications such as newsletters and journals are likely to use programs that provide facilities for page layout and sophisticated print production and are referred to by the generic name *desktop publishing* (*q.v.*).

Initially developed as specialized products for use in the publishing industry, page layout programs have been scaled down for personal computers and they are now frequently used as adjuncts or replacements for standard text editors.

In page layout systems the capabilities of word processing for publication reach their zenith. The text is formatted on screen and the user has almost all the facilities of a full-sized printing press. Copy may be sized, small or large boxes may be embedded in the text, pictures or other graphics may be created and inserted, and columns may be created. Multiple arbitrarily shaped blocks of text may be put onto the pages and linked together so that a single file may span one or more blocks on different pages (allowing for newspaper and magazine stories that jump to a new page for continuation). Insertions or deletions in any block will be reflected in the others as appropriate. Graphics blocks may be intermixed on a page with text blocks so that it is possible to create full layouts interactively.

Hypertext Editing. Hypertext (*q.v.*), a term coined by Ted Nelson (Nelson, 1967, p. 195) is "the combination of natural language text with the computer's capacities for interactive branching, or dynamic display of . . . a nonlinear text . . . which cannot be printed conveniently on a conventional page." Such texts, which are designed to be read on the computer screen and not on the page, make it possible for the user to jump from the text into other computer sources related to the topic, from there to still other sources, and back to the original place. The jumping-off spots, or *links*, are designated by the author of the text. Certain words or phrases are indicated as *hot buttons*, which may be clicked with a *mouse* (*q.v.*) to view further material. The hypertext format is familiar to millions of computer users through the home pages of the World Wide Web (*q.v.*), which typically contain hot buttons linking outline-like information with more detailed description, or with other sources of related information. It is also being used increasingly in computer-assisted education for various subjects.

Text Editing

Every text editing program has an overarching conceptual model of its user and the computer that guides the design and use of the program. This most modern of methods for generating texts often reaches far back into human history for such conceptual models. Currently, the most common model suggests that the screen is the visible part of a scroll (such as the parchment scrolls used in ancient times), which the user may roll back and forth to make space for the text as it is being created, or to view already existing text. As a user types a new document, more screen space is made available from the bottom to take up the new text. By using the *arrow* keys at the bottom of the keyboard or clicking with the mouse on the scroll bar at the right of the text, the user can *scroll* the completed text through the screen.

In Apple's Macintosh system, in Microsoft Windows and in Unix (*q.v.*) with the X Window System, the user can create *windows*, or screen viewing spaces, for several files or documents at one time, which can be viewed side by side, top to bottom, or as alternating screens as the user wishes (*see* WINDOW ENVIRONMENTS). Commonly used commands appear as *icons*, or graphic symbols, along the top of the screen in a *command bar*. These commands, as well as others that appear in a *pull-down menu* the user may view, are issued by the user's click on the mouse or by the use of *function keys*.

INPUT DEVICES

The text and the operations that the user wishes to perform upon it (spacing, capitalizing, italicizing, etc.) are entered via various input devices. These include the alphanumeric keyboard, which is made up of keys for numbers, letters, and other commonly used symbols; special keys on the keyboard used to issue commands, such as the function keys at the top of the keyboard and the Alt and Control keys, used in combination with alphanumeric keys to issue commands to the program; and locator devices such as a mouse or a *trackball*.

The traditional keyboard (*see* Fig. 1 of INTERACTIVE INPUT DEVICES), called the QWERTY keyboard after the first six characters on the upper left of its configuration, was first used by Christopher Latham Sholes in the 1860s. It was designed to keep commonly used letters as far apart as possible in order to avoid jamming of the mechanical keys. In spite of its inefficiency in principle, it remains the most commonly used keyboard because of sheer inertia: millions of typists, fast and slow, learned to type on its layout and they resist change. For example, an argument may be made for adopting the Dvorak Simplified Keyboard (*see* Fig. 2 of INTERACTIVE INPUT DEVICES), whose keys are arranged to maximize typing speed and minimize fatigue, yet in several decades this has not been done and the Dvorak seems unlikely to become the accepted standard in the foreseeable future.

Hand-held or *palmtop* computers (see PORTABLE COMPUTERS) offer handwriting recognition as a means of text or command entry. The user writes on a special pad using a stylus and the computer converts these handwritten entries into characters on the screen or commands for formatting or location.

Unlike a typewriter, which moves either the paper to be typed on or the mechanism with the inked keys to the next available blank space, a text editor makes the whole document available for typing or retyping, and hence needs to show the user where the next typed character will appear. This is done using a *cursor*, usually a character-sized square that flashes in the space to be filled next, or a vertical line that appears directly to the right of the most recently typed character. The mouse and trackball, which move the cursor on the screen, are the most common for text editing.

A capability to accept *voice input*, text or commands that the user speaks and which are then executed directly by the computer, is still in the early stages of commercial viability and is available on only a few systems. It is easy to see how useful voice input would be to many users, for example, the blind or physically disabled (*see* DISABLED, COMPUTERS AND THE).

OUTPUT DEVICES

The screen displays the text input by the user, formatted according to its standard settings or the user's commands. It is the principal output device, far removed from the paper version originally issued by early teletype-like devices, or even the cathode ray tube (CRT) familiar to users of early personal computers. Today, editing systems run on either character-based displays or graphics (*bitmap*) displays. Often, the user can see on the screen a display of even a complex document, looking like a photographic image of how it would appear printed on paper.

Further, some editors permit linking not only of texts, but of still photographs or other images and even sound and moving pictures (*see* MULTIMEDIA). These of course are designed for real-time display rather than for printing out.

Text Editing: A Conceptual Overview

WHAT IS TEXT?

In order to do text editing, we must first have text. Generally, text is provided not only by typing on the keyboard, but also by *scanning*, or *machine-reading* an existing text into a computer file (*see* OPTICAL CHARACTER RECOGNITION), or by importing it from some other outside source, such as through email.

Text editing then involves adding, deleting, or altering the text. In order to accomplish this, the user must specify exactly where in the existing text the change, addition, or deletion is to take place and what is to be done at that site.

But what exactly is meant by *text*? The answer is not as obvious as it may seem. Do the following three examples represent the same text or are they examples of three different texts?

Example 1:
How now brown cow

Example 2:
How   now   brown   cow

Example 3:
How
now
brown
cow

It could be argued that Examples 1–3 are the same text presented differently, or alternatively that the three examples are three different texts, because the spaces and carriage returns are also text.

A similar issue occurs in the following three examples:

Example 4:
How now brown cow.

Example 5:
How now brown cow.

Example 6:
How now brown cow.

Here the words are the same, as is the arrangement on the page, but the appearance of the individual characters is different. Are Examples 4–6 one text or three?

The appearance of a text is not completely unproblematic, either. Often, how a text appears on the screen is not how it appears on the printed page. In some cases the difference is great. When an editor shows on the screen a faithful image of the text as it will appear on paper, it is referred to as a WYSIWYG (What You See Is What You Get) editor. Non-WYSIWYG editors often have special options allowing the user to preview the text to see how it would look when printed.

Varying interpretations of what constitutes legitimate text are built into text editors. The boundary of what constitutes the *text* and what constitutes attributes of the text's *appearance* are, to a great extent, the determining factor of the difference between simple text editors, word processors, text formatting systems, and desktop publishing systems.

DEFINITION OF TEXT WITHIN THE COMPUTER

Characters are stored in a computer's memory in code. The most common code is ASCII (*see* CHARACTER CODES), which uses seven bits of information for each character, for a total of 128 different characters. That allows for 52 characters for upper and lower case of the standard English alphabet along with the most common other symbols used in English, such as the standard punctuation symbols, numeric digits, parentheses, space, carriage return, etc. When text is defined as consisting exclusively of the characters included in the ASCII code, it is usually called plain text or ASCII text. Extended ASCII Code uses 8 bits and thus allows for 256 different characters. Although this allows for twice as many characters as plain ASCII, it still is not nearly enough to represent multiple fonts with different styles and size such as might be found in this volume, not to mention mathematical symbols or non-Roman alphabets. Hence such things as umlauts or Greek letters must be represented internally by the editor's own code, usually consisting of several Extended ASCII symbols. That is why, whenever you try to print a file created with a word processor as plain text, you may get unexpected symbols.

An example of this appears in Figs. 1–3. Fig. 1 shows a poem that has been typed using the Multi-Edit text editor. An additional window has been created to show the ASCII character codes of the file. The cursor is shown at the end of the second line, which is at character 24 of line 2. Fig. 2 shows the same poem as it might appear on the screen after being typed using Microsoft Word. In Fig. 3, the Word document has then been loaded into Multi-Edit. Again, an extra window has been created to show the ASCII codes. Note that although the cursor of Fig. 3 is again at the end of the second line, it is now at page 5, line 15, character 17 (see lower bar—for this type of file, a page is defined as 36 16-character lines). We can see some of the additional characters in the figure, but most are off the screen. Embedded in the additional characters is formatting information about such things as fonts and margins as well as information about the version of Microsoft Word used, the file format, the date the file was created, and the owner of the software license.

DEFINITION OF TEXT AS A STRUCTURE

Text may be understood as a simple linear sequence of characters, just as it is represented in a computer.

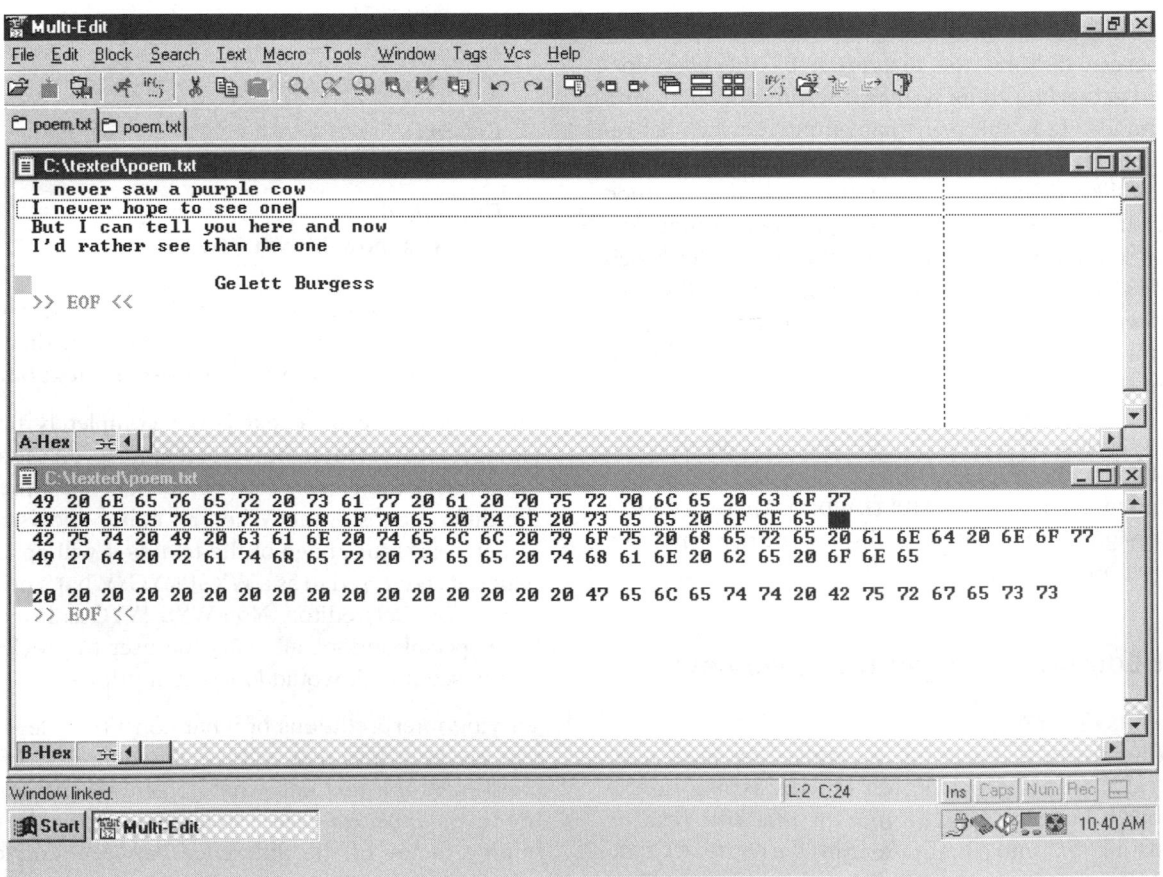

Figure 1.

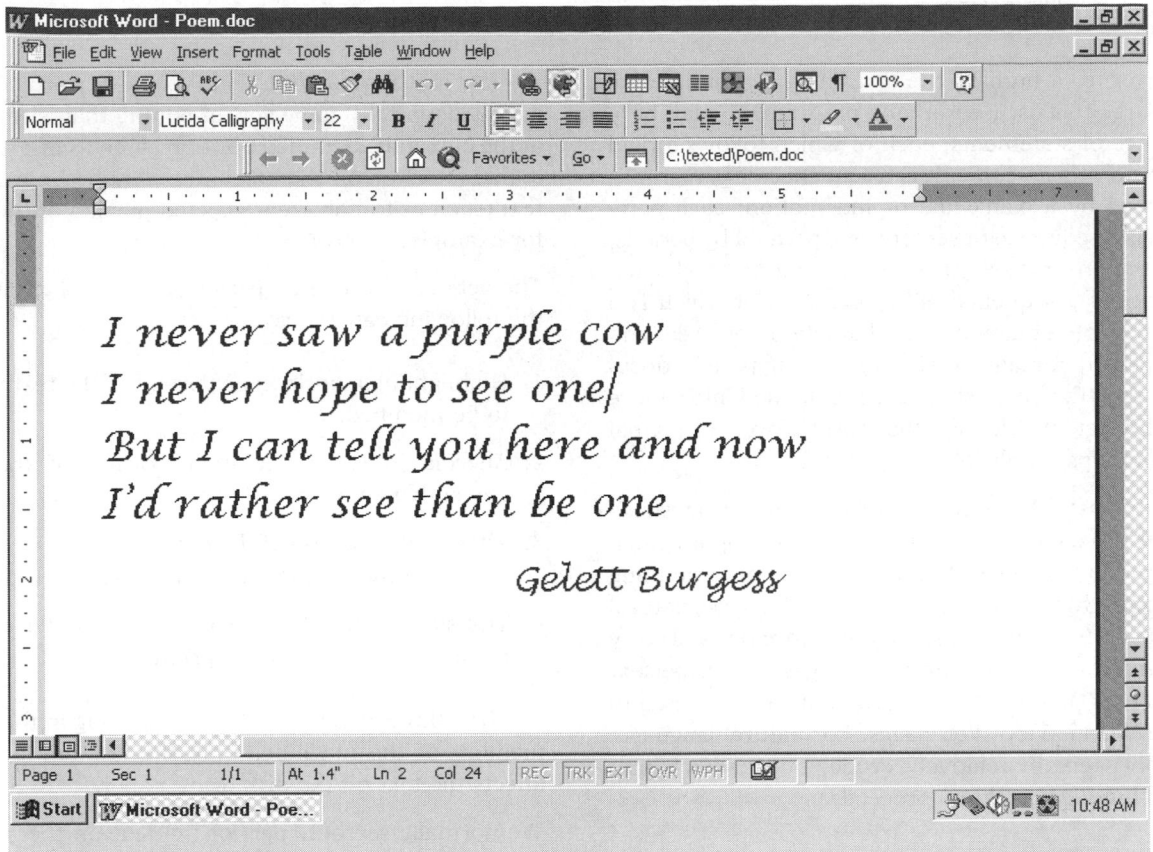

Figure 2.

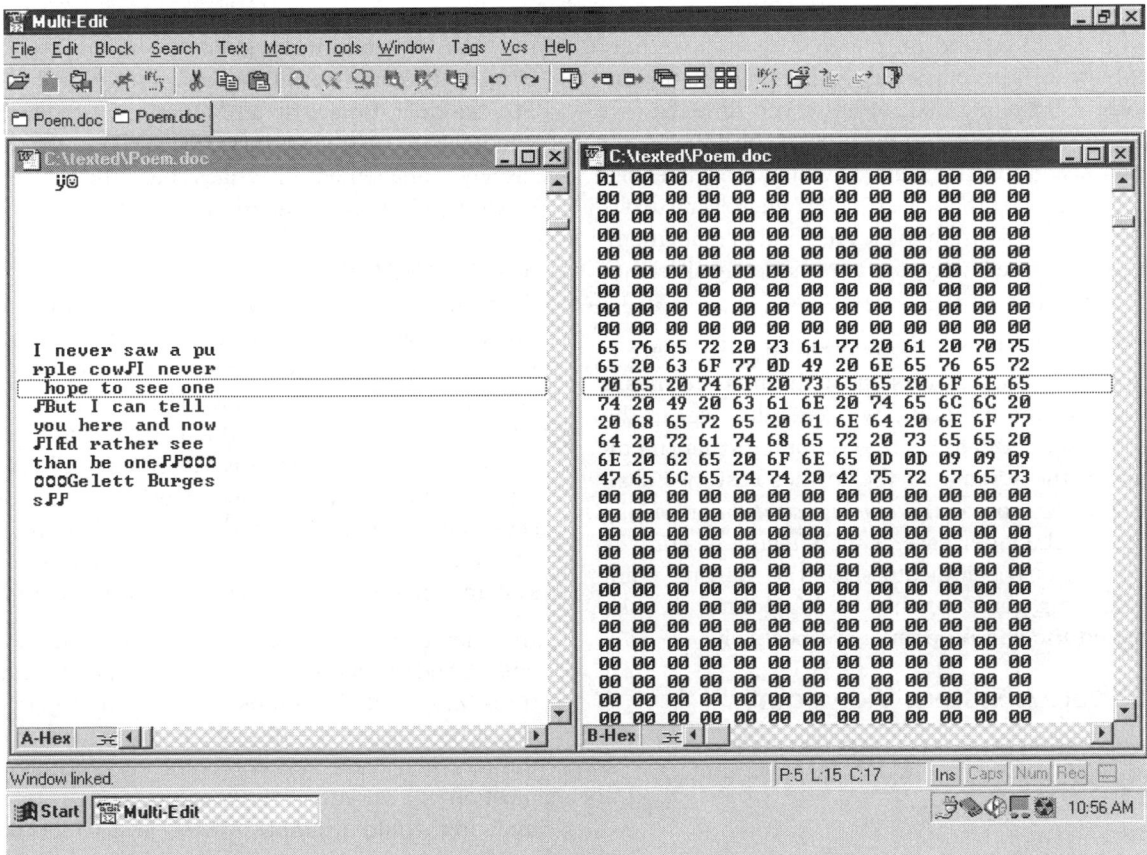

Figure 3.

However, to a human, the text has a certain internal structure. If it is a computer program, it may be a sequence of statements, each of which follows a rigid syntax. If it is an essay, it is a sequence of paragraphs separated by a blank line or indentation; each paragraph is a sequence of sentences separated by periods, exclamation marks, or question marks; and each sentence is a sequence of words, each of which is a sequence of alphanumeric characters followed and preceded by a blank. If the text is a hypertext document, then the linear structure is extended into a more complex set of relations that form a web of textual (and perhaps graphical) components.

The simplest editors recognize only the linear structure of the characters of the text. More sophisticated editors can recognize the structure of programming languages, hypertext, and, to a limited degree, natural language. Structure editors are common and very effective for programming languages and hypertext documents such as HTML documents that are used to define World Wide Web pages. For natural language, the tools remain relatively crude, but research into better *intelligent editors* proceeds.

Where is Text Actually Located?

We can think of text as existing in four different places: on a disk or some other *auxiliary* storage medium (*see* MEMORY: AUXILIARY), in the computer's main memory, on the screen, and on paper. Although we may think of these four places as containing four manifestations of the same text, at any given time the text may vary from one place to the next. If the editor is not a WYSIWYG editor, the printed version may differ significantly from the others. Generally, whenever a text is modified, the versions on the screen and in main memory are both immediately and automatically altered to match each other.

When we speak of a position within the text, there is ambiguity as to which version of the text we mean. When talking about editing, we generally refer to the text as it exists (logically) in the computer's main memory and on the screen. In the former case, we shall refer to the location as the *editing location* or *editing point* and in the latter case as the *viewing location* or *viewing point*. The indicators for the viewing point and the editing point are the viewing pointer (i.e. the cursor) and the editing pointer, respectively.

The Editor: A System Viewpoint

The organization of editors varies widely; Fig. 4 gives a simplified overall view of the organization of a generic editor.

The user provides input via a keyboard or mouse that will identify both a *position* and a *portion of an existing text* and some *action* that is to be performed. The action is typically some sort of editing that is to occur at the currently identified position (such as insertion of a character) or on the currently identified portion of text (such as to italicize a selected portion of the text, for example).

The actions that can be performed fall generally into the following categories:

1. Highlighting a position or portion of the text that is to be modified.

2. Altering in some way that portion of the text currently identified.

3. Altering the portion of the text that is visible on the screen, or the manner in which the text is displayed.

4. Transferring text to or from the computer's main memory (loading, saving, printing).

The first three affect only the text residing in the main memory of the machine. Only the last one actually affects the text on the disk or on paper.

We normally see only part of the text on the screen, which may or may not be a contiguous portion of text. Many editors allow viewing several noncontiguous sections of a text at once or viewing several different texts at the same time on the same screen. The editor may use an underlying *window manager* or it may contain its own internal display management, or both. For example, Emacs on an X Window System has the windowing capabilities of X as well as the internal display management of Emacs that functions within a single window of the X Window System.

Screen Updating

Displaying a full screenful of text creates the potential for unacceptably long delays caused by the time required to update the screen. Large, high resolution screens and complex windowing environments can exacerbate the problem, which in the past was very common, especially for early WYSIWYG editors. A fast typist could type well beyond—perhaps by as much as several lines—what was being displayed on the screen. In some cases, the I/O buffers would fill up, and the system would refuse to allow the typist to continue.

In order to deal with this, the implementors of text editors and word processors developed new data structures (*q.v.*) and algorithms (*q.v.*) for intelligent updating of the computer's display. The idea was to exploit the fact that each new screenful of information was most often a variant of the previous screen. Intelligent updating would attempt to detect just which portions of the screen had changed, and rewrite only those portions.

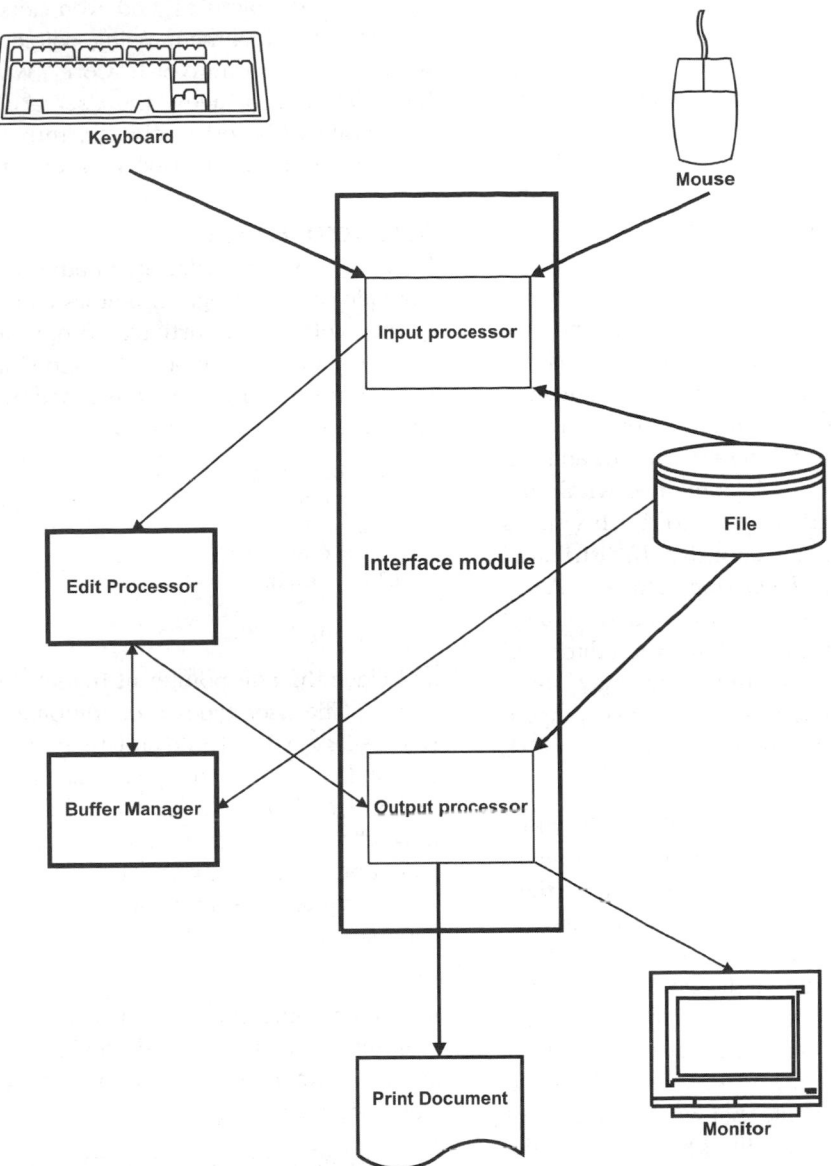

Figure 4.

The *bandwidth* (*q.v.*) of I/O channels and network connections has increased dramatically in recent years, and display monitors (particularly in personal computers—*see* MONITOR, DISPLAY) often have their own memory so that an update of the screen can be accomplished via a memory-to-memory transfer (*see* MEMORY-MAPPED I/O), which is very fast. Thus, in a typical editing environment, screen updates usually appear to be instantaneous.

One problem, particularly in word processors with many fonts and styles, is to match the capabilities of the editor with the capabilities of the hardware being used. There are two main approaches to providing such flexibility. One is for the text editor to use a table that translates logical operations such as *delete line*

into a sequence of commands that relate directly to the device being used. The other is to provide access to programs called *device drivers* (*q.v.*) that are supplied when the device is installed.

FILE FORMATS

As indicated earlier, a text file ultimately consists of a sequence of characters, each most commonly represented in the computer by a sequence of 8-bit Extended ASCII characters. There is now also *Unicode* (*see* CHARACTER CODES), an international standard coding that extends ASCII to 16 bits but this is not yet in common use because of the additional storage required for each character. Although having 16 bits allows for 65,536 different codes, that total would be quickly exhausted by the number of different fonts, styles, sizes, and orientations possible for each character to say nothing of the requirements for non-English alphabets which was the motivation for developing Unicode. In order to manage all this, word processors insert additional information into the file to describe fonts, sizes, etc. This extra information must be coded into the file for proper display and printing.

CONFIGURATIONS

Three types of computing environment may provide the background for text editing: *standalone*, *distributed*, and *time-shared*. In a standalone environment, a single, self-sufficient personal computer or dedicated word processor is used for processing, input, and display. Most often, a disk drive is contained within the unit, and a printer is directly connected. Such systems can be highly interactive and responsive. In distributed computing environments, a *local area network* (LAN—*q.v.*) of personal computers or workstations (*q.v.*) shares disk space and printers. Here, the editor still runs on each personal computer, but may share resources with the other machines, and must compete for some memory or facilities on the network (*see* FILE SERVER).

Although infrequently used now for editing, the *time-sharing* (*q.v.*) environment once characterized mainframes (*q.v.*) and minicomputers (*q.v.*) rather than desktop or personal computers. In time sharing, in which the editor runs on a central processor, users interact with the system through remote terminals. When using *intelligent terminals*, which have their own memory in which editing takes place, some of the processing is performed on the desktop itself. An editor must be able to create a new file that will hold a body of text, open (that is, select for editing) an existing file, and save a file that has been created or edited. The editing operations themselves must include a capability for moving the editing and viewing pointers and for inserting and deleting characters (carriage returns and new lines are considered characters).

CUTTING AND PASTING

One of the most common text-editing features involves a reservoir that holds text. When the user deletes a block of text, the text does not disappear entirely, but moves into that reservoir. The text may then be brought from the reservoir into the current document at any place within the document. Similarly, the command to copy a block of text actually copies it into the reservoir. Then it may be pasted into the document. Some computer environments provide a general reservoir for that purpose (called the *clipboard* in Microsoft Windows) that will allow cutting and pasting across various applications. Hence, objects other than text—

such as charts, pictures, and even video clips—may be put into the document being edited. Some editors, such as Microsoft Word, Corel WordPerfect, and Lotus Word Pro, allow the user access to software for editing those other objects, thus further blurring the distinction between what is text and what is not.

ADVANCED FEATURES

Many editors have a variety of advanced features. For example, *smart* program editors can be made aware of the syntax of a particular programming language and can supply templates for individual statements. For example, if the word *if* is typed into a Pascal program the screen may display

```
if <condition> then
    begin
    <S>
    end
else begin
    <S>
    end
```

and place the edit pointer at the left side of `<condition>`. The user types a conditional expression that replaces `<condition>` and then skips (typically via the tab key) to `<S>` to type a sequence of Pascal statements. In addition to knowing the syntax, the editor may allow the user to choose from a selection of indenting styles and may even do some simple additional syntax checking such as verifying that all variables have been declared.

Given the changing landscape of computer software, an editor could not recognize all the different programming languages and environments, so many editors allow the user to extend the capabilities of the editor via *macros* (*q.v.*).

Virtually all word processing programs include facilities for choosing various fonts and character sizes and styles. They may even include the capability to write text right to left, up to down, upside down, on a slanted line, or along a circular arc. Other programs, such as TEX, LATEX, and *troff* also provide for text formatting and typesetting facilities. Since these programs are not editors, they will not be discussed further here.

Text Editing: A User Viewpoint

MANAGING EDIT POINTERS

The user will frequently want to *move* through a document, causing the *current editing* and *viewing pointers* to be moved. Simple movement, such as arrow key traversals, as well as more complex pattern searches and hypertext jumps, are possible. Early editing systems were designed for transcription of editing changes from paper copy and provided only simple capabilities.

Modern systems, however, are oriented toward online reading and writing and allow the user to browse, organize, rewrite, and study, rather than just to compose and proofread.

SIMPLE MOVEMENT

Graphical, mouse-based text editors typically substitute for a cursor an *insertion point*, a flashing bar that can be positioned only between two characters. In some editors, the user may move the cursor or editing pointer separately from the viewing pointer, which allows the user to browse through all or parts of the document and then to jump back directly to the pre-browsing location where the cursor has stayed. By contrast, other text editors support only cursor movement, and alter the viewing window as necessary.

Text editors that allow the user to see and work with an entire screen of text are called *full-screen editors*. Other text editors, called *line editors*, require the user to work with the text one line at a time. Line editors are no longer common.

POINT SETTING

Most point setting is accomplished by simple movements. Sometimes, though, the user wishes to jump around to various places within a document. One way of doing that is by placing special marks in the document, often called *bookmarks* or *paperclips*. Such marks may be numbered or named so that a *goto* or *jump* command can be given the name or number of the mark in question, setting the edit and view pointers to that location.

PATTERN SEARCHING

Pattern searching commands (usually called *search*, *find*, or *locate*) will locate and display (and sometimes select) the next occurrence of the pattern specified.

Shortcuts have been developed so that the user does not have to type the entire pattern. The *ellipsis* (...), for example, can abbreviate a long pattern by indicating simply a few characters of context at the beginning and end of the pattern. Thus, the text string

```
Four score and seven years ago,
```

might be located with the command:

```
locate /Four...ago/,
```

More complex patterns may be specified in many editors (usually text editors intended for programmers) via *regular expressions* (*q.v.*). For example, in the Unix regular expression format, the string

```
[ab]*[^abyz][yz]*
```

would be interpreted as follows:

◆ [...] represents any of the characters between the square brackets. Hence [abc] represents any one of *a* or *b* or *c*;

◆ * represents any number, including zero, of instances of the previous symbol or set of symbols;

◆ [^...] represents any character other than the ones between the square brackets.

Thus the pattern given would match *k* and *abkzz* but not *akkz* or *akzk*.

INTERFILE MOVEMENT

Sometimes it is useful to be able to move between two or more files, for example to examine multiple sources while writing, to compare versions of the text being edited or other texts, and so forth. Here the user needs the ability to switch the file being edited. Most conveniently, the text editor will be integrated into the computer's operating system so that a large number of editing windows can be opened and worked on simultaneously. Many text editors provide this capability, and some, such as Emacs, even provide *directory editing*—file editing, renaming, and deleting.

A windowing system will provide support for displaying multiple documents. For example, in Microsoft Windows users can open documents for editing, and the corresponding editor windows will be opened automatically. Hypertext links between various files may be made permanent or semipermanent, so that the writer, editor, or reader may quickly jump to other sections or other documents.

FORMATTING

In a text-only editor, the text is shown exactly as it is stored in the internal buffer, with the exception of the carriage return and linefeed characters, which are translated into a new line on the display. However, this formatting is typically sufficient only for a simple programmer's editor. Editors intended for manuscript work need additional formatting capabilities, or must provide an interface to a formatting system. Early text processing systems provided *formatting* codes (such as *.pp* for *paragraph*, *.in 5* for *indent five spaces*, *.ce* for *center*) that were typed in as literal text and subsequently compiled by a text formatter to produce formatted pages; no online feedback was available.

Later, *soft-copy* or *proof-copy* facilities could display (but did not permit editing of) *monospaced output* (i.e. with each character taking the same amount of space on the screen and page) on the alphanumeric terminal. High-resolution graphics displays allowed even *proportionally spaced* typeset text to be previewed.

The next major step in formatting was the creation of the interactive editor/formatter. Today, most editors, especially commercial word processors, instantly display the results of commands such as *indent*, *tab*, *bold*, and *center* as they are entered or changed. Interactive editor/formatters make possible an especially useful view in which all operations on the document are shown immediately on a displayed facsimile of the printed page.

The latest commercial graphical word processors offer interactive editing of multiple column pages, embedded graphics, footnotes, and equations. Some products offer only limited WYSIWYG, but other editors, such as Microsoft Word, Corel WordPerfect, or Lotus Word Pro, have more complete WYSIWYG, down to on-screen columns, page numbers, and footnotes.

FORMATTING COMMANDS

In most word processing systems, the user can give commands for the desired formatting directly. For example, in many text editors the user can select one or more lines and then issue a *center* command to center the lines. An on-screen simulation of a typewriter margin and tab controls, containing margin settings, fonts, tabs, and so forth is called a *ruler*. In other editors, formatting specifications are entered as textual formatting codes in the same manner as normal (literal) text. In some systems, these codes must be entered on separate lines to distinguish them from literal text; in other systems, a special character is used as a *delimiter* (*q.v.*) so that the codes can be embedded in the text.

Format specifications can be *procedural* and *declarative*. In a procedural specification, the user indicates the exact formatting choices (e.g. put this text in 12 point Times Roman, skip two lines). In a declarative system, *tags* or *styles* are used to identify or mark elements of the document, such as paragraphs, items in a numbered list, chapter headings, and running heads. These attributes can be named *paragraph* and subsequently used for all standard paragraphs. Any subsequent revision of the *paragraph* definition would change the appearance of all the text that had been marked as *paragraph*. Styles can be grouped and saved as *stylesheets* and reused to format documents that are to have a common appearance.

EDITING OPERATIONS

Creating. Text editors make computer-based typing far more flexible than typing on a typewriter. First, the backspace or delete key can be used to erase the last character typed. Second, typing a carriage return at the end of each line is unnecessary, thanks to automatic *wordwrap*. As the end of each line is reached, it breaks the line at the first blank space before overflowing and automatically pushes the continuing text to the next line.

Text editors that are not mouse-based generally accept typed input in two ways: *typeover mode* or *insert mode*. In typeover mode, any character typed replaces the character under the cursor, whether this is a blank space or an already typed character. In insert mode, by contrast, each typed character is inserted in front of any text that follows the cursor. Many text editors provide both typeover mode and insert mode as a *toggle* function so that the user may switch between them.

In mouse-based text editors, the insertion point is always between two characters, and typing adds characters at that point. If characters are selected by highlighting them using the mouse button, new typing will replace the selected characters.

Glossaries or *abbreviations* are frequently available to the users of text editors. This allows words specified by the user to be entered in an abbreviated form and then automatically expanded. For example, the words *time zones* could be abbreviated as *tz* and then automatically expanded upon entry. *Variables* allow the user to specify named variables, such as *company*, which may be inserted into the text at any point. If *company* is set to *General Electric*, then *General Electric* will appear in all places in which *company* has been typed. This allows standard letters to be customized if used with a *mailmerge* system, in which the editor reads from a *data file* (for example, a mailing list) and substitutes information in the *source file* (i.e. a form letter being sent out to many companies).

Files or parts of files may be inserted into the document being edited, thus recycling previously created material. The user can create *boilerplate* documents, as is often done with proposals, contracts, and specifications, by using bits and pieces from user files on the computer. Similarly, some editors allow *template* files to be copied automatically into a new file when it is opened.

Deleting. The *delete* command requires that the user select the scope of the operation in order to indicate how much is to be deleted. Some text editors ask for confirmation before actually deleting text; others provide an *undo* command (see also below), making the last deletion reversible. For the delete command, as well as the copy and move operations described below, many systems provide *delete buffers*, the text reservoirs mentioned earlier. The deleted text can be used later as the object of *paste* (also called *insert* or *put*) operations, which put the elements from the delete buffer back into the text. Some text editors provide multiple delete buffers for more complex manipulations.

Changing. The simplest change is the replacement of one letter with another, often to correct a mistyping. In an editor's typeover mode, the user simply types the new character over the erroneous one. In the insert mode, the user must type the new character and then delete the old character (or vice versa).

Similarly, changing a word in typeover mode simply involves typing over the erroneous word. In cases where the replacement word is not the same length as the original word, a delete or insert character function may also be needed. In insert mode, a word is changed by inserting the new word and then deleting the old word. On mouse-based systems, the user selects the word to be replaced and types its replacement over the old word.

Line editors require the user to specify what character(s) to replace. These editors have a change or substitute command that takes as arguments both the scope of the change and the replacement string.

Global changes are those that take place throughout an entire document, such as from single to double spacing, to a new typeface, or replacing every instance of a particular word with a substitute word.

A *transpose* command is not available in most editors, although it is extremely convenient to correct mistypings such as *teh* for *the*. In Emacs, for example, the *transpose-character* (Ctrl-T) command will exchange the character at which the cursor points with the one directly to its left; the *transpose-word* command will do the same for words.

Moving. To move a block of text, the user specifies the scope of text to be copied and the place where the text is to be pasted. In an editor in which the scope is specified by pointing, the user defines the source by selecting the beginning and end of the text to be moved, and then defines the destination by pointing to the location at which it should be placed. (*See* Fig. 5 for an example of cutting and pasting.)

Miscellaneous Capabilities

RELIABILITY

Backup Capability. Text editors often offer *backup* to minimize the possibility of the accidental erasure or destruction of the document. This is sometimes done by having the user work with copies of the files, rather than the original, so that the file cannot be destroyed by a system crash. In some editors, *autosave* or *checkpointing* automatically saves the file after a certain number of keystrokes or on a time schedule.

Undo Facility. The *undo* facility, in its most basic form, allows the user to retract the command most recently

(a)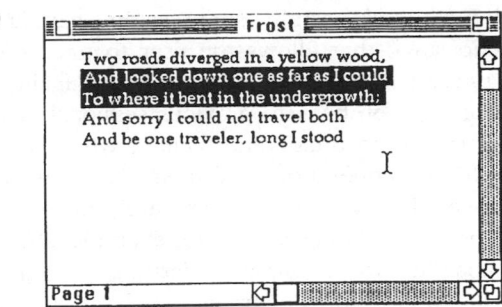

(b)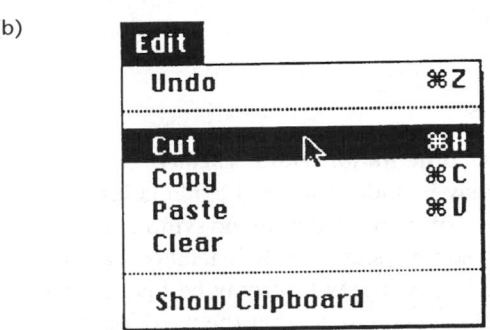

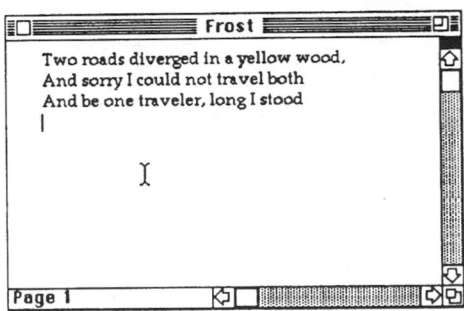

(c)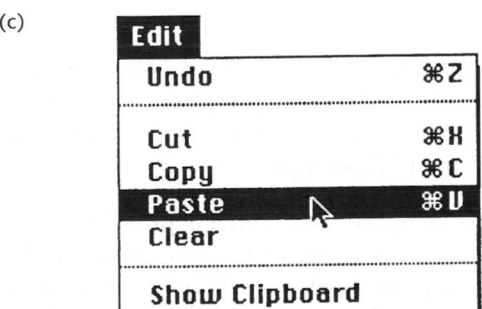

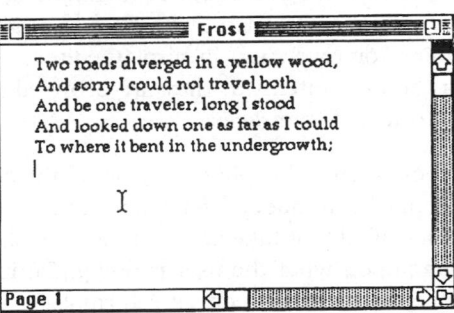

Figure 5. Reordering of a poem using Cut and Paste. (a) Select the two lines out of order; (b) Remove them using Cut; (c) Insert them in the correct place using Paste.

entered. Even more usefully, some systems have an *n-level* undo stack that allows the user to undo commands *n*-levels back (sometimes to the beginning of the session or even back to previous sessions). Some systems provide an undo/redo facility, which allows the user to undo operations and then redo them with a keystroke. However, editors can rarely undo every kind of command. Many editors, for example, offer no undo capability for commands causing a complex transformation of the document, such as a global search/replace.

USER AIDS

Online Documentation/Help Facility. Online *help facilities* may include expanded explanations of error messages, a summary of command syntax, or an online manual. In some systems the help facility is available in a separate help window that may be opened into the document being edited, so that the user does not have to leave the document in order to search for help advice.

In a *context-sensitive* help system, the user can get instant information particularly on commands recently issued. Other systems enable the user to ask for the meaning of any function key or menu item.

Unfortunately, online help facilities are all too often described by users as not helpful, because they are incomplete and because keywords chosen for indexing are not intuitively clear to users.

Feedback to the User. Feedback from the system to the user is necessary to the editing process, for specifying operations and scope and for showing the results of an operation in the updated view.

Editors with typing-oriented interfaces provide immediate feedback on both operation and scope by displaying the typed command on the screen, whereas function key interfaces provide no inherent feedback. Feedback techniques include such things as highlighting a selection in progress (with such techniques as brightening, underlining, or reversing) in display editors, or highlighting the menu items as they are browsed through in menu-oriented interfaces.

Audio cues, such as beeping, may signal the user that an error has been made. User-programmable cursors may be specified that take on different symbolic forms depending upon what the user is doing. During time-consuming operations such as reformatting or loading a large file, a small icon, such as a watch or an hourglass, may signal the user that the system is still working.

Customization: Profiling. A *profiling* or *preferences* facility allows the user to customize the editor environment. Frequently used or preferred settings can be saved and restored automatically for each document.

User Defined Commands (Macros). An editor *macro language* allows the user to define *macros* or *editing scripts* based on the system operation repertoire. The user can thus package under one name sequences of commands that are frequently executed together. In some systems, these commands prompt for or simply accept parameters (operands) and even provide conditional execution for maximum power and flexibility. The less flexible *keystroke macros* offered by some systems capture a set of keystrokes typed in by the user and can then repeatedly execute those keystrokes as if they were typed as one command.

Extensibility. User extension of the editor's command set, using the programming language in which the editor is written, is a feature targeted to advanced users. In Emacs, for instance, the editor can be used to modify or create a function, and this function can be linked into the editor without the user having to leave the editing environment.

Historical Development of Editors

Over the years, editing systems have evolved from simple tools meant primarily for systems programmers into polished products for use by specialized workers in many fields. The history of this technological development is one of many complementary developments occurring almost simultaneously. An accurate chronology is difficult to provide because there are so many text editors and their relationship to each other is cloudy. The following is simply a brief overview of some of the important milestones.

Punched cards (*q.v.*) provided the first stage in non-interactive computerized editing. The basic unit of information on punched cards was the 80-column line; corrections of mispunched cards could be made only by retyping the entire line and the entire card. Yet punched cards, so inflexible by the standards of today's infinitely correctable screen image, represented a step forward in ease of use compared with toggling bits at the system console. The information on a punched card could be read both by the computer and by a human, since the characters punched onto the card appeared in ink on the top line of the card.

Card or *batch editors* were created to address the deficiencies of the punched card. The programmer's initial deck of cards was stored as a tape or disk file, each card numbered for reference. An *edit deck*, composed of cards containing editing requests, was run through the batch editor to make changes. For example, the request to change a misspelled word *rata* in card 35 would be made by typing

```
35 CHANGE/RATA/RATE/
```

Batch editors removed the problems of dropped cards and of retyping (in many cases), and, in some versions, provided options such as global replacement of a pattern. However, some of the advantages of cards, such as the easy visual inspection of a properly sequenced, color-coded, and well-labeled card box, were lost.

With the advent of time-sharing environments in the mid-1960s, interactive line editors allowed the user to create and modify disk files from terminals. These editors attached numbers to lines of limited length, initially 80 characters. Simple command languages allowed the user to make corrections within a line or even within a group of contiguous lines, using a syntax similar to that of batch editors.

But these and subsequent *context-driven line editors* and *variable-length line editors* did not address three basic problems in manuscript editing: truncation when the line length was exceeded, inability to edit a string crossing line boundaries, and inability to search for a pattern crossing line boundaries. The *stream editor* solved all three problems by eliminating line boundaries altogether: the entire text was considered a single stream or string that was broken into screen lines by display routines. An arbitrary string between any two characters could be defined for searching and editing.

Multiline display screens with cursor adressability and local buffers made possible *full-screen, display,* or *cursor editors* (the three terms are synonymous). An early example of a time-shared display editor is Stanford University's TVEDIT (Tolliver, 1965). Commands, represented by control character sequences, could be interspersed with the input of normal text. Users could move the cursor to the point of editing, rather than having to describe text arguments using a programming language syntax. The TVEDIT concepts and similar work (Irons and Djorup, 1972) form the basis of many screen editors in use today.

In 1959, Douglas Engelbart at Stanford Research Institute introduced a major conceptual change with his NLS (oNLine System). It was implemented in the 1960s using display terminals, multicontext viewing, flexible file viewing, and a consistent user interface (Engelbart, 1963; Engelbart and English, 1968; Engelbart *et al.,* 1973). One of its many important contributions was the mouse, which, however, did not achieve popular acceptance until the 1980s. NLS provided support for text *structure* and *hierarchy*: users could manipulate documents in terms of their outline struc-

ture, not only their content. NLS and related editors view the editor as an *author's tool*, an interactive means for organizing and browsing through information, rather than simply as a way to alter characters in a single file. EMILY (Hansen, 1970) extended the concept of the structure editor and developed the *syntax-directed editor*, which imposed on the program being edited the structure of the programming language itself, giving users the power to manipulate logical constructs such as do–while loops and their nested contents as single units.

In the late 1960s, it was usual for general-purpose time-sharing facilities to support only simple interactive line editing and batch formatting facilities for line printer output, adequate for no more than creation and modification of programs and rudimentary documentation. Early in the next decade, *minicomputers* offered dedicated text processing facilities that provided comprehensive editing and formatting/typesetting, as well as facilities usually not available on general-purpose systems, for database management (*q.v.*), information retrieval (*q.v.*), workflow management, and print and job queue management.

The Unix (*q.v.*) system developed in the early 1970s and generally accepted by the middle of the decade, became an important milestone in text editing and text processing. Unix was the first general-purpose computing environment in which text utilities were given as much weight as programming utilities. Unix's suite of utilities (the *ed* text editor, the *troff* text formatter, the *eqn* equation formatter, the *tbl* table formatter, the *refer* bibliographic database and formatter, the *spell* spell checker, and the *style* and *diction* text analyzers; Kernighan and Lesk, 1982) became the benchmark for text tools.

In the area of computer graphics (*q.v.*), picture editors were being designed to allow the user to manipulate graphical elements. Interactive drawing techniques from Sutherland's pioneering Sketchpad system (Sutherland, 1963) were later incorporated into editor interfaces. In the Carnegie Mellon *tablet* editor (Coleman, 1969), hand-drawn proofreader's symbols were used to edit displayed text. For a *delete* or *substitute* operation, for instance, the user drew a line through the text to be deleted.

The Bravo editor and the Smalltalk environment developed at Xerox's Palo Alto Research Center (Xerox PARC) were the major innovations of the 1970s in text handling and the user interface. These systems blended text and graphics on a high-resolution bitmapped raster graphics screen, using a dynamic graphical interface provided by a dedicated personal computer and using the mouse as a pointing device. These systems displayed the text on a bitmapped screen in a facsimile of the document's final appearance, and were thus the first *interactive editor/formatters*.

Throughout the 1980s, the ideas developed at Xerox PARC spread even farther as the WYSIWYG concept influenced the personal computer industry. These new computers, exemplified by the Apple Macintosh, introduced in 1984, put a priority on ease of use, user interface consistency, and interactive type-setting/editing throughout their operating environment. With the proliferation of word processing technology, content and editing have become so intertwined that very little computer-assisted text processing is now distinct from formatting. It is now common for a single piece of software to be used for everything from word processing to typographical style selection, page placement, and updating of the table of contents, index and bibliography.

Several systems now allow the creation of fully editable *composite documents*, which may contain blocks or subdocuments of various types—graphics, text, spreadsheet—each of which may be created and edited by a different editor. For example, a single document might contain data from both a spreadsheet and a word processor.

These systems are exemplified by Quill, an editing system developed at IBM's Almaden Research facility. The developers of this system call it "an extensible system for editing documents of mixed type" (Chamberlain *et al.*, 1988). Another system with related functions is Hewlett-Packard's NewWave operating environment. In this system, which is overlaid on Microsoft Windows, users create *objects*—documents or part of documents—that can be placed in any document, regardless of their type.

Conclusion

Since its appearance in the 1940s, the computer has changed from a tool of a small scientific community to an appliance of the mass market. Text editing, starting with the punched card, has evolved steadily with interactive editors for programs, simple editors for documentation, and sophisticated editors for word processing and page layout. Now, 50 years later, we have inexpensive but powerful editor/formatters that can be used on desktop computers to create the mixed text and graphics necessary in the highest-quality magazine pages.

Editing systems are likely to change in an evolutionary, rather than a revolutionary, manner for the foreseeable future. Still, a few major changes may be in store. First, composite document editors for editing text, graphics, spreadsheets, charts, etc., will become more prevalent. Second, the emerging technologies of lightweight portable computing and handwriting recognition will make it easier for casual users to put large amounts of text and nontext information into a computer without typing. Finally, as speech recognition continues to improve, users will be able to dictate text into the computer, making it possible for more users than ever before to use a computer effectively to create, edit, organize, and browse textual material.

Bibliography

1963. Engelbart, D. C. "A Conceptual Framework for the Augmentation of Man's Intellect," in *Vistas in Information Handling* (ed. P. Howerton), 1–29. Washington, DC: Spartan Books.

1963. Sutherland, I. E. "THOR: A Display Based Timesharing System," in *Proc. Spring Jt. Computer Conf.*, **23**, 329. Baltimore, MD: Spartan Books.

1965. Tolliver, B. "TVEDIT," Stanford Time-Sharing Memo. No. 32, Dept. of Computer Science, Stanford University, Palo Alto, CA.

1967. Tolliver, B. *QED Reference Manual*. Ann Arbor, MI: Com-Share Inc.

1967. Nelson, T. H. "Getting It Out of Our System," in *Information Retrieval: A Critical Review* (ed. G. Schecter), 191–210. Washington, DC: Thompson Book Co.

1968. Engelbart, D. C., and English, W. K. "A Research Center for Augmenting Human Intellect," in *Proc. Fall Joint Computer Conf.*, **33**, 395–410. Arlington, VA: AFIPS Press.

1969. Coleman, M. "Text Editing on a Graphic Display Device Using Hand-drawn Proofreader's Symbols," in *Pertinent Concepts in Computer Graphics* (eds. M. Faiman and J. Nievergelt), 282–290. Urbana, IL: University of Illinois Press.

1970. Hansen, W. J. "Creation of Hierarchic Text with a Computer Display," *Rep. ANL7818*. Argonne National Laboratory, Argonne, IL.

1972. Irons, E. T., and Djorup, F. M. "A CRT Editing System," *Comm. of the ACM*, **15**, 1 (January), 16–20.

1973. Engelbart, D. C., Watson, R. W., and Norton, J. C. "The Augmented Knowledge Workshop," in *Proc. National Computer Conf.*, **42**, 9–21. Arlington, VA: AFIPS Press.

1982. Kernighan, B. W., and Lesk, M. E. "UNIX Document Preparation," in *Document Preparation Systems. A Collection of Survey Articles* (eds. J. Nievergelt, G. Coray, J. Nicoud, and A. Shaw), 1–20. Amsterdam: North-Holland.

1988. Chamberlain, D. D., Hasselmeier, H. F., Luniewski, A. W., Paris, D. P., Wade, B. W., and Zolliker, M. L. "Quill: An Extensible System for Editing Documents of Mixed Type," *Proceedings of the 21st Hawaii International Conference on System Sciences*, Kailu-Kona, Hawaii (January), 317–326.

1990. Lamb, L. *Learning the vi Editor*, 5th Ed. Sebastopol, CA: O'Reilly & Associates.

1990. Smith, P. D. *An Introduction to Text Processing*. Cambridge, MA: MIT Press.

1991. Finseth, C. A. *The Craft of Text Editing: Emacs for the Modern World*. New York: Springer-Verlag.

1993. Apple Computer, Inc. *Inside Macintosh: Text*. Reading, MA: Addison-Wesley.

1996. Stanek, W. R., and DeRose, S. J. *HTML, CGI, SGML,, VRML: Java Web Publishing Unleashed*. Indianapolis, IN: Sams.

1997. Snell, N. *The Comprehensive Guide to Microsoft Office 97*. Research Triangle Park, NC: Ventana Communications Group Inc.

1997. Meade, J. G. *The Comprehensive Guide to Smartsuite 97.* Research Triangle Park, NC: Ventana Communications Group Inc.

1997. Neibauer, A. *Corel WordPerfect Suite 8: The Official Guide.* Berkeley, CA: Osborne McGraw-Hill.

Websites

Yahoo! site for HTML editors:
```
http://www.yahoo.com/Computers_and_Internet/
Software/Reviews/Titles/Internet/Web_
Authoring_Tools/HTML_Editors/.
```
Yahoo! site for word processors:
```
http://www.yahoo.com/Business_and_Economy/
Companies/Communications_and_Media_Services/
Desktop_Publishing/Software/Word_Processing/.
```
Yahoo! site for text editors:
```
http://www.yahoo.com/Computers_and_Internet/
Software/Text_Editors/.
```
Tom Magliery—List of HTML editors:
```
http://www.hypernews.org/HyperNews/get/www/
html/editors.html.
```

Alton F. and Ruth H. Sanders (with material from the 3rd edition article by Norman Meyrowitz and David Temkin)

THEOREM PROVING

For articles on related subjects *see* ARTIFICIAL INTELLIGENCE; EXPERT SYSTEMS; HARDWARE VERIFICATION; HEURISTIC; LOGIC PROGRAMMING; LOGICS OF PROGRAMS; MODEL CHECKING; NONMONOTONIC LOGIC; and PROGRAM VERIFICATION.

The two approaches to automated *theorem proving* are *proof finding* and *consequence finding*. A proof-finding program attempts to find a proof for a certain given theorem. A consequence-finding program is given some axioms and then tries to deduce consequences from the axioms and to select "interesting" consequences.

Purposes

Some of the purposes of programming a computer to prove theorems concern artificial intelligence and deduction. Artificial intelligence researchers point out that proving a nontrivial theorem is an intellectually difficult problem. Except where otherwise stated, the theorem-proving programs we mention in this article use mathematical logic or, to be specific, the *first-order predicate calculus*, which is also called *quantification theory*. In mathematical logic, one can express fairly conveniently almost all kinds of deductive arguments. Writing a theorem-proving program that uses mathematical logic allows the researcher to study deduction in its purest form. Deduction is important because it plays a major role in solving many kinds of problems (not just in mathematics). A program that can prove theorems has what John McCarthy has called *common sense*; i.e. it has the ability to make deductions from given facts. This kind of common sense is an important part of human intelligence. Programs that use math-

ematical logic to find proofs have been extended to deduce answers to questions.

The other purposes of programming a computer to prove theorems concern mathematics and mathematical logic. Mathematicians point out that a program that could prove new and interesting theorems would be useful in itself. It would be a tremendous achievement if some program of the future could prove or disprove the Goldbach conjecture (that every even integer greater than 2 is the sum of two primes), for example. Mathematical logic is well suited to computers, since logicians have striven for decades to make their inference rules "mechanical." It is an attractive idea to write a program based on mathematical logic, since this is a well-formulated and well-studied branch of mathematics. In addition, programming a computer to prove theorems is a way to study mathematical logic. For example, the programmer may develop powerful, natural, and intuitive inference rules to which heuristics can be added easily.

Techniques

ORIGINS

We begin the history of automated theorem proving by mentioning some programs that have proved theorems in areas other than the first-order predicate calculus. A 1957 program called the "Logic Theorist," or simply LT, by Allen Newell, J. C. Shaw, and Herbert Simon (*q.v.*) proves theorems in *propositional calculus* (also called *sentential calculus*, or *Boolean algebra—q.v.*). It performs at approximately the level of a fair-to-good college student on the same theorems. A 1959 program mainly due to Herbert Gelernter proves geometry theorems at the level of a good high school student. A program called ADEPT proves theorems in group theory. It performs at approximately the level of an intelligent college student.

A program of R. Boyer and J. Moore (1979), later renamed Nqthm (for New Quantified Theorem Prover), proved the correctness of one of the fastest string-searching algorithms, the correctness of a simple expression parser, the correctness of the prime factorization theorem, the soundness and completeness of a simple mechanical theorem prover, the correctness of an arithmetic simplifier, and the correctness of a microprocessor. As an integral part of the success of each of these proofs, the user of the theorem prover had to suggest useful intermediate theorems to prove.

RESOLUTION IN FIRST-ORDER LOGIC

P. Gilmore and Hao Wang, as well as Martin Davis and Hilary Putnam, were among the first to program a computer to find proofs in the first-order predicate calculus. Each of these programs substitutes many constant terms for the variables and then checks to see if the theorem has been proved. If not, more constant terms are added and another check is made, etc.

After these programs had been written, J. A. Robinson developed an inference rule which he called the *resolution principle*. Roughly speaking, the resolution principle draws the most general, possible conclusion from two given statements, where the conclusions and the two statements generally contain variables. The resolution principle is more natural, more intuitive, and easier for people to use than are the inference rules used by the previous predicate calculus programs. Furthermore, it is easier to think of heuristics to add to the resolution principle.

A procedure that uses the resolution principle for proof finding tries to show that the negation of the given theorem to be proved is unsatisfiable (contradictory, inconsistent). The resolution principle is complete for proof finding in the sense of the following theorem, first proved by J. A. Robinson: "If a finite set of clauses [statements] is unsatisfiable, a contradiction can be found in a finite number of applications of the resolution principle." This means that there is, in principle, a computer program that, for any true theorem in first-order predicate calculus, can find a proof using the resolution principle. In practice, however, limitations of computer time and memory space prevent programs from finding proofs for many theorems. However, people have written proof-finding programs embodying the resolution principle. These programs are more powerful than the previous predicate calculus programs.

The resolution principle is complete for consequence finding in the sense of the following theorem, first proved by R. Lee: "If a clause *C* is a consequence of a finite nonempty set of clauses, a clause *T* can be found in a finite number of applications of the resolution principle such that *C* is an immediate consequence of *T* alone." Lee wrote a consequence-finding program based on the resolution principle.

Several researchers have strengthened these completeness theorems by showing that certain restricted forms of the resolution principle are still complete. This is of practical importance to automated theorem proving because theoretical considerations and computer experiments indicate that restricted and complete resolution tends to be more efficient than is unrestricted resolution.

Programs using the resolution principle or its restrictions have proved theorems already known (found proofs and found consequences) (e.g. theorems in group theory and abstract algebra). To speed up the search for proofs of theorems involving the equality predicate, complete, valid, and time-efficient inference rules, namely, *paramodulation* and *E-resolution*, were developed for theories with equality. Each of the new rules replaces the equality axioms and is used in addition to the resolution principle. Winker and Wos wrote such a program with paramodulation added, and it answered some open questions in ternary Boolean algebra.

Slagle pointed out the general advantages of building in theories and built in several such theories (e.g. partial and total ordering [Slagle and Norton, 1975]). He advocated clause compiling (replacing axioms by programs; e.g. inference rules) and narrowing (generalized replacement using equations). Stickel later developed a general technique for building in decidable theories (Stickel, 1985). Various other systems translate statements in more powerful logics into first-order statements; for example, McCarthy devised *circumscription* as a technique to perform nonmonotonic reasoning within a first-order framework (*see* NONMONOTONIC LOGIC). Such techniques have also been attempted for temporal (time) and modal (possibility and necessity) logics, though with limited success.

Most existing first-order resolution-based systems also use several strategies to speed up the search for proofs. In general, the strategies can be classified as *simplification* (removing redundant statements), *refinement* (determining on which clauses the resolution principle should be applied), or *ordering* (determining the order in which a set of clauses should have resolution applied to it).

A general theorem-proving program called Organized Techniques for Theorem-Proving and Effective Research (OTTER) (McCune, 1994), written in C (*q.v.*), was orders of magnitude faster than previous programs when it was introduced in 1988. Its speed is attained by using discrimination trees. It has proved many difficult theorems, some formerly unknown. It has also obtained new alternative proofs for existing theorems. The contribution of this theorem prover has ranged from providing insights assisting a human prover to totally automatic proofs. These proofs cover many areas including abstract algebra, group theory, and logical calculi.

Alternatively, the first-order predicate calculus can be restricted to less expressive forms allowing for more efficient proofs. In particular, the restriction of the logic to *Horn Clauses* results in a natural procedural interpretation of the clauses. This interpretation can be captured in a substantially more efficient proof procedure. The logic programming paradigm exploits the Horn Clause restriction to provide a class of programming languages that allow for a procedural semantics within a logical framework. Prolog is the most popular of these languages, and has been used successfully in numerous applications, in the theorem-proving domain as well as in general-purpose applications. Other logic programming languages include those based on temporal logics (Tokio, Tempura), constraint logic programming languages, and those that integrate logic programming and other paradigms such as functional programming (*q.v.*).

CONNECTION METHODS

Recall that the resolution rule attempts to find the most general conclusion from two statements. Proof efficiency is dramatically affected by the algorithm used to select the two statements that are to be resolved. However, a syntactic analysis of the input statements can be used to identify appropriate statement pairs, and *connections* can be made between these statements.

Matrix methods (Bibel, 1993) exploit these connections to guide proofs intelligently, thus providing a global strategy to construct proofs in contrast to the local nature of resolution proof strategies. The negation of the given theorem is first normalized into a form representable as a matrix of Boolean subformulas. The proof then proceeds by exploring paths through the matrix, which correspond to assignments to the variables in the input. If all paths are shown to be contradictory, the given theorem is proven.

TABLEAU METHODS

As with resolution, tableau methods prove a statement by deriving a contradiction from its negation. Unlike resolution, tableau methods apply several expansion rules to generate a tree (*q.v.*) from the input formula. There are expansion rules for each of the logical connectives, and the proof tree corresponds to a decomposition of the input into statements that are subformulas (or variants) of the input statement. The given statement is proven if each path in the proof tree contains a contradiction.

For first-order logic, tableaux are used primarily as a pedagogical device since they are natural, elegant, and simple to understand, but not as efficient as resolution. In contrast, tableau methods are often the method of choice for other logics including various modal, temporal, intuitionistic, nonmonotonic, and many-valued logics (Fitting, 1983; D'Agostino *et al.*, 1998). For most of these logics, resolution methods are either unavailable or complicated. The popularity of temporal and modal logics in other areas such as the semantics of programs, semantics of hardware, formal methods, planning, and scheduling has made tableau methods particularly important for theorem proving.

Connection methods are closely related to tableau methods since matrix paths correspond to tableau branches. Systems that attain many of the benefits of connection methods within the tableau framework have been constructed; for example, Shankar and Slagle introduce a temporal notion of connections that can be used to guide temporal logic tableau proofs (Shankar and Slagle, 1997).

MODEL GENERATION

In tableau systems, each branch corresponds to one set of assignments to the variables in the input (a model). However, these models need not be disjoint or minimal, thus leading to inefficiencies. Theorem provers based on the model generation paradigm apply techniques which generate only minimal models. For first-order logic, a prover called Satisfiability Checking for Model Generation (SATCHMO) (Manthey and Bry, 1988) applied the model generation paradigm as a more powerful technique that greatly reduces the effort spent on generating non-minimal or redundant models. Additionally, SATCHMO compiled first-order clauses into Prolog programs, leading to further efficiency improvements. Model generation theorem provers have achieved substantial efficiency improvements over traditional provers for first-order logic, and their similarity to tableaux make them promising for similar efficiency improvements in other logics.

PROOF ASSISTANTS

The above methods deal mostly with logics that are *complete* (i.e. the proof will halt if the statement is provable) or *decidable* (i.e. the proof will halt for all statements). Higher-order logics are normally incomplete, and no proof procedure that is guaranteed to halt for all provable statements exists. However, such logics have been shown to be of great use for many applications such as formal hardware and software verification, computer security, and protocol (*q.v.*) verification.

Two popular higher-order systems are Higher Order Logic (HOL) (Gordon and Melham, 1993) and Prototype Verification System (PVS) (Owre *et al.*, 1996). These systems include libraries for automatic proofs in decidable theories, along with proof techniques that may be applied at the user's direction. Since these systems generally require experienced users well-versed in the art of proving theorems, they also include features supporting the construction and maintenance of proofs. Although such a system is difficult for the novice user, the approach is popular for applications that require the expressive power of higher-order logics. Since traditional theorem provers also often require user guidance for nontrivial theorems, the need for assistance may not be a serious shortcoming.

Some major accomplishments using these systems include the formal specification of safety-critical hardware and algorithms, and the formal verification of various computer systems including a microprocessor and a division algorithm.

MODEL CHECKERS

In modal and temporal logic theorem proving, the prover attempts to show that the proposed statement holds for any model (i.e. state transition system). The model checking problem is somewhat simpler, in that it considers only the model corresponding to the system being modeled. Verification of a software or hardware system proceeds by identifying the state transition diagram corresponding to the system, and then applying a model checker to that model. Model checkers have been used primarily for temporal logics applied to the verification of circuits and protocols. The Symbolic Model Verifier (SMV) model checker (McMillan, 1993) has been used to verify large systems (10^{100} or more states), and has verified (and found errors in) the IEEE Futurebus protocol.

Applications

Theorem provers have been useful for artificial intelligence, specifying and verifying hardware and software systems, proving mathematical theorems, rigorously verifying existing mathematical proofs, and assisting students being educated on how to construct proofs. Plans are currently under way to construct a single distributed repository that represents all current mathematical knowledge (tentatively titled QED). The users of the system will include students, teachers, mathematicians, and scientists interested in applying, developing, learning, and teaching mathematical knowledge and techniques. Obviously, the system will involve a cooperative long-term effort by hundreds.

Further Study

A recent general introduction to first-order theorem proving is provided by Duffy (1991). Major research problems in automated reasoning are discussed by Wos (1988). A database of provers at `http://www-formal.stanford.edu/clt/ARS/systems.html` has links to the sources of most of the theorem provers mentioned in this article. The home page of the QED project is `http://www.mcs.anl.gov/qed/`.

Bibliography

1975. Slagle, J., and Norton, L. "Automated Theorem-proving for the Theories of Partial and Total Ordering," *Computer Journal*, **18**, 49–54.
1979. Boyer, R. S., and Moore, J. S. *A Computational Logic*. London: Academic Press.
1983. Fitting, M. *Proof Methods for Modal and Intuitionistic Logics*. Dordrecht, Holland: Kluwer.
1985. Stickel, M. E. "Automated Deduction by Theory Resolution," *International Joint Conference on Artificial Intelligence*, 1181–1186.
1988. Manthey, R., and Bry, F. "SATCHMO: A Theorem Prover Implemented in Prolog," *9th Intl. Conference on Automated Deduction*, 415–434.
1988. Wos, L. *Automated Reasoning: 33 Basic Research Problems*. Upper Saddle River, NJ: Prentice Hall.
1991. Duffy, D., *Principles of Automated Theorem Proving*. Chichester, UK: John Wiley.
1993. Bibel, W. *Deduction, Automated Logic*. London: Academic Press.
1993. Gordon, M. J. C., and Melham, T. F. (eds.) *Introduction to HOL*. Cambridge: Cambridge University Press.
1993. McMillan, K. *Symbolic Model Checking*. Dordrecht, Holland: Kluwer.
1994. McCune, W. "OTTER 3.0 Reference Manual and Guide," *Technical Report ANL-94/6*. Argonne, IL: Argonne National Laboratory.
1996. Owre, S., Rajan, S., Shankar, N., and Srivas, M. "PVS: Combining Specification, Proof Checking, and Model Checking," *Computer-Aided Verification '96*, New Brunswick, NJ (Lecture Notes in Computer Science 1102), 411–414. New York: Springer-Verlag.
1997. Shankar, S., and Slagle, J. "Connection-based Strategies for Deciding Propositional Temporal Logic," *Proceedings of the Fourteenth National Conference on Artificial Intelligence*, 172–177.
1998. D'Agostino, M., Gabbay, D., Hähnle, R., and Posegga, J. *Handbook of Tableau Methods*. Dordrecht, Holland: Kluwer.

James Slagle and Subash Shankar

THEORY OF ALGORITHMS

See ALGORITHMS, THEORY OF.

THRASHING

For articles on related subjects *see* OPERATING SYSTEMS; THROUGHPUT; TIME SHARING; VIRTUAL MEMORY; and WORKING SET.

Thrashing is an unstable collapse of throughput of a system of communicating servers, such as disk drives and CPUs, as the load is increased. It occurs when the heavy load shifts the bottleneck from a high-throughput to a low-throughput server. It violates the intuition that leads observers to expect throughput to increase smoothly toward a saturation level as load increases.

Thrashing was first observed in the first-generation multiprogrammed time-sharing systems of the 1960s. Designers had expected system throughput to increase toward a saturation level as the level of multiprogramming (load) increased. To their great surprise, throughput dropped suddenly after a critical load. Moreover, throughput would not return to its former high until the load was reduced below the critical value that triggered the thrashing—a form of hysteresis. This was a serious problem. It portended an unexpected increase of complexity, because dynamic load controllers were needed to prevent it.

Thrashing was explained in 1968 (Denning, 1968). Higher loads in a fixed size memory means that the average partition size decreases, forcing an increase in the rate of page faults. Since the paging server is much slower than the CPU, the increased traffic moves the queue of waiting jobs from the CPU to the paging server. As an example, consider a task that requires 1 second of CPU time on a system with a page fault time of 50 ms. At a small load, the task gets a large partition and generates (say) 10 page faults, which will require a total of 0.5 seconds of disk time; this task is CPU-bound. At a larger system load, the task's partition has been squeezed and the task now generates (say) 200 page faults; its total disk time jumps to 10 seconds and it becomes disk-bound. Within a decade after these early analyses, queueing network models were routinely used to quantify the relationship between throughput and the total demands for devices, and to help design load controllers to prevent thrashing (Courtois, 1977).

All load controllers divide submitted tasks into two sets: the "active set" is allowed to hold space in main memory; additional tasks are held aside in an "overflow" queue. The load controller activates tasks according to a limit criterion applied to the active set. The simplest limit criterion is a fixed, preset largest number of active tasks. The most sophisticated (and also optimal) activates a next overflow task whenever the number of unused page frames in main memory is sufficient to hold its working set. The working-set criterion was found empirically not only to be optimal but to be more robust than the fixed-load criterion (Denning, 1980).

Thrashing has also been observed in packet switched communications where many servers vie for slots in a common medium such as a satellite channel or Ethernet cable. Suppose each server follows this collision-detection protocol: if the medium is busy, wait until it is idle; when it is idle, begin transmitting your packet, and if someone jams you before you finish, stop transmitting and restart the protocol. As the number of contending computers (load) increases, the number of successful packet transmissions increases. Past some threshold of load, however, it becomes highly likely that two or more computers wind up cycling endlessly through the transmit-until-jammed part of their protocol loops; when this happens, few packets are transmitted successfully. These phenomena were first observed with the ALOHA satellite communication network in the late 1960s (Kleinrock, 1976).

Again, a load controller prevents thrashing by limiting when a computer can transmit. Each computer has a value called the *backoff interval* associated with it.

When its transmission is jammed, the computer waits for an amount of time equal to its backoff interval before restarting the protocol. The backoff interval can be adjusted dynamically: when a computer finds the medium idle and transmits successfully, its backoff interval is decreased; when the computer is jammed, its backoff interval is increased; otherwise its backoff interval is unchanged. Backing off reduces the frequency at which computers attempt transmissions when there is too much jamming. Kleinrock (1976) gives a full treatment of a variety of strategies for load control in packet-oriented communication systems.

Thrashing can occur in any network where the bottleneck shifts as the load is increased. It can be avoided by a load controller.

Bibliography

1968. Denning, P. J. "Thrashing: Its Causes and Prevention," *Proc. AFIPS Conf.*, **32** (1968 FJCC), 915–922.
1976. Kleinrock, L. *Queueing Theory*, Vol. 2, 360–407. New York: John Wiley.
1977. Courtois, P. J. *Decomposability*. New York: Academic Press.
1980. Denning, P. J. "Working Sets Past and Present," *IEEE Trans. Software Engrg.*, **SE-6**, *1* (January), 64–84.
1992. Tanenbaum, A. *Modern Operating Systems*. Upper Saddle River, NJ: Prentice Hall.

Peter J. Denning

THROUGHPUT

For articles on related subjects *see* JOB; PERFORMANCE MEASUREMENT AND EVALUATION; QUEUEING THEORY; and SCHEDULING ALGORITHMS.

The *throughput* of a system is the number of jobs, tasks, or transactions the system completes per unit time. Throughput is often used as a figure of merit, with higher values indicating better performance. System engineers use analytic or simulation models to help determine a system configuration and server capacities that enable the system to meet throughput and response-time targets.

The term throughput suggests a stream of jobs flowing through a system, with rates of arrival and completion being the same. But it is not always the case that the arrival and completion rates are the same. To see this, visualize a black box representing a system. Measure this system for a time T, counting A arrivals and C completions; define the arrival rate as A/T and completion rate as C/T. If $A = C$ the system is flow balanced, arrival rate equals completion rate, and the completion rate is the throughput. If the system is not flow balanced but jobs are repeatedly submitted by a fixed population of users who stop and wait for their jobs to complete, then A and C will differ by only a few per cent when both are much larger than the population size. In this case, we can call the completion rate the throughput without significant error.

Throughput considered alone is often a deceptive measure of performance. This is because a queue must build up at a server in order to force its throughput up toward its saturation level, which may induce an unacceptably high response time. To avoid such problems, the savvy analyst considers the entire system. Throughput is a central factor in the flow, response-time, and queueing laws of system performance. The remainder of this article demonstrates this.

A system consists of one or more servers. Two parameters are associated with each server i: (1) the visit ratio V_i is the mean number of visits a job makes to that server before exiting the system; (2) the per-visit service time S_i is the mean time the server processes a job per visit, not including queueing time. The total time demand of a job for the server is denoted D_i and is simply $V_i S_i$. The response time R_i of the server is the sum of the job's queueing time and its service time. The mean queue length Q_i of the server is the average number of jobs in the queue. Several important laws can be deduced from these definitions (Denning and Buzen, 1978):

1. *Utilization Law* The utilization U_i of a server is the fraction of time the server is busy. Throughput X_i of a server with mean service time S_i per task visit is related to the utilization U_i by the law $U_i = S_i X_i$. Since $U_i \leq 1$, the throughput is limited, $X_i \leq 1/S_i$. The maximum possible throughput $(1/S_i)$ occurs when the queue is full all the time—i.e. the server is saturated.

2. *Little's Law* Named after the queueing theorist who discovered it, this law states that a server's mean queue length Q_i is related to the per-visit response time R_i and the throughput X_i by the law $Q_i = R_i X_i$.

3. *Forced Flow Law* Let X_0 denote the system's throughput; then $X_i = X_0 V_i$. This implies that knowledge of a throughput at any single point in the system is sufficient to know the throughputs everywhere; hence the name of the law. When combined with the utilization law, it also implies that the utilizations are proportional to the products $V_i S_i$.

4. *System response time laws* The response time of a closed system is $R_0 = N/X_0 - Z$, where Z is the average time a user spends thinking before issuing a next request to the system. The response time of an open server is approximately $R_i = S_i/(1 - S_i X_i)$. In both cases, higher throughputs imply higher response times.

5. *Bottleneck Analysis* These laws can be combined to determine which servers limit the system and what the maximum throughput and minimum response time are. System throughput X_0 is limited by the speed of the slowest server in the system (bottleneck). The slowest server is the one with the largest value of the D_i (individual device total time demands); let $D_m = \max \{D_i\}$. Then X_0 rises with increasing load toward a saturation value of $1/D_m$. System throughput can be improved by removing bottlenecks, which can be done either by installing more service capacity at the bottleneck or by reducing the number of visits each job makes to the bottleneck.

An example will help visualize these concepts. Consider a system in which the total CPU demand by a typical job is 2 seconds and a typical job visits a disk server 100 times for 50 milliseconds each. The CPU demand is $D_1 = 2$ seconds and disk demand is $D_2 = 5$ seconds. The disk is the bottleneck, and system throughput is limited to $1/5$ job per second. The CPU utilization cannot be higher than $D_1/D_m = 2/5$. A faster CPU will have a smaller D_1—speeding it up will only reduce its utilization. Speeding up the disk will increase system throughput and CPU utilization.

The bottleneck analysis sketched above is for systems in which the parameters V_i and S_i are independent of the load N in the system. If one of the V_i depends on N, then the upper bound on throughput may depend on N. An example of this occurs in multiprogrammed virtual memories as increasing load generates more traffic to the paging disk, whose total demand eventually becomes larger than the other server demands and forces the throughput down from a peak (*see* THRASHING).

These simple relationships can be extended to systems with multiple job classes and variable rate servers (Menascé *et al.*, 1994).

Bibliography

1978. Denning, P. and Buzen, J. "Operational Analysis of Queueing Network Models," *ACM Computing Surveys*, **25** (September), 225–261.
1994. Menascé, D., Almeida, V., and Dowdy, L. *Capacity Planning*. Upper Saddle River, NJ: Prentice Hall.

Peter J. Denning

TIME SHARING

For articles on related subjects *see* ACCOUNTING SYSTEM, COMPUTER; FILE SERVER; INTERACTIVE SYSTEM; MULTIPLEXING; MULTIPROGRAMMING; MULTITASKING; SCHEDULING ALGORITHMS; SWAPPING; TIME SLICE; UNIX OPERATING SYSTEM; and VIRTUAL MEMORY.

Origins

Time sharing is a technique of organizing a computer so that several users can interact with it simultaneously. The term also refers to multi-user systems in which arbitrary general-purpose computation is performed and users operate independently of one another, often at locations remote from the computer itself. Although time sharing was initially perceived by many as a programming convenience for debugging (*q.v.*), the perception was soon extended to include the provision of a wide variety of online services and the availability of a large central memory shared among the user community.

Time sharing originated in the late 1950s and early 1960s. By then, relatively reliable commercial computers had been available for a few years, high-level languages were easing the task of programming applications, and ever larger programs were being constructed. At the same time, the operating staffs of most large computation centers were trying hard to make more efficient use of the still expensive equipment. Typically, programs and data for a batch of jobs would be prerecorded on magnetic tape, and then, under the supervision of a monitor program, the jobs would run serially without interaction until they terminated or encountered an error condition. While effective in keeping the equipment utilized, batch processing made the debugging of programs increasingly difficult. Not only was the time to correct even the most trivial error a matter of hours, but the problem was aggravated as one wrote larger and more ambitious programs.

This state of affairs for program debugging was particularly frustrating to users in universities and research laboratories, where large programming projects were being attempted, often with computers saturated by near-continuous use. In 1959, Christopher Strachey (*q.v.*), then at the National Research Development Corporation in England, presented a paper at a UNESCO Conference describing the possibility of doing program debugging while time-sharing the computer with the normal production computing load. Independently, that same year, Professor John McCarthy, in an influential but unpublished internal memorandum at MIT, proposed key hardware modifications to an IBM 709 computer that would allow the possibility of time-shared debugging by multiple users. Indeed, it was McCarthy's early advocacy of time sharing that inspired much of the interest in developing such systems.

In retrospect, it is not surprising that the notion of time sharing emerged, for it was in a sense a rediscovery of earlier, more experimental, modes of computer use. Although not widely known, it was in the early 1940s at a mathematics conference that the Stibitz relay computer at the Bell Telephone Laboratories was operated remotely by a single user a few hundred miles away (*see* STIBITZ, GEORGE and BELL LABS RELAY COMPUTERS). Also in the early to mid-1950s, the US Air Defense had the massive SAGE System developed. At each of several sites it had multiple users, each at a terminal interacting independently with information displayed on cathode ray tubes. In addition, in the late 1950s, IBM and American Airlines had begun development of the SABRE System, an online airline reservation system with hundreds of terminals distributed geographically. But these early multiterminal systems were dedicated in purpose to their single applications. What was new and striking in the proposals of Strachey and McCarthy was the vision of a computer used independently and virtually simultaneously by different persons for entirely different programs, each of which might still have serious mistakes or "bugs" in them. In short, the notions were planted of a *computer utility* where users would view the system as a set of services and conveniences provided to them and the primary goal was the larger one of optimizing the effectiveness of the users and equipment rather than just the equipment alone.

It was also particularly fortunate for the development of time sharing that two key technology improvements occurred when they did. These key changes were the replacement of the vacuum tube by the transistor and the availability of large-capacity rotating disk memories. Without transistors, the higher level of reliability required by online systems would have been economically infeasible, and without disk memories, the critical central storage for communal programs and data would not have been possible.

By the early 1960s, work on different implementations of the computer utility vision had begun at various places. The Cambridge (Massachusetts) area was particularly active, largely due to the influence of McCarthy. Some of the first working prototypes were the following: at MIT, the Compatible Time Sharing System (CTSS) of F. J. Corbató, initially on an IBM 709 (1961) and, later, the IBM 7090 and 7094 (1963); also at MIT, the DEC PDP-1 System of J. B. Dennis; and, at the Bolt Beranek and Newman Company in Cambridge a DEC PDP-1-based time-sharing system developed by a team consisting of J. McCarthy, S. Boilen, E. Fredkin, and J. C. R. Licklider. Other early influential prototypes were the Dartmouth College Basic (*q.v.*) System of J. Kemeny and T. Kurtz, initially implemented on a GE 235; the JOSS System implemented at the Rand Corporation by C. Shaw; and, at the System Development Corporation, a time-sharing system developed by J. Schwartz for the AN/FSQ-32 military computer. The emphasis differed in each case. CTSS was oriented toward a general-purpose service offered by a central computing service;

this system was to become the initial research vehicle of Project MAC, an MIT research laboratory organized by R. M. Fano to explore the implications of time-sharing and human-machine interactions. The MIT PDP-1 system was organized to allow each user direct control of input–output (I/O) devices in native machine language, but with protection from other users, so that each user was presented with a virtual machine capable of running arbitrary programs. The BBN PDP-1 system was oriented toward an environment for interactive program development that included the use of a high-performance graphical display. The Dartmouth System focused on introducing computing to nonprofessionals with the constrained, but easy to learn, Basic language; the JOSS system focused on a carefully human-engineered computational programming interface; and the developers of the AN/FSQ-32 system were interested in similar objectives to those of CTSS, but in the context of developing and maintaining large programs for military applications.

The above time-sharing systems, while among the earliest and more significant, were not the only ones developed in the 1960s. Rather, they display some of the variety of objectives and directions taken. With hardware obsolescence, none of the systems has survived in original form. Most time-shared systems are now used either for specialized purposes, such as applications involving common databases or for communal sharing of a high-performance workstation (*q.v.*) among a few users. Nevertheless, the early time-sharing systems have had a direct influence on almost all forms of interactive computing, frequently by the students of one system becoming the designers and implementers of the next.

Particularly important to the early growth of time sharing was J. C. R. Licklider, who, after participating in the implementation of the BBN system, joined the Department of Defense Advanced Research Projects Agency (then called ARPA, now DARPA), where he headed the Information Processing Techniques Branch. Licklider was not only an eloquent advocate of the benefits of time-sharing use, but from his ARPA office was also able to support the development of time-sharing systems at several companies and universities active in computer science research.

By the mid-1960s, time-sharing systems, especially those of MIT's Project MAC and of Dartmouth College, had attracted considerable attention among computer users, managers, and manufacturers, and the obvious impact of time-sharing systems forced these different groups to reevaluate their roles and the desired modes of computer use. Moreover, development of extensive new time-sharing systems had begun. Among the more notable plans were those

for the Multics System (by MIT's Project Mac, the Bell Telephone Laboratories, and the General Electric Company) and the TSS System (by IBM for the IBM 360/67), which were especially comprehensive in their goals. Indeed, this very comprehensiveness led to underestimates of the scale of the software engineering (*q.v.*) required. The Multics System, eventually marketed by Honeywell (which had acquired GE's computer department), took several years longer to develop than initially anticipated. The TSS System, implemented by a much larger group, was not as delayed as Multics, but had disappointing performance and human interfaces when first delivered. But despite these warning signs of engineering complexity, by the end of the decade dozens of time-sharing systems were being implemented both by ambitious users and by major manufacturers, and time sharing was well recognized as a significant mode of computer interaction.

How Time Sharing Works

The basic notion of how a time-sharing system works is straightforward. The computer can be considered to have, in its main high-speed memory, the programs for several users, as well as a master supervisory program (sometimes called an *executive* or *monitor*) under whose control the online system runs. The role of the supervisor is to commute the central processor sequentially through the programs associated with the users, running each for a brief burst of time (often called a *quantum* or *time slice*—*q.v.*). One can imagine a simple form of such a system with n terminals and up to n users, each with a program area in the main computer memory which also contains the supervisor program (*see* Fig. 1). Of course, any program that is waiting for input from its associated user terminal does not need processor time, nor does a program that completes its immediate computation in less than a quantum need the remainder of the quantum allotted to it. In the simplest or *round robin* case, where all the user programs are cycled through in order, the programs appear to their users to proceed as if they each had the computer all alone, albeit one that appears to operate slower on extensive requests.

To carry out the above scheme effectively requires three hardware features beyond the basic von Neumann computer (*q.v.*). The first feature is a program-settable "alarm" clock (an *interval timer*—*q.v.*), which the supervisor can use to interrupt user programs that are not finished after their quantum of time. The second feature is a privileged operation mode for the supervisor, not permitted to the user, which allows only the supervisor to execute the powerful instructions for initiating I/O operations, setting the interval timer, etc.; the effect is that any user-program misbehavior, intentional or unintentional, causes program

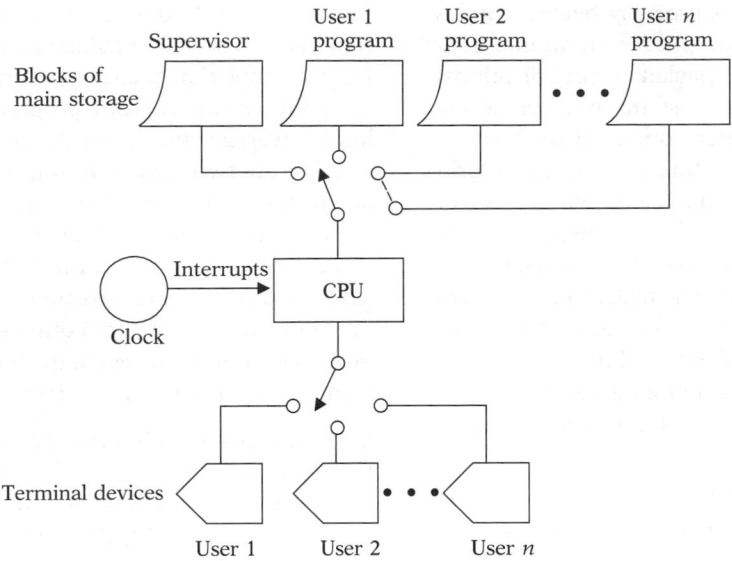

Figure 1. A highly simplified time-sharing system.

control to revert to the supervisory program. The third feature is a pair of *bounds registers*, set by the supervisor, that can be compared with each memory access attempted by the processor. As with the user mode, any attempt by a user program to reference a location outside of its area in memory automatically causes program control to revert or *trap* (*q.v.*) to the supervisor program. The important aspect of these three features is that the supervisor program can never lose control of the computer, no matter how undebugged or misprogrammed a user program might be. Furthermore, one user program can be prevented from interfering with, or even reading, the programs or data of another user.

Implementation Issues

There are several technical and sociological consequences and observations one can make. The first is that, because of user response times, input and output data rates may be limited. With simple text-oriented terminals, telephone lines are usually adequate and allow remote access. However, remoteness introduces anonymity and the need to authenticate user identities. Simple password (*q.v.*) schemes usually suffice, but sensitive data requires cryptographic techniques and secure communications (*see* AUTHENTICATION and CRYPTOGRAPHY, COMPUTERS IN).

A further consequence of time-sharing is that users have centrally stored programs and data representing months or years of work so that extremely reliable and timely backup procedures are vital. Also, to avoid user frustrations, good interactive response times and dependable system reliability and availability are critical requirements. Moreover, a time-sharing system will require resource allocation quotas and usage metering if it is to be operated as a utility.

A basic time-sharing supervisor must manage and share the system resources (e.g. processors, memory, and I/O devices) among the users. It does this using a *scheduling algorithm* and *virtual memory* (*q.v.*) or, in elementary systems, *swapping* (*q.v.*). In more elaborate systems *demand paging* is used to minimize unnecessary paging.

A central *file system* is a key requirement of a time-sharing system. Typically, each user has at least one private directory to hold programs and data and users can share items while specifying the kinds of access (e.g. read-only or none) they wish other users or classes of users to have. In addition, implementation of a file system is much more effective if the system contains a calendar clock. This key hardware component provides users with a unique time stamp for such purposes as branding successive generations of information, preserving event sequences, and facilitating the purging of obsolete files by age or last use.

Time-sharing systems typically provide a large variety of editors, languages, tools, and services. Indeed, many features widely assumed today such as word processing (*q.v.*) and electronic mail (*q.v.*) originated with the early time-sharing systems.

Future Directions

There were several original motivations for time sharing: reducing user costs, interactive program use, and allowing a community of users to share or exchange information, data, and programs. As the costs of both computers and communications continue to decline, time-sharing systems typically become nodes in a large network of other computer systems interconnected with high bandwidth packet communications. Often these other computer systems may be workstations or personal computers operated by a single user. With the growth of the Internet and the World Wide Web, along with the almost universal use of visual displays, new modes of user interaction are rapidly evolving as remote *servers* provide user-operated *browsers* with text, graphics, programs, and data on demand. The overall interactive goals and inner structures of time-sharing still persist but the partitioning of system responsibilities and configurations have taken on a rich new variety of still-evolving forms.

Bibliography

1962. McCarthy, J. "Time-sharing Computer Systems," in *Computers and the World of the Future* (ed. M. Greenberger) (originally published as *Management of the Computer of the Future*). Cambridge, MA: MIT Press.

1975. Wilkes, M. V. *Time Sharing Computer Systems*, 3rd Ed. New York: Elsevier.

1983. Christian, K. *The Unix Operating System*. New York: John Wiley.

1997. Tanenbaum, A. W. *Operating Systems: Design and Implementation*, 2nd Ed. (with A. Woodhull). Upper Saddle River, NJ: Prentice Hall.

F. J. Corbató

TIME SLICE

For articles on related subjects *see* MULTIPLEXING; MULTITASKING; SCHEDULING ALGORITHMS; SWAPPING; and TIME SHARING.

In the late 1950s and early 1960s, computer systems were envisioned that could be used simultaneously by several people, each at a typewriter-like terminal, each appearing to have exclusive use of the computer. The computer was to take advantage of the typing time of one user by turning its attention to another. If the computational tasks requested were short enough, then all users could be serviced, and the illusion of a single-user private computer would be maintained. Early systems served less than a dozen people, whereas modern systems service 10 to 1,000 or more. But what if there were one or more very long computational tasks?

Time slicing provided a part of the answer. At the end of each time slice (or *quantum)* of, say, 10 ms, the operating system interrupts the current user program and turns its attention to other user requests, usually held in a FIFO queue, before returning to the interrupted program for another slice of time. A variety of scheduling algorithms were developed whose purpose was to maintain high-speed response to terminal requests with reasonable computer efficiency. Multiplexing among compute-bound programs (i.e. ones

that require I/O only at relatively long intervals) by time slicing uses the machine less efficiently than serial run-to-completion because a certain amount of time is required to switch from program to program. Also, longer average start-to-finish turnaround times occur: serially run, two equal jobs finish at time n and $2n$ (for an average turnaround of $3n/2$); with time slicing, both finish in somewhat more than $2n$ for an average of somewhat more than $2n$. But the important characteristics of time sharing and time slicing are high-speed response to many short computational requests and nearly continuous access to the machine; total problem turnaround time is a secondary consideration.

Early systems, which often took care of the low-speed terminal I/O with a separate front-end computer (*q.v.*) were driven exclusively by the time-slice clock and ignored the loss of CPU time incurred by the inability to overlap it with I/O to disk file and tape. The loss became more pronounced as time-sharing system applications became more sophisticated. Explicit interrupt signals from the I/O hardware, together with the later introduction of multiple programs in memory, combined to give the new operating systems both knowledge of possible overlaps of I/O and CPU execution, and means of making use of these periods of time. Modern systems achieve 95% CPU use together with significant concurrent use of swapping and I/O devices. Separate front-end processors, which were not popular during the rise of personal desktop systems and client–server (*q.v.*) technology, have now returned as "terminal server" front ends to the computational network or as *firewalls* that guard against unauthorized access to the network.

Event-driven systems, which required the operating system to make a scheduling decision (for each time slice, I/O, and other events), ran the risk of spending too much time deciding and not enough time doing. To solve this problem, Xerox's UTS (1969–1975) and CP-V (1971–1985), and later CP-6 (1979–present) on Honeywell Bull computers, adopted two control quanta in addition to the primary time-slicing quantum. One of these established a minimum interval between changes from program to program, regardless of the importance of the intervening events; it thus established a lower bound on the system overhead incurred in such changes. The second provided corresponding control and minimums for swapping, allowing a program to execute for a minimum period (if needed) before swapping is permitted. (The event-driven schedulers of these systems were patterned after JOSS, an early time-sharing system developed at the Rand Corporation in 1962-64. They were later used in the DEC VMS system for VAXes in the late 1970s, and from DEC they traveled to Microsoft for use in Windows NT.) In many systems compute-bound tasks are prioritized into different queues with the high-priority tasks being serviced before the lower or serviced for longer time-slice quanta, techniques especially important and well developed in real-time systems, where "guaranteed" completion times are used to control quanta.

Modern workstations (*q.v.*) for individual users have much higher performance than the time-sharing systems of the 1970s and 1980s that were so carefully shared, so the need for algorithmic care is much reduced. However, the algorithms are being rediscovered and reused as multitasking workstations evolve to serve the individual with multiple concurrently executing processes. The Macintosh System 7 and Microsoft's Windows 95 and its successors have brought this to the desktop with threads, and Windows NT implements a much more robust version.

Bibliography

1997. Silberschatz, A., and Galvin, P. B. *Operating System Concepts*, 5th Ed. Reading, MA: Addison-Wesley.

1997. Tanenbaum, A. S. and Woodhull, A. *Operating Systems: Design and Implementation*, 2nd Ed. Upper Saddle River, NJ: Prentice Hall.

G. Edward Bryan

TOMOGRAPHY, COMPUTERIZED

For articles on related subjects *see* BIOCOMPUTING; COMPUTER GRAPHICS; IMAGE PROCESSING; MEDICAL APPLICATIONS; MEDICAL IMAGING; OPTIMIZATION METHODS; and PATTERN RECOGNITION.

Tomography is defined as "a diagnostic technique using X-ray photographs in which the shadows of structures before and behind the section under scrutiny do not show." The origin of the word *tomography* is Greek, in which "tomos" means "section." *Computerized tomography* (CT) is a relatively recent development in which only the section under scrutiny is irradiated, and a computer (rather than an X-ray film) is used to produce an image of the section. (An alternative abbreviation used for the process is CAT, for *computer-assisted tomography*, and hence the result of applying the technology is called a CAT-Scan.) CT produces images of cross-sections of the human body from measured attenuation of X-rays through the cross-section. Since the appearance of the first commercial CT scanner in 1972 (built by EMI, Ltd), CT has revolutionized diagnostic radiology. The 1979 Nobel prize in medicine was awarded to Allan M. Cormack and Godfrey N. Hounsfield for their pioneering contributions to the development of CT.

An engineering drawing of a typical CT scanner (one built by the General Electric Company) is shown in Fig. 1. The patient lies on the table, and the table's sliding top moves into the hole of the gantry, which in turn houses the X-ray tube and collimator on one side (the collimator limits the X-ray beam to the section under scrutiny) and the data acquisition/detector unit on the other side. The detector unit contains a large number of detectors (typically about a thousand) arranged on an arc of a circle centred at the X-ray source. X-rays travel along straight lines between the source and the detectors. From the strength of the X-ray beam reaching the detector, we can estimate the total X-ray attenuation along the line between the source and the detector. Since tissues and tumors of different types attenuate X-ray differently, such measurements provide information regarding the cross-section of the body which lies in the plane of the X-ray source and the detectors.

If we keep the X-ray source and detector assembly stationary and slide the patient through the gantry, we can obtain an image similar to images obtained in traditional X-ray film radiography. Such an image is shown at the top left of Fig. 2. Intensities in this image are representative of total X-ray attenuation between source and detector. The image is built up row by row, each row corresponding to a separate incremental position of the patient through the gantry. The intensities in each row correspond to the total X-ray attenuations as measured by the array of detectors. The difficulty with such an output as a diagnostic tool is that images of bones, organs, air spaces, and any existing tumors overlap. It is often impossible to determine the exact nature, or even presence, of a tumor.

In CT, the body is kept stationary while the gantry rotates around it. This way, we obtain an image of the type shown at the top right of Fig. 2. This image is also built up row by row, but now each row corresponds to a separate incremental position of the gantry as it rotates around the patient. The interpretation of intensities in each row is the same as before.

The total X-ray attenuation between a source and a detector is the integral of a physical parameter called the *X-ray attenuation coefficient* along the line from the source to the detector. Since the X-ray attenuation coefficient at a point in the cross-section is indicative of the tissue (or tumor) type at that point, it is diagnostically useful to obtain a distribution of the X-ray attenuation coefficient in cross-sections of the human body. Measurements by the CT scanner (as represented by Fig. 2 top right) provide us with estimates of the integrals of this distribution along a large number of lines of known location.

A schematic representation of such a situation is shown in Fig. 3. The distribution of X-ray attenuation coefficients is indicated by a function of two polar variables $f(r, \varphi)$. The X-ray source moves in a circle around the

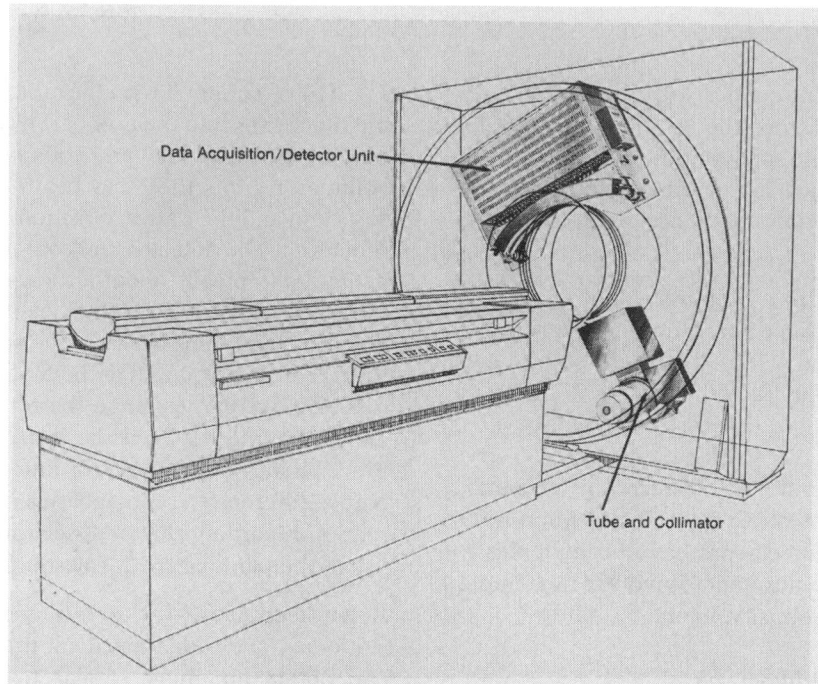

Figure 1. Engineering drawing of a typical CT scanner. (Courtesy General Electric Co.)

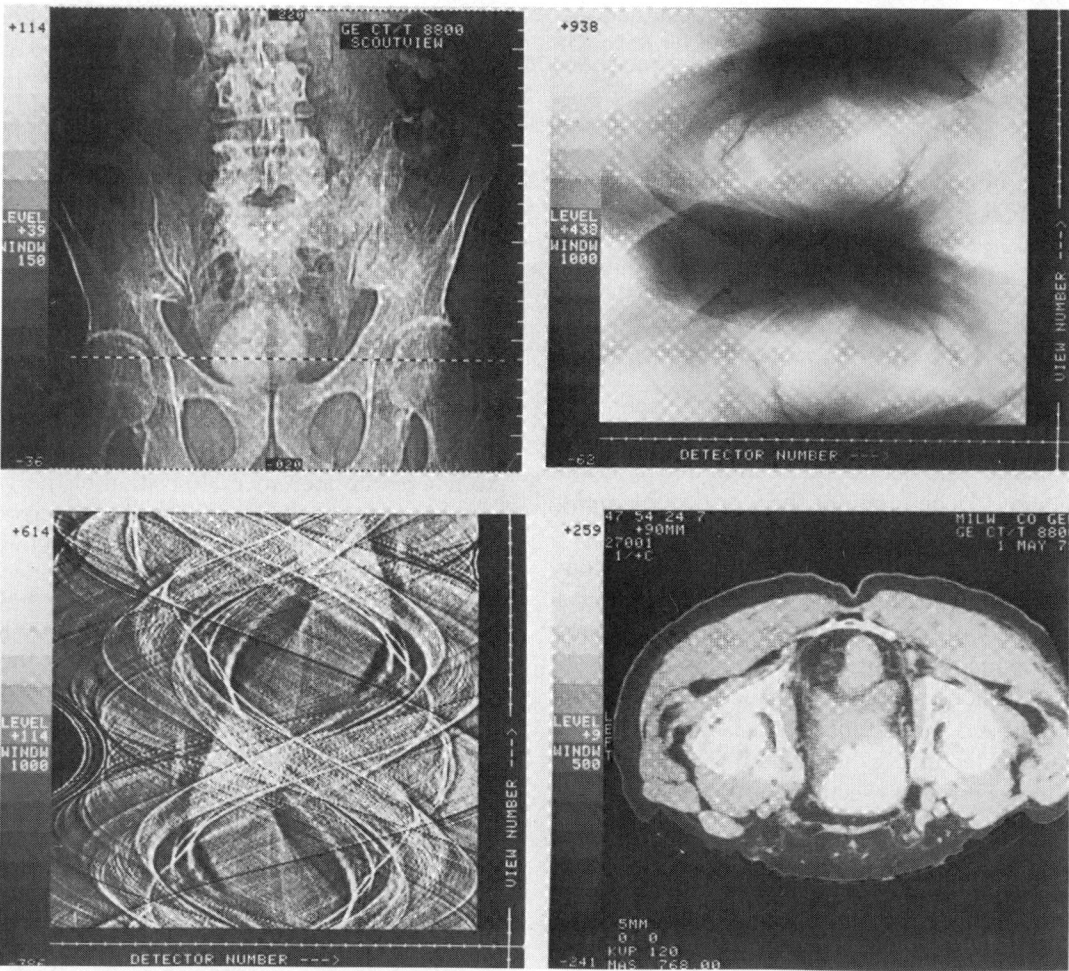

Figure 2. *Top left*: Scout View (a General Electric Trademark) obtained by sliding a patient through the stationary gantry of a CT scanner. The cross-section of interest is marked by a broken line. *Top right*: Projection data for the cross-section indicated on the left, obtained by rotating the gantry around a stationary patient (see also Fig. 3). This data is referred to in the text as $g'_{j,n'}$. *Bottom left*: The modified projection data referred to in the text as $g'_{j,n}$. *Bottom right*: The CT reconstruction of the cross-section of interest. (Illustration provided by G. H. Glover.)

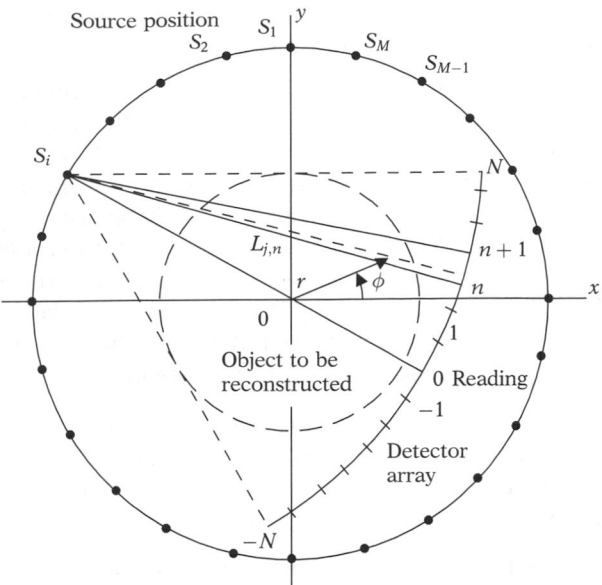

Figure 3. A schematic drawing showing the lines along which integrals of the X-ray attenuation coefficient distribution in the cross-section are assumed to be collected. (*Reprinted with the permission of G. T. Herman and A. Naparstek, from "Fast Image Reconstruction Based on a Radon Inversion Formula Appropriate for Rapidly Collected Data," SIAM J. Appl. Math.,* **33**, 511–533, 1977.)

origin 0, taking projections at M distinct locations $S_1, \ldots, S_M$. Let $L_{j,n}$ denote the line from S_j to the center of the nth (of an array of $2N + 1$) detectors. Then the measurement for the jth position of the X-ray source at the nth detector is approximately the line integral

$$\int_{L_{j,n}} f(r, \varphi)\, ds$$

where ds is the incremental distance from source to detector. Hence we are faced with the following computational problem: given estimates of the integrals of an unknown function of two variables along a number of lines of known location, estimate the values of the function at a number of points of given location.

The desired clinical information mandates that we estimate the function at a large number (typically, 10^5–10^6) of closely spaced (typically less than 1 mm in each direction) points. Accordingly, data is collected for 10^5–10^6 source/detector positions. For such a device to be useful, computational turnaround has to be rapid, and computational costs (which are eventually paid by the patients) have to be kept low. Thus, we are faced with an unusually large computational problem that has to be solved rapidly and inexpensively. Ingenious computational procedures have made the state of the art such that an image of a cross-section (such as shown at the bottom right of Fig. 2) can be produced from the data in less than a second by a minicomputer complemented by a standard array processor.

An example of a reconstruction method is the following. Mathematical analysis of the problem leads to three functions, p, q, and w, such that

$$f(r, \varphi) \simeq \sum_{j=1}^{M} w(r, \varphi, \beta_j) \left[\sum_{n=-N}^{N} q(p(r, \varphi, \beta_j) n\sigma) g_{j,n} \right],$$

where the $g_{j,n}$ form the measurement data (approximations to the line integrals defined above) and $f(r, \varphi)$ is the distribution to be reconstructed. The functions p, q, and w are chosen independently of data; the important fact is that they can be chosen so that the approximation indicated above is close for the class of functions $f(r, \varphi)$ that we desire to reconstruct.

The approximation as shown above implies that a separate double sum has to be calculated for each point (r, φ) at which the reconstructed value is to be obtained. Significant speed-up is obtained by the following observation: for a fixed j, the value of the inner sum is the same for all points (r, φ) that lie on the same line $L_{j,n}$. For $1 \le j \le M$ and $-N \le n' \le N$,

$$g'_{j,n'} = \sum_{\substack{n=-N \\ (r, \varphi) \in L_{j,n'}}}^{N} q(p(r, \varphi, \beta_j), n\sigma) g_{j,n}.$$

The bottom left of Fig. 2 is a pictorial representation of g', in the same way as the top right of Fig. 2 is a pictorial representation of g. In practice, for each j, the $g'_{j,n'}$ are calculated from the $g_{j,n}$ by the formula given above. Note that this can be done independently for the different js. Special-purpose array processors are usually used for the independent calculations of these sums. The estimation of $f(r, \varphi)$ is then done by using interpolation of the $g'_{j,n'}$ to estimate the values of the inner sum for a given j, r, and φ. These processes are usually implemented in firmware (*q.v.*).

The field of study dedicated to such computer algorithms is referred to as *image reconstruction from projections* (Herman, 1980). The usefulness of image reconstruction goes way beyond CT. Essentially the same computational procedure has been found useful in many other areas of science and medicine, such as radioastronomy, solar physics, nuclear medicine, and physiology (see Herman, 1979). There are a number of journals that are largely or wholly devoted to CT; two examples are *Computerized Tomography* and the *Journal of Computer-Assisted Tomography.*

Probably the clinically most significant recent development in CT has been the introduction of the so-called helical or spiral CT scanners, in which the body of the patient slides through the gantry while the gantry rotates around it. This increases patient throughput, but requires computer processes in addition to those indicated above, since the data are no longer collected from all directions for a single slice through the patient. Other developments include scanners that are fast enough (both physically and computationally) to reconstruct the beating heart inside the intact thorax and display of the appearance of organs, using computer graphics, based on a sequence of computerized tomograms. (See Udupa and Herman (2000) for details, and Fig. 4, Color Page CP-16, for an example.) These capabilities justify describing the medical procedures with such machines as *noninvasive vivisection.*

Bibliography

1979. Herman, G. T. (ed.) *Image Reconstruction from Projections. Implementation and Applications.* Berlin: Springer-Verlag.

1980. Herman, G. T. *Image Reconstruction from Projections: The Fundamentals of Computerized Tomography.* New York: Academic Press.

2000. Udupa, J. U., and Herman, G. T. *3-D Imaging in Medicine,* 2nd Ed. Boca Raton, FL: CRC Press.

Gabor T. Herman

TORRES QUEVEDO, LEONARDO

For articles on related subjects *see* CALCULATING MACHINES; and COMPUTER CHESS.

Don Leonardo Torres Quevedo was born on 28 December 1852 in Santa Cruz de Inguña, Santander, northern Spain. He grew up in Bilbao in the Spanish Basque Country and was educated there up to secondary school level. He spent two years at a Catholic school in France before joining the exclusive *Escuela de Caminos,* in Madrid, organized on the model of the French École de Ponts et Chaussées. He graduated from there in 1876.

A bequest from distant relatives allowed him to develop his scientific interests without financial worries. After extensive travelling in Europe, he alternated life in Madrid and at his country home in the north with occasional journeys abroad, mainly to France, where he became friendly with several leading scientists. One of them, Maurice d'Ocagne, publicized Torres Quevedo's work on calculating machines.

In the early 1890s Torres Quevedo became interested in the mechanical representation of general algebraic and transcendental expressions. By 1893, he had designed a machine based on a series of devices, called *arithmophores,* capable of handling monomial expressions. Polynomials were constructed by an original use of a mechanical analog of Gauss's additive logarithms. A quite large range for the argument was made accessible through an ingenious use of logarithmic scales. To preserve high accuracy, all contacts between parts of

his machine were geometric, i.e. dependent only on the geometry of the mechanisms.

His machine was theoretically capable of estimating the real (positive) roots of any given algebraic equation. He also showed how to proceed in the cases of complex roots and in that of special types of transcendental equations. A prototype, capable of solving trinomial equations of degree less than 10, was built in France on his orders and shown in 1895 at a meeting of the French Association for the Advancement of Science. Details of this machine were reported in the proceedings of the French Academy of Science in 1895.

The design of Torres Quevedo's early calculating machines is closely related to d'Ocagne's ideas on *nomography,* which he interpreted in mechanical terms with remarkable originality.

His designs rested on a new, more comprehensive *kinematic* definition of machines, which departed from the classical one given by A. M. Ampère and also from the more modern one of R. Willis. Theoretical questions became central to Torres Quevedo's interests; in 1901, he read a paper at the Academy of Sciences, Madrid, in which he dealt with the question of the definition of algebraic machines. His paper was

Figure 1. Torres Quevedo.

translated into French the following year. In 1914, at the same Academy, he read his interesting *Essay on Automatics* (Randell, 1973). Like Babbage, Torres Quevedo confronted the problem of describing complicated pieces of machinery; in 1906 he proposed a system of notations and symbols to facilitate such descriptions.

In later work, Torres Quevedo moved away from geometrically modeled calculating machines, making use of electrical and electromechanical devices. In 1903, he started a series of experiments in telecontrol by radio signals with a machine he called the *Telekino*. He was able to control the movements of a small boat at sea from a distance of several kilometers. This work was related to the design of radio-controlled torpedoes.

By 1906, a group of leading Spanish scientists and scholars requested official support for Torres Quevedo's research work. This initiative resulted in the creation of a national Institute of Applied Mechanics, later called the Institute of Automatics, in Madrid.

In 1910, he read a paper on electromechanical calculating machines at the National Engineering Society, in Buenos Aires, Argentina, in which he stressed the importance of discussing an *abstract* automatic machine, rather than a specific practical implementation. An enlarged version of this paper was published in the proceedings of the French Academy of Science in 1920.

These ideas were later implemented in a number of mechanical and electromechanical calculating devices built at his Institute in Madrid in the 1910s and 1920s. An advanced electromechanical calculator was shown in Paris in 1920. It operated with numbers of three to five digits. Depending on the operation, the result was a number of up to seven digits. It stored numbers in electromechanical units and had an electrical device to compare the size of numbers. The latter was useful for accelerating divisions. Output and input were effected through one or several typewriters that could be at some distance from the machine. A central station controlled the sequence of operations from input to calculation and printing.

In 1912, Torres Quevedo finished a working model of his well known electromechanical chess playing machine, which he showed in Paris two years later. A more elaborate model was built with the help of his son Gonzalo in 1920. Torres Quevedo's interest in chess-playing and calculating machines was, again, influenced by his desire to show the possibilities that existed in the field of electromechanical automation.

He also did substantial work in other fields of engineering, particularly on aerial cablecars and large airships. His best known design for aerial cablecars is the one over the Whirlpool of the Niagara River in Ontario, Canada, near Niagara Falls, which was commissioned in 1916, and is still operational.

Torres Quevedo had close contact with the industrial and financial community of the Basque Country, where industry was developing fast by the turn of the century. Some of his projects were financially supported by colleagues and friends from that area. In the early years of the 20th century, a private mechanical engineering company was formed in Bilbao to develop his inventions. Calculating machines, however, remained outside his commercial interests.

He began experiments with airships with a flexible structure in Spain at a state institute created for him near Madrid. Later models were built in France by the company Astra under the name Astra-Torres; they played a role in the First World War. Torres Quevedo was also interested in problems of scientific and technical documentation. As a member of the Royal Spanish Academy of Science, where he concentrated a substantial part of his scientific activities, he promoted the publication of a dictionary of new scientific and technical terms with the aim of unifying their use in the Spanish-speaking world. He died in Madrid in 1936.

Bibliography

1982. Randell, B. (ed.) *The Origins of Digital Computers*, 3rd Ed. New York: Springer-Verlag.

Eduardo L. Ortiz

TRACE

For articles on related subjects *see* BUG; DEBUGGING; and PROCEDURE-ORIENTED LANGUAGES: PROGRAMMING.

A *trace* is a debugging aid consisting of a display that chronicles the actions and results of individual steps in a program; the term is sometimes used for a control program that produces this kind of display.

The debugging process precipitates countless problems whose identification and correction may require a detailed stepwise record of a program's execution path. A trace is designed to provide this type of information by taking the user's program and placing it under control of a special routine that monitors its progress. Continuous execution of the user's program is replaced by a process whereby the trace program intercedes between steps of the user's program, displaying a variety of material before permitting execution of the next step. Of course, the type of information varies with the particular trace facility; however, the contents of most traces are characterized by such items as a copy of the instruction (or statement for high-level language programs), its location (or line number), and operand (*q.v.*) and register (*q.v.*) values before and after execution. In addition, some trace facilities are concerned with the sequence of events in a program, as well as with the history of various data items. In this case, the display will include indications as to whether certain branches have been followed, information about cyclic processes, etc.

Since these facilities are intended specifically for debugging, they are designed so that their insertion and subsequent deletion are straightforward. In many systems, a trace is superimposed by explicit specifications external to the program itself, in which case the request is communicated via the command language to the operating system under which the program functions. In other systems, the trace facilities are packaged in a separate program (a *debugger*), which, when activated, controls the execution of the program under scrutiny.

Because of its iterations, branches, and calls, the execution of even a modest-sized program may involve millions of individual steps. Consequently, an unfettered trace routine can easily generate hundreds of screenfuls of information most of which is of no interest. Accordingly, all trace facilities include provisions for damping their zeal. For example, the user may limit the trace to a certain section of the program, allowing the rest of it to execute normally. In addition, one may choose to examine certain variables; if so, the trace output will show only those steps in which the selected variables are affected. Moreover, the user's primary interest may be in the flow of logic, in which case the trace can be restricted to a record of branches, subroutine calls, and other sequence changes.

Seymour V. Pollack

TRANSACTION PROCESSING

For articles on related subjects *see* ADMINISTRATIVE APPLICATIONS; DATABASE MANAGEMENT SYSTEM; ELECTRONIC FUNDS TRANSFER; REAL-TIME SYSTEMS; and TELEPROCESSING SYSTEMS.

Introduction

In broadest computing terms, *transaction processing* describes the activity performed by a computer upon the introduction of an external stimulus, usually data. A *transaction* consists of a collection of functionally related data elements in combination with a signal that is either explicit (often referred to as a *transaction code*) or implied through the context of the application. The transaction code requests that a particular operation be performed in regard to the associated data elements.

A *transaction process* is the action (or series of actions) performed upon an object. Similar to a sentence, a transaction process requires a noun or object (data) and a verb (action). Data without an action is just inactive or stored data. An action may not be taken unless there is an object upon which to act. A transaction process is often referred to as a *unit of work*.

Transaction processing may be roughly divided into two modes of operation: batch processing and interactive or *real-time* processing.

BATCH PROCESSING

In a batch processing mode, transactions are collected into a group, called a *batch*, and processed together in a job initiated by an operator. Batch processing is appropriate where large volumes of data must be processed, the immediacy of the data is not critical, and user interaction is not required. Batch processing of transactions is also useful where a number of relatively static reports must be produced. A classic business example of batch processing is payroll. Individual time documents, which may be reported instantly through a time-capture mechanism, daily or weekly, are collected and periodically processed in scheduled jobs to produce checks, registers, and audit reports. A personal example of batch processing is the manner in which many people collect their bills and pay them at the end of the month. Each bill or invoice (itself the result of a transaction process) is a request that an action (payment) be performed on the associated data. Someone who sits down to write the checks at the end of the month is in effect processing a batch of transactions. The check resulting from the processing of each transaction is itself a transaction request to the bank to pay the person to whom the check is written the amount of money specified.

ONLINE REAL-TIME PROCESSING

In contrast to batch transaction processing, real-time processing is *event-driven*. In a real-time processing mode, transactions are acted upon as soon as they are entered into the computing system, thus allowing the user and machine to operate in the same time frame. In this interactive mode, errors may be detected by the system and reported back to the user, who may then take corrective action. The user may ask for help in entering the data, and the results of the transaction process may be instantly reported back to the user. In order for this process to take place, the user must have online access to the computer. The computer with which the individual is interacting may be a personal computer or network computer in a client–server or Web application (*see* CLIENT–SERVER COMPUTING and WORLD WIDE WEB).

Originally, on-line real-time transaction processing was accommodated through the use of a video display monitor based on a cathode ray tube (CRT) much like a television receiver (*see* MONITOR, DISPLAY). A list of actions which an operator was allowed to perform was displayed on the face of the screen in a form called a *menu*. The operator selected an action by indicating the appropriate option using an attached keyboard or mouse (*q.v.*). Depending upon the complexity of the underlying application, one or more secondary menu screens would be processed before an operator was presented with a screen into which specific data for a transaction could be displayed and entered. Data was then typed onto the screen and, when the Enter key was depressed, the content of the screen image was sent via a telecommunications link to the central computer, where it was edited for completeness and accuracy. If an error condition was detected, a screen was sent back down the telecommunications link to the user with an appropriate error message. The user then made the required correction and sent the new data back to the central computer. This interactive process, often referred to as a dialogue, continued until the transaction information was complete and correct. Depending upon how the application was written, the operator might again be presented with the transaction input and asked to verify the data. After the transaction dialogue was complete, the transaction was processed and the results were presented back to the user along with a request for the user to indicate further action. This is the same approach used today with "thin client" servers or network computers.

Hybrid Processing

Transactions may also be processed in a hybrid mode where the dialogue portion of the transaction is processed in a real-time environment and the data entered by the user is stored in a data file for subsequent batch processing. An easily identifiable example of this type of online (but not real-time) process may be found with the ubiquitous automated teller machine (ATM). The user is identified to the computer as a result of identification data read from the magnetic strip on the back of the user's ATM access card. The user's legitimacy is verified by entry of a personal identification number (PIN). After the user passes the verification test, a *menu* screen showing the available options of transaction types is displayed. By indicating the desired option using the keypad of the ATM, the user may inquire about account balances, transfer funds between accounts, enter deposits, or make withdrawals. Each of these options is an implied transaction type. When the user indicates that no further transactions are required, a receipt is printed that verifies the transaction, the ATM card is returned, and money is dispensed if

the transaction is a withdrawal. This same service has been extended to allow personal computers to perform many of the same tasks via the Internet.

In the ATM example above, the user's account balances are not normally updated during the transaction process, but rather the transaction data is written to a holding file where the activity is posted to the user's account in a subsequent batch job. This process is often referred to as a *shadow file* update. After the transactions are posted to the accounts, a new shadow file is produced against which subsequent transaction activity is recorded. This type of hybrid transaction processing mode has merit in certain types of activities in that the amount of work performed to meet the end user's needs (in our example, the dialogue verification, and perhaps provision of money) is separated from the operational requirements of the organization, which need not be performed in a real-time mode (again in our example, the daily account balancing, posting of interest, audit reports, etc.). This approach allows more mainframe (*q.v.*) computing resources to be dedicated to maintaining high service levels for the on-line network and allows those functions not requiring interactive response by the end user to be performed when the demand for the online system is low.

Online processing of transactions is useful in applications where the number of transactions from any one point of input at any one time is small, the timeliness of the process is important, and interaction with the user is desirable. Online transaction processing also allows data to be captured at the source from geographically widespread areas.

Characteristics of Transactions

Transactions fall roughly into two types: inquiry and file maintenance.

INQUIRY TRANSACTIONS
Inquiry transactions, which are requests that information be displayed, are most commonly requested and serviced online. They may be as simple as looking up a telephone number or as complex as calculating an employee's pension benefit, which requires the examination and analysis of monthly earnings for the past 10 years and extensive calculation. Inquiry transactions may also produce a printed report, which may be produced in a batch environment.

FILE MAINTENANCE TRANSACTIONS
File maintenance transactions generally involve modifications to a *master file* or database. The user has the ability to add data to the file, delete data from the file, or change or update data currently on file. Whether it is better to perform these transactions in a batch or

real-time mode depends upon the application. For example, updating a telephone directory might best be served in a batch update, due to the large volume of transaction data and the large number of telephone directories that must be produced. Additionally, the transactions are relatively simple, little user interaction is required, and the immediacy of the update is not critical. Making an airline reservation is a good use of real-time transaction processing in that the person making the reservation has decisions to make based on available data and timeliness is critical.

Transaction Structure

An online transaction process consists of several different steps:

◆ *Obtain access.* This step gets the computer's attention and is normally performed once in a session in which multiple transactions may be processed. Teleprocessing applications continuously poll terminals to see if any users are out there waiting for service or, in the case of a dial-up network, a new terminal has entered the network. Obtaining access may involve dialing a telephone number, entering a card such as an ATM card, depressing the Enter key on a keyboard, or any other action that starts the process.

◆ *Verify.* With online applications, the application must assure that the person at the terminal is authorized to have access to the information being requested. The user is asked to enter a password (such as a PIN) or some other piece of information to which only the specific user should have access. Normally, this step is performed only once, but, depending upon the complexity of the application, may be done when a user crosses major functional areas of the application.

◆ *Dialogue.* Once the user has obtained access to the system and the identity of the user has been verified, the transaction process presents a screen or series of screens to determine the type of transaction the user wishes to perform and collect the data required to perform the transaction. During the dialogue, data entered by the user is edited and, where errors are detected, the user is given an opportunity to enter corrections. Many applications also allow the user to request help screens, which provide additional information to aid the user in entering the transaction data.

◆ *Process the transaction.* When the data has been entered and edited and the process has been determined, the central computer performs the requested action, either processing the update or retrieving the data that is to be displayed.

◆ *Confirmation.* Once the transaction has been processed, the user is presented with the results of the transaction (as in the case of an inquiry transaction) or confirmation that the transaction process has been completed. The application then returns control to the dialogue portion of the process to allow additional transactions to be entered and operated upon. The user is also presented with an option that there are no further transactions to be processed in which case the application disconnects the user.

The time required for an online system to complete the processing of a transaction and return the results to the user on a terminal is called *response time*. While the user is entering data, the computer is idle (in relation to the transaction being entered). When the Enter key is depressed and the data is sent to the computer for processing, the user is idle while the transaction is being processed. Only when one transaction is complete may the user commence work on another. By separating a transaction into smaller discrete units of work, the amount of work to be performed by the mainframe with each exchange of data over the teleprocessing link is smaller, resulting in faster response to the user. This separation of function into smaller units of work enhances transaction throughput (the number of transactions that may be processed in a given period of time).

Scanning devices used in grocery stores and retail outlets are also examples of on-line transaction processing (*see* UNIVERSAL PRODUCT CODE). Many hotels now allow their guests to complete the room checkout process using the television screen and the remote control keypad in the room.

The current trend in business is moving away from simple display and entry type of non-programmable or *dumb* terminals, such as those discussed above, and increasingly towards the use of programmable or *intelligent* terminals. These intelligent terminals (often called programmable workstations) are actually personal computers that are connected to mainframe computers via telecommunication links These devices allow information to be displayed using graphical images, called *icons*, and capture information using a pointing device such as a mouse (*q.v.*) or, for the more casual user, touch-sensitive screens. One major advantage of using icons is that they allow applications to be written in a manner that is much more intuitive to users. Traditional transaction processing requires the user to perform a series of actions (such as menu selections) before an object (such as a screen) is presented, where in the real world, users are presented with an object and then determine the action to be taken.

The use of the intelligent workstation (*q.v.*) in transaction processing also permits the work performed in the processing of a transaction to be shared between a central application server, which must service many users at the same time, and the workstation, which is a resource dedicated to a single user at a time. Just as transaction processing as described in the ATM example has been broken down into smaller units of work, the use of intelligent workstations can break the process down to still smaller units. If the dialogue portion of the transaction process, with its requirement to gather and display data and perform a variety of edits, may be performed on a workstation rather than the mainframe, then those computing resources previously oriented towards servicing a single user by formatting displays and performing the edits may be reallocated to more users. Where editing is performed on a workstation, the telecommunications link need not pass data back and forth to report on error conditions and receive the corrections. Transaction processing cycles performed on a workstation are also less expensive than those performed on a central server.

Bibliography

1992. Gray, J., and Reuter, A. *Transaction Processing: Concepts and Techniques*. New York: Academic Press/Morgan Kaufmann.
1997. Bernstein, P. A., and Newcomer, E. *Principles of Transaction Processing*. New York: Academic Press/Morgan Kaufmann.

Nelson G. Russell

TRANSFER RATE

See BANDWIDTH; BAUD; and MEMORY: AUXILIARY.

TRANSISTOR

See INTEGRATED CIRCUITRY.

TRANSLATION, LANGUAGE

See MACHINE TRANSLATION.

TRANSPARENCY

For articles on related subjects *see* COMPATIBILITY; and SOFTWARE PORTABILITY.

When changes are made to a computer's hardware or software configuration that do not require any action on a user's part, the changes are said to be *transparent* to the user. The usage derives from the concept of something (such as a pane of glass) that is so clear that one can look right through it as if it weren't there. This does not mean that the user will see no effect of the change, just that no action is required by the user to experience it. If, for example, a computing center replaces its mainframe (*q.v.*) with a faster version of the same series, users will notice that their programs run faster. Similarly, a software vendor might issue a new version of a compiler or a word processor which, given exactly the same input in the same form, functions identically to the prior version. In each case, the change would be said to be "transparent to the user."

Edwin D. Reilly

TRAP

For articles on related subjects *see* DEBUGGING; EXCEPTION HANDLING; and INTERRUPT.

When the occurrence of an exceptional event in a processor results in an automatic transfer to a special routine for handling that event, this transfer is called a *trap*.

Some practitioners consider *trap* and *interrupt* to be synonyms, while others use trap in a somewhat narrower context, i.e. the range of exceptional events that occur within the central processor, in contrast to externally triggered interrupts. Whatever the categorization, the point is that when an exceptional condition (such as an attempt to divide by zero) occurs in a processor equipped with trapping facilities, the hardware automatically executes a transfer to a software routine whose address has been stored in a location that is permanently assigned for that particular contingency. It is the responsibility of the systems programmer (*see* SYSTEMS PROGRAMMING) to write such routines and store their addresses at these specified locations, called *trap vectors*.

Although an exceptional condition may produce circumstances that cannot be remedied by a programmed procedure, there are other conditions from which it is possible to recover. (For example, in some contexts it may be appropriate to set an underflow value to zero without undue harm to the process.) Accordingly, pertinent address information is preserved automatically so that a proper return can be made, once the trapping routine has been completed.

Several such locations might be reserved depending on the types of conditions the processor is designed to recognize. Typically, separate trapping addresses would be provided for overflow, underflow, illegal address, and illegal operation, in addition to division by zero.

Prior to the introduction of trapping facilities (generally associated with second-generation computers), the programmer had to include explicit test instructions at each point where some exceptional condition might possibly occur. The need to do this is obviated by the trapping facility, since it can operate over an entire program. However, software trapping facilities still exist to give the programmer additional control over the program's behavior when confronted by an exceptional condition. For instance, many Pascal implementations include facilities whereby the compiler can be directed to include instructions that override the system's automatic trapping activity. In its place, the program produces a signal (e.g. a predefined value in a special variable) that can be detected and used as a basis for a response.

Systems equipped with trapping facilities usually include a machine instruction that allows the user to force one of several kinds of traps, thereby providing the opportunity to simulate a given type of exceptional condition. This capability has been used to considerable advantage in developing a variety of debugging aids and special features in software programs. Certain trapping facilities may also be explicitly turned off (disabled) by the programmer for all or part of a procedure, whereupon the system ignores the precipitating event and refrains from intervention.

Seymour V. Pollack and Theodor D. Sterling

TREE

For articles on related subjects *see* COMPUTER GAMES: TRADITIONAL; DATA STRUCTURES; GRAPH THEORY; and POLISH NOTATION.

A tree, or more precisely a *rooted tree*, is a special form of directed graph with the following properties: (1) either it has no vertices or it has a distinguished vertex called the *root*, which has no predecessors; and (2) every vertex other than the root has a unique predecessor.

Vertices (or *nodes*) of a tree that have successors are called *nonterminal vertices*, or *parent nodes*, while vertices that have no successors are called *terminal vertices* or *leaves*. Fig. 1 illustrates a tree with root vertex *a*; two nonterminal vertices *a*, *c*; and three leaves *b*, *d*, *e*. Nodes *b* and *c*, since they have the same parent, are said to be *sibling nodes*, as are nodes *d* and *e*. Similarly, all nodes that have a parent (all those other than the root)—*b*, *c*, *d*, and *e* in Fig. 1—are said to be *child nodes*.

Trees in which each nonterminal vertex has at most *n* successors are called *n-ary* trees. Trees in which each nonterminal vertex has at most two successors would

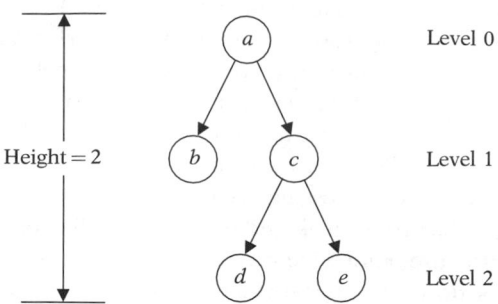

Figure 1. A tree showing terminal and nonterminal vertices.

then be 2-ary trees, but such structures have little or no application in computer science without the additional restriction that children are either *left child nodes* or *right child nodes*. Such trees are very useful; they are called *binary* trees. The tree in Fig. 1 is an example of a binary tree.

Each node of a tree determines a subtree whose root is the given node and whose vertices include all descendants of the node. In a binary tree, each nonterminal node has an associated left subtree and right subtree.

A tree is said to be *unordered* if there is no special significance to the order in which the descendants of a given node are listed, and is said to be *ordered* if the order of descendant nodes is significant.

The root of a tree is said to be at level 0, the children of the root at level 1, the grandchildren at level 2, etc. The highest numbered level is called the *height* (or depth) of the tree (*see* Fig. 1).

Binary trees are a natural data structure for expressing the operator–operand structure of arithmetic expressions. The expression $x + (y * z)$ may be represented by the tree structure in Fig. 2, where the operators are represented by nonterminal vertices and the operands of an operator are represented by successor subtrees of the operator vertex. Thus, the operands of $+$ are x and $y * z$, and are represented by successor subtrees of the vertex $+$.

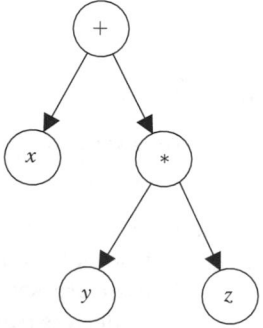

Figure 2. A tree representing an operator–operand structure.

There are four fundamentally different ways to list the nodes of a binary tree. When applied to an expression tree such as that in Fig. 2, the first three yield a recognizable variation of the original expression.

1. *Preorder (or depth-first) traversal*   Visit (print) the root. Traverse the left subtree (if any). Traverse the right subtree (if any). When applied recursively, this algorithm yields

$$+ x * y z$$

which is the *Polish prefix* form of the original expression (*see* POLISH NOTATION).

2. *Inorder (or symmetric) traversal*   Traverse the left subtree. Visit (print) the root. Traverse the right subtree. This yields

$$x + y * z,$$

which recaptures the original *infix* form of the expression.

3. *Postorder (or endorder) traversal*   Traverse the left subtree. Traverse the right subtree. Visit the root. This yields

$$x y z * +$$

which is the *reverse Polish* or *Polish postfix* form of the expression.

Given the diagram of a binary tree, its preorder, inorder, and postorder traversals can be immediately determined, but the converse is not necessarily true. No one of the three traversals alone is sufficient to allow unambiguous reconstruction of the tree that produced that traversal, nor will knowledge of just the combination of preorder and postorder traversals. Knowledge of the preorder and inorder traversals, however, or the inorder and postorder traversals, *is* sufficient to allow deduction of the corresponding binary tree.

A fourth way to list the nodes of a binary tree would be *breadth-first*, that is, level by level. For Fig. 2, the result obtained, $+ x * y z$, happens to be the same as obtained via preorder traversal, but for more complex binary trees, this would not usually be the case.

Binary trees play an important role in computer science. Of particular importance in various applications are *height-balanced* trees, in which the height (maximum distance from the root to a leaf) of the left subtree of any node differs from that of the right subtree by, at most, one. Such trees are also called AVL trees after their inventors G. M. Adel'son-Vel'skii and E. M. Landis (1962). Keeping a tree balanced in this way provides far superior search time as compared to trees that become highly unbalanced through a pre-

ponderance of insertions into one or the other of the left or right subtrees.

The concept of height balancing can also be extended to *n*-ary trees. When data is stored in an external medium, such as a disk file, disk accesses are expensive relative to the reading of the data once an access is completed. Accordingly, it is reasonable to organize the data into a tree structure having a large number of keys per node so that the nodes have a large branching factor. Such trees were called B-trees by R. Bayer and E. McCreight (1972), who were the first to propose use of multiway balanced trees for external searching. For a comprehensive survey of B-trees, see Comer (1979).

Now consider the 5-ary tree in Fig. 3. For *n*-ary trees ($n > 2$), inorder traversal has no meaning, but preorder and postorder traversals still do if the subtrees are visited left to right. The preorder traversal of this tree yields

$$a\,b\,e\,f\,g\,c\,h\,i\,d\,j\,k\,l\,m\,n$$

which coincides with the ordering obtained by the *depth first search (DFS)* algorithm. (An alternative strategy is *breadth-first search* (BFS), in which nodes at the same level are listed from left to right, starting at the root. For the above example, BFS yields $a\,b\,c\,d\,e\,f\,g\,h\,i\,j\,k\,l\,m\,n$.)

Surprisingly, a binary tree can be used to represent an *n*-ary tree. This is done by linking all children of a given node and forming them into a left subtree of their parent in such a way that each left child in the original tree becomes the parent of a linear chain of its siblings. The binary tree equivalent to the 5-ary tree of Fig. 3 is given in Fig. 4.

This tree is equivalent to the original 5-ary tree in the sense that their preorder traversals are identical and the inorder traversal of the binary tree is the same as the postorder traversal of the 5-ary tree. Unlike the case of a binary tree, which in some sense contains more information than an *n*-ary tree because of the chirality ("handedness") of its subtrees, an *n*-ary tree *can* be reconstructed from knowledge of its preorder and postorder traversals. Since these traversals can be obtained from the binary tree of Fig. 4, there is just

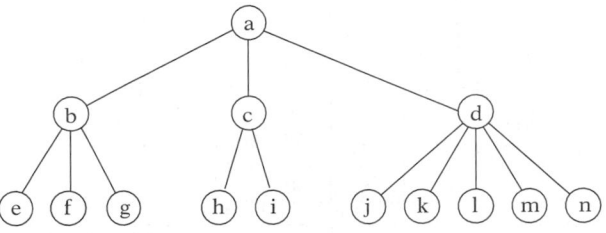

Figure 3.   A 5-ary tree.

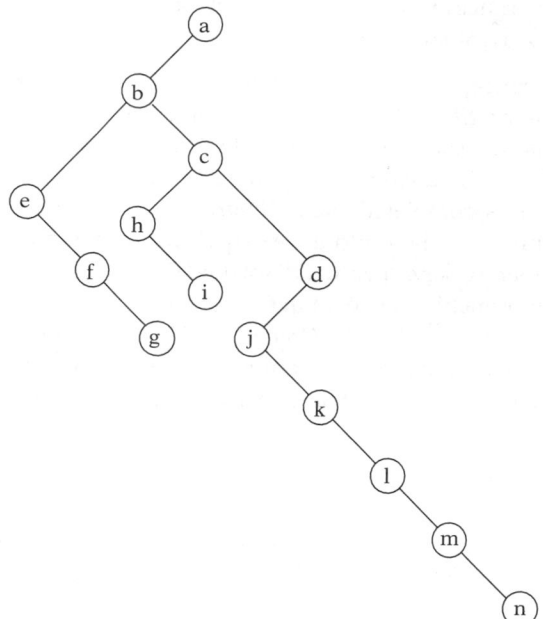

Figure 4. The binary tree equivalent of Fig. 3.

as much information in Fig. 4 as in Fig. 3, justifying the claim that every *n*-ary tree has an "equivalent" binary tree.

A special kind of *n*-ary tree called a *trie* (from re*trie*val, but pronounced "try") has a letter at each node, and any path from its root to a leaf represents a valid word in a given dictionary of entries. Imagine that the trie is used with a spelling checker (*q.v.*). If a "word" cannot be found in the trie, it is probably misspelled (though it may merely be missing from that particular dictionary).

A trie is a kind of search tree in which, instead of checking whole keys (words) against a target item, constituent letters are checked one by one until either a leaf is reached (success) or no further branch can be taken whose root matches the next letter of the target word (failure). Fig. 5 shows a small trie taken from

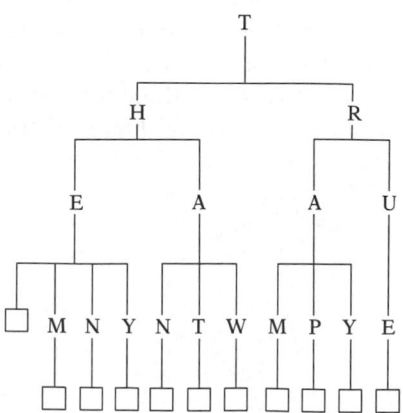

Figure 5. A small trie.

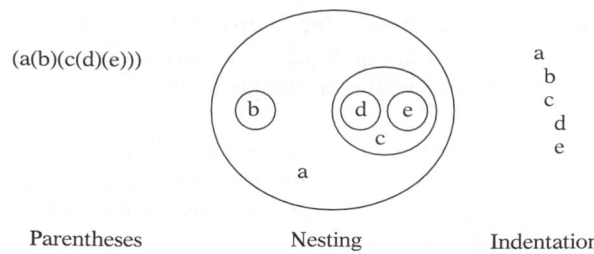

| Parentheses | Nesting | Indentation |

Figure 6. Alternative representations of the tree of Fig. 1.

Reilly and Federighi (1989) in which leaves, the ends of successful search paths, are represented by squares. The trie shown contains the words THE, THEM, THEN, THEY, THAN, THAT, THAW, TRAM, TRAP, TRAY, and TRUE.

Trees are a natural data structure for any data objects whose components stand in a hierarchical relation to each other. For example, the organization chart of a company may be represented by a tree structure, and family trees are, as their name implies, representable by a tree structure.

Tree structures may be indicated by parentheses, nesting, or indentation, as illustrated in Fig. 6 which shows alternative representations of the tree of Fig. 1.

The representation (a)(b) (c(d) (e)) may be viewed as a list structure in which the successor nodes of a are represented by the sublists (b) and (c(d) (e)). This representation is used to represent trees in languages such as Lisp (*q.v.*).

Tree structures are convenient for storing sets of lexicographically ordered objects for purposes of alphabetically-oriented information retrieval. For example, the five words "dog," "cat," "lion," "fox," "tiger" can be stored in the tree structure shown in Fig. 7. A word in this tree structure can be found by comparing it to successive nodes, starting at the root node and taking the left successor if the word occurs earlier in a dictionary ordering or the right successor if it occurs later. Success is reported if the word matches; failure is

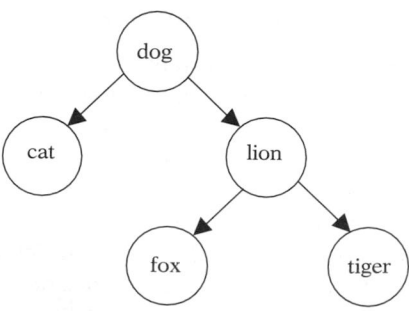

Figure 7. Tree used for information retrieval.

reported if there is no successor of the kind required for the next search step. The failure signal may be used to trigger a procedure for adding the new word to the tree as a new successor at the point of failure.

Example

(1) Assume that we want to determine whether the word "fox" is in the tree. The word "fox" is compared with the word "dog," and since 'f' occurs later in the alphabet than 'd', the right branch is taken. Then "fox" is compared with "lion," and since 'f' occurs earlier in the alphabet than 'l', the left branch is taken. The third comparison results in a match.

(2) Determine whether the word "chicken" is in the tree; if absent, add it to the tree. First compare "chicken" with "dog" and take the left branch. Then compare "chicken" with "cat" and take the right branch. Then report failure because there is no right successor of "cat." Add "chicken" as the new right successor of "cat."

The tree structure representing a given set of sorted words depends on the order in which the words are presented during the construction of the tree. However, the tree representation of the sorted words is convenient, both because of the ease with which new words may be added to the structure and because the number of accesses in general depends on the logarithm of the number of words in the tree. An important problem in computer science is how to convert *unbalanced* sorting trees (i.e. those in which one subtree has height at least 2 greater than the other) into *balanced* (i.e. AVL) trees which can still be sorted by inorder traversal.

Trees are often used in the analysis of strategies for games such as chess and checkers (draughts) (*see* COMPUTER GAMES: TRADITIONAL). In this case, the vertices of the tree represent positions in the game, and a given vertex has as its successors all vertices that can be reached in one move from the given position. The set of all continuations of a game from a given position can be represented by a tree having the given position as its root vertex. The set of all games can be represented by a tree having the initial position as its root vertex. Each path through the tree from the root vertex to a terminal vertex represents a complete game.

It has been estimated that the complete game tree for checkers has about 10^{40} vertices, while the complete game tree for chess has about 10^{120} vertices. Complete game trees for most nontrivial games are much too large to be exhaustively searched or even stored in a computer. In developing strategies for playing games such as chess and checkers, *tree-pruning strategies* must be used to prune the complete game tree, creating subtrees that explore a limited number of continuations for a limited number of moves. Strategies for playing chess and checkers on a computer are effectively strategies for deciding how the complete game tree should be pruned, and for choosing a move on the basis of information in the pruned game tree.

Bibliography

1962. Adel'son-Vel'skii, G. M., and Landis, E. M. "An Algorithm for the Organization of Information," *Soviet Mathematics Doklady*, **3**, 1259–1263.

1972. Bayer, R., and McCreight, E. M. "Organization and Maintenance of Large Ordered Indexes," *Acta Informatica*, **1**, 3, 173–189.

1979. Comer, D. "The Ubiquitous B-tree," *ACM Computing Surveys*, **11**, 2, 121–137.

1989. Reilly, E. D., and Federighi, F. D. *Pascalgorithms*. Boston: Houghton-Mifflin.

1990. Cormen, T. H., Leiserson, C. E., and Rivest, R. L. *Introduction to Algorithms*. Cambridge, MA: MIT Press, and New York: McGraw-Hill.

Peter Wegner, revised by Edwin D. Reilly

TROJAN HORSE

See COMPUTER VIRUS.

TURING AWARD WINNERS

For an article on a related subject *see* MCDOWELL AWARD WINNERS.

The A. M. Turing Award is made annually by the Association for Computing Machinery (ACM—*q.v.*) "for contributions of a technical nature in the computing community." The award, which currently includes a prize of $25,000, memorializes the extraordinary genius Alan M. Turing (*q.v.*) and recognizes his unique and original contribution to the beginning of computing with automatic machinery. Each recipient gives a lecture that is published in an ACM periodical. The first 22 have been collected into a single volume (Ashenhurst and Graham, 1987). ACM's almost exclusive devotion to software and computing theory is reflected in the fact that none of the awards has been for strictly hardware contributions, a field dominated by the IEEE Computer Society (*see* MCDOWELL AWARD WINNERS). Awards made since its inception in 1966 have been:

1966 Alan J. Perlis (1922–1990) (*q.v.*) for his work in programming language definition and design and programming techniques, and for his leadership in computer science education.

1967 Maurice V. Wilkes (1913–) (*q.v.*) for his leadership in the early development of stored program computers; his invention of labels, macros and microcode, and for his co-invention of subroutines.

1968 Richard W. Hamming (1915–1998) (*q.v.*) for his invention of the error-detecting/correcting codes that bear his name (*see* ERROR CORRECTING AND DETECTING CODE), and for his famous aphorism, "The purpose of computing is insight, not numbers."

1969 Marvin M. Minsky (1927–) for his contributions to the theory of computation, programming languages, education, and the beginnings of artificial intelligence (*q.v.*).

1970 James H. Wilkinson (1919–1986) (*q.v.*) for his contributions to numerical analysis, particularly in the fields of matrix computations and error analysis.

1971 John McCarthy (1927–) for his contributions to artificial intelligence (*q.v.*), particularly the invention of Lisp (*q.v.*).

1972 Edsger W. Dijkstra (1930–) for his style and his pervasive influence on programming, of which his memorable indictment of the GO TO statement is most famous.

1973 Charles W. Bachman (1924–) for his work in database technology, particularly the creation of both the Integrated Data Store (IDS), which is the basis of the CODASYL database systems, and a powerful method for displaying data relationships.

1974 Donald Knuth (1938–) for his contributions to the analysis of algorithms (*see* ALGORITHMS, ANALYSIS OF), the design of programming languages, and his series of classic texts, *The Art of Computer Programming*.

1975 Allen Newell (1927–1992) and Herbert A. Simon (1916–) (*q.v.*) for their basic contributions to artificial intelligence, the psychology of human cognition, and their invention of list processing (*q.v.*).

1976 Michael O. Rabin (1931–) and Dana S. Scott (1932–) for their contributions to the course of theoretical computer science which set a standard of clarity and elegance for the entire field.

1977 John W. Backus (1924–) for leading the development of Fortran and the creation of the syntax description language Backus–Naur Form (*q.v.*).

1978 R. W. Floyd (1936–) for helping to found the theory of parsing, the semantics of programming languages, automatic program verifica-

tion (*q.v.*), automatic program synthesis, and analysis of algorithms (*q.v.*).

1979 Kenneth E. Iverson (1920–) for his pioneering efforts in programming languages and mathematical notation, resulting in the language APL (*q.v.*).

1980 C. A. R. Hoare (1934–) for his fundamental contributions to the definition and design of programming languages, specifically their definitions using axiomatic semantics; his development of ingenious algorithms and advanced data structuring techniques; and his contributions to operating systems (*q.v.*).

1981 Edgar F. Codd (1923–) for his contributions to the theory and practice of database management systems (*q.v.*) and the creation of the relational model (*see* RELATIONAL DATABASE).

1982 Stephen A. Cook (1939–) for his contributions to the theory of computational complexity (*q.v.*), which laid the foundations for the theory of NP-completeness (*see* NP-COMPLETE PROBLEMS).

1983 Dennis M. Ritchie (1941–) and Kenneth L. Thompson (1943–) for their development and implementation of the Unix operating system (*q.v.*) and the language C (*q.v.*).

1984 Niklaus E. Wirth (1934–) for his development of a sequence of innovative computer languages: Euler, Algol-W, Modula-2, and Pascal (*q.v.*), particularly the last.

1985 Richard M. Karp (1935–) for his fundamental contributions to complexity theory (*see* NP-COMPLETE PROBLEMS), which extended the earlier work of Stephen Cook.

1986 John Hopcroft (1939–) and Robert E. Tarjan (1938–) for their fundamental achievements in the design and analysis of algorithms (*q.v.*) and data structures (*q.v.*).

1987 John Cocke (1925–) for his contributions to the design and theory of compilers (*q.v.*) and to the architecture of high-performance computers.

1988 Ivan E. Sutherland (1938–) for his contributions to interactive computer graphics (*q.v.*), exemplified by his invention of Sketchpad, which established and defined the field.

1989 William M. Kahan (1933–) for his drive and determination to establish and have adopted the current standards for binary and radix-independent floating-point computations (*see* ARITHMETIC, COMPUTER).

1990 Fernando J. Corbató (1926–) for formulating the concepts and leading the development of the Compatible Time-Sharing System (*see* TIME SHARING) (CTSS) and Multics (Multiplexed Information and Computer Service).

1991 A. J. R. G. Milner (1934–) for three developments: LCF, the mechanization of Scott's logic of computable functions; ML, the first language to contain polymorphic type-inference together with a type-safe exception-handling mechanism; and CCS, a general theory of concurrency (*see* CONCURRENT PROGRAMMING and PROGRAMMING LANGUAGE SEMANTICS).

1992 Butler Lampson (1943–) for his contributions to the development of distributed, personal computing environments and the technology for their implementation: workstations (*q.v.*), networks, operating systems (*q.v.*), programming systems, displays, security, and document publishing.

1993 Juris Hartmanis (1928–) and Richard Stearns (1936–) for their seminal paper which established the foundations for the field of computational complexity (*q.v.*).

1994 Edward A. Feigenbaum (1936–) and Raj Reddy (1937–) for leading in defining the emerging field of applied artificial intelligence and in demonstrating its technological significance.

1995 Manuel Blum (1938–) for his contributions to the foundations of computational complexity (*q.v.*) and its application to cryptography (*q.v.*) and program checking.

1996 Amir Pnueli (1941–) for his seminal work introducing temporal logic into computing science and for outstanding contributions to system and program verification (*q.v.*).

1997 Douglas Englebart (1925–) for an inspiring vision of the future of interactive computing and the invention of key technologies to help realize this vision.

1998 James Gray (1944–) for seminal contributions to database and transaction processing research and technical leadership in system implementation.

1999 Frederick P. Brooks, Jr. (1931–) for landmark contributions to computer architecture (*q.v.*), operating systems (*q.v.*), and software engineering (*q.v.*).

Bibliography

1987. Ashenhurst, R. L. and Graham, S. (eds.) *ACM Turing Award Lectures, The First Twenty Years.* New York: ACM Press.

Eric A. Weiss

TURING MACHINE

For articles on related subjects *see* ALGORITHMS, THEORY OF; AUTOMATA THEORY; CHOMSKY HIERARCHY; FORMAL LANGUAGES; SEQUENTIAL MACHINE; TURING TEST; and TURING, ALAN M.

A *Turing machine* is an abstract computing device invented by Alan M. Turing in 1936. A reprint of his original paper appears in Davis (1965). A Turing machine consists of (1) a *control unit*, which can assume any one of a finite number of possible states; (2) a *tape*, marked off into discrete squares, each of which can store a single symbol taken from a finite set of possible symbols; and (3) a *read–write head*, which moves along the tape and transmits information to and from the control unit (*see* Fig. 1).

The Basic Model

A Turing machine computes via a sequence of discrete steps. Its behavior at a given time is completely determined by the symbol currently being scanned by the read–write head, and by the internal state of the control unit. On a given step, it will write a symbol on the tape, move along the tape at most one square to the left or right, and enter a new internal state. The new symbol is permitted to be the same as the current symbol; similarly, it is permissible to stay on the same tape square on a given step and/or to reenter the same state. Certain symbol-state situations may cause the machine to halt.

For example, on a single step the machine in Fig. 1 could begin in state q_3, change the A under scan to an E, move left one square and enter state q_5. It would now be scanning a T; its next action would be uniquely determined by the new state q_5 and the fact that it was scanning a T. It would continue indefinitely in this step-by-step fashion unless it reached a state-symbol combination causing it to halt.

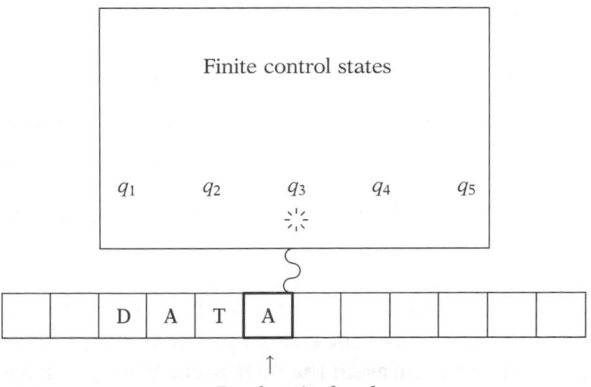

Figure 1. Architecture of a Turing machine.

Table 1. Program for M.

Present state	B is scanned write/shift/state	0 is scanned write/shift/state	1 is scanned write/shift/state	Comment
q_1	1, L, q_7	0, R, q_1	1, R, q_2	Is x 0?
q_2	B, R, q_3	0, R, q_2	1, R, q_2	$x \neq 0$
q_3	0, L, q_4	0, R, q_3	Error	Write a new 0
q_4	B, L, q_5	0, L, q_4	Error	Go back to x
q_5	Error	1, L, q_5	0, L, q_6	Decrease x
q_6	B, R, q_1	0, L, q_6	1, L, q_6	Go to starting position
q_7	Halt	B, L, q_7	Error	Clean up

The tape of a Turing machine is often depicted as infinite, and some persons view this idealization as hopelessly unrealistic. A better approach is to view the tape as finite but indefinitely extendible; i.e. new blank squares can be attached to either end of the tape at will to prevent the machine from running off the tape. Thus, there is no uniform bound on either the time or space used by a Turing machine; both are allowed to grow indefinitely.

The *program* of a Turing machine defines its action for the various state-symbol combinations that are possible. This program can be presented in a number of different ways (e.g. state transition diagrams, assembly-like languages). The two most common ways are a tabular form and representation as a set of quintuples. Each state-symbol combination is represented by either an entry in the table or a single quintuple in the set. In the quintuple convention, the action described above would have been due to the presence of the quintuple

$$\langle q_3, A, E, L, q_5 \rangle$$

where we abbreviate left, right, and no-shift by L, R, and N, respectively.

We now present an example of a Turing machine in tabular form. The state set of this machine M corresponds to rows in Table 1 and the symbol set (alphabet) to columns. The blank symbol is denoted by B. M will compute the function $f(x) = 2^x$ according to the following conventions:

1. x and $f(x)$ are written as binary integers.

2. The tape initially contains x and is blank elsewhere.

3. M begins in state q_1 scanning the leftmost bit of x.

4. When it halts, $f(x)$ will be the only non-blank item on the tape.

The algorithm used is given by the flowchart in Fig. 2. Essentially, each time the string that initially represents x is changed to represent the next smaller integer, a 0 is written on the tape to the right of x. When x has been decreased to 0, a 1 is written to the left of the generated

string of x zeros. The zeros to the left of the 1 are then erased, and M halts. As is often the case, the algorithm is best thought of as an exercise in symbol manipulation rather than as arithmetic.

The entries in Table 1 labeled *error* cannot occur in a normal computation. By convention, M would halt if started in such state-symbol situations.

An *instantaneous description* (total machine configuration) of a machine consists of the entire set of machine conditions at a given point in a computation (i.e. the contents of the tape, the position of the read–write head on the tape and the internal state of the machine). A computation, then, is simply an entire history of instantaneous descriptions beginning with the start configuration and ending with a halt configuration. Table 2 gives the computation of the machine M when started in state q_1 on the input 10 (binary 2). The symbol scanned is set in bold type. Note that, when M

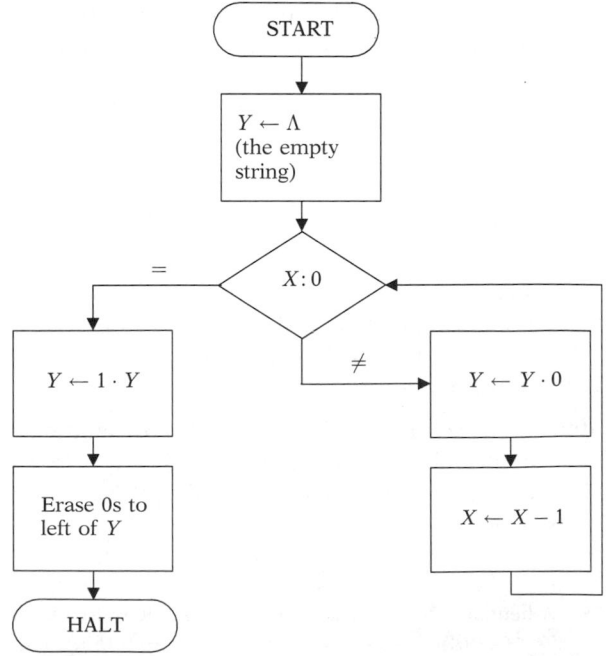

Figure 2. Flowchart for M.

Table 2. Computation of 2^2 by M.

Time	State	Non-blank portion of tape					
0	q_1		**1**	0			
1	q_2		1	**0**			
2	q_2		1	**0**	B		
3	q_3		1	0	B	**B**	
4	q_4		1	0	**B**	0	
5	q_5		1	**0**	B	0	
6	q_5		**1**	1	B	0	
7	q_6	B	**0**	1	B	0	
8	q_1	B	**0**	1	B	0	
9	q_1	B	0	**1**	B	0	
10	q_2	B	0	1	**B**	0	
11	q_3	B	0	1	B	**0**	
12	q_3	B	0	1	B	0	**B**
13	q_4	B	0	1	B	**0**	0
14	q_4	B	0	1	**B**	0	0
15	q_5	B	0	**1**	B	0	0
16	q_6	B	0	**0**	B	0	0
17	q_6	**B**	0	0	B	0	0
18	q_1	B	**0**	0	B	0	0
19	q_1	B	0	**0**	B	0	0
20	q_1	B	0	0	**B**	0	0
21	q_7	B	0	**0**	1	0	0
22	q_7	B	**0**	B	1	0	0
23	q_7	**B**	B	B	1	0	0
24	Halted	No change					

halts, its read–write head is not scanning the leftmost digit of the output 100; the reader is invited to add one more state to M and get it to do this.

Modified Turing Machines

Turing's original model has been altered in a number of ways by a number of different authors. In each of the cases discussed below, it has been proved that the altered model and the original model can each compute the same class of functions. This is done by showing that, for every machine of a given type, there exists a standard Turing machine that can simulate its behavior, and conversely. Turing machines have also been shown capable of defining exactly the same classes of functions definable by the formal systems of Kleene, Church (*q.v.*), Rosser, Markov, and others. *Church's Thesis* and *Turing's Thesis* assert that their respective models correctly capture the mathematical notion of *effective computability* (i.e. of explicit algorithmic processes). Since the models are equivalent in the sense given above, the two theses are equivalent.

The following list contains some of the more common variations that do not affect the classes of functions that can be computed (although the efficiency of a computation may change with the model).

1. *Post-Davis* The machine cannot both change the symbol under scan and move along the tape on the same step (Davis, 1958).

2. *One-ended Tape* The tape can be extended to the right, but not to the left. Thus the read–write head could fall off the left end of the tape.

3. *Paper Tape* A blank square can have a non-blank symbol written on it, but this symbol cannot be changed thereafter.

4. *Two-Symbol* Only the symbols B (blank) and 1 are allowed, although the number of states may be large.

5. *Two-State* Only two states are permitted, although the number of symbols may be large. The generality of this and the previous case is due to Shannon (Shannon and McCarthy, 1956).

6. *Multitape* More than one tape is permitted, each tape having its own read–write head. In this case, the action of the machine depends upon the internal state and the symbols scanned by each of the read–write heads; i.e. for a k-tape machine, the action depends upon the state and an ordered k-tuple of symbols. The tape motions are independent; on a given step some heads could move left, some right, and some could remain in place.

7. *Multihead* More than one head is allowed per tape. Again, the action of the machine is determined by the state and the ordered set of symbols scanned by the various read–write heads as they crawl around their shared tapes. Usually, the machine is allowed access to information concerning which heads are currently scanning the same tape square.

8. *Multidimensional* The "tapes" are multidimensional structures. In the two-dimensional case, the plane is marked off into squares and the permissible head motions are north, south, east, west, and no move. For higher dimensions one uses a coordinate system, and a move changes at most one of the coordinates by ± 1.

Advantages of Turing's Model

The usefulness of the Turing model of computation lies in its simplicity despite which it has all the fundamental properties that a computing system must possess: a finite program, a large data store, and a deterministic step-by-step mode of computation. In particular, one can show that any computer can be simulated (albeit rather slowly) by a Turing machine. The converse is also true, provided that provisions are made to handle larger amounts of storage as needed.

For example, it is true that a minicomputer (*q.v.*) with an accumulator and "sufficiently large" storage can do any computation with only the instructions SUBTRACT, STORE, and TRANSFER ON MINUS, if one assumes the usual conventions of a single-address von Neumann machine (*q.v.*). It is much easier to prove this by showing how to simulate a Turing machine on the minicomputer, rather than by attempting to simulate all of the instructions of a large-scale computer.

Since a Turing machine can simulate any computing device, it follows that anything that cannot be computed on a Turing machine cannot be computed at all. The fact that there are such unsolvable problems motivated Turing to devise his abstract machine. This has also given rise to the theory of algorithms.

Turing machines can also simulate each other by interpretive procedures. In particular, it is possible to program a Turing machine to accept the description of the program and input data of any other Turing machine computation, and to simulate that computation. Such a machine is called a *universal Turing machine*.

Although Turing machines have probably been studied theoretically more than other abstract computing devices, two other models deserve mention. A *random-access machine* looks much like a single-address computer and stores its data in a finite number of cells. The idealization used here is that each cell can store any integer, and hence must have an unbounded number of bits. An *iterative array* consists of a network of finite-state sequential machines. Again, an unbounded memory is needed; this is achieved by allowing the network to be expanded in the middle of a computation, if necessary. Iterative arrays are useful in studying certain kinds of parallel processes.

Time Complexity of Turing Machine Computations

A number of theoretical results have shown that studying the complexity of Turing machine computations can yield insight into the efficiency of computations on real hardware. Within a broad range of conditions, the cost of a computation on a Turing machine (e.g. the number of steps required) is within a polynomial function of the cost on any machine with a finite number of processors. If the real Turing machine has at least two tapes, the relationship to cost on a real machine will often be linear.

On the other hand, Turing machine time studies are insensitive to a constant factor—i.e. computations on a multitape Turing machine can always be sped up by a factor of 2 by increasing the symbol set so as to pack at least two symbols of the original alphabet on a tape square. (Some additional programming is required to make this work in all cases.) Doubling the speed of real machines, on the other hand, cannot be achieved without either a technological breakthrough or an increase in the cost of the hardware, and hence the cost per machine hour.

The Post-Davis, one-ended tape, and two-state variants introduced in the preceding section can be made to run as fast as ordinary (one-tape) Turing machines. The two-symbol variant will run within a constant factor of the others, but since the number of symbols is fixed, the speed-up trick may not be employed.

Although the multihead variant appears to be more powerful than the multitape model, P. Fischer, A. Meyer, and A. Rosenberg have shown that the two variants are equivalent in a very strong sense: any multihead machine can be replaced by an equally fast equivalent multitape machine (but with perhaps a greater total number of heads).

On the other hand, one-tape Turing machines cannot always simulate multitape machines without loss of time. There exist examples for which the time on the one-tape machine must be the square of the multitape machine time. Thus, multitape (and multihead and multidimensional) machines are more efficient than ordinary Turing machines. For this reason, the multitape model is probably the most useful model for efficiency studies, although the one-tape version is better for computability–noncomputability investigations because of its greater simplicity.

The squaring of time to go from a multitape machine to a one-tape machine is never exceeded. In fact, any variant of a Turing machine with a bounded number of processors requiring time t for a computation can be simulated by an ordinary Turing machine in time at most t^2.

When considering multitape Turing machines with different numbers of tapes, some interesting questions remain unsolved. Aanderaa has shown that, for any k, certain problems can be solved faster on a k-tape machine than on a $(k-1)$-tape machine. However, the amount of saving cannot be large, since Hennie and Stearns have shown that any multitape machine requiring time t can be simulated by a two-tape Turing machine in time at most $t(\log_2 t)$. Whether this bound can be improved is still an open question.

Bibliography

1956. Shannon, C. E., and McCarthy, J. (eds.) *Automata Studies*. Princeton, NJ: Princeton University Press.
1958. Davis, M. *Computability and Unsolvability*. New York: McGraw-Hill.
1963. Trachtenbrot, B. *Algorithms and Automatic Computing Machines*. Boston: D. C. Heath.
1965. Davis, M. (ed.) *The Undecidable*. Hewlett, NY: Raven Press.
1978. Hartmanis, J. *Feasible Computations and Provable Complexity Properties*. Philadelphia: Society for Industrial and Applied Mathematics.

1989. Dewdney, A. K. *The Turing Omnibus*, Ch. 48. Rockville, MD: Computer Science Press.

1997. Lewis, H. R., and Papadimitriou, C. H. *Elements of the Theory of Computation*, 2nd Ed. Upper Saddle River, NJ: Prentice Hall.

Patrick C. Fischer

TURING TEST

For articles on related subjects *see* ARTIFICIAL INTELLIGENCE; NONMONOTONIC LOGIC; TURING, ALAN M.; and TURING MACHINE.

Can machines think? This question is difficult to answer because the words "machines" and "think" and even the word "can" are open to different interpretations. Alan Turing thought that the question was "too meaningless to deserve discussion" and suggested that we replace consideration of this question with a contest that is now called the "Turing Test." In a famous article published in 1950, Turing described an "imitation game" in which an interrogator tries to determine solely on the basis of a written interrogation of a man and a woman which is the man and which is the woman. The man in the imitation game tries to imitate a woman and answers the questions as he believes a woman would answer. Turing suggested that we apply the idea of the imitation game to computers and people. Could a human interrogator who uses a teletypewriter to communicate with a human and with a computer determine from the conversation which is the human and which is the computer respondent? The objective for the computer program in the game is to imitate a human. The computer might say that it had curly hair, liked chocolate ice cream, and preferred skiing to skating. Turing believed that the processes generating intelligent behavior could be understood in terms of computable functions, functions that his Turing machines could compute. Hence, Turing believed that an actual computer, if properly programmed, perhaps programmed to learn as a child does, might one day pass the test. Such a computer would produce verbal behavior that was indistinguishable from that of a human being. Turing did not give full details of his proposed test and variations are possible, but it is usually assumed that the interrogator is an intelligent human who asks numerous, penetrating questions and the human subject is a typical, normal, adult respondent.

The Turing Test provides an objective, repeatable test that eliminates prejudice based on the appearance of the respondents and focuses on sustained, sophisticated verbal communication that might naturally be taken as a good indicator of intelligence and thinking. Turing did not believe that passing the test constitutes a necessary condition for a computer to think or to be intelligent. He knew that the test requires a certain acting ability upon the part of the computer. For example, Turing suggested that if a computer in the test were asked to add two large numbers, it might pause for thirty seconds and then give an incorrect answer. In principle, a computer might be very intelligent and yet incapable of deceiving a human interrogator into believing that it was a human thinker.

Nor does passing the Turing Test provide a logically sufficient condition for a computer to think or to be intelligent. For it is logically possible, though extremely unlikely, that a computer could pass the test by generating a random output of characters that just by chance happen to constitute perfectly good answers to the questions being asked. In such a situation the computer would pass the test but would not be intelligent.

A common misunderstanding of the Turing Test is to regard it as an operational or behavioral definition, i.e. a definition that tries to define mental properties completely in terms of overt behavior or dispositions to behave. The Turing Test is more plausibly understood as an inductive test. The Turing Test, like other scientific tests, permits the gathering of evidence that may support or fail to support the tested hypothesis. In the Turing Test convincing evidence can be gathered for or against the existence of various aspects of thinking and intelligence, such as understanding, learning, and problem solving. Inductive evidence does not guarantee the truth or falsity of the hypothesis but indicates a level of probability for or against it. Inductive reasoning is defeasible (sometimes called *nonmonotonic*) reasoning. No matter how much evidence is gathered for a given scientific hypothesis, future evidence may defeat it. At best the results of the Turing Test will provide high probabilities, but never logical guarantees, that a computer can think.

Initially, the Turing Test may seem to be an easy test for a computer to pass. Many computer programs exist that can maintain limited conversations. ELIZA, a classic conversation program written by Joseph Weizenbaum to appear to emulate a non-directive therapist, is probably the most famous. ELIZA contains a language analyzer and a script that allows it to carry out conversations in English on a particular theme. The program can take an input from a human and syntactically rephrase it to make it appear to be giving a human response. If a human says to ELIZA, "I'm very excited!", ELIZA may respond, "Is it because you are very excited that you came to me?". When ELIZA cannot produce a syntactical reformulation of the previous sentence entered by a human, it responds with a generic response such as "Please go on." Weizenbaum does not believe that ELIZA really understands in any significant way and has been astonished at how some people have been deluded into thinking that ELIZA does understand. In fact, neither ELIZA nor any other computer program has come close to passing a Turing Test.

Turing himself knew the test was going to be difficult for a computer to pass, but predicted in 1950 that in about fifty years "an average interrogator will not have more than a 70 per cent chance of making the right identification after five minutes of questioning." Turing's prediction was too optimistic. After about fifty years no computer has yet come close to passing a Turing Test in which the scope of questioning is unrestricted. Hugh Loebner has offered a $25,000 prize to the creator of any computer program that can pass an unrestricted Turing Test and a $100,000 prize to any computer that can pass a Turing Test using audiovisual input. The Loebner Prize contests based on conversations have been run each year since 1991, though during the first four years of these contests conversations were restricted to specific topics. In the Loebner contest human interrogators interview a set of unknown respondents (some human and some computers), and rank those that seem the most human. Over the years the interrogators have reliably identified which respondents were human.

Many philosophical criticisms have been made of the Turing Test. Two of the best known are the Jukebox Objection and the Chinese Room Objection. The Jukebox Objection, given by Ned Block, goes as follows: The Turing Test lasts for some given finite amount of time, and hence, only a finite number of finite strings of characters can be entered to form a conversation in that period of time. At the start of the test there is a large, but finite, number of finite strings of characters a human interrogator might enter. Then for each of these strings, there is large, but finite, number of responses a computer might make. And for each of these a large, but finite, number of responses the human interrogator might make, and so on. In principle, if a computer stored all the finitely possible conversations for the given time, it could look up a plausible response to make to any interrogator's remark at any point in a tree of possible conversations. The objection claims that in this situation the computer would be operating as a giant jukebox of remarks and would pass the Turing Test for a given period of time, but would in fact understand nothing. The Jukebox Objection, however, may be less forceful than it initially appears. Selecting exactly the set of all strings of words that form acceptable branches of a complete tree of possible conversations, and continually updating the remarks in this tree to reflect changes in common knowledge would be a daunting task for a programmer. A program that could perform such selecting and updating automatically would be doing more than just storing a large set of fixed responses.

If the Jukebox Objection is regarded simply as a thought experiment, it would at most show that passing the Turing Test is not a logically sufficient condition for establishing computer mentality, a claim to which even a proponent of the Turing Test can agree.

John Searle has proposed the Chinese Room Objection. Searle, who understands no Chinese, imagines himself in a room into which Chinese symbols are passed. He imagines further that he has a rulebook in English that tells him how to form Chinese expressions so that he can write out and return appropriate responses in Chinese to the symbols coming in. Searle claims that, although from the point of view of a Chinese speaker outside the room, the room or its inhabitant might appear to understand Chinese, neither the room nor its inhabitant (Searle) really understands Chinese at all. Similarly, any computer that passed the Turing Test by merely formally manipulating symbols, as computer programs do, might appear to understand but would not actually understand at all. Searle maintains that syntax is not sufficient for semantics. This objection, however, may also be less forceful than it first appears. Searle may underrate the consequences of complex transformations of syntactic structures, as human understanding itself may be generated from syntactical operations such as the patterns of neurons firing in the human brain.

The Turing Test has been a controversial test for nearly a half century. Whether a computer will some day pass it is an open empirical question. And what conclusions should be drawn if a computer does pass it remains a hotly debated philosophical issue.

Bibliography

1950. Turing, A. M. "Computing Machinery and Intelligence," *Mind*, **59**, 433–460.
1976. Weizenbaum, J. *Computer Power and Human Reason.* San Francisco: Freeman.
1980. Searle, J. R. "Minds, Brains, and Programs," *Behavioral and Brain Sciences*, **3**, 417–457.
1990. Block, N. "The Computer Model of the Mind," in *Thinking: An Invitation to Cognitive Science* (eds. D. N. Osherson, and E. E. Smith). Cambridge, MA: MIT Press.
1994. Shieber, S. M. "Lessons from a Restricted Turing Test," *Comm. of the ACM*, **37**, 70–84.
1998. Moor, J. H. "Assessing Artificial Intelligence and its Critics," in *The Digital Phoenix: How Computers are Changing Philosophy* (eds. T. W. Bynum, and J. H. Moor). Oxford: Blackwell.
1999. Krol, M. "Have We Witnessed a Real-life Turing Test?," *IEEE Computer*, **32**, 27–30.

Websites

Turing WWW page: `http://www.turing.org.uk/turing/`.
Loebner Prize homepage: `http://www.acm.org/~loebner/loebner-prize.html`.

James H. Moor

TURING, ALAN M.

For articles on related subjects *see* ALGORITHMS, THEORY OF; CHURCH, ALONZO; DIGITAL COMPUTERS, HISTORY OF: EARLY; KILBURN, TOM; TURING MACHINE; TURING TEST; and WILLIAMS, SIR FREDERIC C.

Alan Mathison Turing (1912–1954) was born in London, the son of Julius Mathison Turing of the Indian Civil Service and of Ethel Sara Turing (née Stoney). The Stoneys were a family of considerable scientific distinction, three of them having been Fellows of the Royal Society.

From an early age, Alan Turing showed an extraordinary aptitude for science and mathematics, and, in 1931, he entered King's College, Cambridge, as a Mathematical Scholar. He was clearly bored with the rather trivial first-year course, and gained only a second class in Part I of the Mathematics Tripos. At the end of the third year, however, he was a Wrangler, and gained a distinction in the advanced papers. He was elected a Fellow of King's in 1935 for a dissertation on the Central Limit Theorem of Probability. Characteristically, he rediscovered this, being quite unaware of previous work. The following year he was awarded a Smith's prize for his thesis on the same topic.

It was in 1935 that he first became interested in mathematical logic, and in 1937 he published his now celebrated paper "On Computable Numbers with an Application to the Entscheidungsproblem," in which he introduced the concept of a Turing machine. This paper attracted immediate attention and led to an invitation to Princeton, where he worked with Alonzo Church (*q.v.*). He took his Ph.D. there in 1938, the subject of his thesis being "Systems of Logic Based on Ordinals." Turing contemplated staying in the USA and was offered a post as assistant to John von Neumann (*q.v.*), but he decided to return to Cambridge in 1938. Until the outbreak of war, he worked on "A Method for the Calculation of the Zeta-Function," a topic to which he was to return in later years.

During the Second World War, Turing (being of military age) was required to work on government scientific research. He spent 1939–1945 at Bletchley Park (*see* COLOSSUS), the center of British code-breaking work during the Second World War. For many years this work was kept confidential by the British government, but it has now been described by Hodges (1983); Turing's principal role in cracking the codes of the German Enigma cipher machine is now well established. In 1996 the US National Security Agency released Turing's report on his methods, which is currently (1999) being edited for publication (*see* http://www.turing.org.uk/turing/scrapbook/treatise.html). For his work on code-breaking Turing was awarded the Officer Order of the British

Figure 1. Alan Mathison Turing (courtesy of the National Archive of the History of Computing, University of Manchester).

Empire (OBE). It is certain that in this period he gained a detailed knowledge of pulse techniques, and this was to have a decisive influence on his subsequent career. In 1942, he visited the USA on official business. During this visit he had the opportunity to see the latest work on computers and to renew old contacts at Princeton.

In 1945, he declined an offer of a Fellowship at King's in favor of joining the newly formed Mathematical Division at the National Physical Laboratory (NPL). His early work on computability, combined with his wartime experience in electronics, had fired him with an enthusiasm for working on the design of an electronic computer. The machine he designed, which was called the Automatic Computing Engine (ACE) in recognition of Babbage's pioneering work, was characteristically original. Although Turing knew something of the von Neumann proposals for EDVAC (*q.v.*), he was not unduly influenced by them. The ACE, as Turing conceived it, was too ambitious a project, considering the current state of electronic techniques. Therefore he left NPL in 1948, dissatisfied with the rate of progress.

While in the Mathematics Division of NPL, Turing became keenly interested in numerical analysis (*q.v.*). His paper, "Rounding-off Errors in Matrix Processes," showed that the acute anxiety about the effect of rounding errors in Gaussian elimination was largely unjustified. This paper has been overshadowed to some extent by the von Neumann and Goldstine paper on matrix inversion, but is is a brilliant piece of work and would have repaid closer study at the time. After Turing left NPL, it was decided to build a pilot model embodying Turing's ideas (the Pilot ACE), and this was completed in 1950. It was a highly successful computer, and some 30 engineered versions of it were subsequently constructed by the English Electric Company under the name DEUCE. The original Pilot ACE is in the Science Museum in Kensington, London.

On leaving NPL, Turing was appointed to a Readership at Manchester University, where he worked in close collaboration with F. C. Williams (*q.v.*) and T. Kilburn (*q.v.*), both pioneers in the electronic computer field. He was elected a Fellow of the Royal Society in 1951. Papers published while he was at Manchester include further work on the Riemann zeta function, a remarkable discussion on computing machinery and intelligence (*see* TURING TEST), and on the chemical basis of morphogenesis. The latter was his main interest at that time, and he left uncompleted another substantial paper on the same topic.

Turing died tragically in 1954 at the age of 41, a probable suicide. His publications, impressive though some of them are, give only the merest hint of his extraordinary originality and versatility. In recognition of his outstanding pioneering work, the ACM has named its most prestigious award the Turing Award (*q.v.*), awarded annually for outstanding contributions to computer science of a technical nature.

A definitive biography of Turing has been written by Hodges (1983). *Breaking the Code*, a play based on Hodges' book written by Hugh Whitemore, was performed in London and New York in the late 1980s.

Bibliography

1955. Newman, M. H. A. *The Biographical Memoirs of Fellows of the Royal Society*, **1**, 253–263. London: The Royal Society.

1959. Turing, S. *A. M. Turing*. Cambridge: Heffer & Sons.

1970. Wilkinson, J. H. "Some Comments from a Numerical Analyst" (The 1970 A. M. Turing lecture), *JACM*, **18**, 2, 137–147.

1983. Hodges, A. *Alan Turing: The Enigma*. New York: Simon & Schuster. (Reprinted by Walker and Co., New York, 2000.)

1986. Turing, A. M. *A. M. Turing's Ace Report of 1946 and Other Papers* (eds. B. E. Carpenter and R. W. Doran). Cambridge, MA: MIT Press.

1992. Turing, A. M. *Collected Works of A. M. Turing. Vol. 1: Machine Intelligence* (ed. D. C. Ince). *Vol. 2: Morphogenesis* (ed. P. T. Saunders). *Vol. 3: Pure Mathematics* (ed. J. L. Britton). Amsterdam: North-Holland.

Website

http://www.turing.org.uk.

James H. Wilkinson

TYPEFONT

For articles on related subjects *see* METAFONT; MONITOR, DISPLAY; POSTSCRIPT; PRINTERS; T$_E$X; and WORD PROCESSING.

Introduction

The terms *font* and *typeface* are not quite synonyms. To a professional typesetter, a font is a specific typeface at a specific size. In computing, however, the distinction is often lost because the user can resize any typeface at will. But for the purposes of this article, a *typeface* is a character set having a particular styled appearance, regardless of size or attributes such as italic or bold. A *typefont*, or just *font*, is a typeface of specific size and attribute, such as 12-point italic Helvetica. A *point* is 1/72 of an inch. Common typefonts used with personal computers are the italic and bold variants of the *Times Roman*, *Arial*, *Chicago*, and *Courier New* typefaces, but there are literally hundreds of specialized fonts that can be added to the menu of those available for use with word processors, Web browsers, and other software.

Serifs are the tiny picks or tails that, subjectively, make typefonts more readable. Times Roman and the typeface used for the narrative parts of this article are serif fonts. Fonts based on typefaces such as Arial whose letters (like this) do not have serifs are called *sans serif* fonts. Serif fonts are typically used for narrative, and sans serif fonts, because they are arguably more eye-catching at the expense of readability, are typically reserved for headings.

A typefont such as Courier or Courier New in which all characters have the same width is called *monospaced*. A typefont in which each character is allotted a width commensurate to its shape is called *proportional*. Proportional typefonts are more readable, but for printing computer code and numeric output where vertical alignment of data is important, a monospaced format is the usual choice.

Bitmapped vs. Outline Fonts

All printers, whether dot matrix, ink jet, laser, dye sublimation, or solid ink, accomplish essentially the same task: they create a pattern of dots on a sheet of paper. The dots may be sized differently or composed of different inks that are transferred to the paper by different means, but all of the images for text and graphics are made up of dots. The smaller the dots, the more attractive the printout. Regardless of how the dots are created, there must be a common method for determining where to place them. The most common schemes are *bitmapped fonts* and *outline fonts*. Bitmapped fonts come in predefined sizes and weights. Outline fonts can, on the fly, be scaled and given special attributes, such as bold, italic, and underlined. Each method has its advantages and disadvantages, depending on what type of output is wanted.

BITMAPPED FONTS

Bitmapped images are the computer's equivalent of Gutenberg's type. Bitmaps are generally limited to text and are a fast way to produce a printed page that uses only a few typefonts. Bitmapped fonts are typefaces of a specific size and with specific *attributes* or characteristics, such as bold or italic. The bitmap is a record of the pattern of dots needed to create a specific character in a certain size and with a certain attribute. The bitmaps for a 36-point Times Roman medium capital A, for a 36-point Times Roman bold capital A, and for a 30-point Times Roman medium capital A are all different and specific (*see* Fig. 1). Most printers—whether impact dot matrix, laser, or ink jet—come with a few bitmapped fonts, usually *Courier* and *Line Printer* (essentially *Times Roman*) in both normal, italic, and bold varieties as part of their permanent memory (ROM). In addition, many printers have random access memory (RAM) to which the computer can send bitmaps for other fonts.

When a document is sent to a printer using bitmapped fonts, the computer first tells the printer which of the *bitmap tables* contained in the printer's memory it should use. Then for each letter, punctuation mark, or paper movement—such as a tab or carriage return—the computer sends an *ASCII code*. Extended ASCII codes consist of *hexadecimal* numbers that are matched against the table of bitmaps (*see* CHARACTER CODES). If, for example, the hexadecimal number 41 (65 decimal) is sent to the printer, the printer's processor looks up hex 41 in its table and finds that it corresponds to a pattern of dots that creates an uppercase A in whatever typeface, type size, and attribute is in the active table. The printer uses that bitmap to determine which

instructions to send to its other components to reproduce the bitmap's pattern on paper. Each character, one after the other, is sent to the printer.

OUTLINE FONTS

Outline, or *vector* fonts, are used with a *page description language*, such as Adobe *PostScript* or Microsoft *TrueType*, that treats everything on a page—even text—as a graphic. The text and graphics used by the software are converted to a series of commands that the printer's page description language interpreter uses to determine where each dot is to be placed on a page. Page description language interpreters are no longer much slower than matrix printers. Outline fonts are more versatile at producing different sizes of type with different attributes or special effects, and they create more attractive results.

Unlike bitmapped fonts, outline fonts are not limited to specific sizes and attributes of a typeface. Instead, they consist of mathematical descriptions of each character and punctuation mark in a typeface. They are called *outline fonts* because the outline of a Times Roman 36-point capital A is proportionally the same as that of a 24-point Times Roman capital A (*see* Fig. 2). Some printers come with a page description language, most commonly PostScript or Hewlett-Packard Printer Command Language, in *firmware* (*q.v.*)—a computer program contained on a microchip. The language can translate outline font commands from the computer's software into the instructions the printer needs to control where it places dots on a sheet of paper. For printers that do not have a built-in page description language, software can translate the printer language commands into the instructions the printer needs.

When a print command from a software application is issued to a printer using outline fonts, the application sends a series of commands which the page description

Bitmapped Fonts

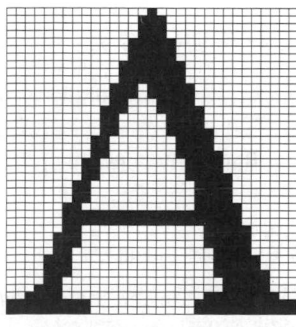

36pt. medium

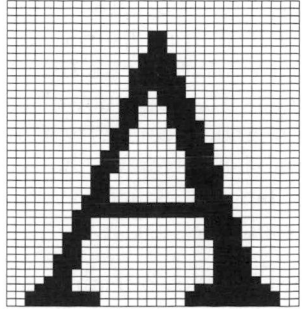

30pt. medium

Figure 1. Bitmaps for, respectively, a 36-pt. Times Roman medium capital A, a bold version of the same size letter, and a 30-pt version of the first letter.

Outline Fonts

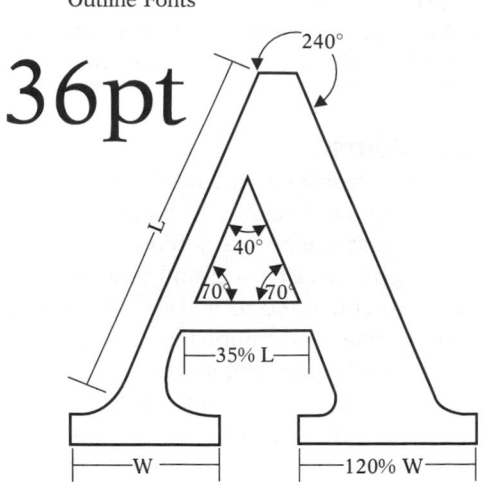

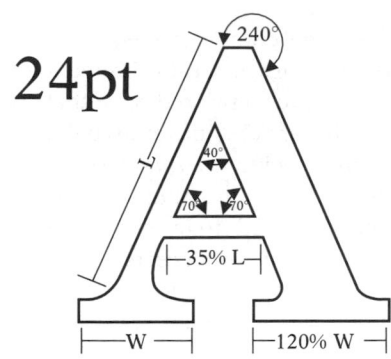

Figure 2. Two differently sized versions of a Times Roman capital A.

language interprets through a set of algorithms (*q.v.*) expressed as mathematical formulas. The algorithms describe the lines and arcs that make up the characters in a typeface. The algorithms for some typefaces include *hints*, special alterations to the details of the outline if the type is to be either extremely big or extremely small. The commands insert variables into the formulas to change the size or attributes of the outline font. The results are commands to the printer that say, in effect, "Create a horizontal line 3 points wide which begins 60 points from the bottom and 20 points to the right." The page description language turns on all the bits that fall inside the outline of the letter—unless the font includes some special shading effect within the outline.

Specialized Typefonts

Through the method described in METAFONT or similar ones, ever newer and more specialized typefonts are being designed and made available. Some may be downloaded free from certain Websites; others are proprietary and licensed for a fee. One of the features that contributed to the early success of the Apple Macintosh was its use of a distinctive sans serif typefont called Chicago **which looks like this** (even when not emboldened). The font is downloadable as freeware for Wintel PCs. And, of course, typefonts exist for most of the natural languages of the world, as well as for computer languages such as APL (*q.v.*) that use a specialized typefont.

One can now, for a fee of course, submit samples of one's own handwriting to a company that will return a special typefont that, when used, will mimic that handwriting. A sample of one of the authors' handwriting produced this way is

now is the time for all good Parties to come to the aid of the people.

Finally, one of the more intriguing special freeware fonts is a TrueType font called *Dancingmen*. It was designed for use in enciphering messages in the substitution cipher used by Sherlock Holmes in "The Adventure of the Dancing Men." The "handwritten" message above in the Dancingmen typefont is

Using a word processor into which the special font has been installed, one may highlight the message and decipher it by changing to a font such as Times Roman or Arial to read its corresponding plaintext. Doing so has amusement value, but since the cipher is mono-alphabetic (one to one correspondence of font symbols), it is, as Holmes showed, cryptographically insecure.

Bibliography

1989. Binns, B. *Better Type*. New York: Watson-Guptill Publications.
1993. Aaron, B., and Aaron, A. *TrueType Display Fonts*. San Francisco: Sybex.
1998. White, R. *How Computers Work*, 4th Ed. Indianapolis, IN: Que.

Ron White and Edwin D. Reilly

TYPES, THEORY OF

For articles on related subjects *see* ABSTRACT DATA TYPE; CLASS; COERCION; DATA STRUCTURES; FUNCTIONAL PROGRAMMING; OBJECT-ORIENTED PROGRAMMING; PROCEDURE-ORIENTED LANGUAGES; and PROGRAMMING LANGUAGES.

A *type* is a collection of computable values that have certain properties in common. Some examples are the type of integers, the type of alphanumeric characters, the type of arrays of integers, and the type of all functions with integer arguments and integer values. Many programming languages keep track of the type of each expression in order to avoid meaningless calculations such as multiplying an integer by a function. A system for keeping track of the types of expressions is called a *type system*.

One way of understanding the role of types in programming is by comparison with the way units are used in calculating physical quantities. In calculations that involve *velocity*, *distance* and *time*, for example, we know that *velocity* × *time* = *distance*. Just as relationships between units can be used to check the consistency of scientific calculations, types may be used in programming to check that a computation is meaningful.

Uses of Types in Programming Languages

There are three main uses for types in programming languages:

- Program organization and documentation
- Preventing the execution of erroneous operations
- Guaranteeing the correctness of optimizations

PROGRAM ORGANIZATION AND DOCUMENTATION

A well-designed program uses concepts related to the problem. For example, a banking program will be organized around concepts common to banks, such as accounts, customers, deposits, withdrawals, and transfers. In modern programming languages, these can be represented as separate types and type checking will be used to make sure that accounts and customers are treated separately, with account operations applied to accounts but not used to manipulate customers. Using types (or classes) to organize a program makes it easier for someone to read, understand and maintain the program. Types therefore serve an important purpose in documenting the design and intent of program designers.

An important tool for program design is the ability to define new types that reflect the structure of data to be used with the program. Most programming languages let the user define types that are built out of language primitives like arrays, records, and basic values such as integers and strings. Thus a programmer could define a type name `account` that would be a record containing information such as customer name, account number, and balance. Such user-defined types may include complex structures like arrays of records (the collection of all bank accounts), or records containing lists of records (an account together with the history of all its transactions).

TYPE ERRORS

Type checking is used to prevent type errors. A *type error* occurs when an operation is applied incorrectly to some operand (*q.v.*). For example, a function that uses integer operations on its arguments should not be applied (called) with an argument that is not an integer. (Most compilers (*q.v.*) would catch such an error.)

Hardware errors. Some erroneous sequences of machine instructions will be detected by the computer hardware and cause the program to stop. For example, when a computer executes a function call, there is a jump to the first location in memory that contains the instructions associated with the function. If a program confuses integers and functions, for example, then a program might jump to a location that does not contain a legal instruction or may be outside the range of memory that is allocated to the program. This will not happen, however, if type checking is used to make sure that every function call is to a correctly defined function.

Unintended semantics. Other forms of type error might not cause a program to halt, but are just as dangerous since they imply that the program is not computing the answer it was intended to. Consider an example drawn from machine language. On most machines, the instruction for adding integers is different from the instruction for adding floating-point numbers. This is because these two kinds of numbers are stored differently. If location x is being used as a floating-point number, then it would be a type error to use integer addition to add x to another number, y. The hardware performing the integer addition would not be able to detect this error, since the sequence of bits (binary digits, 0 or 1) used to represent a floating-point number could also be used to represent an integer. However, the result of addition would not make any sense, since the sequence of bits used to represent a number x in floating-point would represent an integer that is very different from x.

TYPES AND OPTIMIZATION

Types can be used for many kinds of optimization. One example is in finding components of records, or *structs*, as they are called in C (*q.v.*) and C++ (*q.v.*). Essentially the same issues arise in all object-oriented languages. A record consists of a sequence of entries of different types. For example, a student record may contain a student name of type string and a student number of type int. A related type is the type of undergraduate students, with components listed here in a type expression:

```
Student = {name:string, number:int}
Undergrad = {name:string, number:int,
                                year:int}
```

In a program manipulating records, there might be an expression of the form r.name, meaning the name field of the record r. A compiler must generate machine code that, given the location of record r in memory, finds the location of the field name. If the type of the record is known to the compiler, then it is possible to associate a fixed offset with each type and use this at compile time. For example, if the type of r is Student, then the compiler could build a little table saying that name occurs before number in each Student record. Using this table, the compiler could determine that the name is in the first location allocated to the record r. However, for records of a different type, the name field might appear second or third. Therefore, if the type is not known at compile time, the compiler must generate code to compute the location of name at run time.

In some object-oriented programming languages, the type of an object may similarly be used to find the relative location of parts of the object. In other languages, however, the type system does not give this kind of information and run-time search must be used.

Run-time vs. Compile-time Type Checking

RUN-TIME CHECKING

Some programming languages use run-time type checking. In these languages, the compiler generates code so that whenever an operation is performed, the program checks to make sure that the operands have the correct type. For example, the Lisp (*q.v.*) language operation car returns the first element of a list. Since it is a type error to apply car to something that is not a list, Lisp programs are compiled (or interpreted) so that before evaluating (car x) a check is made to make sure that x is a list. An advantage of run-time type checking is that it catches type errors. A disadvantage is the run-time cost associated with making these checks.

COMPILE-TIME CHECKING

Many modern programming languages are designed so that it is possible to check the syntax of expressions for potential type errors. In these languages, it is common to reject programs that do not pass the compile-time type checks. An advantage of compile-time type checking is that it catches errors earlier than run-time checking: a program developer is warned about the error before the program is given to other users or

shipped as a product. Since compile-time checks may eliminate the need to check for certain errors at run time, compile-time checking can make it possible to produce more efficient code.

A disadvantage of compile-time type checking is that the compiler must be conservative. In any sufficiently expressive programming language, there are programs that will run without error but will fail a compile-time test. The reason is that it is *undecidable* whether or not an expression contains a run-time type error. This means that there is no algorithm that always terminates which determines whether a program will produce a run-time type error.

COMBINING COMPILE-TIME AND RUN-TIME CHECKING

Most programming languages actually use some combination of compile-time and run-time type checking. For example, it is common to differentiate arrays from integers at compile time, but to check array bounds errors (which can be considered a form of type error) at run time. In some languages, such as C, array bounds are not checked at run time, making it possible to execute programs with type errors.

Overloading, Polymorphism, and Subtyping

There are several ways that a single expression could have more than one type.

IMPLICIT CONVERSION

Most programming languages provide some form of implicit conversion. The most common example is the conversion between integer and floating-point numbers. For example, the expression

```
(n + 4) + 1.212
```

involves two forms of addition. If n is an integer variable, then the first + can be integer addition. However, the second addition has one operand, 1.212, that is not an integer. An expression like this is usually interpreted so that the first two numbers are added as integers. Then, the result is converted to a floating-point number and added to 1.212 using floating-point addition. The conversion from integer to float is implicit since the expression does not explicitly contain any conversion operation. Implicit conversion is called *coercion* (*q.v.*).

OVERLOADING

Overloading occurs when one symbol or name refers to more than one operation or function (*see* OPERATOR OVERLOADING). A common example is +, which may refer to integer addition or floating-point addition.

Inside the computer, these two operations work in very different ways, since integers and floating-point numbers are represented differently. However, since both are related to the same mathematical operation (addition), it is convenient to use the same symbol for both. In general, overloading is resolved at compile time, using the types of each operand to decide which operation is intended. Therefore overloading generally relies on compile-time type checking. In some languages, however, run-time tests may be used to select the appropriate operation. This is called *multiple dispatch*, and has very different behavior from conventional overloading.

POLYMORPHISM

A function is *polymorphic* if it has one algorithm or implementation, but may be applied to arguments of many different types. This kind of polymorphism is sometimes called *parametric polymorphism*, to distinguish it from *ad hoc polymorphism*, another term for overloading. An example of a polymorphic function is a sorting function that, given a list and an order relation on the elements of the list, returns a sorted list. In many languages, the type of a list element would be passed as an argument to sort. Therefore, sort would have three parameters, a type t, a list of elements of type t, and a function less of type $t \times t \rightarrow boolean$ that reports whether its first argument is less than its second one. Notice that the types of the second and third arguments depend on the first (type) arguments. This dependency is typical of polymorphic functions. In C++ function templates, the type (or class) parameters all occur in a separate parameter list. In some languages, such as ML, the type parameter to a polymorphic function can be inferred automatically by the compiler, using type inference (see below).

SUBTYPING

Subtyping is used in many object-oriented languages. In general terms, type A is a *subtype* of B if every expression of type A may be used where the syntactic (and typing) rules of the language require an expression of type B. In other words, if A is a subtype of B, this means that "A"s are substitutable for "B"s. In many object-oriented languages, subtyping is correlated with subclassing: if A is a subclass of B, then A objects may be used in place of B objects. However, there are many subtle aspects of this correspondence, as discussed in current research on the subject.

Recursive Types

Modern programming languaes allow types to be defined recursively (*see* RECURSION). An example

recursive type definition, from the ML language, is the following definition of a type of binary tree ·

```
datatype bintree =
    Empty
  | Node of string * bintree * bintree
```

This declaration states that a value of type bintree is either the primitive value Empty, representing the empty tree, or a compound tree formed from a string and two subtrees that are also bintrees. Recursive types are useful in programming with various kinds of data structures, allowing programmers to define general types of data without making dealing explicitly with implementation details like pointers.

Type Inference

Type inference is the process of determining the types of expressions based on the known types of some or all of their subexpressions. The difference between type inference and type checking is a matter of degree. In type checking, we assume that programs contain enough declarations to determine the type of every expression. A type-checking algorithm generally goes through the program to check that the types declared by the programmer agree with what the language rules require. In type inference, some information may not be specified and some form of logical inference may be needed to determine the types of identifiers from the way they are used.

Here is a simple example, written in the programming language ML. The declaration

```
fun f(x) = x + 2;
```

defines a function f that adds 2 to its argument. The ML compiler infers that, since the function adds 2 to x, x must be an integer and the operator + must mean integer addition. Since integer plus integer returns an integer, the type of f is $int \rightarrow int$, the ML way of writing "function from integers to integers." Although practical type inference was developed for the programming language ML, the idea can be applied to a variety of programming languages.

Type Parameterization

Type parameterization supports *generic programming*, in which data structures and operations can be defined for many types of constituent data. A generic set data type, for example, would provide a single set implementation that could be used to construct sets for any type of set elements. Using type parameterization, the ML definition of a tree type containing strings could be generalized to trees of arbitrary elements:

```
datatype α tree =
    Empty
  | Node of α * α tree * α tree
```

where α stands for any element type. In languages like C++, generic data structures are represented by templates that must be instantiated to specific types before they are used. In ML, type inference is used to eliminate the need for instantiating generic functions and data structures. For example, a function to search for an element in a tree could then be a polymorphic function in which the element type would be determined by the type inference algorithm. Type systems with generic functions and generic data structures support good software design by combining the security of compile-time checking with reusable standard software components.

Bibliography

1996. Mitchell, J. *Foundations for Programming Languages.* Cambridge, MA: MIT Press.
1996. Sethi, R. *Programming Languages: Concepts and Constructs.* Reading, MA: Addison-Wesley.

John C. Mitchell

ULTRASONIC MEMORY

For articles on related subjects *see* EDSAC; EDVAC; MEMORY: MAIN; SEAC; and UNIVAC I.

Ultrasonic memories played an important role in the early development of digital computers, but are now only of historical interest. The report on the EDVAC drafted by von Neumann in June 1945 on behalf of the group at the Moore School of Electrical Engineering, Philadelphia, clearly envisaged this type of memory, although it did not describe the physical principles on which it operated. Of the early machines, the EDSAC, SEAC, Pilot ACE, EDVAC, and UNIVAC I all had ultrasonic memories.

The principle is illustrated in Fig. 1. A train of pulses representing the number to be stored is modulated onto a carrier and applied to a piezoelectric crystal in contact with a column of mercury. The ultrasonic pulses so generated travel along the column until they reach another crystal at the far end. This converts them back into electric signals, which are amplified and rectified. The resulting pulses are applied to a gate

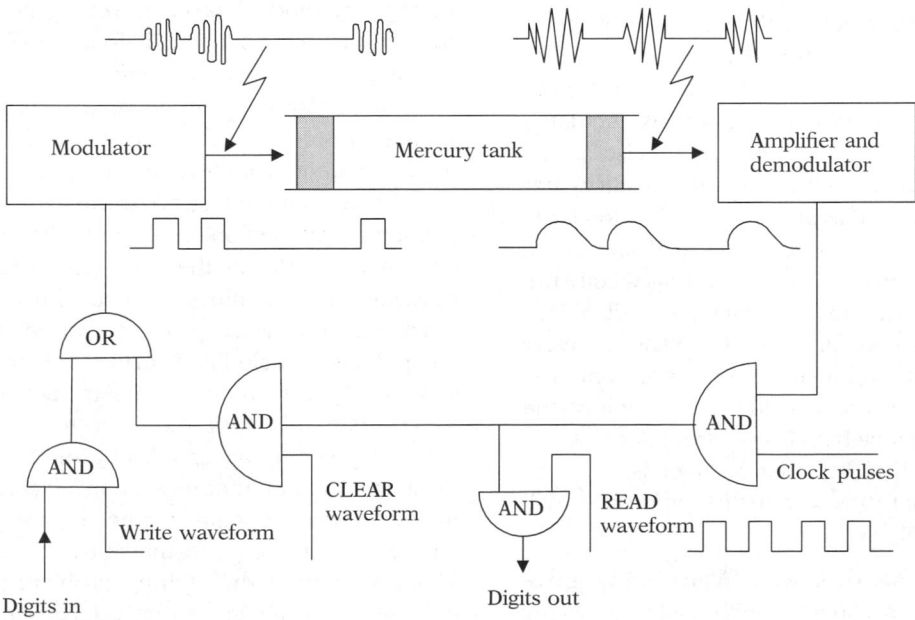

Figure 1. Ultrasonic memory.

together with pulses from a continuously running clock pulse generator. This gating operation serves the twin purposes of regeneration and synchronization. The emerging pulses, which are exact replicas of the original pulses, are reapplied to the modulator and continue to circulate. The operations of reading, clearing, and writing can be performed by applying to the gates shown suitable waveforms accurately synchronized with the clock. A typical main memory consisted of a group of 32 tanks, as the columns were called, each between 0.5 and 1.5 meters long and giving a delay of between one-third and 1 ms.

In the mid-1950s, ultrasonic memories using a fine nickel wire in the form of a coil as the propagation medium appeared in some low-cost computers. The waves were excited by making use of the magnetostrictive properties of the nickel.

Bibliography

1956. Wilkes, M. V. *Automatic Digital Computers.* New York: John Wiley.
1985. Wilkes, M. V. *Memoirs of a Computer Pioneer.* Cambridge, MA: MIT Press.

Maurice V. Wilkes

UNDECIDABLE PROBLEMS

For articles on related subjects *see* ALGORITHMS, THEORY OF; CHURCH, ALONZO; LAMBDA CALCULUS; NP-COMPLETE PROBLEMS; TURING, ALAN M.; and TURING MACHINE.

One of this century's major intellectual discoveries is that there are some perfectly precise problems that can never be solved. This is a technical result, not a mystical one. There is nothing ineffable about these problems; indeed, one can give specific examples of them. Nor should this result be confused with the claim that some problems (e.g. what is the meaning of life?) are too imprecise to be solved computationally. Actually, these unsolvable problems are just as precise as the problem of computing a sum. Also, the result is not based on the fact that some problems are just too large to solve in practical terms. Rather, these problems are unsolvable even under the assumption that wholly unreasonable amounts of time and space are available for their solution. By way of contrast, it is a trivial matter under such an assumption to write a program that plays a perfect game of chess: just explore all of the possibilities systematically. (There are only a finite number of possibilities, but that number is so astronomically large that this exhaustive approach will never be of practical use.)

In the 1930s, the mathematician Alan Turing introduced a conceptual automaton, now called a *Turing machine*, to model the process by which a computer carries out a computational task. At that time, "computer" meant "one who computes" (i.e. a person who carries out a calculation), but the model applies equally well to modern electronic computers. Turing then proved rigorously that no Turing machine can solve the so-called Halting Problem, the problem of determining whether Turing machines eventually halt. Some do, some don't: the problem is, given a Turing machine along with its input data, to determine whether or not it will ever finish its task and halt. Of course, one can run the Turing machine step by step, and, if it halts, one would see that it had. The difficulty is that if it does not halt then this method will not reveal that fact; no matter how long one continues the simulation, it is conceivable that the machine would have halted if processing had continued an additional few moments.

Turing's proof is a formalization of the following idea. Establish a *pairing* between all possible Turing machines (there are infinitely many) and all possible sets of input data (also infinitely many) in a systematic way. Now suppose there were a Turing machine H that could solve the Halting Problem. Starting from H, one could build a "perverse" machine P that acts as follows: P takes its input data x and determines (by using H as a subroutine) whether the particular machine M, which is paired with x, would halt or run forever on input x; and P then perversely either halts or enters an infinite loop, whichever causes it to behave differently from M. Now P has succeeded in behaving differently from *every* machine; specifically, it differs from machine M on the particular input data x that is matched with M in the pairing. But this is impossible, since P would have to differ even from itself. So H cannot exist after all.

Turing's method of proof is very general. It applies equally well to show that it is impossible to write a Pascal program, say, that can test Pascal programs for infinite loops. If this were the end of the story, Turing's result would merely establish certain limits on self-referential application, suggesting, for example, that if one wants to test programs written in a particular language, then one must write the tests in a different language. But at the same time that Turing was describing his machines, Alonzo Church and various other logicians were proving that many models of computation (including Turing machines) that are superficially very different are in fact all equivalent. As a result of this work, the *Church–Turing Thesis* has become generally accepted: any method of performing a computation that might conceivably be proposed in the future, no matter how apparently powerful, will turn out to be performable by a Turing machine. This implies that the Halting Problem is unsolvable, not merely in the sense that no Turing machine can solve it, but that more generally, no computational procedure of any type can. Similarly, one cannot test Pascal programs for termination no matter what present or future programming language one is willing to use for the task.

The unsolvability of the Halting Problem can be used to prove a celebrated result of the logician Kurt Gödel, who showed in 1931 that it is impossible to capture a significant portion of mathematics with any finite number of axioms, thus demonstrating a fundamental limitation of the axiomatic method. The idea is that by carefully encoding both Turing machines and data as integers, one can turn the statement "Turing machine i halts on input j in k steps" into an arithmetic statement $T(i, j, k)$ about i, j, and k. (By this is meant a statement involving addition, multiplication, and logical quantifiers: working out the details of this is the tedious part of the proof.) Now suppose that this Turing machine runs forever on its input. Then the statement "There is no integer k satisfying the arithmetic relation $T(i, j, k)$" would be a true statement of arithmetic. But if enough of mathematics could be axiomatized to make all true statements of arithmetic provable from the axioms, then the futile process of observing the machine as it runs forever could be short-circuited by instead giving a finite-length proof that it never halts. Yet this cannot always be possible, since it would contradict the unsolvability of the Halting Problem.

The proof of the Gödel Incompleteness Theorem just outlined differs in some details from Gödel's original proof, which predated Turing's result, but which used the same idea of arithmetic encoding. The Gödel and Turing results are closely related. In essence, Gödel proved that any sufficiently rich axiomatic system contains undecidable but nonetheless true propositions. Turing proved that one cannot write a computer program that, fed an axiomatic system and an arbitrary proposition as input, can determine whether the proposition is undecidable (*see* Hofstadter, 1985, 484–487).

The unsolvability of the Halting Problem can also be used to prove that various other problems are unsolvable. Suppose that one wants to prove that Problem X is unsolvable. If one can write a procedure for solving the Halting Problem with the assistance of a hypothetical subprocedure for solving X, one can be sure that X in fact cannot be solved (otherwise, the Halting Problem could be). This is called *reducing* the Halting Problem to Problem X. By reducing a problem known to be unsolvable to a new problem, one can prove that the new problem is also unsolvable. In this way, many problems of interest in computer science have been shown to be unsolvable, which establishes that any attempt to write a program to solve all cases of the problem is doomed to fail. Often, an appropriate response is to seek solutions for special cases.

When the solution to a problem requires a yes or no answer to each problem instance, the problem is called a *decision* problem; if it is unsolvable, it is said to be *undecidable*.

Undecidability plays an important role in many theoretical areas of computer science, such as in the study of formal languages (*q.v.*). A typical problem is the *membership* problem for a language: determine, for each given word, whether or not the word is in the language. Languages for which this problem is decidable are called *recursive* languages. As a general rule, almost all problems about regular languages are decidable, while most problems about context-sensitive languages are undecidable (one exception: they are recursive); for context-free languages it is difficult to give any guidelines. For example, the problem of determining whether a context-free grammar generates infinitely many strings is decidable, but determining whether it generates all strings is not. (Of course, it is possible to tell whether or not certain context-free grammars generate all strings; what is impossible is to find a method that works for all context-free grammars.) Similarly, it is undecidable in general to determine whether two context-free grammars generate the same language.

As was mentioned earlier, a problem is solvable if it can be solved in principle, even though the amount of time required to compute the solution may be totally infeasible. More recent research has attempted to divide solvable problems into those that are feasibly solvable and those that are not: *see* NP-COMPLETE PROBLEMS.

Bibliography

1974. Brainerd, W. S., and Landweber, L. H. *Theory of Computation*. New York: John Wiley.
1982. Kfoury, A. J., Moll, R. N., and Arbib, M. A. *A Programming Approach to Computability*. New York: Springer-Verlag.
1984. Tourlakis, G. J. *Computability*. Reston, VA: Reston Publishing Co.
1985. Hofstadter, D. R. *Metamagical Themas*. New York: Basic Books.
1997. Lewis, H. R., and Papadimitriou, C. H. *Elements of the Theory of Computation*, 2nd Ed. Upper Saddle River, NJ: Prentice Hall.

Jonathan Goldstine

UNICODE

See CHARACTER CODES.

UNIVAC I

For articles on related subjects *see* DIGITAL COMPUTERS, HISTORY OF: EARLY; ECKERT, J. PRESPER; and MAUCHLY, JOHN WILLIAM.

UNIVAC I (Universal Automatic Computer) was the first commercially available computer in the USA.

Figure 1. UNIVAC I.

Work on the prototype was begun by the Eckert–Mauchly Computer Corporation in 1948 and completed in 1951, when it was delivered to the US Bureau of the Census. During this period, Eckert–Mauchly was acquired by Remington Rand Inc. (subsequently merged with the Sperry Corporation in 1955 to form the Sperry–Rand Corporation).

A total of 46 UNIVAC I computers were delivered to a wide variety of customers during the period 1951–1958.

The UNIVAC I, a high-speed general-purpose electronic data processing system, was different from earlier computers in that it handled both numbers and alphabetical characters equally well. One of the innovative features of this computer was that it divorced the complex problems of input and output from the actual computational facility.

The program, which was stored in mercury delay lines (*see* ULTRASONIC MEMORY), circulated within the lines in the form of acoustical pulses that could be read from the line and written into it. Information could be accessed at a speed of 40 to 400 microseconds.

Raw data was transcribed to magnetic tape by a key-to-tape device. Data on punched cards (*q.v.*) was transcribed to magnetic tape with a card-to-tape converter. Magnetic tape was the principal input medium and was also used for permanent storage of data. Input could also be effected from the keyboard of the control console during the processing of a program.

Output was recorded on magnetic tape. Data on output tapes was transcribed to punched cards by a tape-to-card converter or to printed copy by a printer. Alphabetical, numeric, and symbolic characters were accommodated in any combination in reading, writing, and processing operations.

Buffered storage registers permitted the central computer to continue processing while other data was being read from or recorded on magnetic tape. The system featured many automatic self-checking techniques, including duplicate circuits for all computing operations.

The operating characteristics were as follows: circuitry—chiefly serial, 2.25 MHz bit rate; Internal Operating Code—7 bits (four numeric pulses in excess-three notation (*see* CODES), two zone pulses, and one parity pulse); word length—12 characters including sign; block length—60 words; program code—single address, automatic sequencing; internal storage capacity—1,000 words or 12,000 characters.

The speeds of the basic arithmetic functions were: addition or subtraction, 0.525 ms; multiplication, 2.150 ms; division, 3.890 ms; comparison, 0.365 ms.

Bibliography

1981. Stern, N. *From ENIAC to UNIVAC*. Bedford, MA: Digital Press.

Michael M. Maynard

UNIVERSAL PRODUCT CODE

For articles on related subjects *see* CODES; OPTICAL CHARACTER RECOGNITION; and PATTERN RECOGNITION.

Symbols such as that shown in Fig. 1 now appear on almost all retail products for use in electronic checkout procedures. The code is designed to be read by an optical scanner, and is obviously non-secret, since the numbers used are interpreted just below the code.

The five leftmost digits identify the manufacturer through a code assigned by the Uniform Code Council. The five rightmost digits are assigned by the manufacturer to identify various individual products; thus, the price itself is not encoded, but instead a product identification number, from which a computer (online to the scanner) can obtain the price by *table lookup* (*see* SEARCHING). The digit 0 appearing at the left of the pattern is called the *code symbol*; it will be 0 for grocery products, but some other digit for other types

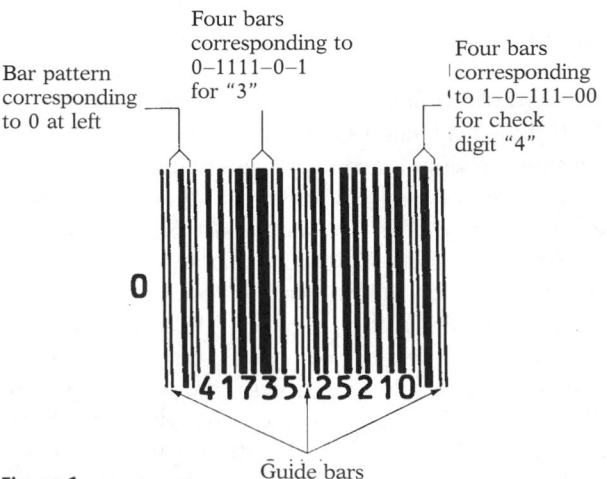

Bar pattern corresponding to 0 at left

Four bars corresponding to 0–1111–0–1 for "3"

Four bars corresponding to 1–0–111–00 for check digit "4"

Guide bars

Figure 1.

of enterprise. Since it will also participate in a checksum calculation to be described later, it is incorporated into the bar pattern itself (but not reprinted as an underlying digit).

Disregarding the guide bars at the left and right and the two center bars separating the two five-digit groups, all of which are longer than the bars over the interpreted digits, each digit is encoded by a sequence of four alternating light and dark bars of one of four different thicknesses. Each digit will have a unique sequence of bars, or, more precisely, a pair of such sequences, since the pattern of a digit on the right-hand side is the encoded 1s complement (*q.v.*) of the pattern it would have had on the left. This is done so that the program processing the scanner's input can detect whether the product was passed over the reading aperture right-to-left or left-to-right. Using 0 and 1 to represent the thinnest light and dark stripes, respectively, and 0000 and 1111 for the thickest such stripes, the code is as follows:

Digit	Left representation	Right representation
0	0001101	1110010
1	0011001	1100110
2	0010011	1101100
3	0111101	1000010
4	0100011	1011100
5	0110001	1001110
6	0101111	1010000
7	0111011	1000100
8	0110111	1001000
9	0001011	1110100

Thus, for example, the code for 4 on the left is, sequentially, the thinnest light bar (0), the thinnest dark bar (1), the next to thickest light bar (000), and the next to thinnest dark bar (11).

Certain patterns can be ascertained in the code assignments. First, note that all left-hand codes have odd *parity* (*q.v.*) (i.e. an odd number of 1s), so of course their right-hand complements have even parity. Second, the first bit of the left codes is always 0 and bit 7 is always 1, so that these code patterns always begin with a light bar and end with a dark one (and vice versa on the right). Of the 32 patterns that could have been assigned to the interior 5 bits, 16 (half) have the desired odd parity. But only 10 of these 16—the 10 selected—consist of exactly two light and two dark stripes. This will allow the scanner to make the further check that the pattern read contains exactly 30 dark and 29 light stripes, 59 in total, originating as follows:

10 interpreted digits × 4 stripes each	= 40
2 uninterpreted digits × 4 stripes each	= 8
2 dark-light-dark side guides	= 6
1 light-dark-light-dark-light center guide	= 5
Total	59

Since each of the 12 digits has a 7-bit representation and each of the 11 guide stripes a 1-bit representation, these 59 stripes would correspond to a string of 95 bits. The uninterpreted check digit is positioned between the guide bars on the right and the last interpreted digit. For further accuracy, the scanner verifies that the check digit read has a value such that

$3 \times$ [code symbol + 2nd + 4th + 6th + 8th + 10th printed digit]

$+$ [check digit + 1st + 3rd + 5th + 7th + 9th printed digit]

is a multiple of 10. Thus, if the product is a grocery item (code symbol at left = 0) whose identification number is 4173525210 (as in Fig. 1), its check digit must be 4 so that

$$3 \times [0 + 1 + 3 + 2 + 2 + 0] + [4 + 4 + 7 + 5 + 5 + 1] = 50$$

which is a multiple of 10.

In the early 1970s, the first scanners to be widely used by retailers were called *pen* (or *wand*) *scanners*. They used a light-emitting diode (LED) at their tip and a light detector in their barrel and had to actually touch the bar code in order to read it. But laser scanners do not need contact: some can even read a bar code from several feet away rather than the few inches needed for a supermarket scanner, and they are much better able to read a bar code imprinted on a curved surface. Early laser scanners were unreliable, frustrating customers who watched clerks swipe and re-swipe,

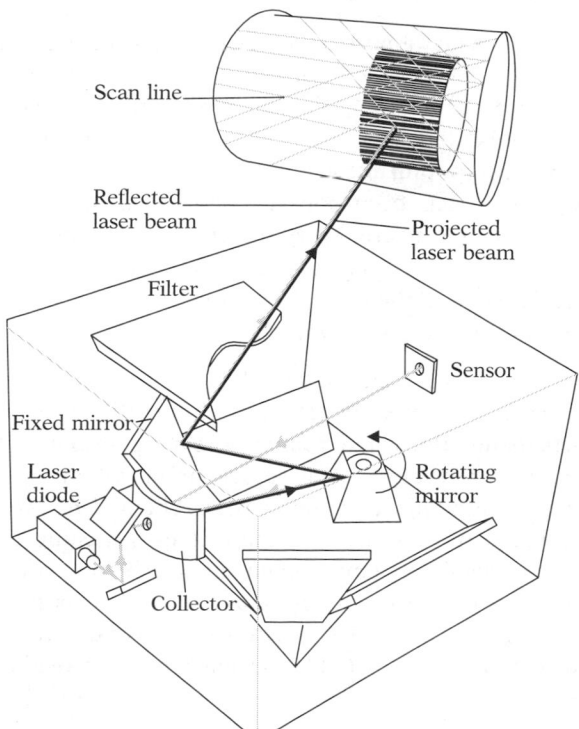

Figure 2. Inside a typical supermarket bar code reader. (Diagram courtesy of *New York Times*.)

often having to give up and enter a code manually. But current models have much higher resolution and usually succeed if an item is brought anywhere near it, regardless of the product's orientation. The inner workings of a typical supermarket bar code reader are shown in Fig. 2.

Bar code readers have applications other than for retail checkout, inventory control and library circulation being obvious candidates. For this purpose, a pen scanner or a small handheld laser scanner is a very effective tool.

Bibliography

1977. Mellen, G. E. "Universal Product Code," *The Cryptogram*, **42**, *1*, 1–3, 23–24.
1980. Helmers, C. "Bar Codes, Revisited," *Byte*, **5**, *4*, 6–10.
1991. Gallian, J. A. "The Mathematics of Identification Numbers," *The College Mathematics Journal*, **22**, *3* (May), 194–202.
1998. Greenman, C. "There's More than One Way to Scan a Bar Code," *New York Times*, 20 August, G11.

Edwin D. Reilly

UNIX OPERATING SYSTEM

> For articles on related subjects *see* C; DIRECTORY; FILE SERVER; INTERACTIVE SYSTEM; INTERNET; KERNEL; MULTITASKING; OPERATING SYSTEMS; REGULAR EXPRESSION; SCRIPTING LANGUAGES; SHELL; VIRTUAL MEMORY; WINDOW ENVIRONMENTS; and WORKSTATION.

Unix is a general-purpose time-sharing system developed in the early 1970s at Bell Laboratories by Ken Thompson and Dennis Ritchie. Almost three decades later, Unix stands as one of the most influential systems in computing history, and its popularity continues to grow. It has been ported to dozens of hardware platforms, and nearly every major vendor supports a product line based on Unix. In 1983, Thompson and Ritchie received the ACM Turing Award (*q.v.*) for their contributions to the computing field.

The roots of Unix can be found in the Multics project of the 1960s, in which Thompson and Ritchie were participants. But where Multics was a high-profile collaborative project involving several organizations, government funding, and many researchers, Unix was developed more quietly by individuals searching for a more hospitable environment in which to perform their activities. Indeed, the name Unix is a pun on Multics; where Multics attempted to explore many alternatives, Unix would concentrate on providing just one.

Unix began in 1969 with Thompson's file system experiments on a Digital Equipment (*q.v.*) PDP-7. The first production version appeared in 1971 and ran on a PDP-9. In 1973, Unix became the first operating system to be written in a high-level language when all but a small part of the system was rewritten in C, a programming language developed specifically for Unix. The first widely available public release, version 6, was released in 1976 and ran on a PDP-11. Version 7, the first portable Unix system, came two years later and ran on several different hardware platforms, including the PDP-11, Interdata 8/32, and the Digital Equipment VAX. The ease with which Unix could be modified led to development efforts at many universities and research laboratories. The most influential of the non-AT&T development sites was the University of California at Berkeley, which produced the Berkeley Software Distributions (BSD) versions of Unix. Berkeley also ported Unix to the VAX architecture and added support for virtual memory, demand paging, and the TCP/IP (*q.v.*) network protocols. Today, many parts of Unix and the C language have been standardized by international standards committees, and Unix has become the operating system of choice for RISC architecture workstations (*see* REDUCED INSTRUCTION SET COMPUTER).

Structure

Unix is a multitasking, multiuser operating system. With the help of terminals, many users can utilize a single computer simultaneously, each of them having in effect a personal machine environment, each as though having a personal workstation. Any computer running Unix can provide the same services, from small portable computers (*q.v.*) to the largest mainframes (*q.v.*), the only difference being speed and storage capacity.

THE UNIX KERNEL

Unix carefully distinguishes between the operating system *kernel* and user applications. Each user program runs as a separate *process*, making system calls into the kernel to perform such tasks as accessing files or allocating additional memory. The kernel itself was deliberately kept small; Thompson (1978) reports: "The kernel is the only Unix code that cannot be substituted by a user to his own liking. For this reason, the kernel should make as few real decisions as possible. This does not mean to allow the user a million options to do the same thing. Rather, it means to allow only one way to do one thing, but have that way be the least-common divisor of all the options that might have been provided." This design philosophy paved the way for the evolution of Unix. By implementing services in processes, users could easily replace an existing implementation of a service with an entirely new one by replacing the utility providing the service. As programmers experimented with new services, services evolved into superior ones. Modern flavors of Unix have adopted symmetric multiprocessor technology with multi-threaded kernels for efficient processing of services (symmetric multiprocessing allows any process to run on any CPU in a multiprocessor system). This allows systems to increase their throughput (*q.v.*) nearly in proportion to the number of available CPUs. Thus for some tasks, computing power comparable to the best mainframes is available on relatively cheap hardware.

UNIX SHELLS

The original user interface for Unix was a command interpreter, called a *shell*. A shell processes keyboard input and performs user-requested tasks. In Unix, the shell is a normal (albeit sophisticated) program executing as its own process. Running the shell as a process has two benefits. First, users can modify the shell as easily as any other program. Several shells, including the C shell and Korn shell, have become popular in addition to the original Bourne shell. Each subsequent shell provided new features that its predecessor lacked. The Bourne shell, for example, supports the creation of multiple simultaneous jobs, but provides limited means of controlling them once they have been started. The C shell permits users to suspend and later resume jobs, and to move jobs from foreground to background. Having shell commands run as regular processes also makes it possible for ordinary users to write *command scripts*, files containing arbitrary commands. In Unix, the shell can process commands contained in a file as easily as those entered at the keyboard.

COMMAND NAMES

Unix command names are highly abbreviated, some would say cryptic (for instance, cp for *copy*, df for *show disk free space*); they arose from the early era where keyboard entry was slow and painful. Since then, graphical user interfaces (GUIs) have been developed to offer a more user-friendly interface for simple operations. These provide users with mouse and menu control, together with multiple windows, screens, and virtual desktops. The X Window System, developed originally by the Massachusetts Institute of Technology, solved not only the problem of building GUI-based systems, but also of how to display windows and data from programs running on hardware at different physical locations. This follows Unix's tradition of remote execution and distributed systems (*q.v.*), based on the client–server (*q.v.*) model. Although some have predicted the demise of the shell interface, it continues to prove itself superior to graphical interfaces in a wide range of situations. The main reason for this is that GUIs permit a user to choose between a limited number of predetermined options, whereas for experts a language interface admits a virtually unlimited mode of expression and enquiry.

FILE SYSTEM

Unix provides a hierarchical file system in which directories hold files and other (sub)directories. The resulting file tree is shared by all users, making it straightforward to name and find files, including those belonging to other users. A file can be named by its full path name, which lists the directories on the path from the root of the tree to the file, or by its short name, in which case the file is assumed to be in the current directory. Symbolic links, or aliases to files, allow a given filename to appear in several places at once in the hierarchy. Each user has his or her own files. A user can lock files so that other users cannot access them; a system of protection bits sets the rights of other users. Other users can be granted access to the files on a read-only or a read–write basis. Unix does not enforce a naming convention on particular file types (such as executable programs and text files). Instead, protection bits and "magic numbers" (codes at the start of the file) are used by the system to recognize file contents if desired.

Unix provides a single, uniform way of accessing file contents. Programs process all files in exactly the same manner; they need not concern themselves with record sizes or differing access methods (*q.v.*) if they do not wish to. File operations treat the data in files as an uninterpreted bit stream. In addition, Unix uses *device independence* to make such devices as terminals and printers appear the same as files, allowing programs to read from either a file or terminal without knowing where the data actually comes from. The shell interface exploits this abstraction by allowing a program to receive input from any source without prejudice: from the keyboard, a file or even the output of another program. Redirection operators <, > and | provide the shell user with powerful tools to control the flow of data between programs and files. For example, the command sort reads lines from the terminal (until the user signals end of input) sending the sorted contents back to the terminal. To sort the data in a file, the same utility is invoked, but its input is redirected from the specified file (here input):

```
sort < input
```

Output can then be redirected to an arbitrary file (here *output*) as follows:

```
sort < input > output
```

Unix provides a service called *pipes*, which allows users to connect the output of one program to the input of another without using an intermediary file. For example, entering:

```
ps -aux | sort
```

invokes the command ps -aux, which displays the names of logged in users, and the processes which they are running. It then pipes the output from `ps` into `sort`. The result is a sorted list of user processes. The two commands of a pipeline execute *concurrently*, with each process running just long enough to fill its output or empty its input pipe. Any number of programs can be chained together with pipes. This is one of the most powerful features of the Unix shell. This possibility has led to the development of many small programs designed to read and write via file streams and perform one function in the most optimal and powerful fashion. Unix commands typically have many optional *switches* which alter their default behavior. These (as in the `ps -aux` example above) are recognized by a leading hyphen.

Tools

Unix is not just an operating system; it is an environment complete with a rich set of powerful tools. The operating system kernel itself runs on a bare machine, controlling access to such resources as memory, devices, and the central processing unit (*q.v.*). Although the kernel is a crucial part of the system, users interact with it only indirectly. Instead, they invoke editors, compilers, text processors, and other utility programs that in turn request kernel services when accessing files. Unix introduced many tools now taken for granted in the computing world, including document formatters and spell checkers (*q.v.*). Several utilities in particular deserve special mention.

The `make` utility takes a recipe describing the exact steps needed to build one complex system of files from another complex set of files. Typically `make` directs a compiler or text processor to build a program or format a document. If changes occur in the source files, `make` rebuilds only those parts of the system that have changed since the last time the system was built. In a large system constructed from hundreds of files, for example, a change in a single important program file might require recompiling the entire system, while a change in another file might require only rebuilding one component of the system. This results in a considerable saving in system resources.

The `lex` and `yacc` utilities provide "meta-tools" for the construction of compilers (*q.v.*) and other text translation programs. Programmers specify patterns and structures which they wish to recognize and respond to in a text stream. In modern parlance, these programs then build event-loops for detecting generalized patterns. The utilities generate actual C program source code which can be incorporated into their own programs to recognize the specified events. They then arrange for the user-supplied actions to be performed. The tools increase programmer productivity by eliminating the need for every programmer to implement difficult code which is commonly required in a wide range of scenarios.

The `grep` utility searches text files for lines matching a specified *regular expression* (*q.v.*). `Grep` makes it possible to locate quickly all references to a particular variable or keyword in a collection of files. The `awk` utility extends this idea, providing a quick way to extract or modify the information in text files. The Perl language has recently been introduced as a modern replacement for `awk`, providing structured programming (*q.v.*), optimized for text processing.

For document processing, Unix provides a set of utilities for formatting text (`nroff`, `troff`, `TeX`—*q.v.*), drawing pictures (`gimp`, `xpaint`, `xfig`) and graphs (`gnuplot`, `xmgr`), creating tables, displaying equations (`TeX`), and managing bibliographic references. Other utilities include spelling checkers and tools for analyzing the grammar and style of documents. The document-processing tools demonstrate the power of using pipes to create an application from a set of smaller applications. Many of them are standalone translation programs, acting as preprocessors (*q.v.*) for the main formatting program, `troff` or `TeX`. Each filter interprets the commands it understands, passing the remaining commands unchanged to the next filter.

The source code control system (*SCCS*) and later the revision control system (*RCS*) were introduced to solve the problem of code editing in a multiuser environment (*see* SOFTWARE CONFIGURATION MANAGEMENT). By checking files in and out of a repository, and placing locks on busy files, these systems prevent teams of workers from working against one another by editing the same file simultaneously. They also admit the analysis of new versions and the recovery of old versions in a structured way.

Evaluation

Why has Unix been so successful? First, it was the first operating system to focus entirely on interactive use. Unix was written *by* programmers *for* programmers, and interactive systems (*q.v.*) provide the most productive environment for them. By using the system as it was being developed, its strengths and weaknesses quickly became apparent to those developing it. They were then able to correct them before it was too late. Unix's unique ability to change and evolve in response to feedback from its user community and to exploit changes in hardware technology has been a major factor in its success. Indeed, Ritchie (1978) reports: "the success of the Unix system is largely due to the fact that it was not designed to meet any predefined objectives."

The command line interface is the part of Unix which has changed the least. The old cryptic abbreviated commands are often cited as a source of irritation to new users who have grown up with GUI-based systems. Ironically, in spite of its initial goals Unix has been slow to focus on user interfaces, since experienced users have always been able to solve their problems using the extremely powerful command line interface. While Unix was focusing on system excellence, personal microcomputers promoted attractive graphical user interfaces and Unix was restricted to mainly professional computer installations. Free software and research has done much to recapture this lost ground, as the international community has implemented GUI systems for Unix far more powerful and at least as attractive as the commercial ones available for personal computers.

Most important though, Unix was made available at almost no cost to universities and other research labs, putting it into the hands of those in the best position to appreciate its features. Moreover, most of the Unix kernel and its support utilities were written in the portable C programming language, and source code was distributed with the system. The openness of the Unix system, together with its popularity in academic circles, has always encouraged its users to fix bugs and to add new tools freely in the spirit of mutual cooperation. Important and useful utilities were frequently replaced by more sophisticated and extended versions. For example, through the GNU ("GNU's Not Unix") project (*see* FREE SOFTWARE FOUNDATION) many of the user commands have been enhanced and limitations have been removed to make the best use of changing hardware technology. The GNU *emacs* text editor is one of the most powerful text editing system available today. Its importance lies as much in its use of an internal language for extensibility as in its popularity. It has paved the way for the development of numerous specialized languages. The GNU C/C++ compiler is a *de facto* reference compiler which runs on almost all systems. Also Unix is perhaps the most adaptable of operating systems. Today there is almost no part of it which cannot be customized to a specific purpose.

One of the main goals for the Free Software Foundation (FSF) is the creation of an improved Unix-like operating system. The GNU Linux operating system, a first step, is a hugely popular freeware system which runs on Intel PCs. Other popular systems for PCs, not part of the GNU effort, include FreeBSD and Net-BSD, based on the BSD 4.4 source code. A vast number of tools and languages have derived from the spirit of free software. Many vendors have adopted the fruits of free software themselves and some have even contributed.

Finally, because Unix was written in C, it was the first system to run on machines of vastly differing architectures. This allowed the core system to take advantage of new hardware technologies as they came along.

The use of C's abstract data types (*q.v.*) allowed Unix to avoid the pitfall of built-in limitations, such as processor register size or memory addressability, which has plagued other systems. When Unix became available on VAX systems in the late 1970s, their large virtual address space made the VAX/Unix combination particularly popular among computer scientists. Another boost was received in the early 1980s when Berkeley released its 4BSD versions of Unix, one of the first widely available systems to support the TCP/IP network protocols. At the same time, vendors introduced local area networks (LANs—*q.v.*) such as the Ethernet, and the availability of cheap LAN hardware created a huge demand for Unix. More recently, Unix was adopted for use by workstation manufacturers, making it the first system to exploit the performance of RISC-based microprocessors. The efficiency and reliability of Unix on PC hardware has also made it enormously cost-effective. More important, Unix has accelerated the spread of the Internet by empowering ordinary users to create tools for true network sharing. These include the World Wide Web (*q.v.*), telnet, ftp, X Window System, and the most advanced distributed file systems of the day.

Bibliography

1978. Ritchie, D. M., and Thompson, K. "The UNIX Time-sharing System," *The Bell System Technical Journal*, **57**, *6*, 1905–1930. Special issue devoted to the Unix time-sharing system.

1978. Thompson, K. "UNIX Implementation," *The Bell System Technical Journal*, **57**, *6*, 1931–1946.

1984. Kernighan, B. W., and Pike, R. *The Unix Programming Environment*. Upper Saddle River, NJ: Prentice Hall.

1985. Quartermain, J., Silberschatz, A., and Peterson, J. "4.2bsd and 4.3bsd as Examples of the Unix System," *ACM Computing Surveys*, **17**, *4*, 379–418.

1986. Bach, M. J. *The Design of the UNIX Operating System*. Upper Saddle River, NJ: Prentice Hall.

1994. Salus, P. *A Quarter Century of UNIX*. Reading, MA: Addison-Wesley.

1996. McKusick, M. K., Bostik, K., Karels, M. J., and Quartermain, J. S. *The Design and Implementation of the 4.4.BSD UNIX Operating System*. Reading, MA: Addison-Wesley.

1999. Cooke, D., Urban, J., and Hamilton, S. "Unix and Beyond: An Interview with Ken Thompson," *Computer*, **32**, *5* (May), 58–64.

Thomas Narten, revised by Mark Burgess

USER GROUPS

For articles on related subjects *see* ELECTRONIC FRONTIER FOUNDATION; FREE SOFTWARE FOUNDATION; and FREEWARE AND SHAREWARE.

Computer user groups began in the 1950s because the manufacturers did not understand how to support the hardware they produced. A forceful, activist community arose. As a manufacturer's products mature and a support infrastructure emerges, the need for a user group diminishes. The oldest, largest user groups have developed a bad case of stagnation; the newer groups continue to grow and thrive.

History

The precise origin in 1955 of the first user group, SHARE, is clear. Users of the IBM 701 in the Los Angeles area worked cooperatively on a primitive automatic programming system. While working on its successor for the soon-to-be-delivered IBM 704, the users felt the need for a united front against a proposed IBM assembler. The first formal user group meeting was held in a basement room at the Rand Corporation's headquarters in Santa Monica, CA, during the week of 22 August 1955 (Armer, 1956).

Installations represented were a cross-section of the scientifically-oriented computer community of that era. There was one government agency (NSA—National Security Agency), three government-sponsored research establishments (Rand, Los Alamos, and Livermore), eight aerospace organizations (Boeing, Curtiss-Wright, Hughes, North American, United Aircraft, and three Lockheed divisions), three industrial giants (General Electric, General Motors, and Standard Oil of California), and IBM (Steel, 1956).

A few months after the founding of SHARE, a group of users of IBM commercial computers (the 702 and the undelivered 705) recognized the merit in the user group idea and founded GUIDE. Since 1965, when IBM's System 360 was announced, membership requirements for SHARE and GUIDE have been almost identical. GUIDE appeals to the banks, insurance companies, retailers, and other large commercial establishments, while SHARE retains the loyalties of universities, engineering organizations, and research establishments. Direct SHARE spin-offs included VIM for the CDC 6600 and successors, as well as now-defunct groups that supported the GE 600 series and the Philco Transac equipment.

The user group idea has spread beyond computers. Today there are groups that support such widely diverse products and services as copiers, printers, programming languages, operating systems such as Unix (*q.v.*) and Linux, and many commercial spreadsheet (*q.v.*), database, and word processing (*q.v.*) products. While DECUS is probably the largest of all user groups, some of the most active groups are those supporting a single software product or one piece of hardware on a regional basis.

Purposes

Before software was sold, a major role of a user group was exchanging home-grown software. Before manufacturers supplied utilities, users had little but their own ingenuity on which to rely for routines to keep a system running. A memory dump from Phillips Petroleum, an internal sort from UCLA, and an assembly program from United Aircraft all crossed and recrossed the USA, spread by word of mouth and the SHARE library, founded and operated by Ben Faden of North American Aviation Corporation.

Early on, user groups generated specifications and did most of the implementation for an entire operating system. One such was SOS, the SHARE operating system, designed for the IBM 709. The complexity of today's systems has made it virtually impossible for a loosely organized, volunteer association to implement a large project. To survive, user group purposes had to be altered. SHARE's purpose is now stated as ". . . to foster the development, free exchange and public dissemination of research data pertaining to SHARE companies . . . in the best scientific tradition." It implies that the group exists to generate a climate for the exchange of information, rather than for pressuring vendors.

Membership

Membership in user groups is generally confined to installations and persons who have installed or have on order the specific hardware, program, or service around which the group is organized. Some groups relax this requirement of eligibility to permit attendance by all who express interest in the "system." Although softening attendance rules invites extended participation, a broader membership base may lead to more emphasis on marketing than on the interests of real customers. This sales device is a perversion of the reasons that users organize.

Membership counts vary widely. DECUS claims over 10,000 individual members. SHARE, the oldest, counts over 2,500 installations. Local, regional, or one-product groups may be as small as 50 members. Usually, acquiring and retaining membership requires little more than a declaration of interest and installing a particular product. However, some more formal groups require meeting attendance on at least a biennial basis.

Legal Status

The legal status of user groups is vague. Some US user groups have incorporated to obtain the protections of corporate law for their officers. From a tax viewpoint, a user group should be a not-for-profit, tax-exempt organization of a scientific and/or educational nature, but the US Internal Revenue Service (IRS) does not necessarily agree with this position. The point of contention is the restrictive nature of the membership rules. The IRS emphasized this in withdrawing the 501(c)(3) tax exemption from several user groups.

Accomplishments

What is actually accomplished by user groups? The record is erratic. The group effectiveness curve seems to be dipping. The vastness of today's systems, the size of the vendors, the difficulties of sustaining voluntary action, and the rising expenses involved have combined to squeeze the user group's effectiveness.

Today's user has almost no opportunity to affect the primary thrust of product developmental efforts; those lines are set by marketing requirements, competitive timings, and product life cycles. The user group can do minor cosmetic surgery on the specifications, detect and note the gross functional errors, and flag basic implementation faults after the product is released.

But user groups tend not to fade away, even when their original incentive is gone. SHARE, 44 in 1999, is older than most who attend its national meeting. As each grows too large or as the vendor with whom it is dealing becomes too rigid, new groups form to deal more specifically with a single product. The vendors recognize the value of even superficial cooperation as a marketing tool, and both sides enjoy the social amenities.

Judged by number, the concept of a user group continues to thrive. As of mid-1998, a request submitted to a popular search engine for "user groups" yielded references to over 100,000 Web pages.

Bibliography

1956. Armer, P. "SHARE—A Eulogy to Cooperative Effort," *RAND Report* P-969 (October).
1956. Steel, T. B. *SHARE Reference Manual*, pp. 0.1–01.

Websites

SHARE (IBM mainframes) www.share.org.
Guide (E-commerce) www.guide.org.
DECUS (Compaq—formerly DEC user group) www.decus.org.
The Association of Personal Computer User Groups www.apcug.org.
The Java Lobby www.javalobby.org.
The International Macintosh Users Group www.imug.org.
COMMON (IBM technology) www.common.org.
Unix user group www.usenix.org.
Linux user group www.linux.org/users/.

Philip H. Dorn

USER INTERFACE

For articles on related subjects, *see* HUMAN FACTORS IN COMPUTING; INTERACTIVE INPUT DEVICES; INTERACTIVE SYSTEM; and WINDOW ENVIRONMENTS.

A *user interface* is that portion of an interactive computer system that communicates with the user. Design of the user interface includes any aspect of the system that is visible to the user. Once, all computer users were specialists in computing, and interfaces consisted of jumper wires in patch boards, punched cards (*q.v.*) prepared offline, and batch printouts. Today a wide range of nonspecialists use computers, and keyboards, mice, and graphical displays are the most common interface hardware. The user interface is becoming a larger and larger portion of the software in a computer system—and a more important portion, as broader groups of people use computers. As computers become more powerful, the critical bottleneck in applying computer-based systems to solve problems is more often in the user interface rather than in the computer hardware or software.

Because the design of the user interface includes anything that is visible to the user, interface design extends deep into the design of the interactive system as a whole. A good user interface cannot be applied to a system after it is built, but must be part of the design process from the beginning. Proper design of a user interface can make a substantial difference in training time, performance speed, error rates, user satisfaction, and the user's retention of knowledge of operations over time. The poor designs of the past are giving way to elegant systems. Descriptive taxonomies of users and tasks, predictive models of performance, and explanatory theories are being developed to guide designers and evaluators. Haphazard and intuitive development strategies with claims of "user friendliness" are yielding to a more scientific approach. Measurement of learning time, performance, errors, and subjective satisfaction is now a part of the design process.

Design of a User Interface

Design of a user interface begins with task analysis—an understanding of the user's underlying tasks and the problem domain. The user interface should be designed in terms of the users' terminology and conception of their jobs, rather than the programmer's. A good understanding of the cognitive and behavioral characteristics of people in general as well as the particular user population is thus important. Good user interface design works from the user's capabilities and limitations, not the machine's; this applies to generic interfaces for large groups of people as well as to designing special interfaces for users with physical or other disabilities. Knowledge of the nature of the user's work and environment is also critical. The task to be performed can then be divided and portions assigned to the user or machine, based on knowledge of the capabilities and limitations of each.

Levels of Design

It is useful to consider the user interface at several distinct levels of abstraction and to develop a design and implementation for each. The design of a user interface is often divided into the conceptual, semantic, syntactic, and lexical levels. The conceptual level describes the basic entities underlying the user's view of the system and the actions possible upon them. The semantic level describes the functions performed by the system. This corresponds to a description of the functional requirements of the system, but it does not address how the user will invoke the functions. The syntactic level describes the sequences of inputs and outputs necessary to invoke the functions described. The lexical level determines how the inputs and outputs are actually formed from primitive hardware operations.

The syntactic–semantic object–action model is a related approach; it, too, separates the task and computer concepts (i.e. the semantics in the previous paragraph) from the syntax for carrying out the task. For example, the task of writing a scientific journal article can be decomposed into the subtasks of writing the title page, the body, and the references. Similarly, the title page might be decomposed into a unique title, one or more authors, an abstract, and several keywords. To write a scientific article, the user must understand these task semantics. To use a word processor, the user must learn about computer semantics, such as directories, filenames, files (*q.v.*), and the structure of a file. Finally, the user must learn the syntax of the commands for opening a file, inserting text, editing, and saving or printing the file. Novices often struggle to learn how to carry out their tasks on the computer and to remember the syntactic details. Once learned, the task and computer semantics are relatively stable in human memory, but the syntactic details must be frequently rehearsed. A knowledgeable user of one word processor who wishes to learn a second one needs to learn only the new syntactic details.

User Interface Management Systems

A user interface management system (UIMS) is a software component that is separate from the application program that performs the underlying task (*see* Fig. 1).

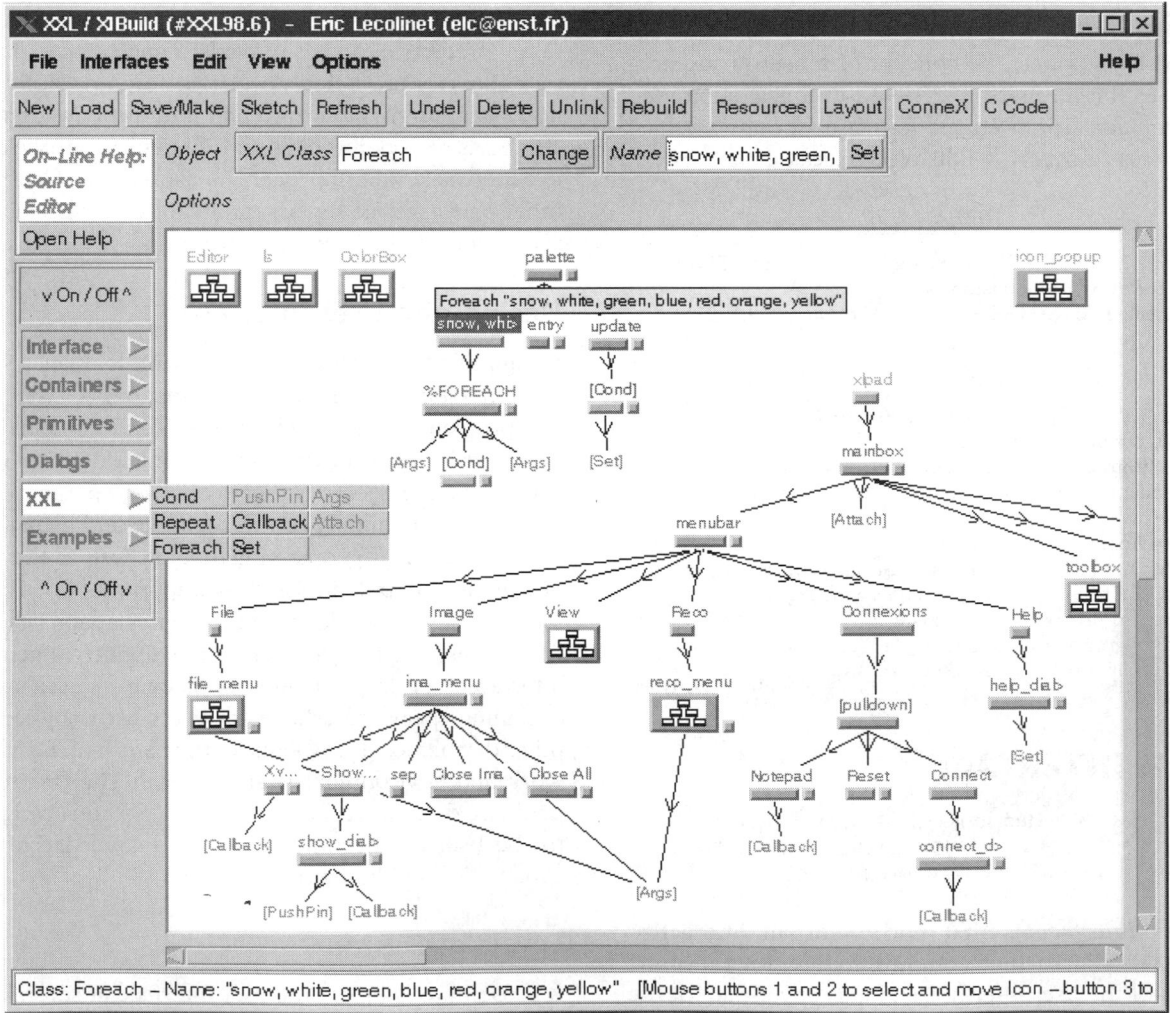

Figure 1. An example of a current User Interface Management System: the XXL builder. (Courtesy of Eric Lecolinet, Ecole Nationale Supérieure des Télécommunications, Paris, France.)

The UIMS conducts the interaction with the user, implementing the syntactic and lexical levels, while the rest of the system implements the semantic level. Like an operating system or graphics library, a UIMS separates functions used by many applications and moves them to a shared subsystem. It centralizes implementation of the user interface and permits some of the effort of designing tools for user interfaces to be amortized over many applications and shared by them. It also encourages consistent "look and feel" in user interfaces to different systems, since they share the user interface component. A UIMS also supports the concept of dialogue independence, where changes can be made to the interface design (the user–computer dialogue) without affecting the application code. This supports the development of alternative user interfaces for the same application (semantics), which facilitates both iterative refinement of the interface through prototyping (*see* SOFTWARE PROTOTYPING) and testing and, in the future, alternative interfaces for users with different physical or other disabilities. A UIMS requires a language or method for specifying user interfaces precisely; this also allows the interface designer to describe and study a variety of possible user interfaces before building any. UIMSs are emerging as powerful tools that not only reduce development effort, but also encourage exploratory prototyping.

Syntactic Level Design: Interaction Styles

The principal classes of user interfaces currently in use are command languages, menus, forms, natural language, direct manipulation, virtual reality, and combinations of these. Each interaction style has its merits for particular user communities or sets of tasks. Choosing a style or a combination of styles is a key step, but within each there are numerous minute decisions that determine the efficacy of the resulting system.

COMMAND LANGUAGE
Command language interfaces (CLIs) use artificial languages, much like programming languages. They are concise and unambiguous, but they are often difficult for a novice to learn and remember. However, since they usually permit a user to combine constructs in new and complex ways, they can be more powerful for advanced users. For them, command languages provide a strong feeling that they are in charge and that they are taking the initiative rather than responding to the computer. Command language users must learn the syntax, but they can often express complex possibilities rapidly without having to read distracting prompts. However, error rates are typically high, training is necessary, and retention may be poor. Error messages and online assistance are difficult to provide because of the diversity of possibilities and the complexity of relating tasks to computer concepts and syntax. Command languages and lengthier query or programming languages are the domain of the expert frequent users (power users—*q.v.*), who often derive satisfaction from mastering a complex set of concepts and syntax. Command language interfaces are also the style most amenable to programming, that is, writing programs or scripts of user input commands (*see* SCRIPTING LANGUAGES).

MENU
Menu-based user interfaces explicitly present the options available to a user at each point in a dialogue. Users read a list of items, select the one most appropriate to their task, type or point to indicate their selection, verify that the selection is correct, initiate the action, and observe the effect. If the terminology and meaning of the items are understandable and distinct, users can accomplish their tasks with little learning or memorization and few keystrokes. The menu requires only that the user be able to recognize the desired entry from a list rather than recall it, placing a smaller load on long-term memory. The greatest benefit may be that there is a clear structure to decision making, since only a few choices are presented at a time. This interaction style is appropriate for novice and intermittent users. It can also be appealing to frequent users if the display and selection mechanisms are very rapid. A principal disadvantage is that they can be annoying for experienced users who already know the choices they want to make and do not need to see them listed. Well-designed menu systems, however, can provide bypasses for expert users. Menus are also difficult to apply to "shallow" languages, which have large numbers of choices at a few points, because the option display becomes too big. For designers, menu selection systems require careful task analysis to ensure that all functions are supported conveniently and that terminology is chosen carefully and used consistently. Software tools to support menu selection help in ensuring consistent screen design, validating completeness, and supporting maintenance.

FORM FILL-IN
Menu selection usually becomes cumbersome when data entry is required; form fill-in (also called fill-in-the-blanks) is useful here. Users see a display of related fields, move a cursor among the fields, and enter data where desired, much as they would with a paper form for an invoice, personnel data sheet, or order form. Seeing the full set of related fields on the screen at one time in a familiar format is often very helpful. Form fill-in interaction does require that users understand the field labels, know the permissible values, be familiar with typing and editing fields, and be capable of

responding to error messages. These demands imply that users must have some training or experience.

NATURAL LANGUAGE

The principal benefit of natural language user interfaces is, of course, that the user already knows the language. The hope that computers will respond properly to arbitrary natural language sentences or phrases has engaged many researchers and system developers, but with limited success thus far. Natural language interaction usually provides little context for issuing the next command, frequently requires a "clarification dialogue," and may be slower and more cumbersome than the alternatives. Therefore, given the state of the art, such an interface must be restricted to some subset of natural language, and the subset must be chosen carefully—both in vocabulary and range of syntactic constructs. Such systems often behave poorly when the user veers even slightly away from the subset. Since they begin by presenting the illusion that the computer can understand natural language the systems can trap or frustrate novice users. For this reason, the techniques of human factors engineering can help. A human factors study of the task and the terms and constructs people normally use to describe it can be used to restrict the subset of natural language in an appropriate way, based on empirical observation. Human factors study can also identify tasks for which natural language input is good or bad. Although future research in spoken natural language offers the hope of human–computer communication that is so natural it is "just like talking to a person," such conversation may not always be the most effective way of commanding a machine (*see* SPEECH RECOGNITION AND SYNTHESIS). It is often more verbose and less precise than computer languages. In settings such as surgery, air traffic control, and emergency vehicle dispatching, people have evolved terse, highly formatted languages, similar to computer languages, for communicating with other people. For a frequent user, the effort of learning such an artificial language is outweighed by its conciseness and precision, and it is often preferable to natural language.

GRAPHICAL USER INTERFACES

In a graphical user interface (GUI), a set of objects called *icons* is presented on a screen, and the user has a repertoire of manipulations that can be performed on any of them. This means that the user has no command language to remember beyond the standard set of manipulations, few cognitive changes of mode, and a reminder of the available objects and their states shown continuously on the display. Examples of this approach include painting programs, spreadsheets (*q.v.*), manufacturing or process control systems that show a schematic diagram of the plant, air traffic control systems, some educational and flight simulations,

videogames (*q.v.*), and the Xerox Star desktop and its descendants (Macintosh, Windows, and various X Window file managers). By pointing at objects and actions, users can rapidly carry out tasks, immediately observe the results, and, if necessary, reverse the action. Keyboard entry of commands or menu choices is replaced by cursor motion devices, such as a lightpen, joystick, touchscreen, trackball, or mouse (*q.v.*), to select from a visible set of objects and actions. Direct manipulation is appealing to novices, is easy to remember for intermittent users, encourages exploration, and, with careful design, can be rapid for power users. The key difficulty in designing a GUI is to find suitable manipulable graphical representations or visual metaphors for the objects of the problem domain, such as the desktop and filing cabinet. A principal drawback of direct manipulation is that it is often difficult to create scripts or parameterized programs in such an inherently dynamic and ephemeral language.

In a well-designed GUI, the user's input actions should be as close as possible to the user's thoughts that motivated those actions; the gap between the user's intentions and the actions necessary to input them into the computer should be reduced. The goal is to build on the equipment and skills humans have acquired through evolution and experience and exploit these for communicating with the computer. Direct manipulation interfaces have enjoyed great success, particularly with new users, largely because they draw on analogies to existing human skills (pointing, grabbing, moving objects in space), rather than trained behaviors. GUIs have become so popular that it may be that some future version of Microsoft Windows will no longer allow dropping back to a command line interface, MS-DOS in current versions.

VIRTUAL REALITY

Virtual reality (*q.v.*) environments carry the user's illusion of manipulating real objects and the benefit of natural interaction still further. By coupling the motion of the user's head to changes in the images presented on a head-mounted display, the illusion of being surrounded by a world of computer-generated images, or a virtual environment, is created. Hand-mounted sensors allow the user to interact with these images as if they were real objects located in the surrounding space. Augmented reality interfaces blend the virtual world with a view of the real world through a half-silvered mirror or a TV camera, allowing virtual images to be superimposed on real objects and annotations or other computer data to be attached to real objects. The state of the art in virtual reality requires expensive and cumbersome equipment and provides very low resolution display, so such interfaces are currently used mainly where a feeling of "presence" in the virtual world is of paramount importance, such as training of firefighters or treatment of phobias.

Virtual reality interfaces, like direct manipulation interfaces, gain their strength by exploiting the user's preexisting abilities and expectations. Navigating through a conventional computer system requires a set of learned, unnatural commands, such as keywords to be typed in, or function keys to be pressed. Navigating through a virtual reality system exploits the user's existing, natural "navigational commands," such as positioning the head and eyes, turning the body, or walking toward something of interest. The result is a more natural user interface, because interacting with it is more like interacting with the rest of the world.

Other Issues

Blending several styles may be appropriate when the required tasks and users are diverse. Commands may lead the user to a form fill-in where data entry is required, or pop-up (or pull-down) menus may be used to control a direct manipulation environment when a suitable visualization of operations cannot be found. The area of computer-supported cooperative work extends the notion of a single user computer interface to an interface that supports the collaboration of a group of users.

Although interfaces using modern techniques such as direct manipulation are often easier to learn and use than conventional ones, they are considerably more difficult to build. Appropriate higher-level software engineering (q.v.) concepts and abstractions for dealing with these new interaction techniques are still needed. Specialized techniques for the actual design and building of direct manipulation interfaces are one solution. Specifying the graphical appearance of the user interface (the "look" via direct manipulation is relatively straightforward and provided by many current tools, such as Visual Basic, but describing the behavior of the dialogue (the "feel") is more difficult and not yet well supported; predefined or "canned" controls and widgets represent the current state of the art.

Lexical Level Design: Interaction Tasks, Devices, and Techniques

Lexical design begins with the interaction tasks necessary for a particular application. These are low-level primitive inputs required from the user, such as entering a text string or choosing a command. For each interaction task, the designer chooses an appropriate interaction device and interaction technique (a way of using a physical device to perform an interaction task). There may be several different ways of using the same device to perform the same task. For example, one could use a mouse to select a command by using a pop-up menu, a fixed menu (palette or toolbox), multiple clicking, circling the desired command, or even writing the name of the command with the mouse.

Input Devices

Input operations range from open-ended word processing or painting programs to simple repeated Page Up or Page Down key presses for page turning in an electronic document. While keyboards and mice have been the standard computer input devices, there are increasingly attractive alternatives for many tasks. High-precision touchscreens have made this durable device more attractive for public access, home control, process control, and other applications. Joysticks, trackballs, and data tablets with styluses with numerous variations are also useful for various pointing and manipulation tasks. Speech input for voice mail and speech recognition (q.v.) for commands are effective, especially over the telephone and for the physically disabled (see DISABLED, COMPUTERS AND THE). Other techniques for input include keys that can be dynamically labeled, speech, 3D pointing, hand gesture, whole body motion, and visual line of gaze. Fig. 2 shows a glove input device.

Output Devices

Output mechanisms must be successful in conveying to the user the current state of the system and what

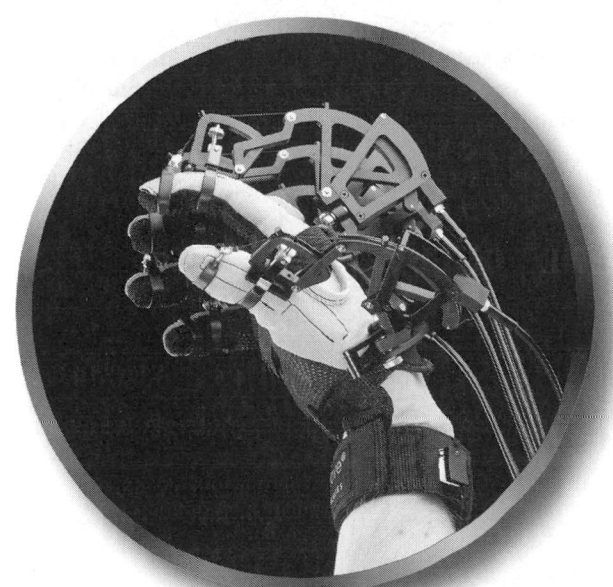

Figure 2. A Cyberglove (® Virtual Technologies, Inc., Palo Alto, CA).

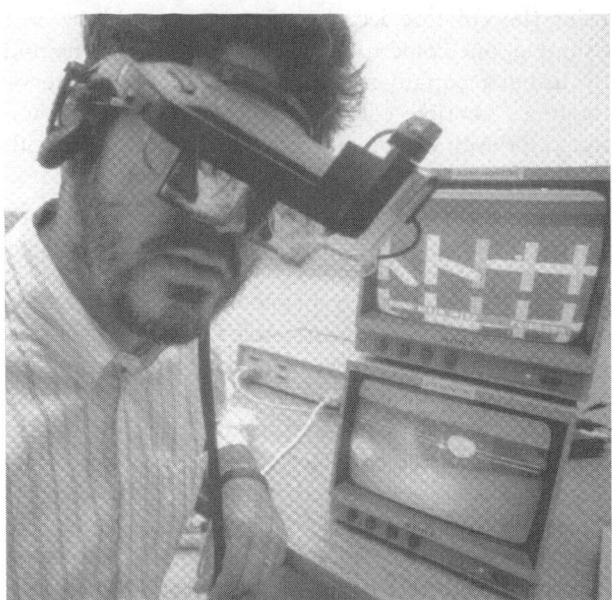

Figure 3. A head-mounted virtual reality display combined with an eye tracker. The 3D tracker attached above the user's left eye reports the position and orientation of the head. The computer uses this information to update the viewpoint of the display constantly. This unit also measures the position of the user's eye, by monitoring it through the mirror located in front of the left eye. (Courtesy Tufts University.)

actions are currently available. The CRT display has become the standard approach, but flat panel (LED, LCD, plasma, electroluminescent, and others) and hard copy devices are alternatives. Current high-resolution screens provide in excess of 1000×1000 pixels; but their resolution (in dots per inch) is still far cruder than a typical paper printout or photograph, and their size is far smaller than a typical user's desk, bulletin board, or other work surface. High-resolution displays can improve the readability of textual displays so that performance can match that of typewritten documents. Synthesized or digitized voice output is effective and economical, especially in telephone applications and for the physically disabled. Voice mail systems that store and forward digitized voice messages continue to grow in popularity. Other output media include animated graphics, audio, windows, icons, active value displays, manipulatable objects, hypertext (*q.v.*), multimedia (*q.v.*), and head-coupled displays. Fig. 3 shows a head-mounted virtual reality display.

Conclusions

Human engineering, once seen as the paint put on at the end of a project, is now more often becoming the steel frame on which the structure is built. Academic and industrial researchers are exploiting the power of empirical observation and traditional scientific method in human–computer interaction. The classic experimental methods of psychology are being applied to deal with the complex cognitive tasks of human performance with information and computer systems. A reductionist approach required for controlled experimentation yields small but reliable results. Through multiple replications with similar tasks, subjects, and experimental conditions, generality and validity can be enhanced. Each small experimental result becomes a tile in the mosaic of human performance with computerized information systems. The goal of successful user interface design is that computer-related idiosyncrasies vanish, and users are free to concentrate on their tasks.

Bibliography

1983. Shneiderman, B. "Direct Manipulation: A Step Beyond Programming Languages," *IEEE Computer*, **16**, *8*, 57–69.
1986. Hutchins, E. L. Hollan, J. D., and Norman, D. A. "Direct Manipulation Interfaces," in *User Centered System Design: New Perspectives on Human-Computer Interaction* (eds D. A. Norman and S. W. Draper), 87–124. Hillsdale, NJ: Lawrence Erlbaum.
1986. Jacob, R. J. K. "A Specification Language for Direct Manipulation User Interfaces," *ACM Transactions on Graphics*, **5**, *4*, 283—31. http://www.eecs.tufts.edu/~jacob/papers/tog.txt (ASCII); http://www.eecs.tufts.edu/~jacob/papers/tog.ps/ (PostScript).
1987. Foley, J. D. "Interfaces for Advanced Computing," *Scientific American*, **257**, *4*, 127–135.
1989. Hartson, H. R., and Hix, D. "Human–Computer Interface Development: Concepts and Systems for its Management," *Computing Surveys*, **21**, *1*, 5–92.
1989. Johnson, J. *et al.* "The Xerox Star: A Retrospective," *IEEE Computer*, **22**, *9*, 11–29.
1990. Foley, J. D., van Dam, A., Feiner, S. K., and Hughes, J. F. *Computer Graphics: Principles and Practice.* Reading, MA: Addison-Wesley.
1992. Olsen, D. R. *User Interface Management Systems: Models and Algorithms.* San Francisco: Morgan Kaufmann.
1992. Shneiderman, B. *Designing the User Interface: Strategies for Effective Human–Computer Interaction*, 2nd Ed. Reading, MA: Addison-Wesley.
1995. Myers, B. A. "User Interface Software Tools," *ACM Transactions on Computer–Human Interaction*, **2**, *1*, 64–103.
1999. Stephenson, N. *In the Beginning Was the Command Line.* New York: Avon Books.

Robert J. K. Jacob

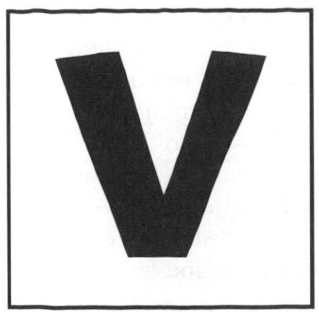

VARIABLE

See GLOBAL AND LOCAL VARIABLES.

VDT, VDU

See MONITOR, DISPLAY.

VECTOR GRAPHICS

See COMPUTER GRAPHICS.

VECTOR PROCESSOR

See PARALLEL PROCESSING; and SUPERCOMPUTERS.

VERIFICATION

See FORMAL METHODS FOR COMPUTER SYSTEMS; HARDWARE VERIFICATION; and PROGRAM VERIFICATION.

VIDEODISC

See OPTICAL STORAGE.

VIDEOGAMES

For articles on related subjects *see* COMPUTER GAMES: ARCADE GAMES; PERSONAL COMPUTING; and VIRTUAL REALITY.

Before personal computers began to appeal to people who were not computer professionals, the only way to play a "computer game" was to buy a videogame console and attach it to an ordinary television set. The first console of this kind was Odyssey, invented by Ralph Baer and marketed by Magnavox. The game played ping pong, hockey and similar games. In each game, a square ball moved across the screen. Players had to keep the ball from reaching their side of the screen by controlling a rectangle that could be moved to intercept the ball. If it was successfully intercepted, the ball bounced off the rectangle and headed to the other side. Odyssey sold 100,000 units in 1972, and in the same year, Nolan Bushnell's company, Atari, released Pong as an arcade game.

Early Standalone Games

In 1974, as microchips became cheaper and with financing provided by Sears, Atari developed Pong for the home market. Because the game had not yet been patented, over a dozen competing versions of Pong were released.

In 1976, Fairchild Instruments released Channel F, a two-player console with multipurpose controllers and, for the first time, the ability to play different games by inserting game cartridges.

In 1977, Milton Bradley developed a game called CompIV which was very similar to the "Mastermind" board game. It was played as a standalone game—it did not require a TV set. Hand-held games by other toy manufacturers soon proliferated as a result of

CompIV's success. During the same year, the Atari Video Control System (VCS) was released. Many Atari cartridges played the same games as Atari's arcade games—a marketing advantage. During Christmas, 1977, sales of handheld games cut deeply into videogame sales, and at the same time, programmable consoles using the Z80 chip were beginning to spell the end of the dedicated console. Many manufacturers went out of business.

In 1978, Magnavox released the Odyssey2, which was similar to the VCS except that the Odyssey2 also had a keyboard. Bally introduced Basic (*q.v.*) on its Professional Arcade, allowing owners to write their own game programs, which could be stored on magnetic tape using an ordinary audio tape player.

The VCS became more popular than ever when Atari released the home version of Space Invaders. However, the VCS faced some serious competition when Mattel released its Intellivision console. It featured better graphics and more sports titles than the existing systems.

In 1981, Activision, the first independent videogame software company, released four games to run on the VCS.

By 1982, manufacturers had developed more ambitious videogame consoles, with new versions of game controllers and more storage. Milton Bradley's Vectrex had a built-in black and white monitor, 64 KB RAM and an 8-bit processor. Emerson's Arcadia 2001 had 28 KB RAM. Coleco's Colecovision had 32 KB for code, 48 KB RAM, and 48 moving objects. Atari released its 5200 Super Game System to compete with the Colecovision. Voice modules became available for the Intellivision and Odyssey2 consoles. Strategy games increased in popularity. Third party vendors proliferated in 1982, providing titles for the VCS (renamed the 2600) and Intellivision consoles.

Modern Videogames

Seven million consoles and 75,000,000 game cartridges were sold in 1983, prior to a big shakeout in which many manufacturers left the videogame market or went out of business. At the same time Nintendo developed its Famicom (Family Computer) for the Japanese market. And at about this time the first interesting games for PCs began appearing.

Mattel sold Intellivision to a new company called Intellivision, Inc. in 1984. Coleco was concentrating on development of the Adam computer, which eventually failed and helped force the company into bankruptcy. Atari was sold to Jack Tramiel, the founder of Commodore computers.

Nintendo sold 2,500,000 Famicoms and 15,000,000 cartridges in Japan and released an American version called the Nintendo Entertainment System (NES) in 1985. Nintendo had a huge success with "Super Mario Brothers," an expanded version of their "Mario Bros." arcade game, which itself was an indirect sequel to "Donkey Kong" (*see* COMPUTER GAMES: ARCADE GAMES). Intellivision, Inc., became INTV Corp.

In 1986, Atari reentered the videogame market by introducing the 7800 console along with "Pole Position II" "Joust," "Ms. Pacman," and "Deluxe Asteroids." Sega introduced its Master System.

In 1988 NEC released the PC Engine in Japan. This was the first machine to support a CD-ROM drive.

In 1989, NEC began selling a version of the PC Engine called TurboGrafx-16 in the USA. Sega introduced Genesis, the first 16-bit machine. Nintendo began to sell its monochrome, 8-bit hand-held game machine, Gameboy. Packaged with "Tetris," the Gameboy became a worldwide success. Atari's 16-bit color Lynx quickly followed.

By 1991, Sega controlled a large share of the videogame market, thanks largely to a game called "Sonic the Hedgehog."

Capcom produced "Street Fighter 2" as a home videogame in 1992. "Street Fighter" had been a very popular arcade game and had undergone many upgrades to sustain player interest. The 16 megabit cartridge for "Street Fighter" cost about $75. Huge numbers of pirate copies of videogame cartridges began to come from Asia. The estimated revenue loss to US companies was $1 billion per year.

Nintendo released its 16-bit Super Nintendo Entertainment System (SNES) to compete with the Genesis. Sega retaliated by releasing a CD-ROM add-on to the Genesis, but it was not popular.

Nintendo sold more than 1,000,000 copies of "Starfox" in 1993. Game Genie and similar add-ons were built to intercept key variables in a game to slow it down or make it easier to play. Videogames made an appearance on the backs of commercial aircraft seats. Acclaim released "Mortal Kombat" for the home but reduced the violence found in the arcade equivalent. Multimedia consoles proliferated. Home computers with multimedia (*q.v.*)—CD-ROM, sound input and output, high-resolution graphics, etc.—began to grab some of the videogame action as game and tutorial software titles were developed, particularly for the IBM PC (*q.v.*) and its clones.

During 1994, Nintendo's Gateway system was installed in 5,000 airplane seats and 10,000 hotel rooms.

Sega introduced the 32-X, which in effect turned the 16-bit Genesis into a 32-bit machine. One week later, Sega announced its forthcoming 32-bit CD-ROM-based Saturn, and most customers elected to wait for it rather than switch to the Genesis. Sony announced its 32-bit Playstation. Acclaim's "Mortal Kombat II" and Nintendo's "Donkey Kong Country" for SNES were very popular introductions, the latter becoming the most popular game to date. Nintendo announced Project Reality, a joint project with Silicon Graphics to develop a 64-bit system.

In 1995, Sega and Sony competed to be first to release their new systems. Sega won by four months, but the Sony Playstation proved more popular. Nintendo released its Virtual Boy system, which displayed games in 3D, but it did not sell well. Project Reality was renamed Ultra 64 and was delayed until 1996.

Nintendo once again renamed its 64-bit console to Nintendo 64 in 1996, selling over a million consoles between its release in September and the end of the year. Activision, Williams, and Namco released home versions of their most famous games.

At the time of this writing, a few percentage points more console games than computer games were sold per year. The advent of multimedia personal computers brought with it the possibility of attractive games for PCs and Macintoshes, but the cost of a PC is roughly 10 times that of a dedicated game machine, so it is not likely that the PC will take over. Instead, the trend is toward faster, better game consoles. Future game consoles will continue to stretch the state of the art, which is 64-bit bandwidth (*q.v.*), multiprocessors (*q.v.*), 3D graphics, DVD, and high-quality sound and picture. New peripherals to facilitate virtual reality (*q.v.*) games are in the works, and imaginative games continue to be produced (*see* Fig. 1 on Color Page CP-16).

Keith S. Reid-Green and Leonard Herman

VIDEOTEX

For articles on related subjects *see* BULLETIN BOARD; COMMUNICATIONS AND COMPUTERS; DATA COMMUNICATIONS; ELECTRONIC MAIL; INTERNET; ONLINE CONVERSATION; and WORLD WIDE WEB.

Introduction

Videotex is a generic term referring to systems that give users access to information and services located in remote computers and databases through public telecommunication services or television broadcasting (whether via radio waves or cable).

The use of either public telecommunication services or a TV-based network results in two basic types of videotex systems: *interactive videotex*, permitting two-way communications between the user and a remote computer, and *broadcast videotex* or *teletext*, which is a one-way system that uses portions of the bandwidth (*q.v.*) of a TV or cable television (CATV) signal.

Interactive videotex (also named "viewdata" by its original developers in the UK) is often simply called *videotex*, while *broadcast videotex* is usually referred to as *teletext*. This terminology will be used in the remainder of this article.

In the early to mid-1970s, the UK was the first to develop videotex and teletext. At just about the same time, the French and the Canadians were experimenting with similar systems, but using different technologies (Gecsei, 1983). Today, videotex and teletext systems are found in many countries around the globe: France has implemented the largest videotex service in the world (called Télétel) with more than 6.5 million households having access to over 26,000 services through a simple videotex terminal called Minitel (*q.v.*). In North America, most of the proprietary online services (America Online, Prodigy, CompuServe, etc.) now provide access to the Internet, which can be considered an advanced form of videotex.

System Architecture

In an interactive videotex system (Fig. 1), users access services through simple, low-cost videotex terminals or through microcomputers equipped with special emulation software. The end user connects to a videotex gateway via public telecommunication services (dial-up telephone lines or high-speed switched data lines). The gateway (*q.v.*) acts as an intermediary between the user and the information/service provider that manages services on remote servers. It can provide a directory of services, and it connects the end user to the selected remote server in addition to handling billing functions. Remote servers are linked to the videotex gateway via a data network. In some systems, however, information/service providers must have their data stored in central computers managed by the videotex network operator.

In a teletext system (Fig. 2), data is continuously and cyclically transmitted to all receivers—typically TV sets equipped with specialized decoders. Information/service providers have their data transmitted and stored in a centralized teletext center which broadcasts the data cyclically on unused portions of the TV or CATV bandwidths. The user selects the required information via a keypad and the decoder captures and stores locally the portion of data of interest to the user. While teletext is actually a one-way broadcast system, the user nevertheless has the impression of

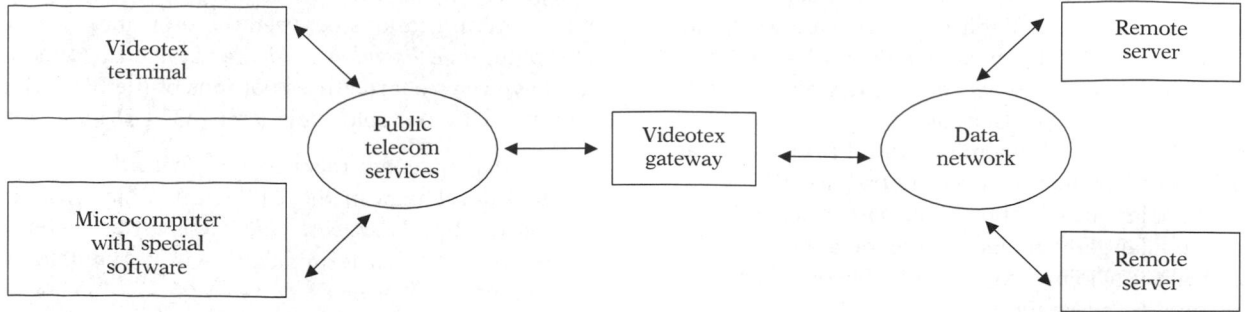

Figure 1. Generic interactive videotex system.

interacting with the system. Because of the cyclical nature of teletext, the amount of data available to the end user is limited, and true interactivity, such as in teleshopping and telebanking, is better achieved through interactive videotext.

Applications

The application programs offered by information/services providers fall under four main categories:

◆ Information retrieval applications, which allow users to query general or specialized databases, and to obtain up-to-date reports on such information as airline schedules, stock quotations, and driving conditions.

◆ Transactional applications, which enable subscribers to purchase tickets, pay bills, order goods, etc.

◆ Messaging applications, which allow for the exchange of messages with a single person or a group of people, through electronic mail (q.v.), bulletin boards and chat lines.

◆ Recreational applications, intended for entertainment and consisting of single- and multiplayer games such as chess and quizzes.

Information retrieval (q.v.) and recreational applications are present in both videotex and teletext systems, while transactional and messaging applications are generally available in interactive videotex systems only. In practice, most services offer a combination of applications. For example, it is not uncommon to find information retrieval and transactional applications incorporated within a single videotex service.

While a videotex/teletext service may present textual information only, it is often desirable to display graphics and multimedia (q.v.) information in addition to basic text. This is particularly true with residential users, where the service offered should be pleasant and user-friendly.

Conclusion

The use of videotex and the World Wide Web is growing rapidly worldwide. This growth will continue as long as the services offered are easy to use and appealing

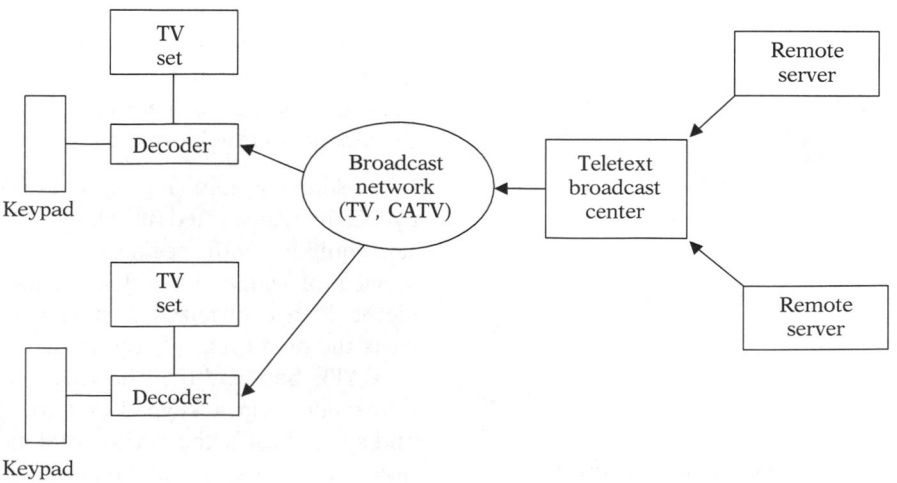

Figure 2. Generic teletext system.

to computer-literate and non-computer-literate users alike, and as long as they can provide the capability to perform either completely new tasks, or current tasks faster or at a lower cost than through other media, such as television, newspapers, and the telephone.

In the upcoming years, we should see the further development of multimedia interactive services, as well as the availability of the so-called "Web TVs" and "network computers" which will provide an inexpensive way to access the Internet.

Bibliography

1983. Gecsei, J. *The Architecture of Videotex Systems.* Upper Saddle River, NJ: Prentice Hall.

1997. *IEEE Communications Magazine,* issues on "Residential Broadband Services and Networks", and on "The Global Internet" (June).

Joseph Chammas

VIENNA DEFINITION LANGUAGE

For articles on related subjects *see* BACKUS–NAUR FORM; METALANGUAGE; PROGRAMMING LANGUAGE SEMANTICS; PROGRAMMING LINGUISTICS; and SYNTAX, SEMANTICS, AND PRAGMATICS.

The *Vienna Definition Language* (VDL) is a language for defining the syntax and semantics of programming languages. It consists of a *syntactic metalanguage* for defining the syntax of program and data structures (*q.v.*) and a *semantic metalanguage* that specifies programming language semantics "operationally" in terms of the computations to which programs give rise during execution.

Syntactic structures in VDL may be graphically represented by means of unordered trees (*q.v.*) whose edges are labeled by *selectors*. For example, the expression $a + b$ might be represented in VDL by any one of a set of equivalent unordered trees such as those in Fig. 1.

These tree (t) structures may in turn be represented in linear notation as

$$t = (\langle s_1{:}a \rangle \langle s_2{:}b \rangle, \langle s{-}\text{op}{:} + \rangle)$$

or

$$t = (\langle s_1{:}a \rangle, \langle s{-}\text{op}{:} + \rangle, \langle s_2{:}b \rangle)$$

Selectors in a VDL syntactic structure serve the same role as pointers (*q.v.*) in a list structure and may be used to select components of the syntactic structure by "applying" the selector to the syntactic structure. In the preceding example, $s_1(t), s_2(t), s{-}\text{op}(t)$ yield the respective components $a, b, +$.

Syntactic objects may be either *elementary* (*atomic*) *objects* with no components (such as the objects $a, b, +$ above) or *composite objects* (such as the tree t above) whose components may be selected by selectors.

The syntactic metalanguage of VDL is illustrated by the following definition of a simple class of arithmetic expressions:

```
expr = const ∨ var ∨ binary
binary = (⟨s₁:expr⟩,⟨s₂:expr⟩,⟨s-op:op⟩)
op = {+, *}
```

This definition specifies that an expression can be a *constant* (`const`), a *variable* (`var`), or a `binary`, where constants and variables are elementary objects with no components, and a binary is a composite object with two components of a type "expr" selectable by the selectors s_1, s_2, and a third component of the type "op" selectable by $s{-}\text{op}$. The expression $a + b * c$ may be represented in terms of the preceding syntax by a tree structure whose edges are labeled by selectors as shown in Fig. 2.

If the tree structure in Fig. 2 is denoted by t, then $s_1(t) = a$, $s_2(t) = b * c$, $s{-}\text{op}(t) = +$, $s_1 \cdot s_2(t) = b$, $s_2 \cdot s_2(t) = c$, and $s{-}\text{op} \cdot s_2(t) = *$.

The example illustrates that syntactic objects in VDL are represented by trees whose edges are labeled by selectors, and that components of a tree-structured syntactic object may be selected by specifying the sequence of selectors along the path from the root to the selected subtree.

It is instructive to contrast syntactic specification in VDL with syntactic specification of a corresponding class of expressions in BNF (Backus–Naur form). The previously given class of arithmetic expressions could be specified in BNF as follows:

```
⟨expr⟩ ::= ⟨const⟩|⟨var⟩|⟨binary⟩
⟨binary⟩ ::= ⟨expr⟩⟨op⟩⟨expr⟩
⟨op⟩ ::= +|*
```

The difference between the BNF and VDL syntactic metalanguages is brought out by comparing the two

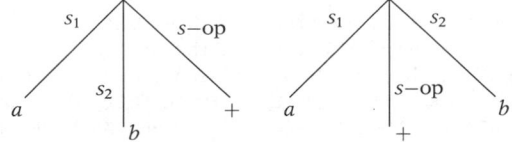

Figure 1.

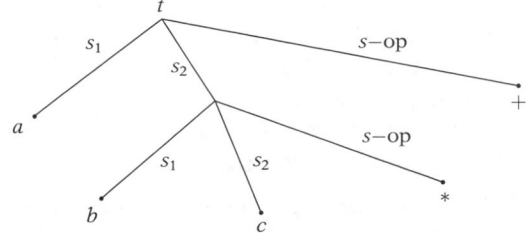

Figure 2.

specifications of `binary`. In BNF a `binary` is a string consisting of an expression followed by an operator followed by a second expression. In VDL a `binary` is a structure with three components selectable by the selectors s_1, s_2, and $s-$op. If the representation for expressions were changed from infix to prefix notation, so that $a + b * c$ were written as $+a * bc$, then the BNF specification would have to be modified to reflect this change in order, but the VDL representation could remain the same. Because VDL specifies structure independently of the order in which components appear in a specific representation, a VDL syntactic specification is sometimes referred to as an *abstract syntax*.

The *semantics* of a programming language is defined in VDL in terms of the sequences of information-structure transformations to which programs give rise during execution. Every computation starts with an initial configuration ξ_0, which contains a syntactic representation of both the program structure and the data structure on which the program is to operate. Terminating computations consist of a finite sequence of configurations $\xi_0 \rightarrow \xi_1 \rightarrow \cdots \rightarrow \xi_n$, where ξ_{j+1} is obtained from ξ_j by the execution of an instruction. The configurations ξ_j are referred to as *instantaneous descriptions*, *snapshots*, or *states*. The instructions form the heart of the semantic specification of a programming language and have the following general form of definition:

$$\text{instruction-name } (x_1, x_2, \ldots, x_n) = p_1 \rightarrow a_1$$
$$p_2 \rightarrow a_2$$
$$\cdots$$
$$p_m \rightarrow a_m$$

where $p_1, p_2, \ldots, p_m$ are a sequence of predicates, $a_1, a_2, \ldots, a_m$ are a sequence of actions to be performed, and $x_1, x_2, \ldots, x_n$ are a sequence of formal parameters that may appear in the predicate specifications p_i and action specifications a_i.

Example

$$\text{abs}(x) = x > 0 \rightarrow x$$
$$x = 0 \rightarrow 0$$
$$x < 0 \rightarrow -x$$

When an instruction of this form is executed with given actual parameters, the current configuration is tested to see whether it satisfies successive predicates p_i for $i = 1, 2, \ldots, n$. The action a_i corresponding to the first true predicate p_i is then executed. Actions a_i specify transformations of the current configuration ξ_j into the next configuration ξ_{j+1}.

The VDL instruction execution cycle differs from that of conventional computers. At any moment of execution, there is a tree of executable instructions called a

control tree, and the next executable instruction may be *any* terminal vertex of the control tree. This leads to a certain amount of nondeterminacy in the instruction execution process, which allows VDL to model nondeterminacy in specifying (for example) guarded command (*q.v.*) execution, and also to model nondeterminacy of execution in certain kinds of multitasking (*q.v.*).

There are two kinds of instructions in VDL:

1. Self-replacing instructions, which, when they are executed, replace the terminal vertex of the control tree at which they occur by a subtree of instructions.

2. Value-returning instructions, which return a computed value to predecessor vertices of the control tree and delete the executed instruction from the control tree.

A computation in VDL generally starts with a control tree consisting of a single vertex containing an instruction such as interpret-program (t), where t is the syntactic specification of the program to be executed. The first few executed instructions are generally self-replacing instructions that generate successively larger control trees (determined by the abstract syntax of t) until terminal vertices corresponding to value-returning instructions are generated. Execution terminates when an empty control tree is generated.

The Vienna Definition Language was developed by Peter Lucas, Kurt Walk, and others at the IBM Vienna Laboratory. It has been applied to the definition of PL/I (Lucas and Walk, 1969), Basic (Lee, 1972), and a number of other programming languages. A more detailed introduction to the basic concepts of VDL may be found in Wegner (1972).

Bibliography

1969. Lucas, P., and Walk, K. "On the Formal Description of PL/I," *Annual Review of Automatic Programming*, **6**, 3, 105–182.
1972. Lee, J. A. N. *Computer Semantics*. New York: Van Nostrand Reinhold.
1972. Wegner, P. "The Vienna Definition Language," *Computing Surveys*, **4**, 5–63.
1997. Harry, A. *Formal Methods Fact File: VDM and Z*. New York: John Wiley.

Peter Wegner

VIRTUAL MEMORY

For articles on related subjects *see* ASSOCIATIVE MEMORY; CACHE MEMORY; DISTRIBUTED SYSTEMS; INTERNET; MEMORY HIERARCHY; MEMORY MANAGEMENT; MEMORY PROTECTION; MULTIPROGRAMMING; OBJECT-ORIENTED PROGRAMMING; OPERATING SYSTEMS; SCHEDULING ALGORITHMS; WORKING SET; AND WORLD WIDE WEB.

Virtual memory is the simulation of a storage space so large that programmers do not need to reprogram or recompile their works when the capacity of a local memory or the configuration of a network changes. The name, borrowed from optics, recalls the virtual images formed by mirrors and lenses—images that are not there but behave as if they are. The designers of the Atlas Computer at the University of Manchester invented virtual memory in the 1950s to eliminate a looming programming problem: planning and scheduling data transfers between main and secondary memory and recompiling programs for each change of size of main memory. Virtual memory is even more useful in the computers of the 1990s, which have more things to hide—on-chip caches, separate RAM chips, local disk storage, network file servers (*q.v.*), large numbers of separately compiled program modules, other computers on the local bus or local network, or the Internet. The story of virtual memory from then to now is a story about machines helping programmers solve problems in storage allocation, protection of information, sharing and reuse of objects, and linking of program components. Virtual memory, common in all computers and operating systems from the smallest microprocessor to the largest supercomputer, is now invading the Internet.

Thirty years ago virtual memory was the subject of intense controversies (Denning, 1970). Virtual memory is now so ordinary that few people think much about it. That this has happened is one of the engineering triumphs of the computer age.

Virtual memory designers have three major concerns: (1) address mapping, the process of translating virtual addresses to memory addresses, should easily accommodate the kinds of program objects that programmers are working with; (2) address mapping should cost no more than a few per cent of memory access time; (3) overall system throughput (*q.v.*) and response time should be within a few per cent of the best possible performance attainable for a given workload.

Mapping

There are many ways to translate virtual addresses to memory addresses. They depend on whether program and data objects are stored as fixed-size pages or variable-size segments, whether each segment is divided into pages, and whether objects are individually protectable and sharable. Although virtual memory was invented before object-oriented programming, its early designers anticipated the structures and benefits of objects; thus, virtual memory is very useful in managing objects and is discussed here in this context. All the varieties depend on a two-level table structure of the kind shown in Fig. 1.

The mapping from a two-dimensional processor address (object s, byte-within-object b) to a one-dimensional memory location address operates in two stages. The objects table maps an object number s to a *handle* (t, a, x) signifying that the object is of type t, the accessing process is allowed accesses only of kind a, and the object's system-wide unique name is x. The descriptor table maps a unique name x to a descriptor for the object. The descriptor contains a presence bit with $P = 1$ meaning the object is in main memory, a usage bit with $U = 1$ meaning that the object has been

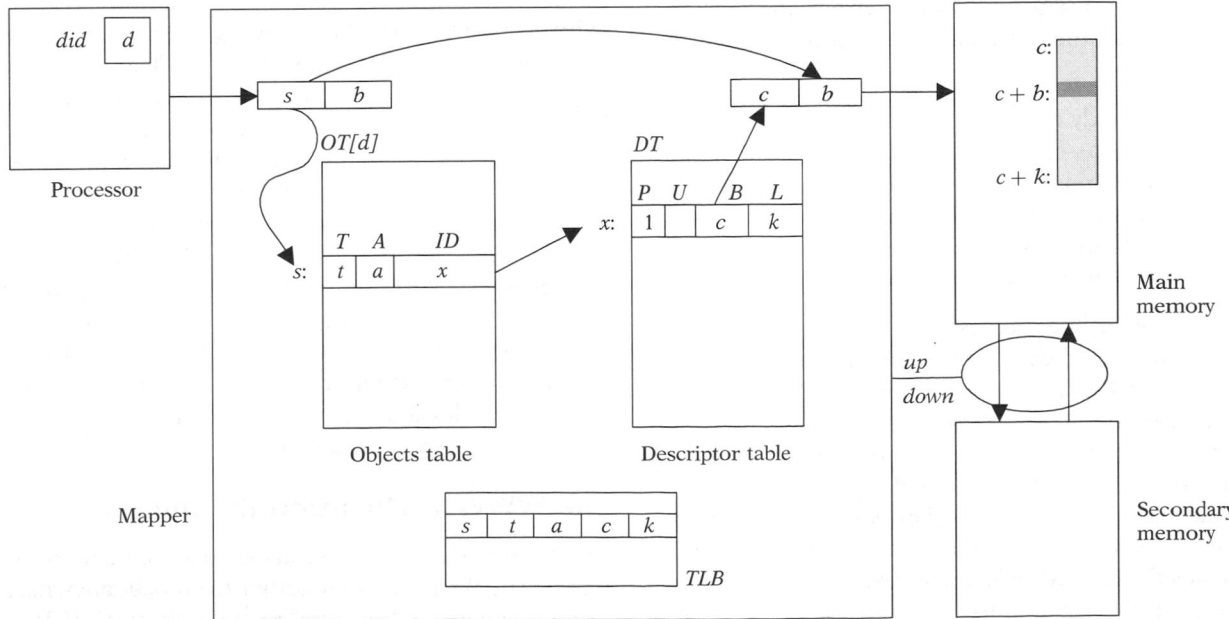

Figure 1. Object-oriented virtual memory.

recently used, a base address c, and length k of the main memory region holding the object.

There is one object table for each protection domain; in fact, the domain's object table *defines* the privileges of any process operating within it. A *domain identifier register* (*did*) in the processor tells the mapper which object table to use. There is only one descriptor for every object; a single system-wide descriptor table holds them all. A shared object can be listed in several domains, each with its own local object number; all those handles point to the same descriptor. When an object is relocated—by removing it from main memory or by moving it to a new region of main memory—only its descriptor is updated to show the change. A translation lookaside buffer (TLB) (*see* ASSOCIATIVE MEMORY) accelerates mapping by bypassing the tables on repeat accesses to the same object location path. The mapper's basic operating cycle is:

```
processor places (s,b) in address register
if ((t,a,c,k) = LOOKUP(s) undefined)
  then
      (t,a,x) ← OT[d,s]
      (P,c,k) ← DT[x]
      if (P = 0) then ADDRESS FAULT endif
      DT[x].U ← 1
      LOAD(s,t,a,c,k)
  endif
if (b ≥ k) then BOUNDS FAULT endif
if (request not allowed by (t,a)) then
                        PROTECTION FAULT endif
place c + b in memory address register
```

The operation LOOKUP(s) scans all the TLB cells in parallel and returns the contents of the cell whose key matches s. The operation LOAD replaces the least recently used cell of TLB with (s,t,a,c,k). The mapper sets the usage bit U to 1 whenever the entry is accessed so that the replacement algorithm can detect unused objects.

If the TLB already contains the path being attempted, the mapper bypasses the lookups in the object and descriptor tables. In practice, small TLBs (e.g. 64 or 128 cells) give high enough hit ratios that address translation efficiency goals are easy to meet (Hennessey, 1990). The TLB is a powerful and cost-effective accelerator.

Sooner or later the processor will generate an unmapped object address (P = 0). The mapping unit will detect this and halt, issuing the signal *address fault*. In response, the operating system interrupts the running program and invokes an *address fault handler routine* that (1) locates the needed object in the secondary memory, (2) selects a region of main memory to put that object in, (3) empties that region if need be, (4) copies the needed object into that region, and then (5) restarts the interrupted program, allowing it to complete its reference.

The processor will encounter a *bounds fault* if it attempts an offset larger than the length of a segment. It will encounter a *protection fault* if it attempts an access type not enabled by the access code—for example, attempting to write into a read-only page. Since they signify major unrecoverable errors, these faults invoke fault-handlers that normally abort the running process.

The replacement policy (above) frees memory by removing objects. The objective is to minimize "mistakes"—replacements that are quickly undone when the process recalls the object replaced. This objective is met ideally when the object selected for replacement will not be used again for the longest time among all the loaded objects. A variety of non-lookahead replacement policies have been studied extensively to see how close they come to this ideal in practice. When the memory space allocated to a process is fixed in size, this usually is LRU (least recently used); when space can vary, it is WS (working set) (Denning, 1980).

This structure provides the memory partitioning needed for multiprogramming. A process can refer *only* to the objects listed in its object table. The operating system can adjust the size of the main memory region allocated to a process so that the rate of address faults stays within acceptable limits. If too many processes are active at once, the average space available to any one of them will fall below the limit, the average fault rate will overload the queue at the secondary memory device, and the system throughput will drop sharply—the condition known as *thrashing* (*q.v.*). System throughput will be near-optimal when the virtual memory guarantees each active process just enough space to hold its working set (Denning, 1980).

With virtual memory, the operating system can restrict every process to a domain of least privilege. Only the objects listed in a domain's object table can be accessed by a process in that domain, and only then in accord with the access codes stored in the object's handle. In effect, the operating system walls each process off, giving it no chance to read or write the private objects of any other process. This has important benefits for system reliability. Should a process run amok, it can damage only its own objects: a program crash does not imply a system crash. This benefit is so important that many systems use virtual memory even if they allocate enough main memory to hold the entire address space of a process.

The WWW: Virtualizing the Internet

The World Wide Web extends virtual memory to the world. The Web allows an author to embed, anywhere in a document, a "uniform resource locator" (URL), which is the Internet address of a file. By clicking the

URL string, the user triggers the operating system to map the URL to the file and then bring a copy of that file from the remote server to the local workstation for viewing. The WWW appeals to many people because it replaces the traditional processor-centered view of computing with a data-centered view that sees computational processes as navigators in a large space of shared objects.

A URL is invalidated when the object's owner moves or renames the object. To overcome this problem, Kahn and Wilensky have proposed a scheme that refers to mobile objects by location-independent "handles" and, with special servers, tracks the correspondence between handles and object locations (Kahn and Wilensky, 1995). Their method is equivalent to that described earlier in the figure: first it maps a URL to a handle and then it maps the handle to the Internet location of the object.

The WWW is being extended to programs as well as documents. Sun Microsystems has taken the lead with its Java (*q.v.*) language. The URL of a Java program can be embedded in another program; exercising the link brings the Java program to a local interpreter, which executes it. The Java interpreter is encapsulated so that imported programs cannot access local objects other than those given it as parameters (*see* ENCAPSULATION).

Conclusion

Virtual memory is one of the great engineering triumphs of the computing age. Virtual memory systems are used to meet one or more of these needs:

◆ *Automatic storage allocation* Solving the overlay problem that arises when a program exceeds the size of the computational store available to it. This includes the problems of relocation and partitioning arising with multiprogramming.

◆ *Protection* Each process is given access to a limited set of objects—its protection domain. The operating system enforces the rights granted in a protection domain by restricting references to the memory regions in which objects are stored and by permitting only the types of reference stated for each object (e.g. read or write). These constraints are easily checked by the hardware in parallel with the main computation. These same principles are being used for efficient implementations of object-oriented programs.

◆ *Modular programs* Programmers should be able to combine separately compiled, reusable, and sharable components into programs without prior arrangements about anything other than interfaces, and without having to link the components manually into an address space.

◆ *Object-oriented programs* Programmers should be able to define managers of classes of objects and be assured that only the manager can access and modify the internal structures of objects (Myers, 1982). Objects should be freely sharable and reusable throughout a distributed system (Chase *et al.*, 1994; Tanenbaum, 1995). (This is an extension of the modular programming (*q.v.*) objective.)

◆ *Data-centered programming* Computations in the World Wide Web tend to consist of many processes navigating through a space of shared, mobile objects. Objects can be bound to a computation only on demand.

◆ *Parallel computations on multicomputers* Scalable algorithms that can be configured at run time for any number of processors are essential to mastery of highly parallel computations on multicomputers. Virtual memory can join the memories of the component machines into a single address space and can reduce communication costs by eliminating some of the copying inherent in message-passing. This is known as *distributed virtual memory* (Tanenbaum, 1995).

Bibliography

1970. Denning, P. J. "Virtual Memory," *Computing Surveys*, **2**, 3 (September), 153–189.

1979. Wilkes, M. V., and Needham, R. *The Cambridge CAP Computer and Its Operating System*. Amsterdam: North-Holland.

1980. Denning, P. J. "Working Sets Past and Present," *IEEE Transactions on Software Engineering*, **SE-6**, 1 (January), 64–84.

1982. Myers, G. J. *Advances in Computer Architecture*, 2nd Ed. New York: John Wiley.

1990. Hennessey, J., and Patterson, D. *Computer Architecture: A Quantitative Approach*. San Francisco: Morgan Kaufmann.

1994. Chase, J. S., Levy, H. M., Feeley, M. J., and Lazowska, E. D. "Sharing and Protection in a Single-address-space Operating System," *ACM Transactions on Computer Systems*, **12**, 4 (November), 271–307.

1995. Kahn, R., and Wilensky, R. "A Framework for Distributed Digital Object Services," *Technical Note 95-01*, Corporation for National Research Initiatives. http://www.cnri.reston.va.us.

1995. Tanenbaum, A. S. *Distributed Operating Systems*. Upper Saddle River, NJ: Prentice Hall.

1996. Denning, P. J. "Virtual Memory," *Computing Surveys*, **28**, 4 (December), 213–216.

Peter J. Denning

VIRTUAL REALITY

For articles on related topics *see* ARTIFICIAL LIFE; COMPUTER-AIDED DESIGN/COMPUTER-AIDED MANUFACTURING; COMPUTER ART; COMPUTER GRAPHICS; CYBERSPACE; HUMAN FACTORS IN COMPUTING; SCIENTIFIC VISUALIZATION; SIMULATION; TELEROBOTICS; and USER INTERFACE.

The Beginning

The term *virtual reality* (VR) can be traced to the work of Jaron Lanier and his co-workers at VPL Research in the late 1980s. It represented Lanier's vision of a new type of computer experience. Another early VR researcher, Steve Bryson, has proposed the following as a standard definition for VR: "The creation of the *effect of immersion* in a computer-generated *three-dimensional environment* in which objects have *spatial presence.*" Bryson simplifies this strict definition to mean "things as opposed to pictures of things."

The implementation of this new experience used advanced computer graphics hardware, interactive software worlds, and immersive interface devices. The interface devices made famous by VPL, and which are the best known icons of VR, are the head-mounted display (HMD) and an electronic glove (DataGlove). The HMD and gloves together are the view of VR which has captured the public's imagination through their use in TV commercials, movies, and magazines.

The field of VR research is actually an agglomeration of various areas of computer science, human factors, and training simulators. Some of the earliest work in VR was that of the US military at the beginning of the Second World War. As the military increasingly used aircraft technology, there was a rising need for pilot training that was too costly and too dangerous to perform using real planes. So the military began to build ground-based, mechanical simulators for teaching pilots how to operate the planes, how to acquire and track targets, and how to escape from downed aircraft. As the USA entered the war and foresaw the need for increased pilot training, these trainers became widely used.

During the 1960s, 1970s, and 1980s, much of the computer technology required to build nonmechanical simulators was developed. The military was again a major sponsor and adopter of early computer-based simulators. Some of this early work was funded by the Defense Advanced Research Projects Agency (DARPA) as well as by the more mission-based arms of the military. As before, the high cost and operational danger of actual weapons systems motivated the creation and use of the mechanical simulators

One of the first major systems built was SIMNET, a tank simulator which also allowed networked simulations. The SIMNET system borrowed from previous mechanical simulators in the way that it used physical mockups of the inside of the tank. SIMNET systems were built to scale and replicated the inside of a tank to present the tank operators with a physical simulation of their environment. These physical manifestations of tanks were accompanied by the use of advanced computer hardware, displays, software, and networks.

Modern VR

In the late 1990s, the price of the technology required to build VR systems came down rapidly, allowing greater access for nonresearchers. Desktop workstations, HMDs for less than $200, joysticks that let a user feel parts of the environment (force-feedback), and low-cost or free VR software led to a dramatic increase in the number of universities, students, and companies working on VR. The development of lower cost technology, while useful for the VR aficionado, was not, in fact, driven by VR itself.

Developments in all areas of computing were spurred by the increased interest in and use of computers by business and the general consumer. Engineering communities working with computer-aided design (CAD) and three-dimensional display technology have influenced the development of software and display systems. Videogame companies and players developed VR technology in their quest for the next blockbuster game. Low-cost HMDs, interesting new game controllers, and low-cost hardware are all products of this consumer-oriented field.

Much of this technological development was enhanced by the VR research and user communities. In addition, as with the earlier military technology, VR research from the early 1990s has itself been a spur for advancements in other fields. For example, the Nintendo 64 game system is actually a product whose genesis was in the VR community. The system was developed by Silicon Graphics, Inc. (SGI), an early producer of VR computer hardware and software and supporter of VR research. The Nintendo 64 graphics are a combination of hardware and software that was only available to the best-funded researchers in 1994. By 1997 this system could be purchased at toy stores for $150.

Technology

There are a number of different technologies which underlie work on VR. Much of this work is also of interest to researchers and users in other computer fields. Because of this, the items to be discussed here are not necessarily being developed solely within the field of VR.

GRAPHICS AND HARDWARE

There are a number of aspects of computer graphics that are used by VR researchers. Some of the most important work centers around three-dimensional real-time systems (*q.v.*). Computer users in the 1990s were accustomed to computers that display two-dimensional graphics. Two-dimensional systems are best exemplified by the desktop metaphors of the Apple Macintosh or Microsoft Windows operating systems. These systems display two-dimensional windows (using only x and y coordinates) on a two-dimensional display, namely, a standard computer monitor. Three dimensional graphics are based on object prototypes that are created using three-dimensional data (x, y, and z) in true three-dimensional space. By mapping the computer graphics to the real world, the user's ability to view, interact, and manipulate the environment becomes similar to these actions in the real world. As an analogy, imagine trying to play baseball with a drawing of a baseball. While the representation of the object in two dimensions could be extremely good, the function of the object is not preserved.

The ability to build and display complex three-dimensional graphics was beyond the ability of all personal computers until the mid-1990s. Before that time researchers wanting to do work with VR worlds needed to find the fastest computers built for other three-dimensional uses, most often computer-aided design, and try to push these machines to their limits. The first generation of VR computers were mostly advanced computers with specialized graphics hardware. The circuits designed to manipulate and display three-dimensional models were different from what most computer users required. A number of companies responded to this need for special hardware dedicated to VR work. One of the early dominant suppliers was Silicon Graphics (SGI), which began to develop graphics hardware boards for its workstations (q.v.) that excelled at three-dimensional mathematics, texturing, and display. By the late 1990s, as the market began to expand, SGI encountered competition from a variety of companies such as Microsoft, Intergraph, and a plethora of video board manufacturers.

INTERFACE DEVICES

With the creation of three-dimensional worlds, researchers and users quickly realized that the tools that they normally used to interact with personal computers, namely keyboards and mice, did not work well in these new worlds. VPL was one of the pioneers in the creation of new interface devices with their glove. The glove was only one of the interfaces that researchers began to experiment with in the quest to find better devices. Fig. 1 shows a haptic feedback device that interacts with the user's sense of touch. The interface between the user and the computer is one of most poorly researched areas in VR in the late 1990s.

NETWORKING

The early military simulator, SIMNET, was built with networks in mind. The SIMNET systems did not do much as standalone units. But when two of these units

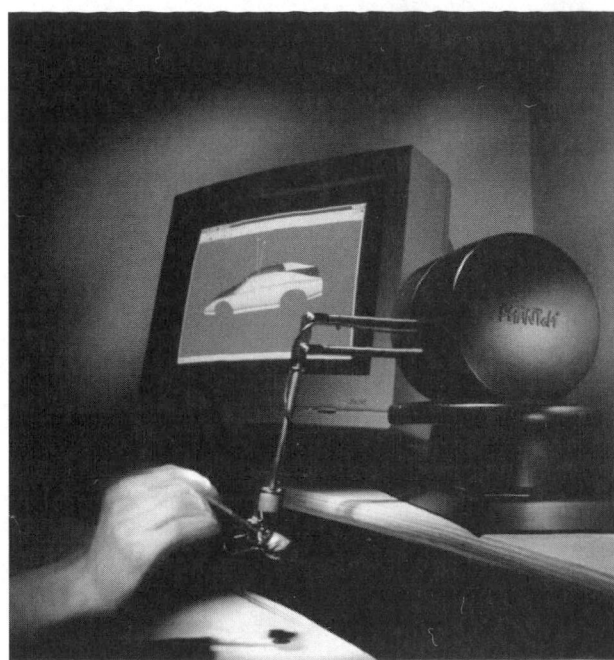

Figure 1. Using the PHANTOM 1.5 haptic device, users can "touch" and manipulate objects that exist within the computer. Applications include surgical stimulation, "digital clay" modeling and seismic data analysis. (Photo courtesy of SensAble Technologies, Inc.)

are connected using a network, though the ability of users to interact with each other and the virtual world around them makes the simulation much more interesting. As the number of units connected to the network increases, the possible interactions and scenarios that could be considered increases as well. Fig. 2 shows an application of a networked virtual environment. Because of this early experience with networked VR worlds and the military's impression that these systems were invaluable training devices, the ability to organize simulators in a network became a design criterion for all military simulators.

However, the use of networks to allow multiple users to interact in virtual worlds was, throughout the 1980s, reserved mostly to military simulators. But by the mid-1990s, there existed a small number of research projects, mostly at universities, interested in studying and advancing the use of networked virtual environments. Despite this academic research, large-scale implementation was still dominated by the military. This began to change as the Internet (q.v.) became more accessible to the public and the costs of VR systems decreased. With the proliferation of low-cost VR systems, more users began to develop simple worlds. These users soon realized that, while a VR world is interesting to build and move around in, showing the world to others and interacting with them in the virtual space is revolutionary. As the number of VR systems connected to the Internet began to

Figure 2. The Virtual Space Devices Omni Directional Treadmill, which uses the NPSNET-IV networked virtual environment, and the Boston Dynamics BDI-Guy human. (Image courtesy of Michael Zyda, Naval Postgraduate School.)

increase, people began talking about all the amazing new products that could be developed. The Internet became a playground for researchers and students interested in building and showing off their latest VR worlds or technology developments. Both of these groups saw the potential for using their work in computer games.

As this revelation was occurring in the VR world, computer games companies had begun to exploit the growing number of company networks to test out their ideas for multiplayer games. The computer gamers began looking for new ways to use networks to allow multiple people to participate, while the VR people began to look for more interesting worlds to show each other. The result of this can be seen in the second generation of network games. These systems build on the research done in networked virtual worlds and the development of interesting story lines and characters in the games world. Still the use of networks in VR is still largely a research issue. But the general VR community and the large number of gamers in society are all convinced that this will be one of the key components of all future VR systems and game systems.

Areas of Study

Virtual reality was developed in order to deliver new worlds to the user, so, unlike what happened during the development of the desktop computer, the user

has always been considered an active part of VR systems. This was the impetus behind the development of the novel interface devices discussed previously. The tight integration of the human into VR systems is also the cause of the largest problems faced by VR researchers. As with much leading edge technology, the technology itself can overshadow its use, so the user, although not an afterthought, may be viewed as a problem to be addressed later. This tendency began about 1994 and grew as more researchers entered the field. We consider now a few of the major issues being addressed by VR specialists in which the human is the main cause of the problem and must be studied extensively to find the solution.

INTERACTIVITY

The creation of VR worlds was driven by the desire to let users interact with real and imagined environments in new and interesting ways. The interaction was driven by the need to present the user with a compelling environment to operate in, whether this environment was for learning, entertainment, or sales. In the real world, people can interact with anything that they see, hear, touch or smell. They can interact using a variety of methods and senses. Picking up a glass, smelling a rose, talking to a friend are all common ways by which people interact with the real world. In attempting to duplicate the real world or, more simply, the experience of that world, the need for this level of interaction comes into focus. Researchers quickly realized that this was a hard problem, related itself to a number of more refined issues.

PRESENCE AND IMMERSION

People in the real world implicitly know that they are there. For example, you know that when you want to reach out and pick up a glass, your hand will be at the end of your arm, and that your arm is attached to your shoulder. You also know that this arrangement can reach objects within a certain distance from your body. People generally understand their bodies and the presence of those bodies in the environment they inhabit. Until now, this realization has not been extensively studied. Few researchers in any scientific field had been forced to think about human operation in this manner or that this manner of operation would have such large repercussions on a user's desire or ability to use a system.

A portion of this issue has been addressed by VR practitioners who built their systems to "remove" the user from the real world. If a user is going to experience a discontinuity in perception when both the real world and the virtual environment can be seen at the same time, one solution is to restrict the user from seeing any of the real world. One advantage to HMDs, in addition to bringing an image close to the user and moving with the user, is that the HMD often limits the user's ability to see the real world.

The user is immersed physically in the VR environment, with the hope that this will contribute to an overall sense of presence. There are a lot of assumptions in this design, and few of them have been adequately explored. There are no definitive answers to questions of presence and immersion, nor are they expected soon. But the research being done in these areas is discovering interesting issues related to humans and how they function in the real world as well as in the virtual world.

LATENCY

One aspect of a user's experience that has been studied extensively and to which researchers have a few answers is that of *latency*. Latency is the delay that exists between the completion of an action and another's initiation. It is simply the time it takes for something to occur. The study of latency related to humans existed prior to VR research, most notably in the field of human factors. People have a well-developed ability to notice time discrepancies. Talking on the phone to another person halfway around the world is an obvious example—people at both ends notice a lag between the end of a sentence and the start of the other person's response. The time between these two events is the latency. Anyone who has experienced this delay knows how unsettling it can be. This is an issue that pervades VR systems and hinders the user's feeling of immersion, and thereby interactivity. When a user turns his or her head in a VR world, the world should respond. If the world takes half a second to begin turning, the user will notice this. Since this latency rarely occurs in the real world, the user not only recognizes the latency but may also stop to think about it. Anyone acquainted with the theater knows that inaccuracies in the actors timing or a set's layout will decrease the user's suspension-of-belief. This theatrical suspension-of-belief is strongly related to the VR world's issue of presence.

The Future

Virtual reality is still a young field. At the beginning of the 21st century, the field is faced with more questions than answers. It is through these questions that today's researchers are beginning to address real world problems using VR technology. The field of VR, its related fields, and its base hardware and software, will continue to evolve and increase in power, function, and versatility.

Bibliography

1989. Laurel, B. (ed.) *The Art of Human–Computer Interface Design*. Reading, MA: Addison-Wesley.

1995. Durlach, N., and Mavor, A. (eds.) *Virtual Reality: Scientific and Technological Challenges*. Washington, DC: National Academy Press.
1997. Cockayne, W. "The Failings and Future of VR," *Final Program and Abstracts of Papers, IS&T/SPIE Symposium on Electronic Imaging: Science and Technology*. Springfield, VA: IS&T.
1999. Singhal, S., and Zyda, M. *Networked Virtual Environments: Design and Implementation*. Reading, MA: Addison-Wesley.

Website

On the Net: Virtual Reality Online. http://www.hitl. washington.edu/projects/knowledge_base/ onthenet.html.

William R. Cockayne

VIRUS, COMPUTER

For articles on related subjects *see* COMPUTER CRIME; DATA SECURITY; HACKER; and LEGAL ASPECTS OF COMPUTING.

A *virus* is a piece of program code that attaches copies of itself to other programs, incorporating itself into them so that the modified programs, while possibly still performing their intended functions, surreptitiously do other things. Programs so corrupted seek others to which to attach the virus, and so the "infection" spreads. Successful viruses lie low until they have thoroughly infiltrated the system, and only reveal their presence when they cause damage. The effect of a virus is rarely traceable back to its originator, so viruses make attractive weapons for vandals.

Viruses work by altering disk files that contain otherwise harmless programs. When an infected program is invoked, it seeks other programs stored in files to which it has write permission and infects them by modifying the files to include a copy of the virus code and inserting an instruction to branch to that code at the old program's starting point. Then the virus starts up the original program so that the user is unaware of its intervention.

A virus can spread when information is shared: on a multi-user system with shared disk facilities, or on a personal computer environment where users download programs from bulletin boards (*q.v.*) or the Internet (*q.v.*) or if they share diskettes (*q.v.*) or other exchangeable media. If A executes one of B's programs that is infected, A's programs risk becoming infected, since programs that A invokes normally have permission to alter A's own files. Even when they never execute one another's programs, infection can spread from A to B through an intermediary. In practice, it is hard to guard against infection in an environment that encourages program sharing. In personal computer environments, viruses easily spread from one diskette to another once having infiltrated the system.

Many applications interpret their data in the same way as programs. Spreadsheets, email programs, and word processors typically have "macro programs" to provide extra functionality. Viruses can therefore infect even the data which is handled by such applications. Viruses can be spread, then, by users sharing a word processor text file (e.g. by email or using diskettes).

Other Malicious Programs

The term "virus" is a popular catch-all for other kinds of malicious software. A *logic bomb* or *time bomb* is a destructive program activated by a certain combination of circumstances, or on a certain date. A *Trojan horse* is any bug (*q.v.*) inserted into a computer program that takes advantage of the trusted status of its host by surreptitiously performing unintended functions. A *worm* is a distributed program that invades computers on a network. It consists of several processes or "segments" that keep in touch through the network; when one is lost (e.g. by a workstation being rebooted), the others conspire to replace it on another processor—they search for an idle workstation, load it with copies of themselves, and start it up. Like viruses, worms spread by replication; unlike them, they may run as independent processes rather than as part of a host program, and can occupy volatile memory rather than disk storage. It is unproductive to be pedantic over the precise terms; the main distinction is that viruses replicate themselves, and Trojan horses explicitly deceive users. Of course, viruses may include Trojan components.

To escape detection, viruses normally reside in binary rather than source code and thus do not survive recompilation or reinstallation of a backup. Just as worms are destroyed by shutting down and then rebooting all affected machines, viruses are eradicated by simultaneously recompiling all affected programs. However, under special circumstances a virus can survive recompilation. In a language compiler that is written in the language it compiles (a common bootstrapping practice), it is possible to implant a virus that reinserts itself into the binary code whenever the compiler is recompiled. Such a virus need never be visible in source form.

History and Examples

The idea of a maliciously self-propagating computer program originated in Gerrold's 1972 novel *When Harlie Was One*, in which a computer program called telephone numbers at random until it found another computer into which it could spread. Worms were also presaged in science fiction by Brunner's 1975 novel *The Shockwave Rider*. The first published report of a worm program, done by Shoch and Hupp (1982) as an experiment in distributed computing, included a quotation from this book. The first actual virus program seems to have been created in 1983 as the result of a discussion in a computer security seminar and described at the AFIPS Computer Security Conference the following year. In 1984, Ken Thompson, in his Turing Award (*q.v.*) lecture, showed how a self-replicating virus can infect a compiler or other language processor, as noted above.

Virus attacks were not reported until a few years thereafter, and so far have been more in the nature of electronic vandalism than serious subversion. One of the first occurred in late 1987 when, over a two-month period, a virus quietly insinuated itself into IBM PC (*q.v.*) programs at a Jerusalem university. It was noticed because it caused programs to grow longer (owing to a bug, it repeatedly reinfected files). Once discovered, it was analyzed and an antidote devised. It was designed to slow processors down on certain Fridays, and to erase all files on Friday, the 13th of May.

At about the same time, another PC virus invaded Lehigh University, and a much-publicized "chain letter" Christmas message spread itself by self-replication, clogging the Bitnet network. The latter was eradicated only by a massive network shutdown. Early 1988 saw a relatively harmless Macintosh virus designed to distribute a "message of peace," and a number of other viruses appeared for this and other personal computers. By that time talk about viruses had invaded the news media.

At 9 p.m. on 2 November 1988, a worm program was inserted into the Internet computer network by Cornell graduate student Robert T. Morris. It exploited several security flaws in systems running Unix (*q.v.*) to spread itself from system to system. Although discovered within hours, it required a huge effort (estimated at 5,000 hours and $200,000) by programmers at affected sites to counteract and eliminate the worm over a period of weeks. Again, it was unmasked by a bug: under some circumstances it replicated itself so fast that it seriously slowed down the infected host. Morris was subsequently indicted on charges that exposed him to a possible sentence of five years imprisonment and a fine of up to $250,000. On 21 January 1990, Morris was convicted and in May 1990 he was sentenced to three years probation and fined $10,000. In addition, he was ordered to perform 400 hours of community service.

On 6 March 1992, the Michelangelo virus (so named because 6 March is Michelangelo's birthday), although widely heralded as a worldwide threat to computer systems, actually did little damage.

More recent viruses have no distinct identity, but "mutate" each time they copy themselves to other files. This, combined with various cryptographic techniques, makes modern viruses difficult to detect. Some viruses have "stealth" code, and behave differently when a user attempts to detect them. False alarms have become an increasing problem, particularly with users sending "chain email" warnings about supposed virus problems; ironically, the panic may cause more problems than the viruses it warns about!

Defenses

The obvious, but generally impractical, defense against viruses is never to use anyone else's software and never to connect with anyone else's computer—assuming you could guarantee that your computer never had an infection to start with. Another is to implement a check in the operating system that queries users whenever a program they have invoked attempts to write to disk. In practice, however, this imposes an intolerable burden because users do not generally know which files their software writes legitimately. Given a particular virus, one can write an *antibody program* that spreads itself in the same way, removing the original virus from infected programs, and ultimately removing itself too. However, this approach cannot protect against viruses in general, since it is not possible to tell whether a particular piece of code is a virus or not.

Digital signatures (*q.v.*) can help prevent the corruption of files. Each file as it is written is sealed by attaching an encrypted checksum. Also, before it is used, the checksum is decrypted and checked against the file's actual checksum. Such a scheme may engender unacceptable overhead, however, both in execution time and in the logistics of handling encryption keys. Moreover, it also assumes that the file is not infected *before* it is signed, and that the checking system itself has not been compromised (e.g. by a Trojan horse).

A more practical approach is regularly (or continuously) to run programs that recognize viruses, and which try to eliminate virus infections before they do too much damage. Because new viruses are being devised every day, it is important to keep detection programs up to date (e.g. by regular subscription from a reputable company), and to minimize risky procedures (e.g. sharing information as infrequently as possible). All approaches are trade-offs. The only real hope is eternal vigilance on the part of users, and, above all, education of users to the possible consequences of their actions.

Bibliography

1972. Gerrold, D. *When Harlie Was One*. Mattituck, NY: Æonian Press.
1975. Brunner, J. *The Shockwave Rider*. New York: Harper & Row.
1982. Shoch, J. F., and Hupp, J. A. "The 'Worm' Programs—Early Experience with a Distributed Computation," *Comm. of the ACM*, **25**, *3* (March), 172–180.
1989. Spafford, E. H. "The Internet Worm: Crisis and Aftermath," *Comm. of the ACM*, **32**, *6* (June), 678–687 (reprinted in Denning, 1990).
1989. Stoll, C. *The Cuckoo's Egg: Tracking a Spy Through the Maze of Computer Espionage*. New York: Doubleday.
1990. Denning, P. J. (ed.) *Computers Under Attack: Intruders, Worms and Viruses*. New York: ACM Press.
1991. Hafner, K., and Markoff, J. *Cyberpunk: Outlaws and Hackers on the Computer Frontier*. New York: Simon and Schuster.
1994. Cohen, F. B. *A Short Course on Computer Viruses*, 2nd Ed. New York: John Wiley.

Ian H. Witten and Harold Thimbleby

VISION, COMPUTER

See COMPUTER VISION.

VISUALIZATION

See SCIENTIFIC APPLICATIONS; and SCIENTIFIC VISUALIZATION.

VLIW (VERY LONG INSTRUCTION WORD) COMPUTER

See INSTRUCTION-LEVEL PARALLELISM.

VLSI (VERY LARGE SCALE INTEGRATION)

See COMPUTER CIRCUITRY; and INTEGRATED CIRCUITRY.

VOICE RECOGNITION AND SYNTHESIS

See SPEECH RECOGNITION AND SYNTHESIS.

VON NEUMANN MACHINE

For articles on related subjects *see* PROGRAM COUNTER; STORED PROGRAM CONCEPT; and VON NEUMANN, JOHN.

The most influential paper in the history of computer science, whether or not anyone else expressed similar ideas earlier, was written in 1946 by John von Neumann, then on the staff of the Institute for Advanced Study at Princeton University, in collaboration with Arthur W. Burks and Herman H. Goldstine. Its title is "Preliminary Discussion of the Logical Design of an Electronic Computing Instrument," and the ideas it contains, collectively known as the *von Neumann machine*, have provided the foundation for essentially all computer system developments since that date.

Central to the von Neumann machine is the concept of the stored program—the principle that instructions and data are to be stored together in a single, uniform storage medium rather than separately, as was previously the case. Not only can computations proceed at electronic speeds, but instructions as well as data can be read and written under program control. From this basic idea it follows that an element in storage has an ambiguous quality with respect to its interpretation; this ambiguity is resolved only temporarily when it is fetched and either executed as an instruction or operated on as data. One exploitation of this ambiguity results in the technique of instruction modification in which a datum, created as the result of some operations in the arithmetic-logic unit (*q.v.*) of the computer, is placed in storage as would be any other datum, but is then fetched and executed as an instruction. Iteration (*q.v.*) is realized by refetching the instruction as a datum, modifying it by operating on its address field, and then storing it and refetching and reexecuting it as an instruction. Contemporary programming practice, particularly in a multiprogramming (*q.v.*) environment, precludes the physical modification of instructions in storage. However, the basic idea of logical instruction modification is still central in computer science, but is supported by more recent developments such as index registers (*q.v.*), base registers, and indirect addressing, which provide similar effects, but leave instructions unchanged.

Another concept central to the von Neumann machine is the *program counter*, a register that is used to indicate the location of the next instruction to be executed and that is automatically incremented by each instruction fetch. With the rare exception at one time of machines with rotating memory devices for main storage, essentially all computers use this technique, since it clearly reduces the storage space that would otherwise be necessary if each instruction contained a field to indicate the address of its successor. The idea of branching can in this context become obvious in that it is effected merely by the replacement of the contents of the program counter (*q.v.*) from some other source, often, but not always, a field in the current instruction.

Since no short article can do justice to these and the many other ideas expressed so clearly by von Neumann and his colleagues in 1946, every computer scientist should read the original report (*see*, for example, Taub, 1963, or Stern, 1981).

Bibliography

1963. Taub, A. H. (ed.) *The Collected Works of John von Neumann*, Vol. 5, 34–79. New York: Macmillan.
1971. Bell, C. G., and Newell, A. *Computer Structures: Principles and Examples*, 92–119. New York: McGraw-Hill.
1981. Stern, N. *From ENIAC to UNIVAC*. Bedford, MA: Digital Press.

Robert F. Rosin

VON NEUMANN, JOHN

For articles on related subjects *see* DIGITAL COMPUTERS, HISTORY OF: EARLY; EDVAC; ENIAC; STORED PROGRAM CONCEPT; and VON NEUMANN MACHINE

John von Neumann (b. 28 December 1903, Budapest, Hungary; d. 8 February 1957, Washington, DC) has become one of the legendary figures of 20th century mathematics. The stories of his quickness of mind, power of absolute recall, linguistic range, and sense of humor abound in the literature and among his former associates. During his career he made significant contributions to logic, to quantum physics, to the theory of high-speed computing machines, and to economics through the mathematical theory of games and strategy. His work in any one of the fields would have secured him a distinguished position in present-day science.

Von Neumann received his early education at the Lutheran gymnasium in Budapest from 1911 through 1921. Toward the end of this period he was also privately tutored by M. Fekete, later to become another well-known Hungarian mathematician, with whom von Neumann published his first paper before he reached the age of 18.

There is a story that von Neumann's father opposed his desire to study mathematics. So, although he enrolled in the University of Budapest, he studied chemistry in Berlin (1921–1923) and Zurich (1923–1925), where he received his diploma in chemical engineering. In 1926, however, he received a Budapest Ph.D. in mathematics with a dissertation concerning the axiomatization of set theory.

During the late 1920s, he was Privatdozent at Berlin and Hamburg. He quickly established a reputation

Figure 1. John von Neumann with the IAS computer (courtesy of the archives of the Institute for Advanced Study, Princeton, NJ).

with publications in set theory, algebra, and quantum mechanics in this period. In 1928, he proved the minimax theorem of game theory. This was later elaborated and applied in his work (with Oskar Morganstern), *The Theory of Games and Economic Behavior* (1944).

In 1930, he was invited to be a visiting lecturer at Princeton University. When the Institute for Advanced Study was founded in 1933, he was appointed one of the original professors of its School of Mathematics. He kept this position for the rest of his life.

Von Neumann's work in the 1930s firmly established his already high reputation as a mathematician. In 1931, he published a book on the mathematical foundation of quantum mechanics, and in that same decade he formulated and proved the mean ergodic theorem for unitary operators. He published a series of papers (some with F. J. Murray) in the latter half of the 1930s, on what he called "rings of operators" (now known as von Neumann algebras), which led him to work in what he called "continuous" geometry.

The Second World War was a watershed in von Neumann's career. Prior to 1940, his work fell primarily into the area of theoretical mathematics and physics, but for the remainder of his career he appeared as an applied mathematician. The citation on his honorary D.Sc. from Princeton (1947) identified him as a mathematician, but the encomium described him in terms of his impact as a physicist, engineer, and patriot. His papers from 1940 on were mainly on statistics, hydrodynamics, ballistics, problems of detonation, meteorology, the applicability of game theory, and the theory and design of computers.

Although von Neumann had the ability to perform incredible mental calculations, his research led him to examine the possibility of machine assistance. His work on the hydrogen bomb in 1944 and the problem of implosion led him to make use of the computational ability of Howard Aiken's Automatic Sequence Control Calculator (Mark I—*q.v.*) at Harvard. During the late summer of 1944, a chance encounter with Herman Goldstine made him aware of the world's first electronic computer being built under the direction of John Mauchly (*q.v.*) and J. Presper Eckert (*q.v.*) at the Moore School of Electrical Engineering of the University of Pennsylvania. His first visit to the ENIAC project occurred in August of that year, and this marked the beginning of his role in the theory of electronic computers and automata.

Von Neumann's role in the next level of conception and implementation is difficult to assess. There is evidence that Eckert and Mauchly were involved in discussions that included the development of a mercury delay line memory with the ability to store both numbers and instructions. Shortly before von Neumann's first visit in 1944, the group had already committed itself to the construction of a successor to ENIAC as soon as time permitted. While von Neumann's authorship of the first EDVAC proposal in mid-1945 may not entitle his admirers to claim for him stored program conceptual priority, it is indicative of the great impact of his presence as a consultant to the group, his probing questions, and his ability to synthesize critical ideas. With the EDVAC paper, the modern era of electronic computers took a major stride forward.

By late 1945, von Neumann had decided to build a high-speed, general-purpose electronic computer at the Institute for Advanced Study. His documents of the period clearly articulate his vision on the ability of the proposed computer to "... revolutionize the purely mathematical approach to the theory of nonlinear differential equations ... extend quantum theory to systems of more particles and more degrees of freedom ... render a computational approach ... to the phenomenon of turbulence ... remove many bottlenecks in the computing approach to ordinary and electron optics ... Such a machine if intelligently used will completely revolutionize ... the field of approximation mathematics." (Memorandum on the Program of the High Speed Computer, 8 November 1945.) The impact of the IAS computer and its progeny (such as Illiac, Maniac, and Johnniac) is well known. The whole family is still generally referred to as *von Neumann machines*.

Von Neumann's clarity and precision of thought had a profound impact in many areas from which we will continue to benefit in the decades ahead. He was clearly one of the major scientific figures of this century.

Bibliography

1972. Goldstine H. H. *The Computer from Pascal to von Neumann*, 167–183. Princeton: Princeton University Press.
1980. Heims, S. J. *John von Neumann and Norbert Wiener: From Mathematics to the Technologies of Life and Death.* Cambridge, MA: MIT Press.
1990. Aspray, W. *John von Neumann and the Origins of Modern Computing.* Cambridge, MA: MIT Press.
1990. Heppenheimer, T. A. "How von Neumann Showed the Way," *American Heritage of Invention & Technology,* **6**, 2, 8–16.
1992. Macrae, N. *John von Neumann.* New York: Pantheon Books.
1992. Poundstone, W. *Prisoner's Dilemma/John von Neumann, Game Theory and the Puzzle of the Bomb.* New York: Doubleday.

Henry S. Tropp

VRML

See VIRTUAL REALITY.

WAIT STATE

For articles on related subjects *see* ACCESS TIME; CACHE MEMORY; CENTRAL PROCESSING UNIT; and INTERLEAVING.

The suspension of a microprocessor's CPU activity for one or more clock cycles while memory access catches up is called a *wait state*. The central processing unit depends upon an internal clock for the critical timing needed to optimize performance. This clock typically operates at millions of cycles per second. One million cycles per second is called a *megahertz* (MHz). An older 80286 chip operating at 10 MHz would have a window of 100 nanoseconds (ns) between ticks of the clock during which a memory access could be effectuated. RAM chips with access times of 100 ns or less might seem to be fast enough to do the job, but reality is more complicated.

RAM is usually composed of chips that store information in tiny capacitors. As with any capacitor, the ability to hold a charge for a period of time depends upon the quality of the insulator that separates the two charged surfaces. In a typical RAM chip, the charge breaks down after a few milliseconds and must be electrically refreshed. Since the information must be maintained dynamically, these chips are called *dynamic random access memory chips* (DRAMs). While it may take only 100 ns to access a DRAM chip under optimum circumstances, this can occur only if the capacitors have been refreshed recently. The actual access time is a combination of the refresh cycle time and the access cycle time. If these two times exceed the

CPU clock cycle window between clock ticks, the CPU must wait another clock cycle for the information or instruction to be retrieved from memory. We then say that a wait state has been introduced. If two CPU clock cycles are needed, then the computer is a two-wait-state machine.

The introduction of wait states can severely reduce the performance of even the fastest CPU chips. Designers try to eliminate wait states. There are several ways to do this. One way is to use faster RAM chips. DRAM chips faster than 70 ns are available but raise the cost of a machine. Static RAM chips called SRAM do not need to be refreshed because capacitors are not used for storage. These chips use latches or flip-flops and can therefore be accessed during their rated cycle times, but these are too expensive for large memories.

Manufacturers use sophisticated memory management (*q.v.*) techniques to reduce wait states. Schemes such as memory caching where only a small piece of memory is made up of very fast chips are used. Another strategy is to break the memory up into pages that operate as small caches. This is called **Page-Mode RAM**. Yet another strategy is to interleave or bank the memory and store sequential information in alternate banks. While one bank is being accessed, the other is being refreshed (*see* INTERLEAVING).

Conventional **DRAM** chips are asynchronous and have no clock input. This asynchronous circuitry cannot sustain speeds beyond 66 MHz. This limits even Pentium processors to a 66 MHz memory bus. A new type of

Synchronous RAM—SDRAM—has been introduced. It was originally designed as a low cost alternative to expensive video RAM—VRAM. SDRAMs are built on a standard DRAM core but the chip can synchronize to the CPU clock and receive data at a specified clock point. Though the time to process data internally hasn't really changed, the delivery of data is much more efficient. This new efficiency reduces cycle time to as low as 5 ns and raises the maximum memory bus speed to 200 MHz. Pipeline addressing for SDRAM also allows a second data access to begin before the first has been completed. As SDRAM becomes part of the installed base of PCs, memory performance will progress to keep up with ever-increasing CPU clock speeds that have now routinely reached 700 MHz. The first GHz PC is within sight.

Memory access is not the only system attribute subject to degradation through the need to use wait states, but it is the most critical to system performance. The efficiency of a machine can be reduced by as much as 50% when wait states need to be used.

Stephen J. Rogowski

WATSON, THOMAS J., SR.

For articles on related subjects *see* DIGITAL COMPUTERS, HISTORY OF: EARLY; ECKERT, WALLACE; ENTREPRENEURS; HOLLERITH, HERMAN; and IBM CORPORATION.

Thomas John Watson was born in East Campbell, Steuben County, New York, on 17 February 1874, of Scots–Irish descent. The son of Thomas and Jane White Watson, he was educated at the Addison Academy and the School of Commerce in Elmira, New York.

He started work in May 1892 as a bookkeeper in Painted Post, NY, at a salary of $6.00 a week. Following this first job, he sold sewing machines and musical instruments in the same village before joining the National Cash Register Company in Buffalo, New York, as a salesman. Four years later, National Cash Register promoted him to manager in Rochester. Promotion to special representative followed, and four and a half years later he was appointed the company's general sales manager.

It was at this time that Watson, bent on inspiring a dispirited NCR sales force, introduced the motto "THINK." He is quoted (THINK, 1956) as having told a meeting of salesmen that the phrase "I didn't think" had cost the world millions of dollars. Overnight, framed placards with the single word "THINK" sprouted throughout the offices of the company. Later, when he took the helm at IBM, he reintroduced this motto.

Figure 1. Thomas John Watson.

Watson resigned from NCR in 1913, a few months after his marriage to Jeannette M. Kittridge, to assume the presidency of the ailing Computing-Tabulating-Recording Company, a 1911 merger of the Computing Scale Company of America, The Tabulating Machine Company, and the International Time Recording Company.

From 1913 until his death 43 years later, Thomas J. Watson built the C-T-R Company, which became the International Business Machines Corporation in 1924, into the leading manufacturer first of automatically operated electromechanical business machines and then of electronic computers and business machines. It became one of the largest, most successful corporations in the world. During this time he always placed heavy emphasis on education, research, and engineering in order to insure the growth of the company. Under his leadership, IBM's history was a succession of technical innovations and inventions that included new applications of punched cards (*q.v.*) to business, government, and education, the introduction of the first commercially successful electric typewriter in 1934, opening the electronic computer era commercially in 1948 with the marketing of the 604 programmable electronic calculator, and the top position in the electronic computing and data processing field from the 1950s to the mid-1980s.

A great deal of Watson's success was due to his understanding of customers' needs, which resulted in steady improvements in IBM's product lines.

One of Watson's lifelong interests was in education, and he sought to put his business acumen at the service of universities and their faculties, giving equipment for the Columbia University Statistical Bureau (1928) and the Astronomical Computing Bureau at Columbia (1934); designing and building as a gift the first large-scale computer, the IBM Automatic Sequence Controlled Calculator (the Mark I—*q.v.*) for Harvard (1944); and dedicating the Selective Sequence Electronic Calculator to "assist the scientist in institutions of higher learning, in government, and in industry to explore the consequences of man's thought to the outermost reaches of time, space, and physical conditions" (1948). In the early 1930s he began serving as a trustee of various universities including Lafayette College, which always remained a sentimental favorite, partly because it was there that he received the first of over 30 honorary degrees he would accumulate before his death. He also served for many years as a trustee of Columbia University.

A month before he died on 19 June 1956, Watson turned over the post of chief executive officer of IBM to his eldest son, Thomas J. Watson, Jr, who in 1952 had succeeded his father as president of the corporation.

Bibliography

1956. Anon. *THINK* (July-August-September), 4-48.
1962. Belden, T., and Belden, M. *The Lengthening Shadow.* Boston: Little, Brown.
1969. Rodgers, W. *THINK—A Biography of the Watsons and IBM.* New York: Stein and Day.
1990. Watson, T. J. Jr, and Petre, P. *Father, Son, and Company: My Life at IBM.* New York: Bantam.

John C. McPherson

WEB

See WORLD WIDE WEB.

WELL-FORMED FORMULA (WFF)

For articles on related subjects *see* FORMAL LANGUAGES; GRAMMARS; PRODUCTION; PROGRAMMING LINGUISTICS; and REGULAR EXPRESSION.

A *well-formed formula* (WFF) is a string of symbols that is grammatically (syntactically) correct by virtue of belonging to some language of interest. The problem of testing whether a string is in the language must be decidable (*see* UNDECIDABLE PROBLEMS). Examples of such languages include WFFs in the propositional calculus, WFFs in the predicate calculus, syntactically correct expressions in most programming languages, arithmetic expressions, and grammatically correct sentences in English.

A set of WFFs (i.e. a language) may be defined either top-down as the set of strings formed by a generative grammar (*see* GRAMMAR) or bottom-up by a recursive definition. The former approach is more common when the set is called a formal language (*q.v.*); the latter is more common when the strings are called WFFs.

As an example of the latter, we may recursively define a set of strings that form fully parenthesized arithmetic expressions, such as $(a*((b+c)/d))$, as follows:

1. Single lower-case letters of the alphabet are variables. A single variable is a WFF.

2. If W and X are WFFs, then $(W+X)$, $(W-X)$, $(W*X)$, and (W/X) are WFFs. (Here, W and X are string variables and " (", ") ", "+", "−", "*", "/" are individual symbols.)

3. No string is a WFF unless it can be obtained by a sequence of applications of the first two rules.

Patrick C. Fischer

WHIRLWIND

For an article on a related subject *see* DIGITAL COMPUTERS, HISTORY OF: EARLY.

Project *Whirlwind* was sponsored at the Massachusetts Institute of Technology by the Special Devices Division of the Office of Research and Inventions, US Navy. It was originally started in 1944 to investigate the solution of aircraft stability and control problems associated with flight simulation by analog methods. By 1946, it had become apparent that the use of an analog computer (*q.v.*) would lead to excessive complexity, and therefore other computing techniques should be studied. Thus, in 1946, a proposal was made for a 16-bit binary general-purpose computer using electrostatic storage and a 1 MHz pulse rate. Although initially proposed as serial, the requirement for 20,000 multiplications per second led eventually to a parallel machine.

Whirlwind was constructed under the leadership of J. W. Forrester. When first put in service during the third quarter of 1949, the computer had 3,300 tubes and 8,900 crystal diodes (germanium point-contact diodes). By June of 1950, one hour of error-free operation with 256 words of electrostatic storage had been achieved. In March of 1951, it was operational on a routine basis on a 35-hour per week schedule. During 1953, a magnetic tape system and a magnetic drum system were installed, and electrostatic storage was replaced by two banks of magnetic core memory consisting of 1,024 words of 16 bits each. By December 1954, the computer had grown to 12,500 vacuum tubes and 23,800 crystal diodes.

Figure 1. The Whirlwind Computer (courtesy MIT Museum, Cambridge, MA).

Whirlwind occupied a two-story building. The CPU, control console, and CRT displays occupied the second floor. One bit of the arithmetic-logic unit was a bay of equipment 2 ft wide and 12 ft high. The drum storage system and data communications interface occupied the ground floor. The basement was filled with power supplies, and the roof of the building was covered with air-conditioning equipment to remove the heat generated by a power consumption on the order of 150 KW.

Whirlwind was a 16-bit parallel, single-address, binary computer. Instructions as well as data occupied 16-bit memory words. The operation code had 5 bits and the address had 11 bits. Eventually, all 32 possible operation codes were used. Multiplication and division were included in the instruction set (*q.v.*). The initial program-load problem was solved by the use of a bank of 32 registers of toggle switches. In routine operation, various bootstrap programs were stored in the toggle-switch memory (see BOOTSTRAP).

Automatic marginal checking was initiated during the fourth quarter of 1949. The computer had the ability to select any section of itself, vary the voltages to that section, and test for failure. By comparing the results from day to day, it was possible to determine whether trends toward failure were developing in the components.

Whirlwind used magnetic tape and magnetic drum auxiliary memory. Input–output equipment included large cathode ray tubes, photoelectric tape readers, and Flexowriters, and, in connection with the Air Force semi-automatic ground-environment air defense system (SAGE), data communication links were established with a number of radar sets and with other computers. One of the cathode ray tubes had a microfilm camera attached so that large-volume output could be displayed on a CRT and microfilmed. This was a common method of obtaining memory dumps (*q.v.*). Prints of the microfilm were available the next morning. With electrostatic storage, the computer was capable of approximately 20,000 operations per second, which increased to 40,000 per second when the magnetic core memory system was installed.

On the software side, there were pioneering efforts in the development of a symbolic assembler (*q.v.*), an interpretive system that provided a comprehensive mathematical package, including floating-point operations, a batch operating system, and an offline printout system that permitted recording the results at high speed on magnetic tape and later printing the results offline.

Despite its physical size, Whirlwind was, in modern terms, a 16-bit minicomputer (*q.v.*). It was, however, a most important project in the development of parallel, binary computers. The Whirlwind project itself and those it spawned (the Memory Test Computer, the TX-0 and TX-2 computers at the Lincoln Laboratory of MIT, and the AN/FSQ-7 manufactured by IBM for the SAGE system) led to many hardware and software developments, most notably magnetic core memories and the first operating systems (*q.v.*). Whirlwind influenced the early IBM 700 series computers and the computers developed by the Digital Equipment Corporation (*q.v.*), much of whose initial staff came from the Lincoln Laboratory.

Whirlwind operated until 1959. Parts of it are now in the Smithsonian Institution in Washington, DC, and the Computer Museum History Center in Mountain View, CA.

Bibliography

1980. Redmond, K. C., and Smith, T. A. *Project Whirlwind: The History of a Pioneer Computer.* Bedford, MA: Digital Press.

John N. Ackley

WIENER, NORBERT

For articles on related subjects *see* CYBERNETICS; and DIGITAL COMPUTERS, HISTORY OF: EARLY.

Norbert Wiener (b. Columbia, Missouri, 26 November 1894; d. Stockholm, Sweden, 18 March 1964) was one of America's most important mathematicians, and a controversial scientist who left a rich heritage of accomplishments, not only through his more than one hundred publications, but also through his personal contacts with scientists throughout the world.

Of his boyhood, Wiener said: "I got my classical education from my father, who was professor of Slavic languages at Harvard. My scientific education I got for myself." (*Current Biography*, 1950.)

Figure 1. Norbert Wiener (courtesy of American Mathematical Society).

Wiener received his A.B. degree from Tufts College in 1909 and his Ph.D. from Harvard in 1913 with a thesis in mathematical logic. The years 1913 to 1915 were significant ones. Traveling under Harvard's Sheldon Fellowship, he worked under Alfred North Whitehead, Bertrand Russell, G. H. Hardy, and J. E. Littlewood in Cambridge, and David Hilbert and Edmund Landau at Göttingen.

After America's entry into the First World War, Wiener joined the facility at Aberdeen Proving Ground, where he worked on designing artillery range tables. In 1919, with the help of Harvard Professor W. F. Osgood, he secured an appointment as an instructor at MIT, an association he maintained until his retirement in 1960.

He was a Guggenheim Fellow at Copenhagen and Göttingen in 1926, and he was also a visiting lecturer at Cambridge (1931–1932) and at Tsing Hua University in Peiping (now Beijing), China (1935–1936). Many significant influences occurred during the pre-war era. At Cambridge, Bertrand Russell encouraged him to read Rutherford's work on the theory of the electron and the nature of matter. At MIT he formed a close friendship with Harold Hazen, and was early exposed to the theory of feedback and servomechanisms. It was also during this period that he met Arturo Rosenblueth, who was engaged in neurophysiological research.

Wiener's direct contributions to the early development of electronic digital computers are difficult to determine. His wartime work on prediction theory and the research in radar and fire control were all to have a major impact by the end of the 1940s. By then, however, his name was synonymous with cybernetics (Wiener, 1948). In his writings on cybernetics, Wiener laid the foundation for the philosophical relations between mechanistic and mathematical scientific

theories. This work may not have directly contributed to the actual machine developments, but it did much to stimulate research in automata theory (*q.v.*) and in attempts to simulate human thought processes. Wiener was also very conscious of the long-range impact of the computer on humans and society. In *The Human Use of Human Beings* (Wiener, 1950), he warned of the dangers that could be caused by selfish exploitation of the computer's potential.

Norbert Wiener was active in professional societies both in the United States and abroad. He also received many honors, such as the Bôcher Prize of the American Mathematical Society (1933). His major publications, in addition to the above, include works on the Fourier integral and its application, Brownian motion, time series, relativity and quantum theory, vector and differential spaces, and potential theory.

Bibliography

1948. Wiener, N. *Cybernetics, or Control and Communication in the Animal and Machine.* Cambridge, MA: MIT Press.
1950. Anon. *Current Biography,* 615–617.
1950. Wiener, N. *The Human Use of Human Beings; Cybernetics and Society.* Boston, MA: Houghton Mifflin.
1953. Wiener, N. *Ex-Prodigy.* Cambridge, MA: MIT Press.
1956. Wiener, N. *I Am A Mathematician.* Cambridge, MA: MIT Press.
1980. Heims, S. J. *John von Neumann and Norbert Wiener: From Mathematics to the Technologies of Life and Death.* Cambridge, MA: MIT Press.
1990. Masari, P. R. *Norbert Wiener, 1894–1964.* Boston: Birkhauser.
1997. Wiener, N., Strook, D. W., Singer, I. M., and Jerison, D. *Legacy of Norbert Wiener.* Proceedings of a 1994 MIT Centenary Symposium. Providence, RI: American Mathematical Society.

Henry S. Tropp

WILKES, SIR MAURICE V.

For articles on related subjects *see* DIGITAL COMPUTERS, HISTORY OF: EARLY; EDSAC; and MICROPROGRAMMING.

Maurice Vincent Wilkes (b. 1913) (Fig. 1) studied mathematics and physics at Cambridge and conducted research on the ionsphere. He worked on radar during the Second World War, and then directed the Mathematical Laboratory (now the Computer Laboratory) of the University of Cambridge from 1945 onward throughout the whole development of stored program (*q.v.*) computers. It was here that the first of these to go into service, the Electronic Delay Storage Automatic Calculator (EDSAC), built by Wilkes and his team, began operating in May 1949. He became a Fellow of the Royal Society in 1956, was the first president of the British Computer Society 1957–1960, and the first UK member of the Council of IFIP 1960–1963. He was the ACM Turing Lecturer in 1967 and received the Harry Goode Award from AFIPS in 1968. He was made a

Figure 1. Maurice Vincent Wilkes.

Distinguished Fellow of the British Computer Society in 1973, a foreign Honorary Member of the American Academy of Arts and Sciences in 1974, and in 1976 was elected to the Fellowship of Engineering, London. He became a foreign Associate of the US National Academy of Engineering in 1977, a Foreign Corresponding Member of the Royal Spanish Academy of Sciences in 1979, and a Foreign Associate of the US National Academy of Sciences in 1980.

In 1980, he retired from Cambridge as Emeritus Professor of Computer Technology and became Senior Consulting Engineer at Digital Equipment Corporation. He received the Eckert–Mauchly Award of the Association for Computing Machinery and IEEE Computer Society in 1980, and the IEEE Computer Society's McDowell Award (*q.v.*) and the IEE Faraday medal in 1981. In 1982, he received the Pender Award of the University of Pennsylvania and in 1988 the C&C Prize (Tokyo). He also received the ITALGAS Prize for Research and Innovation in 1991, and the Kyoto Prize in 1992. From 1981–1985, he was an Adjunct Professor of Electrical Engineering and Computer Science at MIT; in 1986, he returned to the UK and became Member for Research Strategy of the Olivetti Research Board where he remained until February 1999 when he became a Staff Consultant for AT&T. He was knighted in 1999.

Wilkes led the first practical development of programming for stored program machines, including the first program library. He originated labels (which he called "floating addresses"), an early form of macros (which he called "synthetic orders"), and microprogramming (which was used in the design of the second Cambridge

machine, EDSAC II). He later became interested in machine-independent computing, and in this connection developed a simple list-processing (*q.v.*) language known as Wisp. He contributed to the development of time-sharing (*q.v.*) systems, both as a visiting member of Project MAC at MIT and through a system developed in his own laboratory during 1965–1970. In particular, he and his colleagues introduced many ideas relating to facilities for filing and editing for the ordinary user.

In addition to numerous papers and articles, he has written the following books: *Oscillations of the Earth's Atmosphere* (1949), *Preparation of Programs for an Electronic Digital Computer* (joint author; 1951, 2nd Ed. 1958), *Automatic Digital Computers* (1956), *A Short Introduction to Numerical Analysis* (1966), *Time-Sharing Computer Systems* (1966, 2nd Ed. 1972), and *The Cambridge CAP Computer and its Operating System* (joint author 1979).

Bibliography

1985. Wilkes, M. V. *Memoirs of a Computer Pioneer.* Cambridge, MA: MIT Press.

Stanley Gill, revised by the Editors

WILKINSON, JAMES H.

For articles on related subjects *see* DIGITAL COMPUTERS, HISTORY OF; ERROR ANALYSIS; and TURING, ALAN M.

James Hardy Wilkinson (Fig. 1) was born in Strood in Kent, England on 27 September 1919, and died at his home in Teddington, England on 5 October 1986. At

Figure 1. James Hardy Wilkinson.

school, he quickly exhibited an exceptional ability in mathematics and, at the age of only 16, won a Trinity Major Scholarship, thus enabling him to enter Cambridge University. He graduated with Distinction, gaining a First Class Honours degree in 1939 when he was still only 19. In common with many mathematicians during the Second World War, Wilkinson was then drafted into military work, where his interest in computational mathematics started. It was during this period that he met his future wife Heather Nora Ware, herself a mathematician with a First Class Honours degree. They married in 1945 and Heather remained an important source of support and encouragement throughout his life.

In 1946, Wilkinson joined the Mathematics Division of the National Physical Laboratory (NPL) in Teddington, working half his time for the Desk Computing Section and the other half for Alan Turing on the design of an electronic computer, the Automatic Computing Engine (ACE, later called Pilot ACE). When Turing left, Wilkinson was largely responsible for seeing the project through to fruition. Pilot ACE first operated in May 1950 and continued to do much useful computing over the next five years. Wilkinson remained at the NPL until his formal retirement in 1980. By this time he had become a Special Merit Chief Scientific Officer, a very rare distinction in the UK Civil Service and a position that allowed him to continue his research unhindered by administrative duties. Despite retirement, Wilkinson remained actively involved in numerical analysis (*q.v.*) until his untimely death.

Wilkinson's understanding of hardware and software issues through his intimate knowledge of Pilot ACE, his earlier involvement with the Desk Computing Section, his enthusiasm for numerical work, and his knowledge of mathematics were unique at that time and he soon began to produce papers that were to have an important influence on numerical analysis, particularly in the area of numerical linear algebra. In the first of three books cited in the bibliography, Wilkinson developed a fundamental theory called *backward error analysis* that increased understanding of the behavior of many numerical algorithms. The second has become the classic reference for algorithms for the algebraic eigenvalue problem and related topics, and the third, co-edited with Christian Reinsch and commonly referred to simply as "The Handbook," presented the algorithms as properly documented quality software. Both through his publications and his personal interest, Wilkinson influenced a number of software projects, such as the Numerical Algorithms Group Library in the UK and EISPACK in the USA (*see* SOFTWARE LIBRARIES, NUMERICAL AND STATISTICAL).

Wilkinson was a frequent visitor to the USA and over the years held a number of visiting positions at institutions such as the University of Michigan, Argonne National Laboratory, and Stanford University. Although he never held a full-time academic post, it was through such visits and through many invited lectures that he influenced and encouraged a great number of students and fellow researchers, who bear witness to the quality of his lectures and the generosity with which he gave his time.

Wilkinson received many awards in recognition of his outstanding contributions, including a Doctor of Science from Cambridge in 1963; Fellowship of the Royal Society in 1969; both the Turing Award (*q.v.*) of the Association for Computing Machinery and the Von Neumann award of the Society for Industrial and Applied Mathematics (SIAM) in 1970; Honorary Fellowship of the Institute of Mathematics and its Applications in 1977; and the Chauvenet Prize of the Mathematical Association of America in 1987.

His memory is honored through a Fellowship at Argonne National Laboratory and two prizes, one sponsored by SIAM for numerical analysis and scientific computing and the other jointly sponsored by Argonne, NPL, and NAG for numerical software. Aside from his scientific contributions, Wilkinson will long be remembered for his warmth, kindness, and sense of humor.

Bibliography

1964. Wilkinson, J. H. *Rounding Errors in Algebraic Processes.* Upper Saddle River, NJ: Prentice Hall.

1965. Wilkinson, J. H. *The Algebraic Eigenvalue Problem.* Oxford: Clarendon Press.

1971. Wilkinson, J. H., and Reinsch, C. *Handbook for Automatic Computation, Vol. 2, Linear Algebra.* Berlin: Springer-Verlag.

1971. Fox, L. *James Hardy Wilkinson—Biographical Memoirs of Fellows of the Royal Society*, **33**, 671–708. Cambridge: Cambridge University Press.

1985. Nash, J. C. "The Birth of a Computer: An Interview with James H. Wilkinson on the Building of a Computer Designed by Alan Turing," *Byte*, **10**, 2, 177–194.

Sven Hammarling

WILLIAMS TUBE MEMORY

For articles on related subjects *see* MEMORY: MAIN; ULTRASONIC MEMORY; and WILLIAMS, SIR FREDERIC C.

The first stored-program computers were based on two kinds of memory: ultrasonic delay lines and a cathode ray tube (CRT) system named after F. C. Williams of Manchester University. Experimentation with both schemes was being carried on in 1947 in the UK and in the USA, and by 1949–1950 computers of both types were operational. By 1954, magnetic core memories had superseded both delay line and Williams tube memories.

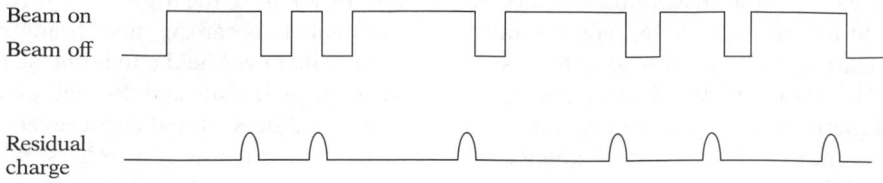

Figure 1. Williams tube charge storage pattern.

Storage of information at a spot on the inside of the face of the CRT was determined by the relative charge level. The secondary emission ratio for phosphors (and for glass) is greater than 1. Thus, if the face is bombarded with a primary electron beam (1,000–2,000 volt acceleration), then the spot becomes positively charged because more low-energy secondary electrons are emitted by the surface than arrive in the primary electron beam. Equilibrium is reached when the relatively positive charge of the spot attracts enough electrons to balance the flow. If a spot is charged, then the nearby area is "discharged" by the secondary electrons from the primary spot.

Williams used the CRTs in a bit-serial mode. To write information on the tube, the electron beam is deflected along a horizontal line, and at each point where the beam is turned off, a residual positive charge remains (Fig. 1). To read the information from the CRT, an electrode is placed on the outside of the face of the CRT (Fig. 2). As the beam again sweeps over a line, the change of potential on the inside face is capac-

itively picked up by the electrode. Since the spots of positive charge occur just before the turn-off points, the resulting signal occurs in time to turn off the beam again at the same place. (Williams called this an "anticipation" pulse.) As the beam sweeps a horizontal line, the induced potential on the electrode is amplified, and via the gating circuits and the control grid of the CRT (Fig. 2), the beam is turned off in a pattern identical to that of the previous sweep. Thus, the line being read is not destroyed by the reading process. However, since reading a given line tended to discharge the neighboring lines, it was necessary to regenerate the whole array systematically. A typical scheme was to regenerate during odd-word times and to access information during even-word times.

The beam, being on or off at a given position (or clock time), can represent the zeros or ones of a binary number. Alternative storage schemes involved using focus/defocused spots, or dots and dashes, at grid points on the face of the cathode ray tube. By changing the vertical or word deflection (Fig. 2), several different

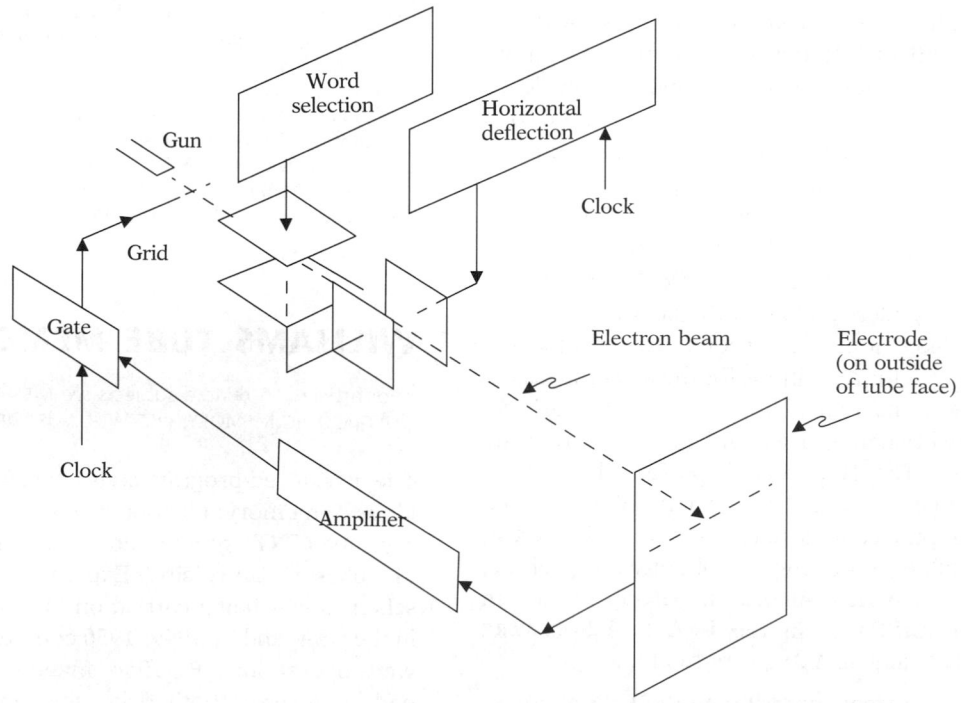

Figure 2. Williams CRT information storage system.

numbers can be stored on one CRT. (Williams stored thirty-two 32-bit numbers.)

The SWAC (*q.v.*) at the Institute for Numerical Analysis at UCLA used the Williams tube in a parallel mode with the kth bit of the memory words stored in the kth CRT. Williams tubes in the parallel mode were also used in the computer at the Institute for Advanced Study in Princeton, NJ. Parallel systems stored 256 to 1,024 bits per tube.

Other memory systems (e.g. Whirlwind—*q.v.*) used special tubes with a second "flooding gun" to maintain the storage. Jan Rajchman (RCA) designed a special memory tube called the "Selectron" which was originally intended to be used in the computer at the Institute for Advanced Study.

Commercially, Ferranti (England) marketed the Williams serial scheme, and IBM used the parallel mode in its 701 computers in 1953.

Bibliography

1949. Williams, F. C., and Kilburn, T. "A Storage System for Use with Binary Digital Computing Machines," *J. Inst. Elect. Engrs.*, **96**, Part III, 81–100.

1980. Lavington, S. *Early British Computers.* Bedford, MA: Digital Press.

1998. "The Williams Tube," The Virtual Museum of Manchester Computing. `http://www.computer50.org/kgill/ williams/williams.html`.

Harry D. Huskey

WILLIAMS, SIR FREDERIC C.

For articles on related subjects *see* KILBURN, TOM; MANCHESTER UNIVERSITY COMPUTERS; WILKES, MAURICE; and WILLIAMS TUBE MEMORY.

Frederic Calland Williams, the inventor of the Williams tube, was born on 26 June 1911 at Romiley, near Stockport, England, and died at Manchester on 11 August 1977. He was educated at Manchester University, graduating with first class honors in engineering in 1932. He received a doctorate in 1936 at Oxford University before returning to Manchester as an assistant lecturer. During the Second World War, Williams conducted important work on radar at the Telecommunications Research Establishment (TRE) at Great Malvern, where he also became interested in the problem of electronic storage for computers. In December 1946, Williams was appointed to the Chair of Electro-technics at Manchester University. Here, his work on cathode ray tube storage, which he had begun at the TRE, was brought to a successful conclusion with his invention of the Williams tube. This was the first successful electrostatic random access memory, and it was used by Williams and his collaborator, Tom Kilburn, to build a

small, working machine. This device, which became operable on 21 June 1948, was the world's first stored-program computer.

Financial support from the government and the technical resources of Ferranti Ltd resulted in a commercial version of this machine, the Manchester Mark I, which was delivered in February 1951—another world first. In addition to the CRT store, the machine pioneered the use of index registers (*q.v.*) and the magnetic drum back-up store. Although the patents were controlled by the National Development Research Corporation, the Williams tube was used under license by IBM in the 701 computer and by the Princeton University team in the Institute of Advanced Study (IAS) computer. By the end of 1956, the Williams–Kilburn partnership and their collaborators had generated 81 computer patents.

After 1962, Williams handed over supervision of the Manchester University computer projects to his colleague, Tom Kilburn. Henceforth, he pursued other aspects of electrical engineering, particularly linear induction motor design.

Figure 1. Sir Frederic Calland Williams (courtesy of National Archive on the History of Computing, University of Manchester).

F. C. Williams was a member of numerous technical societies and committees. Among his many honors and awards were election as a Fellow of the Royal Society in 1950, the John Scott Award of the City of Philadelphia in 1960, and a knighthood in 1976.

Bibliography

——. Papers of F. C. Williams, National Archive for the History of Computing, Manchester University.

1975. Lavington, S. H. *A History of Manchester Computers.* Manchester: National Computer Centre.

1978. Kilburn, T., and Piggott, L. S. "Frederic Calland Williams 1911–1977," *Biographical Memoirs of Fellows of the Royal Society,* **24** (November).

1993. *IEEE Annals of the History of Computing,* **15**, *3* (Special Issue on Computing at the University of Manchester).

1998. "Frederic Calland Williams," The Virtual Museum of Manchester Computing. http://www.computer50.org/mark1/williams.html.

Geoffrey Tweedale

WINDOW ENVIRONMENTS

For articles on related subjects *see* DESKTOP PUBLISHING; HUMAN FACTORS IN COMPUTING; INTERACTIVE INPUT DEVICES; INTERACTIVE SYSTEM; SOFTWARE ENGINEERING; USER INTERFACE; and WORKSTATION.

A *window environment* is an interactive system that supports the now ubiquitous style of graphical user interface (GUI) in which multiple centers of user activity (individual documents, for example) are presented visually as rectangular areas (*windows*) within a graphical display device. (Fig. 1 shows a typical display.) The *window system* in such an environment manages details of user interaction and provides functionality shared among application programs. The advantages of this approach, both for users and application developers, are a significant factor in the rapid expansion of computing to serve more people and a broader range of activities. For most computer users today, it is the window environment that defines the computing platform.

Historical Trends

Users of early computers dealt intimately with the internal details and idiosyncrasies of each system. As computing power has grown, and the breadth of application areas increased, it has become both economically attractive and technically feasible to dedicate more resources to user interface design. An increased focus on human factors replaces machine details in the interface with more abstract notions that are more closely related to users' work. The window-based approach to graphical user interface design grew out of laboratory research and was enabled by the development of affordable bitmapped graphics (*see* COMPUTER GRAPHICS).

Broad commercial exposure to windows came first in 1981 as part of the pioneering Xerox Star (Johnson *et al.*, 1989) and in 1984 with the Apple Macintosh (Apple, 1985). The network-based X Window System (Scheifler and Gettys, 1992) eventually became standard on Unix operating systems, as did Microsoft Windows on IBM PC and PC-compatible computers (Microsoft, 1995). The adoption of window-based interaction is so complete that few users distinguish the window environment from the rest of a computer, even for Unix and IBM-PC (*q.v.*) and compatible machines, where window systems have been distinct additions to their underlying operating systems.

Closely related to the dominance of window environments is the growth of applications software that they support. Desktop publishing and CAD/CAM were among the first such areas, joined more recently by applications (for example, built by Microsoft Visual Basic) that are defined by their graphical user interfaces. This latter trend has been enhanced by the appearance of component software (*q.v.*) in which applications can be at least partially constructed using software units (typically purchased) that are also defined as visual components with supporting program logic, and which can themselves be combined using window-based tools. Widespread adoption of the graphics-rich World Wide Web (*q.v.*), made convenient by window-based Web browsers, has further increased the centrality of window environments in computing.

Advantages

Window environments have dramatically improved the usability of computers. Users alternate among multiple work tasks conveniently by switching attention between windows; windows typically display documents being read and written, electronic mail messages being received and written, World Wide Web pages being browsed, and interfaces to other task-related programs. Users organize work with the direct manipulation style of user interface to manage windows: simple mouse (*q.v.*) actions move, reshape, expose, and hide windows. Window-management functions are supported by a single underlying window system, leading to consistent behavior that enhances usability. This consistency, combined with an industry-wide trend toward similar user interaction styles, has led to the prospect, unprecedented in computing history, that any experienced computer user can perform useful work on almost any standard platform with very little additional learning.

Developers of applications software benefit as well. Window systems typically provide many kinds of built-in support for graphical interaction with users, so that a significant and growing portion of the functionality of window-based applications need not be implemented at

Figure 1. Snapshot of a display with several open windows.

all by the application programmer. This support comes in several forms, as summarized in the layered reference model appearing in Fig. 2: *graphics libraries* enable rich visual presentations; a *base system* provides interfaces to interactive input devices that hide hardware details; an implementation of the shared *window management* behavior described above; and *toolkits* of predefined interactive parts, commonly called *widgets*, such as menus, buttons, and scrollbars. A significant trend in software engineering is toward application development by a combination of prebuilt *components*, and many such components in use today are fundamentally interactive and window-based.

- Application
- User Interface Toolkit
- Window Manager
- Base Window System
- Graphics Library
- Hardware

Window system

Figure 2. A multi-layer model of a computer system.

Portability, the ability to run programs unchanged on many computing platforms, has always been desirable for both users and developers. This engineering challenge has traditionally been especially difficult in the device-dependent realm of interactive window-based computing. Efforts to standardize the support needed for window-based applications, for example the Java (*q.v.*) language and associated libraries (Campione and Walrath, 1998), are beginning to address this challenge.

Window Systems

Although implementations vary, window systems share a number of goals and implementation techniques for managing resources and providing shared functionality.

GRAPHICAL DISPLAY

The most obvious resource is the display device, whose viewing area must be shared among multiple applications programs. In X this is managed using a *window tree*, a hierarchical data structure (*see* TREE) that represents nested rectangles of screen real estate.

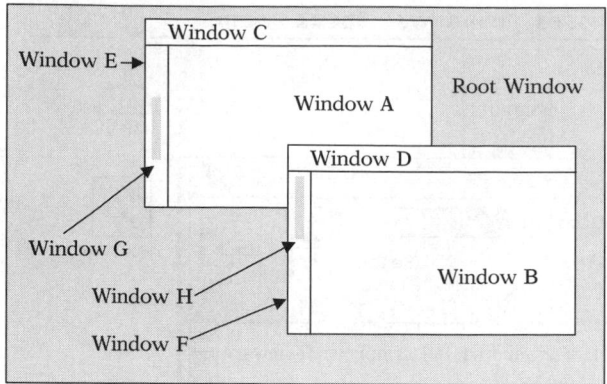

Figure 3. A typical X Window System hierarchy.

In Fig. 3, for example, toolbar C and scrollbar E are nested within window A (*every* independently managed rectangle in X Windows is called a *window*). Fig. 4 represents the corresponding window tree. A window tree also contains geometric information (allowing easy coordinate transformation, so that applications can specify graphical commands independent of their window locations), stacking order (which window should appear in case of overlap), and references to parts of the application program and widgets responsible for painting each rectangle. Efficient algorithms coordinate repainting of the screen in response to user actions such as uncovering or opening windows, determining what is actually visible (*clipping*) and translating painting coordinates into absolute display locations.

INTERACTIVE INPUT DEVICES

Equally important are the devices with which users control window-based applications, most often a keyboard and mouse. Software interaction with such devices varies considerably and can involve subtle time-based effects. A typical base window system supplies an abstract interface to these devices that captures user actions and translates them into easily managed *events*. A typical window event records the kind of action (keyboard press or release, mouse button press or release, mouse motion), the state (up or down) of modifier keys such as Shift and Control, and mouse location.

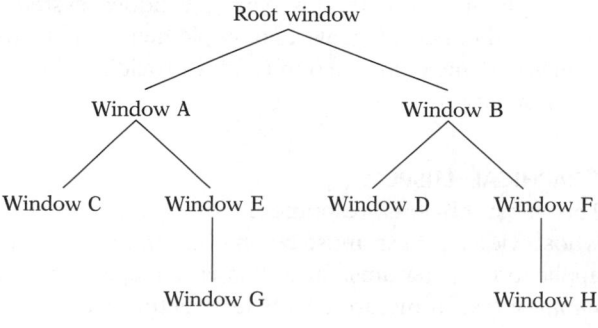

Figure 4. Window tree for Fig. 3.

EVENT MANAGEMENT

In contrast to traditional procedural programs, window-based software is typically event-driven: an application consists of a collection of program fragments, each of which responds to a particular kind of event and then stops so that the next event can be handled. Arriving events wait in a system-managed FIFO queue for dispatch to the appropriate program fragment. The dispatch decision is uniform across all applications; it is based on the geometry of the window tree (over what rectangle(s) is the mouse currently positioned?), toolkit policy (does a particular widget react to this kind of event?), specifications from the application (should a widget implement a particular behavior?), and *keyboard focus* (to which window is the window manager currently routing keystrokes?).

SHARED SERVICES

Window environments also support shared services in which applications collaborate. For example, both a system-wide *clipboard* (where application data can be "copied to" and "pasted from") and global *drag and drop* (where application data can be "moved" from source to destination) enable data supplied by one application to be incorporated into another. The window system coordinates the activity so that applications need not negotiate directly with one another and so that the user sees uniform behavior.

OBJECT-ORIENTED PROGRAMMING

The event-driven programming style leads to close association between the data that describe a visible window element and the code that implements responses to relevant events. Toolkits and applications have thus benefited greatly from the maturing of object-oriented programming (*q.v.*) in which this relationship is fundamental. In fact, one of the earliest interactive graphical programs, Ivan Sutherland's "Sketchpad" in 1963, was organized in ways that significantly anticipated objects.

REMOTE SERVICES

Although most window environments are closely tied to computation on the underlying (or *local*) computer, the NeWS (Gosling *et al.*, 1989) and subsequent X Window systems (Scheifler and Gettys, 1992) both embody a fundamental architectural separation between computation and interaction. This permits users to run applications interchangeably and simultaneously, independent of their location (on the local computer or on one across the world) or platform (workstation or supercomputer—*q.v.*). Limited forms of remote interaction have been added to other window environments, but without the smooth integration and full functionality made possible by the architectural approach.

Bibliography

1985. Apple Computer. *Inside Macintosh.* Reading, MA: Addison-Wesley.

1989. Gosling, J., Rosenthal, D. S. H., and Arden, M. J. *The NeWS Book.* New York: Springer-Verlag.

1989. Johnson, J., Roberts, T. L., Verplank, W., Smith, D.C., Irby, C. H., Beard, M., and Mackey, K. "The Xerox Star: A Retrospective," *IEEE Computer,* **22**, *9* (September), 11–29.

1992. Scheifler, R. W., and Gettys, J. *X Window Systems,* 3rd Ed. Bedford, MA: Digital Press.

1995. Microsoft Corporation. *The Windows Interface Guidelines for Software Design.* Redmond, WA: Microsoft Press.

1998. Campione, M., and Walrath, K. *The Java Tutorial: Object-Oriented Programming for the Internet,* 2nd Ed. Reading, MA: Addison-Wesley.

Michael L. Van De Vanter

Figure 1. Betty Jennings (left) inserting a card deck into the ENIAC, and Frances Bilas (right) removing a deck with the results of a computation (courtesy of the Charles Babbage Institute).

WIZARD

For articles on related subjects *see* GURU; HACKER; and POWER USER.

As first used in computing, a *wizard* was a programmer who knew a particular piece of software—a compiler (*q.v.*), operating system (*q.v.*), or text editor (*q.v.*), perhaps—so well that he or she could modify or enhance its code on short notice to accomplish an important objective. The term still applies, and a wizard is now accorded the admiration and respect that the *hacker* (*q.v.*) once enjoyed. But unlike the latter term, which now has mixed and opposing connotations, *wizard* has no pejorative overtone. Wizards are generally quiet, competent people who operate with surgical precision in a restricted local environment. Wizards seldom aspire to the world stage of the *guru* (*q.v.*). Gurus know things; wizards do things.

The term *wizard* has now been appropriated for use by software developers to refer to what is effectively an automaton rather than a human; namely, that portion of a setup program that guides the user through the decisions needed to complete installation of new software. More generally, any program that tries to automate mundane tasks that would otherwise have to be done tediously—properly formatting a business letter, perhaps—is called a "wizard."

Edwin D. Reilly

WOMEN AND COMPUTING

For articles on related subjects *see* COMPUTER SCIENCE—PH.D. STATISTICS; EDUCATION IN COMPUTER ENGINEERING; EDUCATION IN COMPUTER SCIENCE; PERSONNEL IN THE COMPUTER FIELD; and SOCIETY, COMPUTERS IN.

Women have played a primary role in computer programming since its origins in the mid-1800s. Augusta Ada Byron, Countess of Lovelace (*q.v.*) introduced many concepts of computer programming, such as arrays, loops, and subroutines, in the context of Babbage's Analytical Engine (*q.v.*). When computers became a reality in the late 1940s, the world's first programmers were women. Using nothing but the machine's specifications, six women programmed the ENIAC (*q.v.*): Kathleen Mauchly Antonelli, Frances Bilas (Fig. 1), Betty Jean Bartik, Frances E. Holberton, Ruth Teitelbaum, and Marlyn Meltzer. In addition, Grace Murray Hopper (*q.v.*) was the first programmer of the Mark I at Harvard University, Ethel Marden (Fig. 2) wrote the first program on the SEAC (*q.v.*) at the National Bureau of Standards, and Ida Rhodes wrote the first program on the UNIVAC I, which was used by the US Social Security Administration.

Figure 2. Ethel Marden at the SEAC console (courtesy of the National Institute of Standards and Technology).

Women also made substantial contributions in transforming programming from writing low-level machine code to symbolic representations. Holberton's 1951 Sort-Merge Generator was a vital stepping stone toward Hopper's invention of the world's first business programming language, Flow-Matic, a precursor to Cobol. Beatrice Worsley at the University of Toronto was one of the two designers of Transcode, one of the first compilers for a symbolic programming language. In applying computers to real world problems, Thelma Estrin designed and developed one of the first analog-to-digital conversion (*see* ANALOG-TO-DIGITAL AND DIGITAL-TO-ANALOG CONVERTERS) systems for electroencephalograms in 1960, early in her still-active career in biomedical engineering.

Two reasons that so many of the first programmers were women were their participation in the war effort and the belief that women were better-suited than men to be programmers. However, once programming became more prestigious and more men entered the field in the late1950s, the environment for women became markedly less hospitable, and women's participation fell, as it did in other professional fields, although it increased again in the late 1960s.

Despite biases, women continue to make valuable contributions to computer science. Some American female leaders in computer science are:

◆ Dr. Fran Allen, IBM Fellow and Member of the National Academy of Engineering (NAE) and American Academy of Arts and Sciences, credited with establishing the theory and practice of program optimization.

◆ Dr. Ruzena Bajcsy, a Fellow of the American Association for Artificial Intelligence (AAAI) and Institute of Electrical and Electronics Engineers (IEEE) and Member of the NAE, known for her work in machine perception, particularly her "Active Perception" paradigm.

◆ Dr. Adele Goldberg, researcher and laboratory manager at Xerox Palo Alto Research Center (PARC), and co-inventor of Smalltalk (one of the key sources of the widely used object-oriented programming (*q.v.*) paradigm), then Chair and Founder of ParcPlace Systems. She received the ACM 1987 Systems Software Award and PC Magazine's 1990 Lifetime Achievement Award for her contributions to the personal computer industry. She is a Fellow and former president of the ACM.

◆ Dr. Shafi Goldwasser, winner of the Gödel prize in theoretical computer science and the Association for Computing Machinery (ACM) Hopper Award for her pioneering work in computational complex-

ity (*q.v.*), cryptography (*q.v.*), and computational number theory.

◆ Dr. Barbara J. Grosz, a Fellow of the American Association for the Advancement of Science and Fellow and former president of AAAI, widely regarded as having established the research field of computational modeling of discourse.

◆ Dr. Anita Jones, Chair of the Computer Science Department at the University of Virginia, then Director of Defense Research and Engineering for the United States government (1993–1997), a researcher in computer software systems. She is an NAE Member, ACM Fellow, and IEEE Fellow.

◆ Dr. Nancy G. Leveson, ACM Fellow and former Editor-in-Chief of *IEEE Transactions on Software Engineering*, a founder of software safety (*q.v.*) research.

◆ Dr. Barbara Liskov, Member of the NAE, Fellow of the ACM and the American Academy of Arts and Sciences, widely recognized for her contributions toward the methodology of data abstraction (*see* ABSTRACT DATA TYPES).

◆ Jean E. Sammet, long-time IBM employee and member of the NAE, recognized for many contributions to the development of programming languages including her involvement in the early work on Cobol and her authorship of an influential book on this subject. She is an ACM Fellow and a former president of ACM.

◆ Dr. Mary Shaw, recipient of the 1993 Warnier prize for contributions to software engineering (*q.v.*) and Fellow of the American Association for the Advancement of Science, ACM, and IEEE.

◆ Steve Shirley, founder and life president of the influential information technology group F. I. Group plc. This accomplishment as well as her emphasis on ethics and professional standards in industry led to her being awarded the OBE (Officer of the Order of the British Empire) in 1980 and the Freedom of the City of London in 1987. She also served as President of the British Computer Society (*q.v.*) in 1989–1990.

Despite these women's presence in leadership positions, women are greatly underrepresented in computer science. As Fig. 3 shows, women received 29% of the bachelor's degrees and 27% of the master's degrees awarded in computing sciences in 1995 in the USA, and 14% of the computer science and computer engineering doctoral degrees in American and Canadian universities in 1998. While women's participation increased in the 1970s and early 1980s, it has since

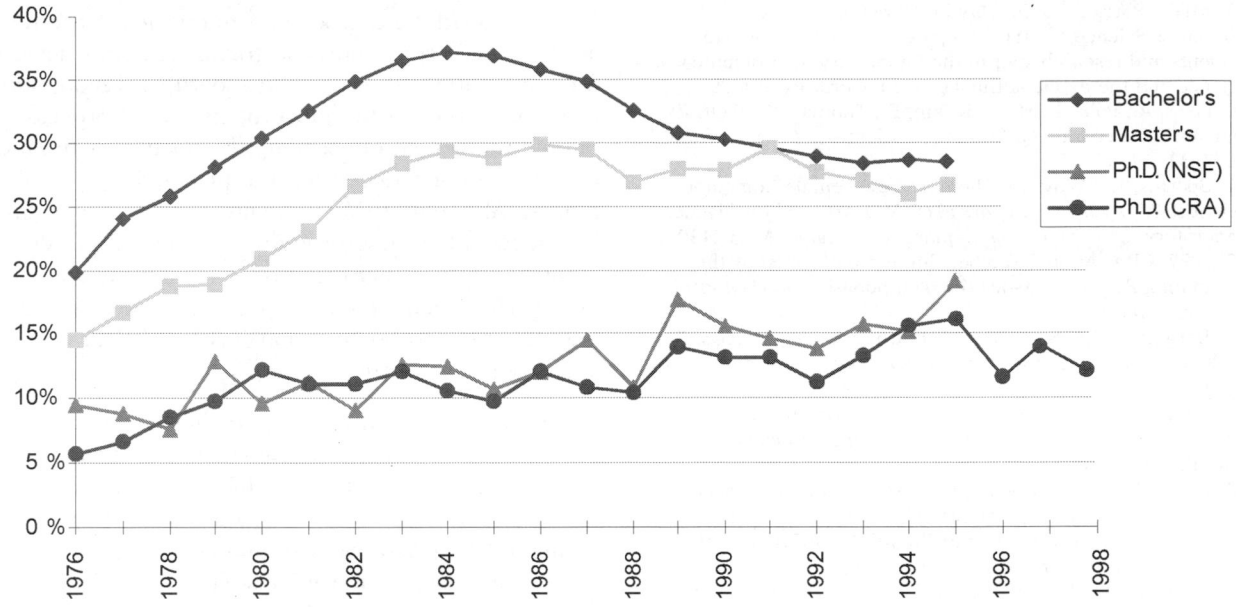

Figure 3. Percentage of computer science degrees awarded to women. US bachelor's, master's, and Ph.D. degrees (denoted by triangles) are from NSF (1996, 1999). The other Ph.D. data is for degrees in the USA and Canada from CRA (1992–1999).

been declining at the bachelor's and master's level. In Ph.D.-granting computer science and computer engineering departments in the USA and Canada, women comprise 19% of assistant professors, 10% of associate professors, and 7% of full professors (CRA, 1997).

While women are underrepresented in all fields of science and engineering (NSF, 1996), there are some factors that are specific to computer science (Pearl *et al.*, 1990; Spertus, 1991):

◆ Computer games and educational software are geared to the preferences and interests of boys, such as war and sports.

◆ Parents appear to be more willing to send their sons than daughters to expensive computer camps. According to one camp director, "Mothers bring their boys to the classes. Girls have to beg to enroll."

◆ Some women find the overwhelmingly male hacker (*q.v.*) culture offensive or intimidating.

◆ Boys tend to monopolize the use of computers in schools.

Since the early 1980s, sparked by the release of a report by the women of MIT's computer science labs (MIT, 1983), there has been a growing awareness of sexual bias in computer science and an interest in activities to counter it. A few of the many recent programs are:

◆ Minerva's Machine (Frenkel, 1995), a widely broadcast documentary on women and computing, sponsored by the Association for Computing Machinery (ACM—*q.v.*).

◆ Systers (Borg, 1993), an electronic mailing list that helps more than 2500 women in computer science reduce their isolation and share advice on how to deal with the problems they face.

◆ The ACM Committee on Women in Computing, which sponsors projects to enhance the environment for women in computing both in academia and industry and to encourage more girls to pursue computer science careers.

◆ The Ada Project, an online clearing house of information on women and computing, created by Yale graduate students Elisabeth Freeman and Susanne Hupfer.

◆ The Grace Hopper Celebrations of Women in Computing, national conferences designed to encourage girls and women in computing by highlighting women's successes.

◆ The CRA committee on the Status of Women in Computing Research, which has a number of projects to advance women in computing research and education, such as the Distributed Mentor Project, which arranges and provides funds for female undergraduates to spend summers working on research with female professors at research universities.

Bibliography

1983. MIT. "Barriers to Equality in Academia: Women in Computer Science at MIT," prepared by female graduate students and research staff in the Laboratory for Computer Science and the Artificial Intelligence Laboratory at MIT.

1990. Pearl, A., Pollack, M. E., Riskin, E., Thomas, R., Wolf, E., and Wu A. "Becoming a Computer Scientist," *Comm. of the ACM*, **33**, *11*, 47–57.

1991. Spertus, E. "Why Are There So Few Female Computer Scientists?," *Technical Report 1315.* MIT Artificial Intelligence Laboratory, 545 Technology Square, Cambridge, MA 02139.

1992–1999. CRA. Annual Taulbee Surveys performed by the Computing Research Association and published in *Computing Research News.*

1993. Borg, A. "Why Systers?," *Computing Research News*, **5**, *4* (September), 3. Also at `http://www.systers.org/keeper/whysys.html`.

1995. Frenkel, K. A. "Minerva's Machine: Women and Computing" (videotape). Available from the Association for Computing Machinery.

1995. Gürer, D. W. "Pioneering Women in Computer Science," *Comm. of the ACM*, **38**, *1* (January), 45–54.

1996. Fritz, W. B. "The Women of ENIAC," *IEEE Annals of the History of Computing*, **18**, *3* (Fall), 13–28.

1996. Gürer, D. W. "Women's Contributions to Early Computing at the National Bureau of Standards," *IEEE Annals of the History of Computing*, **18**, *3*, 29–35.

1996. National Science Foundation (NSF). *Women, Minorities, and Persons with Disabilities in Science and Engineering* (NSF 96-311). Washington DC: National Science Foundation.

1997. Camp, T. "The Incredible Shrinking Pipeline," *Comm. of the ACM*, **40**, *10* (October), 103–110.

1999. National Science Foundation (NSF). *Women, Minorities, and Persons with Disabilities in Science and Engineering: 1998* (NSF 99-338). Washington DC: National Science Foundation.

Websites

ACM-W. `http://www.acm.org/women/`.
CRA-W. `http://www.cra.org/Activities/craw/`.
The Ada Project. `http://www.cs.yale.edu/~tap/tap.html`.

Ellen Spertus and Denise Gürer

WORD PROCESSING

For articles on related subjects *see* DESKTOP PUBLISHING; ELECTRONIC OFFICE; METAFONT; TEXT EDITING SYSTEMS; SPELLING CHECKER; TEX; TYPEFONT; USER INTERFACE; and WINDOW ENVIRONMENTS.

The term *word processing* was invented by IBM as a way to market a new product, a Selectric typewriter that could record words on magnetic tape. Characters, punctuation, and some limited formatting instructions, such as tabs, margins, underline, and double space, could be saved on tape as the typist typed them, and then typed out automatically. The recording capability meant that corrections and revisions could be made in the recorded text by re-recording over the original error. It also meant that unlimited perfect copies of the original could be produced, to all appearances personalized and hand-typed, without manually retyping the document.

Early Systems

IBM marketed word processors to business customers as dedicated, single-purpose (or standalone) devices for the creation (through a keyboard), revision, storage, and output of text documents. Word processors offered the benefit of speeding the document production process and increasing the productivity of office typists. Although IBM originally expected only limited success for these products, by the mid-1970s an enthusiastic customer response led to a burgeoning industry. New vendors of word processors, such as Wang Laboratories and others, soon surpassed IBM in sales and product innovation.

Vendors enlarged and improved their word processing system's storage media from magnetic tape to magnetic cards to magnetic diskettes. Cathode ray tube (CRT) display screens were added that allowed documents to be viewed, revised, and corrected on screen before final hard copy versions were printed. For the sake of economy and efficiency, vendors developed clustered systems, in which, by employing minicomputer technology, several word processors were linked in centralized groups, sharing a central processor and peripherals such as printers. Word processors moved from hard-wired (fixed function) systems to software-programmable general-purpose computing systems.

Although it did not restrain their popularity, the dedicated word processors of this period were far from cheap. A standalone fully functioned display word processor with diskette storage and a printer ranged in price from about $8,000 to about $15,000, including training and vendor support. A multi-user dedicated word processing system installation ranged from $8,000 to $15,000 for the first few workstations; additional workstations cost considerably less.

To help justify the cost of expensive word processing equipment and accommodate its capabilities, a large organization's clerical staff would frequently be reorganized into specialized functions: those who typed, using centralized word processing equipment, and those who were employed in non-typing administrative support tasks. Thus, *word processor* became a term used as a job description, as well as a reference to computer-based typing equipment.

Although the intention was to relieve secretaries of time-consuming typing tasks and generally to improve the productivity of office workers, this reorganization could become the source of conflict. Traditional office staff tended to view the word processing function with disdain, as little different from a typing pool. Word processing operators worried about the possible health risks imposed by long-term daily use of CRT display screens, leading to some scattered litigation regarding their use (limiting operators' hours between work breaks, for example), as well as to some, largely unsuccessful attempts to organize clerical workers. Nevertheless, word processing was established as a familiar and valuable office tool.

Word processing gained further acceptance in the office environment through another and different route. Investigations conducted by universities and the research centers of some large data processing vendors, such as Xerox and IBM, suggested that the productivity of highly paid managerial and professional personnel could be improved if supported by computer technology, by sharing applications, storage and processing power residing on a centralized computer via linked desktop terminals.

Minicomputer builders such as Digital Equipment Corporation (*q.v.*), Data General, Wang, and IBM (*q.v.*) introduced Office Automation systems. Word processing was a software application included on these systems as an essential function. For many users, the comparable worth of these systems could be judged by the functionality and ease of use of their word processing features, since their other functions (typically, file and records sharing, electronic mail—*q.v.*, appointment calendars, financial forecasting tools, etc.) were less important.

Personal Computer Word Processing

The IBM Personal Computer (IBM PC—*q.v.*), introduced in 1981, changed the character of word processing. Once the PC became a widely accepted office tool, virtually all word processing products became software applications for personal computers rather than cumbersome, dedicated word processors.

Microprocessor-based personal computer products were commercially available before the introduction of the IBM PC, but were regarded as chiefly of interest to very small businesses with little need of computer processing power, or to hobbyists. Early microcomputers lacked storage capacity, normally included an inapt, data processing-oriented keyboard design, offered small screen size with poor resolution, could not be linked in clusters, and were almost exclusively based on limited 8-bit central processor technology. Furthermore, they were typically manufactured and marketed by obscure start-up companies, not the major mainframe or minicomputer vendors in whom business customers had built confidence over years of contact.

The IBM PC, however, was based on a 16-bit processor and the MS-DOS operating system, which provided software developers with a sufficiently powerful and flexible platform on which to write software applications. The PC could run word processing as well as

other programs, and, as it became the popular standard among personal computer products in a growing business market, developers were encouraged to write an increasing number of applications for it.

In addition to the inducement of a growing number of software applications, the PC, at the time of its introduction, was one-half or less the cost of a standalone dedicated word processing product. Furthermore, PCs did not require the commitment to a single vendor or the expense of installation that a mini-based system required. Finally, the IBM name established the credibility of the PC in the skeptical mainstream business community, particularly since most business computer users were already IBM customers. Consequently, as the PC market boomed, the dedicated word processor quickly became obsolete.

SOFTWARE

Since the introduction of the PC, most word processing application packages for personal computers have been written and marketed by independent software vendors (ISVs). Although these organizations are independent of the hardware vendors, the applications are written specifically for certain personal computer platforms. Each advance in hardware or operating system has been followed by improved and enhanced software products that take advantage of the new capabilities.

Unlike some other kinds of personal computer applications, spreadsheets (*q.v.*) or databases for example, the word processing market has never been dominated for very long by a single vendor's product. A new hardware platform or technological innovation has often led to a new market, and the lead among word processing products, in terms of market share, has changed many times. As of 1999, the most popular PC word processing programs were Microsoft (*q.v.*) Word, followed at some distance by Corel's WordPerfect and Lotus Word Pro. Although ISVs may convert a popular product, or port it, to a new platform, it is also possible that a brand new product may capture the market. However, Microsoft Word has maintained its market dominance in the move from Windows 3.x to Windows 95 and 98, but is at risk again as the market considers Java and component software (*q.v.*).

The success of current word processing products depends upon the set of useful features they include and the ease with which it can be learned and used. Clearly, certain features will appeal to certain users for certain tasks, and ISVs may aim a product specifically at users with special needs. In a business environment, success also favors a product that employees are able to learn quickly, minimizing training and support costs. Price, naturally, will also play a role in a product's acceptance. Most fully featured word processing packages currently cost about $300. Products offering fewer features typically cost less. A two-tier pricing model operates in many PC application software markets, including word processing. Since most customers for word processing already use a word processor they pay a much smaller (typically 20–25% of list price) upgrade price, even when moving to a new brand of word processing product.

Current word processing products can be expected to provide a feature set far beyond the standard document creation and error correction of the early systems. Few features that could be useful to a document author have been overlooked. They will search for certain words or phrases; merge letters with lists of names and addresses; move blocks of text; display italic, bold, underlining, and superscripts and subscripts; display page breaks; allow text to be arranged in multiple columns; display multiple pages on screen at one time; combine text and graphic images; offer shortcuts for keyboard commands; count characters, words, and paragraphs; provide automatic hyphenation and justification; create footnotes, tables of contents, and indexes; correct spelling errors; provide a thesaurus; and, in a few cases, correct grammar and evaluate the readability of a document according to the reading level of the intended document recipients. The foregoing is a random, partial list; not all word processors offer all of these features.

USER INTERFACES

Early MS-DOS word processors used a character-based *user interface*—the interaction (commands and responses) between user and computer. In a character-based interface, the commands (or instructions) given by the user to the computer are made via the keyboard via specific keys or key combinations. The user must know these commands or refer to a manual to find them. As character commands may differ from product to product, each new word processing package must be learned.

Today, most word processing users benefit by the widespread use of the graphical user interface (GUI), invented by the Xerox Corporation in the mid-1970s, but popularized by Apple Computer's Macintosh personal computer, introduced in 1984. Starting in the mid-1980s, Microsoft began to introduce versions of a GUI interface, modeled on the Xerox/Apple design, on top of MS-DOS, called Windows. In 1990, with the introduction of Windows 3.0, it hit gold and the market began a migration from character-based to GUI systems. Today, virtually all new personal computers use a GUI interface.

In a GUI-based system, pop-up or pull-down menus listing command selections are available to an opera-

tor at all times, regardless of what else may be displayed on the screen. There is no need, for example, to close a document and return to a main menu in order to select functions and issue commands. Menus can be activated and functions selected by pointing to them with a cursor controlled by a hand-operated mouse (*q.v.*) rather than by striking keys. Training, beyond identifying proper commands and basic eye–hand mouse operation, is minimal. Training remains minimal from one GUI-based application to the next, as all follow the same basic approach.

Another advantage of a GUI is the so-called WYSIWYG (What You See Is What You Get) display. In the older MS-DOS word processors, the characters displayed on the screen are monospaced; each character, space, or punctuation mark is assigned an equal amount of space, regardless of typeface or size. A WYSIWYG display shows the user proportional typefaces, in different fonts and type sizes, almost exactly as they will appear when printed on paper. A GUI with WYSIWYG display also allows graphic images to be created, positioned, and incorporated with text in compound documents on screen as they will look when printed.

GUI-based systems also simplify the creation of style sheets (prerecorded formats for text and graphics), including charts and tables. An operator can create a new document by using the recorded margins, tabs, centering, justification, graphics position, etc., and entering only new or altered text. In a character-based system, the creation of style sheet formatting for repetitive formats is an operation accomplished only with great difficulty, by employing obscure operating system commands and menus.

The powerful advantages offered by the GUI, ease of use, WYSIWYG display, and graphics capability have exerted a strong influence on the way software developers design products. All fully featured word processing products now reflect this influence.

DESKTOP PUBLISHING

The GUI influence can be seen in other developments as well. The first is in the features increasingly found in word processing products that until the early 1990s were found almost exclusively in desktop publishing (DTP) systems (*q.v.*).

DTP, also pioneered by the Apple Macintosh, is only practicable with the GUI. DTP applications typically include many of the text entry features of word processors, but add highly sophisticated typesetting and layout functions, such as variable text and display fonts, type styles and sizes, graphics capabilities, and page layout and design features. Where the purpose of word processors is the flexible creation of standard business documents, DTP is intended for the commercial quality design and production of newsletters, brochures, and books.

Although word processing and DTP products are currently distinctly different applications, under normal circumstances either application could be substituted for the other. GUI word processors can and do include DTP functions, such as the integration of graphic images with text, and columnar page design. Word processors now include about 75% of the function of a DTP package, and whether you use one or the other largely depends upon whether you are mainly doing word processing or mainly doing page layout. Some high-end features are reserved for the DTP products, which require substantially more training and technical support.

The influence of the GUI advantage can also be seen in the introduction of graphical operating environments, such as Microsoft Windows. Microsoft introduced its GUI environment as a shell interface on top of MS-DOS but now offers Windows 95, 98 and 2000, a 32-bit operating system with a full GUI environment.

Microsoft has permitted users to protect their investments in character-based applications at the same time they move to GUI environments; old applications, should you still need them, can run in a DOS Window.

In addition, this environment allows the exchange of information between applications; not only can a section of a spreadsheet (*q.v.*), for example, be copied, moved, and incorporated into a word processing document, but if the data contained in the original spreadsheet is changed, the change will automatically appear in the section included in the document. Microsoft started this process with DDE (Dynamic Data Exchange) in Windows 3.0, continued it with OLE and is now supporting it with its ActiveX technology. Using multiple applications has also become progressively easier; if the user needs to edit data in the embedded spreadsheet or graphic in a word processed document, clicking in that embedded area changes the toolbar to one appropriate for the embedded applications, for in-context editing, rather than moving the user and the embedded document to the application in which it was created and then moving the user back, which takes longer and is much more confusing.

NETWORKING

Traditionally, personal computer word processing packages have been designed for and sold to single users. An individual user of an individual computer uses an individual package to produce his or her own documents. Changes or corrections are rekeyed by the same user on the same system.

Sharing a document in editable, electronic form between personal computer users has been possible in two ways. Another user, with the same software package and the same or fully compatible computer, can borrow the storage medium containing the document. With a dialup network connection, files can also be communicated via telephone lines to another user's computer, provided the remote user has compatible software. But, in either case, the data is processed on different computers by users at different times.

In recent years, the trend in office computing has been toward networked computers, typically in local area networks (LANS—*q.v.*). In a LAN, the personal computers within a department or workgroup are linked so that, typically, they are able to communicate electronic messages and share applications and data files. The applications and shared files are stored on a *file server* (*q.v.*) dedicated to this purpose. Unlike the earlier Office Automation model, however, the processing power resides in the users' personal computers, not in a shared minicomputer. The result is many of the advantages offered by the mini-based system but with more flexibility (in adding or subtracting users, for example) and without the higher cost of the minicomputer.

Along with the conveniences of networking, however, come limitations. First, users of LAN word processing are limited to the application that is stored on the network, which may not be their preference. Second, shared data files and documents typically can be accessed and worked on only by one user at one time. To see document changes or to make copies of the document for their personal use, other network users must access the file individually. In a workgroup situation where a document may be the product of several authors, it would be more efficient for several users, working separately or simultaneously, to have access to shared applications and documents.

Several word processing products are now supporting collaborative work, assuming multiple users working on the same documents simultaneously or sequentially. They do this through supporting multiple versions of the same document, permitting users to mark up documents for approval, and letting multiple users work on different sections of a document simultaneously. This has occurred by building function into the personal word processing products used on PCs, but linked together by shared files on network servers, now managed by a server-level application such as Lotus Notes or Microsoft's Outlook and Exchange. Users need not be on a single LAN, either. Intranets may cross multiple geographies or the users may be connected across the Internet (*q.v.*) itself.

Most word processing products today are not sold alone, but rather in software bundles called office suites, together with other personal productivity products such as spreadsheets, databases, personal information managers (calendar, scheduler, Rolodex), and graphics/presentation managers. Vendors may also add licensed software such as browsers (*see* WORLD WIDE WEB). Perhaps 90% of all word processors are sold in such suites. In fact, the suite is sometimes thought of by vendors, by other ISVs, and by the users themselves as a kind of mini-platform, where customizations can be created and to which other applications can be added. This means word processing sales are affected not just by how good the word processor is (although the value of its word processor is a significant measure of the success of an office suite), but also by the other elements of the suite.

This, too, may change. With the rise of the Internet and corporate Intranets, a new kinds of software, *componentware* (*see* COMPONENT SOFTWARE) is becoming popular. Small and lightweight, components are designed to be focused on particular tasks, be downloadable over networks, and be very easy to use. A number of the initial application components are word processors, so if the move to Java and the Internet represents a market break and an opportunity for a new word processing style to arise, components may play an important role in the next round of this constantly renewing market.

Bibliography

1984. McWilliams, P. *The Word Processing Book*. New York: Putnam.
1990. Ruhl, J. *The Writer's Toolbox: Buying and Using a Computer for the Literary Life.* Upper Saddle River, NJ: Prentice Hall.

Amy Wohl

WORKING SET

For articles on related subjects *see* MEMORY MANAGEMENT; MEMORY PROTECTION; MULTIPROGRAMMING; OPERATING SYSTEMS; SCHEDULING ALGORITHMS; THRASHING; and VIRTUAL MEMORY.

From their beginnings in the 1940s, electronic computers had two-level storage systems. In the 1950s, main memory was magnetic core RAM (today it is semiconductor RAM) and the secondary memory was magnetic drums (today it is disks). The processor (CPU) could address only the main memory. A major part of a programmer's job was to devise a good way to divide a program into blocks and to schedule their moves between the levels. The blocks were called *segments* or *pages* and the movement operations overlays or swaps. The contents of main memory were called the "set of working information," or *working set* for short.

In the late 1950s, the designers of the Atlas Computer at the University of Manchester introduced virtual memory, which made programming considerably easier by automating the arduous acts of planning and implementing overlays. They also invented multiprogramming, a method of partitioning main memory among several active programs; multiprogramming increased system throughput by maintaining a reserve of ready-to-execute programs. By the middle 1960s, the term "working set" had come to mean the smallest subset of a program's address space that needed to be present in multiprogrammed main memory to maintain acceptable processing efficiency. Within this understanding, the size as well as the content of the working set can vary over time; and multiprogramming can be run with dynamic partitions.

The first precise definition of working set was given in 1968—the set of pages referenced in a sampling window extending from the current time backwards into the past (Denning, 1968). The idea of sampling for used pages was already familiar with usage-bit-based paging algorithms. What was new was that the window was defined in the virtual time of the program—i.e. CPU time with all interrupts removed—so that the same program with the same input data would have the same working set measurements no matter what the memory size, multiprogramming level, or scheduler policy. The window size was the lone parameter: the larger the window, the larger the working set, the lower the probability of paging, and the greater the processing efficiency.

This definition enabled easy measures of the paging rate and size of the working set memory policy as a function of its window size (Denning, 1980). The measures could be computed from the easily measured histogram of intervals between successive references to the same page. Working set theory explained what caused thrashing; it also gave a method to prevent thrashing by loading more programs only as long as memory can accommodate their working sets (Rodriguez-Rosell and Dupuy, 1973). Under a working set policy, the multiprogramming level could rise and fall with the variations in working set sizes without saturating the secondary storage system. With the right setting of the window size, the multiprogramming level would dynamically adjust to stay near the optimum throughput possible for the system.

Although the hardware needed to measure working sets dynamically was more expensive than most designers were willing to tolerate, a number of very good approximations based on sampling usage bits were made. One of the simplest is the "clock" strategy, so-called because it can be visualized with the aid of a clock face. Imagine that the names of all the blocks in

RAM are noted around the circumference of a clock, and that the clock's minute hand is pointing to one of them. When a running program generates a request to move a new block into RAM, the clock hand begins scanning for a block whose usage bit is off. The block thus selected is removed from RAM to make way for the incoming block.

In some systems, working sets can be deduced from a program's structure rather than by measurement of usage bits. For example, on machines using block-structured programming languages such as Ada, the working set can be defined as the current procedure segment, the stack, and all other data structures (*q.v.*) accessible from activated procedures.

The success of working set policies derives from the dynamic property called *locality of reference*. In each phase of virtual time, a program refers to only a subset of the blocks in its address space. This is a direct consequence of software design: programmers usually organize algorithms to work with subsets or regions of their data space during specific algorithmic phases. The working set estimates the set of blocks used by the program during the current phase. When most virtual time is covered by phases that are long compared with the secondary memory access time, the working set is an excellent predictor of memory demand in the immediate future.

In paging systems it can be advantageous to "restructure" a program by clustering small, logical segments of the same locality on large pages. By preserving in the page references the locality originally present in the segment references, this strategy can yield the smallest possible working sets and efficient performance in systems with large page size. Restructuring is less important in systems with smaller page sizes.

Bibliography

1968. Denning, P. J. "The Working Set Model for Program Behavior," *Communications of the ACM*, **11**, 5 (May), 323–333.

1973. Rodriguez-Rosell, J., and Dupuy, J. P. "The Design Implementation, and Evaluation of a Working Set Dispatcher," *Communications of the ACM*, **16**, 4 (April), 247–353.

1980. Denning, P. J. "Working Sets Past and Present," *IEEE Trans. Software Engineering*, **SE-6**, 1 (January), 64–84.

1992. Tanenbaum, A. *Modern Operating Systems.* Upper Saddle River, NJ: Prentice Hall.

Peter J. Denning

WORKSTATION

For articles on related subjects *see* COMPUTER-AIDED DESIGN/COMPUTER-AIDED MANUFACTURING; COMPUTER ANIMATION; COMPUTER GRAPHICS; FILE SERVER; LOCAL AREA NETWORK; SCIENTIFIC VISUALIZATION; USER INTERFACE; VIRTUAL REALITY; and WINDOW ENVIRONMENTS.

A *workstation* is a powerful graphics-oriented microcomputer intended for a single user. When workstations were introduced in the early 1980s they were distinguished by their large bitmapped displays and their use of a mouse (*q.v.*) for input, at a time when most systems had relatively small ASCII terminals connected to time-shared mainframes (*q.v.*) or to low-power personal computers with keyboard input. By 1999, every PC had a powerful processor and high-resolution displays, and the distinction between workstation and PC has become more a matter of function than of hardware.

Workstations are designed to connect to local area networks, using software that allows them to access files located on remote *file servers* as easily as if the files resided on a disk attached to the local workstation. Network access is facilitated by the use of an operating system (*q.v.*) that hides the details of accessing remote files from user programs. They use the TCP/IP (*q.v.*) Internet protocol for easy access to services provided by machines attached to the network. Users send electronic mail (*q.v.*) to persons on remote machines, establish interactive login sessions with remote machines, and send and retrieve files. They commonly run versions of the Unix (*q.v.*) or Windows NT operating systems, which support concurrent processes (*see* CONCURRENT PROGRAMMING). Used initially by scientists and engineers, workstations have become commonplace in educational and business settings where graphics applications and data visualization are important.

Output displayed on a graphics-oriented bitmapped display allows applications to show pictures, graphics, program output, and text containing arbitrary typefonts (*q.v.*). Window-manager utilities divide the display screen into multiple independent windows, with individual applications controlling one or more windows (*see* WINDOW ENVIRONMENTS). The window manager allows a user to control the size and location of windows in a uniform way, while the application focuses on updating a window's contents rather than its location. Workstations provide high-resolution color graphics with hardware support for computationally intensive operations such as are typical of computer animation and CAD/CAM applications.

The idea of a personal workstation originated at Xerox PARC (Palo Alto Research Center) during the 1960s. It was not until the development of microprocessor technology, however, that workstations became commonly available. Early workstations were sometimes *diskless*, having not only application programs but the operating system itself loaded from the networked file server. As high-capacity hard drives became cheaper, diskless systems became less popular, due to the load that they placed on a network. In 1999 workstations were equipped with 32- or 64-bit microprocessors, an operating system with virtual memory (*q.v.*), a large main memory of at least 128 MB, and auxiliary memory of several to several hundred gigabytes.

In the early 1980s, workstations frequently used the same Motorola 68000 series of processors used in the Apple (*q.v.*) Macintosh. Since the end of the 1980s, they have become a primary beneficiary of reduced instruction set computing (RISC—*q.v.*) technology, in which the instruction set (*q.v.*) of the central processor is stripped down to its bare essentials in order to achieve greater speed (at the expense of physically longer programs, memory now being quite inexpensive). The raw processing power of high-end workstations approaches that of mainframes, but their input–output capabilities are typically significantly less than those of mainframes. Physically, they require space comparable to that of a desktop PC.

Until very recently, it was considered an essential characteristic of a workstation that its software run under Unix on a RISC microprocessor. The leading machines were made by Sun Microsystems, using its Sparc chip, and Silicon Graphics Incorporated (SGI), which used a MIPS chip (*see* Figs. 1 and 2). Depending on configuration, such workstations were priced from $3,000 to $20,000 in 1999, while powerful PCs with memory and displays comparable to those of workstations cost from $2,000 to $6,000.

In the late 1990s then, the processing power and storage capacity of high-end PCs overlapped that of many workstations. In addition to cost, another factor in the growing attractiveness of the PC is the maturation of the Windows NT multitasking (*q.v.*) operating system,

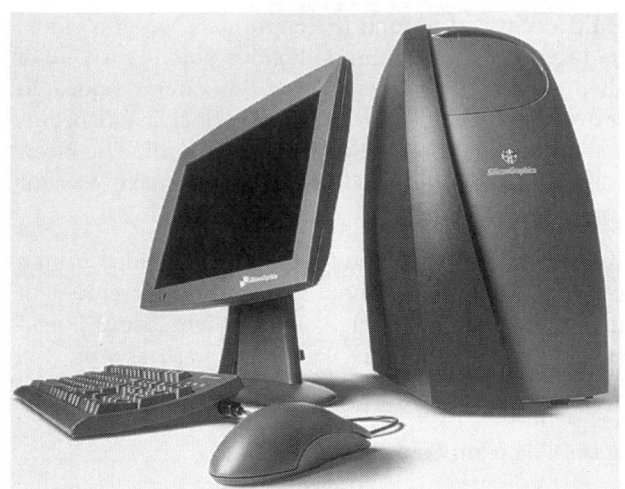

Figure 2. The Silicon Graphics 320 (courtesy of Silicon Graphics, Inc.).

as well as the availability of the Linux PC version of Unix. Unix had a long head-start as a workstation operating system, but now there is virtual parity in capability. Even though there is considerable Unix-based software for workstations, there is, conversely, much desirable PC software that has not yet been ported to the Unix environment. Since neither processing power nor operating system nor networked environment distinguishes a workstation sharply from a PC, the remaining distinction, which is readily blurred, can be made only on the basis of function. A workstation is typically still used for scientific and engineering applications that require computational speed and high-quality displays, while a personal computer is a system used primarily for word processing (*q.v.*), databases, and as an interface to the World Wide Web—with many systems used for both sets of purposes.

The dynamics of this highly competitive computing environment are explored in a comprehensive survey article by Linthicum (1998). In that article extensive benchmark (*q.v.*) comparisons are given for nine systems manufactured by Compaq, DEC, HP, IBM, Intergraph, Micron, NeTpower, SGI, and Sun. According to the survey, dual-processor Pentium II PCs running Windows NT performed as well as or better than Unix workstations for many computational tasks.

Bibliography

1994. Bjelland, H. *Configuring a Customized Engineering Workstation.* New York: Windcrest.

1996. Haramundanis, K. *Exploring Workstation Applications with CDE and Motif.* Bedford, MA: Digital Press.

1998. Linthicum, D. S. "Graphics Workstations," *PC Magazine,* **17**, *4* (24 February), 148–177.

1998. *Laboratory Information Management Systems (LIMS) for Workstations,* special issue of *Scientific Computing & Automation,* **15**, *5* (April).

Thomas Narten (revised by the editors)

Figure 1. The Sun Microsystems Ultra 80 Workstation (courtesy of Sun Microsystems, UK).

WORLD WIDE WEB

For articles on related subjects *see* CLIENT–SERVER COMPUTING; CYBERSPACE; ELECTRONIC COMMERCE; ELECTRONIC MAIL; ENTREPRENEURS; HYPERTEXT; INTERNET; JAVA; MARKUP LANGUAGES; NETWORKS, COMPUTER; PACKET SWITCHING; and TCP/IP.

Introduction

The *World Wide Web*, or just "Web" for short, is a rapidly growing collection of over 800 million *pages* (in 1999) linked together in a seemingly disorganized topology which is densest over the Western Hemisphere and western Europe, but is nonetheless worldwide in scope.

A Web page resides on a *server*, a host computer (*q.v.*) which allows general access for computers connected to the host network. The largest network, the Internet, is a collection of thousands of other networks which are interconnected via common network protocols (*q.v.*) (see below). The networks which form the Internet may be either local area networks (LANs—*q.v.*) or wide area networks (WANs) and public (e.g. community Freenets) or private (e.g. Internet Service Providers—ISPs—such as America Online). While each network has different characteristics owing to its individual role and user community, all share the characteristic of supporting mainstream Internet software, including, but not limited to, that which enables the Web.

A *Website* is a coherent cluster of one or more pages (on one or more servers) whose *home page* is accessed using a *Uniform Resource Locator* (URL). Websites store information according to the tagging conventions of the HyperText Markup Language (HTML). HTML is an application of Standard Generalized Markup Language (SGML) which is a popular document definition language within the publishing community. HTML has one important extension of SGML: *hyperlinks* (*see* HYPERTEXT), usually called just *links*. They are conduits to other resources including offsets within documents, other documents, imagery, animation and motion pictures, executable programs called Server-Side Includes (SSIs), Java applets etc. Typically hyperlinks appear in Web documents either as sensitized text (in color) or as sensitized icons, where "sensitized" means that selecting a link (usually by a mouse (*q.v.*) click) produces some navigational effect. The link uses a URL to specify the location of the hyperlinked resource. The time to access a remote resource depends upon the network bandwidth (*q.v.*) available to its location.

WEB Perspectives

NETWORK PERSPECTIVE

The World Wide Web represents a major paradigm shift in networked computing both in terms of delivery of information and inter-personal, though not in-person, communication. It is the first form of digital communication that has rendering and browsing utilities adequate to allow any person or group with network access to share media-rich information with anyone else. As such, it represents an important departure from more traditional network communications protocols (*q.v.*) such as Telnet and FTP. Where prior network protocols were special purpose in terms of both function and media formats, the Web is highly versatile.

Formally, the Web is a client–server model for packet-switched (*q.v.*), networked computer systems that use a few key Internet protocols. The client handles all of the interaction with other components of the computing environment (i.e. other desktop applications and the server) and temporarily retains information for perusal. The networked servers are information repositories which host software to serve client requests. The procedural "glue" which makes the client–server interactivity possible is the concurrent support, by both client and server, of the protocol-pair HyperText Transfer Protocol (HTTP) and HyperText Markup Language (HTML). The former establishes the basic handshaking (*q.v.*) procedures between client and server, while the latter defines the organization and structure of Web documents to be exchanged. As of July 1999, the current HTTP version remained 1.0, although the draft standard for HTTP 1.1 has been approved by the Internet Engineering Task Force (IETF—http://www.ietf.org). Version 4 of HTML is the recommended standard by the World Wide Web Consortium and is in widespread use.

As a historical aside, according to NSFNET Backbone statistics, the Web moved into first place both in terms of the percentage of total packets moved (21%) and percentage of total bytes moved (26%) along the NSF backbone in the first few months of 1995. This placed the Web well ahead of the traditional Internet activity leaders, FTP (14%/21%) and Telnet (7.5%/2.5%), as the most popular Internet service. A comparison of the evolutionary patterns of the Web, Gopher and FTP is graphically depicted in Fig. 1. The trends speak for themselves. There are no corresponding statistics after 1995 since, after that, there was no single backbone from which to monitor traffic, but by 1999 it is likely that Web access accounts for more than 99% of Internet traffic and all other modes less than a collective 1%.

The rapid growth of the Web is the result of a unique combination of characteristics:

1. *The Web is an enabling technology*. It was the first widespread network technology to extend the notion of virtual network machine to multimedia

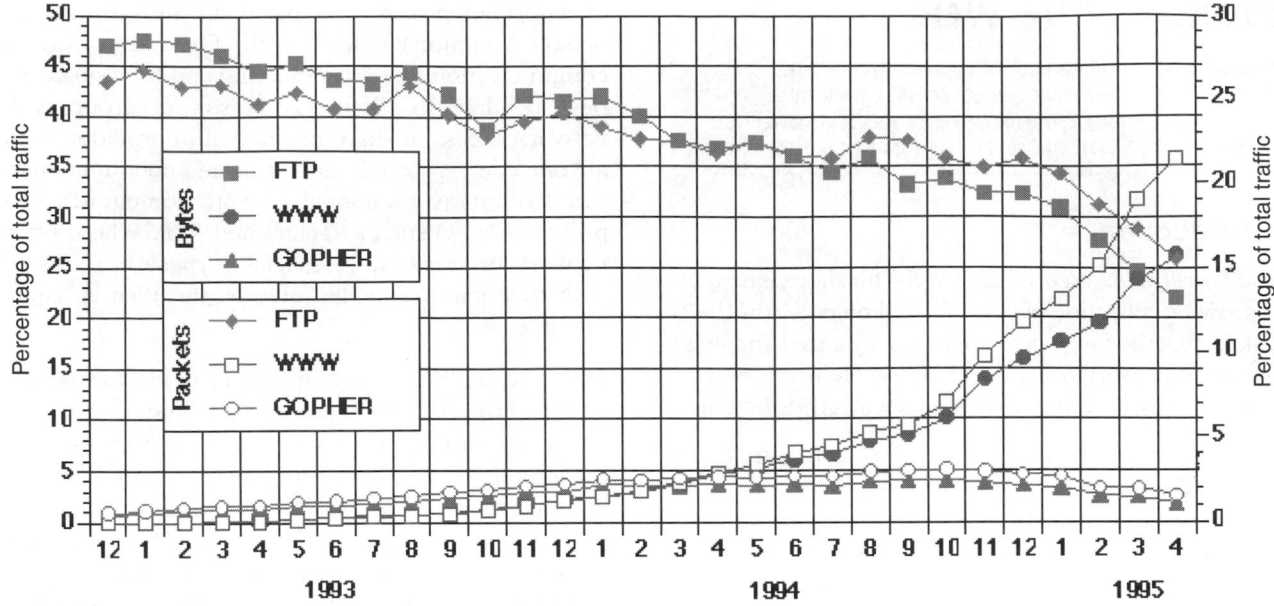

Figure 1. Merit NIC Backbone statistics for the Web, Gopher and FTP from 1993–1995 in terms of both packets and bytes (source: Merit NIC and Jim Pitkow, used with permission; *see* `http://www.cc.gatech.edu/gvu/stats/NSF/merit.html`).

(*q.v.*). While the ability to execute programs on, and retrieve content from, distributed computers was not new (e.g. Telnet and FTP were already in wide use by the time the Web was conceived), the ability to produce and distribute media-rich documents via a common platform-independent document structure was new with the Web.

2. *The Web is a unifying technology.* This occurred through the Web's accommodation of a wide range of multimedia formats. Since such audio (e.g. .WAV, .AU), graphics (e.g. .GIF, .JPG) and animation (e.g. MPEG) formats (*see* Appendix I for meaning of acronyms) are all digital, they were already unified in desktop applications prior to the Web. The Web, however, unified them for distributed network applications. Web "browsers," as they later were called, would correctly render dozens of media formats regardless of network source.

3. *The Web is a social phenomenon.* This aspect evolved in three stages. Stage one was the phenomenon of Web "surfing" (*see* the later section *Surfing the Web*). The richness and variety of Web documents and the novelty of the experience made Web surfing the *de facto* standard for curiosity-driven networking behavior in the 1990s. The second stage involved such Web interactive communication forums as Internet Relay Chat (IRC—*see* ONLINE CONVERSATION), which provided a new outlet for interpersonal but not-in-person communication. The third stage, which is in its infancy as of this writing, involves the notion of *virtual community*. The widespread popularity and social implications of such network-based, interactive communication

is gradually moving out of the research arena and into practice. At the end of this article there is further discussion of the Web as a social phenomenon and of virtual communities.

4. *The Web can significantly reduce transaction friction and the expense of commerce.* The commercial potential of the Web is being highly touted and widely exploited worldwide. A broad base of electronic commerce vendors is already established in the areas of bookselling and music sales, software and hardware sales, electronics, travel, online brokerages and banking, and auctioning, to name but a few. The explosion of valuation of NASDAQ "Internet stocks" in early 1999 was to a great degree due to the online commerce start-ups (e.g. Amazon. com, eBay, E*trade) that continued throughout the first half of that year with exceptionally high stock price/earnings ratios without precedent. This gives some estimate of the investor's perception of the enormous potential of electronic commerce. Perhaps not surprisingly, the pornography industry was the first to pioneer the widespread use of electronic commerce. Although, of course, the nature of the content was objectionable, electronic commerce vendors profited extensively from the pornography experience for insights into electronic transactions.

END USER PERSPECTIVE

Extensive reporting on Web use and Web users may be found in a number of Web survey sites, perhaps the most thorough of which is the biannual, self-selection World Wide Web Survey which began in January 1994. Some general summary information from the tenth survey in July 1999 is reported in Table 1.

Table 1. Summary information on Web uses from the tenth (1999) WWW User Surveys at the Georgia Institute of Technology (`http://www.cc.gatech.edu/user_surveys/`). Since this is data from a self-selection survey in which users decide whether or not to participate, the sample is likely to be biased toward experienced users.

- Average age of Web user = 37.6 years
- Male : female ratio of users = 66 : 34
- Education: college degrees = 33.9%; Masters = 17.2%; Doctorate = 3.4%
- Users in private (public) sector = 62.4% (19.4%)
- Users for whom English is the primary language = 92.2%
- Client operating systems: Microsoft Windows = 70.7%; Apple = 23.7%; Unix = 3.1%)
- Browser preference: Netscape Communicator = 61.6%; Internet Explorer = 56%
- Source of browser: free download = 36.4%; bundled with hardware or software = 23.4%; provided by Internet Service Provider = 17.3%
- Geographical distribution of Web use: USA = 84.7%; Europe = 7.3%; Canada = 3.8%
- Connection speed: 56 Kb/sec or less = 66.3%; 1 Mb/sec or more = 23.5%
- Respondents who reported Web purchases exceeding $100 = 71%
- Average income of respondents = $57,300

HISTORICAL PERSPECTIVE

The Web was conceived by Tim Berners-Lee and his colleagues at CERN (now called the European Laboratory for Particle Physics) in 1989 as a shared information space which would support collaborative work. Berners-Lee defined HTTP and HTML at that time; see his profile in ENTREPRENEURS. As a proof of concept prototype, he developed the first Web client navigator–browser in 1990 for the NeXTStep platform.

Nicola Pellow developed the first cross-platform Web browser in 1991 while Berners-Lee and Bernd Pollerman developed the first server application—a phone book database. By 1992, the interest in the Web was sufficient to produce four additional browsers—Erwise, Midas, and Viola for the X Window system, and Cello for Windows. The following year, Marc Andreessen of the National Center for Supercomputing Applications (NCSA) wrote Mosaic for the X Window system, which soon became the browser standard against which all others would be compared. For the more recent history of browsers, see the subsection on *Commercial Products* in the *Browsers* section later in this article.

Despite the original design goal of supporting collaborative work, Web use has become highly variegated. The Web has been extended into a wide range of products and services offered by individuals and organizations, for commerce, education, entertainment, "edutainment," and even propaganda. A partial list of popular Web applications includes:

- Individual and organizational *home pages*
- Sales prospecting via interactive forms-based surveys
- Advertising and the distribution of product promotional material
- Corporate record-keeping and databases—usually via local area networks (LANs) and Intranets
- Data warehousing (*q.v.*)
- Electronic commerce:
  - —Web-centric commerce, where the entire transaction is conducted on the Web (e.g. book sales, electronic banking and brokering, online reservation systems, online publishing)
  - —Web-augmented commerce, where the Web provides ancillary support for the transaction (e.g. catalogs, product support, manuals, frequently asked question (FAQ) sites)
  - —Web-mediation, where the Web connects the information consumer and information provider directly (e.g. media kiosks and edutainment, electronic auctioning, information agency)
- Religious proselytizing
- Propagandizing
- Digital politics and electioneering (*see* POLITICAL APPLICATIONS)
- Creation of information portals (e.g. Web search engines)
- Low-bandwidth teleconferencing

Most Web resources remain for the most part non-interactive, multimedia downloads (e.g. non-interactive Java animation applets, movie clips, real-time audio transmissions, text with graphics) augmented with Common Gateway Interface (CGI) forms (*see* SCRIPTING LANGUAGES), and frames for added control of layout. This "rectified" information flow will change in the next decade as software developers and Web content-providers shift their attention to the quality of content as well as the interactive and participatory capabilities of the Internet, the Web, and their successor technologies. However, in 1999 the dominant Web theme still seemed to emphasize form over function and esthetics over content.

Support of CGI within HTTP in 1993 was the first major step toward adding interactive capability to the Web. Though modest by comparison with modern desktop productivity applications, CGI forms provide a simple mechanism for input from the Web user-client to be passed to the server for processing without any programming expertise. This opened the area of interactive Web development to the majority of computer users, while the broader use of CGI programming remains within the province of computer programmers. While, in theory, CGI programs can provide server-side support for virtually any Web need, network bandwidth constraints and transmission delays make some heavily interactive and voluminous applications infeasible.

A second major advance was the advent of "plug-in" technology. This increased the media-rendering capability of browsers while avoiding the time-consuming spawning of so-called "helper apps" (applications) through the browser's launchpad. The speed advantage of the plug-ins, together with the tight coupling that exists between the plug-ins and the media formats which they render, make them a highly useful extension. As with helper apps, plug-ins also have the advantage of currency—they can be developed by third-party vendors in parallel with the development of new browsers.

Third, the advent of executable content added a high level of animated media rendering and interactive content on the client side. Such object-oriented network programming languages as Java (*q.v.*) produce platform-independent program modules which are executable on enabled Web browsers. Not surprisingly, this latest extension, which involves executing foreign programs which have been downloaded across the networks, is not without some security risk, although the same is true of such pedestrian applications as email, as was demonstrated by the Melissa virus that spread via email in early 1999 (*see* VIRUS, COMPUTER).

Fourth, we have seen advanced information-gathering strategies which go beyond the original "information-pull" concept behind the Web. Where most users, perhaps through autonomous software agents, currently seek to draw information to them, solicited *push technology* attempts to dispense information routinely and automatically to selected consumers (*see* Fig. 2). Several prototypes of solicited push "netcasting" have been deployed. Some, like Pointcast, consolidate and distribute information via a proprietary server called a *transmitter*. In this case, the client-side software behaves as a dedicated "peruser" for the transmissions. Other solicited push technology, such as Marimba's Castanet, contain a "tuner" which allows the client to connect to an arbitrary number of different servers. Each connection from the client to the transmitter is called a *channel*.

Although somewhat in disfavor as of 1999 because of the initial curiosity-driven abuse of bandwidth (*q.v.*) in 1997–1998, push-phase technology will continue to play an important, though different, role on the Web, especially within Intranet and Enterprise environments.

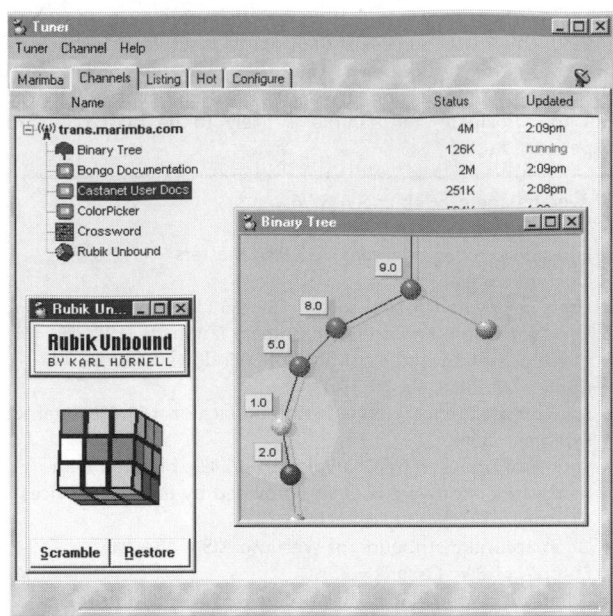

Figure 2. Marimba Corporation's Castanet tuner with two channels open, one which animates binary tree growth as random values are inserted, and the other which supports interactive Rubik cube play.

Finally, the concept of a relying on a single predefined document-structure language has been challenged. Motivated by the rapid and seemingly uncontrolled movement of HTML standards away from structure and toward format, new languages like the eXtensible Markup Language (XML) are undergoing development. XML is an application tool which seeks to render both HTML and Standard Generalized Markup Language (SGML) interoperable on the Web. In a sense, XML is an attempt to reunite HTML with its SGML roots by overcoming the former's penchant for format considerations while supporting a broader range of page design for multimedia applications. By incorporating "personal" or "group-oriented" tags, XML also overcomes a fundamental weakness in HTML, namely that HTML document structure is static between users. XML overcomes this by allowing individualized document designs. (*See* http://www.w3.org/XML/).

CGI, plug-ins, executable content, push technology, and HTML extensions represent significant departures from the original browser-centric paradigm of Web information exchange, and add considerably to Web capabilities.

Surfing the Web

The Web itself, as well as its growth and development, would have been impossible without programs called *browsers* which allow access to the pages of the Web, but in order to search for information efficiently it was necessary to develop utilities called *search engines*. The use of browsers and search engines together is often called *surfing* the Web. Actually, since the Web is now used for many applications (e.g. financial applications, telephony) in addition to searching for information, these search engines have now become *portals* to the services available on the Web.

BROWSERS

General properties. The central software for browsing the Web is the navigator/browser, or simply, the *browser*. A browser is a client-side program which provides the interface capability to the Web. This software opens a window on the desktop which handles the information exchange with the relevant server. Specifically, this includes the formal request of information from the server (via the URL) and the rendering of that information on the desktop. In the earliest days of the Web, this rendering was restricted to text. Since the early 1990s, rendering has been extended to virtually the full range of multimedia.

A Website may contain a cluster of documents and resources. When a document or resource fits within a single browser window (which may be larger than the browser's viewing window), it is referred to as a Web page or Web document. When this Web page is the primary page of an entire Web site, it is called a home page for that site. Examples of home pages include splash pages, which are best seen as multimedia "enticements" to the site, and pass-through pages which serve as navigational or routing menus for visitors. The advantage of home pages is that they are frequently mnemonically associated with the host (e.g. `http://www.ibm.com`, `http://www.acm.org`) and thus provide a unifying effect on the entire Website.

Other pages on the site and which are linked (perhaps indirectly) to the home page are said to be *derivative* of the home page. As an example, the homepage for the XYZ Corporation might be `http://www.XYZ.com/homepage.html`. If no HTML page is specified, the default page or file is assumed to be `index.html`. Thus, the links `http://www.XYZ.com/index.html` and `http://www.XYZ.com` will have the same effect on the browser. It is common to structure Web sites hierarchically, either in terms of the contained links, or in terms of the underlying file structure on the server, or both. In this manner, the URL `http://www.XYZ.com/corporate_officers/` would refer to the subdirectory "`corporate_officers`" beneath the root directory of the Website (named `public_html` on the server machine). A browser would look for a file called "`index.html`" in that subdirectory for information on what to display. However, more complex Websites may eschew the simplicity of hierarchical organization for more complex network models.

Commercial products. In its earliest days, the popularity of the World Wide Web was inextricably linked to one browser, Mosaic, developed at the National Center for Supercomputing Applications. While Mosaic was but one of several competing Web-based browsers available at that time, it quickly displaced the others as the dominant environment for taking in the Web experience. By 1993 Mosaic had more than 90% of the browser market and became the design standard against which all other browsers would be compared for years to come. In 1994, the primary designer and developer of Mosaic, Marc Andreessen, went on to co-found Netscape Communications, whose Netscape Communicator became the *de facto* standard for second-generation Web browsers (*see* Fig. 3). In 1999, the browser market was about evenly split between Netscape and the latest entry into the so-called browser war, Microsoft's Internet Explorer. Both products are currently available as standalone products or bundled with other programs like text editors, email facilities, graphics packages, and office productivity applications. (For information on the history of browser features, see the World Wide Web Test Pattern at `http://www.uark.edu/~wrg/`). The "findings of fact" in November 1999 by Judge Thomas Penfield Jackson in the US Department of Justice prosecution of Microsoft may result in a lessening of Microsoft's advantages in its "browser war" with Netscape (*see also* MICROSOFT).

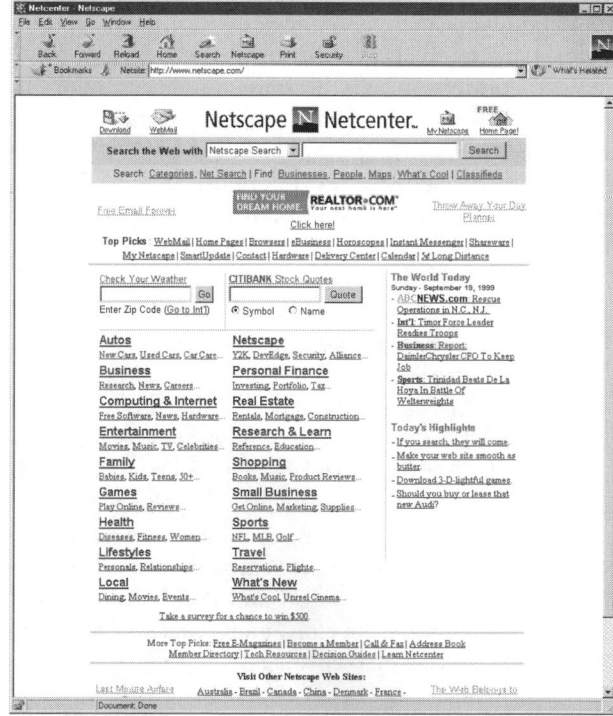

Figure 3. Netscape Navigator 4.5 is a recent generic "navigator/browser" from Netscape Corporation. Displayed is Netscape's Netcenter portal page, which acts as a gateway to Web content.

SEARCH ENGINES

With millions of Websites and Web pages and an astonishing growth rate, a major issue for users is finding relevant information. To meet the need, several search engines have evolved, such as Yahoo!, Excite, AltaVista, Lycos, Webcrawler, Northern Light, Infoseek, Hotbot, Snap, Google, and many others. (Some search engines, such as Yahoo!, whose information is compiled by human editors who search the Web, are perhaps better called *directories* to distinguish them from others whose information is compiled from automated searches of the Web.) Each browser contains a "search" link that leads to a particular search engine, or list of engines. Alternatively, the user who wants to call a particular engine can either recall a link to it from a list of *bookmarked* sites or, if known not to be there, enter its URL from the keyboard.

Users may query search engines using keywords or key phrases. Most engines support complex Boolean operations. For example, one can ask to find all Websites that refer to "strike AND delivery BUT NOT (baseball OR bowling)." Some engines also have proximity operators that allow one to search for occurrences of "encyclopedia NEAR computer." The exact syntax of the request depends on the search engine; there is as yet no standard query format. In addition to the general search engines, there are also search engine sites that specialize in searches for a host of applications in such areas as law, medicine, and health.

To maximize effective service to their users, search engines cruise or "crawl through" the Internet, more or less continuously, searching for information in Websites. Information may be sought in the complete text of the site or just on its page headers; thus Website developers can attract the attention of more search engines by placing certain keywords or phrases at or near the top of their Web pages in attempts to attract more "hits," that is, accesses of their Website. Some search engine companies, most notably Yahoo!, enhance their database of Websites through use of human editors who also create taxonomies and directories in which Websites are catalogued. To gain the attention of these human catalogers, Website creators may also formally register their site with particular search engines, either one by one or by using the services of a third party Internet company which, for a fee, will register a Website with many search engines. Through a combination of registration and their own exploration, search engines develop many pages of information about millions of Websites.

There is an indication, however, that search engine data collection cannot keep pace with the rapid growth of the Internet. The research of Lawrence and Giles (1999) indicates that there are now at least 800 million Web pages, and that the leading search engine (Northern Light at the time of their survey) had indexed only 16% of them. Only two years before, Hotbot, the leading engine of 1997, had indexed 34% (of a far smaller number of pages). In desperation, many users turn to "meta engines" which delegate queries to a number of engines and collect and merge their results, raising coverage to about 42% of the Web. Among these are http://www.metacrawler.com, http://www.metasearch.com, and http://www.dogpile.com.

Another way to manage the growth of information on the Web is to classify its importance to enable users to find the most useful sites. Yahoo's human-constructed directories are one attempt to do this. The experimental CLEVER project explores the graph-like structure of the Web to find sites that are frequently linked-to ("authorities") and those that contain numerous links to such sites ("hubs"). CLEVER can then respond to a query by giving a list of hubs and authorities for the topic, and thus help to guide a search. See http://www.almaden.ibm.com/cs/k53/clever.html and (Clever Project, 1999).

The Lawrence-Giles data also shows the diversification of categories of Web sites. The leading category was "Scientific/Educational," at 6%. "Health" was next at 3%, with categories called "Personal" and "Societies" at about 2% each. What will be surprising to many readers and users (because of the disproportionate amount of email spamming (junk mail) that they generate) is that "pornography" servers account for less than 2% of all Websites.

Most search engine companies base their revenue on the sale of advertising which, in turn, is based upon the number of downloads or page hits that they can offer to an advertiser. The more popular the engine, the higher the price charged.

The Web as a Social Phenomenon

The social effect of the Web remains poorly understood. Not surprisingly, the zeal to harness and exploit the richness of Web resources and technology, combined with the desire to capitalize on commercial Web services, have taken precedence over efforts to understand the social dimensions of Web use.

Much of what little we know of Web behavior seems to be derived from two disparate sources. Descriptive statistics produced by the Web surveys are most useful to measure isolated events and independent activities such as, for example, the number of Windows users who use Netscape, Explorer, or some other browser.

The second source is the study of the use of email. Email's status as a *de facto* paradigm of "interpersonal though not-in-person communication" makes it a useful testbench for testing hypotheses about network behavior, generally. Since email and the Web share several characteristics (e.g. they both minimize the effects of geographical distance between users; they are both based on user-centric models of communication; both rely on self-imposed interrupts, both are paperless and archivable by default, both create potential security and privacy problems, and neither requires continuous endpoint-to-endpoint network connectivity), email can teach us something about Web behavior.

However, both sources provide incomplete views of Web behavior. Descriptive statistics tell us little about either the causes of emerging trends or the connections and associations between various aspects of Web use (e.g. to what extent, if any, do anonymous Web engagements promote discussion of controversial topics?).

There are differences between email and the Web as well. Email deals with network, peer-to-peer communication partnerships, whereas the present Web remains primarily an information-delivery system. Email, in its most basic form at least, exemplifies *push technology*, while the current Web is mostly *pull* oriented. Of course, the onset of new technologies such as Web teleconferencing and virtual communities will change the nature of such comparisons.

While definitive conclusions about the social aspects of Web use remain elusive, at least some central issues have been identified for future study (*see* Table 2).

We are slowly coming to understand the capabilities of the Web for selected applications and venues. To illustrate, early use convincingly demonstrated that the Web was a popular and worthwhile medium for presenting distributed multimedia, even though we cannot yet quantify the social benefits and institutional costs which result from this use. As CGI was added to the Web, it became clear that the Web would provide important location-independent, multi-modal interactivity, although we know little about the motivations behind such interactivity, and even less about how one would measure the long-term utility for the participants and their institutions.

Virtual Communities

The Web's primary utility at the moment is as an information delivery device, what some authors have called the "document phase" of the Web. However, more powerful and robust Web applications are beginning to take hold. Perhaps the most significant future application will involve the construction of *virtual communities*. Virtual, or electronic, communities, are examples of interactive and participatory forums conducted over digital networks for the mutual benefit of participants and sponsors. They may take on any number of forms. The first attempts to establish virtual communities dates back to the mid-1980s with the community, "freenet" movement. While early freenets offered few services beyond email and Telnet, many quickly expanded to offer access to documents in local libraries and government offices, Internet relay chats, community bulletin boards (*q.v.*), and so forth, thereby giving participants an enhanced sense of community through another form of connectivity. Virtual communities of the future are likely to have both advantages and disadvantages when compared to their conventional counterparts (Table 3).

Table 2. Social issues and Web behavior.

- To what extent can the effects of information overload be avoided by advanced information retrieval methods?
- To what extent will future interactive and participatory Web engagements become enticing and immersive?
- What are the advantages and disadvantages of anonymous engagement?
- What virtues are there in quasi-independent and relative-identity environments ?
- To what extent will Web use enhance or supplement alternative modes of information exchange?
- To what extent will the Web increase intellectual quality and economy?
- To what degree will complete geographical transparency be realized? How long will it take before Web access moves beyond technologically advanced nations and regions?
- What rules will govern self-organizing and self-administering virtual communities of the future? How will that affect socialization?
- How will electronic communities of the future enhance and complement their physical counterparts?

Table 3. Potential advantages and disadvantages of electronic communities.

Advantages
- Potential for dynamic involvement where membership may be transitory and the infrastructure of the community informally defined.
- Location transparency for members, as all electronic communities are potentially global.
- Capability of self-administration and self-organization by a membership in continuous flux.
- Creation of "thought swarms" through the continuous, interactive stimulation of participants.
- Increased attention on content.

Disadvantages
- Quality of experience may not justify the participation, or may degrade over time.
- Potential loss of privacy by invasive Web technologies such as cookies, CGI environment variable recording, and the like.
- Some forms of electronic communication lack intensity, and some may lack content (e.g. more information exchange does not imply better information exchange).
- Not all experiences translate well into the electronic realm, as documented by the easy misinterpretation of email and the "flaming" that can ensue.

Conclusion

The World Wide Web represents the closest technology to the ideal of a completely distributed network environment for multiform communication. As such, it may be thought of as a paradigm shift away from earlier network protocols. Many feel that the most significant impact of the Web will not be felt until later in the 21st century, when technologies are added to make the Web fully interactive, participatory, and immersive by default.

Bibliography

1996. Berners-Lee, T. "WWW: Past, Present and Future," *Computer*, **29**, *10*, 69–77.

1997. Berghel, H. "Email: The Good, the Bad and the Ugly," *Comm. of the ACM*, **40**, *4*, 11–15.

1997. Reid, R. H. *Architects of the Web*. New York: John Wiley.

1999. Berghel, H. "The Client Side of the Web," in *Encyclopedia of Library and Information Science*. **24**, 39–51. Marcel Dekker: New York.

1999. Berghel, H., and Blank, D. "The World Wide Web," in *Advances in Computing* (ed. M. Zaelkowitz), **48**, 178–218. New York: Academic Press.

1999. Berners-Lee, T., with Fischetti, M. *Weaving the Web: The Original Design and Ultimate Destiny of the World Wide Web*. New York: HarperCollins.

1999. Comer, D. E., and Droms, R. E. *Computer Networks and Internets*, 2nd Ed. Upper Saddle River, NJ: Prentice Hall. (An excellent source for the Internet and the Web.)

1999. Lawrence, S., and Giles, C. L. "Accessibility of Information on the Web," *Nature*, **400**, *6740* (8 July), 107–109.

1999. Members of the *Clever* Project. "Hypersearching the Web," *Scientific American*, **280**, *6* (June), 54–60.

Hal Berghel

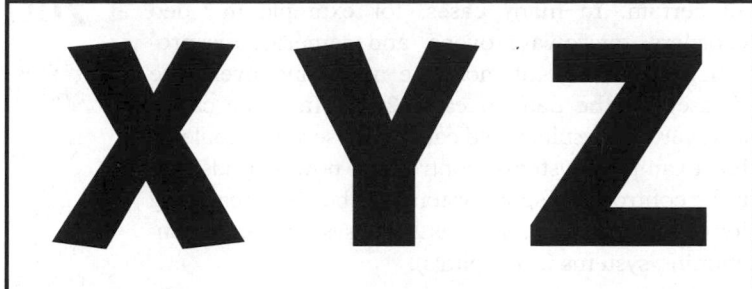

XML

See MARKUP LANGUAGES.

Y2K PROBLEM

For articles on related subjects *see* BUG; and ERRORS.

When explaining this problem (though also called the Millennium Bug, it is not really a bug but is a result of poor design of computer systems), it is difficult to believe that it could happen at all, let alone be one of the major computing problems for the end of the 20th century. Estimates of the cost of rectifying the problem vary, but figures of hundreds of billions of dollars worldwide are often quoted.

The problem is extremely simple. In many early computer systems, the year was represented by two digits in order to save space. The fact that the century digits were "19" was implicit. It is ironic that non-character representations (e.g. binary) would have saved the space without producing the problem. However, character representations were easier and also made debugging (*q.v.*) programs simpler since dates could easily be seen in alphanumeric dumps (*q.v.*). Much of today's problem can also be attributed to the limited capacity of 1940s and 1950s vintage punched cards (*q.v.*); to devote two more of a card's precious 80 columns to hold "19" seemed extravagant to data processing personnel of that era.

Forty years ago a byte of storage cost *one million times* what it does now. As storage became cheaper, it would not have been difficult to use four digits for the year. Not only did this rarely happen, but many old programs which were not originally expected to be in use for more than a few years are still being used, 10, 20 or 30 years after they were written.

The above problem is only one of many date problems which might occur around the turn of a century. Another one is that the solar year and calendar year do not coincide, the former being about 365.25 days long. To correct for this, "leap years" were introduced adding an extra day every four years. But this was still inexact, so century years are generally not leap years. However, to make yet another correction, a year which is a multiple of 400 *is* a leap year. Thus 1800 and 1900 are not leap years, whereas 2000 will be. In this case, a little knowledge is dangerous—not being aware of the century rule would have led to the correct result in 2000.

Various other software uses different means of calculating time. For example, the Unix (*q.v.*) operating system counts in seconds from the beginning of 1970. On a computer with 32-bit words, this will lead to overflow in 2038.

To solve these date problems (especially "the Y2K problem"—or "the Year 2000 problem") requires examining each piece of hardware and software in use. Although it is obvious that computers, including PCs, may be affected, there are also a very large number of devices and systems in which computer chips are embedded. In some cases, the chips don't even use the date but may have it built in; in such cases, it is unlikely that this would cause problems—but it is not certain. In many cases, for example in video recorders, microwave ovens, and cameras, the problem would cause at most the minor inconvenience of resetting the date in early 2000. In some cases, however, the results could cause very serious problems (for example, systems controlling power grids, air traffic control, transport systems) or be life-threatening (for example, devices such as X-ray systems or air conditioning systems in hospitals).

At the time of writing (mid-1999) it is almost certainly too late to complete all the work required to check all systems for "Year 2000" compliance, so many companies are not only checking just their major systems but are putting into place contingency plans. For some time, credit card companies would not issue cards with an expiration date of "00". Airlines said that they might cancel flights near 1 January 2000.

The cost may be enormous. The UK Government has estimated that the total cost to the UK would be about $50 billion. A report by Software Productivity Research in the USA estimates that initial software repairs are likely to cost $71 billion, but with other costs, including hardware replacement, this is likely to rise to $176 billion with a potential $100 billion extra in litigation and damages. But such estimates must be viewed with a great deal of caution, and on detailed examination, many estimates have been reduced.

Obviously the cost worldwide could be higher than the above, and all to save two characters in the representation of dates and times.

Bibliography

There are a number of books on the topic, and their number is likely to increase significantly up to 2000 and perhaps for years afterwards when the problem is analyzed in retrospect.

1997. Ulrich, W. M., and Hayes, I. S. *The Year 2000 Software Crisis: Challenge of the Century.* Upper Saddle River, NJ: Prentice Hall.
1999. Fallows, J. "Hurry Up Please, It's Time," *The New York Review of Books,* **XLVI**, 14 (23 September), 29–34.
1999. Unhelkar, B., Zamir, S., and Due, R. *After the Y2K Fireworks.* Boca Raton, FL: CRC Press.

Websites

The Year 2000 Information Center. http://www.year2000.com.
Year 2000 Technical Audit Center. http://www.auditserve.com.
Institute of Electrical Engineers (UK). http://www.iee.org.uk/2000risk/.
Computer Professionals for Social Responsibility. http://www.cpsr.org/program/y2k/.
UK National Health Service. http://www.imc.exec.nhs.uk/2000/.

Adrian Stokes

ZUSE COMPUTERS

For articles on related subjects *see* DIGITAL COMPUTERS, HISTORY OF; and ZUSE, KONRAD.

Konrad Zuse and the computer company he headed designed and built a number of computers between 1938 and 1969. The first four, which he called Z1 through Z4, have a special place in the history of computing.

Because the Second World War isolated him from the Anglo-American computing mainstream, Zuse's early machines embody genuinely different design alternatives to those produced in that mainstream. Thus, study of the Zuse designs raises the historical question of the extent to which the nature of modern computer architecture reflects "laws" of computer science that are independent of social and cultural forces.

The Z1, begun in 1936 and completed in 1938, used an arrangement of slotted metal plates through which pins passed to store, read, and write binary digits. Calculation was effected by similar mechanical interlocks that provided the fundamental Boolean operations. Zuse knew of binary arithmetic before he turned to building computers and then independently discovered its relation to Boolean logic while working on the arithmetic unit of the Z1. This computer never worked properly, however, due to difficulties he had in joining its arithmetic and memory units.

The failure of Z1 led Zuse to use surplus telephone relays instead of mechanical devices to perform arithmetic for his second machine, the Z2. The Z2, completed in 1939, was built in a workshop at Zuse's parents' Berlin apartment and was successfully demonstrated before the German Aerodynamics Research Institute (AVA) that same year.

With funds from the German military, Zuse built the Z3 (finished in 1941), the first of his machines to work reliably in all respects. The Z3 used 1,800 telephone relays for memory, 600 for calculation, and 200 for sequence control. Sequences were encoded in 8-bit code by manually punching holes onto strips of discarded 35 mm movie film. The computer executed linear sequences with no provision for conditional jumps. Operations included ordinary arithmetic, square root, store and recall from memory, and binary–decimal conversion. The Z3 had a memory of 64 22-bit floating-point numbers consisting of 7 bits for the base-2 exponent, 1 bit for the sign, and 14 for the mantissa. Clock speed was about 4 to 5 Hz, with one multiplication taking about 3 to 5 seconds. The Z3 was completed in early December 1941, and essentially ran only test programs until its destruction in a bombing raid on Berlin in 1944.

Figure 1. The Zuse Z4 computer.

From 1942 to 1945, Zuse built the Z4, a much more capable machine and one that stands with the Harvard Mark I and the Bell Labs relay computers (*q.v.*) as a mature and sophisticated digital computer. For the Z4, Zuse returned to the mechanical memory of his first two computers.

When the Z4 was finally completed in 1949, it had a memory of 64 32-bit words and a very sophisticated instruction set (*q.v.*) (Fig. 1). Although it did not store its programs internally, it nonetheless served as the inspiration for much theoretical work in programming and programming languages, by Zuse himself as well as by Heinz Rutishauser and a number of other continental European researchers. This was at a time when operational digital computers were rare or inaccessible, especially for those not in England or the United States.

Zuse's computers were characterized by electromechanical technology, binary floating-point arithmetic, and a simple and clean logical structure. Their existence supports the argument that binary logic and a separation of memory and processing units are fundamental to computer science, regardless of cultural heritage.

Bibliography

1980. Speiser, A. P. "The Relay Calculator Z4," *IEEE Annals of the History of Computing*, **2**, 3 (July), 242–245.
1997. Rojas, R. "Konrad Zuse's Legacy: The Architecture of the Z1 and Z3," *IEEE Annals of the History of Computing*, **19**, 2 (April–June), 5–16.

Websites

Zuse, H. *The Life and Work of Konrad Zuse*:
  http://www.cs.tu-berlin.de/~zuse/hc.html.
  http://www.epemag.com/zuse.

Paul E. Ceruzzi

ZUSE, KONRAD

For articles on related subjects *see* DIGITAL COMPUTERS, HISTORY OF: ORIGINS, and EARLY; and ZUSE COMPUTERS.

Figure 1. Konrad Zuse at the rebuilt Z3 computer, 1984. (Courtesy of Dr. Ing. Horst Zuse, Berlin.)

Konrad Zuse (b. 1910 in Berlin, d. 1995 in Bonn) (Fig. 1) studied construction engineering at the Technische Hochschule Berlin-Charlottenburg and received the degree Dipl. Ing. in 1935. In 1934, he had already started development work on program-controlled computing machines with electromechanical and mechanical elements. He felt that the tiresome calculations required in this field should be done by a machine. In 1938, he had completed his first model (Z1). In 1941, his first fully working machine (Z3) was operational; it used the binary number system with floating-point arithmetic. Zuse invented a relay adder in which four relays produced the sum of two binary places and that, in an *n*-place binary adder, yields the *n*-place sum in one switching step.

During the next four years, Zuse built a number of special machines and the all-purpose relay computer Z4. The Z3 was destroyed by bombs in 1944 (it was reconstructed in the 1960s), but the Z4 was saved, and in 1950 it was installed at the Eidgenössische Technische Hochschule in Zürich. In 1954, the Z4 was moved to St. Louis, near Basel, where it was operated for five years. Around 1945, when facilities for circuit development were not available to Zuse, he turned to programming and designing an algorithmic language, which he called Plankalkül (Bauer and Wössner, 1972). Its notation was in a kind of matrix form, and it could be used for both numerical and nonnumerical problems (Zuse used it to describe a full chess program).

In 1949, Zuse formed his own company ZUSE KG, and went into manufacturing. In 1952 he built the largest relay computer in West Germany, the Z5, which consisted of 2400 relays and a 12-word memory with a word length of 36 bits. His first successful serial product was Z11, a relay computer for geodetical and optical applications. His second product was Z22, a vacuum-tube computer (later replaced by its transistorized version Z23); it had an extremely flexible instruction code, achieved by a set of functional bits, an early form of microprogramming (*q.v.*). The first of 50 Z22 computers was delivered in 1958; it was the first tube computer sold commercially in Germany. There were 98 installations of its succesor, the Z23. In 1958, Zuse published one of his ideas that was ahead of his time. This was the field computer, a parallel processor (*q.v.*) especially suited for differential equations. In the same year, he designed a computer-controlled plotter called Z64, or Graphomat.

After a number of financial difficulties, Zuse left ZUSE KG, which was absorbed by Siemens AG in 1969. Three years before he had become a professor at the University of Göttingen.

In 1956, Zuse received his first honorary doctoral degree of Dr.-Ing. from the Technische Universität Charlottenburg in Berlin. In Bonn in 1964, he received the Werner von Siemens Ring; in 1965, the Harry Goode Memorial Award from AFIPS; in 1969, the German Diesel Medal; in the same year, the Austrian Exner Medal; and, in 1975, on his 65th birthday, appointment as an Honorary Citizen of Huenfeld. Zuse has received eight honorary doctoral degrees (Berlin 1956, Hamburg 1979, Dresden 1981, Reykjavik 1986, Dortmund 1991, ETH-Zurich 1991, Hochschule Weimar 1991 and Sienna 1992) and he is an Honorary Professor at the Göttingen University. The IEEE Pioneers Award was presented to him in 1982.

Zuse received four high German distinctions: two federal, one of Berlin, and one Bavarian. He was an Honorary Member of the Academia Leopoldina in Halle, a Foreign Associate of the US National Academy of Engineering, and an Honorary Member of the German Society for Informatics (GI).

The achievements of Zuse can be properly evaluated only if his isolation is taken into account. His background was construction engineering, and he knew practically nothing about other computer developments (in Germany or abroad, in his time or earlier) until a very late stage. During all his life, Zuse received too little understanding and support. The German military had no interest in his work, and while the German Research Council after the war did its best to support him, their efforts were not enough to keep his company alive.

Two ZUSE medals are awarded every year, one by the German Building Industry and one by the Gesellschaft für Informatik (GI).

From 1970 until his death in 1995, Zuse became an accomplished painter of abstract art. Some of his paintings and his work on computing may be viewed at:

```
http://www.rtd-net.de/Zusepictures.html
http://www.rtd-net.de/Zusepictures2.html.
```

Two other examples of his art may be seen on Color Page CP-16.

The editors and the author are grateful to Horst Zuse for new information used in this profile of his father.

Bibliography

1972. Bauer, F. L., and Wössner, H. "The Plankalkül of Konrad Zuse: A Forerunner of Today's Programming Languages," *Comm. of the ACM*, **15**, 678–685.
1978. *Proceedings of the SEAS Anniversary Meeting in West Berlin:* "General Considerations of the Evolution of Computers."
1983. Ceruzzi, P. "Computers in Germany," in *Reckoners*, 10–42. Westport, CO: Greenwood Press.
1986. Zuse, K. *Memoirs (Der Computer—mein Lebenswerk)*, 2nd Ed. Berlin: Springer-Verlag.
1993. Zuse, K. *The Computer—My Life*. New York: Springer-Verlag.

Websites

Zuse, H. *The Life and Work of Konrad Zuse*:
```
http://www.cs.tu-berlin.de/~zuse/hc.html.
http://www.epemag.com/zuse.
```

Heinz Zemanek

Appendix I

ABBREVIATIONS AND ACRONYMS

Computing people abbreviate terms and coin acronyms at a rapid rate. The first list that follows contains acronyms used in this Encyclopedia but not necesarily all of those invented by authors strictly for local use in their articles. It also contains additional entries that are in common use in computer magazines and more formal computing literature, but not abbreviations for common units of measurement. Acronyms are alphabetized without regard for special characterssuch as hyphens and solidi since they are not usually pronounced; for example, A/D is listed just ahead of ADAPSO, not ahead of AAAI as it would have if they were ASCII-significant. A bracketed letter used as a suffix, OOP[S] for example, means that a variant that includes that letter is sometimes used and sometimes not. Inside braces, exactly one of the items separated by "|" ("or") must be chosen, e.g. PB{D|E} means that both PBD and PBE are valid acronyms with similar meanings. Parenthesized terms such as (logic) are used to indicate context. Readers should also be alert to the many acronyms that have multiple meanings. Certain acronym explications contain another acronym in the list in order to stress the interrelationship. The second list contains commonly used file extensions. Websites that maintain extensive acronym lists are http://www.ucc.ie/cgi-bin/acronym/ and http://www.cis.columbia.edu/glossary.html.

AAAI	American Association of Artificial Intelligence
AAF	Advanced Authoring Format
ABC	Atanasoff–Berry Computer
ABET	Accreditation Board for Engineering and Technology
ABI	Application Binary Interface
ABR	Available Bit Rate
AC(C)	Accumulator
ACDI	Asynchronous Communications Device Interface
ACE	Automatic Computing Engine
ACH	Association for Computing in the Humanities
ACH	Automated Clearing House
ACID	Atomicity, Consistency, Isolation, and Durability
ACK	Acknowledgement
ACL	Association for Computational Linguistics
ACM	Association for Computing Machinery
ACP	Accelerated Graphics Port

ACPI	Advanced Configuration and Power Interface
ACTRAN	Analog Computer Translator
A/D	Analog to Digital
ADAPSO	Association of Data Processing Service Organizations
ADB	Apple Desktop Bus
ADI	American Documentation Institute
ADO	ActiveX Data Object
ADP	Automatic Data Processing
ADPCM	Adaptive Differential Pulse Code Modulation
ADSL	Asymmetric Digital Subscriber Line
ADT	Abstract Data Type
AED	Automated Engineering Design
AEDS	Association for Educational Data Systems
AESC	American Engineering Standards Committee
AFCET	Association Française pour la Cybernétique Économique et Technique
AFDW	Active Framework for Data Warehousing
AFIPS	American Federation of Information Processing Societies
AFS	Andrew File System (Carnegie Mellon)
AGP	Accelerated Graphics Port
AHPL	A Hardware Programming Language
AI	Artificial Intelligence
AIAA	American Institute of Aeronautics and Astronautics
AIEE	American Institute of Electrical Engineers
AIML	Astronomical Instrument Markup Language
AL	Artificial Life
AL	Assembly Language
ALGOL	ALGOrithmic Language
ALLC	Association for Literary and Linguistic Computing
ALP	Abductive Logic Programming
ALPAC	Automatic Language Processing Committee
ALU	Arithmetic-Logic Unit
ALWAC	Axel L. Wenner-(Gren) Automatic Computer
AM	Amplitude Modulation
AMI	Alternate Mark Inversion
AMLCD	Active Matrix Liquid Crystal Display
AMP	Access Module Processor
AMPS	Advanced Mobile Phone Service
AMS	American Mathematical Society
AMT	Address Mapping Table
ANN	Artificial Neural Network
ANSI	American National Standards Institute
ANSVIP	American National Standard Vocabulary for Information Processing
AOL	America OnLine
AP	Argument Pointer
APA	All Points Addressable
APC	Asynchronous Procedure Call
APCUG	Association of PC User Groups
APEC	Automated Procedures for Engineering Consultants
API	Applications Programming Interface
APL	A Programming Language
APM	Advanced Power Management
APPC	Advanced Program to Program Communication
APS	American Physical Society
APSE	Ada Program Support Environment
APT	Automatic Programmed Tool
ARIES	Automated Reliability Estimation Program

ARP	Address Resolution Protocol
ARPA	Advanced Research Projects Agency
ARPANET	ARPA NETwork
ARQ	Automatic Repeat Request
ART	Advanced Reasoning Tool
ASA	American Standards Association
ASA	American Statistical Association
ASC	Accredited Standards Committee
ASC	Advanced Scientific Computer
ASCI	Accelerated Strategic Computing Initiative
ASCII	American Standard Code for Information Interchange
ASF	Active Streaming Format
ASIC	Application-Specific Integrated Circuit
ASIP	Application-Specific Integrated Processor
ASIS	American Society for Information Science
ASL	Available Space List
ASM	Association for Systems Management
ASP	Active Server Page
ASTM	American Society for Testing Materials
AT&T	American Telephone & Telegraph
ATC	Address Translation Cache
ATDM	Asynchronous Time-Division Multiplexing
ATM	Asynchronous Transfer Mode
ATM	Automated Teller Machine
ATS	Administrative Terminal System
ATSU	Association of Time-Sharing Users
AUP	Acceptable Use Policy
AUUA	America's Univac Users Association
AVI	Audio/Video Interface
AVL	Adel'son-Vel'skii and Landis (tree)
AWC	Association for Women in Computing
AWK	Aho, Weinberger, and Kernighan (Unix tool)
B2B	Business to Business
BASIC	Beginners' All-Purpose Symbolic Instruction Code
BBN	Bolt Beranek and Newman
BB[S]	Bulletin Board [System]
BCD	Binary-Coded Decimal
BCNF	Boyce-Codd Normal Form
BCPL	Basic Combined Programming Language
BCS	British Computer Society
BCTIC	Biomedical Computing Technology Information Center
BDAM	Basic Direct Access Method
BDD	Binary Decision Diagram
BDP	Business Data Processing
BEDO	Burst EDO
BEMA	Business Equipment Manufacturers Association
BeOS	Be (Corporation) OS
BER	Bit Error Rate
BFS	Breadth-First Search
BGP	Border Gateway Protocol
BICS	Brigham (and Women's Hospital) Integrated Computing System
BINAC	BInary Northrop Automatic Computer
BIOS	Basic Input–Output System
BIP	Block-Iterative Projection
BISAC	Book Industries Systems Advisory Committee

BISAM	Basic Indexed Sequential Access Method
B-ISDN	Broadband ISDN
BISYNC	Binary Synchronous Communications Protocol
BIT	Binary digIT
BITNET	Because Its Time NET
BJT	Bipolar Junction Transistor
BLISS	Basic Language for Implementation of System Software
BMD	Biomedical (Computer Programs)
BMDP	Biomedical (Computer Programs—P Series)
BMP	BitMap Picture
BMTI	Block Mode Terminal Interface
BNF	Backus–Naur Form
BOA	Basic Object Adapter
BOC	Bell Operating Company
BOCA	Borland Object Component Architecture
BSAM	Basic Sequential Access Method
BSD	Berkeley Software Distribution (version of Unix)
BSML	BioSequence Markup Language
BSP	Bulk Synchronous Parallel (model)
BSP	Burroughs Scientific Processor
BTAM	Basic Telecommunications Access Method
BTL	Branching Temporal Logic
CA	Cellular Automaton
CACM	Communications of the Association for Computing Machinery
CAD	Computer-Aided Design
CAD/CAM	Computer-Aided Design/Computer-Aided Manufacturing
CADD	Computer-Aided Design and Drafting
CADMIUM	Computer Assisted Decision Making for Image Understanding in Medicine
CAE	Computer-Aided Education
CAE	Computer-Aided Engineering
CAI	Computer-Assisted Instruction
CAL	Computer-Assisted Learning
CALS	Computer-Aided Acquisition in Logistic Support
CALT	Computer-Assisted Learning and Teaching
CAM	Computer-Aided Manufacturing
CAN	Computer Architecture News
CAPP	Computer-Aided Process Planning
CAPTAIN	Character And Pattern Telephone Access Information Network
CAR	Contents of Address part of Register (Lisp)
CARE	Computer-Aided Reliability Estimation
CART	Classification and Regression Tree
CAS	Communicating Applications Specification
CASE	Computer-Aided Software Engineering
CAT	Computer-Assisted Teaching
CAT	Computerized Axial Tomography
CATV	CAble TeleVision
CAUSE	College and University System Exchange
CAV	Constant Angular Velocity
CAVE	Computer Automatic Virtual Environment
CBCT	Customer-Bank Communication Terminal
CBE	Computer-Based Education
CBEMA	Computer and Business Equipment Manufacturers Association
CBF	Charles Babbage Foundation
CBI	Charles Babbage Institute
CBIS	Computer-Based Information System

CBL	Computer-Based Learning
CBR	CASE-Based Reasoning
CBR	Constant Bit Rate
CBT	Computer-Based Training
CC	Compiler-Compiler
CC	Computer Conferencing
CC	Courtesy Copy (formerly Carbon Copy)
CCD	Charge-Coupled Device
CCIIT	Comité Consultatif Internationale Télégraphique et Téléphonique
CC-NUMA	Cache Coherent NUMA
CCP	Certified Computer Professional
CCR	Conditional Critical Region
CCS	Calculus of Communicating Systems
CCS	Common Channel Signaling
CCS	Common Communications Services
CCS	Computer Conferencing System
CD	Compact Disc
CDB	Command Descriptor Block
CDC	Control Data Corporation
CD-I	Compact Disc—Interactive
CDL	Command Definition Language
CDL	Computer Description Language
CDL	Computer Design Language
CDM	Code Division Multiplexing
CDMA	Code Division Multiple Access
CD-MO	Compact Disc—Magneto Optical
CDO	Collaboration Data Object
CDP	Certificate in Data Processing
CDPD	Cellular Digital Packet Data
CDR	Contents of Decrement part of Register (Lisp)
CD-R	Compact Disc—Recordable (WORM drive)
CD-R/E	Compact Disc—Recordable/Erasable
CD-ROM	Compact Disc—Read Only Memory
CD-RW	Compact Disc—ReWritable
CDT	Center for Democracy and Technology
CE	Consumer Electronics
CE	Compact Environment (operating system)
CEPA	Civil Engineering Programming Applications
CEPT	European Council of Postal and Telecommunications administration
CEPTA	Council of European Postal Telecommunications Authorities
CERN	Conseil Européan pour la Recherche Nucléaire
CERT	Computer Emergency Response Team
CG	Computer Graphics
CGA	Color Graphics Adapter
CGI	Common Gateway Interface
CGI	Computer Graphics Interface
CGM	Computer Graphics Metafile
CGRM	Computer Graphics Reference Model
CHAP	Challenge Handshake Authentication Protocol
CHIPS	Clearing House Interbank Payments System
CHRP	Common Hardware Reference Platform
CICS	Customer Information Control Systems
CID	Connected Internet Device
CIDR	Classless InterDomain Routing
CIE	Computer-Integrated Enterprise
CIFS	Common Internet File System

CII	Compagnie Internationale pour Informatique
CIM	Computer Input from Microfilm
CIM	Computer-Integrated Manufacturing
CIPS	Canadian Information Processing Society
CIR	CORBA Interface Repository
CIS	Cybernetic Information Systems
CISC	Complex Instruction Set Computer
CISI	Compagnie Internationale de Services et Informatique
CIX	Commercial Internet Exchange
CJK	Chinese–Japanese–Korean script
CL	Command Language
CLI	Command Language Interface
CLOS	Common Lisp Object System
CLP	Cell Loss Priority
CLP	Constraint Logic Programming
CLSR	Computer Law Service Reporter
CLV	Constant Linear Velocity
CMC	Computer-Mediated Communications
CMCS	Computer-Mediated Communications System
CMI	Computer-Managed Instruction
CMIP	Common Management Information Protocol
CML	Chemical Markup Language
CMM	Capability Maturity Model
C.mmp	Carnegie Multi-Mini Processor
CMOS	Complementary Metal-Oxide Semiconductor
CMOT	CMIP Over TCP/IP
CMP	Chemical Mechanical Polishing
CMS	Conversational Monitor System
CMY(K)	Cyan–Magenta–Yellow (–blacK)
CNC	Computerized Numerical Control
COBOL	COmmon Business-Oriented Language
COCOMO	COnstructive COst MOdel
CODASYL	Conference on Data Systems Languages
CODE	Client–server Open Development Environment
COGO	COordinate GeOmetry
COM	Common Object Module
COM	Component Object Model
COM	Computer Output on Microfilm
COMDEX	COMputer Dealers EXposition
COMSAT	Communications Satellite Corporation
CONLAN	CONsensus LANguage
CONTU	Commission on New Technological Uses of Copyrights
COP	Communications Processor
CORBA	Common Object Request Broker Architecture
COSATI	Committee on Scientific and Technical Information
COSMIC	Computer Software Management and Information Center
COTS	Commercial-Off-The-Shelf
COW	Cluster Of Workstations
CPAN	Comprehensive PERL Archive Network
CPC	Card Programmed Calculator
CPE	Customer Premises Equipment
CPLD	Complex Programmable Logic Device
CP/M	Control Program for Microcomputers
CPM	Critical Path Method
CPSR	Computer Professionals for Social Responsibility
CPU	Central Processing Unit

CR	Computed Radiosity
CRAM	Card Random Access Memory
CRC	Class-Responsibility-Collaboration (card)
CRC	Cyclic Redundancy Check
CRT	Cathode Ray Tube
CRT	Chinese Remainder Theorem
CRUD	Create-Retrieve-Update-Delete
CS	Collaborative {Coordination} System
CSA	Canadian Standards Association
CSA	Carry-Save Adder
CSAB	Computer Science Accreditation Board
CSCW	Computer-Supported Cooperative Work
CSE	Computer Science and Engineering
CSL	Computer Structure Language
CSMA	Carrier-Sense Multiple Access
CSMA/CD	CSMA with Collision Detect
CSMP	Continuous System Modeling Program
CSNET	Computer Science Network
CSP	Communicating Sequential Processes
CSSL	Continuous Systems Simulation Language
CT	Computerized Tomography
CTL	Computation Tree Logic
CTS	Carpal Tunnel Syndrome
CTSS	Compatible Time-Sharing System (MIT)
CUA	Common User Access
CUMREC	College and University Machine Record Conference
CVF	Compressed Volume File
CWA	Closed World Assumption
D2T2	Dye Diffusion Thermal Transfer
D/A	Digital-to-Analog (conversion)
DAA	Data Access Arrangement
DAC	Digital to Analog Conversion
DAG	Directed Acyclic Graph
DAI	Distributed Artificial Intelligence
DAM	Direct Access Method
DAO	Data Access Object
DAP	Distributed Array Processor
DARPA	Defense Advanced Research Projects Agency
DASD	Direct Access Storage Device
DAT	Digital Audio Tape
DAT	Dynamic Address Translation
DAX	Data Acquisition and Control
DB	DataBase
DBA	DataBase Administrator
DBM	DataBase Management
DBMS	DataBase Management System
DBS	Direct Broadcast Satellite
DBTG	Database Task Group
DCA	Digital Computer Association
DCD	Data Carrier Detected
DCE	Data Communications Equipment
DCE	Distributed Computing Equipment
DCG	Definite Clause Grammar
DCOM	Distributed Component Object Model
DCS	Distributed Control System

DCT	Direct Cosine Transform
DD	Data Definition
DD	Device Driver
DDA	Digital Design Automation
DDB	Deductive DataBase
DDBMS	Distributed DBMS
DDE	Dynamic Data Exchange
DDL	Data Definition Language
DDL	Dynamic Data Link
DDP	Distributed Data Processor
DDS	Dataphone Digital Service
DEC	Digital Equipment Corporation
DECUS	Digital Equipment Corporation Users Society
DEQUE	Double-Ended QUEue
DES	Data Encryption Standard
DETAB	DEcision TABle (Language)
DFS	Depth First Search
DFS	Distributed File System
DFT	Discrete Fourier Transform
DFT	Distributed Function Terminal
DHCP	Dynamic Host Configuration Protocol
DHP	Directed Hamiltonian Path
DIA	Document Interchange Architecture
DIB	Device Independent Bitmap
DICOM	Digital Imaging and COmmunications in Medicine
DIF	Data Interchange Format
DII	Dynamic Invocation Interface
DIMM	Dual In-line Memory Module
DIP	Dual-In-line Package
DIVX	DIgital Video eXpress
DLAT	Directory Look-Aside Table
DLCL	Doubly-Linked Circular List
DLE	Data Link Escape
DLL	Dynamic Link Library
DLLL	Doubly-Linked Linear List
DLT	Digital Linear Tape
DMA	Direct Memory Access
DMC	Dynamic Markov Compression
DMD	Digital Micromirror Display
DMI	Desktop Management Interface
DMIS	Distributed Multimedia Information System
DML	Data Manipulation Language
DMP	Data Management Program
DMTF	Desktop Management Task Force
DNA	DeoxriboNucleic Acid
DNA	Digital Network Architecture
DNA	Distributed Network Architecture
DNC	Direct Numerical Control
DNS	Domain Name Service
DOC	Distributed Object Computing
DOCSIS	Data Over Cable Service Interface Specification
DoD	Department of Defense (in USA)
DoE	Department of Energy (in USA)
DOM	Document Object Module
DOS	Disk Operating System
DPMA	Data Processing Management Association

DQDB	Distributed Queue, Dual Bus
DRAM	Dynamic Random Access Memory
DRAW	Direct Read After Write
DRDW	Direct Read During Write
DRO	Destructive Read Out
DSDD	Double-Sided Double Density (diskette)
DSL	Digital Subscriber {Line|Loop}
DSL	Domain-Specific Language
DSOM	Distributed System Object Model
DSP	Digital Signal Processing
DSR	Data Set {Ready|Reading}
DSS	Decision Support System
DSU	Disk Storage Unit
DSVD	Digital Simultaneous Voice and Data
DTD	Document Type Definition
DTE	Data Terminal Equipment
DTF	Define The File
DTL	Diode-Transistor Logic
DTMF	Dual Tone Multi-Frequency (dial tone)
DTP	DeskTop Publishing
DTPM	Distributed Transaction Processing Middleware
DTSS	Dartmouth Time-Sharing System
DUN	Dial-Up Networking
DVA	Distributed Voting Algorithm
DVD	Digital {Versatile|Video} Disc
DVD-E	DVD-Erasable
DVI	Digital Versatile Interactive (disc)
DVST	Direct View Storage Tube
DYANA	Dynamic Analyzer
EAI	Electronic Associates, Inc.
EAI	Enterprise Application Integration
EARN	European Academic Research Network
EBCDIC	Extended Binary-Coded Decimal Interchange Code
EBNF	Extended BNF
ECC	Error-Correcting Code
ECL	Emitter-Coupled Logic
ECMA	European Computer Manufacturers Association
ECP	Extended Capabilities Port
ECPA	Electronic Communications Privacy Act
ECR	Electronic Cash Register
ECS	Embedded Control System
ECS	Extended Core Storage
EDA	Electronic Design Automation
EDB	Extensional DataBase
EDF	Earliest Deadline First
EDI	Electronic Data Interchange
EDIF	Electronic Design Interchange Format
EDIFACT	Electronic Data Interchange for Administration, Commerce, and Transportation
EDO	Extended Data Output
EDP	Electronic Data Processing
EDS	Electronic Data Systems
EDSAC	Electronic Delay Storage Automatic Calculator
EDUCOM	EDUcation COMmunications (Interuniversity Communications Council)
EDVAC	Electronic Discrete Variable Automatic Computer
EEPROM	Electronically Erasable Programmable ROM

EFF	Electronic Frontier Foundation
EFM	Eight to Fourteen Modulation
EFT	Electronic Funds Transfer
EGA	Enhanced Graphics Adapter
EGP	External Gateway Protocol
EIA	Electronic Industries Association
EIDE	Enhanced Integrated Drive Electronics
EIP	Elementary Information Proces
EIS	Electronic Information System
EISA	Extended International Standard Architecture (bus)
ELI	Extensible Language I
EMS	Electronic Meeting System
EMS	Expanded Memory Specification
ENIAC	Electronic Numerical Integrator and Computer
EO	Erasable Optical (auxiliary memory)
EOF	End-Of-File
EOL	End-Of-Line
EOM	End-Of-Message
EOR	End-Of-Record
EOT	End-Of-Transmission
EPIC	Explicitly Parallel Instruction Computing
EPP	Enhanced Parallel Port
EPROM	Erasable Programmable ROM
EPS	Encapsulated PostScript (file)
EPSS	Experimental Packet Switching System
ERA	Engineering Research Associates
ERP	Enterprise Resource Planning
ESDI	Enhanced System Device Interface
ESI	Enhanced Serial Interface
ESMTP	Extended Simple Mail Transfer Protocol
ESS	Electronic Switching System
ETX	End-of-TeXt
EULA	End-User License Agreement
EVGA	Extended Video Graphics Array
EWG	Environmental Working Group
FAP	Fortran Assembly Program
FAQ	Frequently Asked Questions
FAST	Flow Analysis Software Tookit
FAT	File Allocation Table
FAX	FAXsimile
FCC	Federal Communications Commission
FCL	Fibre (sic) Channel Loop
FCS	Fiber Channel Standard
FCT	File Control Table
FDDI	Fiber Distributed Data Interface
FDE	Fetch–Decode–Execute (cycle)
FDHP	Full-Duplex Handshaking Protocol
FDIS	Final Draft International Standard
FDM	Frequency Division Multiplexing
FEC	Forward Error Correction
FED	Field Emission Display
FEM	Finite Element Method
FET	Field-Effect Transistor
FF	Flip-Flop
FFT	Fast Fourier Transform

FHD	Fixed-Head Disk
FIACC	Five International Associations Coordinating Committee
FIFO	First-In-First-Out
FIG	Forth (language) Interest Group
FIMS	Forms Interface Management System
FIPS	Federal Information Processing Standards
FIR	Fast InfraRed (port)
FIR	Finite Impulse Response
FIX	Federal Internet eXchange
FLOPS	FLoating-Point Operations Per Second
FM	Frequency Modulation
FMS	Flexible Manufacturing System
FMS	Fortran Monitor System
FNC	Federal Networking Council
FOI{A|L}	Freedom of Information {Act|Law}
FOPC	First Order Predicate Calculus
FORMAC	FORmula MAnipulation Compiler
FORTRAN	FORmula TRANslator
FOSDIC	Film Optical Sensing Device for Input to Computer
FP	Frame Pointer
FP	Functional Programming (language)
FPAP	Floating Point Array Processor
FPD	Full-Page Display
FP DRAM	Fast Page DRAM
FPGA	Field Programmable Gate Array
FPM	Fast Page Mode
FPS	Floating Point Systems
FPU	Floating Point Unit
FRAM	Ferromagnetic RAM
FSA	Finite State Automaton
FSF	Free Software Foundation
FSK	Frequency-Shift Keying
FSM	Finite State Machine
FTA	Fault Tree Analysis
FTMP	Fault Tolerant MicroProcessor
FTP	Fault-Tolerant Processing
FTP	File Transfer Protocol
FTPP	Fault-Tolerant Parallel Processing
FTSC	Fault Tolerant Spaceborne Computer
FTTH	Fiber To The House
GAMM	Gesellschaft für angewandte Mathematik und Mechanik
GASP	General Activity Simulation Program
GCD	Greatest Common Divisor
GDI	Graphics Device Interface
GDSS	Group Decision Support System
GE	General Electric
GEM	Graphical Environment Manager
GENESYS	GENeral Engineering SYStem
GFC	Generic Flow Control
GGP	Gateway to Gateway Protocol
GIF	Graphics Interchange Format
GIGO	Garbage In, Garbage Out
GILC	Global Internet Liberty Campaign
GIMPS	Great Internet Mersenne Prime Search
GIPSY	General Information Processing System

GIS	{Geographical	Geospatial	Graphical} Information System
GIT	Global Interface Table
GKS	Graphical Kernel System
GNAT	GNU Ada Translator
GNOME	GNU Network Object Model Environment
GNU	GNU is Not Unix
GPF	General Protection Fault
GPL	General Purpose Language
GPM	General Purpose Macrogenerator
GPS	Global Positioning System
GPSS	General Purpose Systems Simulator
GR	Global Router
GRAPE	GRAvity PipE (supercomputer)
G/RE/P	Globally [find] Regular Expression and Print
GRIPHOS	General Retrieval and Information Processing for Humanities-Oriented Studies
GSAM	Generalized Sequential Access Method
GSI	Giga-Scale Integration
GSM	Generalized Sequential Machine
GSM	Global System for Mobile communications
GTK	GUI ToolKit
GUI	Graphical User Interface
GUIDE	Guidance of Users of Integrated Data Processing Equipment

HB	Honeywell–Bull
HCI	Human–Computer Interaction
HDAM	Hierarchical Direct Access Method
HEC	Header Error Checksum
HDL	Hardware Description Language
HDLC	High-level Data Link Control
HDSL	High-speed DSL
HDTV	High-Definition TeleVision
HEP	Heterogeneous Element Processor
HFC	Hybrid Fiber-Coaxial (line)
HGA	Hercules Graphics Adapter
HIF	Hardware Interchange Format
HIPAC	Hitachi Parametron Automatic Computer
HIPO	Hierarchy plus Input–Process–Output
HIPPI	High-Performance Parallel Interface
HIS	Honeywell Information Systems
HIS	Hospital Information System
HLL	High-Level Language
HMA	High-Memory Area
HOL	Higher Order {Language	Logic}
HOLWG	High-Order Language Working Group
HOPP	Half-Object Plus Protocol
HP	Hewlett-Packard
HPC	Handheld PC
HPF	High-Performance Fortran
HPFS	High-Performance File System
HPPA	High-Performance Precision Architecture
HSB	Hue-Saturation-Brightness (image enhancement)
HSM	Hierarchical Storage Manager
HTML	HyperText Markup Language
HTTP	HyperText Transfer Protocol
HWIM	Hear What I Mean

IAB	Internet Activity Board
IAC	International Apple Core
IAG	International Applications Group (of IFIP)
IAHC	Internet Ad Hoc Coalition
IAL	International Algebraic Language
IANA	Internet Assigned Numbers Authority
IAPR	International Association for Pattern Recognition
IASC	International Association for Statistical Computing
IBC	Information-Based Complexity
IBG	Inter-Block Gap
IBM	International Business Machines (Corporation)
IC	Instruction Counter
IC	Integrated Circuit
ICANN	Internet Corporation for Assigned Names and Numbers
ICCA	International Computer Chess Association
ICCCM	Inter-Client Communications Conventions Manual
ICCP	Institute for the Certification of Computing Professionals
ICL	International Computers Ltd.
ICMP	Internet Control Message Protocol
ICP	International Computer Programs (company)
ICR	Intelligent Character Recognition
ICSU	International Council of Scientific Unions
ICT	International Computers and Tabulators
ID	Instruction Decoder
ID	Irvine Dataflow (language)
IDB	Intensional DataBase
IDC	International Data Corporation
IDE	Integrated Development Environment
IDEA	International Data Encryption Algorithm
IDEF	Integrated Data Engineering Facility
IDFT	Inverse Discrete Fourier Transform
IDL	Interface Definition Language
IDN	Integrated Digital Network
IDS	Integrated Data Store
IDT	Interrupt Descriptor Table
IDU	Instruction Decoding Unit
IEEE	Institute of Electrical and Electronics Engineers
IEEE-CS	IEEE-Computer Society
IETF	Internet Engineering Task Force
IFAC	International Federation of Automatic Control
IFEA	Internet Free Expression Alliance
IFIP	International Federation for Information Processing
IFORS	International Federation of Operations Research Societies
IFP	InterFace Processor
IGES	Initial Graphical Exchange Specification
IIL	Integrated Injection Logic
IIOP	Internet Inter-ORB Protocol
ILLIAC	ILLinois Automatic Computer
ILP	Instruction Level Parallelism
IMACS	International Association for Mathematics and Computing in Simulation
IMAP	Internet {Mail|Message} Access Protocol
IMDB	In-Memory DataBase
IMIA	International Medical Informatics Association
IMP	Interface Message Processor
IMS	Information Management System
IMSL	International Mathematical and Statistical Libraries

INS	Internet Naming Service
I/O	Input–Output
IOCS	Input–Output Control System
ION	I/O Node
IOP	Input–Output Processor
IP	Instruction Processor
IP	Internet Protocol
IPC	Interprocess Communication
IPL	Information Processing Language
IPPS	Integrated Power Protection System
IPS	Information Processing System
IPX	Internet Packet eXchange
IR	Information Retrieval
IR	Instruction Register
IRC	Internet Relay Chat
IRE	Institute of Radio Engineers
IRG	Inter-Record Gap
INRIA	Institut National de Recherche en Informatique et en Automatique
IRQ	Interrupt ReQuest
IS	Information Science
ISA	Industry Standard Architecture
ISA	Instruction Set Architecture
ISA	Instrument Society of America
ISAM	Indexed Sequential Access Method
ISAPI	Internet Server Application Programming Interface
ISBN	International Standard Book Number
ISDN	Integrated Systems Digital Network
ISETL	Interactive SETL
ISI	Inter-Symbol Interference
ISIS	Image and Scanner Interface Standard (driver)
ISO	International Organization for Standardization (formerly International Standards Organization)
ISOC	Internet SOCiety
ISODATA	Interactive Self-Organizing DATA analysis technique
ISP	Internet Service Provider
ISP	Instruction Set Processor
ISPL	Instruction Set Processor Language
ISPS	Instruction Set Processor Specifications
ISSMB	Information Systems Standards Management Board
ISTE	International Society for Technology in Education
ISV	Independent Software Vendor
IT	Information Technology
ITAA	Information Technology Association of America
ITC	International Typeface Corporation
ITI	Interactive Terminal Interface
ITU-T	International Telecommunications Union-Telecom
IWIM	Idealized Worker—Idealized Manager
JACM	Journal of the Association for Computing Machinery
JBIG	Joint Bi-level Image Experts Group
JCL	Job Control Language
JOD	Journal of Development
JOVIAL	Jules' Own Version of the International Algebraic Language
JIT	Just In Time
JPEG	Joint Photographic Experts Group
JPL	Jet Propulsion Laboratory
JTP	Job Ticket Processor

JUG	Joint Users Group
JVM	Java Virtual Machine

KBSA	Knowledge-Based Software Assistant
KBSE	Knowledge-Based Software Engineering
KDD	Knowlege Discovery in Databases
KDE	K-Desktop Environment (Linux)
KEE	Knowledge Engineering Environment
KIF	Knowledge Interchange Format
KLOC	KiloLine Of Code (thousand [K] Lines Of program Code)
KSR	Keyboard Send-Receive
KWIC	Keyword-In-Context
KWOC	Keyword-Out-of-Context

LALR	LookAhead Left-to-right, Rightmost derivation (parser)
LAN	Local Area Network
LARC	Livermore Automatic Research Computer
LASER	Light Amplification by Stimulated Emission of Radiation
LAT	Local Area Transport
LBA	Linear Bounded Automaton
LCC	Leadless Chip Carrier
LCD	Liquid Crystal Display
LCD	Lowest Common Denominator
LCF	Least Common Factor
LCP	Link Control Protocol
LCS	Large Core Storage (IBM)
LDAP	Lightweight Directory Access Protocol
LD-ROM	Laser Disc ROM
LEC	Local Exchange Carrier
LECS	LAN Emulation Configuration Server
LED	Light-Emitting Diode
LEO	Lyons Electronic Office (computer)
LEP	Light-Emitting Polymer
LIFO	Last-In-First-Out
LILO	LInux LOader
LIMS	Laboratory Information Management System
LINC	Laboratory Instrument Computer
LINUX	LINus (Torvalds) UniX
LIS	Library Information System
LISP	LISt Processor
LIU	{Line|LAN} Interface Unit
LL	Left-to-right, Leftmost derivation (parser)
LLO	Logical Link Control
LMS	Least Mean Square
LO	Laser Optical (disc)
LOCIS	Library Of Congress Information System
LOINC	Logical Observation Identifier Names and Codes
LP	Linear Programming
LPC	Linear Predictive Coding
LPCVD	Low-Pressure Vapor Deposition
LPT	Line Printer Terminal
LR	Left-to-right, Rightmost derivation (parser)
LRC	Longitudinal Redundancy Check
LRU	Least Recently Used
LS	Laser Servo

LS	Least Squares
LS{b|B|C|D}	Least Significant {bit | Byte | Character | Digit}
LSI	Large Scale Integration
LSTTL	Low-Power Schottky Transistor-Transistor Logic
LT	Logic Theorist (AI program)
LTL	Linear Temporal Logic
LTM	Long-Term Memory
LU	Logic Unit
LUTDAC	Look-Up Table DAC
MAA	Mathematical Association of America
MAC	{Machine-Aided Cognition | Man And Computer} (MIT Project MAC)
MAC	Media Access Code
MACSYMA	MAC SYmbol MAnipulation
MAD	Michigan Algebraic Decoder
MAE	{Market | Metropolitan} Area Exchange
MAN	Metropolitan Area Network
MANIAC	Mathematical Analyzer Numeric Integrator And Calculator
MAP	Manufacturing Automation Protocol
MAR	Memory Address Register
MARC	MAchine-Readable Cataloging
MBQ	Modified Biquinary Code
MBR	Master Boot Record
MCA	MicroChannel Architecture
MCGA	Multi-Color Graphics Array
MCP	Master Control Program
MDA	Message Delivery Agent
MDA	Monochrome Display Adapter
MDC	Magnetic Drum Calculator (IBM)
MDI	Multiple Document Interface
MEDIX	MEdical Data Interchange
MEDLARS	MEDical Literature Analysis and Retrieval System
MEDLINE	Medlars On-Line System
MFM	Modified Frequency Modulation
MFT	Multiprogramming with a Fixed Number of Tasks
MHD	Moving-Head Disk
MHMP	Moving Head Multiple Platter (disk)
MHS	Message Handling System
MHSP	Moving Head Single Platter (disk)
M-HTML	Multimedia HTML
MIB	Management Information Base
MIB	Medical Information Bus
MICR	Magnetic Ink Character Recognition
MIDAC	MIchigan Digital Automatic Computer
MIDI	Musical Instrument Digital Interface
MII	Medical Imaging Informatics
MIMD	Multiple-Instruction—Multiple-Data (architecture)
MIME	{Multipurpose | Multimedia} Internet Mail Extensions
MIMR	Magnetic Ink Mark Recognition
MIN	Multistage Interconnection Network
MIPS	Microprocessor with Interlocked Pipeline Stages
MIPS	Million Instructions Per Second
MIS	Management Information Systems
MISD	Multiple-Instruction–Single-Data (architecture)
MITS	Micro-Instrumentation and Telemetry System
MJPEG	Multimedia JPEG

ML	{Machine | Meta} Language
MLA	Modern Language Association
MLOCR	MultiLine OCR
MMU	Memory {Management | Mapping} Unit
MMX	MultiMedia eXtension {(according to Intel) Matrix Math eXtension}
MO	Magneto-Optical (auxiliary memory)
MODEM	MOdulator-DEModulator
MOLAP	Multidimensional OnLine Analytical Processing
MOM	Message-Oriented Middleware
MOO	MUD-Object-Oriented
MOS	Metal-Oxide Semiconductor
MOSFET	Metal-Oxide Semiconductor Field Effect Transistor
MP3	MPEG audio layer 3
MPC	Multimedia PC
MPEG	Moving Picture Experts Group
MPI	Message Passing Interface
MPMD	Multiple Processor—Multiple Data architecture
MPP	Massively Parallel Processor
MPU	Microprocessing Unit
MPW	Macintosh Programmer's Workshop
MQ	Multiplier–Quotient (register)
MRI	Magnetic Resonance Imaging
MRI	Modeling, Rendering, and Interaction
MRP	Manufacturing Resource Planning
MS	MicroSoft
MSB	Most Significant Byte
MSb	Most Significant bit
MSC	Most Significant Character
MSD	Most Significant Digit
MSI	Medium Scale Integration
MSM	Message Switching Multiplexing
MSMQ	MicroSoft Message Queue server
MSN	Microsoft Network
MSS	Mass Storage System
MSS	Multimedia Systems Services
MSUDC	Michigan State University Discrete Computer
MSW	Machine Status Word
MT	Machine Translation
MTA	Message Transfer Agent
MTBF	Mean Time Between Failures
MTS	Microsoft Transaction Server
MTTF	Mean Time to Failure
MTTR	Mean Time to Repair
MUD	Multi-User Dimension (formerly "Dungeon")
MULTICS	Multiplexed Information and Computing Service
MUMPS	Massachusetts (General Hospital) Utility MultiProgramming System
MUSH	Multi-User Shared Hallucinations
MUX	MUltipleXer
MVS	{Multiple | Multiprogrammed} Virtual Storage
MVT	Multiprogramming with a Variable Number of Tasks
MX	Mail eXchange
NACHA	National Automated Clearing House Association
NAG	Numerical (formerly Nottingham) Algorithms Group
NAIF	Navigation and Ancillary Information Facility (toolkit)
NAK	Negative AcKnowledgement

NaN	Not a Number
NAND	Not AND
NAP	Network Access Point
NAPLPS	North American Presentation Level Protocol Syntax
NAS	Network Attached Storage
NASA	National Aeronautics and Space Administration
NASDAQ	National Association of Securities Dealers Automatic Quotation
NATS	National Activity to Test Software
NC	Numerical Control
NC	Network Computer
NCC	National Computer Conference
NCEFT	National Commission on Electronic Funds Transfers
NCIC	National Crime Information Center
NCITS	National Center for Information Technology Standardization
NCLIS	National Commission on Libraries and Information Science
NC-NUMA	Non-Cache-coherent NUMA
NCR	National Cash Register (Corporation)
NCSA	National Center for Supercomputing Applications
NCSA	National Computational Science Alliance
NDRO	Non-Destructive Read-Out
NEC	Nippon Electric Corporation
NELIAC	Navy Electronics Laboratory International Algol Compiler
NeWS	Network/extensible Window System
NFF	Negation as Finite Failure
NFS	Network File System
NGI	Next Generation Internet
NGIO	Next Generation I/O (bus)
NIC	Network Information Center
NIS	Network Information System
NISO	National Information Standards Organization
NLP	Natural Language Processing
NLP	NonLinear Programming
NLQ	Near Letter Quality
NMA	National Micrographics Association
NMOS	Negative Metal-Oxide Semiconductor
NMR	N-Modular Redundancy
NNI	Network-Network Interface
NNTP	Network News Transfer Protocol
NOR	Not OR
NORC	Naval Ordinance Research Computer
NORMA	NO Remote Memory Access
NOW	Network Of Workstations
NP	Nondeterministic Polynomial
NPACI	National Partnership for Advanced Computational Initiatives
NPL	National Physical Laboratory (UK)
NPL	New Product Line (IBM)
NREN	National Research and Education Network
NRZ	Non-Return to Zero
NSF	National Science Foundation
NSFNET	NSF NETwork
NSI	Network Solutions, Inc.
N-ISDN	Narrowband ISDN
NSTL	National Software Testing Laboratories
NTM	Nondeterministic Turing Machine
NTSC	National Television Standards Committee
NUMA	Non-Uniform Memory Access

NVRAM	Non-Volatile Random Access Memory
NWI	New Work Item
OA	Office Automation
OBDD	Ordered Binary Decision Diagram
OBR	Optical Bar Code
OCR	Optical Character {Recognition | Reader}
OCRS	Online Computing Reviews Service
ODBC	Open DataBase Connectivity specification
ODE	Ordinary Differential Equation
ODMG	Object Database Management Group
ODP	Open Distributed Processing
ODS	Open Distributed System
OECD	Organization for Economic Cooperation and Development
OEM	Original Equipment Manufacturer
OHP	Open Hypertext Protocol
OLAP	OnLine Analytical Processing
OLCP	OnLine Complex Processing
OLE	Object Linking and Embedding
OLED	Organic LED
OLTP	OnLine Transaction Processing
OMG	Object Management Group
OMIBAC	Ordinal Memory Inspecting Binary Automatic Calculator
OMR	Optical Mark Reading
OMT	Object Modeling Technique
ONA	Open Network Architecture
ONC	Open Network Computing
OOAD	Object-Oriented Analysis and Design
OOD	Object-Oriented Design
OOP[S]	Object-Oriented Programming [System]
OOPSLA	Object-Oriented Programming Systems, Languages, and Applications
OPC	Organic Photoconducting Cartridge
ORB	Object Request Broker
ORC	Organic Photoconducting Cartridge
ORDVAC	ORDinance Variable Automatic Computer
OS	Operating System
OSF	Open Software Foundation
OSG	Open Service Gateway
OSI	Open Systems Interconnection
OS/MFT	Operating System/Multiprogramming with a Fixed Number of Tasks
OS/MVS	Operating System/Multiprogramming with Virtual Storage
OS/MVT	Operating System/Multiprogramming with a Variable Number of Tasks
OSPF	Open Shortest Path First
OSSI	Open Storage Systems Interconnection
OTA	Office of Technology Assessment
OTA	Open Terminal Architecture
OTTER	Organized Techniques for Theorem-proving and Effective Research
OWL	Object Windows Library
PACI	Partnership for Advanced Computational Infrastructure
PACS	Picture Archiving and Communications System
PAD	Packet Assembler-Disassembler
PAL	Phase Alternate Line (disc)
PAM	Pluggable Authentication Module
PAN	Personal Area Network
PAP	Password Authentication Protocol

PARC	Palo Alto Research Center (Xerox)
PAS	Publicly Available Specification
PB{D|E}	Programming By {Demonstration | Example}
PBX	Private Branch eXchange
PC	Personal Computer
PC	Program Counter
PCB	Printed Circuit Board
PCI	Peripheral Component Interconnect
PCI	Peripheral Controller Interface
PCL	Printer Control Language
PCM	Plug Compatible Mainframe
PCM	Pulse Code Modulation
PCMCIA	Personal Computer Memory Card International Association
PCS	Personal Communications System
PCTE	Portable Common Tool Environment
PDA	Personal Digital Assistant
PDE	Partial Differential Equation
PDES	Product Data Exchange Specification
PDF	Portable Document Format
PDL	Page Description Language
PDL	Process Design Language
PDP	Parallel Distributed Processing
PDP	Plasma Display Panel
PDP	Programmed Data Processor
PE	Processing Element
PERL	Practical Extraction and Report Language
PERT	Program Evaluation and Review Technique
PET	Positron Emission Tomography
PF	Page Fault
PGA	Programmable Gate Array
PGP	Pretty Good Privacy
PHIGS	Programmer's Hierarchical Interactive Graphics System
PICS	Platform for Internet Content Selection
PID	Processor ID
PID	Proportional-Integral-Derivative (control system)
PIM	Personal Information Manager
PIN	Personal Identification Number
PIN	Positive-Intrinsic-Negative (diode)
PJTP	Portable Job Ticket Processor
PKC	Public Key Cryptosystem
PLA	Programmable Logic Array
PLATO	Programmed Logic for Automatic Teaching Operation
PLC	Programmable Logic Controller
PLCC	Plastic Leadless Chip Carrier
PM	Phase Modulation
PM	Presentation Manager
PMOS	Positive Metal-Oxide Semiconductor
PMS	Processor-Memory-Switch (notation)
PNG	Portable Network Graphics
POL	Problem-Oriented Language
POL	Procedure-Oriented Language
POP	Point Of Presence
POP3	Post Office Protocol version 3
POS	Point-of-Sale
POSIT	Profiles for Open Systems Internetworking Technology
POSIX	Portable Operating System Interface for uniX

POST	Power-On Self-Test
POTS	Plain Old Telephone Service
PP	Peripheral Processor
PPL	Polymorphic Programming Language
PPM	Prediction by Partial Mapping
PPP	Point-to-Point Protocol
PRAM	Parallel Random-Access Machine
PREMO	Presentation Environment for Multimedia Objects
PRI	Primary Rate Interface
PROM	Programmable Read-Only Memory
PR/SM	Processor Resource/Systems Manager
PSA	Pushdown Stack Automaton
PSE	Packet Switching Exchange
PSF	Point-Spread Function
PSL/PSA	Problem Statement Language/Problem Specification Analyzer
PSM	Probabilistic Sequential Machine
PSS	Packet Switching Service
PSTN	Public Switched Telephone Network
PSW	Program Status Word
PTI	Payload Type Identifier
PTO	Patent and Trademark Office
PTT	Post-Telephone-Telegraph
PUFFT	Purdue University Fast Fortran Compiler
PUG	Pascal Users Group
PVC	Permanent Virtual {Circuit|Connection}
PVM	Parallel Virtual Machine
PVS	Prototype Verification System
QAM	Quadrature Amplitude Modulation
QAM	Queued Access Method
QBE	Query By Example
QC	Quantum Computing
QED	Quod Erat Demonstratum (that which was to be proved)
QFT	Quantum Fourier Transform
QIC	Quarter-Inch Cartridge
QISAM	Queued Indexed Sequential Access Method
QoS	Quality of Service
QPSX	Queued Packet Switched eXchange
QSAM	Queued Sequential Access Method
QTAM	Queued Telecommunications Access Method
RAD	Rapid Application Development
RADIUS	Remote Authentication Dial-In Service
RAID	Redundant Array of {Inexpensive|Independent} Disks
RAM	Random Access Memory
RAMAC	Random Access Method for Accounting and Control
RAMDAC	Random Access Memory Digital to Analog Converter
RARP	Reverse Address Resolution Protocol
RAS	Remote Access {Server|Service}
RAT	Robust Audio Tool
RAW	Read After Write
RCS	Revision Control System
RDA	Remote Database Access
RDB	Relational DataBase
RDBMS	Relational DataBase Management System
RDD	Responsibility Driven Design

RDF	Relational Data File
RDF	Resource Description Framework
RF	Radio Frequency
RFC	Request For Comments (Internet)
RFD	Request For Discussion
RFID	Radio Frequency Identification Device
RGB	Red-Green-Blue (color system)
RIE	Reactive Ion Etching
RIP	Raster Image Processor
RIP	Routing Information Protocol
RISC	Reduced Instruction Set Computer
RJE	Remote Job Entry
RLE	Run Length Encoding
RLIN	Research Libraries Information Network
RLL	Run-Length Limited (recording)
RMI	Remote {Message|Method} Invocation
RMM	Read Mostly Memory
RMS	Root Mean Square
ROLAP	Relational OnLine Analytical Processing
ROM	Read-Only Memory
ROOM	Real-time Object-Oriented Modeling
ROT	Running Object Table
RPC	Remote Procedure Call
RPG	Report Program Generator
RPN	Reverse Polish Notation
RPS	Rotational Position Sensing
RRSP	Resource Reservation Setup Protocol
R-S	Reset-Set (Flip-Flop)
RSA	Rivest-Adleman-Shamir (encryption algorithm)
RSFQ	Rapid Single Flux Quantum (logic)
RSL	Requirements Specification Language
RSVP	Resouce reSerVation Protocol
RT	Register Transfer
RTF	Rich Text Format
RTFM	Read the eFfing Manual
RTL	Register Transfer Language
RTL	Register-Transistor Logic
RTM	Register Transfer Module
R/W	Read/Write
SAA	Systems Application Architecture
SAFE	Security And Freedom through Encryption
SAGE	Semi-Automatic Ground Environment
SAM	Sequential Access Method
SAN	Storage Area Network
SAP	Symbolic Assembly Program
SAS	Statistical Analysis System
SASOS	Single Address Space OS
SAX	Simple API for XML
SCALD	Structured Computer-Aided Logic Design
SCC	Serial Communications Controller
SCCS	Source Code Control System
SCI	Simulation Councils Incorporated
SCP	System Control Program
SCS	Society for Computer Simulation
SCSI	Small Computer Systems Interface

SDC	System Development Corporation
SDH	Synchronous Digital Hierarchy
SDI	Selective Dissemination of Information
SDK	Software Development Kit
SDLC	Synchronous Data Link Control (protocol)
SDRAM	Synchronous Dynamic Random Access Memory
SDS	Scientific Data Systems
SEAC	Standards Eastern Automatic Computer
SEI	Software Engineering Institute
SEMATECH	SEmiconductor MAterials TECHnology
SEPP	Software Engineering for Parallel Processing
SET	Secure Electronic Transaction protocol
SETL	SET Language
SGML	Standard Generalized Markup Language
S-HTML	Secure HTML
SIAM	Society for Industrial and Applied Mathematics
SID	Society for Information Display
SIFT	Software-Implemented Fault Tolerance
SIG	Special Interest Group
SIMD	Single-Instruction–Multiple-Data (architecture)
SIMM	Single In-line Memory Module
SIP	Single Inline Package
SIPP	Single Inline Pinned Package
SISAL	Streams and Iteration in a Single-Assignment Language
SISD	Single-Instruction—Single-Data (architecture)
SJF	Shortest Job First
SL	Symbolic Logic
SLAM	Simulation Language for Alternative Modeling
SLCL	Singly-Linked Circular List
SLD	Selection rule with Linear resolution for Definite clauses
SLDL	System Level Description Language
SLDNF	SLD with Negation by Failure
SLI	Symmetic Level Index
SLIP	Serial Line Internet Protocol
SLLL	Singly-Linked Linear List
SLR	Simple LR parser
SLT	Solid Logic Technology
SMDS	Switched Multimedia Data Service
SMIS	Society for Management Information Systems
SMDS	Switched {Multimedia | Multi-megabit} Data Service
SML	Standard Meta Language
SMP	Symmetric MultiProcessor
SMT	Surface Mount Technology
SMTP	Simple Mail Transfer Protocol
SMV	Symbolic Model Verifier
SNA	System Network Architecture
SNMP	Simple Network Management Protocol
SNOBOL	StriNg-Oriented symBOlic Language
SNOMED	Systematized NOmenclature of human & veterinary MEDicine
SOAP	Symbolic Optimizer and Assembly Program
SOC	System On a Chip
SOHO	Small Office / Home Office (computer)
SONET	Synchronous Optical NETwork
SOR	Successive Overrelaxation
SOS	Share Operating System
SOS	Silicon On Sapphire

SOS	Structured Operational Semantics
SP	Stack Pointer
SP	Structured Programming
SPAP	Special Purpose Array Processor
SPARC	Scalable Processor ARChitecture (Sun)
SPARC	Standards Planning and Requirements Committee
SPC	Statistical Process Control
SPEC	System Performance Evaluation Cooperative
SPICE	Simulation Program with Integrated Circuit Emphasis
SPL	Simple Programming Language
SPMD	Single Program – Multiple Data (architecture)
SPOOL	Simultaneous Peripheral Operations On Line
SPSS	Statistical Programs for the Social Sciences
SPX	Sequential Packet eXchange (protocol)
SQA	Software Quality Assurance
SQC	Statistical Quality Control
SQL	Structured Query Language
SQUID	Superconducting QUantum Interference Device
S-R	Set-Reset (Flip-Flop)
SRAM	Static Random Access Memory
SRAPI	Speech Recognition Applications Programming Inteface
SRI	Stanford Research Institute
SRTF	Shortest Remaining Time First
SRPT	Shortest Remaining Processing Time (first)
SSEC	Selective Sequence Electronic Calculator
SSI	Server-Side Include
SSI	Small-Scale Integration
SSL	Secure Sockets Layer
SSM	Soft Systems Methodology
SSP	Scientific Subroutine Package
STAR	Self Testing and Repair (Computer)
STDM	Synchronous Time-Division Multiplexing
STEP	STandard for Exchange of Product (Model Data)
STL	Schottky Transistor Logic
STM	Short-Term Memory
STN	Super Twist Nematic
STRESS	Structural Engineering Systems Solver
STRUDL	STRUctural Design Language
STT	Secure Transaction Technology
SUNYAT-SEN	State University of NY at Albany Time-Shared Executive Network
SVC	Switched Virtual Circuit
SVGA	Super VGA
SVID	System V Interface Definition (Unix)
SWAC	Standards Western Automatic Computer
SWIFT	Society for Worldwide Interbank Financial Telecommunications
SWISH	Simple Web Indexing System for Humans
SYSOP	SYStem OPerator
TAC	Tokyo Automatic Computer
TACACS	Terminal Access Controller Access Control System
TAO	Truth and Action Osmosis
TAXIR	Taxonomic Information Retrieval
TBM	Terabit Memory
TCM	Trellis Code Modulation
TCOS	Technical Committee on Operating Systems (IEEE)
TCP/IP	Transmission Control Protocol/Internet Protocol

TDD	Telecommunications Device for the Deaf
TDM	Time-Division Multiplexing
TEI	Text Encoding Initiative
TERC	Technology Education Research Center
TFT	Thin-Film Transistor
TFTP	Trivial FTP
TI	Texas Instruments
TIA	Telecommunications Industries Association
TICCIT	Time-Shared Interactive Computer-Controlled Informational Television
TIES	Total Integrated Engineering System
TIFF	Tagged Image File Format
TIP	Terminal Interface (message) Processor
TLB	Translation Lookaside Buffer
TM	Turing Machine
TMR	Triple Modular Redundancy
TN	Twisted Nematic
TOCS	Transactions on Computer Systems (ACM)
TODS	Transactions on Database Systems (ACM)
TOG	Transactions on Graphics (ACM)
TOIS	Transactions on Information Systems (ACM)
TOMS	Transactions on Mathematical Software (ACM)
TOPLAS	Transactions on Programming Languages and Systems (ACM)
TOPS	Transcendental Operating System
TP	Transaction Processing
TPC	Transaction Processing Council
TPM	Tape Processing Machine (IBM)
TSAPI	Telephony Services Applications Programming Interface
TSR	Terminate and Stay Resident
TSS	Time-Shared System
TTF	TrueType Font
TTL	Transistor–Transistor Logic
TTY	Teletype
TUG	TEX Users Group
TUG	Transac (S/2000) Users Group
TWAIN	Technology Without An Interesting Name
UA	User Agent
UAE	Unrecoverable Applications Error
UART	Universal Asynchronous Receiver/Transmitter
UBR	Unspecified Bit Rate
UDP	{Universal|User} Datagram Protocol
UHF	Ultra-High Frequency
UI	User Interface
UID	User ID
UIMS	User Interface Management System
ULSI	Ultra Large Scale Integration
UMA	Uniform Memory Access
UML	{Unified|Universal} Modeling Language
UNC	Uniform Naming Convention
UNI	User-Network Interface
UNIVAC	UNIVersal Automatic Computer
UPC	Universal Product Code
UPD	Ultrasonic Positioning Device
UPS	Uninterruptible Power Supply
URC	Uniform Resource Citation
URI	Uniform Resource Identifier

URL	Uniform Resource Locator
URN	Uniform Resource Name
USASCII	USA Standard Code for Information Interchange
USASI	United States of America Standards Institute
USB	Universal Serial Bus
USE	Univac Scientific Exchange
USENET	(Unix) USEr NETwork
USM	Unifying Semantic Model
USRT	Universal Synchronous Receiver-Transmitter
UTC	Universal Time Coordinate
UTM	Universal Turing Machine
UUA	Univac Users Association
UUCP	Unix-to-Unix Copy Protocol
VAL	Vicarm Arm Language
VAN	Value-Added Network
VAR	Value-Added Reseller
VAX	Virtual Address eXtension
VB	Visual Basic
vBNS	very-high-speed Backbone Network Service
VBR	Variable Bit Rate
VC	Virtual {Connection | Circuit}
VCI	Virtual Channel Identifier
VCPI	Virtual Control Program Interface
VCSEL	Vertical-Cavity Surface-Emitting Laser
VDD	Virtual Display Device
VDL	Vienna Definition Language
VDM	Video Display Metafile
VDT	{Video | Visual} Display Terminal
VDU	{Video | Visual} Display Unit
VESA	Video Electronics Standards Association
VFAT	Virtual FAT
VGA	Video Graphics Adapter
VHDL	VHSIC-HDL
VHF	Very High Frequency
VHSIC	Very High Speed Integrated Circuit
VIM	VI (Roman 6) M (Roman 1000) (CDC Users' Association)
VLAN	Virtual LAN
VLIW	Very Long Instruction Word
VLSI	Very Large-Scale Integration
VM	Virtual {Machine | Memory}
VMEbus	VersaModule Eurocard bus
VMM	Virtual Machine Manager
VMS	Virtual Memory System (DEC VAX operating system)
VMT	Virtual Methods Table
VOD	Video On Demand
VPI	Virtual Path Identifier
VPN	Virtual Private Network
VRAM	Video Random Access Memory
VRC	Vertical Redundancy Check
VRML	Virtual Reality Modeling Language
VSAM	Virtual Storage Access Method
VSAT	Very Small Aperture Terminal
VSE	Virtual Storage Extended
VTAM	Virtual Telecommunications Access Method
VTP	Virtual Terminal Protocol

VUP	VAX Unit of Processing
V[&]V[&A]	Verification {& | ,} Validation [,][and Accreditation]

W3C	WWW Consortium
WAIS	Wide Area Information Server
WAN	Wide Area Network
WAP	Wireless { Access | Application } Protocol
WATFIV	WATerloo Fortran IV
WATFOR	WATerloo FORtran
WATS	Wide Area Telephone Service
WBEM	Web-Based Enterprise Management
WCS	Writable Control Store
WDM	Wavelength Division Multiplexing
WELL	Whole Earth 'Lectronic Link
WFF	Well-Formed Formula
WIMP	Windows-Icons-Menus-Pointers
WINE	WINdows Emulator
WIPO	World Intellectual Property Organization
WISC	Wisconsin Integrally Synchronized Computer
WML	Wireless Markup Language
WMRM	Write-Many Read-Many
WORM	Write-Once Read-Many
WP	Word Processing
WWW	World Wide Web
WYSBYGI	What You See Before You Get It
WYSIWYG	What You See Is What You Get

XDR	eXternal Data Representation
XGA	eXtended Graphics Array
XML	eXtensible Markup Language
XMS	eXtended Memory Specification
XNS	Xerox Network System (architecture)
XOR	eXclusive OR

Y2K	Year 2K (2000)
YACC	Yet Another Compiler-Compiler
YAHOO	Yet Another Hierarchical Officious Oracle

Common File Extensions

See main list for uppercase acronyms used in the definitions. For a more comprehensive list of over 800 extensions, see `http://camalott.com/~rebma/filex.html`.

.4th	Forth language source code
.ada	Ada source file
.aif	Audio Interchange Format
.ald	ALDus Pagemaker file
.ani	ANImation file
.api	Adobe Acrobat API file
.arc	ARChive
.art	AOL, Crayola, and Ashton-Tate image format
.asc	ASCii text file
.asm	ASseMbly language source code
.asp	Active Server Page
.au	AUdio format
.awk	AWK program (Unix)

.bak	BAcKup file
.bas	BASic language source file
.bat	BATch file
.bib	BIBliography
.bin	BINary file
.bmp	BitMaP image
.c	C language source file
.cat	CATalog file
.cbl	CoBoL source file
.cdf	Comma-Delineated data File
.cdr	Corel DRaw file
.cfg	ConFiGuration file
.cgi	CGI script
.cgm	Computer Graphics Metafile
.chk	CHecK disk MS file
.clp	CLiPboard
.cmd	OS/2 CoMmanD batch file
.cmf	Creative Music Format
.cob	COBol source file
.com	COMmand file
.cpp	C++ source file
.dat	DATa file
.dbf	DataBase File—several vendors
.dct	DiCTionary file
.dib	Device Independent Bitmap
.dll	DLL file
.doc	DOCument word processing file—several vendors
.dot	DOcument Template
.drv	DRiVer
.drw	DRaW file—Corel Designer
.dwg	DraWinG file—Autocad
.emf	Enhanced MetaFile
.eps	Encapsulated PostScript file
.err	ERRor file
.exe	EXEcutable file
.fax	FAX file
.fif	Fractal Image Format file
.for	FORtran source file
.fpx	Flash PiX
.gif	Graphics Image Format
.glo	LaTeX GLOssary file
.gly	MS Word GLossarY file
.hgl	H-p Graphics Language
.hlp	HeLP file
.htm or .html	HTML text file
.idx	LaTeX and FoxPro InDeX file
.iff	Image File Format—Sun Microsystems
.ini	INItialization file
.jpg or .jpeg	JPEG image format
.js	JavaScript browser information

.lgo	LOGO file
.lib	C++ LIBrary file
.lst	LiSTing
.log	LOG file
.lsp	LiSP source code
.mac	MACpaint graphic file
.mai or .mail	MAIL file
.man	MANual
.map	image MAP
.me	used with self-descriptive file read.me
.mic	Microsoft Image Composition
.mid or .midi	MIDI music file format
.mix	Microsoft Image piX - Picture It! image file
.mme	MIME file
.mpe	MPEG animation file
.mp3	MP3 animation file
.msg	MeSsaGe
.obj	OBJect code file
.ole	MS OLE file
.ovl	OVerLay file
.pas	Pascal language source file
.pcd	Kodak image format
.pct	Macintosh PiCTure file
.pcx	PC paintbrush file
.pdf	Adobe Portable Document Format
.pic	PICture file
.png	Portable Network Graphic image format
.prg	dBase and FoxPro source program
.pro	PROlog source file
.ps	PostScript file
.psd	Adobe PhotoShop Document
.rgb	Silicon Graphics RGB image format
.rtf	Rich Text Format
.scr	SCRipt
.src	SouRCe code
.sty	STYle sheet
.sys	SYStem file
.tar	Tape ARchive
.tbk	ToolBooK
.tex	TeX or LaTeX file
.tga	Truevision GraphicsArray image format
.ths	THeSaurus
.tif or .tiff	Tagged Image File Format
.tmp	TeMPorary file
.ttf	TrueType Font
.uue	UUEncoded compressed file

.wav	WAVefront music file
.wmf	Windows MetaFile
.wps	MS Works word processing file
.wri	MS WRIte word processing file
.xbm	X-windows BitMap file
.xls	Excel spreadsheet file
.zip	ZIPped (compressed) file

Appendix II

NOTATION AND UNITS

Mathematical Notation

Symbol	Meaning

GENERAL

$\sum$ Summation $\left(\sum_{i=1}^{n} a_i = a_1 + a_2 + \cdots a_n \right)$

$\int$ Integral

$|\ |$ Absolute value ($|a| = a$ if $a \geq 0$, $= -a$ if $a < 0$)

$\lfloor\ \rfloor$ Floor function (greatest integer less than or equal to: $\lfloor 2.4 \rfloor = 2$, $\lfloor -2.4 \rfloor = -3$)

$\lceil\ \rceil$ Ceiling function (least integer greater than or equal to: $\lceil 2.4 \rceil = 3$, $\lceil -2.4 \rceil = -2$)

$[\ ]$ Closed interval ($[a, b]$ includes all x such that $a \leq x \leq b$)

$(\ )$ Open interval [$\langle a, b \rangle$ includes all x such that $a < x < b$]

$[\ ), (\ ],$ Half-open (half-closed) interval {$[a, b)$ includes all x such that $a \leq x < b$}

$\approx, \simeq, \cong, \doteq$ Approximately equal

$\sim$ Asymptotic to

$\times$ Set product [$A \times B$ consists of all pairs (a, b) where $a \in A$, $b \in B$]

Modulo (or mod)   Remainder (x mod y is remainder when x is divided by y; thus, $8 \bmod 3$ is 2)

$\circ$ Binary operation (i.e., denotes any operation like $+$ which requires two operands)

fl   Floating point ($\mathrm{fl}(x + y)$ denotes the floating-point sum of x and y)

iff   If and only if

$\lg(x)$ $\log_2(x)$

$\ln(x)$ $\log_e(x)$

wrt   With respect to

LOGIC

$\vee$ Or

$\wedge$ And

$\oplus$ Exclusive or (XOR)

$\sim, \neg$ Not

$\supset, \Rightarrow$	Implication
$\equiv, \Leftrightarrow$	Equivalence
$\not\equiv$	Inequivalence
$\forall x$	For all x (universal quantifier)
$\exists x$	There exists an x *or* some x (existential quantifier)

SET NOTATION

Let S, S_1, S_2 be sets and P be a predicate:

$x \in S$	x is a member of set S
$\bar{S}$	The complement of S relative to a domain; the set of elements of that domain that are not in S
$S_1 \cup S_2$	The union of S_1 and S_2: $\{x \mid x \in S_1 \lor x \in S_2\}$
$S_1 \cap S_2$	The intersection of S_1 and S_2: $\{x \mid x \in S_1 \land x \in S_2\}$
$S_1 - S_2$	The set-difference of S_1 and S_2; the elements of S_1 not in S_2: $\{x \mid x \in S_1 \land x \notin S_2\}$
$\{x \mid P(x)\}$	The set of all x such that P is true of x

Notes
1. For a description of the notation used in describing computer language constructs, *see* BACKUS–NAUR FORM.
2. For symbols used in logical circuitry, *see* COMPUTER CIRCUITRY.

Asymptotic Growth Notation Used in the Analysis of Algorithms

If $f(n)$ and $g(n)$ are functions defined on the natural numbers, and are eventually nonnegative, their asymptotic relative growth rates are expressed by the "big-O" and related notations.

$f(n) = O(g(n))$	There are positive constants c, n_0 such that for all $n > n_0$, $0 \le f(n) \le cg(n)$ ($f(n)$ eventually grows no faster than $g(n)$).
$f(n) = \Omega(g(n))$	There are positive constants c, n_0 such that for all $n > n_0$, $0 \le cg(n) \le f(n)$ ($f(n)$ eventually grows at least as fast as $g(n)$).
$f(n) = \Theta(g(n))$	There are positive constants c_1, c_2, n_0 such that for all $n > n_0$, $0 \le c_1 g(n) \le f(n) \le c_2 g(n)$ ($f(n)$ eventually grows at least as fast as $g(n)$).
$f(n) = o(g(n))$	For every constant $c > 0$, there is an $n_0 > 0$ such that for all $n > n_0$, $0 \le f(n) < cg(n)$ ($f(n)$ eventually grows more slowly than $g(n)$).
$f(n) = \omega(g(n))$	For every constant $c > 0$, there is an $n_0 > 0$ such that for all $n > n_0$, $0 \le cg(n) < f(n)$ ($f(n)$ eventually grows faster than $g(n)$).

Units of Measure

This list contains abbreviations of units of measure used in the *Encyclopedia*; these usually appear in their abbreviated form.

General

K	1,000 or 1024 ($= 2^{10}$)
M	1,000,000 or 1,048,576 ($= 2^{20}$)
G	2^{30} (approximately 1 US billion)
T	2^{40}
	The powers of two are used primarily in measures of computer main memory.

Time

ms, msec	millisecond (10^{-3} s)
μs, μsec	microsecond (10^{-6} s)
ns, nsec	nanosecond (10^{-9} s)
ps, psec	picosecond (10^{-12} s)
fs, fsec	femtosecond (10^{-15} s)

as, asec	attasecond (10^{-18} s)
zs, zsec	zeptosecond (10^{-21} s)
ys, ysec	yoctosecond (10^{-24} s)

Speed

Megaflops or Mflops	Million floating-point operations per second
Gigaflops or Gflops	Billion floating-point operations per second
Teraflops or Tflops	Trillion floating-point operations per second
BIPS	Billion instructions per second
MIPS	Million instructions per second
LIPS	Logical inferences per second

Electricity

Hz	Hertz (cycles/s)
KHz	Kilohertz (10^3 cycles/s)
MHz	Megahertz (10^6 cycles/s)
GHz	Gigahertz (10^9 cycles/s)
μW	Microwatt (10^{-6} watts)
mW	Milliwatt (10^{-3} watts)
kW	Kilowatt (10^3 watts)
mV	Millivolt (10^{-3} volt)
mA	Milliamp (10^{-3} amp)
μF	Microfarad (10^{-6} farad)
nF	Nanofarad (10^{-9} farad)
pF	Picofarad (10^{-12} farad)
fF	Femtofarad (10^{-15} farad)
aF	Attafarad (10^{-18} farad)

Storage

Kb	Kilobit (10^3 bits)
Mb	Megabit (10^6 bits)
Gb	Gigabit (10^9 bits)
Tb	Terabit (10^{12} bits)
Pb	Petabit (10^{15} bits)
Eb	Exabit (10^{18} bits)
KB	Kilobyte (10^3 bytes)
MB	Megabyte (10^6 bytes)
GB	Gigabyte (10^9 bytes)
TB	Terabyte (10^{12} bytes)
PB	Petabyte (10^{15} bytes)
EB	Exabyte (10^{18} bytes)
ZB	Zettabyte (10^{21} bytes)
YB	Yottabyte (10^{24} bytes)
L(x)	Location of x (in main memory)
C(A), [A]	Contents of location A (in main memory)

I/O

bps	Bits per second
bpi	Bits per inch
chps	Characters per second
chpi	Characters per inch
lpm	Lines per minute
rpm	Revolutions per minute
KB/s or Kbytes/s	Kilobytes per second

MB/s or Mbytes/s	Megabytes per second
GB/s or Gbytes/s	Gigabytes per second
TB/s or Tbytes/s	Terabytes per second

Miscellaneous

μ Micron (10^{-6} meter)

Table of important numerical constants

	Decimal (rounded)					Hexadecimal (truncated)				
$\frac{1}{10}$	0.10000	00000	00000	00000	00000	0.1999	9999	9999	9999	9999
$\sqrt{2}$	1.41421	35623	73095	04880	16887	1.6A09	E667	F3BC	C908	B2FB
$\sqrt{3}$	1.73205	08075	68877	29352	74463	1.BB67	AE85	84CA	A73B	2574
$\sqrt{5}$	2.23606	79774	99789	69640	91737	2.3C6E	F372	FE94	F82B	E739
$\sqrt{10}$	3.16227	76601	68379	33199	88935	3.298B	075B	4B6A	5420	9457
$\sqrt[3]{2}$	1.25992	10498	94873	16476	72106	1.428A	2F98	D728	AE22	3DDA
ln 2	0.69314	71805	59945	30941	72321	0.B172	17F7	D1CF	79AB	C9E3
ln 10	2.30258	50929	94045	68401	79915	2.4D76	3776	AAA2	B05B	A95B
$\log_{10} 2$	0.30102	99956	63981	19521	37389	0.4D10	4D42	7DE7	FBCC	47C4
$\log_2 10 = 1/\log_{10} 2$	3.32192	80948	87362	34787	03194	3.5269	E12F	346E	2BF9	24AF
$\log_2 e = 1/\ln 2$	1.44269	50408	88963	40735	99247	1.7154	7642	B82F	E177	7D10
$\log_{10} e = 1/\ln 10$	0.43429	44819	03251	82765	11289	0.6F2D	EC54	9B94	38CA	9AAD
$1° = \pi/180$	0.01745	32925	19943	29576	92369	0.0477	D1AB	94A7	4E45	7076
π	3.14159	26535	89793	23846	26434	3.243F	6A88	85A3	08D3	1319
$1/\pi$	0.31830	98861	83790	67153	77675	0.517C	C1B7	2722	0A94	FE13
π^2	9.86960	44010	89358	61883	44910	9.DE9E	64DF	22EF	2D25	6E26
$\sqrt{\pi}$	1.77245	38509	05516	02729	81675	1.C5BF	891B	4EF6	AA79	C3B0
e	2.71828	18284	59045	23536	02875	2.B7E1	5162	8AED	2A6A	BF71
1/e	0.36787	94411	71442	32159	55238	0.5E2D	58D8	B3BC	DF1A	BADE
e^2	7.38905	60989	30650	22723	04275	7.6399	2E35	376B	730C	E8EE
$\sqrt{e}$	1.64872	12707	00128	14684	86508	1.A612	98E1	E069	BC97	2DFE
γ (Euler's constant)	0.57721	56649	01532	86060	65121	0.93C4	67E3	7DB0	C7A4	D1BE
$\varphi = (1 + \sqrt{5})/2$ (Golden Ratio)	1.61803	39887	49894	84820	45868	1.9E37	79B9	7F4A	7C15	F39C

— Appendix III —

COMPUTER JOURNALS AND MAGAZINES

Though very extensive, this compendium of computer-related publications cannot be regarded as "complete" for at least two reasons. First, the number of such publications is approaching 1,000 and publications are born and die with regularity. Second, editorial judgment was exercised as to the degree to which a candidate journal was "computer-related." Publication titles were gathered through library research and Web browsing, particularly at the sites maintained by computer societies and publishers. Many of these journals can be reached through links in the online lists maintained by the *Internet Electronic Library Project* and the other abstract and review sources cited in the first of the many lists that follow. The URLs cited were valid in late 1999 but are volatile. For brevity, "http://" has been omitted from the start of URLs. Other prefixes (e.g. "ftp://") are retained. Certain journals appear in more than one category.

Abstract and Review Publications

Computer Abstracts: www.csa2.com/jnlsV3/sscomputab.html
Computer and Control Abstracts: tolomeo.cisi.unige.it/erl/in.html
Computer and Information Systems Abstracts: www.csa2.com/siteV3/printjcomp.html
Computing Reviews: www.acm.org/reviews/
Internet Electronic Library Project: elib.cs.sfu.ca/Collections/CMPT/cs-journals/
Microcomputer Abstracts: www.csa2.com/siteV3/printjcomp.html

Research Journals, Theoretical and General

Acta Informatica: link.springer-ny.com/link/service/journals/00236/index.htm
Acta Polytechnica Scandinavica, Mathematics and Computer Science: elib.cs.sfu.ca/cs-journals/P-SomePub/J-SomePub-APSMCSS.html
BIT (Nordisk Tidskrift for Informationsbehandling): www.sztaki.hu/services/library/catalogue/b.html
Chicago Journal of Theoretical Computer Science: cs-www.uchicago.edu/publications/cjtcs/
Computational Complexity: www.birkhauser.ch/fields/journals/3700/3700_tit.htm
Computer Journal: www3.oup.co.uk/jnls/list/comjnl/
Computing: www.springer.at/springer.py?Page=40&cat=3&id_journal=8
Concurrency: www.computer.org/concurrency/
Concurrency: Practice and Experience: www.informall.org/Wiley/CPE/CPE.html
Electronic Notes in Theoretical Computer Science: www.elsevier.nl/cas/tree/store/tcs/free/noncas/pc/menu.htm
Formal Aspects of Computing: www.bcs.org.uk/publicat/journals/formasp/formasp.htm
Formal Methods in System Design: kapis.www.wkap.nl/journalhome.htm/0925-9856/
Fundamenta Informaticae: alfa.mimuw.edu.pl/FI/
Information and Computation: www.academicpress.com/www/journal/ic.htm
INFORMS Journal on Computing: www.informs.org/Pubs/JOC/
Journal of the ACM: www.acm.org/jacm/
Journal of Automated Reasoning: kapis.www.wkap.nl/journalhome.htm/0168-7433/
Journal of Computer and System Sciences: www.apnet.com/www/journal/ss.htm
Journal on Computing: www.informs.org/Pubs/Jocforth.html

Journal of Computing and Information: `phoenix.trentu.ca/jci/`

Journal of Universal Computer Science: `www.iicm.edu/jucs/`

Mathematical Structures in Computer Science: `www.cup.cam.ac.uk/Journals/JNLSCAT/msc/msc.html`

SIAM Journal on Computing: `www.siam.org/journals/sicomp/sicomp.htm`

Theoretical Computer Science: `www.elsevier.nl/locate/tcs/`

Theory of Computing Systems: `link.springer-ny.com/link/service/journals/00224/index.htm`

ACM Publications

TRANSACTIONS

Transactions on Computer-Human Interaction: `www.acm.org/tochi/`

Transactions on Computer Systems: `www.acm.org/tocs/`

Transactions on Computer Logic: `info.acm.org/tocl/`

Transactions on Database Systems: `www.acm.org/tods/`

Transactions on Design Automation of Electronic Systems: `www.acm.org/todaes/`

Transactions on Graphics: `www.acm.org/tog/`

Transactions on Information and System Security: `www.acm.org/tissec/`

Transactions on Information Systems: `www.acm.org/tois/`

Transactions on Mathematical Software: `www.acm.org/toms/`

Transactions on Modeling and Computer Simulation: `www.acm.org/tomacs/`

Transactions on Networking (with IEEE): `www.acm.org/ton/`

Transactions on Programming Languages and Systems: `www.acm.org/toplas/`

Transactions on Software Engineering and Methodology: `www.acm.org/tosem/`

SPECIAL INTEREST GROUP (SIG) PUBLICATIONS

SIGACT News (Algorithms and Computation Theory): `sigact.acm.org/sigactnews/`

SIGAda Ada Letters (Ada language): `www.acm.org/sigada/`

SIGAPL APL Quote Quad (APL and J languages): `www.acm.org/sigapl/qq.htm`

SIGAPP Applied Computing Review (APPlications): `www.acm.org/sigapp/acr/index.html`

SIGARCH News (Computer ARCHitecture): `www.acm.org/sigarch/sigarch_fact_sheet.html`

SIGART Bulletin (ARTificial intelligence): `sigart.acm.org/bulletin/`

SIGBIO Newsletter (BIOmedical computing): `www.acm.org/sigbio/`

SIGCAPH Newsletter (Computers And the Physically Handicapped): `www.acm.org/sigcaph/`

SIGCAS (Computers And Society): `heart.engr.csulb.edu/~sigcas/`

SIGCHI Bulletin (Computer–Human Interaction): `www.acm.org/sigchi/bulletin/`

SIGCOMM Computer Communication Review (data COMMunications): `www.acm.org/sigcomm/ccr/index.html`

SIGCPR Computer Personnel (Computer Personnel Research): `www.acm.org/sigcpr/cpr_pub.html`

SIGCSE Bulletin (Computer Science Education): `www.acm.org/sigcse/bulletin/`

SIGCUE Outlook (Computer Uses in Education): `www.acm.org/sigcue/sigcue_fact_sheet.html`

SIGDA Transactions on Design Automation of Electronic Systems: `www.sigda.acm.org/About/Newsletter/`

SIGDOC Journal of Computer Documentation: `www.acm.org/sigdoc/journal.html`

SIGGRAPH Newsletter (Computer GRAPHics): `www.siggraph.org/publications/newsletter/archive.html`

SIGGROUP (Groupware, etc.): `www.acm.org/siggroup/`

SIGIR Forum (Information Retrieval): `www.acm.org/sigir/Forum.html`

SIGLINK Review (hypertext and hypermedia): `www.acm.org/siglink/newsletter.html`

SIGMETRICS (performance evaluation): `www.cs.du.edu/per/index.html`

SIGMICRO (MICROcomputers): `www.acm.org/sigmicro/`

SIGMIS Data Base (Management Information Systems): `www.cis.gsu.edu/~dbase/`

SIGMM (Multimedia): `www.acm.org/sigmm/`

SIGMOBILE (Mobile Communications and Communications Review): `www.acm.org/sigmobile/MC2R/`

SIGMOD Record (Management of Data): `www.cs.umd.edu/areas/db/record/`

SIGNUM Newsletter (NUMerical mathematics): `www.acm.org/signum/`

SIGOPS Newsletter (OPerating Systems): `www.acm.org/sigops/`

SIGPLAN Notices (Programming LANguages): `www.rowan.edu/sigplan/`

SIGSAC Review (Security, Audit, and Control): `www.acm.org/sigsac/sigsacRv.html`

SIGSAM Bulletin (Symbolic and Algebraic Manipulation): `pineapple.apmaths.uwo.ca/~rmc/sigsam/`

SIGSIM Simulation Digest (SIMulation and modeling): `www.acm.org/sigsim/main/frame.html`

SIGSOFT Software Engineering Notes (SOFTware engineering): `www.acm.org/sigsoft/SEN/index.html`

SIGSound (Sound technology): `www.acm.org/sigsound/sigsound_fact_sheet.html`

SIGUCCS Newsletter (University and College Computing Services): `www.acm.org/siguccs/siguccs_fact_sheet.html`

OTHER ACM PUBLICATIONS

3C Online: `www.acm.org/sig3c/members/images/3conline.htm`

Collected Algorithms: `www.acm.org/calgo/`

Communications of the ACM: `www.acm.org/cacm/`

Computing Reviews: `www.acm.org/reviews/`

Computing Surveys: `www.acm.org/surveys/`

Crossroads: `www.acm.org/crossroads/`

Interactions: `www.acm.org/interactions/`

Journal of Experimental Algorithmics: `www.jea.acm.org`

Journal of Graphics Tools: `www.acm.org/jgt/`

NetWorker: `www.acm.org/networker/`

Performance Evaluation Review: `www.cs.du.edu/per/index.html`

StandardView: `www.acm.org/catalog/journals/121.html`

Publications of the British Computer Society (BCS)

Computer Bulletin: `www.bcs.org.uk/publicat/journals/bulletin/calendar/cbullist.htm`

Computer Journal: `www.bcs.org.uk/publicat/journals/journal/cjournal.htm`

Distributed Systems Engineering: `www.bcs.org.uk/publicat/journals/disteng/disteng.htm`

Formal Aspects of Computing: `www.bcs.org.uk/publicat/journals/formasp/formasp.htm`

Interacting with Computers: `www.bcs.org.uk/publicat/journals/interact/interact.htm`

Journal of Digital Information: `jodi.ecs.soton.ac.uk`
Software – Proceedings: `www.bcs.org.uk/`
 `publicat.journals/softeng/softeng.htm`
Software Quality Management Journal (SQM): `www.bcs.org.`
 `uk/siggroup/sg48.htm`
Vector – Journal of the BCS APL Specialist Group: `www.bcs.`
 `org.uk/siggroup/sg02.htm`

IEEE Publications

TRANSACTIONS

Transactions on Automatic Control: `www.ieee.org/pubs/`
 `pub_preview/ac_toc.html`
Transactions on Communications: `www.ieee.org/pubs/`
 `pub_preview/comm_toc.html`
Transactions on Computer-Aided Design of Integrated Circuits
 & Systems: `www.ieee.org/pubs/pub_preview/`
 `cad_toc.html`
Transactions on Computers: `www.computer.org/tc/`
Transactions on Evolutionary Computation: `www.ieee.org/`
 `pubs/pub_preview/evc_toc.html`
Transactions on Image Processing: `www.ieee.org/pubs/`
 `pub_preview/ip_toc.html`
Transactions on Information Theory: `www.ieee.org/pubs/`
 `pub_preview/it_toc.html`
Transactions on Knowledge and Data Engineering: `www.`
 `computer.org/tkde/`
Transactions on Medical Imaging: `www.ieee.org/pubs/`
 `pub_preview/mi_toc.html`
Transactions on Networking: `www.ccrc.wustl.edu/~ton/`
Transactions on Neural Networks: `www.ieee.org/pubs/`
 `pub_preview/nn_toc.html`
Transactions on Parallel and Distributed Systems: `www.`
 `computer.org/tpds/`
Transactions on Pattern Analysis and Machine Intelligence:
 `www.computer.org/tpami/`
Transactions on Robotics and Automation: `www.ieee.org/`
 `pubs/pub_-preview/ra_toc.html`
Transactions on Signal Processing: `www.ieee.org/pubs/`
 `pub_preview/sp_toc.html`
Transactions on Software Engineering: `www.computer.`
 `org/tse/`
Transactions on Systems, Man and Cybernetics A: Systems &
 Humans: `www.ieee.org/pubs/pub_preview/`
 `smca_toc.html`
Transactions on Systems, Man and Cybernetics B: Cybernetics:
 `www.ieee.org/pubs/pub_preview/smcb_toc.html`
Transactions on Visualization and Computer Graphics: `www.`
 `computer.org/tvcg/`
Transactions on VLSI Systems: `www.ieee.org/pubs/`
 `pub_preview/vlsi_toc.html`

OTHER IEEE PUBLICATIONS

Annals of the History of Computing: `www.computer.org/`
 `annals/`
Computational Science and Engineering:
 `www.computer.org/cse/`
Computer: `www.computer.org/computer/`
Computer Applications in Power: `www.ieee.org/`
 `magazines/cap.htm`
Computer Graphics and Applications: `www.computer.`
 `org/cga/`
Concurrency: `www.computer.org/concurrency/`
Control Systems Magazine: `www.ieee.org/magazines/`
 `cs.htm`
Design and Test of Computers: `www.computer.org/dt/`
IEEE Potentials: `www.ececs.uc.edu/~paw/potentials/`
Intelligent Systems and their Application: `www.computer.`
 `org/intelligent/`

Internet Computing: `www.computer.org/internet/`
Journal on Selected Areas in Communications: `www.ieee.`
 `org/pubs/pub_preview/jsac_toc.html`
looking.forward: `www.computer.org/student/looking/`
Micro: `www.computer.org/micro/`
Multimedia: `www.computer.org/mulitmedia/`
Network: `www.comsoc.org/socstr/techcom/ntwrk/`
Proceedings: `www.ieee.org/pubs/pub_preview/`
 `proc_toc.html`
Robotics & Automation Magazine: `www.ieee.org/`
 `magazines/rob.htm`
Signal Processing Letters: `www.ieee.org/pubs/pub_`
 `preview/spl_toc.html`
Signal Processing Magazine: `www.ieee.org/magazines/`
 `sp.htm`
Software: `www.computer.org/software/`
Spectrum: `www.spectrum.ieee.org`

Proceedings of the Institution of Electrical Engineers (IEE—UK)

Circuits, Devices and Systems: `www.iee.org.uk/publish/`
 `journals/profjrnl/ieeproc.html#procccts`
Computing and Control Engineering Journal: `www.iee.org.`
 `uk/publish/journals/magsnews/compconj.html`
Computers and Digital Techniques: `www.iee.org.uk/`
 `publish/journals/profjrnl/ieeproc.html#`
 `proccomp`
Control Theory and Applications: `www.iee.org.uk/`
 `publish/journals/profjrnl/ieeproc.html#`
 `proccont`
Software: `www.iee.org.uk/publish/journals/`
 `profjrnl/ieeproc.html#procse`
Vision, Image and Signal Processing: `www.iee.org.uk/`
 `publish/journals/profjrnl/ieeproc.html#`
 `procvis`

Publications of the Society for Industrial and Applied Mathematics (SIAM)

SIAM Journal on Applied Mathematics: `www.siam.org/`
 `journals/siap/siap.htm`
SIAM Journal on Computing: `www.siam.org/journals/`
 `sicomp/sicomp.htm`
SIAM Journal on Control and Optimization: `www.siam.org/`
 `journals/sicon/sicon.htm`
SIAM Journal on Discrete Mathematics: `www.siam.org/`
 `journals/sidma/sidma.htm`
SIAM Journal on Mathematical Analysis: `www.siam.org/`
 `journals/sima/sima.htm`
SIAM Journal on Matrix Analysis and Applications:
 `www.siam.org/journals/simax/simax.htm`
SIAM Journal on Numerical Analysis: `www.siam.org/`
 `journals/sinum/sinum.htm`
SIAM Journal on Optimization: `www.siam.org/journals/`
 `siopt/siopt.htm`
SIAM Journal on Scientific Computing: `www.siam.org/`
 `journals/sisc/sisc.htm`
SIAM Review: `www.siam.org/journals/sirev/sirev.`
 `htm`

Industrial Journals

Adobe Magazine: `www.adobe.com/publications/`
 `adobemag/`
AT&T Network Edge: `www.att.com/network_edge/`
Bell Labs Technical Journal: `www.lucent.com/minds/`
 `techjournal/`

Control Data World: www.cdc.com
Digital Technical Journal: www.dec.com
Hewlett-Packard Journal: www.hp.com/hpj/journal.html
Honeywell Monthly: www.honeywell.com
HP World: www.interex.org/hpworldnews/
IBM Journal of Research and Development: www.research.ibm.com/journal/
IBM Systems Journal: www.almaden.ibm.com/journal/
Microsoft Magazine: www.microsoft.com/magazine/
Microsoft Systems Journal: www.msj.com
NetscapeWorld: www.netscapeworld.com
Unisys World: www.unisys.com
SunExpert: www.cpg.com/se/
Sun World: www.sunworld.com

Journals of Specific Countries or Regions

Acta Polytechnica Scandinavica, Mathematics and Computer Science: elib.cs.sfu.ca/cs-journals/P-SomePub/J-SomePub-APSMCSS.html
Asian Journal of Business and Information Systems: www.wspc.com.sg/journals/journals.html
Asian Journal of Control: ajc.csie.ntu.edu.tw
Australian Computer Journal: www.acs.org.au/journal/index0.htm
Australian Journal of Information Systems: www.uow.edu.au/ajis/ajis.html
Australian PC Magazine: apcmag.com
Canadian Artificial Intelligence: elib.cs.sfu.ca/Collections/CMPT/cs-journals/P-CSCSI/J-CSCSI-CAI.html
Chinese Journal of Advanced Software Research: www.ios.ac.cn/xuebao/esy.html
ComputerScene Magazine (New Mexico): www.cscene.com
Computers and Artificial Intelligence (Slovak): nic.savba.sk/logos/journals/libr/libr.html#comp
Computing Japan Magazine Online: www.cjmag.co.jp
European Journal of Information Systems: www.stockton-press.co.uk/ejis/index.html
Information Technology and Control (Lithuania): itc.soften.ktu.lt/
Journal of the Brazilian Computer Society: www.dcc.unicamp.br/~jbcs/
Nordic Journal of Computing: www.porsas.cs.helsinki.fi/njc/
Objekt Spektrum (Germany): www.sigs.com/publications/obsp/
Scandinavian Journal of Information Systems: www.iesd.auc.dk/general/IS/SJIS/
South African Computer Journal: www.cs.up.ac.za/sacj/
Studies in Informatics and Control (Romania): www.cef.pub.ro/raist/scientific/studies.htm
Systems and Computers in Japan: www3.interscience.wiley.com/cgi-bin/jtoc?ID=51986

International Journals

All begin "International Journal of" (or "on" or "for").

Adaptive Control and Signal Processing: www.interscience.wiley.com/jpages/0890-6327/
Algebra and Computation: www.wspc.com.sg/journals/journals.html
Applied Expert Systems: www.abdn.ac.uk/~acc025/ijaes.html
Artificial Intelligence in Education: www.cbl.leeds.ac.uk/ijaied/
Artificial Intelligence Tools: www.wspc.com.sg/journals/journals.html
Bifurcation and Chaos: www.wspc.com.sg/journals/journals.html

Circuit Theory and Applications: www.interscience.wiley.com/jpages/0098-9886/
Clinical Monitoring and Computing: kapis.www.wkap.nl/journalhome.htm/0167-9945/
Communications Systems: www3.interscience.wiley.com/cgi-bin/jtoc?ID=5996
Computational Acoustics: www.wspc.com.sg/journals/journals.html
Computational Engineering Science: www.wspc.com.sg/journals/journals.html
Computational Fluid Dynamics: www.gbhap-us.com/journals/722/
Computational Geometry and Applications: www.wspc.com.sg/journals/journals.html
Computational Intelligence and Organizations: www.ecst.csuchico.edu/~ijcio/
Computer Mathematics: www.gbhap.com/Computer_Mathematics/
Computer Simulation: www.cs.umr.edu/ijcs/
Computer Vision: kapis.www.wkap.nl/journalhome.htm/0920-5691/
Computers and Applications: http://elib.cs.sfu.ca/Collections/CMPT/cs-journals/P-IASTED/J-IASTED-IJCA.html
Computer-Aided Engineering & Systems: www.mcb.co.uk/cgi-bin/journal1/ec/
Computer-Integrated Manufacturing: www.tandf.co.uk/E-pub/cwonline.htm#cim/
Computers and Mathematics in Electrical and Electronic Engineering: www.mcb.co.uk/cgi-bin/journal1/compel/
Computers for Mathematical Learning: kapis.www.wkap.nl/journalhome.htm/1382-3892/
Control: www.tandf.co.uk/E-pub/cwonline.htm#cona/
Cooperative Information Systems (IJCIS) WSJ: www.wspc.com.sg/journals/ijcis/ijcis.html
Cooperative Intelligent Systems: www.wspc.com.sg/journals/journals.html
Digital Libraries: www.springer-ny.com/compsci/ijodl.htm
Document Analysis and Recognition: documents.cfar.umd.edu/IJDAR/
Engineering Intelligent Systems: info.gte.comftp/doc/dimitris/EIS/EIS.html
Expert Systems: www.coginst.uwf.edu/IJES/
Flexible Automation & Integrated Manufacturing: www.begellhouse.com/faim.html
Forensic Computing: www.forensic-computing.com/info2.html
Foundations of Computer Science: www.wspc.com.sg/journals/journals.html
General Systems: www.gbhab.com/General_Systems/
Geographical Information Systems: www.tandf.co.uk/E-pub/cwonline.htm#gis/
High Performance Computing: ca28.sagepub.com/sac.htm
High Speed Computing: www.wspc.com.sg/journals/journals.html
Human–Computer Interaction: www.hcirn.com/res/publish/lea.html
Human–Computer Studies: www.hbuk.co.uk/ap/journals/hc/
Imaging Systems and Technology: www.interscience.wiley.com/jpages/0899-9457/
Information Technology: www.maruzen.co.jp/g-ri-iji%281%29.htm
Intelligent Control and Systems: www.wspc.com.sg/journals/journals.html
Intelligent Engineering Applications: www.gwu.edu/~aisoc/ijiea.html

Intelligent Systems: www3.interscience.wiley.com/cgi-bin/jtoc?ID=36062

Intelligent Systems in Accounting, Finance, and Management: www.usc.edu/dept/sba/atisp/AI/IJISAFM/forthcom.htm

Intelligent Systems: www.interscience.wiley.com/jpages/0884-8173/

Law and Information Technology: www.oup.co.uk/jnls/list/inttec/

Mathematical Algorithms: www.gbhap-us.com/journals/262/262-top.htm

Microwave and Millimeter-wave CAE: www.interscience.wiley.com/jpages/1050-1827/

Modelling and Simulation: www.iasted.com/editinfo.htm

Modern Physics C (IJMPC): Physics and Computers: www.wspc.com.sg/journals/journals.html

Multiple-Valued Logic: www.ghab.com/Multiple_Valued_Logic/

Network Management: www.interscience.wiley.com/jpages/1055-7148/

Neural Systems: www.wspc.com.sg/journals/journals.html

Numerical and Analytical Methods in Geomechanics: www.interscience.wiley.com/jpages/0363-9061/

Numerical Methods for Heat & Fluid Flow: www.mcb.co.uk/cgi-bin/journal1/hff/

Numerical Methods in Engineering: www.interscience.wiley.com/jpages/0029-5981/

Numerical Methods in Fluids: www.interscience.wiley.com/jpages/0271-2091/

Numerical Modelling: www.interscience.wiley.com/jpages/0894-3370/

Parallel and Distributed Systems and Networks: www.iasted.com/editinfo.htm

Parallel Programming: www.plenum.com/cgi/getarec?ple20000085/

Pattern Recognition and Artificial Intelligence: www.wspc.com.sg/journals/journals.html

Real-Time Automation: www.elsevier.nl/inca/publications/store/9/7/5/

Robotics and Automation: www.iasted.com/editinfo.htm

Robotics Research: www.sagepub.com

Shape Modeling (computer graphics): www.wspc.com.sg/journals/journals.html

Software Engineering and Knowledge Engineering: www.wspc.com.sg/journals/journals.html

Software Tools for Technology Transfer: link.springer-ny.com/link/service/journals/10009/index.htm

Supercomputer Applications and High Performance Computing: mitpress.mit.edu/journal-home.tcl?issu=10783482/

Systems Science: www.tandf.co.uk/default.htm

Uncertainty, Fuzziness, and Knowledge-Based Systems: www.wspc.com.sg/journals/journals.html

Very Large Databases (VLDB Journal): link.springer-ny.com/link/service/journals/00778/index.htm

Visual Computing: www.intellect-net.com/journals/ijvc.htm

Wireless Information Networks: www.plenum.com/cgi/getarec?ple20000092/

Specialized Journals and Magazines

ALGORITHMS

Algorithmica: link.springer-ny.com/link/service/journals/00453/index.htm

Collected Algorithms: www.acm.org/calgo/

Journal of Algorithms: www.apnet.com/www/journal/al.htm

Journal of Experimental Algorithmics: www.acm.org/jea/

Journal of Graph Algorithms and Applications: www.cs.brown.edu/publications/jgaa/

Numerical Algorithms: www.math.psu.edu/dna/contents/na.html

Parallel Algorithms and Applications: www.gbhap.com/Parallel_Algorithms_Applications/

Random Structures and Algorithms: www.interscience.wiley.com/jpages/RandomStructAlg/

ARTIFICIAL INTELLIGENCE AND EXPERT SYSTEMS

Adaptive Behavior: mitpress.mit.edu/journal-home.tcl?issn=10597123/

AI Communications: www.iospress.nl/html/node316.html#SECTION00041000000000000000

AI Expert: drtavel.com/CompuPub.htm

AI Magazine: www.aaai.org

AI and Society: link.springer-ny.com/link/service/journals/00146/index.htm

AIXpert: www.developer.ibm.comsdp/library/aixpert/

Annals of Mathematics and Artificial Intelligence: www.baltzer.nl/amai/amai.html

Applied Artificial Intelligence: www.tandf.co.uk/E-pub/cwonline.htm#aai/

Artificial Intelligence: www.elsevier.nl/locate/artint/

Artificial Intelligence in Engineering: www.elsevier.com/inca/publications/store/4/2/2/9/1/7/

Artificial Intelligence for Engineering, Design, Analysis, and Manufacturing: www.hmc.edu/~dym/aiedam.html

Artificial Intelligence and Law: kapis.www.wkap.nl/journalhome.htm/0924-8463/

Artificial Intelligence in Medicine: www.elsevier.nl/estoc/publications/store/7/09333657/

Artificial Intelligence Review: www.wkap.nl/journalhome.htm/0269-2821/

Artificial Life: mitpress.mit.edu/journal-home.tcl?issn=10645462/

Artificial Life and Robotics: link.springer-ny.com/link/service/journals/10015/index.htm

Autonomous Agents and Multi-Agent Systems: kapis.www.wkap.nl/journalhome.htm/1387-2532/

Canadian Artificial Intelligence: elib.cs.sfu.ca/Collections/CMPT/cs-journals/P-CSCSI/J-CSCSI-CAI.html

Cognition: www.elsevier.nl/locate/cognit/

Computational Intelligence: calypso.cs.uregina.ca/CI/ci.html

Computers and Artificial Intelligence (Slovakia): nic.savba.sk/logos/journals/libr/libr.html#comp

Consciousness and Cognition: www.apnet.com/www/journal/cc.htm

Data and Knowledge Engineering: www.elsevier.nl/locate/datak/

Data Mining and Knowledge Discovery: kapis.www.wkap.nl/journalhome.htm/1384-5810/

Engineering Applications of Artificial Intelligence: www.elsevier.com/inca/publications/store/3/0/5/7/6/

Evolutionary Computation: mitpress.mit.edu/journal-home.tcl?issn=10636560/

Expert Systems: www.psyc.abdn.ac.uk/Expertsys/Expertsys.htm

Expert Systems with Applications: www.bus.orst.edu/faculty/brownc/eswa/ESWA.HTM

Intelligent Systems and their Application: www.computer.org/intelligent/

International Journal of Artificial Intelligence in Education: cbl.leeds.ac.uk/ijaied/home.html

International Journal of Intelligent Systems: www3.
  interscience.wiley.com/cgi-bin/jtoc?ID=36062
Journal of Artificial Intelligence Research: www.cs.
  washington.edu/research/jair/home.html
Journal of Automated Reasoning: www-unix.mcs.anl.
  gov/JAR/
Journal of Experimental & Theoretical Artificial Intelligence:
  www.tandf.co.uk/E-pub/cwonline.htm#eta/
Journal of Heuristics: kapis.www.wkap.nl/journalhome.
  htm/1381-1231/
Journal of Intelligent Systems: www.brunel.ac.uk/
  ~hssrjis/
Knowledge-Based Systems: www.elsevier.nl/locate/
  knosys/
Knowledge Engineering Review, The: www.cup.org/
  Journals/JNLSCAT/ker/ker.html
Machine Learning: www.wkap.nl/journalhome.htm/
  0885-6125/
Machine Learning Online: kapis.www.wkap.nl/
  journalhome.htm/1383-7915/
Machine Translation: kapis.www.wkap.nl/journalhome.
  htm/0922-6567/
Minds and Machines: kapis.www.wkap.nl/journalhome.
  htm/0924-6495/
New Review of Applied Expert Systems: www.abdn.ac.uk/
  ~acc025/nraes.htm
PC AI: www.pcai.com/pcai/
Transactions on Pattern Analysis and Machine Intelligence:
  www.computer.org/tpami/

AUTOMATION, CYBERNETICS, AND ROBOTICS

Artificial Life and Robotics: link.springer-ny.com/link/
  service/journals/10015/index.htm
Automatica: www.elsevier.com/inca/publications/
  store/2/7/0/
Autonomous Robots: kapis.www.wkap.nl/journalhome.
  htm/0929-5593/
Biological Cybernetics: link.springer-ny.comlink/
  service/journals/00422/index.htm
Control Theory and Applications: www.iee.org.uk/
  publish/journals/profjrnl/ieeproc.html#
  proccont
Cybernetics and Systems: www.tandf.co.uk/E-pub/
  cwonline.htm#cbs/
Cybernetics and Systems Analysis: www.plenum.com/cgi/
  getarec?ple20000043/
Industrial Robot: www.mcb.co.uk/cgi-bin/
  journal1/ir/
Journal of Automata, Languages, and Combinatorics: fuzzy.
  cs.uni-magdeburg.de/theo/jalc/
Journal of Automation and Information Sciences: www.
  begellhouse.com/jais.html
Journal of Automation and Remote Control: www.plenum.
  com/cgi/getarec?ple20000015/
Journal of Cybernetics & Systems Analysis: www.plenum.com/
  cgi/getarec?ple20000043/
Journal of Intelligent Manufacturing: www.chapmanhall.
  com/ji/default.html
Journal of Intelligent and Robotic Systems: kapis.www.
  wkap.nl/journalhome.htm/0921-0296/
Journal of Robotic Systems: www.interscience.
  wiley.com/jpages/0741-2223/
Kybernetes: www.mcb.co.uk/cgi-bin/journal1/k/
Presence: Teleoperators and Virtual Environments:
  mitpress.mit.edu/journal-home.tcl?issn=
  10547460/
Robotica: www.cup.cam.ac.uk/Journals/JNLSCAT/rob/
  rob.html
Robotics and Autonomous Systems: www.elsevier.nl/
  locate/robot/

*Transactions on Systems, Man and Cybernetics, Part A: Systems
  & Humans*: www.ieee.org/pubs/pub_preview/
  smca_toc.html
*Transactions on Systems, Man and Cybernetics, Part B:
  Cybernetics*: www.ieee.org/pubs/pub_preview/
  smcb_toc.html
Transactions on Automatic Control: www.ieee.org/pubs/
  pub_preview/ac_toc.html
Transactions on Robotics and Automation: www.ieee.org/
  pubs/pub_preview/ra_toc.html

COMPUTATIONAL LINGUISTICS

Computational Linguistics: mitpress.mit.edu/journal-
  home.tcl?issn=08912017/
Grammars: kapis.www.wkap.nl/journalhome.htm/
  1386-7393/
Journal of Pragmatics: www.elsevier.com:80/inca/
  publications/store/5/0/5/5/9/3/
Journal of Quantitative Linguistics: www.ldv.uni-trier.
  de:8080/%7Eiqla/jql.html
Literary and Linguistic Computing: www.oup.co.uk/jnls/
  list/litlin/
Natural Language and Linguistic Theory: kapis.www.wkap.
  nl/journalhome.htm/0167-806X/

COMPUTER GRAPHICS, IMAGING, PATTERN
RECOGNITION, AND VISUALIZATION

Computer Graphics World: www.cgw.com/cgw/Archives/
  index.asp
Computer Vision and Image Understanding:
  www.apnet.com/www/journal/iv.htm
Computers and Graphics: www.elsevier.nl/inca/
  publications/store/3/9/1/index.htt
Fractals: www.wspc.com.sg/journals/journals.html
Graphical Models and Image Processing: www.apnet.com/
  www/journal/ip.htm
Image Communications: www.elsevier.nl/locate/
  image/
Image and Vision Computing: www.elsevier.nl/locate/
  imavis/
Journal of Electronic Imaging: www.spie.org/web/
  journals/jei_home.html
Journal of Flow Visualization and Image Processing: www.
  begellhouse.com/jfv.html
Journal of Graphics Tools: www.acm.org/jgt/
Journal of Mathematical Imaging and Vision: kapis.www.
  wkap.nl/journalhome.htm/0924-9907/
Journal of Visual Communication and Image Representation:
  www.apnet.com/www/journal/vc.htm
Journal of Visualization: www.iospress.nl/html/
  node344.html#SECTION00042900000000000000
Journal of Visualization and Computer Animation: www3.
  interscience.wiley.com/cgi-bin/jtoc?Type=
  DD&ID=14204
Machine Graphics and Vision: www.ipipan.waw.pl/MGV/
  MGV.html
Machine Vision and Applications: link.springer-ny.com/
  link/service/journals/00138/index.htm
Pattern Analysis and Applications: www.soc.plym.ac.uk/
  soc/sameer/paa.htm
Pattern Recognition: www.elsevier.com:80/inca/
  publications/store/3/2/8/
Pattern Recognition Letters: www.elsevier.nl/locate/
  patrec/
Real-Time Imaging: www.hbuk.co.uk/ap/journals/ri/
Signal Processing: Image Communication:
  www.elsevier.nl:80/inca/publications/store/
  5/0/5/6/5/1/
Transactions on Graphics: www.acm.org/tog/

Transactions on Image Processing: `www.ieee.org/pubs/pub_preview/ip_toc.html`
Transactions on Visualization and Computer Graphics: `www.computer.org/tvcg/`
Videre: A Journal of Computer Vision Research: `mitpress.mit.edu/journal-home.tcl?issn=10892788/`
Vision, Image and Signal Processing: `www.iee.org.uk/publish/journals/profjrnl/ieeproc.html#procvis`
Visualization and Computer Animation: `www.wiley.com/journals/vis/`

DATABASE DESIGN AND MANAGEMENT

Database: `www.onlineinc.com/database/index.html`
Database Programming & Design: `www.dbpd.com`
Data Based Advisor: `www.talsoft.com.au/dbinfo.html`
DB2 Magazine : `www.mfi.com`
DBMS: `www.dbmsmag.com`
Distributed and Parallel Databases: `kapis.www.wkap.nl/journalhome.htm/0926-8782/`
Information Systems: `www.elsevier.com/inca/publications/store/2/3/6/`
Journal of Database Management: `www.idea-group.com/jdm.htm`
Oracle Magazine: `www.oramag.com`
Transactions on Database Systems: `www.acm.org/tods/`
VLDB – Journal of Very Large Databases: `link.springer-ny.com/link/service/journals/00778/index.htm`

DISCRETE MATHEMATICS

Annals of Combinatorics: `link.springer-ny.com/link/service/journals/00798/index.htm`
Combinatorica: `gopher://trick.ntp.springer.de/11/TOC/493/`
Combinatorics, Probability, and Computing: `www.cup.cam.ac.uk/Journals/JNLSCAT/cpc/cpc.html`
Cryptosystems Journal: `ourworld.compuserve.com/homepages/crypto/`
Designs, Codes, and Cryptography: `kapis.www.wkap.nl/journalhome.htm/0925-1022/`
Discrete and Computational Geometry: `link.springer-ny.com/link/service/journals/00454/index.htm`
Discrete Applied Mathematics: `www.elsevier.nl/locate/dam/`
Discrete Mathematics: `www.elsevier.nl/locate/disc/`
Discrete Mathematics and Theoretical Computer Science: `www.compscinet.com`
Electronic Journal of Combinatorics: `www.combinatorics.org`
European Journal of Combinatorics: `www.hbuk.co.uk/ap/journals/ej/`
Graphs and Combinatorics: `link.springer-ny.com/link/service/journals/00373/index.htm`
Journal of Algebraic Combinatorics: `www.wkap.nl/journalhome.htm/0925-9899/`
Journal of Combinatorial Designs: `www.emba.uvm.edu/~colbourn/jcd.html`
Journal of Combinatorial Optimization: `kapis.www.wkap.nl/journalhome.htm/1382-6905/`
Journal of Combinatorial Theory Series A: `www.apnet.com/www/journal/ta.htm`
Journal of Combinatorial Theory Series B: `www.apnet.com/www/journal/tb.htm`
Journal of Cryptology: `link.springer-ny.com/link/service/journals/00145/index.htm`
Journal of Difference Equations and Applications: `www.gbhap-us.com/journals/731/`
Journal of Graph Theory: `www.interscience.wiley.com/jpages/JgraphTheory/`

Journal of Integer Sequences: `www.research.att.com/~njas/sequences/JIS/`
Journal of Number Theory: `math.ohio-state.edu:80/Groups/JNT/`
SIAM Journal on Discrete Mathematics: `www.siam.org/journals/sidma/sidma.htm`

DISTRIBUTED COMPUTING AND PARALLEL SYSTEMS

Application Development Advisor: `www.appdevadvisor.com`
Cluster Computing: `www.baltzer.nl/cluster/cluster.html`
Collaborative Computing: `www.crg.cs.nott.ac.uk/~oklee/collab_computing.html`
Component Strategies: `www.componentmag.com`
Distributed Computing (Springer): `link.springer-ny.com/link/service/journals/00446/index.htm`
Distributed Engineering Journal: `www.bcs.org.uk/publicat/journals/disteng/disteng.htm`
Distributed Systems Engineering: `www.iop.org/Journals/ds/`
Distributed and Parallel Databases: `kapis.www.wkap.nl/journalhome.htm/0926-8782/`
Electronic Journal on Networks and Distributed Processing: `rerir.univ-pau.fr`
Journal of Parallel and Distributed Computing: `www.apnet.com/www/journal/pc.htm`
Parallel and Distributed Systems: `www.computer.org/tpds/`
Parallel Algorithms and Applications: `www.gbhap.com/Parallel_Algorithms_Applications/`
Parallel Computing: `www.elsevier.nl/locate/parco/`
Parallel Processing Letters: `www.wspc.com.sg/journals/journals.html`
Transactions on Parallel and Distributed Systems: `www.computer.org/tpds/`

EDUCATION

Archives and Museum Informatics: `www.wkap.nl/journalhome.htm/1042-1467/`
Bits & Bytes Review: `www.publist.com/cgi-bin/show?PLID=4009290`
Compute~Ed: `www.education.uts.edu.au/projects/comped/`
Computer Applications in Engineering Education: `www3.interscience.wiley.com/cgi-bin/jtoc?ID=38664`
Computer-Assisted Language Learning: `www.publist.com/cgi-bin/show?PLID=4266195`
Computer Education: `www.publist.com/cgi-bin/show?PLID=1274880`
Computer Learning: `www.publist.com/cgi-bin/show?PLID=4979448`
Computers and Education: `www.publist.com/cgi-bin/show?PLID=1640963`
Computers in Education Journal: `www.publist.com/cgi-bin/show?PLID=1565394`
Computers in the Schools: `www.publist.com/cgi-bin/show?PLID=369334X`
Education and Information Technologies: `www.chapmanhall.com/ei/default.html`
International Journal of Artificial Intelligence in Education: `cbl.leeds.ac.uk/ijaied/home.html`
Journal of Computer-Assisted Learning: `www.blacksci.co.uk/products/journals/jcal.htm`
Journal of Computers in Mathematics and Science Teaching: `www.aace.org/pubs/jcmst/index.html`
Journal of Computing in Childhood Education: `www.aace.org/pubs/child/index.html`
Journal of Computing in Higher Education: `www-unix.oit.umass.edu/~carolm/jche/`

Journal of Educational Computing Research: `www.publist.com/cgi-bin/show?PLID=372976X`

Journal of Science Education and Technology: `www.plenum.com/cgi/getarec?ple20000164/`

Lecture Notes in Computer Science: `www.springer.de/comp/lncs/index.html`

SIGCSE Bulletin (Computer Science Education): `www.acm.org/sigcse/bulletin/`

SIGCUE Outlook (Computer Uses in Education): `www.acm.org/sigcue/sigcue_fact_sheet.html`

Software and Networks for Learning: `www.publist.com/cgi-bin/show?PLID=1528993`

ENGINEERING APPLICATIONS

Applied Signal Processing: `elib.cs.sfu.ca/Collections/CMPT/cs-journals/P-Springer/J-Springer-ASP.html`

Applied and Computational Harmonic Analysis: `www.academicpress.com/www/journal/ha.htm`

Artificial Intelligence for Engineering Design, Analysis, and Manufacturing: `www2.hmc.edu/~dym/aiedam.html`

Cadence: `www.cadence-mag.com`

Communications in Numerical Methods in Engineering: `www.interscience.wiley.com/jpages/1069-8299/`

Computational Fluid Dynamics: `www.gbhap.com/Computational_Fluid_Dynamics/`

Computational Materials Science: `www.elsevier.nl/inca/publications/store/5/2/3/4/1/2/`

Computational Mechanics: `link.springer-ny.com/link/service/journals/00466/index.htm`

Computational Mechanics Advances: `www.elsevier.nl/locate/cmad/`

Computational Science and Engineering: `www.computer.org/cse/`

Computer-Aided Geometric Design: `www.elsevier.nl/locate/comaid/`

Computer Applications in Engineering Education: `www.journals.wiley.com/cae/`

Computer Methods in Applied Mechanics and Engineering: `www.elsevier.nl/locate/cma/`

Computer Methods in Biomechanics and Biomedical Engineering: `www.gbhap-us.com/journals/291/291-top.htm`

Computing and Control Engineering Journal: `www.iee.org.uk/publish/journals/magsnews/compconj.html`

Computers and Electrical Engineering: `www.elsevier.nl/inca/publications/store/3/6/7/`

Computers and Fluids: `www.elsevier.nl/inca/publications/store/3/6/5/`

Computers and Industrial Engineering: `www.elsevier.nl/inca/publications/store/3/9/9/`

Control and Computers: `www.iasted.com/editinfo.htm`

Design Automation for Embedded Systems: `kapis.www.wkap.nl/journalhome.htm/0929-5585/`

Discrete Event Dynamic Systems: `kapis.www.wkap.nl/journalhome.htm/0924-6703/`

Dynamics and Control: `apis.www.wkap.nl/journalhome.htm/0925-4668/`

Engineering Applications of Artificial Intelligence: `www.elsevier.com/inca/publications/store/3/0/5/7/6/`

Engineering with Computers: `link.springer-ny.com/link/service/journals/00366/index.htm`

Finite Elements in Analysis and Design: `www.elsevier.nl/locate/finel/`

Integrated Computer-Aided Engineering: `www.iospress.nl/html/node333.html#SECTION 00041800000000000000`

Journal of Computational Acoustics: `www.wspc.com.sg/journals/journals.html`

Journal of Computer-Aided Materials Design: `kapis.www.wkap.nl/journalhome.htm/0928-1045/`

Journal of Dynamical & Control Systems: `www.plenum.com/cgi/getarec?ple20000121/`

Journal of Technology & Computer-Aided Design: `www.ieee.org/journal/tcad/`

Technical Computing Magzine: `www.adeptscience.co.uk/as/tcm/`

Telecommunications and Radio Engineering: `www.begellhouse.com/tre.html`

Telecommunication Systems: `www.baltzer.nl/telsys/telsys.html`

Theoretical and Computational Fluid Dynamics: `link.springer-ny.com/link/service/journals/00162/index.htm`

HARDWARE AND COMPUTER ENGINEERING

Analog Integrated Circuits and Signal Processing: `www.wkap.nl/journalhome.htm/0925-1030/`

Chips: `www.chips.navy.mil/chips/`

Circuits, Systems & Signal Processing: `www.birkhauser.com/journals/cssp/`

Computer Standards and Interfaces: `www.elsevier.nl/locate/csi/`

Computers and Digital Techniques: `www.iee.org.uk/publish/journals/profjrnl/ieeproc.html#proccomp`

Computing Systems: `mitpress.mit.edu/journal-home.tcl?issn=08956340/`

Digital Signal Processing: `www.apnet.com/www/journal/sp.htm`

Discrete & Computational Geometry: `link.springer-ny.com/link/service/journals/00454/index.htm`

Integration, the VLSI Journal: `www.elsevier.nl/locate/vlsi/`

Journal of Circuits, Systems, and Computers: `www.wspc.com.sg/journals/journals.html`

Journal of Information Storage and Processing Systems : `www.birkhauser.com/journals/jisps/`

Journal of Systems Architecture: `www.elsevier.com:80/inca/publications/store/5/0/5/6/1/6/`

Journal of VLSI Signal Processing Systems for Signal, Image, and Video Tech: `kapis.www.wkap.nl/journalhome.htm/0922-5773/`

Microcomputer Applications: `www.iasted.com/editinfo.htm`

MicroComputer Journal: `www.midengr.com/micro.htm`

Microelectronics Engineering: `www.elsevier.nl/locate/mee/`

Microelectronics Journal: `www.elsevier.com/inca/publications/store/4/0/5/9/0/4/`

Microprocessing and Microprogramming: `www.elsevier.nl/locate/micpro/`

Microprocessors and Microsystems: `www.elsevier.com:80/inca/publications/store/5/2/5/4/4/9/`

Multidimensional Systems and Signal Processing: `kapis.www.wkap.nl/journalhome.htm/0923-6082/`

Problems of Information Transmission: `www.plenum.com/cgi/getarec?ple20000211/`

Real-Time Systems: `kapis.www.wkap.nl/journalhome.htm/0922-6443/`

Reliable Computing: `kapis.www.wkap.nl/journalhome.htm/1385-3139/`

Signal Processing: `www.elsevier.com/inca/publications/store/5/0/5/6/6/2/`

Transactions on VLSI Systems: `www.ieee.org/pubs/pub_preview/vlsi_toc.html`

VLSI Design: `www.gbhap.com/VLSI_Design`

INFORMATION SYSTEMS and MANAGEMENT

Australian Journal of Information Systems: www.uow.edu.au/ajis/subscr.html

Cutter IT Journal (American Programmer): www.cutter.com/itjournal

Data Base for Advances in Information Systems: www.cis.gsu.edu/~dbase/

European Journal of Information Systems: www.stockton-press.co.uk/ejis/index.html

Informatik—Forschung und Entwicklung: link.springer-ny.com/link/service/journals/00450/index.htm

Informatik—Spektrum: link.springer-ny.com/link/service/journals/00287/index.htm

Information and Computation: www.apnet.com/www/journal/ic.htm

Information Infrastructure and Policy: www.iospress.nl/html/node330.html#SECTION 000415000000000000000

Information and Management: www.elsevier.nl:80/estoc/publications/store/6/03787206/

Information Management and Computer Security: www.mcb.co.uk/cgi-bin/journal1/imes/

Information Processing Letters: www.elsevier.nl/locate/ipl/

Information Processing and Management: www.elsevier.com/inca/publications/store/2/4/4/

Information Retrieval: kapis.www.wkap.nl/journalhome.htm/1386-4564/

Information Science Abstracts: www.plenum.com/cgi/getarec?ple20000077/

Information Sciences: www.elsevier.nl/inca/publications/store/5/0/5/7/3/0/index.htt

Information Society, The: www.tandf.co.uk/E-pub/cwonline.htm#tis/

Information Systems: www.elsevier.com/inca/publications/store/2/3/6/

Information Systems Journal: www.blacksci.co.uk/~cgilib/jnlpage.bin?Journal=isj&File=isj&Page=aims

Information Systems Management: www.auerbach-publications.com/catalog/a3.htm

Information Systems Research: www.informs.org/Pubs/ISR/

Information Technology and the Law: www.wkap.nl/journalhome.htm/0925-9872/

Information Technology and Management: www.baltzer.nl/itm/itm.html

Information Technology and People: www.mcb.co.uk/cgi-bin/journal1/itp/

Interfaces: www.informs.org/Pubs/Interfaces/

Journal of the American Society for Information Science: www.interscience.wiley.com/jpages/0002-8231/

Journal of Global Information Management: www.idea-group.com/jgim.htm

Journal of Information Systems Security: www.auerbach-publications.com/catalog/ziss.htm

Journal of Information Technology: www.chapmanhall.com/jt/

Journal of Intelligent Information Systems: kapis.www.wkap.nl/journalhome.htm/0925-9902/

Systems Research and Information Systems: www.gbhap.com/Systems_Research_Information_Systems

Transactions on Information Systems: www.acm.org/tois/

LANGUAGE-ORIENTED PUBLICATIONS
(Sorted alphabetically by language cited in title)

Ada Letters: www.acm.org/sigada/

APL Quote Quad: www.acm.org/sigapl/qq.htm

Vector – Journal of the British APL Association, BCS Specialist Group: www.bcs.org.uk/siggroup/sg02.htm

Visual Basic Programmer's Journal: www.vbpj.com/

Journal of C Language Translation: wheat.uwaterloo.ca/bibliography/Compiler/jclt.html

C/C++ Users Journal: www.cuj.com

C++ Report: www.creport.com

Visual C++ Journal: www.vcdj.com

Journal of Forth Application and Research: dec.bournemouth.ac.uk/forth/jfar/

Fortran Forum: www.fortran.com/acm_ff.html

FoxPro Advisor: www.advisor.com

Java Developer's Journal: www.JavaDevelopersJournal.com

Java and E-Commerce: www.distributedcomputing.com/jec/index.html

Java Pro: www.java-pro.com

Java Report: www.objectpeople.on.ca/software/java-report/index.html

Java Spektrum: www.sigs.com/html/publications.shtml

Java World: www.javaworld.com

Lisp and Symbolic Computation: kapis.www.wkap.nl/journalhome.htm/0892-4635/

MapleTech: www.birkhauser.com/journals/mapletech/summary.htm

Mathematica in Education and Research: www.telospub.com/journal/MIER/index.html

The Perl Journal: www.tpj.com

Smalltalk Report: www.sigs.com/publications/srpt/

LOGIC

Annals of Pure and Applied Logic: www.elsevier.nl/locate/apal/

Archive for Mathematical Logic: link.springer-ny.com/link/service/journals/0000153/index.htm

Bulletin of the Interest Group in Pure and Applied Logics: ftp://ftp.mpi-sb.mpg.de/pub/igpl/Bulletin/HTML/general.html

Bulletin of Symbolic Logic: www.math.ucla.edu/~asl/bslcontents.html

International Journal of Multiple-Valued Logic: www.yhab.com/Multiple_Valued_Logic/

Journal of Functional and Logic Programming: mitpress.mit.edu/journal-home.tcl?issu=10805230/

Journal of Logic Programming: www.elsevier.nl/locate/jlogpro/

Journal of Logic and Computation: www.oup.co.uk/jnls/list/logcom/

Journal of Logic, Language & Information: kapis.www.wkap.nl/journalhome.htm/0925-8531/

Journal of Symbolic Logic: www.press.uillinois.edu/journals/jsl.html

Transactions on Computer Logic: info.acm.org/pubs/tocl/

Transactions on Fuzzy Systems: www.ieee.org/pub-preview/fuzz_toc.html

MATHEMATICAL TECHNIQUES AND APPLICATIONS

Advances in Computational Mathematics: www.baltzer.nl/adcom/adcom.html

Applicable Algebra in Engineering, Communications, and Computing: link.springer-ny.com/link/service/journals/0000200/index.htm

Applied and Computational Mathematical Anaysis: scs.org/pubs/siminfo.html

Applied Mathematics and Computation: www.elsevier.nl/locate/apmathcomp/

Computational and Applied Mathematics: www.birkhauser.com/journals/cam/

Computational Geometry: www.elsevier.nl/locate/comgeo/

Computational & Mathematical Organization Theory: kapis.
www.wkap.nl/journalhome.htm/1381-298X/
Computational Statistics: comst.wiwi.hu-berlin.de
Computational Statistics & Data Analysis: www.elsevier.
nl/inca/publications/store/5/0/5/5/3/9/
Computers and Mathematics with Applications:
www.elsevier.com/inca/publications/store/
3/0/1/
Experimental Mathematics: www.expmath.com
Journal of Computational and Applied Mathematics: www.
elsevier.nl/locate/cam/
Journal of Computational and Graphical Statistics: www.
maths.uq.oz.au/~gks/webguide/alfjourn.html
Journal of Symbolic Computation: www.hbuk.co.uk/ap/
journals/sy/
Mathematical Methods of Operations Research: gopher://
trick.ntp.springer.de/11/TOC/186/
Mathematical Structures in Computer Science: www.cup.
cam.ac.uk/Journals/JNLSCAT/msc/msc.html
Mathematical and Computer Modelling: www.elsevier.
com/inca/publications/store/6/2/3/
Mathematics of Computation: www.ams.org/mcom/
Mathematics and Computers in Simulation: www.elsevier.
com/inca/publications/store/5/0/5/6/1/5/
Statistics & Computing: www.chapmanhall.com/sc/

NETWORKS – GENERAL
Computer Networks and ISDN Systems: www.elsevier.nl/
locate/comnet/
Electronic Journal on Networks and Distributed Processing:
rerir.univ-pau.fr/
First Monday: www.firstmonday.dk
Internet Computing: www.computer.org/internet/
Internet Research: www.mcb.co.uk/cgi-bin/journal3/
intr/
Internet Week: www.phillips.com/iw/
Internet World Magazine: www.internetworld.com
Interoperable Computer Networks: www.baltzer.nl/icon/
icon.html
Intranet Design Magazine: www.innergy.com/index.html
Journal of High Speed Networks: www.iospress.nl/html/
node254.html#SECTION000419000000000000000
Journal of Network and Computer Applications: www.hbuk.
co.uk/ap/journals/ma/
Journal of Network and Systems Management: www.plenum.
com/cgi/getarec?ple20000146/
LAN Times: www.lantimes.com
LAN Magazine: www.lanmag.com
Mobile Networks and Applications: www.baltzer.nl/
monet/monet.html
Net Magazine: www.netmag.co.uk
Net NP Professional: www.netprolive.com
Netnomics: www.baltzer.nl/netnomics/index.html
Netsurfer Focus Magazine: www.netsurf.com/nsf/
Network Computing: www.NetworkComputing.com
Network Computation in Neural Systems: www.iop.org/EJ/
S/Unreg/?MIval=journal&key=0954-898X/
NetWorker: www.acm.org/networker/
Networking and Information Systems Journal:
www.prism.uvsq.fr/~nis/
Networks: www.interscience.wiley.com/jpages/
0028-3045/
Transactions on Networking: www.acm.org/ton/
Web Developer: www.webdeveloper.com
Web Technique: www.webtechnique.com
Web Week: www.webweek.com
WebMaster: www.cio.com/WebMaster/
WebServer: www.cpg.com/ws/
WebSight: www.websight.com

Wireless Communications: www.baltzer.nl/wirlesscd/
cd.html
Wireless Networks: www.baltzer.nl/winet/winet.html
Wireless Networks: www.plenum.com/cgi/getarec?ple
20000092/
Wireless Personal Communications: kapis.www.wkap.nl/
journalhome.htm/0929-6212/
World Wide Web Journal: www.baltzer.nl/www/
index.html

NEURAL NETWORKS
Neural Computation: mitpress.mit.edu/journal-home.
tcl?issu=08997667/
Neural Computing and Applications: neural-server.
aston.ac.uk/NCAF/journal/index.html
Neural Networks: www.elsevier.nl/inca/
publications/store/8/4/1/
Neural Processing Letters: kapis.www.wkap.nl/
journalhome.htm/1370-4621/
Neurocomputing: www.elsevier.nl/locate/neucom/
Transactions on Neural Networks: www.ieee.org/pubs/
pub_preview/nn_toc.html

NUMERICAL ANALYSIS AND METHODS
Annals of Numerical Mathematics: www.baltzer.nl/
anuma/anuma.html
Applied Numerical Mathematics: www.elsevier.nl/
locate/apnum/
Communications in Numerical Methods in Engineering:
www.interscience.wiley.com/jpages/1069-8299/
Electronic Transactions on Numerical Analysis: etna.mcs.
kent.edu
IMA Journal of Numerical Analysis: www.oup.co.uk/jnls/
list/imanum/
Interval Computations (now *Reliable Computing*): www.wkap.
nl/journalhome.htm/1385-3139/
Numerical Algorithms: www.math.psu.edu/dna/
contents/na.html
Numerical Methods for Partial Differential Equations: www.
interscience.wiley.com/jpages/NumerMethods
PartialDifferentialEq/
Numerische Mathematik: link.springer-ny.com/link/
service/journals/00211/index.htm

OPERATING SYSTEMS
Linux Focus: mercury.chem.pitt.edu/~tiho/
LinuxFocus/
Linux Journal: www.linuxjournal.com
Linux Today: linuxtoday.com
NT Advantage: www.ntadvantage.com
Unix Review: www.unixreview.com
Unix World: www.wcmh.com/uworld/index.html
Win98 Magazine: www.win98mag.com
Windows Developers Journal: www.wdj.com
Windows NT Systems: www.ntsystems.com
Windows Sources NT: www.winsources.com
X Journal, The: www.sigs.com/publications/txjr/
X Resource: A Practical Journal of the X Window System:
www.cs.sfu.ca/projects/ElectronicLibrary/
Collections/CMPT/cs-journals/P-OReilly/
J-OReilly-XR.html
X Spot, The: www.sigs.comxspot/aboutxspot.html

OPTIMIZATION AND PERFORMANCE EVALUATION
Computational Optimization and Applications: kapis.www.
wkap.nl/journalhome.htm/0926-6003/
Journal of Global Optimization: www.wkap.nl/
journalhome.htm/0925-5002/

Journal of Optimization Theory & Applications: www.plenum.com/cgi/getarec?ple20000150/
Optimization: www.gbhap.com/Optimization
Optimization Methods and Software: www.ghab.com/Optimization_Methods_Software/
Performance Computing Magazine: www.performance-computing.com
Performance Evaluation: www.elsevier.nl/locate/peva/

PROGRAMMING PRACTICE
Computer Languages: www.elsevier.com/inca/publications/store/3/5/0/
Embedded Systems Programming: www.embedded.com/mag.shtml
Journal of Functional and Logic Programming: mitpress.mit.edu/journal-home.tcl?issu=10805230/
Journal of Functional Programming: www.cup.cam.ac.uk/Journals/JNLSCAT/jfp/jfp.html
Journal of Logic Programming: www.elsevier.nl/locate/jlogpro/
Journal of Object-Oriented Programming (JOOP): www.joopmag.com
Journal of Programming and Computer Software: www.plenum.comcgi/getarec?ple20000212/
Journal of Programming Languages: www.compscinet.com
Journal of Visual Languages and Computing: www.hbuk.co.uk/ap/journals/vl/
Object Currents: www.sigs.com/objectcurrents/
Object Expert: www.sigs.com/publications/obex/
Object Magazine: www.sigs.com/publications/objm/
Object Oriented Systems: www.compscinet.com
Objekt Spektrum: www.sigs.com/publications/obsp/
Theory and Practice of Object Systems: www.interscience.wiley.com/jpages/1074-3227/
Transactions on Programming Languages and Systems: info.acm.org/toplas/
Visual Developer: www.visual-developer.com
Visual Programming: www.visualprogramming.com

SCIENTIFIC AND MEDICAL APPLICATIONS
Bioinformatics: www3.oup.co.uk/bioinformatics/
Biological Cybernetics: link.springer-ny.com/link/service/journals/00422/index.htm
Complexity: www.journals.wiley.com/complexity/
Complexity International: www.csu.edu.au/ci/ci.html
Computational Geosciences: www.baltzer.nl/comgeo/comgeo.html
Computational Science and Engineering: www.computer.org/cse/
Computer-Aided Surgery: www.journals.wiley.com/cas/
Computer Applications in the Biosciences: www.bio.net:80/bioarchives/BIO-JOURNALS/CABIOS/
Computer Physics Communications: www.elsevier.com/inca/publications/store/5/0/5/7/1/0/
Computers and Biomedical Research: www.apnet.com/www/journal/co.htm
Computers and Chemistry: www.elsevier.nl/inca/publications/store/3/7/9/index.htt
Computing in Science and Engineering: www.computer.org/CSE
Computing and Visualization in Science: link.springer-ny.com/link/service/journals/00791/index.htm
Journal of Clinical Monitoring and Computing: kapis.www.wkap.nl/journalhome.htm/1387-1307/
Journal of Cognitive Neuroscience: mitpress.mit.edu/journal-home.tcl?issn=0898929X/
Journal of Complexity: www.apnet.com/www/journal/cm.htm

Journal of Computational Chemistry: www.journals.wiley.com/jcc/
Journal of Computational Neuroscience: kapis.www.wkap.nl/journalhome.htm/0929-5313/
Journal of Computational Physics: www.apnet.com/www/journal/cp.htm
Journal of Computer-Aided Molecular Design: kapis.www.wkap.nl/journalhome.htm/0920-654X/
Journal of Computer-Assisted Tomography: www.rad.bgsm.edu/jcat/
Journal of Molecular Modeling: www.ccc.uni-erlangen.de/jmolmod/
Journal of Scientific Computing: www.plenum.com/cgi/getarec?ple20000165/
Journal of Supercomputing: www.wkap.nl/journalhome.htm/0920-8542/
Scientific Computing and Instrumentation: www.scimag.com
Scientific Computing World: www.iop.org/Mags/SCW/
Scientific Programming: www.iospress.nl/html/node353.html#SECTION0004380000000000000000
SIAM Journal on Scientific and Statistical Computing: www.siam.org/journals/sisc/sisc.htm

SIMULATION, MODELING, AND GAMING
Applied Mathematical Modelling: www.elsevier.nl/locate/apmathmodel/
Applied Mathematics and Optimization: hplus.harvard.edu/ejournals/sv_appmat.html
Journal of Computation and Simulation: www.gbhap.com/Statistical_Computation_Simulation
Journal of Computational Methods & Modeling: www.plenum.com/cgi/getarec?ple20000040/
Journal of Statistical Computation and Simulation: www.gbhap-us.com/journals/164/
Simulation: scs.org/pubs/siminfo.html
Simulation and Gaming: www.univ-com/piegne.fr/tsh/sg/revue/
Simulation Practice and Theory: www.elsevier.nl/locate/simpra/
Systems Analysis Modelling Simulation: www.gbhap.com/Systems_Analysis_Modelling_Simulation

SOFTWARE ENGINEERING
Annals of Software Engineering: www.baltzer.nl/catalogue.html#soft/
Annual Reviews in Control: www.elsevier.com/inca/publications/store/4/2/9/index.htt
Automated Software Engineering: www.wkap.nl/journalhome.htm/0928-8910/
Chinese Journal of Advanced Software Research: www.ios.ac.cn/xuebao/esy.html
Empirical Software Engineering: kapis.www.wkap.nl/journalhome.htm/1382-3256/
Information and Software Technology: www.elsevier.nl/locate/infsof/
Journal of Software Maintenance: www.interscience.wiley.com/jpages/1040-550X/
Journal of Systems and Software: www.elsevier.com:80/inca/publications/store/5/0/5/7/3/2/
Mathematical Software: www.acm.org/toms/
Programming Languages and Systems: www.acm.org/toplas/
Rapid Prototyping Journal: www.mcb.co.uk/cgi-bin/journal1/rpj/
Science of Computer Programming: www.elsevier.nl/locate/scico/
Software: www.iee.org.uk/publish/journals/profjrnl/ieeproc.html#procse
Software – Concepts and Tools: link.springer-ny.com/link/service/journals/00378/index.htm

Software Development: www.sdmagazine.com
Software Engineering: www.computer.org/tse/
Software Engineering Journal: www.bcs.org.uk/publicat/
  journals/softeng/softeng.htm
Software Engineering and Methodology: www.acm.org/
  tosem/
Software Engineering Notes: www.acm.org/sigsoft/SEN/
  index.html
Software Magazine: www.softwaremag.com
Software: Practice and Experience: www.interscience.
  wiley.com/jpages/0038-0644/
Software Process: www.interscience.wiley.comjpages/
  1077-4866/
Software Quality Journal: www.chapmanhall.com/sq/
  default.html
Software Quality Management Journal (SQM): www.bcs.org.
  uk/siggroup/sg48.htm
Software Testing, Verification and Reliability:
  www.interscience.wiley.com/jpages/0960-0833/
Software World: www.ap-publications.co.uk
Transactions on Software Engineering: www.computer.
  org/tse/
Transactions on Software Engineering and Methodology:
  www.acm.org/tosem/

MISCELLANEOUS

Advanced Systems: www.elsevier.nl/estoc/
  publications/store/8/00664138/
Applied Categorical Structures: kapis.www.wkap.nl/
  journalhome.htm/0927-2852/
Applied Stochastic Models and Data Analysis: www3.
  interscience.wiley.com/cgi-bin/jtoc?ID=15783
Behaviour and Information Technology: www.tandf.co.uk/
  E-pub/cwonline.htm#bit/
Computational Economics: kapis.www.wkap.nl/
  journalhome.htm/0927-7099/
Computer Communications: www.elsevier.nl/locate/
  comcom/
Computer-Mediated Communication: www.december.com/
  cmc/mag/current/toc.html
Computer Music Journal: mitpress.mit.edu/journal-
  home.tcl?issu=01489267/
Computer Speech and Language: www.hbuk.co.uk/ap/
  journals/la/
Computer Supported Cooperative Work: kapis.www.
  wkap.nl/journalhome.htm/0925-9724/
Computers in Human Behavior: www.elsevier.com/inca/
  publications/store/7/5/9/
Computers and the Humanities: kapis.www.wkap.nl/
  journalhome.htm/0010-4817/
Computers in Industry: www.elsevier.com:80/inca/
  publications/store/5/0/5/6/4/6/
Cybermetrics: www.cindoc.csic.es/cybermetrics/
  cybermetrics.html
Data Communications: www.data.com
Desktop Journal: desktop-journal.com
Displays: www.elsevier.nl/locate/displa/
eMedia Professional: www.onlineinc.comemedia/
  index.html
Future Generation Computer Systems: www.elsevier.nl/
  locate/future/
GeoInformatica: kapis.www.wkap.nl/journalhome.htm/
  1384-6175/
Human–Computer Interaction: www.parc.xerox.com/
  istl/projects/HCI/
Intelligent Data Analysis: www-east.elsevier.com/ida/
  Menu.html
Intelligent Enterprise: www.intelligententerprise.
  com

Interacting with Computers: www.elsevier.nl/locate/
  intcom/
Interface Monthly: www.InterfaceMonthly.com
Journal of Computational Intelligence in Finance: ourworld.
  compuserve.com/homepages/FTPub/jcif.htm
Journal of Computer-Mediated Communication: cmc.huji.
  ac.il
Journal of Computer Security: www.iospress.nl/html/
  node339.html#SECTION000424000000000000000
Journal of Documentation: bubl.ac.uk/journals/lis/
  fj/jdocumentation/
Journal of Electronic Publishing: www.press.umich.edu:
  80/jep/
Journal of Information Recording: www.gbhap-us.com/
  journals/614/614-top.htm
Journal of MUD Research: journal.tinymush.org/~jomr/
Journal of Organizational Computing: cism.bus.utexas.
  edu/CISM/JOC/Joc.html
Journal of Systems Integration: kapis.www.wkap.nl/
  journalhome.htm/0925-4676/
Mathematical Intelligencer: www.springer-ny.com/
  journals/283/
Mobile Computing: www.mobilecomputing.com
Multimedia Systems: ink.springer-ny.com/link/
  service/journals/00530/index.htm
Multimedia Tools and Applications: kapis.www.wkap.nl/
  journalhome.htm/1380-7501/
Music and Computers: www.music-and-computers.com/
New Generation Computing: link.springer.de/ol/csol/
  index.htm
Open Systems and Information Dynamics: kapis.www.wkap.
  nl/journalhome.htm/1230-1612/
Soft Computing: link.springer-ny.com/link/service/
  journals/00500/index.htm
Speech Communication: www.elsevier.nl/locate/
  specom/
Telematics and Informatics: www.elsevier.com:80/inca/
  publications/store/7/0/3/
Transputer Communications: unix.hensa.ac.uk/
  parallel/journals/trcom/transputer-
  communications.cfp/
Visual Computer, The: link.springer-ny.com/link/
  service/journals/00371/index.htm
VRS Journal: www.vrs.org.uk/public/journal.html

Magazines

3D Artist: www.3dartist.com
3D Design: www.3D-design.com
Amiga Computing: drtavel.com/CompuPub.htm
AS/400 Magazine: as400magazine.com
Beyond Computing: www.beyondcomputingmag.com
Boardwatch Magazine: www.boardwatch.com
Byte: www.byte.com
CIO WebBusiness: webbusiness.cio.com
ComputerLife: www.computerlife.com
Computer-Mediated Communication Magazine: www.hcirn.
  com/res/period/cmcmag.html
Computer Shopper: www.zdnet.comshopper
Computerist: www.p3p.com
Computerworld: www.computerworld.com
Datamation: www.datamation.com
Desktop Publishers Journal: www.dtpjournal.com
Dr. Dobbs' Journal: www.ddj.com
EDP Weekly: www.erols.com/millin/other/edp.htm
Family PC: www.familypc.com
Home Office Computing: www.smalloffice.com
Home PC: www.homepc.com
HotWired Online Magazine: www.wired.com
InfoWorld: www.infoworld.com
InformationWeek: www.informationweek.com

Inter@active Week: www.interactive-week.com
InterFace Magazine: www.interface.com
Internet Computing: www.icomputing.com
MacCentral Online: www.maccentral.com
Mac Addict: www.macaddict.com
Mac Home Journal: www.fun-net.com/magazines/
  Mmags/machomjourn.html
Mac Net Journal: www.blol.com/web_mnj/080196/
  Abouttx.html
Mac Street Journal Online: www.nymug.org/msjol/
MacHome: www.machome.com
MacTech: www.mactech.com
MacToday: www.mactoday.com
MacUser: www.macuser.com
MacNet Journal: www.macnet.com
MacWeek: www.macweek.com
Macworld: www.macworld.com
Microprocessor Report: www.chipanalyst.com/q/report/
  mpr.html
Nature: www.nature.com
NetGuide: www.netguide.com
Online: www.onlineinc.com/onlinemag/index.html
Online Magazine: www.online-magazine.com/sub.htm
PC Computing: www.pccomputing.com
PC Gamer: www.pcgamer.com
PC Graphics and Video: www.pcgv.com
PC Magazine: www.pcmag.com
PC Today: www.pctoday.com
PC Week: www.pcweek.com
PC World: www.pcworld.com
Pen Computing: pencomputing.com
Robotics Science and Technology Magazine: www.robotmag.
  com/default.htm
Smart Computing: www.smartcomputing.com
Web Developers Journal: www.webdevelopersjournal.com
Windows Magazine: www.winmag.com
Windows NT Magazine: www.winntmag.com
Windows Sources: www.winsources.com
Wired: www.wired.com
WWWiz: wwwiz.com
Yahoo! Internet Life: www.yil.com
ZDNet: www.zdnet.com

General Publications with Frequent Articles on Computing

American Scientist: www.amsci.org
Discover: www.discover.com
Nature: www.nature.com
Popular Science: www.popularscience.com
Scientific American: www.sciam.com

Publishers

Ablex Publishers: www.hcirn.com/res/publish/
Association for Computing Machinery (ACM): www.acm.org
Auerbach: www.auerbach-publications.com
Birkhauser: www.birkhauser.com
Chapman & Hall: www.hcirn.com/res/publish/
  chaphall.html
CRC Press: www.crcpress.com/jour/
Lawrence Erlbaum: www.hcirn.com/res/publish/
  lea.html
Gordon and Breach: www.gbhap.com
Human–Computer Interaction Resources Network:
  www.hcirn.com
IBM: www.ibm.com
IEEE Computer Society: computer.org
John Wiley & Sons: www3.interscience.wiley.com/
  cgi-bin/browsepj/
Kluwer Academic: kapis.www.wkap.nl
Lippincott Raven: www.lrpub.com/lrpub/
Microsoft: www.microsoft.com
Miller Freeman: www.mfi.com
Morgan Kaufmann Publishers: www.mkp.com
Netscape: www.netscape.com
O'Reilly: www.oreilly.com
Society of Industrial & Applied Mathematics (SIAM):
  www.siam.org
WSJ World Scientific Journals: www.wspc.com.sg/
  journals/journals.html
Z-D Ziff Davis: www.zd.com

— Appendix IV —

UNIVERSITIES IN THE UNITED STATES, CANADA, AND THE UNITED KINGDOM THAT OFFER THE PH.D. DEGREE IN COMPUTER SCIENCE AND/OR COMPUTER ENGINEERING

The two lists that follow include departments at universities in the United States, Canada, and the United Kingdom that offer a Ph.D. (or Sc.D.) in computer science or computer engineering or both. A key to departmental codes follows the second list.

UNITED STATES AND CANADA

This list is an augmented version of the *Forsythe List*, named after George Forsythe, one of the founders of academic computer science. The Forsythe List is compiled and maintained by the Computing Research Association (*q.v.*). For a searchable online version, see http://www.cra.org/reports/forsythe.html. Almost all institutions listed offer the master's degree and have undergraduate major programs in computer science and/or computer engineering. In addition to

the programs listed here, some departments of mathematics and electrical engineering also offer doctorates in computer science or computer engineering or with an option in one or the other. In the list given here, but not in the actual Forsythe list, programs at multi-campus state universities (e.g. California, New York) are alphabetized under the *state* in the form *state* at *location* (e.g. *California* at *Irvine*).

University	Department code	Home page
Alabama at Birmingham, University of	CIS	www.cis.uab.edu
Alabama at Tuscaloosa, University of	CS	www.cs.ua.edu
Alabama in Huntsville, University of	ECE	www.eb.uah.edu/ece/
Alberta, University of	CS	www.cs.ualberta.ca
Arizona State University	CSE	www.eas.asu.edu/~csedept/
Arizona, University of	CS	www.cs.arizona.edu
Auburn University	CSE	www.eng.auburn.edu/department/cse/
Boston University	CS	www.cs.bu.edu
Brandeis University	CS	www.cs.brandeis.edu
Brigham Young University	CS	www.cs.byu.edu
British Columbia, University of	CS	www.cs.ubc.ca
Brown University	CS	www.cs.brown.edu
Calgary, University of	CS	www.cpsc.ucalgary.ca
California at Berkeley, University of	CS	www.cs.berkeley.edu

University	Department code	Home page
California at Davis, University of	CS	www.cs.ucdavis.edu
California at Irvine, University of	ICS	www.ics.uci.edu
California at Los Angeles, University of	CS	www.cs.ucla.edu
California at Riverdale, University of	CS	www.cs.ucr.edu
California at San Diego, University of	CSE	www.cs.ucsd.edu
California at Santa Barbara, University of	CE	www.ece.ucsb.edu
California at Santa Barbara, University of	CS	www.cs.ucsb.edu
California at Santa Cruz, University of	CE	www.cse.ucsc.edu
California at Santa Cruz, University of	CIS	www.cse.ucsc.edu
California Institute of Technology	CS	www.cs.caltech.edu
Carnegie Mellon University	CS	www.cs.cmu.edu
Case Western Reserve University	EECS	www.eecs.cwru.edu
Central Florida, University of	ECE	www.ece.engr.ucf.edu
Chicago, University of	CS	www.cs.uchicago.edu
Cincinnati, University of	ECECS	www.ececs.uc.edu
Clemson University	CE	www.ece.clemson.edu
Clemson University	CS	www.cs.clemson.edu
Colorado School of Mines	MCS	www.mines.edu/academic/macs/
Colorado State University	CS	www.cs.colostate.edu
Colorado Technical University	CS	www.colotechu.edu/newdegree.html
Colorado, University of	CS	www.cs.colorado.edu
Columbia University	CS	www.cs.columbia.edu
Concordia University	CS	www.cs.concordia.ca
Connecticut, University of	CSE	www.eng2.uconn.edu/cse/
Cornell University	CS	www.cs.cornell.edu
Dartmouth College	CS	www.cs.dartmouth.edu
Delaware, University of	CIS	www.cis.udel.edu
Denver, University of	MCS	www.cs.du.edu
DePaul University	CS	www.cs.depaul.edu
Drexel University	CE	www.ece.drexel.edu/ECE/
Duke University	CS	www.cs.duke.edu
Florida Atlantic University	CSE	www.cse.fau.edu
Florida Institute of Technology	CS	www.cs.fit.edu
Florida International University	CS	www.cs.fiu.edu
Florida State University	CS	www.cs.fsu.edu
Florida, University of	CISE	www.cis.ufl.edu
George Mason University	ITE	www.ite.gmu.edu
George Washington University	EECS	www.seas.gwu.edu/seas/eecs/
Georgia Institute of Technology	CS	www.cc.gatech.edu
Georgia Institute of Technology	ECE	www.ece.gatech.edu
Georgia State University	CIS	www.cis.gsu.edu
Georgia, University of	CS	www.cs.uga.edu
Harvard University	CS	www.deas.harvard.edu
Hawaii, University of	ICS	www.ics.hawaii.edu
Houston, University of	CS	www.cs.uh.edu
Houston, University of	ECE	www.egr.uh.edu/ece/
Idaho, University of	CS	www.cs.uidaho.edu
Illinois at Chicago, University of	EECS	www.eecs.uic.edu
Illinois at Urbana–Champaign, University of	CE	www.ece.uiuc.edu
Illinois at Urbana–Champaign, University of	CS	www.cs.uiuc.edu
Illinois Institute of Technology	CS	www.cs.iit.edu
Indiana University	CS	www.cs.indiana.edu
Iowa State University	EECE	www.ee.iastate.edu
Iowa State University	CS	www.cs.iastate.edu
Iowa, University of	CS	www.cs.uiowa.edu
Iowa, University of	ECE	www.eng.uiowa.edu
Johns Hopkins University	CS	www.cs.jhu.edu
Kansas State University	CIS	www.cis.ksu.edu
Kansas, University of	EECS	www.eecs.ukans.edu
Kent State University	MCS	www.mcs.kent.edu
Kentucky, University of	CS	www.cs.engr.uky.edu
Lehigh University	EECS	www.eecs.lehigh.edu
Louisiana State University	CS	www.csc.lsu.edu
Louisville, University of	CSE	www.cs.louisville.edu

University	Department code	Home page
Manitoba, University of	CS	www.cs.umanitoba.ca
Maryland–Baltimore County, University of	CSEE	www.csee.umbc.edu
Maryland at College Park, University of	CS	www.cs.umd.edu
Massachusetts at Amherst, University of	CS	www.cs.umass.edu
Massachusetts at Amherst, University of	ECE	www.ecs.umass.edu/ece/
Massachusetts at Lowell, University of	CS	www.cs.uml.edu/curriculum/Grad.html
Massachusetts Institute of Technology	EECS	www-eecs.mit.edu
McGill University	CS	www.cs.mcgill.ca
Michigan State University	CSE	www.cps.msu.edu
Michigan Technological University	CS	www.cs.mtu.edu
Michigan, University of	EECS	www.eecs.umich.edu
Minnesota, University of	CS	www.cs.umn.edu
Mississippi State University	CS	www.cs.msstate.edu
Mississippi, University of	CS	www.cs.olemiss.edu
Missouri at Columbia, University of	CSE	www.cecs.missouri.edu
Missouri at Rolla, University of	CS	www.cs.umr.edu
Montreal, University of	CSOR	www.fas.umontreal.ca
Naval Postgraduate School	CS	www.cs.nps.navy.mil
Nebraska at Lincoln, University of	CSE	www.cse.unl.edu
Nevada at Las Vegas, University of	CS	www.cs.unlv.edu
New Hampshire, University of	CS	www.cs.unh.edu
New Mexico Institute of Mining & Technology	CS	www.cs.nmt.edu
New Mexico State University	CS	www.cs.nmsu.edu
New Mexico, University of	CS	www.cs.unm.edu
New Mexico, University of	ECE	www.eece.unm.edu
New York at Albany, State University of	CS	www.cs.albany.edu
New York at Binghamton, State University of	CS	www.cs.binghamton.edu
New York at Buffalo, State University of	CSE	www.cse.buffalo.edu
New York at Stony Brook, State University of	CS	www.cs.sunysb.edu
New York University	CS	www.cs.nyu.edu
New York, City University of (CUNY)	CS	www.gc.cuny.edu
North Carolina at Chapel Hill, University of	CS	www.cs.unc.edu
North Carolina State University	CE	www.ece.ncsu.edu
North Carolina State University	CS	www.csc.ncsu.edu
North Dakota State University	CS	www.cs.ndsu.nodak.edu
North Texas, University of	CS	www.cs.unt.edu
Northeastern University	CS	www.cs.neu.edu
Northeastern University	ECE	www.ece.neu.edu
Northwestern University	CS	www.cs.nwu.edu
Northwestern University	EECS	www.eecs.nwu.edu
Notre Dame, University of	CSE	www.cse.nd.edu
Oakland University	ECS	www.secs.oakland.edu
Ohio State University	CIS	www.cis.ohio-state.edu
Oklahoma State University	CS	www.cs.okstate.edu
Oklahoma, University of	CS	www.cs.ou.edu
Oklahoma, University of	ECE	www.ou.edu/engineering/ece/
Old Dominion University	CS	www.cs.odu.edu
Oregon Graduate Institute of Sci & Tech	CSE	www.cse.ogi.edu
Oregon State University	CS	www.cs.orst.edu
Oregon State University	ECE	www.ece.orst.edu
Oregon, University of	CIS	www.cs.uoregon.edu
Ottawa, University of	CS	www.site.uottawa.ca/dept/grad/csi.html
Pennsylvania State University	CSE	www.cse.psu.edu
Pennsylvania, University of	CIS	www.cis.upenn.edu
Pittsburgh, University of	CS	www.cs.pitt.edu
Polytechnic University of Brooklyn	CIS	cis.poly.edu
Princeton University	CS	www.cs.princeton.edu
Purdue University	CS	www.cs.purdue.edu
Purdue University	ECE	www.ece.purdue.edu
Quebec at Montreal, University of	CS	saturne.info.uqam.ca
Regina, University of	CS	www.cs.uregina.ca
Rensselaer Polytechnic Institute	CS	www.cs.rpi.edu
Rhode Island, University of	ECE	www.ele.uri.edu
Rice University	CS	www.cs.rice.edu

University	Department code	Home page
Rochester, University of	CS	www.cs.rochester.edu
Rutgers, State University of New Jersey	CS	www.cs.rutgers.edu
Santa Clara University	CSE	www.cse.scu.edu
Saskatchewan, University of	CS	www.cs.usask.ca
Simon Fraser University	CS	www.cs.sfu.ca
South Carolina, University of	ECE	www.ece.sc.edu
South Carolina, University of	CS	www.cs.sc.edu
South Florida, University of	CSE	www.csee.usf.edu
Southern California, University of	CS	www.usc.edu/dept/cs/
Southern California, University of	EES	www.usc.edu/dept/ee/
Southern Methodist University	CSE	www.seas.smu.edu
Southwestern Louisiana, University of	CSE	www.cacs.usl.edu
Stanford University	CS	www.cs.stanford.edu
Stevens Institute of Technology	CS	stewks.ece.stevens-tech.edu/newece/
Syracuse University	CIS	www.cis.syr.edu
Syracuse University	EECS	uplink.syr.edu/Dept/eecs/
Temple University	CIS	joda.cis.temple.edu
Tennessee at Knoxville, University of	CS	www.cs.utk.edu
Texas A&M University	CS	www.cs.tamu.edu
Texas at Arlington, University of	CSE	www.cse.uta.edu
Texas at Austin, University of	ECE	www.ece.utexas.edu
Texas at Austin, University of	CS	www.cs.utexas.edu
Texas at Dallas, University of	EECS	www.utdallas.edu/dept/eecs/
Texas Tech University	CS	www.coe.ttu.edu
Toronto, University of	CS	www.cs.utoronto.ca
Toronto, University of	ECE	www.ece.toronto.edu
Tulane University	EECS	www.cs.tulane.edu
Tulsa, University of	MCS	www.mcs.utulsa.edu
Utah, University of	CS	www.cs.utah.edu
Vanderbilt University	CS	cswww.vuse.vanderbilt.edu
Virginia Polytechnic Institute	CS	www.cs.vt.edu
Virginia, University of	CS	www.cs.virginia.edu
Washington State University	EECS	www.eecs.wsu.edu
Washington University (St Louis)	CS	www.cs.wustl.edu
Washington, University of	CSE	www.cs.washington.edu
Waterloo, University of	CS	www.cs.uwaterloo.ca
Wayne State University	CS	www.cs.wayne.edu
Wayne State University	ECE	www.ece.eng.wayne.edu
West Virginia, University of	CS	www.cs.wvu.edu
West Virginia, University of	CSEE	www.csee.wvu.edu
Western Michigan University	CS	www.cs.wmich.edu
Western Ontario, University of	CS	www.csd.uwo.ca
William & Mary, College of	CS	www.cs.wm.edu
Wisconsin at Madison, University of	CS	www.cs.wisc.edu
Wisconsin at Milwaukee, University of	EECS	www.cs.uwm.edu
Worcester Polytechnic Institute	CS	www.cs.wpi.edu
Wright State University	CS	www.cs.wright.edu
Wyoming, University of	CS	www.cs.uwyo.edu
Yale University	CS	www.cs.yale.edu

UNITED KINGDOM

In the UK, almost all universities have research students who may earn a Ph.D. in any subject taught there. Those listed below are the ones whose research in computer science is rated most highly by the Higher Education Funding Council. Computer Engineering degrees in the UK are generally awarded within departments of electrical engineering. For a database of UK departments with computer science programs, see http://www.doc.mmu.ac.uk/CPHC/cphc-imap.html.

University	Department code	Home page
Aberdeen, University of	CS	www.csd.abdn.ac.uk
Bath, University of	CG	www.maths.bath.ac.uk
Belfast, Queen's University of	CS	www.cs.qub.ac.uk
Birmingham, University of	CS	www.cs.bham.ac.uk
Bradford, University of	CG	www.comp.brad.ac.uk
Brighton, University of	IT	www.it.bton.ac.uk
Bristol, University of	CS	www.cs.bris.ac.uk
Cambridge, University of	CL	www.cl.cam.ac.uk
Canterbury, University of Kent at	CL	www.cs.ukc.ac.uk
Dundee, University of	ACS	www.computing.dundee.ac.uk
Durham, University of	CS	www.dur.ac.uk/~dcs0www/
East Anglia, University of	IS	www.sys.uea.ac.uk
Edinburgh, University of	CS	www.dcs.ed.ac.uk
Essex, University of	CS	cswww.essex.ac.uk
Exeter, University of	CS	www.dcs.ex.ac.uk
Glasgow, University of	CS	www.dcs.gla.ac.uk
Heriot-Watt University	CEE	www.cee.hw.ac.uk
Lancaster, University of	CG	www.comp.lancs.ac.uk
Leeds, University of	C-S	agora.leeds.ac.uk
Liverpool, University of	CS	www.csc.liv.ac.uk
London, City University of	CS	www.soi.city.ac.uk/doc/
London, Birkbeck College	CS	www.dcs.bbk.ac.uk
London, Imperial College	CG	www.doc.ic.ac.uk
London, Queen Mary and Westfield College	CS	www.dcs.qmw.ac.uk
London, Royal Holloway & Bedford College	CS	www.cs.rhbnc.ac.uk
London, University College	CS	www.cs.ucl.ac.uk
Loughborough University	C-S	www.lboro.ac.uk/departments/
Manchester Institute of Science & Technology	C	www.co.umist.ac.uk
Manchester, University of	CS	www.cs.man.ac.uk
Newcastle, University of	CS	www.cs.ncl.ac.uk
Nottingham, University of	CS	www.cs.nott.ac.uk
Oxford, University of	CL	www.comlab.ox.ac.uk
Reading, University of	CS	www.cs.rdg.ac.uk
Sheffield, University of	CS	www.dcs.shef.ac.uk
Southampton, University of	ECS	www.ecs.soton.ac.uk
St Andrews, University of	MCS	www.dcs.st-andrews.ac.uk
Stirling, University of	CS	www.cs.stir.ac.uk
Strathclyde, University of	CS	www.cs.strath.ac.uk
Sussex, University of	CCS	www.cogs.susx.ac.uk
Wales at Aberystwyth, University of	CS	www.aber.ac.uk/~dcswww/
Wales at Cardiff, University of	CS	www.cs.cf.ac.uk
Wales at Swansea, University of	CS	www.swan.ac.uk/compsci/
Warwick, University of	CS	www.dcs.warwick.ac.uk
York, University of	CS	www.cs.york.ac.uk

Department codes

ACS	Applied Computer Studies	CSOR	Computer Science and Operations Research
CCS	Cognitive and Computing Sciences	ECE	Electrical and Computer Engineering
CE	Computer Engineering	ECECS	Electrical and Computer Engineering and
CEE	Computer and Electrical Engineering		Computer Science
CIS	Computer and Information Science	ECS	Engineering (or Electronics) and Computer Science
CISE	Computer and Information Science and Engineering	EECS	Electrical Engineering and Computer Science
CG	Computing/Computing Group	EES	Electrical Engineering Systems
CL	Computing Laboratory	ICS	Information and Computer Science
CN	Computation	IS	Information Systems
CS	Computer Science	IT	Information Technology
C-S	Computer Studies	ITE	Information Technology and Engineering
CSE	Computer Science and Engineering	MCS	Mathematics and Computer Science
CSEE	Computer Science and Electrical Engineering		

Appendix V

PRESIDENTS OF MAJOR COMPUTING SOCIETIES

American Federation of Information Processing Societies (AFIPS)

NATIONAL JOINT COMPUTER COMMITTEE
Morton M. Astrahan, 1956–1958
Harry H. Goode, 1959–1960
Morris Rubinoff, 1960–1961

AMERICAN FEDERATION OF INFORMATION PROCESSING SOCIETIES
Willis Ware, 1961–1962
J. D. Madden, 1963
Edwin L. Harder, 1964–1965
Bruce Gilchrist, 1966–1967
Paul Armer, 1968
Richard I. Tanaka, 1969–1970
Keith W. Uncapher, 1971
Walter L. Anderson, 1972
George Glaser, 1973–1975
Anthony Ralston, 1975–1976
Theodore J. Williams, 1976–1978
Albert S. Hoagland, 1978–1980
J. Ralph Leatherman, 1980–1981
Sylvia Charp, 1982–1983
Stephen S. Yau, 1984–1985
Jack Moshman, 1986
Eddie Ashmore, 1987
Howard Funk, 1988–1990

American Association for Artificial Intelligence (AAAI)

Allen Newell, 1979–1980
Edward A. Feigenbaum, 1980–1981
Marvin Minsky, 1981–1982
Nils Nilsson, 1982–1983
John McCarthy, 1983–1984
Woodrow Bledsoe, 1984–1985
Patrick Winston, 1985–1987
Raj Reddy, 1987–1989
Daniel Bobrow, 1989–1991
Patrick Hayes, 1991–1993
Barbara J. Grosz 1993–1995
Randall Davis, 1995–1997
David L. Waltz, 1997–1999

Association for Computing Machinery (ACM)

EASTERN ASSOCIATION FOR COMPUTING MACHINERY
John H. Curtiss, 1947–1948
John W. Mauchly, 1949–1950
Franz L. Alt, 1950–1952
Samuel B. Williams, 1952–1954

ASSOCIATION FOR COMPUTING MACHINERY
Alston S. Householder, 1954–1956
John W. Carr III, 1956–1958
Richard W. Hamming, 1958–1960
Harry D. Huskey, 1960–1962

Alan J. Perlis, 1962–1964
George E. Forsythe, 1964–1966
Anthony Oettinger, 1966–1968
Bernard A. Galler, 1968–1970
Walter M. Carlson, 1970–1972
Anthony Ralston, 1972–1974
Jean E. Sammet, 1974–1976
Herbert R. J. Grosch, 1976–1978
Daniel D. McCracken, 1978–1980
Peter J. Denning, 1980–1982
David H. Brandin, 1982–1984
Adele Goldberg, 1984–1986
Paul W. Abrahams, 1986–1988
Bryan S. Kocher, 1988–1990
John R. White, 1990–1992
Gwen Bell, 1992–1994
Stuart H. Zweben, 1994–1996
Charles H. House, 1996–1998
Barbara Simons, 1998–

Association of Information Technology Professionals (AITP)

NATIONAL MACHINE ACCOUNTANTS ASSOCIATION

Robert L. Jenal, 1952
Gordon C. Couch, 1953
Richard L. Irwin, 1954
Robert O. Cross, 1955
Donald L. Gerighty, 1956
Willis L. Daniel, 1957
Lester E. Hill, 1958
D. B. Paquin, 1959
L. W. Montgomery, 1960
Alfonso G. Pia, 1961

DATA PROCESSING MANAGEMENT ASSOCIATION

Elmer F. Judge, 1962
Robert S. Gilmore, 1963
John K. Swearingen, 1964
Daniel A. Will, 1965
Billy R. Field, 1966
Theodore Rich, 1967
Charles L. Davis, 1968
D. H. Warnke, 1969
James D. Parker, Jr, 1970
Edward O. Lineback, 1971
Herbert B. Safford, 1972
James Sutton, 1973
Edward J. Palmer, 1974
J. Ralph Leatherman, 1975–1976
Robert J. Marrigan, 1977
Delbert W. Atwood, 1978
George R. Eggert, 1979
Robert A. Finke, 1980
P. Roger Fenwick, 1981
Donald E. Price, 1982

J. Crawford Turner Jr, 1983
Carroll L. Lewis, 1984
Eddie M. Ashmore, 1985
David R. Smith, 1986
Robert A. Hoadley, 1987
Christian G. Meyer, 1988
Georgia B. Miller, 1989
Terence Felker, 1990
Louis J. Berzai, 1991
Ralph E. Jones, 1992
Howard L. Smith, 1993
Dorothy J. Smith, 1994
William R. Reaugh, 1995
William R. Lackey, 1996

ASSOCIATION OF INFORMATION TECHNOLOGY PROFESSIONALS

Gary D. Keller, 1997
Ernest E. Nolan, 1998
Larry Schmitz, 1999

British Computer Society (BCS)

M. V. Wilkes, 1957–1960
F. Yates, 1960–1961
D. W. Hooper, 1961–1962
R. L. Michaelson, 1962–1963
Sir Edward Playfair, 1963–1965
Sir Maurice Banks, 1965–1966
The Earl Mountbatten of Burma, 1966–1967
S. Gill, 1967–1968
B. Z. de Ferranti, 1968–1969
The Earl of Halsbury, 1969–1970
A. d'Agapeyeff, 1970–1971
A. S. Douglas, 1971–1972
G. J. Morris, 1972–1973
R. L. Barrington, 1973–1974
E. L. Willey, 1974–1975
C. P. Marks, 1975–1976
G. A. Fisher, 1976–1977
P. A. Samet, 1977–1978
F. H. Sumner, 1978–1979
J. L. Bogod, 1979–1980
F. J. Hooper, 1980–1981
P. D. Hall, 1981–1982
HRH The Duke of Kent, 1982–1983
D. Firnberg, 1983–1984
E. S. Page, 1984–1985
R. A. McLaughlin, 1985–1986
Sir John Fairclough, 1986–1987
E. P. Morris, 1987–1988
B. W. Oakley, 1988–1989
V. S. Shirley, 1989–1990
A. Rousell, 1990–1991
S. C. T. Matheson, 1991–1992
R. G. Johnson, 1992–1993

J. P. Leighfield, 1993–1994
D. W. Mann, 1994–1995
G. W. Robinson, 1995–1996
R. J. McQuaker, 1996–1997
Sir Brian Jenkins, 1997–1998
I. Ritchie, 1998–1999
D. Hartley, 1999–

Computer Society (IEEE-CS)

CHAIRMEN OF THE AIEE COMMITTEE ON LARGE-SCALE COMPUTING DEVICES AND OF THE IRE PROFESSIONAL GROUP ON ELECTRONIC COMPUTERS

Charles Concordia, 1946–1949, AIEE
John Grist Brainerd, 1949–1951, AIEE
Walter H. MacWilliams, 1951–1953, AIEE
Morton M. Astrahan, 1951–1953, IRE
John H. Howard, 1953–1954, IRE
Frank Maginniss, 1953–1955, AIEE
Harry Larson, 1953–1955, IRE
Jean H. Felker, 1955–1956, IRE
Edwin L. Harder, 1955–1957. AIEE
Jerre D. Noe, 1956–1957, IRE
Werner Buchholz, 1957–1958, IRE
Morris Rubinoff, 1957–1959, AIEE
Willis H. Ware, 1958–1959, IRE
Richard Endres, 1959–1960, IRE
Ruben Imm, 1959–1961, AIEE
Arnold A. Cohen, 1960–1962, IRE
Claude A. Kagan, 1961–1963
Walter M. Anderson, 1962–1964, IRE
Gerhard L. Hollander, 1963–1964

CHAIRMEN OF THE IEEE COMPUTER GROUP

Keith W. Uncapher, 1964–1965
Richard I. Tanaka, 1965–1966
Samuel Levine, 1966–1967
Charles L. Hobbs, 1968–1969
Edward J. McCluskey, 1970–1971

PRESIDENTS AFTER TAKING THE NAME OF THE IEEE COMPUTER SOCIETY

Edward J. McCluskey, 1971
Albert S. Hoagland, 1972–1973
Stephen S. Yau, 1974–1975
Dick B. Simmons, 1976
Merlin G. Smith, 1977–1978
Tse-yun Feng, 1979–1980
Richard E. Merwin, 1981
Oscar N. Garcia, 1982–83
Martha Sloan, 1984–1985
Roy L. Russo, 1986–1987
Edward A. Parrish, Jr, 1988
Kenneth R. Anderson, 1989
Helen M. Wood, 1990

Duncan H. Lawrie, 1991
Bruce D. Shriver, 1992
James H. Aylor, 1993
Laurel V. Kaleda, 1994
Ronald G. Hoelzeman, 1995
Mario R. Barbacci, 1996
Barry W. Johnson, 1997
Doris L. Carver, 1998

Gesellschaft für Informatik e.V. (GI)

Manfred Paul, 1971–1973
Heinz Gumin, 1973–1977
Wilfried Brauer, 1977–1979
Clemens Hackl, 1980–1983
Gerhard Krüger, 1984–1985
Fritz Krückeberg, 1986–1989
Heinz Schwärtzel, 1990–1991
Roland Vollmar, 1992–1993
Wolfgang Glatthaar, 1994–1995
Wolffried Stucky, 1996–1997
Gerhard Barth, 1998–1999

International Federation for Information Processing (IFIP)

Isaac L. Auerbach (USA), 1960–1965
Ambros P. Speiser (Switzerland), 1965–1968
A. A. Dorodnicyn (USSR), 1968–1971
Heinz Zemanek (Austria), 1971–1974
Richard I. Tanaka (USA), 1974–1977
Pierre A. Bobillier (Switzerland), 1977–1980
K. Ando (Japan), 1983–1986
A. W. Goldsworthy (Australia), 1986–1989
Bl. Sendov (Bulgaria), 1989–1992
A. Rolstadås (Norway), 1992–1995
K. Bauknecht (Switzerland), 1995–1998
P. Bollerslev (Denmark), 1998–2001

Information Processing Society of Japan (IPSJ)

Hideo Yamashita, 1960–1963
Mochinori Goto, 1963–1965
Jiro Yamauchi, 1965–1967
Yujiro Degawa, 1967–1969
Hidetoshi Takahashi, 1969–1971
Takeshi Kiyono, 1971–1973
Hanzou Omi, 1973–1975
Toshio Kitagawa, 1975–1977
Mamoru Hosaka, 1977–1979
Koji Kobayashi, 1979–1981
Hiroshi Inose, 1981–1983
Toshiyuki Sakai, 1983–1985
Masanori Ozeki, 1985–1987
Yutaka Ohno, 1987–1989
Takeo Miura, 1989–1991

Hiroshi Hagiwara, 1991–1993
Yukio Mizuno, 1993–1995
Shoichi Noguchi, 1995–1997
Iwao Toda, 1997–1999

Internet Society (ISOC)

(President in 1992–1995, Chair of the Board
since then)
Vinton G. Cerf, 1992–1995
Lawrence Landweber, 1995–1997
Frode Greisen, 1997–98
Geoff Huston, 1999–

International Society for Technology in Education (ISTE)

Dennis Bybee and Paul Resta (jointly), 1989–1990
Gary Bitter, 1990–1991
Bonnie Marks, 1991–1992
Sally Sloan, 1992–1993
Lajeane Thomas, 1993–1994
M. G. Peggy Kelly, 1994–1995
Dave Brittain, 1995–1997
Lynne Schrum, 1997–1999
Heidi Rogers, 1999–2001

Society for Computer Simulation International (SCSI)

Robert M. Howe, 1956–1957
B. Dov Abramis, 1958–1959
Stanley Rogers, 1959–1960
J. E. Sherman, 1960–1962
Maughan S. Mason, 1962–1964
P. J. Hermann, 1964–1966
James E. Wolle, 1966–1968
David R. Miller, 1968–1969
Francis C. Rieman, 1969–1971
Jon N. Mangnall, 1971–1972
George A. Rahe, 1972–1973
Robert D. Brennan, 1973–1975
Paul A. Berthiaume, 1975–1976

Per A. Holst, 1976–1977
Donald C. Martin, 1977–1979
Stewart I. Schlesinger, 1979–1981
Walter J. Karplus, 1982–1984
Norbert E. Pobanz, 1985–1986
Ralph C. Huntsurgh, 1987–1988
Roy E. Crosbie, 1989–1990
Carl Malstrom, 1990–1991
Jordan Chou, 1992–1993
Mitch Sisle, 1994–1996
Wayne Ingalls, 1996–1998
Axel Lehmann, 1998–2000

South East Asia Regional Computer Confederation (SEARCC)

Robert Iau (Singapore), 1976
P. Baraoiden (Philippines), 1978
General Hardijono (Indonesia), 1980
Fong Ah Ngo (Malaysia), 1982
Richard Li (Hong Kong), 1984
Boonrod Binson (Thailand), 1986
F. C. Kohli (India), 1988
Wee Tew Lim (Singapore), 1989
Ms. Octaviano (Philippines), 1990
J. Basri (Indonesia), 1991
Lee Poh Ann (Malaysia), 1992
Agnes Mak (Hong Kong), 1993
Y. Karunaratne (Sri Lanka), 1994
Ahmed Allaudin (Pakistan), 1995
T. Thangsuphanich (Thailand), 1996
S. Ramani (India), 1997
Prins Ralston (Australia), 1998
Alex Siow (Singapore), 1999

USENIX Association

Lou Katz, 1975–1982
Alan Nemeth, 1982–1990
Deborah K. Scherrer, 1990
Marshall Kirk McKusick, 1990–1992
Stephen C. Johnson, 1992–1996
Andrew Hume, 1996–1998

— Appendix VI —

KEY HIGH-LEVEL LANGUAGES

INTRODUCTION

The following list of languages represents the author's personal view of the (approximately 50) high-level languages that are deemed most significant (in 2000) from among the over 1,000 high-level implemented languages (not counting dialects) that have been defined since work in computing started. The defined characteristics of a high-level language are given in this author's article on PROGRAMMING LANGUAGES in this *Encyclopedia*. The languages selected had to satisfy (in the author's personal judgment) one or more of these criteria: significant usage, influence on language design, overall impact on the computing environment, novelty (first of its kind), uniqueness, and existing or potential standard. The principal change from the 1993 edition of the list is the addition of the Java language.

The languages have been grouped into two major categories: (1) those not really in significant use in 1999 (although perhaps a few hardy souls may continue to use them) and (2) those believed to be in significant use, where "significant" is judged relative to the size of the expected user community for that type of language. Within the second group, the languages have been listed by name under the *primary* application areas for which they are intended. This is because of the author's firm belief that the *most important characteristic* of any programming language is the application area for which it is intended to be used.

Of the application areas, the first five (i.e. numerical scientific, business data processing, string and list processing, formula manipulation, and multipurpose) are relatively common or well known. The remainder are narrow, specialized areas. Following this list, each language is listed in alphabetical order, with the following entries:

Name

Meaning of the acronym (when there is one)

Date of first publication (described below)

Reference(s) (described below)

Computers on which the language has been implemented

The primary application area

A comment to indicate very briefly something about the language and/or why it is on the list.

For the date of first publication, this means the earliest dissemination of the following (although sometimes labeled "draft" or "preliminary"): published paper, official technical report, language manual, etc. In many cases, the date refers to a much earlier version of the current language. Thus, the 1956 publication on Fortran has little resemblance to the 1978 ANSI standard or to the 1997 ISO/IEC standard. Where a question mark is used, it means the author is not certain of the date. In a few cases, a specific date has been omitted entirely because of lack of knowledge.

Specific references are not listed (aside from the standards numbers, if they exist). For older references and information (including history) on most of these languages, there are five main sources, and they are referred to with the indicated abbreviations in the listings:

Roster: "Roster of Programming Languages for 1976–77." J. E. Sammet, *ACM SIGPLAN Notices* **13**, *No. 11.*
HOPL: *History of Programming Languages*, R. L. Wexelblat (Ed.). New York: Academic Press, 1981.
HOPL-II: *History of Programming Languages—II*, T. J. Bergin and R. G. Gibson (Eds). Reading, MA: Addison-Wesley, 1996.
PL: *Programming Languages: History and Fundamentals*, J. E. Sammet. Englewood Cliffs, NJ: Prentice Hall, 1969.
ANSI, ISO: For any language that is an ANSI or ISO standard, the appropriate number has been shown. Where both standards exist, the initial or primary location is used wherever possible. In those cases where standardization is under way, the organization is shown without any number. Further details on programming language standards are in the article PROGRAMMING LANGUAGE STANDARDS, which contains a complete list of standards including languages which are not in the list below.

For any language contained in more than one of the above sources, all relevant references have been given. The reader should note that there may be more current references for some of these languages (including, but not limited to, articles in this encyclopedia). In a very few cases, these have been included.

The computers are described either as specific family, or as "many" or "most" where there are too many to list. More implementations may exist but are not known to the author. Implementations include mainframes, mincomputers, and personal computers, and an entry of "many computers" can apply to any or all of these categories. An entry of "most computers" applies to all sizes. An entry of "some" means that there is more than one implementation, but it is not practical to provide a specific list.

The list of computers on which the language has been implemented, and, to a lesser extent, the comment and the implicit value judgment in including the language at all, stem primarily from the author's old language roster, mentioned above, and some updating of that information based on more recent research. However, time has not permitted a thorough updating of implementation and/or usage details.

Jean E. Sammet

List of Languages by Application Area

HISTORICALLY IMPORTANT BUT *NOT* IN *SIGNIFICANT* CURRENT USE

Algol 60
Algol 68
Comit [II]
Flow-Matic
Formac
IPL-V
IT
Joss
Jovial
Mad
Neliac
Simula 67

CURRENT USAGE—BROAD APPLICATION AREAS

Numerical scientific
Basic
Fortran
Speakeasy

Business data processing
Cobol

String and list processing
Icon
Lisp
Snobol4

Formula manipulation
Macsyma
Mathematica
Reduce

Multipurpose
Ada
APL
C++
M (previously called Mumps)
Pascal
PL/I
Prolog
Smalltalk

Social science and/or statistics
OMNITAB II
SPSS

Systems programming (including debugging aids)
Bliss
C
Java

CURRENT LANGUAGES FOR SPECIALIZED APPLICATION AREAS

Computer-assisted instruction
Coursewriter III
PILOT
TUTOR

Circuit design
ECAP II
SCEPTRE

Civil, mechanical, structural engineering
COGO
ICES

Computer hardware design (including simulation)
ISPL
VHDL

Equipment checkout
ATLAS

Machine tool control
APT

Mathematical/linear programming
MPSX
PDS/MaGen

Simulation (continuous)
CSMP
CSSL
DYNAMO III

Simulation (discrete)
GPSS
SIMSCRIPT 11.5

Description of Languages

ADA
1979
HOPL-II, ANSI/ISO/IEC 8652-1995.
Many computers.
Multipurpose.
Very powerful language developed over many years with much public commentary. Sponsored by US Department of Defense, but designed by French language team. Used primarily in embedded computer systems (e.g. military, FAA, NASA), but also in numerous commercial applications.\

ALGOL 60
ALGOrithmic Language 1960
May 1960
Roster, HOPL, PL.
Many computers.
Numerical scientific.
Suitable for problems involving numeric computation and/or logical processes. Its predecessor (Algol 58) had several significant languages based on it (e.g. Jovial, Mad, Neliac).

ALGOL 68
ALGOrithmic Language 1968
1968
Roster, HOPL-II.
Many computers.
Multipurpose.
Very powerful language but not very upward-compatible from Algol 60.

APL
A Programming Language
1962
Roster, HOPL, PL, ISO 8485-1989.
Many computers.
Multipurpose.
Has unusual character set and cryptic syntax, but has very powerful, concise primitive array operations.

APT
Automatically Programmed Tools
1957
Roster, HOPL, PL, ANSI X3.37-1995.
Most computers.
Machine tool control.
Language for programming numerically controlled machine tools. Was first language developed for a specialized application area.

ATLAS
Abbreivated Test Language for "All" Systems
1968
Roster, ANSI/IEEE Standard 416-1988.
Most computers in differing versions.
Equipment checkout.
For test engineers to control automatic test equipment.

BASIC
Beginners All Purpose Symbolic Instruction Code
1964
Roster, HOPL, PL, ANSI X3.113-1987.
Almost all computers.
Numerical scientific.
Very simple language but with some advanced features. Available on many micro- and personal computers for uses beyond just numerical scientific.

BLISS
Basic Language for Implementation of System Software
1970
Roster.
Several computers.
Systems programming.
For writing compilers and operating systems.

C

1973
Roster, HOPL-II, ANSI/ISO 9899-1990.
Many computers.
Systems programming.
Used to write the Unix operating system and most of its application software.

C++

1980
ANSI, HOPL-II.
Many computers.
Multipurpose.
An extension of C with facilities for object-oriented programming.

COBOL

*CO*mmon *B*usiness-*O*riented *L*anguage
1960
Roster, HOPL, PL, ANSI X3.23-1985.
Most computers.
Business data processing.
English-like in style, developed and maintained by committee of users and manufacturers under Codasyl. One of the most widely used languages.

COGO

*CO*ordinate *GeO*metry
1963 (?)
Roster, PL.
Several computers.
Civil engineering.
Useful for solving coordinate geometry problems in civil engineering.

COMIT [II]

1957
Roster, PL.
IBM System/360.
String processing.
First major language for string handling and pattern matching.

COURSEWRITER III

1966 (?)
Roster.
IBM System/360.
Computer-assisted instruction.
Simple language for preparing computer-assisted instruction courses.

CSMP

*C*ontinuous *S*ystem *M*odeling *P*rogram
1968
Roster.
Several computers.
Simulation (continuous).
General name for two languages (statement- and block-oriented) used to simulate the dynamics of continuous systems describable by ordinary differential equations.

CSSL

*C*ontinuous *S*ystems *S*imulation *L*anguage
1967
Roster.
CDC 6400 and XDS Sigma 7.
Simulation (continuous).
Statement-oriented language to simulate dynamics of continuous systems describable by ordinary differential equations. Many varying versions with different names are implemented.

DYNAMO III

1959 (?)
Roster.
Most large and medium-sized computers.
Simulation (continuous).
Used to construct large models of economic and social systems.

ECAP II

*E*lectronic *C*ircuit *A*nalysis *P*rogram *II*
1966
Roster.
Several computers.
Circuit design.
Simple language for analyzing electrical networks.

FLOW-MATIC

1958
PL.
UNIVAC I, II.
Business data processing.
Was first English-like language for business data processing and was a major input to design of Cobol.

FORMAC

*FOR*mula *MA*nipulation Compiler
1964
Roster, PL, HOPL-II.
IBM System/360, 370.
Formula manipulation.
First language to be widely used for formal algebraic manipulation.

FORTRAN

*FOR*mula *TRAN*slation
1956
Roster, HOPL, PL, ANSI X3.198-1992,
    ISO/IEC 1539: 1991

Almost all computers.
Numerical scientific.
First language to be widely used and remains in wide use.

GPSS

General Purpose Systems Simulator
1961
Roster, HOPL, PL.
Several computers.
Simulation (discrete).
Based on block-diagram approach, with statements used for computer input.

ICES

Integrated Civil Engineering System
1967 (?)
Roster.
Several computers.
Civil engineering.
General system for engineering which has internal languages for subsystem development and includes languages such as COGO and STRUDL.

ICON

1978
HOPL-II.
Many computers.
String processing.
Based on concepts from SNOBOL for string processing, but is broader and has different syntax.

IPL-V

Information Processing Language V
1958.
PL.
Many second-generation computers.
List processing.
Was used heavily in the 1960s for list processing applications. Has close notational resemblance to an assembly language.

ISPL

Instruction Set Processor Language
1971
Roster.
DEC PDP-10.
Computer hardware design.
Used to describe general register transfer systems and digital computer architecture.

IT

Internal Translator
1957

IBM 650.
Numerical scientific.
First language implemented on small computer; inspired much compiler research.

JAVA

1995
Many computers.
Multipurpose.
An object-oriented language for machine-independent programming and program execution over a network. Resembles C++ in appearance, but without some of its low-level features.

JOSS

JOHNNIAC Open Shop System
1964
Roster, HOPL, PL.
Many computers in different versions.
Numerical scientific.
First language designed for online use. Is very simple. Had many dialects under differing names.

JOVIAL

Jules Own Version of International Algebraic Language
1960
Roster, HOPL, PL.
Many computers in many versions.
Multipurpose.
Based on Algol 58 (originally called International Algebraic Language) and had many versions. Newest version is Jovial J73, Many early Jovial compilers were written in some version of Jovial.

LISP

LISt Processing
1960
Roster, HOPL, HOPL-II, PL, ANSI X3.226-1994.
Many computers.
List processing.
Sophisticated and theoretically oriented with many dialects, of which most prominent are Common Lisp (the standard) and Scheme (for teaching). Used for much artificial intelligence research.

MACSYMA

Project *MAC's SYmbol MAnipulation*
1972
Roster.
PCs, Unix systems.
Formula manipulation.
Very powerful language for doing formal algebraic manipulation.

MAD

*M*ichigan *A*lgorithm *D*ecoder
1960
Roster, PL.
Several computers.
Systems programming.
Original version was based on Algol 58 and designed
for numerical computation. Later version was
extended significantly.

MATHEMATICA

1986
Formula manipulation.
Many computers.
Powerful language for doing formal algebraic
manipulation that contains many mathematical
built-in functions and powerful graphics facilities.

MPSX

*M*athematical *P*rogramming *S*ystem E*X*tended
1966
Roster.
IBM System/360, 370.
Mathematical programming.
Controls solution strategy for mathematical
programming problems. Other similar languages
run on different computers.

M/MUMPS

*M*assachusetts General Hospital *U*tility
*M*ulti-*P*rogramming *S*ystem
1969
Roster, ANSI X11.1-1995.
Several computers.
Multipurpose.
Fairly general language with emphasis on string
handling and complex file handling. Used heavily
in medical areas, but also in commercial
applications. Name changed from Mumps to M
in 1993.

NELIAC

*N*avy *E*lectronics *L*aboratory *I*nternational *A*lgol
*C*ompiler
1960
PL.
Many second-generation computers.
Numerical scientific.
Was based on Algol 58 and was used to write its own
compilers.

OMNITAB II

1966
Roster.
Most large computers.
Statistics.

Primarily for nonprogrammers, using desk
calculator-type operations, but also containing
powerful mathematical facilities (e.g. regression,
matrix inversion).

PASCAL

1971
Roster, HOPL-II, ANSI/ISO/IEC 7185-1990.
Most computers.
Multipurpose.
Small but elegant language with many significant
features. Used heavily for teaching programming.
Many Pascal compilers are written in Pascal.

PDS/MAGEN

*P*roblem *D*escriptor *S*ystem
1973 (?)
Roster.
Many computers.
Mathematical programming.
Facilitates generation of matrices and reports for
mathematical programming systems.

PILOT

IEEE 1154 1991.
Roster.
Many computers.
Computer-assisted instruction.
Simple language that has been written in Basic,
APL\360, Algol, Fortran, and PL/I.

PL/I

(Not an acronym, although often erroneously
thought to stand for *P*rogramming *L*anguage *I*.)
1964
Roster, HOPL, PL, ANSI X3.53-1976.
Several computers.
Multipurpose.
First of the very large, powerful languages,
combining many features from Algol, Cobol,
Fortran, and other languages.

PROLOG

1971
HOPL-II, ISO 13211–1995.
Many computers.
Multipurpose.
For use in logic programming, which can itself be
applied to many scientific applications. Has a
major use in artificial intelligence.

REDUCE

1967
Roster.
Many computers.

Formula manipulation.
Algol-like language written in itself and using Lisp as an intermediate language.

SCEPTRE

1960s (?)
Roster.
Several computers.
Cicruit design.
Used for designing and analyzing circuits.

SIMSCRIPT 11.5

1963 (?)
Roster.
Many computers.
Simulation (discrete).
Advanced language for large discrete simulation problems. Several previous numbered versions exist.

SIMULA 67

*Simu*lation *L*anguage, 1967
1967
Roster, HOPL, PL.
Many computers.
Multipurpose.
An extension of Algol 60 and quite distinct from its predecessor (Simula I), which was primarily a simulation language. Introduced the important concept of classes.

SMALLTALK

1971
HOPL-II.
Many computers.
Multipurpose.
Design allows object-oriented programming, and is first language with that facility to be significantly used. Has developed as several distinct versions (1971, 1972, 1976, 1980).

SNOBOL4

*StriNg-O*riented Sym*BO*lic *L*anguage
1963
Roster, HOPL.
Most large computers.
String processing.
Emphasizes string processing and pattern matching.

SPEAKEASY

1968
Roster.
Several computers.
Numerical scientific.
Easily learned but powerful array processing language with built-in matrix algebra and powerful library-oriented system.

SPSS

*S*tatistical *P*rograms for the *S*ocial *S*ciences
1975 (?)
Roster.
Most computers.
Statistics.
Is really a language (albeit simple) and is implemented in batch and interactive versions.

TUTOR

1971 (?)
Roster.
CDC 6500, Cyber series.
Computer-assisted instruction.
Runs under PLATO.

VHDL

*V*HSIC *H*ardware *D*escriptor *L*anguage
1983
IEEE Standard #1076 (1993)
Many computers.
Computer hardware design.
International standard used to describe input–output transformations and interconnections of components for a digital electronic system.

— Appendix VII —

GLOSSARY OF TERMS IN FIVE LANGUAGES

English	French	German	Spanish	Russian
Access time	Temps d'accès	Zugriffszeit	Tiempo de acceso	Время выборкн, время обращения
Accumulator	Accumulateur	Akkumulator	Acumulador	Накопитель
Adder	Additionneur, addeur	Addierer, Addierwerk	Sumador	Сумматор
Address	Adresse	Adresse	Dirección	Адрес
Algorithm	Algorithme	Algorithmus	Algoritmo	Алгоритм
Alphanumeric	Alphanumérique	Alphanumerisch	Alfanumérico	Алфавитно-цифровой
Analog computer	Calculateur analogique	Analogrechner	Computador analógico	Аналоговая вычислч-тельная машина, аналоговый компьютер
Architecture (computer)	Architecture (de système informatique)	Architektur (Rechnerarchitektur)	Arquitectura (de computadores)	Структура
Argument	Argument	Argument, Parameter, Aktualparameter	Argumento	Переменная, аргумент
Array	Tableau	Feld	Arreglo	Массив
Artificial intelligence	Intelligence artificielle	Künstliche Intelligenz	Inteligencia artificial	Искусственный разум, искусственный интеллект
Assembler	Assembleur	Assemblierer, Assembler	Ensamblador	Ассемблер
Associative memory	Mémoire associative	Assoziativspeicher	Memoria asociativa	Ассоциативная память
Automation	Automatisation	Automation, Automatisierung	Automatización	Автоматнзация
Automaton	Automate	Automat		Автомат
Bandwidth	Largeur de bande	Bandbreite	Ancho de banda	Диапазон частот
Base register	Registre de base	Basisregister, Basisaddressregister	Registro base	Регнстр Базы, Базовый регистр
Benchmark	Banc d'essai	Benchmark	Banco de pruebas	Зталон, начало отсчёта
Binary	Binaire	Binär	Binario	Двоичный
Bit	Bit	Bit	Bit, digito binario	Бит
Bit map	Bit map	Bitmap	Mapa de bits	Битовая карта
Block	Bloc	Block, physischer Satz	Bloque	Блок
Boot	Démarrer	Starten	Arrancar, iniciar	Загружать (систему), выполнять начальную загрузку

English	French	German	Spanish	Russian
Branch instruction	Branchement	Verzweigungsbefehl, Sprungbefehl	Instrucción de bifurcación	Команда перехода (передача управления)
Browser	Navigateur	Browser, Stöberhilfe	Navegador, visualizador	Программа просмотра (файла)
Buffer	(Mémoire) Tampon	Puffer, Zwischenspeicher	Memoria intermedia	Буфер
Bug	Erreur, défaut, panne	Fehler, Programmfehler	Error	Ошибка
Bulletin board	Les news	Schwarzes Brett	Cartel de anuncios	Информационный листок
Bus	Bus	Bus, Ubertragungsleitung	Barra, enlace común	Шина
Byte	8 Bit byte: octet 6 Bit byte: sextet	Byte	Octeto	Байт
Cache memory	Mémoire à cache	Pufferspeicher, schneller Pufferspeicher	Memoria de cache	Память
Calculator	Calculatrice	Taschenrechner	Calculador	Ќалькулятор
Calling sequence	Séquence d'appel	Aufruffolge (eines Unterprogrammes)	Sequencia de llamada	Вызывающая последовательность
Card	Carte	Karte, Lochkarte	Tarjeta, ficha	Карта
Central processing unit	Unité centrale	Zentrale Recheneinheit, Prozessor	Unidad central de proceso	Ценеральный процессор
Channel	Canal	Kanal	Canal	Канал
Character	Caractère	Zeichen, Schriftzeichen	Carácter, simbolo	Символ
Chip	Puce	Baustein	Oblea, plaqueta	Чип, микросхема
Code	Code	Code	Código	Код
Combinatorics	Combinatoire	Kombinatorik	Métodos combinatorios	Комбинаторика
Compiler	Compilateur	Kompilierer, Compiler, Übersetzer	Compilador	Компилятор
Complement	Complément	Komplement	Complemento	Дополнение
Computability	Calculabilité	Berechenbarkeit	Computabilidad	Вычислимость
Computation	Calcul-traitement	Berechnung	Computación, cálculo	Вычисление
Computer	Ordinateur	Rechner, Datenverarbeitungsanlage, Computer	Computador	Вычислительная машина, компьютер
Computer algebra	Calcul formel	Computer-Algebra	Álgebra de computadoras	Компьютерная алгебра
Computer graphics	Informatique graphique	Computergrafik	Gráficos de computador	Машинная графика
Computer science	Informatique	Informatik	Informática, ciencia de la computación	Вычислительная математика и вычислительная техника
Concatenation	Concaténation	Verkettung	Concatenación	Сцепление
Concurrent programming	Programmation parallèle	Nebenläufige Programmierung	Programación concurrente	Параллельное программирование
Constant	Constante	Konstante	Constante	Постоянная, константа
Control structure	Structure de contrôle	Kontrollstruktur	Estructura de control	Управляющая конструкция (языка программирования)
Control unit	Unité de contrôle	Steureinheit, Steurewerk, Leitwerk, Kommandowerk	Unidad de control	Блок (устройство управления)
Core memory	Mémoire à tores	Kernspeicher	Memoria de núcleos	Оперативная память
Cybernetics	Cybernétique	Kybernetik	Cibernética	Кибернетика
Cycle time	Cycle de base	Zykluszeit	Tiempo de ciclo	Время цикла, время выборки
Data	Donnée	Daten	Datos	Данные
Data bank	Banque de données	Datenbank	Banco de datos	Банк данных
Data communications	Transmission de données	Datenübermittlung	Communicación de datos	Передача данных
Data compression	Compression de données	Datenkompression	Compresión de datos	Сжатие данных
Data encryption	Codage	Datenverschlüsselung	Codificación de datos	Кодирование данных
Data mining	Extraction de données	Data Mining	Minado de datos	Извлечение знаний из данных
Data processing	Traitement de l'information, informatique	Datenverarbeitung	Proceso de datos	Обработка данных
Data structure	Structure de données	Datenstruktur	Estructura de datos	Структура данных
Data type	Type de données	Datentyp	Tipo de datos	Тип данных
Database	Base de données	Datenbasis, Datenbank	Banco de datos	База данных

English	French	German	Spanish	Russian
Database management system	Système de gestion de bases de données	Datenbankbetriebssystem	Gerencia de bancos de datos	Система управления базами данных, СУБД
Deadlock	Bloquage	Verklemmung, Systemverklemmung, Deadlock	Punto muerto, bloquero	Стоп, полная остановка, тупиковая ситуация
Debugging	Mise au point (d'un programme), dépannage (d'une machine)	Fehlerbeseitigung, Fehlerkorrektur, Programm-debugging	Depuración, corrección	Отладка
Delimiter	Borne	Begrenzer, Begrenzungssymbol, Trennzeichen	Delimitar	Ограничитель
Desktop publishing	Publication assistee par ordinateur	Desktop Publishing	Editora de escritoro	Подготовка публикаций с использованием настольных редакционно-издательских средств
Diagnostic	Diagnostic	Diagnoseprogramm	Diagnóstico	Диагностический
Directory	Catalogue	Verzeichnis	Directorio	Директория; каталог
Disk Memory	Mémoire à disque	Plattenspeicher	Memoria de disco	Дисковая память
Diskette	Disquette	Diskette	Disquete, disco flexible	Дискета, гибкий диск, флоппи-диск
Distributed system	Système distribué	Verteiltes System	Sistema distribuído	Распределенная система
Drum memory	Mémoire à tambour	Magnettrommel, Trommelspeicher	Memoria de tambor	Память на барабане
Dump	"Dump" (cliché)	Speicherabzug, Speicherauszug	Vaciado de memoria	Копировать память на внешнее запоминающее устройство
Electronic funds transfer	Transfert de fonds électronique	Elektronische Überweisung	Transferencia electrónica de fondos	Электронные платежи
Electronic mail	Courrier électronique	Elektronische Post	Correo electrónico	Электронная почта
Embedded system	Système embarqué	Eingebettetes System	Sistema empotrado, sistema encastrado	Встроенная система
Emulation	Émulation	Emulation, Nachbildung	Emulación	Эмуляция (программная реализация отсутствующих аппаратных средств)
Encapsulation	Encapsulation	Kapselung	Encapsulación	Инкапсуляция, скрытие ланных (зашита описания реализации модуля)
Expert system	Systeme expért	Expertensystem	Sistema experto	Экспертная система
Exponent	Exposant	Exponent	Exponente	Показатель степени
Expression	Expression	Ausdruck	Expresión	Выражение
Extensible language	Langage extensible	Erweiterbare Sprache	Lenguaje extensible	Свободная грамматика
Fiber optics	Fibre optique	Glasfaser, Lichtleiter	Óptica de fibras	Волоконная оптика, оптоволокно
Field	Champ (for an instruction field), domaine (for a field of interest)	Feld	Campo	Поле
File	Fichier	Datei	Archivo	Файл, массив
Finite state machine	Machine d'états finis	Endlicher Automat	Máquina de estados finitos	Конечный автомат
Fixed point	Virgule fixe	Festpunkt(zahl)	Punto fijo	Фиксированная запятая
Flag	Drapeau	Kennzeichen, Marke	Señalador, indicador	Флаг, признак
Flip-flop	Flipflop	Flipflop, bistabiles Kippglied	Circuito biestable, circuito basculante	Триггер
Floating point	Virgule flottante	Gleitpunkt(zahl)	Punto flotante	Плавающая запятая
Floppy disk	Disquette	Diskette	Disco flexible	Гибкий диск
Flowchart	Organigramme, ordinogramme	Flussdiagram, Datenflussplan, Programmablaufplan	Carta de flujo	Блок-схема
Font	Police	Zeichensatz	Fuente, tipografía	шрифт; гарнитура
Fractal	Fractal	Fraktale	Fractal	Фракталь
Function	Fonction	Funktion	Función	Функция
Gate	Porte	Gatter, Verknupfungsglied	Puerta	Электронный переключатель, логический элемент

English	French	German	Spanish	Russian
Gateway	Passerelle	Gateway, Knoten	Pasarela, puerta	Шлюз (компьютер, управляющий доступом к внешнеи сети)
Global variable	Variable globale	Globale Variable	Variable global	Глобальная переменная
Grammar	Grammaire	Grammatik	Gramática	Грамматика
Hacker	Hacker	Hacker	Jáquer, pirata informático	Хэкер (программист-энтузиаст, стремящийся к абсолютному знанию компъютера и его возможностей)
Handshaking	Rendez-vous	Quittung	Enlace, conexión	Подтверждение связи, квитирование
Hard disk	Disque dur	Festplatte	Disco rígido	Жесткий диск
Hardware	Matériel	Hardware, Maschinen-ausrüstung, Apparatur	Equipo físico, componentes físicos	Аппаратура
Hashing	Hashing, hash code	Streuspeicher verfahnen, Hashing		Контрольное суммирование, хеширование
Heuristic	Heuristique	Heuristische, Heuristisches Verfahren, Heuristik	Método heurísico	Эвристический
Hexadecimal	Hexadécimal	Sedezimal, Hexadezimal (coll)	Hexadecimal	Шестнадцатиричный
Hybrid computer	Calculateur hybride	Hybridrechner	Computadora híbrida	Гибридный компьютер
Icon	Icône	Sinnbild, Symbol	Ícono	Иконка, пиктограмма (условное изображение объекта или операции)
Identifier	Identificateur	Identifikator, Identifizierer, Bezeichner, Name	Identificador	Идентификатор
Image processing	Traitement d'images	Bildverarbeitung	Procesamento de imágenes	Обработка изображений
Index register	Registre d'index	Indexregister	Registro de indice	Индексный регистр
Indirect address	Adresse indirecte	Indirekte Adresse	Dirección indirecta	Косвенный Адрес
Infinite loop	Boucle infinie	Endlosschleife	Bucle infinito	Бесконечный цикл
Information hiding	Masquage d'information	Information Hiding	Encapsulamiento	Скрытие данных
Information processing	Informatique, traitement de l'information	Datenverabeitung, Infor-mationsverarbeitung	Procesamiento de la información	Обработка информации
Information retrieval	Recherche d'information	Informationsrück-gewinnung	Recolección de datos	Извлечение данных
Information science	Informatique	Informationswissenschaft	Ciencia de la información	Теория информации
Information theory	Théorie de l'information	Informationstheorie	Teoría de la información	Теория информации
Inheritance	Héritage	Vererbung	Herencia	Наследование
Input	Entrée	Eingabe, Eingang, eingeben (v), einlesen (v)	Entrada	Ввод, входные данные
Instruction	Instruction	Befehl, Instruktion	Instrucción	Команда
Interface	Interface	Schnittstelle	Interface, conexión	Интерфейс
Integrated circuit	Circuit intégré	Integrierter Schaltkreis, integrierte Schaltung	Circuito integrado	Интегральная схема
Internet	Internet	Internet	Red, internet	Сеть сетей; межсетевой
Interoperability	Interopérabilité	Kompatibilität, Interoperabilität	Interoperabilidad	Возможность, взаимодействия (сетей)
Interpreter	Intrepréteur	Interpretierer, Interpretier Programm, Interpreter	Interpretador	Интерпретирующая программа
Interrupt	Interruption	Unterbrechung, Interrupt	Interrupción	Прерываеь
Iteration	Itération	Iteration	Iteración	Итерация
Job	Tâche, travail	Job, Auftrag	Trabajo	Задание
Joystick	Manche à balais	Steuerknüppel	Palanca de juego	Джойстик

English	French	German	Spanish	Russian
Kernel	Noyau	Kern	Grano	Ядро
Key	Clé	Schlüssel, Kennbegriff, Taste	Llave, clave	Ключ, клавиша
Keyboard	Clavier	Tastatur	Teclado	Клавиатура
Knowledge representation	Représentation de connaissances	Wissensrepräsentation	Representatión del conocimiento	Представление знаний
Label	Etiquette	Marke, Label, Etikett, Kennsatz	Etiqueta	Метка
Language processor	Compilateur	Sprachprozessor, Sprach-übersetzer, Übersetzer	Procesador de lenguaje, compilador	Транслятор языка
Laptop computer	Ordinateur portable	Tragbarer Rechner	Computador portátil	Лаптоп
Laser printer	Imprimante laser	Laserdrucker	Impresora láser	Лазерный принтер
Latency	Latence	Wartezeit, Latenzzeit	Latencia	Время задержки (часть времени выборки)
Lightpen	Crayon optique	Lichtgriffel	Pluma luminosa	Световое перо
Linker	Editeur de liens	Binder	Linker	Редактор связей, линкер
List processing	Traitement de liste	Listenverabeitung	Procesamiento de listas	Обработка списков
Loader	Chargeur	Lader, Ladeprogramm, Programmlader	Cargador	Загрузчик
Local area network	Réseau local	Lokales Netzwerk	Red de area local	Локальная сеть
Local variable	Variable locale	Lokale Variable	Variable local	локальная переменная
Logic design	Conception logique	Logik-Design	Diseño lógico	логическое проектирование
Logic programming	Programmation logique	Logische Programmierung	Programación lógica	логическое программирование
Login	Login	Anmeldung	Registrar, conectar	вход в систему, начало сеанса
Loop	Boucle	Schleife	Ciclo iterativo	Цикл
Machine language	Language machine	Maschinensprache	Lenguaje de máquina	Машинный язык
Machine-readable form	Format machine	Maschinenlesbare Form	Formulario leído a máquina	Машино-читаемая форма
Macroinstruction	Macroinstruction	Makroinstruktion, Makrobefehl, Makro (coll)	Macroinstrucción	Макрокоманда
Magnetic core	Tore magnétique	Magnetkern	Toroide magnético, núcleo magnético	Магнитная память
Magnetic tape	Bande magnétique	Magnetband	Cinta magnética	Магнитная лента
Mainframe	Serveur	Großrechner	Computador central	Большая машина, универсальная вычислитульная машина
Mantissa	Mantisse	Mantisse	Mantisa	Мантисса
Mass storage	Mémoire de masse	Massenspeicher	Almacén de gran volumen	ЗУ большой емкости
Memory	Mémoire	Speicher, Gedächtnis	Memoria	Память
Memory protection	Protection de mémoire	Speicherschutz, Speicher-schreibsperre	Protectión de memoria	Защита памяти
Menu	Menu	Menü, Auswahl	Menú	Меню
Microcomputer	Micro-ordinateur	Mikrocomputer, Mikro (coll)	Microcomputador	Микрокомпьютер
Microprocessor	Microprocesseur	Mikroprozessor	Microprocesador	Микропроцессор
Microprogramming	Microprogrammation	Mikroprogrammierung	Microprogrammación	Мнкропрогаммирование
Microsecond	Microseconde	Mikrosekunde	Microsegundo	Микросекунда
Millisecond	Milliseconde	Millisekunde	Milisegundo	Мнллисекунда
Minicomputer	Mini-ordinateur	Kleinrechner, Minicomputer, Mini (coll)	Minicomputador	Миникомпьютер
Modem	Modem	Modem, Signalumsetzer	Modulador-demodulador, modem	Модем (модулятор-демодулятор)
Monitor	Moniteur	Monitor, Überwachungs-programm, Überwachen (v)	Monitor	Монитор
Mouse	Souris	Maus	Ratón, mouse	Мышъ, мышка

English	French	German	Spanish	Russian
Multimedia	Multimédia	Multimedia	Multimedia	Мулътимедиа, синтетическая система (средства комплексного представления информации: текст, графика и звук)
Multiplexer	Multiplexeur	Multiplexer (Communications Multiplexor: Datenübertragungs-steuereinheit)	Multiplexor	Мультиплексор
Multiprocessor	Multiprocesseur	Mehrprozessorsystem	Procesador múltiple	Мультипроцессор
Multiprogramming	Multiprogrammation	Mehrprogrammbetrieb, Multiprogrammierung	Multiprogramación	Мультипрограммиро-вание
Multitasking	Multitâche	Multitasking	Multitarea	Многозадачность, многозадачный режим
Nanosecond	Nanoseconde	Nanosekunde	Nanosegundo	Наносекунда
Network	Réseau	Netzwerk, Rechnernetz	Red (de computadores)	Сеть
Neural network	Réseau neuronal	Neuronales Netz	Red neural	Нейронная сеть
Numerical analysis	Analyse numérique	Numerische Analyse	Análisis numérico	Численный анализ
Object program	Programme objet	Objektprogramm, Maschinencode-Programm, Zeilprogramm	Programa objeto	Рабочая программа (Объектна программа, программа на машинном языке)
Object-oriented programming	Programmation orientée objet	Objektorientierte Programmierung	Programmación orientada por objetos	Объектно-ориентированное программирование
Octal	Octal	Oktal	Octal	Восьмеричный
Office automation	Bureautique	Büroautomatisierung	Automatización de oficina	Автоматизация конторы, учреждения
Operand	Opérande	Operand	Operando	Операнд
Operating system	Système d'exploitation	Betriebssystem	Sistema operativo	Операционная система
Operator	Opérateur	Bediener, Operator	Operador	Олерация; оператор
Optical computing	Traitement optique	Optisches Rechnen	Computación óptica	Оптические вычисления, вычисленич с помощью оптического коипъютера
Output	Sortie	Ausgabe, ausgeben (v)	Salida	Выход. выходные данные, выдача ptpekmnfnjd
Overflow	Dépassement de capacité	Überlauf	Sobrecarga, desbordamiento de carga	Переполнение
Packet switching	Commutation de paquets	Paketvermittlung	Commutación de paquetes	Коммутация пакетов
Paper tape	Bande perforée	Lochstreifen, Papierstreifen	Cinta de papel	Перфолента
Parallel processing	Traitement parallèle	Parallelverarbeitung, Simultanverabeitung	Procesamiento en paralelo	Параллельная обработка
Parameter	Paramètre	Parameter	Parámetro	Параметр
Parity	Parité	Parität, Parigkeit	Paridad	Уетность
Parsing	Analyse syntaxique	Syntaxanalyse, Parsing	Tabulación, análisis sintáctico	Лексический анализ; синтаксический анализ
Password	Mot de passe	Paßwort	Contraseña, clave de acceso	Пароль
Pattern recognition	Reconnaissance de formes	Mustererkennung	Recononcimiento de formas	Распознавание образов
Peripheral	Périphérique	Peripher	Equipo periférico	Периферическнй
Personal computer	Ordinateur personnel	PC	Computador personal	Персональная вычислительная мащина (компьютер)

English	French	German	Spanish	Russian
Pipelining	Traitement par flôt	Parallelverarbeitung, Befehlsverknüpfung	Serialización	конвейеризация, конвейерный режим
Pixel	Pixel	Bildelement, Pixel	Píxel	пиксель, пиксел, точка растра
Platform	Plate-forme	Plattform	Plataforma	Платформа
Plotter	Traceur	Kurvenschreiber, Kurvenzeichner, Plotter, Zeichengerät	Graficador	Графопостроитель
Pointer	Pointeur	Zeiger	Puntero	Указатель
Port	Port	Anschluß	Puerto, conexión	Порт; переносить (программу) на другую машину
Portability	Portabilité	Übertragbarkeit, Portabilitat	Portabilidad	Портативность
Precision	Précision	Genauigkeit, Stellenzahl	Precisión	Точность
Printer	Imprimante	Drucker	Impresora	Печатающее устройство
Procedure	Procédure	Prozedur	Procedimiento	Процедура
Procedure-oriented language	Langage procédural	Prozedurale Sprache	Lenguaje procedural	Процедурно-ориентированный язык
Processor	Processeur	Prozessor, zentrale Recheneinheit, verarbeitiende Funktionseinheit in Hardware oder Software	Procesador	Процессор
Program	Programme	Programm, programmieren (v)	Programa	Прогорамма
Program counter	Comptcur ordinal	Programmzähler	Contador de programa	Счетчик команд
Programmer	Programmeur	Programmierer	Programador	Программист
Programming language	Langage de programmation	Programmiersprache	Lenguaje de programación	Язык программирования
Queue	File d'attente	Warteschlange	Cola	Очередь
Random access	Accès direct	Direktzugriff, direkter Zugriff, wahlfreier Zugriff	Acceso directo	Произвольный доступ прямой доступ
Random number	Nombre aléatoire	Zufallszahl	Número aleatorio	Случайное число
Record	Enregistrement	Datensatz, Satz, Aufzeichnung	Registro	Запсь
Recursion	Récurrence	Rekursion	Recursión	Рекурсиия
Register	Registre	Register	Registro	Регистр
Regular expression	Expression régulière	Regulärer Ausdruck	Expresión regular	Правильное выражение
Relational database	Base de données relationelle	Relationale Datenbank	Banqo de datos relacionales	Реляционная база данных
Response Time	Temps de réponse	Antwortzeit (Ansprechzeit, Analaufzeit)	Tiempo de respuesta	Время ответа
Robotics	Robotique	Robotik	Robótica	Робототехника
Roundoff error	Erreur d'arrondi	Rundungsfehler	Error de redondeo	Ошибка округления
Run time	Temps d'execution	Laufzeit, Durchlaufzeit	Tiempo de ejecución	Время выполнения
Scanner	Balayage	Abtaster, Abtast-vorrichtung, Scanner	Explorador	Сканнирующее устройство
Scheduler	Régulateur, planificateur	Scheduler	Regulador, planificador	Планировщик
Search engine	Moteur de recherche	Suchmaschine	Buscador, motor de búsqueda	Поисковый механизм
Semantics	Sémantique	Semantik	Semántica	Семантика
Sequential circuit	Circuit séquentiel	Schaltwerk	Circuito secuencial	Последовательная схема, цепь
Serial port	Port série	Serieller Anschluß	Puerto en serie	Последовательный порт (для подключения устройства с последовательным интерфейсом)
Shifting	Décalage	Verschieben, Schieben Stellenversetzen, Schiften (coll)	Desplazamiento	Сдвиг

English	French	German	Spanish	Russian
Side effect	Effet secondaire, effet de bord	Nebenwirkung, Seiteneffekt	Efecto secundario	Побочный эффект
Simulation	Simulation	Simulation, Nachbildung	Simulación	Моделирование
Software	Logiciel	Software, Programm-ausrüstung	Software, componentes lógicos	Программное обеспечение
Software engineering	Ingéniérie du logiciel	Software-engineering, Software-technologie	Ingenieria de software	Разработка программного обеспечения
Sorting	Tri	Sortieren, Sortierung	Ordenar, clasificar	Сортировка
Source program	Programme source	Quellprogramm, Quellen-programm, Primär-programm, Quelle, Sourceprogramm	Programa fuente	Исходная программа
Speech recognition	Reconnaissance de la parole	Spracherkennung	Reconocimiento de lenguaje	Распознавание речи
Spelling checker	Vérificateur orthographique	Rechtschreibhilfe	Verificador de ortograffa	Корректор
Spreadsheet	Tableur	Tabellenkalkulation	Planilla electrónica	Электронная таблица
Stack	Pile	Keller, Kellespeicher, Stapelspeicher	Pila	Набор, пакет, буфер, стек
Statement	Instruction	Anweisung	Sentencia, instrucción	Команда, утверждетне, оператор
Storage	Mémoire	Speicher, Speicherung	Almacén, memoria	Запоминающее устройство, память
Stored program	Programme enregistré	Speicherprogrammiert	Programa almacenado	Хранимая программа
String	Chaîne	Zeichenreihe, Zeichenfolge Kette, Folge, String	Cadena, serie, tira	Строка
Structured programming	Programmation structurée	Strukturierte Programmierung	Programación estructurada	Структурное программирование
Subroutine	Sous-programme	Unterprogramm, Subroutine	Subrutina	Подпрограмма
Subroutine library	Bibliothèque de sous-programmes	Funktionsbibliothek	Biblioteca de subrutinas	Библиотека подпрограмм
Subscript	Indice	Index, indizieren (v)	Subindice	Индекс
Supercomputer	Super-calculateur	Supercomputer	Supercomputador	Супер-компъютер (сверхвысокой производительности)
Swapping	Swapping	Auslargern	Intercambio, conmutación	Подкачка; обмен (местами); свопинг
Switching theory	Théorie de la commutation	Theorie der Scheltwerke	Teoría de circuitos	Теоря переключательных схем
Symbol	Symbole	Symbol	Simbolo	Символ
Symbol manipulation	Manipulation de symboles	Symbolverarbeitung, Symbolmanipulation	Manipulación de simbolos	Обработка символов
Syntax	Syntaxe	Syntax	Sintaxis	Синтаксис
Systems analysis	Analyse fonctionnelle	Systemanalyse	Análisis de sistemas	Системный анализ
Systems programming	Programmation système	Systemprogrammierung	Programacion de sistemas	Системное программирование
Task	Tâche	Task, Aufgabe	Tarea	Задание, задача
Teleprocessing	Télétraitement	Datenfernverarbeitung	Teleprocesamiento	Телеобработка, дистанционная обработка
Terminal	Terminal	Terminal, Endgerät, Datensichtgerät	Terminal	Терминал, устройство Ввода/вывода
Thrashing	Thrashing	Überlastung	Recolección selectiva	Пробуксовка (из-за неэффективной организации механизма)
Throughput	Débit	Durchsatz	Productividad, throughput	Пропускная способность
Time sharing	Temps partagé	Teilnehmerbetrieb, Zeit-multiplex Verarbeitung, zeitlich verzahne Verarbeitung	Tiempo compartido	Система с разделением времени

English	French	German	Spanish	Russian
Touch screen	Écran tactile	Touchscreen	Pantalla de contacto	Сенсорный экран
Trace	Trace, historique	Protokoll, Ablaufprotokoll, Ablaufverfolgung, Ausführungsprotokoll, Trace	Rastreo	След
Trackball	Boule roulante	Steuerkungel	Esfera de pista, seguibola	Координатный шар, трекбол (перевернутая мышъ)
Tree	Arborescence	Baum	Arbol	Дерево
Turing machine	Machine de Turing	Turing-Maschine	Máquina de Turing	Машина тюринга
User friendly	Convivial	Benutzerfreundlich	De uso fácil	Дружественный по отношению к пользователю
User interface	Interface utilisateur	Benutzerschnittstelle	Interface del usuario	Пользовательскнй интерфейс
Variable	Variable	Variable	Variable	Переменная
Virtual memory	Mémoire virtuelle	Virtueller Speicher	Memoria virtual	Виртуальная память
Virtual reality	Réalité virtuelle	Virtuelle Realität	Realidad virtual	Виртуальная реальность
Virus	Virus	Virus	Virus	Вирус
Visual programming	Programmation visuelle	Visuelle Programmierung	Programación visual	Визуальное программирование
Volatile memory память	Mémoire volatile	Flüchtiger Speicher	Memoria volátil	Энергозависимая (с разрушением информации при отключении питания)
Window	Fenêtre	Fenster	Ventana	Окно
Word	Mot	Wort	Palabra	Слово
Word processing	Traitement de texte	Textverarbeitung	Procesamento de texto	Редактор
Workstation	Station de travail	Arbeitsplatzrechner	Estación de trabajo	Автоматизированное рабочее место, АРМ; рабочая станция
World Wide Web	Toile	World Wide Web	Red mundial, malla mundialq	Всемирная паутина

| | PHILLIPPE L. DREYFUS | HORST HÜNKE | ENRIQUE I. OVIEDO | VICTOR YA. PAN |
| | PHILLIPPE JORRAND | THOMAS STROTHOTTE | | BORIS YAMROM |

Appendix VIII

ARTICLES DELETED FROM PREVIOUS EDITIONS

In a discipline which changes as rapidly as Computer Science, it is inevitable that topics once considered important become obsolete although they may still be of interest for historical research. In addition, in order to keep this Encyclopedia to a manageable size, some articles in one edition have had to be merged into other articles in later editions. This Appendix lists all articles which appeared in one of the first three editions but were dropped or merged in a later edition. Often, even when there is not a cross-reference to a related article, a subject listed below will be found in the Index to this edition.

Article title	Last edition in which appeared	Related article(s) in this edition
Acoustic Coupler	2	
Address Modification	2	
Addressless Instructions	2	
American Association for Artificial Intelligence	3	_See_ Computer Societies
American Federation of Information Processing Societies	3	_See_ Computer Societies
American Society for Information Science	3	_See_ Computer Societies
Analog Computer	3	Much shorter article in 4th Ed.
Arithmetic Scan	3	_See_ Compiler
ARPA Network	2	_See_ Networks, Computer
Arts Applications	2	_See_ Computer Art, Computer Music
Artspeak	2	
ASCII	3	_See_ Character Codes
Association for Educational Data Systems	2	
Association for Systems Management	2	
Association Française pour la Cybernétique Économique et Technique	3	_See_ Computer Societies
Associative Languages	2	
Audio Terminals	2	
Authoring Languages and Systems	3	_See_ Computer-Assisted Learning and Teaching
Backtracking	2	_See_ Algorithms, Design and Classification of
Banking Applications	3	_See_ Electronic Commerce, Electronic Funds Transfer
Base Register	3	_See_ Computer Architecture
Binary-Coded Decimal	3	_See_ Codes

Article title	Last edition in which appeared	Related article(s) in this edition
Binary Search	2	*See* Searching
Block Diagram	2	*See* Flowchart
Breakpoint	2	*See* Debugging
Burroughs B5000 Series	2	
Canadian Information Processing Society	3	*See* Computer Societies
Card Reading and Punching Techniques	2	
CD-ROM	3	*See* Optical Storage
Character Set	2	*See* Character Codes
Checkpoint and Restart	3	*See* Checkpoint
CODASYL	3	
Collating Sequence	2	*See* Sorting
Colleges and Universities, Computers in	2	
Command and Job Control Language	3	
Compiler-Compiler	3	*See* Compiler
Compiler Construction	3	*See* Compiler
Compiler, Incremental	2	
Compiler, Syntax-Directed	2	
Computability	2	*See* Algorithms, Theory of
Computer-Assisted Instruction	3	*See* Computer-Assisted Learning and Teaching
Computer-Integrated Manufacturing	3	*See* Computer-Aided Design/Computer-Aided Manufacturing
Computer-Managed Instruction	3	
Computer Utility	2	*See* Time Sharing
Computer, Using a	1	
Computing Center	3	
Computing Economics: Acquisition and Operation	1	
Concatenation	3	*See* String Processing
Concurrency Control	3	*See* Concurrent Programming
Control Point	2	
Controlled Variable	2	*See* Iteration
Copyrights and Patents, Computer Aspects of	1	*See* Legal Protection of Software
Credit Systems Applications	2	
CUBE	2	
Current Awareness System	3	*See* Information Retrieval; Online Information Systems
Cursor	2	*See* Interactive Input Devices; Text Editing Systems
Dangling ELSE	1	*See* Syntax, Semantics and Pragmatics
Data Bank	2	*See* Database Management Systems
Data Acquisition Computer	3	
Data Communication Networks	2	*See* Data Communications; Networks, Computer
Data Communications: Software	3	
Data Definition Languages	2	
Data Preparation Devices	2	*See* Optical Character Recognition; Punched Card Machinery
Data Processing Management Association	3	*See* Computer Societies
Data Set	2	
Data Structures, Set Concepts for	2	
Data Tablet	2	*See* Computer Graphics
Database Administrator	2	
Database Computer	3	
Database, On-line	2	
Deadlock	2	*See* Database Concurrency Control
Decidability	2	*See* Algorithms, Theory of; Undecidable Problems
Decision Table	3	
Decrement	2	
DECUS	2	*See* User Groups
Digital Computers: History: Personal Computers	3	*See* Digital Computers, History of: Since 1950
Digital Equipment Corporation PDP Series	2	*See* Digital Equipment Corporation
Digital Equipment Corporation VAX Series	3	*See* Digital Equipment Corporation
Direct Access	3	*See* Memory: Auxiliary
Disassembler	3	*See* Assembler
EBCDIC	3	*See* Character Codes
Econometric Applications	2	

Article title	Last edition in which appeared	Related article(s) in this edition
Education in Computer Science: Japan	3	*See* Education in Computer Science: Asia
Engineering Applications	2	*See* Computer-Aided Engineering
Errors, Absolute and Relative	2	*See* Errors
Feasibility Study	2	
FIFO-LIFO	3	*See* Data Structures; Stack
Fix	2	
Flow Diagram	2	*See* Flowchart
GIGO	2	
Glitch	2	
Grammar, Generative	1	*See* Grammars
Grammar, Reductive	1	*See* Grammars
Grosch's Law	3	*See* Laws, Computer
GUIDE	2	*See* User Groups
Hard Copy	2	
Hardware Monitor	3	
Hashing	2	*See* Searching
Higher Education, Computers in	1	*See* Education in Computer Science
Hybrid Computers	3	*See* Analog Computer
IBM Card	2	*See* Punched Card
Indirect Address	3	*See* Addressing
Information and Data	3	
Information Systems Methodology	3	*See* Information Systems
Input-Output Devices	2	*See* Printers; Punched Card Machinery
Instruction and Data Representation	3	*See* Addressing, Instruction Set
Intelligent Terminal	1	*See* Terminals
Intensive Care, Computers in	3	*See* Medical Applications
Interactive Systems, Using	2	*See* Time Sharing
Interface Message Processor	2	*See* Networks, Computer
Intergovernmental Bureau for Informatics	2	
International Association for Analog Computation	1	
International Association for Mathematics and Computers in Simulation	2	
International Federation of Automatic Control	3	
International Society for Technology in Education	3	*See* Language Processors
Joint Users Group	2	
Joystick	2	*See* Interactive Input Devices
Key	2	*See* Sorting
Keyboard Standards	3	
Keyword-in-Context Index	2	*See* Information Retrieval
Label	2	*See* Control Structure
Latency	3	*See* Memory: Auxiliary
Lightpen	2	*See* Interactive Input Devices
Load-and-Go Compiler	3	*See* Compiler; Language Processors
Local Store	3	*See* General Register
Loop	3	*See* Control Structure
Macro Languages	2	
Manufacturers, Computer	1	*See* Computer Industry
Markov Algorithms	2	
MEDLARS/MEDLINE	3	*See* Medical Applications
Metacharacter	2	
Metavariable	2	
Models	2	*See* Simulation
Modula-2	3	*See* Procedure-oriented Languages
MUMPS	3	*See* Appendix VI
NCR Computers	3	
New York Times Information Bank	2	
Ninety Column Card	2	*See* Punched Card
Noise	2	
Nucleus	1	*See* Kernel

Article title	Last edition in which appeared	Related article(s) in this edition
Office Automation	2	*See* Electronic Office
One-Level Memory	3	*See* Virtual Memory
Open and Closed Shop	2	
Operation Code	1	*See* Instruction Set
Operations Research	3	
Optical Mark Readers	2	*See* Optical Character Recognition
Original Equipment Manufacturer	3	*See* Digital Computers, History of: Since 1950
Overlay	2	*See* Storage Allocation
Parsing	2	*See* Grammars
Patch	2	*See* Debugging
PERT/CPM	3	
Pictures, Basic Structure	2	*See* Computer Graphics
Pingpong	2	
Planning Systems, Characteristics of	1	
Planning, Computer Applications in	2	*See* Automated Planning
PMS Notation	1	
Point-of-Sale Terminal	2	*See* Terminals
Printing Techniques	2	*See* Printers
Procedure	3	*See* Subprogram
Processing Modes	3	
Program Status Words and State Vectors	2	*See* Interrupt
Programming Language Models	1	*See* Programming Language Semantics
Proprietary Program	1	*See* Legal Protection of Software
Publishing, Computers in	2	*See* Desktop Publishing
Queueing Network Models	2	
RAMAC	2	*See* IBM Corporation
Rand Tablet	1	
Real Time Business Applications	3	*See* Administrative Applications
Regression Analysis	3	*See* Statistical Applications
Remote Job Entry	2	
Report Generators	2	
Ring	2	
Scratch File	3	
Security of Computer Installations, Physical	2	
Semaphore	2	*See* Concurrent Programming
Service Bureaus, Data Processing	2	
SHARE	2	*See* User Groups
Significance Arithmetic	3	
Simplex Method	3	*See* Mathematical Programming
Society for Computer Simulation	3	*See* Computer Societies
Society for Industrial and Applied Mathematics	3	*See* Computer Societies
Society for Management Information Systems	2	
Software Complexity	2	
Software Flexibility	3	*See* Software Reusability
Software Packages	2	*See* Software Libraries, Numerical and Statistical
Software Personalization	3	
Software Science	2	*See* Software Metrics
Sort/Merge Packages	2	*See* Sorting
Special-Purpose Computers	2	
Spooling	2	*See* Operating Systems
Stochastic Process	2	*See* Information Theory
Storage Management Structures	2	
Storage Organization	2	*See* Machine and Assembly Language Programming
String	2	*See* String Processing
Subprograms, Calling	2	*See* Parameter Passing
Subroutine	2	*See* Subprogram
System Chart	2	*See* Flowchart
System Generation	2	
Table Look-up	2	*See* Searching
Tape Label	2	
Task	2	*See* Multitasking

Article title	Last edition in which appeared	Related article(s) in this edition
Transputer	3	
Turnaround Time	3	
Turnkey	3	
Unbundling	2	*See* Software
Univac 1100 Series	2	
Univac Scientific Exchange	1	
Update	2	
Utility Program	2	*See* Computer System
Videodisc	3	*See* Optical Storage
Viewdata	2	*See* Videotex
VIM	2	
Volume	3	*See* Directory
Word Length, Variable	2	

— Appendix IX —

TIMELINE OF SIGNIFICANT COMPUTING MILESTONES

The basic idea of this timeline is that those who have seen close to five decades of computing evolve will enjoy the nostalgia of seeing certain developments pass before their eyes as they read. Some mathematics, physics, and electrical engineering milestones are included because the discoveries or events listed are significant antecedents to the development of the science and technology of computing. Cipher machines are mentioned because cryptography provided so much of the driving force that inspired creation of ever-better computing machines. And the inventions that relate to communications are cited because their use has become such an integral part of computing.

For years that mark multiple accomplishments, there has been no attempt to list these accomplishments in any order of perceived importance. The names of computers, languages, algorithms, methods, books, movies, software, etc. have been italicized. Emboldened phrases indicate the names of articles (or portions thereof) that appear in this *Encyclopedia*.

The entries were compiled from a number of secondary sources and certainly should not be used to settle questions of priority; these sources often disagree by one or two years in their dating of an event.

The editors are grateful to Martin Campbell-Kelly of the University of Warwick for a critical reading of a draft of this timeline. Readers who suspect errors of commission or omission are encouraged to email the editors so that appropriate corrections can be made in the fifth edition: ar9@doc.ic.ac.uk; reilly@cs.albany.edu or hemmendd@union.edu.

We trust that readers will be tolerant of the light-hearted nature of some of the early dates, and of the speculations opposite dates later than 2000.

15 billion BC	Universal computer boots up with a Big Bang.
5 billion BC	First full-scale **analog computer** computes planetary orbits.
500 million BC	First cell, address unknown.
200 million BC	Cells assembled into first **memory** and attached to a rudimentary **central processing unit**.
50,000 BC	Earliest evidence of counting.
2500 BC	Positional number system used in Mesopotamia.
2400 BC	Babylonians use abacus and approximate π as 3 1/8.

1900 BC	Stonehenge erected.
1650 BC	In the Rhind Papyrus, the Egyptian Ahmes the Scribe states that $\pi = 256/81 \cong 3.1\underline{60}\ldots$.
870 BC	A symbol for zero is used in India.
800 BC	I-Ching exhibits binary properties.
600 BC	Abacus used in Greece.
550 BC	Pythagoras gets credit for a theorem known to the Chinese a thousand years earlier. When his student Hippasus discovers irrational numbers, Pythagoras, believing the universe to be strictly rational, acts contrarily and has him drowned for heresy.
450 BC	Hippocrates of Chios rediscovers the irrationals but is saved from drowning by clinging to floating-point numbers.
300 BC	Euclid's *Elements*.
230 BC	*Sieve of Eratosthenes*, an early **algorithm.**
215 BC	Archimedes approximates π as $21,1872/67,441 \cong 3.14159\underline{0}$. Then he discovers the naked truth and shouts "Eureka."
140 BC	Hipparchus of Rhodes, knowing all the angles, invents trigonometry.
100 BC	Chinese use positive and negative powers of 10 to express magnitudes.
80 BC	The Antikythera calendar mechanism.
44 BC	Caesar, lacking an Antikythera, fails to beware the Ides of March.
AD 150	Ptolemy's *Almagest*.
250	Diophantus' *Arithmetica*.
450	Tsu Ch'ung-chih and his son Tsu Keng-chih compute π as $355/133 \cong 3.14159\underline{29}\ldots$, an accuracy unsurpassed for 1,000 years.
600	Decimal number system used in India.
850	*Algebra* of al-Khowarizmi transmits Hindu art of reckoning to the Arabs and thus to Europe; invention of astrolabes.
1050	Chinese scholars arrange the 64 I-Ching hexagrams in a 6-bit binary order called the Fu Hsi arrangement.
1202	Fibonacci sequence.
1261	Yang Hui anticipates "**Pascal**'s" triangle.
1274	Raymond Lull's logic machine.
1430	Baptista Alberti's cipher machine.
1435	Jamshid ben Mas'ud ben Mahmud Ghiath ed-Din al-Kashi invents several special-purpose astronomical calculators, calculates π to 16 places, and is first to express a fraction as a positional decimal.
1489	Use of plus and minus signs by Widmann.
1492	Pellos invents decimal point. Columbus, all at sea, doesn't notice.
1500	Leonardo DaVinci draws sketch of a 13-wheel odometer-like counter, but historians disagree as to whether this was intended to be used in what would have been the first mechanical calculator; Aldus Manutius develops an italic **typefont**.

1518	First known book of cryptology, *Polygraphiae libri sex* (Six books of polygraphy), by Johannes Trithemius, published posthumously, is later placed on the Falwell Index of Forbidden Books.
1527	Apian publishes "**Pascal**'s" triangle.
1540	Robert Recorde invents the equal sign, "=," and, as a matter of recorde, turns over in his grave when it is ambiguously used as the replacement operator in *Fortran* and *C++*.
1580	Francois Vieta causes a sensation by using letters to stand for numerical parameters, thus inventing the concept of a variable; Rabbi Judah ben Loew's automaton.
1610	Edmund Gunter invents several surveying instruments and names the trig functions cosine and cotangent; Ludolph van Ceulen computes π to 35 decimals.
1614	**John Napier**'s *Canon of Logarithms*.
1617	Napier's *Rabdologia* describes "Napier's bones."
1624	Wilhelm Schickard's calculator does automatic addition and subtraction and semiautomatic multiplication and division. Henry Briggs' error-ridden table of logarithms.
1629	William Oughtred and Richard Delamain invent circular slide rule. Adrian Vlacq's first complete set of modern logarithms.
1631	Oughtred's *Clavis Mathematicae* is first to use symbol × for multiplication and *sin* and *cos* as abbreviations for *sine* and *cosine*.
1637	*Fermat's Last Theorem* is of marginal interest but keeps mathematicians busy for 357 years; Descartes' *Discours de la Méthode* describes analytic geometry, which is indispensable for modern work in computer graphics.
1642	**Blaise Pascal**'s calculator, which he names "Pascaline."
1646	Sir Thomas Browne coins the word "electricity" and is first to describe a person who computes as a "computer."
1665	Newton invents calculus but does not publish his discovery.
1666	**Gottfried Wilhelm Leibniz**'s *De Arte Combinatorica*; Gaspard Schott's *Organum Mathematicum*, a mechanical aid that improves on "Napier's Bones."
1672	Samuel Morland's *The Description and Use of Two Arithmetic Instruments*.
1673	René Grillet's adding machine; **Leibniz** invents calculus independently of Newton and, in his spare time, develops the Leibniz "wheel," a calculator that can add, subtract, multiply, and divide, all automatically. He believes that he has invented binary numbers but is later stunned when he learns of the 11th Century Fu Hsi arrangement of the I-Ching.
1687	Newton's *Principia*.
1699	Abraham Sharp computes π to 72 decimal places using the first Sharp calculator (pencil and paper and his head).
1706	Use of the symbol π by William Jones; John Machin computes π to 100 decimal places.

1714	Brook Taylor shows that most basic mathematical functions can be expanded into an infinite series of terms that require only pure arithmetic for their computation; Henry Mill receives an English patent for a typewriter.
1730	Stirling's formula for $n!$ which is now so indispensable for the **analysis of algorithms**.
1736	Vaucanson's automata; Euler generalizes and solves the *Seven Bridges of Königsberg* problem and thereby inaugurates modern **Graph Theory**.
1752	Ben Franklin is told to go fly a kite. He does and experiences an electrifying moment.
1761	J. H. Lambert proves that π is irrational.
1774	Phillipp-Matthaus Hahn builds and sells a 12-digit calculator.
1777	Buffon's Needle Problem is first **Monte Carlo** simulation; Earl of Stanhope's "Logic Demonstrator" is first mechanical logic machine.
1786	J. H. Muller's automatic difference engine; Gripenstierna's cipher machine
1801	Gauss's *Disquisitiones Arithmeticae*; Jacquard's punched-card-controlled loom.
1811	Luddites destroy machines that threaten jobs.
1814	J. H. Hermann's planimeter.
1820	Charles Xavier Thomas (Thomas de Colmar's) Arithmometer.
1822	**Charles Babbage**'s design and partial construction of a **Difference Engine**.
1829	William Austen Burt is first American to patent a typewriter; Wheatstone uses punched paper tape to store data.
1832	**Babbage** designs his **Analytical Engine**; Menabrea advocates use of parallel processing; 20-year old Évariste Galois, on the eve of his death in a duel with the fiancé of his beloved groupie Stéphanie-Félicie Poterine du Motel, frantically writes out an an outline of his *group theory*, one of the mathematical foundations for the ultimate proof of *Fermat's Last Theorem*. Ever since, the inns of the kind to which Évariste and Stéphanie journeyed to their trysts by coach are called "motels."
1843	Menabrea's memoir with commentary by **Ada Augusta**, the Countess of Lovelace; Hamilton's quaternions.
1844	Morse sends telegraph message from Washington to Baltimore; Joseph Liouville finds first transcendental number; Johann Dase, a 20-year-old calculating prodigy, occupies himself for two whole months by computing π to 200 decimal places in his head.
1850	Amedee Mannheim designs the logarithmic slide rule that dominated mechanical calculation for the next 100 years.
1853	Pehr Georg and Edvard Scheutz's Tabulating Machine.
1854	**George Boole**'s *Laws of Thought*.
1855	James Clerk Maxwell's improved planimeter.
1860	**Boole**'s *Finite Differences* is first text on subject.

1867	Wheatstone's cipher machine.
1873	Hermite proves that e is transcendental; William Shanks publishes 707 decimal places of π, but only the first 526 prove to be correct.
1876	Alexander Graham Bell's telephone; Lord Kelvin's harmonic analyzer and tide predictor devices.
1878	Thomas Edison, in a letter to a friend, uses "**bug**" in its modern context 65 years before the legendary moth invades a Harvard **Mark I** relay circuit.
1880	Baudot's punched paper tape telegraph code, **Baudot Code**; Ramon Verea's calculator is first to perform direct multiplication rather than using repeated addition.
1882	*Towers of Hanoi* problem invented by Edouard Lucas; Lindemann proves that π is transcendental.
1884	**W. S. Burroughs'** first adding machine.
1885	Marquand's mechanical logic machine; Dorr Felt invents the comptometer, though he calls it a "Macaroni Box."
1890	**Punched card** machines patented by John Shaw Billings and implemented by **Herman Hollerith**; **Leonardo Torres Quevedo** builds an electromechanical machine for solving certain endgame problems in chess.
1893	Chess-playing machine envisioned by Ambrose Bierce in his short story "Moxon's Master"; Charles Proteus Steinmetz uses complex arithmetic as a basis for practical calculations in alternating current theory, and develops a Law of Hysteresis that becomes the basis of magnetic core **memory** a half-century later.
1894	Variable-toothed gear invented by Odhner and Baldwin and becomes basis for the Monroe calculator.
1895	Marconi transmits radio signals.
1896	**Hollerith** founds Tabulating Machine Company which later became Computing, Tabulating, and Recording Co. (CTR) in 1911 and then the **IBM Corporation** in 1924; Hadamard and de la Vallée Poussin independently prove the prime number theorem.
1899	Founding of **Burroughs** Adding Machine Company.
1901	Marconi transmits first transatlantic wireless message but neglects to credit Jagadis Chandra Bose for inventing the "coherer" (receiver) that made it possible.
1904	Diode vacuum tube invented by J. A. Fleming.
1906	Triode vacuum tube invented by Lee De Forest.
1908	Percy Ludgate's analytical engine; through his will, Paul Wolfskehl establishes a prize of 100,000 marks for whoever is able to prove *Fermat's Last Theorem* no later than 2007.
1910	H. P. Babbage assembles mill of his father's design and builds a printer to go with it; **James Powers** develops mechanical **punched card machinery** for use with 1910 census and later forms Powers Accounting Machine Company; Russell and Whitehead's *Principia Mathematica*.

1911	Founding of Computing, Tabulating, and Recording Co. (CTR), the forerunner of IBM; discovery of superconductivity by Kammerlingh Onnes.
1912	Wireless operators on the *Titanic* are first to send a meaningful S.O.S. signal. The *Carpathia*, 58 miles away, responds; the *Californian*, 15 miles away, does not.
1913	**Torres Quevedo**'s electrified arithmometer; Ramanujan develops formulas that form the basis of the fastest algorithms for computing π known to this day.
1917	Armstrong's superheterodyne radio receiver.
1919	Eccles and Jordan's flip-flop circuit.
1921	Karel Čapek coins the word "robot" in his play *R.U.R.*
1924	Computing, Tabulating, and Recording Company is renamed International Business Machines (IBM).
1925	Formal establishment of Bell Telephone Laboratories; first public television demonstrations by Philo Farnsworth and, independently, by John Logie Baird.
1926	As a sequel, Baird invents radar, fiber optics, and an infrared device for enhancing night vision; early versions of the Hagelin and German *Enigma* cipher machines.
1927	J. A. O'Neill patents magnetic coated tape; newly formed Remington Rand buys Powers Accounting Machine Company.
1928	IBM introduces 80-column **punched card**; **L. J. Comrie** uses **punched card machinery** to compute Moon orbits.
1929	Vladimir Zworykin of RCA patents first Cathode Ray Tube (CRT); first demonstration of color television; station WRGB in Schenectady, NY begins first regularly scheduled TV broadcasts; Lukasiewicz uses parenthesis-free notation (**Polish notation**) in his logic text *Elements of Mathematical Logic*.
1930	**Vannevar Bush**'s **Differential Analyzer**.
1931	R. B. Johnson invents mark-sensed test scoring; Kurt Gödel stuns the mathematical world by enunciating an *Incompleteness Theorem* that states that in any sufficiently rich axiomatic system there are propositions which can neither be proved nor disproved.
1933	Edwin Armstrong and Michael Pupin invent FM broadcasting.
1935	IBM 601 multiplying card punch.
1936	**Alonzo Church**'s **lambda calculus** and Emil Post's production systems, each of which, together with the following year's **Turing machine**, equivalently embodies the concept of effective computation as enunciated in Church's Thesis; **Konrad Zuse**'s Z1 is first binary (though mechanical) computer.
1937	**Bell Labs relay computer** project under the direction of **George Stibitz**; In his paper "On Computable Numbers," **Alan Turing** describes what is now called a **Turing Machine**, which, nine years before the **stored program concept** is credited to **von Neumann**, stores its program on tape (i.e. in memory) in a form indistinguishable from data.

1938   Early computer entrepreneurs William Hewlett and David Packard form the Hewlett-Packard Corporation; xerography invented by Chester F. Carlson; Benford's Law of first digits.

1939   **Atanasoff–Berry Computer (ABC)** is first electronic computing device to use binary arithmetic; *Zuse Z2*.

1940   **Claude Shannon**'s first paper on communications theory; the Bell Labs Complex Number Calculator is demonstrated by Remote Job Entry, first use of that technique.

1941   **Konrad Zuse**'s electromechanical computer *Z3* uses binary and floating-point **computer arithmetic**; Helmut Hoelzer invents first all-electronic general-purpose analog computer.

1942   Mary Cartwright and John Littlewood encounter "chaos" in their solutions to van der Pol's equation but fail to call it that. Their work is ignored, and the concept lies dormant for 20 years; the actress Hedy Lamarr (!) and her husband George Antheil obtain a patent for secure "spread spectrum" communications but fail to call it that. Their work is ignored, and the concept lies dormant for 20 years.

1943   **Colossus**, a large vacuum tube computer, developed by the British to break the German Lorenz cipher; McCulloch and Pitts' concept of artificial neurons; Curt Herzstark designs the Curta calculator while imprisoned at Buchenwald; first issue of influential journal *Mathematical Tables and Other Aids to Computation*.

1944   *Mark I* relay computer developed at Harvard under direction of **Howard Aiken**; development of the **Monte Carlo method** by Stanislaw Ulam and **John von Neumann**; von Neumann and Morganstern's *Theory of Games and Economic Behavior*.

1945   **Zuse** builds *Z4* and envisions *Plunkalkul*, a high-level **programming language** that was never implemented; **Turing** gives a clear exposition of nested subroutines (subprograms) whose calling sequences are based on a pushdown **stack**, floating-point arithmetic, and remote use of a computer over a telephone line; **Vannevar Bush** predicts development of **personal computers** and **hypertext** in his historic essay "As We May Think."

1946   **ENIAC**, the first large general-purpose electronic computer, developed by J. Presper Eckert and John Mauchly; publication of the "Princeton Reports" by Burks, Goldstine, and **von Neumann** defines **stored-program concept** and uses "flow diagrams" (**flowcharts**); **F. C. Williams** applies for patent on what is now called **Williams Tube Memory**; Warren Weaver and Andrew Booth propose **machine translation** of one natural language to another; founding of Engineering Research Associates (ERA); Harvard *Mark II*; IBM 603 Calculating Punch; AIEE appoints Charles Concordia chairman of its Large Scale Computing subcommittee, the forerunner of the **IEEE Computer Society**.

1947   Founding of the **Association for Computing Machinery (ACM)**; Dantzig's Simplex Method; **Hamming** invents **error correcting and detecting codes**; Harvard *Mark II*; first magnetic drum memories; Eckert–Mauchly Computer Corporation, the first company formed with the sole intent to market an electronic digital computer.

1948   The **Manchester University** "baby" machine, a prototype of its later *Mark I*, is built by **F. C. Williams** and **Tom Kilburn** using **Williams**

Tube Memory and becomes first electronic stored program computer to run a complete program; **index register** (B-box) invented by Newman and **Kilburn**; transistor invented at Bell Labs by Bardeen, Brattain, and Shockley; **Norbert Wiener**'s **Cybernetics**; IBM's Selective Sequence Electronic Calculator (SSEC); **Claude Shannon** founds **Information Theory** through publication of his *Mathematical Theory of Communication.*

1949   *EDSAC*, first practical stored-program computer, becomes operational at Cambridge and uses a "relocating loader"; work begins on *LEO*, an extension of *EDSAC*; Harvard *Mark III*; *BINAC*, first stored-program computer built in USA; Zipf's Law; Grosch's Law; An Wang and Jay Forrester independently invent magnetic core memory; Edmund Berkeley's *Giant Brains*; *ENIAC* is converted to a stored-program computer by Richard Clippinger and used to compute π to 2,037 decimal places.

1950   Pilot Ace computer; **Wilkes**, Wheeler, and Gill develop concepts of subroutines and subroutine libraries for *EDSAC*; *SEAC*; *Whirlwind*; **Turing test** for machine intelligence; Asimov's "Three Laws of **Robotics**"; Harry Huskey builds *SWAC* for NBS at UCLA; *ERA 1101*; MIT Lincoln Laboratory founded to develop S*AGE*; K. H. Davis builds a **speech recognition** machine.

1951   *Ferranti Mark I* and **Univac I**, first commercial computers; Holberton's sort-merge generator; founding of the Computer Group of the Institute of Radio Engineers (renamed the **IEEE Computer Society** in 1971); **Grace Hopper** proposes use of word "compiler" for her *A-0* programming system.

1952   *EDVAC*; *Autocode*, the first working high-level language, is developed by Alick Glennie; *MANIAC* at Los Alamos under direction of Nicholas Metropolis; *ORDVAC* at Aberdeen Proving Grounds; *IAS* under leadership of Julian Bigelow at Institute for Advanced Study at Princeton; *RAYDAC* at NBS; *ABNER* at NSA; Svoboda's *SAPO* in Czechoslovakia is first **fault-tolerant computer**; *ILLIAC I* at University of Illinois; Harvard *Mark IV*; core memory installed on **Whirlwind** and **ENIAC**; Sidney Fernbach heads computer group at Lawrence Livermore National Laboratory that uses a **Univac I** to predict Eisenhower's election; Arthur Samuel begins development of a program to play checkers; Huffman encoding.

1953   Nathaniel Rochester's symbolic **assembler**; **von Neumann** demonstrates the possibility of a self-reproducing automaton; *IBM 701*; *OMIBAC*; *ERA 1103*, first commercial computer to use **interrupts**; *BESM1* and *STRELA* in Russia; *JOHNNIAC* at Rand Corporation; **Maurice Wilkes** recommends use of **microprogramming**; A firm founded in 1896 is renamed Burroughs; B. V. Bowden's *Faster than Thought.*

1954   Eiichi Goto's *Parametron*; *DYSEAC*, first computer to use **interrupt**s for I/O; *NORC*; *DEUCE*; Laning and Zierler implement first operational compiler for **Whirlwind**; *IBM 650*; Masterson's *Uniprinter* prints 600 lines per minute.

1955   *Alwac III-E*, an early minicomputer, time-shares four remote terminals at NSA but its 15-minute time quantum does not create illusion of simultaneity; **index registers** added to *EDSAC*; first optical character reader (OCR); *IBM SAGE* is first computer to use direct memory access (DMA); Sperry Gyroscope absorbs Remington Rand to form Sperry Rand; SHARE becomes first of many **user groups**.

1956   *IBM 704* and *Univac 1103* are first commercial computers to use magnetic core storage; **Chomsky hierarchy**; *Ferranti Pegasus* is first computer to use general (purpose) registers; first **operating system** is developed for the *IBM 704* through cooperative effort of General Motors and North American Aviation; *TAC* (Tokyo Automatic Computer) under direction of Hideo Yamashita; *Logic Theorist* of Newell, Shaw, and **Simon** is the first **heuristic** program and first to exploit linked lists; John McCarthy coins "**artificial intelligence**"; work on *ATLAS* begins at **Manchester University** under direction of **Tom Kilburn**; A. I. Dumey publishes first paper on hashing; Kruskal's minimum spanning-tree algorithm; Doug Ross's *APT* language for numerical control of machine tools becomes an early successful **problem-oriented language**.

1957   *Fortran* developed under leadership of John Backus; Harlan Herrick names its unconditional transfer a *GOTO*; Roy Nutt introduces FORMAT statement into the language; Herb Bright is first *Fortran* user to receive an error message; Yngve's Comit is first **string-processing** language; Bill Norris leaves Sperry to form Control Data Corporation (CDC); Fairchild Semiconductor formed by a group led by Gordon Moore and **Robert Noyce**; **Digital Equipment Corporation (DEC)** founded by Ken Olsen and Harlan Anderson. *IBM 305 RAMAC* is first commercial computer to use disk drives; Lejaren Hiller creates first **computer music** composition, the "ILLIAC Suite"; first issue of *Datamation*.

1958   First decision table system developed by Orren Evans at Hunt Foods; Bernstein's **computer chess** program; CDC 1604; Philco *Transac S-2000* forms base for first family of upward-compatible computers; Jack Kilby's **microcomputer chip**; I/O **interrupt** developed by Morton Astrahan of IBM; Daniel McCracken writes first *Fortran* textbook; **Grace Hopper**'s *Flow-Matic* is first business-oriented high-level language.

1959   *IBM 1400*, *7070*, and *7090*; *DEC PDP-1*; CODASYL; **University of Manchester**'s **ATLAS** is first computer to use a paged **virtual memory**; *RPG*; *ERMA*; McCarthy's *Lisp* **list processing** language based on the **lambda calculus** of **Alonzo Church**; oblivious of antecedents, John McCarthy and **Christopher Strachey** independently propose "**time-sharing**"; Herb Gelernter's program proves high-school geometry problems; Rabin and Scott introduce notion of computational nondeterminism; Donald Shell's *Shellsort* **sorting** algorithm; first Xerox copier.

1960   *Algol* 60 language popularizes concepts of **recursion** and **block structure**; **Algol 60** Report introduces notation initially called Backus Normal Form (BNF) in honor of John Backus but later renamed **Backus–Naur Form** to give equal honor to Peter Naur; *Cobol*; *IBM 1620*; first **integrated circuit** patent applied for by **Robert N. Noyce** of Fairchild; Soviet *KIEV* computer; E.H. Fredkin's *trie* data structure; M. D. McIlroy describes high-level language **macro** expansion; Donald Bitzer's *Plato* learning system; Odo Struger's *programmable logic controller*, which made modern factory automation possible; Paul Baran of RAND proposes a global distributed network based on transmission of what would later be called "packets" of information.

1961   MIT's *Compatible Time Sharing System* (CTSS) under direction of Fernando Corbató; Licklider's DEC **time-sharing** system; E. T. Irons' syntax-directed compiler; Newell's *IPL V* **list processing** language; first "**supercomputers**" are IBM's ***Stretch***, the first pipelined computer, and Univac's ***LARC***; Rosenblatt's self-organizing ***perceptron***, an early **neural network** used for **pattern recognition**; Samuel's checker-playing program attains master rank and is routinely able to defeat its inventor; AFIPS founded; C. A. R. Hoare publishes *Quicksort* **sorting** algorithm that he invented while a visiting British student at Moscow State University; Unimation markets first industrial robot designed by George Devol; Meteorologist Edward Lorenz of MIT rediscovers chaos theory; Daniel Shanks and John Wrench use an *IBM 7090* to compute π to 100,000 decimal places.

1962   **University of Manchester**'s ***ATLAS*** computer is first to use **Tom Kilburn**'s idea of a two-level memory; Stanford and Purdue establish first departments of **computer science**; Green's question-answering program Baseball anticipates modern **database** queries; *Univac 1100* series begun; Steve Russell's *Space War* for the *PDP-1* is the first interactive video game; Iverson's *A Programming Language*; Werner Buchholz's *Planning a Computer System*; Adel'son-Vel'skii and Landis (AVL) **tree**; Ross Perot founds Electronic Data Systems (EDS); J. C. R. Licklider describes a "Galactic Network," anticipating the **Internet**.

1963   *Burroughs B-5000*, specified by Ted Glaser and designed by Bob Barton; *Snobol*; **Forth**; Weizenbaum's *Eliza*; *LINC*; *SABRE*, American Airlines reservation system; NEC *SX-1* and *SX-2*; Ivan Sutherland's *Sketchpad*, first interactive **computer graphics** system; Cliff Shaw's *JOSS* interactive system at RAND; Lotfi Zadeh begins work on ***fuzzy logic***; Paul Cohen demonstrates that the continuum hypothesis is independent of the other axioms of set theory.

1964   ***IBM 360***, the first byte-addressable machine; in conjunction with its description, IBM is first to use term "**computer architecture**"; *CDC 6600*, essentially the first **RISC** computer, 16 years prior to coinage of the acronym; Kemeny and Kurtz develop Dartmouth **time-sharing** system and ***Basic*** programming language; *DEC PDP-8*; *RCA Spectra* series; *Honeywell 200* series; Böhm and Jacopini's paper on the sufficiency of canonical **control structures** is basis for **structured programming**; development of *Formac*, first **computer algebra** program, by an IBM team led by Jean Sammet; *Dendral* is first diagnostic **expert system** program; Robert Floyd and John Williams invent *Heapsort* **sorting** algorithm.

1965   Moore's Law; **Wilkes** proposes use of a **cache memory**, attributing the idea to Gordon Scarrott; *PL/I*; *SPSS*; Dijkstra's semaphores advance state of the art of **concurrent programming**; K. C. Knowlton's *buddy system* for **multiprogramming** storage management; Bachman's Integrated Data Store is forerunner of **database management systems (DBMS)**; Project MAC at MIT; Englebart invents **mouse** at SRI; IBM develops **diskettes** for use with 370 series; Cooley and Tukey's **Fast Fourier Transform (FFT)** algorithm; Donald Davies coins "*packet switching*" to describe a distributed network similar to that of Paul Baran; Ted Nelson coins "**hypertext**"; Gregory Chaitin's formal definition of a random sequence; first Ph.D. in **computer science** is awarded to Richard Wexelblat by the University of Pennsylvania.

1966	Iverson and Falkoff's *APL* language incorporates elastic **data structures** and absence of levels of **operator precedence**; Flynn's classification scheme for **computer architectures**; Hoare invents the "case" **control structure**; IBM **Stretch** is used to compute π to 250,000 decimal places.
1967	*LOGO*; Greenblatt's chess-playing program, *Mac Hack VI*, is made an honorary member of the US Chess Federation; S. G. Tucker coins term **emulation** to mean hardware-assisted **simulation**; *IBM 360/85* is first commercial computer to use a **cache memory**; Ole-Johan Dahl and Kristen Nygaard's *Simula*, later considered to have been the first **object-oriented programming** (OOP) language; Fred Brooks' **virtual reality** lab at University of North Carolina.
1968	Dijkstra's letter "Goto considered harmful"; a US federal information processing standard that encourages a YYMMDD date standard really *is* harmful, engendering the **Year 2000 (Y2K) problem** of the late 1990s; ACM Curriculum 68; *NCR Century* series; Denning's **working set** model; Arthur C. Clarke's HAL in *2001* alerts world to the possibility of highly intelligent machines; *CDC 7600*; *Algol 68*; *Speakeasy*; *Multics* **operating system** on the *GE* (later *Honeywell*) *645* at MIT; Intel founded by **Robert Noyce**, Andrew Grove, and Gordon Moore; NATO conference introduces term "**software engineering**"; Alan Kay's *Dynabook*; Volume 1 of Knuth's *Art of Computer Programming*; Jon Postel begins his three decades of service administering the *Internet Assigned Numbers Authority* (IANA).
1969	*Unix*; Seymour Papert and Marvin Minsky solidify computational limits of the Rosenblatt **perceptron**; *Mumps*; *RS232-C* communications standard; IBM "unbundles," pricing software separately from hardware, a decision that spawns a multibillion dollar independent software industry; first use of ARPANET.
1970	*IBM 370*; DEC *PDP-11* uses *Unibus*, first multivendor **bus**; *Bliss*; Conway's *Game of Life*, a popular **cellular automaton**; Codd's first paper on **relational database** systems; Gene Amdahl leaves IBM to form corporation bearing his name; first "smart" terminal, Jack Frassanito's *Datapoint 2200*; DEC *PDP 11/20*; Sinclair *ZX-80*.
1971	Wirth defines *Pascal* language; *Intel 4004* chip inaugurates era of *very large-scale integration* (VLSI); *CDC Cyber 70*; appearance of electronic handheld **calculators**; Harlan Mills advocates use of the **chief programmer team**; Stephen Cook in the USA and Leonid Levin in Russia independently formulate the concept of **NP-complete problems**; Weinberg's *The Psychology of Computer Programming*; formation of the **IEEE Computer Society**.
1972	Founding of Cray Research; Joel Moses's *MACSYMA*; *B-tree* invented by Bayer and McCreight and later proves indispensable for efficient **database management**; David Parnas proposes

"**information hiding**"; first vector computers, the *CDC STAR-100* and the Texas Instruments *Advanced Scientific Computer (ASC)*; Ken Thompson of Bell Labs invents a language called *B*; Dennis Ritchie extends it to form *C*; Colmerauer's *Prolog*; HP-35 calculator; *PDP 11/45*; Nolan Bushnell founds Atari featuring his *Pong* video game; Ray Tomlinson invents **electronic mail**. His choice of @ to separate portions of email addresses causes consternation among some users because the symbol had been used to signal "kill prior characters on this line," but his choice endures.

1973   Alan Kay's language *Smalltalk* inaugurates **object-oriented programming** systems (OOPS), but idea doesn't catch fire for 13 more years; first international **computer chess** tournament; Gary Kildall forms Digital Research Corporation in order to market *CP/M* microcomputer **operating system**; Robert Metcalfe's **local area network (LAN) Ethernet** protocol.

1974   Hewlett-Packard's **programmable calculator**; Texas Instrument's *SR-50* and *SR-51* calculators; Alto **workstation** at Xerox PARC; Roland Moreno invents "smart cards"; July issue of Radio Electronics describes first home computer, Jonathan Titus' *Mark 8*, which uses an *8008* chip; British cryptologists Ellis, Cocks, and Williamson invent a Public Key Cryptosystem based on the difficulty of **factoring integers** but are not permitted to publish it.

1975   MITS' *Altair*, first **personal computer** kit; *ILLIAC IV*; Rubik's Cube; TCP/IP protocols; Fred Brooks' classic *The Mythical Man-Month*; first laser printer developed by an **Apple** group led by Gary Starkweather; Mitchell Feigenbaum discovers a new fundamental constant, 4.669201609103... , which plays an important role in chaos theory.

1976   Introduction of the *CRAY-1* **supercomputer**; Appel and Haken's computer-aided proof of the four-color theorem; Diffie and Hellman rediscover the Public Key Cryptosystem; *Electric Pencil*, Michael Shrayer's **word processing** program for the *Altair* microcomputer; first network **gateway**; First Edition of the *Encyclopedia of Computer Science*.

1977   IEEE Curriculum in Computer Science and Engineering; Mandelbrot's **Fractals**; DEC VAX-11/780; IBM 303x series; Erwin Tomash founds the **Charles Babbage Institute**; Data Encryption Standard (DES); Knuth–Morris–Pratt string pattern matching algorithm; Gates and Allen form **Microsoft Corporation**.

1978   *Apple II* and *Radio Shack TRS-80* achieve wide sales and inaugurate the **personal computer** era; *DEC VAX-11*; *VISICALC* **spreadsheet** program; Rivest–Shamir–Adleman (RSA) trapdoor function for use with public key cryptosystems; first **bulletin board** developed by Ward Christensen and Randy Suess; Intel *8086*.

1979   *IBM 4300* series; ACM Curriculum 78; Allan M. Cormack and Godfrey N. Hounsfield receive Nobel Prize in Medicine for work in **computerized tomography**; Boston Computer Museum founded by C. Gordon Bell and Gwen Bell; Knuth's **TEX** and **Metafont**; first Hayes **modem**; Intel 8088; Compuserve; Philips invents audio CD.

1980   *Ada* (language); Patterson and Ditzel coin term **Reduced Instruction Set Computer (RISC)** and advocate this approach to **computer architecture**; Tarjan, Sleator, and Driscoll invent the *persistent data structure*.

1981	**IBM PC**; *MS-DOS*; *CDC Cyber-205*; Commodore VIC-20; Japan's announcement of a "Fifth Generation" based on **artificial intelligence** is greeted with great skepticism.

1982 AT&T antitrust suit is settled; *Osborne* is first luggable computer; *Turbo Pascal* for the **IBM PC**; *AutoCad*; John Hopfield's theory of **neural networks**; commercial **email** to 25 cities; Compaq; Sun Microsystems; Shoch and Hupp publish first account of an Arpanet worm.

1983 *Cray X-MP*; *Fujitsu VP100* and *VP200*; first **CD-ROM** storage; *IBM PC-XT*; *Lotus 1-2-3* **spreadsheet**; π is computed to 16 million decimal places; Microsoft Word 1.0; Second Edition of the *Encyclopedia of Computer Science and Engineering*.

1984 Introduction of **Apple Computer**'s *Macintosh* popularizes use of a **mouse**-driven **graphical user interface (GUI)** as inspired by earlier research at XEROX PARC; Knuth's **Literate Programming**; *IBM PC-AT* and *Tandy 2000* use *Intel 80286* chip; William Gibson coins "**cyberspace**"; Dell Computer founded; introduction of 3.5″ **diskette** and the HP laser printer.

1985 John Warnock's **PostScript**; Paul Brainard's *PageMaker* for the *Macintosh*, first **desktop publishing** software; *Intel 80386* chip; Inmos Transputer; *Windows 1.0*; Thinking Machines Corporation's *Connection Machine*.

1986 Commodore *Amiga*; Burroughs and Sperry merge to form Unisys; *Cray XM-P* **supercomputer** reaches 700 Mflops.

1987 *C++* language stimulates growth of **object-oriented programming**; π is computed to 134 million decimal places by Yasumasa Kanada of the University of Tokyo using a Nippon Electric *SX-2* supercomputer.

1988 Foundation of SPEC, the System Performance Evaluation Cooperative, for development and registration of **benchmarks**; widespread use of **workstation** networks popularizes use of **client/server architecture** in general and **file servers** in particular; *IBM AS/400*; *Motorola 88000* RISC processor; Barry Boehm's *spiral model* of software development; Robert T. Morris releases **Internet** worm; Wolfram's *Mathematica*.

1989 Stardent corporation begins to ship computers that combine **RISC** architecture with vector processing; *Intel 80486* chip; *Soundblaster* sound card.

1990 **Window environments**, long popular on the Apple *Macintosh*, begin to take hold on the **IBM PC** and compatibles (*Windows 3.0*); James Gosling of Sun Microsystems invents a language called *Oak*, later renamed **Java**; first all-optical processor demonstrated at Bell Labs.

1991 IBM and **Apple Computer** announce joint venture; NCR and Tandy market "clipboard" computers that allow input of handwritten printed characters; working version of the original Babbage **Difference Engine** is displayed at the Science Museum in London; Gopher; *Cray Y-MP C90* **supercomputer** reaches 16 Gflops; brothers David and Gregory Chudnovsky, mathematicians at Columbia University, use a formula of their discovery and a low-budget supercomputer of their design and construction to compute π to 2.1 billion decimals.

1992	Increasing popularity of lightweight notebook and pen-based computers; widespread use of **data compression** software to double effective capacity of microcomputer **hard disks**; Michelangelo **virus** causes media frenzy but does little actual damage; discovery of 32nd Mersenne Prime by Slowinski and Gage.
1993	Apple *Newton* PDA; Intel announces *Pentium* chip (*Intel 80586*) and Andrew Wiles announces a proof of Fermat's Last Theorem, but both turn out to be flawed; Leonard Adleman demonstrates DNA computing (**molecular computing**), using it to solve a small traveling salesman problem; Windows NT; Third Edition of the *Encyclopedia of Computer Science*.
1994	Clark and Andreessen's **World Wide Web** browser, *Mosaic* (later *Netscape*); Thomas Nicely, a number theorist at Lynchburg College in Virginia, discovers a *Pentium* bug whereby, for certain operands, quotients of floating-point divisions are accurate to only three decimals rather than the normal 16. Intel, slow to react, ultimately agrees to a multimillion dollar chip replacement program and its profits continue to rise quite nicely. Following suit, Andrew Wiles, using all the ingenuity that his last name implies, submits a revised proof of Fermat's Last Theorem that withstands scrutiny of the mathematical community.
1995	*Windows 95*; *Lycos, Yahoo!, Webcrawler,* and *AltaVista* search engines; *Toy Story* is first full-length computer-generated movie; Bailey, Borwein, and Plouffe discover a "shocking" formula which allows generation of the nth hexadecimal digit of π without computing all or any prior digits.
1996	Web TV; Yasumasa Kanada temporarily regains world record by computing π to six billion decimal places, but the Chudnovsky brothers reach eight billion shortly thereafter; Joel Armengaud, a member of GIMPS (Great Internet Mersenne Prime Search) uses spare computer time on his PC to find the largest prime known to that date, $2^{1398269} - 1$, a Mersenne prime of over 400,000 digits.
1997	Gordon Spence, also a member of GIMPS, uses a program written by George Woltman to discover a still larger Mersenne prime, the 895,932 digit number $2^{2976221} - 1$; Intel 80686 (*Pentium II*); MMX chip; IBM's *Deep Blue*, a 32-node RS/6000 supercomputer, defeats World Chess Champion Garry Kasparov; Japan, abandoning the "Fifth Generation," announces the "Sixth Generation" based on **neural networks**; a "farm" of thousands of PCs coordinated over the Internet use **cooperative computing** to decipher a message enciphered in the 56-bit key DES in 140 days; on June 27, Andrew Wiles accepts the Wolfskehl prize of $50,000, a mere ten years before the deadline; Kanada forges ahead again by using 29 hours of time on a *Hitachi SR2201* to compute π to 51.5 billion decimal places. In tribute, the Chudnovsky brothers record "Oh Kanada" on **CD-ROM** and vow to reach a trillion places.
1998	Windows 98; *Apple iMac*; IBM Enterprise series; Compaq buys **Digital Equipment Corporation** for ten gigabucks, becoming, after IBM, the world's second-largest computer company; In a three-way deal, WorldCom acquires Compuserve and America Online's network service company and AOL acquires Compuserve's **database** and subscriber list. Then AOL buys Netscape with Sun as

matchmaker. GIMPS member Roland Clarkson discovers 37th Mersenne Prime, the 909,526 digit number $2^{3021377} - 1$.

1999	Intel and Hewlett Packard jointly design and market a 600 MHz chip, the first 64-bit chip and the first Intel chip that is not based on *80x86* architecture. Pentium III; *GNOME* GUI positions Linux as a potentially formidable challenger to Windows. Judge Thomas Penfield Jackson makes "findings of fact" that are adverse to Microsoft. GIMPS member Nayan Hajratwala discovers 38th Mersenne prime, the two-million digit number $2^{6972593} - 1$. NSF asks the President to budget more money for "Information Science," but he replies "It all depends on what the meaning of IS is."
2000	New Year's Day comes and goes with no serious **Y2K problem**s; Intel/HP and AMD begin to ship gigahertz **microcomputer chips**; AOL announces merger with Time-Warner. Internet users gradually switch from **modems** to cable TV or DSL connectivity; Windows 2000; Love Bug **virus** infects 45 million computers in 20 countries within 24 hours. Fourth Edition of the *Encyclopedia of Computer Science*.
2001	HAL writes a bestselling novel about a man named ARTHUR, raising the possibility of there being highly intelligent humans.
2013	Abandoning the "Sixth Generation," Japan announces the "Seventh Generation" based on ESP.
2095	Pentium XCI (Intel 809586); Windows 95 redux.
2768	100th Edition of the *Encyclopedia of Computer Science*, the first not edited by Anthony Ralston.
5432	The *Sugan 5000* is used to compute π to "billions and billions" of places beyond the prior record. The middle ten trillion places are found to encode the entire Library of Congress exclusive of certain still-classified works of an obscure 20th Century Congressman whose papers are marked "For eye of Newt only."
9500	Windows 9.5K.
9999	Work begins on the Y10K problem.

Name Index

This index contains the names of those referred to in the text, including article authors, but not necessarily those cited in Bibliographies. Certain historical figures (Ampère, Cornell, Eiffel, Faraday, Guggenheim, Sperry, Volta, etc.) are present only through physical units, companies, universities, computers, or computer languages named for them. A leading boldface page number indicates a biographical article or a profile in ENTREPRENEURS. The editors would appreciate comments on errors and omissions, information regarding missing first names or initials, and missing dates for persons who have died. See page xiv for our email addresses.

General Index

Subjects of biographical articles and names of fictional persons are included in this index. For actual persons cited, see the preceding Name Index. A citation such as CP-3 refers to Color Plate 3. A parenthesized item such as (catalog) indicates an approximate synonym of the indexed term to which it is affixed. A bracketed term such as [Lisp], [MT] (for "Machine Translation"), or [op sys] (for "operating system") indicates the context in which the indexed term appears. Names of books, other publications, movies, games, ships, and commercial computer programs are italicized, and titles beginning with "The" are not permuted. Universities are indexed under their usual full name, e.g. "Harvard University" and "University of Illinois." Boldface entries are article titles. Initial boldface page numbers indicate that the term is defined or explained thereon; a sequence of page numbers none of which are in boldface indicates that the term is referred to on those pages, or that the pages denote the beginning of a relevant article. Most acronyms use "*See*" to refer to the spelled-out form; see Appendix I for help if necessary.